CHILTON'S
IMPORT CAR
REPAIR
MANUAL 1985

Cars Imported to the U.S. and Canada from 1978 through 1985

Editorial Director	Alan F. Turner
Executive Editor	Kerry A. Freeman, S.A.E.
Senior Editor	Richard J. Rivele, S.A.E.
Project Coordinator	A. Lindsay Brooke
Editorial Staff	John M. Baxter
	Martin Gunther
	Tony Molla, S.A.E.
	W. Calvin Settle, Jr.
	Ron Webb
Production Manager	John J. Cantwell
Manager, Editing and Design	Dean F. Morgantini, S.A.E
Production Coordinator	Robin S. Miller
Mechanical Artists	Margaret A. Stoner
	Cynthia Fiore
	William Gaskins

OFFICERS

President	Lawrence A. Fornasieri
Vice President & General Manager	John P. Kushnerick

CHILTON BOOK COMPANY
Chilton Way, Radnor, PA 19089

Manufactured in USA
© 1984 by Chilton Book Company
ISBN 0-8019-7473-9
Library of Congress Card No. 80-68280
ISSN No. 0271-3608
234567890 321098765

ACKNOWLEDGMENTS

AB Volvo, Göteborg, Sweden
American Honda Motor Company, Moorestown, New Jersey
American Isuzu Motors, Inc., Whittier, California
A Pierburg Auto- & Luftfahrt/Geratebau KG (Zenith Carburetors), Neuss-Rhein, Germany
Arnolt Corporation (Solex Carburetors), Warsaw, Indiana
BMW of North America, Inc., Montvale, New Jersey
Champion Spark Plug Company, Toledo, Ohio
Chicago Rawhide Mfg. Company (Fuel/Water Separators), Elgin, Illinois
Chrysler Motors Corporation, Detroit, Michigan
Gabriel Division, Maremont Corporation, Carol Stream, Illinois
International Automobile Importers (Bertone, Pininfarina), Montvale, New Jersey
Mazda Motors of America, Inc., Compton, California
Mercedes-Benz of North America, Inc., Montvale, New Jersey
Mitsubishi Motor Sales, Inc., Fountain Valley, California
Nissan Motor Corporation of USA, Carson, California
Peugeot, Inc., Clifton, New Jersey
Porsche-Audi, Troy, Michigan
Racor Industries (Fuel/Water Separators), Modesto, California
Renault, Inc., Detroit, Michigan
Robert Bosch Corporation, Long Island City, New York
SAAB-Scania, New Haven, Connecticut
Subaru of America, Inc., Cherry Hill, New Jersey
Toyo Kogyo, Ltd., Hiroshima, Japan
Toyota Motor Sales, USA, Inc., Torrance, California
Volkswagen of America, Inc., Troy, Michigan
Volvo Inc., Rockleigh, New Jersey

CONTENTS

Car Section

Unit Repair Section

8903056

INDEX

R & I: Removal and Installation

INDEX

R & I: Removal and Installation

HOW TO USE THIS MANUAL

This manual is arranged in two sections:

Car Section

Car sections are grouped by manufacturer (Audi, BMW, etc.) and arranged in alphabetical order. The text and illustrations that comprise the service procedures in each Car Section are arranged in the following order of systems and components: Tune-Up, Engine Electrical, Engine Mechanical, Engine Lubrication, Engine Cooling, Emission Controls, Fuel System, Manual Transmission, Clutch, Automatic Transmission, Transaxle, Drive Axle, Rear Suspension, Front Suspension, Steering, Brakes, Heater, Radio, Windshield Wiper, Instrument Panel and Fuse Box.

Specification charts are always located at the front of each section. All illustrations are located as close as possible to the pertinent text. Procedures are for all models in the particular section unless specifically noted otherwise.

Unit Repair Section

The Unit Repair Section contains troubleshooting and overhaul procedures for the major components and systems of your car. This portion of the book is intended to be used in conjunction with the Car Sections.

For example: If your car's engine is misfiring and you do not know the cause, use the "Troubleshooting" portion of the Unit Repair Section to find the cause and its remedy. If the cause should prove to be defective piston rings which are allowing oil to foul the spark plugs, the remedy is to overhaul the engine. Then turn to the proper Car Section to find the procedure for removing the engine from the car. After you have removed the engine, turn to the "Engine Rebuilding" chapter in the Unit Repair Section and follow the steps listed there to overhaul the engine.

Every major Unit Repair Section contains an Identification or Application chart to correlate the information contained in that section. The sections are usually arranged by brands, manufacturers or types of components rather than models of cars.

All overhaul procedures in the Unit Repair Section begin with the component removed from the car. The reason for this division of material is an economic one. The steps involved in overhauling an engine are virtually the same for all engines. However, the operation of removing the engine from the car varies greatly from model to model. By combining where possible, and separating where necessary, we are able to publish the maximum amount of information.

Locating Information

The Table of Contents, at the front of the book, lists the beginning of each Car and Unit Repair Section in the manual.

The Index, also at the front of the book, is a comprehensive listing of all major mechanical sections and systems for every section in the book. The Index contains listings for Car Sections as well as for corresponding Unit Repair Sections. Car Section pages are prefixed with the letter "C." Unit Repair Sections are prefixed with the letter "U."

To find where a particular Car Section is located in the book, you need only look in the Table of Contents. Once you have found the proper section, you may wish to find where specific procedures are located in that section. Turn to the Index and read across the top of the page until you reach the appropriate Car Section. When the proper manufacturer's column has been found, read down the side column to the procedure or system for which you are looking. The intersection of the two columns will provide the page number(s) where the procedure is located.

Safety Notice

Proper service and repair procedures are vital to the safe, reliable operation of all motor vehicles, as well as the personal safety of those performing repairs. This manual outlines procedures for servicing and repairing vehicles using safe effective methods. The procedures contain many NOTES, CAUTIONS and WARNINGS which should be followed along with standard safety procedures to eliminate the possibility of personal injury or improper service which could damage the vehicle or compromise its safety.

It is important to note that repair procedures and techniques, tools and parts for servicing motor vehicles, as well as the skill and experience of the individual performing the work vary widely. It is not possible to anticipate all of the conceivable ways or conditions under which vehicles may be serviced, or to provide cautions as to all of the possible hazards that may result. Standard and accepted safety precautions and equipment should be used when handling toxic or flammable fluids, and safety goggles or other protection should be used during cutting, grinding, chiseling, prying, or any other process that can cause material removal or projectiles.

Some procedures require the use of tools specially designed for a specific purpose. Before substituting another tool or procedure, you must be completely satisfied that neither your personal safety, nor the performance of the vehicle will be endangered.

Part Numbers

Part numbers listed in this book are not recommendations by Chilton for any product by brand name. They are references that can be used with interchange manuals and aftermarket supplier catalogs to locate each brand supplier's discrete part number.

Audi
Fox, 4000, Coupe, 4000S Quattro, 5000, Quattro

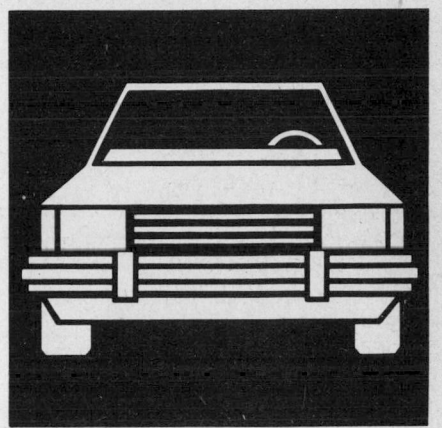

SERIAL NUMBER IDENTIFICATION

Vehicle

5000

The chassis number is on the plate on top of the instrument panel, clearly visible through the driver's side of the windshield. It is also stamped into the upper right corner of the firewall. The vehicle identification plate is mounted on the right wheel housing.

4000

The vehicle identification number (VIN) is located on the left (driver's side) windshield pillar and in the engine compartment on the ledge.

FOX

The chassis number is on a plate on the left windshield pillar, clearly visible through the driver's side of the windshield. It is also stamped into the top center of the firewall. The vehicle identification plate is on the right wheel housing.

Engine

5000

The engine number is stamped on the left side of the engine block (clutch housing).

In addition to the engine number, an engine code number is also stamped on the starter end of the cylinder block, just below the cylinder head. This number indicates the exact cylinder bore of the particular engine.

4000

The engine number is located on the left side of the cylinder block, below the cylinder head and next to the distributor.

FOX

The engine number is stamped on the left side of the engine block, just above the fuel pump.

In addition to the engine number, an engine code number is also stamped into the left front side of the cylinder block, just above the water pump. This number indicates the exact cylinder bore of the particular engine.

GENERAL ENGINE SPECIFICATIONS

Year and Model	Engine Displacement Cu. In. (cc)	Fuel Delivery	Horsepower @ rpm	Torque @ rpm (ft. lbs.)	Bore × Stroke (in.)	Compression Ratio	Normal Oil Pressure (psi)①
'78–'79 Fox	97 (1588)	F.I.	79 @ 5500	89 @ 3300	3.13 × 3.15	8.0:1	64–74
'80 4000	97 (1588)	F.I.	78 @ 5500 (76 Calif.)	84 @ 3200 (83 Calif.)	3.13 × 3.15	8.0:1	28②
'81–'83 4000	105 (1715)	F.I.	74 @ 5000	89.6 @ 3000	3.13 × 3.40	8.0:1③	29②
'84–'85 4000	109 (1780)	F.I.	88 @ 5500	96 @ 3250	3.19 × 3.40	9.0:1	29②

GENERAL ENGINE SPECIFICATIONS

Year and Model	Engine Displacement Cu. In. (cc)	Fuel Delivery	Horsepower @ rpm	Torque @ rpm (ft. lbs.)	Bore × Stroke (in.)	Compression Ratio	Normal Oil Pressure (psi)①
'82–'83 4000 Diesel	97 (1588)	F.I.	52 @ 4800	71.5 @ 2000	3.01 × 3.40	23.0:1	29②
'83–'85 4000 Turbodiesel	97 (1588)	F.I.	68 @ 4500	98 @ 2800	3.01 × 3.40	23.0:1	29②
'80–'85 Coupe 4000 5 cyl.	130.8 (2144)	F.I.	100 @ 5100	112.3 @ 3000	3.12 × 3.40	8.0:1③	29②
'84–'85 4000 Quattro (5 cyl.)	130.8 (2144)	F.I.	115 @ 5500	126 @ 3000	313. × 3.40	8.5:1	29②
'78–'83 5000	130.8 (2144)	F.I.	103 @ 5500④ (100 Calif.)	110 @ 4000⑤	3.13 × 3.40	8.0:1③	29②
'84–'85 5000	130.8 (2144)	F.I.	100 @ 5500⑥	112 @ 3000⑥	3.13 × 3.40	8.2:1	29②
'79–'81 5000 Diesel	121 (1986)	F.I.	67 @ 4800	86.4 @ 3000	3.09 × 3.40	23.0:1	28②
'82–'84 5000 Turbodiesel	121 (1986)	F.I.	84 @ 4500	127 @ 2800	3.01 × 3.40	23.0:1	22②
'80–'83 5000 Turbo	130.8 (2144)	F.I.	130 @ 5400	142 @ 3000	3.12 × 3.40	7.0:1	29②
'84–'85 5000 Turbo	130.8 (2144)	F.I. Turbo	140 @ 5500	149 @ 2500	3.13 × 3.40	8.3:1	29②
'82–'85 Quattro	130.8 (2144)	F.I.	160 @ 5500	170 @ 3000	3.12 × 3.40	7.0:1	29②

F.I.—Fuel injection
① Idle—5,500 rpm
② Min @ 2,000 rpm
③ 1982–84: 8.2:1
④ 1980–83: 100 @ 5,100
⑤ 1980–81: 122.3 @ 4,000
   1982–83: 112.3 @ 3,000
⑥ '85–110 @ 5500 HP
   '85–120 @ 3000T

GASOLINE ENGINE TUNE-UP SPECIFICATIONS

Year and Model	Engine Displacement Cu. In. (cc)	Spark Plugs Type	Gap (in.)	Distributor Point Dwell (deg)	Point Gap (in)	Ignition Timing (deg)	Intake Valve Opens (deg)	Pressure Fuel Pump (psi)	Idle Speed (rpm)	Valve Clear (in.) In	Ex
'78–'79 Fox	97 (1,588)	N8Y	.028	44–50	.016	3A @ Idle	4B	4.8–5.4	850–1000	.008–.012	.016–.020
'80 4000	97 (1,588)	N8Y ①	.028	44–50②	.016②	3A @ Idle	4B	64–74	850–1000③	.008–.012	.016–.020
'81–'83 4000	105 (1,715)	N8Y ①⑨	.028	ELECTRONIC		3A @ Idle⑩	6B	64–74	850–1000③	.008–.012	.016–.020

GASOLINE ENGINE TUNE-UP SPECIFICATIONS

Year and Model	Engine Displacement Cu. In. (cc)	Spark Plugs Type	Spark Plugs Gap (in.)	Distributor Point Dwell (deg)	Distributor Point Gap (in)	Ignition Timing (deg)	Intake Valve Opens (deg)	Pressure Fuel Pump (psi)	Idle Speed (rpm)	Valve Clear (in.) In	Valve Clear (in.) Ex
'84–'85 4000	109 (1,780)	N8GY N281BY	.028	ELECTRONIC		6B@ Idle⑭	N.A.	64–74	850–1000	Hyd.	Hyd.
'80–'85 4000 5 cyl	130.8 (2,144)	N8Y ①	.028 ⑤	ELECTRONIC		3A @ Idle⑦⑩	6B⑯	64–74	850–1000④	.008–⑮ .012	.016–⑮ .020
'78–'85 5000	130.8 (2,144)	N8Y ①	.035 ⑥	ELECTRONIC⑧		3A @ Idle⑦⑩	6B	64–74	850–1000④	.008–⑮ .012	.016–⑮ .020
'80–'85 5000 Turbo	130.8 (2,144)	N8Y ⑪	.028	ELECTRONIC		21B @ 3,000⑬	N.A.	72–82	880–1000⑫	.008–⑮ .012	.016–⑮ .020
'82–'85 Quattro	130.8 (2,144)	N6GY	.028	ELECTRONIC		⑬	N.A.	75–85	790–910	.008–.012	.016–.020

NOTE: The underhood specifications sticker often reflects tune-up specification changes made in production. Sticker figures must be used if they disagree with those in this chart.

N.A. Not available at time of publication
IN Intake
EX Exhaust
A After top dead center
B Before top dead center
① Calif: N8GY
② Calif: Electronic ignition system; not adjustable
③ Calif: 920–960

④ 1980–81 Calif: 880–1000
1982–85 All: 775–925
⑤ 1980: .035
⑥ 1981–84: .028
⑦ 1982: 49 States and Calif. w/MT—6B
⑧ 1978–80 models have adjustable air gap; set to .01 in.
⑨ Canada: N10Y
⑩ 1983–85: 6B (USA only)—'83 MT only; '84

Canada 5000S, GT Coupe—34
⑪ 1983–85: N8GY
⑫ 1983–85: 790–910
⑬ Distributor housing aligned with mark on Quattro and '84–'85 5000 Turbo
⑭ Supply hose to idle by-pass pinched shut
⑮ Models after Jan '84 have hydraulic lash adjusters—no adjustment is necessary.
⑯ '84–'85: 1.5° BTDC

DIESEL ENGINE TUNE-UP SPECIFICATIONS

Model/ Year	Engine Displacement Cu. In. (cc)	Warm Valve Clear (in) In	Warm Valve Clear (in) Ex	Intake Valve Opens (deg)	Injection Pump Setting (deg)	Injection Nozzle Pressure (psi) New	Injection Nozzle Pressure (psi) Used	Idle Speed (rpm)	Compression Pressure (psi)
'79–'81 5000 Diesel	121 (1,986)	.008–.012	.016–.020	N.A.	Align Marks	1849	1706	700–800	398–483
'82–'83 5000 Turbodiesel	121 (1,986)	.008–.012	.016–.020	N.A.	Align Marks	2306	2139	700–800	493
'82–'83 4000 Diesel	97 (1,588)	.008–.012	.016–.020	N.A.	Align Marks	1885	1740	770–870	398–483
'83–'85 4000 Turbodiesel	97 (1,588)	.008–.012	.016–.020	N.A.	Align Marks	2306	2139	900–1000	493

N.A. Not available at time of publication

FIRING ORDER

NOTE: To avoid confusion, always replace spark plug wires one at a time.

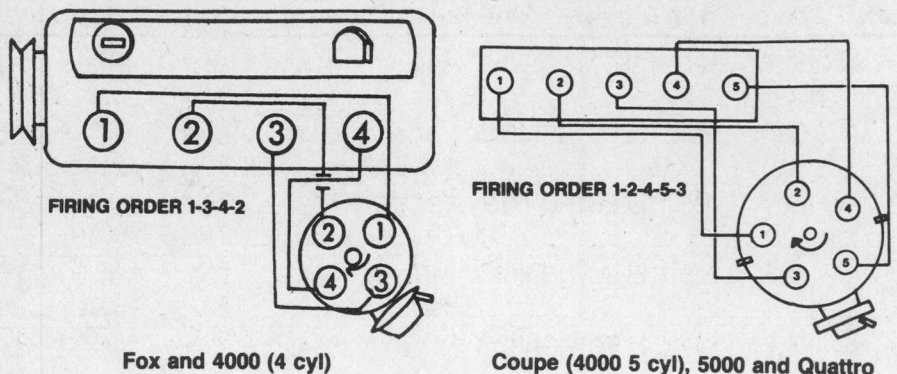

FIRING ORDER 1-3-4-2

Fox and 4000 (4 cyl)

FIRING ORDER 1-2-4-5-3

Coupe (4000 5 cyl), 5000 and Quattro

CAPACITIES

Year/ Model	Engine Displacement cu.in.(cc)	Crankcase (qts) With Filter	Without Filter	Transmission (pts) Manual 4-spd	5-spd	Automatic	Gasoline Tank (gals)	Cooling System (qts)
'78–'79 Fox	97 (1,588)	3.7	3.2	3.4	—	6.4	12.0	6.3
'80–'83 4000	105 (1,715)	3.7③	3.2④	3.4	3.4	6.4	15.9	7.4
'84–'85 4000	109 (1,780)	4.7	4.2	3.4	3.4	6.4	15.9	9.8
'80–'85 Coupe 4000 5cyl	130.8 (2,144)	4.8⑤	4.3⑥	—	5.5⑦	6.4	15.9	8.6
'82–'85 4000 Diesel/ Turbodiesel	97 (1,588)	3.7	3.2	—	3.4	6.4	15.9	6.6
'78–'85 5000	130.8 (2,144)	4.8⑧	4.3⑨	3.4	5.2①	6.4	19.8②	8.6
'79–'83 5000 Diesel/ Turbodiesel	121 (1,986)	4.8	4.3	—	5.2①	6.4	19.8	9.9
'80–'85 5000 Turbo	130.8 (2,144)	4.8⑧	4.3⑨	—	—	6.4	19.8	9.9
'82–'85 Quattro	130.8 (2,144)	4.5	4.0	—	7.6	—	23.8	9.8

① 1980–85: 5.5 ④ 1983–85: 3.0 ⑦ 1983–85: 3.4
② 1978: 15.9 ⑤ 1983–85: 4.0 ⑧ 1983–85: 5.0
③ 1983–85: 3.5 ⑥ 1983–85: 3.5 ⑨ 1983–85: 4.5

CRANKSHAFT AND CONNECTING ROD SPECIFICATIONS
(All measurements are given in inches)

Year/ Model	Crankshaft				Connecting Rod		
	Main Brg. Journal Dia.①	Main Brg. Oil Clearance	Shaft End-Play	Thrust on No.	Journal Diameter①	Oil Clearance	Side Clearance
'78–'79 Fox	2.1260	.0010–.0030	.003–.007	3	1.8110	.0011–.0034	.010
'80 4000	2.1587	.0010–.0030	.003–.007	3	1.8387	.0011–.0034	.015
'81–'83 4000	2.1247	.001–.003	.003–.007	3	1.8098	.0011–.0034	.015
'84–'85 4000	2.1260	0.001–0.003	0.003–0.007	3	1.811	0.001–0.003	.015
'82–'85 4000 Diesel/ Turbodiesel	2.1248	.001–.003	.003–.007	3	1.8807	.0011–.0034	.014
'78–'85 4000 5 cyl, 5000, Coupe, Turbo, Quattro	2.2834②	.0006–.0030	.003–.007	4	1.8110③	.0006–.0020	.016
'79–'83 5000 Diesel/ Turbodiesel	2.3187	.0006–.0030	.003–.007	4	1.9107	.005–.0024	.015

①Standard size
②1982–85: 2.2822
③1982–85: 1.8098

VALVE SPECIFICATIONS

Model	Seat Angle (deg)	Face Angle (deg)	Stem-to-Guide Clearance (in.)		Stem Diameter (in.)	
			Intake	Exhaust	Intake	Exhaust
Fox, 4000 & 5000 (All)	45	45	0.039① MAX.	0.051 MAX.	0.3140	0.3130

NOTE: Valve guides are removable.
①5000 Diesel: 0.051

PISTON AND RING SPECIFICATIONS
(All measurements in inches)

Year/ Model	Piston Clearance	Ring Gap			Ring Side Clearance		
		Top Compression	Bottom Compression	Oil Control	Top Compression	Bottom Compression	Oil Control
'78–'85 Fox, 4000	.0011	.012–.018	.012–.018	.012–.018①	.0008–.002	.0008–.002	.0008–.002
'82–'85 4000 Diesel/ Turbodiesel	.0011	.012–.020	.012–.020	.010–.016	.002–.004	.002–.003	.001–.002
'78–'85 5000, 4000 (5 cyl), Turbo, Quattro	.0011	.010–.020	.010–.020	.010–.020	.0008–.003	.0008–.003	.0008–.003

PISTON AND RING SPECIFICATIONS
(All measurements in inches)

Year/ Model	Piston Clearance	Ring Gap			Ring Side Clearance		
		Top Compression	Bottom Compression	Oil Control	Top Compression	Bottom Compression	Oil Control
'79–'85 5000 Diesel/ Turbodiesel	.0011	.012–.020	.012–.020	.010–.016	.002–.0035	.002–.003	.001–.002

NOTE: Three oversizes of pistons are available to accommodate overbores of up to .040 in.
①Fox: .010–.016

TORQUE SPECIFICATIONS
(All readings in ft. lbs.)

Year/ Model	Cylinder Head Bolts*	Rod Bearing Bolts①	Main Bearing Bolts	Crankshaft Pulley Bolt	Flywheel-To- Crankshaft Bolts	Manifold	
						Intake	Exhaust
'78–'83 Fox, 4000	②	25	47	58	36③	18	18
'84–'85 4000	③	33	47	145	54	18	18
'82–'85 4000 Diesel/Turbodiesel	②	25	47	58⑥	54	18	18
'78–'85 4000 5 cyl, 5000, Coupe Turbo, Quattro	②	36④	47	250	54	18	18
'79–'83 5000 Diesel/Turbodiesel	⑤	33	47	253	54	18	18

* Cold
①Use new bolts
②In sequence: 1) 29 ft. lbs.; 2) 43 ft. lbs.; 3) Tighten ½ turn more (180°)
③1981 and later: 54 ft. lbs.
④Turbo and Quattro: 47 ft. lbs.
⑤Step 1; 29 ft. lbs. Step 2; 43 ft. lbs. Step 3; Tighten ½ turn more (180°).

Warm engine and tighten head bolts an additional ¼ turn (90°)
⑥Replacement bolt and washer: 108 ft. lbs.
Models with a built–in lug: 145 ft. lbs.

BRAKE SPECIFICATIONS
(All measurements given are in. unless noted)

Model	Lug Nut Torque (ft. lbs.)	Master Cylinder Bore	Brake Disc②		Brake Drum			Minimum Lining Thickness	
			Minimum Thickness	Maximum Run-Out	Diameter	Max. Machine O/S	Max. Wear Limit	Front	Rear
'78–'85 Fox, 4000	65	0.825	0.413①	0.002	7.870	7.890	7.910	0.078	0.098
'78–'85 5000 (all but Turbo and Quattro)	80	0.875	0.807	0.004	10.157	9.005	9.094	0.078	0.098

BRAKE SPECIFICATIONS
(All measurements given are in. unless noted)

Model	Lug Nut Torque (ft. lbs.)	Master Cylinder Bore	Brake Disc②		Brake Drum			Minimum Lining Thickness	
			Minimum Thickness	Maximum Run-Out	Diameter	Max. Machine O/S	Max. Wear Limit	Front	Rear
'80–'85 Turbo and Quattro	80	0.875	0.807	0.002	9.645③	0.335④	0.002⑤	0.551	0.472

NOTE: Minimum lining thickness is as recommended by the manufacturer. Due to variations in state inspection regulations, the minimum allowable thickness may be different than recommended by the manufacturer.

① With ventilated discs — 0.768 after refinishing 0.728 in. —discard thickness
② Federal law requires that the minimum rotor thickness be stamped in the disc
③ Rear disc diameter
④ Rear disc min. thickness
⑤ Rear disc max. runout

WHEEL ALIGNMENT

Model	Caster		Camber		Toe-in (in.)	Wheel Pivot Ratio	
	Range (deg)	Pref Setting (deg)	Range (deg)	Pref Setting (deg)		Inner Wheel	Outer Wheel
'78–'79 Fox	0 to 1 P	½P	0 to 1P	½P	5/64	20	18¾
'80–'85 4000	0 to 1P	½P	1 5/32N to 5/32N	21/32N	5/64	N.A.	N.A.
'78–'80 5000 (to VIN-430016066)	13/16N to ½P	5/32N	1N to 0	½N	0	N.A.	N.A.
'80–'85 5000 (from VIN-430016066)	½P to 1 13/16P	1 5/32P	1N to 0	½N	0	N.A.	N.A.
'83–'85 Quattro (2144)	27/32P to 2 5/32P	1½P	1 11/32N to 11/32N	27/32N	0	20	18¾

N Negative
P Positive
N.A. No application

TUNE-UP PROCEDURES

All the tune-up steps should be followed, as each adjustment complements the effects of the other adjustments. If the tune-up specifications sticker in the engine compartment disagrees with the ''Tune-up Specifications'' chart, the sticker figures must be followed.

Spark Plugs

1. Disconnect each spark plug wire by pulling on the rubber cap, not on the wire.
2. Wipe the wires clean with a cloth dampened in kerosene and wipe them dry. If the wires appear to be cracked, they should be replaced.
3. Blow or brush the dirt away from each of the spark plugs.

4. Remove each spark plug with a spark plug socket.
5. Evaluate the condition of the plugs. In general, a tan or medium gray color on the business end of the plug indicates normal combustion conditions.
6. If the plugs are to be reused, file the center and side electrodes with a small, fine file. Check the gap between the two electrodes with a spark plug gap gauge. The round wire type is the most accurate. If the gap is not as specified, use the adjusting device on the gap gauge to bend the outside electrode to correct. Be careful not to bend the electrode too far, because excessive bending may cause it to weaken and possibly fall off into the engine.
7. Clean the plug threads with a wire brush. Crank the engine with the starter to blow out any dirt particles from the cylinder head threads.
8. Put a drop of oil on the threads and screw the plugs in finger tight. Tighten them with the plug socket. If a torque wrench is available, tighten them to 22 ft. lbs.

9. Reinstall the wires. If there is any doubt as to their proper locations, refer to ''Firing Order.''

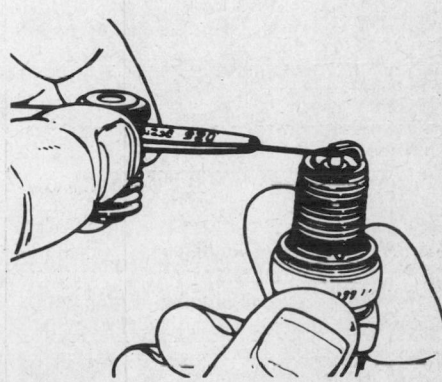

Check the spark plugs with a wire feeler gauge

AUDI

Breaker Points and Condenser

ADJUSTMENT

Fox and 1980 4000 (49 States Only)

The condenser should be replaced each time the points are replaced. After every breaker point adjustment or replacement, the ignition timing must be checked and, if necessary, adjusted. No special equipment other than a feeler gauge is required for point replacement or adjustment, although a dwell meter should be used to ensure the accuracy of the adjustment.

1. Detach the two spring clips securing the distributor cap. Remove the cap.

2. Clean the cap inside and out. Check for cracks and carbon paths. A carbon path shows up as a dark line, usually from one of the cap sockets or inside terminals to ground. Check the condition of the button inside the center of the cap and the four inside terminals. Replace the cap if necessary.

3. Pull the rotor up and off the shaft. Clean off the metal end if it is burned or corroded. Replace the rotor if necessary. Remove the dust cap if there is one.

4. The manufacturer states that the points must be replaced, not reconditioned. Experience also shows that it is more economical and reliable in the long run to replace the point set while the distributor is open, than to have to do this at a later (and possibly more inconvenient) time.

5. Pull off the flat plug terminal on the wire from the point set. Remove the point set hold-down screw, being very careful not to drop it into the inside of the distributor. Remove the point set.

6. Remove the condenser.

Lubricate at (1) with a drop of oil and at (2) with a high melting point grease

7. Install the new condenser, attaching the lead to the coil.

8. Apply a small amount of high melting point grease to the pivot side of the point set rubbing block.

9. Replace the point set and tighten the screw tightly. Replace the flat plug terminals.

10. Check that the contacts meet squarely.

If they do not, bend the tab supporting the fixed contact.

11. Turn the engine until a high point on the cam that opens the points contacts the rubbing block on the point arm. This is easier if the spark plugs have been removed.

12. There is a screwdriver slot and two raised lugs near the contacts. Insert a screwdriver and lever the points open or closed until they appear to be open about the correct gap.

13. Insert the correct size feeler gauge and adjust the gap with the screwdriver until you can push the gauge in and out between the contacts with a slight drag but without moving the point arm. Another check is to try the gauges 0.001–0.002 in. larger and smaller than the setting size. The larger one should disturb the point arm, whereas the smaller one should not drag at all. Tighten the point set hold-down screw snugly. Recheck the gap.

14. After all the point adjustments are complete, pull a white business card through (between) the contacts to remove any traces of oil. Oil will cause rapid point burning.

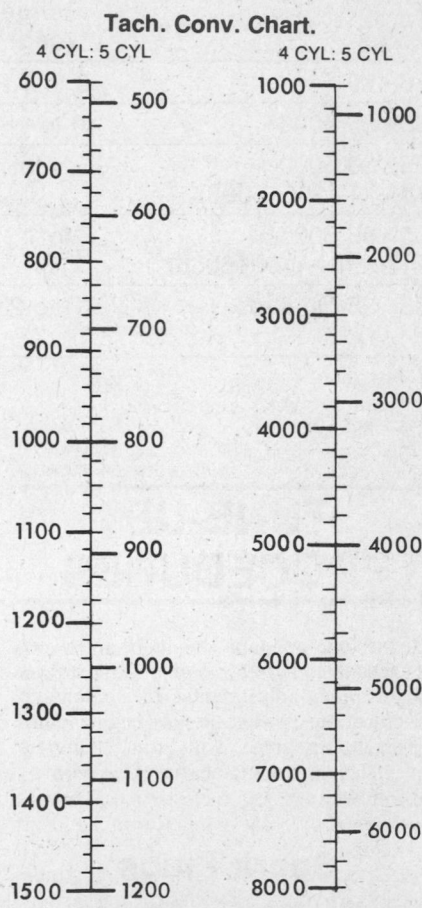

Adjust the point gap with a screwdriver

15. Replace the dust cap.

16. Push the rotor firmly down into place. It will go on only one way. If it is not installed properly, it will probably break when the starter is operated.

17. Replace the distributor cap and install the spring clip.

18. Check the dwell with a meter. Dwell can be checked with the engine running or cranking. Decrease dwell by increasing the point gap; increase by decreasing the gap. Dwell angle is simply the number of degrees of distributor shaft rotation during which the points stay closed. Theoretically, if the point gap is correct, the dwell should also be correct or nearly so. However, dwell is a more accurate setting. If dwell varies more than 3 degrees from idle speed to 2500 engine rpm, the distributor is worn.

NOTE: Some tachometers, dwell meters, and oscilloscopes will not work with the capacitive discharge ignition system. Some may be damaged. Check with the manufacturer of your test equipment if there is any doubt.

19. After the first 200 miles on a new set of points, the point gap often closes up due to initial rubbing block wear. For best performance, recheck the gap or dwell at this time.

20. Since changing the point gap affects the ignition timing setting, the timing should be checked and adjusted if necessary after each point replacement or adjustment.

Electronic Ignition

With the exception of the Fox and the 1980 4000 (49 state), all gasoline engined Audis are equipped with electronic ignition. Audi used two different types of electronic ignition systems between 1978 and 80. The 5000 used an electronic ignition system that consisted of a distributor with an impulse generator, an ignition coil and an electronic control unit. As of 1981, all Audis use an electronic ignition system with a Hall generator instead of an impulse generator. The Hall generator was also used on the 4000 (Calif.), the 5000 Turbo and the 4000 (5 cyl.) in 1980.

Tach. Conv. Chart.

Use this chart to convert the 4-cylinder tachometer reading to the true idle speed on 5-cylinder 5000 models

Because no points or condenser are used and the dwell is determined by the control unit, no adjustments are necessary. Ignition timing is checked in the usual way, but

unless the distributor has been disturbed it is unlikely to change.

Service consists of an inspection of the distributor cap, rotor and ignition wires. In addition, the air gap between the impulse rotor and the permanent magnet should be checked periodically. The air gap on the models equipped with a Hall generator is not adjustable.

AIR GAP ADJUSTMENT

1978-80 5000

1. Release the two clips with a screwdriver and remove the distributor cap.
2. Remove the ignition rotor (not the impulse rotor) by pulling straight up.
3. Rotate the engine by the starter or by turning a wrench on the crankshaft pulley bolt and align the impulse rotor tooth with the tooth on the permanent magnet.
4. Using a non-metallic gauge, the gap should measure 0.010 in. (.25mm). If adjustment is necessary, carefully bend the tooth on the impulse rotor until the proper gap is achieved.

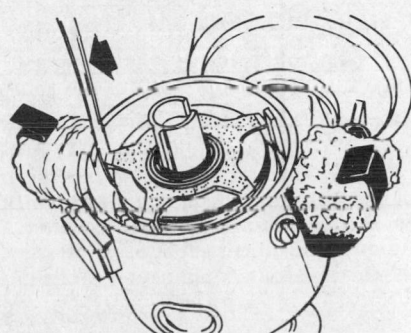

Checking the air gap on the impulse generator; the arrow indicates the feeler gauge

ELECTRONIC IGNITION PRECAUTIONS

When working on the Hall ignition, observe the following precautions to prevent damage to the ignition system.

1. Connect and disconnect test equipment only when the ignition switch is OFF.
2. Do not crank the engine with the starter for compression tests, etc., until the high tension coil wire (terminal 4) is grounded.
3. Do not replace the original equipment coil with a conventional coil.
4. Do not install any kind of condenser to coil terminal 1.
5. Do not use a battery booster for longer than 1 (one) minute.
6. Do not tow cars with defective ignition systems without disconnecting the plugs on the idle stabilizer at the ignition control unit.

Ignition Timing

NOTE: Production changes are noted on the underhood specifications sticker. If the procedure differs from below, follow sticker instructions.

STATIC

A basic timing adjustment can be made in the following manner. Turn the engine until the basic ignition timing mark is aligned with the ignition timing pointer and the distributor rotor points towards the No. 1 cylinder mark on the rim of the distributor body. Timing marks are on the flywheel on the 4000, 5000 and Fox. This will put the No. 1 cylinder at TDC (0°T). Connect a 12 volt test lamp between the ignition coil terminal, No. 1 connected to the distributor, and a ground. Rotate the distributor clockwise until the lamp goes out. Turn the distributor counterclockwise until the lamp just lights, and tighten the clamp on the distributor at that point. The ignition timing is now approximately set. As soon as possible, check the adjustment with a timing light.

DYNAMIC

To check with a timing light, connect a timing light to the No. 1 cylinder and connect a tachometer.

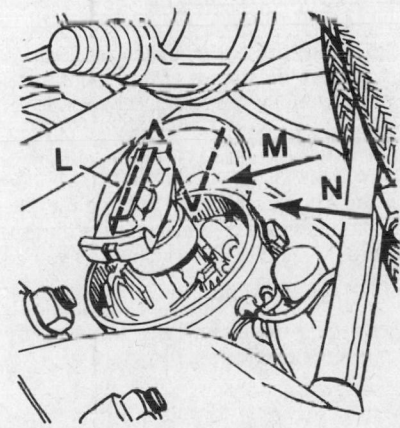

The distributor rotor (L) aligned with the No. 1 cylinder mark (M) on the rim of the distributor body. The dust cap is removed

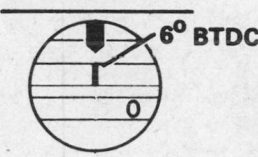

Timing mark alignment—typical of the 1.8L engine

NOTE: Some tachometers, dwell-meters and oscilloscopes will not work with the capacitive discharge ignition system. Some may be damaged. Check with the manufacturer of your test equipment if there is any doubt.

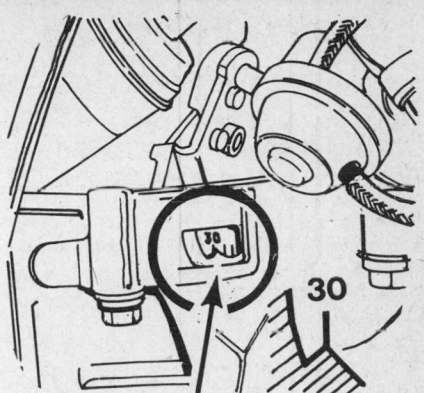

Fox timing marks—5000 series similar

Loosen the distributor clamp screw until it is just possible to turn the distributor by hand. Run the engine at idle speed and point the timing light at the timing window on the flywheel housing. Turn the distributor until the specified notch on the flywheel aligns with the pointer.

NOTE: 5000S Turbo and Quattro models are timed by aligning the distributor housing and reference marks.

Disconnect the vacuum hoses (if required).

NOTE: 4000S and 5000S models require the vacuum hoses to be connected when checking or adjusting the timing or curb idle speed.

On most 1981 and later models the idle stabilizer must be bypassed. To bypass the idle stabilizer, disconnect its two electrical leads and plug them together. *This must be done with the ignition turned off or it could ruin the entire system.* Check the timing at 2500, 2750 or 3000 rpm if specified. Adjust as necessary.

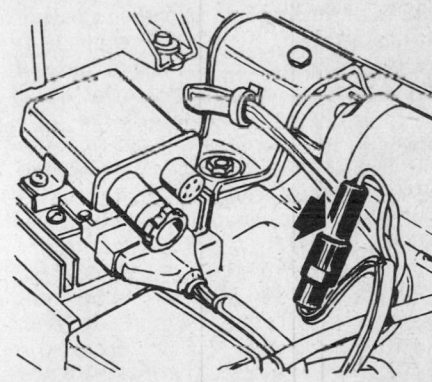

Bypass the idle stabilizer unit by connecting the two plugs together (arrow)

NOTE: Certain late models have an impedance transformer installed on top of the ignition control unit in place of an idle stabilizer. DO NOT disconnect the plugs of the transformer when setting the timing.

NOTE: Timing should always be checked both at idle and at 2500, 2750 or 3000 rpm if specified.

Valve Lash

ADJUSTMENT

NOTE: The 4000 S (built after Jan. 1984) and 5000S series are equipped with hydraulic valve lash adjusters which eliminate the need for periodic valve clearance adjustment. Intermittent valve noises are normal with a cold engine. Should valve noise persist, check cam lobes and lifter for wear, replace as necessary.

Test the hydraulic lash adjuster by pushing down against the lifter with a suitable wooden dowel—if the lifter can be pushed down, replacement is indicated

Audi recommends checking the valve clearance at 1000 miles and then every 15,000 miles thereafter. The overhead cam acts directly on the valves through cam followers which fit over the springs and valves. Adjustment is made with an adjusting disc which fits into the cam follower. Different thickness discs result in changes in valve clearance.

NOTE: Audi recommends that two special tools be used to remove and install the adjustment discs. One is a pry bar (VW 546 or equivalent) to compress the valve springs and the other a pair of special pliers (US 10-208 or equivalent) to remove the disc. If the purchase of these tools is not possible, a flat metal plate can be used to compress the valve springs if you are careful not to gouge the camshaft lobes. The cam follower has two slots which permit the disc to be lifted out. Again, you can improvise with a thin bladed screwdriver. An assistant to pry the spring down while you remove the disc would be the ideal way to perform the operation if you must improvise your own tools.

Valve clearance is checked with the engine moderately warm (coolant temperature should be about 95°F (35°C).

1. Remove the cylinder head cover. Valve clearance is checked in the firing order (1-3-4-2 for the four cylinder and 1-2-4-5-3 for the five cylinder engines) with the piston of the cylinder being checked at TDC of the compression stroke. Both valves will be closed at this position and the cam lobes will be pointing straight up.

NOTE: When adjusting the clearances on the diesel engine, the pistons must not

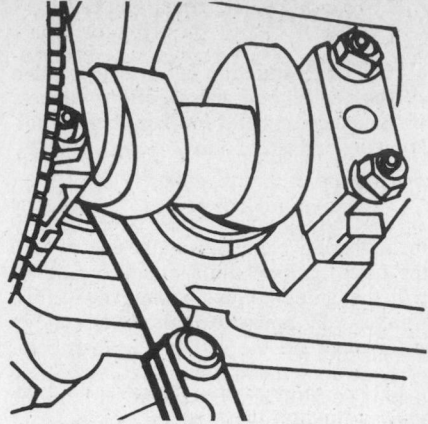

Checking valve clearance with a feeler gauge—4000, 5000 and Coupe

be at TDC. Turn the crankshaft ¼ turn past TDC so that the valves do not contact the pistons when the tappets are depressed.

2. Turn the crankshaft pulley bolt with a socket wrench to position the camshaft for checking.

———————— CAUTION ————————

Do not turn the camshaft by the camshaft mounting bolt, this will stretch the drive belt. When turning the crankshaft pulley bolt, turn it clockwise only.

3. With the No. 1 piston at TDC (¼ turn past for the diesel) of the compression stroke, determine the clearance with a feeler gauge.

4. Continue on to check the other cylinders in the firing order, turning the crankshaft to bring each piston to the top of the compression stroke (¼ turn for the diesel). Record the individual clearances as you go along.

5. If measured clearance is within tolerance levels (0.002 in.), it is not necessary to replace the adjusting discs.

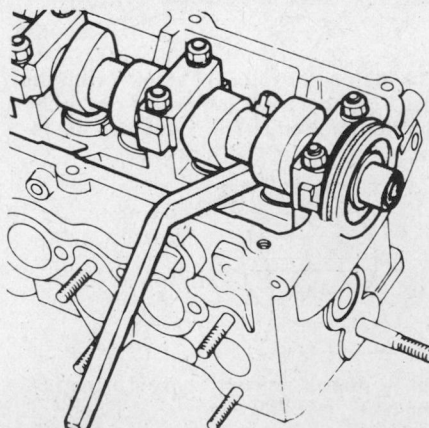

Remove the adjusting discs with a special pry bar and pliers—don't press on the disc itself, but on the lip of the disc holder. Note the position of the camshaft lobes on no. 1 cylinder. This is the correct position for measuring valve clearance

6. If adjustment is necessary, the discs will have to be removed and replaced with thicker or thinner ones which will yield the correct clearance. Discs are available in 0.002 in. increments from 0.12 in. to 0.17 in.

NOTE: The thickness of the adjusting discs are etched on one side. When installing, the marks must face the cam followers. Discs can be reused if they are not worn or damaged.

7. To remove the discs, turn the cam followers so that the grooves are accessible when the pry bar is depressed.

8. Press the cam follower down with the pry bar and remove the adjusting discs with the special pliers or the screwdriver.

9. Replace the adjustment discs as necessary to bring the clearance within the 0.002 in. tolerance level. If the measured clearance is larger than the given tolerance, remove the existing disc and insert a thicker one to bring the clearance up to specification. If it is smaller, insert a thinner one.

10. Recheck all valve clearances after adjustment.

11. Install the cylinder head cover with a new gasket.

Idle Speed/Mixure— Gasoline Engines

ADJUSTMENT

NOTE: On later models, the idle speed should be adjusted in conjunction with the % CO. In these cases, it is suggested that the adjustment not be attempted unless the necessary equipment is available.

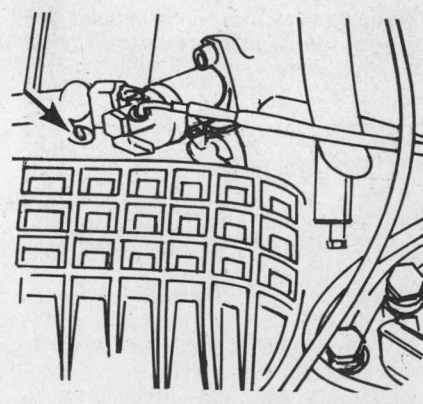

Idle speed adjustment screw—4000 and Fox

Fox

1. Operate the engine at normal operating temperature.

2. With high beams on and A/C on, ignition timing set to 3A with the vacuum hose connected, adjust to 850–1000 rpm.

4000 and 5000 Except Turbo, Quattro and Calif. Models

NOTE: The timing must be set to specifications before adjusting the idle speed.

NOTE: On 1984 and later 4000S 1.8L models: Check idle with all vacuum hoses attached. If adjustment is necessary the oxygen sensor should be connected, the crankcase vent hose to the valve cover should be disconnect and opened to outside air. The evaporative canister cap should be removed. On 4000S Quattro 2.2L models: Check idle with all vacuum hoses connected. If adjustment is necessary the oxygen sensor should be connected, the crankcase vent hose to the valve cover should be disconnect and plugged and the evaporative canister cap should be removed.

On 5000S series models; Check the idle with the oxygen sensor and all vacuum hoses connected. If adjustment is necessary, disconnect the crankcase vent hoses and plug them. Remove the cap from the evaporative canister and on the 5000S (non-turbo) and Quattro, disconnect the purge line. Idle speed stabilizer is by-passed on models so equipped.

1. Connect a dwell/tachometer according to the manufacturer's instructions.
2. Run the engine until the oil temperature is above 140°F (60°C). The radiator fan must come on at least once.
3. Turn the headlights on high beam.
4. Disconnect the PCV valve.
5. Locate the idle adjusting screw in the throttle valve housing on the back of the intake manifold and adjust the idle to specifications.

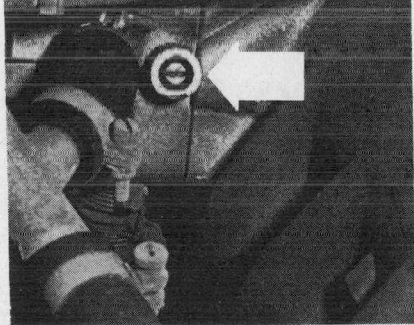

Idle speed adjustment screw—5000

NOTE: The radiator fan must not run while adjusting the idle.

6. Adjust the % CO.

4000 and 5000 Calif. Models, Turbo and Quattro

NOTE: The timing must be set to specifications before adjusting the idle speed.

NOTE: Refer to above note on the 4000S and 5000S models (1984 and later).

1. Connect a dwell/tachometer, according to the manufacturer's instructions.

2. Turn off all electrical accessories.
3. Run the engine until the oil temperature is above 175°F (80°C). The radiator fan must come on at least once.
4. Turn the ignition off.
5. Disconnect the PCV valve.
6. Disconnect the plug for the oxygen sensor wire by the manifold.
7. Unplug both wire leads at the idle stabilizer and connect them together.
8. Start the engine.
9. Locate the idle adjusting screw in the throttle valve housing on the back of the intake manifold and adjust the idle to specifications.

NOTE: The radiator fan must not run while adjusting the idle.

10. Turn off the engine and reconnect the PCV valve, the oxygen sensor wire and the idle stabilizer.
11. Recheck the idle speed. If it has changed, the idle stabilizer will probably require replacement.
12. Adjust the % CO.

CO ADJUSTMENT

4000 and 5000

NOTE: An exhaust gas analyzer or a CO meter will be required for this procedure. These are not common, everyday tools; adjustment of the CO is impossible without one of them.

Idle Stabilizer

The idle stabilizer is located on top of the ignition control unit. The idle stabilizer controls idle speed by either advancing or retarding the distributor timing in accordance with engine load (air conditioner on, lights on, etc.) If idle speed is erratic or if the engine fails to start, try bypassing the idle stabilizer by disconnecting the two plugs at the idle stabilizer and plugging them together. If idle improves, the idle stabilizer should probably be replaced.

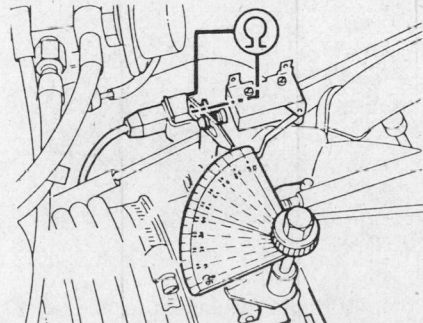

Tool 3084 mounted on the 1st stage throttle valve

Throttle Valve Switches.

NOTE: To check and adjust the idle and full throttle switch on various 1984

and later models, Special Tool No. 3084 and an ohmmeter are necessary.

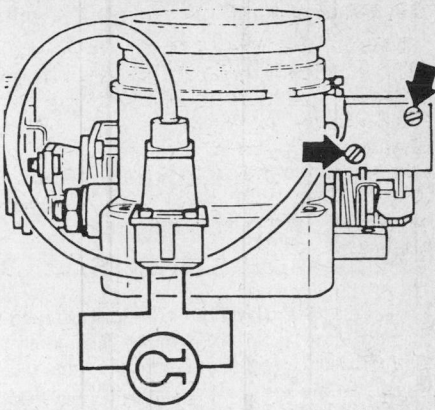

Ohmmeter connection and adjusting points for idle switch adjustment

IDLE SWITCH

1. Loosen the upper left bolt from the throttle valve housing and install the pointer for Tool 3084. Tighten bolt.
2. Attach the protractor (Tool 3084) to the first stage throttle valve shaft (remove the nut if necessary).
3. Disconnect the switch wire plug and connect the ohmmeter.
4. Adjust the protractor to "zero". Open the throttle approximately 20°, close throttle slowly.
5. Ohmmeter should show "zero" when the pointer indicates the throttle position is at 1° to 2.5°. If not within specs, remove housing cover and adjust idle switch position. The ohmmeter must indicate continuity (0 ohms) before the throttle reaches the idle position.

FULL THROTTLE SWITCH

1. Mount pointer as in Idle Switch procedure Step 1.
2. Attach the protractor (Tool 3084) to the second stage throttle valve shaft (remove the nut if necessary).
3. Remove the full throttle switch connectors and connect the ohmmeter.
4. Open the second stage throttle fully and "zero" the protractor.
5. Close the throttle to approximately 30°.

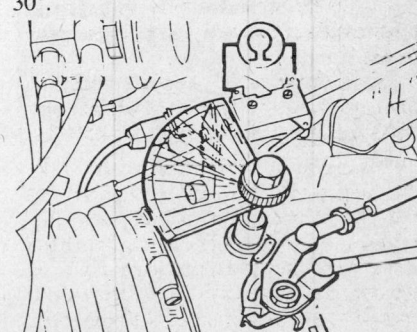

Tool 3084 mounting and ohmmeter connections for the full throttle switch adjustment

6. Open the throttle valve slowly and watch the protractor and ohmmeter. The ohmmeter should read "zero" ohms when the protractor is at 12° to 8° before full throttle.

7. Adjust throttle switch position as necessary. The ohmmeter must indicate zero ohms at full throttle.

Diesel Fuel Injection
IDLE SPEED/MAXIMUM SPEED ADJUSTMENTS.

Diesel engines have both an idle speed and a maximum speed adjustment. The maximum engine speed adjustment prevents the engine from over-revving and self-destructing. The adjusters are located side by side on top of the injection pump. The screw closest to the engine is the idle speed adjuster, while the outer screw is the maximum speed adjuster.

The idle and maximum speed must be adjusted with the engine warm (normal operating temperature). Because the diesel engine has no conventional ignition, you will need a special adaptor to connect your tachometer, or use the tachometer in the instrument panel, if equipped. You should check with the manufacturer of your tachometer to see if it will work with diesel engines. Adjust all engines to the specified idle speed.

When adjustment is correct, lock the locknut on the screw and apply non-hardening thread sealer (Loctite® or similar) to prevent the screw from vibrating loose.

The maximum speed for all engines is between 5500 and 5600 rpm (through 1980) or 5300–5400 rpm (1981 and later). If it is not in this range, loosen the screw and correct the speed (turning the screw clockwise decreases rpm). On 5000 series turn dash control knob counterclockwise until it stops prior to adjustment. Lock the nut on the adjusting screw and apply a dab of thread sealer in the same manner as you did on the idle screw.

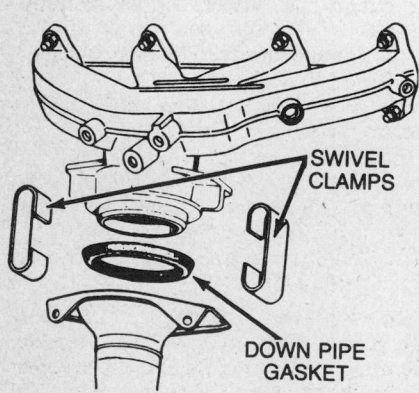

Swivel-type exhaust pipe mounting used on various late models

Do not attempt to squeeze more power out of your engine by raising the maximum speed (rpm).

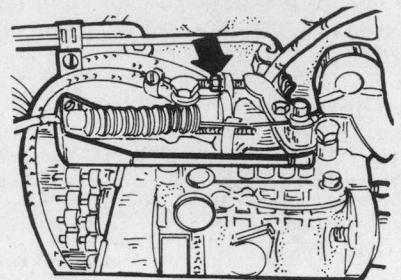

Idle speed adjustment screw—diesel

ENGINE ELECTRICAL

Distributor

REMOVAL & INSTALLATION
Fox

Remove the air cleaner. Pry back the retaining clips and remove the distributor cap. Mark the relationship between the distributor body and the engine block. Make a mark on the distributor body to denote the position of the rotor tip. Disconnect the wiring at the ignition coil. Detach the vacuum line, being careful not to damage the plastic tube. Remove the bolt at the retaining clamp and pull the distributor from the housing. If the distributor is difficult to remove, the rubber seal is probably sticking. Carefully pry the distributor loose.

Distributor installation is the reverse of removal.

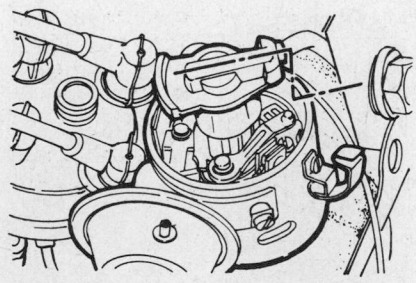

Rotor/distributor alignment for the No. 1 cylinder

The gear-driven Fox distributor has a slot at the bottom which mates with a dog on top of the oil pump driveshaft. Lubricate the seal with a small amount of oil before installation. Align the marks made on removal, then tighten the clamp bolt.

NOTE: If the engine has been turned while the distributor was out, or if a new distributor is being installed, refer to the "Static Ignition Timing" procedure.

All Other Models

1. Disconnect the wiring harness connector and any other connectors from the distributor cap.

2. Remove the static shield (if so equipped).

3. Disconnect and note the position of the vacuum lines.

4. Undo the two retaining spring clips and remove the distributor cap.

5. Note the position of the rotor in relation to the base. Scribe a mark on the base of the distributor and on the engine block to facilitate reinstallation. Align the marks with the direction the metal tip of the rotor is pointing. Note the approximate position of the vacuum advance unit in relation to the engine.

6. Remove the distributor hold-down bolt and clamp.

7. Lift the distributor assembly from the engine.

To install:

1. Insert the distributor shaft and assembly into the engine.

2. Line up the marks on the distributor and on the engine with the metal tip of the rotor.

3. Make sure the vacuum advance unit is pointed in the same direction as it was pointed originally. If the marks on the distributor and the engine are lined up properly, this will be done automatically.

4. Install the distributor hold-down clamp and bolt.

5. Install and secure the distributor cap.

6. Install the vacuum lines in their original places.

7. Install the static shield.

8. Install the wiring harness connector and any other connectors previously removed.

9. Start the engine. Adjust the dwell angle (breaker point ignitions) and set the ignition timing.

NOTE: If the crankshaft has been turned or the engine has been disturbed in any manner (i.e. disassembled and rebuilt) while the distributor was removed, or if the marks were not drawn, it will be necessary to initially time the engine. Follow the procedure given below.

1. It is necessary to place the No. 1 cylinder in the firing position to correctly install the distributor. To locate this position, the ignition timing marks on the flywheel and the clutch housing are used.

2. Remove the spark plug from the No. 1 cylinder. Turn the crankshaft until the piston in the No. 1 cylinder is moving up on the compression stroke. This can be determined by placing your thumb over the spark plug hole and feeling the air being forced out of the cylinder. Stop turning the

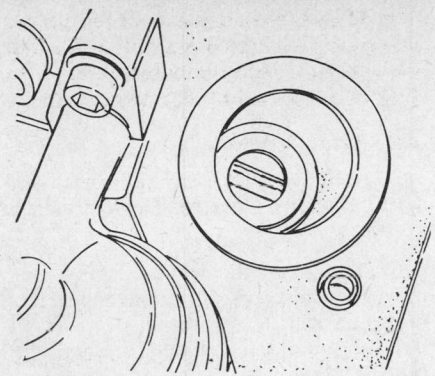

The oil pump driveshaft must be parallel to the crankshaft on the 4000

engine when the timing mark on the fly-wheel is aligned with the lug on the fly-wheel housing.

3. Remove the upper drive belt cover.

4. Align the mark on the camshaft sprocket with the upper edge of the drive belt cover or with the upper edge of the cylinder head cover gasket.

5. Align the oil pump drive pinion lug so that it is parallel to the crankshaft (4000 only).

6. Oil the distributor housing lightly where it bears on the cylinder block.

7. Install the distributor so that the rotor, which is mounted on the shaft, points to the mark on the distributor housing for the No. 1 cylinder.

8. When the distributor shaft has reached the bottom of the hole, move the rotor back and forth slightly until the drive lug on the oil pump shaft enters the slots cut into the end of the distributor shaft, and the distributor assembly slides down into place (4000 only).

9. Clean the distributor cap and check for signs of cracking or carbon tracks. Replace the cap and continue from Step 6 of the installation procedure, engine undisturbed.

Alternator
PRECAUTIONS

All Audi models are equipped with alternators. When performing any service to the alternator or alternator system the following precautions should be observed:

a. Leads or cables to any part of the charging circuit should be disconnected only after the engine has been switched off and has stopped running.

b. When working on the electrical system, always disconnect the lead from the negative battery terminal.

c. When performing tests with the engine running, the battery must always be connected.

d. Temporary connections should never be made to the alternator. Always make firm connections.

The alternator warning light on the instrument panel should go out when the engine reaches idle speed, or shortly after.

REMOVAL & INSTALLATION

1. Disconnect the battery ground strap.

2. Disconnect all the leads to the alternator, tagging them first. Various arrangements of plug-in or bolt-on connections have been used. On some models the wiring may be unplugged from the back of the alternator; on others, it must be unplugged at the voltage regulator on the right front wheel-housing.

NOTE: Current models have a voltage regulator built into the alternator.

3. Remove the belt tensioning bolt from the slotted adjusting bracket.

4. Remove the drive belt.

5. Unbolt and remove the alternator. To install the unit:

6. Install the pivot bolts.

7. Install the drive belt and the belt tensioning bolt.

8. Adjust the belt tension.

9. Replace all the electrical connections, making sure that they are installed in their original locations.

10. Connect the battery ground strap.

BELT TENSION ADJUSTMENT

The alternator drive belt is correctly tensioned when the longest span of belt between pulleys can be depressed about ½ in., by moderate thumb pressure, except as noted below. To adjust, loosen the slotted adjusting bracket bolt on the alternator. If the alternator hinge bolts are very tight, it may be necessary to loosen them slightly to move the alternator. Move the alternator in or out by hand to get the correct tension, then tighten the adjusting bolt.

NOTE: Due to higher alternator output on 4000 and 5000 models, V-belt tension should be adjusted as follows: on belts up to 40 in. long, belt deflection at the longest point should be ⅛ in. (2mm) max. with a new belt, ¼ in. (5mm) with a previously run belt. Belts over 40 in. long should have a ⁷⁄₁₆ in. (10mm) max. deflection when new, and a ⅝ in. (15mm) deflection when previously run.

NOTE: Be careful not to overtighten the belt, as this may damage the alternator bearings.

Regulator

The earlier models have a voltage regulator on the right front wheelhousing in the engine compartment. If there is none there, as on current models, it is built into the alternator.

REMOVAL & INSTALLATION

To remove the regulator, disconnect the battery ground cable, disconnect the three-pronged plug, and unscrew the unit from the wheelhousing. Be careful to make a good ground connection on reinstallation. The manufacturer does not recommend any adjustments to the regulator.

Starter
REMOVAL & INSTALLATION

1. Disconnect the negative battery cable.

2. Jack up the right front of the car and support it with jack stands.

3. Mark with tape and then disconnect the two small wires from the starter solenoid. One wire connects to the ignition coil and the other to the ignition switch.

4. Disconnect the large cable which comes from the battery.

5. Remove the starter support bracket bolts (4000 only). Remove the starter mounting bolts from the back of the starter (all models).

6. Remove the starter.

7. Installation is in the reverse.

STARTER DRIVE REPLACEMENT

NOTE: In order to complete this procedure you will need a pair of circlip pliers and Special Tool US 1078; a gear puller.

1. Remove the starter.

2. Remove the solenoid.

3. Remove the two long housing screws and remove the end plate.

4. Lift the brushes to free them from the commutator and remove the brush holder.

5. Tap the field coil housing lightly with a wooden mallet and remove it from the starter drive housing.

6. Remove the nut and bolt that serves as a pin for the shift lever. Be careful to retain all the associated washers.

7. Remove the shift lever.

8. Slide the armature/starter drive assembly out of the starter drive housing.

9. Press the stop ring down and remove the circlip from the end of the armature shaft.

10. Remove the stop ring using the Special Tool US 1078.

11. Slide the starter drive off of the armature shaft. To install the drive:

1. Lubricate the drive pinion lightly with multi-purpose grease and slide the starter drive onto the armature shaft.

2. Install the stop ring and press it over the circlip groove.

NOTE: When installing the stop ring, the groove must always be on the side closest to the front of the starter (the side nearest the starter drive).

3. Install the circlip and using the Special Tool US 1078, pull the stop ring up into place against the circlip.

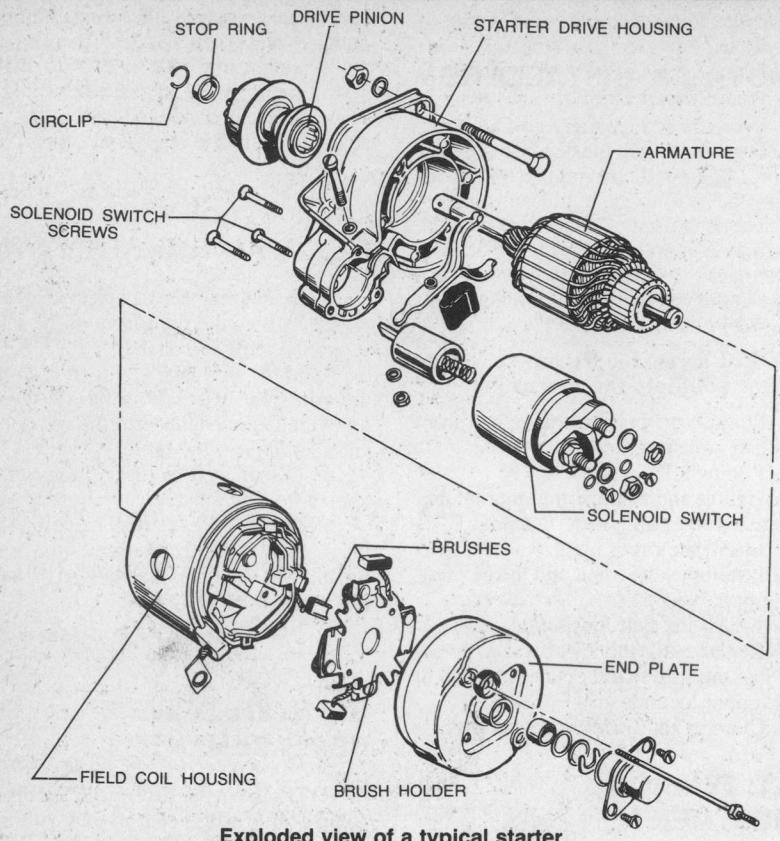

STOP RING — DRIVE PINION — STARTER DRIVE HOUSING — CIRCLIP — SOLENOID SWITCH SCREWS — ARMATURE — SOLENOID SWITCH — BRUSHES — END PLATE — FIELD COIL HOUSING — BRUSH HOLDER

Exploded view of a typical starter

4. Lightly grease the shaft.

5. Install the armature/starter drive assembly into the starter drive housing.

6. Install the shift lever.

7. Ease the field coil housing over the armature assembly and fit it into the starter drive housing.

8. Install the brush holder and the end plate.

9. Install the solenoid.

ENGINE MECHANICAL

Engine

REMOVAL & INSTALLATION

Fox

This procedure explains how to lift the engine out of the chassis. If the car has air-conditioning, it will be necessary to lower the engine, transmission, and front suspension from the car as a unit.

1. Remove the hood and disconnect the battery ground cable. Detach the starter wires.

2. Remove the air cleaner.

3. Disconnect the accelerator linkage and the fuel cutoff solenoid wire.

4. Disconnect the ignition coil primary and secondary wires, the oil pressure sending unit, and the coolant temperature sending unit.

5. Loosen the clutch cable adjusting nuts and disconnect the cable. Disconnect the fuel line at the pump. Unplug the alternator.

6. Remove the grille.

7. Remove the bolts holding the panel. On air-conditioned models, it is necessary to lower the engine, transmission, and front suspension from the car as a unit.

1. Raise the car, allowing the front wheels to hang down. Disconnect the battery ground cable.

2. Drain the coolant.

3. Disconnect all connections between the engine, transmission, and body as explained for models without A/C.

4. Remove the radiator.

5. Disconnect the gearshift rod coupling at the transmission.

6. Detach the front engine mount at the engine block.

7. Use a removal tool to separate the tie–rod ends from the steering levers.

8. Push the brake pedal down about 1½ in. and fasten it in place to keep the system from draining. Disconnect and plug the brake lines at the brackets on the wheel housing.

9. Attach a framework to keep the assembly steady to a sturdy floor jack and clamp it to the crossmember. Lift slightly and disconnect both coil spring units from the wheel housings. Unbolt the crossmember.

10. Disconnect the back–up light switch wire and lower the engine, transmission, and front suspension assembly.

11. On installation, tighten the coil spring units to the body to 16 ft. lbs. and the crossmember to the body to 33 ft. lbs.

4000 Except Coupe, Quattro and Diesels

NOTE: Though not necessary, removal of the hood will make engine removal easier. Be sure to mark the location of each hood hinge to facilitate reinstallation.

1. Disconnect the negative battery cable. Steps 2-13 refer to cars equipped with air conditioning.

2. Remove the two clips on the top of the grille. Remove the screw on the bottom and remove the grille.

3. Loosen the right and left sides of the condenser and tilt it away from the radiator.

4. Remove the air duct from the throttle valve housing.

5. Remove the hose from the air duct to the auxiliary air regulator.

6. Remove the fuel distributor, the air flow sensor, the fuel injectors and the air cleaner as one unit.

NOTE: Leave all fuel lines connected; protect injectors and cold start valve with caps.

7. Remove the front engine mount bolts and remove the mount.

8. Loosen the nuts on the outer half of the crankshaft pulley and remove the V-belt.

9. Discharge the refrigerant.

10. Remove all lines from the compressor and plug all open connections.

11. Remove the crankcase ventilation hose from the valve cover.

12. Move the air conditioning hoses away from the engine.

13. Remove the mounting bolts (2 upper and 3 lower) and remove the compressor.

14. Open the heater control valve all the way (cold position).

15. Remove the cap on the expansion tank and drain the coolant.

16. Remove the upper and lower radiator hoses from the radiator.

17. Disconnect the plug from the radiator fan.

18. Disconnect the plug from the radiator thermoswitch.

19. Remove the radiator complete with the fan and shroud.

20. Disconnect the clutch cable.

21. Tag and disconnect all wiring from the engine.

22. Remove the control pressure regulator (above the oil filter) leaving all the fuel lines connected.

23. Remove the air hose from the back of the alternator if so equipped.

24. Unplug the blue wire from the alternator at the plug located between the battery and the rear of the engine.

25. Remove the charcoal filter hose at the intake air duct.

26. Remove the heater hoses.

27. Remove the throttle cable.

28. Tag and remove all vacuum hoses.

29. Pull out the fuel injectors and remove the cold start valve from the top of the intake manifold.

NOTE: Leave all fuel lines connected; protect the injectors and the cold start valve with caps.

30. Remove the hose running from the auxiliary regulator to the air duct.

31. Remove the three upper engine/transmission bolts.

32. Remove the right and left engine mount nuts.

33. Remove the exhaust pipe attaching bolts from the manifold and remove the exhaust pipe.

34. Remove the cover plate bolts and remove the cover plate.

35. Remove the front engine mount bolts and remove the mount.

36. Tag and disconnect the starter cables and remove the starter.

37. Remove the two lower engine/transmission bolts.

38. Loosen the right and left engine mount nuts on the sub-frame.

39. Remove the bolt from the front exhaust pipe support.

40. Support the transmission.

41. Lift the engine until the weight is taken off of the engine mounts and carefully pry the engine and transmission apart.

42. Remove the engine.

Proceed in the reverse order for installation and note the following:

1. Tighten the engine/transmission bolts to 40 ft. lbs.

2. Tighten the bolt for the front exhaust pipe support to 18 ft. lbs.

3. Tighten the starter bolts to 14 ft. lbs.

4. Hand-tighten the front engine mount bolts.

5. Tighten the front cover plate bolts to 7 ft. lbs.

6. Hand-tighten the right and left engine mount nuts.

7. Tighten the cold start valve bolts, the control pressure regulator bolts and the radiator mounting bolts to 7 ft. lbs.

NOTE: Tighten the engine and subframe mounting bolts while the engine is running at idle. Tighten the front engine mount bolts to 18 ft. lbs. and the right and left engine mount bolts to 25 ft. lbs.

4000 Diesel and Turbodiesel

1. Disconnect the negative battery cable.

2. Remove the engine and transmission cover plates.

3. Open the heater control valve fully and then open the cap on the expansion tank.

4. Drain the coolant.

5. Detach the radiator cowl from the radiator and remove complete with both fans (A/C models only).

6. Remove the grille and then detach the condenser from the radiator (A/C models only).

7. Disconnect the plugs from the fan and the thermoswitch. Remove the radiator with the fan.

8. Disconnect and remove:
   a. fuel supply and return lines from the injection pump
   b. accelerator cable from pump lever and bracket from pump body
   c. cold start cable at pin
   d. wire from fuel shut-off solenoid
   e. gear shift light switch complete with all wiring from the bracket.

9. Tag and disconnect the wiring from the:
   a. oil pressure switch
   b. coolant temperature sensors
   c. glowplugs
   d. thermoswitch.

10. Disconnect the coolant hose.

11. Loosen the clutch cable and unhook it from the clutch lever.

12. Loosen the right and left engine mounts at top.

13. Disconnect the vacuum hose from the vacuum reservoir.

14. Disconnect and remove the alternator.

15. Remove the front engine stop bolts.

16. On models with A/C, remove the front engine stop bolts. Detach the compressor belt after removing the pulley nuts. Remove the top and bottom compressor brackets. Remove the compressor and position it out of the way.

17. Remove the exhaust pipe from the manifold.

18. Disconnect the starter cable and detach it from the intermediate plate.

19. Remove the exhaust pipe from the front transmission support.

20. Remove the starter.

21. Remove the bottom two transmission-to-engine bolts. Remove the flywheel cover plate.

22. Support the transmission with a jack or install transmission support bar VW 785/1B.

23. Attach a lifting apparatus to the engine and raise the engine/transmission until the transmission housing touches the steering rack.

24. Raise the transmission jack or adjust the support bar and then remove the upper three transmission-to-engine bolts.

25. Pry the engine/transmission apart and lift the engine out of the engine compartment.

26. Installation is in the reverse order of removal. Please note the following:
   a. place the intermediate plate on the dowel sleeves and stick it to engine block with grease
   b. place the starter on the engine carrier before installing the engine

---
CAUTION

Do not interchange fuel supply and return pipe union screws. For identification, the fuel return pipe union screw is marked OUT on the screw head.

   c. connect the starter cable so it cannot touch the engine
   d. install the engine mounts free of tension.

27. Tightening torques for installation are as follows:
   a. cover plate-to-transmission/engine—7 ft. lbs.
   b. exhaust pipe-to-transmission—18 ft. lbs.
   c. front engine stop-to-engine block—18 ft. lbs.
   d. stop housing-to-front cross member—18 ft. lbs.
   e. engine mounts—25 ft. lbs.
   f. engine-to-transmission (12 M)—40 ft. lbs.
   g. starter bolts—14 ft. lbs.

5000 (All Models) and 4000 (Coupe and Quattro)

1. Disconnect the negative battery cable.

2. Open the heater control valve all the way (cold position).

3. Remove the cap on the expansion tank and drain the coolant.

4. Remove all radiator and heater hoses. Disconnect the intercooler from the turbocharger on the Quattro.

5. Remove the control pressure regulator.

CAUTION

Do not disconnect any fuel lines.

6. Remove the cold start valve.

7. Pull out the fuel injectors and lay them aside.

NOTE: Protect the fuel injectors and the cold start valve with caps.

8. Loosen the air duct and vacuum hoses from the throttle valve assembly.

9. Remove the air cleaner cover with the filter.

10. Pull the hood latch cable guide off of its bracket.

11. On cars equipped with air conditioning, remove the two clips on the top of the grille and the screw on the bottom and remove the grille, then loosen the condenser mounting bolts and tilt it away from the radiator.

12. Remove the power steering pump leaving the hose connected.

13. Remove the vacuum amplifier.

14. Remove the ignition coil.

15. Remove the EGR control valve.

16. Remove the windshield washer reservoir from its holder.

17. Remove the power steering reservoir from its holder.

18. Remove the distributor cap, the rotor and the ignition wires.

NOTE: Tape the distributor dust cap on to prevent it from falling off.

19. On cars equipped with a manual

transmission, take off the circlip and remove the throttle cable.

20. On cars equipped with an automatic transmission, remove the throttle pushrod.

21. Disconnect the oil pressure and the water temperature senders.

22. On air-conditioned cars, remove the compressor mounting bolts. Leaving the hoses connected, tie back the compressor with wire.

23. Remove the exhaust pipe-to-manifold bolts. On turbocharged models, remove the exhaust pipe-to-wastegate connector.

24. Remove the exhaust pipe support bracket from the transmission.

25. Remove the front engine mount bolts and remove the mount.

26. Tag and disconnect all wires from the starter and remove the starter.

27. Tag and disconnect all wires leading from the alternator and remove the alternator.

28. On cars equipped with an automatic transmission, remove the torque converter mounting bolts from the drive plate. This can be done through the starter hole.

29. Remove the lower engine/transmission bolts.

30. Support the transmission.

31. Remove the upper engine/transmission bolts.

32. Remove the left engine support bracket.

33. Loosen the right engine bracket from the right engine mount.

34. Lift the engine until the V-belt pulley is behind the grille opening.

35. Carefully detach the engine from the transmission.

36. Remove the engine completely, turning it to the right as you lift it out.

Proceed in the reverse order for installation and note the following:

1. Tighten the engine/transmission bolts to 43 ft. lbs.

2. Tighten the bolt for the exhaust pipe support bracket to 22 ft. lbs.

3. Tighten the torque converter-to-drive plate bolts to 4 ft. lbs.

4. Tighten the starter bolts to 14 ft. lbs.

5. Hand tighten all engine mount bolts.

6. Tighten the air conditioner mounting bolt to 29 ft. lbs.

7. Tighten the power steering pump bolts and the control pressure regulator bolts to 14 ft. lbs.

NOTE: Tighten the engine and subframe mounting bolts while the engine is running at idle. Tighten all bolts to 32 ft. lbs. (51 ft. lbs. for Quattro).

5000 Diesel and Turbodiesel

1. Disconnect the negative battery cable.

2. Remove the air cleaner.

3. Remove the cover plates underneath the engine and the transmission.

4. Remove the front grille.

5. Remove the windshield washer reservoir from its holder.

6. Remove the hydraulic fluid reservoir

from its holder.

7. Pull the hood latch cable guide out of its bracket.

8. Remove the cap on the expansion tank and drain the radiator.

9. Remove all radiator and heater hoses.

10. Remove the V-belt for the power steering pump and remove the power steering pump with the hoses connected.

11. On cars equipped with air conditioning, loosen the condenser mounting bolts and tilt it away from the radiator.

12. Remove the auxiliary radiator.

13. Remove the fuel filter and plug the fuel lines.

14. Detach the accelerator cable.

15. Tag and disconnect all electrical wiring coming from the cylinder head.

16. Loosen the fuel return pipe on the injection pump.

17. Disconnect the idle speed control cable from the injection pump lever.

18. Remove the cover plate for the right engine mount.

19. Remove the front engine mount bolts and remove the mount from the crossmember.

20. Tag and disconnect all wiring from the alternator and then remove the alternator and its bracket.

21. Remove the exhaust pipes from the manifold.

22. Remove the exhaust pipe support bracket from the transmission.

23. Tag and disconnect all wiring from the starter and remove the starter.

24. On cars equipped with air conditioning, remove the compressor mounting bolts along with the mount. Leave the hoses connected and tie the compressor out of the way with wire.

25. Remove the lower engine/transmission bolts.

26. Remove the flywheel cover plate from the transmission.

27. Support the transmission.

28. Remove the left engine bracket.

29. Lift the engine/transmission up until the transmission housing touches the steering housing.

30. Remove the upper engine/transmission bolts.

31. Carefully pry the engine/transmission apart.

32. Turn the engine to the right and lift up at the same time.

33. Turn the engine 90 degrees and lift it completely out.

Proceed in the reverse order for installation and note the following:

1. Tighten the engine/transmission bolts to 43 ft. lbs.

2. Tighten all engine mount bolts to 33 ft. lbs.

3. Tighten the exhaust pipe-to-manifold bolts to 22 ft. lbs.

Cylinder Head

NOTE: Before removing or installing the cylinder head, align the engine timing

marks at TDC, then turn the crankshaft mark away about ¼ turn (BTDC). This will prevent the valves from hitting the piston heads. Be sure to turn the crankshaft to the proper position after cylinder head installation.

REMOVAL & INSTALLATION

Fox

1. Disconnect the battery ground cable.

2. Drain the coolant. Disconnect the hoses.

3. Unbolt the exhaust pipe from the manifold.

4. Disconnect the electrical wires. Detach the accelerator linkage.

5. Remove the alternator belt and the timing belt.

6. Loosen the cylinder head bolts in the reverse of the order shown for tightening. Remove the bolts. A metric Allen wrench is required for the head bolts.

—————— CAUTION ——————

Don't loosen the head bolts until the engine is thoroughly cool. Don't loosen the camshaft bearing cap nuts.

7. Remove the head. If it sticks, loosen it by compression or rap it upward with a soft hammer. Do not force anything between the head and block. Check the head for warpage.

—————— CAUTION ——————

Do not attempt to remove the camshaft from the head without checking the "Camshaft Removal and Installation" procedure. Special tools are required.

8. On installation, make sure that the head gasket is installed with the word OBEN up and to the left side of the engine. Put the head in place and install the right front and left rear head bolts first.

9. Tighten the bolts in the sequence shown in four stages until the proper torque is reached. The bolts should be torqued again after the first 300 miles.

10. On overhaul, valve guides must be pressed out or in from above. The cylinder head must be heated to 176–212°F in an oil bath or an oven to install new valve guides.

NOTE: New cylinder head bolts and a new, soft head gasket are available to correct coolant leakage problems. The new bolts are marked 12.9 and should be torqued to normal specifications. Anytime there is a leakage problem, both the head and block should be checked for warpage.

NOTE: Later model Fox cars come equipped with a new type head bolt. These bolts have a 12 point recessed "polygon" head. The manufacturer states that these bolts require no retorquing during their service life. These bolts may be used as replacements on older engines, but only in complete sets.

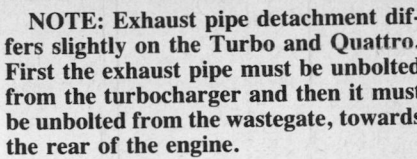
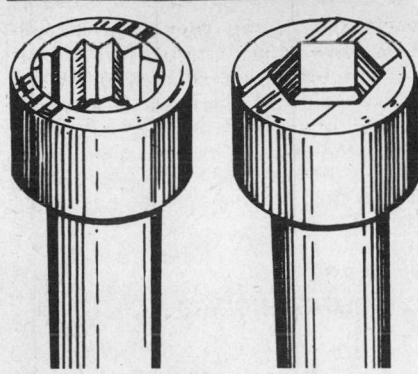

Left, new style, right old style Fox head bolts

11. Make sure to align the timing belt and sprockets as explained under "Timing Belt Removal and Installation."

— CAUTION —

Do not attempt to start the engine until you are sure of this alignment.

4000 and 5000
GASOLINE ENGINES

NOTE: Cylinder head removal should not be attempted unless the engine is cold.

1. Disconnect the negative battery cable.
2. Drain the cooling system.
3. Disconnect the air duct from the throttle valve assembly on all models except the Turbo and Quattro. On the Turbo and Quattro, remove the hose which runs between the air duct and the turbocharger.
4. Disconnect the throttle cable from the throttle valve assembly.
5. Remove the air duct for the injector cooling fan on the Turbo and Quattro.
6. Clean and remove the fuel injectors and all other fuel lines.

NOTE: Protect the fuel injectors and the cold start valve with caps.

7. Tag and disconnect all vacuum and PCV lines.
8. Remove the hose which runs from the intake manifold to the turbocharger on the Turbo and Quattro.
9. Tag and disconnect all electrical lines leading to the cylinder head.
10. Unbolt and remove the intake manifold.
11. Disconnect all radiator and heater hoses where they are attached to the cylinder head. Position them out of the way.
12. Tag and remove all spark plug wires and then remove the spark plugs.
13. For all models but the 4000, remove the distributor. To aid in reinstallation, scribe a mark on the body of the distributor and the cylinder head.
14. Unbolt and separate the exhaust manifold from the exhaust pipe.

NOTE: Exhaust pipe detachment differs slightly on the Turbo and Quattro. First the exhaust pipe must be unbolted from the turbocharger and then it must be unbolted from the wastegate, towards the rear of the engine.

15. Disconnect the EGR valve and the oxygen sensor (if so equipped) from the exhaust manifold.
16. Remove the heat deflector shield on the 4000 models.
17. Unbolt and remove the oil lines (2) from the turbocharger.
18. Unbolt and remove the exhaust manifold.

NOTE: When removing the exhaust manifold on the Turbo and Quattro, the manifold, turbocharger and wastegate should all be removed as one unit.

19. Remove the air hose cover from the back of the alternator (if so equipped) on the 4000.
20. Tag and disconnect all wires coming from the back of the alternator and then remove the alternator and the V-belt.
21. Disconnect and plug the hoses coming from the power steering pump (if so equipped).
22. Remove the power steering pump and the V-belt (if so equipped).
23. Remove the drive belt cover and the drive belt.
24. Remove the cylinder head cover.
25. Loosen the cylinder head bolts in the reverse order of the tightening sequence.
26. Remove the bolts and lift the cylinder head straight off.

— CAUTION —

If the head sticks, loosen it by compression or rap it upward with a soft rubber mallet. Do not force anything between the head and the engine block to pry it upward; this may result in serious damage.

27. Clean the cylinder head and engine block mating surfaces thoroughly and then install the new gasket without any sealing compound. Make sure the words TOP or OBEN are facing up when the gasket is installed.
28. Place the cylinder head on the engine block and install bolts No. 8 and 10 first. These holes are smaller and will properly locate the gasket and the head on the engine block.
29. Install the remaining bolts. Tighten them in three stages as follows; Step 1: 29 ft. lbs. Step 2: 43 ft. lbs. Step 3: Tighten ½ turn more (180°).

— CAUTION —

Do not retorque the cylinder head bolts at the 1000 mile maintenance nor at the 1000 mile interval following repairs.

30. Installation of all other components is in the reverse order of removal.

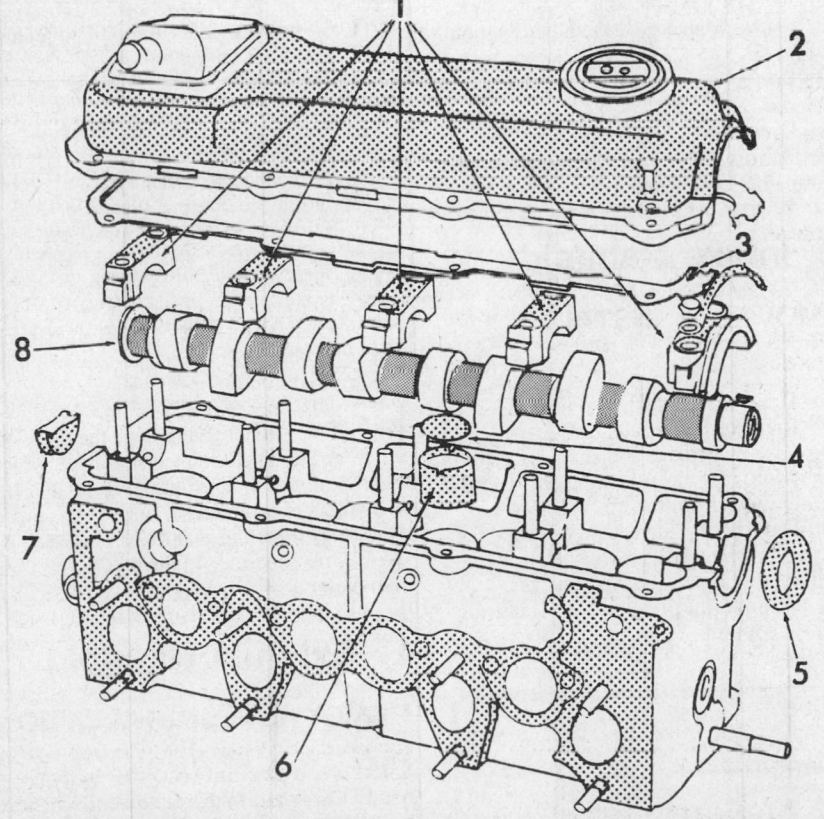

1. Camshaft bearing caps	3. Gasket	5. Oil seal	7. End plug
2. Camshaft cover	4. Valve adjusting disc	6. Cam follower	8. Camshaft

Exploded view of the Fox cylinder head—4000 similar

DIESEL ENGINES

NOTE: Cylinder head removal should not be attempted unless the engine is cold.

1. Disconnect the negative battery cable.
2. Drain the cooling system.
3. Remove the air cleaner.
4. Clean and disconnect the fuel (injector) lines.
5. Tag and disconnect all electrical wires and leads.
6. Disconnect and plug all lines coming from the brake booster vacuum pump and remove the pump.
7. Disconnect the air supply tubes (Turbo Diesels only) and then unbolt and remove the intake manifold.
8. Disconnect and plug all lines coming from the power steering pump and remove the pump and V-belt (if so equipped).
9. Disconnect and remove the oil supply and return lines from the turbocharger (if applicable).
10. Remove the exhaust manifold heat shields (if so equipped).
11. Separate the exhaust pipe from the exhaust manifold or turbocharger and then remove the manifold.

NOTE: On Turbodiesels, the exhaust manifold is removed with the turbocharger and wastegate still attached.

12. Disconnect all radiator and heater hoses where they are attached to the cylinder head and position them out of the way.
13. Remove the drive belt cover and the drive belt.
14. Remove the injection pump belt cover and remove the belt.
15. Remove the PCV hose.
16. Remove the cylinder head cover.
17. Loosen the cylinder head bolts in the reverse order of the tightening sequence shown in the illustration (gas engines).
18. Remove the bolts and lift the cylinder head straight off.

─────── CAUTION ───────
If the head sticks, loosen it by compression or rap it upward with a soft rubber mallet. Do not force anything between the head and the engine block to pry it upward; this may result in serious damage.

19. Clean the cylinder head and engine block mating surfaces thoroughly and then install the new gasket without any sealing compound. Make sure the words TOP or OBEN are facing up when the gasket is installed.

NOTE: Depending upon piston height above the top surface of the engine block, there are three gaskets of different thicknesses which can be used. Be sure that the new gasket has the same number of notches and the same identifying number as the one being replaced.

20. Place the cylinder head on the engine block and install bolts No. 8 and 10 first. These holes are smaller and will properly locate the gasket and the head on the engine block.
21. Install the remaining bolts. Tighten them in three stages as follows; Step 1: 29 ft. lbs. Step 2: 43 ft. lbs. Step 3: Tighten ½ turn more (180°).
22. Installation of all other components is in the reverse order of removal.
23. After reassembly, start the engine and let it run until it reaches normal operating temperature (when the radiator fan switches on). Stop the engine, remove the cylinder head cover and tighten the head bolts an additional ¼ turn (90°), following the tightening sequence.

─────── CAUTION ───────
On all diesel engines using M12, 12 point cylinder head bolts, never reinstall old bolts. Always replace cylinder head bolts.

24. After about 1000 miles, remove the cylinder head cover and retighten the cylinder head bolts, turning the bolts in sequence ¼ turn (90°) WITHOUT loosening them first. This is done one bolt at a time, in the proper sequence, without interruption.

OVERHAUL

For all cylinder head overhaul procedures, please refer to "Engine Rebuilding" in the Unit Repair section.

Intake Manifold

REMOVAL & INSTALLATION

Fox

1. Drain the coolant.
2. Remove the air cleaner.
3. Disconnect the coolant hoses from the manifold and the automatic choke. Remove the wire from the electric choke.
4. Disconnect the vacuum hose and the lead to the idle cutoff valve. Detach the fuel line and the accelerator linkage.
5. Remove the manifold nuts and the manifold support.

6. Pull the manifold off the studs. If it sticks, rap it lightly with a rubber mallet. Do not force anything between the manifold and the cylinder head. Discard the gaskets.
7. Installation is the reverse of the removal procedure. New gaskets must be used. Tighten the nuts to 18 ft. lbs. After refilling the cooling system, start the engine and check for leaks.

4000 and 5000
GASOLINE ENGINES

1. Disconnect the negative battery cable.
2. Drain the cooling system.
3. Disconnect the air duct from the throttle valve assembly on all normally aspirated models. On turbocharged models, remove the hose which runs between the air duct and the turbocharger.
4. Disconnect the throttle cable from the throttle valve assembly.
5. Remove the air duct for the injector cooling fan on the Turbo.
6. Clean and remove the fuel injectors.
7. Disconnect the cold start valve.

NOTE: Protect the fuel injectors and the cold start valve with caps.

8. Tag and disconnect all vacuum and PCV lines.
9. Tag and disconnect all electrical lines leading to the cylinder head.
10. Remove the hose which runs from the intake manifold to the turbocharger (intercooler on the Quattro) on the Turbo.
11. Remove the auxiliary air regulator.
12. Remove the manifold.
13. Installation is in the reverse order of removal.

DIESEL ENGINES

1. Disconnect the negative battery cable.
2. Drain the cooling system.
3. Disconnect the hose that runs between the air duct and the turbocharger (Turbo Diesel only).
4. Remove the air cleaner.
5. Disconnect and plug all lines coming from the brake booster vacuum pump and remove the pump.
6. Disconnect the PCV line.
7. Disconnect and remove the blow-off valve and then disconnect the hose which runs from the intake manifold to the turbocharger (Turbo Diesel only).
8. Remove the manifold.
9. Installation is in the reverse order of removal.

Exhaust Manifold

REMOVAL & INSTALLATION

Fox

1. Disconnect the heated air intake hose from the manifold.
2. Unbolt the exhaust pipe from the manifold.
3. Remove the sheet metal cover.

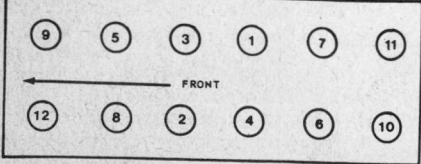

Torque sequence for all 5 cylinder engines

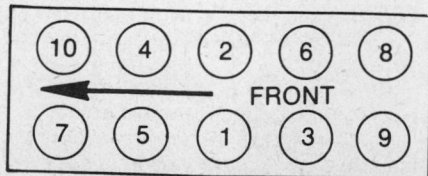

Torque sequence for all 4 cylinder engines

4. Remove the manifold nuts. Pull the manifold off of the studs. If it sticks, rap it lightly with a rubber mallet. Do not force anything between the manifold and the cylinder head. Discard the gaskets.

5. Installation is the reverse of the removal procedure. New gaskets must be used. If the gaskets are the type with round openings, they must be installed with the beaded side outward from the head and the notched edge down. Gaskets with oval openings must be installed with the beaded edge outward from the head. Tighten the manifold nuts to the specified torque. Torque the front exhaust pipe flange nuts to 18–22 ft. lbs. in steps. A new gasket should also be used between the exhaust pipe and the manifold.

4000 and 5000
ALL EXCEPT TURBO, QUATTRO AND TURBODIESELS

Although it is not imperative to remove the intake manifold in order to remove the exhaust manifold, you may find that it makes everything more accessible.

1. Unbolt and separate the exhaust pipe from the exhaust manifold.

2. Disconnect the EGR valve and the oxygen sensor (if so equipped) from the manifold.

3. Remove the heat deflector shield on the 4000.

4. Disconnect the CO probe receptacle tube (if so equipped).

5. Remove the manifold.

6. Installation is in the reverse order of removal.

NOTE: Always replace old gaskets.

TURBO, QUATTRO AND TURBODIESELS

1. Remove the hose which runs between the air duct and the turbocharger.

2. If the intake manifold has not been removed, disconnect the hose which runs from the intake manifold to the turbocharger or intercooler.

3. Unbolt the exhaust pipe from the turbocharger.

4. Unbolt the exhaust pipe from the wastegate on the rear of the manifold (gasoline engines only).

5. Disconnect the EGR valve and the oxygen sensor from the manifold on gasoline engined models.

6. Remove the oil lines (2) from the turbocharger.

7. Remove the line from the bottom of the turbocharger to the intercooler (Quattro only).

NOTE: The manifold, the turbocharger and the wastegate can all be removed as one unit.

8. Remove the manifold.

9. Installation is in the reverse order of removal.

Turbocharger

For more information on turbochargers, please refer to "Turbocharging"in the Unit Repair section.

REMOVAL & INSTALLATION
Except 5000 Turbo

1. Removal of the intake manifold (as detailed earlier) is not absolutely necessary but will greatly aid in the accessibility of all related nuts and bolts.

2. Loosen the hose clamps and remove the hose which leads to the intake manifold or intercooler.

3. Loosen the hose clamps and remove the hose which leads to the air cleaner.

4. Unbolt the oil supply (upper) and return (lower) lines and position them out of the way.

5. Remove the exhaust pipe mounting nuts and pull the exhaust pipe away from the turbocharger.

6. Remove the turbocharger mounting nuts and pull the turbocharger off of the exhaust manifold.

7. Installation is in the reverse order of removal. Note the following:

   a. Use new gaskets.

   b. Tighten the turbocharger-to-exhaust manifold bolts to 43 ft. lbs. (33 ft. lbs. on 4000 Turbodiesel). Coat bolt threads with high temperature grease before installation.

   c. Tighten the turbocharger-to-exhaust pipe bolts to 18–29 ft. lbs.

5000 Turbo

1. Disconnect the negative battery cable. If the battery interferes with space requirements, remove from car.

2. Spray all mounting bolts with a rust solvent.

3. Remove any components that are in the way (grille etc.).

4. Remove the vacuum tube between the intake air boot and turbocharger.

5. Remove the intake boot and crankcase ventilation hose. Remove the hose assembly between the intake manifold and throttle housing.

6. Remove the air filter housing cover.

7. Remove the engine mount heat shield.

8. Remove the oil supply pipe from the turbocharger. Remove the exhaust pipe from the corrugated pipe and loosen the exhaust pipe at the transmission mount and catalytic converter.

9. Remove the retaining clamp from the starter housing and sensor air hose.

10. Remove the exhaust pipe from the turbocharger.

11. Remove the alternator support bolt and position the alternator to the side.

12. Remove the oil return pipe from the turbocharger. Remove mounting bolts and turbocharger.

13. Install in reverse order.

NOTE: Always change the oil and oil filter after turbocharger service.

Turbocharger Wastegate

REMOVAL & INSTALLATION
Turbo and Quattro

1. As suggested in the turbocharger removal procedure, intake manifold removal is a prudent idea for wastegate accessibility.

2. Remove the wastegate-to-exhaust pipe connecting tube (three bolts top and three bolts bottom).

3. Remove the mounting bolt for the tube leading from the wastegate to the exhaust manifold.

4. Remove the vacuum line from the end of the wastegate.

5. Remove the four mounting bolts and remove the wastegate from the exhaust manifold.

6. Installation is in the reverse order of removal.

Turbodiesels

The wastegate on the 4 cylinder engine is a press–fit and cannot be removed. The wastegate on the 5 cylinder engine is removed by disconnecting the air hose and then unbolting it from the turbocharger itself.

Timing Belt Cover

REMOVAL & INSTALLATION
Fox and 4000 (4 Cylinder)

1. Loosen the alternator adjusting bolts. Pivot the alternator over and slip the V-belt off.

2. If equipped with air conditioning, loosen the compressor mounting bolts and slip off the V-belt.

3. Unscrew the retaining nuts and remove the upper timing belt cover. Take care not to lose any of the washers or spacers.

4. Using the large bolt on the crankshaft sprocket, turn the engine until the No. 1 cylinder is at TDC of the compression stroke. At this point, both of the valves will be closed and the 0 mark on the flywheel will be aligned with the pointer on the clutch housing.

5. Unscrew the crankshaft pulley retaining bolts (4) and then loosen the crankshaft sprocket bolt.

NOTE: To remove the crankshaft sprocket bolt, you will need a friend. Put the car in 4th gear and apply the brake, this will enable you to loosen the bolt.

6. Remove the crankshaft pulley.

7. Unscrew the water pump pulley retaining bolts (3) and remove the pulley.

8. Unscrew the retaining nuts and re-

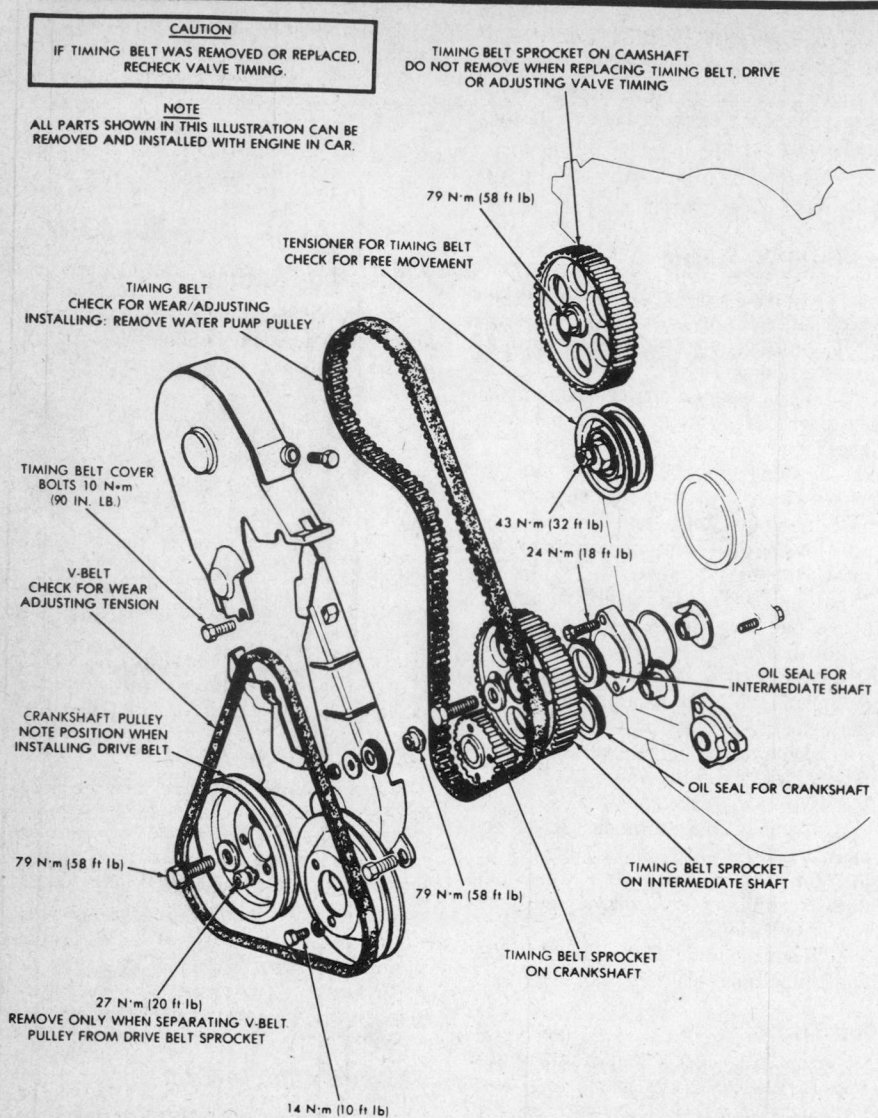

> **CAUTION**
> IF TIMING BELT WAS REMOVED OR REPLACED, RECHECK VALVE TIMING.

> **NOTE**
> ALL PARTS SHOWN IN THIS ILLUSTRATION CAN BE REMOVED AND INSTALLED WITH ENGINE IN CAR.

TIMING BELT SPROCKET ON CAMSHAFT
DO NOT REMOVE WHEN REPLACING TIMING BELT, DRIVE OR ADJUSTING VALVE TIMING

79 N·m (58 ft lb)

TENSIONER FOR TIMING BELT
CHECK FOR FREE MOVEMENT

TIMING BELT
CHECK FOR WEAR/ADJUSTING
INSTALLING: REMOVE WATER PUMP PULLEY

TIMING BELT COVER
BOLTS 10 N·m (90 IN. LB.)

V-BELT
CHECK FOR WEAR
ADJUSTING TENSION

CRANKSHAFT PULLEY
NOTE POSITION WHEN
INSTALLING DRIVE BELT

79 N·m (58 ft lb)

27 N·m (20 ft lb)
REMOVE ONLY WHEN SEPARATING V-BELT
PULLEY FROM DRIVE BELT SPROCKET

14 N·m (10 ft lb)

43 N·m (32 ft lb)
24 N·m (18 ft lb)

OIL SEAL FOR
INTERMEDIATE SHAFT

OIL SEAL FOR CRANKSHAFT

TIMING BELT SPROCKET
ON INTERMEDIATE SHAFT

79 N·m (58 ft lb)

TIMING BELT SPROCKET
ON CRANKSHAFT

4 cylinder engine—timing belt drive components and gear alignment

REMOVAL & INSTALLATION

Fox

1. Remove the grille.
2. Remove the alternator belt and the timing belt cover.
3. Loosen the belt tensioner locknut and turn the tensioner counterclockwise (facing it) to release the belt tension.

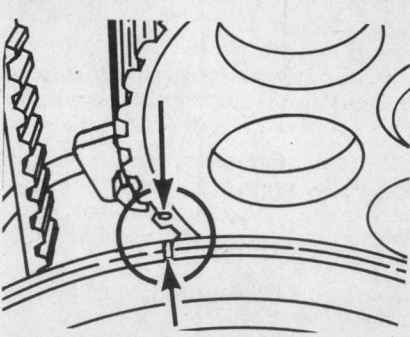

Crankshaft pulley and intermediate shaft sprocket alignment on the Fox and 4000

4. Slide the belt off the camshaft sprocket.
5. Belt installation is easier if the water pump pulley is removed.
6. Set the flywheel timing mark at TDC (0°T).
7. Make sure that the camshaft is positioned so that the No. 4 cylinder valves are overlapping; i.e. the exhaust valve is opening and the intake closing. If there is a punch mark on the back of the camshaft sprocket, align it with the camshaft cover gasket (left side).
8. Turn the intermediate shaft so that the distributor rotor points to the No. 1 cylinder mark on the rim of the distributor body. If there is a notch on the crankshaft pulley, it should now align with the punch mark on the front of the intermediate shaft sprocket.
9. Taking care not to disturb any of the three sprockets, install the timing belt.

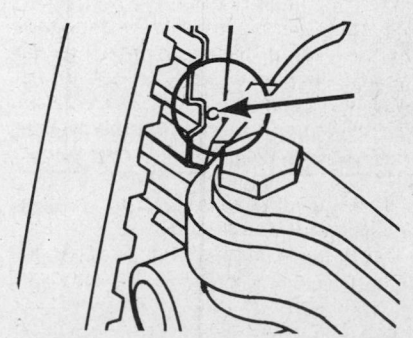

Camshaft sprocket alignment on the Fox and 4000

NOTE: Special tools are available, which can be used to hold the sprockets

---

move the lower timing belt cover. Take care not to lose any of the washers or spacers.

9. Installation is in the reverse order of removal.

4000 (5 Cylinder), 5000, Turbo and Quattro

1. Loosen the alternator adjusting bolts and remove the V-belt.
2. Loosen the power steering pump adjusting bolts and remove the V-belt (if so equipped).
3. If equipped with air conditioning, loosen the compressor adjusting bolts and remove the V-belt.
4. Unscrew the retaining nuts and remove the timing belt cover. Take care not to lose any of the washers or spacers.
5. Installation is in the reverse order of removal.

4000 and 5000 Diesel and Turbo-diesel

There are two drive belts on the 5000 Die-

sels; one at the front of the engine and one at the rear, therefore there are two covers to remove. The front cover on all models is removed in the same manner as the gasoline engined 5000's with two exceptions, the cover has an upper and a lower half. To remove the upper half, follow the procedure for the 5000 above. To remove the lower half, use the following procedure.

1. Remove the upper cover.
2. Unscrew the crankshaft pulley retaining bolts and remove the pulley.
3. Unscrew the retaining nuts and remove the lower cover.
4. Installation is in the reverse order of removal.

To remove the rear timing belt cover on 5000 Diesels, use the following procedure.

1. Remove the outside half of the vacuum pump pulley and remove the V-belt.
2. Unscrew the retaining bolts and remove the rear timing belt cover. Take care not to lose any of the washers or spacers.
3. Installation is in the reverse order of removal.

in alignment. It can also be used to check alignment on early engines which do not have the punch mark on the back of the camshaft sprocket and the notch on the crankshaft sprocket.

10. Recheck that the No. 1 (and 4) cylinder is at TDC, that the camshaft is in the No. 4 cylinder overlap position, and that the distributor rotor is in the No. 1 cylinder firing position.

11. Turn the belt tensioner clockwise (facing it) until it is just possible to turn the longest span of belt about 90°. Lock the tensioner in place.

NOTE: It is not necessary to recheck the belt tension during the normal life span of the belt (about 60,000 miles).

12. Again recheck the alignment as in Step 10 and replace the belt cover, water pump pulley, alternator belt, and grille. Check the ignition timing when the job is complete.

4000 (4 Cylinder)

1. Remove the upper and lower timing belt covers.

2. While holding the large hex nut on the tensioner pulley, loosen the smaller pulley lock nut.

3. Turn the tensioner counterclockwise to relieve the tension on the timing belt.

4. Carefully slide the timing belt off of the three sprockets and remove the belt.

5. Using the large bolt on the crankshaft sprocket, turn the engine until the No. 1 cylinder is at TDC of the compression stroke. At this point, both valves will be closed and the 0 mark on the flywheel will be aligned with the pointer on the clutch housing.

6. Check that the timing mark on the rear face of the camshaft sprocket is aligned with the upper edge of the rear timing belt cover. If it's not, turn the sprocket until they align.

7. Replace the crankshaft pulley and check that the notch on the pulley is aligned with the mark on the intermediate shaft sprocket. If not, turn them until they align.

— CAUTION —
If the timing marks are not correctly aligned with the No. 1 piston at TDC of the compression stroke and the belt is installed, valve timing will be incorrect. Poor performance and possible engine damage can result from the improper valve timing.

8. Remove the crankshaft pulley. Observe its location on the crankshaft sprocket so that it can be replaced in the same position. Hold the large nut on the tensioner pulley and loosen the smaller locknut. Turn the tensioner counterclockwise to loosen and remove the belt.

9. Slide the timing belt back onto the sprockets and check for the proper tension (see "Tension Adjustment").

10. Installation is in the reverse order of removal.

4000 (5 Cylinder), 5000, Turbo and Quattro

1. Remove the alternator and air conditioning compressor from their mounting brackets and position them out of the way.

2. Remove the front cover bolts and lift off the cover.

3. Loosen the water pump bolts and turn the pump clockwise.

4. Slide the drive belt off the sprockets.

5. Turn the camshaft until the notch on the back of the sprocket is in line with the left side edge of the camshaft housing flange.

6. Align the TDC "0" mark on the flywheel with the lug cast on the clutch housing.

V-belt pulley alignment on the 5000

7. Install the drive belt and turn the water pump counterclockwise to tighten the belt. Tighten the water pump bolts to 14 ft. lbs.

NOTE: The belt is correctly tensioned when it can be twisted 90° with the thumb and index finger along the straight run between the camshaft sprocket and the water pump.

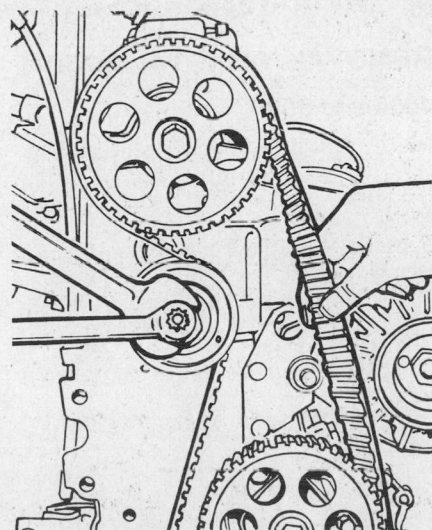

The timing belt on all models is correctly tensioned when it can be twisted 90° with the thumb and forefinger

8. Install the front cover and tighten the bolts to 7 ft. lbs.

9. Install the alternator and compressor and tighten the belts. These belts are correctly tensioned when they can be depressed ⅜ along their longest straight run.

4000 Diesel and Turbodiesel

NOTE: This procedure will require a number of special tools and a certain expertise with diesel engines.

1. Remove the timing belt cover. Remove the cylinder head cover.

2. Turn the engine so that No. 1 cylinder is at TDC and fix the camshaft in position with tool 2065A. Align the tool as follows:
—turn the camshaft until one end of the tool touches the cylinder head
—measure the gap at the other end of the tool with a feeler gauge
—take half of the measurement and insert a feeler gauge of this thickness between the tool and the cylinder head; turn the camshaft so that the tool rests on the feeler gauge
—insert a second feeler gauge of the same thickness between the other end of the tool and the cylinder head.

3. Lock the injection pump sprocket in position with pin 2064.

4. Check that the marks on the sprocket, bracket and pump body are in alignment (engine at TDC).

5. Loosen the timing belt tensioner. Remove the V-belt from the crankshaft.

6. Remove the timing belt.

To install:

7. Check that the TDC mark on the flywheel is aligned with the reference marks.

8. Loosen the camshaft sprocket bolt ½ turn and then loosen the gear from the camshaft end by tapping it with a rubber mallet.

9. Install the timing belt and remove pin 2064 from the injection pump sprocket.

10. Tension the belt by turning the tensioner to the right. Check the belt tension as detailed later in the section.

11. Tighten the camshaft sprocket bolt to 33 ft. lbs.

12. Remove the tool from the camshaft.

13. Turn the crankshaft two turns in the direction of engine rotation (clockwise) and then strike the belt once with a rubber mallet between the camshaft sprocket and the injection pump sprocket.

14. Check the belt tension again. Check the injection pump timing.

5000 Diesel and Turbodiesel

NOTE: This procedure will require the use of a number of special tools.

1. Remove all V-belts on the front of the engine.

2. Remove the outside half of the vacuum pump pulley and remove the V-belt.

3. Remove the front timing belt covers.

4. Remove the rear timing belt cover.

5. Remove the cylinder head cover.

6. Using the large bolt on the crankshaft sprocket, turn the engine until the No. 1 cylinder is at TDC of the compression stroke. At this point, both of the valves will be closed and the mark on the flywheel will be aligned with the pointer on the clutch housing.

7. Align the marks on the injection pump sprocket mounting plate.

8. Using special tool 2064 (a pin), lock the injection pump sprocket in place so that it cannot move and change the valve timing.

9. Using special tool 3036, hold the remaining (inside) half of the vacuum pump pulley and the injection pump drive sprocket in place. Remove the center retaining bolt and take off the pulley half and the drive sprocket along with the timing belt.

10. Using special tool 2084 to hold the crankshaft pulley in place, attach special tool 2079 to a ratchet and *loosen* the crankshaft pulley center bolt.

11. Attach special tool 2065A to the rear of the camshaft so that it will not move and alter the valve timing.

12. Loosen the adjusting bolts (2) on the water pump and turn it counterclockwise to relieve the tension on the timing belt.

13. Unbolt and remove the crankshaft pulley and slide the timing belt off of the sprockets.

To install the front timing belt:

14. Check that the No. 1 cylinder is still at TDC and the mark on the flywheel is still aligned with the pointer on the clutch housing.

15. Loosen the camshaft sprocket bolt approximately 1 turn and lightly tap the gear loose from the camshaft with a rubber mallet.

16. Install the timing belt and check the tension (see "Tension Adjustment").

17. Tighten the camshaft sprocket bolt to 33 ft. lbs. and remove special tool 2065A.

To install the rear timing belt:

18. Install the injection pump drive sprocket along with the timing belt.

19. Check that the No. 1 cylinder is still at TDC.

20. Tighten the injection pump drive sprocket retaining bolt until it is just possible to turn the sprocket by hand.

21. Check for proper tension (see "Tension Adjustment").

22. Retighten the retaining bolt to 7 ft. lbs.

23. Attach the rear timing belt cover and the outside half of the vacuum pump pulley along with the V-belt and check for proper tension.

24. Remove special tool 2064 from the injection pump.

25. Check the injection timing, and adjust if necessary.

26. Installation of the remaining components is in the reverse order of removal.

TENSION ADJUSTMENT

4000 (4 Cylinder)

1. Holding the large bolt on the tensioner pulley, loosen the small nut and turn the tensioner clockwise to tighten and counterclockwise to loosen.

2. The belt is correctly tensioned when it can be twisted 90 degrees with the thumb and forefinger, midway between the camshaft and the intermediate shaft drive sprockets.

4000 (5 Cylinder), 5000, Turbo and Quattro

1. Loosen the water pump adjusting bolts (2) and turn the pump clockwise to tighten and counterclockwise to loosen.

2. The belt is correctly tensioned when it can be twisted 90 degrees with the thumb and forefinger, midway between the camshaft drive sprocket and the water pump.

4000 and 5000 Diesel and Turbo Diesel

NOTE: Special tool VW210 will be required for this procedure.

Tension adjustment on the front timing belt is performed in the same manner as with the other four or five cylinder engines. Deflection is also checked in the same position, but with the special tool VW210 rather than your fingers. Proper tension is achieved when the scale reads 12–13.

Tension on the rear timing belt (5 cyl. engines only) is also checked with VW210, in between the two drive sprockets. The scale should read between 12 and 13. To adjust the tension, loosen the injection pump mounting bracket bolts and move the pump toward the engine to loosen and away from the engine to tighten.

Timing Gears

REMOVAL & INSTALLATION

4000 and 5000

All of the drive sprockets are located by keys on their respective shafts (with the exception of certain diesel engine camshaft sprockets which are a taper fit or crankshaft sprockets which have a built-in lug) and each is retained by a bolt. To remove any or all of the sprockets, first remove the timing belt covers and belts and then use the following procedure.

1. Remove the center retaining bolt for the particular drive sprocket.

2. Gently pry the sprocket off of the shaft.

3. If the sprocket is stubborn in coming off, use a gear puller. *Don't hammer on the sprocket as you may crack it.*

NOTE: On certain 4 cylinder diesel engine camshafts, loosen the center bolt 1 turn and then tap the rear of the sprocket

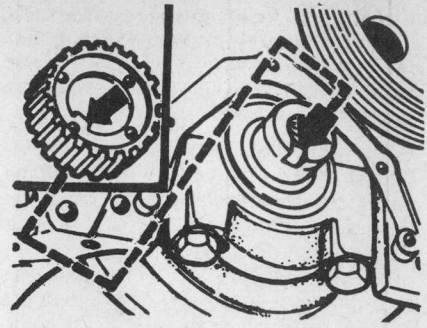

Various late models have the crankshaft pulley locating lug contained by the pulley

with a rubber mallet. When the sprocket loosens, remove the bolt and sprocket.

4. Remove the sprocket being careful not to lose the key.

5. Installation is in the reverse order of removal.

NOTE: Always check valve timing after removing the drive sprockets.

Camshaft

REMOVAL & INSTALLATION

100

Fox and 4000 (4 Cyl.)—All Engines

NOTE: The manufacturer says that the Fox camshaft must not be removed unless a special removal tool is used. This device bolts to the cylinder head and presses down on the camshaft at two places: between the lobes for cylinder 3 and between the lobes for cylinder 2. The following alternate procedure may be used, but great caution must be exercised. THE ALTERNATE PROCEDURE IS NOT RECOMMENDED BY Audi (for the Fox).

1. Remove the timing belt.

2. Remove the PCV line.

3. Remove the cylinder head cover.

4. Remove the camshaft drive sprocket.

5. Unscrew and remove the Nos. 1, 3 and 5 bearing caps (No. 1 is at the front of the engine).

6. Diagonally loosen bearing caps Nos. 2 and 4.

7. Remove the camshaft from the cylinder head.

8. Remove the camshaft journals, lobes, bearing shells and the contact faces of the caps with assembly lube or gear oil before reinstallation.

9. Replace the camshaft oil seal. If necessary, replace the end plug also.

10. Install the Nos. 1, 3 and 5 bearing caps and tighten the nuts to 14 ft. lbs.

NOTE: Tighten the bearing caps diagonally. Observe off center bearing position; numbers on bearing caps are not always on the same side.

11. Install the Nos. 2 and 4 bearing caps and tighten the nuts to 14 ft. lbs.

12. Replace the seal in the No. 1 bearing cap.

13. Installation of the remaining components is in the reverse order of removal.

NOTE: Always recheck the valve clearance after the camshaft has been removed.

4000 (5 Cylinder), 5000, Turbo and Quattro

1. Remove the camshaft cover.

2. Remove the drive belt and camshaft sprocket.

3. Remove bearing caps 2 and 4.

4. Diagonally loosen bearing caps 1 and 3.

5. Lift out the camshaft.

6. When installing, lightly oil the camshaft and bearings with clean engine oil.

7. Position the caps on the same journals from which they were removed.

8. Lightly tighten the nuts of caps 2 and 4.

9. Tighten all nuts to 14 ft. lbs.

10. Install the drive belt and sprocket and the camshaft cover. The sprocket bolt is torqued to 58 ft. lbs.; the cover bolts to 7 ft. lbs.

5000 Diesel and Turbodiesel

1. Remove the front and rear timing belts.

2. Remove the cylinder head cover.

3. Remove the camshaft drive sprocket.

4. Remove the injection pump drive sprocket.

5. Set cylinder No. 1 to TDC of the compression stroke.

6. Remove bearing cap Nos. 1 and 4.

7. Diagonally loosen bearing cap Nos. 2 and 3 and remove.

8. Remove the camshaft from the cylinder head.

9. Lubricate the camshaft journals, lobes, bearing shells and the contact faces of the caps with assembly lube or gear oil before reinstallation.

10. Replace both camshaft oil seals.

NOTE: The cam lobes for the No. 1 cylinder must face upward.

11. Install bearing caps Nos. 2 and 3, tightening alternately and diagonally.

12. Install bearing caps Nos. 1 and 4.

13. Replace the seal in the No. 1 bearing cap.

14. Installation of the remaining components is in the reverse order of removal.

NOTE: Always recheck the valve clearance after the camshaft has been removed.

Pistons and Connecting Rods

REMOVAL & INSTALLATION

Gasoline Engines

1. Follow the instructions under "Timing Belt" and "Cylinder Head" removal.

2. Remove the oil pan.

3. Turn the crankshaft until the piston to be removed is at the bottom of its travel.

4. Make sure the connecting rod and cap are marked for reference as to cylinder location and position match (scribe across the rod end and cap so that the cap will be installed in mating position). Mark the piston heads from front to back, in order, for reinstallation identification.

5. Place a rag down the cylinder bore on the head of the piston to be removed. Remove the cylinder ridge and carbon deposits with a ridge reamer; following instructions of the reamer's manufacturer.

——————— CAUTION ———————

Do not cut too deeply or remove more than 1/32 inch from the ring travel area when removing the ridge.

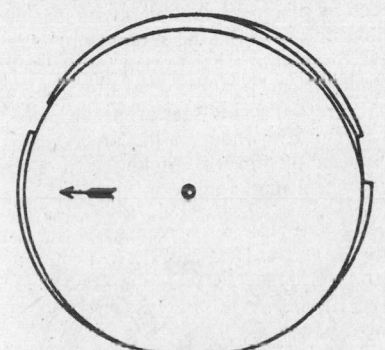

Arrow on pistons must face forward

6. Remove the rag and metal cuttings from the cylinder bore. Remove the connecting rod cap and bearing insert.

7. Push the connecting rod up the bore slightly and remove the upper bearing insert.

8. Push the connecting rod and piston assembly up and out of the cylinder with a wooden hammer handle.

9. Wipe any dirt or oil from the connecting rod bearing saddle and rod cap. Install the bearing inserts (if to be reused) in the connecting rod and cap. Install the cap and secure with rod bolts.

10. Remove the rest of the rod and piston assemblies in a like manner.

11. Lubricate the piston, rings and cylinder wall. Install and lubricate the upper bearing insert. Install a piston ring compressor over the rings and top of the piston; be sure the piston ring ends are staggered. Lower the piston and rod assembly into the cylinder bore with the arrow on the piston head facing the front of the engine. When the ring compressor contacts the top of the

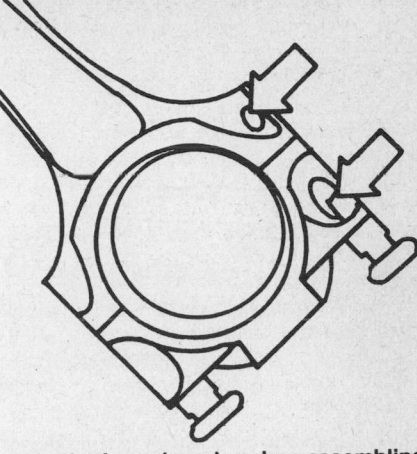

Align the forged marks when assembling the connecting rods and caps

engine block, use a wooden hammer handle to tap the piston into the box.

NOTE: If unusual resistance is encountered when starting the piston into the cylinder bore, it is possible that a ring slipped out of the compressor and is caught at the top of the cylinder. Remove the piston and reinstall compressor.

Guide the connecting rod down the cylinder bore and over the crankshaft journal taking care not to score the wall or shaft. Install the lower bearing insert into the connecting rod cap. Lubricate the insert and mount the cap on the rod with match marks aligned. Install the rod bolts and tighten to specifications.

NOTE: 1.8L engines using rod bolts with a smooth surface between threads and short knurled shank and having a round head containing six notches are stretch type bolts and cannot be reused. Always use new bolts when servicing.

12. Install the remaining piston and rod assemblies in a like manner, turning the crankshaft each time so the crank journal of the piston being installed is at the bottom of travel.

Diesel Engines

The same installation procedures apply to the diesel as to the gas engine. However, whenever new pistons or a short block are installed, the piston projection must be checked.

A spacer (Tool 385/17) and bar with a micrometer are necessary, and must be set up to measure the maximum amount of piston projection above the deck height. A head gasket of suitable thickness must be used. Head gasket thickness is coded by the number of notches located on the edge. Always install a gasket with the same number of notches as the one removed. Consult your dealer if new pistons are installed.

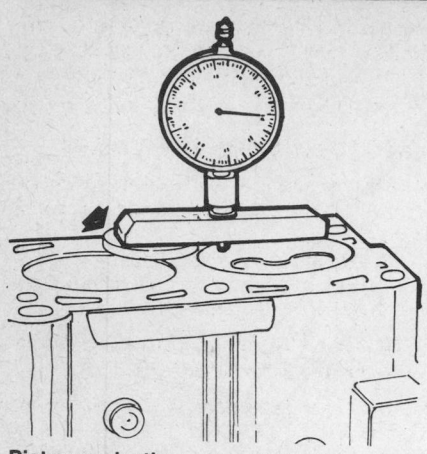

Piston projection measurement on diesel engines—note spacer (arrow)

ENGINE LUBRICATION

Oil Pan

REMOVAL & INSTALLATION

Fox

The front crossmember has to be lowered to remove the oil pan.

1. Raise the car, allowing the front wheels to hang down. Drain the oil.
2. Disconnect the engine vacuum line from the power brake vacuum line T fitting. Pull the vacuum line from the cylinder head on automatic transmission cars.
3. Support the rear of the engine at the cast lifting eye in the cylinder head.
4. From underneath, unbolt the lower left and right engine mounts. Carefully and evenly loosen and remove the four crossmember-to-body bolts and lower the crossmember.
5. Remove the pan bolts. Tap it lightly with a soft hammer to break it loose. Remove the pan and clean it out thoroughly while it is off the engine.
6. On installation, use a new gasket with no sealer. Torque the pan bolts in a criss-cross pattern, in steps, to 6 ft. lbs. Torque the crossmember bolts to 33 ft. lbs.

4000 and 5000—All Models

1. Raise and support the vehicle.
2. Drain the oil.
3. Remove the oil pan bolts while supporting the pan.

NOTE: To remove the two bolts at the rear of the oil pan on the diesel engine, turn the flywheel so that the recesses are pointing down. This will afford you access to the two bolts.

4. Lower the pan from the engine. Discard the gasket.
5. Coat both sides of a new gasket with sealer and install the gasket and oil pan.
6. Torque the bolts to 7 ft. lbs. (14 ft. lbs. on 4000 Diesels).

Rear Main Bearing Oil Seal

REPLACEMENT

When this seal fails, the usual result is oil leakage onto the clutch. This of course, causes clutch slippage or failure to disengage.

Fox

1. Remove the engine.
2. Remove the transmission (and clutch) from the engine.
3. Remove the flywheel. Some method of preventing the flywheel from turning will have to be devised.

NOTE: Mark the relationship between the flywheel and crankshaft to preserve balance.

4. The circular seal may now be removed by placing a suitable tool under the sealing lip or behind the support ring carefully. Be cautious not to damage the seal bearing surface.
5. Press the new seal evenly in place.
6. The remainder of the procedure is the reverse of removal. Make sure to align the flywheel marks made in Step 3.

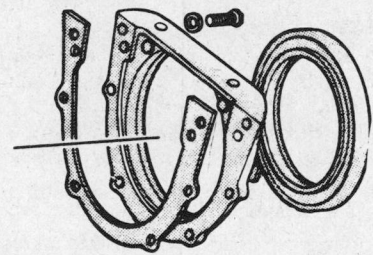

Rear main oil seal (circular)—4000 and 5000

4000 and 5000—All Models

The rear main oil seal is located at the rear of the engine block. It can be found in a housing behind the flywheel. To replace the seal it is necessary to remove the transmission.

1. Remove the transmission.
2. Unscrew the six bolts and remove the flywheel.
3. Using special tool VW2086 or a suitable tool, pry the old seal out of its housing.
4. To install, lightly oil the replacement seal then press it into place using a canister top or other circular piece of flat metal.

CAUTION
Be careful not to damage the seal or score the crankshaft.

---

5. Install the flywheel and the transmission.

Oil Pump

REMOVAL & INSTALLATION

Fox and 4000

1. Drain the oil and remove the oil pan.
2. Remove the oil pump mounting bolts and pull the pump down and out of the engine.
3. Unscrew the two bolts and separate the pump halves (4000).
4. Clean the lower half in solvent.
5. To remove the oil strainer for cleaning, bend out the metal rim of the oil strainer cover plate and remove it (4000).
6. Examine the gears and the driveshaft for any wear or damage. Replace them if necessary (4000).
7. Reassemble the pump halves (4000).
8. Prime the pump with oil and install in the reverse order of removal.

NOTE: Turbocharged diesel engines may use an oil cooler mounted between the oil filter and engine. Always check tightness of the cooler retaining nut when changing the oil filter. Nut should be torqued to 18 ft. lbs.

5000—All Models

1. Loosen and remove the crankshaft bolt.
2. Remove the drive belt guard.
3. Loosen the water pump bolts and turn the pump body clockwise.
4. Remove the drive belt and V-belt pulley with the drive belt sprocket.
5. Remove the dipstick and drain the engine oil.
6. Remove the front bolts on the sub frame and remove the oil pan.
7. Remove the oil suction pipe from the base of the oil pump and bracket to the engine block.
8. Remove the oil pump bolts and remove the oil pump from the front of the engine.

ENGINE COOLING

NOTE: When replacing or adding coolant, use only a phosphate-free coolant/antifreeze.

Radiator

NOTE: Various late models have the radiator retained by locating tabs at the bottom and two mounting brackets at the top. Disconnect hoses, wiring connectors and top brackets. Remove the radiator and fan assembly.

REMOVAL & INSTALLATION

Fox

1. Drain the coolant. Remove the grille.
2. Remove the bolts holding the panel at the side of the radiator through the grille opening.
3. Disconnect the lower radiator hose and the radiator fan switch at the bottom of the radiator. Remove the lower radiator panel and the lower radiator mounting nuts.
4. Loosen the mounting bar and slide the upper radiator panel toward the center of the car to remove it. Unbolt the upper radiator mounts and detach the upper radiator hose.
5. Disconnect the heater and intake manifold coolant hoses at the fan shroud. Remove the radiator side mounting bolt and remove the radiator and electric fan together.

4000 (4 Cylinder)—All Models

1. Drain the cooling system.
2. If equipped with air conditioning, remove the grille and detach the condenser from the radiator.
3. Remove the upper and lower radiator hoses, the expansion tank supply hose and the expansion tank vent hose. Being careful not to crimp them, tie all hoses back out of the way.

NOTE: All disconnections should be done at the radiator end of the particular hose.

4. Disconnect the wiring at the temperature switch (two switches if air conditioning) and the rear of the fan motor.
5. Unscrew the fan shroud retaining bolts and remove the fan, motor and shroud as one assembly.
6. Unscrew the radiator retaining bolts and remove the radiator.
7. Installation is in the reverse order of removal.

4000 (Coupe and Quattro) and 5000 (All Models)

1. Drain the cooling system.
2. Remove the three pieces of the radiator cowl and the fan motor assembly. Take care in removing the fan motor connectors to avoid bending them.
3. Remove the upper and lower radiator hoses and the coolant tank supply hose.
4. Disconnect the coolant temperature switch located on the lower right side of the radiator.
5. Remove the radiator mounting bolts and lift out the radiator.

6. Installation is the reverse of removal Torque radiator mounting bolts to 14 ft. lbs. and cowl bolts to 7 ft. lbs.
The 5000 Diesel and Turbodiesel is equipped with an auxiliary radiator which must also be removed. To remove the auxiliary radiator:
1. Remove the grille and detach the condenser (air conditioning only).
2. Remove all hoses from the auxiliary radiator.
3. Remove the radiator retaining bolts and remove the radiator.
4. Installation is in the reverse order of removal.

Water Pump

REMOVAL & INSTALLATION

Fox

1. Drain the coolant.
2. Remove the alternator.
3. Remove the timing belt cover.
4. Loosen the clamps and detach the hoses from the pump.
5. Unbolt the pump, turn it slightly, and lift it out.
6. On installation, use a new pump-to-block seal and torque the pump bolts to 14 ft. lbs.

4000 and 5000—All Models

1. Drain the cooling system.
2. Remove the V-belts, timing belt covers and timing belts as outlined earlier in this section.
3. On the 4000, unscrew the water pump pulley retaining bolts (3) and remove the pulley. On 1.8L engine, remove the four pump retaining bolts (take note of various lengths and locations). Turn the pump slightly and lift from engine block.
4. On the 4000, unscrew the intermediate shaft drive sprocket retaining bolt and remove the sprocket.
5. Unscrew the water pump retaining bolts and remove the pump from its housing on the 4000 or from the engine block on all other models.
6. Always replace the old gasket with a new one.
7. Installation is in the reverse order of removal.

Thermostat

REMOVAL & INSTALLATION

Fox

1. Drain the coolant from the radiator.
2. The thermostat is inside a cast housing on the engine or the water pump, connected to the upper radiator hose. Unbolt the cover and remove the gasket and the thermostat.
3. Some thermostats have an arrow on

the bar which should also point at the projection. In any case, the bar should be up. The housing bolts should be torqued to 7 ft. lbs. Always use a new gasket.

4000 (4 cylinder)—All Models

The thermostat is located in the lower radiator hose neck on the bottom of the water pump housing.
1. Drain the cooling system.
2. Remove the two retaining bolts from the lower water pump neck.

NOTE: It is not necessary to disconnect the lower radiator hose.

3. Move the neck, with the hoses attached, out of the way.
4. Carefully pry the thermostat out of the water pump housing. Install with new gasket or "O"-ring.

4000 (Coupe and Quattro) and 5000 (All Models)

The thermostat is located in the lower radiator hose neck, on the left side of the engine block, behind the water pump housing.
Follow Steps 1–3 of the 4000 procedure.
1. Carefully pry the thermostat out of the engine block.
2. Install a new O-ring on the water pump neck.
3. Install the thermostat.

NOTE: When installing the thermostat, the spring end should be pointing toward the engine block.

4. Reposition the water pump neck and tighten the retaining bolts.

Thermostat housing—5000

EMISSION CONTROLS

Several emission control devices are used to control different sources of emissions. Engine crankcase emissions are controlled by routing them directly into the carburetor air cleaner or into the fuel vapor control system, which is connected to the air cleaner.
Fuel vapor emissions from the carburetor float bowl and the fuel tank are handled by the fuel vapor control system. The system has an activated carbon container in the

engine compartment to store vapors until they can be drawn in through the air cleaner and burned.

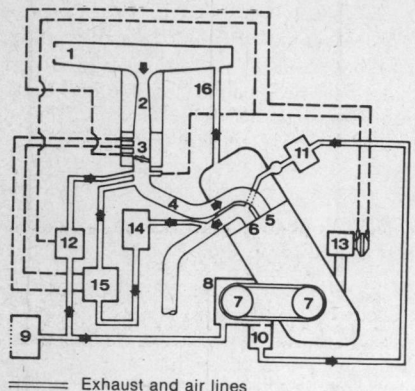

—— Exhaust and air lines
- - - Vacuum control lines

1. Air cleaner
2. Carburetor venturi
3. Throttle valve
4. Intake manifold
5. Cylinder head intake port
6. Cylinder head exhaust port
7. Belt drive for air pump
8. Air pump
9. Air pump filter
10. Pressure relief valve
11. Check valve
12. Diverter valve
13. Distributor
14. EGR filter
15. EGR valve
16. Crankcase ventilation

Emission control schematic for Fox

Fox

The Fox uses emission control systems very similar to those on the 100 series. The fuel evaporation control system differs only in that it does not require a fuel recirculation line.

4000 and 5000

A closed, positive crankcase ventilation system (PCV) is employed on all 4000 and 5000 models. This system cycles incompletely burned fuel which works its way past the piston rings back into the intake manifold for reburning with the fuel/air mixture. The oil filler cap is sealed and the air is drawn from the top of the crankcase into the intake manifold through a valve with a variable orifice (commonly known as a PCV valve).

The evaporative emission control system on these models includes: a sealed filler cap, a gravity vent valve, an activated charcoal canister, a charcoal canister control valve and a fuel pump check valve. All models are equipped with a dual diaphragm distributor. The purpose of the distributor is to reduce exhaust emissions during idling.

All Audis, with the exception of the Turbo, the 4000 5 cylinder and any 1979 and later car built for use in California are equipped

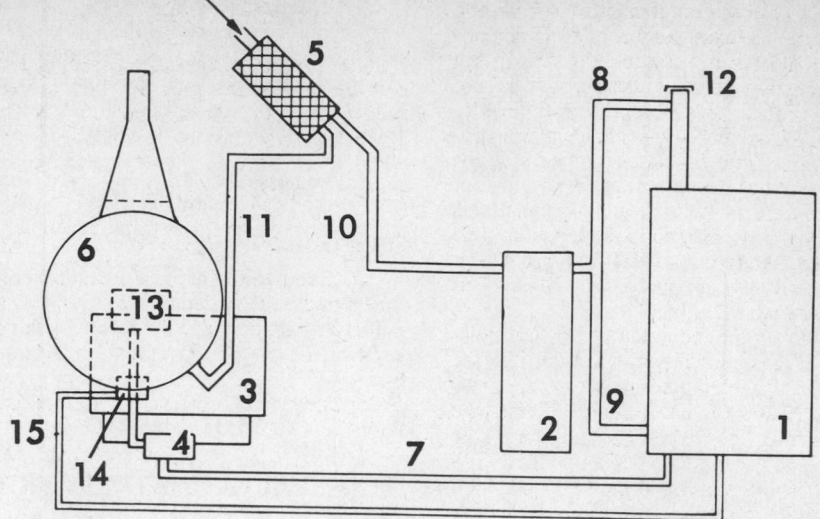

1. Fuel tank
2. Vapor expansion container
3. Engine
4. Fuel pump
5. Activated carbon container
6. Air cleaner
7. Fuel line from tank to pump
8. Breather line from neck to expansion container
9. Breather line from tank to expansion container
10. Breather line to carbon container
11. Line from carbon
11. Line from carbon container to air cleaner
12. Non-vented tank filler cap
13. Carburetor
14. Fuel return valve
15. Line from return valve to tank

Fuel vapor emission control system—typical

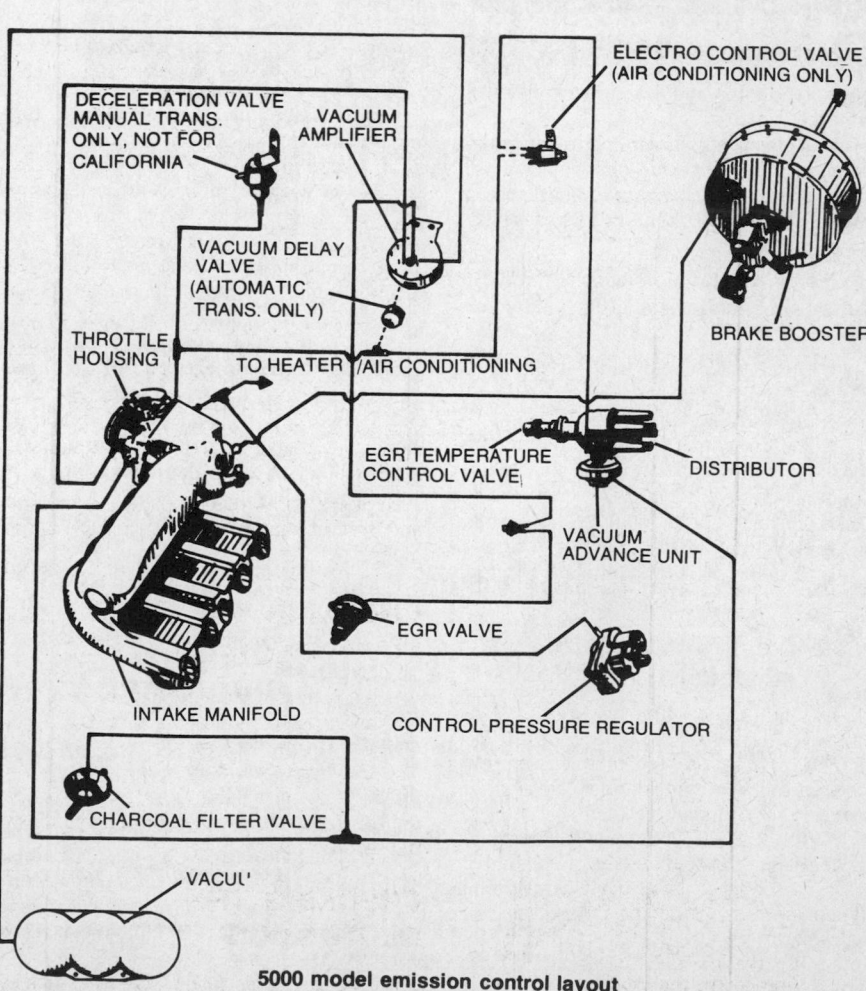

5000 model emission control layout

with an EGR system to control part throttle exhaust emissions. Audi uses a vacuum operated EGR valve controlled primarily by a connection near the throttle plate where the vacuum is only present at part throttle. The EGR system also includes a temperature valve (two on cars equipped with air conditioning) which acts on engine coolant temperature, a vacuum amplifier that acts basically like a relay and a deceleration valve (found only on certain models) that aids in the fuel/air mixture adjustment on deceleration.

To aid in the reduction of exhaust emissions a catalytic converter is built into the exhaust system. There are two types of catalytic converters used: An oxidizing type and a three way type. The oxidizing type is used on the 1978 5000 (Calif.), the 1979–81 5000 (49 state) and the 1980–81 4000 (49 state). The three way type is used on the Turbo, the 4000 5 cylinder, and all 1982 and later models.

FUEL SYSTEM

Fuel Pump

REMOVAL & INSTALLATION

Fox

An electric pump is located on a bracket in the right rear wheel well.
1. Disconnect and plug the hoses.
2. Remove the mounting bolts and lift off the pump.
3. Installation is the reverse of removal.

4000 and 5000—All Models

An electric pump is used, mounted on a bracket near the right rear wheel well.
1. Disconnect the battery ground.
2. Clean all fuel and electrical connections.
3. Disconnect the pump wiring.
4. Disconnect the fuel lines.
5. Unbolt and dismount the pump.
6. Installation is the reverse of removal. Torque the mounting bolts to 14 ft. lbs.

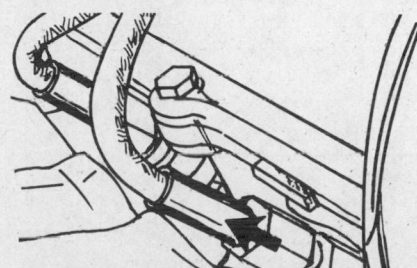

Removing the injector

Fuel Injection

For all fuel injection system repair and service procedures not detailed below, please refer to "Fuel Injection" in the Unit Repair section.

FUEL INJECTORS

Removal & Installation

1. Grasp the injector where it touches the engine block and pull firmly. It should pop right out.
2. Unscrew the injector from the fuel line.
3. Screw the injector back into the fuel line.
4. Moisten the rubber seal with fuel and then press the injector firmly into the injector seat.

Diesel Fuel Injection

For more information on diesel engines, please refer to "Diesel Service" in the Unit Repair section.

The diesel fuel injection system is an extremely complex and sensitive system. Very few repairs or adjustments are possible by the owner. Any service other than that listed here should be referred to an authorized Audi dealer or a diesel specialist. The injection pump itself is not repairable; it can only be replaced.

Any work done to the diesel injection system should be done with absolute cleanliness. Even the smallest specks of dirt can have a disastrous effect on the diesel injection system.

We would advise not attempting to remove the fuel injectors. They are very delicate and must be removed with a special tool to prevent damage. The fuel in the system is also under tremendous pressure, so it's not too wise to loosen any of the lines with the engine running. Exposing your skin to the spray from the injector at working pressure can cause fuel to penetrate the skin. The only component of the injection system that we would suggest performing any sort of maintenance on are the glow plugs.

CHECKING THE GLOW PLUG CURRENT SUPPLY

1. Connect a test light between the No. 4 cylinder glow plug and a ground.
2. Turn the key to the heat position. The test light should light up.
3. If the test light doesn't light, check the glow plug relay, the ignition switch or the fuse box relay plate.

CHECKING THE GLOWPLUGS

This check can be made only after it has

first been established that there is current to the glow plugs.
1. Remove the wire and the glow plug bus bar.
2. Connect a test light between the positive battery terminal and each glow plug in turn.
3. If the test light lights, the glow plug is alright. If it does not, the glow plug is defective and will require replacement.

MANUAL TRANSMISSION

The transmission is combined with the differential in a transaxle.

REMOVAL & INSTALLATION

NOTE: If the flywheel has been removed from the crankshaft for any reasons (4000 and 5000 models) torque the mounting bolts to: Bolt without shoulder-72 ft. lbs; bolt with shoulder-54 ft. lbs. Coat all threads with a locking compound.

Fox

The transaxle can be lowered from the car, leaving the engine in place.
1. Disconnect the battery ground cable. Raise the car.
2. Detach and wire up the entire exhaust system.
3. Release the lockplates and remove the axle shaft bolts. Wire the shafts up.
4. Use pliers to unscrew the speedometer cable nut.
5. Support the transaxle. Remove the engine–to–transaxle bolts and the clutch guard plate.
6. Remove the lock wire and unscrew the gearshift rod coupling square headed bolt. Pull off the gearshift rod.
7. Disconnect the gearshift strut at the transmission and unbolt the small cross-member at the rear of the transmission.
8. Disconnect the back–up light and seat belt system wires at the transmission.
9. Separate the transaxle from the engine and lower it. Reverse the procedure on installation. Torque the engine-to-transaxle bolts to 40 ft. lbs. and the axle shaft bolts to 28 ft. lbs.

4000—All Models

This procedure can be performed with the engine installed.
1. Disconnect the negative battery cable.
2. Unplug the two electrical connectors for the back-up lights. They can be found between the ignition coil and the fuel distributor filter.
3. Remove the upper engine/transmission bolts.

4. Using special tool 3016 or a pair of pliers, detach the speedometer cable where it attaches to the transaxle.

5. Detach the clutch cable from the clutch lever.

6. Unbolt the exhaust pipe from the exhaust manifold.

7. Unscrew the three mounting bolts and remove the center engine mount.

8. Unbolt the front exhaust pipe from the support bracket and then unbolt it from the catalytic converter (muffler on Canadian models).

9. Unscrew the six screws and remove the left halfshaft from the transaxle. Wire the halfshaft up and out of the way. Repeat the procedure for the right halfshaft.

CAUTION

When wiring the halfshaft, tighten the wire only enough so as to relieve any downward pressure on them.

10. Remove the cover plate. On Quattro models you must also disconnect the front/rear driveshaft at the rear output shaft of the transmission and secure out of the way.

11. Tag and disconnect all wires leading to the starter and remove the starter.

12. Remove the bolt from the shift rod coupling.

13. Pry off the linkage coupling.

14. Pull the shift rod coupling off of the shift rod.

15. Loosen the left (chassis) bolt on the rear transmission support. Remove the two bolts (some models have one) from the right (transmission) side of the support and pivot the support out of the way.

16. Remove the rubber mounting block.

17. Unscrew three bolts and remove the front transmission support.

18. Remove the lower engine/transmission bolts.

19. Carefully pry the transmission apart from the engine and remove it.

20. Installation is in the reverse order of removal.

Note the following:

a. Make sure that all engine/transmission mounts are correctly aligned and free of tension.

b. Check for proper adjustment of the gear shift lever.

c. Secure the bolt on the shift rod coupling with wire.

d. Tighten the engine/transmission bolts to 40 ft. lbs.

e. Tighten the halfshaft-to-drive flange bolts to 33 ft. lbs.

f. Tighten the subframe-to-body bolts to 51 ft. lbs.

g. Tighten the front transmission support-to-transmission bolts to 18 ft. lbs.

h. Tighten the rubber mount-to-body bolts to 29 ft. lbs. (new mount, 80 ft. lbs.).

i. Tighten the rubber mount-to-transmission bolts to 40 ft. lbs.

j. Tighten the rubber mount-to-crossmember bolts to 18 ft. lbs.

5000—All Models

The manual transaxle may be removed with the engine in place.

1. Disconnect the battery ground.

2. Remove the air filter (Diesel only).

3. Remove the windshield washer bottle.

4. Remove the upper engine-transmission bolts.

5. Raise and support the car.

6. Disconnect the speedometer cable at the engine.

7. Disconnect all wires and hoses connected to the transaxle.

8. Drive out the clutch slave cylinder lockpin and remove the slave cylinder. Leave the hydraulic line connected.

9. Support the engine, either from above with a hoist or from below with a jack.

10. Remove the heat shield.

11. Remove the lower engine/transmission splash shield (Diesel only).

12. Disconnect the exhaust pipe from the manifold.

13. Remove the right side guard plate.

14. Disconnect the driveshafts from the flanges and support them out of the way with wires. On the Quattro, you must also disconnect the front/rear driveshaft at the rear output shaft on the transmission and wire it out of the way.

15. Disconnect the back–up light switch.

16. Pry off the shift and adjusting rods.

17. Remove the lower engine-transmission bolts.

18. Remove the starter.

19. Remove the subframe skid plate.

20. Install a jack under the transmission and lift it slightly.

21. Remove both transmission-to-subframe bolts.

22. Remove the right side transmission bracket.

23. Slide the transmission back off the locating dowels and remove it from the car.

24. When installing, place the driveshafts on top of the subframe; tighten the lower bolts first, then tighten the transmission bracket, subframe and upper bolts. Driveshaft bolts are torqued to 32 ft. lbs.; transmission bracket bolts to 29 ft. lbs.; subframe support bolts to 29 ft. lbs.; subframe to body bolts to 80 ft. lbs. and the transmission to engine bolts to 40 ft. lbs.

Install all other parts in reverse order of removal.

LINKAGE ADJUSTMENT

Fox

1. Remove the rubber boot at the base of the shift lever.

2. Loosen the two bolts at the base of the lever and move the lever to the far right of the Neutral slot against the stop. Tighten the bolts.

3. If there is a problem with the lever sticking or jamming, loosen the two shift gate bolts from under the car and adjust the gate backward or forward. Tighten the bolts.

4000—All Models

NOTE: This procedure will require Special Tool VW 3014.

1. Place the shift lever in the Neutral position.

2. Working under the car, loosen the clamp nut on the shift rod.

3. Inside the car, remove the shift knob and the boot. It is not necessary to remove the console.

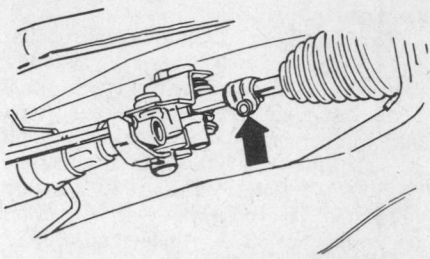

Loosen the clamp nut on the shift rod—4000

4. Align the holes in the shifter base with the holes in the bearing plate directly below it and tighten the bolts.

5. Install the Special Tool VW 3014 with the locating pin toward the front.

6. Push the shift lever to the left side of the tool cutout and tighten the lower knurled knob to secure the tool.

7. Move the top slide of the tool to the left side stop and tighten the upper knurled knob.

8. Push the shift lever into the right cutout of the slide. Align the shift rod and the shift finger under the car and tighten the clamp nut.

9. Remove the special tool.

10. Place the shift lever in the first gear position. Press the lever to the left side against the stop. Release the lever; it should spring back ¼ to ½ in. If not, move the lever housing slightly sideways to correct. Check that all gears can be engaged easily.

Shifter base plate bolts—5000

5000—All Models

1. Remove the gear shift boot.
2. Position the shift lever in neutral.
3. The seam on the plastic stop bracket should line up with the center hole in the curved stop plate. If not, proceed below:
4. Loosen the four bolts at the base of the shifter.
5. Align the holes in the shifter base with the holes in the bearing plate directly below it.

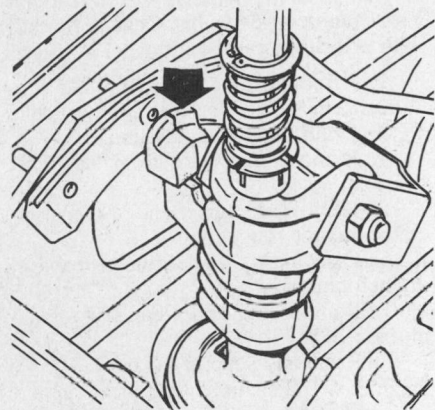

The plastic stop bracket should align with the curved stop plate—5000

6. Tighten the bolts.
7. Loosen the clamp between the front and rear shift rods.
8. Make certain that the front shift rod is in the neutral position.
9. Clamp the shifter securely in the neutral position and tighten the shift rod clamp.
10. Release the shifter and check its operation in all gears.
11. Install the shifter boot, making sure that the top of the boot is in contact with the shift knob.

OVERHAUL

For all overhaul procedures, please refer to "Manual Transaxle Overhaul" in the Unit Repair section.

CLUTCH

REMOVAL & INSTALLATION

1. Remove the transaxle.
2. Mark the relationship of the pressure plate to the flywheel (only if it is to be reused).
3. Unbolt the pressure plate from the flywheel, loosening the bolts alternately, a little at a time, to prevent warpage.
4. To install the clutch, place the driven plate on the pressure plate, making sure that it is facing the right way.
5. Hold the clutch assembly against the

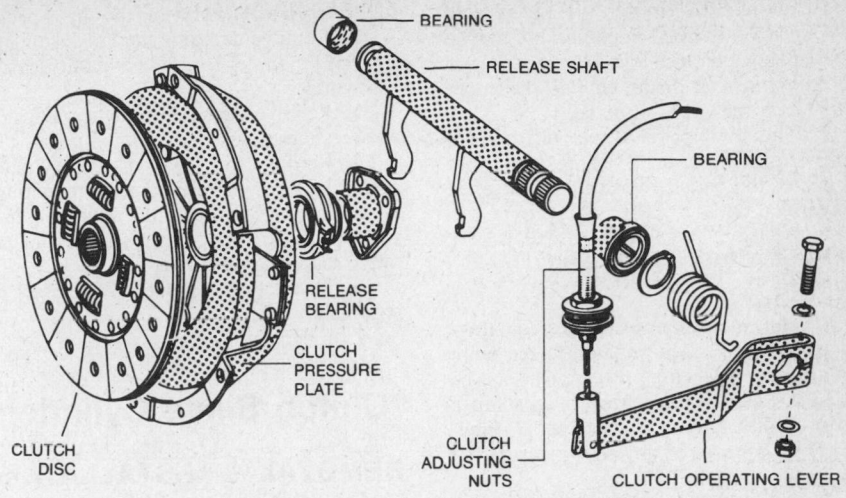

Exploded view of the 4000 clutch—Fox similar

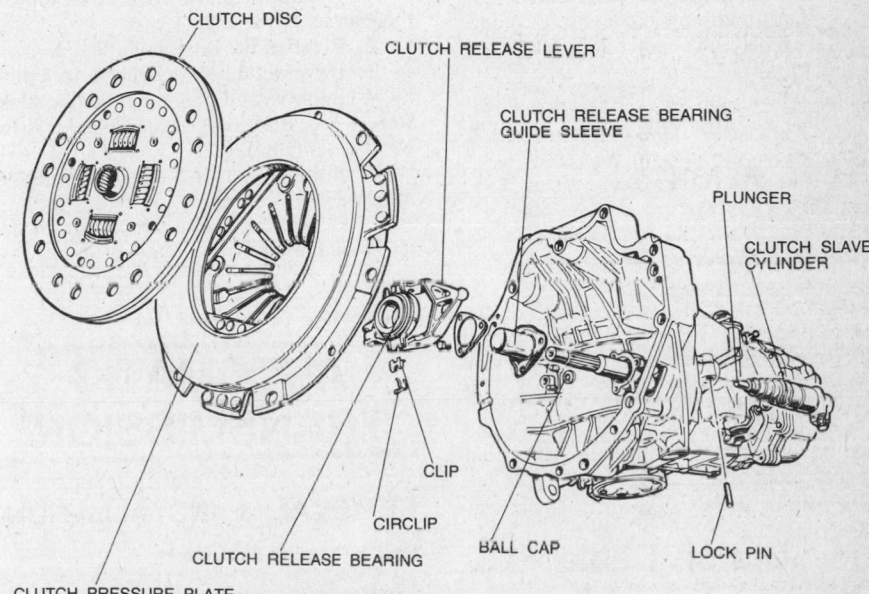

Exploded view of the 5000 clutch

flywheel, aligning the marks made in Step 2 and the three dowel pins on the flywheel with the pressure plate, and insert a dummy shaft through the pressure plate and the driven plate into the crankshaft pilot bearing.

6. Install the pressure plate bolts finger tight. Then tighten the bolts evenly, in rotation, to avoid distortion. Torque the bolts to 24 ft. lbs. Remove the dummy shaft.
7. The clutch release bearing in the front of the transaxle should be checked before reassembly. It is retained by two springs.
8. Replace the transaxle. Torque the engine-to-transaxle bolts to 40 ft. lbs. and the axle shaft to 28 ft. lbs.

PEDAL FREE-PLAY ADJUSTMENT

The pedal free-play is adjusted at the clutch end of the cable. Free-play is the distance that the pedal travels from the released po-

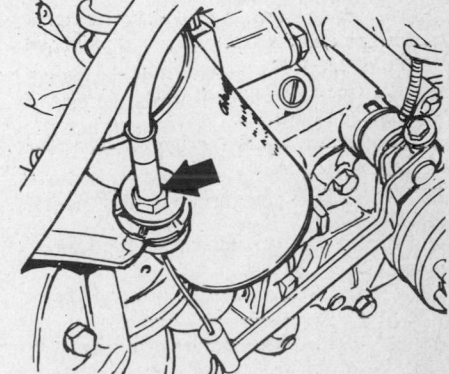

Clutch pedal free-play adjustment nut on the 4000—100 and Fox similar

sition to the point at which clutch spring pressure can be felt. This can be measured by placing a yardstick alongside the clutch pedal. Play should be 0.6–0.8 in.

1. On the 100, loosen the upper cable nut. Turn both nuts clockwise to reduce play, and counterclockwise to increase. After the adjustment is made, tighten the upper nut to lock the cable in place.

2. The total pedal travel on the 100 series should be at least 6.1 in. If it is not adequate, the pedal pivot can be loosened and moved up.

4000—Except Coupe and Quattro

Free-play is the distance that the pedal travels from the released position to the point at which clutch spring pressure can first be felt. This can be measured by placing a yardstick alongside the clutch pedal. Free-play should be ⅝ of an inch, measured at the pedal.

1. Locate the clutch cable bracket by the oil filter.
2. Loosen the upper cable nut.
3. Turn both nuts clockwise to reduce pedal free-play or counterclockwise to increase it.
4. When adjustment is correct, tighten the upper nut to lock the cable in position.

PEDAL HEIGHT ADJUSTMENT

4000 (Coupe and Quattro) and 5000 (All Models)

The clutch pedal should be at rest ⅜ inch above the brake pedal. To adjust the pedal height, remove the cotter pin holding the clutch master cylinder clevis to the pedal, loosen the locknut on the clevis shaft and turn the shaft to give the required pedal height. Tighten the locknut and install the clevis on the pedal.

Clutch Cable

REMOVAL & INSTALLATION

1. Loosen the adjustment.
2. Disengage the cable from the clutch arm.
3. Unhook the cable from the pedal. Remove the threaded eye from the end of the cable. Remove the adjustment nut(s).
4. Remove the C-clip which holds the outer cable at the adjustment point. Remove all the washers and bushings, first noting their locations.
5. Pull the cable out of the firewall toward the engine compartment side.
6. Install and connect the new cable. Adjust the pedal free-play.

Clutch Master Cylinder

REMOVAL & INSTALLATION

5 Cylinder Models Only

1. Locate the master cylinder under the instrument panel and behind the clutch pedal.
2. Remove and plug the line leading to the slave cylinder from the end of the master cylinder.
3. Remove the circlip and the pin which attaches the clevis to the clutch pedal.
4. Remove the two master cylinder mounting screws from the pedal mounting.
5. Remove and plug the remaining line which leads to the fluid reservoir and remove the master cylinder.
6. Installation is in the reverse order of removal.
7. Bleed the system.

Clutch Slave Cylinder

REMOVAL & INSTALLATION

5 Cylinder Models Only

1. Locate the slave cylinder on top of the transaxle housing.
2. Remove the retaining yoke.
3. Drive out the slave cylinder lock pin.
4. Remove and plug the fluid line (this step is necessary only if the cylinder is to be disassembled).
5. Installation is in the reverse order of removal.
6. If the fluid line was removed, bleed the system as described earlier.

AUTOMATIC TRANSMISSION

REMOVAL & INSTALLATION

Fox

The transaxle can be lowered from the car, leaving the engine in place.

1. Disconnect the battery ground cable.
2. Raise and support the car.
3. Remove the lockplates and remove the axle shaft bolts. Wire the shafts up.
4. Disconnect the vacuum hose. Remove the torque converter guard plate. Disconnect the kickdown switch wire.
5. Unscrew the speedometer cable nut.
6. Support the transaxle.
7. Remove the upper engine-to-transaxle bolts.
8. Remove the starter and remove the three torque converter bolts through the starter opening.
9. Unbolt the small crossmember at the rear of the transmission.
10. Lower the transaxle slightly.
11. Detach the shift linkage cable at the transmission.
12. Remove the lower engine-to-transaxle bolts.
13. Separate the transaxle from the engine and lower it. Secure the torque converter in the transmission with a strap. Re-

verse the procedure on installation. Torque the engine-to-transaxle bolts to 40 ft. lbs. and the torque converter bolts to 20–23 ft. lbs. New torque converter bolts and washers must be used. Torque the axle shaft bolts to 28 ft. lbs.

14. Check the shift linkage adjustment.

4000 and 5000

NOTE: If the torque converter drive plate is removed from the crankshaft for any reason, torque the mounting bolts to: Bolt without shoulder—73 ft. lbs; bolt with shoulder—54 ft. lbs. Coat all threads with a locking compound.

1. Disconnect the battery ground.
2. Remove the windshield washer bottle.
3. Drain the cooling system.
4. Remove the hoses from the transmission cooler.
5. Remove the upper end of the accelerator linkage rod.
6. Disconnect the speedometer cable at the bell housing.
7. Remove the upper engine-to-transmission bolts.
8. Raise and support the car.
9. Using a chain hoist or jack, support the engine and raise it just enough to take the weight off of the mounts.
10. Remove the skid plate from the subframe.
11. Disconnect the exhaust pipe from the transmission and the manifold.
12. Remove the right halfshaft guard plate.
13. Remove the right and left halfshafts.
14. Remove the starter.
15. Remove the selector lever cable and holder from the transmission.
16. Remove the lower accelerator linkage rod.
17. Remove the accelerator cable from the transmission support.
18. Remove the right side guard plate from the subframe.
19. Remove both transmission mounts from the subframe.
20. Rotate the torque converter and remove each bolt as it appears in the starter opening.
21. Place a jack under the transmission and raise it slightly.
22. Remove the lower engine-to-transmission bolts.
23. Remove the rear subframe mounting bolts.
24. Swing both halfshafts rearward out of the way.
25. Separate the transmission from the engine and carefully lower the transmission on the jack.
26. Installation is the reverse of removal.

CAUTION

Be sure that the torque converter is fully seated on the one-way clutch support. When the converter is properly seated, the distance between the converter cover nose and the end of the bell housing should be 0.393 in. (10mm).

27. Install the lower engine-to-transmission bolts first, then the transmission-to-subframe bolts.

28. Observe the following torques: converter bolts 22 ft. lbs.; transmission-to-engine bolts 40 ft. lbs.; starter bolts 40 ft. lbs.; subframe to body 80 ft. lbs.

29. Adjust the throttle kickdown switch.

Transmission Pan

REMOVAL & INSTALLATION

The automatic transmission fluid should be changed and the pan cleaned out every 20,000 miles. The interval should be shortened to 12,000 miles under severe use such as city driving or trailer towing.

To change the fluid:

1. Run the engine in Neutral for a minute or two.

2. Make sure that the vehicle is parked on level ground. Stop the engine.

3. Place a pan of at least four quarts capacity under the transmission.

4. Remove the plug from the transmission bottom pan, after wiping the area clean.

5. Remove and clean out the pan.

6. Replace the pan, using a new gasket. Torque the bolts to 7 ft. lbs. Wait ten minutes and retorque the bolts.

7. Clean off the plug, particularly the threads, and replace it.

8. Pour in fluid through the dipstick filler tube. The proper transmission fluid is Dexron® or Dexron®II.

9. Start the engine and shift through all the lever positions.

10. The level should reach the tip of the dipstick. Add fluid until the level reaches this point.

11. Take a short test drive. Fill the transmission until the level is between the marks on the dipstick. Retorque the bolts.

NOTE: If the transmission is overfilled, the excess must be drained.

KICKDOWN SWITCH

Fox

The kickdown switch is mounted behind the accelerator pedal. With the ignition switch on, the switch should make an audible click when the pedal is pressed all the way down.

The transmission should downshift when the accelerator is depressed to the wide open throttle position at speeds between 39 and 65 mph for second gear, and 16 and 36 mph for first gear.

4000 and 5000

1. Position the accelerator pedal in the fully released position.

2. Check the distance between the pedal lower edge and the pedal stop. Clearance should be 3.0 in.

3. If not, loosen the lockbolt which holds

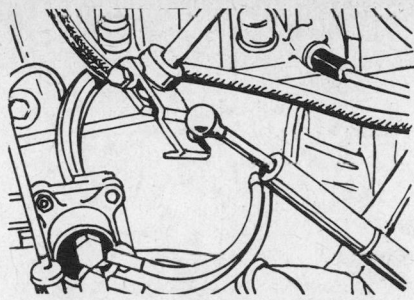

Kickdown detent linkage—4000 and 5000

the cable at the pedal and place the pedal to give the three inch clearance. Tighten the lockbolt.

4. Press the pedal to the full throttle position but not into the kickdown detent. The kickdown take-up spring should not be compressed and the throttle valve should be wide open.

5. Adjust the shift linkage.

NEUTRAL SAFETY SWITCH ADJUSTMENT

The neutral safety switch prevents the engine from being started with the transmission in any position other than Park or Neutral. It also activates the back-up lights. The switch is at the base of the shift lever, inside the floorshift console.

To replace or adjust the switch:

1. Remove the four screws which hold the console to the floor.

2. Shift into Neutral. Remove the two screws which hold the shift position indicator plate to the console. Remove the shift knob and the console.

3. Disconnect the switch electrical leads. These are: red/black—neutral safety; black—back-up lights; blue/red—back-up lights. The back-up light wires are at the front.

4. Remove the two switch retaining screws. Remove the switch.

5. Install the new switch so that the neutral safety switch contacts are together.

6. Install the electrical connectors. Hold the footbrake while making sure that the engine will start only in Neutral and Park. Make sure that the back-up lights operate only in Reverse. If the switch does not operate properly, it may have to be moved on its slotted mounting bracket.

7. Replace the console cover.

SHIFT LINKAGE ADJUSTMENT

The function of this adjustment is to make sure that the transmission is fully engaged in each shift position. If this is not done, the transmission may be only partially engaged in a certain range position. This would result in severe damage due to slippage.

1. Place the selector lever in Park.

2. Loosen the cable clamp nut at the transmission end. On the Fox, remove the rubber cover from the bottom of the shifter

(underneath the car) and loosen the cable clamp screw.

3. Press the selector lever on the transmission back to the stop.

4. Tighten the clamp nut or screw.

BAND ADJUSTMENTS

Fox

FIRST GEAR BAND

1. Loosen the locknut.

2. Tighten first gear band adjusting screw to 7 ft. lbs.

3. Loosen the adjusting screw and retighten to 3.5 ft. lbs.

4. Back off the screw 3.25 to 3.5 turns and tighten the locknut.

SECOND GEAR BAND

1. Loosen the locknut.

2. Tighten the adjusting screw to 7 ft. lbs.

3. Loosen the screw and retighten to 3.5 ft. lbs.

4. Back off the screw exactly 2.5 turns and tighten locknut.

NOTE: Transmission must be horizontal when adjusting bands or bands may jam.

4000 and 5000

SECOND GEAR BAND

1. Loosen the locknut.

2. Tighten the adjusting screw to 7 ft. lbs.

3. Loosen the adjusting screw and retighten it to 4 ft. lbs.

4. Loosen the screw exactly 2½ turns.

5. Hold the screw and tighten the locknut.

DRIVE AXLES

Halfshafts

REMOVAL & INSTALLATION

Fox

1. With the wheels on the ground, remove the front wheel spindle nut.

2. Unbolt the inner halfshaft coupling. If you are removing the right shaft, disconnect the front exhaust pipe at the manifold and the support on the transaxle. Push the inner end of the shaft up and let it rest on the transaxle.

3. Turn the steering wheel all the way in the direction of the side being worked on. Pull the halfshaft out of the steering knuckle.

4. Only the outer joint is available for replacement. If the inner joint is damaged, a new halfshaft must be installed. The outer joint can be removed by removing the snap-

AUDI

ring (inboard side) and hitting the axle end with a soft hammer.

5. On installation, torque the halfshaft coupling bolts to 25 ft. lbs.

4000—All Models

─────── **CAUTION** ───────
Never remove or install the axle nut with the wheel off the ground. The vehicle must be resting on the ground for these operations.

1. Remove the axle nut.
2. Unbolt and remove the six halfshaft retaining bolts from the drive flange.
3. Mark the position of the ball joint on the control arm, remove the two retaining nuts and remove the ball joint.

NOTE: On cars with manual transmissions, remove only the right side ball joint.

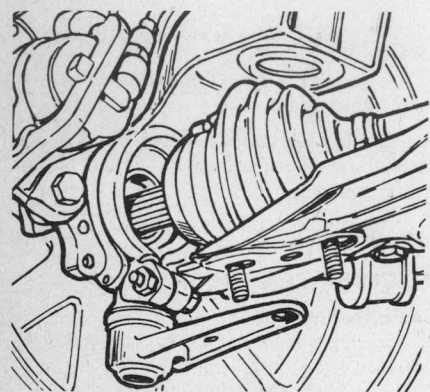

Remove the halfshafts

4. Pull the pivot mounting outward and remove the halfshaft.
5. Installation is the reverse of removal.
6. Tighten the ball joint–to–control arm nuts to 47 ft. lbs.
7. Always replace the self-locking axle nut with a new one and tighten to 167 ft. lbs.
8. Check for proper camber adjustment.

5000—All Models

─────── **CAUTION** ───────
Never remove or install the axle shaft nut with the wheel off the ground. The vehicle must be resting on the ground for these operations. A puller is required for this job.

1. Remove the axle nut.
2. Raise and support the vehicle and remove the wheels.
3. On the right side, remove the half-shaft skid plate.
4. Disconnect the halfshaft from the transmission.
5. Using a 4-armed puller mounted on the wheel hub, press the halfshaft out of the hub.
6. Guide the inside end of the shaft up over the transmission and out of the hub.

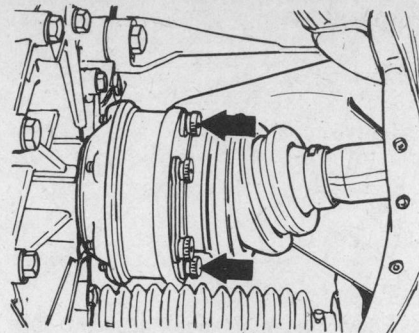

Removing the halfshaft

7. When installing a shaft, make certain that the splines are clean and free of grease. Apply a ⅛ inch bead of RTV silicone sealant around the leading edge of the splines. Allow it to harden at least one hour. Torque the shaft-to-transmission bolts to 32 ft. lbs. and the axleshaft nut to 203 ft. lbs.

CV–Joints

For all CV–Joints removal, installation and overhaul procedures, please refer to "U–Joint/CV–Joint Overhaul" in the Unit Repair section.

REAR SUSPENSION

Rear Axle Beam

REMOVAL & INSTALLATION

Fox

1. Remove the rear wheels. Support the axle, but don't put any load on the springs.
2. Remove the rear muffler and tailpipe.
3. Disconnect the parking brake cable at the yoke where the two cables merge into one. Detach the cable holders from the underbody.
4. Detach both rear brake lines.
5. Unbolt the control arms and the diagonal arm from the body.
6. Unbolt the bottom of the shock absorber struts from the axle.
7. Remove the axle.
8. On installation, torque the control arm-to-body bolts to 32 ft. lbs., and the diagonal arm-to-body bolts to 61 ft. lbs. Torque the lower shock absorber strut-to-axle bolts to 43 ft. lbs. Bleed the brakes.

4000 (exc. Quattro)

1. Raise the rear of the car and support it with jack stands.
2. Remove the wheels.
3. Unhook the exhaust system hangers located at either side of the muffler, lower the exhaust system and secure it.
4. Remove the nut on the parking brake equalizer bar.

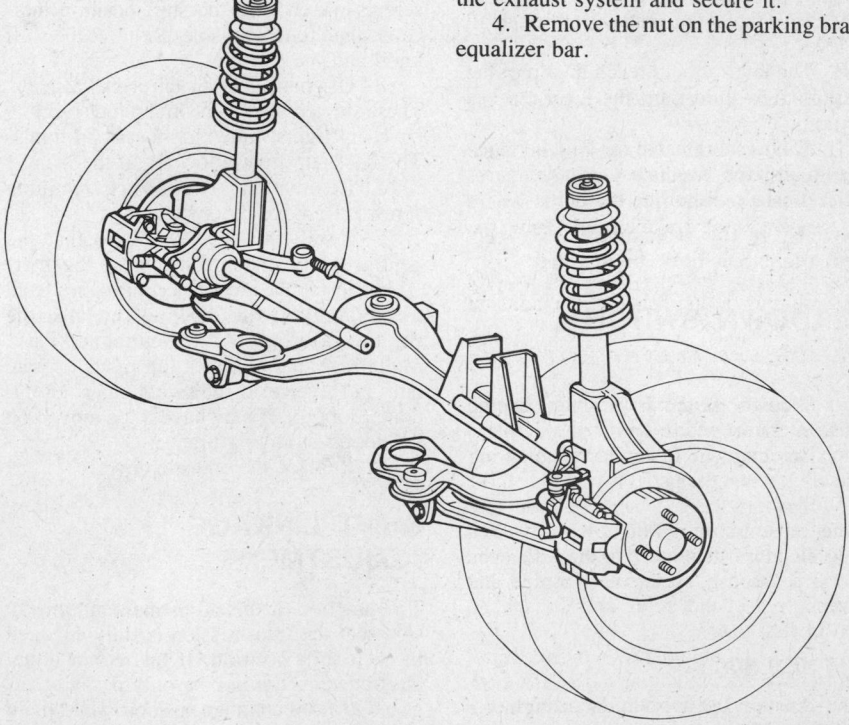

4000S Quattro rear suspension

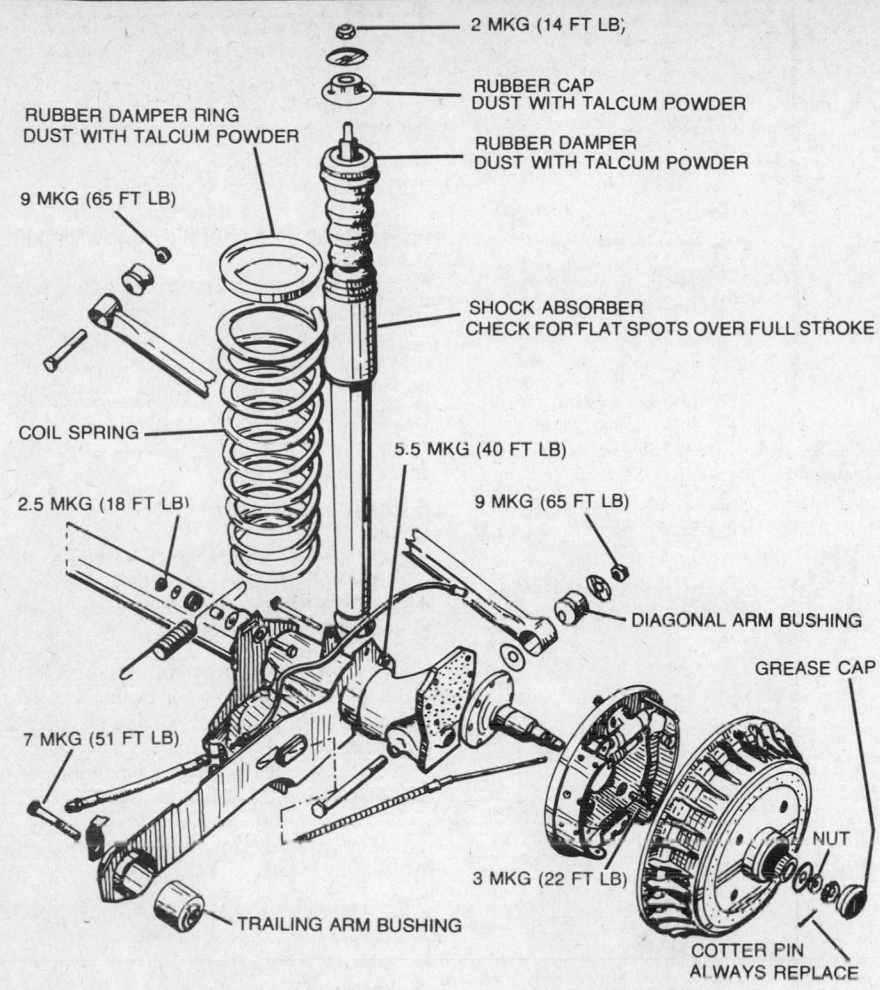

2 MKG (14 FT LB)

RUBBER CAP
DUST WITH TALCUM POWDER

RUBBER DAMPER RING
DUST WITH TALCUM POWDER

RUBBER DAMPER
DUST WITH TALCUM POWDER

9 MKG (65 FT LB)

SHOCK ABSORBER
CHECK FOR FLAT SPOTS OVER FULL STROKE

COIL SPRING

5.5 MKG (40 FT LB)

2.5 MKG (18 FT LB)

9 MKG (65 FT LB)

DIAGONAL ARM BUSHING

GREASE CAP

7 MKG (51 FT LB)

3 MKG (22 FT LB)

NUT

TRAILING ARM BUSHING

COTTER PIN
ALWAYS REPLACE

Rear suspension on the 5000 (exc. Quattro)—4000 similar

5. Pry the parking brake cable sleeves out of their brackets.

6. Remove both parking brake cables at their retaining brackets.

7. Disconnect both brake hoses where they connect to the brake lines and plug the lines.

8. Remove the nuts from the trailing arm mounting bolts, leaving the bolts in place.

9. Disconnect the spring from the brake pressure regulator.

10. Remove the Panhard rod mounting bolt from the axle beam.

11. Remove the lower strut mounting bolts.

12. Support the axle and pull out the trailing arm mounting bolts.

13. Remove the axle while guiding the parking brake cable over the tail pipe and muffler.

To install:

14. Place the axle in position and install both trailing arm mounting bolts and both lower strut mounting bolts. Hand tighten.

15. Install the wheels.

16. Lower the car so that the wheels are on the ground and tighten the trailing arm bolts to 72 ft. lbs. and the lower strut bolts to 51 ft. lbs.

17. Install the Panhard rod, the brake hoses, the spring for the brake pressure regulator and the parking brake cables.

18. Bleed the brakes and adjust the parking brake.

5000 (exc. Quattro)

NOTE: Three persons will be required for installation.

1. Loosen the wheel lugs, but do not remove the wheels. Raise and support the car. Support the rear axle with a jack.

2. Disconnect the Panhard rod at the chassis.

3. Disconnect the right brake hose at the chassis.

4. Disconnect the brake pressure regulator spring.

5. Disconnect the left brake hose at the chassis.

6. Remove the right fuel tank retaining strap.

7. Remove the parking brake from the guide on the fuel tank.

8. Loosen the left side parking brake cable bolt.

9. Loosen the parking brake compensator and disconnect the cable.

10. Remove the exhaust system from the car.

11. Disconnect the struts at the upper end.

12. Lower the axle on the jack until the struts are clear.

13. Remove the struts and the rear wheels.

14. Remove the trailing arm mounting bolt and lower the axle from the car.

15. Place the axle in position on the jack.

16. Install the trailing arm bolts lightly.

17. Install the wheels.

18. Install both rear struts at the same time while raising the axle into position.

19. Connect the shock absorbers.

20. Installation of the remaining parts is the reverse of removal.

21. Torque the strut upper bolts to 14 ft. lbs., the Panhard rod-to-chassis bolt to 65 ft. lbs.; the trailing arm bolts to 51 ft. lbs.

22. Bleed the brakes.

Wheel Bearings and Stub Axles

REMOVAL & INSTALLATION

1. Depress the brake pedal approximately 1.2 in. and hold it in that position to close the master cylinder compensating bore.

2. Detach the brake lines on both sides and plug the lines.

3. Pry off the grease cap and remove the cotter pin, castellated nut, and washer. Remove the wheel and brake drum.

4. Remove the bearing inner race from the brake drum.

5. Carefully (the spring can fly out) pry out the brake shoe retaining spring. Remove the brake shoes complete with pressure rod and spring, bottom bracket first. Disconnect the handbrake cable.

6. Unbolt the rear stub axle and brake backing plate.

7. Pry out the shaft seal (which should be replaced) and remove the inner race of the roller bearing.

8. Drive the roller bearing outer race from the brake drum. Remove the snapring and drive the outer roller bearing race from the drum.

9. Replace the snap-ring and drive in the outer race of the outer roller bearing.

10. Press in the outer race of the inner roller bearing.

11. Lightly coat the inner race of the inner roller bearing with wheel bearing grease and push it into the outer race.

12. Drive a new shaft seal into position (the open side of the seal should face the roller bearing). Fill the space between the two roller bearings with approximately 10 oz. of wheel bearing grease.

13. Coat the inner race of the outer roller bearing with grease and install the inner race.

14. Replace the stub axle and brake backing plate with the groove in the stub

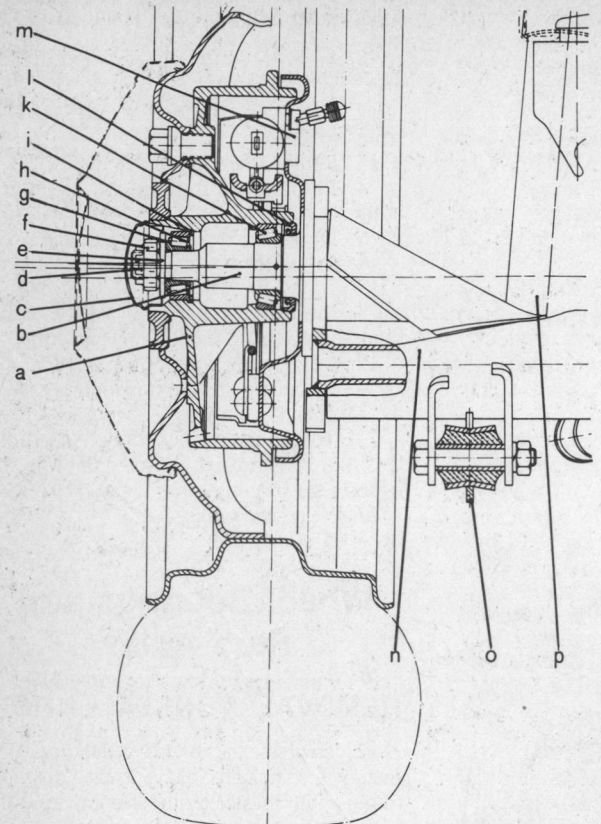

(a)—Brake drum
(b)—Rear stub axle
(c)—Cap
(d)—Cotter pin
(e)—Nut

(f)—Castellated nut
(g)—Washer
(h)—Roller bearing
(i)—Snap-ring
(k)—Roller bearing

(l)—Shaft seal
(m)—Brake assembly
(n)—Rear axle
(o)—Suspension arm
(p)—Shock absorber

Rear wheel bearing and stub axle assembly

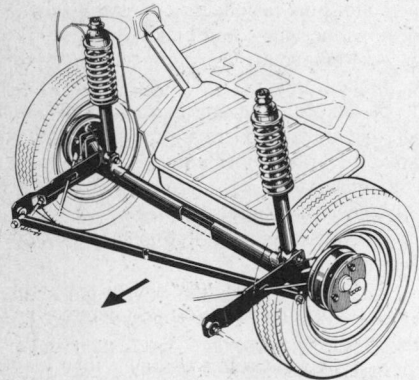

Rear suspension—Fox and 100

axle facing upward. Bolt torque is 14–15 ft. lbs. for 8G bolts and 22 ft. lbs. for 10K bolts.

15. Assemble the brake shoes, connect the handbrake cable, and insert the brake shoes on the bottom bracket first, then at the wheel cylinder. Replace the retaining spring.

16. Replace the brake drum and wheel, special washer, nut, castellated nut, and a new cotter pin. Wheel bearing play should be 0.001–0.002 in. It can be measured with a dial indicator. Fill the dust cap with approximately 10 oz. of wheel bearing grease and replace it.

Struts

For all spring and shock absorber removal and installation procedures and any other strut overhaul procedures, refer to "Strut Overhaul" in the Unit Repair section.

REMOVAL & INSTALLATION
Fox

1. Remove the bottom cushion of the rear seat. Release the mounting tabs at the bottom of the seatback and pull it forward to detach its upper clips.

2. Support the rear of the chassis. Support the axle. Do not put any load on the springs. Remove the rubber guard from the top of the strut, from inside the trunk.

3. Peel back the insulation on the bulkhead to expose the access hole.

4. Remove the mounting nut, washer, and rubber disc.

5. Unbolt the strut from the axle and remove it.

6. Reverse the procedure for installation and torque the lower strut mount bolt to 43 ft. lbs. and the upper mount nut to 23 ft. lbs.

4000 (exc. Quattro)

NOTE: Always remove and install the suspension struts one at a time. Do not

allow the rear axle to hang in place as this may cause undue damage to the brake lines.

1. With the car at ground level, open the trunk and remove the sheet metal trim from around the shock tower.
2. Remove the rubber cap.
3. Remove the strut mounting nut.
4. Raise the rear of the car and support it with jack stands.
5. Remove the lower strut mounting bolt from the axle beam and remove the strut.
6. Installation is the reverse of removal. Torque the upper strut mounting bolt to 14 ft. lbs. and the lower strut mounting bolt to 43 ft. lbs.

5000 (exc. Quattro)

NOTE: The struts must be removed with the weight of the vehicle on the rear wheels. If not, a spring compressor must be used on the rear springs.

1. Remove the upper strut mounting nut.
2. If the vehicle is not on its wheels, install the spring compressor and compress the spring.
3. Remove the lower strut mounting nut.
4. Remove the shock absorber.
5. Installation is the reverse of removal. Torque the lower mounts to 40 ft. lbs. and the upper to 14 ft. lbs.

Quattro

1. Loosen the lug nuts and remove the axle nut cover.
2. Remove the axle nut and then raise and support the rear of the vehicle. Remove the wheels.
3. Using a tie-rod end puller, remove the tie-rod end.
4. Remove the brake caliper mounting bolts. Disconnect the brake line from its bracket and then position the caliper out of the way.
5. Remove the brake disc and the ball joint clamp bolt and then pry the ball joint out of the hub.
6. Using a four-armed puller, remove the stub axle.
7. Have a helper hold the strut assembly and remove the upper strut mounting nut. Remove the strut.

NOTE: The rear axle assembly must be under no tension while removing the strut.

8. Installation is in the reverse order of removal. Please note the following torque figures:
- Tie-rod nut — 43 ft. lbs.
- Axle nut — 203 ft. lbs.
- Upper strut mounting nut — 43 ft. lbs.
- Ball joint clamp bolt — 47 ft. lbs.

FRONT SUSPENSION

The Fox, 4000 and 5000 use MacPherson struts. The strut unit, steering arm, and steering knuckle are all combined in one assembly; there is no upper control arm. The system is designed with negative roller-radius; this stabilizes the car when different retarding forces are applied to the front wheels, as would happen if one front tire were on wet pavement and the other on dry.

NOTE: Exercise extreme caution when working with the front suspension. Coil springs and torsion bars are under great tension and can cause severe injury if released suddenly.

MacPherson Strut

For all spring and shock absorber removal and installation procedures and any other strut overhaul procedures, please refer to "Strut Overhaul" in the Unit Repair section.

REMOVAL & INSTALLATION

Fox

1. With the car resting on its wheels, remove the axle nut.
2. Raise the car and remove the wheels.
3. Unbolt the brake caliper, remove the brake line clip, and rest the caliper on the lower control arm.

1. Cotter pin
2. Tie-rod
3. Axle driveshaft
4. Circlip
5. Retainer nut
6. Brake caliper
7. Wheel bearing
8. Hub
9. Brake disc
10. Axle nut

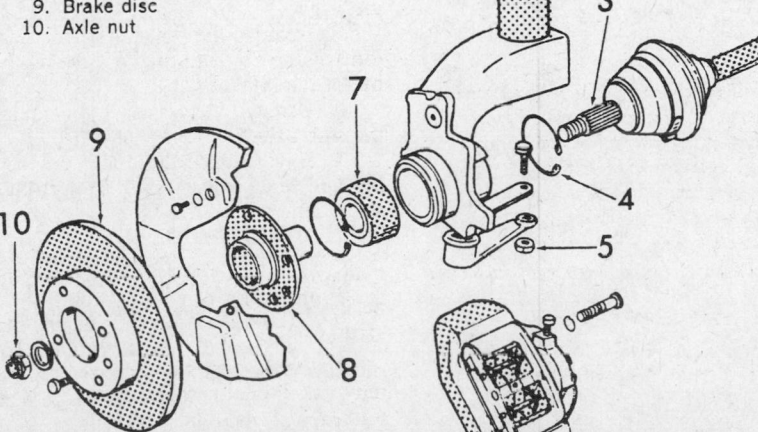

4000 front suspension—Fox similar

4. Remove the bolt holding the steering knuckle to the lower control arm.
5. Detach the steering arm from the tie-rod end.
6. Unbolt the stabilizer bar pivots from the lower control arm. Disconnect the lower control arm from the steering knuckle by removing the bolt at the ball joint.
7. Remove the strut mounting nuts in the engine compartment and remove the strut.
8. It is not recommended that the strut unit be disassembled unless the necessary special tools to do this safely are available. The units should be serviced in pairs to maintain equal shock qualities and ride height.
9. When replacing the strut unit, use a new nut and bolt to attach the lower control arm to the steering knuckle. Torque the strut-to-body bolts to 16 ft. lbs., the control arm-to-steering knuckle bolt to 16 ft. lbs., the brake caliper mounting bolts to 43 ft. lbs., and the stabilizer bar pivots to 7 ft. lbs.
10. Torque the axle nut to 180 ft. lbs. and check the wheel alignment.

4000 and 5000

1. With the car on the ground, remove the front axle nut and loosen the wheel bolts.
2. Raise and support the front of the car and remove the wheels.
3. Remove the brake caliper mounting bolts and the brake line bracket. Remove the brake caliper with the line still attached to it and wire it out of the way.

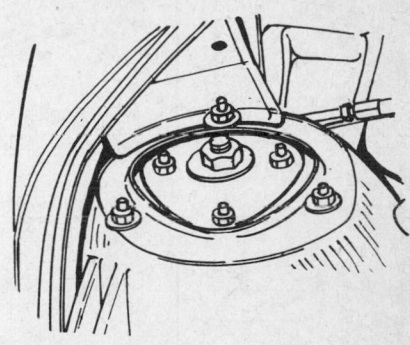

Front strut upper mounting nut—5000

4. Remove the wheel bearing housing/ball joint clamp bolt.
5. Remove the retaining nut and press off the tie-rod end.
6. Unscrew the retaining bolt and remove the stabilizer bar end clamps. Pivot the stabilizer bar downward. (4000 only)
7. Remove the two center stabilizer bar clamps and then unbolt it from the lower control arm. Remove the stabilizer bar (5000 only).
8. Pry the lower control arm down and remove the ball joint from the wheel hub.
9. Remove the halfshaft from the wheel hub.
10. While holding the shock absorber piston rod with an internal socket wrench, remove the retaining bolt and then remove the strut assembly (4000 only).
11. Remove the spring strut cover (Quattro and Turbo) and remove the three strut retaining nuts, then remove the strut assembly (5000 series only).
12. Installation is in the reverse order of removal. Note the following:
   a. When installing the stabilizer bar on the 4000, the positioning is correct if the clamps are difficult to install in the rubber bushings. Attach the clamps loosely, take a short test drive to bring the bushings into the correct position and then tighten to 18 ft. lbs.
   b. Tighten the ball joint bolt to 36 ft. lbs. on the 4000 and 47 ft. lbs. on the 5000.
   c. Tighten the axle nut to 167 ft. lbs. on the 4000, 202 ft. lbs. on the Quattro and Turbo and 203 ft. lbs. on all other 5000 models.

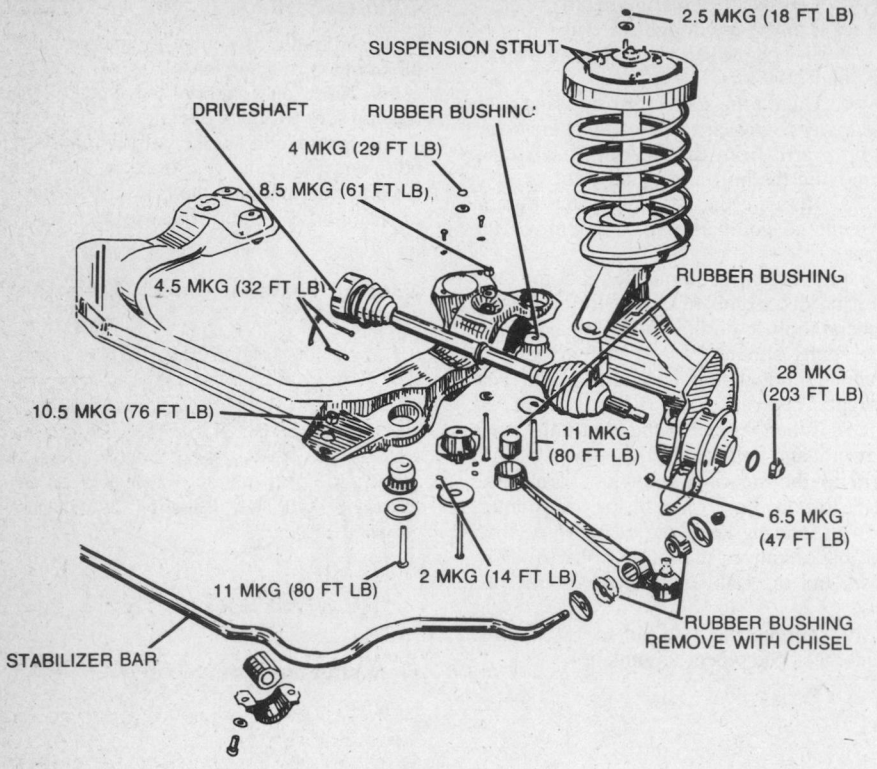

2.5 MKG (18 FT LB)

SUSPENSION STRUT

DRIVESHAFT   RUBBER BUSHING

4 MKG (29 FT LB)

8.5 MKG (61 FT LB)

RUBBER BUSHING

4.5 MKG (32 FT LB)

28 MKG
(203 FT LB)

10.5 MKG (76 FT LB)

11 MKG
(80 FT LB)

6.5 MKG
(47 FT LB)

11 MKG (80 FT LB)

2 MKG (14 FT LB)

STABILIZER BAR

RUBBER BUSHING
REMOVE WITH CHISEL

5000 front suspension

Lower Control Arm and Ball Joint

REMOVAL & INSTALLATION

5000 (exc. Quattro)

1. Remove the ball joint clamp nut.
2. Pry the control arm down and out of the clamp.
3. Remove the nut on the end of the stabilizer bar.
4. Loosen the control arm-to-subframe mounting bolts and then pull the control arm off of the end of the stabilizer bar.
5. Remove the bolts and remove the control arm.

NOTE: The ball joint and control arm are one unit and can only be replaced as a unit.

6. Installation is the reverse of removal.
7. Check the toe and camber adjustments.

Track Control Arm and Ball Joint

REMOVAL & INSTALLATION

Fox

1. Remove the bolts securing the control arm to the subframe. Before removing the ball joint, mark its position on the subframe.
2. Pull the ball joint retaining clamp and pull the ball joint from the knuckle.
3. Remove the bolts securing the ball joint flange to the control arm.
4. To install, position the new ball joint on the control arm and tighten the bolts to 45 ft. lbs.
5. Install the control arm in the reverse of the above. Torque the control arm-to-subframe bolts to 32 ft. lbs.

Ball Joints

REMOVAL & INSTALLATION

4000 and Quattro

1. Mark the position of the ball joint flange on the lower control arm.
2. Remove the ball joint retaining clamp nut and pull the ball joint/control arm down and out of the retaining clamp.
3. Unscrew the two ball flange retaining nuts and remove the ball joint.
4. Installation is the reverse of removal. Tighten the clamp nut to 47 ft. lbs. and tighten the ball joint flange nuts to 47 ft. lbs.

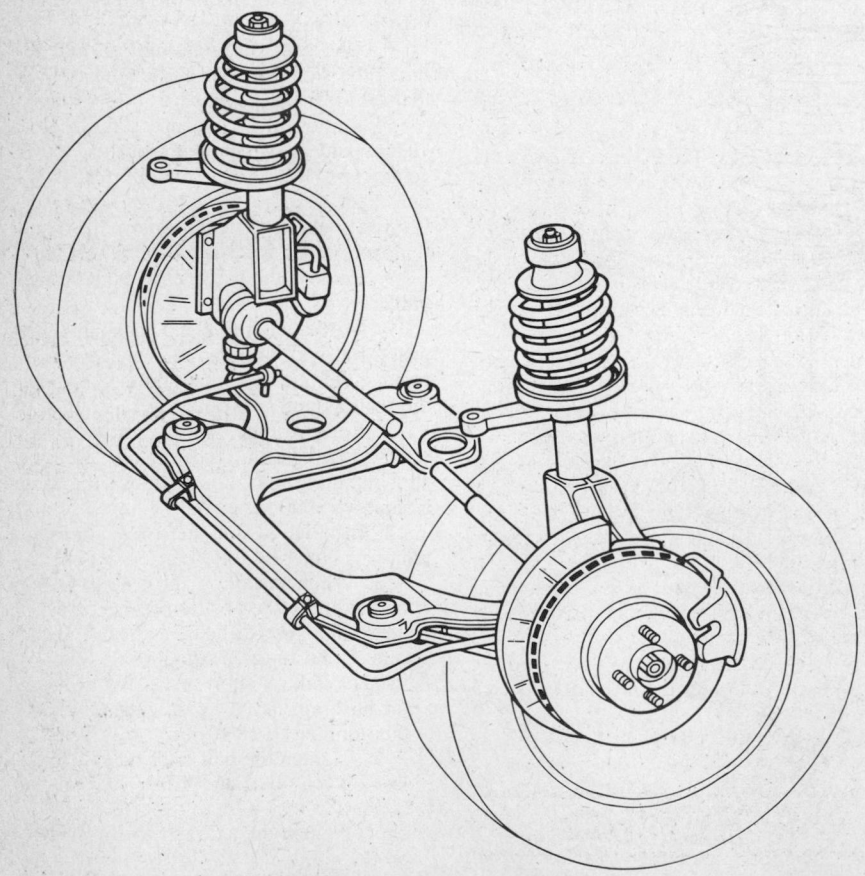

4000S Quattro front suspension

Lower Control Arm

REMOVAL & INSTALLATION

4000 and Quattro

1. Raise the front of the car and support it with jack stands.
2. Remove the ball joint as detailed earlier.
3. Unbolt the end of the stabilizer bar and pull it down.
4. Remove the two control arm-to-subframe bolts and remove the control arm.
5. Installation is in the reverse order of removal. Check control arm bushings for cracking or undue wear. Tighten the control arm-to-subframe bolts to 43 ft. lbs. and the stabilizer bar mounting bolts to 18 ft. lbs.

Wheel Alignment

Before checking wheel alignment, tire pressures should be brought up to specifications and the front ride height checked. The car should be bounced and settled before each alignment check or adjustment. The adjustments should be made in this order: caster, camber, toe-in.

CASTER

Caster is set at the factory on these models and is not adjustable other than the replacement of damaged suspension parts.

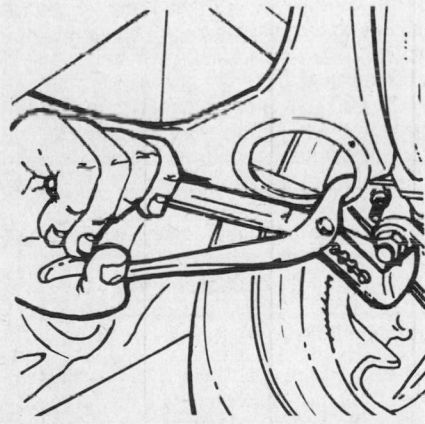

Adjusting the camber on the 4000 and Quattro without the special tool

CAMBER

Camber is checked with the wheels straight ahead.

Fox

1. Loosen the two nuts holding the ball joint to the lower control arm.
2. Push the ball joint in or out to adjust the camber. A special tool is available to lever the ball joint in or out, using the holes in the control arm.
3. Tighten the nuts to 47 ft. lbs.

4000 and Quattro

1. Loosen both ball joint flange mounting bolts on the control arm.
2. Using the special tool US 4490, or by just moving the ball joint with your hands, adjust the camber to specifications.

5000

1. Loosen the spring strut plate mounting bolts.
2. Attach a socket wrench to the top piston rod nut and move the assembly in the slots until the camber is correct.
3. Tighten all bolts.

TOE-IN

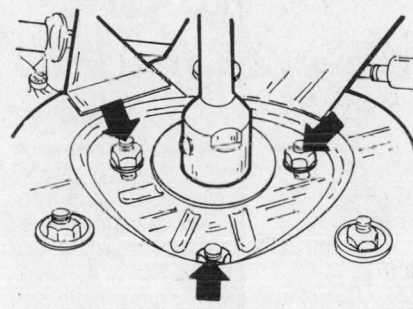

To adjust the camber on the 5000, move the strut assembly in the slots of the spring strut mounting plate

Toe-in is checked with the wheels straight ahead.

1. Toe-in can be determined by measuring and comparing the distance between the center of the tire tread, front and rear, or by measuring and comparing the distance between the inside edges of the wheel rims, front and rear. If the wheel rims are used as the basis of measurement, the car should be rolled forward slightly and a second set of measurements taken. This avoids any error induced by bent wheels. If at all possible, a toe-in gauge should be used; it will give a much more accurate measurement.
2. Toe-in is adjusted at the steering tie-rods. On the Fox, simply loosen the clamp and locknut on the adjustable left tie-rod.
3. Turn both rods to lengthen or shorten them an equal amount. If the tie-rods are not adjusted equally, the steering wheel will be crooked and the turning arcs of the front wheels will be changed. On the Fox, only the left tie-rod is adjustable. If the steering wheel is crooked, it must be removed and repositioned.
4. Tighten the clamps.

STEERING

The steering is a rack and pinion type. The

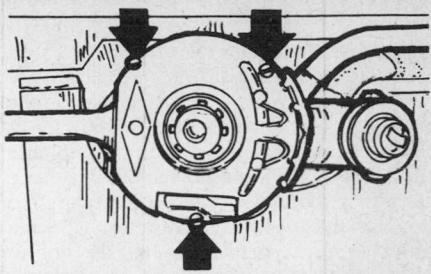

Steering column switch mounting screws—4000

steering geometry is designed to give a variable ratio effect, giving faster steering response as the steering wheel is turned toward either right or left lock. The steering column and linkage is arranged so as to break away and telescope safely in an accident, rather than penetrating into the passenger compartment.

Steering Wheel

REMOVAL & INSTALLATION

1. Center the wheel. Disconnect the battery ground cable.
2. Pry off the wheel pad (horn button).
3. Unbolt and remove the wheel. A steering wheel puller should not be necessary.
4. On installation, torque the bolt to 36 ft. lbs. (100, Fox and 5000) and 29 ft. lbs. (4000, Quattro and Turbo). Do not pound on the wheel, as the collapsible column may be damaged.

Turn Signal and Headlight Dimmer Switch Replacement

Fox

1. Disconnect the battery ground cable.
2. Remove the steering wheel.
3. Remove the screws in the top of the switch housing, lift off the housing and unplug the connectors, and remove the switch housing along with the wiper and turn signal levers.

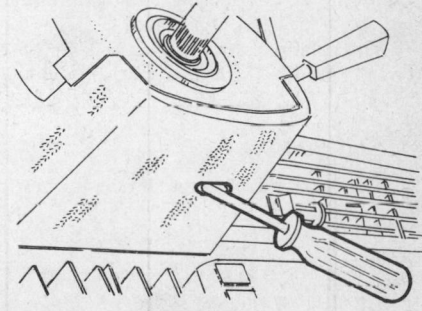

To remove the switch housing on the 5000, insert a screwdriver and loosen the screw

4000 and 5000

1. Disconnect the negative battery cable.
2. Remove the steering wheel.
3. Remove the screws and remove the steering column cover on the 4000.
4. Remove the steering column switches. On the 4000, remove the three screws and pull the switches off enough to unplug the electrical connectors. On the 5000, insert a screwdriver into the slot on the bottom of the switch housing, loosen the screw and pull the housing off enough to unplug the electrical connectors.
5. Installation is in the reverse of removal.

Ignition and Steering Lock Switch

REMOVAL & INSTALLATION
4000

1. Disconnect the negative battery cable.
2. Remove the steering wheel, the steering column covers and the steering column switches.

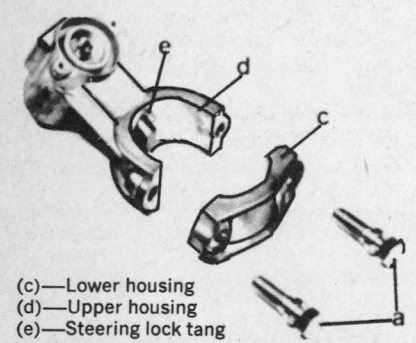

(c)—Lower housing
(d)—Upper housing
(e)—Steering lock tang

The ignition and steering lock switch is held in place by two bolts (a) whose heads shear on installation to deter theft

3. Pry the lock washer off the steering column and discard it.
4. Remove the spring and pull off the contact ring.
5. Unplug the electrical connector.
6. Unscrew the retaining bolt and slide the ignition switch/steering lock assembly off of the steering column tube.
7. Installation is in the reverse order of removal. Replace the old lock washer with a new one.

Fox and 5000

1. Remove the column shroud for access to the screws.
2. Drill out the special shear bolt heads.

--- CAUTION ---
These bolts also support the steering column. Support the column while removing the bolts.

3. On installation, make sure the two projections on the lock clamp assembly engage the two depressions in the columns. Tighten the new bolts until their heads shear off.

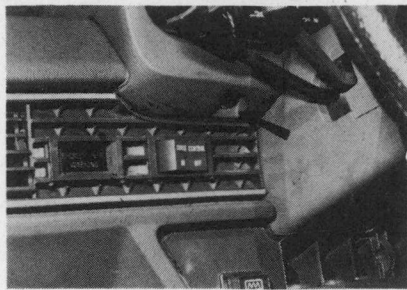

Instrument panel trim pad screw, left side—5000

Steering Gear

REMOVAL & INSTALLATION
Fox and 5000

1. Pry off the lock plate and remove both tie–rod mounting bolts from the steering rack, inside the engine compartment. Pry the tie–rods out of the mounting pivot.
2. Remove the lower instrument panel trim.
3. Remove the shaft clamp bolt, pry off the clip, and drive the shaft toward the inside of the car with a brass drift.
4. Remove the steering gear mounting bolts at both ends. There is a single bolt at the right end.
5. Turn the wheels all the way to the right and remove the steering gear through the opening in the right wheel housing.
6. For installation, temporarily install the tie–rod mounting pivot to the rack with both mounting bolts. Remove one bolt, install the tie–rod, and replace the bolt. Do the same on the other tie–rod. Make sure to install the lock plate. Torque the tie–rod to 39 ft. lbs., the mounting pivot bolt to 15 ft. lbs., and the steering gear-to-body mounting bolts to 15 ft. lbs.

Power Steering Pump

REMOVAL & INSTALLATION

1. Remove the hoses from the pump. Plug the openings.
2. Remove the belt adjusting bolt, push the pump to one side and remove the belt.
3. Support the pump, remove the mounting bolts and lift out the pump.

Steering Linkage

TIE–ROD REMOVAL AND INSTALLATION

NOTE: A puller or press is required for this job.

1. Raise the car and remove the front wheels.
2. Disconnect the outer end of the steering tie–rod from the steering knuckle by removing the cotter pin and nut and pressing out the tie–rod end. A small puller or press is required to free the tie–rod end.
3. Under the hood, pry off the lock plate and remove the mounting bolts from both tie–rod inner ends. Pry the tie–rod out of the mounting pivot.
4. First install the mounting pivot to the rack with both mounting bolts. Remove one bolt, install the tie–rod, and replace the bolt. Do the same on the other tie–rod. Make sure to install the lock plate. The inner tie–rod end bolts should be torqued to 40 ft. lbs. on the Fox and 4000, 43 ft. lbs. on the 5000.

Power steering pump adjusting bolt— 5000

5. If you are replacing the adjustable left tie–rod, adjust it to the same length as the old one. Check the toe-in when the job is done.
6. Use new cotter pins when installing the outer tie–rod ends. Torque the nut to 22 ft. lbs. on the Fox and 4000 and 43 ft. lbs. on the 5000.

BRAKES

All models have dual circuit hydraulic brakes with front disc brakes and rear drum brakes except the Turbo and Quattro, which utilize disc brakes at all four wheels. All models have a brake pad lining thickness warning light. The 5000 brakes are nearly identical to those used on the Fox.

For all brake system repair and service procedures not detailed below, please refer to "Brakes" in the Unit Repair section.

Adjustment

FRONT DISC BRAKES

The front disc brakes are self-adjusting.

REAR DRUM BRAKES

Fox and 1978 5000

The rear drum brakes must be adjusted periodically, or whenever free travel is one third or more of the total pedal travel.

1. Raise the rear of the car.
2. Block the front wheels and release the parking brake. Step on the brake pedal hard to center the linings.
3. On the Fox turn the front adjusting nut on the brake backing plate until the wheel can't be rotated forward by hand. On the 5000, remove the rubber plug and turn the adjuster with a screwdriver to lock the wheel.
4. Loosen the adjusting nut until the wheel can be turned freely without drag.
5. Repeat Steps 3 and 4 for the rear adjusting nut on the Fox.
6. Repeat Steps 3, 4, and 5 for the other rear wheel.
7. Step on the brake pedal hard and make sure the wheels still rotate without drag.

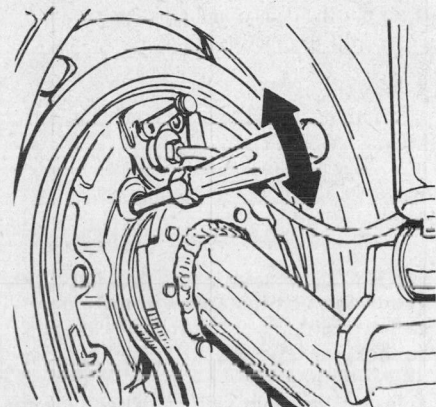

Adjusting the rear drum brakes—1978 5000

4000 and 5000 (Except 1978)

The rear drum brakes are equipped with automatic adjusters actuated by the parking

When adjusting the rear brakes, turn adjustin nuts (A) toward (a) to tighten and (b) to loosen

brake mechanism (as are the rear disc brakes on the Turbo and Quattro). No periodic adjustment of the rear brakes is necessary if this mechanism is working properly. If the brake shoe to drum clearance is incorrect and applying the parking brake a few times does not adjust it properly, the parts will have to be disassembled for repairs.

Master Cylinder

REMOVAL & INSTALLATION

1. Have an assistant hold the brake pedal down about 1½ in. Disconnect the brake lines nearest the firewall.
2. Hold a container under the fitting disconnected in Step 1 and have the assistant release the pedal. The contents of the reservoir will drain into the container. Discard the used fluid.
3. Disconnect the other brake line.
4. Disconnect the stoplight switch from the master cylinder.
5. Unbolt and remove the master cylinder from the power brake unit. Be careful not to lose the sealing ring between the two units.

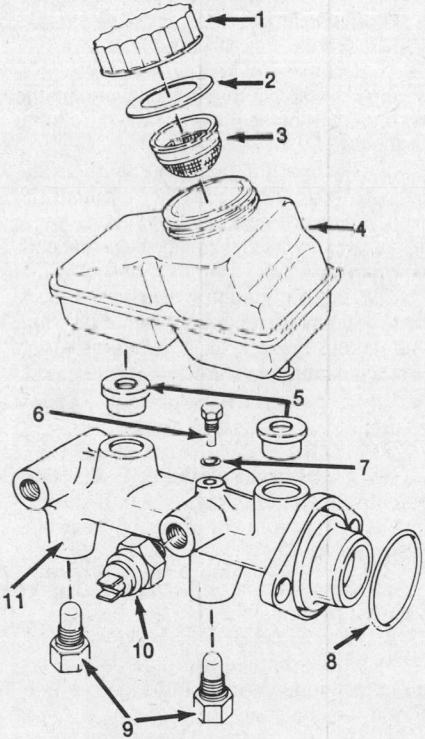

1. Reservoir cap
2. Washer
3. Filter screen
4. Reservoir
5. Master cylinder plugs
6. Stop screw
7. Stop screw seal
8. Master cylinder seal
9. Residual pressure valves
10. Warning light sender unit
11. Brake master cylinder housing

4000 master cylinder—5000 similar

6. Installation is the reverse of removal. Master cylinder bolt torque is 17 ft. lbs. Fill and bleed the system. There should be a pedal free-play of 0.2 in. It can be adjusted on the linkage, inside the car.

Proportioning Valve

CHECKING

1. With the wheels on the ground, depress the brake pedal firmly.
2. Release the pedal suddenly and check that the lever on the proportioning valve moves.
3. If the lever does not move, the valve will probably require replacement.

5000 brake proportioning valve; when checking, the lever (arrow) should move

NOTE: It is normal for small quantities of brake fluid to escape through the vent hole.

REMOVAL & INSTALLATION

1. Remove and plug the four brake lines leading from the proportioning valve.
2. Disconnect the spring which is attached to the valve and the axle beam.
3. Remove the two mounting bolts and remove the valve.

NOTE: Do not disassemble the valve.

4. Installation is in the reverse order of removal.
5. Bleed the brakes.

Front Wheel Bearings

ADJUSTMENT

There is no front wheel bearing adjustment. The bearing is pressed into the steering knuckle. Axle nut torque is 180 ft. lbs. for the Fox, 167 ft. lbs. for the 4000, 203 ft. lbs. for the 5000 and 202 ft. lbs. for the 5000 Turbo and Quattro. The axle nut should be tightened only with the wheels resting on the ground.

REMOVAL & INSTALLATION

1. Raise the front of the car and support it with jackstands.
2. Remove the wheels.
3. Remove the caliper assembly.
4. Remove the brake disc.
5. Unscrew two retaining screws and remove the splash shield.
6. Remove the halfshaft.
7. Press off the wheel hub.
8. Remove the inner and outer circlips and press out the wheel bearing.

NOTE: The wheel bearing will be damaged upon removal and must be replaced.

9. Installation is in the reverse order of removal.

Wheel Cylinders

REMOVAL & INSTALLATION

1. Remove the brake shoes.
2. Depress the brake pedal about 1½ in. to block the master cylinder compensating port and prevent leakage. Secure the pedal in this position.
3. Disconnect the brake line and plug the opening.
4. Remove the two mounting screws from the backing plate.

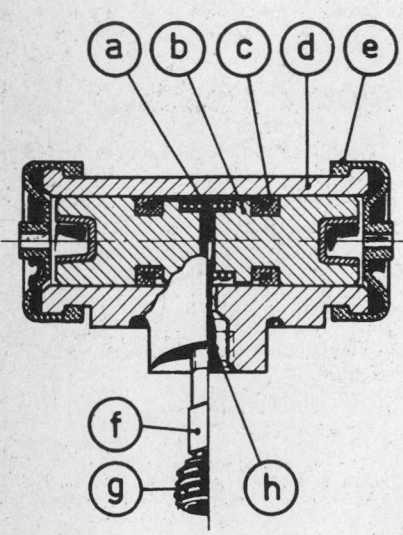

(a)—Spring
(b)—Piston
(c)—Grooved cup
(d)—Cylinder
(e)—Cap
(f)—Bleeder valve
(g)—Dust cap
(h)—Brake line connection

Cross-section of a rear wheel cylinder

5. Remove the cylinder.
6. Reverse the procedure for installation.

Parking Brake

ADJUSTMENT

Fox and 1978 5000

The handbrake (parking brake) must be adjusted periodically to compensate for lining wear and cable stretching. The adjuster is at the cable junction, under the center of the car.

1. Block the front wheels. Raise and support the rear of the vehicle. Do not use a jack under the rear axle tube.
2. Pull the brake up to the first notch.
3. If the wheels will not rotate freely, loosen the adjusting nut.
4. Tighten the adjusting nut until neither wheel can be turned by hand.
5. Check that there is no drag when the brake handle is fully released.

4000 and 1979 and Later 5000 (Except Turbo and Quattro)

NOTE: Because of self-adjusting rear brakes, adjustment is only necessary after replacement of any of the brake components.

1. Raise the rear of the car and support it with jack stands.
2. Release the parking brake lever.
3. Depress the brake pedal once.
4. Pull the parking brake lever onto the second tooth in the 4000 and the third tooth in the 5000.
5. Tighten the adjusting nut on the parking brake cable equalizer bar until the wheels can just be turned by hand.
6. Release the lever and check that both wheels rotate freely.
7. Turn the ignition switch on and check that the brake warning light comes on when the parking brake lever is pulled up to the first tooth and goes out when it is released.

Turbo and Quattro

NOTE: Because of the self-adjusting rear brakes, adjustment is only necessary after replacement of any of the brake components.

1. Raise the rear of the car and support it with jackstands.
2. Release the parking brake lever.
3. Check that the parking brake levers at the rear calipers stay on the stop. If not, loosen the adjusting nut.
4. Depress the brake pedal approximately 40 times and pull the parking brake lever to the third tooth.
5. Tighten the adjusting nut on the parking brake equalizer bar until the rear wheels can just be turned by hand.
6. Release the brake and check that both wheels rotate freely and that the parking brake levers at the rear calipers stay on the stops.
7. Turn the ignition switch on and check that the brake warning light comes on when

the parking brake is pulled to the first tooth and goes out when it is released.

CABLE REMOVAL AND INSTALLATION

Fox

1. Jack up the rear of the car.
2. Block the front wheels and release the handbrake.
3. Remove the rear brake shoes.
4. Remove the cable adjusting nut(s) and detach the cable guides from the floor pan.
5. Replace the cable and brake shoes. Check the parking brake adjustment.

4000 and 5000

1. Raise and support the rear of the car. Release the parking brake.
2. Remove the rear brake drums on all but the Turbo and Quattro.
3. Disconnect the cable from the shoe assembly by pushing the spring forward and removing the cable from the adjusting arm on all but the Turbo and Quattro.
4. Pull the parking brake cable out of its retaining clip on the caliper (Turbo and Quattro only).
5. Remove the cable compensating spring.
6. Back off the equalizer nut and guide the cable through the trailing arms and supports.
7. Installation is the reverse of removal.

NOTE: When installing the parking brake cables on the Turbo and Quattro, the long cable goes on the left side and the short one goes on the right side. The cable coupling should connect the two cables on the right side of the equalizer bar.

8. Adjust if necessary.

CHASSIS ELECTRICAL

Heater

REMOVAL & INSTALLATION

4000

1. Disconnect the negative battery cable.
2. Drain the engine coolant.

NOTE: Save the coolant for reuse.

3. Trace the heater hoses coming from the firewall and disconnect them. One leads to the back of the cylinder head and the other leads to the heater valve located above and behind the oil filter.
4. Detach the cable for the heater valve.
5. Remove the center console.

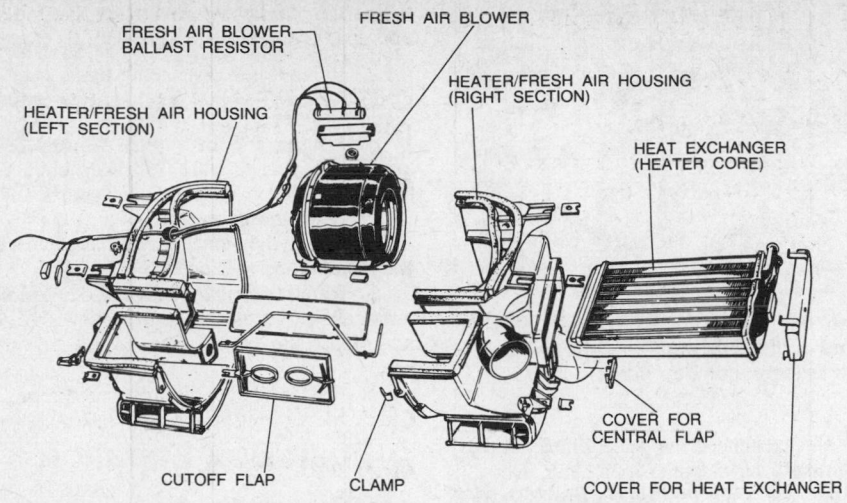

FRESH AIR BLOWER
BALLAST RESISTOR

FRESH AIR BLOWER

HEATER/FRESH AIR HOUSING
(RIGHT SECTION)

HEATER/FRESH AIR HOUSING
(LEFT SECTION)

HEAT EXCHANGER
(HEATER CORE)

CUTOFF FLAP

CLAMP

COVER FOR
CENTRAL FLAP

COVER FOR HEAT EXCHANGER

Exploded view of the 4000 heater assembly

6. Remove the left and right covers below the instrument panel.

7. Pull off the fresh air/heater control knobs.

8. Pull off the trim plate.

9. Remove the screws (2) for the controls.

10. Remove the center cover mounting screws (2 top and 2 bottom) and remove the cover.

11. Detach the right, left and center air ducts.

12. Remove the heater housing retaining spring.

13. Remove the cowl for the air plenum which is located under the hood and in front of the windshield.

14. Remove the heater housing mounting screws (4) and remove the heater housing. The mounting screws are under the hood where the air plenum was.

15. Installation is in the reverse order of removal. Be sure to replace all sealing material.

5000

NOTE: Blower or core removal requires removal and disassembly of the entire unit.

1. Disconnect the battery ground.
2. Drain the cooling system.

— CAUTION —

If the vehicle is equipped with air conditioning, the A/C system must be discharged. This procedure should be left to a trained technician.

3. Discharge the air conditioning system.

4. Disconnect the:
   a. Temperature sensor connector.
   b. Evaporator/heater connector clamp.
   c. Temperature control cable.
   d. Fresh air door vacuum hose.

5. Disconnect the main harness connector.

6. Loosen the case retaining strap.

7. Remove the coolant hoses at the heater core tubes.

8. Remove the yellow, green and red vacuum hoses from the heater case.

9. Remove the air duct hoses.

10. Remove the heater case mounting screws (two in the passenger compartment, one in the engine compartment). On A/C equipped cars, remove the four evaporator housing mounting screws in the passenger compartment.

11. Support the heater/evaporator unit and pull it away from the firewall.

12. Remove the control cable grommet to facilitate case removal.

13. The case halves may be separated by removing the clips at the top and bottom with a small pry bar.

14. Installation is the reverse of removal. Replace all sealing material. Evacuate, charge and leak test the system. This last procedure should be performed by a trained technician.

Fox

The heater must be removed and disassembled to service the heater or the core.

1. Remove the windshield washer container. Remove the ignition coil.

2. Disconnect the two hoses from the heater core connections at the firewall.

3. Unplug the electrical connector.

4. Remove the heater control knobs on the dash.

5. Remove the controls from the dash complete with brackets.

6. Pull the cable connection off the electric motor.

7. Disconnect the cable from the lever on the round knob.

8. Using a small pry bar, pry the retaining clip off the fresh air housing (the front portion of the heater).

9. Remove the fresh air housing complete with the controls.

10. Detach the left and right air hoses.

11. Lower the heater assembly.

12. Pull out the two pins and remove the heater cover. Unscrew and remove the fan motor.

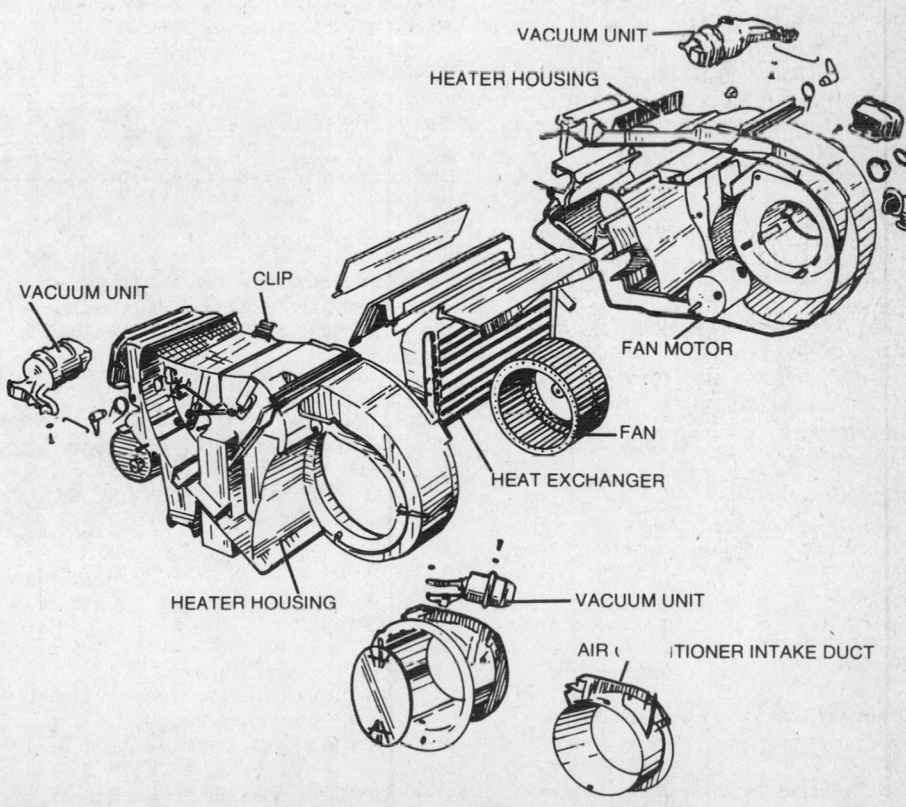

VACUUM UNIT

HEATER HOUSING

VACUUM UNIT

CLIP

FAN MOTOR

FAN

HEAT EXCHANGER

HEATER HOUSING

VACUUM UNIT

AIR CONDITIONER INTAKE DUCT

Exploded view of the 5000 heater assembly

13. Separate the heater halves to remove the heater core.

14. Installation is the reverse of removal.

Radio

The radio is usually a dealer installed or aftermarket unit. Thus no specific removal and installation procedures can be given. The following information applies generally to all car radios.

Care should be taken during installation to avoid reversing the ground and power leads. Reversal of these leads will cause serious damage to the radio. The power lead usually has an in-line fuse.

If the speaker needs replacement, it should be replaced with one of the same impedance, measured in ohms. Mismatched impedance can cause rapid transistor failure as well as poor radio performance. This should also be taken into consideration when adding a second speaker.

The radio should never be operated without a speaker connected or with the speaker leads shorted. This will result in transistor failure.

Windshield Wiper Motor and Linkage

REMOVAL & INSTALLATION

1. Pry off the wiper arms and remove the nuts from the studs in the cowl.

2. Remove the brace-to-body screws.

3. Disconnect the multiple connector at the wiper motor.

4. Remove the motor mounting screw, and pry off the connecting rod.

5. Remove the linkage followed by the motor.

Instrument Cluster

For further information on the instruments, please refer to "Gauges and Indicators" in the Unit Repair section.

REMOVAL & INSTALLATION

Fox

1. Disconnect the battery ground cable.

2. Remove the lower instrument panel trim.

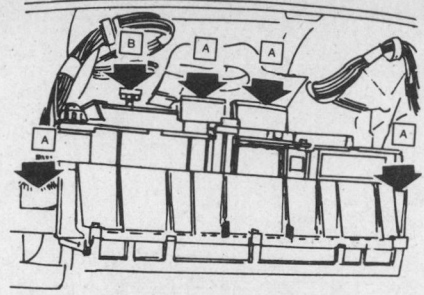

From the top of the instrument cluster, remove the four multi-point connectors and the speedometer cable—4000

3. Disconnect the speedometer cable from the back of the speedometer. Detach the electrical plug at the back of the fuel and temperature gauge.

4. Detach the spring at either end and pull the cluster forward.

4000

1. Disconnect the negative battery cable.

2. Remove the retaining screws for the instrument cluster cover. Remove the cover and the trim strip.

3. From the top of the instrument cluster, remove the four multi-point connectors.

4. Unscrew the speedometer cable.

5. Remove each switch panel from the side of the instrument cluster.

6. Remove the instrument cluster retaining screws and remove the cluster.

7. Installation is in the reverse order of removal.

5000

1. Disconnect the negative battery cable.

2. Remove the instrument panel trim.

3. Remove the instrument cluster cover retaining screws and remove the cover.

4. Loosen the instrument cluster retaining screws and slide it forward enough to remove the multi-point connectors and the speedometer cable.

5. Remove the cluster retaining screws and remove the cluster.

6. Installation is in the reverse order of removal.

Fuse Box Location

The fuse box for all 4000 models can be found underneath the left side of the dashboard, behind the rear panel of the package tray. The fuse box for all 5000 models is located under the hood, at the left rear of the engine compartment. The relays for both models are also plugged into the fuse box. In the cover of each fuse box (and in the Owner's Manual) is a chart which tells which circuit the fuse protects and its correct amperage. The chart also tells which circuit the relays are connected to. Each model also uses in-line fuses for certain circuits: fuel pump, battery, air conditioning and power door locks (if so equipped), 4000; air conditioning, power windows, and heated seats, 5000; glow plug, 5000 Diesel; cigar lighter, power windows and the cooling fan for the injectors, 5000 Turbo and Quattro.

Fuse box—5000

BMW
318i, 320i, 325e, 528e, 528i, 530i, 533i, 630CSi, 633CSi, 733i

SERIAL NUMBER IDENTIFICATION

Manufacturer's Plate

The manufacturer's plate is located in the engine compartment on the right side inner fender panel or support, or on the right side of the firewall.

Vehicle Identification Number

The VIN is located on a plate on the upper left of the instrument panel, visible through the windshield.

Chassis Number

The chassis number can be found in the engine compartment on the right inner fender support or facing forward on the right side of the heater bulkhead. A label is also attached to the upper steering column cover inside the vehicle.

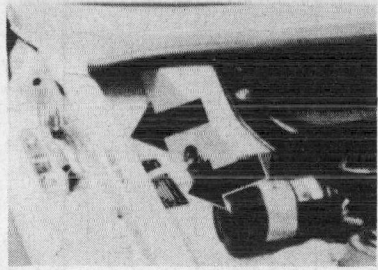

Under hood serial number location—typical

Engine Number

The engine number is located on the left rear side of the engine, above the starter motor.

Engine serial number location

GENERAL ENGINE SPECIFICATIONS

Year	Model	Engine No. Cyl.— Displacement cu. in. (cc)	Carburetor or Injection Type	Horsepower @ rpm	Torque @ rpm (ft. lbs.)	Bore × Stroke (in.)	Compression Ratio	Oil Pressure @ rpm (psi)
'78–'79	320i	4-121 (1990)	Bosch K-Jetronic	110 @ 5800	112 @ 3750	3.504 × 3.150	8.2:1	57 @ 4000
'80–'83	320i	4-108 (1766)	Bosch K-Jetronic	101 @ 5800	100 @ 4500	3.504 × 2.793	8.8:1	57 @ 4000

GENERAL ENGINE SPECIFICATIONS

Year	Model	Engine No. Cyl.— Displacement cu. in. (cc)	Carburetor or Injection Type	Horsepower @ rpm	Torque @ rpm (ft. lbs.)	Bore × Stroke (in.)	Compression Ratio	Oil Pressure @ rpm (psi)
'84–'85	318i	4-108 (1766)	Bosch L-Jetronic	101 @ 6000	103 @ 4500	3.504 × 2.795	9.0:1	54 @ 4000
'78	530i	6-182 (2985)	Bosch L-Jetronic	176 @ 5500	188 @ 4500	3.504 × 3.150	8.1:1	71 @ 6000
'79–'81	528i	6-170 (2788)	Bosch L-Jetronic	169 @ 5500	166 @ 4500	3.390 × 3.150	8.2:1	71 @ 4000
'82–'85	325e, 528e	6-165 (2693)	Bosch Motronic	121 @ 4250	170 @ 3250	3.307 × 3.189	9.0:1	71 @ 5000
'78–'79	633CSi, 733i	6-196 (3210)	Bosch L-Jetronic	176 @ 5500	192 @ 4000	3.504 × 3.386	8.0:1	71 @ 6000
'80–'81	633CSi 733i	6-196 (3210)	Bosch L-Jetronic	174 @ 5200	184 @ 4200	3.504 × 3.386	8.0:1	71 @ 6000
'82–'85	533i, 633CSi, 733i	6-196 (3210)	Bosch Motronic	181 @ 6000	195 @ 4000	3.504 × 3.386	8.8:1	64 @ 6000

TUNE-UP SPECIFICATIONS

Year	Model	Spark Plugs Type	Gap (in.)	Dwell (deg.)	Point Gap (in.)	Ignition Timing (deg.)① MT	AT	Intake Valve Opens (deg.)•	Fuel Pump Pressure (psi)	Idle Speed (rpm) MT	AT	Cold Valve Clearance (in.)
'78–'79	320i	Bosch W125T30②	.024③	62	.014	25B@ 2200 (2400)	25B@ 2200 (2400)	4B	64–74	950	950	.007
'80–'83	320i	Bosch WR9DS	.024	Electronic④		25B@ 2200	25B@ 2200	4B	64–74	850	900	.007
'78	530i	Bosch W145T30	.024	38	.014	22B@ 1700 (2700)	22B@ 1700 (2700)	14B	35	950	950	.011
'79–'81	528i	Bosch WR9DS⑤	.024	Electronic④		22B@ 2100	22B@ 2100	7B	35	900	900	.011
'82–'85	325e, 528e	Bosch WR9LS	.024	Electronic		⑥	⑥	NA	43	⑥	⑥	.010
'78–'79	633CSi, 733i	Bosch W145T30	.024	Electronic		22B@ 2400 (2750)	22B@ 2400 (2750)	14B	37	950	950	.011
'80–'81	633CSi, 733i	Bosch WR9DS	.024	Electronic④		22B@ 1650	22B@ 1650	14B	35	900	900	.011
'82–'85	533i, 633CSi, 733i	Bosch WR9LS	.024	Electronic		⑥	⑥	14B	35	⑥	⑥	.011
'84–'85	318i	Bosch WR9DS	.024	Electronic		⑥	⑥	NA	43	⑥	⑥	.008

•.02 in. clearance cam base circle and rocker
NA Not available at time of publication
① Figures in parenthesis are for California
② 1978–79: W145T30

③ 1979: .027
④ Air gap 0.012–0.028 in.
   Dwell 42° ± 10°@ 15 rpm
   52° ± 5° @ 4500 rpm

⑤ 1979: W125T30
⑥ Motronic injection system; controlled by computer

FIRING ORDERS

NOTE: To avoid confusion, always replace spark plug wires one at a time.

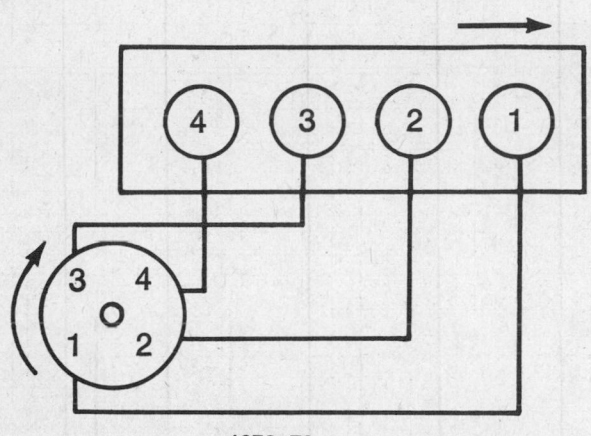

1978–79
4 cylinder firing order: 1-3-4-2

1980–'85
4 cylinder firing order: 1-3-4-2

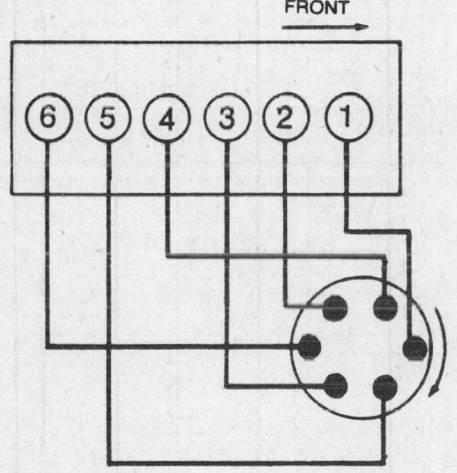

528i, 530i, 630CSi and 1978–81 633CSi and
733i firing order: 1–5–3–6–2–4

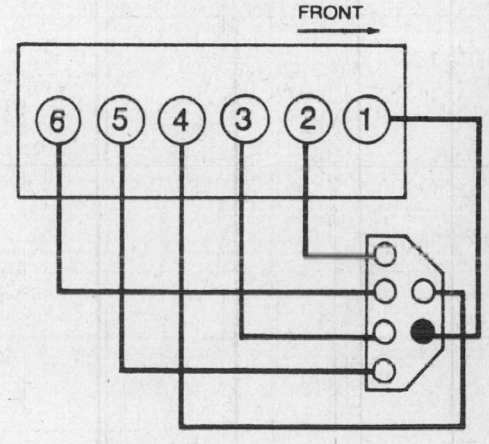

325e, 528e, 533i and 1982 and later 633CSi
and 733i firing order: 1-5-3-6-2-4

CAPACITIES

Year	Model	Engine Crankcase (qts)		Transmission, Refill After Draining (pts)		Drive Axle (pts)	Gasoline Tank (gals)	Cooling System (qts)
		With Filter Change	Without Filter Change	Manual	Automatic			
'78–'79	320i	4.5	4.25	2.2	4.2	2.0	15.9	7.4
'80–'83	320i	4.5①	4.25②	2.2	4.2	1.9	15.3	7.4
'78	530i	6.0	5.25	2.3	4.2	3.4	16.4	12.7
'78–'85	733i	6.0	5.25	2.4	4.0	3.8	22.5	12.7

CAPACITIES

Year	Model	Engine Crankcase (qts) With Filter Change	Without Filter Change	Transmission, Refill After Draining (pts) Manual	Automatic	Drive Axle (pts)	Gasoline Tank (gals)	Cooling System (qts)
'78–'85	633CSi	6.0	5.25	2.4	4.2	3.2	16.5	12.7
'79–'81	528i	6.0	5.25	2.3	4.2	3.4	16.4	12.7
'82–'85	528e	4.5	4.2	3.4	4.2	3.6	16.6	12.7
'83–'85	533i	6.0	5.3	2.65	6.3	3.6	16.6	12.7
'84–'85	318i	4.5	4.2	2.4	6.3	1.9	14.5	7.4
'84–'85	325e	4.5	4.2	2.4	6.3	3.4	14.5	7.4

①With chrome plated guide tube for dipstick:
  4.25
②With chrome plated guide tube for dipstick:
  4.0
③'83–'85 models—6.3
④'83–'85 models—3.6

CRANKSHAFT AND CONNECTING ROD SPECIFICATIONS

(All measurements are given in inches)

Model	Year	Engine Displacement Cu In. (cc)	Crankshaft Main Brg Journal Dia	Main Brg Oil Clearance	Shaft End-Play	Thrust on No.	Connecting Rod Journal Diameter	Oil Clearance	Side Clearance
All	'78–'85	All	2.3622④	.0012–.0027	.003–.007	①	1.8898②	③	.0016

①Four cylinder models: 3
  Six cylinder models: 4
②528e: 1.7717
③1978–82:528i, 530i, 533i, 630CSi and
    633CSi: .0009–.0027
    320i, 733i: .0009–.0031
    528e: .0013–.0027
  1983–85, All Models: .0012–.0028
④318i—2.1654

VALVE SPECIFICATIONS

Model	Year	Engine Displacement Cu In. (cc)	Seat Angle (deg)	Face Angle (deg)	Spring Test Pressure (lbs @ in.)	Spring Free Height (in.)	Stem-to-Guide Clearance (in.) Intake	Exhaust	Stem Diameter (in.) Intake	Exhaust
All exc. 528e	'78–'85	All	45	45½	64 @ 1.48	1.71①	.0010–.0020②	.0015–.0030②	.3149	.3149
325e, 528e	'82–'85	165 (2693)	45	45	—	—	.006	.006	.276	.276

—Not available at time of publication
①A dimension of 1.8110 applies to some springs, depending upon the manufacturer.
  Test pressure is the same.
②Wear limit: .006 in.

PISTON AND RING SPECIFICATIONS
(Measurements in inches)

Model	Year	Piston to Bore Clearance	Ring Gap			Ring Side Clearance		
			Top Compression	Bottom Compression	Oil Control	Top Compression	Bottom Compression	Oil Control
318i	'84–'85	.0008–.0020	.012–.028	.008–.016	.010–.020	.0024–.0035	.0012–.0028	.0008–.0024
320i	'78–'83	.0018	.012–.018	.008–.016	.010–.020	.002–.004	.002–.003	.001–.002
530i	'78	.0018②	.012–.020	.008–.016	.010–.020③	.0024–.0036	④	.001–.002
528i	'79–'81	.0018	.012–.020	.012–.020	.010–.020	.0024–.0036	.0012–.0024	.0008–.0020
633CSi, 733i	'78–'82	.0018	.012–.020	.008–.016	.0024–.0036	⑥	⑤	
533i, 633CSi, 733i	'83–'85	.0008–.0020	.012–.028	.008–.016	.010–.020	.0020–.0032	.0016–.0028	.0008–.0028
325e, 528e	'82–'85	.0004–.0016	.012–.020	.012–.020	.010–.020	.0016–.0028	.0012–.0024	.0008–.0017

② Early Pistons: .0016
③ Bevelled ring: .010–.016
④ Mahle: .0012–.0024
   KS: .0016–.0028
⑤ Mahle: .0008–.0020
   KS: .0012–.0024
⑥ Mahle: .0020–.0032
   KS: .0016–.0028

TORQUE SPECIFICATIONS
(All reading in ft lbs)

Model	Year	Engine Displacement Cu In. (cc)	Cylinder Head Bolts	Rod Bearing Bolts	Main Bearing Bolts	Crankshaft Pulley Bolt	Flywheel-to-Crankshaft Bolts●	Mainfolds	
								Intake	Exhaust
318i	'84–'85	10.8	④	38–41	42–46	130–145	75–83⑦	16–17	22–24
320i	'78–'83	All	①	38–41	42–46	101–108	72–83	15–20	22–24
528i, 530i, 633CSi, 733i	'78–'82	All	①	38–41	42–46	②	72–83	—	22–24
533i, 633CSi, 733i	'83–'85	All	④	38–41	42–46	318–333	75–83⑦	16–17	22–24
528e	'82	165 (2693)	③	14	43–48	282–311	71–82	—	22–24●
325e, 528e	'83–'85	165 (2693)	⑤	14⑥	43–48	282–311	75–83⑦	16–17	22–24

●Install with Loctite®
① Step 1—25–32
   2—49–52
   3—56–59
   4—56–59 (after warm-up)
② Flat hex nut: 174–188
   Shoulder hex nut: 318–333
③ Step 1—22–25
   2—43–47

④ Step 1—25–29
   2 42–45
   Wait 20 minutes
   3—56–59
   4—20°–30°
⑤ Step 1—22–25
   Wait 20 minutes
   2—43–47

Warm engine fully
   3—20°–30°
⑥ Then turn additional 70°
⑦ First coat w/Loctite® 270 or equivalent

ALTERNATOR AND REGULATOR SPECIFICATIONS

| Year | Engine Displacement cu. in. (cc) | Alternator | | Regulator | |
		Bosch Model or Part No.	Maximum Output (Amps)	Bosch Model or Part No.	Regulated Voltage @68°F
'78–83	4-108 (1766)	K1/14V/55A 0 120 489 608	55	0 192 052 004	13.9–14.3
'84–'85	4-108 (1766)	14V 910W 80A	80	—	13.5–14.6
'78–83	6-170 (2788) 6-182 (2985)	14V/55A	55	AD1/14V	13.5–14.2
'78–83	6-196 (3210)	14V/65A 0 120 489 619	65	EE14/V3 0 192 052 006	13.5–14.2
'82–'83	6-165 (2693)	—	65		13.5–14.6
'84–'85	6-164 (2693)	14V 1120W 80A	80	—	13.5–14.6
'84–'85	6-196 (3210)	14V 1120W 80A	80	—	13.5–14.6

Since March 1983

BATTERY AND STARTER SPECIFICATIONS

| Year | Engine Displacement cu. in. (cc) | Battery (12 Volt, Negative Ground) Ampere Hour Capacity | Bosch Model or Part No. | Starter No-Load Test | | |
				Amps	Volts	rpm
'78–'83	4-108 (1766)	55	GF(R)12V1.0 hp 0 001 311 045	210	9.6	1300
'78–'83	6-170 (2788) 6-182 (2985)	55①	GF12V1.2 hp	270	9.1	10,000
'78–'83	6-196 (3210)	66	GF12V1.8 hp 0 001 311 042	340	9.1	10,000
'82–'85	4-108 (1766)	50	GF1.1KW		②	
'84–'85	6-164 (2693)	66	GF1.1KW		②	
'84–'85	6-196 (3210)	66	GF1.5KW		②	

① 633CSi—65 amp hour
② These starters are tested under load at 13V, and should produce nominal power.

BRAKE SPECIFICATIONS

(Measurements in inches)

| Year | Model | Lug Nut Torque (ft. lbs.) | Master Cylinder Bore | Disc | | Drum | | Minimum Lining Thickness | |
				Minimum Thickness	Maximum Runout (installed)	Diameter	Maximum Machined Oversize	Front	Rear
'78–'79	320i	59–65	.812	.827	.008	9.84	9.89	.12	.12
'80–'83	320i	59–65	.812	.827	.008	10.00	10.04	—	—
'84–'85	318i	65–79	—	.595F/.331R	.008	—	—	.079	.079
'85	325e	65–79	—	.9213F/.331R	.008	—	—	.079	.079

BRAKE SPECIFICATIONS

(Measurements in inches)

Year	Model	Lug Nut Torque (ft. lbs.)	Master Cylinder Bore	Disc		Drum		Minimum Lining Thickness	
				Minimum Thickness	Maximum Runout (installed)	Diameter	Maximum Machined Oversize	Front	Rear
'78–'79	530i, 633CSi	59–65	.936	.460F/.334R	.008	—	—	—	—
'79–'81	528i	59–65	.936	.840F/.340R	.008	—	—	—	—
'84–'85	533i	65–79	—	.9213F/.331R	.008	—	—	.079	.079
'82–'85	528e	65–79	—	.138F/.138R	.002	—	—	—	—
'80–'85	633CSi	65–79	.936	.840F①/.720R	.008	—	—	—	—
'78–'79	733i	60–66	.874	.827	.006	—	—	—	—
'80–'85	733i	65–79	.874	.840F①/.360R	.008	—	—	—	—

F Front
R Rear
① '84 and '85 models—.9213F

WHEEL ALIGNMENT SPECIFICATIONS

Year	Model	Front Suspension			Steering Axis Inclination (deg.)	Rear Suspension	
		Caster (deg.)	Camber (deg.)	Toe-In (in.)		Camber (deg.)	Toe-In (in.)
'84–'85	318i, 325e	9P	11/16N	3/32P	14½P	1 13/16N	3/32P
'84–'85	528e, 533i, 733i	8¼P	5/16N	3/32P	12 3/16P	2N	3/32P
'83–'85	633CSi	8¼P	5/16N	5/64P	12 3/16P	2 5/16N	5/64P
'83	528e	8¼P	5/16N	5/64P	12 3/16P	1 13/16N	5/64P
'83	733i	9P	0	1/64	11 9/16P	1½N	5/64P
'83	533i	8¼P	5/16N	5/64P	12 3/16P	2 5/16N	5/64P
'82	528e	8¼P	11/32N	11/64	12 5/32P	1 27/32N	11/64P
'78–'83	320i	8 5/16P	0	1/16	10 15/16P	2N	1/32P
'79–'81	528i	7 11/16P	0	1/16	8½P	2N	5/64P
'78–'82	733i	9P	0	3/64P	11 9/16P	1½N	3/16P
'80–'82	633CSi	7 11/16P	0	1/8P	8P	2N	5/64P
'78	530i	7 11/16P	0	1/16	8½P	2N	1/32P
'78–'79	633CSi	7 11/16P	0	1/16	8P	2N	5/64P

N Negative
P Positive
320i, 528i, 530 and 733 models aligned
with 150 lbs. in each front seat, 150 lbs.
in rear seat and 46 lbs. in trunk.
630, 633 aligned with 150 lbs. in each front
seat and 30 lbs. in trunk on left side.

TUNE-UP PROCEDURES

Spark Plugs

REMOVAL & INSTALLATION

NOTE: Before removing spark plugs clean any dirt from the base area of the spark plugs with compressed air or a stiff brush.

— CAUTION —

Grasp the plug wire by the boot and twist slightly to loosen, before pulling on the boot (not the wire) to remove the wire from the spark plug. Bending or pulling on the wire breaks the internal conductive material.

1. Mark or tag the wires for correct reinstallation, then remove the wires from the spark plugs.
2. Using a $^{13}/_{16}$ in. deep-well sparkplug socket and a swivel head rachet wrench, remove the spark plugs.
3. Inspect spark plugs for cracked and damaged insulators or threads, worn electrodes, damaged gasket and carbon or other fouling deposits.
4. If plugs are to be reused, file the electrodes square.
5. Regap old spark plugs or check the gap on new spark plugs.
6. Install the spark plugs in the head and torque to 18–21 ft. lbs. (25–28 Nm).

NOTE: The cylinder head is made of aluminum. Be very careful to avoid overtightening of the plug. It's best to use a torque wrench and tighten to 17–20 ft. lb. The threads in the head are easily stripped.

7. Install the plug wires on the proper spark plugs.

Breaker Points and Condenser

REPLACEMENT

1. Remove the distributor cap, rotor and the point guard, if equipped.
2. Disconnect the primary wire at the inner side of the distributor body terminal.
3. Remove the point set retaining screw and lift the point set from the breaker plate.

NOTE: Some distributors have the condenser mounted on the outside of the distributor body, while others have the condenser mounted inside the housing. The condenser lead will either be attached to the distributor outside terminal or to the inside terminal. Disconnect the condenser lead wire if necessary to replace the point set or condenser.

Examining the condition of the breaker points. Mild pitting (1) is acceptable. Excessive transfer (2) is unacceptable

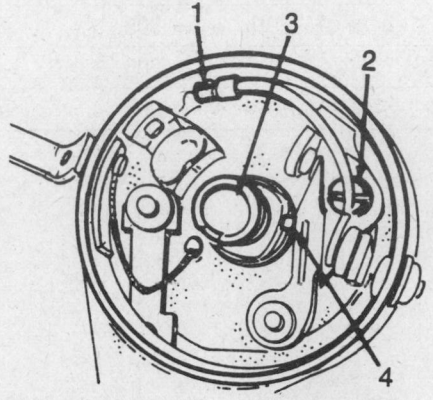

Breaker point attachment and lubrication points: (1) primary connection, (2) holddown screw, (3) advance mechanism lubricating wick, (4) breaker arm rubbing block

4. To install the new point set, clean the old grease from the cam and distributor plate. Put a small amount of special cam lubricant on the distributor cam and install the point set and condenser in the reverse of the removal.
5. Align the point faces to meet squarely and "bump" the engine until the rubbing block is on the high point of the distributor cam.
6. Adjust the point gap by moving the point set until a feeler gauge of the specified size can be inserted in the gap.

Install the point set on the breaker plate, then attach the wires

7. Tighten the retaining screw and recheck the gap.
8. Start the engine and check the dwell.

Electronic Ignition

Breaker points and condensers are not used with the electronic ignition. The air gap between the rotating teeth and the stator teeth can be checked with a brass or plastic feeler gauge. No adjustment is possible. If the gap is not 0.012–0.028 in., the unit should be replaced.

— CAUTION —

All repair work to the electronic ignition system should be done with the engine stopped and the ignition switch Off.

For 1982 and later, some models are equipped with a Motronic engine control system. This system uses various engine sensors including an oxygen sensor in the exhaust to monitor engine conditions. The monitored information is fed to a Motronic (computer) unit, which in turn controls the air fuel mixture entering the engine.

Ignition Timing

The engine should be at normal operating temperature. Adjust the idle speed (except on cars with Motronic injection. See note below). Remove and plug distributor vacuum lines. Connect a timing light to the

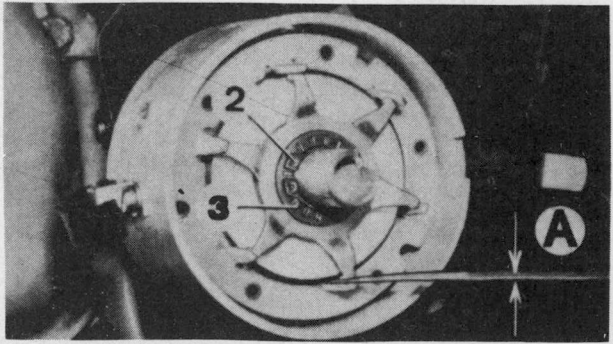

2. Circlip
3. Expander

Measuring rotor to stator clearance (A)

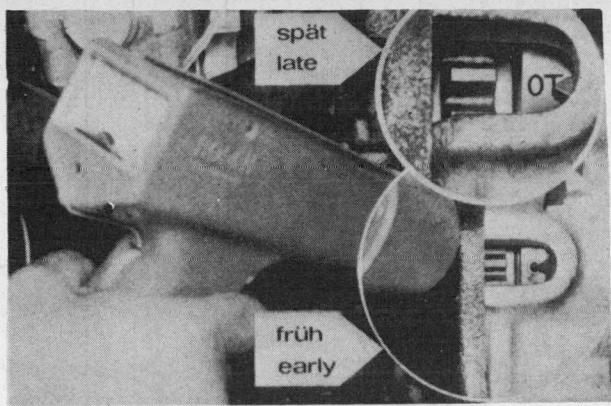

Ignition timing marks at flywheel

No. 1 spark plug wire and start the engine. Align the marks on the flywheel with the bell housing indicator, by rotating the distributor body. Tighten the distributor body clamp.

NOTE: The flywheel mark is either a pressed-in steel ball or a long tapered peg on the side of the starter ring gear.

NOTE: Setting the ignition timing on cars with Motronic emission control requires special test equipment.

Valve Clearance

All BMW engines are equipped with an overhead camshaft operating the intake and exhaust valves through rocker arm linkage.

NOTE: The valves must be adjusted cold.

1. Remove the rocker cover.
2. Rotate the engine until the No. 1 cylinder is at TDC on the compression stroke.

NOTE: Locate No. 1 cylinder firing position by the distributor rotor–to–cap position, or by observing the valve action in the opposite cylinder. Refer to following charts:

Cylinder Firing-Piston at TDC	Exhaust Valve Closing, Intake Valve Opening On Opposite Cylinder
6 CYLINDER	
1	6
5	2
3	4
6	1
2	5
4	3
4 CYLINDER	
1	4
3	2
4	1
2	3

3. Measure the valve clearance between the valve stem end and the rocker arm on the No. 1 cylinder (refer to the specifications for valve clearances).

4. Adjust the clearance by loosening the locknut on the rocker arm and turning the eccentric with a bent rod inserted through a hole provided on the surface of the eccentric.

5. When the proper clearance is obtained, tighten the locknut and recheck the valve clearance. Complete the adjustment on both valves.

6. Rotate the engine crankshaft to the

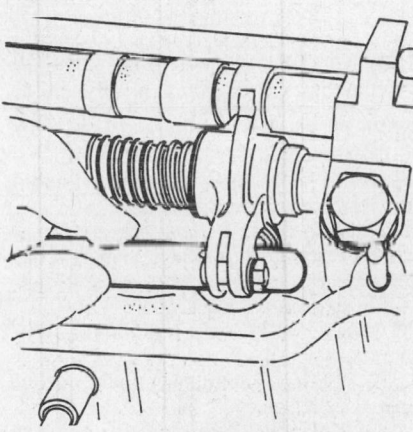

Checking valve clearance with a flat feeler gauge

next cylinder in the firing order, adjust the valves and repeat the procedures until all the valves are adjusted.

7. Replace the rocker cover, using a new gasket.

Fuel Injection

IDLE SPEED AND MIXTURE ADJUSTMENT

NOTE: The idle speed and mixture can be adjusted ONLY with the aid of a CO meter. If you do not have access to this tool, do not attempt any of the following procedures. On late model BMWs with electronic control of idle speed and ignition timing (Motronic Injection Systems), CO adjustment can only be done with a special BMW Service Test Unit or equivalent.

530i

1. Run engine to normal operating temperature.
2. Disconnect the hose from the collector to the charcoal filter. Do not plug the line.

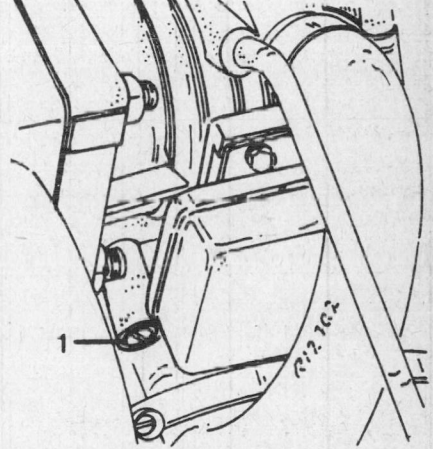

530i idle speed adjustment screw

Adjusting of engine valve clearance with bent rod after loosening the locknut (1)

NOTE: The hose is located between the first and second air induction tubes.

3. Disconnect the air pump hose at the air pump and plug the line.

4. Adjust the idle speed by turning the screw on the side of the throttle housing.

5. The CO level should be between 1.5–3.0% at idle speed.

6. If necessary, adjust the CO to specifications with the idle air screw located on the air volume control, by turning the screw to the left or right.

7. Reconnect the hoses.

NOTE: A plug in the anti-tamper cover of the air flow sensor must be removed in order to adjust the CO level. This should only be done if no other faults or problems are found in the ignition and injection systems and the CO% is not within specification.

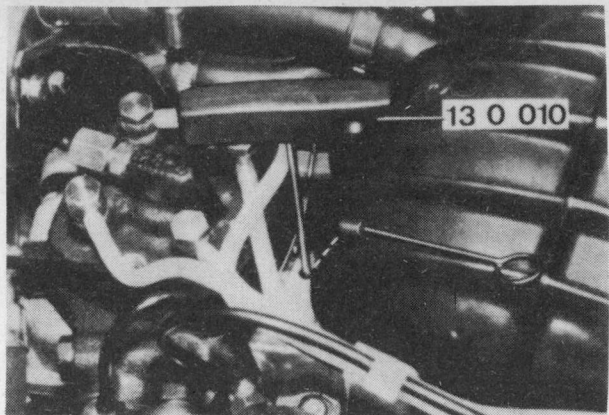

Adjusting CO level with special tool. Hole plug shown—320i

Idle speed screw location—320i

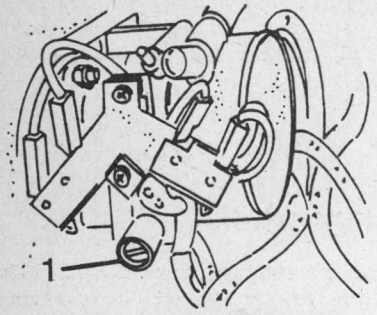

528i idle speed adjustment screw

320i

1. Run the engine to normal operating temperature.

2. Adjust the engine idle speed with the screw located near the throttle valve linkage.

3. Detach the exhaust check valve and plug the hose.

4. To adjust the CO, remove the plug from the fuel distributor and with a special wrench, adjust the CO level to a maximum of 2.0% for the 49 state vehicles or 3.5% for California cars.

5. Reconnect the exhaust check valve hose and check the idle speed.

528i

1. Adjust the idle speed to the proper specifications. The idle screw is on the side of the throttle body housing. Turning it clockwise will decrease the idle and counterclockwise will increase it.

2. Remove the CO test plug at the rear of the exhaust manifold and connect a CO meter. Start the engine and run it until operating temperature is reached. Measure the CO reading. CO must be .2–.8% (by volume).

3. Disconnect the connector for the oxygen sensor from the wiring harness. The connector is on the right side of the firewall in the engine compartment. The CO value

should not change.

4. If CO is not to specification, adjust the mixture by turning the adjusting screw, located low on the airflow meter. Adjust for .5% CO.

5. Reconnect the oxygen sensor and check CO again. If CO does not meet specification, have the car checked by someone professionally trained to troubleshoot the injection system.

6. Disconnect the test probe and reinstall the test plug into the exhaust manifold.

7. Recheck the idle speed.

1978–81 633CSi and 733i

1. Run the engine to normal operating temperature.

2. Disconnect the throttle housing-to-activated carbon filter hose. Disconnect and plug the air hose at the air pump.

3. Adjust the idle speed to specifications with the idle adjusting screw, located in the side of the throttle housing.

4. Adjust the CO to 1.5–3.0% at idle. Remove the cap from the air flow sensor and with the aid of a special tool, or short screwdriver, turn the bypass air screw located in the air flow sensor, until the CO level is as specified.

5. Reconnect the 2 hoses.

318i, 325e, 528e, 533i and 1982 and later 633CSi and 733i

NOTE: The idle speed on these models is controlled by computer and is not adjustable. If the idle speed is not within specifications, the idle speed control unit will require replacement.

ENGINE ELECTRICAL

Distributor

REMOVAL & INSTALLATION
4 Cylinder Engines

1. On all engines so equipped, remove

Remove plug (3) and use special tool 13-1-060 or equivalent to adjust the CO level with the screw in the bottom of the air intake sensor—530i, 528i, 528e, 630CSi, 633CSi and 733i

the weather-proof rubber cap protecting the distributor cap and wires from moisture. Prior to removal, using paint, chalk or a sharp instrument, scribe alignment marks showing the relative position of the distributor body to its mount on the rear of the cylinder head.

2. Following the firing order illustration at the beginning of this section, mark each spark plug wire with a dab of paint or chalk noting its respective cylinder. It will be easier and faster to install the distributor and get the firing order right if you leave the plug wires in the cap.

3. Pull up and disconnect the secondary wire (high tension cable leading from the coil to the center of the distributor cap), and remove the spark plug loom retaining nut(s) from the cylinder head cover. Disconnect the vacuum line(s) from the vacuum advance unit.

4. Disconnect the primary wire (low tension wire running from one of the coil terminals to the side of the distributor) at the distributor.

5. Unsnap the distributor retaining clasps and lift off the cap and wire assembly. On all engines equipped with a dust cap under the rotor, remove the rotor, remove the dust cap and reinstall the rotor.

6. Now, with the aid of a remote starter switch or a friend, "bump" the starter a

Distance (A) rotor moves from the housing mark during the removal of the electronic distributor

few times until the No. 1 piston is at Top Dead Center (TDC) of its compression stroke. At this time, the notch scribed on the metal tip of the distributor rotor must be aligned with a corresponding notch scribed on the distributor case. Before removing the distributor, make sure that these two marks coincide as per the illustration.

7. Loosen the clamp bolt at the base of the distributor (where it slides into its mount) and lift the distributor up and out. You will notice that the rotor turns clockwise as the distributor is removed. This is because the distributor is gear driven and must be compensated for during installation.

8. Reverse the above procedure to install. Remember to rotate the rotor approximately 1.4 in. counterclockwise (see illustration) from the notch scribed in the distributor body. This will ensure that when the distributor is fully seated in its mount, the marks will coincide. Adjust the ignition timing as described earlier. Tighten the clamp bolt to 8.0 ft. lbs.

6 Cylinder Engines—1978–81

1. Pull the vacuum hoses for advance and retard off the distributor, as required.

2. With chalk or paint, mark the relationship between the distributor body and the cylinder head. Then, rotate the engine until the line on the tip of the rotor is directly in line with the notch in the distributor housing (this puts the engine at TDC for No. 1 cylinder). Make sure that the TDC timing marks on the flywheel or balancer pulley are in line.

3. Loosen the clamp bolt at the bottom of the distributor.

4. Unscrew the mounting bracket screw for the electrical connector on the distributor body, pulling the mounting bracket off, and unplug the connector.

5. Pull the distributor out of the cylinder head.

6. To install, first position the rotor about 1½ in. counterclockwise from the notch in the distributor housing. Then, position the distributor body so the alignment marks you

made in Step 1 are aligned. Insert the distributor into the head. If necessary, shift the tip of the rotor just slightly one way or the other to get the distributor and camshaft gears to mesh properly; otherwise, the distributor cannot be inserted into the head.

7. When the distributor is fully seated, reconnect the electrical connector and all vacuum lines and install the cap. Adjust the ignition timing as described earlier.

6 Cylinder Engines— 1982 and Later

1982 and later 6 cylinder engines are equipped with the new Motronic (DME) engine control system. The distributor on these models is contained within the engine itself. Other than distributor cap and rotor removal and installation, no general service is possible.

INSTALLING THE DISTRIBUTOR IF TIMING HAS BEEN DISTURBED

Sometimes, the engine is accidentally turned over while the distributor is removed; in this case, it will be necessary to find TDC position for No. 1 cylinder before installing the distributor. First, go to the "Valve Lash Adjustment" procedure, remove the cam cover, and set the position of the engine as described there for adjustment of the valves for No. 1 cylinder. Check the exact position of the crankshaft via the timing marks on the flywheel or front pulley, and obtain exact alignment as indicated by them. Then, proceed to install the distributor as described above.

Alternator

PRECAUTIONS

Several precautions must be observed with alternator equipped vehicles to avoid damaging the unit. They are as follows:

1. If the battery is removed for any reason, make sure that it is reconnected with the correct polarity. Reversing the battery connections may result in damage to the one-way rectifiers.

2. When utilizing a booster battery as a starting aid, always connect it as follows: positive to positive, and negative (booster battery) to a good ground on the engine of the car being started.

3. Never use a fast charger as a booster to start cars with alternating-current (AC) circuits.

4. When servicing the battery with a fast charger, always disconnect the battery cables.

5. Never attempt to polarize an alternator.

6. Avoid long soldering times when replacing diodes or transistors. Prolonged heat is damaging to alternators.

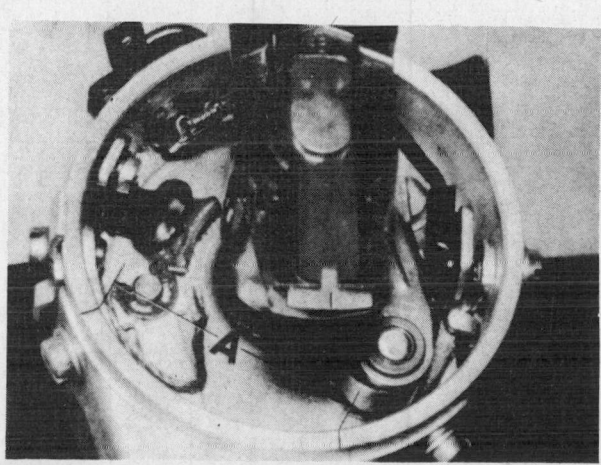

Distance (A) rotor moves from the housing mark during the removal of the conventional distributor—typical

Aligning rotor with the mark on the conventional distributor housing before removing the distributor

4. Transmitter and holder	O/T = TDC
5. Contact pin	
6. Gauge	

Electronic transmitter being gauged into position (left), and TDC mark on the balancer (right)

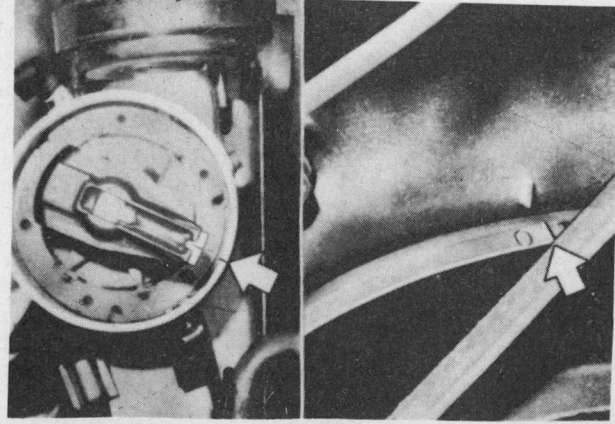

Alignment of the rotor with the electronic distributor housing and alignment of the balancer pulley TDC mark with the timing housing lug, before distributor removal

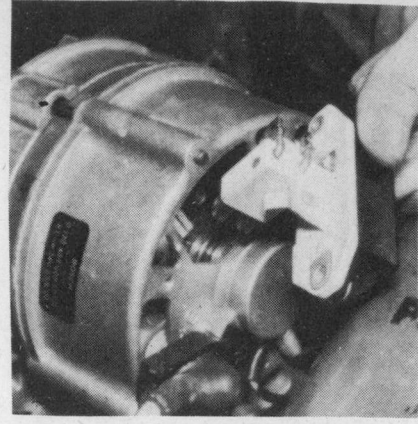

Removal of the voltage regulator and brush holder assembly—typical

7. Do not use test lamps of more than 12 volts (V) for checking diode continuity.

8. Do not short across or ground any of the terminals on the alternator.

9. The polarity of the battery, alternator, and regulator must be matched and considered before making any electrical connections within the system.

10. Never operate the alternator on an open circuit. Make sure that all connections within the circuit are clean and tight.

11. Disconnect the battery terminals when performing any service on the electrical system or charging the battery. This will eliminate the possibility of accidental reversal of polarity.

12. Disconnect the battery ground cable if arc welding is to be done on any part of the car.

REMOVAL & INSTALLATION

1. Disconnect the battery ground cable.

2. Disconnect the wires from the rear of the alternator, marking them for later installation.

3. Loosen the adjusting and pivot bolts, and remove the alternator.

4. Installation is the reverse of removal. Adjust the belt tension to approximately ⅜ in., measured between the balancer and the alternator pulley. On the 318i, position the alternator to create proper belt tension, tighten the adjusting bolt (which is threaded into the alternator housing), and hold it while tightening the locknut.

Starter

REMOVAL & INSTALLATION

1. Disconnect the battery ground cable.

2. On fuel injection 6 cylinder models, you may have to remove No. 6 intake tube for clearance. On injected 4 cylinder models, remove the intake cowl from the mixture control unit. On the 318i, remove the wire holding bracket. On the 325e, disconnect the positive terminal at the junction box on

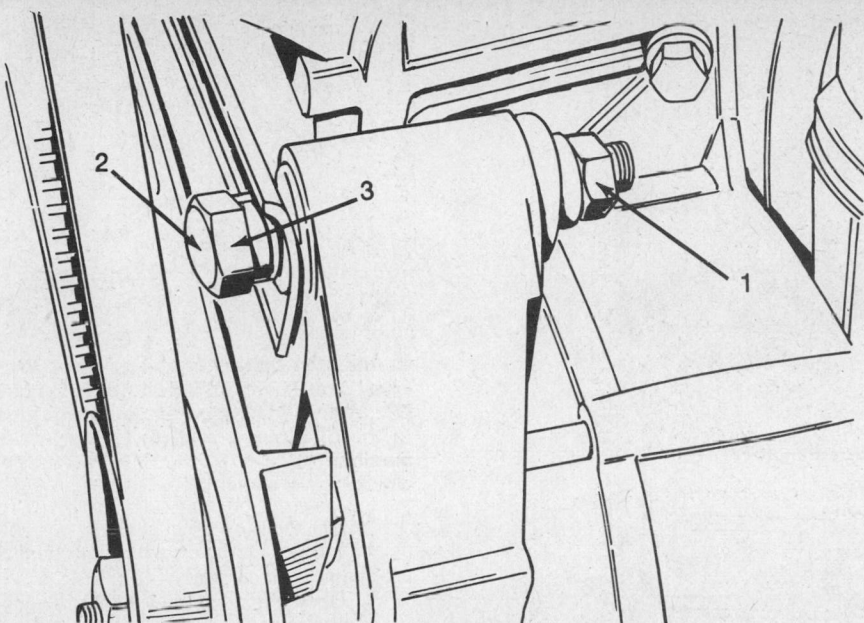

Loosen the locknut (1) at the rear of the alternator, and then turn the bolt (3) and tighten to 4.0–4.3 ft. lb. Hold the bolt in position while tightening the nut—318i

3. Remove the small dust cap from the end of the motor.

4. Remove the C-clip, shims and gasket from the end of the starter motor shaft.

5. Remove the two long pole housing screws from the housing. Lift off the pole housing cap, the brushes and the brush plate.

6. Remove the intermediate bearing screws and remove the pole housing.

7. Remove the rubber seal and washer from the engaging lever housing.

8. Remove the engaging lever screw and pull the armature out of the drive bearing.

9. Push back the thrust washer on the drive pinion end of the motor shaft in order to remove the C-clip retainer.

10. Remove the starter drive pinion and bracket.

11. Install the starter pinion and bracket. Secure them on the shaft with the thrust washer and C-clip. Lubricate the coarse threads, engaging ring and bearing with high temperature silicone grease.

12. Install the armature and shaft into the drive bearing, making sure that the tabs of the engaging lever are installed over the engaging ring. Lubricate the engaging lever with silicone grease.

13. Install the washer and rubber seal into the engaging lever housing, making sure the tabs on the seal and washer point toward the armature.

14. Position the pole housing so that the groove faces toward the rubber pad and install the pole housing into the drive bearing. Secure the screws with Loctite® No. 270.

15. Check the commutator bearing for looseness and then guide the field coil wires into the rubber seal.

16. Install the pole housing screws through the pole housing cap and locating slots in the brush plate. Install the brushes and pole housing cap on the starter.

17. Check armature axial play to 0.004–0.006 in. (0.1–0.15mm) (0.004–0.008 in. on 1983 and later models) and correct any excessive play with additional shims.

18. Install end gasket, shims and C-clip on the end of the motor shaft. Install the dust cover on the end of the starter motor (over the shaft, end gasket and shims).

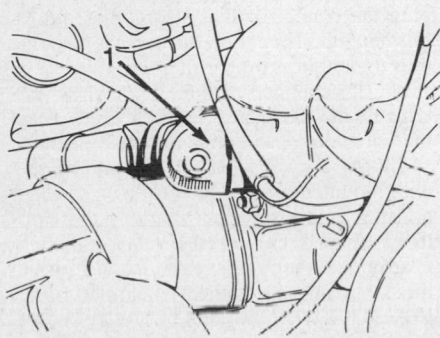

In 318i starter removal, remove the nut and detach the bracket (1)

the fender well. Then, remove the air cleaner with the flow sensor.

3. Remove the starter solenoid wire leads, marking them for later installation. On 4 cylinder models, disconnect the mounting bracket at the block. On the 325e, drain the coolant and disconnect the heater hoses.

4. Unbolt and remove the starter. On the 325e, the lower nut can be removed more easily from underneath.

NOTE: Remove the accelerator cable holder on automatic transmission equipped vehicles.

5. Installation is the reverse of removal.

STARTER DRIVE GEAR REPLACEMENT

The starter must be disassembled to replace the starter drive. A circlip retains the drive gear on the armature shaft and must be removed before the drive gear can be replaced.

1. Remove the field coil wires from the solenoid and remove the solenoid mounting bolts.

2. Disengage the solenoid plunger from the starter drive and remove the solenoid from the starter motor.

Disassembled view of starter brush plate—typical

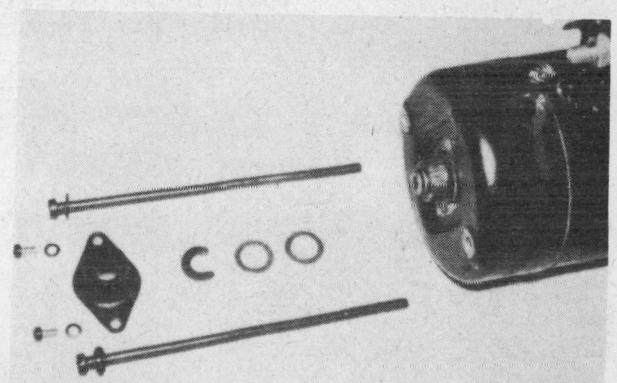

Disassembled view of end cap, retainer clip and through-bolts of starter—typical

Removal of starter solenoid

19. Install the solenoid on the starter and attach the field coil wires to the solenoid.

ENGINE MECHANICAL

Engine

REMOVAL & INSTALLATION

318i

1. Remove the transmission as detailed later.

2. Scribe hood hinge locations on the hood, and then remove it.

3. Detach the two mounting bolts and remove the power steering pump with hoses attached. Suspend the pump securely so that hoses will not be damaged.

4. Looking at the top of the air conditioning compressor, loosen the two outer bolts (bolts screwing nto the compressor) and remove the two bolts fastening the mounting bracket to the engine. Then, support the unit and remove the hinge nut and bolt form the bottom of the unit. Finally, support the unit to avoid putting strain on refrigerant hoses.

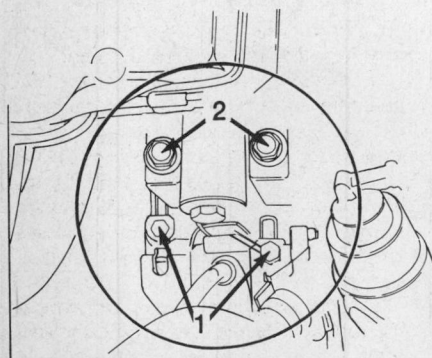

Remove bolts (1 and 2), then remove the bolt at the base of the A/C compressor—318i

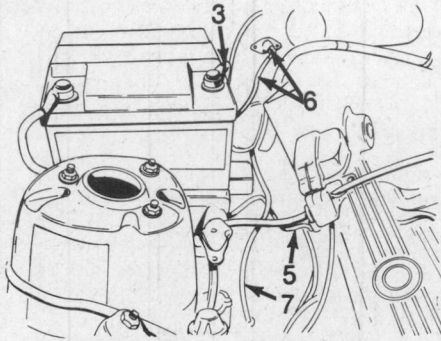

Disconnect wire (3) and ground (5), pull off plugs on temperature sensor (6), and on oxygen sensor (7)—318i

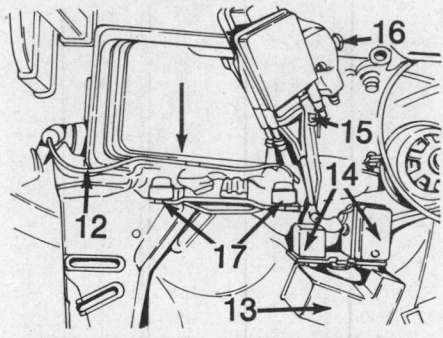

Disconnect wire (12), lift off cap (13) and remove relay (14), disconnect plug (15), open hose strap (16). Loosen nuts (17) and remove the air cleaner—318i

NOTE: Do not disconnect any air conditioning hoses!

5. Remove the radiator cap and drain coolant. Detach radiator hoses. Then, on air conditioned cars, disconnect the wires at the temperature switches. Unscrew and remove the cover located at the left side of the radiator (driver's side). Unscrew and disconnect transmission oil cooler lines at the radiator (automatic only), and plug openings. Finally, remove the mounting bolt located at the top, lift the radiator upward until it clears the rubber mounts on the bottom, and remove it.

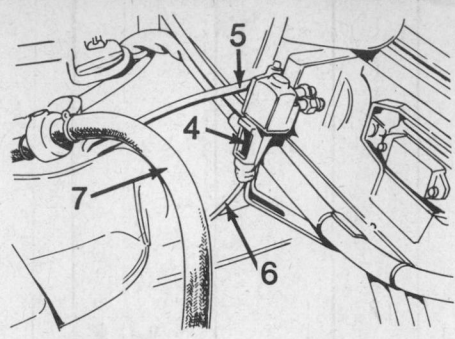

On the 318i, pull off the plug (4) and vacuum hoses (5 and 6). Detach vacuum hose (7). When installing, make sure (5) goes to the distributor, and (6) to the intake manifold.

6. Disconnect both battery leads and the battery-to-alternator wire. Disconnect the engine ground strap.

7. Open clips that hold the wiring harness running along the fender just behind the battery. Disconnect plugs from the temperature sensor and oxygen sensor.

8. Remove glovebox liner. Unplug plugs at the idle control and L-Jetronic units. Unplug the connector that also comes out of this harness. Then, pull the harness through into the engine compartment.

9. Disconnect all three coil wires and wire to the electronic ignition unit. Take the wires out of the clips mounted nearby.

10. At the air cleaner, disconnect the wire mounted on the side of the air cleaner housing, and disconnect the plug. Lift off the L-shaped cap of the relay mounted nearby, and then remove the relay. Loosen the strap and disconnect the inlet hose. Loosen the two mounting nuts and remove the air cleaner.

11. Go to the relay box mounted in between the cowl and suspension strut on the driver's side. Remove the top of the box and lift out and disconnect the plug on the outboard side. Remove the rubber guard from the TCI control unit nearby and pull off the plug connected to that. Open both associated wire straps.

12. Going to the rear of the intake manifold, unscrew the clamp and pull off the large vacuum hose. Label and then disconnect the small vacuum hoses running to the distributor and intake manifold.

13. Disconnect the throttle cable. Remove the hose clamp and hose nearby.

14. Detach fuel hoses at the injection system, and with them the associated hose holder. Collect fuel in a metal pan.

15. Attach a suitable hoist to hooks at front and rear of the engine and support the engine securely.

16. Detach both engine mounts and the vibration damper. Lift out the engine, taking care not to permit the engine to shift and hit anything on the way out.

17. Install the engine in reverse order, keeping these points in mind:

    a. The locating mandrel on the front

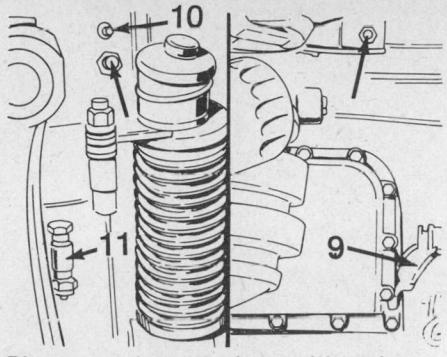

Disconnect the ground strap (9), and engine shock absorber (11) on the 318i. During installation, note that the pin (10) must fit into a bore in the axle carrier.

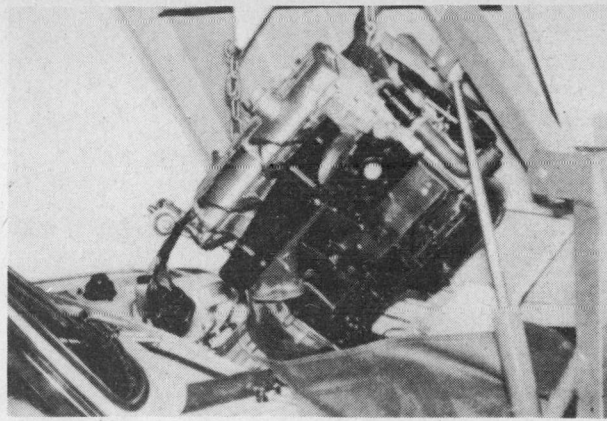

Removal and/or installation of four cylinder engine—typical

of the engine must be guided into the front suspension carrier.

b. Adjust the throttle cable for smooth operation.

c. Adjust the fan, A/C compressor, and power steering pump drive belts.

320i

1978–79

1. Raise and support the vehicle. Remove the transmission (Refer to "Manual Transmission Removal and Installation"). Remove the exhaust pipe from the exhaust manifold.

2. Remove the hood, after scribing the hinge locations.

3. Drain the cooling system, disconnect the hoses and remove the radiator. Remove the intake air panel.

4. Disconnect the lines to the injector valves.

5. Disconnect all electrical wires from the engine, marking them for installation.

6. Disconnect all fuel and vacuum lines and mark them for installation.

7. Disconnect the accelerator cable. Disconnect the battery cables and remove the battery.

8. Attach a lifting sling to the engine. Remove the retaining nuts from the left and right engine mounts and the upper engine damper, located on the left side of the engine.

9. Carefully raise and remove the engine.

10. Installation is the reverse of removal.

1980 AND LATER

1. Remove the transmission as detailed later.

2. Scribe lines, around the hood hinges and then remove the hood.

3. Disconnect the upper and lower radiator hoses and then remove the radiator.

4. Unscrew and remove the air filter housing.

5. On models equipped with air conditioning, detach the compressor and position it out of the way with wires. Do not disconnect the refrigerant lines.

6. Disconnect the battery cables (negative cable first) and remove the battery.

7. Disconnect all fuel lines at the fuel distributor. Pull the hose off the charcoal canister. Disconnect the ground wire from the front axle carrier.

8. Unscrew the retaining nut and lift the accelerator cable from the holders toward the side. Push the nipple out toward the rear and then disconnect the cable.

9. Tag and disconnect all remaining wires and hoses which may interfere with engine removal.

10. Lift out the relay socket and then pull out the two relays to the side of the housing. Disconnect the plug underneath and then lift out the wire harness from its holder on the wheel arch.

11. Open the glove box and disconnect the plug on the left-hand side. Pull the harness out through the hole in the firewall (into the engine compartment). Pull the harness out of its holders.

12. Attach an engine hoist or the like to the front and rear of the engine.

13. Unbolt the left engine mount and the upper engine damper.

14. Unbolt the right engine mount and lift out the engine.

15. Installation is in the reverse order of removal. When installing the accelerator cable, push the cable through the eye on the lever, attach it and then press the nipple into the eye. Attach the cable on the holder.

325e

1. Disconnect the battery ground cable. Remove the transmission as described in the appropriate section.

2. Without disconnecting hoses, loosen and remove the three power steering pump bolts and remove the pump and belts and support the pump out of the way.

3. Remove the drain plug and remove the coolant from the radiator. Then, remove the radiator (see the appropriate procedure).

4. Without disconnecting hoses, remove the three mounting bolts and remove the air conditioner compressor and drive belt and support it out of the way.

5. Disconnect and support the engine hood supports and then open the hood and support it securely.

6. Remove the trim panel inside the

glovebox. Disconnect the plugs going to the engine control computer; two are located in the wiring, and one directly on the unit.

7. Unscrew the idle control unit near the main control computer and pull off its plugs. On automatic transmission-equipped cars, disconnect the plug leading to the vehicle wiring harness.

8. Lift out and disconnect the plug for the oxygen sensor and two additional wires nearby. Pull off the temperature sensor plug. Loosen the straps and pull this harness into the engine compartment.

9. Remove the coolant expansion tank. Pull off the ignition coil high tension and low tension wires. Disconnect the wiring harness.

10. Disconnect the accelerator cable and cruise control cable. Pull off the vacuum hoses going to the throttle body. Loosen the clamp and pull off the large air intake hose.

11. Disconnect the plugs near the air cleaner. Lift out the relay. Disconnect the wiring harness. Unscrew the mounting nuts and remove the air cleaner.

12. Pull off the cover and disconnect the wiring harness plug at the fusebox.

13. Unscrew the fuel lines, pull off the hose and disconnect the fuel filter.

14. Disconnect both heater hoses. Unbolt the engine mounts.

15. Lift out the engine with a suitable hoist, using hooks at front and rear.

16. To install, reverse the removal procedure, keeping these points in mind:

a. When the engine is positioned, the guide pin must fit in the bore of the axle carrier. Torque the mounting bolts on the front axle carrier (small bolt) to 18–20 ft. lb.; the larger bolt to 31–35 ft. lb. The mount-to-bracket bolts are torqued to 31–35 ft. lb. Engine-to-bracket mounts are torqued to (small bolt) 16–17 ft. lb., (large bolt) 31–35 ft. lb.

b. Use new hose clamps to connect the fuel lines to the fuel lines to the fuel filter.

c. Adjust the accelerator cable and cruise control cable.

d. Use a new hose clamp on the cool-

ant expansion tank.

e. When installing hood supports, make sure the plastic portion of the support connects properly to the hood.

f. Install and adjust the V-belts on the air conditioner compressor and power steering pump.

g. Make sure all fluid levels are correct before starting the engine. Bleed air from the cooling system.

530i and 528i

1. Raise and support the vehicle and remove the transmission. Remove the exhaust pipe from the exhaust manifold.

2. Remove the power steering pump and place it out of the way along the inner fender panel. Leave the hoses attached.

3. Lower the vehicle, scribe the hood hinge location and remove the hood.

4. Remove the air cleaner with the duct work attached. Disconnect and remove the air volume control.

5. Disconnect and remove the battery.

6. Disconnect all electrical wires and connectors. Mark the wires and connectors for installation.

7. Disconnect all vacuum hoses, marking them for installation.

8. Drain the cooling system, disconnect the hoses and remove the radiator.

9. Disconnect the accelerator linkage.

10. Install a lifting sling on the engine.

11. Remove the left and right engine mount retaining nuts and washers.

12. Carefully lift the engine from the engine compartment.

13. Installation is the reverse of removal.

528e

1. Remove the transmission as detailed later. Disconnect the exhaust pipe from the exhaust manifold.

2. Remove the splash guard.

3. With the hoses still attached, remove the power steering pump and position it out of the way.

4. Unscrew the drain plug on the engine block, remove the upper and lower radiator hoses and drain the cooling system. After draining, remove the radiator.

5. With the refrigerant hoses still connected, remove the air conditioning compressor and position it out of the way.

6. Disconnect the gas pressure springs, scribe around the hinges and then remove the hood.

7. Disconnect the battery cables (negative first) and remove the battery.

8. Disconnect the accelerator and cruise control cables. Disconnect all hoses from the throttle housing (make sure you tag them all). Disconnect the air duct.

9. Remove the air filter housing along with the air flow sensor.

10. Tag and disconnect all remaining lines, hoses and wires which may interfere with engine removal.

11. Tag and dsiconnect all plugs and wires attached to the control unit in the glove box.

Removal and/or installation of six cylinder engine—typical

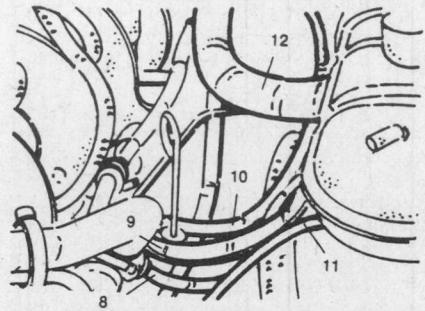

On the 630CSi and 633CSi, also disconnect the hoses shown, which are routed and coded as follows: 8–white from the booster blowoff valve to the white capped valve; 9–black from the booster blowoff valve to the blue capped valve; 10–blue from the booster blowoff valve to the blue capped valve; 11–red from the pressure converter to the EGR valve. Also detach the overflow tank hose (12)

Unscrew the straps on the firewall and pull the wire harness through to the engine compartment.

12. Disconnect the engine ground strap and then loosen both engine mounts.

13. Attach an engine lifting hoist to the front and rear of the engine, remove the engine mount bolts and then lift out the engine.

14. Installation is in the reverse order of removal.

533i and 633CSi

1. Raise and support the vehicle and remove the transmission. Remove the exhaust pipe from the exhaust manifold and reactor.

2. Remove the power steering pump and place it out of the way. Leave the hoses attached.

3. If equipped with air conditioning, remove the compressor and move it aside. *Do not remove the hoses.*

4. Scribe the hood hinge locations and remove the hood.

5. Drain the cooling system, disconnect the hoses and remove the radiator.

6. Remove the air cleaner housing at the wheelhouse.

7. Remove the electrical wires and connectors from the engine components. Tag the wires and connectors.

NOTE: The fuel injection control box is located either in the glove box or behind the right side kick panel. Remove the plug and thread the wire and connector through the hole in the firewall and into the engine compartment.

8. Install a lifting sling on the engine.

9. Remove the right and left engine mount retaining nuts and washers.

10. Remove the engine.

11. Installation is the reverse of removal.

733i

1. Raise and support the vehicle and remove the transmission. Remove the exhaust pipe from the exhaust manifold and reactor.

2. Remove the clutch housing from the engine.

3. Remove the power steering pump and place it out of the way. Do not disconnect the hoses.

4. If equipped with air conditioning, remove the compressor and place it out of the way. Do not disconnect the hoses.

5. Remove the damper bracket from the crankcase and lower the vehicle.

6. Scribe the hood hinge locations and remove the hood.

7. Drain the cooling system, disconnect the hoses and remove the radiator.

8. Remove the windshield washer reservoir and the air filter housing located on the inner fender panel.

9. Remove the electrical wiring from the engine components. Tag all wires.

10. Disconnect and remove the battery.

11. Remove and tag all vacuum hoses.

NOTE: Some vacuum hoses are color coded.

12. Disconnect the throttle linkage.

13. Remove the right kick panel from the passenger compartment, remove the fuel injection control unit wire connector and thread the connector and wire through the hole in the firewall.

14. Attach a lifting sling to the engine. Remove the left and right engine mount retaining nuts and washers. Lift the engine from the engine compartment.

15. Installation is the reverse of removal.

Cylinder Head

REMOVAL & INSTALLATION

318i

NOTE: In order to perform this procedure, you must have a special tool (angle gauge) that will accurately measure the angle at which the cylinder head bolts are torqued.

1. Disconnect exhaust pipes at the exhaust manifold and remove the pipe clamp on the transmission.

2. Disconnect the battery ground cable. Remove the drain plug and drain coolant.

3. Disconnect the wire and plug on the air cleaner. Loosen the clamp and disconnect the air intake hose. Then unscrew the nuts and remove the air cleaner.

4. Disconnect the throttle cable. Remove the dipstick tube locating bracket.

5. Disconnect the throttle position electronic plug. Disconnect the coolant and vacuum hoses nearby. Unscrew the support for the throttle body nearby.

6. Detach the fuel supply and return hoses and the hose mounting clamp.

7. Disconnect the intake manifold, distributor, and power brake unit vacuum hoses.

8. Disconnect the diagnosis plug, alternator wiring, and other plugs (2) nearby. Disconnect the coolant hoses at the cylinder head.

9. Disconnect any electrical plugs on the starter and injection system. This includes pulling off each injection plug and opening up the wiring straps.

10. Remove the distributor cap, disconnect distributor wiring plugs, wiring harness, and all plug wires.

11. Disconnect the coolant hoses going into the firewall.

12. Remove the cylinder head cover. Remove the bracket near the upper timing case over. Then, remove bolts and remove the upper timing case cover.

13. Rotate the engine until the TDC mark on the front pully is aligned with the mark on the front cover and the distributor rotor is aligned with the mark on the side of the distributor (No. 1 cylinder is at TDC). Then, remove the distributor.

14. Remove the timing chain tensioner piston as described below.

15. Remove the retaining bolts and pull off the upper timing chain sprocket. *Do not rotate crankshaft while the sproket is off!*

16. Loosen the cylinder head bolts in reverse order of the torquing sequence and remove. Lift off the cylinder head.

17. Install in reverse order, noting these points:

    a. Use a new head gasket

    b. Lightly oil all head bolts, keeping oil out of the threaded holes in the block.

    c. Torque in the sequence shown in four stages:

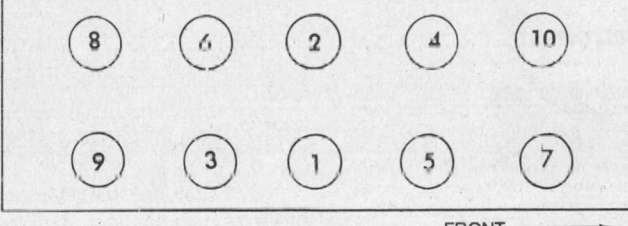

4-cylinder head torque sequence

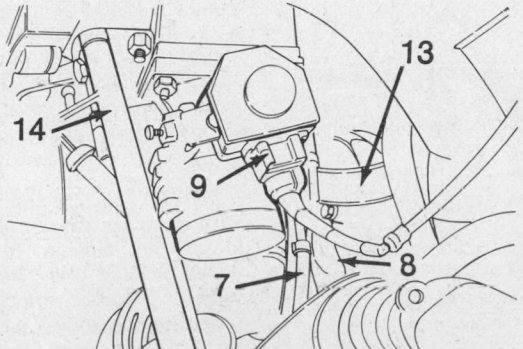

When removing the cylinder head on the 318i, disconnect the coolant hoses (7 and 8), disconnect the plug (9) and vacuum hose (13), and unscrew the support (14)

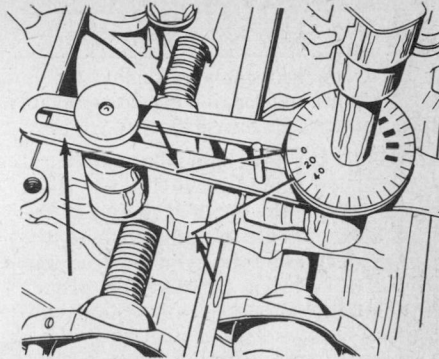

On the final torquing step for 318i cylinder head bolts, tighten head bolts the specified angle, as shown

- 25–29 ft. lb.
- 42–45 ft. lb.
- Wait 20 minutes—adjust the valves during this time
- 56–59 ft. lb.
- Run the engine until it is warm
- Torque bolts to 25° (on the angle gauge)

    d. When installing the timing chain sprocket, first make sure the notch in the camshaft flange is aligned with the cast tab on the cylinder head. The dowel pin will then align with the bore in the sprocket at the 6 o'clock position.

    e. When installing the upper timing cover, pack sealer into the crevices between block and the top of lower cover. Install all bolts *finger tight*. Tighten outer bolts first, from top to bottom on left, and top to bottom on right. Finally, torque the two front bolts.

Sprocket to camshaft torque—5 ft. lb
Chain tensioner plug—22–29 ft. lbs.
Timing case cover—7–8 ft. lb.

320i

1. Remove the air cleaner and disconnect the breather tube. Remove the intake manifold.

2. Disconnect the battery ground cable and drain the cooling system.

3. Remove the choke cable, if so equipped.

4. Disconnect the throttle linkage. Pull the torsion shaft towards the firewall until the ball is free of the torsion shaft.

5. Remove and tag the vacuum hoses.

6. Disconnect the coolant hoses from the cylinder head.

7. Disconnect the electrical wiring and connectors from the cylinder head and engine components.

8. Remove the cylinder head cover and the front upper timing case cover.

9. Rotate the engine until the distributor rotor points to the notch on the distributor body edge and the timing indicator points to the first notch on the belt pulley. No. 1 piston should now be at TDC on its firing stroke.

10. Remove the timing chain tensioner piston by removing the plug in the side of the block.

BMW

CAUTION

The plug is under heavy spring tension.

11. Open the lockplates, remove the retaining bolts and remove the timing chain sprocket from the camshaft.

NOTE: The dowel pin hole on the camshaft flange should be in the 6 o'clock position while the notch at the top of the cam flange should be aligned with the cast projection on the cylinder head and in the 12 o'clock position for proper installation.

Alignment of distributor rotor and belt pulley notch—typical

Timing chain tensioner plug removal or installation—typical

Alignment of dowel pin hole and camshaft flange notch with the cast projection of the cylinder head—four cylinder engine

12. Remove the exhaust pipe from the exhaust manifold and remove the dipstick holder.

13. Unscrew the cylinder head bolts in the reverse of the tightening sequence and remove the cylinder head.

14. Installation is the reverse of removal but note the following points:

a. Tighten the cylinder head bolts in three stages, following the illustrated sequence. Adjust the valves, start the engine and bring to normal operating temperature. Stop the engine and allow it to cool to approximately 95°F (35°C). Retorque the cylinder head bolts to specifications and readjust the valves.

NOTE: The cylinder head bolts should be retorqued after 600 miles (1000 km) of driving.

b. Check the projection of the cylinder head dowel sleeve in the cylinder block mating surface. Maximum height is 0.20 in.

c. Match the cylinder head gasket to the cylinder block and head to verify coolant flow passages are correct.

d. Adjust timing and idle speed.

e. Bleed the cooling system. Set the heater valve to the warm position and fill the cooling system. Run the engine to normal temperature and when the thermostat has opened, release the pressure cap to the first position. Squeeze the upper and lower radiator hoses in a pumping effect, to allow trapped air to escape through the radiator. Recheck the coolant level and close the pressure cap to its second catch position.

325e, 528e, 528i, 530i, 633CSi and 733i

NOTE: Small variances may be encountered among models due to model changes, difference in electrical wiring, vacuum hoses and fuel line routings, but all are basically alike.

1. Disconnect the battery ground cable.
2. Disconnect the wire connectors. Loosen the clamps and remove the air flow sensor with the air filter on the fuel injected models, or remove the air cleaner from carburetor equipped models.
3. Disconnect the rocker cover vent hose, ignition line tube and electrical wiring.
4. Remove the rocker cover.
5. Drain the cooling system and remove the coolant hoses.

NOTE: Do not interchange the heater hoses.

6. Rotate the engine so that the distributor rotor points to the notch on the distributor body edge and the timing indicator points to the notch on the belt pulley. This will place number one piston at TDC on its firing stroke.
7. Remove the upper timing housing cover after removing the distributor and thermostat housing.
8. Remove the timing chain tensioner piston.

NOTE: The 325e and 528e are equipped with a rubber drive and timing belt. To loosen belt tension, loosen the tension roller bracket pivot bolt and adjusting slot bolt. Push the roller and bracket away from the belt to release the tension.

CAUTION

The retaining plug is under heavy spring tension.

9. Open the camshaft sprocket bolt

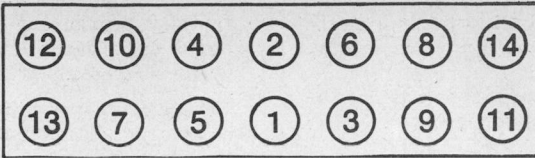

528e—6 cylinder torque sequence

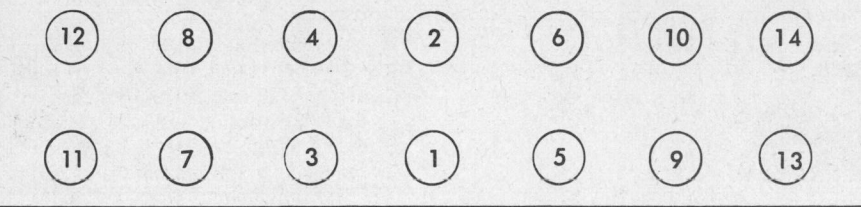

FRONT →

6-cylinder head torque sequence (except 528e)

lockplates and remove the bolts. Remove the sprocket.

NOTE: For installation purposes, the sprocket dowel pin should be located at the lower left, between 7 and 8 o'clock, while the upper bolt bore must align with the threaded bore of the camshaft and the cylinder head cast tab, visable through the two bores, when at the 12 o'clock position.

NOTE: Align the timing marks when installing the timing belt. The crankshaft sprocket mark must point at the notch in the flange of the front engine cover. The camshaft sprocket arrow must point at the alignment mark on the cylinder head. Also, the No. 1 piston must be at TDC of the compression stroke.

10. Remove and tag the electrical wiring and connectors.

11. Remove and tag the vacuum lines.

12. Remove the intake tube at No. 6 cylinder (530i only).

13. Remove the wiring harness by pulling it upward through the opening in the intake neck.

14. Disconnect the fuel lines.

15. Disconnect the exhaust line at the exhaust manifold. Remove the exhaust filter.

16. Remove the cylinder head bolts in the reverse order of the tightening sequence and install locating pins in four head bolt bores to prevent the rocker shafts from turning.

17. Remove the cylinder head.

18. Installation is the reverse of removal. Note the following points:

a. Tighten the cylinder head bolts in three stages, following the illustrated sequence. Adjust the valves, start the engine and bring it to normal operating temperature. Stop the engine and allow it to cool to approximately 95°F (35°C). Retorque the cylinder head bolts to specifications and readjust the valves.

NOTE: The cylinder head bolts (except those on the 325e and 528e) should be retorqued after 600 miles (1000 km) of driving.

b. Check the projection of the cylinder head dowel sleeve in the cylinder block mating surface. Maximum height is 0.20 in. (5.0mm).

c. Match the cylinder head gasket to the cylinder block and head to verify that the coolant flow passages are correct.

d. Adjust the timing and idle speed.

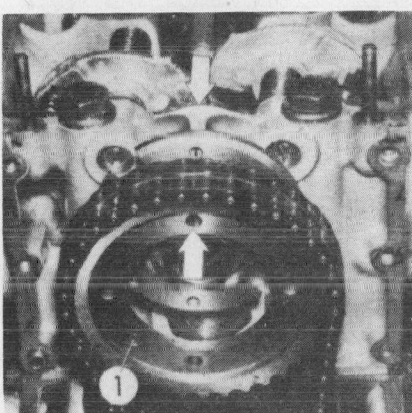

Alignment of dowel pin (1) with the sprocket and upper bolt hole and cylinder head cast tab—six cylinder engines

e. Bleed the cooling system. Set the heater valve in the Warm position and fill the cooling system. Start the engine and bring to normal operating temperature. A venting screw is located on the top of the thermostat housing. Run the engine at fast idle and open the venting screw until the coolant comes out free of air bubbles. Close the bleeder screw and refill the reservoir with coolant.

OVERHAUL

For all cylinder head overhaul procedures, please refer to "Engine Rebuilding" in the Unit Repair section.

Rocker Arms and Shaft

REMOVAL & INSTALLATION

All Models Except 325e and 528e

1. Remove the cylinder head.

2. Remove the camshaft.

3. Slide the thrust rings and rocker arms rearward and remove the circlips from the rocker arm shafts.

4. On 4-cylinder engines:

a. Remove the distributor flange from the rear of the cylinder head.

b. Using a long punch, drive the rocker arm shaft from the rear to the front of the cylinder head.

NOTE: Be sure all circlips are off the shaft before attempting to drive the shaft from the cylinder head.

c. The intake rocker shaft is not plugged at the rear, while the exhaust rocker shaft must be plugged. Renew the plug if necessary, during the installation.

5. On 6-cylinder engines:

a. Unscrew the rocker shaft locking bolts from the cylinder head.

b. Install a threaded slide hammer into the ends of the front rocker shafts and remove the shafts from the cylinder head.

Installation of locating pins in the cylinder head bolt bores to prevent rocker shafts from turning—six cylinder engines

Circlip location on the rocker arm shaft

Removal of camshaft and rocker arm retainer plate from the cylinder head, showing the dowel pin hole on four cylinder engine

11 1 060 and 00 1 490 or equivalent. Secure the head to the stand with one head bolt.

3. Remove the camshaft sprocket bolt and remove the camshaft distributor adapter and sprocket. Reinstall the adapter on the camshaft.

4. Adjust the valve play to the maximum allowable on all valves.

5. Remove the front and rear rocker shaft plugs and lift out the thrust plate.

6. Remove the spring-clips from the rocker arms by lifting them off.

7. Remove the exhaust side rocker arm shaft:

    a. Set the No. 6 cylinder rocker arms at the valve overlap position (rocker arms parallel), by rotating the engine through the firing order.

    b. Push in on the front cylinder rocker arm and turn the camshaft in the direction of the intake rocker shaft, using a ½ inch drive breaker bar and a deep well socket to fit over the camshaft adapter. Rotate the camshaft until all of the rocker arms are relaxed.

    c. Remove the rocker arm shaft.

8. Remove the intake side rocker arm shaft:

    a. Turn the camshaft in the direction of the exhaust rocker arm.

    b. Use a deep well socket and ½ inch drive breaker bar on the camshaft adapter to turn the camshaft until all of the rocker arms are relaxed.

    c. Pull out the rocker arm shaft.

9. Installation is the reverse of removal. Installation notes:

    a. The rocker arm thrust plate must be fit into the grooves in the rocker shafts.

    b. The straight side of the spring-clips must be installed in the grooves in the rocker arm shafts.

    c. The large oil bores in the rocker shafts must be installed down to the valve guides and the small oil bores must face inward toward the center of the head.

    d. Adjust the valve clearance.

Rocker arm shaft locking bolt (2) location—six cylinder engine

Removing the rocker arm shaft with special tool—four cylinder engine

NOTE: Be sure all circlips have been removed from the rocker shafts before removal.

    c. Remove the end cover from the rear of the cylinder head.

    d. Install a threaded slide hammer into the ends of the rear rocker shafts and remove.

6. The rocker arms, springs, washers, thrust rings and shafts should be examined and worn parts replaced. Special attention should be given to the rocker arm cam followers. If these are loose, replace the arm assembly.

The valves can be removed, repaired or replaced, as necessary, while the shafts and rocker arms are out of the cylinder head.

7. Installation is the reverse of removal. Note the following procedures:

    a. Design changes of the rocker arms and shafts have occurred with the installation of a bushing in the rocker arm and the use of two horizontal oil flow holes drilled in the rocker shaft for improved oil supply. Do not mix the previously designed parts with the later designed parts.

    b. When installing the rocker arms and components to the rocker shafts, install locating pins in the cylinder head bolt bores to properly align the rocker arm shafts.

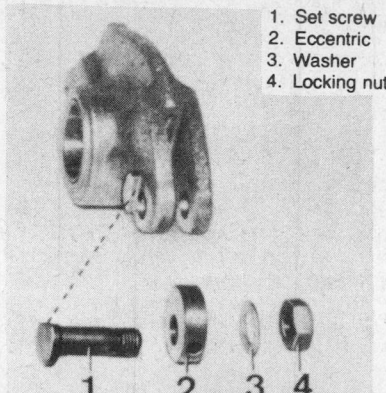

1. Set screw
2. Eccentric
3. Washer
4. Locking nut

Rocker arm valve adjusting mechanism

    c. Install sealer on the rocker arm shaft locking bolts and rear cover.

    d. On the 4-cylinder engines, position the rocker shafts so that the camshaft retaining plate ends can be engaged in the slots of shafts during camshaft installation.

    e. Adjust the valve clearance.

325e and 528e

The cylinder head must be removed before the rocker arm shafts can be removed.

1. Remove the cylinder head.

2. Mount the head on BMW stand

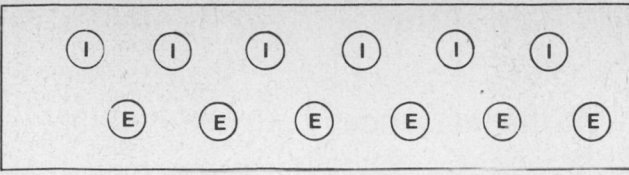

6-cylinder valve location

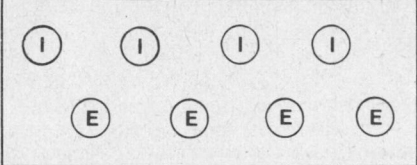

4-cylinder valve location

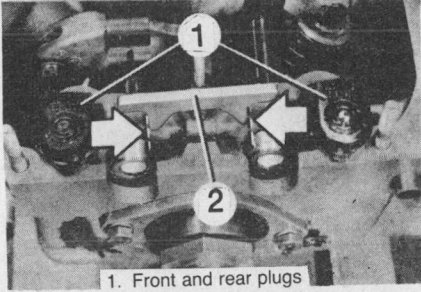

1. Front and rear plugs
2. Rocker arm thrust plate

Removing the thrust plate from rocker shafts—528e

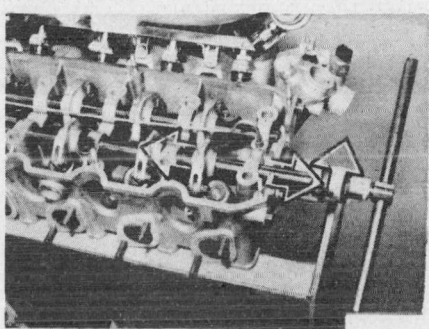

Using adapter and breaker bar to rotate the camshaft on 528e during rocker shaft removal

3. Spring   5. Rocker arm
4. Washer   6. Thrust ring

Installed position of rocker arm components

Intake Manifold

REMOVAL & INSTALLATION

318i and 320i

1. Remove the air cleaner and drain the cooling system.
2. Disconnect the accelerator cable and remove the vacuum hoses from the air collector. Tag the hoses.
3. Remove the injection line holder from No. 4 intake tube.
4. Remove the No. 3 intake tube and disconnect the vacuum and coolant lines from the throttle housing.
5. Disconnect the hoses at the EGR valve and remove the wire plugs at the temperature timing switch.
6. Remove the cold start valve from the air collector.
7. Disconnect the vacuum hose and electrical connections at the timing valve.
8. Disconnect the remaining intake tubes at the collector. Disconnect the collector brackets at the engine and remove the collector.

9. Remove the air intake tubes from the manifold and remove the injector valves.
10. Remove the intake manifold.
11. Installation is the reverse of removal.

All 6 Cylinder Models

NOTE: Slight variations may exist among models due to model changes and updating but basic removal and installation remains the same.

1. Disconnect the battery ground cable and drain the cooling system.
2. Disconnect the wire harness at the air flow sensor. Remove the air cleaner and sensor as an assembly.
3. Remove and tag the vacuum hoses and electrical plugs. Disconnect the accelerator linkage from the throttle housing.
4. Disconnect the coolant hoses from the throttle housing.
5. Working from the rear of the collector housing, disconnect the vacuum lines, and starting valve connector, fuel line and air line. Tag the hoses and lines for ease of assembly.
6. Remove the EGR valve and line.
7. Remove all intake pipes.
8. Remove the air collector housing from the engine.
9. Disconnect the plugs at the injector valves and remove the valves.
10. Disconnect the wire plugs at the coolant temperature sensor, the temperature time switch and the temperature switch.
11. Pull the wire loom upward through the opening in the intake manifold neck.
12. Remove the coolant hoses from the intake neck.

NOTE: Mark the heater hoses for proper reinstallation.

13. Remove the retaining bolts or nuts and remove either front, rear or both intake manifold necks.
14. Installation of the manifolds is the reverse of removal. Use new gaskets on the manifolds and air intake tubes.

Exhaust Manifold

REMOVAL & INSTALLATION

The exhaust manifolds are referred to as exhaust gas recirculation reactors. Refer to the ''Emission Control'' section for operation.

The removal and installation procedures are basically the same for all models. The four cylinder manifold (used on the 320i model), is a one piece, one outlet unit, while

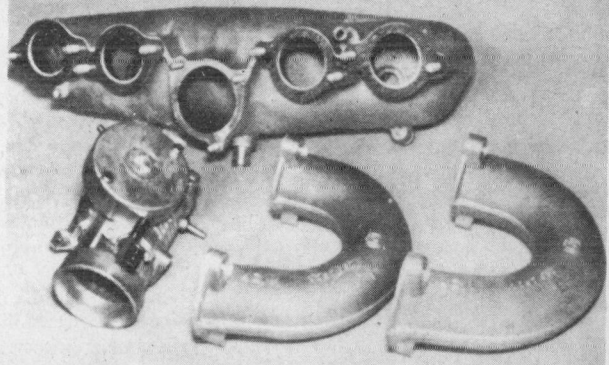

Induction system with induction tubes secured with nuts and washers

the six cylinder manifold assembly consists of a two piece, double outlet to the exhaust pipe. One piece can be replaced independently of the other.

1. Remove the air volume control and if necessary, air cleaner.

2. Disconnect the exhaust pipe at the reactor outlet(s).

3. Remove the guard plate from the reactor(s).

4. Disconnect the air injection pipe fitting, the EGR counterpressure line, EGR pressure line and any supports.

NOTE: An exhaust filter is used between the reactor and the EGR valve and must be disconnected. Replace the filter if found to be defective.

5. Remove the retaining bolts or nuts at the reactor and remove it from the cylinder head.

6. Installation is the reverse of removal. Use new gaskets.

Valve Guide

REMOVAL & INSTALLATION

The valve guides are shrunk-fit into the cylinder head. This procedure requires special tools for measuring valve guide bores, installing guides, reaming guides and guide bores, and heating the head to 450°F. The procedure is included here for reference purposes.

1. Remove the cylinder head.

2. Using a suitable valve spring compressor, compress the spring and remove the split keepers. Remove the spring and check it against specifications.

3. Check the valve stem-to-valve guide clearance by holding the valve about ⅛ in. from the valve seat and rocking it sideways. Movement of the valve head across the seat must not exceed the figure shown in the specifications.

4. If the clearance is excessive, the guide must be driven out (into the combustion chamber) with a drift of the proper diameter and replaced. Check the bore dimension in the cylinder head. If specs (13.0mm) are exceeded, ream the bore out and install an oversize guide.

5. To install a new valve guide, the cylinder head must be heated to 450°F so the new guide can be pressed in without excessive pressure. The guide is then pressed in until it protrudes 0.571–0.611 in. On the 3.3 litre engine, a new type of shorter guide is available, which is pressed in 0.511–0.551 in. BMW special tool 11 1 20 (or the equivalent), incorporates a recess which provides the proper protrusion. The same is true of the 318 engine—use tool 11 1 160 or equivalent. With the shorter guide, a washer is used to create the proper dimension (3.3L only). After installation, the guide must be reamed out to the proper dimension.

Timing Chain (Front) Cover

REMOVAL & INSTALLATION

318i and 320i

There are two timing chain covers, one upper and one lower, which must be removed to service the timing chain and sprocket assemblies.

1. Remove the cylinder head cover. Disconnect the negative battery cable. Disconnect the air injection line at the front of the thermal reactor (if so equipped). On the 318i, disconnect the bracket located on the driver's side of the upper cover.

2. Remove the 8 bolts which retain the upper timing gear cover to the cylinder head and lower timing gear cover. Remove the upper cover, taking note of the placement of the alternator ground wire.

3. Drain the cooling system and remove the radiator, preheater intake air assembly (carburetor equipped cars only) and radiator hoses as outlined under "Radiator Removal and Installation."

4. Bend back the lockplates for the fan retaining bolts. Remove the bolts and lift off the fan.

5. Loosen the alternator retaining bolts. Push the alternator toward the engine and remove the fan pulley and the alternator drive (fan) belt. On the 318i, remove the alternator and tensioning bar. Remove the four mounting bolts from the air pump bracket (where it attaches to the block), and remove the pump and bracket; then remove the bolt attaching the tensioning bar to the block and remove the tensioning bar.

6. Disconnect the coolant hoses from the water pump. Remove the six retaining bolts and copper sealing washers and lift off the water pump.

7. Unscrew the plug and remove the spring from the cam chain tensioner assembly, taking care to cushion the sudden release of spring tension. Remove the plunger (piston).

8. On the 320i, disconnect the multiple plug and cable lead from the alternator. Remove the alternator with its bearing block and clamping strap.

9. Remove the flywheel inspection plate and block the ring gear from turning with a small prybar.

10. Unscrew the crankshaft pulley nut and pull off the belt pulley.

11. Remove the bolts which retain the lower cover to the cylinder block and oil pan. On the 318i, remove the bolts retaining the brace plate and remove it. Also on the 318i, loosen the oil pan lower retaining bolts not directly involved with the lower cover. With a sharp knife, carefully separate the lower edge of the timing cover from the upper edge of the oil pan gasket at the front.

12. Remove the lower timing cover. At this time, it is advisable to replace the tim-

ing cover seal (sealing ring) with a new one. The sealing ring is a press fit into the cover.

13. Clean the mating surfaces of the timing covers, oil pan, cylinder head, and cylinder block. Replace all gaskets (except the oil pan gasket), and seal them at the corners with sealing compound such as Permatex® No. 2. If the oil pan gasket has been damaged, remove the oil pan and replace the gasket.

14. Reverse the above procedure to install, taking care to tighten the upper timing gear cover retaining bolts in the following sequence (as per the illustration): hand-tighten 1 and 2, then torque 3–8 in numerical order, and finally 1 and 2 to 6.5–7.9 ft. lbs. Note that on the 318i, the mounting web for the tensioning piston must be in the oil pocket. On the 318i, also make sure to pack the bores between the lower cover (at the top) and block with sealer.

6 Cylinder Models (Except 325e, 528e)

NOTE: On 533i, 633CSi, and 733i series engines, this procedure requires the use of a special gauge, to be made to a certain dimension, as in Step 16.

1. Remove the cylinder head cover. Remove the distributor as described earlier in this chapter. On 530i, and all 3.3 litre models, detach the distributor guard and the air line going to the thermal reactor.

2. Drain the coolant to below the level of the thermostat and remove the thermostat housing cover.

3. Remove the eight bolts and remove the upper timing case cover with the worm drive which drives the distributor.

4. Remove the piston which tensions the timing chain, *working carefully because of very high spring pressure*.

5. Remove the cooling fan and all drive belts.

6. Remove the flywheel housing cover and lock the flywheel in position with an appropriate special tool.

7. Unscrew the nut from the center of the pulley and pull the pulley/vibration damper off the crankshaft.

8. Detach the TDC position transmitter on 733i, 633CSi and certain 528i models.

9. Loosen all the oil pan bolts, and then unscrew all the bolts from the lower timing case cover. Use a knife to separate the gasket at the base of the lower timing cover. Then, remove the cover.

10. To install the lower cover, first coat the surfaces of the oil pan and block with sealer. Put it into position on the block, making sure the tensioning piston holding web (cast into the block) is in the oil pocket. Install all bolts; then tighten the lower front cover bolts evenly; finally, tighten the oil pan bolts evenly.

11. Inspect the hub of the vibration damper. If the hub is scored, install the radial seal so the sealing lip is in front of or to the rear of the scored area. Pack the seal with grease and install it with a sealer installer.

12. Install the pulley/damper and torque the bolt to specifications. When installing, make sure the key and keyway are properly aligned.

13. Remove the flywheel locking tool and reinstall the cover. Reinstall and tension all belts.

14. Before installing the upper cover, use sealer to seal the joint between the back of the lower timing cover and block at the top. On 528i, 533i and 733i models, there are sealer wells which are to be filled with sealer. Check the cork seal at the distributor drive coupling, and replace it if necessary.

15. See the illustration for four cylinder engines above, and tighten bolts 1 and 2 (the lower bolts) slightly. Then, tighten bolts 3–8. Finally, fully tighten the lower bolts.

16. Install the TDC position transmitter loosely, if so equipped. With the engine at exactly 0 degrees Top Center, as shown by the marker on the front cover, adjust the position of the transmiter with a gauge which should be made to conform to the dimensions shown in the illustration: i.e. it must fit the curve on the outside of the balancer, and incorporate a notch (for the pin on the balancer) and a ridge against which the transmitter must rest. The straight line distance between the center of the notch and bottom of the ridge must be exactly 37.5 mm. Then, tighten the transmitter mounting screw.

17. Reverse the remaining removal procedures, making sure to bleed the cooling system.

Timing Housing Cover Oil Seal

REMOVAL & INSTALLATION

All Models (Except 325e and 528e)

1. Position the No. 1 piston at TDC on the beginning of its compression stroke.

2. Remove the flywheel guard and lock the flywheel with a locking tool.

3. Remove the drive belts and the fan.

4. Remove the retaining nut and remove the vibration damper from the crankshaft.

NOTE: The Woodruff key should be at the 12 o'clock position on the crankshaft.

5. Remove the seal from the timing housing cover with a small pry bar.

6. Using a special seal installer or equivalent, lubricate and install the seal in the cover. This tool is used to press the seal into the bore with even pressure around the entire perimeter.

NOTE: If the balancer hub has serious scoring on the sealing surface, position the seal in the cover so that the sealing lip is in front of or behind the scored groove.

7. Lubricate the balancer hub and in-

Position of crankshaft woodruff key (1)

stall it on the crankshaft, being careful not to damage the seal.

8. Complete the assembly, using the reverse of the removal procedure. Be sure to remove the flywheel locking tool before attempting to start the engine.

325e and 528e

The 325e and 528e have two oil seals on the front engine cover. One is on the crankshaft and the other is on the intermediate shaft.

1. Remove the front engine cover (see the "Timing Belt and Front Cover" procedure).

2. Press the two radial oil seals out of the front engine cover.

3. Install the oil seals flush with the front engine cover using BMW tools 24 1 050, 33 1 180 and 005 5 500 or equivalents.

4. Install the front engine cover.

Timing Chain and Tensioner

REMOVAL & INSTALLATION

All Models Except 325e and 528e

1. Rotate the crankshaft to set the No.

1 piston at TDC, at the beginning of its compression stroke.

2. Remove the distributor (6-cylinder engines only).

3. Remove the cylinder head cover, air injection pipe and guard plate.

4. Drain the cooling system and remove the thermostat housing.

5. Remove the upper timing housing cover. See the "Timing Chain Cover Removal and Installation" procedure above.

6. Remove the timing chain tensioner piston.

NOTE: The piston is under heavy spring tension.

7. Remove the drive belts and fan.

8. Remove the flywheel guard and lock the flywheel with a locking tool.

9. Remove the vibration damper assembly.

NOTE: The crankshaft woodruff key should be in the 12 o'clock position.

10. Remove upper and lower timing covers as described above.

11. On the 318i, turn the crankshaft so that the No. 1 cylinder is at firing position and the top sprocket locating pin is at 6 o'clock. Open the camshaft lockplates if so equipped, remove the bolts and remove the camshaft sprocket.

12. On 4-cylinder engines (except 318i):

a. Remove the bottom circlip holding the chain guide rail to the block. Loosen the upper pivot pin until the guide rail rests against the forward part of the cylinder head gasket.

b. Remove the timing chain from the sprockets and remove the guide rail by pulling downward and swinging the rail to the right.

c. Remove the chain from the guide rail and remove it from the engine.

On the 318i engine:

a. Take the timing chain off top and bottom sprockets and remove carefully from the guide rail.

13. On 6-cylinder engines:

a. Remove the chain from the lower sprocket, swing the chain to the right front and out of the guide rail and remove the chain from the engine.

Location of upper (1) and lower (3) guide rail retainers

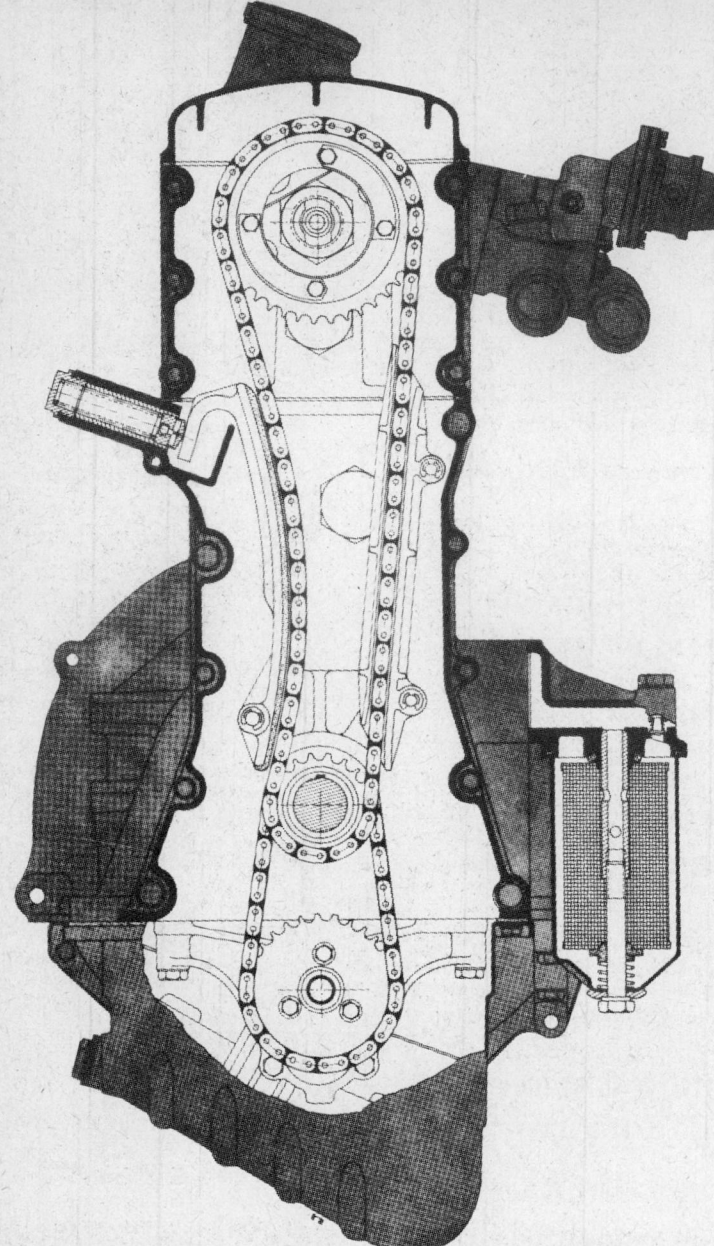

Typical timing chain arrangement—four cylinder engine illustrated

Bleeding the chain tensioner

14. Installation is the reverse of removal, but note the following:

15. Be sure that No. 1 piston remains at the top of its firing stroke and the key on the crankshaft is in the 12 o'clock position.

16. On 4-cylinder engines:

a. Position the camshaft flange so that the dowel pin bore is located at the 6 o'clock position and the notch in the top of the flange aligns with the cast tab on the clyinder head.

b. On all models but the 318i, position the chain in the chain guide rail and move the rail upward and to the left, engaging the lower locating pivot pin and threading the upper pivot pin into the block. Install the circlip on the lower guide pin. On the 318i, simply locate the chain carefully in the guide rail.

c. Engage the chain on the crankshaft sprocket and fit the camshaft sprocket into the chain.

d. Align the gear dowel pin to the camshaft flange and bolt the sprocket into place. Use new lockplates (where so equipped), and secure the bolt heads.

17. On 6-cylinder engines:

a. Position the camshaft flange so that the dowel pin bore is between the 7 and 8 o'clock position and the upper flange bolt hole is aligned with the cast tab on the cylinder head.

b. Position the chain on the guide rail and swing the chain inward and to the left.

c. Engage the chain on the crankshaft gear and install the camshaft sprocket into the chain.

d. Align the gear dowel pin to the camshaft flange and bolt the sprocket into place. Torque the sprocket bolts to 5 ft.lbs.

18. Install the chain tensioner piston, spring and cap plug, but do not tighten.

19. To bleed the chain tensioner, fill the oil pocket, located on the upper timing housing cover, with engine oil and move the tensioner back and forth with a screwdriver until oil is expelled at the cap plug. Tighten the cap plug securely.

20. Complete the assembly in the reverse order of removal. Check the ignition timing and the idle speed. Be sure the fly-

Installation of the timing cover housing showing special sealing locations

wheel holder is removed before any attempt is made to start the engine.

Timing Belt and Front Engine Cover

REMOVAL & INSTALLATION

325e and 528e

The 325e and 528e are equipped with a rubber drive and timing belt and the distributor guard plate is actually the upper timing belt cover.

1. Remove the distributor cap and rotor. Remove the inner distributor cover and seal.

2. Remove the two distributor guard plate attaching bolts and one nut. Remove the rubber guard and take out the guard plate (upper timing belt cover).

3. Rotate the crankshaft to set No. 1 piston at TDC of its compression stroke.

NOTE: At TDC of No. 1 piston compression stroke, the camshaft sprocket arrow should align directly with the mark on the cylinder head.

4. Remove the radiator.

5. Remove the lower splash guard and take off the alternator, power steering and air conditioning belts.

6. Remove the crankshaft pulley and vibration damper.

7. Hold the crankshaft hub from rotating with special BMW tool 11 2 150 or equivalent. Remove the crankshaft hub bolt.

8. Install the hub bolt into the crankshaft about three turns and use BMW tools 00 7 501 and 11 2 132 or a gear puller, to remove the crankshaft hub.

9. Remove the bolt from the engine end of the alternator bracket. Loosen the alternator adjusting bolt and swing the bracket out of the way.

10. Lift out the TDC transmitter and set it out of the way.

11. Remove the remaining bolt and lift off the lower timing belt cover.

12. Loosen the two tensioner pulley bolts and release the tension on the belt by pushing on the tensioner pulley bracket.

13. Mark the running direction of the timing belt and remove the belt.

14. Remove the three bolts across the front of the oil pan and loosen the remaining oil pan bolts. Try not to damage the oil pan gasket. Remove the six front engine cover bolts and remove the front engine cover.

15. Installation is the reverse of removal. Installation notes:

   a. To tighten the timing belt, turn the engine in the direction of normal engine operation, with a ½ inch drive rachet wrench on the crankshaft bolt. When the timing belt is tight, then torque the two tensioner bolts.

   b. Align the hub centering pin through the hole in the vibration damper for proper installation.

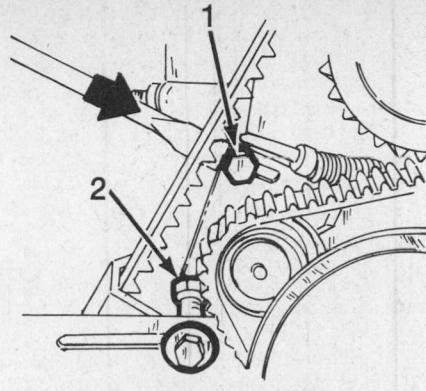

1. Tensioner adjusting slot bolt
2. Tensioner bracket pivot bolt

Releasing the tension on timing belt—528e

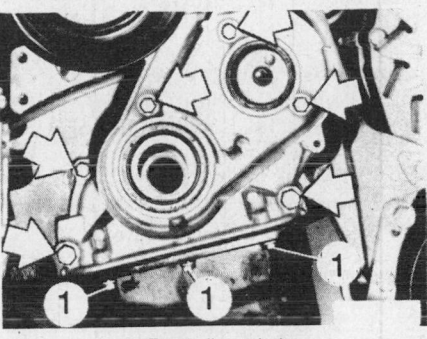

1. Front oil pan bolts

Bolt location for front engine cover—528e

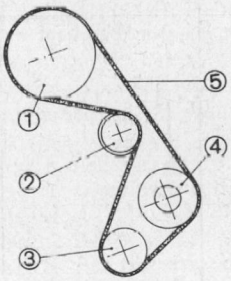

1. Camshaft sprocket
2. Tensioner roller
3. Crankshaft sprocket
4. Intermediate shaft sprocket
5. Timing drive belt

Location of timing belt sprockets and belt tensioner—528e

   c. Align the timing marks when installing the timing belt. The crankshaft sprocket mark must point at the notch in the flange of the front engine cover. The camshaft sprocket arrow must point at the alignment mark on the cylinder head. Also, the No. 1 piston must be at TDC of the compression stroke.

   d. If the oil pan gasket is damaged, it must be replaced.

   e. Check and replace front cover oil seals if needed.

   f. Use BMW tools 11 2 211 (crankshaft seal aligner) and 11 2 212 (inter-

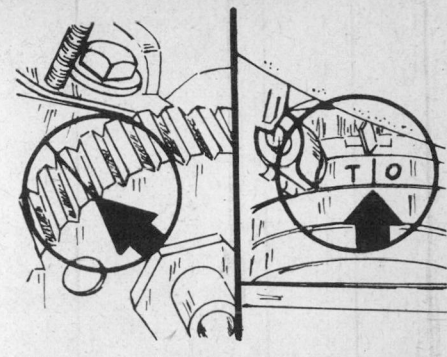

Aligning marks for timing belt installation—528e

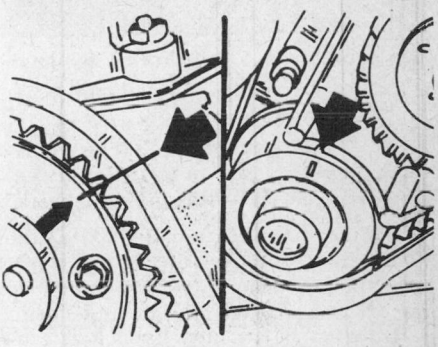

Crankshaft sprocket timing marks aligned for installation of timing belt—528e

mediate shaft seal aligner) or equivalent to install the front engine cover without damaging the oil seals.

   g. Check the engine oil level.

   h. Install engine coolant and bleed the cooling system. Bring the engine up to operating temperature and loosen the bleed screw on top of the thermostat housing. Continue to bleed until escaping coolant is free of bubbles. Add coolant to the expansion tank if needed.

Camshaft

REMOVAL & INSTALLATION

All Models (Except 325e and 528e)

1. Remove the oil line from the top of the cylinder head.

NOTE: Observe the location of the seals when removing the hollow oil line studs. Reinstall the seals in the same position.

2. Remove the cylinder head. Support the head in such a way that the valves can be opened during camshaft removal.

3. Adjust the valve clearance to the maximum clearance on all rocker arms.

4. Remove the fuel pump and pushrod on carbureted engines.

5. On 4-cylinder engines:

   a. Special tools are used to hold the rocker arms away from the camshaft lobes. On the 320i, use tool 11 1 040; on the 318i, use 11 0 040. You can use these

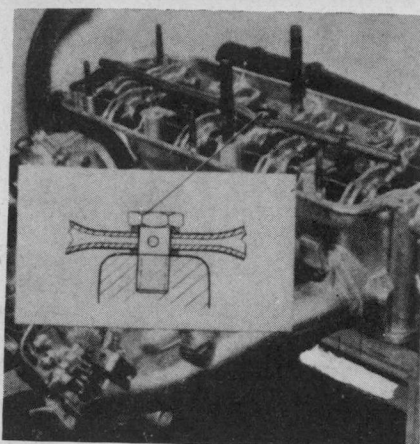

Location of seals at hollow oil line stud

numbers to shop for tools from independent sources also.

NOTE: The proper tool or its equivalent, must be used on fuel injection engines to avoid distorting the valve heads.

NOTE: On the 320i and 318i, the clamping bolt for the special tool is off-center. The clamp must be mounted so the shorter end faces the exhaust side of the engine, or the valve heads may contact each other. On the 318i, install two dowel pins in the head.

On 6-cylinder engines:

a. A special tool (11-2-060) or its equivalent, is used to hold the rocker arms away from the camshaft lobes. When installing the tool, move the intake rocker arms of No. 2 and 4 cylinders forward approximately ¼ in. and tighten the intake side nuts to avoid contact between the valve heads.

6. Remove the camshaft.

On 4-cylinder engines:

a. Turn the camshaft until the flange is aligned with the cylinder head boss. Remove the guide plate retaining bolts and move the plate downward and out of the slots on the rocker arm shafts.

b. Carefully remove the camshaft from the cylinder head.

c. Remove the two plugs behind the guide plate (at top), coat with Loctite® No. 270 or equivalent, and replace them.

On 6-cylinder engines:

a. Rotate the camshaft so that the two cutout areas of the camshaft flange are horizontal and remove the retaining plate bolts.

b. Carefully remove the camshaft from the cylinder head.

c. The flange and guide plate can be removed from the camshaft by removing the lockplate and nut from the camshaft end.

7. Install the camshaft and associated components in the reverse order of removal, but observe the following:

a. After installing the camshaft guide plate, the camshaft should turn easily. Measure and correct the camshaft end play.

b. The camshaft flange must be properly aligned with the cylinder head before the sprocket is installed. Refer to the disassembly procedure.

c. Install the oil tube hollow stud washer seals properly, one above and one below the oil pipe.

d. Adjust the valves.

325e and 528e

The cylinder head and the rocker arm shafts must be removed before the camshaft can be removed.

1. Remove the cylinder head (see "Cylinder Head Removal and Installation").

2. Mount the head on a stand. Secure the head to the stand with one head bolt.

3. Remove the camshaft sprocket bolt and remove the camshaft distributor adapter and sprocket. Reinstall the distributor adapter on the camshaft.

4. Adjust the valve play to the maximum allowable on all valves.

5. Remove the front and rear rocker shaft plugs and lift out the thrust plate.

6. Remove the clips from the rocker arms by lifting them off.

7. Remove the exhaust side rocker arm shaft:

a. Set the No. 6 cylinder rocker arm to the valve overlap position (both rocker arms parallel).

b. Push in on the rocker arm on the front cylinder and turn the camshaft in the direction of the intake rocker shaft, using a ½ in. breaker bar and a deep well socket to fit over the camshaft adapter. Rotate the camshaft until all of the rocker arms are relaxed.

c. Remove the rocker arm shaft.

8. Remove the intake side rocker arm shaft:

a. Turn the camshaft in the direction of the exhaust valves.

b. Use a deep well socket and ½ inch drive breaker bar on the camshaft adapter to turn the camshaft until all of the rocker arms are relaxed.

c. Pull out the rocker arm shaft.

9. Remove the camshaft thrust bearing cover. Check the radial oil seal and round cord seal, replace them if needed.

10. Pull out the camshaft.

11. Installation is the reverse of removal. Installation notes:

a. Use BMW tool 11 2 212 or equivalent over the end of the camshaft during installation of the thrust bearing cover; this will protect the oil seals and guide the cover on.

b. The rocker arm thrust plate must be fit into the grooves in the rocker shafts.

c. The straight side of the springclip must be installed in the groove of the rocker arm shafts.

d. The large oil bores in the rocker shafts must be installed down to the valve guides and the small oil bores must face inward toward the center of the head.

e. Adjust the valve clearance.

Removing camshaft thrust bearing cover—528e

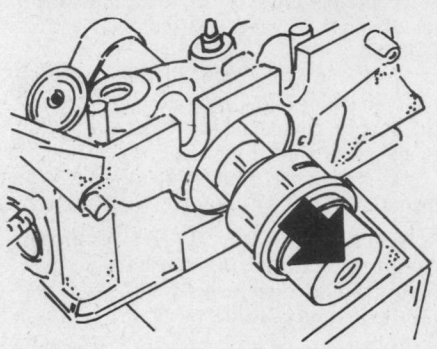

Pulling out the camshaft—528e

Intermediate Shaft

REMOVAL & INSTALLATION

325e and 528e

1. Remove the front cover as detailed previously.

2. Remove the intermediate shaft sprocket.

3. Loosen and remove the two retaining screws and then remove the intermediate shaft guide plate.

4. Carefully slide the intermediate shaft out of the block.

5. Installation is in the reverse order of removal.

Pistons and Connecting Rods
REMOVAL & INSTALLATION

The pistons and connecting rods may be removed from the engine after the cylinder head, oil pan and oil pump are removed. It may be necessary to first remove a ridge worn into the cylinder above the top ring. See the engine rebuilding section. The connecting rods and caps are marked for each cylinder with No. 1 cylinder at the sprocket end of the engine. However, you should mark the exact relationship between each rod and the crankshaft to ensure replacement in the exact same position, in case the bearings can be re-used.

All reference numbers on the pistons and connecting rods must be located on the same

Location of piston in the cylinder bore with ring gaps located 180° apart

When removing the upper oil pan on the 318i, remove the arrowed bolts from the bell housing and reinforcing plate, and remove the plate

Proper piston ring installation—typical

side, with the arrow on the piston top facing the front of the engine. Measurement, ring fitting and installation procedures are outlined in the Engine Rebuilding section. Note the following points, however:

a. To disassemble rods and pistons, remove the circlip and press out the piston pin. Note that pistons and piston pins come as a matched set. *Do not mix them up*.

b. A piston pin must always slide through the connecting rod under light pressure.

c. If replacing pistons, make sure all are of the same make and weight class (marked "+" or "−" on the crown).

d. Piston installed clearance must meet specifications. On the 318i, check installed clearance at a point measured up from the lower skirt edge, depending on the piston manufacturer: Mahle—0.551 in.; KS—1.215 in.; Alcan—0.610 in.

e. Lubricate the piston and rings with engine oil prior to installation. Offset ring gaps 120° apart.

ENGINE LUBRICATION
Oil Pan
REMOVAL & INSTALLATION
530i and 528i

1. Raise and support the vehicle. Drain

the engine oil.

2. Remove the stabilizer bar.

3. Remove the alternator and remove the power steering pump, but do not disconnect the hoses.

4. Remove the lower power steering bracket bolt and remove the remaining bolts to remove the oil pan retaining bolts.

5. Loosen the engine support bracket.

6. Remove the oil pan bolts and loosen the oil pan from the engine block.

7. Rotate the crankshaft until the No. 6 crankpin is above the bottom of the engine block.

8. Lower the front of the oil pan, turn the rear of the pan towards the support bracket and remove the pan.

9. Reverse the procedure to install the oil pan, using new gaskets.

320i

1. Raise and support the vehicle. Drain the engine oil.

2. Loosen the steering gear bolts and pull the steering box off the front axle carrier.

3. Remove the oil pan bolts and separate the pan from the engine block.

4. Swing the oil pan downward while rotating the crankshaft to allow the pan to clear the crankpin and remove the pan toward the front.

5. Reverse the procedure to install the oil pan, using new gaskets.

318i

1. Remove the dipstick. Remove the

lower pan by draining oil, removing pan bolts, and removing the lower pan.

2. Remove the oil pump, as described under "Oil Pump Removal & Installation", below.

3. Unscrew the ground strap, located at the right rear of the upper pan.

4. Remove the bottom three flywheel housing bolts, and two reinforcement plate bolts, and remove the reinforcement plate.

5. Remove upper pan bolts, and remove the upper pan.

6. Clean all four sealing surfaces. Replace both gaskets. Coat the mating surfaces on the timing case and end covers with sealer.

7. Install in reverse order, torquing upper pan bolts to 7–8 ft. lb.

533i and 633CSi

1. Raise and support the vehicle. Drain the engine oil.

2. Remove the front stabilizer bar.

3. Disconnect the wire terminal at the oil level switch.

4. Disconnect the power steering pump, but do not disconnect the hoses. Loosen all the power steering bracket bolts, and remove the bottom bolt.

5. Remove the engine oil pan bolts, separate the oil pan from the engine block and lower the front of the pan.

6. Rotate the crankshaft until the No.

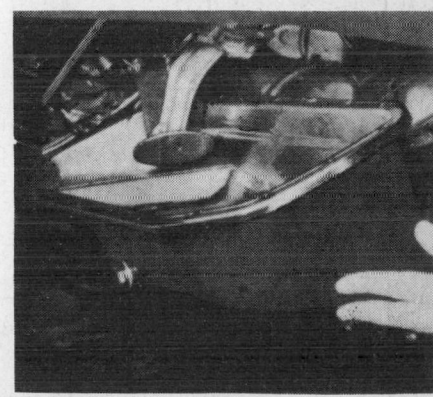

Removal of engine oil pan—typical

6 crankpin is above the bottom of the engine block.

7. Lift the engine slightly at the clutch housing while removing the pan to the right side.

8. Reverse the procedure to install the oil pan, using new gaskets.

733i

1. Raise and support the vehicle. Drain the engine oil.

2. Remove the power steering pump, but do not disconnect the hoses.

3. Remove the lower power steering bracket bolt. Loosen the upper bracket bolts in order to move the bracket away from the oil pan.

4. Disconnect the oil level switch wire terminal.

5. Remove the oil pan bolts and separate the oil pan from the engine block.

6. Disconnect the left and right engine mounts.

7. Remove the engine vibration damper.

8. Lower the vehicle and remove the fan housing from the radiator.

9. Attach a lifting sling and raise the engine until the oil pan can be removed.

10. Reverse the procedure to install the oil pan, using the new gaskets.

325e and 528e

1. Raise the vehicle and support it. Drain the engine oil.

2. Remove the front lower splash guard.

3. Disconnect the electrical terminal from the oil sending unit.

4. Remove the flywheel cover.

5. Remove the oil pan bolts and lower the oil pan. Remove the oil pump bolts and take out the oil pump and oil pan.

6. Installation is the reverse of removal. Installation notes:

  a. Clean the gasket surfaces and use a new gasket on the oil pan.

  b. Coat the joints on the ends of the front engine cover with a universal sealing compound.

  c. Install the sending unit wire and the engine oil.

Rear Main Bearing Oil Seal

REMOVAL & INSTALLATION

The rear main bearing oil seal can be replaced after the transmission, clutch/flywheel or the converter/flywheel has been removed from the engine.

Removal and installation, after the seal is exposed, is as follows.

1. Drain the engine oil and loosen the oil pan bolts.

2. Remove the two rear oil pan bolts.

3. Remove the end cover housing from the engine block and remove the seal from the housing.

Rear main bearing oil seal and end cover housing showing special sealing locations

4. Install a new seal into the end cover housing with a special seal installer or equivalent.

NOTE: Fill the cavity between the sealing lips of the seal with grease before installing.

5. On the 318i, coat the mating surface between the oil pan and end cover with sealer. Using a new gasket, install the end cover on the engine block and bolt it into place.

6. Reverse the removal procedure to complete the installation.

Oil Pump

REMOVAL & INSTALLATION

All Models (Except 325e and 528e)

1. Remove the oil pan. On the 318i, only the lower section of the pan need be removed.

2. Remove the bolts retaining the sprocket to the oil pump shaft and remove the sprocket.

3. On 4 cylinder engines:

  a. Remove the oil pump retaining bolts and lower the oil pump from the engine block.

  b. Note the location of the O-ring seal, between the housing and the pressure safety line.

  c. Be sure that the oil bore in the shim is correctly positioned during the oil pump installation.

4. On 6 cylinder engines:

  a. Remove the oil pump retaining bolts and lower the oil pump from the engine block.

  b. Do not loosen the chain adjusting shims from the two mounting locations.

5. Install the oil pump in the reverse order of removal. On 6 cylinder engines and 318i, add or subtract shims between the oil pump body and the engine block to obtain a slight movement of the chain under light thumb pressure.

―――― **IMPORTANT** ――――
When used, the two shim thicknesses must be the same. Tighten the pump holder at the pick-up end after shimming is completed to avoid stress on the pump.

6. On 6 cylinder engines, after the main pump mounting bolts are torqued, loosen the bolts at the bracket on the rear of the pick-up, allowing the pick-up to assume its most natural position. This will relieve tension on the bracket. Tighten the bolts.

325e and 528e

1. Raise the vehicle and support it. Drain the engine oil.

2. Remove the front lower splash guard.

3. Disconnect the electrical terminal from the oil sending unit.

4. Remove the flywheel cover.

5. Remove the oil pan bolts and lower the oil pan. Remove the oil pump bolts and take out the oil pump and oil pan.

6. Installation is the reverse of removal. Installation notes:

  a. Clean the gasket surfaces and use a new gasket on the oil pan.

  b. Coat the joints on the ends of the front engine cover with a universal sealing compound.

  c. Install the sending unit wire and the engine oil.

ENGINE COOLING

Bleeding the Cooling System

WITH BLEEDER SCREW ON THERMOSTAT HOUSING

Set the heater valve in the WARM position, start the engine and bring it to normal operating temperature. Run the engine at fast idle and open the venting screw on the thermostat housing until the coolant comes out free of air bubbles. Close the bleeder screw and refill the cooling system.

WITHOUT BLEEDER SCREW

Fill the cooling system, place the heater valve in the WARM position, close the pressure cap to the second (fully closed) position. Start the engine and bring to normal operating temperature. Carefully release the pressure cap to the first position and squeeze the upper and lower radiator hoses in a pumping action to allow trapped air to escape through the radiator. Recheck the coolant level and close the pressure cap to its second position.

Radiator

REMOVAL & INSTALLATION

The radiator can be removed after draining the cooling system, removal of the coolant hoses, disconnecting of the automatic transmission oil cooler lines, disconnecting of the temperature switch wire connectors and removing the shroud from the radiator core. On the 318i, remove the cover from the left side of the radiator. Remove the radiator retaining bolts (or single bolt on some

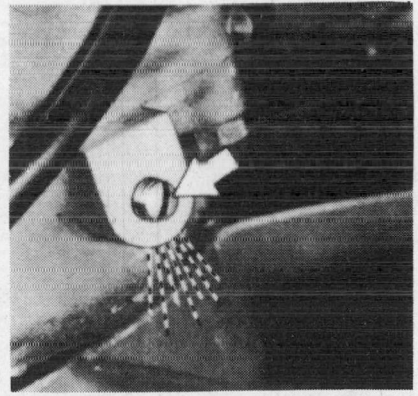

Bleeding of the cooling system with bleeder screw

models) and lift the radiator from the vehicle. The shroud will remain in the vehicle, resting on the fan. The radiator is installed in the reverse order of removal. Fill and bleed the cooling system.

Thermostat

REMOVAL & INSTALLATION

The thermostat is located near the water pump, either on the cylinder head or intake manifold on some models and is located between two coolant hose sections on other models.

The removal and installation of the thermostat is accomplished in the conventional manner.

Water Pump

REMOVAL & INSTALLATION

All Models (Except 325e and 528e)

1. Drain the cooling system and remove the radiator.
2. Remove the fan blades, loosen the drive belts and remove as necessary. On the 318i, this requires holding the fan pulley via the locating posts, and then turning the coupling nut *clockwise* (left hand threads) to remove the fan and clutch. Store in a vertical position.
3. Loosen the alternator bolts. Remove the belt pulley from the pump flange and disconnect the coolant hoses.
4. Remove the retaining bolts and remove the water pump from the engine.
5. The installation is in the reverse of the removal procedure. Use a new gasket and bleed the cooling system.

325e and 528e

1. Drain the cooling system.
2. Remove the distributor cap and rotor. Remove the inner distributor cap and rubber sealing ring.
3. Hold the fan pulley from turning with BMW tool 11 5 030 or equivalent. Remove the fan coupling nut (left hand thread—turn clockwise to remove).
4. Remove the belt and pulley.
5. Remove the rubber guard and distributor and or upper timing belt cover.
6. Compress the timing tensioner spring and clamp pin with BMW special tool 11 5 010 or equivalent.

NOTE: Observe the installed position of the tensioner spring pin on the water pump housing for reinstallation purposes.

7. Remove the water hoses, remove the three water pump bolts and remove the pump.

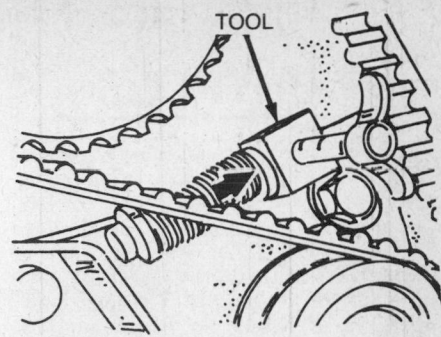

Compress tensioner spring with special tool during water pump removal—528e

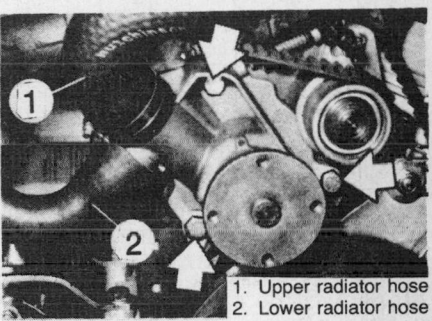

1. Upper radiator hose
2. Lower radiator hose

Removing water pump retaining bolts—528e

8. Clean the gasket surfaces and use a new gasket.
9. Installation is the reverse of removal.
10. Add coolant and bleed the cooling system.

BELT TENSION ADJUSTMENT

The fan belt tension is adjusted by moving the alternator on the slack adjuster bracket. The belt tension is adjusted to a deflection of approximately ½ in. under moderate thumb pressure in the middle of its longest span.

Measuring belt deflection

EMISSION CONTROLS

The BMW emission controls are composed of three major systems to control engine emissions of hydrocarbons (HC), carbon monoxide (CO), and oxides of nitrogen (NOx).

The 3 systems are (1) Crankcase Emissions Control System, (2) Exhaust Emission Control System and (3) Evaporative Emission Control System.

Differences may exist between the systems used on California models or Federal models depending upon the year of production and the vehicle model.

The Emission Control Information Label attached to the vehicle should be consulted before any repairs or specification changes are made to the engine.

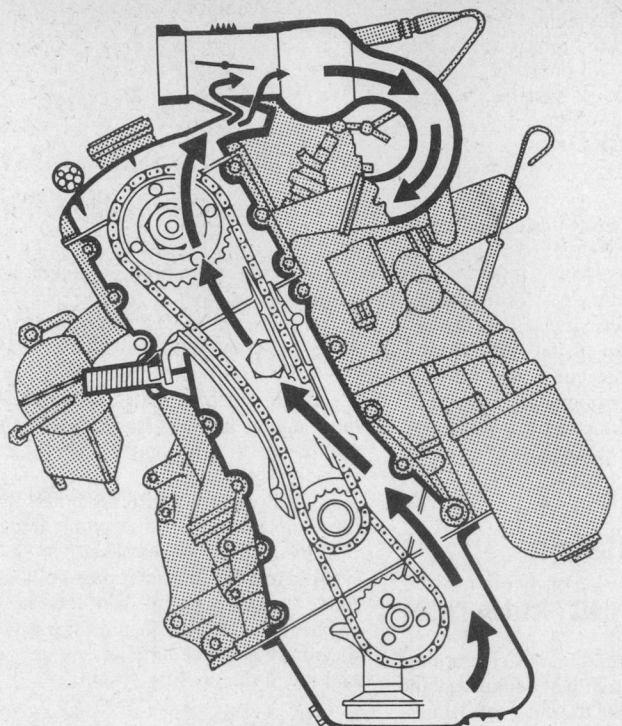

Crankcase emission control system (with Electronic Fuel Injection)

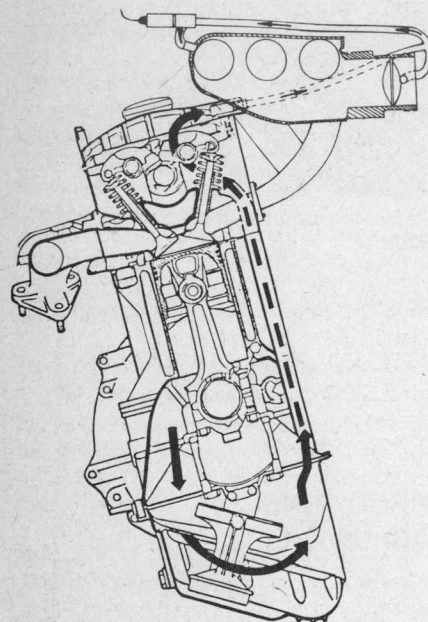

The 528e crankcase emission control system

Crankcase Emission Control System

This system is considered a "sealed" system. No fresh air is allowed to enter the crankcase and the blow-by emissions are routed to the air collector and blended with the air/fuel mixture to be burned through normal combustion.

TESTING

The Crankcase Emission Control System is virtually maintenance free. The connecting tube from the top engine cover of the air collector should be inspected during the routine maintenance services and replaced if cracked, distorted or plugged.

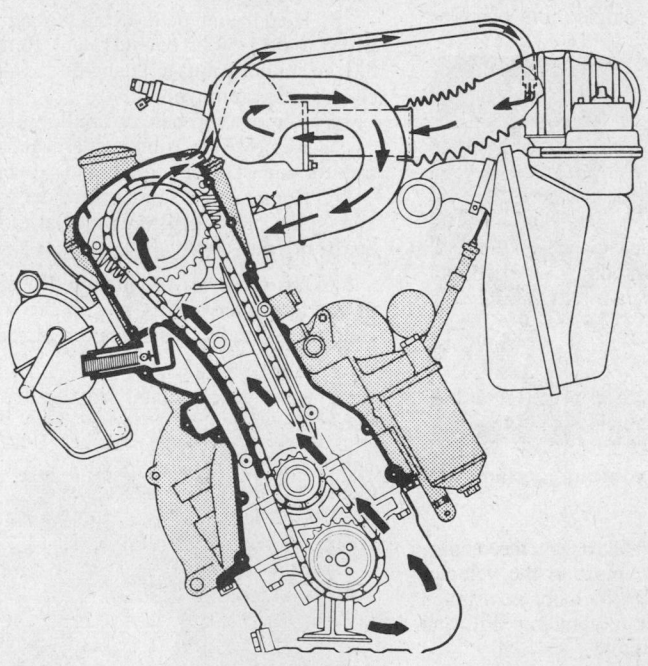

Crankcase emission control system (with Continuous Fuel Injection)

With the engine operating and the connecting tube disconnected, a vacuum should be noted at the air collector side of the hose. If vacuum is not present, an air leak or plugged air induction system may be the cause.

Air Injection System

The Air Injection system is used to add oxygen to the hot exhaust gases in the Thermal Reactor which replaces the exhaust manifold. The introduction of fresh air (oxygen) aids in more complete combustion of the air/fuel mixture lessening the hydrocarbons and the carbon monoxide emissions. A belt driven air pump is used to force air into the exhaust system, through a series of valves and tubing.

TESTING

318i, 320i, 530i, 533i, 633CSi and 733i

AIR PUMP

Disconnect the outlet hose and start the engine. The air velocity should increase as the engine speed increases. If not, the air pump drive belt could be slipping, the check valve or the air pump may be defective and would have to be adjusted or replaced.

BLOW-OFF VALVE

If backfiring occurs when releasing the accelerator or the air pump seems to be overloading, the blow-off valve may be defective.

The valve must release and blow-off during a coasting condition and the internal safety valve must open at 5 psi. The vacuum line must have suction when the engine is running and must allow the air to be blown off when reattached to the valve at idle.

ELECTRIC CONTROL VALVE— WHITE CAP

This control valve governs the blow-off valve and must be open at temperatures below 113°F (45°C) and closed above 113°F (45°C) of the coolant.

With the coolant temperatures above 113°F (45°C), the ignition switch on and the engine off, disconnect both vacuum hoses, attach a test hose to one nipple and blow air into the valve. The valve is functioning properly if air cannot flow through the valve. Turn the ignition switch off and blow into the valve again. Air should flow through the valve.

CHECK VALVE

The check valve must be replaced if air can be blown through the valves in both directions. Air should more towards the reactors only.

BLOW-IN PIPES

The air enters above the reactors, directly into the exhaust ports, behind the exhaust valves. The pipes can be replaced by removing the distribution tube assembly.

THERMAL REACTOR

The reactors have a double casing and have internally vented flame deflector plates. Spontaneous combustion, due to high temperatures, and the introduction of oxygen into the exhaust gas flow maintains the afterburning of the gases.

A warning light marked "Reactor" alerts the driver to have the unit inspected for external heat damage every 25,000 miles. A triggering device, located behind the dash

1. Black   2. Red   3. Blue

Electronic control valves with attaching bolt locations

and operated by the speedometer cable, can be reset to open the electrical contacts and extinguish the warning light.

NOTE: Two different sized buttons are mounted side by side on the triggering device. The small button is for the reactor and the large button is for the EGR valve. Press the button to reset.

Exhaust Gas Recirculating System

The EGR valve is vacuum operated by the position of the injection system throttle plate in the throttle bore during vehicle operation. A metered amount of exhaust gas enters the combustion chamber to be mixed with the air/fuel blend. The effect is to reduce the peak combustion temperatures, which in turn reduces the amount of nitrous oxides (NO_x), formed during the combustion process.

TESTING

318i, 320i, 530i, 533i, 633CSi and 733i

The EGR valve is vacuum controlled from a pressure transmitter which regulates the amount of vacuum applied to the valve from signals originating at the intake manifold and from a back-pressure signal from the exhaust system.

The interior of the EGR valve consists of two diaphragms, the lower one to control the amount of exhaust gas to be recirculated and the upper one to interrupt or shut off the exhaust gas recirculation under conditions of idle, deceleration, full engine load, engine speed over 3750 rpm or coolant temperature below 113°F.

ELECTRIC CONTROL VALVE— RED CAP

The electric control valve should stop the EGR valve operation at coolant temperatures below 113°F (45°C), and speeds above 3000 rpm. Tag and disconnect both vacuum

hoses at the control valve with the engine off and the coolant temperature below 113°F (45°C). Connect a test hose to one of the nipples and blow through the hose. The valve is functioning properly when there is air flowing through the valve with the ignition OFF and no air flow through the valve with the ignition ON.

Connect the vacuum hoses to the valve and operate the engine until the coolant is heated over 113°F (45°C). Disconnect the hoses and check for air flow through the valve. Air should now flow through the valve.

COOLANT TEMPERATURE SWITCH AND CONTROL RELAY

1. With the coolant temperature below 113°F (45°C), turn the ignition ON, but do not start the engine. Remove the wire plug at the control valve and connect a test lamp to the plug.

   a. The test lamp should light. If the test lamp does not light, connect the test lamp to ground. If the lamp now operates, the ground wire to the control valve has an open circuit.

   b. If the test lamp still does not light, disconnect the wire terminal at the coolant temperature switch and connect it to ground. If the test lamp still does not light, replace the control valve.

2. With the coolant temperature above 113°F (45°C), turn the ignition switch ON but do not start the engine. Disconnect the wire terminal plug at the control valve and connect a test lamp. The lamp should be off. If the lamp is on, the coolant temperature switch or control relay is defective.

3. With the engine running at temperatures above 113°F (45°C), connect the test light to the disconnected plug of the control valve. The test lamp should be on over an engine speed of 3000 rpm. If the test lamp does not light, the speed switch is defective.

EGR WARNING LIGHT

A warning light marked EGR is triggered at 25,000 miles, to alert the driver to service

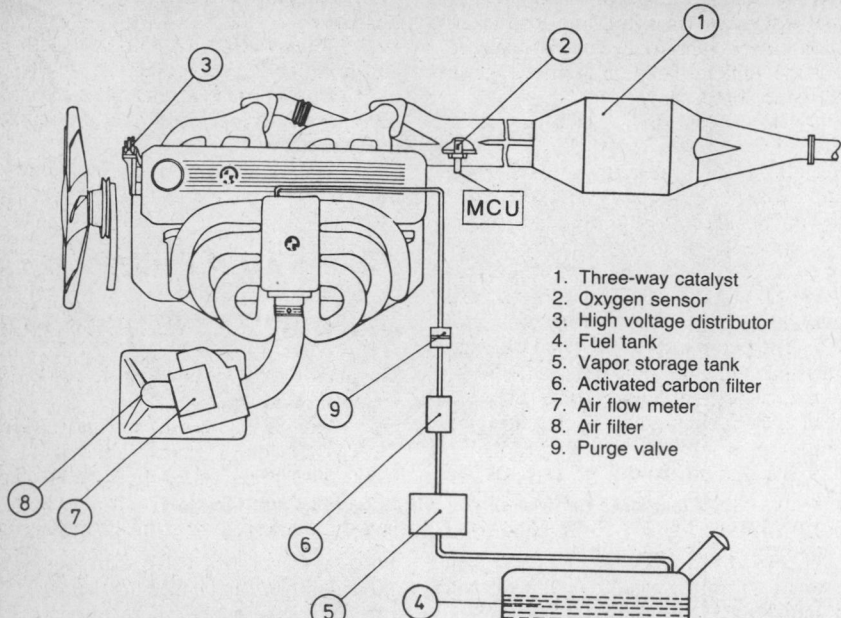

1. Three-way catalyst
2. Oxygen sensor
3. High voltage distributor
4. Fuel tank
5. Vapor storage tank
6. Activated carbon filter
7. Air flow meter
8. Air filter
9. Purge valve

Main components of the exhaust emission system—528e

Triggering device with REACTOR (1) and the EGR (2) resetting buttons shown

the exhaust gas recirculation system filter.

A triggering device, located under the dash and driven by the speedometer cable, can be reset to open the electrical contacts and extinguish the EGR warning light.

NOTE: Two different sized buttons are mounted side by side on the triggering device. The small button is for the reactor light and the large button is for the EGR light. Press the button to reset.

Distributor Advance/ Retard Units

A vacuum advance and retard unit is at- tached to the distributor and is controlled by engine vacuum. The advance can be checked with a strobe light and increasing the engine speed while observing the action of the timing mark during the increase in engine speed. The retard side can be checked at idle by removing the retard vacuum line and noting the increase in engine speed of at least 300 rpm.

NOTE: Models 733i, 633CSi, 320i California and High Altitude vehicles equipped with manual transmissions, have the vacuum advance in operation only when the high gear is engaged. This is controlled by an electrical switch connected to the shifting linkage. Automatic transmission 633CSi for California and High Altitude, have the vacuum advance inoperative. Late model 530i vehicles are equipped with a vacuum retard unit only.

Electric Control Valve
TEST

Black Cap—California Equipment Only

This control valve stops the retard distrib- utor control over speeds of 3000 rpm.

Remove the outer hose (to distributor) and start the engine. At engine rpm lower than 3000 rpm, vacuum should be present in the distributor retard unit hose and not present when the engine speed is increased above 3000 rpm.

Disconnect the wire terminal end at the control valve and have the engine operating at idle. Connect a test lamp to the terminal and check for presence of current. If current is present, the speed switch is defective.

Increase the engine speed to 3000 rpm or above, and the test lamp should light. If the test lamp does not light, the speed switch is defective.

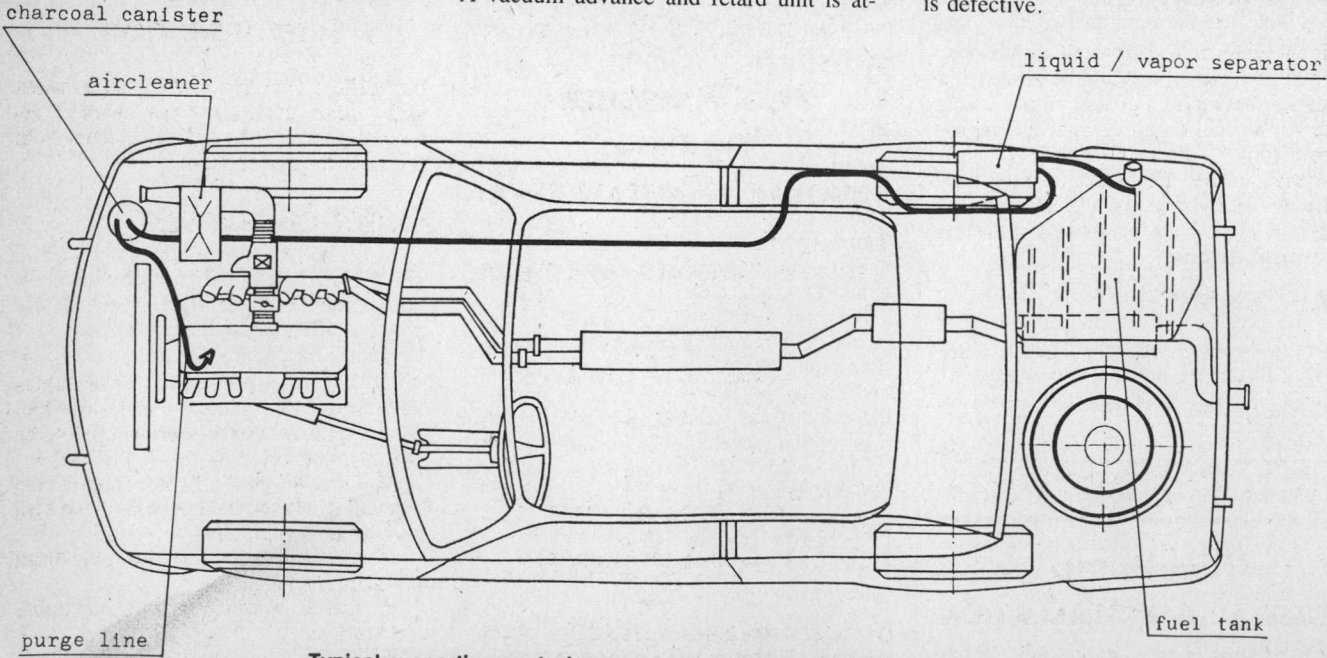

charcoal canister

aircleaner

liquid / vapor separator

purge line

fuel tank

Typical evaportive control system—six cylinder engine illustrated

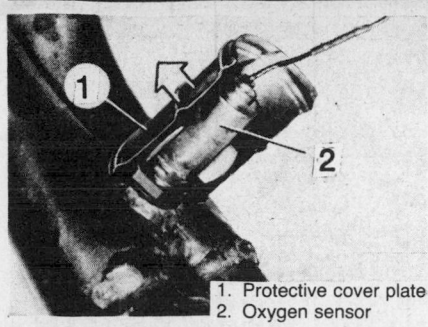

1. Protective cover plate
2. Oxygen sensor

Removing the oxygen sensor plate and the oxygen sensor—528e

Oxygen Sensor

REMOVAL & INSTALLATION

All Models

The oxygen sensor light on the dash will light the first time the mileage reaches 30,000. Replace the oxygen sensor and remove the light bulb from the dash. The bulb lights the first time only, however the sensor must be changed every 30,000 miles.

1. Disconnect the oxygen sensor wire connector and remove the wires from the clip.
2. Pull off the sensor protective plate.
3. Unscrew the oxygen sensor.
4. Before installation coat the threads of the new sensor with CRC® copper paste.
5. Install the sensor unit.
6. Remove the call unit from the dash by unscrewing the bolt and pushing the unit to the right, and remove the oxygen sensor display bulb. On some models, the bulb must be broken off to remove it.

Evaporative Control System

This system is designed to collect and store the raw gasoline vapors (hydrocarbons) and to direct the vapors into the engine along with the air/fuel mixture when the engine is operating.

A maintenance free vapor storage tank is located in the trunk while an activated carbon filter canister is mounted in the engine compartment.

MAINTENANCE

The only repairs or checks that can be made are to maintain the hoses and to change the canister unit if it becomes saturated with raw gasoline.

FUEL SYSTEM

Fuel Pump
REMOVAL & INSTALLATION

The fuel pump is an electrical unit, deliv-

ering fuel through a pressure regulator, to a fuel distributor or a ring-line for the injection valves. The fuel pump is mounted under the vehicle, near the fuel tank, or in the engine compartment.

1. Disconnect the electrical connector(s).
2. If the fuel lines are flexible, pinch them closed with an appropriate tool. Disconnect the fuel lines and plug the ends.
3. Remove the retaining bolts and remove the pump and expansion tank as an assembly. On the 318i, the pump and mounting bracket come off together.
4. The pump can be separated from the expansion tank after removal. On the 318i, separate the pump from the mounting bracket and slide the rubber mounting ring from the pump.
5. Installation is the reverse of removal. Use similar types of hose clamps, if any need replacing. The wrong type clamp can damage the pressure lines.

PRESSURE CHECKING

318i and 320i

1. Connect a pressure gauge in the line leading from the fuel distributor on top of the injector pump to the warm–up regulator. Plug the open end of the line leading to the warm–up regulator, and make sure the gauge will read the pressure coming from the distributor.
2. Disconnect the wire plug on the mixture control unit, and turn on the ignition. The pressure should read 64–74 psi, or the fuel pump will have to be replaced.

325e, 528e, 528i, 530i, 533i, 633CSI and 733I

1. Connect a pressure gauge in the line leading to the cold start valve from the injector feed circuit. With the engine idling, the pressure must be 33–38 psi, or the fuel pump (or filter) is defective.

Fuel Pressure Regulator

REMOVAL & INSTALLATION

318i

1. Remove the vacuum hose from the unit.

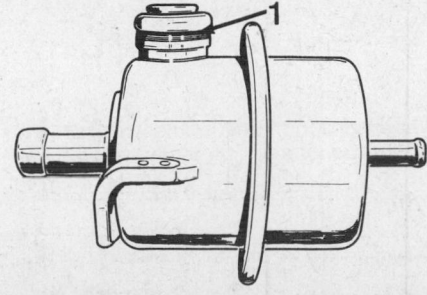

On the 318i fuel pressure regulator, check the seal (1) and replace it if necessary

2. Loosen the clamp and pull off the fuel hose.
3. Remove the two bolts and pull the unit from the injection tube.
4. Inspect the seal that seals the connection with the injection tube and replace it, if necessary.
5. Install in reverse of the removal procedure.

Fuel Filter

REMOVAL & INSTALLATION

The inline fuel filters on all models of BMW are easily removed.

1. Disconnect the inlet and outlet hoses. Remove the hose clamps if necessary.
2. The filters will usually be attached to a frame, floor pan or wheel well by a bracket. Loosen the bracket and remove the filter.
3. Observe the instructions on the inlet and outlet during installation.

LOCATION BY MODEL

320i, 318i, 325e, 528e and 733i

The inline filter is located directly above the final drive assembly and attached to the underside of the floor pan.

528i, 533i and 633CSi

The inline filter is located behind the passenger side wheel, near the frame. Above the final drive shaft.

530i

The inline filter is located above the driver's side front wheel housing and below the fuse box.

Fuel Injection

For all fuel injection testing, adjustment and repair procedures not detailed below, please refer to "Fuel Injection" in the Unit Repair section.

INJECTION VALVES

The injection valves must open at a minimum fuel pressure of 47 psi.

Testing

1. Connect a pressure valve and shut-off valve in the pressure line to the fuel distributor, with the pressure gauge on the fuel distributor side of the shut-off valve.
2. Open the shut-off valve, remove the injectors from the intake manifold and turn the ignition switch ON.
3. Disconnect the terminal plug from the mixture control unit.
4. Lift the sensor plate for a maximum of 4 seconds.
5. The pressure should not drop more

Electric fuel pump assembly—typical

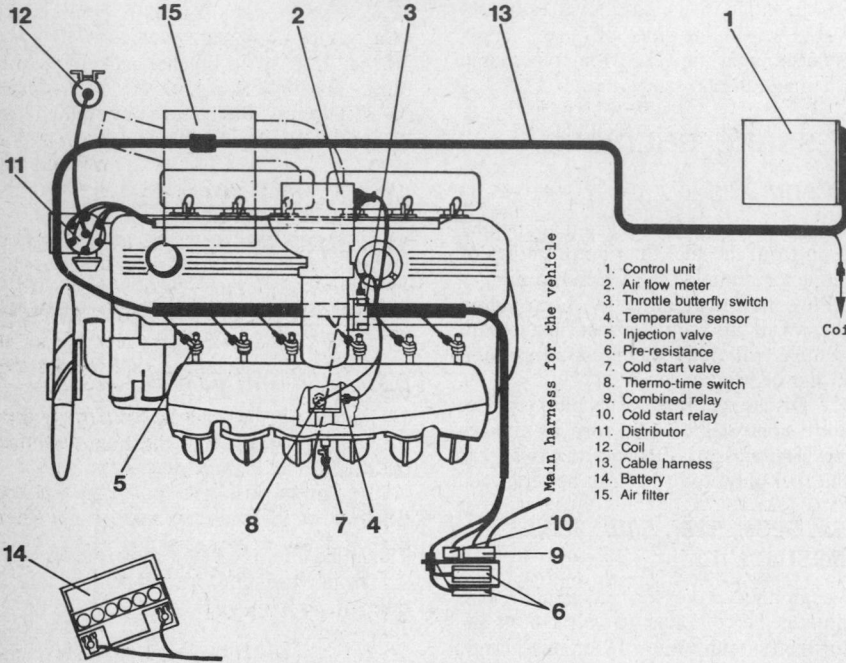

1. Control unit
2. Air flow meter
3. Throttle butterfly switch
4. Temperature sensor
5. Injection valve
6. Pre-resistance
7. Cold start valve
8. Thermo-time switch
9. Combined relay
10. Cold start relay
11. Distributor
12. Coil
13. Cable harness
14. Battery
15. Air filter

Bosch L-Jetronic® Fuel Injection System

than 4 psi. If the pressure drops more than the specifications, the fuel filter is clogged; fuel pump rate is inadequate or the fuel tank is empty.

Removal & Installation
318i

1. Loosen the two injection tube screws (arrowed).

2. Pull the injection tube up so as to pull the injectors out of the fittings in the intake manifold (injectors are lightly pressed in).

3. Each injector that must be replaced can now be disconnected by pulling off its electrical plug, lifting out its retainer, and then pulling it from the injection tube. If an injector is to be reused, make sure to check O-rings at both ends and the plastic washer just under the connector and replace worn or damaged parts.

4. Install in reverse order.

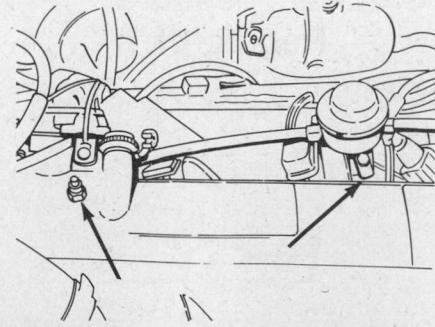

When replacing 318i fuel injectors, loosen the arrowed screws on the injection tube

320i

1. Remove the rubber intake hose leading from the mixture control unit to the throttle unit. Remove the four retaining nuts for each, and then remove No. 2 and No. 3 (the two center cylinders) intake pipes.

2. The injector valves incorporate union nuts and a flatted section on each valve to permit the lines to be attached to the valves. However, the injection lines *need not* be disconnected to remove the valves, which are simply pressed into the intake ports. To remove each valve, simply pass a screwdriver blade downward between the intake header and the cam cover, insert the blade into the groove between the fuel line nut and flatted portion of the injection valve, and pry out. After the valve is out of the port, hold the flatted section of the valve with a wrench, use another wrench to unscrew the union nut, and disconnect the fuel line.

3. On installation, first press the white insulating bushing back into the intake port, if it came out with the valve. Then, press the rubber seal into the groove. Finally, snugly press in the injection valve. Reinstall the intake pipes, using new gaskets.

530i and 533i

1. With the air collector removed, disconnect the electrical connector plugs from the 6 injection valves.

2. Remove the valve retaining bolts and remove the injector tube with all the valves attached.

3. Remove the retaining clamps and remove the valves from the injector tube.

4. To install, reverse the removal procedure.

528i, 633CSi AND 733i

1. With the injector tube and injector valves removed from the engine, cut the metal hose clamp sleeve and remove the sleeve.

2. Heat the hose with a soldering iron and remove the injector hose from the tube.

3. To install the injector valve assembly on the tube, clean the tube adapter and coat the inside of the hose with fuel.

4. Install the fuel injector hose with the hose sleeve on the injector tube and push against the stop, with the electrical terminal facing up.

5. Complete the installation in the reverse of the removal procedure.

325e AND 528e

1. Unscrew the four injection tube mounting bolts.

2. Push up on the injection tube until the injectors have been taken out of the guide on the intake manifold.

3. Disconnect the electrical plug from each injector, lift off the lock and then pull the injector out of the injection tube.

4. Installation is in the reverse order of removal.

Fuel Tank

REMOVAL & INSTALLATION
318i

1. Disconnect the battery. Remove the

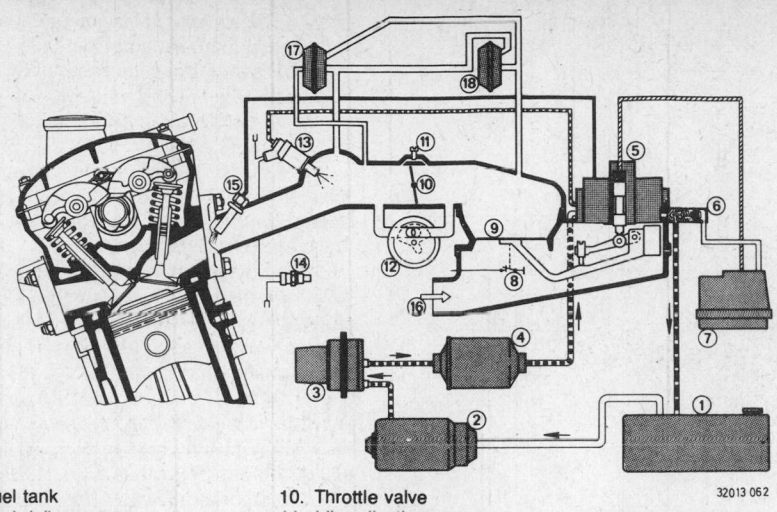

1. Fuel tank
2. Fuel delivery pump
3. Pressure reservoir
4. Fuel filter
5. Fuel distributor
6. System pressure regulator
7. Warm-up regulator
8. Safety switch
9. Sensor plate
10. Throttle valve
11. Idle adjusting screw
12. Auxiliary air regulator
13. Start valve
14. Thermo timing valve
15. Injection valves
16. Air Inlet
17. Vacuum regulator
18. Auxiliary air valve

————— Injection press.
••••••••• System pressure
▬ ▬ ▬ Return
////////// Control pressure

32013 062

Bosch K-Jetronic® Fuel Injection System

panels around the rear seat and remove the seat.

2. Remove the cover that gives access to fuel tank connections. Then, disconnect the in-tank pump electrical connectors and fuel lines and two additional hose connections. Turn the fuel intake assembly counterclockwise and remove it from the tank.

3. Safely siphon or pump all fuel out of the tank.

4. Disconnect the filler pipe which is located near the rear spring.

5. Remove the muffler and disconnect and remove the driveshaft (see appropriate proceudres below).

6. Remove the five bolts holding the right tank in place, and then lift the tank out.

7. Disconnect the hose from the left side tank and remove adhesive strips. Then, remove the left side tank similarly.

8. Install in reverse order. Make sure to replace the seal on the fuel intake assembly. Use new hose clamps on all connections. If a tank is being replaced, make sure to transfer the heat shield.

320i

1. Disconnect the battery negative terminal and drain the fuel.

2. Remove the rear seat. Remove the black guard plate to gain access to fuel lines and the sending unit.

3. Disconnect the electrical connector and the suction and return lines at the sending unit. Disconnect the vent line at the tank.

4. Disconnect the filler neck at the lower end.

5. Remove the mounting screw and remove the guard from behind the connecting

hose (which goes to the left side tank).

6. Disconnect the connecting hose. Then, remove the two mounting screws on the inboard side of the tank at the bottom, and lower the tank out of the car.

7. For the tank on the left side, perform Steps 5 and 6 in a similar way, but before lifting the tank out of the car, disconnect the small vent line from the top of the tank. If this line should have to be replaced, limit the length of the replacement hose section to 23.6 in.

8. Install the fuel tanks in reverse order.

325e

1. Remove the rear seat cushion. Remove the left and right tank covers and the unscrew bolts.

2. Pull off the insulating sheet. Unscrew the fuel intake cover. Pull off both electrical plugs.

3. Label, and then pull off all four hoses.

4. Safely drain the fuel by removing the tank drain plug or pumping the fuel out of the tank from the top.

5. Loosen the hose clamp on the line near the rear spring and disconnect the fuel line.

6. Remove the muffler.

7. Matchmark and remove the driveshaft.

8. Loosen the hose clamps and disconnect the hoses from the fuel filter.

9. Securely support the tank and then remove the two bolts on the fuel filter side and three bolts on the opposite side. First lower the right side of the tank and then remove the tank from underneath.

10. Install the tank in reverse order, using new hose clamps on all connections.

528e

1. Open the tank cap, lift off the rubber cover and disconnect the three vent hoses. Drain the fuel.

2. Remove the trunk mat and unscrew the tank cover.

3. Disconnect the two electrical plugs and the two hoses.

4. Unscrew the bolts and disconnect the exhaust suspension parts on the rear axle carrier. Position the exhaust assembly out of the way and secure it with wire.

5. Unscrew the retaining strap mounting bolt, remove the liner and then remove the strap.

6. Unscrew the mounting bolt and remove the fuel tank.

7. Installation is in the reverse order of removal.

528i and 530i

1. Disconnect the battery ground cable. Siphon the fuel out of the tank.

2. Fold the floor mat out of the way for access. Remove the three screws and remove the round black cover which permits access to the sending unit.

3. Disconnect the wires at the sending unit (Brown—ground, Brown/Yellow—G, Brown/Black—W). Detach the (unclamped) vent line.

4. Detach the feed and return lines at the filter and return pipe (both under the car).

5. Detach the front and rear mounting bushings of the rearmost muffler, and then remove the rear bracket from the body.

6. Loosen the tank mounting bolts at the front and right sides, remove the filler cap, and remove the tank.

7. Install in reverse order.

533i and 633CSI

1. Disconnect the negative battery cable, and siphon fuel from the tank. Lift the rear compartment rug out of the way. Remove the round access cover.

2. Disconnect the electrical plug and the two fuel lines from the top of the sending unit.

3. Remove the fuel tank filler cap and the rubber seal which surrounds the filler neck. Then, disconnect the four vent hoses.

4. Remove the bushings from the rear muffler at front and rear, and then remove the mounting bracket at the rear.

5. Bend the taps down, remove the mounting bolts, and remove the heat shield. Remove the nut and bolt, and remove the stone guard.

6. Remove the three mounting bolts from the right side panel, and lower the tank, right side first, and then remove it, being careful to avoid pinching any of the hoses.

7. Install in reverse order.

733i

1. Unscrew the filler cap and siphon out the tank.

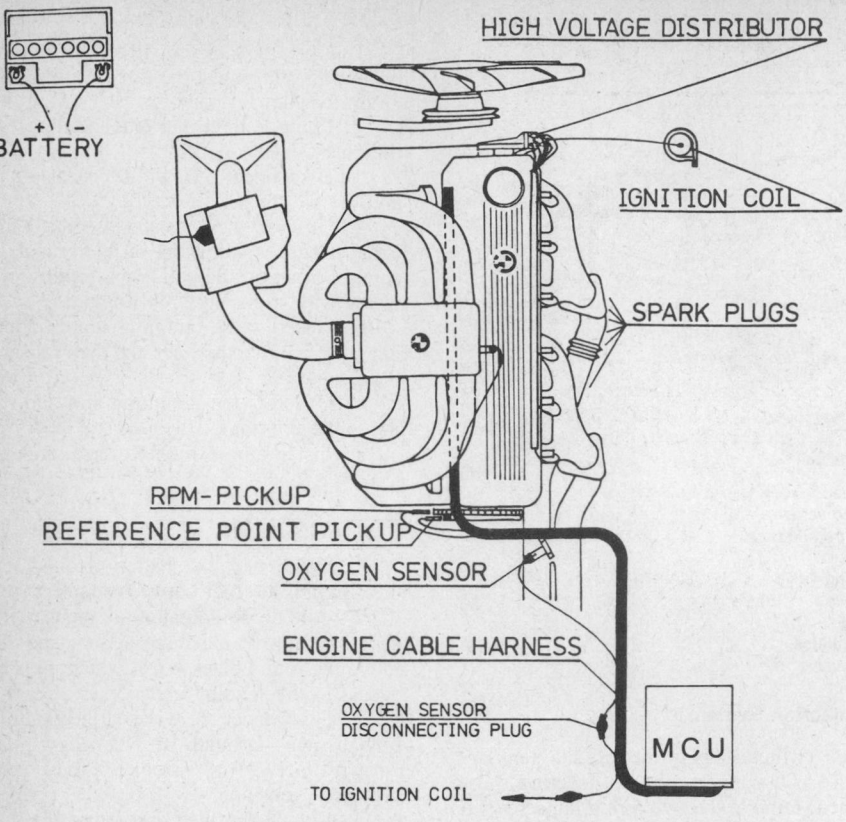

BATTERY

HIGH VOLTAGE DISTRIBUTOR

IGNITION COIL

SPARK PLUGS

RPM-PICKUP
REFERENCE POINT PICKUP
OXYGEN SENSOR

ENGINE CABLE HARNESS

OXYGEN SENSOR
DISCONNECTING PLUG

MCU

TO IGNITION COIL

Main components of the Motronic injection system—528e

1. Support plate
2. Rubber ring
3. Cup flange
4. Rubber ring

Injector valve and sealing components

2. Disconnect the negative battery cable. Fold the rug in the rear compartment out of the way, and remove the round access panel.

3. Disconnect inlet and outlet hoses at the sending unit.

4. Disconnect the sending unit electrical connector at the plug, located near the wiring harness in the trunk.

5. Remove the mounting bolts from the straps and lower the tank slightly and support it. Pull off the (4) vent hoses. Then, lower the tank out of the car.

6. Install in reverse order, making sure the rubber bumpers against which the tank is held by the mounting straps are in good shape, or replace them, as necessary.

MANUAL TRANSMISSION

For manual transmission overhaul procedures, please refer to "Manual Transmission Overhaul" in the Unit Repair section.

REMOVAL & INSTALLATION
320i, 325e and 318i

1. Drain the transmission. On 320i only, unscrew all transmission mounting bolts (4)

accessible from above. Swing up the bracket mounted to the top/left bolt.

2. Disconnect the exhaust system support at the rear of the transmission.

3. Detach the exhaust pipe at the manifold.

4. Detach the driveshaft at the transmission by pulling out bolts from the rear of the coupling (the coupling remains attached to the driveshaft).

5. Remove the heat shield. Remove the bolts for the center bearing bracket, and pull the bracket downward. Bend the driveshaft downward and pull it out of the bearing journal.

6. Remove the bolt and disconnect the speedometer drive cable. Disconnect the back–up light switch wire, and pull the wire out of the clips on the transmission.

7. Remove the two Allen bolts at the top and pull the console off the transmission.

8. Disconnect the gearshift selector rod by pulling off the circlip, removing the washer and pulling the rod off the pin.

9. Detach the clutch slave cylinder line bracket at the front of the transmission, remove the mounting bolts from the slave cylinder mounting, and remove the slave cylinder.

10. Remove the flywheel housing cover.

11. Support the transmission securely at the center with a floor jack and wooden block.

12. Detach the crossmember by removing the nuts attaching it to the body at either end. On 318i, remove all front mounting bolts. Remove the three remaining front mounting bolts on the 320i, and pull the transmission out toward the rear.

13. Reverse the removal procedure to install. Bear the following points in mind:

  a. Front mounting bolts are torqued to 18–19 ft. lbs. on the M8 transmissions; 34–37 on the M10 transmissions. Torque the crossmember rubber mounts to 31–35 ft. lbs.

  b. On the 318i, the console has self-locking bolts which must be replaced for reassembly.

  c. When reinstalling the clutch slave

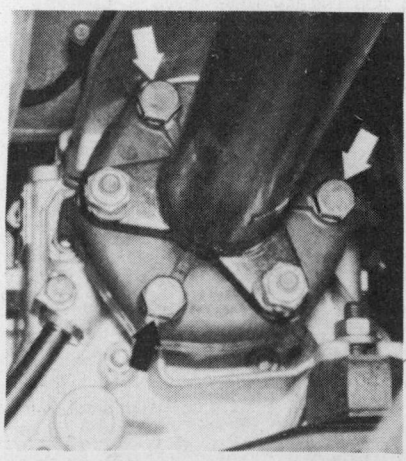

Disconnecting driveshaft at transmission

cylinder, make sure the bleeder screw faces downward.

d. When installing the driveshaft center support bearing, preload it forward .078 in. on 320i, 0.079–0.157 in. on 318i.

c. Replace the locknuts on the driveshaft coupling and tighten the nuts only—not the bolts to 31–35 ft.lb.

f. Inspect the gasket at the joint between the exhaust manifold and pipe and replace it if necessary.

g. When reattaching exhaust system support at the rear, leave the attaching nut/bolt slightly loose; loosen the two nuts/bolts attaching the support via slots to the transmission; push the support toward the exhaust pipe until all tension is removed and then secure nuts and bolts.

All 6 Cylinder Models (Except 325e and 733i)

1. Remove the exhaust system. Drain the transmission.

2. Remove the circlip and washer at the selector rod and disengage the rod at the transmission.

3. Unzip the leather boot surrounding the gearshift lever. With a pointed object such as an ice pick, release the circlip at the bottom of the gearshift lever and then pull the lever upward and out of the transmission. Lubricate the nylon bushings at the bottom of the lever mechanism with a permanent lubricant for reassembly.

4. Remove the three bolts from the coupling at the front of the driveshaft out through the rear of the coupling, leaving the nuts/bolts attaching the driveshaft to the coupling in place.

5. Remove the heat shield. Remove the mounting bolts and remove the center bearing support bracket. Bend the driveshaft downward at the front and slide the spline out of the center bearing.

6. Support the transmission securely between the front axle carrier and oil pan with a floorjack and wooden block.

7. Remove the attaching bolt and pull out the speedometer cable. Disconnect the back-up light wiring electrical connectors and pull the wire out of the clips on the transmission.

8. Loosen the connection to the rubber bushing at the transmission, remove the mounting nuts at either end, and remove the crossmember. On the 633CSi, lower the transmission to the front axle carrier.

9. On the 633CSi, disconnect the mount for the clutch hydraulic line at the front of the transmission. Then, on all models, unscrew the mounting nuts and detach the clutch slave cylinder (with the line connected).

10. Remove the mounting nuts at the clutch housing and separate the transmission and clutch housing.

11. Pull the gearbox to the rear and out of the car.

12. Install the transmission in reverse order, keeping the following points in mind:

a. Use the slave cylinder to move the clutch throwout arm to the correct position. Align the throwout bearing. Grease the guide sleeve and groove in the throwout bearing with a permanent lubricant.

b. Put the transmission into gear before installing.

c. Make sure, when installing the clutch slave cylinder, that the hose connection faces downward.

d. Preload the center bearing .08 in. toward the front.

e. When tightening the coupling, hold the bolt heads and torque only the nuts only to 75 ft. lbs. Use new nuts. Torque the transmission-to-engine bolts to 16–17 ft. lbs. (M8 transmission) or 31–35 ft. lbs. (M10 transmission); torque the bolt for the rubber bushing on the crossmember to 18 ft. lbs.

325e

Raise the car and support it securely.

1. Remove the exhaust system. Remove the cross brace and heat shield.

2. Hold the nuts on the front with one wrench, and remove bolts from the rear with another to disconnect the flexible coupling.

3. Loosen the threaded sleeve on the driveshaft. You'll need a special tool such as BMW 261040 to hold the splined portion of the shaft while turning the sleeve.

4. Remove its mounting bolts and remove the center mount. Support the transmission securely.

5. Remove mounting bolts and remove the crossmember holding the transmission to the body. Lower the transmission and then pull the driveshaft off the centering pin.

6. Remove the retainer and washer, and pull out the shift selector rod.

7. Lift off the gearshift leather boot, and the insulating sheet. Pull out the cover sleeve that seals between the body and shift console. Then, lift out the circlip and remove the shift lever.

8. Remove the console supporting bolts.

9. Mark, and then unplug sensor mounting plugs (near the flywheel). Unscrew the mounting bolts for the speed sensor and reference mark sensor and remove both sensors.

10. Unscrew and remove the clutch slave cylinder and support it so the hydraulic line can remain connected.

11. Pull off wires from the reverse gear switch and pull the wiring out of the harnesses.

12. Using a Torx® socket, remove the Torx® bolts holding the transmission to the engine at the front. Lower the transmission.

13. Install the transmission in reverse order, keeping the following points in mind:

a. Torque front mounting bolts to 46–58 ft.lb.

b. Install the clutch slave cylinder with the bleeder screw downward.

c. Install the speed sensor with no identification ring to align with starter ring gear, while the reference mark sensor (with identification ring) aligns with the flywheel. Clean the faces of the sensors, check the O-rings and coat them with a sealer such as Molykote® Longterm 2 before installation.

d. When installing the gearshift lever, make sure the cover sleeve is sealing all around. Coat spherical working surfaces with Molykote® Longterm.

e. When installing the driveshaft center bearing, preload it forward .079–.157 in. Check the driveshaft alignment with an appropriate tool such as BMW 26 1 030. Torque the center mount bolts to 16–17 ft. lb.

f. Torque the flexible coupling bolts to 83–94 ft. lb.

g. When reinstalling the heat shield mount, install the holder on the right side.

733i

NOTE: This procedure requires a special tool for clamping the flexible drive coupling.

1. Remove the circlip and washer from the front end of the selector rod, and disconnect it from the lower end of the shift lever.

2. Push up the dust cover, and with needle nose pliers, remove the circlip which holds the gearshift lever in place. Lubricate the nylon bushings surrounding the socket with a permanent lubricant for reassembly.

3. Disconnect the back-up light plug near the gearshift lever. Remove the large circlip which surrounds the gearshift mount.

4. Drain the transmission. Raise the car and support it. Install the special tool (BMW 26 1 011 or equivalent) which clamps around the flexible coupling. Then, unscrew the three nuts on the forward side of the coupling, withdraw the bolts out the rear. This requires tightening the clamping tool until the bolts can be pulled out by hand.

5. Remove the web type crossmember located under the driveshaft. Then, loosen the mounting nuts for the center bearing bracket and detach it. Bend the driveshaft downward and pull it off the centering pin.

6. Support the transmission securely with a floor jack working through a wooden block. Then, remove the mounting nut from the crossmember rubber bushing, the nuts and bolts from either end of the crossmember where it bolts to the body, and remove the crossmember.

7. Detach the exhaust system bracket both at the transmission and at the exhaust pipes and remove it.

8. Detach the mounting bracket for the clutch slave cylinder hydraulic line at the transmission and then remove the two mounting bolts and remove the slave cylinder. Detach the fourth gear switch wires, if so equipped.

9. Detach the transmission at the clutch housing and remove it toward the rear.

10. Install the transmission in reverse order, keeping the following points in mind:

a. Use the clutch slave cylinder to put the release lever in position for transmission installation. Align the clutch bearing and lubricate the lubrication groove inside it with Molykote® BR2-750 or its equivalent.

b. Put the transmission into gear prior to installation.

c. Install the guide sleeve of the transmission into the bearing carefully, then turn the output flange until the drive shaft slides into the drive plate. Then, remove the slave cylinder while mounting the transmission. Torque transmission-to-clutch housing bolts to 54–59 ft. lbs.

d. When installing the clutch slave cylinder, make sure the bleeder screw faces downward.

e. When remounting the exhaust system bracket, make sure there is no torquional strain on the system.

f. Preload the center driveshaft bearing toward the front of the car .08 in.

g. When reassembling the flexible drive coupling, use new self-locking nuts. Leave the special tool in the compression while installing the bolts, and then install the nuts, holding the bolts in position and turning only the nuts.

h. Torque the transmission mount-to-crossmember bolt to 36–40 ft. lbs., and the crossmember-to-body nuts to 16–17 ft. lbs.

i. When installing the shift lever, note that the tab on the damper plate nuts engage in the opening in the shift arm.

CLUTCH

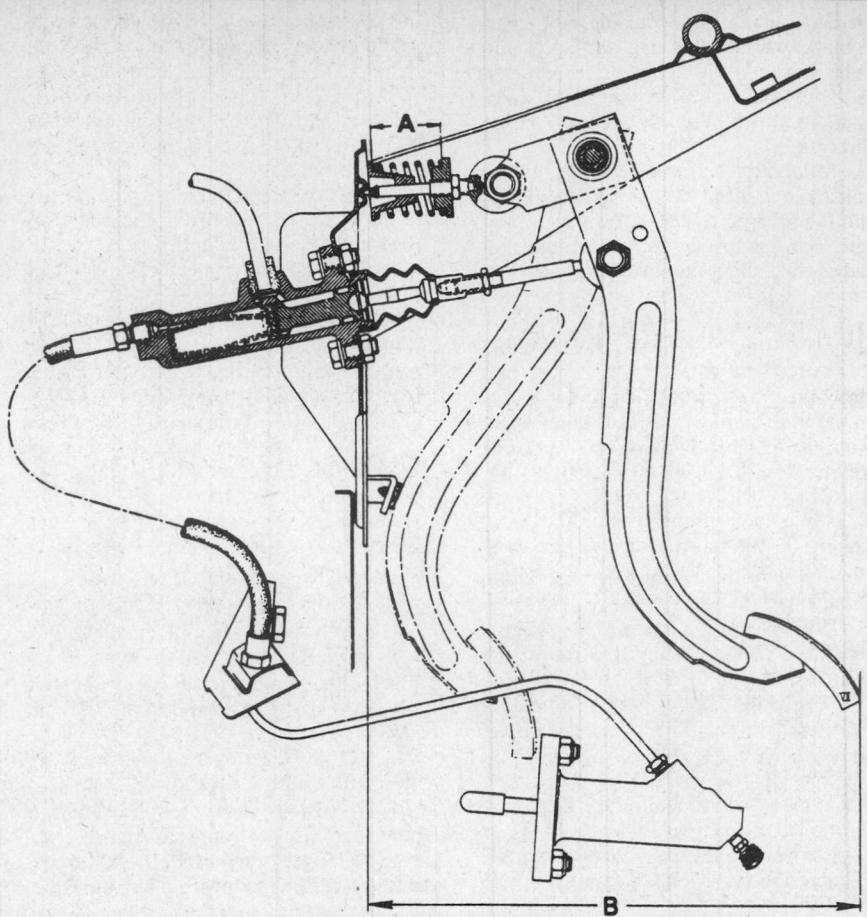

Adjusting the pedal height and over–center spring on 6 cylinder model

PEDAL HEIGHT AND OVER–CENTER SPRING ADJUSTMENTS

All 6 Cylinder Models (except 325e)

Measure the length of the over–center spring (Dimension "A") and, if necessary, loosen the locknut and rotate the shaft as necessary to get the proper clearance. Measure the distance (Dimension "B") from the firewall to the tip of the clutch pedal and move the pedal in or out, if necessary, by loosening the locknut and rotating the shaft. Specifications for the various models are shown below:

Models	Dimension "A"	Dimension "B"
733i	1.338 in.	10.472–10.787 in.
630CSi, 633CSi	1.138–1.358 in.	9.644–9.960 in.
528e, 530i	1.283–1.302 in.	10.078–9.764 in.

All 4 Cylinder Models (and 325e)

Measure the distance between the bottom edge of the clutch pedal and the firewall (A). It should be 9.920–10.197 in. except on 325e. 325e—9.743–10.276. If out of specification, loosen the locknut and rotate the piston rod (1) to correct it.

REMOVAL & INSTALLATION

1. Remove the transmission and clutch housing.

2. Prevent the flywheel from turning, using a locking tool.

3. Loosen the mounting bolts one after another gradually to relieve tension from the clutch.

4. Remove the mounting bolts, clutch, and drive plate.

5. To install, reverse the removal procedure. Torque the clutch mounting bolts to 16–17 ft. lbs.

Clutch Master Cylinder

REMOVAL & INSTALLATION

1. Remove the necessary trim panel or carpet.

2. On the 320i, disconnect the accelerator cable and pull it forward out of the engine firewall.

3. Disconnect the pushrod at the clutch pedal.

4. Remove the float container (if equipped) and remove enough brake fluid from the tank until the level drops below the refill line.

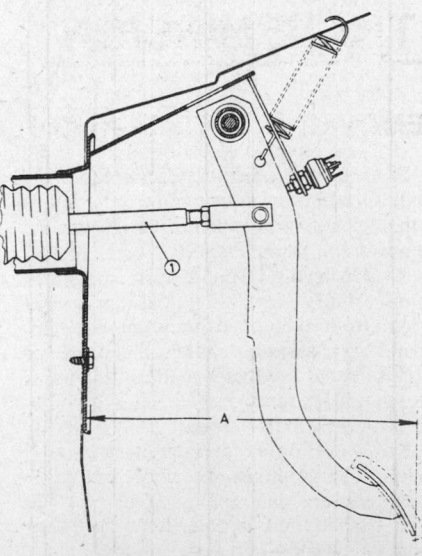

Adjusting the pedal height on the 320i

5. Disconnect the windshield washer fluid tank without removing the hoses on model 733i.

6. Disconnect the lines and retaining bolts and remove the master cylinder from the firewall.

7. Installation is the reverse of removal. On the 318i and 325e, the piston rod bolt should be coated with Molykote® Longterm 2 or equivalent. Bleed the system and adjust the pedal travel with the pushrod to 6 in.

Clutch Slave Cylinder

REMOVAL & INSTALLATION

1. Remove enough brake fluid from the reservoir until the level drops below the refill line connection.

2. Remove the circlip or retaining bolts depending on the model and pull the unit down.

3. Disconnect the line and remove the slave cylinder.

4. Installation is the reverse of removal. Make sure to install the cylinder with the bleed screw facing downward. Bleed the system.

BLEEDING CLUTCH HYDRAULIC SYSTEM

1. Fill the reservoir.

2. Connect a bleeder hose from the bleeder screw to a container filled with brake fluid so that air cannot be drawn in during bleeding procedures.

3. Pump the clutch pedal about 10 times then hold it down.

4. Open the bleeder screw and tighten when no more air bubbles escape.

5. Release the clutch pedal and repeat the above procedure until no more air bubbles can be seen.

AUTOMATIC TRANSMISSION

REMOVAL & INSTALLATION

1. Disconnect the accelerator cable.

2. On the 4 cylinder engine remove all of the transmission mounting bolts which are accessible from above.

3. Detach the oil filler neck and drain the oil.

4. On 4 cylinder engines remove the exhaust pipe support bracket and separate the pipe from the exhaust manifold. On the 318i and 325e, remove the exhaust system and detach the heat shield.

5. On all 6 cylinder engines except model 733i, remove the entire exhaust system.

6. Detach the oil cooler lines from the transmission and drain fluid.

7. Disconnect the propeller shaft at the

Remove the 4 torque convertor retaining bolts

transmission. On model 733i, use special clamping tool. On the 318i and 325e, disconnect the selector rod.

8. Disconnect the speedometer cable.

9. Remove the heat guard and center bearing and bend down and pull off the propeller shaft.

10. Remove the torque converter cover and remove the four bolts that attach the torque converter to the drive plate. Turn the engine for this procedure, using the vibration damper.

NOTE: On 1982 and later 325e, 528e, 533i, 633CSi and 733i models, the speed transmitter and reference transmitter must be removed from the flywheel housing. For installation, the speed transmitter faces the gear ring. The reference transmitter has a plug with a grey ring and faces the flywheel. The engine will not start if the plugs are mixed up.

11. Support the transmission and disconnect the crossmember at the body.

12. Remove the remaining transmission mounting bolts.

13. Srparate the transmission from the engine and take off the torque converter at the same time. On the 318i, lower the transmission onto the front axle carrier. Remove the grill from the torque converter housing and gently pry the torque converter backwards as the transmission is pulled off.

14. Installation is the reverse of removal. Push the torque converter back against the stop on the main transmission and rotate it to align bolt holes with the drive plate holes before installing. Torque drive plate bolts to 16–17 ft.lb. Install the exhaust suspension without twisting. When installing the propeller shaft preload the center bearing by 0.08 in. in the forward direction. Make sure the torque converter is positioned correctly before installing. Replenish drained fluid with new fluid, only.

SELECTOR LEVER ADJUSTMENT

1. Detach the selector rod (1) at the selector lever lower section (2).

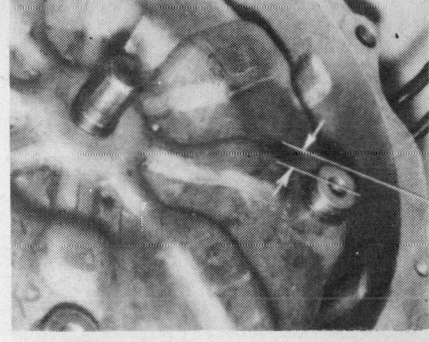

The torque converter is installed correctly if the drive shell mounting parts are located underneath the converter housing

2. Move the selector lever (3) on the transmission to position 0 or N.

3. Press the selector lever (4) against the stop (5) on the shift gate.

4. Adjust the length of the selector rod (1) until the pin (6) aligns with the bore in the selector lever lower section (2). Shorten the selector rod length by: 1 turn—320i, 1–2 turns—318i and 325e, 633CSi, 733i; 2–2½ turns—530i.

NOTE: If equipped with air conditioning on the 4 cylinder models, plates (7) must be installed between the bearing bracket and float plate and selector rod (1) must be attached in bore (K) of selector level (3).

ACCELERATOR LINKAGE AND ACCELERATOR CABLE ADJUSTMENT

530i

1. Synchronize the idle speed with the engine at operating temperature.

2. Detach linkage (1).

3. Detach the accelerator cable at the operating lever (2).

4. Adjust linkage (1) so that the operating lever (2) rests on stop (3).

NOTE: Make sure that linkage (1) is not pulled down into the kickdown position.

5. The swivel joint (5) must align with the hole in the operating lever (2) leaving a play (0.009–0.019 in.) between nipple (4) and the end of the cable sleeve.

6. The accelerator must not sag. Press lever (6) against the acceleration stop (7) and adjust linkage (8) until the distance between nipple (4) and the end of the cable sleeve is 1.456 in. When in kickdown, the nipple (4) must be at least 1.69 in. from the end of the cable sleeve.

NOTE: If the idle speed is altered, repeat the above procedure.

ACCELERATOR CABLE ADJUSTMENT

533i, 633CSi and 733i

1. Adjust play (S) to 0.010–0.030 in.

P Parking
R Reverse
O Neutral
A 1st, 2nd and 3rd gear
2. 1st, and 2nd gear; 3rd gear locked out
1. 1st gear; 2nd and 3rd gear locked out

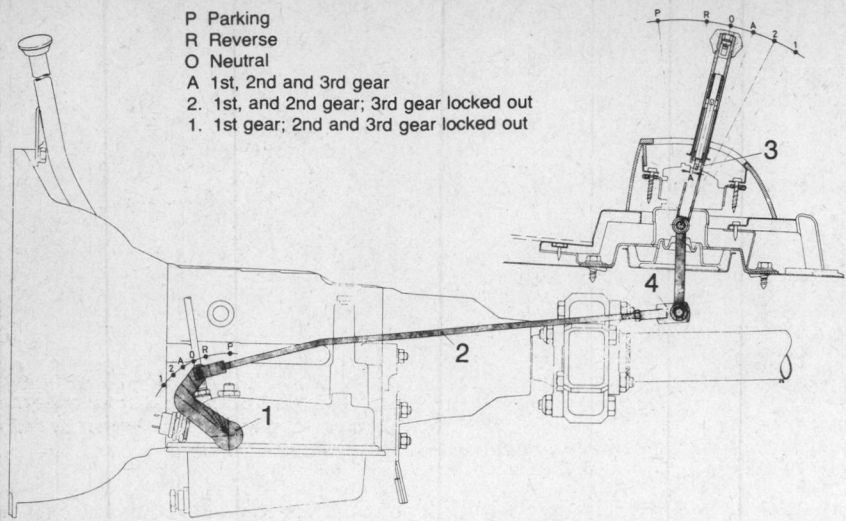

Selector lever adjustment—typical all models

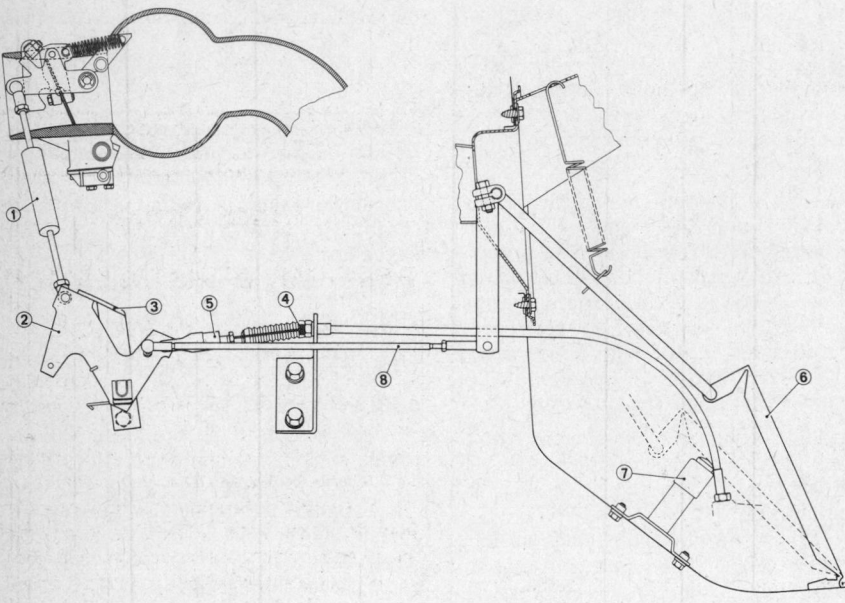

Accelerator linkage and cable adjustment on the 530i

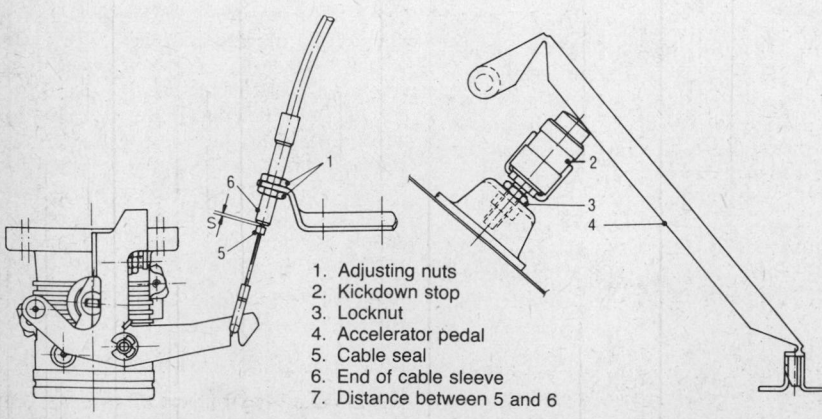

1. Adjusting nuts
2. Kickdown stop
3. Locknut
4. Accelerator pedal
5. Cable seal
6. End of cable sleeve
7. Distance between 5 and 6

Automatic transmission accelerator cable adjustment—528e

with nuts when in Neutral.

2. Press the accelerator pedal against the stop.

3. Adjust the pressure rod (7) until the distance from the seal (3) to the end of the cable (4) is 633CSi—(1.732–2.008 in.). 733i—(1.722–2.057 in.).

320i

1. Adjust the accelerator cable at nuts (1) until the accelerator cable eye (2) has a play of 0.008 in.–0.012 in.

2. Depress the accelerator pedal (3) to the full throttle stop screw (4).

3. There must be 0.020 in. play between the operating lever (5) and stop nut (6).

4. Adjust by the full throttle stop screw (4).

318i and 325e

1. Adjust the cable for zero tension with the throttle closed and accelerator pedal released.

2. Loosen the locknut on the throttle stop bolt. Now adjust the bolt inward just until it suspends the accelerator pedal at the point where the throttle just reaches wide open position. On automatic transmission—equipped cars, make sure the throttle is in full detent position. Now, turn the stop screw 1½ turns lower to get a clearance of 0.020 in. between the accelerator pedal and stop bolt at full throttle. Tighten the locknut.

528e

1. Adjust the freeplay (s) of the cable in N position to 0.010–0.030 in. (0.25–0.75mm). Use cable adjuster nuts (1) to adjust the freeplay.

2. In the passenger compartment, loosen the kickdown switch. Screw in the kickdown stop (2) all the way in the direction of the floor pan.

3. Press down on the accelerator pedal (4) to the transmission pressure point. Unscrew the kickdown stop (2) until it contacts the accelerator pedal.

4. Press the accelerator to the kickdown (wide open throttle) position.

5. In kickdown position, the distance (s) must be 1.732 in. (44.0mm). The distance (s) equals the distance from the cable seal (5) to the end of the cable sleeve (6).

TRANSMISSION CABLE ADJUSTMENT

320i

NOTE: The accelerator cable must be correctly adjusted.

1. With the transmission in the Neutral position, adjust play to 0.010–0.030 in. with the screw.

2. Depress the accelerator pedal to kickdown stop; play must now be 1.712–2.027 in. Make corrections with screw (4).

318i and 325e

1. Adjust the play in the cable "S" to

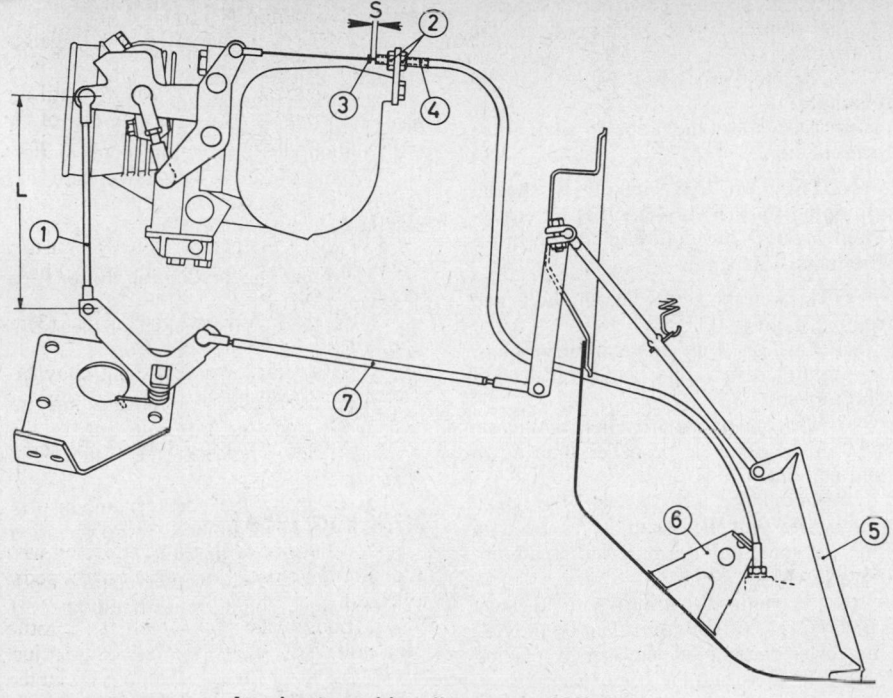

Accelerator cable adjustment—630i, 733i

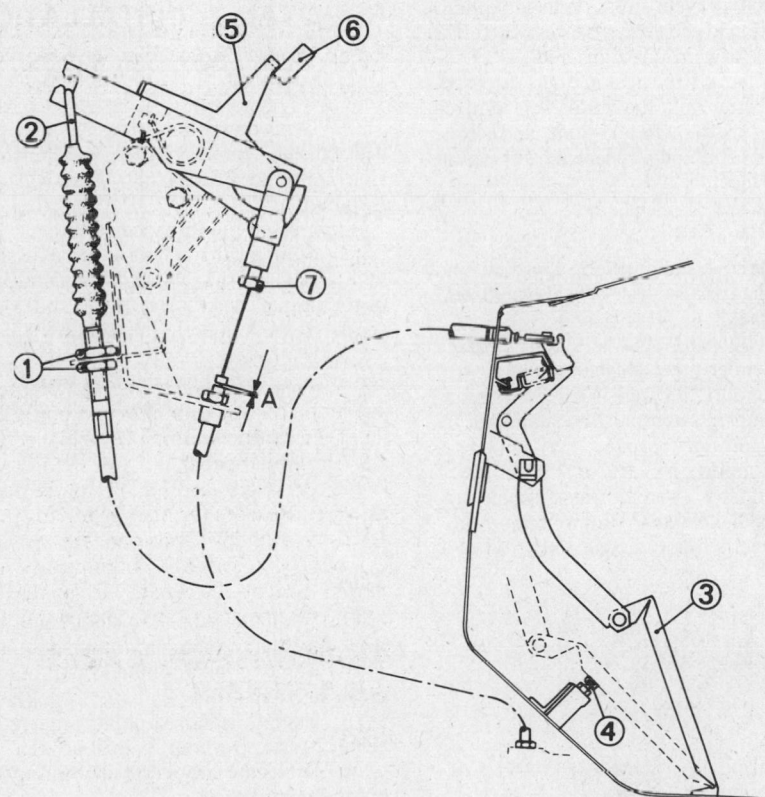

Accelerator cable and transmission cable adjustment—320i

.010–.030 in. Make sure both cable lock-nuts are loose.

2. Back off the accelerator pedal kick-down stop and then depress the accelerator

pedal until the transmission just reaches the detent and some resistance is felt.

3. Run the kickdown stop out until it just touches the bottom of the pedal.

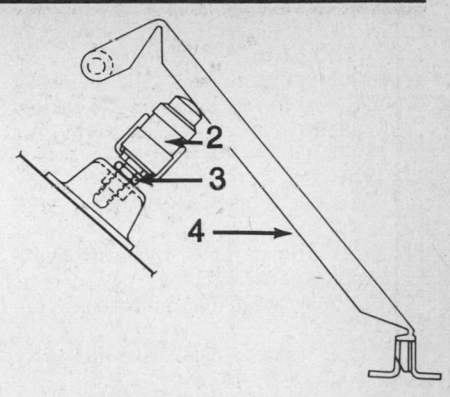

When adjusting the 318i kickdown stop, unscrew the locknut (3), screw in the stop (2) and depress the accelerator pedal (4) to kickdown—see text

4. Depress the accelerator through the detent and hold while measuring distance "S" from the lead seal to the end of sleeve. It must be at least 1.732 in. Adjust further, if necessary.

5. Tighten all locknuts.

DRIVE AXLES

Final Drive

REMOVAL & INSTALLATION

1. Disconnect the universal shaft.

2. Disconnect the output shafts at the CV-joint bolts and tie them up overhead.

3. Detach the self aligning support at the final drive on 320i.

4. Support the final drive unit. Disconnect the final drive from the rear axle carrier.

5. On the 318i and 325e, unscrew the front bolts on both sides. Disconnect the speed pulse wiring on models so equipped.

6. Loosen the rubber mounting screw on 6 cylinder models and the 318i and remove the final drive.

7. Installation is the reverse of re-

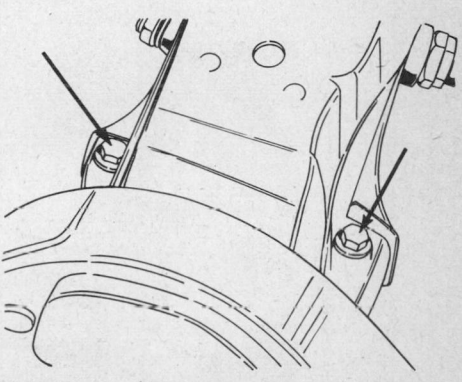

When removing the final drive on the 318i, unscrew the front bolts (arrowed) on both sides, with the drive securely supported

moval. Replace all self-locking nuts. Observe the following torque figures:

U-joint to rear axle—49–55 ft. lbs.
CV-joint to rear axle—22–25 ft. lbs.
Final drive to rear axle carrier:
All but 733i—80–89 ft. lbs.
733i—74–82 ft. lbs.
Vibration damper-to-body (320i, 318i, and 325e)—58–63 ft. lbs.
Final drive-to-rubber mount (6 cylinder models)—58–63 ft. lbs.
Electronic speed transmitter-to-cover—6.5–7.0 ft. lbs.
Output shaft-to-final drive and drive flange—42–46 ft. lbs.

OVERHAUL

For all final drive rebuilding procedures, please refer to "Drive Axles" in the Unit Repair section.

Output Shaft

REMOVAL & INSTALLATION

1. Detach the output shaft at the final drive and drive flange.
2. On 733i, support the control arm if the spring strut and shock absorber are detached.
3. The spring strut serves as a retaining strap and the trailing arm must be supported if the spring strut is detached.
4. Replace the bellows as follows:
   a. Take off the sealing cover.
   b. Remove the circlip.
   c. Remove the clamp.
   d. Press the output shaft out of the joint then slide off the bellows.
5. Installation is the reverse of removal.

Driveshaft

REMOVAL & INSTALLATION

Except 318i and 325e

1. On the 530i, 630CSi, 528i and 528e remove the entire exhaust system.

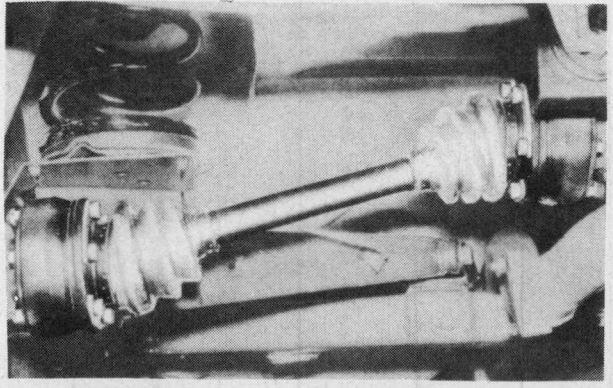

Constant velocity type output shaft

2. On the 320i, detach the outer pipe at the manifold and support it at the transmission.
3. Remove the heat shield if so equipped.
4. Disconnect the propeller shaft at the transmission.

NOTE: On 733i, install a special clamping tool (BMW-261011) or equivalent around the coupling and remove the bolts.

5. Loosen the center bearing bolts and remove them.
6. On 733i, with manual transmission, loosen the crossmember and push the left end forward.
7. Disconnect the propeller shaft at the final drive. Bend the propeller shaft down and pull out.
8. Installation is the reverse of removal.
9. The propeller shaft is balanced in line and must only be renewed as a complete assembly.
10. Align the driveshaft with a gauge (BMW-21-1-000) or equivalent by moving the center bearing sideways or by placing washers underneath the center bearing.
11. On 733i, remove the special coupling tool only after the nuts have been tightened to prevent stress on the coupling.
12. Preload the center bearing by 0.078 in. in the forward direction.
13. Wherever self-locking nuts are used, replace them. Hold the nut or bolt in place where it runs through a U-joint, and torque at the opposite end—where the driveshaft flange is located.

318i and 325e

1. Remove the mufflers. Unscrew and remove the exhaust system heat shield near the fuel tank.
2. Unbolt and remove the cross brace the runs under the driveshaft.
3. Support the transmission. The automatic transmission must be supported by the case and *not* the pan. BMW makes a jig and support (No. 24 0 120 and 00 2 020) for this. Loosen all transmission support bolts and remove. Remove the transmission rear support crossmember.

4. Lower the transmission and remove the driveshaft bolts from the front coupling.
5. Unscrew and remove bolts at the coupling near the final drive.
6. Loosen the threaded sleeve on the driveshaft with a tool such as BMW 26 1 040. Unbolt and remove the center mount.
7. Bend the driveshaft downward and remove it, being careful not to allow it to rest on the connecting line on the fuel tank.
8. Upon installation:
   a. Mount the holder for the oxygen sensor plug.
   b. Make sure the heat shield clears the fuel tank.
   c. Wherever self-locking nuts are used, replace them. On the transmission-end flange, tighten the nuts/bolts only on the flange side, holding the other end stationary.
   d. Preload the center mount to 0.079–0.157 in. in the forward direction before tightening the bolts.
   e. Lubricate the center bearing with Molykote® Longterm 2 or equivalent if it is dry.

Center Bearing

REMOVAL & INSTALLATION

528e, 528i, 530i, 533i, 633CSi, and 733i

1. Bend down the driveshaft and pull it out of the centering pin on the transmission (refer to "Driveshaft Removal and Installation").
2. Loosen the threaded bushing.
3. Mark the driveshaft position on slide with a punch mark and pull the front half of the propeller shaft out of the slide.
4. Remove the circlip and dust guard.
5. Using a standard puller remove the center bearing without the dust guard.
6. Use a puller and remove the grooved ball bearing in the center bearing.
7. Installation is the reverse of removal. Drive the center bearing onto the grooved ball bearing with tool (BMW-24-1-050) or equivalent.

320i

1. With the propeller shaft removed, mark the shaft's location to the coupling.
2. Remove the circlip and pull out the propeller shaft.
3. Using a standard puller remove the center bearing without its dust cover.
4. Drive the grooved ball bearing out of the center bearing.
5. Installation is the reverse of removal.

318i and 325e

1. Remove the driveshaft as described above. Since the shaft is a balanced assembly, matchmark both halves so it can be reassembled in the same position.
2. Unscrew the threaded sleeve (1), and remove the front propshaft section. Re-

Remove circlip (2) and dust guard (3)

Preload center bearing—(A)=0.08 in.

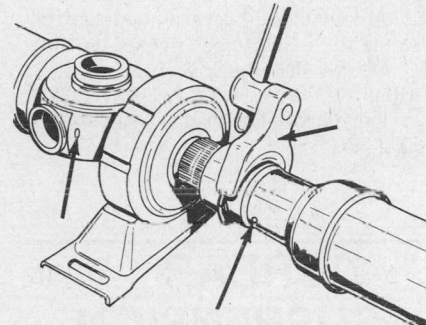

In replacing the center mount on the driveshaft on the 318i, unscrew the threaded sleeve as shown. Matchmark the assembly prior to taking it apart as shown by the arrows.

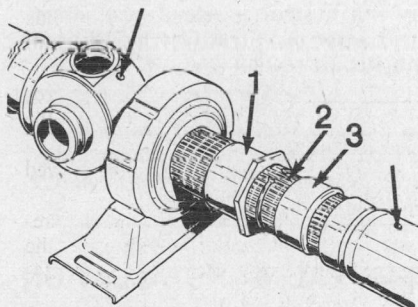

When assembling the driveshaft on the 318i, push on the threaded sleeve (1), washer (2), and rubber ring (3)

move the washer (2) and rubber ring (3). A BMW special tool is shown, but you can loosen the sleeve with an ordinary wrench, provided you carefully devise a way to hold the propshaft against the torque required to loosen the sleeve without damaging it.

3. Lift out the circlip and remove the dustguard behind it.

4. Pull out the center mount and ball bearing with a puller.

5. Lay the center mount on a flat plate and press the new ball bearing in with even pressure all around the outer race.

6. Install the dust guard and then drive the center mount onto the splined portion of the shaft. Make sure the dust guard is installed flush with the center mount and that the center mount will operate with adequate clearance.

7. Assemble the shaft with matchmarks aligned. Push on the threaded sleeve, washer, and rubber ring (do not tighten the threaded sleeve yet).

8. Install the driveshaft as described above. Then, tighten the threaded sleeve.

Centering Ring

REMOVAL & INSTALLATION

1. Fill the center with grease and using a 14mm (0.551 in.) dia. mandrel, drive out the ring.

2. Installation is the reverse of removal.

NOTE: The shaft ring faces out.

Preload center bearing in the forward direction

Rear Axle Shaft, Wheel Bearings and Seals

REMOVAL & INSTALLATION

6 Cylinder Models except 325e

1. Remove the wheel.
2. Loosen the brake caliper and leave the brake line connected.
3. Remove the brake disc.
4. Remove the driving flange as follows:
  a. Disconnect the output shaft.
  b. Remove the bookplate.
  c. Loosen the collared nut and pull off the drive flange.
5. Tighten the collared nut and drive off the rear axle shaft.
6. Drive off the wheel bearings and seals toward the outside.
7. Installation is the reverse of removal.

4 Cylinder Models (Except 318i)

1. Remove the wheel.
2. Remove the cotter pin from the castellated nut.
3. Apply the handbrake.
4. Loosen the castellated nut.
5. Release the handbrake.
6. Remove the brake drum.
7. Pull off the drive flange with a puller.
8. Disconnect the output shaft and tie it up.
9. Drive out the halfshaft with a plastic hammer using the castellated nut to protect the end of the shaft.
10. Drive out the bearing and sealing ring.
11. Take out the spacer sleeve and shim.
12. Installation is the reverse of removal.

318i and 325e

1. Lift out the lockplate and remove the retaining nut from the output flange. Remove the flange.
2. Disconnect the output shaft from the final drive and suspend it.
3. Press out the output shaft with a special tool set 33 2 110 or equivalent. Bolt

Drive center bearing onto grooved ball bearing

Wheel bearing with rear axle shaft removed—
6 cylinder models

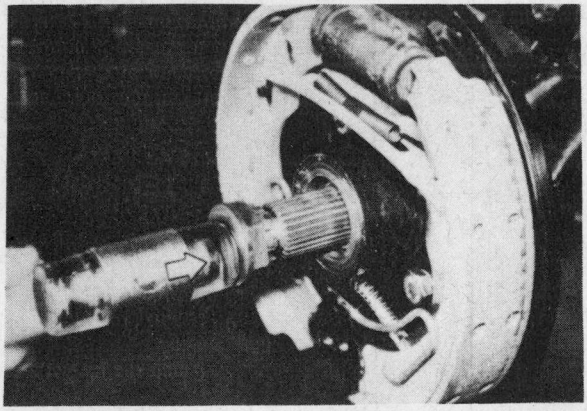

Driving out rear axle shaft—4 cylinder models

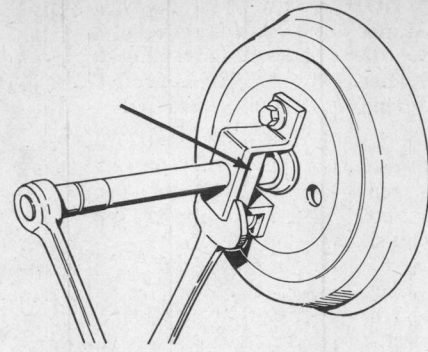

Removing the output shaft on the 318i. Use two wheel bolts to fasten the bridge (33 2 112), and then press the shaft out as shown.

000 or equivalent, knock in the lockplate. Use the following torque figures:

Output shaft to drive flange—42–46 ft. lb.

Drive flange hub to output shaft—140–152 ft. lb.

REAR SUSPENSION

Strut Assembly

For all spring and shock absorber removal and installation procedures and any other strut overhaul procedures, please refer to "Strut Overhaul" in the Unit Repair section.

CAUTION
MacPherson strut springs are under tremendous pressure and any attempt to remove them without proper tools could result in serious personal injury.

REMOVAL & INSTALLATION

1. On model 733i remove the rear seat and back rest.
2. Jack up the car and support the control arms.

NOTE: On the 318i and 325e, the spring and shock absorber are separate. The control arm must be securely supported throughout this procedure.

CAUTION
The coil spring, shock absorber assembly acts as a strap so the control arm should always be supported.

3. Remove the lower shock retaining bolt.
4. Disconnect the upper strut retaining nuts at the wheel arch and remove the assembly.

the bridge to the brake drum with two wheel bolts and hold it with an open-end wrench. Force the output shaft toward the center of the car via the spindle by turning the threaded portion of the tool.

4. Drive out the rear axle shaft with tool 33 4 010 or equivalent.
5. Lift out the circlip. Then, pull out the wheel bearings with special tool 33 4 040 or equivalent.
6. Pull out the seal with a tool such as 33 4 045.
7. If the inner bearing shell is damaged, pull it off with a puller and thrust pad.

8. To install, pull in the wheel bearing assembly, pull in the seal, insert the circlip and then pull in the rear axle shaft, all in reverse of steps above. Install the axle shaft seal with a tool such as 33 4 045.
9. To install the output shaft, screw the threaded spindle into the shaft all the way, and then use the nut and washer against the outside of the bridge.
10. Reconnect the output shaft to the final drive.
11. Lubricate the bearing surface of the outer nut with oil. Then install and torque the nut.
12. Using installers 33 4 050 and 00 5

NOTE: On the 318i and 325e, this is located behind the trim panel in the trunk. On these models only, the shock absorber, because it is separate from the spring, may now be replaced.

5. Using the appropriate spring compressor, compress the coil spring far enough to remove the centering cup, then release the coil spring and separate the spring, boot and shock absorber.

6. Install in reverse order, using new gaskets between the unit and the wheel arch, and new self-locking nuts on top of the strut. Torque the shock-to-body nuts to 16–17 ft. lb.; spring retainer-to-wheel house nuts (6 cyl.) to 16–17 ft. lb.; lower bolt to 52–63 ft. lb. (4 cyl.), 90–103 ft. lb. (6 cyl.).

Rear Spring

REMOVAL & INSTALLATION

318i and 325e

1. Disconnect the rear portion of the exhaust system and hang it from the body.

2. Disconnect the final drive rubber mount, push it down, and hold it down with a wedge.

3. Remove the bolt that connects the rear stabilizer bar to the strut on the side you're working on. Be careful not to damage the brake line.

NOTE: Support the lower control arm securely with a jack or other device that will permit you to lower it gradually, while maintaining secure support.

4. Then, to prevent damage to the output shaft joints, lower the control arm *only* enough to slip the coil spring off the retainer.

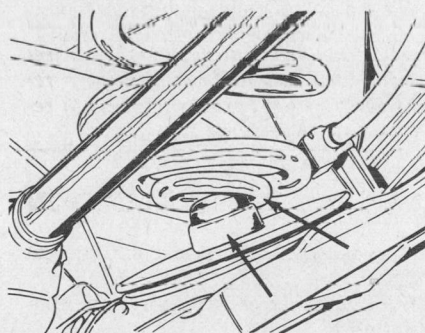

On the 318i, lower the trailing arm just enough to get the spring off the locating tang

5. Make sure, in replacing the spring, that the same part number, color code, and proper rubber ring are used. Reverse all removal procedures to install, making sure that the spring is in proper position, keeping the control arm securely supported until the shock bolt is replaced, and tightening stabilizer bar and lower shock mount bolts with the control arm in the normal ride position. Torque the stabilizer bolt to 22–24 ft. lb., and the shock bolt to 52–63 ft. lb.

Stabilizer

REMOVAL & INSTALLATION

1. Disconnect the stabilizer from the trailing arm by removing the connect bolt.

2. Disconnect the stabilizer on the crossmember.

3. Check the rubber bushings for wear and replace as necessary.

Rear Control Arm

REMOVAL & INSTALLATION

528e, 528i and 530i

1. Remove the parking brake lever.

2. Plug the front hose to prevent loss of brake fluid in the reservoir.

3. Support the body.

4. Disconnect the brake line at the brake hose.

5. Disconnect the driveshaft.

6. Disconnect the stabilizer and coil spring at the control arm.

Rear axle shaft seal (1), bearing (2), ring (3), spacer (4)

7. Disconnect the control arm at the axle carrier.

8. Installation is the reverse of removal. Bleed brake system.

733i

1. Remove the rear wheel.

2. Pull up the parking brake lever and disconnect the output shaft at the drive flange.

3. Remove the parking brake lever.

4. Remove the brake fluid from the reservoir.

5. Disconnect the brake line.

6. Disconnect the control arm from the rear axle carrier.

7. Disconnect the shock absorber and remove the control arm.

8. Installation is the reverse of removal. Bleed the brake system.

Trailing Arm

REMOVAL & INSTALLATION

533i and 633CSi

1. Remove the parking brake lever.

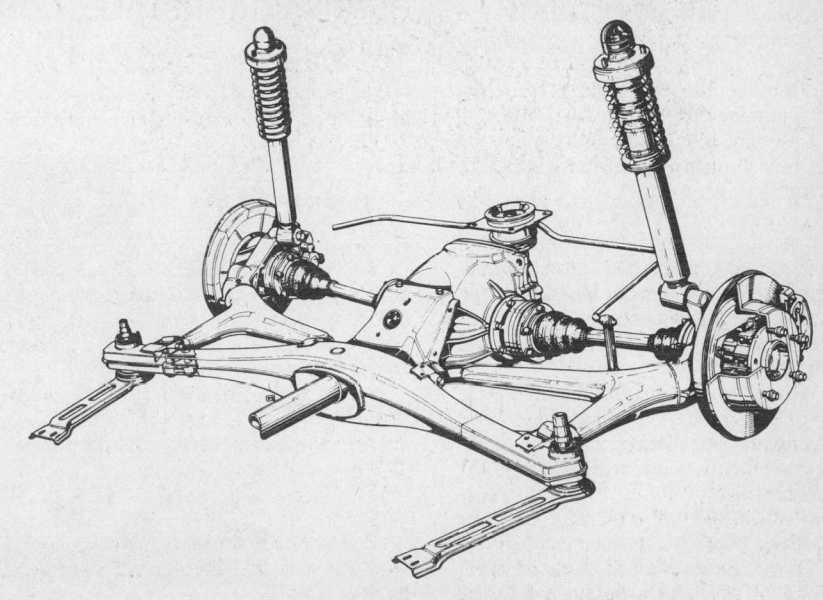

Rear suspension—528e

1. Spacer ring   2. Washer   3. Wishbone

Detaching the lower arm at front axle beam

2. Remove the rear wheel.

3. Using vise grips, clamp the front hose to prevent loss of fluid.

4. Support the body.

5. Pull the parking brake cable out of the pipe.

6. Disconnect the stabilizer and spring strut at the trailing arm.

7. Disconnect the brake line at the brake hose.

8. Disconnect the trailing arm at the rear axle support.

9. Detach the output shaft.

10. Disconnect the brake pad wear indicator wire at the right trailing arm and take the wire out of the clamps.

11. Installation is the reverse of removal. Bleed the system.

318i, 320i, and 325e

1. Raise the vehicle and remove the rear wheel. Apply the parking brake and disconnect the output shaft at the rear axle shaft. Then, on the 320i, disconnect the parking brake cable at the handbrake. On the 318i and 325e, remove the parking brake lever.

2. Remove the brake fluid from the master cylinder reservoir on the 318i and 325e. Disconnect the brake line connection on the rear control arm on both types of car. Plug the openings.

3. Support the control arm securely. Disconnect the shock absorber at the control arm. On 318i and 325e, lower the control arm slowly and remove the spring. On the 320i, the control arm need not be lowered slowly because the spring is integral with the strut.

4. Remove the nuts and then slide the bolts out of the mounts where the control arm is mounted to the axle carrier.

5. Install in reverse order. Torque the bolts holding the trailing arm to the axle carrier to 48–54 ft. lb. On the 318i and 325e, make sure the spring is positioned properly top and bottom. Torque the strut bolt to 52–63 ft. lb. Reinstall the handbrake or reconnect the cable and adjust. Then ap-

ply the brake and reconnect the output shaft. Reconnect the brake line, replenish with the proper brake fluid, and bleed the system.

FRONT SUSPENSION

Strut Assembly

For removal of springs from struts and all strut overhaul procedures, please refer to "Strut Overhaul" in the Unit Repair section.

CAUTION
Macepherson strut springs are under tremendous pressure and any attempt to remove them without proper tools could result in serious personal injury.

REMOVAL & INSTALLATION

318i and 325e

1. Remove the front wheel. Disconnect the brake pad wear indicator plug and ground

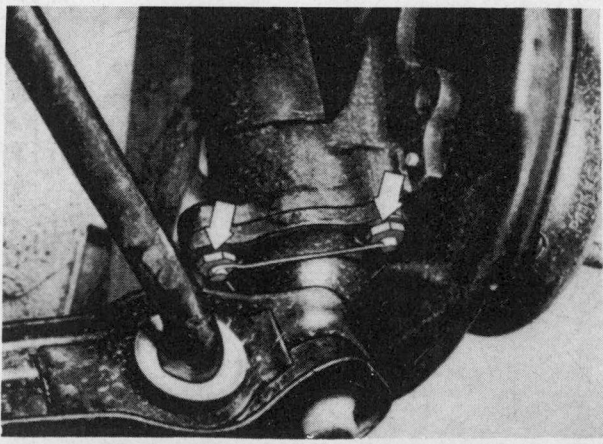

Lock wire location at strut assembly

wire. Pull the wires out of the holder on the strut.

2. Unbolt the caliper and pull it away from the strut, suspending it with a piece of wire from the body. Do not disconnect the brake line.

3. Remove the attaching nut and then detach the push rod on the stabilizer bar at the strut.

4. Unscrew the attaching nut and press off the guide joint.

5. Unscrew the nut and press off the tie rod joint.

6. Press the bottom of the strut outward and push it over the guide joint pin. Support the bottom of the strut.

7. Unscrew the nuts at the top of the strut (from inside the engine compartment) and then remove the strut.

Install in reverse order, keeping the following points in mind:

a. Replace the self-locking nuts that fasten the top of the strut.

b. Tie rod and guide joints must have both pins and both bores clean for reassembly. Replace both self-locking nuts.

c. Torque the control arm to spring strut attaching nut to 43–51 ft. lb. Torque the spring strut to wheel well nuts to 16–17 ft. lb.

320i

1. Raise the vehicle and support safely. Remove the wheel.

2. Detach the bracket at the strut assembly.

3. Disconnect and suspend the brake caliper with a wire from the vehicle body. Do not disconnect the brake line.

4. Remove the cotter pin and castle nut. Press the tie–rod off the steering knuckle.

5. Remove the three retaining nuts and detach the strut assembly at the wheel house.

6. Installation is the reverse of removal.

530i, 528i, 528e, 533i, and 633CSi

1. Raise the vehicle and support safely. Remove the wheel.

2. Disconnect the bracket at the strut assembly.

3. Disconnect the brake caliper and suspend from the vehicle body with wire. Do not remove the brake hose.

4. Remove the lock wire and disconnect the tie rod arm at the strut assembly.

5. Remove the three retaining nuts and detach the strut assembly at the wheelhouse.

6. Installation is the reverse of removal.

733i

1. Raise the vehicle and support safely. Remove the wheel.

2. Disconnect the vibration strut from the control arm.

3. Disconnect the bracket and clamps from the strut assembly.

4. Disconnect the wire connection and press out the wire from the clamp on the spring strut tube.

5. Remove the brake caliper and suspend it from the vehicle body with a wire. Do not remove the brake hose.

6. Disconnect the tie-rod from the shock absorber.

7. Remove the three retaining nuts and disconnect the strut assembly from the wheelhouse.

8. Installation is the reverse of removal.

Control Arm

REMOVAL & INSTALLATION

528e, 528i, 530i, 533i and 633CSi

1. Raise the vehicle and support safely. Remove the wheel.

2. Disconnect the stabilizer at the control arm.

3. Remove the tension strut nut on the control arm.

4. Disconnect the control arm at the front axle support and remove it from the tension strut.

5. Remove the lock wire, remove the bolts and take the control arm off the spring strut.

6. Remove the cotter pin and nut.

7. Using special tool BMW 00-7-500 or equivalent, pull the guide joint from the tie-rod arm.

8. Installation is the reverse of removal.

318i and 325e

1. Remove the front wheel. Disconnect the rear control arm bracket where it connects to the body by removing the two bolts.

2. Remove the nut and disconnect the thrust rod on the front stabilizer bar where it connects to the center of the control arm.

3. Unscrew the nut which attaches the front of the stabilizer bar to the crossmember and remove the nut from above the crossmember. Then, use a plastic hammer to knock this support pin out of the crossmember.

4. Unscrew the nut and press off the guide joint where the control arm attaches to the lower end of the strut.

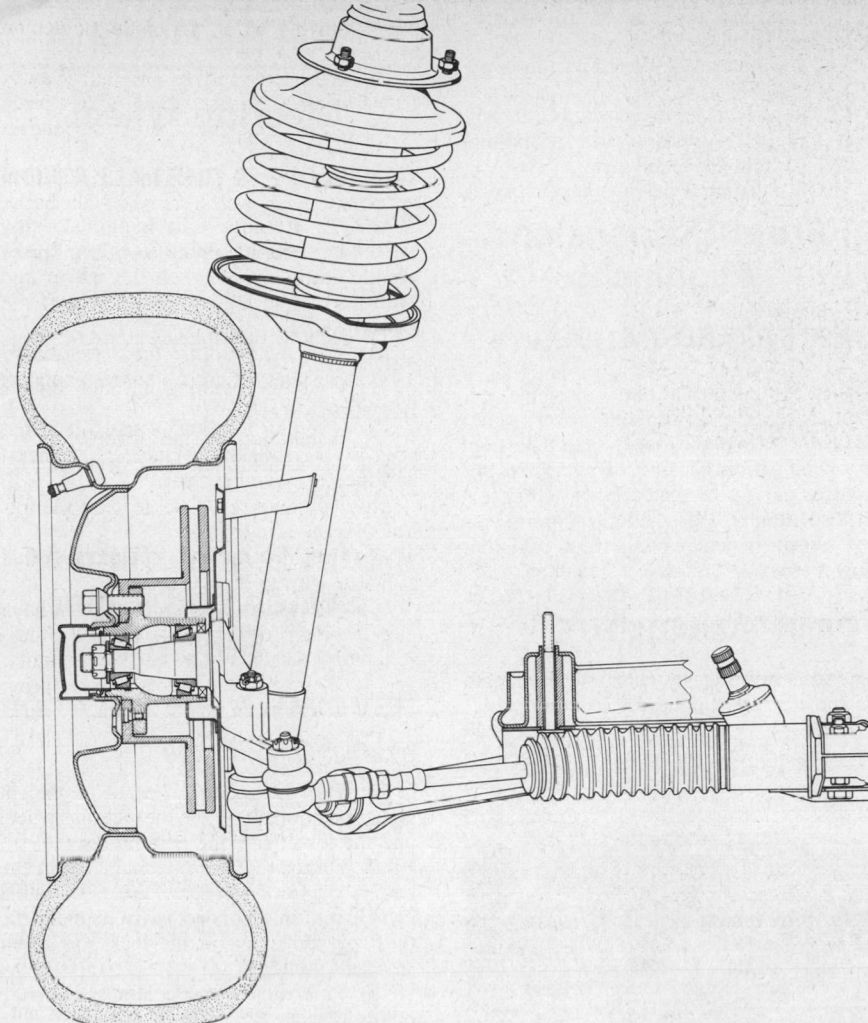

Front suspension—320i

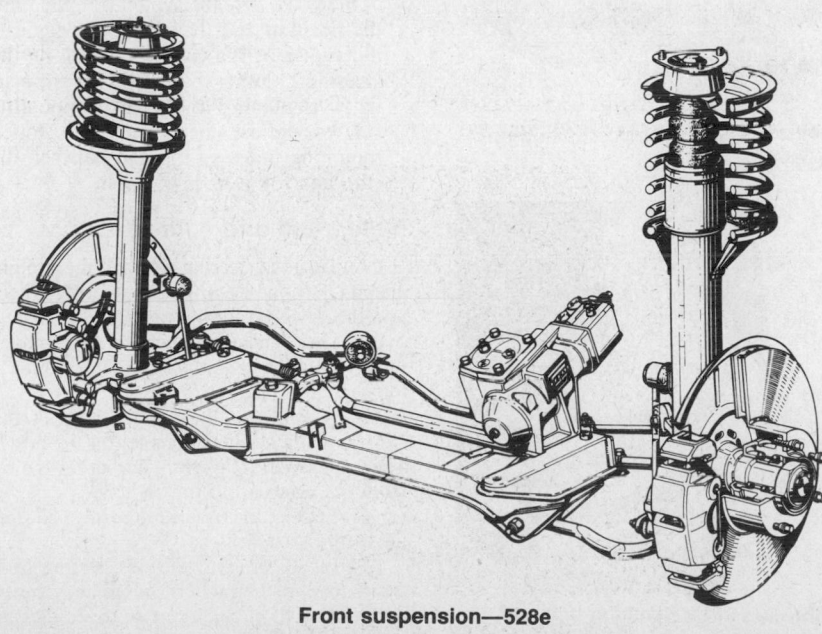

Front suspension—528e

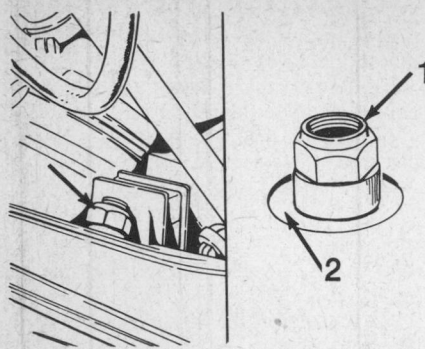

In replacing the nut located in the center of the control arm, use a replacement nut (1) and washer (2) of the type shown

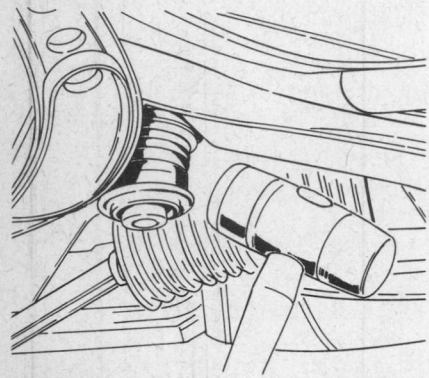

On the 318i, knock the pin loose with a soft hammer, as shown

5. Reverse the procedure to install. Keep these points in mind:

   a. Replace the self-locking nut that fastens the guide joint to the control arm.

   b. Make sure the support pin and the bore in the crossmember are clean before inserting the pin through the crossmember. Replace the original nut with a replacement nut and washer equivalent to those shown in the illustration.

   c. Torque the control arm-to-spring strut nut to 43–51 ft. lb. Torque the control arm support to crossmember nut to 29–34 ft. lb. Torque the push rod on the stabilizer bar to 29–34 ft. lb.

320i

1. Disconnect the stabilizer at the control arm.

2. Disconnect the control arm at the front axle support.

3. Remove the cotter pin and castle nut.

4. Press the control arm off the steering knuckle with special tool BMW 31-1-100 or equivalent.

5. Installation is the reverse of removal.

733i

1. Raise the vehicle and support safely. Remove the wheel.

2. Disconnect the vibration strut from the control arm.

3. Disconnect the control arm from the axle carrier.

4. Disconnect the tie rod arm from the shock absorber.

5. Remove the cotter pin and castle nut. Press off the control arm with special tool BMW 31-1-110 or equivalent.

6. Installation is the reverse of removal.

Front Suspension Alignment

CASTER AND CAMBER

Caster and camber are not adjustable, except for replacement of bent or worn parts.

On the 318i and 325e, camber that is out of specification because of excessive tolerances can be corrected by installing eccentric mounts. This cannot be done to correct misalignment caused by a collision, however.

TOE-IN ADJUSTMENT

Toe-in is adjusted by changing the length of the tie rod and tie rod end assembly. When adjusting the tie rod ends, adjust each by equal amount (in the opposite direction) to increase or decrease the toe-in measurement.

Stabilizer-to-control arm attaching nut —530i, 630i

Vibration strut attaching bolt—733i

STEERING

Steering Wheel

REMOVAL & INSTALLATION

NOTE: Remove and install steering wheel in straight ahead position. Mark the relationship between the wheel and spindle.

1. Remove steering wheel pad or BMW emblem.

2. Unscrew retaining nut and remove the wheel.

3. Installation is the reverse of removal. Replace the self-locking nut on 318i and 325e.

Turn Signal/Dimmer Switch and Wiper Switch

REMOVAL & INSTALLATION

318i, 320i, and 325e

1. Turn the steering wheel to the straight ahead position. Remove the steering wheel and the lower steering column cover.

2. Disconnect the (−) cable from the battery. Disconnect the direction signal switch multiple connector from under the dash by squeezing in the locks on either side and pulling it off.

3. Remove the cable straps from the column.

4. Loosen the mounting screws and remove the switch and harness.

5. Install in reverse order, noting the following points:

   a. Make sure to mount the ground wire.

   b. Make sure the switch is in the middle position and that the follower faces the center of the cancelling cam on the steering column shaft. Then, before finally tightening the switch mounting screws, adjust the switch on slotted mounting holes so the gap between the cam and follower is 0.118 in.

528e, 528i and 530i

1. Turn the steering wheel to the straight ahead position. Remove the steering wheel and the lower column cover.

2. Disconnect the battery (−) cable. Disconnect the parking light cable connector near the column.

3. Disconnect the supply plug at the center of the connector panel on the cowl. Then, loosen the clips from the harness going from the cowl up to the switch.

4. Loosen the mounting screws and remove the switch.

5. Install in reverse order. Before final tightening of the switch mounting screws, slide the switch on its slots to adjust the

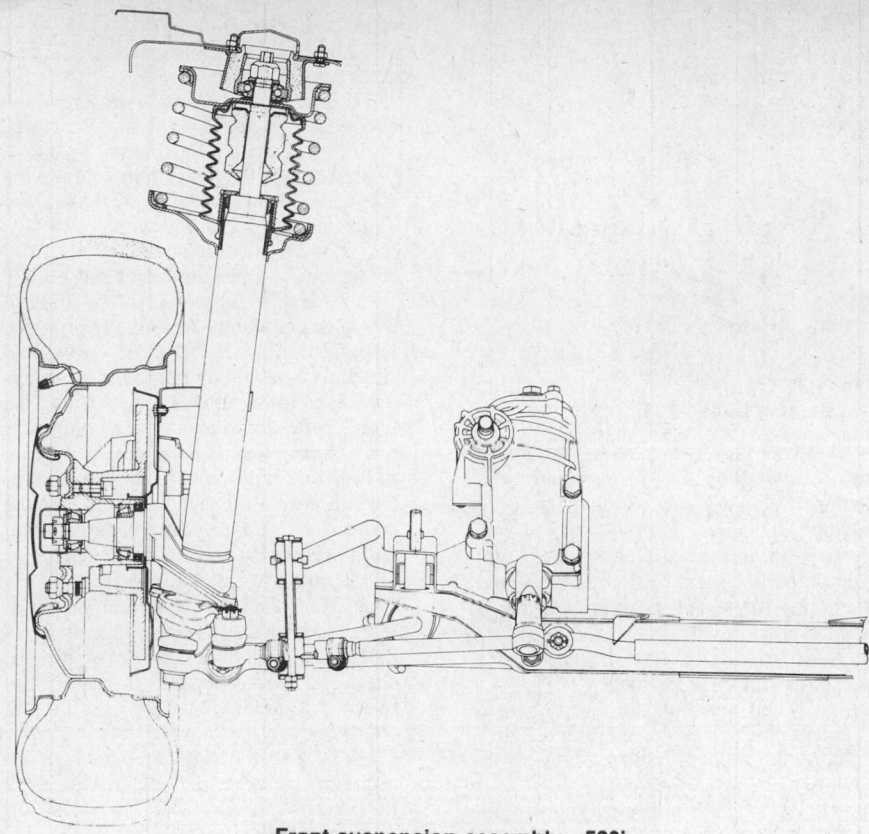

Front suspension assembly—530i

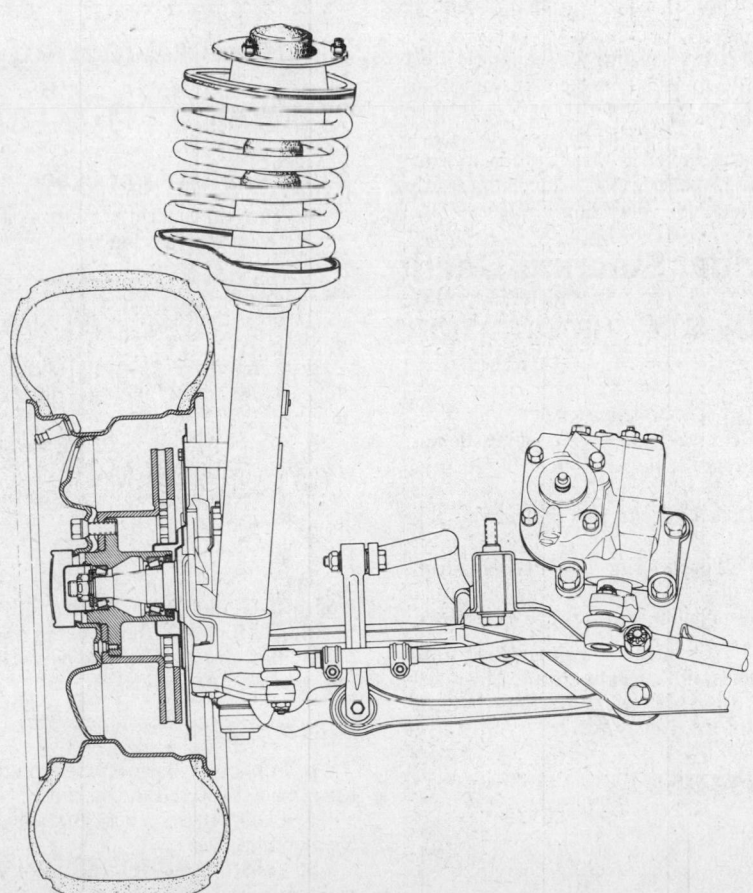

Front suspension—733i

Turn signal switch adjustment

gap between the cancelling cam and cam follower as follows:

    a. Make sure the switch is in its middle position and that it points to the middle of the cancelling cam.

    b. Adjust the gap to 0.012 in.

533i and 633CSi

1. Follow the procedure above exactly; when adjusting the gap between the cancelling cam and the switch follower, use the dimension 0.118 in.

733i

1. Remove the steering wheel and disconnect the battery ground cable.

2. Remove the trim from below the steering column. Remove the mounting screws and detach the switch from the switch plate.

3. Loosen the straps holding the switch cable to the steering column. Pull the center plug out of the panel on the cowl and remove the switch.

4. Install in reverse order.

Ignition Switch

REMOVAL & INSTALLATION

All Except 318i and 325e

1. Disconnect negative battery terminal.

2. Remove lower steering column casing.

3. On 320i, 630i, 633CSi, 733i, 528i and 528e models the shear off the four tamperproof screws with a chisel or other tool.

4. Unscrew the set screw and remove the switch.

5. Disconnect the central fuse/relay plate plug.

6. Installation is the reverse of removal.

NOTE: Turn ignition key all the way back and set the switch at the "O" position before installing. Marks on the switch must be opposite each other.

318i and 325e

1. Disconnect the battery ground cable. Remove the steering wheel.

Tie rod arm-to-shock absorber retaining bolts—733i

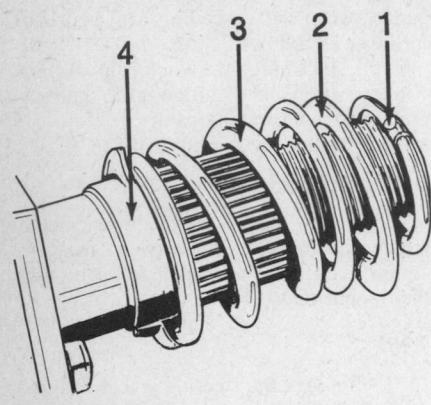

When removing the 318i steering lock, remove the snap ring (1), washer (2), spring (3), and seating ring (4)

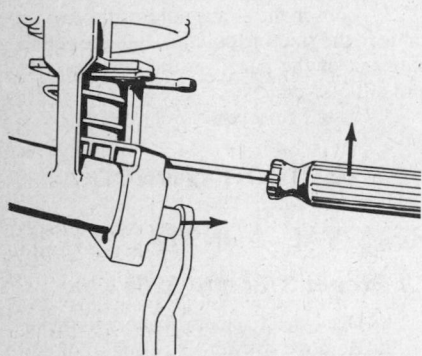

On the 318i, press down the locking hook with a screwdriver, as shown, and remove the ignition switch

2. Remove the four screws, and remove the lower steering column cover.

3. Disconnect the turn signal/wiper switch by removing the four screws and disconnecting the wires.

4. Remove the collar from the steering column shaft. Then, remove the snap ring (1), washer (2), spring (3) and seating ring (4).

5. Pry off the steering spindle bearings with two screwdrivers. *Pry by the inner race only.*

6. Disconnect the main electrical plug at the bottom of the steering column.

7. Use a chisel to remove the tamperproof screw. Pull the lock assembly with the upper section of the casting off the outer column.

8. With a screwdriver, press downward on the lock and then slide the switch off, noting the switch position and that of the lock assembly.

9. To install, reverse the above procedure, noting these points:

a. When installing the switch, make sure its position is the same in relationship with the lock, so the actions of the two will be synchronized.

b. Use a Torx® screwdriver for the tamperproof screw.

c. Drive the steering spindle bearings back on by the inner races only.

d. When installing the seating ring that goes on the shaft, make sure the spring seat faces outward. Use a piece of pipe slightly larger than the shaft and tap it with a hammer to install the snap ring. Then, make sure the collar that goes on next locks the snap ring in place.

Manual Steering Gear

REMOVAL & INSTALLATION

320i

1. Loosen the front wheels.
2. Remove the cotter pin and castle nut.
3. Press the tie rods off of the steering knuckles.
4. Detach the steering at the front axle support.
5. Pull the steering gear off of the steering spindle.
6. Installation is the reverse of removal.

NOTE: Turn the steering wheel until the wheels point straight ahead. The mark on the dust seal must be between the marks on the gear box.

ADJUSTMENT

320i

1. Remove the steering gear from the car.
2. Clamp the special tool 32-1-100, or equivalent, in a vise and place the steering gear assembly into the tool.

3. Unscrew the nut on the steering damper and slide it back.

4. Remove the cap and unscrew the socket head cap about ½ inch.

5. Pressure pad adjustment:

a. Remove the cotter pin. Tighten the set screw with special 32-1-040, or equivalent, and a torque wrench, to 4 ft. lbs. Loosen the set screw by one full castle slot to align the cotter pin bore.

b. Use special tools 32-1-000 and 00-2-000 or equivalent to move rack to the left and right over the entire stroke and check for sticking and hooking. If this is the case, loosen the set screw by one more castle slot and insert the cotter pin.

c. Repeat test. If there is still sticking or hooking, replace rack, drive pinion or the entire steering gear. Never loosen the screw by 2 castle slots regardless of circumstances.

6. Turning torque adjustment:

a. Move rack to the center position. Place special tools 00-2-000 and 32-1-000 or equivalent on the drive pinion, check the turning torque. If it is not between 7.8 and 11.2 ft. lbs., adjust the set screw.

b. Turn to the right to increase friction, and turn to the left to decrease friction.

c. Install cap.

Power Steering

REMOVAL & INSTALLATION

All Except 318i and 325e

1. Turn the steering to left lock.
2. Drain the steering fluid.
3. Remove the cotter pin and loosen the castle nut.
4. Press the center tie rod off the steering drop arm.
5. Remove the screw and slide the coupling flange with the steering column upward.
6. Disconnect the hoses at the steering gear and plug the openings.
7. Detach and remove the steering gear at the front axle carrier.
8. Installation is the reverse of removal.

NOTE: System must be bled and the front wheels must be in the straight ahead position. Marks on the housing and propeller shaft must align. Use new self locking nuts on all models.

318i and 325e

1. Support the car securely and remove front wheels. Remove the pinch bolt (1) and loosen bolt (2). Press the spindle off the steering gear.

2. Loosen the clamp and pull off the hydraulic fluid return line from the power steering unit. Discard drained fluid.

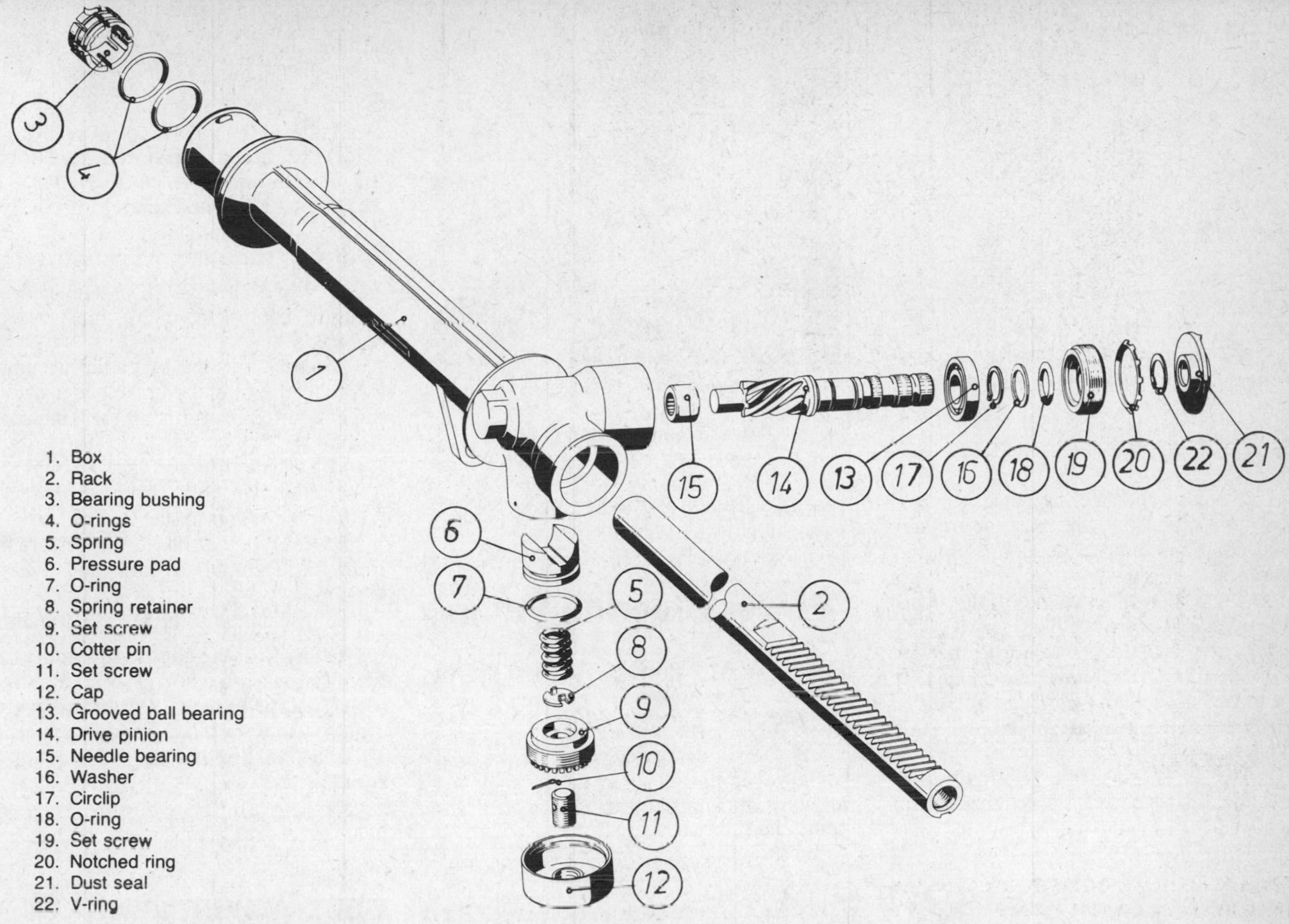

1. Box
2. Rack
3. Bearing bushing
4. O-rings
5. Spring
6. Pressure pad
7. O-ring
8. Spring retainer
9. Set screw
10. Cotter pin
11. Set screw
12. Cap
13. Grooved ball bearing
14. Drive pinion
15. Needle bearing
16. Washer
17. Circlip
18. O-ring
19. Set screw
20. Notched ring
21. Dust seal
22. V-ring

Rack and pinion steering gear—typical

Steering adjustment 320i

Turning torque adjustment—320i

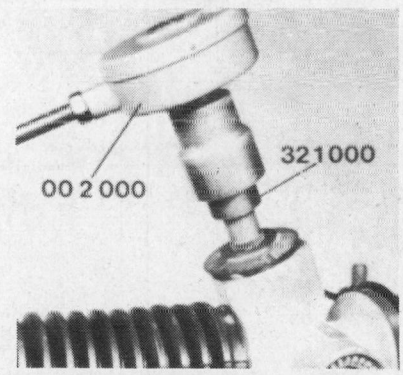

Pressure pad adjustment—320i

3. Detach the pressure line (arrowed). Seal off openings.

4. Unscrew left and right side nuts, and press off the tie rods where they connect to the spring struts.

5. Remove the bolts attaching the steering unit to the front axle carrier and remove it.

6. Install in reverse order, keeping the following points in mind:

   a. The steering unit bolts to the rear holes of the axle carrier. Use new self-locking nuts and torque them to 29–34 ft. lb.

   b. When reconnecting tie rods to the spring struts, make sure tie rod pins and strut bores are clean. Replace self-locking nuts, coat threads with Loctite 270® or equivalent, and torque to 40–48 ft. lb.

   c. Replace the seals on the power steering pump connection, and torque the bolt to 29–32 ft lb.

   d. Refill the fluid reservoir with specified fluid. Idle the engine and turn the steering wheel back and forth until it has reached right and left lock two times each. Then, turn off the engine and refill the reservoir.

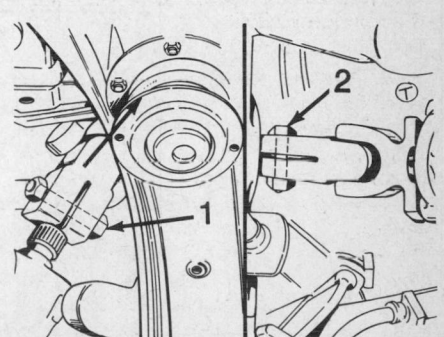

On the 318i, remove the pinch bolt (1), and through bolt (2)

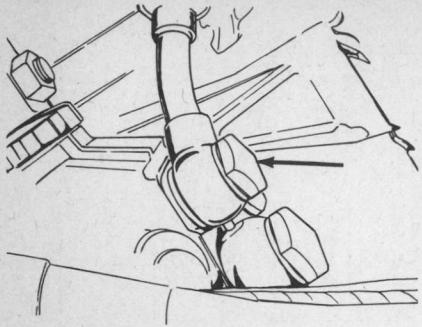

On the 318i power steering pump, disconnect the pressure line (arrowed)

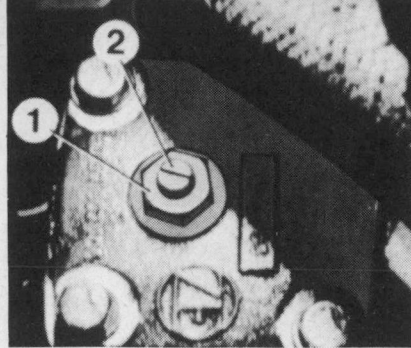

1. Locknut   2. Adjusting nut

Power steering adjustment

ADJUSTMENT

1. Remove the steering wheel center.
2. With the front wheels in the straight ahead position, remove the cotter pin and loosen the castle nut.
3. Press the center tie rod off the steering drop arm.
4. Turn the steering wheel to the left about one turn. Install a friction gauge and turn the wheel to the right, past the point of pressure and the gauge should read 10.4 ft. lbs.
5. To adjust, turn the steering wheel about one turn to the left. Loosen the counter nut and turn the adjusting screw until the specified friction is reached when passing over the point of pressure.

Power Steering Pump

REMOVAL & INSTALLATION

All Models Except 733i

1. Detach the steering pump hoses. Seal off all openings. Loosen the locknut and turn the adjusting bolt to release belt tension, and remove the belt.

1. Screw
2. Hose
3. Hose

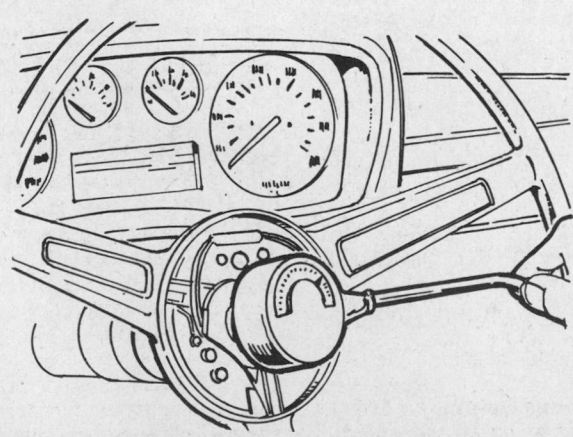

Coupling flange and steering box

Friction gauge installation

2. Remove bolts from the brackets holding the front and rear of the pump.
3. Installation is the reverse of removal. Torque pump mounting bolts to 16–17 ft. lbs.

NOTE: Bleed the system and torque the hose connections to 35 ft. lbs. (29–32 ft. lb—318i and 325e).

733i

1. When the pump is damaged, the pressure control regulator must also be replaced.
2. Discharge the hydraulic accumulator, by depressing the brake pedal with the force required for full stop breaking (about 20 times).
3. Detach all hoses at the pump.
4. Remove bolts from the brackets holding the pump in place.
5. Remove the brake booster return hose from the accumulator tank and plug the opening.
6. Installation is the reverse of removal.

NOTE: Run the engine 10 minutes and turn the steering wheel several times from stop to stop. Operate the brake booster quickly, to obtain hard resistance, about 10 times to discard the oil leaving the return hose.

7. Stop the engine, drain the oil from the tank and connect the booster return hose on the tank.

BELT ADJUSTMENT

Tighten the belt so that when pressure is applied to the belt, the distance between both belt pulleys is 5–10mm.

SYSTEM BLEEDING

1. Fill the reservoir to the edge with the proper fluid.
2. Start the engine and add oil until the oil level remains constant.
3. Turn the steering wheel from lock to lock quickly until air bubbles are no longer present in the reservoir.
4. On the 733i, operate the brake pedal to discharge the hydraulic accumulator until

Power steering reservoir—typical

Power steering belt adjustment

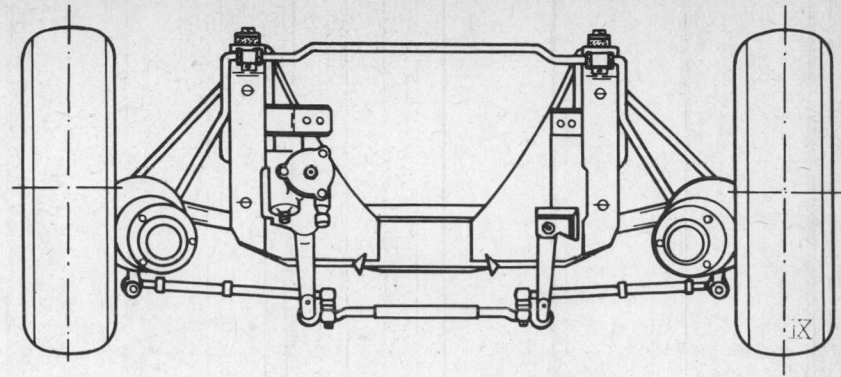

Recirculating-ball type steering linkage—all except 318i and 320i

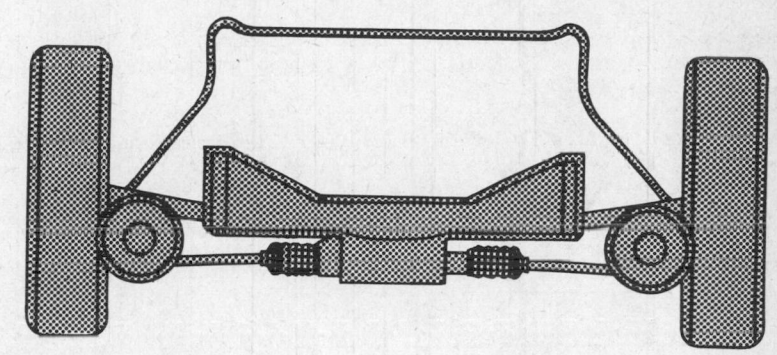

Rack and pinion steering linkage—318i and 320i

the oil level stops rising or noticeable resistance on the brake pedal is felt.

Steering Linkage

REMOVAL & INSTALLATION

All Models Except 318i, 320i and 325e

TIE-ROD ARM

1. Remove the front wheel.
2. Detach the wishbone at the front axle beam. Detach the trailing link from the wishbone.
3. Remove the cotter pin and castle nut.
4. Press the outer tie-rod off the tie-rod arm, and press the stabilizer off the control arm.
5. Remove the lock wire and detach the tie-rod arm at the shock absorber.
6. Press the tie-rod arm off the control arm.
7. Installation is the reverse of removal.

OUTER TIE-ROD

1. Remove the cotter pin, castle nut and press the outer tie-rod off of the center tie-rod.
2. Remove the cotter pin, loosen the castle nut and press the outer tie-rod off the tie-rod arm.
3. Installation is the reverse of removal.
4. Align the front axle.

CENTER TIE-ROD

1. On the 733i, remove the heat guard.
2. Remove the cotter pins, loosen the castle nuts and press the left and right tie-rods off center tie-rod.
3. Press the center tie-rod off of the steering control arm.
4. Installation is the reverse of removal.
5. Align the front axle.

318i, 320i, and 325e

LEFT AND RIGHT TIE-RODS

1. Support the car securely and remove the front wheel. On the 320i, remove the cotter pin and remove the castellated nut from the end of the tie-rod at the steering

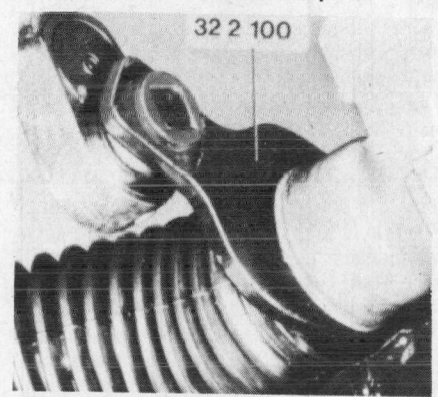

Tie rod removal—320i

knuckle. On the 318i and 325e, remove the self-locking nut at the steering knuckle and discard it.

2. Press the tie-rod off the steering knuckle.

3. On the 318i, 325e and on the 320i on the left side, detach the clamp fastening the rubber bellows and slide it back. On the 320i right side, unscrew the nut and slide back the steering damper.

4. Bend open the tang on the lock plate. Use pliers only. Run the rack in far enough to permit access to the notches on the inner tie-rod end (on 320i, left side only slide the tie-rod in for access).

NOTE: Inner tie-rod ends have a dimpled area for access by a thin, open end wrench with either straight or convex

jaws. Use BMW tool 32 2 100 or equivalent except for 320i on the right side. On the 320i, use 32 2 110 or equivalent. You may be able to fashion some sort of tool of your own for this job.

Using a special tool or one you have fashioned, unscrew the inner tie-rod end and remove the assembly.

5. To install, reverse the procedure above. Make sure the tie-rod pin and steering knuckle bore are clean and grease-free. Bend the lock-plate tang over against the flat on the steering rack. Tie-rod-to-rack torque is 50–56 ft. lb., and nut torque is 25–29 ft. lb. Replace the self-locking nuts on 318i and 325e. Adjust the toe in on the front end.

BRAKE SYSTEM

For all brake system repair and service procedures not detailed below, please refer to "Brakes" in the Unit Repair section.

All BMW models incorporate dual, fluid-circuit, tandem arrangement master cylinders in their brake systems, which are similar in design and function. However, even though they are similar to one another, they are not identical to one another in design or function.

By dual circuit, tandem arrangement we mean that the master cylinder is comprised of two (dual) integrally joined fluid chambers (each supplying a predetermined com-

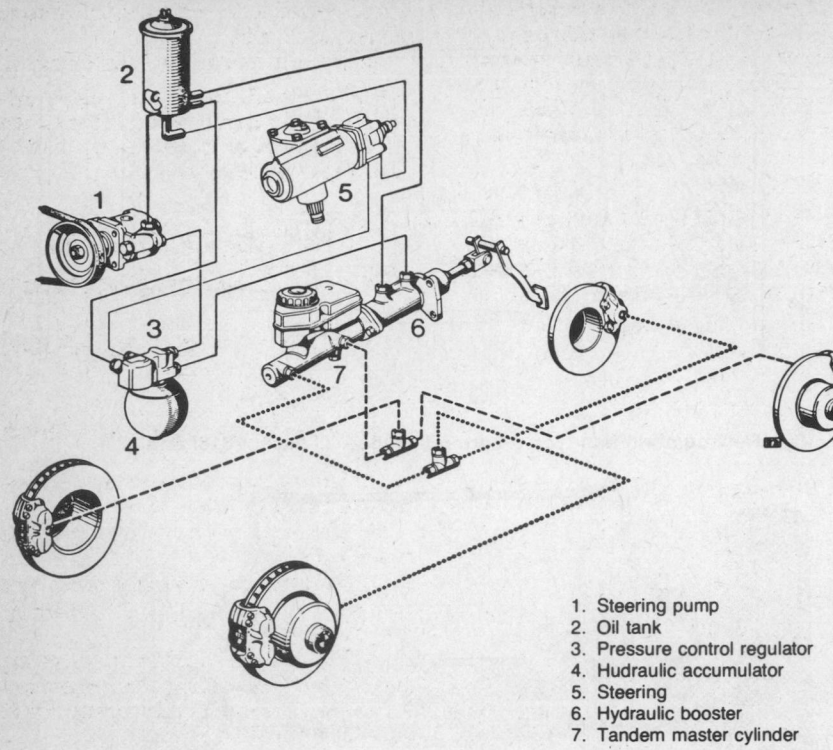

1. Steering pump
2. Oil tank
3. Pressure control regulator
4. Hudraulic accumulator
5. Steering
6. Hydraulic booster
7. Tandem master cylinder

Diagonally split, dual circuit brake system—733i

bination of wheel brakes) which are positioned one in front of the other (tandem).

Two variations of the standard dual circuit system are the double dual circuit system and the diagonally split, dual circuit system.

In the case of the standard dual circuit system, one chamber supplies the front brakes while the other chamber supplies the rear brakes. In the case of the double dual circuit system, one chamber supplies the circuit to the front brakes while the other supplies a circuit to the front and rear brakes combined. In the case of the diagonally split, dual circuit system, one chamber supplies the left front and right rear brakes while the other chamber supplies the right front and left rear brakes.

A brief list of brake-system-according-to-model follows.

Model 318i and 320i: Standard dual circuit; (front) Ate caliper type disc brakes with automatic adjustment for pad wear; (rear) inside shoe brakes with simplex shoes; (park) mechanical, with action on rear wheels.

Model 530i: 528i, 528e and 325e Double Dual Circuit; (front) Ate four piston with fixed caliper discs and automatic adjustment, (rear) Ate two piston, fixed caliper discs with automatic adjustment, (park) Duo servo drums.

Models 533i and 633CSi; Double dual circuit brakes with brake pressure booster and governor, and brake pad wear indicator, (front) Ate four piston caliper disc brakes

with automatic adjustment, (rear) Ate two piston caliper disc brakes with automatic adjustment, (park) Dual hydraulic drum brakes with cable operation on rear wheels only.

Model 733i: Diagonally split, dual circuit brake system with hydraulic brake pressure boost and mutual hydraulic pump for brakes and steering as well as pressure accumulator for brakes including brake fluid reservoir. Equipped with an indicator for brake fluid level and brake pad wear, (front) Ate four piston caliper disc brakes with automatic adjustment, (rear) Ate two piston caliper disc brakes with automatic adjustment, (park) Dual power drum brakes with bowden cable acting on the rear wheels.

NOTE: In the hydraulically boosted power brake system, pressure developed in the booster is transferred to the standard master cylinder which is bolted to the booster unit.

The hydraulic pressure to the power booster is regulated between the power steering pump and the power booster by a pressure control regulator. The fluid is pumped through the regulator at an approximate flow rate of 7 quarts per minute, and into a fluid accumulator where it is stored (charged) at 510–810 psi. This charge is sufficient to operate the brake system several times if the power steering pump fails. When the reserve pressure is depleted the brake system will remain operational, however, considerably more force will be required to stop the vehicle.

Master Cylinder

REMOVAL & INSTALLATION
All Models Except 318i, 320i, 325e and 733i

1. Remove the air cleaner if necessary.
2. Drain and disconnect the brake fluid reservoir from the master cylinder. The brake fluid reservoir will be mounted in one of two ways: (1) assembled directly on top of the master cylinder; it is removed by tilting the reservoir to one side and lifting it off of the master cylinder, or (2) the reservoir is mounted in the engine compartment where it is attached to the inner fender sheet metal by means of attaching bolts; carefully disconnect hoses leading to the master cylinder and allow the reservoir to drain.
3. Disconnect all brake lines from the master cylinder.
4. Remove the master cylinder–to–power booster attaching nuts, and remove the master cylinder.

NOTE: Observe the correct seating of the master cylinder-to-power booster seals.

To install:
1. Bench-bleed the master cylinder.

NOTE: Check for proper seating of the master cylinder–to–power booster O-ring. Check clearance between the master cylinder piston and push rod with Plastigage® or equivalent, and, if necessary, adjust to 0.002 inch by placing shims behind the head of the push rod.

2. Position the master cylinder onto the studs protruding from the power booster; install and tighten the attaching nuts.
3. Connect all brake lines.
4. Install the brake fluid reservoir and fill with brake fluid.

NOTE: An alternate method to bench bleeding the master cylinder is to bleed the master cylinder in the vehicle by opening (only slightly) the brake line fitting at the master cylinder, and allowing the fluid to flow from the master cylinder into a container, however, this method should be considered as an ALTERNATE METHOD ONLY as it is more difficult to control the fluid leaving the master cylinder during bleeding, thereby increasing the chance of accidentally splashing brake fluid onto the painted surface of the vehicle.

5. Bleed the brake system.

318i, 320i and 325e

1. Remove the fuel mixture control unit on the 320i. Disconnect the fluid level indicator plug.
2. Disconnect the hose at the clutch connection.
3. Drain and disconnect the brake fluid reservoir.

4. Disconnect the brake lines from the master cylinder.

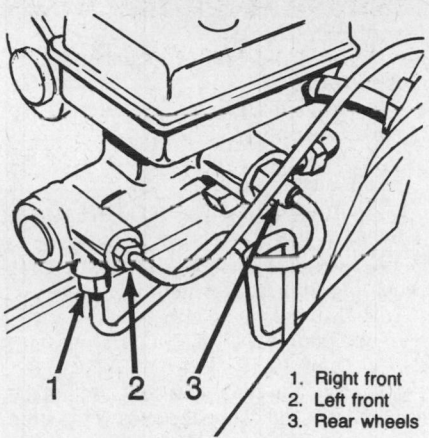

1. Right front
2. Left front
3. Rear wheels

Master cylinder—320i

5. On the 320i, working from the underside of the left-side inner fender panel (wheel opening area) remove the two master cylinder support bracket attaching nuts.

6. Remove the master cylinder–to–power booster attaching nuts, and remove the master cylinder.

7. Install in the reverse order of removal.

NOTE: Bench bleed the master cylinder prior to installation. Refer to the aforementioned note concerning an ALTERNATE bleeding procedure.

8. Bleed the brake system.

733i

1. Drain and disconnect the fluid reservoir.

2. Disconnect the brake lines at the master cylinder.

3. Remove the master cylinder–to–hydraulic booster attaching bolts, and remove the master cylinder.

4. Install in the reverse order of removal.

NOTE: Bench bleed the master cylinder prior to installation. Refer to the aforementioned note concerning an ALTERNATE bleeding procedure.

Vacuum Operated Power Brake Booster

REMOVAL & INSTALLATION

318i and 325e

1. Draw off brake fluid in the reservoir and discard.

2. Remove the reservoir and disconnect the clutch hydraulic hose.

3. Disconnect all brake lines from the master cylinder.

4. Remove the instrument panel trim from the bottom/left inside the passenger compartment.

5. Remove the return spring from the brake pedal. Press off the clip and remove the pin which connects the booster rod to the brake pedal.

6. Remove the four nuts and pull the booster and master cylinder off in the engine compartment.

7. If the filter in the brake booster is clogged, it will have to be cleaned. To do this, remove the dust boot, retainer, damper, and filter, and clean the damper and filter. Make sure when reinstalling that the slots in the damper and filter are offset 180 degrees.

8. Install in reverse order. Adjust the stoplight switch for a clearance of 0.197–0.236 in.

320i

1. Remove the master cylinder.

2. Disconnect the vacuum line at the power booster.

3. Remove the brake pedal apply-rod to power booster push rod pin.

4. Remove the power booster attaching nuts, and remove the power booster.

5. Install in the reverse order of removal.

NOTE: If the original power booster unit is to be reused, remove the dust boot and clean the silencer and filter. Position the slots in the silencer 180 degrees away from the slots in the filter.

6. Adjust the extended visible length of the brake light switch head to 0.20–0.24 inch.

528e, 528i, 530i, 533i and 633CSi

1. Remove the coolant reservoir.

2. Remove the master cylinder.

3. Disconnect the vacuum hose at the power booster.

4. Disconnect the power booster apply rod at the brake pedal.

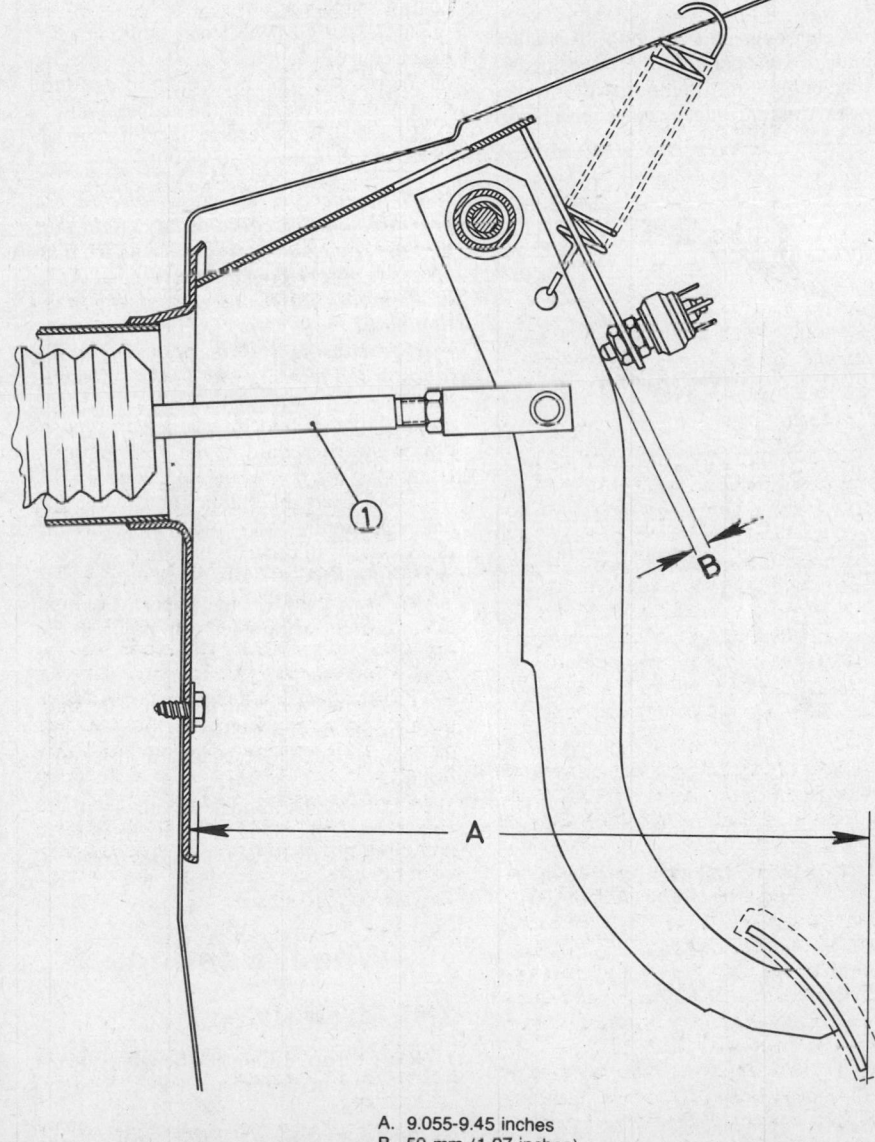

A. 9.055-9.45 inches
B. 50 mm (1.97 inches)

Brake pedal adjustment 530i, 630CSi, 528i, 528e and 633CSi

5. Remove the power booster attaching bolts.

6. Remove the power booster.

7. Install in the reverse order of removal.

NOTE: If the original power booster unit is to be reused, remove the dust boot and clean the silencer and filter. Position the slots in the silencer 180 degrees away from the slots in the filter.

8. Adjust the brake pedal distance to 9.055–9.450 in. Adjust the stop light switch distance to 0.197–0.237 in.

Hydraulically Operated Power Brake Booster

REMOVAL & INSTALLATION

733i

1. Release the pressure in the hydraulic accumulator by operating the brake pedal (with the engine not running) with a force equivalent to that necessary to bring the vehicle to a full and complete stop.

2. Remove the lower left instrument panel trim.

3. Disconnect the power booster apply-rod at the brake pedal.

4. Remove the master cylinder.

5. Disconnect the fluid lines at the brake booster.

6. Remove the power booster to pedal base assembly attaching bolts, and remove the power booster.

7. Install in the reverse order of removal.

8. Adjust the distance between the brake pedal and the bulk head to 9.882–10.236 in.

9. Adjust the extended visible length of the brake light switch head (plunger) to 0.197–0.237 in.

Hydraulic Accumulator

REMOVAL & INSTALLATION

733i

1. Release the pressure in the hydraulic accumulator by operating the brake pedal (with the engine not running) with a force equivalent to that necessary to bring the

vehicle to a full and complete stop.

2. Disconnect the electrical lead at the indicator switch.

3. Disconnect the hydraulic fluid lines from the pressure control regulator:

   a. from the control regulator to the fluid reservoir.

   b. from the control regulator to the power steering gear box.

   c. from the control regulator to the power steering pump.

   d. from the control regulator to the power brake booster.

4. Fabricate a circular removing strap according to the following dimensions:

   a. 110mm (4.33 in.)

   b. 50mm (1.97 in.)

   c. 5mm (0.197 in.)

5. Place the removing strap around the accumulator and clamp the ends of the strap in a vise, thereby locking the accumulator, so as to prevent the accumulator from turning when torque is applied to the pressure control regulator.

6. Install BMW special tool 34-3-200 or an equivalent removing device directly on the pressure control regulator, and turn the regulator free from the accumulator.

7. Install in the reverse order of removal.

CAUTION

When connecting the fluid lines to the pressure control regulator be certain that all lines are clean and free from dirt. The presence of foreign particles trapped in the fluid circuit can seriously impair the functioning of the pressure control regulator, thereby causing failure of power assistance to the steering and brake systems.

---

8. Fill the fluid reservoir with type A power steering fluid to a level approximately ⅜ in. below the top edge of the reservoir. Start the engine; and, while the engine is running, add fluid to the reservoir, if necessary, in order to maintain the level at the full mark.

9. Turn the steering wheel from stop to stop, until air bubbles stop rising in the reservoir.

10. Stop the engine.

11. Operate the brake pedal until the fluid level in the reservoir stops rising, or until there is noticeable resistance at the brake pedal.

12. Check the fluid level in the reservoir. Correct the level to approximately ⅜ in. below the top edge of the reservoir.

Wheel Bearings

ADJUSTMENT

NOTE: The 318i and 325e wheel bearings cannot be adjusted.

320i, 533i, 633CSi and 733i

1. Raise the vehicle, support it and remove the front wheel.

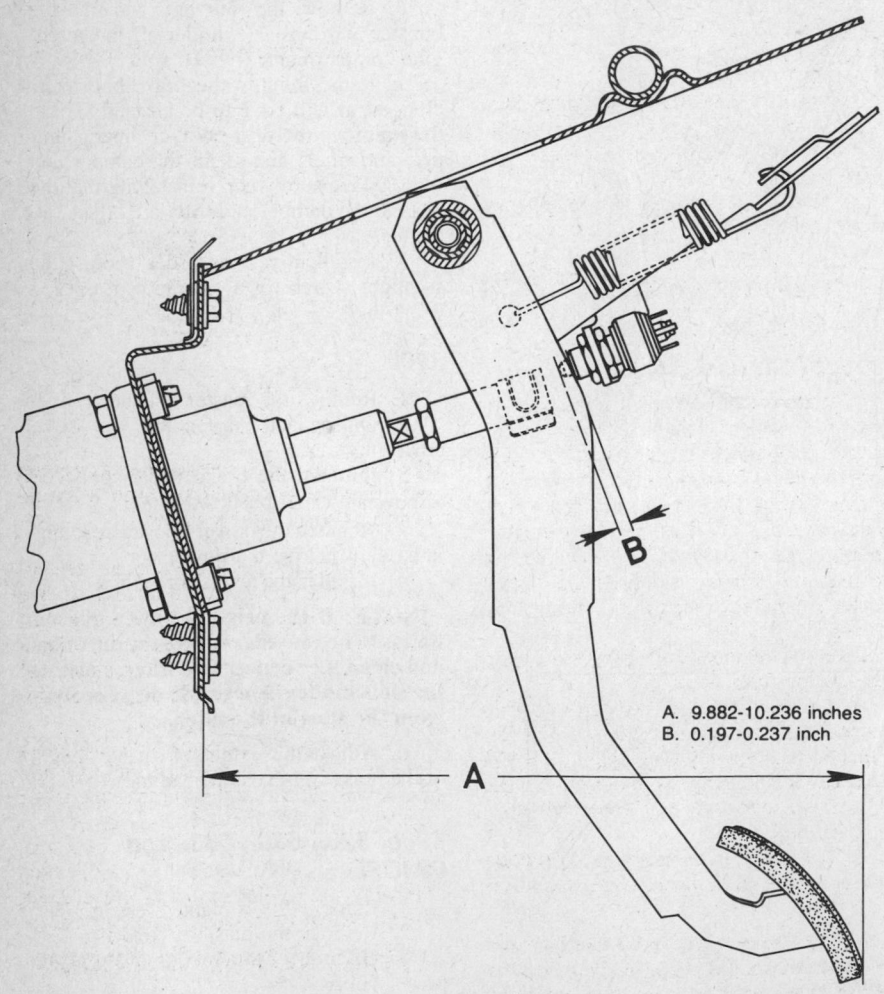

A. 9.882–10.236 inches
B. 0.197–0.237 inch

Brake pedal adjustment—733i

1. From the control regulator to the fluid reservoir
2. From the control regulator to the power steering gear box
3. From the control regulator to the power steering pump
4. From the control regulator to the power brake booster

Pressure control regulator—733i

2. Remove the end cap, and then straighten the cotter pin and remove it. Loosen the castellated nut.

3. While continuously spinning the brake disc, torque the castellated nut down to 22–24 ft. lbs. Keep turning the disc thru–out this and make sure it turns at least two turns after the nut is torqued and held.

4. Loosen the nut until there is end play and the hub rotates with the nut.

5. Torque the nut to no more than 2 ft. lbs. Finally, loosen slowly just until castellations and the nearest cotter pin hole line up and insert a new cotter pin.

6. Make sure the slotted washer is free to turn without noticeable resistance; otherwise, there is no end play and the bearings will wear excessively.

528i and 530i

1. Remove the wheel. Remove the locking cap from the hub by gripping it carefully on both sides with a pair of pliers.

2. Remove the cotter pin from the castellated nut, and loosen the nut.

3. Spin the disc constantly while torquing the nut to 7 ft. lbs. Continue spinning the disc a couple of turns after the nut is torqued and held.

4. Loosen the castellated nut ¼–⅓ turn—until the slotted washer can be turned readily.

5. Fasten a dial indicator to the front suspension and rest the pin against the wheel hub. Preload the meter about 0.039 in. to remove any play.

6. Adjust the position of the castellated nut while reading the play on the indicator. Make the play as small as possible while backing off the castellated nut just until a new cotter pin can be inserted. The permissible range is 0.0008–0.004 in.

7. Install the new cotter pin, locking cap, and the wheel.

528e

1. Raise the vehicle and support it safely. Remove the front wheels.

2. Remove the bearing cap and the selflocking nut.

3. Install a new nut and tighten it to specified torque.

4. Lock the nut by hitting it with a round punch several times on the outer lip.

5. Install bearing cap and front wheels. Lower the vehicle.

REMOVAL & INSTALLATION (PACKING)

Except 318i and 325e

1. Remove the wheel. Unbolt and remove the caliper. Hang it from the body. Do not disconnect or stress the hose. On models with a separate disc, remove the locking cap by gripping carefully on both sides with a pair of pliers, remove the cotter pin from the castellated nut, and remove the nut and, where equipped, the slotted washer. Then, remove the entire hub and bearing.

2. Remove the shaft sealing ring and take out the roller bearing.

3. On most models, the outer bearing race may be forced out through the recesses in the wheel hub. A BMW puller 00 8 550 or the equivalent may also be used. On the 733i, the recesses are not provided and a puller is necessary.

4. Clean all bearings and races and the interior of the hub with alcohol, and allow to air dry.

NOTE: Do not dry with compressed air as this can damage the bearings by rolling them over one another unlubricated or force one loose from the cage and injure you.

5. Replace *all* bearings and races if there is any sign of scoring or galling.

6. Press in the outer races with a suitable sleeve. Pack a new shaft seal with graphite grease and refill the hub with fresh grease.

7. Assemble in this order: outer race; inner race; outer race; inner race; shaft seal.

8. Adjust the wheel bearing play as described above.

318i and 325e

NOTE: The bearings on the 318i and 325e are only removed if they are worn. They cannot be removed without destroying them (due to side thrust created by the bearing puller). They are not periodically disassembled, repacked, and adjusted.

1. Remove the front wheel and support the car. Remove the attaching bolts and remove and suspend the brake caliper, hanging it from the body so as to avoid putting stress on the brake line.

2. Pull off the brake disc and pry off the dust cover with a small prybar. Remove the setscrew.

3. Using a chisel, knock the tab on the collar nut away from the shaft. Unscrew and discard the nut.

4. Pull off the bearing with a puller and discard.

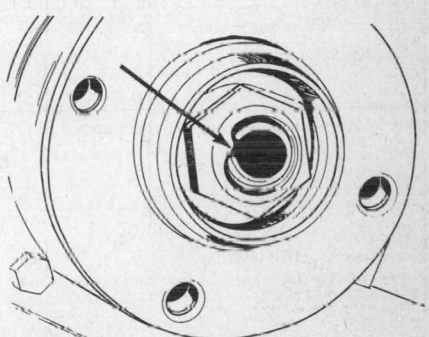

On 318i, unlock the collar nut as shown with a chisel, by applying force in the direction shown by the arrow

5. If the inside bearing inner race remains on the stub axle, unbolt and remove the dust guard. Bend back the inner dust guard and pull the inner race off with a special tool capable of getting under the race (BMW 00 7 500 and 33 1 309 or equivalent. Reinstall the dust guard.

6. Then install a special tool (BMW 31 2 120 or equivalent) over the stub axle and screw it in for the entire length of the guide sleeve's threads. Press the bearing on.

7. Reverse the remaining removal procedures to install the disc and caliper. Torque the wheel hub collar nut to 188 ft. lb. Lock the collar nut by bending over the tab.

Rear Wheel Cylinder
REMOVAL & INSTALLATION

1. Remove the rear brake drum.

2. Loosen the wheel cylinder bleeder screw. DO NOT remove the bleeder screw.

3. Disconnect the brake line from the wheel cylinder.

4. Turn the brake shoe adjusting cams as far to the outside as possible.

5. Remove the wheel cylinder attaching bolts, and remove the wheel cylinder.

6. Install in the reverse order of removal.

Parking Brake

ADJUSTMENT

Vehicles Equipped with Rear Drum Brakes

1. Support the rear of the vehicle in a raised position.

2. Fully release the handbrake.

3. On vehicles with adjustable brakes, while rotating the tire and wheel assembly, turn the left hand eccentric adjustment nut counterclockwise and the right-hand eccentric adjustment nut clockwise until the brake shoes are tight against the drum and the wheel will no longer rotate. On vehicles with self-adjusting brakes, simply operate the brake pedal hard several times to ensure automatic adjusters have taken up the slack.

4. Loosen the eccentric nuts by 1/8 of a turn, so that the wheel is just able to turn, on vehicles with adjustable brakes.

5. Push up the rubber sleeve on the handbrake lever until the locknut is visible.

6. Loosen the locknut.

7. Pull up on the handbrake lever for a distance of five notches. Measure the distance between the middle of the handle and propeller shaft tunnel. This distance should be approximately 4.5 ± 0.2 in.

8. Tighten the adjustment nut until the wheels are locked, and retighten the locknut. On the 318i, the wheels must be just beginning to drag, and resistance on both sides must be equal.

9. Release the handbrake. Make sure that the wheels turn freely when the handbrake is released.

Vehicles Equipped with Rear Disc Brakes—Except 325e

The procedure for adjusting the handbrake on vehicles equipped with rear disc brakes is similar to the procedure for adjusting the handbrake on vehicles equipped with rear drum brakes with one exception.

The mechanism for adjusting the brake shoes is a star wheel type adjuster. Insert a screwdriver through the 0.6 in. hole, and turn the adjusting star wheel until the brake disc can no longer be moved. Proceed as though adjusting the handbrake on vehicles equipped with rear drum brakes.

325e

1. Remove one bolt on each rear wheel with the vehicle securely supported. Make sure the handbrake is off and cable properly adjusted.

2. Turn the wheels until the bolt hole is about 30 degrees behind the 12 o'clock position. You can then reach the star wheel adjuster with a long screwdriver.

3. Turn the left side adjusting nut up, or the right side nut down, to tighten the adjustment until the shoes prevent the disc from being turned by hand. Now loosen the adjustment 3–4 threads. Make sure the disc turns easily.

REMOVAL & INSTALLATION

318i and 320i

1. Remove the brake drum as described above. Pull off the rubber boot at the handbrake lever, loosen and remove the locknuts on the appropriate side, and disconnect the cable at the handbrake lever.

2. Remove the brake shoes as described in Unit Repair.

3. Then, on 320i, pull the cable out of the holder toward the rear of the car. On 318i, disconnect the cable on the rear suspension arm, compress the locking clamp, and disconnect the cable on the backing plate and pull it out.

4. Install in reverse order, making sure the cable holders are both located properly—one in the protective tube, and the other in the backing plate. On the 318i, make sure the clamp which locates the tube is properly connected. Adjust the brakes as described at the front of this chapter.

325e

1. Remove the rubber boot at the base of the handbrake by pulling up the clamp at the front and lifting it out at the rear.

2. Lift out the ashtray at the rear of the console. Remove the bolt located under the ashtray. Then, pull the console to the rear to disconnect it and remove it.

3. Unscrew and remove the parking brake cable nuts.

4. Remove the parking brake shoes. See the "Brakes" Unit Repair section. Locate the cable spread outboard of the brake disc. Pull the outer portion of the spreader to the rear and remove it. Then, press out the pin and pull the unit off.

5. Disconnect the brake cable at the trailing arm. Then, pull the cable out of the protective tube. Disconnect the cable support at the rear disc and then pull the assembly out.

6. Install in reverse order. The sliding surfaces of the cable spreader should be coated with Molykote® G paste or equivalent. Make sure the cable holder rests on the protective tube. To adjust the cable, pull the brake up just five notches, and then tighten the nuts until the right and left rear wheels just begin to drag uniformly. Release the brake and make sure the wheels turn freely.

All Others

1. Remove the parking brake shoes as described in the Unit Repair section.

2. Disconnect the negative battery cable, loosen the mounting screw and pull off the footwell nozzle.

3. Unscrew mounting bolts, and pull the tray at the front of the footwell out far enough to disconnect the wires. Then, remove the tray.

4. Remove the rubber boot from the handbrake lever. Unscrew the locknuts and remove them and pull the cable out of the brake lever.

5. Working under the car, detach the brake cable at the suspension arm. Remove the two mounting nuts at the brake backing plate, and then pull the cable out of the protective tube.

6. Reverse the removal procedure to install.

CHASSIS ELECTRICAL

Heater Assembly, Core and Blower

REMOVAL & INSTALLATION

320i

1. Disconnect the battery ground.

2. Move the selector lever to the WARM position.

3. Drain the cooling system.

4. Loosen the hose clamp, and remove the heater core return hose.

5. Disconnect the heater hose between the hot water control valve and the engine.

6. Remove the package tray.

7. Remove outer tube casing.

8. Remove the lower center trim panel.

9. Remove the left side outer trim panel.

10. Remove the upper section of the steering tube casing.

11. Remove the heater control knobs.

12. Remove the heater control trim panel.

13. Remove the right side trim panel.

14. Disconnect the heater electrical lead.

15. Remove the heater housing retaining nuts.

16. Disconnect the left side distribution duct, and move the steering tube outer casing retaining bracket out of the way.

17. Remove the glove box lower trim panel.

18. Disconnect the left side distribution duct, and lift out the heater housing.

19. Remove the housing rivets.

20. Remove the housing clamps, and separate the housing halves.

21. Disconnect the bowden cable from the hot water control valve.

22. Remove the hot water control valve and hose from the water valve bracket on the heater housing.

23. Remove the rubber sleeves from the heater core inlet and outlet tubes.

24. Disconnect the electrical leads at the blower motor.

25. Disconnect the electrical leads at the blower resistor in the heater housing.

26. Open the blower motor support clamps, and remove the blower motor and fan as an assembly.

27. Install in the reverse order of removal.

28. Check operation of the heater controls. Adjust if necessary.

528e, 528i and 530i (533i and 633CSi Similar)

1. Remove the center tray and instrument panel trim to bottom right of tray.

2. Remove the glove box and remove heater controls at water valve and at air doors. Remove center console if equipped.

3. Disconnect the battery ground.

4. Push the selector lever to the WARM position.

5. Drain the coolant and remove the air conditioning evaporator:

  a. Drain the refrigerant slowly out of the low side Schrader® valve.

  b. Take off the no-drip tape and disconnect both refrigerent lines from the evaporator.

NOTE: Plug the refrigerant lines immediately to prevent moisture and contaminants from entering the system.

  c. Pull the temperature sensor out of the evaporator housing.

  d. Disconnect the evaporator/heater control electrical connector.

  e. Remove the right and left screw from the housing (from area where the housing meets the passenger compartment carpeting).

  f. Remove the floor pan to evaporator housing bracket. Lift the housing slightly and pull it from under the dash.

———— CAUTION ————
Do not bend the temperature sensor or it will have to be replaced.

  g. Disconnect the blower wires and the blower resistor wire. Lift the evaporator slightly and pull the adapter and evaporator from under the dash.

6. Disconnect the heater hoses from the heater core, and remove the rubber seal.

7. Remove the lower instrument panel center trim.

8. Disconnect the heater controls at the instrument panel.

9. Disconnect the control shafts at the joints.

10. Disconnect the multiple electrical connector at the heater.

11. Remove the instrument panel center cover.

12. Working from inside the engine compartment, remove the upper section of the fire shield.

13. Remove the heater assembly retaining nuts, and lift out the heater.

14. Open the heater housing clips, and separate the housing halves and remove the heater core.

15. Disconnect the electrical leads at the blower motor, and remove the motor.

16. Install in the reverse order of removal.

733i

1. Drain the coolant from the system.

2. Discharge the refrigerant from the air conditioner.

3. Remove the instrument trim panel.

4. Remove the cowl fresh air grille.

5. Remove the heater assembly cover attaching screws, and remove the cover.

6. Disconnect the heater hoses at the heater core.

7. Disconnect the vacuum lines at the heater.

8. Bend open the heater duct mounting clamp.

9. Disconnect the central electrical lead.

10. Pull the duct cover downward, and remove it.

11. Remove the center strut attaching bolts (4).

12. Remove the insulation from the refrigerant lines.

13. Disconnect the refrigerant lines from the evaporator.

14. Disconnect the evaporator drain tube.

15. Remove the heater assembly retaining bolts, remove the heater and the heater core.

16. Install in the reverse order of removal.

Heater Core

REMOVAL & INSTALLATION

318i and 325e

1. Disconnect the negative battery cable. Remove the package tray. Remove bolts and remove the left/lower dash trim panel.

2. Drain the coolant, loosen the bolt and remove the clamp bracing the two lines going to the heater core.

3. Remove the left side duct carrying air from the heater to the rear seat duct.

4. Unscrew the bolts and remove the lower heater discharge duct.

5. Unscrew the bolts fastening the water lines from the engine compartment to the lines coming down from the heater core. Remove and discard the O-ring seals.

6. Unscrew the bolts, separate the halves of the core housing, and pull the core out of the housing.

7. Installation is the reverse of removal. Replace the O-ring seals for the water lines.

Heater Blower

REMOVAL & INSTALLATION

318i and 325e

1. Disconnect the negative battery cable. The blower is accessible by removing the cover at the top of the firewall in the engine compartment. To remove the cover, pull off the rubber strip, cut off the wire

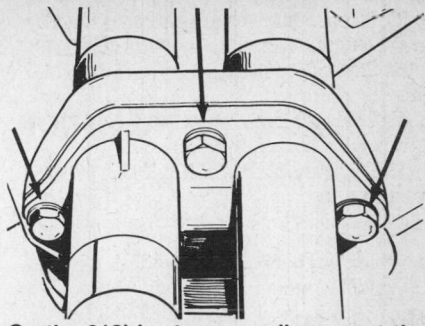

On the 318i heater core, disconnect the water lines by removing the arrowed bolts

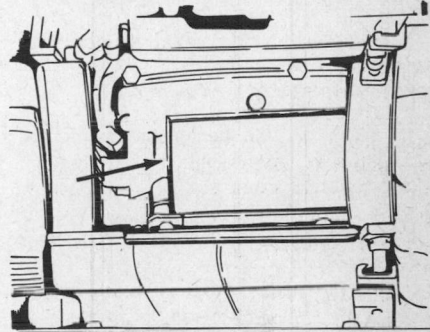

In removing the 318i heater motor, be careful not to damage the damper (arrowed)

that runs diagonally across the cover, unscrew and remove the bolts, and pull the cover aside.

2. Open the retaining straps, swing them aside, and then remove the blower cover.

3. Pull off both connectors. Disengage the clamp that fastens the assembly in place by pulling the bottom toward you. Now, lift out the motor/fan assembly, being careful not to damage the air damper underneath.

Radio

REMOVAL & INSTALLATION

NOTE: The following procedure is a general one, which applies to all models.

1. Pull off the radio knobs and ornamental rings.

2. Push up on spring catches and remove them from the control shafts. Remove the radio mask.

3. Remove the bolts from supports on both sides of the radio.

4. Disconnect the automatic antenna lead, the antenna, the right and left speaker wires and the power supply.

5. Installation is the reverse of removal.

Windshield Wiper Motor

The electric wiper motor assembly is located under the engine hood, at the top of the cowl panel. A few models have covers over the wiper motor assembly, while others have the motors exposed. Link rods op-

erate the left and right wiper pivot assemblies from a drive crank bolted to the wiper motor output shaft.

REMOVAL & INSTALLATION

320i, 528e, 528i, 530i, 533i and 633CSi

1. Remove the cowl cover to expose the wiper motor (320i and 530i).
2. Disconnect the wiper motor crank arm from the motor output shaft.
3. Remove the motor retaining screws and disconnect the electrical connector.
4. Remove the wiper motor from the vehicle.
5. Reverse the procedure to install the motor.

318i and 325e

1. Remove the heater motor, as described above. Remove the bracket bracing the windshield wiper motor, which is now visible.
2. Disconnect the electrical connector for the motor.
3. Lift out the grill located at the top of the cowl and disconnect the linkages to both wiper arms at the left side shaft mounts.
4. Disconnect both wiper arms from their shafts, by lifting the cover, unscrewing the nut, and pulling the arm off. Then, remove the cover, nut, and washer surrounding the shafts and holding the console in place. Now remove the entire console and remove the motor from the console.
5. Installation is the reverse of removal.

733i

1. Remove the cowl fresh air intake grill and tilt rearward.
2. Remove the cover from the windshield wiper motor and remove the electrical plugs.
3. Remove the left and right wiper arms. Loosen the left and right pivot bearings.
4. Turn the rubber pad at the motor, counterclockwise and disconnect the right wiper linkage.
5. Remove the motor bracket retaining screws. Separate the spacers and remove the wiper motor assembly.

NOTE: Do not lose the shims.

6. The wiper motor can be removed from the bracket after the removal.
7. Reverse the removal procedure to install.

Windshield Wiper Switch

REMOVAL & INSTALLATION

The wiper switch is located on the steering column and in most cases the steering wheel will have to be removed, along with the lower steering column trim panels, to gain access to the switch.

After the retaining screws and electrical connectors are removed, the switch can be lifted from the plate of the steering column.

─── **CAUTION** ───
To avoid possible electrical short-circuits, the negative battery cable should be removed before the repairs are attempted.

Windshield Washer Motor

The windshield washer motor is attached to the washer reservoir and controlled from the wiper switch. A double motor is present on some models to pump the washer solution to both the windshield washers and to the headlamp cleaners.

To remove the washer pump, the reservoir should be removed from the vehicle to avoid damage to the reservoir.

A delaying relay is used on some models, to control the spraying of the washer solution for a period of five seconds, stop briefly and then recycle.

Instrument Cluster

REMOVAL & INSTALLATION

318i and 325e

1. Remove the attaching screws and remove the lower instrument panel trim from under the steering column.
2. Remove the mounting nuts for the trim just under the instrument carrier, and remove it.
3. Unscrew the four screws underneath and two above the instrument carrier, and remove trim that surrounds the instrument carrier.
4. Remove the two screws at the top of the carrier, lift it out of the instrument panel, and then disconnect the plugs. To disconnect the combination plug, first pull the sliding clamp off the center.
5. Installation is the reverse of removal.

320i

1. Disconnect the negative battery cable.
2. Remove the steering wheel assembly.
3. Remove the bottom center instrument trim panel.
4. Disconnect the speedometer cable, loosen the knurled nut and pull the instrument assembly outward.
5. Remove the electrical plugs and wires.
6. Remove the instrument cluster from the dash.
7. Reverse the removal procedure to install.

528e, 528i and 530i

1. Remove the negative battery cable.
2. Remove the lower instrument trim panel.

3. Disconnect the speedometer cable.
4. Loosen the knurled nuts on the cluster back.
5. Loosen the steering column to dash screws.
6. Pull the instrument cluster outward and remove the electrical wires and connectors.
7. Remove the cluster from the dash panel.
8. Reverse the removal procedure to install the cluster.

533i and 633CSi

1. Disconnect the negative battery cable.
2. Remove the steering wheel assembly.
3. Remove the bottom center instrument trim panel.
4. Remove the cover from the "INQUIRY" unit.
5. Remove the three retaining screws and remove the "INQUIRY" printed circuit board.
6. Remove the light switch, leaving the wiring connected.
7. Remove the left air control knob and remove the bezel cover.
8. Remove the fog lamp switch and leave the wiring attached.
9. Remove the screws from the instrument cluster and loosen the steering column control base screws.
10. Disconnect the speedometer cable.
11. Push downward on the upper section casing and the steering column, so that the instrument cluster can be removed at an angle. Disconnect the electrical wiring and connectors.
12. Reverse the removal procedure to install the instrument cluster.

733i

1. Remove the negative battery cable from the battery post.
2. Remove the instrument panel trim section at the left bottom of the dash.
3. Remove the upper bezel retaining screws.
4. Loosen the steering column control and pull the steering housing all the way out.
5. Pull the instrument cluster outward, remove the electrical wires and plugs, after removal of the speedometer cable.
6. Turn the cluster assembly towards the right rear and pull it away from the dash.
7. The installation is in the reverse of the removal procedure.

Fuse Box Locations

The fuse box is located under the engine hood on the left side, near the upper strut housing or near the battery, on the remaining models.

Various relays are also mounted on the fuse box for easy accessibility.

Chrysler Corp.
Arrow, Colt, Champ, Challenger, Conquest, Sapporo, Vista

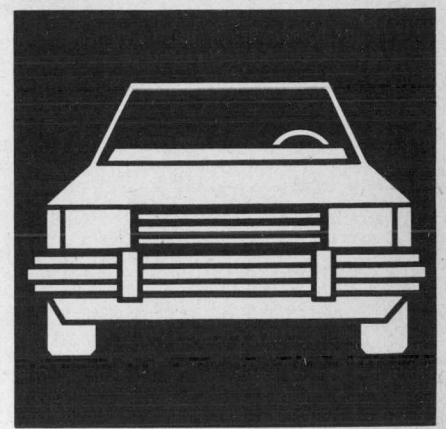

SERIAL NUMBER IDENTIFICATION

Vehicle Number

The vehicle identification plate is mounted on the instrument panel, adjacent to the lower corner of the windshield on the driver's side, and is visible through the windshield. The thirteen digit vehicle number is composed of a seven digit identification code, and a six digit sequential number.

Starting for 1981 and later, a standardized 17 digit Vehicle Identification Number (VIN) was used. The number continues to be visible from the outside of the lower driver's side windshield area.

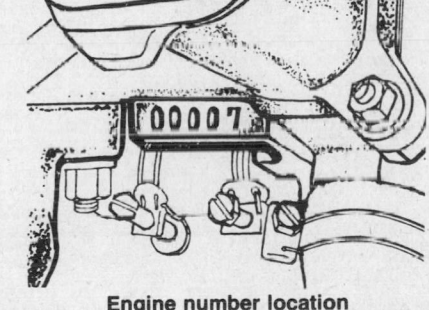

Engine number location

Engine model number

Engine Number

The engine model number in embossed on the lower left side of the block.

The engine model number is stamped near the serial number of the upper right front side of the engine block. The serial number is stamped on a pad at the upper right front of the engine adjacent to the exhaust manifold.

Vehicle Identification Plate

7 H 24 K 87 2 0 0 0 1 1

1st Digit	2nd Digit	3rd & 4th Digit	5th Digit	6th Digit	7th Digit	8th Digit	9th to 13th Dight

Car line	Price class	Body type	Engine displacement	Model year	Transmission code	Trim code	Sequence number
5—Plymouth 21, 41 & 45 6—Dodge 21, 41 & 45 7—Plymouth 24 8—Dodge 24	L—Low M—Medium H High P—Premium	21—2 door Coupe 24—2 door Hatchback 41—4 door Sedan 45—Station Wagon	K—97.5 CID (1600c.c.) U—121.7 CID (2000c.c.) F—155.9 CID (2600c.c.)	8—1978	49 states 1—4 speed M/T 4—5 speed M/T 7—Automatic California 2—4 speed M/T 5—5 speed M/T 8—Automatic Canada 3—4 speed M/T 6—5 speed M/T 9—Automatic	1—Low 2—Medium 3—High 6—Premium or GT 7—Estate package	00011

Serial number location

Vehicle I.D. plate—typical 1980 and earlier

J B 3 B E 4 4 3 9 C U 4 0 0 0 0 1

	1st Digit	2nd Digit	3rd Digit	4th Digit	5th Digit	6th Digit	7th Digit	8th Digit	9th Digit	10th Digit	11th Digit	12th Digit	13th to 17th Digits
	Manufacturing country	Sales channel	Vehicle type	Other	Vehicle line	Trim code	Body type	Engine displacement	*Check digit	Model year	Assembly plant	Transmission code	Sequence number
	J—Japan	B—Dodge P—Plymouth	3—Passenger car	B—Manual seat belt	E—Colt/ Champ	2—Low 3—Medium 4—High, High (RS, LS)	4—2 door hatchback	2—1.4 litre (86.0 CID) 3—1.6 litre (97.5 CID)	1 2 . . 9 X	C—1982	U— MIZUSHIMA Plant	1—4 speed M/T Federal 2—4 speed M/T California 3—4 speed M/T Canada 4—4 x 2 speed M/T Federal 5—4 x 2 speed M/T California 6—4 x 2 speed M/T Canada 7—3 speed A/T Federal 8—3 speed A/T California 9—3 speed A/T Canada	00001 to 99999

NOTE: *"Check Digit" means a single number or letter X used to verify the accuracy of transcription of vehicle identification number.
M/T is an abbreviation for manual transaxle.
A/T is an abbreviation for automatic transaxle.
RS is an abbreviation for "Rally Sports".
LS is an abbreviation for "Luxury Sports".

Typical 1981 and later 17 digit vehicle identification number

GENERAL ENGINE SPECIFICATIONS

Year	Engine Displacement cu. in. (cc)	Carburetor Type	Horsepower @ rpm	Torque @ rpm (ft. lbs.)	Bore × Stroke (in.)	Compression Ratio	Oil Pressure (psi)
'78①	97.5 (1600)	1 × 2 bbl	83 @ 5500	89 @ 3500	3.03 × 3.39	8.5:1	57–71
	97.5 (1600)②	1 × 2 bbl	83 @ 5500	89 @ 3500	3.03 × 3.39	8.5:1	50–64
	121.7 (2000)②	1 × 2 bbl	96 @ 5500	109 @ 3500	3.31 × 3.54	8.5:1	50–64
'79–'82	86.0 (1400)	1 × 2 bbl	70 @ 5200	78 @ 3000	2.91 × 3.23	8.8:1	50–64
	97.5 (1600)②	1 × 2 bbl	77 @ 5200	87 @ 3000	3.03 × 3.39	8.5:1	50–64
	121.7 (2000)②	1 × 2 bbl	93 @ 5200	108 @ 3000	3.31 × 3.54	8.5:1	50–64
	155.9 (2600)② ③	1 × 2 bbl	105 @ 5000	139 @ 2500	3.59 × 3.86	8.2:1	50–64
'83	86.0 (1400)	1 × 2 bbl	64 @ 5000	78 @ 3000	2.91 × 3.23	8.8:1	63
	97.5 (1600)②	1 × 2 bbl	72 @ 5000	85 @ 3000	3.03 × 3.39	8.5:1	63
	155.9 (2600)②	1 × 2 bbl	100 @ 5000	137 @ 2500	3.59 × 3.86	8.2:1	56

GENERAL ENGINE SPECIFICATIONS

Year	Engine Displacement cu. in. (cc)	Carburetor Type	Horsepower @ rpm	Torque @ rpm (ft. lbs.)	Bore × Stroke (in.)	Compression Ratio	Oil Pressure (psi)
'84–'85	86.0 (1400)	1 × 2 bbl	64 @ 5000	78 @ 3000	2.91 × 3.23	8.8:1	64
	97.5 (1600)②	1 × 2 bbl	72 @ 5000	85 @ 3000	3.03 × 3.39	8.5:1	64
	97.5 (1600)②	EFI (Turbo)	102 @ 5000	122 @ 3000	3.03 × 3.39	7.6:1	64
	121.7 (2000)②	1 × 2 bbl	88 @ 5000	108 @ 3500	3.31 × 3.54	8.5:1	49
	155.9 (2600)④	EFI	145 @ 5000	185 @ 2500	3.59 × 3.86	7.0:1	56

MT—Manual transmission
AT—Automatic transmission
EFI—Electronic Fuel Injection
NA—Not available at time of publication
① California emission:
97.5 (1600) MT: 80 @ 5500 HP
87 @ 3500 torque
AT: 78 @ 5500 HP
83 @ 3500 torque

121.7 (2000) All: 93 @ 5500 HP
106 @ 3500 torque
② Silent shaft
③ Specifications also apply to 1978 Challenger/Sapporo
④ Conquest

TUNE-UP SPECIFICATIONS

(When analyzing compression test results, look for uniformity among cylinders, rather than specific pressures.)

Year	Engine Displace. cu. in. (cc)	Spark Plugs Type	Spark Plugs Gap (in.)	Distributor Point Dwell (deg)	Distributor Point Gap (in.)	Ignition Timing (deg) MT	Ignition Timing (deg) AT	Intake Valve Opens (deg) BTDC	Fuel Pump Pressure (psi)	Idle Speed (rpm)	Valve Clear (in)● In.	Valve Clear (in)● Ex.
'78	97.5 (1600)	BPR6ES	0.028–0.031	49–55	0.018–0.022	5B ②	5B ②	24 M 19 A	3.7–5.1	①	0.006	0.010
	121.7 (2000)	BPR6ES	0.028–0.031	49–55	0.018–0.022	5B ②	5B ②	24	4.6–6.0	③	0.006	0.010
	155.9 (2600)	BPR6ES	0.039–0.043	52 ± 3	0.018–0.021	7B	7B	25	4.6–6.0	④	0.006⑤	0.010
'79–'82	86.0 (1400)	BPR6ES-11⑫	0.039–⑫ 0.043	52 ± 3	0.018–0.021 ⑧	5B	—	18	3.7–5.1	700⑨	0.006⑤	0.010
	97.5 (1600)	BPR6ES-11⑫	0.039–⑫ 0.043	52 ± 3	0.018–0.021 ⑧	5B ⑥	5B ⑥	20	3.7–5.1	650 M 700 A	0.006⑤	0.010
	121.7 (2000)	BPR6ES⑫	0.039–⑫ 0.043	Electronic		5B	5B	25	4.6–6.0	650 M 700 A	0.006⑤	0.010
	155.9 (2600)	BRP6ES⑫	0.039–⑫ 0.043	Electronic		7B ⑦	7B ⑦	25	4.6–6.0	④ ⑩	0.006⑤	0.010

TUNE-UP SPECIFICATIONS

(When analyzing compression test results, look for uniformity among cylinders, rather than specific pressures.)

Year	Engine Displace. cu. in. (cc)	Spark Plugs		Distributor		Ignition Timing (deg)		Intake Valve Opens (deg) BTDC	Fuel Pump Pressure (psi)	Idle Speed (rpm)	Valve Clear (in)●	
		Type	Gap (in.)	Point Dwell (deg)	Point Gap (in.)	MT	AT				In.	Ex.
'83–'85	86.0 (1400)	BUR6EA-11⑫	0.039–⑫ 0.043	Electronic		⑪	⑪	18	2.7–3.7	⑪	0.006⑤	0.010
	97.5 (1600)	BUR6EA-11⑫	0.039–⑫ 0.043	Electronic		⑪	⑪	20	2.4–3.4	⑪	0.006⑤	0.010
	121.7 (2000)	BUR6EA-11	0.039– 0.043	Electronic		5B	5B	19	NA	⑭	0.006	0.010
	155.9 (2600)	BPR5ES-11⑫	0.039–⑫ 0.043	Electronic		7B ⑪	7B ⑪	25	4.6–6.0	⑪	0.006⑤	0.010
	155.9⑬ (2600)	BUR6EA-11	0.039– 0.043	Electronic		10B	—	NA	35.6	850	0.006	0.010

NOTE: The underhood specifications sticker often reflects tune-up specifications changes made in production. Sticker figures must be used if they disagree with those in this chart.

B Before top dead center
NA—Not available at time of publication
● All clearances set hot
① Fed: 800–900
  Alt: 900–1000
  Calif.: 900–1000 man.
    800–900 auto.
② Altitude (TDC)
  Calif.: 5A
③ Fed.: 900–1000 man.
  800–900 auto.
  Calif.: 900–1000
④ Fed.: 850 ± 50 rpm—both MT and AT
  Calif. & High Alt.: 700 ± 50 rpm—MT
  Calif.: 750 ± 50 rpm—AT
⑤ Jet valve clearance: 0.006 inch
⑥ High altitude only: 10B
⑦ Actual timing with dual diaphragm advance,
  Calif.: 3 ATDC
  High Alt.—2 BTDC

⑧ 1980 California cars and all 1981 cars:
  electronic reluctor gap not adjustable
⑨ Fed.: 4 speed man. trans. (not available in
  California) 650 rpm
⑩ 1982–83: Man. trans., 50 states 750 rpm
  Auto. trans., 50 states 800 rpm
⑪ See underhood specification sticker
⑫ Canada: 1400—BPR6ES; .028–.031
        1600—BPR6ES; .028–.031
        2000—BPR6ES; .028–.031
        2600—BPR5ES; .028–.031
⑬ 1984 and later Conquest
⑭ Man. Trans.: with AC—750
        without AC—700
  Auto. Trans.: with AC—850
        without AC—750

FIRING ORDERS

NOTE: To avoid confusion, always replace spark plug wires one at a time.

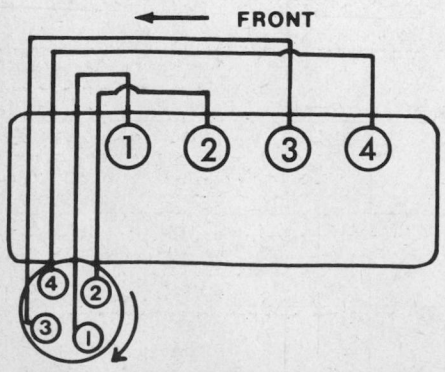

1400cc, 1600cc and 1984 and later 2000cc engines

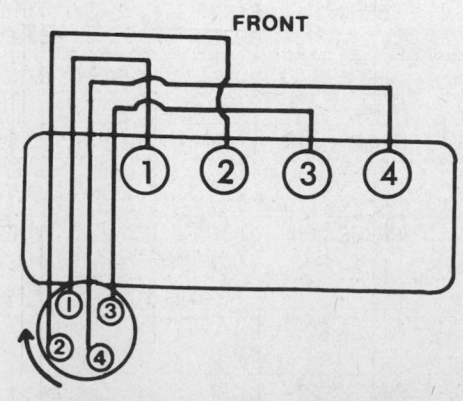

2600cc and 1978–83 2000cc engines

CAPACITIES
Rear Wheel Drive Cars

| Year | Model | Engine Displacement (cc) | Engine Crankcase (qts) | | Transmission (qts) | | | Drive Axle (pts) | Gasoline Tank (gals) | Cooling System (qts) | |
| | | | With Filter | Without Filter | Manual | | Automatic | | | W/AC | W/O AC |
					4-spd	5-spd					
'78	All	1600	4.2	3.7	1.8	2.1	6.8	1.2	15.8	7.7	7.7
		2000	4.5	4.0	—	2.4	6.8	1.2	15.8	9.5	9.5
		2600	4.5	4.0	—	2.4	6.8	1.2	15.8	9.7	9.7
'79–'85	All	1600	4.2	3.7	—	2.1	7.2	1.2	①	7.7	7.7
		2000	4.5	4.0	—	2.4	7.2	1.2	①	9.5	9.5
		2600	4.5	4.0	—	2.4	7.2	1.4②④	①③	9.5	9.5

①Colt Coupe, Sedan and Arrow: 13.2
  Challenger and Sapporo: 15.8
  Sta. Wgn.: 14.0 (1979) 13.2 (1980)
②'81–'84: 2.7
③'81–'84: 15.8; Conquest: 19.8
④Conquest: on complete refills include 4-oz.
  of Mopar Hypoid Gear Additive, No.
  4318060

CAPACITIES
Front Wheel Drive Cars

| Year | Model | Engine Displacement (cc) | Engine Crankcase (qts) | | Transaxle (qts) | | | Gasoline Tank (gals) | Cooling System (qts) | |
| | | | With Filter | W/O Filter | Manual | | Automatic | | W/AC | W/O AC |
					4-spd	Twin Stick				
'79	All	1400	3.7	3.17	2.2	2.2	—	10.6	—	5.2
		1600	4.2	3.67	2.2	2.2	—	10.6	6.9	6.9
'80	All	1400	3.7	3.17	2.3	2.3	—	10.6	—	4.7
		1600	4.2	3.67	2.3	2.3	6.0	10.6	4.7	4.7
'81–'85	All	1400	3.7	3.17	2.4	2.4	—	10.6①	—	4.7
	All	1600	4.2	3.67	2.4	2.4	6.0	10.6①	4.7	4.7
	Vista	2000	4.2	—	2.4	2.4	6.1	13.2	7.4	7.4

①RS, LS: 13.2

CRANKSHAFT AND CONNECTING ROD SPECIFICATIONS
(All measurements are given in inches)

| Year | Engine Displace (cu. in.) | Crankshaft | | | | Connecting Rod | | |
		Main Brg. Journal Dia.	Main Brg. Oil Clearance	Shaft End-Play	Thrust on No.	Journal Diameter	Oil Clearance	Side Clearance
All	86.0	1.8898	0.0008–0.0028	0.002–0.007	3	1.6535	0.0004–0.0024	0.004–0.010
	97.5	2.2441	0.0008–0.0028	0.002–0.007	3	1.7717	0.0004–0.0028	0.004–0.010
	121.7	2.5984	0.0008–0.0028④	0.002–0.007	3	2.0866	0.0008–0.0028④	0.004–0.010
	155.9	①	0.0008–0.0028②	0.002–0.007	3	2.0866	0.0008–0.0028③	0.004–0.010

①1978–79: 2.5984
  From 1980: 2.3622
②Conquest: 0.0008–0.0020
③Conquest: 0.0008–0.0024
④Colt Vista: 0.0008–0.0020

VALVE SPECIFICATIONS

Year	Engine Displacement cu. in. (cc)	Seat Angle (deg)	Face Angle (deg)	Spring Test Pressure (lbs @ in.)	Spring Installed Height (in.)	Stem–To–Guide Clearance (in.)		Stem Diameter (in.)	
						Intake	Exhaust	Intake	Exhaust
'78–'85	86.0 (1400)	45	45	69 @ 1.417	1.417	0.0012–0.0024	0.0020–0.0035	0.315	0.315
	97.5 (1600)	45	45	61 @ 1.470	1.470	0.0010–0.0022①	0.002–0.0033②	0.315	0.315
	121.7 (2000)	45	45	61 @ 1.590	1.590	0.0010–0.0022①	0.002–0.0033②	0.315	0.315
	155.9 (2600)	45	45	61 @ 1.590	1.590	0.0012–0.0024	0.0020–0.0035	0.315	0.315
'78–'85	Jet valve	45	45	5.5 @ .846	.846	—	—		0.1693

① 1984 and later: 0.0012–0.0024
② 1984 and later: 0.0020–0.0035

PISTON AND RING SPECIFICATIONS
(All measurements in inches)

Year	Engine Displace. cu. in. (cc)	Piston Clearance	Ring Gap			Ring Side Clearance		
			Top Compression	Bottom Compression	Oil Control	Top Compression	Bottom Compression	Oil Control
'78–'85	86.0 (1400)	0.0008–0.0016	0.008–0.016	0.008–0.016	0.008–0.020	0.0012–0.0028	0.0008–0.0024	—
	97.5 (1600)	0.0008–0.0016	0.008–0.016	0.008–0.016	0.008–0.020	0.0012–0.0028	0.0008–0.0024	—
'78–'83	121.7 (2000)	0.0008–0.0016	0.010–0.017	0.010–0.017	0.008–0.035	0.0024–0.0039	0.0008–0.0024	—
	155.9 (2600)	0.0008–0.0016	0.010–0.017①	0.010–0.017①	0.008–0.035	0.0024–0.0039	0.0008–0.0024	—
'84–'85	121.7 (2000)	0.0008–0.0016	0.010–0.018	0.008–0.016	0.008–0.028	0.0020–0.0035	0.0008–0.0024	—
	155.9 (2600)	0.0008–0.0016	0.012–0.020	0.010–0.016	0.012–0.031	0.002–0.004	0.001–0.002	—

① '82–'83 (2600): 0.010–0.018

TORQUE SPECIFICATIONS
(All readings in ft. lbs.)

Year	Engine Displace. (cu. in.)	Cylinder Head Bolts	Rod Bearing Bolts	Main Bearing Bolts	Crankshaft Pulley Bolt	Flywheel–to–Crankshaft Bolts	Manifold	
							Intake	Exhaust
'78–'85	86.0, 97.5	51–54 (cold)	24–25	37–39	44–50① ③	94–101②	11–14	11–14
	121.7	65–72 (cold)	33–34⑥	55–61⑦	80–94	94–101②	11–14	11–14
	155.9	65–72 (cold)④	33–34	55–61	80–94	94–101② ⑤	11–14	11–14

① 1600 cc w/silent shaft—44–50 ft. lbs.
② AT drive plate—84–90 ft. lbs.
③ 86.0: 37–43
④ Front bolts on 1984–'85 Conquest: 11–15
⑤ 1984–'85 Conquest: 94–110
⑥ 1984 and later Colt Vista: 37–38
⑦ 1984 and later Colt Vista: 37–39

ALTERNATOR, REGULATOR AND BATTERY SPECIFICATIONS

		Alternator			Regulator③				Battery Capacity Ampere-Hour
							Charging Light Relay		
Year	Engine	Rated Output	Rotation (Viewed from Pulley)	No Load Adjusted Voltage	Cover Temperature		Off Voltage	On Voltage	
'78–'85	1400, 1600	45A @ 12V	Clockwise	14.1 to 14.7V	68°F–20°C		4.0 to 5.8V	0.5 to 3.5V	①④
	2000, 2600	50A @ 12V⑤	Clockwise	14.1 to 14.7V	68°F–20°C		4.2 to 5.2V	0.5 to 3.0V	①④
	2600⑥	65A @ 12V	Clockwise	14.1 to 14.7V	68°F–20°C		—	—	45

①Coupe 1600 MT: 45 A.H.
    AT: 60 A.H.
 Sedan all models: 60 A.H.
 Hatchback 1600 MT, AT: 60 A.H.
     2000 MT: 45 A.H.
      AT: 60 A.H.
 Station wagon 1600 MT, AT: 60 A.H.
    2000, 2600 All: 65 A.H.
②1600 W/SS, off voltage: 4.0 to 5.8V
    on voltage: 0.5 to 3.5V
③All models are equipped with sealed voltage regulators which cannot be adjusted if the readings vary from the specifications.
④'82 and later USA: Colt/Champ, Vista—45 amp
    Challenger/Sapporo—50 amp
 '82 and later Canada: Clt/Champ—60 amp
    Challenger/Sapporo—55 amp
⑤'83: 55A @ 12V; '84 and later 65A @ 12V
⑥1984 and later Conquest

STARTER SPECIFICATIONS

Year	Engine (cc) and Transmission	No Load Test			Load Test				Stall Test			Brush Spring Tension (lbs.)
		Amp①	Volts	rpm②	Amp①	Volts	Torque②③	rpm②	Amp①	Volts	Torque③	
'78–'81	1400 1600 MT	53	10.5	5000	150	8.6	2.53	1600	400	6.0	6.73	3.3
	1600 AT 2000 MT	55	11.0	6500	150	9.6	2.24	2200	560	6.0	10.85	3.3
	2000 AT 2600 All	62	11.0	4500	200	9.2	3.83	1600	730	6.0	18.08	3.3
'82–'85	All	60④	11.5	6500	—	—	—	—	—	—	—	3.3

MT: Manual transmission
AT: Automatic transmission
Brush length, all
 Max.: 669 in.
 Min.: .453 in.
Pinion drive to stopper gap, all: 0 to .079 in.
① Less than
② More than
③ Ft. lbs.
④ Reduction drive starter 90 amp.

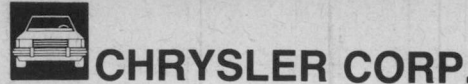

BRAKE SPECIFICATIONS
Rear Wheel Drive Cars
(All measurements given are in. unless noted)

Year	Lug Nut Torque ft. lbs.	Master Cylinder Bore	Brake Disc Thickness			Brake Drum			Lining Thickness			
			Max.	Min.	Runout	Diameter	Maximum	Maximum Wear	Front		Rear	
									Max.	Min. ⑤	Max.	Min. ⑤
'78–'85	51–58 ⑨	13/16 ⑩	0.510 ①⑥⑪	0.450 ②⑦⑪	0.006⑪	9.0	9.060	9.079	0.38③	0.08④	0.157	0.04⑧

① '78–'79 Station wagon and '82 all rear drive: 0.490 in.
② '78–'79 Station wagon and '82 all rear drive: 0.430 in.
③ '78–'79 Station wagon: 0.41 in.
④ '78–'79 Station wagon and '82 all: 0.04 in.
⑤ Due to variations in state inspection regulations, the minimum allowable lining thickness may be different from that recommended by the manufacturer.
⑥ '80–'81—0.380
⑦ '80–'81—0.08
⑧ Rear drum and disc same
⑨ Steel wheel: 51–58 ft. lbs.
   Aluminum wheel: 58–72 ft. lbs.
⑩ '82–'85 vehicles: 0.875 in.
⑪ Rear brake disc:
   max. 0.390–min. 0.330—runout 0.006

BRAKE SPECIFICATIONS
Front Wheel Drive Cars
(All measurements given are in. unless noted)

Year	Model	Lug Nut Torque ft. lbs.	Master Cylinder Bore	Brake Disc Thickness			Brake Drum			Lining Thickness			
				Max.	Min.	Runout	Diameter	Maximum	Maximum Wear	Front②		Rear②	
										Max.	Min.	Max.	Min.
'79	All	51–58①	13/16	0.510	0.450	0.006	7.0	7.060	7.079	0.382	0.08	0.201	0.04
'80–'83	All	51–58①	13/16	0.510	0.450	0.006	7.1	7.160	7.200	0.382	0.08③	0.201	0.04
'84–'85	Colt	51–58①	13/16	0.510	0.450	0.006	7.0	7.1	7.2	0.038	0.04	0.20	0.04
	Colt Turbo	51–58①	7/8	0.700	0.640	0.006	7.0	7.1	7.2	0.041	0.04	0.20	0.04
	Colt Vista	51–58①	0.875	0.710	0.650	0.006	8.0	8.1	8.2	0.041	0.04	0.16	0.04

① Aluminum wheels: 58–72
② Due to variations in state inspection regulations, the minimum allowable lining thickness may be different from that recommended by the manufacturer.
③ '82–'83 minimum pad thickness: 0.04 in.

WHEEL ALIGNMENT
Rear Wheel Drive Cars

Year	Model	Caster (degrees)	Camber (degrees)	Toe-in (in.)	Steering Angle Inner Wheel (degrees)	Outer Wheel (degrees)	King Pin Angle (degrees)
'78	All exc. Sta. Wgn.	$2^1/_{16} \pm 1/_2$	$1 \pm 1/_2$	$1/_{32}$ to $1/_8$	35	36	9
	Station Wagon	$2^5/_8 + 1/_2$	$1^7/_{16} \pm 1/_2$	$1/_{32}$ to $3/_{10}$	39	$30^1/_2$	$8^7/_{16}$
'79	Colt Coupe & Sedan, Arrow	$2^1/_{16} \pm 1/_2$	$1 \pm 1/_2$	$1/_{32}$ to $1/_8$	35	30	9
	Challenger & Sapporo	$2^5/_8 \pm 1/_2$	$1^7/_{16} \pm 1/_2$	$1/_{32}$ to $3/_{16}$	37	32	$8^7/_8$
	Colt Sta. Wagon	$2^5/_8 \pm 1/_2$	$1^7/_{16} \pm 1/_2$	$1/_{32}$ to $3/_{16}$	39	$30^1/_2$	$8^7/_8$
'80	Arrow	$2^1/_{16} + 1/_2$	$1 \pm 1/_2$	$1/_{32}$ to $1/_8$	35	30	9
	Challenger & Sapporo	$2^5/_8 \pm 1/_2$	$1^1/_4 \pm 1/_2$	$1/_{32}$ to $3/_{16}$	37	32	$8^7/_8$
	Colt Sta. Wagon	$2^5/_8 \pm 1/_2$	$1^1/_4 \pm 1/_2$	$1/_{32}$ to $3/_{16}$	37	32	$8^7/_8$
'81–'83	Challenger, Sapporo	$2^{11}/_{16}$	$1^3/_{16}$	0 to $1/_8$	37	32	$9^1/_2$
'84–'85	Conquest	$5^5/_{16}$	0	$1/_8$ to $1/_{32}$	39	31	—

WHEEL ALIGNMENT
Front Wheel Drive Cars

Year	Model	Caster (degrees)	Camber (degrees)	Toe-in (in.)	Steering Angle Inner Wheel (degrees)	Outer Wheel (degrees)	King Pin Angle (degrees)
'79–'83	All	$^{13}/_{16} \pm 5/_{16}$	$1/_2 \pm 1/_2$	$3/_{32}$ in to $1/_{32}$ out	$35^{11}/_{16}$	$29^5/_{16}$	$12^{11}/_{16}$
'84–'85	Colt	$^{13}/_{16} \pm 5/_{16}$	$1/_2 \pm 1/_2$	$3/_{32}$ in to $1/_{32}$ out	$35^{11}/_{16}$	$29^5/_{16}$	$12^{11}/_{16}$
	Colt Vista	$^{13}/_{16} \pm 1/_2$	$^7/_{16} \pm 1/_2$	$0 \pm 3/_{16}$	—	—	—

TUNE-UP PROCEDURES

NOTE: For all procedures involving the 1984 and later Conquest, please refer to the Starion procedures in the Mitsubishi section.

Spark Plugs

REMOVAL & INSTALLATION

NOTE: Before removing spark plugs clean any dirt from the base area of the spark plugs with compressed air or a stiff brush.

—— CAUTION ——

Grasp the plug wire by the boot and twist slightly to loosen, before pulling on the boot (not the wire) to remove the wire from the spark plug. Bending or pulling on the wire breaks the internal conductive material.

1. Mark or tag the wires for correct reinstallation, then remove the wires from the spark plugs.
2. Using a $^{13}/_{16}$ inch deep-well spark-plug socket and a swivel head rachet type wrench, remove the spark plugs.
3. Inspect spark plugs for cracked and damaged insulators or threads, worn electrodes, damaged gasket and carbon or other fouling deposits.
4. If plugs are to be reused, file the electrodes square.
5. Regap old spark plugs or check the gap on new spark plugs with a wire feeler gauge.
6. Install the spark plugs in the head and torque to 18–21 ft. lbs. (25–28 Nm).
7. Install the plug wires on the proper spark plug.

Breaker Points and Condenser

Snap off the two retaining clips on the distributor cap. Remove the cap and examine it for cracks, deterioration, or carbon tracking. Replace the cap, if necessary, by transferring one wire at a time from the old cap to the new one. Examine the rotor for corrosion or wear. Check the points for pitting and burning. Slight imperfections on the contact surface may be filed off with a point file (fine emery paper will also do), but it is best to replace the breaker point set when tuning. Always replace the condenser when you replace the point set.

To replace the breaker points.
1. Remove the rotor.
2. Observe which screws retain the ground and primary wires. Remove the two retaining screws and lift out the lubricator wick plate and the point set.

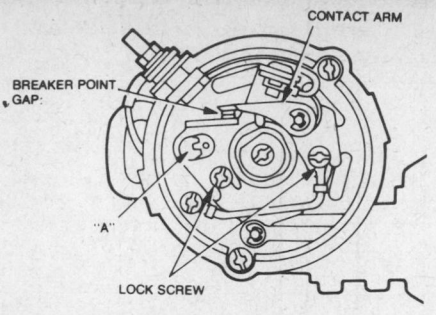

Point gap adjustment is made by twisting a flat bladed screwdriver in slot (A)

3. Install the new point set, making sure that the pin on the bottom engages the hole in the breaker plate.
4. Install the lubricator wick plate, primary and ground wires, and then the two retaining screws (hand-tight).
5. Turn the crankshaft pulley until the breaker arm rubbing block is on the high point of one of the cam lobes.
6. The correct size feeler gauge should just slip through the points. If the gap is incorrect, adjustment is made by inserting a screwdriver in the slot and pivoting it to correct the gap.
7. When the gap is correct, tighten the two retaining screws.
8. Lubricate the distributor cam wick with engine oil or silicone grease.
9. Install the rotor and distributor cap.
10. Check the dwell angle and the ignition timing as outlined in the following sections.
11. The condenser is mounted on the outside of the distributor. Undo the mounting screw and the terminal screw to replace the condenser.

Dwell Angle

The dwell angle or cam angle is the number of degrees that the distributor cam rotates while the points are closed. There is an inverse relationship between dwell angle and point gap. Increasing the point gap will decrease the dwell angle and vice versa. Checking the dwell angle with a meter is a far more accurate method of measuring point opening then the feeler gauge method.

After setting the point gap to specification with a feeler gauge, check the dwell angle with a meter. Attach the dwell meter according to the manufacturer's instruction sheet. The negative lead is grounded and the positive lead is connected to the primary wire that runs from the coil to the distributor. Start the engine, let it idle and reach operating temperature, and observe the dwell on the meter. The reading should fall within the allowable range. If it does not, the gap will have to be reset.

Electronic Ignition System

This system consists of the battery, ignition switch, breaker (pointless type), electronic control unit, spark plugs and wiring. Primary circuit is switched by the electronic control unit responding to timing signals produced by a magnetic pick-up (which replaces the breaker points). Any malfunction in this system should be serviced by a qualified serviceman. The only adjustment necessary is ignition timing, dwell is adjusted electronically. Plug wires, distributor cap and rotor are inspected and serviced as on breaker type distributors.

Ignition Timing

—— CAUTION ——

When performing this or any other adjustment with the engine running, be very careful of the fan belt and pulley.

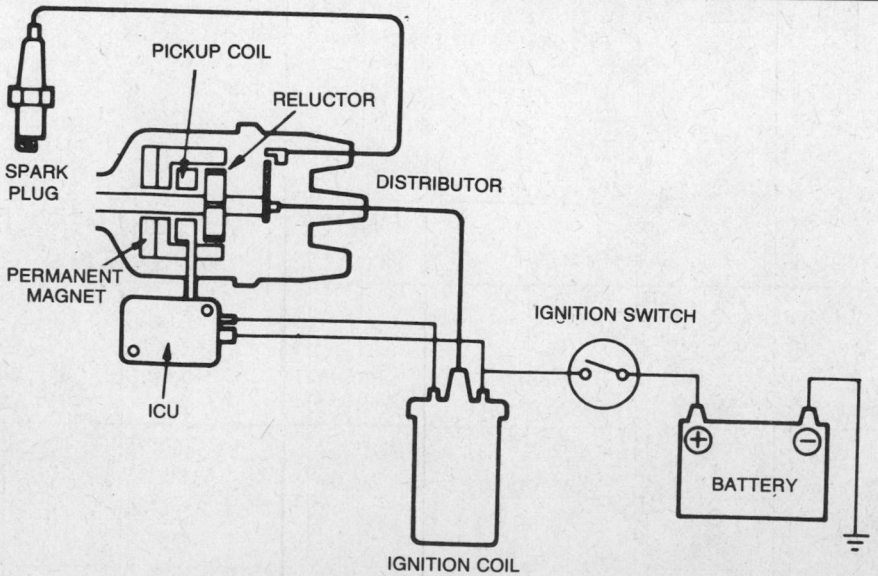

Typical electronic ignition circuit

1977–78

The distributor is equipped with either a single or dual-diaphragm vacuum advance unit, depending upon the locale in which the car is sold, due to emission control regulations.

The retard section of the dual-diaphragm unit is located on the distributor side, with the advance section located on the opposite side of the advance mechanism. The retard section is activated during the engine idle and de–acceleration cycles.

At idle the basic ignition timing is retarded to 5 degrees ATDC by the vacuum retard unit. Basic timing is checked with the rubber plug removed from the advance/retard unit, the vacuum lines are *not* re-

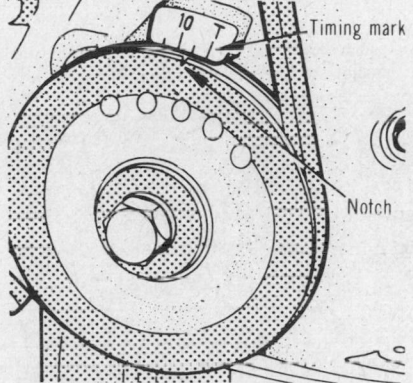

Timing mark—1400cc and 1600cc engines (1984 and later 2000cc similar)

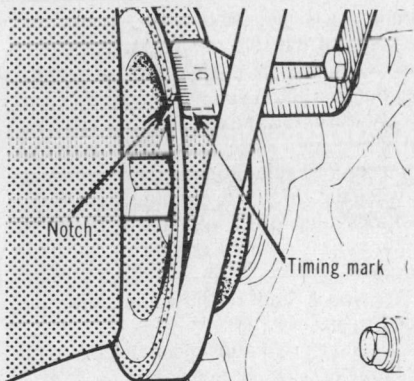

Timing mark—1978–83 2000cc engine (2600cc similar)

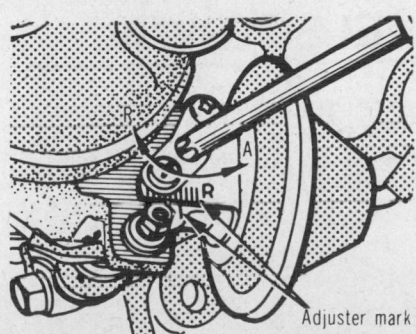

Vacuum advance adjustment

moved and plugged as on the single unit diaphragm equipped distributor.

To adjust the timing:

1. Attach the timing light according to the instructions that came with the light.
2. Locate the timing tab line on the front of the engine and the notch on the crankshaft pulley. Mark them with chalk.
3. Remove the rubber plug on dual diaphragm unit, or remove and plug the line on single units.
4. Start the engine and allow it to reach operating temperature.
5. Shine the timing light at the crankshaft pulley marks. The marked line should align with the pulley notch.
6. If the marks do not align, loosen the distributor mounting nut and rotate the distributor slowly in either direction to align the timing marks.
7. Tighten the mounting nut when the ignition timing is correct.
8. Replace the rubber plug (dual diaphragm) and check the retarded timing. Adjustment is made by loosening the two diaphragm mounting screws and turning the phillips adjusting screw as necessary to bring timing into specs. Shut off the engine and remove the timing light.

1979 and Later

Point fired or electronic ignition:

1. Attach the timing light according to the instructions that came with the light.
2. Locate the timing tab line on the front of the engine and the notch on the crankshaft pulley. Mark them with chalk.
3. Start the engine and allow it to reach operating temperature.
4. Shine the timing light at the crankshaft pulley marks. The marked line should align with the pulley notch.
5. If the marks do not align, loosen the distributor mounting nut and rotate the distributor slowly in either direction to align the timing marks.
6. Tighten the mounting nut when the ignition timing is correct. Shut off the engine and remove the timing light.

Valve Lash

ADJUSTMENT

NOTE: A jet valve is added (from 1978) on USA models. The jet valve adjuster is located on the intake valve rocker arm and must be adjusted before the intake valve.

1. Start the engine and allow it to reach normal operating temperature.

NOTE: Do not run the engine with the rocker arm cover removed—oil will be sprayed on to the hot exhaust manifold.

2. Shut off engine and remove the rocker arm cover.
3. Watch the valve operation on No. 1 cylinder (No. 1 cylinder on transverse mounted engines is on the driver's side) while turning the crankshaft to close the exhaust valve and have the intake valve just begin to open. This places the No. 4 cylinder on TDC of its firing stroke and permits the adjustment of the valves.

Exhaust Valve Closing	Adjust
No. 1 cylinder	No. 4 cylinder valves
No. 2 cylinder	No. 3 cylinder valves
No. 3 cylinder	No. 2 cylinder valves
No. 4 cylinder	No. 1 cylinder valves

NOTE: On 1980 and later front wheel drive models with the "K" engine (1600 cc) a crankshaft pulley access hole is located on the left side fender shield. Remove the covering plug and use a ratchet extension to turn the crankshaft when adjusting the valves.

4. Jet valves must be adjusted before the intake valve.

To adjust the jet valves:

a. Loosen the intake valve lock nut

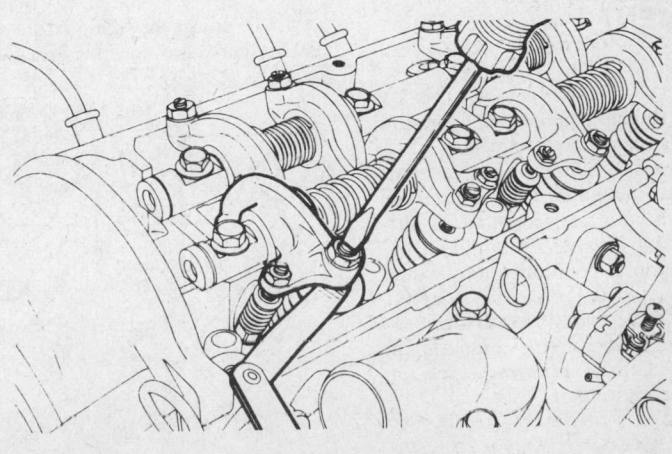

Adjusting valve clearance all engines

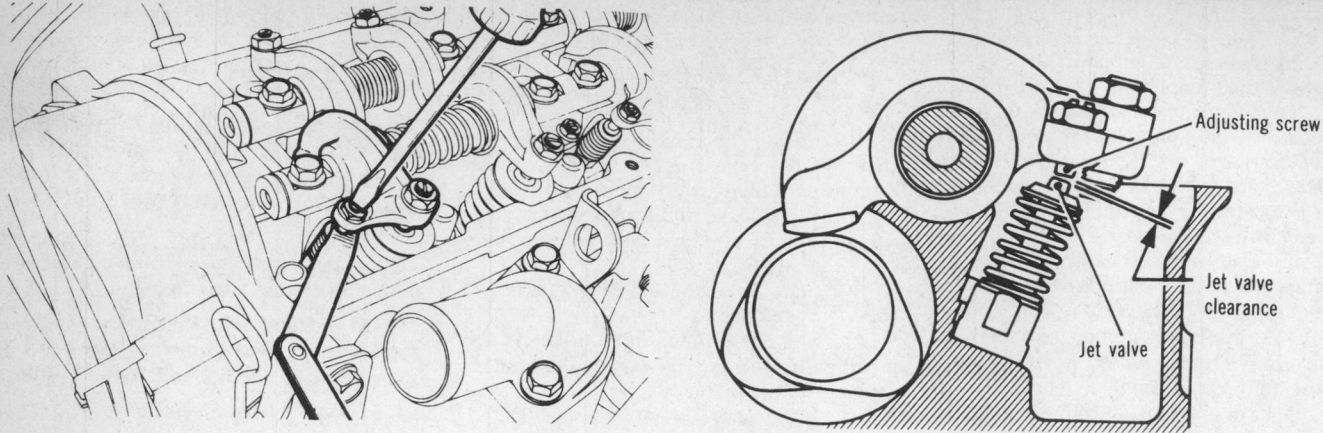

Jet valve clearance adjustment

and back off the adjustment screw two or more turns.

b. Loosen the lock nut on the jet valve adjusting screw. Turn the jet valve adjusting screw counterclockwise and insert a 0.006 in. feeler gauge between the valve stem and the adjusting screw.

c. Tighten the adjusting screw until it touches the feeler gauge.

NOTE: The jet valve spring is weak, be careful not to force the jet valve in.

d. After adjustment is made, hold the adjusting screw with a screwdriver and tighten the lock nut.

5. Proceed to adjust the intake and the exhaust valves on the same cylinder as the jet valve you finished adjusting. Adjust by loosening the locknut and passing a feeler gauge of the correct thickness between the bottom of the rocker arm and top of the valve stem. If the clearance is too great or too small, turn the adjusting screw until the gauge will pass through with a slight drag. Tighten the locknut and proceed to the next valve. Refer to the chart in Step 3 for the adjusting sequence.

Idle Speed

ADJUSTMENT

1978–81

1. Have the engine at normal operating temperature. Connect a tachometer.

2. Position the manual altitude compensator knob (if equipped) with the lugs and the slot in a vertical position for altitudes over 4000 ft. and the lugs and the slot in a horizontal position for less than 4000 ft.

3. Adjust the engine speed to the specifications listed on the engine compartment sticker, using the idle adjusting screw on the base of the carburetor.

1982 and Later

Set the idle with all accessories off and the transmission in neutral.

1. Run the engine until normal operating temperature is reached.

2. Run the engine at 2,000–3,000 rpm for over 5 seconds, then run the engine at idle for 2 minutes.

3. Using a tachometer, set the idle to specifications, using the idle screw on the base of the carburetor.

Mixture

ADJUSTMENT

1. Start and run the engine at idle until normal operating temperature is reached.

2. Check the underhood decal for the correct curb idle speed.

3. Connect a tachometer (follow the instructions that came with the meter) and adjust the idle speed screw until the correct rpm is reached.

4. Idle mixture adjustments should only be made using a CO meter. However, a small amount of adjustment is possible (within the limits of the idle mixture screw limiter cap which must not be removed).

NOTE: Some late model carburetors have a tamper-proof, sealed idle mixture screw.

5. To adjust the idle mixture; first, adjust the curb idle speed. Next, watch the

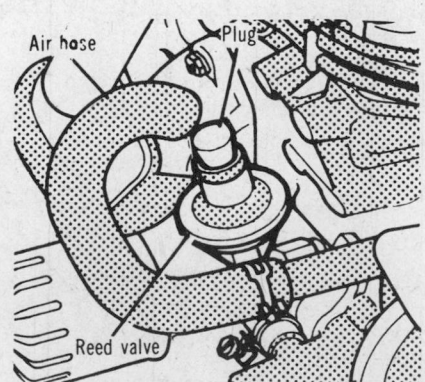

Air hose removal (typical)

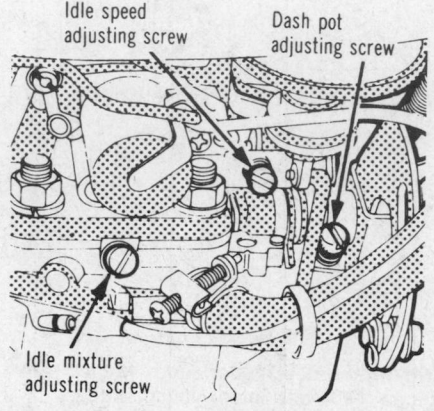

Idle speed adjusting screw

tachometer scale, listen to the engine and slowly turn the idle mixture screw clockwise. A drop in engine rpm or engine roughness will tell you when to stop. Then, slowly turn the mixture screw counterclockwise until once again you encounter rpm drop or engine roughness. A point in-between the clockwise or counterclockwise positions, that gives you the highest rpm or smoothest running engine, is the best setting.

6. Check and readjust the curb idle speed, if necessary.

7. Have your adjustment checked with a CO meter as soon as possible.

ENGINE ELECTRICAL

NOTE: For all procedures involving the 1984 and later Conquest, please refer to the Starion procedures in the Mitsubishi section.

Distributor

REMOVAL & INSTALLATION

Although the distributor can be removed

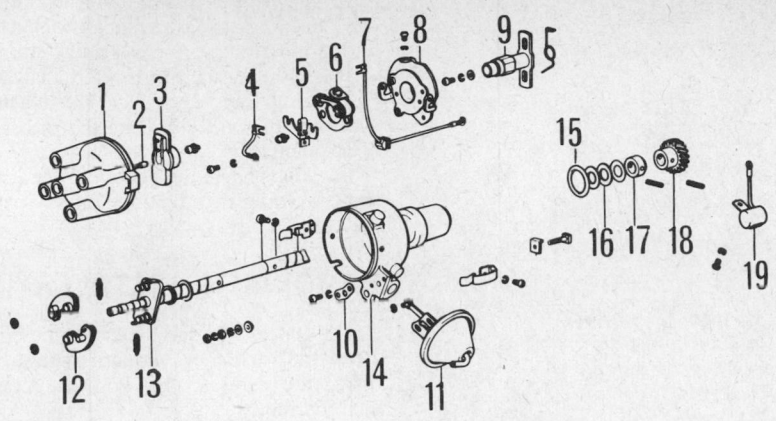

1. Cap
2. Carbon
3. Rotor
4. Ground wire
5. Cam felt
6. Arm support
7. Lead wire
8. Breaker base
9. Cam
10. Locking plate
11. Vacuum control
12. Governor weight
13. Shaft
14. Housing
15. O-ring
16. Washer
17. Thrust collar
18. Gear
19. Condenser

Exploded view of the distributor—typical through 1983

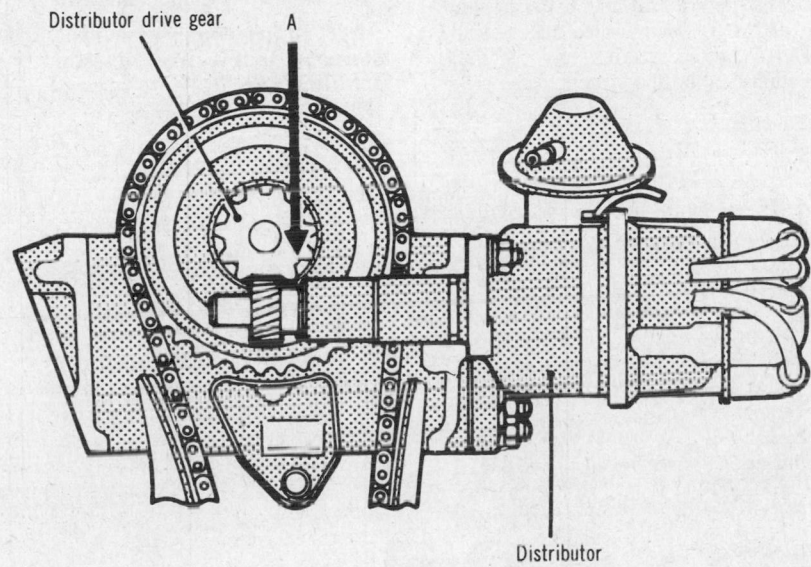

Distributor installation—cylinder head mounted distributors

of removal. Carefully align the match-marks. Always check the ignition timing whenever the distributor has been removed.

If the engine has been disturbed, i.e. rotated while the distributor was out, proceed as follows:

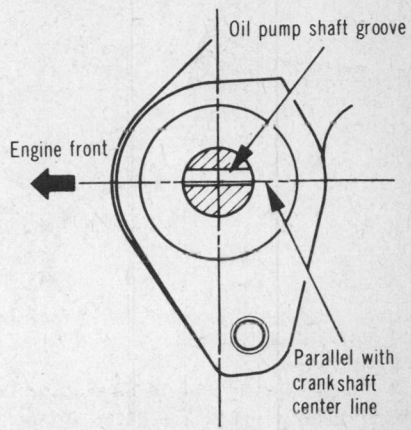

Positioning the oil pump driveshaft groove—1978–83 2000cc engine

7. Turn the crankshaft so that the No. 1 piston is on the compression stroke and the timing marks are aligned.

8. Turn the distributor shaft so that the rotor points approximately 15 degrees before the rotor position that you marked on the distributor.

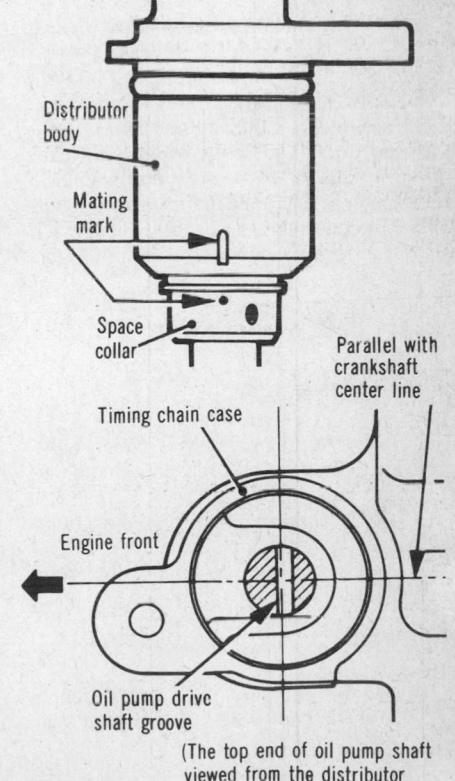

1600cc block mounted distributor installation

from the engine no matter which cylinder is about to fire, it is a good idea to have No. 1 cylinder at TDC on the compression stroke and the timing marks aligned before distributor removal.

1. Unsnap the two clips or unfasten (press down and turn clockwise) the two screws that hold on the distributor cap. Position the cap out of the way or remove the spark plug wires from the spark plugs (twist and pull on the boots), the coil wire from the coil and remove the cap and wires from the car.

2. Turn the engine (use a wrench on the crank pulley or bump the starter) until the rotor points to the No. 1 cylinder position and the timing marks on the crankshaft pulley and the timing tab are aligned at TDC.

3. Mark the distributor body to the exact place the rotor points. Matchmark both the distributor mounting flange and the engine block.

4. Disconnect the negative battery cable from the battery.

5. Disconnect the distributor primary wire or wiring harness. Remove the vacuum line (lines) from the advance unit. Loosen and remove the retaining nut from the mounting stud. Lift the distributor straight from the engine. The rotor may turn away slightly from your mark on the distributor body, make note of how far. When you reinstall the distributor this is the point to position the rotor.

6. If the engine has not been disturbed, i.e. the crankshaft was not turned, then reinstall the distributor in the reverse order

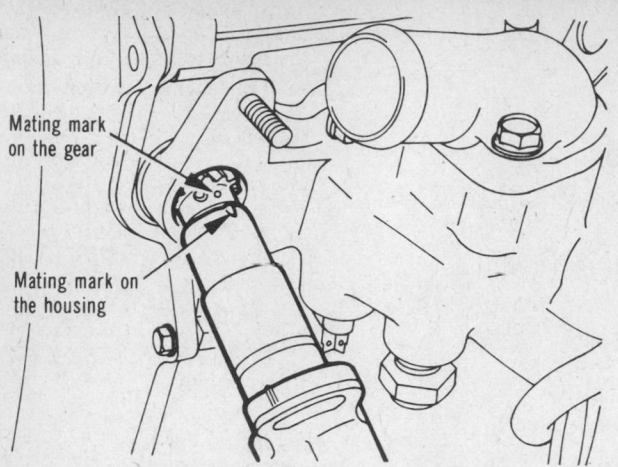

Aligning mating marks for installation of cylinder head mounted distributors

If you did not mark the distributor, line up the factory marks on the shaft and housing.

9. Insert the distributor into the engine. On block-mounted distributors, if you meet resistance and slight wiggling of the rotor shaft does not help seat the distributor, the oil pump gear is probably out of alignment.

NOTE: Do not force the distributor.

Remove the distributor, and using a long screwdriver, turn the oil pump shaft so that it is vertical to the centerline of the crankshaft on 1600cc engines; parallel on 2000cc engines.

10. When the distributor seats against the engine block or head, align the matchmarks and install the retaining nut. Do not tighten the retaining nut all the way, you still have to check the engine timing. Reinstall the rotor, cap, plug wires, coil lead, primary lead (or harness) and connect the vacuum hoses. Connect the negative battery cable. Start the engine, allow it to reach operating temperature and check the ignition timing.

Alternator

PRECAUTIONS

There are several precautions which must be strictly observed in order to avoid damaging the unit. They are:

1. Reversing the battery connections will result in damage to the diodes.

2. Booster batteries should be connected from negative to ground on dead vehicle, and positive to positive.

3. Never use a fast charger as a booster to start the car.

4. When servicing the battery with a fast charger, always disconnect the car battery cables.

5. Never attempt to polarize an alternator.

6. Avoid long soldering times when replacing diodes or transistors. Prolonged heat is damaging to alternators.

7. Do not use test lamps of more than 12 volts (V) for checking diode continuity.

8. Do not short across or ground any of the terminals on the alternator.

9. The polarity of the battery, alternator, and regulator must be matched and considered before making any electrical connections within the system.

10. Never operate the alternator on an open circuit. Make sure that all connections within the circuit are clean and tight.

11. Disconnect the battery terminals when performing any service on the electrical system. This will eliminate the possibility of accidental reversal of polarity.

12. Disconnect the battery ground cable if arc welding is to be done on any part of the car.

REMOVAL & INSTALLATION

1. Disconnect the battery cables (negative first) and the alternator wires. Note or tag the wires so that you can reinstall them correctly.

2. Loosen and remove the top mounting bolt.

3. Loosen the elongated lower mounting nut. Slide the alternator over in its attaching bracket and remove the fan belt.

4. Remove the lower mounting nut and bolt, being sure not to lose any mounting shims (if equipped).

5. Remove the alternator.

NOTE: Remember when installing the alternator that it is not necessary to polarize the system.

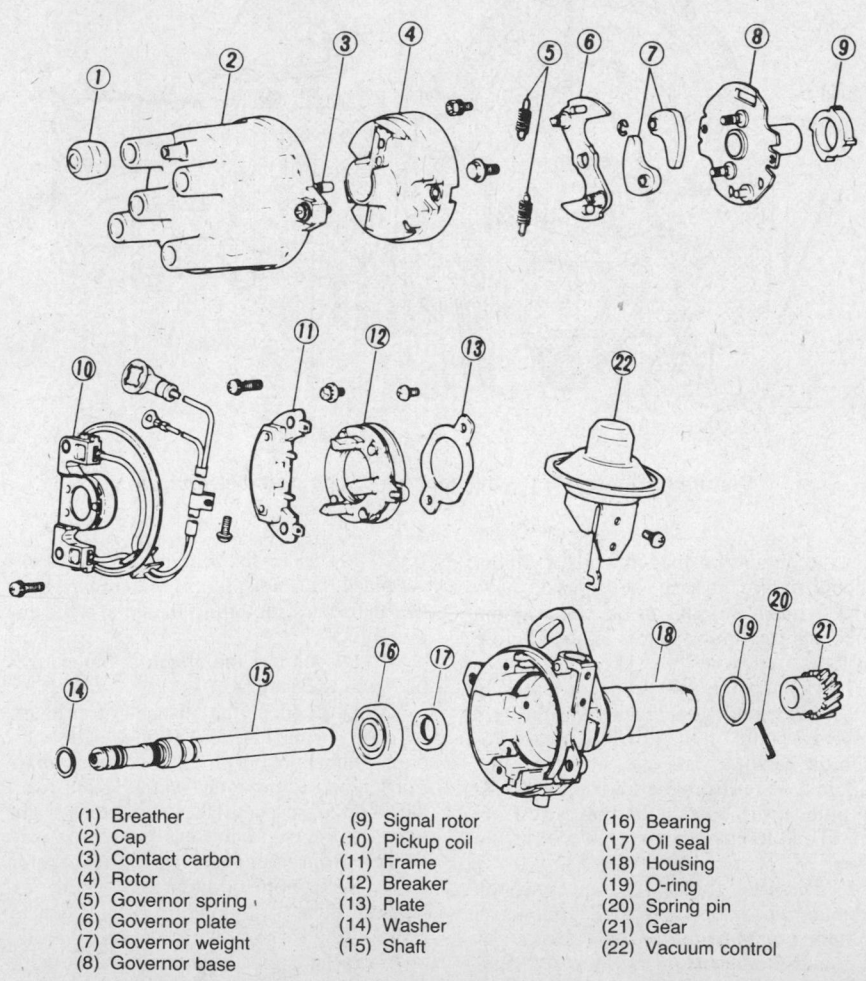

(1) Breather	(9) Signal rotor
(2) Cap	(10) Pickup coil
(3) Contact carbon	(11) Frame
(4) Rotor	(12) Breaker
(5) Governor spring	(13) Plate
(6) Governor plate	(14) Washer
(7) Governor weight	(15) Shaft
(8) Governor base	

(16) Bearing
(17) Oil seal
(18) Housing
(19) O-ring
(20) Spring pin
(21) Gear
(22) Vacuum control

Exploded view of distributor, models with turbocharger—1984 and later

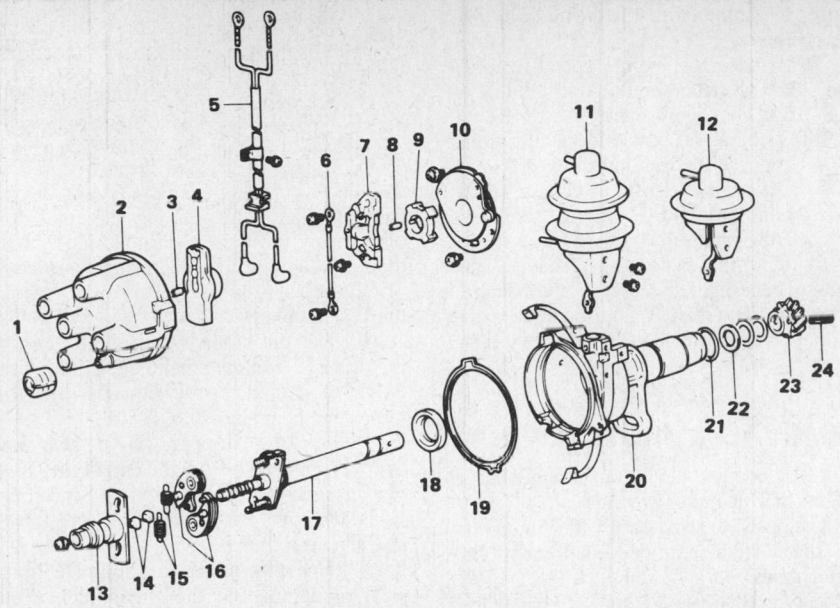

1. Breather
2. Cap
3. Contact carbon
4. Rotor
5. Lead wire
6. Earth wire
7. Igniter
8. Pin
9. Rotor
10. Breaker base
11. Vacuum controller for dual diaphragm
12. Vacuum controller for single diaphragm
13. Rotor shaft
14. Spring retainer (2)
15. Governor spring (2)
16. Governor weight (2)
17. Distributor shaft
18. Oil seal
19. Packing
20. Distributor housing
21. O-ring
22. Washer
23. Gear
24. Pin

Exploded view of distributor, models without turbocharger—1984 and later

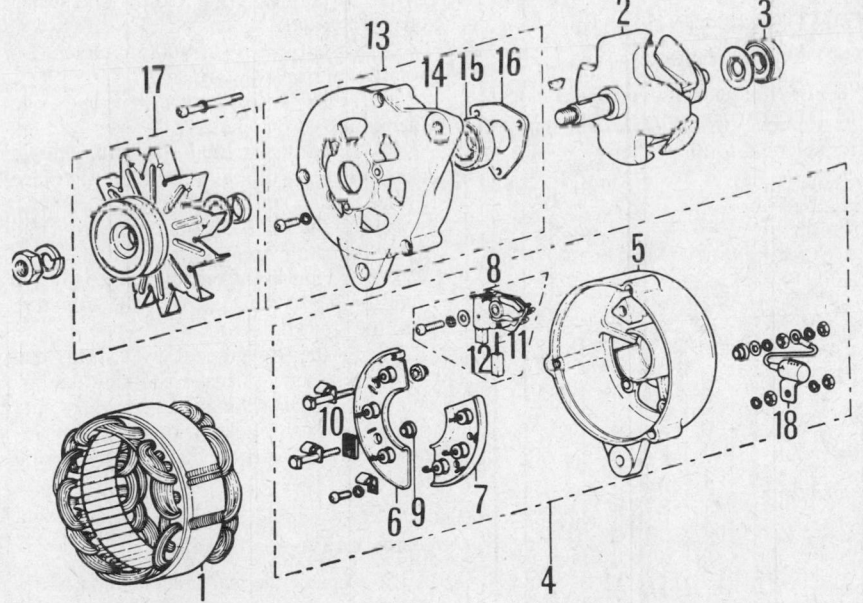

1. Stator
2. Rotor
3. Ball bearing
4. Rear bracket assembly
5. Rear bracket
6. Heat sink complete (+)
7. Heat sink complete (−)
8. Brush holder assembly
9. Insulator
10. Insulator
11. Brush spring
12. Brush
13. Front bracket assembly
14. Front bracket
15. Ball bearing
16. Bearing retainer
17. Pulley
18. Condenser

Exploded view of the typical alternator

6. Trial fit the alternator on the engine. The shims are installed on the inside of both alternator mounting legs. Add more shims, if necessary, for a tight fit.

7. Install the lower mounting bolt and nut. Do not completely tighten it yet.

8. Fit the fan belt over the alternator and crankshaft pulleys.

9. Loosely install the top mounting bolt and pivot the alternator over until the fan belt is correctly tensioned as outlined in the next procedure.

10. Finally tighten the top and bottom bolts.

11. Connect the alternator wires and the battery cables.

BELT REPLACEMENT AND TENSIONING

1. Check the drive belt(s) for cracking, fraying, and any other deterioration. Replace it if it is at all suspect.

2. To replace the belt, loosen the mounting bolts and pivot the driven component in its bracket. Remove the old belt and slip the replacement belt over the pulleys.

3. Move the drive component over until the belt can be deflected ¼ to ⅜ inch at its midpoint.

4. Tighten the mounting bolts.

Regulator

REMOVAL & INSTALLATION

The voltage regulator, on late models, is a solid state unit built into or mounted on the alternator. The regulator is non-adjustable and is serviced, when necessary, by replacement.

1. On non–solid state regulators, disconnect the ground cable from the battery.

2. Disconnect the electrical connector plug.

3. Loosen and remove the two mounting screws. Remove the regulator.

4. Clean the attaching area for proper grounding of the regulator.

5. Install the regulator. Do not overtighten the mounting screws or you will distort the case.

6. Connect the electrical plug and the battery cable.

——————— CAUTION ———————
Never operate the engine with the regulator disconnected.

ADJUSTMENT

Late model cars have a solid-state regulator built into, or mounted on, the alternator.

1. Connect a voltmeter to the A and E terminals of the regulator connector plug.

NOTE: Do not disconnect the plug.

2. Disconnect one of the battery ter-

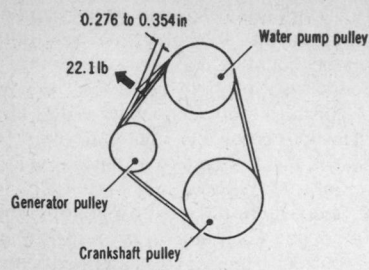

0.276 to 0.354in

Water pump pulley

22.1lb

Generator pulley

Crankshaft pulley

Belt tension adjustment

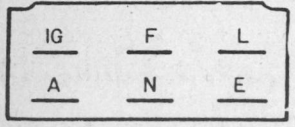

IG	F	L
A	N	E

Regulator terminals

Terminal ID for testing

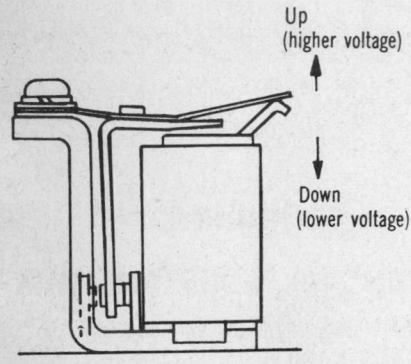

Up
(higher voltage)

Down
(lower voltage)

Adjusting the voltage

minals while the engine is idling to unload the alternator.

3. Increase the engine speed to 2000 rpm. The voltmeter should show a value of 14.3–15.8 V at room temperature.

If the reading is not within specifications:

4. Remove the regulator cover.

5. Adjust the constant voltage relay (located on the left) by bending the end of the coil side plate up or down.

Bending the plate down reduces the voltage, bending it up increases the voltage.

6. The field relay is adjusted in the same manner as the voltage relay.

Starter
REMOVAL & INSTALLATION

1. Disconnect the battery ground cable and the starter motor wiring.

2. Loosen the two starter attaching bolts and brace (if so equipped). Remove the starter motor.

NOTE: With air conditioning or large steering gear box, disconnect the pitman arm from the starter motor attaching bolts and remove the starter from under the car.

3. Position the starter in the housing opening.

4. Install the attaching bolts and brace (if so equipped). Tighten evenly to avoid binding.

5. Install the starter wiring and connect the battery cable.

STARTER OVERHAUL
Direct Drive Stater

NOTE: Starter removed from car

1. Remove the wire connecting the starter solenoid to the starter.

2. Remove the two screws holding the starter solenoid on the starter-drive housing and remove the solenoid.

3. Remove the two long through bolts at the rear of the starter and separate the armature yoke from the armature.

4. Carefully remove the armature and the starter drive engagement lever from the front bracket, after making a mental note of the way they are positioned along with the attendant spring and spring retainer.

5. Loosen the two screws and remove the rear bracket.

6. Tap the stopper ring at the end of the drive gear engagement shaft in towards the drive gear to expose the snap ring. Remove the snap ring.

7. Pull the stopper, drive gear and overrunning clutch from the end of the shaft. For 1979 models with automatic transmissions, remove the center bracket, spring and spring retainer.

Inspect the pinion and spline teeth for wear or damage. If the engagement teeth are damaged, visually check the flywheel ring gear through the starter hole to insure that it is not damaged. It will be necessary to turn the engine over by hand to completely inspect the ring gear.

Check the brushes for wear. Their service limit length is 0.453 in. Replace if necessary.

Assembly is performed in the following manner. For 1979 models with automatic transmissions, fit the spring retainer, spring and center bracket on the shaft.

8. Install the spring retainer and spring on the armature shaft.

9. Install the overrunning clutch assembly on the armature shaft.

10. Fit the stopper ring with its open side facing out on the shaft.

11. Install a new snap ring and, using a gear puller, pull the stopper ring into place over the snap ring.

12. Fit the small washer on the front end of the armature shaft.

13. Fit the engagement lever into the overrunning clutch and refit the armature into the front housing.

14. Fit the engagement lever spring and spring retainer into place and slide the armature yoke over the armature. Make sure you position the yoke with the spring retainer cut-out space in line with the spring retainer.

NOTE: Make sure the brushes are seated on the commutator.

15. Replace the rear bracket and two retainer screws.

16. Install the two though bolts in the end of the yoke.

17. Refit the starter solenoid, making sure you fit the plunger over the engagement lever. Install the screws and connect the wire running from the starter yoke to the starter solenoid.

Reduction Gear Type

NOTE: Starter removed from car.

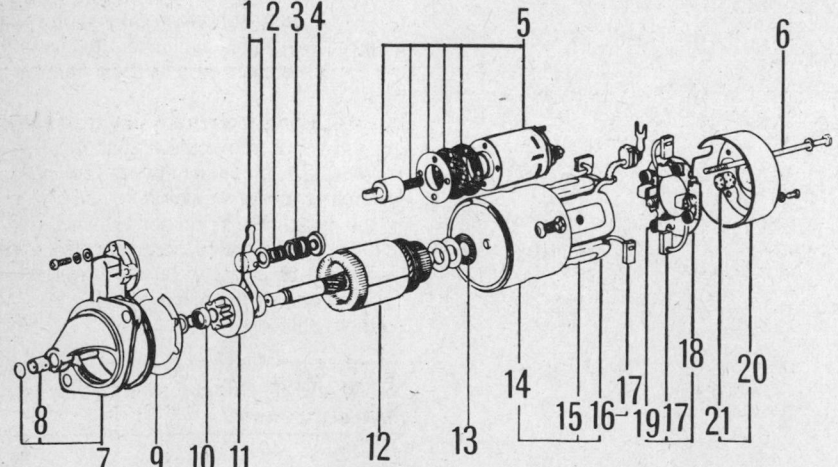

1. Lever assembly
2. Lever spring (A)
3. Lever spring (B)
4. Spring retainer
5. Electromagnetic switch
6. Through bolt
7. Front bracket
8. Front bracket bearing
9. Plate
10. Stop ring
11. Overrunning clutch
12. Armature
13. Insulating washer
14. Yoke assembly
15. Pole piece
16. Field coil
17. Brush
18. Brush holder
19. Brush spring
20. Rear bracket
21. Rear bracket bearing

Exploded view of the typical starter

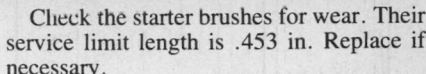

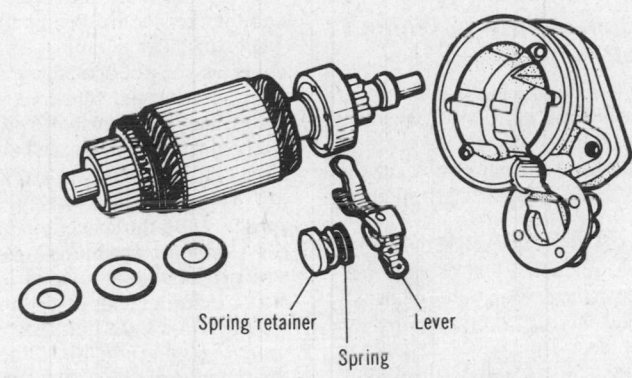

Installing the snap-ring stopper

Check the starter brushes for wear. Their service limit length is .453 in. Replace if necessary.

Assembly is the reverse of disassembly procedure. Be sure to replace all the adjusting and thrust washers that you removed. When replacing the rear bracket, fit the conical spring pinion washer with its convex side facing out. Make sure that the brushes seat themselves on the commutator.

ENGINE MECHANICAL

NOTE: For all procedures involving the 1984 and later Conquest, please refer to the Starion procedures in the Mitsubishi section.

Engine

REMOVAL & INSTALLATION

For engine removal and installation procedures, please refer to the Mitsubishi car section.

Cylinder Head

The timing chain and gear should be attached together in correct timing position and hung on wire except on 1400cc engines where only the timing belt needs to be removed.

--- **CAUTION** ---
Never remove the cylinder head unless the engine is absolutely cold; the cylinder head could warp.

Removing the starter armature and lever

1. Remove the wire connecting the starter solenoid to the starter.

2. Remove the two screws holding the solenoid and, pulling out, unhook it from the engagement lever.

3. Remove the two through bolts in the end of the starter and remove the two bracket screws. Pull off the rear bracket.

NOTE: Since the conical spring washer is contained in the rear bracket, be sure to take it out.

4. Remove the yoke and brush holder assembly while pulling the brush upward.

5. Pull the armature assembly out of the mounting bracket.

6. On the side of the armature mounting bracket there is a small dust shield held on by two screws, remove the shield. Remove the snap ring and washer located under the shield.

7. Remove the remaining bolts in the mounting bracket and separate the reduction case.

NOTE: Several washers will come out of the reduction case when you separate it. These adjust the armature end play; do not lose them.

8. Remove the reduction gear, lever and lever spring from the front bracket.

9. Use a brass drift or a deep socket to knock the stopper ring on the end of the shaft in toward the pinion. Remove the snap ring. Remove the stopper, pinion and pinion shaft assembly.

10. Remove the ball bearings at both ends of the armature.

NOTE: The ball bearings are pressed into the front bracket and are not replaceable. Replace them together with the bracket.

Inspect the pinion and spline teeth for wear or damage. If the pinion drive teeth are damaged, visually check the engine flywheel ring gear. Check the flywheel ring gear by looking through the starter motor mounting hole. It will be necessary to turn the engine over by hand to completely inspect the ring gear.

REMOVAL & INSTALLATION

1. Disconnect the battery ground cable, remove the air cleaner assembly, and the attached hoses.

2. Drain the coolant, remove the upper radiator hose, and the heater hoses.

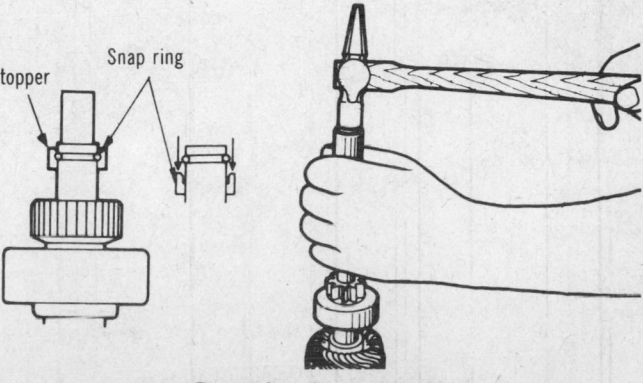

Removing the starter drive

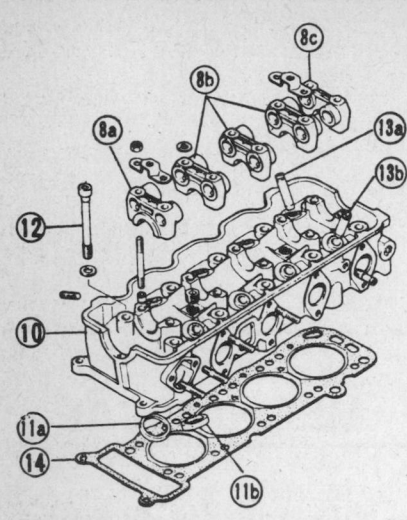

8a. Camshaft bearing cap
8b. No. 2, 3 and 4 caps
8c. Camshaft bearing cap (rear)
10. Cylinder head
11a. Intake valve seat ring
11b. Exhaust valve seat ring
12. Cylinder head bolt
13a. Exhaust valve guide
13b. Intake valve guide
14. Cylinder head gasket

Exploded view of the cylinder head

3. Remove the fuel line, disconnect the accelerator linkage, distributor vacuum lines, purge valve, and water temperature gauge wire.

4. Remove the spark plug wires and the fuel pump. Remove the distributor, where necessary.

5. Disconnect the exhaust pipe from the exhaust manifold flange.

6. Remove the exhaust manifold assembly.

7. Remove the intake manifold and carburetor as a unit.

8. Turn the crankshaft to put No. 1 piston at TDC on the compression stroke.

NOTE: During the following procedures, do not turn the crankshaft after locating TDC.

1400cc Engine

a. Remove the timing belt cover. Be sure that the knockout pin is at 12 o'clock and the cam sprocket mark and cylinder head pointer are aligned at 3 o'clock.

b. Loosen the timing belt tensioner mounting. Move the tensioner toward the water pump and secure it in that position. Remove the timing belt from the pulley.

c. Remove the rocker arm cover.

NOTE: The cam pulley need not be removed.

1600cc Engine—With or Without Silent Shaft

a. Align the timing mark on the upper under cover of the timing belt with that of the camshaft sprocket.

b. Match-mark the timing belt and the timing mark on the camshaft sprocket with a felt tip pen.

c. Remove the sprocket and insert a 2 inch piece of timing belt or other material between the bottom of the camshaft sprocket and the sprocket holder on the timing belt lower front cover, to hold the sprocket and belt so that the valve timing will not be changed.

d. Remove the timing belt upper under cover and the rocker arm cover.

2000cc and 2600cc Engines

a. Remove the rocker arm cover.

b. Position the camshaft sprocket dowel pin at the 12 o'clock position with the crankshaft pulley notch aligned with the timing mark "T" at the front of the timing chain case.

c. Match the timing chain with the timing mark on the camshaft sprocket.

d. Remove the camshaft sprocket bolt, distributor, gear and the sprocket from the camshaft.

All Engines

9. Loosen and remove the cylinder head bolts in two or three stages to avoid cylinder head warpage.

10. Remove the cylinder head from the engine block.

11. Clean the cylinder head and block mating surfaces, and install a new cylinder head gasket.

12. Position the cylinder head on the engine block, engage the dowel pins front and rear, and install the cylinder head bolts.

13. Tighten the head bolts in three stages and then torque to specifications.

14. Install the timing belt upper under cover on the 1600cc engine.

15. Locate the camshaft in original position. Pull the camshaft sprocket and belt or chain upward, and install on the camshaft.

NOTE: If the dowel pin and the dowel pin hole does not line up between the sprocket and the spacer or camshaft, move the camshaft by bumping either of the two projections provided at the rear of No. 2 cylinder exhaust cam of the camshaft, with a light hammer or other tool, until the hole and pin align. Be certain the crankshaft does not turn.

16. Install the camshaft sprocket bolt and the distributor gear, and tighten. (The gear is used on 1977–83 2000cc and 2600cc engines).

17. Install the timing belt upper front cover and spark plug cable support.

18. Apply sealant to the intake manifold gasket on both sides. Position the gasket and install the intake manifold. Tighten the nuts to specifications.

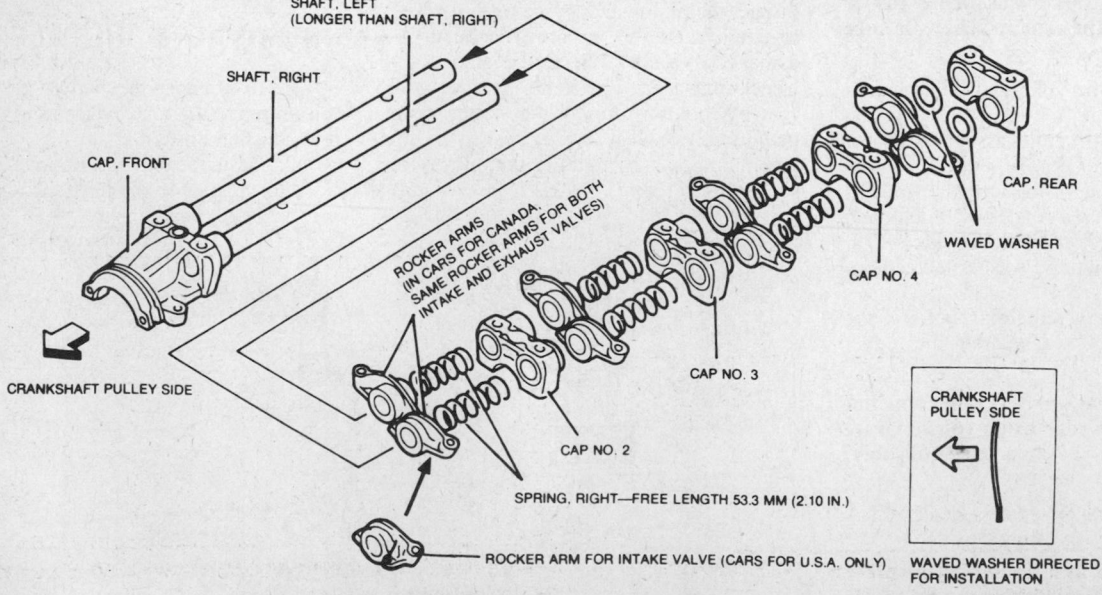

Typical late model rocker arm shaft assembly

— CAUTION —

Be sure that no sealant enters the jet air passages, when equipped.

19. Install the exhaust manifold gaskets and the manifold assembly. Tighten the nuts to specifications.
20. Connect the exhaust pipe to the exhaust manifold and install the fuel pump. Install the purge valve.
21. Install the water temperature gauge wire, heater hoses and the upper radiator hose.
22. Connect the fuel lines, accelerator linkage, vacuum hoses, and the spark plug wires.
23. Fill the cooling system and connect the battery ground cable. Install the distributor.
24. Temporarily adjust the valve clearance to the cold engine specifications.

COLD ENGINE SPECIFICATIONS

	Inch.	MM
Jet valve, if equipped	.003	.07
Intake valve	.003	.07
Exhaust valve	.007	.17

25. Install the gasket on the rocker arm cover and temporarily install the cover on the engine.
26. Start the engine and bring it to normal operating temperature. Stop the engine and remove the rocker arm cover.
27. Adjust the valves to hot engine specifications.

HOT ENGINE SPECIFICATIONS

	Inch	MM
Jet valve, if equipped	.006	.15
Intake valve	.006	.15
Exhaust valve	.010	.25

28. Reinstall the rocker arm cover and tighten securely.
29. Install the air cleaner, hoses, purge valve hose, and any other removed unit.

OVERHAUL

For all cylinder head overhaul procedures, please refer to "Engine Rebuilding" in the Unit Repair section.

Intake Manifold

REMOVAL & INSTALLATION

— CAUTION —

The intake manifold is cast aluminum.

1. Remove the air cleaner.
2. Disconnect the fuel line and EGR lines on models so equipped.
3. Disconnect the throttle positioner solenoid and fuel cut-off solenoid wires.
4. Disconnect the accelerator linkage and, if equipped with automatic transmission, the shift cables at the carburetor.
5. Drain the coolant.
6. Remove the water hose from carburetor and cylinder head.
7. Remove the heater and water outlet hoses.
8. Disconnect the water temperature sending unit.
9. Remove the manifold and carburetor.
10. Clean all mounting surfaces. Before reinstalling the manifold, coat both sides with gasket sealer.

— CAUTION —

If the engine is equipped with the jet air system, take care not to get any sealer into the jet air intake passage.

11. Installation is the reverse of removal.

Exhaust Manifold

REMOVAL & INSTALLATION

1. Remove the carburetor air cleaner assembly.

2. Remove the manifold heat stove and hose. Disconnect the EGR lines and reed valve, if equipped.
3. Disconnect the exhaust pipe bracket from the engine block.
4. Remove the exhaust pipe flange bolts (one bolt and nut may have to be removed from under the car.).
5. Remove the manifold flange stud nuts and remove the manifold from the cylinder head.
6. Installation is the reverse of removal. Port liner gaskets may be used along with the exhaust manifold gaskets on some engine models.

Turbocharger

REMOVAL & INSTALLATION

NOTE: Before disconnecting any of the exhaust system make sure the engine is cool.

1. Remove the heat protector.
2. Remove the oxygen sensor from the catalytic converter.
3. Remove the catalytic converter-to-turbocharger nuts.
4. Disconnect the oil hose from the oil return pipe and timing chain case.
5. Remove the oil pipe from the turbocharger and oil filter bracket.
6. Remove the air intake pipe connecting bolt.
7. Remove the turbocharger mounting nuts and remove the turbocharger from the exhaust manifold.
8. Installation is the reverse of removal with the following precautions:
   a. Torque all parts to specifications (see chart below).
   b. Before installing the oil pipe flare nut (at the top of the turbocharger) pour

Description	Torque ft. lbs. (Nm.)
Turbocharger-to-exhaust manifold	37–50(49–68)
Oil pipe joint	16.5–19.5(22–26)
Oil pipe flare nut	12–17(16–23)
Oil return pipe to turbocharger	6–7(8–9.5)
Catalytic converter to turbocharger	37–50(49–68)
Exhaust manifold to engine	11–14(15–19)
Coolant temperature sensor	22–28(30–39)

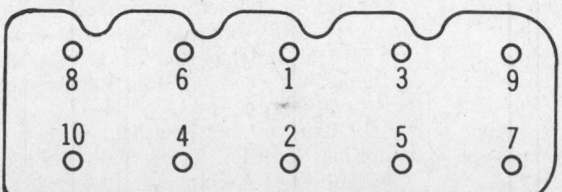

Cylinder head bolt tightening sequence—1400cc, 1600cc and 1984 and later 2000cc engines

Cylinder head bolt tightening sequence—2600cc and 1978–83 2000cc engines

⟵ Front

clean engine oil into the oil pipe feed line hole in the turbocharger.

   c. Securely clamp all oil and air hoses.

   d. Do not reuse a heat damaged, corroded or deformed exhaust manifold gasket or turbocharger gasket (made of stainless steel).

TROUBLESHOOTING

For further details on turbochargers, please refer to "Turbocharging" in the Unit Repair section.

Camshaft and Rocker Arm

REMOVAL & INSTALLATION

All Except 1400cc Engine

1. Match-mark the rocker arm bearing caps to the cylinder head.

2. Remove the bearing cap bolts from the cylinder head, but do not remove them from the bearing caps and shafts. Lift the rocker arm assembly from the cylinder head.

3. Remove the camshaft from the bearing saddles.

NOTE: On some engines, a distributor drive gear and spacer are used on the front of the camshaft.

4. The valves, valve springs, and valve guide seals can now be removed from the cylinder head.

NOTE: Refer to the cylinder head overhaul procedures in the "Engine Rebuilding" section. Valve guides are a shrink fit, with oversize guides available. Valve seats are replaceable, with oversize seats available.

5. The rocker arm assembly can be disassembled by the removal of the bolts from the bearing caps and shafts.

   a. Keep the rocker arms and springs in proper order. The left and right springs have different tension ratings and free lengths.

   b. Observe the location of the mating marks of the right and left rocker arm shaft in relation to the front bearing cap mating marks.

6. Observe the mating marks and reassemble the units in the reverse order of the removal.

1400cc Engine

1. Remove the cylinder head. Remove the cylinder head rear cover.

2. Remove the camshaft thrust case tightening bolt, located on top of the rear mounting boss.

3. Carefully slide the camshaft and thrust case (attached to the rear of the cam) out the rear of the cylinder head.

4. Installation is the reverse of removal. Coat all parts with clean engine oil prior to installation.

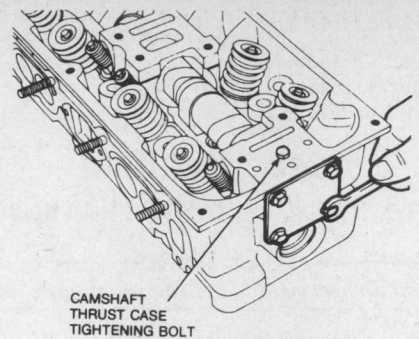

CAMSHAFT
THRUST CASE
TIGHTENING BOLT

Rear cam cover—1400 cc engine

Jet Valves

The jet valve can be removed from the cylinder head with the rocker arm either in place or removed. Care must be exercised not to twist the socket while removing or replacing the valve, so as not to break it. Torque the valve to 13.5–15.5 ft. lbs.

Timing Gear Cover, Chain, Counterbalance Shafts, and Tensioner

NOTE: The timing chain case is cast aluminum, so exercise caution when handling this part.

The following outlines are the recommended removal and installation procedures for the timing chain or belt. Some modifications to the procedures may be necessary due to added accessories, sheetmetal parts, or emission control units and connecting hoses.

REMOVAL & INSTALLATION

1400 Engine—Belt Equipped

1. Turn the engine until the No. 1 piston is on TDC with the timing marks aligned.

2. Disconnect the ground (negative) battery cable.

3. Remove the fan drive belt, the fan blades, spacer and water pump pulley.

4. Remove the timing belt cover.

5. Loosen the timing belt tensioner mounting bolt and move the tensioner toward the water pump. Temporarily secure the tensioner.

6. Remove the crankshaft pulley and slide the belt off of the camshaft and crankshaft drive sprockets.

7. Inspect the drive sprockets for abnormal wear, cracks or damage and replace as necessary. Remove and inspect the tensioner. Check for smooth pulley rotation, excessive play or noise. Replace tensioner if necessary.

8. Reinstall the tensioner, if it was removed, and temporarily secure it close to the water pump.

9. Make sure that the timing mark on

the camshaft sprocket is aligned with the pointer on the cylinder head and that the crankshaft sprocket mark is aligned with the mark on the engine case (see illustration).

10. Install the timing belt on the crankshaft sprocket.

11. Install the belt counterclockwise over the camshaft sprocket making sure there is no play on the tension side of the belt. Adjust the belt fore and aft so that it is centered on the sprockets.

12. Loosen the tensioner from it's temporary position so that the spring pressure will allow it to contact the timing belt.

13. Rotate the crankshaft two complete turns in the normal rotation direction to remove any belt slack. Turn the crankshaft until the timing marks are lined up. If the timing has slipped, remove the belt and repeat the procedure.

14. Tighten the tensioner mounting bolts, slotted side (right) first, then the spring side.

15. Once again rotate the engine two complete revolutions until the timing marks line up. Recheck the belt tension.

NOTE: When the tension side of the timing belt and the tensioner are pushed in horizontally with a moderate force (about 11 lbs.) and the cogged side of the belt covers about a quarter of an inch of the tensioner right side mounting bolt head, (across flats) the tension is correct.

16. Reinstall the timing belt cover, the water pump pulley, spacer, fan blades and drive belt.

17. Connect the battery ground cable.

1600 Engine—Standard
1600 Engine—W/Silent Shaft Belt Equipped

1. Drain the coolant and remove the radiator. Disconnect the battery cable.

2. Remove the alternator and accessory belts.

3. Rotate the crankshaft to bring No. 1 piston to TDC on the compression stroke. Align the notch on the crankshaft pulley with the "T" mark on the timing indicator scale and the timing mark on the upper under cover of the timing belt with the mark on the camshaft sprocket. Mark and remove the distributor.

4. Remove the crankshaft pulley and bolt.

5. Remove the fan blades.

6. Remove the timing belt covers, upper front and lower front.

7. Remove the crankshaft sprocket bolt.

8. Loosen the tensioner mounting nut and bolt. Move the tensioner away from the belt and retighten the nut to keep the tensioner in the off position. Remove the belt.

9. Remove the camshaft sprocket, crankshaft sprocket, flange, and tensioner.

10. Silent shaft engines:

   a. Loosen the counterbalance shaft sprocket mounting bolt.

   b. Remove the belt tensioner and remove the timing belt.

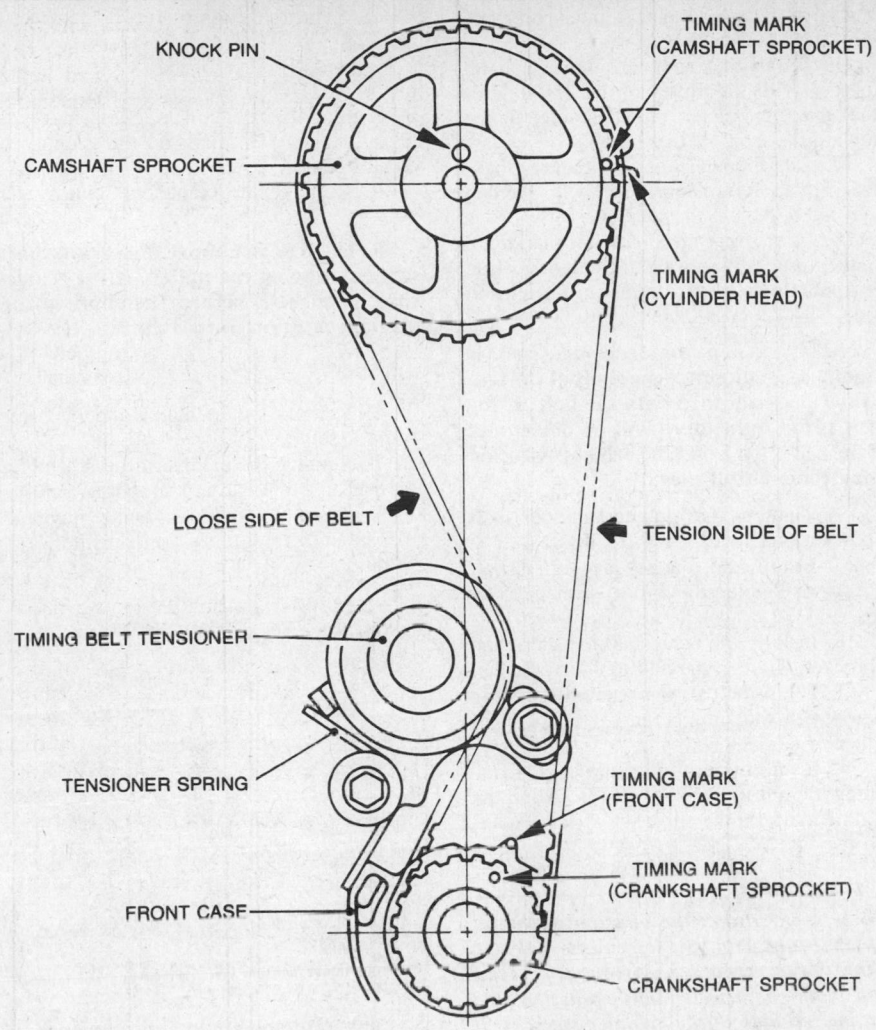

Timing belt system—1400cc engine

c. Remove the crankshaft sprocket (inner) and counterbalance shaft sprocket.

d. Remove the upper and lower under timing belt covers.

11. The water pump or cylinder head may be removed at this point, depending upon the type of repairs needed.

12. Raise the front of the car and support it safely. Remove any interfering splash pans.

13. Drain the oil pan and remove the pan from the block.

14. Remove the oil pump sprocket and cover.

NOTE: On the silent shaft engines, remove the plug at the bottom of the left side of the cylinder block and insert a screwdriver to keep the left counterbalance shaft in position while removing the sprocket nut.

15. Remove the front cover and oil pump as a unit, with the left countershaft attached, if equipped.

16. Remove the oil pump gear and left counterbalance shaft.

NOTE: To aid in removal of the front cover, a driver groove is provided on the

cover, above the oil pump housing. Avoid prying on the thinner parts of the housing flange or hammering on it to remove the case.

17. Remove the right counterbalance shaft from the engine block.

TO INSTALL—STANDARD ENGINE

1. Install a new front seal in the cover. Install a new gasket on the front of the cylinder block and using a seal protector on the front of the crankshaft, install the front cover on the engine block.

2. Tighten the front case mounting bolts to 11–13 ft. lbs.

3. Install the oil screen, and using a new gasket, install the oil pan. Tighten bolts to 4.5–5.5 ft. lbs.

4. If the cylinder head and/or water pump had been removed, reinstall them, using new gaskets.

5. Install the upper and lower under covers.

6. Install the spacer, flange and crankshaft sprocket and tighten the bolt to 43.5–50 ft. lbs.

7. Align the timing mark on the crank-

shaft sprocket with the timing mark on the front case.

8. Align the camshaft sprocket timing mark with the upper under cover timing mark.

9. Install the tensioner spring and tensioner. Temporarily tighten the nut. Install the front end of the tensioner spring (bent at right angles) on the projection of the tensioner and the other end (straight) on the water pump body.

10. Loosen the nut and move the tensioner in the direction of the water pump. Lock it by tightening the nut.

11. Ensure that the sprocket timing marks are aligned, and install the timing belt. The belt should be installed on the crankshaft sprocket, the oil pump sprocket, and then the camshaft sprocket, in that order, while keeping the belt tight.

12. Loosen the tensioner mounting bolt and nut and allow the spring tension to move the tensioner against the belt.

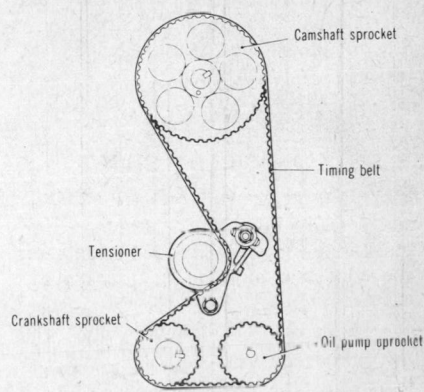

Timing system—1600cc engine

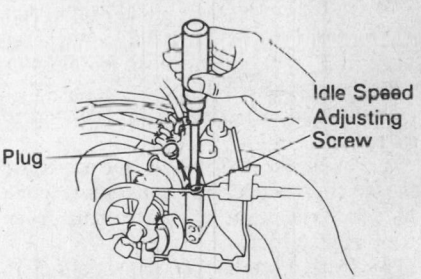

Camshaft sprocket timing mark—1600cc engine

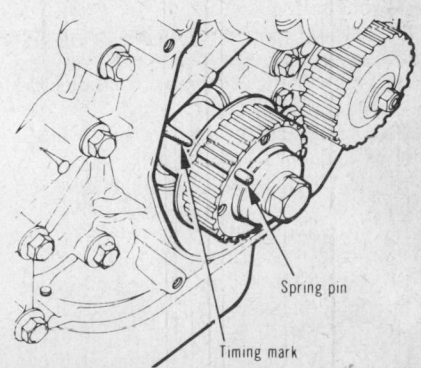

Crankshaft sprocket timing mark—1600cc engine

NOTE: Make sure the belt comes in complete mesh with the sprocket by lightly pushing the tensioner up by hand toward the mounting nut.

13. Tighten the tensioner mounting nut and bolt.

NOTE: Be sure to tighten the nut before tightening the bolt. Too much tension could result from tightening the bolt first.

14. Recheck all sprocket alignments.
15. Turn the crankshaft through a complete rotation in the normal direction.

CAUTION

Do not turn in a reverse direction or shake or push the belt.

16. Loosen the tensioner bolt and nut. Retighten the nut and then the bolt.
17. Install the lower and upper front outer covers.
18. Install the crankshaft pulley and tighten the bolts to 7.5–8.5 ft. lbs.
19. Install the alternator and belt and adjust. Install the distributor.
20. Install the radiator, fill the cooling system, and inspect for leaks.

TO INSTALL—SILENT SHAFT ENGINES

1. Install a new front seal in the cover. Install the oil pump drive and driven gears in the front case, aligning the timing marks on the pump gears.
2. Install the left counterbalance shaft in the driven gear and temporarily tighten the bolt.
3. Install the right counterbalance shaft into the cylinder block.
4. Install an oil seal guide on the end of the crankshaft, and install a new gasket on the front of the engine block for the front cover.
5. Install a new front case packing, if equipped.
6. Insert the left counterbalance shaft into the engine block and at the same time, guide the front cover into place on the front of the engine block.
7. Insert a screwdriver at the bottom of the left side of the block and hold the left counterbalance shaft and tighten the bolt. Install the hole plug.
8. Install an O-ring on the oil pump cover and install it on the front cover.
9. Tighten the oil pump cover bolts and the front cover bolts to 11–13 ft. lbs.
10. Install the oil screen, and using a new gasket, install the oil pan.
11. Install the water pump and/or the cylinder head, if removed previously.
12. Install the upper and lower under covers.
13. Install the spacer on the end of the right counterbalance shaft, with the chamfered edge toward the rear of the engine.
14. Install the counterbalance shaft sprocket and temporarily tighten the bolt.
15. Install the inner crankshaft sprocket

and align the timing marks on the sprockets with those on the front case.

16. Install the inner tensioner (B) with the center of the pulley on the left side of the mounting bolt and with the pulley flange toward the front of the engine.
17. Lift the tensioner by hand, clockwise, to apply tension to the belt. Tighten the bolt to secure the tensioner.
18. Check that all alignment marks are in their proper places and the belt deflection is approximately ¼–½ in. on the tension side.

NOTE: When the tensioner bolt is tightened, make sure the shaft of the tensioner does not turn with the bolt. If the belt is too tight there will be noise, and if the belt is too loose, the belt and sprocket may come out of mesh.

19. Tighten the counterbalance shaft sprocket bolt to 22–28.5 ft. lbs.
20. Install the flange and crankshaft sprocket. Tighten the bolt to 43.5–50.5 ft. lbs.
21. Install the camshaft spacer and sprocket. Tighten the bolt to 44–57 ft. lbs.
22. Align the camshaft sprocket timing mark with the timing mark on the upper inner cover.
23. Install the oil pump sprocket, tightening the nut to 25–28.5 ft. lbs. Align the timing mark on the sprocket with the mark on the case.

CAUTION

To be assured that the phasing of the oil pump sprocket and the left counterbalance shaft is correct, a screwdriver or a metal rod should be inserted in the plugged hole on the left side of the cylinder block. If it can be inserted more than 2⅜ inches, the phasing is correct. If the tool can only be inserted approximately one inch, turn the oil pump sprocket through one turn and realign the timing marks. Keep the screwdriver or metal rod inserted until the installation of the timing belt is completed. Remove the tool from the hole and install the plug, before starting the engine.

24. Refer to Step 9 of the belt installation for the standard engine.
25. If the timing belt is correctly tensioned, there should be about 0.5 in. clearance between the outside of the belt and the edge of the belt cover. This is measured about halfway down the side of the belt opposite the tensioner.
26. Complete the assembly by installing the upper and lower front covers.
27. Install the crankshaft pulley, alternator, and accessory belts, and adjust to specifications.
28. Install the radiator, fill the cooling system, and start the engine.

1600 Engine—Chain Equipped

1. Drain the coolant and remove the radiator. Disconnect the battery ground cable.

2. Remove the alternator and accessory belts.
3. Rotate the crankshaft to bring No. 1 piston to TDC on the compression stroke, by aligning the notch on the crankshaft pulley with the "T" mark on the timing indicator scale.
4. Remove the crankshaft pulley and bolt.

NOTE: Do not move the crankshaft when removing the pulley. If the crankshaft is turned, return the shaft to the original position as in Step 3.

5. Remove the crankshaft pulley and bolt.
6. Remove the fan blades and the water pump assembly.
7. Remove the cylinder head assembly.
8. Raise the car and support it safely.
9. Drain the engine oil and remove the oil pan, oil pressure switch, oil filter, and oil pump.

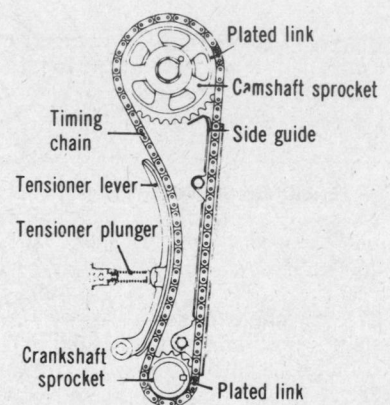

1600 cc timing chain and tensioner

NOTE: Undercar splash pans may have to be removed to gain access to the oil pan.

10. Remove the chain tension holder, spring, and plunger, on the right side of the chain cover.
11. Remove the timing chain cover from the engine block.
12. Remove the oil slinger and crankshaft gear from the crankshaft. Do not misplace the Woodruff key from the crankshaft.
13. Remove the crankshaft and camshaft sprockets with the chain attached, from the engine block.
14. If needed, remove the chain tensioner lever and side guide.
15. If removed, install the chain tensioner lever and the side guide, with the jet of the guide toward the chain and sprocket meshing point.
16. Be sure the No. 1 piston is at TDC. Using a new gasket, install the cylinder head assembly.
17. Rotate the camshaft until the dowel pin is between the 1 and 2 o'clock position.
18. Position the crankshaft sprocket and the camshaft sprocket so that the punch marks on the sprockets align with the chrome or buff plated links of the timing chain.

19. Install the Woodruff key on the crankshaft and while holding the timing chain and sprockets in position, install the sprockets onto the camshaft and the crankshaft.

20. If the dowel pin does not align with the hole in the camshaft sprocket, bump the camshaft on the projections provided to align the two. Install the camshaft sprocket bolt and torque to 36–43 ft. lbs.

NOTE: The chain must be fitted in the guide groove and against the tensioner lever.

21. Install the Woodruff key, crankshaft gear with the "F" mark toward the front. The oil slinger must be installed with its concave side facing the front of the engine.

22. Install a new gasket and seal on the front timing cover case and install the case on the engine block. Torque the bolts to 11–13 ft. lbs.

23. Install the tensioner lever plunger and spring into the case and torque to 29–36 ft. lbs.

—————— CAUTION ——————

Because the timing chain is supported and stretched by the tensioner lever, it is important to align the marks on the sprockets and chain.

24. Install the oil screen and oil pump.

25. Install the oil pan, oil filter, and the oil pressure gauge sender. Fill the oil pan.

26. Reinstall any splash pans and lower the car to the floor.

27. Align the oil pump shaft in a vertical position. Align the distributor marks to fire No. 1 cylinder, and install the distributor.

28. Install the crankshaft pulley and torque the bolt to 43–50 ft. lbs.

29. Install the water pump, fan blades, alternator and belt. Adjust the belt.

30. Install the radiator, add coolant to the system, and connect the battery ground cable.

31. Refer to the "Cylinder Head Installation" section and adjust the valves as for a cold engine. Temporarily install the rocker arm cover, start the engine, and warm it up.

32. Stop the engine and remove the rocker arm cover. Adjust the valves to the hot specifications.

2000 & 2600 Engine—W/Silent Shaft (Chain Equipped)

1. Drain the coolant and remove the radiator. Disconnect the battery ground cable.

2. Remove the alternator and accessory belts.

3. Rotate the crankshaft to bring No. 1 piston to TDC, on the compression stroke.

4. Mark and remove the distributor.

5. Remove the crankshaft pulley.

6. Remove the water pump assembly.

7. Remove the cylinder head, if necessary.

8. Raise the front of the car and support it safely.

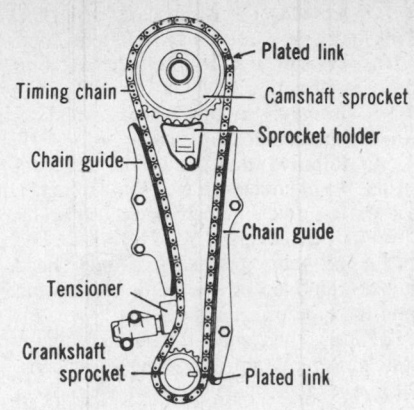

2000 cc timing chain and tensioner

9. Drain the engine oil and remove the oil pan and screen.

10. Remove the timing case cover.

11. Remove the chain guides. Side (A), Top (B), Bottom (C), from the "B" chain (outer).

12. Remove the locking bolts from the "B" chain sprockets.

13. Remove the crankshaft sprocket, counterbalance shaft sprocket and the outer chain.

14. Remove the crankshaft and camshaft sprockets and the "A" (inner) chain.

15. Remove the camshaft sprocket holder and the chain guides, both left and right. Remove the tensioner spring and sleeve from the oil pump.

16. Remove the oil pump by first removing the bolt locking the oil pump driven gear and the right counterbalance shaft, and then remove the oil pump mounting bolts. Remove the counterbalance shaft from the engine block.

NOTE: If the bolt locking the oil pump driven gear and the counterbalance shaft is hard to loosen, remove the oil pump and the shaft as a unit.

17. Remove the left counterbalance shaft

thrust washer and take the shaft from the engine block.

18. Install the right counterbalance shaft into the engine block.

19. Install the oil pump assembly. Do not lose the Woodruff key from the end of the counterbalance shaft. Torque the oil pump mounting bolts to 6–7 ft. lbs.

20. Tighten the counterbalance shaft and the oil pump driven gear mounting bolt.

NOTE: The counterbalance shaft and the oil pump can be installed as a unit, if necessary.

21. Install the left counterbalance shaft into the engine block.

22. Install a new O-ring on the thrust plate and install the unit into the engine block, using a pair of bolts without heads, as alignment guides.

—————— CAUTION ——————

If the thrust plate is turned to align the bolt holes, the O-ring may be damaged.

23. Remove the guide bolts and install the regular bolts into the thrust plate and tighten securely.

24. Rotate the crankshaft to bring No. 1 piston to TDC.

25. Install the cylinder head, if removed.

26. Install the sprocket holder and the right and left chain guides.

27. Install the tensioner spring and sleeve on the oil pump body.

28. Install the camshaft and crankshaft sprockets on the timing chain, aligning the sprocket punch marks to the plated chain links.

29. While holding the sprocket and chain as a unit, install the crankshaft sprocket over the crankshaft and align it with the keyway.

30. Keeping the dowel pin hole on the camshaft in a vertical position, install the camshaft sprocket and chain on the camshaft.

NOTE: The sprocket timing mark and the plated chain link should be at the 2 to 3 o'clock position when correctly installed.

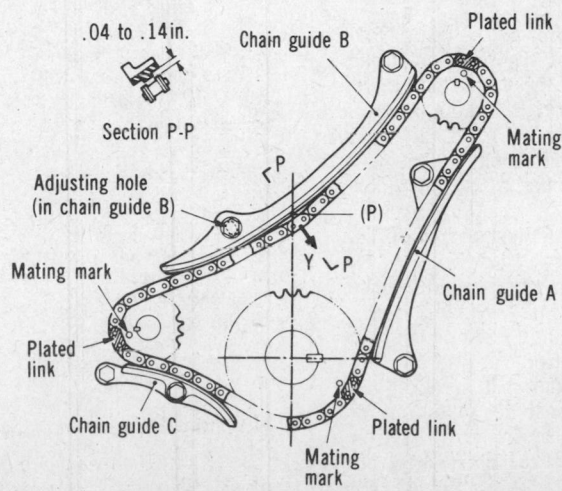

Silent shaft balancing system

---— **CAUTION** ———

The chain must be aligned in the right and left chain guides with the tensioner pushing against the chain. The tension for the inner chain is predetermined by spring tension.

---

31. Install the crankshaft sprocket for the outer or "B" chain.

32. Install the two counterbalance shaft sprockets and align the punched mating marks with the plated links of the chain.

33. Holding the two shaft sprockets and chain, install the outer chain in alignment with the mark on the crankshaft sprocket. Install the shaft sprockets on the counterbalance shaft and the oil pump driver gear. Install the lock bolts and recheck the alignment of the punch marks and the plated links.

34. Temporarily install the chain guides, Side (A), Top (B), and Bottom (C).

35. Tighten Side (A) chain guide securely.

36. Tighten Bottom (B) chain guide securely.

37. Adjust the position of the Top (B) chain guide, after shaking the right and left sprockets to collect any chain slack, so that when the chain is moved toward the center, the clearance between the chain guide and the chain links will be approximately 9/64 inch. Tighten the Top (B) chain guide bolts.

38. Install the timing chain cover using a new gasket, being careful not to damage the front seal.

39. Install the oil screen and the oil pan, using a new gasket. Torque the bolts to 4.5–5.5 ft. lbs.

40. Install the crankshaft pulley, alternator and accessory belts, and the distributor.

41. Install the oil pressure switch, if removed, and install the battery ground cable.

42. Install the fan blades, radiator, fill the system with coolant and start the engine.

2000—Silent Shaft (Belt Driven)

1. Drain the coolant and remove the radiator. Disconnect the battery cable.

2. Remove the alternator and accessory belts.

3. Rotate the crankshaft to bring No. 1 piston to TDC on the compression stroke. Align the notch on the crankshaft pulley with the "T" mark on the timing indicator scale and the timing mark on the upper under cover of the timing belt with the mark on the camshaft sprocket. Mark and remove the distributor.

4. Remove the crankshaft pulley and bolt.

5. Remove the fan and mounting bracket assembly if necessary for working room.

6. Remove the timing belt covers, upper front and lower front.

7. Remove the crankshaft sprocket bolt.

8. Loosen the tensioner mounting nut and bolt. Move the tensioner away from the belt and retighten the nut to keep the tensioner in the off position. Remove the belt.

9. Remove the camshaft sprocket, crankshaft sprocket, flange, and tensioner.

10a. Loosen the counterbalance shaft sprocket mounting bolt.

b. Remove the belt tensioner and remove the timing belt.

c. Remove the crankshaft sprocket (inner) and counterbalance shaft sprocket.

d. Remove the upper and lower under timing belt covers.

11. The water pump or cylinder head may be removed at this point, depending upon the type of repairs needed.

12. Raise the front of the car and support it safely. Remove any interfering splash pans.

13. Drain the oil pan and remove the pan from the block.

14. Remove the oil pump sprocket and cover.

NOTE: Remove the plug at the bottom of the left side of the cylinder block and insert a screwdriver to keep the left counterbalance shaft in position while removing the sprocket nut.

15. Remove the front cover and oil pump as a unit, with the left counter shaft attached, if equipped.

16. Remove the oil pump gear and left counterbalance shaft.

NOTE: To aid in removal of the front cover, a driver groove is provided on the cover, above the oil pump housing. Avoid prying on the thinner parts of the housing flange or hammering on it to remove the case.

17. Remove the right counterbalance shaft from the engine block.

18. Install a new front seal in the cover. Install the oil pump drive and driven gears in the front case, aligning the timing marks on the pump gears.

19. Install the left counterbalance shaft in the driven gear and temporarily tighten the bolt.

20. Install the right counterbalance shaft into the cylinder block.

21. Install an oil seal guide on the end of the crankshaft, and install a new gasket on the front on the engine block for the front cover.

22. Install a new front case packing, if equipped.

23. Insert the left counterbalance shaft into the engine block and at the same time guide the front cover into place on the front of the engine block.

24. Insert a screwdriver at the bottom of the left side of the block and hold the left counterbalance shaft and tighten the bolt. Install the hole plug.

25. Install an O-ring on the oil pump cover and install it on the front cover.

26. Tighten the oil pump cover bolts and the front cover bolts to 11–13 ft. lbs.

27. Install the oil screen, and using a new gasket, install the oil pan.

28. Install the water pump and/or the cylinder head, if remove previously.

29. Install the upper and lower under covers.

30. Install the spacer on the end of the

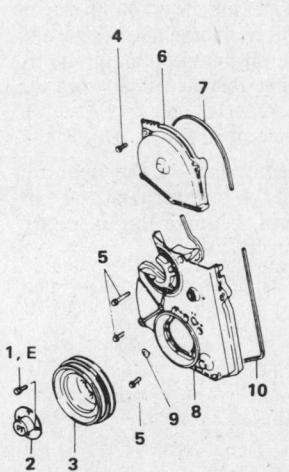
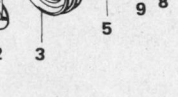
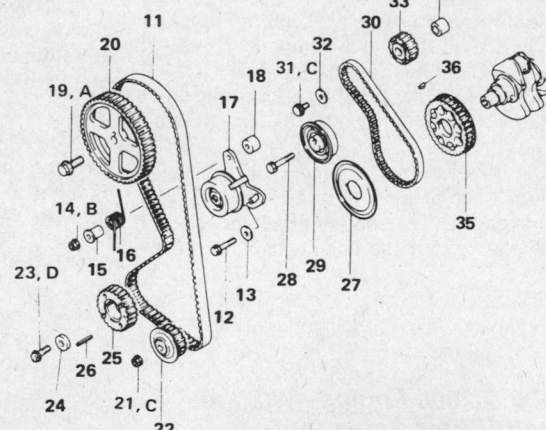

1. Bolt (4)	12. Flange bolt	24. Special washer
2. Cranking adapter	13. Washer	25. Crankshaft sprocket
3. Crankshaft pulley	14. Flange nut	26. Spring pin
4. Flange bolt (8)	15. Spacer	27. Flange
5. Flange bolt (3)	16. Tensioner spring	28. Bolt
6. Timing belt upper cover	17. Tensioner	29. Tensioner "B"
7. Gasket	18. Spacer	30. Timing belt "B"
8. Timing belt lower cover	19. Flange bolt	31. Flange bolt
9. Access cover (2)	20. Camshaft sprocket	32. Washer
10. Gasket	21. Nut	33. Right silent shaft sprocket
11. Timing belt	22. Oil pump sprocket	34. Spacer
	23. Crankshaft sprocket bolt	35. Crankshaft sprocket "B"
		36. Key

Disassembled view of timing belt train—2000cc engine (1984 and later)

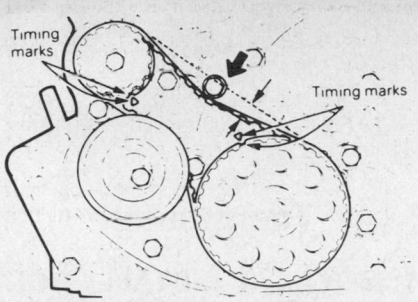

Timing marks—belt "B" (2000cc engine)

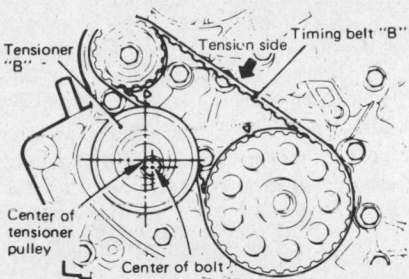

Installation of timing belt and tensioner "B"—2000cc engine

right counterbalance shaft, with the chamfered edge toward the rear of the engine.

31. Install the inner counterbalance shaft sprocket and temporarily tighten the bolt.

32. Install the inner crankshaft sprocket and align the timing marks on the sprockets with those on the front case.

33. Install the inner tensioner (B) with the center of the pulley on the left side of the mounting bolt and with the pulley flange toward the front of the engine.

34. Lift the tensioner by hand, clockwise, to apply tension to the belt. Tighten the bolt to secure the tensioner.

35. Check that all alignment marks are in their proper places and the belt deflection

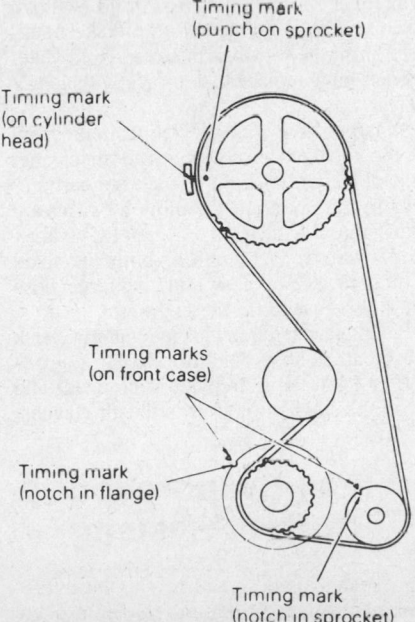

Timing marks—2000cc engine

is approximately ¼–½ inch on the tension side.

NOTE: When the tensioner bolt is tightened, make sure the shaft of the tensioner does not turn with the bolt. If the belt is too tight there will be noise, and if the belt is too loose, the belt and sprocket may come out of mesh.

36. Tighten the counterbalance shaft sprocket bolt to 22–28.5 ft. lbs.

37. Install the flange and crankshaft sprocket. Tighten the bolt to 43.5–50.5 ft. lbs.

38. Install the camshaft spacer and sprocket. Tighten the bolt to 44–57 ft. lbs.

39. Align the camshaft sprocket timing mark with the timing mark on the upper inner cover.

40. Install the oil pump sprocket, tightening the nut to 25–28.5 ft. lbs. Align the timing mark on the sprocket with the mark on the case.

─────── **CAUTION** ───────

To be assured that the phasing of the oil pump sprocket and the left counterbalance shaft is correct, a screwdriver or a metal rod should be inserted in the plugged hole on the left side of the cylinder block. If it can be inserted more than 2⅜ inches, the phasing is correct. If the tool can only be inserted approximately one inch, turn the oil pump sprocket through one turn and realign the timing marks. Keep the screwdriver or metal rod inserted until the installation of the timing belt is completed. Remove the tool from the hole and install the plug, before starting the engine.

41. Install the tensioner spring and tensioner. Temporarily tighten the nut. Install the front end of the tensioner spring (bent at right angles) on the projection of the tensioner and the other end (straight) on the water pump body.

42. If the timing belt is correctly tensioned, there should be about 0.5 in. clearance between the outside of the belt and the edge of the belt cover. This is measured about halfway down the side of the belt opposite the tensioner.

43. Complete the assembly by installing the upper and lower front covers.

44. Install the crankshaft pulley, alternator, and accessory belts, and adjust to specifications.

Pistons and Connecting Rods

REMOVAL & INSTALLATION

For procedures concerning pistons, piston rings and connecting rods, please refer to the Mitsubishi car section.

ENGINE LUBRICATION

NOTE: For all procedures involving the 1984 and later Conquest, please refer to the Starion procedures in the Mitsubishi section.

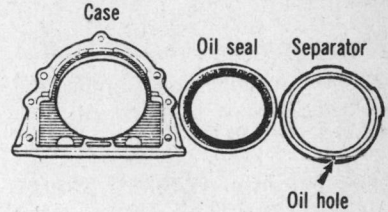

Rear main oil seal

Oil Pan

REMOVAL & INSTALLATION

The engine must be raised off its mount for the pan to clear the suspension crossmember. However, on front wheel drive models there is usually enough room without raising the engine.

1. Remove the underbody splash shield.
2. Unbolt the left and right engine mounts (except front wheel drive).
3. Jack up the engine under the bell housing (except front wheel drive).
4. Remove the oil pan.
5. Installation is the reverse of removal.

Rear Main Oil Seal

REMOVAL & INSTALLATION

The rear main oil seal is located in a housing on the rear of the block. To replace the seal, remove the transmission and do the work from underneath the car (except front wheel drive models) or remove the engine and do the work on the bench.

1. Remove the housing from the block.
2. Remove the separator from the housing.
3. Pry out the oil seal.
4. Lightly oil the replacement seal. The oil seal should be installed so that the seal plate fits into the inner contact surface of the seal case. Install the separator with the oil holes facing down.

Oil Pump

LOCATION

1400cc Engine

A gear drive oil pump is mounted in the front case and driven directly by the crankshaft.

1600cc—Standard (Timing Chain)

A rotor type oil pump is located in the timing chain case and driven by a crankshaft gear.

Standard-(Timing Belt)

A rotor type oil pump is located on the lower left side of the front case, driven by the timing belt.

2000cc Engine—W/Silent Shaft

A gear type oil pump is on the front of the right counterbalance shaft, driven by the timing chain or belt.

2600cc Engine—W/Silent Shaft

A gear type oil pump is on the front of the right counterbalance shaft, driven by the timing chain.

REMOVAL & INSTALLATION

1400cc Engine

1. Remove the timing belt. See "Timing Belt Removal" section.
2. Remove the engine oil pan and oil screen.
3. Remove the front case assembly (seven bolts).

The oil pump is mounted in the rear of the front case. Turn the front case over and remove the oil pump cover. Service as required.

All Other Engines

To remove the rotor type pumps that are located behind the front timing cover, refer to the "Timing Gear Cover, Chain, Counterbalance Shaft and Tensioner" section and follow the procedure to remove the pump.

To remove the oil pumps that are located in the oil pan, the following procedures should be followed.

1. Place No. 1 piston at TDC on the compression stroke.
2. Loosen the left and right engine mounts and raise the engine off the mount brackets.
3. Remove the front splash shields. Drain the oil and remove the oil pan.
4. Remove the screen and the oil pump from the engine block.
5. To install, be sure that No. 1 piston is still on the compression stroke.
6. Remove the distributor cap and make sure the rotor is pointing to the No. 1 position.

NOTE: This should align the distributor pawl parallel with the crankshaft center line.

7. Align the mating marks of the distributor gear and body and insert the oil pump assembly with a new gasket, into the engine block until the oil pump shaft gear is in mesh with the crankshaft gear and is engaged with the distributor pawl.

8. Using a new gasket, install the oil pan, connect the engine mounts, and install the front splash shields.
9. Install the oil, start the engine and check the ignition timing.

COOLING SYSTEM

NOTE: For all procedures involving the 1984 and later Conquest, please refer to the Starion procedures in the Mitsubishi section.

Radiator

REMOVAL & INSTALLATION

1. Remove the splash panel from the bottom of the car. Drain the radiator by opening the petcock. Remove the shroud on models so equipped.
2. Disconnect the radiator hoses at the engine. On automatic transmission cars, disconnect and plug the transmission lines to the bottom of the radiator.
3. Remove the two retaining bolts from either side of the radiator. Lift out the radiator. On front wheel drive models, disconnect the electric fan wiring harness. Do not remove the fan motor, blades or bracket—remove as a unit with the radiator.
4. Install the radiator in the reverse order of removal. Tighten the retaining bolts gradually in a criss-cross pattern.

CAUTION
Work around the electric cooling fan when the engine is cold or disconnect the negative battery cable. The fan will run to cool the engine even when the ignition is off.

Water Pump

REMOVAL & INSTALLATION

1. Drain the cooling system.
2. Remove the fan shroud and radiator if necessary for working room.
3. Remove the alternator belt and accessory belts.
4. On J and K engines:
   a. Place the piston in No. 1 cylinder at TDC of the compression stroke.
   b. Remove the crankshaft pulley, timing belt upper and lower covers, timing belt and timing belt tensioner.
   c. Remove the four water pump mounting bolts and remove the water pump.
5. On U and F engines:
   a. Remove the fan blades and/or automatic hub, if equipped.

b. Remove the water pump assembly from the timing chain case or the cylinder block.
6. Installation is the reverse of removal.
7. Fill the radiator with coolant and test for leaks.

Thermostat

REMOVAL & INSTALLATION

The thermostat is located in the intake manifold under the upper radiator hose.

1. Drain the coolant below the level of the thermostat.
2. Remove the two retaining bolts and lift the thermostat housing off the intake manifold with the hose still attached.

NOTE: If you are careful, it is not necessary to remove the upper radiator hose.

3. Lift the thermostat out of the manifold.
4. Install the thermostat in the reverse order of removal. Use a new gasket and coat the mating surfaces with sealer.

EMISSION CONTROLS

Crankcase Emission Control System

A closed-type crankcase ventilation system is used to prevent engine blow-by gases from escaping into the atmosphere.

A hose connects the rear of the rocker arm cover and the intake manifold. A small fixed orifice is located in the intake manifold or on the rocker arm cover. Some later models have replaced the orifice with a PCV valve.

A larger hose is connected from the front of the rocker arm cover to the air cleaner assembly. Under light to medium carburetor throttle opening, the blow-by gases are drawn through the fixed orifice or PCV valve. Under heavy acceleration, both the fixed orifice or PCV valve and the large hose route the gases into the engine.

Maintenance required is to regularly check the breather hose condition, clean the orifice or PCV valve (replace if clogged) and clean the steel wool filter in the air cleaner.

Fuel Evaporation Control System

This system is designed to prevent hydrocarbons from escaping into the atmosphere from the fuel tank, due to normal evaporation.

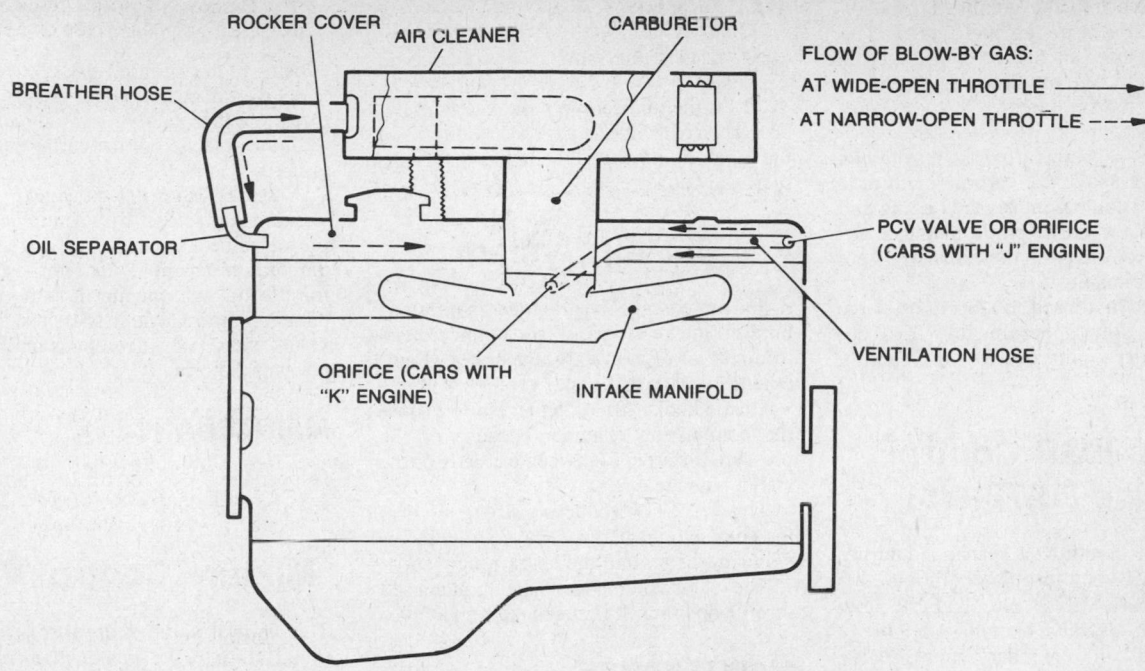

Late model crankcase ventilation system (typical)

The parts of the system are as follow:

Separator Tank—Located near the gasoline tank, used to accommodate expansion, and to allow maximum condensation of the fuel vapors.

Bowl Vent System (1980–85)—Controls carburetor bowl vapors between canister and carburetor.

Carbon Element (1980–85)—Element is located in air cleaner to store vapors generated in the carburetor. Replace if clogged or dirty.

Canister—Either one or two, located in the engine compartment to trap and retain gasoline vapors while the engine is not operating. When the engine is started, fresh air is drawn into the canister, removing the stored vapors, and is directed to the air cleaner.

Two-Way Valve (1978–85)—Because of different methods of tank venting and the use of a sealed gasoline tank cap, the two-way valve is used in the vapor lines. The valve relieves either pressure or vacuum in the tank.

Purge Control Valve (1978–85)—The purge control valve replaces the check valve used in previous years. During idle, the valve closes off the vapor passage to the air cleaner.

Fuel Check Valve (1978–85)—This valve is used to prevent fuel leakage in case of roll over. It is installed in the vapor line between the two-way valve and the canister on the coupe, sedan, and hatchback and between the separator and the two-way valve on the station wagon.

MAINTENANCE

Be sure that all hoses are clamped and not dry-rotted or broken. Check the valves for cracks, signs of gasoline leakage, and proper operating condition.

The canister air filter (if equipped) should be inspected and changed at least every 24,000 miles.

Heated Air Intake System

All models are equipped with a temperature regulated air control valve in the air cleaner snorkel.

When the underhood air temperature is 41 degrees or lower, the air control valve allows preheated air to flow through the heat cowl of the exhaust manifold, via a flexible hose, to the air cleaner and into the carburetor.

When the underhood temperature is 108 degrees or above, the air flow is directed through the air cleaner snorkel.

At intermediate temperatures, the carburetor intake air is a blend of the direct underhood and preheated air.

MAINTENANCE

Visually check the control valve assembly when the engine is cold to be sure that the valve is closed.

Warm up the engine and check that the control valve opens to the outside air.

Secondary Air Supply System

This system supplies air for the further combustion of unburned gases in the thermal reactor (if equipped) or exhaust manifold and consists of a reed valve, air hoses, and air passages built into the cylinder head.

The reed valve is operated by exhaust pulsations in the exhaust manifold. It draws fresh air through the air cleaner and supplies it to the exhaust ports.

MAINTENANCE

Check for damage to the air hoses and air pipes. Make sure the air passages are open in the head.

Pulse Air Feeder System (1981–85)

This system supplies "secondary air" into the exhaust system between the front and rear catalytic converters to promote oxidation of exhaust emissions in the rear converter. The system consists of a main reed valve, a sub–reed valve, air hoses and crankcase passages.

The main reed valve is actuated by pressures created by No. 3 piston. The sub-reed valve is actuated by exhaust pulsations. Fresh air is drawn through the air cleaner.

INSPECTION

Remove the hose connecting the "reed valve" at the air cleaner. Start the engine and check for vacuum in the hose. Check the hose for leaks if no vacuum is felt.

Exhaust Gas Recirculation System

The EGR system recirculates part of the

exhaust gases into the combustion chambers. This dilutes the air/fuel mixture, reducing formation of oxides of nitrogen in the exhaust gases by lowering the peak combustion temperatures.

The parts of the EGR system are:

EGR Valve—Operated by vacuum drawn from a point above the carburetor throttle plate. The vacuum controls the raising and lowering of the valve pintle to allow exhaust gases to pass from the exhaust system to the intake manifold.

Thermo Valve—Used to stop EGR valve operation below approximately 131 degrees, in order to improve cold driveability and starting.

Dual EGR Control Valve (1978–85)

The EGR vacuum flow is suspended during idle and wide open throttle operation.

The primary valve controls EGR flow when the throttle valve opening is relatively narrow, while the secondary control valve operates at wider openings.

Sub-EGR Control Valve—Linked to the throttle valve to closely modulate the EGR gas flow.

EGR Maintenance Warning Light (1978)

A light in the speedometer assembly to alert the driver to the need for EGR system maintenance.

This device has a mileage sensor to light the visual signal at 15,000 mile intervals.

Upon completion of the required EGR system maintenance, the warning light can be turned off by resetting the switch. It is in the speedometer cable, under the instrument panel.

MAINTENANCE

1. Check all vacuum hoses for cracks, breakage and correct installation.
2. Check EGR valve operation by applying vacuum to the EGR valve vacuum nipple with the engine idling. The idle should become rough.
3. Check the passages in the cylinder head and intake manifold for clogging. Clean as necessary.
4. Cold start the engine. The EGR port nipple should be open. When the coolant is warmed to over 131 degrees, the port should be closed.

Catalytic Converter

This unit or units (two used from 1981) replaces the thermal reactor. It is filled with catalyst to oxidize hydrocarbons and carbon monoxide in the exhaust gases.

MAINTENANCE

1. Check the core for cracks and damages.
2. If the idle carbon monoxide and hydrocarbon content exceeds specifications and the ignition timing and idle mixture are correct, the converter must be replaced.

Jet Air System

A jet air passage is provided in the carburetor, intake manifold, and cylinder head to direct air to a jet valve, operated simultaneously with the intake valve.

On the intake stroke, jet air is forced into the combustion chamber because of the pressure difference between the ends of the air jet passage.

This jet of air produces a strong swirl in the combustion chamber scavenging the residual gases around the spark plug.

The jet air volume lessens with increased throttle opening. It is at a maximum at idle.

MAINTENANCE

NOTE: Refer to "Valve Lash Adjustment" for adjusting the jet valve clearance.

No maintenance is required other than clearance adjustment during valve adjustment. The valve can be removed from the cylinder head for service or replacement.

Ignition Timing Control System

When the engine is idling or operating at low speeds under light load or deceleration, the exhaust gas temperature is low, resulting in incomplete combustion of the air/fuel mixture. To prevent this, ignition timing is retarded under these conditions to maintain high exhaust gas temperature.

The units in the Ignition Timing Control system are as follow:

Dual-diaphragm distributor—This distributor has both retard and advance mechanisms operated by vacuum.

Thermo valve—This valve is used to protect the engine from overheating. When coolant temperature reaches 203 degrees, the advance unit is allowed to operate, causing an increase in engine speed and a decrease in coolant temperature.

Single diaphragm distributor—This distributor has a single diaphragm vacuum advance unit, which advances the ignition timing as engine vacuum dictates. The single diaphragm distributor must not be interchanged with the dual diaphragm distributor. The distributor operating curves are different and would cause increased emissions. A thermo valve is *not* used with this type of distributor.

Deceleration Device

Closing of the throttle valve on deceleration is delayed in order to burn the air/fuel mixture more thoroughly. A vacuum controlled dashpot, attached to the carburetor linkage is used.

A servo valve detects intake manifold vacuum and closes if vacuum exceeds a preset value. Since the air in the dashpot diaphragm chamber can not escape, the throttle linkage opening is temporarily retained. If the vacuum is below the preset value, the servo valve opens and the dashpot works normally.

MAINTENANCE

Inspect the hoses for breaks and damage, and the valve body for cracks.

Mixture Control Valve

This control valve is used to supply additional air into the intake manifold to decrease manifold vacuum during deceleration, and is activated by the intake manifold vacuum level.

Manual Altitude Compensation System

An off-on valve is used to increase the air supply to the carburetor to lean the mixture and decrease the EGR flow for high altitude operation.

MAINTENANCE

The required maintenance is to inspect any vacuum hoses and routing for kinks, breakage and cracks. The off-on valve should be on for high altitude and off for driving under 4000 ft.

FUEL SYSTEM

NOTE: For all procedures involving the 1984 and later Conquest, please refer to the Starion procedures in the Mitsubishi section.

Fuel Pump

TESTING

Without Fuel Injection

Disconnect the fuel line from the carburetor and attach a pressure tester to the end of the line. Crank the engine. The tester should agree with the figure given in the "Tune-Up Specifications" chart.

With Fuel Injection

There is a connector for checking the fuel function in the engine compartment, under the battery. The fuel pump can be operated by connecting the terminals with jumper wires.

1. Connect jumper wires to terminals 1 and 2 of fuel pump check connector, and check to ensure that when operating sound of fuel pump can be heard.

2. When no operating sound can be heard, check for defective connector, wiring, etc.

3. If there is nothing wrong with connector and wiring, disconnect the fuel pump connector at the pump and energize the pump. If pump still fails to operate, replace it.

REMOVAL & INSTALLATION

Without Fuel Injection

The pump is mounted on the front side of the engine and is driven by an eccentric on the camshaft.

1. Remove the fuel lines.
2. Unbolt the pump mounting bolts, and remove the pump, insulator, and gasket.
3. Coat both sides of a new insulator and gasket with sealer, and install the pump in the reverse order of removal.

With Fuel Injection

The fuel pump on these models is mounted on the underside of the rear floor.

1. Before disconnecting the fuel lines, the fuel line pressure must be relieved by using the following procedure:

a. Start the engine, then disconnect the electric fuel pump connector.

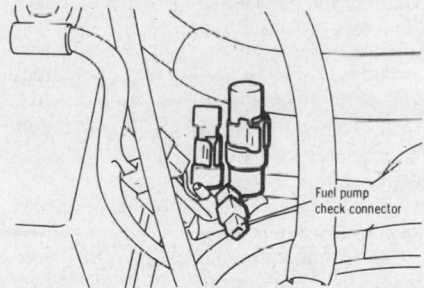

Fuel pump check connector, located in engine compartment—fuel injected models

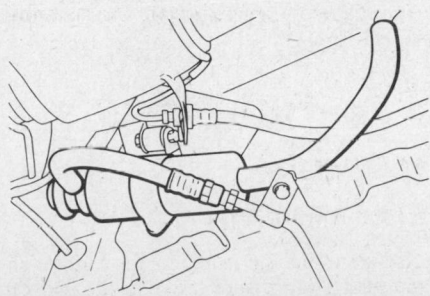

Fuel pump location—fuel injected models

b. Stop the engine, and turn the ignition key to the off position.

c. Disconnect the negative battery cable from the battery.

2. Disconnect the fuel lines and remove the fuel pump.

Fuel Filter

REPLACEMENT

The fuel filter should be replaced every 12,000 miles. The filter is usually located on the left-hand inner fender near the master cylinder. Loosen both hose clamps and remove the lines from the filter. Pull the filter from its bracket and discard it. Snap the replacement filter into the bracket. Install the lines on the filter and tighten the hose clamps. Start the engine and check for leaks.

NOTE: On models with fuel injection (Turbo), relieve fuel system pressure before removing filter. Follow Step 1 of "Fuel Pump Removal," fuel injected engines.

Carburetors

REMOVAL & INSTALLATION

1. Remove the solenoid valve wiring.
2. Disconnect the air cleaner breather hose, air duct and vacuum tube.
3. Remove the air cleaner.
4. Remove the air cleaner case.
5. Disconnect the accelerator and shift cables (automatic transmission) at the carburetor.
6. Disconnect the purge valve hose; remove the vacuum compensator, and fuel lines.
7. Drain the coolant.
8. Remove the water hose between the carburetor and the cylinder head.
9. Remove the carburetor.
10. Installation is the reverse of removal.

OVERHAUL

For all carburetor overhaul procedures, please refer to "Carburetor Service" in the Unit Repair section.

THROTTLE LINKAGE ADJUSTMENT

Adjust the stopper bolt to a distance of .75 ± 0 to 0.04 inch from the inside of the bolt holding bracket, to the contact point of the pedal lever while holding the carburetor throttle plates closed. The yoke at the carburetor end of the accelerator rod is serrated to allow the yoke to be loosened and moved so that a minimal readjustment of the stopper adjusting bolt is needed to give the proper throttle release and opening.

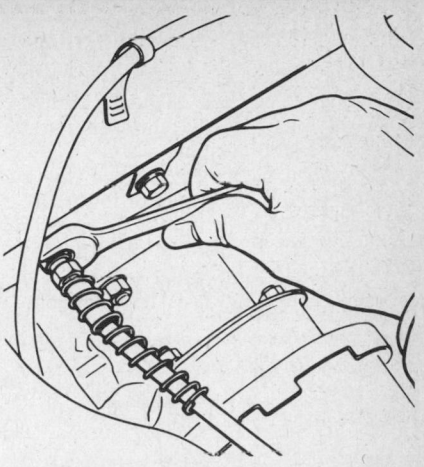

Throttle linkage adjustment (typical)

FLOAT LEVEL ADJUSTMENT

1978–83

A sight glass is fitted at the float chamber and the fuel level can be checked without disassembling the carburetor. Normal fuel level is within the level mark on the sight glass.

The fuel level adjustment is corrected by increasing or decreasing the number of needle valve packings. The float level may be off 0.160 inch, above or below the level mark and the operation of the engine would not be affected.

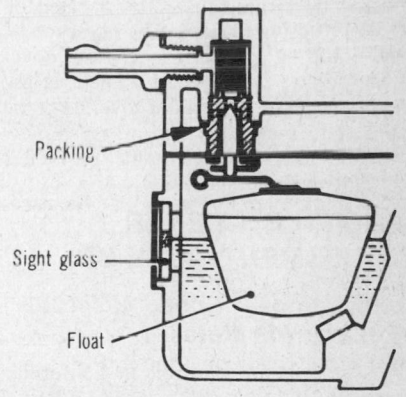

Float level adjustment—models through 1983

1984 and Later (Dry Setting)

1. Invert the float chamber cover assembly without a gasket.
2. Position a universal float level gauge and measure the distance from the bottom of the float to the surface of the float chamber cover. The distance should be 0.787 in. (20mm) ± 0.0394 in. (1mm).
3. If the reading is not within this range, the shim under the needle seat must be changed. Shim kits are available which contain 3 shims; 0.0118 in. (0.3mm), 0.0157 in. (0.4mm) and 0.0196 in. (0.5mm).

FAST IDLE ADJUSTMENT

1. Start the engine and open the throttle valve about 45 degrees. Manually close the choke valve and slowly return the throttle valve to the stop position.

2. With a tachometer, check that the fast idle speed is 2000 rpm or lower. (Not less than 1700 rpm). Adjust the speed as necessary with the fast idle speed screw.

3. Cold start the engine and check the automatic choke and fast idle operation.

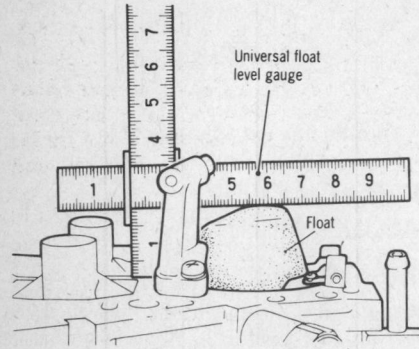

Dry float level adjustment—1984 and later

AUTOMATIC CHOKE ADJUSTMENT

The choke case has five small projections. Align the center projection with the yellow punch mark of the bimetal case.

On 1980 and later models, the choke is adjusted by turning the screw located on the choke spring bracket. The latest model years could have a tamper resistant cover on the screw. If choke adjustment is absolutely necessary, then the cover could be removed to make the adjustment. A new cover should be installed on the screw after the adjustment is made.

THROTTLE OPENER ADJUSTMENT (IDLE-UP)

Colt/Champ—4 Speed M/T 1982 and Later (49 states)

This system is not available in California.

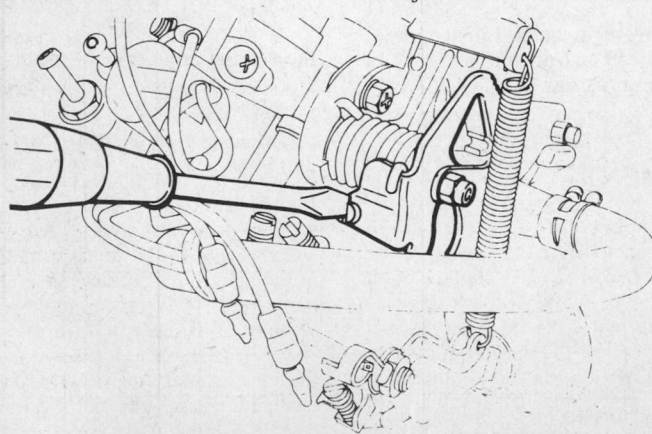

Adjusting the choke on 1980 and later vehicles

The throttle opener increases engine rpm if it drops below a specified amount. The system can be adjusted.

1. Check and adjust curb idle if needed.

2. Turn off all accessories and disconnect the electric radiator fan and hook a tachometer to the engine.

3. If equipped with air conditioning, switch the system on.

4. Warm up the engine and set the transaxle in neutral.

5. Remove the pressure on throttle opener by lifting on the unit with a finger.

——————— CAUTION ———————

Do not push up on the throttle opener lever or rod.

6. Adjust the throttle opener screw to obtain 800–900 rpm.

NOTE: Turn the A/C switch on and off several times to check the throttle opener operation (lever up/down).

Fuel Injection Unit

For troubleshooting and disassembly of the injection unit, please refer to "Fuel Injection" in the Unit Repair section.

REMOVAL & INSTALLATION

1. Relieve the fuel system pressure as outlined in the "Fuel Pump" removal and installation procedure.

2. Disconnect the negative battery cable.

3. Drain the coolant down to the intake manifold level or lower.

4. Disconnect the air intake hose from the injection unit.

5. Disconnect the throttle cable from the throttle lever of the injection unit.

6. Disconnect the fuel inlet pipe and return hose from the injection unit.

7. Disconnect the harness connectors at the injectors.

8. Disconnect the ISC servo and throttle position sensor connectors.

9. Disconnect all vacuum hoses.

10. Remove the four bolts and remove the injection unit from the intake manifold.

11. Installation is the reverse of removal.

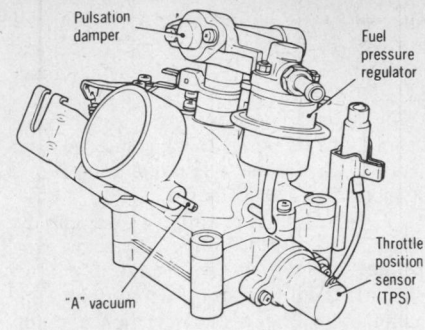

Fuel injection unit

IDLE SPEED CONTROL (ISC) SERVO AND THROTTLE POSITION SENSOR ADJUSTMENT

NOTE: When the ISC servo, throttle position sensor, mixture body or throttle body has been removed or replaced, performing the following adjustment is extremely important since car driveability is dependant on it.

1. Run the cold engine at fast idle until the coolant temperature is raised to 85–90°C (185–205°F), then stop the engine.

2. Disconnect the accelerator cable from the throttle lever of the injection mixer.

3. Loosen the two throttle position sensor retaining screws, turn the sensor fully clockwise then retighten the screws.

4. Turn the ignition switch to the "ON" position for 15 seconds, then turn it off. This sets the ISC servo to the specified position.

5. Disconnect the ISC servo harness connector, then start the engine.

6. Check the engine speed, and adjust the engine speed to 600 rpm with the adjusting screw. Stop the engine.

7. Disconnect the throttle position sensor harness connector.

8. Connect the adapter and digital voltmeter between throttle position sensor connector.

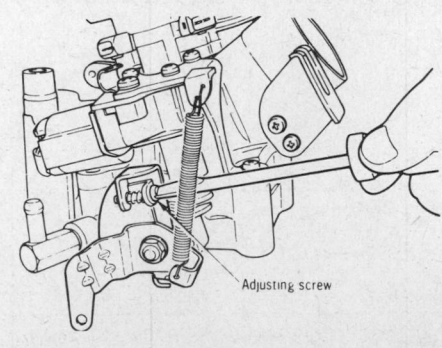

Adjusting engine speed—fuel injection unit

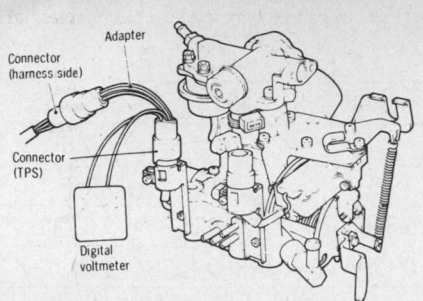

Voltmeter connection—fuel injection unit

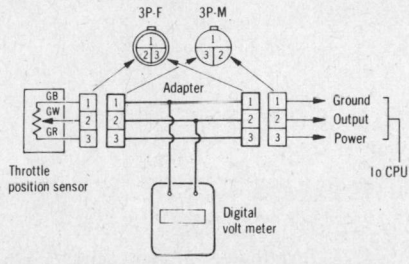

Voltmeter connection—fuel Injection unit

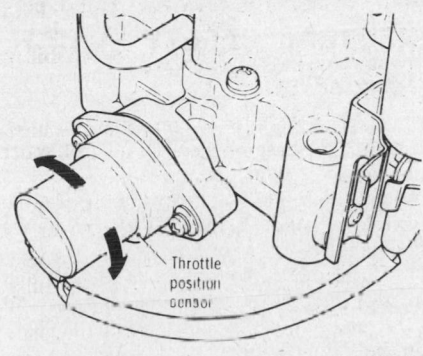

Throttle position sensor adjustment

9. Ignition switch ''ON''. Do not start the engine.

10. Read the throttle position sensor output voltage.

11. If the measurement of the output voltage does not agree with $0.48 \pm 0.03V$, loosen the throttle position sensor mounting screws, and turn the sensor clockwise or counterclockwise to gain the specified output voltage; $0.48 \pm 0.03V$. And tighten the screws after applying sealant to them.

12. Fully open the throttle valve once, return it to its original position and check for proper output voltage.

Make readjustment if necessary.

13. Remove the adapter and voltmeter, and reconnect ISC servo harness connector.

14. Make sure that curb idle speed is normal.

15. Stop the engine.

16. Turn ignition switch from OFF to ON position, and after lapse of 15 seconds, return it to OFF positon.

17. Connect accelerator cable to throttle lever of injection mixer and adjust accelerator cable.

MANUAL TRANSMISSION

REMOVAL & INSTALLATION

Please refer to the Mitsubishi car section for removal and installation procedures.

For all overhaul procedures, please refer to "Manual Transmission Overhaul" in the Unit Repair section.

CLUTCH

REMOVAL & INSTALLATION

Please refer to the Mitsubishi car section for clutch replacement procedures.

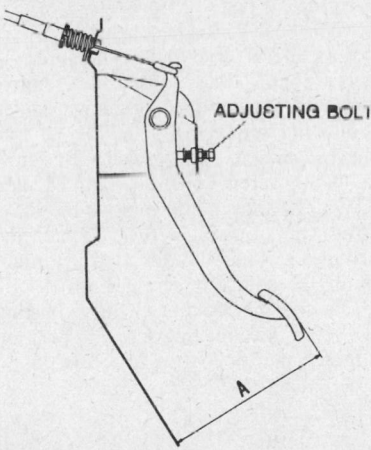

Measure dimension A between these points

Clutch Cable

REMOVAL & INSTALLATION

1. On all models except the Colt Vista, loosen the cable adjusting wheel inside the engine compartment.

2. Loosen the clutch pedal adjusting bolt locknut and loosen the adjusting bolt.

3. Remove the cable end from the clutch throwout lever.

4. Remove the cable end from the clutch pedal.

5. Installation is the reverse of removal.

NOTE: Lubricate the cable with engine oil and after installation, install pads isolating the cable from the intake manifold and from the rear side of the engine mount insulator on coupe, sedan, and hatchbacks only.

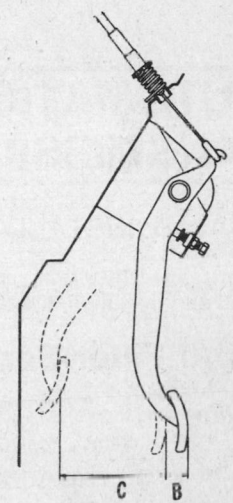

Dimension B and C

ADJUSTMENT

1. Adjust the clutch pedal height by the adjusting bolt to the distance shown in the following specifications. (Dimension A.)

2. Draw the outer cable from the cable holder on the toe-board and adjust its free-play by means of the adjusting nut. (Dimension D.)

3. Check clutch pedal free-play. (Dimension C), and the correct pedal stroke distance, (Dimension B), as outlined in the specifications.

CLUTCH ADJUSTMENT SPECIFICATIONS
Front Wheel Drive Cars

	Vista	All Exc. Vista
Pedal height from toe board	7.1–7.3	7.1–7.3
Pedal stroke	—	5.7
Clearance between adjusting nut & cable	0–.04	0.20–0.24
Clearance between pedal and floor board (pedal depressed)	2.2	—
Pedal free play	.6–.8	.8–1.2

CLUTCH AND PEDAL ADJUSTMENT SPECIFICATIONS
Rear Wheel Drive Cars

	Dimension	1978	1979	1980	1981	1982–85
Pedal height from toe board	A	6.8 inch	6.8 ④	6.8 ④	7.1	7.5
Pedal stroke	B	5.5 inch ①	5.5 ①	5.9	5.8	6.0
Clutch pedal free-play	C	0.8–1.2 inch ②	0.6–0.08 ⑤	0.6–0.8 ⑤	0.6–0.8	0.6–0.8
Adjusting nut to cable holder clearance	D	0.2–0.24 inch ③	0.12–0.16	0.12–0.16	0.12–0.16	0.12–0.16 ⑥
Clearance between release bearing face and pressure plate	E	0.080 inch	—	—	—	—

① 2600 cc engine: 5.9 inch
② Station wagon: 0.4 to 0.6 inch
③ Station wagon w/2000 cc engine: 0.14 to 0.18 inch
④ 2600 cc engine: 7.2
⑤ Arrow: 0.8–1.2
⑥ Measured between adjusting wheel and insulator

AUTOMATIC TRANSMISSION

REMOVAL & INSTALLATION

Please refer to the Mitsubishi car section for removal and installation procedures.

Pan and Filter Service

TorqueFlite

1. Raise and support the vehicle.
2. Loosen the pan bolts from one end to the other allowing the fluid to drain out.
3. Unbolt the old filter from the pan.
4. Clean the pan and install a new filter. Tighten filter bolts to 35 in. lbs.
5. Install the pan and new gasket. Torque pan bolts to 6–9 ft. lbs.
6. Add four quarts of Dexron® II fluid, start the engine and move the lever through all positions, pausing momentarily in each. Add enough fluid to bring the level to the full mark on the dipstick.

BAND ADJUSTMENTS

TorqueFlite Kickdown Band

The kickdown band adjusting screw is located on the left-side of the transmission case.

1. Loosen the locknut and back off approximately 5 turns. Test the adjustment screw for free turning in the transmission case.
2. On models through 1980, use an in. lb. torque wrench and tighten the adjusting screw to 72 inch pounds. On 1981 and later models, tighten the adjusting screw to 69 inch pounds (the torque specifications shown are true torque with no adapter on the wrench).

3. On models through 1980, back off the adjusting screw 3 full turns. On 1981 and later models, back off the adjusting screw 3½ turns.
4. Hold the adjusting screw to prevent turning and secure the locknut to 30–40 ft. lbs.

TorqueFlite—Low & Reverse Band

1. Raise and safely support the front of the car. Drain the transmission fluid and remove the oil pan.
2. The allen socket head adjusting screw is located at the servo end of the strut. On models through 1980, loosen and remove the locknut from the adjusting screw. Tighten the adjusting screw to 41 in. lbs. of true torque (no adapter on wrench). Back off the adjusting screw 7½ turns. On 1981 and later models, loosen and remove the locknut from the adjusting screw. Tighten the adjusting screw to 43 in. lbs. of true torque. Back off the adjusting screw 7 turns.
3. Install the locknut on the adjusting screw. Hold the adjusting screw in position and tighten the locknut to 25–35 ft. lbs.

4. Reinstall the oil pan using a new gasket. Refill the transmission with the proper amount of transmission fluid.

NEUTRAL SAFETY SWITCH

TorqueFlite

1. The inhibitor (Neutral) switch is located at the base of the shift control under the console cover.
2. Loosen the set screw that retains the shift lever handle to the shift lever. Remove the handle.
3. Remove the screws at the top and rear of the console, place the shift lever in "L" and remove the console. Put the lever in the "P" position.
4. Remove the top and side shift indicator panel mounting screws and pull the panel up. The inhibitor switch can now be disconnected and removed if necessary.
5. Adjust the switch by moving the selector lever to the "N" position. Loosen the mounting screws and adjust the inhibitor switch so that the pin on the forward end of the rod assembly will be in the position near the lobe of the detent plate and

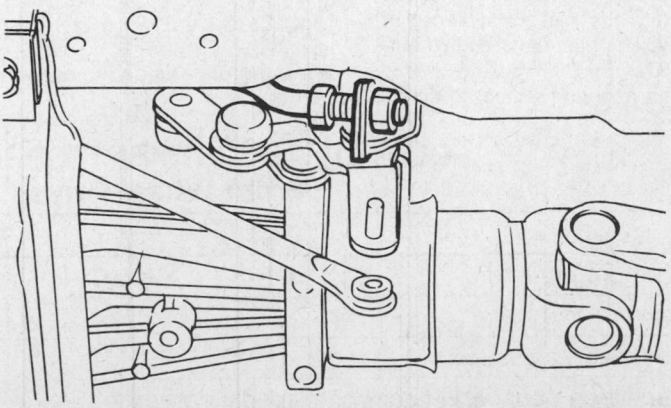

Transmission rod linkage adjustment on rear wheel drive vehicles

that this position will be at the front end of the range of the N connection of the switch. Temporarily tighten the switch mounting screws. After adjusting the selector lever clearance to 0.059 in., tighten the mounting screws.

6. To test the switch, disconnect the wiring connector and set the selector lever in each of its positions. With a continuity tester connected, current should be available in the "P," "N" and "R" positions only. Replace the switch if necessary. Install the console and shift handle.

SHIFT LINKAGE ADJUSTMENT

TorqueFlite

1. Disconnect the control cable at the transaxle (control rod on rear drive vehicles).
2. Place the selector lever in neutral and the inhibitor switch on the transaxle in neutral position (the manual control lever in neutral position on rear drive vehicles).
3. Install the control cable on the transaxle or control rod on the transmission and check for slack.
4. Turn the adjusting nut to remove any slack from the cable or rod.
5. Confirm the smoothness of lever operation and that the red indicator moves to show each gear.
6. Move the selector slowly upward until it clicks into the "P" position. Check to see if the starter will operate in park. After checking park, move the selector toward "N" until the lever drops at the end of the selector gate. If the starter also operates at this point, the gearshift linkage is properly adjusted.

THROTTLE ROD ADJUSTMENT

TorqueFlite

Warm the engine until it reaches the normal operating temperature. With the carburetor automatic choke off the fast idle cam, adjust the engine idle speed by using a tachometer. Then make the throttle rod adjustment.

1. Install each linkage. Loosen its bolts so that the rods B and C can slide properly.
2. Lightly push the rod A or the transmission throttle lever and the rod C toward the idle stopper and set the rods to idle position. In this case the carburetor automatic choke must be fully released. Tighten the bolt securely to connect the rods B and C.
3. Make sure that when the carburetor throttle valve is wide-open, the transmission throttle lever smoothly moves from idle to wide-open position (operating angle; 45°–54°) and that there is some room in the lever stroke.

NOTE: Make sure that when the throttle linkage alone is returned slowly from the fully open throttle position, that

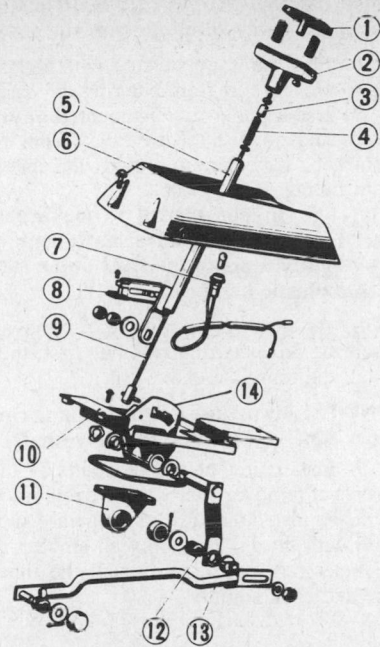

1. Push button
2. Shift handle
3. Rod adjusting nut
4. Rod return spring
5. Selector lever assembly
6. Position indicator assembly
7. Indicator lamp socket assembly
8. Inhibitor switch
9. Shift lever rod
10. Shift lever bracket assembly
11. Lever bracket cover
12. Transmission control arm
13. Transmission control rod

Exploded view of Torqueflite automatic transmission control

the transmission throttle lever completely returns to the idle position by spring force.

TRANSAXLE

REMOVAL & INSTALLATION

Please refer to the Mitsubishi car section for removal and installation procedures.

For all overhaul procedures, please refer to "Manual Transaxle Overhaul" in the Unit Repair section.

PAN AND FILTER SERVICE

Automatic Transaxle Only

1. Raise and support the vehicle.
2. Loosen and remove the transmission pan drain plug and the differential drain plug.
3. Remove the pan to install a new filter. Clean the pan and reinstall with a new gasket.
4. Add four quarts of Dexron® II fluid through the dipstick after replacing the two (2) drain plugs. Start the engine and move

selector lever through all positions: allow engine to run for at least two minutes.

5. Add sufficient fluid to bring level up to the lower dipstick. Recheck after transmission is at normal operating temperature.

KICKDOWN BAND ADJUSTMENT

1. Remove all dirt from the kickdown servo cover. Location is to right of dipstick; the large bump with a round cover.
2. Remove the snap-ring that retains the cover. Use a pair of pliers that fit into the notches of the cover and remove.
3. Loosen the locknut. Hold the kickdown servo piston from turning and tighten the adjusting screw to 7 ft. lbs., then back it off. Repeat the tightening and backing off two times. This will assure the seating of the kickdown band on the drum.
4. Tighten the adjusting screw to 3.5 ft. lbs. and back off 3.5 turns (counterclockwise).
5. Hold the adjusting screw and tighten the locknut to 12 ft. lbs.
6. Install a new cover seal ring "D"-shaped section in the groove. Install the servo cover and snap-ring.

INHIBITOR SWITCH ADJUSTMENT

1. Place the control lever in the "N" position.
2. Make sure the short end of the manual control lever covers the switch body flange. Loosen the switch mounting bolts (2) and adjust switch as necessary. Tighten the bolts.
3. Check the switch operation by attempting to start the engine in gears other than the P and N positions.

THROTTLE CONTROL CABLE ADJUSTMENT

All Models

Warm the engine to normal operating temperature and make sure the throttle is at curb idle position. Turn engine off.

1. Raise the cover on the throttle control cable to expose the nipple.
2. Loosen the lower cable bracket mounting bolt.
3. Move the lower cable bracket until the distance between the nipple and the cover nearest the mounting bracket is adjusted to 0.04 inches (1.0 mm).
4. Tighten the lower cable bracket mounting bolt to 9.0–15.0 ft. lbs. (12.0–14.0 Nm).
5. With the throttle lever in wide-open position (engine off), pull the cable further upward to confirm the cable has freedom of movement.

Halfshafts

REMOVAL & INSTALLATION

1. Remove the hub center cap and loosen

the driveshaft (axle) nut. Loosen the wheel lug nuts.

2. Lift the car and support it on jack stands. Remove the front wheels. Remove the engine splash shield.

3. Remove the lower ball joint and strut bar from the lower control arm.

4. Drain the transaxle fluid.

NOTE: On models with turbocharger, remove the snap ring which secures the center bearing.

5. Insert a pry bar between the transaxle case (on the raised rib) and the driveshaft double off-set joint case (DOJ) or tripod joint (T.J.). Do not insert the pry bar too deeply or you will damage the oil seal. Move the bar to the right to withdraw the left driveshaft; to the left to remove the right driveshaft.

NOTE: In the case of the T.J.-R.J. drive shaft be sure to hold the T.J. case and pull out the shaft straight. Simply pulling the shaft out of position could cause damage to the T.J. boot or the spider assembly slipping from the case.

6. Plug the transaxle case with a clean rag to prevent dirt from entering the case.

7. Use a puller-driver mounted on the wheel studs to push the driveshaft from the front hub. Take care to prevent the spacer from falling out of place.

NOTE: On models with turbocharger, after forcing out the drive shaft, remove it by lightly tapping the DOJ outer race with a plastic hammer.

8. Assembly is the reverse of removal. Insert the driveshaft into the hub first, then install the transaxle end.

NOTE: Always use a new retaining ring every time you remove the driveshaft.

9. Installation of the old parts is the reverse of removal after you have regreased them. To install the kit, use the grease supplied with the kit and apply an amount to the inner race and cage. Install the inner race and cock slightly.

10. Apply grease to the balls and install them in the cage. Place the inner race on the driveshaft and install the snap-ring. Apply grease to the outer race and install. Install the boots and bands.

11. Install the driveshaft using a new retainer ring.

OVERHAUL

For all CV–Joint removal, installation and overhaul procedures, please refer to "U–Joint/CV–Joint Overhaul" in the Unit Repair section.

DRIVE AXLE

NOTE: For all procedures involving the 1984 and later Conquest, please refer to the Starion procedures in the Mitsubishi section.

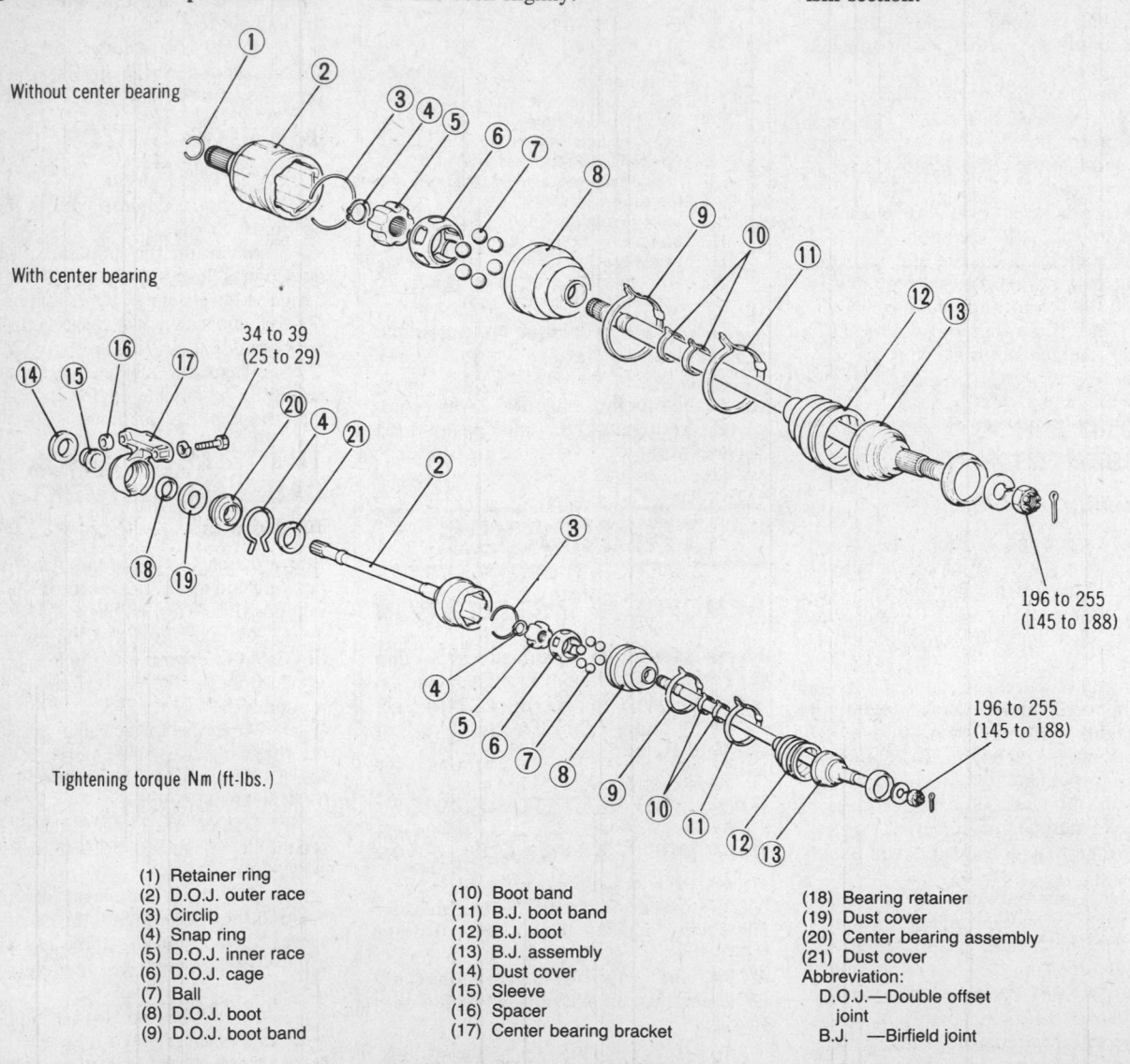

Without center bearing

With center bearing

34 to 39
(25 to 29)

196 to 255
(145 to 188)

196 to 255
(145 to 188)

Tightening torque Nm (ft-lbs.)

(1) Retainer ring
(2) D.O.J. outer race
(3) Circlip
(4) Snap ring
(5) D.O.J. inner race
(6) D.O.J. cage
(7) Ball
(8) D.O.J. boot
(9) D.O.J. boot band

(10) Boot band
(11) B.J. boot band
(12) B.J. boot
(13) B.J. assembly
(14) Dust cover
(15) Sleeve
(16) Spacer
(17) Center bearing bracket

(18) Bearing retainer
(19) Dust cover
(20) Center bearing assembly
(21) Dust cover
Abbreviation:
  D.O.J.—Double offset joint
  B.J. —Birfield joint

Exploded view of front drive shaft—Type D.O.J. and B.J.

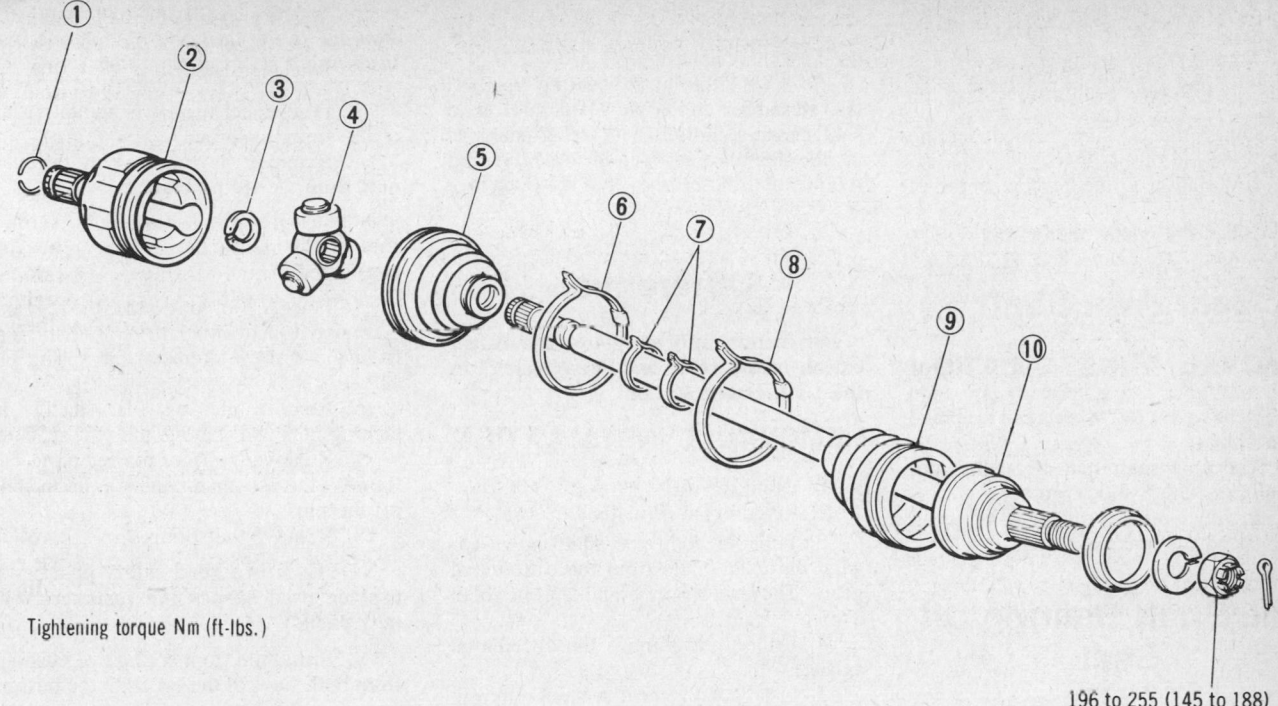

Tightening torque Nm (ft-lbs.)

196 to 255 (145 to 188)

(1) Retainer ring
(2) T.J. case
(3) Snap ring
(4) Spider assembly
(5) T.J. boot

(6) T.J. boot band
(7) Boot band
(8) R.J. boot band
(9) R.J. boot

(10) R.J. assembly
Abbreviation:
T.J.—Tripod joint
R.J.—Rzeppa joint

Exploded view of front drive shaft—Type T.J. and R.J.

DRIVESHAFTS AND U-JOINTS

REMOVAL & INSTALLATION

1. Matchmark the rear flange yoke and the differential pinion flange.

2. On late models with a two piece driveshaft, remove the center support mounting bolts. Remove the bolts from the rear flange. Remove the driveshaft by pulling it from the rear of the transmission extension housing.

NOTE: Place a container under the transmission extension housing to collect any oil leakage when the driveshaft is removed.

3. To install the shaft, align the front sleeve yoke with the splines of the transmission output shaft, and push the driveshaft into the extension housing.

NOTE: Be careful not to damage the rear transmission seal lip upon installation.

4. Align the matchmarks on the rear yokes, install the bolts, and tighten securely. Secure center support mounting bolts.

5. Inspect the oil level of the transmission.

Center Bearing and Support

REMOVAL & INSTALLATION

1. After removing the driveshaft from the car, put mating marks on the front shaft flange, center yoke and rear shaft flange for reinstallation alignment.

2. Disconnect the front and rear shaft sections by disassembling the universal joint.

3. Remove the center yoke from the front shaft by removing the center retaining nut. Remove the center support bracket; the support will slide off of the bearing by applying alternate side pressure.

4. Remove the center bearing, if necessary, with a two armed puller.

5. Inspect the center support: the bracket for damage, the rubber for deterioration and the bearing for noise, looseness or rough rotation. Replace as necessary.

6. Fill the groove on the inside center of the bearing with a multi–purpose grease (NLGI Grade 2). Partially install the bearing onto the driveshaft and install the center bearing bracket over the bearing. Make sure the bearing is securely fitted in the rubber mount. Slide the assembly into place on the driveshaft. Install the yoke and rear driveshaft.

NOTE: Always use a new self locking nut to secure the center yoke.

U–JOINT OVERHAUL

For all removal, installation and overhaul procedures, please refer to "U–Joint/CV–Joint Overhaul" in the Unit Repair section.

Rear Axle

REMOVAL & INSTALLATION

Leaf Spring Type

1. Raise and support the car safely.
2. Remove the rear wheels.
3. Remove the driveshaft.
4. Disconnect all rear brake lines.
5. Remove the rear U-bolts and the shock absorbers.
6. Remove the spring shackle pin nuts and the shackle plate. With the axle housing resting on the jack, remove the rear springs.
7. To replace the axle assembly, reverse the removal procedure. Bleed the brakes.

Coil Spring Type

1. Raise the car and support it safely.
2. Remove the rear wheels and the driveshaft.
3. Disconnect the parking brake cable and the hydraulic brake hose.
4. Remove the shock absorbers from the rear housing.

5. Lower the housing and remove the coil springs.

6. Position the housing and remove the lower and upper control arms and the assist link.

7. Guide the housing from under the car with the aid of a helper.

8. Installation is the reverse order of removal.

9. Bleed the brakes thoroughly.

Rear Axle Shaft

REMOVAL & INSTALLATION

1. Remove the rear wheels and the brake backing plate.

2. The axle shaft may be pulled out manually or with a slide hammer.

3. Installation is the reverse of removal.

4. Bleed the brake system.

Axle Shaft Bearing/Oil Seal

REMOVAL & INSTALLATION

NOTE: Front wheel drive models use an inner and outer bearing contained in the rear brake drum hub. Refer to front wheel bearing servicing, in the brake section, for removal and installation.

1. Remove the axle shaft.

2. Grind a small notch on the inner bearing retainer and split the retainer at that point with a chisel.

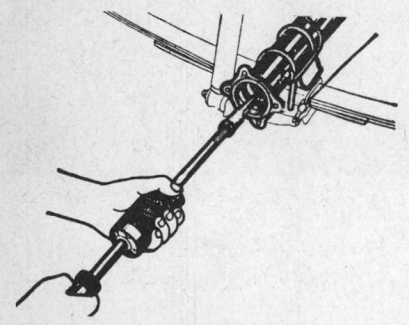

Oil seal removal

3. Remove the bearing with a puller.

4. The oil seal can be removed after the axle shaft is removed.

5. Install the outer bearing retainer (raised surface facing the wheel hub), axle shaft bearing and retainer. Using packing, set the clearance between the outer bearing retainer and the bearing to 0.00–0.01 in.

Differential

For further information on the differential, please refer to "Drive Axles" in the Unit Repair section.

REMOVAL & INSTALLATION

1. Drain the oil.

2. Remove the driveshaft.

3. Pull out both axle shafts to disengage the axle shafts from the differential gears. They need only be pulled out about 2 in.

4. Unbolt and remove the differential carrier.

5. Installation is the reverse of removal.

REAR SUSPENSION

NOTE: For all procedures involving the 1984 and later Conquest, please refer to the Starion procedures in the Mitsubishi section.

Leaf Springs

REMOVAL & INSTALLATION

1. Remove the hub cap or wheel cover. Loosen the lug nuts.

2. Raise the rear of the car. Install a stand at the exact point of the sill shown in the drawing. Two dimples locate the support point on the sill flange.

---CAUTION---
Damage to the unit body can result from installing a stand at any other location.

3. Disconnect the lower mounting nut of the shock absorber.

4. Remove the four U-bolt fastening nuts from the spring seat.

NOTE: It's not necessary to remove the shock absorber, leave the top connected.

5. Place a floor jack under the rear axle and raise it just enough to remove the load from the springs. Remove the spring pad and seat.

6. Remove the two rear shackle attaching nuts and remove the rear shackle.

7. Remove the front pin retaining nut. Remove the two pin retaining bolts and take off the pin.

8. Remove the spring.

NOTE: It is a good safety practice to replace used suspension fasteners with new parts.

9. Install the front spring eye bushings from both sides of the eye with the bushing flanges facing out.

10. Insert the spring pin assembly from the body side and fasten it with the bolts. Temporarily tighten the spring pin nut.

11. Install the rear eye bushings in the same manner as the front, insert the shackle pins from the outside of the car, and temporarily tighten the nut after installing the shackle plate.

12. Install the pads on both sides of the spring, aligning the pad center holes with the spring center bolt collar, and then install the spring seat with its center hole through the spring center collar.

13. Attach the assembled spring and spring seat to the axle housing with the axle housing spring center hole meeting with the spring center bolt and install the U-bolt nuts. Tighten the nuts to 33–36 ft. lbs.

14. Tighten the lower shock absorber nut to 12–15 ft. lbs. on all models.

15. Lower the car to the floor, jounce it a few times, and then tighten the spring pin and shackle pin nuts to 36–43 ft. lbs.

Coil Springs

REMOVAL & INSTALLATION

1. Raise and support the car safely allowing the rear axle to hang unsupported.

2. Place a jack under the rear axle, and remove the bottom bolts or nuts of the shock absorbers.

3. Lower the rear axle and remove the left and right coil springs.

4. Installation is the reverse of removal.

NOTE: When installing the spring, pay attention to the difference in shape between the upper and lower spring seats.

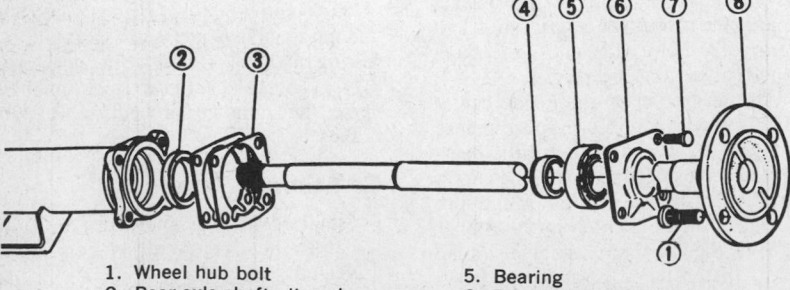

1. Wheel hub bolt	5. Bearing
2. Rear axle shaft oil seal	6. Bearing retainer (outer)
3. Packing	7. Bearing retainer bolt
4. Bearing retainer (inner)	8. Rear axle shaft

Exploded view of axle shaft

Shock Absorbers

REMOVAL & INSTALLATION

1. Remove the hub cap or wheel cover. Loosen the lug nuts.
2. Raise the rear of the car. Support the car with jack stands.

NOTE: The body sill is marked with two dimples to locate the support position. Never place a stand anywhere but between these marks or you'll damage the body.

3. Remove the upper mounting bolt and nut.
4. While holding the bottom stud mount nut with one wrench, remove the locknut with another wrench.
5. Remove the shock absorber.
6. Check the shock for:
   a. Excessive oil leakage; some minor weeping is permissable;
   b. Bent center rod, damaged outer case, or other defects.
   c. Pump the shock absorber several times, if it offers even resistance on full strokes it may be considered serviceable.
7. Install the upper shock mounting nut and bolt. Hand tighten the nut.
8. Install the bottom eye of the shock over the spring stud. Tighten the lower nut to 12–15 ft. lbs.
9. Finally, tighten the upper nut to 47–58 ft. lbs. on all models except station wagons, which are tightened to 12–15 ft. lbs.

Lower Control Arm— Rear Drive Vehicle

REMOVAL & INSTALLATION

1. Support the vehicle body on safety

Left side......L or white paint
Right side......R or no marking

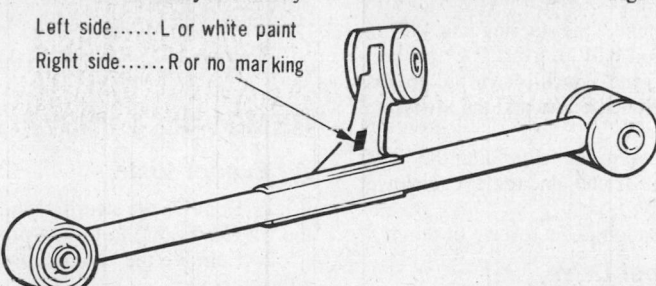

Rear wheel drive lower control arm mark to identify left and right sides

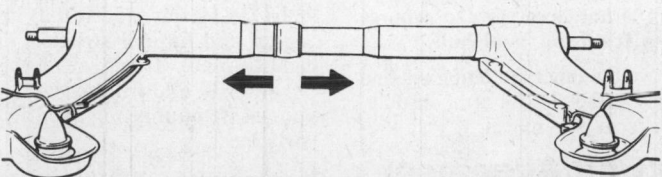

Rear lower control arm removed from front wheel drive type vehicle

stands. Use a jack under the rear axle to raise the rear axle assembly slightly.
2. Remove the wheel and the upper control arm rod.
3. Detach the parking brake rear cable from the lower arm.
4. Remove the lower arm from the rear axle housing and from the bracket attached to the body.
5. Temporarily install the lower arm (check for marking on left side arm) and torque the bolts to 94.0–108.0 ft. lbs. (127.0–147.0 Nm). Torque the assist link bushing bolt to 47.0–58.0 ft. lbs. (64.0–78.0 Nm).
6. With the special nut assembly placed securely against the rear axle housing bracket, install the upper control arm rod to the bracket. Torque the bolt to 94.0 ft. lbs. (127.0–147.0 Nm).

— CAUTION —
Always use new bolts.

Lower Control Arm— Front Drive Vehicle

REMOVAL & INSTALLATION

1. Support the side frame on jack stands and remove the rear wheels. Remove the rear brake assembly.
2. Remove the muffler and jack the control arm just enough to raise it slightly.
3. Remove the shock absorber and lower the jack. Remove the coil spring and temporarily install the shock absorber to the control arm.
4. Disconnect the brake hoses at the rear suspension arms and remove the rear suspension from the body as an assembly.
5. Install the fixture–to–body bolts and torque to 36.0–51.0 ft. lbs. (49.0–69.0 Nm).
6. Install the coil springs and loosely install the shock absorbers. Tighten the shock

absorber bolts to specification after the vehicle is lowered to the floor.
7. Install the rear brake assembly.
8. Lower the vehicle and tighten the suspension arm end nuts all except Colt Vista: to 36.0–51.0 ft. lbs. (49.0–69.0 Nm) Colt Vista: 94–108 ft. lbs. (130–150 Nm) and the shock bolts to 47.0–58.0 ft. lbs. (64.0–78.0 Nm), for all models.
9. Install the brake drums and wheels.
10. Bleed the brake system and adjust the rear brake shoe clearance.

FRONT SUSPENSION

NOTE: For all procedures involving the 1984 and later Conquest, please refer to the Starion procedures in the Mitsubishi section.

Strut

For all spring and shock absorber removal and installation procedures, and any other strut overhaul procedures, please refer to "Strut Overhaul" in the Unit Repair section.

REMOVAL & INSTALLATION

Rear Wheel Drive

1. Remove the front wheel and caliper. Remove the front hub with disc and dust cover.
2. Disconnect the stabilizer linkage and the lower arm. Remove the strut assembly, knuckle arm and strut insulator retaining bolts and remove the strut assembly from the wheelhouse.
3. Installation is the reverse of removal.

Front Wheel Drive

1. Jack up and support the front of the car.
2. Remove the front wheel. Remove the brake line from the strut.
3. Remove the four upper and two lower mounting nuts/bolts and remove the strut.
4. Installation is the reverse of removal. Be sure to bleed the brakes after installation.

Ball Joint

REMOVAL & INSTALLATION

NOTE: The ball joint on front wheel drive models may be replaced by removing the mounting nut from the front hub, separating the stud from the hub and removing the two control arm

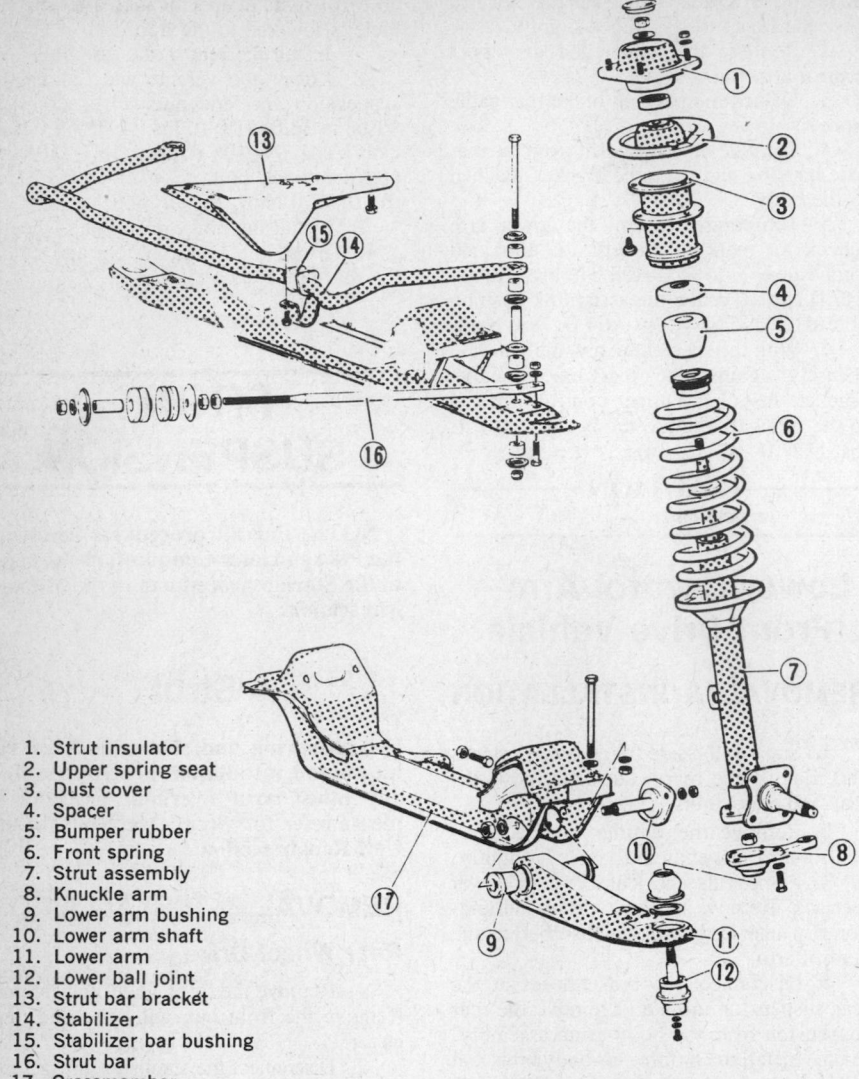

1. Strut insulator
2. Upper spring seat
3. Dust cover
4. Spacer
5. Bumper rubber
6. Front spring
7. Strut assembly
8. Knuckle arm
9. Lower arm bushing
10. Lower arm shaft
11. Lower arm
12. Lower ball joint
13. Strut bar bracket
14. Stabilizer
15. Stabilizer bar bushing
16. Strut bar
17. Crossmember

Arrow front suspension

mounting nuts and bolts. Installation is reverse of removal.

1. Remove the strut assembly and tie rod.

2. Remove the lower arm ball joint dust seal by prying up the dust seal ring evenly with a screwdriver.

3. Remove the snap-ring using snap-ring pliers.

4. Using a ball joint remover and installer tool, press off the ball joint.

5. To install the ball joint, press the ball joint properly into the burred hole, with the ball joint and lower arm mating marks aligned.

Lower Control Arm

REMOVAL & INSTALLATION
Rear Wheel Drive

1. After disconnecting the stabilizer ring from the lower arm, remove the strut assembly.

2. Disconnect the steering knuckle arm and the tie rod ball joint.

3. Using the knuckle arm puller, disconnect the knuckle arm and the lower arm ball joint.

4. Remove the bolts holding the lower arm to the sub-frame, and remove the lower arm assembly.

5. Installation is the reverse of removal.

Front Wheel Drive

1. Remove lower ball joint (two bolts) and strut bar (two bolts) from the lower control arm.

NOTE: It is not necessary to remove the ball joint from the front hub.

2. Remove the inner mounting nut and bolt and remove the control arm. Installation is the reverse of removal.

Front End Alignment
CASTER AND CAMBER

Caster is preset at the factory. It requires adjustment only if the suspension and steering linkage components are damaged, in which case, repair is accomplished by replacing the damaged part. A slight caster adjustment can be made by moving the nuts on the front anchors of the strut bars.

TOE-IN

Toe-in is the difference in the distance between the front wheels, as measured at both the front and the rear of the front tires.

Toe-in is adjusted by turning the tie rod turnbuckles as necessary. The turnbuckles should always be tightened or loosened the same amount for both tie rods; the difference in length between the two tie rods should not exceed 0.2 in. On the Challenger and Sapporo, only the left tie rod is adjustable.

STEERING

NOTE: For all procedures involving the 1984 and later Conquest, please refer to the Starion procedures in the Mitsubishi section.

Steering Wheel

REMOVAL & INSTALLATION

1. Pry off the steering wheel center foam pad.

2. Remove the steering wheel retaining nut.

3. Using a steering wheel puller, remove the wheel.

4. Be sure the front wheels are in a straight ahead position. Reverse the removal procedure.

Turn Signal Switch

REMOVAL & INSTALLATION

All Except Vista

1. Remove the steering wheel and have the tilt handle in the lowest position.

2. Remove the combination meter and column cover.

3. Remove the connectors from the column switch, and the column switch from the column tube.

NOTE: Early models may have the turn signal and hazard switches mounted on a base plate. Removal of the attaching screws will allow these switches to be removed without removal of the remaining switches.

4. Switch installation is the reverse of removal. Be sure that the switch is centered in the column or self-cancelling will be affected.

Ignition Lock and Switch

REMOVAL & INSTALLATION

1. Cut a notch in the lock bracket bolt head with a hacksaw.
2. Remove the bolt and lock.
3. Remove the column cover and unbolt and remove the ignition switch.
4. Install both lock and switch in reverse of removal.

NOTE: When replacing the ignition switch or key reminder switch only, remove the column cover, remove the screw holding the switch, and pull out the switch.

NOTE: When installing the lock, the bolt should be tightened until the head is crushed. When installing the switch, install the switch bolt loosely and insert and work the key a few times to make sure everything checks out before tightening the bolt.

Manual Steering Gear

REMOVAL & INSTALLATION

1. Remove the clamp bolt connecting the steering shaft with the steering gear housing mainshaft. Check for or make mating marks for the assembly.
2. Using appropriate pullers, disconnect the pitman arm and the relay rod at the linkage connection.
3. Remove the gearbox from the frame by removal of the attaching bolts.
4. Remove the pitman arm from the cross shaft. Check for mating marks.
5. Installation is the reverse of removal.

ADJUSTMENT

1. Measure the mainshaft preload with an inch/pound torque wrench. The allowable torque is 3–4.8 in. lbs.
2. The preload torque is corrected by reducing or increasing the number of shims under the end plate.
3. Seat the cross shaft and bearings by turning the steering mainshaft and the adjusting bolt two or three times.
4. Tighten the adjusting bolt to obtain zero free-play with the cross shaft in the center position. Tighten the locknut on the adjusting bolt.

Power Steering Gear

The power steering consists of a belt driven pump, a separate fluid reservoir, pressure and return lines, and a steering gear assembly with an integral control valve.

REMOVAL & INSTALLATION

1. Matchmark and disconnect the steering shaft from the gearbox main shaft.

1. Stabilizer
2. Lower arm **shaft**
3. Lower arm
4. Strut insulator
5. Spacer
6. Rubber bumper
7. Front spring
8. Strut assembly
9. Knuckle arm
10. Lower ball joint

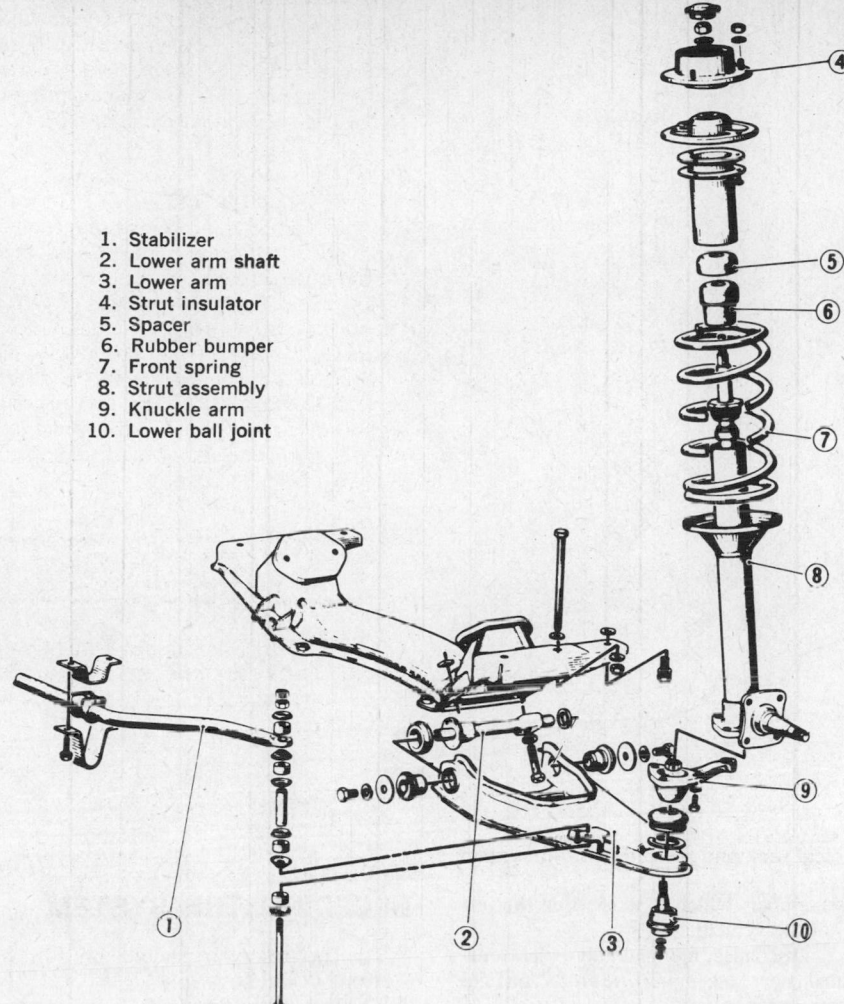

Colt front suspension—typical

1. Steering wheel
2. Tilt bracket
3. Steering shaft
4. Gear box
5. Tie rod assembly (right)
6. Relay rod
7. Tie rod assembly (left)
8. Idler arm

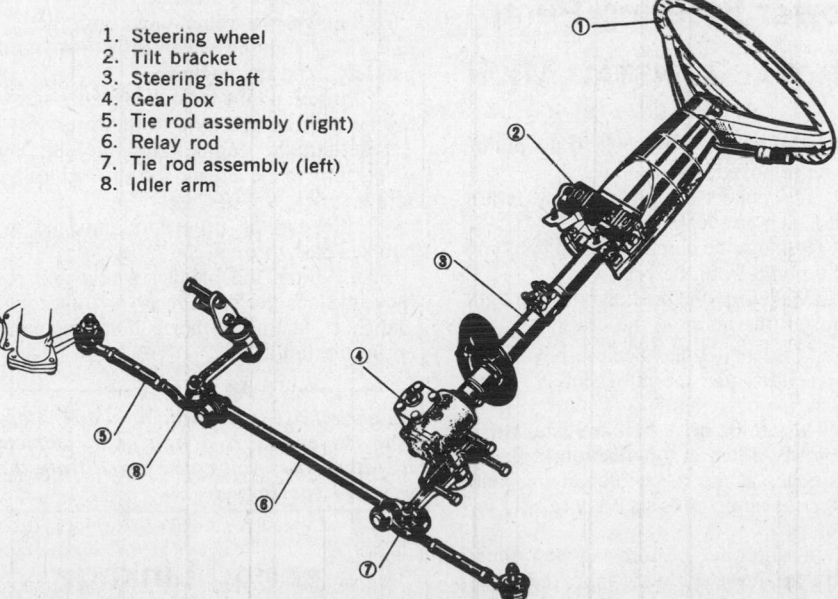

Steering system—gear type

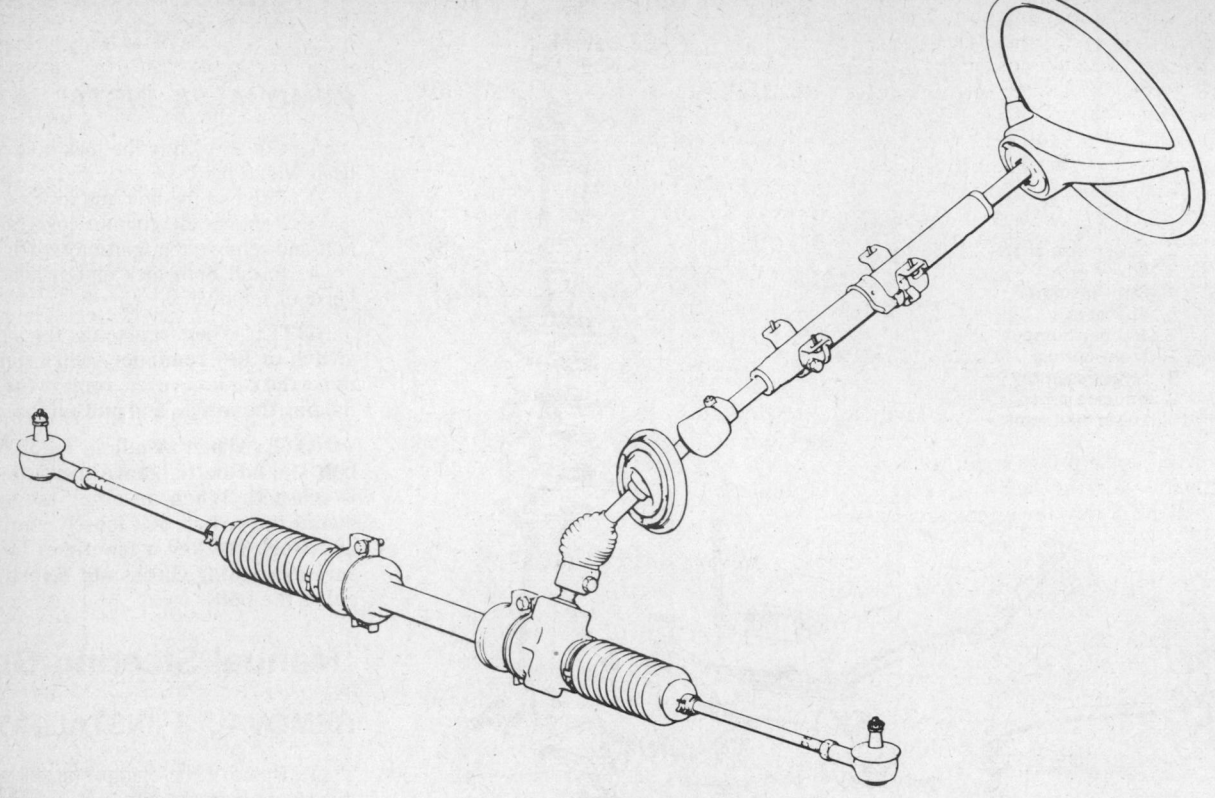

Typical rack and piston steering system

2. Disconnect the tie rod end and pit-man arm from the relay rod.

3. Remove the air cleaner and disconnect the pressure and return lines from the steering gear assembly.

4. Remove any interfering splash pans from underneath the vehicle.

5. If necessary, remove the kickdown linkage splash pan shield and bolts. Move the fuel line aside to avoid damage during removal.

6. Remove the frame bolts from the gearbox and lower the unit from the vehicle.

7. Install in reverse order.

Rack and Pinion Steering

REMOVAL & INSTALLATION

1. Jack up the car and support it on jack stands. Remove the front wheels.

2. Remove the bolt connecting the steering shaft universal joint with the steering gear. Before removing the bolt, mark its location and be sure the wheels are pointed straight.

3. Remove the tie–rod ends from the hub kuckles. Disconnect the mounting bolts (four) located near the inner tie–rods on the crossmember.

4. On the Colt Vista, remove the crossmember support bracket from the No. 2

crossmember, which is located on the left side of the vehicle.

5. Disconnect the mounting bolts (four) located near the inner tie rods on the crossmember.

6. Installation is the reverse of removal.

Power Steering Pump

REMOVAL & INSTALLATION

1. Remove the drive belt. If the pulley is to be removed, do so now.

2. Disconnect the pressure and return lines. Catch any leaking fluid.

3. Remove the pump attaching bolts and lift the pump from the brackets.

4. Make sure the bracket bolts are tight and install the pump to the brackets.

5. If the pulley has been removed, install it and tighten the nut securely. Bend the lock tab over the nut.

6. Install the drive belt and adjust to a tension of 22 lbs. at a deflection of 0.28–0.39 inches at the top center of the belt. Tighten the pump bolts securely to hold the tension.

7. Connect the pressure and return lines and fill the reservoir with approved fluid. (Dexron® type A).

8. Bleed the system (refer to the "Bleeding" procedure.)

BLEEDING THE SYSTEM

1. The reservoir should be full of Dexron® A fluid.

2. Jack up the front wheels and support the vehicle safely.

3. Turn the steering wheel fully to the right and left until no air bubbles appear in the fluid. Maintain the reservoir level.

4. Lower the vehicle and with the engine idling, turn the wheels fully to the right and left. Stop the engine.

5. Install a tube from the bleeder screw on the steering gear box to the reservoir.

6. Start the engine, turn the steering wheel fully to the left and loosen the bleeder screw.

7. Repeat the procedure until no air bubbles pass through the tube.

8. Tighten the bleeder screw and remove the tube. Refill the reservoir as needed, and check that no further bubbles are present in the fluid.

CAUTION

An abrupt rise in the fluid level after stopping the engine is a sign of incomplete bleeding. This will cause noise from the pump or control valve.

Steering Linkage

The steering linkage except on cars equipped with rack and pinion steering is of the conventional type, using tie rods, tie rod ends, relay rod, and idler arm assembly. The tie rods and tie rod ends are adjustable for length, and are locked in position by locking nuts. Front wheel drive models have adjustable outer tie rod ends. On later models, heat shields are used over ball sockets located near the engine to avoid heat loss of lubricating grease.

Lubricating grease is used in the dust cover and the sealer is used to join the cover to the ball socket body.

BRAKES

For all brake system repair and service procedures not detailed below, please refer to "Brakes" in the Unit Repair section.

System

Front disc brakes are used on all models. Depending on year and model, rear brakes are either drum or disc.

Adjustment

The front disc brakes require no periodic adjustment. All models equipped with rear drum brakes are self-adjusting.

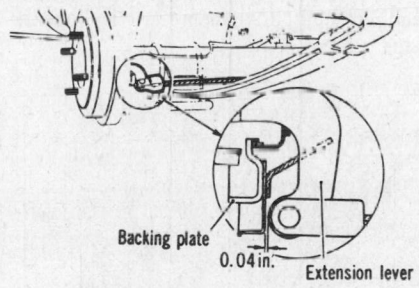

Parking brake adjustment

Backing plate
0.04 in.
Extension lever

1. Parking brake lever cover
2. Parking brake lever assembly
3. Parking brake cable
4. Clip
5. Bolt
6. Clip
7. Bushing
8. Clevis pin

Exploded view of parking brake linkage—rear wheel drive models

Master Cylinder/Brake Booster

REMOVAL & INSTALLATION

1. Remove all brake lines to the master cylinder. Slowly depress the brake pedal and catch the brake fluid in a container. Remove the power brake booster vacuum line if servicing the booster.
2. Remove the clevis pin from the pushrod at the brake pedal connection.
3. Remove the master cylinder from the brake booster or firewall.
4. Remove the brake booster from the firewall.
5. Install in the reverse order of removal. Completely bleed the brake system after filling the master cylinder with fresh brake fluid.

Wheel Cylinders

REMOVAL & INSTALLATION

1. Remove the brake shoes.
2. Place a bucket or some old newspapers under the brake backing plate to catch the brake fluid that will run out of the wheel cylinder. Disconnect the brake line and remove the cylinder mounting bolts. Remove the cylinder from the backing plate.
3. Install new or rebuilt wheel cylinder. Install brake shoes, etc. Bleed the brake system.

Parking Brake Cable

REMOVAL & INSTALLATION

Except Front Wheel Drive Models

1. Block the front wheels, jack up the rear of the car and support with jackstands.
2. Release the parking brake. Pull off the clevis pins from both sides of the rear brake. Disconnect the cable from the extension lever.

3. On drum brake models (through 1980); loosen the parking brake lever mounting bolts and disconnect the front end of the rear cable from the equalizer. On 1981 and later models, remove the brake drums and disconnect the cable from the lever. Remove the retaining clip and push the cable through the hole in the backing plate. Remove the front cable after disconnecting the parking brake lever. On rear disc brake models: Remove the rubber hanger from the center of the axle housing. Remove the parking brake lever and clevis pin linking the lever and cable. Remove the clips under the floor and remove the cable.

4. Installation is the reverse of the removal. When installing, make sure that the cable clips do not interfere with a rotating part. Adjust the extension lever to stop first. Then adjust the left cable, then the right on the Challenger/Sapporo and Wagons.

Front Wheel Drive Models
ALL EXCEPT COLT VISTA

1. Block the front wheels, raise the rear of the car and support on jackstands.
2. Disconnect the brake cable at the parking brake lever (brakes released). Remove the cable clamps inside the driver's compartment (two bolts). Disconnect the clamps on the rear suspension arm.
3. Remove the rear brake drums and the brake shoe assemblies. Disconnect the parking brake cable from the lever on the trailing (rear) brake shoe. Remove the brake cables.

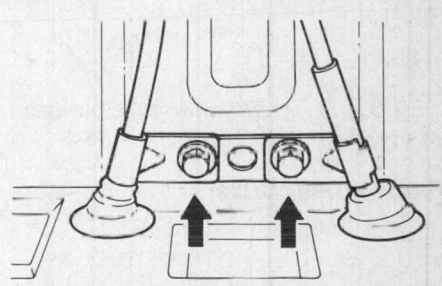

Location of cable clamp attaching bolts in passenger compartment—all except Vista

4. Installation is the reverse of removal.

COLT VISTA

1. Remove the console box and parking brake cover.
2. Take out the front, second and third seats.
3. Remove the floor carpet.
4. Remove the cable adjuster, and then disconnect the front parking brake cable and parking brake lever.
5. Remove the equalizer cover, and then remove the coupling of the parking cable at the interior side.
6. Remove the parking brake cable clamp on the rear suspension arm.
7. Remove the rear brake drum.
8. Remove the snap ring of the rear side of the backing plate.

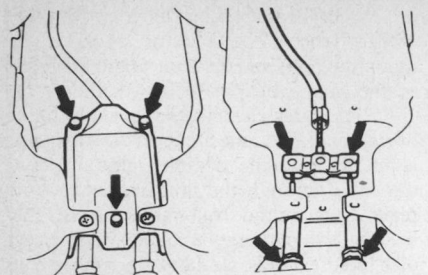

Parking brake equalizer cover bolts and cable coupler—Colt Vista

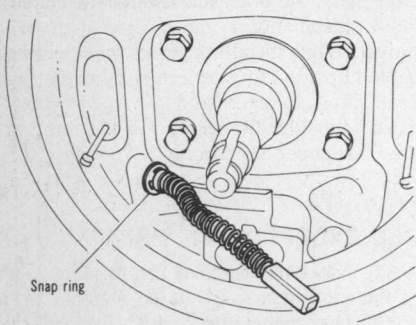

Cable snap ring on backing plate

9. Disconnect the lever and cable and take out the cable.

10. Installation is the reverse of removal. The parking brake lever stroke is 5–7 clicks. The switch should be adjusted so that the light goes on when the brake lever is pulled one notch.

ADJUSTMENT

NOTE: Overtightening of the parking brake will result in dragging brakes.

Front Wheel Drive

1. Release the parking brake.
2. Adjust the extension lever to backing plate clearance to .008–.080 inch, by moving the adjustment nut on the cable.
3. Check the brake lever free stroke. Brake drag should occur at 6–8 notches (Colt Vista: 5–7).

NOTE: On all models except the Colt

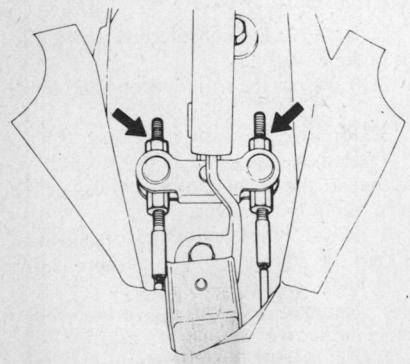

Cable adjusting nuts—front wheel drive models except Vista

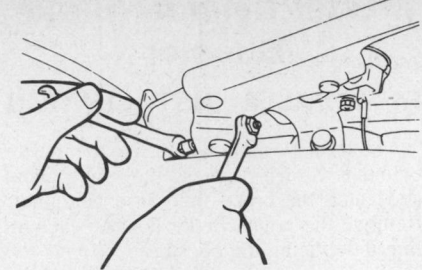

Lever adjustment—Colt Vista

Vista, adjust the right and left cables so that when the lever is pulled, their lengths will almost be eqaul.

Rear Wheel Drive

1. Release the parking brake.
2. Adjust the extension lever to stopper clearance to 0.100 inch by loosening both cable lever attaching bolts and adjusting the nut. Move the cable lever to the right. Set the left cable first and then the right.
3. Check the brake lever free stroke. Brake drag should occur at 5–7 notches.

Wheel Bearings

REMOVAL & INSTALLATION

Except Front Wheel Drive

1. Remove the caliper (pin type) or the caliper and support (sliding type).

NOTE: On sliding type calipers, remove the caliper and support as a unit by unfastening the bolts holding it to the adapter ("backing plate"). Support the caliper with wire, do not allow the weight to be supported by the brake hose.

2. Pry off the dust cap. Tap out and discard the cotter pin. Remove the locknut.
3. Being careful not to drop the outer bearing, pull off the brake disc and wheel hub.
4. Remove the grease inside the wheel hub.
5. Using a brass drift, carefully drive the outer bearing race out of the hub.
6. Remove the inner bearing seal and bearing.
7. Check the bearings for wear or damage and replace them if necessary.
8. Coat the inner surface of the hub with grease.
9. Gease the outer surface of the bearing race and drift it into place in the hub.
10. Pack the inner and outer wheel bearings with grease. (see repacking).

NOTE: If the brake disc has been removed and/or replaced, tighten the retaining bolts to 25–29 ft. lbs.

11. Install the inner bearing in the hub. Being careful not to distort it, install the oil seal with its lip facing the bearing. Drive

the seal on until its outer edge is even with the edge of the hub.

12. Install the hub/disc assembly on the spindle, being careful not to damage the oil seal.

13. Install the outer bearing, washer, and spindle nut. Adjust the bearing as follows.

Front Wheel Drive Models

1. Remove the brake caliper assembly.
2. Remove drive axles.

NOTE: When removing the drive axle from the hub, do not lose the shims or mix them with the opposite side.

3. Use a puller and disconnect the ball joint and tie-rod end form the steering knuckle. Unfasten the two bolts that mount the knuckle to the strut and remove the knuckle, hub and rotor.

4. Remove the hub assembly from the knuckle. On all models except the Colt Vista and models equipped with a turbocharger, mount the knuckle in a vise, support the rotor and hub, and drive out the hub with a soft hammer. On the Colt Vista and models equipped with a turbocharger, remove the hub assembly from the knuckle with these special tools: Front Hub Remover and Installer (MB990998) and Knuckle Arm Bridge (MB991001).

5. On models with a turbocharger, remove the bearing spacer from the hub.

6. Remove the brake disc rotor from the hub.

7. Clean and inspect the bearings and races (cups), replace if necessary.

8. If the inner and outer races (cups) need replacing, drive them from the knuckle using a brass drift.

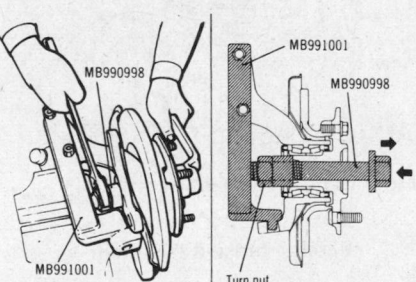

Using special tools to remove the hub from the knuckle

NOTE: On the Colt Vista, remove the outer bearing inner race from the hub using special tool (MB990781).

9. Install new races (cups), if necessary, pack the bearings (see repacking) and reinstall in the reverse manner of removal.

BEARING SERVICE

1. Clean the inner and outer bearings and the wheel hub with a suitable solvent. Remove all old grease.
2. Thoroughly dry and wipe clean all components.

3. Clean all old grease from the spindle or steering knuckle.

4. Carefully check the bearings for any sign of scoring or other damage. If the roller bearings or bearing cages are damaged, the bearing and the corresponding bearing cup in the rotor or knuckle must be replaced. The bearing cups must be driven out of the rotor or knuckle to be removed. The outer bearing cup is driven out of the front of the rotor or knuckle from the rear and vice versa for the inner bearing cup.

5. Whether you are reinstalling the old bearings or installing new ones, the bearings must be packed with wheel bearing grease. To do this, place a glob of grease in your left palm, then, holding one of the bearings in your right hand, drag the edge of the bearing heavily through the grease. This must be done to work as much grease as possible through the roller bearings and cage. Turn the bearing and continue to pull it through the grease until the grease is packed between the bearings and the cage all the way around the circumference of the bearing. Repeat this operation until all of the bearings are packed with grease.

6. Pack the inside of the hub with a moderate amount of grease, between the bearing cups. Do not overload the hub with grease.

7. Apply a small amount of grease to the spindle.

8. Place the knuckle or rotor, face down, on a protected surface and install the inner bearing.

9. Coat the lip of a new grease seal with a small amount of grease and position it on the knuckle.

10. Place a block of wood on top of the grease seal and tap on the block with a hammer to install the seal. Turn the block of wood to different positions to seat it squarely in the hub.

ADJUSTMENT

Rear Drive Models

1. Remove the wheel and dust cover. Remove the cotter pin and lock cap from the nut.

2. Torque the wheel bearing nut to 14.5 ft. lbs. (19.6 Nm) and then loosen the nut. Retorque the nut to 3.6 ft. lbs. (4.9 Nm) and install the lock cap and cotter pin.

3. Install the dust cover and the wheel.

Front Drive Models

1. Remove the wheel, the dust cover and the cotter pin.

2. Torque the axle shaft nut to 1980–82—87.0–130.0 ft. lbs. (118.0–177.0 Nm), 1983 and later—144–188 ft. lbs. (200–260 Nm).

3. Back off the nut to the nearest point where the slot in the nut will align with the hole in the shaft. Install the cotter pin and dust cover.

4. Install the wheel.

Rear Wheel Bearings

FRONT WHEEL DRIVE

The rear wheel, on front wheel drive models, rides on bearings contained in the hub of the rear brake drum. The axle is similar to a conventional front wheel spindle. Refer to "Brakes" in the Unit Repair section of this manual for bearing removal and service.

CHASSIS ELECTRICAL

NOTE: For all procedures involving the 1984 and later Conquest, please refer to the Starion procedures in the Mitsubishi section.

Heater Blower

REMOVAL & INSTALLATION

Coupe, Sedan, and Hatchback

1. Remove the instrument cluster (coupe and sedan). Remove the instrument cluster and the glove box (hatchback).

2. Remove the heater control bracket assembly.

3. Remove the motor assembly and disconnect the wire connection.

4. (Coupe and sedan) Remove the motor in a horizontal position while holding the control bracket down.

5. (Hatchback) Remove the motor through the glove box opening.

6. Installation is the reverse of removal.

Colt Vista

1. Remove the upper and lower glove boxes.

2. Disconnect the connectors and remove the mounting bolts and remove the blower motor.

NOTE: To remove the blower case assembly the instrument panel must be removed.

3. Installation is the reverse of removal.

1977–80 Challenger, Sapporo and Station Wagon

1. Remove the instrument cluster and the meter cluster.

2. Disconnect the wiring to the motor.

3. Remove the motor assembly.

4. Installation is reverse of removal.

1981 and Later Challenger/Sapporo

1. Remove the lower instrument pad cover assembly from under the glove box.

2. Remove the passenger side console cover.

3. Remove the glove box–to–center support attaching screw.

4. Loosen the stops at either side of the glove box so that the glove box swings free.

5. Disconnect the glove box light.

6. Remove the glove compartment assembly from the instrument pad.

7. Remove the ducts, heater fan switch connector and control cables.

8. Remove three attaching bolts and lift out the blower assembly.

9. Remove the wiring bracket and the motor connector. Remove the vent tube and three motor attaching screws. Lift out the motor and remove the fan from the motor assembly.

10. Installation is the reverse of removal.

Heater Core

REMOVAL & INSTALLATION

Coupe, Sedan and Hatchback

1. Drain the cooling system.

2. Disconnect the battery ground cable.

3. Place the water valve in the OFF position.

4. Remove the under tray, defroster nozzle and console box.

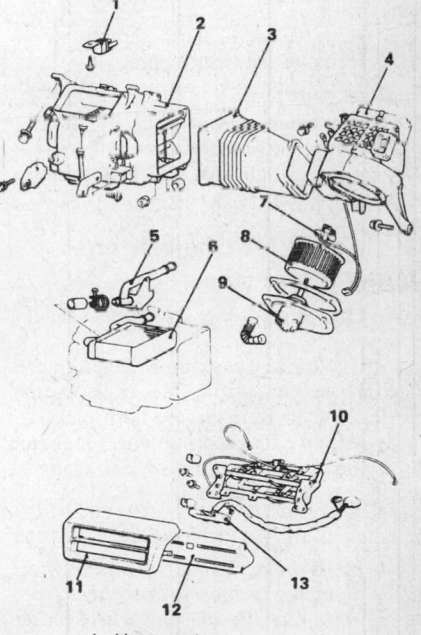

1. Heater relay
2. Heater unit
3. Duct
4. Blower case
5. Water control assembly
6. Heater core
7. Resistor
8. Fan
9. Fan motor assembly
10. Heater control assembly
11. Heater control panel cover
12. Heater control panel
13. Fan switch

Heating system—Colt Vista

5. Disconnect each heater control wire and connectors at the heater assembly.

6. Disconnect the water hoses, heater duct and wiring harness.

7. Remove the heater assembly.

8. Remove the heater core.

9. Installation is the reverse of removal.

Colt Vista

1. Disconnect the negative battery cable.

2. Move the warm water flow control lever to the "WARM" side and drain the engine coolant.

3. Remove the instrument panel.

4. Remove the duct between the heater unit and the blower assembly.

5. Disconnect the heater hose at the heater unit and remove the heater unit.

6. Remove the cover, disconnect the links and clamps and remove the heater core from the heater unit.

7. Installation is the reverse of removal.

1977–80 Hardtop and Station Wagon

1. Drain the cooling system.

2. Remove the glove box, instrument cluster and console assembly.

3. Disconnect the heater control wires at the heater box.

4. Remove the heater control assembly.

5. Disconect all heater hoses and air ducts.

6. Remove the heater assembly.

7. Remove the heater core.

8. Installation is the reverse of removal.

NOTE: Upon removal of the heater control box, the heater core is removable. Replace all gaskets and insulation in its proper place.

1981 and Later Challenger/ Sapporo

1. Disconnect the negative battery terminal.

2. Remove the steering wheel horn pad attaching screws, from the back of the steering wheel. Remove the horn pad.

3. Remove the steering wheel lock nut and remove the steering wheel using a steering wheel puller tool.

CAUTION

Do not apply impact to the column or wheel with a hammer to loosen the wheel from the column. Use the steering wheel puller tool.

4. Loosen the tilt lock lever and lower the steering column fully.

5. Remove the meter (instrument cluster) hood. Remove the meter (instrument cluster) assembly and disconnect the electrical and cable connectors.

6. Remove the inner box from the console accessory box. Press on the spring catch, to remove the remote control mirror switch from the accessory box.

7. Remove the accessory box assembly

and disconnect the electrical connector.

8. Pull off the heater control knob, pull out the control panel and take out the illumination harness.

9. Pull off the radio knobs and remove the radio to panel attaching nuts. Remove the radio panel.

10. Remove the cover assembly attaching screws from below the glove box and remove the cover assembly.

11. Remove the console side covers (both sides).

12. Remove the shift knob on manual transmission vehicles and remove the center console.

13. Remove the instrument pad bolt

covers at both ends of the instrument pad and remove the attaching nuts.

14. Take off the hood lock release knob and remove the release cable attaching screws. Remove the hood lock release assembly from the instrument pad.

15. Remove the defroster garnish.

16. Remove the screws attaching the glove compartment to the center dash reinforcement.

17. Remove all remaining instrument pad attaching bolts.

18. Disconnect the clock, glove box, chime and dimmer control and remove the instrument pad.

19. Disconnect the defogger switch, ra-

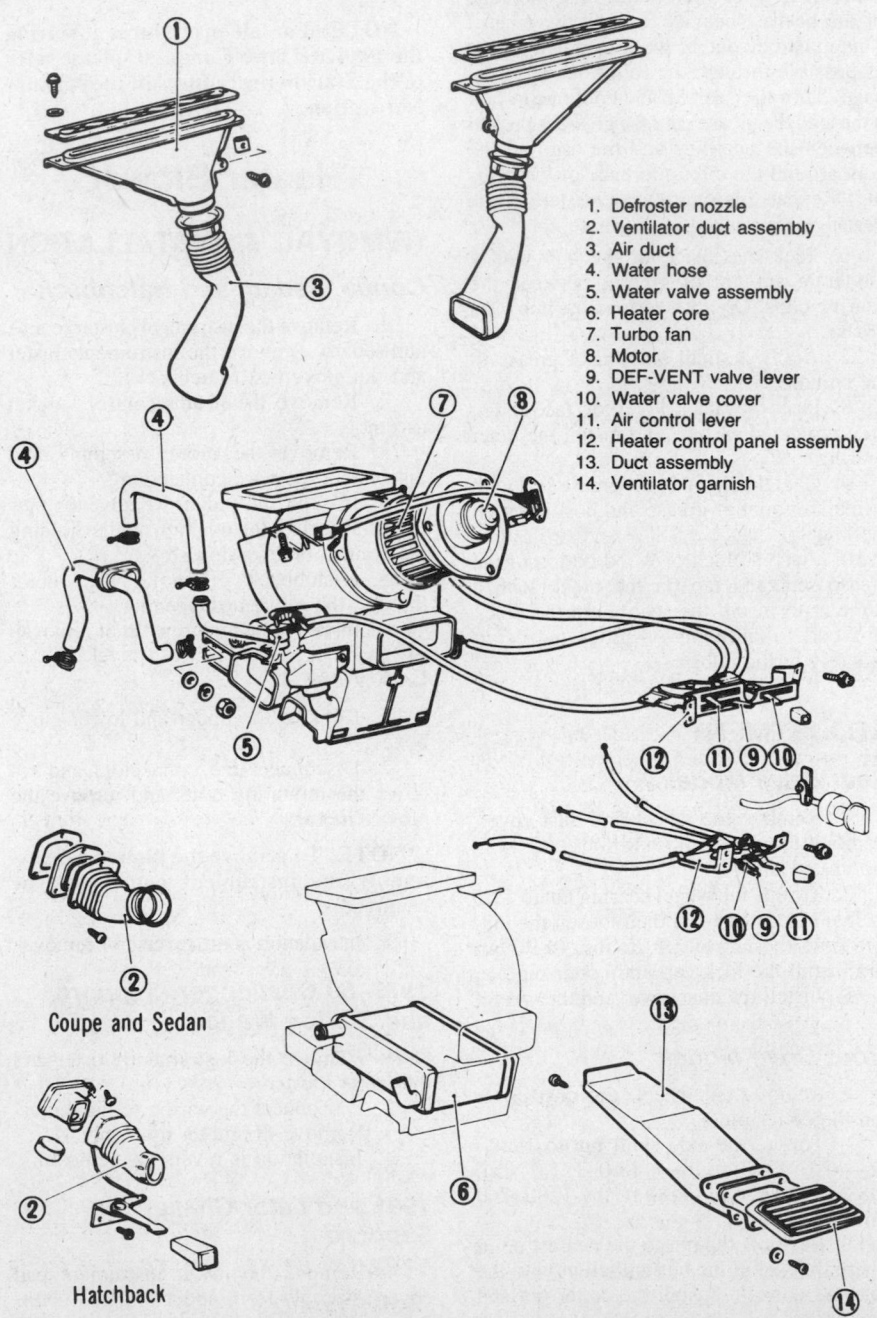

1. Defroster nozzle
2. Ventilator duct assembly
3. Air duct
4. Water hose
5. Water valve assembly
6. Heater core
7. Turbo fan
8. Motor
9. DEF-VENT valve lever
10. Water valve cover
11. Air control lever
12. Heater control panel assembly
13. Duct assembly
14. Ventilator garnish

Coupe and Sedan

Hatchback

Exploded view of heater assembly—typical of coupe, sedan and hatchback vehicles

dio, chime driver, defogger relay connectors and the antenna feeder end.

20. Remove the center reinforcement.

21. Set the heater temperature control to "WARM" position and drain the coolant from the radiator.

22. From the engine compartment, remove the heater hoses from the heater assembly.

23. From under the dash, remove the heater ducts from the heater assembly. To remove the rear seat heater duct, move the outlet control link to the "VENT" side, insert a finger into the outlet and remove the duct from inside heater.

24. Disconnect the power relay connector, remove three attaching bolts and remove the heater assembly. Remove the heater core.

25. The installation is the reverse of removal.

26. Connect the heater hoses in a fully seated position on the inlet and outlet fittings of the heater core assembly, so they will not leak.

27. Adjust the heater control cable by setting the control panel to "COOL" and heater unit lever on "COOL" and tighten the cable at that position.

NOTE: In order to fill the engine cooling and heating system completely it may be necessary to open the water valve fully, run the engine to circulate the coolant and then stop the engine and add more coolant.

Windshield Wiper Motor and Linkage

REMOVAL & INSTALLATION

The wiper motor may be located on either the right or left side of the front deck, depending upon the year and model. A wiper removing hole is provided to gain access to the linkage for removal purposes.

1. Remove the wiper arms. Remove the arm shaft locknuts and push in the shafts. Disconnect the electrical wiring.

2. Remove the bolts holding the motor bracket to the body and pull the wiper assembly outward and away from the body.

3. Hold the motor shaft and the linkage at right angles to each other and disconnect them. Remove the motor.

4. The linkages can be pulled from the opening in the front deck.

5. The installation is in the reverse of the removal, being sure to insert the linkage shaft bracket positioning boss positively in the hole provided in the body before tightening the wiper shaft nut.

6. Locate the wiper blades in the stopped position approximately ½ to ¾ inch above the bottom moulding or sealer of the windshield.

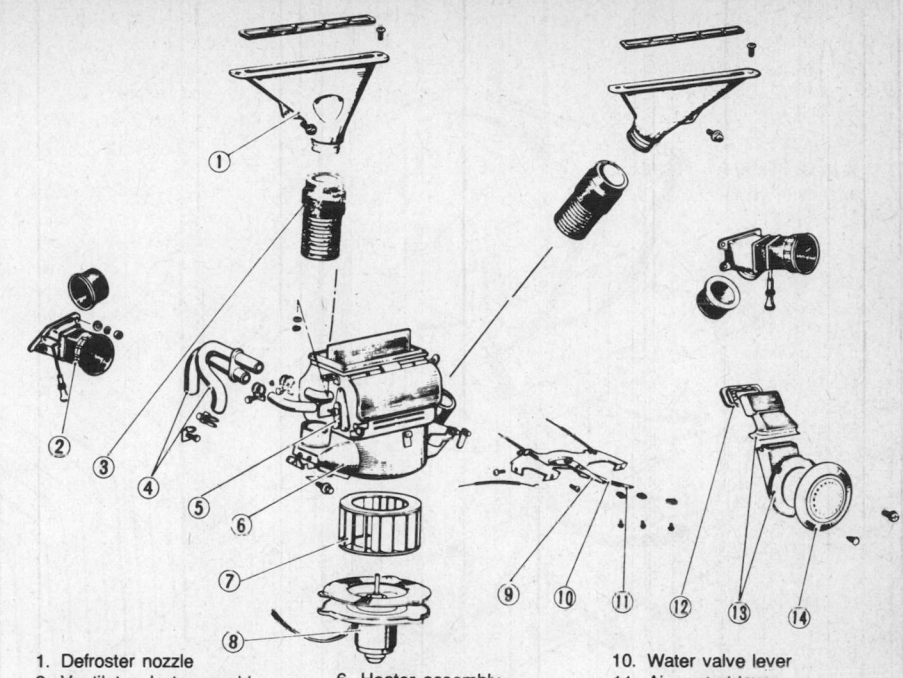

1. Defroster nozzle
2. Ventilator duct assembly
3. Air duct
4. Water hose
5. Water valve assembly
6. Heater assembly
7. Turbo fan
8. Motor
9. Heater-defroster lever
10. Water valve lever
11. Air control lever
12. Valve (Hardtop)
13. Duct assembly (Hardtop)
14. Ventilator garnish (Hardtop)

Exploded view of heater assembly—typical of hardtop and station wagon vehicles

Radio

REMOVAL & INSTALLATION

Rear Wheel Drive

1. Remove glove box then loosen the knobs and attaching nuts on the front of the radio.

2. Remove speaker, antenna, and power wires from the back of the radio. Remove the radio attaching bracket and take out the radio.

3. Installation is the reverse of removal.

Front Wheel Drive

1. Remove the instrument panel trim.

2. Remove the radio knobs from the radio panel.

3. Remove the nuts from behind the knobs, the screw from the bracket and remove the radio (AM radio). Remove the bolts from under the brackets and remove the radio (AM/FM radio).

NOTE: The AM radio circuit fuse block is located on the right rear side of the radio, the AM/FM circuit fuse block is installed in the line with the power cable.

Instrument Cluster

For further information on the instrument cluster, please refer to "Gauges and Indicators" in the Unit Repair section.

REMOVAL & INSTALLATION
Colt/Champ

NOTE: Disconnect the battery ground cable before cluster removal.

1. Loosen screws at the upper and lower part of the instrument cluster. Loosen the screws holding the heater control knobs, ash tray, and cigarette lighter from their respective brackets. Remove the blind cover on the right side of the glove box and remove the attaching screws on the right side of the cluster.

2. Remove the harness cover at the bottom of the instrument panel and disconnect the lighting switch and the instrumental panel harness.

3. Pull the instrument panel cluster a little toward you, disconnect multiple connector, antenna feeder, speaker connector, heater fan connector and meter cables and then remove the instrument cluster assembly.

4. Installation is the reverse of removal.

After the instrument cluster has been installed, draw out the meter cables as long as the marking tape can be seen from the engine compartment.

Arrow

1. Remove the air intake control knob, the ash tray and heater control knobs and the radio knobs and retaining nuts.

2. Remove the three upper screws and a lower screw, a screw located behind the blind cover above the air intake control panel, and the three screws behind and in the upper inside part of the ash tray.

3. Pull the ash tray out a little and disconnect the heater, meter and speedometer connectors.

4. Remove the ground cable which is attached to the body by a screw and remove the cluster.

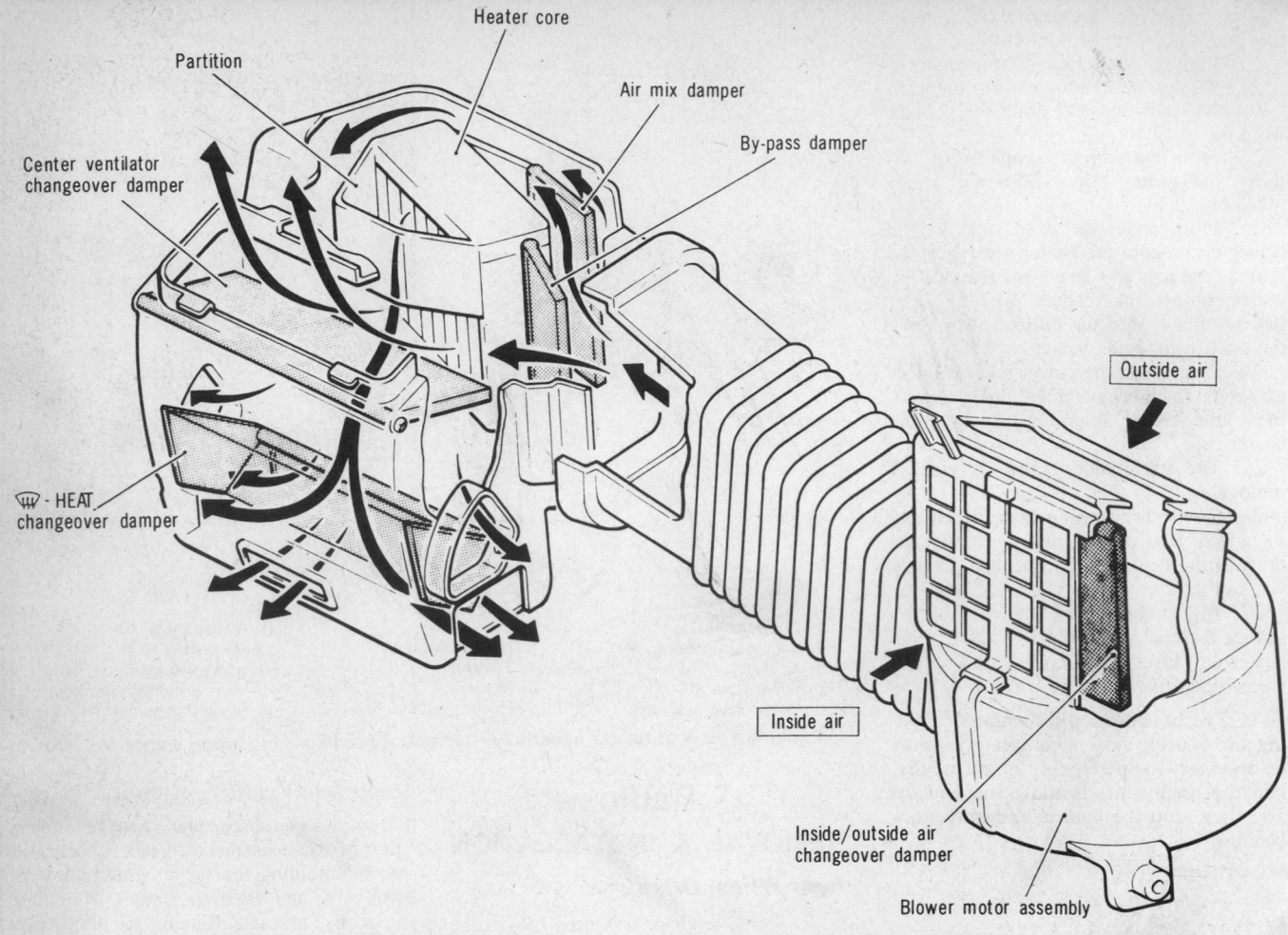

Heater system on 1981 and later Challenger and Sapporo vehicles

5. To install reverse the removal procedure.

Challenger/Sapporo

1. Remove the battery ground cable.
2. Remove three screws from the top and three screws from the bottom of the cluster assembly.

NOTE: Two of the bottom screws are located behind the "brake warning" an "fasten seat belt" lens and the third bottom screw is located at the ash tray opening. A thin tipped screwdriver or a wire hook is required to remove the lenses to gain access to the screws.

3. Move the instrument cluster away from the dash and disconnect the meter connections, heater fan connections, speedometer cable and any other connector or ground cables.
4. Remove the cluster assembly from the dash.
5. Installation is the reverse of removal.

1978–81 Station Wagon

The instrument cluster hood is removed separately to expose the instrument cluster attaching screws. Remove the screws, attaching wires and cables, and remove the cluster from the dash. Install in the reverse of the removal procedure.

Fuse Box Location

Front Wheel Drive

The fuse block is located up under the instrument panel on the driver's side of the steering column.

All Other Models

The fuse block is located on the lower part of the driver's side front piller post.

Datsun/Nissan
200SX, B210, 210, 280Z, 280ZX, 300ZX, 310, 510, 810, F10, Maxima, Pulsar, Sentra, Stanza

SERIAL NUMBER IDENTIFICATION

Engine Number

The engine number is stamped on the right side top edge of the cylinder block, except on the 1984 and later 200SX, and the 1984 and later 300ZX V6. On the V6, the number is stamped on the right rear edge of the right cylinder bank, facing up. On the 1984 and later 200SX (CA20E and CA18ET engines), the number is stamped on the left rear edge of the block, next to the bellhousing. The engine serial number is preceded by the engine model code.

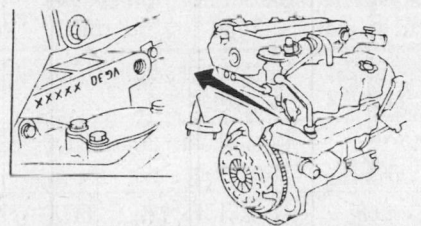

Engine identification number location—1984 and later V6

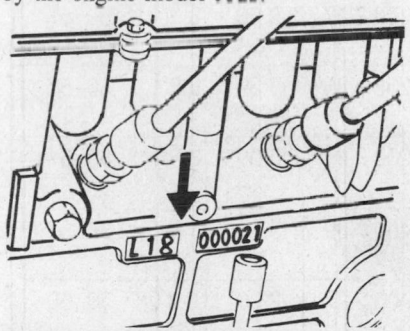

Engine serial and code number, all except V6, CD17 and CA20/CA18ET

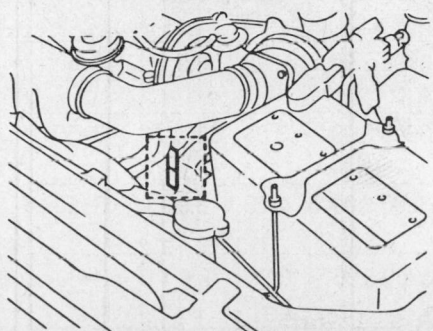

CD17 1.7L diesel engine serial number location

Chassis Number

The chassis number is on the firewall under the hood. Late model vehicles also have the chassis number on a plate attached to the top of the instrument panel on the driver's side. The chassis serial number is preceded by the model designation. Late models also have an Emission Control information label on the firewall under the hood.

ENGINE I.D. TABLE

Number of Cylinders	Displacement cu. in. (cc)	Type	Engine Model Code
4	119.1 (1952)	OHC	L20B
4	85.24 (1397)	OHV	A14
6	146 (2393)	OHC	L24, L24E
6	168 (2753)	OHC	L28, L28E, L28ET
6	170 (2793)	OHC	LD28①
4	75.48 (1237)	OHV	A12A
4	90.80 (1488)	OHV	A15
4	90.8 (1488)	OHC	E15
4	90.8 (1488)	OHC	E15T, E15ET
4	97.6 (1597)	OHC	E16
4	103.7 (1680)	OHC	CD17①
4	119.1 (1952)	OHC	Z20S, Z20E
4	133.4 (2181)	OHC	Z22E
4	120.4 (1974)	OHC	CA20, CA20E, CA20S
4	110.3 (1809)	OHC	CA18ET
V6	180.6 (2960)	OHC	VG30E, VG30ET

① Diesel

DATSUN/NISSAN

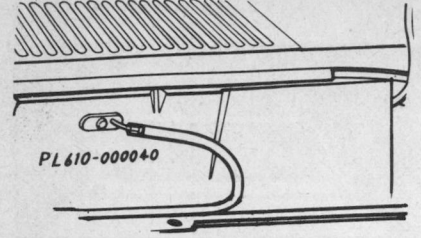

PL610-000040

Chassis number location

DATSUN	TYPE	HLS30
ENGINE CAPACITY		2,393 cc
MAX. HP at RPM		151 HP at 5,600 rpm
WHEEL BASE		2,305 mm
ENGINE NO.		L24- ▢▢▢▢▢▢
CAR NO.		HLS30- ▢▢▢▢▢

NISSAN MOTOR CO., LTD.
YOKOHAMA JAPAN

Vehicle identification plate

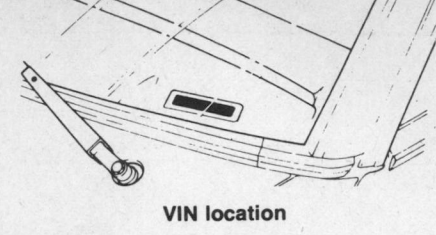

VIN location

VEHICLE IDENTIFICATION PLATE

The vehicle identification plate is attached to the hood ledge or the firewall. This plate is mounted on the left hood ledge panel at the back of the strut housing on the 280Z (on the front of the left strut housing on the 300ZX) and on the right side of the firewall, behind the battery, on the 280ZX. The identification plate gives the vehicle model, engine displacement in cc., SAE horsepower rating, wheelbase, engine number and chassis number.

GENERAL ENGINE SPECIFICATIONS

Year	Model	Type (Model)	Engine Displacement cu. in. (cc)	Carburetor Type	Horsepower @ rpm	Torque @ rpm (ft. lbs.)	Bore × Stroke (in.)	Compression Ratio	Normal Oil Pressure (psi)
'78	B210	OHV 4 (A14)	85.2 (1397)	Dual throat downdraft	80 @ 6000	83 @ 3600	2.99 × 3.03	8.5:1	43–50
	F10	OHV 4 (A14)	85.2 (1397)	Dual throat downdraft	80 @ 6000	83 @ 3600	2.99 × 3.03	8.5:1	43–50
'78	280Z	OHC 6 (L28)	168 (2753)	EFI	170 @ 5600	177 @ 4400	3.39 × 3.11	8.3:1	50–57
'78	200SX	OHC 4 (L20B)	119.1 (1952)	Dual throat downdraft	97 @ 5600	102 @ 3200	3.35 × 3.39	8.5:1	50–57
	810	OHC 6 (L24)	146 (2393)	EFI	154 @ 5600	155 @ 4400	3.27 × 2.90	8.6:1	50–57
'78	510	OHC 4 (L20B)	119.1 (1952)	Dual throat downdraft	97 @ 5600	102 @ 3200	3.35 × 3.39	8.5:1	50–57
'79	200SX, 510	OHC 4 (L20B)	119.1 (1952)	Dual throat downdraft	92 @ 5600	107 @ 3200	3.35 × 3.39	8.5:1	50–57
	280ZX	OHC 6 (L28)	168 (2753)	EFI	135 @ 5200	144 @ 4400	3.39 × 3.11	8.3:1	50–57
'79–'80	810	OHC 6 (L24)	146 (2393)	EFI	120 @ 5200	125 @ 4400	3.27 × 2.90	8.9:1 ①	50–60
	310	OHV 4 (A14)	85.2 (1397)	Dual throat downdraft	65 @ 5600	75 @ 3600	2.99 × 3.03	8.9:1	43–50
'79–'82	210	OHV 4 (A12A)	75.5 (1237)	Dual throat downdraft	58 @ 5600	67 @ 3600	2.95 × 2.75	8.5:1	43–50
		OHV 4 (A14)	85.3 (1397)	Dual throat downdraft	65 @ 5600	75 @ 3600	2.99 × 3.03	8.5:1 ②	43–50
		OHV 4 (A15)	90.8 (1488)	Dual throat downdraft	67 @ 5200	80 @ 3200	2.99 × 3.23	8.9:1	43–50
'80	200SX	OHC 4 (Z20E)	119.1 (1952)	EFI	100 @ 5200	112 @ 3200	3.35 × 3.39	8.5:1	50–60
	510	OHC 4 (Z20S)	119.1 (1952)	Dual throat downdraft	92 @ 5200	112 @ 2800	3.35 × 3.39	8.5:1	50–60

C150

GENERAL ENGINE SPECIFICATIONS

Year	Model	Type (Model)	Engine Displacement cu. in. (cc)	Carburetor Type	Horsepower (SAE) @ rpm	Torque @ rpm (ft. lbs.)	Bore × Stroke (in.)	Com- pression Ratio	Normal Oil Pressure (psi)
'80	280ZX	OHC 6 (L28)	168 (2753)	EFI	132 @ 5200	144 @ 4000	3.39 × 3.11	8.3:1	50–57
'81	310	OHV 4 (A15)	90.8 (1488)	Dual throat downdraft	65 @ 5200	82 @ 2800	2.99 × 3.23	8.9:1	43–50
	510	OHC 4 (Z20)	119.1 (1952)	Dual throat downdraft	92 @ 5200	112 @ 2800	3.35 × 3.39	8.5:1	50–60
	200SX	OHC 4 (Z20)	119.1 (1952)	EFI	100 @ 5200	112 @ 3200	3.35 × 3.39	8.5:1	50–60
'81–'85	810, Maxima	OHC 6 (L24E)	146 (2393)	EFI	120 @ 5200	134 @ 2800	3.27 × 2.90	8.9:1	50–60
	810, Maxima (Diesel)	OHC 6 (LD28)	170 (2793)	DFI	80 @ 4600	120 @ 2400	3.33 × 3.27	22.7:1	③
'81–'83	280ZX	OHC 6 (L28E)	168 (2753)	EFI	145 @ 5200	156 @ 4000	3.39 × 3.11	8.8:1	50–57
	280ZX (Turbo)	OHC 6 (L28ET)	168 (2753)	EFI	180 @ 5600	202 @ 2800	3.39 × 3.11	7.4:1	④
'82–'83	310, Sentra	OHC 4 (E15)	90.8 (1488)	Dual throat downdraft	67 @ 5200	85 @ 3200	2.92 × 3.23	9.0:1	50–57
'83–'85	Sentra, Pulsar	OHC 4 (E16,E16S)	97.6 (1597)	Dual throat downdraft	69 @ 5200	92 @ 3200	2.99 × 3.46	9.4:1	50–57
'83–'85	Sentra (Diesel)	OHC 4 (CD17)	103.7 (1680)	DFI	55 @ 4800	104 @ 2800	3.15 × 3.31	22.2:1	28 @ 1000
'83–'85	Pulsar Turbo	OHC 4 (E15ET)	90.8 (1488)	EFI	100 @ 5200	152 @ 3200	2.92 × 3.23	7.8:1	50–57
'82–'83	200SX	OHC 4 (Z22,Z22E)	133.4 (2181)	EFI	102 @ 5200	129 @ 2800	3.43 × 3.62	8.5:1	50–60
	Stanza	OHC 4 (CA20)	120.4 (1974)	Dual throat downdraft	88 @ 5200	112 @ 2800	3.33 × 3.46	8.5:1	50–60
'84–'85	300ZX	OHC V6 (VG30E)	180.6 (2960)	EFI	160 @ 5200	173 @ 4000	3.43 × 3.27	9.0:1	43 @ 2000
	300ZX (Turbo)	OHC V6 (VG 30ET)	180.6 (2960)	EFI	200 @ 5200	227 @ 3600	3.43 × 3.27	7.8:1	43 @ 2000
'84–'85	Stanza (Canada)	OHC 4 (CA20S)	120.4 (1974)	Dual throat downdraft	88 @ 5200	112 @ 2800	3.33 × 3.46	8.5:1	57 @ 4000
	200SX, Stanza (U.S.)	OHC 4 (CA20E)	120.4 (1974)	EFI	102 @ 5200	116 @ 3200	3.33 × 3.46	8.5:1	57 @ 4000
'84–85	200SX (Turbo)	OHC 4 (CA18ET)	110.3 (1809)	EFI	120 @ 5200	134 @ 3200	3.27 × 3.29	8.0:1	71 @ 4000

NA: Not available at time of publication
EFI: Electronic Fuel Injection
DFI: Diesel Fuel Injection
① 1980 Calif.: 8.6:1
② 1981–84: 8.9:1
③ 10–20 at idle; 40–50 max. when fully warm
④ 10–15 at idle; up to 80 max. when fully warm

GASOLINE ENGINE TUNE-UP SPECIFICATIONS

(When analyzing compression test results, look for uniformity among cylinders, rather than specific pressures)

Year	Model	Spark Plugs		Distributor		Ignition Timing (deg)		Fuel Pump Pressure (psi)	Idle Speed (rpm)		Valve Clearance (in.)●	
		Type	Gap (in.)	Dwell (deg)	Air Gap (in.)	MT	AT		MT	AT▲	In	Ex
'78	F10	BP5ES	.039–.043	Electronic	.008–.016	10B	—	3.8	700	—	.014	.014
'78	B210 Exc. FU	BP5ES	.039–.043	Electronic	.008–.016	10B	8B①	3.9	700	650	.014	.014
'78–'79	B210, 210 FU	BP5EQ	.043–.051	Electronic	.012–.020	5B	—	3.9	700		.014	.014
'79–'80	210 Exc. FU	BP5ES	.039–.043	Electronic	.012–.020	10B②③	8B②	3.9	700	650	.014	.014
'81–'82	210	BP5ES-11 BPR5ES-11	.039–.043	Electronic	.012–.020	5B④	5B	3.8	700	650	.014	.014
'79	310	BP5ES⑤	.039–.043	Electronic	.012–.020	10B②	—	3.8	700	—	.014	.014
'80	310	BP5ES⑤	.039–.043	Electronic	.012–.020	8B	—	3.8	750	—	.014	.014
'81	310	BP5ES-11⑤	.039–.043	Electronic	.012–.020	5B	—	3.8	750	—	.014	.014
'82	310	BP5ES-11⑤	.039–.043	Electronic	.012–.020	2A⑦	2A⑦	3.8	750	750⑧	.011	.011
'78–'79	510	BP6ES	.039–.043⑨	Electronic	.012–.020	12B⑩	12B	3.8	600	600	.010	.012
'80	510	BPR6ES⑪	.031–.035	Electronic	.012–.020	12B⑫	12B⑫	3.8	600	600	.010⑬	.012
'81	510	BP6ES⑭	.031–.035	Electronic	.012–.020	6B	6B	3.8	600	600	.012	.012
'78–'79	200SX	BP6ES	.039–.043⑮	Electronic	.012–.020	9B⑯	12B	3.8	600	600	.010	.012
'80	200SX	BP6ES	.031–.035	Electronic	.012–.020	8B⑰	8B⑰	37	700	700	.012	.012
'81	200SX	BP6ES⑭	.031–.035	Electronic	.012–.020	6B⑱	6B⑱	37	750	700	.012	.012
'82–'83	200SX	BPR6ES⑲	.031–.035	Electronic	.012–.020	8B	8B	37	750	700	.012	.012
'78–'85	810 Maxima	BP6ES㉑	.039–.043	Electronic	.012–.020	10B⑳	10B⑳	36	700	650	.010	.012
'78	280Z	BP6ES-11㉓	.039–.043㉔	Electronic	.012–.020	10B	10B	36	800	700	.010	.012
'79	280ZX	B6ES-11㉓	.039–.043	Electronic	.012–.020	10B	10B	36	800㉕	700	.010	.012
'80–'83	280ZX	BP6ES-11⑭	.039–.043	Electronic	.012–.020	10B㉖	10B㉖	36	700	700	.010	.012
'81–'83	280ZX Turbo	BPR6ES-11	.039–.043	Electronic	.012–.020	20B㉟	20B㉟	36	650	650	.010	.012
'82	Sentra	BPR5ES-11	.039–.043	Electronic	.012–.020	4A	6A	3.8	750	650	.011	.011

GASOLINE ENGINE TUNE-UP SPECIFICATIONS

(When analyzing compression test results, look for uniformity among cylinders, rather than specific pressures)

Year	Model	Spark Plugs Type	Gap (in.)	Distributor Dwell (deg)	Air Gap (in.)	Ignition Timing (deg) MT	AT	Fuel Pump Pressure (psi)	Idle Speed (rpm) MT	AT▲	Valve Clearance (in.)● In	Ex
'83	Sentra (E15)	BPR5ES-11	.039–.043	Electronic	.012–.020	2A	2A	3.8	700	700	.011	.011
'83–'85	Sentra, Pulsar (E16)	BPR5ES-11㉘	.039–.043	Electronic	.012–.020	5A㉙	5A㉙	3.8	750㉚	650	.011	.011
'82–'84	Stanza	㉗	.039–.043	Electronic	.012–.020	0	0	3.8	650㉛	650㉛	.012	.012
'84–'85	200SX	BCPR6ES-11㉜	.039–.043	Electronic	.012–.020	OB	OB	37	750	700㉝	.012	.012
'84–'85	200SX Turbo	BCPR6ES-11㉜	.039–.043	Electronic	.012–.020	15B	15B	37	750	700㉝	.012	.012
'84–'85	300ZX	BCPR6ES-11	.039–.043	Electronic	NA	20B	20B	37	700	650	㉞	㉞
'84–'85	300ZX Turbo	BCPR6E-11	.039–.043	Electronic	NA	20B	20B	37	700	650	㉞	㉞

NOTE: Emission control requires a very precise approach to tune-up. Timing and idle speed are peculiar to the engine and its application, rather than to the engine alone. Data for the particular application is on a sticker in the engine compartment on all late models. If the sticker disagrees with this chart, use the sticker figure. The results of any adjustments or modifications should be checked with a CO meter.

●Set hot
▲In Drive
MT: Manual trans.
AT: Automatic trans.
NA: Not available
FU: Hatchback with 5 spd. sold in 49 states but not in Calif.
A: After Top Dead Center
B: Before Top Dead Center
①Calif.: 10B
②Calif.: 5B
③1980 A14 engine: 8B
④A12A with MT and Canada: 10B
⑤Canada: BPR5ES-11; gap: .031–.035 in.
⑥1980
⑦Canada: 4A
⑧Canada: 650
⑨Canada: .031–.035 in.
⑩1979 49 states cars; 11B
⑪Z20S engine: BP6ES
⑫Z20S engine: 49 states, 8B; Calif./, 6B
⑬Z20S engine: .012 in.
⑭Canada and 1981 280ZX: BPR6ES-11
⑮Canada: .031–.035 in.
⑯Calif. and Canada: 12B
⑰Calif.: 6B
⑱Canada: 8B
⑲Intake side; exhaust side: BPR5ES
⑳1978 Calif. and 1982–85 all: 8B
㉑1978–79; B6ES; 1984 and later BPR6ES-11
㉒1980–81: BP6ES-11
㉓1982–83: BPR6ES-11

㉔Canada: BR6ES
㉕Canada: .028–.031
㉖1981–83 U.S.: 8B
㉗Intake side plugs: BPR6ES-11. 1984 and later: BCPR6ES-11 Exhaust side plugs: BPR5ES-11. 1984 and later: BCPR5ES-11
㉘Canada: BPR5ES; gap: .031–.035
㉙1983 models. 1984 and later:
  5A @ 750 rpm MT, Calif., Canada
  5A @ 650 rpm AT, Calif., Canada
  15B @ 800 rpm MT, 49 states
  8B @ 650 rpm AT, 49 states
㉚1984 and later 49 states w/MT: 800 rpm
㉛1982–83 all models, and 1984 and later Canadian specs. 1984 and later U.S. models (CA20E): 750 MT, 700 AT
㉜Intake side; Exhaust side BCPR5ES-11
㉝630 rpm high altitudes
㉞Hydraulic valve lifters—no adjustment necessary
㉟1983: 24B

DIESEL ENGINE TUNE-UP SPECIFICATIONS

Year Model	Engine Displacement cu. in. (cc)	Warm Valve Clearance (in.)		Intake Valve Opens (deg)	Injection Pump Setting (deg)	Injection Nozzle Pressure (psi)		Idle Speed (rpm)	Compression Pressure (psi)
		In	Ex			New	Used		
'81–'85	170 (2,793)	0.010	0.012	NA	align marks	1,920–2,033	1,778–1,920	650	455
'83–'85	102 (1681)	0.010	0.018	NA	See Text	1,920–2,033	1,778–1,920	750	455

NA: Not Available

FIRING ORDERS

NOTE: To avoid confusion when replacing spark plug wires, always remove them one at a time.

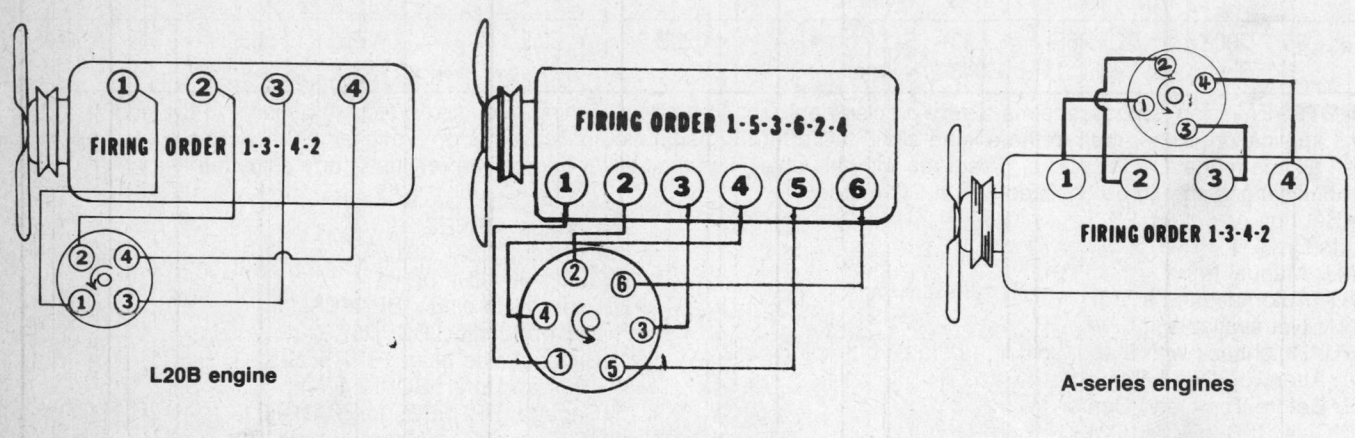

L20B engine

L24, L28 engines

A-series engines

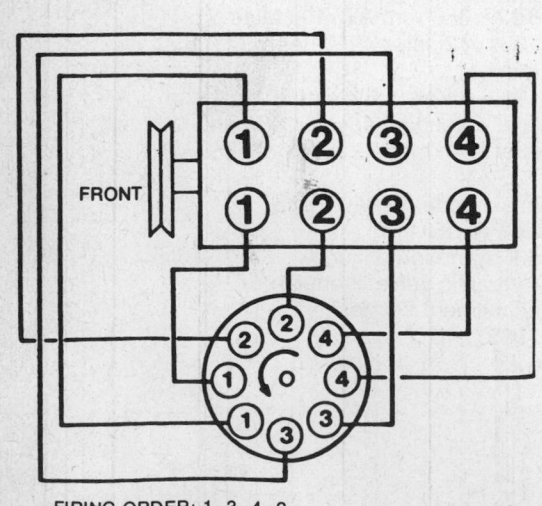

FIRING ORDER: 1-3-4-2
DISTRIBUTOR ROTATION: COUNTERCLOCKWISE

Z20, Z22, Z22E engine—1980 (Calif.), 1981 and later (all)

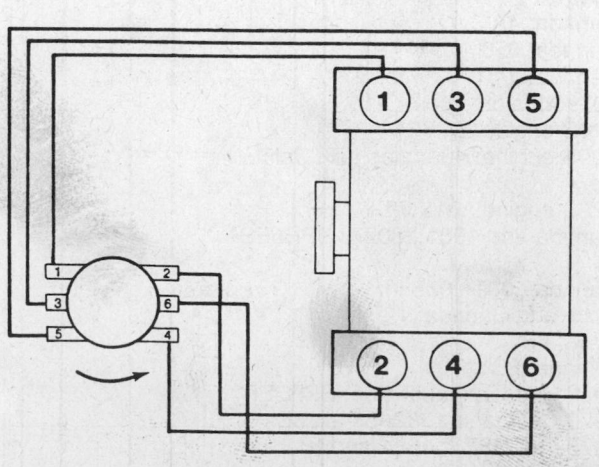

V6 engine firing order: 1-3-5-4-6-2

FIRING ORDERS

NOTE: To avoid confusion when replacing spark plug wires, always remove them one at a time.

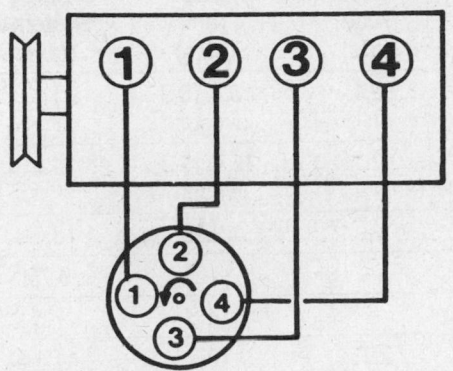

FIRING ORDER: 1–3–4–2
DISTRIBUTOR ROTATION: COUNTERCLOCKWISE

Z20 engine—1980 (49 states)

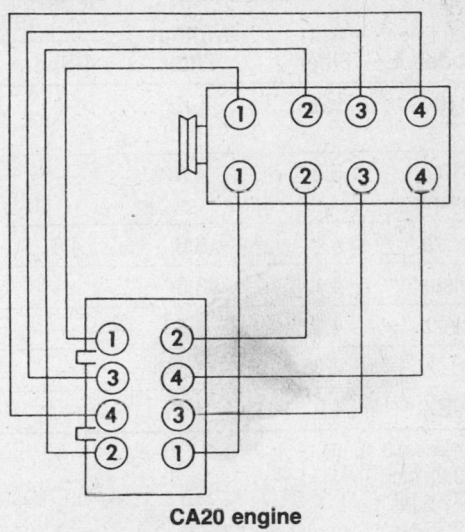

CA20 engine

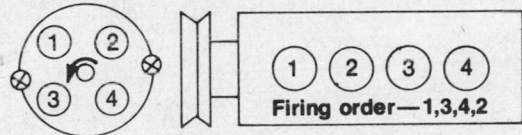

Firing order—1,3,4,2

E15, E16 engine

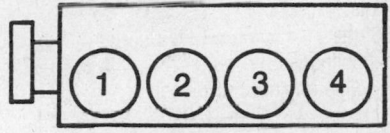

Firing order 1-3-4-2—CD 17

CAPACITIES

Year	Model	Engine Crankcase (Qts)		Transmission (pts)		Automatic (Total Capacity)	Drive Axle (pts)	Gas Tank (gals)	Cooling System (qts)
		With Filter	Without Filter	4-Spd	5-Spd				
'78	B210	3.8	3.4	2.75	3.6	11.8	1.8	11.5	6.25③
	F10	3.6	3.2	4.90	4.9	—	—	10.6/9.1 (wagon)	7.00
'78	810	6.0	5.5	3.60	—	11.8	2.75/2.2 (wagon)	15.9/14.5 (wagon)	11.0
'78	280Z	5.0	4.25	3.63	4.25	11.8	2.75	17.25	11.0
'78–'79	200SX	4.5	4.0	—	3.6	11.8	2.75	15.9	7.90
'78–'79	510	4.5	4.0	3.6	3.6	11.8	2.4	13.2	9.40
'79–'82	210	①	—	②	2.5	11.8	1.8	13.25	6.25③
'79–'81	310	3.4	2.8	4.9	4.9	—	—	13.25	6.25
'79–'80	810	5.9	5.25	3.7	4.25	11.8	2.0	15.9/14.5 (wagon)	11.00
'79–'83	280ZX	4.75⑤	4.25⑤	3.63	4.25	11.8	2.75	21.12	11.12
'80–'81	510	④	—	3.15	3.6	11.8	2.4	13.25	9.25
'80–'83	200SX	4.4	4.1	—	4.25	11.8	2.4	14/15.9 (hatchback)	10
'82	310	4.12	3.6	4.9	5.74	12.75	—	13.25	6.50

DATSUN/NISSAN

CAPACITIES

Year	Model	Engine Crankcase (Qts) With Filter	Engine Crankcase (Qts) Without Filter	Transmission (pts) 4-Spd	Transmission (pts) 5-Spd	Automatic (Total Capacity)	Drive Axle (pts)	Gas Tank (gals)	Cooling System (qts)
'81	810	5.25	4.75	—	4.25	11.8	2.1	16.4/15.9 (wagon)	11.6
'82–'85	810, Maxima	5.0⑥	4.5⑧	—	4.25	11.8	2.1	16.4/15.9 (wagon)	11.6⑦
'82–'85	Sentra	4.1	3.6	4.8	5.75	13.1	—	13.25	5.0
'83–'85	Pulsar	4.1	3.6	—	5.75	13.1	—	13.25	5.75
'82–'85	Stanza	4.1	3.75	—	5.75	12.75	—	14.3	7.8
'84–'85	300ZX	4.25	3.5	—	4.0	14.5	2.75	19	11.1⑧
'84–'85	200SX	4.0	3.75	—	4.25	14.5	⑨	14	9.1

① A12A, A14 engines: 3.46 qts.
  A15 engine: 3.25 qts.
② A12A engine: 2.5 pts.
  A14 engine: 2.75 pts.
③ Automatic transmission: 6 qts.
④ L20B engine: 4.5 qts.
  Z20S engine: 4.65 qts.
⑤ Turbo: 5.5 with, 5.0 without
⑥ Figures are for gasoline engine. For diesel engine: w/filter—6.5 qts., w/o filter—6.0 qts.
⑦ Figure is for gasoline engine. For diesel engine: 11.0 qts.
⑧ Non-turbo model; turbo 11.5
⑨ Solid rear axle: 2.1 pt
  IRS: 2.75 pt.

VALVE SPECIFICATIONS

Model	Seat Angle (deg)	Spring Test Pressure lbs @ in. Outer	Spring Test Pressure lbs @ in. Inner	Spring Installed Height (in.) Outer	Spring Installed Height (in.) Inner	Stem-to-Guide Clearance (in.) Intake	Stem-to-Guide Clearance (in.) Exhaust	Stem Diameter (in.) Intake	Stem Diameter (in.) Exhaust
L20B	45	108 @ 1.16	56.2 @ 0.965	1.575	1.378	0.008– 0.0021	0.0016– 0.0029	0.3136– 0.3142	0.3128– 0.3134
A14 (1978)	45	52.9 @ 1.52	—	1.83	—	0.0006– 0.0018	0.0016– 0.0028	0.3138– 0.3144	0.3128– 0.3134
A12A, A14, A15 (1979–82)	45°30'	52.7 @ 1.19	—	1.83	—	0.0006– 0.0018	0.0016– 0.0028	0.3138– 0.3144	0.3128– 0.3134
E15, E15ET	45°30'	128 @ 1.19	—	1.543	—	0.0008– 0.0020	0.0018– 0.0030	0.2744– 0.2750	0.2734– 0.2740
E16	45°30'	128 @ 1.19	—	1.543	—	0.0008– 0.0020	0.0018– 0.0030	0.2744– 0.2750	0.2734– 0.2740
CA20, CA20E, CA20S	45°30'	47 @ 1.575 ③	24.3 @ 1.378 ④	1.575	1.378	0.0008– 0.0021	0.0016– 0.0029	0.2742– 0.2748	0.2734– 0.2740
L24	45	108 @ 1.16②	56.2 @ 0.965②	1.575	1.378	0.001– 0.002	0.002– 0.003	0.3136– 0.3142	0.3128– 0.3134
L28, L28E, L28ET	45①	108 @ 1.16	56 @ 0.965	1.575	1.378	0.0008– 0.0021	0.0016– 0.0029	0.3136– 0.3142	0.3128– 0.3134

VALVE SPECIFICATIONS

Model	Seat Angle (deg)	Spring Test Pressure lbs @ in.		Spring Installed Height (in.)		Stem-to-Guide Clearance (in.)		Stem Diameter (in.)	
		Outer	Inner	Outer	Inner	Intake	Exhaust	Intake	Exhaust
LD28	45	115.3 @ 1.18	—	1.575	—	0.0008–0.0021	0.0016–0.0029	0.3136–0.3142	0.3128–0.3134
Z20E, Z20S, Z22E	45	115.3 @ 1.16	57 @ 0.98	1.575	1.378	0.0008–0.0021	0.0016–0.0029	0.3136–0.3142	0.3128–0.3134
CD17	45°30′	33.7 @ 156	19.2 @ 1.41	1.8268	1.7008	0.0008–0.0021	0.0016–0.0029	0.2742–0.2748	0.2734–0.2740
VG30E, VG30ET	45°30′	118 @ 1.18	56.2 @ .965	1.575	1.378	0.0008–0.0021	0.0016–0.0029	0.2742–0.2748	0.3128–0.3134
CA18ET	45	118.2 @ 1.00	66.6 @ 1.00	⑤	⑤	0.0008–0.0021	0.0016–0.0029	0.2742–0.2748	0.2734–0.2740

① 45°30′, 1979 and later
② Figure is for Exhaust; for Intake:
   Outer 105.2 @ 1.181
   Inner 54.9 @ 0.984
③ CA20E pressure: 118.2 @ 1.00
④ CA20E pressure: 66.6 @ 1.00
⑤ Free height: 1.967 outer, 1.736 inner

CRANKSHAFT AND CONNECTING ROD SPECIFICATIONS

(All measurements given in inches)

Engine Model	Crankshaft				Connecting Rod Bearings		
	Main Brg. Journal Dia.	Main Brg. Oil Clearance	Shaft End-Play	Thrust on No.	Journal Diameter	Oil Clearance	Side Clearance
L20B	2.3599–2.360	0.0008–0.0024	0.002–0.007	3	1.9660–1.9670	0.001–0.002	0.008–0.012
L24, L24E	2.1631–2.1636	0.001–0.003	0.002–0.007	center	1.9670–1.9675①	0.001–0.003	0.008–0.012
L28 (1978)	2.1631–2.1636	0.008–0.0028	0.002–0.007	center	1.9670–1.9675	0.0010–0.0022	0.0079–0.0118
L28E, L28ET (1979–84)	2.1631–2.1636	0.0008–0.0026	0.002–0.007	center	1.9670–1.9675	0.0009–0.0026	0.0079–0.0118
A14 (1978)	1.966–1.967	0.0008–0.002	0.002–0.006	3	1.7701–1.7706	0.0008–0.002	0.008–0.012
A12A, A14, A15 (1979–82)	1.9666–1.9671	0.001–0.0035	0.002–0.0059	3	1.7701–1.7706	0.0012–0.0031	0.008–0.012
Z20S, Z20E, Z22E	2.1631–2.1636	0.0008–0.0024	0.002–0.0071	3	1.9670–1.9675	0.001–0.0022	0.008–0.012
LD28	2.1631–2.1636	0.0008–0.0024	0.0020–0.0071	center	1.9670–1.9675	0.0008–0.0024	0.008–0.012
E15, E15ET	1.9663–1.9671	②	0.002–0.007	3	1.5730–1.5738	0.0012–0.0024	0.004–0.0146
E16	1.9663–1.9671	②	0.002–0.007	3	1.5730–1.5738	0.0012–0.0024	0.004–0.0146
CA20, CA20E, CA20S	2.0847–2.0852	0.0016–0.0024	0.012	3	1.7701–1.7706	0.0008–0.0024	0.008–0.012

CRANKSHAFT AND CONNECTING ROD SPECIFICATIONS
(All measurements given in inches)

Engine Model	Crankshaft				Connecting Rod Bearings		
	Main Brg. Journal Dia.	Main Brg. Oil Clearance	Shaft End-Play	Thrust on No.	Journal Diameter	Oil Clearance	Side Clearance
CD17	2.0847–2.0852	0.0015–0.0026	0.0020–0.0071	center	1.7701–1.7706	0.0009–0.0026	0.008–0.012
VG30E, VG30ET	2.4790–2.4793	0.0011–0.0022	0.0020–0.0067	4	1.9670–1.9675	0.0004–0.0020	0.0079–0.0138
CA18ET	2.0847–2.0852	0.0016–0.0024	0.0020–0.0071	3	1.8898–1.8903	0.0008–0.0024	0.0118

① L24E: 1.7701–1.7706
② #1 & 5: 0.0012–0.0030
   #2, 3, 4: 0.0012–0.0036

CAMSHAFT SPECIFICATIONS
(All measurements in inches)

Engine	Journal Diameter					Bearing Clearance	Lobe Lift		Camshaft End Play
	1	2	3	4	5		Intake	Exhaust	
L18, L20B	1.8878–1.8883	1.8878–1.8883	1.8878–1.8883	1.8878–1.8883	—	0.0015–0.0026	0.276	0.276	0.0031–0.0150
Z20E, Z20S, Z22E	1.2967–1.2974	1.2967–1.2974	1.2967–1.2974	1.2967–1.2974	—	0.0018–0.0035	NA	NA	0.008
L24, LD28	1.8878–1.8883	1.8878–1.8883	1.8878–1.8883	1.8878–1.8883	1.8878–1.8883	0.0015–0.0026	0.262	0.276	0.0031–0.0150
CA20E, CA18ET	1.8085–1.8092	1.8085–1.8092	1.8085–1.8092	1.8085–1.8092	1.8077–1.8085	0.004①	0.354	0.354	0.0028–0.0055
E15, E15ET	1.6515–1.6522	1.6498–1.6505	1.6515–1.6522	1.6498–1.6505	1.6515–1.6522	0.0014–0.0030②	NA	NA	0.016
E16, CD17	1.1795–1.1803	1.1795–1.1803	1.1795–1.1803	1.1795–1.1803	1.1795–1.1803	0.0008–0.0024	NA	NA	0.0024–0.0067
VG30E VG30ET	1.8478–1.8486	1.8478–1.8486	1.8478–1.8486	1.8478–1.8486	1.8478–1.8486	0.0018–0.0035	NA	NA	0.0012–0.0024

NA Not available
① Clearance limit
② Journals No. 1,3,5. Journals 2 and 4:
   0.0031–0.0047

PISTON AND RING SPECIFICATIONS
(All measurements in inches)

Engine Model	Piston Clearance	Ring Gap			Ring Side Clearance		
		Top Compression	Bottom Compression	Oil Control	Top Compression	Bottom Compression	Oil Control
L20B	0.001–0.002	0.010–0.016	0.012–0.020	0.012–0.035	0.002–0.003	0.001–0.003	—
L24, L24E	0.001–0.002	0.009–0.015	0.006–0.012	0.012–0.035	0.002–0.003	0.001–0.003	0.001–0.003

PISTON AND RING SPECIFICATIONS
(All measurements in inches)

| Engine Model | Piston Clearance | Ring Gap | | | Ring Side Clearance | | |
		Top Compression	Bottom Compression	Oil Control	Top Compression	Bottom Compression	Oil Control
L28 (1978)	0.001–0.0018	0.0098–0.0157	0.0118–0.0197	0.0118–0.0354	0.0016–0.0019	0.0012–0.0028	0
L28 (1979–80)	0.001–0.0018	0.0098–0.0157	0.0118–0.0197	0.0118–0.0354	0.0016–0.0029	0.0012–0.0025	0
L28E (1981–85)	0.001–0.0018	0.0098–0.0157	0.0050–0.0118	0.012–0.035	0.0016–0.0029	0.0012–0.0025	—
L28ET (1981–83)	0.0010–0.0018	0.0075–0.0130	0.0059–0.0118	0.012–0.035	0.0016–0.0029	0.0012–0.0025	0.0009–0.0028
LD28 (1981–84)	0.0020–0.0028	①	0.0079–0.0138	0.0118–0.0177	0.0024–0.0039	0.0016–0.0031	0.0012–0.0028
Z20E, Z20S, Z22E	0.001–0.002	0.0098–0.016	0.006–0.012	0.012–0.035	0.002–0.003	0.001–0.0025	0
A14 (1978)	0.0009–0.002	0.008–0.014	0.006–0.012	0.012–0.035	0.002–0.003	0.001–0.002	Combined ring
A12A, A14, A15 (1979–82)	0.001–0.002	0.008–0.014	0.006–0.012	0.012–0.035	0.002–0.003	0.001–0.002	Combined ring
E15, E16 (1982–85)	0.0009–0.0017	0.0079–0.0138	0.0059–0.0018	0.0118–0.0354	0.0016–0.0029	0.0012–0.0025	0.0020–0.0057
CA20 (1982–83)	0.0009–0.0017	0.0079–0.0138	0.0059–0.0118	0.0118–0.0354	0.0016–0.0029	0.0012–0.0025	0.002–0.0057
CD17 (1983–85)	0.0020–0.0028	0.0079–0.0138	0.0079–0.0138	0.0118–0.0177	0.0024–0.0039	0.0016–0.0031	0.0012–0.0028
CA20S, CA20E (1984–85)	0.0010–0.0018	0.0098–0.0138	0.0059–0.0098	0.0079–0.0236	0.0016–0.0029	0.0012–0.0025	—
CA18ET (1984–85)	0.0010–0.0018	②	0.0059–0.0098	0.0079–0.0236	0.0016–0.0029	0.0012–0.0025	—
VG30E, VG30ET (1984–85)	0.0010–0.0018	0.0083–0.0173	0.0071–0.0173	0.0079–0.0299	0.0016–0.0029	0.0012–0.0025	0.0006–0.0075

① Without mark—0.0079–0.0014
  With mark—0.0055–0.0087
② Piston grades No. 1 and No. 2: 0.0098–0.0126 in.
  Piston grades No. 3, 4, and 5: 0.0075–0.0102 in.

TORQUE SPECIFICATIONS
(All readings in ft. lbs.)

| Engine Model | Cylinder Head Bolts | Main Bearing Bolts | Rod Bearing Bolts | Crankshaft Pulley Bolt | Flywheel to Crankshaft Bolts | Manifolds | |
						Intake	Exhaust
L20B	51–61	33–40	33–40	87–116	101–116	9–12	9–12
L24	51–61	33–40	33–40	101–116	94–108	④	④
L28, L28E, L28ET	54–61⑤	33–40	33–40	94–108②	94–108	③	③
LD28	87–94	51–61	33–40	101–116	101–116	⑥	⑥
Z20E, Z20S, Z22E	51–58	33–40	33–40	87–116	101–116	12–15	12–15

TORQUE SPECIFICATIONS
(All readings in ft. lbs.)

Engine Model	Cylinder Head Bolts	Main Bearing Bolts	Rod Bearing Bolts	Crankshaft Pulley Bolt	Flywheel to Crankshaft Bolts	Manifolds	
						Intake	Exhaust
A12A, A14, A15 E15, E16	51–54 ⑧	36–43	23–27	108–145 ⑦	58–65 ①	11–14	11–14
CA20, CA20E, CA20S	51–61 ⑨	33–40	22–27	90–98	72–80	13–16	13–17
CD17	72–80	23–27	33–40	90–98	72–80	13–16	13–16
CA18ET	⑨	33–40	24–27	90–98	72–80	14–19	14–22
VG30E, VG30ET	40–47	67–74	33–40	90–98	72–80	⑩	13–16

① 1978 A14: 54–61 ft. lbs.
② 1978: 87–116; 1979–83: 101–116
③ 8 mm bolts: 10–13; 10 mm bolts: 25–36
④ 8 mm bolts: 11–18; 10 mm bolts: 25–33; 8 mm nut: 9–12
⑤ Tighten in three steps: 1st, 30; 2nd, 44; 3rd, 54–61
⑥ Upper bolt (M10): 24–27 ft. lbs. Lower nut and bolt (M8): 12–18 ft. lbs.
⑦ E15, E16: 83–108
⑧ Tighten in two steps: 1st, 33; 2nd, 51–54
⑨ Tighten in two steps: 1st, 22; 2nd, 58. Then loosen all bolts completely. Final torque in two steps: 1st, 22; 2nd, 54–61. If angle torquing, turn all bolts 90–95 degrees clockwise.
⑩ Intake bolt: 12–14; intake nut: 17–20

BRAKE SPECIFICATIONS
(All measurements given are in inches unless noted)

Model	Year	Lug Nut Torque (ft. lbs.)	Brake Disc			Drum		Minimum Lining Thickness	
			Master Cylinder Bore	Minimum Thickness	Maximum Run-Out	Diameter	Max. Wear Limit	Front	Rear
510	1978–81	58–72	0.8125	0.331	0.0047	9.000	9.060	0.080	0.059
810	1978–80	58–72	0.8125	0.413	0.0059	9.000	9.060	0.080	0.059
Maxima	1981–85	58–72	0.8125	0.630 ①	0.0059 ②	9.000	9.060	0.079	0.059
B210	1978	58–65	0.750	0.331	0.0047	8.000	8.051	0.063	0.059
200SX	1978–79	58–65	0.750	0.331	0.0047	9.000	9.060	0.059	0.059
	1980–83	58–72	0.8750	③	④	—	—	0.079	0.079
	1984–85	58–72	0.938	0.630 ⑦	0.0028	—	9.060	—	—
F-10	1978	58–65	0.750	0.339	0.0059	8.000	8.050	0.063	0.039
210	1979–82	58–65	0.8125	0.331	0.0047	8.000	8.050	0.063	0.059
280Z	1978	58–65	0.8750	0.413	0.0039	9.000	9.060	0.079	0.059
280ZX	1979–83	58–72	0.9375	0.709 ①	0.0039 ②	—	—	0.080	0.080
300ZX	1984–85	58–72	0.938	0.787	0.0028	—	—	—	—
310	1979–82	58–72	0.8125	0.339	0.0047	8.000	8.050	0.079	0.059

BRAKE SPECIFICATIONS
(All measurements given are in inches unless noted)

Model	Year	Lug Nut Torque (ft. lbs.)	Brake Disc			Drum		Minimum Lining Thickness	
			Master Cylinder Bore	Minimum Thickness	Maximum Run-Out	Diameter	Max. Wear Limit	Front	Rear
Sentra	1982–85	58–72	0.750	0.433⑤	0.0047⑥	7.09	7.13	0.079	0.059
Stanza	1982–85	58–72	0.8125	0.633	0.0059	8.000	8.050	0.080	0.059
Pulsar	1983–85	58–72	0.750	0.394	0.0028	7.09	7.13	0.079	0.059

NOTE: Minimum lining thickness is as recommended by the manufacturer. Due to variation in state inspection regulations, the minimum allowable thickness may be different than recommended.
— Not Applicable
① Rear disc: 0.339
② Rear disc: 0.0059
③ Front disc: 0.413; Rear disc: 0.339
④ Front disc: 0.0047; Rear disc: 0.0059
⑤ 0.394 in. 1983–85
⑥ 0.0028 in. 1983–85
⑦ Rear disc: 0.354

BATTERY AND STARTER SPECIFICATIONS
(All cars use 12 volt, negative ground electrical systems)

Year	Model	Battery Amp Hour Capacity	Starter						Brush Spring Tension (oz.)	Min. Brush Length (in.)
			Lock Test			No Load Test				
			Amps	Volts	Torque (ft. lbs.)	Amps	Volts	rpm		
All	710	50, 60	430 MT	6.0	6.3	60	12	7000	49–64	0.47
			540 AT	5.0	6.0	60	12	6000	49–64	0.47
All	F10	60	Not Recommended			60	12	7000	49–64	0.47
All	B210	60	420	6.3	6.5	60	12	7000	49–64	0.47
			Not Recommended			60	12	6000	29	0.37
			Not Recommended			100	12	4300 RG	56–70	0.43
'78	280Z	65	Not Recommended			100	12	4300	63.4	0.43
'78	200SX	60	Not Recommended			60 MT	12	7000	49–64	0.47
			Not Recommended			60 AT	12	6000	49–64	0.47
			Not Recommended			100 RG	12	4300	56–70	0.43
'79	280ZX	60①	Not Recommended			100	12	4300	63.4	0.43
'80–'83	280ZX	60①	Not Recommended			100	11	3900	63.4	0.43
'84–'85	300ZX	60①	Not Recommended			100	11	3900	63.4	0.43
'79–'83	510, 200 SX, Stanza	60				60 MT	11.5	7000	50–64	0.47
			Not Recommended							
			Not Recommended			60 AT	11.5	6000	50–64	0.47
			Not Recommended			100 RG	11	3900	56–70	0.43
'84–'85	200SX	60①	Not Recommended			60	11.5	7000	64–78.4	0.43
		60①				100RG	11	3900	56–70	0.43
All	210, 310, Sentra, Pulsar	60⑤	Not Recommended			60	11.5	7000	50–64	0.47
			Not Recommended			100 RG	11	3900	56–70	0.43

BATTERY AND STARTER SPECIFICATIONS

(All cars use 12 volt, negative ground electrical systems)

Year	Model	Battery Amp Hour Capacity	Starter							Brush Spring Tension (oz.)	Min. Brush Length (in.)
			Lock Test			No Load Test					
			Amps	Volts	Torque (ft. lbs.)	Amps	Volts	rpm			
'78–'79	810	60①	Not Recommended			100 RG	12	4300		56–70	0.43
'80–'85	810, Maxima	60①②	Not Recommended			100 RG⑥	11	3900		56–70③	0.43④

MT: Manual Transmission
AT: Automatic Transmission
RG: Reduction Gear type starter
① Canada and optional in USA: 70 amps
② Diesel: 80
③ Diesel: 96–117
④ Diesel: 0.35
⑤ Sentra, Pulsar: Canada and optional USA:
  65 amps
⑥ Diesel: 140 RG

ALTERNATOR AND REGULATOR SPECIFICATIONS

Model	Year	Alternator Identification Number	Rated Output @ 5000 rpm (amps)	Output @ 2500 rpm (not less than) (volts)	Brush Length (in.)	Brush Spring Tension (oz.)	Regulated Voltage (volts)
F-10	1978	LR150–36①	50	40	0.295	8.99–12.7	14.3–15.3
		LR160–46①②	60	45	0.295	8.99–12.17	14.4–15.0
B210	1978	LR150–36①	50	40	0.295	9.0–12.2	14.3–15.3
210	1979–80	LR150–36①	50	40	0.295	8.99–12.17	14.4–15.0
210	1980–82	LR150–99①④	50	40	0.28	8.99–12.17	14.4–15.0
310	1979–80	LR160–46①	60	40	0.295	8.99–12.17	14.4–15.0
310 USA	1980–82	LR160–125①	50	35	0.295	8.99–12.17	14.4–15.0
310 Canada	1980–82	LR150–99①	50	35	0.295	8.99–12.17	14.4–15.0
Sentra	1980–85	LR150–125B①⑩	50	42	0.28	8.99–12.17	14.4–15.0
	1984–85	LR150–402⑪	50	42	0.236⑫	6.35–12.7	14.4–15.0
		LR160–401⑪	60	50	0.236⑫	6.35–12.7	14.4–15.0
Pulsar	1983–85	LR150–125B①⑬	50	42	0.28	8.99–12.17	14.4–15.0
	1984–85	LR160–121⑭	60	60	0.276⑫	8.99–12.17	14.4–15.0
510	1978–79	LR150–35①	50	40	0.295	8.99–12.17	14.4–15.0
		LR160–47①③	60	41	0.295	8.99–12.17	14.4–15.0
	1980–81	LR150–52①⑤	50	40	0.295	8.99–12.17	14.4–15.0
Stanza	1982–85	LR160–104①	60	40	0.295	8.99–12.17	14.4–15.0
810 Maxima	1978–79	LT160–42①	60	40	0.280	8.99–12.17	14.4–15.0
	1980	LR160–42B①	60	50	0.295	8.99–12.17	14.4–15.0
	1981–85⑥	LR160–82①⑧	60	50	0.280	8.99–12.17	14.4–15.0
	1981–83⑦	LR160–97①⑨	60	52	0.240	10.79–14.60	14.4–15.0

ALTERNATOR AND REGULATOR SPECIFICATIONS

Model	Year	Alternator Identification Number	Rated Output @ 5000 rpm (amps)	Output @ 2500 rpm (not less than) (volts)	Brush Length (in.)	Brush Spring Tension (oz.)	Regulated Voltage (volts)
200SX	1978–79	LR150-35①	50	40	0.295	8.99–12.17	14.4–15.0
	1980	LR160-47①	60	45	0.295	8.99–12.17	14.4–15.0
	1981	LR260-78①	60	50	0.280	8.99–12.17	14.4–15.0
	1982–83	LR160-78B①	60	50	0.280	8.99–12.17	14.4–15.0
	1984–85	LR160-104⑬	60	50	0.276⑫	8.99–12.17	14.4–15.1
		LR170-706⑭	70	50	0.217⑫	5.29–12.7	14.4–15.0
280Z	1978	LT160-42①	60	45	0.280	8.99–12.17	14.4–15.0
280ZX	1979–80	LR160-42B①	60	50	0.276	8.99–12.17	14.4–15.0
	1981–83	LR160-82①	60	50	0.276	8.99–12.17	14.4–15.0
300ZX	1984–85	LR170-701B⑬	70	50	0.217⑫	5.29–12.7	14.1–14.7
		A2T48195⑭	70	50	0.31⑫	10.93–15.17	14.1–14.7

① Uses integral voltage regulator
② With air conditioning
③ Optional in USA; standard in Canada
④ 1982: LR150-99B
⑤ 1981: LR150-98
⑥ Gasoline
⑦ Diesel
⑧ 1982–85 LR160-82B
⑨ 1982–85 LR160-97B
LR160-97C
⑩ Gasoline engine model
⑪ Diesel engine model
⑫ Wear limit
⑬ Non-turbo models
⑭ Turbo models

WHEEL ALIGNMENT SPECIFICATIONS

		Caster		Camber				Wheel Pivot Ratio (deg)	
Year	Model	Range (deg)	Preferred Setting (deg)	Range (deg)	Preferred Setting (deg)	Toe-In (in.)	Steering Axis Inclination (deg)	Inner Wheel	Outer Wheel
1978–80	810 (Front)	1 3/16–2 11/16	2 1/4	0–1 1/2	3/4	1/8	7 29/32	20	18 29/32
	810 (Rear)	—	—	—	—	3/16	—	—	—
1981–83	810 (Front)	2 15/16–4 7/16	3 11/16	– 5/16–1 3/16	7/16	1/32	12 1/8	20	18 11/16
	810 (Rear)	—	—	15/16–2 7/16	1 11/16	7/32	—	—	—
1984–85	Maxima (Front)	2 15/16–4 7/16	3 11/16	– 5/16–1 3/16	7/16	1/32	12 1/8	20	18 11/16
	Maxima (Rear)	—	—	1 1/4–2 3/4	2	5/32	—	—	—
1978–79	200SX	1 1/16–2 9/16	1 13/16	5/16–1 13/16	17/16	1/8	7 13/16	35	30
1980–83	200SX	1 3/4–3 1/4	2 1/2	– 11/16–13/16	1/16	3/64	8 5/32	20	18 45/64
1984–85	200SX	2 3/4–4 1/4	3 1/2	– 3/8–1 1/16	1 7/8	3/64	11 11/16	20	18 11/16
1978–81	510 Station Wagon	15/16–2 7/16	1 9/16	1/16–1 9/16	3/4	1/16	8 5/32	20	19 1/2
1979–81	510	1 1/16–2 9/16	1 13/16	– 1/4–1 1/4	1/2	1/16	8 27/32	20	19 1/2
1978	F10 (Radials)	1/4–1 3/4	1	13/16–2 1/4	1 1/2	0–3/32	10	32 1/2	36 1/2
	(Bias Ply)	1/4–1 3/4	1	13/16–2 1/4	1 1/2	1/8–7/32	10	32 1/2	36 1/2
1979–81	310	7/16–1 15/16	1 1/4	1/4–1 3/4	1	0–3/32	11 27/32	18 13/32	20
1982	310	7/16–1 15/16	1 1/4	1/4–1 3/4	1	0–3/32	11 27/32	19	20
1978	280ZX	2 1/16–3 7/16	1 1/4	5/16–1 13/16	17/16	0–1/8	12	34	33
1979	280ZX Power Steering	4–5 1/2	1 1/2	– 1/2–1	1/4	1/16–1/8	9 11/32	34	26 1/2

WHEEL ALIGNMENT SPECIFICATIONS

Year	Model	Caster Range (deg)	Caster Preferred Setting (deg)	Camber Range (deg)	Camber Preferred Setting (deg)	Toe-In (in.)	Steering Axis Inclination (deg)	Wheel Pivot Ratio (deg) Inner Wheel	Outer Wheel
1979	280ZX Man. Steering	4–5½	1½	−½–1	¼	1/16–1/8	9 11/32	35½	31
	Rear, All			−29/32–1¼		1/32–1/8			
1980–83	280ZX Power Steering	4 3/16–5 11/16		−9/16–15/16	3/16	3/64–1/8	9 11/32	20	18 7/16
	280ZX Man.-Steering	4 3/16–5 11/16		−9/16–15/16	3/16	3/64–1/8	9 11/32	20	18 45/64
	Rear, All			−1/16–1 7/16	¾	5/64–5/32			
1984–85	300ZX	5 13/16–7 5/16		−9/16–15/16	3/16	1/32–1/8	13	22½	20
	Rear			−1 15/16–7/16		1/16–1/16			
1978	B210	1–2½	1½	7/16–1 15/16	1 1/8	3/32–5/32	8¼	38	32
1979–82	210 Except Wagon, Canadian	1 11/16–3 7/16		0–1½	¾	3/64–1/8	8 19/32	20	19 19/64
	Wagon	1 15/16–3 7/16		0–1½	¾	3/64–1/8	8 19/32	20	19 19/64
	1.2L Canadian	1 11/16–3 3/16		−¼–1 3/32		0–3/32	8 13/32	20	19 19/64
1982–84	Stanza	11/16–2 3/16	1 3/8	−¾–¾	0	0–5/64	14 13/32	20	18½
	Rear			0–1½	¾	0–5/64			
1983–84	Pulsar	¾–2¼	1½	−9/16–1 1/16	¼	0–5/64	12¾	20	17½
1983–84	Sentra	¾–2¼	1½	−9/16–1 1/16	¼	1/8–3/16	12 15/16	20	17½

TUNE-UP PROCEDURES

Number the spark plug wires and clean any foreign material from around the spark plugs prior to removing them. Use a spark plug socket with a rubber insert to remove the plugs. This will prevent cracking the porcelain insulator. Each spark plug should be individually inspected and, if necessary, re-placed. Refer to "Troubleshooting" in the Unit Repair section for an analysis of plug tip conditions. Clean reusable spark plugs and file the center electrode flat. Adjust the spark plug gap, according to the "Tune-Up-Specifications" chart, with a wire–type feeler gauge. Lightly oil the threads and torque the spark plugs to 11–15 ft.lbs. Do not overtorque; the cylinder heads are aluminum, and the plug threads are easily stripped.

Electronic Ignition

AIR GAP ADJUSTMENT

1978

Reluctor air gap should be checked periodically. Standard air gap is 0.008–0.016 in. for both single and dual gap distributors. If the gap is incorrect, adjustment may be made by loosening the pick-up coil screws and inserting a feeler gauge.

NOTE: The use of a non-magnetic feeler gauge such as plastic or brass, is recommended for accurate gapping.

Remove the rubber cap from the tip of the rotor shaft. Add grease if necessary.

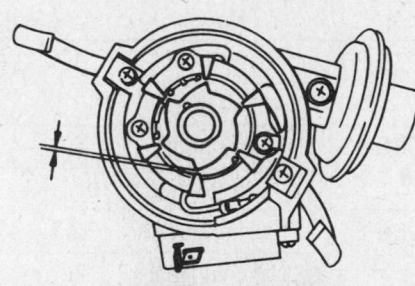
Checking the air gap—1979 and later with ring-type pick-up

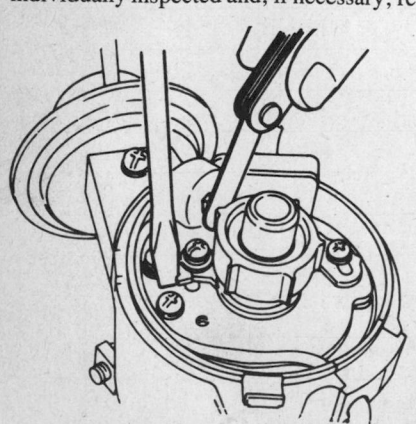
Checking the air gap—1978-79

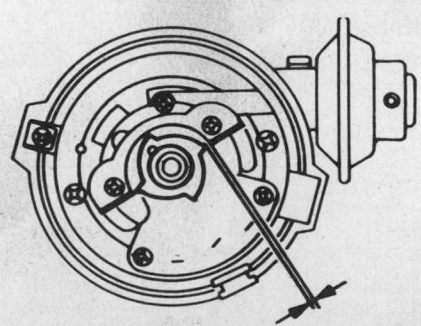
Checking the air gap—1979 and later with stator

The reluctor cannot be removed. To remove the pick-up coil, take out the two pick-up coil assembly and core screws clamping the primary wire. Reverse the sequence to install.

1979 and Later
WITH RING-TYPE PICK-UP

All models built in 1979 and later with the exception of those listed under "With Stator" use the ring-type of electronic ignition system.

Adjustment of these models is made by simply loosening the pick-up coil (toothed stator ring) retaining screws and centering the ring around the reluctor until the proper gap is achieved.

WITH STATOR

Models using this type of electronic ignition system include: 1980–83 510 and 200SX (W/Z20 and Z22, Z22E engine), 1984 and later 200SX (CA20E and CA18ET engines) 1982 210 (USA models only), 1982–84 310, Sentra Pulsar and Stanza.

Adjustment of these models is made by simply loosening the stator mounting screws and moving the stator until the proper gap is achieved.

Ignition Timing

Timing settings for each model are given in the "Tune-Up Specifications" chart.

NOTE: Datsun does not give ignition timing adjustments for 1980 California models or for any 1981 and later models, except those specified below. These models are not covered in this section. If the ignition timing requires adjustment, please refer to the underhood specifications sticker for applicable procedures.

ADJUSTMENT

All Except 1983 and Later 200SX

1. Set the dwell to the proper specification.
2. Locate the timing marks on the crankshaft pulley and the front of the engine.
3. Clean off the timing marks so that you can see them.
4. Use chalk or white paint to color the mark on the crankshaft pulley and the mark on the scale which will indicate the correct timing when aligned with the notch on the crankshaft pulley.
5. Attach a tachometer to the engine.
6. Attach a timing light to the engine, according to the manufacturer's instructions.
7. Leave the vacuum line connected to the distributor vacuum diaphragm on all models except the 1979 210 wagons with automatic transmission, the A15 engine and 1980 and later A series engines; disconnect and plug the hose on those models. On 1980 810s, disconnect the throttle valve switch harness connector and plug the purge hose from the intake manifold. Plug the opening

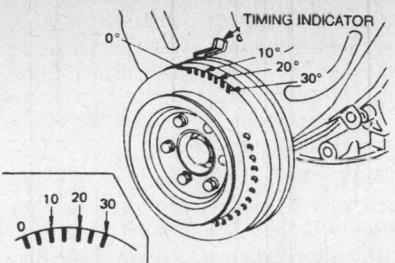

300ZX V6 timing marks

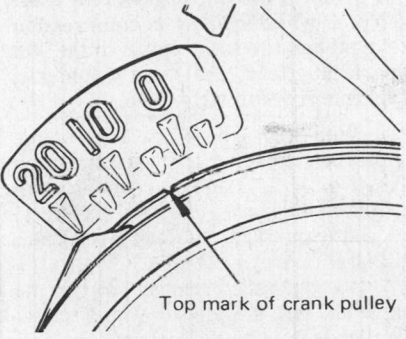

Top mark of crank pulley

Typical timing marks

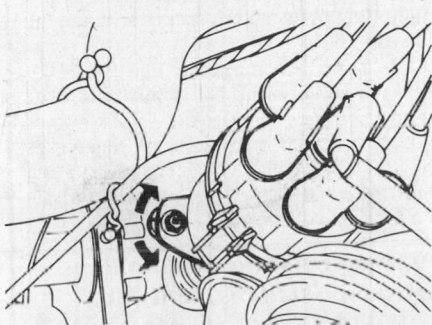

Loosen the distributor lockbolt and turn the distributor slightly to advance (upper arrow) or retard (lower arrow) the timing

in the intake manifold. On 1980 49 States models, also disconnect the hose from the air induction pipe and cap the pipe, and disconnect and plug the vacuum advance hose at the distributor. Note that the disconnect and plug instructions for the air induction pipe and the distributor vacuum advance do not apply to 1980 models sold in Canada.

8. Check to make sure that all of the wires clear the fan and then start the engine. Allow the engine to reach normal operating temperature.
9. Adjust the idle to the correct setting.
10. Aim the timing light at the timing marks. If the marks that you put on the pulley and the engine are aligned when the light flashes, the timing is correct. Turn off the engine and remove the tachometer and the timing light. If the marks are not in alignment, proceed with the following steps.
11. Turn off the engine.
12. Loosen the distributor lockbolt just enough so that the distributor can be turned with a little effort.

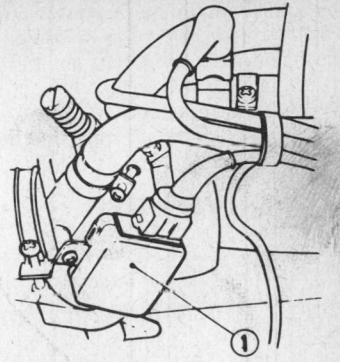

1980 and later throttle valve switch

13. Start the engine. Keep the wires of the timing light clear of the fan.
14. With the timing light aimed at pulley and the marks on the engine, turn the distributor in the direction or rotor rotation to retard the spark, and in the opposite direction of rotor rotation to advance the spark. Align the marks on the pulley and the engine with the flashes of the timing light. Tighten the hold-down bolt.

NOTE: See the "Emission Controls" section for adjustment of phase difference on dual point models.

1983 and Later 200SX

NOTE: When checking ignition timing on air conditioner-equipped cars, make sure that the air conditioner is "off" when proceding with the check.

— CAUTION —

Automatic transmission-equipped models should be shifted into "D" for idle speed checks. When in "Drive" the parking brake must be fully applied and both front and rear wheels checked. When racing the engine on automatic transmission-equipped models, make sure that the shift lever is in the "N" or "P" position, and always have an assistant in the driver's seat with his or her foot on the brake pedal. After all adjustments are made, shift the car to the "P" position and remove the wheel chocks.

1. Run the engine up to normal operating temperature.
2. Open the hood, and run the engine up to 2,000 rpm for about 2 minutes under no-load (all accessories "off").
3. Run the engine at idle speed. Disconnect the hose from the air induction pipe, and cap the pipe.
4. Race the engine two or three times under no-load, then run the engine for one minute at idle.
5. Check idle speed. Manual transmission cars should be idling at 750 rpm (plus 50 rpm, or minus 150). Automatic transmission cars should be idling in the "D" position at 750 rpm (plus 50 rpm, or minus 150 rpm). Adjust the idle speed by turning the idle speed adjusting screw.
6. Connect the timing light according to the light's manufacturer's instructions.

Ignition timing should be 8° plus or minus 2° BTDC. Adjust the timing by loosening the distributor hold-down bolts and turning the distributor clockwise to advance and counter-clockwise to retard.

7. Reconnect the air induction pipe hose.

Valve Lash

ADJUSTMENT

B210, F10, 210, 310, Sentra, and Pulsar

1. Run the engine until it reaches normal operating temperature. Oil temperature, not water temperature, is critical to valve adjustment. With this in mind, make sure the engine is fully warmed up since this is the only way to make sure the parts have reached their full expansion. Generally speaking, this takes around fifteen minutes. After the engine has reached normal operating temperature, shut it off.

2. Purchase a new valve cover gasket before removing the valve cover. The new silicone gasket sealers are just as good or better if you can't find a gasket.

3. Note the location of any hoses or wires which may interfere with valve cover removal, tag and disconnect them and move them aside. Then, remove the bolts which hold the valve cover in place.

4. After the valve cover has been removed, the next step is to get the number one piston at TDC on the compression stroke. There are at least two ways to do it; you can bump the engine over with the starter or turn it over by using a wrench on the front pulley attaching bolt. The easiest way to find TDC is to turn the engine over slowly

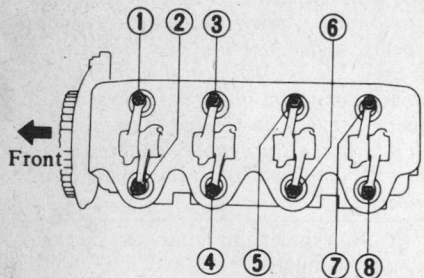

Valve adjustment—E-series engines

A-series engines valve adjustment order

with a wrench (after first removing No. 1 plug) until the piston is at the top of its stroke and the TDC timing mark on the crankshaft pulley is in alignment with the timing mark pointer. At this point, the valves for No. 1 should be closed.

NOTE: Make sure both valves are closed with the valve springs up as high as they will go. An easy way to find the compression stroke is to remove the distributor cap and see toward which spark plug lead the rotor is pointing. If the rotor points to the No. 1 spark plug lead, the No. 1 cylinder is on its compression stroke. When the rotor points to the No. 2 spark plug lead, the No. 2 cylinder is on its compression stroke etc.

5. With No. 1 piston at TDC of the compression stroke, check the clearance on valves No. 1, 2, 3 and 5 (counting from the front to the rear). Adjust valves No. 1, 2, 3 and 6 on 1982 and later 310 Sentra and Pulsar.

6. To adjust the clearance, loosen the locknut and turn the adjuster with a screwdriver while holding the locknut. The correct size feeler gauge should pass with a slight drag between the rocker arm and the valve stem.

7. Turn the crankshaft one full revolution to position the No. 4 piston at TDC of the compression stroke. Adjust valves No. 4, 6, 7 and 8 in the same manner as the first four. Adjust valves No. 4, 5, 7 and 8 on 1982 and later 310 Sentra and Pulsar.

8. Replace the valve cover.

1978–80 510 and 200SX (49 State models only) and 710

1. The valves are adjusted with the engine at normal operating temperature. Oil temperature, and the resultant parts expansion, is much more important than water temperature. Run the engine for at least fifteen minutes to ensure that all the parts have reached their full expansion. After the engine is warmed up, shut if off.

2. Purchase either a new gasket or some silicone gasket seal before removing camshaft cover. Note the location of any wires and hoses which may interfere with cam cover removal, disconnect them and move them aside. Then remove the bolts which hold the cam cover in place and remove the cam cover.

3. Place a wrench on the crankshaft pulley bolt and turn the engine over until the valves for No. 1 cylinder are closed. When both cam lobes are pointing up, the valves are closed. If you have not done this before, it is a good idea to turn the engine over slowly several times and watch the valve action until you have a clear idea of just when the valve is closed.

4. Check the clearance of the intake and exhaust valves. You can differentiate between them by lining them up with the tubes of the intake and exhaust manifolds. The correct size feeler gauge should pass between the base circle of the cam and the

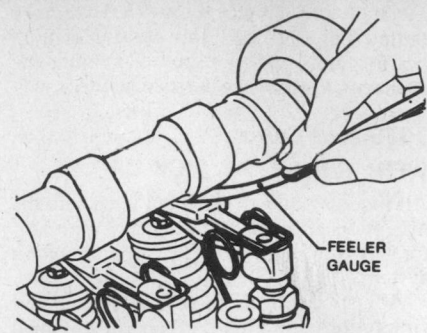

Checking the valve lash with a flat feeler gauge—L-series engines

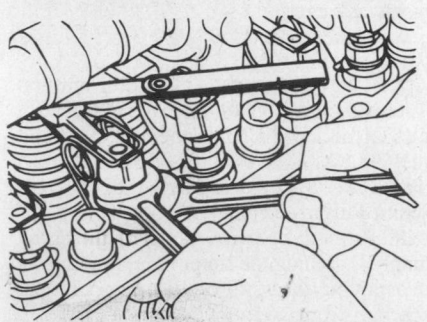

Loosen the locknut and turn the pivot adjuster to change the clearance

rocker arm with just a slight drag. Be sure the feeler gauge is inserted *straight* and not on an angle.

5. If the valves need adjustment, loosen the locking nut and then adjust the clearance with the adjusting screw. You will probably find it necessary to hold the locking nut while you turn the adjuster. After you have the correct clearance, tighten the locking nut and recheck the clearance. Remember, it's better to have them slightly loose than too tight, especially exhaust valves.

6. Repeat this procedure (Steps 3–5) until you have checked and/or adjusted all the valves. (Be sure to adjust in the firing order.) Keep in mind that all that is necessary is to have the valves closed and the camshaft lobes pointing up. It is not particularly important what stroke the engine is on.

7. Install the cam cover gasket, the cam cover and any wires and hoses which were removed.

810 (Maxima) and 280Z, ZX

1978–85 810 and Maxima engines and all 1978–83 Z and ZX engines are adjusted hot.

NOTE: Skip Steps 7–8 if you have a 1978–85 810 or a 1978–84 280Z, ZX.

1. Note the locations of all hoses or wires that would interfere with valve cover removal disconnect them and move them aside. Then, remove the six bolts which hold the valve cover in place.

2. Bump one end of the cover sharply to loosen the gasket and then pull the valve cover off the engine vertically.

3. Place a wrench on the crankshaft pulley bolt and turn the engine over until the first cam lobe is pointing straight up. The timing marks on the crankshaft pulley should be lined up approximately where they would be when the No. 1 spark plug fires.

NOTE: If you decide to turn the engine by "bumping" it with the starter, be sure to disconnect the high tension wire from the coil to prevent the engine from accidentally starting and spewing oil all over the engine compartment.

— CAUTION —

Never attempt to turn the engine by using a wrench on the camshaft sprocket bolt; this would put a tremendous strain on the timing chain.

4. See the illustration for primary adjustment and check the clearance for valves (1), (3), (7), (8), (9) and (11) using a flat-bladed feeler gauge. The feeler gauge should pass between the cam and the cam follower with a very slight drag. Insert the feeler gauge *straight*, not at an angle.

5. If the clearance is not within the specified limits, loosen the pivot locking nut and then insert the feeler gauge between the cam and the cam follower. Adjust the pivot screw until there is a very slight drag on the gauge, tighten the locking nut, recheck the adjustment and correct as necessary.

6. Turn the engine over so that the first cam lobe is pointing straight down. See the illustration for secondary adjustment and then check the clearance on valves (2), (4), (5), (6), (10) and (12). If clearance is not within specifications, adjust as detailed in Step 5.

7. Repeat the entire valve adjustment procedure using the gauges specified in the "Tune-Up" chart, but do not loosen the locking nuts unless the gauge indicates that adjustment is required.

8. When all valves are at hot specifications, clean all traces of old gasket material from the valve cover and the head. Install the new gasket in the valve cover with sealer and install the valve cover. Tighten the valve cover bolts evenly in several stages going around the cover to ensure a good seal. Reconnect all hoses and wires securely and operate the engine to check for leaks.

1980–83 510, 200SX (with Z20 and Z22) Engines and 1982 and Later Stanza

1. The valves must be adjusted with the engine warm, so start the car and run the engine until the needle on the temperature gauge reaches the middle of the gauge. After the engine is warm, shut it off.

2. Purchase either a new gasket or some silicone gasket sealer before removing the camshaft cover. Counting on the old gasket to be in good shape is a losing proposition; always use new gaskets. Note the location

of any wires and hoses which may interfere with cam cover removal, tag and disconnect them and move them to one side. Remove the bolts holding the cover in place and remove the cover. Remember, the engine will be hot, so be careful.

3. Place a wrench on the crankshaft pulley bolt and turn the engine over until the first cam lobe behind the camshaft timing chain sprocket is pointing straight down.

NOTE: If you decide to turn the engine by "bumping" it with the starter, be sure to disconnect the high tension wire from the coil(s) to prevent the engine from accidentally starting and spewing oil all over the engine compartment.

— CAUTION —

Never attempt to turn the engine by using a wrench on the camshaft sprocket bolt; there is a one-to-two turning ratio between the camshaft and the crankshaft which will put a tremendous strain on the timing chain.

4. See the illustration for primary adjustment and adjust valves (1), (4), (6), and (7) using a flat-bladed feeler gauge. The feeler gauge should pass between the valve stem end and the rocker arm screw with a very slight drag. Insert the feeler gauge *straight*, not an angle.

5. If the clearance is not within specified value, loosen the rocker arm lock nut and turn the rocker arm screw to obtain the

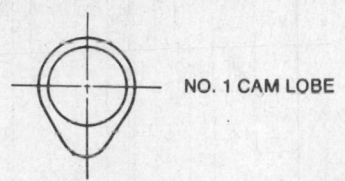

Secondary valve adjustment, No. 1 cam lobe pointing down—810, Maxima and 280Z and ZX

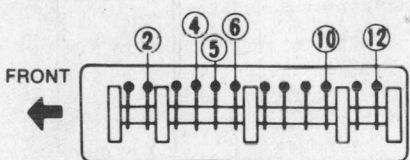

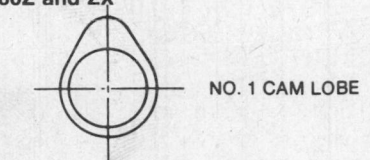

Primary valve adjustment, No. 1 cam lobe pointing up—810, Maxima and 280Z and ZX

proper clearance. After correct clearance is obtained, tighten the lock nut.

6. Turn the engine over so that the first cam lobe behind the camshaft timing chain sprocket is pointing straight up and adjust valves marked (2), (3), (5), and (8) in the secondary adjustment illustration. They, too, should be adjusted to specification as in Step 5.

7. Install the cam cover gasket, the cam cover and any wires and hoses which were removed.

1984 and Later 200SX

Follow the procedure above for 1980–83 models, with the following exceptions: on step 4, check and adjust the clearance on valves 1, 2, 4 and 6 as shown in the accompanying illustration. This is with No. 1 cylinder at TDC on compression. On step 6, check and adjust the clearance on valves 3, 5, 7 and 8 with the No. 4 cylinder at TDC on compression.

1984 and Later 300ZX

The V6 engines in these models are equipped with hydraulic lash adjusters, which continually take up excess clearance in the valve train. No routine adjustment is necessary or possible.

CD17 Diesel

NOTE: The CD17 diesel valve train differs from the other Datsun/Nissan engines in that the valves are operated directly off of the camshaft via bucket-type cam followers; valve adjustment is performed by compressing the follower removing the adjusting shim and replacing it with either a thicker shim (when clearance is too large) or a thinner shim (when clearance is small). The shim is located on top of the bucket directly underneath each cam lobe. A valve spring compressor, Kent-Moore part no. KV 101092S0, is necessary for this job. A magnet is also very useful for removing the shims.

1. Warm the engine up to operating temperature.

2. Set the No. 1 piston at TDC following the procedure under "B210, etc." valve adjustment.

3. Remove the camshaft (valve) cover.

4. Measure the clearance between the cam follower (actually the top of the shim) and the cam lobe using a feeler gauge. If clearance is beyond specification (see the "Tune-Up Specifications" chart), install a new adjustment shim according to the amount of clearance needed or in excess. Shims are available in varying thicknesses from Datsun/Nissan dealers. Mike up the old shims and mark down the measurement of each, or keep the shims in order and take them to the dealer for miking so you'll know the proper sizes to buy.

5. After replacing the adjustment shims, recheck valve clearances.

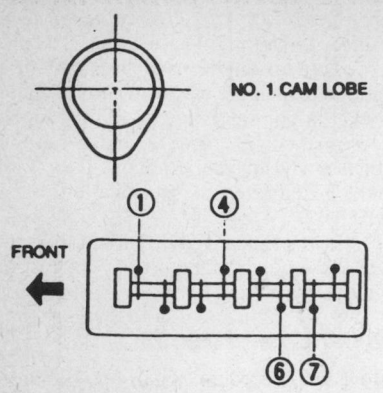

Primary valve adjustment, No. 1 cam lobe pointing down—all dual-plug engines

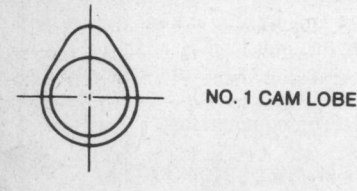

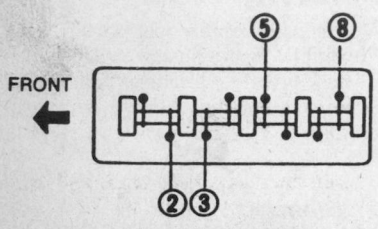

Secondary valve adjustment, No. 1 cam lobe pointing up—all dual-plug engines

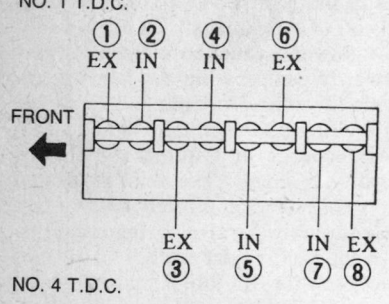

CD17 valve adjustment sequence

NOTE: The adjustment shims that have been removed may be reused if not excessively worn or damaged. Mark the sizes on each for later reference.

Carburetor

IDLE SPEED & MIXTURE ADJUSTMENT

NOTE: 1980 and later Datsuns/Nissans require a CO meter to adjust their mixture ratios, therefore, no procedures concerning this adjustment are given. Also, many California model Datsuns have a plug over their mixture control screw.

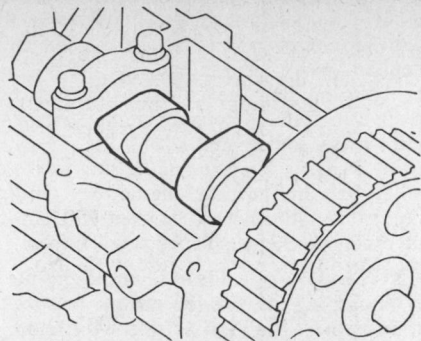

Position of No. 1 cylinder camshaft lobes at TDC

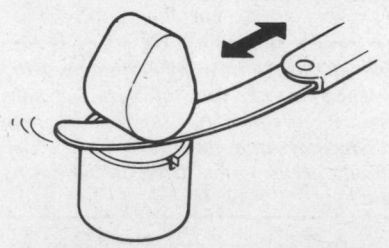

Insert the feeler gauge between the cam lobe and the top of the cam follower on the CD17

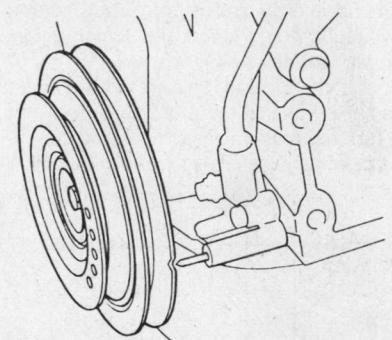

Timing marks and pointer at TDC—CD17 diesel

1. Start the engine and allow it to run until it reaches normal operating temperature.
2. Allow the engine idle speed to stabilize by running the engine at idle for at least one minute.
3. If it hasn't already been done, check and adjust the ignition timing to the proper setting.

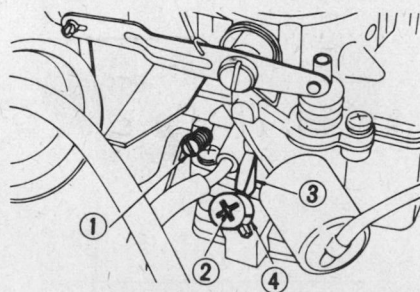

1. Throttle adjusting screw
2. Idle adjusting screw
3. Stopper
4. Idle limiter cap

Downdraft carburetor idle adjustment screw

4. Shut off the engine and connect a tachometer.
5. Disconnect and plug the air hose between the three way connector and the check valve, if equipped. On 1980 and later models, disconnect the air induction hose and plug the pipe. With the transmission in Neutral, check the idle speed on the tachometer. If the reading is correct, continue onto Step 6 for 1978–79 models. For 1980 and later and certain California models, proceed to Step 8 below if the idle is correct. If not, turn the idle speed adjusting screw clockwise with a screwdriver to increase idle speed or counterclockwise to decrease it.
6. With the automatic transmission in Drive (wheels blocked and parking brake on) or the manual transmission in Neutral, turn the mixture screw out until the engine rpm starts to drop due to an overly rich mixture.
7. Turn the screw in past the starting point until the rpm starts to drop due to an overly lean mixture. Turn the mixture screw in until the idle speed drops 35–45 rpm with manual transmission or 10–20 with automatic for 1978 B 210; 35–45 rpm (all transmissions) for 1978 F 10 and 1978–79 510, 200 SX. If the mixture limiter cap will not allow this adjustment, remove it, make the adjustment, and reinstall it. Go on to Step 8 for 1978–79 models.
8. Install the air hose. If the engine speed increases, reduce it with the idle speed screw.

Electronic Fuel Injection

IDLE SPEED ADJUSTMENT

NOTE: See the "Fuel Injection" Unit Repair Section for specifics on the electronic fuel injection systems on all Datsun and Nissan models covered here.

To adjust the mixture controls on these units requires a CO meter and several special tools, therefore we will confine ourselves to idle speed adjustment.

1. Start the engine and run it until the water temperature indicator points to the middle of the temperature gauge. It might be quicker to take a short spin down the road and back.
2. Open the hood. Run the engine at about 2,000 rpm for a few minutes with the

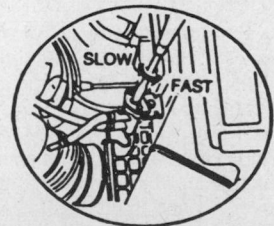

Idle speed adjusting screw—fuel injected 200SX

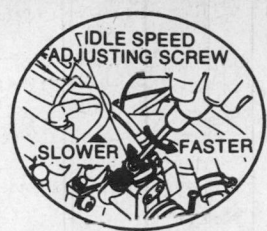

Idle speed adjusting screw—1978-80 810 and Maxima

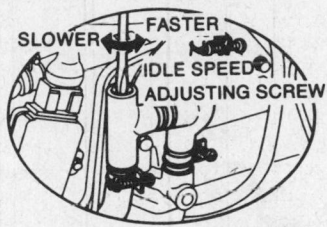

Idle speed adjusting screw—1981 and later 810

transmission in Neutral and all accessories off. If you have not already done so, check the ignition timing and make sure it is correct. Hook up a tachometer. For automatic transmission, set the parking brake, block the wheels and set the shift selector in the Drive position.

3. Run the engine at idle speed and disconnect the hose from the air induction pipe, then plug the pipe. Allow the engine to run for about a minute at idle speed.

4. Check the idle against the specifications given earlier in this section. Adjust the idle speed by turning the idle speed adjusting screw. Turn the screw clockwise for slower idle speed and counterclockwise for faster idle speed.

5. Connect the hose and disconnect the tachometer. If the idle speed increases, adjust it with the idle speed adjusting screw.

Diesel Fuel Injection

IDLE SPEED ADJUSTMENT

NOTE: A special tachometer compatible with diesel engines will be required for this procedure. A normal tachometer will not work.

1. Make sure all electrical accessories are turned off.

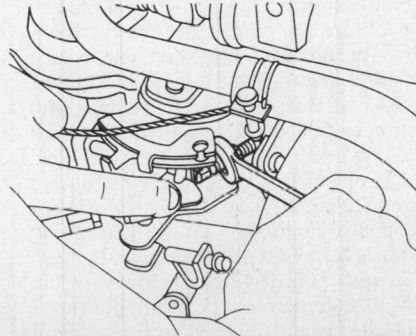

Loosen the idle screw locknut while holding the control lever—diesel engine

2. The automatic transmission (if so equipped) should be in 'D' with the parking brake on and the wheels blocked.

3. Start the engine and run it until it reaches the normal operating temperature.

4. Attach the diesel tachometer's pick-up to the No. 1 injection tube.

NOTE: In order to obtain a more accurate reading of the idle speed, you may wish to remove all the clamps on the No. 1 injection tube.

5. Run the engine at about 2,000 rpm for two minutes under no-load conditions.

6. Slow the engine down to idle speed for about 1 min. and then check the idle.

7. If the engine is not idling at the proper speed, turn it off and disconnect the accelerator wire from the injection pump control lever.

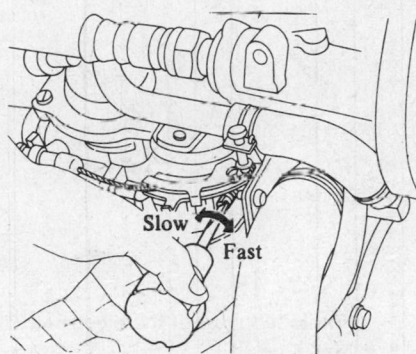

Idle speed adjusting screw—diesel engines

8. Move the control lever to the full acceleration side, and then loosen the idle screw lock nut while still holding the control lever.

NOTE: It is not necessary to disconnect the accelerator wire on the CD17.

9. Start the engine again and turn the adjusting screw until the proper idle is obtained. Stop the engine.

10. Tighten the idle adjusting screw lock nut while still holding the control level to the full acceleration side and then connect the accelerator wire.

ENGINE ELECTRICAL

Distributor

REMOVAL

1. Unfasten the retaining clips and lift the distributor cap straight up. *It will be easier to install the distributor if the wiring is not disconnected from the cap.* If the wires must be removed from the cap, mark their positions to aid in installation.

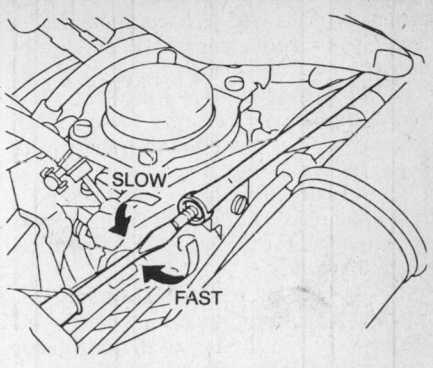

CD17 idle speed adjustment

2. Disconnect the distributor wiring harness.

3. Disconnect the vacuum lines.

4. Note the position of the rotor in relation to the base. Scribe a mark on the base of the distributor and on the engine block to facilitate reinstallation. Align the marks with the direction the metal tip of the rotor is pointing.

5. Remove the bolt(s) which holds the distributor to the engine.

6. Lift the distributor assembly from the engine.

INSTALLATION

1. Insert the distributor shaft and assembly into the engine. Line up the mark on the distributor and the one on the engine with the metal tip of the rotor. Make sure that the vacuum advance diaphragm is pointed in the same direction as it was pointed

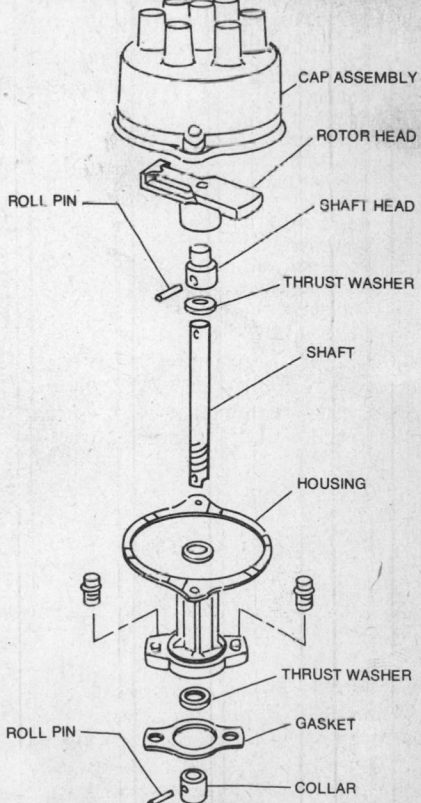

Exploded view of the electronic distributor—280ZX Turbo

originally. This will be done automatically if the marks on the engine and the distributor are lined up with the rotor.

2. Install the distributor hold-down bolt and clamp. Leave the screw loose enough so that you can move the distributor with heavy hand pressure.

3. Connect the primary wire to the coil. Install the distributor cap on the distributor housing. Secure the distributor cap with the spring clips.

4. Install the spark plug wires if removed. Make sure that the wires are pressed all the way into the top of the distributor cap and firmly onto the spark plug.

5. Adjust the point dwell and set the ignition timing.

NOTE: If the crankshaft has been turned or the engine disturbed in any manner (i.e., disassembled and rebuilt) while the distributor was removed, or if the marks were not drawn, it will be necessary to initially time the engine. Follow the procedure given below.

INSTALLATION—ENGINE DISTURBED

1. It is necessary to place the No. 1 cylinder in the firing position to correctly install the distributor. To locate this position, the ignition timing marks on the crankshaft front pulley are used.

2. Remove the No. 1 cylinder spark plug. Turn the crankshaft until the piston in the No. 1 cylinder is moving up on the compression stroke. This can be determined by placing your thumb over the spark

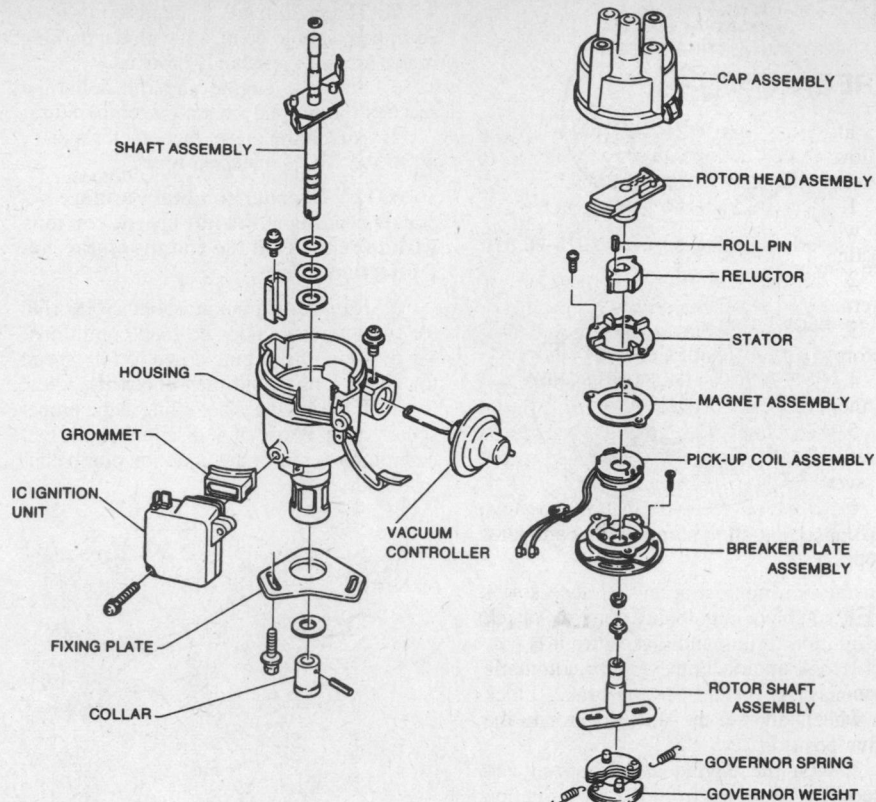

Exploded view of the electronic distributor—with ring-type pick-up

plug hole and feeling the air being forced out of the cylinder. Stop turning the crankshaft when the timing marks that are used to time the engine are aligned.

1. Cap
2. Rotor head
3. Rollpin
4. Reluctor
5. Pick-up coil
6. Contactor
7. Breaker plate assembly
8. Packing
9. Rotor shaft
10. Governor spring
11. Governor weight
12. Shaft assembly
13. Cap setter
14. Vacuum controller
15. Housing
16. Fixing plate
17. O-ring
18. Collar

Exploded view of the electronic distributor—1978

3. Oil the distributor housing lightly where the distributor bears on the cylinder block.

4. Install the distributor so that the rotor, which is mounted on the shaft, points toward the No. 1 spark plug terminal tower position when the cap is installed. Of course, you won't be able to see the direction in which the rotor is pointing if the cap is on the distributor. Lay the cap on the top of the distributor and make a mark on the side of the distributor housing just below the No. 1 spark plug terminal. Make sure that the rotor points toward that mark when you install the distributor.

5. When the distributor shaft has reached the bottom of the hole, move the rotor back and forth slightly until the driving lug on the end of the shaft enters the slots cut in the end of the oil pump shaft and the distributor assembly slides down into place.

6. When the distributor is correctly installed, the breaker points should be in such a position that they are just ready to break contact with each other; or, on engines with electronic ignition, the reluctor teeth should be aligned with the pick-up coil. This can be accomplished by rotating the distributor body after it has been installed in the engine. Once again, line up the marks that you made before the distibutor was removed.

7. Install the distributor hold-down bolt.

8. Install the spark plug into the No. 1 spark plug hole and continue from Step 3 of the preceding distributor installation procedure.

Alternator

PRECAUTIONS

An alternator is used on all models. The following precautions must be observed to prevent alternator and regulator damage:

1. Be absolutely sure of correct polarity when installing a new battery, or connecting a battery charger.

2. Do not short across or ground any alternator or regulator terminals.

3. Disconnect the battery ground cable before replacing any electrical unit.

4. Never operate the alternator with any of the leads disconected.

5. When steam cleaning the engine, be careful not to subject the alternator to excessive heat or moisture.

6. When charging the battery, remove it from the car or disconnect the alternator output terminal.

REMOVAL & INSTALLATION

1. Disconnect the negative battery terminal.

2. Disconnect the two lead wires and connector from the alternator.

3. Loosen the drive belt adjusting bolt and remove the belt.

4. Unscrew the alternator attaching bolts and remove the alternator from the vehicle.

5. Installation is in the reverse order of removal.

BELT TENSION ADJUSTMENT

The correct belt tension for all alternators gives about ½ in. play on the longest span of the belt.

1. Loosen the alternator pivot and mounting bolts.

2. Pry the alternator toward or away from the engine until the tension is correct. Use a hammer handle or wooden prybar.

3. When the tension is correct, tighten the bolts and check the adjustment. Be careful not to overtighten the belt, which will lead to bearing failure.

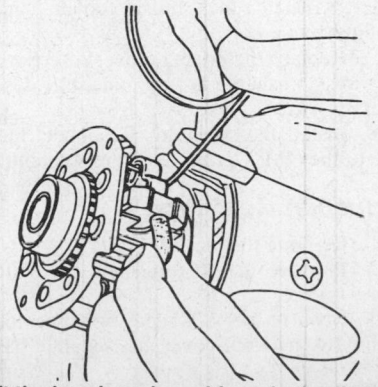

Lift the brush spring with a wire hook and remove the brush on non-reduction starters

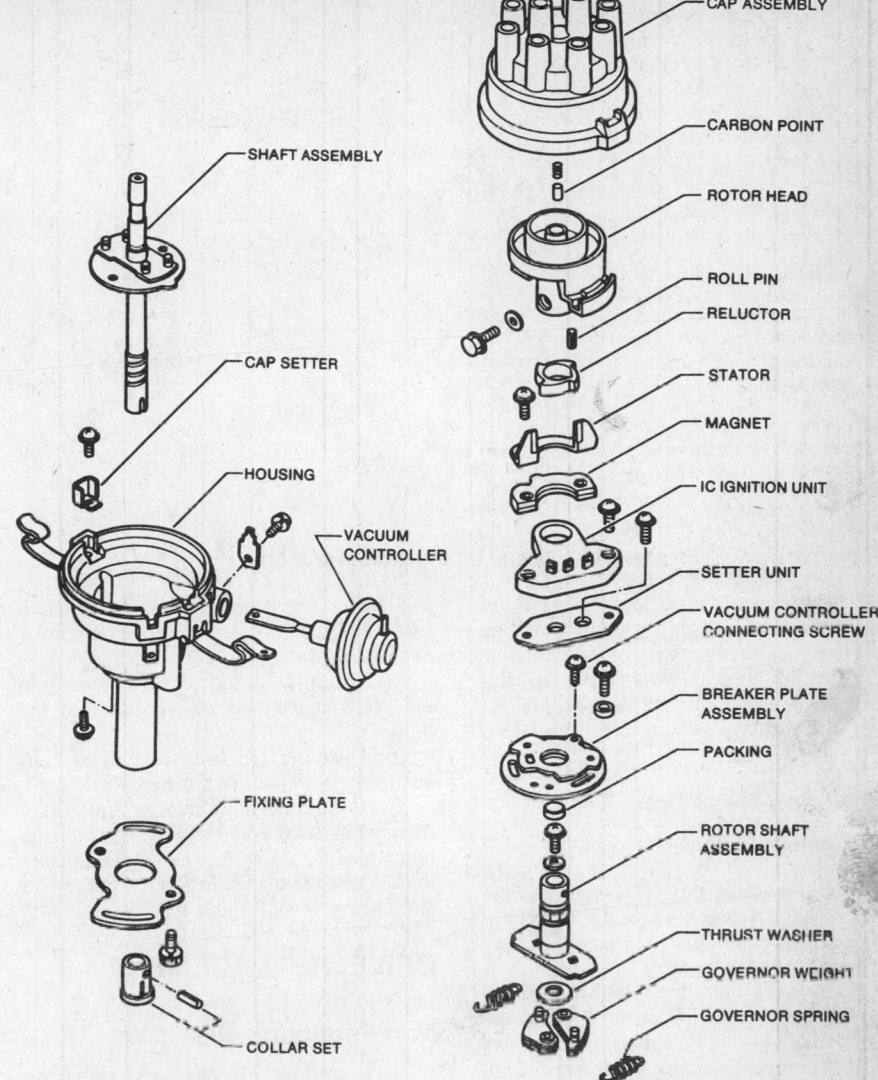

Exploded view of the electronic distributor—with stator

Regulator

REMOVAL & INSTALLATION

NOTE: All models covered here are equipped with integral regulator alternators. Since the regulator is part of the alternator, no adjustments are possible or necessary.

Starter

The starter is mounted at the right rear of the engine. The solenoid is mounted on top of the starter and engages the drive pinion through a pivot yoke shift lever.

REMOVAL & INSTALLATION

1. Disconnect the negative battery cable.

2. Disconnect and label the wires from the terminals on the solenoid.

3. Remove the two bolts which secure the starter to the flywheel housing and pull the starter forward and out. To install, reverse the removal procedure.

BRUSH REPLACEMENT

Non-Reduction Gear Type

1. Remove the starter. Remove the dust cover (if so equipped), the E-ring, and the two thrust washers from the rear cover. Remove the two brush holder set screws from the rear cover.

2. On all models, remove the two thru-bolts and remove the rear cover.

3. Remove the brushes from their holders by lifting the brush spring away from the brush; you can use a hook fabricated from wire to do this.

4. Unsolder the brush electrical connections.

5. Remove the brushes.

To install:

6. Insert the brushes into the holder.

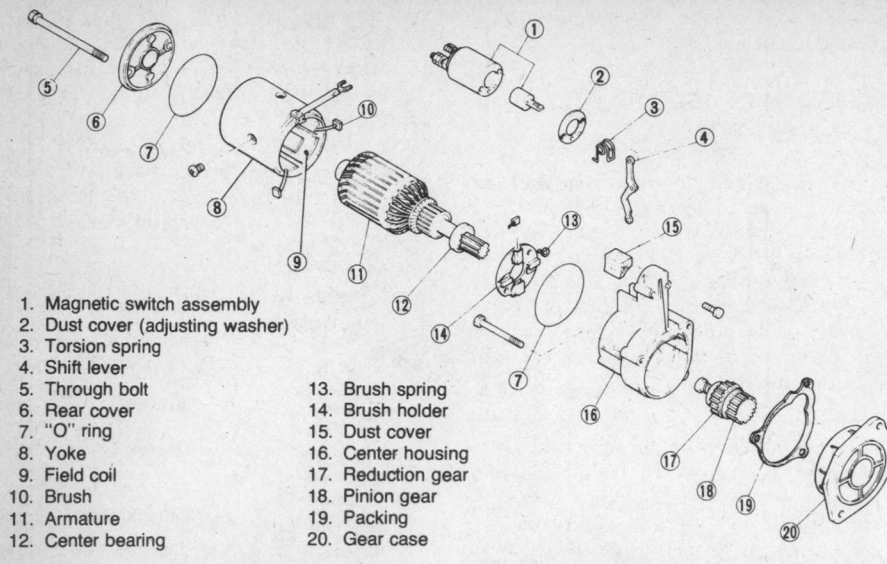

1. Magnetic switch assembly
2. Dust cover (adjusting washer)
3. Torsion spring
4. Shift lever
5. Through bolt
6. Rear cover
7. "O" ring
8. Yoke
9. Field coil
10. Brush
11. Armature
12. Center bearing
13. Brush spring
14. Brush holder
15. Dust cover
16. Center housing
17. Reduction gear
18. Pinion gear
19. Packing
20. Gear case

Exploded view of a reduction gear starter

Solder the brush electrical connections. Raise the brushes far enough to permit installing the brush holder over the commutator.

7. Install the rear cover thru–bolts. Replace the brush holder set screws, and replace the thrust washers, E-ring, and the dust cover.

Reduction Gear Type

1. Remove the starter. Remove the solenoid.

2. Remove the thru–bolts and the rear cover. The cover can be pried off with a small prybar or the like, but be careful not to damage the O-ring.

3. Remove the starter housing, armature, and brush holder from the center housing. They can be removed as an assembly.

4. Remove the positive side brush from its holder. The positive brush is insulated from the brush holder, and its lead wire is connected to the field coil.

5. Carefully lift the negative brush from the commutator and remove it from the holder.

6. Unsolder the brush electrical connections. Remove the brushes.

7. Install the new brushes and solder their wires to the connections. Install the brush holder, armature, and starter housing to the center housing. Install the rear cover and O-ring. Install the solenoid.

DRIVE REPLACEMENT

Non-Reduction Gear Type

1. Loosen the locknut and remove the connection going to the "M" terminal of the solenoid. Remove the securing screws and remove the solenoid.

2. Remove the dust cover, E-ring, thrust washers, and the two screws retaining the brush holder assembly. Remove the brush cover thru–bolts and remove the cover assembly (all models).

3. Lift the brushes to free them from the commutator and remove the brush holder.

4. Tap the yoke assembly lightly with a wooden hammer and remove it from the field and case.

5. Remove the nut and bolt which serve as a pin for the shift lever, carefully retaining the associated washers.

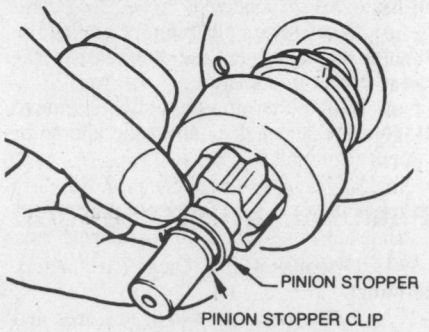

PINION STOPPER
PINION STOPPER CLIP

Pinion stopper removal

6. Remove the armature assembly and shift lever.

7. Push the stop ring (located at the end of the armature shaft) toward the clutch and remove the snap-ring. Remove the stop ring.

8. Remove the clutch assembly from the armature shaft.

To install the drive:

1. Install the clutch assembly onto the armature shaft.

2. Put the stop ring on and hold it toward the clutch while installing the snap-ring.

3. Install the armature assembly and shift lever into the yoke.

4. Install the washers, nut and bolt which serve as a shift lever pivot pin.

5. Install the field back onto the yoke assembly.

6. Lift the brushes and install the brush holder. Install the brush cover and throughbolts.

7. Replace the brush holder set screws, the thrust washers, E-ring, and the dust cover.

8. Install the solenoid. Reconnect the wire to the "M" terminal of the solenoid.

Reduction Gear Type

1. Remove the starter.

2. Remove the solenoid and the shift lever.

3. Remove the bolts securing the center housing to the front cover and separate the parts.

4. Remove the gears and the starter drive.

5. Installation is the reverse.

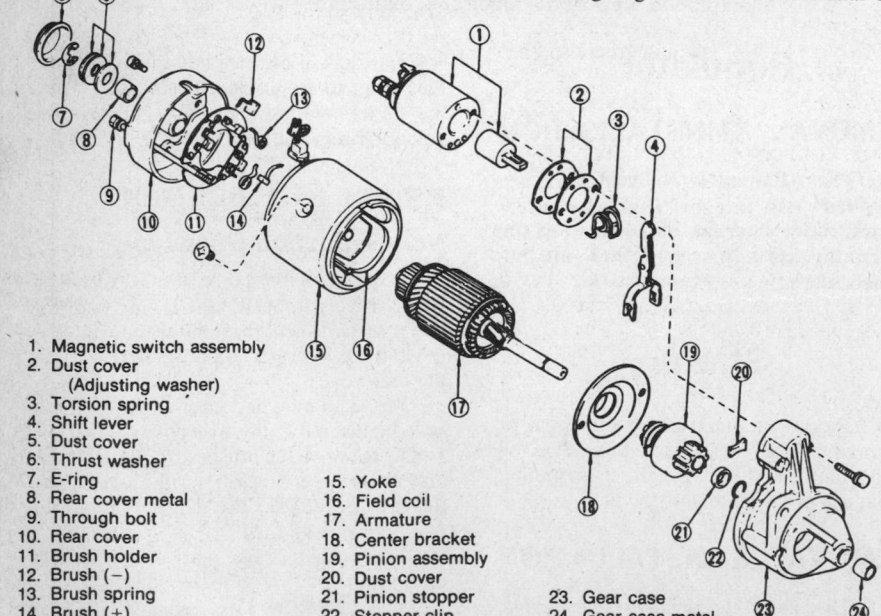

1. Magnetic switch assembly
2. Dust cover (Adjusting washer)
3. Torsion spring
4. Shift lever
5. Dust cover
6. Thrust washer
7. E-ring
8. Rear cover metal
9. Through bolt
10. Rear cover
11. Brush holder
12. Brush (−)
13. Brush spring
14. Brush (+)
15. Yoke
16. Field coil
17. Armature
18. Center bracket
19. Pinion assembly
20. Dust cover
21. Pinion stopper
22. Stopper clip
23. Gear case
24. Gear case metal

Exploded view of a non-reduction gear starter

SOLENOID REPLACEMENT

All Models

1. Loosen the locknut and remove the connection going to the "M" terminal of the solenoid.

2. Remove the three securing screws and remove the solenoid.

3. To install, reverse the removal procedures.

Auto-Glow System— Diesel Engines

The glow plug circuit is used on diesel engines to initially start the engine from cold. The glow plugs heat up the combustion chambers prior to cranking the engine. This heat, combined with the first "squirt" of fuel from the injectors and the extremely high cylinder pressures, fires the engine during cold starts. After normal operating temperature is reached, the water temperature sensor wired in the glow plug system changes the system's electrical resistance and cancels glow plug operation during hot starting.

Glow Plug

REMOVAL

LD28 and CD17 Engines

1. Diconnect the glow plug electrical leads. Remove the glow plug connecting plate.

2. Remove the glow plugs by unscrewing them from the cylinder head.

3. Inspect the tips of the plugs for any evidence of melting. If even one glow plug tip looks bad, all the glow plugs must be replaced. This is a general rule-of-thumb which applies to all diesel engines.

TESTING

Glow plugs are tested by checking their resistance with an ohmmeter. The plugs can be tested either while removed from the cylinder head or while still in position. To test them while removed, connect the ground side of the ohmmeter to the threaded section of the plug, and the other side to the plug's tip as shown in the accompanying illustration. If a minimum of continuity is shown on the meter, the plug is OK. If no continuity whatsoever is shown, the plug must be replaced. To check the glow plugs without removing them from the cylinder head, connect the ground side of the ohmmeter to the engine block (or any other convenient ground) and the other end to the glow plug tip. Likewise, a minumum of continuity shown signifies that the plug is OK; a lack of continuity and the plug must be replaced.

INSTALLATION

To install the glow plugs, reverse the removal procedure. Torque the glow plugs to 14–18 ft. lbs. and the glow plug connecting plate bolts to 1 ft. lb.

CHECKING GLOW PLUG CONNECTIONS

A diesel engine's reluctance to start can often be traced to the glow plug busbar (the wire connections to the plugs). Because diesel engines have a certain degree of vibration when running, they tend to loosen the glow plug busbars. This causes hard starting, as the plugs are not receiving their full current. Periodically tighten the wire connection to all glow plugs.

—————— CAUTION ——————

The Datsun/Nissan glow plug system is a 12 volt system equipped with a dropping resistor and fast glow control unit. The resistor reduces the amount of current flowing through the plugs during the after-glow period, and the glow plug control unit stops the after-glow when more than 7 volts is detected flowing through the glow plugs.

Fast Glow Control Unit

OPERATION

The fast glow control unit on the Sentra, 810 and Maxima diesels has multiple functions, controlling various components of the glow plug system. It has a total of ten terminals:

① Terminal:
A terminal at which voltage being applied to the glow plug is measured. It serves two functions:
1. Determines the pre-glow time (approx. 4 to 12 seconds)
2. Stops after-glow operation when a voltage of more than 7 volts is detected after pre-glow operation

② Terminal:
Control unit's power source terminal

③ Terminal:
Control unit's ground terminal

④ Terminal:
A terminal that controls the ON-OFF operation of glow plug relay-1.

⑤ Terminal:
A terminal connected to the water temperature sensor to serve three functions:
1. Determines the period that the warning lamp remains illuminated (approx. 1 to 9 seconds)
2. Determines the after-glow time (approx. 5 to 32 seconds)
3. Stops pre-glow operation when coolant temperature is higher than 50°C (122°F)

⑥ Terminal:
A terminal connected to the "START" position of the ignition switch (When the ignition key is returned from "START" to "ON", after-glow operation begins.)

⑦ Terminal:
Controls the ON-OFF operation of glow plug relay-2.

⑧ Terminal:
A grounding terminal for the water temperature sensor

⑨ Terminal:
A terminal for the glow/fuel filter warning lamp

⑩ Terminal:
A terminal used to determine whether the engine has started or not (Glow plug relay is turned "OFF" by means of terminal ④ immediately after the engine has started.)

CHECKING
Pre-Glow System

1. Connect a test light to the blue/yellow wire leading to the glow control unit. Measure the length of time that the test light is lighted.

Standard operation (except re-start operation within 60 seconds):

Engine coolant temperature °C (°F)	Glow plug terminal voltage	Time (sec.)
Below 50 (122)	8V	Approx. 13
50 (122)	10.5V	Approx. 6
Above 50 (122)		Approx. 0

Re-start operation (within 80 seconds): The length of time the light is "ON" should be less than 6.5 seconds. For example, when re-starting the engine 5 seconds after the ignition switch is turned off, the lamp should be "ON" for 1.5 seconds (with engine coolant temperature below 122°F and glow plug voltage 10.5 volts).

After-Glow Operation

1. Connect a test light to the blue/red wire leading to the glow control unit. Measure the length of time that the light is lighted.

Normal condition, when the ignition switch is turned "ON" from "ST" or "OFF":

Engine coolant temperature °C (°F)	Time (sec.)
Below −25 (−13) (approx.)	Approx. 31
Approx. 20 (68)	Approx. 17
Approx. 40 (104)	Approx. 9
Above 50 (122) (approx.)	0

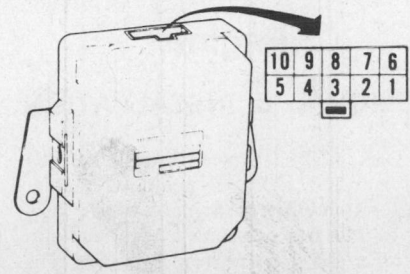

Diesel fast glow control unit

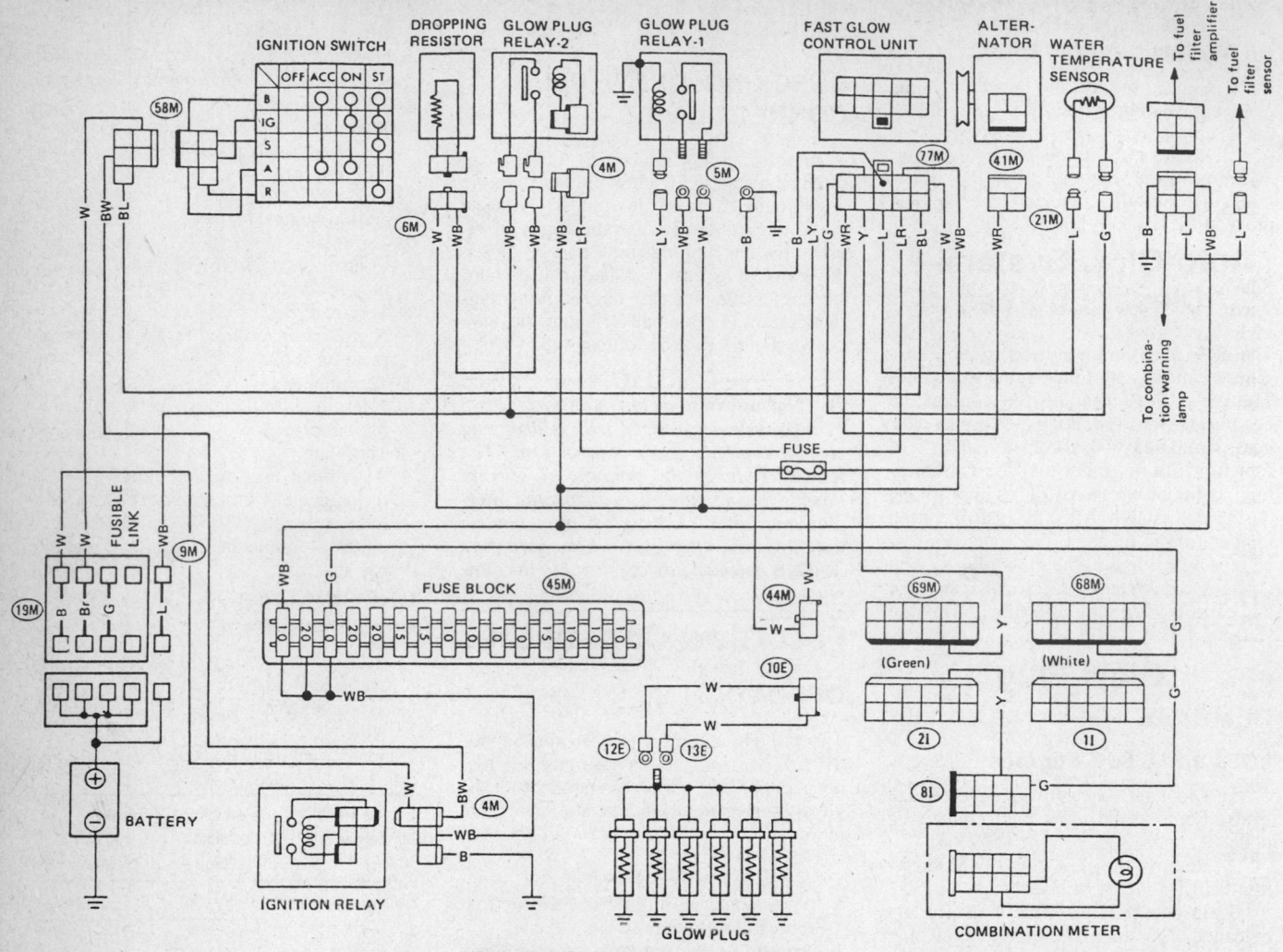

LD28 diesel glow plug wiring diagram

TESTING

The sensor is tested by measuring resistance while removed from the engine and inserted in a vessel of water as shown in the illustration. Replace the sensor if resistance figures vary greatly from those shown.

Ignition switch in "ST", the test light is on continuously. Refer to the accompanying illustration.

2. After the pre-glow system turns off, check the operation of the test light in the accompanying illustration; (test light no. one in the illustration in OFF).

Glow plug terminal voltage	Test lamp ②
Above 7V	OFF
Below 7V	ON

Water Temperature Sensor

OPERATION

The water temperature sensor is connected to the fast glow control unit. Sensor resistance varies with changes in the temperature of the engine coolant.

ENGINE MECHANICAL

Engine

REMOVAL & INSTALLATION

All Datsun/Nissan engines, except the 1984 and later 300ZX V6 are inline, with either four or six cylinders. Some have overhead valves with rocker arm valve gear and others have a single overhead camshaft. The 300ZX engine is a single overhead cam V6,

with rocker arm-type valve gear. Refer to the "Engine Identification" chart for identification of engines by model, number of cylinders, displacement, and camshaft location. Engines are referred to by model designation codes throughout this section.

Rear Wheel Drive

It is best to remove the engine and transmission as a unit, except on 300ZX; the engine and transmission are separated before engine removal.

1. Mark the location of the hinges on the hood. Unbolt and remove.
2. Disconnect the battery cable. Remove the battery on California models with the Z20E and Z22E engine with air conditioning.
3. Drain the coolant and automatic transmission fluid, if so equipped.
4. Remove the grille on 510 models. Remove the radiator after disconnecting the automatic transmission coolant tubes.
5. Remove the air cleaner.
6. Remove the fan and pulley.
7. Disconnect:
   a. water temperature gauge wire

b. oil pressure sending unit wire

c. ignition distributor primary wire

d. starter motor connections

e. fuel hose

f. alternator leads

g. heater hoses

h. throttle and choke connections

i. engine ground cable

j. thermal transmitter wire—B210, 280Z

k. fuel cut-off switch wire—B210

l. vacuum cut solenoid wire—B210

NOTE: A good rule of thumb when disconnecting the rather complex engine wiring of today's cars is to put a piece of masking tape on the wire and on the connection you removed the wire from, then mark both pieces of tape 1, 2, 3, etc. When replacing wiring, simply match the pieces of tape.

——— CAUTION ———

On models with air conditioning, it is necessary to remove the compressor and the condenser from their mounts. DO NOT ATTEMPT TO UNFASTEN ANY OF THE AIR CONDITIONER HOSES.

8. Disconnect the power brake booster hose from the engine.

9. Remove the clutch operating cylinder and return spring.

10. Disconnect the speedometer cable from the transmission. Disconnect the back up light switch and any other wiring or attachments to the transmission. On cars with the L20B engine, disconnect the parking brake cable at the rear adjuster.

11. Disconnect the column shift linkage. Remove the floorshift lever. On the Z20, Z20E and Z22E and B210 models, remove the boot, withdraw the lock pin, and remove the lever from inside the car.

12. Detach the exhaust pipe from the exhaust manifold. Remove the front section of the exhaust system.

13. Mark the relationship of the driveshaft flanges and remove the driveshaft.

14. Place a jack under the transmission. Remove the rear crossmember. On B210 models, remove the rear engine mounting nuts.

15. Attach a hoist to the lifting hooks on the engine (at either end of the cylinder head). Support the engine.

16. Unbolt the front engine mounts. Tilt the engine by lowering the jack under the transmission and raising the hoist.

17. Reverse the procedure to install the engine.

On the 300ZX, torque the engine gusset bolts in six stages, as shown in the accompanying illustration.

Front Wheel Drive

It is recommended that the engine and transmission be removed as a unit. If need be, the units may be separated after removal.

1. Mark the location of the hinges on the hood. Remove the hood by holding at

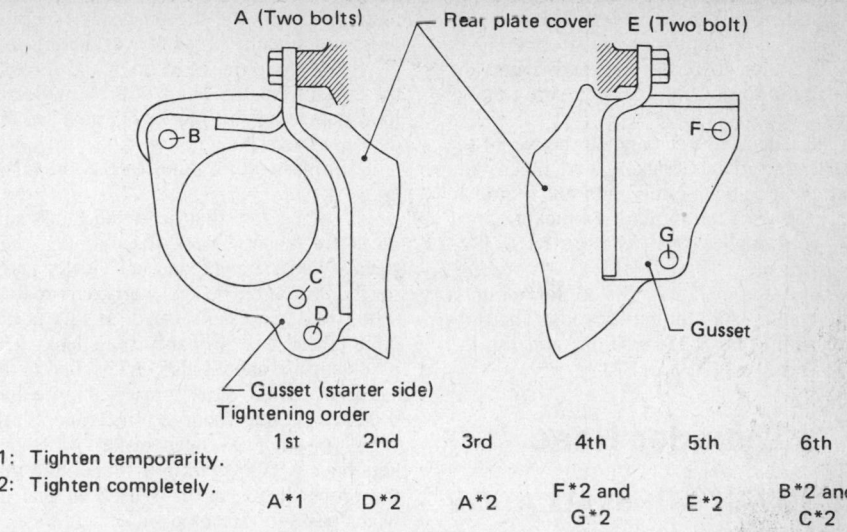

Tightening order

	1st	2nd	3rd	4th	5th	6th
*1: Tighten temporarily.						
*2: Tighten completely.	A*1	D*2	A*2	F*2 and G*2	E*2	B*2 and C*2

Torquing 300ZX engine gussets

both sides and unscrewing bolts. This requires two people.

2. Remove the battery and drain radiator coolant.

3. Remove the air cleaner and disconnect the accelerator wire from the carburetor.

4. Disconnect the following wires and hoses:

a. Ignition wire from the coil to the distributor.

b. Ignition coil ground wire and the engine ground cable.

c. Disconnect the block connector from the distributor.

d. Remove fusible links.

e. Unplug all engine harness connectors.

f. Remove the fuel and fuel return hoses.

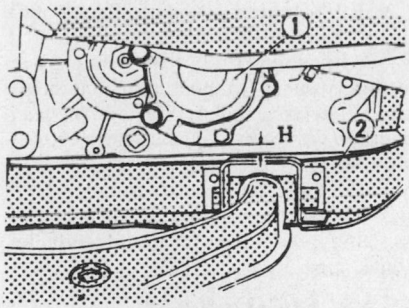

1. Clutch housing
2. Sub-frame

Clearance between frame and clutch housing

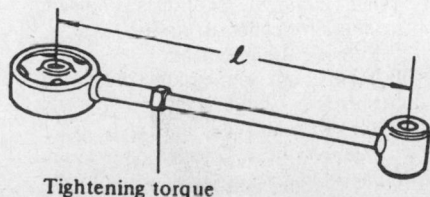

Tightening torque
0.8 to 1.2 kg-m (5.8 to 8.7 ft-lb)

Adjusting buffer rod length

g. Disconnect the upper and lower radiator hoses.

h. Detach the heater inlet and outlet.

i. Remove the Master-Vac vacuum hose.

j. Disconnect the carbon canister hoses and the air pump air cleaner hose.

5. Remove the air pump air cleaner.

6. Remove the carbon canister.

7. Remove the auxiliary fan and the washer tank.

8. Remove the grille and radiator with the fan assembly.

9. Remove the clutch cylinder from the clutch housing.

10. Remove both buffer rods (do not alter the length of the rods) and disconnect the speedometer cable.

11. Remove the spring pins from the transmission gear selection rods.

12. Attach suitable engine slingers to the block and attach chain or cable. Keep the lifting source slack at this point.

13. Disconnect the exhaust pipe at both the manifold connection and the clamp holding the pipe to the engine.

14. On the Sentra, Stanza and Pulsar, remove the lower ball joint.

15. Drain the gear oil.

16. Disconnect the right and left side drive shafts from their side flanges and remove the bolt holding the radius link support.

NOTE: When drawing out the half-shafts on the Sentra, Stanza and Pulsar, it is necessary to loosen the strut head bolts.

17. Lower the shifter and selector rods and remove the securing bolts from the motor mounts.

a. Remove the nuts holding the front and rear motor mounts to the frame.

b. On the Sentra, Stanza and Pulsar, disconnect the clutch and accelerator wires and remove the speedometer cable with its pinion from the transaxle.

18. Lift the engine up and away from the car.

Installation is the reverse of removal with the following cautions and observations.

1. When lowering the engine into the car and onto the frame, make sure to keep it as level as possible.

2. Check the clearance between the frame and clutch housing and make sure that the engine mount bolts are seated in the groove of the mounting bracket.

a. Distance "H" should be 0.394–0.472 in. (F10 and 310).

3. After installing the motor mounts, adjust and install the buffer rods. The right side should be 8.23–8.31 in. and the left 5.39–5.47 in. (F10 and 310).

Cylinder Head

REMOVAL & INSTALLATION

NOTE: To prevent distortion or warping of the cylinder head, allow the engine to cool completely before removing the head bolts.

A14 and A15 Overhead Valve Engines

To remove the cylinder head on OHV engines:

1. Drain the coolant.
2. Disconnect the battery ground cable.
3. Remove the upper radiator hose. Remove the water outlet elbow and the thermostat.
4. Remove the air cleaner, carburetor, rocker arm cover, and both manifolds.
5. Remove the spark plugs.
6. Disconnect the temperature gauge connection.
7. Loosen the rocker arm adjusting nuts and turn the adjusting screws out to disengage the pushrods. Loosen the rocker shaft bolts evenly and remove the rocker shaft

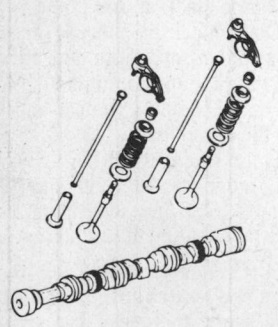

Pushrod, cam and valve assemblies—A series engines

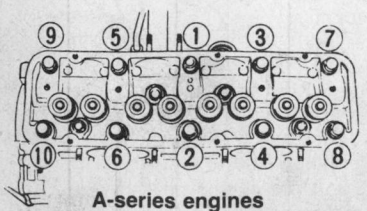

A-series engines

assembly. Remove the pushrods, keeping them in the same order for reassembly.

8. Remove the head bolts and remove the head. Tap the head with a mallet to loosen it from the block. Remove it and discard the gasket.

To replace the cylinder head on OHV engines:

1. Make sure that head and block surfaces are clean. Check the cylinder head surface with a straightedge and a feeler gauge for flatness. If the head is warped more than 0.003 in., it must be trued. If this is not done, there will probably be a leak. The block surface should also be checked in the same way. If the block is warped more than 0.003 in., it must be trued (machined flat).

2. Install a new head gasket. Most gaskets have a TOP marking. Make sure that the proper head gasket is used so that no water passages are blocked off.

3. Install the head. Install the pushrods in their original locations. Install the rocker arm assembly. Loosen the rocker arm adjusting screws to prevent bending the pushrods when tightening the head bolts. Tighten the head bolts finger tight. The single bolt marked T must go in the No. 1 position on the center right side of the engine.

4. Refer to the "Torque Specifications" chart for the correct head bolt torque. Tighten the bolts to one third of the specified torque in the order shown in the head bolt tightening sequence illustration. Torque the rocker arm mounting bolts to 15–18 ft. lbs.

5. Tighten the bolts to two thirds of the specified torque in sequence.

6. Tighten the bolts to the full specified torque in sequence.

7. Adjust the valves. If no cold setting is given, adjust the valves to the normal hot setting.

8. Reassemble the engine. Intake and exhaust manifold bolt torque is 11–14 ft. lbs. Fill the cooling system. Start the engine and run it until normal temperature is reached. Remove the rocker arm cover. Torque the bolts in sequence once more. Check the valve clearances.

9. Retorque the head bolts after 600 miles of driving. Check the valve clearances after torquing, as this may disturb the settings.

E15 and E16 Overhead Camshaft Engines

1. Crank the engine until the No. 1 piston is at Top Dead Center on its compression stroke and disconnect the negative battery cable. Drain the cooling system and remove the air cleaner assembly.

2. Remove the alternator.

3. Number all spark plug wires as to their respective cylinders and remove the distributor, with all wires attached.

4. Remove the EAI pipes bracket and EGR tube at the right (EGR valve) side. Disconnect the same pipes on the front (exhaust manifold) side from the manifold.

5. Remove the exhaust manifold cover

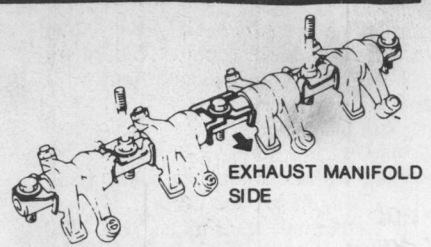

EXHAUST MANIFOLD SIDE

Make sure the cutout on the E–series engine rocker shaft faces the exhaust manifold

and the exhaust manifold, taking note that the center manifold nut has a different diameter than the other nuts.

6. Remove the A/C compressor bracket and the power steering pump bracket (if equipped).

7. Label and disconnect the carburetor throttle linkage, fuel line, and all vacuum and electrical connections.

8. Remove the intake manifold with carburetor.

9. Remove water pump drive belt and pulley. Remove crankshaft pulley.

10. Remove the rocker (valve) cover.

11. Remove upper and lower dust cover on the camshaft timing belt shroud.

12. With the shroud removed, the cam sprocket, crankshaft sprocket, jackshaft sprocket, tensioner pulley, and toothed rubber timing belt are exposed.

13. Mark the relationship of the camshaft sprocket to the timing belt and the crankshaft sprocket to the timing belt with paint or a grease pencil. This will make setting everything up during reassembly much easier if the engine is disturbed during disassembly.

14. Remove the belt tensioner pulley.

15. Mark an arrow on the timing belt showing direction of engine rotation, because the belt wears a certain way and should be replaced the way it was removed. Slide the belt off the sprockets.

16. Carefully remove the cylinder head from the block, pulling the head up evenly from both ends. If the head seems stuck, DO NOT pry it off. Tap lightly around the lower perimeter of the head with a rubber mallet to help break the joint. Label all head bolts with tape or magic marker, as they must go back in their original positions.

To install:

1. Thoroughly clean both the cylinder block and head mating surfaces. Avoid scratching either.

2. Turn the crankshaft and set the No. 1 cylinder at TDC on its compression stroke. This causes the crankshaft timing sprocket mark to be aligned with the cylinder block cover mark.

3. Align the camshaft sprocket mark with the cylinder head cover mark. This causes the valves for No. 1 cylinder to position at TDC on the compression stroke.

4. Place a new gasket on the cylinder block.

5. Install the cylinder head on the block and tighten the bolts in two stages: first to

29–33 ft. lbs. on all bolts, then go around again and torque them all up to 51–54 ft. lbs. After the engine has been warmed up, check all bolts and re-torque if necessary.

6. Reassemble in the reverse order of disassembly, making sure all timing marks are in proper alignment.

L20B Overhead Camshaft Engines

1. Crank the engine until the No. 1 piston is at TDC of the compression stroke and disconnect the negative battery cable, drain the cooling system and remove the air cleaner and attending hoses.

2. Remove the alternator.

3. Disconnect the carburetor throttle linkage, the fuel line and any other vacuum lines or electrical leads, and remove the carburetor.

4. Disconnect the exhaust pipe from the exhaust manifold.

5. Remove the fan and fan pulley.

6. Remove the spark plugs.

7. Remove the rocker cover.

8. Remove the water pump.

9. Remove the fuel pump.

10. Remove the fuel pump drive cam.

11. Mark the relationship of the camshaft sprocket to the timing chain with paint or chalk. If this is done, it will not be necessary to locate the factory timing marks. Before removing the camshaft sprocket, it will be necessary to wedge the chain in place so that it will not fall down into the front cover. The factory procedure is to wedge the timing chain in place with the wooden wedge shown here. The problem with this procedure is that it may allow the chain tensioner to move out far enough to cock itself against the chain. If this happens, you'll find that the chain won't go back over the sprocket after you've put the sprocket back on. In this case, you'll have to remove the front cover and push the tensioner back. After you've wedged the chain, unbolt the camshaft sprocket and remove it.

12. Loosen and remove the cylinder head bolts. You will need a 10 mm allen wrench to remove the head bolts. Keep the bolts in order since they are different sizes. Lift the cylinder head assembly from the engine. Remove the intake and exhaust manifolds as necessary.

13. Thoroughly clean the block and head mating surfaces. Check for warpage; see the preceding A-series engine section for instructions. Install a new head gasket on the block. Do not use sealer on the gasket.

14. With the crankshaft turned so that the No. 1 piston is at TDC of the compression stroke (if not already done so as mentioned in Step 1), make sure that the camshaft sprocket timing mark and the oblong groove in the plate are aligned.

15. Place the cylinder head in position on the cylinder block, being careful not to allow any of the valves to come in contact with any of the pistons. Do not rotate the crankshaft or camshaft separately because

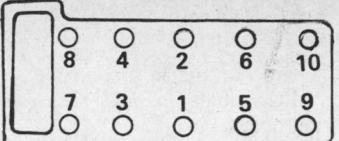

L20B engine

of possible damage which might occur to the valves.

16. Temporarily tighten the two center right and left cylinder head bolts to 14.5 ft. lbs.

17. Install the camshaft sprocket together with the timing chain to the camshaft. Make sure the marks made earlier line up with each other. If you get into trouble, see "Timing Chain Removal and Installation" for timing procedures.

18. Install the cylinder head bolts. Note that there are two sizes of bolts used; the longer bolts are installed on the driver's side of the engine with a smaller bolt in the center position. The remaining small bolts are installed on the opposite side of the cylinder head.

19. Tighten the cylinder head bolts in three stages: first to 29 ft. lbs., second to 43 ft. lbs., and lastly to 47–62 ft. lbs. Tighten the cylinder head bolts on all models in the proper sequence.

20. Install and assemble the remaining components of the engine in the reverse order of removal. Adjust the valves. Fill the cooling system; start the engine and run it until normal operating temperature is reached. Retorque the cylinder head bolts to specification, then readjust the valves. Retorque the head bolts again after 600 miles and recheck the valves at that time.

L24, L28 and LD28 Overhead Cam Engines

1. Crank the engine until the No. 1 piston is at TDC of the compression stroke, disconnect the battery, and drain the cooling system.

NOTE: To set the No. 1 piston at TDC of the compression stroke on the LD28 engine, remove the blind plug from the rear plate. Rotate the crankshaft until the marks on the flywheel and rear plate are in alignment. The No. 1 piston should now be at TDC.

2. Remove the radiator hoses and the heater hoses. Unbolt the alternator mounting bracket and move the alternator to one side.

3. If the car is equipped with air-conditioning or power steering, unbolt the compressor or pump and place it to one side. *Do not disconnect the compressor lines. Severe injury could result.*

4. Remove the fan and the fan pulley.

5. Remove the water pump. Remove the spark plug leads from the spark plugs.

6. Remove the cold start valve and the fuel pipe as an assembly. Remove the throttle linkage.

7. Remove all lines and hoses from the

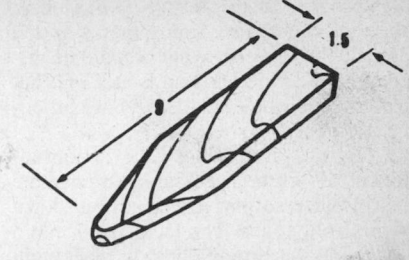

Dimensions of wooden wedge used to hold chain in place

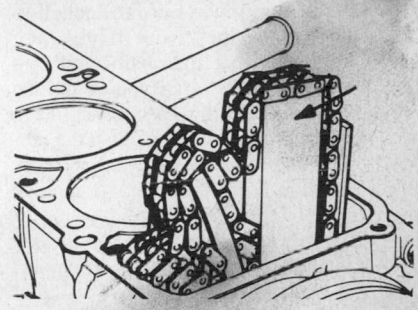

On overhead cam engines, the wedge shown by the arrow can be used to prevent the timing chain from slipping off the crankshaft sprocket.

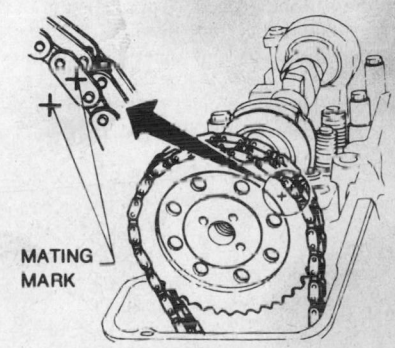

MATING MARK

Matchmark the timing chain to the camshaft sprocket

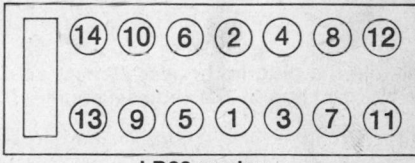

LD28 engine

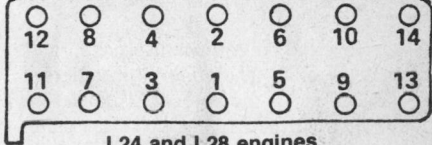

L24 and L28 engines

intake manifold. Mark them first so you will know where they go.

8. Unbolt the exhaust manifold from the exhaust pipe. The cylinder head can be removed with both the intake and exhaust manifolds in place.

9. Remove the camshaft cover.

10. Mark the relationship of the cam-

shaft sprocket to the timing marks chain with paint. There are timing marks on the chain and the sprocket which should be visible when the No. 1 piston is at TDC, but the marks are quite small and not particularly useful.

11. Before removing the camshaft sprocket, it will be necessary to wedge the chain in place so that it will not fall down into the front cover. The factory procedure is to wedge the timing chain in place with a wooden wedge shown here. The problem with this procedure is that it may allow the chain tensioner to move out far enough to cock itself against the chain. If this happens, you'll find that the chain won't go back over the sprocket after you've put the sprocket back on. In this case, you'll have to remove the front cover and push the tensioner back. After you've wedged the chain, unbolt the camshaft sprocket and remove it.

12. Remove the cylinder head bolts; they require an allen wrench type socket adapter. Keep the bolts in order as two different sizes are used.

13. Lift off the cylinder head. You may have to tap it *lightly* with a hammer.

14. Clean the block and head mating surfaces thoroughly and check for warpage according to the procedure described in the A-series engine section. Install a new head gasket on the block and lower the head into position.

15. Install a new head gasket and place the head in position on the block.

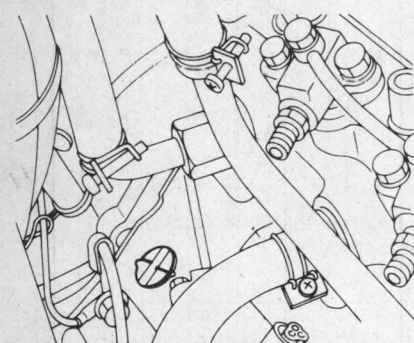

Remove the plug in the rear plate to set the No. 1 piston at TDC—diesel engines

16. Install the head bolts in their original locations.

17. Torque the head bolts in three stages: first to 29 ft. lbs., then to 43 ft. lbs., then to 62 ft. lbs.

18. Reinstall the camshaft sprocket in its original location. The chain is installed at the same time as the sprocket. Make sure the marks made earlier line up. If the chain has slipped, or the engine has been disturbed, correct the timing as described under "Timing Chain Removal and Installation."

19. Reinstall all remaining parts, coolant, etc.

20. Adjust the valves.

21. After 600 miles of driving, retorque the head bolts and readjust the valves.

Z20E, Z20S, Z22E Overhead Camshaft Engine

1. Complete Steps 1–5 under "L24 Overhead Camshaft Engine." Observe the following note for step 5.

NOTE: The spark plug leads should be marked. However, it would be wise to mark them yourself, especially the dual spark plug models.

2. Disconnect the throttle linkage, the air cleaner or its intake hose assembly (fuel injection). Disconnect the fuel line, the return fuel line and any other vacuum lines or electrical leads. On the Z20S, remove the carburetor to avoid damaging it while removing the head.

NOTE: A good rule of thumb when disconnecting the rather complex engine wiring of today's automobiles is to put a piece of masking tape on the wire or hose and on the connection from which you removed the wire or hose, then mark both pieces of tape 1, 2, 3, etc. When replacing wiring, simply match the pieces of tape.

3. Remove the EGR tube from around the rear of the engine.

4. Remove the exhaust air induction tubes from around the front of the engine on Z20S engines and from the exhaust manifold on Z20E engines.

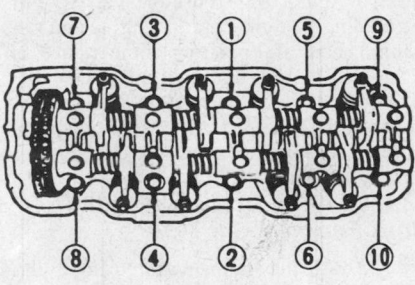

Z20, Z22 engine

5. Unbolt the exhaust manifold from the exhaust pipe. On the Z20S, remove the fuel pump.

6. On the Z20E, remove the intake manifold supports from under the manifold. Remove the PCV valve from around the rear of the engine if necessary.

7. Remove the spark plugs to protect them from damage. Remove the valve cover.

8. Mark the relationship of the camshaft sprocket to the timing chain with paint or chalk. If this is done, it will not be necessary to locate the factory timing marks. Before removing the camshaft sprocket, it will be necessary to wedge the chain in place so that it will not fall down into the front cover. The factory procedure is to wedge the timing chain in place with the wooden wedge shown here. The problem with this procedure is that it may allow the chain tensioner to move out far enough to cock itself against the chain. If this happens, you'll find that the chain won't go back over the sprocket after you've put the

sprocket back on. In this case, you'll have to remove the front cover and push the tensioner back. After you've wedged the chain, unbolt the camshaft sprocket and remove it.

9. Working from both ends in, loosen the cylinder head bolts and remove them. Remove the bolts securing the cylinder head to the front cover assembly.

10. Lift the cylinder head off the engine block. It may be necessary to tap the head *lightly* with a copper or brass mallet to loosen it.

To install the cylinder head:

11. Thoroughly clean the cylinder block and head surfaces and check both for warpage. See "A12, etc. Overhead Valve Engines" cylinder head removal section for procedure (Step 1 of assembly process).

12. Fit the new head gasket. Don't use sealant. Make sure that no open valves are in the way of raised pistons, and do not rotate the crankshaft or camshaft separately because of possible damage which might occur to the valves.

13. Temporarily tighten the two center right and left cylinder head bolts to 14 ft. lbs.

14. Install the camshaft sprocket together with the timing chain to the camshaft. Make sure the marks you made earlier line up with each other. If you get into trouble, see "Timing Chain Removal and Installation" for timing procedures.

15. Install the cylinder head bolts and torque them to 20 ft. lbs., then 40 ft. lbs., then 58 ft. lbs. in the order shown in the illustration.

16. Assemble the rest of the components in the reverse order of disassembly.

NOTE: It is always wise to drain the crankcase oil after the cylinder head has been installed to avoid coolant contamination.

CA20, CA20E, CA20S and CA18ET Overhead Camshaft Engines

1. Turn the crankshaft so that the No. 1 cylinder is at TDC.

2. Drain the cooling system.

3. Remove the drive belts.

4. Remove the front cover.

5. Remove the water pump pulley.

6. Remove the crankshaft pulley.

7. Remove the distributor-to-canister vacuum tube.

8. Remove the alternator adjusting

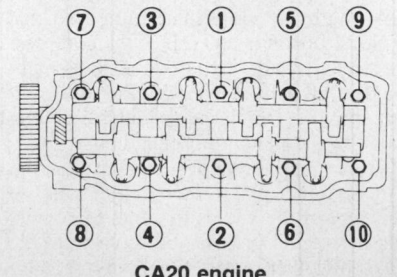

CA20 engine

bracket. On the CA18ET, remove the air intake pipe.

9. Remove the drive belt tensioner and camshaft sprocket.

10. Remove the water pump.

11. Remove the oil pump.

12. Loosen the cylinder head bolts in sequence.

13. Lift off the head.

14. Installation is the reverse of removal. When installing the bolts, tighten the two center bolts temporarily to 15 ft. lbs. Install all the head bolts loosely. After the timing belt and front cover have been installed, torque all the head bolts in the sequence shown to the specification given in the torque chart.

VG30E and VG30ET V6 Engines
REMOVAL

NOTE: Includes camshaft, intake manifold, exhaust manifold, rocker shaft removal procedures.

1. Remove the engine assembly.

2. Remove the timing belt.

3. Set the number 1 cylinder at TDC on its compression stroke.

4. Drain the coolant from the cylinder block.

5. Remove the collector cover and collector.

6. Remove the intake manifold with fuel tube assembly.

7. Remove the power steering pump bracket.

8. Remove the exhaust manifold covers.

9. Disconnect the exhaust manifold connecting tube.

10. Remove the bolts securing the camshaft pulleys and rear timing cover.

11. Remove the compressor and rocker covers.

12. Remove the cylinder head with exhaust manifold.

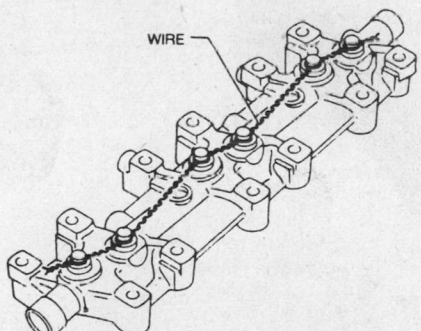

Holding the V6 valve lifters with a wire

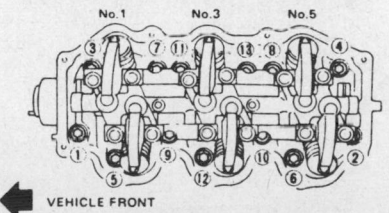

V6 cylinder head bolt removal sequence

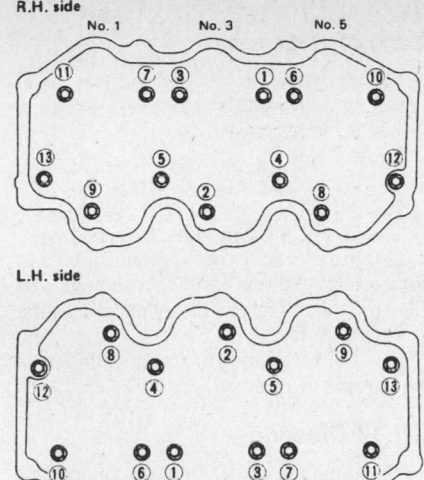

Cylinder head torque sequence—V6

DISASSEMBLY

1. Remove the right and left exhaust manifolds. Loosen the bolts in numerical order as illustrated.

2. Loosen the bolts in two or three stages and remove the rocker shafts with the rocker arms.

3. Remove the hydraulic valve lifters and lifter guide.

NOTE: Hold the valve lifters with wire so that they will not drop from the lifter guide. Put an identification mark on the lifters to avoid mixing them up.

4. Remove the camshaft.

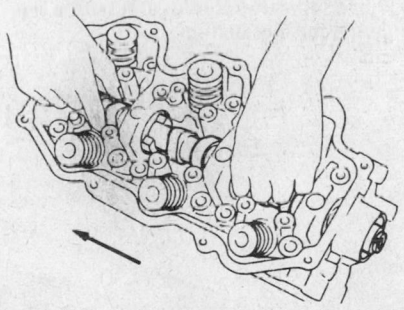

Remove the V6 camshaft in the direction of the arrow

INSPECTION

Camshaft End Play

Using a dial guage measure the camshaft end play. If the camshaft end play exceeds the limit (0.0012–0.0024 in.), select the thickness of a cam locate plate so that the end play is within specification.

Example:

If camshaft end play measures 0.08mm (0.0031 in.) with shim 2 used, then change shim 2 to shim 3 so that the camshaft end play is 0.05mm (0.0020 in).

Camshaft Journal Clearance

Measure the inside diameter of the camshaft

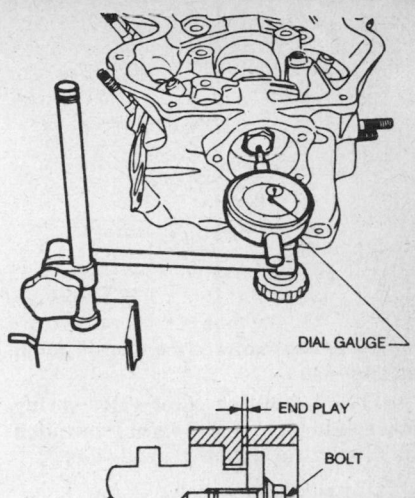

Using a dial indicator to measure camshaft end play—V6

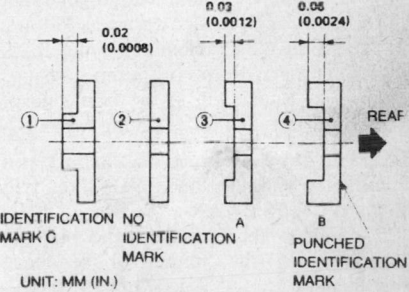

Select shim thickness so that camshaft end play is withing specs—V6

journals in the head and the outside diameter of the camshaft.

Standard Inside Diameter:
- 47.00–47.025mm (1.8504–1.8514in.)

Standard Outside Diameter:
- 46.94–46.96mm (1.8480–1.8488in.)
- Wear Limit: 0.15mm (0.0059in.)
- Valve Dimensions

Check the valve dimensions in each valve. When the valve head has been worn down to .05mm (0.020in.) in margin thickness, replace the valve.

Grinding allowance for the valve stem tip is 0.2mm (0.008in.) or less.

ASSEMBLY

1. Install the valve component parts.

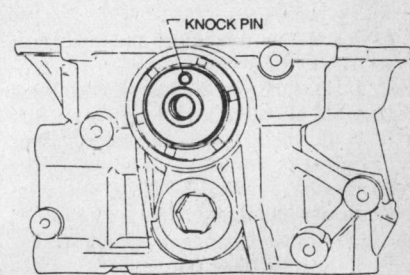

Knock pin of camshaft facing upward—V6

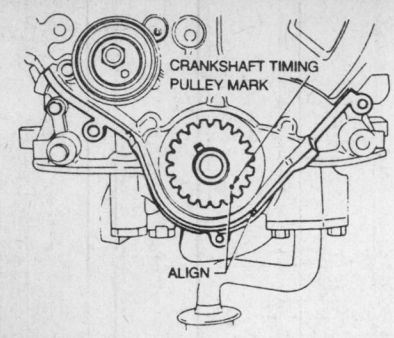

Aligning timing mark and mark on oil pump housing—V6

NOTE: Install the outer valve spring (uneven pitch type) with its narrow pitch side toward the cylinder head side.

2. Install the camshaft.

3. Apply engine oil to the camshaft oil seal and install it in place.

4. Adjust the camshaft end play with the locate plate installed.

INSTALLATION

1. Make sure the No. 1 cylinder is set at TDC on its compression stroke as follows:

   a. Align the crankshaft timing mark with the mark on the oil pump housing.

   b. The knock pin in the front end of the camshaft should be facing upward.

NOTE: Do not rotate crankshaft and camshaft separately because valves will hit piston head.

2. Tighten the cylinder head bolts in five steps in the numerical sequence illustrated.

1st Tighten all bolts to 29 Nm
   (3.0 kg-m, 22 ft. lb.)
2nd Tighten all bolts to 59 Nm
   (6.0 kg-m, 43 ft. lb.)
3rd Loosen all bolts completely.
4th Tighten all bolts to 29 Nm
   (3.0 kg-m, 22 ft. lb.)
5th Tighten all bolts to 54–64 Nm
   (5.5–6.5 kg-m, 40–47 ft. lb.)
or if you have an angle wrench, turn all bolts 60–65 degrees clockwise.

3. Tighten the rear timing cover.

4. Install the camshaft pulley and tighten to 58–65 ft. lbs.

NOTE: The R.H. and L.H. camshaft pulleys are different parts. Install them in the correct positions. The R.H. pulley has an R3 identification mark and the L.H. has an L3.

5. Install the timing belt and adjust the tension.

6. Install the front upper and lower belt covers.

7. Install the valve lifters and lifter guide. Hold all valve lifters with a wire as was done during disassembly and install to their original position.

8. Install the rocker shafts with the rocker arms and tighten the rocker shaft bolts to 13–16 ft. lbs. in two or three stages.

9. Install the rocker cover.

10. Install the intake manifold and fuel tube and tighten in two or three stages.

Nut
   1st 3–5 Nm
      (0.3–0.5 kg-m, 2.2–3.6 ft. lb.)
   2nd 24–27 Nm
      (2.4–2.8 kg-m, 17–20 ft. lb.)
Bolt
   1st 3–5 Nm
      (0.3–0.5 kg-m, 2.2–3.6 ft. lb.)
   2nd 24–27 Nm
      (2.4–2.8 kg-m, 17–20 ft. lb.)

11. Install the exhaust manifolds and connecting tube and torque in sequence to 13–16 ft. lbs. Tighten the connecting tube to 16–20 ft. lbs.

12. The remainder of the installation is the reverse of removal.

CD 17 Diesel

1. Drain the coolant and disconnect the battery.

2. Disconnect the exhaust pipe.

3. Set the No. 1 cylinder at TDC on the compression stroke. Tag and disconnect all hoses and electrical connections.

4. Remove the valve timing belt on the camshaft pulley side of the engine.

5. Remove the injection pump timing belt.

6. Loosen the injection pump pulley and remove it with a suitable puller.

7. Remove the rear engine cover.

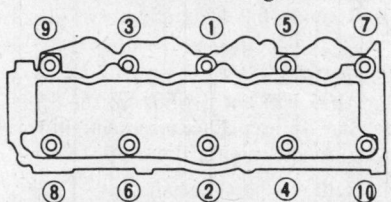

CD17 head torque sequence. Reverse the sequence for installation

8. Tag and remove all fuel injection lines from the injectors.

9. Remove the camshaft (valve) cover and loosen the cylinder head bolts in the reverse of the torque sequence given in this section.

10. Remove the cylinder head, with the manifolds still attached. If the head will not budge, tap around the head-to-block mating

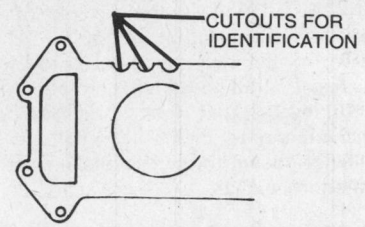

Cylinder head gasket identification

surface with a rubber mallet. The manifolds can be removed on a bench.

11. Reverse the above removal procedure for installation. Head gaskets are selected by measuring the piston projection. See "Piston and Connecting Rod" for an application chart. Torque the head bolts.

OVERHAUL

For all cylinder head overhaul procedures, please refer to "Engine Rebuilding" in the Unit Repair section.

Rocker Shaft

REMOVAL & INSTALLATION

NOTE: All rocker shaft removal and installation procedures other than those

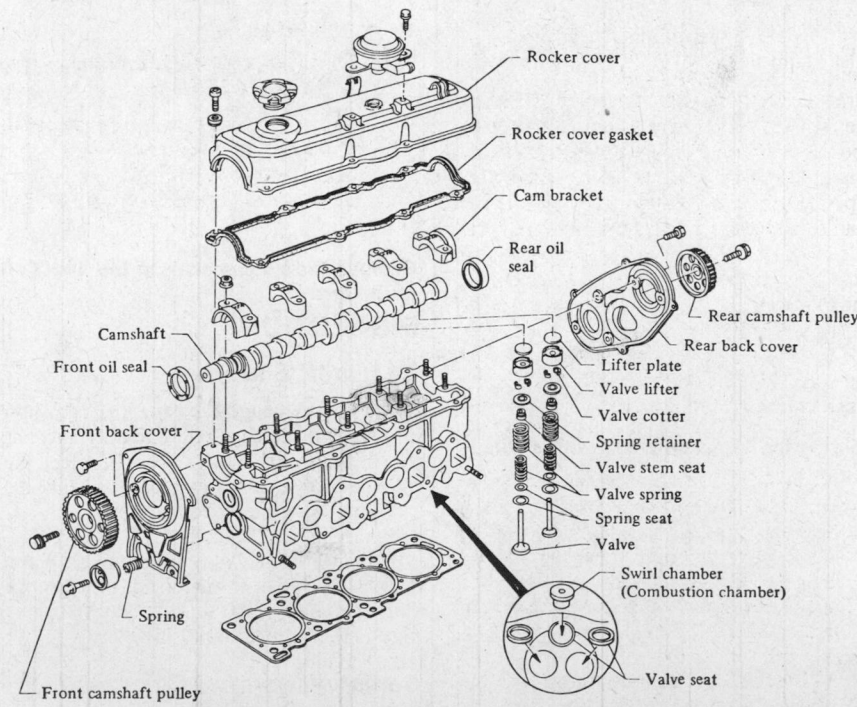

Exploded view of CD17 cylinder head assembly

detailed below (except on the VG30E/ET, which is detailed in the "Cylinder Head" removal and installation procedure), are given in the "Camshaft Removal and Installation" section.

A14 and A15 Engines

1. Remove the rocker cover.
2. Loosen the rocker adjusting bolts and push the adjusting screws away from the pushrods.
3. Unbolt and remove the rocker shaft assembly.
4. To install, reverse the above. Tighten rocker shaft bolts to 14–18 ft. lbs. in a circular sequence. Adjust the valves.

Intake and Exhaust Manifolds

REMOVAL & INSTALLATION

280Z and 280ZX

NOTE: It is important to replace the gasket whenever either manifold is removed. Because the manifolds share a common gasket, it is necessary to remove both manifolds for access to the gasket. Be sure to get the correct replacement gasket for the car. 1979–84 models have square exhaust ports, instead of the round ports used on 1978 models. The gaskets are not interchangeable.

1. Disconnect the air and vacuum hoses from the air cleaner. Disconnect the hose linking the balance tube and the temperature sensor at the balance tube end, on carbureted models.
2. Remove the air cleaner.
3. On carbureted models: disconnect the coolant, air, vacuum, and fuel hoses from the intake manifold and carburetors (drain enough coolant from the bottom of the radiator to perform this without losing coolant). Remove the carburetors from the manifold. Disconnect the rear coolant inlet pipe and the exhaust gas inlet tube at the manifold. Remove the air conditioner fast idle mechanism and bracket from the manifold, if equipped. Remove the securing nut and disconnect the coolant tube from the balance tube.
4. On fuel injected models: relieve fuel line pressure as outlined in the fuel filter replacement procedure. Disconnect the fuel injection wiring harness. Disconnect the hose from the rocker cover to the throttle chamber at the rocker cover. Drain the coolant into a clean container. Disconnect the coolant hose which runs from the heater to the coolant inlet at the inlet. Remove the bolt securing the coolant pipe/fuel pipe to the cylinder head. Remove the tube connecting the heater to the thermostat housing. Disconnect the fuel lines.
5. Disconnect the vacuum hose to the EGR valve, and the EGR tube from the exhaust manifold.

6. On models with an air pump, disconnect the air injection hose from the air injection gallery on the exhaust manifold at the check valve.
7. Disconnect the exhaust pipe from the exhaust manifold or from the exhaust outlet of the turbocharger if so equipped. Remove the exhaust manifold heat shield.
8. Remove the intake and exhaust manifolds.
9. Install the manifolds in the reverse order of removal. *Always use a new gasket:* air leaks will cause burnt valves and misfiring. Tighten the manifold bolts from the center outwards, in two progressive steps, to the proper torque.

Intake Manifold

REMOVAL & INSTALLATION

All Except 810, 300ZX and 1980–85 200SX/510

1. Remove the air cleaner assembly together with all of the attending hoses.
2. Disconnect the throttle linkage and fuel and vacuum lines from the carburetor.
3. The carburetor can be removed from the manifold at this point or can be removed as an assembly with the intake manifold.
4. Disconnect the intake and exhaust manifold unless both are being removed on A-series engines. Loosen the intake manifold attaching nuts, working from the two ends toward the center, and then remove them.
5. Remove the intake manifold from the engine.
6. Install the intake manifold in the reverse order of removal.

810, Maxima

NOTE: Certain procedures may apply only to the gasoline engine.

1. Disconnect all hoses to the air cleaner and remove the air cleaner.
2. Disconnect all air, water, vacuum and fuel hoses to the intake manifold. Re-

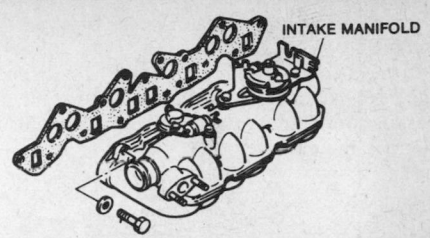

LD28 diesel intake manifold—810 and Maxima

move the cold start valve and fuel pipe as an assembly. Remove the throttle linkage.
3. Remove the B.P.T. valve control tube from the intake manifold. Remove the EGR hoses.
4. Disconnect all electrical wiring to the fuel injection unit. Note the location of the wires and mark them in some manner to facilitate reinstallation.
5. Make sure all wires, hoses, lines, etc. are removed. Unscrew the intake manifold bolts. Keep the bolts in order since they are of two different sizes. Remove the manifold.
6. Installation is the reverse of removal. Use a new gasket, clean both sealing surfaces, and torque the bolts in several stages, working from the center outward.

1980–85 200SX/510

1. Drain the coolant.
2. On the fuel injected engine, remove the air cleaner hoses. On the carbureted engine, remove the air cleaner.

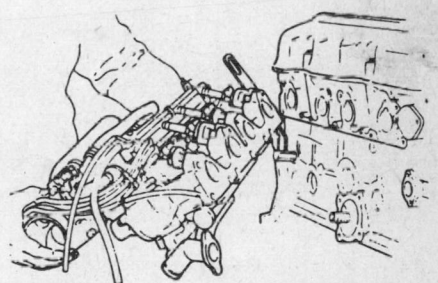

Removing the manifold with injectors, etc., still attached—Z20E, Z22E

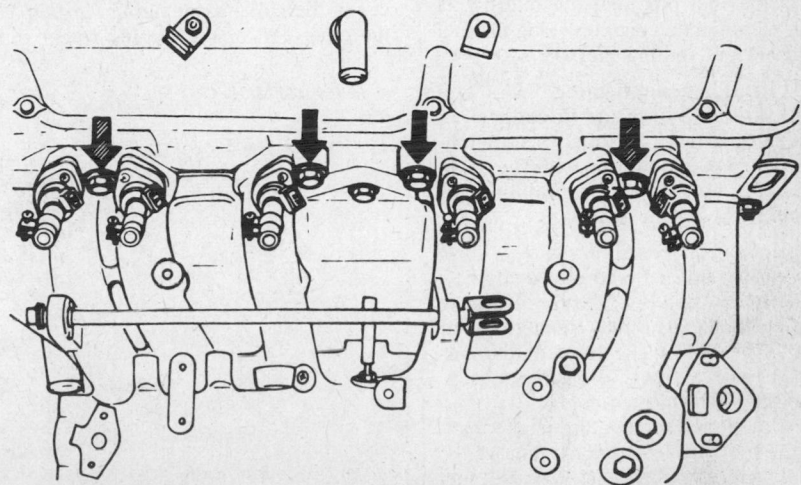

810/Maxima intake manifold mounting bolt locations—gasoline engines

3. Remove the radiator hoses from the manifold.

4. For the carbureted engine, remove the fuel, air and vacuum hoses from the carburetor. Remove the throttle linkage and remove the carburetor.

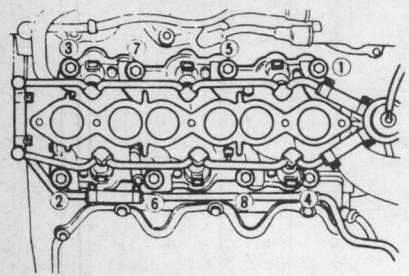

Intake manifold bolt removal sequence—V6

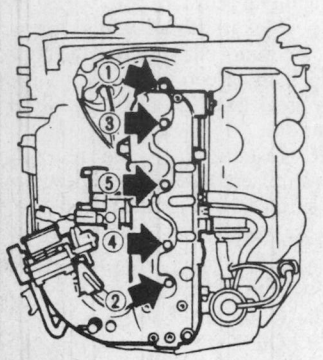

Intake manifold collector cover bolt removal sequence—V6

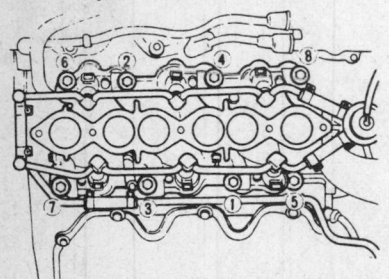

TIGHTEN IN NUMERICAL ORDER.

Intake manifold torque sequence—V6

5. Remove the throttle cable and disconnect the fuel pipe and the return fuel line on fuel injection engines. Plug the fuel pipe to prevent spilling fuel.

NOTE: When unplugging wires and hoses, mark each hose and its connection with a piece of masking tape, then match-code the two pieces of tape with the numbers 1, 2, 3, etc. When assembling, simply match the pieces of tape.

6. Remove all remaining wires, tubes, the air cleaner bracket (carbureted engines) and the E.G.R. and P.C.V. tubes from the rear of the intake manifold. Remove the air induction pipe from the front of the carbureted engine. Remove the manifold supports on the fuel injected engine.

7. Unbolt and remove the intake manifold. On fuel injected engines, remove the manifold with injectors, E.G.R. valve, fuel tubes, etc., still attached.

8. Installation is the reverse of removal. Use a new intake manifold gasket.

Exhaust Manifold

REMOVAL & INSTALLATION

NOTE: You may find that removing the intake manifold will provide better access to the exhaust manifold (on all engines except the V6).

1. Remove the air cleaner assembly, if necessary for access. Remove the heat shield, if present.

2. Disconnect the exhaust pipe from the exhaust manifold. Disconnect the intake manifold from the exhaust manifold (A-series engines only) unless removing both.

3. Remove all temperature sensors, air induction pipes and other attachments from the manifold. Disconnect the EAI and EGR tubes from their fittings on the E-series manifold.

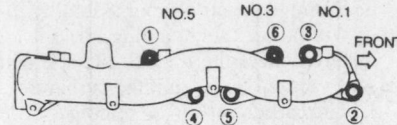

L.H. exhaust manifold

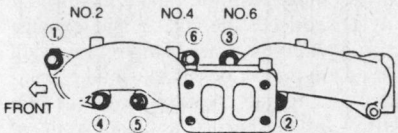

V6 exhaust manifold removal sequence

4. Loosen and remove the exhaust manifold attaching nuts and remove the manifold from the engine.

5. Install the exhaust manifold in the reverse order of removal.

Turbocharger

The turbocharger is installed on the exhaust manifold. This system utilizes exhaust gas energy to rotate the turbine wheel which drives the compressor turbine installed on the other end of the turbine wheel shaft.

The compressor supplies compressed air to the engine to increase the charging efficiency so improving engine output and torque.

For more information on turbochargers, please refer to "Turbocharging" in the Unit Repair section.

REMOVAL & INSTALLATION

280ZX

1. Remove the heat insulator, inlet tube, air duct hose and suction air pipe.

2. Disconnect the exhaust gas sensor harness connector, front tube, oil delivery tube and oil drain pipe.

3. Loosen the nuts which attach the turbocharger unit to the exhaust manifold, then remove the turbocharger.

NOTE: The turbocharger should not be disassembled. The turbocharger is replaced as a unit if found to be defective.

300ZX

Remove the following:

    a. Compressor and compressor bracket.

    b. Exhaust front tube.

    c. Center cable.

    d. Heat insulator for the brake master cylinder.

    e. Air duct and hoses.

    f. Exhaust manifold connecting tube and heat shield plate.

    g. Oil delivery tube and return hose.

2. Remove the exhaust manifold and the turbocharger as an assembly.

NOTE: The turbocharger unit should not be disassembled.

3. Installation is the reverse of removal.

1984 and Later 200SX

1. Drain the engine coolant.

2. Remove the air duct and hoses, and the air intake pipe.

3. Disconnect the front exhaust pipe at the exhaust manifold (exhaust outlet in the illustration).

4. Remove the heat shield plates.

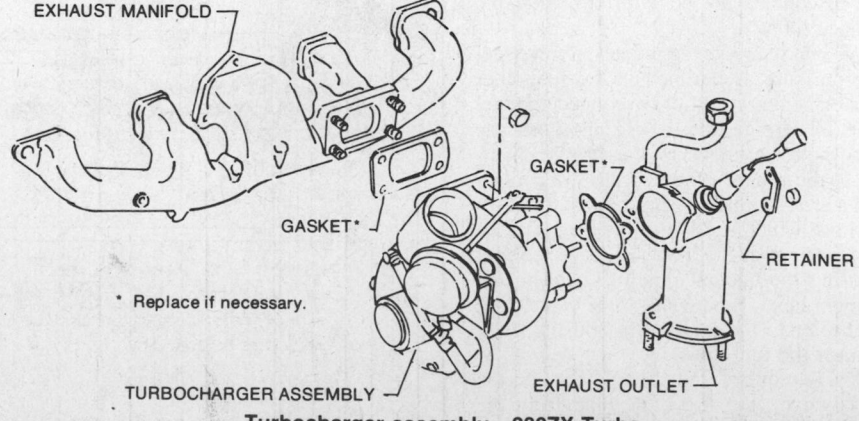

Turbocharger assembly—280ZX Turbo

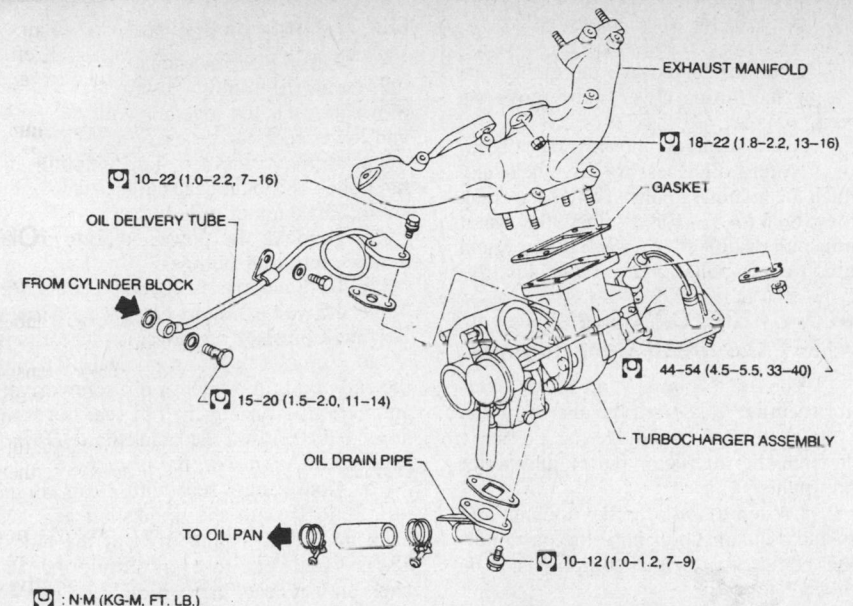

10–22 (1.0–2.2, 7–16)

OIL DELIVERY TUBE

FROM CYLINDER BLOCK

EXHAUST MANIFOLD

18–22 (1.8–2.2, 13–16)

GASKET

15–20 (1.5–2.0, 11–14)

44–54 (4.5–5.5, 33–40)

OIL DRAIN PIPE

TURBOCHARGER ASSEMBLY

TO OIL PAN

10–12 (1.0–1.2, 7–9)

: N·M (KG-M, FT. LB.)

V6 turbocharger assembly

5. Tag and disconnect the oil delivery tube and return hose.

6. Disconnect the water inlet tube.

7. Unbolt and remove the turbocharger from the exhaust manifold.

NOTE: The turbocharger unit should only be serviced internally by an engine specialist trained in turbocharger repair.

8. Reverse the above procedure to install. Torque the turbocharger outlet-to-housing bolts to 16–22 ft. lbs.

Front Cover

REMOVAL, INSTALLATION & OIL SEAL REPLACEMENT

A14 and A15 Overhead Valve Engines

1. Remove the radiator. Loosen the alternator and remove the belt. Loosen the air pump and remove the belt on engines with the air pump system.

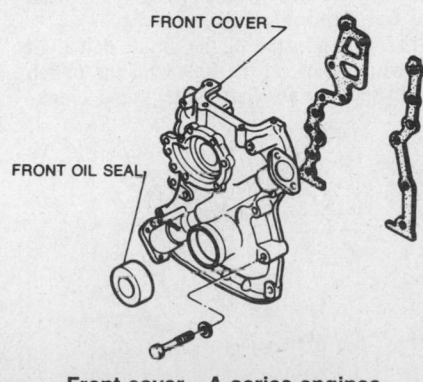

FRONT COVER

FRONT OIL SEAL

Front cover—A-series engines

2. Remove the fan unbolt and remove water pump.

3. Bend back the lock tab from the crankshaft pulley nut. Remove the nut with a heavy wrench. If the nut will not come loose without turning the pulley with it, you may have to fabricate a wooden wedge to place between the pulley and cover in order to hold the pulley. The nut must be unscrewed opposite normal engine rotation. Pull off the pulley.

4. It is recommended that the oil pan be removed or loosened before the front cover is removed.

5. Unbolt and remove the timing chain cover.

6. Replace the crankshaft oil seal in the cover. Most models use a felt seal.

7. Reverse the procedure to install, using new gaskets. Apply sealant to both sides of the timing cover gasket. Front cover bolt torque is 4 ft. lbs., water pump bolt torque is 7–10 ft. lbs., and oil pan bolt torque is 4 ft. lbs.

L20B, L24, L28, Z20 and Z22 Overhead Cam Engines

NOTE: It may be necessary to remove the cylinder head to perform this operation if you cannot cut the front of the head gasket cleanly as described in Step 10. If so, you will need a new head gasket.

1. Disconnect the negative battery cable from the battery, drain the cooling system, and remove the radiator together with the upper and lower radiator hoses.

2. Loosen the alternator drive belt adjusting screw and remove the drive belt. Remove the bolts which attach the alternator bracket to the engine and set the alternator aside out of the way.

3. Remove the distributor.

4. Remove the oil pump attaching

screws, and take out the pump and its drive spindle.

5. Remove the cooling fan and the fan pulley together with the drive belt.

6. Remove the water pump.

7. Remove the crankshaft pulley bolt and remove the crankshaft pulley.

8. Remove the bolts holding the front cover to the front of the cylinder block, the four bolts which retain the front of the oil pan to the bottom of the front cover, and the two bolts which are screwed down through the front of the cylinder head and into the top of the front cover.

9. Carefully pry the front cover off the engine.

10. Cut the exposed front section of the oil pan gasket away from the oil pan. Do the same to the gasket at the top of the front cover. Remove the two side gaskets and clean all of the mating surfaces.

11. Cut the portions needed from a new oil pan gasket and top front cover gasket.

12. Apply sealer to all of the gaskets and position them on the engine in their proper places.

13. Apply a light coating of grease to the crankshaft oil seal and carefully mount the front cover to the front of the engine and install all of the mounting bolts.

Tighten the 8 mm bolts to 7–12 ft. lbs. and the 6 mm bolts to 3–6 ft. lbs. Tighten the oil pan attaching bolts to 4–7 ft. lbs.

14. Before installing the oil pump, place the gasket over the shaft and make sure that the mark on the drive spindle faces (is aligned with) the oil pump hole. Install the oil pump so that the projection on the top of the shaft is located in the exact position as when it was removed or in the 11:25 o'clock position with the piston in the No. 1 cylinder placed at TDC on the compression stroke, if the engine was disturbed since disassembly. Tighten the oil pump attaching screws to 8–10 ft. lbs. See "Oil Pump Removal and Installation."

LD28 Diesel Engine

NOTE: It may be necessary to remove the cylinder head to perform this procedure if you cannot cut the front of the head gasket cleanly as described in Step 16. If so, you will need a new head gasket.

——— CAUTION ———

This procedure requires the removal and subsequent installation of the fuel injection pump. It is a good idea to read through the "Diesel Fuel Injection" section before you continue with this procedure—you may decide that the job is better left to a qualified service technician.

1. Disconnect the negative battery cable. Drain the cooling system and then remove the radiator together with the upper and lower radiator hoses.

2. Remove the fan, fan coupling and fan pulley.

3. Unscrew the retaining bolts on the crankshaft damper pulley. Use a plastic

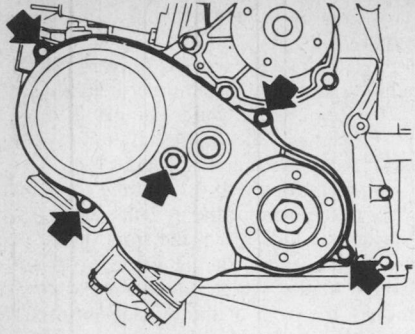

Remove the dust cover on the diesel

mallet and lightly tap around the outer edges of the pulley, this should loosen it enough so that you can pull it off. If not, use a two-armed gear puller.

4. Remove the power steering pump, bracket and idler pulley (if so equipped).

5. Unscrew the five mounting bolts and remove the front dust cover.

6. Remove the thermostat housing and the bottom bypass inlet with the hose.

7. Remove the engine slinger.

8. Tag and disconnect all hoses and lines running from the injection pump. Make sure to plug any hoses or lines to prevent dust or dirt from entering.

9. Drain the engine oil.

10. Remove the oil cooler and coolant hose together with the oil filter.

11. Remove the water inlet, the oil dipstick and the right side engine mounting bracket.

12. Remove the oil pump.

13. Remove the injection pump.

14. Remove the water pump.

15. Loosen the mounting bolt and remove the injection pump drive crank pulley. You will need a two armed gear puller.

16. Remove the bolts holding the front cover to the front of the cylinder block, the four bolts which retain the front of the oil pan to the bottom of the front cover, and the two bolts which are screwed down through the front of the cylinder head and into the top of the front cover.

17. Carefully pry the front cover off the front of the engine.

18. Follow Steps 10–14 of the previous "L20B, etc." procedure.

19. Installation of the remaining components is in the reverse order of removal.

E15 and E16 Overhead Cam Engines

1. Disconnect the battery, drain the cooling system, and remove the radiator together with the upper and lower radiator hoses.

2. Loosen the air conditioner belt and remove.

3. Loosen the alternator adjusting bolt, and remove the alternator belt. Unbolt the alternator mounting bracket and remove the alternator.

4. Remove the power steering belt (if equipped) by loosening the steering pump adjusting bolt.

5. Remove the water pump pulley.

6. Remove crankshaft pulley.

7. Loosen and remove the eight bolts securing the timing cover and remove the cover.

8. Installation is the reverse of removal. Adjust all accessory drive belts and tighten the mounting bolts. Torque the crank pulley bolt to 83–108 ft. lbs.; the water pump pulley bolt to 2.7–3.7 ft. lbs.; and the belt cover bolts to 2.7–3.7 ft. lbs.

CA20, CA20E, CA20S and CA18ET Overhead Cam Engines

1. Loosen the upper and lower alternator securing bolts until the alternator can be moved enough to remove the alternator belt from the alternator pulley and water pump pulley.

2. Loosen the idler pulley locknut and turn the adjusting bolt until the air conditioner compressor belt (if equipped) can be removed.

3. Unbolt and remove the crankshaft pulley, removing the alternator belt along with it. Remove the crankshaft damper.

4. Unbolt and remove the water pump pulley.

5. Remove the lower and upper timing belt covers and their gaskets. If the gaskets are in good condition after removal, they can be reused; if they are in any way damaged or broken, replace them.

6. Reverse the above procedure for installation. Torque the front cover bolts evenly to 2.2–3.6 ft. lbs.; torque the crank pulley damper bolt to 90–98 ft. lbs.; torque the crank pulley bolt to 9–10 ft. lbs.; torque the water pump pulley bolts to 4.3–7 ft. lbs. Adjust tension on all drive belts.

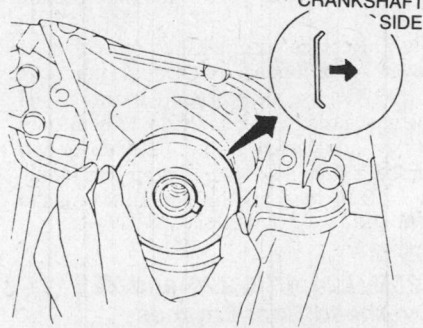

Correct installation of crankshaft pulley plate

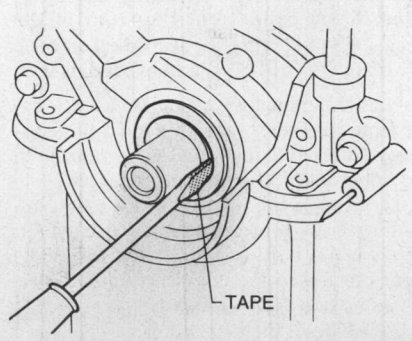

Carefully pry out the front oil seal

CD 17 Diesel Engine

1. Disconnect the negative battery cable. Drain the cooling system and then remove the radiator together with the upper and lower radiator hoses.

2. Remove the fan, fan coupling and fan pulley. Using a gear puller, remove the crankshaft damper pulley.

3. Remove the power steering pump, bracket and idler pulley.

4. Remove the front belt cover. Remove the valve timing belt (see "Timing Belt and Camshaft" removal in this section).

5. Remove the front oil seal by taping the end of a thin prybar or old screwdriver, and carefully prying the old seal out from around the end of the crankshaft. *Do not scratch the shaft with the prybar*.

6. Coat a new seal with clean engine oil. Slide it onto the crankshaft end and back into place in the front of the block. Use a small drift to evenly drive the seal back until it seats in position.

7. Installation is the reverse of removal. Follow the "Timing Belt and Camshaft" removal and installation procedure when installing the timing belt.

Timing Cover and Belt

REMOVAL AND INSTALLATION

V6 Engine (300ZX)

1. Remove the radiator shroud, fan and pulleys.

2. Drain the coolant from the radiator and remove the water pump hose.

3. Remove the power steering, compressor and alternator drive belts.

4. Set the No. 1 cylinder at TDC on its compression stroke.

5. Remove the front upper and lower belt covers.

6. Loosen the timing belt tensioner and return spring then remove the timing belt.

7. Before installing the timing belt confirm that the No. 1 cylinder is set at TDC on its compression stroke.

8. Remove both rocker covers and loosen all rocker shaft retaining bolts.

9. Install tensioner and return spring.

10. Make sure that the timing belt is clean and free from oil or water.

11. When installing the timing belt align the white lines on the belt with the punch mark on the camshaft pulleys and crank-

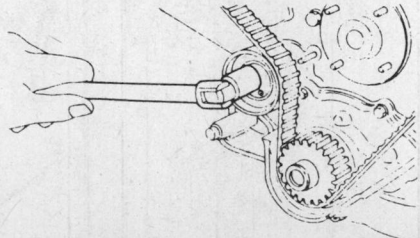

Loosening timing belt tensioner—V6

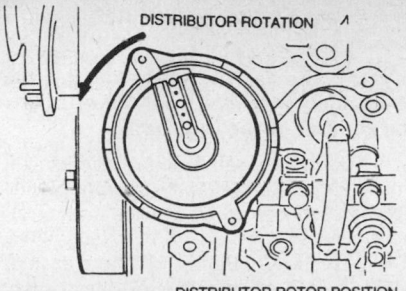

Distributor rotor position for timing belt removal—V6

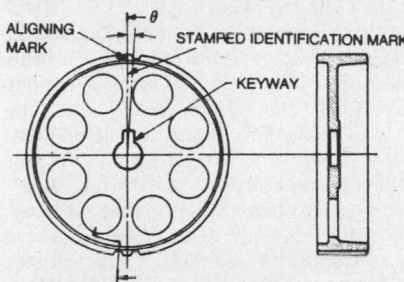

Camshaft pulley alignment marks—V6

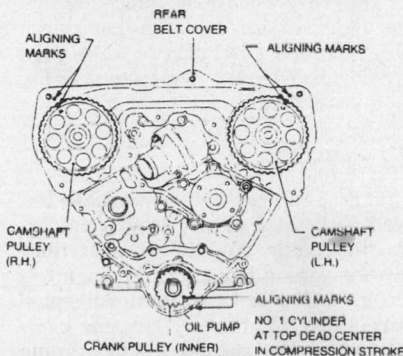

Align camshaft and crankshaft pulley marks—V6

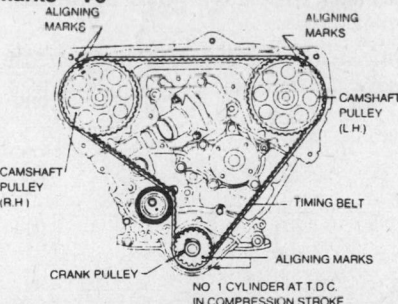

Aligning timing belt white lines with marks on camshaft and crankshaft pulleys—V6

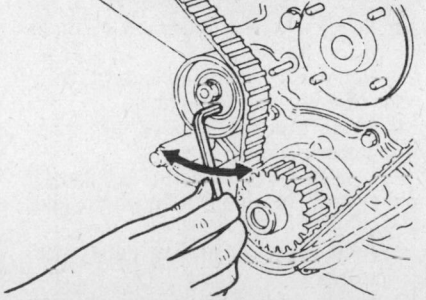

Tightening tensioner locknut—V6

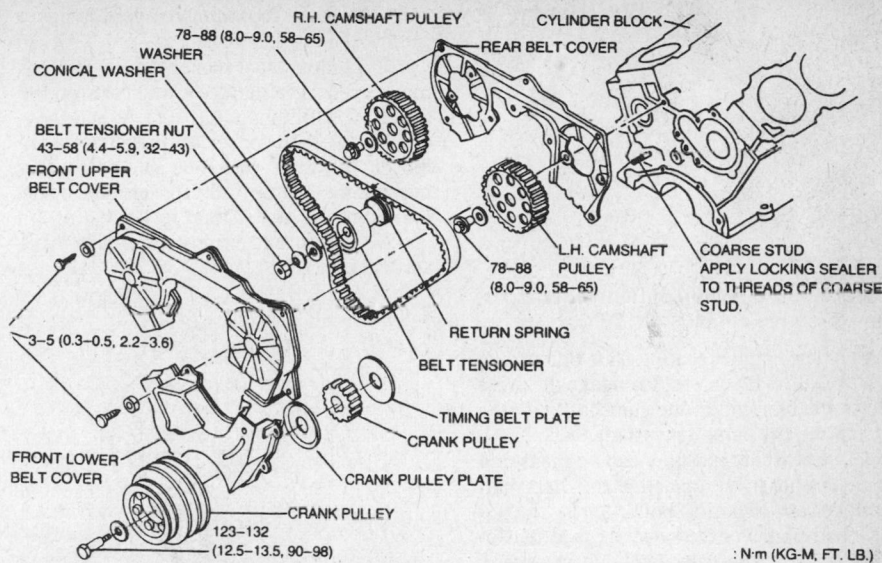

Exploded view of the V6 timing belt assembly, showing timing cover

shaft pulley. Have the arrow on the timing belt pointing toward the front belt covers.

12. Slowly turn the tensioner with a hexagon wrench clockwise and counterclockwise two or three times.

13. Tighten the tensioner lock nut to 32–43 ft. lbs.

14. Tighten the rocker shaft retaining bolts in two or three stages.

NOTE: Before tightening, be sure to set the camshaft lobe at the position where the lobe is not lifted.

15. Install the lower and upper belt covers.

16. The remainder of the installation is the reverse of removal.

Timing Chain and Camshaft

REMOVAL & INSTALLATION

A14 and A15 Overhead Valve Engines

This operation can only be performed with the engine out of the car.

1. Remove the engine.
2. Remove the rocker cover and rocker shaft assembly.
3. Remove the pushrods.
4. Invert the engine.
5. Remove the timing chain cover.
6. Remove the chain tensioner.
7. Remove the camshaft sprocket retaining bolt.
8. Remove the camshaft sprocket, crankshaft sprocket, and timing chain as an assembly. Be careful not to lose the shims (if present) and oil slinger from behind the crankshaft sprocket.
9. Remove the distributor, and distributor drive spindle. Remove the oil pump and pump driveshaft.

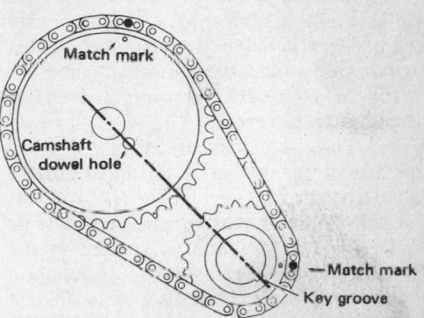

A14 and 15 sprocket and timing chain assembly

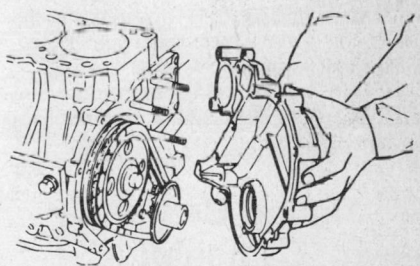

Installing the A-series timing chain cover. Note slinger on end of crankshaft

10. Unbolt and remove the camshaft locating plate. Remove the camshaft carefully. The engine must be inverted to prevent the lifters from falling down into the engine. If the lifters must be removed, remove the oil pan and remove them after withdrawing the camshaft. Keep the lifters in order and return them to their original positions.

11. The camshaft bearings can be pressed out and replaced. They are available in undersizes, should it be necessary to regrind the camshaft journals. The bearings must be line-bored after installation.

12. Coat the bearings and camshaft with engine oil. Reinstall the camshaft. If the locating plate has an oil hole, it should be to the right of the engine. The locating plate is marked with the word LOWER and an

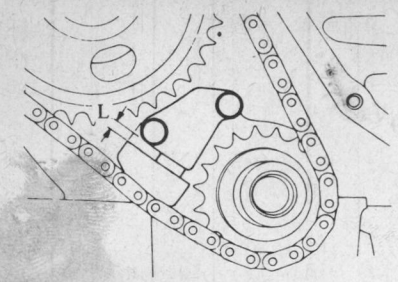

Checking projection of tensioner spindle—A-series engines

arrow. The engine locating plate bolt torque is 3–4 ft. lbs. Be careful to engage the drive pin in the rear end of the camshaft with the slot in the oil pump driveshaft.

13. Camshaft end-play can be measured after temporarily replacing the camshaft sprocket and securing bolt.

If end-play is excessive, replace the locating plate. They are available in several sizes.

14. If the crankshaft or camshaft has been replaced, install the sprockets temporarily and make sure that they are parallel. Adjust by shimming under the crankshaft sprocket.

15. Assemble the sprockets and chain, aligning them.

16. Turn the crankshaft until the keyway and No. 1 piston are at top dead center. Install the sprockets and chain. The oil slinger behind the crankshaft sprocket must be replaced with the concave surface to the front. If the chain and sprocket installation is correct, the sprocket marks must be aligned between the shaft centers when the No. 1 piston is at TDC. Check the projection (''L'') of the timing chain tensioner spindle. If the projection exceeds 0.59 in., replace the timing chain. Engine camshaft sprocket retaining bolt torque is 33–36 ft. lbs.

17. The rest of the reassembly procedure is the reverse of disassembly. Engine chain tensioner bolt torque is 4–6 ft. lbs.

Timing Belt and Camshaft

REMOVAL & INSTALLATION

E15, E16, CA20, CA20E and CA18ET Overhead Cam Engines

1. Removal of the cylinder head from the engine is optional. Crank the engine until the No. 1 piston is at TDC on its compression stroke.

2. Follow the ''Front Cover'' removal procedure and remove the cover. Mark the relationship of the camshaft sprocket to the timing belt and the crankshaft sprocket to the timing belt with paint or a grease pencil. This will make setting everything up during reassembly much easier if the engine is disturbed during disassembly.

3. Remove the distributor.

4. Remove the thermostat housing.

5. Remove the timing belt from the

sprockets, after loosening the belt tensioner pulley.

6. Remove the rocker cover and remove the rocker shaft (rocker shafts on the CA20, CA20E and CA18ET). When loosening the CA20 rocker shaft bolts, evenly loosen the bolts in sequence; before removing the shafts, fully loosen the rocker arm adjusting screws and locknuts.

7. Loosen and remove the cam drive sprocket.

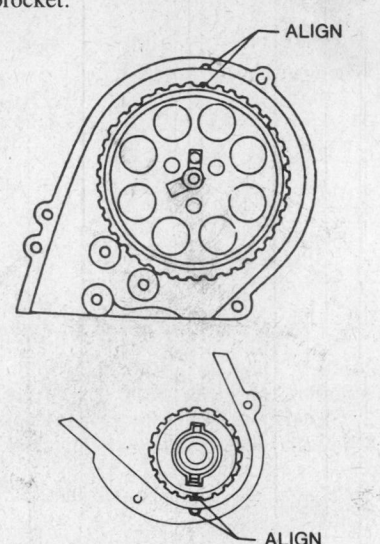

E-series engine valve timing mark alignment

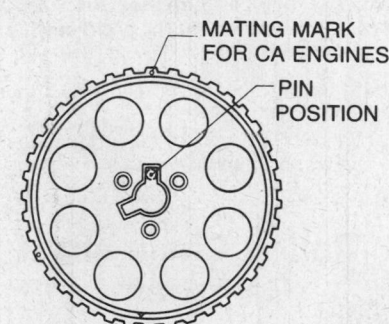

Camshaft sprocket installation—CA20

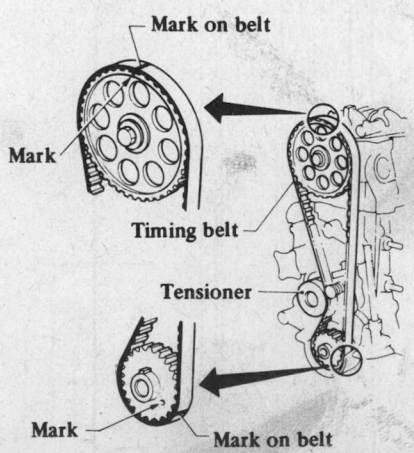

Align the CA20 timing belt mating marks with those of the crankshaft and camshaft sprockets

8. Remove the camshaft front retainer plate.

NOTE: Be careful not to damage the oil seal lip between the front retainer plate and the end of the camshaft.

9. Squirt a small amount of clean oil around the camshaft bearings. Carefully slide the camshaft out of the carrier in the cylinder head.

10. To install, lightly oil the camshaft bearings with clean motor oil and slowly slide the cam into place in the cylinder head.

11. Install the camshaft front retainer plate on the cylinder head.

12. Reassemble the remainder of the head assembly in the reverse order of removal. Check the valve timing after all sprockets and timing belts are installed. Tighten the camshaft drive sprocket on the E15 and E16 to 4.3–5.8 ft. lbs. Torque the CA20 camshaft sprocket bolts to 36–40 ft. lbs. Install a new gasket behind the thermostat housing. Adjust the valves, and adjust all drive belts. Tighten the belt tensioner and assemble the spring. To set the spring, first hook one end on bolt ''B'' side, then hook the other end on the tensioner bracket pawl. Rotate the crankshaft two turns clockwise, then tighten bolt ''B'' then bolt ''A''. At this point, belt tension will automatically be at the specified value.

CD 17 Diesel

NOTE: The camshaft is normally removed with the cylinder head removed from the engine. Follow the procedure below for timing belt removal, then follow the ''Cylinder Head Removal'' procedure earlier in this section; the camshaft removal procedure follows timing belt removal. The injection pump has its own belt drive and is covered later in this section.

1. Support the engine with a jack and remove the right side engine mount, then jack the engine up to allow working clearance.

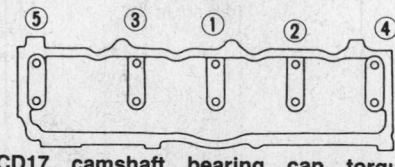

CD17 camshaft bearing cap torque sequence

2. Set the No. 1 cylinder at TDC on its compression stroke.

3. Remove the alternator and A/C compressor (if equipped) drive belts.

4. Using a puller, remove the crankshaft damper pulley.

5. Loosen the tensioner pulley and set it to the ''free'' position. Remove the idler pulley.

6. Remove the crankshaft pulley with the timing belt.

7. Check the belt for damage, missing teeth, wear or saturation with oil or grease.

If damage is evident or if you are in doubt as to the belt's condition, replace the belt.

NOTE: Do not bend, twist or turn the timing belt inside out. Do not allow the belt to come into contact with any grease, oil or solvents.

8. Remove the cylinder head and manifolds.

9. Remove the camshaft bearing caps and check the clearance with Plastigage®. *Do not turn the camshaft.* If the bearing clearance exceeds 0.1 mm (0.004 in.) replace the bearing caps, camshaft or cylinder head.

10. After checking clearances, remove the bearing caps and remove the camshaft with both oil seals. Have the camshaft runout and lobe height checked; if worn beyond specification, replace the camshaft.

11. To install the camshaft, assemble in the reverse order of removal. Before installing the oil seals, lubricate with clean engine oil. Reinstall the cylinder head and check valve clearances; adjust if necessary.

NOTE: There are two different diameter seals used on the camshaft front and rear. Be sure to use the correct seal when installing. (The front seal has an arrow on the outer edge facing clockwise; the rear seal arrow points counterclockwise). If you are replacing the oil seals without removing the camshaft, remove the pulleys and carefully pry the seals out using a small pry bar or an old screwdriver covered with tape. Use care not to scratch the camshaft, cylinder head or bearing cap.

12. Install the timing belt assembly in the reverse order of removal. Align the marks on the timing belt with those on the camshaft and crankshaft pulleys. When tensioning the belt, loosen the tensioner bolt and turn the crankshaft two times in its normal rotating direction, then tighten the tensioner while holding it. Do not allow the tensioner to rotate when tightening, and *NEVER turn the engine against its normal rotating direction.*

Timing Chain and Tensioner

REMOVAL & INSTALLATION

L20B, L24, L28, Z20 and Z22 Overhead Cam Engines

1. Before beginning any disassembly procedures, position the No. 1 piston at TDC on the compression stroke.

2. Remove the front cover as previously outlined. Remove the camshaft cover and remove the fuel pump if it runs off a cam lobe in front of the camshaft sprocket.

3. With the No. 1 piston at TDC, the timing marks on the camshaft sprocket and the timing chain should be visible. Mark both of them with paint. Also mark the

relationship of the camshaft sprocket to the camshaft. There are three sets of timing marks and locating holes in the sprocket for making adjustments to compensate for timing chain stretch. See the following "Timing Chain Adjustment" for more details.

4. With the timing marks on the cam sprocket clearly marked, locate and mark the timing marks on the crankshaft sprocket. Also mark the chain timing mark. Of course, if the chain is not to be re-used, marking it is useless.

5. Unbolt the camshaft sprocket and remove the sprocket along with the chain. As the chain is removed, hold it where the chain tensioner contacts it. When the chain is removed, the tensioner will come apart; *hold on to it and you won't lose any of the parts.* There is no need to remove the chain guide unless it is being replaced.

6. Using a two-armed gear puller, re move the crankshaft sprocket.

7. Install the timing chain and the camshaft sprocket together after first positioning the chain over the crankshaft sprocket. Position the sprocket so that the marks made earlier line up. This is assuming that the engine has not been disturbed. The camshaft and crankshaft keys should both be pointed upward. If a new chain and/or gear is being installed, position the sprocket so that the timing marks on the chain align with the marks on the crankshaft sprocket and the camshaft sprocket (with both keys pointing up). The marks are on the right-hand side of the sprockets as you face the engine. The L20B has 44 pins between the mating marks of the chain and sprockets when the chain is installed correctly. The 1978 L24 and L28 engine has 42 pins between timing marks. The L24 (1979 and later), L28 (1979 and later), Z20 and Z22 engines do not use the pin counting method for finding correct valve timing. Instead, position the key in the crankshaft sprocket so that it is pointing upward and install the camshaft sprocket on the camshaft with its dowel pin at the top using the No. 2 (No. 1—L24 and L28) mounting hole and timing mark. The painted links of the chain should be on the right hand side of the sprockets as you face the engine. See the illustration.

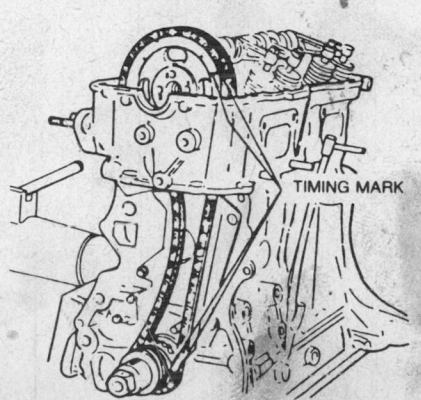

Timing chain and sprocket alignments— Z20 engines

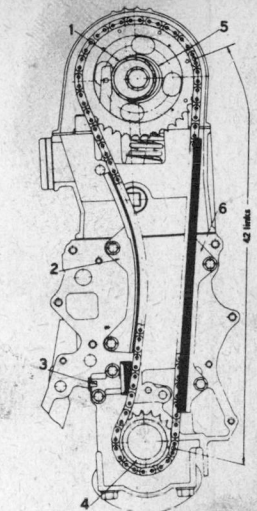

1. Fuel pump drive cam
2. Chain guide
3. Chain tensioner
4. Crankshaft sprocket
5. Camshaft sprocket
6. Chain guide

Camshaft chain installation—all OHC except E-series

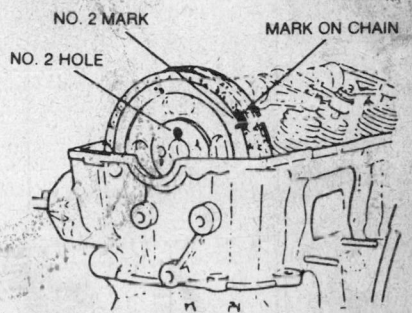

Use the No. 2 mark and hole to align the camshaft—Z20, Z22 series engines

NOTE: The factory manual refers to the pins to be counted in the L-series engines as links, but in America, this is not correct. Count the pins. There are two pins per link. This is an important step. If you do not get the exact number of pins between the timing marks, valve timing will be incorrect and the engine will either not run at all, in which case you may stand the chance of bending the valves, or the engine will run very feebly.

8. Install the chain tensioner. Adjust the protrusion of the tensioner spindle to zero clearance. Install the remaining components in the reverse order of disassembly.

LD28 Diesel Engine

1. Follow Steps 1–6 of the preceding "L20B, etc." procedure. You need not remove the fuel pump as detailed in Step 2.

2. Install the crankshaft sprocket. Make sure that the mating marks on the sprocket face the front of the car.

3. Install the timing chain and the camshaft sprocket together after first positioning the chain over the crankshaft sprocket. Position the cam sprocket so that the marks

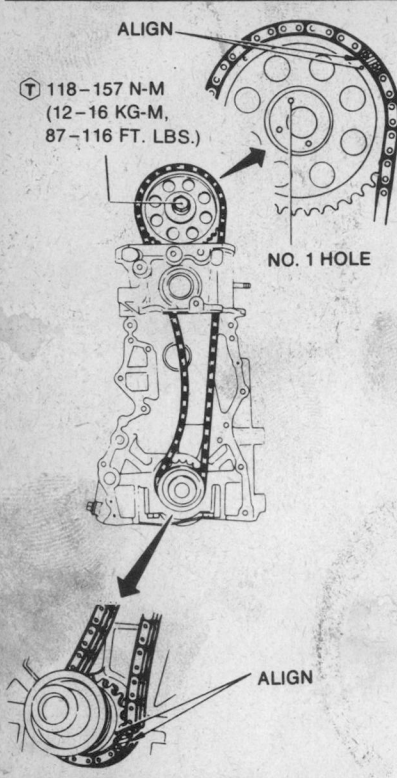

(T) 118–157 N-M
(12–16 KG-M,
87–116 FT. LBS.)

ALIGN

NO. 1 HOLE

ALIGN

Timing chain and sprocket alignment—1979 and later L24 and L28 series

made earlier line up. This is assuming that the engine has not been disturbed. The camshaft and crankshaft keys should be pointing upward. If a new chain and/or gear is being installed, position the sprocket so that the timing marks on the chain align with the marks on the crankshaft and camshaft sprockets (with both keys pointing up). The marks are on the right-hand side of the sprockets as you face the engine. Insert the camshaft dowel pin into the No. 1 hole in the camshaft sprocket. Install and tighten the camshaft sprocket bolt.

4. Install the chain guide (if removed) and the chain tensioner. Tighten the slack side (left side when facing the engine) chain guide mounting bolt so that the protrusion of the chain tensioner spindle is 0 in.

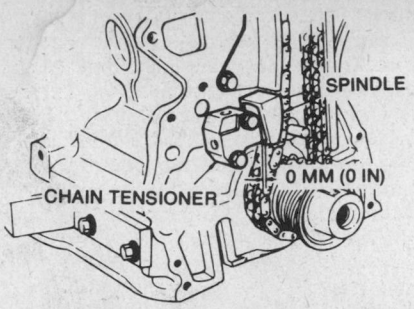

SPINDLE

0 MM (0 IN)

CHAIN TENSIONER

Chain tensioner mounting—1979 and later L24 and L28 series

5. Installation of the remaining components is in the reverse order of removal.

TIMING CHAIN ADJUSTMENT

When the timing chain stretches excessively, the valve timing will be adversely affected. There are three sets of holes and timing marks on the camshaft sprocket.

If the stretch of the chain roller links is excessive, adjust the camshaft sprocket location by transferring the set position of the camshaft sprocket from the factory position of No. 1 or No. 2 to one of the other positions as follows:

1. Turn the crankshaft until the No. 1 piston is at TDC on the compression stroke. Examine whether the camshaft sprocket location notch is to the left of the oblong groove on the camshaft retaining plate. If the notch in the sprocket is to the left of the groove in the retaining plate, then the chain is stretched and needs adjusting.

2. Remove the camshaft sprocket together with the chain and reinstall the sprocket and chain with the locating dowel on the camshaft inserted into either the No. 2 or 3 hole of the sprocket. The timing mark on the timing chain must be aligned with the mark on the sprocket. The amount of modification is 4 degrees of crankshaft rotation for each mark.

3. Recheck the valve timing as outlined in Step 1. The notch in the sprocket should

be to the right of the groove in the camshaft retaining plate.

4. If and when the notch cannot be brought to the right of the groove, the timing chain is worn beyond repair and must be replaced.

Camshaft

REMOVAL & INSTALLATION

NOTE: For VG30E series V6 camshaft removal, please refer to "Cylinder Head Removal" for this engine.

L20B, L24 and L28

1. Removal of the cylinder head from the engine is optional. Remove the camshaft sprocket from the camshaft together with the timing chain.

2. Loosen the valve rocker pivot locknut and remove the rocker arm by pressing down on the valve spring.

3. Remove the two retaining nuts on the camshaft retainer plate at the front of the cylinder head and carefully slide the camshaft out of the camshaft carrier.

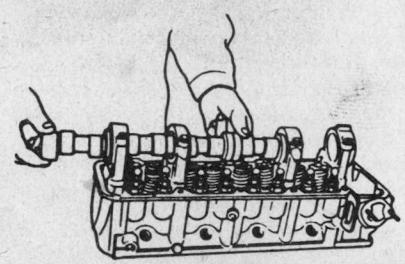

Carefully slide the camshaft out of the carrier

4. Lightly coat the camshaft bearings with clean motor oil and carefully slide the camshaft into place in the camshaft carrier.

5. Install the camshaft retainer plate with the oblong groove in the face of the plate facing toward the front of the engine.

6. Check the valve timing as outlined under "Timing Chain Removal and Installation" and install the timing sprocket on the camshaft, tightening the bolt together with the fuel pump cam to 86–116 ft. lb.

7. Install the rocker arms by pressing down the valve springs with a screwdriver and install the valve rocker springs.

8. Install the cylinder head, if it was removed, and assemble the rest of the engine in the reverse order of removal.

Z20 and Z22

1. Removal of the cylinder head from the engine is optional. Remove the camshaft sprocket from the camshaft together with the timing chain, after setting the No. 1 piston at TDC on its compression stroke.

2. Loosen the bolts holding the rocker shaft assembly in place and remove the six center bolts. Do not pull the four end bolts out of the rocker assembly because they hold the unit together.

① TO ③: TIMING MARK
1 TO 3: LOCATION HOLE

OBLONG GROOVE
LOCATION MATCH

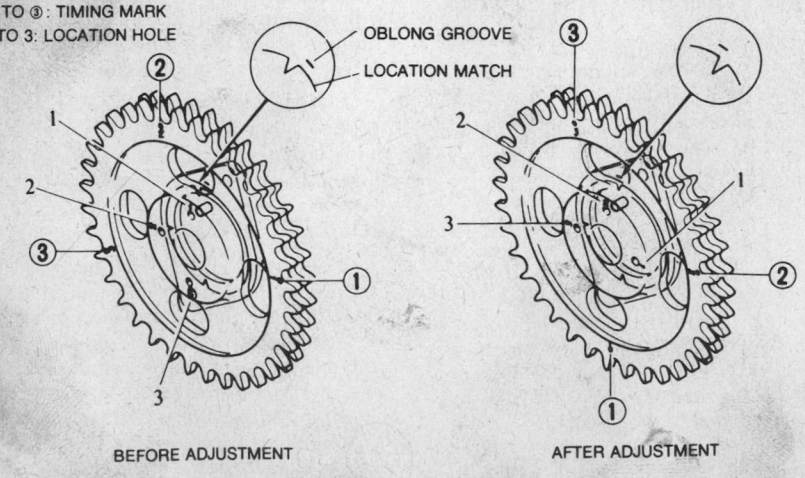

BEFORE ADJUSTMENT

AFTER ADJUSTMENT

Timing chain adjustment

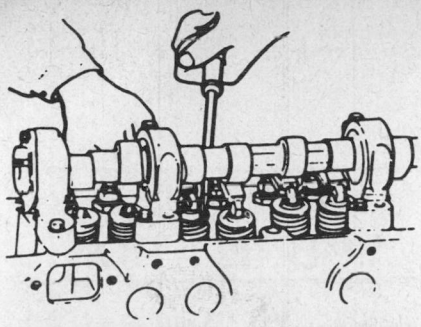

Remove the rocker arm by pressing down on the valve spring

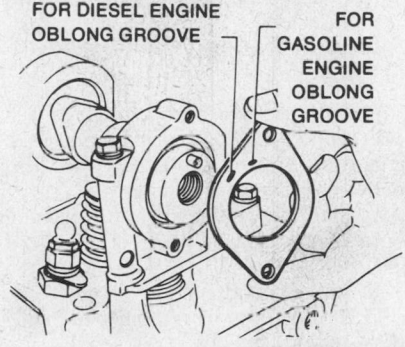

When installing the retaining plate, make sure the oblong groove is facing the front of the engine

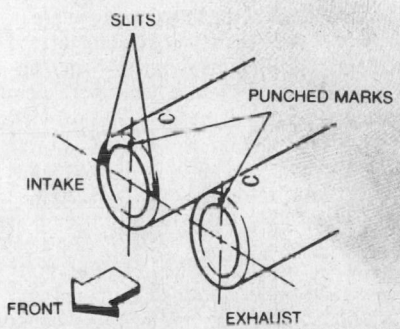

Note the difference in rocker shafts—Z20, Z22 series engines

—————— **CAUTION** ——————
When loosening the bolts, work from the ends in and loosen all of the bolts a little at a time so that you do not strain the camshaft or the rocker assembly. Remember, the camshaft is under pressure from the valve springs.
————————————————————

3. After removing the rocker assembly, remove the camshaft.

NOTE: Keep the disassembled parts in order.

If you need to disassemble the rocker unit, assemble as follows.

4. Install the mounting brackets, valve rockers and springs observing the following considerations.

The two rocker shafts are different. Both have punch marks in the ends that face the front of the engine. The rocker shaft that

goes on the side of the intake manifold has two slits in its end just below the punch mark. The exhaust side rocker shaft does not have slits.

The rocker arm for the intake and exhaust valves are interchangeable between cylinders one and three and are identified by the mark "1". Similarly, the rockers for cylinders two and four are interchangeable and are identified by the mark "2".

The rocker shaft mounting brackets are also coded for correct placement with either an "Λ" or a "Z" plus a number code.

To install the camshaft and rocker assembly:

5. Place the camshaft on the head with its dowel pin pointing up.

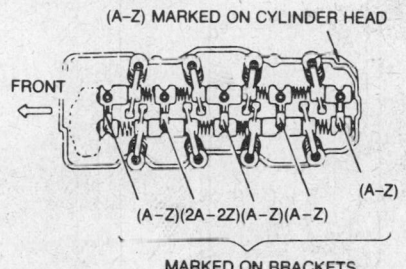

Rocker shaft mounting brackets are assembled in this order—Z20, Z22 series engines

6. Fit the rocker assembly on the head, making sure you mount it on its knock pin.

7. Torque the bolts to 11–18 ft. lbs., in several stages working from the middle bolts and moving outwards on both sides.

NOTE: Make sure the engine is on TDC of the compression stroke for the No. 1 piston or you may damage some valves.

See the section on timing chain installation. Adjust the valves.

Pistons and Connecting Rods

REMOVAL & INSTALLATION

All Engines

1. Remove the cylinder head.
2. Remove the oil pan.
3. Remove any carbon buildup from the cylinder wall at the top of the piston travel with a ridge reamer tool.
4. Position the piston to be removed at the bottom of its stroke so that the connecting rod bearing cap can be reached easily from under the engine.
5. Unscrew the connecting rod bearing cap nuts and remove the cap and lower half of the bearing. Attach a length of rubber hose to each of the connecting rod bolts. These will protect the cylinder bore from being scratched by the rod bolts.
6. Push the piston and connecting rod up and out of the cylinder block with a length of wood. Use care not to scratch the

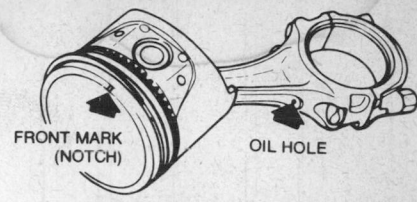

Piston and rod positioning

cylinder wall with the connecting rod or the wooden tool.

7. Keep all of the components from each cylinder together and install them in the cylinder from which they were removed.
8. Coat the bearing face of the connecting rod and the outer face of the pistons with engine oil. Attach a length of rubber hose to each of the connecting rod bolts. These will protect the cylinder bore from being scratched by the rod bolts.
9. See the illustrations for the correct placement of the piston rings.
10. Turn the crankshaft until the rod journal of the particular cylinder you are working on is brought to the TDC position.

NOTE: On the LD28 diesel, the amount of projection of each piston crown above the deck of the block must be measured.

11. On the LD28 diesel, Clean the deck of the cylinder block completely. Set a dial gauge on the cylinder block surface to zero. For every cylinder, measure the piston projection and record the length. Be sure to measure the length of piston projection at least three points for every cylinder. Determine the maximum length of piston projection and select the suitable head gasket according to the chart below. The head gaskets have cut-outs in them for identification

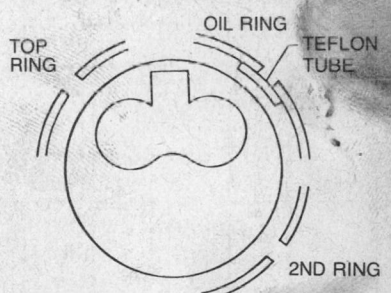

Space CD17 ring gaps 120° apart when installing piston

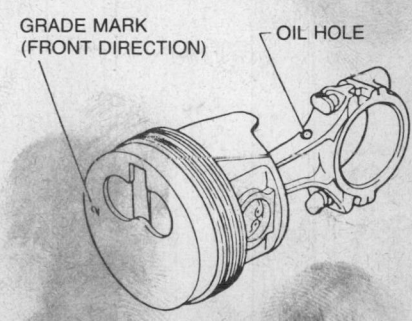

CD17 piston identification marks

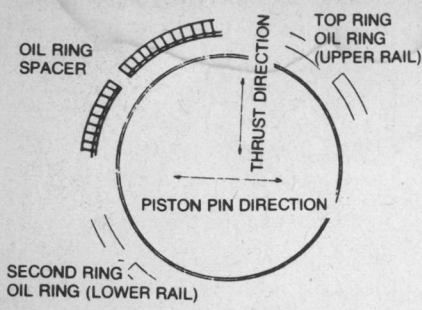

Piston ring placement—A-series engines;
L28, 1981 and later L24E similar

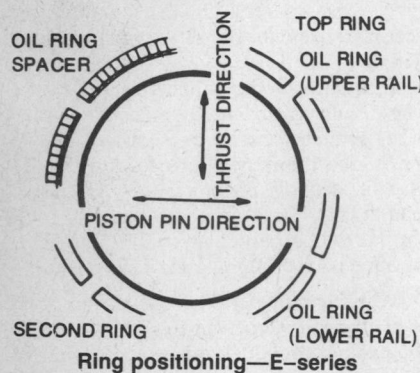

Ring positioning—E-series

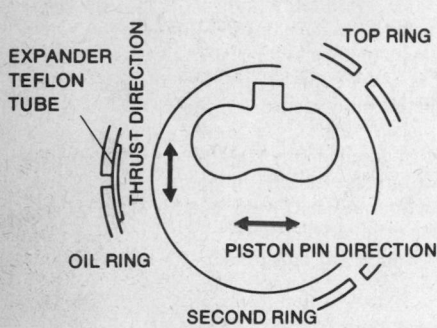

Piston ring placement—LD28 diesel; note
Teflon expander tube

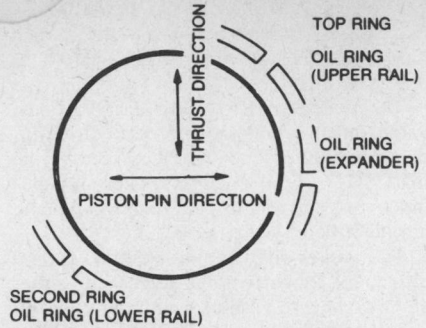

Piston ring placement for installation—
L20B, 1978-80 L24, Z20, Z22 engines

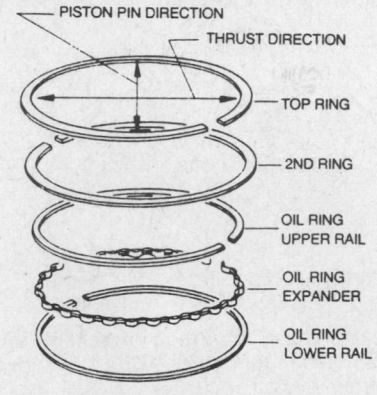

MARK SHOULD BE FACING UPWARD.

V6 piston ring installation

purposes. When the gasket is replaced, always install a gasket of the same thickness.

Piston projection mm (in)	Cylinder head gasket thickness mm (in)	No. of cutouts in cylinder head gasket
Below 0.487 (0.0192)	1.12 (0.0441)	1
0.487–0.573 (0.0192–0.0226)	1.2 (0.047)	2
Above 0.573 (0.0226)	1.28 (0.0504)	3

2. With the piston and rings clamped in a ring compressor, the notched mark on the head of the piston toward the front of the engine, and the oil hole side of the connecting rod toward the fuel pump side of the engine, push the piston and connecting rod assembly into the cylinder bore until the big bearing end of the connecting rod contacts and is seated on the rod journal of the crankshaft. Use the lengths of rubber hose as guides in seating the connecting rod onto the crankpin. Use care not to scratch the cylinder wall with the connecting rod.

13. Push down farther on the piston and turn the crankshaft while the connecting rod rides around on the crankshaft rod journal. Turn the crankshaft until the crankshaft rod journal is at BDC (bottom dead center).

14. Align the mark on the connecting rod bearing cap with that on the connecting rod and tighten the bearing cap bolts to the specifed torque.

15. Install all of the piston/connecting rod assemblies in the manner outlined above and assemble the oil pan and cylinder head to the engine in the reverse order of removal.

IDENTIFICATION & POSITIONING

The pistons are marked with a notch (or F) in the piston head. When installed, the notch (or F) markings are to be facing toward the front of the engine.

The connecting rods are installed with the oil hole facing toward the right side of the engine.

NOTE: It is advisable to number the pistons, connecting rods, and bearing caps in some manner so that they can be rein- stalled in the same cylinder, facing the same direction, from which they are removed.

ENGINE LUBRICATION

Oil Pan

REMOVAL & INSTALLATION

All Models Except VG30E and VG30ET

1. If the engine is in the vehicle, attach a lift, support the engine, and remove the engine mounting bolts as described in "Engine Removal and Installation".

2. Raise the engine slightly, watching to make sure that no hoses or wires are damaged.

3. Drain the engine oil.

4. Remove the oil pan bolts and slide the pan out to the rear.

To install the pan:

1. Use a new gasket, coated on both sides with sealer.

2. Apply a thin bead of silicone seal to the engine block at the junction of the block and front cover, and the junction of the block and rear main bearing cap. Then apply a thin coat of silicone seal to the new oil pan gasket, install the gasket to the block and install the pan.

3. Tighten the pan bolts in a circular pattern from the center to the ends, to 4–7 ft. lbs. Overtightening will distort the pan lip, causing leakage.

4. Reinstall the engine mounting bolts as described under "Engine Removal and Installation," using the specified torque and maintaining support until all mounts are secure.

5. Refill the oil pan to the specified level.

VG30E, VG30ET

1. Drain the engine oil.

2. Raise the vehicle and support it safely with jack stands.

3. Remove the front stabilizer bar retaining bolts and nuts from the suspension crossmember.

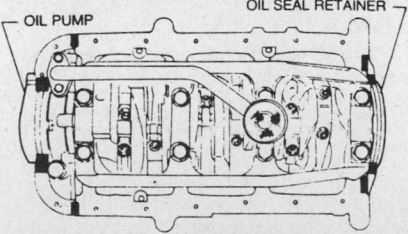

Apply sealant to these areas before installing the oil pan gasket—V6

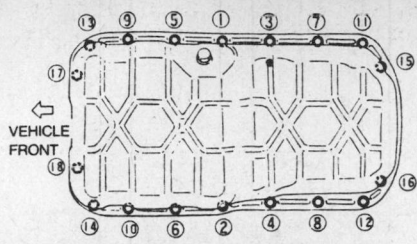

Oil pan tightening sequence—V6

4. Remove the steering column shaft from the gear housing.

5. Remove the tension rod retaining nuts from the transverse link.

6. Lift and support the engine.

7. Remove the rear plate cover from the transmission case.

8. Remove the oil pan retaining bolts.

9. Remove the suspension crossmember retaining bolts.

10. Remove the strut mounting insulator retaining nuts.

11. Remove the screws retaining the refrigerant lines and power steering tubes to the suspension crossmember.

12. Lower the suspension crossmember.

13. Remove the oil pan from the rear side.

14. Installation is the reverse of removal. Apply sealant to the surface points indicated in the illustration and torque the pan retaining bolts in numerical sequence to 3.5–5.1 ft. lbs.

Rear Main Oil Seal

REPLACEMENT

All Models Except CA20 Series and CA18ET

In order to replace the rear main oil seal, the rear main bearing cap must be removed. Removal of the rear main bearing cap requires the use of a special rear main bearing cap puller. Also, the oil seal is installed with a special crankshaft rear oil seal drift. Unless these or similar tools are available to you, it is recommended that the oil seal be replaced by a Datsun/Nissan service center.

1. Remove the engine and transmission assembly from the vehicle.

2. Remove the transmission from the engine. Remove the oil pan.

3. Remove the clutch from the flywheel.

4. Remove the flywheel from the crankshaft.

5. Remove the rear main bearing cap together with the bearing cap side seals (except on CD17).

6. Remove the rear main oil seal from around the crankshaft.

7. Apply lithium grease around the sealing lip of the oil seal and install the seal around the crankshaft using a suitable tool.

8. Apply sealer to the rear main bearing cap, install the rear main bearing cap, and tighten the cap bolts to 33–40 ft. lbs.

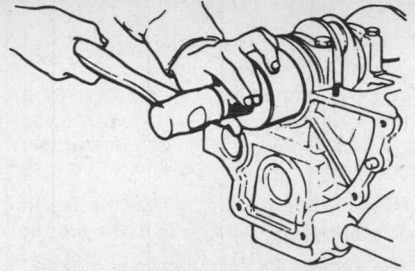

Installing the A–series rear oil seal using a drift; Z20, Z22, L24, L28, LD28 similar

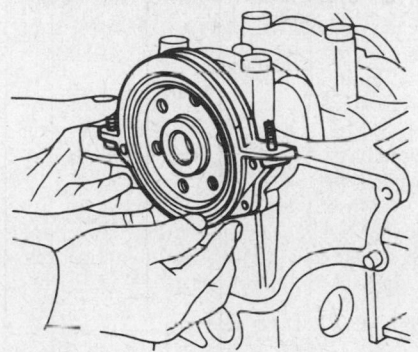

Installing the E–series rear oil seal retainer

9. Apply sealant to the rear main bearing cap side seals and install by driving the seals into place with a suitable drift.

10. Assemble the engine and install it in the vehicle in the reverse order of removal.

CA20E and CA18ET

1. Remove the transmission.

2. Remove the flywheel.

3. Remove the rear oil seal retainer.

4. Using a pair of pliers, remove the oil seal from the retainer.

5. Liberally apply clean engine oil to the new oil seal and carefully install it into the retainer.

6. Install the rear oil seal retainer into the engine, along with a new gasket. Torque the bolts to 2.9–4.3 ft. lbs. Install the flywheel and transmission in the reverse order of removal.

Oil Pump

REMOVAL & INSTALLATION

A14 and A15 Engines

1. Drain the engine oil.

2. Remove the front stabilizer bar if it is in the way of removing the oil pump.

3. Remove the splash shield.

4. Remove the oil pump body with the drive spindle assembly.

5. Install the A-series oil pump in the reverse order of removal.

6. Fill the pump housing with engine oil, then align the punch mark on the spindle with the hole in the oil pump.

7. With a new gasket placed over the drive spindle, install the oil pump and drive

spindle assembly so that the projection on the top of the drive spindle is located in the 11:25 o'clock position.

8. Install the distributor with the metal tip of the rotor pointing toward the No. 1 spark plug tower of the distributor cap.

9. Assemble the remaining components in the reverse order of removal.

E15 and E16 Engines

1. Loosen the alternator lower bolts.

2. Remove the alternator belt and adjusting bar bolt.

3. Move the alternator out of the way and support it safely.

4. Disconnect the oil pressure gauge harness.

5. Remove the pump assembly.

6. For installation, fill the pump with clean engine oil and rotate it several times.

7. Install the pump on the engine using a new gasket. Torque the pump mounting bolts to 7–9 ft. lbs.

CA20, CA20E and CA18ET Engines

1. Remove all accessary drive belts and the alternator.

2. Remove the timing (cam) belt covers and remove the timing belt.

3. On 1984 and later 200SX, unbolt the engine from its mounts and lift or jack the engine up from the unibody.

4. Remove the oil pan.

5. Remove the oil pump assembly along with the oil strainer.

6. If installing a new or rebuilt oil pump, first pack the pump full of petroleum jelly to prevent the pump from cavitating when the engine is started. Apply RTV sealer to the front oil seal end of the pan prior to installation. Install the pump in the reverse order of removal, torquing the mounting bolts to 9–12 ft. lbs.

1978–79 L20B, L24, and L28 Engines

These oil pumps are mounted at the bottom of the engine front cover.

1. Remove the distributor.

2. Drain the oil.

3. Remove the front stabilizer bar.

4. Remove the splash shield.

5. Unbolt and remove the oil pump.

6. Before replacing the pump, prime

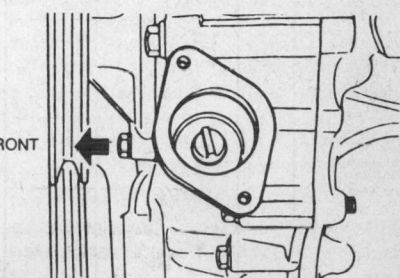

Position of the distributor drive spindle— L-series gas engines

the pump and position the No. 1 cylinder at top dead center. Install the oil pump with the spindle punch mark toward the front. The projection on top of the drive spindle must be in the 11:25 o'clock position, viewed from above. Torque the mounting bolts to 11–15 ft. lbs.

7. Install the distributor with the rotor pointing to the No. 1 spark plug lead in the cap.

8. Reverse the rest of the removal procedure.

1980 and Later L20B, L24, L28, Z20 and Z22 Engines

1. Drain the crankcase.
2. Turn the crankshaft so that the No. 1 piston is at TDC on its compression stroke.
3. Remove the distributor cap and mark the position of the distributor rotor in relation to the distributor base with a piece of chalk.

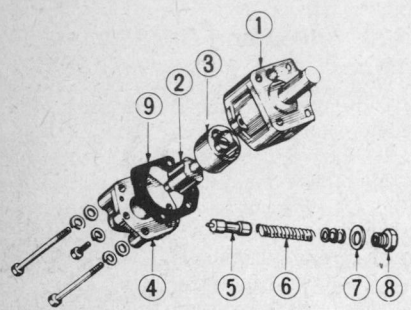

1. Pump body
2. Inner rotor and shaft
3. Outer rotor
4. Pump cover
5. Pressure regulator valve
6. Valve spring
7. Washer
8. Cap
9. Gasket

Oil pump—all inline overhead cam engines similar

4. Remove the front stabilizer bar (if so equipped).
5. Remove the splash shield.
6. Remove the oil pump body with the drive spindle assembly.
7. To install, fill the pump housing with engine oil, align the punch mark on the spindle with the hole in the oil pump. The No. 1 piston should be at (TDC) on its compression stroke.
8. With a new gasket placed over the drive spindle, install the oil pump and drive spindle assembly, making sure the tip of the drive spindle fits into the distributor shaft notch securely. The distributor rotor should be pointing to the match mark.

NOTE: Great care must be taken not to disturb the distributor rotor while installing the oil pump, or the ignition timing may be wrong.

9. Assemble the remaining components in the reverse order of removal.

CD 17 Diesel

1. Remove the valve timing belt.
2. Drain the oil and remove the oil pan.
3. The oil pump is bolted to the front of the engine block, at the front of the crankshaft. Loosen the mounting bolts and remove the oil pump assembly.

NOTE: Remove the crankshaft key to avoid damage to the oil seal on the pump.

4. Remove the oil pump rear cover and check gear clearances using a feeler gauge. Body-to-outer gear clearance should be 0.0043–0.0079 in.; inner gear-to-crescent clearance should be 0.0047–0.0091 in.; outer gear-to-crescent clearance should be 0.0083–0.0126 in.

5. Replace the oil seal in the pump by carefully prying it out. Coat the new seal liberally with clean engine oil before installation.

6. Installation is the reverse of removal. Apply sealer to the four corners of the oil pan and use a new oil pump gasket. Torque the oil pump bolts to 9–12 ft. lbs.

VG30E and VG30ET

1. Drain the oil from the oil pan.
2. Remove the oil pan. (See the Oil Pan removal and installation procedure earlier in this section.)
3. Remove the oil pump retaining bolts and remove the oil pump.

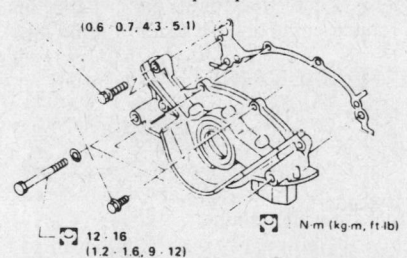

(0.6 0.7, 4.3 · 5.1)

12 · 16
(1.2 · 1.6, 9 · 12)

N·m (kg·m, ft·lb)

Oil pump installation—V6

4. Installation is the reverse of removal. Before installation apply engine oil to the inner and outer gear, use a new oil seal and gasket and make sure the o-ring is properly fitted.

ENGINE COOLING

Water Pump

REMOVAL & INSTALLATION

Except V6 and CD17

1. Drain the engine coolant.
2. Loosen the bolts retaining the fan shroud to the radiator and remove the shroud.
3. Loosen the belt, then remove the fan and pulley from the water pump hub.
4. Remove the bolts retaining the pump and remove the pump together with the gasket from the front cover.
5. Remove all traces of gasket material and install the pump in the reverse order. Use a new gasket and sealer. Tighten the bolts uniformly.

V6

1. Drain the coolant from the right side drain cocks on the cylinder block and radiator.
2. Remove the radiator shroud fan and pulleys.
3. Remove the power steering, compressor and alternator drive belts.
4. Disconnect the water pump hose.
5. Remove the upper and lower timing covers.

NOTE: Be careful not to get coolant on the timing belt.

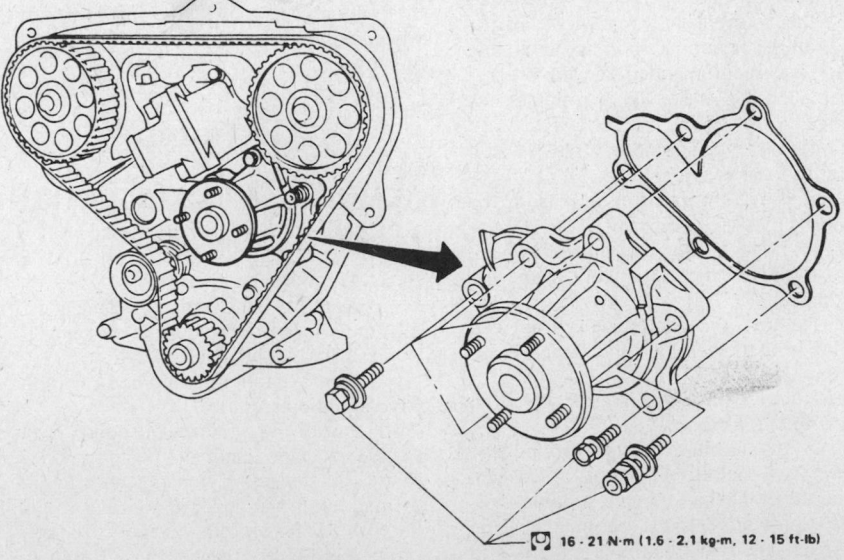

16 · 21 N·m (1.6 · 2.1 kg·m, 12 · 15 ft·lb)

Water pump installation—V6

6. Remove the water pump retaining bolts.

7. Installation is the reverse of removal. Torque the retaining bolts to 12–15 ft. lbs.

CD 17 Diesel

1. Disconnect the negative battery cable. Drain the cooling system.

2. Remove the alternator and A/C compressor drive belts, if equipped.

3. Remove the front crankshaft pulley after first setting the No. 1 cylinder at TDC on the compression stroke.

4. Remove the front engine covers.

5. Remove the timing belt.

6. Loosen the mounting bolts and remove the water pump.

7. Installation is the reverse of removal. Clean all gasket surfaces before reassembly.

NOTE: The water pump cannot be disassembled and must be replaced as a unit. Inspect the timing belt for wear or damage and replace if necessary.

Thermostat

REMOVAL & INSTALLATION

The engine thermostat is housed in the water outlet casting on the cylinder head.

1. Drain the coolant.

2. Remove the upper radiator hose and unbolt the water outlet elbow.

3. The thermostat may now be removed.

4. Reverse the removal procedure to replace the thermostat. When installing, be sure that the side with the spring faces into the engine. Use a new gasket. 1979 and

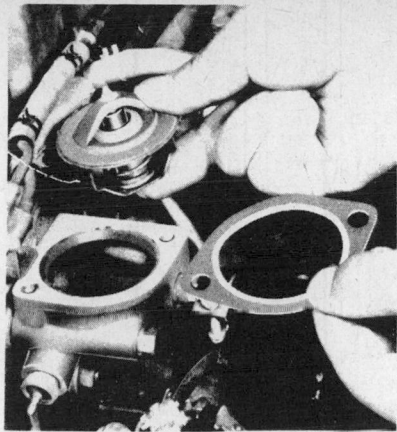

Correct thermostat installation

later models use a thermostat with an air bleed hole. The thermostat should be installed with the hole facing the left side of the engine. When replacing the thermostat, be sure the new one has a bleed hole.

Radiator

REMOVAL & INSTALLATION

To remove the radiator:

1. Drain the coolant.

2. Disconnect the upper hose, lower hose, and expansion tank hose.

3. Disconnect the automatic transmission oil cooler lines after draining the transmission. Cap the lines to exclude dirt.

4. If the fan has a shroud, unbolt the shroud and move it back, hanging it over the fan.

5. Remove the radiator mounting bolts and radiator.

6. Reverse the procedure to replace the radiator. Fill the automatic transmission to the proper level. Fill the cooling system.

EMISSION CONTROLS

Crankcase Ventilation System

The closed crankcase ventilation system is used to route the crankcase vapors to the intake manifold (carburetor equipped) or throttle chamber (fuel injected), to be mixed and burned with the air/fuel mixture.

An air intake hose is connected between the air cleaner assembly or the throttle chamber, and the valve cover. A return hose is connected between a steel net baffle on the side of the crankcase to the intake manifold or throttle chamber, with a metering positive crankcase ventilation (PCV) valve in the hose.

To test the system, allow the engine to idle. With the PCV valve removed from the hose, a hissing sound should be heard, and vacuum should be felt when you cover the engine side of the valve with your finger. The PCV valve should be replaced at regular intervals of 24,000 miles.

Air Injection Reactor System

In this system, an air injection pump, driven by the engine, compresses, distributes, and injects filtered air into the exhaust port of each cylinder. The air combines with unburned hydrocarbons and carbon monoxide to produce harmless compounds. The system includes an air cleaner, the belt driven air pump, a check valve, and an anti-backfire valve.

The air pump draws air through a hose connected to the carburetor air cleaner or to a separate air cleaner. The pump is a rotary vane unit with an integral pressure regulating value. The pump outlet pressure passes through a check valve which prevents exhaust gas from entering the pump in case of insufficient pump outlet pressure. An anti-backfire valve admits air from the air pump into the intake manifold on deceleration to prevent backfiring in the exhaust manifold.

A combined air control (C.A.C.) valve limits injection of secondary air and also controls its supply.

All engines with the air pump system have a series of minor alterations to accommodate the system. These are:

1. Special close-tolerance carburetor. Most engines require a slightly rich idle mixture adjustment.

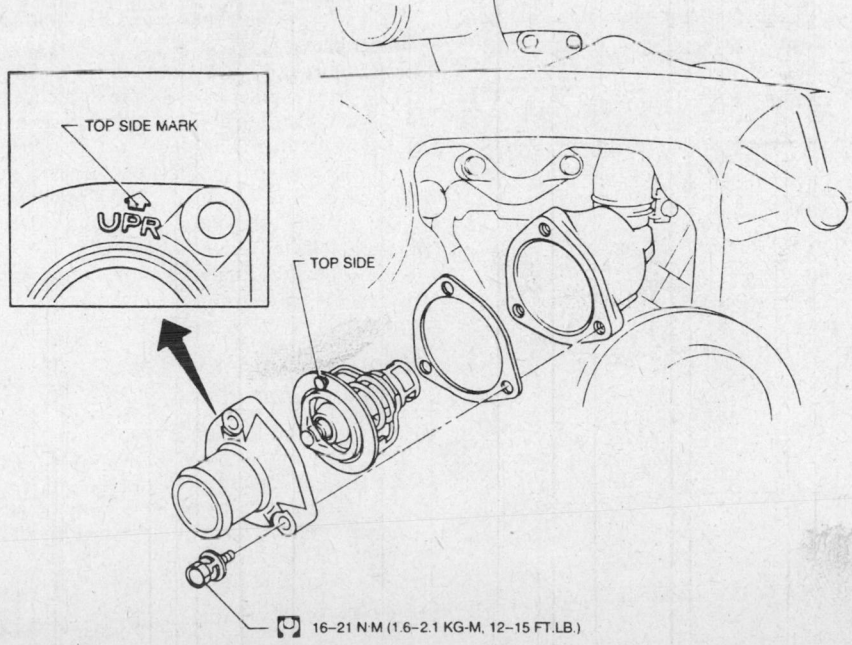

TOP SIDE MARK

UPR

TOP SIDE

16–21 N·M (1.6–2.1 KG-M, 12–15 FT.LB.)

V6 thermostat installation

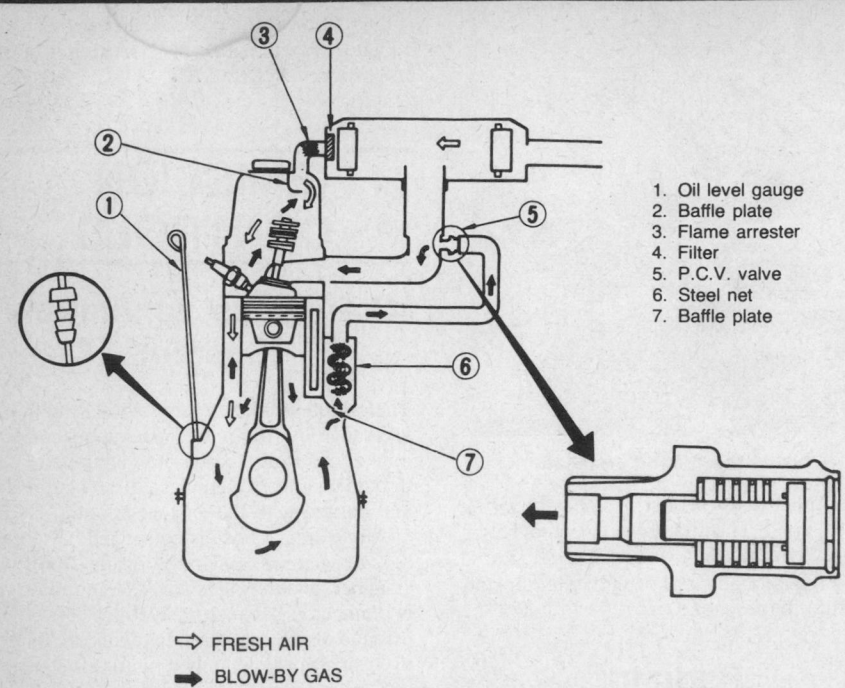

1. Oil level gauge
2. Baffle plate
3. Flame arrester
4. Filter
5. P.C.V. valve
6. Steel net
7. Baffle plate

⇨ FRESH AIR
➡ BLOW-BY GAS

PCV valve air flow

2. Distributor with special advance curve. Ignition timing is retarded about 10° at idle in most cases.

3. Cooling system changes such as larger fan, higher fan speed, and thermostatic fan clutch. This is required to offset the increase in temperature caused by retarded timing at idle.

4. Faster idle speed.

5. Heated air intake on some engines.

The only periodic maintenance required on the air pump system is replacement of the air filter element and adjustment of the drive belt.

AIR PUMP SYSTEM TESTS & REPAIRS

Air Pump Test, Removal and Installation

To test air pump output pressure:

1. The engine must be at normal operating temperature.

2. Stop the engine. Disconnect the air supply hose from the check valve at the exhaust manifold. Disconnect the vacuum hose from the air control valve (Calif. cars only).

3. Start the engine. Check the pump pressure output at 1,500 rpm. With an L24, or L28 engine, the pressure should be 0.063 in. (16 mm.) Hg or more. L20B, A14 and A15, Z20S, L20B engines should have at least 3.94 in. Hg pressure.

4. If air pressure is not as specified, disconnect the air hose at the anti-backfire valve. Plug the hose opening and repeat the pressure test.

5. At 1500 rpm, close the hole of the gauge with a finger. If leaking air is felt at the relief valve, replace the relief valve.

6. Replace the pump if it does not show proper pressure.

To remove and replace the air pump:

1. Disconnect the hoses from the pump.

2. Remove the bolt holding the pump to the belt adjustment arm or adjusting bracket.

3. Unbolt the pump from the mounting bracket. Remove the belt.

4. Remove the pump from the car.

5. Reverse the procedure to install, adjusting the belt to have about ½ in. play under thumb pressure at the longest span between pulleys.

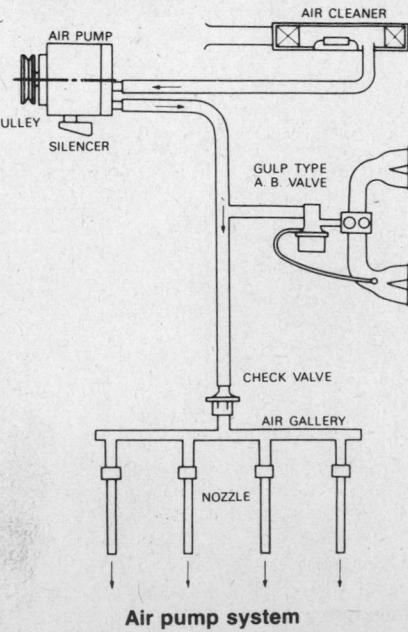

Air pump system

Check Valve Test, Removal and Installation

To test the check valve action:

1. The engine must be at normal operating temperature.

2. Stop the engine. Disconnect the air supply hose from the check valve at the exhaust manifold.

3. The valve plate inside the valve body should be lightly positioned against the valve seat away from the air distributor manifold.

4. Insert a small screwdriver into the valve and depress the valve plate. The plate should reset freely when released.

5. Start the engine. Increase the idle speed to 1500 rpm and check for exhaust leakage. Valve pulsation or vibration at idle is a normal condition.

To remove and replace the check valve:

1. Remove the check valve from the air gallery pipe, holding the air gallery flange with a wrench.

2. On reinstallation, the proper torque is 65–76 ft. lbs.

Air Control Valve Test, Removal and Installation

1. Warm engine to normal operating temperature.

2. Check all hoses for leaks.

3. Disconnect the outlet side hose of the valve and check for air flow. If no air is felt, replace the valve.

4. Disconnect the vacuum hose from the valve. If air flow from the air hose stops, the valve is working correctly, if air flow continues, replace the valve.

5. To replace valve, disconnect hoses and remove from bracket.

Emergency Air Relief Valve Test, Removal and Installation

1. Warm engine to normal operating temperature.

2. Check all vacuum hoses for leaks.

3. Run engine at 2000 rpm and check for air flow at outlet port of valve. If no air is felt, the valve is normal.

4. Disconnect the vacuum hose from the valve. Run engine at 2000 rpm and check for air at the outlet port of the valve. If air is felt, the valve is normal.

5. To remove valve, remove hoses and disconnect valve from mounts.

Anti-Backfire Valve Test, Removal and Installation

To test the anti-backfire valve:

1. The engine must be at normal operating temperature.

2. Disconnect the air hose from the air cleaner at the anti-backfire valve. Plug the hose.

3. Open and close the throttle rapidly. Air flow should be felt at the valve for 1-2 seconds on deceleration. If no air flow is felt or flow is felt continuously for more than 2 seconds, replace the valve.

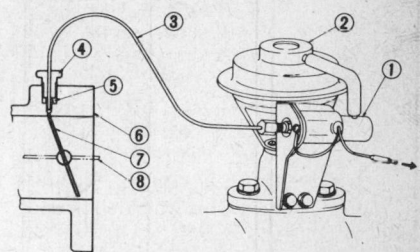
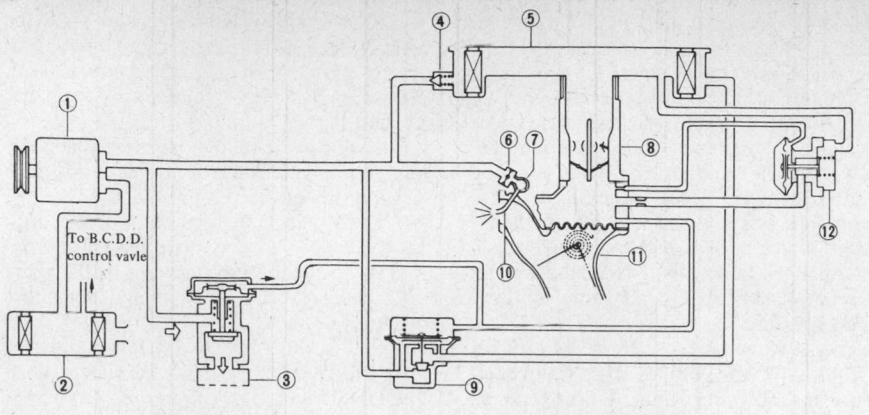

1. Air pump
2. Air pump air cleaner
3. Emergency air relief valve
4. Air relief valve
5. Air cleaner
6. Check valve
7. Air gallery pipe
8. Carburetor
9. Air control valve
10. Injection nozzle
11. Exhaust manifold
12. Anti-backfire valve

Air pump system schematic—typical

To remove the anti-backfire valve, simply disconnect the hoses.

Air Induction System

This system is used on Sentra, Pulsar, Stanza, 210, 310 and 810 models made in USA and Canada except California; 200SX and 510 in all of USA and 280ZX in USA except California.

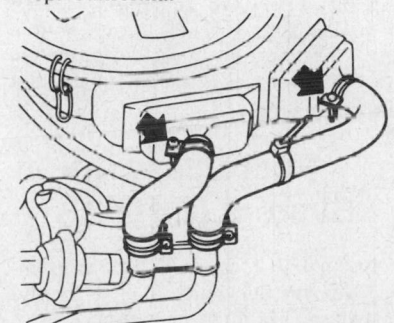

Typical Air Induction system connections

The system is designed to send fresh air into the exhaust manifold without the need of an air pump, utilizing a vacuum caused by exhaust pulsation in the exhaust manifold. The fresh air promotes burning of hot HC and CO gases which otherwise would escape the combustion process.

The only periodic maintenance required is the replacement of the air induction filter, installed at the dust side of the air cleaner at 24,000 mile or 30 month intervals.

Exhaust Gas Recirculation System (EGR)

Oxides of nitrogen (NO_x) are formed in the engine under conditions of high temperature and high pressure. Elimination of one of these two conditions reduces the formation of NO_x. Exhaust gas recirculation is used to reduce combustion temperatures in the engine.

1978 280Z, 1979 and Later 280ZX

All 1978–79 models have EGR, and all 1980 and later models sold in Canada and for 49 State use in the U.S. have EGR; 1980 and later models sold in California do not have the system.

An EGR valve is mounted on the intake manifold. The exhaust gas is drawn from the exhaust manifold, through the EGR valve, and into the intake manifold. The EGR valve is closed when the engine is idling; exhaust gas recirculation would cause a rough idle. As the throttle is opened, vacuum is applied to the EGR valve vacuum diaphragm. When the vacuum reaches about 2 inches of mercury (in. Hg) the diaphragm

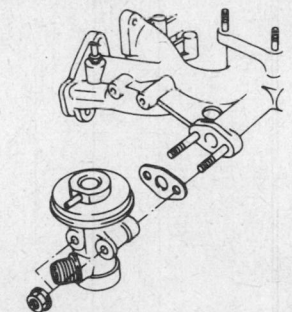

E–series EGR location on side of intake manifold

moves against spring pressure and is fully open at 8 in. Hg of vacuum. As the diaphragm moves up, it pulls the EGR valve pintle from its seat, allowing exhaust gas to be pulled into the intake manifold by intake vacuum. The valve closes at full throttle, when EGR is not needed, as a means of improving fuel economy.

On 1978 and later models, a thermal vacuum valve (TVV) controls the application of vacuum to the EGR valve. When the engine coolant reaches a predetermined temperature, the TVV opens and allows vacuum to be routed to the EGR valve. Below the predetermined temperature, the TVV closes and blocks vacuum to the EGR valve.

1. Solenoid valve
2. EGR valve
3. EGR vacuum tube
4. Attaching nut
5. Sealing nut
6. Rear carburetor
7. Throttle valve
8. Throttle valve fully open

L24 EGR system

All 1978 models, all 1979 U.S. models, and all 1980 and later 49 State U.S. models have a back pressure transducer (BPT) valve installed between the EGR valve and the thermal vacuum valve. The BPT valve has a diaphragm raised or lowered by exhaust back pressure. The diaphragm opens or closes an air bleed, which is connected into the EGR vacuum line. High pressure results in higher levels of EGR, because the BPT diaphragm is raised, closing off the air bleed, which allows more vacuum to reach and open the EGR valve. Thus, the amount of recirculated exhaust gas varies with exhaust pressure.

1978 models sold in California, 1979 models with a catalytic converter, and 1980 and later 49 State models have a vacuum delay valve (VDV) installed in the line between the thermal vacuum valve and the EGR valve. The valve delays rapid drops in vacuum in the EGR signal line, thus effecting a longer EGR time.

INSPECTION

1. Remove the EGR valve. Apply enough vacuum to the EGR valve vacuum connection to raise the diaphragm and open the valve. Pinch off the vacuum connection. The valve should remain open for at least thirty seconds. If not, the diaphragm is leaking and the valve must be replaced.

2. Check the valve for damage (warpage, cracks, etc.) and replace as necessary.

3. Clean the valve seat with a wire brush and compressed air.

4. Install the EGR valve on the engine. Start the engine and allow it to idle. With the engine idling, reach up under the EGR valve and raise the diaphragm by pushing it upwards with your fingers. Wear a glove to protect your hand if the engine is hot. When the diaphragm is raised, the engine idle should become rough, indicating that

exhaust gases are recirculating. If the roughness does not occur, the EGR passages are blocked.

5. To check the operation of the thermal vacuum valve, drain the engine coolant and remove the valve. Connect two lengths of vacuum hose to the two TVV vacuum connections. Place the valve in a container of water together with a thermostat, with the vacuum hoses above the level of the water. Do not allow water to get into the valve. When the water temperature is below 177°F (47°C), the vacuum passage should be closed. You can check this by sucking on one of the vacuum hoses.

6. Heat the water. On 1978–80 models, the valve should open at about 122°F (50°C), and remain open until the water temperature reaches about 203°F (95°C). On 1978 and later models only, the valve should close again when water temperature reaches about 208°F (98°C). Replace the valve if it behaves otherwise.

7. To test the BPT valve installed on some models, disconnect the two vacuum hoses on the valve. Plug one of the ports. While applying pressure to the bottom of the valve, apply vacuum to the unplugged port and check for leakage. If any exists, replace the valve.

8. To check the delay valve installed on some 1977 and later models, remove the valve and blow into the side which connects to the EGR or BPT valve. Air should flow. When air is applied to the other side, air flow resistance should be greater. If not, replace the valve.

All Models Except 280Z and 280ZX

An EGR valve is mounted on the center of the intake manifold. The recycled exhaust gas is drawn into the bottom of the intake manifold riser portion through the exhaust manifold heat stove and EGR valve. A vacuum diaphragm is connected to a timed signal port at the carburetor flange.

As the throttle valve is opened, vacuum is applied to the EGR valve vacuum diaphragm. When the vacuum reaches about 2 in. Hg, the diaphragm moves against spring pressure and is in a fully up position at 8 in. Hg of vacuum. As the diaphragm moves up, it opens the exhaust gas metering valve which allows exhaust gas to be pulled into the engine intake manifold. The system does not operate when the engine is idling because the exhaust gas recirculation would cause a rough idle.

A thermal vacuum valve inserted in the engine thermostat housing controls the application of the vacuum to the EGR valve. When the engine coolant reaches a predetermined temperature, the thermal vacuum valve opens and allows vacuum to be routed to the EGR valve. Below the predetermined temperature, the thermal vacuum valve closes and blocks vacuum to the EGR valve.

All 1978–79 models and the 1980 and later 210, 510 (Canadian), 200SX (Cana-

dian), 310 and 810 have a BPT valve installed between the EGR valve and the thermal vacuum valve. The BPT valve has a diaphragm which is raised or lowered by exhaust back pressure. The diaphragm opens or closes an air bleed, which is connected into the EGR vacuum line. High pressure results in higher levels of EGR, because the diaphragm is raised, closing off the air bleed, which allows more vacuum to reach and open the EGR valve. Thus, the amount of recirculated exhaust gas varies with exhaust pressure.

The 1980 and later 510 (USA), 200SX (USA), 310 (California), 210 (California) and non-California Senta, Pulsar, and all Stanza models use a VVT valve (venturi vacuum transducer valve) instead of the BPT valve. The VVT valve monitors exhaust pressure and carburetor vacuum in order to activate the diaphragm which controls the throttle vacuum applied to the EGR control valve. This system expands the operating range of the EGR unit, as well as increasing the EGR flow rate as compared to the BPT unit.

Many models are equipped with an EGR warning system which signals via a light in the dashboard that the EGR system may need service. The EGR warning light should come on every time the starter is engaged as a test to make sure the bulb is not blown. The system uses a counter which works in conjunction with the odometer, and lights the warning signal after the vehicle has traveled a pre-determined number of miles.

To reset the counter, which is mounted in the engine compartment, remove the grommet installed in the side of the counter and insert the tip of a small screwdriver into the hole. Press down on the knob inside the hole. Reinstall the grommet.

TEST

1. Remove the EGR valve and apply enough vacuum to the diaphragm to open the valve.

2. The valve should remain open for over 30 seconds after the vacuum is removed.

3. Check the valve for damage, such as warpage, cracks, and excessive wear around the valve and seat.

4. Clean the seat with a brush and compressed air and remove any deposits from around the valve and port (seat).

5. To check the operation of the thermal vacuum valve, remove the valve from the engine and apply vacuum to the ports of the valve. The valve should not allow vacuum to pass.

6. Place the valve in a container of water with a thermometer and heat the water. When the temperature of the water reaches 134°–145°F, remove the valve and apply vacuum to the ports; the valve should allow vacuum to pass through it.

7. To test the BPT valve installed on 1978 and later models, disconnect the two vacuum hoses from the valve. Plug one of the ports. While applying pressure to the bottom of the valve, apply vacuum to the unplugged port and check for leakage. If any exists, replace the valve.

8. To test the check valve installed in some 1978 and later models, remove the valve and blow into the side which connects to the EGR valve. Air should flow. When air is applied to the other side, air flow resistance should be greater. If not, replace the valve.

9. To check the VVT valve which replaces the BTP valve on some 1980 and later models, disconnect the top and bottom center hoses and apply a vacuum to the top hose. Check for leaks. If a leak is present, replace the valve.

Early Fuel Evaporation System (E.F.E.)

The 1978–79 A-series and all L-series engines use a system much akin to the old style exhaust manifold heat riser. In this

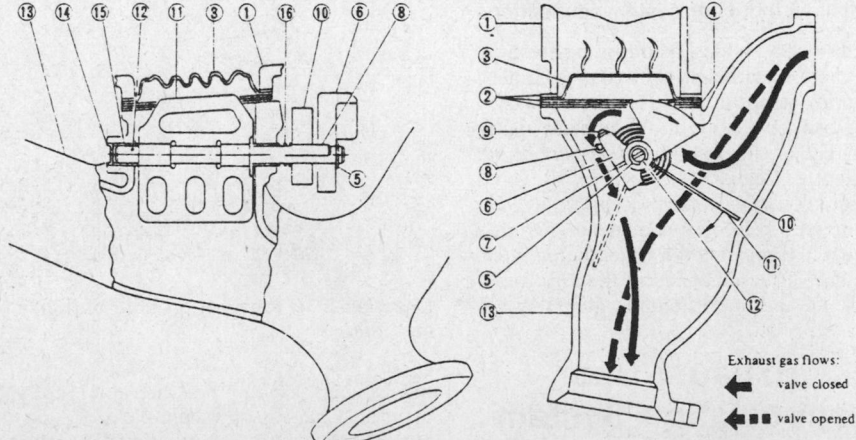

Exhaust gas flows:
→ valve closed
⇢ valve opened

1. Intake manifold	5. Snap ring	9. Screw	13. Exhaust manifold
2. Stove gasket	6. Counterweight	10. Thermostat spring	14. Cap
3. Manifold stove	7. Key	11. Heat control valve	15. Bushing
4. Heat shield plate	8. Stopper pin	12. Control valve shaft	16. Coil spring

Early Fuel Evaporation (EFE) system

system, a control valve is welded to the valve shaft and installed on the exhaust manifold thru–bushing. This heat control valve is actuated by a coil spring, thermostatic spring and counterweight which are assembled on the valve shaft projecting at the rear outside of the manifold. The counterweight is secured to the shaft with a key, bolt and snap-ring. A chamber between the intake and exhaust manifolds above the manifold stove heats the air-fuel mixture by means of exhaust gases. This results in better atomization and lower HC content.

The 1980 and later carbureted engines use coolant water heat instead of exhaust gas heat to pre-warm the fuel mixture. This system should be maintenance-free.

TESTING

1. Run engine and visually check for movement.

2. In cold weather, the counterweight will move counterclockwise until it reaches the stop pin. As the engine warms up the counterweight gradually moves down.

3. As engine speed increases, the flow of exhaust gases causes the counterweight to move clockwise. When the heat control valve is full open the counterweight should again be in contact with the stop pin.

Check for bent stop pin, broken heat valve key, axial clearance between heat control valve and manifold of 0.028–0.059 in., and cracks or flaking at the heat control valve weld.

Boost Control Deceleration Device (BCDD)/Throttle Opener Control System (TOCS)

The Boost Control Deceleration Device (BCDD) used on the L-series engines, and the Throttle Opener Control System (TOCS) used on A-series engines (except 1980 and later California) both accomplish the same purpose: to reduce hydrocarbon emissions during coasting conditions.

High manifold vacuum during coasting prevents the complete combustion of the air/fuel mixture because of the reduced amount of air. This condition will result in a large amount of HC emission. Enriching the air/fuel mixture for a short time (during the high vacuum condition) will reduce the emission of the HC.

However, enriching the air/fuel mixture with only the mixture adjusting screw will cause poor engine idle or invite an increase in the carbon monoxide (CO) content of the exhaust gases. The BCDD consists of an independent system that when the engine is coasting and enriches the air/fuel mixture, which reduces the hydrocarbon con-

tent of the exhaust gases. This is accomplished without adversely affecting engine idle and the carbon monoxide content of the exhaust gases.

The TOCS system used on 1980 A-series non-California models achieves the same end as the BCDD system but uses a slightly different method. The system consists of a servo diaphragm, vacuum control valve, throttle opener solenoid valve, speed detecting switch and amplifier on manual transmission models. Automatic transmission models use an inhibitor and inhibitor relay in the place of the speed detecting switch and amplifier. At the moment when the manifold vacuum increases, as during deceleration, the vacuum control valve opens to transfer the manifold vacuum to the servo diaphragm chamber, and the carburetor throttle valve opens slightly. Under this condition, the proper amount of fresh air is sucked into the combustion chamber. As a result, a more thorough ignition takes place, burning much of the HC in the exhaust gases.

1980 and Later Z20E and Z22E Engine (200SX)

This engine uses a simplified version of the boost control system. In place of the BCDD (see above) is a vacuum control valve which works on manifold vacuum. Service is restricted to replacing the valve.

ADJUSTMENT

Normally, the BCDD never needs adjustment. However, if the need should arise because of suspected malfunction of the system, proceed as follows:

1. Connect a tachometer to the engine.

2. Connect a quick-response vacuum gauge to the intake manifold.

3. Disconnect the solenoid valve electrical leads.

4. Start and warm up the engine until it reaches normal operating temperature.

5. Adjust the idle speed to the proper specification.

6. Raise the engine speed to 3000–3500 rpm under no-load (transmission in Neutral or Park), then allow the throttle to close quickly. Take notice as to whether or not the engine rpm returns to idle speed and if it does, how long the fall in rpm is interrupted before it reaches idle speed.

At the moment the throttle is snapped closed at high engine rpm the vacuum in the intake manifold reaches between −23 to −27.7 in. Hg and then gradually falls to about −16.5 in. Hg at idle speed. The process of the fall of the intake manifold vacuum and the engine rpm will take one of the following three forms:

a. When the operating pressure of the BCDD is too high, the system remains inoperative and the vacuum in the intake manifold decreases without interruption just like that of an engine without a BCDD.

b. When the operating pressure is lower than that of the case given above, but still higher than the proper set pressure, the fall of vacuum in the intake manifold is interrupted and kept constant at a certain level (operating pressure) for about one second and then gradually falls down to the normal vacuum at idle speed.

c. When the set of operating pressure of the BCDD is lower than the intake manifold vacuum when the throttle is suddenly released, the engine speed will not lower to idle speed.

To adjust the set operating pressure of the BCDD, remove the adjusting screw cover from the BCDD mechanism mounted on the side of the carburetor. On 810 models,

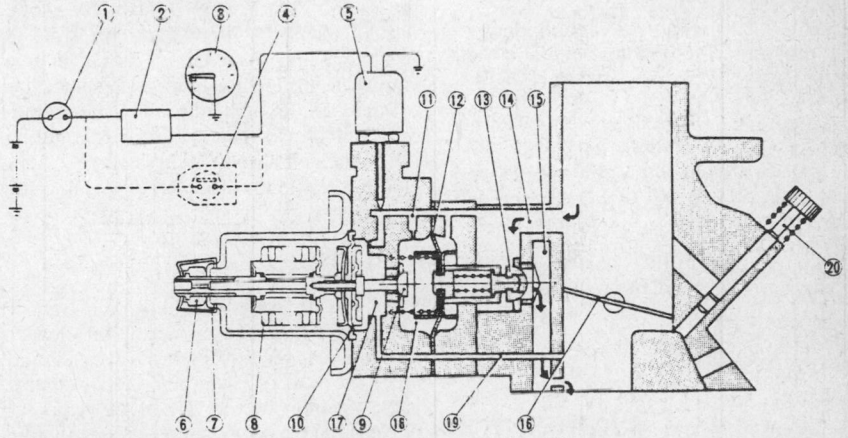

1. Ignition switch	5. Vacuum control solenoid valve
2. Amplifier	
3. Speed detecting switch Blow 10 M.P.H.: ON (For M/T)	6. Adjusting nut
	7. Lock spling
	8. Altitude corrector
4. Inhibitor switch "N" or "P" position: ON (For A/T)	9. Vacuum control valve
	10. Diaphragm I
	11. Air passage
	12. Diaphragm II

13. Air control valve	
14. Air passage	
15. Air passage	
16. Throttle valve	
17. Vacuum chamber I	
18. Vacuum chamber II	
19. Vacuum passage	
20. Idle speed adjusting screw	

BCDD sectional view

the BCDD system is installed under the throttle chamber.

The adjusting screw is a left-hand threaded screw. Late models may have an adjusting nut instead of a screw. Turning the screw 1/8 of a turn in either direction will change the operation pressure about 0.79 in. Hg. Turning the screw counterclockwise will increase the amount of vacuum needed to operate the mechanism. Turning the screw clockwise will decrease the amount of vacuum needed to operate the mechanism.

The operating pressure for the BCDD on most models should be between −19.9 to −22.05 in Hg. The decrease intake manifold vacuum should be interrupted at these levels for about one second when the BCDD is operating correctly.

Don't forget to install the adjusting screw cover after the system is adjusted.

ADJUSTMENT—TOCS

Adjustment procedures for TOCS are the same as those for BCDD. Observe the following pressures.

When snapping the throttle closed as described in Step 6 for BCDD, the vacuum in the intake manifold should reach −23.6 in. Hg or above and then gradually decreases to idle lever.

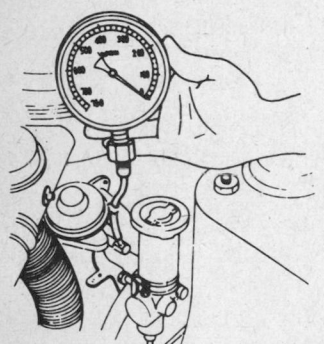

Connect a quick–response vacuum gauge to the intake manifold when checking the Throttle Opener Control System (TOCS)

The operating pressure of the TOCS should be −22.05 ± 0.79 in. Hg.

Turning the adjusting screw clockwise raises the vacuum level. Turning the screw counterclockwise lowers the vacuum level.

NOTE: When adjusting the TOCS, turn the adjusting nut in or out with the lock spring in place. Always set the lock spring properly to prevent changes in the set pressure.

Evaporative Emission Control System

These systems include the positive-seal fuel tank cap and vapor vent line of the earlier system. Additionally, a carbon canister, vacuum signal line, and canister purge line are used. The canister stores fuel vapors until vacuum pressure in the vacuum signal line forces a purge control valve to open. This admits fuel vapor from the canister into the intake manifold to be burnt with the incoming charge. The only maintenance required with this system is to change the carbon canister filter, located in the bottom of the canister, once every two years, and to periodically check the lines for leaks or obstructions.

Automatic Temperature Controlled Air Cleaner

This system is used on all Datsun models, except the 810, Maxima, 280Z, 280ZX, 200SX and 300ZX.

The rate of fuel atomization varies with the temperature of the air that the fuel is being mixed with. The air/fuel ratio cannot be held constant for efficient fuel combustion with a wide range of air temperatures. Cold air being drawn into the engine causes a denser and richer air/fuel mixture, inefficient fuel atomization, and thus, more hydrocarbons in the exhaust gas. Hot air being drawn into the engine causes a leaner air/fuel mixture and more efficient atomization and combustion for less hydrocarbons in the exhaust gases.

The automatic temperature controlled air cleaner is designed so that the temperature of the ambient air being drawn into the engine is automatically controlled, to hold the temperature of the air and, consequently, the fuel/air ratio at a constant rate for efficient fuel combustion.

A temperature sensing vacuum switch controls vacuum applied to a vacuum motor operating a valve in the intake snorkle of the air cleaner. When the engine is cold or the air being drawn into the engine is cold, the vacuum motor opens the valve, allowing air heated by the exhaust manifold to be drawn into the engine. As the engine warms up, the temperature sensing unit shuts off the vacuum applied to the vacuum motor which allows the valve to close, shutting off the heated air and allowing cooler, outside (under hood) air to be drawn into the engine.

TESTING

When the air around the temperature sensor of the unit mounted inside the air cleaner housing reaches 100°F, the sensor should block the flow of vacuum to the air control valve vacuum motor. When the temperature around the temperature sensor is below 100°F, the sensor should allow vacuum to pass onto the air valve vacuum motor thus blocking off the air cleaner snorkle to under hood (unheated) air.

When the temperature around the sensor is above 118°F, the air control valve should be completely open to under hood air.

If the air cleaner fails to operate correctly, check for loose or broken vacuum hoses. If the hoses are not the cause, replace the vacuum motor in the air cleaner.

Dual Spark Plug Ignition System

Some 1980 California and all 1981–85 510, 200 SX (Z20, Z22E and CA20E/CA18ET engines) and Nissan Stanza (CA20) have two spark plugs per cylinder. This arrangement allows the engine to burn large amounts of recirculated exhaust gases without effecting performance. In fact, the system works so well it improves gas mileage under most circumstances.

Both spark plugs fire simultaneously, which substantially shortens the time required to burn the air/fuel mixture when exhaust gases (EGR) are not being recirculated. When gases are being recirculated, the dual spark plug system brings the ignition level up to that of a single plug system which is not recirculating exhaust gases.

ADJUSTMENT

The only adjustments necessary are the regular tune-up and maintenance procedures outlined in the tune-up section.

Spark Timing Control System

There are two types of spark timing control. The first system, Transmission Controlled Spark System (TCS) was used on most Datsuns through 1979. This system consists of a thermal vacuum valve, a vacuum switching valve, a high gear detecting switch, and a number of vacuum hoses. Basically, the system is designed to retard full spark advance except when the car is in high gear and the engine is at normal operating temperature. At all times, the spark advance is retarded to one degree or another.

The 1980 and later Spark Timing Control System replaces the TCS system. The major difference is that it works solely from engine water temperature changes rather than a transmission-mounted switch. The system includes a thermal vacuum valve, a vacuum delay valve, and attendant hoses. It performs the same function as the earlier TCS system; to retard full spark advance at times when high levels of pollutants would otherwise be given off.

INSPECTION & ADJUSTMENTS

Normally the TCS and Spark Timing Control systems should be trouble-free. However, if you suspect a problem in the system, first check to make sure all wiring (if so equipped) and hoses are connected and free from dirt. Also check to make sure the distributor vacuum advance is working properly. If everything appears all right, connect a timing light to the engine and make sure the initial timing is correct. On vehicles with the TCS system, run the engine until it reaches normal operating temperature, and then have an assistant sit in the car and shift the transmission through all the gears slowly. If the system is functioning properly, the timing will be 10 to 15 degrees advanced in high gear (compared to the other gear positions). If the system is still not operating correctly, you will have to check for continuity at all the connections with a test light.

To test the Spark Timing Control System, connect a timing light and check the ignition timing while the temperature gauge is in the "cold" position. Write down the reading. Allow the engine to run with the timing light attached until the temperature needle reaches the center of the gauge. As the engine is warming up, check with the timing light to make sure the ignition timing retards. When the temperature needle is in the middle of the gauge, the ignition timing should advance from its previous position. If the ignition timing does not change, replace the thermal vacuum valve.

Maximum Ratio Rich-Lean and EGR Large-Small Exchange System

This system controls the air-fuel mixture ratio and the amount of recirculated exhaust gas on 1980 California A series engines (manual transmission models only) in accordance with the engine coolant temperature and car speed. The system consists of a vacuum switching valve, a power valve, a speed detecting switch located in the speedometer, a speed detecting switch amplifier and a water temperature switch.

When the coolant temperature is above 122°F and the car is traveling at least 40 miles per hour, the vacuum switching valve is on and acts to lean down the fuel mixture. It also allows a small amount of EGR to be burned on manual transmission cars. When the coolant temperature is above 122°F but the vehicle is traveling less than 40 miles per hour, the vacuum switching valve is off and allows the mixture to richen. It also allows a large amount of EGR to be burned in manual transmission models. When coolant temperature is below 122°F the vacuum switching valve is always on and acts to lean down the fuel mixture.

TESTING

Warm up the engine and jack up the drive wheels of the vehicle. Support the raised end of the car on jack stands and chock the wheels still on the ground. Start the engine and shift the transmission into TOP speed and maintain a speedometer speed higher

than 50 mph. Pinch the hose running from the vacuum switching valve to the air cleaner and see if the engine speed decreases and operates erratically. Shift the transmission into 3RD speed and run the car at a speed lower than 30 mph. Disconnect the vacuum hose running between the vacuum switching valve and the power valve, by detaching it at the power valve and blocking its open end with your finger. The engine should operate erratically. If the expected engine reaction in both of these tests does not happen, check all wiring connections and hoses for breaks and blockage.

Mixture Ratio Feedback System

The need for better fuel economy coupled to increasingly strict emission control regulations dictate a more exact control of the engine air/fuel mixture. Datsun has developed a Mixture Ratio Feedback System in response to these needs. The system is installed on all 1980 and later 280ZX and 810 models sold in California, all twin–plug 200SX models and all late–model 810 Maxima, 280ZX and 300ZX.

The principle of the system is to control the air/fuel mixture exactly, so that more complete combustion can occur in the engine, and more thorough oxidation and reduction of the exhaust gases can occur in the catalytic converter. The object is to maintain a stoichiometric air/fuel mixture, which is chemically correct for theoretically complete combustion. The stoichiometric ratio is 14.7:1 (air to fuel). At that point, the converter's efficiency is greatest in oxidizing the reducing HC, CO, and NOx into CO_2, H_2O, O_2, and N_2.

Components used in the system include an oxygen sensor, installed in the exhaust manifold upstream of the converter; a three-way oxidation-reduction catalytic converter; an electronic control unit, which is part of the electronic fuel injection control unit; and the fuel injection system itself.

The oxygen sensor reads the oxygen content of the exhaust gases. It generates an electrical signal which is sent to the control unit. The control unit then decides how to adjust the mixture to keep it at the correct air/fuel ratio. For example, if the mixture is too lean, the control unit increases the fuel metering to the injectors. The monitoring process is a continual one, so that fine mixture adjustments are going on at all times.

The system has two modes of operation: open loop and closed loop. Open loop operation takes place when the engine is still cold. In this mode, the control unit ignores signals from the oxygen sensor and provides a fixed signal to the fuel injection unit. Closed loop operation takes place when the engine and catalytic converter have warmed to normal operating temperature. In closed loop operation, the control unit uses the oxygen sensor signals to adjust the

mixture; the burned mixture's oxygen content is read by the oxygen sensor, which continues to signal the control unit, and so on. Thus, the closed loop mode is an interdependent system of information feedback.

Mixture is, of course, not readily adjustable in this system. All system adjustments require the use of a CO meter; thus, they should be entrusted to a qualified dealer with access to the equipment and special training in the system's repair. The only regularly scheduled maintenance is replacement of the oxygen sensor at 30,000 mile intervals. This procedure is covered in the following section.

It should be noted that proper operation of the system is entirely dependent on the oxygen sensor. Thus, if the sensor is not replaced at the correct interval, or if the sensor fails during normal operation, the engine fuel mixture will be incorrect, resulting in poor fuel economy, starting problems, or stumbling and stalling of the engine when warm.

OXYGEN SENSOR INSPECTION & REPLACEMENT

An exhaust gas sensor warning light will illuminate on the instrument panel when the car has reached 30,000 miles. This is a signal that the oxygen sensor must be replaced.

Note that the warning light is not part of a repeating system; that is, after the first 30,000 mile service, the warning light will not illuminate again. However, it is important to replace the oxygen sensor every 30,000 miles, to ensure proper monitoring and control of the engine air/fuel mixture.

The oxygen sensor can be inspected using the following procedure:

1. Start the engine and allow it to reach normal operating temperature.

2. Run the engine at approximately 2,000 rpm under no load. Block the front wheels and set the parking brake.

3. An inspection lamp has been provided on the bottom of the control unit, which is located in the passenger compartment on the driver's side kick panel, next to the clutch or brake pedal. If the oxygen sensor is operating correctly, the inspection lamp will go on and off more than 5 times in 10 seconds. The inspection lamp can be more easily seen with the aid of a mirror.

4. If the lamp does not go on and off as specified, the system is not operating correctly. Check the battery, ignition system, engine oil and coolant levels, all fuses, the fuel injection wiring harness connectors, all vacuum hoses, the oil filler cap and dipstick for proper seating, and the valve clearance and engine compression. If all of these parts are in good order, and the inspection lamp still does not go on and off at least 5 times in 10 seconds, the oxygen sensor is probably faulty. However, the

possibility exists that the malfunction could be in the fuel injection control unit. The system should be tested by a qualified dealer with specific training in the Mixture Ratio Feedback System.

To replace the oxygen sensor:

1. Disconnect the negative cable from the battery.

2. Disconnect the sensor electrical lead. Unscrew the sensor from the exhaust manifold.

3. Coat the threads of the replacement sensor with a nickel base anti-seize compound. Do not use other types of compounds, since they may electrically insulate the sensor. Install the sensor into the manifold. Installation torque for the sensor is 29–36 ft. lbs. (4.0–5.0 kg-m). Connect the electrical lead. Be careful handling the electrical lead; it is easily damaged.

4. Connect the negative battery cable.

After the first 30,000 mile replacement, the warning lamp harness connector should be unplugged to extinguish the lamp. The connector is located under the right side of the instrument panel; the harness wire color is green with a yellow stripe.

Catalytic Converter

All 1978 and later models sold in California, some 1979 models sold in the other 49 States of the U.S., and all 1980 and later models sold in the U.S. and Canada have a catalytic converter, which is a muffler-shaped device installed into the exhaust system. The converter is filled with a monolithic substrate coated with small amounts of platinum and palladium. Through catalytic action, a chemical change converts carbon monoxide and hydrocarbons into carbon dioxide and water. All 1980 and later 280ZX and 810 Maxima models sold in California have a three-way catalytic converter. Platinum, palladium, and rhodium are used in an oxidation-reduction process which acts on all three major constituents of exhaust pollution; HC and CO and oxidized in the usual manner into H_2O and CO_2, and oxides of nitrogen are reduced to free hydrogen and nitrogen (H_2 and N_2 respectively).

1978 models (all California models) have a floor temperature warning system, consisting of a temperature sensor installed onto the floor of the car above the converter; a relay, located under the passenger seat; and a light, installed on the instrument panel. The lamp illuminates when floor temperatures become abnormally high, due to converter or engine malfunction. The light also comes on when the ignition switch is turned to Start, to check its operation. 1979 and later models do not have the warning system.

1980 and later 280ZX, 300ZX, 810 California and late–model 200SX and 810 Maxima models have an oxygen sensor warning light on the dashboard, which illuminates at the first 30,000 mile interval, signaling the need for oxygen sensor re-

placement. The oxygen sensor is part of the Mixture Ratio Feedback System. The Feedback System uses the three-way converter as one of its major components.

No regular maintenance is required for the catalytic converter system, except for periodic replacement of the Air Induction System filter on some 1980 and later models. The Air Induction System is described earlier in this section. The Air Induction System is used to supply the catalytic converter with fresh air; oxygen present in the air is used in the oxidation process.

REMOVAL & INSTALLATION

1. Apply the parking brake.

2. Disconnect the temperature sensor connectors (1978 Calif.) and pull the connectors outside of the floor.

3. Block the wheels.

4. Jack and support the car.

5. Remove the temperature sensor protector (1978 Calif.)

6. Remove the catalytic converter shield.

7. Unbolt and remove the catalytic converter. Handle the converter gently; it is very delicate.

8. Installation is the reverse of removal.

FLOOR TEMPERATURE WARNING SYSTEM

1978 California Models

This system employs temperature sensors to warn of impending catalytic converter overheating. The system consists of a floor sensor located in the luggage compartment, a floor sensor relay located under the front passenger seat and a warning lamp located on the left side of the instrument panel.

TESTING

Lamp should light when ignition is turned to ON.

To test sensor, wait until floor temperature is below 80°F. Then heat floor area around sensor to 239°F. Light should come on.

FUEL SYSTEM— GASOLINE ENGINES

Mechanical Fuel Pump

The mechanical fuel pump is driven from the camshaft on all engines. It is mounted on the side of the engine on OHV engines and on the side of the cylinder head on OHC engines. The pump is on the right side of all engines.

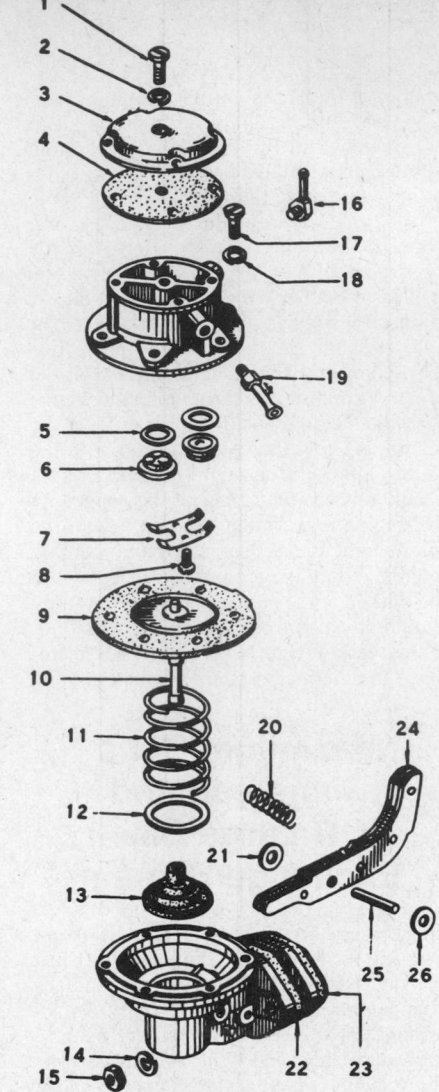

1. Screw
2. Lockwasher
3. Cover
4. Cover gasket
5. Packing
6. Valve
7. Valve retainer
8. Valve retainer screw
9. Diaphragm
10. Pull rod
11. Spring
12. Seal washer
13. Seal
14. Lockwasher
15. Nut
16. Elbow
17. Screw
18. Lockwasher
19. Connector
20. Spring
21. Rocker arm slide spacer
22. Spacer
23. Gasket
24. Rocker arm
25. Pin
26. Rocker arm slide spacer

Typical mechanical fuel pump

REMOVAL & INSTALLATION

1. Disconnect the inlet and outlet lines from the pump.
2. Remove the mounting bolts.
3. Remove the pump and discard the gasket.
4. Lubricate the pump rocker arm, rocker arm pin, and lever pin before reinstallation.
5. Bolt the pump into position, using a new gasket.
6. Connect the fuel lines.

FUEL PUMP TESTS

Static Pressure Test

1. Disconnect the fuel line at the carburetor.
2. Attach an adapter and tee to the fuel line and connect a pressure gauge.
3. Run the engine at varying speeds. Pressure should remain constant, 3–4 psi.

Electric Fuel Pump

DESCRIPTION AND LOCATION

280Z and 280ZX

All 280Z and ZX models are equipped with one electric fuel pump mounted near the fuel tank and the right rear wheel.

810 Maxima and 200SX

The fuel injected 810 and 200SX use an electric fuel pump mounted near the fuel tank on the 810 and near the center of the car on the 200SX. The pump is of wet type construction. A vane pump and roller are directly coupled to a motor filled with fuel. A relief valve in the pump is designed to open when the pressure in the fuel line rises over 64 psi. Normal operating pressure is 36–43 psi. The pump is automatically activated when the ignition switch is turned to the "start" position. If the engine stalls for some reason, the fuel pump is cut off even though the ignition switch remains in the "on" position.

300ZX

The electric fuel pump on the 300ZX is mounted on the fuel tank on the top left side.

PRESSURE TEST

1978 280Z

1. Reduce the fuel line pressure to zero, following Steps 1–3 of the pump removal and installation procedure.
2. Connect a pressure gauge into the fuel line in the engine compartment between the fuel tube and the fuel filter outlet hose.

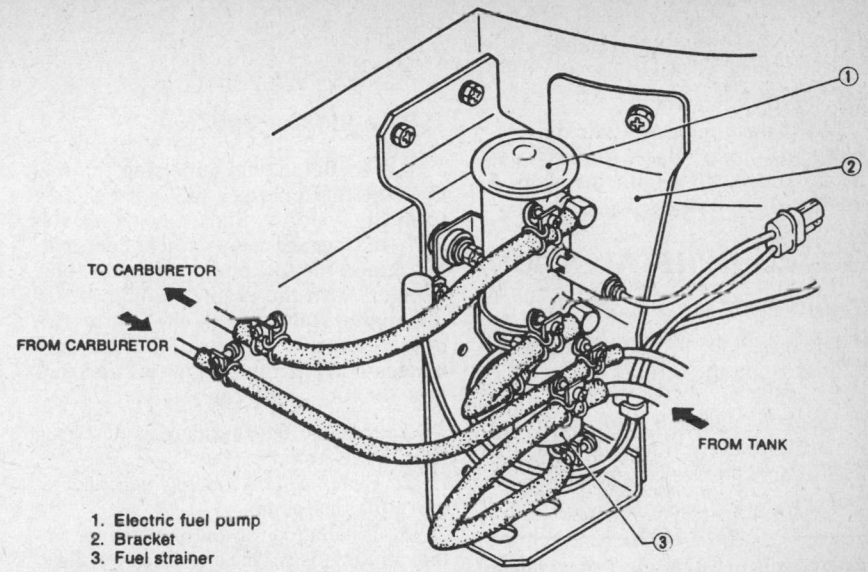

TO CARBURETOR

FROM CARBURETOR

FROM TANK

1. Electric fuel pump
2. Bracket
3. Fuel strainer

280Z electric fuel pump and strainer—typical through 1983

3. Disconnect the wire from the "S" terminal of the starter motor solenoid.
4. Connect the negative battery cable.
5. Turn the ignition key to Start.
6. Pressure should be approximately 36.3 psi (2.55 kg/cm²).
7. If not, replace the pressure regulator (see the replacement procedure following) and repeat the tests. If the pressure is still not correct, check all fuel lines for kinks or blockage, and replace the pump as necessary.

1979 and later 280ZX and 300ZX

1. Reduce the fuel pressure to zero. For 1979 models, follow Steps 1–3 of the 1978 fuel pump replacement procedure. For 1980 and later models, follow Step 1 of the 1980 fuel pump replacement procedure.
2. On 1979 models, connect the negative battery cable.
3. Connect a fuel pressure gauge into the fuel line in the engine compartment between the fuel pipe and the fuel filter outlet hose.
4. Start the engine and read the fuel pressure. It should be approximately 30 psi (2.1 kg/cm²) at idle, and approximately 37 psi (2.6 kg/cm²) at any speed above idle.
5. If the pressure is incorrect, replace the pressure regulator, following the replacement procedure given later in this chapter. After replacement of the regulator, repeat the pressure test. If still incorrect, check the fuel lines for kinks or blockage, and replace the pump as necessary.

810, Maxima and 200SX

1. Fuel pressure must be reduced to zero.
2. Connect a fuel pressure gauge between the fuel feed pipe and the fuel filter outlet.
3. Start the engine and read the pressure. It should be 30 psi at idle, and 37 psi at the moment the accelerator pedal is fully depressed.

4. If pressure is not as specified, replace the pressure regulator and repeat the test. If the pressure is still incorrect, check for clogged or deformed fuel lines, then replace the fuel pump.

FUNCTIONAL TEST

280Z

1. Disconnect the cable from the "S" terminal of the starter motor solenoid.
2. Unplug the cold start valve wiring connector.
3. Turn the ignition key to Start. You should be able to hear the fuel pump running. If not, check the wiring circuits and fuses. If the circuits and fuses are in order, replace the pump.

280ZX

1. Disconnect either the wire to the alternator "L" terminal, or the oil pressure switch connector.
2. Turn the ignition key to Start. You should be able to hear the fuel pump running. If not, check the wiring circuits and fuses; if they are in order replace the fuel pump.

810, Maxima and 200SX

Fuel pressure must be reduced to zero before tests are made.

On 1978–79 810's, disconnect the ground cable from the battery. Disconnect the cold start valve wiring harness at the connector. Connect two jumper wires to the terminals of the cold start valve. Touch the other ends of the jumpers to the positive and negative terminals of the battery for a few seconds to release the pressure.

For 1980 and later 810s, Maximas and 200SXs, start the engine, disconnect the harness connector of fuel pump relay-2 while the engine is running. On 1984 and later 200SXs, the fuel pump connector is inside the tool box on the rear right-hand side of the car. After the engine stalls, crank it over two or three times to make sure all of the fuel pressure is released.

NOTE: If the engine will not start remove the fuel pump relay-2 harness connector and crank the engine for about 5 seconds.

REMOVAL & INSTALLATION

280Z and 280ZX

1. Disconnect the battery ground cable.
2. Disconnect the wiring harness to the cold start valve.
3. Using two jumper wires from the battery, energize the cold start valve for two or three seconds to relieve pressure in the fuel system.

——————— CAUTION ———————
Be careful not to short the two jumpers together.

4. Jack up the rear of the car and safely support it on stands. Have a can and a rag handy to catch any spilled fuel.
5. Clamp the hose between the fuel tank and the fuel pump.
6. Loosen the hose clamps on the fuel lines at both ends of the pump and remove the lines from the pump.
7. Remove the two retaining screws and remove the fuel pump bracket.
8. Disconnect the fuel pump harness connector. On 280Z models, roll back the carpet behind the passenger seat to reach the connector. On 280Z 2 + 2 models, remove the rear seat and remove the harness cover. Disconnect the wiring. On ZX models, remove the mat in the luggage compartment, and disconnect the harness connector at the rear of the compartment.
9. Pull the harness through the rubber grommet in the floor and remove the fuel pump.
10. Install the fuel pump in the reverse order of removal.

1980 and Later 280ZX

1. Reduce the fuel line pressure to zero: start the engine and remove the fuel pump relay No. 2 while the engine is running. After the engine stalls, crank the engine with the starter two or three times. Turn the ignition off.
2. Disconnect the negative battery cable.
3. Remove the luggage compartment mat. Disconnect the fuel pump harness wiring at the connector at the rear of the compartment. Push the wires and grommet through the floor.
4. Raise and support the rear of the car.
5. Clamp the hose between the fuel tank and the pump.
6. Loosen the fuel line clamps and disconnect the hoses from the pump. Have a metal container ready to catch the fuel which will spill from the lines.
7. Remove the bolts which secure the

pump bracket to the body and remove the pump.
8. Installation is the reverse.

1984 and later 300ZX

NOTE: Before disconnecting the fuel line, the fuel pressure must be released from the fuel line. Start the engine. Remove the luggage compartment floor mat. Disconnect the fuel pump connector (blue in color) with the engine running. After the engine stalls, crank the engine two or three times to make sure that pressure is released. Turn the engine off and connect the fuel pump connector.

1. Remove the fuel tank as described later in this section.
2. Remove the retaining bolt and remove the fuel pump.
3. Installation is the reverse of removal. Run the engine and check for leaks.

810, Maxima and 200SX

1. Reduce the fuel pressure to zero. See procedures under the "Testing" section, above.
2. Disconnect the electrical harness connector at the pump. The 810 and Maxima pump is located near the fuel tank. The 200SX pump is located near the center of the car.
3. Clamp the hose between the fuel tank and the pump to prevent gas from spewing out from the tank.
4. Remove the inlet and outlet hoses at the pump. Unclamp the inlet hose and allow the fuel lines to drain into a suitable container.
5. Unbolt and remove the pump. The 200SX pump and fuel damper can be removed at the same time.
6. Installation is the reverse of removal. Use new clamps and be sure all hoses are properly seated on the fuel pump body.

Carburetors

The carburetors used are a two-barrel down-draft type with a low-speed (primary) side and a high-speed (secondary) side.

All models have an electrically-operated anti-dieseling solenoid. As the ignition switch is turned off, the valve is energized and shuts off the supply of fuel to the idle circuit of the carburetor.

REMOVAL & INSTALLATION

1. Remove the air cleaner.
2. Disconnect the fuel and vacuum lines from the carburetor.
3. Remove the throttle lever.
4. Remove the four nuts and washers retaining the carburetor to the manifold.
5. Lift the carburetor from the manifold.
6. Remove and discard the gasket used between the carburetor and the manifold.

7. Install the carburetor in the reverse order of removal, using a a new carburetor base gasket.

FUEL LEVEL ADJUSTMENT

All Nihonkikaki (Nikki) and Hitachi carburetors have a glass float chamber side cover marked with a fuel level line (some have a small window in the side of the float chamber). Fuel level is adjusted by bending the float seat tab with the float cover removed and inverted, and the float fully raised.

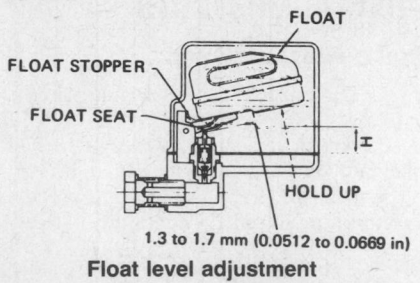

1.3 to 1.7 mm (0.0512 to 0.0669 in)
Float level adjustment

THROTTLE LINKAGE ADJUSTMENT

On all models, make sure the throttle is wide open when the accelerator pedal is floored. Some models have an adjustable accelerator pedal stop to prevent strain on the linkage.

DASHPOT ADJUSTMENT

A dashpot is used on carburetors of cars with automatic transmission as means of slowly closing the throttle valve to prevent stalling. It is also used in later years as an emission control device on models with either automatic or manual transmissions. The dashpot should be adjusted to contact the throttle lever on deceleration at approximately 1900–2100 rpm for manual transmissions, or 1600–1800 rpm for automatic transmission with the L series engines, or 2000–2300 rpm for all models of the A series engine, or 2,300–2,500 rpm for all E15 and E16 engines. The 1980 and later Z20S engine's dashpot contact point should be between 1400–1600 rpm for automatic transmissions.

NOTE: Before attempting to adjust the dashpot, make sure the idle speed, timing and mixture adjustments are correct.

SECONDARY THROTTLE ADJUSTMENT

On the two stage carburetors used on Datsuns and Nissans, the secondary throttle plate begins to open when the primary throttle plate has opened to an angle of approximately 50° (from the fully closed position). This works out to a clearance measurement of approximately 0.28–0.32 in. between the throttle valve and the carburetor body. This

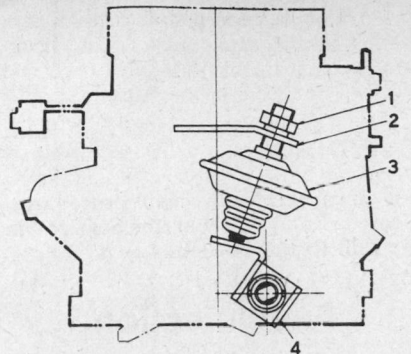

1. Locknut 3. Dashpot
2. Mounting arm 4. Throttle lever

Typical dashpot

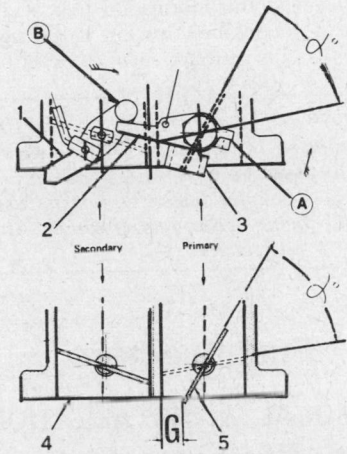

1. Connecting lever
2. Return plate
3. Adjusting plate
4. Secondary throttle chamber
5. Primary throttle valve
a. Primary throttle opening in degrees
G. Primary throttle opening in inches

Secondary throttle adjustment

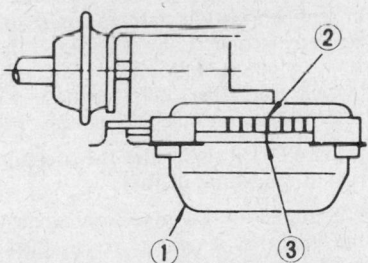

1. Thermostat cover
2. Thermostat housing
3. Groove

Choke index setting

can be measured with a drill bit of the correct diameter. If adjustment is required, bend the connecting link between the two linkage assemblies.

AUTOMATIC CHOKE ADJUSTMENT

1. With the engine cold, make sure the

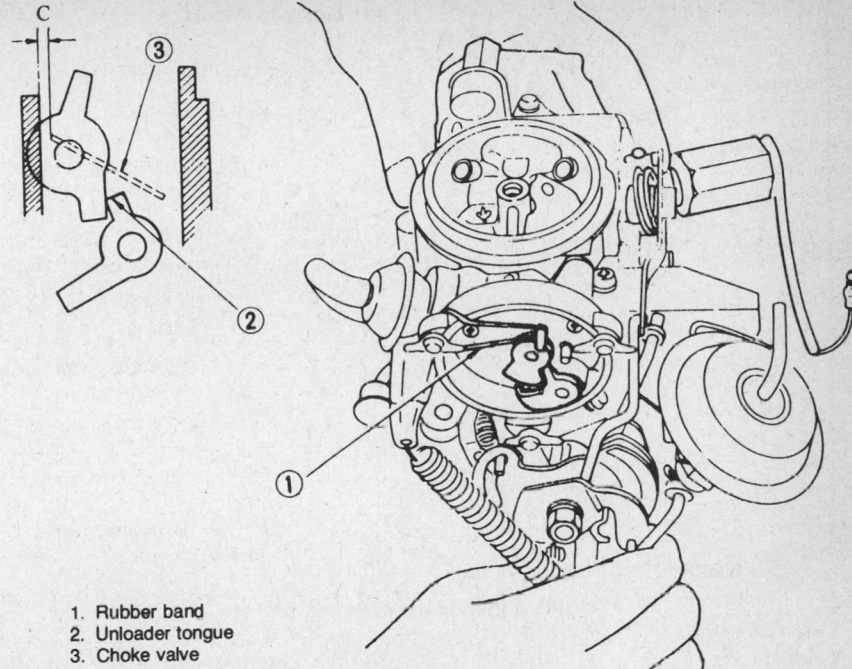

1. Rubber band
2. Unloader tongue
3. Choke valve

Typical choke unloader adjustment

choke is fully closed (press the gas pedal all the way to the floor and release).

2. Check the choke linkage for binding. The choke plate should be easily opened and closed with your finger. If the choke sticks or binds, it can usually be freed with a liberal application of a carburetor cleaner made for the purpose. A couple of quick squirts of the right stuff normally does the trick.

If not, the carburetor will have to be disassembled for repairs.

3. The choke is correctly adjusted when the index mark on the choke housing (notch) aligns with the center mark on the carburetor body. If the setting is incorrect, loosen the three screws clamping the choke body in place and rotate the choke cover left or right until the marks align. Tighten the screws carefully to avoid cracking the housing.

CHOKE UNLOADER ADJUSTMENT

1. Close the choke valve completely.
2. Hold the choke valve by stretching a rubber band between the choke shaft lever and the carburetor.
3. Pull the throttle lever until it completely opens.
4. Adjust the gap between the choke plate and the carburetor body to:
   A-series engines:
   1978–80: 0.0929 in. except:
   1978 and later: Non-Cal. 5 speed hatchback 210, B210 and 1980 and later Canada manual trans. A12A: 0.0854 in.
   L-series engines, 1980 Z20S engine:
   1978–80: 0.0807–0.1122 in.
   E-series engines:

1982–84: 0.0929 in. (E15)
1983–85: 0.1165 in. (E16)
CA–series engines:
1982–85: 0.0965 in.

FAST IDLE ADJUSTMENT

1. With the carburetor removed from the vehicle, place the upper side of the fast idle screw on the second step (first step for 1978–81 L and Z engines) of the fast idle cam and measure the clearance between the throttle valve and the wall of the throttle valve chamber at the center of the throttle valve. Check it against the following specifications:
1978 F10: 0.0287–0.0343 in.
1978 B210:
   0.0287–0.0343 in. M/T
   0.0394–0.0449 in. A/T
1978–79 510, 200SX:
   0.0370–0.0465 in. M/T
   0.0457–0.0551 in. A/T
1979–80 310:
   0.0283–0.0350 in.
1979–82 210, A12A engine:
   0.0248–0.0315 in. M/T
A14 engine:
   0.0283–0.0350 in. M/T
A15 engine:
   0.0386–0.0461 in. A/T
1980–81 510:
   0.0299–0.0354 in. M/T
   0.0378–0.0433 in. M/T
1981 310:
   0.0287–0.0343 in.
1982 310:
   0.0287–0.0343 in. M/T
   0.0393–0.0449 in. A/T
1982 Stanza:
   0.0260–0.0315 in.

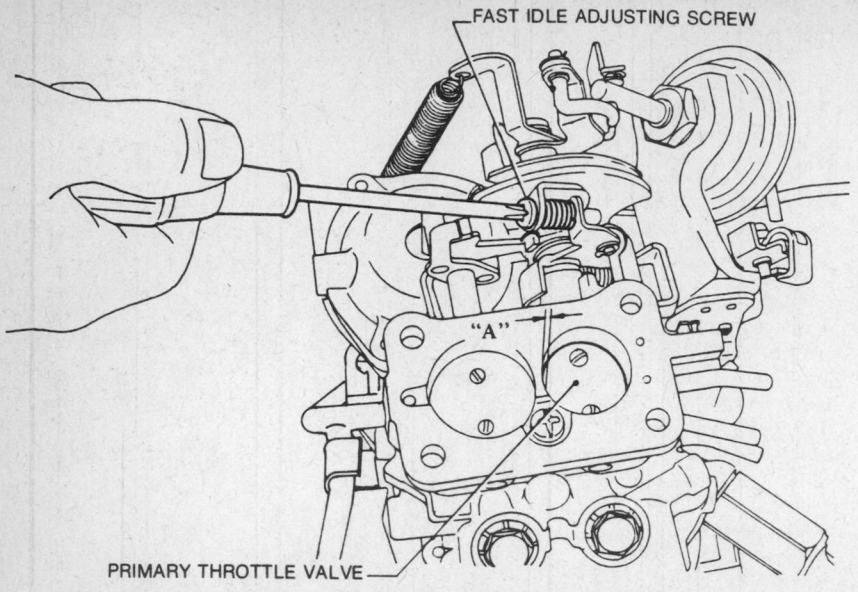

Fast idle adjustment—E-series engines

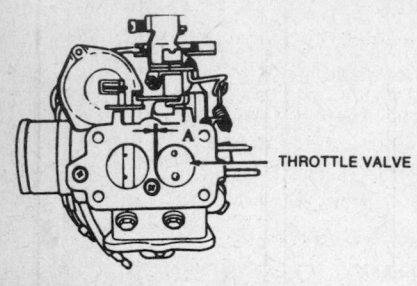

THROTTLE VALVE

FAST IDLE CAM STEPS

4TH
3RD
2ND
1ST

Fast idle adjustment—L-series carbureted engines

1983–85 Stanza:
  0.0260–0.0315 M/T
  0.0319–0.0374 A/T
1982 Sentra:
  0.0315–0.0343 in. M/T
  0.0421–0.0449 in. A/T
1983–84 Sentra (E15):
  0.0315–0.0343 in. M/T
  0.0421–0.0449 in. A/T
1983–84 Sentra, Pulsar (E16):
  USA: 0.0311–0.0367 in. M/T
       0.0425–0.0481 in. A/T
  Canada: 0.0255–0.0311 in. M/T
        0.0366–0.0422 in. A/T
1984–85 Sentra, Pulsar (E16):
  USA: 0.0339–0.0378 in. M/T
       0.0453–0.0492 in. A/T
  Canada: 0.0283–0.0322 in. M/T
        0.0394–0.0433 in. A/T
"M/T" means manual transmission.
"A/T" means automatic transmission.

NOTE: The first step of the fast idle adjustment procedure is not absolutely necessary.

2. Install the carburetor on the engine.
3. Start the engine and measure the fast idle rpm with the engine at operating temperature. The cam should be at the 2nd step. 2nd step.
1978 F10:
  1900–2700 rpm
1978–79 510, 200SX:
  M/T 1,900–2,800 rpm
  A/T 2,200–3,200 rpm
1978 B210:
  M/T 1,900–2,700 rpm
  A/T 2,400–3,200 rpm
1980 and later 210, A12A, A14 engines:
  49 states M/T 2,400 and 3,200 rpm
  California M/T 2,300–3,100 rpm
A15 engines:
  A/T 2,700–3,500 rpm
  M/T 2,300–3,100 rpm
1979–81 310:
  49 states 2400–3200 rpm
  Calif. 2300–3100 rpm
  Canada 1900–2700 rpm
1982 310:
  49 states 2400–3200 rpm
  Calif. 2300–3100 rpm
  Canada 1900–2700 rpm M/T
              2400–3200 A/T
1982 Sentra:
  Calif. 2,300–3,100 rpm
  49 States 2,400–3,200 rpm
  Canada 1,900–2,700 rpm M/T
           2,400–3,200 rpm A/T
1983–84 Sentra (E15):
  2,400–3,200 rpm
1983–85 Sentra (E16), Pulsar:
  Calif. 2,600–3,400 rpm M/T
       2,700–3,700 rpm A/T
  49 States 2,400–3,200 rpm M/T
         2,700–3,500 rpm A/T
  Canada 1,900–2,700 rpm M/T
        2,400–3,200 rpm A/T

4. To adjust the fast idle speed, turn the fast idle adjusting screw counterclockwise to increase the fast idle speed and clockwise to decrease the fast idle speed.

OVERHAUL

For all carburetor overhaul procedures, please refer to "Carburetor Service" in the Unit Repair Section.

Fuel Injection

The fuel injection system on all injected Datsun and Nissan models is an electronic type, using various types of sensors to convert engine operating conditions into electrical signals. The information generated is fed to a control unit, giving it the right figures to set the injector open-valve period.

—————— **CAUTION** ——————
The 1979 and later Electronic Control Unit must not be installed on 1978 or earlier models. Damage to the ECU will result. A special adapter harness must be used with the factory EFI analyzer when testing the 1979 and later ECU.

Fuel Injectors

REMOVAL & INSTALLATION
Z20E and Z22E Engines

1. Release fuel pressure by following the procedure under "Fuel Pump" earlier in this section.
2. Disconnect the accelerator cable.
3. Disconnect the injector harness connector.
4. Tag and disconnect the vacuum hose at the fuel pipe connection end. Disconnect the air regulator and its harness connector, and tag and disconnect any other hoses that may hinder removal of the injector assembly.
5. Disconnect the fuel feed hose and fuel return hose from the fuel pipe.

NOTE: Place a rag under the fuel pipe to prevent splashing of fuel.

6. Remove the vacuum hose connecting the pressure regulator to the intake manifold.
7. Remove the bolts securing the fuel pipe and pressure regulator.
8. Remove the screws securing the fuel injectors. Remove the fuel pipe assembly, by pulling out the fuel pipe, injectors and pressure regulator as an assembly.
9. Unfasten the hose clamp on the injectors and remove the injectors from the fuel pipe.
10. To install, reverse the order of removal, noting the following:
  a. When installing the injectors, check that there are no scratches or abrasion at the lower rubber insulator, and securely install it, making sure it is air-tight.

b. When installing the fuel hose, make sure the hose end is inserted onto the metal pipe until the end contacts the unit, as far as it will go. Push the end of the injector rubber hose onto the fuel pipe until it is one inch from the end of the pipe.

c. Never reuse the hose clamps on the injection system. Always renew the clamps. When tightening clamps, make sure the screw does not come in contact with adjacent parts.

L28E and L28ET Engines

1. Release the fuel system pressure by following the procedure in this section under "Fuel Pump".

2. Disconnect the electric connector from the injector and cold start valve.

3. Disengage the harness from the fuel pipe wire clamp.

4. Disconnect the blow-by hose at the side of the rocker cover.

5. Disconnect the vacuum tube, which connects the pressure regulator to the intake manifold, from the pressure regulator.

6. Remove the air regulator pipe.

7. Disconnect the fuel feed hose and fuel return hose from the fuel pipe.

NOTE: Place a rag underneath the fuel pipe to catch spilled fuel.

8. Remove the bolts securing the fuel pipe and cold start valve. Remove the screws securing the fuel injectors.

9. Remove the fuel pipe assembly by pulling out the fuel pipe, injectors pressure regulator and cold start valve as an assembly.

10. Unfasten the hose clamp on the injectors and remove the injectors from the fuel pipe.

11. To install, reverse the removal procedure, noting the items listed under No. 10 of "Z series Fuel Injector Removal and Installation" above.

CA20E and CA18ET Engines

1. On the CA20E engine, drain the engine coolant. Disconnect the fuel injection wiring harness, the ignition wires, and the collector with the throttle chamber. Tag and disconnect all related hoses.

2. On the CA18ET engine, disconnect the air intake pipe, the fuel injector wiring harness, the ignition wires and accelerator cable. Disconnect the throttle chamber.

3. On all engines, disconnect the fuel hoses and pressure regulator vacuum hoses.

4. Remove the injectors together with the fuel tube assembly. Remove the individual injectors from the fuel tube.

5. Installation is the reverse of removal, noting the items listed under No. 10 of "Z-series Fuel Injector Removal and Installation."

VG30E and VG30ET Engines

1. Release the fuel system pressure as described in this section under "Fuel Tank Removal and Installation."

2. Disconnect the following from the intake collector:

a. Air duct
b. Accelerator wire
c. Blow-by hoses
d. Air regulator hoses
e. EGR tube
f. Harness clamps
g. Harness connectors
h. Intake collector cover

3. Tag and disconnect the fuel hoses.

4. Remove the intake collector.

5. Remove the bolts securing the fuel tube.

6. Remove the bolts securing the injectors and remove the injectors, fuel tubes and pressure regulator as an assembly.

7. Reverse the procedure for installation, making sure all hose and fuel line connections are properly tightened. Check all connection for fuel leakage when the engine is started.

E15ET Engine

1. Release the system fuel pressure.

a. Disconnect the harness connector of the fuel pump relay while the engine is running.

b. After the engine stalls, crank the engine two or three times.

c. Turn the ignition switch "OFF".

d. Reconnect the harness connector of the fuel pump relay. If the engine does not start, remove the fuel pump connector and crank the engine for about 5 seconds.

2. Remove the air inlet pipe and hose.

3. Disconnect the accelerator wire and throttle wire (automatic transmission cars only).

4. Disconnect the throttle valve switch harness connector and remove the throttle chamber.

5. Remove the P.C.V. valve and hose.

6. Loosen the clamps at both ends of the air pipe.

7. Disconnect the I.C.V. and air regulator harness connectors.

8. Remove the air pipe.

9. Disconnect the harness connectors from the injectors.

10. Remove the fuel hoses.

11. Remove the bolts securing the fuel pipe.

12. Remove the fuel injector screws. Remove the fuel pipe assembly by pulling out the fuel pipe along with the injectors.

13. Unfasten the hose clamp on the fuel injector and remove the fuel injector from the fuel pipe.

14. Reverse the removal procedure to install.

NOTE: When installing the injector, check that there are no scratches or abrasion at the lower rubber insulator, and securely install it, making sure it is air-tight.

For all fuel injection system repair and service procedures, please refer to "Fuel Injection" in the Unit Repair section.

FUEL SYSTEM—DIESEL ENGINES

Injection Pump

For further information on diesel injection systems, please refer to "Diesel Service" in the Unit Repair Section.

NOTE: The diesel injection pump is located at the right front side of the engine. In case of pump failure or damage, the pump must be replaced as an assembly, except for certain simple parts on the outside of the pump.

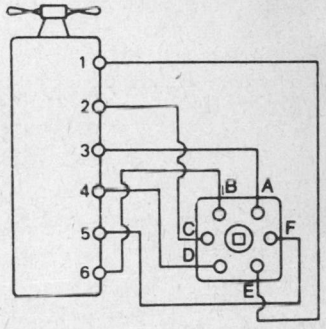

Injection tube routing—diesel engines

REMOVAL & INSTALLATION

LD28 Six Cylinder

1. Disconnect the negative battery cable.

2. Remove the air cleaner duct. Remove the engine under cover.

3. Drain the engine coolant and then remove the radiator and its shroud.

4. Loosen the fan pulley nuts and then remove the drive belts (air conditioning, alternator and power steering pump).

5. Disconnect the power steering oil pump and position it out of the way.

6. Tag and disconnect the accelerator wire, the overflow hose (on the spill tube side), the fuel cut solenoid connector and the fuel return hose.

7. Tag and disconnect the potentiometer, the injection timing control solenoid valve wire, the cold start device water hoses (at the 4-way connector side) and the vacuum modulator (A/T models only).

8. Remove the crank damper pulley. Use a plastic mallet and tap lightly around the sides, if this does not loosen the pulley you will need a two-armed gear puller.

9. Remove the pulley bracket and the idler pulley (if so equipped) and then remove the front dust cover.

10. Loosen the spring set pin, set the tensioner pulley to the "free tension" position and then tighten them.

11. Slide the injection pump drive belt off its pulleys.

12. Loosen the retaining nut and remove

the injection pump drive gear. You may need a two-armed gear puller.

13. Disconnect the injection tubes at the injection nozzle side.

14. Unscrew the injection pump fixing nuts and the bracket bolt.

15. Remove the injection pump assembly with the injection tubes attached.

NOTE: If you plan to measure plunger lift, remove the injection tubes before removing the pump.

Installation is in the reverse order of removal. Observe the following:

1. Set the No. 1 cylinder at TDC of the compression stroke. Make sure that the grooves in the rear plate and the flywheel align and that the No. 1 cam lobe on the camshaft is in the position shown.

2. Install the injection pump and temporarily tighten the mounting bolts.

3. Use the alignment marks as shown in the illustration and install the injection pump drive gear. Tighten the nut to 43–51 ft. lbs. (59–69 Nm).

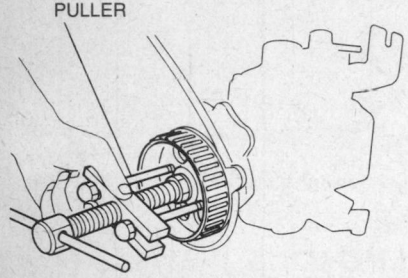

Removing injection pump pulley using puller

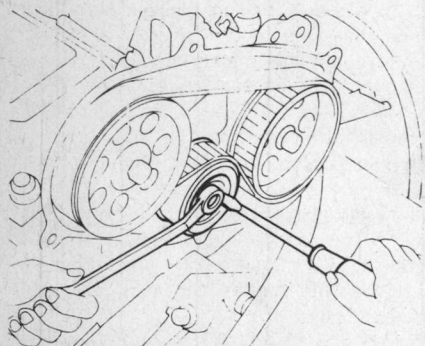

Move the belt tensioner to the free position

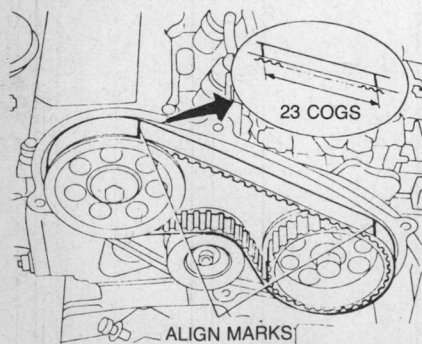

Mark the timing belt before removal

NOTE: The injection pump drive shaft is tapered.

If the drive gear is difficult to install, use a plastic mallet and drive it into place.

4. Make sure that the tensioner pulley is still in the free position and slide the injection drive belt over the pulleys.

5. The drive belt should have two timing marks on it. Align one with the mark on the crank pulley and the other with the mark on the drive gear. If the timing marks on the drive belt are not clear enough to read, set the marks on the drive gear and the crank pulley so that there are 20 cogs of the drive belt between them when it is installed.

6. Loosen the spring set pin and the tensioner so that the belt is automatically set to the "tension" position.

7. Adjust the injection timing as detailed later in this chapter.

8. Tighten the injection pump nuts to 12–15 ft. lbs. (16–21 Nm) and the bracket bolt to 22–26 ft. lbs. (30–35 Nm).

9. Reconnect the injection tubes. Connect them to the cylinders in this order: 4, 2, 6, 1, 5, 3.

10. Bleed the air from the fuel system as detailed later in this chapter.

CD17 Four Cylinder

1. Disconnect the negative battery cable.

2. Drain the radiator coolant. Remove the air cleaner assembly.

3. Tag and disconnect all wires and hoses attached to the injection pump.

4. Remove the injection timing belt by first setting the No. 1 cylinder at TDC on its compression stroke. Matchmark the timing belt to both pulleys using paint or a crayon for later installation. Set the belt tensioner to the "free" position and remove the timing belt.

5. Loosen the nut and remove the injection pump pulley. Remove all injection tubes. Remove the injection pump fixing nuts and bracket bolt, and remove the injection pump.

6. To install the pump, reverse the removal procedure. Make sure the No. 1 cylinder is at TDC on its compression stroke. Install the pump and temporarily tighten the bolts. Torque the pump pulley nut to 43–51 ft. lbs. Install the belt by aligning the match marks on the belt and pulleys. Loosen the tensioner and turn the crankshaft two times in its normal direction of rotation. Tighten the tensioner while holding it.

7. Set the injection timing, and tighten the pump securely. Connect the injection tubes in the order shown. Bleed the injection pump as explained below.

INJECTION PUMP TIMING

LD28 Six Cylinder

1. Remove the under cover and drain the coolant.

2. Remove the coolant hoses that are connected to the coldstart device.

3. Remove the power steering pump.

4. Set the No. 1 cylinder at TDC of its compression stroke. Make sure that the grooves in the rear plate and the drive plate are aligned with each other. Make sure that the No. 1 camshaft lobe is in the position shown in the illustration.

5. Using two wrenches, remove the fuel injection tubes.

6. Loosen the fork retaining screw on the cold start device. Turn the fork 90° and then set the cold start device in the free position.

───── **CAUTION** ─────

Never remove the screw on the cold start device wire. If it should be removed accidentally, the pump assembly should be readjusted at a service shop specified by the manufacturer.

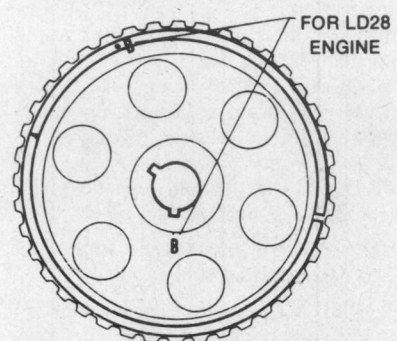

Injection pump drive gear alignment marks—diesel engines

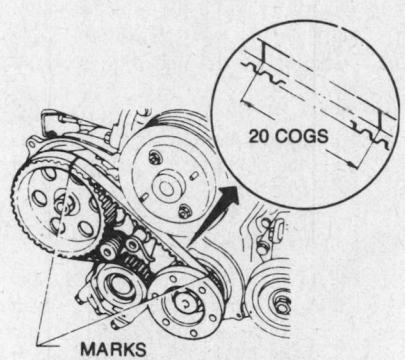

Timing mark alignment on the injection pump drive belt—diesel engines

7. Remove the plug bolt from the rear side of the injection pump and, in its place, attach a dial indicator.

8. Loosen the injection pump mounting nuts and bracket bolt.

9. Turn the crankshaft counterclockwise 15 to 20 degrees from the No. 1 cylinder TDC position.

10. Find the dial indicator needle rest point and set the gauge to zero.

11. Turn the crankshaft clockwise two complete revolutions in order to remove the play in the camshaft mechanism. Loosen the tensioner and then retighten it.

12. Turn the crankshaft clockwise until the No. 1 cylinder is again at TDC and then read the dial indicator.

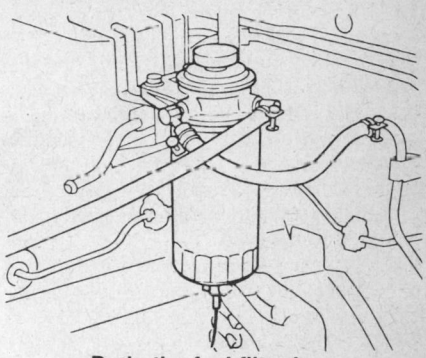

Plunger lift mm (in) For low altitudes	
M/T	0.85 ± 0.03 (0.0335 ± 0.0012)
A/T	0.81 − 0.03 (0.0319 ± 0.0012)
For high altitudes (Non-California model only)	
M/T	0.09 ± 0.03 (0.0354 ± 0.0012)
A/T	0.85 ± 0.03 (0.0335 ± 0.0012)

13. If the dial indicator is not within the above range, turn the injection pump counterclockwise to increase the reading and clockwise to decrease it.

14. Tighten the injection pump mounting nuts and bracket bolt (torque figures are given in the preceding section).

15. Remove the dial indicator and reinstall the plug bolt with a new washer. Tighten the plug bolt to 10–14 ft. lbs. (14–20 Nm).

16. Set the fork at the cold start device in its original position by pulling on the cold start device wire and then tighten the fork screw.

17. Connect the injection tubes as detailed in the preceding section.

18. Install the power steering pump, connect the cold start device water hoses, refill the pump with coolant and replace the under cover.

CD 17 Four Cylinder

1. Set the No. 1 cylinder to TDC on its compression stroke. Make sure the tim-

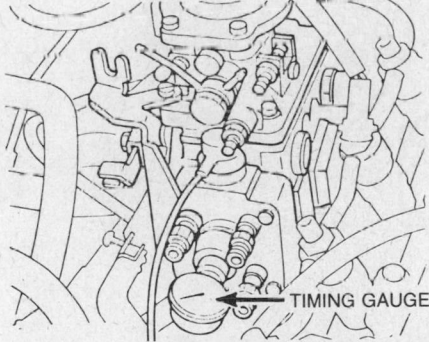

Timing gauge installed in injection pump

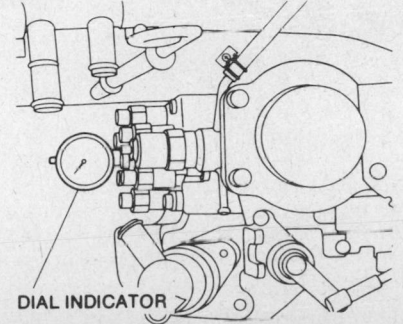

Remove the plug bolt and attach a dial indicator—diesel engines

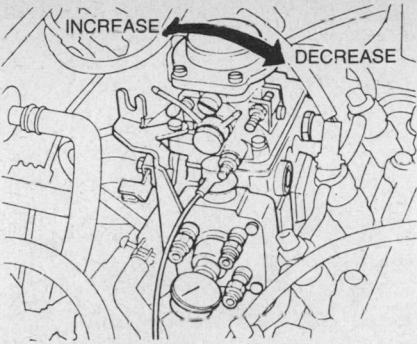

Move the injection pump to adjust plunger lift

ing indicator and crank damper pulley marks are aligned with each other.

2. Tag and remove the fuel injection lines.

3. Turn the cold start device linkage clockwise and set a 0.59 in. block between the cold start device and the linkage.

4. Remove the plug bolt from the fuel injection pump and insert a timing gauge.

5. Turn the crankshaft clockwise 15–20 degrees from TDC. Find the dial gauge needle rest point, then zero the timing gauge.

6. Turn the crankshaft clockwise until the No. 1 cylinder is again at TDC and read the gauge measurement.

Plunger lift for low altitudes	
M/T	0.94 ± 0.03 mm (0.0370 ± 0.0012 in.)
A/T	0.88 + 0.03 mm (0.0346 ± 0.0012 in.)

Plunger lift for high altitudes	
M/T	1.00 ± 0.03 mm (0.0394 + 0.0012 in.)
A/T	0.94 ± 0.03 mm (0.0370 + 0.0012 in.)

BLEED THE FUEL SYSTEM

NOTE: Air should be bled from the fuel system whenever the injection pump is removed or the fuel system is repaired.

1. Loosen the priming pump vent screw and pump a few times. Make sure that the fuel overflows at the vent screw.

2. Tighten the vent screw.

3. Disconnect the fuel return hose and install a suitable hose over the overflow connector. Place a small pan under the overflow hose.

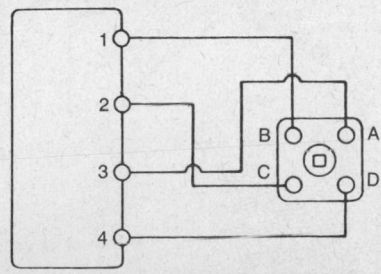

Connect the CD17 injection tubes in the 4,3,2,1 order

4. Prime the priming pump to make sure that the fuel overflows at the open end of the hose.

5. Remove the pan and the overflow hose and then install the return hose.

Drain the fuel filter here

Fuel Injectors

REMOVAL & INSTALLATION

1. Remove the injection tubes at the injector and then remove the spill tube assembly.

2. Unscrew the two mounting bolts and pull out the injectors and their washers.

3. Installation is in the reverse order of removal. Tighten the injector mounting nuts to 12–15 ft. lbs. (16–21 Nm). Tighten the injection tube-to-injector nut to 16–18 ft. lbs. (22–25 Nm). Always use a new injector small washer.

MANUAL TRANSMISSION

REMOVAL & INSTALLATION

The transmission may be removed separately from under the vehicle. Transmission removal and replacement procedure for early models is generally similar.

Rear Wheel Drive

1. Raise and support the vehicle. Disconnect the battery. Disconnect the back-up light switch on all models and neutral switch, if equipped.

2. On the Z and ZX, remove the exhaust system. On models with the A14, L20B, Z20 and Z22 engine, disconnect the exhaust pipe from the manifold. On the 280Z and 280ZX and the 1980 and later Maxima, 810 and 200SX, disconnect the accelerator linkage. Remove the bent shield plate on the 280Z and ZX.

3. Unbolt the driveshaft at the rear and remove. If there is a center bearing, unbolt it from the crossmember. Seal the end of the transmission extension housing to prevent leakage.

4. Disconnect the speedometer drive cable from the transmission.

5. Remove the shift lever.

6. Remove the clutch operating cylinder from the clutch housing.

7. Support the engine with a large wood block and a jack under the oil pan.

8. Unbolt the transmission from the crossmember. Support the transmission with a jack and remove the crossmember.

9. Lower the rear of the engine to allow clearance.

10. Remove the starter.

11. Unbolt the transmission. Lower and remove it to the rear.

12. Reverse the procedure for reinstallation. Check the clutch linkage adjustment.

Front Wheel Drive

You must remove the engine/transmission as a unit.

After removal, remove the bolts holding the transmission to the engine and separate by pulling the transmission towards the clutch housing.

NOTE: The clutch assembly will remain attached to the engine.

Installation is the reverse of removal. The bolts holding the transmission should be torqued to 10–13 ft. lbs.

—————— CAUTION ——————
If the clutch has been removed, it will have to be re-aligned. When connecting driveshafts, insert O-rings between the differential side flanges and driveshafts.

OVERHAUL

For all manual transmission/transaxle overhaul procedures, please refer to "Manual Transmission/Transaxle Overhaul" in the Unit Repair section.

CLUTCH

All models in all years use diaphragm spring pressure plates.

Rear Wheel Drive

REMOVAL & INSTALLATION

1. Remove the transmission from the engine.

2. Insert a clutch aligning bar or similar tool all the way into the clutch disc hub. This must be done so as to support the weight of the clutch disc during removal. Mark the clutch assembly-to-flywheel relationship with paint or a center punch so that the clutch assembly can be assembled in the same position from which it is removed.

L24 clutch release mechanism. (1) is the withdrawal lever, (2) is the return spring and (3) is the release bearing

3. Loosen the bolts in sequence, a turn at a time. Remove the bolts.

4. Remove the pressure plate and clutch disc.

5. Remove the release mechanism. Apply multi-purpose grease to the bearing sleeve inside groove, the contact point of the withdrawal lever and bearing sleeve, the contact surface of the lever ball pin and lever. Replace the release mechanism.

6. Inspect the pressure plate for wear, scoring, etc., and reface or replace as necessary. Inspect the release bearing and replace as necessary. Apply a small amount of grease to the transmission splines. Install the disc on the splines and slide it back and forth a few times. Remove the disc and

remove any excess grease on the hub. Be sure no grease contacts the disc or pressure plate.

7. Install the disc, aligning it with a splined dummy shaft.

8. Install the pressure plate and torque the bolts to 11–16 ft. lbs.

9. Remove the dummy shaft.

10. Replace the transmission.

Front Wheel Drive

REMOVAL & INSTALLATION

F10 and 1979–80 310

Because of the unique configuration of the F10 and 310 transmission/drive shaft system (transaxle), the transmission is impossible to remove from the car without removing the engine.

Due to this problem, Datsun has made provisions for clutch service through an access plate (cover) on the top of the housing. The engine and transmission need not be removed to permit repair or replacement.

NOTE: The clutch cover and pressure plate are balanced as a unit. If replacement is necessary, replace both parts.

1. Disconnect the following cables, wires and hoses:
   a. Battery ground cable
   b. Fresh air duct

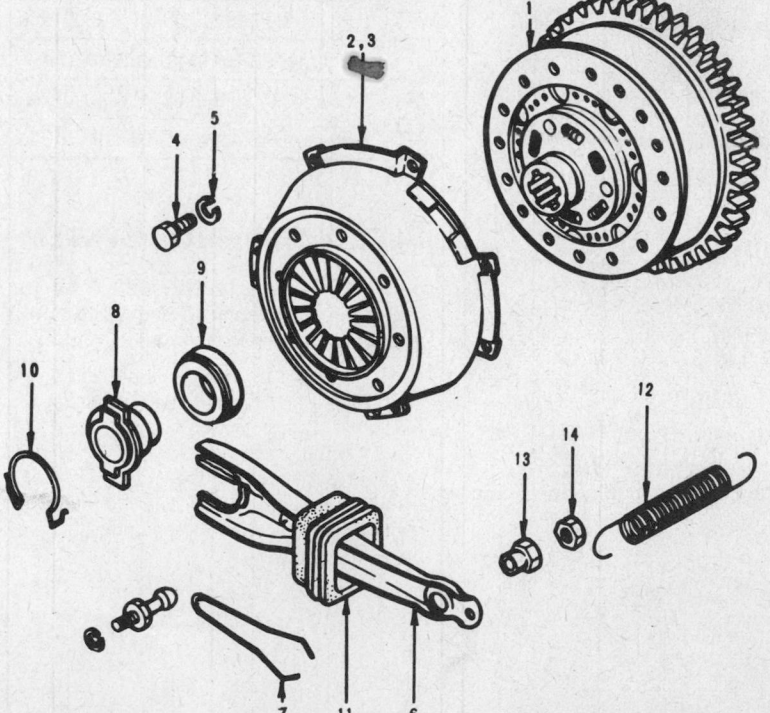

1. Disc
2, 3. Clutch cover assembly with pressure plate
4. Bolt
5. Lockwasher
6. Withdrawal lever
7. Retainer spring
8. Bearing sleeve
9. Release bearing
10. Bearing sleeve holder spring
11. Dust cover
12. Return spring
13. Withdrawal lever push nut
14. Locknut

Diaphragm spring clutch—510 shown

c. Engine harness connectors on the clutch housing

d. Ignition wire between the coil and the distributor

e. Carbon canister hoses

2. Remove the inspection plate from the top of the clutch housing and remove the six bolts holding the clutch cover.

NOTE: To reach all six bolts, jack up the car and rotate the right front wheel with the car in top gear. This will rotate the clutch cover.

——————— **CAUTION** ———————
Be sure to loosen the bolts evenly in order.

3. Rotate the steering wheel all the way to the right and remove the inspection plate inside the right wheel well.

4. Disconnect the withdrawal lever and remove the six bolts on the bearing house. Reaching through the wheel well inspection hole, pull out the primary drive gear assembly.

NOTE: To remove the withdrawal lever pin you must first remove the E-ring that holds it to the bearing housing.

5. After removing the drive gear, go back to the engine compartment and lift the clutch cover and the disc assembly out through the open section of the clutch housing. You may also remove the diaphragm at the same time.

6. Remove the strap holding the pressure plate to the clutch cover and remove the clutch from the center.

NOTE: This strap must be replaced in the same position it had been in before removal. Mark the relative position before removal. Installing it out of position will cause an imbalance.

Installation is the reverse of removal, but observe the following:

1. Paying particular attention to the alignment marks, reassemble the disc and cover to the pressure plate. Tighten the strap bolts to 5–6 ft. lbs. (F10), 7–9 ft. lbs. (310).

2. Put the diaphragm spring and cover assembly onto the flywheel and screw the bolts in with your fingers.

NOTE: These bolts should remain loose enough to shift the assembly when installing the drive gear. There are a pair of aligning pins on the flywheel.

3. Install the drive gear assembly by aligning the disc hub with the gear spline. After alignment, tighten the cover bolts to 5–7.2 ft. lbs.

Sentra, Stanza, Pulsar and 1981–82 310

1. Remove the transaxle.

2. Insert a clutch disc centering tool into the clutch disc hub for support.

3. Loosen the pressure plate bolts evenly, a little at a time to prevent distortion.

4. Remove the clutch assembly.

5. Installation is the reverse of re-

moval. Apply a light coating of chassis lube to the clutch disc splines and the input shaft. Use a centering tool to aid installation. Torque the pressure plate bolts in a criss-cross pattern, to 12–15 ft. lbs.

Clutch Linkage

ADJUSTMENT—HYDRAULIC CLUTCH

Refer to the "Clutch Specifications" chart for clutch pedal height above floor and pedal free-play.

Pedal height is usually adjusted with a stopper limiting the upward travel of the pedal. Pedal free-play is adjusted at the master cylinder pushrod. If the pushrod is nonadjustable, free-play is adjusted by placing shims between the master cylinder and the firewall. On a few models, pedal free-play can also be adjusted at the operating (slave) cylinder pushrod. Pushrods are available in three lengths for the F-10 and 310.

ADJUSTMENT— MECHANICAL CLUTCH

All 1982 and later front wheel drive models use a mechanical clutch. Check pedal height and free travel, adjust if necessary. Refer to the "Clutch Specifications" chart for proper adjustment specifications.

1. Loosen the locknut and adjust the pedal height by means of the pedal stopper. Tighten the locknut.

2. Adjust withdrawal lever play at the lever tip end with the locknuts.

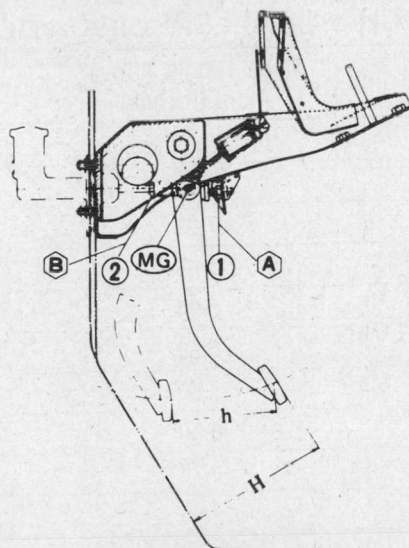

1. Adjust pedal height here
2. Adjust pedal free-play here
MG. Lubricate with multipurpose grease here
H. is pedal height
h. is free play

Clutch adjusting points

3. Depress and release the clutch pedal several times and then recheck the withdrawal lever play again. Readjust if necessary.

4. Measure the pedal free travel at the center of the pedal pad.

Clutch Master Cylinder

REMOVAL & INSTALLATION

1. Disconnect the clutch pedal arm from the pushrod.

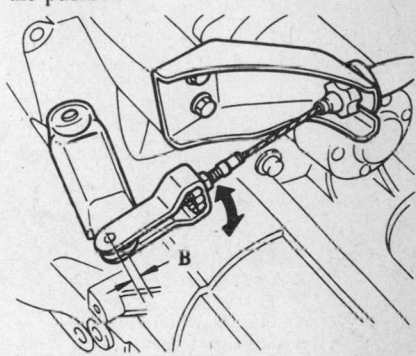

Clutch withdrawal lever adjustment— Sentra, Pulsar, Stanza; arrow shows locknut adjustment

2. Disconnect the clutch hydraulic line from the master cylinder.

NOTE: Take precautions to keep brake fluid from coming in contact with any painted surfaces.

3. Remove the nuts attaching the master cylinder and remove the master cylinder and pushrod toward the engine compartment side.

4. Install the master cylinder in the reverse order of removal and bleed the clutch hydraulic system.

Clutch Slave Cylinder

REMOVAL & INSTALLATION

1. Remove the slave cylinder attaching bolts and the pushrod from the shift fork.

2. Disconnect the flexible fluid hose from the slave cylinder and remove the unit from the vehicle.

3. Install the slave cylinder in the reverse order of removal and bleed the clutch hydraulic system.

HYDRAULIC SYSTEM BLEEDING

Bleeding is required to remove air trapped in the hydraulic system. This operation is necessary whenever the system has been leaking or dismantled. The bleed screw is usually located on the clutch operating (slave) cylinder.

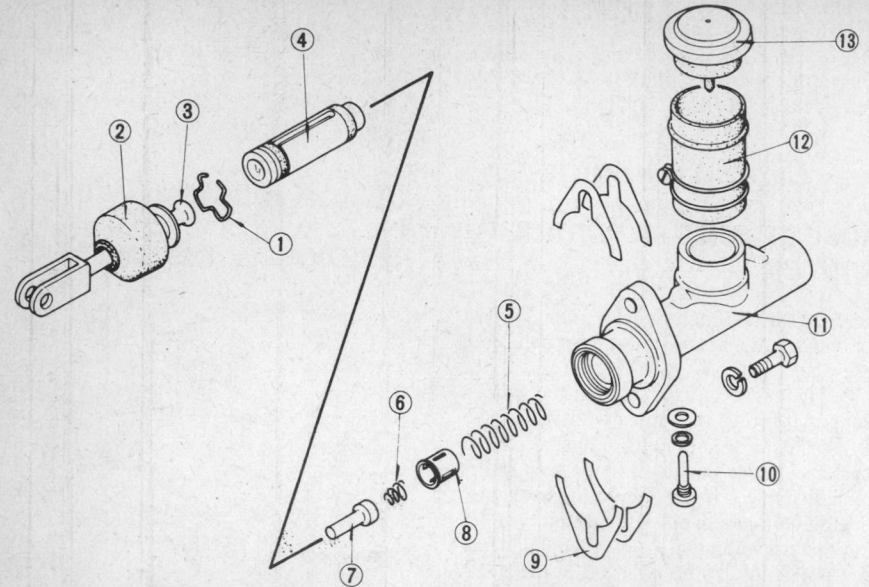

1. Snap-ring
2. Dust cover
3. Pushrod
4. Piston
5. Spring
6. Inlet valve spring
7. Inlet valve
8. Spring retainer
9. Shims
10. Inlet valve release pin
11. Housing
12. Fluid reservoir
13. Reservoir cap

Clutch master cylinder—B210 shown; others similar

1. Remove the bleed screw dust cap.
2. Attach a tube to the bleed screw, immersing the free end in a clean container of brake fluid.
3. Fill the master cylinder with fluid.
4. Open the bleed screw about ¾ turn.
5. Depress the clutch pedal quickly.

Hold it down. Have an assistant tighten the bleed screw. Allow the pedal to return slowly. Bleeder screw torque is 5–6 ft. lbs.
6. Repeat Steps 2 and 5 until no more air bubbles are seen in the fluid container.
7. Remove the bleed tube. Replace the dust cap. Refill the master cylinder.

AUTOMATIC TRANSMISSION

Only external transmission adjustments and repairs, and transmission removal and replacement, are covered in this section.

All models use a JATCO automatic transmission, either model 3N71B or L4N71B (four speed overdrive). This transmission uses Dexron® fluid.

REMOVAL & INSTALLATION

1. Disconnect the battery cable.
2. Remove the accelerator linkage.
3. Detach the shift linkage.
4. Disconnect the neutral safety switch and downshift solenoid wiring.
5. Remove the drain plug and drain the torque converter. If there is no converter drain plug, drain the transmission. If there is no transmission drain plug, remove the pan to drain. Replace the pan to keep out dirt.
6. Remove the front exhaust pipe.
7. Remove the vacuum tube and speedometer cable.
8. Disconnect the fluid cooler tubes.
9. Remove the driveshaft and starter.
10. Support the transmission with a jack under the oil pan. Support the engine also.
11. Remove the rear crossmember.
12. Mark the relationship between the torque converter and the drive plate. Remove the four bolts holding the converter to the drive plate through the hole at the front, under the engine. Unbolt the transmission from the engine.

CLUTCH PEDAL SPECIFICATIONS

Model	Pedal Height Above Floor (inches)	Pedal Free Play (inches)
B210	6.02	0.04–0.12
210 (1980)	5.75	0.04–0.20
310 (1979–81)	7.29	0.04–0.20
710	7.09	0.04–0.20
810, Maxima	6.90	0.04–0.20
F-10	6.90	0.23–0.55
200SX	7.60	0.04–0.12①
510	6.50	0.04–0.20
280Z	8.78	0.039–0.197
280ZX	7.99	0.04–0.20
Stanza	6.50	0.43–0.63
Sentra, 310 (1982–84)	8.00	0.43–0.83
Pulsar	8.03	0.43–0.83
300ZX	7.68	0.04–0.12

① 0.04–0.06 in. 1984 and later

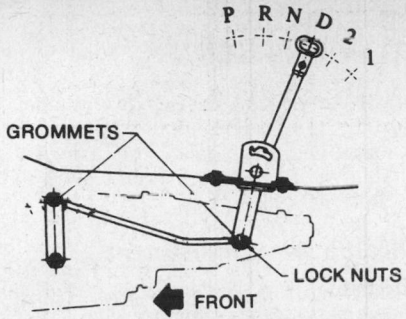

Automatic transmission linkage adjustment—1979 and later

13. Reverse the procedure for installation. If warped, make sure the drive plate has no more than 0.020 in. run—out. Torque the drive plate-to-torque converter and converter housing-to-engine bolts to 29–36 ft. lbs. Drive plate-to-crankshaft bolt torque is 101–116 ft. lbs.

14. Refill the transmission and check the fluid level.

Shift Linkage Adjustment

1978 (All But 280Z)

This adjustment is only necessary on the 1978 B210, 1978 200SX, and the 1978 510.

1. Loosen the trunnion locknuts at the lower end of the control lever. Remove the selector lever knob and console.

2. Place the selector lever in Neutral.

3. Place the transmission shift lever in neutral position by pushing it all the way forward, then pulling it back two stops.

4. Check the vertical clearance between the top of the shift lever pin and transmission control bracket. The clearance ("B") should be 0.1–1.1mm (0.020–0.059 in.). Adjust by turning the nut at the lower end of the selector lever compression rod.

5. Check the horizontal clearance of the shift lever pin and transmission control bracket ("C"). This should be 1.0mm. Adjust with the trunnion locknuts.

6. Replace the console, making sure that the shift pointer is correctly aligned. Install the knob.

280Z

1. Loosen the adjusting nuts ("B").

2. Set both transmission control lever and range selector lever in the "N" position.

3. Tighten the adjusting nuts so that they both just touch the trunnion ("2").

4. Tighten the nuts. Test the shifter for proper operation.

1979 and Later (All Models Except 1984 and later 300ZX)

Adjustment is made at the locknuts at the base of the shifter, which control the length of the shift control rod.

1. Place the shift lever in "D".

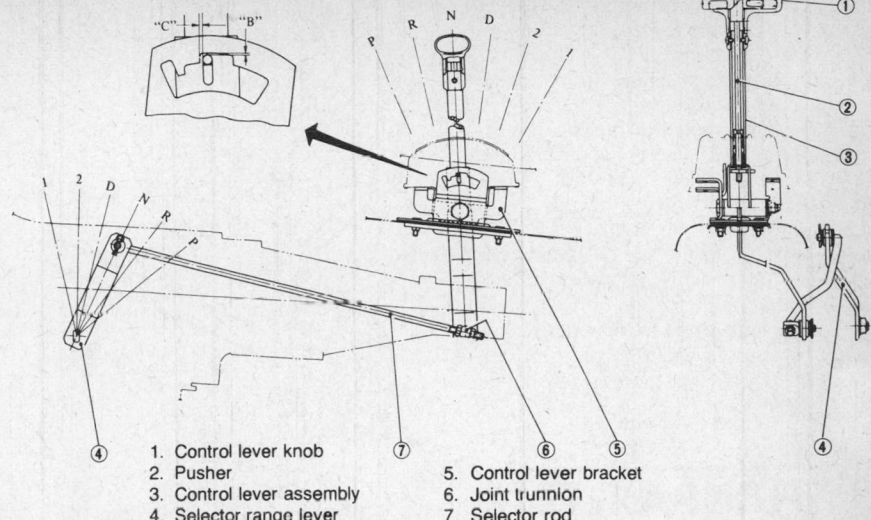

1. Control lever knob
2. Pusher
3. Control lever assembly
4. Selector range lever
5. Control lever bracket
6. Joint trunnion
7. Selector rod

Automatic transmission linkage assembly—1978

2. Loosen the locknuts and move the shift lever until it is firmly in the "D" range, the pointer is aligned, and the transmission is in "D" range.

3. Tighten the locknuts.

4. Check the adjustment. Start the car and apply the parking brake. Shift through all the ranges, starting in "P". As the lever is moved from "P" to "1", you should be able to feel the detents in each range. If proper adjustment is not possible, the grommets are probably worn and should be replaced.

1984 and later 300ZX

If the detents cannot be felt or the pointer indicator is improperly aligned while shifting from the "P" range to range "1", the linkage should be adjusted.

1. Place the shifter in the "N" position.

2. Loosen the locknuts.

3. Move the range selector lever at the transmission to the "N" range.

4. Tighten the lock nuts when the floor control lever is in the "N" range and pushed against the "P" range side.

5. Shift the control lever through the different ranges to make sure it shifts smoothly and without any sliding noises.

Downshift Solenoid Check

The solenoid is controlled by a downshift switch on the accelerator linkage inside the

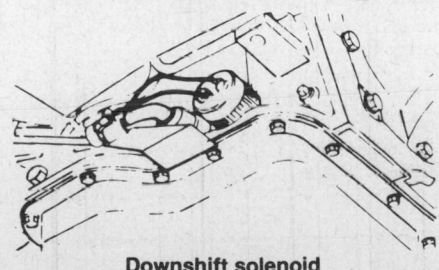

Downshift solenoid

car. To test the switch and solenoid operation:

1. Turn the ignition on.

2. Push the accelerator all the way down to actuate the switch.

3. The solenoid should click when actuated. The solenoid is screwed into the outside of the case. If there is no click, check the switch, wiring, and solenoid.

4. To remove the solenoid, first drain 2–3 pints of fluid, then unscrew the unit.

Neutral Safety and Back—Up Light Switch Adjustment

The switch unit is bolted to the left side of the transmission shift lever. The switch prevents the engine from being started in any transmission position except Park or Neutral. It also controls the back—up lights.

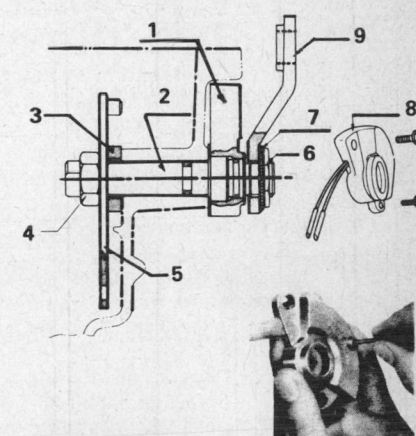

1. Neutral safety switch
2. Manual shaft
3. Washer
4. Nut
5. Manual plate
6. Nut
7. Washer
8. Neutral safety switch
9. Transmission shift lever

Neutral safety and back-up light switch —JATCO transmission

1. Remove the transmission shift lever retaining nut and the lever.

2. Remove the switch.

3. Remove the machine screw in the case under the switch.

4. Align the switch to the case by inserting a 0.059 in. diameter pin through the hole in the switch into the screw hole. Mark the switch location.

5. Remove the pin, replace the machine screw, install the switch as marked, and replace the transmission shift lever and retaining nut.

6. Make sure while holding the brakes on, that the engine will start only in Park or Neutral. Check that the back–up lights go on only in reverse.

TRANSAXLE

Shift Linkage Adjustment

MANUAL TRANSMISSION

F-10 4 Speed

1. Loosen the control lever adjusting nuts.

2. Measure the initial clearance between the case cover and the shift lever when the shift lever is pushed completely into the case cover.

3. Relocate the shift lever to increase the clearance by 8 mm. Move shift lever fully downward (hand lever in 4th gear).

4. Push the select lever fully upward so that the hand lever guide plate touches the detent pin.

5. Turn the upper adjusting nut until it contacts the trunnion plate, then back off one full turn.

6. Tighten the lower adjusting nut.

F-10 5 Speed

1. Loosen all 4 locknuts and move the shift lever completely into the transmission case, then back out 8 mm.

2. Move the shift lever down so that the gears are in 3rd position.

3. Push the select lever fully down so that the hand lever guide plate touches the detent pin.

4. Turn the selector shaft upper adjusting nut until it touches the trunnion plate. Then turn it one complete turn more and tighten the lower nut.

5. Place the hand lever in neutral and adjust the hand lever–to–detent gap to one to two millimeters. Tighten the lock nuts.

310 4 and 5 Speed (1979–81)

Adjustment can be made by adjusting the select lever.

1. Loosen the adjusting nuts at each end of the control rod lever near the bottom of the linkage.

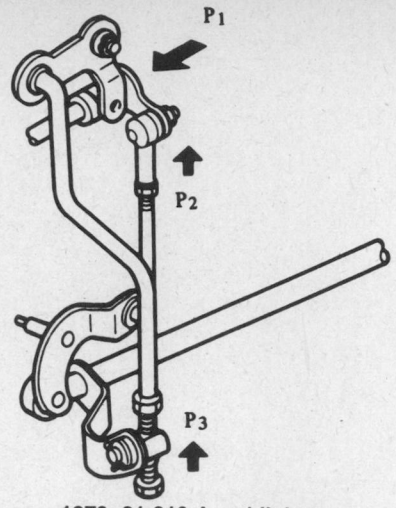

1979–81 310 4 spd linkage

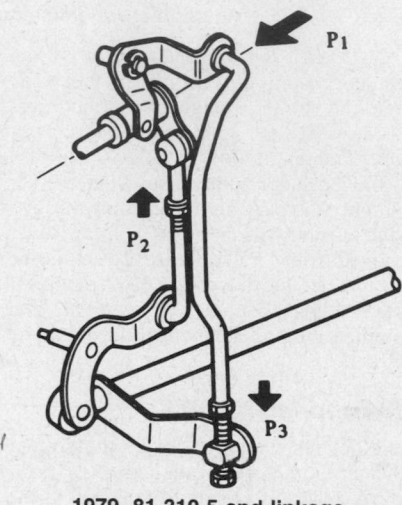

1979–81 310 5 spd linkage

2. Set the shift control lever in the Neutral position.

3. Fully push the shift lever (transmission side) in the direction P1, as shown in the illustration. On the four speed transmission, pull the lever back about 8mm (0.31 in.). On the five speed, pull the shift lever back 11.5mm (0.453 in.). With the select lever held in the above position, move the shift lever in direction P2, which engages third gear on four speed transmissions and second gear on five speed transmissions.

4. Push the control rod select lever as far as it will go in direction P3, then turn the upper adjusting nut until it touches the trunnion. Turn the nut a quarter turn more, and lock the select lever with the other adjusting nut.

5. Operate the shift control lever in the car to see if it shifts smoothly through the gears.

Sentra, Pulsar, Stanza and 310 (1982–84)

No linkage adjustment is either possible or necessary.

AUTOMATIC TRANSMISSION

Of all the vehicles covered in this book, only the 1982 310, Sentra and Stanza are available with an automatic transaxle. This is either the RN3F01A 3-speed unit, or the RL3F01A 3-speed.

Throttle Wire Adjustment

The throttle wire is adjusted by means of double nuts on the carburetor side.

1. Loosen the adjusting nuts.

2. With the throttle fully opened, turn the threaded shaft inward as far as it will go and tighten the first nut against the bracket.

3. Back off the first nut ½ turn and tighten the second nut against the bracket.

4. The throttle wire stroke between the threaded shaft and the cam should be 1.079–1.236 in.

Control Cable Adjustment

1. Place the control lever in Park.

2. Connect the control cable end to the lever in the transaxle unit, and tighten the cable securing bolt.

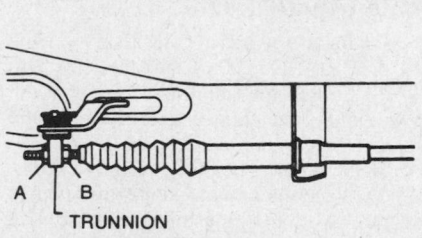

Automatic transaxle cable adjustment— Sentra, Stanza, Pulsar

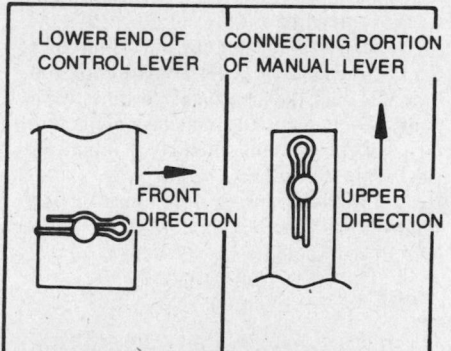

Proper transaxle spring pin position— Sentra, Stanza and Pulsar

3. Move the lever to the 1 position. Make sure that the lever works smoothly and quietly.

4. Place the lever in Park.

5. Make sure that the lever locks in Park. Remove the cable adjusting outer nut and loosen the inner nut. Connect the control cable to the trunnion and install the outer nut.

6. Pull on the cable a couple of times,

then tighten the outer nut until it just contacts the bracket. Tighten the inner nut securely. The length of the cable between the inner end of the rubber boot and the outer end of the rod should be 4.75 in.

7. Check all parts to ensure smooth working order. Check the cable spring cotter pin to make sure that it is assembled as shown.

Band Adjustment

1. Loosen the band adjuster locknut.
2. Tighten the anchor end pin locknut to 3–4 ft. lbs.
3. Back off the anchor end pin lock nut exactly 2½ turns.
4. Tighten the locknut to 12–16 ft. lbs. making absolutely certain that the anchor end pin locknut does not move.

DRIVE AXLE

Driveshaft and U-Joints

REMOVAL & INSTALLATION

510, B210, 200SX with Automatic Transmission, 280Z and ZX

These driveshafts are the one piece type with a U-joint and flange at the rear, and a U-joint and a splined sleeve yoke which fits into the rear of the transmission, at the front. The U-joints must be disassembled for lubrication at 24,000 mile intervals if no grease fittings are present. The splines are lubricated by transmission oil.
1. Release the handbrake.
2. The insulator, pipe, and muffler on the 280Z; the front pipe and the heat shield plate must come off on 280ZX models sold in California, and all 300ZXs.
3. Matchmark the flanges on the driveshaft and differential so that the driveshaft can be reinstalled in its original orientation; this will help maintain driveline balance.
4. Unbolt the rear flange.
5. Pull the driveshaft down and back.

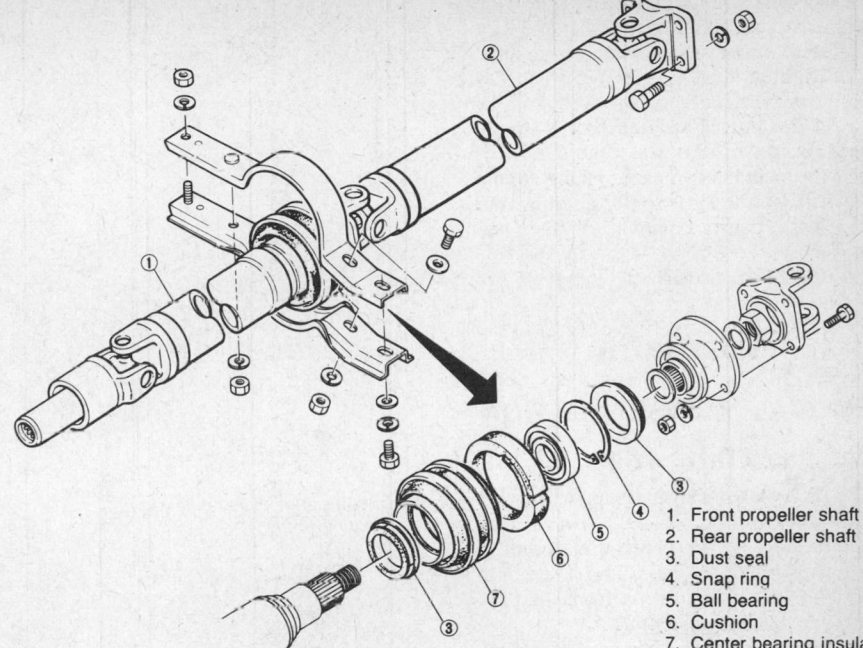

Two piece driveshaft with center bearing and three U-joints

1. Front propeller shaft
2. Rear propeller shaft
3. Dust seal
4. Snap ring
5. Ball bearing
6. Cushion
7. Center bearing insulator

6. Plug the transmission extension housing.
7. Reverse the procedure to install, oiling the splines. Flange bolt torque is 17–24 ft. lbs., except for the 280 and 300Z models, which should be tightened to 25–33 ft. lbs.

200SX with Manual Transmission and Maxima 810

These models use a driveshaft with three U-joints and a center support bearing. The driveshaft is balanced as an assembly. It is not recommended that it be disassembled.
1. Mark the relationship of the driveshaft flange to the differential flange.
2. Unbolt the center bearing bracket.
3. Unbolt the driveshaft flange from the differential flange.
4. Pull the driveshaft back under the rear axle. Plug the rear of the transmission to prevent oil or fluid loss.

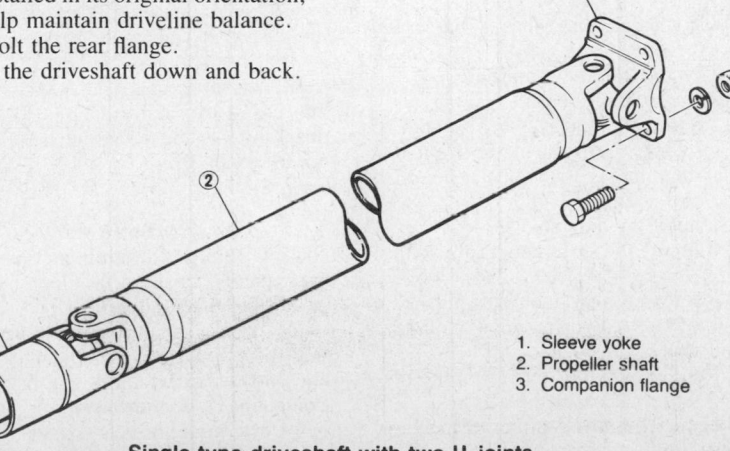

1. Sleeve yoke
2. Propeller shaft
3. Companion flange

Single type driveshaft with two U–joints

5. On installation, align the marks made in Step 1. Torque the flange bolts to 17–24 ft. lbs. Center bearing bracket bolt torque is 26–35 ft. lbs. on the 610.

U-JOINT OVERHAUL

For all overhaul procedures, please refer to "U-Joint/CV-Joint Overhaul" in the Unit Repair section.

CENTER BEARING REPLACEMENT

The center bearing is a sealed unit which must be replaced as an assembly if defective.
1. Remove the driveshaft.
2. Paint a matchmark across where the flanges behind the center yoke are joined. This is for assembly purposes. If you don't paint or somehow mark the relationship between the two shafts, they may be out of balance when you put them back together.
3. Remove the bolts and separate the shafts. Make a matchmark on the front driveshaft half which lines up with the mark on the flange half.
4. Devise a way to hold the driveshaft while unbolting the companion flange from the front driveshaft. Do not place the front driveshaft tube in a vise. The best way is to grip the flange while loosening the nut. It is going to require some strength to remove.
5. Press the companion flange off the front driveshaft and press the center bearing from its mount.
6. The new bearing is already lubricated. Install it into the mount, making sure that the seals and so on are facing the same way as when removed.
7. Slide the companion flange on to the

front driveshaft, aligning the marks made during removal. Install the washer and lock nut. If the washer and locknut are separate pieces, tighten them to 145–175 ft. lbs. If they are a unit, tighten it to 180–217 ft. lbs. Check that the bearing rotates freely around the driveshaft. Stake the nut.

8. Connect the companion flange to the other half of the driveshaft, aligning the marks made during removal. Tighten the bolts securely.

9. Install the driveshaft.

Halfshafts

REMOVAL & INSTALLATION

Front Wheel Drive Only

1. Jack up the car and support it with jackstands.
2. Remove the wheel and tire assembly.
3. Remove the brake caliper assembly.
4. Pry off the cotter pin from the castellated nut on the wheel hub.
5. Loosen, but do not remove, the wheel hub nut from the halfshaft while holding the wheel hub with a suitable tool.
6. Remove the tie–rod ball joint. Remove the lower ball joint. *Do not reuse the nut once it has been removed;* install a new nut during assembly.
7. Drain the gear oil from the transaxle.
8. Remove the bolts holding the halfshaft flange to the transaxle. Remove the halfshaft, along with the wheel hub and knuckle.
9. Insert a suitable bar, wooden dowel or similar tool into the transaxle to prevent the sidegear from dropping inside.

CAUTION

When removing the transaxle, be very careful not to damage the grease seal on the transaxle side.

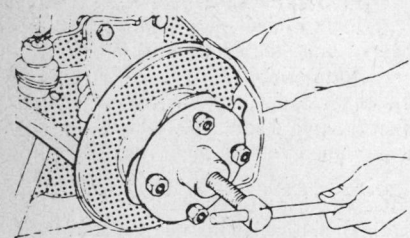

Removing halfshaft

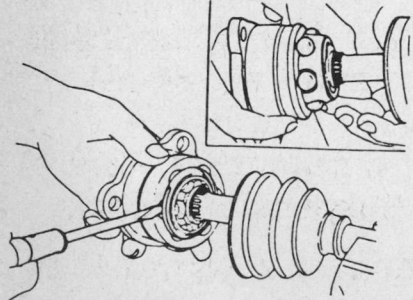

Removing the clip and outer ring

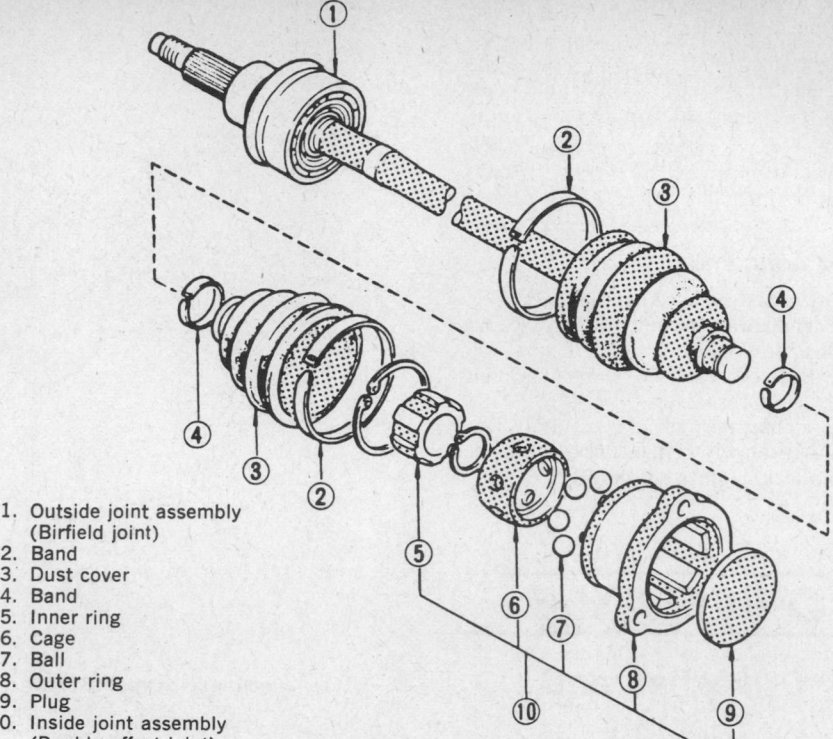

1. Outside joint assembly (Birfield joint)
2. Band
3. Dust cover
4. Band
5. Inner ring
6. Cage
7. Ball
8. Outer ring
9. Plug
10. Inside joint assembly (Double offset joint)

Halfshaft assembly—F10

10. Installation is the reverse of removal. Coat the transaxle-end halfshaft spline with a molybdenum-disulfide grease before insertion. Make sure the rubber gaiters on both ends of the halfshaft are in good shape; if not, replace them (use new metal bands to retain the gaiters).

Final Drive Unit— Independent Rear Suspension

For further information on differentials, please refer to "Drive Axles" in the Unit Repair section.

REMOVAL & INSTALLATION

280Z

1. Chock the front wheels. Raise and support the rear of the vehicle.
2. Remove the main muffler.
3. Unbolt the driveshaft.
4. Loosen the transverse link spindle inner bolts (on the front of the front differential mounting crossmember) enough to free the crossmember.
5. Unbolt the axle shafts.
6. Support the differential unit with a jack.
7. Remove the two mounting nuts from the rear of the rear differential mounting crossmember.
8. Remove the four nuts from the bottom of the front crossmember.
9. Lower the front crossmember and final drive unit together.

10. Unbolt the front crossmember from the differential unit.
11. Reverse the procedure to install. Tighten the transverse link spindle inner bolts with the vehicle lowered to the ground and with two 150 lb. passengers inside.

280ZX and 810 (Maxima) Sedan

1. Jack up the rear of the car and drain the oil from the differential.
2. Disconnect the driveshaft.
3. Disconnect the halfshafts.
4. Remove the side flange fixing bolts, and disconnect the flange yokes together with the halfshafts. Support the case with a jack.
5. Remove the four bolts retaining the case to the suspension carrier.
6. Pull the case backwards on the jack until clear of the car.
7. After the case is removed, support the suspension on a stand to prevent damage.
8. Installation is the reverse. Tighten the rear cover-to-insulator nuts to 65–87 ft. lbs., the case-to-suspension bolts to 43–58 ft. lbs., and the side flange and driveshaft bolts to 36–43 ft. lbs.

300ZX

1. Jack up the rear of the car and drain the oil from the differential. Support with jack stands. Position the floor jack underneath the differential unit.
2. Disconnect the brake hydraulic lines and the parking brake cable.
3. Disconnect the sway bar from the control arms on either sides.
4. Remove the rear exhaust tube.
5. Disconnect the drive shaft.

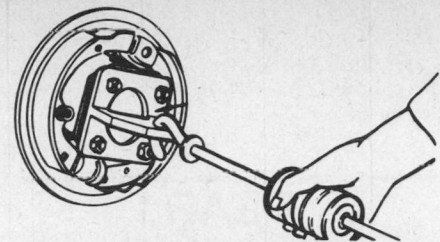
6. Remove the rear shock absorbers from the control arms.

7. Unbolt the differential unit from the chassis, at the differential mounting insulator.

8. Lower the rear assembly out of the car using the floor jack. It is best to have at least one other person helping to balance the assembly.

9. Reverse the procedure to install. Torque the rear cover-to-insulator nuts to 72–87 ft. lbs.; the mounting insulator-to-chassis bolts to 22–29 ft. lbs.; the non-turbo driveshaft-to-flange bolts to 43–51 ft. lbs. Torque the strut nuts to 51–65 ft. lbs.; and the sway bar-to-control arm nuts to 12–15 ft. lbs.

Axle Shaft—Solid Rear Axle Models

REMOVAL & INSTALLATION

NOTE: Bearings must be pressed on and off the shaft with an arbor press. Unless you have access to one, it is inadvisable to attempt any repair work on the axle shaft and bearing assemblies.

1. Remove the hub cap or wheel cover. Loosen the lug nuts.

2. Raise the rear of the car and support it safely on stands.

3. Remove the rear wheel. Remove the four brake backing plate retaining nuts. Detach the parking brake linkage from the brake backing plate.

4. Attach a slide hammer to the axle shaft and remove it. Use the slide hammer and a two-pronged puller to remove the oil seal from the housing.

NOTE: If a slide hammer is not available, the axle can sometimes be pried out using pry bars on opposing sides of the hub.

If end-play is found to be excessive, the bearing should be replaced. Shimming the

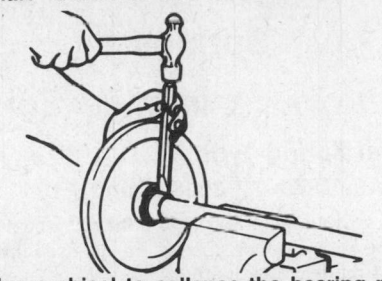

Use a slide hammer to remove the axle shaft—solid rear axle models

Use a chisel to collapse the bearing retainer

bearing is not recommended as this ignores end-play of the bearing itself and could result in improper seating of the bearing.

5. Using a chisel, carefully nick the bearing retainer in three or four places. The retainer does not have to be cut, only collapsed enough to allow the bearing retainer to be slid off the shaft.

6. Pull or press the old bearing off and install the new one by pressing it into position.

7. Install the outer bearing retainer with its raised surface facing the wheel hub, and then install the bearing and the inner bearing retainer in that order on the axle shaft.

8. With the smaller chamfered side of the inner bearing retainer facing the bearing, press on the retainer. The edge of the retainer should fully touch the bearing.

9. Clean the oil seal seat in the rear axle housing. Apply a thin coat of chassis grease.

10. Using a seal installation tool, drive the oil seal into the rear axle housing. Wipe a thin coat of bearing grease on the lips of the seal.

11. Determine the number of retainer gaskets which will give the correct bearing-to-outer retainer clearance of 0.01 in.

12. Insert the axle shaft assembly into the axle housing, being careful not to damage the seal. Ensure that the shaft splines engage those of the differential pinion. Align the vent holes of the gasket and the outer bearing retainer. Install the retaining bolts.

13. Install the nuts on the bolts and tighten them evenly, and in a criss-cross pattern, to 20 ft. lbs.

Half Shaft— Independent Rear Suspension Models

REMOVAL & INSTALLATION

All Except 1982 and Later 810 (Maxima)

1. Raise and support the car.

2. Remove the U-joint yoke flange bolts at the outside. Remove the U-joint center bolt at the differential.

3. Remove the axle shaft.

4. Installation is the reverse. Torque the outside flange bolts to 36–43 ft. lbs. (5.0–6.0 kg-m). Tighten the four differential side flange bolts to 36–43 ft. lbs. (5.0–6.0 kg-m). On axle shafts retained to the differential with a single center bolt, tighten the bolt to 17–23 ft. lbs. (2.4–3.2 kg-m), 1976–77, or 23–31 ft. lbs. (3.2–4.3 kg-m), 1978–83.

1982 and Later 810 (Maxima)

1. Raise and support the rear of the car.

2. Disconnect the half shaft on the wheel side by removing the four flange bolts.

3. Grasp the half shaft at the center and extract it from the differential carrier by prying it with a suitable pry bar.

4. Installation is in the reverse order of removal. Install the differential end first and then the wheel end. Tighten the four flange bolts to 20–27 ft. lbs. (2.3–3.8 kg).

—— **CAUTION** ——
Take care not to damage the oil seal or either end of the half shaft during installation.

Stub Axle (Axle Shaft) and Rear Wheel Bearings— Independent Rear Suspension Models

REMOVAL & INSTALLATION

1. Block the front wheels. Loosen the

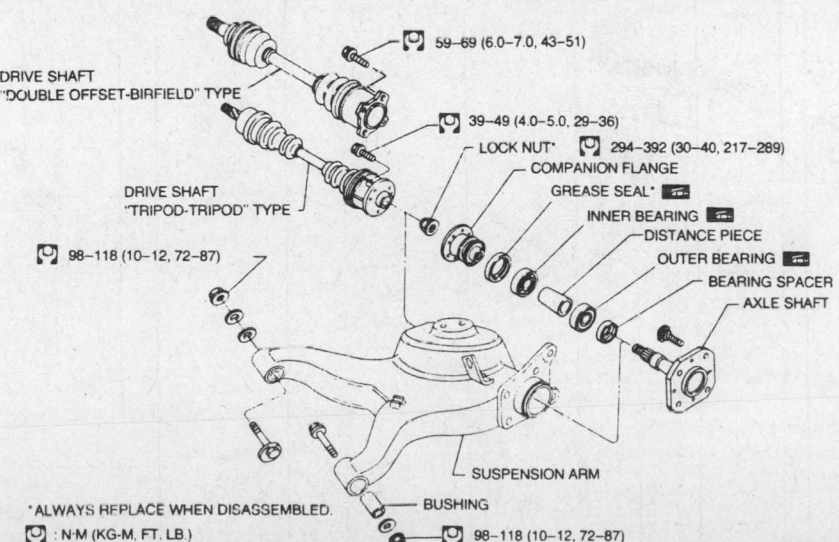

DRIVE SHAFT "DOUBLE OFFSET-BIRFIELD" TYPE

DRIVE SHAFT "TRIPOD-TRIPOD" TYPE

59–69 (6.0–7.0, 43–51)

39–49 (4.0–5.0, 29–36)

LOCK NUT* 294–392 (30–40, 217–289)

COMPANION FLANGE

GREASE SEAL*

INNER BEARING

DISTANCE PIECE

OUTER BEARING

BEARING SPACER

AXLE SHAFT

98–118 (10–12, 72–87)

SUSPENSION ARM

BUSHING

*ALWAYS REPLACE WHEN DISASSEMBLED.

: N·M (KG-M, FT. LB.)

98–118 (10–12, 72–87)

Exploded view of the rear axle shaft shown with either the "Double Off-set Birfield" type drive shaft or the "Tripod-Tripod" type drive shaft

wheel nuts, raise and support the car, and remove the wheel.

2. Apply the parking brake very firmly. This will help hold the stub axle while your remove the axle nut. You will probably also have to hold the stub axle at the outside while removing the nut from the axle shaft side. The nut will require a good deal of force to remove, so be sure to hold the stub axle firmly.

3. On cars with rear disc brakes, unbolt the caliper and move it aside. Do not disconnect the hose from the caliper. Do not allow the caliper to hang by the hose; support the caliper with a length of wire or rest it on a suspension member.

4. Remove the brake disc on models with rear disc brakes. Remove the brake drum on cars with drum brakes.

5. Remove the stub axle with a slide hammer and an adapter. The outer wheel bearing will come off with the stub axle.

6. Remove the companion flange from the lower arm.

7. Remove and discard the grease seal and inner bearing from the lower arm using a drift made for the purpose or a length of pipe of the proper diameter.

The outer bearing can be removed from the stub axle with a puller. If the grease seal or the bearings are removed, new parts must be used on assembly.

8. Clean all the parts to be reused in solvent.

9. Sealed-type bearings are used. When the new bearings are installed, the sealed side must face out. Install the sealed side of the outer bearing facing the wheel, and the sealed side of the inner bearing facing the differential.

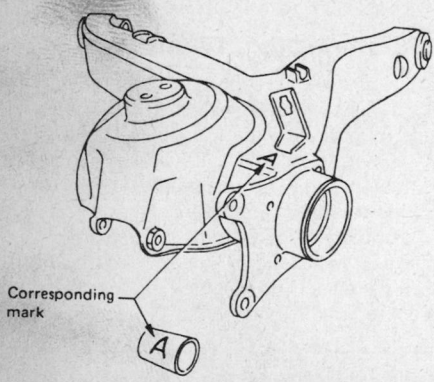

Corresponding mark

Match the bearing housing to the spacer with the proper letter

10. Press the outer bearing onto the stub axle.

11. The bearing housing is stamped with an "A", "B", or "C", through 1978. 1979 and later models have an "N", "M", or "P". Select a spacer with the same marking. Install the spacer on the stub axle.

12. Install the stub axle into the lower arm.

13. Install the new inner bearing into the lower arm with the stub axle in place. Install a new grease seal.

14. Install the companion flange onto the stub axle.

15. Install the stub axle nut. Tighten to 181–239 ft. lbs. (217–289 ft. lbs. on 300ZX).

16. Install the brake disc or drum, and the caliper if removed. Install the wheel and lower the car.

REAR SUSPENSION

Springs

REMOVAL & INSTALLATION

Leaf Spring Type
B210, 1978–79 200SX, and F10

1. Raise the rear axle until the wheels hang free. Support the car on stands. Support the rear axle with a jack.

2. Unbolt the bottom end of the shock absorber.

3. Unbolt the axle from the spring leaves. Unbolt and remove the front spring bracket. Lower the front of the spring to the floor.

4. Unbolt and remove the spring rear shackle.

5. Before reinstallation, coat the front bracket pin, bushing, shackle pin, and shackle bushing with a soap solution.

6. Reverse the procedure to install. The front pin nut and the shock absorber mounting should be tightened after the vehicle is lowered to the floor. Make sure that the elongated flange of the rubber bumper is to the rear.

510 AND 810 STATION WAGONS

1. Raise the rear of the car and support it with jackstands.

2. Remove the wheels and tires.

3. Disconnect the lower end of the shock absorber and remove the U-bolt nuts.

4. Place a jack under the rear axle.

5. Disconnect the spring shackle bolts at the front and rear of the spring.

6. Lower the jack slowly and remove the spring.

7. Installation is the reverse of removal.

Coil Spring Type

Four types of coil spring suspension are used:

Trailing Arm Type—F10, 310, Sentra and Pulsar
Four Bar Link Type—210, 510 and 1980–83 200SX
MacPherson Strut Type—810, Maxima, 280Z and ZX, 300ZX and Stanza
I.R.S. Coil Spring Type—1984 and later 200SX with independent rear suspension

—————— CAUTION ——————

Coil springs are under considerable tension and can exert enough force to cause bodily injury. Exercise extreme caution when working with them.

TRAILING ARM TYPE

1. Raise the rear of the vehicle and support it on jack stands.

2. Remove the wheels.

3. Disconnect the handbrake linkage and return spring.

4. Unbolt the axleshaft flange at the wheel end.

5. Unbolt the rubber bumper inside the bottom of the coil spring.

6. Jack up the suspension arm and unbolt the shock absorber lower mounting.

7. Lower the jack slowly and cautiously. Remove the coil spring, spring seat, and rubber bumper.

8. Reverse the procedure to install, making sure that the flat face of the spring is at the top.

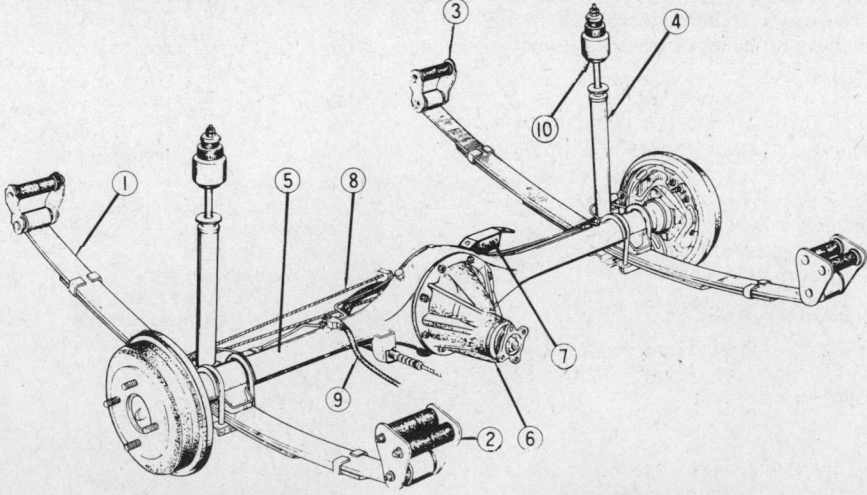

1. Leaf spring	6. Differential carrier
2. Front mounting	7. Torque arrester
3. Shackle	8. Handbrake cable
4. Shock absorber	9. Brake hose
5. Axle housing	10. Bound bumper

Typical leaf spring rear suspension—B210 shown

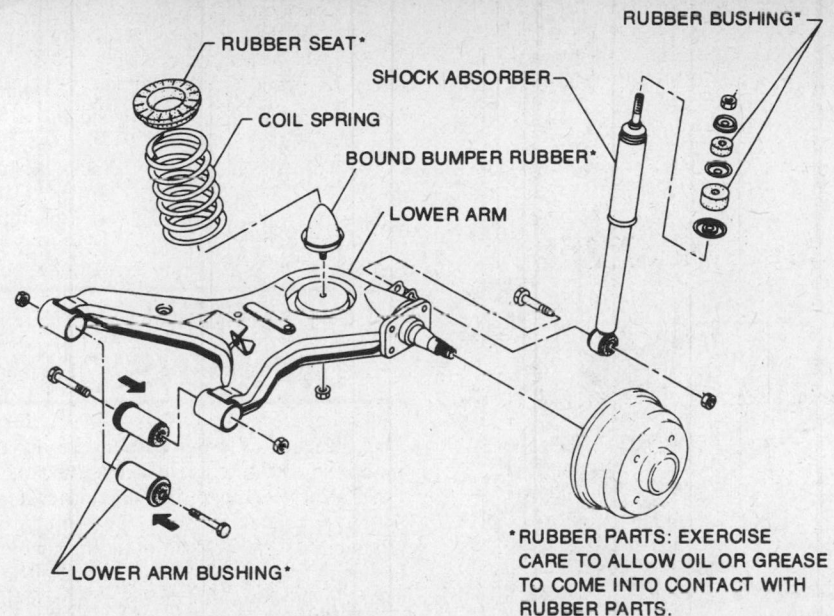

One side of a typical trailing arm rear suspension

* RUBBER PARTS: EXERCISE
CARE TO ALLOW OIL OR GREASE
TO COME INTO CONTACT WITH
RUBBER PARTS.

FOUR BAR LINK TYPE

1. Raise the car and support it with jackstands.
2. Support the center of the differential with a jack or other suitable tool.
3. Remove the rear wheels.
4. Remove the bolts securing the lower ends of the shock absorbers.
5. Lower the jack under the differential slowly and carefully and remove the coil springs after they are fully extended.
6. Installation is in the reverse order of removal.

I.R.S. Coil Spring Type

This suspension is similar to the I.R.S. MacPherson strut type, except this type utilizes separate coil springs and shock absorbers, instead of strut units.

1. Set a suitable spring compressor on the coil spring.
2. Jack up the rear end of the car.
3. Compress the coil spring until it is of sufficient length to be removed. Remove the spring.
4. When installing the spring, be sure the upper and lower spring seat rubbers are not twisted and have not slipped off when installing the coil spring.

MACPHERSON STRUT TYPE

For all strut overhaul procedures, please refer to "Strut Overhaul" in the Unit Repair section.

280Z

1. Raise and support the rear of the car with stands placed under the frame. Remove the wheels.
2. Disconnect and plug the brake hose where it connects to the tube; disconnect the parking brake cable.
3. Disconnect the stabilizer bar at the crossmember and transverse link.

4. Remove the transverse link outer spindle nuts and spindle bolt. Pull the spindle out and separate the transverse link and strut.
5. Disconnect the outer end of the halfshaft.
6. Place a jack under the lower end of the strut. Remove the upper mounting nuts of the strut inside the cargo compartment. Carefully and slowly lower the jack until all spring tension is released, and remove the strut.

7. Installation is the reverse. The spindle is installed with the shorter length (measured from the locking bolt notch) toward the front. Bleed the brakes after installation.
810 (Maxima), 280ZX, 300ZX and Stanza
The shock absorber and spring must be removed as a unit.

1. Block the front wheels. Raise the rear of the car until the suspension hangs free and support the car with stands under the frame members.
2. Remove the upper shock absorber mounting nuts (inside the trunk on the 810 and Maxima, or under covers in the cargo compartment in the ZX).
3. Disconnect the lower end of the shock and remove the assembly.
4. Installation is the reverse. Install the top end of the unit first.

Shock Absorber

REMOVAL & INSTALLATION

200SX and 210, and 510 Sedans

1. Open the trunk and remove the cover panel (if necessary) to expose the shock mounts. Pry off the mount covers, if so equipped. On leaf spring models, jack up the rear of the vehicle and support the rear axle on stands.
2. Remove the two nuts holding the top of the shock absorber. Unbolt the bottom of the shock absorber.
3. Remove the shock absorber.
4. Installation is the reverse of removal.

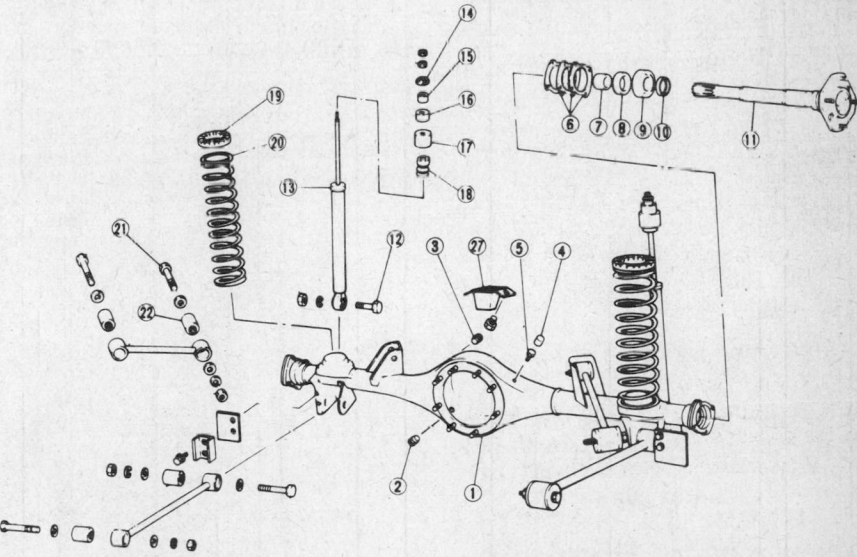

1. Rear axle case	12. Shock absorber lower end bolt
2. Drain plug	13. Shock absorber assembly
3. Filler plug	14. Special washer
4. Breather cap	15. Shock absorber mounting bushing
5. Breather	16. Shock absorber mounting bushing
6. Rear axle case end shim	17. Bound bumper cover
7. Bearing collar	18. Bound bumper rubber
8. Oil seal	19. Shock absorber mounting insulator
9. Rear axle bearing	20. Coil spring
10. Bearing spacer	21. Upper link bushing bolt
11. Rear axle shaft	22. Upper link bushing

Four link rear suspension

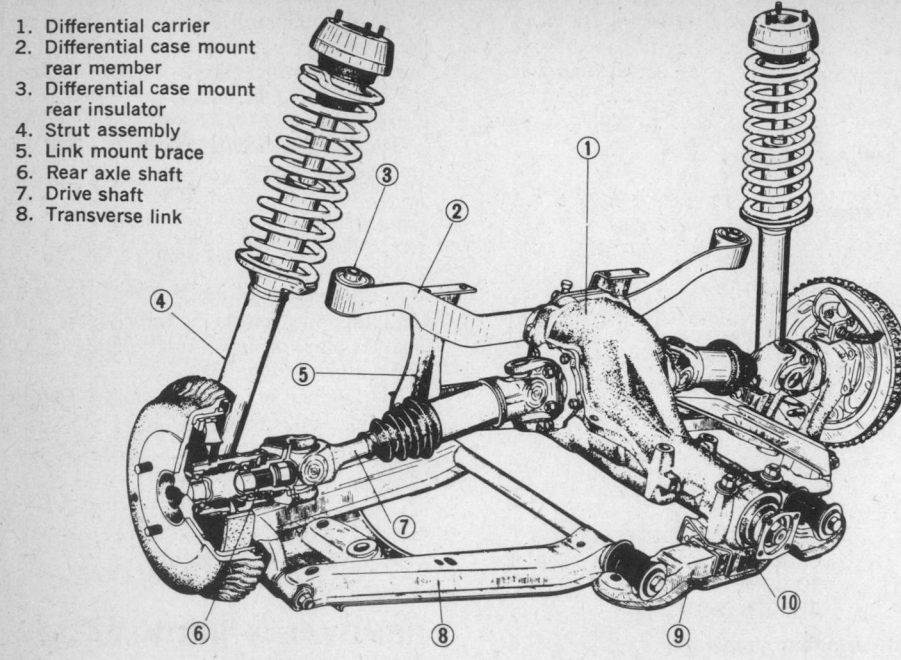

1. Differential carrier
2. Differential case mount rear member
3. Differential case mount rear insulator
4. Strut assembly
5. Link mount brace
6. Rear axle shaft
7. Drive shaft
8. Transverse link
9. Differential case mount front member
10. Differential case mount front insulator

MacPherson strut-type rear suspension—1978 280Z shown (rear drum brake model)

510, 810 (Maxima) Station Wagons

1. Raise the rear of the car and support the axle on jack stands.
2. Remove the lower retaining nut on the shock absorber.
3. Remove the upper retaining bolt(s).
4. Remove the shock from under the car.

F-10, 310, Sentra and Pulsar

1. Raise and support the rear of the car.
2. Remove the wheels.
3. Support the rear arm with a jack at the lower end.
4. Remove the upper and lower shock mounting nuts.
5. Slowly and carefully lower the jack and remove the shock.
6. Installation is the reverse.

810, 280Z and ZX, Maxima, 300ZX and Stanza

For all strut removal and installation procedures and all strut overhaul procedures, please refer to "Strut Overhaul" in the Unit Repair section.

Rear Wheel Bearings

ADJUSTMENT

F-10 and 310

The rear wheel bearings on the F-10 and 310 are adjusted in the same manner as front wheel bearings. Use this procedure for all F-10 and 310 models.

1. Raise the rear of the car.

2. Remove the wheel.
3. Remove and discard the cotter pin.
4. Tighten the wheel bearing lock nut to 18–22 ft. lbs. (F-10) 29–33 ft. lbs. (310).
5. Rotate the drum back and forth a few revolutions to snug down the bearing.
6. On the F-10, loosen the locknut, then tighten handtight.
7. On the 310, after turning the wheel, recheck the torque of the nut then loosen it 90° from its position.

8. Check the drum rotation. If it does not move freely, check for dragging brake shoes, or dirty bearings.
9. Align the cotter pin hole in the spindle with that in the locknut, and install a new cotter pin.
10. Turn the nut slightly clockwise on the F-10 to align the holes. On the 310, tighten the nut no more than 15° to align the holes.

FRONT SUSPENSION

The independent front suspension on all models covered here uses MacPherson struts. Each strut combines the function of coil spring and shock absorber. The spindle is mounted to the lower part of the strut which has a single ball joint. No upper suspension arm is required in this design. The spindle and lower suspension transverse link (control arm) are located fore and aft by the tension rods to the front part of the chassis on most models. Compression rods, which run rearward, are used on the 280Z. A cross-chassis sway bar is used on all models.

Strut

REMOVAL & INSTALLATION

All Models

1. Jack up the car and support it safely. Remove the wheel.

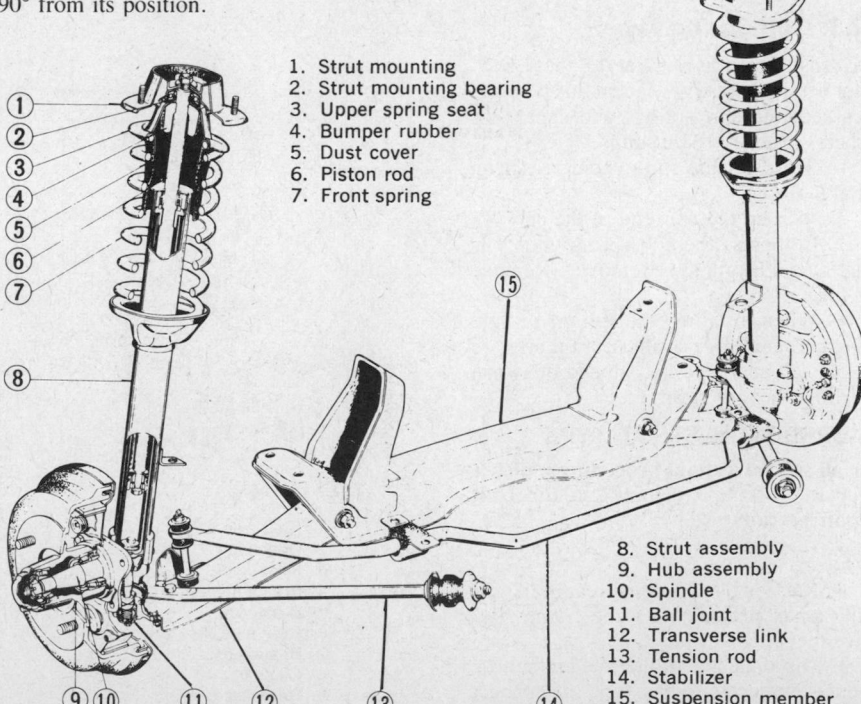

1. Strut mounting
2. Strut mounting bearing
3. Upper spring seat
4. Bumper rubber
5. Dust cover
6. Piston rod
7. Front spring

8. Strut assembly
9. Hub assembly
10. Spindle
11. Ball joint
12. Transverse link
13. Tension rod
14. Stabilizer
15. Suspension member

B210 strut-type front suspension. On the 280Z, the tension rods are replaced by compression rods running to the rear

2. Disconnect and plug the brake hose.

3. Disconnect the tension rod (compression rod on the "Z" series) and stabilizer bar from the transverse link.

4. Unbolt the steering arm.

5. Place a jack under the bottom of the strut.

6. Open the hood and remove the nuts holding the top of the strut.

7. Lower the jack slowly and cautiously until the strut assembly can be removed.

8. Reverse the procedure to install. The self locking nuts holding the top of the strut must be replaced.

OVERHAUL

For all spring and shock absorber removal and installation procedures and any other strut overhaul procedures, please refer to "Strut Overhaul" in the Unit Repair section.

Ball Joint

INSPECTION

The lower ball joint should be replaced when play becomes excessive. Datsun does not publish specifications for this, giving instead a rotational torque figure for the ball joint. However, this requires removal for measurement. An effective way to determine play is to jack up the car until the wheel is clear of the ground. Do not place the jack under the ball joint; it must be unloaded. Place a long bar under the tire and move the wheel up and down. Keep one hand on top of the tire while doing this. If ¼ in. or more of play exists at the top of the tire, the ball joint should be replaced.

Be sure the wheel bearings are properly adjusted before making this measurement. A double check can be made; while the tire is being moved up and down, observe the ball joint. If play is seen, replace the ball joint.

REMOVAL & INSTALLATION

Rear Wheel Drive Models

The ball joint should be greased every 30,000 miles. There is a plugged hole in the bottom of the joint for installation of a grease fitting.

1. Raise and support the car so the wheels hang free. Remove the wheel.

2. Unbolt the tension rod (compression rod on "Z" series) and stabilizer bar from transverse link.

3. Unbolt the strut from the steering arm.

4. Remove the cotter pin and ball joint stud nut. Separate the ball joint and steering arm.

5. Unbolt the ball joint from the transverse link.

6. Reverse the procedure to install a new ball joint. Grease the joint after installation.

F-10

1. Raise the car and support it with safety stands. Remove the wheel and tire.

2. Remove the nut holding the ball stud to the knuckle and force out the stud with a ball joint fork, being careful not to damage the ball joint dust cover.

3. Remove the ball joint bolts and ball joint.

Install the ball joint in the reverse order

of removal. Tighten the ball stud attaching nut to 22–29 ft. lbs., and the ball joint–to–transverse link attaching bolts to 40–47 ft. lbs.

310, Sentra, Stanza and Pulsar

1. Jack up the car and support it on stands.

2. Remove the wheel.

3. Remove the halfshaft.

4. Separate the ball joint from the steering knuckle with a ball joint remover, being careful not to damage the ball joint dust cover if the ball joint is to be used again.

5. Remove the other ball joint from the transverse link and remove the ball joint.

Installation is the reverse of removal. Tighten the ball stud attaching nut (from ball joint–to–steering knuckle) to 22–29 ft. lbs., and the ball joint–to–transverse link bolts to 40–47 ft. lbs.

Lower Control Arm (Transverse Link) and Ball Joint

REMOVAL & INSTALLATION

You'll need a ball joint remover for this operation.

1. Jack up the vehicle and support it with jackstands; remove the wheel.

2. Remove the splash board, if so equipped.

3. Remove the cotter pin and castle nut from the side rod (steering arm) ball joint and separate the ball joint from the side rod. You'll need either a fork type or puller type ball joint remover.

4. Separate the steering knuckle arm from the MacPherson strut.

5. Remove the tension rod and stabilizer bar from the lower arm. Front wheel drive models do not have tension rods. On Z models, 1978 remove the compression rod.

6. Remove the nuts or bolts connecting the lower control arm (transverse link) to the suspension crossmember on all models.

7. On the 810 and Maxima, to remove the transverse link (control arm) on the steering gear side, separate the gear arm from the sector shaft and lower steering linkage; to remove the transverse link on the idler arm side, detach the idler arm assembly from the body frame and lower steering linkage.

8. Remove the lower control arm (transverse link) with the suspension ball joint and knuckle arm still attached.

Installation is the reverse of removal with the following notes.

9. When installing the control arm, temporarily tighten the nuts and/or bolts securing the control arm to the suspension crossmember. Tighten them fully only after the car is sitting on its wheels.

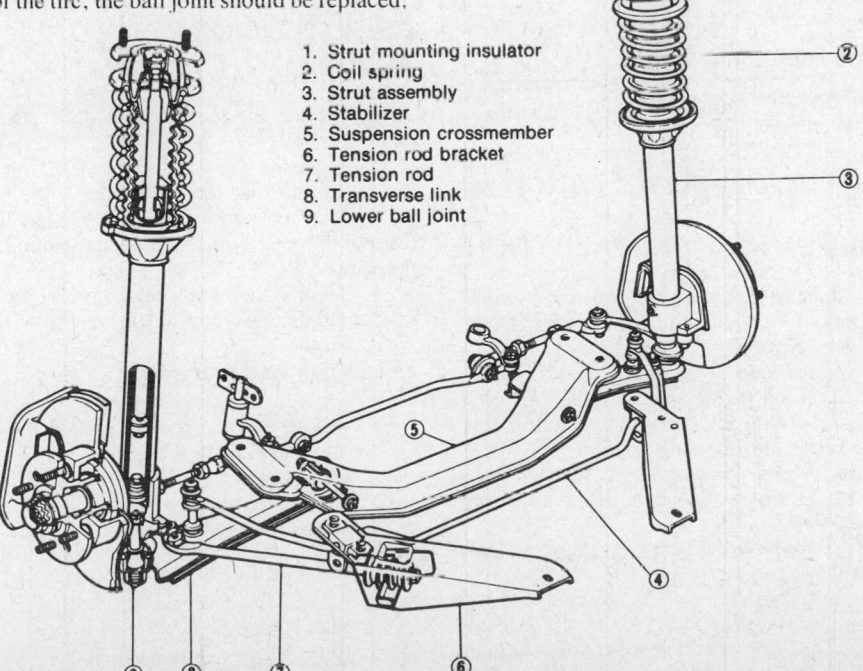

1. Strut mounting insulator
2. Coil spring
3. Strut assembly
4. Stabilizer
5. Suspension crossmember
6. Tension rod bracket
7. Tension rod
8. Transverse link
9. Lower ball joint

Strut-type front suspension, 200SX. 510 and early 810 similar; later 810, Maxima, Sentra, Pulsar, Stanza similar except rack and pinion steering

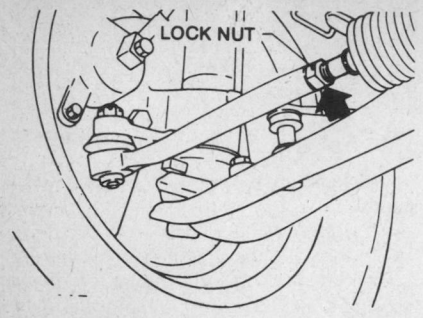

Toe adjustment is made at the tie-rod

10. Lubricate the ball joints after assembly.

Wheel Alignment

Caster and camber angles cannot be adjusted except by replacing worn or bent parts. Suspension height is adjusted by replacing the front springs. Various springs are available for adjustment. Toe-in is adjusted by changing the length of the steering side-rods. The length of these rods should always be equal. Steering angles are adjusted by means of a stop bolt on each steering arm.

STEERING

Steering Wheel

REMOVAL & INSTALLATION

1. Position the wheels in the straight-ahead direction. The steering wheel should be right-side up and level.
2. Disconnect the battery ground cable.
3. Look at the back of your steering wheel. If there are countersunk screws in the back of the steering wheel spokes, remove the screws and pull off the horn pad. Some models have a horn wire running from the pad to the steering wheel. Disconnect it.

There are three other types of horn buttons or rings on Datsuns and Nissans. The first simply pulls off. The second, which is usually a large, semi-triangular pad, must be pushed up, then pulled off. The third must be pushed in and turned clockwise.

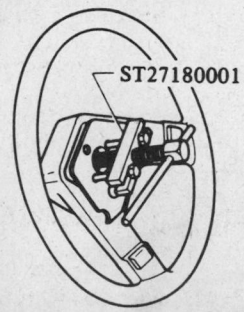

ST27180001

Use a puller to remove the steering wheel

4. Remove the rest of the horn switching mechanism, noting the relative location of the parts. Remove the mechanism only if it hinders subsequent wheel removal procedures.
5. Match-mark the top of the steering column shaft and the steering wheel flange.
6. Remove the attaching nut and remove the steering wheel with a puller.

───── CAUTION ─────
Do not strike the shaft with a hammer; which may cause the column to collapse.

7. Install the steering wheel in the reverse order of removal, aligning the punch marks. Do not drive or hammer the wheel into place, or you may cause the collapsible steering column to collapse; in which case you'll have to buy a whole new steering column unit.
8. Tighten the steering wheel nut to 22–25 ft. lbs. on the B210, 310, 1978–79 200SX. Tighten all other steering wheel nuts to 28–36 ft. lbs.
9. Reinstall the horn button, pad, or ring.

STEERING APPLICATIONS

Model	Type
510, B210, 210, 200SX, 810, 280ZX①	Recirculating ball
280Z, F-10, 280ZX②, 300ZX, 310, Sentra, Pulsar, 810, Maxima 1982 and later Stanza	Rack and pinion

① Power steering
② Manual steering

Turn Signal Switch

REMOVAL & INSTALLATION

On some later models, the turn signal switch is part of a combination switch. The whole unit is removed together.

1. Disconnect the battery ground cable.
2. Remove the steering wheel as previously outlined. Observe the "caution" on the collapsible steering column.
3. Remove the steering column covers.
4. Disconnect the electrical plugs from the switch.
5. Remove the retaining screws and remove the switch.
6. Installation is the reverse of removal. Many models have turn signal switches that have a tab which must fit into a hole in the steering shaft in order for the system to return the switch to the neutral position after the turn has been made. Be

sure to align the tab and the hole when installing.

Steering Lock

The steering lock/ignition switch/warning buzzer switch assembly is attached to the steering column by special screws whose heads shear off on installation. The screws must be drilled out to remove the assembly. The ignition switch is on the back of the assembly, and the warning switch on the side. The warning buzzer, which sounds when the driver's door is opened with the steering unlocked, is located behind the instrument panel.

Steering lock securing screw—1978–79 200SX. Others similar

Power Steering Pump

REMOVAL & INSTALLATION

1. Disconnect and plug the hoses at the pump.
2. Disconnect the pump mounting bolts and remove the drive belt.
3. Remove the pump. Installation is the reverse. Adjust the belt tension after installation, and fill and bleed the system.

BELT TENSION ADJUSTMENT

1. Loosen the tension adjustment and mounting bolts.
2. Move the pump toward or away from the engine so that the belt deflects ¼–½ in. midway between the idler pulley and the pump pulley under moderate thumb pressure.
3. Tighten the bolts and recheck the tension adjustment.

SYSTEM BLEEDING

1. Fill the pump reservoir and allow to remain undisturbed for a few minutes.
2. Raise the car until the front wheels are clear of the ground.
3. With the engine off, quickly turn the wheels right and left several times, lightly contacting the stops.
4. Add fluid if necessary.
5. Start the engine and let it idle.
6. Repeat Steps 3 and 4 with the engine idling.
7. With the steering wheel all the way to the left, open the bleeder screw on the

steering gear to allow the air to bleed. Close the screw when fluid is expelled.

8. Stop the engine, lower the car until the wheels just touch the ground. Start the engine, allow it to idle, and turn the wheels back and forth several times. Check the fluid level and refill if necessary.

BRAKE SYSTEM

Front disc brakes are used on all models, with drum brakes at the rear. 1979 and later 280ZX, 300ZX, 1980 and later 200SX and later model 810 and Maxima models have rear disc brakes. All models have a vacuum booster system to lessen required pedal pressure. The parking brake operates the rear brakes through a cable system.

For all brake system repair and service procedures not detailed below, please refer to "Brakes" in the Unit Repair section.

Adjustment

There are four basic types of brake adjusting systems used. Only drum brakes require periodic adjustment; disc brakes are self-adjusting.

To adjust the brakes, raise the wheels, disconnect the handbrake linkage from the rear wheels, apply the brakes hard a few times to center the drums, and proceed as follows:

BOLT ADJUSTER

Turn the adjuster bolt on the backing plate until the wheel can no longer be turned, then back off until the wheel is free of drag. Repeat the procedure on the other adjuster bolt on the same wheel. Some models may have only one adjuster bolt per wheel.

BOLT ADJUSTER WITH CLICK ARRANGEMENT

The adjuster is located on the backing plate. The adjustment proceeds in clicks or notches. The wheel will often be locked temporarily as the adjuster passes over center for each click. Thus the adjuster is alternately hard and easy to turn. When the wheel is fully locked, back off 1–3 clicks.

STAR WHEEL ADJUSTER

Remove the rubber boot from the backing plate. Insert a screwdriver through the adjusting hole to engage the toothed wheel. Turn the adjuster teeth down until the wheel is locked, then push them up 10-12 notches so that the wheel is free of drag.

SELF-ADJUSTING

No manual adjustment is required. The self-adjusters operate whenever the hand or foot brakes are used.

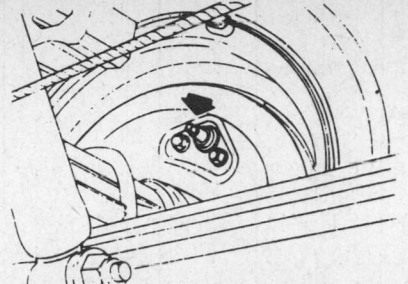

Bolt adjuster

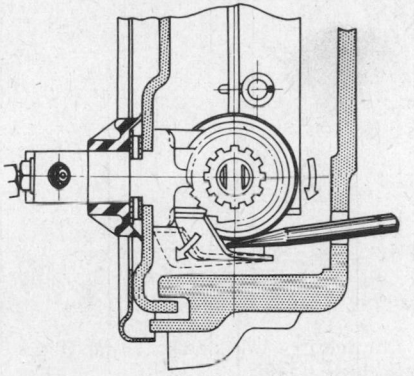

Loosening the "Z" series rear brake adjuster

After Adjustment

After adjusting the brakes, reconnect the handbrake linkage. Make sure that there is no rear wheel drag with the handbrake released. Loosen the handbrake adjustment if necessary.

Master Cylinder

REMOVAL & INSTALLATION

Clean the outside of the cylinder thoroughly, particularly around the cap and fluid

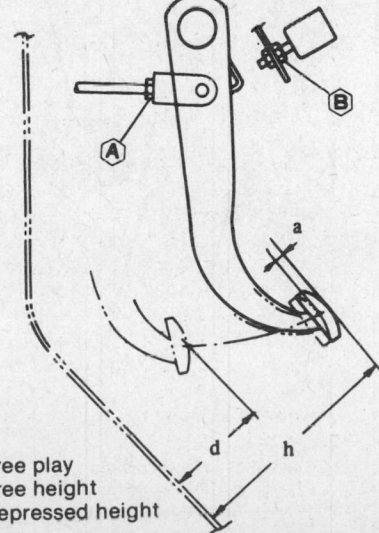

Free play
Free height
Depressed height

Brake pedal adjustment—all models. "B" shows locknut

lines. On ZX models, remove the heat-shield plate. Disconnect the fluid lines and cap them to exclude dirt. On models with a fluid level gauge, disconnect the electrical connector. Remove the clevis pin connecting the pushrod to the brake pedal arm inside the vehicle. This pin need not be removed on models with the vacuum booster. Unbolt the master cylinder from the firewall and remove. If the pushrod is not adjustable, there will be shims between the cylinder and the firewall. These shims, or the adjustable pushrod, are used to adjust brake pedal free-play. After installation, bleed the system and check for pedal free-play. The 1980 and later 200SX's pushrod is not adjustable, as the rod between the brake booster and the master cylinder is secured by adhesion. After installation, bleed the system and check the pedal free-play.

PEDAL ADJUSTMENT

NOTE: Ordinary brake fluid will boil and cause brake failure under the high temperatures developed in disc brake systems. Special fluid meeting DOT 3 or 4 specifications for disc brake systems must be used.

Before adjusting the pedal, make sure that the wheelbrakes are correctly adjusted.

Adjust the pedal free-play by means of an adjustable pushrod or shims between the master cylinder and the firewall. Adjust the pedal height by means of the pedal arm stop pad. Free-play should be approximately 0.04–0.20 in on all models. Pedal height (floorboard to pedal pad) should be approximately 6 in. on all B210s, 1978–80 510s and 1980 and later 200SX and 210 models; 7 in. on all 200SX, 810, Maxima and F-10 models; 8 in. on all Z models, except 7.6 in. on the 300ZX; 8 in. on the Sentra and Pulsar and 6 in. on the Stanza.

Parking Brake

ADJUSTMENT

Handbrake adjustments are generally not needed, unless the cables have stretched.

All Models Except the "Z" Series

There is an adjusting nut on the cable under the car, usually at the end of the front cable and near the point at which the two cables from the rear wheels come together (the equalizer).

1. Adjust the rear brakes with the parking brake fully released.

2. Apply the handbrake lever so that it is approximately 3–3½ in. from its fully released position.

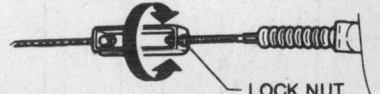

LOCK NUT

Parking brake adjustment turnbuckle, underneath car

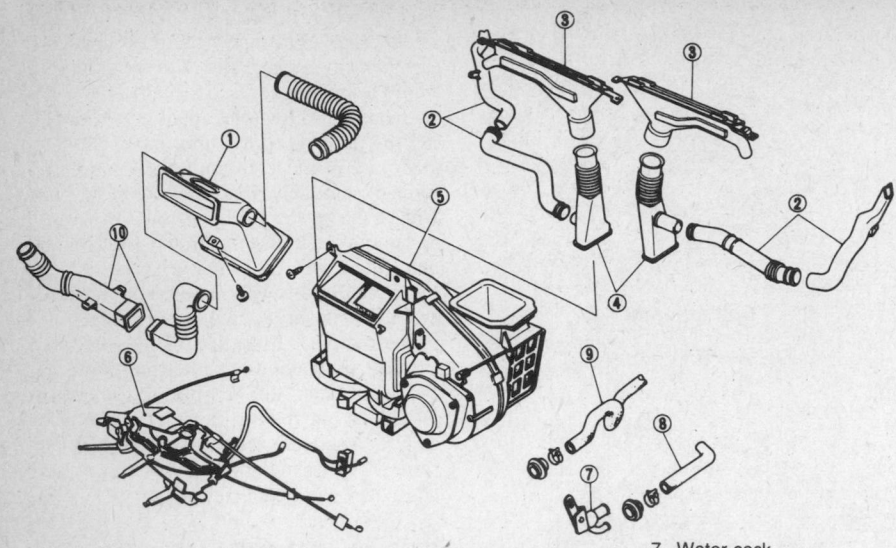

1. Center ventilation duct
2. Side defroster duct
3. Defroster nozzle
4. Defroster duct
5. Heater unit
6. Heater control
7. Water cock
8. Water inlet hose
9. Water outlet hose
10. Air cond. duct

210 heater assembly

3. Adjust the parking brake turnbuckle, locknuts, or equalizer so that the rear brakes are locked.

4. Release the parking brake. The wheels should be free to turn. If not, loosen the parking brake adjuster until the wheels turn with no drag.

280Z

The driveshaft must be removed to gain access to the adjusting nut on the front linkage rod.

1. Release the handbrake fully and block the vehicle wheels.

2. Loosen the locknut at the rear of the front rod.

3. Measure the dimension between the wheel cylinder lever pin hole centers and their respective buffer plates.

4. Rotate the front rod to bring the dimension to 0.453–0.492 in. (11.5–12.5 mm) on both sides.

5. Tighten the locknut at the rear of the front rod.

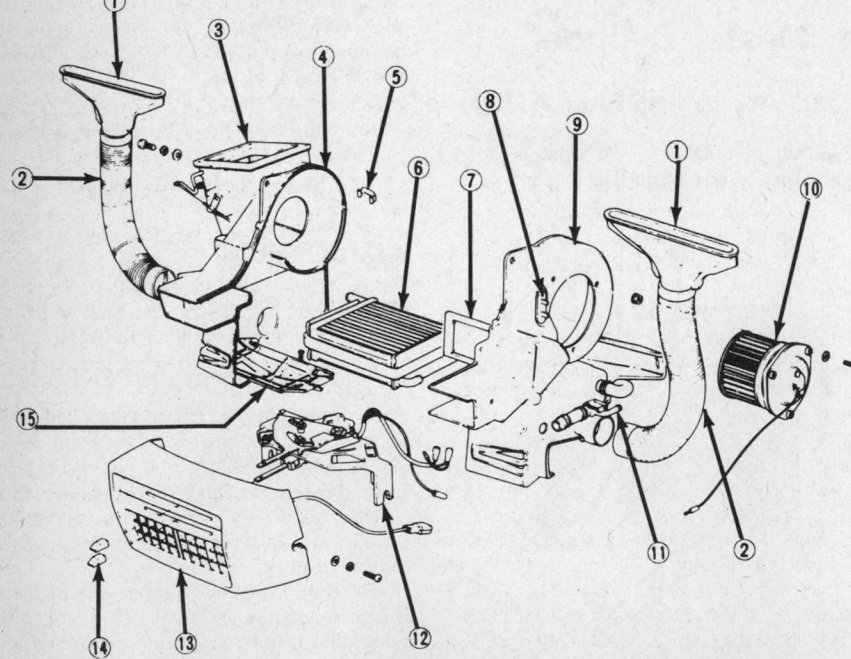

1. Defroster nozzle
2. Defroster hose
3. Air intake box
4. Heater box (L.H.)
5. Clip
6. Heater core
7. Ventilator valve
8. Resistor
9. Heater box (R.H.)
10. Fan and fan motor
11. Heater cock
12. Heater control
13. Center ventilator
14. Knob
15. Heat valve

B210 heater

280ZX and 300ZX

1. Pull up the handbrake lever, counting the number of ratchet clicks for full engagement. Full engagement should be reached in 4–6 notches on the 280ZX, 8–9 notches on the 300ZX.

2. Release the parking brake.

3. Adjust the lever stroke at the cable equalizer under the car: loosen the locknut and tighten the adjusting nut to reduce the number of ratchet clicks necessary for engagement. Tighten the locknut.

4. Check the adjustment and repeat as necessary.

5. After adjustment, check to see that the rear brake levers (at the calipers) return to their full off positions when the lever is released, and that the rear cables are not slack when the lever is released.

6. To adjust the warning lamp, bend the warning lamp switch plate down so that the light comes on when the lever is engaged one notch.

CHASSIS ELECTRICAL

Heater Unit

REMOVAL & INSTALLATION

F-10

1. Disconnect the battery ground cable and drain the coolant.

2. Disconnect the inlet and outlet hoses and remove the defroster hoses from each side of the heater unit.

3. Remove the cable retaining clamps for the heater valve, floor door and intake door.

4. Disconnect the electrical connectors. Remove the four unit retaining screws and remove the heater unit.

5. Installation is the reverse of removal.

B210

1. Disconnect the battery ground strap.

2. Drain the engine coolant.

3. Remove the defroster hose from both sides of the heater unit.

4. Disconnect the electrical wires from the heater unit.

5. Remove the clamps and disconnect the water hose from the right side of the heater.

6. Remove one attaching bolt from each side of the unit and one at the top center and remove the unit by pulling forward and out.

7. Reverse the procedure for installation.

210 and 510

1. Disconnect the ground cable at the battery. Drain the coolant.

2. Remove the console.

3. Remove the driver's side of the instrument panel. See the following section.

4. Remove the heater control assembly: remove the defroster ducts, door cables at the doors, harness connector, and control assembly.

5. Remove the radio.

6. Disconnect the heater ducts, side defrosters, and center vent duct.

7. Remove the screws attaching the defroster nozzle to the unit. Disconnect the blower wire, and the heater hoses

8. Remove the retaining bolts and the heater unit.

9. Installation is the reverse of removal.

310 without A/C

1. Disconnect the battery ground cable.

2. Set the temperature lever to the HOT position and drain the engine coolant.

3. Remove the instrument panel assembly. See the following section for instructions.

4. Disconnect the control cables and rod from the heater unit. Disconnect the heater motor harness.

310 with A/C

1. Disconnect the battery ground.

2. Set the temperature control lever to HOT and drain the cooling system.

3. Remove the instrument panel.

4. Disconnect the hoses at the core.

5. Disconnect all wiring from the unit.

6. Loosen the band seal at the joint between the cooling and heater units.

7. Unbolt and remove the heater.

Sentra and Pulsar

1. Set the "TEMP" lever to the maximum "HOT" position and drain the engine coolant.

2. Disconnect the heater hoses at the engine compartment.

3. Remove the instrument assembly.

4. Remove the heater control assembly.

5. Remove the heater unit assembly. Installation is the reverse of removal.

Stanza without A/C

1. Remove the instrument panel.

2. Disconnect the heater hoses and vacuum tube in the engine compartment.

3. Remove the heater control assembly.

4. Unbolt and remove the heater unit.

5. Installation is the reverse of removal.

1978–79 200SX

1. Disconnect the battery ground cable. Drain the coolant. Disconnect the heater hose clamp at the engine.

2. Inside the car, disconnect the electrical connectors at each side of the instrument panel.

3. Remove the instrument panel: Remove the steering column covers; disconnect the speedometer cable and radio antenna cable; disconnect all electrical

connectors; remove the steering column clamp bolts; remove the package tray; remove the bolts attaching the panel to the side brackets; remove the right windshield pillar moulding and remove the panel bolt there; remove the panel moulding; remove the panel bolts and remove the panel.

4. Remove the defroster hoses. Remove the coolant hoses.

5. On air conditioned models, disconnect the electrical wires between the heater and a/c unit.

6. Remove the three bolts and heater.

7. Installation is the reverse of removal.

1980 and Later 200SX

1. Set the TEMP lever to the HOT position and drain the coolant.

2. Disconnect the heater hoses from the driver's side of the heater unit.

3. At this point the manufacturer suggests removing the front seats. To do this, remove the plastic covers over the ends of the seat runners, both front and back, to expose the seat mounting bolts. Remove the bolts and remove the seats.

4. Remove the console box and the floor carpets.

5. Remove the instrument panel lower covers from both the driver's and passenger's sides of the car. Remove the lower cluster lids.

6. Remove the left hand side ventilator duct.

7. Remove the radio, sound balancer and stereo cassette deck.

8. Remove the instrument panel-to-transmission tunnel stay.

9. Remove the rear heater duct from the floor of the vehicle.

10. Remove the center ventilator duct.

11. Remove the left- and right-hand side air guides from the lower heater outlets.

12. Disconnect the wire harness connections.

13. Remove the two screws at the bottom sides of the heater unit and the one screw and the top of the unit and remove the unit together with the heater control assembly.

Installation is the reverse of removal.

NOTE: You may be able to skip several of the above steps if only certain components of the heater unit need service.

710

1. Disconnect the battery ground strap.

2. Drain the engine coolant. Disconnect the heater hoses at the firewall (engine compartment side).

3. Remove the intake duct hose and defroster duct from both sides of the heater unit. Remove the console box if so equipped.

4. Disconnect the electrical wires at the connectors.

5. Loosen the retaining clamps and remove the control cables.

6. Remove the two bolts on each side of the unit and one on top. Remove the unit from the vehicle.

7. Install in the reverse of the above.

1978–80 810

1. Disconnect the battery ground cable.

2. Drain the engine coolant.

3. Remove the console box and the console box bracket. Remove the front floor mat.

4. Loosen the screws and remove the rear heater duct.

5. Remove the hose clamps and remove the inlet and outlet hoses.

6. Remove the heater duct and remove the defroster hoses from the assembly.

7. Remove the air intake door control cable.

8. Disconnect the wiring harness to the heater.

9. Remove the retaining bolts and remove the heater unit.

10. Installation is the reverse of removal.

1981–85 810 and Maxima

NOTE: You may be able to skip several of the following steps if only certain components of the heater assembly need service.

1. Set the TEMP lever to the HOT position and drain the coolant.

2. Disconnect the heater hoses from the driver's side of the heater unit.

3. At this point the manufacturer suggests removing the front seats. To do this, remove the plastic covers over the ends of the seat runners, front and back, to expose the seat mounting bolts. Remove the bolts and lift out the seats.

4. Remove the front floor carpets.

5. Remove the instrument panel lower covers from both the driver's and passenger's sides of the car.

6. Remove the left side ventilator duct.

7. Remove the instrument panel assembly as detailed later in this chapter.

8. Remove the rear heater duct from the floor of the car.

9. Tag and disconnect the wire harness connectors.

10. Remove the two screws at the bottom sides of the heater unit and the one screw from the top of the unit. Lift out the heater together with the heater control assembly.

11. Installation is the reverse of removal.

280Z without A/C

1. Disconnect the negative battery cable.

2. Remove the clamp at the air intake duct so as to disconnect the air intake box control cable.

3. Disconnect the blower and resistor wires at the connectors.

4. Remove the retaining screws and remove the blower unit.

5. The motor and fan may be separated from the blower unit by removing the three mounting screws. Be careful to retain the washers and spacers.

6. Reassembly is accomplished in reverse order. When reassembling the control

cable for the air intake door, set the AIR lever in the OFF position and position the wire in the clamp so that the door will just be closed.

280Z with A/C

1. Disconnect the battery negative cable. Disconnect the vacuum hose at the intake door actuator.
2. Remove the defroster duct which is located near the passenger seat.
3. Disconnect the connectors at the blower motor and at the resistor.
4. Remove the three housing mounting bolts and remove the housing.
5. The motor may be removed by removing the three bolts and pulling it out. Be careful to retain the three washers and three spacers.
6. Installation is the reverse of removal.

280ZX without A/C

1. Disconnect the negative battery cable.
2. Remove the lower instrument panel cover and the glove box.
3. Remove the floor nozzle, defroster duct, and the side defroster duct on the right side.
4. Remove the heater duct.
5. Disconnect the blower motor wiring harness.
6. Disconnect the control cable at the blower assembly by removing the clip.
7. Remove the bolts securing the blower assembly to the firewall and remove the blower assembly.
8. The motor and fan can be removed by removing the three motor retaining screws. The fan simply bolts onto the motor shaft.

9. Installation is in the reverse order of removal.
The motor and fan can also be removed without removing the entire blower housing assembly:
1. Disconnect the negative battery cable.
2. Remove the lower instrument panel cover and the floor nozzle on the right side.
3. Disconnect the blower motor wiring harness.
4. Remove the three motor attaching screws and remove the motor and fan as a unit from the blower housing.

280ZX with A/C

1. Disconnect the negative battery cable.
2. Remove the instrument panel lower cover on the right side. Remove the glove box.
3. Remove the floor nozzle, the defroster duct, and the side defroster duct on the passenger's side.
4. Disconnect the blower motor electrical harness.
5. Disconnect and label the two vacuum hoses.
6. Remove the three blower assembly mounting bolts and remove the assembly.
7. Installation is the reverse order of removal.
The motor can be removed without removing the blower assembly:
1. Disconnect the negative battery cable.
2. Remove the instrument panel lower cover and the floor nozzle on the right side.
3. Disconnect the blower motor electrical harness.
4. Remove the three blower motor attaching screws and remove the motor and fan as an assembly from the blower housing.

5. Installation is the reverse.

Heater Core

REMOVAL & INSTALLATION

B210 and F-10

1. Remove the heater from the car.
2. Remove the clip and slide the hose from the cock.
3. Pry off the five clips and separate the left and right sides of the heater case.
4. Lift out the heater core.

280Z

1. Remove the heater from the car.
2. Loosen the clamp on the heater cock side.
3. Remove the screws retaining the heater cock and remove from the case.
4. Loosen the clamp on the core side and disconnect the hose.
5. Remove the E-ring from the floor door operating rod.
6. Remove the five screws and take off the side cover. Pull out the heater core with the floor door open.
7. Assembly is the reverse of the above.

1978–79 200SX

1. Remove the heater unit.
2. Remove the control lever assembly. Remove the knobs, disconnect the lamp wire, remove the center vent (4 screws), disconnect the fan wires, remove the clips and cables, remove the retaining screws and the unit.
3. Disconnect the hose from the heater cock.
4. Remove the connecting rod (with bracket) from the air door.
5. Remove the clips on each side of the box, split the box, and remove the core.
6. Installation is the reverse of removal.

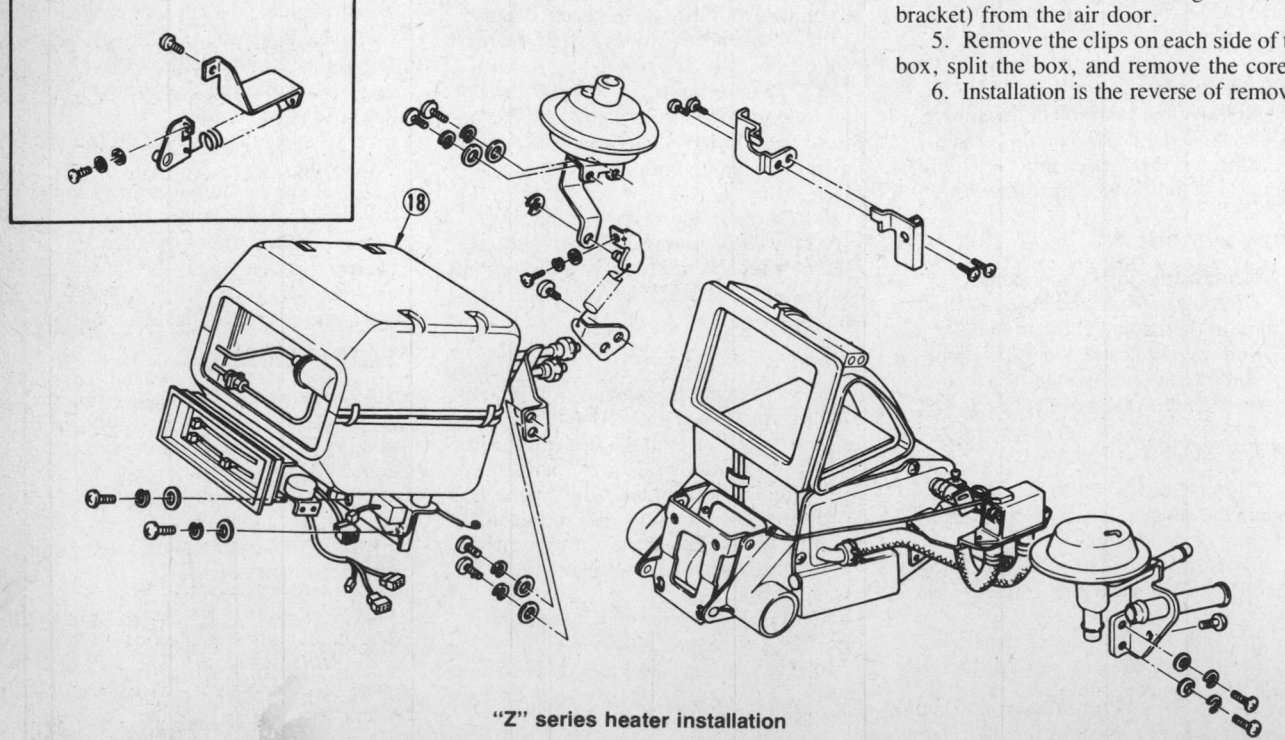

"Z" series heater installation

1980 and Later 200SX

1. Remove the heater unit as described earlier.
2. Remove the hoses from the heater core and remove the core.
3. Installation is the reverse of removal.

1978 and Later 510, 210, Sentra and Pulsar

1. Remove the heater unit.
2. Disconnect the inlet and outlet hoses.
3. Remove the case clips and split the case. Remove the core.
4. Installation is the reverse of removal.

810 and Maxima

1. Remove the heater unit.
2. Remove the center vent cover and heater control assembly, loosening the clips and screws.
3. Remove the screws securing the door shafts.
4. Remove the clips from the case and split the case. Remove the core.
5. Installation is the reverse of removal.

280ZX

1. Remove the heater unit.
2. Remove the water cock.
3. Remove the case clips and split the heater case. Remove the core.

310

1. Remove the heater unit from the vehicle.
2. Disconnect the inlet and outlet hoses from the core if you have not done so already.
3. Remove the clips securing the case halves and separate the halves.
4. Remove the heater core.
5. Installation is the reverse of removal.

Stanza

1. Remove pedal bracket mounting bolts, steering column mounting bolts, brake and clutch pedal cotter pins.

2. Move the pedal bracket and steering column to the left.
3. Disconnect the air mix door control cable and heater valve control lever, then remove the control lever.
4. Remove the core cover.
5. Disconnect the hoses at the core.
6. Installation is the reverse of removal. Be sure to bleed the system.

Windshield Wiper Motor

REMOVAL & INSTALLATION

280Z, 810 and Maxima

The wiper motor and operating linkage is on the firewall under the hood.
1. Lift the wiper arms. Remove the securing nuts and detach the arms.
2. Remove the nuts holding the wiper pivots to the body. Remove the air intake grille for access.
3. Open the hood and unscrew the motor from the firewall.
4. Disconnect the wiring connector and remove the wiper motor with the linkage.
5. Reverse the procedure for installation.

NOTE: If the wipers do not park correctly, adjust the position of the automatic stop cover on the wiper motor.

B210, Sentra and Pulsar

The wiper motor is on the firewall under the hood. The operating linkage is on the firewall inside the car.
1. Detach the motor wiring plug.
2. Inside the car, remove the nut connecting the linkage to the wiper shaft.
3. Unbolt and remove the wiper motor from the firewall.
4. Reverse the procedure for installation.

F-10

1. Disconnect the battery ground cable and remove the meter cover and glove box.

2. Remove the base of the wiper arm from the pivot shaft by raising the wiper blade away from the glass and loosening the attaching nut.
3. Remove the wiper motor by removing the ball joint connecting the motor shaft to the wiper link. Remove the motor from the dash.
4. Remove the pivot bolts and remove the link assembly.
5. Installation is the reverse of removal. Make sure the angle is correct to obtain the right sweeping zone.

1978 and Later 510, 210, 280ZX, 1980 and Later 310, 200SX and Stanza

1. Disconnect the battery ground cable.
2. Disconnect the electrical connector.
3. Remove the motor attaching bolts.
4. Remove the nut securing the arm to the motor shaft. Remove the motor.
5. Installation is the reverse of removal.

1978–79 200SX

1. Remove the wiper arms.
2. Disconnect the motor electrical connector.
3. Remove the cowl top grille.
4. Remove the motor retaining bolts.
5. Pull the motor out a little and disconnect the motor from the linkage.
6. Installation is the reverse of removal.

Instrument Cluster

For more information on the instruments, please refer to "Gauges and Indicators" in the Unit Repair section.

REMOVAL & INSTALLATION

B210

1. Disconnect the battery negative lead.
2. Depress the wiper, light switch, and choke knobs, turning them counterclockwise to remove.
3. From the rear, disconnect the lighter wire. Turn and remove the lighter outer case.
4. Remove the radio and heater knobs.
5. Remove the shell cover from the steering column.
6. Remove the screws which hold the instrument cluster to the instrument panel. Pull out the cluster.
7. Disconnect the wiring connector. Disconnect the speedometer cable by unscrewing the nut at the back of the speedometer.
8. Individual instruments may be removed from the rear of the cluster.

F-10

1. Disconnect the battery ground cable.
2. Disconnect the speedometer cable from the back of the speedometer.
3. Remove the package tray and disconnect the heater control cables from the heater.

Wiper linkage and motor—210; others similar

4. Disconnect all wire harness connectors from the back of the instrument panel after noting their locations and tagging them.

5. Remove the choke knob and nut.

6. Remove the steering column bracket installation bolts.

7. Loosen the instrument panel upper attaching screws.

8. Remove the bolts securing the sides of the instrument panel.

9. Remove the bolts attaching the instrument panel to the pedal bracket.

10. Remove the instrument panel.

11. Installation is in the reverse order of removal.

210

1. Disconnect the battery ground cable.

2. Remove the steering wheel.

3. Remove the steering column cover.

4. Remove the illumination control rheostat.

5. Pull off the heater control knob and remove control panel. Remove the screw attaching the panel to the instrument panel.

6. Pull off the radio knobs; remove the nuts and washers.

7. Remove the ash tray and ash tray holder.

8. Remove the cluster lid screws.

9. Disconnect the electrical connectors.

10. Remove the cluster lid.

11. Remove the cluster gauge screws.

12. Disconnect the speedometer cable by pushing and turning the cap counterclockwise.

13. Disconnect the cluster wires and remove the instrument cluster.

1978 and Later 510

1. Disconnect the battery ground cable.

2. Remove the steering column covers. Disconnect the hazard warning switch connector.

3. Remove the wiper switch. Pull out the ash tray, remove the heater control knobs, and remove the heater control plate by inserting a screwdriver into the fan lever slit and levering the plate out.

4. Remove the finish plate to the left of the glove compartment.

5. Pull off the radio knobs and remove the nuts and washers.

6. Remove the choke and side defroster knobs.

7. Remove the cluster lid screws.

8. Disconnect the electrical connectors.

9. Remove the cluster lid.

10. Remove the instrument cluster retaining screws. Disconnect the speedometer cable by pushing and turning counterclockwise.

11. Disconnect the instrument cluster wire connectors and remove the cluster.

1978–80 810

1. Disconnect the battery ground cable.

2. Remove the knobs and nuts on the radio and the knob on the choke control wire. Remove the ash tray.

3. Remove the steering column covers.

4. Disconnect the harness connectors after noting their location and marking them.

5. Remove the retaining screws and remove the instrument panel.

6. Installation is in the reverse order of removal.

1981 and later 810 and Maxima

1. Disconnect the negative battery cable.

2. Remove the instrument lower cover.

3. Remove the steering wheel.

4. Disconnect the speedometer cable.

5. Remove the six mounting screws and lift out the cluster lid.

6. Unscrew the mounting bolts and lift off the left side instrument pad (this is the hooded part of the dashboard that the instrument cluster sits in).

7. Loosen the instrument cluster mounting screws, pull it out slightly and disconnect all wiring. Remove the cluster.

8. Installation is in the reverse order of removal.

1978–79 200SX

1. Disconnect the battery ground cable.

2. Remove the steering column covers.

3. Disconnect the speedometer cable and the radio antenna.

4. Disconnect all the wires from the back of the panel after noting their location and marking them.

5. Remove the bolts which secure the steering column clamp. Remove the package tray.

6. Unbolt the panel from the brackets on the left and right-hand sides.

7. Remove the right-side windshield pillar trim and remove the bolt which attaches the panel to the pillar.

8. Remove the instrument garnish.

9. Remove the retaining bolts and remove the panel.

10. Installation is in the reverse order of removal.

280ZX

1. Disconnect the battery ground cable.

2. Remove the steering wheel.

3. Remove the steering column cover.

4. Remove the instrument panel lower cover on the left side.

5. Disconnect the speedometer cable at the intermediate connection.

6. Remove the combination switch.

7. Remove the cluster retaining screws, pull out slightly and disconnect the electrical connectors. Remove the instrument cluster.

1980 and Later 200SX

1. Disconnect the battery ground terminal.

2. It may be necessary to remove the steering wheel and covers to remove the instrument cluster.

3. Remove the screws holding the cluster lid in place and remove the lid.

4. Remove the five bolts holding the cluster in place and pull the cluster out, then remove all connections from its back. Make sure you mark the wiring to avoid confusion during reassembly.

310 and Stanza

1. Disconnect the battery terminals.

2. Remove the steering wheel and the steering column covers.

3. Remove the instrument cluster lid by removing its screws.

4. Remove the instrument cluster screws, pull the unit out and disconnect all wiring and cables from its rear. Mark the wires to avoid confusion during assembly. Be careful not to damage the printed circuit.

5. Remove the cluster.

6. Installation is the reverse of removal.

Instruments

REMOVAL & INSTALLATION

280Z

The speedometer and tachometer are both attached at the rear with two wingnuts. Access is from under the instrument panel. After the wingnuts are removed, the instrument can be pulled out through the instrument panel. The other three gauge units are held to brackets by slotted head hex bolts. To gain access, the center console panel must be removed.

FUSE BOX LOCATION CHART

Model	Fuse Box Location	Fusible Link Location
310	Under dash at extreme right	Right fender area of eng. comp.
280ZX 280X 810	Under dash at extreme right	Right rear of engine compartment①
B210, 210	Above brake light switch	Engine compartment below voltage regulator
F-10, 510	Under dash at extreme left	Off of (+) cable on battery
Stanza	Under dash at extreme right	Off of battery (+) cable
Sentra	Under dash at extreme left	Off of battery (+) cable
Pulsar	Under dash at extreme left	Off of battery (+) cable

① A fusing link for the fuel injection is in (+) battery cable

Fiat
124, 128, 131, X1/9,
Azzurra, Spider, Strada

SERIAL NUMBER IDENTIFICATION

Vehicle and Engine

NOTE: The X1/9 and Spider 2000 are no longer imported into the U.S. by Fiat Motors of North America. Since 1984, the X1/9 has been imported from Bertone and the Spider 2000 from Pininfarina.

The vehicle serial number is stamped on a metal plate located on the left front corner of the instrument panel, visible through the windshield. The serial number is also stamped on a non-removable rib or bulkhead of the body.

An identification plate, mounted on the engine compartment wall (front trunk X1/9), carries the chassis number and the spare parts ordering number. The engine number is stamped on a pad on the engine block.

From Sept. 1, 1980, federal regulations require a new format for all vehicle identification numbers. All 1981 and later vehicles have the new 17-digit V.I.N. format.

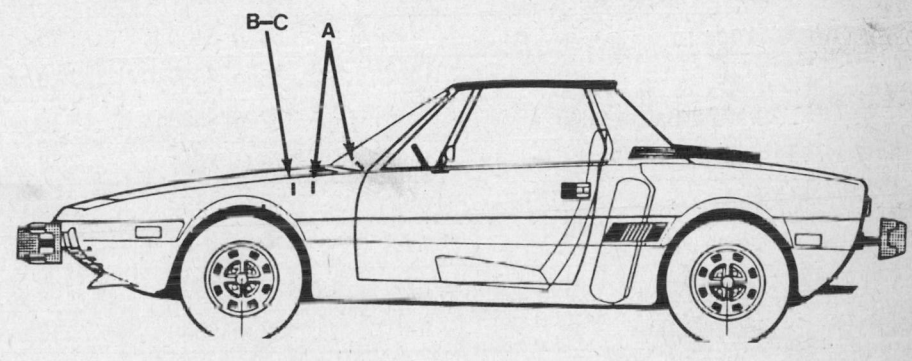

A—Chassis type and serial number
B—Identification plate
C—Engine type and serial number

X1/9 Identification locations

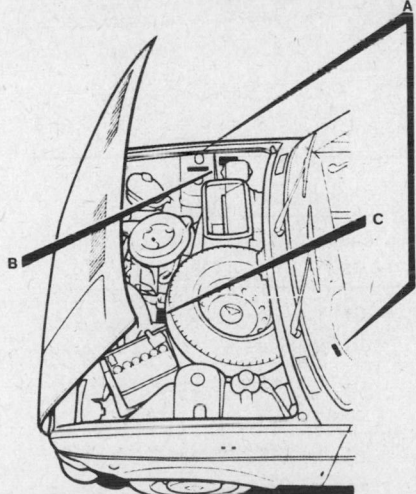

A—Chassis type and serial number
B—Identification plate
C—Engine type and serial number

128 and Strada typical identification locations

A—Chassis type and serial number
B—Engine type and serial number
C—Identification plate

131 and Brava identification locations

GENERAL ENGINE SPECIFICATIONS

Year	Model	Displacement (cc)	Horsepower @ rpm	Torque @ rpm (ft. lbs.)	Bore & Stroke (in.)	Compression ratio
'78	128—all w/SE	1290	62 @ 6000	67 @ 4000	3.39 × 2.19	8.5:1
	128—all w/SE, w/CC	1290	61 @ 5800	67 @ 4000	3.39 × 2.19	8.5:1
	X1/9—w/SE	1290	61.5 @ 5800	67 @ 4000	3.39 × 2.19	8.5:1
	X1/9—w/SE, w/CC	1290	61 @ 5800	67 @ 4000	3.39 × 2.19	8.5:1
	124—w/SE	1756	86 @ 6200	90 @ 2800	3.31 × 3.12	8.0:1
	124—w/SE, w/CC	1756	83 @ 6200	89 @ 2800	3.31 × 3.12	8.0:1
	131—all, Brava—all w/SE	1756	86 @ 6200	90 @ 2800	3.31 × 3.12	8.0:1
	131—all, Brava—all w/SE, w/CC	1756	83 @ 6200	89 @ 2800	3.31 × 3.12	8.0:1
'79	X1/9	1498	66 @ 5250	75.9 @ 4000	3.40 × 2.52	8.5:1
	Brava & Spider 2000	1995	80 @ 5000①	100 @ 3000②	3.31 × 3.54	8.1:1
	Strada	1498	65 @ 5100	75 @ 2900	3.40 × 2.52	8.5:1
'80	X1/9	1498	66 @ 5250	75.9 @ 4000	3.40 × 2.52	8.5:1
	Brava & Spider 2000	1995	80 @ 5000①	100 @ 3000②	3.31 × 3.54	8.1:1
	Strada	1498	65 @ 5100	75 @ 2900	3.40 × 2.52	8.5:1
'81	X1/9	1498	75 @ 5500	79.6 @ 3000	3.40 × 2.52	8.5:1
	Brava & Spider 2000	1995	102 @ 5500	110 @ 3000	3.31 × 3.54	8.1:1
	Strada	1498	75 @ 5500	79.6 @ 3000	3.40 × 2.52	8.5:1
'82–'85	X1/9	1498	75 @ 5500	79.6 @ 3000	3.40 × 2.52	8.5:1
	Strada	1498	75 @ 5500	79.6 @ 3000	3.40 × 2.52	8.5:1
	Spider Turbo	1995	120 @ 6000	130 @ 3600	3.31 × 3.54	8.2:1
	Spider 2000	1995	102 @ 5500	110 @ 3000	3.31 × 3.54	8.1:1

① W/F.I.: 102 @ 5500
② W/F.I.: 110 @ 3000
SE—Standard exhaust
CC—Catalytic Converter

TUNE-UP SPECIFICATIONS

Year	Model	Displacement (cc)	Spark Plug Type ⑨	Spark Plug Gap (in.)	Points Gap (in.)	Points Dwell (deg.)	Ignition Timing (deg.)	Idle Speed (rpm)	Valve Lash Intake (in.)	Valve Lash Exh. (in.)	Intake Valve Opens (deg.)	Mixture (% CO)
'78	128, all	1290	③	.023	.015–.017	52 58	TDC⑥	800–850	.011–.014	.015–.018	10B	1.5–2.5
	X 1/9	1290	④	.027–.031	.015–.017	52–58	TDC⑥	800–850	.016–.019	.018–.021	5B	1.5–2.5
	124	1756	③	.023–.027	.015–.017⑤	52–58	TDC⑥	800–850	.016–.019	.018–.021	5B	1.5–2.5
	131, all	1756	④	.027–.031	.015–.017	52–58	TDC⑥	800–850	.016–.019	.018–.021	5B	1.5–2.5
	Brava, all	1756	④	.027–.031	.015–.017⑦	52–58	TDC⑥	800–850⑦	.018	.020	5B	1.5–2.5

TUNE-UP SPECIFICATIONS

Year	Model	Displacement (cc)	Spark Plug Type ⑨	Spark Plug Gap (in.)	Points Gap (in.)	Points Dwell (deg.)	Ignition Timing (deg.)	Idle Speed (rpm)	Valve Lash Intake (in.)	Valve Lash Exh. (in.)	Intake Valve Opens (deg.)	Mixture (% CO)
'79	X 1/9	1498	③ ④	.023–.027	Electronic		5 BTDC①	800–850	.011–.014	.015–.018	12B	1.0–2.0
	Strada	1498	③ ④	.023–.027	Electronic		MT-5 BTDC① AT-5 BTDC	800–850 700–750	.011–.014	.015–.018	12B	1.0–2.0
	131, Brava	1995	③ ④	.023–.027	Electronic		MT-10 BTDC AT-10 BTDC	800–850 700–750	.016–.019	.018–.021	5B	1.0–2.5
	Spider 2000	1995	③ ④	.023–.027	Electronic		MT-10 BTDC AT-10 BTDC	800–850 700–750	.016–.019	.018–.021	5B	1.0–2.5
'80	X 1/9	1498	④	.027–.031	Electronic		MT-10 BTDC AT-10 BTDC	800–850 700–750	.011–.014	.015–.018	12B	.05–.09
	Strada	1498	④	.027–.031	Electronic		MT-10 BTDC AT-10 BTDC	800–850 700–750	.011–.014	.015–.018	12B	.05–.09
	131, Brava	1995	④	.027–.031	Electronic		MT-10 BTDC AT-10 BTDC	800–850 700–750	.016–.019	.018–.021	5B	.05–.09
	Spider 2000	1005	④	.027–.031	Electronic		MT-10 BTDC AT-10 BTDC	800–850 700–750	.016–.019	.018–.021	5B	.05–.09
'81	Strada	1498	④	.027–.031	Electronic		MT-10 BTDC AT-10 BTDC	800–850 700–750	.011–.014	.015–.018	12B	.05–.09
	131, Brava	1995	④	.027–.031	Electronic		MT-10 BTDC AT-10 BTDC	800–850 700–750	.016–.019	.018–.021	5B	.05–.09

TUNE-UP SPECIFICATIONS

Year	Model	Displace- ment (cc)	Spark Plug Type ⑨	Spark Plug Gap (in.)	Points Gap (in.)	Points Dwell (deg.)	Ignition Timing (deg.)	Idle Speed (rpm)	Valve Lash Intake (in.)	Valve Lash Exh. (in.)	Intake Valve Opens (deg.)	Mixture (% CO)
'81–'85	X 1/9	1498	④	.027– .031	Electronic		MT-10 BTDC	800– 850	.011– .014	.015– .018	12B	.05–.09
							AT-10 BTDC	700– 750				
	Spider 2000	1995	④	.027– .031	Electronic		MT-10 BTDC②	800– 850	.016– .019	.018– .021	5B	.05–.09
							AT-10 BTDC②	700– 750				

NOTE: The underhood specifications sticker often reflects tune-up specification changes made in production. The sticker specifications must be used if they disagree with those in the chart.

DP Dual point distributor; see text for explanation

MT Manual transmission

AT Automatic transmission

① At 800 to 850 rpm

② Spider Turbo timing is 8.5 BTDC @ 800– 850 rpm

③ Regular
  Bosch W175T30
  Marelli CW7LP
  Champion N9Y
  AC 42 XLS

④ Resistor
  Bosch W175TR30
  Marelli CW7LPR
  Champion RN9Y
  AC R42 XLS

⑤ Starting point gap—.012–.019 inch

⑥ w/auto trans—5 BTDC

⑦ Original equipment spark plugs; similar characteristic plugs of different manufacture may be used without damage to the engine

FIRING ORDER

NOTE: The position of No. 1 tower on the distributor cap may vary. To avoid confusion when replacing wires, always replace wires one at a time. The notch cut into the rim of the distributor body always indicates No. 1 cylinder.

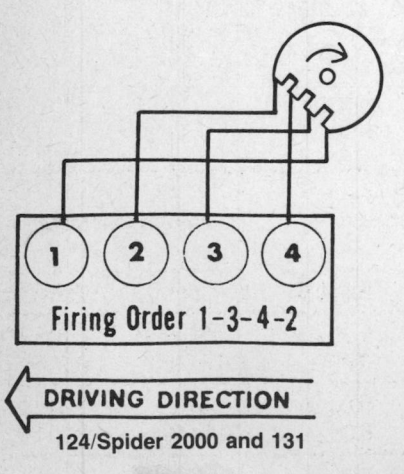

124/Spider 2000 and 131

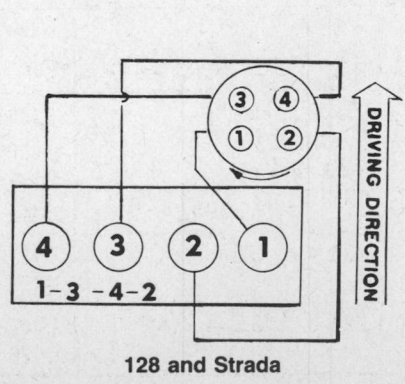

128 and Strada

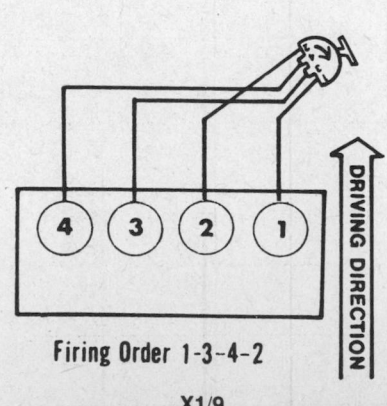

X1/9

CAPACITIES

Year	Model	Engine Disp. (cc)	Crankcase (qts) With Filter	Crankcase (qts) Without Filter	Trans-axle (pts)	Transmission Manual (pts)	Transmission Automatic (pts)	Rear Axle (pts)	Fuel Tank (gals)	Cooling System (qts)
'78–'79	128 Sedan, Wagon	1290	4.5	4.5	6.6	6.6②	—	—	9.5	6.8
	128 SL, 3P	1290	4.5	4.5	6.6	6.6②	—	—	12.5	7.0
'78–'85	X1/9	1290	4.5	4.5	6.6	6.6②	—	—	12.7	11.6
		1498	4.75	4.5	7.0	7.0②	—	—	12.2	11.6
'78	124	1756	4.5	4.0	—	3.5	6.0①	2.8	11.4	8.0
	131 Sedan and Wagon Brava Sedan, Wagon	1756	4.5	4.0	—	3.8	6.0①	2.8	12.2	8.0
'79–'81	Brava	1995	5.5	4.3	—	3.5	6.0①	2.8	12.2	8.5
'79–'85	Spider 2000 and Turbo	1995	5.5	4.3	—	3.5	6.0①	2.8	11.4	8.0
'79–'81	Strada	1498	4.75	3.75	7.0	7.0②	6.0①	—	12.1	7.5

NOTE: Because of the high temperatures associated with turbocharging, a superior grade oil must be used. Fiat recommends only oils with an SF/CC rating for use in the Turbo Spider, preferably straight 30 or 40.
① 12 pints to refill after total disassembly and rebuild
② SAE 90 (not EP)

CRANKSHAFT AND CONNECTING ROD SPECIFICATIONS

(All measurements in inches)

Engine Displacement (cc)	Crankshaft Main Bearing Journal Dia.	Crankshaft Main Bearing Oil Clearance	Crankshaft End-Play	Thrust on No.	Connecting Rod Dia.	Connecting Rod Oil Clearance
1290	1.9994–2.0002	0.0016–0.0033	0.0021–0.0104	5	1.7913–1.7920	0.0014–0.0034
1756	2.0860–2.0868	0.0020–0.0037	0.0021–0.0120	5	1.9997–①2.0001	0.0018–0.0032
1498	1.9990–1.9997	0.0019–0.0037	0.0021–0.0104	5	2.1459–2.1465	0.0014–0.0034
1995	2.0860–2.0868	0.0012–0.0030	0.0021–②0.0120	5	2.2329–2.2334	0.0008–0.0025

① Class "A", 1.9997–2.0001; Class "B", 1.9993–1.9997 in.
② Thrust rings installed

VALVE SPECIFICATIONS

Engine Displacement (cc)	Seat Angle (deg)	Face Angle (deg)	Spring Test Pressure (lbs. @ in.) Inner	Spring Test Pressure (lbs. @ in.) Outer	Stem to Guide Clearance (in.) Intake	Stem to Guide Clearance (in.) Exhaust	Stem Diameter (in.) Intake	Stem Diameter (in.) Exhaust
1290, 1498	45	45.5	32.7 @ 1.220	75.5 @ 1.417	0.0012–0.0026	0.0012–0.0026	0.3139–0.3146	0.3139–0.3146
1756, 1995	45	45.5	32.7 @ 1.220	85.5 @ 1.417	0.0012–0.0026	0.0012–0.0026	0.3139–0.3146	0.3139–0.3146

PISTON AND RING SPECIFICATIONS
(All measurements in inches)

Engine Displacement (cc)	Piston Clearance	Ring Gap			Ring Side Clearance		
		Top Compression	Top Oil Control	Bottom Oil Control	Top Compression	Top Oil Control	Bottom Oil Control
1290	0.0028–0.0035	0.0118–0.0176	0.0118–0.0176	0.0098–0.0157	0.0018–0.0030	0.0016–0.0028	0.0012–0.0024
1756	0.0016–0.0024	0.0118–0.0176	0.0079–0.0138	0.0079–0.0138	0.0018–0.0030	0.0011–0.0027	0.0011–0.0024
1498	0.0011–0.0019	0.0118–0.0177	0.0118–0.0177	0.0098–0.0157	0.0018–0.0030	0.0016–0.0028	0.0011–0.0024
1995	0.0016–0.0024	0.0118–0.0177	0.0118–0.0177	0.0098–0.0157	0.0018–0.0030	0.0011–0.0027	0.0011–0.0024

TORQUE SPECIFICATIONS
(All readings in ft. lbs.)

Displacement (cc)	Cylinder Head Bolts	Rods Bearing Bolts	Main Bearing Bolts	Crankshaft Pulley Bolt Chart	Flywheel to Crankshaft Bolts	Manifolds	
						Intake	Exhaust
1290, 1498	69	36	58	101	61	22	22
1756	61	36	83①	87	61	18	18
1995	61	54	83	181	106	18	18

① Front main bearing cap bolts—58 ft. lbs.

ALTERNATOR AND REGULATOR SPECIFICATIONS

Year	Model	Alternator			Regulator						Armature to Core Gap (in.)
		Part No. or Manufacturer	Output Current @ 14v	Max. Output (amps)	Part No. or Manufacturer	1st Stage		2nd Stage		Contact Gap (in.)	
						Testing Current (amps)	Regulating Voltage (volts)	Testing Current (amps)	Regulating Voltage (volts)		
'78–'79	128	Marelli A124-14V-60A	60	70	Marelli	40–	13.7–	10–	14.2	.018	.059③
'78–'85	X1/9	Variant ①			RC2/12E①	45①	14.2	14			
'78	124	Fiat A12M 124/12/42M⑤	42	53	Marelli RC2/12B	25–35	13.5–14.0	2–12	14.2	.018	.059③
'79–'85	Spider 2000										
'78–'81	131, Brava	Marelli A-124-14V-44A②	43	53	Marelli RC2/12D②	25–35②	13.5–14.0	10–14	14.2	0.18	.059③
'80–'82	Strada with A/C	Bosch K1-14-V65 A21	65	65	Integral Bosch Electronic	20–22	13.8–14.2	20–22	14.2	—	—

ALTERNATOR AND REGULATOR SPECIFICATIONS

| | | Alternator | | | Regulator | | | | | | |
| | | | | | | 1st Stage | | 2nd Stage | | | Armature to Core Gap (in.) |
Year	Model	Part No. or Manufacturer	Output Current @ 14v	Max. Output (amps)	Part No. or Manufacturer	Testing Current (amps)	Regulating Voltage (volts)	Testing Current (amps)	Regulating Voltage (volts)	Contact Gap (in.)	
'79–'80	Strada without A/C	Marelli A125-14V55A	55	55	Integral Fimm Rtt113C Electronic	20–22	13.8–14.2	20–22	14.2	—	—
		Delco-Remy 1101-039-70A	70	70	Integral Delco-Remy Electronic	20–22	13.8–14.2	20–22	14.2	—	—

① Various alternators used: Marelli A124-14V-44A with Marelli RC2/12D regulator (1st stage testing current of 25-35 amps; Marelli A125-14V-55A (55 amp) with FIMM RTT 113 C integral regulator; and Bosch K1-14V-65A 21 (65 amp).

② 131 models equipped with A/C use Marelli A124-14V-60A alternator and Marelli RC2/12E regulator with 1st stage testing current of 40–45 amps

③ 1978 and later models use electronic non-adjustable regulators

④ 1979 Strada with air conditioning modified per P.I.C. 129

⑤ Also used: Bosch K1-14V-55A20 (55 amp), 1977–80; Bosch K1-14V-65A21 (65 amp), 1981 and later

BATTERY AND STARTER SPECIFICATIONS

(All cars use 12 volt, negative ground electrical systems)

| | | | Starter | | | | | | | | |
| | | Battery Amp Hour Capacity | LOCK TEST | | | NO LOAD TEST | | | Brush Spring Tension (oz.) | Manufacturer or Part No. |
Year	Model		Amps	Volts	Torque (ft. lbs.)	Amps	Volts	rpm		
'78–'79	128	50	370	8.3	7.9	35	11.7	7000	40	Fiat E84-0.8/12
'78–	X1/9,	60	370	8.3	7.9	35	11.7	7000	40	Variant 1
'78–	124, 131, Brava Spider 2000	60	530	7	12.6	28	12	5200	35	Fiat/Marelli E100-1.3/12
'79–'82	Strada (Automatic)	60	370	8.5	9①	45	11.5	7000	40	Bosch 0-001-212-210
	Strada (Manual)	60	450	7.5	11①	40	11.5	6500	40	Marelli E95-0,9/12

C233

BRAKE SPECIFICATIONS
(All measurements given are in inches unless noted)

Year	Model	Lug Nut Torque (ft. lbs.)	Master Cylinder Bore	Brake Disc Minimum Thickness	Brake Disc Maximum Run-Out	Brake Drum Diameter	Brake Drum Max. Machine O/S	Brake Drum Max. Wear Limit	Minimum Lining Thickness Front	Minimum Lining Thickness Rear
'78–'79 '80–'82	128 Strada	50	0.75	Regrind 0.368 Wear limit 0.354	0.0006	7.2929– 7.3043	7.3234– 7.3358	7.3554	0.08	0.06
1978 '79–'85	124 Spider 2000 and Turbo	51	0.75	Regrind front—0.368 rear—0.371 Wear limit 0.354	0.006	①	—	—	0.08	0.08
'78–'81	131, Brava Sedan, Wagon	51	0.75	Regrind 0.368 Wear limit 0.354	0.006	8.9882– 9.000	9.0182– 9.0300	9.0551	0.06	0.18
'78–'85	X1/9	50	0.75	Regrind 0.368 Wear limit 0.354	0.006②	①	—	—	0.08	0.08

① Disc brakes on four wheels
② 0.010 in. 1984 and later; measured 2mm from outer edge

WHEEL ALIGNMENT SPECIFICATIONS
(Applies only to unladen vehicle)

Year	Model	Caster Front (deg)	Camber Front (deg)	Camber Rear (deg)	Toe-In Front (in.)	Toe-In Rear (in.)
'78–'81	128 Sedan, Wagon	1⅙P to 2⅙P	1⅙P to 2⅙P	⅔N to ⅓P① ⅙N to 1⅙P②	−⅛ + ³⁄₆₄	+¹⁄₁₆ + ⁷⁄₃₂
'78–'81	128 SL, 3P	1⅙P to 2⅙P	½P to 1½P	⅔N to 1⅔N	−¹⁄₁₆ + ⅛	+⁵⁄₆₄ + ¹⁵⁄₆₄
'79–'81	Strada	1½P to 2½P	1⅙P to 2⅙P	½P to 1½P	−³⁄₁₆ − ³⁄₃₂	0 + ⁵⁄₆₄
'78 '79–'85	124 Spider 2000	2⅔P to 3⅔P	⅓N to ⅔P	Fixed	+⁵⁄₃₂ + ⁵⁄₁₆③	Fixed
'78–'85	X1/9	6½P to 7½P	0 to 1N	④	+⁵⁄₆₄ + ¹⁵⁄₆₄	+⅜ + ½
'78 '79–'81	131 Sedan, Wagon Brava Sedan, Wagon Brava, Super Brava	3¼P to 4¼P	¼P to 1¼P	Fixed	+¹⁵⁄₆₄ + ²⁵⁄₆₄	Fixed

NOTE: Toe-in = + sign Toe-out = − sign
P Positive
N Negative
① Sedan
② Wagon
③ 1979–85 Spider 2000 & Brava +⁵⁄₃₂ to +⁵⁄₁₆
④ 1978: −2⁵⁄₁₆ to −1⅝
   1979: −2¼ to −1¼
   1980 and later: −1¾ to −¾

TUNE-UP PROCEDURES

Spark Plugs

NOTE: Number all spark plug wires before removal. Tighten all plugs to 27 ft. lbs.

Spark plugs should be cleaned and re-gapped at 6000 mile intervals, and replaced every 12,000 miles.

Since all Fiat engines use aluminum alloy cylinder heads, care should be taken to avoid damage to the spark plug threads. Remove the plugs with a 13/16 in. socket wrench and use a feeler gauge to check the electrode gap. When reinstalling used plugs, clean and lightly oil the threads. Thread the plugs in by hand (a short piece of fuel line slipped over the porcelain will facilitate installation) and use the socket to seat the plug snugly against the head, forming a good compression seal. Torque to 27 ft. lbs. Do not overtighten.

NOTE: Use caution when threading plugs, they go in on an angle.

If cross–threaded or stripped threads are encountered, see the engine rebuilding section at the end of the book.

Electronic Ignition

All 1979 and later Fiat engines are equipped with electronic ignition. Strada, 128 and X1/9 models use a Bosch system, 131 and 124 Spider 2000 models use a Marelli system.

Primary voltage is supplied from the battery through the ignition switch to the electronic control module and, through a resistor, to the coil. The resistor functions as a heat dissipator.

NOTE: The Marelli ignition does not use an external resistor.

The ground side of the coil primary circuit is connected to the control module. The control module has a circuit which connects with the magnetic pick-up in the distributor. Primary voltage is controlled by the electronic module to supply a regulated current to the primary windings of the ignition coil.

The control module is triggered by an impulse generated in the distributor. This turns the coil primary circuit on and off. Each time the primary circuit is broken, a high voltage is induced in the coil secondary windings. This voltage is distributed to the spark plugs through the distributor rotor and cap in the conventional manner.

ELECTRONIC IGNITION TEST PRECAUTIONS

DO NOT:
- Energize ignition unless coil support base is properly grounded.
- Ground the tachometer lead.
- Crank the engine with the high voltage wire disconnected from the coil.
- Disconnect the high voltage wire from the coil when the engine is running.
- Ground the primary circuit or use diagnostic equipment to ground the primary circuit.
- Test for current or voltage by flashing terminals with each other or to a ground.
- Disconnect the battery cables with the engine running. The electronic voltage regulator will be damaged.

When required, the distributor pickup assembly may be disconnected when the engine is running, or when cranking for compression testing.

ELECTRONIC IGNITION TEST SPECIFICATIONS

	Bosch	Marelli
Pick up coil resistance—wires from terminal 7 and 31d of module	890 to 1285 ohms	700 to 800 ohms
Pick up insulator—wire from terminal 7 to the distributor body	∞ (Infinity)	∞ (Infinity)
Primary input—positive coil terminal to ground	6 volts or more	6 volts or more
Control module ground—negative battery terminal to module support mount	0.2 ohms or less	0.2 ohms or less
Coil primary resistance—disconnect primary coil wires	1.1 to 1.7 ohms	0.75 to 0.81 ohms
Primary resister—disconnected	0.85 to 0.95 ohms	—
Coil secondary resistance to primary	6,000 to 10,000 ohms	10,000 to 11,000 ohms
Stator pole to reluctor gap	0.3 to 0.5mm (.011 to .019 in.)	0.5 to 0.6mm (0.020 to 0.024 in.)
Control module—check only after all other components have checked out good	Disconnect the coil tower wire. Position wire 5mm—¼in. from ground. Rotate the engine manually and observe spark as each tooth passes the pick up.	Disconnect high voltage wire from distributor. Do not disconnect from coil. While holding wire 5mm from ground. Crank engine and check for spark. If no spark is seen-replace module.

NOTE: Hold all high voltage wires with insulated tool to avoid shock.

ELECTRONIC IGNITION TEST

1. Set key to ON position.
2. Check that voltage at primary coil terminal equals battery voltage.
3. Repeat test at tachometer coil terminal. Voltage should be within 0.3 of battery voltage.
4. If not, check the coil primary winding for open circuits. Disconnect the primary leads from the coil, then connect an ohmmeter to the coil. The meter should read 1.1–1.7 ohms on the Bosch system, and 0.75–0.81 ohms on the Marelli system.
5. Reconnect one ohmmeter lead to the coil high voltage terminal. Check resistance: the Marelli system should read 10,000–11,000 ohms; the Bosch system should read 6,000–10,000 ohms. Replace the coil if not within specifications on any of the above checks.
6. To check the resistor on Bosch systems, disconnect one end of the resistor, then connect the ohmmeter across the resistor. Resistance should be 0.85–0.95 ohms. Replace the resistor if not within these specifications.

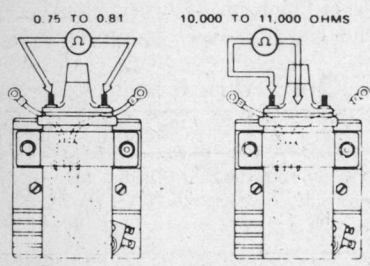

Coil resistance check—Marelli ignition system (Spider shown)

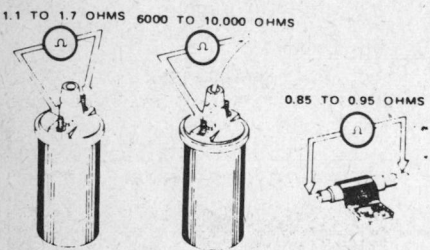

Coil resistance check—Bosch (X1/9) ignition system

CONTROL MODULE CHECK

1. Make sure the coil primary leads are connected, and that the pickup assembly is connected to the control module.
2. Disconnect the high voltage wire from the distributor. Do not disconnect the coil end.
3. Hold the wire using an insulated tool. Hold the wire about 5mm from a ground, crank the engine and check for spark. If no spark appears, replace the module.

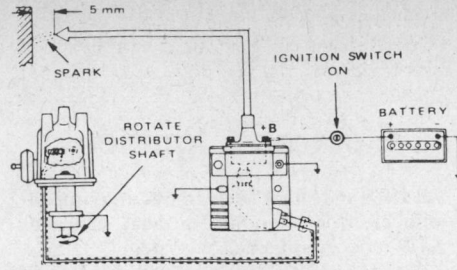

Control module check—Marelli system

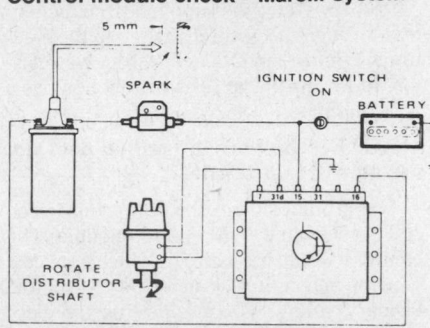

Bosch control module check—X1/9

IGNITION DISTRIBUTOR (PICK-UP ASSEMBLY) TEST

1. With key in OFF position remove connector from module.
2. Place ohmmeter leads on module connector.
3. Reading should be 700–800 ohms (890–1285 ohms on Bosch).
4. Remove distributor cap and check rotor arm resistance.
5. Resistance should be about 5000 ohms.

NOTE: If above tests indicate proper results, module is at fault.

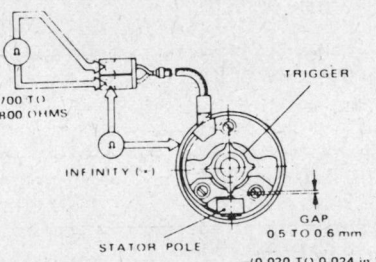

Pickup assembly check—Marelli ignition systems

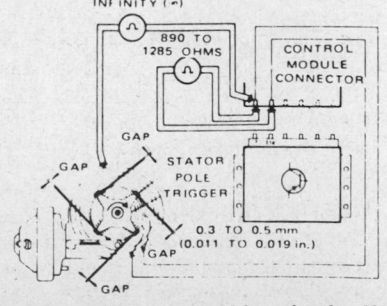

Bosch pickup assembly check—X1/9 shown

Breaker Points and Condenser

REMOVAL & INSTALLATION

Breaker points should be inspected and re-gapped at 6000 mile intervals, and replaced with the condenser(s) at 12,000 mile intervals.

128 and 1978 X1/9

NOTE: Fiat recommends servicing the points and condenser with the distributor removed. See "Distributor Removal and Installation" in the Engine Electrical section.

1. Unsnap the two distributor cap clasps and remove the cap with the spark plug wires connected. On some models, the cap is retained by two screws that stay with the cap.
2. Pull straight up and remove the rotor. It is good practice to apply a few drops of light (10W) oil to the lubricating wick at the top of the distributor shaft.
3. Disconnect the breaker points lead and condenser lead at the primary connection. Remove the condenser bracket retaining screws, and replace the condenser. Remove the breaker point retaining screws (and wire clip on 1978–79 128 and X1/9 models) and remove the points. Apply a light film of silicone–based grease to the distributor cam lobes. Wipe off any excess.
4. Install new breaker points and condenser. To adjust the point gap, rotate the crankshaft pulley until the breaker point rubbing block rests on the high point of the distributor cam lobe. Slightly loosen the breaker point retaining screw and insert the proper sized feeler gauge between the point contacts. Move the fixed arm in or out to obtain the specified clearance. Tighten the retaining screw.
5. Connect the electrical leads for the breaker points and condenser. Install the cap and rotor.
6. Check the dwell angle and ignition timing.

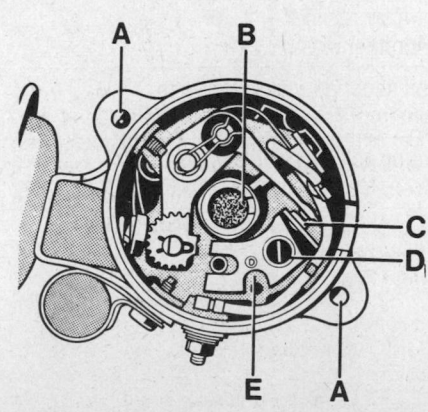

Ignition points—1978 128 and X1/9

131 and 124 (1756 cc)

NOTE: These models are equipped with a dual point distributor. The dual point sets do not operate simultaneously; one set is used for starting, and the other for running. The starting set provides 10 degrees of additional spark advance during starter cranking. The running set returns the spark timing to Top Dead Center. On 1978 models with an automatic choke, the starting set is actuated by

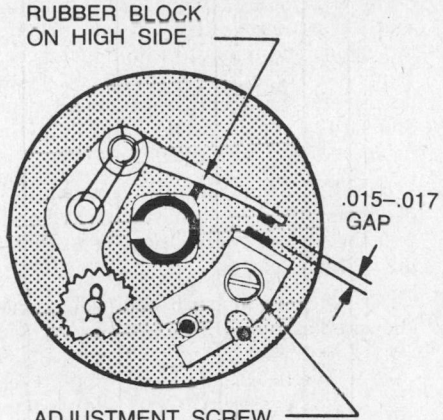

1978 128 and X1/9 point gap adjustment

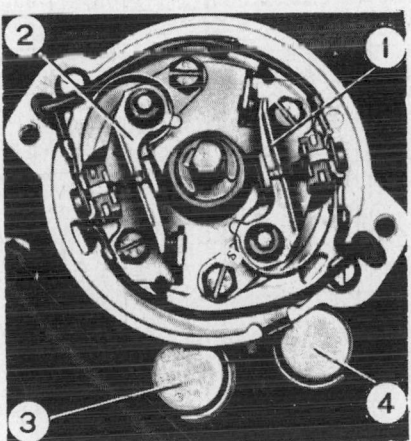

1. Main breaker points
2. Auxiliary breaker points
3. Capacitor, main breaker points
4. Capacitor, auxiliary breaker points

Ignition points—1978 124 and 131

coolant temperatures of 36–46°F or less. On both systems, the starting set cuts out and the running set takes over when full cold oil pressure is reached.

1. Remove the two distributor cap retaining screws. The screws will stay with the cap. Remove the cap.

2. Pull straight up and remove the rotor. Apply a few drops of light (10W) oil to the lubricating wick atop the distributor shaft.

3. Crank the engine over until both point sets open with their rubbing blocks on the high points of the distributor cam lobes.

Disconnect both breaker point and condenser leads at the primary connections. Remove and replace both point sets and condensers. Apply a light film of silicone based grease to the distributor cam lobes. Wipe off any excess.

4. Adjust the point gap for both breaker point sets by inserting the feeler gauge between the point contacts; set both sets for .015–.017 in. gap.

The running points are connected to the green wire and the starting points are connected to the green/black wire. If the points need adjustment, insert a screwdriver in the adjusting slot and twist it one way or the other to change the gap.

NOTE: For longer service, set the gap to the maximum specification, as the rubbing block will wear down in service and slowly close the gap.

5. Install the rotor. Install the distributor cap.

6. Check the dwell angle and ignition timing.

Dwell Angle

NOTE: Dwell angle is not applicable on electronic ignition.

Dwell angle is the amount of degrees of distributor shaft rotation that the points remain closed (making contact). Increasing the point gap decreases dwell, while decreasing the point gap increases dwell. Dwell angle may be checked with the engine running, or with the engine cranking over at starter speed. With a running engine, the dwell angle reading should be fairly constant. When the engine is being cranked over, the dwell angle reading will fluctuate between zero and the maximum figure for that angle.

Dwell angle should always be checked after adjusting or installing new points. Using a dwell meter, connect the negative lead to a good ground (such as an engine bolt) and the positive lead to the primary distributor connection at the coil (the small wire that leads from the distributor to the coil). On 128 and X1/9 models, disconnect and plug the vacuum retard signal line at the distributor.

NOTE: Leave the line connected on high altitude versions.

On all models with dual points, both sets must be checked separately. To check the running set of points, first locate the ignition mode selector relay. Trace the wires from the distributor until you locate it. Usually, it is located on the passenger's side fender well. Remove the relay from the plug and connect a jumper wire between the power side and the running side. Connect the dwell meter positive lead to the green distributor lead. Crank the engine and check the dwell. If the dwell needs adjusting, remove the distributor cap and adjust the point gap. To check the dwell on the

starting set of points, leave one end of the jumper wire on the power side of the relay and connect the other end to the starting side. Connect the dwell meter positive lead to the green/black lead at the distributor. Crank the engine and check the dwell.

On all other Fiat models, dwell is adjusted in the normal manner. Simply connect the dwell meter positive lead to the distributor primary wire and the negative lead to a good ground.

Once you have set the dwell, the ignition timing must be checked. A 1° increase in dwell results in the ignition timing being retarded 2° and vice versa.

Ignition Timing

CAUTION

On Spider Turbo models the ignition timing must be carefully set according to specifications. Altering the timing beyond specifications could cause detonation and serious engine damage.

Fiat recommends that the ignition timing be checked at 6000 mile intervals, or whenever the breaker points, dwell angle setting, or distributor body is disturbed. All timing checks are made with the engine warmed to operating temperature, and idling in neutral (manual transmission cars) or Drive (automatic equipped cars), with the hand brake on, and the drive wheels blocked.

NOTE: The timing marks are located on the front cover. There will be three lines, the longest is TDC, the shortest is 10° BTDC.

ELECTRONIC MODELS

Ignition timing is checked in the conventional manner, using a timing light.

1. Locate the timing marks on the front cover. Clean and highlight the marks with chalk or paint.

2. Start the engine and allow it to warm up to operating temperature. Make sure the idle speed is correct.

3. Connect the timing light according to the manufacturer's instructions.

A = 10° (Adv.)
B = 5° (Adv.)
C = 10° (TDC)

Timing marks—124/Spider 2000 and 131 (early models with marks on shroud)

NOTE: When using a timing light with an inductive pick-up, place the pick-up along the No. 1 spark plug wire at a point where it can be separated from the other wires to eliminate false signals generated by the strong firing impulses.

4. Using the timing light, check the position of the timing mark on the crankshaft pulley. The mark should index with the timing pointer according to specifications. If the timing is within specs, no further adjustment is necessary.

5. If the initial timing needs adjustment, loosen the distributor hold-down locknut and turn the body of the distributor to advance or retard timing.

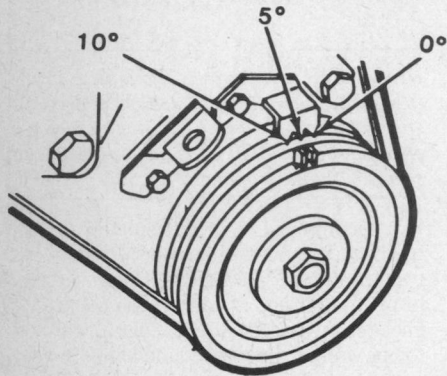

Timing marks on crankshaft pulley and timing pointer—later X1/9s

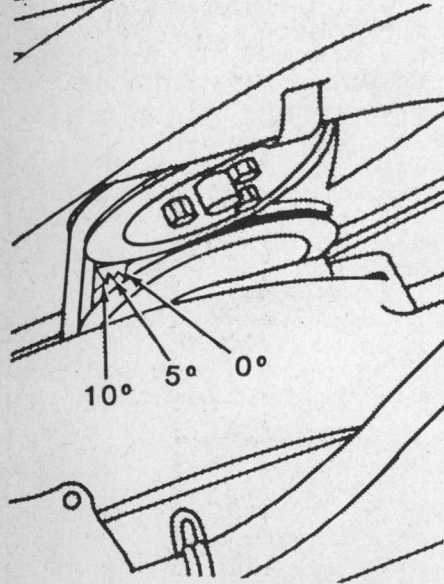

Timing marks on crankshaft pulley and timing pointer—later Spiders

SINGLE POINT MODELS

1. 1978 and later 128's, Strada's, and X1/9's are equipped with two sets of timing marks—one set is in the conventional position on the front cover and the other set is located on the flywheel, visible through a small opening in the bellhousing. On 1978 and later 128's, and Strada's, remove the spare tire to expose the timing marks.

A = 0° (Adv.)
B = 5° (Adv.)
C = 10° (T.D.C.)

Timing marks on flywheel—128, Strada and X1/9. View is through hole in bellhousing

2. Locate the correct mark and highlight it with paint or chalk. If you're timing the engine through the bellhousing, tap the engine over with the starter or turn it over by hand until you can find the punch mark on the flywheel. Put a spot of paint or chalk on it.

3. Connect the timing light according to the manufacturer's instructions.

4. Start the engine and let it warm up. Check the idle speed and make sure it is correct before setting the timing.

5. Disconnect the vacuum line from the distributor and plug it. Remember, this is a vacuum *retard*, not a vacuum advance.

1. TDC   3. 10° BTDC
2. 5° BTDC   4. Crankshaft pulley mark

Timing marks—Strada

Adjusting retard—not for high altitude versions

6. Aim the timing light at the marks. The marks should coincide. Keep in mind that with the vacuum line disconnected, the timing should be 10° BTDC. If the timing needs adjusting, stop the engine, loosen the distributor hold-down clamp and turn the distributor in the engine.

7. Reconnect the vacuum retard line. The timing should now be TDC. You may have to mark the timing marks with different paint colors to distinguish between them.

8. If the retard mechanism has not provided approximately 10 degrees retard, stop the engine and remove the cap and rotor. Depress the retard follower cap and rotate the eccentric star wheel to change the amount of retard. Counterclockwise equals more retard and clockwise equals less retard.

NOTE: On high altitude versions, simply leave the vacuum line connected and time the engine. There is no need to check the ignition retard.

9. After the timing is set, recheck the idle speed as it may have changed.

DUAL POINT MODELS

1. Locate the timing marks on the front cover and mark them with paint. Mark the pulley also. The longest mark is TDC and the shortest mark is 10° BTDC. The middle mark is 5° BTDC.

2. Start the engine and let it warm up. Check to make sure the idle is correct before setting the timing.

3. Locate the ignition mode selector relay. This is generally found on the passenger's side fender well. Remove the top of the relay and connect a jumper wire (with blade ends) between the power and running terminals.

4. Connect the timing light according to the manufacturer's instructions.

5. Start the engine and aim the timing

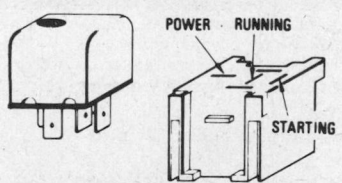

Ignition mode selector relay and terminal—1978 124 and X1/9

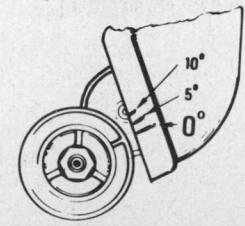

Timing marks aligned at TDC on the running points

light at the marks. The TDC mark on the front cover and the reference mark on the pulley should coincide. If they don't, stop the engine, loosen the distributor hold-down clamp and rotate the distributor as necessary to obtain a reading of TDC. Tighten the hold-down clamp once you get the timing right.

6. Shut the engine off and connect the starting and power terminals in the relay block. Start the engine and check the timing. It should now be 10° BTDC. If it isn't, adjust the amount of advance by changing the dwell angle of the starting points. If the timing is less than 10° BTDC, increase the point gap. If it's more than 10° BTDC, decrease the point gap.

7. Once you have the starting timing correct, remove the jumper wire and replace the relay.

8. Check and reset the idle speed if necessary.

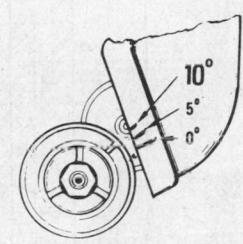

Timing marks advanced 10° on the starting points

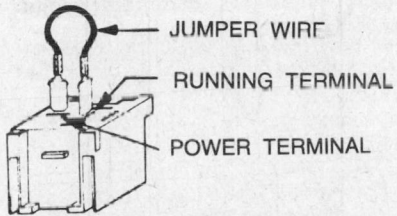

JUMPER WIRE

RUNNING TERMINAL

POWER TERMINAL

Setting timing on running points

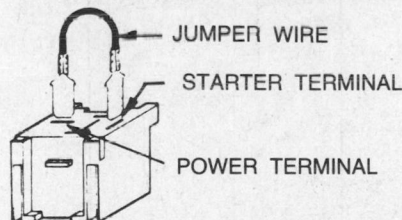

JUMPER WIRE

STARTER TERMINAL

POWER TERMINAL

Checking advance on starting points

Valve Clearance Adjustment

Valve clearances should be checked with the engine cold. Valve clearance should be checked every 12,000 miles—sooner if the head is removed or if excessive valve train noise is noticed. On both single and double overhead cam engines (128, X1/9, 131, 124/Spider 2000 and Strada), valve clearance is adjusted by the thickness of the shim (plate) between the cam lobe and tappet bucket.

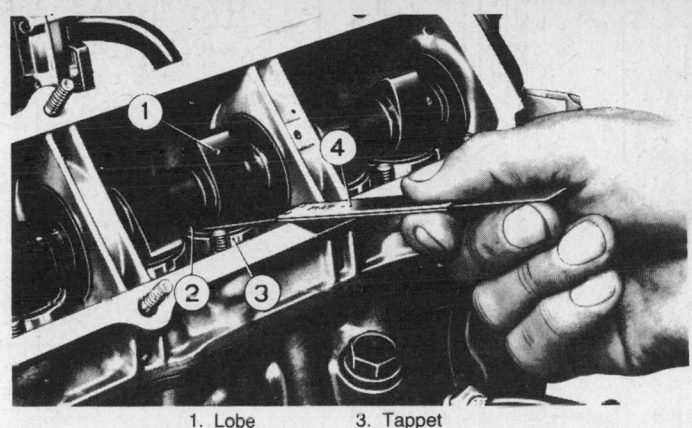

1. Lobe   3. Tappet
2. Plate   4. Feeler gauge

Measuring gap on overhead cam lobe to tappet plate

ALL MODELS

NOTE: Special tools required for this job include a tappet depressor tool #A60421 (128, Strada, X1/9), or #A60422 (124/Spider 2000, 131), a pair of curved tip needle nose pliers (such as #A87001), a lever #A60443 (Twin Cam only), and a compressed air source and air chuck to blow out the old adjusting shim. The engine must be cold for a valve clearance check.

1. Remove the retaining screws and remove the camshaft cover.

2. Turn the crankshaft until the lobe controlling the tappet being checked is pointing upward and is at a right angle to the tappet plate.

NOTE: To simplify crankshaft rotation on the 128, Strada, and X1/9, place the transmission in 4th gear and raise the car so that the right front wheel (right rear wheel on the X1/9) is free to rotate. Turn the free wheel to rotate the engine, in the direction of normal rotation, to the valve adjustment positions.

3. Measure the clearance between the tappet plate and the camshaft lobe with a feeler gauge.

4. If the clearance is not at the proper specification, a tappet plate of the required thickness will have to be installed.

5. To remove the old tappet plate (shim), the tappet must be depressed and held in that position. On the 128, Strada, and X1/9, this is accomplished with special tool #A60421. However, on the 124/Spider 2000 and 131 twin cam engines, this is a two step process. First, depress the tappet with special lever #60443 or rotate the camshaft until the lobe depresses the tappet. Then, install the tappet clamping tool #60422 which will keep the tappet depressed. If the camshaft is rotated to depress the tappet, rotate it again to give clearance for plate removal. Finally, using compressed air through the notch in the tappet or needle nose pliers, or both, remove the old plate.

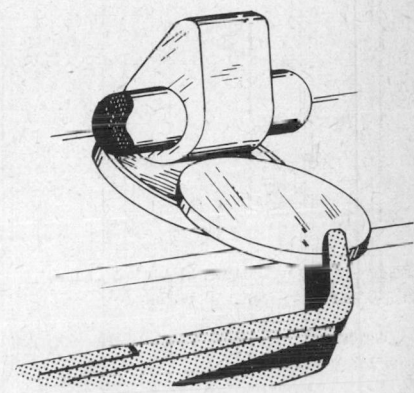

Removing or replacing shim plate

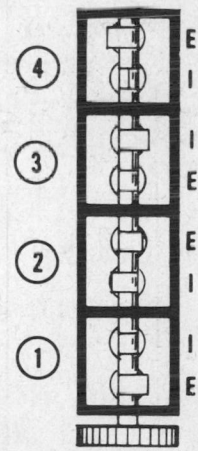

Single overhead cam—cylinder and valve location

NOTE: Use the following charts to help determine valve clearances and the necessary adjusting shims.

Excessive clearance (exhaust valve used as an example):

Valve clearance recorded	0.023 in.
Valve clearance required	0.019 in.
Excessive clearance	+0.004 in.

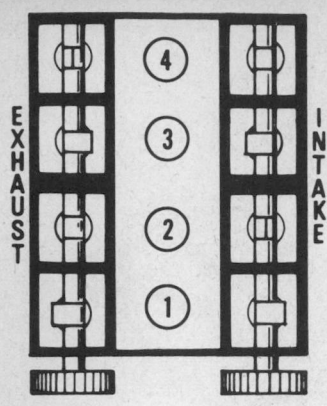

Double overhead cam—cylinder and valve location

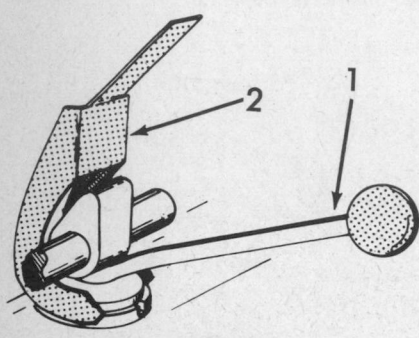

1. Depress Tappet
2. Tappet retaining tool

Preparing to change shim plate—double overhead cam type

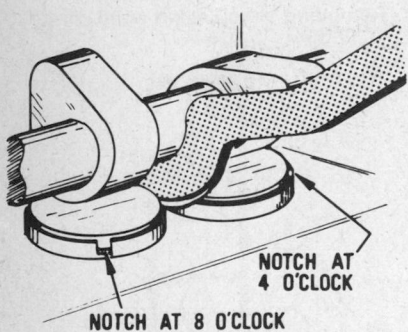

NOTCH AT 4 O'CLOCK

NOTCH AT 8 O'CLOCK

Preparing to change shim plate—single overhead cam type

Shim (plate) thickness
recorded   0.146 in.
New shim thickness required   0.150 in.

Insufficient clearance (intake valve used for example):
Valve clearance recorded   0.013 in.
Valve clearance required   0.017 in.
Insufficient clearance   −0.004 in.
Shim (plate) thickness
recorded   0.165 in.
New shim thickness required   0.161 in.

6. Install a new tappet plate after determining its thickness by comparing it to the clearance measurement taken in Step 3.
Tappet clearance adjustment plates are

available in a range of thicknesses from 0.146 in. to 0.185 in. with a difference between each plate of 0.002 in.

The thickness of the plate is shown on one of the plate's flat sides. This side should be installed facing the tappet. It is recommended that the plate's thickness be checked to make sure that it is actually the thickness specified.

VALVE SHIM SIZE

mm	in.	mm	in.
3.25	0.128	4.02	0.158
3.30	0.130	4.10	0.161
3.40	0.134	4.20	0.165
3.50	0.138	4.30	0.169
3.60	0.142	4.40	0.173
3.70	0.146	4.50	0.177
3.80	0.150	4.60	0.181
3.90	0.154	4.70	0.185
4.00	0.157	4.80	0.189

Carburetor

Often mistaken for an improperly adjusted carburetor is an incorrectly adjusted air cleaner climatic setting. This adjustment provides warmed intake air for cold climated and cool intake air for warm climates. See "Emission Controls" for details.

IDLE SPEED AND MIXTURE ADJUSTMENT

All models

NOTE: On models equipped with a catalytic converter, idle speed and mixture is checked with the air injection hose between the diverter valve and check valve pinched shut with locking pliers.

1. Start the engine and warm to operating temperature (176°F min.). Make sure the choke plate is open.

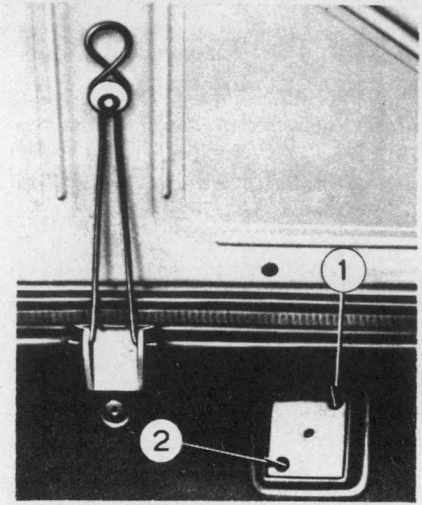

1. Idle speed   2. Idle mixture

Access holes for carburetor adjustment—X1/9 only

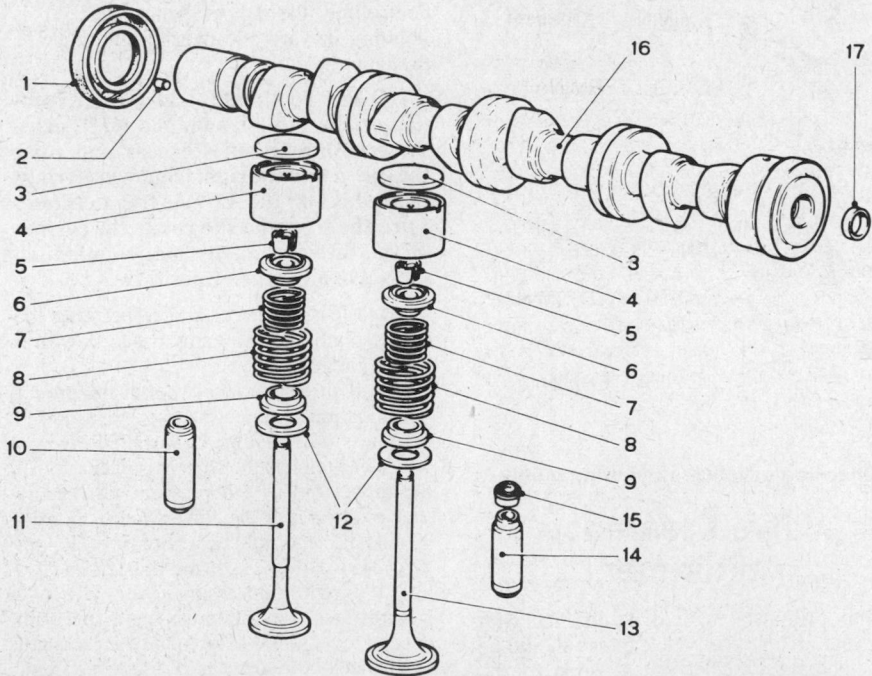

1. Seal	7. Inner spring	13. Intake valve
2. Dowel	8. Outer springs	14. Intake valve guide
3. Plates of adjusting valve clearance	9. Lower cups	15. Oil seal
4. Tappets	10. Exhaust valve guide	16. Camshaft
5. Locks	11. Exhaust valve	17. Welch plug
6. Upper cups	12. Flat washer	

Exploded view of single overhead cam valve mechanism—typical

NOTE: If possible, make all adjustments with the air cleaner on, as removal may artificially lean out the mixture. On 1979 and later 49 State versions, remove the air cleaner lid and block the inlet to the reed valves; replace the lid.

2. Adjust the idle speed to specifications with the idle speed screw. The idle speed is set with the transmission in Neutral on manual transmission cars, and is set in Drive with the parking brake firmly applied on automatic cars.

3. Adjust the idle mixture (% CO) to specifications (see "Tune-up" chart) with the idle mixture metering screw.

NOTE: Fiat recommends the use of a carbon monoxide (CO) meter for setting the mixture. However, if one is not available, a satisfactory setting should be found by first screwing the mixture screw all the way in until it lightly sets, and then backing it out about 2 to 3½ turns. Then adjust the mixture for the highest possible rpm within that range. Screw clockwise to lean (decrease CO), and counterclockwise to richen (increase CO).

4. After adjusting the mixture, recheck the idle speed and adjust if necessary.

ENGINE ELECTRICAL

Distributor

All Fiat distributors use a centrifugal ignition advance system which advances spark timing in direct proportion to increasing engine rpm. In addition, 128 and X1/9 models with the Ducellier distributor utilize a vacuum retard system which retards the ignition timing about 10° under high vacuum situations such as idling and deceleration.

Models with electronic ignition have a vacuum advance mechanism in addition to the centrifugal advance. Turbo Spider models have an advance limiter replacing one of the springs on the centrifugal advance weights.

REMOVAL & INSTALLATION

The quick method of distributor removal is to mark the distributor body and rotor positions relative to some stationary engine component before removal. However, on the 1756 cc engines installed in the 124 and 131 (these are the ones with the distributor located at the right rear of the engine above the exhaust manifold), the distributor drive gear is helical (slanted drive). Therefore, the rotor will rotate about 30–40 degrees during removal or installation. For this reason, mark the position of the rotor before removal and just after removal. When the

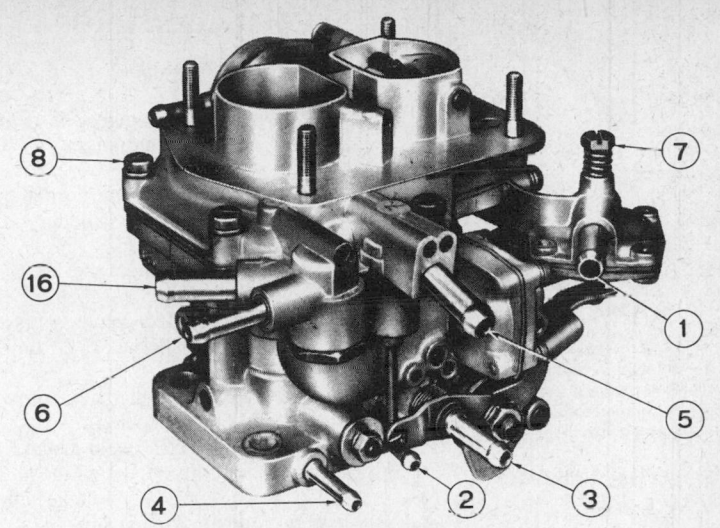

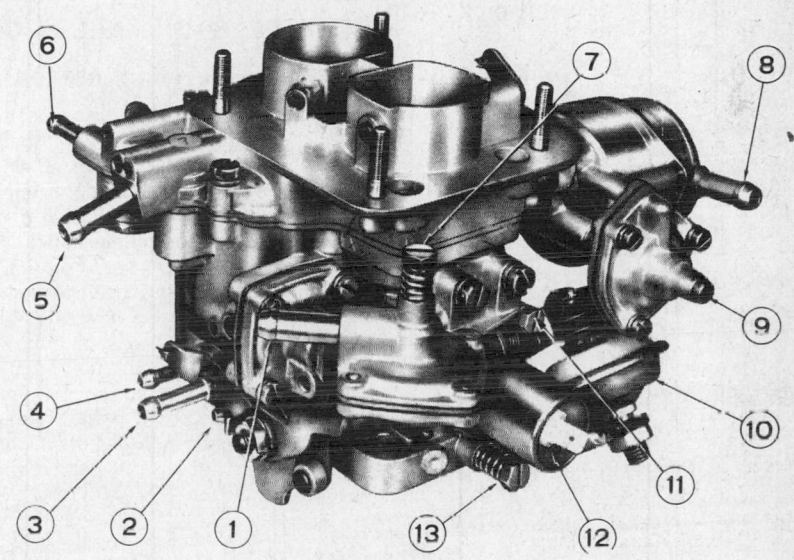

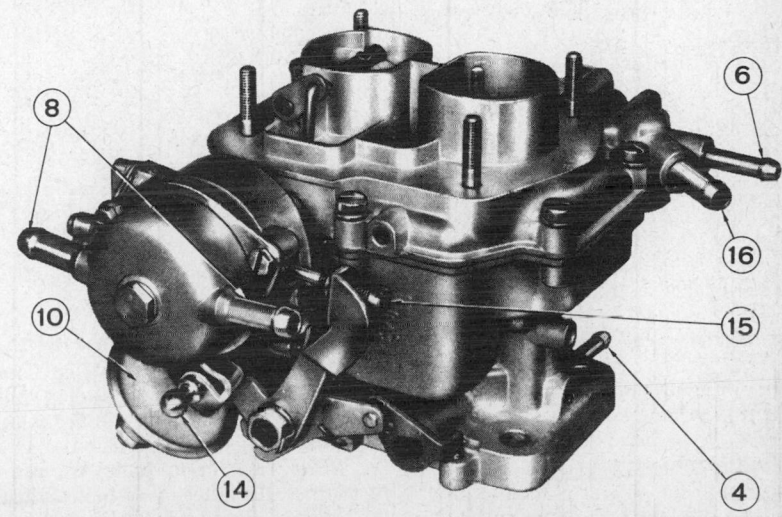

Adjustments and vacuum connections—typical

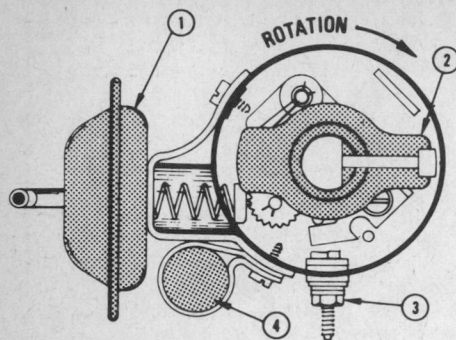

1—Vacuum retard
2—Rotor toward #4 terminal
3—Primary lead facing grille
4—Condenser

Single point distributor

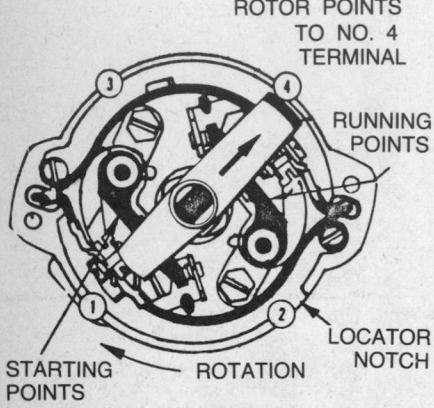

ROTOR POINTS TO NO. 4 TERMINAL

RUNNING POINTS

LOCATOR NOTCH

STARTING POINTS   ROTATION

Dual point distributor

distributor is installed, align the rotor with the mark made just after removal so when the distributor is installed, the rotor will correctly align with the first mark.

The Fiat approved method of distributor removal is the following:

1. Remove the spark plug wires from the distributor.
2. Remove the low tension leads and disconnect the vacuum control (if equipped).
3. Rotate the crankshaft to bring the No. 1 cylinder to Top Dead Center (TDC) of the compression stroke (both valves closed). Align the timing marks.
4. Remove the distributor clamp bolt at the base of the distributor and remove the distributor from the engine. To install:
5. Position the distributor rotor opposite the No. 1 contact in the cap. At this point the contact breaker points are about to open.
6. Fit the distributor into its housing and tighten the clamp bolt.
7. Replace the distributor cap and connect the spark plug wires in the correct firing order.
8. Check the ignition timing with a timing light and the point dwell with a dwell meter.

Alternator

PRECAUTIONS

Certain precautions should be observed when working in this, or any other AC charging system.

1. Never switch battery polarity.
2. When installing a battery, connect the ground cable last.
3. Never disconnect the battery while the engine is running.
4. If the molded connector is disconnected from the alternator, do not ground the hot wire.
5. Never run the alternator with the main output cable disconnected.
6. Never electric weld around the vehicle, without disconnecting the alternator.
7. Never apply any voltage, other than battery voltage, when testing.
8. Never apply more than 12 volts to jump a battery for starting purposes.

REMOVAL & INSTALLATION

NOTE: Disconnect the battery first.

The alternator is removed by disconnecting the electrical leads and unscrewing the nut on the upper bracket and the screw which attaches the bracket to the engine. Remove the two nuts of the lower brackets, alternator and water pump belt. Installation is the reverse of removal.

1981 and later Strada and X1/9 models with air conditioning use a new drive belt system. The system consists of three V-belts and an adjustable crankshaft pulley.

The alternator belt rides on the inner groove of the waterpump pulley. Adjust alternator belt tension to 30–45 lbs. Do not pry on the alternator case or pulley when adjusting belt tension.

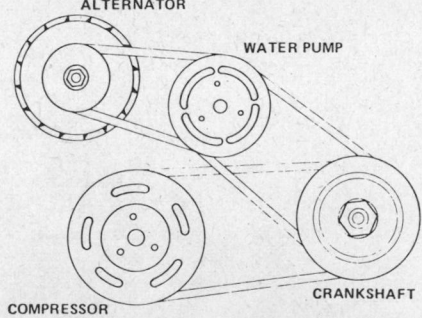

V-belt configuration—1981 and later Strada and X1/9

NOTE: The water pump belt is adjusted by removing the crankshaft outer pulley half and removing or adding shims. A shim change of 0.020 in. (0.5 mm) causes a change in belt tension of 17–22 lbs. If the water pump pulley is removed to replace the alternator belt, reinstall the original shims and check belt tension. Proper water pump belt tension is 60–80 lbs.

Voltage Regulator

Only the electro-mechanical regulator mounted separately from the alternator is adjustable. All later models have integral alternator and voltage regulator.

ADJUSTMENTS

Cut-out

1. Measure the air gap for the cut-out relay between the clapper and the edge of the core nearest the contacts.
2. Make the cut-in adjustment with the unit at 65–95°F.
3. Adjust by bending the spring tension arm until the points close at the proper specification.
4. Check the reverse current by connecting a two-way ammeter in series with the battery lead to the regulator.
5. Run the alternator to 4500 rpm and gradually reduce speed, noting the reverse current at the point where the contacts open. (See specifications for the proper amperage.)
6. The range between cut-in and cut-out action can be adjusted by enlarging or reducing the air gap.

Starter

REMOVAL & INSTALLATION

124/Spider 2000, 128 and 131

1. Jack up the car and place jack stands beneath the frame.
2. Disconnect the battery positive terminal to prevent accidental shorting.
3. Remove the exhaust manifold and muffler to provide clearance.
4. Disconnect the wires from the starter.
5. Remove the mounting bolts and pull the starter from the housing.
6. Installation is the reverse of removal.

X1/9

1. Raise the car at the rear and set it on two stands at the control arms.
2. Disconnect the battery (positive) cable to prevent shorting.
3. Disconnect and remove the lower linings of the compartment.
4. If necessary, remove the exhaust manifold and muffler.
5. Disconnect the wires from the starter.
6. Remove the mounting bolts and the starter.
7. Installation is the reverse of removal.

Strada

1. Disconnect the battery ground cable.
2. Disconnect all electrical leads to the starter.
3. On manual transmission cars, remove three bolts, lockwashers and washers to remove starter (Marelli).
4. On automatic transmission cars, remove two bolts, lockwashers and nut plate.

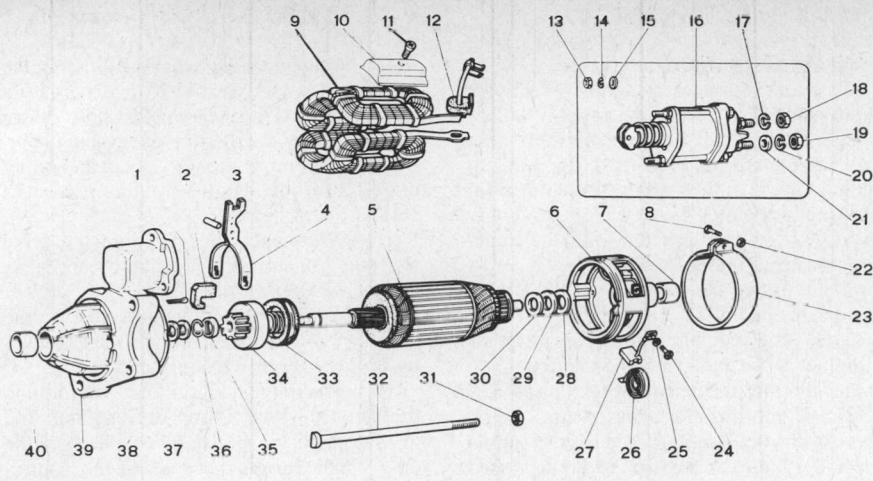

1. Split pin	14. Lock washer	25. Lock washer
2. Rubber pad	15. Plain washer	26. Brush spring
3. Lever pivot pin	16. Solenoid assembly	27. Brush
4. Starter drive pinion shifter fork	17. Lock washer	28-29. Plain washers
5. Armature	18. Nut, current lead clamping	30. Fibre thrust washer
6. Commutator end head	19. Nut, field winding terminal	31. Thru-bolt nut
7. Bushing	20. Lock washer	32. Starter thru-bolt
8. Protection band screw	21. Plain washer	33. Starter drive sleeve
9. Field winding	22. Nut, protection band screw	34. Drive pinion
10. Pole shoe	23. Commutator end head protection band	35. Stop ring
11. Pole shoe attaching screw	24. Screw, brush terminal clamping	36. Snap ring
12. Grommet		37-38. Plain washers
13. Nut, solenoid to drive end head		39. Drive end head
		40. Bushing

Fiat E84-0.8/12 starter—all 128, X1/9—others similar

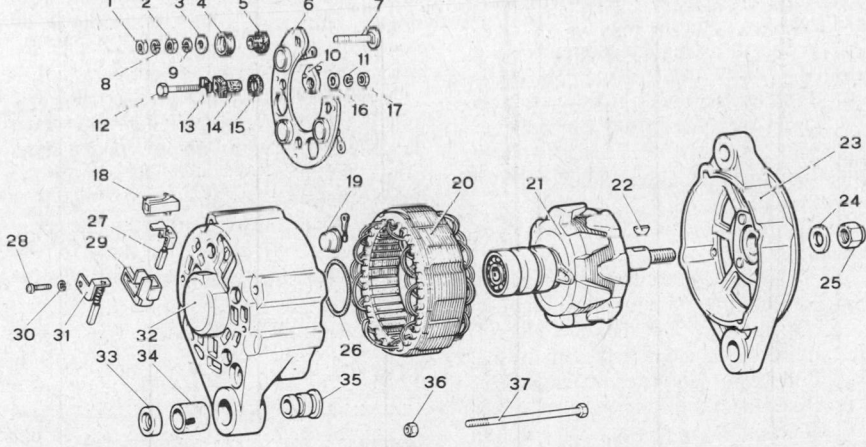

1-2. Nuts	14-15. Insulators	26. Rubber seal, bearing outer race
3. Flat washer	16. Flat washer	27. Positive brush
4-5. Positive clamp insulators	17. Nut	28. Screw
6. Positive diode plate	18. Insulated connector for charge indicator blade plug	29. Brush holder
7. Screw, positive clamp	19. Negative diode	30. Spring washer
8-9. Spring washers	20. Stator	31. Negative brush
10. Diode terminal connector insulator	21. Rotor	32. Diode end frame
11. Spring washer	22. Key	33-34-35. Rubber bushing components
12. Screw, positive diode plate, diode terminals and stator phases ends attachment	23. Drive end frame	36. Nut
13. Plate	24. Spring washer	37. Through-bolt
	25. Pulley nut	

Fiat A12M 124/12/41M alternator—others similar

Remove three bolts, lockwashers and washers to remove starter (Bosch).

5. Reinstall in reverse order.

STARTER DRIVE REPLACEMENT

The starter can be broken down into the following subassemblies; solenoid, commutator end head, frame, armature, drive and pinion end head.

1. To disassemble, disconnect the starter motor lead from the solenoid and remove the solenoid.

2. Remove the brush cover and disconnect the brush holder.

3. Lift the brushes slightly and retain them in their holders by arranging the springs against their sides.

4. Unscrew the two self-locking nuts and take off the brush holder bracket, saving the fiber and steel thrust washers.

5. Slide the frame off the pinion end.

6. Remove the cotter pin from the linkage pivot and remove the pivot. The armature can then be taken out, along with the drive and fork lever.

7. Assembly is the reverse of removal.

ENGINE MECHANICAL

Engine

REMOVAL & INSTALLATION

All 124/Spider 2000 and 131 Models

1. Removal of 124/Spider 2000 and 131 engines is facilitated by removing the radiator and the transmission.

2. Jack up the car and place it on jack stands.

3. Drain the radiator, auxiliary tank, block and heater system by first moving the heater lever to the far right, then opening the radiator drain cock and removing the plug on the right-hand side of the block.

4. Speed drainage by removing the radiator and auxiliary tank caps.

5. Disconnect the battery leads.

6. Disconnect the ignition coil, alternator, starter, low oil pressure and water temperature indicator wires.

NOTE: Tag all wires to avoid confusion during reassembly.

7. Disconnect the accelerator rod, sliding it out of the lever ball joint end toward the dash.

8. Remove the air filter.

9. Detach the choke cable from the carburetor.

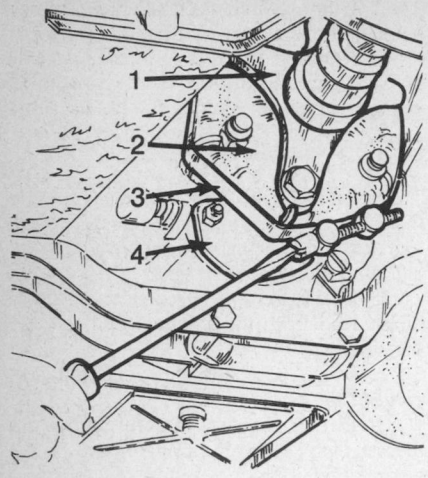

1. Propellor shaft yoke
2. Flexible coupling
3. Clamp
4. Transmission mount

Installation of flex coupling clamp before removal

— CAUTION —

On Fuel Injection models, depressurize fuel system before removing any fuel lines.

10. Disconnect the line from the fuel pump and detach the exhaust pipe from the manifold.

11. Disconnect the radiator and heater hoses.

12. Remove the upper two screws that hold the radiator to the body, then remove the radiator by sliding it from the lower support bracket.

NOTE: On cars with automatic transmission, follow the procedures outlined in the transmission section for removal and installation.

13. Working from inside the car, remove the gearshift lever by pressing down the upper part of the sleeve and, with a screwdriver, releasing the spring ring from its seating in the lower part of the lever. The upper part of the lever can then be slipped from the lower part.

14. Remove the transmission cover.

15. From under the car, disconnect the driveshaft spider and transmission mainshaft from the universal.

NOTE: This is facilitated by placing a 5 inch diameter hose clamp or a band, Tool A70025 or its equivalent, on the coupling itself to compress it slightly.

16. Disconnect the speedometer cable from the transmission and disconnect the flexible cable from the clutch fork.

17. Remove the flywheel cover, electrical ground cable and exhaust pipe bracket clip.

18. Remove the heat shield from the exhaust manifold and the three bolts that hold the starter to the front of the transmission.

19. Position a hydraulic jack under the transmission for support.

20. Remove the four bolts which mount the transmission to the crankcase.

21. Remove the crossmember that holds the transmission to the car floor.

22. Supporting the transmission jack, move it toward the rear of the car so as to withdraw the clutch shaft from the pilot bushing and clutch hub.

23. Lower the jack and pull the transmission from under the car.

24. Remove the starter from the engine compartment.

25. Using a chain hoist, pass the rear sling under the crankcase and the front sling under the thermostat housing.

26. Supporting the engine with a hoist, remove the front mounts and lift the engine clear. Push the car out from under the raised engine, then gently lower the hoist. Make sure the engine is stable before attempting further disassembly.

27. Installation is the reverse of removal.

— CAUTION —

Support the engine in such a manner so as not to damage the oil pan or any cast aluminum parts.

128

NOTE: The engine and transaxle are removed as a unit from below. Make sure the car can be raised high enough to allow sufficient clearance for removal.

1. Place the car on jack stands and be sure the car is in a stable position before removal.

2. Raise the hood and unhook the stay rod. Place covers on the fenders.

3. Loosen the wing nut and remove the spare tire.

4. Take off the lower guards.

5. Drain the water from the radiator, supply tank, cylinder block and passenger compartment heating system in the following way:

   a. Completely lower the heater lever inside the car.

   b. Open the cock at the bottom of the radiator and remove the radiator cap.

   c. Open the cock at the inner side of the engine block and take the cap off the supply tank to help water drainage.

6. Disconnect the battery cables.

7. Disconnect the primary and secondary wires from the coil to the distributor.

NOTE: Tag all wires to avoid confusion during reassembly.

8. Disconnect the wires from the alternator.

9. Disconnect the wires from the starter, the oil pressure sending unit, and the water temperature sending unit.

10. Disconnect the air cleaner.

11. Disconnect the linkage and choke wire from the carburetor.

— CAUTION —

On fuel injection models, depressurize the fuel system before removing any fuel lines.

12. Disconnect the fuel inlet hose from the fuel pump.

13. Disconnect the exhaust pipe from the manifold.

14. Remove the two rubber hoses from the union with the thermostat to the radiator.

15. Disconnect the water inlet and outlet hoses from the engine to the passenger compartment heater.

16. Disconnect the speedometer drive from the transmission housing by unscrewing the retaining ring.

17. Remove the adjustable rod of the flexible cable from the clutch release lever by unscrewing the locknut and nut.

18. Detach the anti-roll bar by removing the screws which clamp the brackets and insulators to the body. Then unscrew the nuts which fasten the ends to the control arms.

19. Remove the exhaust pipe support bracket from the transmission housing.

20. Disconnect the rod from the gearshift control lever.

21. Remove the ground strap from the transmission housing.

22. Take off the left hand wheel. Unscrew the left tie–rod-to-steering nut and disconnect the ball joint.

23. Remove the shock absorber from the pillar.

24. Unscrew the constant-speed joint nuts from both front wheels.

25. From above the car, working in the engine compartment, disconnect the reaction strut.

26. Hook up the engine and put the cable under light tension. Then, working from above, unscrew the engine–to–body clamping bolt and, from below, detach the crossmember from the underbody.

27. Work the shaft of each constant-speed joint out of its seat in the pillars and secure the axle shafts with wire to prevent them from coming away from their seats in the differential.

28. Using a hoist, lower the engine group to remove. Lower slowly and check for any wires, hoses, or linkage that may become snagged.

29. Install in the reverse order.

X1/9

— CAUTION —

Discharge the air conditioning, if installed, before attempting to remove engine assembly.

NOTE: The engine and transaxle are removed as a unit from below. Make sure the car can be raised high enough to allow sufficient clearance for removal.

1. Disconnect the battery and drain the cooling system.

2. Remove the air cleaner assembly.

3. Disconnect the air pump inlet hose and outlet hose from the pump.

4. Disconnect the heater return hose at the coupling joint and disconnect the heater hose from the pump.

5. Disconnect the wires from the alternator.

NOTE: Tag all wires to avoid confusion during reassembly.

6. Remove the two bolts retaining the louvered protection panel below the carbon trap in the rear firewall.

7. Disconnect the manual choke linkage from the carburetor. On models with an automatic choke, remove the water lines.

8. Disconnect all vacuum hoses from the carburetor. Disconnect the electrical leads from the solenoid and the carburetor vent hose from the carburetor.

9. Disconnect the coil wires at the distributor. Disconnect the leads from the oil pressure and water temperature sending units. Disconnect the electrical wires from the starter.

--- CAUTION ---

On fuel injection models, depressurize the fuel system before removing any fuel lines.

10. Remove the clamp securing the fuel lines to the firewall and disconnect the fuel supply and return lines from the firewall.

11. Remove the stopbolt from the accelerator cable, slide the seal off the cable, remove the retainer clip from the cable sheath and remove the cable from the support.

12. Remove the bolts securing the coolant expansion tank, top and bottom, and lift the tank, allowing the water to drain into the engine. Disconnect the hoses from the tank at the thermostat and remove the tank.

13. Remove the hoses from the thermostat.

14. Remove the cotter pin holding the slave cylinder pushrod to the clutch shaft. Loosen the two bolts securing the slave cylinder to the transmission. Open the bleeder screw of the slave cylinder and allow the pushrod to retract. Swing the slave cylinder out of the way.

15. From underneath the vehicle, remove the remaining bolt holding the louvered panel and remove the panel from the firewall. Remove the heat shield located behind the alternator. Remove the three panels from the bottom of the engine compartment and the panel inboard of each rear wheel.

16. Drain the transmission/differential lubricant.

17. Disconnect the electrical connectors for the seatbelt interlock system and the back-up lights. Remove any clamps as necessary to allow the wires to be removed with the engine.

18. Disconnect the speedometer cable from the differential and secure the cable out of the way.

19. Remove the bolts retaining the gearshift linkage to the shifting tube. Loosen the bolt at the transmission end of the flexible link and swing the link to one side.

20. Remove the bolts holding the ground strap to the body.

21. Straighten the lock-tabs on the exhaust manifold flange. Remove the four nuts and lock-tab plates. Remove the 2 bolts from the upper bracket at the left end of the muffler. Remove the two nuts retaining the center support of the muffler to the crossmember and remove the muffler assembly. Remove the two nuts and bolt retaining the upper bracket to the differential case and remove the bracket.

22. Remove the three bolts securing the axle boot retaining ring on the right and left sides and slide the boots away from the differential, draining any excess oil.

23. Remove the handbrake cable bracket at the forward end of each suspension control arm.

24. Take note of and record the number of shims at each suspension control arm mounting point.

25. Remove the four bolts and nuts plus the shims holding the control arms to the body and swing the control arms downward out of their brackets. Move the control arms away from the differential until the axles are free of the differential. Secure the axle assemblies to the control arms.

NOTE: If necessary, the entire suspension assemblies may be removed at this time by removing the wheels and brake calipers and the three nuts securing the top of the shock absorbers.

26. Straighten the lock-tabs on the two bolts on each end of the lower crossmember and loosen the bolts. Lower the vehicle until the engine is resting on a support.

--- CAUTION ---

Support the engine in such a manner so as not to damage the oil pan or any cast aluminum parts.

Remove the bolts from the lower crossmember.

27. From the top of the engine compartment, disconnect the engine torque rod from the bracket on the engine.

28. Remove the bolt from the engine mount, raise the car slightly and rock the engine/transmission assembly in order to clear the front engine mount.

29. Carefully raise the vehicle while supporting the engine. Watch for snags by wires, hoses or linkage.

30. Install the engine in the reverse order of removal.

Strada

NOTE: The engine and transaxle are removed as a unit from below. Make sure the car can be raised high enough to allow sufficient clearance for removal.

1. Remove the hood, jack and spare tire.

2. Disconnect the battery positive and negative leads, starter and ground at engine.

3. Drain the cooling system. Discharge the air conditioning, if equipped.

--- CAUTION ---

The sudden discharge of freon from any A/C system can be extremely dangerous.

4. Remove three nuts and washers to remove air cleaner cover. Remove the four self-locking nuts to remove air cleaner assembly complete with the hoses to the cold air box, exhaust manifold shield, oil separator, reed valve, or check valve for the air pump.

5. Plug the openings to prevent dirt entry.

6. Mark to identify, then remove the electrical leads to engine left and right side sending units, engine bottom side sending unit, reverse gear switch, starter solenoid, intake manifold, idle stop solenoid and A/C compressor.

7. For vehicles with a separate voltage regulator, disconnect the alternator leads at the voltage regulator, and the two leads near the heater box.

8. For vehicles with an integral regulator, disconnect the two alternator leads near the heater box.

--- CAUTION ---

On Fuel Injection models, depressurize fuel system before attempting to remove any fuel lines.

9. Remove any fuel and vapor canister lines from the carburetor. Disconnect the vapor canister hose from the exhaust manifold shield.

10. Disconnect the vacuum hose to the brake booster at the intake manifold and disconnect the air hose to the gulp valve.

11. On A/C cars, disconnect the vacuum hose to the fast idle diaphragm at the carburetor.

12. Disconnect the vacuum hose to the vacuum manifold at the T-fitting. Disconnect the vacuum hose at the electrovalve.

13. On manual transmission cars, disconnect the return spring at the carburetor. Slide the lock ring off the ball socket and remove from the bracket.

14. On automatic transmission cars, loosen the locknuts on the trans linkage (kick-down).

15. Remove the accelerator cable from the bracket and unhook the eyelet from the kick-down lever.

16. On A/C vehicles, disconnect the compressor delivery hose at the condensor and the compressor return hose at the barometric valve.

17. Disconnect the heater hoses at the engine.

18. Disconnect the upper and lower radiator hoses at the engine.

19. Raise the car on a lift and support it safely.

20. Remove the front wheels, left and right splash shields from the fender wells and from the front center.

21. Remove the gearshift control rod, reverse lamp connector, left side reaction rod (manual trans), left side hub support, left side control arm, right side control arm and center rubber mount.

22. Disconnect the power unit support bracket.

23. Remove two nuts and bolts, each side, to separate the strut assembly from the hub carrier.

24. Remove the nut on each side and use Fiat tool A.47038 or equivalent to separate the tie-rod ball joint from the hub carrier.

25. Remove six allen head capscrews and three plates, each side, to separate the axles (halfshafts) from the differential.

NOTE: Discard allen screws and replace with new ones for installation.

26. Make sure that the catalytic converter is cool, then straighten the lock tabs on the mounting nuts and remove the converter.

27. On air pump equipped vehicles, remove two nuts, washers and bolts from the exhaust pipe. Remove the exhaust pipe.

28. Disconnect the speedometer cable.

29. On manual transmission cars, scribe an alignment mark on the shift rod and bracket. Remove two nuts, washers, lockwashers and bolts. Disconnect the shift rod.

30. On automatic cars, place the gear selector in 1. Remove E-clip and washer and then slide the shift cable eyelet off of the pin on the transmission lever.

31. Remove the nut from the cable clamp and lay the cable aside.

32. Attach a lift sling to the engine and transmission assembly.

33. Place a jack under the center engine mount. Remove two bolts and washers to separate the engine mount from the body.

34. Remove two bolts, lockwashers and washers attaching the right engine mount to the mounting bracket.

35. Remove two upper and loosen only lower bolts, lockwasher and washer. Remove the mounting bracket. Do not remove the right engine mount.

36. On automatic transmission models, remove the bolt and washer from the left engine mount. Remove the two bolts and lockwashers to separate the sway bar from its mounting bracket.

37. Remove two bolts and lockwashers to separate the mounting bracket from the body.

38. On manual transmission cars, remove three nuts, lockwashers and bolts to separate the mounting bracket from the body.

39. Slowly remove the jack supporting the center engine mount. Slowly lower the engine out of the engine compartment.

40. Install the engine in reverse order of removal. Refill the cooling system and inspect all lines for tightness.

Cylinder Head

REMOVAL & INSTALLATION

124/Spider 2000 and 131 DOHC Engine

1. Before beginning any dismantling procedures, find the valve timing marks. Turn the engine over until the timing mark on the crank pulley is aligned with the TDC mark on the front cover, and the rotor is pointing at No. 4 in the distributor cap. At this point, the marks on the cam housings should be visible and in line with the holes in the cam gears.

2. Drain the cooling system and disconnect the upper radiator hose.

3. Remove the air cleaner.

--------- CAUTION ---------

On fuel injection models, depressurize the fuel system before removing any fuel lines. See "Fuel Injection" later in this section for the depressurizing procedure.

4. Disconnect all linkage and hoses from the carburetor and cylinder head.

5. Remove the carburetor and intake manifold as an assembly.

6. Disconnect the exhaust manifold from the side of the cylinder head.

7. Remove the timing belt shroud from the front of the engine.

8. Loosen the timing belt tensioner (idler) and remove the timing belt from the camshaft drive pulleys.

9. Remove the spark plug wires from the spark plugs.

10. Unscrew the cylinder head attaching bolts and carefully lift off the cylinder head.

Lift the head straight up so as not to damage any of the open valves.

11. Clean the mating surfaces of all gasket material.

12. Before placing the cylinder head on the block, make sure the holes in the cam gears are aligned with the marks on the cam housings. Once the timing marks are aligned, avoid turning the camshafts until the drive belt has been installed.

13. Carefully place the cylinder head on the block. Do not allow any of the open valves to contact the block.

14. Install the cylinder head bolts and torque to specifications in the proper sequence.

15. Install the belt on the crankshaft pulley, auxiliary shaft pulley, intake camshaft pulley, exhaust cam pulley and the tensioner.

NOTE: Timing belts should never be re-used. Replace the timing belt if removed for any reason.

16. The procedure for tightening the belt is to allow the tensioner to remove the play from the belt.

17. Check the belt tension after turning the crankshaft two or three times.

18. Check for proper valve timing by checking the timing marks. Assemble the

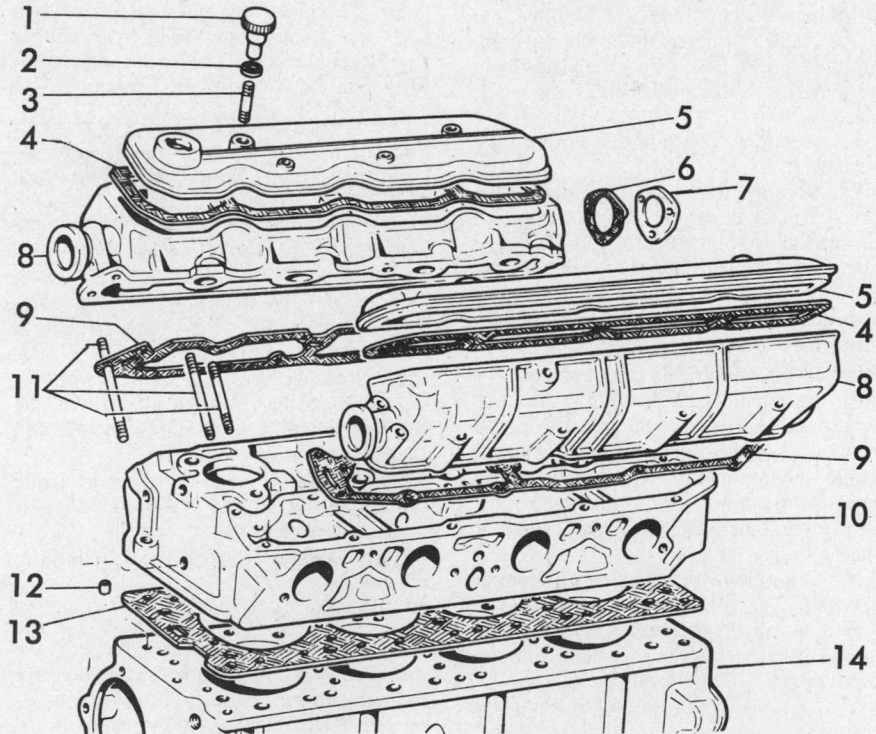

1. Knob
2. Washer
3. Stud
4. Cover gasket
5. Cover
6. End cover gasket
7. End cover
8. Cam housing
9. Cam housing gasket
10. Cylinder head
11. Studs
12. Locating dowel
13. Head gasket
14. Engine block

Exploded view of the 131, 124 and Spider double overhead cam (DOHC) cylinder head

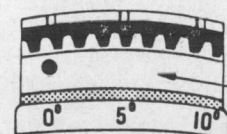

remaining components in the reverse order of removal.

128 and Strada SOHC Engine

NOTE: The aluminum cylinder head sometimes seizes on 128 and X1/9 models. To remove the head, remove all nuts and washers, then saturate the area around the studs with penetrating oil and allow to soak overnight. Before reassembly, clean all oil from the studs and housings and apply anti-seize compound.

1. Drain the cooling system. Disconnect the battery.

2. Remove the spare tire from the engine compartment.

3. Remove the air cleaner.

4. Disconnect the spark plug cables.

5. Disconnect the accelerator control linkage from the carburetor.

CAUTION

On fuel injection models, depressurize the fuel system before removing any fuel lines.

6. Disconnect the fuel line and the choke heater hoses from the carburetor.

7. Disconnect the temperature sending unit electrical lead and thermoswitch leads.

8. Disconnect the heater inlet hose, the upper and lower radiator hoses, and the coolant pump delivery hose from the thermostat housing. On A/C equipped models, remove the distributor.

9. Disconnect the exhaust pipe from the manifold and remove the bracket.

10. Remove the belt guard cover, working from below the vehicle to get at the lower screw after removing a guard. 1978 and later models have a two-piece cover.

11. Loosen the belt tensioner pulley retaining nut and remove the belt from the camshaft sprocket.

NOTE: Timing belts should never be re-used. Replace the timing belt if removed for any reason.

12. Unscrew the belt guard lower screw.

13. Remove the shroud by unscrewing the set screws. Remove the air pump and alternator brackets.

14. Disconnect the reaction rod from the bracket in the cylinder head.

15. Remove the cylinder head retaining screws and nuts and remove the cylinder head along with the intake and exhaust

manifolds, carburetor, and the camshaft housing. Removal of these parts is best performed with the cylinder head out of the vehicle.

CAUTION

Do not allow the cylinder head to rest on any open valves. The proper size cap screws on each corner will ensure enough clearance during bench work.

16. Install the cylinder head, with the intake and exhaust manifolds, carburetor and camshaft housing assembled to it, in the reverse order of removal. Tighten the cylinder head bolts in the proper sequence in two stages; 29 ft. lbs. the first time and to specifications the second time.

X1/9 SOHC Engine

See the note preceding the 128 cylinder head removal section before beginning.

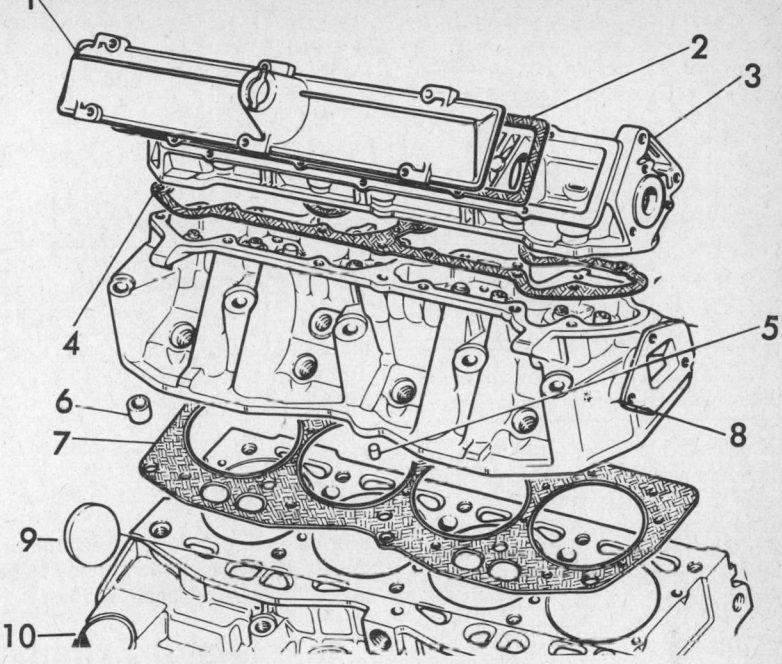

1. Cover
2. Cover gasket
3. Cam housing
4. Cam housing gasket
5. Locating dowel
6. Bushing
7. Cylinder head gasket
8. Cylinder head
9. Welsh plug
10. Engine block

Exploded view of single cam cylinder head—typical

ALIGN CAMSHAFT TIMING MARKS WITH CAM HOUSING MARKS

PULLEY TIMING MARK IS AT 0° (TDC)

Timing mark alignment—DOHC engines

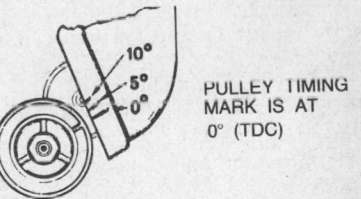

ALIGN CAMSHAFT TIMING MARK WITH BELT COVER POINTER

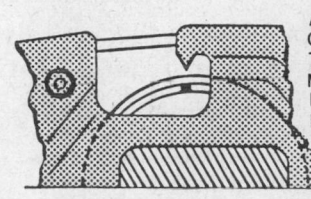

FLYWHEEL TIMING MARK IS AT 0° (TDC) (BELL HOUSING VIEW)

Timing mark alignment—SOHC engines

1. Drain the cooling system and disconnect the battery.
2. Remove the air cleaner assembly.

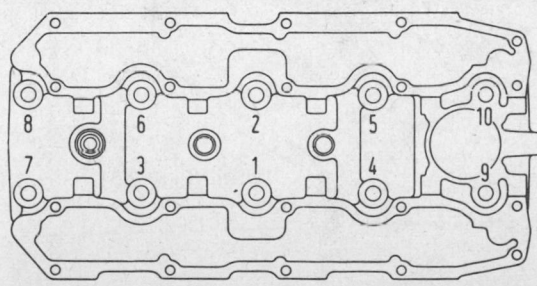

Torque sequence for the 124/Spider 2000 and 131

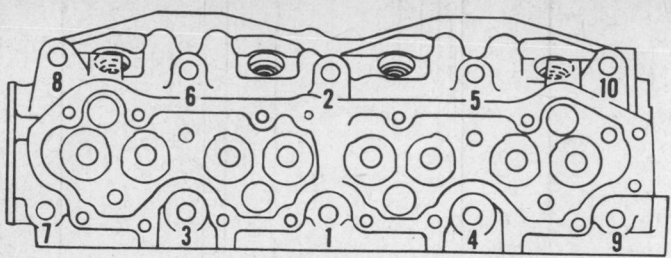

Torque sequence for the 128, X1/9 and Strada

— CAUTION —

On fuel injection models, depressurize the fuel system before removing any fuel lines.

3. Disconnect the fuel hoses from the carburetor and pull the two hoses out of the bracket on the camshaft cover.

4. Disconnect the accelerator linkage leading from the carburetor at the camshaft.

5. Disconnect the spark plug cables from the spark plugs.

6. Disconnect the distributor vacuum hose from the fitting in the cylinder head.

7. Remove the stop-bolt from the accelerator cable.

8. Slide the seal off of the cable and remove the clip retaining the cable to the camshaft cover. Remove the cable.

9. Disconnect the expansion tank hose, water pump inlet and outlet hoses, and the water pump-to-union hose.

10. Remove the bolt retaining the engine torque rod in its bracket and move the rod out of the way.

11. Disconnect the hose from the exhaust shroud.

12. Disconnect the electrical leads of the thermostatic switch on the carburetor.

13. Disconnect the evaporative hose from the carburetor.

14. Remove the air pump hoses.

15. Disconnect the muffler from the exhaust manifold flange.

16. Remove the bolts and washers attaching the timing cover.

17. Remove the lower right shield from under the engine.

18. Remove the alternator and the drive belt.

19. Remove the air pump.

20. Loosen the nut on the timing belt tensioner pulley and remove the timing belt.

NOTE: Timing belts should never be re-used. Replace the timing belt if removed for any reason.

21. Remove the lower bolt through the belt guard.

22. Remove the cylinder head attaching bolts and nuts and lift the cylinder head straight up and off of the engine. The carburetor and intake and exhaust manifolds are removed with the cylinder head as an assembly and removed from the cylinder head on the work bench.

23. Install the cylinder head in the reverse order of removal. Tighten the cyl-

inder head bolts in the proper sequence. The valve timing is adjusted in the same manner as for the 128.

CYLINDER HEAD OVERHAUL

For all cylinder head overhaul procedures, please refer to "Engine Rebuilding" in the Unit Repair section.

Intake and Exhaust Manifolds

REMOVAL & INSTALLATION

All Models

NOTE: Depressurize fuel system on fuel injection models.

1. Remove the air cleaner.

2. Remove the fuel line, all vacuum lines, coolant lines and accelerator linkage from the carburetor.

3. The carburetor can be removed at this point or removed after the manifold is removed from the vehicle.

4. Disconnect the exhaust pipe from the manifold. This is not necessary if removing just the intake manifold on DOHC engines.

5. Remove the manifold retaining bolts from the cylinder head and remove the manifold from the engine.

6. Install the manifold(s) in the reverse order of removal, tighten the retaining bolts to specification in an alternating sequence starting at the center and working toward the ends. Torque all bolts to 20 ft. lbs.

Turbocharger

The Turbo Spider uses an I.H.I.RHB6 turbocharger unit that is calibrated to deliver a maximum boost of 6 psi. The low inertia turbine wheel is connected to a compressor wheel by a shaft. The shaft is supported by two bearings floating on a thin film of engine oil. The turbocharger unit is bolted to a modified exhaust manifold and is driven by exhaust gases that will spin the turbine wheel at up to 100,000 rpm. A wastegate, controlled by boost pressure, prevents damaging overboost by allowing some exhaust to bypass the turbocharger when the pressure exceeds 6 psi.

NOTE: The fuel injection system is modified to allow boost and load enrichment and contains an overboost fail-safe circuit that will shut off the fuel injectors should the wastegate fail and boost pressure reach 9 psi.

REMOVAL & INSTALLATION

1. Remove the air intake and output hoses from the compressor side of the turbocharger.

2. Disconnect the oil feed and return lines.

NOTE: Use a new compression fitting when reinstalling oil lines.

3. Remove the eight allen head bolts attaching the turbocharger flanges to the

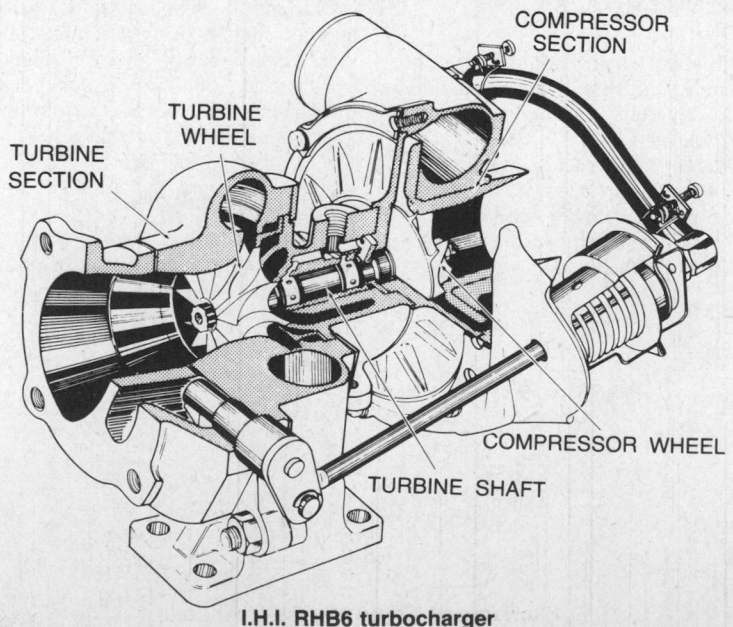

I.H.I. RHB6 turbocharger

exhaust system.

NOTE: Discard the allen bolts. Use new bolts for installation.

4. Disconnect the Lambda sensor.

5. Remove the allen bolts from the exhaust elbow to the support bracket.

6. Remove the bolts from the turbocharger support bracket and remove the turbocharger assembly.

7. Reinstall in reverse order, torquing all bolts to specifications.

NOTE: Turbocharger mounting and flange bolts should be torqued every 15,000 miles.

TURBOCHARGER TORQUE REFERENCE

Description	Torque (ft. lbs.)
Turbocharger to exhaust manifold	20
Exhaust manifold nuts	22
Outlet elbow to turbocharger bolts	22
Outlet elbow to exhaust pipe nuts	22
Outlet elbow support bracket to block bolts	30
Plenum support bracket to plenum bolt	12
Lambda sensor	30
Exhaust manifold heat shield	22

NOTE: Retorque all bolts 1500 miles after reinstalling turbocharger.

Timing Gear Cover

REMOVAL & INSTALLATION

131 and 124/Spider 2000 DOHC

The valve mechanism drive belt cover on these engines is removed by simply removing the retaining screws and lifting the cover from the engine. Install in reverse order.

128 and X1/9

1. On 128 models, loosen the right engine mount and jack the engine up slightly.

2. On X1/9 models, there is no room to jack the engine. Remove the bolts that retain the belt cover and work the cover loose. There is no easy way to do this.

3. On 128 models, remove the bolts and tilt the cover up and out. If the engine is jacked up far enough, the cover should come out intact.

4. Installation is the reverse of removal.

Strada

1. Remove the bolts, lockwashers and washers holding the timing belt covers. Remove the covers.

2. Remove attaching hardware for the inner shields. Remove the shields.

3. Installation is the reverse of removal.

NOTE: Lower cover bolt must be removed from under car.

Timing Belt

NOTE: Fiat recommends that the timing belt not be reused. Whenever belt tension is relieved, the timing belt must be replaced. The belt should also be replaced every 50,000 miles.

REMOVAL & INSTALLATION

124/Spider 2000 and 131 DOHC

1. Before dismantling anything, turn the engine over by hand until the No. 4 cylinder is on TDC and the timing mark on the crank pulley is aligned with the TDC mark on the timing cover. The rotor should be pointing at No. 4 in the distributor cap.

2. At this point, you should be able to see that the holes in the cam pulleys are aligned with the small cast fingers on the cam housing.

3. If the car is equipped with air-conditioning, remove the compressor drive belt.

4. Partially drain the cooling system and remove the upper radiator hose.

5. Remove the thermostat housing.

6. Remove the timing belt cover.

7. Remove the drive belt for the air pump. Remove the alternator drive belt.

8. Loosen the nut on the belt tensioner. Loosen the bolt for the spring support. Pry the tensioner away from the belt and remove the belt.

9. Install a new belt. Allow the tensioner to remove the play from the belt, and tighten the tensioner and the spring support. Rotate the engine a couple of times and recheck the belt tension.

10. Loosely install the belt cover and check to make sure all the valve timing marks line up.

11. If the valve timing is correct, reinstall the timing belt cover.

12. Reinstall the remaining components in the reverse order of removal.

128 SOHC

1. Remove the timing gear cover. The lower retaining screw of the cover must be

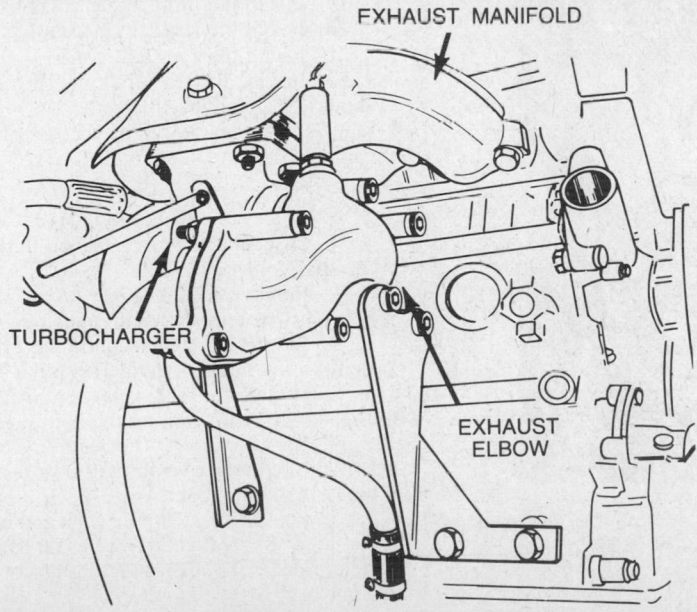

Turbocharger mounting location

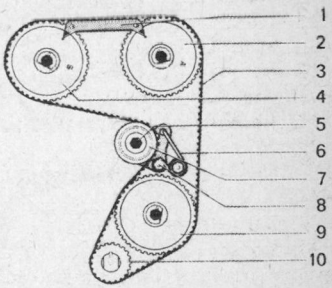

1. Valve timing pointers
2. Intake camshaft drive pulley
3. Timing belt
4. Exhaust camshaft/distributor drive pulley
5. Roller retaining nut
6. Tensioner spring
7. Tensioner roller
8. Tensioner retaining screw
9. Oil pump drive pulley
10. Crankshaft pulley

124/Spider 2000 and 131 engine cam drive

removed from under the car after removing the right side guard.

2. Check the valve timing by aligning the timing mark on the camshaft sprocket with the fixed mark on the engine and making sure that the timing mark on the crankshaft sprocket is simultaneously aligned with its fixed index mark.

3. Remove the water pump and alternator drive belt.

4. Loosen the tensioner pulley retaining nut and relieve the spring pressure to remove the timing belt.

5. Install the new belt, making sure the belt and sprocket teeth engage perfectly.

6. Tighten the tensioner pulley nut to 33 ft. lbs.

X1/9

1. Turn the crankshaft until the No. 4 piston is at TDC of the compression stroke. The timing mark on the front (right) crankshaft pulley should be at TDC and the camshaft timing pulley mark should be aligned with the cast finger of the support, visible through the hole in the camshaft cover.

NOTE: Throughout this entire procedure remember that if the camshaft is turned independently of the crankshaft the valves may hit the pistons causing damage.

2. Remove the bolts attaching the timing cover, remove the right guard from under the engine, remove the lower bolt retaining the timing cover and remove the cover.

3. Loosen the alternator and remove the alternator/water pump drive belt.

4. Remove the drive pulley from the crankshaft.

5. Loosen the air pump and remove the drive belt.

6. Remove the camshaft cover. Check and make sure the cam lobes of the No. 4 cylinder are pointing up.

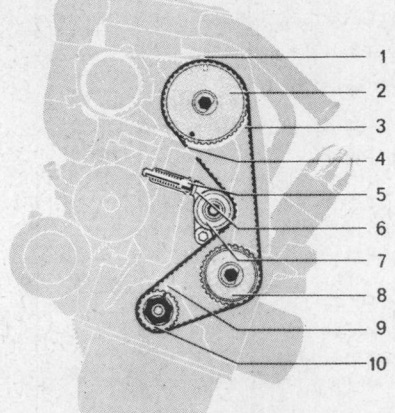

1. Camshaft timing reference mark (engine on car)
2. Camshaft drive pulley
3. Toothed timing belt, driving the camshaft and pulley 8
4. Camshaft timing reference mark (engine on bench)
5. Idler pulley tensioner
6. Idler pulley support
7. Idler pulley
8. Drive pulley for oil pump and ignition distributor
9. Reference mark for pulley 10 setting
10. Crankshaft sprocket

128, X1/9 and Strada engine cam drive

1. Exhaust camshaft sprocket
2. Intake camshaft sprocket
3. Oil dipstick tube
4. Tensioner bracket bolt
5. Spring retaining bolt
6. Hole
7. Bolt
8. Crankshaft sprocket
9. Auxiliary shaft sprocket
10. Spacer
11. Tensioner pulley
12. Belt

124/Spider 2000 and 131 DOHC engine

7. Remove the distributor.

8. Loosen the idler pulley locknut, push it on the support and tighten the locknut. Remove the timing belt, starting at the idler pulley.

9. Install the new timing belt, starting at the crankshaft. Twist the belt gently into position around the crankshaft pulley. Do not kink the belt.

10. Slip the belt over the camshaft pulley. The camshaft pulley may have to be turned slightly to align the slots with the belt cogs.

11. Install the belt over the idler pulley last.

12. Loosen the idler pulley locknut and retighten after tension is on the belt. Turn the crankshaft one half of a turn in the direction of normal rotation by either pushing the car with it in fourth gear or bumping the starter.

13. Release the idler pulley locknut to make sure all slack is removed from the belt and then retighten the locknut.

14. Continue to turn the crankshaft in the direction of normal rotation by either method mentioned in Step 12 until the No. 4 piston reaches TDC of the compression stroke (one and one-half turns).

NOTE: Never push the car backward in gear or allow the engine to rock backward while pushing the car. Slack will develop in the belt, allowing the belt to jump timing.

15. Position the belt cover on the engine and check to make sure the crankshaft timing mark is at TDC and that the camshaft mark is aligned with the pointer. Tighten the tensioner pulley nut to 32 ft. lbs.

16. Install the pulley on the crankshaft.

17. Install the drive belt on the air pump.

18. Install the drive belt for the water pump and the alternator. Adjust the belt tension.

19. Install the timing gear cover.

20. Install the lower right guard.

21. Install the camshaft cover.

22. Install the distributor. The rotor should be pointing toward the No. 4 cylinder spark plug tower of the distributor cap.

Strada

1. Disconnect battery cable. Remove the spark plugs.

2. Remove the timing belt covers (lower bolt must be removed from under car).

3. Rotate the engine until the crankshaft pulley mark is aligned with the TDC indicator and the cam sprocket mark is aligned with the mark on the belt guard.

4. Loosen the alternator (and A/C compressor if equipped) mounting bolts and remove the pulley belt.

5. Loosen the idler pulley nut and move the pulley toward the firewall as far as possible. Secure the idler pulley in place with a nut.

6. Remove the timing belt.

7. Install the new timing belt with slack

on the tensioner side. Make sure that the teeth are perfectly aligned with the sprockets.

8. Loosen the idler pulley nut and the tensioner will tighten the timing belt. Torque the idler pulley nut to 33 ft. lbs.

9. Check that the timing marks are still aligned.

10. Reinstall the covers, spark plugs and battery cable.

Camshafts

REMOVAL & INSTALLATION

128, Strada, and X1/9 SOHC

1. Remove the camshaft drive belt.
2. Remove the camshaft carrier attaching bolts and remove the camshaft carrier assembly from the engine.
3. Remove the camshaft drive sprocket.
4. Remove the camshaft thrust plate from the opposite end (opposite the belt end) of the camshaft carrier.
5. Carefully slide the camshaft out of the camshaft carrier.
6. Install the camshaft in the reverse order of removal, making sure the valve timing marks on the camshaft sprocket and the crankshaft sprocket are properly aligned before installing the timing belt. See "Timing Belt Removal and Installation" procedure.

124/Spider 2000 and 131 DOHC

1. Remove the timing cover and remove the camshaft drive belt.
2. Remove the camshaft housings.
3. Remove the bolts in the center of the cam pulleys. Remove the cam pulleys with a gear puller.
4. Remove the three nuts retaining the front cam covers.
5. Slide the camshafts out from the cam housings.
6. Installation is the reverse of removal. Refer to the "Timing Belt Removal and Installation" procedure.

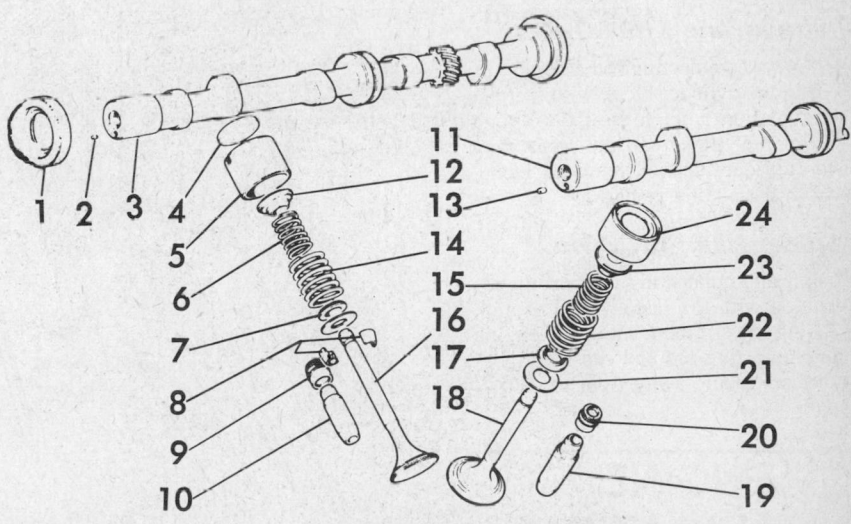

1. Camshaft sprocket
2. Tensioner pulley
3. Drive pulley
4. Auxiliary shaft sprocket
5. Tensioner
6. Belt guard
7. Bracket

Removing the belt tensioner pulley nut

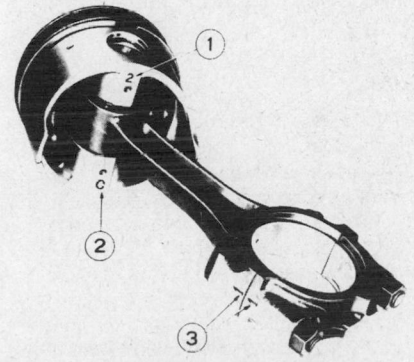

1. Piston pin bore class
2. Piston class
3. Matching number of connecting rod to cylinder

Piston identification marks

1. Camshaft seal
2. Exhaust camshaft dowel
3. Exhaust camshaft
4. Tappet plate
5. Exhaust valve tappet
6. Exhaust valve inner spring
7. Lower cup
8. Locks
9. Exhaust valve oil seal
10. Exhaust valve guide
11. Intake camshaft
12. Upper cup
13. Dowel
14. Exhaust valve outer spring
15. Intake valve inner spring
16. Exhaust valve
17. Lower cup
18. Intake valve
19. Intake valve guide
20. Oil seal
21. Washer
22. Intake valve outer spring
23. Upper cup
24. Intake valve tappet

124/Spider 2000 and 131 DOHC valve mechanism—typical

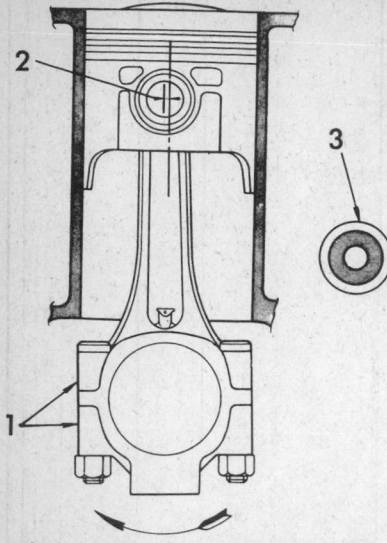

1. Location of the connecting rod and bearing cap identification and cylinder number
2. Piston pin offset 0.08 in.
3. Auxiliary shaft
NOTE: Arrow shows direction of crankshaft rotation

Piston and connecting rod installation for all engines

PISTON AND CONNECTING ROD IDENTIFICATION AND POSITIONING

If the connecting rod and piston assemblies are going to be reinstalled in the engine, they should be clearly identified during disassembly so they can be reinstalled in their original positions.

128, Strada, and X1/9 SOHC

The piston and connecting rod assembly is installed in the cylinder block with the piston identification letter toward the timing belt end of the engine and the connecting rod and cap identification numbers facing away from the auxiliary shaft.

124/Spider 2000, 131 DOHC

The piston and connecting rod assemblies are installed with the piston identification letter facing toward the front of the engine and the connecting rod and cap identification numbers facing away from the auxiliary shaft.

ENGINE LUBRICATION

Oil Pan

REMOVAL & INSTALLATION

124/Spider 2000 and 131

1. Drain the engine oil.

2. Raise the car in the air and support it securely.

3. The engine will have to be raised about six inches in the chassis in order for the oil pan to be removed. Unbolt the motor mounts and raise the engine up about six inches.

4. You will have to fabricate some way of holding the engine in the air while removing the oil pan. Remove the oil pan bolts and remove the pan.

5. Installation is the reverse of removal.

128 and X1/9

1. Raise the car in the air and support it securely. Drain the engine oil.

2. The oil pan can be removed from the bottom only if the engine is raised and supported which will allow the engine mounting crossmember and splash shields to be removed.

3. If a hoist is available, raise the engine high enough to take the strain off, and remove the crossmember and splash shields. The crossmember holds the engine up, so be careful.

4. Unbolt the oil pan and remove it.

5. Installation is in the reverse of removal.

Strada

1. Raise the car and support it safely.

2. Drain the engine oil.

3. Remove the 20 bolts and lockwashers holding the oil pan.

4. Remove the oil pan and gasket.

5. Installation is the reverse of removal. Clean the oil pan and block mating surfaces, use a new gasket.

Oil Pump

REMOVAL & INSTALLATION

All Models

1. Remove the oil pan.

2. Remove the oil pump assembly attaching bolts and remove the oil pump.

3. Install the oil pump in the reverse order of removal.

Crankshaft Oil Seals

REPLACEMENT—REAR

All Models

The transmission must be removed in order to replace the rear main oil seal. The oil seal housing is bolted to the rear of the engine block. With the housing removed, press the old seal out of the housing and press the new seal into place. Oil the lips

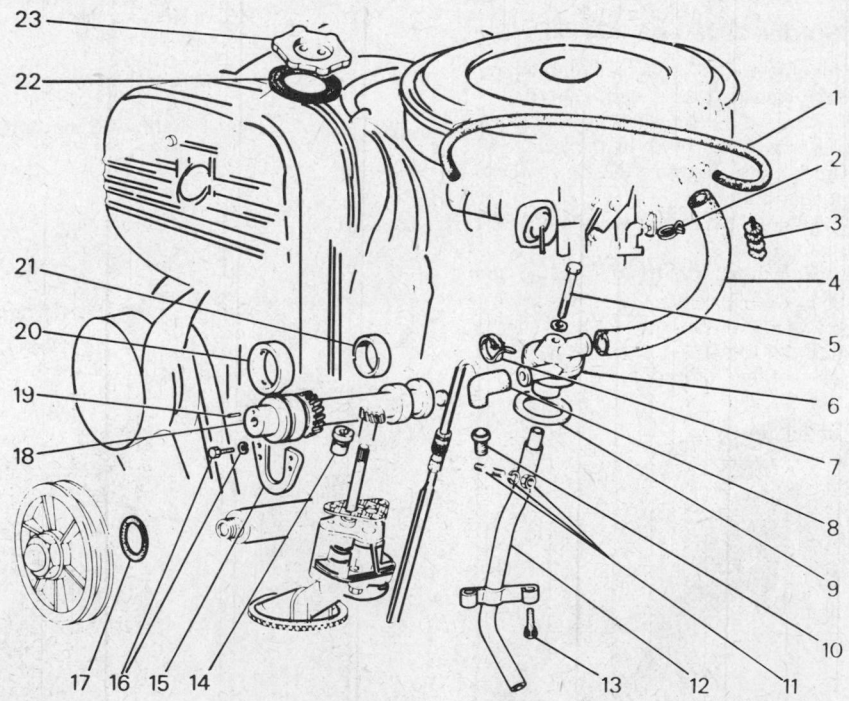

1. Blow-by gas and oil vapor hose
2. Collar
3. Flam trap
4. Breather hose
5. Bolt and washer
6. Breather
7. Collar
8. Hose
9. Seal
10. Vapor return connection
11. Stud, lockwasher, and nut
12. Breather tube
13. Bolt
14. Gear bushing
15. Retaining plate
16. Bolt and lockwasher
17. Spring washer
18. Auxiliary shaft
19. Dowel
20. Front bushing
21. Rear bushing
22. Seal
23. Oil filler cap

124/Spider 2000 and 131 DOHC engine lubrication components

of the seal before installation. All engines use indexing lugs to aid the centering of the seal and housing.

REPLACEMENT—FRONT

All Models

The timing belt and cover assembly must be removed from the front of the engine to expose the front crankshaft seal housing. The seal is pressed into the housing. The housing has indexing lugs to assist the centering of the housing. Lubricate the seal lips before installation.

Auxiliary Shaft Seals

REPLACEMENT

All Models

The auxiliary shaft seal housing is exposed with the removal of the timing belt, cover assembly, and front accessories. Unbolt the housing from the engine, and remove the old seal. Press the new seal into the housing cover, center the cover over the shaft flange, and bolt it into place. Oil the lips of the seal before installation.

ENGINE COOLING

NOTE: All models use an electric cooling fan, operated by a thermoswitch.

Radiator

REMOVAL & INSTALLATION

124/Spider 2000 and 131

1. Open the petcock at the bottom of the radiator and drain the coolant from the radiator and cylinder block.

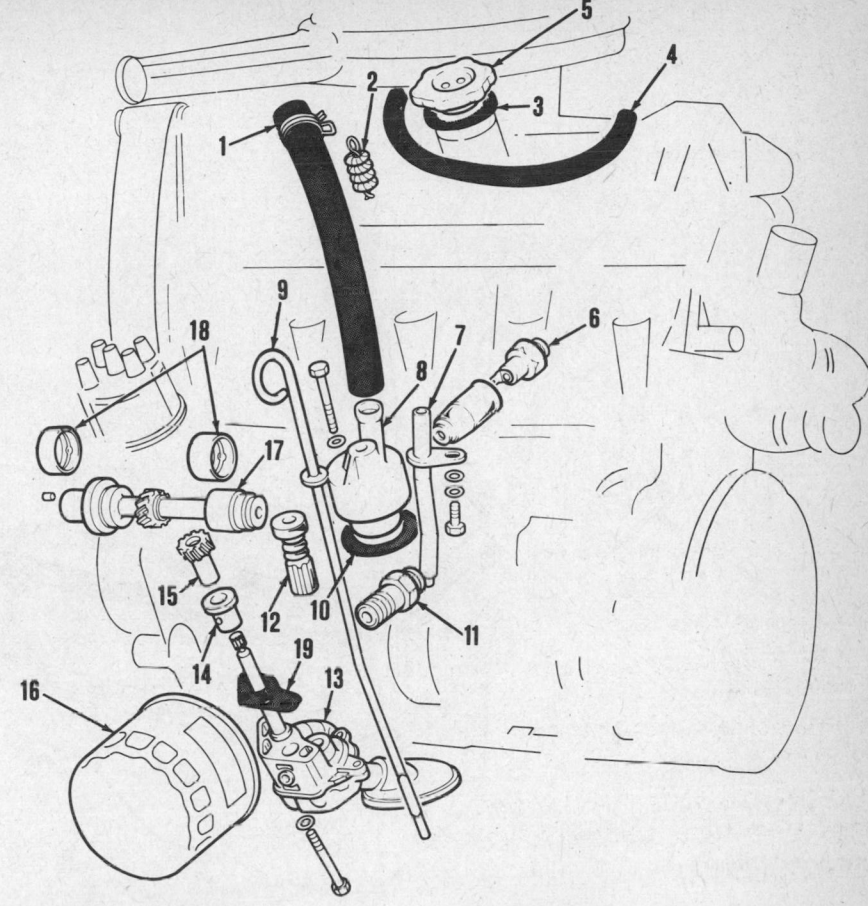

1. Breather hose
2. Flame trap
3. Seal
4. Blow-by gas and oil vapor hose
5. Oil filler cap
6. Oil pressure sw
7. Breather oil return pipe
8. Crankcase breather
9. Dipstick
10. Gasket
11. Oil filter connector
12. Dipstick seal
13. Oil pump
14. Bushing
15. Oil pump drive gear
16. Oil filter
17. Auxiliary shaft
18. Bushings
19. Gasket

Strada and X1/9 engine lubrication components

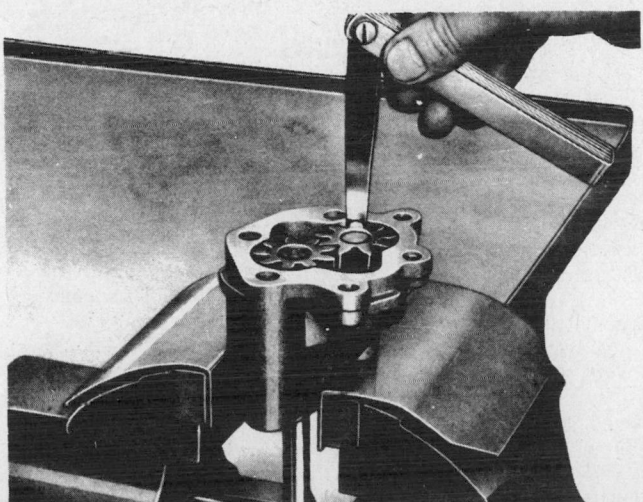

Measuring clearance between gear and housing of oil pump

Measuring clearance between ends of gears and

1. Bolt and lockwasher	8. Bolt and lockwasher	15. Stud, lockwasher, and nut
2. Auxiliary shaft cover	9. Rear cover	16. Bolt and lockwasher
3. Gasket	10. Gasket	17. Front cover
4. Cover	11. Gasket	18. Oil seal
5. Bolt	12. Bolt and lockwasher	19. Bolt and lockwasher
6. Gasket	13. Drain plug	20. Gasket
7. Oil seal	14. Oil sump	21. Oil seal

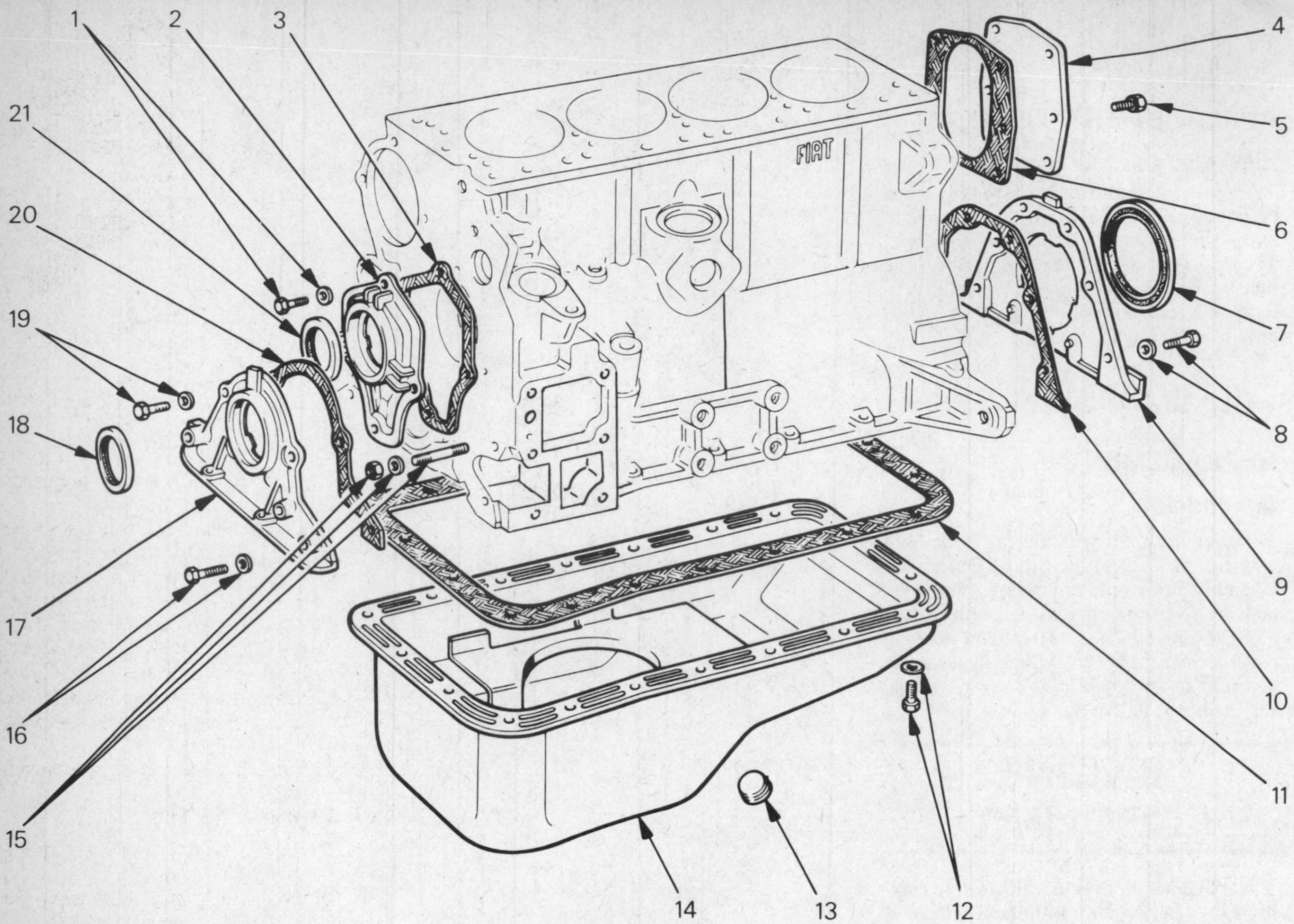

Oil pan and crankshaft seal locations—typical

2. Remove the hose which connects the radiator and thermostat cover.

3. Remove the coolant hoses.

4. When equipped with an automatic transmission, disconnect oil lines.

5. Unbolt and remove the radiator.

6. Installation is the reverse of removal.

128 and Strada

1. Drain the radiator and the cylinder block.

2. Disconnect the thermal fan switch and the fan relay switch.

3. Disconnect the coolant hoses.

4. Remove the screws that attach the top part of the radiator to the brackets fitted on the body, together with the rubber pads, washers, and spacers.

5. Slide the radiator, fan, and shroud out of the top of the engine compartment.

6. Installation is the reverse of removal.

NOTE: Do not use coolant containing sealers or rust inhibitors.

X1/9

1. Drain the cooling system.

2. Remove the three lower screws securing the grille to the crossrail.

3. Remove the four nuts retaining the guard plate to the body and remove the plate.

4. Disconnect the hoses at the radiator.

5. Disconnect the electrical connector for the fan motor and the wires from the thermostatic switch.

6. Remove the bolt and nut holding the bottom crossrail at each side and remove the crossrail.

7. Lower the radiator out from under the car, being careful of the fan. Installation is the reverse of removal.

BLEEDING

The radiator must be bled after it is refilled with coolant. The bleeder valve is on the top of the radiator (accessible through the trunk once the radiator is in place on the X1/9). Start the car and check for leaks. Turn on the heater. Connect a pressure tester to the radiator and pump in no more than 11 psi of air. Open the bleeder valve and repeat the operation until all air is removed from the system.

Water Pump

REMOVAL & INSTALLATION

124/Spider 2000 and 131

1. If necessary, remove the radiator from the vehicle.

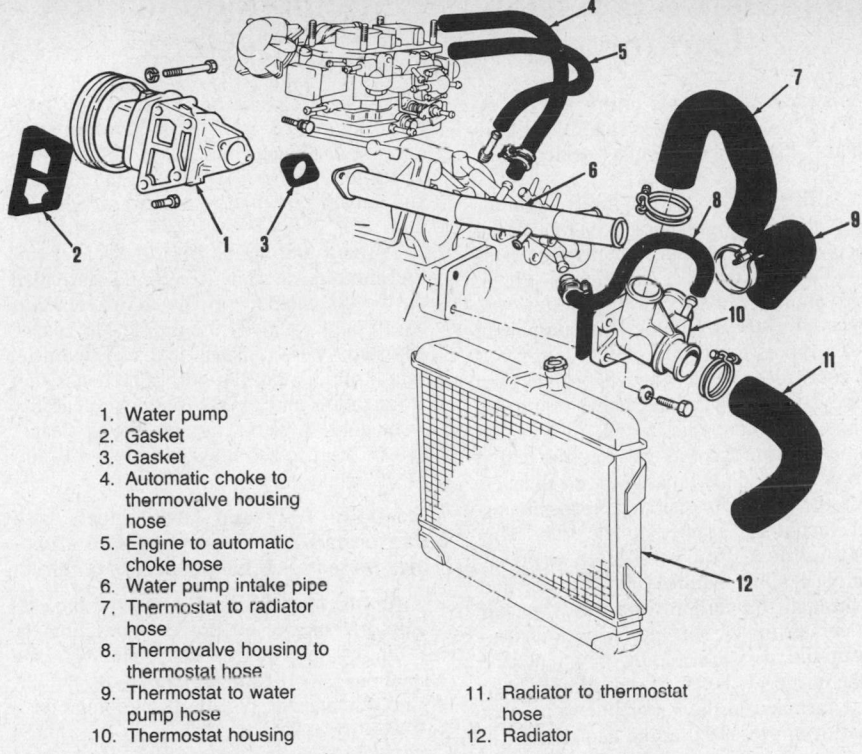

1. Water pump
2. Gasket
3. Gasket
4. Automatic choke to thermovalve housing hose
5. Engine to automatic choke hose
6. Water pump intake pipe
7. Thermostat to radiator hose
8. Thermovalve housing to thermostat hose
9. Thermostat to water pump hose
10. Thermostat housing
11. Radiator to thermostat hose
12. Radiator

Cooling system components—Strada and X1/9

1. Large coolant hoses
2. Thermovalve hose
3. Mounting bolt
4. Thermostat assembly
5. Gasket

Thermostat assembly—typical

2. Unbolt and remove the fan from the water pump flange.

3. Remove the hose which connects the water pump and radiator.

4. Remove the water pump from the mounting.

5. Installation is the reverse of removal.

128

1. Remove the spare wheel.

2. Place protective coverings on the fenders.

3. Drain the water from the cooling system.

4. Disconnect the hot air hose and the accelerator rod from the shroud.

5. Remove the shroud.

6. Disconnect the passenger compartment heater water delivery and return hoses.

7. Slacken the nuts that hold the alternator on the two lower brackets and remove the top bracket.

8. Unscrew the nuts which attach the pump to the crankcase and slide off the pump assembly.

9. Installation is the reverse of removal.

Strada

1. Drain the cooling system.

2. If equipped with an air pump, remove the top half of the timing belt cover.

3. Remove the air pump and drive belt.

4. Remove the alternator, drive belt and alternator mount.

5. If equipped with air conditioning, remove the compressor, drive belt and compressor mount.

6. Remove the two bolts holding the water pipe to the water pump and disconnect the pipe.

7. Remove the four bolts holding the water pump to the block. Remove the pump and gasket.

8. Installation is reverse of removal. Install a new pump gasket.

9. Refill the radiator with approved coolant, start the engine and check for leaks.

10. Stop the engine and bleed the cooling system.

X1/9

1. Drain the cooling system.

2. Remove the protection panels from the bottom right side of the engine.

3. Remove the alternator and drive belt.

4. Disconnect the hoses from the water pump.

5. Remove the three nuts and washers retaining the heater hose pipe to the pump.

6. Remove the bolt holding the support for the air pump to the water pump.

7. Remove the four bolts holding the water pump to the engine and remove the pump.

8. Install the pump in the reverse order of removal.

9. Bleed the cooling system.

Thermostat

REMOVAL & INSTALLATION

124/Spider 2000 and 131

1. Drain off part of the coolant in the radiator (to a level below the inline bypass thermostat).

2. Disconnect the 3 hoses to the inline thermostat and withdraw the thermostat.

Immerse the thermostat in the water and heat the water. When the temperature reaches 185–192°F, the thermostat valve should begin to open. The valve should be completely open when the water temperature reaches 212°F. If the thermostat does not meet specifications, it is defective and must be replaced.

3. Installation is the reverse of removal.

128, X1/9 and Strada

1. Drain the water from the cooling system.

2. Remove the spare wheel from the engine compartment on the 128 and Strada.

3. Disconnect the hoses from the thermostat union.

4. Unscrew the attachment screws and remove the union complete with the thermostat.

5. Unscrew the union cover and slide out the thermostat and its seal.

6. Installation is the reverse of removal.

7. Bleed the cooling system.

EMISSION CONTROLS

Application

Crankcase Ventilation System—All models

Fuel Evaporative System—All models

Engine Modification System—All models except those with fuel injection

Deceleration Throttle Positioner System—All models except those with fuel injection

Air Injection System—All models 1978–79. All California models

Air Induction System—1979 and later 49 States versions

Air Gulp System—1979 and later 49 States versions
Exhaust Gas Recirculation—All models 1977 and later except those with fuel injection
Catalytic Converter—All models 1978 and later, all California models
Fuel Injection—1980 Spider, Super Brava, all models 1981 and later
Turbocharging—1982 and later Spider 2000

Crankcase Ventilation System

This is a closed system in which all crankcase vapors are drawn into the engine's combustion chambers to be consumed, rather than being vented to the atmosphere.

During idle and part-throttle operation, intake vacuum draws the vapors from the crankcase and a connecting hose (with a flame trap) conveys them to the air cleaner and into the carburetor.

During full-throttle engine operation, the crankcase vapors are conveyed directly to the intake manifold downstream of the carburetor by an additional smaller diameter hose; this part of the circuit is controlled by a valve which is activated by the throttle mechanism of the carburetor.

NOTE: The crankcase ventilation system functions much the same way on fuel injection versions. On Turbo models, the crankcase vapor hose is rerouted from the throttle housing to the turbocharger compressor inlet hose.

MAINTENANCE

Every 12,000 miles, this blowby gas and oil vapor recirculation system, including the carburetor, vent valve and flame trap must be cleaned and flushed with solvent.

Evaporative Emission Control

This system is designed to prevent the escape of raw fuel vapors into the atmosphere—that is, in effect, a "sealed" fuel system.

The fuel tank is of the "limited filling" type—that is, it maintains a volume of air space which is normally slightly pressurized. The tank and filler cap are non-vented. Fuel vapors originating in the fuel tank are conveyed to the separator; this component passes vapors but is designed to return liquid fuel to the tank. The vapors are then conveyed to a three-way valve. With the fuel tank slightly pressurized, fuel vapors are passed through this valve to the active carbon trap and become absorbed there.

As the engine is operated, intake manifold vacuum is applied to the trap. This draws warm air from a collector, normally near the exhaust manifold, into the trap and up through the carbon trap; the warm air regenerates the carbon, purifying it and releasing the fuel vapors to be drawn into the intake manifold. Turbo models have a check valve installed in the vapor line to prevent boost from pressurizing the canister.

MAINTENANCE

It is recommended that the components of the system be visually inspected periodically in order to determine that all units and hoses are intact and hose connections are secure. Replace the charcoal canister every 25,000 miles.

NOTE: 1979 and later models use a permanent charcoal canister. The new canister requires no maintenance and should last the life of the car.

Engine Modification System

This system consists of a leaner, more carefully controlled carburetor; a recalibrated distributor that brings in the ignition advance at a higher rpm; a revised camshaft and valve timing; and a lower compression ratio.

To help the engine burn the leaner air/fuel mixture, a climatic setting is provided on the air cleaner (all models except X1/9). In cold weather, the air cleaner can be adjusted to draw in only exhaust manifold heated intake air, providing for better fuel atomization and overall better driveability when cold. In warm climates, the air cleaner can be adjusted to draw in only cool (ambient) intake air.

NOTE: 1979 and later models with thermostatic air cleaner are self-adjusting. No seasonal maintenance is required.

An idle stop solenoid is used on the carburetor linkage to prevent dieseling or "running on" after the key is shut off. The solenoid cuts off the fuel supply to the engine, closing the throttle plate completely.

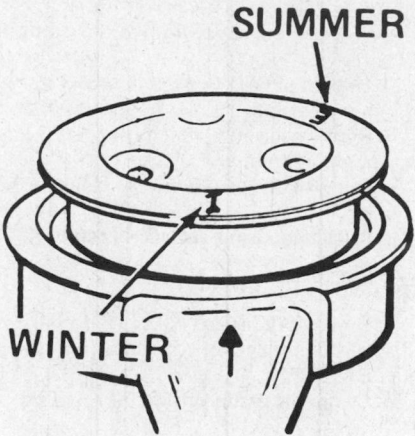

Air cleaner climate settings

MAINTENANCE

The only maintenance item is the air cleaner climatic setting. In temperate zones, the setting is adjusted in spring and autumn. Adjust the air intake as per the following:
1. Remove the air cleaner cover bolts.
2. Lift the air cleaner cover and align the marks with the arrow on the snorkel duct according to climate.
   I—ambient temperature below 60°F
   E—ambient temperature above 60°F

Deceleration Throttle Positioner System

This system, also known as the Fast Idling System, reduces emissions by holding the throttle slightly open when decelerating in

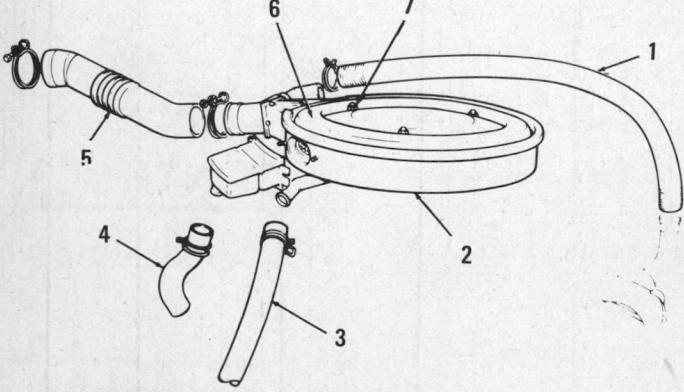

1. Hose to exhaust manifold shield
2. Air cleaner
3. Hose to oil separator
4. Hose to reed valve or check valve
5. Hose to cold air box
6. Air cleaner cover
7. Nut and washer

Thermostatic air cleaner components

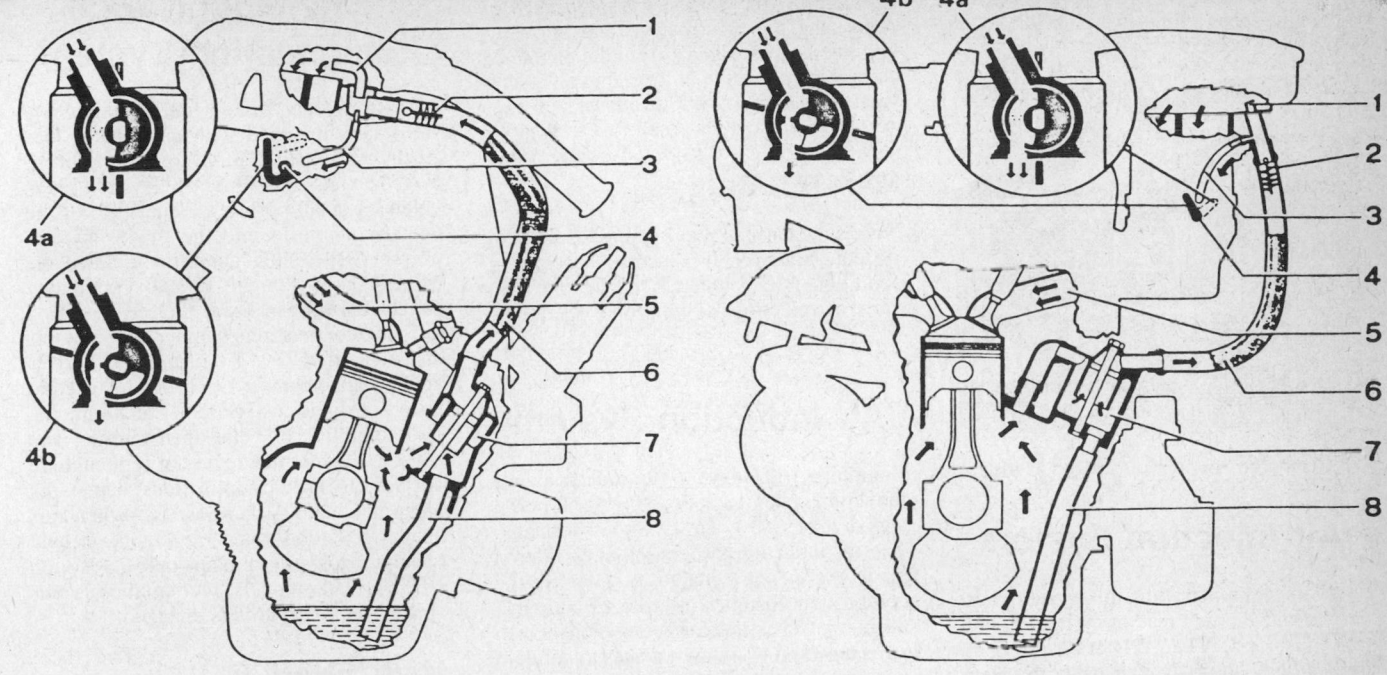

Crankcase emission control systems, carbureted engines—128/X1/9 Strada on left, 124/131/Spider on right.

third or fourth gears (manual transmission), and when decelerating in second or third gears (automatic transmission). If uncontrolled, deceleration from speed causes a high vacuum condition when the throttle plate closes with the engine in the middle to upper rpm range. This high vacuum draws in raw fuel which causes an overrich condition. With the throttle positioner holding the throttle open to the fast idle position, extra air is admitted with the fuel, leaning out the mixture and reducing emissions.

The carburetor is provided with a vacuum-sensitive diaphragm which is linked to the primary throttle plate shaft. Vacuum to operate this diaphragm is derived from the intake manifold through an electropneumatic valve. This valve is mounted on the vehicle firewall or side wall of the engine compartment, depending on car model, and is operated by applying an electrical ground to complete the activating circuit.

One switch is fitted to the transmission, and is closed (activating the circuit) when 3rd or 4th gears are engaged.

Another switch is fitted at the clutch pedal and is connected in series with the first switch. It is closed when the pedal is released and opens as the pedal is depressed. Thus, with 3rd or 4th gear engaged and the clutch pedal released, both switches are closed and the electrovalve is energized. Under such conditions, manifold vacuum is applied to the diaphragm keeping the throttle plate from returning completely to the closed or idle position. If the transmission is in a position other than 3rd or 4th gears, or the clutch pedal is depressed regardless of conditions existing in the transmission, the activating circuit is broken and the device is rendered inoperative.

In order to be able to check and/or adjust the fast idle setting, a pushbutton switch is provided to manually ground, or activate, the electrovalve. This switch is mounted on the firewall or side of the engine compartment, depending on the car model. Fast idle speed is then adjusted with the screw on the vacuum diaphragm unit on the carburetor.

NOTE: This circuitry is fused through the windshield wiper system; therefore, if that circuit is inoperative, the device will not function.

MAINTENANCE

The only adjustment on the system is the fast idle speed, which can be checked after setting normal idle speed and mixture. With the engine warm and idling in neutral, depress and hold down the fast idle electrovalve button (located inside the engine compartment on the firewall, radiator support or fender apron) while accelerating the engine to approximately 2500 rpm. This will activate the system and simulate a deceleration condition. While still depressing the button, allow the engine speed to decrease to the fast idle speed; 1600 rpm on a manual transmission car and 1300 rpm with an automatic. Adjust as necessary with the fast idling adjusting screw on the fast idle diaphragm and recheck. Finally, re-

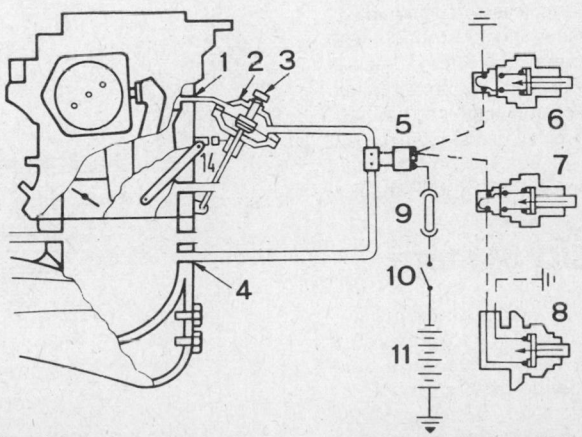

1. Compensating intake
2. Vacuum-sensitive capsule
3. Throttle adjustment screw for fast idle speed
4. Vacuum connection on intake manifold
5. Electrovalve
6. Button switch for fast idle speed control
7. Switch closed when clutch is engaged
8. Switch closed by transmission on 3rd-4th gear
9. Fuse
10. Ignition switch
11. Battery

Deceleration throttle positioner system—typical

FIAT

lease the pushbutton switch and check that the engine speed returns to normal idle speed, within 1–3 seconds.

Fast idle electrovalve button—124 shown

Air Injection System

Fiats are equipped with this system (also known as a thermal reactor system) to control emissions. A belt-driven air pump delivers filtered air to the exhaust ports. Here, the additional oxygen supplied by the vane type pump reacts with the uncombusted fuel mixture, promoting an afterburning effect in the hot exhaust manifold. To prevent a damaging reverse flow in the air injection manifold when exhaust gas pressure exceeds air supply pressure, a non-return check valve is used. Also, to prevent backfiring in the exhaust system during deceleration, a diverter valve is used to divert pump air to the atmosphere under these conditions. The diverter valve also serves to cutout the air pump air during cold temperature starts.

MAINTENANCE

On 128, Strada, and X1/9 models with the Bosch or Nippondenso air pump, replace the air pump filter cartridge at 12,000 mile intervals; sooner if the car is driven in dusty areas. On 124/Spider and 131 models with the Saginaw air pump, the filter is integral with the pump and does not require servicing.

Air pump belt tension cannot be adjusted when the toothed belt is used (V-belts are adjustable). Replace belt if worn. Average belt life should be 25,000–35,000 miles.

Air Gulp System

Beginning with 1979 models, the gulp valve replaces the diverter valve to prevent an overrich situation (backfiring) during deceleration by supplying fresh air to the intake manifold on demand. A vacuum signal from the intake manifold controls the valve. When starting, the gulp valve is held closed by a vacuum signal from the electrovalve which is energized through the starting circuit. If the engine temperature is below 46°F the thermoswitch is closed, energizing the electrovalve and closing the gulp valve.

Above 54°F the thermoswitch opens, de-energizing the electrovalve and allowing varying vacuum signals from the engine to control the operation of the gulp valve. The vacuum signal is strongest during deceleration.

MAINTENANCE

No maintenance is required on the air gulp system, however if a sudden backfiring condition is encountered, check the gulp valve and electrovalve for proper operation.

Air Induction System

Beginning with some 1979 models, the air induction system replaces both the air pump and diverter valve on 49 States versions. The air induction system supplies filtered air to the exhaust charge as it leaves the combustion chamber in order to complete the burning cycle and lower emissions. Fresh air is drawn in by exhaust pulses rather than pumped in under pressure. Inducted air passes through a filter on the air cleaner housing and is supplied to a delivery passage in the cylinder head that feeds all cylinders. Two reed valves mounted on the cylinder head prevent any damaging reverse flow of exhaust gases in the system.

MAINTENANCE

The only required maintenance is to replace the induction system air filter every 30,000 miles. The air filter is mounted on the air cleaner housing and also serves as a silencer for the system.

Exhaust Gas Recirculation System

All Fiat models, except fuel injection versions, are equipped with an Exhaust Gas Recirculation (EGR) System to control nitrogen oxide emissions. The system recirculates a small portion (about 10%) of the exhaust manifold into the intake mixture during past-throttle conditions. Since the exhaust gases contain little oxygen, they cannot burn when fired, thereby lowering the peak combustion chamber temperatures and reducing NOx. To ensure good driveability of the car, an EGR valve is used to prevent exhaust gas recirculation during periods of idling or wide open throttle, and is used to meter the degree of recirculation during part-throttle applications, depending on engine load. A thermostatic switch cuts out recirculation when the engine is cold (catalytic converter models only). Also, on 1978 and later models, recirculation is prevented when 5th gear is engaged.

MAINTENANCE

1978 and later models have no regularly scheduled EGR maintenance specified.

Catalytic Converter System

All models manufactured for sale in California, as well as all 1979 and later models are equipped with a catalytic converter to further reduce emissions. The converter is located in the exhaust system, upstream from the muffler. The converter is filled with a platinum/palladium pellet substrate which

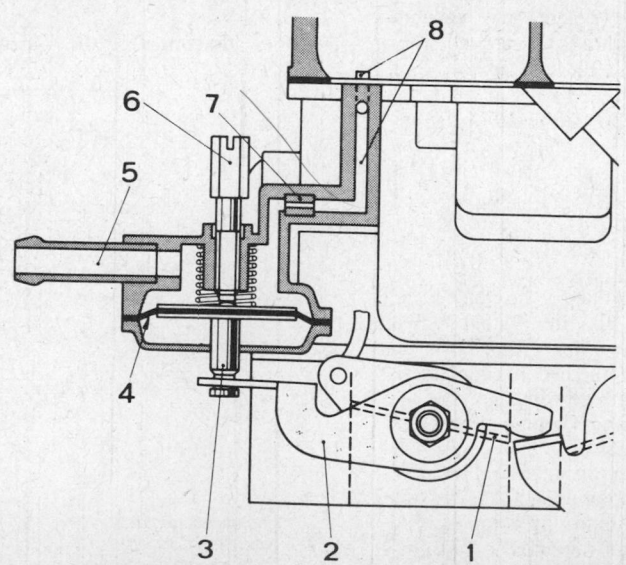

1. Primary throttle
2. Idler lever
3. Tie rod
4. Diaphragm controlling opening of primary throttle
5. Vacuum tapping line on intake manifold
6. Fast idle adjustment screw
7. Calibrated bushing
8. Air suction orifice

Cross section of fast idle adjusting screw and vacuum control

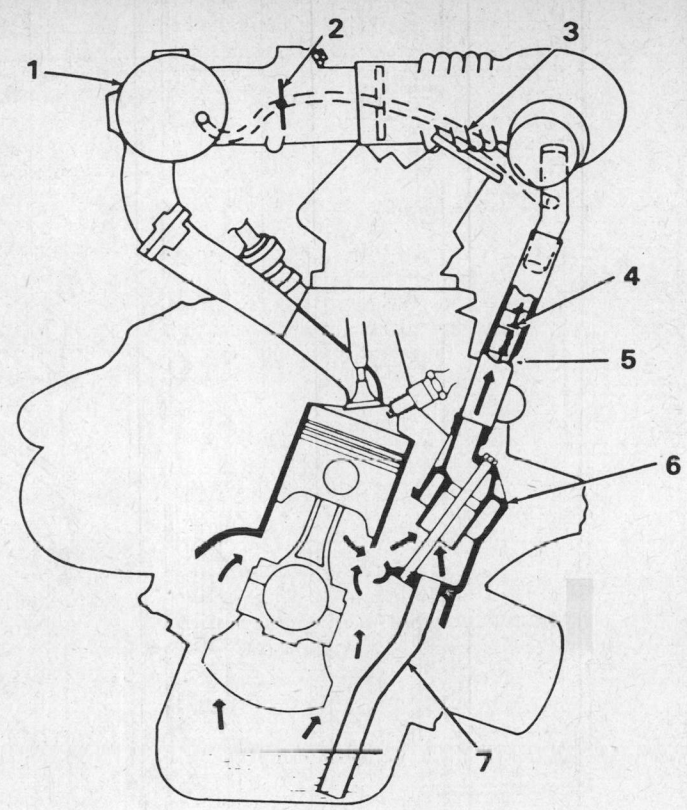

1. Intake manifold
2. Throttle plate
3. Bypass hose
4. Flame trap
5. Hose
6. Cyclonic trap
7. Return line

Crankcase emission control system—fuel injected X1/9

rapidly oxidizes emissions of hydrocarbons and carbon monoxide into carbon dioxide and water.

The converter is certified for 50,000 miles or more, with no regularly scheduled replacement intervals.

FUEL SYSTEM

Mechanical Fuel Pump

A mechanical type fuel pump is used on all models without fuel injection. The pump is located on the engine block and is driven by the auxiliary shaft. A pushrod (128 and 1978–79 X1/9 engine) or pump lever (131 engine) riding on the camshaft or auxiliary shaft eccentric operates the fuel pump diaphragm.

REMOVAL & INSTALLATION

All Models

1. Remove and plug the fuel lines leading to the fuel pump.
2. Remove the mounting nuts and carefully remove the fuel pump from the block (or crankcase).
3. If the pump is equipped with a pushrod, remove the pushrod, gasket and insulator from the mounting.

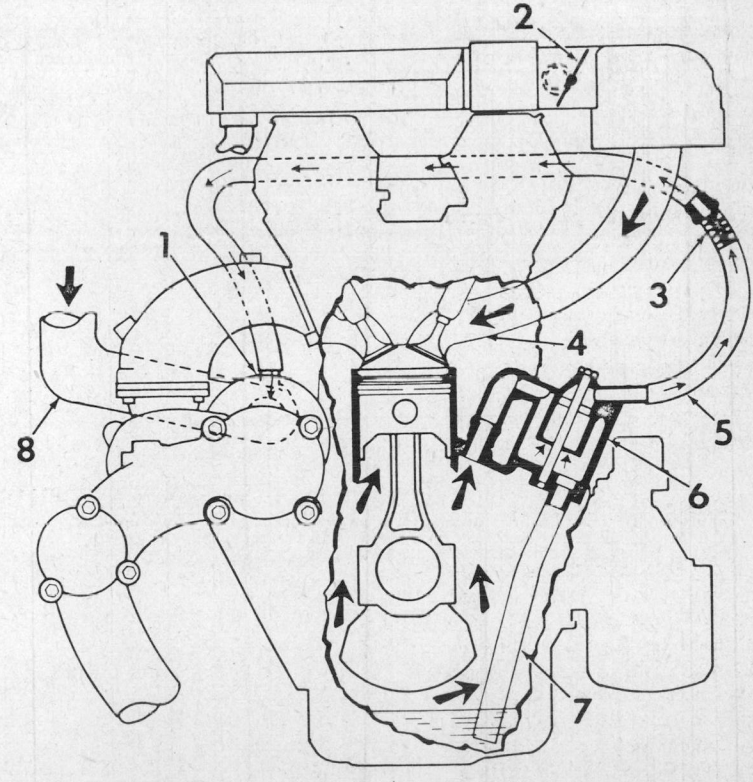

Crankcase emission control system—Spider Turbo

Spider Turbo exhaust emission control system, with catalytic converter

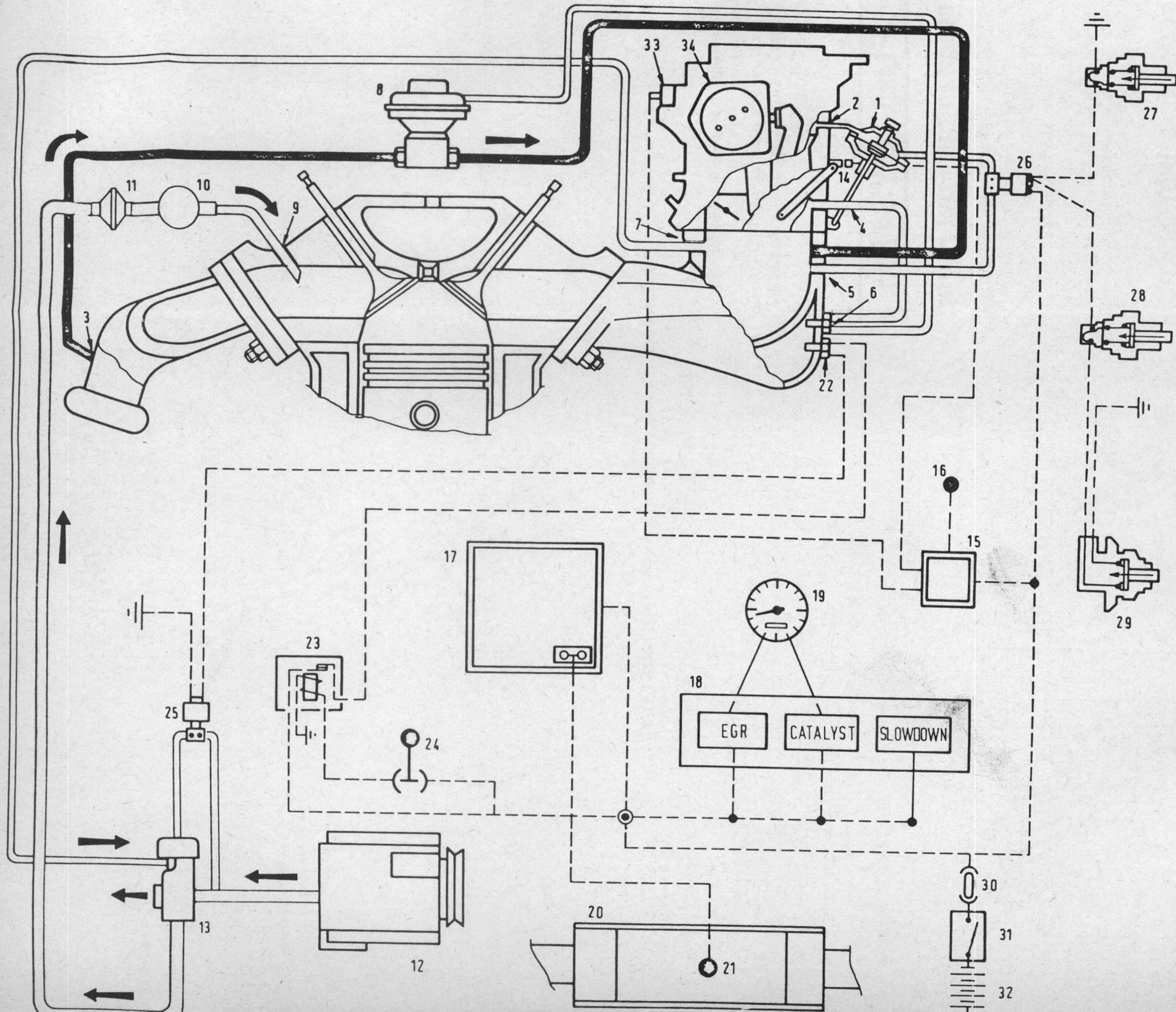

EGR

CATALYST

SLOWDOWN

1. Fast idle capsule
2. Continuity hole
3. Exhaust gas recirculation intake
4. EGR valve control vac- uum intake
5. Fast idle valve control vacuum intake
6. EGR valve control
7. Diverter valve control vac- uum intake
8. EGR valve
9. Air injector
10. Air injection manifold
11. Check valve
12. Air injection pump
13. Diverter valve
14. Inhibitor switch
15. Tachymetric switch (oper- ates at 2650 ± 50 rpm)
16. From ignition coil
17. Control unit
18. Warning device panel*
19. Odometer*
20. Catalytic converter
21. Thermocouple
22. Thermoswitch
23. Magnetic reversing switch
24. Gearshift lever (switch open with transmission in neutral)
25. Electrovalve (normally closed)
26. Electrovalve
27. Fast idle control switch
28. Switch closed when clutch is engaged
29. Switch contacts closed by transmission on 3rd-4th gear
30. Fuse
31. Ignition contact matched switch
32. Battery
33. Idle stop solenoid
34. Automatic choke system

*The maintenance reminder system is no longer neces- sary. If servicing is required, the system should be eliminated.

4. Installation is the reverse of removal. Perform the following additional steps on the 128, Strada, and X1/9.

a. Before replacing the fuel pump, adjust the projection of the pump pushrod.

b. Fit the insulating spacer to its seat with a gasket.

NOTE: On the X1/9, Strada, and 128, the outer gasket used must be 0.012 in. In all cases, adjust pushrod projection only with the inner gasket thickness.

c. Slide in the pushrod. The projection of the pushrod should be 0.59–0.61 in. If the projection is not within specified limits, adjust the projection by replacing the inner gasket with another. Service gaskets are available in the following thicknesses: 0.012 in., 0.027 in., and 0.047 in.

SERVICE

Sludge deposited in the fuel chamber or on the filter may be removed with the pump cover off. Intake and outlet valves should be inspected and replaced if damaged. Check springs for good condition.

Control mechanism for the intake chamber diaphragm should be washed in kerosene and lightly lubricated with thin oil. Lightly coat new fuel pump seals with grease before assembly. If a new diaphragm is to be installed, soak it in kerosene for a few minutes before assembly.

Electric Fuel Pump

NOTE: All fuel injection engines use an electric fuel pump.

An electric fuel pump is used on the later Strada, 128, 131, and all fuel injected models. On the 128 and Strada, the pump is located beneath the floor pan, near the fuel tank. On 124/Spider 2000 and 131 models, the pump is located inside the luggage compartment. On fuel-injected X1/9s, the pump is located behind an access panel in the left rear wheel well. The fuel pump is activated by a relay located in the engine compartment. The system is also protected by an 8 amp fuse located in the fuse box.

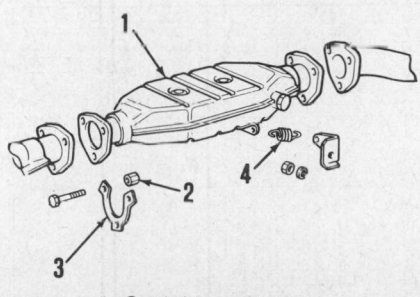

1. Catalytic converter
2. Nut
3. Lock ring
4. Spring

Catalytic converter installation—typical

NOTE: If the fuel pump stops, check the relay and the fuse box before attempting any repairs.

REMOVAL & INSTALLATION

——— CAUTION ———
Depressurize fuel system on fuel injection models.

1. Jack up the rear of the car and place it on stands allowing room to work on the pump.

2. Remove the hot wire from the pump.

3. Remove the ground wire. (If applicable.)

4. Remove and plug the gasoline inlet hose.

5. Remove the outlet gas line.

6. Remove the fuel recirculating lines.

7. Remove the mounting screws and the pump.

NOTE: On models with the pump in the trunk, use the Steps 2–7 given above.

FUEL FILTER

The fuel filter should be replaced every 6000 miles. The filter is an in-line type, located near the carburetor or near the gas tank. Removal is accomplished by loosening the two hose clamps.

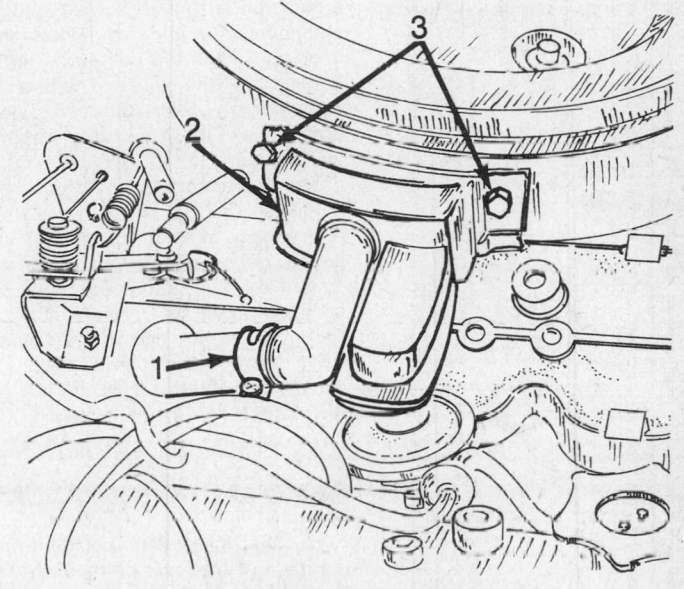

1. Clamp
2. Air induction housing
3. Retainer bolts

Reed valve filter housing

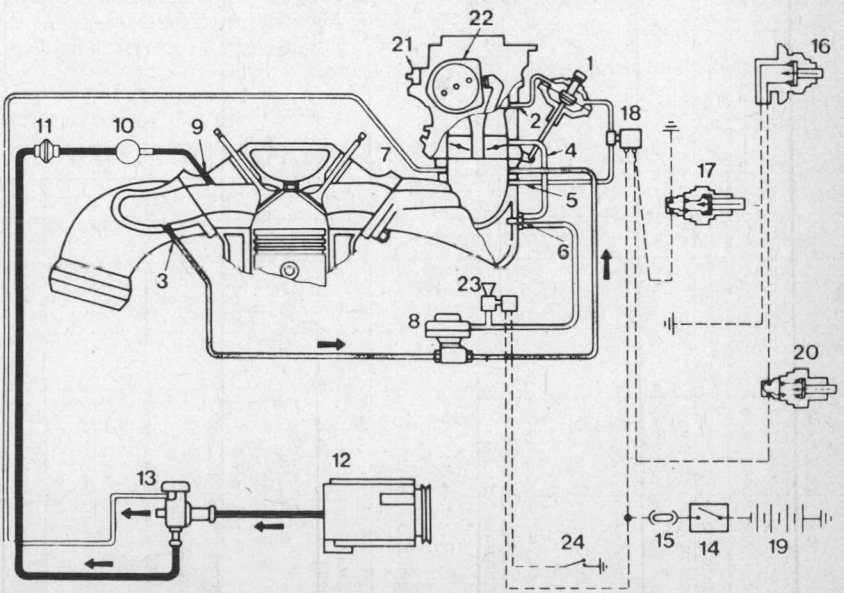

49 state emission control schematic—Spider

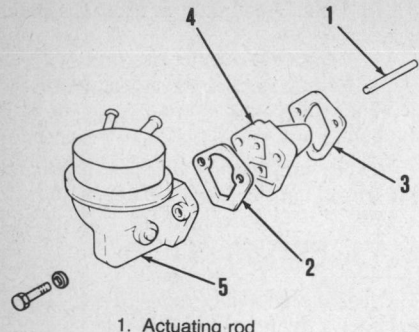

1. Actuating rod
2. Gasket
3. Adjustable gasket
4. Insulator
5. Fuel pump

Mechanical fuel pump assembly—Strada

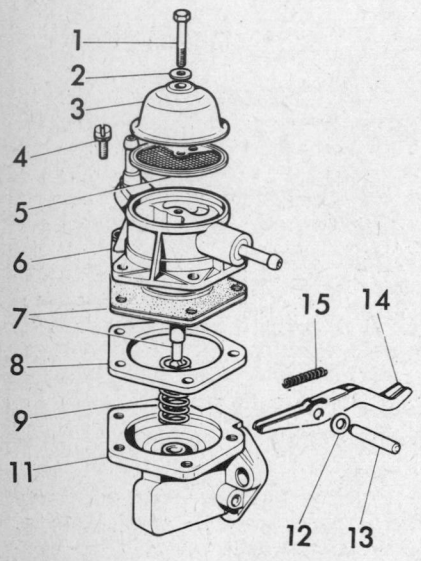

1. Screw	8. Spacer
2. Lockwasher	9. Spring
3. Cover	11. Lower body
4. Screw	12. Flat washer
5. Filter	13. Pivot pin
6. Upper body	14. Operating lever
7. Diaphragm	15. Spring

Mechanical fuel pump—124

CAUTION

Do not use plastic body fuel filters in the engine compartment. Fiat recommends metal body filters for all models.

Be sure to install the new fuel filter with the arrow pointing toward the carburetor. *Never operate any vehicle without a fuel filter in place.*

Carburetors

All carbureted Fiat engines use Weber two-barrel downdraft carburetors with differential opening of the secondary throttle, automatic butterfly valve choke and accelerating pump. An idle stop device comes into operation when the ignition is turned off. If the vehicle is equipped with a catalytic converter, the idle stop device also functions in case of abrupt deceleration above 2600 rpm.

The Weber carburetors are specially calibrated so that the air/fuel ratio allows the best post combustion of exhaust gases by the secondary injected air to help control emissions. The automatic choke is regulated by engine water temperature and the carburetor is provided with a vacuum-sensitive capsule which partially opens the primary barrel throttle from the idle position (fast idle).

REMOVAL & INSTALLATION

1. Disconnect the accelerator rod, sliding it out of the lever ball joint end toward the dashboard.
2. Remove the air filter.
3. Disconnect the fuel line.
4. Disconnect all of the vacuum, electrical and water lines.
5. Remove the mounting bolts or nuts.
6. Remove the carburetor and gasket.
7. Installation is the reverse of the above procedure.

OVERHAUL

For all carburetor overhaul procedures, Please refer to "Carburetor Service" in the Unit Repair section.

THROTTLE LINKAGE ADJUSTMENT

All Fiat models use cable type throttle linkage. Adjustments can be made at the carburetor by loosening the hold-down screw of the eye in which the cable slides. Proper

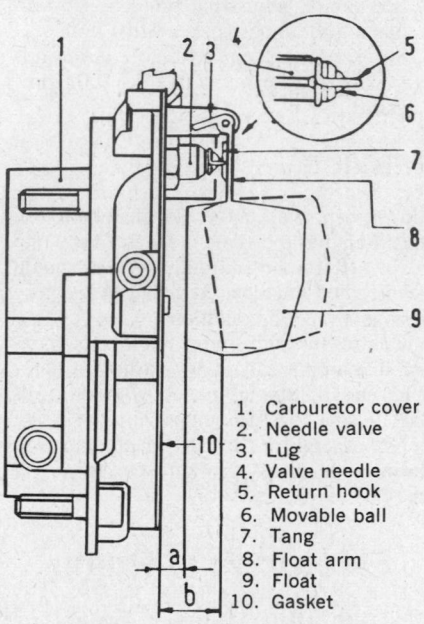

1. Carburetor cover
2. Needle valve
3. Lug
4. Valve needle
5. Return hook
6. Movable ball
7. Tang
8. Float arm
9. Float
10. Gasket

a = 0.236 in. (6mm) = distance between float and cover with gasket, in vertical position
b = 0.590 in. (15mm) = maximum distance of float from cover face with gasket
b-a = 0.354 in. (9mm) = float travel

Float level adjustment—128 engine family

CARBURETOR IDENTIFICATION

Model	Year	Carburetor Number
128	'78–'79	32 DATRA
131	'78	32 ADFA
	'79–'80	28/32 ADHA①
Strada	'79–'80	28/30 DHTA
	'81	Fuel Injection
124, Spider 2000	'78	32 ADFA
	'79–'80	28/32 ADHA①
	'81 & Later	Fuel Injection
X1/9	'78	32 DATRA
	'79–'80	28/30 DHTA①
	'81 & Later	Fuel Injection

① Calif. Models Use Fuel Injection

adjustment will allow the gas pedal to be fully released from the floor boards and at the same time the carburetor will be in the fully-closed position.

NOTE: If the gas pedal suddenly becomes sloppy, before checking the adjustment be sure that the cable housing is securely mounted.

FLOAT LEVEL ADJUSTMENT

1. Remove the air horn section of the carburetor from the rest of the carburetor assembly.

2. Check to make sure that the needle valve is screwed all the way into its seat. Make sure that the float is not dented or punctured and can turn freely on its hinge.

3. Holding the air horn assembly so that the float hangs vertically, the distance between the top side of the float and the cover with the gasket in place should be 0.236 in.

4. Holding the air horn assembly in the normal horizontal position, the float should drop so that the maximum distance between the end of the float and the cover mating surface with the gasket in place is distance "b" (see illustrations). Total float travel is b-a.

5. To adjust the float level, carefully bend the tang of the float that attaches to the needle valve.

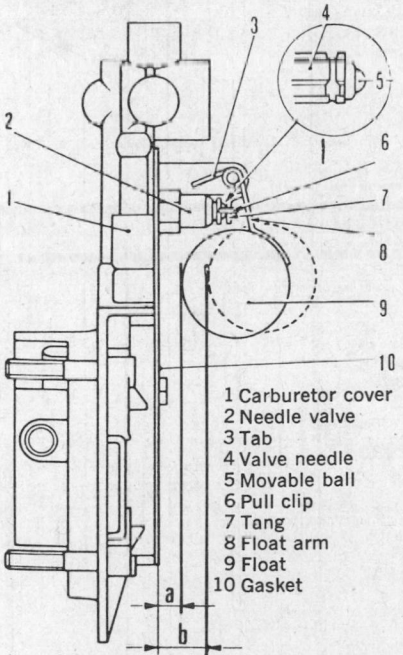

1 Carburetor cover
2 Needle valve
3 Tab
4 Valve needle
5 Movable ball
6 Pull clip
7 Tang
8 Float arm
9 Float
10 Gasket

a = 6 mm (.236 in.) = distance between float and cover with gasket, in vertical position
b = 14 mm (.551 in.) = maximum distance of float from cover face, with gasket
b-a = 8 mm (.315 in.) = float travel

Float level adjustment—131 engine family

Vacuum Accelerator Pump

1979 and Later Models

In addition to the standard accelerator pump operated by throttle linkage, another pump is provided for enrichment of the fuel mixture during cold engine operation. The vacuum pump uses the same output circuit as the mechanical pump. Under high manifold vacuum, the diaphragm is pulled back, compressing the spring and allowing the pump cavity to fill. A drop in vacuum will allow the spring to push the diaphragm, causing a discharge of fuel through the accelerator pump nozzle.

The operation of the vacuum accelerator pump is controlled by a thermovalve which senses coolant temperature. The thermo valve is open when the engine is cold.

AUTOMATIC CHOKE ADJUSTMENT

1. Remove the three screws securing the choke cover to the housing on the carburetor.

2. Make sure the lug on the spring inside the choke cover is properly located in the fork of the choke opening lever.

3. Rotate the choke cover to align the index mark with the mark on the housing.

4. Secure the cover with three screws.

5. With the index marks aligned and the carburetor at room temperature of 77°F, check that the choke plate closes fully and remains closed when the primary throttle is opened.

DASHPOT ADJUSTMENT

1. Use a 0.052 in. wire gauge drill.

2. Open the choke plate and throttle plate fully.

3. Allow the throttle plate to close on the drill while holding the choke plate. Release the choke plate.

4. Loosen the locknut on the dashpot and turn the dashpot until there is clearance between the plunger and the tab.

5. Turn the dashpot clockwise until the plunger just touches the tab, then tighten the locknut.

FAST IDLE SPEED ADJUSTMENT

See the "Deceleration Throttle Positioner Maintenance" portion of the Emission Control section.

Fuel Injection

All Fiat engines equipped with fuel injection use the Bosch L-Jetronic system. The Bosch fuel injection system measures intake air volume and meters the proper fuel to obtain the best air/fuel ratio for emissions and performance under a wide range of driving conditions.

For all overhaul and adjustment procedures not detailed below, please refer to "Fuel Injection" in the Unit Repair section.

RELIEVING FUEL PRESSURE

—————— CAUTION ——————
The fuel system pressure must be relieved before attempting to disconnect or remove any fuel lines or components. Take precautions to avoid any risk of fire while servicing any part of the fuel system.

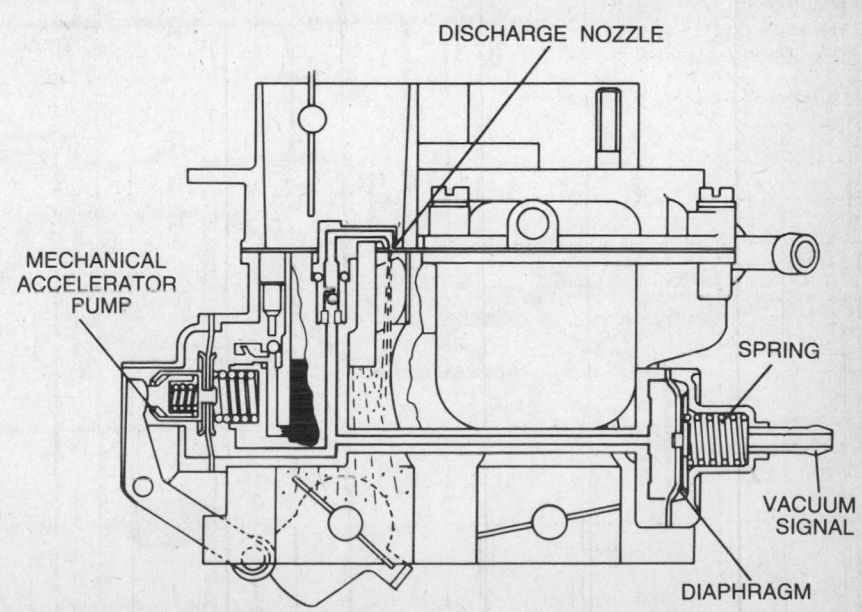

Mechanical and vacuum accelerator pumps—typical

1. Choke plate   2. Housing alignment mark   3. Cover alignment mark
Choke alignment marks—typical

All Models

1. Remove the vacuum hose from the fuel pressure regulator.
2. Connect a hand vacuum pump to the regulator and pump up to 20 inches.
3. Fuel pressure will be vented into the fuel tank.

NOTE: Although the pressure is relieved by this method, some fuel will remain in the lines.

ALTERNATE METHOD FOR RELIEVING FUEL PRESSURE

If a hand vacuum pump is not available, use this procedure to ensure fuel pressure release.

1. Start the engine.
2. Disconnect the connector to the fuel injection relay set while the engine is running.

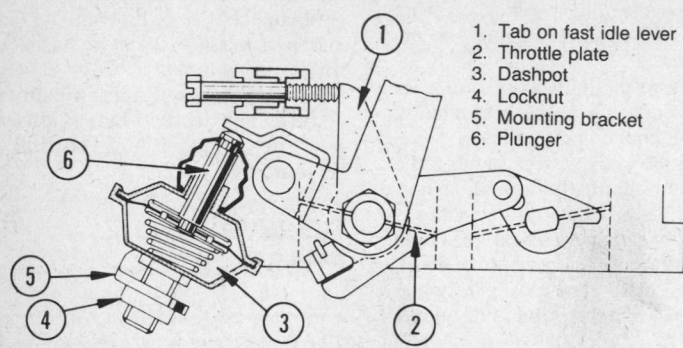

1. Tab on fast idle lever
2. Throttle plate
3. Dashpot
4. Locknut
5. Mounting bracket
6. Plunger

Dashpot adjustment—typical

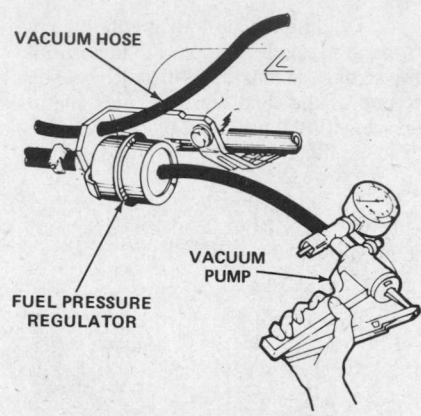

Relieving fuel pressure

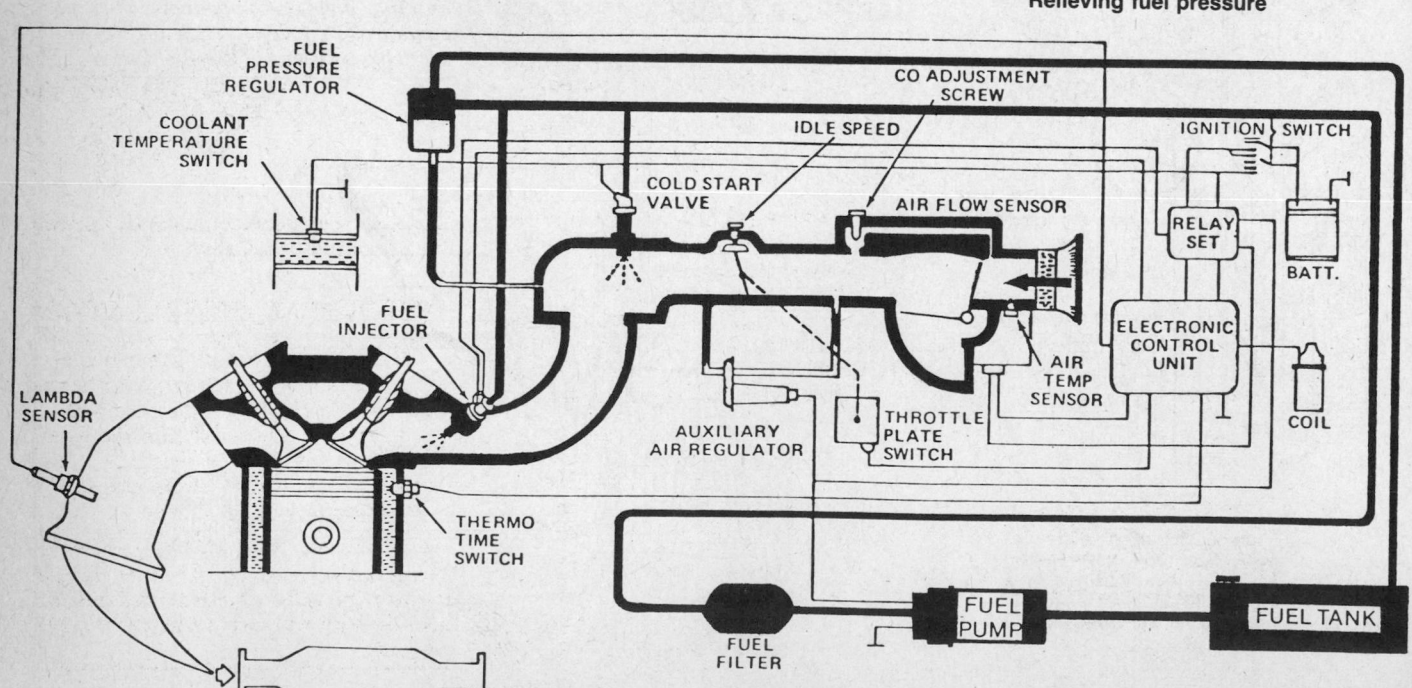

Bosch L-Jetronic fuel injection schematic—Spider shown

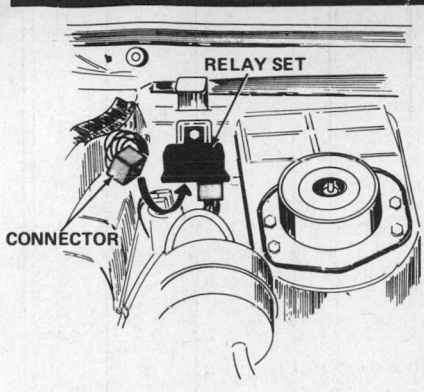

Relieving fuel pressure—alternate method

3. After the engine stalls, crank it over two or three times.

4. Turn the ignition off and reconnect the relay connector.

Fuel Injectors

REMOVAL & INSTALLATION

All Models

1. Relieve the fuel pressure.

2. Disconnect the wire harness from the injectors, remove the fuel supply hose from the fuel manifold, vacuum hose and fuel return hose from the pressure regulator and fuel feed hose to cold start valve.

3. Remove the 10 mm bolts holding the fuel manifold to the intake manifold. Remove the four 10 mm nuts and washers holding the injector retainers to the intake manifold.

4. Remove the fuel manifold complete with the injectors and pressure regulator. Be careful of the rubber bushings in the intake manifold, they may fall out.

5. Remove the four small and four large rubber bushings and retainers from the injectors. Inspect for cracks or damage.

6. Separate the injector from the hose to the fuel manifold. Replace the hose whenever replacing an injector, making sure the hose is tight against the collars at both ends.

7. Reinstall the large and small bushings on the injectors along with the retainers. Reinstall the injectors and fuel manifold, making sure all components seat and seal properly.

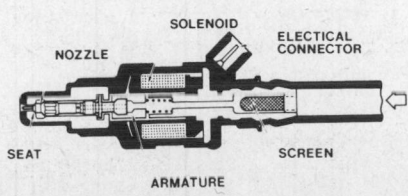

Fuel injector—typical

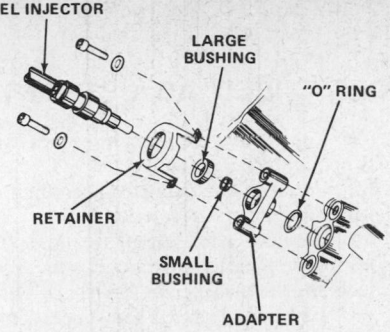

Fuel injector installation—typical

Cold Start Valve

REMOVAL & INSTALLATION

1. Relieve the fuel system pressure.

2. Provide a container to catch any fuel.

NOTE: Take care to prevent dirt from entering the fuel system.

3. Disconnect the electrical connector from the cold start valve.

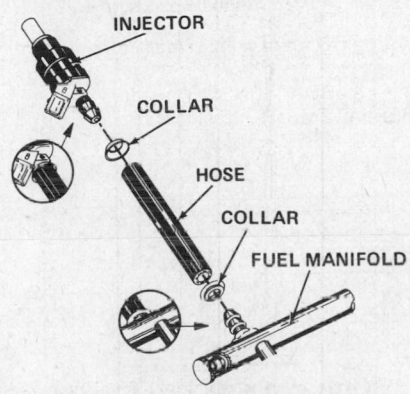

Injector-to-fuel manifold assembly

4. Remove the clamp holding the fuel line on the valve and pull the fuel hose off of the cold start valve.

——— **CAUTION** ———

Use care in removing the fuel hose; the valve body is plastic.

5. Using a 5mm Allen wrench, remove the two screws holding the valve in the intake manifold and remove the valve.

6. Installation is the reverse of removal.

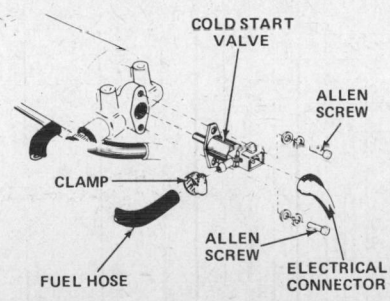

Removing the cold start valve

moval. Make sure the hose clamp is tight and check for leaks.

Lambda (Oxygen) Sensor

The Lambda sensor is a probe with a ceramic body in a protective housing. It measures the oxygen concentration in the exhaust system and provides a feedback signal to the control unit. This signal allows the ECU to adjust the air/fuel mixture for the best combination of performance and exhaust emissions.

The Lambda sensor must be replaced every 30,000 miles. A warning system consisting of a switch unit, speedometer connection and the dash mounted "EX GAS SENSOR" light alerts the driver when the sensor is in need of replacement. The switch must be reset after servicing.

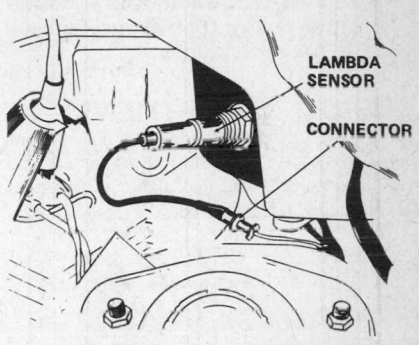

Lambda (Oxygen) Sensor

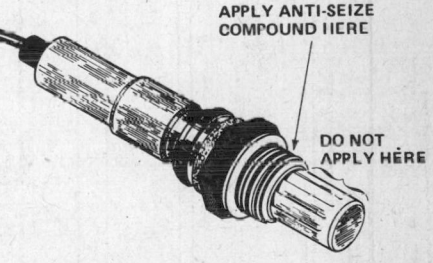

Apply anti-seize compound to the Lambda sensor before installation

REMOVAL & INSTALLATION

1. Allow the exhaust system to cool.

2. Locate the Lambda sensor in the exhaust manifold and disconnect the wire.

3. Remove the sensor from the manifold with a deep socket wrench.

4. Coat the threads of the new sensor with anti-seize, anti-rust grease.

——— **CAUTION** ———

Do not allow grease to get on the sensor surface or it will contaminate and ruin the sensor. Exercise care when coating the threads.

5. Thread the new sensor in by hand, then torque to 30–36 ft. lbs.

6. Connect the wire to the Lambda sen-

FIAT

sor and check the CO. Reset the warning switch.

NOTE: Setting the CO level on fuel injection models requires the use of an infra-red exhaust emissions analyzer with a special adaptor. No attempt should be made to adjust the CO without the proper equipment.

RESETTING THE SERVICE REMINDER

1. Locate the switch unit under the dash.
2. Remove the bore screening cap screw. Remove the screw.
3. Insert a small screwdriver through the housing and gently press on the switch contacts. Contact will reset to a high point on the wheel.
4. Make sure the dash light is out.

NOTE: On the Strada, it is necessary to lower the heater control panel to gain access to the switch unit.

IDLE CO ADJUSTMENT

CO level is pre-set at the factory on all fuel injection models and no further adjustment is necessary unless a fuel injection com-

ponent is replaced. This operation requires the use of an exhaust gas analyzer.

IDLE SPEED ADJUSTMENT

1. Run the engine until it reaches normal operating temperature.
2. Connect a tachometer according to the manufacturer's instructions.
3. On cars with automatic transmission, set the parking brake, chock the front wheels and put the selector lever in DRIVE.
4. Turn the idle speed adjustment screw all the way in.

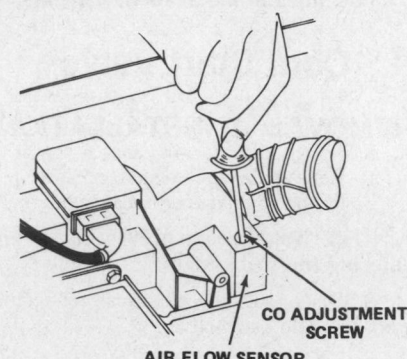

CO ADJUSTMENT SCREW
AIR FLOW SENSOR
Setting CO level on fuel injection—typical

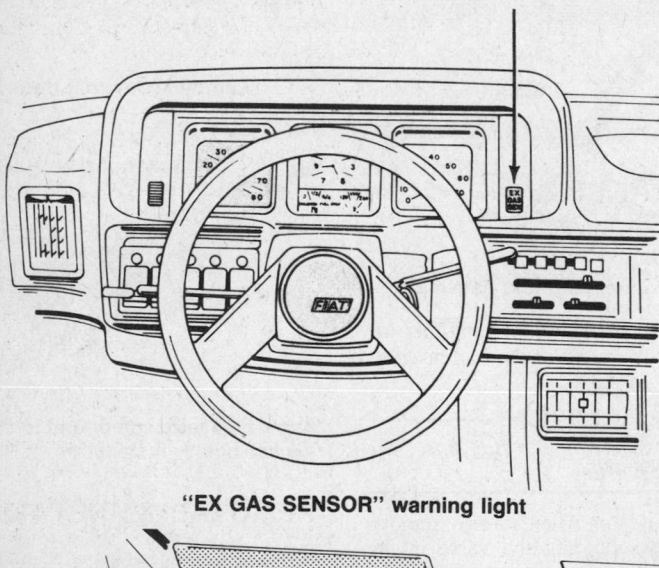

LAMBDA SENSOR REPLACEMENT INDICATOR

"EX GAS SENSOR" warning light

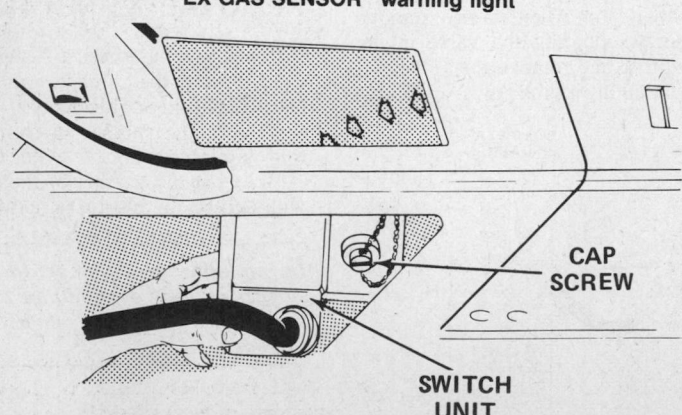

CAP SCREW
SWITCH UNIT
Resetting Lambda service reminder switch unit

5. Loosen the locknut on the accelerator linkage stop screw. Adjust the stop screw to obtain:
Manual transmission 700–800rpm
Automatic transmission 600–700rpm
6. Back out the idle speed adjustment screw to:
Manual transmission 800–900rpm
Automatic transmission 700–800rpm
7. Hold the throttle linkage stop screw and tighten the locknut.

KICK-DOWN CABLE ADJUSTMENT

NOTE: Make sure the idle speed is set correctly.

1. Depress the accelerator cable until the throttle lever contacts the maximum opening stop. Check that the kick-down cable starts to pull.
2. Depress the accelerator fully and check that the kick-down cable extends 3.5–4.25 in. (11mm).

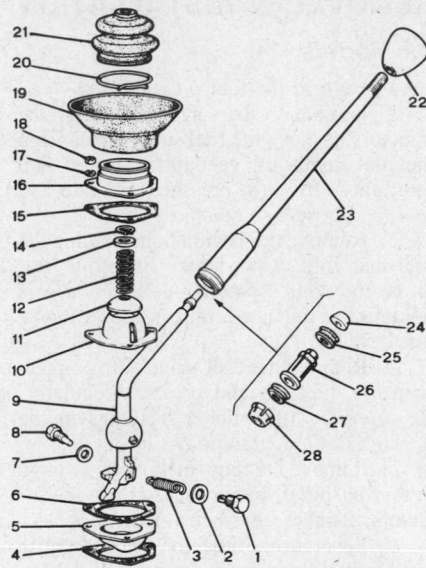

1. Gear lever return spring anchor screw
2. Flat washer
3. Lever return spring
4. Gasket
5. Socket plate
6. Gasket
7. Flat washer
8. Gear lever stop screw
9. Lower part of gear lever with ball
10. Upper socket plate
11. Dome washer
12. Spring
13. Cup washer
14. Retaining snap-ring
15. Gasket
16. Flange
17. Spring washer
18. Nut
19. Grommet
20. Spring clip
21. Rubber boot
22. Knob
23. Upper part of gear lever
24. Shoulder block
25. Rubber bushings
26. Spacer
27. Rubber bushings
28. Spring-ring

Exploded view of the 124/Spider 2000 4-speed shifter assembly

3. If necessary, adjust the nuts on the housing to obtain the correct extension of the cable.

MANUAL TRANSMISSION

REMOVAL & INSTALLATION

124/Spider 2000 and 131 Models

1. Working from the inside of the car,

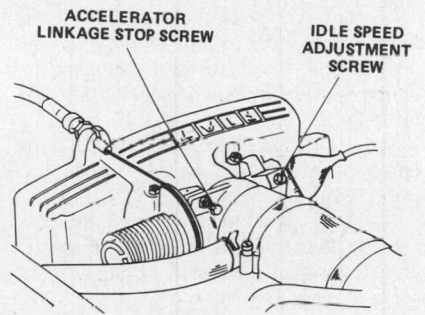

ACCELERATOR LINKAGE STOP SCREW

IDLE SPEED ADJUSTMENT SCREW

Idle speed and linkage adjustments on fuel injection

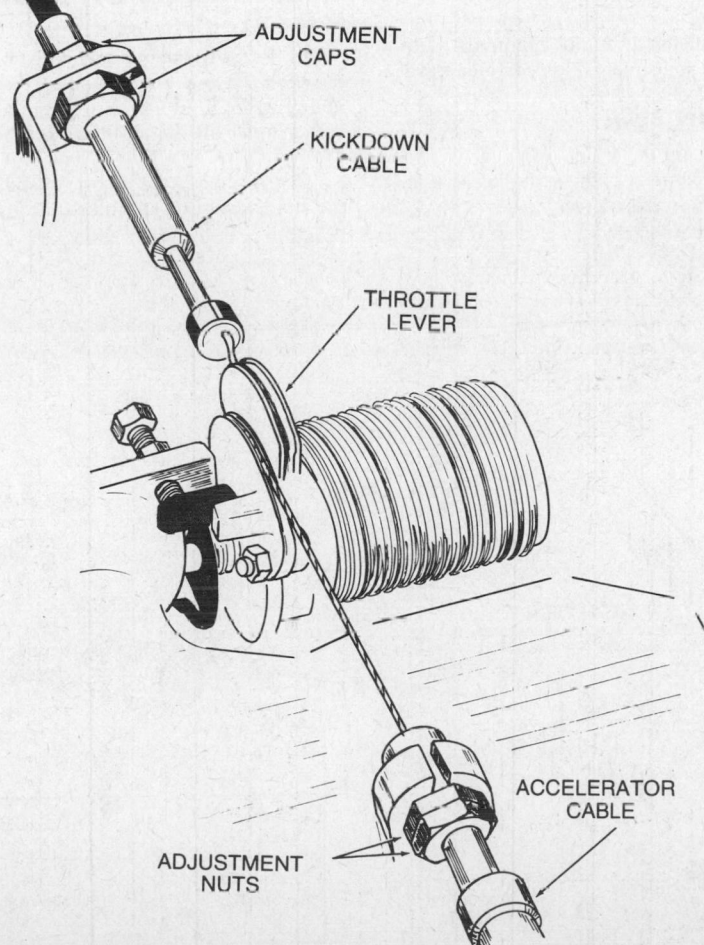

ADJUSTMENT CAPS

KICKDOWN CABLE

THROTTLE LEVER

ACCELERATOR CABLE

ADJUSTMENT NUTS

Adjusting kick-down linkage on fuel injection—typical

remove the gear lever and cover plate.

2. Underneath the car, remove the flexible coupling from the spider on the mainshaft. Remove the drain plug and drain the transmission.

3. Remove the speedometer drive from the support on the transmission.

4. Disconnect the clutch withdrawal fork return spring.

5. Remove the locknut and unscrew the adjusting rod from the flexible clutch cable.

6. Remove the flywheel cover from the bellhousing.

7. Remove the bolt which secures the exhaust pipe bracket to the transmission. On the 131, remove the driveshaft protection bracket.

8. Detach the exhaust piping.

9. Remove the starter motor heat shield and the starter motor. Disconnect the clutch and transmission emission control switch wires.

10. Support the transmission, and disconnect the transmission mount from the underbody. Remove the 4 bolts which secure the transmission to the engine.

11. Move the transmission carefully away from the engine and lower it to the ground. Do not rest the input shaft on the clutch disc or release bearing.

12. To install, reverse the removal procedure.

LINKAGE ADJUSTMENT

124/Spider 2000 and 131

The shifter linkage is integral with the transmission assembly and does not require adjustment.

OVERHAUL

For all overhaul procedures, please refer to "Manual Transmission Overhaul" in the Unit Repair section.

CLUTCH

A single, dry clutch disc and diaphragm spring pressure plate are utilized on all models. Clutch actuation is by cable, except on the X1/9, which uses a hydraulic master and slave cylinder system.

REMOVAL & INSTALLATION

128, Strada, and X1/9

1. Jack up the car and remove the transaxle.

NOTE: It is important that the input shaft never be allowed to rest on the fingers of the pressure plate, as the fingers may be bent.

2. Mark the position of the clutch in relation to the flywheel to facilitate assembly.

3. Remove the bolts (in stages) which secure the clutch cover to the flywheel. The bolts should be removed evenly to prevent distortion of the clutch.

4. Remove the pressure plate and clutch disc.

5. Check the condition of the pilot bushing which is pressed into the crankshaft. If necessary, replace the bushing. Installation of the clutch is the reverse of removal. Use an old input shaft or wooden dummy shaft to center the clutch disc. Tighten the clutch cover bolts diagonally, in rotation, to 11 ft. lbs.

NOTE: Be careful not to get oil or grease on the clutch disc during installation.

124/Spider 2000 and 131

1. Jack up the car and remove the transmission.

2. Before removing the clutch, mark the position of the clutch in relation to the flywheel to facilitate reassembly (if the clutch is to be reused).

3. Remove the bolts which secure the clutch cover to the flywheel. Remove them in stages to prevent distortion.

4. Remove the pressure plate and clutch.

5. Before reinstallation, check the pilot bushing in the crankshaft for wear, replacing as necessary.

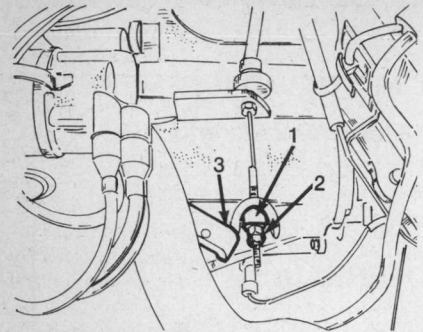

1. Half moon block
2. Adjusting nut
3. Lever

Clutch adjustment location

6. Install the clutch using an alignment tool or an old input shaft to center the clutch disc.

7. With the clutch disc centered, tighten the cover bolts diagonally, in rotation, to 22 ft. lbs.

8. Install the transmission.

CLUTCH PEDAL ADJUSTMENT

NOTE: On all models, check the clutch control cable grommet for damage. A damaged grommet will not allow the cable sheath to react correctly, thus causing a clutch malfunction. To correct this problem, replace the grommet. Lubricate to prevent clutch "shudder".

128

1. Open the hood, remove the spare tire and locate the cable nut and locknut.

2. Adjust the nut until the pedal has one in. of free-play. Tighten the locknut.

Strada

1. Open the hood, remove the spare tire and locate the cable nut and locknut.

2. Loosen the 10mm locknut on the clutch cable and adjust the nut next to the half-moon block until the clutch pedal is one inch below the brake pedal height.

3. Tighten the locknut and check adjustment.

NOTE: As the clutch wears, the clutch pedal will rise. When the clutch pedal is one inch above the brake pedal, the clutch may be worn enough to need replacing.

X1/9

1. Jack up the rear of the car.

2. Clutch pedal free-play (distance before resistance is felt when depressing pedal) should be 1.25 in.

3. If not, adjust as necessary by loosening the locknut and turning the adjusting nut on the slave cylinder pushrod where it contacts the clutch release lever. Tighten the locknut.

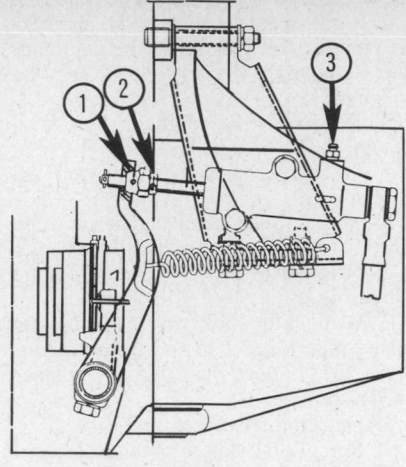

1. Adjusting nut
2. Locknut
3. Bleed nipple

Clutch adjusting location—X1/9

4. Lower the car and recheck the adjustment. If the slave cylinder does not operate at all, check for air in system and bleed the circuit.

131

Clutch adjustment is not required. Automatic wear adjustment. No pedal free travel.

124/Spider 2000

1. Jack up the front of the car.

2. Adjustment is made at the cable nut at the clutch release lever.

3. Adjust the pedal travel to 0.98 in.

Clutch Master Cylinder

REMOVAL & INSTALLATION

X1/9 Only

NOTE: The upper steering column assembly must first be removed to gain access to the clutch master cylinder.

1. Disconnect the battery.

2. Remove the five screws retaining the steering column upper and lower trim halves.

3. Disconnect the column wiring (three connectors and one wire).

4. Remove the two nuts and two bolts retaining the upper column assembly to the underside of the dashboard. Support the column and steering wheel assembly and pull it straight back and out, disconnecting it from the steering box shaft. Remove the complete column and steering wheel assembly from the car.

5. Place absorbant rags over the driver's side floor carpets. Locate the master cylinder up over the clutch pedal. Disconnect and plug the fluid line to the slave cylinder.

NOTE: Use a small length of fuel line with a screw or bolt in one end, just slip it over the flared end of the hydraulic line.

6. Remove the two retaining bolts. Pull the cylinder out far enough to disconnect and plug the fluid line to the reservoir. Pull the cylinder off the pushrod. Remove from car.

7. Reverse Steps 1–6 to install. Refill the fluid reservoir and bleed the hydraulic system.

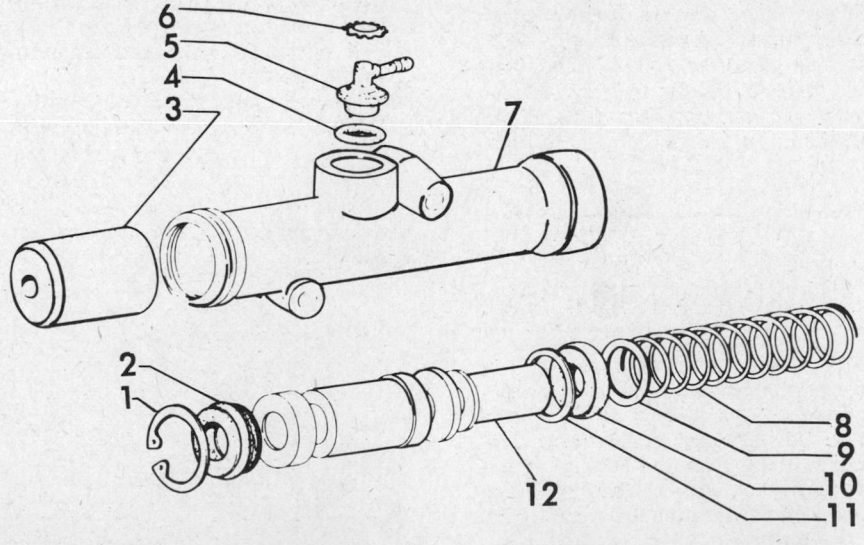

1. Lockring	4. Gasket	7. Cylindetr	10. Seal
2. Seal	5. Connector	8. Spring	11. Gasket
3. Boot	6. Lockplate	9. Seal	12. Plunger

Exploded view of clutch master cylinder—X1/9

Clutch Slave Cylinder

REMOVAL & INSTALLATION

X1/9 Only

1. Disconnect and plug the fluid line banjo connector from the rear of the slave cylinder.
2. Remove the cotter pin from the end of the slave cylinder pushrod.
3. Disconnect the release arm return spring.
4. Remove the two slave cylinder retaining bolts and remove the cylinder.
5. Reverse Steps 1–4 to install, using new copper gaskets at the fluid line banjo connector. Bleed the hydraulic system. Adjust clutch pedal free-play, if necessary.

Hydraulic System

BLEEDING

X1/9 Only

1. Connect a bleeder hose to the slave cylinder bleeder nipple. Place the other end of the hose in a container partially filled with brake fluid. Make sure the hose end is immersed in fluid.
2. Fill up the clutch fluid reservoir with clean brake fluid. Open the bleeder nipple screw.
3. Have an assistant pump the clutch pedal until all air bubbles stop coming out of the hose. Periodically check the reservoir level so that it doesn't run dry.
4. When all air is expelled, close the nipple screw and remove the hose. Discard the old clutch (brake) fluid. Refill the reservoir and check clutch operation.

NOTE: Hydraulic fluid will absorb moisture from the atmosphere if left standing in an open container. Any brake fluid that has been stored in anything other than a tightly sealed container should be considered contaminated and discarded.

AUTOMATIC TRANSMISSION

NOTE: Any model equipped with an automatic transmission may be towed a maximum of 30 miles @ 30 mph with the driveshaft connected. However if the transmission is damaged or if speed and distance will be greater than 30 mi. @ 30 mph, disconnect the driveshaft or lift the drive wheels.

The automatic transmission available in the 124/Spider 2000 and 131 series is the GM/Adam Opel Trimatic. It is a three-speed unit with a variable torque multiplication ratio of between 2.4 to 1 and 1 to 1.

REMOVAL & INSTALLATION

124/Spider 2000 and 131

1. Disconnect the battery.
2. Remove the dipstick, remove the bolts holding the filler tube to the engine bracket and remove the filler tube.
3. Remove the center console in the driver's compartment, disconnect the wiring for the transmission switch and push the connector through the opening in floor.
4. Raise the car and drain the transmission fluid.
5. Remove the three 13mm bolts holding the starter to the transmission. Remove the starter and secure out of the way.
6. Remove the 10mm bolt, nut and washers holding the clamp for the speedometer cable.
7. Disconnect the speedometer cable from the clamp. Remove the safety wire holding the connector for the cable.
8. Remove the 10mm bolt, nut and washers holding the clamp for the cooling lines.
9. Remove two 13mm bolts holding the bracket for the exhaust pipe.
10. Disconnect the vacuum hose from the modulator valve. Disconnect the vacuum tube from the spring clip on the transmission.
11. Remove 13mm bolt holding the bracket for the kick-down cable.
12. Remove the bracket and disconnect the cable from the kick-down valve.
13. Remove 13mm nut holding the lever to the control rod in the transmission. Disconnect the lever.
14. Remove the cooling lines from the fittings in the transmission.
15. Remove the driveshaft.
16. Support the transmission with a removal tool and a jack.
17. Remove two 13mm bolts and washers holding the support to the body.
18. Remove four 10mm bolts and washers holding the flywheel cover.
19. Remove three 15mm bolts holding the flywheel to the torque converter, turn the flywheel to gain access to the bolts.

CAUTION

Support the torque converter while removing or installing the transmission.

20. Remove four 19mm bolts holding the transmission to the engine.
21. Tilt the rear of the transmission down and carefully slide the transmission back.
22. Lower the transmission with the jack.
23. When reinstalling the transmission, feed the connector for the transmission switch up through the floor before positioning the transmission.
24. Position the filler tube up from the bottom.
25. Install the transmission in reverse order.
26. Torque all bolts to the specifications given in the transmission bolt torque chart.

NOTE: After attaching the transmission to the engine, push the torque converter against the flywheel flange. Check that the gap between the boss and attachment point is 0.008–0.048 in. (0.2–1.21mm). Use a feeler gauge to check each point. If the clearance is not correct, replace the flywheel. Attach the flywheel to the converter with three 15mm bolts and washers.

TRANSMISSION INSTALLATION BOLT TORQUE

Description	Torque (ft. lbs.)
Bolt, bell housing to engine	61.5
Bolt, converter to flywheel	47.0
Self-locking nut, gear selection rod lever	14.5
Bolt, starter to engine	14.5
Bolt, support plate to rear housing	36.0

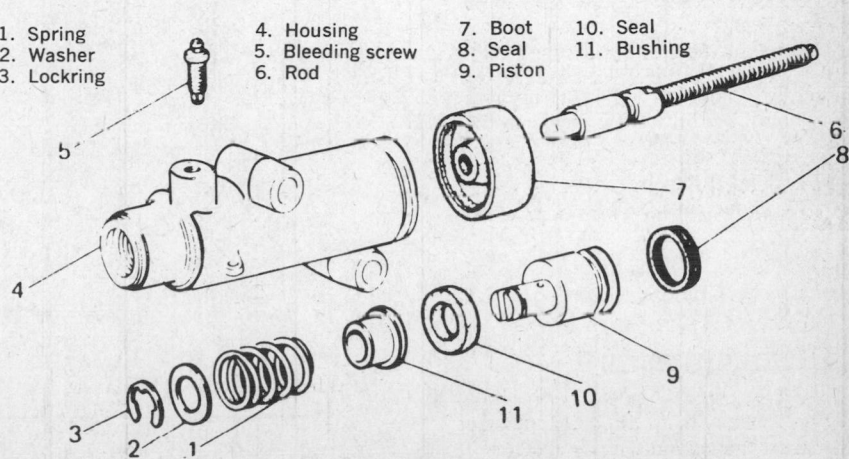

1. Spring
2. Washer
3. Lockring
4. Housing
5. Bleeding screw
6. Rod
7. Boot
8. Seal
9. Piston
10. Seal
11. Bushing

Exploded view of clutch slave cylinder—X1/9

PAN REMOVAL & FILTER SERVICE

124/Spider 2000 and 131

1. Raise the car and support it safely.
2. Drain all fluid from the oil pan.
3. Remove the oil pan and gasket. Discard the old gasket.
4. Remove the strainer assembly and strainer gasket and discard the gasket.
5. Install a new oil strainer gasket. Install a new strainer assembly.
6. Install a new gasket on the oil pan and install the pan. Tighten the attaching bolts to 7–10 ft. lbs.
7. Lower the car and add approximately three (3) pints of transmission fluid (Dexron®) through the filler tube.
8. With the manual control lever in the Park position, start the engine. **DO NOT RACE THE ENGINE.** Move the manual control lever through each range.
9. Immediately check the fluid level with the selector lever in Neutral, engine running, and vehicle on a level surface. (Set the parking brake.)
10. Add additional fluid to a level between the MIN and MAX marks on the dipstick. Do not overfill.

Strada

1. Raise the car and support it safely.
2. Drain all fluid from the oil pan.
3. Remove the oil pan and gasket. Discard the old gasket.
4. Remove the two capscrews holding the oil filter and remove the oil filter and seal. Discard the old oil filter and seal.
5. Install the new oil filter and seal. Torque the oil filter capscrews to 2.2 ft. lbs.
6. Clean the oil pan and install using a new gasket. Torque the oil pan capscrews to 14.5 ft. lbs.
7. Lower the car and add approximately 2½ quarts of Dexron® transmission fluid through the filler tube.
8. Place the gear selector in Park and start the engine. **DO NOT RACE THE ENGINE.** Move the shift lever through all ranges.
9. Allow the engine to idle and check the oil level on the transmission dipstick. If the oil level is below MIN, top up with Dexron® until the oil level is between the marks.

NOTE: The difference between MIN and MAX is one pint. DO NOT OVERFILL.

10. Test drive to heat up transmission fluid and recheck fluid level.

BAND ADJUSTMENT

124/Spider 2000 and 131

1. Drain the transmission.
2. Remove the pan and gasket.
3. Remove the servo brake band cover.

4. Loosen the locknut for the servo brake adjusting screw.
5. Tighten the adjusting screw to 40 *inch pounds*. Then, back off the adjusting screw five full turns.
6. Without disturbing the adjustment, tighten the locknut to 12–15 ft. lbs.
7. Install the servo brake band cover, using a new gasket. Tighten to 17–19 ft. lbs.
8. Install the pan and gasket. Tighten to 7–10 ft. lbs.
9. Fill the transmission with Dexron® automatic transmission fluid. Follow Steps 7–10 under "Pan Removal and Filter Service."

Strada

1. Raise the car and support it safely.
2. Remove the throttle and kick-down lever nut and remove the lever to gain access to the band adjuster screw.
3. Loosen the locknut on the band adjuster screw.
4. Using 5mm hex and socket adapter (Fiat tools A.57140/4 and A.57140/1), torque the band adjuster screw to 7.23 ft. lbs. to remove all slack.
5. Loosen the adjuster screw and retorque to 3.6 ft. lbs., then back off the adjuster 2½ turns and tighten the locknut.
6. Reinstall the throttle and kick-down lever and check the adjustment.

GEAR SELECTOR LINKAGE ADJUSTMENT

124/Spider 2000 and 131

1. With the engine off, place the shift lever in Drive.
2. Raise the front of the car and support it safely.
3. Disconnect the shifter tie-rod at the relay lever (shift lever).
4. Move the cross shaft actuating lever (shift lever on transmission) to the Drive

position, which is the third detent from the front.
5. Without disturbing either of the two levers, try to insert the end of the shifter tie-rod into the relay lever. If necessary, loosen the adjusting nut and rotate until the tie-rod end will just slip into the eye of the relay lever. Then, tighten the adjusting nut. Connect the tie-rod to the relay lever using a new circlip.
6. Remove the jack stands and lower the car. Check the shifter operation.

Strada

1. Remove the shift nameplate by squeezing, then remove the two screws retaining the center console. Remove the console.
2. Place the gearshift lever in the Park position. Rock the car slightly to make sure the lock inside the transmission is engaged.
3. Remove the pin attaching the shift cable to the gearshift lever.
4. Loosen the 8mm locknut on the shift cable. Adjust the clevis until the pin can be freely installed, then tighten the locknut.
5. Reinstall the center console and shift nameplate. Check operation.

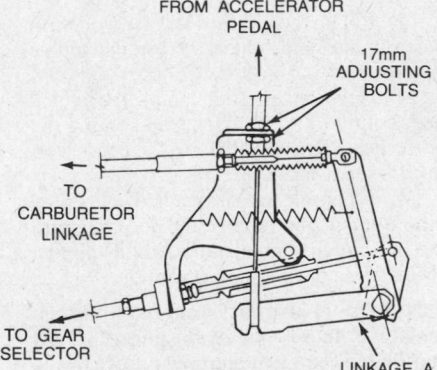

Detail D—transmission linkage

1. Brake band anchoring pin
2. Brake band
3. Transmission main case
4. Brake actuating rod
5. Sleeve
6. Release spring
7. Damping spring seat
8. Damping spring
9. Piston ring
10. Retainer
11. Piston
12. Circlip
13. Adjusting screw
14. Nut

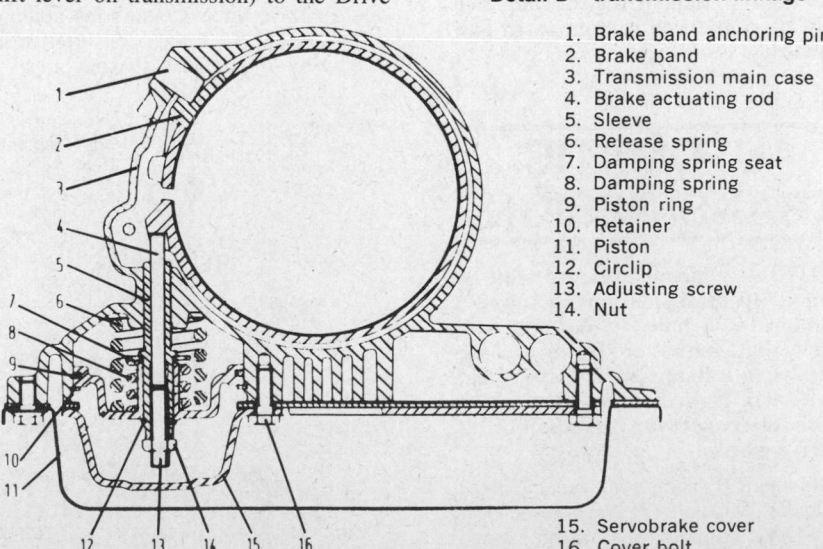

15. Servobrake cover
16. Cover bolt

Band adjustment—124/Spider 2000 and 131 automatic transmission

KICKDOWN LINKAGE ADJUSTMENT

Strada

1. Check accelerator pedal travel, total travel should be 4 in. (10 cm).

2. If pedal travel is incorrect, bend the pedal rod to obtain proper distance.

NOTE: Include floor mat thickness in adjustment.

3. With the accelerator pedal fully depressed, including kickdown, verify that the transmission linkage (A) is at full travel up.

4. If the transmission linkage is not at full travel up, loosen and adjust the 17mm adjuster nuts.

5. Fully depress the accelerator pedal, including kickdown, and verify that the throttle is wide open and the carburetor cable is pulled about ½ in. (13mm) from its stop.

6. If necessary, adjust the 14mm adjuster nuts at the cable brace near the carburetor to obtain proper linkage travel.

7. Release the accelerator pedal and verify that the throttle closes (choke plate open) without binding.

NOTE: Linkage control cables and connections should be lubricated periodically to ensure smooth operation and prevent binding.

124/Spider 2000 and 131

1. Disconnect the telescopic link from the control lever on the transmission.

2. Push the accelerator pedal down until the ball end on the cable is just touching the cable pin.

3. Push the pedal to the floor stop and check that the cable has extended 7–9mm.

4. If cable travel is not correct, adjust the cable nuts to obtain the proper travel.

5. Push the accelerator pedal to the floor stop. Hold the transmission control lever in the full throttle position, extend the telescopic link and check that the link can be connected to the control lever. If the link cannot be connected to trans control lever, loosen the link nuts and adjust.

6. Release the accelerator pedal until the ball end is just touching the cable pin.

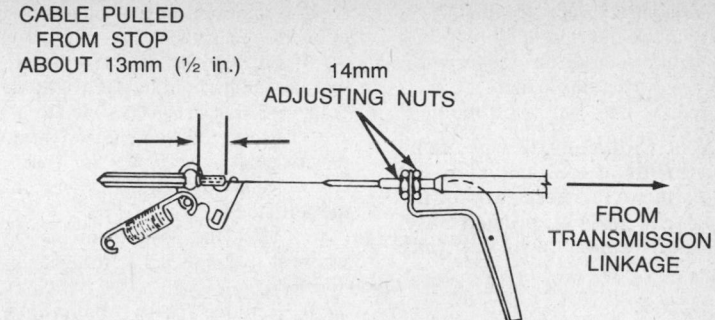

CABLE PULLED FROM STOP ABOUT 13mm (½ in.)

14mm ADJUSTING NUTS

FROM TRANSMISSION LINKAGE

Detail C—carburetor linkage

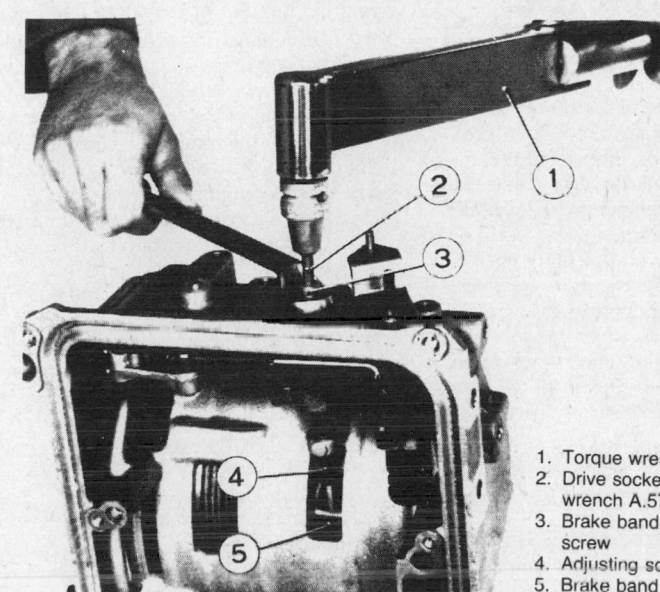

1. Torque wrench
2. Drive socket and hex wrench A.57140/4
3. Brake band adjusting screw
4. Adjusting screw pushrod
5. Brake band

Adjusting brake band on Strada automatic transmission

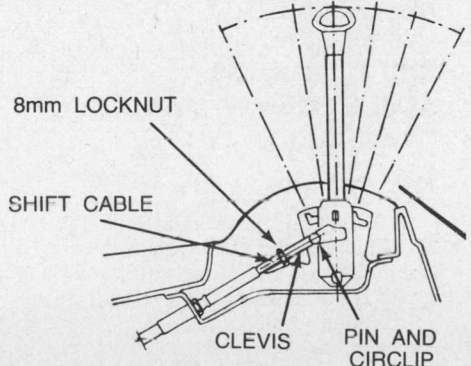

8mm LOCKNUT

SHIFT CABLE

CLEVIS

PIN AND CIRCLIP

Detail A—gear shift selector lever—Strada

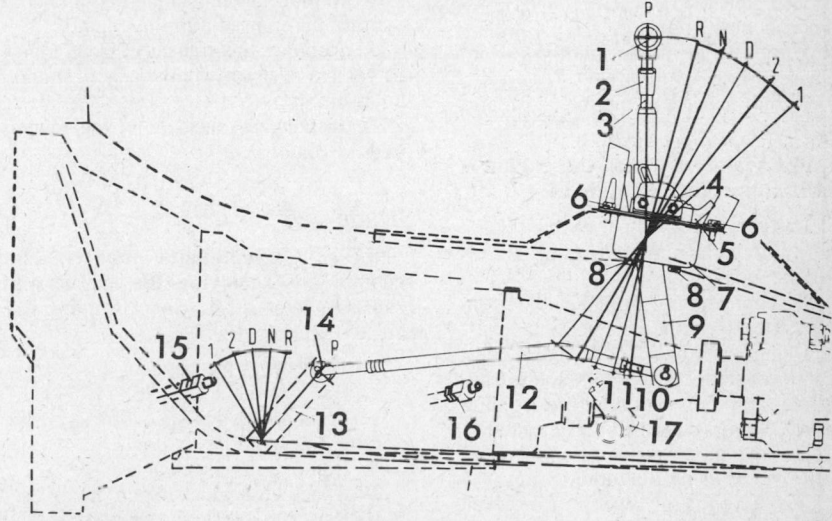

1. Upper handle
2. Lower handle
3. Selector lever
4. Starter inhibitor switch
5. Gear selector
6. Bolt
7. Support
8. Bracket bolt
9. Relay lever
10. Tie rod adjustable end
11. Adjusting nut
12. Tie rod
13. Cross shaft actuating lever
14. Flat washer
15. Oil union
16. Oil union
17. Speedometer drive support
18. Bracket
19. Flat washer
20. Bushing
21. Cotter pin
22. Cotter pin
23. Gear selector bolt

Shift lever linkage adjustment—124/Spider 2000 and 131 automatic

Move the trans control lever to the full throttle position and check that the telescopic link can be connected to the control lever without extending. If the link cannot be connected, loosen the nuts and adjust the link.

NOTE: When adjusting the link, make equal adjustments at each end. For the correct adjustment, it is necessary for the kickdown valve to move its specified travel when the accelerator pedal is fully depressed.

TRANSAXLE

REMOVAL & INSTALLATION
128

1. Disconnect the battery.
2. Remove the spare tire.
3. Remove the speedometer drive.
4. Disconnect the flexible cable adjusting rod from the clutch release lever and unhook the return spring.
5. Unscrew the guard-to-body nut.
6. Unscrew the transaxle-to-crankcase attachment screws and nuts, accessible from above.
7. Attach the engine support crosspiece.
8. Remove the hub caps from the front wheels and unscrew the constant speed joint-to-wheel hub nuts.
9. Remove the left front wheel.
10. Disconnect the left tie-rod from the steering arm.
11. Remove the stabilizer bar.
12. Unscrew the two lower left shock absorber-to-pillar attaching screws and nuts.
13. Remove the two lower guards.
14. Unscrew the nuts which fasten the exhaust clamping bracket to the transaxle.
15. Disconnect the gearshift and selection lever control rod.
16. Unscrew the starter motor-to-transaxle assembly bolts.
17. Remove the engine support crossmember.

NOTE: Make sure that the engine is properly supported from above.

18. Remove the flywheel cover.
19. Unscrew the remaining transaxle-to-engine attachment screws.
20. Disconnect the ground cable from the transaxle assembly.
21. Using wire, fix the axle shafts complete with constant-speed joints, to the transaxle in order to prevent them from coming away from their seats in the differential.
22. Remove the transaxle assembly from beneath the car using a hydraulic jack.
23. Installation is the reverse of removal.

X1/9

1. Remove the air cleaner and the carburetor cooling duct.
2. Disconnect the battery cables from the battery.
3. Disconnect the clutch slave cylinder from the clutch linkage, remove the two slave cylinder attaching bolts and move the cylinder out of the way.
4. Support the engine and remove the nuts and bolts holding the transaxle to the crankcase that are accessible from above.
5. Raise the vehicle and remove the rear wheels.
6. Remove the three lower guards on the left side.
7. Mark the position of the shift tube where it is connected to the gearshift flexible link.
8. Remove the two bolts holding the flexible link to the shift tube, loosen the bolt at the transaxle end of the link and swing the link out of the way.
9. Disconnect the electrical connector for the backup lights and remove the clamp securing the wires to the body.
10. Disconnect the connector for the seat belt system in the transaxle. The connector is located inboard and forward of the transaxle near the engine water hoses.
11. Remove the starter from the transaxle.
12. Disconnect the ground strap.
13. Remove the exhaust pipe.
14. Remove the hub nuts holding the constant speed joints to the wheel hubs.
15. Remove the two bolts and nuts securing the suspension control arms to their supports. Pull the hub off the constant speed joints and attach the axle shafts to the transaxle with wire to prevent them from coming out.
16. Remove the flywheel cover.
17. Remove the crosspiece supporting the engine.

— CAUTION —
Make sure that the engine is properly supported from above.

18. Remove the remaining nuts and bolts securing the transaxle to the engine.
19. Remove the transaxle from below the vehicle. Use a hydraulic jack to support the assembly.
20. Install the transaxle in the reverse order of removal.

Strada

NOTE: On automatic models, Fiat recommends removing the engine and transaxle as a unit. See "Engine Removal" section.

1. Disconnect the battery.
2. Remove the spare tire.
3. Disconnect the speedometer drive from the transaxle.
4. Remove the air cleaner.
5. Attach an engine support crosspiece.
6. Raise the vehicle and support it safely.
7. Remove the front shield and left side shield.
8. Disconnect the ground cable from the transaxle.
9. Disconnect the clutch operating cable at the transaxle end.
10. Disconnect the reverse light switch connector.

11. Remove the three bolts holding the starter to the transaxle.

NOTE: Before removal of the gear selector link, mark the position of the slots in relation to the bolts so that the adjustment will remain the same upon installation.

12. Remove the two nuts and bolts holding the gear selector link to the linkage joint.
13. Remove the six allen head bolts and disconnect the left side halfshaft complete with the CV-joint from the flange.

NOTE: Discard the allen head bolts and replace with new ones upon installation.

14. Remove the six allen head bolts and disconnect the right side halfshaft complete with the CV-joint from the flange.
15. Remove the three bolts and disengage the driveshaft from the transaxle.
16. Place a jack under the transaxle.
17. Remove the center mount bolt.

— CAUTION —
Make sure the engine is supported from above.

18. Remove the three nuts and support the bracket.
19. Remove the three bolts to the flywheel guard and remove the guard.
20. Remove the retaining nut and three bolts holding the transaxle to the engine.
21. Disconnect the left side rubber mount and bracket by removing the two bolts on the rubber mount and four bolts holding the bracket to the transaxle.
22. Lower the transaxle with a jack.
23. Installation is the reverse of removal.

NOTE: If after installation, difficult shifting or jumping out of gear is encountered, adjust the gearshift linkage.

OVERHAUL

For all overhaul procedures, please refer to "Manual Transaxle Overhaul" in the Unit Repair section.

SHIFT LINKAGE ADJUSTMENT—MANUAL TRANSAXLE
128, X1/9 and Strada

1. Place the transaxle in Neutral.
2. Loosen the two adjustment screws at the transaxle end of the shift rod.
3. Place the gear shift lever in the neutral position (centered and straight up and down) and tighten the two adjusting screws at the transaxle end of the shift rod. The holes in the flexible shift rod are slotted to allow for adjustment.

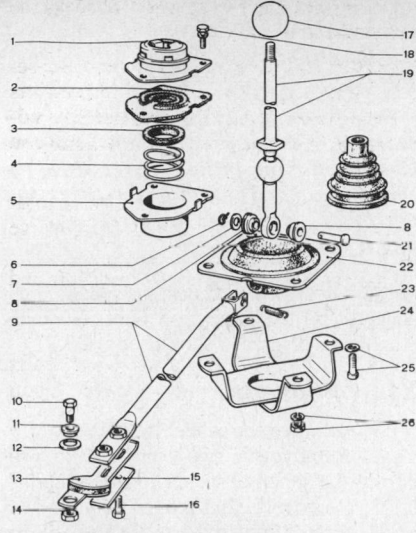

1. Guide plate
2. Upper socket
3. Lower socket
4. Spring
5. Support
6. Cotter pin
7. Flat washer
8. Bushings
9. Rod
10. Screw
11. Bushing
12. Spring washer
13. Flexible rod
14. Nut
15. Plate
16. Screw
17. Knob
18. Screw
19. Lever
20. Dust boot
21. Pin
22. Guard and boot
23. Return spring
24. Guard
25. Screw and washer
26. Nut and spring washer

Gearshift mechanism for 128—X1/9 and Strada similar

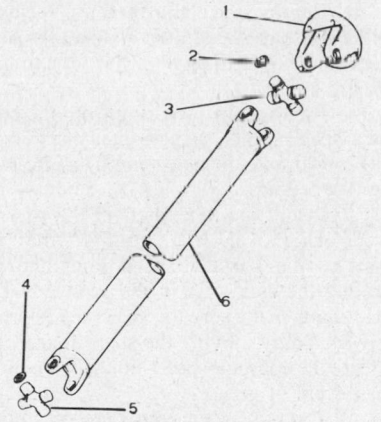

1. Fork connecting rear prop shaft to drive pinion sleeve
2. Spider snap ring
3. Spider assy.
4. Snap ring
5. Spider assy.
6. Rear prop shaft

124/Spider 2000 and 131 driveshaft rear section

DRIVE AXLE

DRIVESHAFT AND U-JOINTS

124/Spider 2000 and 131

Fiat 124/Spider 2000 and 131 driveshafts

1. Flexible coupling
2. Bushing
3. Sleeve
4. Lubrication fitting
5. Slotted sleeve and spring
6. Seal
7. Resilient pad
8. Yoke
9. Nut
10. Disc
11. Lock ring
12. Ball bearing

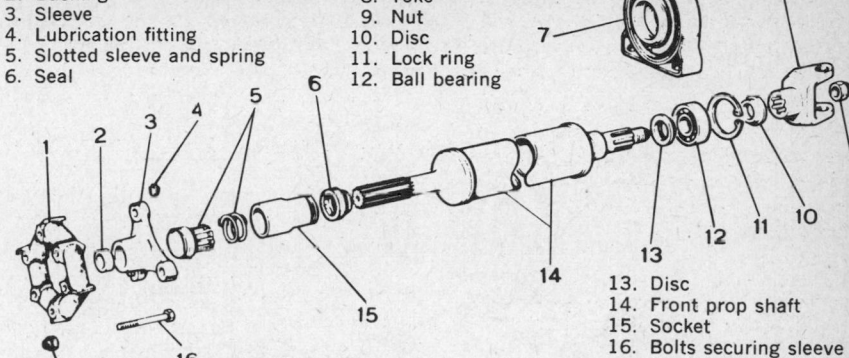

13. Disc
14. Front prop shaft
15. Socket
16. Bolts securing sleeve to flexible coupling
17. Self locking nut

124/Spider 2000 and 131 driveshaft front section

arc in two parts; a splined tubular front piece connected to the transmission through a flexible spider coupling and a solid rear piece, connected to the front piece by a universal joint and to the rear axle by a universal joint.

REMOVAL & INSTALLATION

NOTE: Special tool A.70025 or a 5 in. diameter screw type hose clamp is required to remove the sleeve of the front shaft.

1. Install the special tool or 5 in. diameter hose clamp and unscrew the 3 self-locking nuts and withdraw the bolts.
2. Remove the retaining clip of the brake hose from the rear shaft cover and disconnect the hose from the rear brake pipe.
3. Release the brake pipe from the two clips on the rear shaft cover.
4. Disconnect the rear shaft cover from the differential.
5. Disconnect the handbrake return spring from the central support.
6. Unscrew the nuts holding the central support to the body and slide the shafts toward the front to remove.
7. Install the driveshaft in the reverse order of removal.

DISASSEMBLY & ASSEMBLY

1. Remove the spider of the universal joint.
2. Unscrew the attaching nut of the universal joint fork.
3. Remove the fork and the shield snap-ring.
4. Slide the rear shaft and bearing out of the tubular cover.
5. Remove the bearing from the end of the shaft.
6. When the cover has been removed, the sliding sleeve will come off the front.
7. To assemble, reverse the disassembly procedure using grease to lubricate the couplings.

NOTE: The universal joint fork nut must be tightened to 69 ft. lbs. and then staked with a center punch.

U-JOINT OVERHAUL

For all U–Joint overhaul procedures, please refer to "U–Joint/CV–Joint Overhaul" in the Unit Repair section.

Axle Shafts

REMOVAL & INSTALLATION

124/Spider 2000

1. Jack up the rear of the car. Remove the wheels. Remove the caliper support bracket assembly without disconnecting the brake fluid lines.
2. Remove the snap-ring which retains the bearing dust cover.
3. Using a slide hammer, remove the axle shaft, complete with snap-ring, dust cover, bearing and bearing retained collar.
4. Extract the shaft oil seal and O-ring.

NOTE: Always use a hydraulic press to remove the axle shaft bearing retaining collar.

5. Fit the oil seal and O-ring to the housing.
6. Insert the complete axle shaft and fit the snap-ring to the housing.
7. Fit the brake disc to the axle shaft hub with two centering screws.
8. Fit the caliper support bracket and caliper assembly to the axle.
9. Fit the wheel and lower the car to the ground.

131

1. Jack up the rear of the car and block the front wheels. Release the parking brake. Remove the rear wheel.
2. Remove the two brake drum retaining bolts and pull off the drum.
3. Working through the axle shaft flange, remove the four backing plate bolts.
4. Attach a slide hammer to the axle

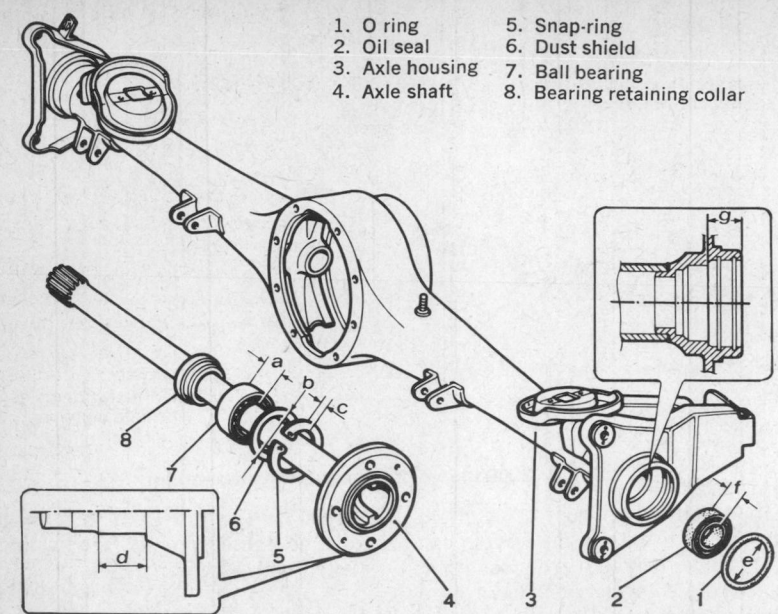

1. O ring
2. Oil seal
3. Axle housing
4. Axle shaft
5. Snap-ring
6. Dust shield
7. Ball bearing
8. Bearing retaining collar

124/Spider 2000 rear axle and axle shaft assembly

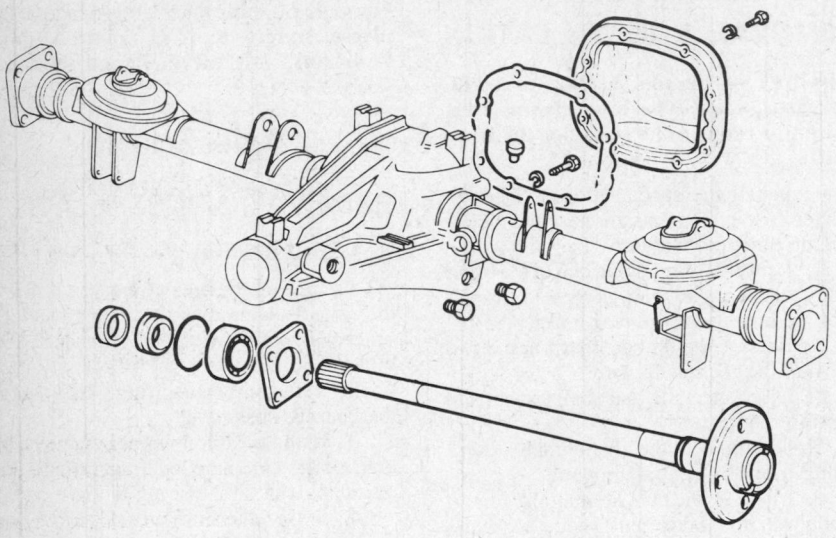

131 rear axle and axle shaft assembly

shaft flange and pull out the axle shaft, bearing and retainer.

NOTE: Do not stretch or bend the brake line.

5. Remove and replace the oil seal in the axle housing.

6. Check that the axle bearing is tight against its retainer and axle shaft shoulder. If replacement is necessary, press off the retainer with an arbor press. Never reuse the retainer. To install the new retainer, heat to 578°F and press on so that the bearing inner race is locked between the retainer and axle shaft shoulder.

7. Install the axle shaft assembly. Install the backing plate bolts, brake drum, and wheel.

128

1. Drain the transmission oil.

2. Unscrew the oil seal boot at the transmission.

3. Remove the outer clamps on the boot at the constant-speed joint and pull back both boots enough to uncover both joints.

4. Clean the grease off both joints.

5. Open the sealing ring on the constant-speed joints and remove the shaft ends from their seats in the joint.

6. Turn the car wheels to enable the shafts to be fully removed from their seats in the differential.

NOTE: Some early cars are equipped with twin–type axle shafts. If it becomes necessary to replace one of these shafts it can be replaced with the later integral–type shaft.

7. Installation is the reverse of the removal procedure, bearing the following in mind.

8. When each axle shaft end has been inserted into the constant-speed joint, check that the snap-ring is lying in its axle shaft groove.

— CAUTION —

Make sure that the axle shaft snap-ring is, in fact, lying in its groove. Move the shaft inward and outward a few times; this operation is necessary as correct ring setting is vital.

9. Grease the constant-speed joint sockets and the protection boot. No more than 3 oz. of grease should be used.

X1/9 (4-Speed)

1. Remove the wheel/tire assembly.

2. Remove the two bolts and nuts securing the shock absorber to the pillar.

3. Remove the nut holding the ball joint of the control arm in the pillar and remove the ball joint from the pillar.

4. Remove the nut retaining the strut ball joint to the pillar and remove the ball joint from the pillar.

5. Drain the transmission.

6. Remove the three bolts and washers retaining the oil seal boot to the differential.

7. Pull the axle shaft and wheel hub from the differential.

8. Remove the brake caliper and support bracket from the pillar.

9. Remove the bolts securing the retaining plate and brake rotor to the hub and remove the plate and rotor.

10. Remove the clamp retaining the boot to the constant-speed joint and pull the boot back to uncover the joint. Clean the grease off the joints.

11. Remove the lock-ring from the constant-speed joints, using a pair of pliers.

12. Remove the axle shaft from the constant-speed unit.

13. Install the axle shaft in the reverse order of removal. After installing the axle shaft in the constant-speed joint and installing the snap-ring in the groove of the axle shaft, make sure the snap-ring is properly seated by moving the shaft in and out. Grease the constant-speed joint with no more than 3 oz. of grease.

Half-Shaft

REMOVAL & INSTALLATION

Strada and X1/9 (5-Speed)

1. Jack up the car and support it safely.

2. Remove the wheel.

3. With the brakes applied, remove the hub nut and washer.

4. Remove the six allen head bolts holding the halfshaft to the driveshaft flange.

NOTE: Discard the allen head bolts and replace with new ones upon installation.

5. Pull the halfshaft out of the hub carrier.

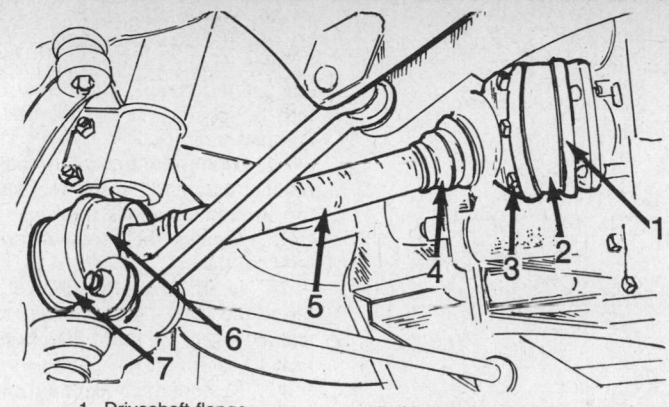

1. Driveshaft flange
2. CV joint
3. Allen head bolts
4. Protective boot
5. Half-shaft
6. Protective boot
7. CV joint

Drive axle assembly—Strada

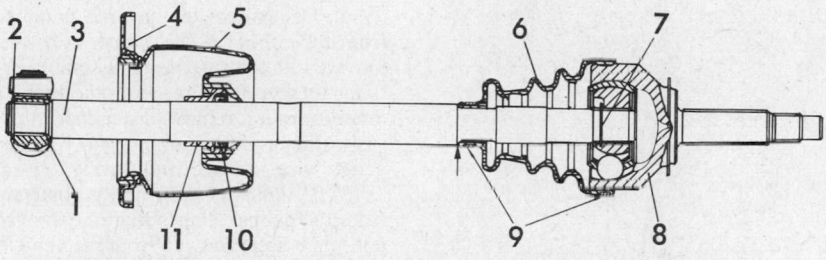

1. Tripod joint
2. Circlip
3. Axle shaft
4. Flange
5. Oil seal boot
6. Boot
7. Snapring
8. Constant-speed joint
9. Boot clamps
10. Sealing ring
11. Bushing

The arrow indicates the shoulder with which the boot
(6) should be in contact after installation

Left axle shaft assembly—128

6. Remove the large clamp holding the protective boot on the CV-joint (drive end).

7. Remove the circlip retaining the CV-joint on halfshaft and slide the CV-joint off.

8. To remove the CV-joint from the hub carrier end, remove the large clamp holding the protective boot and pull the CV-joint from the halfshaft so that the circlip remains in its seat.

9. Reinstall the CV-joints and halfshaft in the reverse order. Torque the new allen head bolts to 31 ft. lbs.

NOTE: Wheel side constant velocity joints are graded into classes and identified by paint marks. They must always be fitted in matched pairs as shown in table.

HALFSHAFT TO CV-JOINT MATING REFERENCE

Half-Shaft		CV Joint	
Class	Color	Class	Color
A	Blue	A	Blue
B	Red	B	White
		C	Red

NOTE: Class B joints can be mated with both half-shaft classes.

Stub Axle

REMOVAL & INSTALLATION
128

1. Raise and support the front of the car.

2. Remove the wheel.

3. Disconnect the shock absorber from the steering knuckle.

4. Disconnect the brake caliper from the steering knuckle.

5. Remove the brake disc and mounting plate from the hub.

6. Disconnect the tie-rod from the steering knuckle.

7. Disconnect the anti-roll bar from the control arm.

NOTE: When removing the anti-roll bar from the control arms, make sure to take note of the number of adjustment shims inserted between the ends of the bar and the control arm bushings so they can be replaced in their original positions.

8. Disconnect the control arm from the body.

9. If necessary, remove the control arm from the steering knuckle.

10. Remove the stub axle from the steering knuckle with a press.

11. Install the stub axle in the reverse order.

X1/9 (4-Speed)

1. Remove the axle shaft.

2. Remove the hub and pillar assembly from the car.

3. Remove the hub nut and washer.

4. Pull the constant-speed joint out of the hub.

5. Press the hub from the pillar.

6. Remove the ring nut securing the bearing in the pillar and remove the bearing from the pillar.

7. Install the new bearing in the pillar.

8. Screw the *new* ring nut into the pillar to hold the bearing. Tighten the nut to 43 ft. lbs. Fiat tool A.57123 is the socket used to tighten the nut.

NOTE: Whenever the bearing in the pillar is replaced, use a new ring nut. It is necessary to replace the bearing every time the hub (stub axle) is removed from the pillar.

9. Press the hub into the pillar.

10. Install the constant-speed joint into the hub.

11. Install the washer and hub nut and tighten the nut to 100 ft. lbs. Stake the nut with a punch.

Differential

REMOVAL & INSTALLATION

124/Spider 2000 and 131

NOTE: A case spreader is required to remove the carrier assembly.

To remove only the differential, use the following procedure.

1. Unscrew the drain plug in the lower part of the axle housing and drain the gear oil.

2. Jack the rear of the car and remove the rear wheels. Disconnect the driveshaft.

3. Withdraw the axle shafts far enough to disengage them from the side gears.

4. Unbolt and remove the differential from the housing.

5. Installation is the reverse of removal. Tighten pinion nut to 14–18 inch lbs.

OVERHAUL

For general differential overhaul procedures, please refer to "Drive Axles" in the Unit Repair section.

REAR SUSPENSION

NOTE: Replacement of shock absorbers requires removal of the rear suspension. On the 131 station wagon only, the

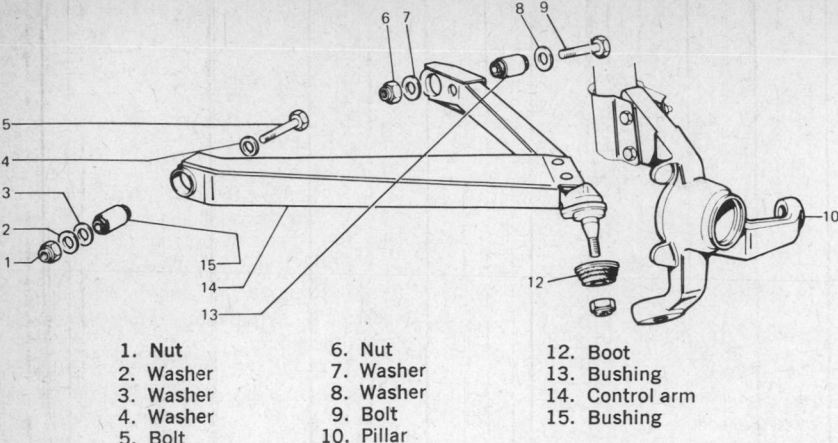

1. Nut
2. Washer
3. Washer
4. Washer
5. Bolt
6. Nut
7. Washer
8. Washer
9. Bolt
10. Pillar
12. Boot
13. Bushing
14. Control arm
15. Bushing

Exploded view of the rear control arm assembly for X1/9

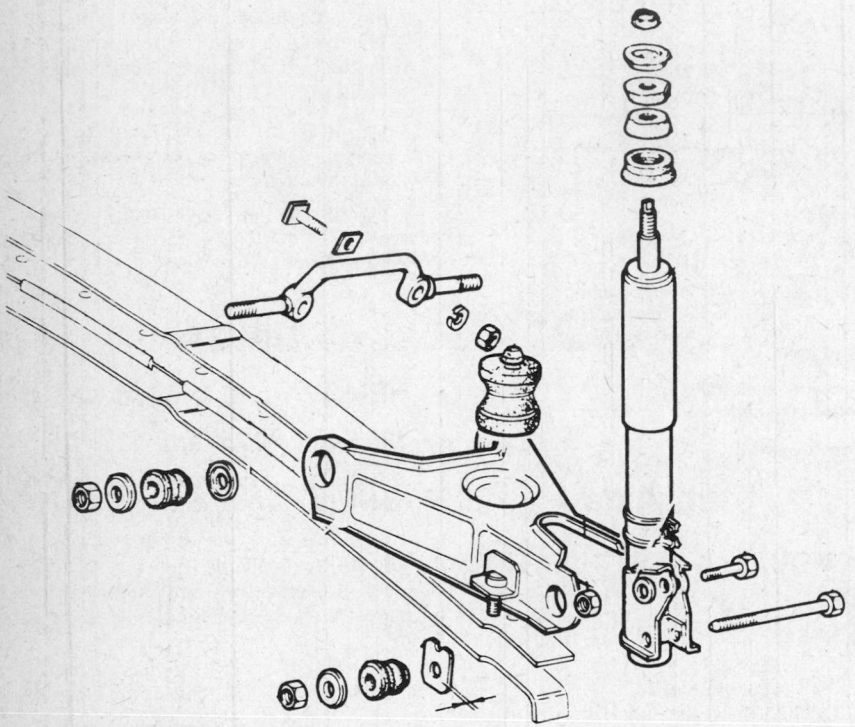

128 rear suspension components—Strada similar

rear shock absorbers are replaced in the conventional manner.

REMOVAL & INSTALLATION

128 and Strada

1. Raise the rear of vehicle and support safely.

2. Remove the rear wheels.

3. Plug the outlet hole of the brake fluid reservoir.

4. Detach the flexible brake fluid hose from the metal pipe.

5. Release the handbrake relay lever and detach the cable from the shoe control levers on the brake backing plate.

6. Disconnect the braking regulator torsion bar from the left control arm.

7. Place a hydraulic jack under the control arm, raise the suspension, and detach the shock absorbers inside the luggage compartment. Remove the jack.

8. Detach the rubber pads which attach the leaf spring to the control arms.

9. Unscrew the nuts that attach the swivels of the control arms to the screws which pass through the plate that mounts the suspension to the body. Keep track of any shims.

10. Attach the control arm to the body by passing the two screws through the plate. Torque the nuts to 36.2 ft. lbs.

11. Reattach the rubber pads used to anchor the leaf spring.

12. Link the braking regulator torsion bar to the left control arm.

13. Slip the bottom rubber bushing onto

the top stud of the shock absorber. Apply a hydraulic jack under the suspension and lift the whole assembly to enable the top stud of the shock absorber to be inserted into the special hole provided in the luggage compartment.

14. Mount the top rubber bushings, the retainer cap, and the self-locking nut to the top stud of the shock absorber.

15. Tighten the shock absorber nuts to 18.1 ft. lbs.

16. Reattach the handbrake control cable to the lever on the brake backing plate and reconnect the brake fluid hose and metal pipe to each other.

17. Restore the brake fluid and bleed the system.

X1/9

1. Raise the vehicle and support it safely. Remove the wheel.

2. Disconnect the flexible brake tube from the caliper if the caliper is to be removed with the suspension assembly or, in order to save from bleeding the brake hydraulic system, remove the caliper from the suspension assembly and support with heavy gauge wire attached to the body.

3. Disconnect the parking brake cable from the caliper, depending on whether or not it is being removed from the vehicle or not.

4. Remove the exhaust pipe.

5. Note the number of shims and their position on the control arm. Remove the nut, washer, and bolt attaching the control arm to the bracket at the front of the suspension. Allow the shims to remain between the arm and bracket.

6. Remove the nut, washer, and bolt securing the arm to the bracket at the rear of the suspension. Take note of the number of shims and their position. Allow the shims to remain between the arm and bracket.

7. Remove the hub nut and washer.

8. Remove the three nuts and washers securing the top of the shock absorber.

9. Slide the suspension assembly off of the constant-speed joint shaft. Position the axle shaft so that it will not come out of the differential.

To install the suspension assembly:

10. Install the shims in their original positions and loosely attach the arm to the brackets.

11. Raise the assembly and mount the hub to the constant-speed joint.

12. Insert the upper attachment of the shock absorber in the holes in the body and install the three attaching nuts and spring washers.

13. Place the washer on the axle shaft and thread a new hub nut onto the shaft. Tighten the nut to 101 ft. lbs. and stake the nut.

NOTE: Always use a new hub nut.

14. Install the exhaust pipe.

15. Install the wheel.

16. Lower the car to the ground.

17. With the vehicle laden (two people

sitting inside or their equivalent weight), tighten the control arm attaching nuts to 72 ft. lbs. Tighten the three upper shock absorber attaching nuts to 43 ft. lbs.

124/Spider 2000 and 131

1. Jack up the rear of the car. Remove the rear wheels after placing the car on jack stands.

2. Disconnect the driveshaft.

3. Disconnect the brake lines.

4. Disconnect the handbrake cables.

5. Free the cables from their clips on the body.

6. Disconnect the shocks from inside the trunk. On 131 wagons, disconnect the shocks from their upper mounts, beneath the car.

7. Disconnect the two stabilizer bar links.

8. Disconnect the brake regulator link.

9. Support the rear axle with a hydraulic jack.

10. Disconnect the anchor rods and the sway bar.

11. Remove the assembly by lowering the jack.

12. Remove the stabilizer bar brackets and the bar.

13. Remove the shocks at the spring mounts, or lower attachment (131 wagon).

14. Remove the anchor rods and sway bar from the axle.

NOTE: Do not tighten any bolts during assembly unless otherwise instructed. Bolts should be tightened in sequence with the vehicle on a level surface.

15. Connect the anchor rods and the sway bar to the housing.

16. Bolt the shocks to the spring seats or lower mount (131 wagon), and tighten them.

17. Bolt up the stabilizer bar with its links, but do not tighten it completely.

18. Seat the springs with pads to the axle plates.

19. Place the jack in position.

20. Connect the axle to the body, but do not fully tighten the anchor rods to their brackets.

21. Connect the stabilizer bar links to

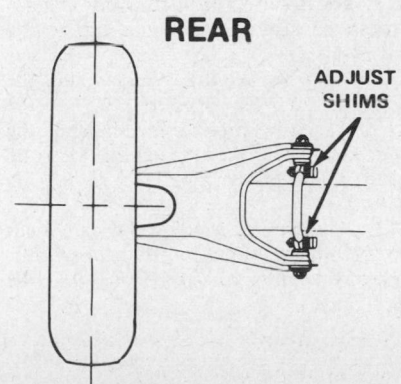

128 and Strada rear suspension adjustment locations

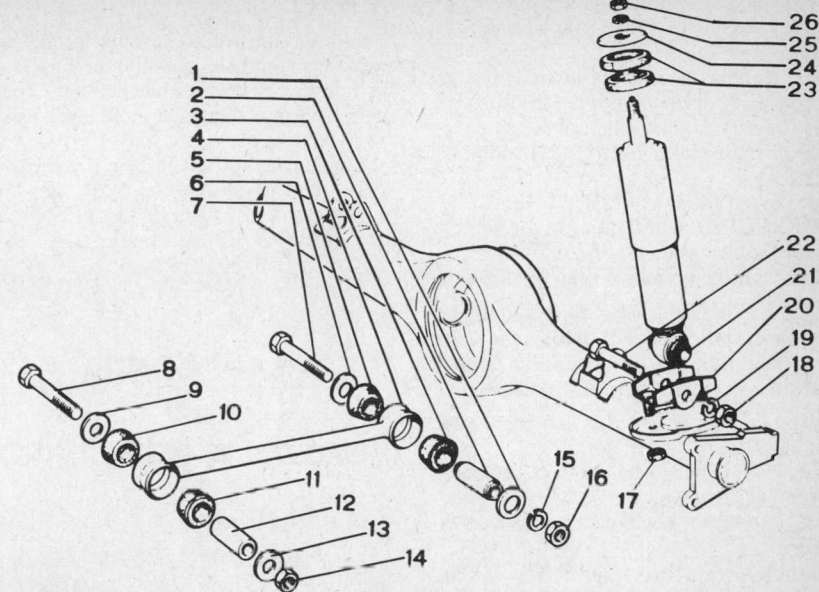

1. Flat washer	9. Flat washer	19. Lock washer
2. Spacer	10. Rubber bushing	20. Lower bracket
3. Rubber bushing	11. Rubber bushing	21. Shock absorber, complete
4. Upper side rod	12. Spacer	22. Bolt fixing shock absorber
5. Rubber bushing	13. Flat washer	to lower bracket
6. Flat washer	14. Nut	23. Rubber bushing
7. Bolt anchoring upper side	15. Lock washer	24. Upper cup
rod to axle housing	16. Nut	25. Lock washer
8. Bolt anchoring upper side	17. Nut	26. Nut
rod to body	18. Nut	

124/Spider 2000 rear suspension shock absorbers

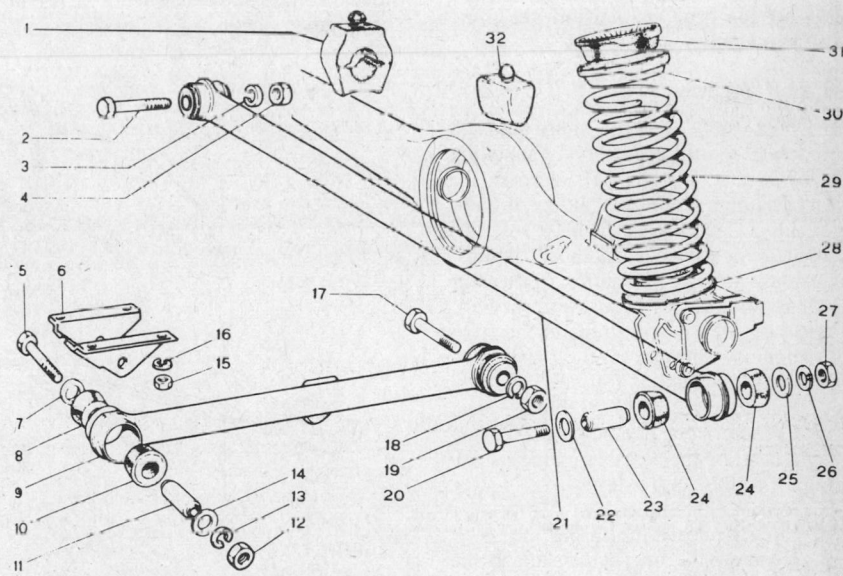

1. Rubber pad	11. Spacer	21. Cross rod
2. Bolt anchoring cross rod	12. Nut	22. Flat washer
to body	13. Lock washer	23. Spacer
3. Lock washer	14. Flat washer	24. Rubber bushings
4. Nut	15. Nut	25. Flat washer
5. Bolt anchoring lower side	16. Lock washer	26. Lock washer
rod to bracket 6	17. Bolt anchoring lower side	27. Nut
6. Bracket	rod to axle housing	28. Lower ring-pad
7. Flat washer	18. Lock washer	29. Coil spring
8. Rubber bushing	19. Nut	30. Upper seating ring
9. Lower side rod	20. Bolt anchoring cross rod	31. Upper rubber ring-pad
10. Rubber bushing	to axle housing	32. Rubber buffer

124/Spider 2000 rear suspension rods and springs

the housing, but do not tighten fully.

22. Connect the brake regulator rod to the housing.

23. Tighten the shocks at the luggage compartment, or upper mount (131 wagon).

24. Install the driveshaft and tighten.

25. Install brake lines and handbrake cables.

26. Bleed the brake system.

27. Install the wheels. Lower the vehicle and torque the wheels to 51 ft. lbs.

28. Tighten the nuts on the pivot bolts.

NOTE: The following bolts should be tightened in the order in which they appear. They should be gradually loaded until the specified torque is obtained.

a. Anchor rod-to-the housing (124/Spider 2000)—72 ft. lbs.

b. Sway bar-to-the axle (124/Spider 2000)—72 ft. lbs.

c. Stabilizer bar links-to-axle—25 ft. lbs.

d. Reaction strut nuts (131)—58 ft. lbs.

e. Transverse strut nuts (131)—58 ft. lbs.

NOTE: The above procedure prevents the rubber bushings from being unduly stressed.

ADJUSTMENTS

NOTE: Camber and toe-in adjustments on the rear suspension are done at the same time.

128 and Strada

Rear wheel camber and toe-in are adjusted at the lower control arm-to-body attaching bolts by means of shims. To increase the negative camber angle, add an equal number of shims. To decrease the negative camber angle, remove an equal number of shims. To increase toe-in, add shims to the rear bolt or remove shims from the front bolt. To decrease toe-in, add shims to the front bolt or remove shims from the rear bolt.

To adjust, proceed as follows:

1. Raise the rear of the vehicle.

2. Compress one end of the leaf spring to shift it from the flexible guide which anchors it to the control arm.

3. Remove the guide.

4. Slowly release the spring.

5. Unscrew the nuts which attach the pivot to the body.

6. Partly remove the screw to free the adjustment shims.

7. Carry out the required variation in the number of shims.

8. Reinsert the screw.

9. Carry out this operation on both control arm-to-body screws.

10. Adjust the other wheel as necessary.

11. Reassemble the two flexible guides which anchor the leaf spring to the control arms and tighten the attachment nuts to 22 ft. lbs.

X1/9

Toe-in is adjusted by turning the reaction rod, thus lengthening or shortening the rod to the desired toe-in specification. Toe-in with the vehicle unladen should be between $+ \frac{3}{16}$ and $\frac{1}{4}$ in.

Camber should be $- 2\frac{5}{16}$ to $-1\frac{5}{8}$ on 1978 models; $-2\frac{1}{4}$ to $-1\frac{1}{4}$ on 1979 models; and $-1\frac{3}{4}$ to $-\frac{3}{4}$ on 1980 and later models.

Leaf Spring

REMOVAL & INSTALLATION

128 and Strada

1. Place car on a hoist or jack stands and support it safely. Rear suspension must be unladen.

2. Disconnect the brake compensator torsion bar from the link.

3. Remove two nuts and bolts to remove the spring guide.

4. Remove four nuts and washers to remove the rubber buffers.

5. Remove the leaf spring. To separate the leaf spring, slowly remove the clamp at the center.

6. Installation is the reverse of removal. Torque buffer nuts to 22 ft. lbs. and spring guide nuts to 25 ft. lbs.

FRONT SUSPENSION

The 124/Spider 2000 model range is equipped with parallel upper and lower control arm front suspension. A coil spring is located between the control arms, along with a shock absorber. The steering knuckles are located in ball joints. A stabilizer bar is used on all models.

The 128, 131, Strada and X1/9 are equipped with MacPherson strut front suspension. The suspension strut acts as a shock absorber, suspension (with a concentric coil

REAR

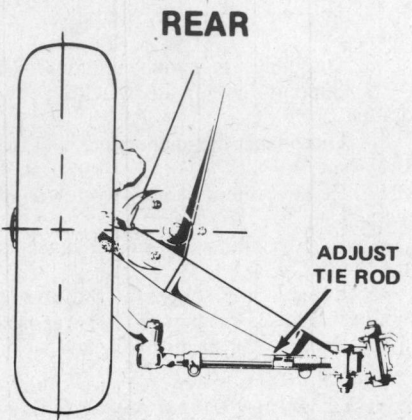

ADJUST TIE ROD

X1/9 rear suspension adjustment locations

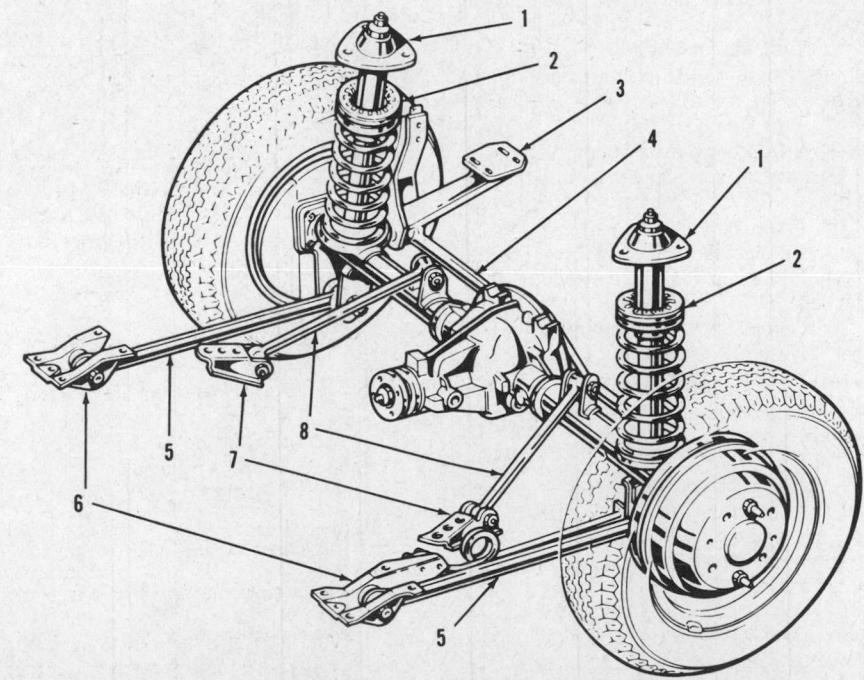

1. Shock absorber
2. Coil spring
3. Transverse strut support
4. Transverse strut
5. Lower reaction strut
6. Lower reaction strut support
7. Upper reaction strut support
8. Upper reaction strut

131 rear suspension

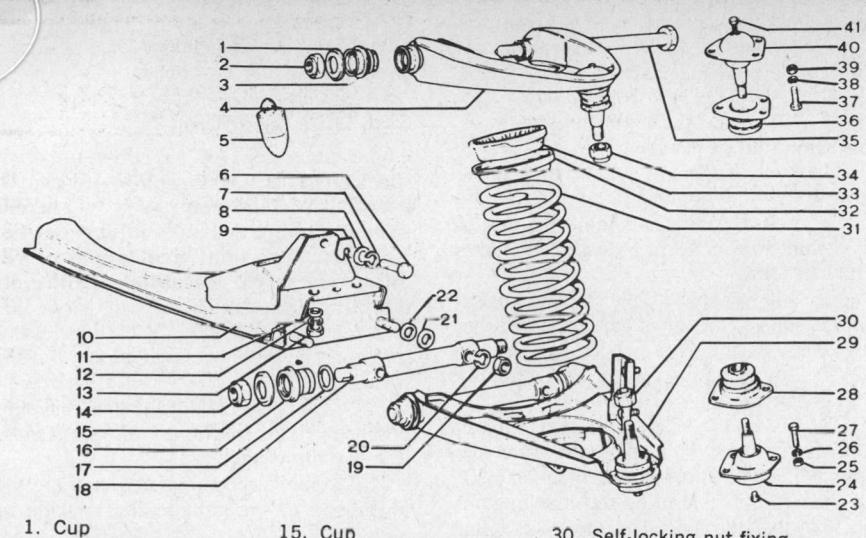

1. Cup
2. Nut fixing upper control arm to body
3. Resilient bushing
4. Upper control arm
5. Buffer
6. Bolt
7. Spring washer
8. Flat washer
9. Tab strip
10. Crossmember
11. Flat washer
12. Spring washer
13. Nut
14. Nut fixing pivot bar 18 to lower control arm
15. Cup
16. Resilient bushing
17. Flat washer
18. Pivot bar
19. Nut fixing lower control arm to crossmember 10
20. Spring washer
21. Flat washer
22. Tab strip
23. Plug
24. Lower ball joint
25. Nut
26. Spring washer
27. Bolt
28. Seal
29. Lower control arm
30. Self-locking nut fixing steering knuckle to lower control arm
31. Spring
32. Spring seat
33. Rubber pad
34. Self-locking nut fixing steering knuckle to upper control arm
35. Bolt
36. Seal
37. Bolt
38. Spring washer
39. Nut
40. Upper ball joint
41. Plug

Exploded view of the 124/Spider 2000 front suspension

spring), and upper locating member. A control arm is located at the bottom of the steering knuckle. A stabilizer bar is used on all models.

REMOVAL & INSTALLATION

124/Spider 2000

1. Support the front of the car with safety stands.
2. Remove the front wheels.
3. Remove the shock.
4. Using a spring compressor, compress the spring until it no longer exerts pressure on the control arm.

──────── CAUTION ────────

Make sure spring compressor is properly attached.

5. Disconnect the stabilizer bar at the lower control arm.
6. Disconnect the brake hoses.
7. Disconnect the tie rod at the steering knuckle arm.
8. Unscrew the fixing nut and remove the pivot bolt to allow the control arm to separate from the body.
9. Remove the nuts which secure the lower control arm to the crossmember. Be sure to mark the number of shims removed and from which stud they were removed.
10. The assembly can now be removed and disassembled.

NOTE: Shims are located between the body and the pivot bar to which the control arm is mounted.

11. Install the stabilizer bar to the body.
12. Insert the shims and install the wishbone assembly, bolting the lower control arm to the crossmember.
13. Insert the spring with the tool attached into its seat in the control arm.
14. Compress the spring until its height will allow the connecting of the upper control arm.
15. Connect the upper control arm, but do not tighten it fully.
16. Connect the stabilizer bar to the control arm.
17. Connect the tie-rod to the steering arm.
18. Connect the brake lines.
19. Bleed the brake system.
20. Seat the spring by unloading the compressor.
21. Remove the compressor and install the shock.
22. Install the tires, lower the car and torque the wheels to 50 ft. lbs.
23. With the vehicle on a level surface, gradually tighten the following bolts in the order in which they appear and to the proper specification.
    a. Nut on the pin connecting the upper control arm to the body—72 ft. lbs.
    b. Nuts retaining the lower control arm to the crossmember—43 ft. lbs.
    c. Nuts fixing the lower control arm to the pin—72 ft. lbs.

128 and Strada

1. Loosen the front wheel stud bolts.
2. Loosen the front wheel hub nuts.
3. Place the vehicle on jack stands.
4. Remove the front wheels.
5. Unscrew the nuts which attach the brake caliper to the pillar and secure the caliper to the body.
6. Unscrew the nut which attaches the tie–rod ball joint to the steering arm and then remove the swivel with a puller.
7. Unscrew the nut which attaches the end of the anti-roll bar to the control arm.
8. Detach the control arm from the body.
9. Remove the hub nut.
10. Release the top attachment of the shock absorber by unscrewing the 3 mounting nuts in the engine compartment and slide the suspension assembly off the constant-speed joint shaft and support the axle shaft in such a way as to prevent it from slipping out of the differential. Remove the suspension assembly for further service.
11. Attach the anti-roll bar to the body.
12. Take up each completely reassembled control arm and mount the hub on the shaft of the constant-speed joint. At the same time, insert the upper attachment of

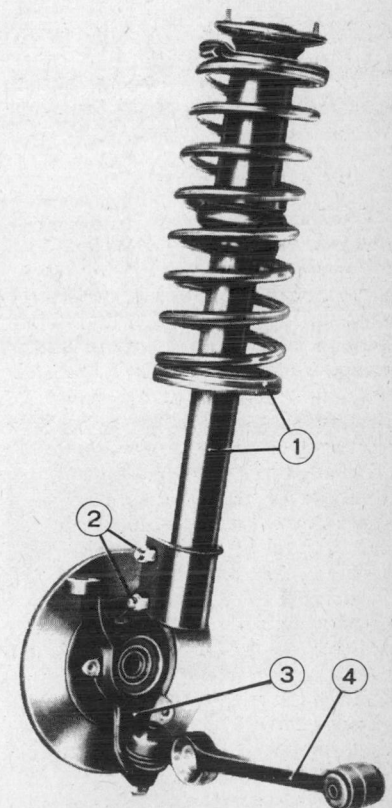

1. Shock absorber and spring
2. Screws and nuts attaching the shock absorber to the pillar
3. Pillar
4. Control arm

Left front suspension assembly on 128–131 and Strada similar

the shock absorber into the holes provided in the body and secure it with the nuts and the spring washers.

13. Place a flat washer on the shaft of the constant-speed joint and screw up the attachment nut. Torque hub nut to 159 ft. lbs.

14. Grease the rubber bushings in the anti-roll bar-to-control arm joint.

15. Using as many shims as were present on disassembly, reattach the end of the anti-roll bar and its flexible pads to the control arm and reinstall the latter on the body.

16. Attach the tie-rod to the steering arm and tighten the nut to 58 ft. lbs.

17. Remount the brake caliper onto the brake disc.

X1/9 and 131

1. Remove the wheel and tire.

2. If the brake caliper is to be removed with the suspension, disconnect the flexible brake line from the caliper and plug it. If

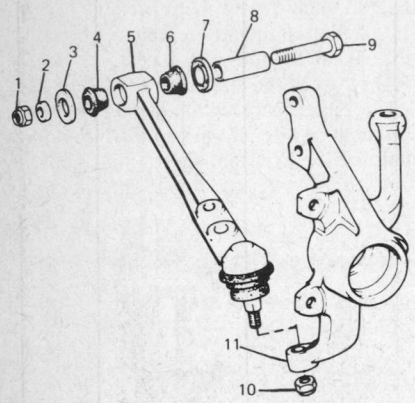

1. Nut	7. Washer
2. Washer	8. Spacer
3. Washer	9. Bolt
4. Rubber bushing	10. Nut
5. Control arm	11. Pillar
6. Rubber bushing	

Exploded view of front control arm assembly—X1/9

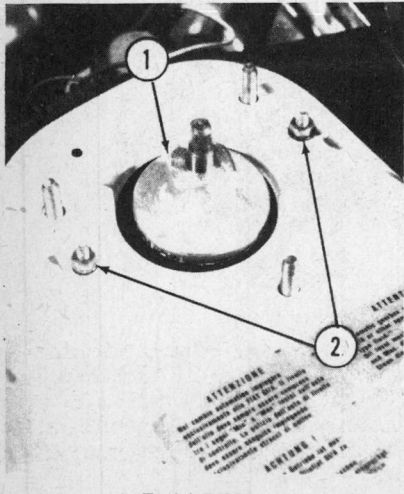

1. Tool A.74375
2. Retainer nuts

Removing shock absorber assembly

the caliper need not be removed from the vehicle, remove it from the suspension and support it with a length of heavy gauge wire.

3. Disconnect the stabilizer strut (sway bar) from the suspension.

4. Remove the bolt holding the control arm to the body mount.

5. Remove the nut holding the tie-rod ball joint to the steering arm and remove the ball joint.

6. Support beneath the steering knuckle. Disconnect the top of the shock absorber by removing the three nuts and washers.

7. Lower the suspension strut assembly out of the car.

8. Install the suspension assembly in the reverse order. Tighten the attaching nuts and bolts with the vehicle under a load. Tighten the knuckle-to-tie-rod attaching nut to 58 ft. lbs.; the control arm-to-lower pillar attaching nut to 51 ft. lbs. (X1/9) 58 ft. lbs. (131); the control arm-to-body attaching bolt to 29 ft. lbs. (X1/9) 65 ft. lbs. (131); and the stabilizer strut bar attaching bolt to 29 ft. lbs. (X1/9) 43 ft. lbs. (131).

Ball Joint

CHECKING

1. Using a jack, raise the control arm slightly to unload the ball joint.

2. Use Fiat gauge A.96505 or equivalent to check that lower lip does not touch the threaded pin on the ball joint.

3. If not as specified, the control arm/ball joint assembly must be replaced. See removal of front suspension.

Shock Absorber

REMOVAL & INSTALLATION

124/Spider 2000

1. Working from inside the engine compartment, disconnect the upper end of the shock.

2. Remove the nut and bolt fixing the shock to the lower control arm.

3. Remove the shock through the lower control arm.

4. Installation is the reverse of the removal procedure to include replacing all the worn bushings and washers.

128, Strada, and X1/9

The replacement of MacPherson strut shock absorber inserts requires the proper use of a spring compressor to prevent serious damage or bodily injury. See the Unit Repair section for overhaul procedures and safety precautions before attempting disassembly.

1. Detach the shock at the top by unscrewing the three nuts that attach it to the body.

2. Jack up the front of the car and support beneath the subframe with jack stands. Remove the wheel.

3. Remove the two bolts retaining the lower end of the strut to the knuckle or pillar.

4. Remove the shock and coil spring (strut assembly) as a unit.

5. Reinstall strut assembly in reverse order.

131

The replacement of MacPherson strut shock absorber inserts requires the proper use of a spring compressor to prevent serious damage or bodily injury. See the Unit Repair section for overhaul procedures and safety precautions before attempting disassembly.

1. With car on the ground, remove the upper nut and washer from the shock absorber shaft.

2. Remove the three nuts and washers and remove rubber mounting assembly.

3. With the car still on the ground, install and tighten tool A.74375 or equivalent on the shock absorber shaft. **THIS TOOL IS A MUST**.

4. Remove the two nuts and washers holding the shock assembly to the body.

5. Jack up the car, support it safely, then remove the wheel.

6. Disconnect the brake hose from the tube in the clip.

7. Remove the nut and washer holding the ball joint. Remove the ball joint.

8. Remove the nut and washer holding the sway bar to the lower support arm. Pry

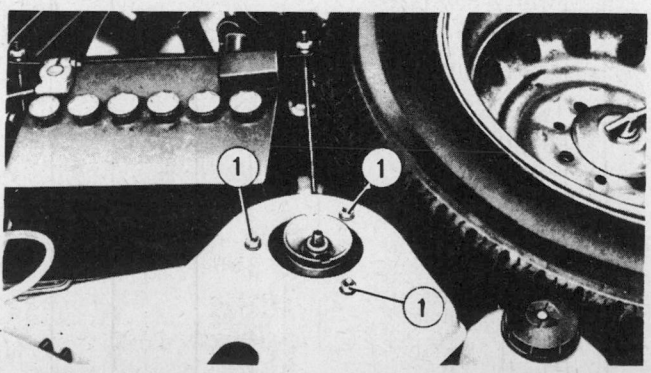

Removing front shock upper attachment—all except 124/Spider 2000

the rubber bushing off the threaded end of the sway bar.

9. Remove the bolt, nut and washers holding the support arm to the bracket on the frame.

10. Remove the arm from the bracket. Push the arm to the rear to remove it from the sway bar.

11. Carefully lower the suspension out of the car. Install in reverse order.

Front End Alignment

CAMBER ADJUSTMENT

124/Spider 2000

Camber angle adjustments are made by changing the number of shims under the two bolts that hold the lower control arm to the frame crossmember. Camber is increased by removing shims and reduced by adding shims. Add or remove the same number for each bolt, otherwise caster will be affected.

X1/9, 131, 128 and Strada

Camber cannot be adjusted and is built into the suspension. Replace weak, worn, or damaged springs or other suspension components to gain the proper camber measurement.

CASTER ADJUSTMENT

124/Spider 2000

Caster angle is increased by moving these shims from the front bolts to the rear and decreased by moving them from the rear bolt to the front.

131

Caster is adjusted by adding or removing shims between the sway bar and lower support (control) arm.

128 and Strada

If the caster angles are incorrect, the necessary corrections must be made by varying the number of shims inserted between the end of the anti-roll bar and the rubber pad of the control arm. The angle is reduced by about 15 minutes for each extra shim.

1. Raise the front of the vehicle.
2. Remove the nut which anchors the anti-roll bar to the control arm.
3. Disconnect the control arm from the body.
4. Withdraw the end of the anti-roll bar from the control arm.
5. Add or remove as many shims as necessary to correct the caster angle.
6. Reassemble the various components. Lower the vehicle and rock it a few times to settle down the suspension before tightening the two attachment nuts to their correct torque values.

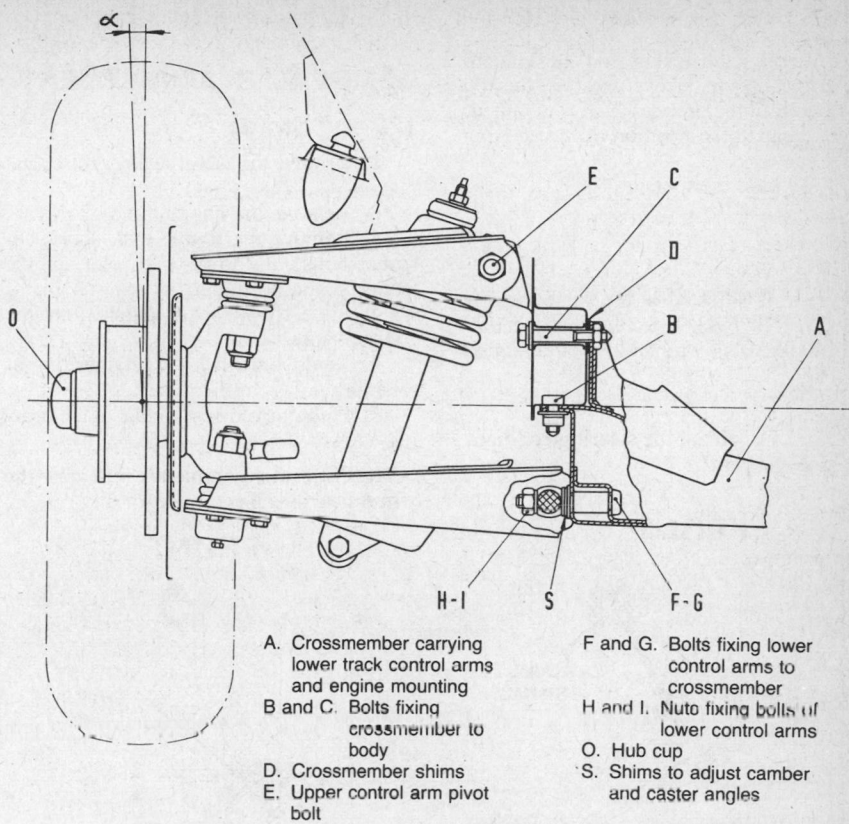

A. Crossmember carrying lower track control arms and engine mounting
B and C. Bolts fixing crossmember to body
D. Crossmember shims
E. Upper control arm pivot bolt
F and G. Bolts fixing lower control arms to crossmember
H and I. Nuto fixing bolts of lower control arms
O. Hub cup
S. Shims to adjust camber and caster angles

124/Spider 2000 front suspension adjustments

1. Tie rod
2. Flats for wrench
3. Locknut
4. Tie rod end

Toe-in adjustment on 128, Strada and X1/9

X1/9

Caster is adjusted on the X1/9 by adding or subtracting shims between the front reaction struts and body-end supports.

TOE-IN

124/Spider 2000

Toe-in is adjusted by loosening the clamp bolts and turning the sleeves to lengthen or shorten the left and right-hand tie–rods. Turn the sleeves in opposite directions and to an equal extent. After adjusting, make sure the gaps in the sleeves and clamps are on the same side and flush.

X1/9, 128 and Strada

1. Set the wheels straight ahead. Make

sure the spokes on the steering wheel are positioned properly.

2. Loosen the locknut on the inboard end of the tie–rod sleeve and turn the rod in or out until the proper toe-in is obtained. Do not change the position of the steering wheel spokes.

3. Tighten the locknut.

131

131 toe-in is adjusted in the same manner as the 128 and X1/9, except that the outboard locknut is loosened to rotate the tie–rod.

NOTE: Lubricate the steering rod boot so it doesn't tear.

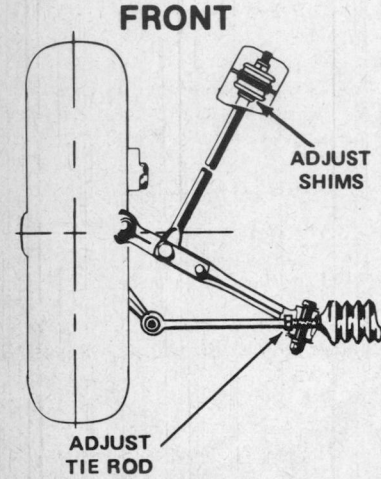

Caster and toe-in adjustments—X1/9

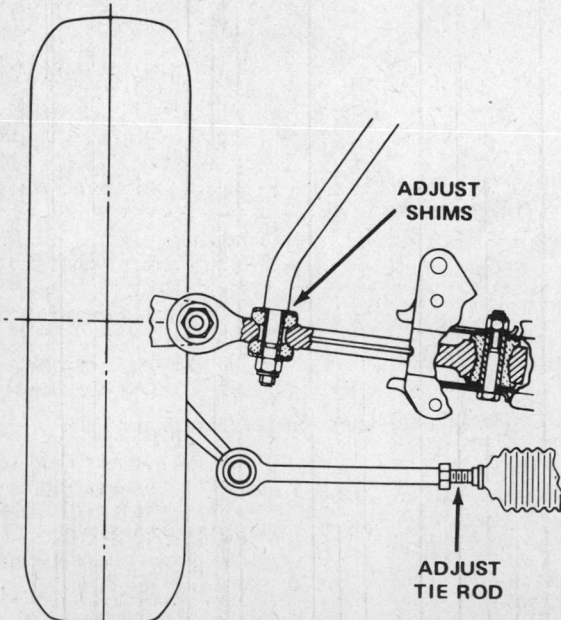

Caster and toe-in adjustments—131

Wheel Bearings

REMOVAL & ADJUSTMENT

128 and Strada

1. Remove the wheel, caliper, disc, and plate.

2. Remove the hub nut and discard.

3. Remove the tie-rod end, shock absorber bolts, and lower ball joint spindle from the knuckle pillar.

4. Slide the knuckle pillar from the constant-speed joint.

5. Remove the bearing retainer ring or retaining nut from the pillar.

6. Press the old bearing out of the bearing cavity.

NOTE: Fiat recommends replacing the wheel bearings if removed for any reason.

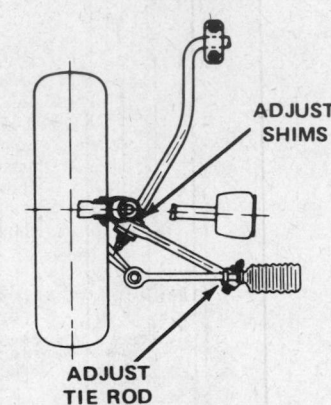

Caster and toe-in adjustments—128 and Strada

7. Press the new bearing into the bearing cavity.

8. Reinstall the snap-ring or retaining nut. Torque the retaining nut to 44 ft. lbs. Stake to the knuckle pillar.

9. Complete the assembly in the reverse of removal. Torque the hub attachment nut to 100 ft. lbs. and stake the collar of the nut.

X1/9

1. Jack up the front end of the vehicle and remove the wheel.

2. Disconnect the brake calipers and support bracket from the steering pillar.

3. Remove the bolt and centering stud holding the brake rotor and plate and remove the rotor and plate.

4. Remove the nut securing the tie-rod to the pillar and remove the ball joint from the pillar.

5. Remove the nut holding the control arm to the pillar and remove the control arm ball joint from the pillar.

6. Remove the two nuts and bolts holding the shock absorbers to the pillar and remove the pillar from the vehicle.

7. Remove the nut and washers holding the hub to the pillar and press the hub out of the pillar.

8. Remove the ring nut holding the bearing in the pillar and pull the bearing out of the pillar.

NOTE: The removal and installation of the bearing is facilitated by using special Fiat tools A.57123 socket to remove the bearing ring nut and 8015 bearing puller/installer or their equivalents remove and install the bearing.

9. Discard the old bearing.

10. Install the new bearing.

11. Screw a *new* ring nut into the pillar. Tighten the nut to 43 ft. lbs. Always use a new ring nut.

12. Stake the ring nut with a punch.

13. Install the hub in the pillar and press it into place with a press. Install the two washers and a nut and tighten the nut to 100 ft. lbs. Stake the nut with a punch.

14. Install the steering pillar to the car in the reverse order of removal.

124/Spider 2000 and 131

NOTE: A puller is required to remove the wheel hub.

1. Raise and support the front of the car. Remove the wheel, caliper assembly, disc and plate.

2. Remove the hub nut and discard.

3. Remove the hub from the spindle using a puller.

4. The inner and outer bearings can be driven or pressed from the hub and new or repacked ones installed. Pack the bearings and the area between the bearings with grease.

NOTE: Some replacement bearings are of the sealed type and do not require

lubrication. Follow the instructions on the package.

5. Install the hub on the spindle and tighten the new hub nut to 15 ft. lbs. while turning the hub back and forth.

6. Back off the nut and retighten to 5 ft. lbs.

7. Back the nut off 30 degrees and check the hub end-play. It should measure between 0.001–0.004 in.

8. Stake the nut to the spindle and reverse the removal process to complete assembly.

STEERING

Steering Wheel

REMOVAL & INSTALLATION

128, X1/9 and 131

1. Disconnect the battery. Remove the screws attaching the horn button cover.

2. Remove the screws holding the steering column masking sleeves and remove the sleeves.

3. Unscrew the steering wheel attaching nut and remove the steering wheel.

4. Install in the reverse order.

124/Spider 2000

1. Disconnect the battery. Pry off the horn button by inserting a small prybar between the button and the wheel hub.

2. Disconnect the horn wire at the button.

3. Unscrew and remove the steering wheel attaching nut and remove the steering wheel from the shaft.

1. Bolt	19. Lockwasher
2. Washer	20. Bolt
3. Retainer	21. Shaft
4. Support	22. Clamp
5. Nut	23. Pad
6. Lockwasher	24. Clamp
7. Washer	25. Lockwasher
8. Steering wheel	26. Nut
9. Nut	27. Pad
10. Bushing	
11. Steering column	
12. Bushing	
13. Cover	
14. Screw	
15. Pad	
16. Gasket	
17. Steering box	
18. Nut	

Exploded view of steering column and steering gear—X1/9

4. Install the steering wheel in the reverse order.

Strada

1. Center the steering wheel and front wheels.

2. Disconnect the battery.

3. Pry the horn button from the steering wheel.

4. Remove the two horn button springs.

5. Remove the nut holding the wheel to the shaft. Mark the steering wheel and steering shaft for reinstallation. Pull the wheel off of the shaft.

6. Reinstall in reverse order. Torque wheel retaining nut to 36 ft. lbs.

Horn/Directional/Light Switch Assembly

REMOVAL & INSTALLATION

1. Remove the horn button and steering wheel.

2. Disconnect the switch wiring. Remove the shroud.

3. Remove the attaching clamp and slide off the switch.

4. Installation is the reverse of removal.

Steering Gear

REMOVAL & INSTALLATION

128

1. Disconnect the battery leads.

2. Rest the front of the car on stands.

3. Unscrew the stud bolts and remove the front wheels.

4. Remove the spare wheel.

5. Disconnect the drive pinion from the lower section of the steering column at the universal joint.

6. Using a puller, remove the tie-rods from the steering arms.

7. Remove the screws which attach the top guard in order to facilitate removal of the steering box.

8. Unscrew the steering box from the mounting bracket and remove it from the rightside of the vehicle.

9. To install, insert the steering box (complete with tie-rods and filled with oil), from the right side of the vehicle.

10. With the steering wheel in the straight ahead position, connect the drive pinion to the steering column lower section, with the universal joints.

11. Mount the assembly on the body by means of the brackets. The rubber cushions must be inserted between the two parts.

12. Connect the tie-rods to the steering arms. Torque the nuts to 58 ft. lbs.

13. Attach the top guard to the body.

14. Replace the front wheels and return the spare wheel to the engine compartment.

X1/9, 131 and Strada

1. Remove the bolt and nuts retaining the universal on the bottom of the steering column to the pinion shaft of the steering box.

2. Remove the three screws securing the gasket cover to the steering box on the floor boards.

3. Jack up the front of the vehicle and remove the two front wheels.

4. Remove the nuts securing the ball joints in both knuckles. Remove the tie-rods from the knuckles.

5. Remove the four bolts securing the steering box to the body and remove the steering box from the vehicle.

6. Install the steering box in the reverse order of removal.

Brava with Power Steering

1. Remove the nut on the tie-rod.

2. Remove the ball joint from the steering knuckle.

3. Repeat for the other side.

4. Remove the hoses and allow the box to drain.

5. Remove the box and nut on the steering shaft.

6. Remove the bolt holding the left side of the box.

7. Remove 2 bolts holding the right side.

8. Remove the steering box from the car.

9. Install the steering box in reverse order of removal.

10. Fill with Dexron® ATF fluid.

124/Spider 2000

1. Disconnect the battery.

2. Remove the horn button and emblem cover.

3. Remove the steering wheel retaining

nut and pull the steering wheel from the shaft, using a wheel puller.

4. Remove the turn signal switch half covers and unscrew the retaining collar of the turn signal switch. This is located on the bracket which fixes the steering column to the body.

5. Disconnect the steering column bracket from the ignition switch (threaded ring) and remove the retaining collar of the turn signal switch.

6. Remove the screw which clamps the steering column to the worm shaft and remove the steering column from inside the car.

7. Unscrew the nuts which fix the left-hand steering arm and intermediate arm pins.

8. Remove the pins with an appropriate puller.

9. Remove the steering box from the body by removing the 3 mounting screws.

NOTE: Shims can be placed on the steering box bolts to ensure proper alignment.

Note the number and placement of such shims.

10. Drain the oil from the steering box.

11. Using a puller, remove the drop arm from the roller shaft.

12. Remove the roller shaft cover, complete with roller shaft adjusting screw, adjusting disc, lockwasher and locknut.

13. Remove the roller shaft assembly from the steering box.

14. Remove the worm shaft thrust cover and the front bearing adjusting shims.

15. Turn the worm shaft to withdraw the front roller bearing.

16. Use a puller and remove the outer race of the rear roller bearing.

17. Remove the worm and shaft from the steering box along with the inner race of the inner roller bearing.

ADJUSTMENTS

124/Spider 2000

1. Measure the amount of free-play in the steering wheel by moving it back and forth until the wheels will not respond. At this point whatever movement is left in the wheel is free-play.

2. To adjust this condition, loosen the locknut and turn the adjusting screw in.

3. Gradually adjust the free-play out of the steering wheel until it becomes minimal.

4. Tighten the locknut while holding the adjustment screw in place.

NOTE: Serious damage may result from turning the adjustment screw in too far. A small amount of free-play should remain to insure against this condition.

128, X1/9, 131 and Strada

Adjustments to the steering gear are not necessary during normal service. Adjustments are performed only as part of overhaul.

Power Steering Pump

REMOVAL & INSTALLATION

1. Remove the two hoses from the pump.

2. Allow the system to drain.

3. Remove the power steering pump tensioner bolt and mounting bolt.

4. Remove the belt and power steering pump.

5. Reinstall in reverse order. Tension the belt and fill the system with Dexron® transmission fluid.

NOTE: There is no rack adjustment on power steering models.

BRAKES

Spider and X1/9 models are equipped with four wheel disc brakes, while the 128, 131 and Strada models use front disc and rear drum brakes. All models use a vacuum-hydraulic power assist booster acting on all four wheels through a dual brake circuit. A proportioning valve or brake compensator provides a pressure differential between front and rear brake systems according to load conditions and deceleration.

For all brake system procedures not detailed below, please refer to "Brakes" in the Unit Repair section.

ADJUSTMENT

Rear Drum Brakes

The rear brakes on all models are self-centering with an automatic clearance adjustment. Periodic inspection of brake linings for wear and the wheel cylinders for leakage is the only required maintenance. No adjustment is necessary.

Master Cylinder

REMOVAL & INSTALLATION

124/Spider 2000 and 131

1. Remove the reservoir cover and plug the fluid outlet port.

2. Disconnect the pipe between the reservoir and master cylinder.

3. Remove the 3 brake lines from the master cylinder.

4. Unbolt the master cylinder from the firewall, or power booster (124 and 131).

5. Reverse the removal procedure to install the master cylinder. Bleed the system after installation.

X1/9

1. Remove the steering column as follows:
   a. Disconnect the battery.
   b. Remove the five screws holding the

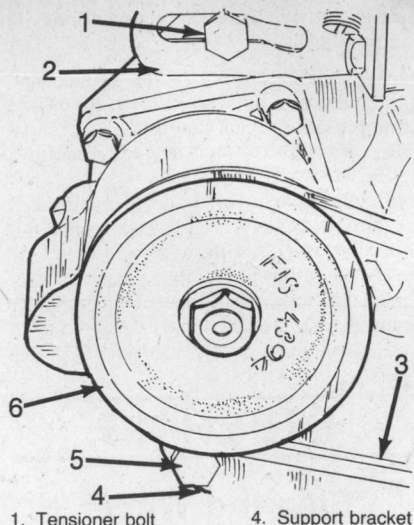

1. Tensioner bolt
2. Tensioner bracket
3. Belt
4. Support bracket
5. Mounting bolt
6. Pump

Power steering pump—Brava

steering column cover halves and remove the covers.

   c. Disconnect the three electrical connectors and one wire.

   d. Remove the two nuts and washers holding the column to the top of the dashboard.

   e. Remove the two bolts and washers holding the column to the bottom of the dashboard.

   f. Slide the shaft off of the steering box shaft and remove the column from the vehicle.

2. Disconnect the hoses from the master cylinder reservoir.

3. Remove the nuts and washers holding the master cylinder to its support.

4. Pull the master cylinder off of the actuating rod. Remove the hoses from the master cylinder and switch assembly.

5. Remove the master cylinder from the vehicle and drain the fluid into an appropriate container.

6. Install the master cylinder and steering column in the reverse order of removal and bleed the brake hydraulic system.

Strada

1. Remove the jack and spare tire. Remove the spare tire support.

2. While holding the brake fluid level switch, unscrew the cover from the reservoir.

3. Drain the reservoir with a syringe.

4. Using gentle side-to-side rocking motion, pull the reservoir from the master cylinder.

5. Disconnect the three brake lines from the master cylinder. Cap the lines to keep out dirt.

6. Remove the two mounting nuts and pull the master cylinder away from the power brake booster.

7. Install in reverse order, making sure all fittings and lines are clean.

8. Bleed the system.

128

1. Remove the spare wheel from the engine compartment.

2. Remove the fluid reservoir cover and plug the outlet to the master cylinder in order to keep the reservoir from draining.

3. Disconnect the reservoir-to-master cylinder tubes.

4. Disconnect the fluid delivery tubing to the front and rear brakes, removing the fastening screws.

5. Remove both nuts and spring washers which secure the master cylinder to the power booster and remove the master cylinder.

6. Installation is the reverse of removal. Bleed the system.

Power Brake Booster

REMOVAL & INSTALLATION

All Models

1. Remove the reservoir and master cylinder as previously outlined.

2. Loosen the clamp and disconnect the vacuum hose from the brake booster.

3. Remove the cotter pin and washer to disconnect the brake booster push rod from the brake pedal.

4. Remove the four nuts and lockwashers holding the booster. Remove the brake booster.

5. Reinstall in reverse order.

Parking Brake

CABLE ADJUSTMENT

All Models

NOTE: The 124/Spider 2000 and 128 cable adjusters are located under the car. The 131 and Strada models have the adjuster located on the underside of the handbrake lever. The X1/9 adjuster is located on the underside of the car underneath an access plate, or on the lever similar to 131.

1. Disengage the handbrake cable, using the lever.

2. Pull the lever up three or four notches.

Parking brake adjustment access window—X1/9

3. Loosen the locknut on the tensioner and turn the adjusting nut until the cable is stretched and the wheels are locked.

4. Tighten the locknut.

5. The cable is correctly tensioned when the car is held by a movement of the lever through 3 notches.

6. Release the lever and check that the wheels are free to turn. Make sure the locking spring presses against a flat side of the adjuster nut.

CHASSIS ELECTRICAL

Heater Assembly

REMOVAL & INSTALLATION

124/Spider 2000

1. Drain the engine cooling system and the heater radiator.

2. The lower heater lever must be moved to the right.

3. Loosen the hose clips on the flow and return pipes to the heater.

4. From the engine compartment, remove the rubber seals on the heater pipes.

5. Remove the valve cable from the clip.

6. Disconnect the yellow cable to the fan.

7. Release the spring clips and remove the fan housing.

8. Lower the radiator and remove the air intake shutter control cable.

9. Remove the heater from the car.

10. Installation is the reverse of removal. Be sure that the gasket between fan and body is positioned correctly. Run the engine and fill the radiator.

128

1. Completely drain the cooling system.

2. Loosen the clips which retain the inlet and outlet hoses.

3. Remove the screw and nut from the air shutter actuating rod.

4. Remove the air conveyor.

5. Slide out the radiator housing spring clips.

6. Withdraw the outside shutter actuating rod.

7. Remove the heater valve control cable.

8. Remove the heater core.

9. Remove the fan housing attaching nuts.

10. Disconnect the cables which feed the motor at the fan switch.

11. Installation is the reverse of removal.

NOTE: Be sure to check all hoses and clamps and the drain cock and gaskets before reinstalling the heater core. Heater disassembly is done easily by removing or prying out the case clips. The electric fan is also mounted with clips.

X1/9

1. Drain the cooling system. Make sure you have drained it thoroughly, or there will be water left in the heated radiator.

2. The heater assembly is located behind the console in the center of the car. Remove the console.

3. Remove the hoses from the heater assembly.

4. The heater assembly box is a two piece unit which is held together with clips.

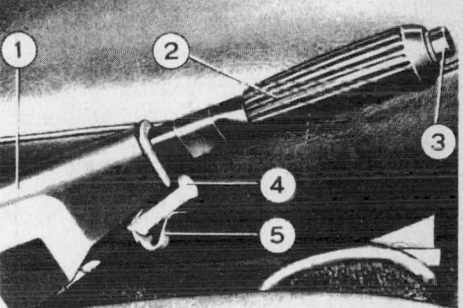

1. Cover   4. Adjustment nut
2. Lever   5. Spring
3. Release button

Parking brake adjustment—131 and Strada

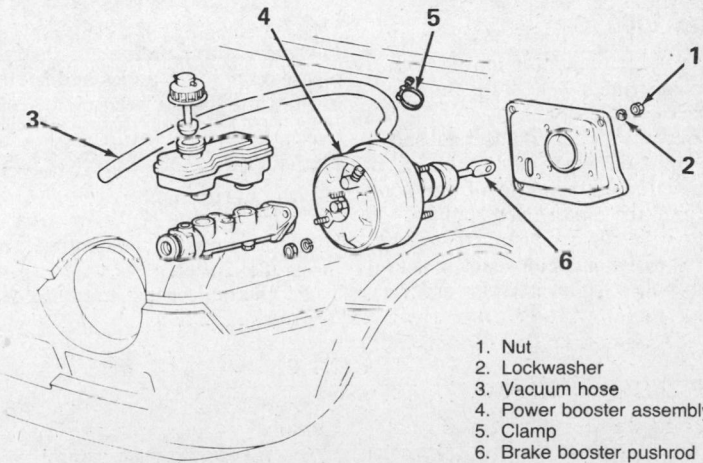

1. Nut
2. Lockwasher
3. Vacuum hose
4. Power booster assembly
5. Clamp
6. Brake booster pushrod

Removing brake booster—typical

Remove all attached components and remove the heater assembly.

5. Installation is the reverse of removal.

131

1. Drain the cooling system. Make sure you have drained it thoroughly or there will be water left in the heater radiator.

2. The heater assembly is located in the center of the dashboard behind the console (if equipped).

3. Remove all hoses and control cables from the heater. The heater is a two piece unit, held together with clips. Remove the heater assembly.

4. Installation is the reverse of removal.

Strada

1. Disconnect the battery cable.

2. Drain the cooling system.

3. Remove the spare tire and air cleaner.

4. Remove the four nuts and carefully pull the control console down from the dash.

5. Remove the three screws to separate the control panel from the control console.

6. Loosen the two clamps to remove the feed and return hoses from the heater core connections.

7. Remove the two nuts and one bolt holding the heater box to the firewall. Carefully lift the heater box from its mounting until electrical leads to the blower motor can be disconnected.

8. Remove the heater box by slowly feeding the control panel through the dash and firewall.

9. Installation is reverse of removal.

10. After installation and refill of cooling system, bleed the heater core. Run the engine at fast idle with the heater knob turned to full hot position, slowly open the bleed valve next to the feed hose inlet on the heater box.

Windshield Wiper Motor

REMOVAL & INSTALLATION

124/Spider 2000

The windshield wiper motor is removed from the engine compartment side in the following manner:

1. Unscrew the left hand spacer nut and remove the left hand wiper blade and arm.

2. Remove the retaining nuts from the bracket and pull the motor back slightly.

3. Remove the clip connecting the right half-link to the motor and remove the motor.

4. Installation is the reverse of removal.

128

1. Remove the wiper blades and arms.

2. Back out the attaching nuts and remove the wiper blade pivot spacers.

3. Remove the spare wheel.

4. Remove the speedometer cable clip from the body.

5. Remove the screws which attach the wiper assembly to the mounting bracket.

6. Disconnect the connector block and remove the unit completely.

7. Installation is the reverse of removal.

X1/9

1. The X1/9 wiper motor is located on the driver's side under a screen on the cowling.

2. Remove the cowl screen. The wiper motor and linkage will then be visible.

3. Unbolt the wiper motor to remove it.

4. Installation is the reverse of removal.

131

1. The wiper motor is located under a plastic cover on the firewall.

2. Remove the plastic cover.

3. Unbolt and remove the motor.

4. Installation is the reverse of removal.

Strada—Front

NOTE: Wipers should be in Park position.

1. Disconnect the electrical connector.

2. Remove the shaft nut.

3. Remove three bolts holding the motor assembly. Remove the motor.

4. Installation is reverse of removal.

Strada and 131 Wagon—Rear

1. Swing the wiper arm up to the locked position and remove it.

2. Remove the nut at the shaft base.

3. Remove the bolt holding the motor assembly.

4. Remove the motor and disconnect the electrical connector.

5. Installation is reverse of removal.

Instrument Cluster

For more information on instruments, please refer to "Gauges and Indicators" in the Unit Repair section.

REMOVAL & INSTALLATION

124/Spider 2000

1. Unscrew the 4 mounting screws securing the cluster.

2. Disconnect the speedometer cable.

3. Disconnect the 5 cluster connectors.

4. Remove the cluster.

5. Install the cluster in the reverse order of removal.

131

1. Remove the screws which hold the instrument cluster to the panel.

2. Pull the cluster out a short way and disconnect the electrical connections and the speedometer cable.

3. Remove the instrument cluster.

4. Installation is the reverse of removal.

128

1. Open the hood and remove the spare wheel.

2. Back out the speedometer cable retainer plate screw.

3. Remove the instrument cluster retainer screw from inside the car.

4. Withdraw the instrument cluster.

5. To install, reverse the removal procedure.

X1/9

1. Remove the five screws retaining the instrument cluster to the instrument panel.

2. Slide the cluster out enough to disconnect the three electrical connectors and the speedometer cable.

3. Remove the instrument cluster from the instrument panel.

4. Install the instrument cluster in the reverse order of removal.

Strada

1. Disconnect the battery.

2. Remove the jack and spare tire.

3. Remove the steering wheel.

4. From the spare wheel recess area, remove the bolt on the firewall holding the instrument cluster.

5. Release the tabs on both sides of the instrument cluster and carefully pull the cluster out of the housing.

6. Disconnect the electrical connectors and the speedometer cable, then remove the cluster completely.

7. Installation is the reverse of removal.

Fuse Box Location

On all Fiat models, the fuse box will be in one of three possible locations:

1. Under the left side dash.

2. Under the right side glove box.

3. Under the hood on the right side next to the relay assembly.

Honda
Accord, Civic, CRX, Prelude

SERIAL NUMBER IDENTIFICATION

Vehicle Identification (Chassis) Number

Honda vehicle identification numbers are mounted on the top edge of the instrument panel and are visible from the outside. In addition, there is a Vehicle/Engine Identification plate under the hood on the cowl.

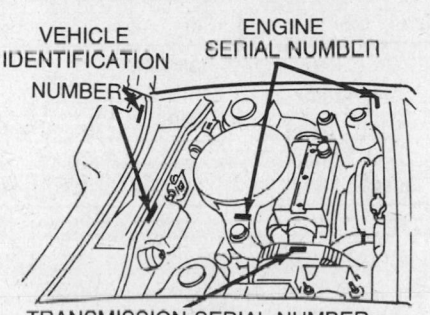

Honda identification numbers

Transmission Serial Number

The transmission serial number is stamped on the top of the transmission/clutch case.

Engine Serial Number

The engine serial number is stamped into the clutch casing. The first three digits indicate engine model identification. The remaining numbers refer to production sequence. This same number is also stamped onto the Vehicle/Engine Identification plate mounted on the hood bracket.

GENERAL ENGINE SPECIFICATIONS

Year	Model	Engine Displacement (cc)	Carburetor Type	Horsepower @ rpm	Bore x Stroke (in.)	Compression Ratio	Torque @ rpm (ft. lbs.)
'78–'79	Civic Exc. CVCC	1237	Hitachi 2 bbl	N.A.	2.83 × 2.99	8.1:1	N.A.
'78–'83	Civic 1.5	1487	Keihin 3 bbl	63 @ 5000	2.91 × 3.41	7.9:1②	77 @ 3000
'78	Accord	1600	Keihin 3 bbl	68 @ 5000	2.91 × 3.66	8.0:1	85 @ 3000
'79–'82	Accord, Prelude	1751	Keihin 3 bbl	72 @ 4500	3.03 × 3.70	8.0:1①	94 @ 3000
'80–'83	Civic 1.3	1335	Keihin 3 bbl	60 @ 5500	2.83 × 3.23	7.9:1③	68 @ 4000
'83	Accord	1751	Keihin 3 bbl	75 @ 4500	3.03 × 3.70	8.8:1	96 @ 3000

GENERAL ENGINE SPECIFICATIONS

Year	Model	Engine Displacement (cc)	Carburetor Type	Horsepower @ rpm	Bore x Stroke (in.)	Compression Ratio	Torque @ rpm (ft. lbs.)
'83–'85	Prelude	1829	Keihin Dual Sidedraft	100 @ 5500 ④	3.15 × 3.58	9.4:1 ⑤	104 @ 4000
'84–'85	Civic 1.3	1342	Keihin 3 bbl	60 @ 5500	2.91 × 3.02	10.0:1	73 @ 3500
'84–'85	Civic 1.5	1488	Keihin 3 bbl	76 @ 6000	2.91 × 3.41	9.2:1	84 @ 3500
'84–'85	Accord	1829	Keihin 3 bbl	86 @ 5800	3.15 × 3.58	9.0:1	99 @ 3500

N.A. Not available
① '80 8.8:1 in Calif, '81 8.9:1 in Calif, '82–8.8:1
② '80–9.0:1, 8.9:1 Calif, '81–8.8:1, '82–'83–9.3:1
③ '81–8.8:1, '82–'83–9.3:1
④ 95 HP with auto. trans.
⑤ '84–'85–9.1:1

TUNE-UP SPECIFICATIONS

(When analyzing compression test results, look for uniformity among cylinders, rather than specific pressures.)

Year	Model	Engine Displacement (cc)	Original Equipment Spark Plugs Type	Gap (in.)	Distributor Point Dwell (deg)	Point Gap (in.)	Basic Ignition Timing (deg) MT	AT	Intake Valve Fully Opens (deg)	Fuel Pump Pressure (psi)	Idle Speed (rpm) MT	AT	Valve Clearance (in.) Intake (cold)	Auxiliary (cold)	Exhaust (cold)
'78–'79	Civic	1237	BP6ES or W20EP	0.028–0.032	49–55	0.018–0.022	2B ④	2B ④	10A	2.56	650–750 ①	650–750 ②	0.004–0.006	—	0.004–0.006
'78–79	Civic CVCC	1487	B6EB or W20ES-L	0.028–0.032	49–55	0.018–0.022	6B ⑥	6B ⑥	10A	1.85–2.56	650–750 ①	600–700 ②	0.005–0.007	0.005–0.007	0.007–0.009
'78	Accord	1600	B6EB or W20ES-L	0.028–0.032	49–55	0.018–0.022	6B ⑤ ⑥	6B ⑤ ⑥	10A	2.13–2.84	750–850 ①	650–750 ②	0.005–0.007	0.005–0.007	0.007–0.009
'79	Accord Prelude	1751	B7EB	0.028–0.032	Electronic		6B ⑤ ⑧	4B ⑨ ⑦	10A	2.13–2.84	650–750 ①	650–750 ①	0.005–0.007	0.005–0.007	0.010–0.012
'80	Civic	1487	B7EB-11	0.042	Electronic		15B⑤ ⑩	TDC ⑪	—	2.5	700–800 ①	700–800 ②	0.005–0.007	0.005–0.007	0.007–0.009
	Civic	1335	B6EB-11	0.042	Electronic		2B⑤ ⑰	—	10A	2.5	700–800 ①	—	0.005–0.007	0.005–0.007	0.007–0.009
	Accord	1751	B7EB	0.030	Electronic		TDC ⑯	TDC ⑰	—	2.5	750–850 ①	750–850 ①	0.005–0.007	0.005–0.007	0.010–0.012
	Prelude	1751	B7EB	0.030	Electronic		TDC ⑰	TDC ⑰	—	2.5	750–850 ①	750–850 ②	0.005–0.007	0.005–0.007	0.010–0.012
'81	Civic	1487	B6EB-11	0.042	Electronic		10B⑫ ⑤	2A	10A	2.5	700–800 ①	700–800 ②	0.005–0.007	0.005–0.007	0.007–0.009
	Civic	1335	B6EB-11	0.042	Electronic		2B ⑤	—	10A	2.5	700–800 ①	—	0.005–0.007	0.005–0.007	0.007–0.009

TUNE-UP SPECIFICATIONS

(When analyzing compression test results, look for uniformity among cylinders, rather than specific pressures.)

Year	Model	Engine Displacement (cc)	Original Equipment Spark Plugs Type	Gap (in.)	Distributor Point Dwell (deg)	Point Gap (in.)	Basic Ignition Timing (deg) MT	AT	Intake Valve Fully Opens (deg)	Fuel Pump Pressure (psi)	Idle Speed (rpm) MT	AT	Valve Clearance (in.) Intake (cold)	Auxiliary (cold)	Exhaust (cold)
'81	Accord	1751	B6EB-L11	0.042	Electronic		TDC ⑰	TDC ⑰	10A	2.5	750–850 ①	750–850 ②	0.005–0.007	0.005–0.007	0.010–0.012
	Prelude	1751	B6EB-L11	0.042	Electronic		TDC ⑰	TDC ⑰	10A	2.5	750–850 ①	750–850 ②	0.005–0.007	0.005–0.007	0.010–0.012
'82	Civic	1487	BR6EB-11	0.042	Electronic		18B ⑤	18B ⑤	10A	2.5	650–750 ①	650–750 ②	0.005–0.007	0.005–0.007	0.007–0.009
	Civic	1335	BR6EB-11	0.042	Electronic		20B ⑤	—	10A	2.5	650–750 ①	—	0.005–0.007	0.005–0.007	0.007–0.009
	Accord	1751	BR6EB-L11	0.042	Electronic		16B⑬	16B	10A	2.5	750–850 ①	750–850 ②	0.005–0.007	0.005–0.007	0.010–0.012
	Prelude	1751	BR6EB-L11	0.042	Electronic		12B⑭	16B	10A	2.5	700–800 ①	700–800 ②	0.005–0.007	0.005–0.007	0.010–0.012
'83	Civic	1487	BR6EB-11	0.042	Electronic		18B⑤	18B⑤	10A	2.5	650–750 ①	650–750 ②	0.005–0.007	0.005–0.007	0.007–0.009
	Civic	1335	BR6EB-11	0.042	Electronic		18B⑮ ⑤	—	10A	2.5	600–750 ①	—	0.005–0.007	0.005–0.007	0.007–0.009
	Accord	1751	BR6EB-L11	0.042	Electronic		16B⑬	16B ⑤	10A	2.5	700–800 ①	650–750 ②	0.005–0.007	0.005–0.007	0.010–0.012
	Prelude	1829	BUR6EB-11	0.042	Electronic		10B⑬ ⑤	12B ⑤	N.A.	2.5	750–850 ①	700–800 ②	0.005–0.007	0.005–0.007	0.010–0.012
'84–'85	Civic	1488	BUR6EB-11	0.042	Electronic		⑤	⑤	N.A.	3.0	650–750	650–750	0.007–0.009	0.007–0.009	0.009–0.011
	Civic	1342	BUR6EB-11	0.042	Electronic		⑤	⑤	N.A.	3.0	650–750	—	0.007–0.009	0.007–0.009	0.009–0.011
	Accord	1829	BUR6EB-11	0.042	Electronic		22B ⑱	18B	N.A.	2.5	700–800	650–750	0.005–0.007	0.005–0.007	0.010–0.012
	Prelude	1829	BPR6EY-11	0.042	Electronic		20B	12B	N.A.	2.5	750–850	750–850	0.005–0.007	0.005–0.007	0.010–0.012

NOTE: The underhood specifications sticker often reflects tune-up specification changes made in production. Sticker figures must be used if they disagree with those in this chart.

TDC—Top Dead Center
B—Before top dead center
A—After top dead center
—Not applicable
N.A. Not available
① In neutral, with headlights on
② In drive range, with headlights on
④ Aim timing light at red notch on crankshaft pulley with distributor vacuum hose(s) connected at specified idle speed

⑤ Aim timing light at red mark (yellow mark, '78–'79 Accord M/T) on flywheel or torque converter drive plate distributor vacuum hose connected at specified idle speed
⑥ California (KL) and High Altitude (KH) models: 2B
⑦ Aim light at blue mark (49 states models)
⑧ California (KL) and High Altitude (KH) models: TDC (white mark)
⑨ California (KL) and High Altitude (KH) models: 2A (black mark)

⑩ 49 States Wagon 10B
⑪ California and High Altitude TDC
⑫ Wagon/Sedan—4B, Calif-2A
⑬ Calif.—12B
⑭ Calif.—16B
⑮ 4 speed 20B
⑯ California models: 4A, Aim timing light at red mark
⑰ Aim timing light at white mark
⑱ California models: 18B

FIRING ORDERS

NOTE: To avoid confusion, always replace spark plug wires one at a time.

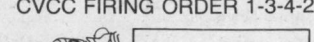

CVCC FIRING ORDER 1-3-4-2

Firing order—1829cc Accord (1984 and later)

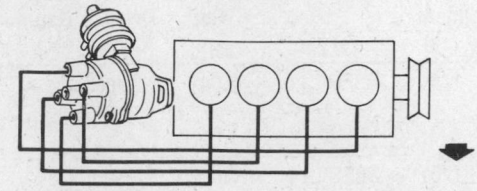

Firing order—1342 & 1488cc Civic (1984 and later)

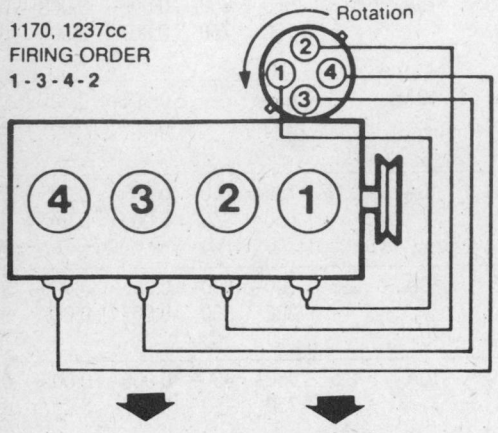

1170, 1237cc
FIRING ORDER
1 - 3 - 4 - 2

Rotation

Front of car

Non–CVCC firing order

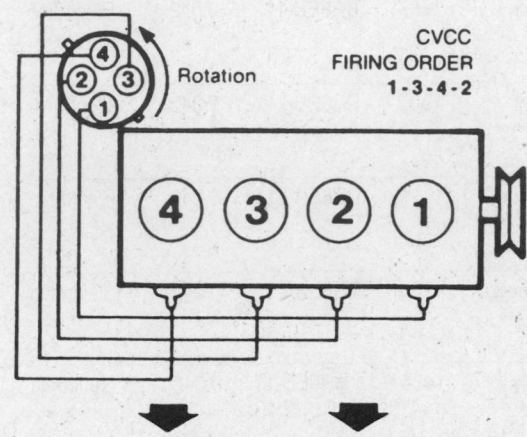

CVCC
FIRING ORDER
1 - 3 - 4 - 2

Rotation

Front of car

Firing order—1978–83 CVCC (exc. 1829cc Prelude)

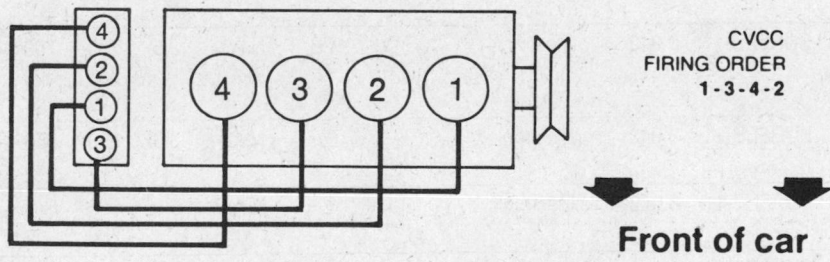

CVCC
FIRING ORDER
1 - 3 - 4 - 2

Front of car

Firing order—1983 and later 1829cc Prelude

CAPACITIES

Year	Model	Engine Displacement (cc)	Engine Crankcase (qts)②	Transmission (pts) Manual 4-sp	5-sp	Auto.③	Gasoline Tank (gals)	Cooling System (qts)
'78	Civic	1237	3.8	5.2	—	5.2	10.6	4.2
	Civic CVCC	1487	3.8	5.2	5.2	5.2	10.6①	4.2
	Accord	1600	3.8	5.2	5.2	5.2	13.2	4.2
'79	Civic	1237	3.8	5.2	—	5.2	10.6	4.8
	Civic	1487	3.8	5.2	5.6	5.2	10.6①	4.8

CAPACITIES

Year	Model	Engine Displacement (cc)	Engine Crankcase (qts)②	Transmission (pts) Manual 4-sp	5-sp	Auto.③	Gasoline Tank (gals)	Cooling System (qts)
'79	Accord	1751	3.8	5.2	5.2	5.2	13.2	6.4
	Prelude	1751	3.8	5.2	5.2	5.2	13.2	6.0
'80–'81	Civic	1335, 1487	3.8	5.2	5.2	5.2	10.8④	4.8⑤
	Accord & Prelude	1751	3.8	5.0	5.0	5.2	13.2	6.4
'82	Civic	1335, 1487	3.7	5.2	5.2	5.2	10.8④	4.8⑤
	Accord	1751	3.7	5.0	5.0	5.2	15.8	6.0
	Prelude	1751	3.7	5.0	5.0	5.2	13.2	6.0
'83	Civic	1335, 1487	3.7	5.2	5.2	5.2	10.4④	4.8⑤
	Accord	1751	3.7	5.0	5.0	6.0	15.8	6.0
	Prelude	1829	3.7	—	5.0	5.8	15.9	6.3
'84–'85	Civic	1342, 1488	3.7	5.0	5.0	6.0	11.9⑥	4.8⑦
	Accord	1829	3.7	—	5.0	6.0	15.8	6.4
	Prelude	1829	3.7	—	5.0	5.8	15.9	6.3⑧

① Sta. Wgn.: 11.0
② Includes filter
③ Does not include torque converter.
④ 4 Door Sedan: 12.1
⑤ 1335cc: 4.0
⑥ 4 Door Sedan: 12.1, CRX: 10.8
⑦ 1342cc: 3.6
⑧ Auto. trans.: 7.1 qts.

CRANKSHAFT AND CONNECTING ROD SPECIFICATIONS

(All measurements given in in.)

Year	Engine Displacement (cc)	Crankshaft Main Brg Journal Dia	Main Brg Oil Clearance	Shaft End-Play	Thrust on No.	Connecting Rod Journal Dia	Oil Clearance	Side Clearance
'78–'79	1237	1.9685–1.9673	0.0009–0.0017	0.0039–0.0138	3	1.5736–1.5480	0.0008–0.0015	0.0079–0.0177
'80–'83	1335	1.9676–③ 1.9685	0.0009–0.0017	0.004–0.014	3	1.5739–1.5748	0.0008–0.0015	0.006–0.012
'84–'85	1342	1.7707–1.7717	0.0009–0.0017	0.004–0.014	3	1.4951–1.4961	0.0008–0.0015	0.006–0.012
'78–'83	1487, 1600, 1751	1.9687–② 1.9697	0.0010–0.0022	0.0039–① 0.0138	3	1.6525–1.6535	0.0008–0.0015	0.006–0.012
'84–'85	1488	1.9676–1.9685	0.0009–0.0017	0.004–0.014	3	1.7707–1.7717	0.0008–0.0015	0.006–0.012
'83–'85	1829	1.9685–1.9694	0.0010–0.0022	0.004–0.014	3	1.7707–1.7717	0.0008–0.0015	0.006–0.012

① '81–'83 with 1487, 1751—.004–.014
② '81 with 1487—1.9676–1.9685, '82–'83 with 1487—1.9687–1.9803
③ '80—1.9687–1.9697

PISTON AND RING SPECIFICATIONS
(All measurements are given in inches)

Year	Engine Displacement (cc)	Piston Clearance	Ring Gap			Ring Side Clearance		
			Top Compression	Bottom Compression	Oil Control	Top Compression	Bottom Compression	Oil Control
'78–'79	1237	0.0012–0.0039	0.0098–0.0157	0.0098–0.0157	0.0118–0.0394	0.0008–0.0018	0.0008–0.0018	Snug
'78	1487 CVCC, 1600	0.0012–0.0039	0.0079–0.0157	0.0079–0.0157	0.0079–0.0354 ①	0.0008–0.0018	0.0008–0.0018	Snug
'79	1487 CVCC	0.0012–0.0060	0.0079–0.0157	0.0079–0.0157	0.0079–0.0354	0.0008–0.0018	0.0008–0.0018	Snug
'80–'81	1335, 1487	0.0004–0.0020	0.006–0.014	0.006–0.014	0.012–0.035	0.0008–0.0018	0.0008–0.0018	Snug
'82–'83	1335, 1487	0.0004–0.0020	0.006–0.014	0.006–0.014	0.012–0.035	0.0012–④ 0.0020	0.0012–④ 0.0020	Snug
'84–'85	1342, 1488	0.0004–0.0016	0.006–0.014	0.006–0.014	0.008–0.024	0.0012–0.0024	0.0012–0.0022	Snug
'79–'83	1751 CVCC	0.0008–0.0028 ②	0.006–0.014	0.006–0.014	0.012–0.035	0.0008–0.0018	0.0008–0.0018	Snug
'83–'85	1829 CVCC	0.0008–0.0016	0.008–0.014	0.008–0.014	0.008–0.035	0.0008–0.0018	0.0008–0.0018	Snug

① 1600 engine oil control ring gap—0.0118–0.0354
② 0.0004–0.0024–'80–'84
③ 1335–0.0004–0.0024
④ 1335–0.0012–0.0024

VALVE SPECIFICATIONS

Year	Engine Displacement (cc)	Seat Angle (deg)	Face Angle (deg)	Spring Installed Height (in.)	Stem To Guide Clearance (in.)			Stem Diameter (in.)		
					Intake	Exhaust	Auxiliary	Intake	Exhaust	Auxiliary
'78–'79	1237	45	45	Inner—1.6535 Outer—1.5728①	0.0004–0.0020	0.0020–0.0031	—	0.2591–0.2594	0.2579–0.2583	—
'78	1600 CVCC	45	45	Intake inner—1.6654 Intake outer—1.6649 Exhaust inner—1.9882 Exhaust outer—2.1181 Auxiliary: (CVCC)—1.1457	0.0008–0.0020	0.0020–0.0032	0.0008–0.0020	0.2591–0.2594	0.2579–0.2583	0.2157–0.2161
'78–'79	1487	45	45	Intake inner—1.401 Intake outer—1.488 Exhaust inner—1.358 Exhaust outer—1.437 Auxiliary—0.906	0.0004–0.0016	0.0020–0.0031	0.0008–0.0021	0.2592–0.2596	0.2580–0.2584	0.2162–0.2166

VALVE SPECIFICATIONS

Year	Engine Displacement (cc)	Seat Angle (deg)	Face Angle (deg)	Spring Installed Height (in.)	Stem To Guide Clearance (in.)			Stem Diameter (in.)		
					Intake	Exhaust	Auxiliary	Intake	Exhaust	Auxiliary
'80–'83	1335, 1487	45	45	Intake inner—1.402 Intake outer—1.488 Exhaust inner—1.402 Exhaust outer—1.488 Auxiliary—0.984①	0.0008–0.0020	0.0025–0.0037	0.0009–0.0023	0.2591–0.2594	0.2574–0.2578	0.2587–0.2593
'84–'85	1342, 1488	45	45	Intake—1.690 Exhaust–1.690 Auxiliary–0.980	0.001–0.002	0.002–0.003	0.001–0.002	0.2591–0.2594	0.2579–0.2583	0.2587–0.2593
'79–'80	1751	45	45	Intake inner—1.402 Intake outer—1.488 Exhaust inner—1.402 Exhaust outer—1.488 Auxiliary—0.984	0.0008–0.0020	0.0024–0.0035	0.0009–0.0023	0.2748–0.2751	0.2732–0.2736	0.2587–0.2593
'81–'83	1751	45	45	Intake inner—1.402 Intake outer—1.488 Exhaust inner—1.402 Exhaust outer—1.488 Auxiliary—0.984	0.001–0.002	0.002–0.004	0.0009–0.0023	0.2748–0.2751	0.2732–0.2736	0.2587–0.2593
'83–'85	1829	45	45	Intake—1.660 Exhaust inner—1.460 Exhaust outer—1.670 Auxiliary—0.984	0.001–0.002	0.002–0.004	0.001–0.002	0.2591–0.2594	0.2732–0.2736	0.2587–0.2593

① '80 1335cc—0.906

TORQUE SPECIFICATIONS

(All readings are given in ft. lbs.)

Year	Engine Displacement (cc)	Cylinder Head Bolts	Main Bearing Bolts	Rod Bearing Bolts	Crankshaft Pulley Bolts	Flywheel to Crankshaft Bolts	Manifold		Spark Plugs	Oil Pan Drain Bolt
							In	Ex		
'78–'79	1237	30–35① 37–42②	27–31	18–21	34–38	34–38	13–17	13–17	9–12	29–36
'78	1487 CVCC, 1600	40–47	30–35	18–21	34–38	15–17	15–17	15–17	11–18	29–36

TORQUE SPECIFICATIONS
(All readings are given in ft. lbs.)

Year	Engine Displacement (cc)	Cylinder Head Bolts	Main Bearing Bolts	Rod Bearing Bolts	Crankshaft Pulley Bolts	Flywheel to Crankshaft Bolts	Manifold		Spark Plugs	Oil Pan Drain Bolt
							In	Ex		
'79–'83	1335, 1487	43③	29–33	21	61④	51	18	18	15⑤	33
'84–'85	1342, 1488	43③	36	20	83	86⑨	16	23	13	33
'79–'83	1751	43③	48	23⑥	61⑦	51	18	18	15⑤	33
'83–'85	1829	49③	48	23	83	76⑨	16	20	13	33

①To engine number EB 1-1019949
②From engine number EB 1-1019950
③Two step procedure—see text
④'80–'83—80 ft. lbs.
⑤'80–'83—13 ft. lbs.
⑥'82–'83—21 ft. lbs.
⑦'81–'83—83 ft. lbs, '82—195 ft. lbs.
⑧'81–'83—76 ft. lbs.
⑨auto. trans.—54 ft. lbs.

BATTERY AND STARTER SPECIFICATIONS
(All cars use 12 volt, negative ground electrical systems)

Year	Model (cc)	Battery Amp Hour Capacity	Starter							Brush Spring Tension (oz.)	Min. Brush Length (in.)
			Lock Test			No Load Test					
			Amps	Volts	Torque (ft. lbs.)	Amps	Volts	rpm			
'78–'79	(1237)	45	380 (max.)	5.5	6.15	70 (max.)	11	6000		56–57	0.16
'80–'83	CVCC (1335, 1487)	47	230④	8.0	4.7⑤	90②	11.5①	3000③		N.A.	0.33⑦
'78–'79	CVCC (1487)	47	160	9.6	N.A.	less than 80	11.5	N.A.		N.A.	0.39
'84–'85	CVCC (1342, 1488)	47	350	8.0	4.7⑤	90②	11.5①	3000③		N.A.	0.33⑦
'78	CVCC (1600)	47	300 (max.)	2.5	5.0	90 (max.)	11.5	3000		53–67	0.35
'79–'83	CVCC (1751)	47	400 (max.)	2.4	7.9	90 (max.)	11.5	3500		N.A.	0.47⑥
'83–'85	CVCC (1829)	50	450 (max.)	2.4	7.9	90 (max.)	11.5	3500		N.A.	0.47⑥

N.A. Not available
①Cal. Nippon Denso; Hitachi 11.0
②Cal. Nippon Denso; Hitachi 70
③Cal. Nippon Denso 5000; Hitachi 6000
④Cal. Nippon Denso; Hitachi: 200
⑤Cal. Nippon Denso; Hitachi: 3.3
⑥Reduction type Nippon Denso: 0.33
⑦Cal. Nippon Denso: 0.39; Hitachi: 0.47

ALTERNATOR AND REGULATOR SPECIFICATIONS

| | | Alternator | | | Regulator | | | | | | |
| | | | | | Field Relay | | | | Regulator | | |
Year	Engine Displacement (cc)	Part No. or Manufacturer	Field Current @ 12V (amps)	Output (amps) @ 5,000 rpm	Part No. or Manufacturer	Yoke Gap (in.)	Point Gap (in.)	Volts to Close	Yoke Gap (in.)	Point Gap (in.)	Volts @ 5,000 rpm
'78–81	1237	Hitachi	2.5	40① 35②	Hitachi	0.008– 0.018	0.0016– 0.0472	4.5– 5.8	0.008– 0.024	0.010– 0.018	13.5– 14.5
'78–'83	1487 CVCC	Nippon Denso	2.5	35③ 45④	Nippon Denso	N.A.	0.016– 0.047	4.5– 5.8	0.020	0.016– 0.020	13.5– 14.5
'78	1600 CVCC	Nippon Denso	2.5	50	Nippon Denso	N.A.	0.016– 0.047	4.5– 5.8	0.020	0.016– 0.047	13.5– 14.5
'80–'83	1335 CVCC	Nippon Denso	2.5	45	Nippon Denso	0.008– 0.018	0.020– 0.050	N.A.	0.020	0.016– 0.047	13.5– 14.5
'79–'83	1751 CVCC	Nippon Denso	2.5	50⑤	Nippon Denso ⑥	0.008– 0.024	0.016– 0.047	N.A.	0.020	0.016– 0.047	13.5– 14.5
'84–'85	1342 CVCC	Nippon Denso Mitsubishi	2.5	55	Nippon Denso Mitsubishi⑦	N.A.	N.A.	N.A.	N.A.	N.A.	13.5– 14.5
'84–'85	1488 CVCC	Nippon Denso Mitsubishi	2.5	55	Nippon Denso Mitsubishi⑦	N.A.	N.A.	N.A.	N.A.	N.A.	13.5– 14.5
'83–'85	1829 CVCC	Nippon Denso	2.5	60	Nippon Denso ⑥	N.A.	N.A.	N.A.	N.A.	N.A.	13.5– 14.5

① From no. 1011759
② Up to no. 1011158
③ Without A/C
④ With A/C
⑤ '82–'83 60
⑥ '82 and later Solid State
⑦ Solid State Internal Regulator
N.A. Not applicable

BRAKE SPECIFICATIONS

(All measurements given are in in. unless noted)

| Year | Model | Lug Nut Torque (ft. lbs.) | Brake Disc | | Brake Drum | | Minimum Lining Thickness | |
			Minimum Thickness	Maximum Run-Out	Inner Diameter	Max. Machine O/S	Front	Rear
'78–'83	Civic Sedan, Hatchback, (Wagon '80–'83)	51–65	0.354①	0.006	7.087⑥	7.126⑦	0.063	0.079
'78–'79	Civic Wagon	51–65	0.449	0.006	7.874	7.93	0.300	0.08
'78–'82	Accord, Prelude	51–65⑧	0.433③	0.006	7.087④	7.126⑤	0.039②	0.079
'83	Accord	80	0.60	0.006	7.87	7.91	0.063	0.079
'83	Prelude	80	0.59	0.004	7.87	7.91	0.118	0.079
'84–'85	Civic	80	0.59⑨	0.006	7.09⑥	7.13⑦	0.120	0.080
'84–'85	Accord	80	0.67	0.006	7.87	7.91	0.120	0.080
'84–'85	Prelude	80	0.67⑩	0.004	N.A.	N.A.	0.120	0.060

N.A. Not applicable
① '81–'83—0.394 exc.'83 1500—0.60 '80 Wagon—0.394
② 0.063—'80–'82
③ '80—0.4126, '81—0.4134, '82—0.60
④ '82—7.87
⑤ '82—7.91
⑥ Wagon—7.87
⑦ Wagon—7.91
⑧ Prelude: 80
⑨ Civic: 1300 CRX 0.35, 1300 Hatchback 0.39
⑩ Rear disc: 0.31

HONDA

WHEEL ALIGNMENT SPECIFICATIONS

Year	Model	Caster Range (deg)	Caster Preferred Setting (deg)	Camber Range (deg)	Camber Preferred Setting (deg)	Toe-In (in.)	Steering Axis Inclination (deg)
'78–'79	Civic—all exc. Station Wagon	¼P–1¼①	¾②	0–1P	½P	³⁄₆₄③	9⁵⁄₁₆
'78–'79	Civic Station Wagon	O–1P	½P	0–1P	½P	³⁄₆₄④	9⁵⁄₁₆
'80–'81	Civic—all exc. Station Wagon	¾P–2¾P	1¾P	1N–1P	0	0	12⁵⁄₁₆
'80–'81	Civic Station Wagon	0–2P	1P	1N–1P	0	0	12⁵⁄₁₆
'82–'83	Civic—all exc. Station Wagon	1½P–3½P	2½P	1N–1P	0	0	12¹¹⁄₃₂
'82–'83	Civic Station Wagon	⁵⁄₁₆P–2⁵⁄₁₆P	1⁵⁄₁₆P	1N–1P	0	0	12¹¹⁄₃₂
'84–85	Civic—all exc. Station Wagon	1⁵⁄₁₆P–3⁵⁄₁₆P	2⁵⁄₁₆P	1N–1P	0	0	12¹³⁄₁₆
'84–'85	Civic Station Wagon	1⅛P–3⅛P	2⅛P	1N–1P	0	0	12
'78	Accord	1P–3P	2P	¼N–1¾P	¾P	³⁄₆₄	12³⁄₁₆
'79–'80	Accord	¾P–1¾P	1¼P	0–1P	½P	¹⁄₃₂	12³⁄₁₆
'81	Accord	¹¹⁄₁₆P–2¹¹⁄₁₆P	1¹¹⁄₁₆	¹¹⁄₁₆N–1⁵⁄₁₆P	⁵⁄₁₆	³⁄₆₄	12½
'82–'85	Accord	⁷⁄₁₆P–2⁷⁄₁₆P	1⁷⁄₁₆	1N–1P	0	0	12½
'79–'82	Prelude	½P–2½P	1½P	1N–1P	0	0	12¹³⁄₁₆
'83–'85	Prelude	1N–1P	0	1N–1P	0	0	6¹³⁄₁₆

P—Positive
N—Negative
①'78 CVCC 0–1P
②'78 CVCC ½P
③'78 CVCC ¹⁄₃₂
④'78 CVCC Wagon ¹⁄₃₂

TUNE-UP PROCEDURES

Spark Plugs

REMOVAL

1. Place a piece of masking tape around each plug wire and number it according to its corresponding cylinder.

2. Pull the wires from the spark plugs, grasping the wire by the end of the rubber boot and twisting off.

NOTE: Avoid spark plug removal while the engine is hot. Since the cylinder head spark plug threads are aluminum, the spark plug becomes tight due to the different coefficients of heat expansion. If a plug is too tight to be removed even while the engine is cold, apply asolvent around the plug followed with an application of oil once the solvent has penetrated the threads. Do this only when the engine is cold.

3. Loosen each spark plug with a ¹³⁄₁₆ in. spark plug socket. When the plug has been loosened a few turns, stop to clean any material from around the spark plug holes. Compressed air is preferred; however, if air is not available, simply use a rag to clean the area.

NOTE: In no case should foreign matter be allowed to enter the cylinders. Severe damage could result.

4. Finish unscrewing the plugs and remove them from the engine.

INSPECTION & CLEANING

Before attempting to clean and re-gap plugs, be sure that the electrode ends aren't worn or damaged and that the insulators (the white

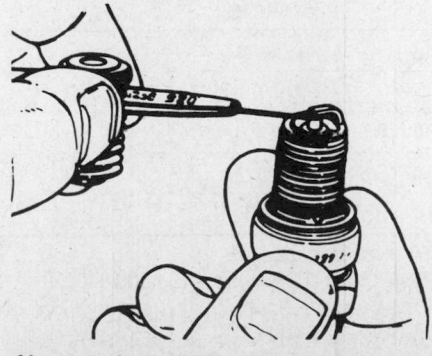

Always use a round wire gauge to check spark plug gap

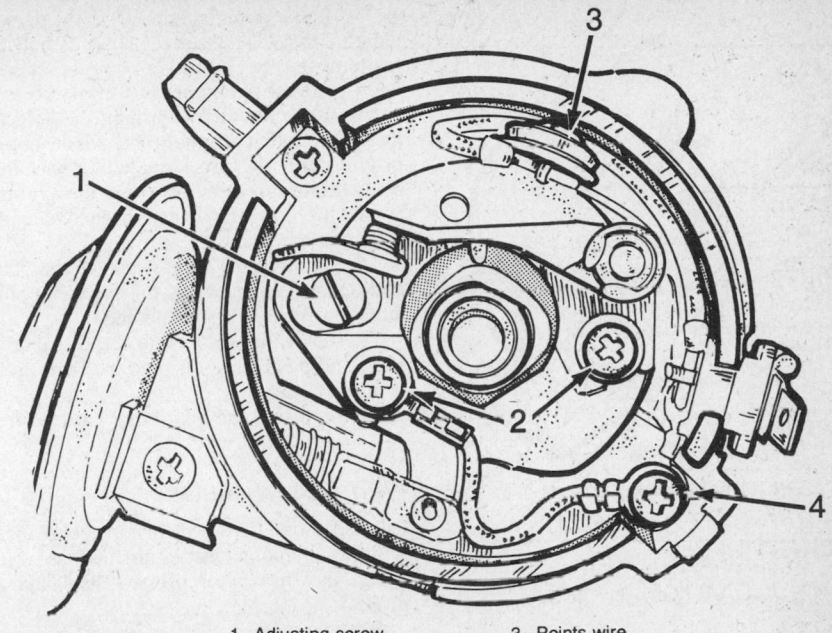

porcelain covering) are not cracked. Replace the plug if this condition exists.

Clean reusable plugs with a plug cleaner or a wire brush. The plug gap should be checked and readjusted, if necessary, by bending the ground (side) electrode with a spark plug gapping tool.

NOTE: Plugs removed from a Honda CVCC engine may have more carbon build-up than plugs from conventional engines. This is a normal condition caused by a spark plug igniting the rich mixture supplied to the pre-combustion chamber.

NOTE: Do not use a flat gauge to check plug gap; an incorrect reading will result. Use a wire gauge only.

INSTALLATION

1. Lightly oil the spark plug threads and hand tighten them into the engine.
2. Tighten the plugs securely with a spark plug wrench (about 10–13 ft. lbs. of torque).

——— CAUTION ———
Do not overtighten because of the aluminum threads.

3. Reconnect the wires to the plugs, making sure that each is securely fitted.

Breaker Points and Condenser

1979 Accords and all 1980 and later models have electronic ignition, eliminating the breaker points and condenser. No routine maintenance is required.

NOTE: There are two rules that should always be followed when adjusting or replacing points. The points and condenser are a matched set; never replace one without replacing the other. If you change the point gap (or dwell) of the engine, you also change the ignition timing. Therefore, if you adjust the points, you must also adjust the timing.

INSPECTION

1. Disconnect the high-tension wire from the coil.
2. Unfasten the two retaining clips to remove the distributor cap.
3. Remove the rotor from the distributor shaft by pulling it straight up. Examine the condition of the rotor; if it is cracked or the metallic tip is excessively burned, replace it.
4. Pry the breaker points open and examine the condition of the contact points. If the points are excessively worn, burned, or pitted they should be replaced.

NOTE: Contact points which have been used for several thousand miles will have a gray, rough surface, but this is not necessarily an indication that they are

1. Adjusting screw	3. Points wire
2. Hold-down screws	4. Ground wire

Internal components of the distributor

malfunctioning. The roughness between the points matches so that a large contact area is maintained.

5. If the points are in good condition, polish them with a point file. If the points are to be filed, they should be removed from the distributor to keep the grit from falling into it.

NOTE: Do not use emery cloth or sandpaper as they may leave particles on the points which could cause them to arc.

After polishing the points, refer to the section following the breaker point replacement procedures for proper adjustment. If the points need replacing, refer to the following procedure.

REMOVAL & INSTALLATION

1. Remove the small nut from the terminal screw located in the side of the distributor housing and remove the nut, screw, condenser wire, and primary wire from the terminal. Remove the terminal from the slot in the distributor housing.
2. Remove the screw(s) which attaches the condenser to the outside of the distributor housing (most models), or to the breaker plate inside the distributor (CVCC Hondamatic models), and remove the condenser.
3. Unscrew the Phillips head screw which holds the ground wire to the breaker point assembly and lift the end of the ground wire out of the way.
4. Remove the two Phillips head screws which attach the point assembly to the breaker plate and remove the point assembly.

NOTE: You should use a magnetic or locking screwdriver. Trying to locate one of these tiny screws after you've dropped it can be an excruciating affair.

5. Wipe all dirt and grease from the distributor plate and cam with a lint-free cloth. Apply a small amount of heat resistant lubricant to the distributor cam. Although the lube is supplied with most breaker point kits, you can buy it at any auto parts store if necessary.
6. Properly position the new points on the breaker plate of the distributor and secure with the two point screws. Attach the ground wire, with its screw, to the breaker plate assembly. Screw the condenser to its proper position on the distributor housing, or breaker plate.
7. Fit the terminal back into its notch in the distributor housing and attach the condenser and primary wires to the terminal screw and fasten with the nut. Adjust the gap using the following procedure.

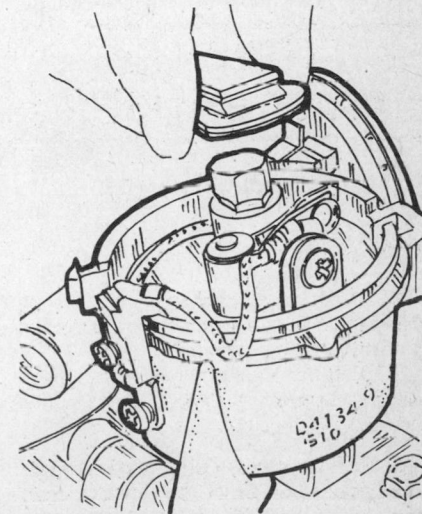

Pull straight up to remove the rotor

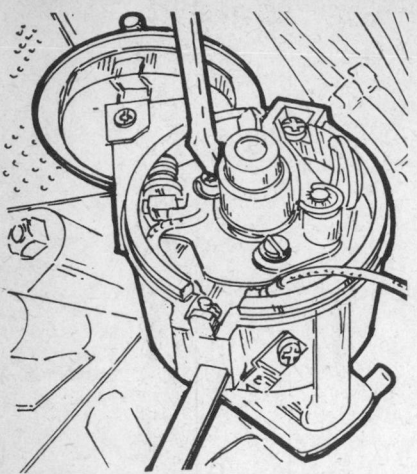

Point set screw removal

ADJUSTMENT

With a Feeler Gauge

1. Rotate the crankshaft pulley until the point gap is at its greatest (where the rubbing block is on the high point of the cam lobe). This can be accomplished by using either a remote starter switch or by rotating the crankshaft pulley by hand.

2. At this position, insert the proper sized feeler gauge between the points. A slight drag should be felt. Point gap should be 0.018–0.022 in.

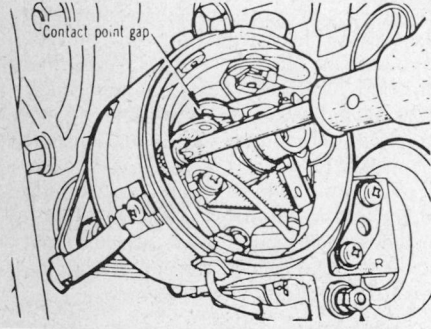

Adjust the point gap with a flat feeler gauge

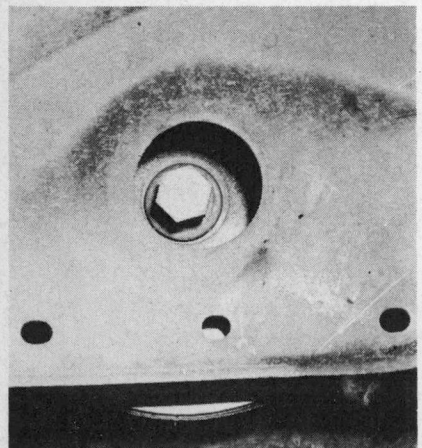

Crankshaft pulley bolt access window on left front fender—CVCC models

3. If no drag is felt, or if the feeler gauge cannot be inserted, loosen, but do not remove the two breaker point screws.

4. Adjust the points as follows:
Insert a screwdriver through the hole in the breaker point assembly and into the notch provided on the breaker plate. Twist the screwdriver to open or close the points. When the correct gap has been obtained, retighten the point set screws.

5. Recheck the point gap to be sure that it did not change when the breaker point attaching screws were tightened.

6. Align the rotor with the distributor shaft and push the rotor onto the shaft until it is fully seated.

7. Reinstall the distributor cap and the coil high tension wire.

With a Dwell Meter

Connect a dwell/tachometer, in accordance with its manufacturer's instructions, between the distributor primary lead and a ground.

With the engine warmed up and running at the specified idle speed (see the tune-up chart), take a dwell reading.

If the point dwell is not within specifications, shut the engine off and adjust the point gap, as outlined above.

NOTE: Increasing the point gap decreases the dwell angle and vice versa.

Install the dust cover, rotor, and cap. Check the dwell reading again and adjust it, as required.

Ignition Timing

Honda recommends that the ignition timing be checked at 15,000 mile intervals. Also, the timing should always be adjusted after installing new points or adjusting the dwell angle. On all non-CVCC engines, the timing marks are located on the crankshaft pulley, with a pointer on the timing belt cover; all visible from the driver's side of the engine compartment. On all CVCC engines, the timing marks are located on the flywheel (manual transmission) or torque converter drive plate (automatic transmission), with a pointer on the rear of the cylinder block; all visible from the front right-side of the engine compartment after removing a special rubber access plug in the timing mark window. In all cases, the timing is checked with the engine warmed to operating temperature (176°F), idling in Neutral (manual trans.) or Drive (automatic), and with all vacuum hoses *connected*.

1. Stop the engine, and hook up a tachometer according to the manufacturer's instructions.

NOTE: On some models you will have to pull back the rubber ignition coil cover to reveal the terminals.

2. Hook up a timing light to the engine according to the manufacturer's instructions.

3. Make sure that all wires are clear of

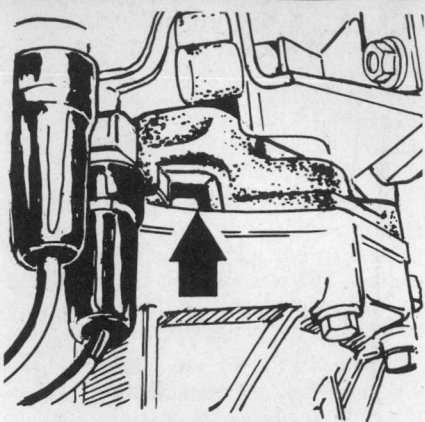

CVCC timing mark window

the cooling fan and hot exhaust manifolds. Start the engine. Check that the idle speed is set to specifications with the transmission in Neutral (manual transmission) or 2nd gear (Hondamatic). If not, adjust as outlined later. At any engine speed other than the specified idle speed, the distributor advance or retard mechanisms will actuate, leading to an erroneous timing adjustment.

— CAUTION —

Make sure that the parking brake is firmly applied and the front wheels blocked to prevent the car from rolling forward when the automatic transmission is engaged.

4. Point the timing light at the timing marks. On non-CVCC cars, align the pointer with the "F" or red notch on the crankshaft pulley. On CVCC cars, align the pointer with the red notch on the flywheel or torque converter drive plate (except on cars where the timing specifications is TDC in which case the "T" or white notch is used).

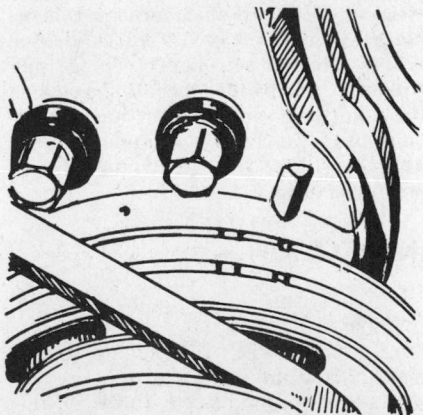

Non-CVCC timing marks. The white notch is TDC

NOTE: Different colors are used in different years; see the footnotes below the "Tune-Up Specifications" chart for details.

5. If necessary, adjust the timing by loosening the larger distributor hold-down (clamp) bolt and slowly rotate the distributor in the required direction while observing the timing marks.

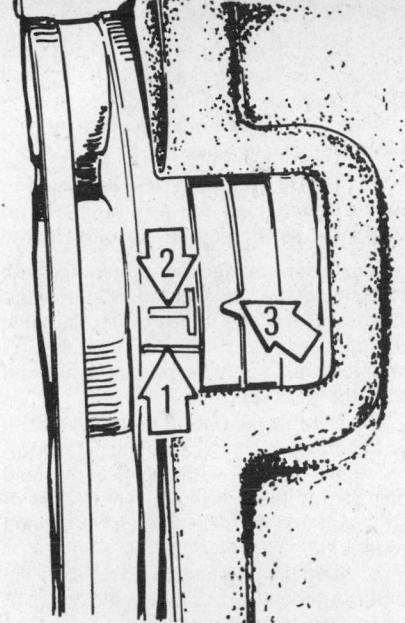

1. Ignition timing mark
2. TDC mark
3. Timing pointer

CVCC timing marks

On non-CVCC engines, align the marks on the cam sprocket with the top of the cylinder head.

─────── **CAUTION** ───────

Do not grasp the top of the distributor cap while the engine is running as you might get a nasty shock. Instead, grab the distributor housing to rotate.

After making the necessary adjustment, tighten the hold-down bolt, taking care not to disturb the adjustment.

NOTE: There are actually two bolts which may be loosened to adjust ignition timing. There is a small bolt on the underside of the distributor swivel mounting plate. This smaller bolt should not be loosened unless you cannot obtain a satisfactory adjustment using the upper bolt. Its purpose is to provide an extra range of adjustment, such as in cases where the distributor was removed and then installed one tooth off.

Valve Lash Adjustment

Honda recommends that the valve clearance be checked at 15,000 mile intervals.

NOTE: While all valve adjustments must be as accurate as possible, it is better to have the valve adjustment slightly loose than slightly tight, as burned valves may result from overly tight adjustments.

NON-CVCC

1. Adjust valves when the engine is cold (100°F or less).
2. Remove the valve cover and align the TDC (Top Dead Center) mark on the crankshaft pulley with the index mark on the timing belt cover. The TDC notch is the one immediately following the red 5° BTDC notch used for setting ignition timing.
3. When No. 1 cylinder is at TDC on the compression stroke, check and adjust the following valves (numbered from the crankshaft pulley end of the engine):

Intake—Nos. 1 and 2 cylinders
Exhaust—Nos. 1 and 3 cylinders
Adjust the valve as follows:

a. Check valve clearance with a flat feeler gauge between the tip of the rocker arm and the top of the valve. There should be a slight drag on the feeler gauge;

b. If there is no drag or if the gauge cannot be inserted, loosen the valve adjusting screw locknut;

c. Turn the adjusting screw with a screwdriver to obtain the proper clearance;

d. Hold the adjusting screw and tighten the locknut;

e. Recheck the clearance.

4. Then rotate the crankshaft 360° and adjust:

Intake—Nos. 3 and 4 cylinders
Exhaust—Nos. 2 and 4 cylinders

CVCC

1. Make sure that the engine is cold (cylinder head temperature below 100°F).
2. Remove the valve cover. From the front of the engine, take a look at the forward face of the camshaft timing belt gear. When No. 1 cylinder is at Top Dead Center (TDC), the word "UP" will be at the top of the gear on all models except the 1980–

On CVCC engines, except: 1980–83 Civic; 1983 Accord; and the 1984 and later 1829cc Accord/Prelude, when the No. 1 piston is set at TDC, the word "up" will be on the top position on the pulley. NOTE: The marks are slightly off in this photo.

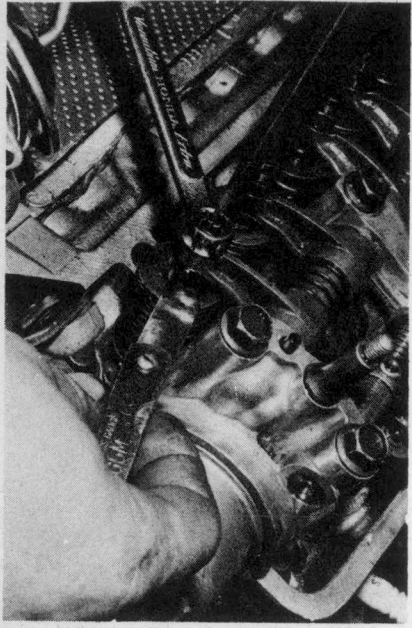

Valve adjustment—all models

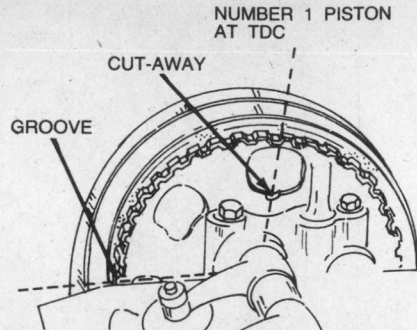

NUMBER 1 PISTON
AT TDC

CUT-AWAY

GROOVE

On the 1980–83 Civic and the 1983 Accord, when the No. 1 piston is set at TDC, the cut-away in the pulley is at the top and the groove on the pulley is aligned with the top of the cylinder head.

83 Civics, the 1983 and later Accords and the 1984 and later Preludes. On the Civic and 1983 Accord models the cut-away in the pulley will be at the top. On the 1984 and later Accord and Prelude models the round mark on the pulley will be at the top. You can doublecheck this by distributor rotor position. Take some chalk or crayon and mark where the No. 1 spark plug wire goes into the distributor cap on the distributor body. Then, remove the cap and check that the rotor points toward that mark.

3. With the No. 1 cylinder at TDC, you can adjust the following valves (numbered from the crankshaft pulley end of the engine):

Intake(s)—Nos. 1 and 2 cylinders
Auxiliary Intake—Nos. 1 and 2 cylinders
Exhaust—Nos. 1 and 3 cylinders
Adjust the valve as follows:

a. Check valve clearance with a flat feeler gauge between the tip of the rocker arm and the top of the valve. There should be a slight drag on the feeler gauge;

b. If there is no drag or if the gauge cannot be inserted loosen the valve adjusting screw locknut;

c. Turn the adjusting screw with a screwdriver to obtain the proper clearance;

d. Hold the adjusting screw and tighten the locknut;

e. Recheck the clearance.

4. To adjust the remaining valves, rotate the crankshaft to the No. 4 cylinder TDC position. To get the No. 4 cylinder to the TDC position, rotate the crankshaft 360 degrees. This will correspond to an 180 degree movement of the distributor rotor and camshaft timing gear. The rotor will now be pointing opposite the mark you made for the No. 1 cylinder. The camshaft timing gear "UP" mark, cut-away, or round mark will now be at the bottom (6 o'clock position). At this position, you may adjust the remaining valves:

Intake(s)—Nos. 3 and 4 cylinders
Auxiliary Intake—Nos. 3 and 4 cylinders
Exhaust—Nos. 2 and 4 cylinders

Distributor rotor at TDC (#1 cylinder)

Carburetor

IDLE SPEED & MIXTURE ADJUSTMENT

NOTE: All carburetor adjustments must be made with the engine fully warmed up to operating temperature (176°F.)

Non-CVCC (1237 cc Engine)

1. The idle speed is adjusted with the headlights on and the radiator cooling fan off. To make sure that the cooling fan stays off while you are making your adjustments, disconnect the fan leads.

NOTE: Do not leave the cooling fan leads disconnected for any longer than necessary, as the engine may overheat.

Manual transmission cars are adjusted with the transmission in Neutral. On Hondamatic cars, the idle adjustments are made with the car in gear "1." As a safety precaution, firmly apply the parking brake and block the front wheels.

2. Remove the plastic limiter cap from the idle mixture screw. Hook up a tachometer to the engine with the positive lead connected to the distributor side (terminal) of the coil and the negative lead to a good ground.

3. Start the engine and adjust first the mixture screw (turn counterclockwise to richen), and then the idle speed screw for the best quality idle at 870 rpm (Hondamatic in gear).

4. Then, lean out the idle mixture (turn mixture screw clockwise), until the idle speed drops to the correct idle speed, according to the "Tune-Up Specifications" chart or the emission control decal in the engine compartment.

5. Replace the limiter cap, connect the cooling fan, and disconnect the tachometer.

CVCC with Keihin 3-bbl and Keihin Dual Side Draft
1978–79

1. The idle speed is adjusted with the headlights on and the radiator cooling fan on. With the engine warmed to operating temperature and idling, the cooling fan should come on. But, if it doesn't, you can load the engine's electrical system (for purposes of adjusting the idle speed), by turning the high-speed heater blower on instead. Do not have both the cooling fan and heater blower operating simultaneously, as this will load the engine too much and lower the idle speed abnormally. Manual transmission cars are adjusted with the transmission in Neutral. On Hondamatic cars,

Valve adjustment—CVCC auxiliary valve

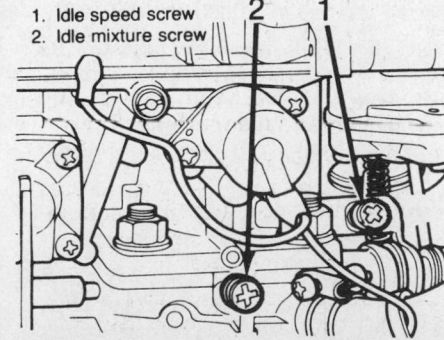

1. Idle speed screw
2. Idle mixture screw

Idle speed and mixture screws—Keihin 3 bbl carburetor

the idle adjustments are made with the car in gear "2" (that's right, Hi-gear). As a safety precaution, apply the parking brake and block the front wheels.

2. Remove the plastic cap from the idle mixture screw. Hook up a tachometer to the engine with the positive lead connected to the distributor side (terminal) of the coil and the negative lead to a good ground.

3. Start the engine and rotate the idle mixture screw counterclockwise (rich), until the highest rpm is achieved. Then, adjust the idle speed screw to 910 rpm (manual transmission), or 810 rpm (Hondamatic in Second gear) for the Civic. Adjust the idle to 880 rpm (manual) or 730 rpm (automatic) for the Accord and Prelude.

4. Finally, lean out the idle mixture (turn mixture screw in clockwise), until the idle speed drops to the correct idle speed, according to the "Tune-Up Specifications" chart or the emission control decal in the engine compartment

5. Replace the limiter cap and disconnect the tachometer.

1980 and Later

NOTE: Changes in the carburetors and emission controls have made the adjustment of the idle speed and mixture impossible without a propane enrichment system not available to the general public.

ENGINE ELECTRICAL

Distributor

REMOVAL & INSTALLATION

1. Disconnect the high tension and primary lead wires that run from the distributor to the coil.

2. Unsnap the two distributor cap retaining clamps or remove the two hold-down screws, and remove the distributor cap. Position it out of the way.

3. Using chalk or paint, carefully mark the position of the distributor rotor in relation to the distributor housing, and mark the relation of the distributor housing to the engine block. When this is done, you should have a line on the distributor housing directly in line with the tip of the rotor, and another line on the engine block directly in line with the mark on the distributor housing.

NOTE: This aligning procedure is very important because the distributor must be reinstalled in the exact location from which it was removed, if correct ignition timing is to be maintained.

4. Note the position of the vacuum line(s) on the vacuum diaphragm with masking tape and then disconnect the lines from the vacuum unit.

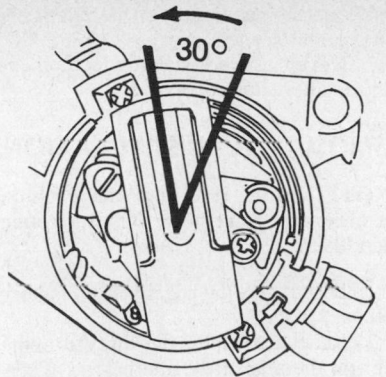
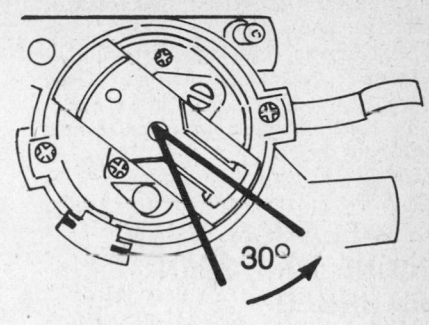

During removal and installation, the rotor will move 30 degrees. Take this into account when positioning the distributor. The illustration shows two typical installations, left is with manual transaxle; right is with automatic transaxle

5. Remove the bolt which attaches the distributor to the engine block or distributor extension housing (CVCC), and remove the distributor from the engine.

— CAUTION —
Do not disturb the engine while the distributor is removed. If you attempt to start the engine with the distributor removed, you will have to retime the engine.

6. To install, place the rotor on the distributor shaft and align the tip of the rotor with the line that you made on the distributor housing.

7. With the rotor and housing aligned, insert the distributor into the engine while aligning the mark on the housing with the mark on the block, or extension housing (CVCC).

NOTE: Since the distributor pinion gear has helical teeth (except 12 valve engines), the rotor will turn slightly as the gear on the distributor meshes with the gear on the camshaft. Allow for this when installing the distributor by aligning the mark on the distributor with the mark on the block, but positioning the tip of the rotor slightly to the side of the mark on the distributor.

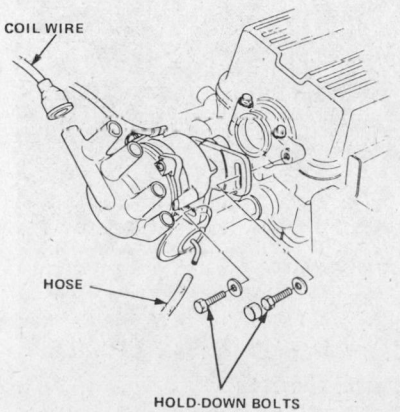

Distributor mounting—1983 and later Prelude

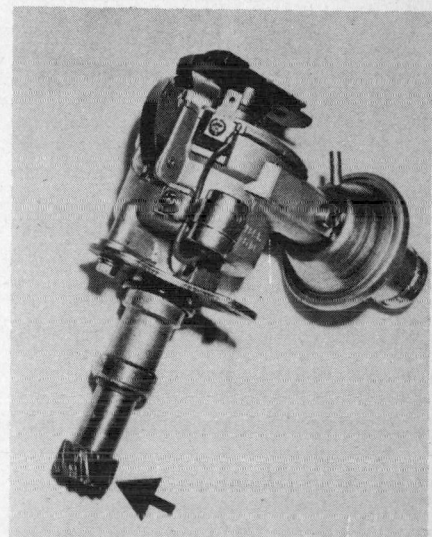

Distributor—arrow points to the helical drive gear

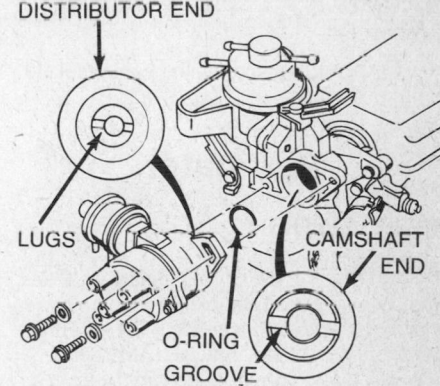

Distributor lug positioning—1342, 1488, and 1829cc engines

NOTE: On the 1342, 1488 and 1829cc CVCC 12 Valve engines, the distributors are equipped with a coupling that connects it to the camshaft. The lugs at the end of the coupling and its mating grooves in the end of the camshaft are offset to prevent installing the distributor 180° out of time.

8. When the distributor is fully seated in the engine, install and tighten the distributor retaining bolt.

9. Align and install the distributor cap and snap the retaining clamps into place or install the two hold–down screws.

10. Install the high-tension and primary wires onto the coil.

11. Check the ignition timing.

INSTALLATION WHEN ENGINE HAS BEEN DISTURBED

If the engine was cranked with the distributor removed it will be necessary to retime the engine. If you have installed the distributor incorrectly and the engine will not start, remove the distributor from the engine and start from scratch.

1. Install the distributor with No. 1 cylinder at the top dead center position on the compression stroke (the "TDC" mark on the crankshaft pulley or flywheel aligned with the index mark on the timing belt cover or crankcase and both intake and exhaust valves closed).

2. Line up the metal end of the rotor head with the protrusion on the distributor housing.

3. Carefully insert the distributor into the cylinder head opening with the attaching plate bolt slot aligned with the distributor mounting hole in the cylinder head. Then secure the plate at the center of the adjusting slot. The rotor head must face No. 1 cylinder.

NOTE: Since the distributor pinion gear has helical teeth (except 12 valve engines), the rotor will turn slightly as the gear on the distributor meshes with the gear on the camshaft. Allow for this when installing the distributor by positioning the tip of the rotor to the side of the protrusion.

4. Inspect and adjust the point gap and ignition timing.

Alternator

PRECAUTIONS

1. Observe the proper polarity of the battery connections by making sure that the positive (+) and negative (−) terminal connections are not reversed. Misconnection will allow current to flow in the reverse direction, resulting in damaged diodes and an overheated wire harness.

2. Never ground or short out any alternator or alternator regulator terminals.

3. Never operate the alternator with any of its or the battery's leads disconnected.

4. Always remove the battery or disconnect its output lead while charging it.

5. Always disconnect the ground cable when replacing any electrical components.

6. Never subject the alternator to ex-

cessive heat or dampness if the engine is being steam-cleaned.

7. Never use arc-welding equipment with the alternator connected.

REMOVAL & INSTALLATION

NOTE: On the 1983 and later Prelude it is necessary to remove the air cleaner assembly.

1. Disconnect the negative (−) battery terminal.

2. Label and unplug the wires from the plugs on the rear of the alternator.

3. Loosen and remove the alternator mounting bolts and remove the V-belt and alternator assembly.

4. To install, reverse the removal procedure. Adjust the alternator belt tension according to the "Belt Tension Adjustment" section below.

BELT TENSION ADJUSTMENT

The initial inspection and adjustment to the alternator drive belt should be performed after the first 3,000 miles or if the alternator has been moved for any reason. Afterwards, you should inspect the belt tension every 12,000 miles. Before adjusting, inspect the belt to see that it is not cracked or worn. Be sure that its surfaces are free of grease and oil.

1. Push down on the belt halfway between pulleys with a force of about 24 lbs. The belt should deflect ½–⅜ in.

2. If the belt tension requires adjustment, loosen the adjusting link bolt and move the alternator with a pry bar positioned against the front of the alternator housing.

Check belt tension midway between pulleys

— CAUTION —
Do not apply pressure to any other part of the alternator.

3. After obtaining the proper tension, tighten the adjusting link bolt.

— CAUTION —
Do not overtighten the belt; damage to the alternator bearings could result.

Voltage Regulator

REMOVAL & INSTALLATION

The regulator is inside the engine compartment, attached to the right fender wall just above the battery, except the 1982–83 Accord, which is located just below the main fuse plate and the 1984 and later Accord and Civic, which have solid state regulators mounted in the alternator.

All except 1982–83 Accord

1. Disconnect the negative (−) terminal from the battery.

2. Remove the regulator terminal lead wires.

NOTE: You should label these wires to avoid confusion during installation.

3. Unscrew the two regulator retaining bolts and remove the regulator from the car.

4. To install, reverse the removal procedure.

1982–83 Accord

1. Disconnect the negative (−) terminal from the battery.

2. Remove the four main fuse plate retaining bolts and remove the main fuse plate to gain access to the solid state regulator.

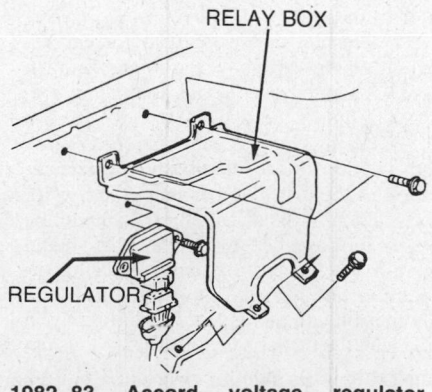

1982–83 Accord voltage regulator mounting

3. Remove the regulator terminal plug from the regulator.

4. Unscrew the regulator retaining bolts and remove the regulator from the car.

5. To install, reverse the removal procedure.

Starter

REMOVAL & INSTALLATION

1. Disconnect the ground cable at the battery negative (−) terminal, and the starter motor cable at the positive terminal.

2. Disconnect the starter motor cable at the motor.

3. Remove the two attaching bolts and remove the starter.

4. Reverse the removal procedure to install the motor. Be sure to tighten the attaching bolts to 29–36 ft. lbs. and make sure that all wires are securely connected.

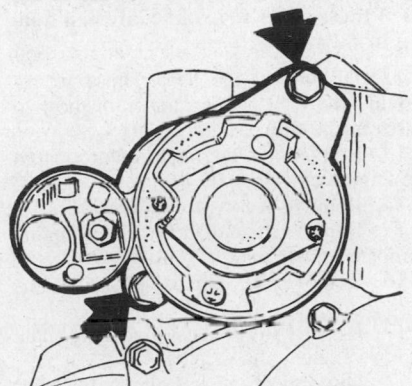

Mounting bolts—non-CVCC starter

STARTER DRIVE REPLACEMENT

Direct Drive Type

1. Remove the solenoid by loosening and removing the attaching bolts.

2. Remove the two brush holder plate retaining screws from the rear cover. Also pry off the rear dust cover along with the clip and thrust washer(s).

3. Remove the two thru–bolts from the rear cover and lightly tap the rear cover with a mallet to remove it.

4. Remove the four carbon brushes from the brush holder and remove the brush holder.

5. Separate the yoke from the case. The yoke is provided with a hole for positioning, into which the gear case lock pin is inserted.

6. Pull the yoke assembly from the gear case, being sure to carefully detach the shift lever from the pinion.

7. Remove the armature unit from the yoke casing and the field coil.

8. To remove the pinion gear from the armature, first set the armature on end with the pinion end facing upward and pull the

Removing pinion gear from armature

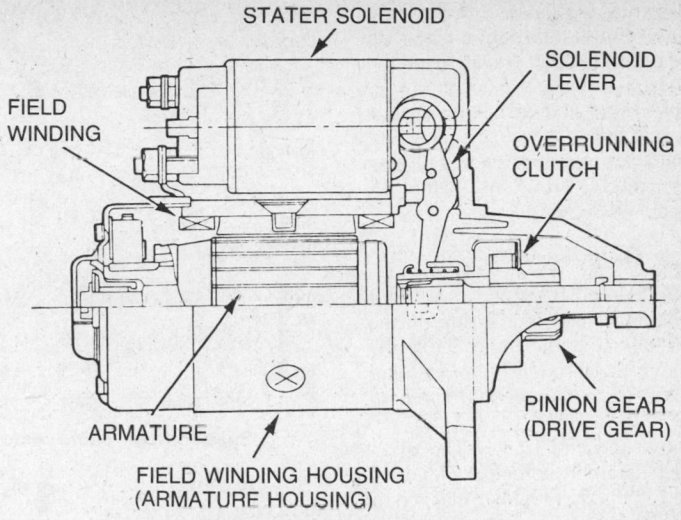

Direct drive starter—typical

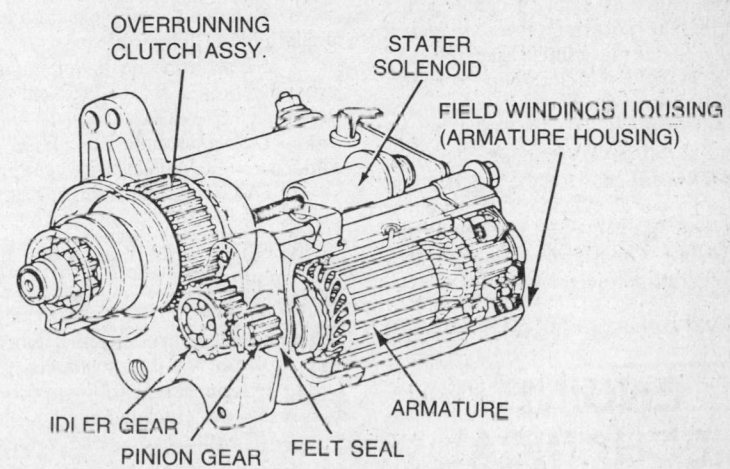

Reduction gear starter—typical

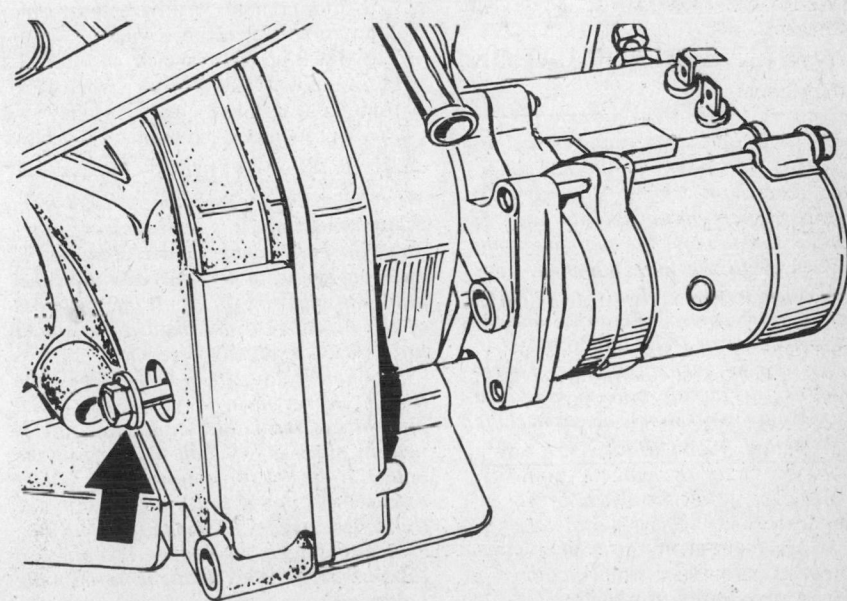

The rear mounting bolt on some CVCC starters is installed from the opposite side of the starter mounting

clutch stop collar downward toward the pinion. Then remove the pinion stop clip and pull the pinion stop and gears from the armature shaft as a unit.

9. To assemble and install the starter motor, reverse the disassembly and removal procedures. Be sure to install new clips, and be careful of the installation direction of the shift lever.

Reduction Gear Type

1. Remove the solenoid end cover. Pull out the solenoid. There is a spring on the shaft and a steel ball at the end of the shaft.

2. Remove the through bolts retaining the end frame to the motor and solenoid housing.

3. Remove the end frame. The overrunning clutch assembly complete with drive gear can be removed. The idler and motor pinion gears can be removed separately. The idler gear retains five steel roller bearings.

4. The clutch assembly is held together by a circlip. Push down on the gear against the spring inside the clutch assembly and remove the circlip with a circlip expander. Slide the stopper ring, gear, spring, and washer out of the clutch assembly.

5. Assembly is the reverse. The stopper ring is installed with the smaller end with the lip towards the clutch. Be sure that the steel ball is in place at the end of the solenoid shaft. Grease all sliding surfaces of the solenoid before reassembly.

ENGINE MECHANICAL

Engine

REMOVAL & INSTALLATION

——— CAUTION ———

If any repair operation requires the removal of a component of the air conditioning system (on vehicles so equipped), do not disconnect the refrigerant lines. If it is impossible to move the component out of the way with the lines attached, have the air conditioning system evacuated by a trained serviceman. The air conditioning system contains freon under pressure. This gas can be very dangerous. Therefore, under no circumstances should an untrained person attempt to disconnect the air-conditioner refrigerant lines.

1237 cc Models

1. Raise the front of the car and support it with safety stands.

2. Remove the front wheels.

3. Drain the engine, transmission, and radiator.

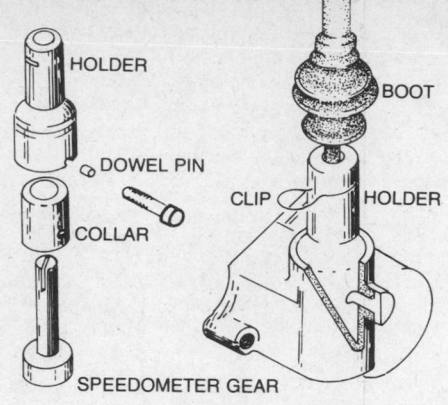

Speedometer cable removal

4. Remove the front turn signal lights and grille.

5. Remove the hood support bolts and the hood. Remove the fan shroud, if so equipped.

6. Remove the air cleaner case, and air intake pipe at the air cleaner.

7. Disconnect the battery and engine ground cables at the battery and the valve cover.

8. Disconnect the hose from the fuel vapor storage canister at the carburetor.

9. Disconnect the fuel line at the fuel pump.

NOTE: Plug the line so that gas does not siphon from the tank.

10. Disconnect the lower coolant hose at the water pump connecting tube and the upper hose at the thermostat cover.

11. Disconnect the following control cables and wires from the engine:

   a. Throttle and choke cables at the carburetor;

   b. Clutch cable at the release arm;

   c. Ignition coil wires at the distributor;

   d. Starter motor positive battery cable connection and solenoid wire;

   e. Back-up light switch and T.C.S. (Transmission Control Spark) switch wires from the transmission casing;

   f. Speedometer and tachometer cables;

——— CAUTION ———

When removing the speedometer cable from the transmission, it is not necessary to remove the entire cable holder. Remove the end boot (gear holder seal) and the cable retaining clip and then pull the cable out of the holder. Do not disturb the holder unless it is absolutely necessary.

The holder consists of three pieces: the holder, collar, and a dowel pin. The dowel pin indexes the holder and collar and is held in place by the bolt that retains the holder. If the bolt is removed and the holder rotated, the dowel pin can fall into the transmission case, necessitating transmission disassembly to remove the pin. To insure that this does not happen when the holder must be removed, do not rotate the holder more than 30° in either direction when removing it. Once removed, make

sure that the pin is still in place. Use the same precaution when installing the holder.

   g. Alternator wire and wire harness connector;

   h. The wires from both water temperature thermal switches on the intake manifold;

   i. Cooling fan connector and radiator thermoswitch wires;

   j. Oil pressure sensor;

   k. Vacuum hose to throttle opener at opener, and vacuum hose from carburetor insulator to throttle opener;

   l. By-pass valve assembly and bracket.

NOTE: It would be a good idea to tag all of these wires to avoid confusion during installation.

12. Disconnect the heater hose by removing the "H" connector from the two hoses in the firewall.

13. Remove the engine torque rod from the engine and firewall.

14. Remove the starter motor.

15. Remove the radiator from the engine compartment.

16. Remove the exhaust pipe-to-manifold clamp.

17. Remove the exhaust pipe flange nuts and lower the exhaust pipe.

18. Disconnect the left and right lower control arm ball joints at the knuckle, using a ball joint remover (or special tool 07941-6340000).

19. Hold the brake disc and pull the right and left drive shafts out of the differential case.

20a. Manual transmission only: Drive out the gearshift rod pin (8 mm) with a drift and disconnect the rod at the transmission case.

NOTE: Do not disconnect the shift lever end of the gearshift rod and extension.

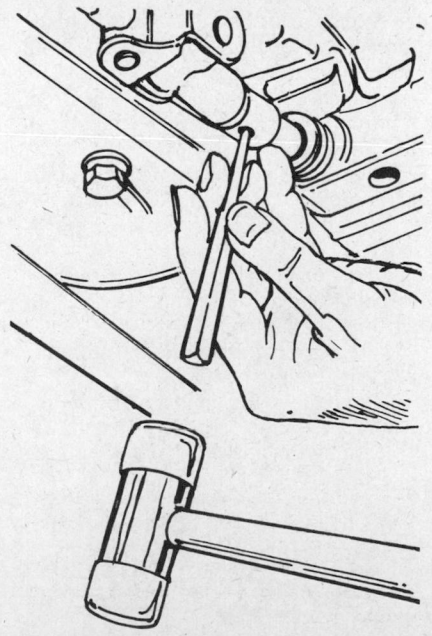

Driving out gearshift rod pin

20b. Hondamatic only: Disconnect shift cable at console and cooler line at transmission.

21. Disconnect the gearshift extension at the engine (man. trans. only).

22. Screw in two engine hanger bolts in the torque rod belt hole and the bolt hole just to the left of the distributor. Then, engage the lifting chain hooks to the hanger bolts and lift the engine just enough to take the load off the engine mounts.

23. After being sure that the engine is properly supported, remove the two center mount bracket nuts.

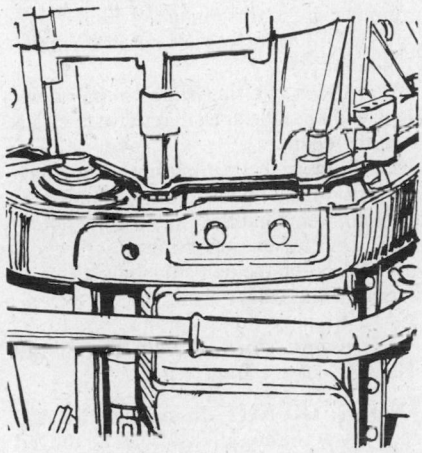

Center mount nuts

24. Remove the left engine mount.

25. Lift the engine out slowly, taking care not to allow the engine to damage other parts of the car.

26. To install, reverse the removal procedure. Pay special attention to the following points:

a. Lower the engine into position and install the left mount. Do not attach mounting bolts at this time.

b. Align the center mount studs with the beam and tighten the nuts and washer several turns (just enough to support the beam).

c. Lower the engine so it rests on the lower mount. Torque the lower mount nuts to 7–12 ft. lbs.

d. Use a new shift rod pin;

e. After installing the driveshafts, attempt to move the inner joint housing in and out of the differential housing. If it moves easily, the driveshaft end clips should be replaced;

f. Make sure that the control cables and wires are connected properly;

g. When connecting the heater hoses, the upper hose goes to the water pump connecting pipe and the lower hose to the intake manifold;

h. Refill the engine, transmission, and radiator with their respective fluids to the proper levels;

i. On Hondamatic cars, check shift cable adjustment.

1335 and 1487cc Civic CVCC

1. Raise the front of the car and support it with jackstands. On models through 1979, remove both front wheels.

2. Disconnect the battery and on 1980 and later models, remove the battery, hold-down equipment, tray and mount.

3. Remove the headlight rim attaching screws and the rims.

4. Remove the lower grill molding and remove the six grille retaining bolts and the grille.

5. Disconnect the windshield washer hose and remove it from the underside of the hood.

6. Remove the upper torque (engine locating) arm.

7. Disconnect the vacuum hose at the power brake booster, thermosensors "A" and "B" at their wiring connectors, and the coolant temperature gauge sending unit wire.

8. Drain the radiator. After all coolant has drained, install the drain bolt finger tight.

9. Disconnect all four coolant hoses. Disconnect cooling fan motor connector and the temperature sensor. Remove the radiator hose to the overflow tank.

10. On Hondamatic cars only, remove both ATF cooler line bolts.

NOTE: Save the washers from the cooler line banjo connectors and replace if damaged.

11. Remove the radiator.

12. Label and disconnect the starter motor wires. Remove the two starter mounting bolts (one from each end of the starter), and remove the starter.

13. Label and disconnect the spark plug wires at the plug. Remove the distributor cap and scribe the position of the rotor on the side of the distributor housing. Remove the top distributor swivel bolt and remove the distributor (the rotor will rotate 30° because the drive gear is beveled).

14. On manual transmission cars, remove the C-clip retaining the clutch cable at the firewall. Then, remove the end of the clutch cable from the clutch release arm and bracket. First, pull up on the cable, and then push it out to release it from the bracket. Remove the end from the release arm.

15. Disconnect the back-up light switch wires. Disconnect the control valve vacuum hose, the air intake hose, and the preheat air intake hose. Disconnect the air bleed valve hose from the air cleaner. Label and disconnect all remaining vacuum hoses from the underside of the air cleaner. Remove the air cleaner.

16. Label and disconnect all remaining emission control vacuum hoses from the engine. Disconnect the emission box wiring connector and remove the black emission box from the firewall.

17. Remove the engine mount heat shield.

18. Disconnect the engine-to-body ground strap at the valve cover.

19. Disconnect the alternator wiring connector and oil pressure sensor leads.

20. Disconnect the vacuum hose from the start control and electrical leads to both cut-off solenoid leads.

21. Disconnect the vacuum hose from the charcoal canister and both fuel lines to the carburetor. Mark the adjustment and disconnect the choke and throttle cables at the carburetor.

22. On Hondamatic cars only, remove the center console and disconnect the gear selector control cable at the console. This may be accomplished after removing the retaining clip and pin.

23. Drain the transmission oil.

CAUTION

On cars with air conditioning, be sure to use the following procedure.

a. Disconnect the heater hose with the heater valve cable attached.

b. Remove the compressor belt cover, then loosen the adjusting nut.

c. Loosen the belt on the compressor hose bracket at the radiator.

d. Remove the compressor mounting bolt then lift the compressor out of the bracket with the hoses attached and wire it up to the firewall.

NOTE: The system does not have to be discharged.

e. Remove the compressor bracket (5 bolts).

24. Remove the fender well shield under the right fender, exposing the speedometer drive cable. Remove the set screw securing the speedometer drive holder. Then, slowly pull the cable assembly out of the transmission, taking care not to drop the pin or drive gear. Finally, remove the pin, collar, and drive gear from the cable assembly.

25. Disconnect the front suspension stabilizer bar from its mounts on both sides. Also, remove the bolt retaining the lower control arm to the subframe on both sides.

26. Remove the forward mounting nut on the radius rod on both sides. Then, pry the constant velocity joint out about ½ in. and pull the stub axle out of the transmission case. Repeat for other side.

27. Remove the six retaining bolts and remove the center beam.

28. On manual transmission cars only, drive out the pin retaining the shift linkage.

29. Disconnect the lower torque arm from the transmission.

30. On Hondamatic cars only, remove the bolt retaining the control cable stay at the transmission. Loosen the two U-bolt nuts and pull the cable out of its housing.

31. Disconnect the exhaust pipe at the manifold. Disconnect the retaining clamp also.

32. Remove the rear engine mount nut.

33. Attach a chain pulley hoist to the engine. Honda recommends using the threaded bolt holes at the extreme right and left ends of the cylinder head (with special hardened bolts) as lifting points, as opposed to wrapping a chain around the entire block

and risk damaging some components such as the carburetor, etc.

34. Raise the engine enough to place a slight tension on the chain. Remove the nut retaining the front engine mount. Then, remove the three bolts retaining the front mount. While lifting the engine, remove the mount.

35. Remove the three retaining bolts and push the left engine support into its shock mount bracket to the limit of its travel.

36. Slowly raise the engine out of the vehicle.

37. Install the engine in the reverse order or removal, making the following checks:

a. Make sure the clip at the end of the driveshaft seats into the groove in the differential. You should hear a click as they seat themselves.

NOTE: Always use new spring clips.

b. Bleed the air from the cooling system.

c. Adjust the throttle cable tension.

d. Check the clutch for the correct free play.

e. Make sure the transmission shifts properly.

1342 and 1488cc Civic CVCC

1. Apply the parking brake and place blocks behind the rear wheels. Raise the front of the car and support it on jackstands.

2. Disconnect both battery cables from the battery. Remove the battery, and then remove the battery tray from the engine compartment.

3. Scribe a line where the hood brackets meet the inside of the hood. This will help realign the hood during the installation. Unbolt and remove the hood.

4. Remove the engine and wheelwell splash shields.

5. Drain the oil from the engine, the coolant from the radiator, and the transmission oil/fluid from the transmission.

NOTE: Removal of the filler plug or cap will speed the draining process.

6. Remove the air cleaner using the following procedure:

a. Disconnect and label all hoses leading to the air cleaner.

b. Remove the air cleaner cover and filter.

c. Remove the three bolts holding down the air cleaner. Lift up the air cleaner and disconnect the temperature sensor wire and the remaining two hoses. Remove the air cleaner.

7. Disconnect the following hoses and wires:

a. The engine compartment sub-harness connector

b. The engine secondary cable

c. The brake booster vacuum hose

d. On engines with A/C, remove the idle control solenoid hoses from the valve and remove the valve.

8. Disconnect the control box connector(s). Remove the control box(es) from the bracket(s), and let it hang next to the engine.

9. Disconnect the purge control solenoid valve vacuum hose at the charcoal canister.

10. Remove the air jet controller (if so equipped).

11. Loosen the throttle cable locknut and adjusting nut, then slip the cable end out of the throttle bracket, removing the cable.

12. Disconnect the fuel line hose from the fuel pump. Remove the fuel pump cover and the pump.

13. Remove the spark plug wires and the distributor from the engine.

14. Remove the radiator and heater hoses from the engine.

NOTE: Label the heater hoses so they will be reinstalled in their original locations.

15. On manual transmission cars:

a. Disconnect the transmission ground cable

b. Loosen the clutch cable adjusting nut and remove the cable from the release arm

c. Disconnect the shift lever torque rod from the clutch housing

d. Slide the shift rod pin retainer out of the way, then with a pin punch, drive the pin out and remove the shift rod.

16. On automatic transmission cars:

a. Remove the oil cooler hoses at the transmission, let the fluid drain from the hoses then prop the hoses up out of the way near the radiator

b. Remove the center console from the inside of the car

c. Put the shift lever in reverse and remove the lock pin from the end of the shift cable

d. Unbolt and remove the shift cable holder

e. Disconnect the throttle control cable end from the throttle lever. Loosen the lower locknut on the throttle cable bracket and remove the cable from the bracket.

NOTE: Do not move the upper locknut as it will change the transmission shift points.

17. Remove the speedometer cable clip, then pull the cable out of the holder.

NOTE: Do not remove the holder from the transmission as it may cause the speedometer gear to fall into the transmission.

18. Squirt penetrating oil on the 7 nuts (5 front and 2 rear) holding the exhaust header pipe in place. Loosen and remove the nuts and pipe.

19. Remove the driveshafts as follows:

a. Remove the jackstands and lower the car. Loosen the 32mm spindle nuts with a socket. Raise the car and resupport on jackstands

b. Remove the front wheel, and the spindle nut

c. Place a floor jack under the lower control arm, then remove the ball joint cotter pin and nut

NOTE: Be certain the lower control arm is positioned securely on top of the floor jack so that it doesn't suddenly jump or spring off when the ball joint remover is used.

d. Using a ball joint puller, separate the ball joint from the front hub

e. Slowly, lower the floor jack to lower the control arm. Pull the hub outward and off the driveshaft

f. Using a small pry bar, pry out the inboard CV-joint approximately ½ in. in order to release the spring clip from the groove in the differential

g. Pull the driveshaft out of the transmission case.

20. Attach a lifting sling to the engine block and raise the hoist to remove the slack from the chain.

21. Remove the rear transmission mount, and remove the bolts from the front transmission mount and the engine side mount.

22. On A/C equipped cars:

a. Loosen the belt adjusting bolts and remove the belt

b. Remove the mounting bolts to the A/C compressor, then wire it up out of the way on the front beam

NOTE: DO NOT disconnect the A/C freon lines; the compressor can be moved without discharging the system.

c. Remove the lower compressor mounting bracket.

23. Disconnect the alternator wiring harness connectors. Remove the alternator belt. Remove the alternator mounting bolts and remove the alternator.

24. Check that the engine and transaxle are free from any hoses or electrical connectors.

25. Slowly raise the engine up and out of the car.

26. To install, reverse the removal procedures. Pay special attention to the following:

a. Torque the engine mounting bolts in the proper sequence

b. Be sure that the spring clip on the end of each driveshaft "clicks" into the differential

NOTE: Always use new spring clips on installation.

c. Bleed the air from the cooling system

d. Adjust the belt(s) tension, and the throttle cable tension

e. Check the clutch pedal free play.

Accord 1600 and Accord/Prelude 1751

1. Disconnect the negative battery terminal.

2. Drain the radiator of coolant, and drain the engine and transmission oil.

3. Jack up the front of the car and remove the front wheels. Be sure to support the car with safety stands.

4. Remove the air cleaner.

5. Remove the following wires and hoses:

a. The coil wire and the ignition primary wire from the distributor.

b. The engine subharness and the starter wires (mark the wires before removal to ease installation).

c. The vacuum tube from the brake booster.

d. On Hondamatic models, remove the ATF cooler hose from the transmission.

e. The engine ground cable.

f. Alternator wiring harness.

g. Carburetor solenoid valve connector.

h. Carburetor fuel line.

i. On 1981 and later models with California and high altitude disconnect the hoses at the air controller.

6. Remove the choke and throttle cables.

7. Remove the radiator and heater hoses.

8. Remove the emission control "black box."

9. Remove the clutch slave cylinder with the hydraulic line attached.

10. Remove the speedometer cable. Pull the wire clip from the housing, and remove the cable from the housing. Do not, under

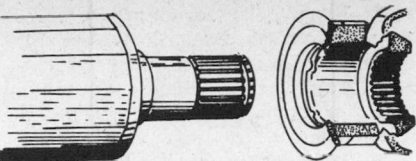

Accord driveshaft removal

any circumstances, remove the housing from the transmission.

11. Attach an engine hoist to the engine block, and raise the engine just enough to remove the slack from the chain.

12. Disconnect the right and left lower ball joints, and the tie rod ends. You will need a ball joint remover tool for this operation. An alternative method is to leave the ball joints connected, and remove the lower control arm inner bolts, and the radius rods from the lower control arms.

13. Remove the driveshafts from the transmission by prying the snap-ring off the groove in the end of the shaft. Then, pull the shaft out by holding the knuckle.

14. Remove the center engine mount.

15. Remove the shift rod positioner from the transmission case.

16. Drive out the pin from the shift rod using a small pin driver.

Emission control box

17. On Hondamatics, remove the control cable.

18. Disconnect the exhaust pipe.

19. Remove the three engine support bolts and push the left engine support into the shock mount bracket.

20. Remove the front and rear engine mounts.

21. Raise the engine carefully and remove it from the car.

22. Install the engine in the reverse order of removal, making the following checks:

a. Make sure that the clip at the end of the driveshaft seats in the groove in the differential. *Failure to do so may lead to the wheels falling off.*

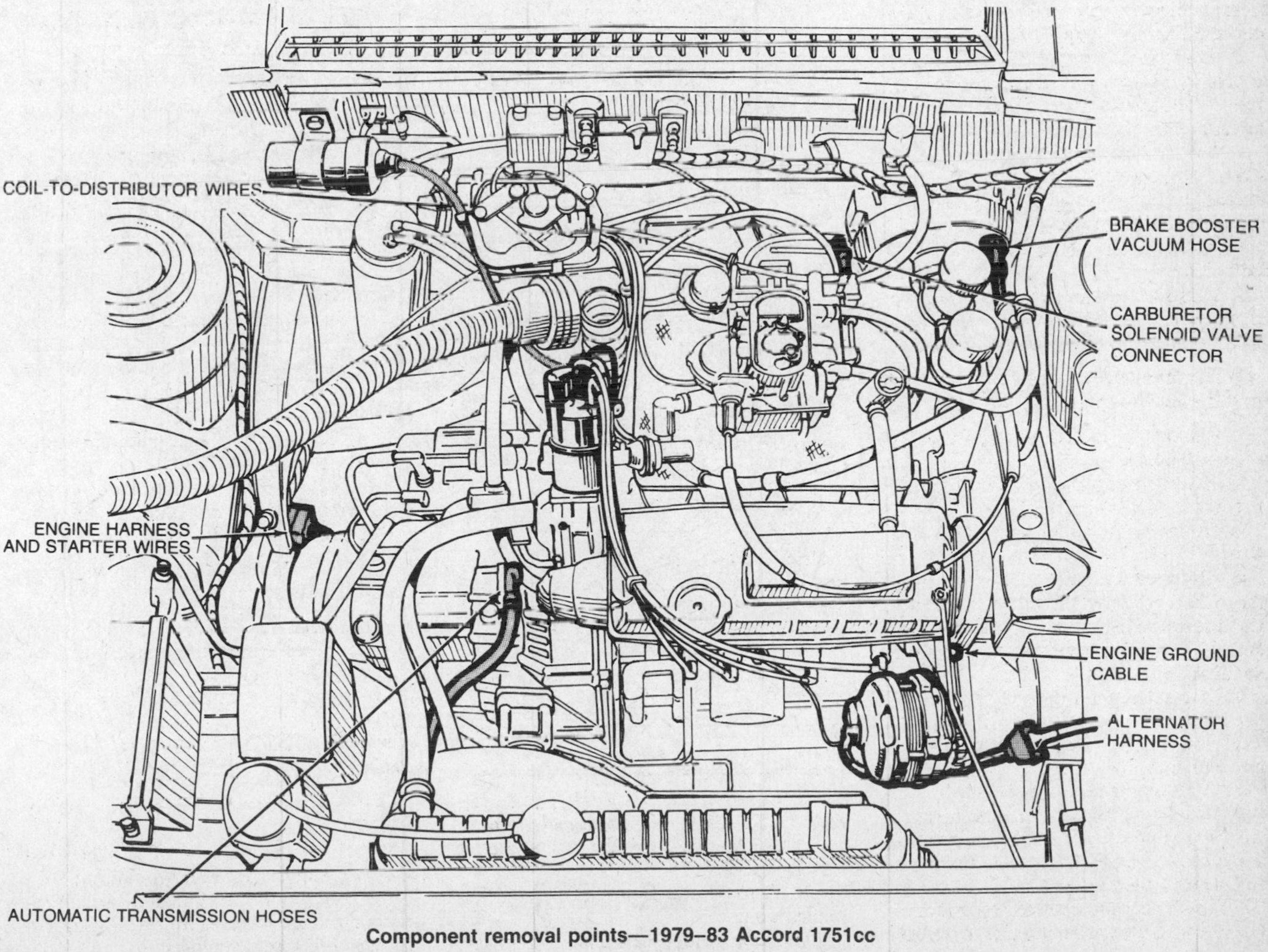

COIL-TO-DISTRIBUTOR WIRES

BRAKE BOOSTER VACUUM HOSE

CARBURETOR SOLENOID VALVE CONNECTOR

ENGINE HARNESS AND STARTER WIRES

ENGINE GROUND CABLE

ALTERNATOR HARNESS

AUTOMATIC TRANSMISSION HOSES

Component removal points—1979–83 Accord 1751cc

NOTE: Always use new spring clips.

b. Bleed the air from the cooling system.

c. Adjust the throttle and choke cable tension.

d. Check the clutch for the correct free play.

e. Make sure that the transmission shifts properly.

Accord/Prelude 1829cc

1. Disconnect the negative and then the positive battery terminal.

2. Remove the knob caps covering the headlight manual retracting knobs, then turn the knobs to bring the headlights to the on position (Prelude only).

3. Remove the five screws retaining the grille and remove the grille (Prelude only).

4. Remove the splash guard from under the engine. Unbolt and remove the hood.

5. Remove the oil filler cap and drain the engine oil.

NOTE: When replacing the drain plug be sure to use a new washer.

6. Remove the radiator cap, then open the radiator drain petcock and drain the coolant from the radiator.

7. Remove the transmission filler plug, then remove the drain plug and drain the transmission.

8. Label and then remove the wires at the coil and the engine secondary ground cable located on the valve cover.

9. Remove the air cleaner cover and filter.

10. Remove the air intake ducts. Remove the two nuts and two bolts from the air cleaner, remove the air control valve, then remove the air cleaner (Accord only).

11. Loosen the locknut on the throttle cable and loosen the cable adjusting nut, then slip the cable end out of the carburetor linkage.

NOTE: Be careful not to bend or kink the throttle cable. Always replace a damaged cable.

12. Disconnect the No. 1 control box connector. Remove the control box from its bracket, and let it hang next to the engine.

13. Disconnect the fuel line at the fuel filter and remove the solenoid vacuum hose at the charcoal canister.

14. On California and high altitude models, remove the air jet controller.

15. Disconnect the radiator and heater hoses at the engine. Label the heater hoses so they can be installed correctly.

16. On automatic models, disconnect the transmission oil cooler hoses at the transmission, let the fluid drain from the hoses, then hang the hoses up near the radiator.

17. On manual transmission models, loosen the clutch cable adjusting nut and remove the clutch cable from the release arm.

18. Disconnect the battery cable at the transmission and the starter cable at the starter motor terminal.

19. Disconnect both engine harness connectors.

20. Remove the speedometer cable clip, then pull the cable out of the holder.

NOTE: DO NOT remove the holder as the speedometer gear may drop into the transmission.

21. On models equipped with power steering:

a. Remove the speed sensor complete with the hoses.

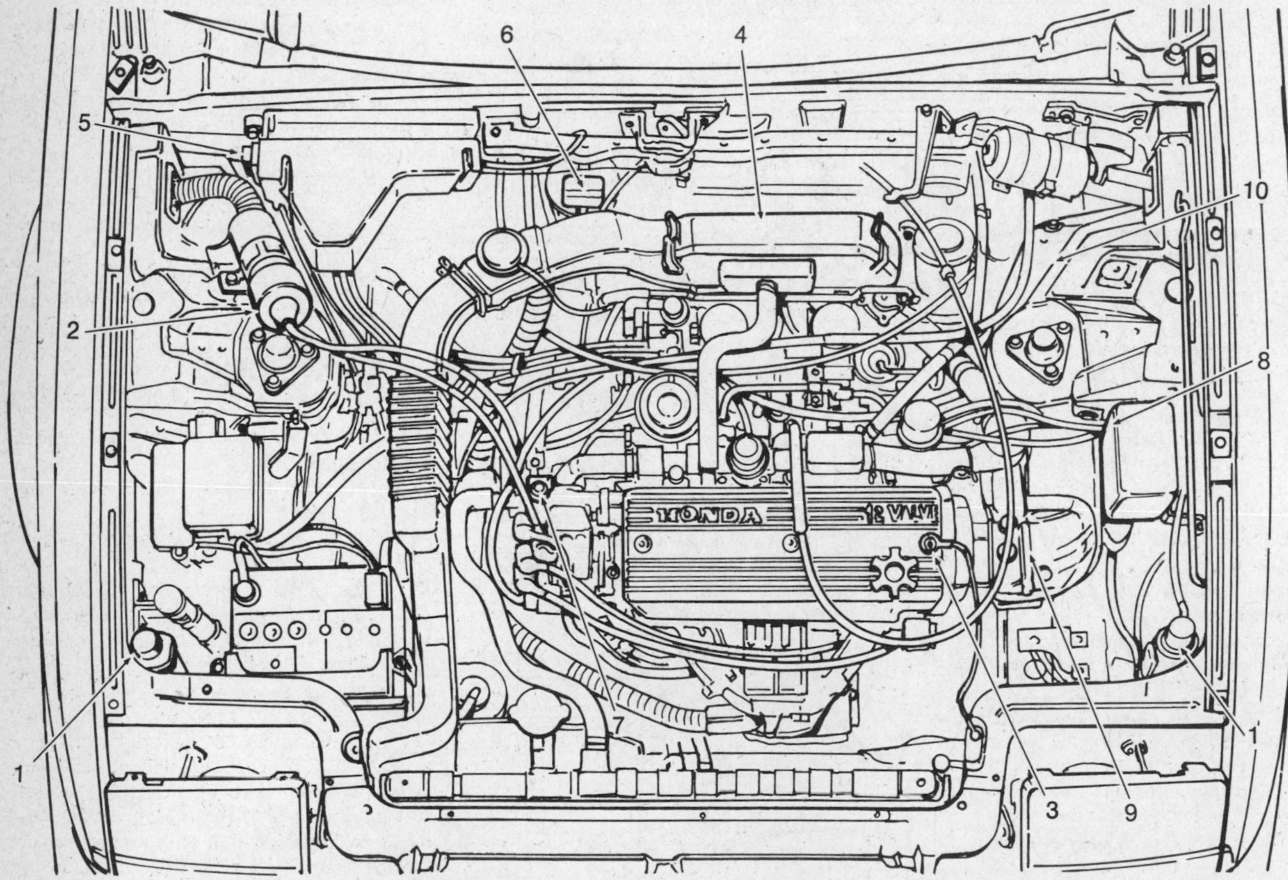

① Headlight retracting knobs
② Ignition coil wires
③ Secondary ground cable
④ Air cleaner assembly
⑤ No. 1 control box connector
⑥ Charcoal canister
⑦ Air bleed bolt for cooling system
⑧ No. 2 control box connector
⑨ Air chamber location (if so equipped)
⑩ Air jet controller location (if so equipped)

Component removal points—1983 and later Prelude 1829cc

b. Remove the adjusting bolt and the V-belt.

c. Without disconnecting the hoses, pull the pump away from its mounting bracket and position it out of the way.

d. Remove the power steering hose bracket from the cylinder head.

22. Remove the center beam beneath the engine. Loosen the radius rod nuts to aid in the later removal of the driveshafts (Accord only).

23. On models equipped with air conditioning:

a. Remove the compressor clutch lead wire.

b. Loosen the belt adjusting bolt.

NOTE: DO NOT remove the air conditioner hoses. The air conditioner compressor can be moved without discharging the air conditioner system.

c. Remove the compressor mounting bolts, then lift the compressor out of the bracket with the hoses attached, and hang it to the front bulkhead with a piece of wire.

24. On models with manual transmission, remove the shift rod yoke attaching bolt and disconnect the shift lever torque rod from the clutch housing.

25. On models with automatic transmission:

a. Remove the center console.

b. Place the shift lever in reverse, then remove the lock pin from the end of the shift cable.

c. Unscrew the cable mounting bolts and remove the shift cable holder.

d. Remove the throttle cable from the throttle lever. Loosen the lower locknut, then remove the cable from the bracket.

NOTE: DO NOT loosen the upper locknut as it will change the transmission shift points.

26. Disconnect the right and left lower ball joints and the tie-rod ends.

27. Remove the driveshafts as follows:

a. Remove the jackstands and lower the car. Loosen the 32mm spindle nuts with a socket. Raise the car and resupport on jackstands.

b. Remove the front wheel, and the spindle nut.

c. Remove the damper fork and damper pinch bolts. Remove the damper fork (Prelude only).

d. Remove the ball joint bolt and separate the ball joint from the front hub (Accord) or lower control arm (Prelude).

e. Disconnect the tie rods from the steering knuckles.

f. Remove the sway bar bolts (Accord only).

g. Pull the front hub outward and off the driveshafts.

h. Using a small pry bar, pry out the inboard CV-joint approximately ½ in. in order to release the spring clip from the differential, then pull the driveshaft out of the transmission case.

NOTE: When installing the driveshaft, insert the shaft until the spring clip clicks into the groove. Always use a new spring clip when installing driveshafts.

28. Remove the exhaust header pipe.

29. Attach a chain hoist to the engine and raise it just enough to remove the slack.

30. Disconnect the No. 2 control box connector, lift the control box off of its bracket, and let it hang next to the engine (if so equipped).

31. On models with air conditioning, remove the idle control solenoid valve.

32. Remove the air chamber (if so equipped).

33. Remove the three engine mount bolts located under the air chamber, then push the engine mount into the engine mount tower.

34. Remove the front engine mount nut, then remove the rear engine mount nut.

35. Loosen and remove the alternator belt. Disconnect the alternator wire harness and remove the alternator.

36. Remove the bolt from the rear torque rod at the engine, then loosen the bolt in the frame mount and swing the rod up and out of the way.

37. Raise the engine carefully from the car checking that all wires and hoses have been removed from the engine/transaxle. Raise the engine all the way up and remove it from the car.

38. Install the engine in the reverse order of removal, making the following checks:

a. Torque the engine mounting bolts in the proper sequence.

b. Bleed the air from the cooling system.

c. Adjust the clutch pedal free play.

d. Adjust the throttle cable tension.

e. Make sure the transmission shifts properly.

Cylinder Head

REMOVAL & INSTALLATION

NOTE: You will need a 12 point socket to remove and install the head bolts on the CVCC engine.

Removal Precautions

1. To prevent warping, the cylinder head should be removed when the engine is cold.

2. Remove oil, scale or carbon deposits accumulated from each part. When decarbonizing take care not to score or scratch the mating surfaces.

3. After washing the oil holes or orifices in each part, make sure they are not restricted by blowing out with compressed air.

4. If parts will not be reinstalled immediately after washing, spray parts with a rust preventive to protect from corrosion.

All Except 1342, 1488, 1751 and 1829cc Engines

NOTE: If the engine has already been removed from the car, begin with Step 12 in the following procedure.

1. Disconnect the negative battery cable.

2. Drain the radiator.

3. Disconnect the upper radiator hose at the thermostat cover.

a. On CVCC models, remove distributor cap, ignition wires and primary wire. Also, loosen the alternator bracket and remove the upper mounting bolt from the cylinder head.

b. On CVCC models with A/C, remove the compressor drive belt cover, then loosen the drive belt adjusting nut. Remove the compressor mounting bolts and move the compressor to one side without discharging it. Remove the compressor bracket.

4. Remove the air cleaner case.

5. Disconnect the tube running between the canister and carburetor at the canister.

6. Disconnect the throttle and choke control cables. Label and disconnect all vacuum hoses.

7. Disconnect the heater hose at the intake manifold.

8. Disconnect the wires from both thermoswitches.

9. Disconnect the fuel line.

a. On CVCC models, disconnect the temperature gauge sending unit wire, idle cut-off solenoid valve, and primary/main cut-off solenoid valve.

10. Disconnect the engine torque rod.

11. Disconnect the exhaust pipe at the exhaust manifold.

12. Remove the valve cover bolts and the valve cover.

13. Remove the two timing belt upper cover bolts and the cover.

14. Bring No. 1 piston to TDC. Do this by aligning the notch next to the red notch you use for setting ignition timing, with the index mark on the timing belt cover (1237 cc) or rear of engine block (CVCC).

15. Loosen, but do not remove, the timing belt adjustment bolt and pivot bolt.

16. On 1237 cc models only, remove the camshaft pulley bolt. Do not let the woodruff key fall inside the timing cover. Remove the pulley with a pulley remover (or special tool 07935-6110000).

— CAUTION —

Use care when handling the timing belt. Do not use sharp instruments to remove the belt. Do not get oil or grease on the belt. Do not bend or twist the belt more than 90°.

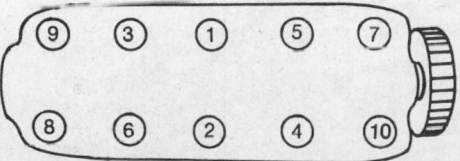

Cylinder head torque sequence—All except: 1342, 1488 and 1829cc engines

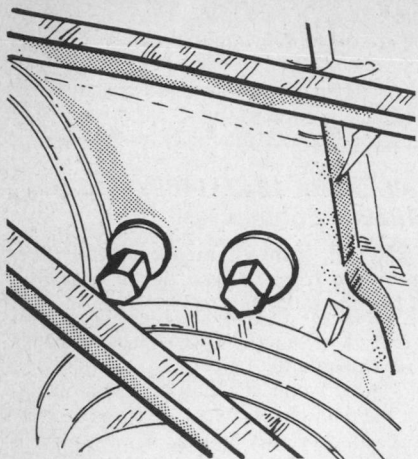

Timing belt pivot and adjustment bolts

Hidden bolt next to the oil pump gear

17. On 1237cc models only, remove the fuel pump and distributor.

18. On 1237cc models only, remove the oil pump gear holder and remove the pump gear and shaft.

19. Loosen and remove the cylinder head bolts in the *reverse* order given in the head bolt tightening sequence diagram. The number one bolt is hidden underneath the oil pump. On CVCC engines, to prevent warpage, unscrew the bolts ⅓ turn each time and repeat sequence until loose.

20. Remove the cylinder head with the carburetor and manifolds attached.

21. Remove the intake and exhaust manifolds from the cylinder heads.

NOTE: After removing the cylinder head, cover the engine with a clean cloth to prevent materials from getting into the cylinders.

22. To install, reverse the removal procedure, being sure to pay attention to the following points:

a. Be sure that No. 1 cylinder is at top dead center before positioning the cylinder head in place;

b. Use a new head gasket and make sure the head, engine block, and gasket are clean.

c. The cylinder head aligning dowel pins should be in their proper place in the block before installing the cylinder head;

d. Tighten the head bolts in three progressive steps to the proper torque according to the diagram. On the 1335 and 1487cc engine, tighten the head bolts in two steps. First to 22 ft. lbs. in sequence then to 43 ft. lbs. in the same sequence;

e. After the head bolts have been tightened, install the woodruff key and camshaft pulley (if removed), and tighten the pulley bolt according to specification. On the 1237cc and the 1335cc engine, align the marks on the camshaft pulley so they are parallel with the top of the head and the woodruff key or cutout is facing up; on the 1487 engine, the word "UP" or cut out should be facing upward and the mark on the cam sprocket

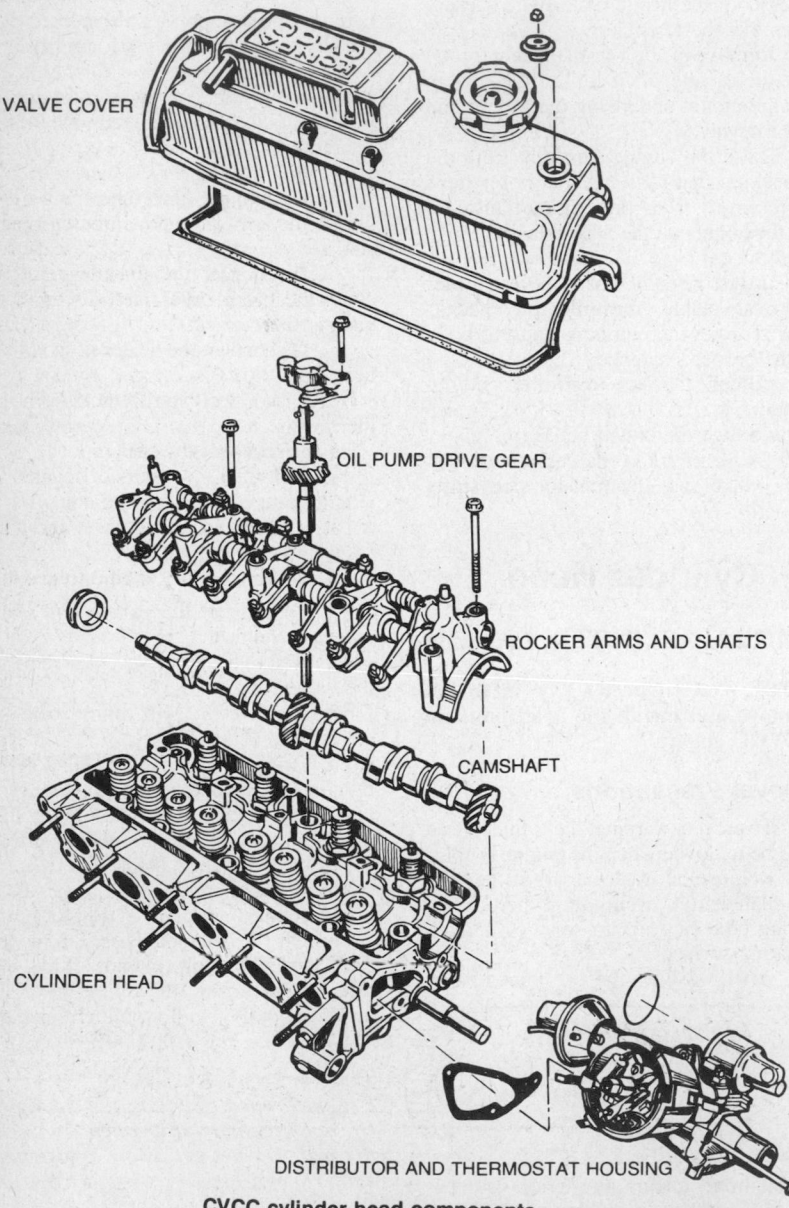

VALVE COVER

OIL PUMP DRIVE GEAR

ROCKER ARMS AND SHAFTS

CAMSHAFT

CYLINDER HEAD

DISTRIBUTOR AND THERMOSTAT HOUSING

CVCC cylinder head components

Remove the non-CVCC camshaft sprocket with the woodruff key facing up

should be aligned with the arrow on the cylinder head;

f. After installing the pulley (if removed), install the timing belt. Be careful not to disturb the timing position already set when installing the belt.

1342 & 1488cc Civic

1. Disconnect the negative battery cable.
2. Drain the radiator.
3. Remove the air cleaner:
   a. Remove the air cleaner cover and filter.
   b. Disconnect the hot and cold air intake ducts, and remove the air chamber hose.
   c. Remove the 3 bolts holding the air cleaner.
   d. Lift up on the air cleaner housing, then remove the remaining hoses and the air temperature sensor wire.
   e. Remove the air cleaner.
4. Remove the brake booster vacuum tube from the intake manifold.
5. Remove the engine ground wire from the valve cover and disconnect the wires from the fuel cut-off solenoid valve, automatic choke and the thermosensor.
6. Disconnect the fuel lines
7. Disconnect the spark plug wires from the spark plugs, then remove the distributor assembly.
8. Disconnect the throttle cable from the carburetor.
9. Disconnect the hoses from the charcoal canister, and from the No. 1 control box at the tubing manifold.
10. Disconnect the air jet controller (California and high altitude only).
11. Disconnect the idle control solenoid hoses (w/air conditioning only).
12. Disconnect the upper radiator heater and bypass hoses.
13. Remove the thermostat housing-to-intake manifold hose.
14. Remove the exhaust manifold bracket and manifold bolts, then remove the manifold.
15. Remove the bolts from the intake manifold and bracket.
16. Disconnect the hose from the breather chamber to the intake manifold.
17. Remove the valve and timing belt covers.
18. Loosen the timing belt tensioner adjustment bolt, then remove the belt.
19. Remove the cylinder head bolts in the reverse order given in the head bolt torque sequence.

NOTE: Unscrew the bolts ⅓ of a turn each time and repeat the sequence to prevent cylinder head warpage.

20. Carefully remove the cylinder head from the engine.
21. To install reverse the removal procedure, being sure to pay attention to the following points:
   a. Always use a new head gasket and make sure the head, engine block, and gasket are clean.

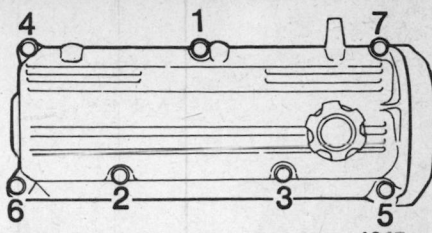

ADJUSTMENT BOLT

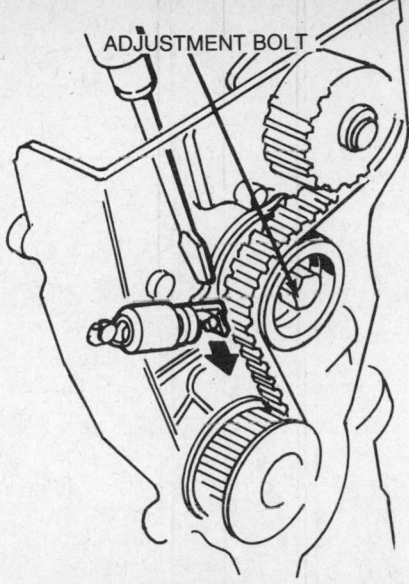

Timing belt tensioner adjustment bolt—1342 and 1488cc engines

   b. Be sure the No. 1 cylinder is at top dead center and the camshaft pulley "UP" mark is on the top before positioning the head in place.
   c. The cylinder head dowel pins and oil control jet must be aligned.
   d. Tighten the cylinder head bolts in two progressive steps as shown in the torque sequence diagram. First to 22 ft. lbs. in sequence, then to 43 ft. lbs. in the same sequence.
   e. On the 1342cc engine torque the valve cover two turns at a time in the sequence shown to 9 ft. lbs.
   f. After installation, check to see that all hoses and wires are installed correctly.

Accord and Prelude 1751cc

———— CAUTION ————
Cylinder head temperature must be below 100°F.

1. Disconnect the battery ground cable.
2. Drain the cooling system.
3. Remove the air cleaner, tagging all hoses for installation.

Valve cover torque sequence—1342cc engine

4. Disconnect the wires from the thermosenser temperature gauge sending unit, idle cut-off solenoid valve, primary/main cut-off solenoid valve, and the automatic choke.
5. Disconnect the fuel lines and throttle cable from the carburetor.
6. Tag all emission hoses going to the carburetor then remove them and the carburetor.
7. Disconnect all wires and hoses from the distributor, tagging them for installation, and remove the distributor.
8. Remove all coolant hoses from the head.
9. Disconnect the hot air ducts and head pipe from the head. Loosen the exhaust manifold-to-engine bracket bolts to ease assembly.
10. If equipped with power steering, loosen the adjustment bolt and remove the belt. Disconnect the hoses and plug the hoses and fitting to prevent contamination. Remove the pump mounting bolt and swing the pump to the right side of the engine.
11. On cars without A/C, remove the bolt holding the alternator bracket to the head. Loosen the adjustment bolt.
12. On cars with A/C, remove the alternator and bracket from the car.
13. Disconnect the brake booster vacuum hose at the one-way valve.
14. Remove the valve cover and timing bolt upper cover.
15. Loosen the timing belt pivot and adjust bolts and slide the belt off the pulley.
16. Remove the oil pump gear cover and pull the oil pump shaft out of the head.
17. Remove the head bolts in sequence working from the ends, across the head, toward the center. This is the reverse of the tightening sequence. To prevent warpage,

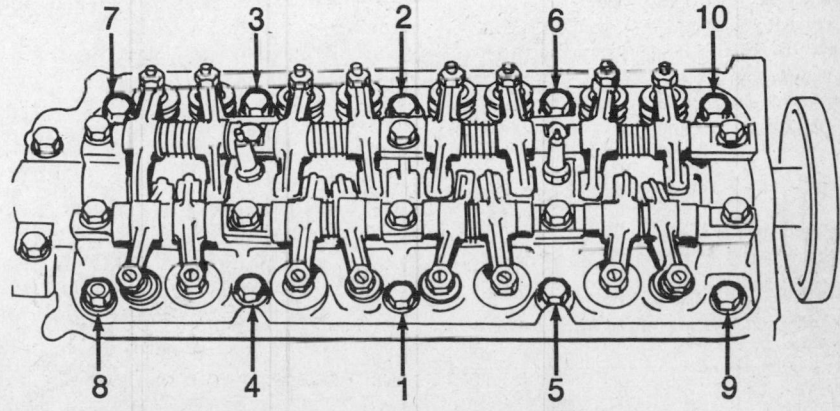

Cylinder head torque sequence—1342 and 1488cc engines

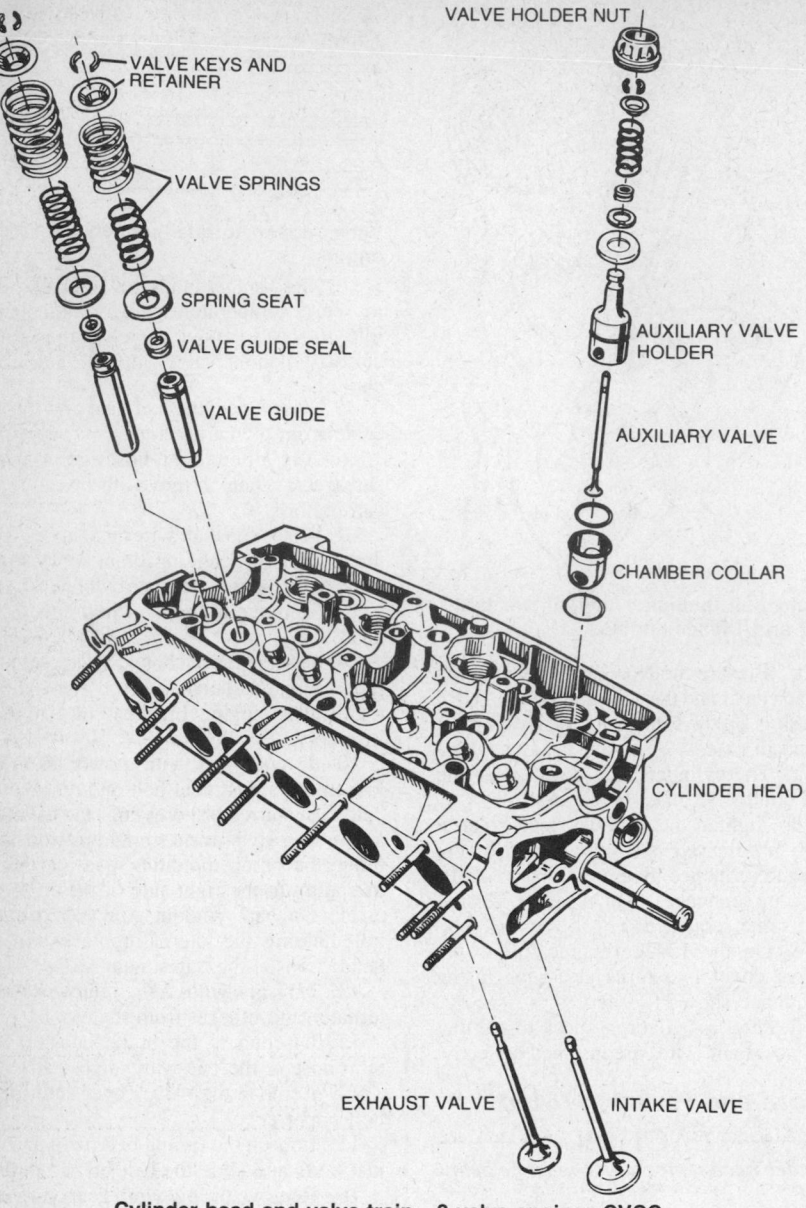

VALVE KEYS AND RETAINER

VALVE SPRINGS

SPRING SEAT

VALVE GUIDE SEAL

VALVE GUIDE

VALVE HOLDER NUT

AUXILIARY VALVE HOLDER

AUXILIARY VALVE

CHAMBER COLLAR

CYLINDER HEAD

EXHAUST VALVE   INTAKE VALVE

Cylinder head and valve train—8-valve engines CVCC

7. Disconnect the wires from the automatic choke and the fuel cut-off solenoid valve.

8. Disconnect the throttle cable and the fuel lines.

9. Disconnect the connecter and hoses from the distributor.

10. Disconnect the No. 1 control box hoses from the tubing manifold.

11. On California and high altitude models, disconnect the air jet controller hoses.

12. Disconnect the cooling system hoses at the cylinder head.

13. Remove the power steering pump (on models so equipped) but DO NOT disconnect the pump hoses. Also, remove the hose clamp bolt on the cylinder head.

14. Remove the power steering pump bracket.

15. Disconnect the No. 2 control box connector. Lift the control box from its bracket, and let it hang next to the carburetor (if so equipped).

16. Remove the air chamber, and on models with air conditioning, disconnect the idle boost solenoid hoses.

17. Remove the engine splash guard from under the car (if so equipped).

18. Remove the exhaust header pipe and pull it clear of the exhaust manifold.

19. Remove the air cleaner base mount bolts and disconnect the hose from the intake manifold to the breather chamber.

20. Remove the valve cover, upper timing belt cover and then loosen the belt tensioner to remove the belt.

21. Remove the cylinder head bolts and remove the head.

NOTE: Unscrew the cylinder head bolts ⅓ of a turn in the reverse order of the torque sequence each turn until loose to prevent warpage to the cylinder head.

22. Installation is the reverse of the removal procedure, taking note of the following items:

a. Make sure the cylinder head gasket surfaces are clean.

b. Make sure the "UP" mark on the timing belt pulley is at the top.

c. Make sure the head dowel pins are aligned.

d. Adjust the valve timing.

e. Torque the cylinder head bolts in two steps. Torque all bolts in sequence

unscrew the bolts ⅓ turn each time and repeat the sequence until loose.

18. Carefully lift the head from the block.

19. Thoroughly clean the mating surfaces to the head and block.

20. Always use a new gasket.

21. Install the head in reverse order of the removal procedure. Make sure the head dowel pins are aligned. Make sure that the UP mark or cut-out on the timing belt pulley is at the top. Torque the cylinder head bolts in two equal steps. Tighten all bolts to 22 ft. lbs. in sequence, then to 43 ft. lbs. in the final step.

Accord and Prelude 1829cc

————— **CAUTION** —————

Cylinder head temperature must be below 100°F.

1. Disconnect the battery ground cable.
2. Drain the cooling system.

3. Remove the vacuum hose from the brake booster.

4. Remove the air intake ducts from the air cleaner case.

5. Remove the secondary ground cable from the valve cover.

6. Remove the air cleaner, tagging all hoses for installation.

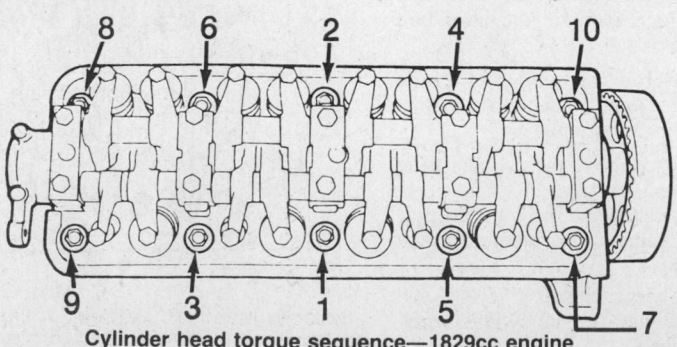

Cylinder head torque sequence—1829cc engine

Rocker arm assembly—8-valve engines CVCC

to 22 ft. lbs., then to 49 ft. lbs. in the final step.

OVERHAUL

For all cylinder head overhaul procedures, please refer to "Engine Rebuilding" in the Unit Repair section.

Camshaft and Rocker Shafts

REMOVAL & INSTALLATION

NOTE: To facilitate installation, make sure that No. 1 piston is at Top Dead Center before removal of camshaft.

1. Follow the "Cylinder Head" removal procedure before attempting to remove the camshaft.
2. Loosen the camshaft and rocker arm shaft holder bolts in a crisscross pattern, beginning on the outside holder.
3. Remove the rocker arms, shafts, and holders as an assembly.
4. Lift out the camshaft and right head seal (or tachometer body if equipped).
5. To install, reverse the removal procedure, being sure to install the holder bolts in the reverse order of removal.

NOTE: Back off valve adjusting screws before installing rockers. Then adjust valves as outlined earlier.

Intake Manifold

REMOVAL & INSTALLATION

Non-CVCC

1. Drain the radiator.
2. Remove the air cleaner and case.
3. Remove the carburetor from the intake manifold.
4. Remove the emission control hoses from the manifold T-joint. One hose leads to the condensation chamber and the other leads to the charcoal canister.
5. Remove the hose connected to the intake manifold directly above the T-joint and underneath the carburetor, leading to the air cleaner check valve.
6. Remove the thermo-switch wires from the switches.

7. Remove the solenoid valve located next to the thermo-switch.
8. Remove the six (6) intake manifold attaching nuts in a crisscross pattern, beginning from the center and moving out to both ends. Then remove the manifold.
9. Clean all old gasket material from the manifold and the cylinder head.
10. If the intake manifold is to be replaced, transfer all necessary components to the new manifold.
11. To install, reverse the removal procedure, being sure to observe the following points:
    a. Apply a water-resistant sealer to the new intake manifold gasket before positioning it in place;
    b. Be sure all hoses are properly connected;
    c. Tighten the manifold attaching nuts in the reverse order of removal.

1983 and Later 1342, 1488 and 1829cc CVCC

1. Drain the coolant from the radiator.
2. Remove the air cleaner and case from the carburetor(s).
3. Remove the air valve, EGR valve, air suction valve and air chamber (if so equipped).
4. Label and remove any wires running to the intake manifold.
5. Remove the intake manifold attaching nut in a crisscross pattern, beginning from the center and moving out to both ends. Then remove the manifold.
6. Clean all the old gasket material from the manifold and the cylinder head.
7. If the intake manifold is to be replaced, transfer all the necessary components to the new manifold.

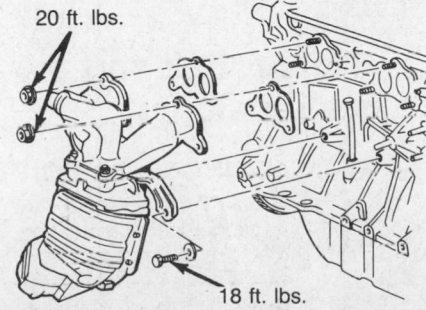

Exhaust manifold mounting—1342 and 1488cc engines

8. To install, reverse the removal procedures, being sure to observe the following points.:
   a. Always use a new gasket.
   b. Tighten the nuts in a crisscross pattern in 2–3 steps, starting with the inner nuts.
   c. Be sure all hoses and wires are correctly connected.

Exhaust Manifold

REMOVAL & INSTALLATION

Non-CVCC

——————— CAUTION ———————
Do not perform this operation on a warm or hot engine.

1. Remove the front grille.
2. Remove the three (3) exhaust pipe-to-manifold nuts and disconnect the exhaust pipe at the manifold.
   a. Disconnect the air injection tubes from the exhaust manifold and remove the air injection manifold.
3. Remove the hot air cover, held by two bolts, from the exhaust manifold.
4. Remove the eight (8) manifold attaching nuts in a crisscross pattern starting from the center, and remove the manifold.
5. To install, reverse the removal procedure. Be sure to use new gaskets and be sure to tighten the manifold bolts in the reverse order of removal to the proper tightening torque.

1983 and Later 1342, 1488 and 1829cc Engines

——————— CAUTION ———————
Do not perform this operation on a warm or hot engine.

1. Remove the header pipe or catalytic converter to exhaust manifold attaching bolts.
2. Remove the oxygen sensor (if so equipped).
3. Remove the EGR and the air suction tubes (if so equipped).
4. Remove the exhaust manifold shroud.
5. Remove the exhaust manifold bracket bolts.
6. Remove the exhaust attaching nuts in a crisscross pattern starting from the center, and remove the manifold.
7. To install, reverse the removal procedure. Use new gaskets and tighten the manifold bolts in a crisscross pattern starting from the center.

Combination Manifold

REMOVAL & INSTALLATION

1978–83 CVCC Models

1. Drain the radiator. Disconnect manifold coolant hoses.

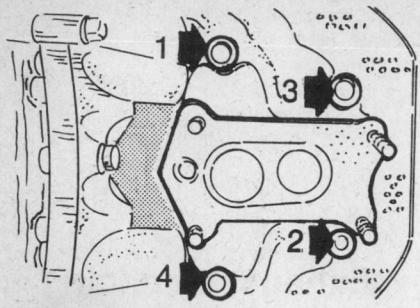

When installing the CVCC combination manifold, tighten the four bolts after the manifolds have been installed to avoid cracking the manifold ears

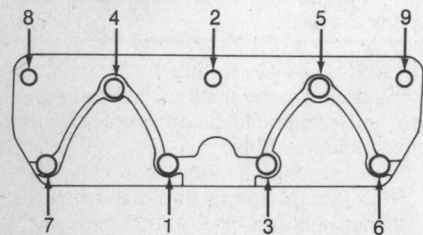

Combination manifold torque sequence—1978–79 1487cc, 1979 1751cc, 1980 1751cc (exc. Calif.), and 1980 1335cc engines

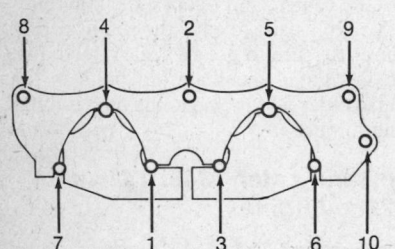

Combination manifold torque sequence—1980–81 1487cc, 1981 1335cc, 1980 1751cc (Calif.), and all 1981 1751cc engines

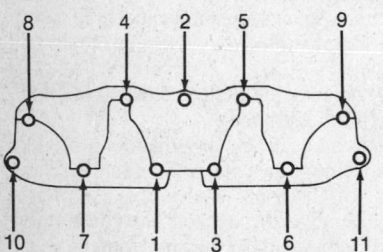

Combination manifold torque sequence—1982–83 1751cc engine

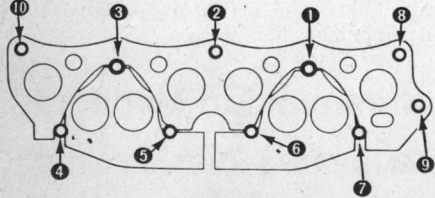

Combination manifold torque sequence—1982–83 1335 and 1487cc engines

2. Remove the air cleaner assembly.
3. Label and disconnect all emission control vacuum hoses and electrical leads.
4. Disconnect the fuel lines, throttle, and choke linkage.
5. Remove the carburetor from the intake manifold.
6. Remove the upper heat shield. Loosen, but do not remove the four bolts retaining the intake manifold to the exhaust manifold.
7. Disconnect the exhaust pipe from the exhaust manifold.
8. Remove the nuts retaining the intake and exhaust manifolds to the cylinder head. The two manifolds are removed as a unit.
9. Reverse the above procedure to install, using new gaskets. The thick washers used beneath the cylinder head-to-manifold retaining nuts must be installed with the dished (concave), side toward the engine. Tighten in sequence shown to specifications given in the "Torque Specifications" chart. Readjust the choke and throttle linkage and bleed the cooling system.

Timing Gear Cover

REMOVAL & INSTALLATION

1. Align the crankshaft pulley (1237 cc), or flywheel pointer (CVCC), at Top Dead Center (TDC).
2. Remove the bolt(s) which hold the timing belt upper cover and remove the cover.
3. Loosen the alternator and air pump (if so equipped), and remove the pulley belt(s).
4. Remove the water pump pulley bolts and the water pump pulley (except 1984 and later Civic).
5. Remove the crankshaft pulley attaching bolt. Use a two-jawed puller to remove the crankshaft pulley.

NOTE: The crankshaft bolt cannot be reused. It must be replaced whenever removed.

6. Remove the timing gear cover retaining bolts and the timing gear cover.
7. To install, reverse the removal procedure. Make sure that the timing guide plates, pulleys and front oil seal are properly installed on the crankshaft and before replacing the cover.

Timing Belt and Tensioner

REMOVAL & INSTALLATION

1. Turn the crankshaft pulley until No. 1 is at Top Dead Center of the compression stroke. This can be determined by observing the valves (all closed) or by feeling for pressure in the spark plug hole (with your thumb or a compression gauge) as the engine is turned.

2. Remove the pulley belt, water pump pulley (if so equipped), crankshaft pulley, and timing gear cover. Mark the direction of timing belt rotation.
3. Loosen, *but do not remove*, the tensioner adjusting bolt and pivot bolt.
4. Slide the timing belt off the camshaft sprocket, crankshaft sprocket and the water pump sprocket (if so equipped), then remove it from the engine.
5. To remove the camshaft timing sprocket, first remove the center bolt and then remove the sprocket with a pulley remover or a brass hammer. This can be accomplished by simply removing the timing belt upper cover, loosening the tensioner bolts, and sliding the timing belt off to expose the sprocket for removal.

NOTE: If you remove the timing sprocket with the timing belt cover in place, be sure not to let the woodruff key fall inside the timing cover when removing the sprocket from the camshaft.

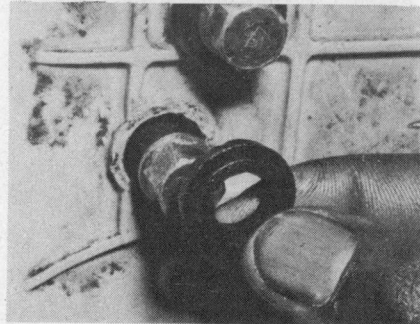

Remove the washers behind the tensioner and adjuster bolts to allow removal of the cover without removing the bolts.

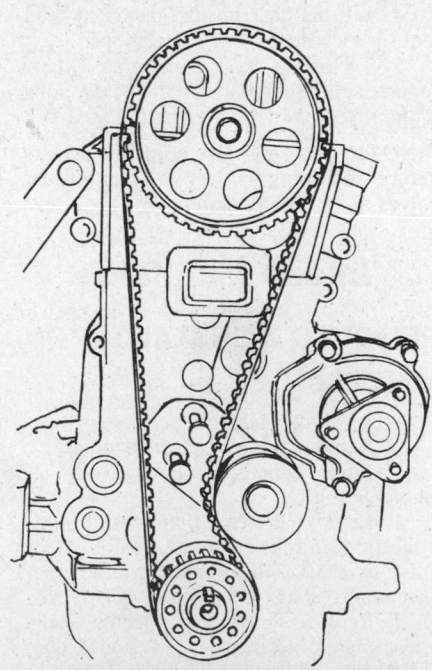

Non CVCC engine timing bolt installation. The crankshaft key is straight up and the cam sprocket marks are parallel with the cylinder head

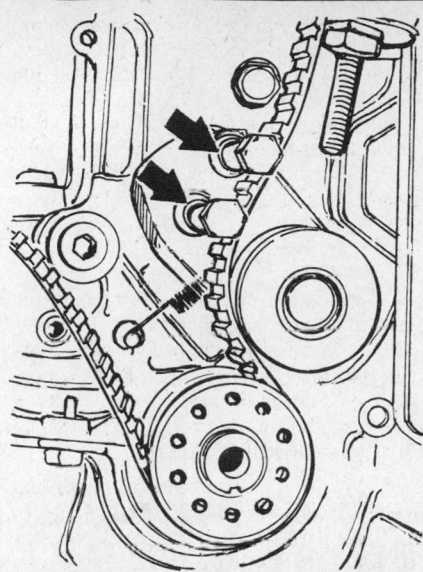

Typical timing belt tensioner adjustment

Inspect the timing belt. Replace if over 10,000 miles old, if oil soaked (find source of oil leak also), or if worn on leading edges of belt teeth.

6. To install, reverse the removal procedure. Be sure to position the crankshaft and camshaft timing sprockets in the top dead center position. On the non-CVCC engine, align the marks on the camshaft timing gear so they are parallel with the top of the cylinder head and the Woodruff key is facing up. On CVCC engines, refer to "Valve Lash" Adjustment for camshaft gear positioning at No. 1 TDC.

When installing the timing belt, do not allow oil to come in contact with the belt. Oil will cause the rubber to swell. Be careful not to bend or twist the belt unnecessarily, since it is made of fiberglass; nor should you use tools having sharp edges when installing or removing the belt. Be sure to install the belt with the arrow facing in the same direction it was facing during removal.

After installing the timing belt, adjust the belt tension by first rotating the crankshaft counterclockwise ¼ turn or 3-teeth on the camshaft pulley. Then, retighten the adjusting bolt and finally the tensioner pivot bolt.

— **CAUTION** —
Do not remove the adjusting or pivot bolts, only loosen them. When adjusting, do not use any force other than the adjuster spring. If the belt is too tight, it will result in a shortened belt life.

Pistons and Connecting Rods

REMOVAL & INSTALLATION

For removal with the engine out of the car, begin with Step 8.

1. Drain the radiator.
2. Drain the engine oil.
3. Raise the front of the car and support it with safety stands.
4. Attach a chain to the clutch cable bracket on the transmission case and raise just enough to take the load off the center mount.
5. Remove the lower splash pan.

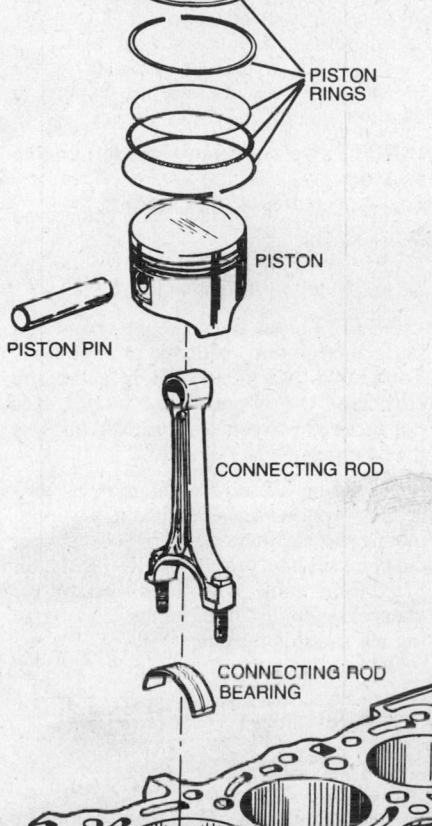

PISTON RINGS

PISTON

PISTON PIN

CONNECTING ROD

CONNECTING ROD BEARING

NOTE: Do not remove the left engine mount.

6. Remove the center beam and engine lower mount.
7. Remove the cylinder head.
8. Loosen the oil pan bolts and remove the oil pan and flywheel dust shield. Loosen the oil pan bolts in a criss-cross pattern beginning with the outside bolt.

To remove the oil pan, lightly tap the corners of the oil pan with a mallet. It is not necessary to remove the gasket unless it is damaged.

— **CAUTION** —
Do not pry the oil pan off with the tip of a screwdriver.

9. Remove the oil passage block and the oil pump assembly.

— **CAUTION** —
As soon as the oil passage block bolts are loosened, the oil in the oil line may flow out.

NOTE: Before removing the pistons, check the top of the cylinder bore for carbon build-up or a ridge. Remove the carbon or use a ridge-reamer to remove the ridge before removing the pistons.

10. Working from the underside of the car, remove the connecting rod bearing caps. Using the wooden handle of a hammer, push the pistons and connecting rods out of the cylinders.

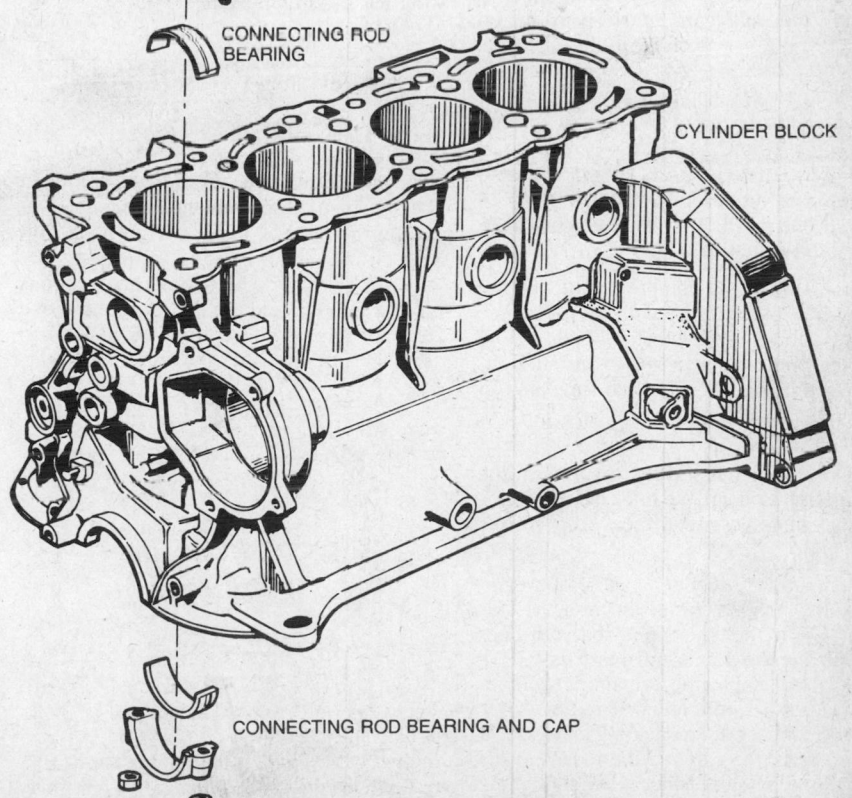

CYLINDER BLOCK

CONNECTING ROD BEARING AND CAP

Typical CVCC engine block and piston

NOTE: Bearing caps, bearings, and pistons should be marked to indicate their location for reassembly.

11. When removing the piston rings, be sure not to apply excessive force as the rings are made of cast iron and can be easily broken.

NOTE: A hydraulic press is necessary for removing the piston pin.

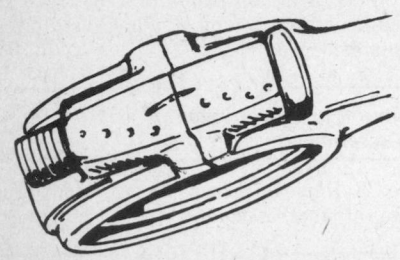

Mark the pistons and rods if they are not marked from the factory

12. Observe the following points when installing the piston rings:

a. When installing the three-piece oil ring, first place the spacer and then the rails in position. The spacer and rail gaps must be staggered 0.787–1.181 in. (2–3 cm);

b. Install the second and top rings on the piston with their markings facing upward;

c. After installing all rings on the piston, rotate them to be sure they move smoothly without signs of binding;

d. The ring gaps must be staggered 120° and must NOT be in the direction of the piston pin boss or at right angles to the pin. The gap of the three-piece oil ring refers to that of the middle spacer.

NOTE: Pistons and rings are also available in four oversizes, 0.010 in. (0.25 mm), 0.020 in. (0.50 mm), 0.030 in. (0.75 mm), and 0.040 in. (1.00 mm).

13. Using a ring compressor, install the piston into the cylinder with the skirt protruding about ⅓ of the piston height below the ring compressor. Prior to installation, apply a thin coat of oil to the rings and to the cylinder wall.

NOTE: When installing the piston, the connecting rod oil jet hole or the mark on the piston crown faces the intake manifold.

14. Using the wooden handle of a hammer, slowly press the piston into the cylinder. Guide the connecting rod so it does not damage the crankshaft journals.

15. Reassemble the remaining components in the reverse order of removal. Install the connecting rod bearing caps so that the recess in the cap and the recess in the rod are on the same side. After tightening the cap bolts, move the rod back and forth on the journal to check for binding.

ENGINE LUBRICATION

Oil Pan

REMOVAL & INSTALLATION

1. Drain the engine oil.
2. Raise the front of the car and support it with safety stands. Remove the lower splash pan (if so equipped).
3. Attach a chain to a bracket on the transmission case and raise just enough to take the load off the center mount.

NOTE: Do not remove the left engine mount.

4. Remove the center beam and engine lower mount.
5. Loosen the oil bolts and remove the oil pan flywheel dust shield.

NOTE: Loosen the bolts in a criss-cross pattern beginning with the outside bolt. To remove the oil pan, lightly tap the corners of the oil pan with a mallet. It is not necessary to remove the gasket unless it is damaged.

6. To install, reverse the removal procedure. Apply a coat of sealant to the entire mating surface of the cylinder block, except the crankshaft oil seal, before fitting the oil pan. Tighten the bolts in a circular sequence, beginning in the center and working out towards the ends.

Rear Main Oil Seal

REPLACEMENT

The rear oil seal is installed in the rear main bearing cap. Replacement of the seal requires the removal of the transmission, flywheel and clutch housing, as well as the oil pan. Refer to the appropriate sections for the removal and installation of the above components. Both the front and rear main seal are installed after the crankshaft bear-

Oil pump retaining bolt under screen

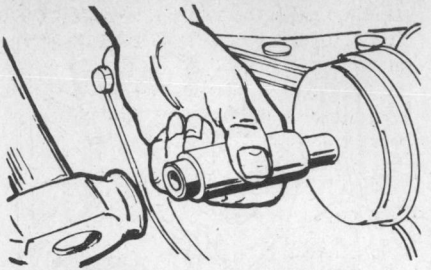

Driving in the rear main seal

ing caps have been torqued, if the crankshaft has been removed. Special drivers must be used.

Oil Pump

REMOVAL & INSTALLATION

All Models Except 1342, 1488 and 1829cc CVCC Engines

To remove the oil pump, follow the procedure given for oil pan removal and in-

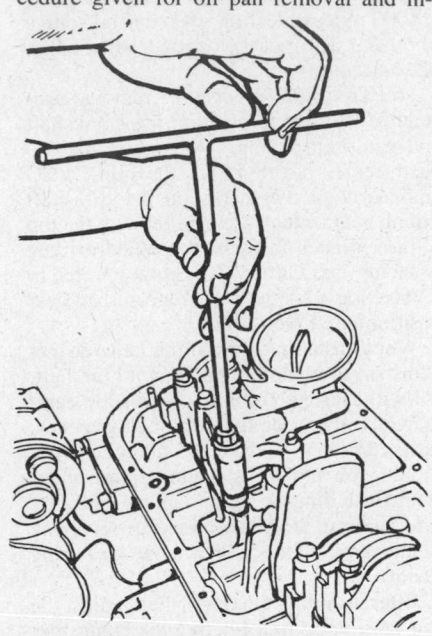

Oil pump removal; there is a bolt under the screen

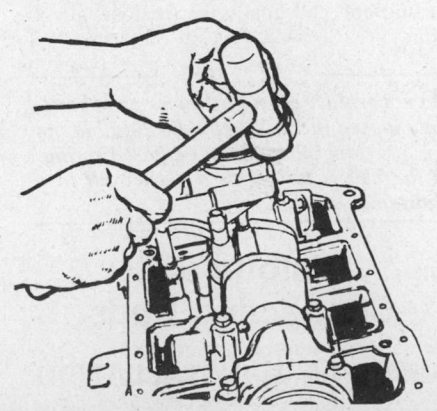

Use a soft mallet when installing the oil pump screen

stallation. After the oil pan has been dropped, simply unbolt the oil passage block and oil pump assembly from the engine. Remove the oil pump screen to find the last bolt. When installing the pump, tighten the bolts to no more than 8 ft. lbs.

1342, 1488 and 1829cc CVCC Engines

To remove the oil pump, follow the procedure given to remove the timing gear cover. After removing the cover, remove the timing belt and unbolt the oil pump and remove it from the block. When installing the pump, tighten the bolts to 9 ft. lbs. and the nuts to 5 ft. lbs. To remove the oil pump pick-up screen, follow the procedure to remove the oil pan.

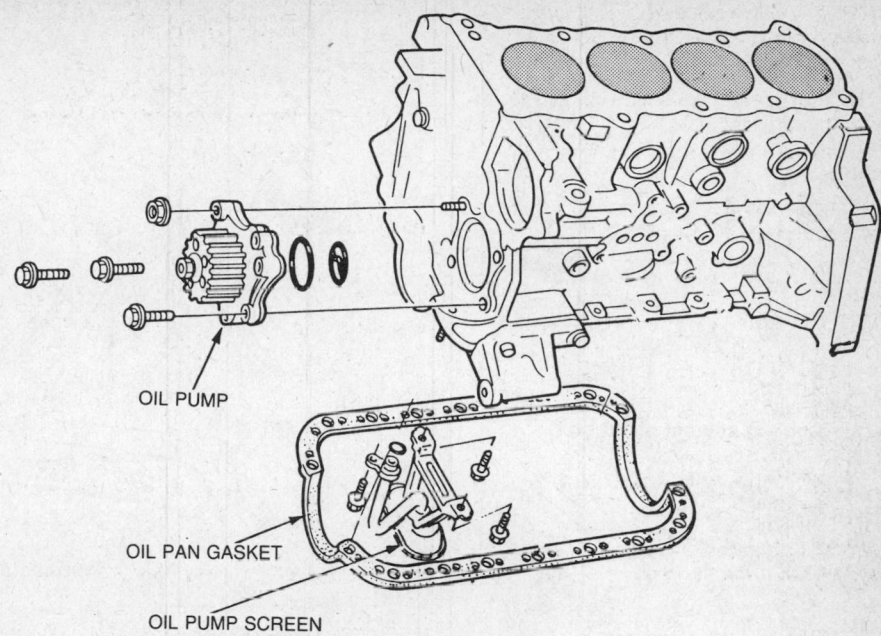

OIL PUMP

OIL PAN GASKET

OIL PUMP SCREEN

Oil pump mounting—1829cc engine

ENGINE COOLING

Radiator

REMOVAL & INSTALLATION

NOTE: When removing the radiator, take care not to damage the core and fins.

1. Drain the radiator.
2. Disconnect the thermo switch wire and the fan motor wire. Remove the fan shroud (if so equipped).
3. Disconnect the upper coolant hose at the upper radiator tank and the lower hose at the water pump connecting pipe. Disconnect and plug the Hondamatic cooling lines at the bottom of the radiator (if so equipped).
4. Remove the hoses to the coolant reservoir (if so equipped).
5. Detach the radiator mounting bolts and remove the radiator with the fan attached. The fan can be easily unbolted from the back of the radiator.
6. To install, reverse the removal procedure. Bleed the cooling system.

Water Pump

REMOVAL & INSTALLATION

All Except 1342, and 1488cc CVCC

1. Drain the radiator.
2. On 1237cc cars only, loosen the alternator bolts. Move the alternator toward the cylinder block and remove the drive belt.
3. Loosen the pump mounting bolts and remove the pump together with the pulley and the rubber seal.
4. To install, reverse the removal procedure using a new gasket. Bleed the cooling system.

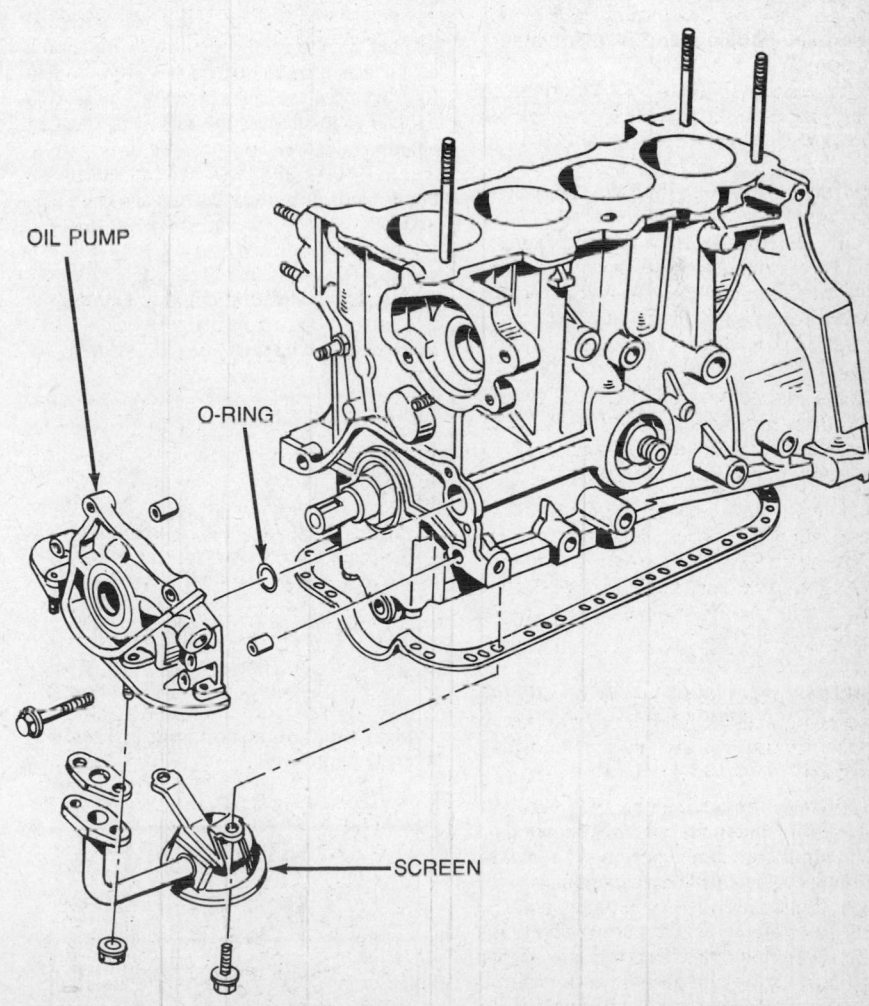

OIL PUMP

O-RING

SCREEN

Oil pump mounting—1342 and 1488cc engines

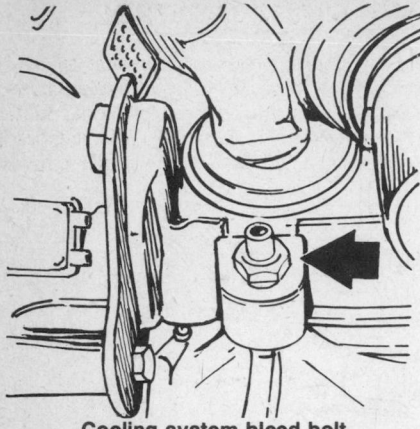

Cooling system bleed bolt

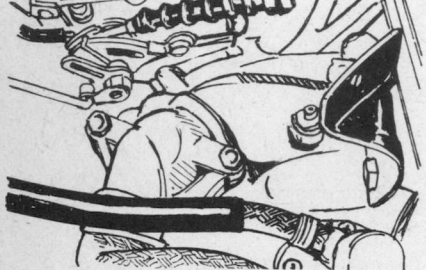

Thermostat housing and coolant bleed bolt, non-CVCC

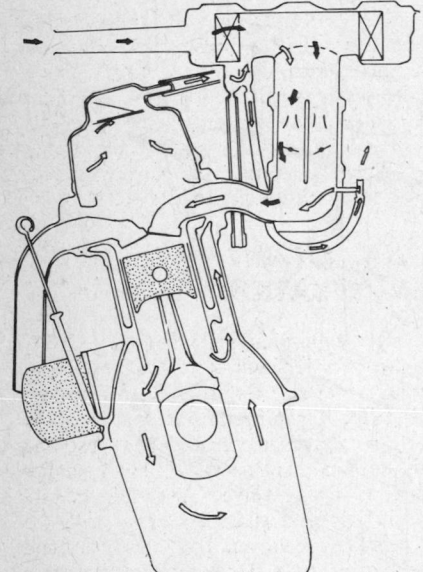

Crankcase ventilation system operation—1237 cc engine (CVCC similar)

1342 and 1488cc CVCC

1. Drain the radiator.
2. Following the procedures shown under "Timing belt and Tensioner" remove the timing belt from the water pump drive sprocket.
3. Loosen the water pump mounting bolts and remove together with the drive sprocket.
4. To install, reverse the removal procedure using a new O-ring. Bleed the cooling system.

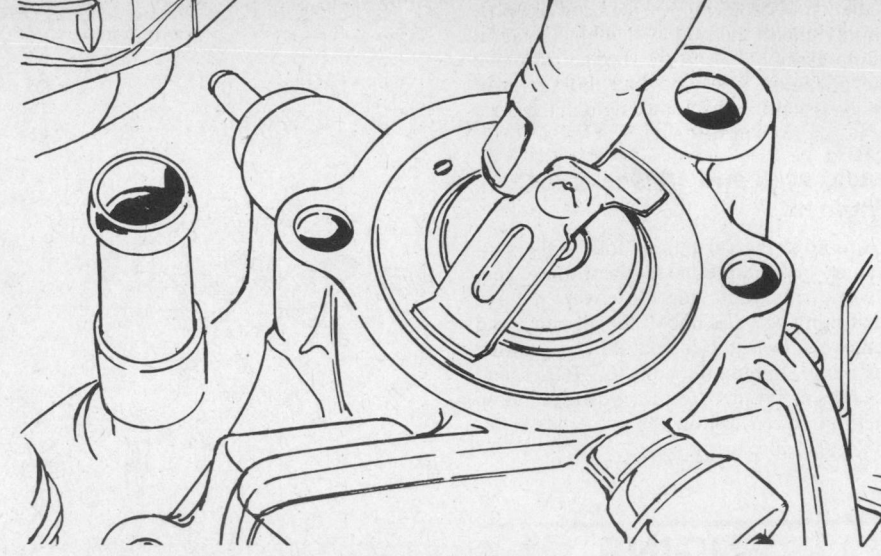

Thermostat installation

Thermostat

REMOVAL & INSTALLATION

1. On 1237cc cars, the thermostat is located on the intake manifold, under the air cleaner nozzle, so you will first have to remove the air cleaner housing. On CVCC cars, it is located at the rear near the distributor housing.
2. Unbolt and remove the thermostat cover and pull the thermostat from the housing.
3. To install, reverse the removal procedure. Always install the spring end of the thermostat toward the engine. Tighten the two cover bolts to 7 ft. lbs. Always use a new gasket. Bleed the cooling system.

Typical thermostat housing and cooling system bleed bolt

EMISSION CONTROLS

Emission controls fall into three basic systems: Crankcase Emission Control System, Exhaust Emission Control System and Evaporative Emission Control System.

Crankcase Emission Control System

All engines are equipped with a "Dual Return System" to prevent crankcase vapor emissions. Blow-by gas is returned to the combustion chamber through the intake manifold and carburetor air cleaner. When the throttle is partially opened, blow-by gas is returned to the intake manifold through breather tubes leading into the tee orifice located on the outside of the intake manifold. When the throttle is opened wide and vacuum in the air cleaner rises, blow-by gas is returned to the intake manifold through an additional passage in the air cleaner case.

Exhaust Emission Control System

Control of exhaust emissions, hydrocarbon (HC), carbon monoxide (CO), and Oxides of nitrogen (NOx), is achieved by a combination of engine modifications and special control devices. Improvements to the combustion chamber, intake manifold, valve timing, carburetor, and distributor comprise the engine modifications. These modifications, in conjunction with the special control devices, enable the engine to produce low emission with leaner air-fuel mixtures while maintaining good driveability. The special control devices consist of the following:

a. Intake air temperature control;
b. Throttle opener;
c. Transmission and temperature controlled spark advance (TCS) for the 4-speed transmission.

INTAKE AIR TEMPERATURE CONTROL

Intake air temperature control is designed

to provide the most uniform carburetion possible under various ambient air temperature conditions by maintaining the intake air temperature within a narrow range. When the temperature in the air cleaner is below 100°F (approx.), the air bleed valve, which consists of a bimetallic strip and a rubber seal, remains closed. Intake manifold vacuum is then led to a vacuum motor, located on the snorkel of the air cleaner case, which moves the air control valve door, allowing only preheated air to enter the air cleaner.

When the temperature in the air cleaner becomes higher than approx. 100°F, the air bleed valve opens and the air control valve door returns to the open position allowing only unheated air through the snorkel.

THROTTLE OPENER

When the throttle is closed suddenly at high engine speed, hydrocarbon (HC) emissions increase due to engine misfire caused by an incombustible mixture. The throttle opener is designed to prevent misfiring during deceleration by causing the throttle valve to remain slightly open, allowing better mixture control. The control valve is set to allow the passage of vacuum to the throttle opener diaphragm when the engine vacuum is equal to or greater than the control valve preset vacuum (21.6 ± 1.6 in. Hg) during acceleration.

Under running conditions, other than fully closed throttle deceleration, the intake manifold vacuum is less than the control valve set vacuum; therefore the control valve is not actuated. The vacuum remaining in the throttle opener and control valve is returned to atmospheric pressure by the air passage at the valve center.

IGNITION TIMING RETARD UNIT

When the engine is idling, the vacuum produced in the carburetor retarder port is communicated to the spark retard unit and the ignition timing, at idle, is retarded.

TCS SYSTEM

The transmission and temperature controlled spark advance for 4-speed transmissions is designed to reduce NOx emissions during normal vehicle operation.

The vacuum is cut off to the spark advance unit regardless of temperature when First, Second, or Third gear is selected. Vacuum advance is restored when Fourth gear is selected.

TEMPERATURE CONTROLLED SPARK ADVANCE

Temperature controlled spark advance on cars equipped with Hondamatic transmission is designed to reduce NOx emissions

by disconnecting the vacuum to the spark advance unit during normal vehicle operation.

When the coolant temperature is approximately 120° or higher, the solenoid valve is energized, cutting off vacuum to the advance unit.

Air Injection System

NON-CVCC

An air injection system is used to control hydrocarbon and carbon monoxide emissions. With this system, a belt-driven air pump delivers filtered air under pressure to injection nozzles located at each exhaust port. Here, the additional oxygen supplied by the vane-type pump reacts with any uncombusted fuel mixture, promoting an afterburning effect in the hot exhaust manifold. To prevent a reverse flow in the air injection manifold when exhaust gas pressure exceeds air supply pressure, a non-return check valve is used. To prevent exhaust afterburning or backfiring during deceleration, an anti-afterburn valve delivers air to the intake manifold instead. When manifold vacuum rises above the preset vacuum of the air control valve and/or below that of the air by-pass valve, air pump air is returned to the air cleaner.

THROTTLE CONTROLS

This system controls the closing of the throttle during periods of gear shifting, deceleration, or anytime the gas pedal is released. In preventing the sudden closing of the throttle during these conditions, an overly rich mixture is prevented which controls excessive emissions of hydrocarbons and carbon monoxide. This system has two main parts; a dashpot system and a throttle positioner system. The dashpot diaphragm and solenoid valve act to dampen or slow down the throttle return time to 1–4 seconds. The throttle positioner part consists of a speed sensor, a solenoid valve, a control valve and an opener diaphragm which will keep the throttle open and predetermined minimum amount any time the gas pedal is released when the car is traveling 15 mph or faster, and closes it when the car slows to 10 mph.

IGNITION TIMING CONTROLS

A variety of ignition timing control systems are used on various models to reduce hydrocarbons and oxides of nitrogen emissions. These timing controls combined with centrifugal advance affect the time at which each spark plug ignites the air/fuel mixture. The ignition spark is controlled according to the engine's speed, load and coolant temperature.

HOT START CONTROL

This system is designed to prevent an overrich mixture condition in the intake manifold due to vaporization of residual fuel when starting a hot engine. This reduces hydrocarbon and carbon monoxide emissions.

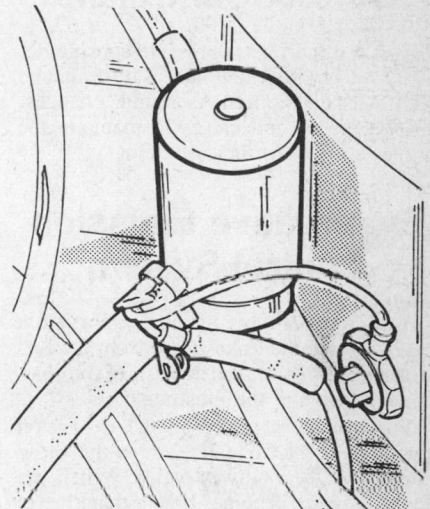

Start control solenoid valve

ANTI-AFTERBURN VALVE

Various 1979 and later models have an anti-afterburn valve. The valve lets fresh air into the intake manifold when it senses sudden increases in manifold vacuum. The valve responds only to sudden increases in vacuum and the amount of time it stays open is determined by an internal diaphragm which is acted on by the vacuum level.

CVCC ENGINE MODIFICATIONS

By far, the most important part of the CVCC engine emission control system is the Compound Vortex Controlled Combustion (CVCC) cylinder head itself. Each cylinder has three valves: a conventional intake and conventional exhaust valve, and a smaller auxiliary intake valve. There are actually *two* combustion chambers per cylinder: a precombustion or auxiliary chamber, and the main chamber. During the intake stroke, an extremely lean mixture is drawn into the main combustion chamber. Simultaneously, a very rich mixture is drawn into the smaller precombustion chamber via the auxiliary intake valve. The spark plug, located in the precombustion chamber, easily ignites the rich pre-mixture, and this combustion spreads out into the main combustion chamber where the lean mixture is ignited. Due to the fact that the volume of the auxiliary chamber is much smaller than the main chamber, the overall mixture is very lean (about 18 parts air to one part fuel). The result is low hydrocarbon emissions due to the slow, stable combustion of the lean mixture in the main chamber; low

carbon monoxide emissions due to the excess oxygen available; and low oxides of nitrogen emissions due to the lowered peak combustion temperatures. An added benefit of burning the lean mixture is the excellent gas mileage.

Air Jet Controller

This is a atmospheric pressure sensing device used on 1981 and later California and High Altitude models. As altitude changes, a valve opens and closes to maintain the proper air flow to the carburetor.

Evaporative Emission Control System

This system prevents gasoline vapors from escaping into the atmosphere from the fuel tank and carburetor and consists of the components listed in the illustration.

Fuel vapor is stored in the expansion chamber, in the fuel tank, and in the vapor line up to the one-way valve. When the vapor pressure becomes higher than the set pressure of the one-way valve, the valve opens and allows vapor into the charcoal canister. While the engine is stopped or idling, the idle cut-off valve in the canister is closed and the vapor is absorbed by the charcoal.

At partially opened throttle, the idle cut-off valve is opened by manifold vacuum. The vapor that was stored in the charcoal canister and in the vapor line is purged into the intake manifold. Any excessive pressure or vacuum which might build up in the fuel tank is relieved by the two-way valve in the filler cap.

MAINTENANCE & SERVICE

Components Pertaining To Emission Controls

The proper control of exhaust emissions depends not only on the primary components of the emission controls mentioned above, but also on such related areas as ignition timing, spark plugs, valve clearance, engine oil, cooling system, etc. Before tackling the primary emission controls, you should determine if the related components are functioning properly, and correct any deficiencies.

Crankcase Emission Control System

1. Squeeze the lower end of the drain tube and drain any oil or water which may have collected.
2. Make sure that the intake manifold T-joint is clear by passing the shank end of a No. 65 (0.035 in. dia.) drill through both ends (orifices) of the joint.
3. Check for any loose, disconnected, or deteriorated tubes and replace if necessary.

Exhaust Emission Control System
INTAKE AIR TEMPERATURE CONTROL SYSTEM (ENGINE COLD)

1. Inspect for loose, disconnected, or deteriorated vacuum hoses and replace as necessary.
2. Remove the air cleaner cover and element.
3. With the transmission in Neutral and the blue distributor disconnected, engage the starter motor for approximately two (2) seconds. Manifold vacuum to the vacuum motor should completely raise the air control valve door. Once opened, the valve door should stay open unless there is a leak in the system.
4. If the valve door does not open, check the intake manifold port by passing a No. 78 (0.016 in. dia.) drill or compressed air through the orifice in the manifold.
5. If the valve door still does not open, proceed to the following steps:

   a. Vacuum Motor Test—Disconnect the vacuum line from the vacuum motor inlet pipe. Fully open the air control valve door, block the vacuum motor inlet pipe, then release the door. If the door does not remain open, the vacuum motor is defective. Replace as necessary and repeat Steps 1–3;

   b. Air Bleed Valve Test—Unblock the inlet pipe and make sure that the valve door fully closes without sticking or binding. Reconnect the vacuum line to the vacuum motor inlet pipe. Connect a vacuum source (e.g. hand vacuum pump) to the manifold vacuum line (disconnect at the intake manifold fixed orifice) and draw enough vacuum to fully open the valve door. If the valve door closes with the manifold vacuum line plugged (by the vacuum pump), then vacuum is leaking through the air bleed valve. Replace as necessary and repeat Steps 1–3;

CAUTION
Never force the air bleed valve (bi-metal strip) on or off its valve seat. The bi-metal strip and the valve seat may be damaged.

---

   c. Check Valve Test—Again draw a vacuum (at the manifold vacuum line) until the valve door opens. Unplug the line by disconnecting the pump from the manifold vacuum line. If the valve door closes, vacuum is leaking past the check valve. Replace as necessary and repeat Steps 1–3.
6. After completing the above steps, replace the air cleaner element and cover and fit a vacuum gauge into the line leading to the vacuum motor.
7. Start the engine and raise the idle to 1500–2000 rpm. As the engine warms, the vacuum gauge reading should drop to zero.

NOTE: Allow sufficient time for the engine to reach normal operating temperature—when the cooling fan cycles on and off.

If the reading does not drop to zero before the engine reaches normal operating temperature, the air bleed valve is defective and must be replaced. Repeat Step 3 as a final check.

TEMPERATURE AND TRANSMISSION CONTROLLED SPARK ADVANCE (ENGINE COLD)—ALL MODELS

1. Check for loose, disconnected, or deteriorated vacuum hoses and replace as necessary.
2. Check the coolant temperature sensor switch for proper operation with an ohmmeter or 12V light. The switch should normally be open (no continuity across the switch terminals) when the coolant temperature is below approximately 120°F (engine cold). If the switch is closed (continuity across the terminals), replace the switch and repeat the check.
3. On manual transmission models, check the transmission sensor switch. The switch should be open (no continuity across the connections) when Fourth gear is selected, and closed (continuity across the connections) in all other gear positions. Replace if necessary and repeat the check.
4. Remove the spark control vacuum tube, leading between the spark advance/retard unit and the solenoid valve, and connect.

Evaporative Emission Control System (Engine at Normal Operating Temperature)
CHARCOAL CANISTER

1. Check for loose, disconnected, or deteriorated vacuum hoses and replace where necessary.
2. Pull the free end of the purge air guide tube out of the body frame and plug it securely.
3. Disconnect the fuel vapor line from the charcoal canister and connect a vacuum gauge to the charcoal canister vapor inlet according to the diagram.
4. Start the engine and allow it to idle. Since the vacuum port in the carburetor is closed off at idle, the vacuum gauge should register no vacuum. If vacuum is available, replace the charcoal canister and recheck for no vacuum. A vacuum reading indicates that the charcoal canister idle cut-off valve is broken or stuck.
5. Open the throttle to 2000 rpm and make sure that the charcoal canister idle cutoff valve is opening by watching the vacuum.

   a. Disconnect the vacuum signal line and connect the vacuum gauge to the carburetor T-joint orifice formerly occupied by the signal line. The vacuum reading at 2000 rpm should be greater than 3 in. Hg. If vacuum is now available (with the throttle open), replace the charcoal canister and repeat Steps 4 & 5. If vacuum is still not available, or is below 3 in. Hg proceed to the next step.

b. If vacuum is less than 3 in. Hg (with the throttle open), the carburetor vacuum port or T-joint might be plugged. Clear the passages with compressed air. If vacuum is now available, repeat Steps 4 & 5. If vacuum is not available, or below 3 in. Hg, the carburetor vacuum port is blocked. Repair or replace as necessary and repeat Steps 4 & 5. If vacuum is *still* not available, proceed to the next step.

c. Plug the solenoid valve vacuum line (the other line to the carburetor T-joint) and recheck for vacuum. If vacuum is now available, the leak is in the advance/retard solenoid valve. Repair or replace as necessary and repeat Steps 4 & 5.

FUEL SYSTEM

All 1978–79 Civics with the 1237cc engine use a two-barrel downdraft Hitachi carburetor. Fuel pressure is provided by a camshaft-driven mechanical fuel pump. A replaceable fuel filter is located in the engine compartment in-line between the fuel pump and carburetor.

On all other models except the 1983 and later Prelude a Keihin three-barrel carburetor is used. On this carburetor, the primary and secondary venturis deliver a lean air/fuel mixture to the main combustion chamber. Simultaneously, the third or auxiliary venturi which has a completely separate fuel metering circuit, delivers a small (in volume) but very rich air/fuel mixture to the precombustion chamber. The 1983 and later Prelude uses two Keihin side draft carburetors. Between the two side draft carburetors is a small third carburetor used to supply fuel to the rich mixture chambers in the CVCC head. Fuel pressure is provided by an electric fuel pump (except the '84 and later Civic models) which is actuated when the ignition switch is turned to the "on" position. The electric pump is located under the rear seat beneath a special access plate on Civic sedan and hatchback models, and located under the rear of the car adjacent to the fuel tank on all other models. Fuel pressure on the 1984 and later Civic models with the 1342 & 1488cc engines is provided by a camshaft-driven mechanical fuel pump located next to the distributor.

Fuel Filter

REPLACEMENT

— CAUTION —
Before disconnecting any fuel lines, be sure to open the gas tank filler cap to relieve any pressure in the system. If this is not done, you may run the risk of being squirted with gasoline.

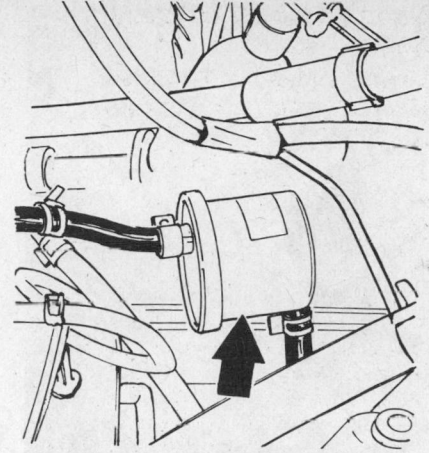

Fuel filter (non-CVCC Civic)

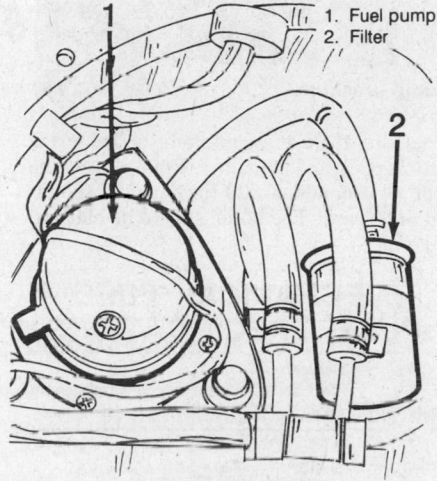

1. Fuel pump
2. Filter

Rear fuel filter location—CVCC sedan

All models use a disposable-type fuel filter which cannot be disassembled for cleaning. The filter is replaced after the first 15,000 miles, and every 30,000 miles (through 1980) 60,000 miles (1981 and later) thereafter.

On 1978–79 Civics with the 1237cc engine, the filter is located in the engine compartment, inline between the fuel pump and carburetor. Replacement is a simple matter of pinching the lines closed, loosening the hose clamps and discarding the old filter.

On all 1980–83 Civic Sedan models, the rear filter is located beneath a special access cover under the rear seat on the driver's side. The rear seat can be removed after removing the bolt at the rear center of the cushion and then pivoting the seat forward from the rear. Then, remove the four screws retaining the access cover to the floor and remove the cover. The filter, together with the electric fuel pump, are located in the recess. Pinch the lines shut, loosen the hose clamps and remove the filter.

On all 1984 and Civic Sedans, Coupes, and Wagons and the Accord and Prelude models, the rear filter is located under the car, in front of the spare tire. To replace the fuel filter, you must raise the rear of

the car, support it with jackstands, and clamp off the fuel lines leading to and from the filter. Then, loosen the hose clamps and, taking note of which hose is the inlet and which is the outlet, remove the filter. Some replacement filters have an arrow embossed or printed on the filter body, in which case you want to install the new filter with the arrow pointing in the direction of fuel flow. After installing the new filter, remember to unclamp the fuel lines. Check for leaks.

All 1982 and later models are also equipped with a front in-line desposible fuel filter, located at the carburetor. Replacement is the same as the others.

Mechanical Fuel Pump

REMOVAL & INSTALLATION

1237cc Engine

The fuel pump in the Civic is located in back of the engine, underneath the air cleaner snorkle.

1. Remove the air cleaner and cover assembly.
2. Remove the inlet and outlet fuel lines at the pump.
3. Loosen the pump nuts and remove the pump.

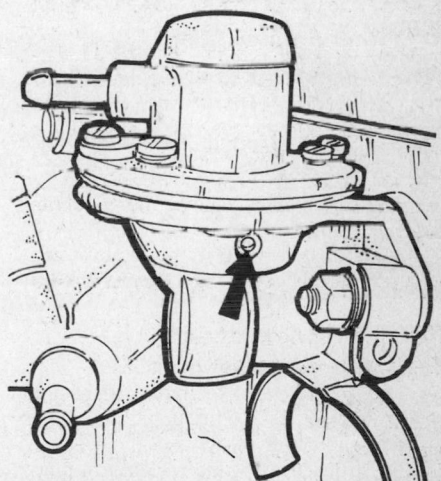

Mechanical fuel pump, 1237cc engine. Arrow indicates air hole

NOTE: Do not disassemble the pump. Disassembly may cause fuel or oil leakage. If the pump is defective, replace it as an assembly.

4. To install the fuel pump, reverse the removal procedure.

1342 & 1488cc Engines

1. Pinch the fuel lines closed at the pump.
2. Remove the inlet and outlet fuel lines at the pump.

NOTE: When removing the fuel lines, slide the clamps back and twist the lines as you pull, to avoid damaging them.

Checking fuel pump pressure.

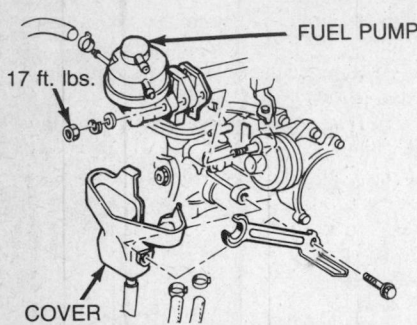

Mechanical fuel pump mounting—1342 and 1488cc engines

3. Loosen and remove the mounting bolts. Remove the pump.

4. To install, reverse the removal procedure. Start the engine and check for leaks.

Inspection

1. Check the following items:
   a. Looseness of the pump connector.
   b. Looseness of the upper and lower body and cover screws.
   c. Looseness of the rocker arm pin.
   d. Contamination or clogging of the air hole.
   e. Improper operation of the pump.

2. Check to see if there are signs of oil or fuel around the air hole. If so, the diaphragm is damaged and you must replace the pump.

3. To inspect the pump for operation, first disconnect the fuel line at the carburetor. Connect a fuel pressure gauge to the delivery side of the pump. Start the engine and measure the pump delivery pressure.

4. After measuring, stop the engine and check to see if the gauge drops suddenly. If the gauge drops suddenly and/or the delivery pressure is incorrect, check for a fuel or oil leak from the diaphragm or from the valves.

5. To test for volume, disconnect the fuel line from the carburetor and insert it into a one quart container. Crank the engine for 64 seconds at 600 rpm, or 40 seconds at 3000 rpm. The bottle should be half full (1 pint).

MECHANICAL FUEL PUMP SPECIFICATIONS

Engine rpm	Delivery Pressure (lb. in.²)	Vacuum (in.Hg.)	Displacement (in.³/minute)
600	2.56	17.72	27
3,000	2.56	7.87–11.81	43
6,000	2.56	7.87–11.81	46

Electrical Fuel Pump

REMOVAL & INSTALLATION

All Except 1237, 1342 and 1488cc Engines

1. Remove the gas filler cap to relieve any excess pressure in the system.

2. Obtain a pair of clothes pins or other suitable clamps to pinch shut the fuel lines to the pump.

3. Disconnect the negative battery cable.

4. Locate the fuel pump. On Civic sedan and hatchback models (1978–82 only), you will first have to remove the rear seat by removing the bolt at the rear center of the bottom cushion and pivoting the seat forward from the rear. The pump and filter are located on the driver's side of the rear seat floor section beneath an access plate retained by four Phillips head screws.

On station wagon and 1983 sedan & hatchback models and the Accord and Prelude, you will probably have to raise the rear of the car to obtain access. On Accord and Prelude models, remove the left rear wheel. In all cases, make sure, if you are

crawling under the car, that the car is securely supported. *Do not venture beneath the car when it is supported only by the tire changing jack.*

5. Pinch the inlet and outlet fuel lines shut. Loosen the hose clamps. On station wagon and Accord models, remove the filter mounting clip on the left hand side of the bracket.

6. Disconnect the positive lead wire and ground wire from the pump at their quick disconnect.

7. Remove the two fuel pump retaining bolts, taking care not to lose the two spacers and bolt collars.

8. Remove the fuel lines and fuel pump.

9. Reverse the above procedure to install. The pump cannot be disassembled and must be replaced if defective. Operating fuel pump pressure is 2–3 psi.

Carburetor

REMOVAL & INSTALLATION

1. Disconnect and label the following:
   a. Hot air tube.
   b. Disconnect all vacuum hoses and lines.
   c. Breather chamber (on air cleaner case) to intake manifold at the breather chamber.
   d. Hose from the air cleaner case to the valve cover.
   e. Hose from the carbon canister to the carburetor—at the carburetor.
   f. Throttle opener hose—at the throttle opener.
   g. On the 1829cc Prelude, drain the coolant and remove the coolant hoses from the thermowax valve and the right end of the intake manifold.

2. Disconnect the fuel line at the carburetor. Plug the end of the fuel line to prevent dust entry.

3. Disconnect the choke and throttle control cables.

4. Disconnect the fuel shut-off solenoid wires.

5. Remove the carburetor retaining bolts or loosen the insulator bands and then remove the carburetor. Leave the insulator on the manifold.

NOTE: After removing the carburetor, cover the intake manifold parts to keep out foreign materials.

OVERHAUL

For all carburetor overhaul procedures, please refer to "Carburetor Service" in the Unit Repair section.

THROTTLE LINKAGE ADJUSTMENT

1237cc Models

1. Check the gas pedal free-play (the amount of free movement before the throt-

tle cable starts to pull the throttle valve). Adjust the free-play at the throttle cable adjusting nut (near the carburetor) so the pedal has 0.04–0.12 in. (1.0–3.0 mm) freeplay.

2. Make sure that when the accelerator pedal is fully depressed, the primary and secondary throttle valves are opened fully (contact the stops). If the secondary valve does not open fully, adjust by bending the secondary throttle valve connecting rod.

CVCC Models

1. Remove the air cleaner assembly to provide access.

2. Check that the cable free-play (deflection) is ³⁄₁₆ to ⅜ in. (4–10 mm). This is measured right before the cable enters the throttle shaft bellcrank.

3. If deflection is not to specifications, rotate the cable adjusting nuts in the required direction.

4. As a final check, have a friend press the gas pedal all the way to the floor, while you look down inside the throttle bore checking that the throttle plates reach the wide open throttle (WOT) vertical position.

5. Install the air cleaner.

FLOAT AND FUEL LEVEL ADJUSTMENT

1237cc Models

1. Check the float level by looking at the sight glass on the right of the carburetor. Fuel level should align with the dot on the sight glass. If the level is above or below the dot, the carburetor must be disassembled and the float level set.

NOTE: Try to check float level with the dot at eye level.

2. Remove the carburetor from the engine and disconnect the air horn assembly from the carburetor body.

NOTE: When removing the air horn, do not drop the float pin.

3. Invert the air horn and raise the float.

4. Measure the distance between the float tang and the needle valve stem. The distance should be 0.051–0.067 in. (1.3–1.7 mm). Adjust by bending the float stop tang.

5. Remove and invert the air horn until the float arm just touches the needle valve, or there is about 0.1 mm (0.004 in.) clearance between them. Measure the distance between the bottom of the air horn (gasket installed) and the center of the bottom of the float. The distance should measure 36.4 mm (1.39–1.47 in.). Adjust by turning the needle valve seat. Be careful not to allow the valve seat to protrude from the seat attaching boss, which would allow the valve to fall. If this is the case, bend the float arm slightly until the proper clearance can be obtained.

6. When the carburetor is installed, re-

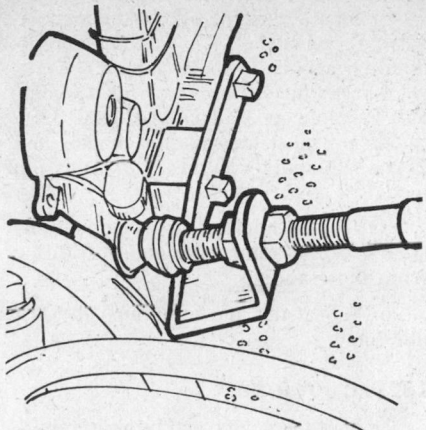

CVCC throttle cable adjusting location

check the float level by looking into the carburetor float sight glass. Fuel level should be within the range of the dot on the glass.

1335, 1342, 1487, 1488, 1600 and 1751cc CVCC Models
1978–81

Due to the rather unconventional manner in which the Keihin 3 bbl carburetor float level is checked and adjusted, this is one job best left to the dealer, or someone with Honda tool No. 07501-6570000 (which is a special float level gauge/fuel catch tray/drain bottle assembly not generally available to the public). This carburetor is adjusted while mounted on a running engine. After the auxiliary and the primary/secondary main jet covers are removed, the special float gauge apparatus is installed over the jet apertures. With the engine running, the float level is checked against a red index line on the gauge. If adjustment proves necessary, there are adjusting screws provided for both the auxiliary and the primary/secondary circuits atop the carburetor.

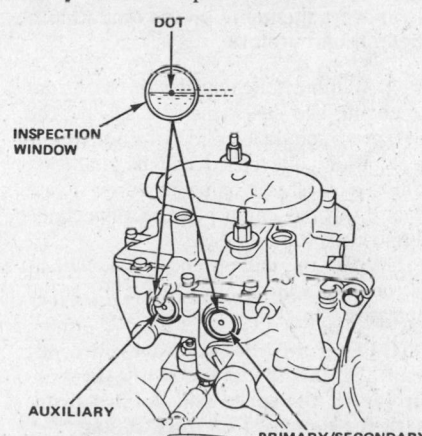

Inspection window showing the fuel level on the 1982 and later models, except 1829cc Prelude

1982 and Later Except 1829cc Prelude

With the car on level ground and at normal operating temperature, check the primary

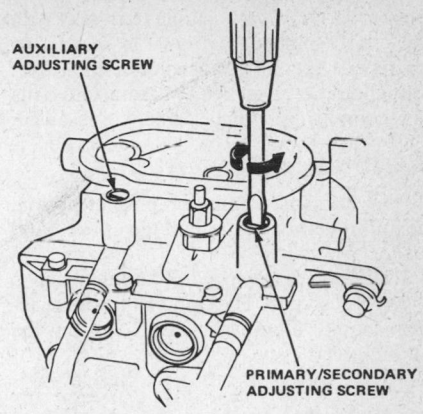

Float level adjustment screw—1982 and later models, except 1829cc Prelude

and secondary fuel level inspection windows. If the fuel level is not touching the dot, adjust it by turning the adjusting screws.

NOTE: Do not turn the adjusting screws more than ⅛ turn every 15 seconds.

1829cc Prelude

1. Remove the side draft carburetors from the engine and remove the float chambers from the carburetors.

2. Using a float level gauge, measure the float level with the float tip lightly touching the float valve and the float chamber surface tilted about 30° from vertical. The float level should be 16 mm or 0.04 in.

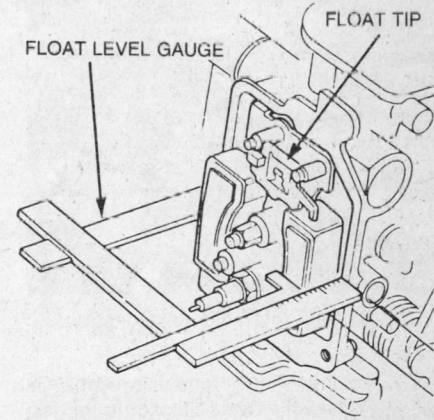

Float level measurement on the dual Keihin sidedraft carburetors—1829cc Prelude

3. To adjust the float level on the sub carburetor, remove the float chamber. Using a float level gauge, measure the float level as described above.

NOTE: The float level of the sub carburetor cannot be adjusted. If the float level is incorrect the float must be replaced.

FAST IDLE ADJUSTMENT

During cold engine starting and the engine warm-up period, a specially enriched fuel mixture is required. If the engine fails to

run properly or if the engine over-revs with the choke knob pulled out (on models so equipped) in cold weather, the fast idle system should be checked and adjusted. This is accomplished with the carburetor installed.

1237cc Models

1. With the engine running at normal operating temperature, pull the choke knob all the way out.

2. The engine speed should increase to 1400–2200 rpm. The arm of the choke lever should align with the boss on the carburetor.

3. Adjust by bending the link lever.

1487 and 1600cc CVCC Models
1978–79

1. Run the engine until it reaches normal operating temperature.

2. Place the choke control knob in its second detent position (two clicks out from the dash). With the choke knob in this position, run the engine for 30 seconds and check that the fast idle speed is 3000 rpm plus or minus 500 rpm.

CVCC fast idle adjusting location

3. To adjust on all models except 1978 and later Accords, bend the slot in the fast idle adjusting link. Narrow the slot to lower the fast idle, and widen the slot to increase. Make all adjustments in small increments.

4. On 1978–79 Accord and Prelude, adjust the fast idle by means of the fast idle adjusting screw, located on the throttle arm below the choke housing.

1335, 1342, 1487 (1980–83) 1488, 1751 and the Accord 1829cc

1. Run the engine to normal operating temperature.

2. Connect a tachometer according to the manufacturer's specifications.

3. Disconnect and plug the hose from the fast idle unloader.

4. Shut the engine off, hold the choke valve closed, and open and close the throttle to engage the fast idle cam.

5. Start the engine, run it for one minute. Fast idle speed should be 2300–3300 rpm for manual transmission models and 2200–3200 rpm for automatic transmission models.

NOTE: Underhood specifications sticker figures must be used if they differ from those above.

6. Adjust the idle by turning the fast idle screw.

1829cc Prelude

1. Start the engine and bring it to normal operating temperature. Shut off the engine.

2. Remove the E-clip and flat washer from the thermo-wax valve linkage, then slide the linkage past the fast idle cam.

NOTE: Be careful not to bend the linkage or the fast idle speed will be changed.

3. While holding open the throttle, turn the fast idle cam counterclockwise until the fast idle lever is on the third step.

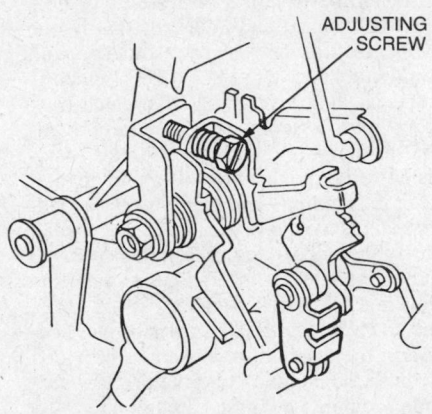

Idle speed adjustment on the dual Keihin sidedraft carburetors

4. Without touching the throttle, start the engine and check the idle speed. The idle speed should be 2,000 rpm. Adjustment of the idle speed can be made by turning the fast idle adjusting screw.

5. Stop the engine and reconnect the thermo-wax valve linkage.

6. Start the engine and check that as the engine warms up, the idle speed decreases.

NOTE: If the idle speed doesn't drop, clean the linkage along with the carburetor. If the speed still doesn't drop, check for damaged or stuck linkage.

CHOKE ADJUSTMENT

1237cc Models

The choke valve should be fully open when the choke knob is pushed in, and fully closed with the choke knob pulled out. The choke valve is held in the fully closed position by

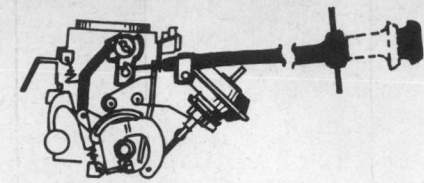

Choke adjustment—1237 cc engines

spring action. Pull the choke knob to the fully closed position and open and close the choke valve by rotating the choke valve shaft. The movement should be free and unrestricted.

If adjustment is required, adjust the cable length by loosening the cable clamp bolt.

PRECISION ADJUSTMENT

1. Using a wire gauge, check the primary throttle valve opening when the choke valve is fully closed. The opening should be 0.050–0.066 in. (1.28–1.68mm).

2. If the opening is out of specification, adjust it by bending the choke rod. After installing, make sure that the highest fast idle speed is 2500–2800 rpm while the engine is warm.

NOTE: When adjusting the fast idle speed, be sure the throttle adjusting screw does not contact the stop.

1487 and 1600cc CVCC Models
1978–79

1. Push the choke actuator rod towards the diaphragm, so it does not contact the choke valve linkage.

2. Pull the choke knob out to the first detent (click) position from the dash. With the knob in this position, check the distance between the choke butterfly valve and the venturi opening with a 3/16 in. drill (shank end).

3. Adjust as necessary by bending the relief lever adjusting tang with needle nose pliers.

4. Now, pull out the choke knob to its second detent position from the dash. Again, make sure the choke actuator rod does not contact the choke valve linkage.

5. With the choke knob in this position, check that the clearance between the butterfly valve and venturi opening is 1/8 in. using the shank end of a 1/8 in. drill.

6. Adjust as necessary by bending the stop tab for the choke butterfly linkage.

1335, 1487 (1980–83) and 1751cc Models

The choke plate should close to less than 3 mm (1/8 in.) clearance when the engine is cold (ignition on) on models with the automatic choke.

1. Remove the choke cover (3 screws) and check free movement of the linkage. Repair or replace as necessary.

2. Install the choke cover and adjust so that the index marks on the cover and ther-

1. Stop tab
2. Relief lever adjusting tang
3. Actuator rod
4. Choke opener diaphragm

CVCC choke adjustment components

mostat body align. If the choke still does not close properly, replace the cover and retest.

CHOKE CABLE ADJUSTMENT

NOTE: Perform the adjustment only after the throttle plate opening has been set.

1237cc Models

Turn the adjusting nut until there is zero clearance between the choke lever and stay plate. The choke should be fully closed when the knob is pulled all the way out, and fully opened when the knob is pushed all the way in.

All 1487cc CVCC Civics

1. Remove the air cleaner assembly.
2. Push the choke knob all the way in at the dash. Check that the choke butterfly valve (choke plate) is fully open (vertical).
3. Next, have a friend pull out the choke knob while you observe the action of the butterfly valve. When the choke knob is pulled out to the second detent position, the butterfly valve should just close. Then, when the choke knob is pulled all the way out, the butterfly valve should remain in the closed position.
4. To adjust, loosen the choke cable locknut and rotate the adjusting nut so that with the choke knob pushed flush against

the dash (open position), the butterfly valve just rests against its positioning stop tab. Tighten the locknut.

5. If the choke butterfly valve is notchy in operation, or if it does not close properly, check the butterfly valve and shaft for binding. Check also the operation of the return spring.

ACCELERATOR PUMP ADJUSTMENT

1237cc Models

Check the pump for smooth operation. See if fuel squirts out of the pump nozzle by

operating the pump lever or the throttle lever. When the pump is operated slowly, fuel must squirt out until the pump comes to the end of its travel. If the pump is defective, check for clogging or a defective piston. Adjust the pump by either repositioning the end of the connecting rod arm in the pump lever, or the arm itself.

1487 and 1600cc CVCC Models 1978–79

1. Remove the air cleaner assembly.
2. Check that the distance between the tang at the end of the accelerator pump lever and the lever stop at the edge of the throttle body is 0.57–0.6 in. (14.5–15.1 mm). This corresponds to effective pump lever travel.
3. To adjust, bend the pump lever tang in the required direction.
4. Install the air cleaner.

1335, 1487 (1980–83) and 1751cc Models

1. Remove the air cleaner.
2. Make sure that the pump shaft is moving freely throughout the pump stroke.
3. Check that the pump lever is in contact with the pump shaft.
4. Measure between the bottom end of the pump lever and the lever stop tang. The gap should be $9/16$ to $19/32$ inch (through 1980), $29/64$ to $31/64$ inch (1981 and later). If not, bend the tang to adjust.

MANUAL TRANSAXLE

REMOVAL & INSTALLATION

Four and Five Speed Except Prelude and Civic (1980 and Later)

1. Disconnect the battery ground cable at the battery and the transmission case.

1. Choke butterfly valve
2. Adjusting nut
3. Locknut

CVCC choke cable adjustment

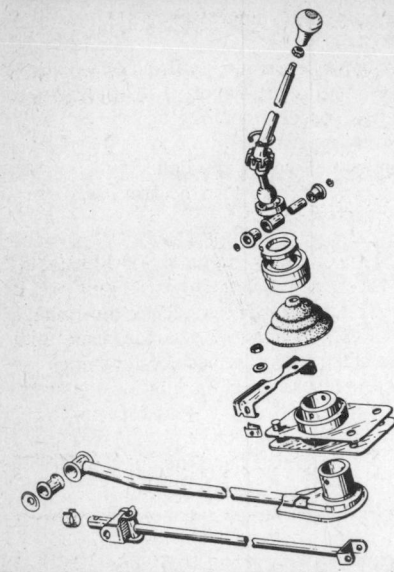

Exploded view of the gearshift mechanism

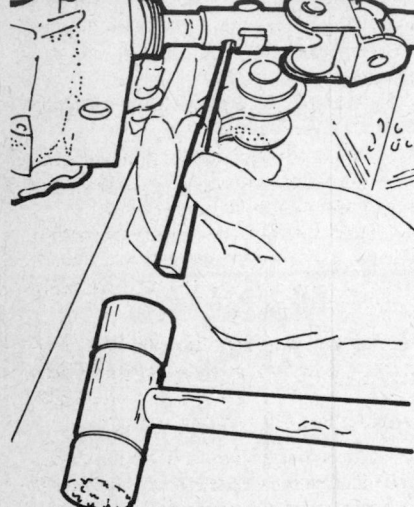

Driving out the gearshift rod pin

Unlock the steering column; place the transmission in neutral.

2. Drain the transmission.

3. Raise the front of the car and support it with safety stands.

4. Remove the front wheels.

5. Remove the starter motor positive battery cable and the solenoid wire. Then remove the starter.

6. Disconnect the following cables and wires:

    a. Clutch cable at the release arm (Civics) (Accord 1982 and later);

    b. Back-up light switch wires;

    c. TCS (Transmission Controlled Spark) switch wires;

    d. Speedometer cable;

    e. Hydraulic hose at slave cylinder (Accord 78–81).

CAUTION

When removing the speedometer cable from the transmission, it is not necessary to remove the entire cable holder. Remove the end boot (gear holder seal), the cable retaining clip and then pull the cable out of the holder. In no way should you disturb the holder, unless it is absolutely necessary. For further details, see the Engine Removal section.

---

7. Disconnect the left and right lower ball joints at the knuckle, using a ball joint remover.

8. Pull on the brake disc and remove the left and right driveshafts from the differential case.

9. Drive out the gearshift rod pin (8 mm) with a drift and disconnect the rod at the transmission case.

10. Disconnect the gearshift extension at the clutch housing.

11. Screw in the engine hanger bolts (see the "Engine Removal" section) to the engine torque rod bolt hole and to the hole just to the left of the distributor. Hook a chain onto the bolts and lift the engine just enough to take the load off the engine mounts.

12. After making sure that the engine is properly supported, remove the two center beam-to-lower engine mount nuts. Next, remove the center beam, followed by the lower engine mount.

13. Reinstall the center beam (without mount) and lower the engine until it rests on the beam.

14. Place a jack under the transmission and loosen the 4 attaching bolts. Using the jack to support the transmission, slide it away from the engine and lower the jack until the transmission clears the car.

15. To install, reverse the removal procedure. Be sure to pay attention to the following points:

    a. Tighten all mounting nuts and bolts.

    b. Use a new shift rod pin;

    c. After installing the driveshafts, attempt to move the inner joint housing in and out of the differential housing. If it moves easily, the driveshaft end clips should be replaced;

    d. Make sure that the control cables and wires are properly connected;

    e. Be sure the transmission is refilled to the proper level.

Prelude and Civic (1980 and later)

1. Disconnect the battery ground.

2. Unlock the steering and place the transmission in neutral.

3. Disconnect the following wires in the engine compartment:

    a. battery positive cable

    b. black/white wire from the solenoid

    c. temperature gauge sending unit wire

    d. ignition timing thermo-sensor wire

    e. back-up light switch

    f. distributor wiring

    g. transmission ground cable.

4. Unclip and remove the speedometer cable at the transmission. *Do not disassemble the speedometer gear holder!*

5. Remove the clutch slave cylinder with the hydraulic line attached, or disconnect the clutch cable at the release arm.

6. Remove the side and top starter mounting bolts. Loosen the front wheel lug nuts. Remove the front wheels.

7. Raise and support the car.

8. Drain the transmission.

9. Remove the splash shields from the underside.

10. Remove the stabilizer bar.

11. Disconnect the left and right lower ball joints and tie rod ends, using a ball joint remover.

CAUTION

In 1984 and later Civics use caution when removing the ball joints. Place a floor jack under the lower control arm securely at the ball joint. Otherwise, the lower control arm may "jump" suddenly away from the steering knuckle as the ball joint is removed.

---

12. Turn the right steering knuckle out as far as it will go. Place a prybar against

Engine center mount nuts

the inboard CV joint, pry the right axle out of the transmission about ½ inch. This will force the spring clip out of the groove inside the differential gear splines. Pull it out the rest of the way. Repeat this procedure on the other side.

13. Disconnect the shift lever torque rod from the clutch housing.

14. Remove the bolt from the shift rod clevis.

15. Raise the transmission jack securely against the transmission to take up the weight.

16. Remove the engine torque rods and brackets.

17. Remove the remaining starter mounting bolts and take out the starter.

18. Remove the remaining transmission mounting bolts and the upper bolt from the engine damper bracket.

19. Start backing the transmission away from the engine and remove the two lower damper bolts.

20. Pull the transmission clear of the engine and lower the jack.

21. To ease installation, fabricate two 14 mm diameter dowel pins and install them in the clutch housing.

22. Raise the transmission and slide it onto the dowels. Slide the transmission into position aligning the mainshaft splines with the clutch plate.

23. Attach the damper lower bolts when the positioning allows. Tighten both bolts until the clutch housing is seated against the block.

24. Install two lower mounting bolts and torque them to 33 ft. lbs.

25. Install the front and rear torque rod brackets. Torque the front torque rod bolts to 54 ft. lbs., the front bracket bolts to 33 ft. lbs., the rear torque rod bolts to 54 ft. lbs. and the rear bracket bolts to 47 ft. lbs.

26. Remove the transmission jack.

27. Install the starter and torque the mounting bolts to 33 ft. lbs.

28. Turn the right steering knuckle out far enough to fit the end into the transmission. Use new 26 mm spring clips on both axles. Repeat procedure for the other side.

— CAUTION —
Make sure that the axles bottom fully so that you feel the spring clip engage the differential.

29. Install the lower ball joints. Torque the nuts to 32 ft. lbs.

30. Install the tie rods. Torque the nuts to 32 ft. lbs.

31. Connect the shift linkage.

32. Connect the shift lever torque rod to the clutch housing and torque the bolt to 7 ft. lbs.

33. Install the stabilizer bar.

34. Install the lower shields.

35. Install the front wheels and torque the lugs to specifications.

36. Install the remaining starter bolts and torque to 33 ft. lbs.

37. Install the clutch slave cylinder or install the clutch cable at the release arm.

38. Install the speedometer cable using a new O-ring coated with clean engine oil.

39. Connect all engine compartment wiring.

40. Fill the transmission with SAE 10W-40 engine oil.

OVERHAUL

For all overhaul procedures, please refer to "Manual Transaxle Overhaul" in the Unit Repair section.

Halfshaft (Driveshaft)

REMOVAL & INSTALLATION

The front driveshaft assembly consists of a sub-axle shaft and a driveshaft with two universal joints.

A constant velocity ball joint is used for both universal joints, which are factory-packed with special grease and enclosed in sealed rubber boots. The outer joint cannot be disassembled except for removal of the boot.

1. Remove the hubcap from the front wheel and then remove the center cap.

2. Pull out the 4 mm cotter pin (if so equipped) and loosen, but do not remove, the spindle nut.

3. Raise the front of the car and support it with safety stands.

4. Remove the wheel lug nuts and then the wheel.

5. Remove the spindle nut.

6. Drain the transmission.

7. Remove the lower arm ball joints at the knuckle by using a ball joint remover.

— CAUTION —
On 1984 and later Civic models, make sure that a floor jack is positioned securely under the lower control arm, at the ball joint. Otherwise, the lower control arm may "jump" suddenly away from the steering knuckle as the ball joint is removed.

On 1983 and later Prelude models, remove the damper fork bolt and damper locking bolt. Remove the damper fork.

8. To remove the driveshaft, hold the front hub and pull it toward you. Then slide the driveshaft out of the front hub. Pry the CV-joint out about ½ in. Pull the inboard joint side of the driveshaft out of the differential case.

9. To install, reverse the removal procedure. If either the inboard or outboard joint boot bands have been removed for inspection or disassembly of the joint (only the inboard joint can be disassembled), be sure to repack the joint with a sufficient amount of bearing grease.

— CAUTION —
Make sure the CV joint sub-axle bottoms so that the spring clip may hold the sub-axle securely in the transmission.

CV–JOINT OVERHAUL

For all overhual procedures, please refer to "CV–Joint Overhaul" in the Unit Repair section.

SHIFT LINKAGE ADJUSTMENT

The Honda shift linkage is non-adjustable. However, if the linkage is binding, or if there is excessive play, check the linkage bushings and pivot points. Lubricate with light oil, or replace worn bushings as necessary.

CLUTCH

All models use a single dry disc with a diaphragm spring type pressure plate. The Civic, the (1982 and later) Accord and the (1983 and later) Prelude clutch is cable operated. However, on the Accord (1978–81) and Prelude (1979–82), a hydraulic master and slave cylinder system is used.

REMOVAL & INSTALLATION

1. Follow the transaxle removal procedure, previously given. Matchmark the flywheel and clutch for reassembly.

2. Hold the flywheel ring gear with a tool made for the purpose, remove the retaining bolts and remove the pressure plate and clutch disc.

NOTE: Loosen the retaining bolts two turns at a time in a circular pattern. Removing one bolt while the rest are tight may warp the diaphragm spring.

3. The flywheel can now be removed, if it needs repairing or replacing. Inspect it for scoring and wear, and reface or replace as necessary. Torque to the specifications shown in the "Torque Specification" chart. Tighten in a criss-cross pattern.

4. To separate the pressure plate from the diaphragm spring, remove the 4 retracting clips.

5. To remove the release, or throwout bearing, first straighten the locking tab and remove the 8 mm bolt, followed by the release shaft and release arm with the bearing attached.

NOTE: It is recommended that the release bearing be removed after the release arm has been removed from the casing. Trying to remove or install the bearing with the release arm in the case will damage the retaining clip.

6. If a new release bearing is to be installed, separate the bearing from the holder, using a bearing drift.

7. To assemble and install the clutch, reverse the removal procedure. Be sure to pay attention to the following points:
   a. Make sure that the flywheel and the

end of the crankshaft are clean before assembling;

b. When installing the pressure plate, align the mark on the outer edge of the flywheel with the alignment mark on the pressure plate. Failure to align these marks will result in imbalance.

c. When tightening the pressure plate bolts, use a pilot shaft to center the friction disc. The pilot shaft can be bought at any large auto supply store or fabricated from a wooden dowel. After centering the disc, tighten the bolts two turns at a time, in a criss-cross pattern to avoid warping the diaphragm springs; tighten to 7 ft. lbs.;

d. When installing the release shaft and arm, place a lock tab washer under the retaining bolt;

e. When installing the transmission, make sure that the mainshaft is properly aligned with the disc spline and the aligning pins are in place, before tightening the case bolts (17–22 ft. lbs.).

PEDAL HEIGHT ADJUSTMENT

Civic

1978–79

Check the clutch pedal height and if necessary, adjust the upper stop, so that the clutch and brake pedals rest at approximately the same height from the floor. First, be sure that the brake pedal free-play is properly adjusted.

1980–81

The pedal height should be $1\frac{3}{16}$ in. minimum from the floor.

Accord (1978–81) and Prelude (1979–82)

1. Pedal height should be 184 mm (7.24 in.) measured from the front of the pedal to the floorboard (mat removed).

2. Adjust by turning the pedal stop bolt in or out until height is correct. Tighten the locknut after adjustment.

FREE-PLAY ADJUSTMENT

Civic, Accord (1982 and Later) and Prelude (1983 and Later)

Adjust the clutch release lever so that it has 0.12–0.16 in. (3–4 mm) through 1980, $\frac{7}{16}$–$\frac{9}{16}$ in. (4.4–5.4 mm) 1981–83 or $\frac{5}{32}$–$\frac{13}{64}$ in. (4.0–5.0 mm) 1984 and later for Civics; $\frac{1}{5}$–$\frac{1}{4}$ in. (5.2–6.4 mm) for all 1982 and later Accords and 1983 and later Preludes, of play when you move the clutch release lever at the transmission with your hand. Or 15–20 mm (0.6–0.8 in.) through 1979 or 10–30 mm ($\frac{3}{8}$–$\frac{13}{16}$ in.) 1980 and later Civics and 1982–83 Accords or 23–28 mm ($\frac{7}{8}$–$1\frac{1}{8}$ in.) 1984 and later Accords, and 1983 and later Prelude, at the pedal. This adjustment is made at the outer cable housing adjuster, near the release lever on all models except the 1487 cc engine (through 1979). Less than $\frac{1}{8}$ in. of free-play may lead to clutch slippage, while more than $\frac{1}{8}$ in. clearance may cause difficult shifting.

—— CAUTION ——
Make sure that the upper and lower adjusting nuts are tightened after adjustments.

On 1487cc models through 1979, the free-play adjustment is made on the cable at the firewall. Remove the C-clip and then rotate the threaded control cable housing until there is sufficient free-play at the release lever.

Accord (1978–81) and Prelude (1979–82)

1. Free-play should measure 2.0–2.6 mm (0.08–0.1 in.) at the clutch release fork.

2. Adjust by loosening the locknut on the slave cylinder pushrod. Turn the pushrod in or out to adjust. Standard adjustment is made by turning the pushrod in until all play is removed, then backing out the pushrod $1\frac{3}{4}$–2 turns to achieve specified free-play. Tighten the locknut after adjustment.

Clutch Master Cylinder

REMOVAL & INSTALLATION

Accord (1978–81) and Prelude (1979–82)

1. The clutch master cylinder is located on the firewall in the engine compartment next to the brake master cylinder. Remove the hydraulic line. Either plug the port to prevent leakage or drain the reservoir prior to removing the hydraulic line.

2. Remove the cotter pin which retains the pivot pin in the yoke of the pushrod (under the instrument panel at the clutch pedal).

3. Detach the pushrod from the clutch pedal.

4. Remove the two bolts retaining the master cylinder to the firewall. Remove the master cylinder.

5. Installation is the reverse. Bleed the system after installation.

OVERHAUL

1. Remove the snap ring which retains the stopper plate. Note the installed position of the stopper plate before removal.

2. Apply compressed air to the inlet port to remove the piston assembly. Note the order of all components.

3. Check the cylinder bore for corrosion or wear. Light scores or scratches can be removed with crocus cloth or a brake cylinder hone. The cylinder should be replaced if heavily worn.

4. Replace the piston and spring with new ones. Reassemble in correct order. Coat the inside of the cylinder and the piston with clean brake fluid before installation.

5. Install the cylinder and bleed the system.

Clutch Slave Cylinder

REMOVAL & INSTALLATION

Accord (1978–81) and Prelude (1979–82)

1. The slave cylinder is retained by two bolts. Disconnect and plug the hydraulic line at the slave cylinder and remove the two mounting bolts. Remove the return spring and remove the slave cylinder.

2. Installation is the reverse. Bleed the system after installation.

Accord slave cylinder locknut and adjusting nut

OVERHAUL

1. Apply compressed air to the inlet port to remove the piston and seal.

2. Inspect the cylinder bore for pitting, corrosion, or wear. Replace the cylinder if worn.

3. Coat the parts with clean brake fluid and reassemble.

CLUTCH HYDRAULIC SYSTEM BLEEDING

Accord (1978–81) and Prelude (1979–82)

The hydraulic system must be bled whenever the system has been leaking or dismantled. The bleed screw is located on the slave cylinder.

1. Remove the bleed screw dust cap.

2. Attach a clear hose to the bleed screw. Immerse the other end of the hose in a clear jar half filled with brake fluid.

3. Fill the clutch master cylinder with fresh brake fluid.

4. Open the bleed screw slightly and have an assistant slowly depress the clutch pedal. Close the bleed screw when the pedal reaches the end of its travel. Allow the clutch pedal to return slowly.

5. Repeat Steps 3 and 4 until all air bubbles are expelled from the system.

6. Discard the brake fluid in the jar. Replace the dust cap. Refill the master cylinder.

AUTOMATIC TRANSAXLE

REMOVAL & INSTALLATION

The automatic transmission is removed in the same basic manner as the manual transmission. The following exceptions should be noted during automatic transmission removal and installation.

1. Remove the center console and control rod pin.
2. Remove the front floor center mat and control cable bracket nuts.
3. Jack and support the front of the car
4. Remove the two selector lever bracket nuts at front side.
5. Loosen the bolts securing the control cable holder and support beam and disconnect the control cable.
6. Disconnect the transmission cooler lines at the transmission.
7. Remove the throttle control cable, by loosening only the lower cable locknut. Otherwise the transmission shift points will be changed.
8. Remove the engine [to transmission] mounts and torque converter case cover.
9. Remove the starter motor and separate the transmission from the engine.
10. Installation of the automatic transmission is the reverse of removal. Close attention should be paid to the following points.
11. Be sure that the stator hub is correctly located and moves smoothly. The stator shaft can be used for this purpose.
12. Align the stator, stator shaft, main shaft and torque converter turbine serrations.
13. After installation of the engine-transmission unit in car, make all required adjustments.

Shift Lever

INSPECTION

1. Pull up fully on the parking brake lever and run the engine at idle speed, while depressing the brake pedal.

— CAUTION —
Be sure to check continually for car movement.

2. By moving the shift selector lever slowly forward and backward from the "N" position, make sure that the distance between the "N" and the points where the D clutch is engaged for the "2" and "R" positions are the same. The D clutch en-

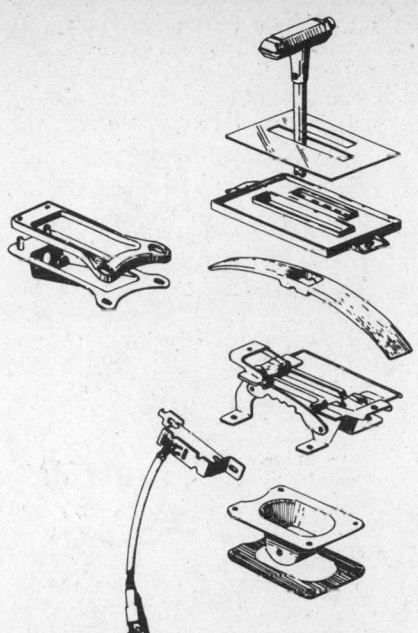

Exploded view of Hondamatic gearshift mechanism

gaging point is just before the slight response is felt. The reverse gears will make a noise when the clutch engages. If the distances are not the same, then adjustment is necessary.

ADJUSTMENT

1. Remove the center console retaining screws, and pull away the console to expose the shift control cable and turnbuckle.

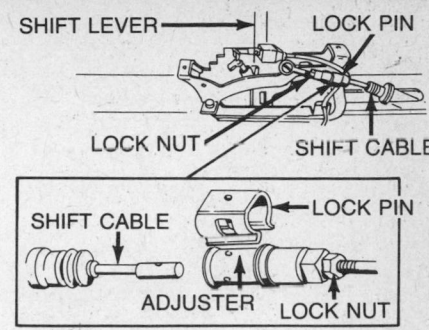

Automatic shift lever adjustment

2. Adjust the length of the control cable by removing the lock pin, (if so equipped) loosening the lock nut and turning the turnbuckle, located at the front bottom of the shift lever assembly. After adjustment, the cable and turnbuckle should twist toward the left (driver's) side of the car when shifted toward the "R" position and toward the right-side when shifted into the "2" position. The hole in the cable end should be perfectly aligned with the holes in the selector lever bracket (pin removed).

REAR SUSPENSION

All Civic sedan, hatchback and 1984 and later station wagon models and the Accord and Prelude utilize an independent MacPherson strut arrangement for each rear

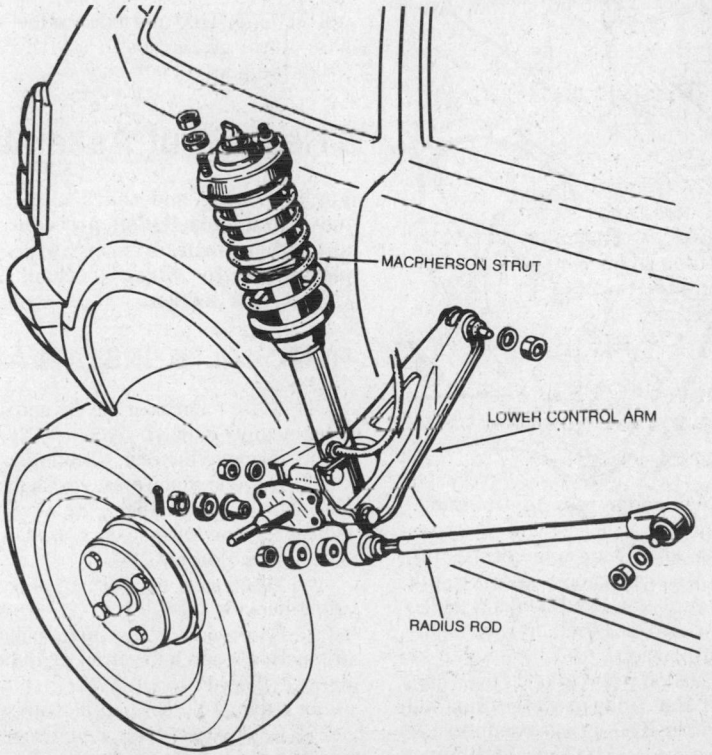

Civic sedan and hatchback rear suspension through 1979

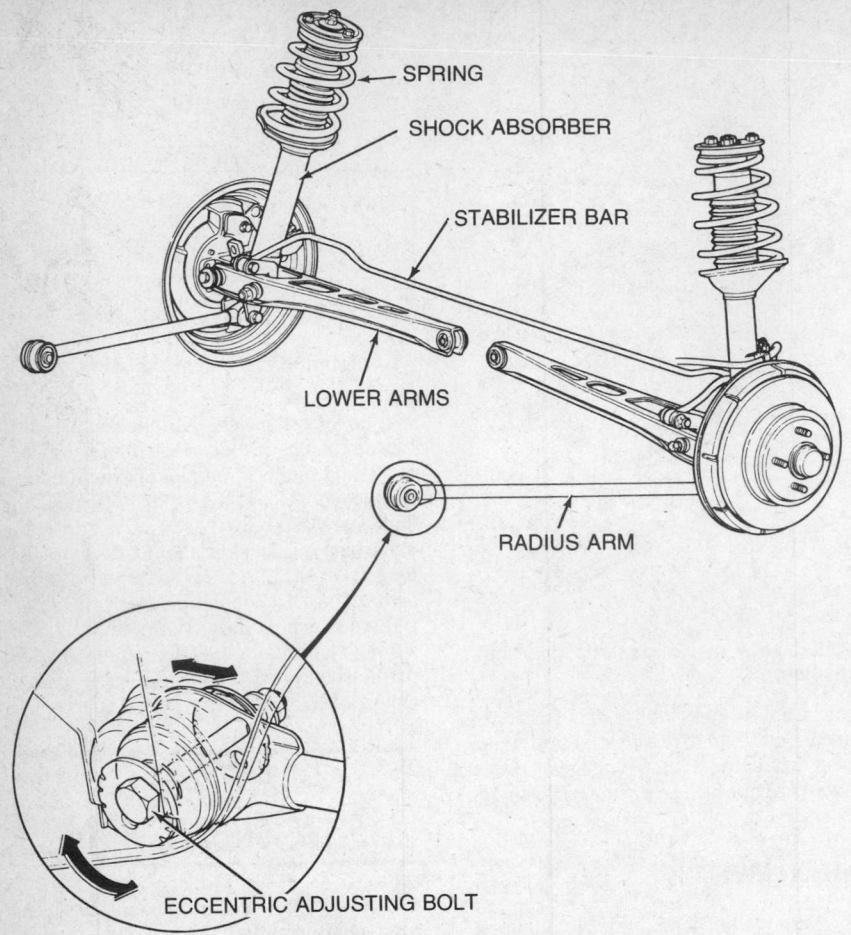

ECCENTRIC ADJUSTING BOLT

Rear suspension—Accord and Prelude 1983 and later

1978–83 Civic sedan rear control arm

wheel. Each suspension unit consists of a combined oil spring/shock absorber strut, a lower control arm, and a radius rod or arm. The Accord and Prelude have adjustable rear suspension.

1978–83 station wagon models use a more conventional leaf spring rear suspension with a solid rear axle. The springs are three-leaf, semi-elliptic types located longitudinally with a pair of telescopic shock absorbers to con-

trol rebound. The solid axle and leaf springs allow for a greater load carrying capacity for the wagon.

Rear Strut Assembly

For all spring and shock absorber removal and installation procedures and any other strut overhaul procedures, please refer to "Strut Overhaul" in the Unit Repair section.

REMOVAL & INSTALLATION

1. Raise the rear of the car and support it with safety stands.
2. Remove the rear wheel.
3. Disconnect the brake line at the shock absorber (if so equipped). Remove the retaining clip and separate the brake hose from the shock absorber.
4. Disconnect the parking brake cable at the backing plate lever.
5. Remove the lower strut retaining bolt or pinch bolt and hub carrier pivot bolt. To remove the pivot bolt, you first have to remove the castle nut and its cotter pin.
6. Remove the upper strut retaining nuts and remove the strut from the car.
7. To install, reverse the removal pro-

cedure. Be sure to install the top of the strut in the body first. After installation, bleed the brake lines.

Lower Control Arm and Radius Arm

REMOVAL & INSTALLATION
Except 1978–83 Station Wagon

1. Raise the rear of the car and support it with safety stands.
2. Remove the rear wheels and brake drums.
3. Disconnect the hydraulic brake line and parking brake cable.
4. Remove the backing plate assembly.
5. Remove the radius arm nuts and bolts, and remove the radius arm. Unscrew the stabilizer bolt and remove the stabilizer bar (if so equipped).
6. Remove the shock absorber pinch bolt, then separate the hub carrier from the shock absorber.
7. Remove the lower control arm retaining bolts, then remove the arm.

Rear Wheel Alignment

Caster and camber are fixed as on the front suspension. However, toe-out is adjustable (except 1984 and later Civics) by means of an eccentric adjusting bolt at the forward anchor of the radius rod.

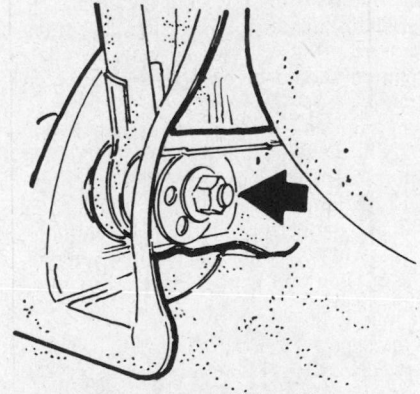

Rear toe adjustment location—1978–82 Accord

Leaf Spring

REMOVAL & INSTALLATION
1978–83 Station Wagon Only

1. Raise the rear of the car and support it on stands placed on the frame. Remove the wheels.
2. Remove the shock absorber lower mounting bolt.
3. Remove the nuts from the U-bolt and remove the U-bolts, bump rubber, and clamp bracket.

4. Unbolt the front and rear spring shackle bolts, remove the bolts, and remove the spring.

5. To install, first position the spring on the axle and install the front and rear shackle bolts. Apply a soapy water solution to the bushings to ease installation. Do not tighten the shackle nuts yet.

6. Install the U-bolts, spring clamp bracket and bump rubber loosely on the axle and spring.

7. Install the wheels and lower the car. Tighten the front and rear shackle bolts to 33 ft. lbs. Also tighten the U-bolt nuts to 33 ft. lbs., after the shackle bolts have been tightened.

8. Install the shock absorber to the lower mount. Tighten to 33 ft. lbs.

Shock Absorbers

REMOVAL & INSTALLATION

1978–83 Station Wagon Only

1. It is not necessary to jack the car or remove the wheels unless you require working clearance. Unbolt the upper mounting nut and lower bolt and remove the shock absorber. Note the position of the washers and lock washers upon removal.

2. Installation is the reverse. Be sure the washers and lock washers are installed correctly. Tighten the upper mount to 44 ft. lbs. and the lower mount to 33 ft. lbs.

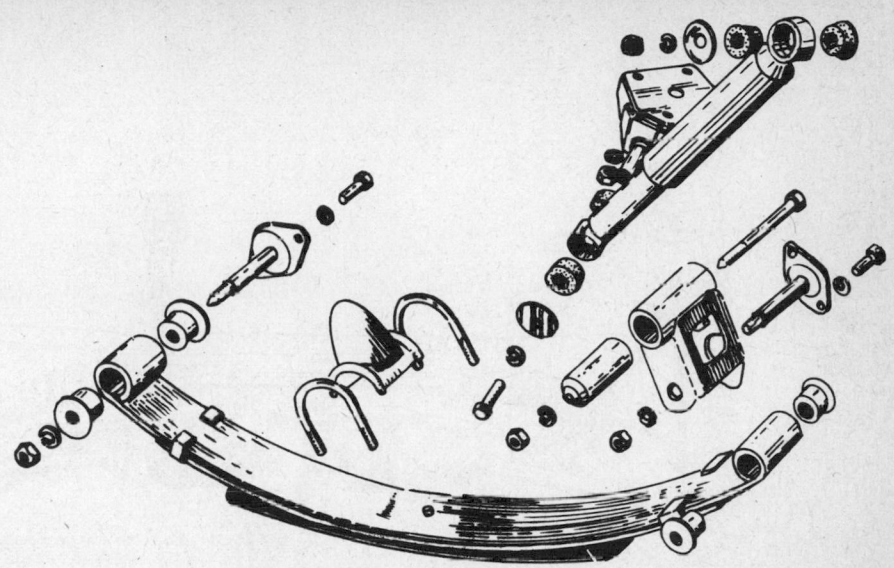
Rear suspension—station wagon 1978–83

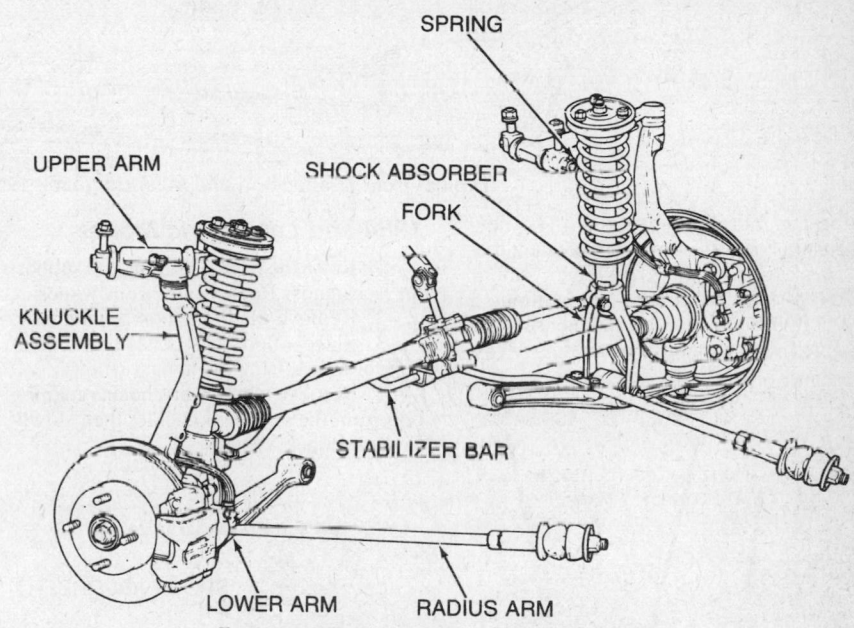
Front suspension—1983 and later Prelude

FRONT SUSPENSION

All models except the 1983 and later Prelude, and the 1984 and later Civic models use a MacPherson strut type front suspension. Each steering knuckle is suspended by a lower control arm at the bottom and a combined coil spring/shock absorber unit at the top. A front stabilizer bar, mounted between each lower control arm and the body, doubles as a locating rod for the suspension. Caster and camber are not adjustable and are fixed by the location of the strut assemblies in their respective sheet metal towers.

The 1983 and later Prelude uses a completely redesigned front suspension. A double wishbone system, the lower wishbone consists of a forged transverse link with a locating stabilizer bar. The lower end of the shock absorber has a fork shape to allow the driveshaft to pass through it. The upper arm is located in the wheel well and is twist mounted, angled forward from its inner mount, to clear the shock absorber.

The 1984 and later Civic models also use a redesigned front suspension. This change was made to lower the hood line, thus mak-

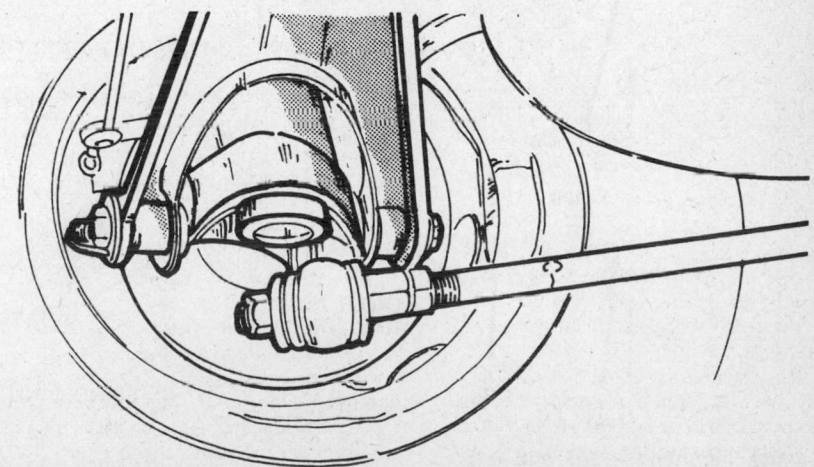
Rear toe adjustment location—Civic 1978–83

Typical front suspension and steering gear—1978–82

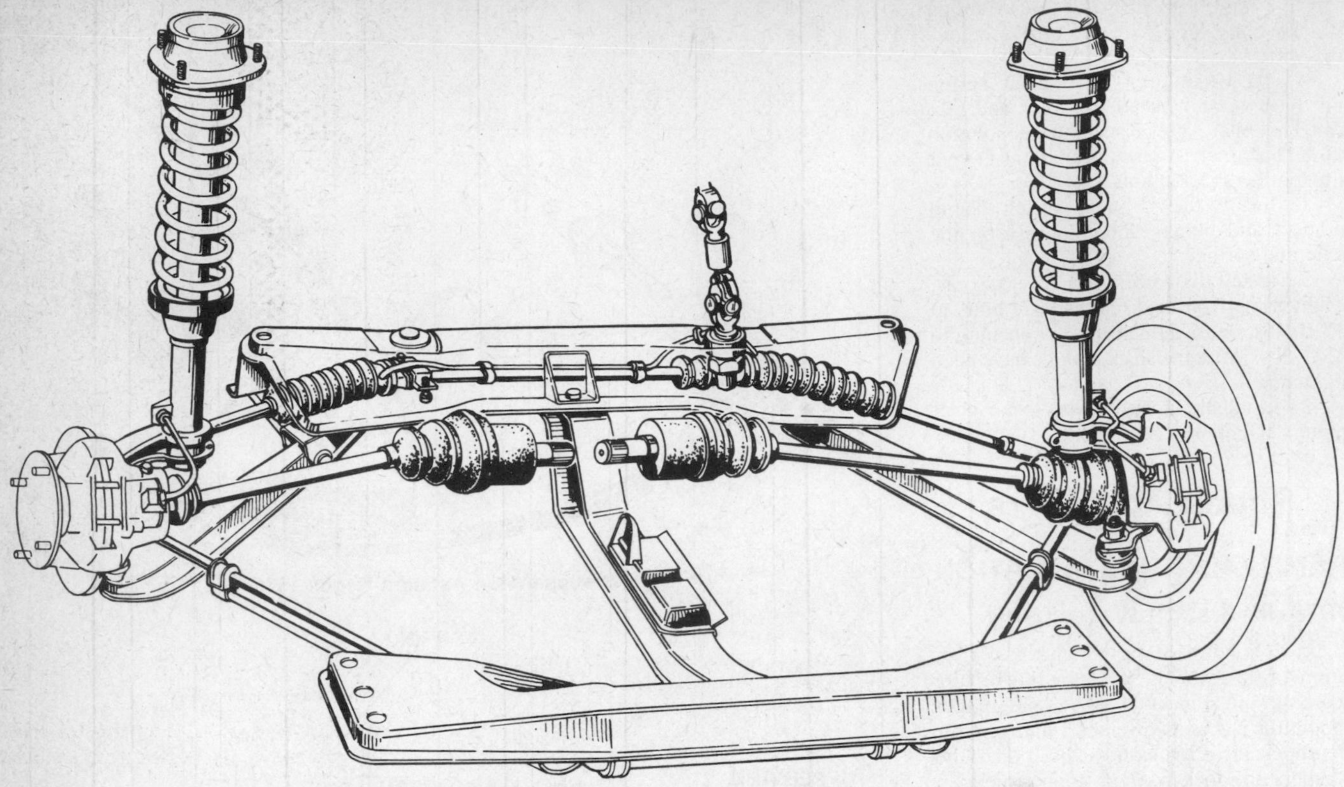

ing the car more aero-dynamic. The new suspension consists of two independent torsion bars and front shock absorbers similar to a front strut assembly, but without a spring. Both lower forged radius arms are connected with a stabilizer bar.

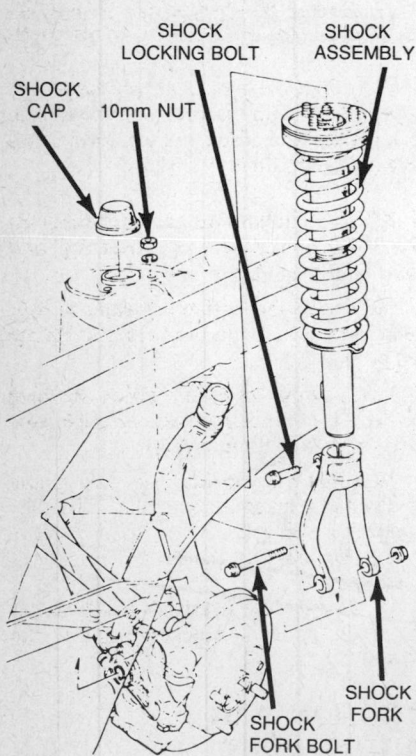

Front shock mounting—1983 and later Prelude

1984 and Later Civic Models

1. Raise the front of the car and support on jackstands. Remove the front wheels.
2. Remove the brake hose clamp bolt.
3. Place a floor jack beneath the lower control arm to support it.
4. Remove the lower shock retaining bolt from the steering knuckle, then slowly lower the jack.

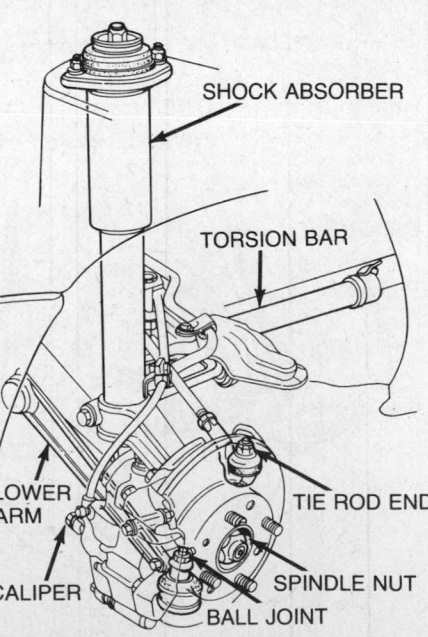

Front suspension—1984 and later Civic

Shock Absorbers

REMOVAL & INSTALLATION

1983 and Later Prelude

1. Raise the front of the car and support on jackstands. Remove the front wheels.
2. Remove the shock absorber locking bolt.
3. Remove the shock fork bolt and remove the shock fork.
4. Remove the shock absorber assembly.

NOTE: For spring and shock absorber disassembly procedures, please refer to "Strut Overhaul" in the Unit Repair section.

5. Installation is the reverse of the removal procedure, taking note of the following:
   a. Align the shock absorber aligning tab with the slot in the shock absorber fork.
   b. The mounting base bolt should be tightened with the weight of the car placed on the shock.
   c. Torque the upper mounting bolts to 29 ft. lbs., the shock locking bolt to 32 ft. lbs. and the shock fork bolt to 47 ft. lbs.

— **CAUTION** —
Be sure the jack is positioned securely beneath the lower control arm at the ball joint. Otherwise, the tension from the torsion bar may cause the lower control arm to suddenly "jump" away from the shock absorber as the pinch bolt is removed.

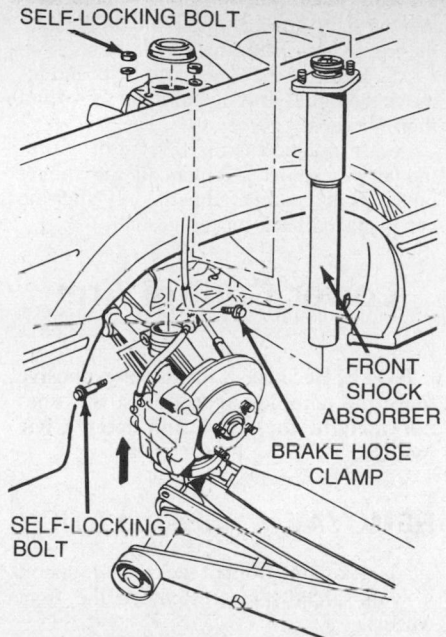

Front shock mounting—1984 and later Civic

5. Compress the shock absorber by hand, then remove the two upper lock nuts and remove from the car.

6. Installation is the reverse of the removal procedure, taking note of the following:

a. Use new self locking nuts on the top of the shock assembly and torque to 28 ft. lbs.

b. Tighten the lower pinch bolt to 47 ft. lbs.

c. Install and tighten the brake hose clamp to 16 ft. lbs.

Strut Assembly

For all spring and shock absorber removal and installation procedures and any other strut overhaul procedures, please refer to "Strut Overhaul" in the Unit Repair section.

INSPECTION

1. Check for wear or damage to bushings and needle bearings.

2. Check for oil leaks from the struts.

3. Check all rubber parts for wear or damage.

4. Bounce the car to check shock absorber effectiveness. The car should continue to bounce for no more than two cycles.

REMOVAL & INSTALLATION

1. Raise the front of the car and support it with safety stands. Remove the front wheels.

2. Disconnect the brake pipe at the strut and remove the brake hose retaining clip.

3. Remove the caliper and carefully hang

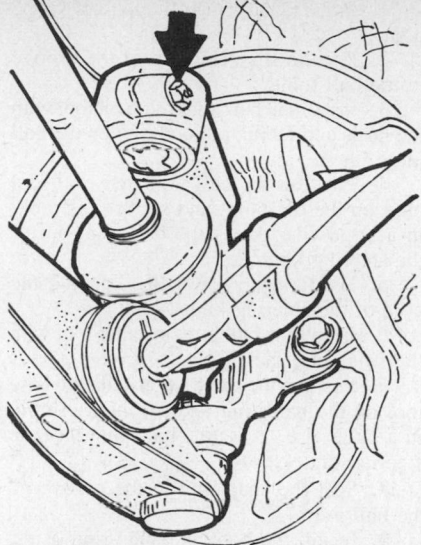

Lower strut retaining (pinch) bolt

from the undercarriage of the car with a piece of wire.

4. On Accord models, disconnect the stabilizer bar from the lower arm.

5. Loosen the bolt on the knuckle that retains the lower end of the shock absorber. Push down firmly while tapping it with a hammer until the knuckle is free of the strut.

6. Remove the three nuts retaining the upper end of the strut and remove the strut from the car.

7. To install, reverse the removal procedure. Be sure to properly match the mating surface of the strut and the knuckle notch. Tighten the knuckle bolt to 40 ft. lbs. (43-51 ft. lbs.—Accord).

Torsion Bar Assembly

REMOVAL & INSTALLATION

1984 and Later Civic Models

1. Raise the front of the car and support on jackstands.

2. Remove the height adjusting nut and the torque tube holder.

3. Remove the 33mm circlip.

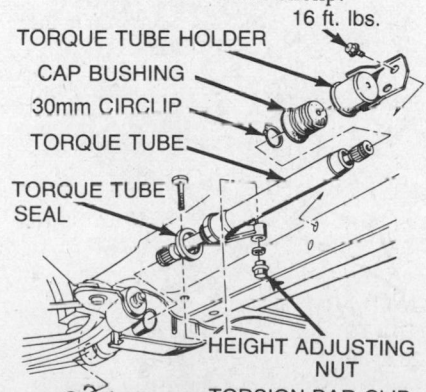

Torsion bar assembly—1984 and later Civic

Typical strut upper mounting nuts

4. Remove the torsion bar cap, then remove the torsion bar clip by tapping the bar out of the torque tube.

NOTE: The torsion bar will slide easier if you move the lower arm up and down.

5. Tap the torsion bar backward, out of the torque tube and remove the torque tube.

6. Install a new seal onto the torque tube. Coat the torque tube seal and torque with grease, then install them on the rear beam.

7. Grease the ends of the torsion bar and insert into the torque tube from the back.

8. Align the projection on the torque tube splines with the cutout in the torsion bar splines and insert the torsion bar approximately (10mm) 0.394 in.

NOTE: The torsion bar will slide easier if the lower arm is moved up and down.

9. Install the torsion bar clip and cap, then install the 30mm circlip and the torque tube cap.

NOTE: Push the torsion bar to the front so there is no clearance between the torque tube and the 30mm circlip.

10. Coat the cap bushing with grease and install it on the torque tube. Install the torque tube holder.

11. Temporarily tighten the height adjusting nut.

12. Remove the jackstands and lower the car to the ground. Adjust the torsion bar spring height.

TORSION BAR ADJUSTMENT

1. Measure the torsion bar spring height

C333

between the ground and the highest point of the wheel arch.

COUPE(CRX) 25.35 + or − 0.20in.
HATCHBACK 25.43 + or − 0.20in.
SEDAN 25.63 + or − 0.20in.
WAGON 25.55 + or − 0.20in.

2. If the spring height does not meet the specifications above, make the following adjustment.

a. Raise the front wheels off the ground.

b. Adjust the spring height by turning the height adjusting nut. Tightening the nut raises the height, and loosening the nut lowers the height.

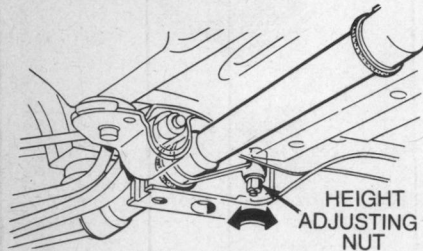

Torsion bar adjustment—1984 and later Civic

NOTE: The height varies 0.20 in. per turn of the adjusting nut.

c. Lower the front wheels to the ground, then bounce the car up and down several times and recheck the spring height to see if it is within specifications.

Lower Ball Joints

INSPECTION

Check ball joint play as follows:

a. Raise the front of the car and support it with safety stands.

b. Clamp a dial indicator onto the lower control arm and place the indicator tip on the knuckle, near the ball joint;

c. Place a pry bar between the lower control arm and the knuckle. Replace the lower control arm if the play exceeds 0.020 in.

REMOVAL & INSTALLATION

All Except the 1983 and Later Prelude

If the ball joint play exceeds 0.020 in. the ball joint and lower control arm or lower radius arm (1984 and later Civics) must be replaced as an assembly.

1983 and Later Prelude

NOTE: This procedure is performed after the removal of the steering knuckle and requires the use of the following special tools or their equivalent: Honda part no. 07965-SB00100 Ball Joint Remover/ Installer, 07965-SB00200 Ball Joint Removal Base, 07965-SB00300 Ball Joint Installation Base, and 07974-SA50700 Clip Guide Tool.

1. Pry the snap-ring off and remove the boot.

2. Pry the snap-ring out of the groove in the ball joint.

3. Install the ball joint removal tool with the large end facing out and tighten the ball joint nut.

4. Position the ball joint removal tool base on the ball joint and set the assembly in a large vise. Press the ball joint out of the steering knuckle.

5. Position the new ball joint into the hole of the steering knuckle.

6. Install the ball joint installer tool with the small end facing out.

7. Position the ball joint installation base tool on the ball joint and set the assembly in a large vise. Press the ball joint into the steering knuckle.

8. Seat the snap-ring in the groove of the ball joint.

9. Install the boot and snap-ring using the clip guide tool.

Radius Arm

REMOVAL & INSTALLATION

1984 and Later Civic Models Only

1. Raise the front of the car off the ground and support on jackstands. Remove the front wheels.

2. Place a floor jack beneath the lower control arm, then remove the ball joint cotter pin and nut.

——————— CAUTION ———————
Be sure to place the jack securely beneath the lower control arm at the ball joint. Otherwise, the tension from the torsion bar may cause the arm to suddenly "jump" away from the steering knuckle as the ball joint is removed.

3. Using a ball joint remover, remove the ball joint from the steering knuckle.

4. Remove the radius arm locking nuts

STABILIZER LOCKING NUT 16 ft. lbs.
SELF LOCKING NUT 60 ft. lbs.
SELF LOCKING NUTS
LOWER ARM BOLTS 28 ft. lbs.
RADIUS ARM

Radius arm—1984 and later Civic

and the stabilizer locking nut, then separate the radius arm from the stabilizer bar.

5. Remove the lower arm bolts and remove the radius arm by pulling it down and then forward.

6. Installation is the reverse of the removal procedure. Tighten all the rubber bushings and dampered parts only after the car is placed back on the ground.

Lower Control Arm

NOTE: Because of the use of expensive tools and complex procedures, this does not include the 1984 and later Civic models.

REMOVAL & INSTALLATION

1. Raise the front of the car and support it with safety stands. Remove the front wheels.

2. Disconnect the lower arm ball joint. Be careful not to damage the seal.

3. Remove the stabilizer bar retaining brackets, starting with the center brackets.

4. Remove the lower arm pivot bolt.

5. Disconnect the radius rod and remove the lower arm.

6. To install, reverse the removal procedure. Be sure to tighten the components to their proper torque.

Steering Knuckles

REMOVAL & INSTALLATION

1. Pry the spindle lock nut tab away from the spindle, then loosen the spindle nut.

2. Raise the front of the car and support it with safety stands. Remove the front wheel.

3. Remove the spindle nut cotter pin and the spindle nut.

4. Remove the two bolts retaining the brake caliper and remove the caliper from the knuckle. Do not let the caliper hang by the brake hose, support it with a length of wire.

NOTE: In case it is necessary to remove the disc, hub, bearings and/or outer dust seal, use Steps 5 and 6 given below. You will need a hydraulic press for this (see the Brakes Section). If this is unnecessary, omit Steps 5 and 6.

5. Install a hub puller attachment against the hub with the lug nuts.

6. Attach a slide hammer in the center hole of the attachment and pull out the hub, with the disc attached, from the knuckle.

7. Remove the tie-rod from the knuckle using the ball joint remover. Use care not to damage the ball joint seals.

CAUTION

On the 1984 and later Civic models, make sure a floor jack is positioned securely under the lower control arm, at the ball joint. Otherwise the tension from the torsion bar may cause the lower control arm to suddenly "jump" away from the steering knuckle as the ball joint is removed.

8. Remove the lower arm from the knuckle using the ball joint remover. On the 1983 and later Prelude, also remove the upper ball joint from the steering knuckle using the ball joint remover.

9. Loosen the lockbolt which retains the strut in the knuckle. Tap the top of the knuckle with a hammer and slide it off the shock.

10. Remove the knuckle and hub, if still attached, by sliding the driveshaft out of the hub.

11. To install, reverse the removal procedure. If the hub was removed, refer to Brake Disc Removal, for procedures with the hydraulic press. Be sure to visually check the knuckle for visible signs of wear or damage and to check the condition of the inner bearing dust seals.

Front End Alignment

CASTER & CAMBER ADJUSTMENT

Caster and camber cannot be adjusted on any Honda except the 1983 and later Prelude. If caster, camber or kingpin angle is incorrect or front end parts are damaged or worn, they must be replaced.

1983 and Later Prelude

NOTE: Wheel alignment adjustments must be performed in the following order: camber, caster and then toe-in.

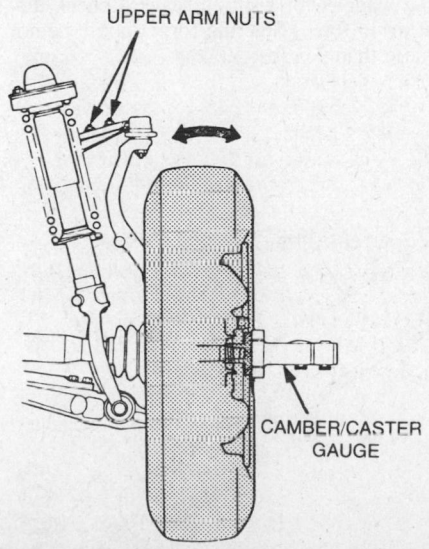

Camber adjustment—1983 and later Prelude

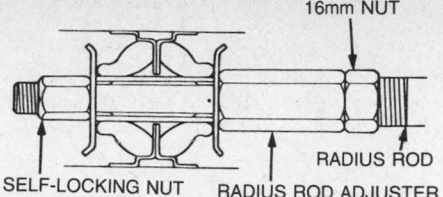

Caster adjustment—1983 and later Prelude

The camber adjustment can be made by loosening the two nuts on the upper control arm and sliding the ball joint until the camber meets specifications. The caster adjustment can be made by loosening the 16mm nuts on the front beam radius rods and then turning the locknut to make the adjustment. Turning the nut clockwise decreases the caster and turning it counterclockwise increases the caster. After adjusting to specifications, hold the nylon locknut and lightly tighten the adjuster. Tighten the 16mm nut to 58 ft. lbs., then tighten the locknut to 32 ft. lbs. while holding the 16mm nut.

TOE-OUT ADJUSTMENT

Toe is the difference of the distance between the forward extremes of the front tires and the distance between the rearward extremes of the front tires. On Hondas, the fronts of the tires are further apart than the rear to counteract the pulling-together effect of front wheel drive.

Toe-out can be adjusted on all Hondas by loosening the locknuts at each end of the tie rods. To increase toe-out, turn the right tie rod in the direction of forward wheel rotation and turn the left tie rod in the opposite direction. Turn both tie rods an equal amount until toe-out meets specifications.

STEERING

Steering Wheel

REMOVAL & INSTALLATION

1. Remove the steering wheel pad by lifting it off.
2. Remove the steering wheel retaining

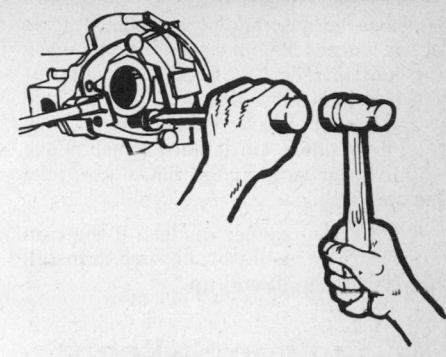

Loosening the turn signal cam nut screw

nut. Gently hit the backside of each of the steering wheel spokes with equal force from the palms of your hands.

CAUTION
Avoid hitting the wheel or the shaft with excessive force. Damage to the shaft could result.

3. Installation is the reverse of the removal procedure. Be sure to tighten the steering wheel nut to 22–36 ft. lbs.

Combination Switch

REMOVAL & INSTALLATION

1. Remove the steering wheel.
2. Disconnect the column wiring harness and coupler.

CAUTION
Be careful not to damage the steering column or shaft.

3. Remove the upper and lower column covers.
4. On models so equipped, remove the cruise control slip ring.
5. Remove the turn signal cancelling sleeve.
6. On later models, remove the switch retaining screws, then remove the switch.
7. Loosen the screw on the turn signal switch cam nut and lightly tap its head to permit the cam nut to loosen. Then remove the turn signal switch assembly and the steering shaft upper bushing.
8. To assemble and install, reverse the above procedure. When installing the turn

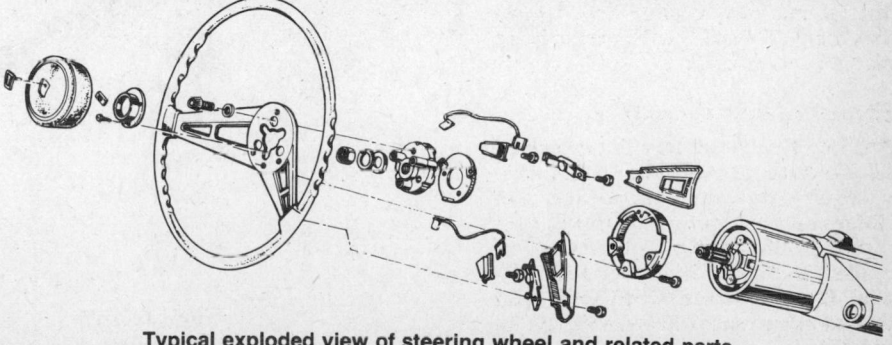

Typical exploded view of steering wheel and related parts

signal switch assembly, engage the locating tab on the switch with the notch in the steering column. The steering shaft upper bushing should be installed with the flat side facing the upper side of the column. The alignment notch for the turn signal switch will be centered on the flat side of the bushing.

NOTE: On earlier models, if the cam nut has been removed, be sure to install it with the small end up.

Ignition Switch

REMOVAL & INSTALLATION

1. Remove the steering column housing lower cover.
2. Disconnect the ignition switch wiring at the couplers.
3. The ignition switch assembly is held onto the column by two shear bolts. Remove these bolts, using a drill, to separate and remove the ignition switch.
4. To install, reverse the removal procedure. You will have to replace the shear bolts with new ones.

On 1982 and later Accords, 1983 and later Preludes, and 1984 and later Civics, the mechanical part of the switch does not have to be removed to replace the electrical

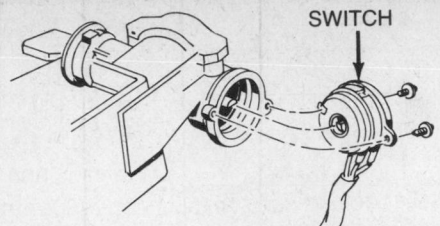

Ignition switch removal—1982 and later Accord, 1984 and later Civic and 1983 and later Prelude.

part. To remove the electrical part or base of the switch proceed as follows:
1. Remove the steering column lower cover.
2. Disconnect the electrical connector at the switch.
3. Insert the key and turn it to lock position.
4. Remove the two switch retaining screws, then remove the switch (base) from the rest of the switch.

Steering Gear

TESTING

1. Remove the dust seal bellows retaining bands and slide the dust seals off the left and right side of the gearbox housing.
2. Turn the front wheels full left and,

using your hand, attempt to move the steering rack in an up-down direction.
3. Repeat with the wheel turned full right.
4. If any movement is felt, the steering gearbox must be adjusted.

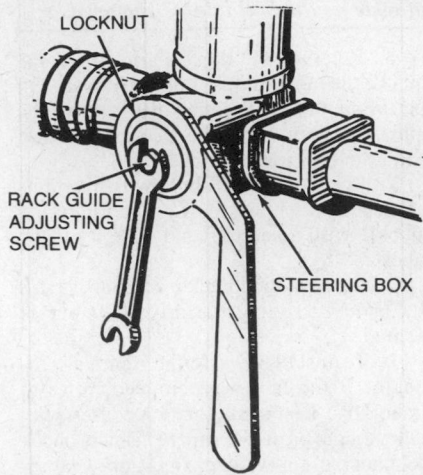

Steering box adjustment

ADJUSTMENT

1. Make sure that the rack is well lubricated.
2. Loosen the rack guide adjusting locknut.
3. Tighten the adjusting screw just to the point where the front wheels cannot be turned by hand.
4. Back off the adjusting screw 45 degrees and hold it in that position while adjusting the locknut.
5. Recheck the play, and then move the wheels lock-to-lock, to make sure that the rack moves freely.
6. Check the steering force by first raising the front wheels and then placing them in a straight-ahead position. Turn the steering wheel with a spring scale to check the steering force. Steering force should be no more than 3.3 lbs.

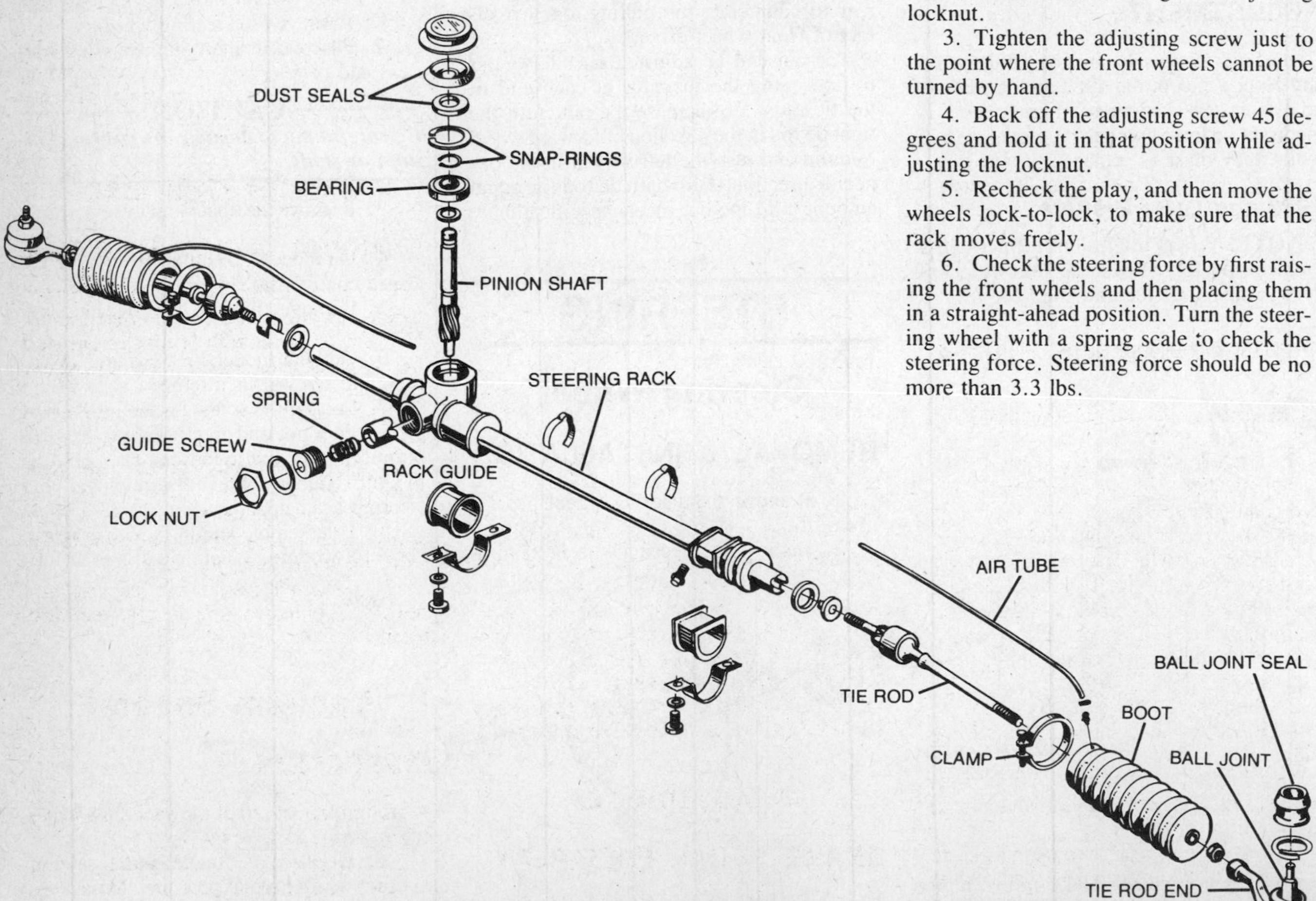

Steering box and linkage

Tie Rods

REMOVAL & INSTALLATION

1. Raise the front of the car and support it with safety stands. Remove the front wheels.

2. Use a ball joint remover to remove the tie rod from the knuckle.

3. Disconnect the air tube at the dust seal joint. Remove the tie rod dust seal bellows clamps and move the rubber bellows on the tie rod rack joints.

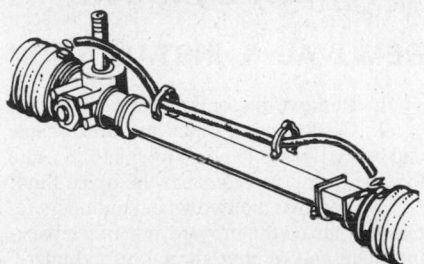

Separate the air tube from the dust boot

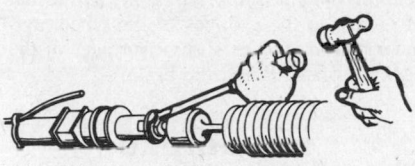

Tie—rod lockwasher removal

4. Straighten the tie-rod lockwasher tabs at the tie rod-to-rack joint and remove the tie rod by turning it with a wrench.

5. To install, reverse the removal procedure. Always use a new tie rod lockwasher during reassembly. Fit the locating lugs into the slots on the rack and bend the outer edge of the washer over the flat part of the rod, after the tie rod nut has been properly tightened.

Power Steering Pump

REMOVAL & INSTALLATION

1. Drain the fluid from the system: Disconnect the cooler return hose from the reservoir and place the end in a large container. Start the engine and allow it to run at fast idle. Turn the steering wheel from lock to lock several times, until fluid stops running from the hose. Shut off the engine and discard the fluid. Reattach the hose.

2. Disconnect the inlet and outlet hoses at the pump.

3. Remove the drive belt.

4. Remove the bolts and remove the pump.

5. To install, install the pump on its mounts, install the belt, adjust belt tension, and install the fluid hoses.

6. Fill the reservoir with fresh fluid, to the full mark. Use only genuine Honda power steering fluid; ATF or other brands of fluid will damage the system.

7. Start the engine and allow to fast idle. Turn the steering wheel from side to side several times, lightly contacting the stops. This will bleed the system of air. Check the reservoir level and add fluid if necessary.

BELT ADJUSTMENT

1. Loosen the bolt on the adjuster arm.

2. Move the pump toward or away from the engine, until the belt can be depressed approximately ⁹⁄₁₆ in. at the midpoint between the two pulleys under moderate thumb pressure. If the tension adjustment is being made on a new belt, the deflection should only be about ⁷⁄₁₆ in., to allow for the initial stretching of the belt.

There is a raised bump on the top of the adjusting arm. If the belt has stretched to the point where the adjustment bolt is at or beyond the bump, the belt should be replaced.

3. Tighten the bolt and recheck the adjustment.

STEERING TORQUE SPECIFICATIONS

Components	Ft. Lbs.
Tie-rod locknut	29–35
Tie-rod ball joint nut	29–35
Bask guide locknut	29–36
Steering wheel retaining nut(s)	22–36

BRAKE SYSTEM

Honda uses a dual hydraulic system, with the brakes connected diagonally. In other words, the right front and left rear brakes are on the same hydraulic line and the left front and right rear are on the other line. This has the added advantage of front disc emergency braking, should either of the hydraulic systems fail. The diagonal rear brake serves to counteract the sway from single front disc braking.

A leading/trailing drum brake is used for the rear brakes except the 1984 and later Prelude which has 4 wheel disc brakes. All models are equipped with front disc brakes. All Hondas are equipped with a brake warning light, which is activated when a defect in the brake system occurs.

For all brake system repair and service procedures not detailed below, please refer to "Brakes" in the Unit Repair section.

Adjustments

BRAKE PEDAL FREE-PLAY

Free-play is the distance the pedal travels from the stop (brake light switch) until the pushrod contacts the vacuum booster, which actuates the master cylinder.

To check free-play, first measure the distance (with the carpet removed) from the floor to the brake pedal. Then push down the pedal until contact is felt and again measure the distance from the floor to the brake pedal. The difference between the two measurements is the pedal free-play. The specified free-play is 0.04–0.20 in. Free-play adjustment is made by loosening the lock nut on the brake light switch and rotating the switch body until the specified clearance is obtained.

FRONT/REAR DISC BRAKES

Disc brakes are inherently self adjusting. No adjustments are either necessary or possible.

REAR DRUM BRAKES

1. Block the front wheels, release the parking brake and raise the rear of the car, supporting it with safety stands.

2. Depress the brake pedal two or three times and release.

3. The adjuster is located on the inboard side, underneath the control arm. Turn the adjuster clockwise until the wheel no longer turns.

4. Back off the adjuster two (2) clicks and turn the wheel to see if the brake shoes are dragging. If they are dragging, back off the adjuster one more click.

Master Cylinder

REMOVAL & INSTALLATION

——— CAUTION ———
Before removing the master cylinder, cover the body surfaces with fender covers and rags to prevent damage to painted surfaces by brake fluid.

1. Disconnect and plug the brake lines at the master cylinder.

2. Remove the master cylinder-to-vacuum booster attaching bolts and remove the master cylinder from the car.

3. To install, reverse the removal procedure. Before operating the car, you must bleed the brake system.

Vacuum Booster

INSPECTION

A preliminary check of the vacuum booster can be made as follows:

a. Depress the brake pedal several times using normal pressure. Make sure that the pedal height does not vary;

b. Hold the pedal in the depressed po-

sition and start the engine. The pedal should drop slightly;

c. Hold the pedal in the above position and stop the engine. The pedal should stay in the depressed position for approximately 30 seconds.

d. If the pedal does not drop when the engine is started or rises after the engine is stopped, the booster is not functioning properly.

REMOVAL & INSTALLATION

1. Disconnect the vacuum hose at the booster.

2. Disconnect and plug the brake lines at the master cylinder.

3. Remove the brake pedal-to-booster link pin and the four nuts retaining the booster. The pushrod and nuts are located inside the car under the instrument panel.

4. Remove the booster with the master cylinder attached.

5. To install, reverse the removal procedure. Check the vacuum booster pushrod-to-master cylinder piston clearance as outlined in the master cylinder removal procedure. Don't forget to bleed the brake system before operating the car.

Front Wheel Bearings

REMOVAL & INSTALLATION

NOTE: The following procedure for wheel bearing removal and installation necessitates the use of a hydraulic press. You will have to go to a machine or auto shop equipped with a press. Do not attempt this procedure without a press.

1. Remove the steering knuckle and front hub as outlined earlier. Please refer to "Steering Knuckles" for these procedures.

2. Remove the wheel bearing dust cover on the inboard side of the knuckle.

3. Remove the four bolts which hold the brake disc onto the hub. Remove the splashguard by removing the three retaining screws.

4. Remove the outer bearing retainer.

5. Remove the wheel bearings by supporting the knuckle in a hydraulic press, using two support plates. Make sure that the plates do not overlap the outer bearing race. Now use a proper sized driver and handle to remove the bearings.

NOTE: Whenever the wheel bearings are removed, always replace with a new set of bearings and outer dust seal.

6. Pack each bearing with grease before installing (see below).

7. To install the bearings, press them into the knuckle using the same support plates as above, plus the installing base. Use the same driver and handle you used to remove the bearing.

NOTE: The front wheel bearings are the angular contact type. It is important that they be installed with the manufacturer's markings facing inward (towards each other).

8. Use the press to install the front hub (see above).

9. The rest of installation is the reverse of the removal procedure.

CLEANING & REPACKING

1. Clean all old grease from the driveshaft spindles on the car.

2. Remove all old grease from the hub and knuckle and thoroughly dry and wipe clean all components.

3. When fitting new bearings, you must pack them with wheel bearing grease. To do this, place a glob of grease in your left palm, then, holding one of the bearings in your right hand, drag the face of the bearing heavily through the grease. This must be done to work as much grease as possible through the ball bearings and the cage. Turn the bearing and continue to pull it through the grease, until the grease is thoroughly packed between the bearing balls and the cage, all around the bearings. Repeat this operation until all of the bearings are packed with grease.

4. Pack the inside of the rotor and knuckle hub with a moderate amount of grease. Do not overload the hub with grease.

5. Apply a small amount of grease to the spindle and to the lip of the inner seal before installing.

6. To install the bearings, check the above procedures.

CHECKING & ADJUSTING

The front wheel bearings should be inspected and repacked (or replaced) every 30,000 miles. To check the wheel bearings for any play, jack up each wheel and shake it to check the bearings for any play. If any play is felt, tighten the castellated spindle nut to the specified torque (87–130 ft. lbs.) and reinspect. If play is still present, replace the bearing.

NOTE: Overtightening the spindle nuts will cause excessive bearing friction and will result in rough wheel rotation and eventual bearing failure.

Wheel Cylinders

REMOVAL & INSTALLATION

1. Remove the brake drum and shoes.

2. Disconnect the parking brake cable and brake lines at the backing plate. Be sure to have a drip pan to catch the brake fluid.

3. Remove the two wheel cylinders retaining nuts on the inboard side of the backing plate and remove the wheel cylinder.

4. To install, reverse the removal procedure. When assembling, apply a thin coat of grease to the grooves of the wheel cylinder piston and the sliding surfaces of the backing plate. Bleed the brakes.

Handbrake

CABLE REMOVAL & INSTALLATION

1. Remove the adjusting nut from the equalizer mounted on the rear axle, or in the console on ('82 and later Accords, '83 and later Preludes and '84 and later Civics) and separate the cable from the equalizer.

2. Set the parking brake lever to a fully released position and remove the cotter pin from the side of the brake lever.

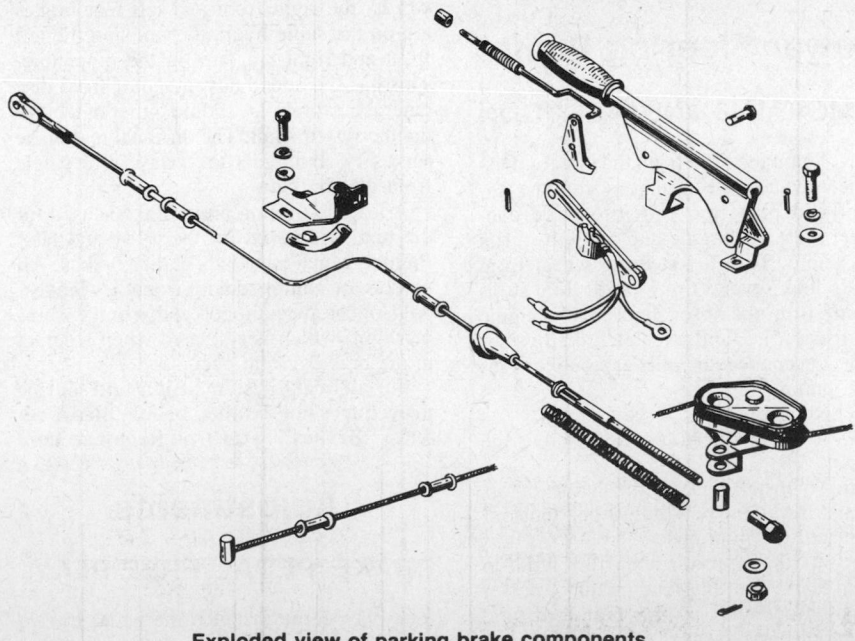

Exploded view of parking brake components

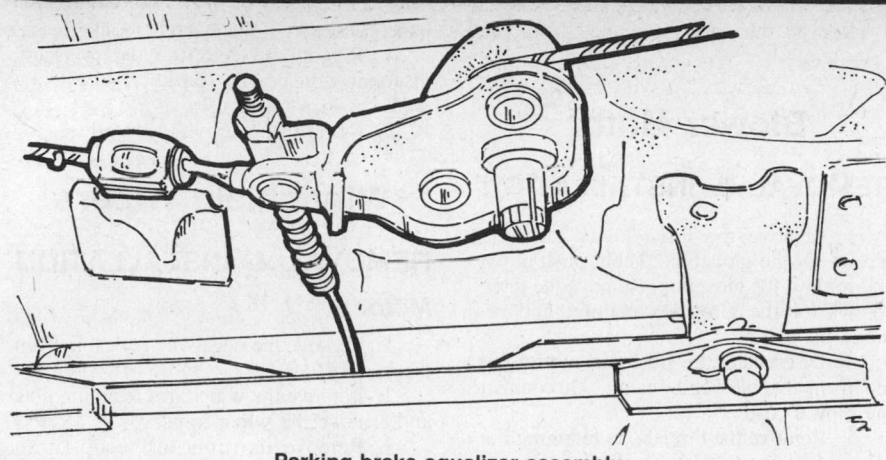

Parking brake equalizer assembly

3. After removing the cotter pin, pull out the pin which connects the cable and the lever.

4. Detach the cable from the guides at the front and right side of the fuel tank and remove the cable.

5. To install, reverse the removal procedure, making sure that grease is applied to the cable and the guides.

ADJUSTMENT

Inspect the following items:

    a. Check the ratchet for wear;

    b. Check the cables for wear or damage and the cable guide and equalizer for looseness;

    c. Check the equalizer cable where it contracts the equalizer and apply grease if necessary;

    d. Check the rear brake adjustment.

1. Block the front wheels and jack up the rear of the car. Support the car on jack stands.

2. Loosen the adjusting nut, located in the console on ('82 and later Accords, '83 and later Preludes and '84 and later Civics) and at the equalizer, between the lower control arms on the other models.

3. Pull the parking brake lever up one notch.

4. Tighten the adjusting nut until the rear brakes drag slightly.

5. Release the brake lever and check that the rear brakes do not drag.

6. The rear brakes should be locked when the handbrake lever is pulled 4–8 notches.

Rear Wheel Bearings

ADJUSTMENT

Rear wheel bearings are not adjustable on the 1978–79 or 1984 and later Civic models. Tighten the castle nut to 83 ft. lbs. and install a new cotter pin whenever removed.

To adjust the bearings on all other models.

1. Tighten the castle nut to 18 ft. lbs.

2. Rotate the drum a few times.

3. Back off the castle nut about 100°.

4. Tighten the castle nut to 2–4 ft. lbs.

5. Install the lock nut with its slots as close as possible to the spindle hole. Tighten the castle nut/lock nut just enough to align the slots and the hole, and install a new cotter pin.

CHASSIS ELECTRICAL

Heater

REMOVAL & INSTALLATION

NOTE: These procedures do not apply to cars equipped with air conditioning. On cars equipped with air conditioning, heater removal may differ from the procedures listed below. Only a trained air conditioning specialist should tamper with A/C equipped units. Air conditioning units contain pressurized Freon which can be extremely dangerous (e.g. burns and/or blindness) to the untrained.

Civic

1978–79

1. Drain the radiator.

2. Disconnect the right and left defroster hoses.

3. Disconnect the inlet and outlet water hoses at the heater assembly.

NOTE: There will be a coolant leakage when disconnecting the hoses. Catch the coolant in a container to prevent damage to the interior.

4. Disconnect the following items:

    a. Fre-Rec control cable;

    b. Temperature control rod;

    c. Room/Def. control cable;

    d. Fan motor switch connector;

    e. Upper attaching bolts;

    f. Lower attaching bolts;

    g. Lower bracket.

5. Remove the heater assembly through the passenger side.

6. To install the heater assembly, reverse the removal procedure. Pay attention to the following points:

    a. When installing the heater assembly, do not forget to connect the right side of the upper bracket;

    b. Connect the inlet and outlet water hoses SECURELY;

NOTE: The inlet hose is a straight type, and the outlet hose is an L-type.

    c. Install the defroster nozzles in the correct position;

    d. Connect the control cables securely. Operate the control valve and lever to check for proper operation.

    e. Be sure to bleed the cooling system.

1980 AND LATER

1. Drain the radiator.

2. Remove the dashboard.

3. Disconnect both heater hoses at the firewall and drain the coolant into a container.

4. Remove the heater lower mounting nut on the firewall.

5. Remove the two heater duct retaining clips or bolts.

6. Disconnect the control cables from the heater.

7. Remove the heater valve cable cover and remove the heater assembly.

8. Installation is the reverse of removal. Bleed cooling system and make sure cables are properly adjusted.

Accord

NOTE: To remove the heater core, it is necessary to first remove the entire instrument panel and heater assemblies.

1. Drain the cooling system.

2. Remove the steering column lower trim cover.

3. Remove the two nuts and two bolts retaining the column to the firewall support.

4. Remove the instrument wire harnesses from cabin wire harness couples.

5. Reach behind the instrument cluster and disconnect the speedometer cable and four wiring harness connectors at rear of cluster. Pry out the lock tabs to disconnect.

6. Disconnect radio lead and antenna wire.

7. Remove the heater fan switch knob, heater lever knobs and heater control bezel. Remove heater control center panel. Disconnect cigarette lighter and blower motor leads.

8. Disconnect clock leads.

9. Remove the seven sheet metal screws retaining the instrument panel to the firewall. There are two at each end of the dash (adjacent to windshield pillar), two beneath the radio and one adjacent to the clock.

10. Pull out the instrument panel and support. Check for any wires still connected.

11. Inside the engine compartment, disconnect the two heater hoses at the firewall. Remove the nut retaining the heater unit to the firewall.

12. Disconnect the three heater control cables from the heater unit. Disconnect the cable clip from the heater valve.

13. Remove the heater unit lower mounting bolt and the right and left upper mounting bolts. Separate the blower hose from the heater.

14. Lay some towels underneath to catch residual coolant leakage. Remove the heater unit.

15. To service the heater core, separate the heater housing halves.

16. Reverse the above to install. Bleed the cooling system using the bleed bolt located near the ignition distributor.

Prelude
1979–82

1. Remove the blower by removing the instrument panel side cover.

2. Remove the glove box and the three blower mounting bolts.

3. Remove the blower from the heater case.

4. Drain the coolant.

5. Remove the lower dash panel.

6. Place a drain pan under the case and disconnect both heater hoses at the core tubes.

7. Remove the heater lower mount nut on the firewall.

8. Disconnect the cable at the water valve.

9. Remove the control cables from the heater case.

Heater Core

REMOVAL & INSTALLATION

NOTE: Only the 1983 and later Prelude models may have the heater core replaced without removing the heater assembly.

1983 and later Prelude

1. Drain the cooling system. Remove the heater pipe cover and heater pipe clamps.

2. Remove the heater core retaining plate.

3. Pull the cotter pin out of the hose clamp joint and separate the heater pipes.

NOTE: Engine coolant will drain from the heater pipes when they are disconnected. Place a drip pan under the pipes to catch the coolant.

4. When all the coolant has drained from the heater core, remove it from the heater housing.

5. Installation is the reverse of the removal procedure, please note the following:

a. Replace the hose clamps with new ones.

b. Turn the cotter pin in the hose clamps tightly to prevent leaking coolant.

c. Fill the cooling system with coolant and open the bleed bolt until coolant begins to flow from it. Tighten the bolt

when all the air has escaped from the system.

Blower Motor

REMOVAL & INSTALLATION

1. Remove the three lower retaining screws for the glovebox. Then, push down and remove the glovebox. Remove the three screws for the glovebox ceiling, and remove the ceiling.

2. Disconnect the fresh air control cable from the blower housing. Disconnect the blower leads.

3. Remove the three bolts retaining the blower housing to the firewall. Separate heater duct hose from the blower housing, and remove the blower housing.

4. To service the blower motor, separate the blower housing halves.

5. Reverse the above procedures to install.

Radio

REMOVAL & INSTALLATION

—— CAUTION ——

Never operate the radio without a speaker; severe damage to the output transistors will result. If the speaker must be replaced, use a speaker of the correct impedance (ohms) or else the output transistors will be damaged and require replacement.

Civic

1. Remove the screw which holds the rear radio bracket to the back tray underneath the instrument panel. Then remove the wing nut which holds the radio to the bracket and remove the bracket.

2. Remove the control knobs, hex nuts, and trim plate from the radio control shafts.

3. Disconnect the antenna and speaker leads, the bullet type radio fuse, and the white lead connected directly over the radio opening.

4. Drop the radio out, bottom first, through the package tray.

5. To install, reverse the removal procedure. When inserting the radio through the package tray, be sure the bottom side is up and the control shafts are facing toward the engine. Otherwise, you will not be able to position the radio properly through its opening.

Accord and Prelude

1. Remove the center lower trim panel beneath the radio. Then remove the three radio lower bracket retaining screws.

2. Pull off the radio knobs and remove the radio shaft nuts.

3. Remove the heater fan switch knob, the heater lever knobs, the heater control bezel, and the heater control center trim

panel. Disconnect the cigarette lighter leads.

4. Pull out the radio from the front, and disconnect the power, speaker, and antenna leads.

5. Reverse the above to install.

Windshield Wipers

REMOVAL & INSTALLATION

Motor

1. Remove the negative (−) cable from the battery.

2. Remove the wiper arm retaining nuts and remove the wiper arms.

3. Remove the front air scoop (if so equipped) and hood seal located over the wiper linkage at the bottom of the windshield.

4. Disconnect the linkage from the wiper motor.

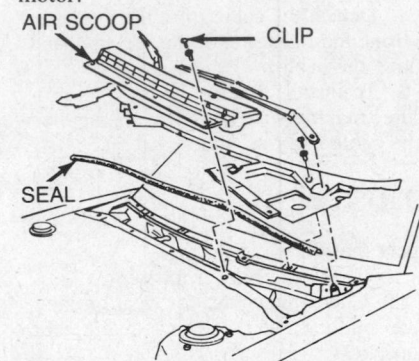

Front air scoop removal—typical

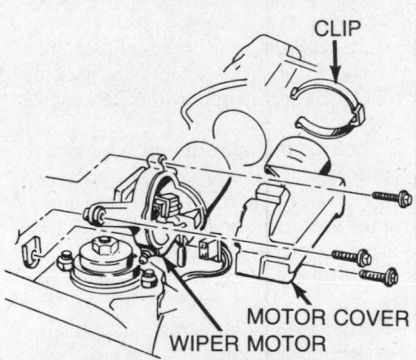

Windshield wiper motor installation

5. Remove the wiper motor water seal cover clamp, and remove the cover (if so equipped).

6. Disconnect the wiper motor electrical connector, remove the motor mounting bolts and remove the motor.

7. Installation is the reverse of the removal procedure. Coat the linkage joints with grease and make sure the linkage moves smoothly.

Instrument Cluster

For more information on instruments, please refer to "Gauges and Instruments" in the Unit Repair section.

REMOVAL & INSTALLATION

All except 1980 and later Civics, 1982 and later Accord and 1983 and later Prelude

METER CASE ASSEMBLY

1. Remove the three meter case mounting wing nuts from the rear of the instrument panel.

2. Disconnect the speedometer and tachometer drive cables at the engine.

3. Pull the meter case away from the panel. Disconnect the meter wires at the connectors.

NOTE: Be sure to label the wires to avoid confusion during reassembly.

4. Disconnect the speedometer and tachometer cables at the meter case and remove the case from the car.

5. To install, reverse the removal procedure.

SWITCH PANEL

1. Loosen the four steering wheel column cover screws and remove the upper and lower covers.

2. Remove the four steering column bolts (remove the upper two bolts first) and rest the steering assembly on the floor.

3. Remove the four switch panel screws from the rear of the instrument panel.

4. To release the switch panel, remove the switches in the following manner:

   a. Remove the light switch by prying the cover off the front of the knob. Pinch the retaining tabs together and pull off the knob;

   b. Remove the wiper switch by pushing the knob in and turning counterclockwise. Then remove the retaining nut;

   c. Remove the choke knob by loosening the set screw. Then remove the retaining nut.

5. To install, reverse the removal procedure.

Civic 1980–83

1. On 1980–81 models remove the steering column.

2. On 1982–83 models lower the steering column.

3. On 1980–81 models remove the bulb access panel and remove the two upper mounting screws through the access panel; then the lower mounting bolt and screws.

4. On 1982–83 models, remove the four screws and trim cover.

5. Disconnect the speedometer cable and tachometer cable if so equipped.

6. Disconnect any remaining mount screws and wire connecters and remove the instrument panel.

7. Installation is the reverse of removal.

1984 and later Civic Coupe (CRX)

1. Remove the screws and clips that retain the lower dash panel and remove the panel.

2. Remove the heater lower control knob and the lower panel.

3. Remove the heater control mount screws and the upper screws in the instrument panel.

4. Pull the panel out and disconnect the wire connectors. Remove the instrument panel.

5. Remove the 4 screws, then lift out the gauge assembly so that you can disconnect the wire connectors.

6. Disconnect the speedometer cable, then remove the gauge assembly.

7. To install, reverse the removal procedure.

1984 and later Civic Hatchback and Sedan

1. Remove the upper instrument panel caps and the 4 screws, then remove the panel.

2. Remove the 4 screws retaining the gauge assembly, then lift out the gauge assembly so you can disconnect the wire connectors.

3. Disconnect the speedometer cable and remove the gauge assembly.

4. To install, reverse the removal procedure.

1984 and later Civic Wagon

1. Remove the screws and the dashboard lower panel, this allows access to the four instrument panel retaining bolts.

2. Remove the four instrument panel retaining bolts, raise the panel and disconnect the wire connectors and the speedometer cable. Remove the instrument panel with the gauge assembly.

3. The gauge assembly may be separated from the instrument panel by removing the four screws.

4. To install, reverse the removal procedure.

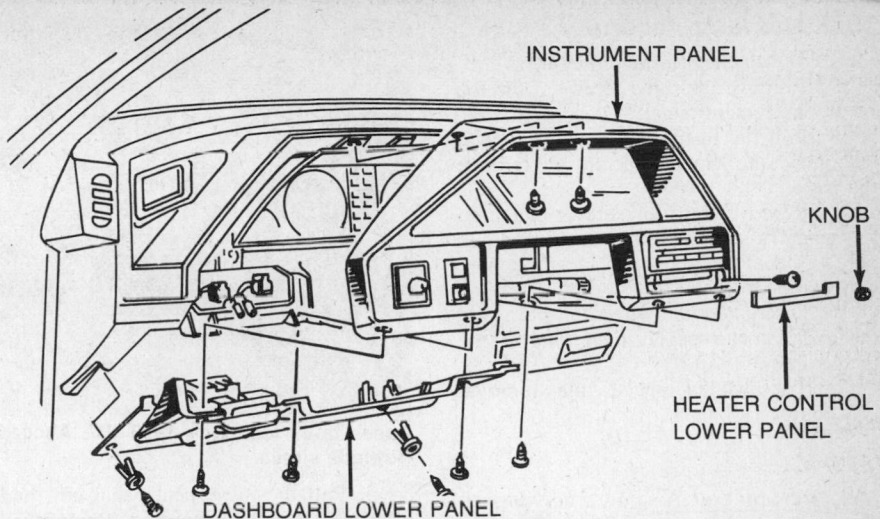

Instrument panel removal—1984 and later Civic Coupe (CRX)

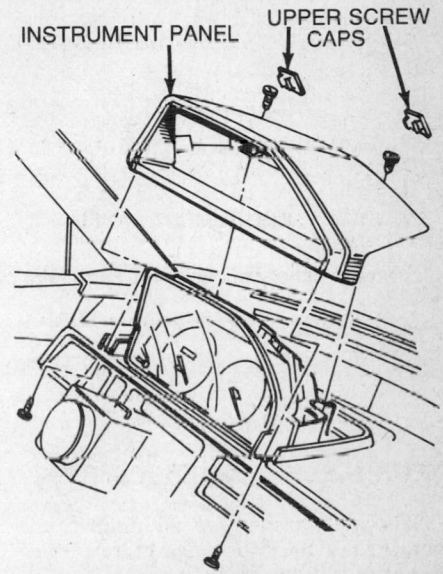

Instrument panel removal—1984 and later Civic Hatchback & Sedan

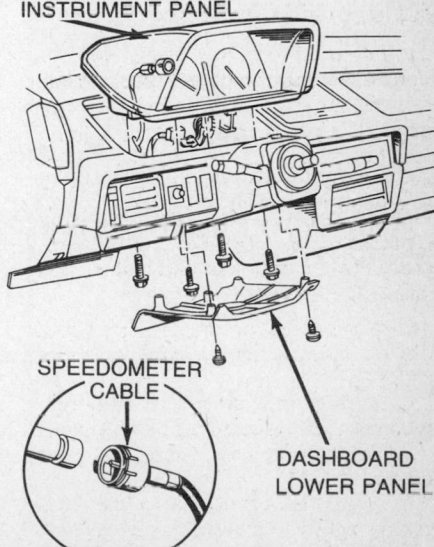

Instrument panel removal—1984 and later Civic Wagon

1982 and later Accord

1. Lower the steering column.
2. Remove the three screws at the top of the instrument panel.
3. Pull the instrument panel out, then disconnect the wire connectors and remove the panel.
4. Remove the four screws that hold the gauge assembly in place, then lift up on the panel so you can reach the wire connectors.
5. Disconnect the wire connectors and the speedometer cable, then remove the gauge assembly.
6. To install, reverse the removal procedure.

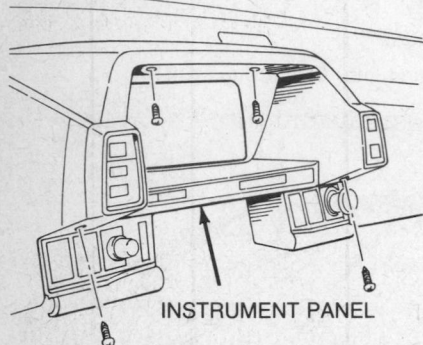

Instrument panel removal—1983 and later Prelude

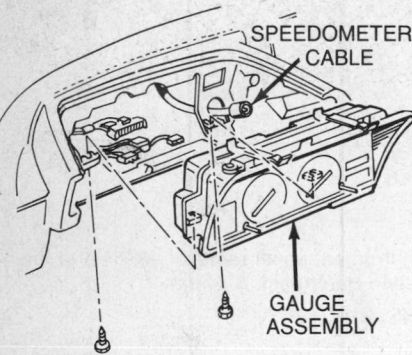

Gauge assembly removal—1983 and later Prelude

1983 and later Prelude

1. Lower the steering column, and remove the lower dashboard panel.
2. Remove the four instrument panel retaining screws.

Fuse box location—1978–81 Accord (Prelude similar)

3. Pull the instrument panel out, and disconnect the wire connectors. Remove the panel.
4. Remove the two screws retaining the gauge assembly, then lift out the assembly and remove the wire connectors and speedometer cable.
5. Installation is the reverse of the removal procedure.

Fuses and Fusible Links

All models are equipped with a fusible link connected between the starter relay and the main wiring harness of the car, located next to the battery.

The 1978–83 Civic fuse box is located below the glove compartment, on the right bulkhead. The 1984 and later Civic fuse box is located under a flip down door, under the dashboard on the left side of the in-

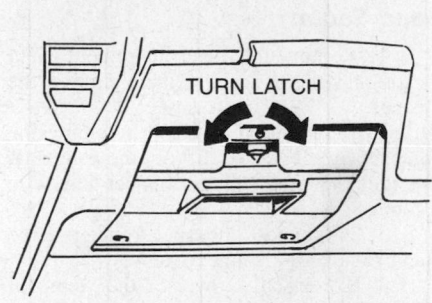

Fuse box location—1983 and later Prelude

Fuse box location—1978–83 Civic

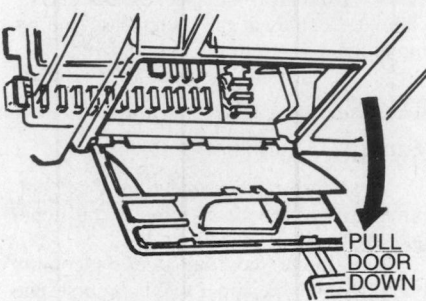

Fuse box location—1982 and later Accord, 1984 and later Civic

strument panel. The rating and function of each fuse is posted inside the fuse box cap for quick reference.

The 1978–82 Accord and Prelude fuse box is a flip down affair, located under the left side of the instrument panel. The 1983 and later Accord and Prelude fuse box is located behind a flip down door, under the dashboard on the left side of the instrument panel.

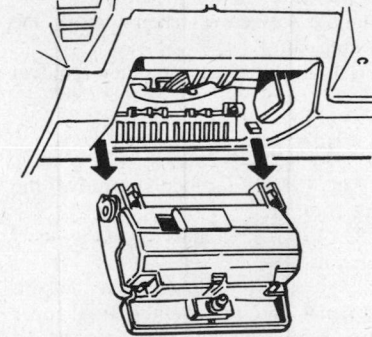

Isuzu
I-Mark, Impulse

SERIAL NUMBER IDENTIFICATION

Vehicle

The vehicle identification number is embossed on a plate attached to the top left of the instrument panel. The number is visible through the windshield from outside the car.

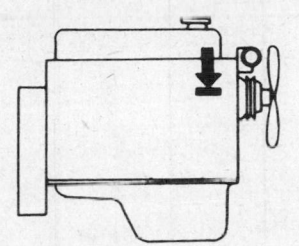

Engine serial number location—gasoline

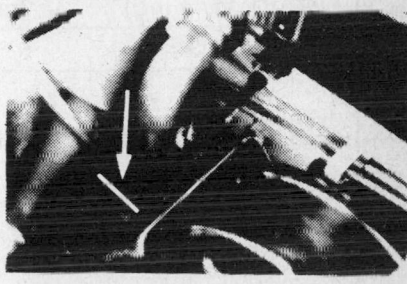

Engine serial number location—diesel

Engine

The engine serial number is stamped on the top right front corner of the engine block on gasoline engines. On diesel models, the engine serial number is stamped on the left rear corner of the engine block.

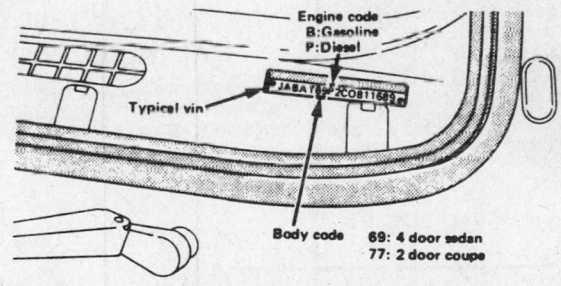

Vehicle identification plate location

Transmission

Both manual transmissions have their serial numbers on the side of the main case. The automatic location is similar.

GENERAL ENGINE SPECIFICATIONS

Year	Engine Displacement (cu. in.)	Carburetor Type	Horsepower (@ rpm)	Torque @ rpm (ft. lbs.)	Bore × Stroke (in.)	Compression Ratio	Oil Pressure @ rpm (psi)
'81–'85	110.8	Hitachi DCH340	80 @ 4800	95 @ 3000	3.31 × 3.23	8.5:1	57 @ 1400
	111	Diesel	51 @ 5000	72 @ 3000	3.31 × 3.23	22.0:1	64 @ 1400
'83–85	118.9	E.F.I.	90 @ 5000	108 @ 3000	3.43 × 3.29	9.3:1	60 @ 1400

E.F.I.—Electronic Fuel Injection

GASOLINE ENGINE TUNE-UP SPECIFICATIONS

(When analyzing compression test results, look for uniformity among cylinders, rather than specific pressures)

Year	Engine Displacement (cu. in.)	Spark Plugs		Distributor		Ignition Timing (deg)		Intake Valve Opens (deg)	Fuel Pump Pressure (psi)	Idle Speed (rpm)	Valve Clear (in.) (cold)	
		Type	Gap (in.)	Point Dwell (deg)	Point Gap (in.)	MT	AT				In	Ex
'81–'85	110.8	NGK-BPR6ESII	0.040	Electronic		6B	6B	21	3.6	900	0.006	0.010
'83–'85	118.9	NGK-BPR6ESII	0.040	Electronic		12B	12B	28	2.0–2.5	900	0.006	0.010

NOTE: The underhood specifications sticker often reflects tune-up specification changes made in production. Sticker figures must be used if they disagree with this chart.
B Before top dead center

DIESEL ENGINE TUNE-UP SPECIFICATIONS

Year	Injector Opening Pressure (psi)	Low Idle (rpm)	Valve Clearance		Intake Valve Opens (deg.)	Injection Timing (deg.)	Firing Order
			Intake	Exhaust			
'81–'85	2133③	625①	0.010	0.014	32B	18B②	1-3-4-2

①A/T: 725 rpm
②12B on 1982 and later
③1770–1984 and later

Firing Orders

NOTE: To avoid confusion, always remove spark plug wires one at a time.

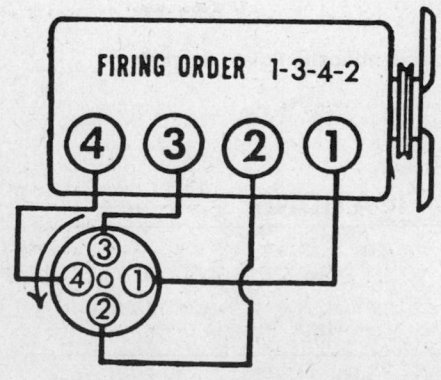

Firing order—gasoline engine

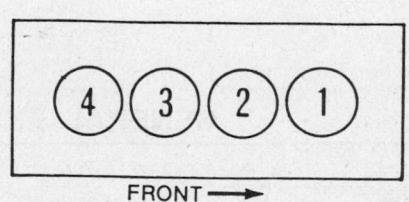

Firing order—diesel engine, 1-3-4-2

CAPACITIES

Year	Model	Engine Displacement (cu.in.)	Engine Crankcase (qts)		Transmission (pts)			Drive Axle (pts)	Gasoline Tank (gals)	Cooling System (qts)	
			With Filter	Without Filter	Manual 4-spd	Manual 5-spd	Automatic			W/ AC	W/O AC
'81–'85	Gas	110.8	3.8	3.4	2.7	3.2	14①	2.5	13.7	6.4	6.4
	Diesel	111	5.5	5.0	2.7	3.2	14①	2.5	13.7	7.4	7.4
'83–'85	Gas	118.9	3.8	3.4	—	3.2	13.4	2.1	15.1	6.6	6.6

① 26.8 pts with torque converter

CRANKSHAFT AND CONNECTING ROD SPECIFICATIONS

All measurements are given in inches

Year	Engine Displacement (cu.in.)	Crankshaft				Connecting Rod		
		Main Brg. Journal Dia.	Main Brg. Oil Clearance	Shaft End-Play	Thrust on No.	Journal Diameter	Oil Clearance	Side Clearance
'81–'85	110.8 (Gas)	2.2050	0.0008–0.0025	0.0117	3	1.929	0.0007–0.0030	0.0137
	111 (Diesel)	2.2020	0.0012–0.0027	0.0018	3	1.925	0.0016–0.0027	0.0137
'83–'85	118.9	2.205	0.0008–0.0025	0.0017	3	1.929	0.0007–0.0029	0.0137

VALVE SPECIFICATIONS

Year	Engine Displacement (cu.in.)	Seat Angle (deg)	Face Angle (deg)	Spring Test Pressure (lbs. @in.)	Spring Installed Height (in.)	Stem-to-Guide Clearance (in.)		Stem Diameter (in.)	
						Intake	Exhaust	Intake	Exhaust
'81–'85	110.8 (Gas)	45①	45	outer—34.5 @ 1.614 inner—20 @ 1.516	outer—1.61 inner—1.51	0.009–0.0022	0.0015–0.0031	0.315	0.315
	111 (Diesel)	45①	45	outer—34.6 @ 1.614 inner—20 @ 1.515	outer—1.85 inner—1.78	0.0015–0.0027	0.002–0.003	0.313	0.313
'83–'85	118.9	45	45	55 @ 160	1.60	0.009–0.0022	0.0015–0.0031	0.315	0.315

① Because of the aluminum head and valve seat inserts, cut the valve seat with 15, 45 or 75 degree cutters. Use the minimum necessary to remove dents or damage, leaving the contact width inside the 0.0472–0.063 range.

PISTON AND RING SPECIFICATIONS

(All measurements in inches)

Year	Engine Displacement (cu. in.)	Piston Clearance	Ring Gap			Ring Side Clearance		
			Top Compression	Bottom Compression	Oil Control	Top Compression	Bottom Compression	Oil Control
'81–'85	110.8 (Gas)	0.0018–0.0026	0.008–① 0.016	0.008–① 0.016	0.008–0.035	0.0059	0.0059	0.0059
	111 (Diesel)	0.0002–0.0017	0.008–0.016	0.008–0.016	0.008–0.016	0.0059	0.0059	0.0059
'83–'85	118.9	0.0018–0.0026	0.011–② 0.019	0.008–② 0.016	0.008–0.035	0.001–0.0024	0.001–0.0024	0.0008

① 1983–85—0.012–0.018
② 1984–85—0.014–0.019

TORQUE SPECIFICATIONS
(All readings in ft. lbs.)

Year	Engine Displacement (cu. in.)	Cylinder Head Bolts	Rod Bearing Bolts	Main Bearing Bolts	Crankshaft Pulley Bolt	Flywheel to Crankshaft Bolts	Manifolds	
							Intake	Exhaust
'81–'84	110.8②	72①	43	72	87	69	13	15
	111③	⑥	58	72	108	43	26	15
'83–'85	118.9	④	33	72	87	69⑤	NA	16

① Install head bolts according to pattern: 1st step: 61 ft. lbs., 2nd step: 72 ft. lbs.
② Gasoline engine
③ Diesel engine
④ 1st Step—61
  Final Step—72
⑤ 1984 and later—75
⑥ Tighten in sequence—New bolts: 90 ft. lbs., used bolts 97 ft. lbs.

BATTERY AND STARTER SPECIFICATIONS
(All cars use 12 volt, negative ground electrical systems)

Year	Engine Cu. in.	Battery Amp Hour Capacity	Starter						Brush Spring Tension (oz)	Min. Brush Length (in.)
			Lock Test			No Load Test				
			Amps	Volts	Torque	Amps	Volts	rpm		
'81–'85	All	50	NOT RECOMMENDED						56	0.472

ALTERNATOR AND REGULATOR SPECIFICATIONS

Year	Alternator		Voltage Regulator						
	Manufacturer or Part Number	Output Amps @ rpm	Charge Indicator Relay		Regulator			Regulated Voltage	
			Back Gap (in.)	Point Gap (in.)	Back Gap (in.)	Air Gap (in.)	Point Gap (in.)		
'81–'85	LT140-126	40	0.036	0.020	0.015	0.014	0.012	13.8–14.8	
	L150-144	50	0.036	0.020	0.015	0.014	0.012	13.8–14.8	
	LT150-131B	50	0.036	0.020	0.015	0.014	0.012	13.8–14.8	
	Impulse	60	Integral					13.8–14.4	

WHEEL ALIGNMENT SPECIFICATIONS
(All settings at curb weight)

Year	Model	Caster		Camber		Toe-In (in.)
		Range (deg)	Preferred Setting (deg)	Range (deg)	Preferred Setting (deg)	
'81–'85	Exc. Impulse	4P–6P	5P	½N–½P	0	⅛
'83–'85	Impulse	3½P–6P	4¾P	1N–1½P	½N	⅛

Note: Caster angle is pre-set and cannot be serviced

BRAKE SPECIFICATIONS

(All measurements given are in. unless noted)

Year	Model	Lug Nut Torque (ft. lbs.)	Master Cylinder Bore	Brake Disc		Brake Drum			Minimum Lining Thickness	
				Minimum Thickness	Maximum Run-Out	Diameter	Max. Machine O/S	Max. Wear Limit	Front	Rear
'81–'85	Exc. Impulse	50①	0.875	.339	.006②	9.00	9.04	9.06	.067	.040
'83–'85	Impulse	87	0.874	0.654	0.0051	—	—	—	0.12	0.12

① 86 ft. lbs. on aluminum wheels
② Front wheel bearings properly adjusted

TUNE-UP PROCEDURES

All Isuzu models come equipped with a tune-up label in the engine compartment. This label has information developed during production. Should the following information in any way disagree with the specifications label, follow the label information for proper settings.

Spark Plugs

REMOVAL & INSTALLATION

NOTE: Spark plugs should be replaced every 30,000 miles and inspected every 15,000 miles.

Grasp each ignition wire by the boot around the plug and pull straight out. Do not pull on the wire lead itself. Check the condition of the boot and wire and replace if necessary. Slowly back out the plug, being careful not to damage the threads in the cylinder head. Be sure to keep the socket straight on the plug to avoid breaking the ceramic insulator. If the insulator is cracked or damaged in any way, the spark plug should be replaced.

Inspect the plugs for signs of wear or abnormal combustion. Discard plugs that are fouled badly or have a damaged electrode. Clean and regap all plugs before installation. Use a wire gauge to set the correct plug gap, according to the tune-up chart. The wire should pass through the electrode gap with a slight drag. Never attempt to adjust the center electrode. Lightly oil the threads of the plug before reinstalling in the head. Start the plugs in by hand to avoid cross-threading, then tighten the plugs with the socket to 18–21 ft. lbs. If cross-threaded plug holes are encountered, see the cylinder head overhaul section. Install the ignition wires firmly on the plugs, being careful not to cross any wires.

Electronic Ignition

AIR GAP ADJUSTMENT

All models of gasoline engines have electronic ignition. The only adjustment possible on this ignition system is the setting of the air gap inside the distributor.

1. Remove the distributor cap and O-ring.
2. Remove the rotor.
3. Use a feeler gauge (brass) to measure the air gap at the pick up coil projection. The gap should be 0.008–0.016 in. Adjust if necessary.
4. Loosen the screws and move the signal generator until the gap is correct. Tighten the screws and recheck the gap.

NOTE: The electrical parts in this system are not repairable. If found to be defective they must be replaced.

The signal generator can be checked for proper operation by using an ohmmeter to determine its resistance. It should be 140–180 ohms. If the resistance is not correct, replace the signal generator.

Ignition Timing

ADJUSTMENT

NOTE: The timing marks are located at the front of the crankshaft pulley and consist of a graduated scale attached to the engine block and a notch in the crankshaft pulley. Check and adjust the timing every 30,000 miles.

1. Locate and clean off the timing marks. Highlight the marks with paint or chalk.
2. Connect a timing light according to the manufacturer's instructions. The spark plug connection may be made at either No. 1 or No. 4 cylinder.
3. Start the engine and allow it to reach operating temperature. Make sure the engine is idling smoothly.
4. Aim the timing light at the marks and check the position of the crankshaft pulley notch on the timing scale. If necessary, adjust the timing by loosening the distributor clamping bolt and turning the distributor to the specification in the "Tune-Up" chart.

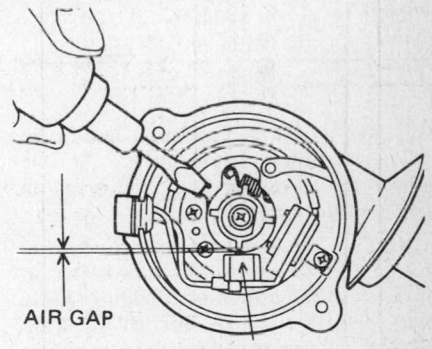

AIR GAP

PICK-UP COIL

Distributor air gap adjustment

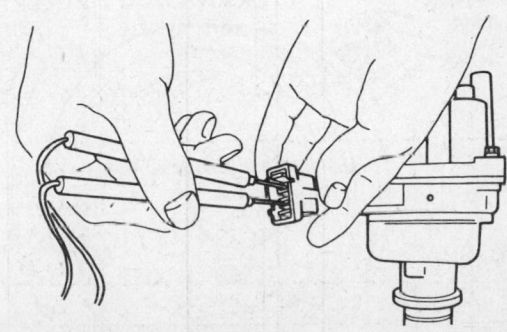

Checking resistance in signal generator with ohmmeter

5. After timing is set to specifications, tighten the distributor clamping bolt and remove the timing light connections.

Valve Lash

ADJUSTMENT

1. Remove the air cleaner and rocker shaft cover.

NOTE: Engine should be cold for adjustment. Adjust the valves every 15,000 miles.

2. Check the rocker arm shaft bracket nuts for tightness before adjusting the valves. Torque the bracket nuts to 16 ft. lbs.

3. Bring either No. 1 or No. 4 piston up to top dead center on the compression stroke. Align the timing mark with the pointer on the crankshaft pulley by turning the crankshaft.

4. Once the engine is set up at TDC, adjust the valves for the cylinder at TDC, then move down in order after turning the crankshaft one revolution for each cylinder.

5. Measurements should be taken at the clearance between the rocker arm and valve stem. Standard valve clearances at low temperatures are:

	Diesel	Gasoline
Intake	0.25mm (0.010 in)	0.15mm (0.006 in)
Exhaust	0.35mm (0.014 in)	0.25mm (0.010 in)

6. To adjust the clearance, loosen the locknut and use a screwdriver to turn the adjusting stud until a slight drag is felt on the feeler gauge.

NOTE: While all valve adjustments must be made accurately, it's better to have the valve adjustment slightly loose than slightly tight. A burned valve or warped valve stem can result from overly tight adjustments.

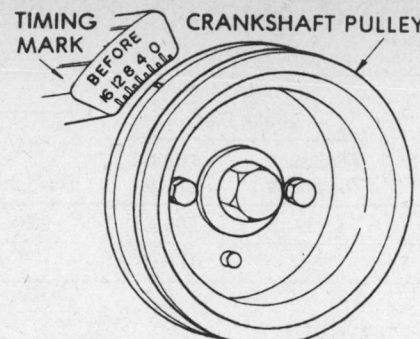

TDC timing mark alignment

7. Tighten the locknut and recheck the adjustment.

8. When all valves are correctly adjusted, replace the rocker arm cover using a new gasket. Check for oil leaks.

Idle Speed

ADJUSTMENT

Gasoline Engine (110.8 cu. in.)

NOTE: Idle speed should be adjusted every 30,000 miles.

1. Set the parking brake and block the drive wheels.

2. Place the transmission in Neutral, start the engine and allow it to reach normal operating temperature.

NOTE: If the engine is idling for more than five minutes, precede all adjustments with a clear-out blip of the throttle for a few seconds.

3. The adjustments should be made with the choke open, air conditioner off, air cleaner installed, and distributor vacuum line, canister purge line and EGR vacuum line disconnected and plugged, and the idle compensator vacuum line closed by bending the rubber hose.

4. Turn the throttle adjusting screw to

adjust the engine to 900 ± 50 rpm if the car is an automatic, and 800 ± 50 rpm if the car has a manual transmission.

5. If the car has an air conditioner, turn the A/C on Max Cold and High blower. Open the throttle to approximately ⅓ and allow the throttle to close. (This allows the speed–up solenoid to reach full travel.) Adjust the speed–up solenoid adjusting screw to set the idle at 900 ± 50 rpm.

Gasoline Engine (118.9 cu. in.)

Measuring valve clearances

Adjusting valve clearance

1. Run the engine to the normal operating temperature.

2. Set the parking brake and block the drive wheels.

3. Place the transmission in neutral or park.

4. With the air conditioner turned off and the harness of the pressure regulator V.S.V. disconnected, adjust the idle adjustment screw to specifications.

NOTE: It is important to check and clean the idle port as necessary, as restrictions in the port can cause fluctuations in idle speed.

Ignition timing marks

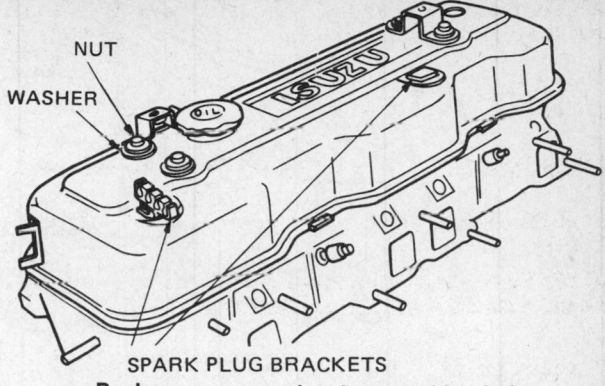

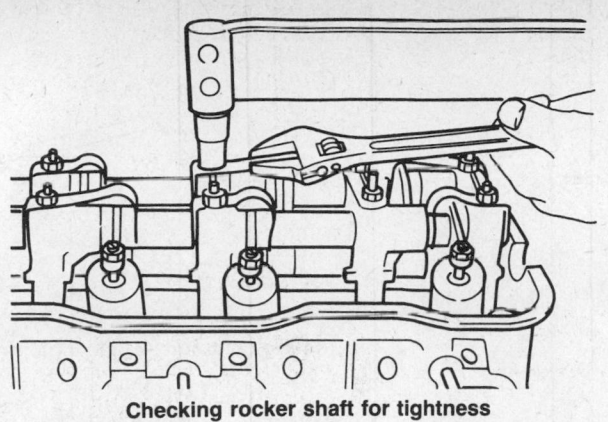

Checking rocker shaft for tightness

NUT
WASHER
SPARK PLUG BRACKETS
Rocker arm cover showing attaching bolts

Diesel Engines

NOTE: Idle speed should be adjusted every 30,000 miles.

1. Set the parking brake and block the drive wheels.
2. Place the transmission in Neutral.
3. Start the engine and allow it to warm up to operating temperature.
4. Connect a tachometer according to the manufacturer's instructions.
5. If the idle speed deviates from the specified range, loosen the idle adjusting screw lock nut and turn the screw in or out until the idle speed is correct.

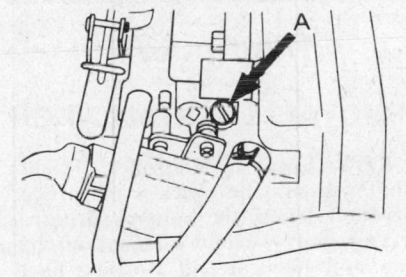

Idle adjustment screw (A) on the throttle body—118.9 cu. in. engine

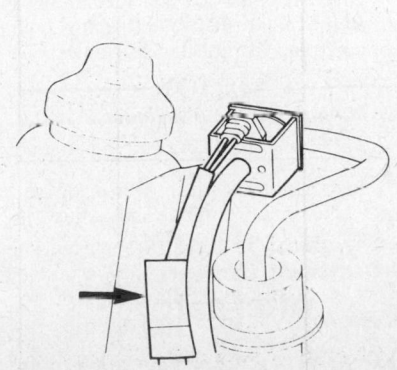

VSV wire connection—118.9 cu. in. engine

Idle Mixture

ADJUSTMENT

Carburetted Engines Only

1. Set the parking brake and block the drive wheels.
2. Place the transmission in neutral and remove the carburetor assembly (see carburetor section for R&R procedures).
3. Remove the plug for the idle mixture screw using a screwdriver which is inserted into the slit on the lower carburetor flange.
4. Reinstall the carburetor assembly.
5. Make the engine idle speed adjustments with the engine at normal operating temperature, choke open, A/C off, distributor vacuum line and EGR vacuum line disconnected and plugged, and idle compensator vacuum line closed by bending the rubber hose.

NOTE: The exact fuel mixture can only be set with the use of an emissions analyzer. While these adjustments will get you in the ballpark, all adjustments must be double-checked and fine-tuned with the proper test equipment.

6. Turn the idle mixture screw all the way in and back out one turn on California models and two turns on 49 states models

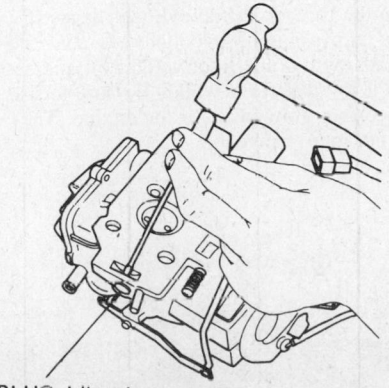

PLUG; Idle mixture screw

Removing mixture plug

(1981). On 1982 and later models, back out the screw 1½ turns.
7. Check that engine idle is still at specifications. Adjust if necessary.
8. Adjust the setting of the idle mixture screw to achieve the maximum rpm, then reset the idle to specs using idle adjusting screw (clockwise is lean).
9. Fine-tune the mixture adjustment to achieve the correct idle speed.
10. Replace the idle mixture plug.

Diesel Injection Timing

ADJUSTMENT

1. Check that the notched line on the injection pump flange is in alignment with the notched line on the injection pump front bracket.
2. Bring the piston in No. 1 cylinder to TDC on the compression stroke by turning the crankshaft as necessary.
3. With the timing pulley housing cover removed, check that the timing belt is properly tensioned and that the timing marks are aligned (see timing belt adjustment).
4. Disconnect the injection pipe from the injection pump and remove the distributor head screw, then install a static timing gauge (special tool J-29763).
5. Use a wrench to hold the delivery holder when loosening the sleeve nuts on the injection pump side.
6. Bring the piston in No. 1 cylinder to a point 45–60 degrees before top dead center by turning the crankshaft, then calibrate the dial indicator to zero.
7. Turn the crankshaft pulley slightly in both directions and check that gauge indication is stable.
8. Turn the crankshaft in the normal direction of rotation (clockwise) and take the reading on the dial indicator when the timing mark on the crankshaft pulley is in alignment with the pointer.
9. If the reading on the dial indicator deviates from the specified range, hold the crankshaft in position 18 degrees before top

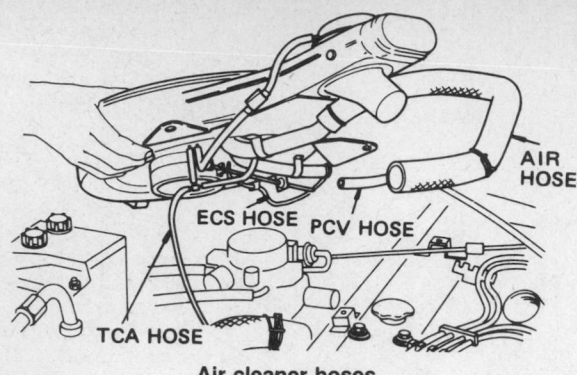

Air cleaner hoses

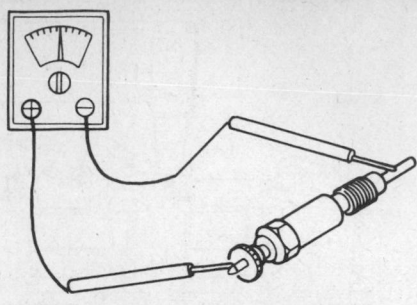

Testing continuity of glow plug

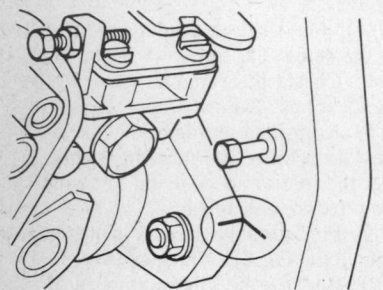

Correct injection pump alignment

dead center (12 degrees 1982 and later) and loosen the two nuts on the injection pump flange.

10. Move the injection pump to a point where the dial indicator gives a reading of 0.5 mm (0.020 in) then tighten the pump flange nuts to 42–52 ft. lbs.

Static timing gauge J-29763

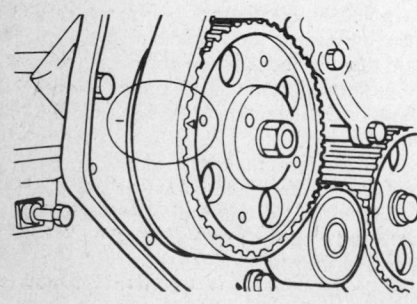

Correct alignment of timing marks

Fast Idle Speed

ADJUSTMENT

Diesel Only

1. Start and warm up the engine.
2. Connect a tachometer according to the manufacturer's instructions.
3. Disconnect the hoses from the vacuum switch valve, then connect a pipe (4 mm diameter) in position between the hoses.
4. Loosen the adjusting nut and adjust the idle speed. Fast idle should be around 900–950 rpm.
5. Tighten the adjusting nut and remove the tachometer.

Glow Plugs

REMOVAL & INSTALLATION

The glow plugs are designed to preheat the combustion chambers so that the diesel engine will have sufficient temperature to fire the fuel on initial starting. They resemble spark plugs and are removed much the same way. Disconnect the wire leads and use a deep socket to remove the glow plug from the cylinder head. Care must be taken not to damage the glow plug in any way or to strip the threads in the cylinder head. If a tight glow plug is encountered, coat the threads with some light weight oil and allow it to soak for a while. Be sure to use the correct glow plug for the engine. They are not interchangeable.

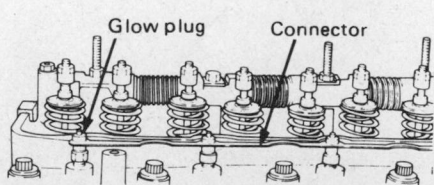

Glow plugs and connector locations

TESTING

NOTE: If the glow plugs should fail to work, check the fusible link before removing the glow plugs. The fusible link wire can be found near the battery, at the left side of the engine compartment.

1. Remove the glow plug.
2. Using a circuit tester, check for continuity across the plug terminals and the body. If no continuity exists, the glow plug should be replaced.

ENGINE ELECTRICAL

Distributor

REMOVAL & INSTALLATION

NOTE: Every 30,000 miles, the distributor should be checked for proper operation. Check the cap and wires, rotor, air gap, vacuum advance mechanism and lubricate all working parts lightly.

1. Disconnect the battery cable.
2. Tag the wires and remove the distributor cap with the ignition wires attached.
3. Disconnect the coil and vacuum line.
4. Remove the distributor clamp bolt and bracket and lift out the distributor.

—————— CAUTION ——————
Never hammer on the distributor housing to tap it loose.

5. Installation is the reverse of removal. Check the timing and adjust if necessary.

Alternator

REMOVAL & INSTALLATION

Removing the alternator is simply a matter of loosening the mounting and adjustment

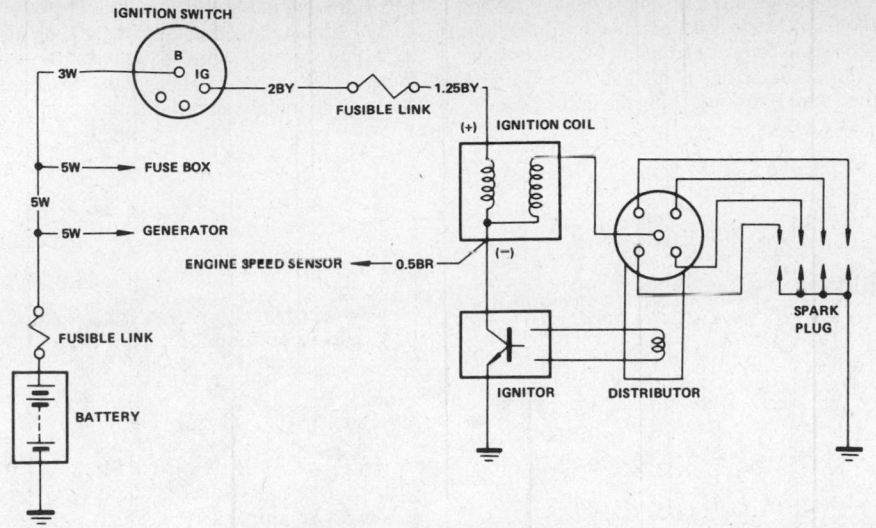

Ignition system schematic—gasoline only

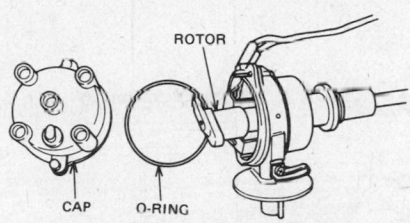

Distributor cap, O-ring and rotor

bolts, removing the belt and lifting out the assembly. Diesel models have a vacuum pump mounted on the front of the alternator assembly. It must be removed along with the alternator for service.

1. Disconnect the battery.

2. Loosen all mounting and adjusting bolts and remove the drive belt.

3. Remove mounting bolts and lift out the alternator.

NOTE: Tag all wires before removing them from the alternator.

4. Installation is the reverse of removal. Proper belt deflection is 0.4 in. (10 mm).

Regulator

TESTING AND ADJUSTING

Externally Mounted Regulator

1. Perform this test with the regulator on the car and the engine running.

2. Connect a voltmeter between the condenser lead and ground with all electrical loads disconnected, including the blower relay connector.

3. The voltage regulator is working properly when the lower side points are closed while the engine is turned off, and when the upper points are closed when the engine is running at idle. If the points are not working normally, chances are that the regulator is out of adjustment, or the voltage coil is open.

4. Check the coil resistance and replace the regulator assembly if found to be malfunctioning. If the coil resistance is normal, adjust the regulator.

5. Start the engine and increase the engine speed gradually. Voltage should increase with engine rpm up to 1400–1850 rpm. A normal condition is indicated when the voltage is within the range of 13.8–14.8 volts. Reconnect the blower relay connector.

6. Remove the regulator cover and check all internal parts for wear or damage. Be careful of all gaskets and seals.

7. Check the points for burning—file if necessary until all burrs are removed. Use an ohmmeter to check the resistance of the regulator and relay coils. The regulator coil resistance should be 102 ohms and the relay coil resistance should be 24 ohms. If an open or shorted coil is indicated, replace the regulator assembly.

8. Check the resistor resistance. It should be 10.5 ohms. If it's not, replace the resistor.

9. Connect a voltmeter between "N" terminal and ground, then increase the engine speed gradually. Voltmeter reading should be 4–5.8 volts when the indicator light goes out. Adjust the cut-in voltage by adjusting the armature core gap and point gap. If the voltage is too high, adjust by bending the core arm "A" down. Bend it up if the cut-in voltage is too low.

10. If adjustment of the core arm does not correct cut-in voltage, proceed with the point gap adjustment.

11. Disconnect the battery. Check the armature core gap with the armature depressed until moving point is in contact with the "B" side point. Armature core gap should be 0.012 in. (0.3mm) or more. Adjust by bending the point arm "B".

12. Release the armature and adjust the gap between the "B" side point and the moving point by bending the point arm "C". Point gap should be 0.016–0.04 in. (0.4–1.2mm).

13. After the point gap adjustment, recheck the cut-in voltage. If not within 4–5.8 volts, repeat the cut-in voltage adjustment.

14. If the no load regulated voltage is not within the 13.8–14.8 range, adjust the voltage regulator setting. If the voltage is too high, bend the core arm "D" down. If the voltage is low, bend it up.

15. If the core arm adjustment does not correct the voltage problem, adjust the regulator point gap. Make sure the battery ground cable is disconnected.

16. Depress the armature until the moving point contacts the "E" side point. Bend the point arm "E" to obtain an armature

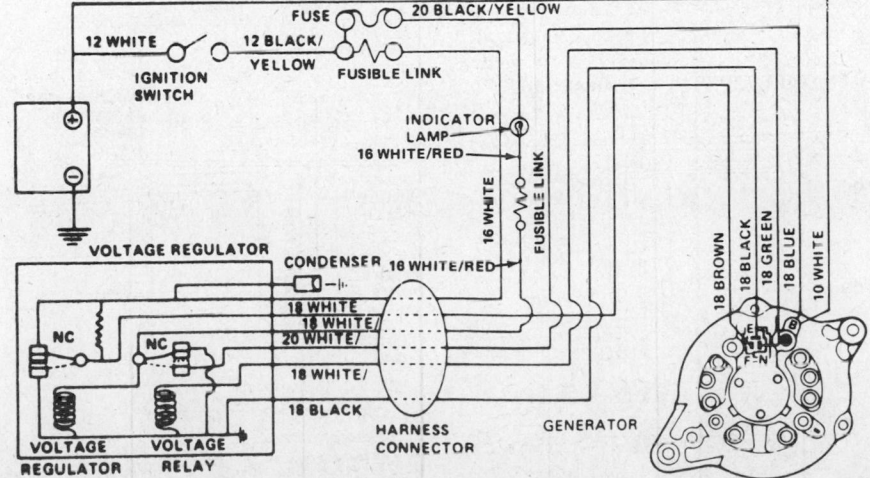

Alternator and regulator wiring schematic

gap of 0.012 in. (0.3mm).

17. Release the armature and adjust the gap between the ''E'' side point and the moving point by bending the point arm ''F''. The gap should be 0.012–0.016 in. (0.3–0.46mm).

18. After the gap adjustment is made, recheck the no load regulated voltage and repeat the core arm adjustment if necessary.

19. Adjust the point gap by loosening the 3 mm screw attaching the upper contact.

Move the contact up or down as desired.

20. Adjust the regulated voltage with the adjusting screw. Turn clockwise to decrease it. Be sure to tighten the lock nut when adjustments are complete.

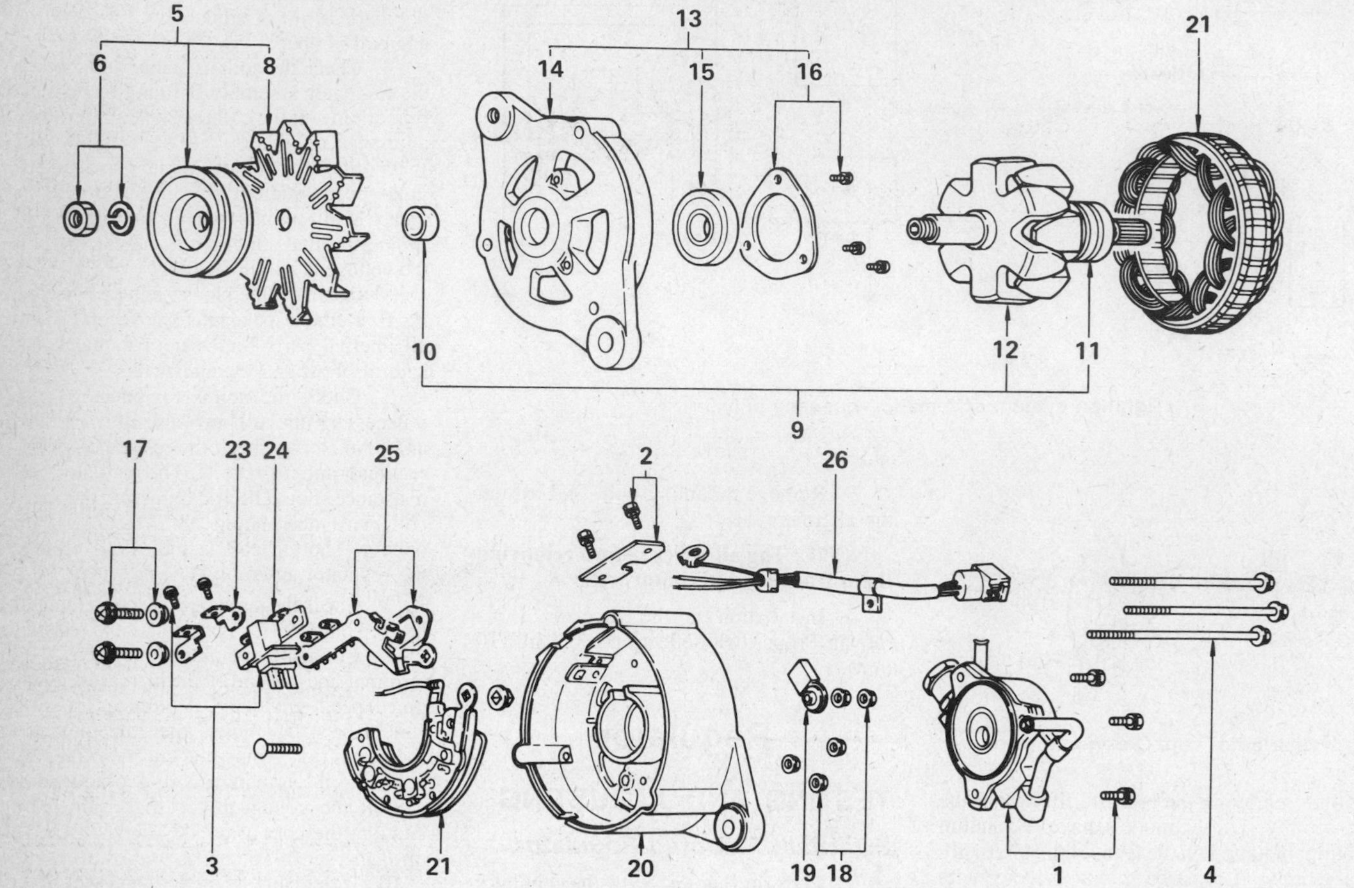

1. Vacuum pump	7. Pulley	12. Rotor	17. Screw	22. Diode
2. Cover	8. Fan	13. Front cover assembly	18. Terminal bolt and nut	23. Holder plate
3. Brush	9. Rotor assembly	14. Front cover	19. Condenser	24. Brush holder
4. Through bolt	10. Spacer	15. Ball bearing	20. Rear cover	25. IC regulator assembly
5. Pulley assembly	11. Ball bearing	16. Bearing retainer	21. Stator	26. Lead wire
6. Pulley nut				

Exploded view of the diesel alternator. Gasoline engine model similar but without vacuum pump.

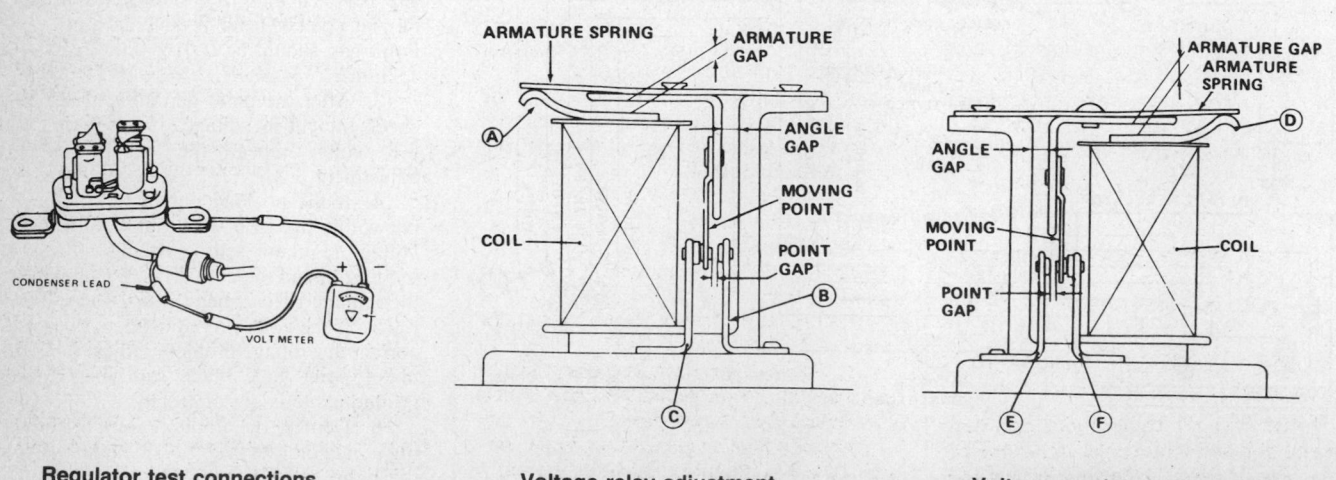

Regulator test connections   **Voltage relay adjustment**   **Voltage regulator adjustments**

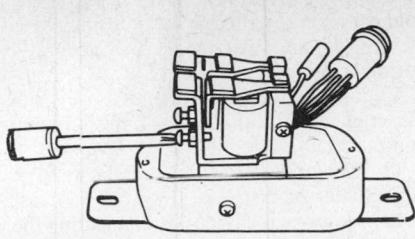

Adjustment of regulator voltage

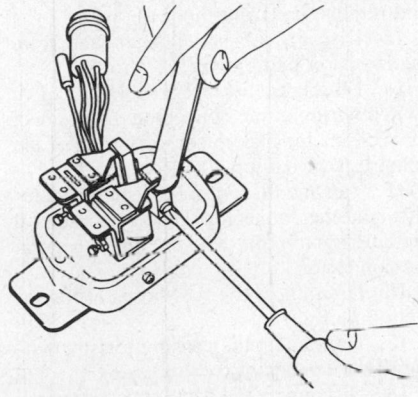

Adjustment of regulator point gap

Starter with magnetic valve removed—gasoline engine

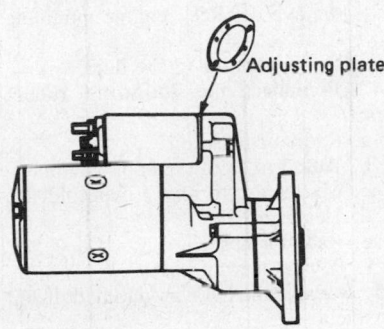

Typical diesel engine starter assembly showing adjustment shims

Starter

REMOVAL & INSTALLATION

Gasoline Engines

1. Disconnect the battery cables at the battery posts.
2. Disconnect the EGR pipe from the EGR valve and exhaust manifold, then remove the EGR pipe.
3. Disconnect the wiring from the starter magnetic switch.

NOTE: Tag all wires before disconnecting.

4. Remove the bolts and nuts attaching the starter to the motor.
5. Remove the starter assembly through the clearance under the intake manifold.
6. Installation is the reverse of removal.

Diesel Engines

1. Open the hood and disconnect the battery cables at the posts.
2. Disconnect the magnetic switch wiring at the connector.

NOTE: Label all wires before disconnecting.

3. Remove the starter motor attaching nut and bolt and remove the starter motor.
4. Installation is the reverse of removal.

ENGINE MECHANICAL

Engine

REMOVAL & INSTALLATION

Gasoline Engine
I-MARK

1. Remove the battery cables.
2. Scribe the position of the hood hinges on the underside of the hood. Remove the four attaching bolts and lift off the hood.
3. Remove the bottom shrouds and drain the crankcase and cooling system.
4. Disconnect the PCV hose from the air cleaner body. Disconnect the air hose from the air pump and remove the air duct from the air cleaner.
5. Remove the bolts attaching the air cleaner and loosen the clamp bolt.
6. Disconnect the thermostatic air cleaner (TAC) hot air hose and remove the manifold cover.
7. Tag and disconnect the generator wires at the connector.
8. Remove the two nuts connecting the exhaust pipe to the exhaust manifold and disconnect the exhaust pipe.
9. Take the tension off the clutch control cable by loosening the adjusting nut.

10. Disconnect the heater hose from the engine to the heater control valve at the engine side.
11. Disconnect the heater hose from the heater unit and joint.
12. Disconnect the control cable from the heater temperature valve and remove the control valve together with the hose.
13. Remove the engine mounting nut.
14. Support the engine with special tool J-26555 or equivalent. Attach the engine hanger using the exhaust manifold stud bolts.
15. Disconnect the cable grounding the cylinder block to the frame.
16. Disconnect the fuel lines and vapor lines from the carburetor and charcoal canister.
17. Remove the high tension cable from the coil. Disconnect the vacuum hose from the rear of the intake manifold at the connector.
18. Disconnect the accelerator control cable from the carburetor.
19. Disconnect the starter motor wiring.

NOTE: Tag all wires before disconnecting.

20. Disconnect the thermo-unit, oil pressure switch and distributor wiring at the connectors.
21. Disconnect the carburetor solenoid valve and the automatic choke wiring at the connectors.
22. Disconnect the back-up light switch and transmission switch wiring at the connector on the rear part of the engine.
23. Disconnect the emission control hose from the oil pan.
24. Remove the engine mounting nut.

— **CAUTION** —
Make sure the engine is well-supported from above.

25. Remove the stopper plate.
26. Connect the engine hoist. Raise the engine slightly and disconnect the left side engine mounting stopper plate.
27. Disconnect the air conditioner hoses.

— **CAUTION** —
Discharge the A/C system before attempting to disconnect any hoses.

28. Disconnect the radiator upper and lower hoses. Remove the bolts attaching the fan shroud and remove the shroud.
29. Remove the radiator attaching bolts and remove the radiator by lifting straight upward.
30. Remove the fan blades from the pulley.
31. Remove the gearshift lever assembly.
32. Disconnect the parking brake return spring and disconnect the cable.
33. Disconnect the propeller shaft from the transmission. Remove the clutch return spring.
34. Disconnect the clutch control cable from the clutch withdraw lever and remove it from the engine stiffener.

35. Remove the front side exhaust pipe bracket from the transmission.

36. Disconnect the front and rear side exhaust pipes at the joint, then remove the front side exhaust pipe.

37. Disconnect the speedometer cable.

38. Remove the rear engine mounting bolts.

NOTE: Check that the engine is slightly lifted before removing the rear mounting bolts.

39. Check to make certain all the parts have been removed or disconnected from the engine and that the parts are tied safely out of the way so as not to snag when the engine is being lifted clear.

40. Lift the engine and slide it toward the front of the car. Remove the transmission from the engine and set it on the floor.

41. Slowly lift the engine clear.

42. Installation is the reverse of removal. Fill the crankcase and cooling system. Check and adjust the clutch pedal free play and check the carburetor and clutch linkage for smooth operation. Start the engine and check for leaks.

IMPULSE

1. Remove the battery cables.

2. Disconnect the headlight cover motor harness, remove the strut-to-hood bolt and the engine hood side bolt and remove the hood.

3. Drain the crankshaft and cooling systems.

4. Disconnect the upper radiator hose.

5. Disconnect the oil cooler line for the automatic transmission (if so equipped).

6. On models with air conditioning, remove the compressor mounting bracket from the engine and position the compressor out of the way without disconnecting the refrigerant lines.

NOTE: If the compressor lines do not have enough slack to move the compressor out of the way without disconnecting the refrigerant lines, the air conditioning system must be evacuated, using the required tools, before the refrigerant lines can be disconnected.

--- CAUTION ---

Do not disconnect any refrigerant lines unless you have experience with air conditioning systems. Escaping refrigerant will freeze any surface it contacts, including your skin and eyes.

7. Remove the rubber air duct hose to the cylinder head cover.

8. Disconnect the accelerator cable.

9. Disconnect and tag the rubber hoses at the following connections:

a. Between the injection pipe and the pressure regulator.

b. Fuel pipe to injection pipe.

c. Canister (purge) to common chamber.

d. Canister (VC) to 3-way.

e. VSV to common chamber.

f. VSV to 3-way.

g. Solenoid fast idle to common chamber.

h. Solenoid fast idle to thermal valve.

10. Disconnect the cable harness between the fender skirt and the cylinder head.

11. Disconnect and tag the connectors at the following locations:

a. Oil pressure switch.

b. Water temperature sensor.

c. Knock sensor.

d. I-TEC harness.

e. Crank angle distributor sensor.

f. Starter terminal.

g. Cable harness, engine rear to cross-member front.

h. Automatic transmission control.

i. O₂ Sensor.

12. Remove the R.H. engine mounting nut.

13. Remove the air intake duct.

14. Disconnect the following rubber hoses.

a. Radiator reservoir.

b. Auto cruise to common chamber.

c. Master vac to intake manifold.

d. Heater hoses.

e. Radiator hoses.

f. Power steering hoses.

15. Remove the L.H. mounting bolt and heat shield.

16. Remove the cover from under the engine.

17. Disconnect the propeller shaft and install a plug in the transmission rear cover to prevent the oil from draining.

18. On models with automatic transmission remove the pin from the transmission select lever.

19. Disconnect the speedometer cable.

20. On models equipped with manual transmissions remove the clutch slave cylinder.

21. Remove the converter mounting bracket.

22. Remove the exhaust pipe nut to manifold.

23. Disconnect the rear engine mounting bracket.

24. Install an engine hoist and remove the engine and transmission from the vehicle.

25. Installation is the reverse of removal.

Diesel Engine

1. Open the hood and remove the battery cables at the posts. Remove the battery.

2. Scribe the position of the hinges on the underside of the hood and remove the hood.

3. Remove the bottom shrouds.

4. Drain the radiator and crankcase.

5. Remove the fan shroud attaching screws and remove the shroud. Remove the radiator attaching bolts and remove the radiator after disconnecting the upper and lower hoses.

6. Remove the air connecting hose.

7. Disconnect the heater hoses at the thermostat housing pipe and water inlet pipe.

8. Disconnect the quick start and silent idle (Q.S.S.I.) thermo switch, fast idle thermo switch, thermo unit wiring at the connector on the thermostat housing.

9. Tag and disconnect the generator wiring at the connector.

10. Disconnect the vacuum hose from the connector at the rear of the vacuum pump.

11. Disconnect the vacuum hose from the actuator of fast idle.

12. Remove the two nuts connecting the exhaust pipe to the exhaust manifold and separate the pipe from the manifold, then remove the two nuts connecting the exhaust front pipe to the exhaust mounting bracket and separate the front pipe from the bracket and remove the front pipe.

13. Disconnect the accelerator cable from the injection pump lever.

14. Disconnect the fuel cut colenoid valve switch wiring at the connector. Disconnect the tachometer pickup sensor wiring at the connector (if equipped).

15. Tag and disconnect the starter motor wiring at the connector. Disconnect the oil pressure switch, oil pressure unit wiring at the connector.

16. Disconnect the fuel hoses at the injection pump.

17. Disconnect the sensing resistor wiring at the connector.

18. Disconnect the back-up lamp switch and the top/third switch wiring at the connector on the rear of the engine.

19. Remove the return spring and disconnect the clutch control cable from the hook on the withdraw lever.

20. Disconnect the speedometer cable at the transmission side.

21. Remove the four bolts connecting the propeller shaft with the extension shaft and disconnect the propeller shaft flange yoke from the extension shaft, then pull the propeller shaft rearward. When the propeller shaft has been removed, wrap a small plastic bag around the rear transmission housing to prevent any leakage of fluid.

22. Untie the strings on the console boot and remove the screws on each side of the console box. Remove the grommets between the floor carpet and floor panel.

23. Pry off the edge of the gearshift lever dust boot and remove the gearshift lever assembly upward.

NOTE: Plug the gearshift lever fitting hole to prevent entry of dust or foreign material.

24. Remove the bolts and nuts attaching the rear mounting bracket, then remove the bolts attaching the exhaust mounting bracket.

25. Using a chain, engine lifting fixtures or other suitable means, lift the engine slightly.

26. Remove the engine mount nuts and disconnect the engine damper from the frame.

27. Check to make certain all parts have been removed or disconnected and tied out of the way so as not to snag on the motor when it is lifted clear.

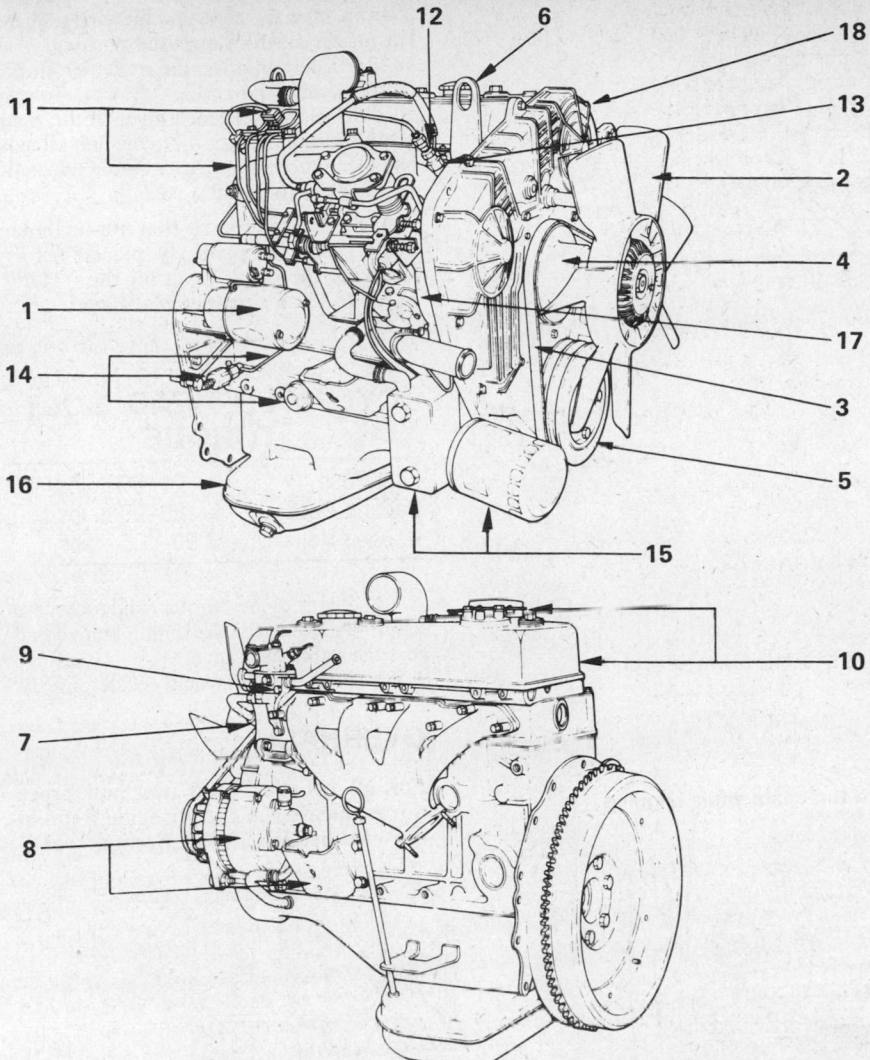

Diesel engine major components

1. Starter motor assembly
2. Cooling fan
3. V-belt
4. Fan pulley
5. Damper pulley
6. Engine hanger
7. Water by-pass hose
8. Generator assembly and engine foot
9. Thermostat housing
10. Cam cover with positive crankcase ventilation valve
11. Injection pipe and clip
12. Nozzle holder assembly
13. Glow plug and connector
14. Oil pressure switch, unit and oil pipe
15. Oil cooler and oil filter
16. Oil pan
17. Tension spring
18. Dust cover

5. Drain the cooling system.

6. Lower the car.

7. Disconnect the heater hoses at the intake manifold and at the rear of the cylinder head.

8. Disconnect the accelerator linkage, all necessary electrical connections, spark plug wires and necessary vacuum lines.

NOTE: Tag all wires and hoses before disconnecting them from the engine.

9. Rotate the camshaft until No. 4 cylinder is in firing position. Remove the distributor cap and mark the rotor–to–housing relationship. This simple act will save untold grief when trying to get the distributor back in correctly.

10. Lock the timing chain adjuster by depressing and turning the automatic chain adjuster slide pin 90° clockwise.

11. Remove the timing sprocket–to–camshaft bolt and remove the sprocket from the camshaft. Keep the sprocket on the chain damper and tensioner. Do not remove the sprocket from the chain.

12. Disconnect the air pump hose and check valve at the exhaust manifold.

13. Remove the cylinder head–to–timing cover bolts.

14. Remove the cylinder head bolts using an extension bar with socket. Remove bolts in progressive sequence, beginning with the outer bolts.

NOTE: Use light oil to free frozen bolts.

15. With the aid of an assistant, remove the cylinder head, intake and exhaust manifolds as an assembly.

16. Clean all gasket material from the cylinder head and block surfaces. Check for nicks or heavy scratches on the mating surfaces.

17. Installation is the reverse of removal. Cylinder bolt threads in the block and threads on the bolts must be cleaned. Dirt will affect head torque.

18. Torque all head bolts to specifications according to the sequence in the front of the chapter. Torque bolts to half normal value in sequence, then to specifications on the second pass.

28. Attach the engine hoist and remove the engine assembly with the transmission attached. Slowly lift the engine clear of the chassis.

29. Installation is the reverse of removal. Fill the crankcase, cooling system and check all cable adjustments.

30. Bleed the fuel system by filling the filter with diesel fuel and operating the priming pump handle several times. The force needed to operate the priming pump becomes greater as the filter fills up.

31. Start the engine and check for leaks.

Cylinder Head

REMOVAL & INSTALLATION

Gasoline Engines

1. Remove the cam cover.

2. Remove the EGR pipe clamp bolt at the rear of the cylinder head.

3. Raise the vehicle and safely support it.

4. Disconnect the exhaust pipe at the exhaust manifold.

CYLINDER HEAD BOLT TORQUE

First Pass	61 ft. lbs.
Second Pass	72 ft. lbs.

Diesel Engines

1. Drain the cooling system by opening the drain plug on the cylinder block.

2. Remove the camshaft.

3. Remove the sensing resistor assembly.

4. Remove the six screws attaching the injection pipe clip and remove the injection pipe clip.

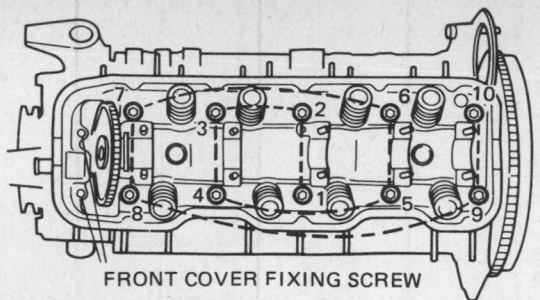

FRONT COVER FIXING SCREW

Cylinder head bolt torque sequence—gasoline engine

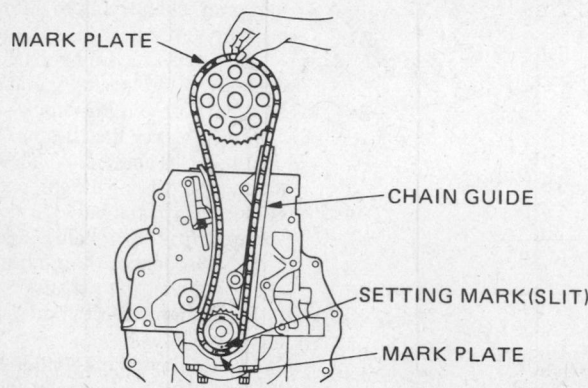

MARK PLATE

CHAIN GUIDE

SETTING MARK (SLIT)

MARK PLATE

Keep the timing sprocket attached to the chain while aligning or removing

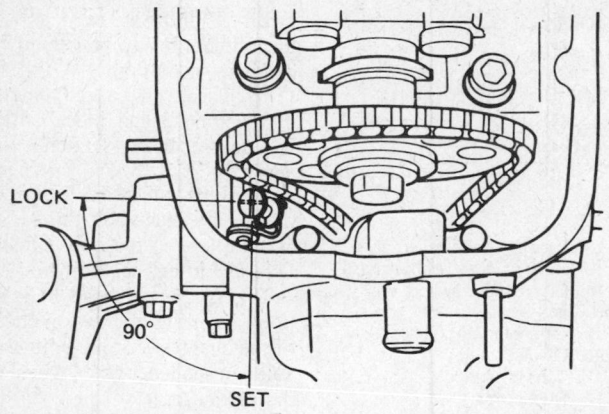

LOCK

90°

SET

Locking the timing chain adjuster—110.8 cu. in. engine

5. Remove the eight sleeve nuts attaching the injection pipes and separate the injection pipes.

6. Remove the clip attaching the fuel leak off hose and separate the hose from the return pipe.

7. Remove the two nuts connecting the exhaust manifold to the exhaust pipe and separate the pipe from the manifold.

8. Disconnect the joint bolt attaching the oil feed line to the head side.

9. Disconnect the heater hose at the thermostat housing pipe.

10. Remove the cylinder head bolts by loosening them in sequence, then remove the cylinder head and gasket.

NOTE: Use light oil to free stubborn bolts.

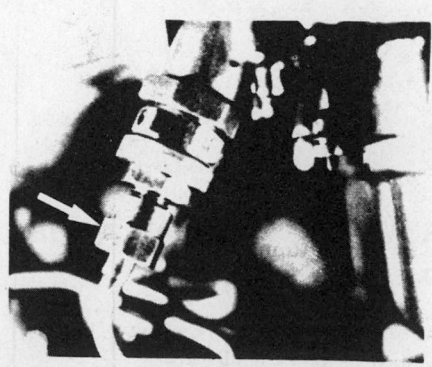

Diesel fuel injector showing injection pipe union

11. Clean the head and block of all gasket material before reassembly.

12. Installation is the reverse of removal. Refill the cooling system. Torque all bolts in the sequence given at the front of this section. Apply oil to the bolt threads and clean them thoroughly before reinstalling them in the head.

NOTE: Make sure that the cylinder head gasket is properly placed before lowering the head. Look for the "TOP" mark to assure proper placement.

CYLINDER HEAD BOLT TORQUE

First Pass	21–36 ft. lbs.
Second Pass	83–98 ft. lbs.
Reused Bolt	90–105 ft. lbs.

13. Reinstall the camshaft and rocker arm assembly. Reinstall the timing belt and adjust the valve clearance.

14. Start the engine and check for leaks.

OVERHAUL

For all cylinder head overhaul procedures, please refer to "Engine Rebuilding" in the Unit Repair Section.

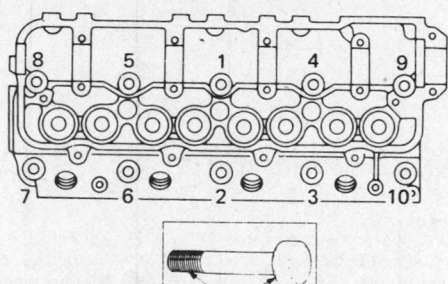

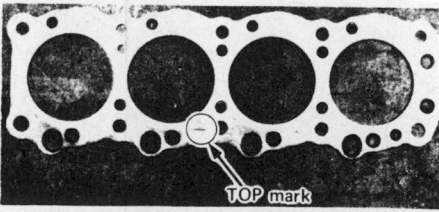

Lubricate with engine oil

Cylinder head bolt torque sequence—diesel engine

TOP mark

Location of TOP mark

Rocker Arms/Shaft

REMOVAL & INSTALLATION
All Engines

1. Remove the cam cover.

2. On the 118.9 cu. in. engine release the tension on the automatic adjuster prior

to removal of the rocker shaft assembly as follows:

a. With a screwdriver or equivalent depress the lock lever on the automatic adjuster rearward.

b. Push on the automatic adjuster shoe and lock it in the retracted position by releasing the lever.

3. Loosen the rocker arm shaft bracket nuts a little at a time, in sequence, commencing with the outer brackets.

4. Remove the nuts from the rocker arm shaft brackets.

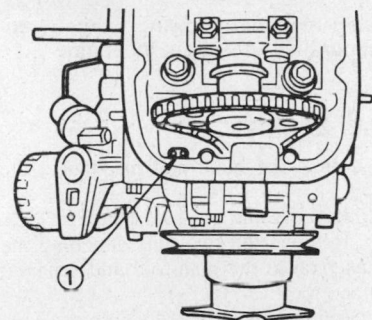

Timing chain automatic adjuster lock lever (1)—118.9 cu. in. gasoline engine

Push in on the automatic adjuster shoe (1) and lock it in the retracted position by releasing lever (2)—118.9 cu. in. gasoline engine

5. Disassemble the rocker arm shaft assembly by removing the spring from the rocker arm shaft and then removing the rocker arm brackets and arms.

6. Inspect the rocker arm shaft for runout. Support the shaft on V-blocks at each end and check runout by slowly turning it with the probe of a dial indicator. Replace the shaft with a new one if the runout exceeds 0.0156 in. (0.4mm). Runout should not exceed 0.0079 in. (0.2mm).

7. Inspect the rocker arm shaft for wear, replace the shaft if obvious signs of wear are encountered.

8. Installation is the reverse of removal. Use a liberal amount of clean engine oil to coat the shaft, rocker arms and valve stems. Install the longer shaft on the exhaust valve side, shorter shaft on the intake side, so that the aligning marks on the shafts are turned to the front of the engine.

9. Torque the rocker arm shaft bracket stud nuts to 16–22 ft. lbs. (110.8 cu. in. engine), 15–17 ft. lbs. (118.9 cu in. engine). Hold the rocker arm springs with an adjustable wrench while torquing nuts to prevent damage to the springs. Torque nuts

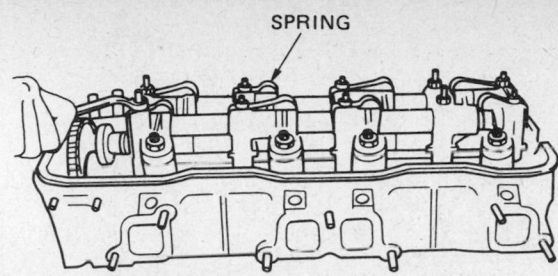

Rocker arm assembly—gasoline engine

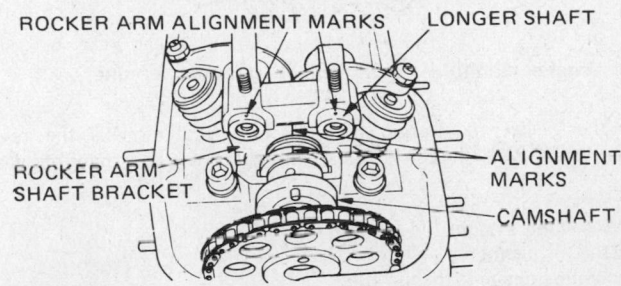

Rocker arm shaft installation—gasoline engine

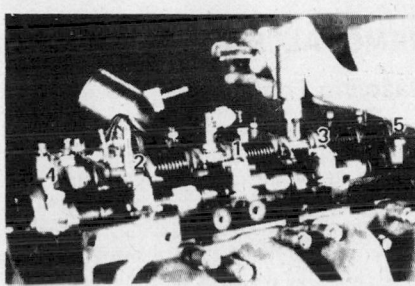

Rocker shaft torque sequence—diesel engine

a little at a time in sequence, beginning with the center bracket and working outward.

10. Adjust valve clearances, reinstall the cam cover and check for leaks.

Intake Manifold

REMOVAL & INSTALLATION

Gasoline Engines
I-MARK

1. Drain the cooling system.

NOTE: Before removing the intake manifold, check to make certain the engine coolant is completely drained. If any water remains in the block it will flow into the cylinders when the intake manifold is removed.

2. Remove the air cleaner assembly.

3. Disconnect the radiator hose from the front part of the intake manifold.

4. Disconnect the fuel lines, all vacuum lines and the carburetor control cable.

5. Disconnect the heater hoses from the rear part of the manifold and from the connector under the dashboard.

6. Disconnect the distributor vacuum

hose and all thermo-valve wiring. Disconnect the electric choke or solenoid wires.

NOTE: Tag all wires before disconnecting them.

7. Disconnect the PCV hose from the rocker cover. Disconnect the EGR valve from the EGR pipe and disconnect the air injection vacuum hose from the three-way connector.

8. Remove the eight nuts attaching the intake manifold and lift it clear, being careful not to snag any loose lines.

9. Installation is the reverse of removal. Check the manifold for cracks or damage. The manifold head surfaces can be checked for distortion by using a straight edge and a feeler gauge. Distortion should be no more than 0.0157 in. (0.4mm), if it is beyond the limit, the distortion has to be corrected with a surface grinder.

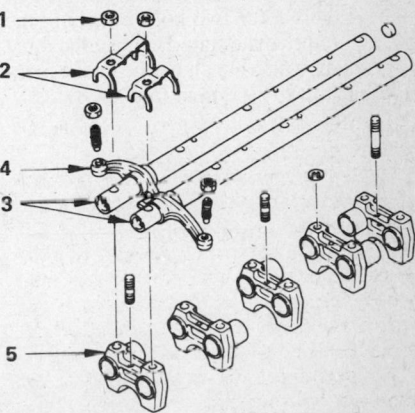

1. Rocker arm bracket nut
2. Rocker arm spring
3. Rocker arm shaft
4. Rocker arm
5. Rocker arm shaft bracket

Rocker arm and shaft assembly—118.9 cu. in. engine

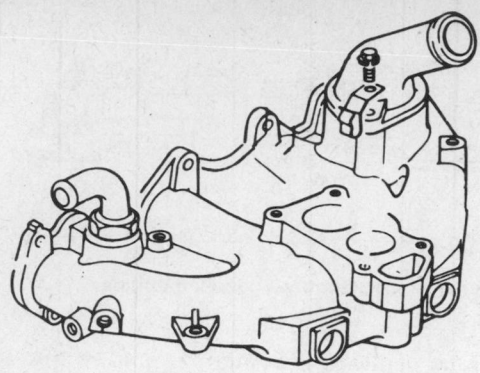

Intake manifold—110.8 cu. in. gasoline engine

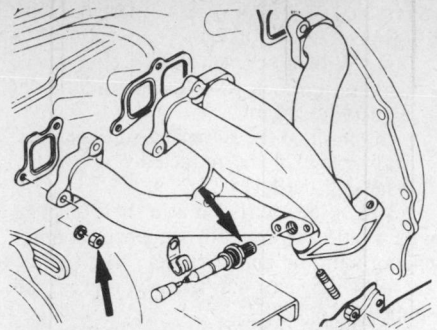

Exhaust manifold showing oxygen sensor mounting—118.9 cu. in. engine

10. Replace the gasket and torque all nuts in sequence to 25–32 ft. lbs.

IMPULSE

1. Drain the cooling system.
2. Remove the air cleaners.
3. Disconnect the linkage to the throttle valve.
4. Tag and disconnect all wires and hoses.
5. Remove the eight manifold attaching bolts and remove the manifold and common chamber as an assembly.
6. Installation is the reverse of removal.

Diesel Engine

1. Open the hood and disconnect the battery. Remove the air cleaner assembly.
2. Remove the connecting hose and PCV hose.
3. Remove the sensing resistor assembly.
4. Remove the six screws attaching the injection pipe clips and remove the injection pipe.
5. Remove the ten bolts attaching the upper dust cover and remove the upper dust cover.
6. Remove the two bolts attaching the engine hanger and remove the engine hanger.
7. Remove the two bolts attaching the stay and remove the stay. Remove the three bolts and two nuts attaching the intake manifold and lift off the manifold.

8. Installation is the reverse of removal. Use a new manifold gasket. Torque to 25–32 ft. lbs.

Exhaust Manifold

REMOVAL & INSTALLATION

Gasoline Engines

1. Remove the bolts attaching the air cleaner and loosen the clamp bolt.
2. Lift the air cleaner slightly and remove the hot air hose.
3. Remove the bolts attaching the manifold cover and remove the manifold cover.
4. Remove the EGR pipe clip from the upper portion of the transmission and disconnect the EGR pipe from the exhaust manifold.
5. Remove the two nuts connecting the exhaust pipe with the exhaust manifold and disconnect the exhaust pipe from the manifold.
6. Remove the seven nuts mounting the exhaust manifold and remove the manifold.
7. Installation is the reverse of removal. Use a straightedge to check for distortion as described in the intake section. Use new gaskets and torque to 11–18 ft. lbs.

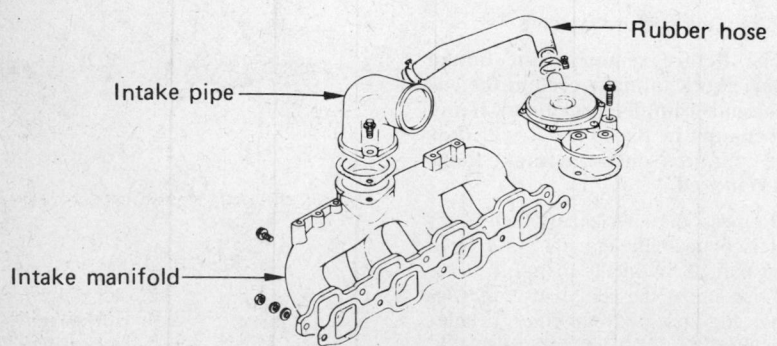

Intake manifold—diesel engine

Diesel Engines

1. Open the hood and disconnect the battery.
2. Remove the oil level gauge.
3. Remove the two nuts attaching the exhaust pipe to the manifold and separate the pipe.
4. Remove the six bolts and two nuts attaching the exhaust manifold to the cylinder head. Remove the distance tube, manifold and gaskets.
5. The gasket surfaces should be cleaned and inspected for nicks or deep scratches. Use a new gasket when installing with the "TOP" mark turned to the manifold side.
6. Installation is the reverse of removal. Torque all manifold nuts and bolts to 11–18 ft. lbs.

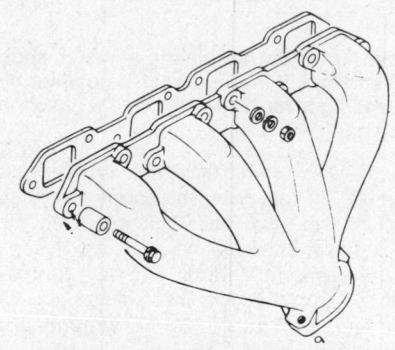

Exhaust manifold—diesel engine

Timing Chain

REMOVAL & INSTALLATION

Gasoline Engines Only

1. Open the hood and disconnect the battery. Drain the cooling system.
2. Disconnect the radiator inlet and outlet hoses. Remove the radiator.
3. Remove the generator and the A/C drive belts.
4. Remove the engine fan.
5. Remove the crankshaft pulley center bolt and remove the pulley and hub assembly.
6. Remove the cylinder head.

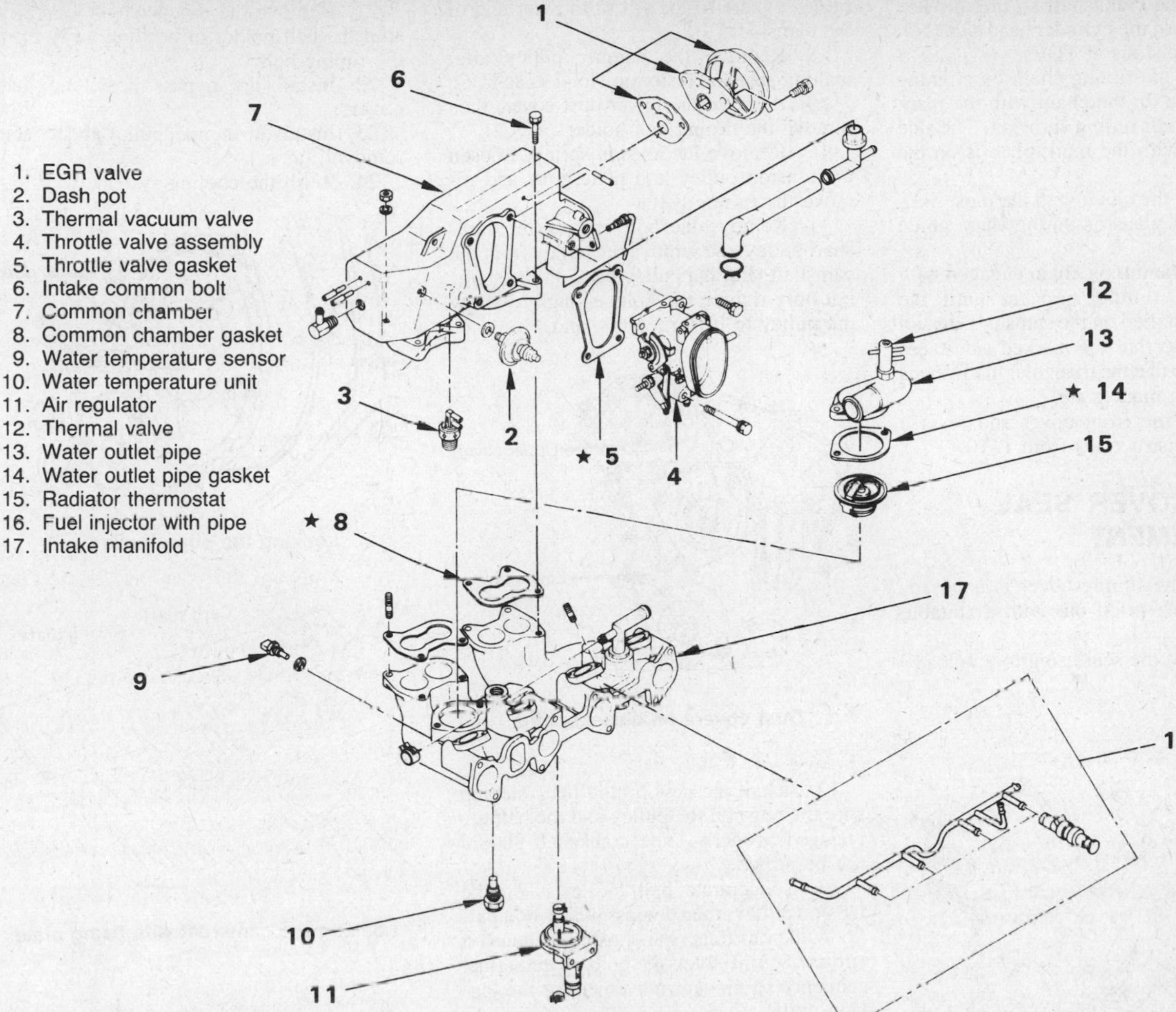

1. EGR valve
2. Dash pot
3. Thermal vacuum valve
4. Throttle valve assembly
5. Throttle valve gasket
6. Intake common bolt
7. Common chamber
8. Common chamber gasket
9. Water temperature sensor
10. Water temperature unit
11. Air regulator
12. Thermal valve
13. Water outlet pipe
14. Water outlet pipe gasket
15. Radiator thermostat
16. Fuel injector with pipe
17. Intake manifold

Intake manifold and common chamber—118.9 cu. in. engine

CHAIN GUIDE
AUTOMATIC ADJUSTER
CHAIN TENSIONER
TIMING CHAIN
PINION GEAR
TIMING SPROCKET

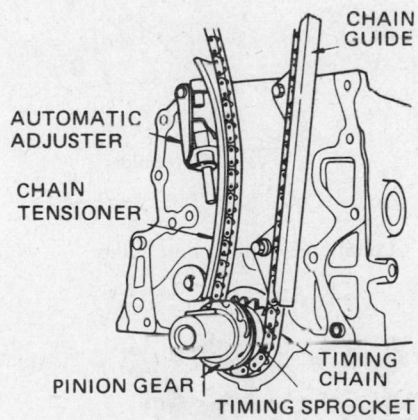

Removing the timing chain

7. Remove the oil pan.
8. Remove the oil pick–up tube from the pump.
9. Remove the air pump belt, remove the compressor (if equipped with A/C) and lay it to one side. Remove the compressor mounting brackets.
10. Remove the distributor.
11. Remove the front cover attaching bolts and remove the front cover.
12. Remove the timing chain from the crankshaft sprocket. Check sprockets for damage or wear. If the sprocket on the crankshaft must be replaced, a gear puller will be necessary to remove it.
13. Inspect the automatic chain adjuster for wear or damage. Replace any component that is doubtful. Make sure that the adjuster is freely rotating on its pins.

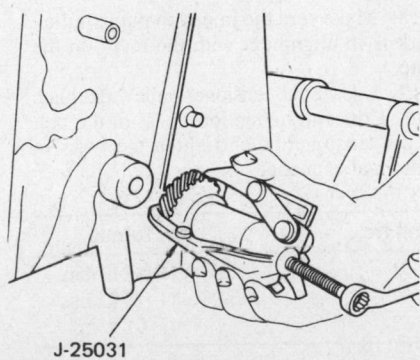

J-25031

Using a puller to remove crankshaft sprocket

MARK PLATE
CHAIN GUIDE
SETTING MARK (SLIT)
MARK PLATE

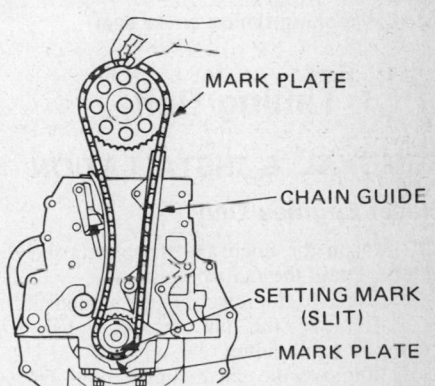

Timing chain alignment—gasoline engines

14. Install the timing sprocket and pinion gear (groove side toward front cover). Align the key grooves with the key on the crankshaft and then drive it into position with special tool J-26587 or equivalent.

15. Turn the crankshaft so that the key is turned toward the cylinder head side (No. 1 and No. 4 pistons at TDC).

16. Install the timing chain by aligning the mark plate on the chain with the mark on the crankshaft timing sprocket. The side of the chain with the mark plate is on the front side.

The side of the chain with the most links between mark plates is on the chain guide side.

17. Keep the timing chain engaged with the camshaft timing sprocket until the sprocket is installed on the camshaft. Install the sprocket so that the marked side faces forward and so that the triangular mark aligns with the chain mark plate.

18. Install the front cover and reverse the removal instructions from 1–10.

TIMING COVER SEAL REPLACEMENT

1. Once the timing cover is exposed, the seal can be pried out with a suitable screwdriver.

2. Replace the seal using tool J-26587 or equivalent.

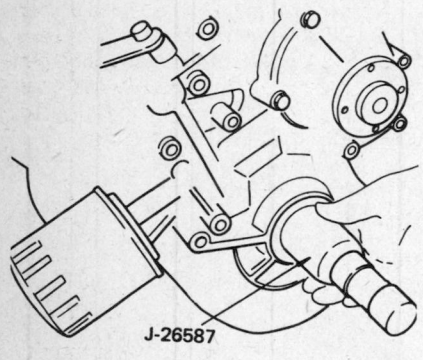

J-26587

Installing timing cover seal

Timing Belt

REMOVAL & INSTALLATION

Diesel Engines Only

1. Open the hood and disconnect the battery. Drain the radiator system.

2. Remove the lower engine shrouds.

3. Remove the fan shroud, v-belt, cooling fan and pulley.

4. Remove the ten retaining bolts on the upper dust cover and remove the cover.

5. Remove the bypass hose.

6. With the piston in the No. 1 cylinder at TDC, make sure the setting mark on the pump pulley is in alignment with the front plate, then lock the pulley with an 8mm 1.25 pitch bolt.

7. Remove the cam cover. Loosen the adjusting screws so that the rocker arms are held in a free state. Lock the camshaft by

fitting a plate to the slit in the rear end of the camshaft.

8. Remove the damper pulley after making sure the piston in No. 1 is at TDC.

9. Remove the lower dust cover, then remove the timing belt holder.

10. Remove the tension spring. Loosen the tension pulley and plate bolts and remove the timing belt.

11. Remove the bolt locking the camshaft pulley and remove the pulley from the camshaft. Put the pulley back on the shaft, but only tighten the bolts enough to allow the pulley to be turned by hand.

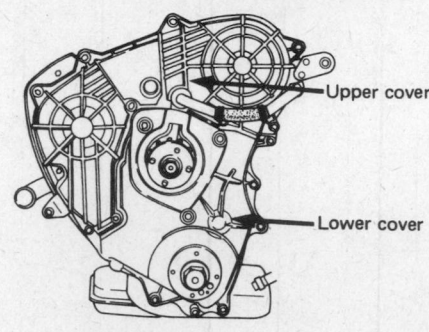

← Upper cover

← Lower cover

Dust covers on diesel engine

12. Install the new timing belt, making sure the cogs on the pulley and the belt are engaged properly. The crankshaft should not be turned.

13. Concentrate belt looseness on the tension pulley, then depress the tension pulley with your fingers and install the tension spring. Semi-tighten the bolts in numerical sequence to prevent movement of the tension pulley.

14. Tighten the camshaft pulley bolts.

15. Remove the injection pump pulley lock bolt.

16. Remove the locking plate on the end of the camshaft.

17. Install the damper pulley on the hub and make sure the No. 1 piston is still at TDC.

CAUTION
Do not turn the crankshaft in an attempt to make an adjustment.

---

18. Make sure the injection pump pulley mark is in alignment with the mark on the plate.

19. Loosen the tensioner pulley and plate bolts. Concentrate the looseness of the belt on the tensioner, then tighten the bolts in numerical sequence. Torque the bolts to:

Bolt No.	Torque
1	11–18 ft. lbs.
2	11–18 ft. lbs.
3	47–61 ft. lbs.

20. Check valve adjustment and install the cam cover.

21. Remove the damper pulley and install the belt holder in position away from the timing belt.

22. Install the bypass hose and dust covers.

23. Install the damper pulley and reverse removal Steps 1–5.

24. Refill the cooling system.

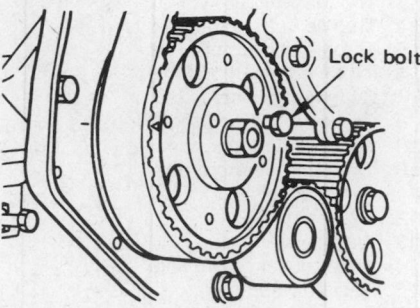

← Lock bolt

Locking the pump pulley

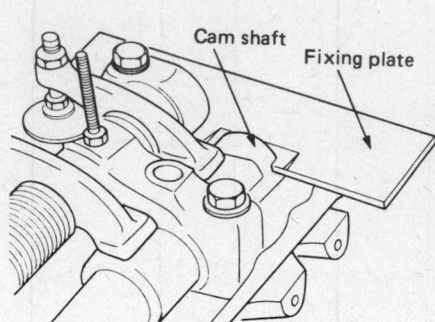

Cam shaft

Fixing plate

Locking the camshaft with fixing plate

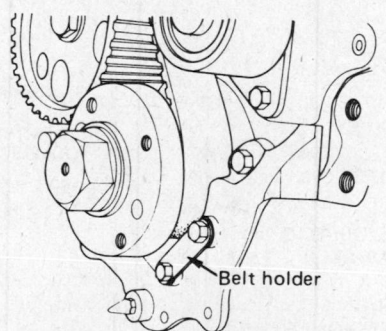

Belt holder

Location of timing belt holder

Install timing belt in numerical sequence

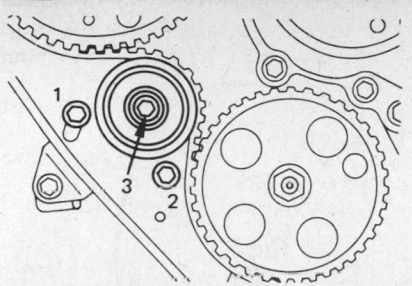

Tensioner pulley bolt tightening sequence

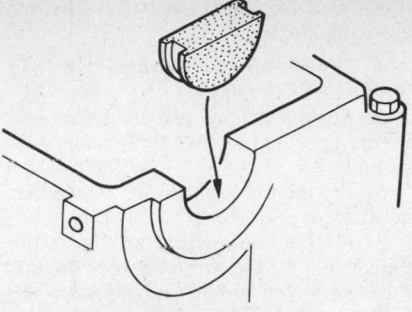

Half-moon seal

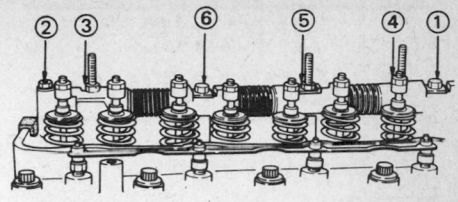

Bolt loosening sequence for removing rocker arm assembly

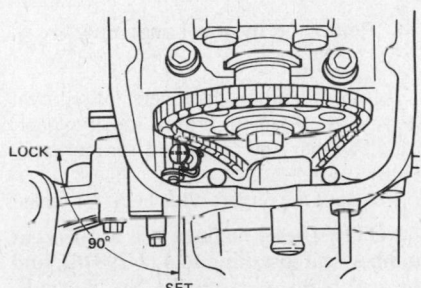

Locking the timing chain adjuster—110.8 cu. in. gasoline engine

Camshaft

REMOVAL & INSTALLATION

Gasoline Engines

1. Remove the cam cover.
2. Rotate the camshaft until No. 4 cylinder is in firing position. Remove the distributor cap and mark the rotor-to-housing position.
3. On the 110.9 cu. in. engine, lock the timing chain adjuster by depressing and turning the automatic adjuster slide pin 90° in a clockwise direction. After locking the chain adjuster, check that the chain is loose.
4. On the 118.9 cu. in. engine, release the tension on the automatic adjuster as follows:

    a. With a screwdriver or equivalent depress the lock lever on the automatic adjuster rearward.

    b. Push in the automatic adjuster shoe and lock in the retracted position by releasing the lever.

5. Remove the timing sprocket-to-camshaft bolt and remove the sprocket on the chain damper and tensioner without removing the chain from the sprocket.
6. Remove the rocker arm, shaft and the bracket assembly.
7. Remove the camshaft.
8. Installation is the reverse of removal. Use a liberal amount of clean oil to coat the camshaft before installing. Check that the mark on the No. 1 rocker arms shaft bracket is in alignment with the mark on the camshaft and that the crankshaft pulley groove is aligned with the TDC mark ("O" mark) on the front cover.

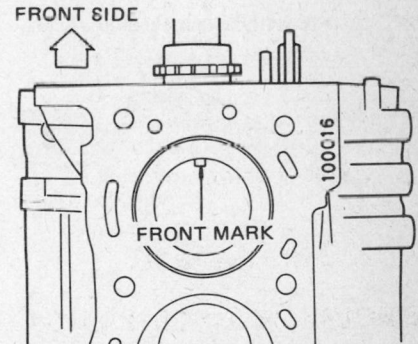

Removing camshaft pulley with gear puller

9. Assemble the timing sprocket to the camshaft by aligning it with the pin on the camshaft. Use care not to remove the chain from the sprocket.
10. Install the sprocket retaining bolt. Remove the half-moon seal in the front end of the head, insert a torque wrench and torque the bolt to 58 ft. lbs. Apply sealant and replace the half-moon seal in the head.
11. Set the automatic adjuster by turning the adjuster slide pin 90° counterclockwise with a screwdriver.
12. Check the valve timing and the rotor mark alignment on the distributor. Reinstall the distributor cap.

Diesel Engines

1. Remove the cam cover.
2. Remove the timing belt.
3. Remove the rear plug and hold the shaft by attaching the fixing plate (J-29761 or equivalent) into the slit at the rear of the camshaft.
4. Remove the camshaft pulley bolt, then remove the pulley with a gear puller.
5. Remove the rocker arm and shaft.
6. Remove the bolts attaching the front head plate and remove the plate.
7. Remove the bolts attaching the camshaft bearing caps. Remove the caps and bearings.
8. Remove the camshaft oil seal, then remove the camshaft.
9. Installation is the reverse of removal. Use a liberal amount of clean oil to coat the camshaft and journals during assembly.
10. Install a new oil seal and apply Permatex® or equivalent gasket compound to the cylinder head fitting face of the No. 1 camshaft bearing cap.
11. Torque the rocker arm shafts and camshaft bearing caps to specifications.

Piston and Connecting Rod

All Engines

It is not advisable to remove the piston from the connecting rod unless part replacement is necessary. Whenever a piston is removed, the piston pin should be replaced. When examining a piston, look for scuffs, cracking or wear. The rings should be removed with a ring expander and should be kept separately to avoid interchanging parts. All clearances should be checked with a micrometer or comparable precision gauge. Assemble the piston rings to the piston so that the NPR or TOP marks are turned up. Every piston has a mark to designate proper installation, this "Front Mark" is located on the top edge, in line with the piston pin bore. In addition, the cylinder number that the piston came from is stamped on the connecting rod and the bearing cap.

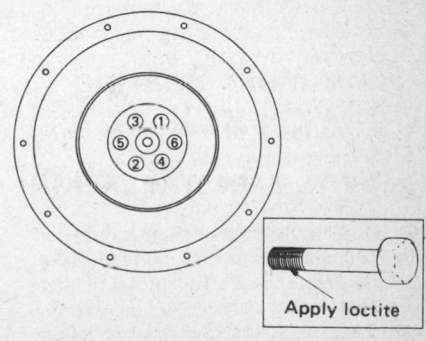

Piston correctly installed

Flywheel torque sequence

C361

ENGINE LUBRICATION

Oil Pan

REMOVAL & INSTALLATION

All Engines

NOTE: Isuzu recommends removing the engine (or at least raising it up) to service the oil pan. There isn't sufficient clearance to remove the pan with the engine bolted down.

1. Remove or raise the engine to allow sufficient room to clear the oil pan.
2. Remove the bolts and nuts attaching the oil pan to the engine block. Remove the oil pan and gasket.
3. Clean the oil pan and engine block gasket surface carefully to remove all traces of the old gasket.
4. Install in reverse order of removal, using a thin coat of Permatex® #2 or equivalent to hold the gasket in place while installing the bolts and to prevent any oil leaks.
5. Torque the oil pan bolts evenly to 4 ft. lbs. Check the edges of the gasket to ensure that it is seated properly. If the gasket projects unevenly around the oil pan flange, remove the gasket and reinstall carefully.

NOTE: Do not overtighten the oil pan bolts. Bolts that are too tight cause as many leaks as bolts that are too loose.

6. Start the engine and check for leaks.

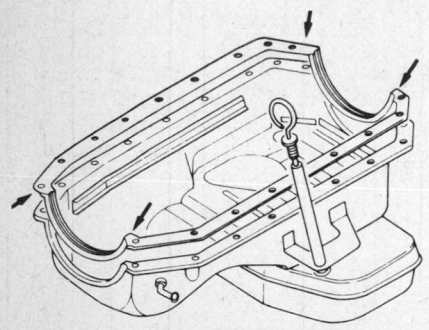

Oil pan and gasket—diesel engine

Rear Main Bearing Oil Seal

REMOVAL & INSTALLATION

1. Remove the transmission and oil pan.
2. On manual transmission models, remove the clutch cover and pressure plate assembly.
3. Remove the starter and lay to one side or wire to the frame.

NOTE: Disconnect the battery before removing starter.

4. Remove the six flywheel bolts and the flywheel assembly.
5. Remove the four rear crankshaft seal retainer bolts and remove the retainer seal assembly.
6. Pry the old seal out of the retainer and discard.
7. Place a new seal in position in the retainer. Fill the clearance between the lips of the seal with grease and lubricate the seal lip with engine oil.
8. Place the retainer on a flat surface and drive the seal into place using installer tool J-22354 or equivalent.

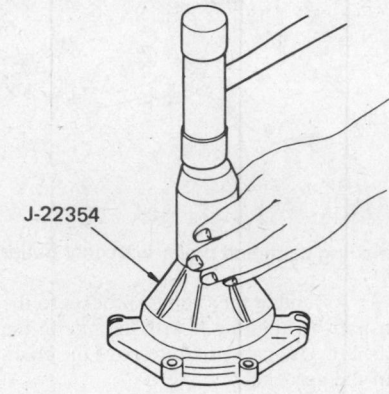

J-22354

Installing crankshaft rear seal with special tool

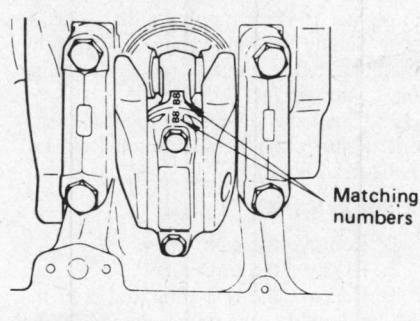

Matching numbers

Cylinder identification on connecting rod and bearing cap

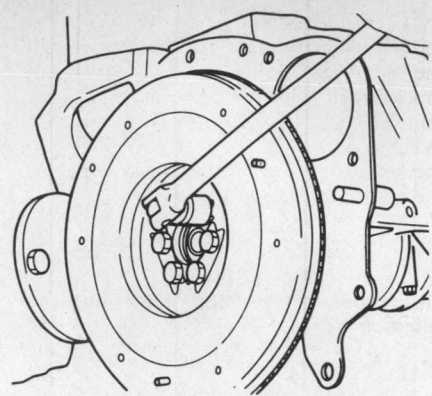

Removing flywheel assembly

9. Installation is the reverse of removal Steps 1–6. When installing the flywheel, install washer and bolts and torque to 69 ft. lbs.
10. Start the engine and check for leaks.

NOTE: Diesel engines use a different number seal installing tool (J-29818), and the seal is installed on the No. 5 crankshaft bearing cap. Other than that, the removal and replacement procedures are identical for all engines.

Oil Pump

REMOVAL & INSTALLATION

Gasoline Engine

NOTE: The oil pump can be serviced with the engine in or out of the vehicle. The procedure below is for the engine in the car.

1. Remove the cam cover.
2. Remove the distributor assembly.
3. Remove the engine oil pan.
4. Remove the bolt attaching the oil pick–up tube to the block and remove the tube from the oil pump.
5. Remove the oil pump mounting bolts and remove the pump assembly.
6. Remove the rubber hose and relief valve from the oil pump.

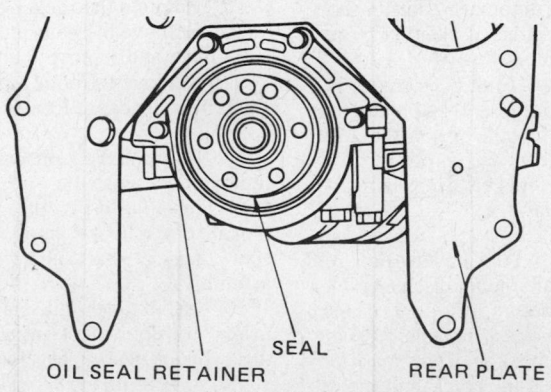

OIL SEAL RETAINER   SEAL   REAR PLATE

Rear main oil seal assembly

7. Installation is in reverse order of removal. Align the mark on the camshaft with the mark on the No. 1 rocker arm shaft bracket. Align the notch on the crankshaft pulley with the ''O'' mark on the front cover. When the two sets of marks are aligned, the No. 4 cylinder is at top dead center on the compression stroke.

8. Install the driven rotor so that the alignment mark lines up with the mark on the drive rotor.

9. Install the oil pump assembly by engaging the oil pump drive gear with the pinion gear on the crankshaft, so that the alignment mark on the drive gear is turned rearward and is away from the crankshaft by approximately 20° in a clockwise direction.

10. When the oil pump is installed, check to assure that the mark on the oil pump drive gear is turned to the rear side as viewed from the clearance between the front cover and the cylinder block and that the slit at the end of the oil pump drive shaft is parallel with the front face of the cylinder block and is off-set forward as viewed through the distributor fitting hole.

11. Check for leaks after assembly. Measure the oil pressure by attaching a pressure gauge to the hole for the oil pressure switch. Correct oil pump pressure is 56–71 psi.

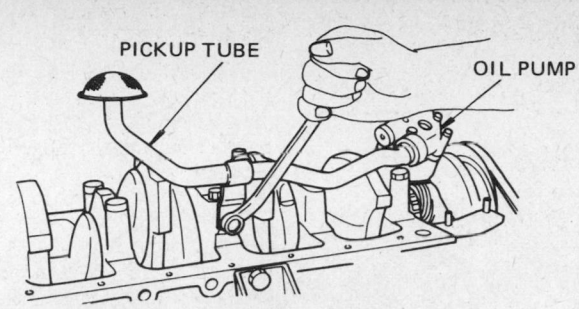

Oil pump assembly (engine upside down)

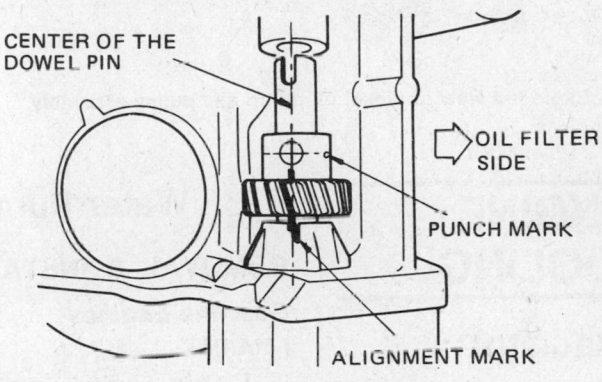

Oil pump alignment

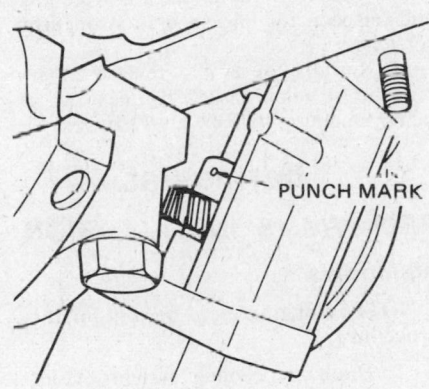

Checking oil pump alignment

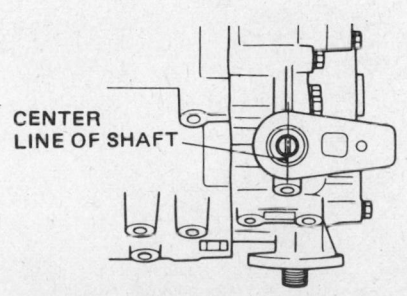

View through distributor fitting hole

Diesel Engine

1. Remove the timing belt.
2. Remove the Allen bolts attaching the oil pump and remove the pump together with the pulley.

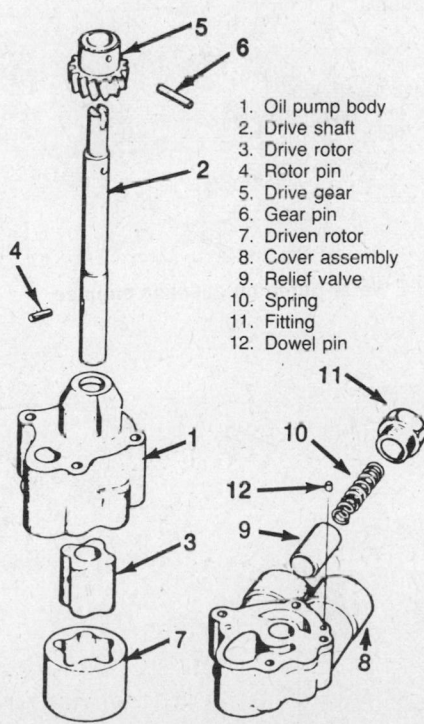

1. Oil pump body
2. Drive shaft
3. Drive rotor
4. Rotor pin
5. Drive gear
6. Gear pin
7. Driven rotor
8. Cover assembly
9. Relief valve
10. Spring
11. Fitting
12. Dowel pin

Exploded view of oil pump

NOTE: The special tool for the Allen bolts is J-29767.

3. Disassemble the oil pump on the workbench. A gear puller may be necessary to remove the pulley.

4. Installation is the reverse of removal. Apply generous amounts of clean engine oil to all components before installation. Install the vane with the taper side toward the cylinder body.

5. Install a new O-ring into the groove in the housing. Lubricate with oil. Install the rotor and then the pump body together with the pulley. Torque the Allen bolts to 11–18 ft. lbs.

Using special tool to remove Allen bolts on oil pump

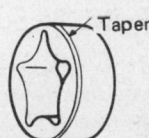

Install vane with taper side toward the cylinder body

1. Nut
2. Oil pump pulley
3. Vane
4. Key
5. Pin
6. Rotor
7. Shaft
8. Housing
9. Oil seal

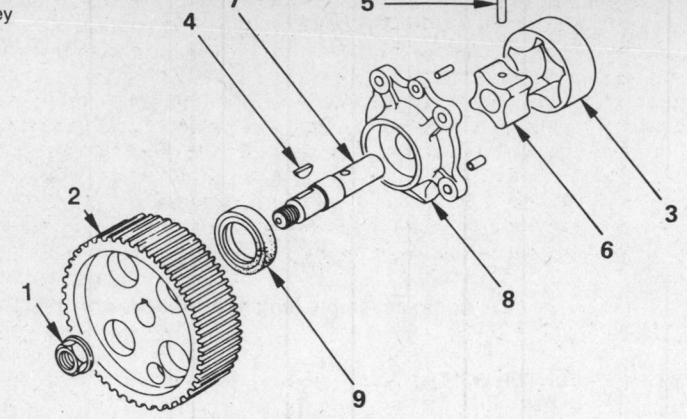

Exploded view of diesel oil pump and pulley assembly

ENGINE COOLING

Radiator

REMOVAL & INSTALLATION

All Models

1. Open the hood and disconnect the battery.
2. Remove the radiator cap and drain the cooling system.

— CAUTION —

The engine should be cold for removal procedures.

3. Loosen the top and bottom hose clamps and remove the radiator hoses.
4. Remove the fan shroud.
5. Remove the bolts and nuts attaching the radiator and remove the radiator assembly.
6. Installation is the reverse of removal. Fill the cooling system with water and the proper proportion of anti-freeze solution. Start the engine and check for leaks.

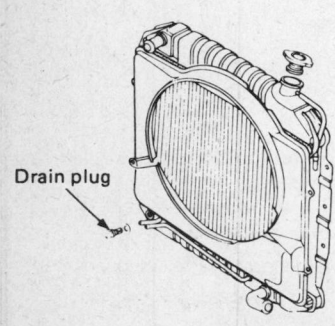

Drain plug

Radiator with shroud attached

Water Pump

REMOVAL & INSTALLATION

Gasoline Engines

I-MARK

1. Open the hood and disconnect the battery. Remove the lower engine cover.
2. Drain the cooling system.
3. On cars without A/C, remove the fan.
4. On cars with A/C, remove the air pump and generator mounting bolts, then remove the fan and air pump drive belt (pivot the generator and air pump in toward the engine). Remove the fan and pulley with set plate. Remove the hoses to the pump.

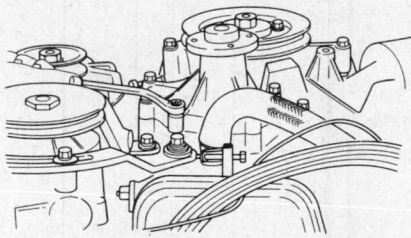

Water pump on gasoline engines

5. Remove the six bolts attaching the water pump and remove the water pump assembly. Clean all gasket surfaces carefully.
6. Installation is the reverse of removal. Fill the cooling system with the correct anti-freeze and water solution and adjust all drive belts. Use a new gasket.
7. Start the engine and check for leaks.

IMPULSE

1. Disconnect the battery and drain the radiator.
2. Remove the fan belt, plate, spacer, and pulley.
3. Remove the water pump and gasket.
4. Before installation, clean the gasket surfaces carefully and torque the water pump retaining bolts to 18 ft. lbs.

Diesel Engines

1. Open the hood and disconnect the battery. Remove the radiator cap.
2. Drain the cooling system and remove the hoses from the pump.
3. Remove the fan and pulley.
4. Remove the four attaching bolts holding the damper pulley. Remove the damper pulley.
5. Remove the engine dust covers.
6. Remove the bypass hose.
7. Remove the five bolts attaching water pump and remove the pump and gasket.
8. Clean all gasket surfaces carefully and inspect for nicks, cracks or deep scratches.
9. Installation is the reverse of removal. Use a new gasket. Torque all water pump mounting bolts to 11–18 ft. lbs.

Thermostat

REMOVAL & INSTALLATION

All Models

NOTE: Engine should be cold for this procedure.

1. Drain the cooling system and remove the air cleaner.

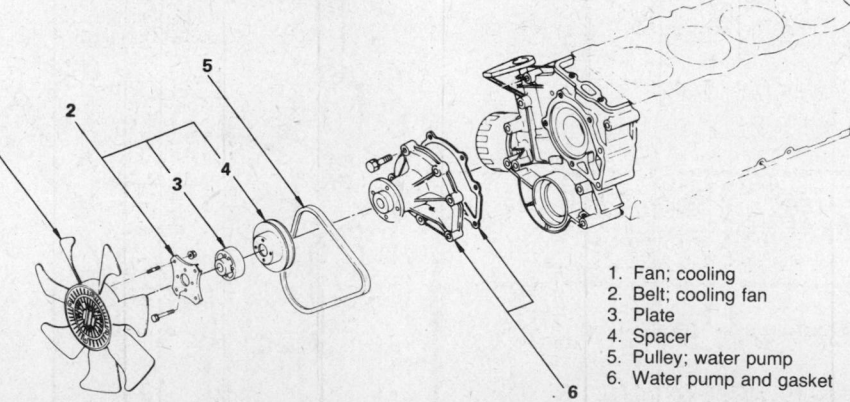

1. Fan; cooling
2. Belt; cooling fan
3. Plate
4. Spacer
5. Pulley; water pump
6. Water pump and gasket

Disassembled view of water pump—118.9 cu. in. engine

2. Remove the two attaching bolts holding the thermostat housing.

3. Lift the housing and remove the thermostat.

4. Remove all traces of old gasket.

5. Reinstall in reverse order using a new gasket. Permatex® is a good idea to avoid leaks. Make sure the thermostat is installed properly (it doesn't work upside-down).

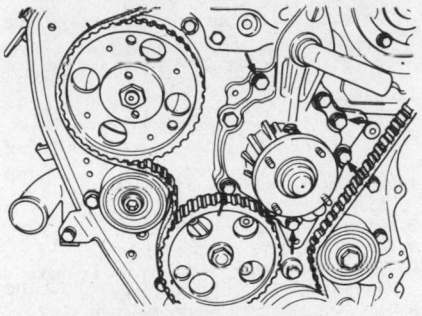

Water pump attaching bolts

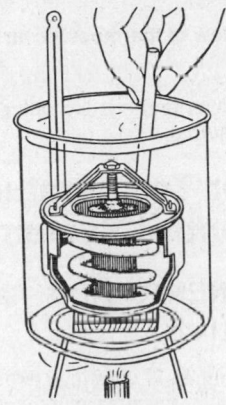

Testing thermostat operation in hot water

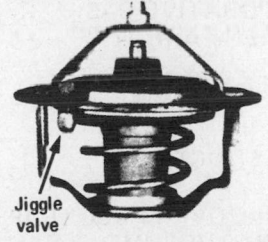

Thermostat—typical for all models

EMISSION CONTROLS

General Information

GASOLINE ENGINE

There are two versions of the Isuzu gasoline engine, the 49 State (Federal) version and the California version. The CO and HC settings are different, so it is wise to check the underhood specifications sticker to verify any settings before adjustment. An exhaust gas analyzer is required to properly adjust emission levels to comply with Federal or Local standards. The adjustment of carbon monoxide and hydrocarbon levels should be left to a qualified repair shop with the proper equipment. All other emission control maintenance can be done by the owner.

EQUIPMENT USED

Positive Crankcase Ventilation System— all models
Evaporative Control System—all models
Thermostatic Air Cleaner—all models
Over Temperature Control System—all models
Coasting Richer System—all models
Air Injection Reactor (Air Pump)—California models only
Exhaust Gas Recirculation System—all models
Oxidizing Catalytic Converter System— all models

Crankcase Emission Control System (PCV)

COMPONENTS AND OPERATION

NOTE: The PCV system is the only emission control device used on the diesel engine.

The positive crankcase ventilation system is designed to force blow-by gases generated in the engine crankcase back into the intake manifold, then deliver them, together with the fuel mixture, to the combustion chambers. This system is a closed type and consists of a baffle plate in the rocker arm cover for separating oil particles from blow-by gases; an orifice in the intake manifold for controlling suction of blow-by gases; a hose connecting these parts and another hose from the air cleaner to allow fresh air into the system. Under normal operating conditions, blow-by gases passing between piston rings and cylinder walls and fuel vapor from the fuel tank air mixed with ambient air supplied from the air cleaner. This mixture of gases is then drawn through the regulating orifice into the intake manifold for burning. When the engine is running with the throttle wide open, part of the blow-by generated is drawn directly into the air cleaner via the rear end of the rocker arm cover.

MAINTENANCE

Clean internal parts of hoses and regulating orifice with solvent and blow out any obstructions with compressed air. Check hoses for cracks, fatigue and swelling; replace if defective. Make sure all connections are tight.

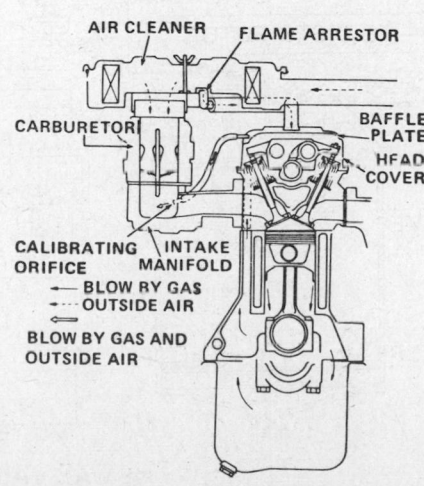

PCV system—gasoline engine

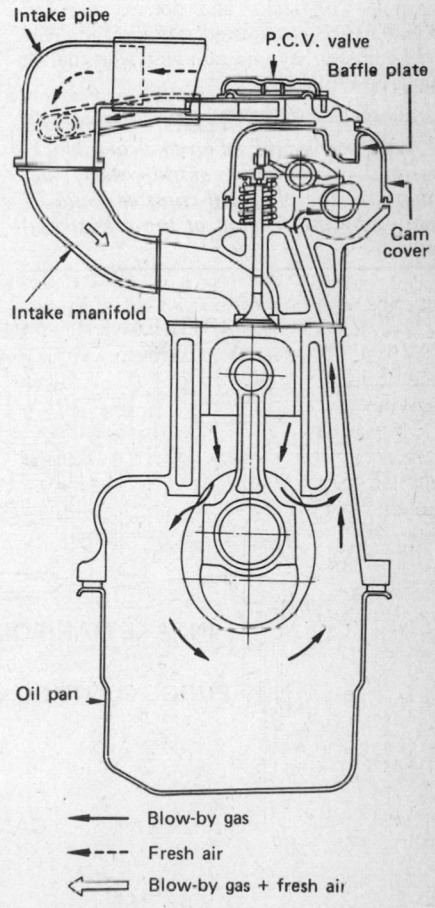

PCV system—diesel engine

Evaporative Emission Control System

COMPONENTS AND OPERATION

The evaporative system is designed to lead the fuel vapors from the tank into the crankcase and the vapors from the carburetor float bowl into the carbon canister. The fuel evaporative system consists of the vapor separator tank, check and relief valve, charcoal (carbon) canister, vent switching valve, ventilation valve and the hoses that connect it all together. The vapors drawn into the engine crankcase are mixed with blow-by gases and drawn into the intake manifold for combustion when the engine is running. The charcoal canister stores the vapors when the engine is off. The stored fuel vapor is purged when the engine is started and the vapors are drawn into the intake manifold. The purge rate is controlled by the manifold pressure and the orifice in the purge control valve.

MAINTENANCE

Aside from checking the hoses and connections for leaks and deterioration no maintenance is required. Should the charcoal canister become saturated with fuel, it must be replaced.

--- CAUTION ---

Never use compressed air to clear a blockage in the evaporative control system. Fuel vapors in the charcoal canister could be ignited by the friction of the pressurized air.

Thermostatic Air Cleaner

COMPONENTS AND OPERATION

The automatic temperature-controlled air cleaner is designed so that the temperature of ambient air is automatically controlled to hold the fuel/air ratio constant for efficient combustion. The system consists principally of the thermo-sensor, vacuum motor, hot air control valve and hot idle compensator. These components are mounted to the air cleaner body and snorkel. The hot air control valve is fully open when the engine is cold, allowing only air heated by the manifold heat stove into the engine. As the engine heats up, the thermo-sensor bleeds off vacuum and gradually closes the hot air control valve. Under conditions of hard acceleration when cold, the vacuum drops low enough to allow the diaphragm spring to open the snorkel passage and allow more air into the engine as required. Under conditions of hot operation (idling, climbing a long grade, etc.) excessive fuel vapors cause an over-rich situation, so the car is equipped with a hot idle compensator mounted in the air cleaner. The idle compensator allows ambient air into the intake manifold to lean out the temporarily rich mixture.

MAINTENANCE

Periodically check the function of the thermostatic air cleaner system by observing component operation when cold through the warm-up cycle. Check all connections for

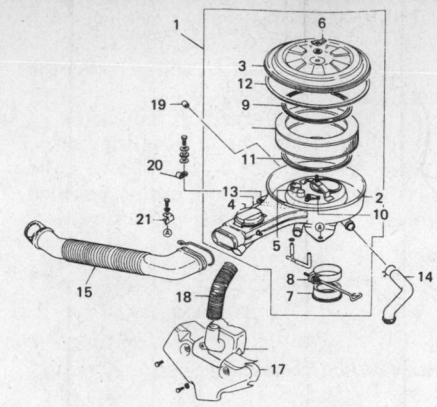

1. Air cleaner assembly	11. Gasket
2. Body assembly	12. Gasket
3. Cover assembly	13. Hose
4. Vacuum control	14. Hose
5. Sensor assembly— thermo	15. Duct—air intake
6. Nut	16. Cover
7. Grommet	17. Protector
8. Clamp	18. Hose
9. Element	19. Cap
10. Idle compensator	20. Clip
	21. Clip

Exploded view of thermostatic air cleaner system

leaks and deterioration. No other maintenance is required.

Over Temperature Control System

COMPONENTS AND OPERATION

When the engine is coasting, the coasting fuel cut device prevents catalytic converter

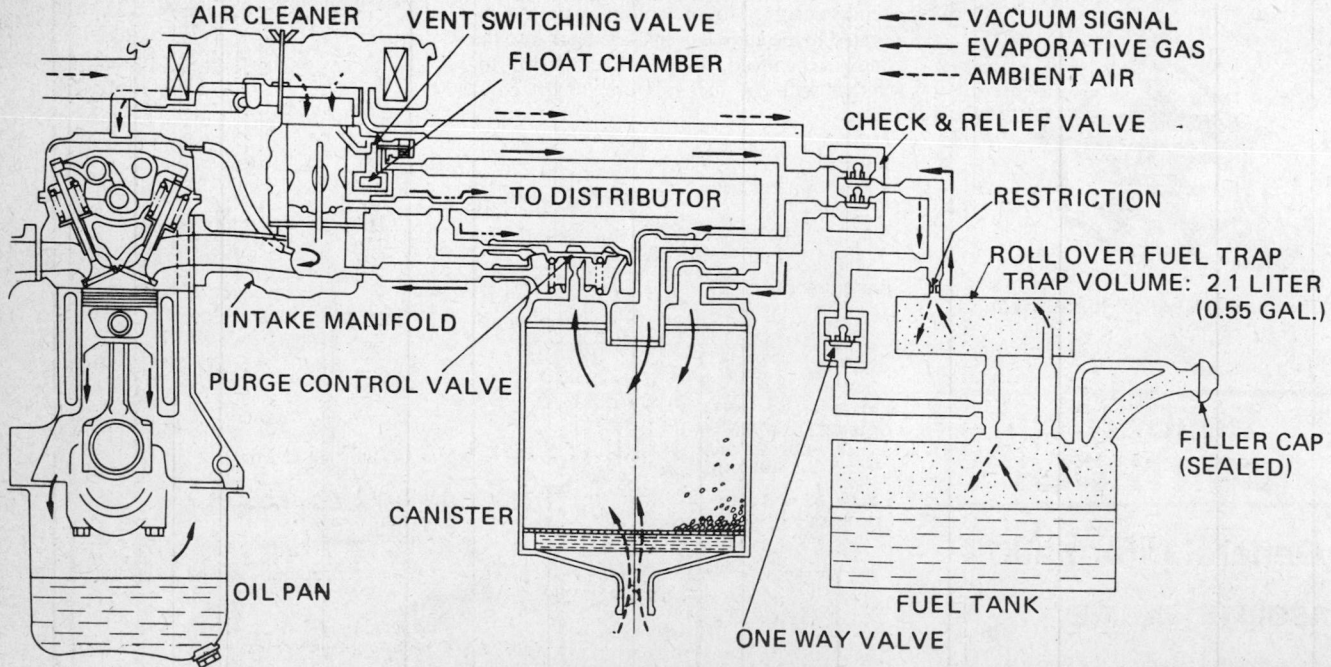

Evaporative control system—typical

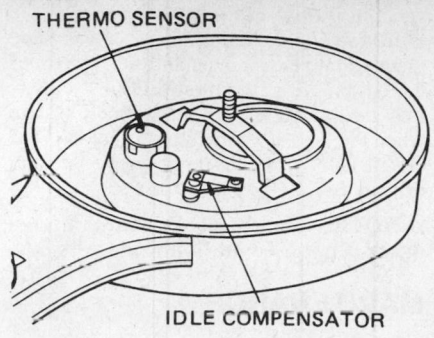

THERMO SENSOR

IDLE COMPENSATOR

Hot air controls mounted in air cleaner

overheating caused by poor combustion. When the catalyst reaches a temperature of 730°C (1350°F) due to high speed and high load driving, the secondary air diverted to the atmosphere to reduce the chemical reaction in the catalyst, lowering the temperature and preventing damage to the converter. A thermo-sensor is installed in the front side of the catalytic converter and monitors the catalyst temperature. The thermo-sensor provides the signal to the vacuum switching valve.

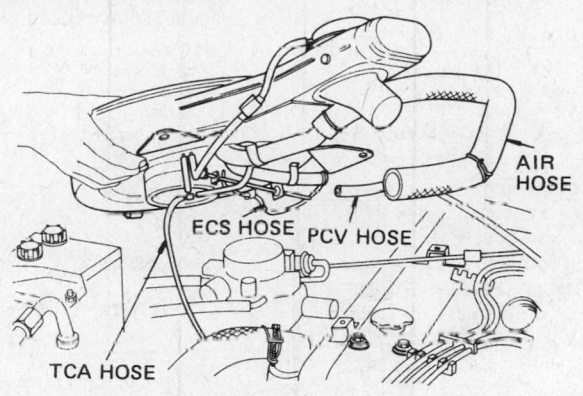

AIR HOSE

ECS HOSE PCV HOSE

TCA HOSE

Typical air cleaner hose connections

Air Injection Reactor System

COMPONENTS AND OPERATION

The AIR system is designed to lower exhaust emissions by injecting ambient air into the exhaust charge from the engine, causing an "afterburner" effect that consumes the unburned fuel in the exhaust manifold (postcombustion). Ambient air is pressurized by the air pump and delivered via a diverter valve and check valve to the injector nozzles mounted in the exhaust manifold. Pump pressure is limited by a relief valve pressed into the pump housing. The check valve mounted on the air injection manifold allows air to pass in one direction and prevents exhaust gas from backing up into the air lines and damaging the system. The diverter valve (mixture control valve) prevents backfiring during deceleration by venting pump air to the atmosphere whenever the intake manifold vacuum increases rapidly.

MAINTENANCE

The air pump drive belt can be adjusted by loosening the mounting bolts and moving

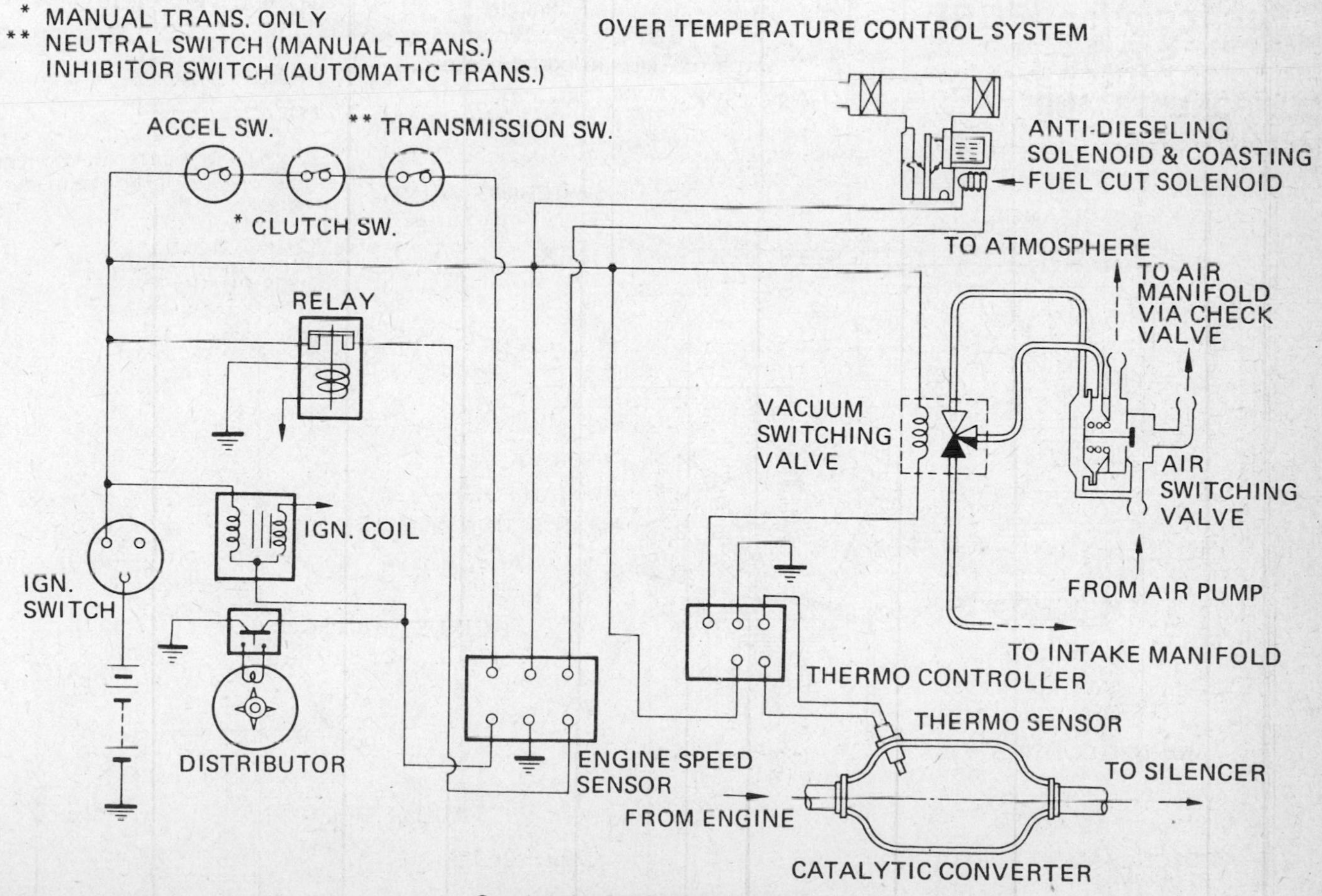

---

* MANUAL TRANS. ONLY
** NEUTRAL SWITCH (MANUAL TRANS.)
  INHIBITOR SWITCH (AUTOMATIC TRANS.)

OVER TEMPERATURE CONTROL SYSTEM

ACCEL SW.   ** TRANSMISSION SW.

* CLUTCH SW.

RELAY

IGN. COIL

IGN. SWITCH

DISTRIBUTOR

ENGINE SPEED SENSOR

FROM ENGINE

VACUUM SWITCHING VALVE

THERMO CONTROLLER

THERMO SENSOR

CATALYTIC CONVERTER

ANTI-DIESELING SOLENOID & COASTING FUEL CUT SOLENOID

TO ATMOSPHERE

TO AIR MANIFOLD VIA CHECK VALVE

AIR SWITCHING VALVE

FROM AIR PUMP

TO INTAKE MANIFOLD

TO SILENCER

Over temperature control system

the pump and adjusting plate. Proper belt tension can be checked by pressing on the belt at a point mid way between pulleys. A belt deflection of 10 mm (0.4 in) indicates proper tension. The air pump itself is non-servicable and must be replaced if found to be defective.

NOTE: Air pumps are normally a little noisy in operation. Before replacing a noisy pump, first try tightening the mounting bolts. A loose belt or worn bushings can also cause pump noise.

The AIR system should be periodically checked for proper operation and any leaks or deterioration in the lines. The air pump output can be checked by removing the delivery hose from the back of the pump and making sure that the air volume increases with engine rpm. The check valve on the air manifold should be removed and blown through to verify one-way operation. The diverter (mixture control) valve may be checked by removing the rubber hose connecting the valve with the intake manifold, then plugging the intake manifold side. If the secondary air continues to blow out from the valve for a few seconds when the accelerator pedal is depressed fully and quickly released, the valve is operating properly. If the air continues to blow out of the valve for more than five seconds, replace the valve.

Exhaust Gas Recirculation (EGR) System

COMPONENTS AND OPERATION

The EGR system is used to lower the peak combustion temperatures by recirculating non-combustible exhaust gases through the intake manifold, thereby lowering the level of oxides of nitrogen in the exhaust. Exhaust gas is drawn into the intake manifold through a steel pipe and EGR valve mounted on the exhaust manifold. The vacuum diaphragm of the EGR valve is attached to a signal port at the carburetor flange through a Back Pressure Transducer responsive to exhaust pressure. This transducer modulates the vacuum signal and a thermal vacuum valve which operates the EGR cold override. As the carburetor throttle is opened, vacuum is applied to the diaphragm of the EGR valve which allows exhaust gas to be metered into the intake manifold. The faster the engine runs, the more EGR. The thermal vacuum valve cuts out the EGR system when the engine temperature is below 54°C (129°F) to improve cold response and driveability.

NOTE: The Back Pressure Transducer is not used on California versions.

MAINTENANCE

The operation of the EGR valve should be checked periodically by applying an outside vacuum source (hand vacuum pump) to the

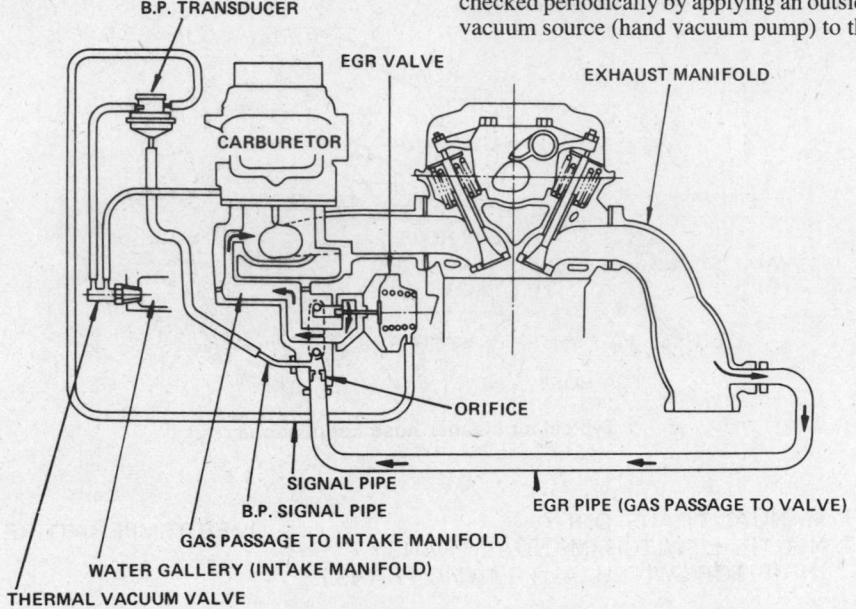

EGR system

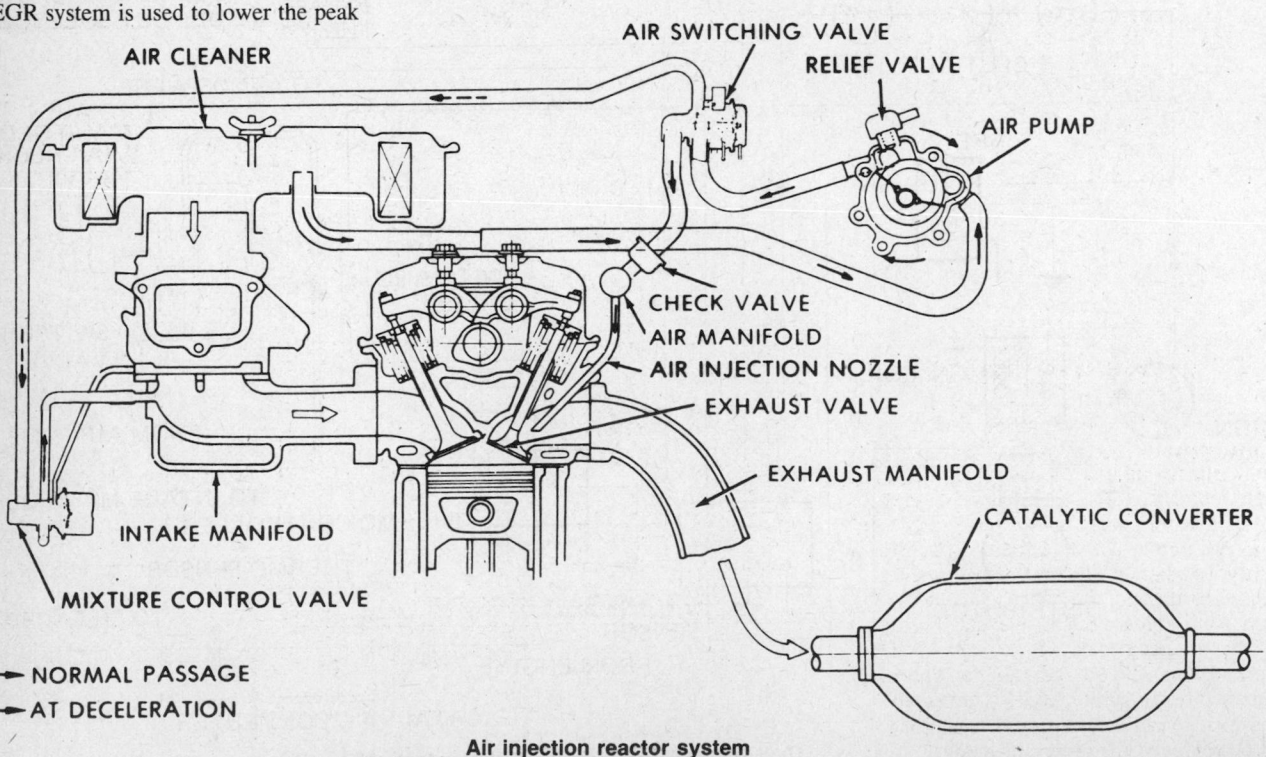

Air injection reactor system

FUEL SYSTEM

Fuel Pump

OPERATION

Gasoline Engines (110.8 cu. in.)

The fuel pump is a lightweight, motor-driven centrifugal type mounted near the bottom of the fuel tank. The pump will shut off immediately if the generator belt breaks, if there is a loss of voltage signal from the generator, or if the fusible link is open. At idle, the shut down is immediate; at fast idle or if the accelerator is partially depressed, the shut down is delayed 30–45 seconds to use up the fuel in the carburetor float bowl.

TESTING DELIVERY PRESSURE

Gasoline Engine (110.8 cu. in.)

1. Disconnect the main fuel hose at the carburetor side and connect a fuel pump pressure gauge using a T-fitting.
2. Start the engine and note the pressure reading on the gauge.
3. Delivery pressure at 900–4800 rpm is 2.4–3.3 psi.
4. If the measured value is different from specifications, replace the fuel pump.

— CAUTION —
Do not operate the fuel pump under no-load conditions and perform all tests with the filter installed.

TRUNK ROOM
TO FUEL TANK
AIR
CHECK & RELIEF VALVE
AIR FILTER
★:ON AIR CLEANER
ROCKER COVER
INTAKE MANIFOLD
CARBURETOR
PCV LINE AIR CLEANER
CANISTER
★VENTILATION VALVE
★PCV PIPE
EGR VALVE (UNDER INTAKE MANIFOLD)
★ IDLE COMPENSATOR
★ THERMO SENSOR
★VACUUM MOTOR
AIR SWITCHING VALVE
THERMAL VACUUM VALVE
BACK PRESSURE TRANSDUCER
DISTRIBUTOR
MIXTURE CONTROL VALVE
FVAP PIPE (OIL PAN)
RADIATOR
VACUUM SWITCHING VALVE

Vacuum circuits—gasoline engine

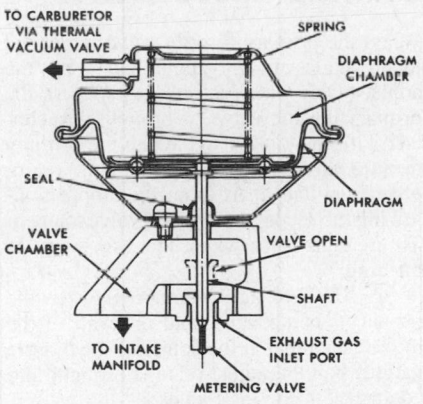

EGR valve

NOTE: Never try to remove carbon deposits with the intake manifold installed on the engine. Clean all metal lines with solvent and a bristle bore brush.

vacuum supply tube at the top of the diaphragm chamber. The diaphragm should not "leak down" and should move to the full up position at about 125mm'(5 in.) of mercury. In addition, the EGR valve should be removed and all carbon deposits sandblasted using a plug cleaning machine. Once the valve is clean, remove any grit with compressed air blown through the valve chamber. If heavy carbon deposits are noted in the intake manifold ports, the manifold must be removed for proper cleaning.

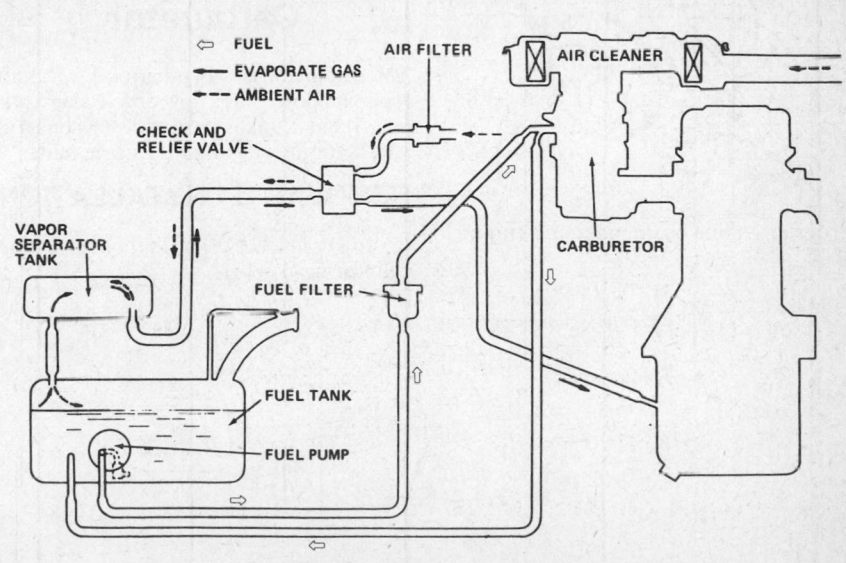

Fuel system schematic

REMOVAL & INSTALLATION

Gasoline Engine (110.8 cu. in.)

1. Disconnect the fuel return hose from the pipe and drain the fuel.

CAUTION

Fire hazard. Take precautions to avoid igniting any spilled fuel. Be particularly careful when using a work light around the fuel system.

---

2. Remove the fuel tank cover.
3. Remove the two screws holding the fuel pipe cover and remove the cover.
4. Disconnect the fuel hose from the fuel pipe.
5. Disconnect the fuel pump wiring.
6. Remove the nine screws attaching the fuel pump and remove the fuel pump assembly from the fuel tank.
7. Installation is the reverse of removal. Check for leaks and cracked hoses.

Gasoline Engine (118.0 cu. in.)

1. Raise the rear seat by hand and disconnect the electrical harness connector under the right side of the seat.
2. Remove the bolts connecting the fuel pump guard to the body.
3. Disconnect and cap the rubber hose at the fuel pump.
4. Remove the fuel pump bracket and fuel pump.

NOTE: The fuel pump cannot be disassembled and must be replaced if found to be defective.

5. Installation is the reverse of removal.

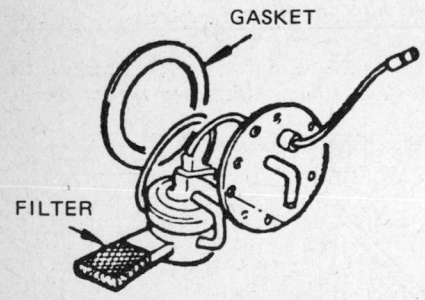

Fuel pump—110.8 cu. in. gasoline engine

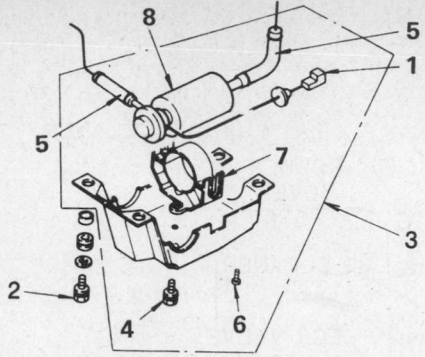

1 Connector; fuel pump harness
2 Bolt; guard to body
3 Bracket; fuel pump, guard and fuel pump assembly.
4 Bolt; guard to fuel pump bracket
5 Hose; rubber
6 Screw; fuel pump bracket
7 Bracket; fuel pump
8 Pump assembly; fuel

Exploded view of fuel pump and attaching parts—118.9 cu. in. engine

Fuel Filter

REMOVAL & INSTALLATION

The fuel system has a cartridge type, inline filter installed on the left side panel in the luggage compartment on all models except the Impulse. On the Impulse it is located in the engine compartment.

1. Remove the bolts attaching the cover on the side of the fuel tank in the luggage compartment, then remove the cover.
2. Disconnect the hoses from the filter.
3. Remove the fuel filter from the clip.
4. Installation is the reverse of removal.

Carburetor

The carburetor is a two barrel down draft type composed of a low-speed side (primary) and a high-speed side (secondary) which are integrated into a single unit.

REMOVAL & INSTALLATION

1. Disconnect the PCV hose from the cylinder head cover.

FUEL RETURN PIPE: TO FUEL TANK

FUEL HOSE; FROM FUEL TANK **FUEL PUMP**

FUEL HOSE: TO CARBURETOR

Fuel pump location—110.8 cu. in. gasoline engine

2. Disconnect the ECS hose from the air cleaner body.
3. Disconnect the AIR hose from the air pump.
4. Remove the bolts attaching the air cleaner and loosen the clamp bolts.
5. Lift the air cleaner slightly and disconnect the TCA vacuum hose and air duct, then remove the air cleaner.
6. Disconnect the vacuum signal hose from the EGR valve.
7. Disconnect the electrical leads connector.
8. Disconnect the accelerator cable.
9. Disconnect the fuel line at the carburetor.

CAUTION

Fire hazard. Use rags to catch any fuel and be careful with work lights. A broken light bulb landing on raw fuel can be quite spectacular.

---

10. Disconnect the ECS hose from the carburetor.
11. Remove the four nuts and lockwashers securing the carburetor to the intake manifold and remove the carburetor.
12. Installation is the reverse of removal. Clean all gasket surfaces before installation and always use a new gasket.
13. Start the engine and adjust the carburetor. Any time the carburetor is removed for inspection or overhaul, the emissions levels must be reset using an exhaust gas analyzer.

LINKAGE ADJUSTMENTS

When the primary throttle valve is opened to an angle of 47° (about half way) the adjust plate, which is interlocked with the primary throttle valve, is brought into contact with the kick lever. When the primary throttle valve is opened further, the return plate is pulled apart from the stopper, allowing the secondary throttle valve to open. To measure just when the secondary is opening:

1. Measure the clearance between the primary throttle valve and the wall of the throttle chamber at the center of the throttle valve when the adjust plate is brought into contact with the kick lever.
2. Standard clearance is 0.24–0.30 in. (6.1–7.6mm). If necessary, make adjustments by bending the kick lever.

PRIMARY THROTTLE VALVE OPENING ADJUSTMENT

Check and make necessary adjustment so that the primary throttle valve is opened, by means of the fast idle adjusting screw, to an angle of 16°MT or 17°AT (1981); 18° AT (1982 and later) when the choke valve is completely closed. To check the opening angle of the primary throttle valve:

1. Close the choke valve completely and measure the clearance between the throttle valve and the wall of the throttle valve chamber at the center part of the valve.

2. Standard clearance is 0.050–0.059 in. (1.28–1.51mm) for manual and 0.055–0.064 in. (1981) or 0.059–0.069 in. (1982 and later) for automatic transmissions. If necessary, adjust by bending the kick lever.

FLOAT LEVEL ADJUSTMENT

The fuel level is normal if it is within the marks on the window glass of the float chamber when the engine is off. If the fuel level is outside of the lines, make adjustment by bending the float seat. The needle valve should have an effective stroke of about 0.59 in. (1.5mm).

The needle valve is adjusted by bending the float stopper, but accomplishing that simple task requires the removal and disassembly of the carburetor. See the Unit Repair Section.

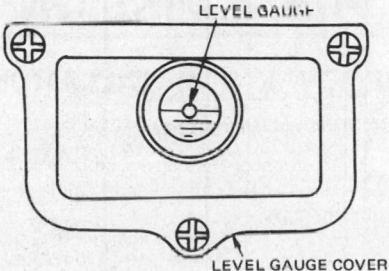

Checking float level

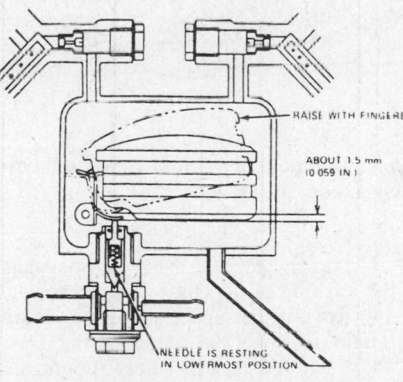

Adjusting float level

AUTOMATIC CHOKE ADJUSTMENT (FAST IDLE)

— CAUTION —

The automatic choke fast idle is adjusted by opening the angle of the throttle valve on the carburetor, NOT by engine speed.

The adjusted throttle valve opening at the first step of the fast idle cam is 16° ± 1°(MT) and 17° ± 1°(AT). The engine fast idle speed becomes approximately 3200 rpm after the engine is warmed up, or if the vacuum line to the distributor, idle compensator and EGR valve is plugged.

OVERHAUL

For all carburetor overhaul procedures, please refer to "Carburetor Service" in the Unit Repair section.

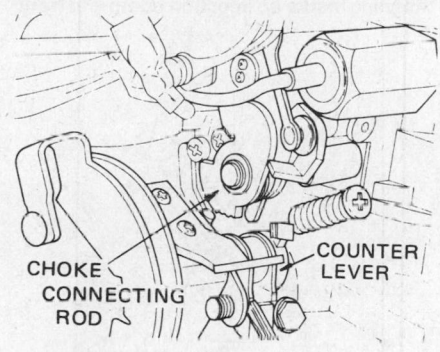

Choke components

Diesel Injection Pump

For additional information on diesel maintenance, etc., please refer to "Diesel Maintenance" in the Unit Repair section.

NOTE: The diesel injection pump is an extremely complicated device, built to tolerances of millionths of an inch. Servicing should be left to a qualified diesel specialist. Never use cold water to clean a hot engine or the diesel injection pump may seize.

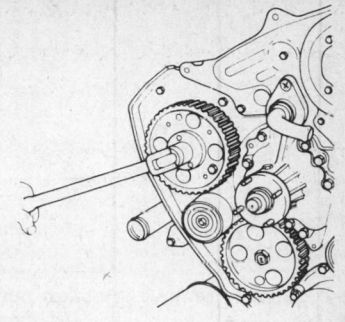

Removing nut on injection pump pulley

REMOVAL & INSTALLATION

1. Remove the timing belt as previously described.

2. Remove the nut attaching the injection pump pulley.

3. Remove the pulley using a suitable puller and remove the lock bolt.

4. Disconnect the fuel cut-off solenoid valve switch wiring and tachometer sensor wiring, if equipped.

5. Disconnect the accelerator cable from the pump lever. (A/T models only)

6. Disconnect the vacuum hose from the actuator of the fast idle device.

7. Disconnect the fuel hoses at the injection pump.

8. Remove the six screws attaching the injection pipe clips and remove the clips.

9. Remove the eight sleeve nuts attaching the injection pipes and remove the pipes.

10. Remove the four bolts attaching the pump rear bracket and remove the rear bracket. Disconnect the spring of the control lever.

11. Remove the two nuts attaching the injection pump flange and remove the in-

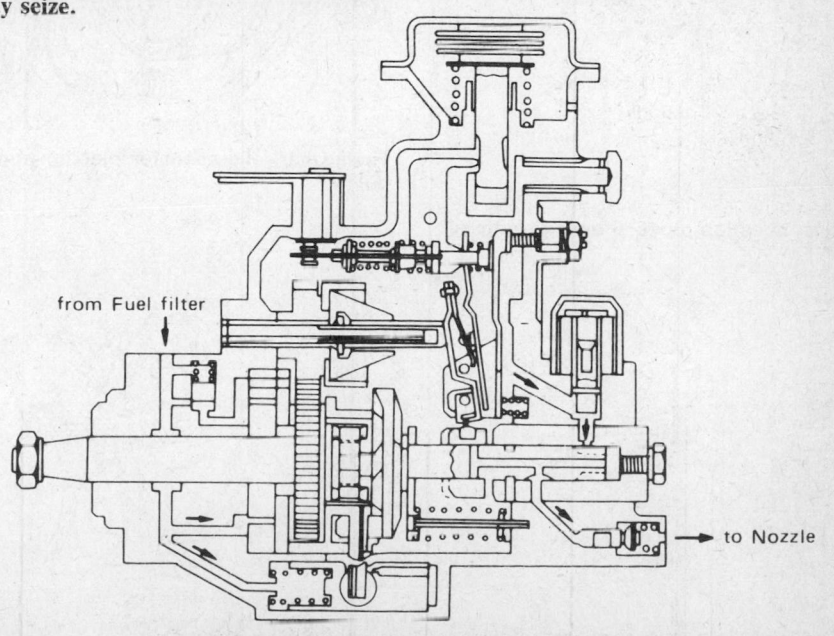

Cross section of diesel injection pump

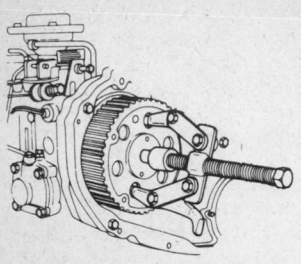

Using a puller to remove injection pump pulley

jection pump together with the fast idle device.

12. Install the injection pump together with the fast idle device by aligning the notched line on the flange with the line on the front plate.

13. Tighten the bolts in sequence. No clearance should be between the rear bracket and injection pump bracket.

14. Install the injection pump pulley by aligning it with the key groove. Align the mark on the pulley with the mark on the front plate, then tighten the nut using the lock bolt to prevent the pulley from turning.

15. Reinstall the timing belt as previously described and set the injection timing.

16. Install the injection pipes, clips and the vacuum hose for the actuator. Connect all control cables and wiring.

17. Fill the filter with fuel by operating the priming handle several times. Adjust the idle speed.

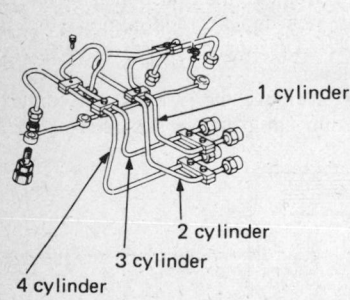

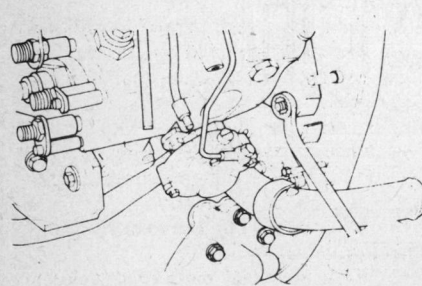

Diesel injection pipes showing routing

Removing pump flange nuts

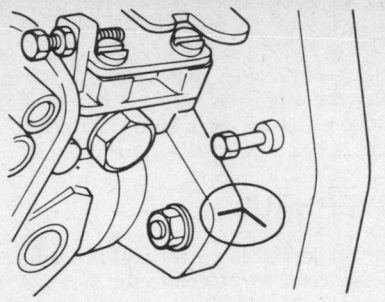

Aligning marks on injection pump and front plate

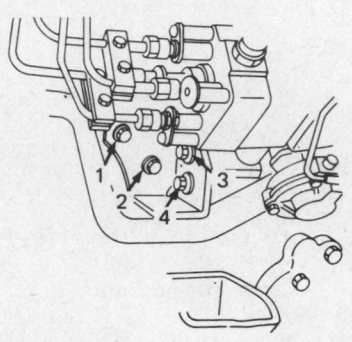

Bolt tightening sequence for injection pump mount

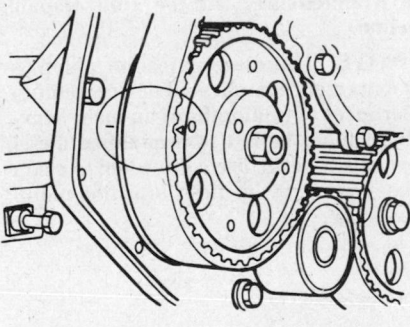

Timing mark alignment for injection pump pulley

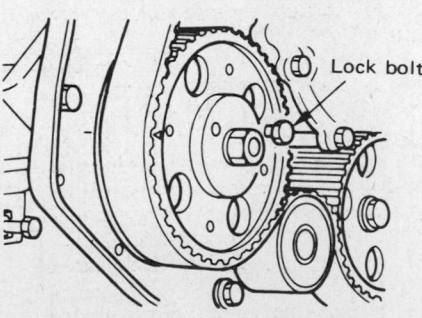

Securing injection pump pulley

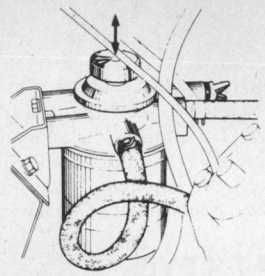

Diesel fuel filter with priming pump (arrows)

Injection Timing

Follow directions outlined under removal and installation of timing belt for proper injection timing procedure.

MANUAL TRANSMISSION

REMOVAL & INSTALLATION
(All Except Impulse)

1. Disconnect the battery ground cable.
2. Remove the shift lever assembly from inside the car.

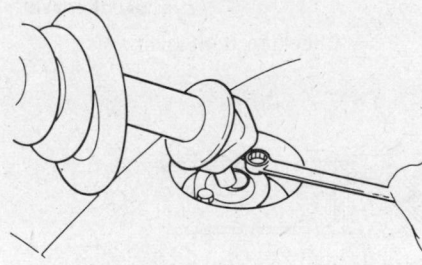

Typical removal of manual shifter assembly—except Impulse

3. Loosen the clutch cable adjusting nuts at the left side of the engine compartment.

4. Remove the upper starter mounting nut and disconnect the starter wiring.

5. Raise the car and safely support it.

6. Remove the driveshaft.

7. Disconnect the speedometer cable.

8. Remove the clutch cable.

9. Remove the starter lower bolt and remove the starter.

10. Disconnect the exhaust pipe from the manifold.

11. Remove the exhaust pipe bracket.

12. Remove the flywheel inspection cover.

13. Remove the rear transmission support mounting bolt.

14. Support the transmission under the

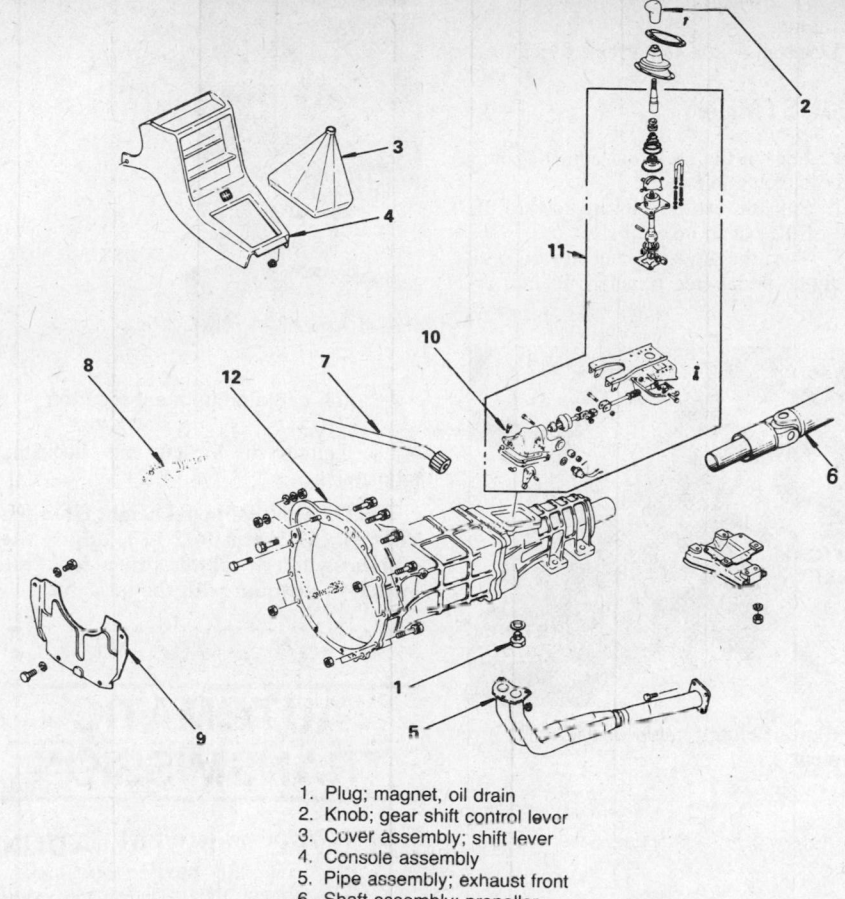

1. Plug; magnet, oil drain
2. Knob; gear shift control lever
3. Cover assembly; shift lever
4. Console assembly
5. Pipe assembly; exhaust front
6. Shaft assembly; propeller
7. Cable assembly;
   speedometer
8. Cylinder assembly; slave
9. Cover; under, transmission
   case
10. Bolts; quadrant cover to case
11. Box assembly; control
12. Transmission assembly

Transmission removal and installation—Impulse

case and remove the rear transmission support from the frame.

15. Lower the transmission approximately four inches. Disconnect the back-up light and coasting fuel cut-off switch (gasoline models only) wires.

16. Remove the transmission housing–to–engine block bolts.

─── **CAUTION** ───

Make sure transmission is supported by a suitable jack.

17. Move the transmission slowly back and lower it clear of the car.

18. Installation is the reverse of removal. Lubricate the drive gear shaft spline with a light coat of grease before installing.

19. Adjust the clutch as described in the clutch section. Fill the transmission with SAE 30 engine oil until it begins to run out the filler hole.

Impulse

1. Disconnect the negative battery cable.
2. Drain the transmission oil.
3. Remove the gearshift control lever knob, cover assembly and console.
4. Disconnect the front exhaust pipe.
5. Disconnect the propeller shaft.
6. Disconnect the speedometer cable assembly.
7. Disconnect the clutch slave cylinder.
8. Remove the cover under the transmission case.
9. Position a jack under the transmission case, remove the engine rear mounting nuts, lower the transmission case slightly, then remove the bolts attaching the quadrant box cover to the transmission case.
10. Disconnect all electrical harness connectors.
11. Remove the control box assembly.
12. Remove the transmission to engine retaining bolts.

NOTE: The starter assembly is mounted in position with the bolts that are used for installing the transmission assembly to the engine. It may be necessary to move the starter assembly forward to prevent it from falling out when the bolts are removed.

13. Installation is the reverse of removal with the following exceptions:

a. Position the transmission assembly with the speedometer cable fitting face turned downward and slide the assembly forward, guiding the gear shaft into the pilot bearing.

b. Install and tighten the quadrant box cover to the transmission case bolts with a gasket fitted in position between the quadrant box cover and the transmission case, then install the engine rear mounting.

c. When reconnecting the propeller shaft, install the bolts from the extension shaft side and the nuts and washers on the propeller shaft side and torque to 20 ft. lbs.

d. After tightening the rear engine mounting nuts to 20 ft. lbs., raise the tab of the washers to prevent the nuts from loosening.

LINKAGE ADJUSTMENT

The shift lever is mounted on top of the transmission extension housing and requires no adjustment. For further details, see the Unit Repair Section.

OVERHAUL

For all overhaul and disassembly procedures, please refer to "Manual Transmission Overhaul" in the Unit Repair section.

CLUTCH

REMOVAL & INSTALLATION

1. Remove the transmission as previously described.

2. Mark the clutch assembly position on the flywheel with paint or a scribe.

3. Install clutch aligning tool J-24547 or equivalent and remove the six retaining bolts. Remove the clutch assembly.

4. Remove the release bearing-to-yoke retaining springs, and then remove the release bearing with its support.

5. Remove the release yoke from the transmission ball stud.

6. Wash all metal parts of the clutch assembly, except the release bearing and friction plate in suitable cleaning solution.

CAUTION

Soaking the release bearing in cleaning solution will ruin the bearing, soaking the clutch plate in cleaning solution will damage the facings.

7. Inspect all parts for wear or deep scoring. Replace any parts that show excessive wear.

8. Installation is the reverse of removal. Lubricate the ball stud when installing the release yoke. Align the clutch with scribe marks and use an aligning tool to assure proper positioning of the clutch.

Clutch Cable

REMOVAL & INSTALLATION

All Except Impulse

1. Loosen the clutch lock and adjusting nuts.

2. Raise the car and support it safely with jackstands.

3. From under the car, remove the clutch cable from the release yoke and slide it forward through the retaining bracket.

4. Disconnect the cable from the pedal and remove.

5. Installation is the reverse of removal.

ADJUSTMENT

1. Loosen the lock and adjusting nuts on the clutch cable.

2. Pull the cable foreward toward the front of the car to take up slack.

3. Turn the adjusting nut inward until the clutch pedal free travel is 16 mm (⅝ in.)

Location of clutch cable under car —typical

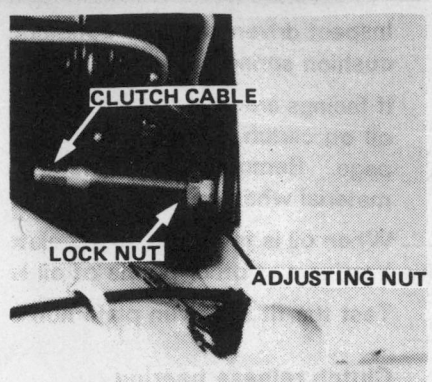

Clutch cable adjustment location

4. Tighten the locknut and check the adjustment.

NOTE: Correct pedal height from the floor is 157.5 mm (6.2 in.), adjust the clutch switch to obtain, then lock the switch in position with the lock nut.

AUTOMATIC TRANSMISSION

REMOVAL & INSTALLATION

1. Disconnect the battery cables and raise the vehicle. Make sure it is supported safely.

2. Remove the transmission dipstick. Drain the fluid into a suitable container and discard.

3. Remove the starter toward the front of the vehicle.

4. Disconnect the propeller shaft from the central joint, then slide the propeller shaft rearward and remove it.

5. Disconnect the shift control rod from the shift lever.

6. Disconnect the speedometer cable.

7. Remove the exhaust pipe bracket.

8. Disconnect the oil cooler lines by loosening the joint nuts at the transmission.

NOTE: Secure the cooler lines closer to the body to avoid damage during transmission removal.

9. Remove the four bolts attaching the converter housing lower cover and remove the cover.

10. Remove the lower cover on the front part of the engine to permit turning of the engine and torque converter.

11. Remove the six bolts fastening the torque converter and drive plate by turning the crankshaft pulley.

12. Remove the bolt on the center part of the rear mounting frame bracket.

13. Raise the engine and transmission using a suitable jack and support the rear end of the engine to hold it in position when the transmission is removed.

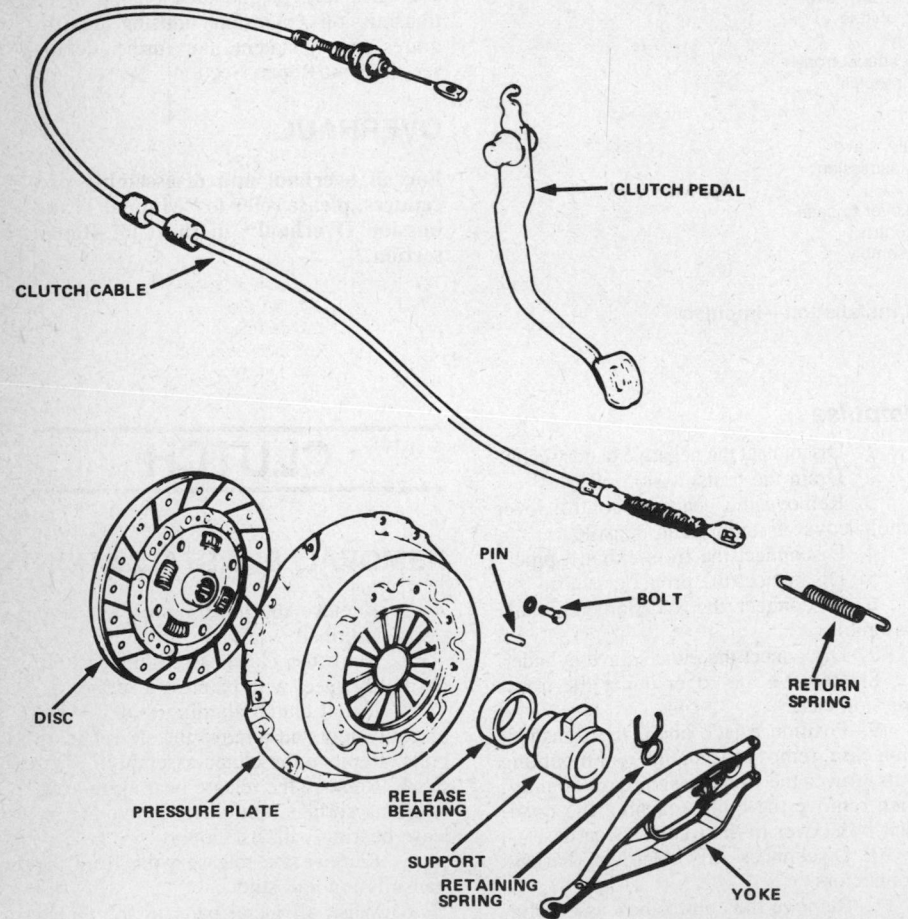

Exploded view of clutch components—all except Impulse

14. Remove the four bolts or nuts securing the rear mounting frame bracket, then remove the bracket.

15. Lower the transmission slightly, then remove the bolts and nuts fixing the converter housing, then remove the transmission toward the rear.

—————— CAUTION ——————
When removing the transmission, exercise care so as not to let the torque converter slide out.

16. Installation is the reverse of removal. Refill the transmission with fluid according to the capacities chart. Adjust the throttle valve control cable.

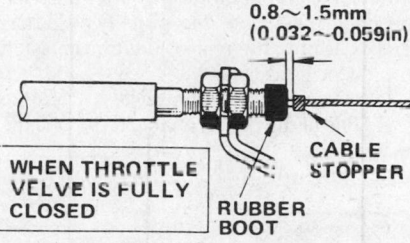

Throttle valve cable adjustment—gasoline engine

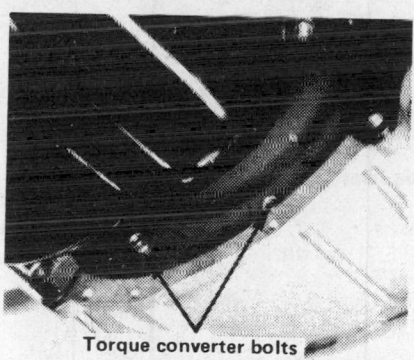

Removing torque converter bolts

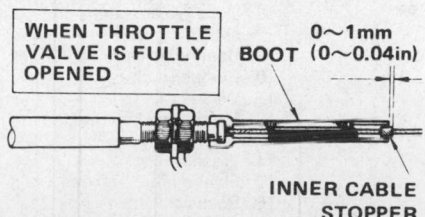

Throttle valve cable adjustment—diesel engine

DRIVE AXLE

Driveshaft and U-Joint

REMOVAL & INSTALLATION

1. Raise the rear of the car and support it safely on jack stands at the rear jack brackets.

2. Disconnect the parking brake return spring from the rod.

3. Mark the mating parts of the U-joint and the drive pinion extension shaft flange.

4. Remove the bolts and nuts connecting the U-joint and the extension shaft flange.

5. Work the propeller shaft slightly forward, lower the rear end of the shaft and slide the assembly rearward. Remove the thrust spring from the front of the shaft.

6. Install a plug (or wrap a small plastic bag) on the transmission extension housing to prevent the loss of oil.

—————— CAUTION ——————
When replacing any fasteners or attaching bolts, be sure to use the proper grade bolt. Substitution of lesser quality hardware could cause failure and serious damage.

7. Installation is the reverse of removal. Make certain that the transmission rear seal is not damaged. Align all marks and torque the bolts to 18 ft. lbs.

8. Connect the parking brake return spring.

OVERHAUL

For all U–Joint overhaul procedures, please refer to "U–Joint/CV–Joint Overhaul" in the Unit Repair Section.

Central Joint

REMOVAL & INSTALLATION

1. Raise and support the rear of the car safely under the axle tubes.

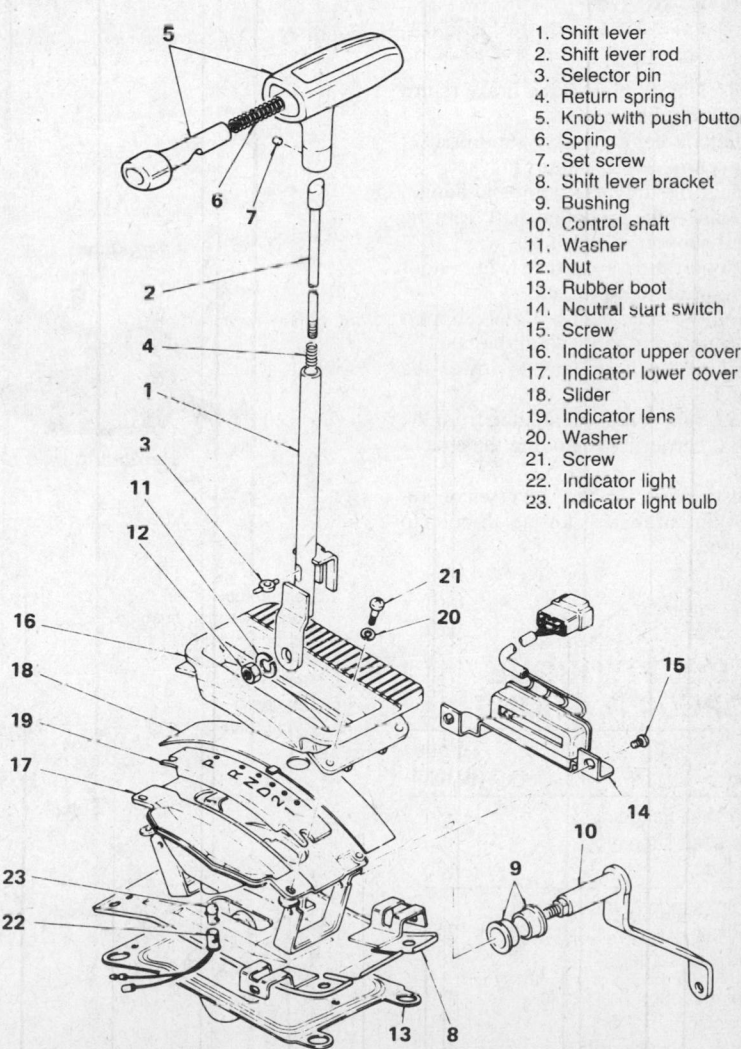

1. Shift lever
2. Shift lever rod
3. Selector pin
4. Return spring
5. Knob with push button
6. Spring
7. Set screw
8. Shift lever bracket
9. Bushing
10. Control shaft
11. Washer
12. Nut
13. Rubber boot
14. Neutral start switch
15. Screw
16. Indicator upper cover
17. Indicator lower cover
18. Slider
19. Indicator lens
20. Washer
21. Screw
22. Indicator light
23. Indicator light bulb

Exploded view of shifter assembly—all except Impulse

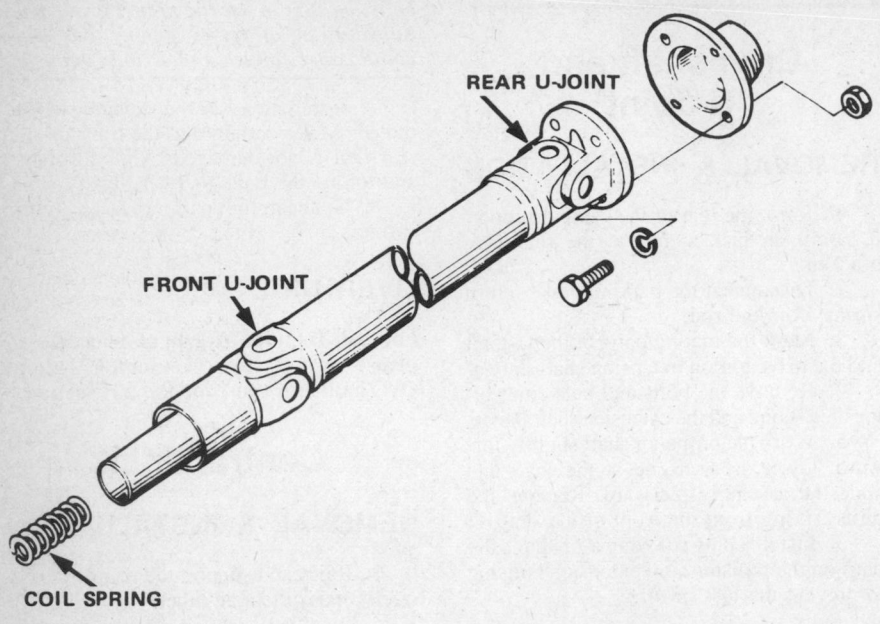

REAR U-JOINT

FRONT U-JOINT

COIL SPRING

Driveshaft assembly

REMOVAL & INSTALLATION

1. Raise the rear of the car and support it safely with jackstands positioned under jack brackets on each side of the car. Loosen the lug nuts and remove the rear wheels.

2. Disconnect the parking brake cable equalizer and the return spring from the brake rod.

3. Remove the clamps securing the rear stabilizer bar to the body and loosen the bolts and nuts connecting the stabilizer bar and axle bracket.

4. Disconnect shock absorbers at the lower end.

5. Disconnect the lateral rod at the left end.

6. Unhook the exhaust system brackets.

7. Disconnect the universal joint from the companion flange and support or tie the propeller shaft out of the way after marking the mating areas. If the propeller shaft is removed, plug the rear of the transmission to prevent fluid loss.

8. Disconnect the brake hose from the brake line at the differential and remove the retainer clip.

2. Disconnect the parking brake return spring from the brake rod.

3. Unhook the exhaust system bracket from the central joint support bracket.

4. Mark the universal joint and flange, then disconnect the propeller shaft from the flange and support it out of the way.

5. Support the torque tube with a floor jack using minimum pressure.

6. Remove the central joint support bracket to underbody attaching bolts.

7. Allow the floor jack to lower the torque tube.

8. Disconnect the torque tube from the differential carrier by removing the attaching bolts.

9. Installation is the reverse of removal. Align all marks, torque all bolts to specifications.

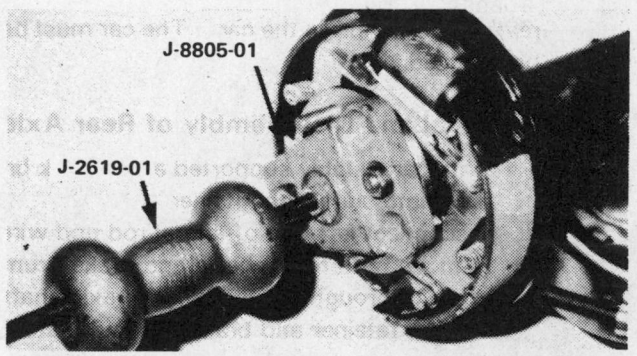

J-8805-01

J-2619-01

Removing axle shaft with slide hammer and adaptor

BOLT TORQUE SPECIFICATIONS

Location	Torque (ft. lbs.)
Extension shaft flange nut	87
Extension shaft flange-to-universal joint	18
Central joint support bracket-to-under body	30
Torque tube-to-carrier	20
Central joint support bracket-to-support cushion	15
Rubber cushion retainer-to-central joint support	10

1. Torque tube
2. Rubber support cushion
3. Support bracket
4. Bearing Assembly
5. Rubber cushion
6. Retainer
7. Rubber cushion ring

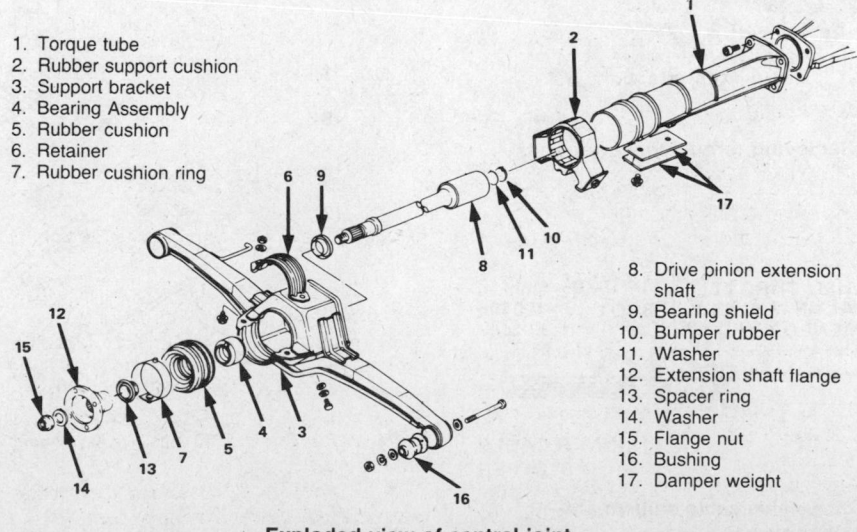

8. Drive pinion extension shaft
9. Bearing shield
10. Bumper rubber
11. Washer
12. Extension shaft flange
13. Spacer ring
14. Washer
15. Flange nut
16. Bushing
17. Damper weight

Exploded view of central joint

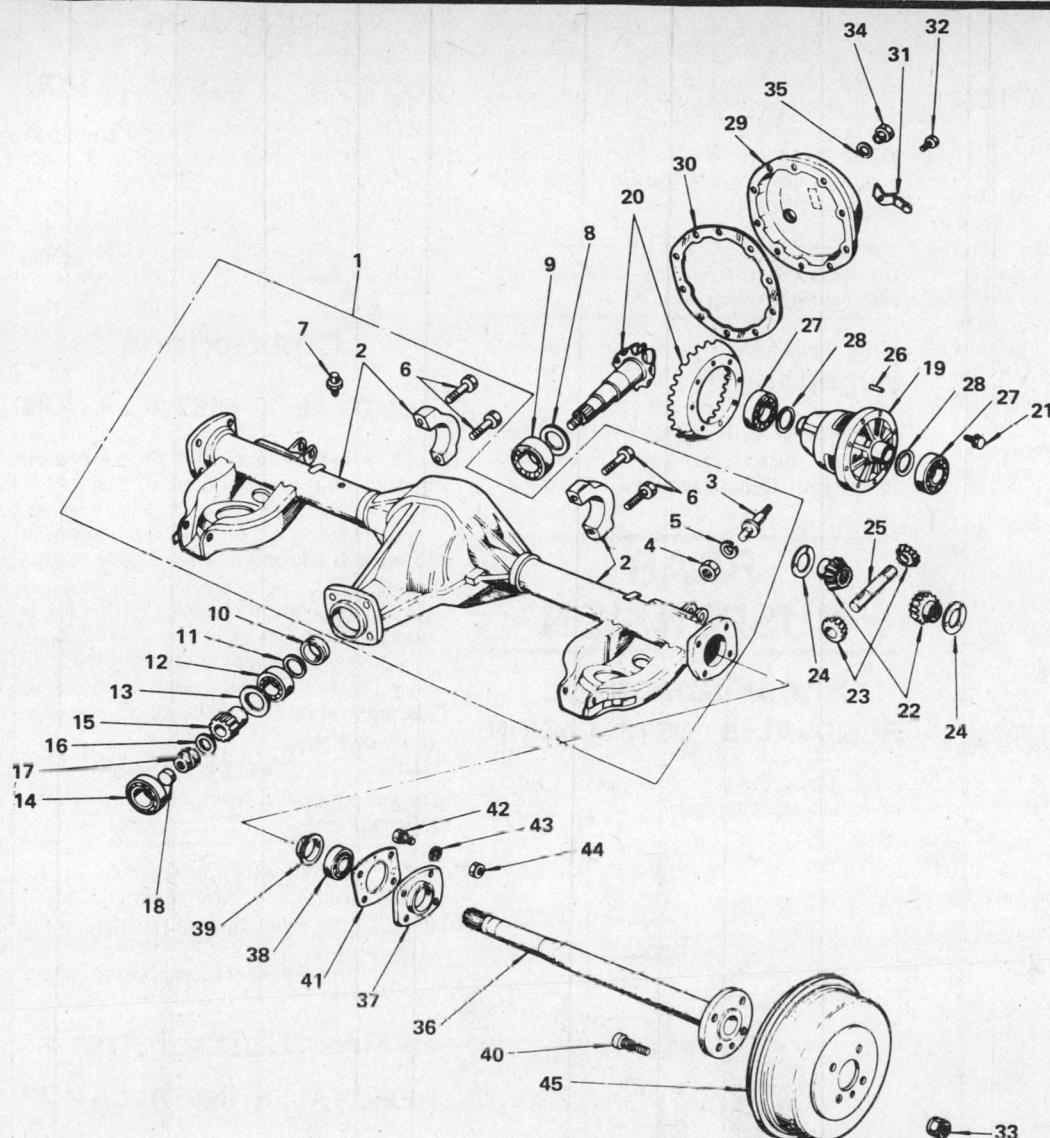

1. Rear axle housing assembly
2. Rear axle case
3. Bolt—axle housing to lateral rod
4. Nut
5. Washer
6. Bolt—bearing cap to axle case
7. Rear axle breather assembly
8. Pinion bearing shim
9. Pinion rear bearing
10. Collapsible distance spacer
11. Shim—distance piece
12. Pinion front bearing
13. Oil deflector plate
14. Sliding sleeve oil seal
15. Barrel spline sleeve
16. Drive pinion washer
17. Pinion nut
18. Pressure cap
19. Differential case
20. Ring gear and pinion
21. Ring gear setting bolt
22. Side gears
23. Pinion gears
24. Side gear thrust washer
25. Rear axle pinion shaft
26. Lock pin
27. Side bearing
28. Side gear shim
29. Differential cover
30. Differential cover gasket
31. Brake pipe union bracket
32. Union bracket bolt
33. Wheel nut
34. Oil filler plug
35. Oil filler gasket
36. Rear axle shaft
37. Axle shaft bearing retainer
38. Axle shaft bearing
39. Axle shaft bearing retaining ring
40. Wheel pin
41. Axle shaft shim
42. Bolt—bearing retainer to axle case
43. Spring washer
44. Nut
45. Rear brake drum

Exploded view of rear axle assembly—typical

9. Lower the rear axle assembly far enough to remove coil springs.

10. Remove the central joint support bracket-to-underbody retaining nuts and bolts.

11. Disconnect the lower control arms at the rear axle assembly bracket and roll the assembly from under the car.

12. Installation is the reverse of removal.

NOTE: If any attaching nuts or bolts must be replaced, be sure to use the proper grade of nut or bolt. Failure to use the proper grade fastener may result in component failure and serious damage.

13. Torque the central joint support bolts to 30 ft. lbs. Torque the universal joint bolts to 18 ft. lbs.

14. Torque the lower control arm-to-axle housing bolts to 29 ft. lbs. Torque the lateral rod-to-rear axle attaching nut to 54

ft. lbs. Torque the shock absorber nuts to 29 ft. lbs. Tighten the stabilizer nuts as tightly as possible.

Axle Shaft

REMOVAL & INSTALLATION

1. Raise the car and support it safely with jackstands at the jack brackets.

2. Remove the wheel and brake drum assembly.

3. Working through the access holes in the axle shaft flange, remove the four nuts and washers that retain the axle shaft and bearing retainer.

4. Install an axle shaft puller (slap-hammer) and remove the axle shaft.

5. To replace the bearing parts, first

remove the retaining ring by cutting it off with a chisel. The bearing must be pressed off with a suitable bench press.

6. Installation is the reverse of removal. Press the new bearing on to the axle shaft with a suitable press.

7. Check the axle shaft end play by using a depth gauge to measure the depth of the rear axle bearing seat in the axle housing with the backing plate in place.

8. Measure the width of the bearing outer race. The difference between the two measurements indicates the required thickness of the shims. If necessary to increase end-play, add shims. To decrease end-play, remove shims. Standard end play is 0–0.008 in. (0–0.2mm). Shims are only available in 0.006 in. (0.15mm) thickness.

9. Coat all rear axle components with gear oil before installation. Torque the lock washers and nuts to 28 ft. lbs.

Differential

REMOVAL & INSTALLATION

1. Raise the car and support it safely at the rear axle.

2. Remove the rear axle cover bolts and drain the lubricant into a suitable container.

3. Disconnect the left end of the lateral rod and wire it to the left shock absorber. Remove the rear wheels.

4. Working through the access holes in the axle shaft flange, remove the four nuts and washers retaining the axle shafts on each side. Loosen the brake backing plate to the axle housing.

5. Using a suitable puller, remove the axle shafts, taking care not to damage the oil seals.

6. Remove the differential cover and discard the gasket.

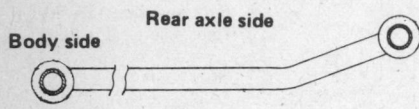

Body side   **Rear axle side**

Installing rear control arm—all except Impulse

1. Control arm
2. Bushing
3. Bushing
4. Lateral rod
5. Bushing
6. Bushing
7. Sleeve
8. Spring
9. Insulator
10. Insulator
11. Shock Absorber assembly
12. Rear stabilizer bar
13. Bushing
14. Clamp
15. Bracket
16. Bushing
17. Sleeve

Exploded view of rear suspension system—all except Impulse

7. Mark the rear axle side bearing caps and carrier so that the caps can be re-installed in their original positions.

8. Remove the rear axle side bearing cap bolts and caps.

9. Using two wooden hammer handles or similar devices, pry the differential case assembly from the carrier.

— **CAUTION** —
Do not drop or interchange the differential side bearing outer races.

10. Installation is the reverse of removal.

OVERHAUL

For general differential overhaul procedures, please refer to "Drive Axles" in the Unit Repair section.

REAR SUSPENSION

Shock Absorbers
REMOVAL & INSTALLATION

1. Raise the car and support it safely under the axle housing.

2. Disconnect the lower end of the shock absorber from the axle.

3. Remove the fuel tank cover from inside the trunk on all models except the Impulse and disconnect the upper end of the shock absorber.

4. Working from under the car, remove the shock absorber.

5. Installation is the reverse of removal. Use lock nuts at each end. Torque all shock absorber nuts to 29 ft. lbs.

Coil Springs
REMOVAL & INSTALLATION

1. Raise the rear of the car on the axle housing and support it at the jack side brackets with jackstands.

2. Position a hydraulic jack under the differential housing, but use a light contact pressure.

3. Disconnect the shock absorber lower mounting bolts.

4. Slowly lower or separate the axle assembly from the car body to the point where the spring becomes loose enough to allow removal.

— **CAUTION** —
Do not stress the brake hoses when lowering the axle.

5. Installation is the reverse of removal. Position the spring correctly. Make sure that the insulator is in position on top of the spring.

6. Torque the shock absorber lower bolts to 29 ft. lbs.

Rear Control Arm
REMOVAL & INSTALLATION

1. Raise the car and support it safely.

2. Remove the bolt connecting the control arm to the axle case.

3. Remove the bolt connecting the control arm to the body.

4. Remove the control arm assembly.

5. Installation is the reverse of removal. Torque the bolts to 29 ft. lbs.

NOTE: When reinstalling the control arm assembly, leave the bolts semi-tight. Lower the car before torquing any nuts. The vehicle weight should be on all suspension components when torquing the nuts.

FRONT SUSPENSION

Front Wheel Bearings
ADJUSTMENT AND REPACKING

1. Raise the car and safely support it

with jackstands. Remove the front wheel.

2. Remove the grease cap. Remove and discard the cotter pin, then remove the spindle nut and washer.

3. Wiggle the hub and the wheel bearing will pop out enough to grab it. Wipe any dirt or old grease off of the spindle.

NOTE: If the rear wheel bearing is to be inspected, the hub will have to be removed. Remove and tie up the brake caliper as outlined in the brake section and the hub will be free to be removed.

4. Inspect the wheel bearing for signs of wear, nicks or obvious damage. Clean the bearings in solvent and blow dry with compressed air.

——————— **CAUTION** ———————

Do not give in to the impulse of spinning the clean bearing with the air nozzle. Running a dry bearing at high rpm while holding it in your hand can damage the bearing.

5. Carefully repack the front wheel bearings with new high temperature wheel bearing grease. Put a glob of grease in your palm and force it into the bearing with a scraping motion until the grease comes out the top. Coat the packed bearing with a covering of grease and install it with the taper side in.

6. Clean and install the washer and spindle nut. Torque the spindle nut to 22 ft. lbs. while rotating the hub. This will seat the bearing.

7. Back off the spindle nut completely, then turn it back all the way using only your fingers. Once the spindle nut is snug, insert a new cotter pin.

NOTE: If the holes on the spindle nut and spindle do not align, tighten the nut only enough to align. A properly adjusted wheel bearing has a small amount of end-play and a slightly loose nut when adjusted in this manner.

Removing spindle nut on front hub

Shock Absorbers

REMOVAL & INSTALLATION

1. Raise the car and support it safely. Remove the front wheel.

2. Disconnect the shock absorber from the upper control arm using two wrenches.

3. Remove the shock absorber nuts from the engine compartment.

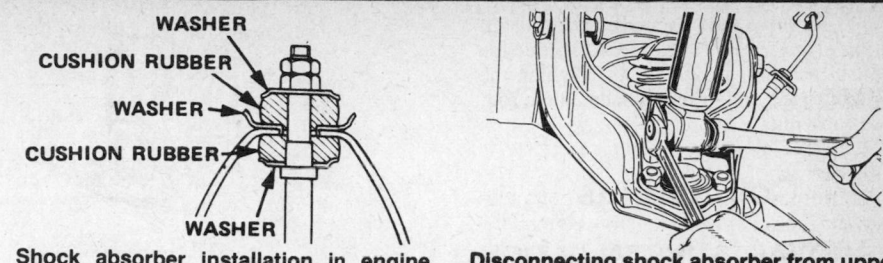

Shock absorber installation in engine compartment

Disconnecting shock absorber from upper control arm—except Impulse

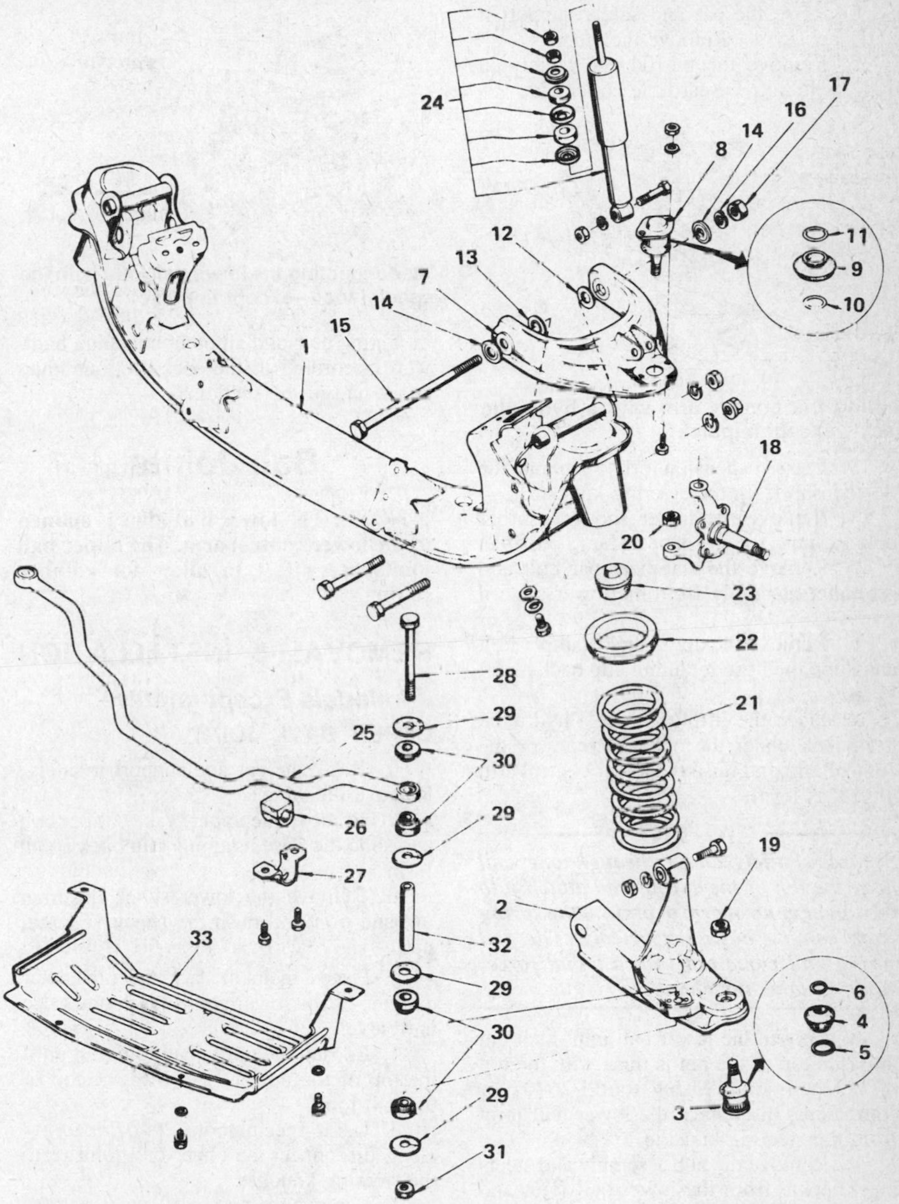

1. Cross member assembly	12. Washer	23. Bumper rubber
2. Lower control arm assembly	13. Washer	24. Shock absorber
3. Lower ball joint assembly	14. Washer	25. Stabilizer bar
4. Boot	15. Through-bolt	26. Rubber bushing
5. Clamp ring	16. Spring washer	27. Clamp
6. Clamp ring	17. Nut	28. Bolt
7. Upper control arm assembly	18. Steering knuckle	29. Retainer
8. Upper ball joint	19. Nut	30. Grommet
9. Boot	20. Nut	31. Nut
10. Clamp ring	21. Front coil spring	32. Distance tube
11. Clamp ring	22. Damper rubber	33. Under cover

Exploded view of front suspension system—all except Impulse

4. Remove the shock absorber. Installation is the reverse of removal. Torque the control arm nut to 29 ft. lbs. Tighten the top nut to the end of the threads on the rod. Use lock nuts.

Coil Springs

REMOVAL & INSTALLATION

All Models Exc. Impulse

1. Raise the car and safely support it with jackstands. Remove the wheel.
2. Remove the tie-rod end cotter pin and castle nut. Discard the cotter pin.

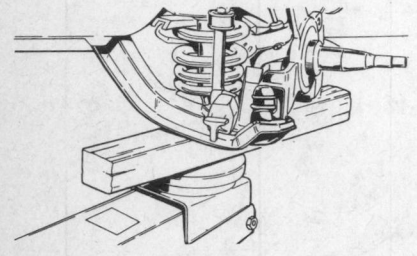

Lifting the control arm with a hydraulic jack—except Impulse

3. Use a suspension fork to separate the tie-rod end from the steering knuckle.
4. Remove the lower shock absorber bolt and push the shock up as far as possible.
5. Remove the stabilizer bar bolt and grommet assembly from the lower control arm.
6. Remove the upper brake caliper bolt and slide the hose retaining clip back about ½ in.
7. Place the lifting pad of a hydraulic floor jack under the outer extreme of the control arm and raise the lower control arm until it is level.

———— CAUTION ————

Secure a safety chain through one coil near the top of the spring and attach it to the upper control arm to prevent the spring from coming out unexpectedly. The coil spring will come out with a lethal force, so don't take any chances.

8. Loosen the lower ball joint lock nut until the top of the nut is flush with the top of the ball joint. Using tool J-26407 or equivalent, disconnect the lower ball joint from the steering knuckle.
9. Remove the hub assembly and steering knuckle from the lower ball joint and support with a wire or rope out of the way.
10. Pry the lower control arm down, using extreme caution so as not to injure yourself. Remove the spring.
11. Installation is the reverse of removal. Properly seat the spring and use the safety chain. Use the hydraulic jack to compress the new spring until the control arm is level.
12. Torque the ball joint lock nut to 58 ft. lbs. Torque the lower shock absorber

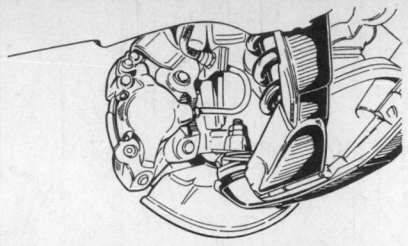

Brake caliper attaching bolts—except Impulse

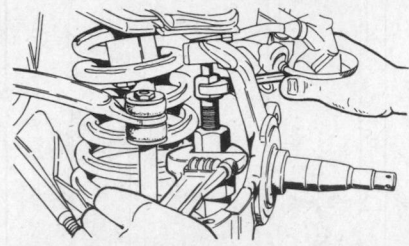

Disconnecting the lower ball joint with the special tool—except Impulse

mounting nuts and all other attaching hardware according to the specifications chart at the end of the section.

Ball Joints

NOTE: **The lower ball joint is splined to the lower control arm. The upper ball joints are offset to allow for camber setting.**

REMOVAL & INSTALLATION

All Models Except Impulse
UPPER BALL JOINT

1. Raise the car and support it safely. Remove the wheel.
2. Remove the upper brake caliper bolt and slide the hose retaining clip back about ½ in.
3. Remove the lower shock absorber nut and bolt and push the shock absorber up.
4. Place a hydraulic jack under the outer extreme of the lower control arm and raise until level.
5. Loosen the upper ball joint nut until the top of the nut is flush with the top of the ball joint.
6. Using special tool J-26407 or equivalent, disconnect the upper ball joint from the steering knuckle.
7. Remove the two bolts connecting the upper ball joint to the upper control arm. Remove the ball joint.
8. Installation is the reverse of removal. Install the new ball joint in the control arm so that the cut-off portion is facing outward. Torque the ball joint lock nut to 40 ft. lbs. Torque all attaching nuts and bolts. For specifications, see the torque chart at the end of the section.

NOTE: **The car should be aligned**

whenever any suspension components are replaced.

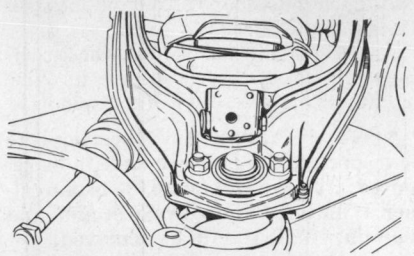

Installing the upper ball joint in the control arm—except Impulse

LOWER BALL JOINT

1. Raise the car and support it safely. Remove the front wheel.
2. Remove the tie-rod end cotter pin and castle nut. Discard the pin and separate the tie-rod end with a suspension fork. Remove the tie-rod from the steering knuckle.
3. Remove the stabilizer bar bolt and grommet assembly from the lower control arm.
4. Remove the upper brake caliper bolt and slide the brake hose retaining clip back about ½ in.
5. Remove the shock absorber lower bolt and push the shock up.

———— CAUTION ————

Secure a safety chain through the upper and lower control arms to prevent the possibility of the spring coming out and causing serious damage or injury. Allow enough room to get the ball joint out.

6. Place a hydraulic jack under the outer extremity of the lower control arm and raise it until level.
7. Loosen the ball joint lock nut until the top of the nut is flush with the top of the ball joint.
8. Using special tool J-26407 or equivalent, disconnect the lower ball joint from the steering knuckle.
9. Remove the hub assembly and steering knuckle from the lower ball joint and support with a wire or rope.
10. Remove the lower ball joint from the control arm using tool J-9519-03 or equivalent.
11. Installation is the reverse of removal. Do not strike the ball joint bottom. Torque the ball joint nut to 50 ft. lbs.
12. Torque all bolts to specifications as listed in the chart at the end of the section.

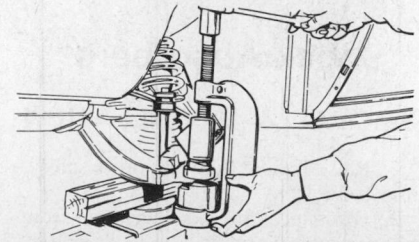

Removing the lower ball joint from the control arm—except Impulse

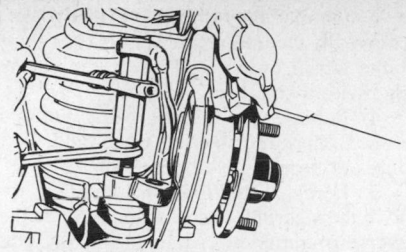

Removing the lower ball joint from the steering knuckle—except Impulse

Control Arms

REMOVAL & INSTALLATION

All Models Except Impulse
UPPER

1. Raise the car and support it safely. Remove the front wheel.
2. Remove the upper brake caliper bolt and slide the brake hose retainer clip back about ½ in.
3. Remove the lower shock bolt and push the shock absorber up.
4. Place a hydraulic jack under the control arm on the outer extreme and raise the control arm until it is level.
5. Loosen the upper ball joint lock nut until the top of the nut is flush with the top of the ball joint. Disconnect the upper ball joint from the steering knuckle using tool J-26407 or equivalent.

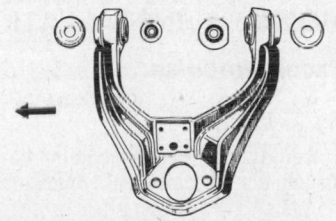

Installation of the upper control arm—except Impulse

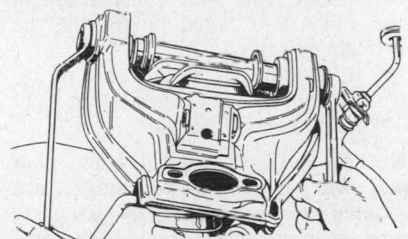

Removing the upper control arm from the crossmember—except Impulse

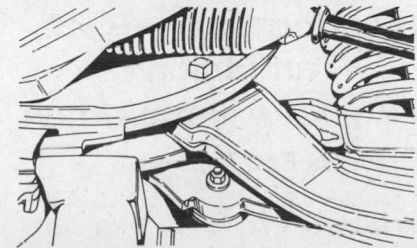

Removing the lower control arm—except Impulse

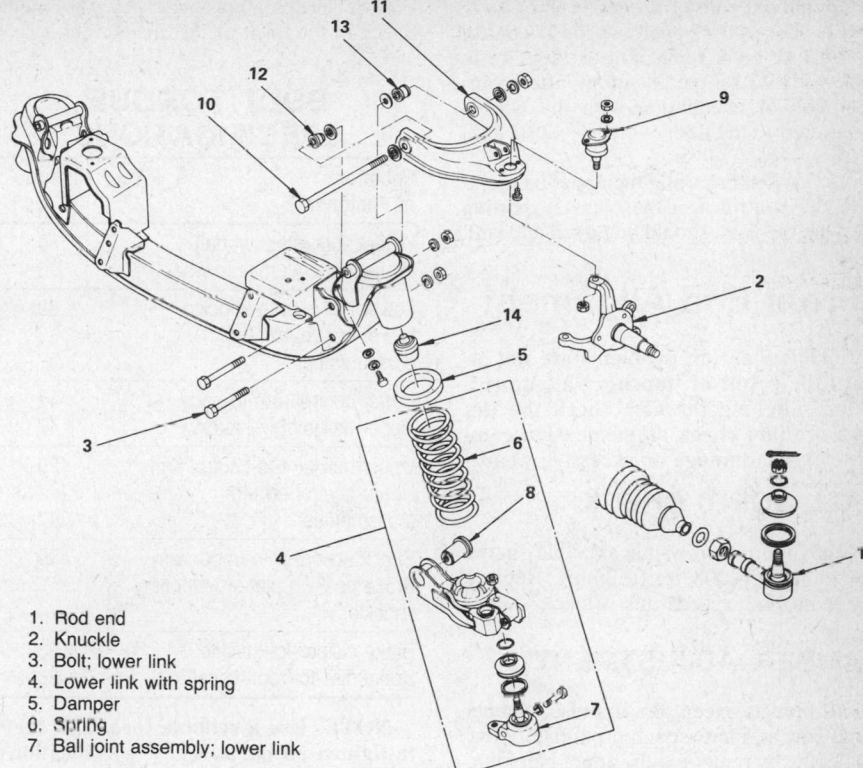

1. Rod end
2. Knuckle
3. Bolt; lower link
4. Lower link with spring
5. Damper
6. Spring
7. Ball joint assembly; lower link

Exploded view of front suspension—Impulse

6. Disconnect and remove the through bolt connecting the upper control arm to the crossmember. Remove the upper control arm.
7. Installation is the reverse of removal. On installation, make sure the smaller washer is on the inner face of the front arm and the larger washer is on the inner face of the rear arm.
8. Torque all attaching hardware to the specifications in the chart at the end of the section. Align the front end.

NOTE: Always check the camber when working around the upper control arm area.

LOWER

1. Follow Steps 1–10 for removal of coil springs.
2. Remove the bolts connecting the lower control arm to the crossmember and the body.
3. Installation is the reverse of removal. Torque all bolts and nuts to specifications.

NOTE: When reinstalling front end components, it's best to snug all the bolts and nuts first, then lower the car so that there is weight on the suspension when final torque adjustments are made.

Control Arms, Knuckles and Coil Springs

REMOVAL & INSTALLATION

Impulse

1. Raise the car and support it safely. Remove the front wheel.
2. Remove the tie-rod end cotter pin and castle nut and remove the tie-rod end using tool J-21687-02.
3. Using coil spring compressor J-33992, compress the coil spring.

— **CAUTION** —
Secure a safety chain through one coil near the top of the spring and attach it to the upper control arm to prevent the spring from coming out.

4. Compress the coil spring until its top end releases from the cushion rubber at the center of the upper link, then remove the coil spring.
5. Remove the lower link bolt, then remove the coil spring together with the lower link.
6. Remove the lower ball joint assembly.
7. Press out the lower link bushing.
8. Remove the upper ball joint assembly.
9. Press out the upper link bushings.
10. Installation is the reverse of removal with the following precautions:
   a. When installing the upper control arm washers install the small washer on

the inboard side of the rear end.

b. Leave the upper and lower control arm link bolts semi-tight as they are to be torqued to specifications after completion of installation with the wheels lowered to the floor. Upper—47 ft. lbs., lower—61 ft. lbs.

c. When installing the upper ball joint to the control arm the cutaway portion of the ball joint should be turned outward.

Front End Alignment

NOTE: Steering problems are not always the result of improper alignment. Before aligning the car, check the tire pressure and check all suspension components for damage or excessive wear.

BALL JOINT CHECK

The maximum permissible axial play in the ball joints is 0.008 in. (0.2mm). Replace any joint that exceeds this value.

CAMBER ADJUSTMENT

On all models except the Impulse, camber angle can be increased approximately one (1) degree by removing the upper ball joint, rotating it ½ turn and reinstalling it with the cut-off portion of the upper flange on the inboard side of the control arm. On the Impulse, camber is not adjustable. Replace parts as necessary to correct alignment.

CASTER ADJUSTMENT

The caster angle is pre-set at the factory and cannot be adjusted.

TOE-IN ANGLE ADJUSTMENT

Toe-in is controlled by adjusting the tie-rod. To adjust the toe-in setting loosen the nuts at the steering knuckle end of the tie-rod. Rotate the rod as required to adjust the toe-in. Retighten the cover and locknuts, check that the rubber bellows is not twisted.

Toe-in adjustment

For all specifications, see the Alignment Specs in the front of the chapter.

BOLT TORQUE SPECIFICATIONS

Location of Fastener	Torque (ft. lbs.)
Wheel nuts (steel wheel)	50
Wheel nuts (aluminum wheel)	90
Lower ball joint-to-knuckle	58
Lower control arm-to-crossmember	47
Lower control arm-to-body	47
Upper ball joint-to-knuckle	47
Upper ball joint-to-control arm	29
Upper control arm-to-crossmember	47
Shock absorber-to-upper arm	29
Brake backing plate-to-steering knuckle	4
Brake caliper-to-knuckle	36
Brake disc-to-front wheel hub	36

NOTE: Use a reliable torque wrench to tighten all parts. These specifications are for clean threads, lightly oiled. Dirty threads produce different torque values by increasing friction and giving a false reading.

STEERING

Steering Wheel

REMOVAL & INSTALLATION

1. Raise the hood and disconnect the battery ground cable.

2. On models with the 2-spoke wheel, remove the two screws retaining the horn shroud and disconnect the horn contact.

3. On models with the 3-spoke wheel, remove the medallion cover from the center of the wheel by prying lightly around the edge with a small screwdriver.

4. Remove the steering wheel nut and washer. Mark the steering wheel and shaft to assure proper positioning later.

5. Using a steering wheel puller, remove the steering wheel. Installation is the reverse of removal. Align the marks you made earlier.

6. Torque the steering wheel nut to 22 ft. lbs.

Removing emblem cover—except Impulse

Combination Switch

REMOVAL & INSTALLATION

All Except Impulse

1. Remove the steering wheel as previously described.

2. Remove the steering column covers and disconnect the electrical connectors to the switches.

3. Remove the washer/wiper switch by removing the two retaining screws.

4. Remove the turn signal/headlight switch and hazard switch by removing the four retaining screws.

5. Installation is the reverse of removal. Make sure the connectors are tight and properly connected.

NOTE: The light, wiper/washer, turn signal switches etc. on the Impulse, are contained in a control panel which is removed as an assembly. Refer to the procedure under "Chassis Electrical."

Steering Gear—Rack an Pinion

REMOVAL & INSTALLATION

All Models Exc. Impulse

1. Raise the car and safely support it with jackstands. Remove the lower engine shrouds.

2. Remove the steering shaft coupling bolt.

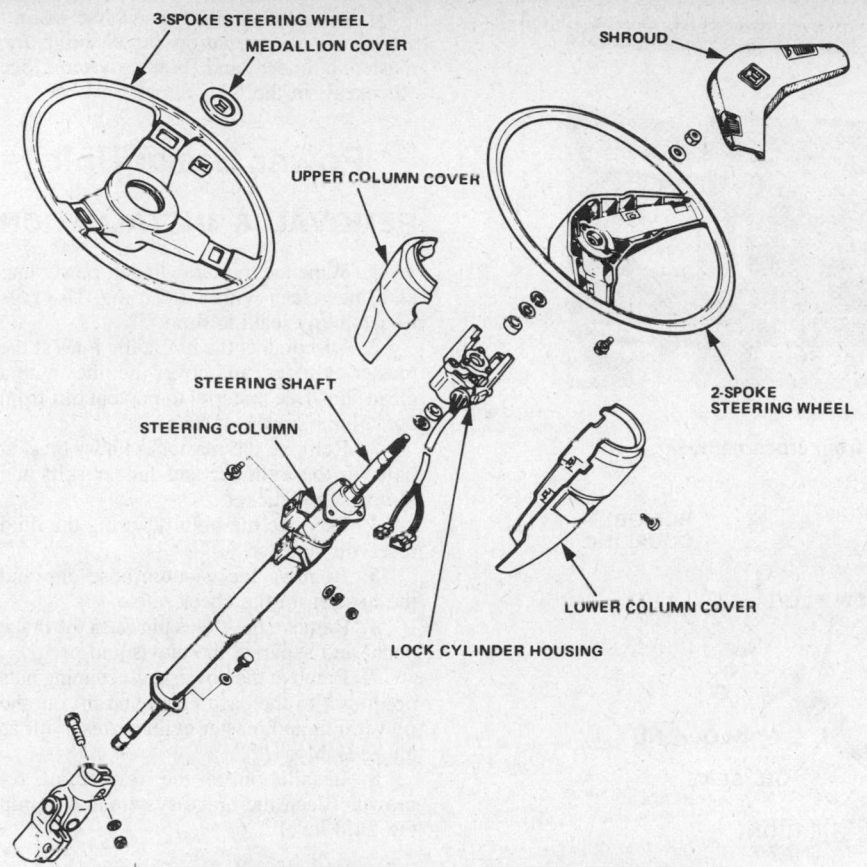

Exploded view of steering column assembly—except Impulse

Removing tie-rod end from knuckle

Power Steering Unit

REMOVAL & INSTALLATION

Impulse

1. Remove the front disc brake hub and rotor.
2. Remove the outer tie rod end with tool J-21687-02.
3. Disconnect and plug the return and feed pipes.
4. Unbolt the brackets at the crossmember and remove the power steering unit.
5. Installation is the reverse of removal.

Removing combination switches

3. Remove both tie-rod ends cotter pin and castle nut. Discard the pins and use tool J-21687-02 or equivalent to disconnect the tie-rod ends from the steering knuckles.

4. Disconnect the rack retaining bolts from the crossmember. Expand the steering shaft coupling and remove the assembly.

5. Installation is the reverse of removal. Before installing the rack assembly, set the steering gear to the high point by positioning the front wheels straight ahead with the steering wheel centered.

6. Torque the crossmember retaining bolts to 14 ft. lbs. Torque the steering shaft coupling bolt to 19 ft. lbs.

ADJUSTMENTS

Adjustment of the steering gear assembly is accomplished by turning the adjusting screw in or out.

1. Set the steering to the high point by positioning the front wheels straight ahead with the steering wheel centered.

2. Thread the adjusting screw into the steering gear housing and torque the adjusting screw to 11 ft. lbs.

3. Back off the adjusting screw slightly, then torque the locknut to 58 ft. lbs.

BRAKES

General Information

The Isuzu brake system on all models consists of a dual master cylinder operating front disc and rear drum brakes (rear disc brakes on the Impulse). The disc brakes are self-adjusting due to the design of the disc brake system. The rear brakes are self-adjusting by virtue of a lever-type mechanism that automatically adjusts the rear brakes whenever the parking brake is applied. The brakes are power-assisted by a power brake unit that operates off of engine vacuum. A combination valve serves both as the failure indicator and pressure control valve (proportioning valve). It is mounted on the left side of the engine compartment. Hydraulic brake fluid with a DOT-3 rating is recommended for normal use.

For all brake system repair and service not detailed below, please refer to "Brakes" in the Unit Repair section.

Master Cylinder

REMOVAL & INSTALLATION

1. Set the parking brake and chock the

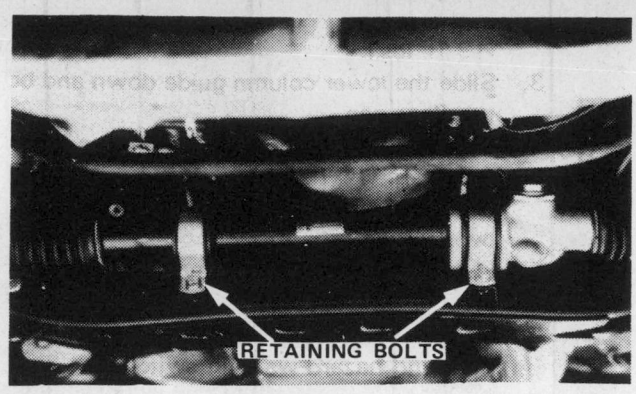

Removing steering rack from crossmember

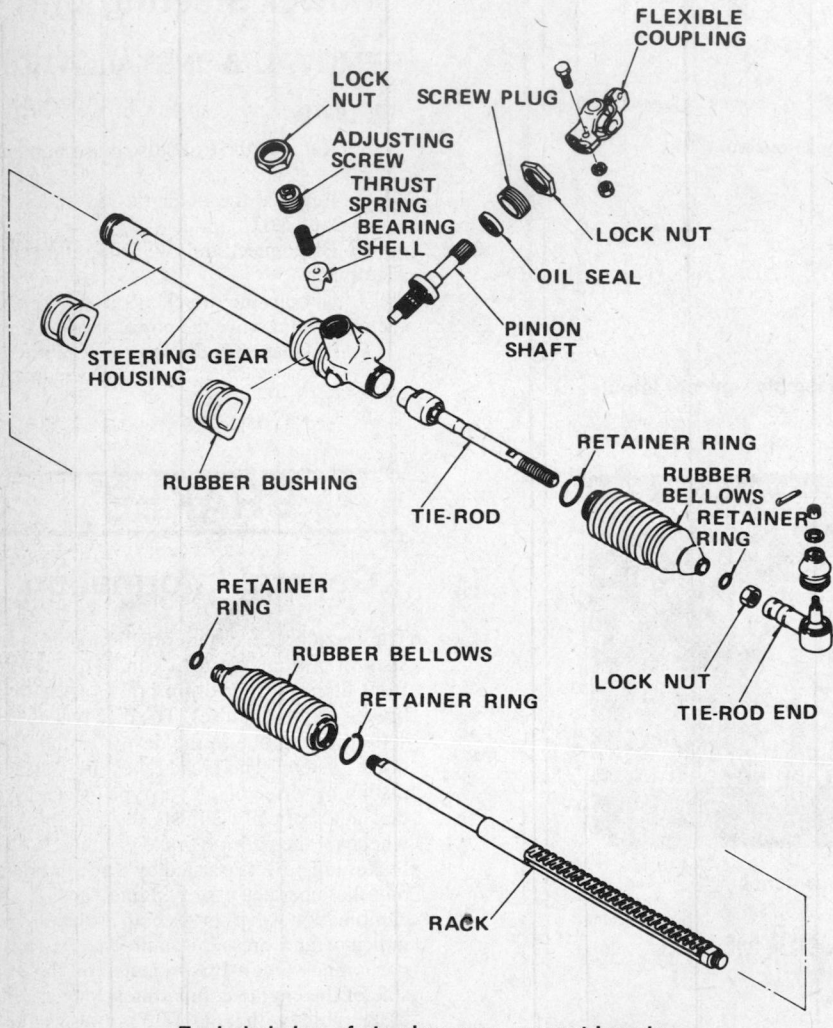

FLEXIBLE COUPLING
LOCK NUT
SCREW PLUG
ADJUSTING SCREW
THRUST SPRING
BEARING SHELL
LOCK NUT
OIL SEAL
PINION SHAFT
STEERING GEAR HOUSING
RUBBER BUSHING
TIE-ROD
RETAINER RING
RUBBER BELLOWS
RETAINER RING
RETAINER RING
RUBBER BELLOWS
RETAINER RING
LOCK NUT
TIE-ROD END
RACK

Exploded view of steering gear—except Impulse

wheels to prevent the car from rolling.

2. Open the hood and disconnect the front and rear brake lines from the master cylinder.

3. Remove the nuts securing the master cylinder to the power brake unit and the support bracket.

4. Remove the nuts securing the fluid reservoir bracket and remove the master cylinder and fluid reservoir as an assembly. (remove the rubber hoses, too)

NOTE: Be careful not to spill brake fluid on any painted surface. Brake fluid acts exactly like paint remover.

5. Installation is the reverse of removal. For information on bleeding the master cylinder and brake system, see "Brakes" in the Unit Repair section.

Power Brake Unit

REMOVAL & INSTALLATION

1. Wipe the master cylinder, power unit and lines clean with a clean rag. Use rags to catch any leaking fluid.

2. Disconnect the hydraulic lines at the master cylinder, and cover the lines with a clean, lint-free material to prevent dirt from contaminating the system.

3. Remove the master cylinder bracket bolts to the cylinder and fender skirt and remove the bracket.

4. Remove the bolts securing the fluid reservoir bracket.

5. Remove the vacuum hose clip and the hose from the check valve.

6. Remove the clevis pin from the brake pedal and separate the clevis and pedal.

7. Remove the power unit retaining nuts holding it to the dash panel and lift out the power unit and master cylinder/reservoir as an assembly.

8. Installation is the reverse of removal. Bleed the brake system and top up the fluid level.

Wheel Bearings

NOTE: For front wheel bearing removal and installation and adjustment refer to "Front Suspension."

Wheel Cylinder

REMOVAL & INSTALLATION

1. Remove the brake shoes.

2. Disconnect the hydraulic brake line at the wheel cylinder.

3. Remove the wheel cylinder attaching bolts from the backing plate.

4. Cap or tape the openings of the brake line and wheel cylinders.

5. Installation is the reverse of removal. Bleed the brake system.

Parking Brake

ADJUSTMENT

All Models Except Impulse

NOTE: Adjustment of the parking brake is necessary every time the rear brake cables are disconnected for any reason.

1. Fully release the parking brake lever and check the cable for free movement.

2. Remove the cable play by turning the brake lever rod adjusting nut.

1. Disc brake; front
2. Hub and rotor; front brake
3. Rod end assembly; outer
4. Shaft; steering, 2nd
5. Pipe assembly; return
6. Pipe assembly; feed
7. Bolt; bracket to crossmember
8. Washer; spring, bracket to crossmember
9. Bracket; steering unit to crossmember

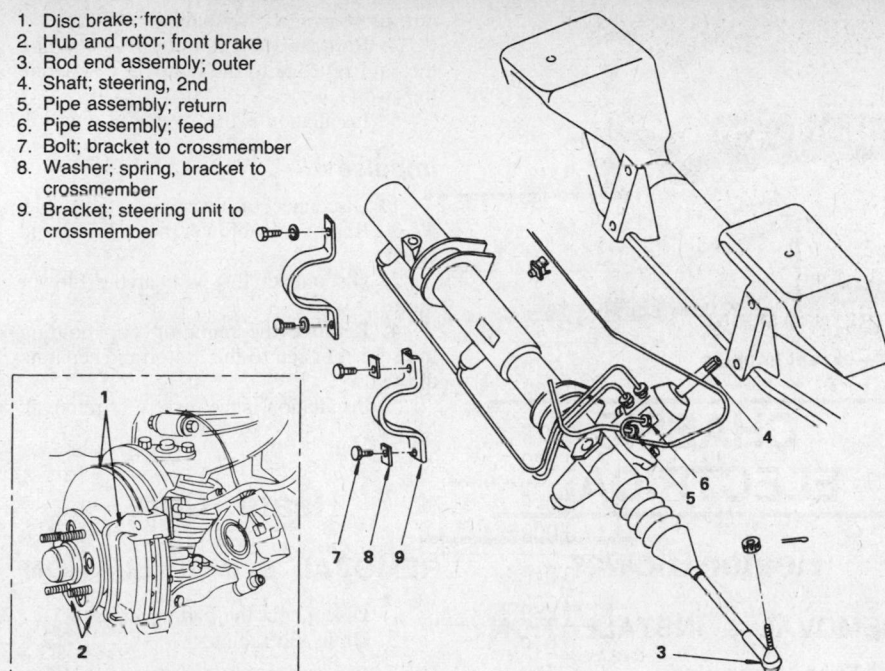

Power steering unit removal and installation—Impulse

3. When adjustment is complete, check that the travel of the parking brake lever is within 8–10 notches from full off to full on. If the travel is incorrect, readjust to specifications.

Impulse

1. The parking brake shoes can be adjusted by turning the adjuster until contact can be felt when turning the wheel manually, then backing off six notches.

2. The parking brake cable can be adjusted by pulling the parking brake lever from full off to full on. The lever travel should be within 11-12 notches. If the travel is incorrect adjust by turning the rod adjusting nut. Make sure the brakes do not drag after adjustment.

Parking Brake Shoe Assembly

REMOVAL & INSTALLATION

Impulse

1. Remove the shoe hold down pins.
2. Remove the shoe hold down spring clips.
3. Remove the anchor to shoe pull-back springs.
4. Remove the adjuster, adjuster spring and the primary shoe assembly.
5. Remove the retainer and washer and remove the secondary shoe and parking brake lever.
6. Installation is the reverse of removal with the following precautions:

a. Apply a thin coat of high temperature light grease to the adjuster assembly and the sliding surfaces of the backing plate.

b. When installing the left side adjuster assembly install the adjuster with the toothed side turned to the front of the vehicle. On the right side install the adjuster in the opposite direction.

1. Tandem master cylinder assembly
2. Cylinder body
3. Primary piston assembly
4. Secondary piston assembly
5. Primary piston spring
6. Secondary piston spring
7. Check valve
8. Connector
9. Check valve spring
10. Washer
11. Gasket
12. Stop—bolt
13. Gasket
14. Snap-ring
15. Connector
16. Clip
17. Gasket
18. Bracket
19. Bolt
20. Washer
21. Fluid reservoir assembly
22. Body
23. Filter
24. Cover
25. Bracket
26. Screw
27. Washer
28. Bolt
29. Washer
30. Front rubber hose
31. Rear rubber hose
32. Clip
33. Nut
34. Washer

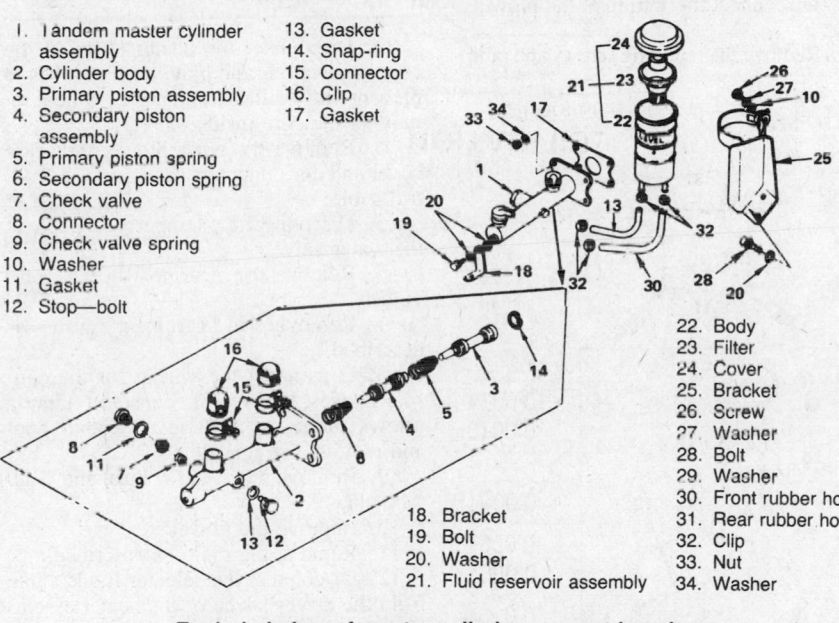

Exploded view of master cylinder—except Impulse

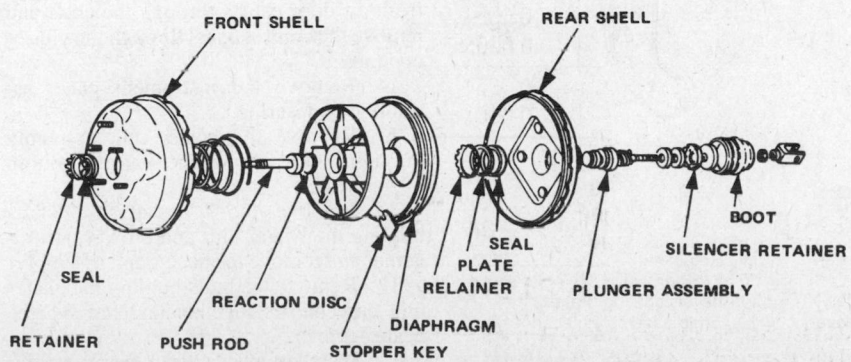

Exploded view of power brake unit—typical

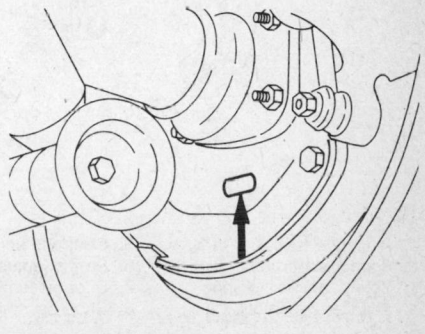

Parking brake shoe adjuster hole—Impulse

C385

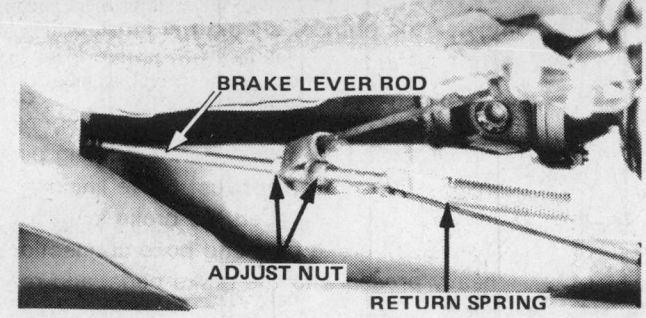

Parking brake adjustment—except Impulse

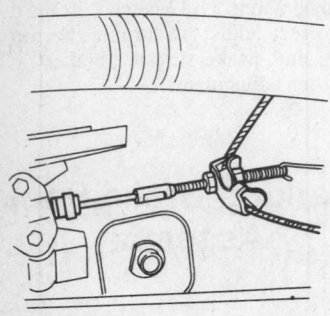

Parking brake cable adjusting nut— Impulse

out the blower motor and squirrel cage.

4. Remove the retaining clip holding the squirrel cage to the motor and separate the two.

5. Installation is the reverse of removal.

Impulse

1. Disconnect the negative battery cable.

2. Remove the blower motor lining and covers.

3. Disconnect the wire at the blower motor.

4. Remove the retaining clip holding the squirrel cage to the motor and separate the two.

5. Installation is the reverse of removal.

CHASSIS ELECTRICAL

Heater Blower

REMOVAL & INSTALLATION

All Except Impulse

1. Disconnect the battery cables.

2. Disconnect the wiring at the blower motor.

3. Remove the retaining screws and pull

Heater Core

REMOVAL & INSTALLATION

1. Disconnect the battery cables.

2. Drain the radiator.

———— CAUTION ————
This operation should only be carried out on a cold engine.

3. Disconnect the heater hoses at the core connections and plug the core tubes to prevent the spillage of coolant when removing the core inside the car.

4. Remove the outer blower unit case cover and disconnect the fresh air door control cable.

5. Disconnect the temperature cable at the water valve.

6. Remove the steering wheel as previously described.

7. Remove the instrument cluster as described.

8. Disconnect the wiring for the console gauges, remove the console retaining screws, untie the shift lever leather boot and remove the console.

9. Remove the heater control and radio face plate.

10. Remove the glovebox.

11. Remove the radio as described.

12. Disconnect the selector mode cable from the driver's side of the heater assembly.

13. Carefully pull the temperature and fresh air door cables through the cowl and remove the control panel through the cluster opening.

14. Remove the instrument panel assembly as described.

15. Remove the heater unit assembly through-bolt located at the rear and bottom of the heater.

16. Remove the four attaching nuts holding the heater unit and blower unit together and remove the heater unit assembly.

17. Remove the bolts holding the heater unit case halves together and remove the heater core.

18. Installation is the reverse of removal. Refill and bleed the cooling system.

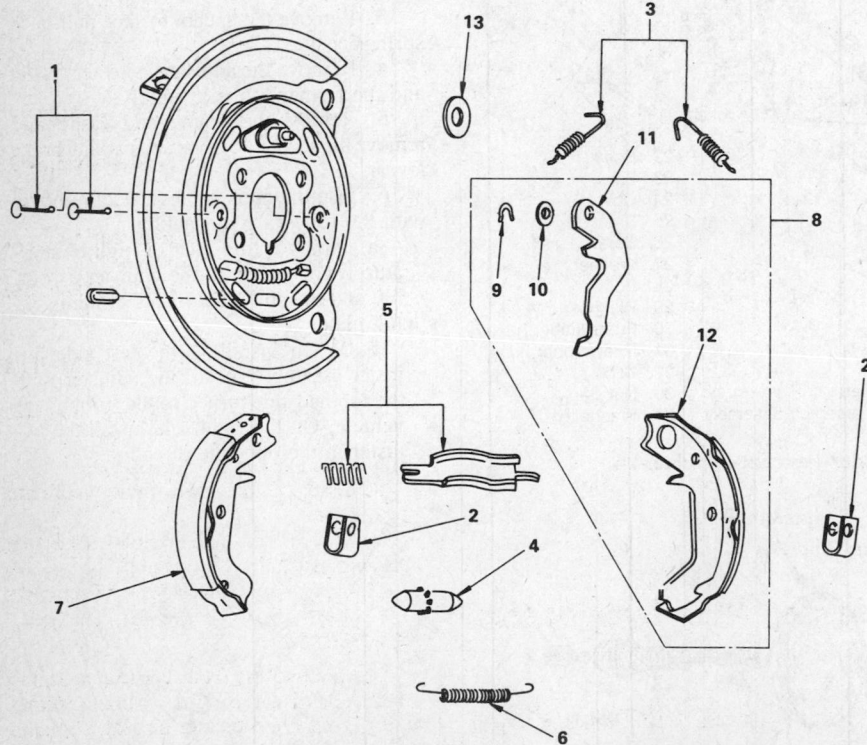

1. Pin; shoe hold	5. Strut and spring	9. Retainer
2. Spring; shoe hold	6. Spring; adjuster	10. Washer; wave
3. Spring; anchor to shoe	7. Shoe assembly (primary)	11. Lever; parking brake
4. Adjuster assembly	8. Shoe assembly with lever	12. Shoe assembly (secondary)
		13. Washer

Exploded view of parking brake shoe assembly—Impulse

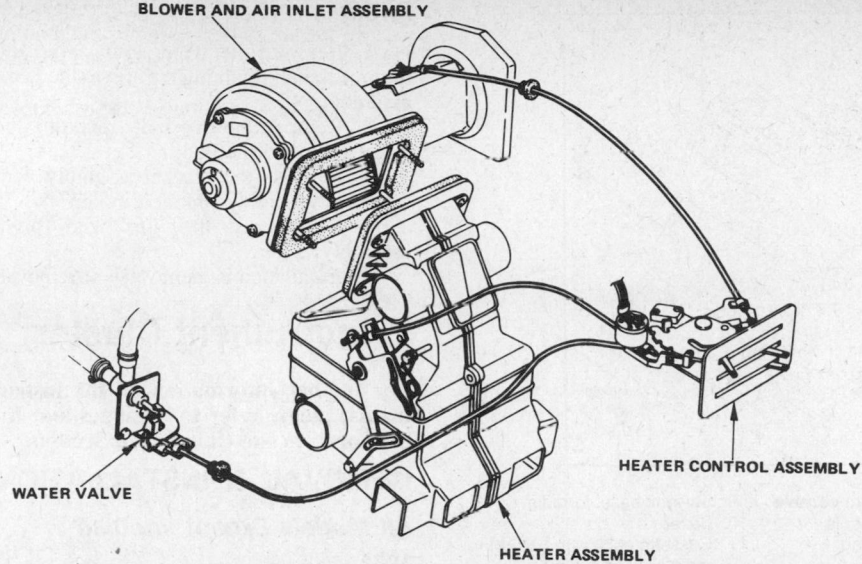

Heater system components—except Impulse

NOTE: **The air conditioning system must be discharged and evacuated, using the required tools, before the refrigerant lines can be disconnected.**

———— CAUTION ————

Do not disconnect any refrigerant lines unless you have experience with air conditioning systems. Escaping refrigerant will freeze any surface it contacts, including your skin and eyes.

3. Disconnect and plug the heater hoses, then remove the blower motor and heater assemblies.

4. The heater core may now be removed by removing the retaining screws.

5. Installation is the reverse of removal.

Radio

REMOVAL & INSTALLATION

All Except Impulse

1981

1. Remove the battery cables.
2. Remove the ash tray and ash tray support.
3. Remove the radio knobs and heater control knobs by pulling them straight back.
4. Remove the radio shaft nuts and trim panel.
5. Remove the radio retainer screws from under the dash board.
6. Disconnect the electrical and speaker connections and antenna cable.
7. Remove the radio down through the back of the dash.
8. Installation is the reverse of removal.

1982 AND LATER

1. Disconnect the battery cables.
2. Pull off the radio knobs.
3. Remove the radio shaft nuts and trim panel.
4. Remove the ash tray.
5. Pull off the A/C control knobs, if so equipped.
6. Remove the four screws, then remove the control panel.
7. Remove the two panel lights.
8. Remove the two radio retaining screws.
9. Disconnect the electrical connectors and lead–in cable.
10. Installation is the reverse of removal.

Impulse

1. Remove the front console retaining screws and disconnect the wiring harnesses at the front console and also at the radio main feed connection. Disconnect the antenna cable and the bolt retaining the ground the ground cable.
2. Remove the flange nuts retaining the front console pad to the front console.
3. Remove the screws retaining the bezel to the radio.

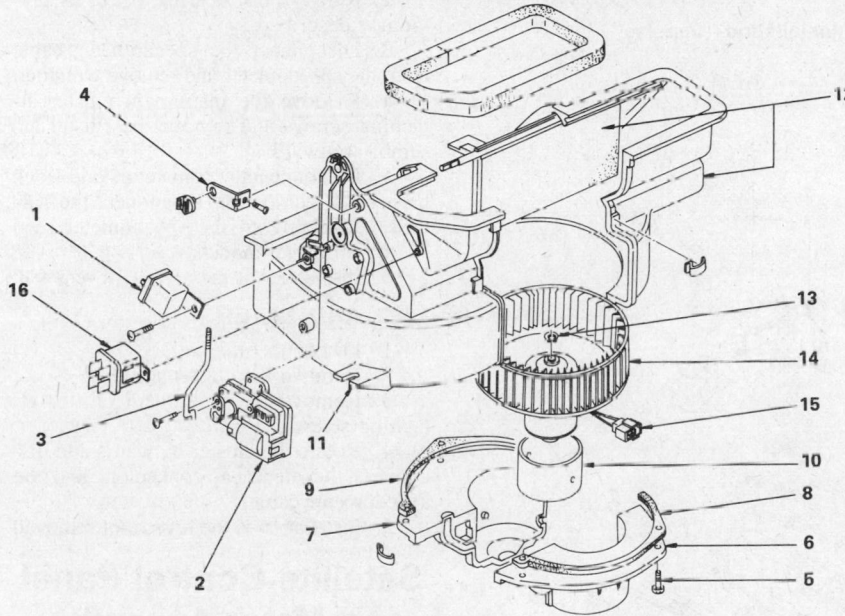

1. Relay; fresh-circulation
2. Actuator; blower unit
3. Rod; actuator
4. Lever; shutter
5. Screw; cover to case
6. Cover; blower unit
7. Cover; blower unit
8. Lining; blower unit
9. Lining; blower unit
10. Isolator; blower unit
11. Case; blower unit rear
12. Case; blower unit front
13. Ring; snap
14. Impeller; motor
15. Motor assembly; fan
16. Relay; blower unit

Blower motor removal—Impulse

Heater And Evaporator Assembly

REMOVAL & INSTALLATION

Impulse

1. Remove the instrument panel and compartment box.
2. Disconnect the A/C lines at the evaporator.

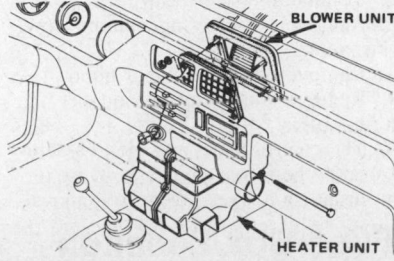

Heater installation—except Impulse

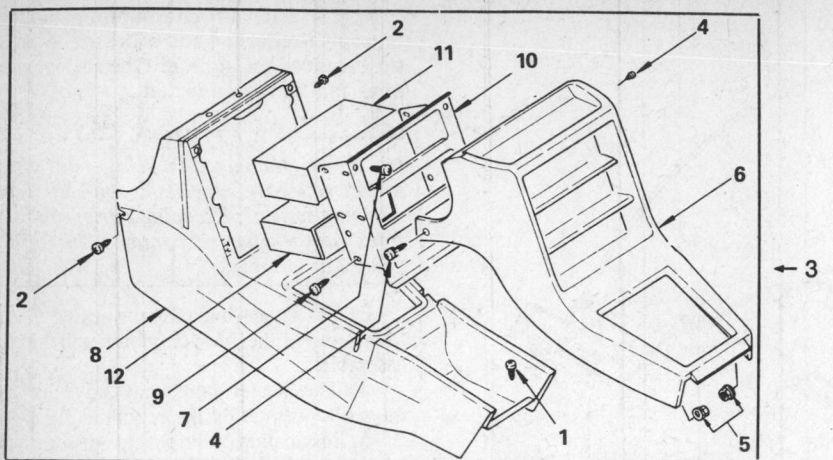

1. Screw; front console to body
2. Screws; front console to bracket
3. Console assembly
4. Screws; front console pad to front console
5. Flange nuts; front console pad to front console
6. Front console pad
7. Screws; bezel to front console
8. Front console
9. Screws; bezel to radio
10. Bezel
11. Cassette deck with FM/AM radio or FM/AM radio
12. Graphic equalizer or cassette deck

Radio and front console removal and installation—Impulse

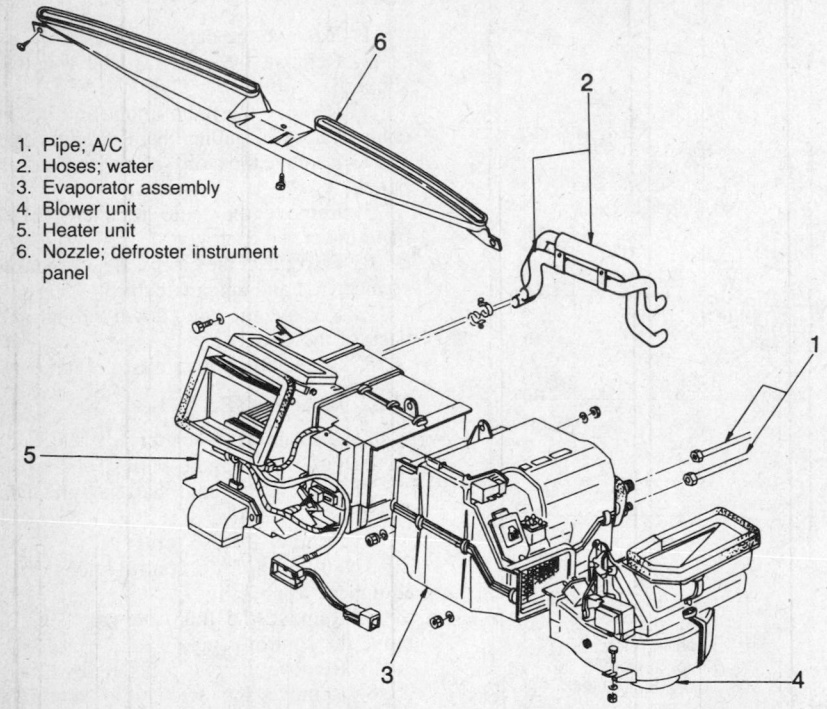

1. Pipe; A/C
2. Hoses; water
3. Evaporator assembly
4. Blower unit
5. Heater unit
6. Nozzle; defroster instrument panel

Heater and evaporator assembly removal and installation—Impulse

4. Disconnect any remaining harnesses and remove the radio assembly.

5. Installation is the reverse of removal. Be sure to properly connect all harnesses and cables before installing the console assembly.

Wiper Motor
REMOVAL & INSTALLATION
All Except Impulse
1. Disconnect the battery cables.

Wiper Motor And Linkage
REMOVAL & INSTALLATION

2. Working under the instrument panel, remove the nut and crank-arm from motor.
3. Disconnect the wiring connector.
4. Remove the three nuts securing the wiper motor and remove the motor.
5. Installation is the reverse of removal.

Impulse

1. Remove the wiper arm cover and remove thenut retaining the arm to the pivot assembly.
2. Remove the two bolts retaining the wiper motor to the body.
3. Remove the bracket assembly with the pivot assembly link and motor.
4. Disconnect the link and pivot assembly.
5. Installation is the reverse of removal.

Instrument Cluster

For further information on the instruments, please refer to "Gauges and Indicators" in the Unit Repair section.

REMOVAL & INSTALLATION

All Models Except Impulse
1981
1. Disconnect the battery.
2. Remove the steering wheel as previously described.
3. Disconnect the speedometer cable from the speedometer and remove wing nut.
4. Remove the instrument cluster attaching screws and remove the cluster assembly outward.
5. Disconnect the connectors and clock harness (if equipped). Disconnect the harness connecting to the speedometer reed switch on diesel models.
6. Installation is the reverse of removal.

1982 AND LATER
1. Disconnect the battery.
2. Remove the cluster panel.
3. Remove the instrument cluster attaching screws.
4. Rotate the cluster outwards and disconnect the electrical connectors and the speedometer cable.
5. Installation is the reverse of removal.

Satellite Control Panel and Meter Assembly

For further information on the instruments, please refer to "Gauges and Indicators" in the Unit Repair section.

REMOVAL & INSTALLATION

Impulse

1. Remove the steering wheel.
2. Remove the steering column cowl set or covers.
3. Remove the upper meter bond.
4. Remove the meter disconnect the wiring couplers.
5. The control panel and meter assembly can now be removed as a unit.
6. Installation is the reverse of removal.

Fuse Box Location

The fuse box is located on the left kick panel, just under the dash.

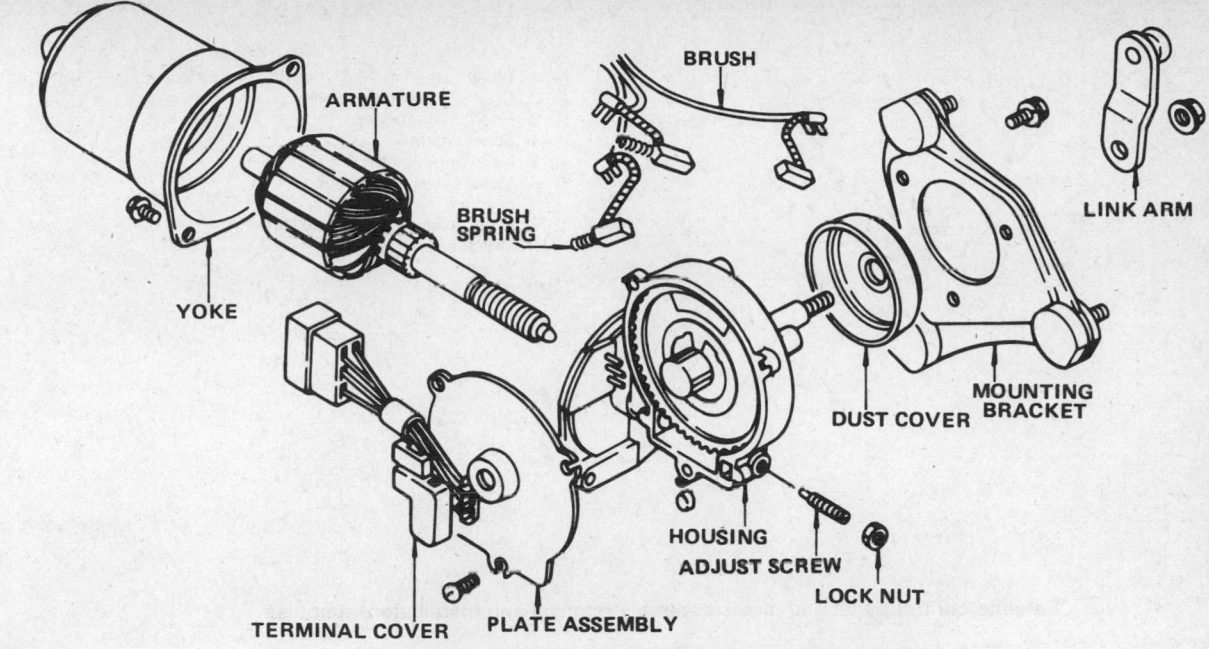

ARMATURE

BRUSH

BRUSH
SPRING

LINK ARM

YOKE

DUST COVER

MOUNTING
BRACKET

HOUSING

ADJUST SCREW

LOCK NUT

TERMINAL COVER

PLATE ASSEMBLY

Exploded view of wiper components—except Impulse

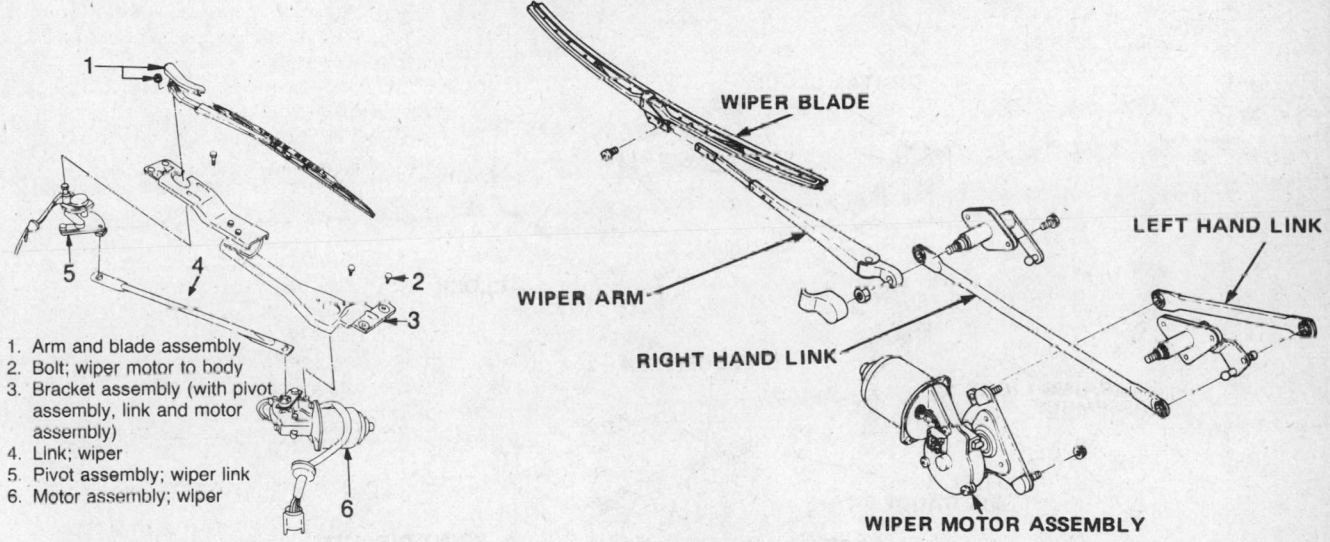

WIPER BLADE

LEFT HAND LINK

WIPER ARM

RIGHT HAND LINK

WIPER MOTOR ASSEMBLY

1. Arm and blade assembly
2. Bolt; wiper motor to body
3. Bracket assembly (with pivot assembly, link and motor assembly)
4. Link; wiper
5. Pivot assembly; wiper link
6. Motor assembly; wiper

Front wiper motor and linkage—Impulse

Wiper system components—except Impulse

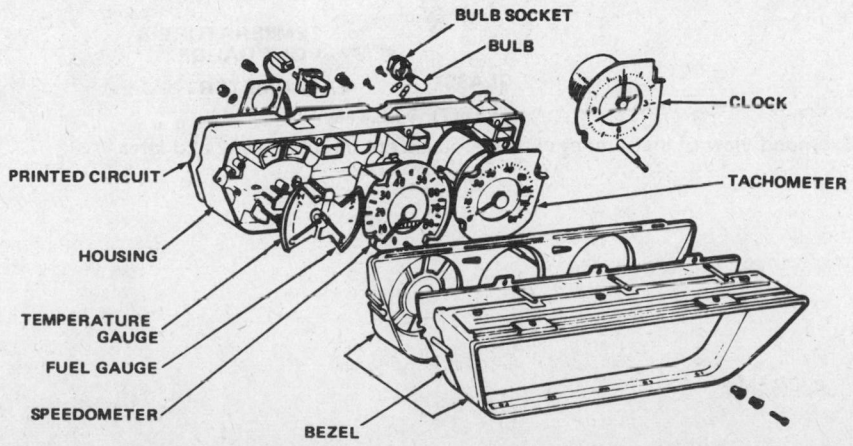

BULB SOCKET

BULB

CLOCK

PRINTED CIRCUIT

TACHOMETER

HOUSING

TEMPERATURE
GAUGE

FUEL GAUGE

SPEEDOMETER

BEZEL

Exploded view of instrument cluster—1981 except Impulse

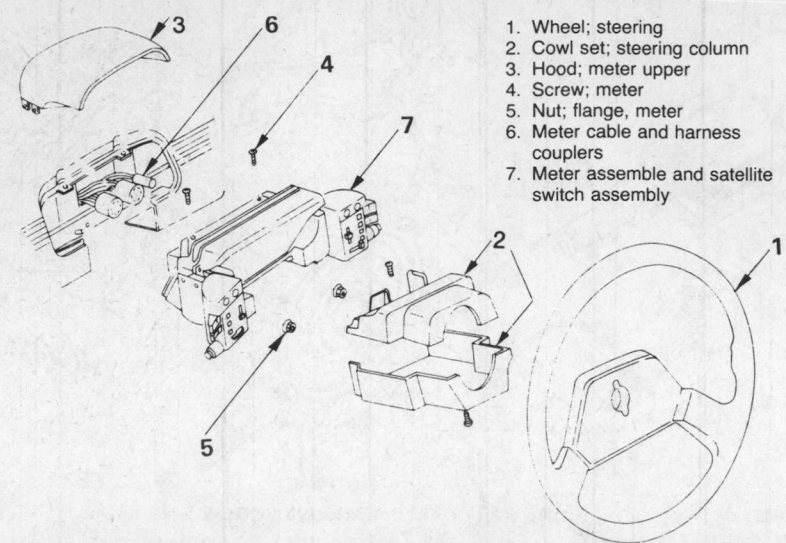

1. Wheel; steering
2. Cowl set; steering column
3. Hood; meter upper
4. Screw; meter
5. Nut; flange, meter
6. Meter cable and harness couplers
7. Meter assemble and satellite switch assembly

Satellite control panel and meter assembly removal and installation—Impulse

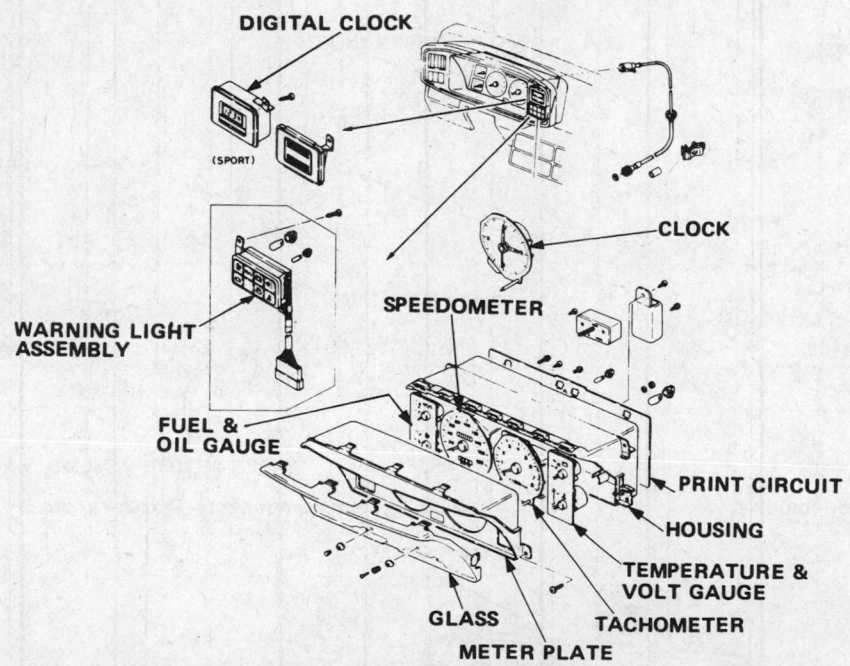

Exploded view of instrument cluster—all except Impulse, 1982 and later

Mazda
Cosmo, GLC, RX-3SP, RX-4, RX-7, 626, 808

SERIAL NUMBER IDENTIFICATION

Vehicle

The serial number is on a plate located on the driver's side windshield pillar and is visible through the glass.

A vehicle identification number (VIN) plate, bearing the serial number and other data, is attached to the cowl.

Engine

The engine number is located on a plate which is attached to the engine housing, just behind the distributor or on a machined pad at the right front side of the engine block.

The engine number consists of an identification number followed by a six-digit production number.

GENERAL ENGINE SPECIFICATIONS—PISTON ENGINE

Year	Model	Engine Displacement cu. in. (cc)	Carb Type	Horsepower (@ rpm)	Torque @ rpm (ft. lbs.)	Bore × Stroke (in.)	Compression Ratio	Oil Pressure (@ rpm)
'79–'82	626	120.2 (1970)	2V	75 @ 4500	105 @ 2500	3.15 × 3.86	8.6:1	50–64 @ 3000
'83–'85	626	121.9 (2000)	2V	83 @ 4800	110 @ 2500	3.39 × 3.39	8.6:1	43–57 @ 3000
'78	GLC	77.6 (1272)	2V	52 @ 5000	65 @ 3000	2.87 × 2.99	9.2:1	50–64 @ 3000
'79–'80	GLC	86.4 (1415)	2V	77 @ 4300	109 @ 2400	3.03 × 2.99	9.0:1	50–64 @ 3000
'81–'85	GLC	90.9 (1490)	2V	68 @ 5000	82 @ 3000	3.03 × 3.15	9.0:1	50–60 @ 3000

GENERAL ENGINE SPECIFICATIONS—ROTARY ENGINE

Model	Engine Displacement cu. in. (cc)	Carburetor Type	Net Horsepower @ rpm	Net Torque @ rpm	Rotor Displacement (cu. in.)	Compression Ratio	Oil Pressure @ rpm (psi)
RX-7 ('78–'84)	70 (1146)	4-bbl	100 @ 6000	105 @ 4000	35	9.4:1	71.1 @ 3000
RX-7 ('84–'85)	80 (1308)	EFI	135 @ 6000	133 @ 2750	40	9.4:1	64–78 @ 3000
RX-3SP	70 (1146)	4-bbl	95 @ 6000	100 @ 4000	35	9.4:1	71.1 @ 3000
RX-4 Cosmo	80 (1308)	4-bbl	110 @ 6000	120 @ 4000	40	9.2:1	71.1 @ 3000

EFI Electronic Fuel Injection

MAZDA

TUNE-UP SPECIFICATIONS—PISTON ENGINE

(When analyzing compression test results, look for uniformity among cylinders, rather than specific pressures)

Year	Engine Displacement (cu. in.)	Spark Plugs Type	Gap (in.)	Distributor Point Dwell (deg)	Distributor Point Gap (in.)	Ignition Timing (deg) MT	Ignition Timing (deg) AT	Intake Valve Opens (deg)	Fuel Pump Pressure (psi)	Idle Speed (rpm)	Valve Clearance (in.) In	Valve Clearance (in.) Ex
'78	77.6	BP6ES	.031	49–55	.020	7B④	11B	13	2.84–3.84	700–750⑤	.010	.012
'79	86.4	BP5ES, BPR5ES	.031	49–55	.020	7B⑥	7B⑦	15	2.8–3.8	700–750 ⑨⑩	.010	.012
	120.2	BP5ES, BPR5ES	.031	Electronic		8B	8B	10	2.8–3.6	650–700	.012	.012
'80	86.4	BP5ES, BPR5ES	.031	Electronic		5B	5B	15	2.8–3.8	700–750⑨	.010	.012
'80–'82	120.2	BP5ES, BPR5ES	⑬	Electronic		5B⑧	5B⑧	10	2.8–3.6	750–700	.012	.012
'81–'85	90.9	BPR5ES, BPR6ES	⑫	Electronic		8B⑭	8B⑭	15	2.8–3.8 ⑯	850⑪	.010	.012
'83–'85	121.9	BPR5ES, BPR6ES	.031	Electronic		6B	6B	17	2.8–3.5 ⑰	750⑮	.012	.012

NOTE: The underhood specifications sticker often reflects tune-up specification changes made in production. Sticker figures must be used if they disagree with those in this chart.

N.A. Information not available
② California: 8B
③ Automatic: 650–700 in Drive
④ California: 11B
⑤ Automatic: 600–650 in Drive
⑥ California: 5B
   Canada: 8A
⑦ California: 5B
   Canada: 8B
⑧ Canada: 8B

⑨ Federal:
   Automatic: 600–650
⑩ Canada:
   Manual: 800–850
   Automatic: 700–750
⑪ Automatic 750 in Drive
⑫ BPR5ES—.031, BPR6ES—.031
⑬ '80—.031, '81–'82 BP5ES, BPR5ES—.031, BP6ES, BPR6ES—.031
⑭ '83–'85—6° BTDC
⑮ Automatic: 700 in Drive
⑯ '84–'85—4.27–5.97
⑰ '84–'85—2.8–4.27

TUNE-UP SPECIFICATIONS—ROTARY ENGINE

(When analyzing compression test results, look for uniformity among cylinders, rather than specific pressures)

Year	Engine Displacement (cu. in.)	Spark Plugs Type	Gap (in.)	Distributors Point Dwell (deg)	Distributors Point Gap (in.)	Ignition Timing (deg) Leading Normal	Ignition Timing (deg) Leading Retarded	Ignition Timing (deg) Trailing Normal	Idle Speed (rpm) MT	Idle Speed (rpm) AT
'78	70②	RN278B	0.039–0.043	58 ± 3	.018	0	—	20A	725–775	725–775①
'78	80	RN278B	0.039–0.043	58 ± 3	.018	5A	—	25A	725–775	725–775①
'79	70	RN280B	0.039–0.043	58 ± 3	.018	0	—	20A	725–775	725–775①
'80	70	RN280B	0.039–0.043	Electronic		0	—	20A	725–775	725–775①

TUNE-UP SPECIFICATIONS—ROTARY ENGINE

(When analyzing compression test results, look for uniformity among cylinders, rather than specific pressures)

Year	Engine Displacement (cu. in.)	Spark Plugs		Distributors		Ignition Timing (deg)			Idle Speed (rpm)	
		Type	Gap (in.)	Point Dwell (deg)	Point Gap (in.)	Leading		Trailing	MT	AT
						Normal	Retarded	Normal		
'81–'85	70④	③	0.053–0.057 ⑤	Electronic		0⑥	—	20A	750⑦	750①

NOTE: The underhood specifications sticker often reflects tune-up specification changes made in production. Sticker figures must be used if they disagree with those in this chart.

TDC—Top dead center
A—After top dead center
B—Before top dead center
MT—Manual transmission
AT—Automatic transmission
deg—degrees
① Transmission in Drive
② Used in RX-3SP only
③ NGK-BR7EQ14, BR8EQ14, BR9EQ14

NIPPONDENSO-W22EDR14, W25EDR14, W27EDR14
④ 13B
eng: 80
⑤ 13B
eng: .055
⑥ 13B
eng: Leading-5A
⑦ 13B
eng: 800

FIRING ORDERS

NOTE: To avoid confusion, always replace spark plug wires one at a time.

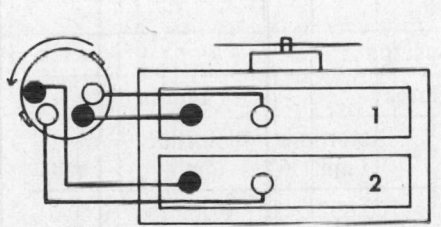

Rotary engine

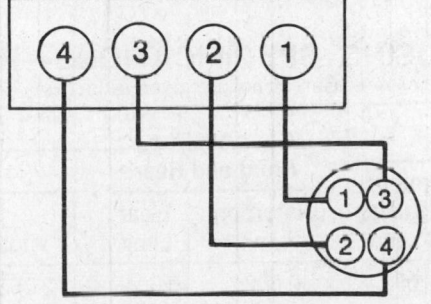

All except 1490 cc engine with front wheel drive

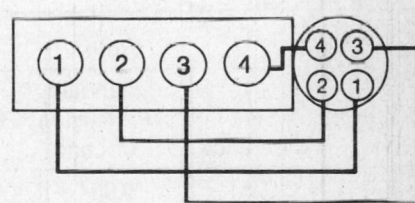

1490 cc engine—GLC front wheel drive

CAPACITIES

Year	Model	Engine Displacement cu. in. (cc)	Engine Crankcase (qts)		Transmission (pts)			Drive Axle (pts)	Gasoline Tank (gals)	Cooling System (qts)
			With Filter	Without Filter	Manual		Automatic			
					4-spd	5-spd				
'78	RX-4, RX-3SP	80 (1308)	6.8	5.3	3.6	4.6	13.2	2.8	16.9②	10.0
	Cosmo	80 (1308)	6.8	5.3	—	3.6	13.2	2.6	17.2	10.0
	GLC	77.6 (1272)	—	3.2	2.8	3.6	12.0	1.6	10.0	6.8
'79–'80	GLC	86.4 (1415)	—	3.2	2.8	3.6	12.0	2.2	10.6③	5.8
'81–'85	GLC	90.9 (1490)	3.9	—	6.8	6.8	12.0	—	11.1	5.8
'79–'82	626	120.2 (1970)	—	4.1④	3.0	3.6	13.2	2.6	14.5	7.9

CAPACITIES

Year	Model	Engine Displacement cu. in. (cc)	Engine Crankcase (qts) With Filter	Engine Crankcase (qts) Without Filter	Transmission (pts) Manual 4-spd	Transmission (pts) Manual 5-spd	Transmission (pts) Automatic	Drive Axle (pts)	Gasoline Tank (gals)	Cooling System (qts)
'83–'85	626	121.9 (2000)	4.8	—	—	7.0	12.0	—	15.8 ⑦	7.4
'79	RX-7	70 (1146)	5.5	4.4	3.6	3.6	13.2	2.6	14.5	7.6
'80–'85	RX-7	70 (1146) ⑥	5.5 ⑨	4.4 ⑧	3.6	3.6 ⑩	13.2 ⑪	2.6	14.5 ⑤ ⑫	10.0

① Station wagon: 10.4
② Station wagon: 17.4
③ Station wagon: 11.9
④ '82—3.8
⑤ '81–'83—16.4

⑥ 13B engine: 80 (1308)
⑦ '84–'85: 15.6
⑧ 13B: 4.9 w/o filter, 6.1 full capacity
⑨ 12A: 4.9 full capacity

⑩ 12A: 4.2
    13B: 4.2
⑪ 15.8 total capacity
⑫ '84–'85: 16.4

ECCENTRIC SHAFT SPECIFICATIONS—ROTARY ENGINE
(All measurements are given in inches)

Model	Journal Diameter Main Bearing	Journal Diameter Rotor Bearing	Oil Clearance Main Bearing	Oil Clearance Rotor Bearing	Eccentric Shaft End-Play Normal	Eccentric Shaft End-Play Limit	Min. Shaft Run-Out
All	1.6929	2.9134	0.0016– 0.0028 ①	0.0016– 0.0031	0.0016– 0.0028	0.0035	0.0008

① '84–'85: .0016–.0031

ROTOR AND HOUSING SPECIFICATIONS—ROTARY ENGINE
(All measurements are given in inches)

Model	Rotor Side Clearance	Rotor Standard Protrusion of Land	Rotor Limit of Protrusion of Land	Housings Front and Rear Distortion Limit	Housings Front and Rear Wear Limit	Housings Rotor Width	Housings Rotor Distortion Limit	Housings Intermediate Distortion Limit	Housings Intermediate Wear Limit
RX-3SP	0.0051– 0.0067	0.004– 0.006	0.003	0.002	0.004	2.7539	0.002	0.002	0.004
RX-7	0.0047– ① 0.0071	—	—	0.0016	0.0039	2.7559 ②	0.0024	0.0016	0.0039
RX-4 Cosmo	0.0039– 0.0083	—	—	0.0016	0.0039	3.150	0.0024	0.0016	0.0039

① 13B: .0047–.0083
② 13B: 3.1497

CRANKSHAFT AND CONNECTING ROD SPECIFICATIONS—PISTON ENGINE
(All measurements are given in inches)

Year	Engine Displacement cu. in.(cc)	Crankshaft Main Brg. Journal Dia.	Crankshaft Main Brg. Oil Clearance	Crankshaft Shaft End-Play	Crankshaft Thrust on No.	Connecting Rod Journal Dia.	Connecting Rod Oil Clearance	Connecting Rod Side Clearance
'78	77.6 (1272)	2.4804	0.0012– 0.0024	0.003– 0.009	5	1.7717	0.0011– 0.0029	0.004– 0.008
'79–'80	86.4 (1415)	1.9685	0.0009– 0.0017	0.004– 0.006	5	1.5748	0.0009– 0.0019	0.004– 0.008

CRANKSHAFT AND CONNECTING ROD SPECIFICATIONS—PISTON ENGINE
(All measurements are given in inches)

Year	Engine Displacement cu. in.(cc)	Crankshaft				Connecting Rod		
		Main Brg. Journal Dia.	Main Brg. Oil Clearance	Shaft End-Play	Thrust on No.	Journal Dia.	Oil Clearance	Side Clearance
'79–'82	120.2 (1970)	2.4804	0.0012– 0.0020	0.003– 0.009	5	2.0866	0.001– 0.003	0.004– 0.008
'81–'84	90.9 (1490)	1.9664	0.0009– 0.0017	0.004– 0.006	5	1.5729	0.0009– 0.0019	0.004– 0.010
'83–'85	121.9 (2000)	2.3590	0.0012– 0.0019	0.0031– 0.0071	3	2.005– 2.006	0.0010– 0.0026	0.004– 0.010

CAMSHAFT SPECIFICATIONS
(All measurements in inches)

Year	Engine Cu. In. (CC)	Journal Diameter			Front & Rear Bearing Clearance	Lobe Lift		Camshaft End Play (New)
		Front	Center	Rear		Intake	Exhaust	
'78	77.6 (1272)	1.6536	1.6536	1.6536	0.0014 0.0030②	1.7369	1.7369	0.001– 0.007①
'79–'82	120.2 (1970)	1.7717	1.7717	1.7717	0.0007–0.0027③	1.7731	1.7718	0.001– 0.007①
'79–'80	86.4 (1415)	1.6536	1.6536	1.6536	0.0014–0.0030②	1.7370	1.7370	0.001– 0.007①
'81④	90.9 (1490)	1.6536	1.6536	1.6536	0.0014–0.0030②	1.7367	1.7367	0.001– 0.007①
'82–'85	90.9 (1490)	1.6515– 1.6522	1.6504– 1.6510	1.6515– 1.6522	0.0014–0.0030②	1.7368	1.7368	0.001– 0.007①
'83–'85	121.9 (2000)	1.257– 1.258	1.256– 1.257	1.257– 1.258	0.0014–0.0033	1.5023	1.5024	0.003– 0.006

① Wear limit 0.008 in.
② Center clearance 0.0026–0.0043 in.
③ Center clearance 0.0011–0.0031 in.
④ Includes 1981–84 GLC Station Wagon

SEAL CLEARANCES—ROTARY ENGINE
(All measurements are given in inches)

Model	Apex Seals				Corner Seal		Side Seal			
	To Side Housing		To Rotor Groove		To Rotor Groove		To Rotor Groove		To Corner Seal	
	Normal	Limit	Normal	Limit	Normal	Limit	Normal	Limit	Normal	Limit
RX-3SP	0.0020– 0.0028 ①	0.0039	0.0014– 0.0029	0.0039	0.0008– 0.0019	0.0031	0.0016– 0.0028	0.0039	0.002– 0.006	0.016
RX-4, Cosmo	0.0051– 0.0067	0.0118	0.0020– 0.0035	0.006	0.0008– 0.0019	0.0031	0.0016– 0.0028	0.0040	0.0020– 0.0059	0.0157
RX-7	0.0051– 0.0075	—	0.0020– 0.0035	0.0059	—	—	0.0012– 0.0031	0.0039	0.0020– 0.0059	0.0157

① Arctic specifications—0.0004–0.0020

MAZDA

SEAL SPECIFICATIONS—ROTARY ENGINE
(All measurements are given in inches)

Model	Apex Seal Normal Height	Apex Seal Height Limit	Corner Seal Width (OD)	Side Seal Thickness	Side Seal Height	Oil Seal Contact Width of Lip Normal	Oil Seal Contact Width of Lip Limit
RX-3SP	0.03937	0.03150	0.2756	0.0394	0.1378	0.008	0.031
RX-4, Cosmo	0.33500	0.27600	0.4331	0.0394	0.1378	0.008	0.031
RX-7	0.33470	0.27560	0.4331	0.0394	0.1378	0.0197	—

VALVE SPECIFICATIONS—PISTON ENGINE

Year	Engine Displacement cu. in. (cc)	Seat Angle (deg)	Face Angle (deg)	Spring Test Pressure (lbs.@in.)	Spring Installed Height (in.)	Stem-to-Guide Clearance(in.) Intake	Stem-to-Guide Clearance(in.) Exhaust	Stem Diameter(in.) Intake	Stem Diameter(in.) Exhaust
'78	77.6 (1272)	45	45	①	③	0.0007–0.0021	0.0007–0.0023	0.3150	0.3150
'78	109.6 (1796)	45	45	④	②	0.0007–0.0021	0.0007–0.0023	0.3150	0.3150
'79–'80	86.4 (1415)	45	45	⑤	③	0.0007–0.0021	0.0007–0.0021	0.3150	0.3150
'79–'82	120.2 (1970)	45	45	⑥	②	0.0007–0.0021	0.0007–0.0021	0.3150	0.3150
'81–'85	90.9 (1490)	45	45	N.A.	N.A.	0.0007–0.0021	0.0007–0.0021	0.3164	0.3163
'83–'85	121.9 (1998)	45	45	N.A.	N.A.	0.0010–0.0024	0.0010–0.0024	0.3177–0.3185	0.3159–0.3165

N.A. Not available at time of publication
① Outer: 43.7 @ 1.319
   Inner: 20.9 @ 1.260
② Outer: 1.339
   Inner: 1.260
③ Outer: 1.319
   Inner: 1.260
④ Outer: 31.4 @ 1.339
   Inner: 20.9 @ 1.260
⑤ Outer: 36.6 @ 1.319
   Inner: 17.9 @ 1.260
⑥ Outer: 31.4 @ 1.339
   Inner: 17.9 @ 1.260

PISTON AND RING SPECIFICATIONS
(All measurements are given in inches)

Year	Engine Displacement cu. in. (cc)	Piston Clearance	Ring Side Clearance Top Compression	Ring Side Clearance Bottom Compression	Ring Side Clearance Oil Control	Ring Gap Top Compression	Ring Gap Bottom Compression	Ring Gap Oil Control
'78–'79	96.8 (1586)	0.0022–0.0028	0.0014–0.0028	0.0012–0.0025	0.008–0.016	0.008–0.016	0.008–0.016	0.008–0.016
'78	77.6 (1272)	0.0021–0.0026	0.0014–0.0028	0.0012–0.0025	0.008–0.016	0.008–0.016	0.008–0.016	0.008–0.016
'79–'80	86.4 (1415)	0.0021–0.0026	0.0012–0.0025	0.0012–0.0025	0.008–0.016	0.008–0.016	0.008–0.016	0.012–0.035
'79–'82	120.2 (1970)	0.0014–0.0030 ①	0.0012–0.0028	0.0012–0.0025	0.008–0.016	0.008–0.016	0.008–0.016	0.012–0.035
'81–'85	90.9 (1490)	0.0010–0.0026	0.0012–0.0028	0.0012–0.0028	0.008–0.016	0.008–0.016	0.008–0.016	0.012–0.035
'83–'85	121.9 (1998)	0.0014–0.0030	0.0012–0.0028	0.0012–0.0028	—	0.008–0.014	0.006–0.012	0.012–0.035

① '82-0.0019–0.0025

TORQUE SPECIFICATIONS—ROTARY ENGINE
(All figures in ft. lbs.)

Engine Displacement cu. in. (cc)	Front Cover	Bearing Housing	Rear Stationary Gear	Eccentric Shaft Pulley Bolt	Flywheel to Eccentric Shaft Nut	Manifolds		Oil Pan	Tension Bolts
						Intake	Exhaust		
70 (1146)	15	15	15	45④	325⑥	15	30②	7	20③
80 (1308)	—	—	—	54–69①	289–362	15	32–43	5–7	23–27

① 1978 and 1984–85—72–87
② RX-7: 35
③ RX-7: 23–27
④ 1984–85—72–87
⑤ 1984–85—23–34
⑥ 1984–85—289–362

TORQUE SPECIFICATIONS—PISTON ENGINE
(All figures in ft. lbs.)

Year	Engine Displacement (cc)	Cylinder Head Bolts (cold)	Rod Bearing Bolts	Main Bearing Bolts	Crankshaft Pulley Bolt	Flywheel to Crankshaft Bolts	Manifolds	
							Intake	Exhaust
'78	1600	56–60	36–40	61–65	101–108	112–118	14–19	16–21
'78	1300	47–51	29–33	43–47	80–87	60–65	14–19	12–17
'79–'80	1415	47–51	22–25	43–47	80–87	60–65	14–19	12–17
'79–'82	1970	59–64①	29–33	61–65	101–108	112–118	14–19	16–21
'81–'85	1490	56–59	22–25	48–51	80–87	60–65②	14–19	14–17
'83–'85	2000	59–64③	37–41	61–65	80–87	71–76	14–19	16–21

① '82—65–69
② Auto
 Trans: 51–61
③ Warm: 69–80

ALTERNATOR AND REGULATOR SPECIFICATIONS

Year	Model	Alternator		Regulator							
				Field Relay			Regulator				
		Field Current @14v	Output (amps)	Air Gap (in.)	Point Gap (in.)	Back Gap (in.)	Air Gap (in.)	Point Gap (in.)	Back Gap (in.)	Volts @75°
'78	All Rotary	—	63	0.035–0.055	0.028–0.043	0.028–0.049	0.028–0.051	0.012–0.018	0.028–0.059	14
'78–'80	GLC, 626	—	30	0.039–0.059	0.020–0.035	0.028–0.059	0.028–0.051	0.012–0.018	0.028–0.059	14–15
'79–'80	RX-7	—	40	0.035–0.055	0.028–0.043	0.028–0.059	0.028–0.051	0.012–0.018	0.028–0.059	14–15
'81–'85	All	—	50	Not Adjustable						

BATTERY AND STARTER SPECIFICATIONS
(All cars use 12 volt, negative ground electrical systems)

Year	Model	Battery Amp Hour Capacity	Starter Lock Test Amps	Lock Test Volts	Lock Test Torque (ft. lbs.)	No Lead Test Amps	No Lead Test Volts	No Lead Test rpm	Brush Spring Tension (oz)	Min. Brush Length (in.)
'78	RX-4 w/MT	70	780	5	7.97	75	11.5	4900	56	.45
	RX-4 w/AT	70①	1100	5	17.36	100	11.5	7800	56	.45
'78	Cosmo w/MT	45	600	5	6.9	50	11.5	5600	56	.45
	Cosmo w/AT	70	1050	5	15.9	100	11.5	6600	56	.45
'78–'80	GLC	45②	310	5	5.4	53	11.5	6800	56	.45
'79–'80	626	45	310	5	5.4	53	11.5	6800	56	.45
'79–'80	RX-7	55	600	5	6.9	50	11.5	5600	56	.45
'81–'82	626 w/MT	45	310	5	5.4	53	11.5	6800	56	.45
	626 w/AT	45	500	5	8.3	60	11.5	6600	56	.45
'83–'85	626	50⑥	310	5	5.4	60	11.5	6500	—	.453
'81–'85	RX-7 w/MT	④	600	5	6.9	50	11.5	5600	71	.45
	RX-7 w/AT	④	1100	4	22.4	100	11.5	3500	71	.45
'81–'85	GLC	⑤	310	5	5.4	53	11.5	6800	—	.45

MT—Manual transmission
AT—Automatic transmission
① 60 amp w/MT
② '77   Canada: 45 amp
      Exc Calif.: 60 amp
      Calif.: 35 amp
  '78   Calif.: 35 amp
  '79–'80 Calif.: 33 amp

③ Calif.: 35
④ Calif.: 45
  MT Exc Calif.: 55 amp optional—1984–85:
  50 or 60
⑤ 33, 45, 50 or 60
⑥ 60 amp optional

WHEEL ALIGNMENT SPECIFICATIONS

Year	Model		Camber Range (deg)	Camber Preferred Setting (deg)	Caster Range (deg)	Caster Preferred Setting (deg)	Toe-In (in.)	Steering Axis Inclination (deg)
'78	RX-3SP		¹⁄₁₆P–2¹⁄₁₆P	1¹⁄₁₆P	1⁷⁄₁₆P–3¹⁵⁄₁₆P	2³⁄₁₆P	0–¼	8¹³⁄₁₆
'78	RX-4							
		Sedan	0P–2P	1P	1¹⁄₁₆P–2⁹⁄₁₆P	1¹³⁄₁₆P	0–¼	9½
		Wagon	¼P–2¼P	1¼P	1¹⁄₁₆P–2⁹⁄₁₆P	1¹³⁄₁₆P	0–¼	9½
'78	Cosmo							
		Man. Str.	0P–2P	1P	1¹⁄₁₆P–2⁵⁄₁₆P	1¹³⁄₁₆P	0–¼	9¾
		Pwr. Str.	0P–2P	1P	1½P–3P	2¼P	0–¼	9¾
'78	GLC		⁵⁄₁₆N–1¹¹⁄₁₆P	¹¹⁄₁₆P	³⁄₁₆P–2⁵⁄₁₆P	1⁹⁄₁₆P	0–¼	8¹³⁄₁₆
'79–'80	GLC							
		Exc. Wagon	¼P–1¼P	¾P	¹⁵⁄₁₆P–2⁷⁄₁₆P	1¹¹⁄₁₆P	0–¼	8¾
		Wagon	½P–1½P	1P	1P–2½P	1¾P	0–¼	8½

WHEEL ALIGNMENT SPECIFICATIONS

Year	Model	Camber Range (deg)	Camber Preferred Setting (deg)	Caster Range (deg)	Caster Preferred Setting (deg)	Toe-In (in.)	Steering Axis Inclination (deg)
'81–'82	GLC						
	Exc. Wagon	7/16P–1 7/16P	15/16P	1 3/16P–2 11/16P	1 15/16P	1/8–1/8	12 3/16
	Wagon	3/4P–1 3/4P	1 1/4P	3/4P–2 1/4P	1 1/2P	0–1/4	8 1/4
'83–'85	GLC						
	Exc. Wagon	7/16P–1 7/16P	15/16P	1 3/16P–2 11/16P	1 15/16P	1/8–1/8	12 3/16
	Wagon (83)	1/4P–1 1/4P	3/4P	13/16P–2 5/16P	1 9/16P	0–1/4	8 3/4
'79–'80	626 (1979; Camber–1 1/4P. Caster; 3 3/4P)	3/4P–1 3/4P	1 1/4P	(Right) 2 29/32P–4 13/32P (Left) 2 7/16P–3 15/16P	3 21/32P 3 3/16P	0–1/4	10 11/16
'81–'82	626	3/4P–1 3/4P	1 1/4P	2 15/16P–3 15/16P	3 7/16P	0–1/4	10 9/16
'83–'85	626	3/16N–11/16P	5/16P	15/16P–2 7/16P	1 11/16P	1/8–1/0	12 15/16
'79	RX7	11/16P–1 11/16P	1 3/16P	3 1/4P–4 3/4P	4P	0–1/4	10 3/4
'80	RX7	11/16P–1 11/16P	1 3/16P	(Right) 4P–5P (Left) 3 1/2P–4 1/2P	4 1/2P 4P	0–1/4	10 3/4
'81–'83	RX7	1/2P–1 1/2P	1P	(Right) 3 11/16P–4 11/16P (Left) 3 3/16P–4 3/16P	4 3/16P 3 11/16P	0–1/4	10 3/4
'84–'85	RX7						
	13" Tires	1/2P–1 1/2P	1P	(Right) 3 11/16P–4 11/16P (Left) 3 3/16P–4 3/16P	4 3/16P 3 11/16P	0–1/4	10 3/4
	14" Tires	1/16P–1 1/16P	9/16P	(Right) 3 11/16P–4 11/16P (Left) 3 3/16P–4 3/16P	4 13/16P 3 11/16P	0–1/4	11 5/16

BRAKE SPECIFICATIONS

(All measurements given are in. unless noted)

Model	Lug Nut Torque (ft. lbs.)	Master Cylinder Bore	Brake Disc Minimum Thickness	Brake Disc Maximum Run-Out	Brake Drum Diameter	Brake Drum Max. Machine O/S	Brake Drum Max. Wear Limit	Minimum Lining Thickness Front	Minimum Lining Thickness Rear
RX-3SP	65	0.875	0.394	0.003	7.874	7.90	7.9135	0.276	0.039
RX-4	65–72	0.875	0.433	0.004	9.0	9.025	9.0395	0.276	0.039
Cosmo	65–72	0.875	0.6693①	0.0024②	—	—	—	0.276	0.276
GLC	65–72④	13/16	0.4724⑤	0.0024⑥	7.874⑦	③	7.9135⑧	0.276⑨	0.039⑩
626	65–80	7/8	0.4724	0.004	7.874⑪	③	7.9135⑫	0.256⑬	0.039
RX-7	65–80	0.8125	0.6693	0.0039	7.8741	⓪	7.9135	0.236	0.039
626⑭	65–80	7/8	0.55	0.004	7.87	—	7.91	0.040	0.040

NOTE: Minimum lining thickness is as recommended by the manufacturer. Due to variations in state inspection regulations, the minimum allowable thickness may be different than recommended by the manufacturer.

① Rear: 0.354
② Rear: 0.004
③ No matching maximum given—remove minimum amount which smooths surface, then ensure drum inner diameter meets specification.
④ 65-80—'79-'85
⑤ 0.43—'81-'85
⑥ 0.004—'81-'85
⑦ 7.09—'81-'85
⑧ 7.13—'81-'85
⑨ 0.04—'81-'85
⑩ 0.04—'81-'85
⑪ 9.0001—'81-'82
⑫ 9.0395—'81-'82
⑬ 0.04—'81-'82
⑭ Front wheel drive

TUNE-UP PROCEDURES

Spark Plugs

REMOVAL & INSTALLATION

NOTE: Before removing spark plugs clean any dirt from the base area of the spark plugs with compressed air or a stiff brush.

———— CAUTION ————
Grasp the plug wire by the boot and twist slightly to loosen, before pulling on the boot (not the wire) to remove the wire from the spark plug. Bending or pulling on the wire breaks the internal conductive material.

1. Mark or tag the wires for correct reinstallation, then remove the wires from the spark plugs.
2. Using a $^{13}/_{16}$ in. deep-well sparkplug socket and a swivel head rachet type wrench, remove the spark plugs.
3. Inspect spark plugs for cracked and damaged insulators or threads, worn electrodes, damaged gasket and carbon or other fouling deposits.
4. If plugs are to be reused file the electrodes square.
5. Regap old spark plugs or check the gap on new spark plugs.
6. Install the spark plugs in the head and torque to 18–21 ft. lbs. (25–28 Nm).
7. Install the plug wires on the proper spark plug.

Compression

ROTARY ENGINE

Because of the unusual shape of the combustion chamber, the lack of valves and because there are three chambers for each rotor, a normal gauge is useless for the measurement of rotary engine compression.

Mazda makes a special recording compression tester which produces a separate graph for each of the three chambers.

This is an expensive piece of equipment; check with a Mazda dealer for availability.

PISTON ENGINE

The compression is checked in the conventional manner.

Compression pressures are considered normal if the lowest reading is within 25% of the highest.

Breaker Points and Condenser

ALL MODELS

Rotary engines are equipped with a single

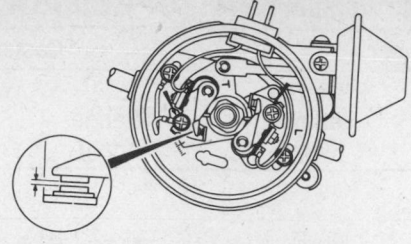
Adjusting the dual point distributor

distributor with either dual or triple point sets. Most piston engines are equipped with breaker point distributors through 1979. GLC models use a breakerless distributor except for some California and Canadian models. The 1979 and later 626 models are equipped with breakerless ignition. On the breakerless distributors there are no points or condenser to replace.

Electronic Ignition

ROTARY ENGINE

1. Spark plugs—rotary engine type with 3 electrodes.
2. Distributor—breakerless type.
   a. Signal rotor—timing teeth
   b. Vacuum and centrifugal advance—standard.
   c. Pick-up coils—1 leading and 1 trailing; generates the signals to the igniter (control unit).
3. Igniter—receives signals from the pick-up coils and switches the primary ignition current off and on.
4. Ignition coils—1 leading and 1 trailing coil; not to be exchanged with standard ignition coils.

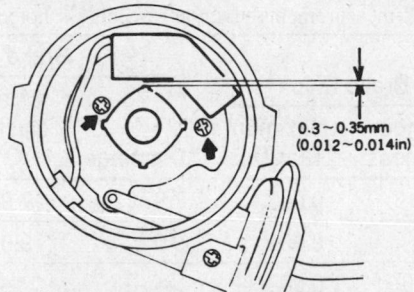
0.3~0.35mm
(0.012~0.014in)

Checking the air gap in the electronic ignition distributor

PISTON ENGINES

In 1979 the 626 and GLC models were equipped with electronic ignition. Unlike the rotary engines the piston engines have a single coil ignition system. As of 1980, all Mazda vehicles sold in the USA were equipped with electronic ignition.

Ignition Timing

ROTARY ENGINE
1978

1. Have the engine at normal operating temperature.

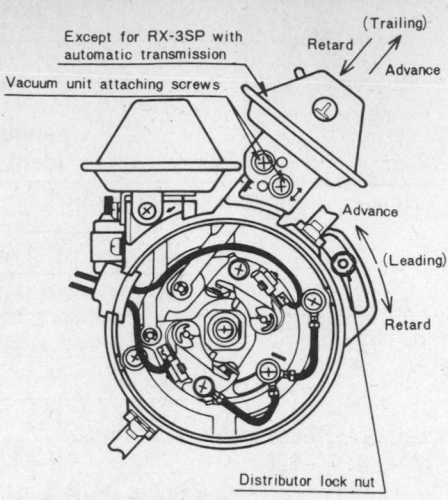
Except for RX-3SP with automatic transmission
Vacuum unit attaching screws
Retard   (Trailing)
          Advance
Advance
(Leading)
Retard
Distributor lock nut

Trailing timing adjustment for 1978-79 rotary engines

2. Connect a timing light to the leading spark plug wire and a tachometer to the engine.
3. Operate the engine at the specified idle speed. On automatic transmission equipped vehicles, place the selector in DRIVE and block the wheels.
4. Check the timing on the crankshaft pulley and if the leading timing is not correct, loosen the distributor body locknut and rotate the distributor housing to correct the timing. Tighten the locknut and recheck the timing.
5. Install the timing light on the trailing spark plug and check the trailing timing.
6. If the trailing timing is not correct, loosen the vacuum unit for the trailing points and move the unit in or out until the correct timing is obtained.
7. Tighten the trailing vacuum unit and recheck the trailing timing.

1979 and Later Except 1979 Automatic Transmission After Chassis No. 522504

1. Warm the engine up until it reaches operating temperature. Connect a tachometer as per the manufacturer's instructions. On automatic transmission cars, securely apply the handbrake, block the wheels, and put the car in Drive. Reading the tach as for a conventional four cylinder engine, verify that the engine is running at its normal idle speed. If not, adjust idle speed to specification.
2. Stop the engine and connect a timing light to the leading (lower) spark plug on the front rotor. Then, restart the engine. Aim the timing light at the pin on the front housing cover, and observe the timing. If the timing pointer does not line up with the first (yellow) notch on the pulley, loosen the distributor locknut and rotate the distributor either way until the timing is correct. Tighten the locknut and check that the timing is still correct.
3. Stop the engine and connect the timing light to the trailing (upper) spark plug

Timing marks—1146cc rotary engine

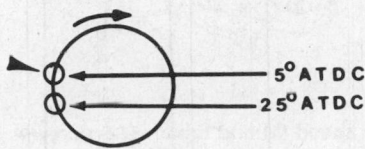

Timing marks—1308cc rotary engine

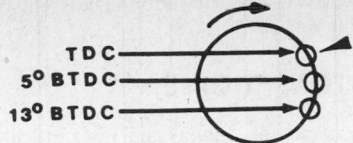

Timing marks—1586cc piston engine (exc. Calif.)

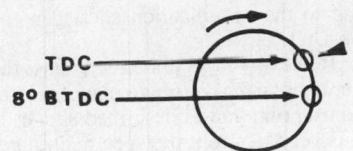

Timing marks—1586cc piston engine (Calif.)

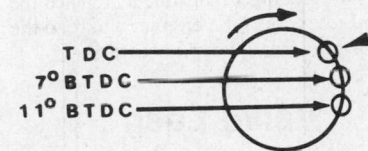

Timing marks—1272cc piston engine

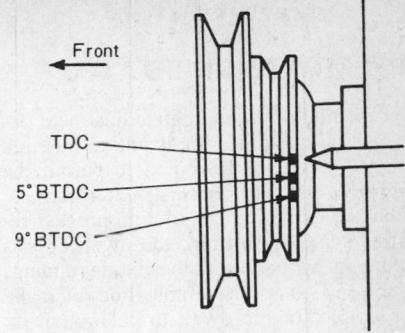

Timing marks—1978–80 GLC (exc. Calif.)

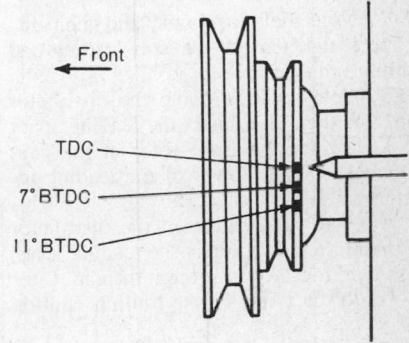

Timing marks—1978–80 GLC (Calif.)

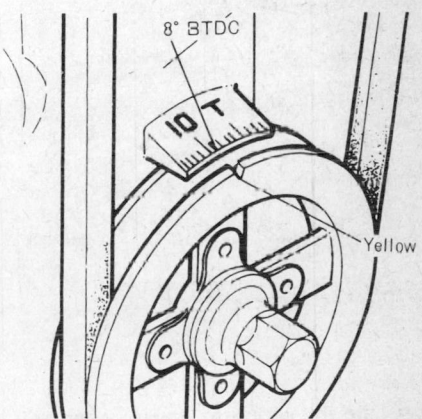

Timing marks—1981 and later GLC

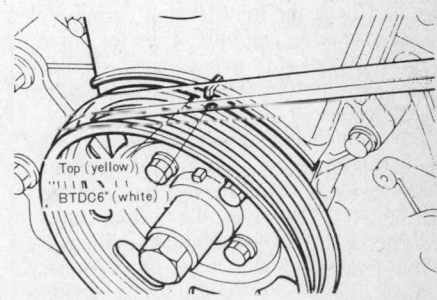

Timing marks—1983 and later 626

on the front rotor. Start the engine (putting automatic transmission cars in Drive), and check the trailing timing. The timing pointer should line up with the second (red) notch in the pulley.

4. If the trailing timing is not correct, loosen the vacuum unit attaching screws (manual transmission) or the adjusting lever attaching screws (automatic transmission) and move the vacuum unit (manual transmission) or adjusting lever (automatic transmission) in or out until the timing pointer lines up with the second mark on the pulley, then tighten the screws and recheck the timing.

1979 Automatic Transmission After Chassis No. 522504

Complete Steps 1–3 under "1979 Models—Automatic Transmission Up To . . . etc."

To adjust the trailing timing, stop the engine and remove the distributor cap and rotor. Slightly loosen the breaker base attaching screws, then reinstall the rotor and distributor cap. Start the engine. Set the selector lever in Drive and run the engine at idle speed. Loosen the external adjusting lever attaching screws and move the adjusting lever in or out until the timing pointer lines up with the second (red) mark on the pulley, then tighten the adjusting lever attaching screws. Stop the engine, remove the distributor cap and rotor and tighten the two breaker base attaching screws. Refit the rotor and distributor and recheck the trailing timing.

PISTON ENGINE

NOTE: Most models require the ignition timing adjusted with the vacuum line connected to the distributor. Refer to the emission sticker (under the hood) to determine if the vacuum line is to be connected or disconnected and plugged.

1. If required, disconnect and plug the distributor vacuum line.

2. Set the parking brake and block the front wheels. Start and run the engine until it reaches the normal operating temperature. Shut off the engine and connect a ta-

chometer. Restart and check engine idle speed. Adjust if necessary. Shut off engine.

NOTE: Prior to starting the engine, clean off any grease or oil that will prevent seeing the timing marks on the crankshaft pulley. Mark the pulley notches with chalk or paint.

3. Connect a timing light to the engine following the manufacturer's instructions. Start the engine and observe the timing by pointing the light at the timing marks on the crankshaft pulley.

NOTE: If the car is equipped with an automatic transmission put the lever in "D"; check emission sticker or tune-up "specs" for requirement.

4. If the timing is not correct, loosen the distributor mounting bolt and rotate the distributor as necessary to produce the correct timing mark alignment. Recheck the timing after tightening the lock bolt. Readjust if necessary. Check the idle speed.

5. On 1978 non-California cars with manual transmissions, the advance timing may be checked by disconnecting the leads to the switch which is operated by the accelerator pedal. If the advance setting is not at 11° BTDC, check the dwell angles of both sets of points. If the advance setting is not correct, it indicates unequal dwell angles, or, more rarely, faulty parts in one or both contact sets or a worn distributor shaft or cam.

NOTE: Some Canadian models require the bullet connectors at the water temperature connector disconnected before timing the ignition; check the emission sticker for requirements.

6. Reconnect the vacuum line, accel-

erator switch or bullet connectors if disconnected. Recheck idle speed, readjust if necessary.

Dwell Angle

ROTARY ENGINES

The method of dwell angle adjustment described here requires that some of the high tension wiring be re-routed to permit the engine to run with the distributor cap and rotor off. While this re-routing process requires some extra time, the dwell adjustment may be made with the engine running, which will save considerable time and make it possible for the dwell to be brought to specification on the first adjustment.

1. Run the engine until it is hot and stop it.

2. Note their locations, and then disconnect high tension leads at leading and trailing ignition coils.

3. Note its location in the distributor cap, and then disconnect the leading spark plug wire for the front rotor at the cap. Connect it to the tower of the leading ignition coil.

4. Note its location in the distributor cap, and then disconnect the leading spark plug wire for the rear rotor at the cap. Connect it to the tower of the trailing ignition coil.

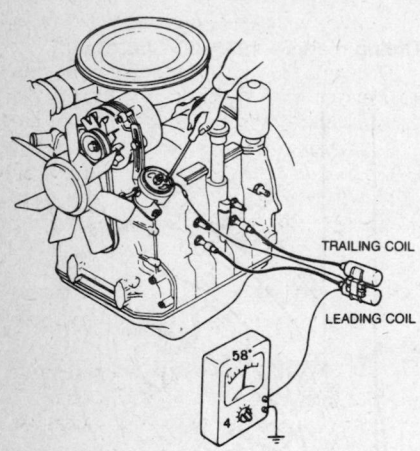

TRAILING COIL

LEADING COIL

58°

Re-route the wiring as shown when setting the dwell on rotary engines

5. Remove the distributor cap and rotor.

6. Check the high tension wiring with the illustration. The plug wires for the top two plugs will still be connected to the rotor, but the bottom two plugs must be wired as shown.

7. Connect the dwell angle tester to the trailing ignition coil. Then, start the engine and read the dwell. If the dwell is incorrect, loosen the set screw for the trailing contact set *only slightly* (or the engine will stop). Then, very gradually move the stationary contact back and forth until dwell is within the specified range (55–61 degrees).

8. When dwell is correct, tighten the set screw and recheck dwell. Readjust it as necessary.

9. Connect the dwell meter to the leading ignition coil and repeat Steps 7 and 8 for the leading contacts.

10. Reconnect all wiring and reinstall the cap and rotor.

PISTON ENGINE

1. Start the engine and run until it is hot and running at normal idle speed.

2. Connect a dwell meter to the ignition coil as described in the manufacturer's instructions. Read the dwell and compare the reading to the specification shown in the "Tune-Up Chart."

3. If the dwell is incorrect, stop the engine, remove the distributor cap and rotor and adjust point gap as described above. If dwell is very far from the specified range, simply set the contacts to the specified gap. If dwell is just a little too high, open the contact gap just slightly; if dwell reading is too low, close the point gap just slightly.

4. After contact adjustment, replace the cap and rotor, start the engine, and read the dwell again. Readjust if necessary.

Valve Lash

PISTON ENGINE ONLY

Models through 1982

Adjust the valves in the firing order 1-3-4-2.

1. Rotate the crankshaft so that the No. 1 cylinder (front) is in the firing position.

2. The clearance is checked between the adjusting screw and valve top.

3. If the valve clearance is incorrect, loosen the adjusting screw locknut and adjust the clearance.

4. Rotate the crankshaft (in the normal direction of rotation), adjusting the valves for each cylinder at TDC of the compression stroke.

1983 and Later

1. Warm-up the engine and tighten the cylinder head bolts in the proper sequence.

2. Rotate the engine until the No. 1 piston is at top dead center.

   a. Adjust No. 1 and No. 2 cylinder intake valve clearance.

   b. Adjust No. 1 and No. 3 cylinder exhaust valve clearance.

3. Rotate the engine one turn, so that the No. 4 piston is at top dead center.

   a. Adjust the No. 1 and No. 4 cylinder intake valve clearance.

   b. Adjust the No. 2 and No. 4 cylinder exhaust valve clearance.

Carburetor

NOTE: For further carburetor adjustments see the "Fuel System."

PISTON ENGINE

Adjustment of the idle mixture requires the

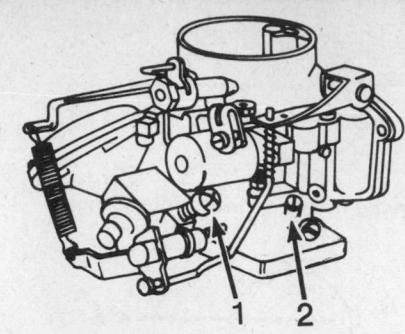

Idle speed (1) and mixture (2) screws —piston engine

1983 and later 626 idle mixture locking procedure

use of an exhaust gas analyzer, a piece of equipment the amateur mechanic does not usually own. The mixture adjustment procedure is given here for those who have access to an exhaust gas analyzer.

Idle Speed

1. Thoroughly warm the engine.

2. Make sure that the choke valve is fully open.

NOTE: On 1983 and later models, disconnect the electric cooling fan motor before setting the idle speed.

3. Connect a tachometer.

4. Adjust the idle speed screw to specifications.

5. The mixture should be checked by a CO meter. The carbon monoxide percentage at idle should be 0.1%–2.0%.

6. Disconnect the tachometer.

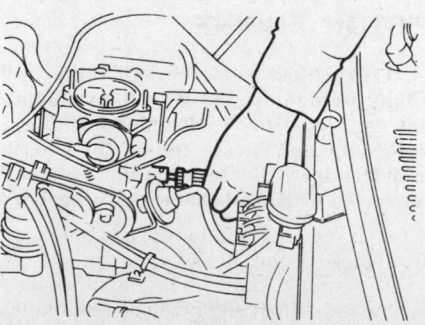

Adjusting 1983 and later 626 idle mixture

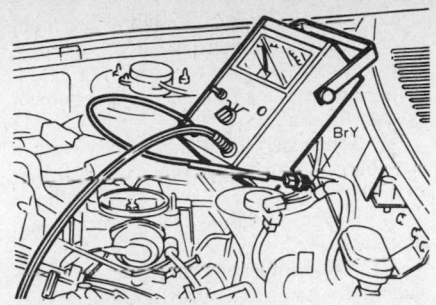

Tachometer hook-up 1983 and later 626—checking and adjusting idle mixture

Mixture Adjustment
THROUGH 1982

If for some reason the idle and throttle screws need adjustment, use the following procedure.

HC/CO Analyzer

1. Adjust the throttle angle opening to specifications. Make the adjustment from the fully closed position.
2. Adjust the idle speed.
3. Using the gas analyzer, check the HC (hydrocarbon) and CO (carbon monoxide) readings. If the HC is less than 200 ppm (parts per million) and the CO is between 0.1–2.0%, no further adjustment is needed.
4. If the HC and CO are not within specifications, adjust the CO reading to as close to 0.1% as possible, keeping the HC reading below 200 ppm. Use the idle fuel screw to make this adjustment.
5. Recheck the idle speed.

1983 AND LATER

Adjustment of the engine idle mixture is normally unnecessary. In case an overhaul is necessary, due to carburetor trouble, adjust the engine idle mixture and pay atention to the following points.

1. Assemble the carburetor in the reverse order of assembly.

---- CAUTION ----
Do not secure the spring pin to lock the mixture adjust screw.

---

2. Install the carburetor in the reverse order of removal.
3. Install the air cleaner onto the carburetor and connect the holes of the idle compensator, thermosensor, and reed valves.
4. Warm up the engine to the normal operating temperature and let it idle.
5. Connect a tachometer to the engine.
6. Set a dwell meter for the four cylinder read-out and connect it to the test terminal on the A/F solenoid valve (the valve is in the carburetor). Check for a dwell of 32–40 degrees at idle.
7. If the dwell reading is not within specifications, adjust the idle mixture screw.

NOTE: If the adjustment cannot be made, it is probably because of a faulty O_2 sensor, or either a broken wire or

short in the wiring between the O_2 sensor and the control unit.

8. Using a hammer and punch, tap the spring pin down into the locked position. This will lock the idle mixture adjustment screw.

ROTARY ENGINE

Through 1980

Idle speed changes with air temperature. It is suggested by Mazda that the idle adjustment be made indoors with a floor fan blowing through the radiator to assist in cooling. Whenever operating an engine indoors, make certain that provision is made for removal of exhaust gases. Idle speed should be adjusted with the engine at normal operating temperature, all accessories off and fuel tank cap removed.

1. Disconnect the idle compensator tube at the air cleaner and plug the end of the tube.
2. Run the engine at normal operating temperature and make sure that the choke is wide open.
3. Check the float level.
4. Connect an exhaust gas analyzer and tachometer.
5. With the engine at idle, check the CO density.
6. Adjust the idle speed to specification with the idle adjusting screw.
7. Turn the mixture adjusting screw clockwise until the engine lopes severely.
8. Turn the screw slowly counterclockwise until the CO density reaches 0.1%, then turn it an additional ¼ turn in the same direction.

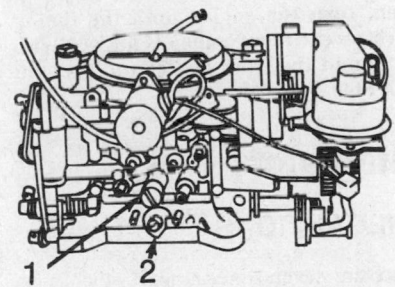

Adjusting the idle speed, rotary engines thru 1979. (1) air adjusting screw, (2) mixture screw

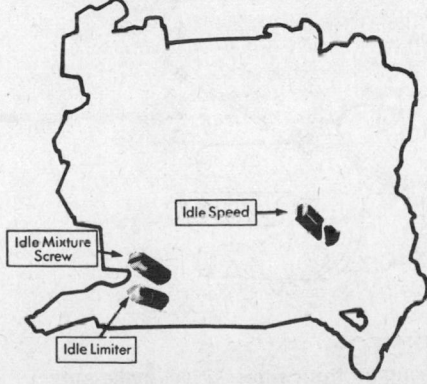

Idle adjustments—rotary engine

From 1981
EXCEPT 13B ENGINE

When adjusting the idle speed and mixture on the 1981 and later rotary engines, take the following steps:

1. Start with a cold engine.
2. Set the parking brake and block the wheels.
3. Remove the fuel filler cap.
4. Switch off all accessories.
5. Disconnect the vacuum line at the idle compensator in the air cleaner and plug the line.
6. Check the dash pot rod and the air conditioner throttle opener. Make certain these devices are not stopping the throttle linkage from returning to a fully seated idle stop position.
7. Connect a tachometer to the negative terminal of the leading coil and a good ground. The leading coil is the rear coil on the driver's side fender well. Disconnect richer solenoid connector, if equipped.
8. Bring the engine up to operating temperature.
9. Set vehicles equipped with automatic transmissions in the drive selector position. Adjust the idle stop screw to obtain 750 rpm in drive. Adjust manual transmission equipped vehicles to 750 rpm in neutral.
10. Adjust the idle mixture by removing the mixture screw limiter cap. Richen the idle mixture to obtain the highest rpm before it starts to drop. Reset the idle speed to specification. Repeat these procedures until both the highest rpm and the idle speed are correct. Install a replacement limiter cap on the idle mixture screw.

13B ENGINE

1. Set the parking brake and block the wheels.
2. Turn off all accessories and remove the fuel filler cap. Connect tachometer.
3. Warm engine to normal operating temperature.
4. Disconnect the vent and vacuum solenoid valve connector.
5. Check idle speed. If not within specification, remove the blind cap and turn the air adjusting screw until specified rpm is reached.
6. Install cap, shut off engine. Connect vent and vacuum solenoid, remove tachometer and replace fuel filler cap.

For further information on the Electronic Fuel Injection system, refer to the "Fuel Injection" Unit Repair section.

ENGINE ELECTRICAL
Distributor
REMOVAL & INSTALLATION
Rotary Engines

1. Rotate the engine in the normal di-

rection of rotation until the first ("TDC" or "Leading") timing mark aligns with the pin on the front cover. Matchmark the body of the distributor and the engine rotor housing.

2. The easiest way to clear the high tension wires out of the way is to simply remove the cap and set it aside with the wires still attached. However, if you wish to keep the cap with the distributor, tag the wires and then pull the wires out of the cap, observing markings.

3. Disconnect the vacuum advance and, if so equipped, retard hoses. Disconnect the primary electrical connector.

4. Remove the distributor adjusting bolt. Pull the distributor vertically out of the engine.

5. To install the distributor, first make sure the engine has not been disturbed. If it has been moved, again turn the crankshaft until the first timing mark lines up with the pin on the front cover. Then align the dimple in the distributor gear with the notch or line cast into the body of the distributor.

6. Insert the distributor carefully and slowly into the engine with the distributor body and rotor housing matchmarks aligned. Avoid allowing the shaft to turn and be careful not to damage the housing when inserting the gear into it.

7. Install the adjusting bolt, but do not tighten. Turn the distributor until the leading points just start to open, and then tighten the locking bolt.

8. Install vacuum hoses, electrical connectors, and high tension wires in reverse of the removal procedure.

9. If the ignition points have been disturbed or replaced, set the dwell as described previously. Set the ignition timing.

Piston Engines

1. Unfasten the clips which hold the distributor cap to the top of the distributor, and remove the cap. Note the location of the wire going to the No. 1 (the front) cylinder where it enters the cap.

2. Rotate the engine with the starter or by using a socket wrench on the bolt which retains the front pulley until the timing mark on the pulley is aligned with the pin on the front cover. Check to see if the contact on the rotor is pointing toward the No. 1 spark plug wire. If the rotor is half a turn away from the No. 1 plug wire, turn the crankshaft ahead one full turn until the timing mark is again aligned with the pin. Match mark the distributor body with the cylinder head.

3. Disconnect the vacuum advance line at the advance unit and disconnect the primary wire at the connector near the distributor.

4. Remove the adjusting bolt, and pull the distributor out of the engine.

5. To install the distributor, first align the dimple on the distributor drive gear with the mark cast into the base of the distributor body by rotating the shaft. Then, being careful not to rotate the shaft, insert the distributor back into the cylinder head with the distributor body and cylinder head match marks aligned and seat it.

6. Install the mounting bolt, but do not tighten it. Rotate the distributor until the points are just opening, and tighten the mounting bolt.

7. Install the distributor cap, and reconnect the vacuum advance line and the primary connector.

8. If the ignition points have been disturbed, set the dwell as described in the previous chapter. Set the timing.

NOTE: If the engine has been rotated while the distributor was removed, it will be necessary to turn the crankshaft until the point where the No. 1 cylinder is just about to fire. To do this, remove the No. 1 spark plug and rotate the engine until you can feel compression pressure building (with your finger over the spark plug hole) as the engine is turned forward. Then, turn the engine until the timing mark on the front pulley is aligned with the pin on the front cover, and proceed with Step 5.

Alternator

PRECAUTIONS

There are several precautions which must be strictly observed in order to avoid damaging the unit. They are:

1. Reversing the battery connections will result in damage to the diodes.

2. Booster batteries should be connected from negative to negative, and positive to positive.

3. Never use a fast charger as a booster to start the car.

4. When servicing the battery with a fast charger, always disconnect the car battery cables.

5. Never attempt to polarize an alternator.

6. Avoid long soldering times when replacing diodes or transistors. Prolonged heat is damaging to alternators.

7. Do not use test lamps of more than 12 volts (V) for checking diode continuity.

8. Do not short across or ground any of the terminals on the alternator.

9. The polarity of the battery, alternator, and regulator must be matched and considered before making any electrical connections within the system.

10. Never operate the alternator on an open circuit. Make sure that all connections within the circuit are clean and tight.

11. Disconnect the battery terminals when performing any service on the electrical system. This will eliminate the possibility of accidental reversal of polarity.

12. Disconnect the battery ground cable if arc welding is to be done on any part of the car.

REMOVAL & INSTALLATION

Disconnect all of the leads. Remove the alternator adjusting link bolt. Do not remove the adjusting link. Remove the drivebelt and remove the alternator.

NOTE: The alternator is removed from under the vehicle on 1981 and later GLC models. If necessary to raise the vehicle, make sure it is safely supported with jack stands.

Installation is the reverse order of removal. Adjust the drive belt.

BELT TENSION ADJUSTMENT

Check tension by applying thumb pressure to the belt, midway between the eccentric shaft and alternator pulleys. The belt should deflect about ½ in.

Regulator

REMOVAL & INSTALLATION

Externally Mounted

Disconnect the wiring and remove the regulator mounting screws. Remove the regulator.

Installation is the reverse of removal.

VOLTAGE ADJUSTMENTS

Models With Ammeters Only

1. Remove the cover.

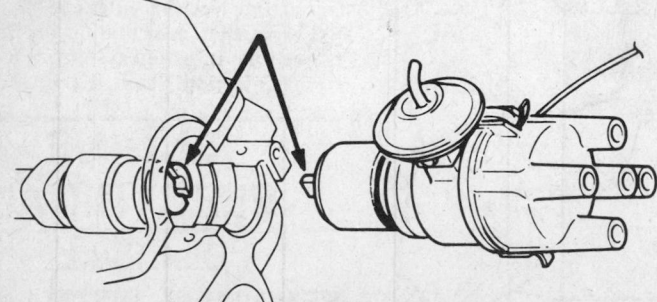

When installing the distributor on the 1490 cc engine front wheel drive, make sure the distributor shaft fits into the groove in the camshaft

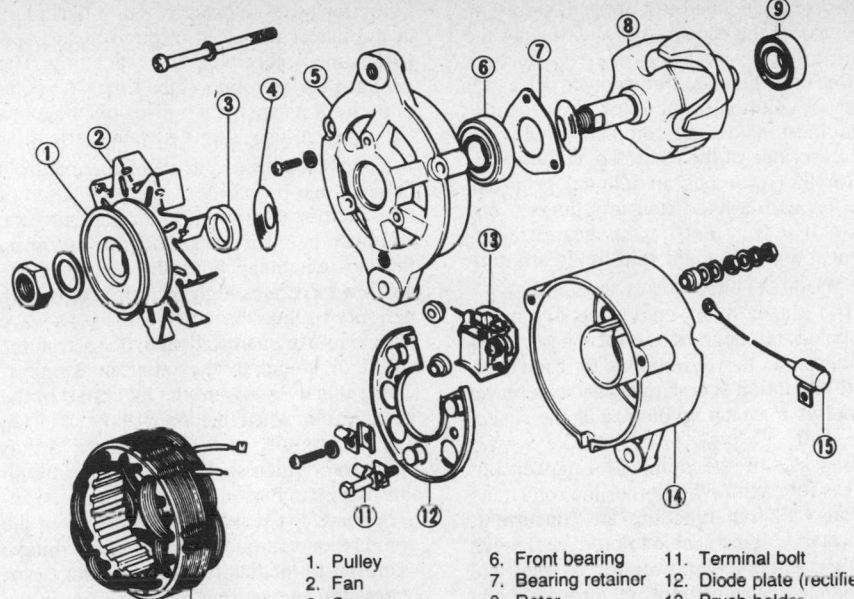

1. Pulley
2. Fan
3. Spacer
4. Slinger
5. Front housing
6. Front bearing
7. Bearing retainer
8. Rotor
9. Rear bearing
10. Stator
11. Terminal bolt
12. Diode plate (rectifiers)
13. Brush holder
14. Rear housing
15. Condenser

Exploded view of typical alternator

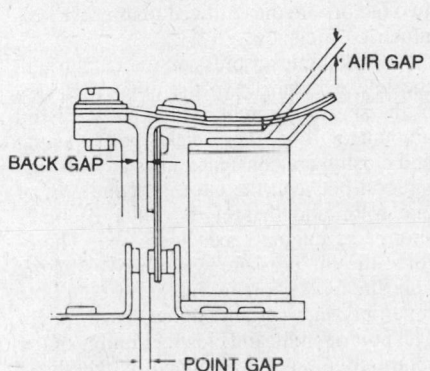

Regulator mechanical adjustments

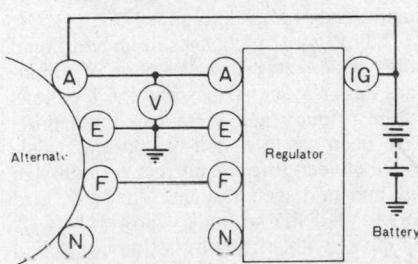

Testing the voltage regulator

2. Check the air gap, the point gap, and the back gap with a feeler gauge.

3. Adjust the gaps by bending the stationary contact bracket.

4. Connect a voltmeter between the "A" and "E" terminal of the regulator.

5. Run the engine at 2000 rpm. The voltmeter reading should be 13.5–14.5 volts.

6. Stop the engine.

7. Bend the upper plate *down* to decrease the voltage setting or *up* to increase the setting, as required.

8. If the regulator cannot be brought within specifications, replace it.

REGULATOR TEST

Models With Warning Light
CONSTANT VOLTAGE RELAY

1. Use an almost fully charged battery and connect a voltmeter between the "A" and "E" terminals of the regulator.

2. Run the engine at 2000 rpm and read

the voltmeter. It should read from 14–15 volts.

3. If not, adjust the voltage relay.

PILOT LAMP RELAY

1. Using a voltmeter and variable resistor, construct a circuit as shown.

2. Light the pilot lamp.

3. Gradually increase voltage.

4. Read the voltage between the "N" and "E" terminals of the regulator. If the voltage is 3.7–5.7 volts, it is operating properly.

5. Decrease the voltage. Note the point on the voltmeter where the light will light again. If the reading is less than 3.5 volts, the unit is working properly.

CONSTANT VOLTAGE RELAY

Air gap: 0.028–0.043 in.
Point gap: 0.012–0.016 in.
Back gap: 0.028–0.043 in.

PILOT LAMP RELAY

Air gap: 0.035–0.047 in.
Point gap: 0.028–0.043 in.
Back gap: 0.028–0.043 in.

Internally Mounted

Late model alternators have the voltage regulator mounted within the unit as part of the brush holder assembly. No adjustments can be made to the regulator assembly and the alternator must be removed and disassembled to replace the voltage regulator.

Starter

REMOVAL & INSTALLATION
Rotary Engine

The starter is removed in the conventional

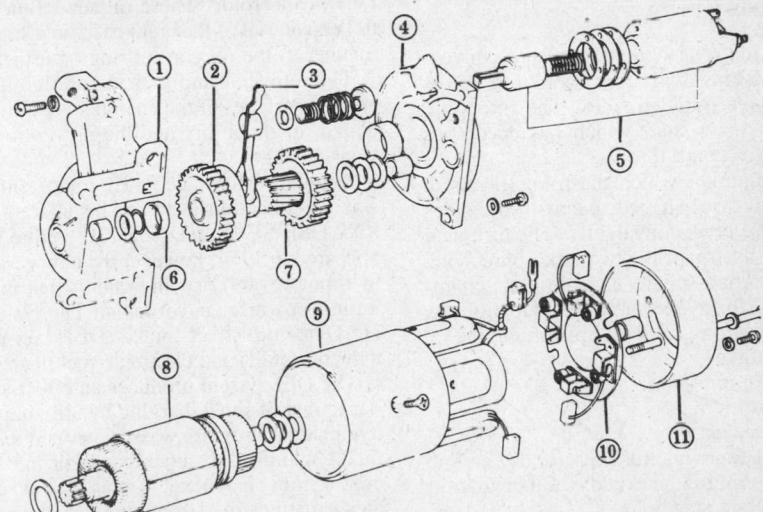

1. Front housing
2. Overruning clutch
3. Engagement fork
4. Center frame
5. Solenoid
6. Stop
7. Idler gear
8. Armature
9. Field coil
10. Brush holder
11. End frame

Typical starter components

manner. If the car is equipped with the lower mounted starter, remove the gravel shield from underneath the engine.

Installation is the reverse of the above.

Piston Engine

The air cleaner/air intake tube must be removed. Remove the starter out below the emission system hoses.

STARTER DRIVE REPLACEMENT

Unless disassembly of the starter is desired, do not remove the thru-bolts.

1. Remove the solenoid.
2. Remove the plunger from the drive engagement fork.
3. Remove the nuts from the thru-bolts.
4. Remove the drive housing.
5. Remove the engagement fork, spring and spring seat.
6. Withdraw the over-running clutch from the armature shaft.

Assembly is the reverse order of disassembly. Check the clearance between the pinion and the stop collar with the solenoid closed. It should be 0.001–0.006 in.

ENGINE MECHANICAL

Rotary Engine

NOTE: Because of the unique design of the Mazda rotary engine, some procedures require the use of special factory tools. The text notes where these tools are necessary.

DESIGN

The Mazda rotary engine replaces conventional pistons with three-cornered rotors which have rounded sides. The rotors are mounted on a shaft which has eccentrics rather than crank throws.

The chamber which the rotor travels in is roughly oval-shaped, but with the sides of the oval bowed in slightly. The technical name for this shape is a two-lobe epitrochoid.

As the rotor travels its path in the chamber, it performs the same four functions as the piston in a traditional piston engine.

1. Intake
2. Compression
3. Ignition
4. Exhaust

But all four functions in a rotary engine are happening concurrently, rather than in four separate stages.

Ignition of the compressed fuel/air mixture occurs each time a side of the rotor passes the spark plugs. Since the rotor has three sides, there are three complete power impulses for each complete revolution of the rotor.

As it moves, the rotor exerts pressure on the cam of the eccentric shaft, causing the shaft to turn.

Because there are three power pulses for every revolution of the rotor, the eccentric shaft must make three complete revolutions for every one of the rotor. To maintain this ratio, the rotor has an internal gear that meshes with a fixed gear in a three-to-one ratio. If it were not for this gear arrangement, the rotor would spin freely and timing would be lost.

The Mazda rotary engine has two rotors mounted 60 degrees out of phase. This produces six power impulses for each complete revolution of both rotors and two power impulses for each revolution of the eccentric shaft.

Because of the number of power impulses for each revolution of the rotor, and because all four functions are concurrent, the rotary engine is able to produce a much greater amount of power for its size and weight than a comparable reciprocating piston engine.

Instead of using valves to control the intake and exhaust operations, the rotor uncovers and covers ports on the wall of the chamber as it turns. Thus, a complex valve train is unnecessary. The resulting elimination of parts further reduces the size and weight of the engine, as well as eliminating a major source of mechanical problems.

Spring-loaded carbon seals are used to prevent loss of compression around the rotor apexes and cast iron seals are used to prevent loss of compression around the side faces of the rotor. These seals are equivalent to compression rings on a conventional piston but must be more durable because of the high rotor rpm to which they are exposed.

Oil is controlled by means of circular seals mounted in two grooves on the side face of the rotor. These oil seals function to keep oil out of the crankcase, in a similar manner to the oil control ring on a piston.

The rotor housing is made of aluminum and the surfaces of the chamber are chrome plated for durability and the prevention of wear damage.

A high performance 13B rotary engine was introduced in 1984 and installed in the RX7 GSL-SE model. The 13B engine first appeared in 1974, however the new version incorporates three main systems that make it more powerful and efficient. The systems are Dynamic Effect Intake (DEI), six port induction (6PI) and electronic fuel injection.

The DEI system produces an effect similar to that of supercharging by utilizing the dynamic air pressure wave generated in the intake manifold to supercharge air into the combustion chambers. A rotary engine creates a distinct and strong dynamic air pressure wave in the intake air because its intake port can open and close much more quickly than the port of a piston engine. Moreover, on the rotary engine there is no valve blocking the free movement of air in the intake port area, and in the standard two-rotor con-

figuration, the air pressure wave generated in the intake manifold of one rotor travels to the other intake port very efficiently. The greater overlap found in the times the ports of both rotors are open is also advantageous for effective use of this dynamic effect.

The pressure wave in the intake manifold is generated primarily by a combination of two factors: First, when air fed into the combustion chamber is suddenly cut off by the closing intake port, the inertia of the air flow generates high pressure. This high pressure bounces back in the form of a wave in the intake manifold and travels at the speed of sound to the other intake port, where it arrives toward the latter part of the intake cycle, when the port is about to close. The air pressure in the intake area is thus increased, which serves to charge more air into the chamber.

Second, the residual gas pressure in the combustion chamber pushes into the intake manifold immediately after the intake port opens, thus generating high pressure in the intake manifold. This pressure travels in the form of a wave to the other intake port and works to charge additional air just before the intake port of the other rotor closes.

The air pressure waves generated by these two factors are thus utilized to improve volumetric efficiency.

The dynamic air pressure travels through the intake manifold to the other port area at the speed of sound, which takes a fixed amount of time. The intake port opening and closing are constant and as a result, the interval between the closing of the port of one rotor and that of the other becomes shorter as engine speed increases. Therefore, the air pressure wave arrives at the opposite intake port area at the best possible time only in a certain engine speed range. The port opening and closing timings of the rotary engine are determined by the shape and location of the port. Therefore, in determining the port design, the engine speed range within which the dynamic effect is maximized is also determined.

The 6PI system consists of an additional port besides the two intake ports of a standard engine. The shapes and the locations of the primary and secondary main ports have been set to obtain the optimum balance between torque and fuel economy in low and mid speed ranges. The new third port, called the secondary power port, is equipped with a rotating valve controlled by exhaust pressure. This port is opened only when high power is required at high engine speeds. In short, the 6PI is designed to improve low-end torque without sacrificing high-end performance.

The dynamic chamber, fitted to the intake manifold, has two inside compartments. One compartment is connected to the primary ports of both rotors and the other is connected to the secondary ports.

The size and shape of the chambers are designed to facilitate the most effective transfer of the dynamic air pressure wave from one intake port to the other. A longer intake manifold also helps maximize the dynamic effect in the desired speed range.

The high performance 13B engine is equipped with electronic fuel injection to ensure good fuel feed over a wider engine speed range. The computer controlled system takes its cues from engine operating conditions and multiple sensors to precisely adjust the fuel flow.

An injection nozzle is placed close to both of the primary ports in order to assure that fuel feed is fully responsive despite the longer intake manifold and dynamic chamber.

REMOVAL & INSTALLATION

All Except RX-7

Be sure that the engine has completely cooled before attempting to remove it.

1. Scribe matchmarks on the hood and hinges. Remove the hood from the hinges.

2. Working from underneath the car, remove the gravel shield then drain the cooling system and the engine oil.

3. Disconnect the cable from the negative (−) battery terminal.

4. Remove the air cleaner, its bracket, and its attendant hoses.

5. Detach the accelerator cable, choke cable, and fuel lines from the carburetor.

6. Remove the nuts which secure the thermostat housing. Disconnect the ground cable from the housing and install the housing again after the cable is removed.

7. Disconnect the power brake vacuum line from the intake manifold.

8. Remove the fan shroud securing bolts and then the shroud itself.

9. Remove the bolts which secure the fan clutch to the eccentric shaft pulley. Withdraw the fan and clutch as a single unit.

— CAUTION —

Keep the fan clutch in an upright position so that its fluid does not leak out.

10. Unfasten the clamps and remove both radiator hoses.

11. Note their respective positions and remove the spark plug cables. Disconnect the primary leads from the distributors and remove both distributor caps.

12. Detach all of the leads from the alternator, the water temperature sender, the oil pressure sender, and the starter motor.

13. Disconnect all of the wiring from the emission control system components.

14. Detach the heater hoses at the engine.

15. Detach the oil lines from the front and the rear of the engine.

16. Disconnect the battery cable from the positive (+) battery terminal and from the engine.

17. Unfasten the clutch slave cylinder retaining nuts from the clutch housing and tie the cylinder up and out of the way.

NOTE: Do not remove the hydraulic line from the slave cylinder.

18. Remove the exhaust pipe and the thermal reactor.

— CAUTION —

Be sure that the thermal reactor has completely cooled; severe burns could result if it has not.

19. Remove the nuts and bolts, evenly and in two or three stages, which secure the clutch housing to the engine.

20. Support the transmission with a jack placed underneath it.

21. Remove the nuts from each of the engine mounts.

22. Attach a lifting sling to the lifting bracket on the rear of the engine housing.

23. Use a hoist to take up the slack on the sling.

— CAUTION —

Be sure that the hoist is secure to prevent personal injury or damage to the engine.

24. Pull the engine forward until it clears the transmission input shaft. Lift the engine straight up and out of the car.

— CAUTION —

Be careful not to damage any of the components remaining in the car.

25. Remove the heat stove from the exhaust manifold.

26. Remove the thermal reactor as outlined below.

27. Mount the engine on a workstand.

NOTE: A special three part workstand, designed for the rotary engine, is available from Mazda.

Engine installation is performed in the reverse order of removal. Remember to refill all fluids according to specifications and to adjust the ignition after installation.

RX-7
EXCEPT 13B ENGINE

— CAUTION —

Be sure that the engine has completely cooled before attempting to remove it.

1. Scribe matchmarks on the hood and hinges and remove the hood. The matchmarks are made so that you can align the hood on its hinges when installing it.

2. Working from underneath the car, remove the gravel shield then drain the cooling system and the engine oil.

3. Disconnect the negative (−) battery cable and disconnect the high tension wires from the center towers of the ignition coils.

NOTE: A good rule of thumb when disconnecting the engine wiring and vacuum hoses, is to put a piece of masking tape on the wire or hose and on the connection you remove the wire or hose from, then mark both pieces of tape, 1, 2, 3, etc. When replacing wiring and hoses, simply match the pieces of tape.

4. Disconnect the distributor wiring, the oil level sensor lead, the water tem-

perature lead and, on all except California models, the coupler from the oil thermo-sensor.

5. On all California models and 1980 and later automatic transmission models, disconnect the vacuum sensing tube for the vacuum switch. Disconnect the evaporative hose.

6. Disconnect the hoses from the oil cooler, located beneath the radiator. Disconnect the radiator coolant level sensor lead from the top of the radiator and disconnect the coolant reservoir hose.

7. Remove the bolts holding the coolant fan and drive unit to the drive pulley and remove. Remove the air cleaner.

— CAUTION —

On models with air conditioning it will be necessary to remove the compressor and the condensor from their mounts. DO NOT ATTEMPT TO UNFASTEN ANY OF THE AIR CONDITIONER HOSES.

8. On 1980 and later models except those for California and Canada, disconnect the connectors from the No. 2 water temperature sensor, located on the radiator next to the radiator cap.

9. Remove the lower and upper radiator hoses. Disconnect the transmission fluid pipes from the radiator (automatic transmission only).

10. Remove the radiator and shroud assembly.

11. Remove the vacuum hose for the brake booster. Disconnect the heat exchanger pipe from the rear of the intake manifold.

12. Disconnect the coupler from the power valve solenoid on 1979 automatic transmission and California manual transmission models and on all 1980 models except Canadian manual transmission.

13. Disconnect the coasting enrichment connector from manual transmission models. Disconnect the leads from the choke heater and the anti-afterburn solenoid. Disconnect the idle switch coupler on manual transmission models.

14. On 1980 and later models except California and Canada, disconnect the lead from the choke return solenoid valve.

15. Remove the two upper transmission–to–engine bolts. Remove the rear cover from the exhaust manifold, if so equipped. Disconnect the accelerator, choke and hot start assist cables.

16. Disconnect the fuel lines from the carburetor and plug the fuel intake line to prevent leaks.

17. Disconnect the sub-zero start assist hose, if so equipped, and disconnect the wiring from the alternator.

18. Disconnect the wiring from the water temperature switch and the air vent solenoid. Disconnect the heater hose from the left side of the engine.

19. From underneath the car, disconnect and remove the starter. Remove the lower engine–to–transmission bolts.

20. On automatic transmission models, remove the converter housing lower cover,

matchmark the drive plate in relation to the torque converter, then remove the torque converter–to–drive plate bolts.

21. Disconnect all interfering exhaust system components. The thermal reactor (1979–80) or the catalysts (1981 and later) may be very hot if the engine is still warm, so use caution.

22. Support the front of the transmission with a floor jack, then remove the left and right side engine mount bolts.

23. Attach a suitable sling to the engine hanger brackets and raise the engine with a hoist slightly.

24. Pull the engine forward until it clears the clutch shaft or torque converter, then lift it out of the car.

25. Mount the engine on a stand.

NOTE: A special hanger and work stand are available from Mazda (engine stand tool number 49 0107 680A, hanger tool number 49 1114 005).

Engine installation is performed in the reverse order of removal. Be sure to refill the engine with all fluids and check the engine timing.

13B ENGINE

NOTE: Do not disconnect any air conditioner lines unless the system has been properly discharged.

1. Scribe mark the hinge locations and remove the hood. Drain the coolant and engine oil.

2. Disconnect the negative battery.

3. From the left side of the engine compartment, remove the spark plug wires and distributor cap. Disconnect the oil pressure gauge, and oil temperature gauge wire harnesses. Disconnect the accelerator cable, fuel lines and evaporator lines. Plug the lines.

4. Disconnect the air conditioner compressor drive belt and remove the compressor. Remove the power steering pump and mounting brackets. Remove the starter wire harness bracket. Disconnect the heater hoses and temperature gauge unit wiring.

5. From the right side of the engine remove or disconnect the following: Remove the air pump hose, the air funnel, air flow meter connector and the air cleaner assembly. Remove the radiator hoses and heater hoses.

6. Disconnect the fan harness and remove the fan and cover. Disconnect the coolant level sensor. Remove the radiator. Disconnect the oil cooler hoses. Disconnect the cruise control cable and the oil pump metering rod connector. Remove water hoses, brake booster hose and air pump hoses.

7. From the top of the engine, remove or disconnect the eight vacuum sensor tubes from the chamber to sensing pipes. Disconnect the intake air sensor connector and the throttle sensor. Remove the mounting nut and disconnect the terminal cover wire. Remove the dynamic chamber from the engine.

8. Disconnect the following wiring connectors: Oxygen sensor, injectors, water temperature sensor, vacuum control solenoid valve, pressure regulator control solenoid, vent solenoid, vacuum valve solenoid, engine ground and the alternator harness and wires.

9. Raise and support the car on jackstands. Remove the exhaust pipe front cover, catalytic converter cover, exhaust pipe bracket, exhaust pipe, disconnect the starter motor harness and remove the starter motor.

10. Remove the converter cover and remove the converter to flywheel mounting bolts. Remove the transmission to engine mounting bolts, and engine mount nuts.

11. Lower the vehicle, attach a suitable lifting sling to a hoist and carefully remove the engine after pulling it forward slightly to disengage the transmission.

12. Reinstall in the reverse order.

DISASSEMBLY

All Models

NOTE: Because of the design of the rotary engine, it is not practical to attempt component removal and installation. It is best to disassemble and assemble the entire engine, or go as far as necessary with the disassembly procedure. Refer to the specification charts for measurements of the components.

EXCEPT 1984 AND LATER 13B ENGINE

1. Mount the engine on a stand.

2. Remove the oil hose support bracket from the front housing.

3. Disconnect the vacuum hoses, air hoses and remove the decel valve.

4. Remove the air pump and drive belt. Remove the air pump adjusting bar.

5. Remove the alternator and drive belt.

6. Disconnect the metering oil pump connecting rod, oil tubes and vacuum sensing tube from the carburetor.

7. Remove the exhaust manifold cover, if equipped. Remove the carburetor and intake manifold as an assembly.

8. Remove the gasket and two rubber rings.

9. Remove the thermal reactor and gaskets, if equipped. Remove the exhaust manifold and engine mount.

10. Remove the distributor.

11. Remove the water pump.

1984 AND LATER 13B ENGINE

1. Mount the engine on a stand.

2. Remove components in the following order:

3. Engine mount, Air outlet hose, Air pump strap bolt.

4. Air pump drive belt, Air pump, Alternator strap bolt, Alternator drive belt, Alternator.

5. Emission devices attaching bolts.

6. Delivery pipe attaching bolts.

7. Remove the emission devices and delivery pipe assembly as one unit.

8. Fuel injection nozzles, Metering oil pump hoses.

9. Intake manifold & gasket, Auxiliary port valves, Exhaust manifold covers, Exhaust manifold & gasket.

10. Distributor, Oil filter & body. Remove the eccentric shaft pulley and Water pump.

ALL ENGINES

1. Invert the engine.

2. Remove the oil pan.

3. Remove the oil strainer and gasket.

4. Identify the front and rear rotor housings with a felt tip pen. These are common parts and must be identified to be reassembled in their respective locations.

5. Turn the engine on the stand so that the top of the engine is up.

6. Remove the engine mounting bracket from the front cover.

7. Remove the eccentric shaft pulley.

8. Turn the engine on a stand so that the front end of the engine is up.

9. Remove the front cover.

10. Remove the O-ring from the oil passage on the front housing.

11. Remove the oil slinger and distributor drive gear from the shaft.

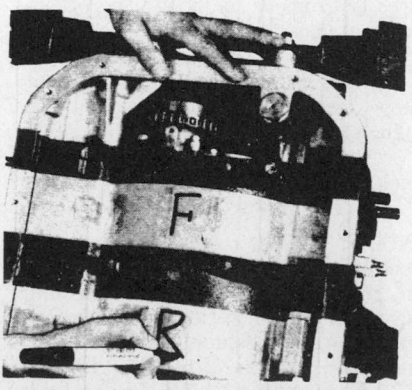

Mark the front and rear rotor housings to prevent confusion during assembly

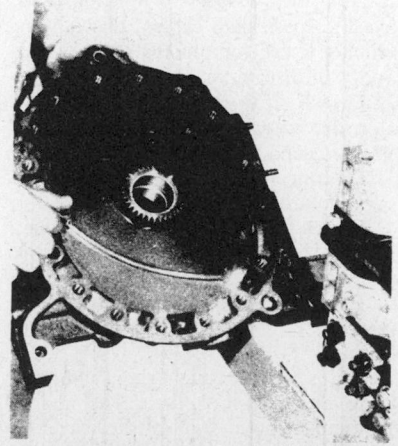

Remove any side seals adhering to the front housing surfaces

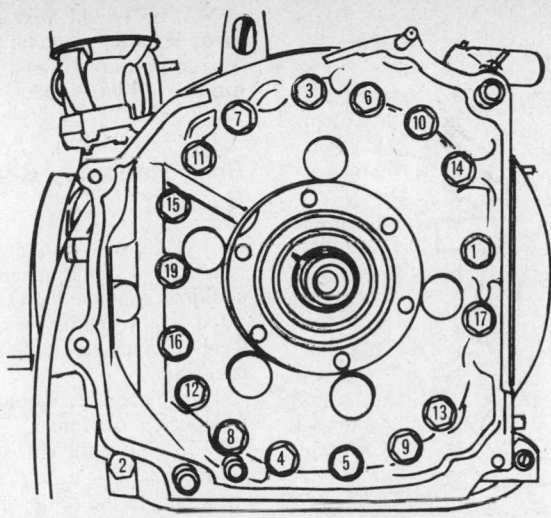

Tension bolt loosening sequence

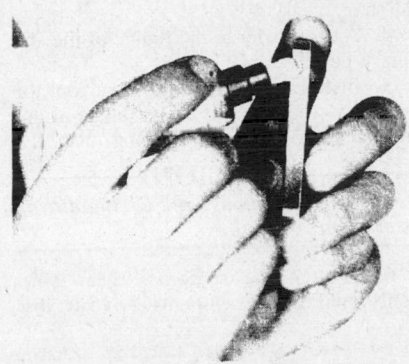

Use a felt-tipped pen to mark the bottom of each apex seal

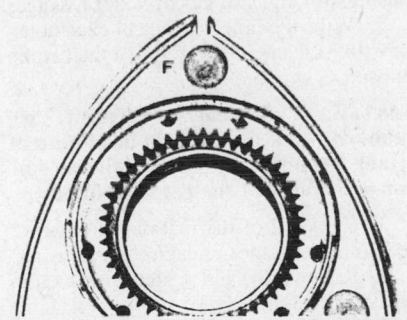

The front rotor is marked with an "F" on its internal gear side; The rear rotor is marked with an "R" in a similar manner.

12. Unbolt and remove the chain adjuster.

13. Remove the locknut and washer from the oil pump driven sprocket.

14. Slide the oil pump drive sprocket and driven sprocket together with the drive chain off the eccentric shaft and oil pump simultaneously.

15. Remove the keys from the eccentric and oil pump shafts.

16. Slide the balance weight, thrust washer and needle bearing from the shaft.

17. Unbolt the bearing housing and slide the bearing housing, needle bearing, spacer and thrust plate off the shaft.

18. Turn the engine on the stand so that the top of the engine is up.

19. If equipped with a manual transmission, remove the clutch pressure plate and clutch disc. Remove the flywheel with a puller. Remove the key from the shaft.

20. If equipped with an automatic transmission, remove the drive plate. Remove the counterweight. Block the weight and remove the mounting nut. Remove the counterweight with a suitable puller.

21. Working at the rear of the engine, loosen the tension bolts.

NOTE: Do not loosen the tension bolts one at a time. Loosen the bolts evenly in small stages to prevent distortion. Mark tension bolts to replace in original holes during reassembly.

22. Lift the rear housing off the shaft.

23. Remove any seals that are stuck to the rotor sliding surface of the rear housing and reinstall them in their original locations.

24. Remove all the corner seals, corner seal springs, side seal and side seal springs from the rear side of the rotor. Mazda has a special tray which holds all the seals and keeps them segregated to prevent mistakes during reassembly. Each seal groove is marked to prevent confusion.

25. Remove the two rubber seals and two O-rings from the rear rotor housing.

26. Remove the dowels from the rear rotor housing.

27. Lift the rear rotor housing away from the rear rotor, being very careful not to drop the apex seals on the rear rotor.

28. Remove each apex seal, side piece and spring from the rear rotor and segregate them.

29. Remove the rear rotor from the eccentric shaft and place it upside down on a clean rag.

30. Remove each seal and spring from the other side of the rotor and segregate these.

31. If some of the seals fall off the rotor,

be careful not to change the original position of each seal.

32. Identify the bottom of each apex seal with a felt tip pen.

33. Remove the oil seals and the springs. Do not exert heavy pressure at only one place on the seal, since it could be deformed. Replace the O-rings in the oil seal when the engine is overhauled.

34. Hold the intermediate housing down and remove the dowels from it.

35. Lift off the intermediate housing being careful not to damage the eccentric shaft. It should be removed by sliding it beyond the rear rotor journal on the eccentric shaft while holding the intermediate housing up and, at the same time, pushing the eccentric shaft up.

36. Lift out the eccentric shaft.

37. Repeat the above procedures to remove the front rotor housing and front rotor.

INSPECTION & REPLACEMENT

Front, Intermediate and Rear Housings

1. Check the housing for signs of gas or water leakage.

2. Remove the carbon deposits from the front housing with extra fine emery cloth.

3. Remove any of the old sealer which is adhering to the housing, using a brush or a cloth soaked in Ketone.

4. Check for distortion by placing a straightedge on the surface of the housing. Measure the clearance between the straightedge and the housing with a feeler gauge. If the clearance is greater than 0.002 in.

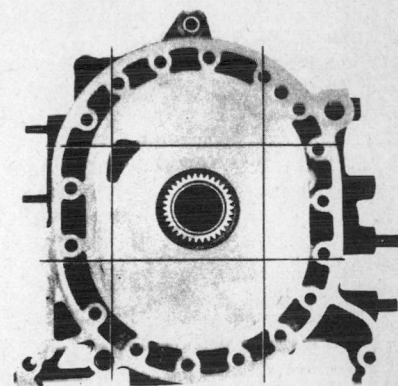

Measure the housing distortion along the axes indicated

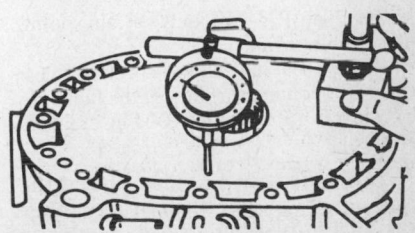

Measuring housing wear with a dial indicator

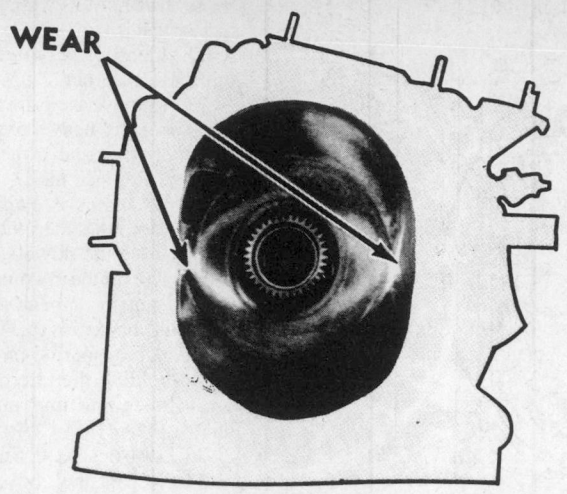

WEAR

Most of the front and rear housing wear occurs at the end of the minor axis as shown.

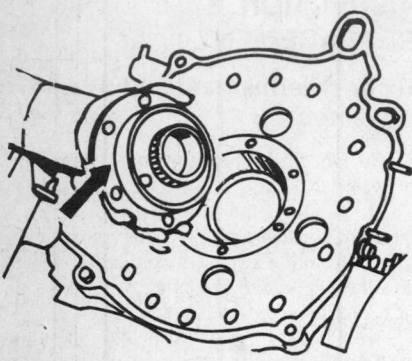

Position the O-ring in the groove on the stationary gear (arrow)

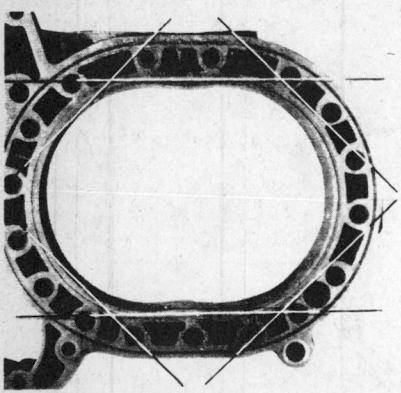

Measure the rotor housing distortion along the axes indicated

(.0016 in. on RX-7 models) at any point, replace the housing.

5. Use a dial indicator to check for wear on the rotor contact surfaces of the housing. If the wear is greater than 0.004 in., replace the housing.

NOTE: The wear at either end of the minor axis is greater than at any other point on the housing. However, this is normal and should be no cause for concern.

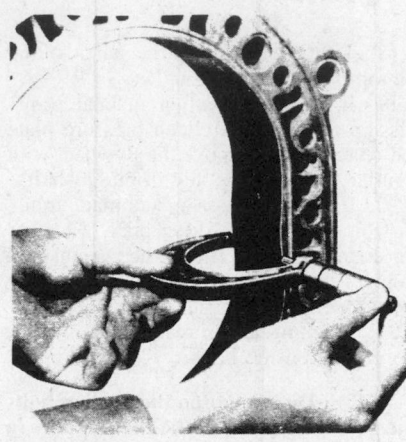

Check the rotor housing width at eight points near the trochoid surface

Front Stationary Gear and Main Bearing

1. Examine the teeth of the stationary gear for wear or damage.
2. Be sure that the main bearing shows no signs of excessive wear, scoring, or flaking.
3. Check the main bearing-to-eccentric journal clearance by measuring the journal with a vernier caliper and the bearing with a pair of inside calipers.

Main Bearing Replacement

1. Unfasten the securing bolts, if used. Remove stationary gear and main bearing assembly, out of the housing, using a suitable puller/installer tool, such as Mazda tool No. 490813235.
2. Press the main bearing out of the stationary gear.
3. Press a new main bearing into the stationary gear so that it is in the same position that the old bearing was.
4. Align the slot in the stationary gear flange with the dowel pin in the housing and press the gear into place. Install the securing bolts, if required.

NOTE: To aid in stationary gear and main bearing removal and installation, Mazda manufactures a special tool, part number 49 0813 235.

Rear Stationary Gear and Main Bearing

Inspect the rear stationary gear and main bearing in a similar manner to the front. In addition, examine the O-ring, which is located in the stationary gear, for signs of wear or damage. Replace the O-ring, if necessary.

To replace the stationary gear, use the following procedure.

1. Remove the rear stationary gear securing bolts.
2. Drive the stationary gear out of the rear housing with a brass drift.
3. Apply a light coating of grease to a new O-ring and fit it into the groove on the stationary gear.
4. Apply sealer to the flange of the stationary gear.
5. Install the stationary gear on the housing so that the slot on its flange aligns with the pin on the rear housing.

— **CAUTION** —
Use care not to damage the O-ring during installation.

6. Tighten the stationary gear bolts evenly, and in several stages, to 15 ft. lbs.

Rotor Housings

1. Examine the inner margin of both housings for signs of gas or water leakage.
2. Wipe the inner surface of each housing with a clean cloth to remove the carbon deposits.

NOTE: If the carbon deposits are stubborn, soak the cloth in a solution of Ketone. Do not scrape or sand the chrome plated surfaces of the rotor chamber.

3. Clean all of the rust deposits out of the cooling passages of each rotor housing.
4. Remove the old sealer with a cloth soaked in Ketone.
5. Examine the chromium plated inner surfaces for scoring, flaking, or other signs of damage. If any are present, the housing must be replaced.
6. Check the rotor housings for distortion by placing a straightedge on the axes.
7. If distortion exceeds 0.002 in., replace the rotor housing.
8. Check the widths of both rotor housings, at a minimum of eight points near the trochoid surfaces of each housing, using a vernier caliper.

If the difference between the maximum and minimum values obtained is greater than 0.0031 in. (RX-3) or 0.0024 in. (RX-4, RX-7), replace the housing. A housing in this condition will be prone to gas and coolant leakage.

Rotors

1. Check the rotor for signs of blow-by around the side and corner seal areas.

2. The color of the carbon deposits on the rotor should be brown, just as in a piston engine.

NOTE: Usually the carbon deposits on the leading side of the rotor are brown, while those on the trailing side tend toward black, as viewed from the direction of rotation.

3. Remove the carbon on the rotor with a scraper or extra fine emery paper. Use the scraper carefully when doing the seal grooves so that no damage is done to them.

4. Wash the rotor in solvent and blow it dry with compressed air.

5. Examine the internal gear for cracks or damaged teeth.

NOTE: If the internal gear is damaged, the rotor and gear must be replaced as a single assembly.

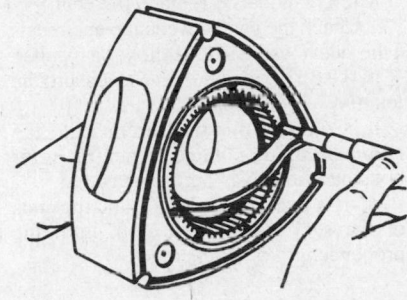

Measure the rotor width at the point indicated

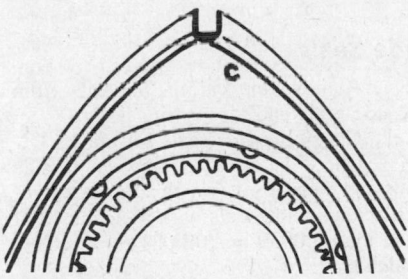

Weight classification letter placement (arrow)

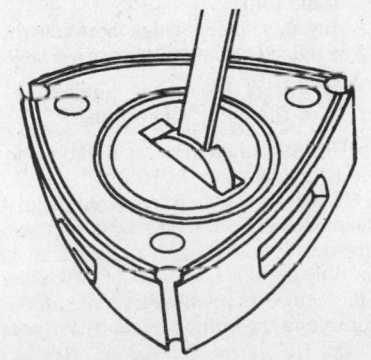

Insert the special bearing expander into the rotor

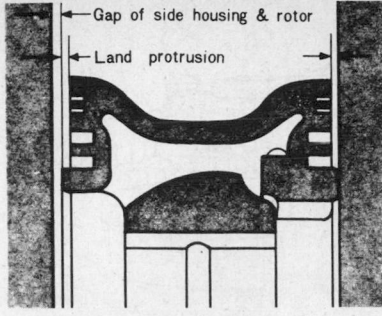

Oil seal protrusion

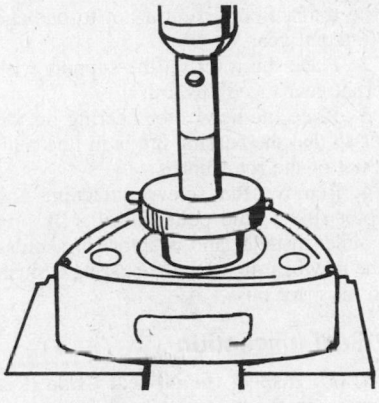

Installing a new rotor bearing

6. With the oil seal removed, check the land protrusions by placing a straightedge over the lands. Measure the gap between the rotor surface and the straightedge with a feeler gauge.

7. Check the gaps between the housings and the rotor on both of its sides

a. Measure the rotor width with a vernier caliper.

b. Compare the rotor width against the width of the rotor housing which was measured above.

c. Replace the rotor, if the difference between the two measurements is not within 0.0051–0.0067 in.; on RX-7 models with 12A engine—0.0047 in.—.0074 in.; 13B engine—0.0047 in.—0.0083 in.

8. Check the rotor bearing for flaking, wearing, or scoring and proceed as indicated in the next section, if any of these are present.

The rotors, except on RX-7 models, are classified into five lettered grades, according to their weight. A letter between A and E is stamped on the internal gear side of the rotor. If it becomes necessary to replace a rotor, use one marked with a "C" because this is the standard replacement rotor, and it can be used in most balancing combinations.

Rotor Bearing Replacement

—————— CAUTION ——————
The use of the special service tools, as indicated in the text, is mandatory, if damage to the rotor is to be avoided.

Check the clearance between the rotor bearing and the rotor journal on the eccentric shaft. Measure the inner diameter of the rotor bearing and the outer diameter of the journal. The wear limit is 0.0039 in.; replace the bearing if it exceeds this.

EXCEPT RX-7

1. Install the bearing expander (Mazda part number 49 0813 245) in the rotor bearing. If the expander is not used, bearing deformation will result when the holes are drilled.

2. Drill a 0.14 in. diameter hole, roughly 0.028 in. deep, into each of the lockscrews which secure the bearings to the rotor. Use a No. 28 drill.

3. Remove the bearing expander.

4. Support the rotor with the internal gear facing upward.

5. Using the rotor bearing remover (Mazda part number 49 0813 240), less the adaptor ring, press the bearing out of the rotor.

—————— CAUTION ——————
Be extremely careful not to damage the internal gear. It cannot be replaced separately from the rotor.

6. If the bore in which the bearing is installed is damaged, dress it with emery paper and blow it clean with compressed air.

7. With the rotor internal gear facing upward, press-fit a new bearing into the bore. Use the bearing replacer with the adaptor screws removed.

NOTE: Be sure that the oil hole in the bearing is aligned with the hole in the apex side of the rotor. Once the bearing is installed, it should be flush with the rotor boss.

8. Insert the rotor bearing expander into the new bearing, as in Step 1.

9. Drill 0.14 in. holes, about 0.28 in. deep, within 0.28 in. of the original lockscrew holes (either to the left or right of them) with a No. 28 drill. The center of the holes must be 0.02 in. from the rotor bore.

NOTE: The new holes should all be in the same direction from the original holes; e.g., if the first hole is drilled to the left of the original hole, drill the remaining holes to the left of the other lockscrew holes.

10. Thread the holes with an M4, P-0.70mm metric tap.

11. Install the bearing lockscrews and stake them with a punch so that they cannot work loose.

12. Wash the rotor and blow it dry with compressed air.

RX-7

1. Place the rotor on the support so that the internal gear is facing downward. Using the puller/installer (part No. 49 0813 240) without adaptor ring, press the bearing out

C411

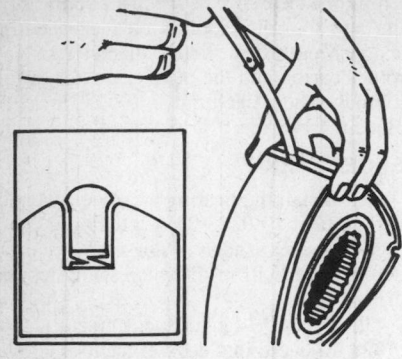

Check the gap between the apex seal and groove with a feeler gauge

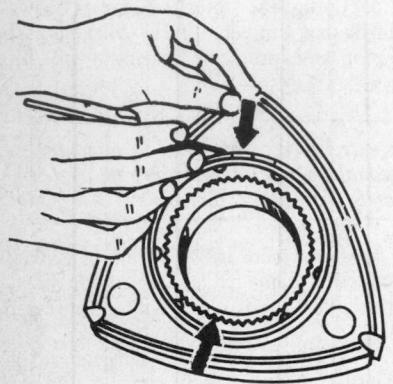

Position the oil seal spring gaps at arrows

Apex seal-to-side housing gap

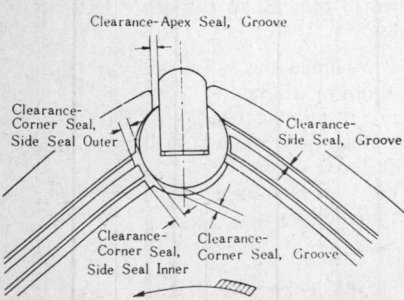

Check the clearance of the seals at the points indicated

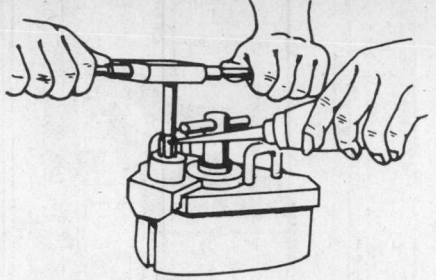

Reaming the corner seal groove

of the rotor. Being careful not to damage the internal gear.

2. Place the rotor on the support with internal gear faced upward.

3. Place the new rotor bearing on the rotor so that the bearing lug is in line with the slot of the rotor bore.

4. Remove the screws attaching the adaptor ring to the puller/installer. Using the puller/installer and adaptor ring, press fit the new bearing until the bearing is flush with the rotor boss.

Oil Seal Inspection

NOTE: Inspect the oil seal while it is mounted in the rotor.

1. Examine the oil seal.

2. If the width of the oil seal lip is greater than 0.031 in. (0.020 in.—RX-7), replace the oil seal.

3. If the protrusion of the oil seal is greater than 0.020 in., replace the seal.

Oil Seal Replacement

NOTE: Replace the rubber O-ring in the oil seal as a normal part of engine overhaul.

1. Pry the seal out by inserting a small prybar into the slots on the rotor.

— **CAUTION** —
Be careful not to deform the lip of the oil seal if it is to be reinstalled.

2. Fit both of the oil seal springs into their respective grooves so that their ends are facing upward and their gaps are opposite each other on the rotor.

3. Insert a new O-ring into each of the oil seals.

NOTE: Before installing the O-rings into the oil seals, fit each of the seals into its proper groove on the rotor. Check to see that all of the seals move smoothly and freely.

4. Coat the oil seal groove and the oil seal with engine oil.

5. Gently press the oil seal into the groove with your fingers. Be careful not to distort the seal.

NOTE: Be sure that the white mark is on the bottom side of each seal when it is installed.

6. Repeat the installation procedure for

the oil seals on both sides of each rotor.

Apex Seals

— **CAUTION** —
Although the apex seals are extremely durable when in service, they are easily broken when they are being handled. Be careful never to drop them.

1. Remove the carbon deposits from the apex seals and their springs. Do not use emery cloth on the seals as it will damage their finish.

2. Wash the seals and the springs in cleaning solution.

3. Check the apex seals for cracks.

4. Test the seal springs for weakness.

5. Use a micrometer to check the seal height. Refer to the specifications chart.

6. With a feeler gauge, check the side clearance between the apex seal and the groove in the rotor. Insert the gauge until its tip contacts the bottom of the groove. If the gap is greater than 0.005 in. (0.0035 in. on RX-7 models), replace the seal.

7. Check the gap between the apex seals and the side housing in the following manner:

a. Use a vernier caliper to measure the length of each apex seal.

b. Compare this measurement to the *minimum* figure obtained when the rotor housing width was being measured.

c. If the seal is too long, sand the ends of the seal with emery cloth until the proper length is reached.

— **CAUTION** —
Do not use the emery cloth on the faces of the seal.

Side Seals

1. Remove the carbon deposits from the side seals and their springs.

2. Check the side seals for cracks.

3. Check the clearance between the side seals and their grooves with a feeler gauge. Replace any side seals with a clearance of more than 0.0039 in. (0.0031 in. on RX-7 models).

4. Check the clearance between the side seals and the corner seals with both installed in the rotor.

a. Insert a feeler gauge between the end of the side seal and the corner seal.

NOTE: Insert the gauge against the direction of the rotor's rotation.

b. Replace the side seal if the clearance is greater than 0.016 in.

5. If the side seal is replaced, adjust the clearance between it and the corner seal as follows:

a. File the side seal on its reverse side, in the same rotational direction of the rotor, along the outline made by the corner seal.

b. The clearance obtained should be 0.002–0.006 in. If it exceeds this, the performance of the seals will deteriorate.

There are four different types of side seals, depending upon location. Do not mix the seals up and be sure to use the proper type of seal for replacement.

Corner Seals

1. Clean the carbon deposits.
2. Examine each of the seals.
3. Measure the clearance between the corner seal and its groove. The clearance should be 0.008–0.0019 in. The wear limit of the gap is 0.0031 in.
4. If the wear between the corner seal and the groove is uneven, check the clearance with the special "bar limit gauge" (Mazda part number 49 0839 165). The gauge has a "go" end and a "no go" end.

   a. If neither end of the gauge goes into the groove, the clearance is within specifications.

   b. If the "go" end of the gauge fits into the groove, but the "no go" end does not, replace the corner seal with one that is 0.0012 in. oversize.

   c. If both ends of the gauge fit into the groove, then the groove must be reamed out. Replace the corner seal with one which is 0.0072 in. oversize, after reaming.

NOTE: Take the measurement of the groove in the direction of maximum wear, i.e., that of rotation.

Corner seal installation

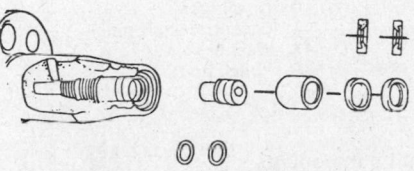

Needle bearing components

Position the dial indicator as shown to measure shaft run-out

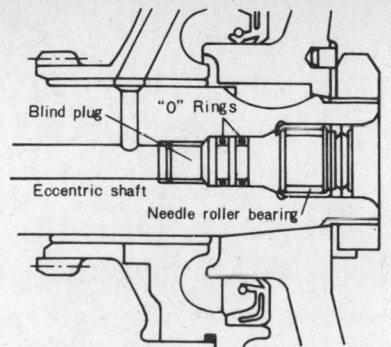

Blind plug   "0" Rings

Eccentric shaft

Needle roller bearing

Eccentric shaft blind plug assembly

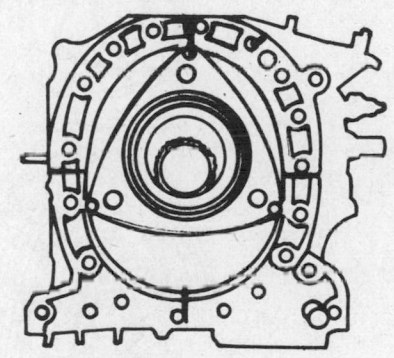

The rear rotor must be positioned as shown during engine assembly

Seal Springs

Check the seal springs for damage or weakness. Be exceptionally careful when checking the spring areas which contact either the rotor or the seal.

Eccentric Shaft

1. Wash the eccentric shaft in solvent and blow the oil passages dry with compressed air.
2. Check the shaft for wear, cracks, or other signs of damage. Make sure that none of the oil passages are clogged.
3. Measure the shaft journals.
Replace the shaft if any of its journals shows excessive wear.
4. Check eccentric shaft run-out. Rotate the shaft slowly and note the dial indicator reading. If run-out is more than specifications, replace the eccentric shaft.
5. Check the blind plug at the end of the shaft. If it is loose or leaking, remove it with an Allen wrench and replace the O-ring.
6. Check the operation of the needle roller bearing for smoothness by inserting a mainshaft into the bearing and rotating it. Examine the bearing for signs of wear or damage. Check the oil jet for spring weakness, sticking or ball damage.
7. Replace the bearings, if necessary, with the special bearing replacer (Mazda part numbers 49 0823 073 and 49 0823 072).

ASSEMBLY

All Models

NOTE: Replace all O-rings, rubber seals, and gaskets with new parts.

1. Place the rotor on a rubber pad or cloth.
2. Install the oil seal rings in their respective grooves in the rotors with the edge of the spring in the stopper hole. The oil seal springs are painted cream or blue in color. The cream colored springs must be installed on the front faces of both rotors. The blue colored springs must be installed on the rear faces of both rotors. When installing each oil seal spring, the painted side (square side) of the spring must face upward (toward the oil seal).
3. Install a new O-ring in each groove. Place each oil seal in the groove so that the square edge of the spring fits in the stopper hole of the oil seal. Push the head of the oil seal slowly with the fingers, being careful that the seal is not deformed. Be sure that the oil seal moves smoothly in the groove before installing the O-ring.
4. Lubricate each oil seal and groove with engine oil and check the movement of the seal. It should move freely when the head of the seal is pressed.
5. Check the oil seal protrusion and install the seals on the other side of each rotor.
6. Install the apex seals without springs and side pieces into their respective grooves so that each side piece positions on the side of each rotor.
7. Install the corner seal springs and corner seals into their respective grooves.

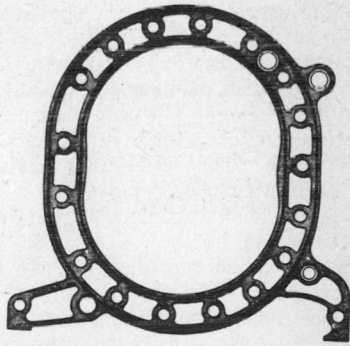

Apply sealer to the grey shadowed areas of the rotor housing

Intermediate housing installation

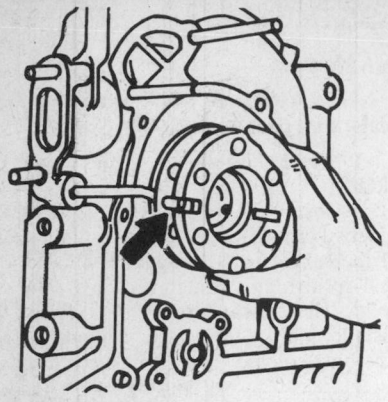

Align the slot in the stationary gear flange with the pin in the housing (arrow)

8. Install the side seal springs and side seals into their respective grooves.

9. Apply engine oil to each spring and check each spring for smooth movement.

10. Check each seal protrusion.

11. Invert the rotor being careful that the seals do not fall out, and install the oil seals on the other side in the same manner.

12. Mount the front housing on a workstand so that the top of the housing is up.

13. Lubricate the internal gear of the rotor with engine oil.

14. Hold the apex seals with used O-rings to keep the apex seals installed and place the rotor on the front housing. Be careful not to drop the seals. Turn the front housing so that the sliding surface faces upward.

15. Mesh the internal and stationary gears so that one of the rotor apexes is at any one of the four places shown and remove the old O-ring which is holding the apex seals in position.

16. Lubricate the front rotor journal of the eccentric shaft with engine oil and lubricate the eccentric shaft main journal.

17. Insert the eccentric shaft. Be careful that you do not damage the rotor bearing and main bearing.

18. Apply sealing agent to the front side of the front rotor housing.

19. Apply a light coat of petroleum jelly onto new O-rings and rubber seals (to prevent them from coming off) and install the O-rings and rubber seals on the front side of the rotor housing.

NOTE: The inner rubber seal is of the square type. The wider white line of the rubber seal should face the combustion chamber and the seam of the rubber seal should be positioned as shown. Do not stretch the rubber seal.

20. If the engine is being overhauled, install the seal protector to only the inner rubber seal to improve durability.

21. Invert the front rotor housing, being careful not to let the rubber seals and O-rings fall from their grooves, and mount it on the front housing.

22. Lubricate the dowels with engine oil and insert them through the front rotor

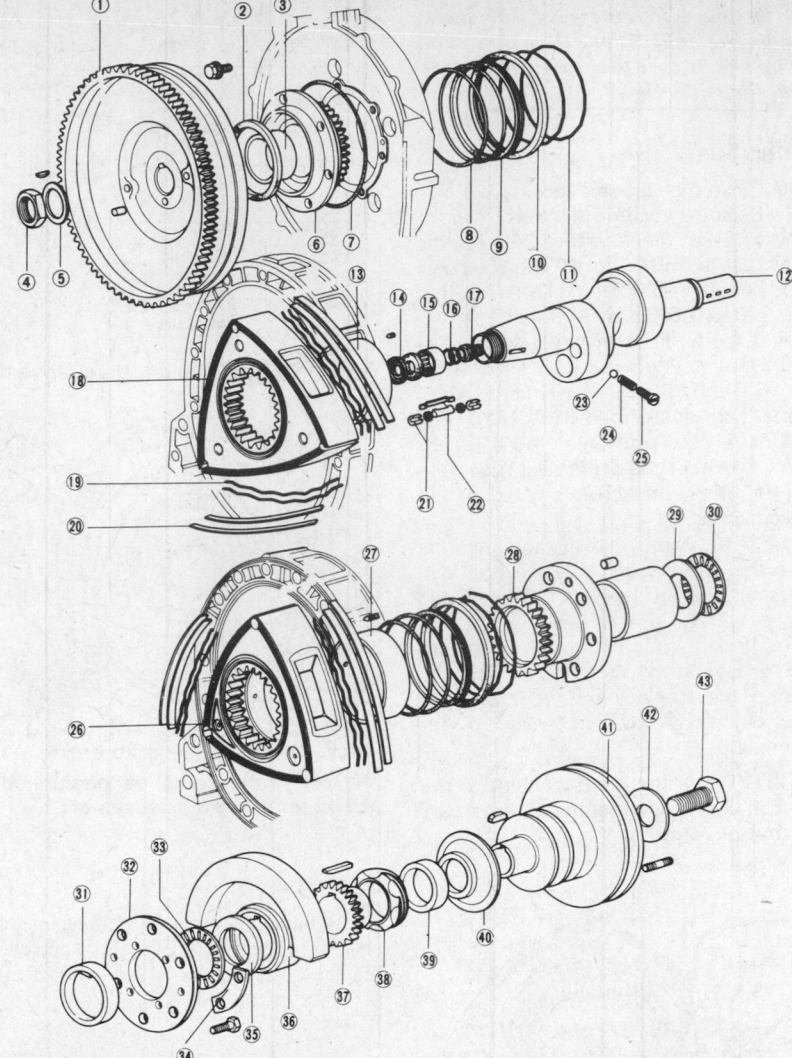

1. Flywheel	16. O-ring	31. Spacer
2. Oil seal	17. Blind plug	32. Bearing housing
3. Main bearing	18. Front rotor	33. Needle bearing
4. Locknut	19. Side seal spring	34. Washer
5. Washer	20. Side seal	35. Thrust plate
6. Rear stationary gear	21. Corner seal and spring	36. Balance weight
7. O-ring	22. Apex seal and spring	37. Oil pump drive sprocket
8. Oil seal O-ring	23. Ball	38. Distributor drive gear
9. Oil seal	24. Spring	39. Spacer
10. Oil seal	25. Oil nozzle	40. Oil slinger
11. Oil seal spring	26. Rear rotor	41. Eccentric shaft pulley
12. Eccentric shaft	27. Rotor bearing	42. Washer
13. Rotor bearing	28. Front stationary gear	43. Pulley bolt
14. Grease seal	29. Thrust washer	
15. Needle bearing	30. Thrust bearing	

Rotor and eccentric shaft components

housing holes and into the front housing.

23. Apply sealer to the front side of the rotor housing.

24. Install new O-rings and rubber seals on the front rotor housing in the same manner as for the other side.

25. Insert each apex spring seal, making sure that the seal is installed in the proper direction.

26. Install each side piece in its original position and be sure that the springs seat on the side piece.

27. Lubricate the side pieces with engine oil. Make sure that the front rotor housing is free of foreign matter and lubricate the sliding surface of the front housing with engine oil.

28. Turn the front housing assembly with the rotor, so that the top of the housing is up. Pull the eccentric shaft about 1 in.

29. Position the eccentric portion of the eccentric shaft diagonally, to the upper right.

30. Install the intermediate housing over the eccentric shaft onto the front rotor hous-

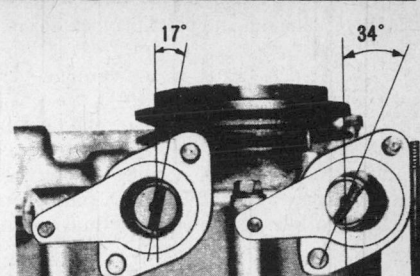

ing. Turn the engine so that the rear of the engine is up.

31. Install the rear rotor and rear rotor housing following the same steps as for the front rotor and the front housing.

32. Turn the engine so that the rear of the engine is up.

33. Lubricate the stationary gear and main bearing.

34. Install the rear housing onto the rear rotor housing. If necessary, turn the rear rotor slightly to mesh the rear housing stationary gear with the rear rotor internal gear.

35. Install a new washer on each tension bolt, and lubricate each bolt with engine oil.

36. Install the tension bolts and tighten them evenly, in several stages following the sequence shown. The specified torque is 23–27 ft. lbs. (23–29 ft. lbs. on 1984 and later 13B engine).

NOTE: Be sure bolts are installed in their original positions. Longer bolts are used in later engines and are not interchangeable.

37. After tightening the bolts, turn the eccentric shaft to be sure that the shaft and rotors turn smoothly and easily.

38. Lubricate the oil seal in the rear housing.

39. On vehicles with manual transmission, install the flywheel on the rear of the eccentric shaft so that the keyway of the flywheel fits the key on the shaft.

40. Apply sealer to both sides of the flywheel lockwasher and install the lockwasher.

41. Install the flywheel locknut. Hold the flywheel SECURELY and tighten the nut to THREE HUNDRED AND FIFTY FT. LBS. (350 ft. lbs.) of torque.

NOTE: 350 ft. lbs. is a great deal of torque. In actual practice, it is practically impossible to accurately measure that much torque on the nut. At least a 3 ft. bar will be required to generate sufficient torque. Tighten it as tight as possible, with no longer than 3 ft. of lever-

age. Be sure the engine is held SECURELY.

42. On vehicles with automatic transmission, install the key, counterweight, lockwasher and nut. Tighten the nut to 350 ft. lbs. SEE STEP 41 AND THE NOTE

Use a dial indicator attached to the flywheel to measure eccentric shaft end-play

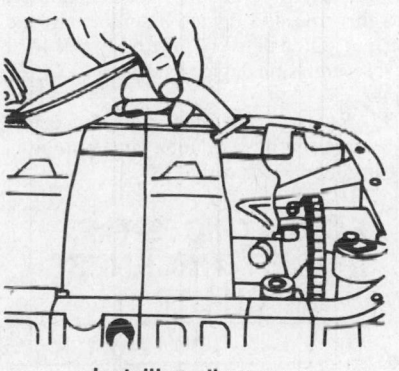

Installing oil pump

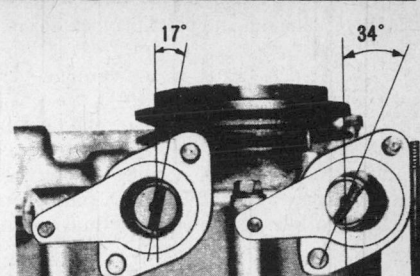

Position the slots in the distributor drive as shown

FOLLOWING STEP 41. Install the drive plate on the counterweight and tighten the attaching nuts.

43. Turn the engine so that the front faces up.

44. Install the thrust plate with the tapered face down, and install the needle bearing on the eccentric shaft. Lubricate with engine oil.

45. Install the bearing housing on the front housing. Tighten the bolts and bend up the lockwasher tabs.

The spacer should be installed so that the center of the needle bearing comes to the center of the eccentric shaft and the spacer should be seated on the thrust plate.

46. Install the needle bearing on the shaft and lubricate it with engine oil.

47. Install the balancer and thrust washer on the eccentric shaft.

48. Install the oil pump drive chain over both of the sprockets. Install the sprocket and chain assembly over the eccentric shaft and oil pump shafts simultaneously. Install the key on the eccentric shaft.

NOTE: Be sure that both of the sprockets are engaged with the chain before installing them over the shafts.

49. Install the distributor drive gear onto the eccentric shaft with the "F" mark on the gear facing the front of the engine. Slide the spacer and oil slinger onto the eccentric shaft.

50. Align the keyway and install the eccentric shaft pulley. Tighten the pulley bolt to 60 ft. lbs. (72–87 ft. lbs. on RX-7 models).

51. Turn the engine until the top of the engine faces up.

52. Check the eccentric shaft end-play in the following manner:

a. Attach a dial indicator to the flywheel. Move the flywheel forward and backward.

b. Note the reading on the dial indicator; it should be 0.0016–0.0028 in.

c. If the end-play is not within specifications, adjust it by replacing the front spacer. Spacers come in four sizes, ranging from 0.3150–0.3181 in. If necessary, a spacer can be ground on a surface plate with emory paper.

d. Check the end-play again and, if it is now within specifications, proceed with the next step.

53. Remove the pulley from the front of the eccentric shaft. Tighten the oil pump

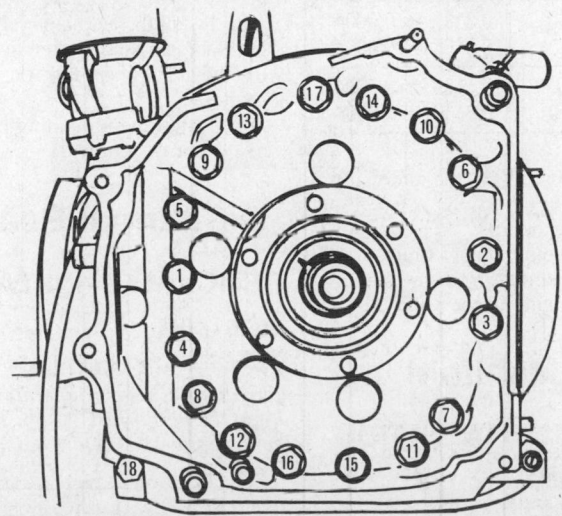

Tension bolt tightening sequence

drive sprocket nut and bend the locktabs on the lockwasher.

54. Fit a new O-ring over the front cover oil passage.

55. Install the chain tensioner and tighten its securing bolts.

56. Position the front cover gasket and the front cover on the front housing, then secure the front cover with its attachment bolts.

57. Install the eccentric shaft pulley again. Tighten its bolt to required torque.

58. Turn the engine so that the bottom faces up.

59. Cut off the excess gasket on the front cover along the mounting surface of the oil pan.

60. Install the oil strainer gasket and strainer on the front housing and tighten the attaching bolts.

61. Apply sealer to the joint surfaces of each housing.

62. Install the oil pan.

63. Turn the engine so that the top is up.

NOTE: On engines except 1984 and later 13B install the following. On 13B engines go to Step 74.

64. Install the water pump.

65. Rotate the eccentric shaft until the yellow mark (leading side mark) aligns with the pointer on the front cover.

66. Align the marks on the distributor gear and housing and install the distributor so that the lockbolt is in the center of the slot.

67. Rotate the distributor until the leading points start to separate and tighten the distributor locknut.

68. Install the gaskets and thermal reactor.

69. Install the hot air duct.

70. Install the carburetor and intake manifold assembly.

71. Connect the oil tubes, vacuum tube and metering oil pump connecting rod to the carburetor.

72. Install the decel valve and connect the vacuum lines, air hoses and wires.

73. Install the alternator bracket, alternator and bolt and check the clearance. If the clearance is more than 0.006 in., adjust the clearance using a shim. Shims are available in three sizes: 0.0059 in., 0.0118 in., and 0.0197 in.

74. **On 13B Engines:** Install the water pump and tighten the nuts in a crisscross sequence. Tighten to 13–20 ft. lbs.

─────── CAUTION ───────

Do not forget to use shims on the side housing contact surfaces indicated by 2 and 4 in the figure. If shims are not used, coolant will leak.

75. Attach two O-rings to the oil filter body. Install the oil filter body.

76. Align the leading timing mark (yellow painted) on the eccentric shaft pulley with the indicator pin on the front cover.

77. Align the tally marks on the distributor housing and driven gear. Install the

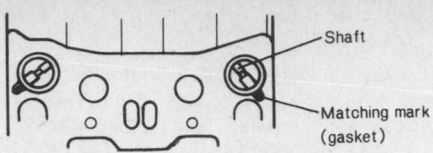

Auxiliary port valve and mounting gasket marks must match

distributor and lock nut. Turn the distributor housing until the projection of the signal rotor aligns with core of the leading side pick-up coil. Tighten the lock nut. Install the distributor rotor and cap.

78. Place the exhaust manifold gasket in position and install the exhaust manifold. Tighten to 23–34 ft. lbs.

79. Install the hot air duct and absorber plate.

80. Install the intake manifold auxiliary ports.

NOTE: Installation should be made so that the bigger sides of the auxiliary port valve shafts align the matching mark on the gasket as shown in the figure.

81. Install the "O" rings. Install the intake manifold and gasket.

82. Connect the metering oil pump pipes. Tighten to 14–19 ft. lbs.

83. Install the fuel-injection nozzles.

84. Refer to the illustration and install the delivery pipe assembly, the chamber, and the emission device assembly as one piece. Tighten delivery pipe body to 14–19 ft. lbs.; emission device assembly to 14–19 ft. lbs.

85. Refer to the illustration and check to be sure that the vacuum sensing tube is not installed incorrectly.

ECCENTRIC SHAFT SPACER THICKNESS CHART

Mark-ing	Thickness	
	mm	in.
X	8.08 ± 0.01	0.3181 ± 0.0004
Y	8.04 ± 0.01	0.3165 ± 0.0004
V	8.02 ± 0.01	0.3158 ± 0.0004
Z	8.00 ± 0.01	0.3150 ± 0.0004

86. On all engines, install the alternator drive belt.

87. Install the air pump.

88. Install the engine hanger bracket.

89. Remove the engine from the stand.

90. Install the engine in the vehicle.

Intake Manifold

REMOVAL & INSTALLATION

Except 1984 and Later 13B Engine

To remove the intake manifold and car-

buretor assembly with the engine remaining in the automobile, proceed in the following manner:

1. Perform Steps 2–7 "Engine Removal and Installation." Do not remove the engine. Do not drain the engine oil; merely remove the metering oil pump hose from the carburetor.

2. Perform Steps 1–4 of "Engine Disassembly."

Install the intake manifold and carburetor assembly in the reverse order of removal.

Intake Manifold and Auxiliary Port Valve

REMOVAL & INSTALLATION

1984 and Later 13B Engine

1. Remove the dynamic chamber by removing or disconnecting the following parts:

a. Negative battery cable; Air funnel; accelerator cable and throttle sensor connector.

b. Metering oil pump connecting rod and water hoses.

c. Terminal cover; vacuum sensing tubes (label for correct reinstallation).

d. Air supply connector; intake air temperature sensor connector.

e. Retaining bolts and nuts and the dynamic chamber.

2. Cover the intake manifold port opening with a clean cloth to prevent dust or dirt from entering.

3. Remove the incline check valve assemblies and vacuum lines.

4. Remove the air hoses from the manifold mounted solenoids.

5. Remove the actuator from the intake manifold.

6. Remove the nuts and bolts that mount the intake manifold to the engine, remove the manifold. Clean all gaskets mounting surfaces.

7. Remove the auxiliary port valve. Check the valve for cracks and breakage.

8. Install the auxiliary valve. Make sure that the bigger side of the valve shafts align with the matching mark on the mounting gasket.

9. Install the remaining parts in the reverse order of removal.

Thermal Reactor

REMOVAL & INSTALLATION

1978–80

─────── CAUTION ───────

The thermal reactor operates at extremely high temperatures. Allow the engine to cool completely before attempting to remove it.

To remove the thermal reactor, which replaced the exhaust manifold:

ENGINE LUBRICATION— ROTARY

A conventional oil pump, which is chain driven, circulates oil through the rotary engine. A full-flow filter is mounted on the top of the rear housing and an oil cooler is used to reduce the temperature of the engine oil.

An unusual feature of the rotary engine lubrication system is a metering oil pump which injects oil into the float chamber of the carburetor. Once there, it is mixed with the fuel which is to be burned, thus providing extra lubrication for the seals. The metering oil pump is designed to work only when the engine is working under a load.

Oil Pan

REMOVAL & INSTALLATION

NOTE: The only component(s) that can be serviced by removing the oil pan are the oil strainer and the oil pressure control valve.

1. Drain the engine oil.
2. Disconnect the oil level sensor and the oil thermo unit, if so equipped.
3. Remove the pan bolts and lower the pan.
4. To install, clean all of the old gasket material off the pan and engine mating surfaces, then apply a continuous bead of sealer (part no. 8527 77 739) to the pan surface. The bead should be from 0.16–0.24 in. (4–6mm) wide and should overlap at the end.
5. Fit the gasket on the pan, then apply an identical bead of sealer on top of the gasket.
6. Fit the gasket and torque the bolts to 6–8 ft. lbs. (0.6–0.9 Nm).
7. Fill the crankcase with oil.

Oil Pump

REMOVAL & INSTALLATION

Oil pump removal and installation is contained in the engine overhaul section above. Perform only those steps needed to remove the oil pump.

Metering Oil Pump

OPERATION

A metering oil pump, mounted on the top of the engine, is used to provide additional lubrication to the engine when it is operating under a load. The pump provides oil to the carburetor, where it is mixed in the float chamber to be burned.

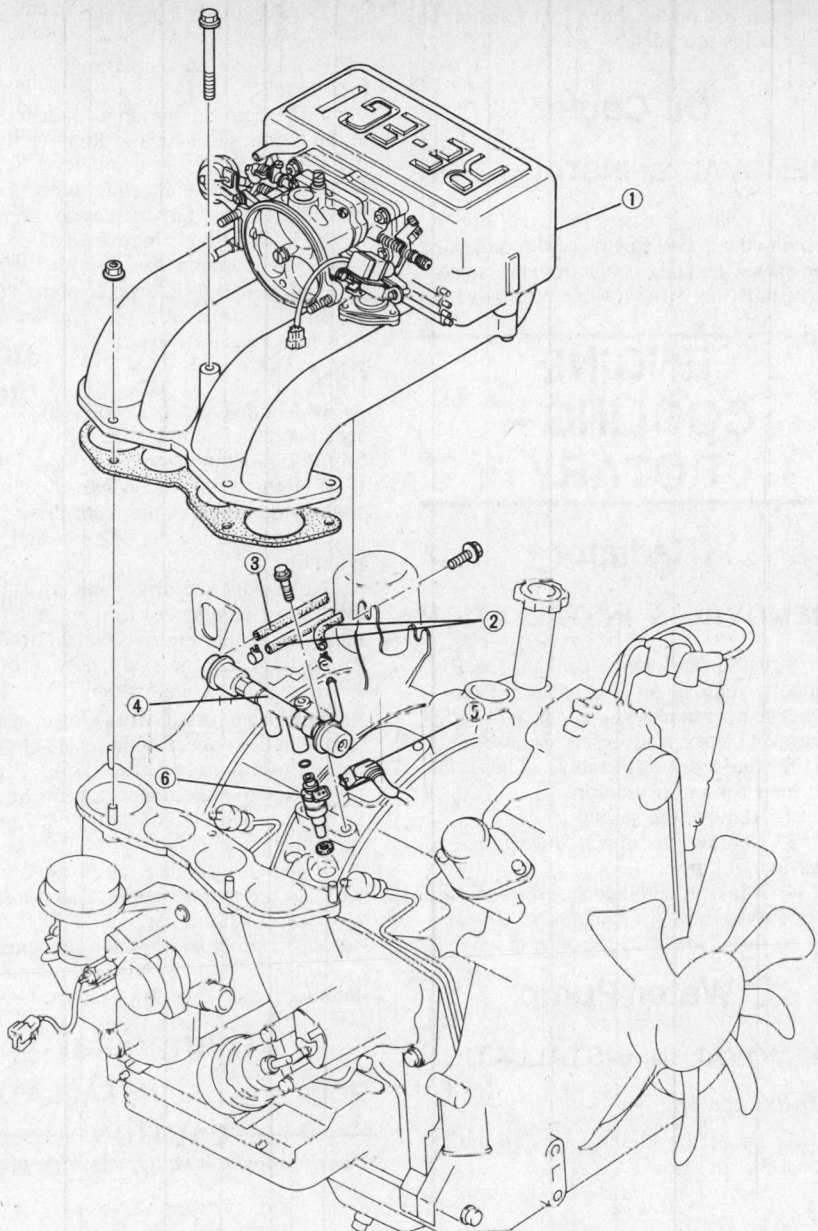

1. Dynamic chamber
2. Fuel hose
3. Vacuum sensing tube
4. Injector connector
5. Delivery pipe
6. Injector

Dynamic chamber, removal and installation

NOTE: The bottom nut is difficult to reach. Mazda makes a special wrench (part number 49 213 001) to remove it. If the wrench is unavailable, a flexible drive metric socket wrench may be substituted.

1. Remove the air cleaner.
2. Unbolt and remove the air injection pump.
3. Remove the intake manifold complete with the carburetor.
4. Remove the heat stove from the thermal reactor.
5. Unfasten the thermal reactor securing nuts, including those on the exhaust pipe flange.
6. Remove the thermal reactor.
7. Installation is the reverse of removal.

1981 and Later

On 1981 and later models, the thermal reactor/heat exchanger system is replaced by two catalytic converters and a special reactive exhaust manifold. See "Emission Control" section for explanation.

Arrow (right) indicates the metering oil pump adjusting screw. The 3 arrows (left) indicate the connecting rod adjusting holes

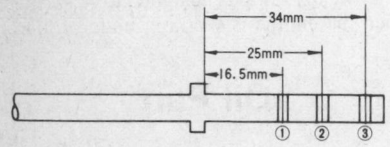

① : 248cc / 6,000rpm / Hr
② : 174cc / 6,000rpm / Hr
③ : 104cc / 6,000rpm / Hr

Connecting rod adjusting holes

The metering pump is a plunger type and is controlled by throttle opening. A cam arrangement, connected to the carburetor throttle lever, operates a plunger. The plunger, in turn, acts as a differential plunger, the stroke of which determines the amount of oil flow.

When the throttle opening is small, the amount of the plunger stroke is small; as the throttle opening increases, so does the amount of the plunger stroke.

TESTING

1. At the carburetor, disconnect the oil lines which run from the metering oil pump to the carburetor.

2. Use a container which has a scale calibrated in cubic centimeters (cc) on its side to catch the pump discharge from the oil lines.

3. Run the engine at 2,000 r.p.m. for six minutes.

4. At the end of this time, 2.4–2.9cc should be collected in the container. If not, adjust the pump.

ADJUSTMENTS

Rotate the adjusting screw on the metering oil pump to obtain the proper oil flow. Clockwise rotation of the screw *increases* the flow; counterclockwise rotation *decreases* the oil flow.

If necessary, the oil discharge rate may be further adjusted by changing the position of the cam in the pump connecting rod. The shorter the rod throw, the more oil will be pumped. Adjust the throw by means of the three holes provided.

Oil Cooler

REMOVAL & INSTALLATION

The oil cooler is easily removed after removing the gravel shield and disconnecting the lines. Unbolt the cooler from the radiator. Installation is the reverse of removal.

ENGINE COOLING— ROTARY

Radiator

REMOVAL & INSTALLATION

1. Drain the engine coolant. On RX7 models, remove or disconnect the No. 2 water temperature switch connector, coolant level sensor lead, reservoir hose, cooling fan and a drive assembly, all hoses and oil lines for automatic trans.

2. Remove the shroud.

3. Remove the upper, lower, and expansion tank hoses.

4. Remove the oil cooler, if interfering.

5. Withdraw the radiator.

6. Install in the reverse order of removal.

Water Pump

REMOVAL & INSTALLATION

All Except RX-7

1. Drain the cooling system and remove the air cleaner.

2. Disconnect the water temperature sending unit.

3. Remove the alternator, air pump and their belts.

4. Disconnect the upper radiator hose at the thermostat housing. Remove the upper fan shroud.

5. Remove the attaching bolts, and remove the fan and fan drive as an assembly.

6. Installation is in reverse order. Coat a new water pump gasket with sealer on both sides, and torque water pump attaching bolts, a little at a time, in the order shown to 13–20 ft. lbs.

RX-7

1. Remove the air cleaner and disconnect the water temperature switch wiring from the radiator.

2. Remove the air conditioner, air pump, power steering, and alternator drive belts.

3. Remove the cooling fan and drive assembly.

4. Remove the drive pulley for the air conditioner compressor from in front of the alternator/air pump drive pulleys (the pulley on the eccentric shaft, not the one on the front of the compressor).

5. Place a pan under the lower radiator hose then disconnect the hose and allow the coolant to drain out of the system.

6. Remove the upper radiator hose.

7. Remove the attaching bolts and remove the water pump.

8. When installing, clean the old gasket from the mating surfaces, and install a new gasket with sealer. Torque the attaching bolts evenly and in the order shown to 13–20 ft. lbs. (17–27 Nm). Remaining installation is the reverse of removal.

Thermostat

REMOVAL & INSTALLATION

—— **CAUTION** ——
The thermostat is equipped with a plunger

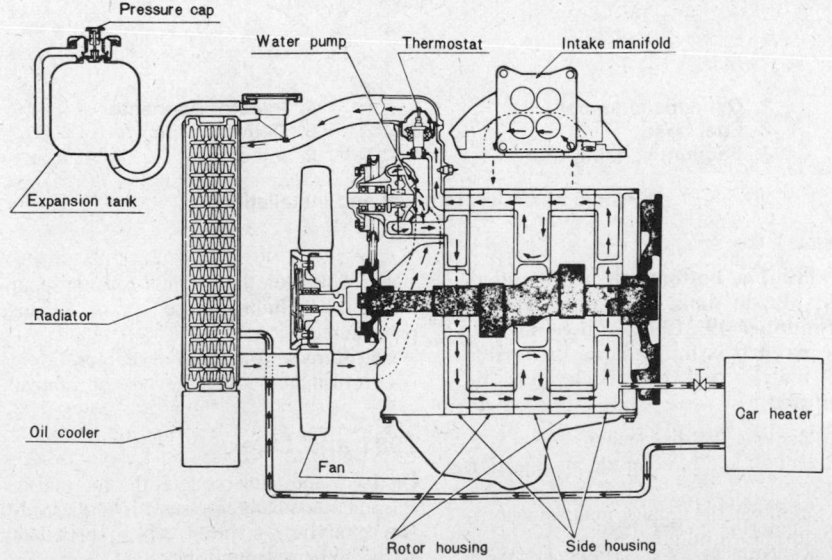

Cooling system

which covers and uncovers a by-pass hole at its bottom. Because of this unusual construction, only the specified Mazda thermostat should be used for replacement. A standard thermostat will cause the engine to overheat.

1. Drain the engine coolant. Remove upper hose from thermostat housing.

2. Remove the thermostat housing and the thermostat.

3. Installation is the reverse of removal, always install a new mounting gasket.

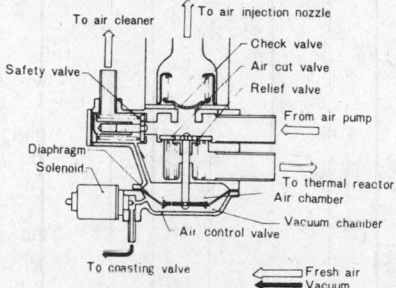

Thermostat installation and by-pass circuit

ENGINE MECHANICAL

Piston Engine

The Mazda piston engines are four cylinder, with a chain driven single overhead camshaft operating double rocker arm assemblies. The engines are water cooled and lubricated by a chain driven oil pump. Five main bearings support the crankshaft. Varied displacement engines are used in the Mazda models.

1. 96.8 cu. in.—1586cc
2. 77.6 cu. in.—1272cc
3. 120.2 cu. in.—1970cc
4. 86.4 cu. in.—1415cc
5. 90.9 cu. in.—1490cc

The varied engines are constructed basically the same, but with many external differences, such as distributor and fuel pump locations, carburetor usages and Emission Control components. Many differences exist internally and the manufacturer sources must be consulted before any attempt is made to interchange internal parts.

REMOVAL & INSTALLATION

Rear Wheel Drive

The engine is removed separately, leaving the transmission in place.

1. Remove the hood.
2. Remove the engine splash shield.
3. Drain the coolant.
4. Drain the engine oil.
5. Disconnect all electrical wires and leads. Remove the battery.

6. Disconnect all fluid lines and hoses.
7. Remove the air cleaner.
8. Unbolt and remove the radiator and cowling.
9. Disconnect the throttle cable from the carburetor and remove the throttle linkage from the rocker cover.
10. Disconnect the choke cable.
11. Remove the starter.
12. Disconnect the exhaust pipe.
13. Remove the clutch cover plate. Support the transmission.
14. Unbolt the right and left engine mounts.
15. Attach a lifting sling to the engine and pull the engine forward until it clears the clutch shaft.
16. Lift the engine from the vehicle.
17. Installation is the reverse of removal.

GLC—Front Wheel Drive

NOTE: **The factory recommends that the engine and transaxle be removed from the car as a unit.**

1. Mark the outline of the hood hinges for reinstallation alignment. Remove the hood.

2. Disconnect the battery cables from the battery; negative cable first. Remove the battery.

3. Loosen the front wheel lugs. Jack up the car and safely support it on jackstands.

4. Remove the two front wheels. Remove the bottom and side splash shields. Drain the coolant, engine oil and transaxle fluid.

5. Remove the air cleaner assembly. Remove the radiator hoses and the radiator shroud and electric fan assembly.

6. Connect an engine lifting sling to the engine. Connect a chain hoist or portable engine crane to the lifting sling and apply slight upward pressure to the engine and transaxle assembly.

7. Remove the mounting bolts from the engine crossmember. Remove the crossmember.

8. Disconnect the lower ball joints. Dismount the steering knuckles and drive axles.

9. Cars equipped with manual transaxles: disconnect the shifting rod and extension bar. Cars equipped with an automatic transaxle: disconnect the selector rod and counter rod.

10. Remove the front and rear transaxle mounting bushings. Disconnect the exhaust pipe from the converter. Remove the transaxle crossmember.

11. Disconnect all wires and hoses from under the engine and transaxle. Label them for identification.

12. Disconnect all wires, heater hoses and vacuum hoses from the upper side of the engine and transaxle. Label them for correct installation.

13. Disconnect the accelerator cable, speedometer cable, clutch cable, power brake booster line and fuel lines.

14. Check to be sure all remaining hoses

and wiring are disconnected. Remove the evaporative canister. Remove the right side upper engine mount through bolt.

15. Lift the engine and transaxle assembly from the car. Take care not to allow the assembly to swing forward into the radiator.

16. If the car must be moved from underneath the engine; remount the steering knuckles, secure the drive axles so that they can still turn, mount the front wheels and lower the car from the jackstand.

17. Installation is in the reverse order of removal.

626—Front Wheel Drive

NOTE: **The factory recommends that the engine and transaxle be removed from the car as a unit.**

1. Mark the outline of the hood hinges for reinstallation alignment. Remove the hood.

2. Disconnect the battery cables, negative cable first. Remove the battery.

3. Loosen the front wheel lugs. Jack up the car and safely support it on jackstands.

4. Remove the two front wheels. Remove the bottom and side splash shields. Drain the coolant, engine oil and transaxle fluid.

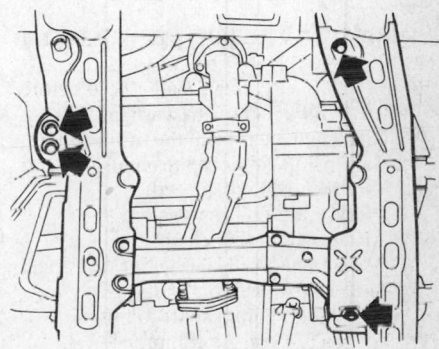

1983 and later 626 engine mounting bolts

5. Remove the air cleaner assembly. Remove the radiator hoses and the radiator shroud and electric fan assembly.

6. Remove the fuel hose, fuel return hose, accelerator cable and speedometer cable.

7. On cars with a manual transaxle, remove the clutch cable, and on those with an automatic transaxle, remove the control cable.

8. Remove the engine ground wire, power brake vacuum hose and three-way valve vacuum switch.

9. Remove the heater hoses, duty solenoid valve and the vacuum sensor.

10. Remove any additional engine or transaxle wiring.

11. Remove the air vent hose and vacuum canister hose.

12. Remove the electric cooling fan and radiator.

13. Remove the washer tank and the radiator overflow tank.

14. On air conditioned models, remove the alternator and the A/C compressor.

NOTE: Do not disconnect the high and low pressure hoses from the compressor. Secure the compressor in the fender well area with a piece of wire or rope.

15. Remove the front wheels and the splash shields.
16. Remove the power steering pump, if equipped.

NOTE: Do not remove the pressure and return hoses from the pump. Raise the pump and allow it to rest on the crossmember.

17. Remove the drive axles.
18. Disconnect the shift control rod on manual transaxle models. Remove the shift control extension bar.
19. Remove the transmission and engine mounting bolts and nuts.
20. Remove the torque stopper mount from the right wheel house area and inside the engine compartment.
21. Carefully remove the engine and transaxle from the vehicle.
22. Installation is the reverse of removal. Refill the engine coolant, engine oil and transaxle fluid.

Cylinder Head

REMOVAL & INSTALLATION

Be sure that the cylinder head is cold before removal. This will prevent warpage. Do not remove the cam gear from the timing chain. The relationship between the chain and gear teeth should not be disturbed.
1. Drain the cooling system.
2. Remove the air cleaner.
3. Disconnect all applicable electrical wires and leads.
4. Rotate the crankshaft to put the No. 1 cylinder at TDC on the compression stroke.
5. Remove the distributor.
6. Remove the rocker arm cover.
7. Raise and support the vehicle. Disconnect the exhaust pipe from the manifold.
8. Remove the accelerator linkage.
9. Remove the nut, washer and the distributor gear from the camshaft.
10. Remove the nut, washer and camshaft gear. On front-wheel drive 1490cc models, remove the tensioner from the timing case cover. Fasten the gear and chain together.
11. Remove the cylinder head bolts and cylinder head-to-front cover bolt.
12. Remove the rocker arm assembly.
13. Remove the camshaft from the camshaft gear.
14. Lift off the cylinder head.
15. Installation is the reverse of removal. Adjust the chain tension, and valves.

OVERHAUL

For all cylinder head overhaul procedures, please refer to "Engine Rebuilding" in the Unit Repair section.

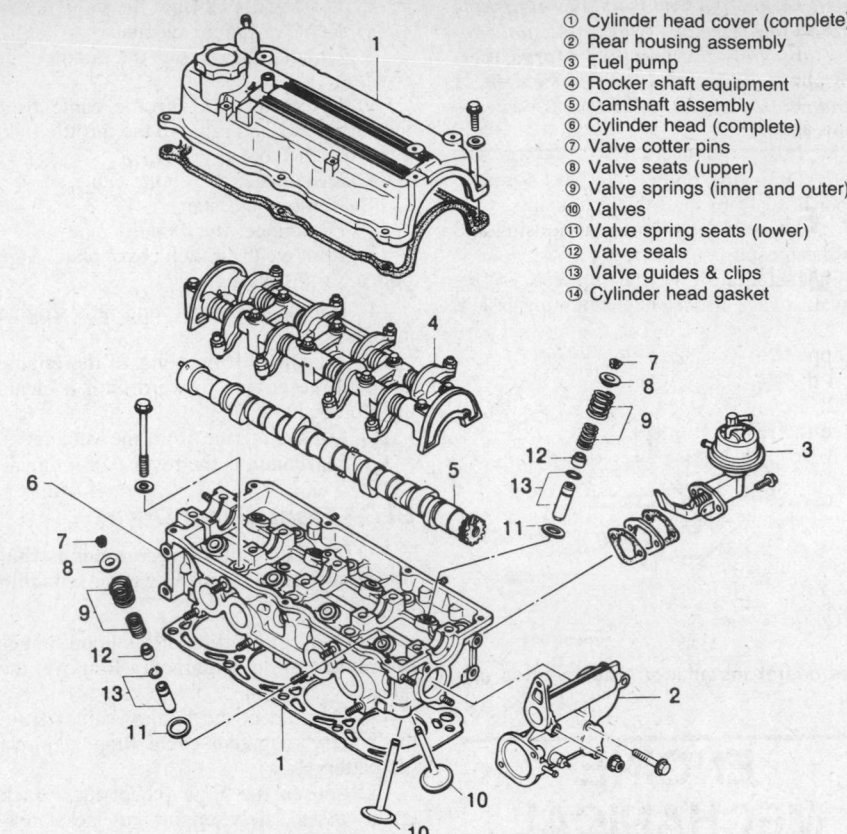

① Cylinder head cover (complete)
② Rear housing assembly
③ Fuel pump
④ Rocker shaft equipment
⑤ Camshaft assembly
⑥ Cylinder head (complete)
⑦ Valve cotter pins
⑧ Valve seats (upper)
⑨ Valve springs (inner and outer)
⑩ Valves
⑪ Valve spring seats (lower)
⑫ Valve seals
⑬ Valve guides & clips
⑭ Cylinder head gasket

Exploded view of 1983 and later 626 cylinder head

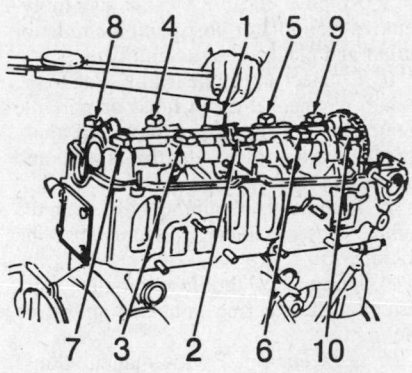

Piston engine cylinder head torque sequence

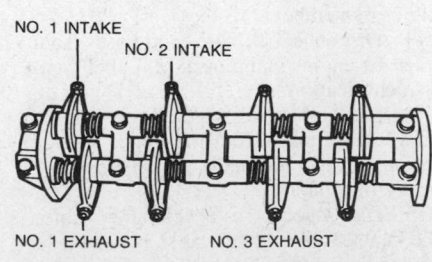

1983 and later 626 valve lash procedures

Rocker Shafts

REMOVAL & INSTALLATION

This operation should only be performed on a cold engine; the bolts which hold the rocker shafts in place also hold the cylinder head to the block.
1. Disconnect the choke cable.
2. If equipped, disconnect the air bypass valve cable.
3. Remove the rocker cover.
4. Remove the rocker arm shaft attaching bolts.
5. Installation is the reverse of removal. Install the rocker arm assemblies on the cylinder head. Temporarily tighten the cylinder head bolts to specifications and offset each rocker arm support 0.04 in. from the valve stem center.

Intake Manifold

REMOVAL & INSTALLATION

1. Drain the cooling system.
2. Remove the air cleaner.
3. Remove the accelerator linkage.
4. Disconnect the choke cable and fuel line.
5. Disconnect the PCV valve hose.

6. Disconnect the heater return hose and by-pass hose.

7. Remove the intake manifold-to-cylinder head attaching nuts.

8. Remove the manifold and carburetor as an assembly.

9. Installation is the reverse of removal.

Exhaust Manifold

REMOVAL & INSTALLATION

1. Remove the heat shield cover (if so equipped). Remove the two attaching nuts from the exhaust pipe at the manifold.

2. Remove the retaining nuts and remove the manifold.

3. Installation is the reverse of removal.

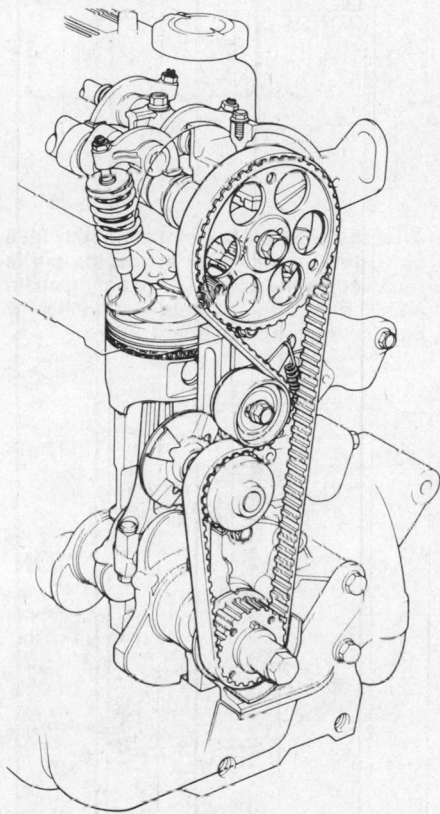

Cutaway view of 1983 and later 626 timing belt

Front Cover, Timing Chain and Tensioner

REMOVAL & INSTALLATION

1983 and Later 626

NOTE: Use Special Tool No. 49E301060 or the equivalent on the engine flywheel gear to stop the engine from rotating during removal and installation of the crankshaft pulley.

1. Turn the crankshaft so that the No. 1 cylinder piston is at TDC.

2. Drain the coolant and remove the alternator belt.

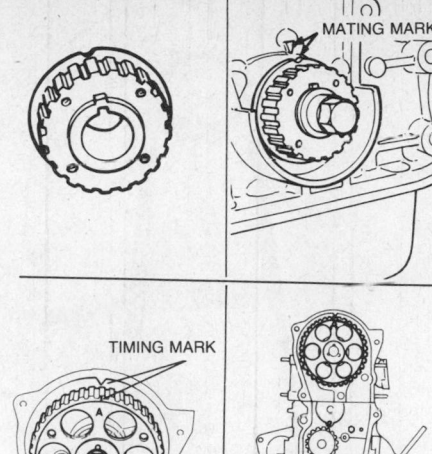

MATING MARK

TIMING MARK

1983 and later 626 timing gear alignment

3. Remove the upper timing belt cover and splash shield.

4. Remove the crankshaft pulley and the lower timing belt cover.

5. Remove the timing belt tensioner and the timing belt.

6. Install the tensioner and tensioner spring.

7. Position the tensioner all the way to the intake side and secure it by tightening the lock bolt.

8. Make sure the camshaft gear timing mark is aligned with the V-notch on the front engine cover. Check that the crankshaft timing marks are aligned.

9. Install the timing belt, making sure that the arrow on the belt points in the direction of engine rotation.

10. Loosen the tensioner lock bolt and allow the spring tension to tighten the belt.

11. Remove the Special Tool from the flywheel gear and turn the crankshaft pulley two full turns in the normal direction of engine operation.

12. Tighten the tensioner lock bolt to 27.5–38.3 ft. lbs. (38–53 Nm).

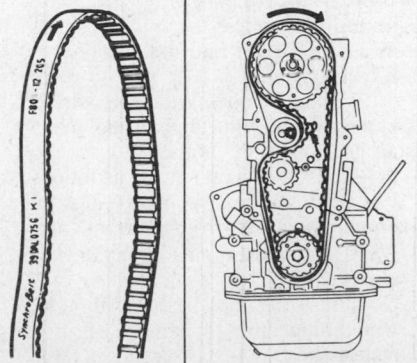

1983 and later 626 timing belt installation

13. Reinstall the upper and lower belt covers with gaskets.

14. Install the crankshaft pulley and the alternator belt.

All Other Models

NOTE: On front wheel drive GLC models, the engine must be removed from the car. Start procedure at Step 5.

1. Bring the No. 1 piston to TDC (timing marks aligned). Drain the cooling system. Remove the radiator hoses, thermostat housing, thermostat, fan, water pump and radiator.

2. Remove all lower and side splash or skid shields. Remove the crankshaft pulley and any driven units (alternator, air pump, etc.) that will interfere with front cover removal.

3. Remove the blind cover (small plate retained by two or three bolts that covers the chain adjuster). Install the special clamping tool or make a simple device to prevent the slipper head of the chain adjuster from popping out.

4. Remove the cylinder head, oil pan and timing chain front cover.

5. On GLC front wheel drive models: Remove the chain tensioner (located on the left upper corner of the timing cover) before removing the cylinder head. Remove the crankshaft pulley and proceed as follows.

6. Remove the oil slinger from the crankshaft. Depending on the engine, remove the oil pump pulley and chain or the timing chain with sprockets first, the remaining sprockets and chain second. Loosen the timing chain guide strip and remove the chain tensioner if necessary.

7. Installation is in the reverse order of removal.

8. When installing the oil pump sprocket and chain, check for excessive slack. Replace the chain if necessary. On the 626 models slack should be 0.015 in. Adjusting shims (between the oil pump and mounting) are available in thicknesses of 0.006 in.

9. Inspect the slipper head of the chain adjuster, the chain guide strip and the vibration damper for wear or damage. Check the adjuster spring for loss of tension. Replace parts as necessary.

10. Place the camshaft sprocket into the timing chain as shown on appropriate illustration. Wire the sprocket and chain in position.

11. Install the timing chain onto the crankshaft sprocket as illustrated. Tighten the chain guide. Install the timing chain tensioner (except GLC—front wheel drive). Make sure the snubber spring is fully compressed. Install clamping tool.

12. Install a new timing cover oil seal. Install the timing chain front cover, oil pan and cylinder head. When installing the front cover, be sure tension is applied to the timing chain to prevent it from coming off of the crankshaft sprocket. If the chain comes off of the sprocket, incorrect timing and engine damage will occur.

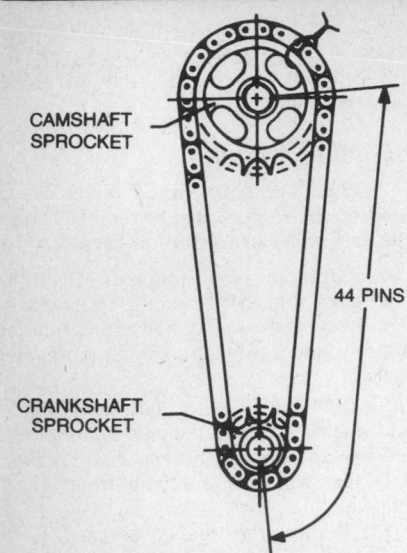

Timing chain installation—1970 cc piston engine, 1979 and later

CAMSHAFT SPROCKET

44 PINS

CRANKSHAFT SPROCKET

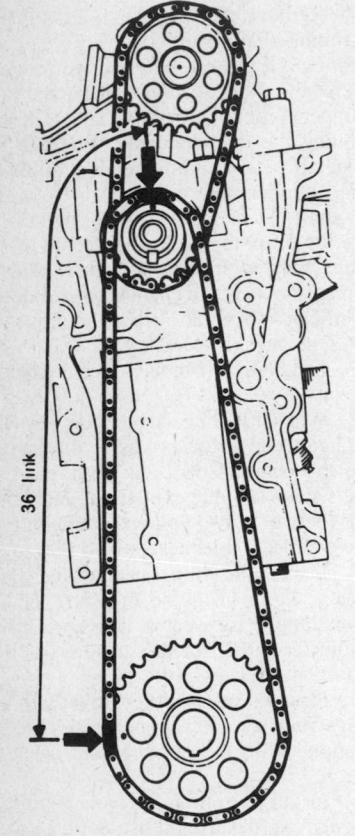

36 link

Timing chain installation—1490 cc engine (front wheel drive). Match the ring plate mark (shiny white) of the timing chain with the timing mark of the crankcase sprocket

13. Install the sprocket and timing chain on the camshaft. Refer to the illustrations. Adjust the timing chain tension.

14. Further installation is the reverse of removal.

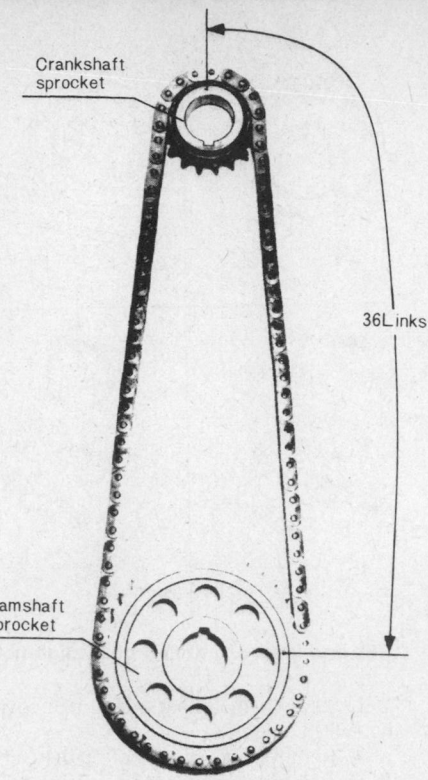

Crankshaft sprocket

36 Links

Camshaft sprocket

Alignment of the timing chain and timing gear marks—1979–80 1415 cc engine, 1978 1300 cc engine and 1981–82 GLC wagon 1490 cc engine

Timing Chain Tensioner

REMOVAL, INSTALLATION AND ADJUSTMENT

All Except GLC (Front Wheel Drive)

FRONT COVER INSTALLED

1. Remove the water pump (early engines).

2. Remove the tensioner cover.

3. Remove the attaching bolts from the tensioner. Remove the tensioner.

To install the tensioner:

4. Fully compress the snubber spring. Insert a screwdriver into the tensioner release mechanism.

5. Without removing the screwdriver, insert the tensioner and align the bolt holes. Install and torque the bolts.

6. Adjust the chain tension as follows:

a. Remove the two blind plugs and aluminum washers from the front cover.

b. Loosen the guide strip attaching screws.

c. Press the top of the chain guide strip through the adjusting hole in the cylinder head.

d. Tighten the guide strip attaching screws.

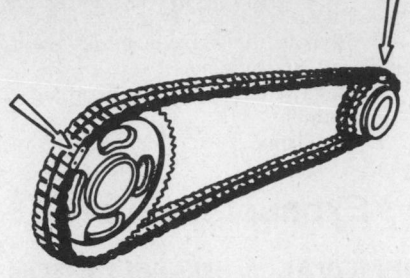

Align the bright links and the marks, 1586 cc piston engine

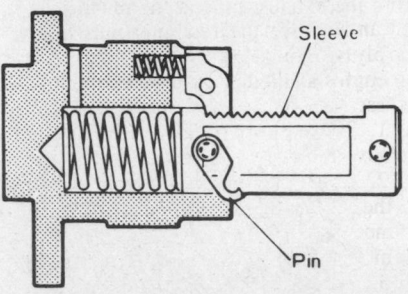

Sleeve

Pin

After the adjuster is installed on the 1490 cc engine (front wheel drive), the pin is removed by the action of the timing chain and the sleeve projects automatically, completing the adjustment

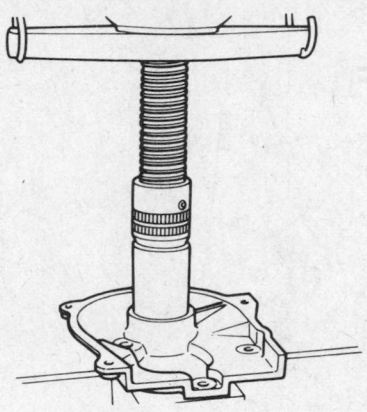

Installation of 626 (1983 and later) front housing assembly seal

e. Remove the screwdriver from the tensioner and let the snubber take up the slack in the chain.

f. Install the blind plugs and aluminum washers.

g. Install the tensioner cover and gasket.

h. Install a new gasket and water pump, if removed. Install the crankshaft pulley and drive belt and adjust the tension. Check the cooling system level.

GLC (Front Wheel Drive)

The chain tensioner is located on the left upper side of the timing case cover. It is operated by spring plus hydraulic pressure. The tensioner has a one-way locking system

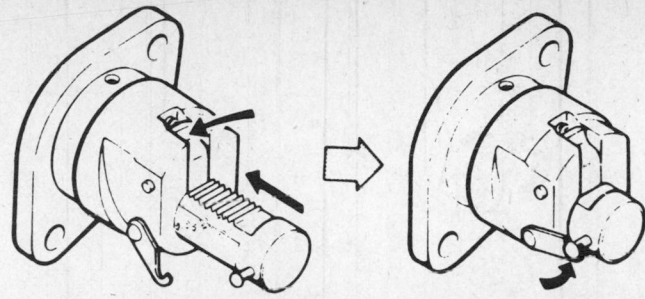

Push the sleeve into the body completely and lock it with pin—1490 cc engine (front wheel drive)

and an automatic release device. After assembly, it will automatically adjust when the engine is rotated one or two times. No disassembly of the tensioner is required.

1. The tensioner is retained by two bolts. Remove the bolts and the tensioner.

2. Check the number of teeth showing on the sleeve of the tensioner. If thirteen or more notches are showing the timing chain is stretched and must be replaced.

3. To install the tensioner, push the sleeve back into the body and lock it with the swivel catch on the tensioner body. Install the tensioner into the timing cover. After installation, the catch is released by the action of the timing chain when the engine is rotated one to two revolutions. The sleeve projects automatically providing the proper chain adjustment.

Front Cover Oil Seal

REMOVAL & INSTALLATION

The front cover oil seal can be replaced, in most cases, without removing the front cover.

1. Drain the cooling system (except GLC front wheel drive).

2. Remove the radiator (except GLC front wheel drive).

3. Remove the drive belts and crankshaft pulley.

4. Pry the front oil seal carefully from the timing case cover.

5. Install the new oil seal. The rest of the installation is in the reverse order of removal.

Camshaft

REMOVAL & INSTALLATION

1983 and Later 626

1. Set the No. 1 piston on TDC of the compression stroke, and drain the coolant.

2. Remove the timing belt.

3. Remove the air cleaner and distributor.

4. Remove the cylinder head cover and gasket.

5. Remove the camshaft timing gear and the front housing cover.

6. Remove the thermostat housing and the rear engine cover assembly.

7. Remove the rocker shaft equipment. Follow the reverse sequence for head bolt installation.

— CAUTION —
Do not remove the head bolts when the engine is hot.

8. Remove the camshaft.

9. Installation is the reverse of removal. Install a new seal in the front cover

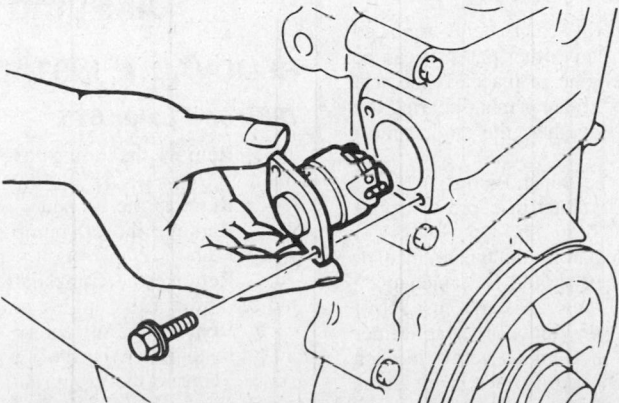

Installing the chain adjuster—1490 cc engine (front wheel drive)

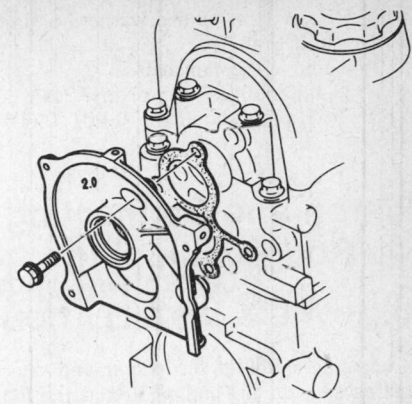

Removal and installation of 626 (1983 and later) engine front housing assembly

housing. Torque the front cover housing bolts to 13.7–18.8 ft. lbs. (19–26 Nm.).

All Other Models

Perform this operation on a cold engine only. Do not remove the camshaft gear from the timing chain. Be sure that the gear teeth and chain relationship is not disturbed. Wire the chain and cam gear to a place so that they will not fall into the front cover.

1. Remove the water pump if necessary.

2. Rotate the crankshaft to place the No. 1 cylinder on TDC of the compression stroke.

3. Remove the distributor.

4. Remove the valve cover.

5. Release the tension on the timing chain.

6. Remove the cylinder head bolts.

7. Remove the rocker arm assembly.

8. Remove the nut, washer and distributor gear from the camshaft.

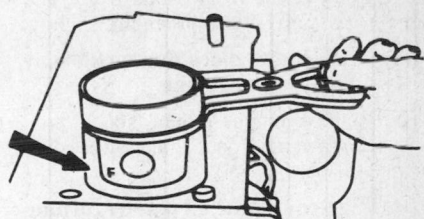

The "F" marks (arrow) face the front of the engine

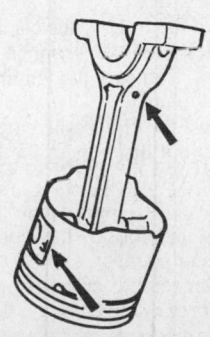

Piston and connecting rod positioning

9. Remove the nut and washer holding the camshaft gear.

10. Remove the camshaft.

11. Installation is the reverse of removal. End-play should be 0.001–0.007 in.

Piston and Connecting Rod Positioning

REMOVAL & INSTALLATION

When assembling the piston and connecting rod, the big end of the rod and the "F" mark on the piston must face in the same direction. The pistons should be installed in the block with the "F" facing the front of the engine.

ENGINE LUBRICATION— PISTON ENGINE

Oil Pan

REMOVAL & INSTALLATION

1983 and Later 626

1. Jack up the vehicle and use safety stands to support it.

2. Drain the engine oil and remove the torque stopper.

3. Remove the right wheel and splash shield.

4. Remove the front exhaust pipe and raise the passenger side of the engine slightly.

NOTE: A chain, block and tackle may be used to raise the engine.

5. Remove engine mount No. 3.

6. Remove the front engine lower cover and the oil pan.

NOTE: Remove the oil pan by turning the front end to the left.

7. Installation is the reverse of removal.

All Other Models

1. Jack up the front of the car and safely support on jackstands. Disconnect negative battery cable. Remove the engine splash shield or skid plate.

2. Remove the clutch slave cylinder, if equipped. Do not disconnect the hydraulic line, let the cylinder hang.

3. Remove the engine rear brace attaching bolts and loosen the bolts on the left side, if equipped.

4. Disconnect the emission line from the oil pan, if equipped.

5. Loosen the front motor mounts, raise the front of the engine and block up to gain

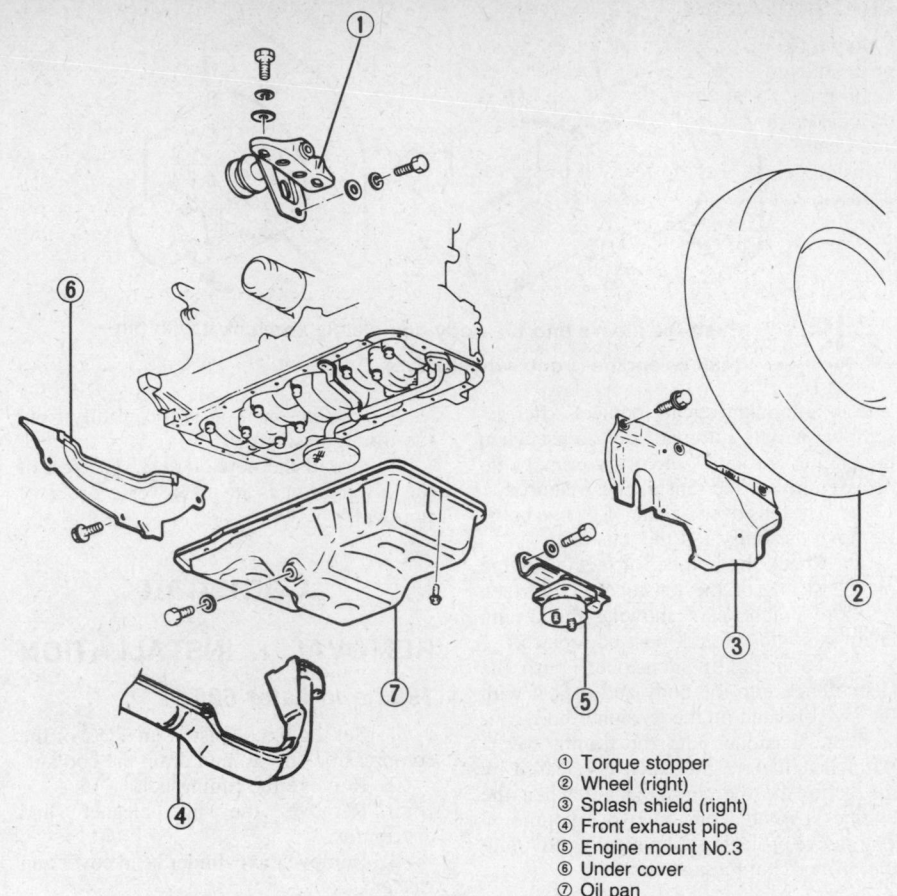

① Torque stopper
② Wheel (right)
③ Splash shield (right)
④ Front exhaust pipe
⑤ Engine mount No.3
⑥ Under cover
⑦ Oil pan

1983 and later 626 oil pan removal and installation

clearance if necessary (except GLC—front wheel drive).

6. Remove the oil pan and allow it to rest on the crossmember. Remove the oil pump pickup tube, if necessary, to remove the oil pan.

7. Install in the reverse order of removal.

Rear Main Oil Seal

REPLACEMENT

If the rear main oil seal is being replaced independently of any other parts, it can be done with the engine in place. If the rear main oil seal and the rear main bearing are being replaced, together, the engine must be removed.

1. Remove the transmission.

2. Remove the clutch disc, pressure plate and flywheel.

3. Punch two holes in the crankshaft rear oil seal. They should be punched on opposite sides of the crankshaft, just above the bearing cap-to-cylinder block split line.

4. Install a sheet metal screw in each hole. Pry against both screws at the same time to remove the oil seal.

5. Clean the oil recess in the cylinder block and bearing cap. Clean the oil seal surface on the crankshaft.

6. Coat the oil seal surfaces with oil. Coat the oil surface and the seal surface on the crankshaft with Lubriplate®. Install the new oil seal and make sure that it is not cocked. Be sure that the seal surface was not damaged.

7. Install the flywheel. Coat the threads of the flywheel attaching bolts with oil-resistant sealer.

8. Install the clutch, pressure plate and transmission.

Oil Pump

REMOVAL & INSTALLATION

1983 and Later 626

1. Remove the timing cover and timing chain.

2. Remove the oil pan.

3. Remove the oil pump strainer and pick-up tube.

4. Remove the crankshaft timing gear and the lower front engine bracket.

5. Remove the oil pump.

6. Installation is the reverse of removal. Torque the crankshaft pulley bolt to 80–87 ft. lbs. (110–120 Nm). Torque the oil pump bolts to 13.7–18.8 ft. lbs. (19–26 Nm). Torque the front engine bracket bolts to 27.5–38.0 ft. lbs. (38–53 Nm).

All Other Models

Remove the oil pan. Remove the oil pump gear attaching nut. Remove the bolts attaching the oil pump to the block. Loosen the gear on the pump. Remove the oil pump and gear.

Installation is the reverse of removal.

ENGINE COOLING— PISTON ENGINE

Radiator

REMOVAL & INSTALLATION

1. Drain the coolant from the radiator.
2. Remove the fan blades and shroud or disconnect the electrical harness from the electric fan motor and remove the fan and cowling mount.
3. Remove the upper and lower hoses. Disconnect the transmission cooler lines, (if so equipped).
4. Remove the radiator mounting bolts and remove the radiator.
5. Install the radiator by reversing the removal procedure.

Water Pump

REMOVAL & INSTALLATION

1983 and Later 626

NOTE: Use Special Tool 49E301060 or equivalent on the engine flywheel gear to stop the engine from rotating during removal and installation of the crankshaft pulley.

1. Turn the crankshaft so that the No. 1 cylinder piston is at TDC on the compression stroke.
2. Drain the coolant and remove the alternator belt.
3. Remove the upper timing belt cover and the splash shield.
4. Remove the crankshaft pulley and the lower timing belt cover.
5. Remove the timing belt tensioner and the timing belt.
6. Make sure the camshaft gear timing mark is aligned with the V-notch on the front engine cover. Check that the crankshaft timing marks are aligned.
7. Remove the water inlet pipe from the water pump.
8. Remove the water pump and gasket.
9. Installation is the reverse of removal. Torque the water pump bolts to 13.7–18.8 ft. lbs. (19–26 Nm).

All Other Models

1. Drain the coolant from the radiator.
2. On GLC front wheel drive models, jack up the front of the car and safely support it on jackstands. Remove the splash shield. Remove the drive belt, lower hose and by-pass pipe with O-ring. Remove the water pump.
3. On other models, remove the air pump if interfering. Remove the fan from the fan pulley if not equipped with electric fan assembly. Loosen and remove the fan drive belt. Remove the radiator hose.
4. Loosen and remove the water pump mounting bolts, remove the water pump.
5. Clean all gasket surfaces. Mount the new water pump and gasket. Tighten the mounting bolts evenly in several stages. The rest of the installation is in the reverse order of removal.

Thermostat

REMOVAL & INSTALLATION

1. Drain several quarts of coolant from the radiator so that the coolant level is below the thermostat.
2. Disconnect the radiator hose from the thermostat housing.
3. Remove the thermostat housing mounting bolts, housing, gasket and thermostat.
4. Clean all gasket surfaces. Install the new thermostat with the temperature sensing pellet downwards. Use a new mounting gasket and install the housing.
5. The rest of the installation is in the reverse order of removal.

EMISSION CONTROLS

The Emission Control System is separated into three different categories.

1. Crankcase emission control system
2. Evaporative emission control system
3. Engine exhaust gas emission control system

The three sub-systems vary in application on the vehicle models, depending upon the areas in which the vehicle is to be operated, such as Federal, California, High Altitude or Canada. The engine/transmission applications will vary the requirements needed to comply with the Federal or State regulations.

EMISSION CONTROL COMPONENTS

Rotary Engine
EXCEPT 1984 AND LATER 13B

1. Anti-Afterburn Valve No. 1—Supplies fresh air into the front primary port

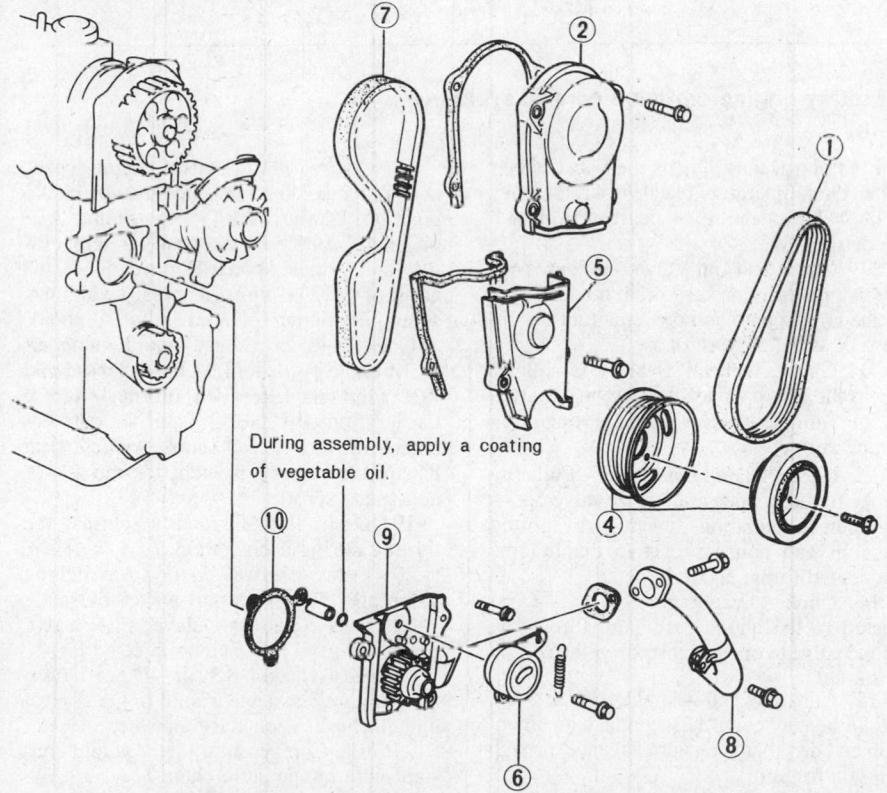

During assembly, apply a coating of vegetable oil.

① V-ribbed belt (for alternator)
② Timing belt cover (upper)
③ Splash shield
④ Crankshaft pulley
⑤ Timing belt cover (lower)
⑥ Tensioner
⑦ Timing belt
⑧ Inlet pipe
⑨ Water pump
⑩ Gasket

Water pump removal 1983 and later 626

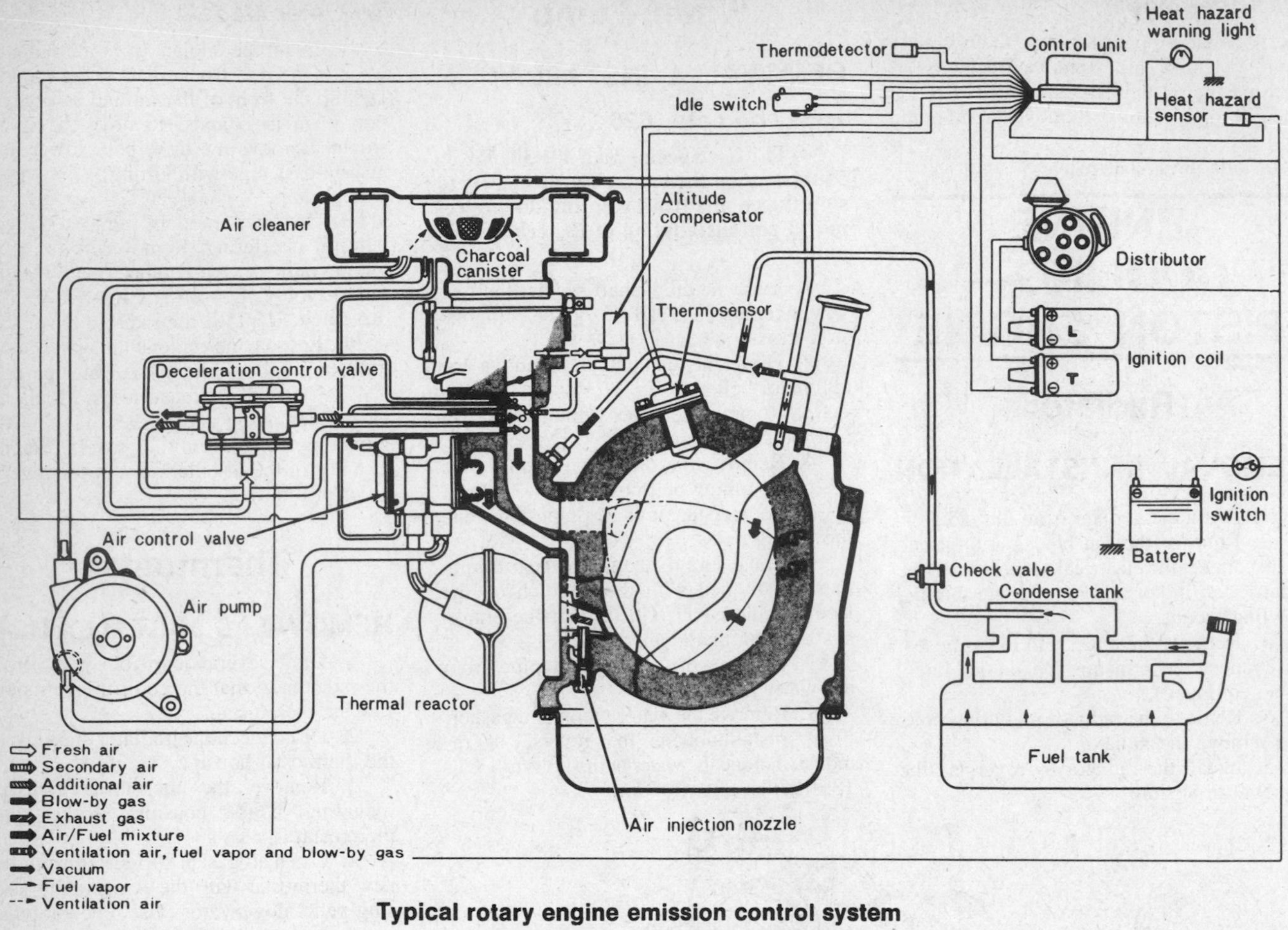

Fresh air
Secondary air
Additional air
Blow-by gas
Exhaust gas
Air/Fuel mixture
Ventilation air, fuel vapor and blow-by gas
Vacuum
Fuel vapor
Ventilation air

Typical rotary engine emission control system

during deceleration. The valve is included in the air control valve and is vacuum operated.

2. Anti-Afterburn Valve No. 2—Supplies fresh air into the rear secondary port during deceleration and is vacuum operated.

3. A/C Solenoid Valve—Applies Vacuum to the throttle opener when the A/C switch is turned on. Coded white.

4. Air Cleaner—Filters air entering the carburetor.

5. Air Control Valve (ACV)—Directs the air to one of three locations: Exhaust port, 3-bed catalyst or back to the air cleaner. The ACV consists of three valves; the air relief valve, air switching valve and No. 1 anti-afterburn valve.

6. Air Pump—Supplies secondary air to the ACV.

7. Air Vent Solenoid Valve—Vents the carburetor float chamber to the canister when the engine is off. When the engine is started, the fumes are drawn into the intake manifold through a purge valve.

8. ALC Valve—Leans the fuel mixture at high altitude, adds air to the carburetor air bleeds.

9. Canister—Stores gas tank and carburetor fumes when the engine is off. Vented to the atmosphere through charcoal and filter.

10. Catalyst Thermo Sensor—Detects exhaust gas temperature and sends the sig-

nal to control unit. Opens the rear catalyst when the temperature reaches 1418 degrees F on MT models; 1364 degrees F on AT models.

11. Check and Cut Valve—Releases excessive pressure or vacuum in the fuel tank to the atmosphere and prevents fuel loss in case of vehicle overturn.

12. Choke Bimetal Heater—Gradually opens the choke valve after engine is started as the engine reaches normal operating temperature.

13. Choke Diaphragm No. 1—Pulls the choke partially open after delay valve opens or when accelerating. Operated by ported vacuum and consists of two diaphragms connected to the choke bimetal.

14. Choke Diaphragm No. 2—Connected to the choke valve and forces the choke valve to open slightly after the engine is started.

15. Choke Switch—Applies power to the choke heater, controls secondary air injection and distributor vacuum advance through the control unit.

16. Clutch Neutral Switch—Detects in-gear condition, prevents vehicle from starting when the clutch is not depressed. Will allow starting when vehicle is in neutral.

17. Coasting Valve—Supplies fresh air into the rear primary port when decelerating to prevent excessive vacuum.

18. Control Unit—Detects engine speed, coolant temperature, throttle opening, choke position, catalyst (floor) temperature, A/C on or off condition, exhaust gas temperature and vehicle speed. Controls the operation of the vacuum solenoids, switching-solenoid, shutter solenoid, relief solenoid, A/C solenoid, port air solenoid, main air bleed control solenoid, richer solenoid and fuel pump relay. Receives information from the ignition coil, No. 2 water temperature switch, throttle sensor, choke switch, heat hazard sensor, A/C switch, thermo sensor and speed sensor.

19. Dash Pot—Gradually closes the throttle during deceleration.

20. Delay Valve—Delays switching valve operation from port air to split air.

21. Delay Valve—Delays relief valve operation from relief air to injected air.

22. Heat Hazard Sensor—Detects floor temperature and sends signal to the control unit. Relieves secondary air when closed.

23. Idle Compensator—Keeps idle constant with temperature change.

24. Main Air Bleed Control Solenoid Valve—Opens air passage and leans the mixture during acceleration.

25. No. 1 Converter—Reduces HC and CO, is an oxidizing catalyst.

26. No. 2 Converter—Reduces HC, CO and NOx, is 3-way catalyst.

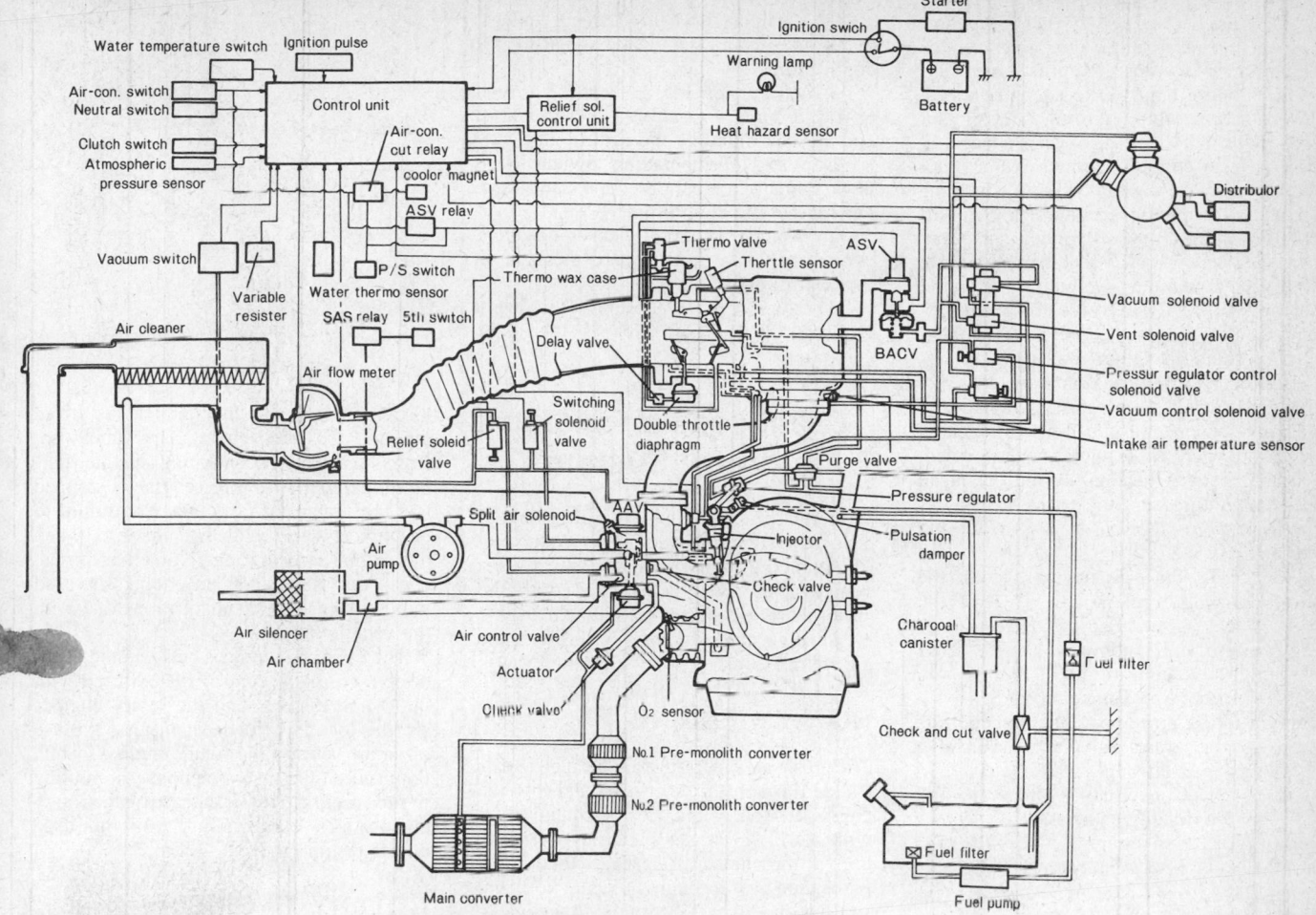

RX7 with 13B rotary engine—emissions controls

27. Port Air Solenoid Valve—Closes port air by-pass passage during acceleration at a certain speed.

28. Purge Valve—Carries evaporative fumes from the gas tank and canister to the intake manifold during open throttle.

29. Relief Solenoid Valve—Relieves secondary air to the air cleaner when unnecessary. Coded blue.

30. Richer Solenoid Valve—On MT models, opens primary fuel passage after deceleration. Operates for 30 seconds when the engine speed becomes 1,100 rpm or less.

31. Shutter Solenoid Valve—Operates the coasting valve during deceleration above 1,100 rpm. Operates shutter valve at the same time. Coded yellow.

32. Shutter Valve—Shuts off the primary port during deceleration.

33. Speed Sensor—Detects vehicle speed. The sensor is a reed switch integrated into the speedometer.

34. Split Air Injection Pipe—Injects secondary air into the main converter between the center and rear at 1,100 rpm with open throttle and choke off.

35. Switching Solenoid Valve—Switches the secondary air to exhaust port or rear catalyst. Coded gray.

36. Throttle Opener—Pulls the throttle partially open when the A/C is on and compensates for load of the compressor during non-A/C operation.

37. Throttle Sensor—Detects the throttle opening angle.

38. Vacuum Advance Diaphragm—Controlled by solenoid valve.

39. Vacuum Control Solenoid Valve—Controls vacuum to the distributor during various engine operating speeds. Coded-Leading; Brown. Trailing; Green.

40. Vacuum Switch—On MT models, detects intake manifold vacuum.

41. Water Temperature Switch No. 1—Hold choke on below 158 degrees F. Operates hot start above 158 degrees F.

42. Water Temperature Switch No. 2—Detects coolant temperature and sends information to control unit.

43. 3-Bed Monolith Converter—Further reduces HC, CO, and NOx. This is the main converter.

1984 AND LATER 13B ROTARY ENGINES

1. Air Cleaner—Filters the air into the throttle chamber.

2. Air Control Valve (ACV)—Directs air to one of three locations; exhaust port, 3-bed catalyst or back to the relief air silencer. The ACV consists of three valves; the air relief valve, air switching valve and the anti-afterburn valve.

3. Air Flow Meter—Detects the amount of intake air and sends the information to the control unit.

4. Air Pump—Supplies secondary air to the ACV.

5. Air Supply Valve—Supplies by-pass air into the dynamic chamber during A/C operation and power steering operation.

6. Anti-Afterburn Valve — Supplies fresh air into the rear port during deceleration, is included in the ACV and is vacuum operated.

7. Atmospheric Pressure Sensor—Detects atmospheric pressure and sends the information to the control unit.

8. By-Pass Air Control Valve (BAC)—Controls the amount of by-pass air to maintain idling speed and other functions. Is controlled by the vent solenoid valve and vacuum source valve.

9. Canister—Stores gas tank fumes when the engine is off and is vented to the atmosphere through charcoal and a filter.

10. Check and Cut Valve—Releases excessive pressure or vacuum from the fuel tank into the atmosphere. Prevents fuel loss

in case of vehicle overturn.

11. Clutch Neutral Switch—Prevents engine starting when in gear unless clutch is depressed or transmission is in neutral.

12. Control Unit—Detects engine speed, coolant temperature, throttle opening, intake manifold vacuum, oxygen concentration, in-gear condition, idle mixture, floor temperature, intake air pressure, cranking signal, atmospheric pressure, A/C on-off condition and amount of intake air. Controls the operation of; Vacuum control valve solenoid, switching solenoid valve, relief solenoid valve, BAC valve (vent and vacuum solenoid valves), pressure regulator control solenoid valve, fuel injection system. Receives information from the ignition coil, water temperature switch, water thermo sensor, throttle sensor, vacuum switch, oxygen sensor, clutch neutral switch, variable resistor, heat hazard sensor, intake air temperature sensor, starter switch, atmospheric pressure sensor, A/C switch and the air flow meter.

13. Dash Pot—Gradually closes the throttle during deceleration.

14. Heat Hazard Sensor—Detects floor temperature and sends signal to the relief solenoid valve control unit.

15. Intake Air Temperature Sensor—Detects intake air temperature and controls the pressure control valve and BAC valve through the control unit.

16. No. 1 Converter—Reduces HC and CO, is an oxidizing catalyst.

17. No. 2 Converter—Reduces HC, CO and NOx, is 3-way catalyst.

18. Overdrive Switch—Controls the ACV solenoid.

19. Oxygen Sensor—Detects exhaust manifold oxygen concentration and sends a signal to the control unit.

20. Pressure Regulator Control Solenoid Valve—Shuts the vacuum passage between the dynamic chamber and pressure regulator to prevent the engine from shutting off.

21. Purge Valve—Carries evaporative fumes from the gas tank and canister to the intake manifold during open throttle operation.

22. Relief Solenoid Valve—Relieves secondary air to the air cleaner when it is unnecessary. Coded blue.

23. Split Air Solenoid Valve—Controls the amount of split air, it operates when the overdrive switch is open and increases split air when the ACV solenoid operates.

24. Split Air Injection Pipe—Injects secondary air between the center and rear sections of the main converter above 1,100 rpm with open throttle.

25. Switching Solenoid Valve—Switches secondary air to the exhaust port or rear catalyst. Coded gray.

26. Throttle Sensor—Detects throttle opening angle.

27. Vacuum Advance Diaphragm—Controlled by the solenoid valve.

28. Vacuum Control Solenoid Valve—Control vacuum to the distributor advance.

Coded green.

29. Vacuum Switch—Detects intake manifold vacuum and sends signal to the control unit.

30. Vent Solenoid Valve and Vacuum Solenoid Valve—Controls the BAC valve and are controlled by the control unit.

31. Water Temperature Switch—Detects coolant temperature and sends the message to the control unit.

32. Water Thermo Sensor—Detects coolant temperature and sends message to the control unit.

33. 3-Bed Converter—Further reduces HC, CO and NOx. This is the main converter.

Crankcase Emission Control System

The crankcase emission control system is a closed system, maintaining a specific ventilation in the crankcase and positively prevents vapors from being emitted to the atmosphere by being recirculated to the combustion chamber for burning with the air/fuel mixture.

ROTARY ENGINE

The fresh air enters the air cleaner and is routed through the inlet hose and into the engine air space. The fresh air then mixes with the blow-by gases and any other vapors in the engine air space. The blow-by gases then pass through the outlet hose and ventilation valve, to be routed to the intake manifold and to be mixed with the air/fuel mixture and be burned.

NOTE: Evaporated fuel from the fuel tank is also held in the crankcase.

PISTON ENGINE

The fresh air enters the air cleaner and is routed through the inlet hose to the rocker arm cover and into the crankcase. There the fresh air mixes with the vapors and blow-by gases. The blow-by gases then pass through the outlet hose and ventilation valve, into the intake manifold to be mixed with the air/fuel mixture and be burned. It should be noted that the ventilation valve can be at valve cover area or at the intake manifold area.

NOTE: When the volume of blow-by gases is very high, such as operating the engine under heavy loads, the gases and vapors may back into the inlet hose and air cleaner.

Evaporative Emission Control System

The evaporative emission control system is designed to control the gasoline vapors from

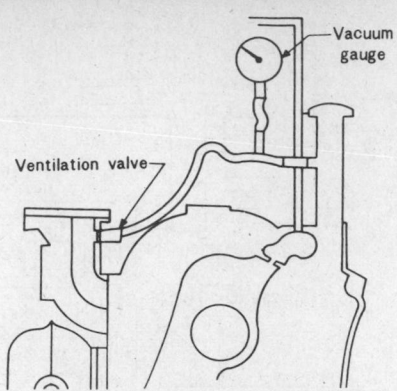

Testing the PCV valve

the carburetor and fuel tank areas, from entering the atmosphere. The vapors are stored in a canister containing activated carbon (charcoal) while the engine is stopped and are drawn into the intake manifold to be burned with the air/fuel mixture, when the engine is operating. Numerous hoses, check valves, and condenser tanks are used in the systems. Size and locations vary with the vehicle models.

The major differences between the evaporative emission control system used with the piston engines and the rotary engines are the locations of the canisters, the use of an air vent on the rotary engines, while not used on the piston engines, the routing of fuel vapors to the crankcase on the rotary engines as a storage point, while not used on the piston engines.

ROTARY ENGINE

An air vent valve is used with the rotary engines and is located on the carburetor float chamber. Its purpose is to control the passage of vapors from the carburetor float chamber, into the canister or air horn. When the engine is stopped, an electrical solenoid is opened, allowing the vapors to pass from the float chamber to the canister in the air cleaner. When the engine is started, the passage is closed and the vapors are directed to the carburetor air horn. The gasoline in the fuel tank that evaporates when the engine is not operating, is held in the tank and lines until a preset pressure is reached. This preset pressure operates the check valve in the ventilation and check valve assembly, allowing the excess gasoline vapors to be routed to the crankcase and to the canister, where it is held until the engine is started and then burned with the air/fuel mixture.

A check and cut valve is used in the vapor line and has three functions. When the pressure in the fuel tank becomes high, the check valve opens to the atmosphere and releases the excess pressure. When the negative pressure in the tank becomes high, the check valve again opens and allows atmosphere pressure to enter and equalize the inner and outer pressures. The third function of the valve is to prevent fuel from flowing out, should the vehicle overturn.

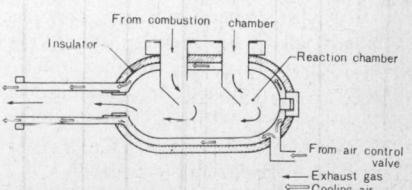
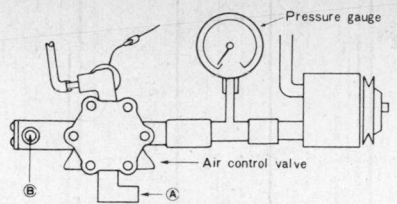

Testing the air control valve

PISTON ENGINES

The system for the piston engines consists of either condensing tanks or spaces for the fuel vapors to be collected and be condensed back into fuel and returned to the fuel tank. The vapors that are not condensed are routed through a check valve and into a canister containing activated charcoal which absorbs the vapors. When the engine is started, the vapors are drawn into the intake manifold, mixed with the air/fuel mixture and burned. The check valve is used to prevent negative pressure in the tank and to open at a specific point to allow atmosphere pressure to flow into the tank. When positive pressures build up in the tank and the canister and lines can accept no more vapors, the check valve will open at a specific pressure and allow a controlled release of the pressure from the tank to avoid tank damage.

Exhaust Emission Control System

AIR INJECTION AND THERMAL REACTOR SYSTEM

Rotary Engines
1978–80 ONLY

This system is designed to direct fresh air (secondary air) into the hot exhaust gases, just released from the combustion chambers and into the thermal reactor, through the exhaust ports. The purpose of the addition of fresh air to the exhaust is to completely burn the HC and CO contained in the exhaust gases. The fresh air is supplied by an air pump, driven by the engine. The air is directed through lines and a check valve, to the thermal reactor. The thermal reactor is a chamber to maintain the temperature of hot gases as high as possible to facilitate reaction between the hot gases and the fresh or secondary air. The check valve also performs the function of preventing the exhaust gases from backflowing into the air pump and causing damage.

The check valve or air control valve, contains three valves. A number one relief valve, a number two relief valve and an anti-afterburn valve. The number one and two relief valves control the air from the air pump according to engine needs, determined by engine speed and load.

Number One Relief Valve Operation

Excessive high heat can cause the thermal reactor to deteriorate rapidly, because of the high temperatures, needed to burn the unburned elements in the exhaust gases. The function of the number one relief valve is to aid in the cooling of the outer jacket of the thermal reactor when air pressure in the system becomes higher than specified. The operation of the number one relief valve is the same for vehicles, so equipped.

Number Two Relief Valve Operation
FEDERAL AND CANADA

The number two relief valve is closed when the engine rpm is below 1500. When the engine speed is increased to over 1500 rpm, the relief valve is opened by intake manifold vacuum, controlled by the engine load. As the relief valve is opened, the air from the air pump is directed to the air cleaner, rather than to the thermal reactor.

CALIFORNIA

The relief valve remains closed under the following conditions.
1. When the engine is below 1500 rpm.
2. When the choke knob is fully pulled.
3. When accelerating in any gears except 4th and 5th within 130 seconds after engine starting with the choke used.
4. When accelerating in any gears except 4th and 5th, after the 130 seconds, with the engine rpm below 3000.

Under any other conditions than those listed above, the valve opens and releases part of the air from the air pump into the air cleaner, according to the vacuum signal to the valve, which is controlled by the load applied to the engine. The result is a balanced air-exhaust gas mixture required for the reburning of the exhaust gases in the thermal reactor.

SPLIT-AIR SYSTEM

Rotary Engines
1981 AND LATER

A new system, using the air injection principle and major components, eliminates the thermal reactor, but uses two catalytic converters in its place. A reactive exhaust manifold is bolted to the engine and acts as a chamber to combust the unburned Hydrocarbons (HC) and Carbon Monoxide (CO) by the addition of fresh or secondary air. The exhaust gases then pass through the first of the two catalysts, a monolith type, and then through the second, which is a two bed, pellet type. The air pump is driven by the engine with the air flow controlled by an air control valve, which directs the fresh air to either the exhaust port, the pellet catalyst or to the engine air cleaner assembly, as required by the engine speed and/or load.

During the operation of the engine at low speeds, when the HC and the CO pollutants are produced in larger amounts, the air is directed to the engine exhaust port to begin the oxidation of the HC and CO in the exhaust port and to continue in the 1st and 2nd catalytic converters.

With the engine operating at mid-range speeds, the air control valve directs the fresh air to the pellet or second converter. The air from the air pump is injected through a nozzle located between the two pellet beds and stopped from entering the exhaust port manifold. The front pellet bed acts as a three way catalyst, primarily taking care of the oxides of nitrogen (NO_x), while the rear bed with the split air continues to oxidize HC and CO pollutants.

The function of the 1st or monolith catalyst, consisting of a small capacity platinum and rhodium base three-way catalyst, is as a back-up unit, for the reactive exhaust manifold to oxidize the increased amounts of HC and CO pollutants. It is also used to heat up the exhaust gases, shorten the warm-up time of the pellet catalyst so that it will reach full operating capacity in a shorter period of time.

Low inherent NO_x emissions are experienced with the rotary engine. With this air injected system used, there is no need for the exhaust gas recirculation (EGR) valve, normally used to control the NO_x.

Piston Engines

The air injection system is used to inject fresh or secondary air into the exhaust manifold for the purpose of reburning the unburned elements in the exhaust gases. The system consists of the air pump, air injection manifold, air injection nozzles (one for each cylinder), port liners, air control valve, control unit and heat hazard sensor.

Certain vehicles do not use the control unit or the sensors, but rely upon the vacuum signal from the engine intake manifold to the control valve, to direct the fresh or secondary air to the injection nozzles or to the air cleaner assembly. A second type of air injection system is used. This system does not use the air pump, but relies upon the pulse of the exhaust gases to draw fresh air into the exhaust manifold through a one-way reed valve.

AIR INJECTION SYSTEM WITH CONTROL UNIT

The air pump is supplied fresh air from the air cleaner and directs the air, under pressure, to the air control valve. The control

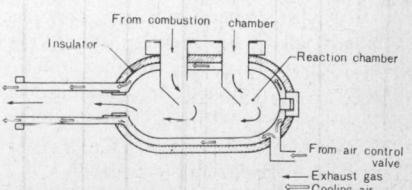

Thermal reactor cooling circuit

valve has two valves, number one relief valve which controls the exhausting of the compressed air to the atmosphere when the engine speed is over 4000 rpm or when the floor temperature reaches 302°F. The Number two relief valve controls the injection of fresh or secondary air into the exhaust manifold by the intake manifold vacuum signals, dependent upon the speed and the load of the engine.

The electric control switch (engine speed switch) sends the electrical signal to the solenoid valve of the air control valve to release the fresh or secondary air and to prevent heat damage to the exhaust system when the engine speed is over 4000 rpm. The heat hazard switch sends an electrical signal to the solenoid valve of the air control valve, to release the fresh or secondary air to the atmosphere to prevent heat damage to the floor when the floor temperature reaches 302°F from the exhaust system burning of the unburned elements in the exhaust gases.

Two check valves are used. The check valve on the injection pipes is used to prevent the backflow of exhaust gases into the air pump, while the check valve for the number one relief valve controls the intake manifold vacuum to the number one relief valve of the air control valve, accordingly to the engine load and speed.

AIR INJECTION AND CATALYTIC CONVERTER SYSTEM

Reed Valve Operation

This system inducts fresh or secondary air into hot gases, flowing into the exhaust system from the cylinder head exhaust ports, for the purpose of reburning the unburned elements of the exhaust gases. A catalytic converter is used to convert the hydrocarbons (HC) and the carbon monoxide (CO), contained in the exhaust gases, into harmless water (H_2O) and carbon dioxide (CO_2).

The system consists of a reed valve, air distribution manifold, air injection nozzles, air silencer and catalytic converter.

The reed valve is operated by the exhaust gas pulsations to induct the fresh or secondary air into the exhaust ports from the air cleaner assembly. A silencer is used in the air cleaner to insulate the noise of the reed valve during its operation. The air manifold divides and distributes the inducted air to the injection nozzles, one for each cylinder, and placed to direct the injected fresh air into the hot gases discharged from the cylinder head exhaust ports. As the exhaust gases are directed through the exhaust system, the gases enter the catalytic converter. The inducted air continues the combustion of the unburned elements in the exhaust gases and the catalytic converter converts the remaining hydrocarbons (HC) and carbon monoxide (CO) into harmless water (H_2O) and carbon dioxide (CO_2).

Air Pump Operation

The operation of the air injection and catalytic converter system, using an air pump is virtually the same as the air injected system, with the exception of the addition of a catalytic converter to the exhaust system. The air pump is used in place of the reed valve to inject a more positive force of fresh air into the exhaust gases. The electric control box may or may not be used in this type of system, along with the floor heat hazard warning system.

HEAT HAZARD WARNING SYSTEM

The heat hazard warning system is used to prevent potential heat hazard to the vehicle due to the excessive heat radiated from the exhaust system and the catalytic converter. A test system for the warning light is provided to warn the vehicle operator should the warning lamp circuit not operate. When the warning lamp is operating properly, it will come on when the ignition switch is turned on and go out when the engine is started. The warning temperature setting varies with vehicle models, but ranges from 212° to 302°F. Should the temperature rise and cause the heat hazard warning system to operate, the fresh or secondary air is directed from the exhaust system to deny the exhaust gases the fresh air to continue the combustion of the unburned elements in the exhaust system and the catalytic converter, which in turn, lowers the heat from the exhaust system.

CATALYTIC CONVERTERS

Various catalytic converter configurations are used from the monolithic (block type) to the pellet type, each containing, but not limited to, platinum, palladium and rhodium as the catalyst. The construction of the various converters differ, depending upon the vehicle model usage, but the main purposes of the units are to reduce the oxides of nitrogens (NO_x) and to oxidize the hydrocarbons (HC) and carbon monoxide (CO) into harmless water H_2O and carbon dioxide (CO_2).

Catalytic Converter Precautions

1. Unleaded fuel must be used to avoid contaminating the converter catalyst.
2. Do not park the vehicle over inflammable materials.
3. Do not operate the engine with the spark plug wires disconnected.
4. Do not coast the vehicle with the ignition switch turned off and the engine internal parts rotating.
5. Avoid driving with the choke control knob (manual) pulled out with the engine warmed up.

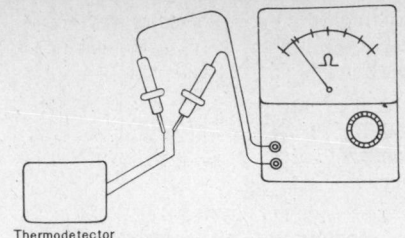

Testing the thermodetector

Deceleration Control System

ROTARY ENGINES

The deceleration control system is designed to maintain a balanced air/fuel mixture and to prevent excessive afterburn in the exhaust system. The system uses a deceleration control valve, idle switch and control unit. The deceleration control valve contains two valves: one, the anti-afterburn valve which prevents the fuel detonation and two, the coasting valve which compensates for the insufficient air/fuel mixtures. Both valves will allow fresh air to enter the intake manifold to prevent the exhaust afterburn, when the ignition switch is turned off. At the beginning of sudden deceleration, rich air/fuel mixture is present in the intake manifold and is supplied to the cylinders. This excessively rich mixture does not completely burn in the combustion chambers and when this unburned rich mixture is discharged into the exhaust manifold and the injected fresh air is mixed with it, an undesirable combustion type explosion occurs in the exhaust system. To prevent this occurence in the exhaust system, the anti-afterburn valve permits fresh air to enter the intake manifold upon sudden increase of the manifold vacuum and the fresh air mixes with the over-rich mixture of air and fuel, reducing the mixture to a combustible mixture so that it can be burned normally in the engine combustion chambers.

The system consists of the following.
1. Anti-afterburn valve—allows fresh air to enter the intake manifold.
2. Coasting valve—allows fresh air to enter the intake manifold.
3. Solenoids—when energized, close the air passages for the anti-afterburn and coasting valves air chambers.
4. Idle switch—detects decelerating conditions and cuts the electric current from the ignition switch to the coasting valve, through the control unit.
5. Control unit—detects the operational mode condition and sends the signals to the solenoids.

The afterburn and coasting valves operate under the following conditions.
1. When the ignition switch is turned off, the solenoids for the two valves are turned off, which allows the air chambers to open. Atmospheric pressure acts on the

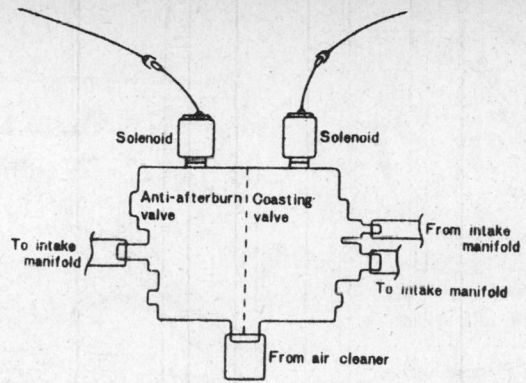

diaphragms to open the valves. As a result, fresh air is allowed to enter the intake manifold for a brief period of time.

NOTE: On California and Federal models with automatic transmissions, the coasting valve is closed and cannot operate.

2. Immediately after deceleration, the anti-afterburn valve is opened by a difference of pressures between the air chamber and the vacuum chamber. The solenoid on the valve is not off, but is turned on by the ignition switch being in the "ON" position. As the intake manifold pressure is increased, the diaphragm is pulled down and the valve is opened to supply fresh air to the intake manifold, momentarily. The metering orifice controls the time of valve operation (open) as the vacuum equalizes through the top of the diaphragm.

3. During deceleration over 1150 rpm of engine speed, the coasting valve is opened by the difference of pressure between the atmospheric pressure in the air chamber and the vacuum pressure in the vacuum chamber. The electrical signals from the idle switch and the control unit are not sent to the coasting valve solenoid, which allows the air passage to be opened to the air chamber of the coasting valve diaphragm. As a result, the coasting valve is opened by the pressure difference between the air chamber and the vacuum chamber, which in turn, allows air to enter the intake manifold.

When the engine speed decreases below 1150 rpm during the deceleration, the electrical signals from the idle switch and the control unit are sent to the solenoid on the coasting valve, closing the air passage and not allowing fresh air to enter the intake manifold.

Shutter Valve (1981 and Later)

To eliminate misfirings and the accompanying emissions of raw hydrocarbons (HC), which is a common characteristic of the early rotary engines, a shutter valve is installed in the primary intake passage for the rear rotor chamber and is closed by vacuum during deceleration and diverts the total air/fuel mixture through a bypass port and into the front rotor chamber. The front chamber continues to run with sufficient air/fuel mixture to eliminate engine misfiring. To avoid an abnormally high manifold vacuum from the rear chamber, a coasting valve, linked to the shutter valve, is opened as the shutter valve closes, allowing fresh air to enter the rear chamber and reducing the vacuum.

PISTON ENGINES

The deceleration control system used on the piston engines is designed to balance the air/fuel mixture during deceleration. The system utilizes an anti-afterburn valve to prevent afterburning of the rich mixture in the exhaust system and coasting richer valve

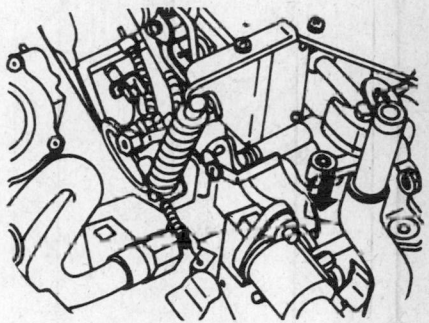

to compensate for lean (insufficient) air/fuel mixtures in automatic transmission equipped vehicles.

At the beginning of sudden deceleration, the engine air/fuel mixture is extremely rich and will not burn completely in the combustion chamber. This overrich mixture is discharged into the exhaust system and when mixed with the fresh air supplied by the air injection system, abnormal combustion and explosions occur within the exhaust system. To prevent this condition, the anti-afterburn valve allows fresh air to be routed to the intake manifold, diluting the overly rich mixture and allowing the mixture to be burned properly in the combustion chambers before entering the exhaust system.

Coasting Richer Valve (Automatic Transmission Equipped Only)

The coasting richer valve is attached to the carburetor and begins to operate during the deceleration and after the anti-afterburn valve has started its operation. The air/fuel mixture is extremely rich before the anti-afterburn valve operates, and after the valve has opened its passage and allowed fresh air to enter the manifold, the mixture becomes too lean. Should this occur, the mixture would not complete its combustion to burn the elements from the exhaust gases and the mixture being too lean, the air injected into the exhaust manifold would be of no value. To avoid this condition, a coasting richer valve, attached to the carburetor, opens and allows fuel passage to the secondary stage of the carburetor to supply an additional amount of fuel, to prevent the mixture from becoming too lean, so that the complete combustion of the mixture can take place in the combustion chambers and the emissions of hydrocarbons (HC) and carbon monoxide (CO) are reduced.

The operation of the coasting richer valve is controlled by the accelerator switch and the vehicle speed switch, and operates only for a duration while both switches are in the circuit for the coasting richer valve. The accelerator switch is mounted on the accelerator linkage and depressing the accelerator pedal opens the circuit. The speed

Combination anti-afterburn and coasting valve connections

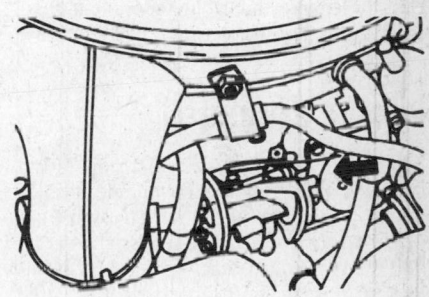

Arrow indicates the position of the anti-afterburn valve

Arrow indicates the position of the coasting valve

switch is mounted on the speedometer and operates when the speed is 16 ± 1.5 m.p.h. and over.

Throttle Opener System

ROTARY ENGINE

Dash Pot

The dash pot is used to slow the throttle valve return upon the release of the accelerator pedal. By slowing the throttle valve, a balanced air/fuel mixture is maintained to prevent engine misfire.

NOTE: Vehicles with automatic transmissions are not equipped with the dash pot or coasting valve, although an anti-afterburn valve is used.

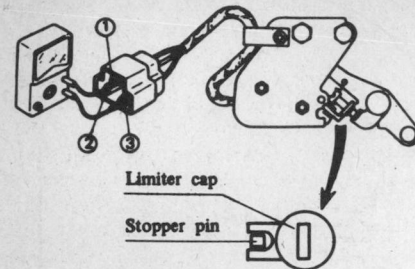

Limiter cap

Stopper pin

Adjusting the idle switch

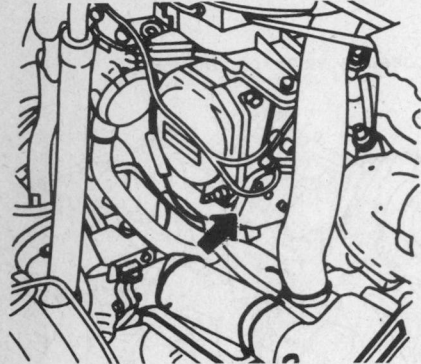

Idle switch position

Typical piston engine emission control system legend:

⇨ Fresh air
➡ Blow-by gas
⊨⇨ Exhaust gas
⇶⇨ Fuel and air mixture
---➤ Evaporative gas
⟶ Intake manifold vacuum

Typical piston engine emission control system

Coasting Valve

The coasting valve allows additional air to enter the intake manifold to prevent misfiring during the deceleration of the engine at speeds over 1150 rpm.

PISTON ENGINES

The throttle opener system is in operation during the deceleration of the engine at times of high engine vacuum, sensed by a vacuum control valve to open a passage so that engine vacuum can react on the servo-diaphragm to open the primary throttle valve slightly, to provide the additional richness to the lean air/fuel mixture. The diaphragm return spring of the vacuum control valve is set to start operating when the intake manifold vacuum exceeds 22.4 in. Hg. Under this vacuum setting, the throttle opener system does not operate, therefore controlling the system only on deceleration. An altitude corrector (bellows) in the vacuum control valve prevents varied responses due to the differences in atmospheric pressure at the different levels of altitude, by adjusting the diaphragm return spring to the proper tension.

NOTE: Canadian vehicles equipped with the throttle opener system operate above 22.0 in. Hg and do not have the altitude correction bellows included in the vacuum control valve.

Dash Pot

The dash pot is used to maintain a balanced air/fuel mixture during gearshifting to prevent excessive hydrocarbons (HC), to ac-cumulate during the deceleration of the engine when the accelerator is released, and to allow the throttle valve to gradually return to normal idle.

A combination of spring pressure and air pressure is used to operate the dash pot. A metered orifice with a check valve connects the two chambers of the dash pot diaphragm with a spring operated assist against the diaphragm and stem during acceleration, to move the stem towards the throttle lever of the carburetor. When the throttle lever is released by the release of the accelerator pedal and the tension of the throttle return spring overcomes the diaphragm return spring pressure, the stem and diaphragm are moved into the dash pot. The metered air orifice connecting the two chambers in the dash pot diaphragm, controls the rate of movement of the stem. The duration of the rod movement of 0.18 in. with a 2.4 lb. load on the stem, is 0.8 seconds, approximately.

Exhaust Gas Recirculation (EGR) System

The increase of exhaust temperatures also increases the emissions of oxides of nitrogen (NO_x) from the exhaust gases. The EGR system is used to dilute the air/fuel mixture in the intake manifold with a small percentage of exhaust gas. The exhaust gas does not burn, but absorbs some of the combustion heat to lower the emissions of NO_x.

1. The EGR system consists of the EGR

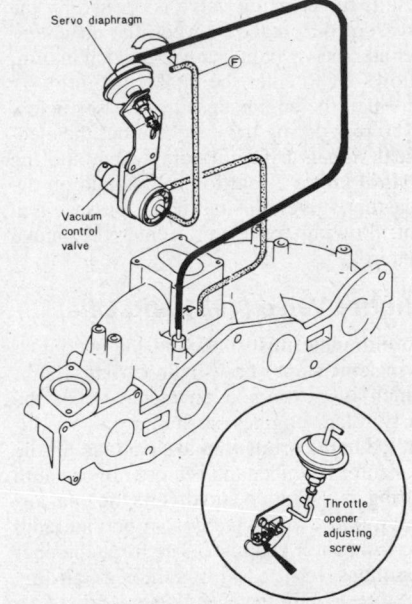

GLC servo diaphragm check; "F" is the vacuum sensing tube. If the idle speed increases to 1400 rpm, the system is ok.

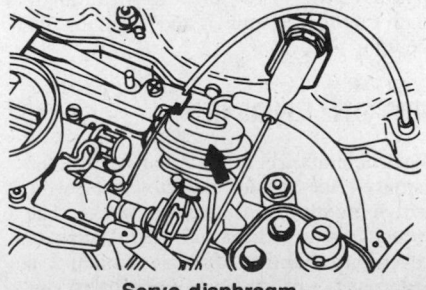

Servo diaphragm

control valve, three way solenoid valve and water temperature switch. The EGR valve is a cone type valve and meters the exhaust gases into the intake manifold in response to the varying vacuum signals of the engine. The three way solenoid valve closes the vacuum line leading to the EGR valve when the coolant temperature is lower than approximately 131°F to provide good driveability of the vehicle when cold. The system operates only on acceleration.

2. EGR relay is used to open or close the electrical current from the number one vacuum switch to the EGR solenoid, accordingly to the signals of the water temperature switch or control unit.

3. The EGR solenoid opens the vacuum sensing passage to the EGR valve when the electrical current is directed from the Number one vacuum switch through the EGR relay.

4. The number one vacuum switch and number one delay valve detect the condition of acceleration by using intake manifold vacuum.

5. The control unit sends the electrical signal to the EGR relay, from the choke switch, according to driving conditions.

Federal Models With Automatic Transmission

The EGR relay is controlled by the water temperature switch. When the temperature of the coolant is higher than 140°F, the relay is allowed to be turned on.

California Models With Automatic Transmission

The EGR relay is controlled by the water temperature switch and control unit so that the relay turns on to close the circuit from the number one vacuum switch to the EGR solenoid, when the engine coolant temperature is more than 140°F or after 130 seconds from starting the engine with the choke knob pulled out.

EGR WARNING SYSTEM

This system is used to alert the operator to either perform or have performed, the EGR maintenance service on the system. A warning lamp on the dashboard will illuminate every 12,500 miles of operation.

To reset the EGR maintenance interval detector, located under the left side of the dash panel, simply reverse the connector to the detector terminals.

Piston Engines

The EGR system used on the piston engines consists of the EGR valve, three way solenoid valve and a coolant temperature switch. The EGR control valve is used to modulate the exhaust gas flow into the intake manifold in response to the varying vacuum signal of the intake manifold when the vehicle is in the acceleration mode. The system is not in operation when the coolant

temperature is less than 131°F. When the coolant temperature is lower than 131°F, the three-way solenoid valve is energized to close the vacuum passage between the three-way valve and the EGR valve. When the coolant temperature is over 131°F, the three-way switch is de-energized and the passage from the three-way solenoid valve to the EGR valve is opened so that vacuum from the carburetor acts on the EGR valve diaphragm to open the EGR valve stem, to allow the exhaust gas to enter the intake manifold.

NOTE: At engine idle and full throttle, the exhaust gas is not mixed with the air/fuel mixture, so that full power and a smooth idle can be obtained.

A vacuum amplifier is used on certain vehicles used in the state of California. The purpose of the vacuum amplifier is to increase or amplify the weak vacuum signal from the carburetor venturi and to give a more positive vacuum signal to the EGR valve.

Automatic Choke Release System

ROTARY ENGINE

Type 1

The automatic choke release system controls the opening and the closing of the choke valve in the air horn of the carburetor, to provide the correct air/fuel mixture at the time of engine start-up. The choke valve is operated manually to restrict the air flow through the carburetor and remains closed while the engine is cranking. As soon as the engine has started, the choke valve opens slightly to allow more air to enter the air horn so as to correct the air/fuel mixture. The choke valve is opened slightly by a vacuum diaphragm and the force of a bi-metal spring. The tension of the bi-metal spring is weakened by the electrical circuit flowing through the choke switch to the choke heater, when the choke lever is pulled.

It should be noted that when the engine is being cranked the intake manifold vacuum is so low that the vacuum diaphragm does not operate. When the engine starts a high intake manifold vacuum is created and is routed to the vacuum diaphragm to open the choke valve in a preset manner. As the carburetor heater for the choke bi-metal spring is heated, the choke valve is gradually opened. This prevents an overly rich mixture during start-ups or while driving with the choke knob pulled out.

Type 2
FEDERAL

To avoid excessively high temperatures in the thermal reactor from an overly rich air/fuel mixture during the engine warm-up period, the manually operated choke control

pull rod is held in place by an electrical magnet, when the coolant temperature is below a specified degree and is released automatically when the coolant temperature rises above the specified degree, governed by a coolant temperature switch.

The choke operation is basically the same as the choke mechanism used on many piston engines, but with wiring differences. The type two rotary engine choke magnet is grounded through the choke switch case or from a case connector lead to ground, while the piston engine choke magnet is grounded through the coolant temperature switch.

CALIFORNIA

To more closely control the automatically returned choke valve to the vertical position, to avoid excessive high temperatures to be developed in the thermal reactor due to an overly rich air/fuel mixture, in addition to the controls of the federal vehicle choke assembly, the following components are required in the state of California.

1. The full choke magnet switch which controls the electric current to the choke magnet according to the number two vacuum switch operation.

2. Number two vacuum switch which stops the electric current to the full choke switch.

3. Number two delay valve which controls the number two vacuum switch operating time.

When the choke knob is pulled half way out, the operation is the same as the Federal choke operation. With the control knob pulled all the way out and the ignition switch turned on, the electric current flows to the choke magnet and holds the control rod in the full closed position. After approximately 30 seconds from engine starting, the vacuum switch cuts or stops the current between the ignition switch and the choke magnet according to the intake manifold vacuum and the choke knob is forcibly returned to the "OFF" position.

PISTON ENGINES

To avoid having the choke valve on for a long period of time and causing an overly rich air/fuel mixture, the choke control pull rod is held in place by an electrical magnet, wired in series with a coolant temperature switch, with the electrical current controlled by the ignition switch. The choke control pull rod can be controlled manually by the vehicle operator, when the magnet is in use.

With the coolant temperature below 131°F, the coolant switch is on and current is allowed to move from the ignition switch, to the magnet and to the temperature switch, energizing the magnet and holding the choke control pull rod in the "ON" position, as set by the operator. As the coolant temperature rises over 131°F the coolant temperature switch contacts open and the flow of electrical current is interrupted, causing

the magnetic field to collapse and release the choke control pull rod. Internal linkage forces the rod to move to the "OFF" position and allows the choke valve to open, thereby allowing more air to enter the carburetor and preventing the air/fuel mixture from becoming too rich.

Intake Air Temperature Control System

ROTARY ENGINES

This system is designed to keep the temperature of the air drawn into the carburetor as even as possible, regardless of the ambient temperature.

When the temperature of the intake air is more than 45°F, the bimetal strip connected to the air duct valve begins to operate. It closes the cold air intake from the engine compartment area and opens the hot air intake from the thermal reactor area.

When the temperature is more than 115°F, the bimetal strip connected to the air duct valve again begins to operate. The hot air duct from the thermal reactor is closed and the duct from the engine compartment is opened to allow the colder air to enter the air cleaner assembly and carburetor.

PISTON ENGINES

Both a thermostat type and a vacuum operated type flapper valve arrangement is used on the piston engine carburetors to control the temperature of the induction air.

The vacuum operated valve has a metered amount of vacuum to operate the flapper valve when cold and a thermostatic valve to overcome the metered vacuum pressure to open the flapper valve when warm.

The fully thermostatic operated flapper valve is controlled by the temperature of the inducted air flowing through the intake tube, to either close or open the air ducts.

Fuel Enrichment System

ROTARY ENGINES

Richer Solenoid

This system is used in two different modes of operation, depending upon the area and the transmission equipment. The richer solenoid is used on Federal and California vehicles, equipped with manual transmissions. The purpose of the system is to supply additional fuel to the intake manifold to prevent engine misfire during the deceleration mode, with engine speeds greater than 1150 rpm. This additional fuel maintains a balanced air/fuel mixture during the deceleration.

During the deceleration over 1150 rpm, the electric signal from the control unit is

sent to the richer solenoid through the idle switch, causing the richer solenoid to open and supply the additional fuel to the intake manifold.

As the engine speed decreases to below 1150 rpm during deceleration, the electrical signal is stopped by the low speed switch in the control unit, and the additional fuel is cut off from entering the intake manifold.

Power Valve Solenoid

This system is used on Federal vehicles using automatic transmissions and on California vehicles using manual or automatic transmissions. The power valve solenoid for California vehicles differs in its function and operation, from that used on the Federal and Canada vehicles. The solenoid appearance is the same, but the timing of the opening and closing of the valve differs.

CALIFORNIA

The power valve solenoid closes the vacuum passage to the power valve so that the additional fuel can be supplied from the power valve to the intake manifold at the following times.

1. When accelerating in any gear except 4th and 5th at any engine speed of 1150 to 3000 rpm.

2. When accelerating over 4600 rpm and when the engine is 1150 to 4600 rpm within 130 seconds from the initial engine starting with the choke used.

FEDERAL AND CANADA

The power valve closes the vacuum passage leading to the power valve during acceleration so that the additional fuel is supplied by the power valve to the intake manifold.

Idle Compensation System

ROTARY ENGINES

The need to stabilize the engine idle under various operating conditions are required and an idle compensator and throttle opener are used.

Idle Compensator

The idle compensator is used to supply a small amount of air into the intake manifold under extremely hot conditions, through an opening of a bimetal valve, located in the carburetor air cleaner, with the air routed to the intake manifold by a tube or hose. The compensator valve opens when the inlet air temperature reaches and exceeds 149°F.

Throttle Opener

The throttle opener system is used to improve the idle stability of an engine in an air condition equipped vehicle with the air conditioning turned on and the engine speed under 1150 rpm.

The system consists of a control unit, housing a low speed switch, an air conditioning relay, an air conditioning solenoid valve and a throttle opener.

When the idle speed is below 1150 rpm and the air conditioning is turned on, current is routed through the low speed switch and the air conditioning relay, to the air conditioning solenoid. As the solenoid is energized, the vacuum passage between the throttle opener and the intake manifold is opened, allowing vacuum to act upon the diaphragm inside the throttle opener. The movement of the diaphragm is controlled and the linkage connecting the diaphragm stem to the throttle valve is moved, causing the primary throttle valve to open slightly more than at idle, causing an increase in the engine rpm and preventing stalling out of the engine.

Kickdown Control System

ROTARY ENGINE

The purpose of the kickdown system is to increase the engine speed when the choke knob is pulled out, by having the automatic transmission in a reduction gear.

When the choke valve is pulled out, the choke switch allows electrical current to flow to the kickdown relay and operates the kickdown valve in the transmission. When the choke knob is released, the transmission is allowed to up-shift into the higher gear ratios.

NOTE: This system is related to the shifting operation of the transmission and not to any other emission control system or device.

Ignition Control System

ROTARY ENGINES

California Models

The ignition control system is used to warm-up the thermal reactor quickly by controlling the operation of the leading and trailing ignition systems.

The methods of ignition controls are as follows.

1. The leading spark plug ignition only (normal and retarded modes).

2. Both leading or trailing spark plug ignition.

The system consists of the following.

1. Trailing ignition relay—controls the trailing ignition circuit.

2. Retard relay—selects the flow of electrical current sent from the leading or trailing coil when the choke knob is pulled out. Usually the leading coil will be connected to the trailing contact points and the trailing coil will be disconnected from the circuit.

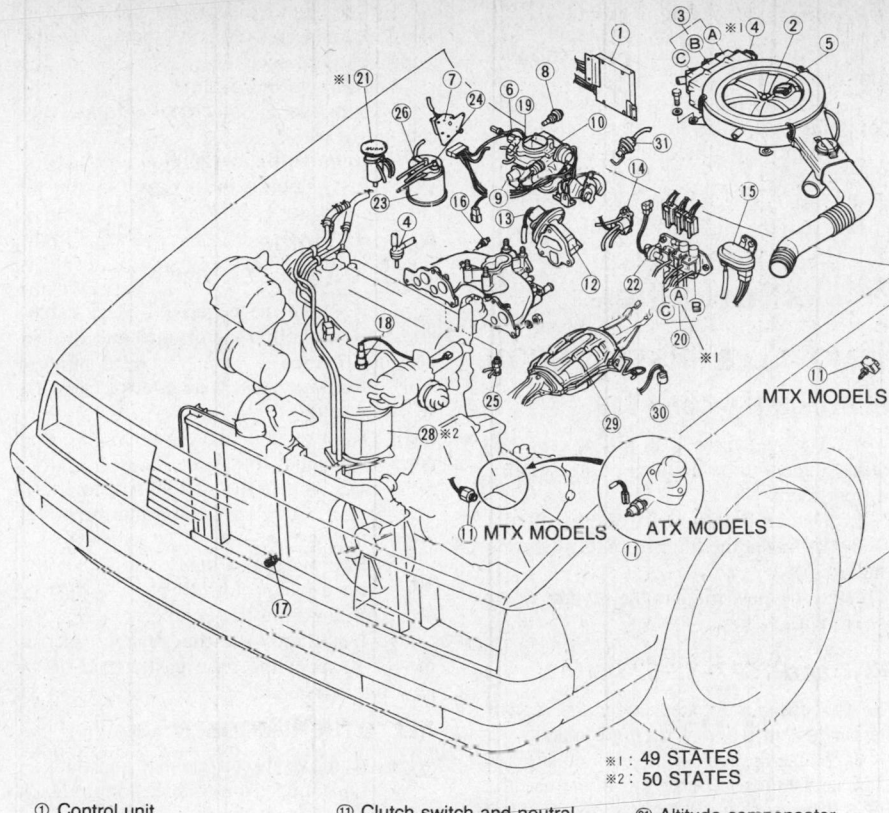

MTX MODELS

MTX MODELS **ATX MODELS**

※1 : 49 STATES
※2 : 50 STATES

① Control unit	⑪ Clutch switch and neutral switch	㉑ Altitude compensator
② Air cleaner	⑫ E.G.R. valve	㉒ Vacuum switch
③ Reed valve	⑬ E.G.R. position sensor	㉓ Canister
④ No. 1 ACV	⑭ Duty solenoid valve	㉔ Purge control valve No.1
No. 2 ACV *1	⑮ Vacuum sensor	㉕ Water thermo valve
⑤ Idle compensator valve	⑯ Water thermo sensor	㉖ Purge control valve No.2
⑥ Air vent solenoid valve	⑰ Water thermo switch	㉗ Check valve
⑦ Idle switch	⑱ O₂ sensor	㉘ Front catalyst
⑧ Dashpot	⑲ A/F solenoid valve	㉙ Rear catalyst
⑨ Coasting richer solenoid	⑳ Three-way solenoid valve	㉚ Power steering switch
⑩ Slow fuel cut solenoid valve		㉛ Servo diaphragm

1983 and later 626 emission control components

3. Idle, choke and overdrive switch—detects the specific conditions such as, deceleration, cold starting or cruising in overdrive. Each electrical signal is sent to the control unit separately.

4. Vacuum control valve—closes the vacuum sensing tube to the trailing vacuum diaphragm, so that under a cold condition, no vacuum advance will occur at the trailing contact points.

5. Control unit—sends the electrical signal to the trailing ignition relay and retard relay.

RETARDED LEADING IGNITION

The following conditions must occur simultaneously to retard the leading ignition timing. When this happens, there is no trailing ignition.

1. Within 130 seconds after the engine starting, with the choke knob pulled out, except during engine deceleration (choke switch and timer are "ON" and idle switch is "OFF").

2. Engine speed is over 1150 rpm and under 4600 rpm.

NOTE: If the choke knob is pushed back in during the 130 seconds, the engine idle speed should be over 1150 and under 4000 rpm.

NORMAL LEADING IGNITION CALIFORNIA MODELS WITH AUTOMATIC TRANSMISSIONS

To have normal leading ignition, the following conditions must occur simultaneously.

1. Engine speed is over 1150 and under 2500 rpm, except while in a deceleration condition.

2. The time span should be more than 130 seconds when the choke knob is pulled out (timer "OFF").

CALIFORNIA MODELS WITH MANUAL TRANSMISSION

To have normal leading ignition, the following conditions must occur simultaneously.

1. Engine speed over 1150 and under 3000 rpm, except while in a deceleration mode.

2. The time span should be more than 130 seconds when the choke knob is pulled out (timer "OFF").

BOTH LEADING AND TRAILING SPARK PLUG IGNITION

The leading and trailing spark plugs will ignite when the trailing ignition relay is "ON", the retard relay is deactivated and the following conditions are occurring.

1. When the engine speed is lower than 1150 rpm and the timer is "OFF".

2. During deceleration.

3. When the engine speed is more than 3000 rpm (manual transmission) or 2500 rpm (automatic transmission) after 130 seconds from starting with the choke knob pulled out or in cases of starting without the choke.

4. During operation of the engine while the transmission is in overdrive gear (5th—manual transmission).

5. When starting the engine with the choke knob pulled out during the 130 seconds and the engine speed is over 4600 rpm.

NOTE: Should the choke knob be pushed back in within the 130 seconds, the engine speed will be altered to 4000 rpm.

PISTON ENGINES

Federal With Electronic Ignition and Manual Transmission

The ignition control system retards or advances the ignition timing as required, with the engine operating under certain conditions. The system consists of a top switch, accelerator switch and the transistorized ignition system. The timing advances normally when the accelerator and top switches are in the "OFF" position and retards when the switches are in the "ON" position.

The accelerator switch is "ON" when the accelerator pedal is depressed to ¾ of its travel, while the top switch is on when the transmission is in the 1st, 2nd, 3rd or reverse gear positions.

Federal and Canada With Dual Point Distributors

The system consists of a dual point distributor, containing a retard and an advance (normal) set of ignition points, a vehicle speed switch (Federal) or a water temperature switch (Canada) to control the retard or advanced sets of ignition points during the operation.

The operating conditions are as follows.

1. The advanced set of ignition points operate when the vehicle speed is higher than 42 mph (Federal) or when the coolant temperature is more than 112–140°F (Canada).

2. The retard set of ignition points operate when the vehicle speed is lower than 42 mph (Federal) or when the coolant temperature is lower than 122–140°F (Canada).

FUEL SYSTEM

Electric Fuel Pump

REMOVAL & INSTALLATION

All Except 1979–1982 626, RX-7, and Station Wagons

1. Remove the rear inside trim panel.
2. Disconnect the wiring and the fuel lines.
3. Remove the pump.
4. Installation is the reverse of removal.

Station Wagons

1. Remove the left-hand cargo compartment trim panel.
2. Disconnect the wiring and fuel lines.
3. Remove the pump.
4. Installation is the reverse of removal.

1979–82 626

1. Disconnect the negative battery cable at the battery.
2. Disconnect the fuel pump lead wire in the luggage compartment.
3. Raise the vehicle and support with jack stands.
4. Disconnect the fuel pump bracket.
5. Disconnect the fuel inlet and outlet hoses and remove the fuel pump.
6. Installation is the reverse of removal.

RX-7

1. Remove the rear floor mat and floor plate.
2. Disconnect the fuel pump electrical connection under the floor plate.
3. Raise the car and support it on jack stands.
4. Remove the fuel pump protecting cover. Remove inlet and outlet lines. Remove the pump.
   Installation is the reverse of removal.

Mechanical Fuel Pump

The mechanical fuel pump is mounted on the right front side of the engine block.

NOTE: The 1981 and later GLC fuel pump is mounted on the left side of the intake manifold.

REMOVAL & INSTALLATION

GLC

1. Slide the two fuel line clips from the pump inlet and outlet hoses. Remove the hoses.
2. Remove the fuel pump mounting bolts and remove the pump, gasket and spacer.
3. The installation is the reverse of the removal procedure.

1983 and Later 626

1. Remove the fuel inlet and return hoses from the pump.
2. Remove the fuel outlet hose and two fuel pump-to-engine attaching bolts.
3. Remove the fuel pump, two gaskets and a spacer.
4. Installation is the reverse off removal. Start the engine and check for leaks.

Fuel Filter

REMOVAL & INSTALLATION

All Except RX-7 and 626

1. The fuel filter is an in-line type, located under the hood in the engine compartment.
2. Detach both hoses from the filter.
3. Unfasten the filter from its mounting bracket.
   Install the new filter in the reverse order of removal.

RX-7 and 1977–82 626

The fuel filter is located under the rear of the car just in front of the fuel tank.

1. Raise the rear of the car and support it on jackstands. Locate the filter; use the illustration as a guide to its shape.
2. Loosen the clips at both ends of the filter and place a collection pan beneath it to catch any of the fuel that is in the lines.
3. Disconnect the fuel filter lines and remove the filter from its retainer.
4. Install the new filter, paying close attention to the direction of the filter in relation to the direction of fuel flow. See the illustration for correct positioning.
5. Turn the starter to ON to activate the fuel pump and check the fuel filter connections for leaks.

NOTE: If the filter is held by spring tension clamps, it would be wise to replace them with new clamps when the filter is changed.

1983 and Later 626

The fuel filter is located in the engine compartment, next to the driver's side shock tower.

1. Remove the screw and wire retaining bracket.
2. Remove the inlet and outlet fuel lines.

NOTE: Install the filter in the proper direction.

Carburetor

REMOVAL & INSTALLATION

Rotary Engine

1. Remove the air cleaner.
2. Detach the choke and accelerator cables.

3. Label and disconnect the fuel and vacuum lines and plug the main fuel line to prevent leakage.
4. Remove the oil line.
5. Remove all electrical wiring from carburetor.
6. Remove the carburetor.
7. Installation is the reverse of removal.

Piston Engine

1983 AND LATER 626

1. Remove the negative battery cable.
2. Remove the air cleaner and the accelerator cable.
3. Remove the cruise control cable (if so equipped).
4. Remove the vacuum hoses and disconnect the fuel line.
5. Disconnect the air/fuel solenoid harness at the wiring connector and the bullet connector.
6. Remove the carburetor and cover the inlet with a clean cloth to prevent dust or dirt from entering the engine.
7. Installation is the reverse of removal. Inspect the base gasket and use a new one if needed.

ALL OTHER MODELS

1. Remove the air cleaner and duct.
2. Disconnect the accelerator shaft.
3. Disconnect the fuel supply and fuel return lines.
4. Disconnect the leads from the throttle solenoid and deceleration valve at the quick-disconnects.
5. Disconnect the throttle return spring.
6. Disconnect the choke cable.
7. Remove the carburetor.
8. Installation is the reverse of removal.

ACCELERATOR LINKAGE ADJUSTMENT

All Models

1. Check the pedal position. The accelerator pedal should be lower than the brake pedal.

Accelerator Pedal Specifications

Model	Distance below brake pedal—in.
Rotary Pickup	2.3
Cosmo	2.2
RX-3SP	1.6
RX-4	1.6
GLC	1.6
RX-7	1.7–0.2
626:	
1979–82	1.7–0.2
1983 & later	①

① The throttle valve fully open with pedal depressed to floor

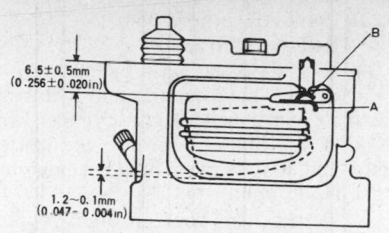

Piston engine float adjustment: bend tab "A" to adjust float drop and bend tab "B" to adjust float level

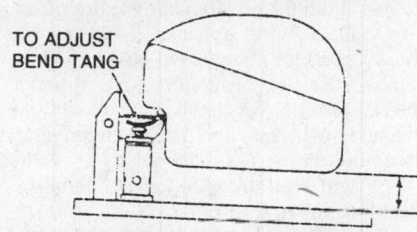

Float level adjustment, float bowl inverted and gasket installed

2. If necessary, adjust the nut on the linkage above the pedal to obtain the proper height.

3. Check the free-play of the cable at the carburetor. It should be 0.04–0.12 in. If not, adjust by turning the clevis nut.

FLOAT AND FUEL LEVEL ADJUSTMENTS

RX-3SP

1. Bend the float stop to adjust the fuel amount through the needle valve. Distance between lowest part of the float and lower air horn face should be 2.1–2.2 in.

2. Invert the air horn (float seat lip contacting needle valve).

3. The distance between float and the surface of the air horn gasket should be 0.47 in.

4. Bend the float seat lip in order to adjust the float setting.

RX-4 and Cosmo

1. With the engine running, check the fuel level in the sight glass, using a mirror.

2. If the fuel levels are not within the specified marks on the sight glass, remove the air horn with the floats.

3. Invert the air horn and let the float hang so that it just contacts the needle valve.

4. Measure the clearance between float and the air horn gasket, which should be 0.100 in. Bend the float seat lip to adjust the clearance if necessary.

1300, 1415, 1490 and 1970cc Engine

1. Remove the carburetor air horn assembly.

2. Invert the air horn and allow the float to hang so that the needle valve contacts the seat.

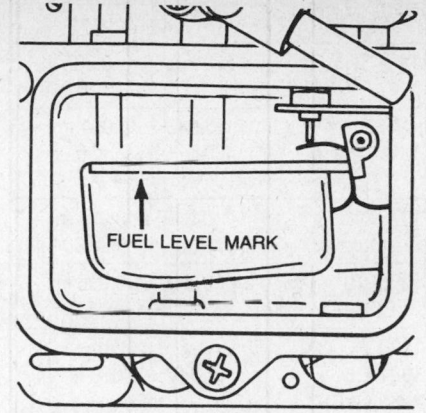

Fuel level mark on sight glass: piston engine

3. Measure the clearance between the float and the air horn without the air horn gasket in place.

4. The clearance should be 0.433 in., except for 1983 and later 626, which is 0.394 in.

5. Adjust by bending the float seat lip.

6. Reassemble and recheck idle.

RX-7

1. Remove the carburetor air horn assembly.

2. Invert the air horn to a position with the float facing upward. The air horn gasket surface must be level. Place the air horn on a carburetor work stand, if available, in order to insure a level position.

3. The distance between the float and the air horn gasket should be 0.63 ± 0.02 in., measured at the top of the float.

4. Install the air horn assembly.

FLOAT DROP

RX-4, Cosmo and RX-3SP

1. Remove the air horn with the floats and allow the floats to hang free.

2. Measure the clearance between the bottom of the float and the air horn gasket. The clearance should be 2.05 in. (2.13 RX-3).

3. If not, adjust the distance by bending the float stop.

GLC

1. With the air horn inverted, lift the float and measure the clearance between the float seat lip and the needle valve.

2. The clearance should be 0.051–0.067 in.

3. Adjust the clearance by bending the float stopper.

1979–80 626 w/1970cc Engine

1. With the engine running, check fuel level in the fuel bowl sight glass.

2. When the fuel level is not at the specified level on the sight glass, remove the carburetor from the vehicle.

3. Remove the fuel bowl sight glass.

4. Invert the carburetor on a stand and allow the float to lower by its own weight.

5. Measure the clearance from the float to the bowl.

6. Bend the float seat lip until a clearance of 8.5mm (0.335 in.) is obtained.

7. Turn the carburetor to its normal position and the float should drop by its own weight.

8. Set the clearance between the bottom of the float and the bowl at 1.0mm (0.039 in.).

9. Install the sight glass on the carburetor.

10. Install the carburetor on the engine.

11. Operate the engine and check for the specified level of fuel at the sight glass.

1981 and Later 626 w/1970cc Engine

1. Measure the distance between the bottom of the float and the air horn bowl. The distance should be 1.811 in. Bend the float stopper to adjust.

2. Turn the air horn to the normal position and allow the float to lower by its own weight.

RX-7

1. Remove the carburetor air horn assembly.

2. Position the air horn in the normal installed position. The air horn gasket surface should be level.

3. The float should be in a fully dropped position. Measure the distance between the lowest part of the float and the air horn gasket.

4. The measured distance should be 2.0 ± 0.02 in. If the distance is not correct, bend the tab on the float to obtain the correct distance.

5. Install the air horn.

FAST IDLE CAM ADJUSTMENT

All Except 1415, 1490 and 1970 cc Engine

1. Remove the carburetor from the engine.

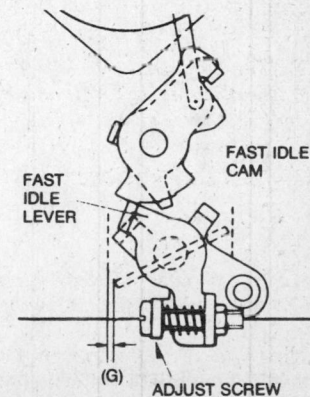

Fast idle cam adjustment—1970 cc engine

C437

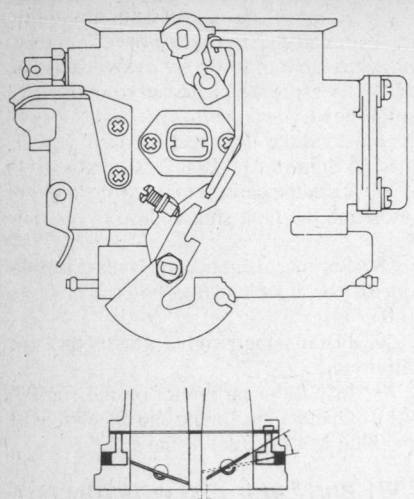

Fast idle adjustments: measure the angle "A" and clearance "B"—rotary engines

2. With the choke valve fully closed, adjust the clearance between the primary throttle valve and the wall of the throttle bore by bending the connecting rod between the choke valve and the throttle valve to the following specifications:

1415, 1490 and 1970cc Engines

1. On the 1415cc engine, remove the bi-metal cover.
2. Using your fingers, close the choke valve fully.
3. Make sure the fast idle cam is on the first position. (Third position-GLC with 1490cc engine).
4. Check the clearance at the throttle valve opening and adjust by turning the adjustment screw.

1998cc Engine

1. Set the fast idle cam on the second position.
2. Adjust the throttle valve clearance by turning the adjusting screw.

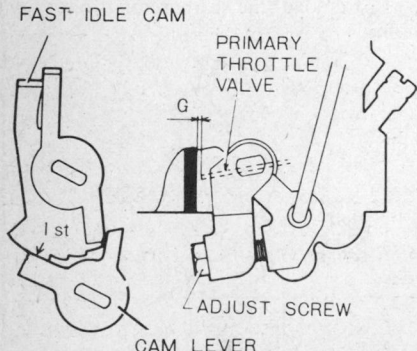

Fast idle cam adjustment showing cam lever in the first position (see text)—1415, and 1490 cc engine

Year/Model	Clearances
RX-3 SP	MT-0.079 ± 0.008 in. (Calif. AT 0.087 ± 0.008 in.)
1978 RX-4	0.043 ± 0.004 in. (Calif. 0.056 ± 0.056 ± 0.004 in.)
1978 Cosmo	0.043 ± 0.004 in. (Calif. 0.056 ± 0.004 in.)
1978–79 GLC	0.054 ± 0.006 in.
1980 GLC	0.043 in.
1981 GLC	0.048–0.060 in.
1982 GLC	0.067 in.
1983–84 GLC	0.0343–0.0035 in.
1983 GLC wagon	0.031–0.038 in.
1979–80 626	0.019–0.026 in. (U.S.A.) 0.035–0.049 in. (Canada)
1981 626	0.019–0.026 in.
1982 626	0.018–0.030 in.
1983–84 626	0.028–0.043 in.
1979 RX-7	0.051–0.059 in. (Calif.) 0.035–0.040 in. (49 states and Canada)
1980 RX-7	0.051–0.059 in. (U.S.A.) 0.035–0.040 in. (Canada)
1981–82 RX-7	0.031–0.039 in.
1983–84 RX-7	0.040–0.047 in.

OVERHAUL

For all carburetor overhaul procedures please refer to "Carburetor Service" in the Unit Repair section.

Fuel Injection

For all fuel injection service and adjustment procedures, please refer to "Fuel Injection" in the Unit Repair section.

MANUAL TRANSMISSION

REMOVAL & INSTALLATION

NOTE: The GLC (front wheel drive) and the 1983 and later 626 are detailed in the "Manual Transaxle" section.

All Except GLC (Rear Wheel Drive) and 1979–83 626

1. Remove the console over the shift lever.
2. Remove the floor mat.
3. Remove shift lever.
4. Tie the clutch release cylinder up out of the way. Do not disconnect the hydraulic line from the clutch release cylinder. On RX-4, RX-7 models, remove the starter motor and loosen the 3 upper engine-to-transmission bolts.
5. Detach the back-up light switch multiconnector which is located near the clutch release cylinder. On RX-4s, RX-7s, remove the brake booster vacuum line bracket from the clutch housing.
6. Drain the oil. Remove the driveshaft.
7. Detach the exhaust pipe from the thermal reactor flange. On RX-4 models, remove the heat insulators first. Remove the converter cover, brackets and lower the exhaust pipe (rear) and the pellet converter assembly on the RX-7 models.
8. Unfasten the speedometer cable.
9. Remove the starter.
10. Support the transmission.
11. Unbolt the transmission support.
12. Remove the bolts which retain the bell housing.
13. Carefully slide the transmission rearward until the input shaft has cleared the clutch disc.
14. Lower the transmission.
15. Transmission installation is the reverse of removal. Align the clutch plate with an arbor or an old input shaft. Adjust the clutch and shift linkage as detailed elsewhere. Refill the transmission with gear oil.

GLC (Rear Wheel Drive)

1. Disconnect the negative (−) battery cable.
2. Put the transmission in neutral and remove the shift lever.
3. Remove the two upper bolts from the clutch housing.
4. Raise the vehicle and support it securely on axle stands or a lift.
5. Drain the transmission oil and replace the plug.
6. Remove the driveshaft, and plug or cover the hole in the extension housing.
7. Disconnect the speedometer cable and back-up light switch wires.
8. Disconnect the exhaust pipe hanger from the bracket on the clutch housing.
9. Remove the exhaust pipe support bracket from the clutch housing. Disconnect the clutch cable at the release lever.
10. Remove the lower clutch housing cover.
11. Remove the starter electrical connections, remove the bolts, and remove the starter.
12. Disconnect the exhaust pipe hanger at the extension housing.
13. Place a jack under the engine, using a block of wood to protect the oil pan. Make sure the jack can securely support the weight of the engine.
14. Disconnect the transmission support member at the transmission.
15. Remove transmission-to-engine attaching bolts.

16. Carefully slide the transmission rearward until the input shaft has cleared the clutch disc, and lower it out of the car.

17. In installation, reverse above procedures, aligning the clutch plate with an arbor or old input shaft. Adjust clutch and shift linkage. Refill the transmission with the proper grade of gear oil.

1979–82 626

1. Remove the gearshift lever knob.
2. Remove the console box.
3. Remove the gearshift lever boot and the gearshift lever.
4. Disconnect the negative battery cable.
5. Raise the vehicle and support it with jack stands.
6. Drain the transmission lubricant.
7. Disconnect the propeller shaft.
8. Disconnect the exhaust pipe hanger.
9. Remove the starter motor.
10. Disconnect the back-up switch wire.
11. Disconnect the speedometer cable.
12. Place a jack under the engine, protecting the oil pan with a block of wood.
13. Remove the transmission attaching bolts and remove the transmission.
14. Transmission installation is performed in the reverse order of removal. Align the clutch plate with an old arbor or an old input shaft. Add lubricant until the level reaches the bottom of the filler plug hole.

SHIFT LEVER ADJUSTMENT

The shift lever may be adjusted during transmission installation by means of the adjusting shims on the three bolts between the cover plate and the packing. The force required to move the shift knob should be 4 4–8.8 lbs.

OVERHAUL

For all transmission overhaul procedures, please refer to "Manual Transmission Overhaul" in the Unit Repair section.

MANUAL TRANSAXLE

REMOVAL & INSTALLATION

1983 and Later 626

1. Disconnect the negative battery cable and remove the speedometer cable from the transaxle.
2. Remove the clutch cable bracket mounting bolts, and disconnect the clutch cable from the release lever.
3. Remove the ground wire and wiring harness clip.
4. Remove the starter.
5. Install the engine support 49–G030–

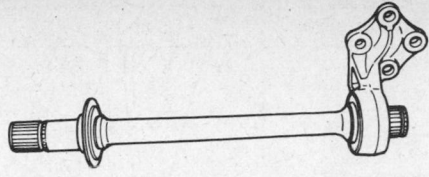

Joint shaft—1983 and later 626

025 or equivalent and support the weight of the engine on the hook.

6. Remove the transaxle–to–engine mounting bolts.
7. Jack up the vehicle and support it with jackstands. Drain the transaxle oil.
8. Remove the front wheels and the splash shields.
9. Remove the stabilizer bar control link. Remove the under cover (if so equipped).
10. Remove the lower arm ball joint and the knuckle coupling bolt, pull the arm downward and separate the lower arm from the knuckle.
11. Remove the driver's side drive shaft from the transaxle.

   a. Insert a lever between the driveshaft and the transaxle case. Tap the end of the lever to uncouple the driveshaft from the differential side gear.

CAUTION

Do not insert the lever too deeply between the shaft and the case or the oil seal lip could be damaged.

---

   b. Pull the front hub forward and separate the driveshaft from the transaxle.

CAUTION

To avoid damage to the oil seal, hold the CV joint at the differential with one hand and pull the driveshaft straight out.

---

12. Remove the passenger side driveshaft and joint shaft.

   a. Insert a lever between the driveshaft and the joint shaft. Pry the lever to uncouple the shafts.

   b. Pull the front hub forward and then separate the driveshaft from the joint shaft.

   c. Remove the joint shaft bracket mounting bolts. Remove the joint shaft and bracket from the transaxle as an assembly.

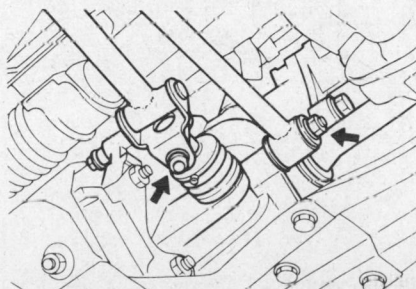

Shift change control rod and extension bar on 1983 and later 626 with manual transaxle

13. Remove the transaxle mounting bracket nuts at the crossmember.
14. Remove the crossmember and the left lower arm as an assembly.
15. Separate the shift change control rod from the shift change rod.
16. Remove the shift control extension bar from the transaxle. Remove the transaxle undercover.
17. Attach a rope to the transaxle mount bracket at two places and to the engine support.
18. Place a board on a garage floor jack and use this to support the transaxle.

CAUTION

Try to center the weight of the transaxle on the board.

---

19. Remove the two remaining transaxle–to–engine bolts and separate the transaxle from the engine.

NOTE: To prevent the transaxle from falling off the jack, loosen the rope while removing the transaxle.

20. Remove the transaxle mounting brackets from the transaxle.
21. Installation is the reverse of removal.

GLC (front wheel drive)

1. Raise the vehicle and support it safely. Disconnect the negative battery cable.
2. Disconnect all electrical wiring and connections, control linkages from the transaxle. Mark these units to aid in reassembling.
3. Remove the front wheels. Disconnect the lower ball joints from the steering knuckles. Pull the driveshafts from the differential gears.

NOTE: A circlip is positioned on the driveshaft ends and engages in a groove, machined in the differential side gears. The driveshafts may have to be forced from the differential housing to release the clip from the groove.

CAUTION

Do not allow the driveshafts to drop. Damage may occur to the ball and socket joints and to the rubber boots. Wire the shafts to the vehicle body when released from the differential.

---

4. Support the engine with a jack. Remove the mounting bolts retaining the transaxle in place. Remove the unit from the vehicle.
5. Installation is the reverse of removal.

CAUTION

Be sure the rubber mounts are not twisted or distorted and not in contact with the body.

---

6. To properly install the driveshafts in the differential side gears, position the open end of the circlip in the up position, and with the driveshaft in a horizontal position, push the driveshafts into the side gears. To be sure the circlip engages the groove, a sound may be heard or attempt to pull the

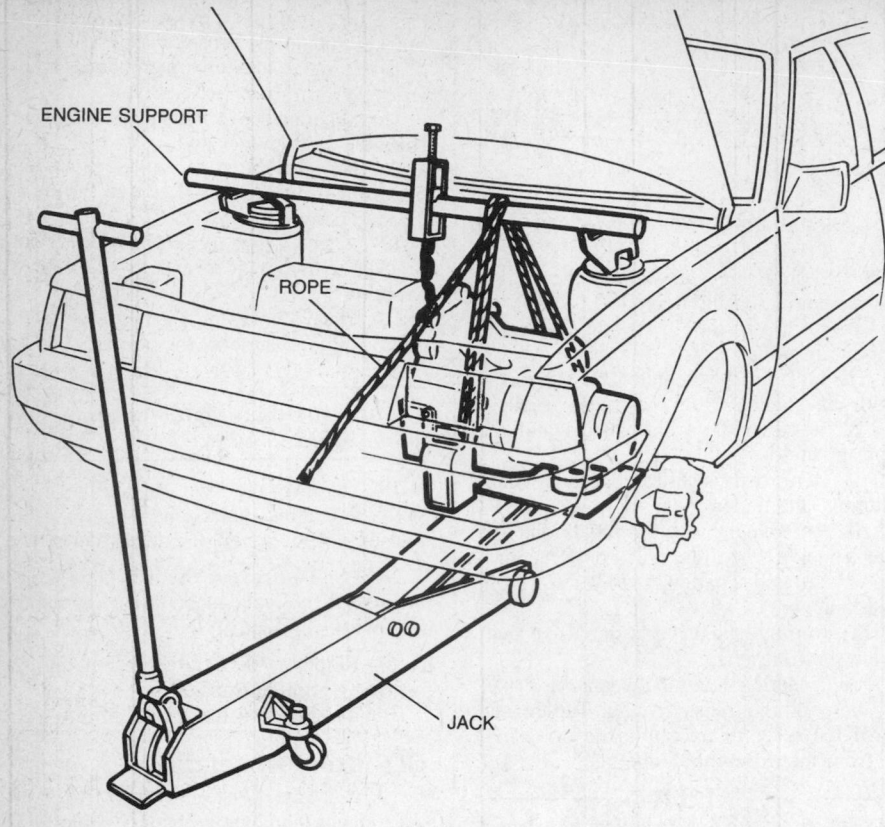

ENGINE SUPPORT

ROPE

JACK

Lowering the transaxle from vehicle with rope and floor jack arrangement—1983 and later 626

1. Clutch disc
2. Bolt
3. Clutch cover and pressure plate assembly
4. Service hole cover
5. Release fork
6. Oil seal
7. Dust boot
8. Reamer bolt
9. Release bearing
10. Spring
11. Clutch housing

Clutch components

cedures, please refer to "Manual Transaxle Overhaul" in the Unit Repair section.

CLUTCH AND FLYWHEEL

REMOVAL & INSTALLATION

The flywheel nut on rotary engine models is tightened to 350 ft. lbs. with no more than a 3 foot extension on the wrench.

1. Remove the transmission or transaxle.
2. Remove the clutch cover (use centering tool).
3. Remove the clutch disc.
4. Remove the flywheel.

From the Clutch Housing:

5. Unhook the return spring from the throwout bearing and remove the bearing.
6. Pull out the release fork until the retaining spring frees itself from the ball stud.

7. Installation is the reverse of removal.
Apply Loctite® (RX-3 only) on the eccentric shaft threads.
Apply sealer to both sides of the flywheel lockwasher and position the lockwasher on the eccentric shaft.
Install the flywheel locknut(s) and tighten

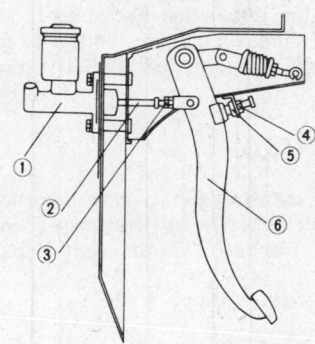

1. Master cylinder
2. Rod
3. Locknut
4. Adjusting bolt
5. Locknut
6. Clutch pedal

Clutch pedal height adjustment

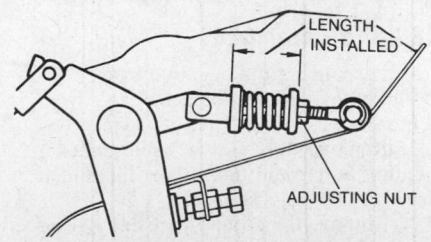

LENGTH INSTALLED

ADJUSTING NUT

Clutch pedal assist spring adjustment

driveshaft from the differential. Reconnect the ball joints at the lower arms.

OVERHAUL
For all manual transaxle overhaul pro-

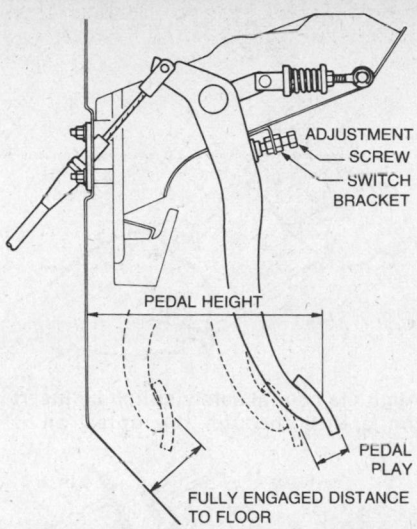

1983 and later 626 clutch pedal arrangement—pedal height and pedal free play shown

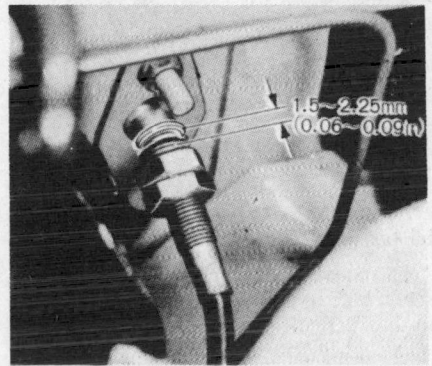

GLC clutch cable adjustment

it to 350 ft. lbs. (Rotary), (112–118 ft. lbs.—Piston)(71–76 ft. lbs.—83 626): then bend the tabs of the lockwasher up around it.

PEDAL HEIGHT ADJUSTMENT

All Models (except 1983 and later 626)

Loosen the locknut on the adjusting bolt. Turn the adjusting bolt until the clearance between the pedal pad and the floormat is 7.28 in. (7.50—RX-7, 7.48—thru '80 GLC, 9.05—'81–'84 GLC, 7.60—626). Carefully tighten the locknut.

1983 and Later 626

1. Measure the pedal-to-dash insulation distance for 7.24 in. (184mm).
2. Remove the air blower duct at the lower part of the dash panel.
3. Adjust the pedal height by turning the stopper bolt on the clutch switch.
4. Adjust the installation length of the assist spring. The pedal assist spring di-

mension should be adjusted to 1.114–1.54 in. (33.5–34.5mm).

PEDAL FREE-PLAY ADJUSTMENT

RX-4 and Cosmo

The free-play of the clutch pedal before the pushrod contacts the piston in the master cylinder should be 0.02–0.12 in.

To adjust the free-play, loosen the locknut and turn the pushrod until the proper adjustment is obtained. Tighten the locknut after the adjustment is complete.

GLC

Loosen the locknut and pull the outer cable away from the engine side of the firewall. Turn the adjusting nut on the cable to obtain a 0.060–0.090 in. clearance between the adjusting nut and the firewall. Tighten the locknut. Adjust the 1981 and later GLC cable to obtain free play of 0.43–0.67 in.

1979 and Later RX-7 and 626

Loosen the locknut on the clutch master cylinder pushrod. Turn the pushrod to obtain 0.02–0.12 in. free play between the pedal and the pushrod. Tighten the locknut on the pushrod. 1983 and later 626 free play is 0.08–0.12 in.

Clutch Master Cylinder

REMOVAL & INSTALLATION

Unfasten the hydraulic line from the master cylinder outlet. Remove the master cylinder.

Installation is the reverse of removal. Bleed the hydraulic system.

Clutch Release Cylinder

REMOVAL & INSTALLATION

1. Unscrew the hydraulic line.
2. Unhook the release fork return spring from the cylinder.
3. Remove the release cylinder.

Installation is the reverse of removal. Bleed the hydraulic system. Adjust the release fork free-play.

Bleeding the Clutch Hydraulic System

1. Remove the rubber cap from the bleeder screw on the release cylinder.
2. Place a bleeder tube over the end of the bleeder screw.
3. Submerge the other end of the tube in a jar half-filled with hydraulic (brake) fluid.
4. Depress the clutch pedal fully and allow it to return slowly.

Loosening the torque converter bolts

5. Keep repeating Step 4, while watching the hydraulic fluid in the jar. As soon as the air bubbles disappear, close the bleeder screw.

NOTE: During the bleeding procedure the reservoir must be kept at least ¾ full.

AUTOMATIC TRANSMISSION

REMOVAL & INSTALLATION

RX3-SP

The automatic transmission is filled with Type F fluid.

1. Remove the heat shroud. Remove the exhaust pipe bracket from the torque converter housing.
2. Detach the exhaust pipe.

————— CAUTION —————
The exhaust system on rotary engine-equipped Mazdas gets considerably hotter than a conventional system; be sure to allow enough time for it to cool.

3. Remove the driveshaft.
4. Detach the speedometer cable.
5. Remove the control rod.
6. Unfasten the vacuum lines from the vacuum modulator.
7. Unfasten the multiconnector from the downshift solenoid and the neutral safety switch.
8. Disconnect the oil cooler lines.
9. Remove the starter.
10. Matchmark the torque converter and the flex-plate.
11. Working through the starter motor mounting hole, remove the four bolts which secure the torque converter to the flex-plate.
12. Support the transmission.
13. Remove the crossmember.
14. Remove the bolts which secure the torque converter housing to the top of the engine.
15. Raise the transmission so that it is level.
16. Use an appropriate prying tool to carefully apply pressure between the torque converter and the flex-plate.

17. Slide the transmission rearward and lower it from the car.

———— **CAUTION** ————

Do not rest the weight of the transmission on the torque converter splines.

18. Automatic transmission installation is the reverse of removal. There are several points which should be noted, however:

19. Before installing the transmission, use a dial indicator to measure flex-plate runout. If runout exceeds 0.020 in., the flex-plate must be replaced.

20. Hand-tighten the four torque converter installation bolts and then lock the flex-plate with a brake. Next, tighten the four bolts evenly, and in several stages, to 29–36 ft. lbs.

Check the fluid level again and road test the car.

RX-4, RX-7 and Cosmo

NOTE: The transmission is filled with Type F fluid.

1. Remove the converter access hole cover. Lock the flex-plate by holding the drive pulley lockbolt with a wrench.

2. Matchmark the converter and flex-plate. Unfasten the four converter-to-flex-plate securing bolts.

3. Remove the exhaust pipe.
4. Remove the driveshaft.
5. Remove speedometer cable.
6. Remove all vacuum lines and electrical leads from the transmission.
7. Remove the starter.
8. Remove the bottom cover from the converter housing.
9. Support the transmission and remove the crossmember.
10. Disconnect the oil cooler.
11. Unbolt the converter housing, raise the transmission to a level place and separate it from the flex-plate.
12. Automatic transmission installation is the reverse of removal. There are several points which should be noted, however.

Before installing the transmission, use a dial indicator to measure flex-plate runout. Runout should be around 0.012 in. If runout exceeds 0.020 in., the flex-plate must be replaced.

Tighten the converter to drive plate attaching bolts to 25–36 ft. lbs.

After completing transmission installation, rotate the eccentric shaft to be sure that there is no interference in the transmission.

1978–80 GLC and 1979–82 626

Use only Type F transmission fluid.
1. Drain the transmission.
2. Remove the heat insulator.
3. Disconnect the exhaust pipe.
4. Disconnect the driveshaft at the rear axle flange.
5. Remove the driveshaft.
6. Disconnect the speedometer cable.
7. Disconnect the shift rod.

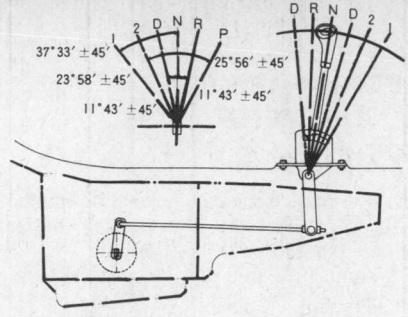

Transmission linkage adjustment

8. Remove all vacuum hoses.
9. Disconnect all wiring.
10. Disconnect the oil cooler lines.
11. Remove the access cover from the lower end of the converter housing.
12. Matchmark the drive plate and torque converter for realignment and remove the converter bolts.
13. Support the transmission with a jack and remove the crossmember.
14. Remove the converter housing-to-engine bolts.
15. Remove the filler tube.
16. Separate the flex-plate and the converter.
17. Remove the transmission and converter as an assembly.
18. To install the transmission, reverse the removal procedure.

SHIFT LINKAGE ADJUSTMENT

All Models Except RX-7

1. Place the transmission selector lever in Neutral.
2. Disconnect the clevis from the lower end of the selector arm.
3. Move the manual lever to the N position.

NOTE: The N position is the third detent from the back.

4. Loosen the two clevis retaining nuts and adjust the clevis so that it freely enters the lever hole.
5. Tighten the retaining nuts.
6. Connect the clevis to the lever and secure with the spring washer, flat washer and retaining clip.

NEUTRAL SAFETY SWITCH ADJUSTMENT

RX3-SP and RX-7

1. Check the shift linkage.
2. Remove the nut from the gear selector lever and the neutral safety switch attaching bolts.
3. Unfasten the screw underneath the switch body.
4. Place the selector shaft in Neutral by using the gear selector lever.

NOTE: If the linkage is adjusted prop-

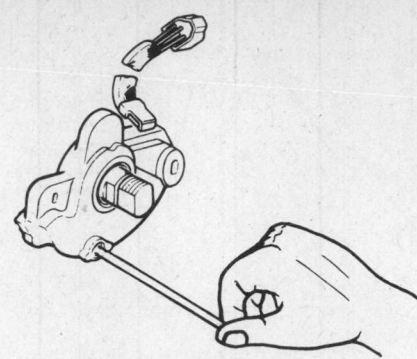

Align the neutral safety switch by inserting a drill through the holes on it.

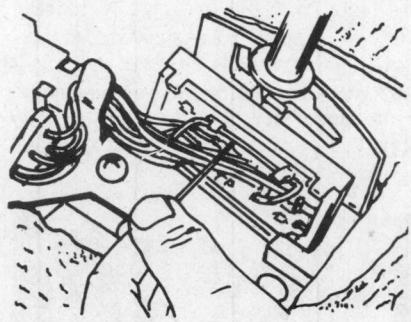

Adjusting the neutral safety switch—RX-4 and Cosmo

erly, the slot in the selector shaft should be vertical.

5. Move the switch body so that the screw hole in the case aligns with the hole in the internal rotor.
6. Check the alignment by inserting an 0.009 in. diameter pin or a No. 53 drill through the holes.
7. Once the proper alignment is obtained, tighten the switch mounting bolts.
8. If it still is not operating properly, i.e., the car starts in position other than P (Park) or N (Neutral) or the back-up lights come on in gears other than R (Reverse), replace the switch.

RX-4 and Cosmo

1. Remove the housing from the shift lever.
2. Adjust the shift lever so that there is 0–0.012 in. clearance between the pin and the guide plate, when the lever is in Neutral.
3. Adjust the neutral safety switch so that the pin hole in the switch body is aligned with the pin hole of the sliding plate when the shift lever is in Neutral.
4. Check the adjustment by trying to start the engine in all gears. It should only start in Park or Neutral.
5. Reinstall the housing on the shift lever.

1978–80 GLC

1. Place the manual lever in N. N is the third detent from the back.

2. Remove the manual lever.

3. Loosen the neutral switch attaching bolts and remove the screw from the alignment hole at the bottom of the switch.

4. Rotate the switch so that the hole in the switch aligns with the hole in the internal rotor. The 0.078 in. diameter pin should be inserted while tightening switch.

5. Install the alignment hole screw and manual lever.

1979–82 626

1. Place the transmission selector lever in the neutral position.

2. Loosen the neutral switch attaching screws.

3. Position the manual shift lever shaft in the neutral position by adjusting the range select lever. The proper neutral position is where the slot of the manual shaft is positioned vertically and the detent positions in the shaft correctly with a click sound.

4. Move the neutral switch so that the identification marks on the switch body and the sliding plate are aligned.

5. Tighten the neutral switch adjusting screws.

6. Check the adjustment by trying to start the engine in all gears. It should only start in Park and Neutral.

KICKDOWN SWITCH AND DOWNSHIFT SOLENOID ADJUSTMENT

All Except 1979–82 626

1. Check the accelerator linkage for smooth operation.

2. Turn the ignition on but do not start the engine.

3. Depress the accelerator pedal fully to the floor. As the pedal nears the end of its travel, a light "click" should be heard from the downshift solenoid.

4. If the kickdown switch operates too soon, loosen the locknut on the switch shaft. Adjust the shaft so that the accelerator linkage makes contact with it when the pedal is depressed 7/8-15/16 of the way to the floor. Tighten the locknut.

5. If no noise comes from the solenoid at all, then check the wiring for the solenoid and the switch.

6. If the wiring is in good condition, remove the wire from the solenoid and connect it to a 12V power source. If the so-

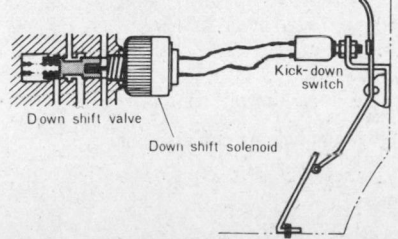

Kickdown switch the downshift solenoid circuit

lenoid does not click when connected, it is defective and should be replaced.

NOTE: When the solenoid is removed, about two pints of transmission fluid will leak out.

1979–82 626

1. Disconnect the wiring connectors from the kickdown switch.

2. Screw out the kick-down switch a few turns.

3. Fully depress the accelerator pedal.

4. Gradually screw in the kick-down switch until you hear a clicking sound then screw it in ½ turn more.

5. Tighten the locknut and connect the wiring connectors.

BAND ADJUSTMENT

JATCO Model 3N71B

1. Raise the vehicle and support safely.

2. Drain the transmission fluid and remove the transmission pan.

3. Loosen the locknut and torque the servo adjusting bolt to 9–11 ft. lbs.

4. Back off the servo bolt two full turns and tighten the locknut.

5. Install the pan assembly and fill with fluid.

JATCO Model R3A

1. Raise the vehicle and support safely.

2. Locate the servo cover and remove from the right side of the transmission case.

3. Loosen locknut and tighten the servo adjusting bolt to 9–11 ft. lbs. torque.

4. Loosen the servo bolt two full turns and tighten the locknut.

5. Install the servo cover and lower vehicle.

AUTOMATIC TRANSAXLE

REMOVAL & INSTALLATION

GLC

1. Raise the vehicle on a hoist and support it safely. Disconnect the negative battery cable.

NOTE: When removing or installing the transaxle assembly the rear end of the power plant (engine) must be lifted and secured with the aid of a chain, or special engine support.

2. Disconnect all electrical wiring and connections, control linkages from the transaxle. Mark these units to aid in reassembling.

3. Remove the front wheels. Disconnect the lower ball joints from the steering knuckles. Pull the driveshafts from the differential gears.

NOTE: A circlip is positioned on the driveshaft ends and engages in a groove, machined in the differential side gears. The driveshafts may have to be forced from the differential housing to release the clip from the groove.

4. Remove the crossmember and disconnect the cooler lines.

5. Remove the starter motor.

—————— CAUTION ——————
Do not allow the driveshafts to drop. Damage may occur to the ball and socket joints and to the rubber boots. Wire the shafts to the vehicle body when released from the differential.

6. Support the transaxle with a jack. Remove the transaxle-to-engine mounting bolts. Remove the unit from the vehicle.

7. Installation is the reverse of removal.

—————— CAUTION ——————
Be sure the rubber mounts are not twisted or distorted and not in contact with the body.

8. To properly install the driveshafts in the differential side gears, position the open end of the circlip in the up position, and with the driveshaft in a horizontal position, push the driveshafts into the side gears. To be sure the circlip engages the groove, a sound may be heard or attempt to pull the driveshaft from the differential. Reconnect the ball joints at the lower arms.

1983 and Later 626

1. Disconnect the negative battery cable and remove the speedometer cable.

2. Remove the shift control cable from the transaxle.

3. Disconnect the ground wire, the inhibitor switch and the kickdown solenoid.

4. Remove the starter motor.

5. Attach the engine support bar and suspend the engine.

6. Remove the line connected to the vacuum diaphragm.

7. Remove the five upper transaxle-to-engine attaching bolts.

8. Remove the transmission cooler lines from the transaxle.

9. Jack up the vehicle and support it with safety stands.

10. Remove the front wheels and the left and right splash shields.

11. Remove the stabilizer bar control link. Remove the undercover.

12. Remove the pinch bolt and separate the ball joint from the steering knuckle.

13. Pull the left driveshaft from the transaxle:

a. Insert a chisel between the driveshaft and the bearing housing. Tap the end of the chisel lightly in order to uncouple the driveshaft and differential side gear.

—————— CAUTION ——————
Do not insert the chisel too far between the shaft and the housing, doing so might

damage the lip of the oil seal or the dust cover.

b. Pull the front hub outward and remove the driveshaft from the transaxle.

NOTE: Support the driveshaft during and after removal to avoid damaging the CV-joints and boots.

14. Pull the right driveshaft from the transaxle:

a. Insert a prybar between the driveshaft and the joint shaft and force the driveshaft coupling open.

b. Pull the front hub out and remove the driveshaft from the joint shaft.

NOTE: Support the driveshaft during and after removal to avoid damaging the CV-joints and boots.

c. Remove the joint shaft assembly from the transaxle.

15. Remove the transaxle undercover and the torque converter-to-drive plate bolts.

16. Remove the crossmember and the left side lower arm together as an assembly.

17. Attach a rope to the transaxle mounting brackets in two places and secure the rope over the engine support bar.

18. Place a board on a floor jack and use it to support the transaxle.

19. Remove the lower two transaxle-to-engine bolts.

20. Lower the transaxle with the floor jack while guiding it with the rope.

NOTE: Do not separate the torque converter from the transaxle during removal.

21. Installation is the reverse of removal.

SHIFT LEVER ADJUSTMENT

The shift lever adjustment should be performed by the forward and backward of the shift lever with the shift lever setting at the "P" range.

VACUUM DIAPHRAGM SWITCH

Intake manifold vacuum controls the vacuum line pressure and the diaphragm varies the position of the throttle valve through the interconnecting rod. No adjustment can be made to the vacuum modulator, the unit must be replaced if it is found to be defective.

DOWNSHIFT SOLENOID

When the accelerator pedal is fully depressed, the kickdown switch becomes active and the downshift solenoid gets power. The downshift valve in the control valve is pushed up to kickdown position 3-to-2 and position 2-to-1 at a given speed.

NEUTRAL SAFETY/ REVERSE LAMP SWITCH

The switch contacts should operate when the switch plunger is moved into its respective operating positions. The switch operates from closed (starter solenoid on) to the neutral (or "off") position and then to the reverse light ("on" position). The switch plunger must operate smoothly otherwise the gear selector will be affected.

DRIVELINE

Driveshaft and U-Joints

REMOVAL & INSTALLATION

1978–80 GLC, RX-3SP and RX-7

Do not remove the oil seals from models with a center bearing unless they are defective.

1. Matchmark the flanges on the driveshaft and pinion so that they may be installed in their original position.

2. Lower the back end of the driveshaft and slide the front end out of the transmission.

3. Plug up the hole in the transmission to prevent it from leaking.

4. Driveshaft installation is the reverse of removal.

RX-4, 1979–82 626 and Cosmo Models

Perform this operation only when the exhaust system is *cold*.

1. Remove the front heat insulator.

2. Remove the nuts which secure the downpipe to the thermal reactor flange.

3. Remove the downpipe from the main muffler flange.

4. Matchmark the pinion and driveshaft flange bolts.

5. Unfasten the center bearing.

6. Remove the driveshaft.

7. Driveshaft installation is the reverse of removal. Tighten the yoke-to-front driveshaft locknut to 116–130 ft. lbs.

OVERHAUL

For all overhaul procedures, please refer to "U-Joint/CV-Joint Overhaul" in the Unit Repair section.

REAR AXLE

Axle Shafts

REMOVAL, INSTALLATION AND ADJUSTMENT

Rear Wheel Drive Only

1. Remove the wheel.

2. Remove the brake shoes.

3. Remove the brake backing plate and the bearing retainer.

4. Withdraw the axle shaft with a puller.

5. Apply grease to the oil seal lips and then insert the oil seal into the axle housing.

6. Check the axle shaft end-play.

a. Temporarily install the brake backing plate on the axle shaft.

b. Measure the depth of the bearing seat and then measure the width of the bearing outer race.

c. The difference between the two measurements is equal to the overall thickness of the adjusting shims required. Shims are available in thicknesses of 0.004 and 0.016 in.

NOTE: The maximum permissible end-play is 0.004 in.

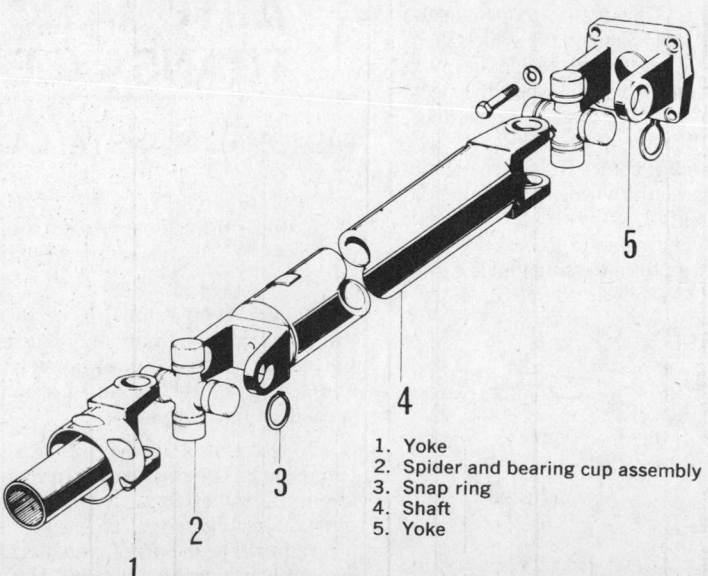

1. Yoke
2. Spider and bearing cup assembly
3. Snap ring
4. Shaft
5. Yoke

Components of a typical driveshaft—RX–4 shown

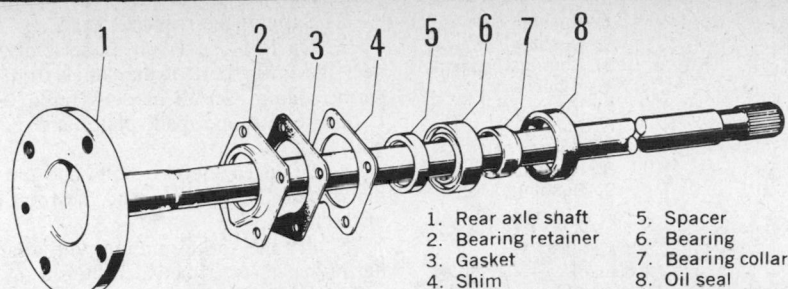

1. Rear axle shaft
2. Bearing retainer
3. Gasket
4. Shim
5. Spacer
6. Bearing
7. Bearing collar
8. Oil seal

Components of the axle shaft assembly

7. Remove the backing plate, apply sealer to the rear axle surfaces and install the backing plate.

8. Install the rear axle shaft, bearing retainer, gasket, and shims. Coat the shims with sealer.

9. Install the brake shoes.

Axle Shaft Bearing and Seal

REPLACEMENT

Rear Wheel Drive Only

1. Install the retainer and spacer on the shaft.

Position the bearing on the shaft with the sealed side toward the shaft flange. Press it on until the spacer comes in contact with the shoulder of the shaft.

Press the bearing retaining collar onto the shaft until it contacts the bearing inner race.

NOTE: If the bearing retaining collar can be press fitted with a force less than 2.5 tons, replace the collar.

2. Remove the rear axle shaft.

3. Press the axle shaft out of the collar and bearing.

NOTE: If the pressure needed to press out the shaft exceeds 10 tons, grind off part of the bearing retaining collar and cut it with a cold chisel.

4. Remove the bearing retainer.

Differential

REMOVAL & INSTALLATION

Rear Wheel Drive Only

1. Drain the lubricant.
2. Remove the driveshaft.
3. Remove both of the axle shafts.
4. Remove the differential carrier.
5. Installation is the reverse of removal.

OVERHAUL

For further information on differential overhaul procedures, please refer to "Drive Axles" in the Unit Repair section.

DRIVEAXLES

Front Wheel Drive Only

INSPECTION

1981 and Later GLC and 1983 and Later 626

1. Loosen the front wheel lugs, raise the car and safely support it on jackstands. Remove the wheels and tires.

2. Check the driveaxle inner and outer boots for cracks or damage, for leaking grease or loose bands. Replace or repair if necessary.

3. Turn the driveaxle by hand, if the splines or joints are excessively loose, replace or repair as necessary.

4. Examine the driveaxle for cracks or twist. Replace if necessary.

REMOVAL & INSTALLATION

1981 and Later GLC

1. See Step 1 of "Inspection". Drain the transaxle fluid after removing the splash shields.

2. Loosen the driveaxle locknut at the center of the disc brake hub after raising the lock tab. Apply brake pressure while loosening.

3. Remove the lower ball joint from the steering knuckle.

4. Remove the driveaxle from the transaxle case by pulling the brake caliper outward with increasing force. While applying outward force, hit the driveaxle shaft with a brass hammer, if necessary, to help in removal.

5. Remove the locknut and pull the drive-axle from the steering knuckle. Remove the driveaxle and plug the transaxle case with a clean rag to prevent dirt from entering.

6. Installation is in the reverse order of removal. Before installing the driveaxle into the transaxle case, check the oil seals for cuts or damage. Replace the oil seals if necessary. Insert the axle into the transaxle case by pushing on the wheel hub assembly. Always install a new clip on the drive-axle.

1983 and Later 626

1. Drain the transaxle fluid and remove the splash shield.

2. Operate the brakes to secure the wheel hub and then loosen the driveshaft lock nut.

NOTE: Raise the tabs before loosening the lock nut.

3. Remove the stabilizer bar control link from the lower arm.

4. Remove the pinch bolt and remove the ball joint from the steering knuckle.

5. Remove the driver's side driveshaft:
   a. On manual transaxles, insert a prybar between the driveshaft and the transaxle case. Remove the driveshaft from the side gear by lightly tapping the end of the prybar.

— CAUTION —
Do not insert the prybar too far, doing so, could damage the lip of the oil seal or the dust cover.

   b. For automatic transaxles, insert a prybar between the driveshaft and the bearing housing. Tap the end of the prybar in order to uncouple the driveshaft and differential side gear.

   c. After removing the driveshaft lock nut, pull the front hub outward and toward the rear. Disconnect the driveshaft from the wheel and the transaxle.

6. Remove the right driveshaft and joint shaft:
   a. Insert a prybar between the driveshaft and the joint shaft and separate them.

   b. Remove the driveshaft lock nut and pull the front hub outward and to the rear, disconnecting the driveshaft from the front hub. Remove the driveshaft from the joint shaft.

7. Installation is the reverse of removal.

JOINT OVERHAUL

NOTE: On GLC, the joint on the wheel side of the driveaxle is non-rebuildable. If worn, the joint and axle must be replaced. The boot may be changed if necessary. Do not interfere with the balancer found on the right axle unless necessary for wheel/joint boot replacement. If balancer is removed it must be reinstalled in the same position 14.45 in. from the front of the wheel joint.

For further information on joint overhaul, please refer to "U-Joint/CV-Joint Overhaul" in the Unit Repair section.

REAR SUSPENSION

Springs

REMOVAL & INSTALLATION

RX-4

1. Remove the wheel.

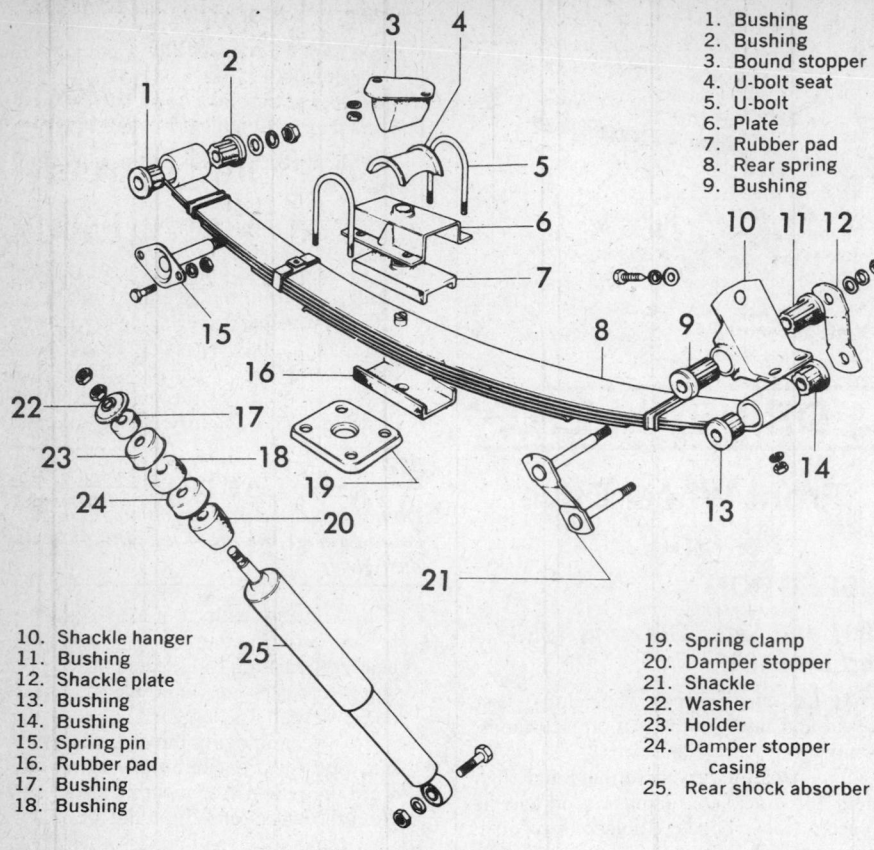

1. Bushing
2. Bushing
3. Bound stopper
4. U-bolt seat
5. U-bolt
6. Plate
7. Rubber pad
8. Rear spring
9. Bushing

10. Shackle hanger
11. Bushing
12. Shackle plate
13. Bushing
14. Bushing
15. Spring pin
16. Rubber pad
17. Bushing
18. Bushing

19. Spring clamp
20. Damper stopper
21. Shackle
22. Washer
23. Holder
24. Damper stopper casing
25. Rear shock absorber

RX–4 rear suspension

1. Crossmember
2. Rear stabilizer bar
3. Lateral link
4. Mounting block
5. Spring upper seat
6. Rubber seat
7. Dust cover
8. Coil spring
9. Shock absorber
10. Rear hub spindle
11. Trailing link

Left side only

Rear suspension assembly—GLC front wheel drive

2. Support the rear axle housing.

3. On RX-4 and 808 models, disconnect the lower part of the shock from the spring clamp. On all models, remove the U-bolt seat, rubber pad, plate, and the U-bolt itself.

4. Unfasten the two bolts and the nut that secure the spring pin to the front end of the rear spring.

5. Pry the spring pin out with a large, flat prybar inserted between the spring pin and its body bracket.

6. Unfasten the nuts and the bolts which attach the rear shackle to the body.

7. Withdraw the rear spring assembly, complete with its shackle.

8. Remove the shackle assembly from the end of the spring.

9. Pull the rubber bushings out from both ends of the spring.

10. Rear spring installation is the reverse of removal. When installing the rubber bushings, do not lubricate them.

Cosmo

1. Remove the rear wheels.

2. Support the lower arms with a jack.

3. Remove the pivot bolt and nut which secures the rear end of the lower arm to the axle housing.

4. Lower the jack to relieve the spring pressure on the lower arm and remove the spring.

5. If replacing one spring only, a suitable adjusting plate will be necessary to give equal road clearance on each side.

6. Install spring in reverse order of removal, but do not tighten bolts while car is on stands.

1978–80 GLC and All GLC Wagons

1. Raise the rear end of the vehicle and place jack stands under the frame side rails.

2. Remove the rear wheel.

3. Remove the upper and lower shock absorber bolts and nuts and remove the shock absorber.

4. Place a jack under the lower arm to support it.

5. Remove the pivot bolt and nut that secures the rear end of the lower arm to the axle housing.

6. Slowly lower the jack to relieve the spring pressure on the lower arm, then remove the spring.

7. Install the spring in the reverse order of removal.

RX-7 and 1979–82 626

1. Raise the rear of the vehicle and support it safely.

2. Remove the rear wheel.

3. Position an hydraulic floor jack under the rear axle housing.

4. Disconnect the shock absorber lower end and the lower link bolt (just to the front of the lower shock bolt). Remove the rear bolt from the upper link.

FRONT SUSPENSION

NOTE: These trailing control arm links run parallel from the front to rear on the vehicle, with the smaller watt links running side to side on the vehicle.

5. Disconnect the front ends of the stabilizer bar (if equipped).

6. Remove the right and left watt links at the rear axle housing.

7. Carefully lower the rear axle housing and remove the coil spring and the rubber seat.

8. The installation is the reverse of the removal.

Shock Absorbers

REMOVAL & INSTALLATION

RX-4, RX-3 SP Coupes and Sedans, 1979–82 626, RX-7 and Cosmo

Remove the trim panel from the rear of the luggage compartment. On RX-4 models it will be necessary to remove the rear seat first.

1. Unfasten the nuts, then remove the washers and rubber bushings from the upper shock absorber mounts.

2. Unfasten the nut and bolt which secure the end of the rear shock to the axle housing.

3. Remove the shock.

4. Installation is the reverse of removal.

RX-4 Wagons

1. Remove the locknuts, washers, and rubber bushings from the bottom shock absorber mount.

2. Compress the shock. Unfasten the bolts which secure the upper shock absorber mount.

3. Withdraw the shock.

4. Shock absorber installation is the reverse of removal.

1978–80 GLC

1. Raise the rear end of the vehicle and place jack stands under the frame side rails.

2. Remove the rear wheel.

3. Remove the upper and lower shock absorber bolts and nuts and remove the shock absorber.

4. Install the shock absorber in the reverse order of removal.

Strut Assembly

REMOVAL & INSTALLATION

1981 and Later GLC and 1983 and Later 626

1. Remove the side trim panels from inside the "trunk," or the rear seat and trim. Loosen and remove the top mounting nuts from the strut mounting block assembly.

2. Loosen the rear wheel lugs, raise the

car and safely support it on jackstands.

3. Remove the rear wheels. Disconnect the flexible brake hose from the strut.

4. Disconnect the trailing arm from the lower side of the strut: Separate the lateral link and strut by removing the bolt assembly.

5. Remove the strut from the lower unit by removing the two through nuts and bolts.

6. Remove the strut and brake assembly.

——— CAUTION ———

The coil springs are retained under considerable pressure. They can exert enough force to cause serious injury. Exercise extreme caution when servicing.

OVERHAUL

For all strut overhaul procedures, please refer to "Strut Overhaul" in the Unit Repair section.

1. Front side bushing
2. Spindle
3. Lower arm
4. Ball joint
5. Mounting block
6. Spring upper seat
7. Rubber seat
8. Dust cover
9. Coil spring
10. Shock absorber
11. Knuckle

FRONT SUSPENSION

MacPherson Struts

REMOVAL & INSTALLATION

1. Remove the wheel cover and loosen the lug nuts.

2. Raise the front of the vehicle and support it with jackstands. Do not jack it or support it by any of the front suspension members. Remove the wheel.

——— CAUTION ———

Be sure the car is securely supported. Remember, you will be working underneath it.

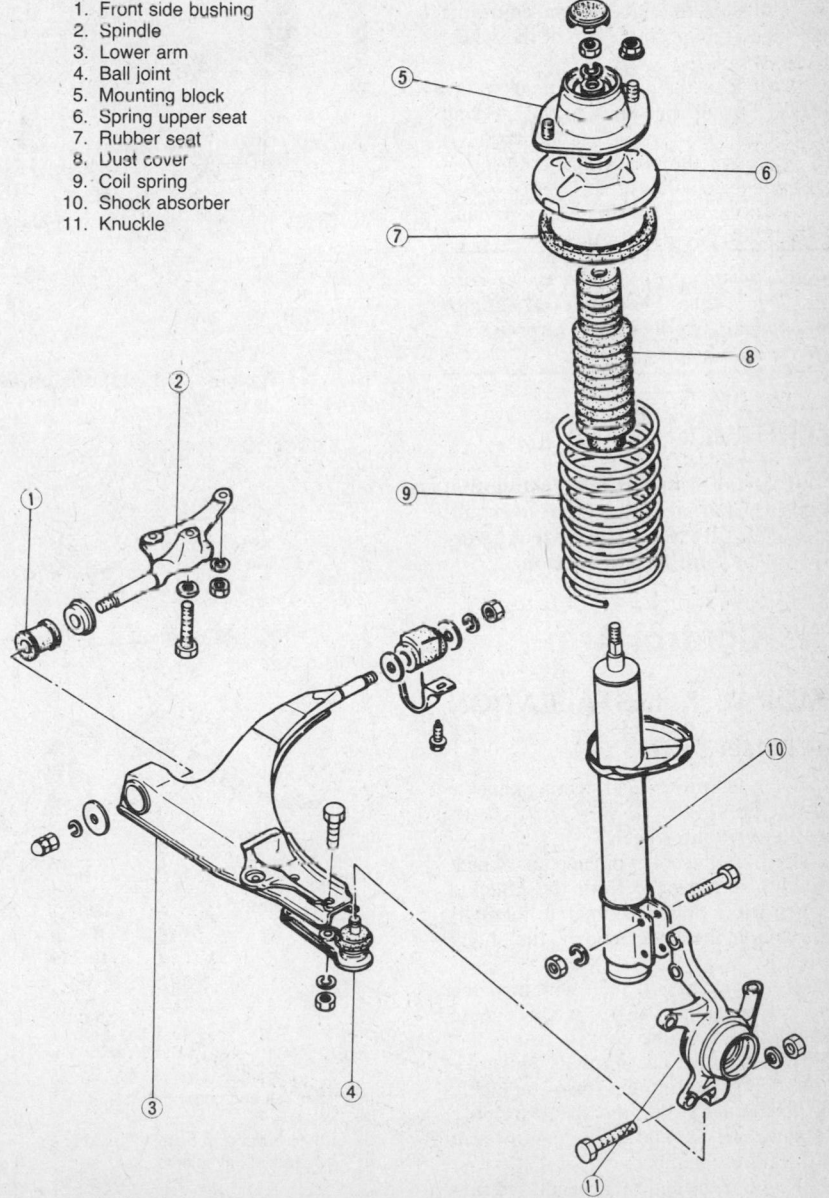

Typical front suspension assembly—front wheel drive models

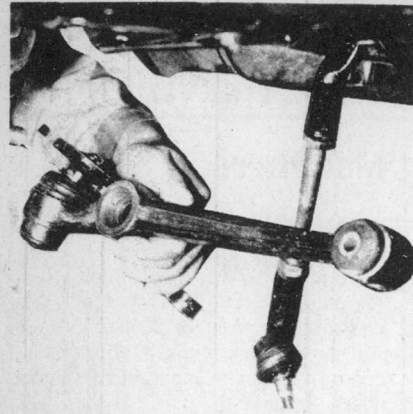

Removing the control arm except GLC front wheel drive

3. Remove the brake caliper and disc on all models except the GLC and 626 with front wheel drive.

4. Unfasten the nuts which secure the upper shock mount to the top of the wheel arch.

5. Unfasten the two bolts that secure the lower end of the shock to the steering knuckle arm.

6. Remove the shock and coil spring as a complete assembly.

7. Installation is in the reverse order.

CAUTION

The coil springs are retained under considerable pressure. They can exert enough force to cause serious injury. Exercise extreme caution when servicing.

OVERHAUL

For all spring removal and installation procedures and any other strut overhaul procedures, please refer to "Strut Overhaul" in the Unit Repair section.

Control Arm

REMOVAL & INSTALLATION

Rear Wheel Drive

Remove the control arm and steering knuckle as an assembly.

1. Remove the wheel.

2. Remove the cotter pin and nut, which secure the tie-rod end, from the knuckle arm; then use a puller to separate them.

3. Unbolt the lower end of the shock absorber.

4. Remove the nut, then withdraw the rubber bushing and washer which secure the stabilizer bar to the control arm.

5. Unfasten the nut and bolt which secure the control arm to the frame member.

6. Push outward on the strut assembly while removing the end of the control arm from the frame member.

7. Remove the control arm and steering knuckle arm as an assembly.

C448

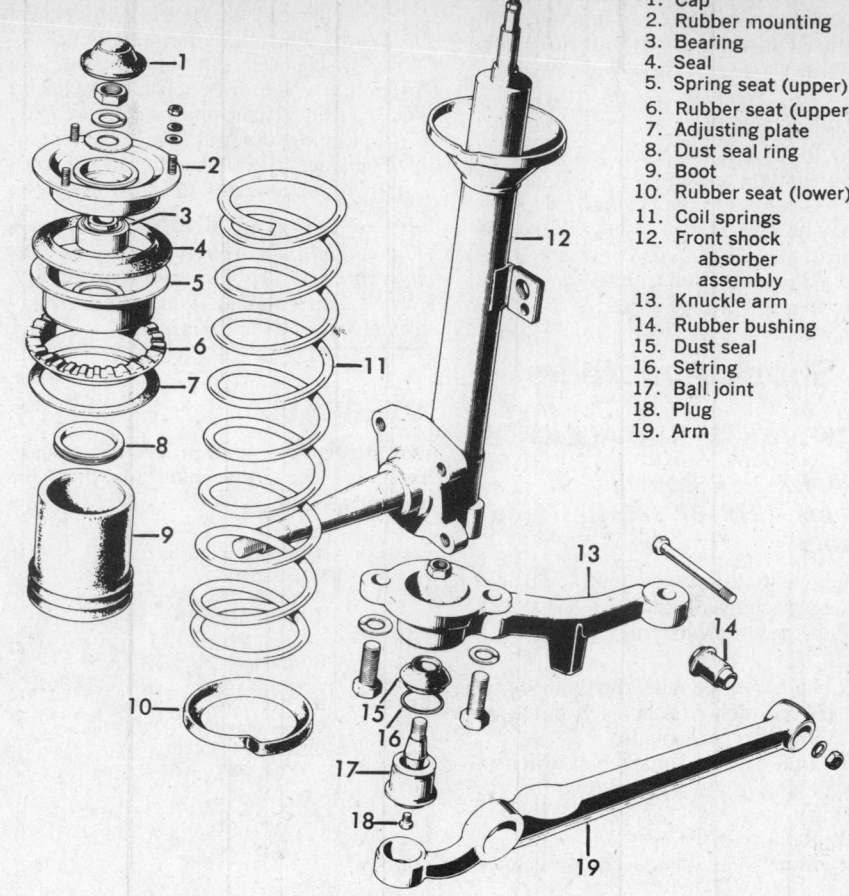

1. Cap
2. Rubber mounting
3. Bearing
4. Seal
5. Spring seat (upper)
6. Rubber seat (upper)
7. Adjusting plate
8. Dust seal ring
9. Boot
10. Rubber seat (lower)
11. Coil springs
12. Front shock absorber assembly
13. Knuckle arm
14. Rubber bushing
15. Dust seal
16. Setring
17. Ball joint
18. Plug
19. Arm

Typical front suspension assembly—rear wheel drive models

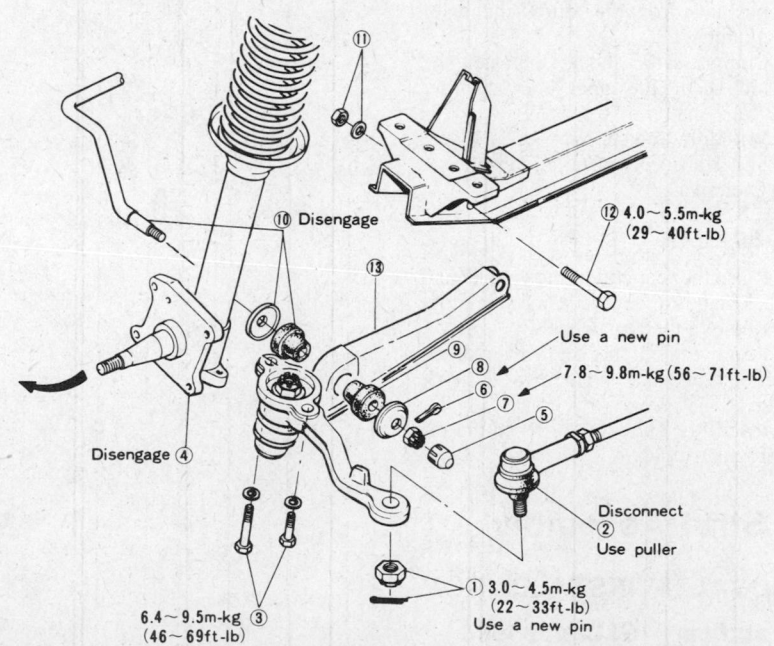

1. Castle nut and cotter pin
2. Tie-rod end
3. Strut to lower arm bolts
4. Strut and wheel spindle
5. Cap nut
6. Cotter pin
7. Castle nut
8. Washer
9. Bushing
10. Anti-roll bar and bushing
11. Nut and washer
12. Suspension arm bolt
13. Suspension arm

GLC rear wheel drive—strut and lower control arm

8. Separate the knuckle arm from the control arm with a puller.

9. Installation of the control arm is the reverse of removal.

Front Wheel Drive

GLC

1. Loosen the wheel lugs, raise the car and safely support it on jackstands. Remove the front wheel.

2. Remove the thru–bolt connecting the lower arm to the steering knuckle.

3. Remove the bolts and nuts mounting the control arm to the body (two inner and three outer).

4. Remove the lower control arm. The ball joint can be serviced at this time if necessary.

5. Installation is in the reverse order of removal.
Mounting Torque;
Ball Joint-to-Steering Knuckle: 32–40 ft. lbs.
Outer Bolts: 43–54 ft. lbs.
Inner Bolts: 69–86 ft. lbs.

1983 AND LATER 626

1. Raise the front end and support it with safety stands.

2. Remove the wheel and splash shield.

3. Remove the stabilizer link from the control arm.

4. Remove the lower control arm-to-frame attaching bolts.

5. Remove the pinch bolt and separate the ball joint from the steering knuckle.

6. Remove the lower control arm.

7. Installation is the reverse of removal. Torque the lower arm mounting bolts to 69–86 ft. lbs, (95–119 Nm).

Front Hub and Steering Knuckle

REMOVAL & INSTALLATION

Front Wheel Drive

1. Loosen the lug nuts, raise the front of the car and safely support it on jackstands. Remove the tire and wheel.

2. Raise the staked tab from the hub center nut, remove the nut from the axle. Apply the brake to help hold the rotor while loosening the nut.

3. Remove the tie-rod end from the steering knuckle. Disconnect the horseshoe clip that retains the brake line to the strut.

4. Remove the mounting bolts that hold the caliper assembly to the knuckle. Wire the caliper out of the way, do not allow the caliper to be supported by the brake hose.

5. Remove the thru–bolt and nut that retains the lower ball joint to the steering knuckle and disconnect the ball joint.

6. Remove the two bolts and nuts retaining the strut to the steering knuckle. Separate the steering knuckle and hub from the strut and drive axle.

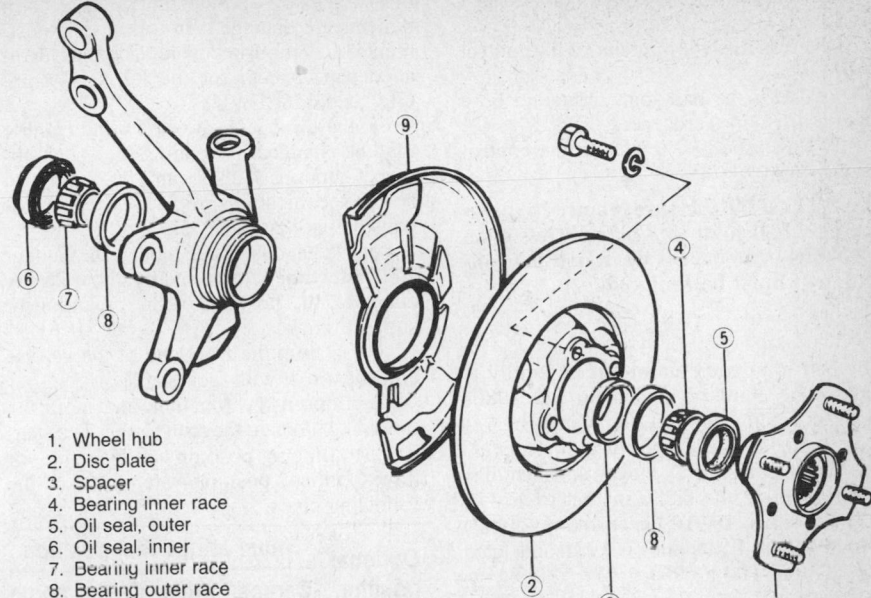

1. Wheel hub
2. Disc plate
3. Spacer
4. Bearing inner race
5. Oil seal, outer
6. Oil seal, inner
7. Bearing inner race
8. Bearing outer race
9. Dust cover

Front hub and knuckle assembly—GLC front wheel drive

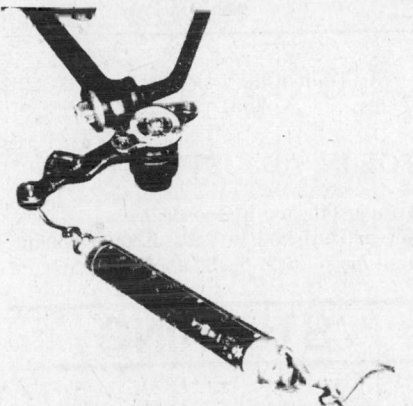

Checking the ball stud rotational torque with a spring scale

7. The hub is pressed through the wheel bearings into the knuckle. Replacement of the wheel bearings or hub removal requires a special puller and the use of a bench press.

8. Remove the inner oil seal and bearing. Remove the wheel hub from the knuckle with a wheel hub puller (Mazda tool 49 F001 726 or equivalent). Remove the outer bearing using a press and Mazda tools 49 F401 368 and 49 F401 365. Drive the outer and inner race from the knuckle with a brass drift and hammer.

9. Install new inner and outer races. Pack the inner and outer bearing and install in knuckle. Use Mazda tool 49 B001 727 or equivalent to tighten the tool nut and measure the preload with a scale connected to the caliper mounting hole on the knuckle. Various spacers are available to increase or decrease the preload. Preload should be 1.7–6.9 ft. lbs.

10. Install the inner and outer grease seals. Press fit the hub through the bearings into the knuckle.

11. Installation of the knuckle and hub is in the reverse order of removal. Always use a new axle locknut and tighten it to 116–174 ft. lbs. Stake the locknut after tightening. Knuckle to strut mounting; 58–86 ft. lbs. Knuckle to ball joint; 33–40 ft. lbs. Knuckle to tie rod end; 22–33 ft. lbs.

Ball Joints

INSPECTION

All Exc. GLC

1. Perform Steps 1–5 of the "Control Arm Removal" procedure.

2. Check the ball joint dust boot.

3. Check the amount of pressure required to turn the ball stud, by hooking a pull scale into the tie rod hole in the knuckle arm. Pull the spring scale until the arm just begins to turn; this should require (4.4–8.8 ft. lbs.—1978–79 Cosmo and RX-4) or (4.6–9.2 ft. lbs.—RX-3SP), or (4.4–7.7 lbs.—626).

If the reading is lower than 14 oz. on the RX-7, replace the ball joint and the suspension arm as a unit.

GLC

1. Check the dust boot for wear.

2. Raise the wheels off the ground and grip the tire at the top and bottom and alternately push and pull to check ball joint end-play. Wear limit is 0.04 in. If necessary, replace the ball joint and control arm assembly.

REMOVAL & INSTALLATION

All Exc. GLC and 1983 and Later 626

Remove the control arm.

1. Remove the set-ring and the dust boot.

2. Press the ball joint out of the control arm.

3. Clean the ball joint mounting bore and coat it with kerosene.

4. Press the ball joint into the control arm.

NOTE: If the pressure required to press the new ball joint into place is less than 3,300 lbs., the bore is worn and the control arm must be replaced.

GLC

The ball joint and control arm assembly is replaced as a unit on models through 1980. On 1981 and later models it may be removed during lower control arm removal. See "Control Arm Removal and Installation." Torque the ball joint nut to 43–51 ft. lbs.—(thru 1980), check the revolving torque of the ball joint on 1981 and later models (63–109 ft. lbs).

1983 and Later 626

The ball joint and control arm assembly is replaced as a unit.

Front End Alignment

CASTER AND CAMBER

Caster and camber are preset by the manufacturer. They require adjustment only if

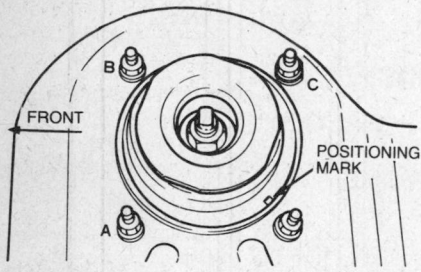

1983 and later 626—a camber and caster position at each nut on the strut tower

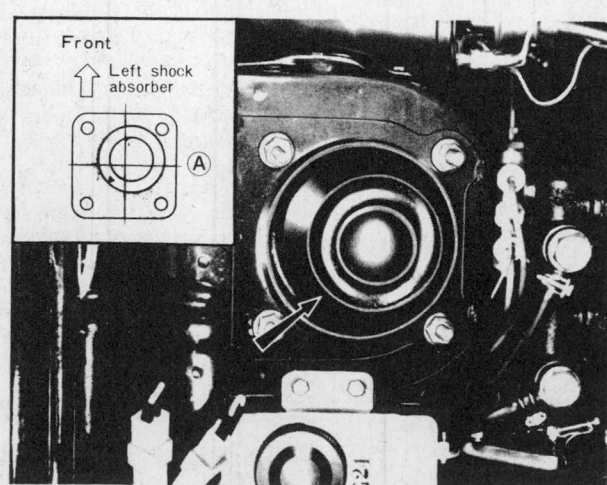

Caster and camber adjustment—RX-4

the suspension and steering linkage components are damaged. In this case, adjustment is accomplished by replacing the damaged part, except for the RX-4, Cosmo, GLC and 626 (FWD).

On these models, the caster and camber may be changed by rotating the shock absorber support. If they can't be brought to within specifications, replace or repair suspension parts as necessary.

On 1983 and later 626 models the camber and caster can be adjusted by about 28′ by changing the position of the mounting or support block.

1. Jack up the front end of the vehicle and support it with jack stands.

2. Loosen the four nuts that hold the mounting block to the strut tower. The standard strut mount position and the value for three optional positions are given in the following chart:

Optional position	Value at optional position	
	Camber angle	Caster angle
A	0°	28′
B	28′	28′
C	28′	0°

3. Tighten the four nuts to 17.0–22.0 ft. lbs. (23–30 Nm).

TOE-IN ADJUSTMENT

To adjust the toe-in, loosen the tie-rod locknuts and turn both tie-rods an equal amount, until the proper specification is obtained.

STEERING

Steering Wheel

REMOVAL & INSTALLATION

1. Remove the crash pad/horn button assembly. On four-spoke steering wheels, pull the center cap toward the wheel top.

2. Punch matchmarks on the steering wheel and steering shaft.

— CAUTION —
Never strike the steering shaft on collapsible steering columns. Always use a suitable puller to remove the steering wheel.

3. Remove the wheel.

4. Installation is the reverse of removal.

Combination (Turn Signal) Switch

REPLACEMENT

RX-3SP and RX-7

1. Remove the steering wheel.

2. Remove the left-hand column shroud.

3. Remove the retaining ring (screw on 808) from the combination (turn signal) switch.

4. Withdraw the switch over the steering column.

5. Installation is the reverse of removal.

RX-4, Cosmo and 1979–82 626

1. Remove the steering wheel.

2. Loosen the nut which secures the vent knob (left side) and allow the knob assembly to drop away from its mounting bracket.

3. Remove choke knob. Remove the choke retaining nut and separate the choke from the panel.

4. Remove the upper column cover.

5. Disconnect the panel light dimmer switch wiring.

6. Disconnect the exhaust temperature warning light wiring.

7. Loosen, but don't remove the screws at either end of the lower panel cover.

NOTE: The left-hand screw is located in the hole which was covered by the upper column cover and the right-hand screw is above the ashtray opening (ashtray removed).

8. Pull the upper column cover away from the instrument panel.

9. Disconnect the combination switch connector.

10. Remove the retaining ring from the steering column.

11. Unfasten the combination switch retaining screw and remove the switch.

12. Installation is the reverse of removal.

GLC and 1983 and Later 626

1. Disconnect the negative battery cable.

2. Remove the horn cap and steering wheel.

3. Remove the steering column covers.

4. Disconnect the wire connectors.

5. Remove the stop ring from the shaft.

6. Remove the attaching screw and remove the combination switch.

7. To install reverse the removal procedure.

Ignition Lock/Switch Assembly

REMOVAL & INSTALLATION

RX-3SP and RX-7

1. Remove the light switch knob.
2. Remove the left and right steering column shrouds.
3. Disconnect the multiconnector from the switch assembly.
4. Use a file or a hacksaw to make slots in the switch securing bolts. Remove the bolts with a screwdriver.
5. Withdraw the switch assembly.
6. To install the switch, reverse the removal procedure. After tightening the switch securing bolts, break their heads off, in order to make the switch difficult for a thief to remove.

RX-4, GLC, Cosmo and 626

1. Follow steps under "Combination Switch Replacement".
2. Remove the instrument frame brace.
3. Disconnect the switch wires.
4. Remove the switch.

NOTE: On the 1983 and later 626, use a chisel to make slots in the lockscrews. Remove the screws with a screwdriver. Install the new screws until the head twists off.

5. Installation is the reverse of removal.

Steering Linkage

REMOVAL & INSTALLATION

All Exc. Front Wheel Drive

The front wheels should point straight ahead. Align the marks on the pitman arm and the sector shaft to ensure proper steering linkage alignment.

1. Remove the cotter pins and the cas-

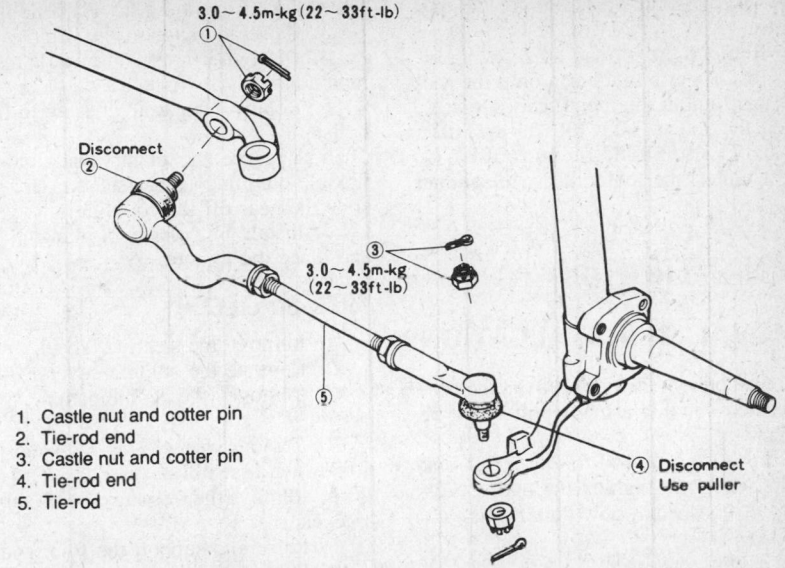

1. Castle nut and cotter pin
2. Tie-rod end
3. Castle nut and cotter pin
4. Tie-rod end
5. Tie-rod

GLC-thru 1980, tie-rod removal; other models similar

tellated nuts which secure the ends of the tie rods to the center link and the steering knuckle.

2. Remove the tie rods.
3. Remove the idler arm.
4. Remove the pitman arm. Remove the center link. On RX-4 models, remove steering damper first.
5. Unfasten the nut which secures the pitman arm to the sector shaft and use a puller to separate them.
6. Installation is the reverse of removal.

Idler Arm

REPLACEMENT

All exc. 1978–80 GLC

1. Remove the front wheels.
2. Disconnect the center link from the idler arm.
3. Unbolt the idler arm bracket from the frame.
4. Hold the assembly in a vise and remove the arm from the bracket by turning

the arm counterclockwise.

5. Check all parts for wear and replace as necessary.
6. Insert the spring into the bracket and screw the idler arm into the bracket until the distance between the lip edge on the idler arm and the leading edge of the bracket is 0.157–0.236 in.
7. Check the revolving torque of the arm with a spring scale. If the torque is less than 0.2 lbs., screw in the arm until the correct reading is obtained. If the torque is greater than 6.6 lbs., unscrew the arm until the correct torque is obtained.
8. If the correct torque cannot be obtained, replace the spring.
9. Grease the assembly through a nipple replacing the plug in the end of the bracket.
10. Attach the idler arm and bracket assembly to the frame.
11. Connect the idler arm to the center link.

1978–80 GLC

1. Remove the front wheels.
2. Disconnect the center link from the idler arm by removing the nut and split pin and using a puller.
3. Unbolt the idler arm bracket from the frame.
4. Remove the split pin and nut from the idler arm at the frame bracket and remove the arm from the bracket.
5. To install reverse the removal procedure. Torque the bracket to frame bolt and nut to 32–40 ft. lbs. and the center link to idler arm nut to 18–25 ft. lbs.

Pitman Arm

REMOVAL & INSTALLATION

1. Remove the wheels.

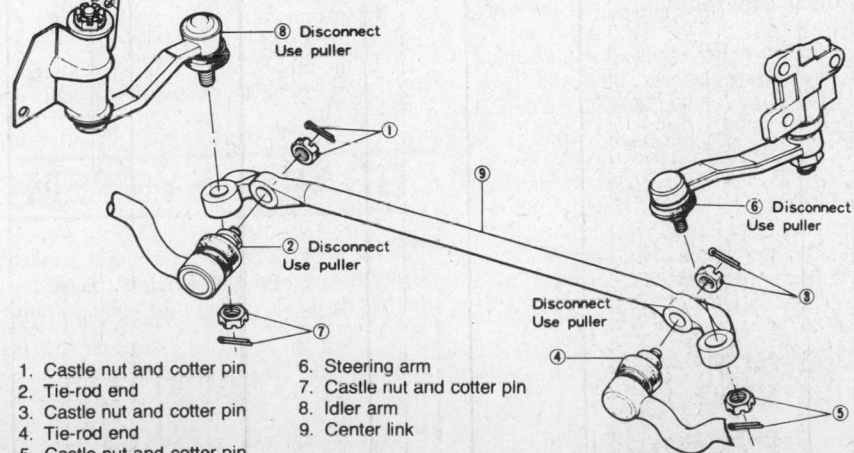

1. Castle nut and cotter pin
2. Tie-rod end
3. Castle nut and cotter pin
4. Tie-rod end
5. Castle nut and cotter pin
6. Steering arm
7. Castle nut and cotter pin
8. Idler arm
9. Center link

GLC-thru 1980, center link removal; other models similar

2. Disconnect the center link at the pitman arm.

3. Remove the pitman arm.

4. Install the pitman arm onto the sector shaft, aligning the identification marks. Tighten the nut to 108–130 ft. lbs. (thru 1979 exc GLC), 58–87 ft. lbs. (GLC).

5. Connect the center link to the pitman arm.

Tie-Rod

REMOVAL & INSTALLATION

1. Disconnect the tie-rod from the center link and knuckle arm. A puller will be necessary.

2. Install the tie-rod to the center link and knuckle arm. Tighten the nuts to 22–32 ft. lbs. and install new cotter pins.

Steering Gear

REMOVAL & INSTALLATION

RX-3SP and RX-7

1. Remove the steering wheel.

2. Remove the column covers.

3. Remove the combination switch assembly.

4. Remove the steering lock and ignition switch assembly.

5. Remove the steering column support bracket.

6. Raise and support the front end.

7. Remove the front wheel.

8. Remove the cotter pin and nut and disconnect the center link from the pitman arm using a ball joint puller.

9. Unbolt the steering gear from the frame, taking note of the presence of any shim for realigning the gear with the shaft.

10. Remove the steering column dust cover and remove the gear housing, column jacket and aligning shim.

11. Reverse the removal for installation. Place the shim in its original position for realignment. Gear housing-to-frame bolt torque is 32–40 ft. lbs.

RX-4, Cosmo and 1979–82 626 (Manual Steering)

1. Remove the front wheel.

2. Remove the nut and cotter pin and disconnect the center link from the pitman arm with a ball joint puller.

3. Unbolt the flexible coupling from the worm shaft.

4. Unclip the speedometer cable from the gear housing and the power brake unit.

5. Unbolt and remove the gear housing.

6. Install in reverse of the above.

RX-4 and Cosmo Power Steering

1. Remove the oil filter cartridge.

2. Mark and disconnect the pressure and return lines from the gear. Plug the lines.

3. Raise and support the vehicle.

4. Disconnect the center link at the pitman arm.

5. Remove the gear housing-to-frame bolts.

6. Remove the clamp that holds the flexible coupling to the steering gear and slide the gear off the coupling.

7. Install in reverse of removal. Fill and bleed the system.

1978–80 GLC

1. Remove the steering wheel.

2. Remove the column covers.

3. Remove the combination switch assembly.

4. Remove the steering lock and ignition switch assembly.

5. Remove the steering column support bracket.

6. Raise and support the front end.

7. Disconnect the center link from the pitman arm using a ball joint puller.

8. Remove the steering gear retaining bolts and check for the existence of a shim. Note its position for realignment.

9. Remove the steering column dust cover.

10. Remove the gear housing, column jacket and aligning shim.

11. Installation is the reverse of removal.

12. Place shim in its original position.

Steering Gear and Linkage

REMOVAL & INSTALLATION

1981 and Later GLC and 1983 and Later 626

1. Raise the front of the vehicle and support it with safety stands.

2. Remove the wheels.

3. Disconnect the tie-rod ends from the knuckles.

NOTE: On models with power steering, place a pan underneath to catch fluid and disconnect the return and pressure lines.

4. Remove the boot band and attaching bolts and remove the gear and linkage from the engine compartment through the tie-rod hole.

5. Installation is the reverse of removal. Make sure the steering wheel is straight forward and tighten to the following torques: Mounting bracket bolts: 23–34 ft. lbs.; tie rod end and knuckle bolts: 21–35 ft. lbs.; Intermediate shaft and pinion connecting bolt: 13–19.5 ft. lbs.

STEERING GEAR ADJUSTMENT

Worm Bearing Preload

1. Remove the gear.

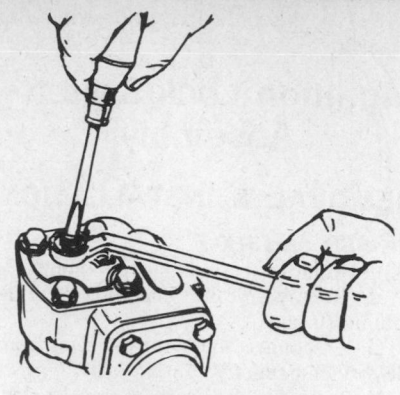

Adjusting backlash

2. Rotate the worm shaft with a torque wrench and check the torque. Rotating torque should be 8–10 in. lbs. for RX-4; 0.44–1.1 in. lbs. for RX-7; 5–11 in. lbs. for Cosmo; 5–7 in. lbs. for GLC. If not, adjust as follows:

3. Remove the end cover and shims.

4. If the preload was too light, remove shims; if too heavy, add shims.

5. Install the end cover.

Backlash

The sector shaft adjusting screw, located in the cover, raises or lowers the sector shaft to provide proper mesh with the sector gear and rack. Adjust as follows:

1. Turn the wormshaft gently and stop it at the center position.

2. Loosen the locknut and turn the adjusting screw in or out. The standard backlash is 0–0.0039 in.

3. Tighten the adjusting screw.

Power Steering Pump

REMOVAL & INSTALLATION

1. Disconnect the fluid hoses from the pump.

2. Loosen the pump belt adjusting bolt, slide the pump to one side and remove the belt.

3. Support the pump, remove the mounting bolts and lift out the pump.

4. Installation is the reverse of removal. Adjust belt to give a ½ in. deflection at the mid-point of its longest stretch. Fill the reservoir and bleed the system.

BRAKE SYSTEM

For all brake system repair and service procedures not detailed below, please refer to "Brakes" in the Unit Repair section.

Adjustments

FRONT DISC BRAKES

Disc brakes are self-adjusting by design.

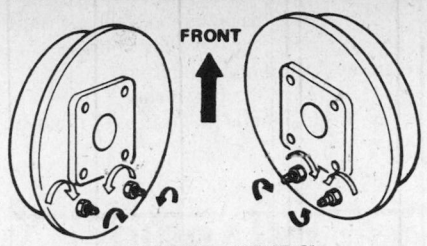

TURNING DIRECTION

∩ — Anchor pin (to expand brake shoe)

∩ — Lock nut (to tighten)

GLC-thru 1980, rear brake adjustment

As the brake pads and disc wear, fluid pressure compensates for the amount of wear. Because this action causes the fluid level to go down, the level should be checked periodically and replenished as necessary.

REAR DRUM BRAKE

All Exc. GLC and 1983 and Later 626

1. Release the parking brake completely.
2. Remove the adjusting hole plugs.
3. Engage the adjuster with a brake spoon. Turn the adjuster in the direction of the arrow stamped on the backing plate until the brake shoes are locked.
4. Pump the brake pedal several times to be sure that the brake shoe contacts the drum evenly.

NOTE: If the wheel turns after you remove your foot from the brake pedal, continue turning the adjuster until the wheel will no longer rotate.

5. Back off on the adjuster, about five notches (2–3 notches—RX-4). The wheel should rotate freely, without dragging.

NOTE: The RX-7 has rear disc brakes as an option. No adjustment is needed.

1978–80 GLC

1. Release the parking brake.
2. Loosen the locknut that secures the anchor pin.
3. Hold the locknut and turn the anchor pin counterclockwise until the wheel is locked.
4. Then release the anchor pin until the wheel just turns freely.
5. Hold the anchor pin in position and tighten the locknut.
6. Repeat the above adjustment for each brake shoe.

1981 and Later GLC and 1983 and Later 626

These models are equipped with self-adjusting rear drum brakes. No adjustment is either necessary or possible.

BRAKE PEDAL

1. Detach the wiring from the brake light switch terminals.

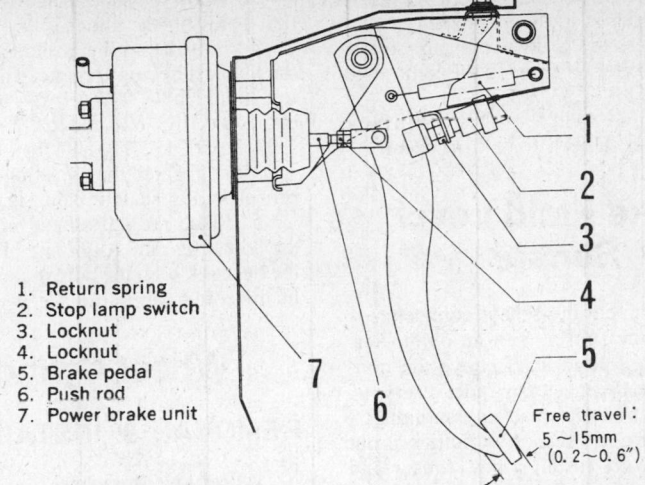

1. Return spring
2. Stop lamp switch
3. Locknut
4. Locknut
5. Brake pedal
6. Push rod
7. Power brake unit

Free travel:
5～15mm
(0.2～0.6")

Brake pedal component

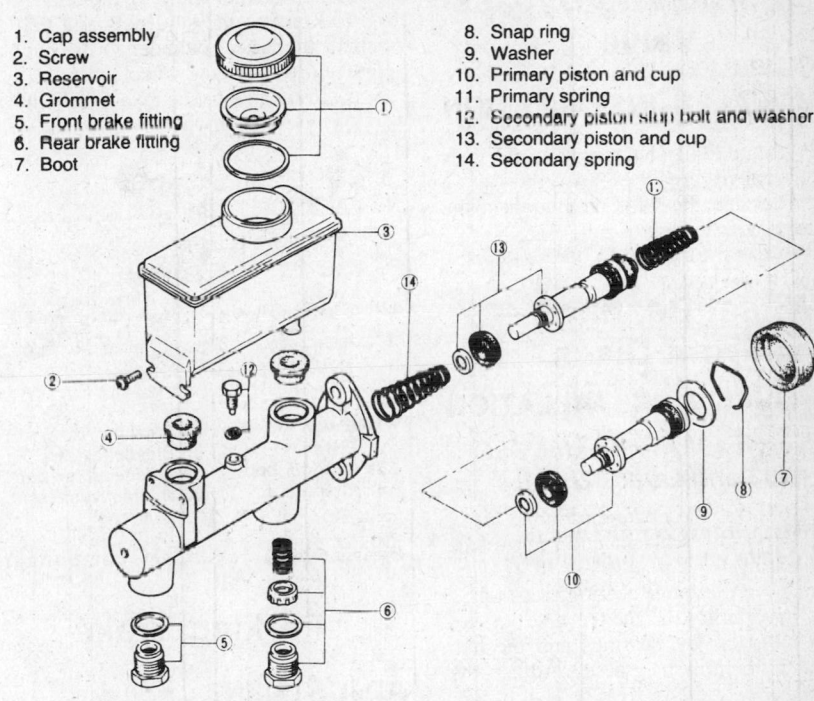

1. Cap assembly
2. Screw
3. Reservoir
4. Grommet
5. Front brake fitting
6. Rear brake fitting
7. Boot
8. Snap ring
9. Washer
10. Primary piston and cup
11. Primary spring
12. Secondary piston stop bolt and washer
13. Secondary piston and cup
14. Secondary spring

GLC-thru 1980, brake master cylinder; other models similar

2. Loosen the locknut on the switch.
3. Turn the switch until the distance between the pedal and the floor is 7.3 in (4.53 in. on 1983 and later 626).
4. Tighten the locknut on switch.
5. Loosen the locknut located on the push rod.
6. Rotate the pushrod, until a pedal free travel of 0.2–0.6 in. (0.28–0.35 in. on 1983 and later 626) is obtained.
7. Tighten the pushrod locknut.

Master Cylinder

REMOVAL & INSTALLATION

NOTE: On models which have a fluid reservoir located separately from the master cylinder, remove the lines which run between the two and plug the lines to prevent leakage.

Detach and plug the lines. Unbolt and remove the master cylinder.

Installation is the reverse of removal.

Brake Failure Warning Valve

CENTRALIZING

1. Turn the ignition switch to the ON position.

2. Make sure that the fluid level in the master cylinder is at the ¾ mark.

3. Depress the brake pedal and the piston will center itself causing the light to go off.

4. Turn the switch to OFF and check the fluid level. Check for a firm pedal.

Brake Fluid Level Sensor

1. Disconnect the sensor connector.

2. Test the sensor with an ohmmeter. With the brake fluid level above the minimum mark in the master cylinder reservoir, the ohmmeter should read no continuity.

3. Replace the sensor by pulling it out of the reservoir. Install a new sensor and connect the electrical wires.

Proportioning Bypass Valve

REMOVAL & INSTALLATION

1. Remove all of the brake fluid lines from the valve.

2. Remove the valve and connect the lines to a new valve.

3. Bleed the system.

Wheel Bearings— Front Discs

REMOVAL & INSTALLATION

All Except 1981 and Later GLC and 1983 and Later 626

1. Remove the brake disc/hub.

2. Drive the seal out and remove the inner bearing.

3. Drive the outer bearing races out.

4. Installation is the reverse of removal. Repack the bearings and the hub cavity with lithium grease. Adjust the bearing.

1981 and Later GLC and 1983 and Later 626

NOTE: On these models refer to the "Front Hub and Steering Knuckle" removal and installation procedure in the Front Suspension section.

ADJUSTMENT

NOTE: This operation is performed with the wheel, grease cap, nut lock, and cotter pin removed.

1. To seat the bearings, back off on the adjusting nut three turns and then rotate the hub/disc assembly while tightening the adjusting nut.

2. Back off on the adjusting nut about ⅙ of a turn.

3. Hook a spring scale in one of the bolt holes on the hub.

4. Pull the spring scale squarely, until the hub just begins to rotate. The scale reading should be 0.9–2.2 lbs.—all passenger cars exc. GLC, 626 and RX-7. GLC: 0.33–1.32 lbs.; 626: 0.77–1.92 lbs.; RX-7: 0.99–1.43 lbs. Tighten the adjusting nut until the proper spring scale reading is obtained.

5. Place the castellated nut lock over the adjusting nut. Align one of the slots on the nut-lock with the hole in the spindle and fit the cotter pin into place.

Wheel Cylinder

REMOVAL & INSTALLATION

1. Remove the wheel.

2. Remove the brake drum and brake shoes.

3. Disconnect and plug the brake line.

4. Remove the stud nuts and bolt attaching the wheel cylinder to the backing plate and remove the wheel cylinder.

5. Installation is the reverse of removal.

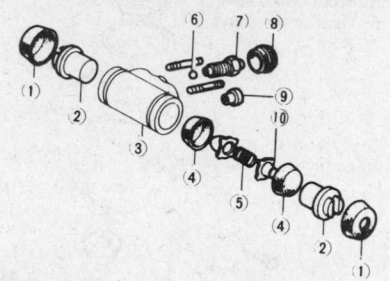

1. Boot
2. Piston
3. Cylinder body
4. Piston cup
5. Return spring
6. Steel ball
7. Bleeder screw
8. Bleeder screw cap
9. Hydraulic line seat
10. Push rod

Rear wheel cylinder components

Parking Brake

ADJUSTMENT

1. Adjust the rear brake shoes.

2. Adjust the front cable with the nut located at the rear of the parking brake handle. The handle should require 3–7 notches for RX-4, GLC (thru 80) and Cosmo models, 6–8 notches for RX-7, 5–7 for the 626 and 5–9 for the GLC (1981 and later) to apply the parking brake. Adjust 1983 and later 626 to 7–9 notches.

3. Operate the parking brake several times; check to see that the rear wheels do not drag when it is fully released.

Parking Brake Shoes

REPLACEMENT

Cosmo Only

1. Remove the brake disc.

2. Remove the brake shoe return springs.

3. Remove the secondary brake shoe retaining spring and guide pin.

4. Remove the brake shoe.

5. Installation is the reverse of removal.

CHASSIS ELECTRICAL

Wiper Motor

REPLACEMENT

1. Remove the wiper arms.

2. Remove the cowl plate screws, move the cowl plate up at the front and disconnect the washer hose. Remove the cowl plate.

3. Disconnect the wires from the wiper motor.

4. Unbolt and remove the motor.

5. Installation is the reverse of removal.

Instrument Cluster

NOTE: For more information on instruments, please refer to "Gauges and Indicators" in the Unit Repair section.

REMOVAL & INSTALLATION

RX-3 SP and RX-7

1. Pull the knob off of the steering column-mounted headlight switch. Remove the halves of the steering column shroud.

2. Open the left-hand (driver's side) door, to gain access to the screw located on the side of the instrument cluster.

3. Remove the three retaining screws which are located underneath the instrument cluster.

4. Tip the top of the cluster toward the steering wheel.

5. Disconnect the wiring and the speedometer cable from the back of the instrument cluster.

6. Remove the cluster.

7. Installation is the reverse of removal.

RX-4, Cosmo, and 1979–82 626

1. Remove the steering wheel.

2. Loosen the nut which secures the vent knob (left side) and allow the knob assembly to drop away from its mounting bracket.

3. Remove choke knob. Remove the choke retaining nut and separate the choke from the panel.

4. Remove the upper column cover.

5. Disconnect the panel light dimmer switch wiring.

6. Disconnect the exhaust temperature warning light wiring.

7. Loosen, but don't remove the screws

at either end of the lower panel cover.

NOTE: The left-hand screw is located in the hole which was covered by the upper column cover and the right-hand screw is above the ashtray opening (ashtray removed).

8. Pull the upper column cover away from the instrument panel.

9. Remove the instrument cluster surround.

10. Unfasten the instrument cluster wiring harness(es).

11. Disconnect the speedometer cable.

12. Tilt the top of the cluster forward, and lift the cluster out.

13. Installation is the reverse of removal.

GLC (Standard Dash) Through 1980

1. Disconnect the negative battery cable.

2. Remove the screw above each meter and remove the instrument cluster outside cover.

3. Remove the woodgrain center panel cover by removing the screw from the left side and unclipping the panel from the right side.

4. Remove the instrument panel pad by removing the three screws located under the front edge of the pad.

5. Disconnect the speedometer cable.

6. Remove the three instrument cluster retaining screws and pull the cluster out of the dash.

7. To install reverse the removal procedure.

GLC (Sport Dash) Through 1980

1. Disconnect the negative battery cable.

2. Remove the tripmeter knob and the cluster cover retaining screws and clips.

3. Remove the woodgrain center panel cover by removing the screw from the left side and unclipping the panel from the right side.

4. Remove the instrument panel pad by removing the three screws located under the front edge of the pad.

5. Remove the three screws and remove the instrument cluster outward.

6. Disconnect the electrical connectors and the speedometer cable.

7. To install reverse the removal procedure.

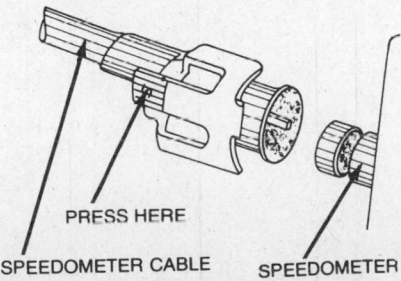

PRESS HERE

SPEEDOMETER CABLE   SPEEDOMETER

Speedometer cable removal, all models

1981 and Later GLC

1. Disconnect the negative battery cable.

2. Remove the steering wheel.

3. Remove the meter hood by removing the four screws.

4. Disconnect the speedometer cable and electrical coupler.

5. Installation is the reverse of removal.

1983 and Later 626

NOTE: Models with switches on either side of the cluster have different removal procedures than the type with no switches. The cluster switches control the wipers, washers, lights and rear defogger. The electronic (LED) meters are removed in the same manner as the regular meters.

WITH CLUSTER SWITCHES

1. Disconnect the negative battery cable and remove the upper meter cover.

2. Remove the meter hood, take out the meter light and wires and cables.

3. Remove the meter cluster screws and lift out the meter cluster.

4. Installation is the reverse of removal.

WITHOUT CLUSTER SWITCHES

1. Remove the light and meter cover.

2. Remove the wire connectors and meter cables.

3. Remove the meter screws and lift out the meter cluster.

4. Installation is the reverse of removal.

Heater Core

REMOVAL & INSTALLATION

All Models

NOTE: On models equipped with air conditioning access to the heater core will be more difficult.

——— CAUTION ———

Do not attempt to discharge the air conditioning system unless you are thoroughly familiar with the system. Escaping refrigerant will freeze any surface it contacts. If you do not have the proper training, have the system discharged and recharged by a professional.

1. Disconnect the negative battery cable. Drain the coolant from the radiator.

2. Disconnect the heater hoses at the engine firewall.

3. Disconnect the duct which runs between the heater box and the blower motor or, depending on the model, remove the crash pad and instrument panel pad from the dash. See preceding section for pad and panel removal.

4. Disconnect the defroster hose(s) if necessary, set the control to the DEF and HOT position and disconnect the control wires if they are in the way.

5. Unfasten the retaining screws that secure the halves of the heater box together

or remove the heater unit and separate the heater box for access to the heater core.

6. Detach the hoses if not already disconnected. Remove the mounting clips and the heater core. Reverse the removal procedure for installation.

Blower Motor

REMOVAL & INSTALLATION

All Models

1. Disconnect the negative battery cable.

2. Remove the dash undercover if equipped. Disconnect the multiconnector to the blower motor.

3. Remove the right side defroster hose for clearance if necessary.

4. If equipped with sliding heater controls, move the control to the HOT position and disconnect the control wire if in the way.

5. Remove the mounting screws and dismount the blower motor.

6. Installation is the reverse of removal.

Fuse Box Location

COSMO

The box is located just above the lower parcel shelf, and uses a back-hinged cover.

Fusible links in the engine compartment–RX–7

Fusible links in the steering column—RX–7

The cover has the location, amperage, and the circuit protected by each individual fuse stamped on it.

The cable running from the positive side of the battery is equipped with a fusible link.

RX-4

The main fuse and secondary fuse block are located next to the battery in the engine compartment. An additional fuse box is located beneath the glove compartment. The amperage of each fuse is printed on the fuse box lids.

RX-3SP, RX-7, GLC AND 626

The main fuse block is mounted under the dash near the driver's side kick panel.

Fusible Links

On all rotary engine cars and the 808, these are located in either one or two boxes next to the battery in the engine compartment. If these links blow, they may be replaced with the specified parts by disconnecting the battery, disconnecting wiring to each link requiring replacement, removing the attaching screws and the link, and installing the new link or links in the reverse of the removal procedure.

On the GLC, there is a connector block located on the radiator panel on the right side of the radiator inside the engine compartment. Two links connected there are color coded red and green and may simply be unplugged to remove them, and replaced by plugging in replacement parts. Make sure to disconnect the battery before replacing them.

Mercedes-Benz
190, 230, 240, 300, 380
450, 500, 6.9—All Series

ENGINE/VEHICLE IDENTIFICATION

Model	Chassis Type	Engine Model	No. of Cyls.	Engine Type	Engine Description (Fuel, Fuel Delivery, Valve Gear, Displacement)	Years
190D	201.122	OM601	4	601.921	Diesel (2197 cc)	1984–85
190E	102.961	M102	4	102.961	Gas, Fuel Inj. SOHC (2299 cc)	1984–85
230	123.023	M115	4	115.954	Gas, Carb., OHC (2307 cc)	1978
240D	123.123	OM616	4	616.912	Diesel (2404 cc)	1978–83
280E	123.033	M110	6	110.984	Gas, Fuel Inj., DOHC (2746 cc)	1978–81
280CE	123.053	M110	6	110.984	Gas, Fuel Inj., DOHC (2746 cc)	1978–81
280SE	116.024	M110	6	110.985	Gas, Fuel Inj., DOHC (2746 cc)	1978–80
300D	123.130	OM617	5	617.912	Diesel (2998 cc) ①	1978–81
	123.133	OM617	5	617.952	Diesel, Turbocharged (2998 cc)	1982–85
300CD	123.150	OM617	5	617.912	Diesel (2998 cc) ①	1978–81
	123.153	OM617	5	617.952	Diesel, Turbocharged (2998 cc)	1982–85
300SD	116.120	OM617	5	617.950	Diesel, Turbocharged (2998 cc)	1978–80
	126.120	OM617	5	617.951	Diesel, Turbocharged (2998 cc)	1981–85
300TD	123.190	OM617	5	617.912	Diesel (2998 cc)	1979–80
	123.193	OM617	5	617.952	Diesel, Turbocharged (2998 cc)	1981–85
380SE	126.032	M116	8	116.963	Gas, Fuel Inj., OHC (3839 cc)	1984–85
380SEC	126.043	M116	8	116.963	Gas, Fuel Inj., OHC (3839 cc)	1982–83
380SEL	126.033	M116	8	116.961	Gas, Fuel Inj., OHC (3839 cc)	1981–83
380SL	107.045	M116	8	116.960	Gas, Fuel Inj., OHC (3839 cc)	1981–85
380SLC	107.025	M116	8	116.960	Gas, Fuel Inj., OHC (3839 cc)	1981–82
450SEL	116.033	M117	8	117.986	Gas, Fuel Inj., OHC (4520 cc)	1978–80
450SL	107.044	M117	8	117.985	Gas, Fuel Inj., OHC (4520 cc)	1978–80
450SLC	107.024	M117	8	117.985	Gas, Fuel Inj., OHC (4520 cc)	1978–80
500SEC	126.044	M117	8	117.963	Gas, Fuel Inj., OHC (4973 cc)	1984–85

ENGINE/VEHICLE IDENTIFICATION

Model	Chassis Type	Engine Model	No. of Cyls.	Engine Type	Engine Description (Fuel, Fuel Delivery, Valve Gear, Displacement)	Years
500SEL	126.037	M117	8	117.963	Gas, Fuel Inj., OHC (4973 cc)	1984–85
6.9	116.036	M100	8	100.985	Gas, Fuel Inj., OHC (6836 cc)	1978–79

NOTE: 1978–85 models are covered in this section. The years given are not necessarily production years.
Engine designations are as follows: C = 1982, D = 1983, E = 1984, F = 1985
  DMB 2.4D6-J501-2.4 liter Diesel
  DMB 3.0D9-J508-3.0 liter Turbodiesel
  DMB 3.8V6-FSE8-3.8 liter V8 (380SEL/SEC)
  DMB 3.8V6-FSL6-3.8 liter V8 (380 SEL)
① 1978: 3005 cc

SERIAL NUMBER IDENTIFICATION

Transmission Identification

Mercedes-Benz cars for the U.S. market have been equipped with either a 4 or 5-speed manual transmission or with a fully automatic 3 or 4-speed unit. The automatic transmissions are equipped with a torque converter.

Serial numbers on the manual transmission are located on a pad on the side cover of the transmission (left side).

Automatic transmission serial numbers are located on a metal plate which is attached to the driver's side of the transmission.

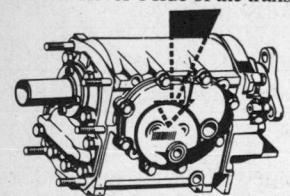

Transmission identification number

1. Catalyst and certification tag (left door pillar)
2. Identification tag (left window post)
3. Chassis no.
4. Body no. and paintwork no.
5. Engine no. on rear engine block
6. Emission control information

Location of important information on the 450SL, 450SLC and 380SL

1. Certification tag (left door pillar)
2. Identification tag (left window post)
3. Chassis no.
4. Body no. and paintwork no.
5. Engine no.
6. Emission control tag
7. Emission control tag catalyst information

Location of important information on the 300SD

1. Certification tag (left door pillar)
2. Identification tag (left window post)
3. Chassis no.
4. Body no. and paintwork no.
5. Engine no. on engine block, rear
6. Emission control information

Location of important information on all models not shown

Example: Engine Family 80.22.45.30

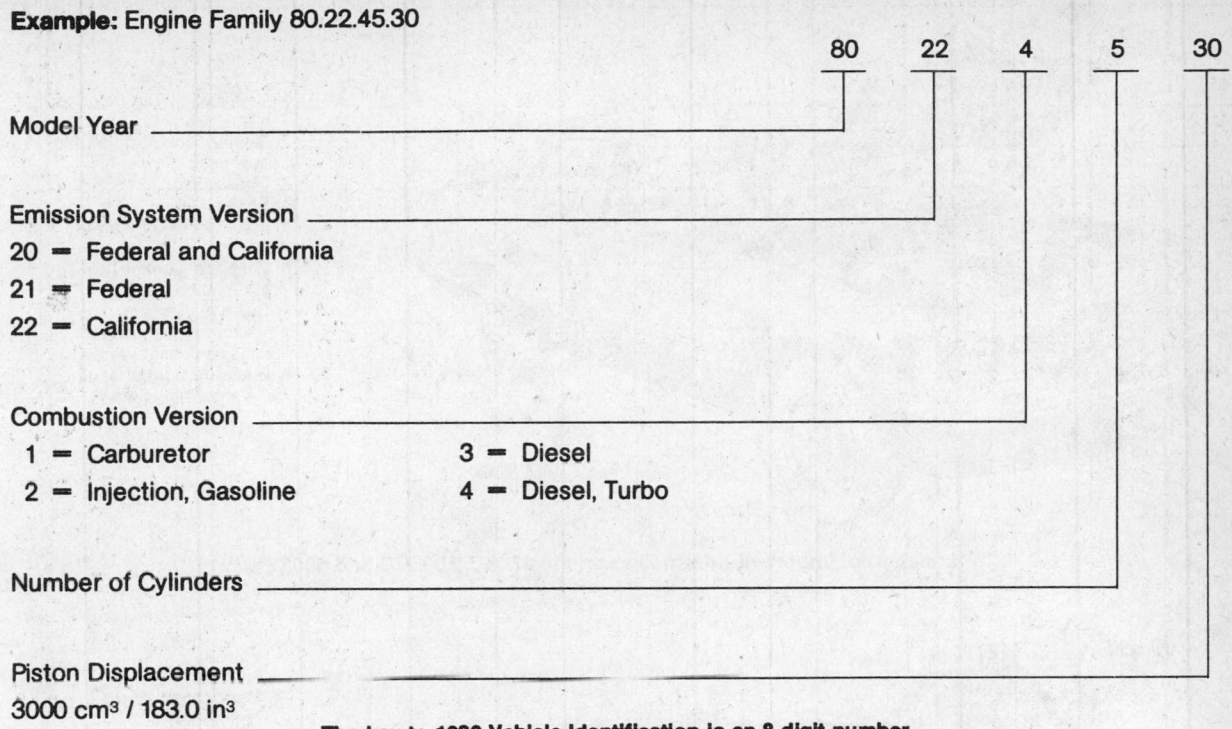

Model Year

Emission System Version
20 = Federal and California
21 = Federal
22 = California

Combustion Version
1 = Carburetor   3 = Diesel
2 = Injection, Gasoline   4 = Diesel, Turbo

Number of Cylinders

Piston Displacement
3000 cm³ / 183.0 in³

The key to 1980 Vehicle Identification is an 8 digit number

Example: Engine Family B MB 3.8 V 6 F B 4

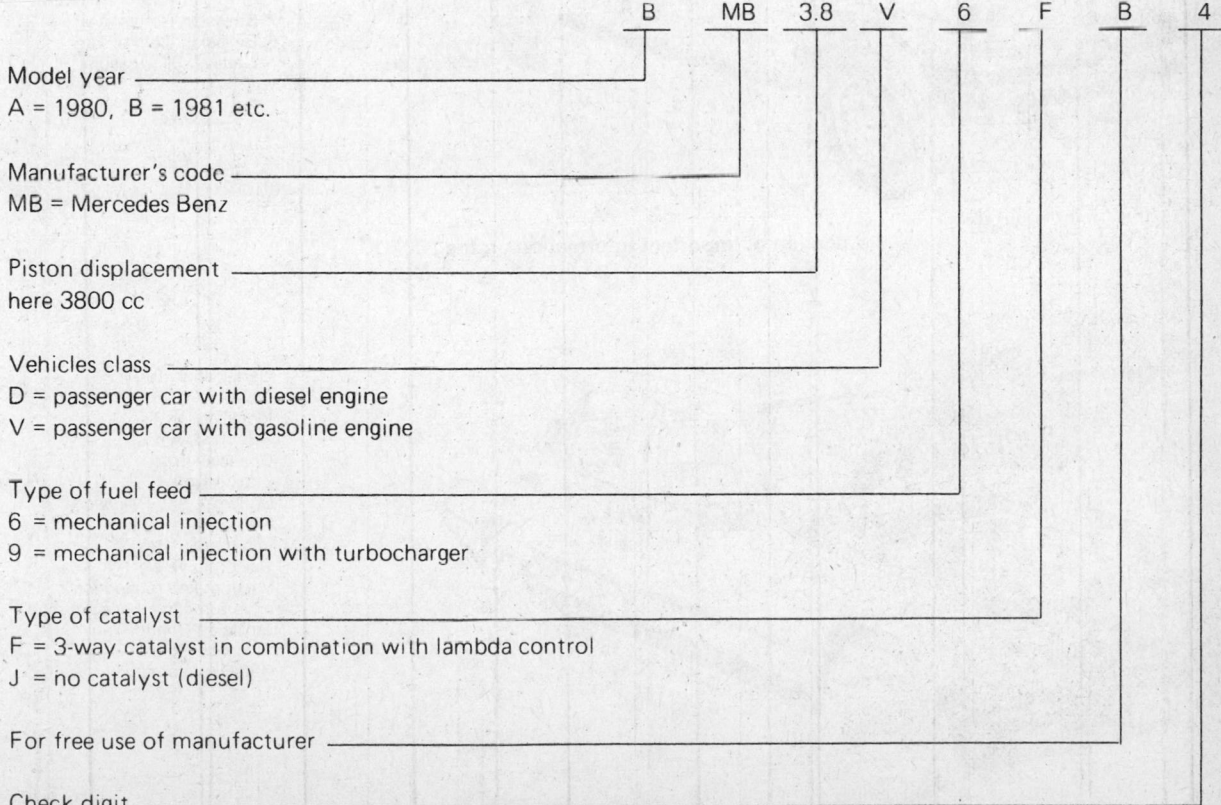

Model year
A = 1980, B = 1981 etc.

Manufacturer's code
MB = Mercedes Benz

Piston displacement
here 3800 cc

Vehicles class
D = passenger car with diesel engine
V = passenger car with gasoline engine

Type of fuel feed
6 = mechanical injection
9 = mechanical injection with turbocharger

Type of catalyst
F = 3-way catalyst in combination with lambda control
J = no catalyst (diesel)

For free use of manufacturer

Check digit

The key to 1981 and later engine identification is a 10 digit number.

1 Certification Tag (left door pillar)
2 Identification Tag (left window post)
3 Chassis No.
4 Engine No.
5 Body No. and Paintwork No.
6 Emission Control Tag
7 Information Tag California version Vacuum line routing for emission control system
8 Emission Control Tag Catalyst Information

Location of important information on the 380SE, 500SEC and 500SEL

1 Certification Tag (left door pillar)
2 Identification Tag (left window post)
3 Chassis No.
4 Engine No.
5 Body No. and Paintwork No.
6 Information Tag California version Vacuum line routing for emission control system
7 Emission Control Tag
8 Emission Control Tag Catalyst Information

Location of important information on the 300TD

1 Certification Tag (left door pillar)
2 Identification Tag (left window post)
3 Chassis No.
4 Engine No.
5 Body No. and Paintwork No.
6 Information Tag California version Vacuum line routing for emission control system
7 Emission Control Tag Emission Control Tag Catalyst Information

Location of important information on the 190D and 190E

MERCEDES–BENZ

TRANSMISSION APPLICATIONS

Model	Automatic Transmission	Manual Transmission
190D	W4A020	GL68/20A-5
190E	W4A020	GL68/20B-5
230	W4B 025	—
240D (thru '80)	W4B 025	G-76/18C(4-spd.)
240D ('81 and later)	W4B 025	GL68/20A (4-spd.)
280E, 280CE	W4B 025	—
280SE	W4B 025	—
300D, 300CD, 300TD	W4B 025	—
300D Turbo. 300CD Turbo	W4A 040	—
300TD Turbo 1981–85	W4A 040	—
300SD 1978–80	W4B 025	—
300SD 1981–85	W4A 040	—
380SL, 380SLC, 380SEL, 380SEC, 380SE	W4A 040	—
450SEL, 450SL, 450SLC	W3A 040	—
500SEC, 500SEL	W4A040	—
6.9	W3B 050	—

GENERAL GASOLINE ENGINE SPECIFICATIONS

Year/Model	Engine Model	Engine Displacement (cc)	Fuel Delivery	Horsepower @ rpm	Torque @ rpm (ft. lbs.)	Bore x Stroke (mm)	Compression Ratio	Firing Order
190E	M102	2299	Fuel Injection	113 @ 5000	133 @ 3500	95.50 × 80.25	8.0:1	1 3 4 2
230	M115	2307	Stromberg 175 CDT	95 @ 4800	128 @ 2500	93.75 × 83.6	8.0:1	1 3 4 2
280E, 280CE, 280SE	M110	2746	Fuel Injection	142 @ 5750 ①	149 @ 4600 ②	86.00 × 78.80	8.0:1	1 5 3 6 2 4
380SL 380SLC 380SE 380SEL 380SEC	M116	3839	Fuel Injection	155 @ 4750	196 @ 2750	88.0 × 78.9	8.3:1	1 5 4 8 6 3 7 2
450SEL 450SL 450SLC	M117	4520	Fuel Injection	180 @ 4750	220 @ 3000	92.00 × 85.00	8.0:1	1 5 4 8 6 3 7 2
500SEC 500SEL	M117	4973	Fuel Injection	184 @ 4500	247 @ 2000	96.5 × 85.0	8.0:1	1 5 4 8 6 3 7 2
6.9	M100	6836	Fuel Injection	250 @ 4000	360 @ 2500	107.0 × 95.0	8.0:1	1 5 4 8 6 3 7 2

NOTE: Horsepower may vary depending on year of application.
① California—137@5750
② California—142@4600

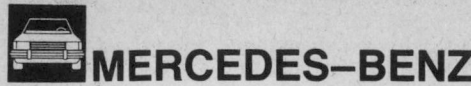

GENERAL DIESEL ENGINE SPECIFICATIONS

Car Model	Engine Model	Engine Displacement (cc)	Fuel Delivery	Horsepower @ rpm	Torque @ rpm (ft. lbs.)	Bore x Stroke (mm)	Compression Ratio	Firing Order
190D	OM601	2197	Fuel Injection	72 @ 4200	96 @ 2800	87.0 × 92.4	22:1	1 3 4 2
240D	OM616	2404	Fuel Injection	62–67 @ 4000	97 @ 2400	91.0 × 92.4	21:1	1 3 4 2
300D ('78–'81) 300CD ('78–'81) 300TD ('79–'80)	OM617	2998①	Fuel Injection	77–83 @ 4000	115–120 @ 2400	90.9 × 92.4②	21:1	1 2 4 5 3
300TD ('81–'85) 300D ('82–'85) 300CD ('82–'85)	OM617	2998	Fuel Inj. Turbocharged	120 @ 4350	170 @ 2400③	90.9 × 92.4	21:1	1 2 4 5 3
300SD	OM617	2998	Fuel Inj. Turbocharged	110–120 @ 4200④	168–170@ 2400③	90.9 × 92.4	21:1⑤	1 2 4 5 3

NOTE: Horsepower may vary depending on year and application.
① 1978: 3005cc
② 1978: 91.0 × 92.4
③ 1984–85: 184 @ 2400
④ 1984–85: 123 @ 4350
⑤ 1984–85: 21.5:1

GASOLINE ENGINE TUNE-UP SPECIFICATIONS
(When analyzing compression test results, look for uniformity among cylinders, rather than specific pressures)

Year	Model	Spark Plugs Type	Gap (in.)	Distributor Point Dwell (deg)	Ignition Timing (deg)	Intake Valve Opens (deg)	Fuel Pump Pressure (psi) Idle●	▲ Idle Speed (rpm)	Valve Clearance* (in.) In (cold)	Ex (cold)
'78–'79	230	N10Y	0.032	Elec.	10B w/vacuum	14B	2–3	850	0.004	0.008
	280E, 280CE, 280SE	N10Y	0.032	Elec.	TDC w/vacuum	7B	75–84 ①	800	0.004	0.010
	450SEL	N10Y	0.032	Elec.	TDC w/vacuum	②	75–84 ①	750	Hyd.	Hyd.
	450SL, 450SLC	N10Y	0.032	Elec.	TDC w/vacuum	②	75–84 ①	750	Hyd.	Hyd.
	6.9	N10Y	0.032	Elec.	TDC w/vacuum	③	75–84 ①	600	Hyd.	Hyd.
'80	280E, 280CE, 280SE	N10Y	0.032	Elec.	10B	7B	④	700–800	0.004	0.010
	450SEL	N10Y	0.032	Elec.	5B	⑤	④	600–700	Hyd.	Hyd.
	450SL, 450SLC	N10Y	0.032	Elec.	5B	⑤	④	600–700	Hyd.	Hyd.

GASOLINE ENGINE TUNE-UP SPECIFICATIONS

(When analyzing compression test results, look for uniformity among cylinders, rather than specific pressures)

Year	Model	Spark Plugs Type	Gap (in.)	Distributor Point Dwell (deg)	Ignition Timing (deg)	Intake Valve Opens (deg)	Fuel Pump Pressure (psi) Idle●	▲ Idle Speed (rpm)	Valve Clearance* (in.) In (cold)	Valve Clearance* (in.) Ex (cold)
'81	280E, 280CE	N10Y	0.032	Elec.	10B	7B	④	700–800	0.004	0.010
	380SEL	N10Y	0.032	Elec.	5B	24A	④	500	Hyd.	Hyd.
	380SL, 380SLC	N10Y	0.032	Elec.	5B	24A	④	500	Hyd.	Hyd.
'82	380SL	N10Y	0.032	Elec.	5B	24A	④	500–600	Hyd.	Hyd.
	380SEL	N10Y	0.032	Elec.	5B	24A	④	500–600	Hyd.	Hyd.
	380SEC	N10Y	0.032	Elec.	5B	24A	④	500–600	Hyd.	Hyd
'83–'84	190E	S12YC	0.032	Elec.	5B	⑥	77–80	700–600	Hyd.	Hyd.
	380SL	N10Y	0.032	Elec.	TDC w/o vacuum	24A	④	500–600	Hyd.	Hyd.
	380SE, 380SEC, 380SEL	N10Y	0.032	Elec.	TDC w/o vacuum	24A	④	500–600	Hyd.	Hyd.
	500SEC, 500SEL	N10Y	0.032	Elec.	TDC w/o vacuum	⑤	④	600–700	Hyd.	Hyd.
'85	All	See Underhood Specification Sticker								

CAUTION: If the specifications listed above differ from those on the tune-up decal in the engine compartment, use those listed on the tune-up decal.

NOTES: 1. On transistor ignitions, only a transistorized dwell meter can be used. Transistor ignitions are recognizable by the "Blue" ignition coil, 2 series resistors and the transistor switchgear.

2. To counteract wear of the fiber contact block, adjust the dwell to the lower end of the range.

A After Top Dead Center
B Before Top Dead Center
w/vacuum—vacuum advance connected
w/o vacuum—vacuum advance disconnected
* Below 0°F; increase valve clearance by 0.002 in.
—Not Available
▲ In Drive
●Timing for test measurements @ 2mm valve lift

① Injection pump pressure
② Right side camshaft—4.5° ATDC
   Left side camshaft—6.5° ATDC
③ Right side camshaft—12° ATDC
   Left side camshaft—10°ATDC

④ Approximately 1 quart In 30 seconds
⑤ Left side—22° ATDC
   Right side—20° ATDC
⑥ New timing chain: 17A
   Used timing chain (12,000 miles): 18A

DIESEL ENGINE TUNE-UP SPECIFICATIONS

Model	Valve Clearance (cold)① Intake (in.)	Valve Clearance (cold)① Exhaust (in.)	Intake Valve Opens (deg)	Injection Pump Setting (deg)	Injection Nozzle Pressure (psi) New	Injection Nozzle Pressure (psi) Used	Idle Speed (rpm) ②	Cranking Compression Pressure (psi)
190D	Hyd.	Hyd.	⑤	15A	1564–1706	1422–1706	700–800	284–327
240D	0.004	0.016	13.5B	24B	1564–1706	1422–1706	750–800	284–327

DIESEL ENGINE TUNE-UP SPECIFICATIONS

Model	Valve Clearance (cold) ①		Intake Valve Opens (deg)	Injection Pump Setting (deg)	Injection Nozzle Pressure (psi)		Idle Speed (rpm) ②	Cranking Compression Pressure (psi)
	Intake (in.)	Exhaust (in.)			New	Used		
300D, 300CD, 300TD (5-cylinder, non-turbo)	0.004	0.012	13.5B	24B④	1635–1750 ③	1422	700–800	284–327
300SD, 300TD (5-cylinder, turbo) '78–'81	0.004	0.014	13.5B	24B④	1958–2074	1740	650–850	284–327
300D, 300CD, 300SD, 300TD (5-cylinder, turbo) '82–'85	0.004	0.014	13.5B	24B④ ⑥	1958–2074	1740	650–850⑦	284–327

B Before Top Dead Center
① In cold weather (below 5°F.), increase valve clearance 0.002 in.
② Manual transmission in Neutral; Automatic in Drive.

③ Difference in opening pressure on injection nozzles should not exceed 71 psi.
④ The injection pump is in start of delivery position when the mark on the pump camshaft is aligned with the mark on the injection pump flange.

⑤ New timing chain: 11A
   Used timing chain (12,000 miles): 12A
⑥ 1984–85: 15A
⑦ 1984–85: 700–800

FIRING ORDERS

NOTE: The position of No. 1 tower on the distributor cap may vary. To avoid confusion when replacing wires, always replace wires one at a time. The notch cut into the rim of the distributor body always indicates No. 1 cylinder.

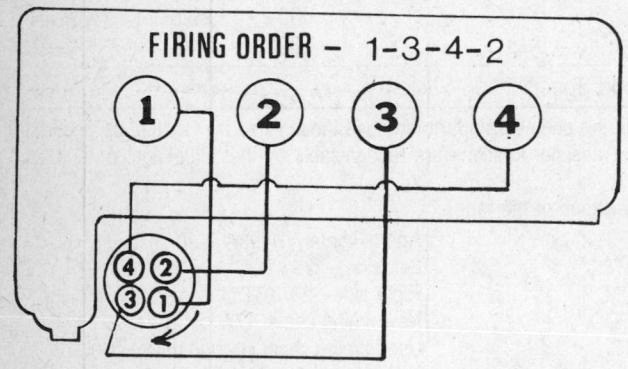

4-cylinder gas engine

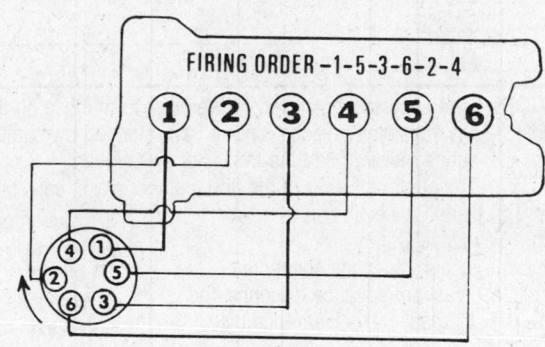

6-cylinder gas engine

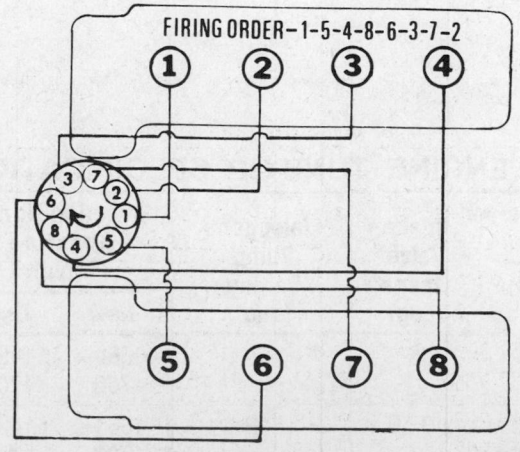

V8 gasoline engines

CAPACITIES

Year	Model	Cooling System (qts)	Engine Crankcase (qts) ▲		Transmission (pts)		Drive Axle (pts)	Steering Gear (pts)		Level Control (qts)
			With Filter	Without Filter	Manual (4-spd)	Automatic		Power	Manual	
'84	190D	9.0	4.8	4.8	3.2	11.6	1.5	1.0	—	—
'84	190E	9.0	6.3	5.8	3.2	11.6	1.5	1.0	—	—
'78	230	10.5	5.8	5.3	—	11.5	②	3.0	⅝	—
'78–'83	240D	10.5	6.3	5.3	3.4	11.5	②	3.0	⅝	—
'78–'81	280E, 280CE	11.5	6.3	5.8	—	12.3	2.1	3.0	—	—
'78–'80	280SE	11.5	6.3	5.8	—	12.3	2.1	3.0	—	—
'78–'81	300D, 300CD	11.7	6.8	5.3	—	11.5	2.1	3.0	—	—
'82–'85	300D, 300CD	13.2	8.0	6.3	—	13.2	2.2	3.0	—	—
'78–'80	300SD, 300TD	12.7④	6.8	5.3	—	11.5	2.1	3.0	—	6.2③
'81–'85	300SD, 300TD	13.2	8.0	6.3	—	13.2	2.2	3.0	—	3.7
'81	380SL, SLC 380SEL	13.7	8.5	8.0	—	13.0	2.7	⑤	—	—
'82 '85	380SL, 380SE	13.2	8.5	8.0	—	16.2	2.7	3.0	—	—
'82–'83	380SEL 380SEC	13.2	8.5	8.0	—	13.0	2.7	2.5	—	—
'78–'80	450SEL, 450SL, 450SLC	16.0	8.5	8.0	—	16.5	①	3.0	—	6.2③
'84–'85	500SEC 500SEL	13.7	8.5	8.0	—	16.2	2.8	2.6	—	—
'78 '79	6.9	16.0	11.5	10.5	—	16.5	2.7	3.0	—	6.2③

▲Add approximately ½ quart if equipped with additional oil cooler
—Not Applicable
① 450SL, 450SLC—2.7 pts
   450SEL—3.0 pts
② See text:1st version—2.4 pts
           2nd version—2.1 pts
③ Approximately 1 qt between dipstick maximum and minimum marks
④ 300SD—13.0 qts
⑤ 380SEL—2.5
   380SL, SLC—3.0

CRANKSHAFT AND CONNECTING ROD SPECIFICATIONS

(All measurements are given in millimeters)

Car Model	Engine Displace (cc)	Engine Model	Crankshaft				Connecting Rod		
			Main Brg. Journal Dia.	Main Brg. Oil Clearance	Shaft End-Play	Thrust on No.	Journal Diameter	Oil Clearance	Side Clearance
190D	2197	OM601	57.960–57.965	0.031–0.073	0.100–0.250	①	47.950–47.965	0.031–0.073	N.A.
190E	2299	M102	57.960–57.965	0.031–0.073	0.100–0.250	①	47.950–47.965	0.031–0.073	N.A.
230	2307	M115	69.955–69.965	0.045–0.065	0.100–0.240	①	51.955–51.965	0.035–0.055	0.110–0.260

CRANKSHAFT AND CONNECTING ROD SPECIFICATIONS

(All measurements are given in millimeters)

Car Model	Engine Displace (cc)	Engine Model	Crankshaft				Connecting Rod		
			Main Brg. Journal Dia.	Main Brg. Oil Clearance	Shaft End-Play	Thrust on No.	Journal Diameter	Oil Clearance	Side Clearance
240D	2404	OM616	69.955–69.965	0.045–0.065	0.100–0.240	①	51.955–51.965	0.035–0.055	0.110–0.260
280E 280CE 280SE	2746	M110	59.96–59.95	0.03–0.07	0.10–0.24	①	47.95–47.96	0.15–0.50	0.11–0.23
300D, 300CD, 300TD, 300SD	2998②	OM617	69.955–69.965	0.045–0.065	0.100–0.240	①	51.955–51.965	0.035–0.055	0.110–0.260
380SE 380SEL 380SL 380SLC 380SEC	3839	M116	63.950–63.965	0.045–0.065	0.100–0.240	①	47.945–47.965	0.045–0.065	0.220–0.359
450SL 450SLC 450SEL	4520	M117	63.955–63.965	0.035–0.075	0.100–0.240	①	51.955–51.965	0.035–0.065	0.220–0.380
500SEC 500SEL	4973	M117	63.950–63.965	0.045–0.065	0.100–0.240	①	47.945–47.965	0.045–0.065	0.220–0.359
6.9	6836	M100	69.945–69.965	0.045–0.065	0.100–0.240	①	54.940–54.600–	0.045–0.065	0.220–0.359–

N.A. Not Available
① Center main on 5 main bearing engines; rear main on 7 main bearing engines; 3rd from front on 300D (5-cylinder)
② 1978: 3005cc

VALVE SPECIFICATIONS

Car Model	Engine Displacement (cc)	Seat Angle (deg)	Spring Test Pressure (mm@KP)	STEM DIAMETER (mm)	
				Intake	Exhaust
190D	2197	45	30.5 @ 85.96–91.98	7.97	8.96
190E	2299	45	27 @ 73.42–78.52	7.97	8.96
230	2307	45 + 15′	39 @ 36①	8.948–8.970	10.918–10.940
240D	2404	30 + 15′	38.4 @ 23–26.4	9.920–9.905	9.918–9.940
280CE 280E 280SE	2746	45 + 15′	84–92 @ 30.5	8.950–8.970	③
300D, 300CD, 300TD, 300SD	2998④	30 + 15′	38.4 @ 23–26.4	9.920–9.940	9.918–9.940
380SE 380SL 380SLC 380SEL 380SEC	3839	45	30.5@88①	8.955–8.970	8.935–8.960

VALVE SPECIFICATIONS

Car Model	Engine Displacement (cc)	Seat Angle (deg)	Spring Test Pressure (mm@KP)	STEM DIAMETER (mm)	
				Intake	Exhaust
450SL 450SLC 450SEL	4520	45 + 15′	42 @ 29.5–32.5 ①	8.955– 8.970	10.940– 10.960
500SEC 500SEL	4973	45 + 15′	30.5 @ 88 ①	8.955– 8.970	8.935– 8.960
6.9	6834	45 + 15′	44.5 2.3	8.948– 8.970	11.932– 11.950

N.A. Not available at time of publication
① Outer spring—the spring should be installed so that the close coils are in contact with the cylinder head
② 1980 and later: 28.0
③ 1978–79: 10.940–10.960
  1980–81: 8.940–8.960
④ 1978: 3005cc

VALVE TIMING SPECIFICATIONS▲

Model	Camshaft Code Number●	Intake Valve		Exhaust Valve	
		Opens ATDC*	Closes ABDC*	Opens BBDC*	Closes BTDC*
190D	05	11/12	17/18	28/27	15/14
190E	20①, 21②	17/18	11/12	17.5/16.5	12/11
230	05	14	20	22	12
240D	02, 06③	11.5/13.5	13.5/15.5	21/19	19/17
280E, 280CE, 280SE	67④, 71④	7	21	30	12
300D ('78–'81), 300CD ('78–'81), 300SD ('78–'79), 300TD ('79–'80)	00, 08③	11.5/13.5	13.5/15.5	21/19	19/17
300D ('82–'85), 300CD ('82–'85), 300SD ('80–'85), 300TD ('81–'85)	05③	9/11	15/17	27/25	16/14
380SEL, 380SL, 380SLC	62/63, 68/69 L R L R	L-24 R-22	L-7.5 R-5.5	L-4 R-6	R-12.5 R-14.5
380SE, 380SEC	70/71 L R	L-16 R-14	L-15 R-13	L-16 R-18	R-17 R-19
450SEL, 450SL, 450SLC ('78–'80)	00/01 L R	L-6.5 R-4.5	L-18.5 R-16.5	L-23 R-25	L- 8 R-10
500SEC, 500SEL	08/09 L R	L-22 R-20	L-21 R-19	L-10 R-12	L-15 R-17
6.9	36/37 L R	L-12 R-10	L-25 R-23	L-32 R-34	L-19 R-21

▲Taken at 2mm valve lift
●Camshaft code number is stamped into rear face of camshaft
*When numbers are separated by a slash, first figure is for a new timing chain and second figure is for a used timing chain (approx. 20,000 km). When no slash is used, the figure is for a new timing chain.
L Left
R Right
ATDC After Top Dead Center
ABDC After Bottom Dead Center
BBDC Before Bottom Dead Center
BTDC Before Top Dead Center
① Camshaft with 32mm bearing diameter (standard)
② Camshaft with 32.5mm bearing diameter (repair version)
③ Camshaft made of chilled cast iron
④ 1st figure: exhaust camshaft
  2nd figure: intake camshaft

TORQUE SPECIFICATIONS
(All readings in ft. lbs.)

Car Model	Engine Model	Cylinder Head Bolts	Rod Bearing Bolts	Main Bearing Bolts	Crankshaft Pulley Bolt	Flywheel To Crankshaft Bolts	Cam Sprocket Bolt(s)	Exhaust Manifold Bolts
190D	OM601	⑦①	⑧	65	195–239	⑨	33	N.A.
190E	M102	⑩①	⑨	65	195–239	⑨	58	N.A.
230	M115	58	①	58③	151–158	①	18	18–21
240D	OM616	65⑬	①	65	151–158	①	18	18–21
280E 280CE 280SE	M110	58	①	58	206–226	①	58	N.A.
300D, 300CD 300TD, 300SD	OM617	65⑬	①	65	195–240	①	18	18–21
380SE 380SL 380SEL 380SLC 380SEC	M116	⑫	30–37 ①	⑤	289	①	74	N.A.
450SL 450SLC 450SEL	M117	⑪	①	④	180–194	①	36	18–21
500SEC 500SEL	M117	⑫	①	④	180–194	①	36	18–21
6.9	M100	65	①	⑤	289	①	72	N.A.

N.A. Not Available at time of publication
① See text
② With cold engine; cylinder head bolts should be tightened in at least 3 stages
③ 65 on M115 engines
④ M 10 bolts—37 ft. lbs.
   M 12 bolts—72 ft. lbs.
⑤ M 10 bolts—43 ft. lbs.
   M 12 bolts—58 ft. lbs.
⑥ Tighten to 22 ft. lbs. then to 45 ft. lbs. in proper sequence. After 10 mins. loosen and tighten again to 45 ft. lbs.
⑦ M10 bolts: 1st step—18 ft. lbs.
          2nd step—29 ft. lbs.
          setting time—10 min.
          3rd step—90° torquing angle
          4th step—90° torquing angle
   M8 bolts: 18 ft. lbs.
⑧ 1st step: 22–25 ft. lbs.
   2nd step: 90–100° torquing angle
⑨ 1st step: 22–29 ft. lbs.
   2nd step: 90–100° torquing angle
⑩ M12 bolts: 1st step—29 ft. lbs.
          2nd step—51 ft. lbs.
          setting time—10 min.
          3rd step—90° torquing angle
          4th step—90° torquing angle
   M8 bolts: 18 ft. lbs.

⑪ 1st step: 22 ft. lbs.
   2nd step: 44 ft. lbs.
   setting time: 10 min.
   3rd step: warm engine, loosen bolts and retighten to 44 ft. lbs.
⑫ 1st step: 22 ft. lbs.
   2nd step: 44 ft. lbs.
   setting time: 10 min.
   3rd step: loosen bolts and retighten to 44 ft. lbs.
⑬ All vehicles manufactured after Feb. 1979:
   1st step:—29 ft. lbs.
   2nd step—51 ft. lbs.
   setting time—10 min.
   3rd step—90° torquing angle
   4th step—90° torquing angle

BATTERY AND STARTER SPECIFICATIONS

(All cars use 12 volt, negative ground electrical systems)

Engine Model	Lock Test Amps	Lock Test Volts	Lock Test Torque (ft. lbs.)	No Load Test Amps	No Load Test Volts	No Load Test rpm	Brush Spring Tension (oz)	Min. Brush Length (in.)
All w/Diesel Engine	650–750	9.0	1000–1200	80–95	12	7500–8500	N.A.	N.A.
All w/Gas Engine	290–300	9.0	1600–1800	50–70	12	9000–11000	N.A.	0.5

N.A. Not specified by manufacturer

BRAKE SPECIFICATIONS

(All measurements given are in inches unless noted. See following summary of Brake Pad Application)

Year	Model	Lug Nut Torque (ft. lbs.)	Master Cylinder Bore (in.)	Front Brake Disc Minimum Thickness (in.)	Front Brake Disc Maximum Run-Out (in.)	Rear Brake Disc Minimum Thickness (in.)	Rear Brake Disc Maximum Run-Out (in.)	Minimum Lining Thickness Front ▲ (in.)	Minimum Lining Thickness Rear ▲ (in.)
'84–'85	190D, 190E	75	⑥	0.35	0.0047 (max.)	0.30	0.0059 (max.)	0.08②	0.08②
'78–'85	230, 240D, 280E, 280CE, 300D, 300CD, 300TD	75	③	①	0.0047 (max.)	0.33	0.0059 (max.)	0.08②	0.08②
'78–'85	280SE, 300SD, 380SE, 380SEC, 380SEL, 380SL, 380SLC, 450SEC, 450SL, 450SLC, 500SEC, 500SEL, 6.9	75	③	④ ⑤	0.0047 (max.)	0.33	0.0047 (max.)	0.08②	0.08②

NOTE: Minimum lining thickness is as recommended by the manufacturer. Due to variations in state inspection regulations, the minimum allowable thickness may be different than recommended by the manufacturer.

▲New thickness of brake lining and back-up plate—0.59 in.
New thickness of backing plate—0.20 in.
New thickness of brake lining—0.39 in.
—Not Applicable
① Caliper w/57 mm piston diameter: 0.44 in.
Caliper w/60 mm piston diameter: 0.42 in.
② 1978 and later brake pads are equipped with electric pad wear indicators

③ Pushrod circuit: 15/16 in.
Floating circuit: ¾ in.
④ Caliper w/57 mm piston diameter: 0.81 in.
Caliper w/60 mm piston diameter: 0.79 in.
⑤ March, 1980 and later: 0.76 in.
⑥ Pushrod circuit: ⅞ in.
Floating circuit: 11/16 in.

SUMMARY OF BRAKE PAD APPLICATION

Model	Arrangement mm/in.	Thickness of Pad mm/in.	Brake Pad Repair Set Part No.	Color Code	Remarks
107 1st version	Front axle Caliper with 57/2.244 dia. piston	15/0.591	001 586 19 42 001 586 31 42	gn-yl-gn-gn gn-gn-gn-gn-bu	—
Without brake pad sensor 107 2nd version 116 1st version	Front axle Caliper with 60/2.362 dia. piston	15/0.591	001 586 18 42 001 586 32 42	gn-yl-gn-gn gn-gn-gn-gn-bu	

SUMMARY OF BRAKE PAD APPLICATION

Model	Arrangement mm/in.	Thickness of Pad mm/in.	Brake Pad Repair Set Part No.	Color Code	Remarks
With brake pad sensor 107 3rd version 116 2nd version 123 1st version	Front axle Caliper with 60/2.362 dia. piston	15/0.591	001 586 33 42 001 586 36 42	gn-yl-gn-gn gn-gn-gn-gn-bu	—
With brake pad sensor 116 123 Beginning '80	Front axle Caliper with 60/2.362 dia. piston	17.5/0.689	002 586 45 42 002 586 46 42	gn-gn-gn-gn-bu gn-yl-gn-gn	These linings must only be combined with the rear axle linings 002 586 47 42 or 002 586 48 42
107 All except 116 '80 models 123	Rear axle Caliper with 38/1.496 dia. piston	15/0.591	000 586 76 42	gn-gn-bu-bu	—
116 123 Beginning '80	Rear axle Caliper with 38/1.496 dia. piston	15.0/0.610	002 586 47 42 002 586 48 42	gn-gn-bu-gn-bu gn-yl-yl-gn-yl	These linings must only be combined with the front axle linings 002 586 45 42 or 002 586 46 42
123.190 All	Rear axle Caliper 2ith 42/1.654 dia. piston	15/0.591	001 586 64 42	gn-gn-bu-bu-bu	—

gn—green yl—yellow bu—blue

WHEEL ALIGNMENT SPECIFICATIONS

Car Model	Front Wheels			Rear Wheels	
	Camber (deg)	Caster (deg) Power Steering	Toe-In (in.)	Camber (deg)	Toe-In (mm)
190D, 190E	5/16 + 1/4 − 7/16	10 3/16 ± 1/2	1/16–5/32	See Chart 7	3 + 1.0 − 0.5
230 240D 280E 280CE 300D 300CD 300TD	0 + 3/16 − 5/16	8 3/4 ± 1/2	3/32–5/32	See Chart 2	See Chart 3
450SL 450SLC	0 + 3/16 − 5/16	3 11/16 ± 5/16	1/32–1/8	See Chart 1	See Chart 3
280SE 300SD (thru '80) 450SEL 6.9	5/16N	9 1/2–10 1/2	3/32–5/32	See Chart 4	See Chart 3
380SL 380SLC	0 + 3/16 − 5/16	3 11/16 ± 5/16	1/32–1/8	3/16–11/16 See Chart 5	0–35
300SD('81 and later) 380SEL, 380SEC 380SEC 500SEC, 500SEL	0 ± 3/16	9 1/4–10 1/4	1/8–1/4	See Chart 6	①

N Negative
① If trailing arm position is   35–50 mm toe-in is .08–.19
    0–35 mm toe-in .06–.18   50–60 mm toe-in is .10–.21

WHEEL ALIGNMENT CHART 1

Control Arm Position mm (in.)	Corresponds to Rear Wheel Camber On: 450SL, 450SLC
+80(3.17")	—
+75(2.98")	—
+70(2.78")	—
+65(2.58")	—
+60(2.38")	—
+55(2.18")	—
+50(1.99")	13/16 ± ½
+45(1.79")	9/16 ± ½
+40(1.59")	5/16 ± ½
+35(1.39")	1/16 ± ½
+30(1.12")	−3/16 ± ½
+25(0.99")	−7/16 ± ½
+20(0.79")	−11/16 ± ½
+15(0.60")	−15/16 ± ½
+10(0.40")	−1 3/16 ± ½
+5(0.20")	−1 7/16 ± ½
0	−1 11/16 ± ½
−5(0.20")	−1 15/16 ± ½
−10(0.40")	−2 3/16 ± ½
−15(0.60")	−2 7/16 ± ½
+20(0.79")	−2 11/16 ± ½

REAR WHEEL CAMBER CHART 2
(230, 240D, 280E, 280CE, 300D, 300CD, 300TD)

Semi-trailing Arm Position mm (inches)	Corresponds to Rear Wheel Camber
+70(+2.76)	1¾ ± ½
+65(+2.56)	1½ + ½
+60(+2.36)	1¼ ± ½
+55(+2.17)	1 ± ½
+50(+1.97)	¾ ± ½
+45(+1.77)	½ ± ½
+40(+1.58)	¼ ± ½
+35(+1.37)	−0 ± ½
+30(+1.18)	−¼ ± ½
+25(+0.98)	−½ ± ½
+20(+0.79)	−¾ ± ½
+15(+0.59)	−1 ± ½
+10(+0.39)	−1¼ ± ½
+5(+0.20)	−1½ ± ½
0(0)	−1¾ ± ½
−5(−0.20)	−2 ± ½
−10(−0.39)	−2¼ ± ½
−15(−0.59)	−2½ ± ½

WHEEL ALIGNMENT CHART 3

Rear Wheel Control Arm Position	Corresponds to Rear Wheel Toe-In of:
0 to +35 mm (0 to +1.38")	0°10' +20'/−10' or 1 +2/−1 mm (0.04" +0.08"/−0.04")
+35 to +50 mm (+1.38" to +1.97")	0°15' +20'/−10' or 1.5 +2/−1 mm (0.06" +0.08"/−0.04")
+50 to +60 mm (+1.97" to +2.36")	0°20' +20'/−10' or 2 +2/−1 mm (0.08" +0.08"/−0.04")
+60 to +70 mm (+2.36" to +2.76")	0°25' +20'/−10' or 2.5 +2/−1 mm (0.10" +0.08"/−0.04")
+70 to +80 mm (+2.76" to +3.15")	0°30' +20'/−10' or 3 +2/−1 mm (0.12" +0.08"/−0.04")

REAR WHEEL CAMBER CHART 4
(450SEL, 300SD, 280SE, 6.9)

Semi-trailing Arm Position mm (inches)	Corresponds to Rear Wheel Camber
+65(2.58")	1¾ ± ½
+60(2.38")	1½ ± ½
+55(2.18")	1¼ ± ½
+50(1.99")	1 ± ½
+45(1.79")	¾ ± ½
+40(1.59")	½ ± ½
+35(1.39")	¼ ± ½
+30(1.12")	0 ± ½
+25(0.99")	−¼ ± ½
+20(0.79")	−½ ± ½
+15(0.60")	−¾ ± ½
+10(0.40")	−1 ± ½
+5(0.20")	−1¼ ± ½
0	−1½ ± ½
−5(0.20")	−1¾ ± ½
−10(0.40")	−2 ± ½
−15(0.60")	−2¼ ± ½
−20(0.79")	−2½ ± ½

REAR WHEEL ALIGNMENT CHART 5
(380SL, 380SLC)

Semi-trailing Arm Position mm	Corresponds to Rear Wheel Camber
35	0 ± ½
30	−¼ ± ½
25	−½ ± ½
20	−¾ ± ½
15	−1 ± ½
10	−1¼ ± ½
5	−1½ ± ½
0	−1¾ ± ½
− 5	−2 ± ½
−10	−2¼ ± ½
−15	−2½ ± ½
−20	−2¾ ± ½

WHEEL ALIGNMENT CHART 6
('81 and Later 300SD, 380SEL, 380SEC, 380SE, 500SEC, 500SEL)

Semi-trailing Arm Position mm	Corresponds to Rear Wheel Camber
+ 65	1½ ± ½
+ 60	1¼ ± ½
+ 55	1 ± ½
+ 50	¾ ± ½
+ 45	½ ± ½
+ 40	¼ ± ½
+ 35	0 ± ½
+ 30	−¼ ± ½
+ 25	−½ ± ½
+ 20	−¾ ± ½
+ 15	−1 ± ½
+ 10	−1¼ ± ½
+ 5	−1½ ± ½
0	−1¾ ± ½
− 5	−2 ± ½
−10	−2¼ ± ½
−15	−2½ ± ½
−20	−2¾ ± ½

REAR WHEEL ALIGNMENT CHART 7

Spring Link Position mm	Corresponds To Rear Wheel Camber
+ 50	−¼ ± ½
+ 40	−½ ± ½
+ 30	−¾ ± ½
+ 20	−1 ± ½
+ 10	−1¼ ± ½
0	−1½ ± ½
− 10	−1¾ ± ½
− 20	−2 ± ½

TUNE-UP

Ignition System Precautions

Mercedes-Benz has determined that some transistorized switching units have been damaged due to improper handling during service and maintenance work. The following precautions should be observed when working with transistorized switching units.

1. Do not shut off a running engine by shorting terminal 15 (terminal 1 or 15 on 1981 6-cylinder engines) of the ignition coil to ground or the transistorized switching unit will be destroyed.

2. Do not steam clean or apply water pressure to transistorized switching units, fuel injection control units, or ignition components, since water may enter these and short them.

3. Do not assume that transistor switching units are defective without checking the plug terminals. The plug terminals are frequently corroded because the rubber boot was not properly seated. In addition, the terminals can become corroded even if the rubber boot is properly seated. Mercedes-Benz recommends that all contacts be cleaned before assuming that a transistorized switching unit is defective.

4. Do not test for spark by holding a spark plug wire at a distance from the plug or pull off a spark plug wire with the engine running.

5. Disconnect test instruments with the engine off.

6. Do not operate the ignition without the harness connected.

7. Do not connect lights or noise suppression devices to terminal 1 of the ignition coil.

8. Do not install adapters (for timing lights, etc.) in series with ignition wires.

Spark Plugs

NOTE: On most models, the plug wires are numbered at the cap and on the wire with small yellow rings.

Prior to removing the plugs, blow dirt away with compressed air. This is especially necessary on 6 cylinder DOHC engines. Remove each plug in turn and measure the gap with a round feeler gauge of the appropriate thickness. Insert the round feeler gauge between the center and side electrode. To adjust the gap, bend the side electrode.

Reinstall and tighten the spark plugs to 18–21 ft. lbs. and install the spark plug wires on their respective plugs.

Check the spark plug wires and replace any that are cracked or brittle. Bend the wires into a loop to check for cracks.

Ignition Timing

ADJUSTMENT

Before setting the ignition timing, be sure that the point gap (dwell angle) is set to the proper specifications since this will influence the timing, while timing will have no influence on the dwell angle.

Before attempting to set the timing, read the ''Ignition Timing Specifications'' chart carefully and determine at what speed the timing should be set and whether the vacuum should be connected or disconnected.

NOTE: It is a good idea to paint the appropriate timing mark with dayglow or white paint to make it quickly and easily visible.

On engines with transistorized coil ignition, the timing light may or may not work depending on the construction of the light.

All Gas Engines

1. Raise the hood and connect a tachometer.
2. Connect a timing light.
3. Run the engine at the specified speed and read the firing point on the balancing plate or vibration damper while shining the light on it.

The typical vibration damper is marked like this (note the pin)

NOTE: The balancer on some engines has 2 timing scales. If in doubt as to which scale to use, rotate the crankshaft (in the direction of rotation only) until the dis- tributor rotor is aligned with the notch on the distributor housing (No. 1 cylinder). In this position, the timing pointer should be at TDC on the proper timing scale.

4. Adjust the ignition timing by loosening the distributor clamp bolt and rotating the distributor. To advance the timing, rotate the distributor in the opposite direction of normal rotation. To retard the timing, rotate the distributor in the direction of normal rotation.

5. Once the timing has been adjusted, recheck the timing once more to be sure that it has not been disturbed.

6. Remove the timing light and tachometer and connect any wires that were removed.

Diesel Engines

The diesel uses no distributor, so requires no ignition timing adjustment.

Valve Clearance

ADJUSTMENT

The valve clearance of all gasoline engines can be checked and, if necessary, adjusted when the engine is hot or cold. Consult the valve location illustrations. The valve clearance on intake and exhaust valves is different, but all valves should be set slightly loose, rather than too tight.

4 and 6-Cylinder Gasoline Engines

NOTE: The 190E has hydraulic valve clearance compensation. No adjustment is either necessary or possible.

The valve clearance is measured between the sliding surface of the rocker arm and the heel of the camshaft lobe. The highest point of the camshaft lobe should be at a 90° angle to the sliding surface of the rocker arm.

NOTE: Prior to rotating 6-cylinder engine manually, disconnect the transmitter-ignition distributor plug (green cable) from the switching unit.

1. Remove the air vent hose and air cleaner from the valve cover. Remove the spark plugs.
2. Remove the valve cover and gasket.
3. Note the position of the intake and exhaust valves.
4. Rotate the crankshaft, using a socket wrench on the crankshaft pulley bolt, until the heel of the camshaft lobe is perpendicular to the sliding surface of the rocker arm.

NOTE: Do not rotate the engine using the camshaft sprocket bolt. The strain will distort the timing chain tensioner rail. Always rotate the engine in the direction of normal rotation only.

5. Some models have holes in the vibration damper plate to assist in crankshaft

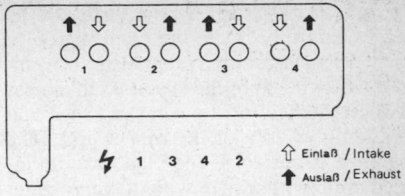

Valve location—4-cylinder engines

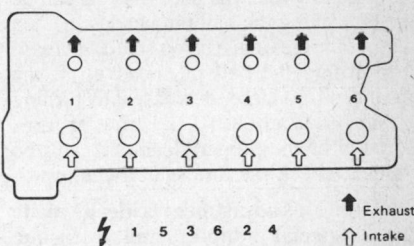

Valve location—DOHC 6-cylinder engine

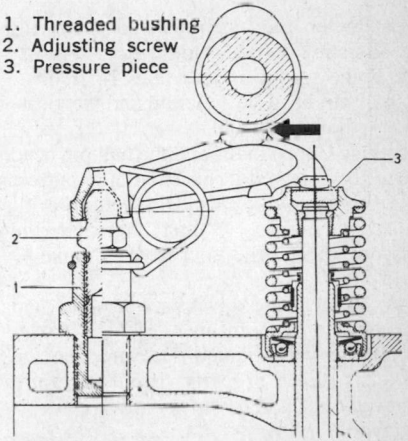

1. Threaded bushing
2. Adjusting screw
3. Pressure piece

Measure the valve clearance between the sliding surface of the rocker arm and the heel of the camshaft lobe on 4 cylinder engines (except 190)

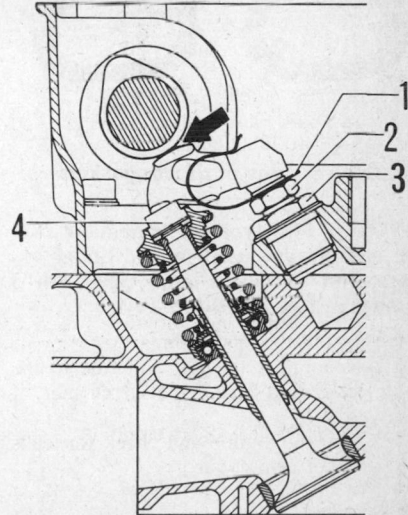

1. Tension spring   3. Threaded bushing
2. Adjusting screw   4. Pressure piece

Check the valve clearance between the sliding surface of the rocker arm and the heel of the camshaft lobe on DOHC—6-cylinder engines

rotation. In this case, a large drift can be used to carefully rotate the crankshaft.

6. To measure the valve clearance, insert a feeler blade of the specified thickness between the heel of the camshaft lobe and the sliding surface of the rocker arm. The clearance is correct if the blade can be inserted and withdrawn with a very slight drag.

7. If adjustment is necessary, it can be done by turning the ball pin head at the hex collar. If the clearance is too small, increase it by turning the ball pin head in. If the clearance is too large, decrease it by turning the ball pin head out. If the adjuster turns too easily or the proper clearance can't be obtained, check the torque of the adjuster.

NOTE: This adjustment is ideally made with a special adapter and a torque wrench. By using it, the torque wrench can be directly aligned with the ball pin head.

8. When the ball pin head is turned, the adjusting torque should be 14–25 ft. lbs. If the torque is less than 14 ft. lbs., the ball pin head will vibrate and the clearance will not remain as set. If the valve clearance is too small, and the ball pin head cannot be screwed in far enough to correct it, a thinner pressure piece should be installed in the spring retainer. To replace the pressure piece, the rocker arm must be removed.

9. After all the valves have been checked and adjusted in the manner described above, install the valve cover. Be sure that the gasket is seated properly. It is best to use a new gasket whenever the valve cover is removed.

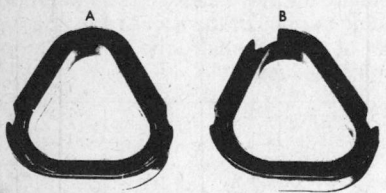

(a)—Spark plug holes 1, 3 and 5
(b)—Spark plug holes 2 and 4
Two versions of rubber gaskets

NOTE: Two types of triangular rubber gaskets are used on 6-cylinder engines, but only the later type with 3 notches are supplied for service.

10. Install the spark plugs.
11. Reconnect the air vent line to the valve cover and install the air cleaner, if removed.
12. Run the engine and check for leaks at the rocker arm cover.

V8 Engines

NOTE: V8 engines use hydraulic valve lifters and require no periodic adjustment.

The valve clearance is measured between the sliding surface of the rocker arm and the heel of the camshaft lobe. The highest

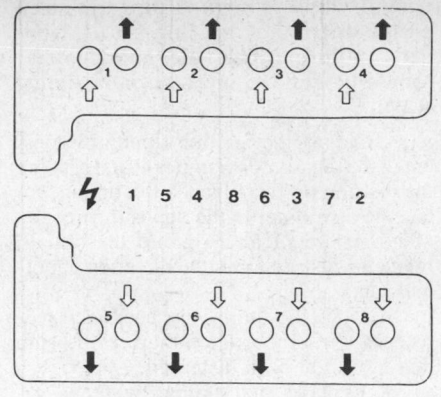

Valve locations—6.9 V8

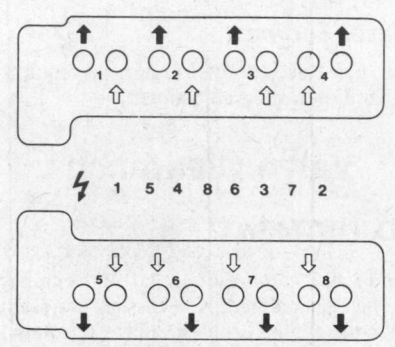

V8 (except 6.9) valve location

point of the camshaft lobe should be at a 90° angle to the sliding surface of the rocker arm.

1. Loosen the venting line and remove the regulating linkage. Remove the valve cover.
2. Disconnect the cable from the ignition coil.
3. Identify all of the valves as intake or exhaust.
4. Beginning with the No. 1 cylinder, crank the engine with the starter to position the heel of the camshaft approximately over the sliding surface of the rocker arm.
5. Rotate the crankshaft by means of a socket wrench on the crankshaft pulley bolt until the heel of the camshaft lobe is perpendicular to the sliding surface of the rocker arm.

NOTE: Do not rotate the engine using the camshaft sprocket bolt. The strain will distort the timing chain tensioner rail. Always rotate the engine in the direction of normal rotation only.

6. Some models have holes in the vibration damper plate to assist in crankshaft rotation. In this case, a small prybar can be used to carefully rotate the crankshaft.
7. To measure the valve clearance, insert a feeler blade of the specified thickness between the heel of the camshaft lobe and the sliding surface of the rocker arm. The clearance is correct if the blade can be inserted and withdrawn with a very slight drag.
8. If adjustment is to be

A valve adjusting wrench (crow's foot) is required to accurately measure torque on all models

done by turning the ball pin head at the hex collar. If the clearance is too small, increase it by turning the ball pin head in. If the clearance is too large, turn the ball pin head out.

NOTE: If the adjuster turns very easily, or if the proper clearance can't be obtained, check the torque on the adjuster using a special adapter ("crow's foot").

9. When the ball pin head is turned, the adjusting torque should be 14–29 ft. lbs. If the torque is lower, either the adjusting screw, the threaded bolt, or both will have to be replaced. If the valve clearance is too small, and the ball pin head cannot be screwed in far enough to correct it, a thinner pressure piece should be installed in the spring retainer. To replace the pressure piece, the rocker arm must be removed. (See the "Engine Mechanical" section.)
10. Install the regulating linkage, valve cover gasket, and valve cover. Be sure the gasket is seated properly.
11. Connect the cable to the coil and the venting line. Run the engine and check for leaks at the valve cover.

Diesel Engines

NOTE: The 190D utilizes hydraulic valve clearance compensators. No adjustment is either necessary or possible.

1. Remove the valve cover and note the position of the intake and exhaust valves.
2. Turn the engine with a socket and breaker bar on the crankshaft pulley or by using a remote starter, hooked to the battery

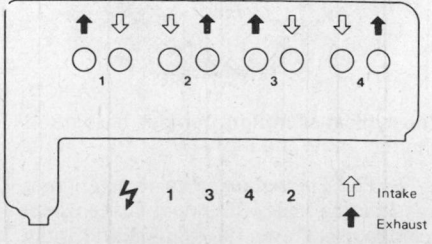

Valve arrangement—4-cylinder diesels

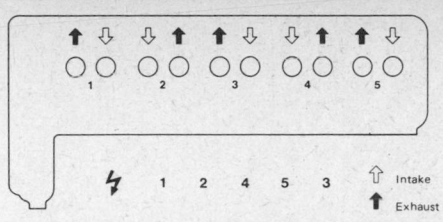

Valve arrangement—5-cylinder diesels

Idle speed adjustment screw (8)—230

CO adjustment—230

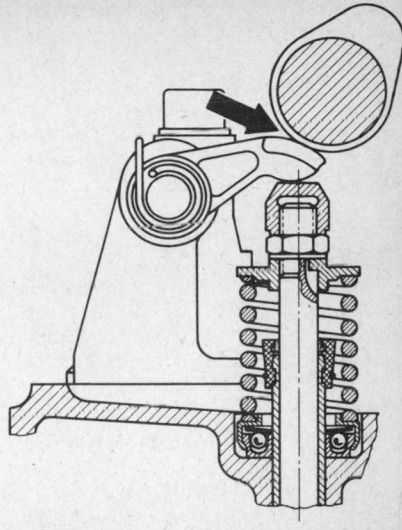

Measure valve clearance on diesel engines at arrow

(+) terminal and the large, uppermost starter solenoid terminal. Due to the extremely high compression pressures in the diesel engine, it will be considerably easier to use a remote starter. If a remote starter is not available, the engine can be bumped into position with the normal starter.

NOTE: Do not turn the engine backwards or use the camshaft sprocket bolt to rotate the engine.

3. Measure the valve clearance when the heel of the camshaft lobe is directly over the sliding surface of the rocker arm. The lobe of the camshaft should be vertical to the surface of the rocker arm. The clearance is correct when the specified feeler gauge can be pulled through with a very slight drag.

4. To adjust the clearance, loosen the cap nut while holding the hex nut. Adjust the valve clearance by turning the hex nut.

5. After adjustment, hold the cap nut and lock it in place with the hex nut. Recheck the clearance.

6. Check the gasket and install the rocker arm cover.

Idle Speed

CATALYTIC CONVERTER PRECAUTIONS

With the exception of diesels, all Mercedes-Benz cars are equipped with catalytic converters. The following points should be adhered to:

1. Use only unleaded gas.
2. Maintain the engine at the specified intervals.
3. Avoid running the engine with an excessively rich mixture. Do not run the engine excessively on fast idle.
4. Prolonged warm-up after a cold start should be avoided.
5. Do not check exhaust emissions over a long period of time without air injection.
6. Do not alter the emission control system in any way.

CARBURETORS

Stromberg 175 CDT

1. Turn off the heater and A/C and run the vehicle to normal operating temperature.
2. Check the throttle valve for ease of operation.
3. Connect a tachometer and adjust the idle speed to specifications with the idle speed adjusting screw.

4. See whether the idle speed stop is resting against the throttle valve lever and not against the vacuum governor. Set the vacuum governor back if required.

5. If an exhaust gas analyzer (CO meter) is available, check the exhaust gas for percentage of CO. Be sure the wheel for altitude compensation is set correctly.

7. Capnut	14. Holding wrench
8. Locknut	16. Adjusting wrench

Adjusting valve clearance on diesel engine

6. If required, adjust the CO by means of the fuel mixture screw. Loosen the locknut while simultaneously holding the nozzle screw and turning the fuel shut off valve. Accelerate a brief moment after each adjustment of the idle speed and fuel control screw, to stabilize the mixture.

7. Check the idle speed again and adjust with the idle speed adjusting screw, if required.

8. Adjust the control linkage as follows:
Run the engine at idle speed. Set the control rod so that it can be attached with no binding.

FUEL INJECTION

Gasoline Engines

1978–79

The mechanical fuel injection is known as C.I.S. (Continuous Injection System) or Bosch K-Jetronic. The idle speed should be adjusted with the air conditioner off and the transmission in Park.

1. Connect a tachometer.
2. Be sure the cruise control cable is connected to the regulating lever with no binding or kinking.
3. Run the engine to normal operating temperature.
4. Be sure the throttle valve rests against the idle speed stop.
5. Set the idle speed to specifications with the idle air screw.

Adjust the idle speed on V8's prior to 1979 at the idle air screw (arrow).

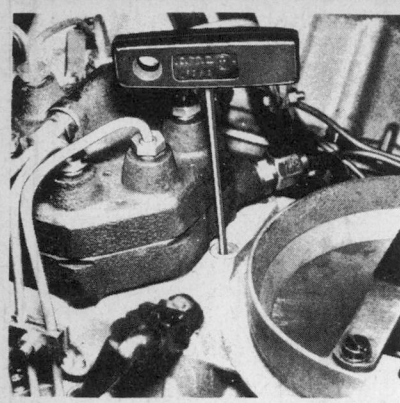

An Allen wrench is necessary to adjust the idle mixture on 1978–79 V8 engines

Idle speed adjusting screw—1980 and later 6-cylinder

6. If possible, check the CO level:

Disconnect the hose at the exhaust back pressure line and connect the CO tester to the line. On Federal V8 engines, check CO with the air injection connected. On all others, disconnect the blue/purple vacuum line from the blue thermal valve and plug the thermo valve to cancel air injection.

7. Adjust the CO valve by unscrewing the plug and inserting the special adjusting tool (Allen wrench). Turn the screw in to richen the mixture and out to lean the mixture.

8. Accelerate briefly and check the speed and CO again.

9. Reconnect the vacuum lines and check the CO value again. It should be below the specified value.

10. Adjust the regulating lever so that the roller rests in the gate lever without binding. Put the transmission in Drive and turn on the A/C. Turn the wheels to full lock and adjust the idle speed so the engine runs smoothly.

1980 6-CYLINDER AND V8

1. Connect a tachometer and remote oil temperature gauge.

2. Run the engine to approximately 176° F oil temperature.

3. The automatic transmission should be in Park and the A/C off.

4. Be sure the throttle valve lever rests against the idle stop.

5. Adjust the Bowden cable with the adjusting screw so there is no tension against the throttle valve lever.

6. Check the idle speed. If necessary, adjust with the idle air adjustment screw.

1981 6-CYLINDER

1. Run the engine to normal operating temperature (167°–185°F oil temperature) and connect a tachometer.

2. The automatic transmission should be in Park and A/C off.

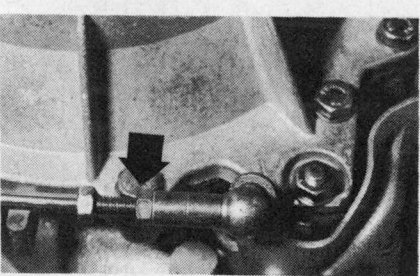

Regulating lever adjustment—1978–79 V8 engines

3. Be sure the throttle valve lever rests against the idle speed stop.

4. Be sure the cruise control actuating rod rests against the idle speed stop. Disconnect the connecting rod and push the lever of the actuating lever clockwise to the idle speed position.

5. Reconnect the connecting rod; make sure that the actuating element is approximately 0.04 in. from the idle speed stop. Adjust this clearance with the pull rod.

6. Check and adjust the idle speed. Idle speed is adjusted at the idle speed air screw.

1981–85 (4 CYLINDER AND V8)

These engines have electronically controlled idle speed, using a solenoid connected to terminals 1 and 5 of the control unit.

Diesel Engines
1978–80 EXCEPT 1980 300SD

Since the diesel engine has no ignition distributor or ignition coil, there is no way to connect a conventional external tachometer to measure idle speed. Using the built-in tachometer on the dash is not the most accurate way to set idle speed. See the "Diesel Services" unit repair section for more accurate methods of measuring idle speed.

1. Turn the knob on the instrument panel completely clockwise and check the distance between the adjusting ring and the specially shaped spring. It should be approximately 0.04 in.

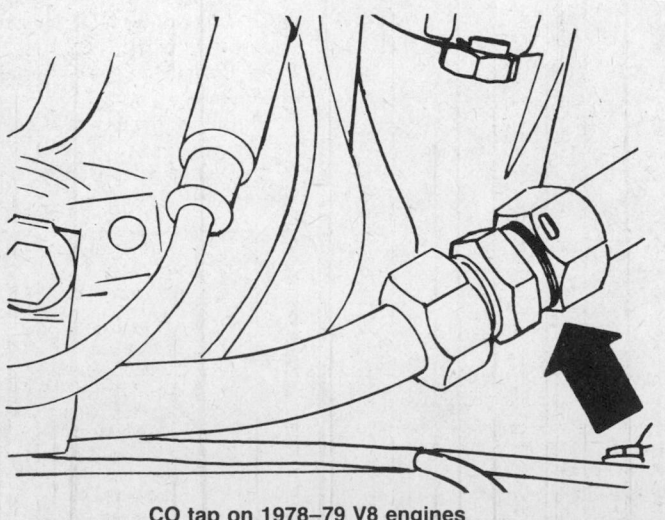

CO tap on 1978–79 V8 engines

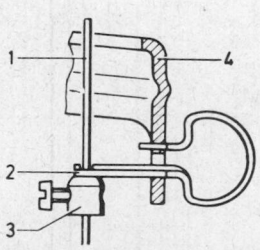

1. Cable
2. Spring
3. Adjusting barrel
4. Lever

Be sure the specially shaped spring is installed as shown

Idle speed adjusting screw—1980 and later V8

Clearance between cam and actuator on switch-over valve—1980 and later except turbodiesel

2. With the engine stopped, depress the accelerator pedal while turning the idle knob counterclockwise.

3. Start the engine. The idle speed should be 1000–1100 rpm. Adjust this with the adjusting screw, but do not exceed 1100 rpm.

4. Be sure the special spring is installed correctly.

5. Run the engine to normal operating temperature.

6. Turn the idle adjusting knob on the dash fully to the right.

7. Disconnect the regulating rod and adjust the idle speed with the idle speed adjusting screw. There is a locknut on the idle speed adjusting screw.

8. Reconnect the regulating rod.

1980 300SD AND ALL 1981−85 DIESELS EXCEPT 1982−83 240D AND 1984−85 190D

1. Run the engine to normal operating temperature.

2. On normally aspirated engines (non-turbocharged), turn the idle speed adjuster on the dash completely to the right.

3. Disconnect the pushrod at the angle lever.

4. Check the idle speed. Adjust by loosening the locknut and adjusting the idle speed screw. Tighten the locknut.

5. On all except turbodiesels, adjust the pushrod so that a clearance of approximately 0.2 in. exists between the cam on the lever and the actuator on the switchover

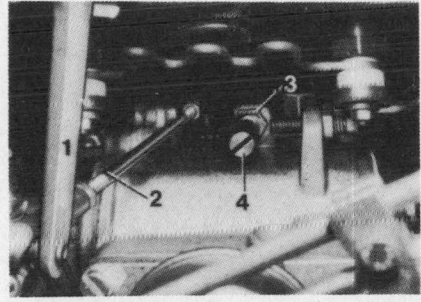

Idle speed adjustment—5 cylinder engines

Idle speed adjustment—240D

Diesel engine idle speed adjustment (4)—300D and 300CD

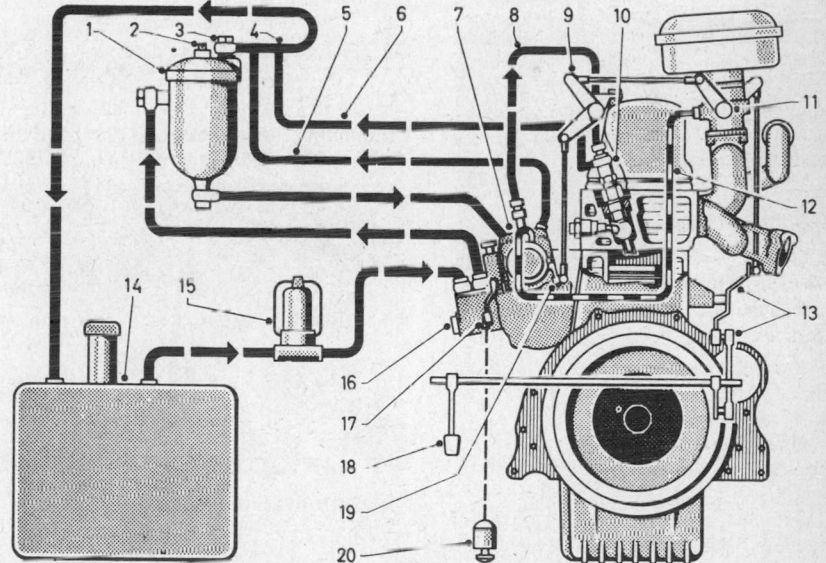

1. Main fuel filter
2. Vent screw
3. Hollow screw with throttle screw
4. Fuel return line
5. Overflow line
6. Injection nozzle leakage line
7. Injection pump
8. Pressure line from injection pump to injection nozzle
9. Angular lever for auxiliary mechanical control
10. Injection nozzle
11. Venturi control unit
12. Vacuum line with throttle screw
13. Linkage and lever for accelerator pedal control
14. Fuel tank
15. Fuel prefilter
16. Fuel feed pump with hand pump
17. Adjusting lever
18. Accelerator pedal
19. Lever for auxiliary mechanical control
20. Heater plug starting switch with starting and stopping cable

Schematic diagram of diesel fuel system

valve. The lever on the fuel injection pump must rest against the idle stop.

6. On all models except the 1981 turbodiesel, depress the stop lever as far as possible. The cruise control Bowden cable should be free of tension against the angle lever. Use the adjusting screw to alter the tension. Let go of the stop lever. The Bowden cable should have a slight amount of play.

7. On turbodiesels, adjust the pushrod so that the roller in the guide lever rests free of tension against the stop.

8. Put the automatic transmission in Drive and turn the steering wheel to full lock. The engine should run smoothly. If not, adjust the idle speed. Disconnect the cruise control connecting rod, and push the lever clockwise to the idle stop. Attach the connecting rod, making sure the lever is about 0.04 in. from the idle speed stop.

———— CAUTION ————

If the engine speed is adjusted higher, it will be above the controlled idle speed range of the governor and the engine can increase in speed to maximum rpm.

1982–83 240D

1. Run the engine to normal operating temperature.

2. Turn the idle speed adjuster knob on the dashboard completely to the right.

3. Disconnect the pushrod at the operating lever.

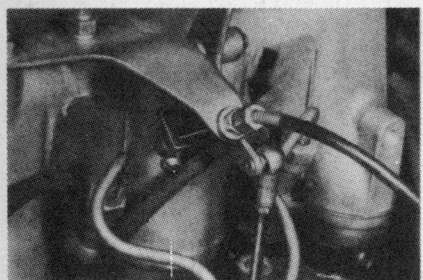

Adjusting nut for dashboard idle speed knob

4. Move the guide lever to the idle speed position. Set the edge of the guide lever at the mark (arrow) on the cap.

5. Check, and if necessary, adjust the idle speed. Use the idle speed adjusting screw.

6. Attach the pushrod to the injection pump lever so that the rod is free of tension when the lever is against the idle speed stop.

7. Check to be sure the cruise control rods are free of tension.

8. Move the automatic transmission into Drive. Turn on the A/C and turn the wheels to full lock. The engine should run smoothly. Adjust the idle speed if necessary.

190D

NOTE: Testing the idle speed on the 190D will require two special tools. A digital tester (Sun-1019, 2110 or All-Test 3610-MB) and a TDC impulse transmit-

ter; not commonly available tools. Without these special tools, idle speed adjustment is impossible and should not be attempted.

1. Run the engine until it reaches normal operating temperature.

2. Connect the digtial tester and the TDC impulse transmitter as indicated in the illustration.

3. Check all linkages for ease of operation.

4. Disconnect the pushrod (204) from the adjusting lever (214).

5. Start the engine and check the idle speed. If required, adjust by loosening the locknut on the vacuum control unit and turning the unit itself in or out.

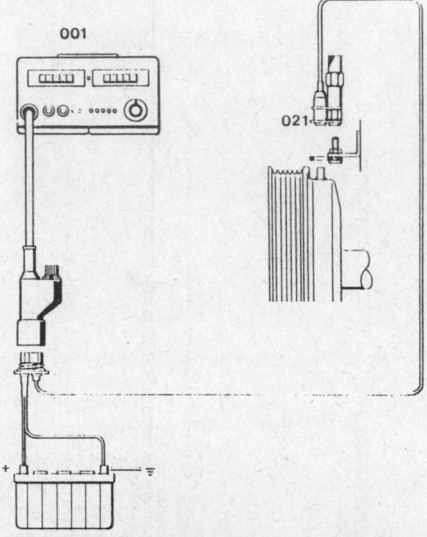

Connecting the digital tester (001) and the TDC impulse transmitter (021) on the 190D

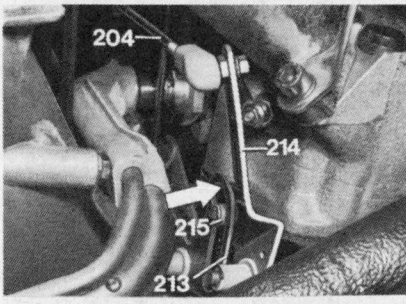

Throttle linkage on the 190D

Loosen the locknut (4A) and turn the vacuum control unit (4) to adjust the idle speed on the 190D

6. After the idle speed is correct, tighten the vacuum control unit locknut and reconnect the pushrod so that it is tension-free when the lever is against the idle speed stop.

7. Switch on all auxiliary power accessories and check that the engine continues to run smoothly. Readjust the idle speed if necessary.

8. Disconnect the two special tools and turn off the engine.

ENGINE ELECTRICAL

Distributor

REMOVAL & INSTALLATION

The removal and installation procedures for all distributors on Mercedes-Benz vehicles are basically similar. Certain minor differences may exist from model to model.

1. The distributor is usually located on the front side or front of the engine.

2. Remove the dust cover, distributor cap, cable plug connections, and vacuum line.

3. Rotating the engine in the normal direction, crank it around until the distributor rotor points to the mark on the rim of the distributor housing. This indicates the No. 1 cylinder.

4. The engine can be cranked with a socket wrench on the balancer bolt or with a pry bar inserted in the balancer.

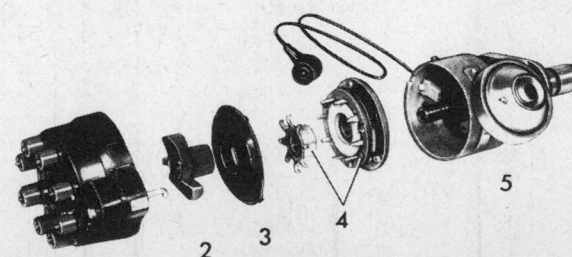

1. Distributor cap
2. Rotor
3. Dust cover
4. Armature and pick-up assembly
5. Distributor housing with pick-up connection

Breakerless ignition distributor—up to 1980

5. Matchmark the distributor body and the engine so that the distributor can be returned to its original position.

6. Remove the distributor hold-down bolt and withdraw the distributor from the engine.

NOTE: Do not crank the engine while the distributor is removed.

7. Installation is the reverse of removal. Insert the distributor so that the matchmarks on the distributor and engine are aligned.

8. Tighten the clamp bolt and check the dwell angle and ignition timing.

Electronic Ignition

TESTING

All Except 1981 6 Cylinder and 1984 and Later 4 Cylinder

1. Check the screw type plug terminals and the plug wires.

2. With the ignition ON, a primary current of about 8 amps will flow continuously through the system.

3. Check the input voltage at the terminal block. Terminal 15 should show 4.5 volts and terminal 1 should show 0.5–2.0 volts. If the voltage at terminal 1 is excessive, replace the switching unit.

4. If there is no spark but terminal 1 voltage is OK, check the armature resistance (terminal 7 and 31d). Resistance should be 450–750 ohms.

5. Test the pick-up coil resistance. There should be infinite resistance between terminal 7 and ground.

6. Check the armature and pick-up coil

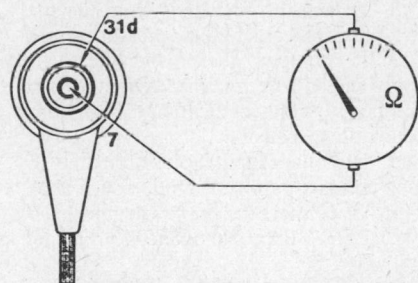

Testing armature resistance—electronic ignition prior to 1980

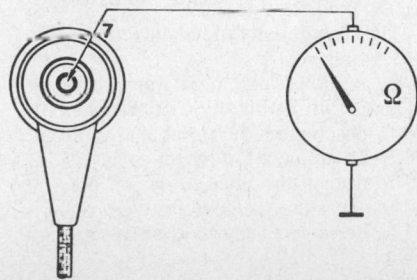

Testing pick-up coil resistance—electronic ignition prior to 1980

for mechanical damage. An air gap should exist between them.

7. Check the dwell angle. Even though it cannot be adjusted, it should be 25–39° at 1400–1500 rpm.

8. If the armature and pick-up coil are functioning, replace the switching unit. If the armature and pick-up coil indicate no damage, replace the switching unit. If the armature or pick-up coil are defective, replace the distributor.

1981 6-Cylinder

This engine uses a new breakerless transistorized ignition system with no preresistance and no current flow unless the engine is running. The new system consists of ignition coil, distributor, harness and switching unit. Do not replace the coil with a previously used coil. Also, see the ignition system precautions given previously.

1. Test the voltage between bushing 5 of the diagnosis plug and ground with the ignition ON. Nominal battery voltage should be indicated. If not, test the voltage via the ignition switch. If voltage is correct, go to Step 2.

2. Test the voltage between bushing 4 and 5 of the diagnosis plug socket. Zero voltage should be indicated. If voltage is more than 0.1 volt, switch off the ignition immediately. Renew the switching unit. Check the pressure relief plug in the ignition coil and the ohmic (resistance) value of the ignition coil between terminals 1 and 15. If the pressure relief plug has popped out or the resistance is not 0.7 ohms, replace the ignition coil.

3. Test the dwell angle. It should be 7–25°. If more than 25°, replace the switching unit. If no reading or the reading is correct, go to Step 4.

4. Disconnect the green control line from the switching unit and test the resistance between terminals 3 and 7. Resistance should be 500–700 ohms. If the resistance is wrong, pull the green cable from the distributor and see that there are 500–700 ohms present at the connector plugs. If so, replace the green cable. If not, replace the distributor.

5. Remove the green cable from the control unit. There should be 200k ohms between terminals 3 or 7 and ground. If not, disconnect the green cable from the distributor and test the resistance between any of the plugs and ground. If 200k ohms are not present, replace the distributor.

1984 and Later 4 Cylinder

The electronic ignition system on the 190E differs from the previous systems with the addition of a small switching unit.

NOTE: The base plate of this switching unit serves as a heat sink; periodic cleaning will ensure proper heat flow between it and the wheel arch.

The ignition coil and all testing procedures are similar to those given for the 1981 6 cylinder engine.

The switching unit (2), cable connector (1) and diagnostic socket (3) distinguish the 190E electronic ignition from that of the 1981 6 cylinder

Alternator

All Mercedes-Benz cars covered in this book use 12 volt electrical systems with alternators, in conjunction with the transistor or electronic ignition system.

PRECAUTIONS

Some precautions that should be taken into consideration when working on this, or any other, AC charging system are as follows:

1. Never switch battery polarity.

2. When installing a battery, always connect the grounded terminal first.

3. Never disconnect the battery while the engine is running.

4. If the molded connector is disconnected from the alternator, do not ground the hot wire.

5. Never run the alternator with the main output cable disconnected.

6. Never electric weld around the car without disconnecting the alternator.

7. Never apply any voltage in excess of battery voltage during testing.

8. Never ''jump'' a battery for starting purposes with more than 12 volts.

REMOVAL & INSTALLATION

Viewing the engine from the front, the alternator is located on either side, usually down low. Because of the location, it is sometimes easier to remove the alternator from below the vehicle. The following is a general procedure for all models.

1. Locate the alternator and disconnect and identify all wires.

2. Loosen the adjusting (pivot) bolt or the adjusting mechanism and swing the alternator in toward the engine.

3. Remove the drive belt from the alternator pulley.

4. The alternator can now be removed from its mounting bracket or the bracket and alternator can be removed from the engine.

5. Installation is the reverse of removal.

6. Tighten all of the drive belts that were loosened.

BELT TENSION ADJUSTMENT

All alternator drive belts should be tensioned to approximately ½ in. deflection under thumb pressure at the middle of the longest span.

NOTE: The 190D utilizes a single V-belt with automatic tensioning. No adjustment is necessary.

Starter

All Mercedes-Benz passenger cars are equipped with 12-volt Bosch electric starters of various rated outputs. The starter is actuated and the pinion engaged by an electric solenoid mounted on top of the starter motor.

When removing the starter, note the exact position of all wires and washers since they should be installed in their original locations. On some models it may be necessary to position the front wheels to the left or right to provide working clearance.

REMOVAL & INSTALLATION

1. Remove all wires from the starter and tag them for location.
2. Disconnect the battery cable.
3. Unbolt the starter from the bellhousing and remove the ground cable.
4. Remove the starter from underneath the car.
5. Installation is the reverse of removal. Be sure to replace all wires and washers in their original locations.

ENGINE MECHANICAL

NOTE: Care should be taken when working on Mercedes-Benz engines, since there are many aluminum parts which can be damaged if carelessly handled.

Engine

REMOVAL & INSTALLATION

NOTE: In all cases, Mercedes-Benz engines and transmissions are removed as a unit.

––––––– **CAUTION** –––––––
Air conditioner lines should not be indiscriminately disconnected without taking proper precautions. It is best to swing the compressor out of the way while still connected to its hoses. Never do any welding around the compressor—heat may cause an explosion. Also, the refrigerant, while inert at normal room temperature, breaks down under high temperature into hydrogen fluoride and phosgene (among other products), which are highly poisonous.

190D, 190E, 230, 240D, 300D, 300CD, 300TD, 300SD

1. First, remove the hood, then drain the cooling system and disconnect the battery. While not strictly necessary, it is better to remove the battery completely to prevent breakage by the engine as it is lifted out.
2. Remove the fan shroud, radiator, and disconnect all heater hoses and oil cooler lines. Plug all openings to keep out dirt.
3. Remove the air cleaner and all fuel, vacuum and oil hoses (e.g., power steering and power brakes). Plug all openings to keep out dirt.
4. Remove the viscous coupling and fan and, on applicable engines, disconnect the carburetor choke cable (if so equipped).
5. On diesel engines, disconnect the idle control starting cables. On the 300SD, loosen the oil filter cover slightly; siphon off the power steering fluid and disconnect the hoses.
6. On all engines, disconnect the accelerator linkage.
7. Disconnect all ground straps and electrical connections. It is a good idea to tag each wire for easy reassembly.
8. Detach the gearshift linkage and the exhaust pipes from the manifolds.
9. Loosen the steering relay arm and pull it down out of the way, along with the center steering rod and hydraulic steering damper.
10. The hydraulic engine shock absorber should be removed.
11. Remove the hydraulic line from the clutch housing and the oil line connectors from the automatic transmission.
12. Unbolt the clutch slave cylinder from the bellhousing after removing the return spring.
13. Remove the exhaust pipe bracket attached to the transmission and place a wood-padded jack under the bellhousing, or place a cable sling under the oil pan, to support the engine. On turbocharged models, disconnect the exhaust pipes at the turbocharger.

1 U-joint flange
2 U-joint plate
3 Wooden block
Supporting a V8 engine

14. Mark the position of the rear engine support and unbolt the two outer bolts, then remove the top bolt at the transmission and pull the support out.
15. Disconnect the speedometer cable and the front driveshaft U-joint. Push the driveshaft back and wire it out of the way.
16. Unbolt the engine mounts on both sides and, on four-cylinder engines, the front limit stop.
17. Unbolt the power steering fluid reservoir and swing it out of the way; then, using a chain hoist and cable, lift the engine and transmission upward and outward. An angle of about 45° will allow the car to be pushed backward while the engine is coming up.
18. Reverse the procedure to install, making sure to bleed the hydraulic clutch, power steering, power brakes and fuel system.

V8 Engines

NOTE: Removal of a V8 engine equipped with air conditioning, may require discharging the air conditioning system. Use caution; Freon is lethal.

1. Remove the hood. On the 380SEC, the hood can be tilted back 90° and does not have to be removed.
2. Drain the cooling system.
3. Remove the radiator and fan shroud.
4. Remove the cable plug from the temperature switch.
5. Remove the battery, battery frame and air filter.
6. Drain the power steering reservoir and windshield washer reservoir.
7. Disconnect and plug the high pressure and return lines on the power steering pump.
8. Detach the fuel lines from the fuel filter, pressure regulator, and pressure sensor.
9. If equipped, loosen the line to the supply and anti-freeze tanks. On models so equipped, disconnect the lines to the hydro-pneumatic suspension.
10. Disconnect the cables from the ignition coil and transistor ignition switchbox.
11. Disconnect the brake vacuum lines.
12. Detach the cable connections for the following:
    a. venturi control unit
    b. temperature sensor
    c. distributor
    d. temperature switch
    e. cold starting valve
    f. speedometer inductance transmitter (3.8 only)
13. Remove the regulating shaft by pushing it in the direction of the firewall.
14. Disconnect the thrust and pullrods.
15. Disconnect the heater lines.
16. Detach the lines to the oil pressure and temperature gauges.
17. Remove the ground strap from the vehicle.
18. Detach the cables from the alternator, terminal bridge, and battery. Remove the battery.

19. On the 6.9, remove the oil line shield and disconnect the oil lines between the oil pan and oil reservoir.

20. Position a lifting sling on the engine and take up the slack in the chain.

21. Remove the left-hand engine mount and loosen the hex nut on the right-hand mount.

22. Remove the exhaust system. Remove the connecting rod chain on the rear level control valve and loosen the torsion bar slightly. Raise the vehicle slightly at the rear and remove the exhaust system in a rearward direction.

23. Disconnect the handbrake cable.

24. Remove the shield plate from the transmission tunnel.

25. Place a block of wood between the transmission and crossyoke so the engine will not sag when the rear mount is removed.

26. Loosen the driveshaft intermediate bearing and the driveshaft slide.

27. Support the transmission with a jack.

28. Mark the installation of the crossmember and remove the crossmember. Remove the rear engine carrier with the engine mount.

29. Unbolt the front U-joint flange on the transmission and push it back. Do not loosen the clamp nut on the intermediate bearing. Support the driveshaft.

30. Disconnect the speedometer shaft, shift rod, control pressure rod, regulating linkage (on automatic transmissions), kickdown switch cable, starter lockout switch cable, and the cable for the back-up light switch.

31. Remove the front engine mounting bolt and remove the engine at approximately a 45° angle.

32. Installation is the reverse of removal. Lower the engine until it is behind the front axle carrier. Place a jack under the transmission and lower the engine into its compartment. While lowering the engine, install the right-hand shock mount.

Fill the engine with all required fluids and start the engine. Check for leaks.

280E, 280CE, 280SE

1. Scribe alignment marks on the hood hinges and remove the hood. Drain the coolant from the radiator and block.

2. Remove the radiator.

3. Disconnect the lines from the vacuum pump.

4. On vehicles with air conditioning, remove the compressor and place it aside.

— CAUTION —
Do not remove the refrigerant lines from the compressor. Physical harm could result.

5. Disconnect and tag all electrical connections from the engine.

6. Disconnect all coolant and vacuum lines from the engine.

7. Disconnect and plug the oil pressure lines from the power steering pump after draining the pump reservoir.

8. Remove the accelerator linkage con-

Engine removal—6-cylinder gas engine. Inset shows lift attaching points.

trol rod by pulling off the lockring and pushing the shaft in the direction of the firewall.

9. Loosen and remove the exhaust pipes from the manifold and transmission supports.

10. Disconnect the transmission linkage and all other connections.

11. Loosen the front right (driving direction) shock absorber from the front axle carrier.

12. Remove the left hand engine shock absorber from the engine mount.

13. Attach a lifting device to the engine and tension the cables.

14. Unbolt the engine and transmission mounts and remove the engine at a 45° angle.

15. Installation is the reverse of removal. Be sure to check all fluids and fill as necessary. Check all adjustments on the engine.

Cylinder Head

REMOVAL & INSTALLATION

4 and 5-Cylinder Engines

This is fairly straightforward but some caution must be observed to ensure that the valve timing is not disturbed.

1. Drain the radiator and remove all

hoses and wires. Tag all wires to ensure easy reassembly.

2. Remove the camshaft cover and associated throttle linkage, then press out the spring clamp from the notch in the rocker arm (all except 190).

NOTE: The cylinder head cover on the 190E is removed with the spark plug cables and distributor cap still attached to it.

3. Push the clamp outward over the ball cap of the rocker, then depress the valve with a large prying tool and lift the rocker arm out of the ball pin head (all except 190).

4. Remove the rocker arm supports (all except 190) and the camshaft sprocket nut.

5. On all 5 cyl. engines and the 190E, the rockers and their supports must be removed together.

6. Using a suitable puller, remove the camshaft sprocket, after having first marked the chain, sprocket and cam for ease of assembly.

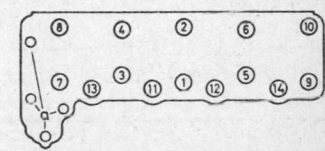

Cylinder head torque sequence—4 cylinder gasoline engines (except 190E)

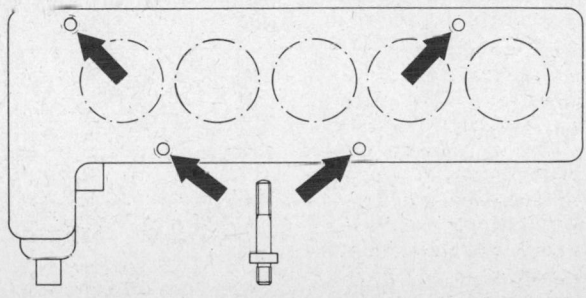

Studs (arrows) on the 5-cylinder engine are for attaching the rocker cover.

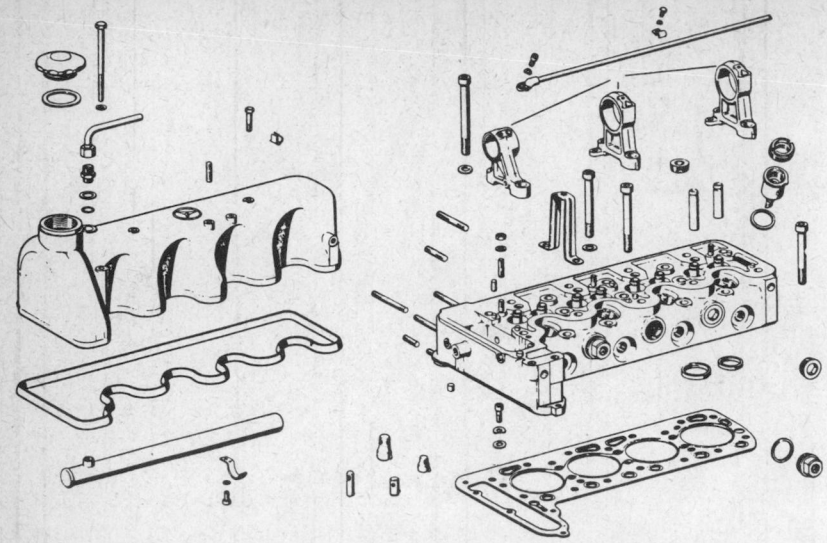

Exploded view of the cylinder head—4 cylinder gasoline engines (except 190E)

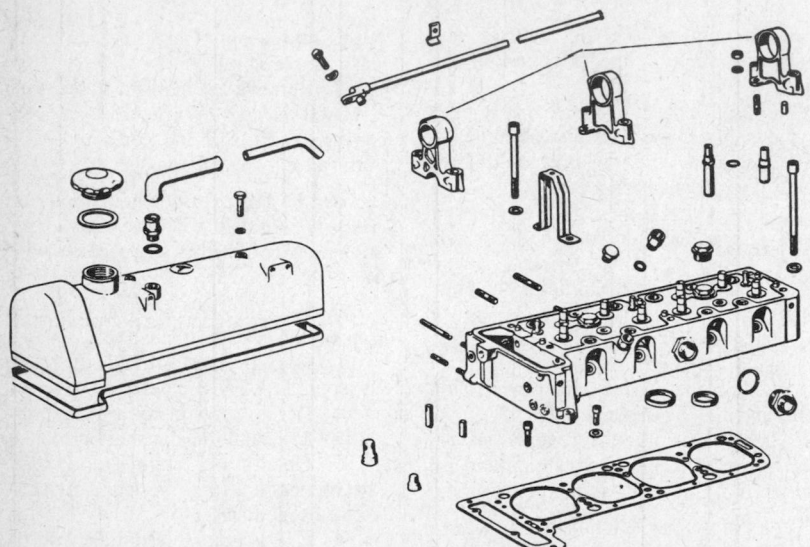

Exploded view of the cylinder head—4 cylinder diesel engines (except 190D); 5 cylinder engines similar

7. Remove the sprocket and chain and wire it out of the way.

— CAUTION —

Make sure the chain is securely wired so that it will not slide down into the engine.

8. Unbolt the manifolds and exhaust header pipe and push them out of the way.

9. Loosen the cylinder head holddown bolts in the reverse order of that shown in

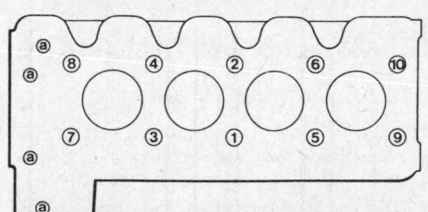

Cylinder head torque sequence—190D (bolts "A" and "B" are tightened to 25 Nm)

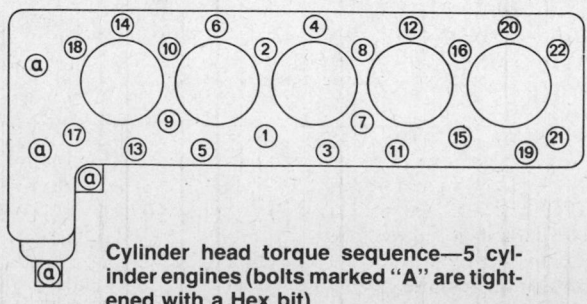

Cylinder head torque sequence—5 cylinder engines (bolts marked "A" are tightened with a Hex bit)

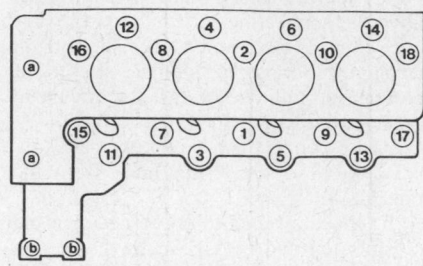

Cylinder head torque sequence—4 cylinder diesel engines (except 190D)

Cylinder head torque sequence—190E (bolts "A" are tightened to 25 Nm)

torque diagrams for each model. It is good practice to loosen each bolt a little at a time, working around the head, until all are free. This prevents unequal stresses in the metal.

10. Reach into the engine compartment and gradually work the head loose from each end by rocking it. Never, under any circumstances, use a screwdriver between the head and block to pry, as the head will be scarred badly and may be ruined.

11. Installation is the reverse of removal.

NOTE: All diesel engines manufactured after February, 1979, utilize cylinder head "stretch" bolts. These bolts undergo a permanent stretch each time they are tightened. When a maximum length is reached, they must be discarded

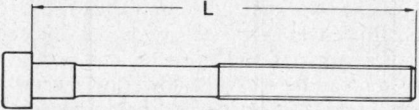

Cylinder head bolt stretch is measured at "L"

and replaced with new bolts. When tightening the head bolts on these engines, it is imperative that the steps listed under "Torque Specifications" are followed exactly. Maximum stretch lengths for the different models are as follows:

Model	Length when new (mm)	Maximum (mm)
190E	119	122
190D	80	83.6
	102	105.6
	115	118.6
240D, 300D, 300CD, 300SD, 300TD	104	105.6
	119	120.5
	144	145.6

Under no circumstances may the older type cylinder head bolts be exchanged with the newer "stretch" bolts.

V8 Engines

NOTE: Before removing the cylinder head from a V8, be sure you have the 4 special tools necessary to torque the head bolts; without them it will be impossible. Do not confuse the left and right-hand head gaskets—the left side has 2 attaching holes in the timing chain cover, the right side has only 1 hole.

Cylinder heads on 3.8, 4.5 and 5.0 liter V8's are not interchangeable.

NOTE: Cylinder heads can only be removed with the engine cold.

1. Drain the cooling system.
2. Remove the battery.
3. Remove the air cleaner. Remove the fan and fan shroud.
4. Pull the cable plug from the temperature sensor.
5. On the 6.9, to remove the right-hand head, remove the alternator (with bracket), windshield washer reservoir and bracket and automatic transmission dipstick tube.
6. Detach the vacuum hose from the venturi control unit.

Be careful removing the cylinder head bolts on a V8. The inner row of cam bolts are the only bolts NOT holding the head on. Note the angle of the bolts.

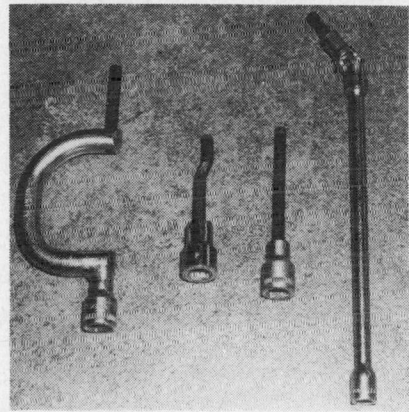

You need these tools to remove or install the V8 cylinder head. Without them it is practically impossible.

7. Remove the following electrical connections:
  a. injection valves
  b. distributor
  c. venturi control unit
  d. temperature sensor and temperature switch
  e. starting valve
  f. temperature switch for the auxiliary fan.
8. Loosen the ring line on the fuel distributor.
9. Loosen the screws on the injection valves and pressure regulator or mixture regulator. Remove the ring line with the injection valves and pressure regulator.
10. Plug the holes for the injection valves in the cylinder head.
11. Remove the regulating shaft by disconnecting the pull rod and the thrust rod.
12. Remove the ignition cable plug.
13. Loosen the vacuum connection on the intake manifold.

14. Loosen the vacuum connection for the central lock at the transmission.
15. Remove the oil filler tube from the right hand cylinder head and remove the temperature connector.
16. Remove the oil pressure gauge line from the left hand cylinder head.
17. Loosen the coolant connection on the intake manifold.
18. Remove the intake manifold. This is not necessary on 3.8 and 5.0 liter V8's although the intake manifold bolts must be removed.
19. Loosen the alternator belt and remove the alternator and mounting bracket.
20. Remove the electrical connections from the distributor and electronic ignition switch-gear
21. Drain some fluid from the power steering reservoir and disconnect and plug the return hose and high pressure supply line.
22. Disconnect the exhaust system. On 3.8 and 5.0 liter V8's, remove the exhaust manifolds.
23. Loosen the right hand holder for the engine damper.
24. Remove the right hand chain tensioner.
25. Matchmark the camshaft, camshaft sprocket, and chain. Remove the camshaft sprocket and chain after removing the cylinder head cover. Be sure to hang the chain and sprocket to prevent it from falling into the timing chain case.
26. Remove the upper slide rail. On 3.8 and 5.0 liter V8's, remove the distributor and remove the inner slide rail on the left cylinder head. Remove the rail after the camshaft sprocket.
27. Unscrew the cylinder head bolts. This should be done with a cold engine. Unscrew the bolts in the reverse order of the torque sequences. Unscrew all the bolts a little at a time and proceed in this manner until all the bolts have been removed. On the 6.9, you'll need to raise the engine to remove No. 12 and 18 bolts on the left side

head. To do this, place the level adjusting switch at "S" (first notch).

NOTE: Cylinder head bolts on the 3.8 and 5.0 liter V8's are nickel plated and 10 mm longer than those for previous engines.

28. Remove the cylinder head. Do not pry on the cylinder head.
29. Remove the cylinder head gasket.
30. Clean the cylinder head and cylinder block joint faces.
31. To install, position the cylinder head gasket.
32. Do not confuse the cylinder head gaskets. The left hand head has two attaching holes in the timing chain cover while the right hand has three.

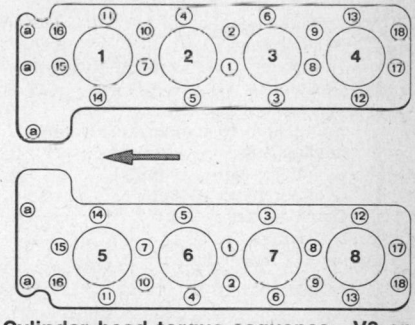

Cylinder head torque sequence—V8 engines (except 6.9)

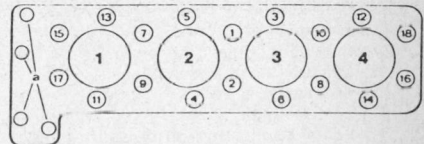

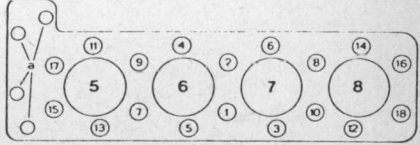

Cylinder head torque sequence—6.9 V8

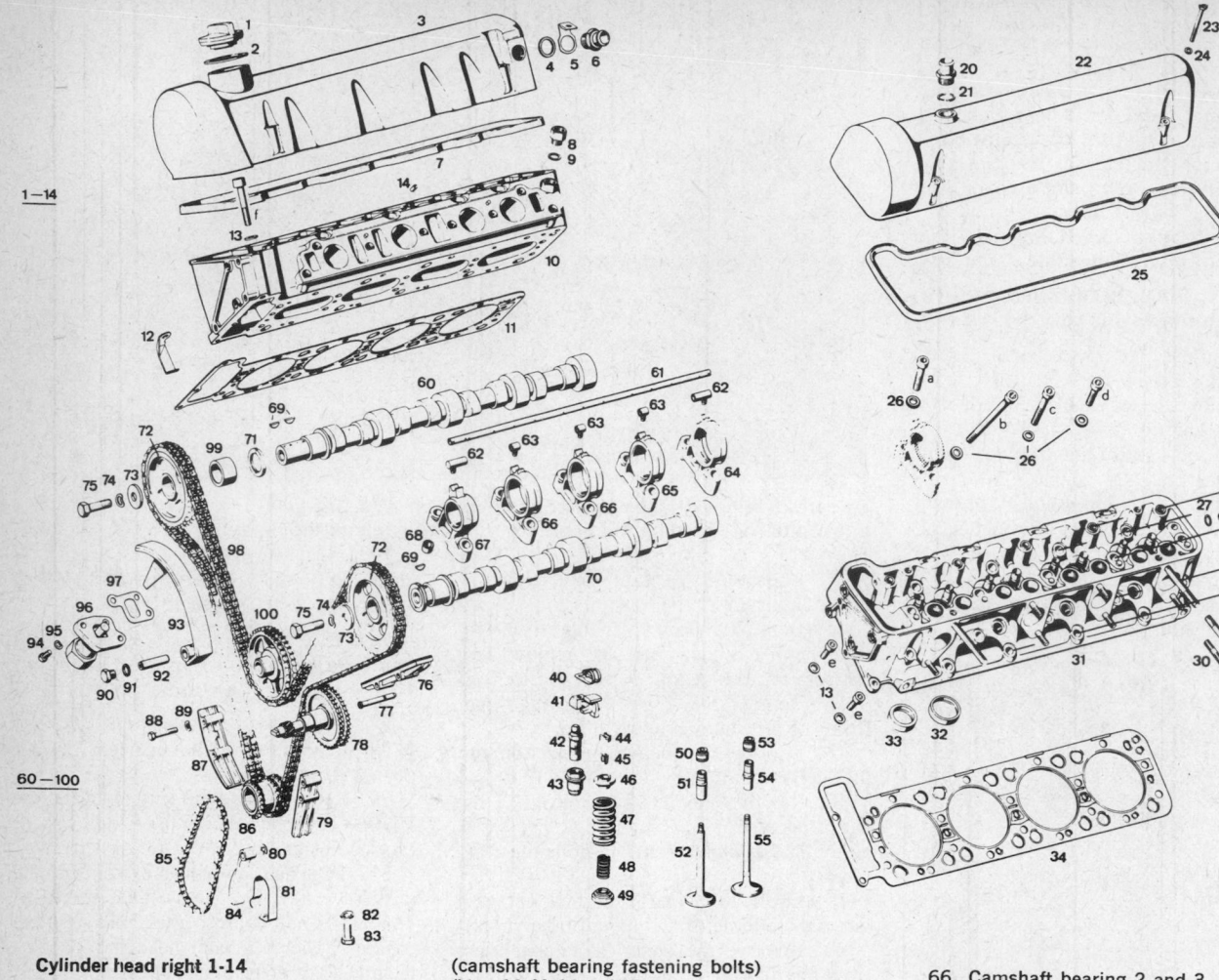

Exploded view of the V8 cylinder head

Cylinder head right 1-14

1. Filler plug
2. Sealing ring
3. Cylinder head cover
4. Sealing ring
5. Holder for cable to injection valves
6. Connection
7. Valve cover gasket
8. Connection to temperature sensor
9. Sealing ring
10. Cylinder head
11. Cylinder head gasket
12. Cable holder
13. 5 Washers
14. Hollow dowel pins

Cylinder head left 20-34

20. Connection
21. Sealing ring
22. Cylinder head cover
23. 8 Screws
24. 8 Sealing rings
25. Cylinder head cover gasket
26. 36 Washers
27. Sealing ring
28. Screw connection oil pressure gauge
29. 3 Studs
30. 13 Studs
31. Cylinder head
32. Valve seat ring—intake
33. Valve seat ring—exhaust
34. Cylinder head gasket

Cylinder head bolts

(a)—10 M 10 x 50chrauben)

(camshaft bearing fastening bolts)
(b)—10 M 10 x 155
(c)—18 M 10 x 80
(d)—8 M 10 x 55
(e)—4 M 8 x 30
(f)—1 M 8 x 70

Valve arrangement 40-55

40. Tensioning spring
41. Rocker arm
42. Adjusting screw
43. Threaded bushing
44. Thrust piece
45. Valve cone piece
46. Valve spring retainer
47. Outer valve spring
48. Inner valve spring
49. Rotator
50. Intake valve seal
51. Exhaust valve guide
52. Intake valve
53. Exhaust valve seal
54. Exhaust valve guide
55. Exhaust valve

Engine timing 60-100

60. Camshaft-right
61. Oil pipe (external lubrication)   Oil pipe to
62. Connecting piece   camshaft
63. Connecting piece   bearing
64. Camshaft bearing-flywheel end
65. Camshaft bearing 4

66. Camshaft bearing 2 and 3
67. Camshaft bearing-cranking end
68. 5 Hollow dowel pins
69. Spring washer
70. Camshaft-left
71. Compensating washer
72. Camshaft gear
73. Washer-camshaft gear
74. Spring washer
75. Bolt
76. 3 Slide rails
77. 6 Bearing bolts
78. Drive gear ignition distributor
79. Guide rail
80. Lockwasher
81. Spring—chain tensioner, oil pump
82. Washer
83. Screw
84. Clamp
85. Single roller chain (oil pump drive)
86. Crankshaft gear
87. Slide rail
88. 4 Screws
89. 4 Spring washers
90. Plug
91. Sealing ring
92. Bearing bolt
93. Tensioning lever
94. 2 Bolts
95. 2 Spring washers
96. Chain tensioner
97. Gasket
98. Double roller chain
99. Spacer ring
100. Idler gear

33. Install the cylinder head and torque the bolts according to the illustrated torque sequence.

34. Further installation is the reverse of removal. On 3.8 and 5.0 liter V8's, insert the rear cam bearing cylinder head bolt before positioning the cylinder head. Also, install the exhaust manifolds only after the cylinder head bolts have been tightened. The camshaft sprocket should be installed so that the flange faces the camshaft. Check the valve clearance and fill the engine with oil. Top up the power steering tank and bleed the power steering system.

35. Run the engine and check for leaks.

6-Cylinder DOHC Engine

NOTE: Two people are best for this job.

NOTE: The head must be removed STRAIGHT up. The 2 bolts in the chain case are removed with a magnet.

To install use 2 pieces of wood ½ in. × 1½ in. × 9 in. to support the head while aligning the bolt holes. The exhaust camshaft gear bolt is 0.2 in. shorter.

1. Completely drain the cooling system.
2. Remove the air filter.
3. Remove the radiator.
4. Remove the rocker arm cover.
5. Remove the battery. Remove the idler pulley and the holding bracket for the compressor.
6. Remove the compressor and bracket and lay it aside without disconnecting any of the lines.

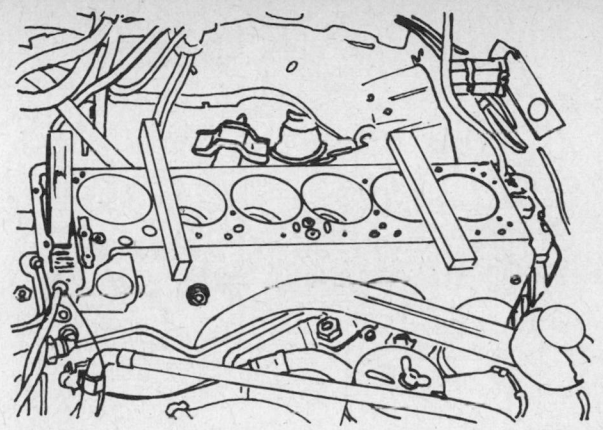

Fabricated tools for installing the cylinder head on DOHC 6-cylinder engines

———— CAUTION ————
Disconnecting any of the refrigerant lines could result in physical harm.

7. Unbolt the cover from the camshaft housing.
8. Disconnect the heating water line from the carburetor, the vacuum line on the starter housing, and the distributor vacuum line.
9. Disconnect all electrical connections, water lines, fuel lines, and vacuum lines which are connected to the cylinder head. Tag these for reassembly.
10. Remove the regulating linkage shaft.
11. Remove the EGR line between the exhaust return valve and the exhaust pipe.

12. Disconnect and plug the oil return line at the cylinder head.
13. At the thermostat housing, loosen the hose which passes between the thermostat housing and the water pump. Unscrew the bypass line on the water pump.
14. Loosen the oil dipstick tube from the clamp and bend it slightly sidewards.
15. Unbolt the exhaust pipes from the exhaust manifolds and bracket on the transmission.
16. Force the tension springs out of the rocker arm with a small pry bar.
17. Remove all of the rocker arms.
18. Crank the engine to TDC. This can be done with a socket wrench on the crankshaft pulley bolt. The marks on the cam-

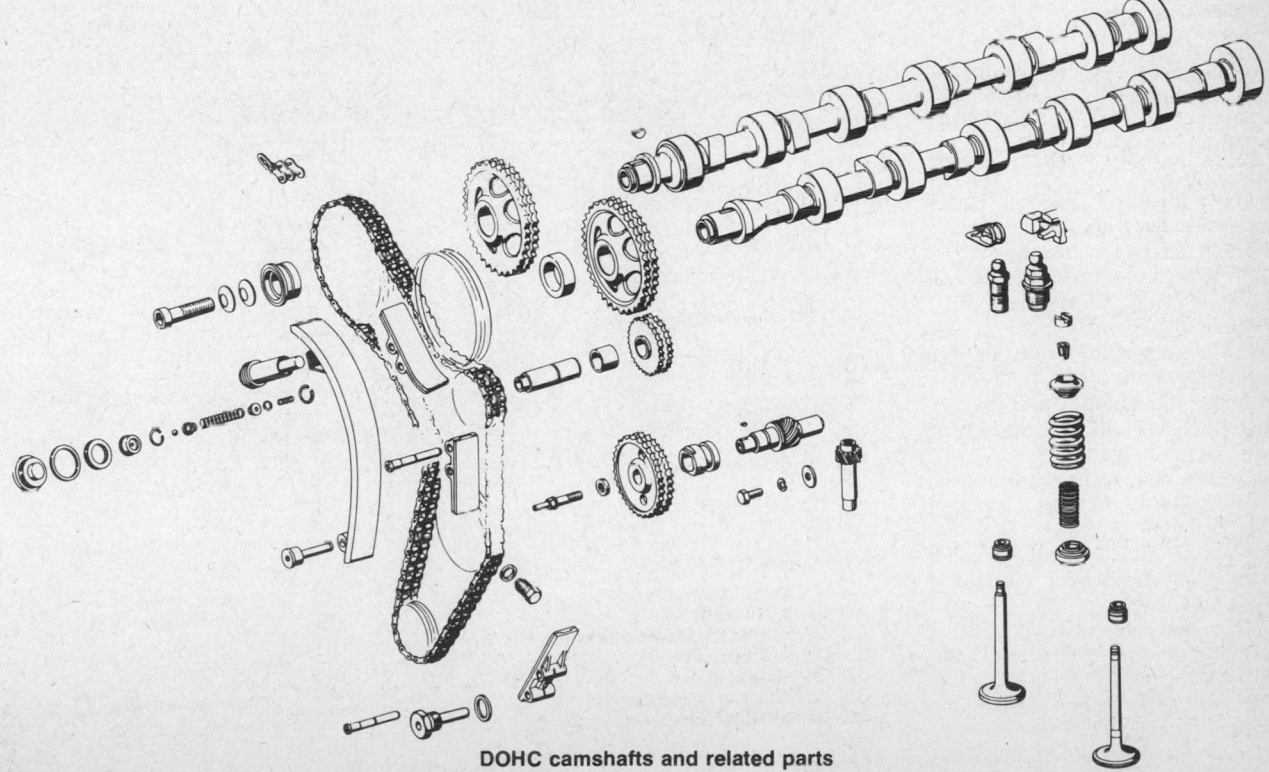

DOHC camshafts and related parts

The marks on the camshaft and bearing housing must align on DOHC 6-cylinder engines when the engine is at TDC

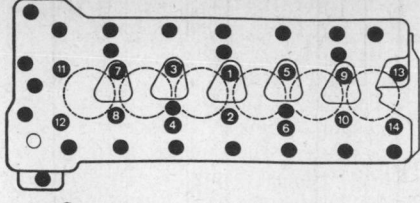

● Tighten   ○ Concealed, cannot be tightened

Cylinder head torque sequence—6 cylinder engines

33. Install the cylinder head in an inclined position so that the timing chain and tensioning rail can be inserted.

34. Lift the cylinder head at the front and remove the front piece of wood toward the exhaust side. Carefully lower the cylinder head until the bolt holes align.

35. Lift the head at the rear so that the board can be removed toward the exhaust side. Carefully lower the cylinder head until all the bolt holes align.

36. Tighten the cylinder head bolts in gradual steps until they are fully tightened. Follow the torque sequence.

37. Check to be sure that both camshafts rotate freely after the bolts are tight.

38. The remainder of installation is the reverse of removal. Be sure that the spacer for the camshaft gear with the engaging lugs for the vacuum pump drive gear is installed on the exhaust side. Also, the washers for the bolts attaching the camshaft gears to the camshafts must be installed with the domed side against the head of the bolt.

While the head is removed from a 6-cylinder engine, always replace this rubber hose, whether it needs it or not; it is impossible to replace with the cylinder head installed.

case with a magnet. *Be careful not to drop the washers.*

29. Pull up on the timing chain and force the tensioning rail toward the center of the engine.

30. Lift the cylinder head up in a vertical direction.

NOTE: Mercedes-Benz recommends two people for this job.

31. Remove the cylinder head gasket and clean the joint faces of the block and head.

32. To install, cut two pieces of wood ½ in. × 1½ in. × 9½ in. Lay one piece upright between cylinders 1 and 2; lay the other flat between cylinders 5 and 6.

shaft sprockets and bearing housings must be aligned.

19. Hold the camshafts and remove the bolt which holds each camshaft gear to the camshaft.

20. Remove the upper slide rail. Knock out the bearing bolts with a puller.

21. Remove the chain tensioner.

22. Push both camshafts toward the rear and remove the camshaft sprockets.

23. Remove the spacer sleeves on both camshafts. The sleeves are located in front of the camshaft bearings.

24. Remove the guide wheel by unscrewing the plug and removing the bearing bolt.

25. Lift off the timing chain and suspend the chain from the hood with a piece of wire. Pull out the guide gear.

26. Remove the slide rail in the cylinder head by removing the bearing pin with a puller.

27. Loosen the cylinder head bolts in small increments, using the reverse order of the tightening sequence. This should be done on a cold engine to prevent the possibility of head warpage.

28. Pull out the two bolts in the chain

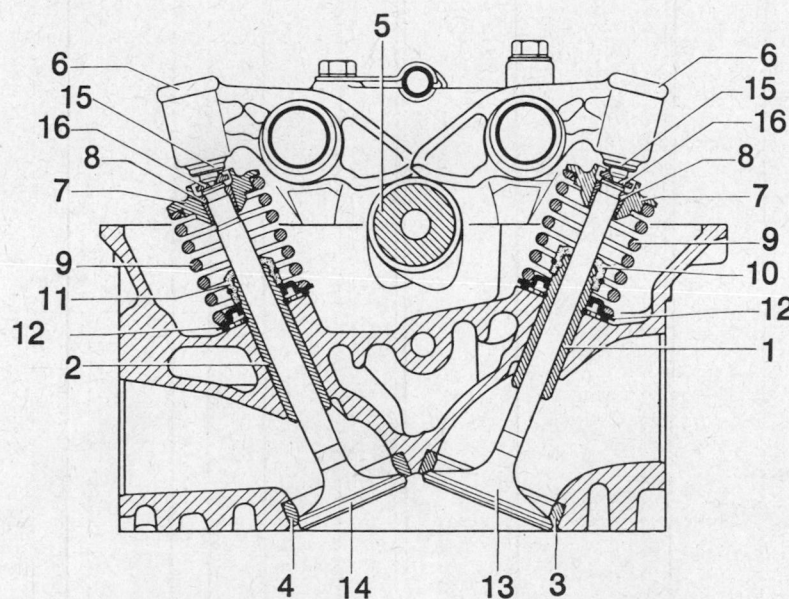

1. Intake valve guide
2. Exhaust valve guide
3. Intake valve seat ring
4. Exhaust valve seat ring
5. Camshaft
6. Rocker arm
7. Valve spring retainer
8. Valve cone halves
9. Valve spring
10. Intake valve stem seal
11. Exhaust valve stem seal
12. Thrust ring
13. Intake valve
14. Exhaust valve
15. Hydraulic valve tappet
16. Ball socket

Valve train on the 190E

39. Note that the attaching bolt for the exhaust camshaft gear is 0.2 in. shorter.

40. Be sure to adjust the valve clearance and fill the cooling system. Run the engine and check for leaks.

OVERHAUL

Overhaul procedures for cylinder heads are contained in "Engine Rebuilding" in the Unit Repair section of this book. Consult this section for detailed overhaul procedures.

Valves and Springs

REMOVAL & INSTALLATION

1. Remove the cylinder head. Remove the rocker arms and shafts (all except 190D). Remove the camshaft (190D only).

On gasoline engines only:

2. Using a valve spring compressor, compress the spring and remove the valve cone halves (be careful not to lose the two valve cone halves).

3. Remove the spring retainer and then lift out the spring.

4. Pry off the valve stem oil seal and lift out the lower spring seat (thrust ring). Remove the valve through the bottom of the cylinder head.

NOTE: When removing the valve stem seal and the thrust ring, a small screwdriver and a magnet may come in handy.

On the 190D:

5. Remove the hydraulic valve tappet with Special Tool # 601 589 05 33 00. After the tappet has been removed, follow the procedures detailed for gasoline engines.

On all other diesel engines:

6. Position an open-end wrench on the valve spring retainer; while holding the retainer, unscrew the capnut with a valve adjusting wrench.

NOTE: A second valve adjusting wrench will be required to hold the counternut while loosening the capnut.

7. Loosen and remove the counternut.

8. Lift out the valve spring and lower spring seat. Remove the valve through the bottom of the cylinder head.

On all engines:

9. Inspect the valve and spring. Clean the valve guide with a cotton swab and solvent. Inspect the valve guide and seat and check the valve guide-to-stem clearance.

10. Lubricate the valve stem and guide with engine oil. Install the valve into the cylinder head through the bottom and position the lower spring seat (thrust ring).

11. Lubricate the valve stem oil seal with engine oil, slide it down over the stem and then install it into position over the spring seat.

NOTE: When installing seals, always ensure that a small amount of oil is able

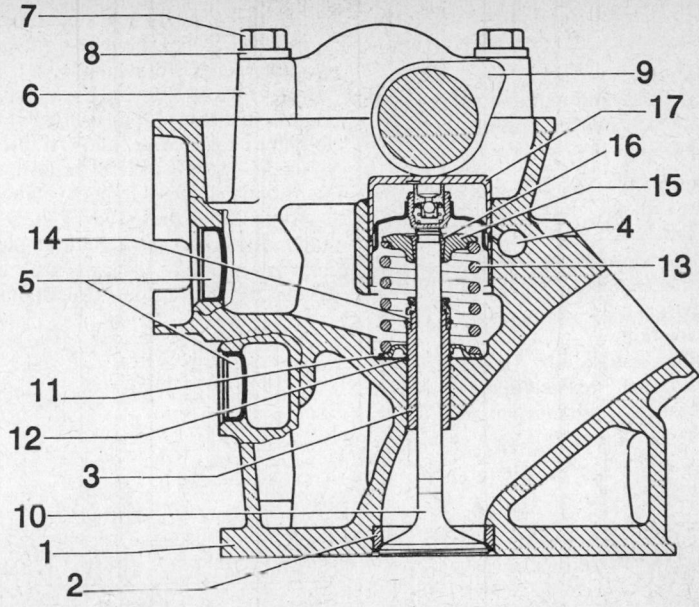

1. Cylinder head
2. Intake valve seat ring
3. Intake valve guide
4. Oil passage
5. Sheet metal plug
6. Bearing cap
7. Screw M 8 × 45
8. Washer
9. Camshaft
10. Intake valve
11. Thrust ring
12. Lock ring
13. Valve spring
14. Intake valve stem seal
15. Valve spring retainer
16. Valve cone halves
17. Hydraulic valve tappets

Valve train on the 190D (intake shown, exhaust similar)

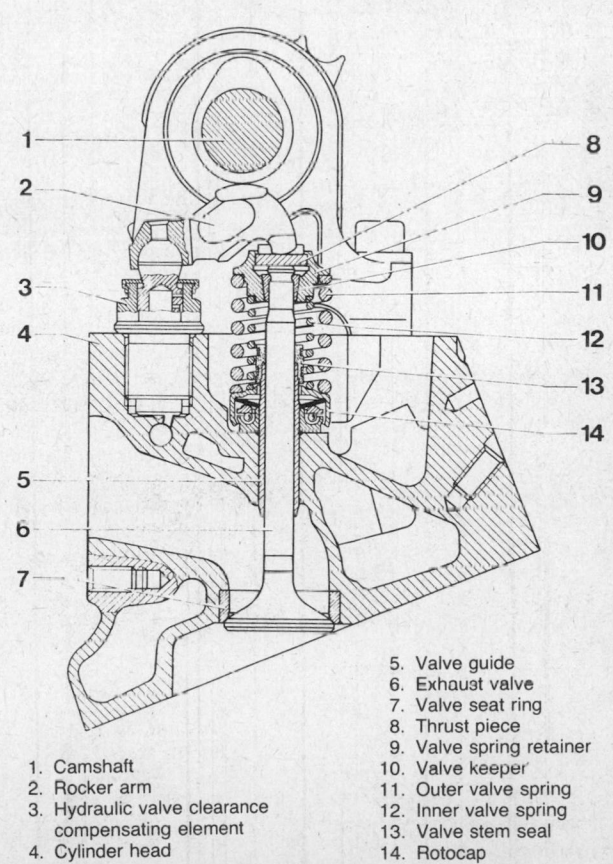

1. Camshaft
2. Rocker arm
3. Hydraulic valve clearance compensating element
4. Cylinder head
5. Valve guide
6. Exhaust valve
7. Valve seat ring
8. Thrust piece
9. Valve spring retainer
10. Valve keeper
11. Outer valve spring
12. Inner valve spring
13. Valve stem seal
14. Rotocap

Valve train on the 3.8 V8 (other V8 engines similar)

to pass the seal so as to lubricate the valve guides; otherwise, excessive wear may result.

NOTE: Intake and exhaust valve stem seals on the 190 series engines are not interchangeable.

12. Position the valve spring onto the spring seat with the tight coils facing the cylinder head.

13. Install the spring retainer. On all diesel engines (except 190D), the lug on the retainer must be seated in the groove on the valve stem.

14. Further installation is the reverse of the removal procedures detailed previously for the individual engine groups.

NOTE: Tap the installed valve stem lightly with a rubber mallet to ensure a proper fit.

INSPECTION

Inspect the valve faces and seats (in the cylinder head) for pits, burned spots and other evidence of poor seating. If the valve face is in such bad shape that the head of the valve must be ground in order to true up the face, discard the valve because the sharp edge will run too hot. The correct angle for valve faces is given in the specification section.

It is recommended that any reaming or resurfacing (grinding) be performed by a reputable machine shop.

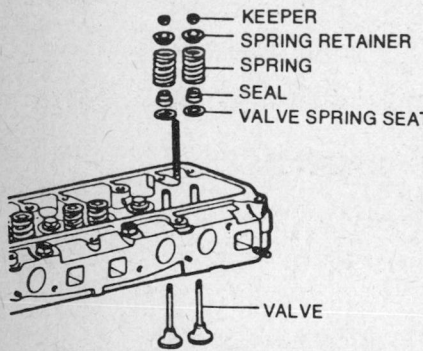

Typical valve and related components

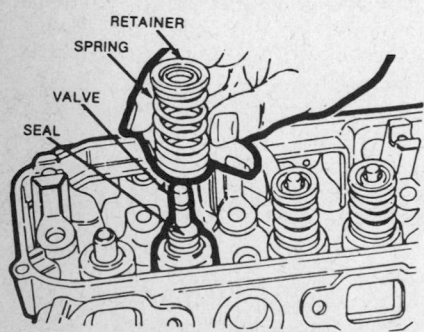

Installing the valve

Check the valve stem for scoring and/or burned spots. If not noticably scored or damaged, clean the valve stem with a suitable solvent to remove all gum and varnish.

Clean the valve guides using a suitable solvent and an expanding wire-type valve guide cleaner (generally available at a local automotive supply store). If you have access to a dial indicator for measuring valve stem-to-guide clearance, mount it so that the stem of the indicator is at a 90° angle to the valve stem and as close to the valve guide as possible. Move the valve off its seat slightly and measure the valve guide-to-stem clearance by rocking the valve back and forth so that the stem actuates the dial indicator.

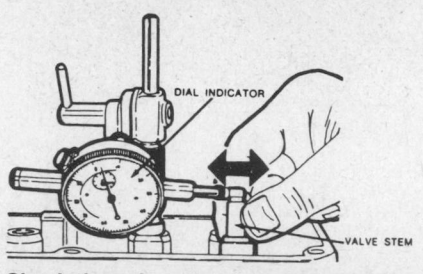

Check the valve stem-to-guide clearance

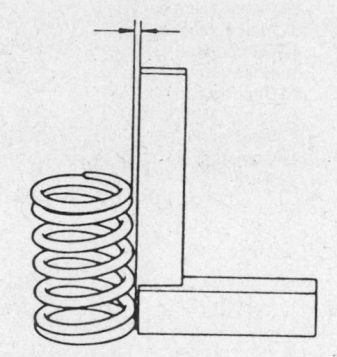

Checking the valve spring for squareness

Measure the valve stem using a micrometer, and compare to specifications in order to determine whether the stem or the guide is responsible for the excess clearance. If a dial indicator and a micrometer are not available, take the cylinder head and valves to a reputable machine shop.

Using a steel square, check the squareness of the valve spring. If the spring is out of square more than the maximum allowable, it will require replacement. Check that the spring free height is up to specifications. Measure the distance between the thrust ring and the lower edge of the spring retainer, and compare to specifications.

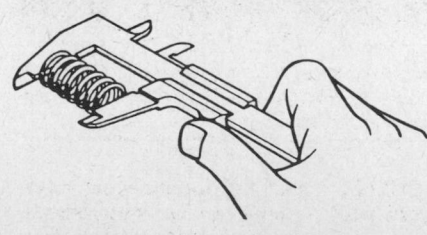

Checking the spring free height

Valve Guides

REMOVAL & INSTALLATION

See "Engine Rebuilding" in the Unit Repair section also.

1. Remove the cylinder head.

2. Clean the valve guide with a brush, knocking away all loose carbon and oil deposits.

3. Knock out the old valve guide with a drift.

4. Check the bore in the cylinder head and clean up any rough spots. Use a reamer for this purpose. If necessary, the valve guide bore can be reamed for oversize valve guides.

5. Clean the basic bores for the valve guides.

6. Heat the cylinder head in water to approximately 176–194°F.

7. If possible cool the valve guides slightly.

8. Drive the valve guides into the bores with a drift. Coat the bores in the cylinder head with wax prior to installation and be sure that the circlip rests against the cylinder head.

9. Let the head cool and try to knock the valve guide out with light hammer blows and a plastic drift. If the guide can be knocked out, try another guide with a tighter fit.

10. Install the cylinder head.

Rocker Arms

REMOVAL & INSTALLATION

Diesel Engines

NOTE: The 190D does not use rocker arms. The camshaft acts directly on the hydraulic valve tappet.

Rocker arms on diesel engines can only be removed as a unit with the respective rocker arm blocks.

1. Detach the connecting rod for the venturi control unit from the bearing bracket lever and remove the bearing bracket from the rocker arm cover.

2. Remove the air vent line from the rocker arm cover and remove the rocker arm cover.

3. Remove the stretchbolts from the rocker arm blocks and remove the blocks with the rocker arms. Turn the crankshaft in each case so that the camshaft does not put any load on the rocker arms.

NOTE: Turn the crankshaft with a socket wrench on the crankshaft pulley bolt. Do not rotate the engine by turning the camshaft sprocket.

4. Before installing the rocker arms, check the sliding surfaces of the ball cup and rocker arms. Replace any defective parts.

5. To install, assemble the rocker arm blocks and insert new stretchbolts.

6. Tighten the stretchbolts. In each case,

Replacing valve guides

position the camshaft so that there is no load on the rocker arms. See the previous NOTE.

7. Check to be sure that the tension clamps have engaged with the notches of the rocker arm blocks.

8. Adjust the valve clearance.

9. Reinstall the rocker arm cover, air vent line, and bearing bracket for the reverse lever. Attach the connecting rod for the venturi control unit to the reversing lever.

10. Make sure that during acceleration, the control cable can move freely without binding.

11. Start the engine and check the rocker arm cover for leaks.

Gasoline Engines—All Except 190E

NOTE: 1976 and later V8's use hydraulic valve lifters.

Before removing the rocker arm(s), be sure that they are identified as to their position relative to the camshaft lobe. They should be installed in the same place as they were before disassembly.

Be very careful removing the thrust pieces. They can easily fall into the engine.

1. Remove the rocker arm cover or covers.

2. Force the clamping spring out of the notch in the top of the rocker arm. Slide it in an outward direction across the ball socket or the rocker arm.

NOTE: Turn the engine over each time to relieve any load from the rocker arm.

3. On V8 models, the clamping spring must be forced from the adjusting screw with a small prybar.

4. Force the valve down to remove load from the rocker arm.

NOTE: Don't depress the spring too far. When the piston is up as it should be, the valve will hit the piston. As the spring goes down, the thrust piece will fall off into the engine.

5. Lift the rocker arm from the ball pin and remove the rocker arm.

6. To install the rocker arm(s), force the rocker arm down until the rocker arm and its ball socket can be installed in the top of the ball pin.

7. Install the rocker arms.

8. Slide the clamping spring across the ball socket of the rocker arm until it rests in the notch of the rocker arm.

9. On V8 models, engage the clamping spring into the recess of the adjusting screw.

10. Check and, if necessary, adjust the valve clearance.

11. After completion of the adjustment, check to be sure that the clamping springs are correctly seated.

12. Install the rocker arm cover and connect any hoses or lines that were disconnected.

13. Run the engine and check for leaks at the rocker arm cover.

190E

Rocker arms on this engine are individually mounted on rocker arm shafts that fit into either side of the camshaft bearing brackets.

1. Remove the cylinder head cover. The cover on the 190E is removed with the spark plug wires and distributor cap still connected.

2. Tag each rocker arm and shaft so that they are identified as to their position relative to the camshaft. They should always be installed in the same place as they were before disassembly.

3. The rocker arm shaft is held axially and rotationally by a bearing bracket fastening bolt. Remove the bolt on the side of the bearing bracket that allows access to the exposed end of the rocker shaft.

4. Thread a bolt (M8) into the end of the rocker arm shaft and slowly ease the shaft out of the bearing bracket.

--- CAUTION ---
Support the rocker arm/lifter assembly while removing the shaft so it will not drop onto the cylinder head.

NOTE: **Carefully forcing the valve down with a small prybar will remove the load on the hydraulic valve tappet and ease the removal of the shaft. Don't**

depress the spring too far. When the piston is up as it should be, the valve will hit the piston. As the spring goes down the thrust piece will fall off into the engine.

To remove the rocker shaft on the 190E, thread a bolt into the hole (D). On installation, the dished groove (arrow) must always line up with the mounting bolt shank

5. Replace the bearing bracket bolt and tighten it to 11 ft. lbs. (15 Nm) until ready to replace the rocker shaft.

6. To install, position the rocker arm between the two bearing brackets and slide the shaft into place.

NOTE: **The circular groove on the end of the rocker shaft must line up with the mounting bolt shank to ensure proper positioning.**

7. Replace the bearing bracket mounting bolt.

8. Repeat Steps 3–7 for all remaining rocker arm/shaft assemblies. Turn the engine over each time to relieve any load from the rocker arm.

9. Replace the cylinder head cover.

Hydraulic Valve Lifters

V8 ENGINES

Hydraulic valve lifters are used with overhead cams. The rocker arm is always in contact with the cam, reducing noise and eliminating operating clearance.

Checking Base Setting

The base setting is the clearance between the upper edge of the cylindrical part of the plunger and the lower edge of the retaining cap (dimension A) when the cam lobe is vertical.

NOTE: **A dial indicator with an extension and a measuring thrust piece (MBNA #100 589 16 63 00) 0.187 in. thick are necessary to perform this adjustment.**

1. Turn the cam lobe to a vertical position, relative to the rocker arm.

2. Attach a dial indicator and tip extension and insert the extension through the bore in the rocker arm onto the head plunger. Preload the dial indicator by 0.08 in. and zero the instrument.

3. Depress the valve with a valve spring compressor. The lift on the dial indicator should be 0.028–0.075 in.

C489

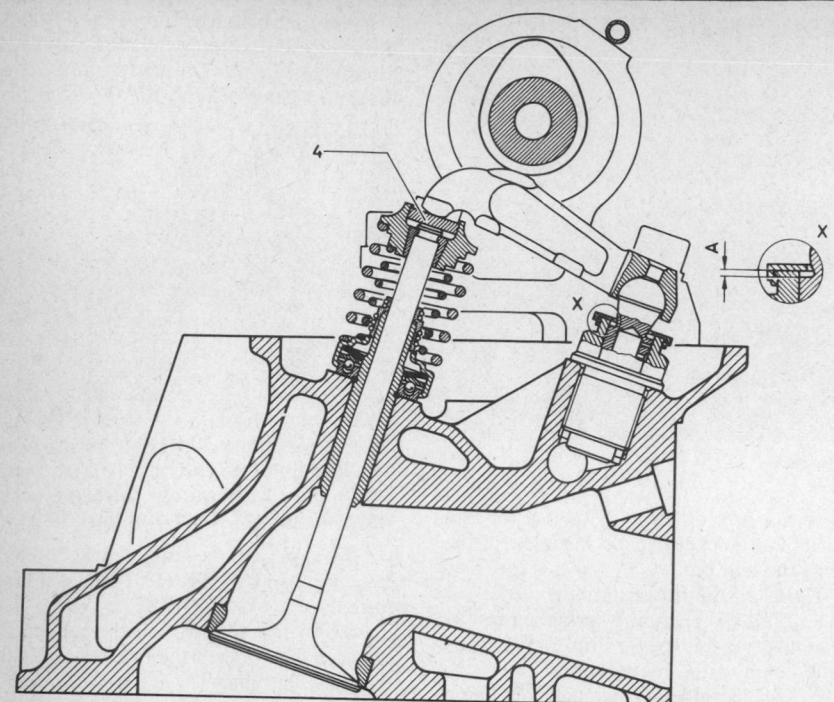

Cutaway of valve train showing hydraulic valve lifter. Dimension "A" is base setting clearance.

4. If the lift is excessive, the base setting can be changed by installing a new thrust piece.

5. Remove the dial indicator.

6. Remove the rocker arm.

7. Remove the thrust piece and insert the measuring disc.

8. Install the rocker arm and repeat Steps 1–3.

9. Select a thrust piece according to the table. If the measured valve was 0–0.002 in. and the 0.2146 in. thrust piece will not give the proper base setting, use the 0.2283 in. thrust piece.

10. Remove the dial indicator and the rocker arm. Install the selected thrust piece.

11. Reinstall the rocker arm and dial indicator and repeat Steps 1–3.

SELECTIVE THRUST PIECES

Measured Value (in.)	Thrust Piece Thickness(s) (in.)
0–0.002	0.2146/0.2283
0.002–0.034	0.2008
0.035–0.066	0.1870
0.067–0.099	0.1732
0.099–0.131	0.1594
above 0.131	0.1457

Removal & Installation

Temporarily removed valve lifters must be reinstalled in their original locations. When replacing worn rocker arms, the camshaft must also be replaced. If the rocker arm,

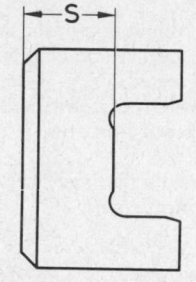

Thrust piece thickness

or hydraulic lifter is replaced, check the base setting.

Remove the rocker arm and unscrew the valve lifter with a 24mm socket.

Intake Manifold

REMOVAL & INSTALLATION

V8 Engine

1. Partially drain the coolant.

2. Remove the air cleaner.

3. Disconnect the regulating linkage and remove the longitudinal regulating shaft.

4. Pull off all cable plug connections.

5. Disconnect and plug the fuel lines on the pressure regulator and starting valve.

6. Unscrew the nuts on the injection valves and set the injection valves aside.

7. Remove the 16 attaching bolts from the intake manifold.

8. Loosen the hose clip on the thermostat housing hose and disconnect the hose.

9. Remove the intake manifold. If a portion of the manifold must be replaced, disassemble the intake manifold. Replace the rubber connections during reassembly.

Replace the rubber connecting pieces on the intake manifold, anytime the manifold is removed.

10. Intake manifold installation is the reverse of removal. Replace all seals and gaskets. Adjust the linkage and idle speed.

Exhaust Manifold

REMOVAL & INSTALLATION

V8 Engine

1. Unbolt the exhaust pipes from the manifolds.

2. Disconnect the rubber mounting ring from the exhaust system.

3. Loosen the shield plate on the exhaust manifold.

4. When removing the left hand exhaust manifold, remove the shield plate for the engine mount together with the engine damper.

5. Unbolt the manifold from the engine.

6. Pull the manifolds off of the mounting.

7. Installation is the reverse of removal.

Turbocharger

NOTE: There is no particular maintenance associated with the turbocharger. It should also be noted that a turbocharger cannot be installed on an engine that was not meant for one without incurring serious engine damage.

The exhaust gas turbocharger is a Garrett Model TA 0301. It uses the aerodynamic energy of the exhaust gases to drive a centrifugal compressor which in turn delivers high pressure air to the cylinders of the diesel engine. The turbine wheel and the compressor wheel are mounted on a common shaft. The turbocharger is mounted between the exhaust manifold and the exhaust pipe. For lubrication and cooling, the turbocharger is connected directly to the engine lubrication system.

A boost pressure control valve (wastegate valve) is attached to the turbine housing to insure that a certain boost pressure is not exceeded. Should the boost pressure control valve malfunction, an engine overload protection system will prevent a failure of the engine.

For further information on turbo-chargers, please refer to "Turbocharging" in the Unit Repair Section.

OPERATION

Turbocharger

The exhaust gases of the engine are routed via the exhaust manifold directly into the turbine housing (6) and to the turbine wheel (7). The velocity of the exhaust gases causes the turbine wheel (7) to turn. This turns the compressor wheel (2) which is directly connected to the turbine wheel via the shaft (5). The turbocharger can obtain a maximum of approximately 100,000 rpm; the fresh air drawn in by the compressor wheel is compressed and delivered to the pistons of the engine.

1. Mounting bracket
2. Intermediate flange
3. Turbocharger

Remove the mounting nuts (arrow) to remove the turbocharger

At idle speed, the engine operates as a naturally aspirated engine. With increasing load and engine rpm, (increasing velocity of the exhaust gases), the turbine wheel (7) accelerates and boost pressure is produced by the compressor wheel (2). The boost pressure is routed via the intake manifold to the individual cylinders.

The exhaust gases produced by the combustion are routed into the turbine housing and from there into the exhaust pipe.

Boost Pressure Control Valve

In order not to exceed the designed boost pressure, a boost pressure control valve (8) is installed on the turbine housing (6). The boost pressure is picked up at the compressor housing (1) and connected to the boost pressure control valve (8) via a connecting hose (9). If the maximum permissible boost pressure is obtained, the boost pressure control valve (8) starts to open the bypass canal (c) for the exhaust gas around the turbine wheel (7). A part of the exhaust gas now flows directly into the exhaust pipe. This keeps the boost pressure constant and prevents it from increasing beyond its designed limits.

REMOVAL & INSTALLATION

1. Remove the air filter.

15. Valve connection
16. Nut
17. Washer
18. Gasket
19. Idle speed air line
20. Screw connection
21. Sealing ring
22. Upper Intake manifold
23. Holder
24. Hex bolt
25. Connection
26. Sealing ring
27. Gasket
28. Screw connection
29. Sealing ring
30. Screw connection
31. Sealing ring
32. Bottom intake manifold
33. Rubber connecting piece
35. Hex bolt
34. Hex bolt
36. Sealing ring
37. Plug
38. Hose

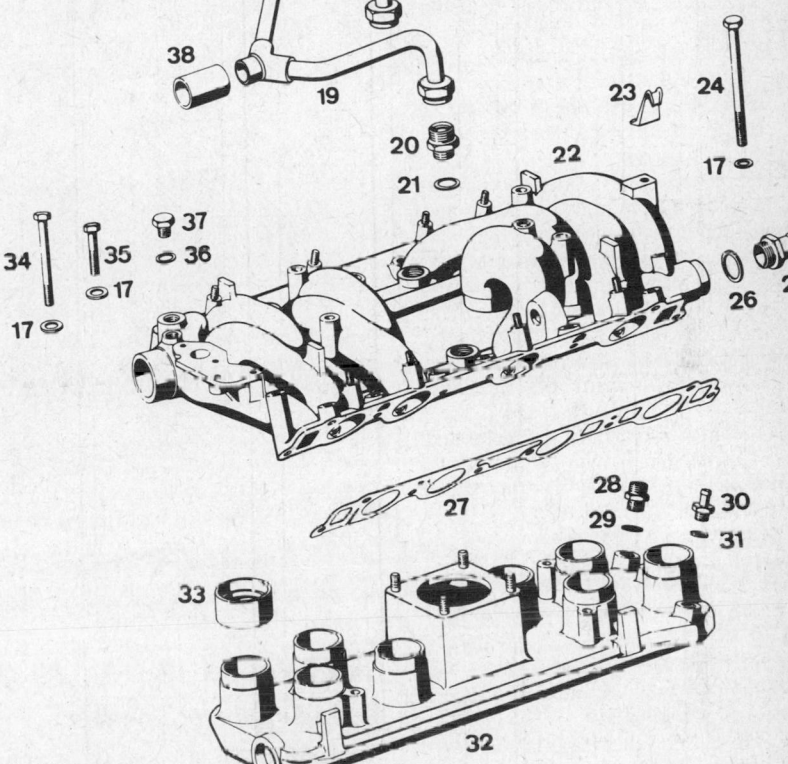

V8 Intake manifold

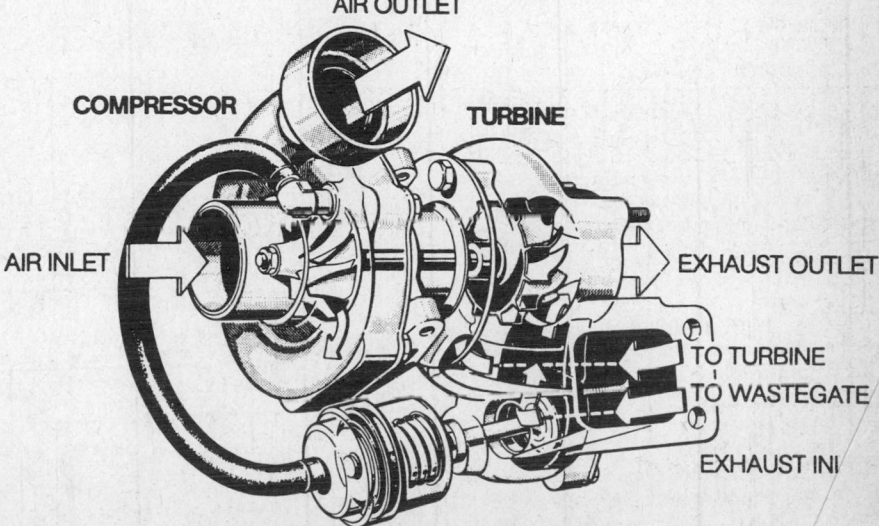

Garret TA0301 turbocharger operation

AIR OUTLET
COMPRESSOR
TURBINE
AIR INLET
EXHAUST OUTLET
TO TURBINE
TO WASTEGATE
EXHAUST INI
WASTEGATE BOOST CONTROL

2. Disconnect the electrical cable from the temperature switch.

3. Loosen the lower hose clamp on the air duct that connects the air filter with the compressor housing.

4. Remove the vacuum line and crankcase breather pipe.

5. Remove the air filter and air intake duct.

6. Disconnect the oil line at the turbocharger.

7. Remove the air filter mounting bracket.

8. Disconnect the turbocharger at the exhaust flange.

9. Disconnect and remove the pipe bracket on the automatic transmission.

10. Push the exhaust pipe rearward.

11. Remove the mounting bracket at the intermediate flange.

12. Unbolt and remove the turbocharger.

13. Remove the intermediate flange and oil return line at the turbocharger.

14. Installation is the reverse of removal. Before installing the turbocharger, install the oil return line and intermediate flange. Install the flange gasket between the turbocharger and exhaust manifold with the reinforcing bead toward the exhaust manifold.

Use only heat proof nuts and bolts and fill a new turbocharger with ¼ pint of engine oil through the engine oil supply bore before operating.

TROUBLESHOOTING

To properly evaluate the turbocharger, the full throttle stop, maximum no-load engine rpm, start of delivery and opening pressure of the injection nozzles must be within specifications.

Complaint: Poor engine performance
Probable cause: Boost pressure too low
Remedy:

1. Clean air filter and check air intake shroud and duct for obstructions.

2. Check turbocharger for leaks at following points:

Between exhaust manifold and turbine housing; tighten nuts.

Between compressor housing discharge and intake manifold.

Between intake or exhaust manifold and cylinder head.

3. Check pressure line between intake manifold and aneroid compensator.

4. Check fuse No. 4 or the black/red wire at the switchover valve for breaks or loose connection.

5. The boost pressure control valve (wastegate) on the turbocharger should close. If not, replace the turbocharger.

Complaint: Engine surges at full load.
Probable cause: Boost pressure control valve does not open.
Remedy: Check the connecting hose between the compressor housing and wastegate. If the hose is leaking or has a kink, replace the hose. If the hose is OK, replace the turbocharger.

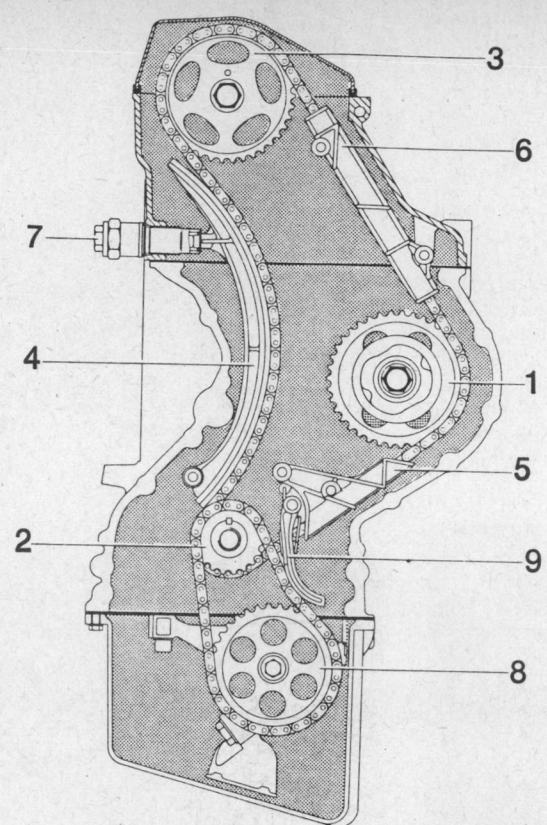

1. Injection timing advance mechanism
2. Crankshaft sprocket
3. Camshaft sprocket
4. Tensioning rail
5. Slide rail
6. Slide rail
7. Chain tensioner
8. Oil pump drive gear
9. Tensioning lever, chain, oil pump drive

Timing chain assembly—190D

Timing Chain Tensioner

REMOVAL & INSTALLATION

4 and 5-Cylinder Engines

There are 2 kinds of timing chain tensioners. One uses an O-ring seal and the other a flat gasket. Do not install a flat gasket on a tensioner meant to be used with an O-ring.

Chain tensioners should be replaced as a unit if defective.

1. Drain the coolant. If the car has air conditioning, disconnect the compressor and mounting bracket and lay it aside. Do not disconnect the refrigerant lines.

On diesel engines, drain the coolant from the block.

2. Remove the thermostat housing.

3. Loosen and remove the chain tensioner. Be careful of loose O-rings. On the 190, you must first remove the tensioner capnut and the tension spring. The ten-

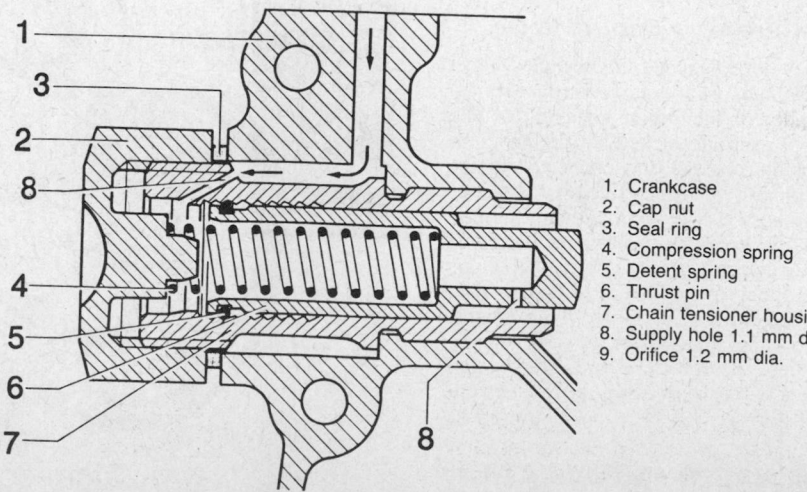

1. Crankcase
2. Cap nut
3. Seal ring
4. Compression spring
5. Detent spring
6. Thrust pin
7. Chain tensioner housing
8. Supply hole 1.1 mm dia.
9. Orifice 1.2 mm dia.

Cross section of the timing chain tensioner—190E (190D similar)

sioner body can then be unscrewed with an Allen wrench.

4. Check the O-rings or gasket and replace if necessary.

5. To fill the chain tensioner, place the tensioner (pressure bolt down) in a container of SAE 10 engine oil, at least up to the flat flange. Using a drill press, depress the pressure bolt slowly, about 7–10 times. Be sure this is done slowly and uniformly.

6. Install the chain tensioner. Tighten the bolts evenly. Tighten the capnut on the 190 to 51 ft. lbs. (70 Nm).

V8 Engines

The chain tensioner is connected to the engine oil circuit. Bleeding occurs once oil pressure has been established and the tensioner is filling with oil.

A venting hole has been installed in the tensioner to prevent oil foaming. If there is a lot of timing chain noise, use this type of tensioner, which is identified by a white paint dot on the cap.

Service procedures for tensioners and rails on the different V8's are similar. Arrangement and shape and size of parts however, is slightly different.

1. On California models, disconnect the line from the tensioner.

2. Remove the attaching bolts and remove the tensioner. The inside bolts will probably require a long, straight 6 mm Allen key to bypass the exhaust manifold. It is a tight fit.

3. Place the tensioner vertically in a container of engine oil. Operate the pressure bolt to fill the tensioner. After filling, it should permit compression very slowly under considerable force. If not, replace the tensioner with a new unit.

4. Install the tensioner and tighten the bolts evenly.

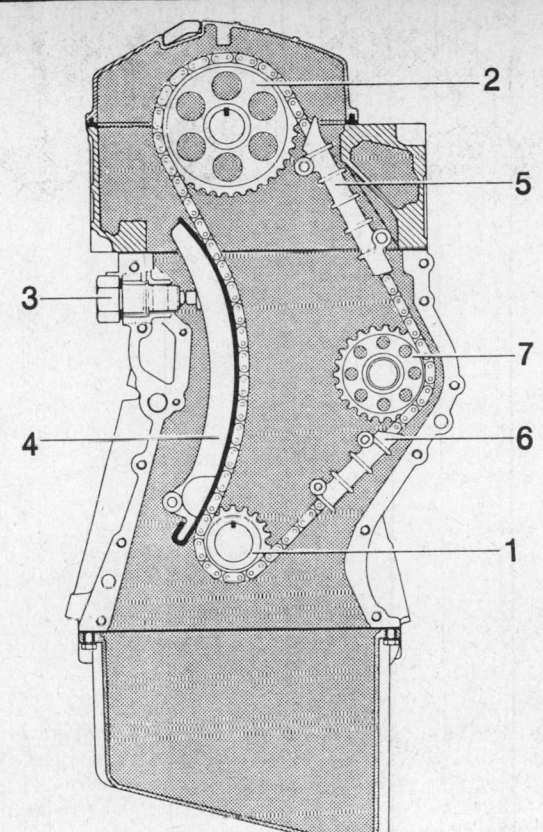

1. Crankshaft sprocket
2. Camshaft sprocket
3. Chain tensioner
4. Tensioning rail
5. Slide rail
6. Slide rail
7. Idler gear

Timing chain assembly—190E

6-Cylinder Engines

1. On A/C vehicles, remove the battery. Unbolt the refrigerant compressor and lay it aside. Do not disconnect the refrigerant lines.

2. Remove the plug with a 17 mm Allen key.

3. Tighten the threaded ring and loosen the ball seat ring.

4. Remove the threaded ring.

5. Remove the chain tensioner with a 10 mm Allen key.

6. Be sure the tight side of the chain is tight.

7. Compress the tensioner and install the chain tensioner with a 10 mm Allen key. Do not bump the Allen key or the tensioner will release.

8. Screw in the threaded ring and tighten it to 44 ft. lbs.

9. Tighten the ball seat ring to 18 ft. lbs. The pressure bolt should jump forward with an audible click. If it does not, the assembly must be removed and the installation repeated until it does click.

10. Install the plug.

11. Reinstall the A/C compressor, battery and air cleaner.

The inside bolt (arrow) on the V8 chain tensioner can only be reached by inserting a long, straight allen key underneath the exhaust manifold.

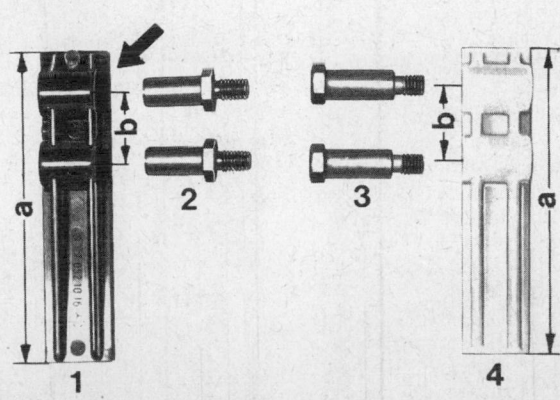

Attachment for tensioning rails for 3.8 V8 (left) and 4.5 V8 (right)

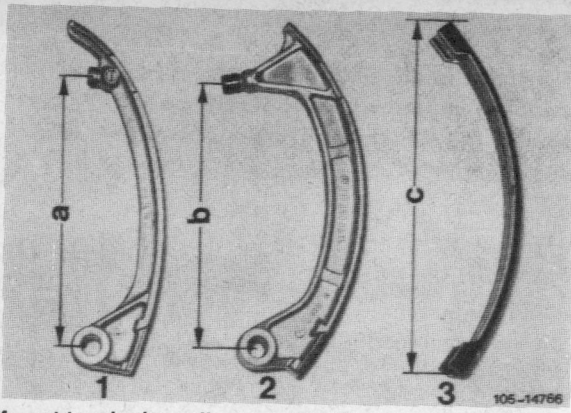

2 different tensioning rails are used. (1) is used on 3.8 V8's and is 133mm (a). (2) is used on 4.5 V8's and is 161.5mm (b). (3) is the lining for the 3.8 V8 rail.

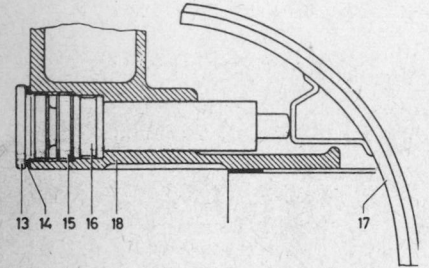

13. Closing plug
14. Sealing ring
15. Threaded ring
16. Chain tensioner
17. Tension rail
18. Cylinder head

6-cylinder timing chain tensioner

Timing Chain

REPLACEMENT

All Models

An endless timing chain is used on production engines, but a split chain with a connecting link is used for service. The endless chain can be separated with a "chain-breaker." Only one master link (connecting link) should be used on a chain.

1. Remove the spark plugs.

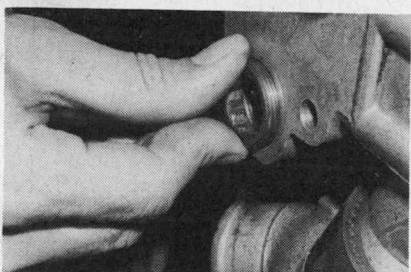

Remove the threaded plug.

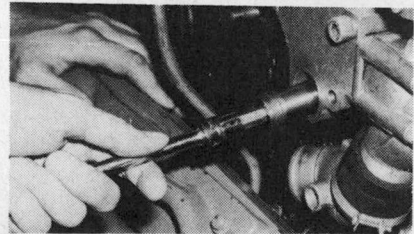

Remove the chain tensioner with a 10 mm allen key

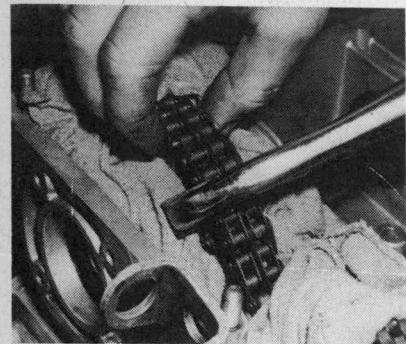

Clamp the chain to the gear and cover the opening with rags

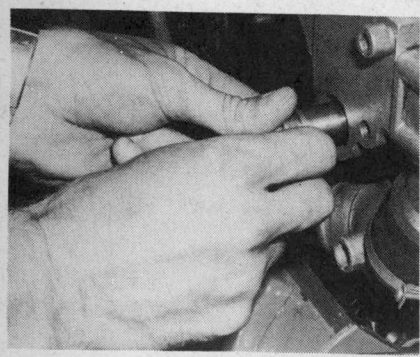

Install the chain tensioner

Remove the plug with a 17 mm allen key

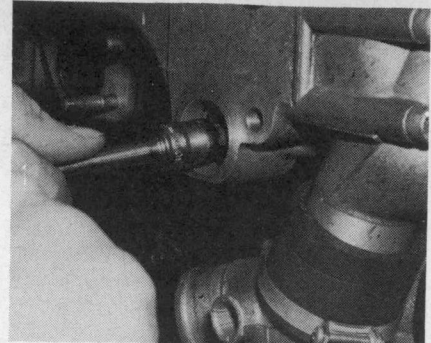

Tighten the tensioner until it "clicks"

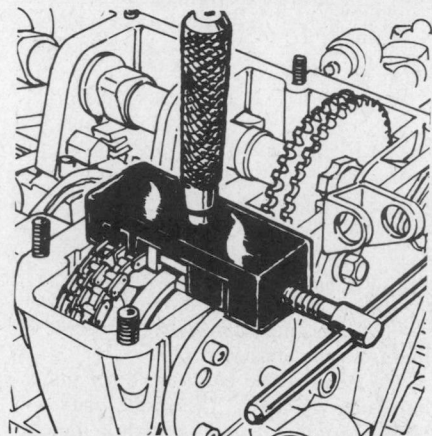

Remove the link with a chain breaker

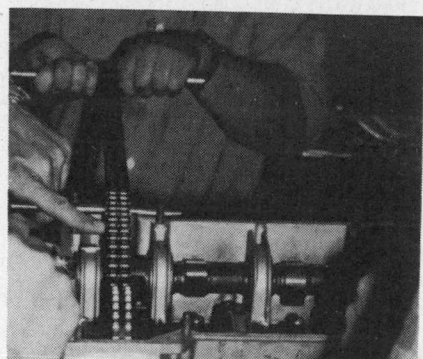

Crank the engine by hand until the new chain has come all the way through the engine. Be sure to keep tension on chain.

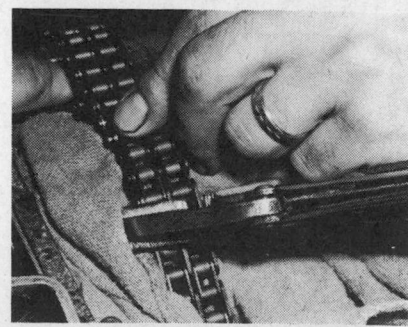

Clamp the chain again, cover the opening and remove the old chain from the master link. Connect both ends of the new chain.

2. Remove the valve cover(s).

3. Clamp the chain to the camshaft gear and cover the opening of the timing chain case with rags. On 6-cylinder and V8 engines, remove the rocker arms from the right hand camshaft.

4. Separate the chain with a chain breaker.

5. Attach a new timing chain to the old chain with a master link.

6. Using a socket wrench on the crankshaft, slowly rotate the engine in the direction of normal rotation. Simultaneously, pull the old chain through until the master link is uppermost on the camshaft sprocket. Be sure to keep tension on the chain throughout this procedure.

7. Disconnect the old timing chain and connect the ends of the new chain with the master link. Insert the new connecting link from the rear so that the lockwashers can be seen from the front.

8. Rotate the engine until the timing marks align. Check the valve timing. Once the new chain is assembled, rotate the engine (by hand) through at least one complete revolution to be sure everything is OK. See valve timing for illustrations.

Camshaft

REMOVAL & INSTALLATION

4 and 5-Cylinder Engines
EXCEPT 190D AND 190E

When the camshaft is replaced, be sure the rocker arms are also replaced.

1. Remove the valve cover.
2. Remove the chain tensioner.
3. Remove the rocker arms.
4. Set the crankshaft at TDC for the No. 1 cylinder and be sure that the camshaft timing marks are aligned.
5. Hold the camshaft and loosen the cam gear bolt. Remove the cam gear and wire it securely so that the chain does not lose tension nor slip down into the chain case.
6. Remove the camshaft.
7. Installation is the reverse of removal. Be sure to check that the valve timing marks align when the No. 1 cylinder is at TDC. Check the valve clearance.

On the 190E, the mark (arrow) on the camshaft collar (B) must always be aligned

Using a puller, remove the pins from the slide rails and remove the slide rails.

190D AND 190E

NOTE: On the 190E it is always a good idea to replace the rocker arms and shafts whenever the camshaft is replaced.

1. Remove the valve cover.
2. Remove the chain tensioner.
3. On the 190E, remove the rocker arms and shafts.
4. Set the crankshaft at TDC for the No. 1 piston and make sure that the timing marks on the camshaft are in alignment.
5. Using a 24mm open-end wrench, hold the rear of the camshaft (flats are provided) and then loosen and remove the camshaft retaining bolt. Carefully slide the gear and chain off the shaft and wire them securely so they won't slip down into the case.

NOTE: Be careful not to lose the woodruff key while removing the gear on the 190E.

6. The camshaft is secured on the cylinder head by means of the bearing caps. Remove them and keep them in their proper order. Each cap is marked by a number punched into its side; this number must match the number cast into the cylinder head.

― CAUTION ―
When removing the bearing caps on the 190D, always loosen the center two first and then move on to the outer ones.

7. Remove the camshaft.
8. Installation is in the reverse order of removal. Always make sure that the No. 1

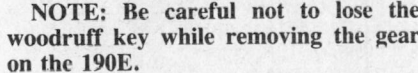

Loosen the camshaft bolts.

Remove the vacuum pump and camshaft cover.

cylinder is at TDC and all timing marks are aligned. Tighten the bearing caps to 15 ft. lbs. (21 Nm) on the 190E and 18 ft. lbs. (25 Nm) on the 190D. The camshaft gear retaining bolt should be tightened to 58 ft. lbs. (80 Nm) on the 190E and 33 ft. lbs. (45 Nm) on the 190D.

NOTE: Be certain not to forget the woodruff key on the 190E.

6-Cylinder Engines

With the engine installed in the car, the camshafts can only be removed together with the camshaft housing. If a new camshaft is installed, be sure to use new rocker arms.

1. Remove the refrigerant compressor but do not disconnect the refrigerant lines.
2. Remove the battery.
3. Remove the vacuum pump from the right-hand cylinder head.
4. Drain the coolant and remove the water hoses.
5. Remove the rocker arm cover.
6. Remove the cover from the front of the camshaft housing.
7. Remove the rocker arm springs.
8. Remove the rocker arms.
9. Crank the engine around in the nor-

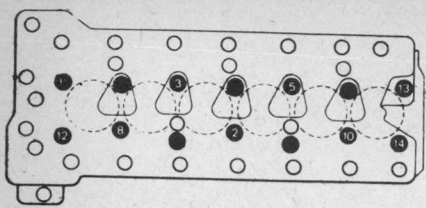

○ Unscrew M 8 bolts

① Unscrew cylinder head bolts in reverse order

● Do not loosen bolts

Bolts to be removed during the camshaft housing removal

mal direction of rotation (using the crankshaft bolt) until the No. 1 piston is at TDC, the pointer aligns with the TDC mark on the crankshaft pulley and the camshaft timing marks are aligned.

10. Hold the camshaft(s) and loosen the camshaft bolts.

NOTE: Wire the camshaft gears up so that tension is applied to the chain. The chain must not be allowed to slip off the camshaft or crankshaft gears.

11. Remove the chain tensioner.

12. Remove the slide rail from the camshaft housing. A small puller is needed for this.

13. Loosen the cover at the right hand rear side of the camshaft housing and push the right hand camshaft toward the rear. Remove the camshaft gear.

14. Loosen the camshaft housing retaining bolts. Do not loosen the 5 lower cylinder head bolts or the 2 M8 bolts.

15. Remove the camshaft housing with the camshafts.

16. Remove the rear covers from the camshaft housing.

17. Hold the left hand camshaft and loosen the attaching bolt.

18. Push the camshaft rearward and remove the camshaft gear. Remove the spacer from the intake camshaft.

19. Remove both camshafts from the housing.

20. Oil the bearings and install the intake camshaft (left hand) with cam gear and spacer. Use a retaining bolt and washer (not springs).

21. Install the exhaust (right hand) camshaft. Do not install the gear until the housing is installed.

22. Install the rear camshaft covers. Do not tighten the one on the right hand side.

23. Install the camshaft housing.

24. Lubricate the bolts and tighten them in 3 stages:

● Starting with bolt No. 2, tighten to 30 ft. lbs.

● Starting with bolt No. 2, tighten to 44 ft. lbs.

● Starting with bolt No. 1, tighten to 67 ft. lbs. First, slightly loosen the 5 lower cylinder head bolts.

25. After torquing the camshaft housing bolts, torque the cylinder head bolts. When all bolts have finally been tightened, the camshafts should rotate easily and freely.

26. Install the righthand camshaft gear. Be sure the cam timing is accurate and the engine is set at TDC on the No. 1 cylinder.

───── CAUTION ─────

Some engines have a scale for BDC as well as one for TDC. The TDC mark is next to the pin in the balancer.

27. Install the timing chain rail.

28. Install the rockers and tension springs. Adjust the valve.

29. Crank the engine by hand and check the valve timing.

30. Tighten the camshaft gear bolts to 59 ft. lbs.

31. Install the chain tensioner.

32. Install the camshaft rear housing covers (if not already done) and the vacuum pump.

33. Install the rocker covers.

V8 Engines

Experience shows that the right hand camshaft is always the first one to require replacement. When the V8 camshaft is removed, keep the pedestals with the camshaft. In particular, make sure that the 2 left hand rear cam pedestals are not swapped. The result will be no oil pressure. Always replace the oil gallery pipe with the camshaft.

NOTE: Arrangement of parts on the 3.8 and 5.0 liter V8 is slightly different compared to the 4.5 liter V8. Service procedures are the same.

1. Remove the valve cover.

2. Remove the tensioning springs and rocker arms.

3. Using a wrench on the crankshaft pulley, crank the engine around until the No. 1 piston is at TDC on the compression stroke. Using some stiff wire, hang the camshaft gear so that the chain will not slip off the gears.

4. Remove the camshaft gear.

5. Unbolt the camshaft, camshaft bearing pedestals and the oil pipe. Note the angle of the bolts holding the cam bearing pedestals to the engine. The inner row of bolts are the only bolts that do not hold the head to the block.

6. Install the bearing pedestals and camshaft. On the left hand camshaft, the outer bolt on the rear bearing must be inserted prior to installing the bearings or it will not clear the power brake unit. Tighten the bolts from the inside out. When finished tightening, the camshaft should rotate freely.

7. Check the oil pipes for obstructions and replace if necessary.

8. When installing the oil pipes, also check the 3 inner connecting pipes.

Remove the rocker arm springs, rocker arms and thrust pieces.

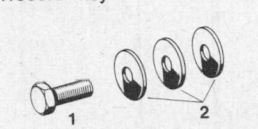
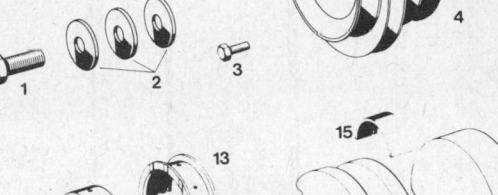
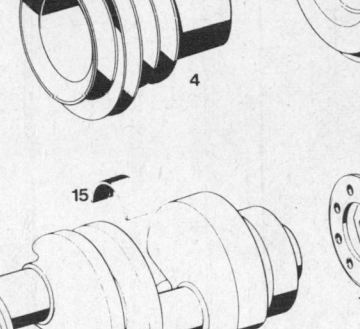
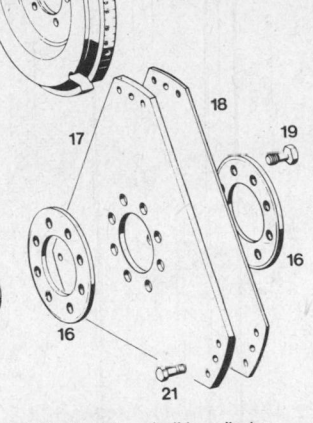
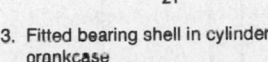

1. Screw
2. Cup washers
3. Screw
4. Pulley
6. Vibration damper
7. Hub
8. Crankshaft sprocket
9. Crankshaft
10. Woodruff key
11. Crankshaft bearing shell in cylinder crankcase
12. Crankshaft bearing shell in bearing cap

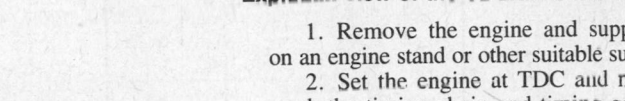

13. Fitted bearing shell in cylinder crankcase
14. Fitted bearing shell in bearing cap
15. Connecting rod bearing shells
16. Discs
17. Flex plate 1.5 mm thick, 296 mm dia.
18. Flex plate 1 mm thick, 287 mm dia
19. Stretch bolt for driven plates
20. Ring gear with welded-on steel ring
21. Fitted screws
22. Spring washer
23. Nut

Exploded view of the V8 crankshaft assembly

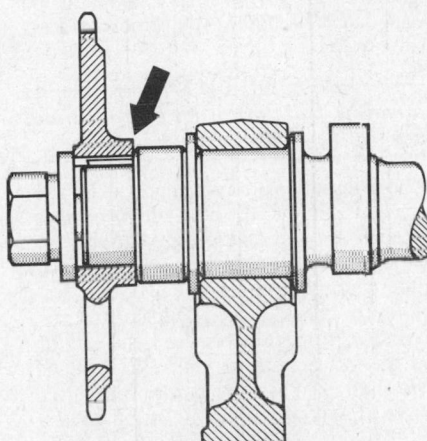

The camshaft flange (arrow) on 3.8 liter V-8's faces rearward

9. Install the compensating washer so that the keyway below the notch slides over the Woodruff key of the camshaft.

10. Install the rocker arms and tensioning springs.

11. Adjust the valve clearance and check the valve timing. See valve timing for illustrations.

Engine Overhaul

DISASSEMBLY

NOTE: This procedure is general and intended to apply to all Mercedes-Benz engines. It is suggested, however, that you be entirely familiar with Mercedes-Benz engines and be equipped with the numerous special tools before attempting an engine rebuild.

1. Remove the engine and support it on an engine stand or other suitable support.

2. Set the engine at TDC and matchmark the timing chain and timing gear(s). Remove the cylinder head(s) and gasket(s).

3. Remove the oil pan bolts and the pan and, on most models, the lower crankcase section.

4. Remove the oil pump.

5. Matchmark the connecting rod bearing caps to identify the proper cylinder for reassembly. Matchmark the sides of the connecting rod and side of the bearing cap for proper alignment. Pistons should bear an arrow indicating the front. If not, mark the front of the piston with an arrow using a magic marker. Also identify pistons as to cylinder so they may be replaced in their original location.

6. Remove the connecting rod nuts, bearing caps, and lower bearing shells.

7. Place small pieces of plastic tubing on the rod bolts to prevent crankshaft damage.

8. Inspect the crankshaft journals for nicks and roughness and measure diameters.

9. Turn the engine and ream the ridge from the top of the cylinders to remove all carbon deposits.

10. Using a hammer handle or other piece of hardwood, gently tap the pistons and connecting rods out from the bottom.

11. The cylinder bores can be inspected at this time for taper and general wear. See "Engine Rebuilding" in the Unit Repair section.

12. Check the pistons for proper size and inspect the ring grooves. If any rings are cracked, it is almost certain that the grooves are no longer true, because broken rings work up and down. It is best to replace any such worn pistons.

Check the oil pipes (arrow) on a V8 engine.

13. The pistons, pins and connecting rods are marked with a color dot assembly code. Only parts having the same color may be used together.

14. If the cylinders are bored, make sure the machinist has the pistons beforehand—cylinder bore sizes are nominal, and the pistons must be individually fitted to the block. Maximum piston weight deviation in any one engine is 4 grams.

15. The flywheel and crankshaft are balanced together as a unit. Matchmark the location of the flywheel relative to the

Pistons normally are marked with an arrow (a) indicating front and a weight or size marking (b).

crankshaft, then remove the flywheel. Stretch bolts are used on some newer flywheels and can be identified by their "hourglass" shape. Once used, they should be discarded and replaced at assembly.

16. Remove the water pump, alternator, and fuel pump, if not done previously.

17. Unbolt and remove the vibration damper and crankshaft pulley. On certain models, it is necessary to clamp the vibration damper with C-clamps before removing the bolts. Otherwise, the vibration damper will come apart.

18. Remove the timing chain tensioner and chain cover.

19. Matchmark the position of the timing chain on the timing gear of the crankshaft.

20. Matchmark the main bearing caps for number and position in the block. It is important that they are installed in their original positions. Most bearing caps are numbered for position. Remove the bearing caps.

21. Lift the crankshaft out of the block in a forward direction.

22. With the block completely disassembled, inspect the water passages and bearing webs for cracks. If the water passages are plugged with rust, they can be cleaned out by boiling the block at a radiator shop.

CAUTION

Aluminum parts must not be boiled out. They will be eroded by chemicals.

---

23. Measure piston ring end gap by sliding a new ring into the bore and measuring. Measure the gap at the top, bottom, and midpoint of piston travel and correct by filing or grinding the ring ends.

24. To check bearing clearances, use Plastigage® inserted between the bearing and the crankshaft journal. Blow out all crankshaft oil passages before measuring; torque the bolts to specification. Plasti-

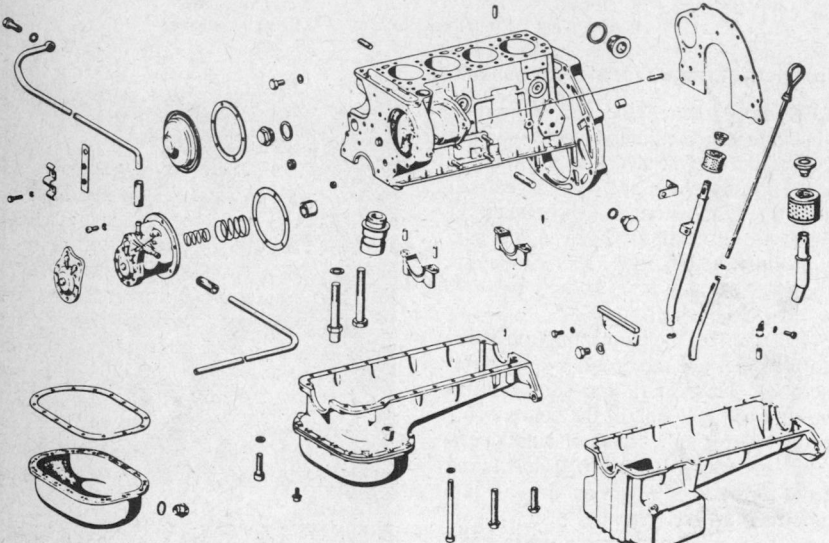

4-cylinder diesel engine cylinder block components (5-cylinder 300D is similar)

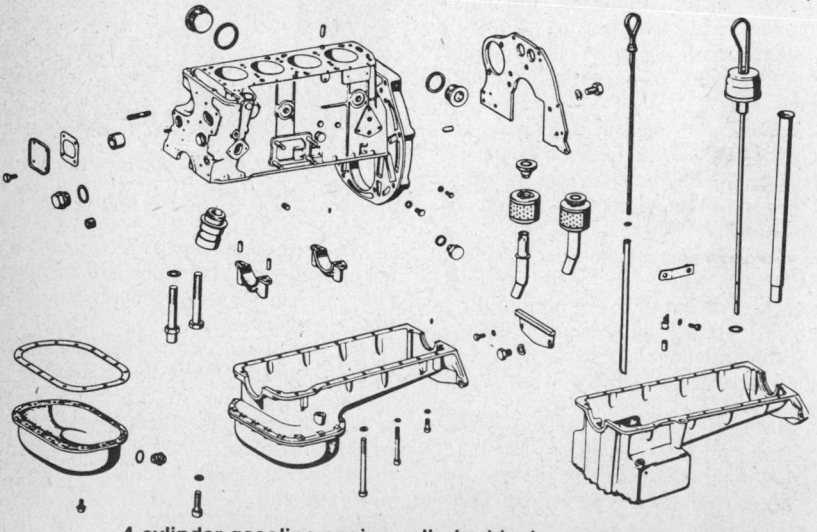

4-cylinder gasoline engine cylinder block components

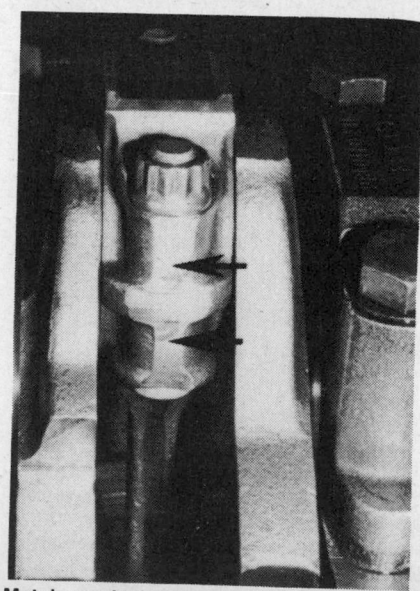

Match mark the connecting rod bearing caps.

gage® is a thin plastic strip that is crushed by the bearing end cap and spreads out an amount in proportion to clearance. After torquing the bearing cap, remove the cap and compare the width of the Plastigage® with the scale.

NOTE: Do not rotate the crankshaft. Bearing shells of various thicknesses are available and should be used to correct clearance; it may be necessary to machine the crankshaft journals undersize to obtain the proper oil clearance.

—————— **CAUTION** ——————

Use of shim stock between bearings and caps to decrease clearance is not a good practice.

———————————————————

25. Check crankshaft end-play using a feeler gauge.

26. When installing new piston rings, ring grooves must be cleaned out, preferably using a special groove cleaner, although a broken ring will work as well. After installing the rings, check ring side clearance.

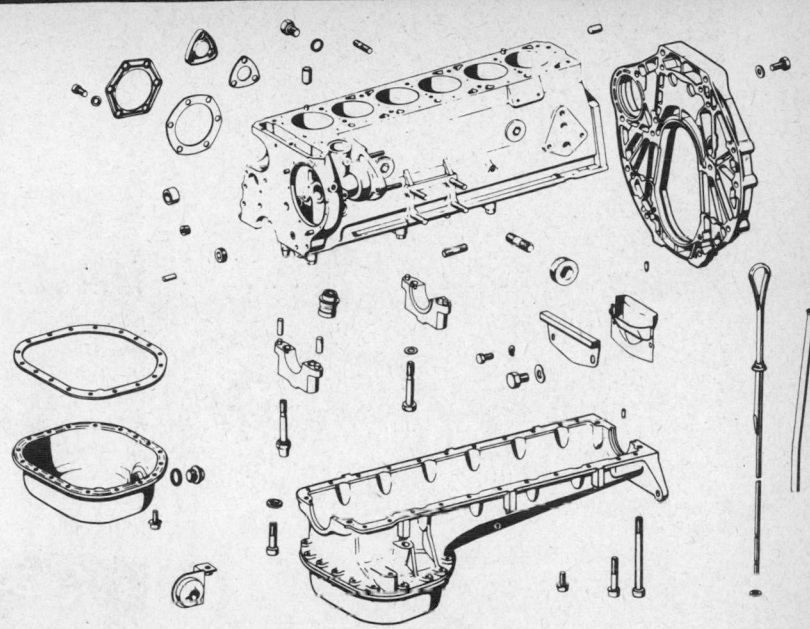

6-cylinder engine block components

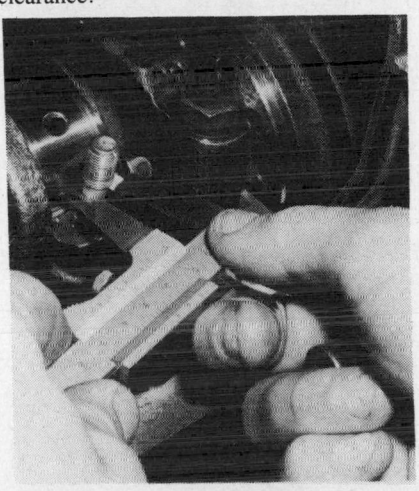

Check the connecting rod bolts

Before removing the flywheel, mark its position. It should be returned to its original position

ASSEMBLY

1. Assemble the engine using all new gaskets and seals and make sure all parts are properly lubricated. Bearing shells and cylinder walls must be lubricated with engine oil before assembly. Make sure no metal chips remain in the cylinder bores or crankcase.

2. To install pistons and rods, turn the engine right side up and insert the rods into the cylinders. Clamp the rings to the piston, with their gaps equally spaced around the circumference, using a piston ring compressor. Gently tap the piston into the bore, using a hammer handle or similar hard wood, making sure the rings clear the edge.

NOTE: Pistons on the 3.8 and 5.0 liter V8 are installed with the arrow facing in the driving direction.

3. Torque the connecting rod bearing and main bearing caps to specification and try to turn the crankshaft by hand. It should turn with moderate resistance, not spin freely or be locked up. Main bearing caps use standard bolts (see specifications chart); stretchbolts are used for the connecting rods (see this step for torquing procedure). These bolts are tightened by angle of rotation rather than by use of a torque wrench. Make sure the stretch section diameter is greater than 0.35 in. (−0.003 in.). Remove the bolt from the rod and measure the diameter at the point normally covered by the rod; it should

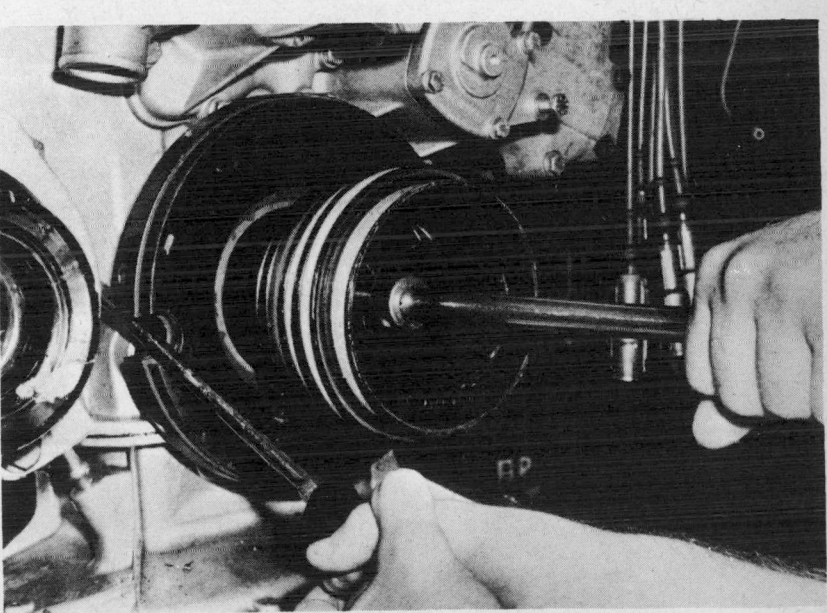

Unbolt and remove the crankshaft pulley (V8 shown)

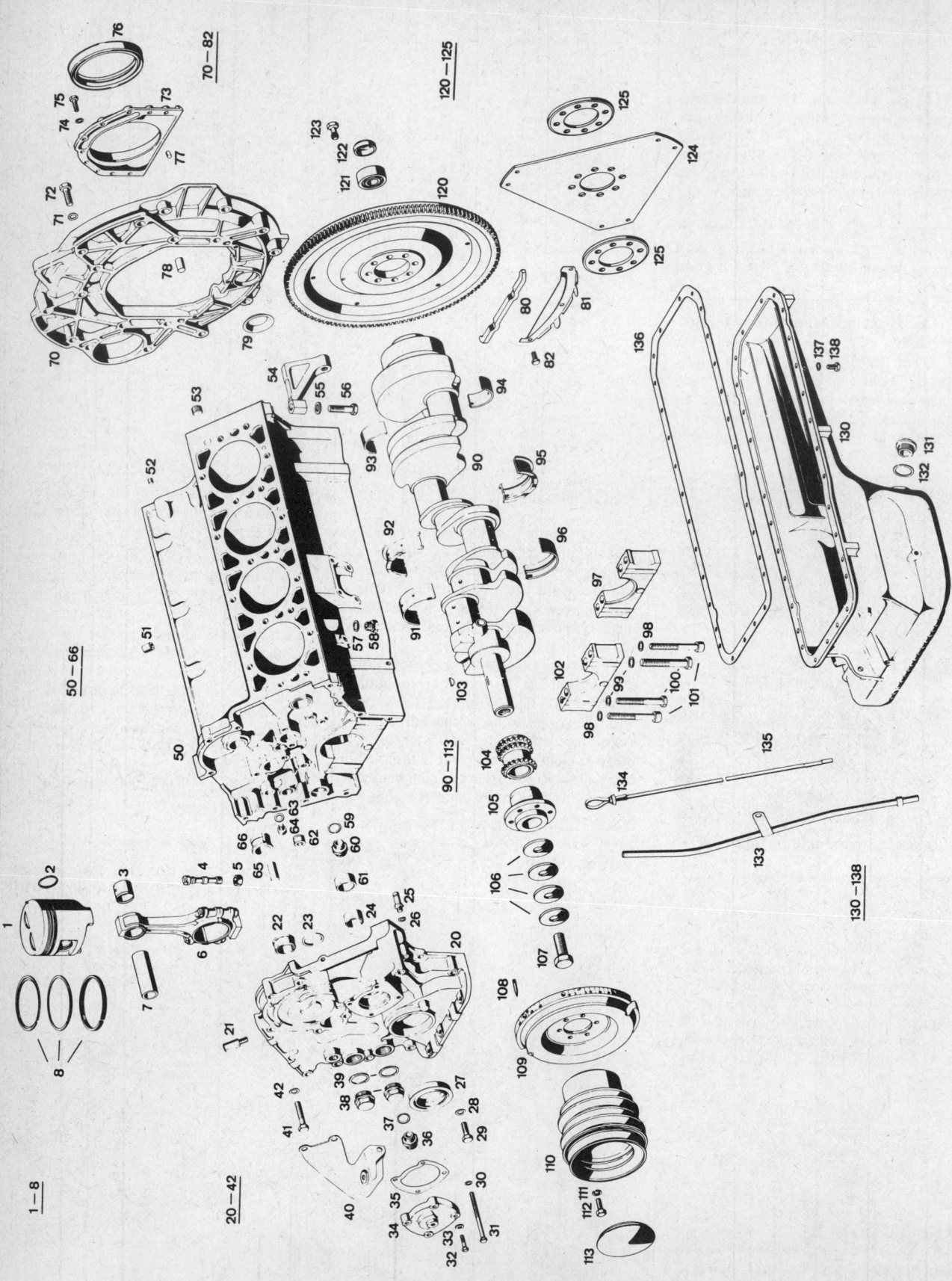

V-8 engine block and crankshaft components

Piston and connecting rod 1-8

1. Piston
2. Circlip
3. Connecting rod bearing
4. Connecting rod bolt
5. Nut
6. Connecting rod
7. Wrist pin
8. Piston rings

Timing housing cover 20-42

20. Timing housing cover
21. Threaded bolts for adjusting lever of ignition distributor
22. Bearing bushing (guidewheel bearing)
23. 2 O-rings
24. Bearing bushing (intermediate gear shaft)
25. Bolt
26. Spring plate
27. Crankshaft sealing ring (front)
28. Washer
29. Screw
30. Washer
31. Screw
32. 4 Screws
33. 4 Washers
34. End cover
35. Gasket
36. Screw connection
37. Sealing ring
38. Plug
39. Sealing ring
40. Holder-engine damper
41. 6 Screws
42. 6 Washers

Cylinder crankcase 50-66

50. Cylinder block

51. 4 Hollow dowel pins
52. 3 Plugs (oil duct)
53. Plug (rear main oil duct)
54. 2 Supporting angle pieces
55. 2 Washers
56. 2 Screws
57. 2 Sealing rings
58. 2 Plugs
59. Sealing ring
60. Screw connection
61. Bearing bushing intermediate gear shaft rear
62. Plug (front main oil duct)
63. Sealing ring
64. Plug
65. 2 Cyl. pins
66. Idler gear bearing

Intermediate flange 70-82

70. Intermediate flange
71. 4 Spring washers
72. 4 Screws
73. Cover (crankcase sealing ring, rear)
74. 8 Washers
75. 3 Screws
76. Crankshaft sealing ring (rear)
77. 2 Cyl. pins
78. 2 Set pins
79. Cover
80. Sealing strip
81. Cover plate
82. 3 Screws

Crankshaft 90-113

90. Crankshaft
91. Main bearing shell (top)
92. Fitted bearing shell (top)
93. Connecting rod bearing shell (top)
94. Connecting rod bearing shell (bottom)
95. Fitted bearing shell (bottom)

96. Main bearing shell (bottom)
97. Crankshaft bearing cap (fitted bearing)
98. 10 Washers
99. 10 Washers
100. 10 Hex bolts
101. 10 Hex socket bolts
102. Crankshaft bearing cap (main bearing)
103. Key
104. Crankshaft gear
105. Vibration damper pulley
106. Plate springs
107. Bolt
108. Indicating needle
109. Vibration damper
110. Pulley
111. 6 Circlips
112. 6 Screws
113. Pulley cover

Flywheel and driven plate 120-125

120. Flywheel
121. Ball bearing 6202
122. Closing ring
123. 8 bolts
124. Driven plate
125. Spacers

Oil pan 130-138

130. Oil pan
131. Oil drain plug
132. Sealing ring
133. Guide tube (oil dipstick)
134. Oil dipstick
135. Stop-ring (oil dipstick)
136. Oil pan gasket
137. 30 washers
138. 30 Screws

V8 engine cylinder block and crankshaft components

be at least 0.31 in. For reasons of standardization, the angle of rotation for all the screw connections tightened according to angle of rotation has been set to 90° + 10°. Initially the bolts should be torqued to 22–35 ft. lbs., then an additional 90°.

NOTE: The bearing shells on the 3rd main bearing of the 190 series engines are fitted with thrust washers. The thrust washers in the bearing cap have two locating tabs to keep them from rotating.

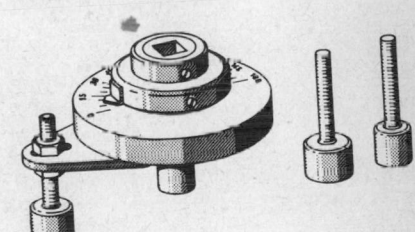

Preferred tools for torquing by angle rotation. A torque wrench is also needed.

On V8 models, dress the inside of the vibration damper hub before reinstalling. This will allow you to "feel" the key when installing. On early models, the key extends only 1/3 of the length of the keyway; on later models, 1/2 the length of the keyway.

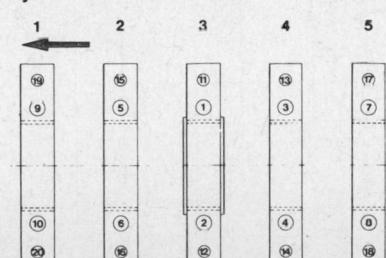

Main bearing cap—4.5 V8

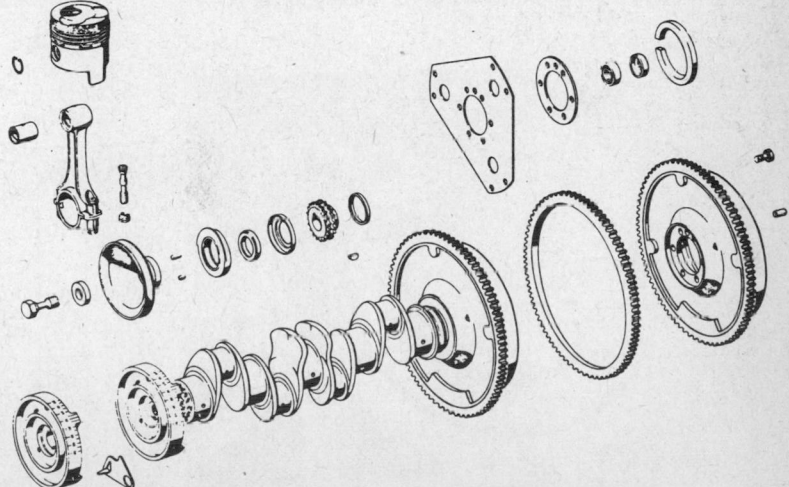

4-cylinder diesel engine components (5-cylinder is similar).

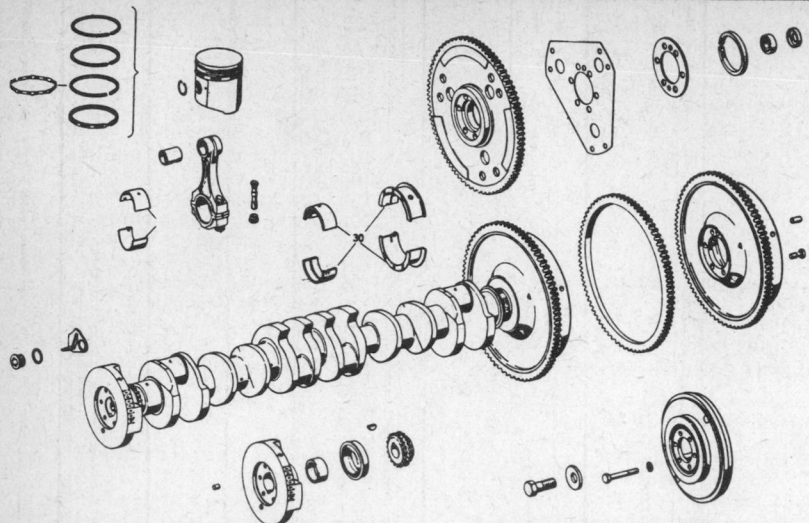

6-cylinder crankshaft and components (4-cylinder engine is similar)

During assembly the grooves in the washers should face the crankshaft thrust surfaces.

4. Disassemble the oil pump and check the gear backlash. Place a straightedge on the cover and check for warpage. Deep scoring on the cover usually indicates that metal or dirt particles have been circulating through the oil system. Covers can be machined, but it is best to replace them if damaged.

5. Install the oil pump.

6. Install the oil pan and lower crankcase and tighten the bolts evenly all around, then turn the engine right side up and install the cylinder head gasket and head. Make sure the gasket surfaces are clean before installation; a small dirt particle could cause gasket failure. Tighten the cylinder head bolts in sequence, in stages, to insure against distortion. Don't forget the small bolts at the front of the head.

7. Install the engine into the vehicle.

NOTE: It is a good practice to use a good break-in oil after an engine overhaul. Be sure that all fluids have been replaced and perform a general tune-up. Check the valve timing.

Valve Timing

Ideally, this operation should be performed by a dealer who is equipped with the necessary tools and knowledge to do the job properly.

Checking valve timing is too inaccurate at the standard tappet clearance; therefore timing values are given for an assumed tappet clearance of 0.4mm. The engines are not measured at 0.4mm but rather at 2mm.

1. To check the timing, remove the rocker arm cover and spark plugs. Remove the tensioning springs. On the 6-cylinder engine install the testing thrust pieces. Eliminate all valve clearance.

2. Install a degree wheel.

NOTE: If the degree wheel is attached to the camshaft as shown, values read from it must be doubled.

On 6 cylinder engines, always replace the thrust piece (arrow) if the front seal is replaced. If you don't it will almost always leak. If a new thrust piece is not available, at least remove it and turn it around. This provides a new surface for the seal because the seal does not ride on the centerline of the thrust piece.

Piston marking on 3.8 V8

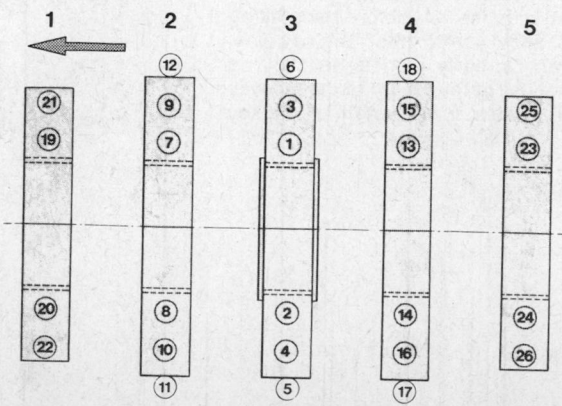

Main bearing cap torque sequence—3.8 liter V-8's

The V8 timing marks on the left-hand cam

The valve timing marks must align (6-cylinder shown)

Note that the timing marks on the right-hand cam do not exactly align. This is because the timing chain travels farther on the right side than on the left.

3. A pointer must be made out of a bent section of ³⁄₁₆ in. brazing rod or coathanger wire, and attached to the engine.

4. With a 22 mm wrench on the crankshaft pulley, turn the engine in the direction of rotation until the TDC mark on the vibration damper registers with the pointer and the distributor rotor points to the No. 1 cylinder mark on the housing.

The camshaft timing marks should align at this point.

NOTE: Due to the design of the chain tensioner on V8 engines, the right side of the chain travels slightly farther than the left side. This means the right-side cam will be almost 7° retarded compared to the left side, and both marks will not simultaneously align.

5. Turn the loosened degree wheel until the pointer lines up with the 0° (OT) mark, then tighten it in this position.

6. Continue turning the crankshaft in the direction of rotation until the camshaft lobe of the associated valve is vertical (e.g., points away from the rocker arm surface). To take up tappet clearance, insert a feeler gauge (thick enough to raise the valve slightly from its seat) between the rocker arm cone and the pressure piece.

7. Attach the indicator to the cylinder head so that the feeler rests against the valve spring retainer of the No. 1 cylinder intake valve. Preload the indicator at least 0.008 in. then set to zero, making sure the feeler is exactly perpendicular on the valve spring retainer. It may be necessary to bleed down the chain tensioner at this time to facilitate readings.

8. Turn the crankshaft in the normal direction of rotation, again using a wrench on the crankshaft pulley, until the indicator reads 0.016 in. less than zero reading.

9. Note the reading of the degree wheel at this time, remembering to double the reading if the wheel is mounted to the camshaft sprocket.

10. Again turn the crankshaft until the valve is closing and the indicator again reads 0.016 in. less than zero reading. Make sure, at this time, that preload has remained constant, then note the reading of the degree wheel. The difference between the two degree wheel readings is the timing angle (number of degrees the valve is open) for that valve.

11. The other valves may be checked in the same manner, comparing them against each other and the opening values given in "Tune-Up Specifications." It must be remembered that turning the crankshaft contrary to the normal direction of rotation results in inaccurate readings and damage to the engine.

12. If valve timing is not to specification, the easiest way of bringing it in line is to install an offset Woodruff key in the camshaft sprocket. This is far simpler than replacing the entire timing chain and it is the factory-recommended way of changing valve timing provided the timing chain is not stretched too far or worn out. Offset keys are available in the following sizes:

VALVE TIMING OFFSET KEYS

Offset	Part No.	For a Correction at Crankshaft of
2° (0.7)	621 991 04 67	4°
3°20⁺ (0.9)	621 991 02 67	6½°
4° (1.1)	621 991 01 67	8°
5° (1.3)	621 991 00 67	10°

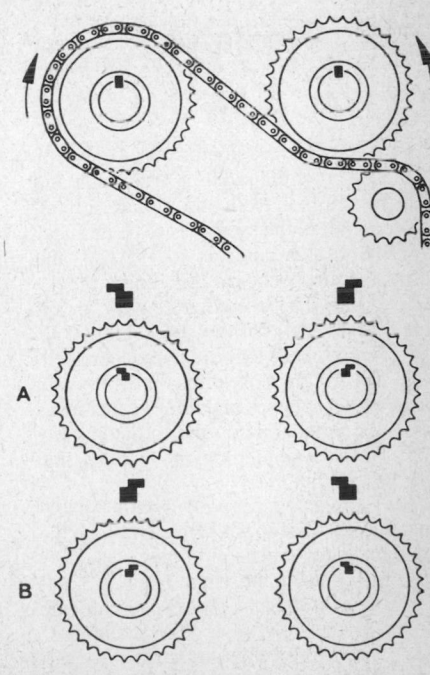

Offset woodruff keys for 6-cylinder engine

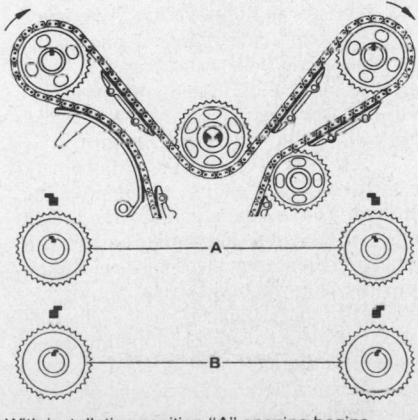

With installation position "A" opening begins earlier
With installation position "B" opening begins later
Offset woodruff keys for V8 engine

13. The Woodruff key must be installed with the offset toward the "right", in the normal direction of rotation, to effect advanced valve opening; toward the "left" to retard.

14. Advancing the intake valve opening too much can result in piston and/or valve damage (the valve will hit the piston). To check the clearance between the valve head and the piston, the crankshaft must be positioned at 5° ATDC (on intake stroke). The procedure is essentially the same as for measuring valve timing.

15. As before, the dial indicator is set to zero after being preloaded, then the valve is depressed until it touches the top of the piston. As the normal valve head-to-piston clearance is approximately 0.035 in., you can see that the dial indicator must be preloaded at least 0.042 in. so there will be enough movement for the feeler.

If the clearance is much less than 0.035 in., the cylinder head must be removed and checked for carbon deposits. If none exist, the valve seat must be cut deeper into the head. Always set the ignition timing after installing an offset key.

ENGINE COOLING

Mercedes-Benz passenger car engines are all equipped with closed, pressurized, water cooling systems. Care should be exercised when dealing with the cooling system. always turn the radiator cap to the first notch and allow the pressure to decrease before completely removing the cap.

Radiator

REMOVAL & INSTALLATION

1. Remove the radiator cap.
2. Unscrew the radiator drain plug and drain the coolant from the radiator. If all of the coolant in the system is to be drained, move the heater controls to WARM and open the drain cocks on the engine block.
3. If the car is equipped with an oil cooler, drain the oil from the cooler.
4. If equipped, loosen the radiator shell.
5. Loosen the hose clips on the top and bottom radiator hoses and remove the hoses from the connections on the radiator.
6. Unscrew and plug the bottom line on the oil cooler.
7. If the car is equipped with an automatic transmission, unscrew and plug the lines on the transmission cooler.
8. Disconnect the right hand and left hand rubber loops and pull the radiator up and out of the body. On 450SL and SLC models, push the retaining springs toward the fenders to remove the radiator from the shell.

9. Inspect and replace any hoses which have become hardened or spongy.
10. Install the radiator shell and radiator (if the shell was removed) from the top and connect the top and bottom hoses to the radiator.
11. Bolt the shell to the radiator.
12. Attach the rubber loops or position the retaining springs, as applicable.
13. Position the hose clips on the top and bottom hoses.
14. Attach the lines to the oil cooler.
15. On cars with automatic transmissions, connect the lines to the transmission cooler.
16. Move the heater levers to the WARM position and slowly add coolant, allowing air to escape.
17. Check the oil level and fill if necessary. Run the engine for about one minute at idle with the filler neck open.
18. Add coolant to the specified level. Install the radiator cap and turn it until it seats in the second notch. Run the engine and check for leaks.

Water Pump

REMOVAL & INSTALLATION

All Except V8

1. Drain the water from the radiator.
2. Loosen the radiator shell and remove the radiator.
3. Remove the fan with the coupling and set it aside in an upright position.
4. Loosen the belt around the water pump pulley and remove the belt.
5. Remove the bolts from the harmonic balancer and remove the balancer and pulley.
6. Unbolt and remove the water pump.
7. Installation is the reverse of removal. Tighten the belt and fill the cooling system.

V8 Models

1. Drain the water from the radiator and block.
2. Remove the air cleaner.
3. Loosen and remove the drive belt.
4. Disconnect the upper water hose from the radiator and thermostat housing.
5. Remove the fan and coupling.
6. Remove the hose from the intake (top) connection of the water pump.
7. Set the engine at TDC. Matchmark the distributor and engine and remove the distributor. Crank the engine with a socket wrench on the crankshaft pulley bolt or with a small prybar inserted in the balancer. Crank in the normal direction of rotation only.
8. Turn the balancer so that the recesses provide access to the mounting bolts. Remove the mounting bolts. Rotate the engine in the normal direction of rotation only.
9. Remove the water pump.
10. Clean the mounting surfaces of the water pump and block.
11. Installation is the reverse of re-

moval. Always use a new gasket. Set the engine at TDC and install the distributor so that the distributor rotor points to the notch on the distributor housing. Fill the cooling system and check and adjust the ignition timing.

Thermostat

REMOVAL & INSTALLATION

4 and 5-Cylinder Engines

The thermostat housing is a light metal casting attached directly to the cylinder head, except on the 190D where it is attached to the side of the water pump housing.

1. Open the radiator cap and depressurize the system.
2. Open the radiator drain cock and partially drain the coolant. Drain enough coolant to bring the coolant level below the level of the thermostat housing.

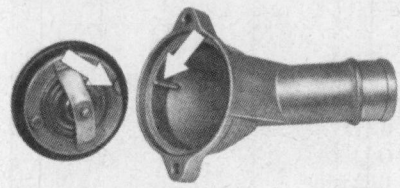

Aligning the thermostat on the 190D

3. Remove the four bolts on the thermostat housing cover and remove the cover.
4. Note the installation position of the thermostat and remove it.
5. Installation is the reverse of removal. Be sure that the thermostat is positioned with the ball valve at the highest point and that the 4 bolts are tightened evenly against the seal. On the 190D, the recess in the thermostat casing should be located above the lug in the thermostat housing.
6. Refill the cooling system and check for leaks.

6-Cylinder Engines

1. Drain the coolant from the radiator.
2. Remove the vacuum pump and put the pump aside.
3. Remove the three bolts on the thermostat housing.
4. Remove the cover and the thermostat.
5. Installation is the reverse of removal. Install the thermostat so that the ball valve is at the highest point. Refill the cooling system.

V8 Engines

1. Drain the coolant from the radiator and block.
2. Remove the air cleaner.
3. Disconnect the battery and remove the alternator.
4. Unscrew the housing cover on the side of the water pump and remove the thermostat. Note that the thermostat used on 4.5 liter V8 models differs from the one

used on other models due to a different positioning of the ball valve.

5. If a new thermostat is to be installed, always install a new sealing ring.

6. Installation is the reverse of removal. Be sure to tighten the screws on the housing cover evenly to prevent leaks. Refill the cooling system and check for leaks.

EMISSION CONTROLS

Unless otherwise specified, the base color of vacuum lines for emission control is white. Lines originating at a vacuum source have only one color stripe. These lines are connected to the center connection of the switchover valve of the same color. Lines terminating at a vacuum operated device have 2 color stripes. Purple is always the second color. The lines are connected to the outer connection of the switchover valve of the same color.

Switchover valve filter caps are color coded as follows:

RED—Valve for ignition advance.
GREY—Valve for throttle lift.
Brown—Valve for EGR.
Blue— Valve for air injection.

1978–79

The following tests should be performed in the order given with the engine at normal operating temperature.

230

Testing the System
EGR

1. Run the engine at idle speed.

1. Carburetor
2. Distributor
5. Fuel evaporation control system purge valve
31. EGR valve
39. Charcoal canister
40. Air pump
41. Diverter valve
42. Check valve
61. 62° F thermo-vacuum valve (blue), for EGR, located at front of engine next to distributor
61. 62° F thermo-vacuum valve (blue), for air injection, located at rear of engine
73. 122° F thermo-vacuum valve
74. Pressure relief valve
78. Air filter for noise suppression
A. To cylinder head
B. To catalyst
C. Air conditioning
D. Central locking system
E. Fuel tank ventilation connection
F. To air filter
    bl = blue
    br = brown
    gr = gray
    rt = red
    vi = purple

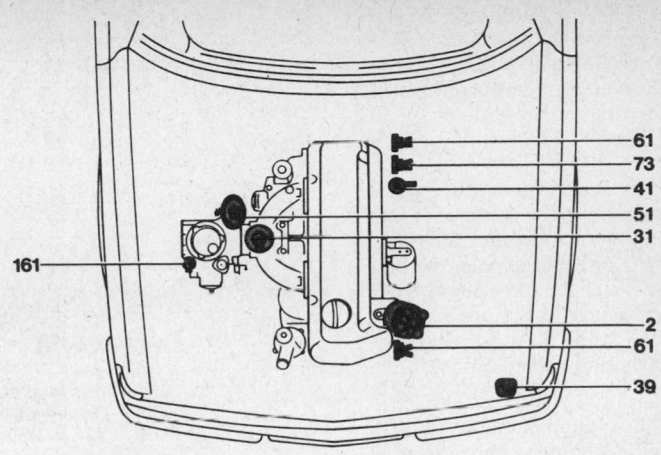

2. Distributor
31. EGR valve
39. Charcoal canister
41. Diverter valve
51. Vacuum governor
61. 62° F thermo-vacuum valve (blue); for EGR, located at front of engine next to distributor
61. 62° F thermo-vacuum valve (blue), for air
73. 122° F thermo-vacuum valve (black with green dot)
161. Float chamber vent valve

230 emission control component location

2. Remove the brown vacuum line at the carburetor and the gray vacuum line at the intake manifold. Connect the brown line at the intake manifold.

3. The engine should run roughly or stall. If the rpm does not change, check the vacuum line connections. Check for leaks and blow through the vacuum connection on the carburetor

4. Check the thermo-vacuum valve (blue plastic portion and "50AB5" stamped in metal housing). Remove the brown/purple vacuum line and race the engine. Vacuum must be present at the open connection when accelerating.

5. Check the EGR valve. Remove the EGR valve. Connect the brown/purple vacuum line to the EGR valve and slowly increase engine rpm. Cover the bores in the intake manifold. The valve stem should lift from its seat; if not replace the EGR valve with a new one.

AIR INJECTION

1. Connect a CO tester to the test connection and remove the vacuum hose from the vertical connection of the thermo-vacuum valve. The air injection thermo-vacuum valve has "50AA" stamped in the metal housing. Plug the connection on the valve. The CO reading should drop noticeably.

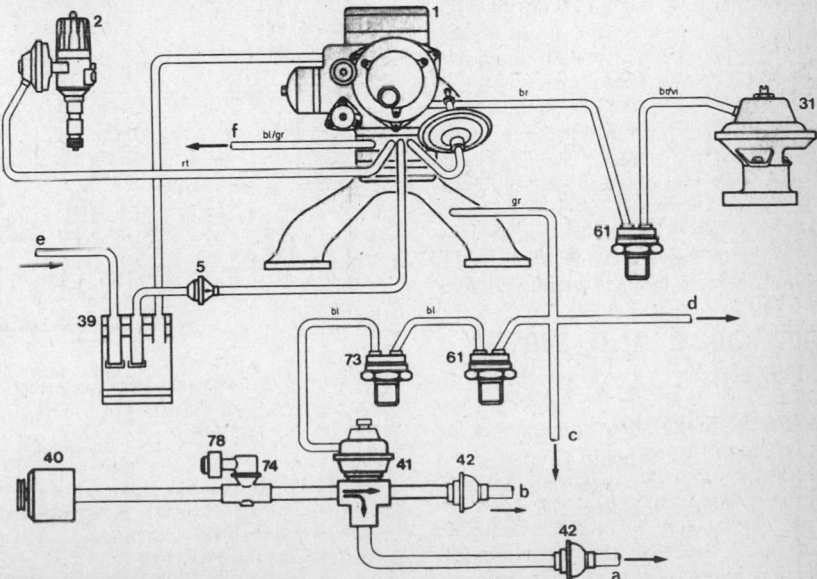

230 emission control schematic

2. If the CO does not drop, and vacuum IS indicated, replace the thermo-valve. If the CO does not drop and vacuum is NOT indicated, clean the vacuum line to the intake manifold with compressed air.

3. Check the connection of the vacuum lines.

4. Check the vertical connection of the thermal-vacuum valve for vacuum. If vacuum is present, replace the diverter valve. If no vacuum is present, remove the blue vacuum line from the thermo-vacuum valve and check for vacuum at the line.

5. If the CO still does not decrease, check that the thermo-valve is open; if not, replace the valve.

NOTE: Below approximately 120°F, the valve should be open; above that, it should be closed.

THROTTLE VALVE LIFT

1. Remove the vacuum hose from the vacuum governor on the carburetor. The idle speed should increase. Reconnect the hose. The idle speed should decrease.

2. If the rpm does not increase, check the connection of the hose. Check the hose for leaks.

3. Run the engine at idle. Remove the vacuum line on the carburetor; the idle speed should increase. If not, replace the vacuum governor.

FUEL EVAPORATION CONTROL SYSTEM

1. Remove the solenoid plug from the float chamber vent valve. Reconnect the solenoid; it should click audibly.

2. If the solenoid does not click, turn on the ignition and connect a test lamp to the plug. The test lamp should light with the ignition ON. If not, check the proper fuse. If the lamp still does not light, replace the solenoid.

3. Remove the middle purge hose to the carburetor from the charcoal canister and cover the hose opening with your finger. Slowly increase engine speed to over 2000 rpm. At idle no vacuum should be present. As engine speed increases, vacuum should increase. If no vacuum is present as the engine speed increases, check the connection of the purge hose. Check the hose for leaks and clean it out with compressed air.

4. On 1978–79 models, remove the hose from the purge valve and repeat the test. If vacuum is present, replace the purge valve.

280E, 280CE AND 280SE (FEDERAL)

Testing the System

The following tests should be performed with the engine at idle speed, at operating temperature and in the order listed.

EGR

1. Remove the brown vacuum line from

the EGR valve and slowly increase engine rpm. At about 1200 rpm, the engine should run roughly or stall.

2. If it does not run roughly or stall, check the vacuum line connections. The connections at the exhaust pressure transducer are marked with colored rings and must be connected to the same color code.

3. Disconnect the vacuum line from the vertical connection of the thermo-vacuum valve marked "50AA4" in the metal housing. Run the engine and increase rpm. Vacuum should be present at the connection.

4. Run the engine at idle and disconnect the brown line between the EGR valve and exhaust pressure transducer. Cover the line with your finger; vacuum must be present at idle. If not, replace the exhaust pressure transducer.

5. Run the engine at idle and remove both vacuum lines from the EGR valve. Connect the brown line to the connection on the red/purple line on the EGR valve. The engine should run roughly or stall. If not, replace the EGR valve.

AIR INJECTION

1. Connect a CO tester to the exhaust back pressure line. Remove and plug the vacuum hose from the vertical connection at the thermo-vacuum valve. The CO should increase.

2. If not, check the vacuum line connections. The (large) cap end connection

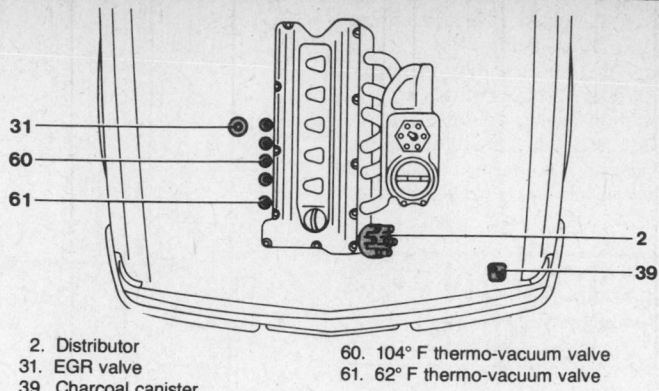

2. Distributor
31. EGR valve
39. Charcoal canister
60. 104° F thermo-vacuum valve
61. 62° F thermo-vacuum valve

1978–79 280E, 280CE, 280SE Federal emission control component location

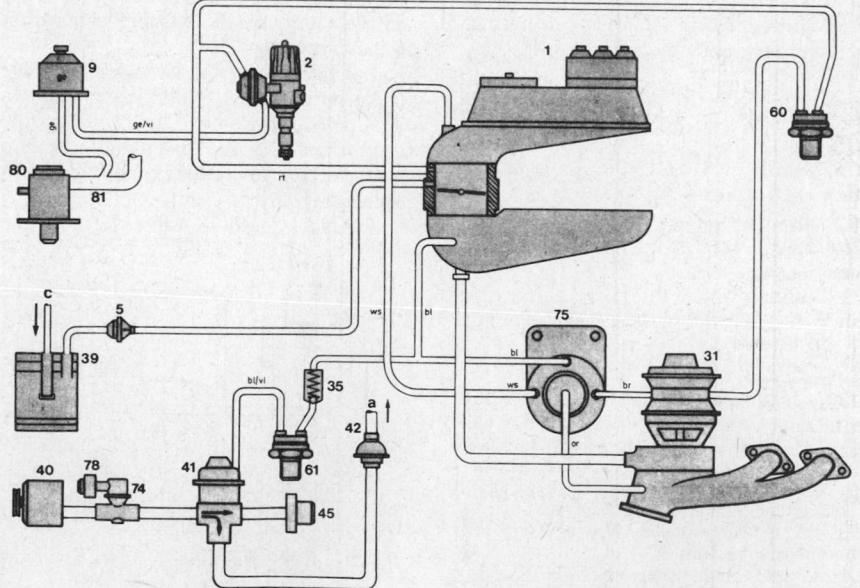

1. Mixture regulator assembly
2. Ignition distributor
5. Purge valve
9. Ignition switch over valve
31. EGR valve
39. Charcoal canister
40. Air pump
41. Diverter valve
42. Check valve
60. 104° F thermo-vacuum valve

61. 62° F thermo-vacuum valve
73. 122° F thermo-vacuum valve
74. Pressure relief valve
75. Exhaust pressure transducer
78. Muffler (air filter)
80. Auxiliary air valve
81. Shaped hose

A. Air injection line, cylinder head
B. Fuel tank vent connection

1978–79 280E, 280CE, 280SE Federal emission control schematic

of the check valve must face the intake manifold (Federal only).

3. Remove the blue vacuum line from the thermo-vacuum valve and cover it with your finger. Vacuum must be present at idle; if not, check for leaks and clean the line with compressed air.

4. If vacuum is present, check the thermo-vacuum valve and replace if necessary.

5. Disconnect the blue/purple line from the thermo-vacuum valve marked "50AB5" on the metal housing. Run the engine. Vacuum should be present at the vertical connection. If not, replace the diverter valve.

FUEL EVAPORATION CONTROL SYSTEM

1. Remove the black purge line from the charcoal canister. Cover the opening with your finger and increase rpm to over 2000 rpm. No vacuum should be present at idle and vacuum should increase with engine speed. If not, check the vacuum line connections, check for leaks and clean the line with compressed air.

If vacuum is still not present, remove the purge line from the front of the purge valve. If vacuum is present, replace the purge valve.

280E, 280CE AND 280SE (CALIFORNIA)

Testing the System
EGR

See 280E and 280SE (Federal).

AIR INJECTION

1. Connect a CO tester to the exhaust pressure transducer. Remove the vacuum line from the vertical connection of the 122°F thermo-vacuum valve and connect it to the vertical connection of the 62°F thermo-vacuum valve. The CO should drop.

2. If not, check the vacuum line connections.

3. Run the engine at idle and check for vacuum at the vertical connection of the 62°F thermo-vacuum valve. If vacuum is present, replace the diverter valve.

If no vacuum is present, remove the blue line from the 62°F thermo-vacuum valve and check for vacuum at the valve. If vacuum is present, replace the thermo-vacuum valve. If no vacuum is present, remove the line from the intake manifold and clean it with compressed air.

4. If the CO still does not drop, check the 122°F thermo-vacuum valve. It will have "50AA13" stamped in the metal housing. Above 122°F, the valve is closed and no vacuum should be present at the vertical connection. Below 122°F, vacuum should be present at the vertical connection. If these conditions are not met, replace the valve.

FUEL EVAPORATION CONTROL SYSTEM

See 280E and 280SE (Federal).

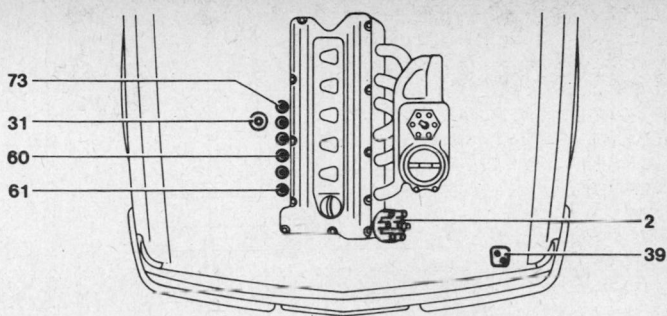

2. Distributor	60. 104° F thermo-vacuum valve
31. EGR valve	61. 62° F thermo-vacuum valve
39. Charcoal canister	73. 122°F thermo-vacuum valve

1978–79 280E, 280CE, 280SE California emission control component location

450SL, 450SLC AND 450SEL (FEDERAL)

Testing the System

The following tests should be performed with the engine running at normal operating temperature in the order given.

EGR

1. Remove the brown line at the EGR valve and slowly increase engine speed. Above 1200 rpm, the engine should run roughly or stall. If not check the vacuum line connections.

2. Check the thermo-vacuum valve with "50AA4" stamped in the metal housing (104° F valve). Remove the red/purple line from the vertical connection, run the engine and accelerate briefly. Vacuum should be present at the vertical connection.

3. Run the engine at idle and remove the brown vacuum line at the EGR valve. If no vacuum is present at idle, replace the exhaust pressure transducer.

4. Run the engine at idle and remove both lines from the EGR valve. Connect the brown line to the connection for the red/purple line. The engine should run roughly or stall. If not, replace the EGR valve.

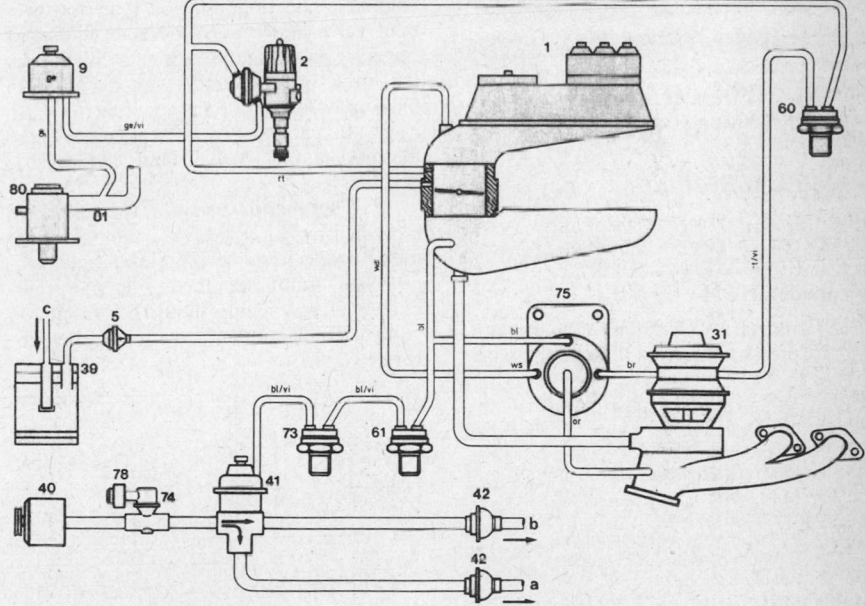

1. Mixture regulator assembly	80. Auxiliary air valve
2. Ignition distributor	81. Shaped hose
5. Purge valve	
9. Ignition switch-over valve	A. Air injection line, cylinder head
31. EGR valve	B. Air injection line, between catalysts
39. Charcoal canister	C. Fuel tank vent connection
40. Air pump	bl = blue
41. Diverter valve	br = brown
42. Check valve	ge = yellow
60. 104° F thermo-vacuum valve	gr = gray
61. 62° F therm 74. Pressure relief valve	or = orange
75. Exhaust pressure transducer	rt = red
78. Muffler (air filter)	vi = purple
	ws = white

1978–79 280E, 280CE, 280SE California emission control schematic

2. Distributor
31. EGR valve
39. Charcoal canister
60. 104° F thermo-vacuum valve (black)
61. 62° F thermo-vacuum valve (blue)

1978–79 4.5 V8 California emission control component location

2. Distributor
31. EGR valve
39. Charcoal canister
60. 104° F thermo-vacuum valve (black)
80. Suction hose to aspirator/check valve

1978–79 4.5 V8 Federal emission control component location

AIR INJECTION

1. Remove the suction hose from the aspirator/check valve in the air cleaner and cover with your finger. Vacuum should be present and a suction noise should be audible. If no vacuum is present, replace the aspirator/check valve.

FUEL EVAPORATION CONTROL SYSTEM

See this test under 280E and 280SE(Federal).

450SL, 450SLC, 450SEL (CALIFORNIA) AND 6.9

Testing the System
EGR

See 450SL, 450SLC, 450SEL (Federal).

AIR INJECTION

1. Connect a CO tester to the exhaust gas back pressure line and remove the blue/purple vacuum line from the vertical connection of the 62°F thermo-vacuum valve. Plug the connection. The CO should increase.

2. If not, check the vacuum line connections. The check valve must be installed with the larger (cap) end toward the intake manifold.

3. Remove the vacuum line from the angular connection of the 62°F thermo-vacuum valve and cover the valve with your finger. If no vacuum is present at idle, check the lines for leaks and clean the vacuum pick-up bore with compressed air.

4. If vacuum is present, check the thermo-vacuum valve and replace if necessary.

5. The thermo-vacuum valve can be identified by the "50AB5" stamped in the metal body. Remove the blue/purple vacuum line, run the engine at idle and accelerate briefly. Vacuum should be present the vertical connection; if not, replace the diverter valve.

FUEL EVAPORATION CONTROL SYSTEM

See this test under 280E and 280SE (Federal).

CATALYST REPLACEMENT WARNING INDICATOR

A warning light in the instrument cluster comes on at 37,500 mile intervals, indicating that the catalyst should be replaced. The catalyst mileage counter is located under the dash and is driven by the speedometer cable. To reset the mileage counter, push the reset pin on the counter.

1980

6-CYLINDER ENGINES

The base color of the emission control vac-

1. Mixture regulator assembly
2. Distributor
5. Purge valve
9. Ignition switch-over valve
31. EGR valve
39. Charcoal canister
60. 104° F thermo-vacuum valve
75. Exhaust pressure transducer
80. Auxiliary air valve
81. Shaped hose

B. Fuel tank vent connection

bl = blue
br = brown
ge = yellow
gr = gray
or = orange
rt = red
vi = purple
ws = white

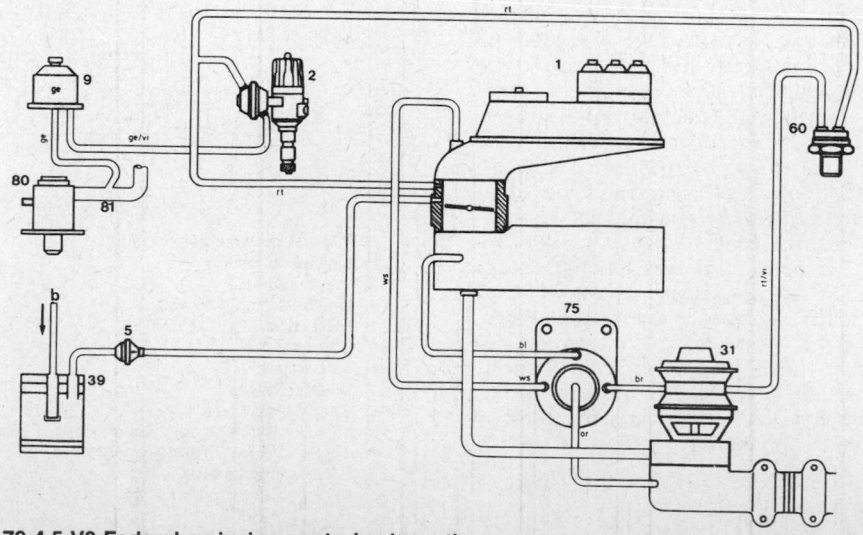

1978–79 4.5 V8 Federal emission control schematic

uum lines is white. Colored stripes identify various functions:

Advanced timing = red
Retarded timing = yellow/purple
Air injection = blue

A Lambda oxygen sensor control system ensures a constant air fuel ratio of approximately 14.5:1. The oxygen sensor is screwed into the front part of the exhaust pipe to constantly monitor the oxygen content of the exhaust gases. An electronic control unit, located behind the kick panel, receives input from a throttle valve switch and oil temperature switch to maintain an ideal fuel mixture in conjunction with the 3-way catalyst. The oxygen sensor must be replaced every 30,000 miles (light on the dash warns driver).

An air injection system is used, the components of which are very similar to those used in 1979.

Testing the System

A special test adaptor that connects to the electronic control unit plug and a special test meter that connects to the adaptor are necessary to properly test the emission system. Do not attempt to try and test electrical components of the system with an ordinary volt-ohmmeter.

The only tests that can be performed without special equipment are as follows:

AIR INJECTION VACUUM TEST

1. Pull the Y-fitting from the angled connections at the thermo-vacuum valves and check for vacuum at the Y-fitting. If no vacuum is present, clean the connection at the intake manifold with compressed air.

2. Be sure the fitting and connecting lines are not plugged. If vacuum is present, the thermo-vacuum valves should be open. If the valves are open, replace the diverter valve.

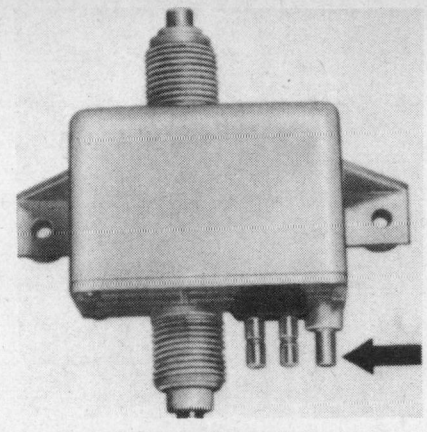

Catalyst elapsed mileage indicator reset button (arrow)

FUEL EVAPORATION CONTROL SYSTEM

1. Remove the purge line from the charcoal canister (connected to the throttle valve housing) and block it with your finger. Slowly increase the engine speed to more than 2000 rpm.

2. There should be no vacuum at idle, but vacuum should increase with rpm.

3. If vacuum does not increase with rpm, test the purge line connection and purge valve. The purge line must be connected to the throttle valve housing, and must not leak. Clean out the throttle valve housing with compressed air. If vacuum is still not present, remove the purge line from the front of the purge valve. If vacuum is present, replace the purge valve.

V8 ENGINES

Color coding of the vacuum lines is identical to the 6-cylinder engines and operation of the Lambda oxygen sensor control system is the same as 6-cylinder engines.

Air injection uses a shut-off valve in a special shaped hose between the air filter and the aspirator valve, which is in the air injection line leading to the cylinder head.

Primary, underfloor and catalyst/muffler combination catalytic converters are used, depending on application.

The fuel evaporation control system is identical to the 1979 system.

Testing the System

A special test adapter that connects to the electronic control unit plug and a special test meter that connects to the adapter are necessary to properly test the emission control system. Do not attempt to try and test electrical components of the system with an ordinary volt-ohmmeter.

The only tests that can be performed without special equipment are as follows:

FREQUENCY VALVE

1. With the engine idling at normal operating temperature, place your hand on the frequency valve.

2. Operation of the frequency valve can be felt. If not replace the valve.

AIR INJECTION

1. Idle the engine and remove the specially shaped hose from the air shut-off valve. A suction sound should be audible.

2. If there is no suction sound, check the vacuum lines and vacuum supply. Check the blue line connected to the air shut-off valve. Disconnect the line at the air shut-off valve. If vacuum is not present, clean out the vacuum connection at the throttle valve housing.

3. If vacuum is present at the air shut-off valve, remove the valve. If the suction

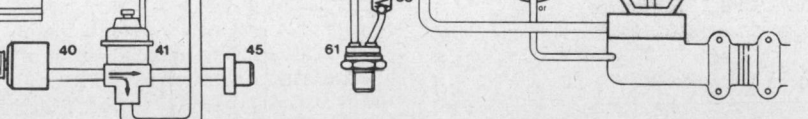

1. Mixture regulator assembly
2. Distributor
5. Purge valve
9. Ignition switch-over valve
31. EGR valve
35. Vacuum check valve
39. Charcoal canister
40. Air pump
41. Diverter valve
42. Check valve
60. 104° F thermo-vacuum valve
61. 62°F thermo-vacuum valve
73. 122°F thermo-vacuum valve
74. Pressure relief valve
75. Exhaust pressure transducer
80. Auxiliary valve
81. Shaped hose

A. Air injection line to cylinder head
B. Fuel tank vent connection

bl = blue
br = brown
ge = yellow
gr = gray
or = orange
rt = red
vi = purple
ws = white

1978-79 4.5 V8 California emission control schematic

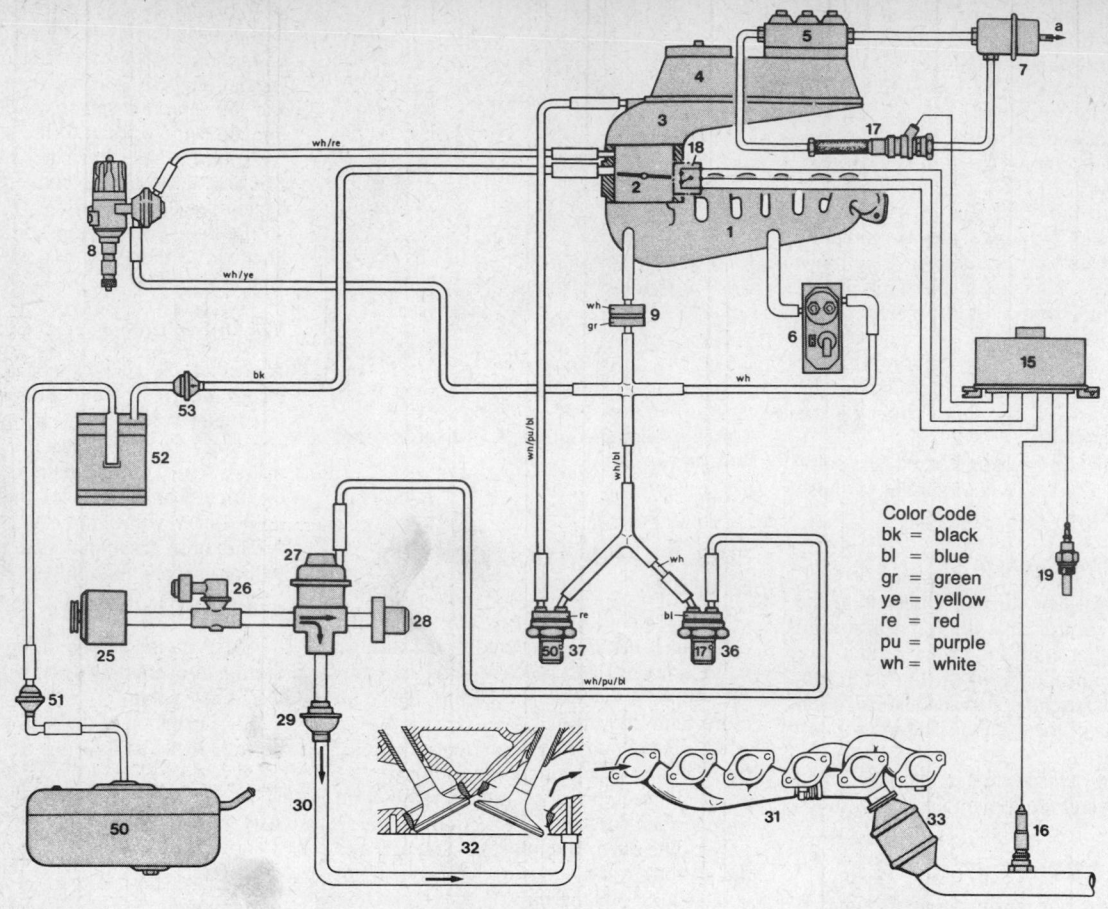

1. Intake manifold
2. Throttle valve housing
3. Air duct housing
4. Air flow sensor
5. Fuel distributor
6. Warm-up enrichment compensator
7. Pressure damper
8. Ignition distributor
9. Restricting orifice
15. Electronic control unit

16. Oxygen sensor
17. Frequency valve
18. Throttle valve switch
19. Temperature switch, oil 60° F
25. Air pump
26. Pressure relief valve
27. Diverter valve
28. Muffler (air filter)
29. Check valve
30. Air injection line

31. Exhaust manifold
32. Cylinder head
33. Primary catalyst
36. Thermo-vacuum valve 63° F
37. Thermo-vacuum valve 122° F
50. Fuel tank
51. Vent valve
52. Charcoal canister
53. Purge valve
a. Leak-off connection

Color Code
bk = black
bl = blue
gr = green
ye = yellow
re = red
pu = purple
wh = white

Emission control schematic—1980 6-cylinder engines

sound is still audible, replace the air shut-off valve. If no suction sound could be heard at the air shut-off valve, replace the aspirator valve.

1981–84

6-CYLINDER ENGINES

The emission control system is the same as 1980, with two exceptions. The air pump intake is connected to the clean side of the air cleaner. A rubber scoop inside the air cleaner facilitates air intake. The second change is that the fuel evaporation control purge system is controlled by a thermo valve and is effective only at temperatures above 122°F.

Color coding of the vacuum lines is as follows:

Device	Color of line originating at a vacuum source	Color of line terminating at a vacuum operated device
Ignition advance	Red	
Ignition retard	Yellow	
Air injection	Blue	Blue/purple
Fuel evaporation thermo valve	Black	Black/purple

Lines originating at a vacuum source have only one color stripe; lines terminating at a vacuum operated device have 2 color stripes and purple is always the second color.

Testing the System

See "Testing the System" under 1980.

V8 ENGINES

Color coding of the vacuum lines is identical to the 6-cylinder engines. Operation of the Lambda oxygen sensor control system is the same as 1980. Only the oxygen sensor itself has been modified for production reasons. All models in 1983 are equipped with a standardized O_2 sensor, with a new plug connection. The plug is no longer below the vehicle, but inside the passenger compartment, accessible after removing the

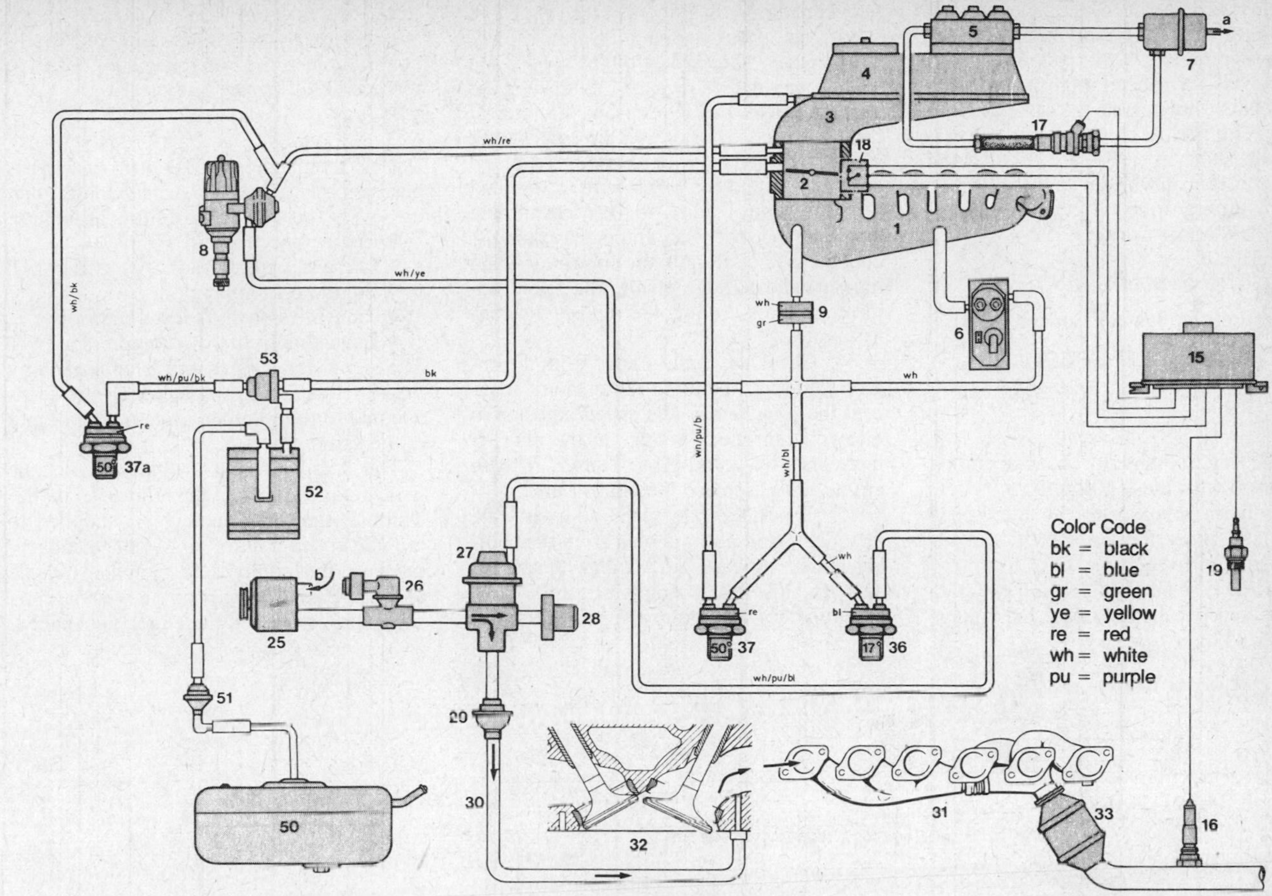

wh/re

wh/ye

wh/bk

wh/pu/bk

53

bk

re

50 37a

52

wh
gr
9

6

wh

15

27

b
26

25

28

wh/pu/gn

wh/bl

re
50 37

bl
17 36

wh/pu/bl

51

20

50

30

32

31

33

19

16

Color Code

bk = black
bl = blue
gr = green
ye = yellow
re = red
wh = white
pu = purple

1.	Intake manifold	17.	Frequency valve	33.	Primary catalyst
2.	Throttle valve housing	18.	Throttle valve switch	36.	Thermo valve 63° F
3.	Air duct housing	19.	Temperature switch, oil 60° F	37.	Thermo valve 122° F
4.	Air flow sensor	25.	Air pump	37a.	Thermo valve 122° F
5.	Fuel distributor	26.	Pressure relief valve	50.	Fuel tank
6.	Warm-up compensator	27.	Diverter valve	51.	Vent valve
7.	Silencer (damper)	28.	Silencer	52.	Charcoal canister
8.	Ignition distributor	29.	Check valve	53.	Purge valve
9.	Orifice	30.	Air injection line		
15.	Control unit	31.	Exhaust manifold	a.	Leak-off connection
16.	Oxygen sensor	32.	Cylinder head	b.	from the air cleaner

Emission control schematic—1981 6 cylinder

19. Temperature switch, 16 °C oil
21. Control unit, electronic idle speed control
23. Idle speed adjuster

a To terminal (a), automatic climate control
b To ignition/starter switch, terminal 50
c To lambda control unit, terminal 6
d To lambda control unit, terminal 7
e To relay, Lambda control with excess
   voltage protection
f To coolant temperature switch 42 °C

Wire color code
bl = blue
br = brown
ge = yellow
gn = green
gr = grey
rt = red
sw = black
vi = purple
ws = white

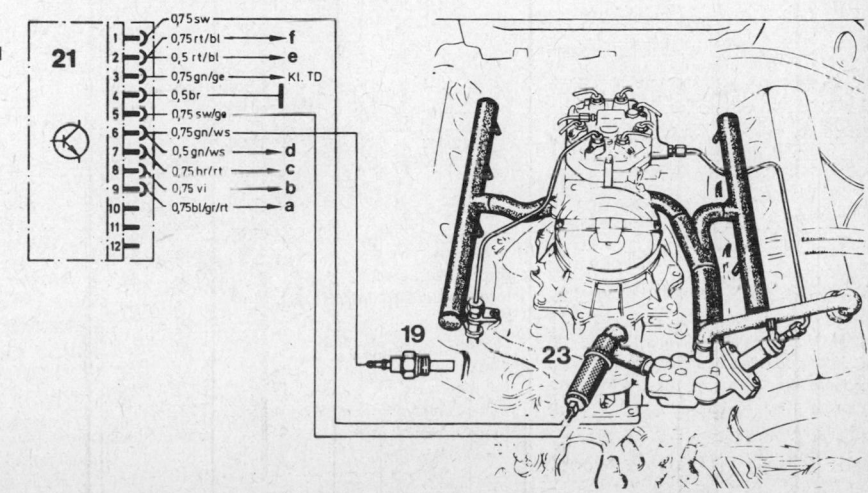

21

1 0,75 sw
2 0,75 rt/bl → f
3 0,5 rt/bl → e
4 0,75 gn/ge → Kl. TD
5 0,5 br
6 0,75 sw/ge
7 0,75 gn/ws
8 0,5 gn/ws → d
9 0,75 br/rt → c
10 0,75 vi → b
11 0,75 bl/gr/rt → a
12

19

23

Electronic idle speed control system—V8 engines

control unit cover plate. The air pump is a maintenance-free vane type pump, similar in operation to the 1980 system. Three-way-catalysts have been slightly modified dimensionally, but operate the same as those in 1980. The fuel evaporation control system is the same as 1980, except that the purge system is controlled by a thermo valve that allows purge only at coolant temperatures below approximately 122°F.

Testing the System

See "Testing the System" under 1980.

ELECTRONIC IDLE SPEED CONTROL

1981–82

1. The engine should be at operating temperature with the ignition ON.
2. Pull the plug from the idle speed adjuster and check the voltage. If 12 volts are present, go to Step 4.
3. If there is no voltage, pull the plug from the control unit and check the voltage

between terminals 2 and 4 (arrows). There should be approximately 12 volts. If there is no voltage, check the voltage supply and replace any defective parts. If 12 volts are present, check the wires from the plug of the idle speed adjuster and the control unit plug (black/yellow wire to terminal 5 of the control unit and the black wire to terminal 1 of the control unit). If there are infinite ohms, replace the wire. If there are 0 ohms, connect the coupling to the control unit and measure the voltage at the idle speed adjuster. If there are 0 volts, replace the control unit.

4. Check the control unit. With the engine idling at operating temperature, connect the plug to the idle speed adjuster so that you can check voltage at the plug. If there are 4–6 volts, go to Step 5. If there are no volts, replace the control unit.

5. Check the idle speed adjuster. Idle the engine and pull the plug from the coolant temperature switch. Bridge the terminals. The idle speed should increase. If not, apply battery voltage to the idle speed ad-

juster (for no more than 5 seconds). If the speed drops or the engine stops, replace the control unit. If the idle speed does not drop, replace the idle speed adjuster.

1983–84

The electronic idle speed control system has been slightly modified. A new control unit on V–8's, processes the following inputs:
- Engine speed (rpm)
- Idle and partial load
- Engine oil temperature
- Transmission shift lever position
- Engagement of A/C compressor

The signal for engine rpm is controlled by the oil temperature switch, which also sends a signal to the Lambda system control unit at the same time.

The A/C compressor clutch has a time delay relay in place of the relay used in '82. Through the relay, voltage is supplied to the idle speed control unit prior to engagement of the compressor clutch. The idle speed solenoid will already be maintaining sufficient rpm when the clutch is engaged.

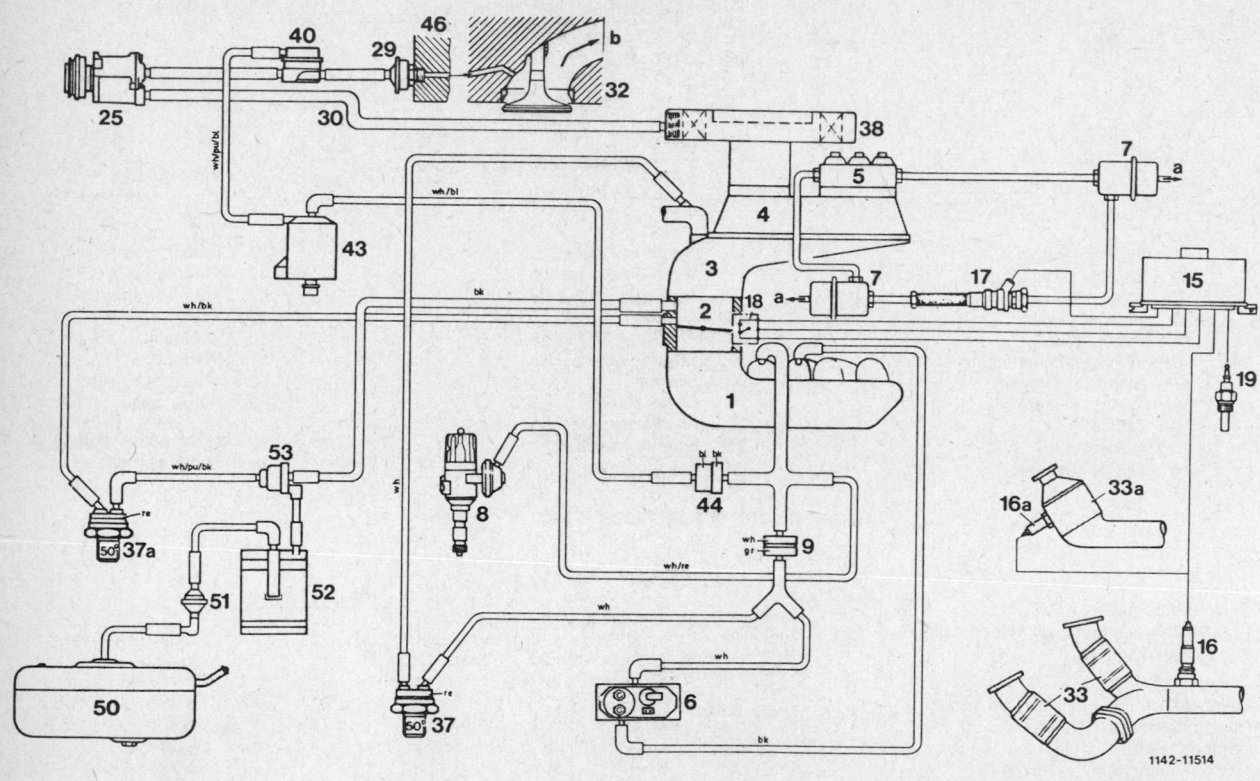

1	Intake manifold	17	Frequency valve	40	Air shutoff valve	bk	= black
2	Throttle valve housing	18	Throttle valve switch	43	Switchover valve	bl	= blue
3	Air guide housing	29	Temperature switch 16°C, oil	44	Check valve (vacuum)	gr	= green
4	Air flow sensor	25	Air pump	46	Timing housing cover	pu	= purple
5	Fuel distributor	29	Check valve (Air injection)	50	Fuel tank	re	= red
6	Warm-up compensator	30	Intake line	51	Vent valve unit	wh	= white
7	Damper	32	Cylinder head	53	Purge valve		
8	Ignition distributor	33	Primary catalyst (model 107)				
9	Throttle (orifice)	33a	Primary catalyst (model 126)	a	Leak connection		
15	Control unit	37	Thermovalve 50°C	b	To exhaust manifold		
16	O₂-sensor (model 107)	37a	Thermovalve 50°C				
16a	O₂-sensor (model 126)	38	Air cleaner				

Emission control system—1984 V8 engines

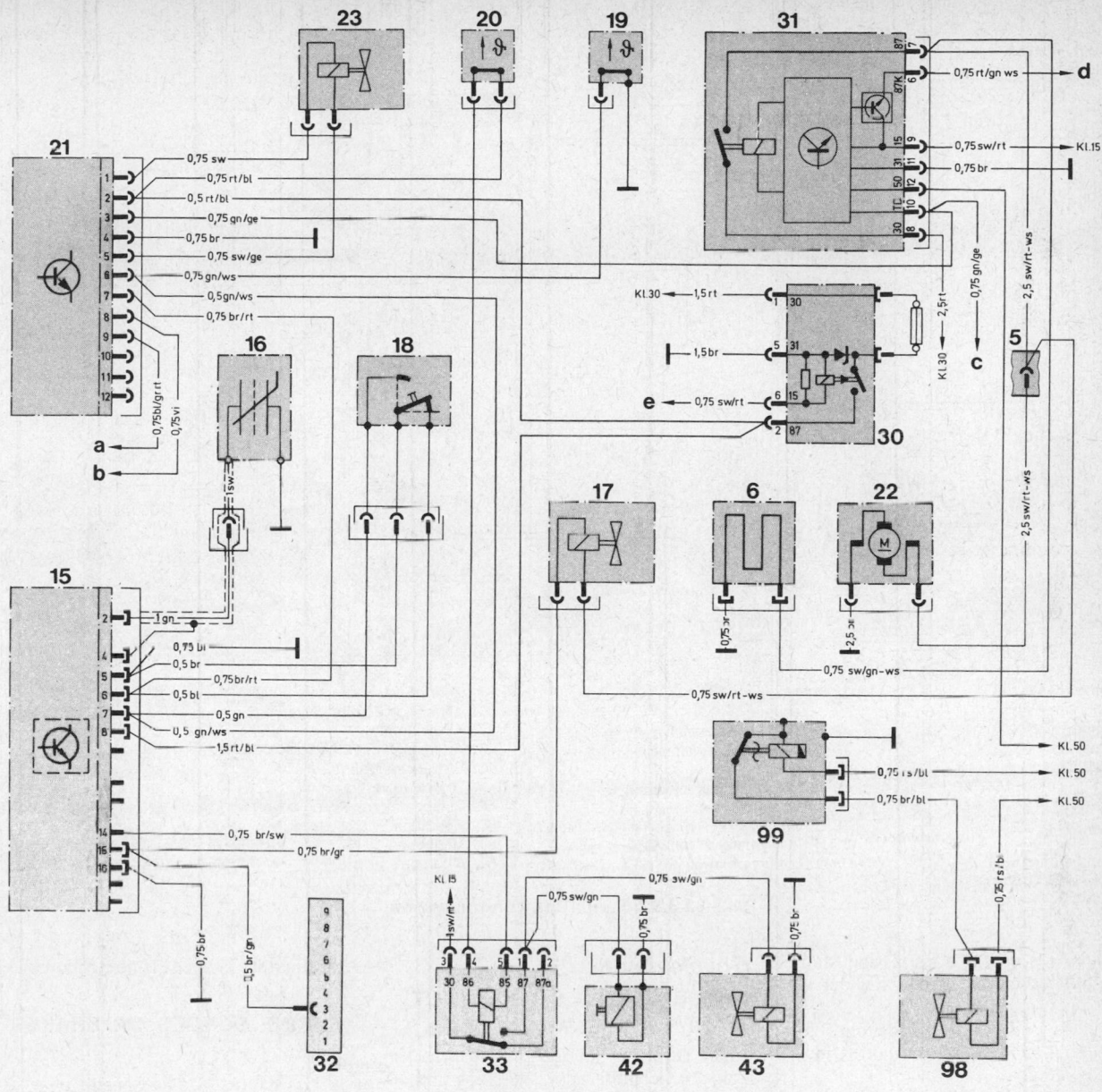

5. Connector, tail lamp harness
6. Warm-up compensator
15. Lambda control unit
16. Oxygen sensor
17. Frequency valve
18. Throttle valve switch
19. Temperature switch, 16 °C oil
20. Temperature switch, 42 °C coolant
21. Electronic idle speed control unit
22. Fuel pump
23. Idle speed control valve
30. Relay, lambda control with excess voltage protection
31. Relay, fuel pump
32. Diagnostic plug
33. Relay, air injection
42. Solenoid clutch, air pump
43. Switch-over valve, air injection
98. Cold start valve
99. Thermo time switch

a to terminal (a), automatic climate control
b to ignition/starter switch, terminal 50
c to terminal block, terminal TD
d to starter lockout/back-up light switch, terminal 7
e 380SL: to fuse Nr. 5, terminal 15
  380SFI , SEC: to fuse Nr. 14, terminal 15

Wire color code
bl = blue
br = brown
ge = yellow
gn = green
gr = grey
rs = pink
rt = red
sw = black
vi = purple
ws = white

2. Frame—transverse
   member
5. Suspension strut
5c. Upper rubber mount
5d. Lower rubber mount
6g. Hex. bolt
5h. Spring washer
5q. Stud
B3. Pressure line (pres-
    sure hose),
    pressure reservoir—
    suspension strut

Lambda control, air injection and electronic idle speed control wiring diagram.

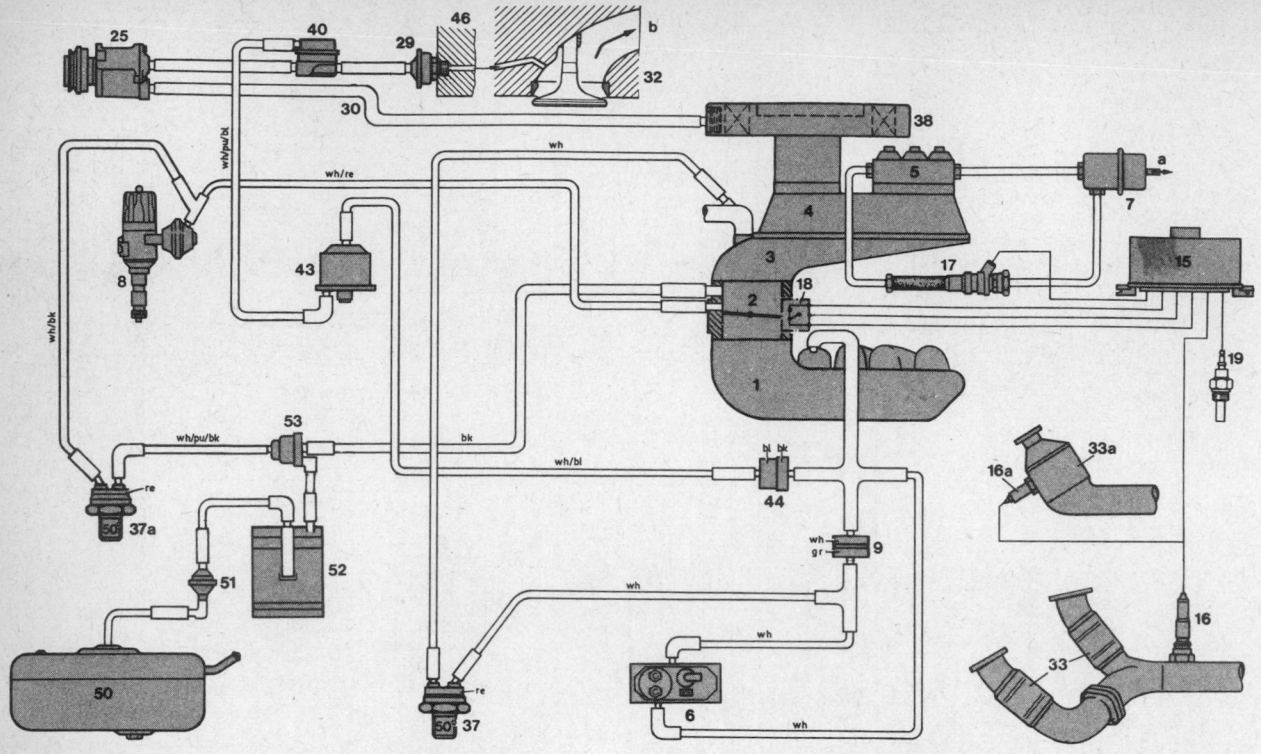

1. Intake manifold
2. Throttle valve housing
3. Air guide housing
4. Air flow sensor
5. Fuel distributor
6. Warm-up compensator
7. Damper
8. Ignition distributor
9. Orifice
15. Lambda control unit
16. O_2 sensor 380 SL

16a. O_2 sensor 380 SEC
17. Frequency valve
18. Throttle valve switch
19. Temperature switch (oil)
25. Air pump
29. Check valve (air injection)
30. Suction line, air pump
32. Cylinder head
33. Primary catalyst 380 SL
33a. Primary catalyst 380 SEC

37. Thermo-vacuum valve 50°C
37a. Thermo-vacuum valve 50°C
38. Air cleaner
40. Air injection shutoff valve
43. Switchover valve
44. Check valve (vacuum)
46. Timing chain housing cover
50. Fuel tank
51. Vent valve
52. Charcoal canister

53. Purge valve
a. Leak-off connection
b. To exhaust manifold
Color code
bk = black
bl = blue
gr = green
pu = purple
re = red
wh = white

1982–83 3.8 V8 emission control system

When the automatic transmission shift lever is in P or N, the starter lockout is closed and the solenoid is ground. When the shift lever is in a driving position, the starter lockout swtich is open and the idle speed is lowered.

This new version of the electronic control unit cannot be used on older model vehicles.

Troubleshooting
ENGINE STALLS OR WILL NOT START

1. Turn the ignition on and off. The idle speed control valve switch on and off noticeably (audibly).

2. If not, remove the valve and see if the aperture is open. If not, follow the Idle Speed Control Test.

ENGINE SURGES OR SHAKES AT IDLE

1. Perform the Idle Speed Control Test.

Time delay relay—380SEL and 380SEC

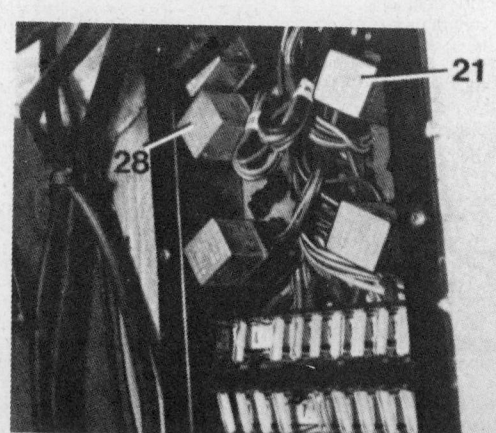

Time delay relay—380SL

Disconnect the wiring harness (arrow) from the idle control solenoid (23).

IDLE SPEED TOO HIGH OR LOW, ENGINE STALLS

1. Disconnect the plug from the idle speed control valve and reconnect it.
2. The idle speed should increase to about 1500 rpm.
3. If no change in idle speed occurs, replace the control valve.
4. Put the transmission in a driving gear. The idle speed should drop to about 500 rpm. If not, perform the Idle Speed Control Test.

IDLE SPEED TO HIGH, ENGINE AT NORMAL TEMPERATURE

1. Disconnect the plug from the temperature switch.
2. If the engine rpm drops with the automatic transmission in P or N, replace the temperature switch. If the engine rpm does not drop, perform the Idle Speed Control Test.

Idle Speed Control Test
CHECK VOLTAGE TO CONTROL VALVE

1. Turn the ignition on and off.
2. The idle speed control valve should switch on and off audibly.

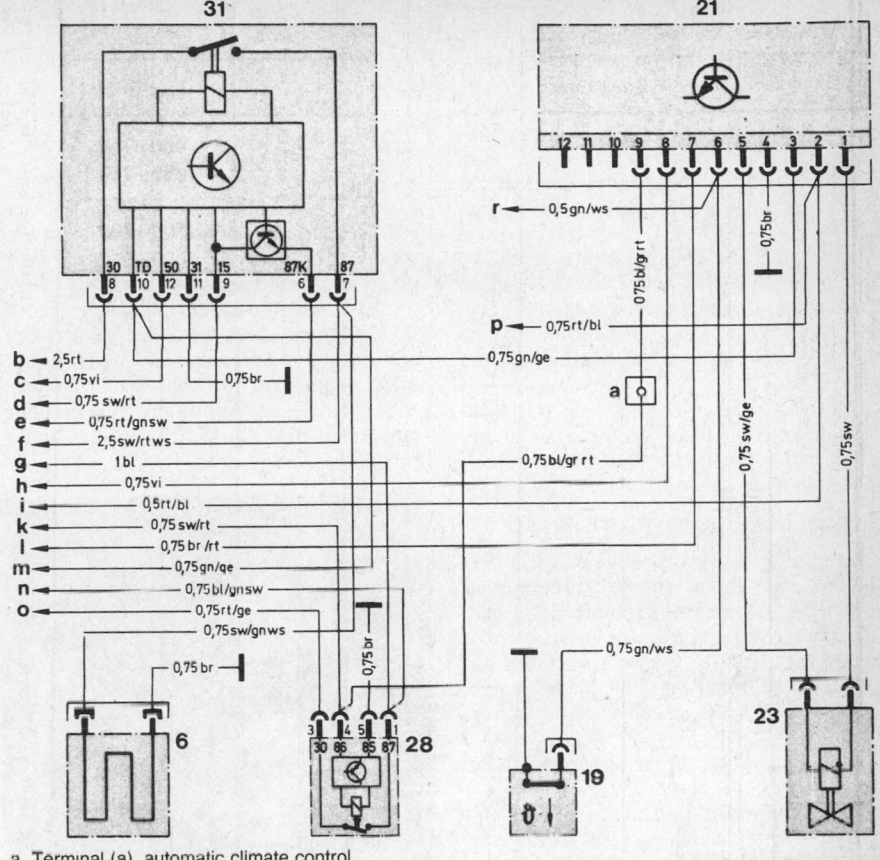

a Terminal (a), automatic climate control
b Model 107: to terminal block engine, terminal 30
   Model 126: to terminal block, terminal 30
c to terminal block engine, terminal 50
d to fuse box, terminal 15
e to starter lockout/back-up lamp switch, terminal 7
f to tail lamp harness, terminal 2
g to connector, A/C compressor
h to ignition/starter switch, terminal 50
i to relay, lambda control unit with excess voltage protection, terminal 2
k to low pressure switch, A/C compressor
l to lambda control unit, terminal 6
m Model 107: to tachometer
   Model 126: to terminal block, terminal TD
n to electronic temperature control unit
o to fuse box, terminal 15 X
p to temperature switch, 42 °C coolant
r to lambda control unit, terminal 7

Wire color codes
bl = blue
br = brown
ge = yellow
gn = green
gr = grey
rt = red
sw = black
vi = purple
ws = white

6. Warm-up compensator
19. Temperature switch, 16 °C
21. Control unit—electronic idle speed control
23. Idle speed control valve
28. Time delay relay—ACC
31. Fuel pump relay

Electronic idle speed control system wiring diagram—V8 engines

Control unit on the 380SL is under a cover on the right side of the passenger compartment.

Control unit location on the 380SEL and 380SEC

3. If it does not, turn the ignition on and disconnect the plug at the idle speed control valve and see if voltage is present. If it is, replace the valve.

4. If no voltage is present, disconnect the plug on the control unit and check battery voltage between pins 2 (positive) and 4 (negative). If no voltage is present, check the power supply according to the wiring diagram.

5. If there is voltage at pins 2 and 4, bridge pins 1 and 2 and 4 and 5 simultaneously for a maximum of 5 seconds. The idle speed valve should switch audibly.

6. If the valve switches, replace the control unit.

7. If the valve does not switch, check the black and the black/yellow wires to the idle speed valve for continuity and repair if necessary.

CHECK IDLE AND PART LOAD

A special M-B test cable is necessary for this test. The engine should be running at idle (with accessories turned off) at normal operating temperature. The transmission should be in P or N. Connect a multimeter to a test cable and connect the test cable between the idle speed valve and the wiring harness.

1. The reading on the meter should be above 400 mA at about 650 rpm.

2. If the reading fluctuates and the engine surges, replace the idle speed valve or the control unit.

3. If the reading is 0 mA, perform the Idle Speed Control Test.

4. Disconnect the throttle valve switch connector and check the idle speed. The idle speed should increase to about 850 rpm.

5. If the idle speed does not increase, turn off the engine and disconnect the plug from the control unit. Set the multimeter on the 0 to infinite ohms scale and connect it to bushings 4 and 7. With the throttle valve against the stop, the meter should read 0 ohms. With the throttle valve slightly opened, the meter should read infinite ohms. If the readings are not present, adjust the throttle valve switch, or if necessary, replace it. Check the wires to the throttle valve switch.

Disconnect the control unit

6. Reconnect the plug to the control unit. Start the engine.

7. The idle speed should increase to approximately 850 rpm.

8. If not, replace the control unit.

CHECK FAST IDLE

The engine should be idling at normal operating temperature with the shift lever in P or N. Connect the plug of the temperature switch to ground to simulate an oil temperature of less than 16°C.

1. If the idle speed increase to about 800–900 rpm, check the temperature switch and replace if necessary. Below an actual oil temperature of 16°C, the switch contacts should be closed. Above an actual oil temperature of 16°C, the switch contacts should be open.

Oil temperature switch (19)

2. If the idle speed does not increase, disconnect the plug from the control unit and check the wire from pin No. 6 to the temperature switch for continuity. If 0 ohms are present, replace the control unit. If infinite ohms are present, check the wire to the temperature switch.

CHECK IDLE SPEED WITH AND WITHOUT THE TRANSMISSION ENGAGED

The engine should be running at idle, at normal operating temperature, and the wheels blocked.

1. Put the car in gear. The idle speed should drop to about 500 rpm.

2. If the idle speed does not drop, disconnect the plug from the control unit. Turn the engine off, then on.

3. Connect a voltmeter betwen pins 8 (negative) and 2 (positive). Battery voltage should be present with the transmission in P or N.

4. If battery voltage is present, replace the control unit. If battery voltage is not present, and no voltage is present at pin No. 2, check the wiring according to the wiring diagram.

5. If no ground is made at pin No. 8, check the wiring to the starter lockout/back-up light switch.

CHECK IDLE SPEED WHEN A/C COMPRESSOR IS ENGAGED

1. Turn the ignition on and engage the A/C compressor. Disconnect the plug from the control unit. Battery voltage should be present at pin No. 9.

2. If battery voltage is not present, check the voltage supply on the wiring diagram.

3. If battery voltage is present, but the idle speed drop is too much when the compressor is engaged, replace the ACC time delay relay or the control unit.

IDLE SPEED TOO HIGH ON WARM ENGINE

The engine should be running at idle, at normal operating temperature. The transmission should be in P or N.

1. Disconnect the plug on the temperature switch.

2. If the idle speed drops to about 500 rpm, replace the temperature switch.

3. If the idle speed does not drop, disconnect the plug from the control unit. Check the wire from pin No. 6 to the temperature switch for continuity.

4. If 0 ohms are present, replace the control unit.

5. If infinite ohms are present, check the wire to the temperature switch.

FUEL SYSTEM

Fuel Filter

FUEL INJECTED ENGINES—ALL MODELS

Two types of filters are used, depending on the car model. Both are located between the rear axle and the fuel tank.

Test Cable

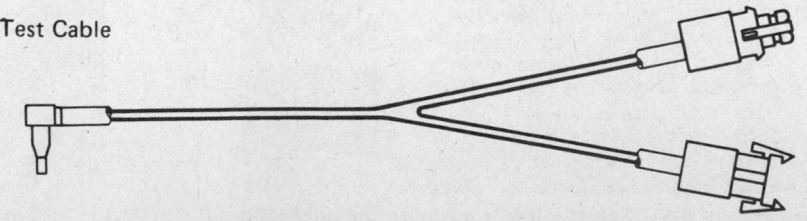

Test cable for testing electronic idle control

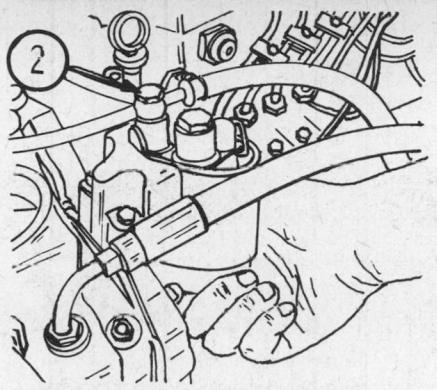

Remove the main diesel fuel filter after removing the center attaching bolt. The bleed screw is (2).

1. Unscrew the cover box.
2. Remove the pressure hoses.
3. Loosen the attaching screws and remove the filter. Remove the connecting plug from the old filter and install it on a new filter using a new gasket.
4. Install a new filter in the direction of flow.
5. Replace the attaching screws.
6. Install the pressure hoses.
7. Install the fuel filter in the holder by positioning it in the center of the transparent holder. Be sure the plastic sleeve between the fuel filter and fuel pump is installed. Galvanic corrosion may occur in cases of direct contact between these components.
8. Replace the cover box and check for proper sealing.

4-CYLINDER CARBURETED ENGINE

1. Loosen the hose clips.
2. Remove the fuel filter.
3. Install a new filter in the direction of flow (arrow) along with new fuel hoses.
4. Replace the hose clips.
5. Check for proper sealing.

DIESEL ENGINES

Main Fuel Filter

Loosen the center attaching bolt and remove the filter cartridge downward. Lubricate the new filter gasket with clean diesel fuel and install a new filter cartridge.

To bleed the fuel filter: Loosen the bleed bolt on the fuel filter housing and release the manually operated delivery pump. Operate the delivery pump until the fuel emerges free of bubbles at the bleed screw. Close the bleed bolt and operate the pump until the overflow valve on the injection pump opens (a buzzing noise will be heard). Close the manual pump before starting the engine. To bleed the injection pump on 4-cylinder diesels, loosen the bleed screw on the injection pump and keep pumping the hand pump until fuel emerges free of bubbles.

NOTE: The 190D uses a self-bleeding fuel pump, therefore the hand pump has been eliminated. No bleeding is necessary.

Diesel Prefilter

Diesel engines use a prefilter in addition to the main fuel filter, since even the most minute particle of dirt will clog the injection system. The prefilter is located in the line just before it enters the injection pump.

To replace it, simply unscrew the clamps on each end and remove the old filter. Install a new filter and bleed the system (see Main Fuel Filter).

Fuel Pump Strainer (Carbureted Engines)

Plunger type fuel pumps on carbureted engines use a strainer located behind the cover.
1. Disconnect and plug the fuel line at the pump.
2. Remove the center screw and remove the cover. A small amount of fuel will run out.
3. Replace the strainer, gasket, screw and aluminum washer, all of which are part of the replacement kit.
4. Replace the cover. There are assembly marks on the cover and fuel pump body.
5. Reconnect the fuel line. Start the engine and check for leaks.

Mechanical Fuel Pump

All Mercedes-Benz carbureted engines use a diaphragm type fuel pump, which is mounted on the side of the block. It is operated by a gear driven eccentric shaft through a rocker arm on the fuel pump.

REMOVAL & INSTALLATION

1. Clean the joint around the fuel pump base and cylinder block.
2. One at a time, remove and plug the intake and outlet lines from the fuel pump.
3. Unbolt the retaining bolts and remove the fuel pump and gasket from the cylinder block.
4. Clean the mating surfaces of the engine and cylinder block.
5. Install a new gasket.
6. Insert the fuel pump into the block and install the retaining bolts. Be sure that the bolts are tightened evenly.
7. Reconnect the intake and outlet lines to the fuel pump.
8. Run the engine and check for leaks.

TESTING DELIVERY PRESSURE

1. Remove the wire from the coil to prevent starting.
2. Connect a pressure gauge into the output line of the fuel pump.

Some diesel injection pumps have a manually operated delivery pump (1)

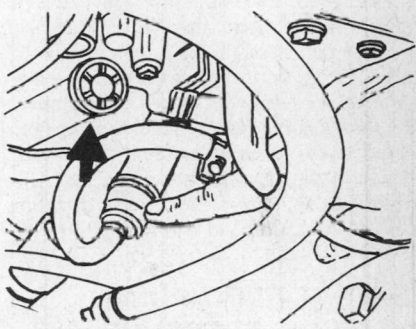

Diesel engines use a pre-filter in addition to the main fuel filter. The arrow indicates the hard operated delivery pump

Testing fuel pump pressure

3. Crank the engine and read the delivery pressure on the pressure gauge. The pressure should be a constant 1.5–2.5 psi.
4. If the pressure is not within specifications or is erratic, remove the pump for service or for replacement with a new or rebuilt unit. No adjustment is provided.

Electric Fuel Pump

NOTE: Do not confuse the electric fuel pump with the injection pump.

All Mercedes-Benz fuel injected engines are equipped with electric fuel pumps. The electric fuel pump is located underneath the rear floor panel. The fuel return line was also eliminated and a check ball installed in its place. Beginning in 1980, the fuel pump uses a replaceable check valve on the outside of the pump which can be replaced separately.

Two types of fuel pumps have been used. One, the large pump, has been replaced with a new small design which has a bypass system to prevent vapor lock.

REMOVAL & INSTALLATION

1. Jack the left rear of the car and support it on jack stands. This will provide sufficient working clearance.

2. Remove and plug the intake, outlet and bypass lines from the pump.

3. Disconnect the electrical leads.

4. Unbolt and remove the fuel pump and vibration pads.

5. Install the fuel pump in the reverse order of removal. Be sure that the electrical leads are connected to the proper terminals. The negative wire (brown) is connected to the negative terminal (brown plastic plate) and the positive wire (black/red) is connected to the positive terminal (red plastic plate). If the terminals are reversed, the pump will operate in the reverse direction of normal rotation and will deliver no fuel.

TESTING FUEL PUMP DELIVERY PRESSURE

Remove the fuel return hose from the fuel distributor. Connect a fuel line and hold the end in the measuring cup. Disconnect the plug from the safety switch on the mixture regulator and turn on the ignition for 30 seconds. If the delivery rate is less than 1

liter in 30 seconds, check the voltage at the fuel pump (11.5) and the fuel lines for kinks. Disconnect the leak off line between the fuel accumulator and the suction damper. Check the delivery rate again. If it is low, replace the accumulator.

Replace the fuel filter and test again. If still low, replace the fuel pump.

Carburetors

REMOVAL & INSTALLATION

Stromberg 175CDT (1978 230)

1. Remove the air cleaner.
2. Remove and plug the fuel lines.

— CAUTION —

Do not pull off the fuel lines. They should be pried off along with the securing discs.

3. Disconnect the control linkage.
4. Remove the vacuum lines.
5. Disconnect the water hoses for the automatic choke.
6. Disconnect the leads for the automatic choke and fuel shut-off valve.
7. Remove the carburetor retaining nuts and remove the carburetor.
8. Installation is the reverse of removal. Adjust the carburetor. See "Tune-Up Specifications".

OVERHAUL

For all carburetor overhaul procedures, please refer to "Carburetor Overhaul" in the Unit Repair section.

ADJUSTMENTS

Stromberg 175CDT
DAMPER FLUID LEVEL

1. Unscrew the top of the damper and check the fluid level.
2. If necessary, top up the reservoir with automatic transmission fluid (ATF).
3. The fluid level should be to the top edge of the piston ring.
4. Replace the top on the reservoir.

FLOAT ADJUSTMENT

1. Remove the carburetor.
2. Remove the float chamber cover and idling speed cut-off valve.
3. Do not loosen the lock screw from the needle or the needle will have to be recentered.
4. Remove the fuel nozzle and compensating element.
5. Push the float down until the float needle valve ball is fully pushed in.

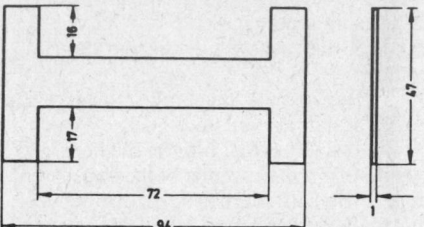

Home-made gauge for measuring Stromberg 175 CDT float level (dimensions in mm)

6. Check the float level with a home-made gauge.
7. To correct the float level, bend the float arm at the tang over the needle valve. The float arm must always remain perpendicular to the needle valve. Also, check the sealing ring under the needle valve for specified thickness (1.5mm) and replace if necessary.
8. Replace the float chamber cover and install the carburetor.
9. Adjust the idle.

AUTOMATIC CHOKE

1. The idle should be set and the engine should be at normal operating temperature.
2. On vehicles with air conditioning, remove the air cleaner and air intake.
3. Check the adjustment of the choke cover. The index marks should be aligned.
4. Raise the throttle linkage slightly and insert a screwdriver through the slot of the starter housing on the carburetor. Push the screwdriver against the engaging lever in the direction of the engine. Release the throttle linkage and engaging lever. This will set the engine at fast idle.
5. The fast idle speed should be 3300–3600 rpm. If the speed requires adjustment, loosen both locknuts on the connecting rod and turn the threaded bolt. ½ turn of the bolt will change the engine rpm by about 200–300 rpm. Decreasing the length of the

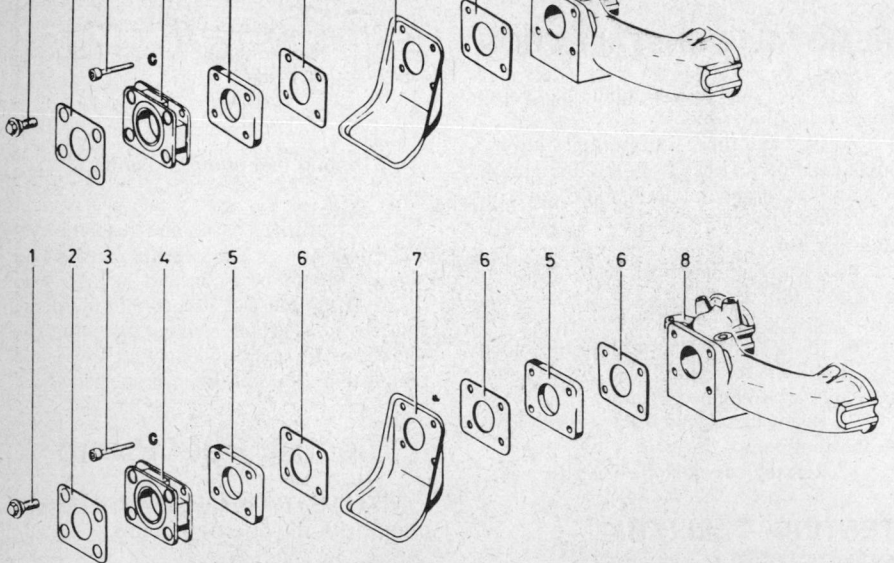

1. Carburetor attachment screw
2. Gasket
3. Rubber flange fastening screw
4. Rubber flange
5. Insulating flange
6. Gasket
7. Shielding plate
8. Intake pipe

Stromberg 175 CDT carburetor gaskets

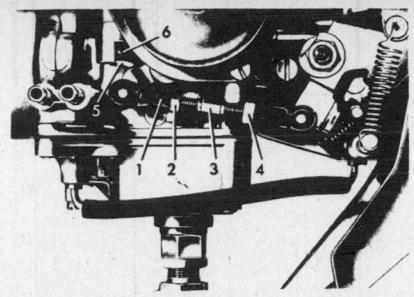

1. Connecting rod
2. Hex nut
3. Threaded bolt
4. Hex nut
5. Actuating lever
6. Venting valve

Stromberg 175CDT automatic choke adjustment

Access slot (arrow) on Stromberg 175CDT—1979 and prior years

bolt will decrease rpm and increasing the length will increase rpm.

FAST IDLE

The fast idle adjustment is done with the cam on the second step.

1. Run the engine to normal operating temperature.

2. With the engine idling, raise the throttle linkage slightly.

3. At the same time, push the engaging lever with a small screwdriver, through the slot of the choke housing in the direction of the engine, against the stop on the pull down diaphragm rod. Do not force it past the stop.

4. Raise the throttle linkage while holding the engaging lever against the stop.

5. Check the CO and fast idle.

6. Adjust the fast idle speed with the upper adjusting screw to 1600–1800 rpm.

7. Adjust the CO with the mixture adjusting screw to 5–8%. To check the CO, the center vacuum line for the air injection switchover valve must be disconnected and plugged.

FULL THROTTLE STOP (CALIFORNIA ONLY)

1. With the accelerator pedal fully depressed, adjust the full throttle stop screw so that a clearance of 0.02 in. exists between the throttle valve lever and carburetor housing.

THERMO AIR VALVE

1. Disconnect the hoses from the thermo-air valve and blow into one hose. If the valve is cold, no air can pass through the valve. If the valve is warm (slightly above room temperature) air should pass through the valve.

Fuel Injection

Mercedes-Benz uses the Bosch K–Jetronic (CIS) fuel injection system on all models except the 190E, which uses a variation of the K-Jetronic, called the KE-Jetronic.

Minor running changes and improvements are made during production, but essential operation and service of the system remains alike on all vehicles equipped with the CIS injection.

The 190E utilizes an electronically controlled version of the K-Jetronic injection system called KE-Jetronic (CIS-E). This system is a further development of the mechanically controlled CIS system. The essential difference between the two is mixture correction by means of electronically controlled correction functions (CIS-E). An electronic control unit sends out impulses which effect the amount of fuel being in-

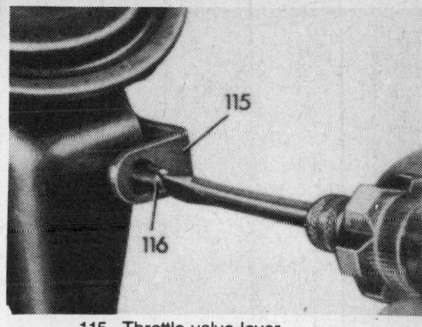

115. Throttle valve lever
116. Full throttle adjusting screw

Full throttle stop adjusting screw

jected. Since only the mixture corrections are controlled by this new system, the vehicle will continue to operate if there is an electronic malfunction.

——————— CAUTION ———————
Even a seemingly minor adjustment, such as idle speed, can necessitate adjustments to other portions of the fuel injection system. Be extremely careful when adjusting the idle. If any difficulty at all is experienced, it will only upset the balance of an already delicate system.

For all fuel injection system service and repair procedures not detailed below, please refer to "Fuel Injection" in the Unit repair section.

TESTING

Delivery Capacity

See "Testing Fuel Pump Output" under Fuel Pump earlier in this section.

Cold Start Valve

1. Disconnect the plugs from the safety switch and mixture control regulator.

2. Remove the cold start valve with fuel line connected.

3. Hold the cold start valve in a container.

4. Turn on the ignition. Connect the valve to battery voltage. It should emit a cone shaped spray.

8. Idle adjusting screw
114. Fast adjusting screw (cold start).

Fast idle adjusting screw (114) on Stromberg 175CDT—1979 and prior years

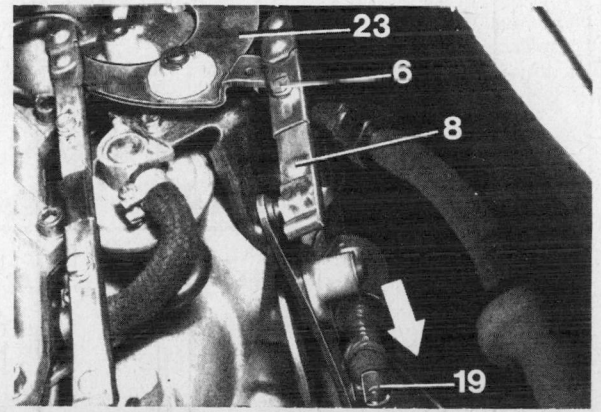

380SEL control pressure adjustment. The clamp screw is (6) and the ball socket (19)

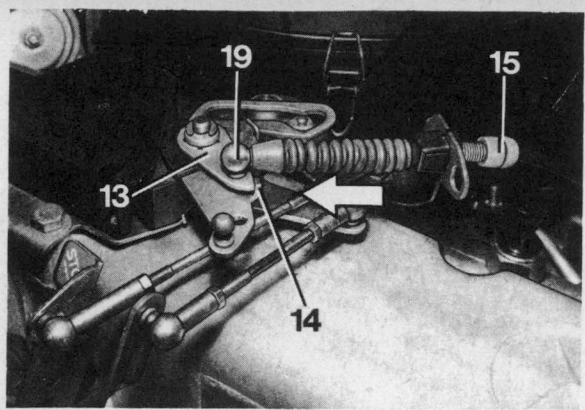

1981 300SD control pressure adjustment. Adjust the ball socket (19) at the adjusting screw (15)

5. Dry the nozzle off. No fuel should leak out.

Hot Start System

Perform the test at coolant temperature 104°–122°F.

1. Remove the coil wire.
2. Connect a voltmeter to hot start terminal 3 and ground.
3. Actuate the starter. In approximately 3–4 seconds, the voltmeter should read about 11 volts for 3–4 seconds.
4. If 11 volts are not indicated, check fuse 10. Connect the plug of the 104°F temperature switch and ground and repeat the test. If 11 volts are now indicated, replace the temperature switch. If 11 volts are not indicated, or if the time periods are wrong, replace the hot start relay.

Fuel Pump Safety Circuit

The pump will only run if the starter motor is actuated or if the engine is running.

1. Remove the air filter.
2. Turn on the ignition and briefly depress the sensor plate.
3. Remove the coil wire from the distributor.
4. Connect a voltmeter to the positive fuel pump terminal and ground.
5. Actuate the starter. Voltmeter should indicate 11 volts.
6. If the fuel pump runs only when the sensor plate is depressed or only when the engine is cranked, replace the fuel pump relay. If the pump is already running when the ignition is turned ON, replace the safety switch.

ADJUSTMENTS

Prior to 1979
CONTROL LINKAGE

1. Check the control linkage for ease of operation.
2. Disconnect the control rod. The throttle valve should rest against the idle stop. Reconnect the control rod.
3. Adjust the control rod so that the roller rests tension free in the gate slot.

FULL THROTTLE STOP

1. With the engine stopped, press the accelerator pedal until it rests against the kickdown switch.
2. The throttle valve lever should rest against the full throttle stop. If necessary, adjust the throttle valve lever.
3. If the full throttle stop is not reached, adjust the control rod (bell crank lever to accelerator pedal) to 4.8 in. (from center to center of ball sockets).
4. Adjust the accelerator pedal linkage if necessary with the fastening screw.
5. Adjust the control pressure rod (at idle) by compressing the adjusting clip, and moving the rod completely to the rear against the stop.

1980 and Later
THROTTLE VALVE SWITCH

1. Set an ohmmeter to 0-infinity.
2. Check the idle speed stop. Push the throttle valve against the idle speed stop. Connect the ohmmeter across terminals 1 and 2. Rotate the throttle valve switch until the ohmmeter reads 0.
3. Advance the throttle valve slightly. The ohmmeter should read 0-infinite ohms.
4. Check the full throttle stop. Push the throttle valve against the full throttle stop and connect an ohmmeter across terminals 2 and 3. The reading should be 0 ohms.
5. Turn the throttle valve back slightly. A reading of infinite ohms should result.

MANUAL TRANSMISSION

REMOVAL & INSTALLATION

With Engine
ALL MODELS

The transmission should only be removed with the engine as a unit, since transmission-to-clutchhousing bolts can only

be reached from the inside. Once the engine/transmission unit has been removed from the vehicle, the transmission and bellhousing must be separated from the engine, as follows:

See the "Engine" section to remove the engine/transmission.

1. After removing the engine/transmission unit, unbolt the bellhousing from the engine. The bolts which hold the transmission to the bellhousing cannot be reached except from inside the bellhousing.
2. Remove the starter from its mounting position and pull the transmission and bellhousing from the engine.
3. The bolts which secure the bellhousing to the transmission are now visible and can be removed to separate the bellhousing and transmission.
4. To install, connect the engine, bellhousing, and transmission, after coating the splines of the mainshaft with grease.
5. Install the starter.
6. Further installation is the reverse of removal.

Without Engine
1978–81 240D

1. Support the car on jackstands.
2. Disconnect the battery.
3. Disconnect the exhaust pipe and/or muffler to provide clearance around the bellhousing.
4. Unhook the slave cylinder hydraulic line at the connection and plug both openings.
5. Unbolt the rear engine mount.
6. Slightly raise the transmission with a jack and remove the lower plate covering the transmission tunnel.
7. Disconnect the speedometer cable from the rear of the transmission.
8. Disconnect the shift rods from the transmission shift leavers.
9. Loosen, but do not remove, the intermediate bearing bolts.
10. Matchmark the U-joint and driveshaft coupling and loosen the U-joint.
11. Matchmark the driveshaft flange and adaptor. Loosen the 3 driveshaft bolts. Remove 2 of the bolts and pivot the driveshaft around enough to reinstall the 2 bolts. Remove the 3rd bolt and position the driveshaft rearward as far as the center bearing permits. Use a piece of wood to block the driveshaft up in the driveshaft tunnel. Reinstall the 3rd bolt. The adaptor plate should remain on the 3-legged transmission flange.
12. Remove the starter.
13. Remove all bolts attaching the transmission to the intermediate flange, but remove the upper 2 bolts last.

NOTE: The clutch housing is heavily ribbed. Because of this, most of the bolts can only be reached with a 17 or 19 mm insert and extension.

14. Turn the transmission 45° to the left so that the starter domes on both sides of the clutch housing do not scrape the transmission tunnel.

15. Keep the transmission level and slide it out.

16. The clutch housing bolts can only be reached from inside. Unbolt the housing and remove it.

17. Installation is the reverse of removal.

1982–83 240D

1. Disconnect the battery.

2. Disconnect the regulating shaft in the engine compartment.

3. Support the transmission with a floor jack.

4. Unbolt the rear engine mount.

5. Unbolt each side of the engine carrier on the floor frame.

6. Unscrew the exhaust mounting bracket on the transmission. *Note the number and positioning of all washers.*

7. Unbolt the retaining strap and remove the exhaust pipe bracket.

8. Loosen the clamp nut on the driveshaft.

9. Loosen, but do not remove, the intermediate bearing bolts.

10. Unbolt the driveshaft on the transmission so that the companion plate remains with the driveshaft.

11. Carefully push the driveshaft as far to the rear as permitted.

12. Loosen and remove the tachometer drive shaft on the rear transmission case cover. Unclip the clip for the tachometer drive shaft from its holder.

13. Unscrew the holder for the line to the clutch housing. Unscrew the clutch slave cylinder and move it toward the rear until the pushrod is clear of the housing.

14. Push off the clip locks and then remove the shift rods from the intermediate levers on the shift bracket. *Note the position of the disc springs.*

— **CAUTION** —

When the shift rods are disconnected, do not move the shift lever into reverse or you risk damaging the back-up light switch.

15. Unbolt the starter and remove it.

16. Remove all transmission-to-intermediate flange screws. Remove the upper two last.

17. Carefully pull the transmission toward the rear of the vehicle and then remove it downward.

— **CAUTION** —

Make sure that the input shaft has cleared the clutch plate before tilting the transmission.

To install:

1. Lightly grease the centering lug and splines on the transmission input shaft.

NOTE: Position the clutch slave cylinder and line above the transmission before beginning installation.

2. Move the transmission into the clutch so that one gear step engages. Rotate the mainshaft back and forth until the splines on the input shaft and clutch plate are aligned.

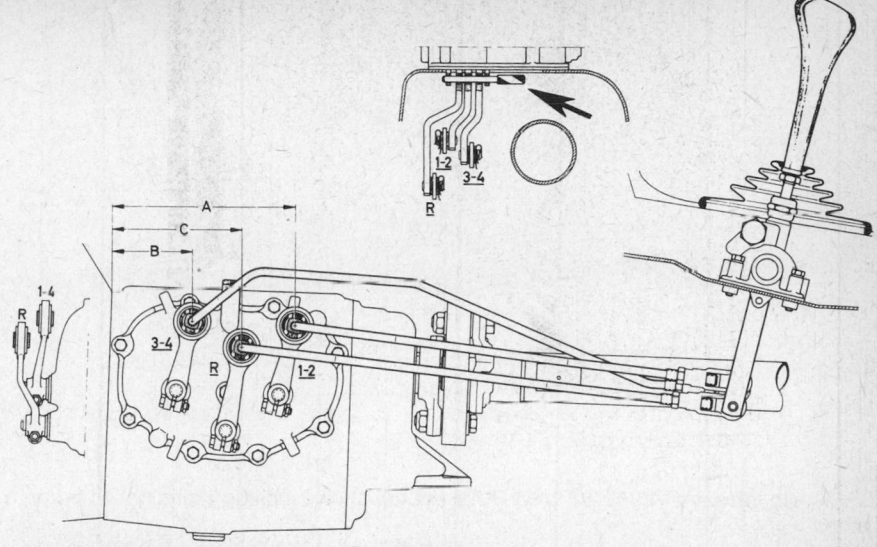

Transmission linkage—1978–81 240D. Arrow at top shows locking pin installed prior to adjustment

3. Move the transmission all the way in and then tighten the transmission-to-intermediate flange screws.

4. Install the starter.

5. Install the clutch slave cylinder with the proper plastic shims.

6. Installation of the remaining components is in the reverse order of removal. Please note the following:

   a. After installing the driveshaft, roll the car back and forth and then tighten the intermediate bearing free of tension.

   b. Tighten the driveshaft clamp nut to 22–29 ft. lbs. (30–40 Nm).

   c. Make sure of the proper positioning of all washers, spacers and shims.

190D AND 190E

1. Disconnect the battery.

2. Cover the insulation mat in the engine compartment to prevent damage.

3. On vehicles equipped with a auxiliary heater, be sure that the water hose is out of the way.

4. Support the transmission with a floor jack.

5. Unbolt the engine mounts at the rear transmission cover.

6. Unbolt the engine carrier on the floor frame.

7. Unscrew the exhaust holder at the transmission. *Note the number and positioning of all washers.*

8. Unscrew the clamping strap and remove the exhaust pipe holder.

9. Remove the intermediate bearing shield plate.

10. Repeat Steps 8–11 of the "1982–83 240D" procedure.

NOTE: On the 190E, the fitted sleeves on the universal flange must be loosened before separating the flange from the companion plate. This will require a cylindrical mandrel.

11. Disconnect the exhaust system at the rear suspension and suspend it with wire.

12. Loosen and remove the input shaft for the tachometer.

13. Repeat Steps 12–16 of the "1982–83 240D" procedure.

14. Rotate the transmission approximately 45° to the left, slide it out of the clutch plate and then remove it downward.

— **CAUTION** —

Make sure that the input shaft has cleared the clutch plate before tilting the transmission.

15. To install, repeat Steps 1–6 (installation) of the "1982–83 240D" procedure. Remember that the transmission must be tilted approximately 45° to the left when installing.

LINKAGE ADJUSTMENT

The only type of shifter used is a floor mounted type.

— **CAUTION** —

On all types of transmissions, never hammer or force a new shift knob on with the shifter installed, as the plastic bushing connected to the lever will be damaged and cause hard shifting.

Proper adjustment of the shift linkage is dependent on both the position of the shift levers at the transmission and the length of the shift rods. The shift levers, rods and bearing block are all located underneath the floor tunnel; the driveshaft shield may have to be removed to gain access to them.

1. With the transmission in neutral and the driveshaft shield removed (if so equipped), remove the clip locks and disconnect the shift rods from the intermediate shift levers under the floor shift bearing bracket.

2. With the shifter still in the neutral position, lock the three intermediate shift levers by inserting a 0.2156 in. rod (a No.

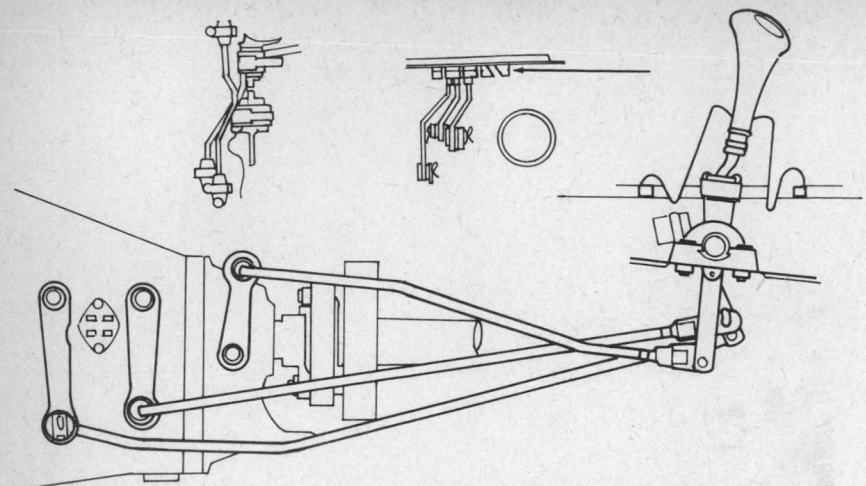

Transmission linkage—1982–83 240D. Arrow at top shows locking rod installed prior to adjustment

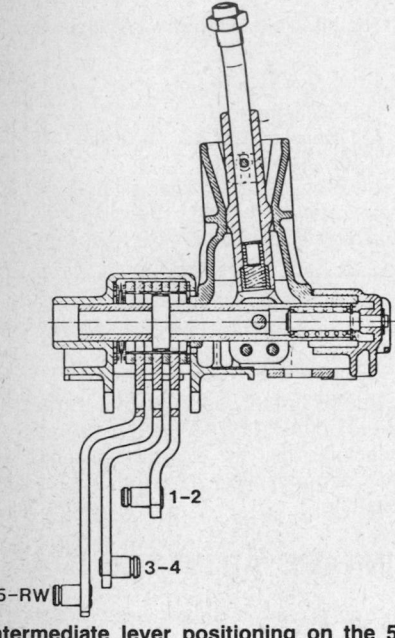

1–2
3–4
5–RW

Intermediate lever positioning on the 5 speed 190. Arrow shows where locking rod goes

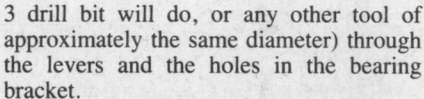

3 drill bit will do, or any other tool of approximately the same diameter) through the levers and the holes in the bearing bracket.

3. Check the positioning of the shift levers at the transmission (see illustrations). Adjust by loosening the clamp bolts and moving the levers.

4. With the intermediate levers locked and the shift levers adjusted properly, try hooking the shift rods back onto their respective intermediate levers. The shift rods may be adjusted by loosening the locknut and turning the ball socket on the end until they are the proper length.

NOTE: When hooking up the shift rods to the intermediate levers, be very careful not to move the transmission shift levers out of their adjusted position.

NOTE: When reattaching the shift rods on 190 models, use only clip locks which have a radiused edge. If the old style clip locks with a square edge are used, there is a possibility that the locks will pop out and the shift rods will drop down.

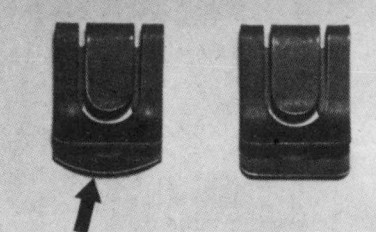

Always use clip locks with curved edges when installing the shift rods on the 190

5. Remove the locking rod from the bearing bracket, start the engine and then shift through the gears a few times. Occasionally slight binding may call for VERY slight further adjustments.

OVERHAUL

For overhaul procedures, refer to the "Manual Transmission Overhaul" in the Unit Repair Section.

CLUTCH

REMOVAL & INSTALLATION

1. To remove the clutch, first remove the transmission and bell housing.

2. Loosen the clutch pressure plate hold-down bolts evenly, 1–1½ turns at a time, until tension is relieved. Never remove one bolt at a time, as damage to the pressure plate is possible.

3. Examine the flywheel surface for blue heat marks, scoring, or cracks. If the flywheel is to be machined, always machine both sides.

4. To reinstall, coat the splines with high temperature grease and place the clutch disc against the flywheel, centering it with a clutch pilot shaft. A wooden shaft, available at automative jobbers, is satisfactory, but an old transmission mainshaft works best.

5. Tighten the pressure plate hold-down bolts evenly, 1–1½ turns at a time, until tight, then remove the pilot shaft.

——— CAUTION ———
Most clutch plates have the flywheel side marked as such (Kupplungsseite). Do not assume that the pressure springs always face the transmission.

CHECKING CLUTCH PLATE WEAR

A spring plate clutch that automatically compensates for wear is used, so no periodic adjustments are required. Apart from the usual slippage which accompanies severe wear of the clutch plate or disc, Mercedes-Benz has a simple tool, which can be purchased from a dealer that mea-

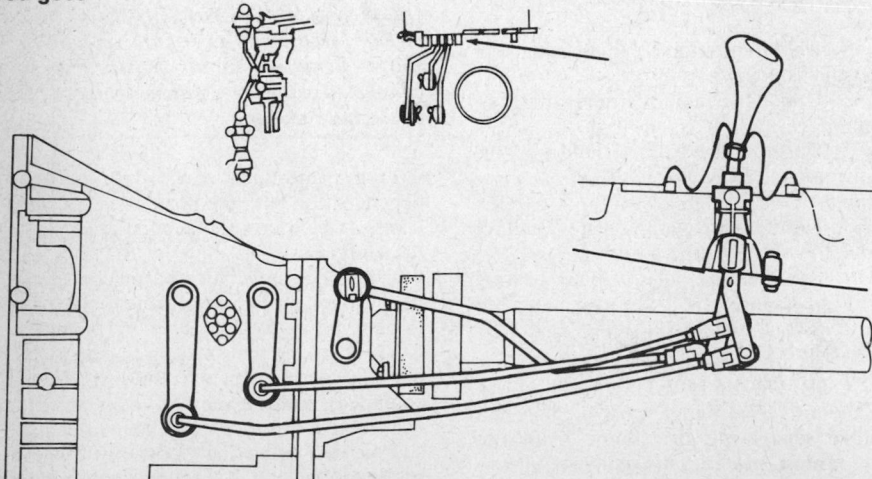

Transmission linkage—190 (4 speed shown, 5 speed similar). Arrow at top shows locking rod installed prior to adjustment

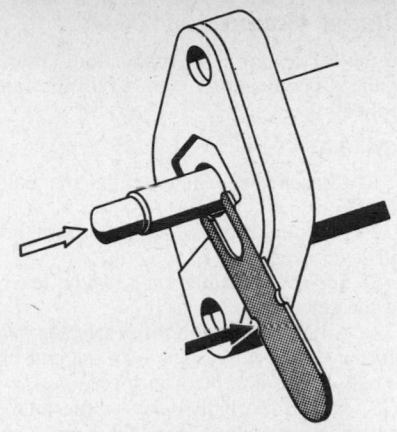

Wear limit has been reached

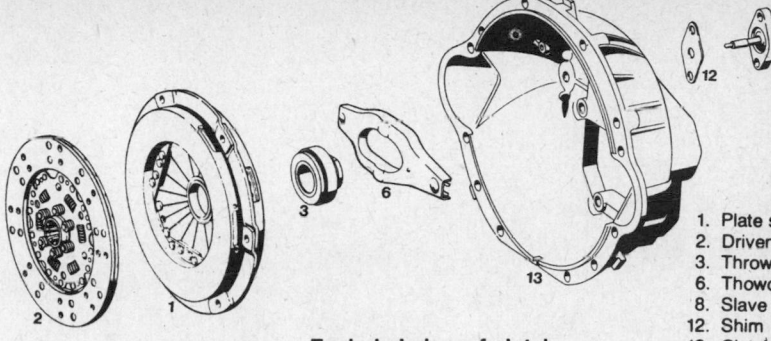

Exploded view of clutch

1. Plate spring clutch
2. Driven plate
3. Throwout
6. Thowout rocker
8. Slave cylinder
12. Shim
13. Clutch housing

sures the amount of war on the clutch plate. Actually, it is a simple "go-no-go" gauge.

1. A plastic shim is installed between the slave cylinder and the bell housing.

2. The shim is provided with two flat grooves running diagonally from bottom to center. When the shim is installed, these grooves appear as slots. Use groove (a) for left hand drive vehicles and groove (b) for right hand drive vehicles.

3. The clutch slave cylinder pushrod has two different diameters. The width of the slot in the test gauge corresponds to the smaller diameter of the pushrod. If the notches on the test gauge disappear when the test gauge is inserted as far as it will go, the clutch plate is still operational.

4. If however, the notches on the test gauge remain visible, this is an indication that the clutch plate is worn severely and should be replaced.

Clutch Slave Cylinder

REMOVAL & INSTALLATION

1. Detach and plug the pressure line from the slave cylinder.

2. Remove the attaching screws from the slave cylinder.

3. Remove the slave cylinder, pushrod, and spacer.

4. To install, place the grooved side of the spacer in contact with the housing and hold it in position.

5. Install the slave cylinder and pushrod into the housing. Be sure that the dust cap is properly seated.

6. Install the attaching screws.

7. Connect the pressure line to the slave cylinder.

8. Bleed the slave cylinder.

BLEEDING THE SLAVE CYLINDER

The same principle is used as in bleeding the brakes.

1. Check the brake fluid level in the compensating tank and fill to maximum level.

2. Put a hose on the bleeder screw of the right front caliper and open the bleeder screw.

3. Have a helper depress the brake pedal until the hose is full and there are no air bubbles. Be sure that the bleeder screw is closed each time the pedal is released.

4. Put the free end of the hose on the bleeder screw of the slave cylinder and open the bleeder screw.

5. Keep stepping on the brake pedal. Close the bleeder screw on the caliper and release the brake pedal. Open the bleeder screw and repeat the process until no air bubbles show up at the mouth of the inlet line of the compensating tank.

Between operations, check and, if necessary, refill the compensating tank.

6. Close the bleeder screws on the caliper and slave cylinder and remove the hose.

7. Check the clutch operation and the fluid level.

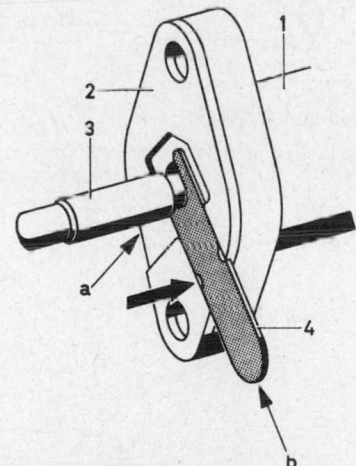

1. Clutch slave cylinder
2. Plastic shim
3. Thrust rod
4. Measuring gauge
    (Part No. 115 589 07 23 00)
(a)—Direction of measuring on lefthand drive vehicle with steering wheel and center shift, as well as on righthand drive vehicles with center shift
(b)—Direction of measuring on righthand drive vehicles with steering wheel shift

Wear limit has not been reached

AUTOMATIC TRANSMISSION

REMOVAL & INSTALLATION

Mercedes-Benz automatic transmissions are removed as a unit with the engine. Consult the "Engine Mechanical" section for removal and installation procedures concerning a given engine.

PAN AND FILTER REPLACEMENT

1. Drain the transmission of all fluid by loosening the dipstick tube.

2. Remove the transmission pan.

3. Remove the bolt or bolts which retain the filter to the transmission.

Bottom view of automatic transmission showing dipstick tube (1), converter drain plug (2) and pan (3)

4. Remove the filter and replace it with a new one.

5. Install the transmission pan, using a new gasket.

6. Refill the transmission to the proper level with the specified brand of fluid.

SELECTOR ROD LINKAGE ADJUSTMENT

NOTE: Before performing this adjustment on any Mercedes-Benz vehicle, be sure that the vehicle is resting on its wheels. No part of the vehicle may be jacked for this adjustment.

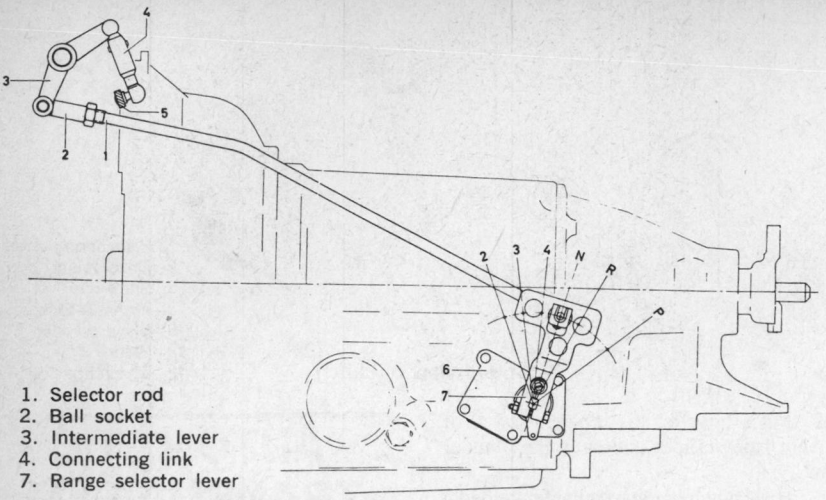

1. Selector rod
2. Ball socket
3. Intermediate lever
4. Connecting link
7. Range selector lever

Column mounted selector rod linkage—W3A 040

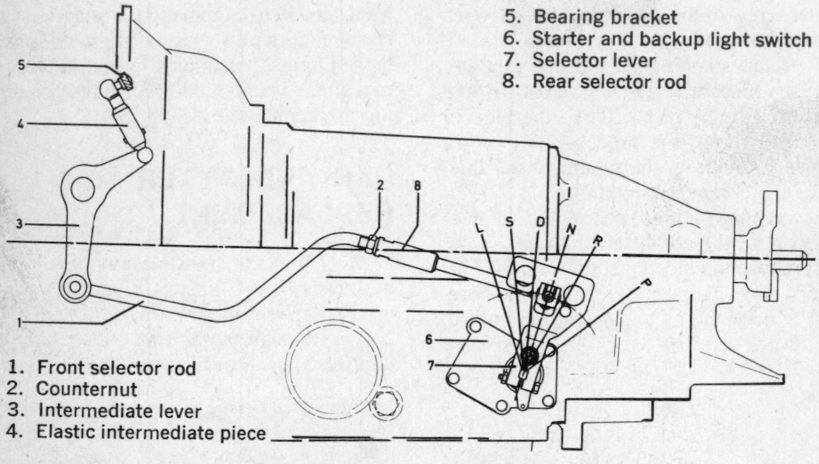

5. Bearing bracket
6. Starter and backup light switch
7. Selector lever
8. Rear selector rod

1. Front selector rod
2. Counternut
3. Intermediate lever
4. Elastic intermediate piece

Selector rod linkage on the W4A 040 and W4B 025

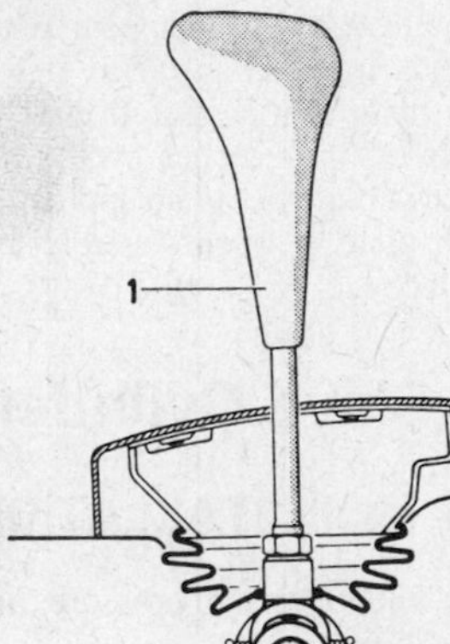

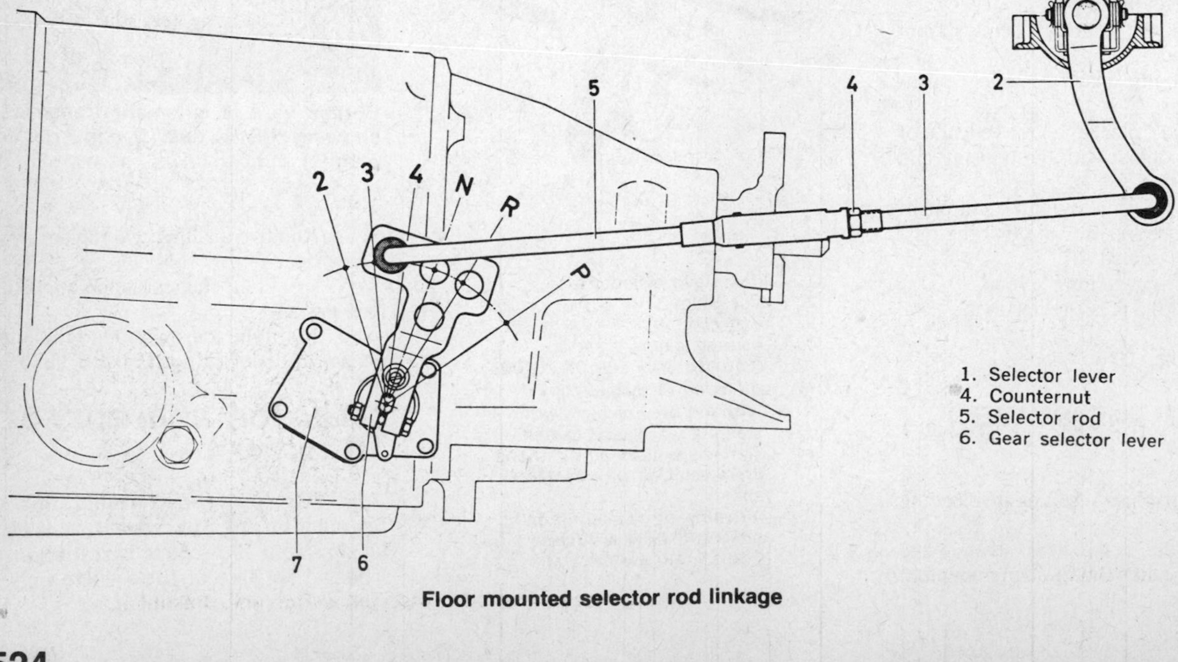

1. Selector lever
4. Counternut
5. Selector rod
6. Gear selector lever

Floor mounted selector rod linkage

Column Mounted Linkage

See the "Transmission Application" chart in the specifications for Transmission Application

W3A 040

1. Loosen the counternut on the ball socket.

2. Disconnect the selector rod from the shift lever bracket.

3. Set the transmission selector lever and the selector rod in Neutral.

4. Adjust the length of the selector rod until the ball socket aligns with the end of the ball on the intermediate lever.

5. Attach the ball socket to the intermediate lever, making sure that the play in the selector lever in position Three (D) and Four (S) is about equal.

6. Tighten the counternut on the ball socket.

W3A 040 (380SEL, 450SE AND 450SEL ONLY), W4B 025 AND W4A 040

1. Loosen the counternut on the rear selector rod while holding both recesses of the front selector rod with an open end wrench.

2. Disconnect the selector rod from the selector lever.

3. Set the selector lever on the transmission and on the column to Neutral.

4. Adjust the selector rod until the bearing pin is aligned with the bearing bushing in the selector lever.

5. Connect the rear selector lever to the selector rod and secure it with the lock. Be sure that the clearance of the selector lever in D and S is equal.

6. Tighten the locknut on the rear selector rod while holding the front selector rod as in Step 1.

Floor Mounted Linkage

NOTE: The vehicle must be standing with the weight normally distributed on all four wheels. No jacks may be used.

1. Disconnect the selector rod from the selector lever.

2. Set the selector lever in Neutral and make sure that there is approximately 1 mm clearance between the selector lever and the N stop of the selector gate.

3. Adjust the length of the selector rod so that it can be attached free of tension.

4. Retighten the counternut.

STARTER LOCKOUT AND BACK-UP LIGHT SWITCH ADJUSTMENT

1. Disconnect the selector rod and move the selector lever on the transmission to position Neutral.

2. Tighten the clamping screw prior to making adjustments.

3. Loosen the adjusting screw and insert the locating pin through the driver into the locating hole in the shift housing.

4. Tighten the adjusting screw and remove the locating pin.

5. Move the selector lever to position N and connect the selector rod so that there is no tension.

6. Check to be sure that the engine cannot be started in Neutral or Park.

KICKDOWN SWITCH

1. The kickdown position of the solenoid valve is controlled by the accelerator pedal.

2. Push the accelerator pedal against the kickdown limit stop. In this position the throttle lever should rest against the full load stop of the venturi control unit.

3. Adjustments are made by loosening the clamping screw on the return lever on the accelerator pedal shaft and turning the shaft. Tighten the clamping screw again.

CONTROL PRESSURE ROD

All Except 190, 1981 and Later 300, 380 and 500 Models

230

1. Remove the vacuum control unit from the carburetor.

1. Control pressure rod
2. Bellcrank
3. Screw
4. Bellcrank

Control pressure rod adjustment—230

2. Disconnect the automatic choke connecting rod so the throttle valve rests against the idle stop.

3. Loosen the screw and turn the levers against each other so the control rod rests against the idle stop.

4. Tighten the screw and depress the accelerator to the kickdown position. The throttle valve must rest against the full throttle stop. If necessary adjust the full throttle stop (see Fuel System).

5. Install the vacuum control unit on the distributor and connect the automatic choke rod.

DIESEL ENGINES

The control pressure rod can only be adjusted with a special gauge available only from Mercedes-Benz dealers.

6-CYLINDER ENGINES

1. Disconnect the control pressure rod.
2. Push the angle lever in the direction of the arrow.
3. Push the control pressure rod rearward against the stop and adjust its length so there is no binding.

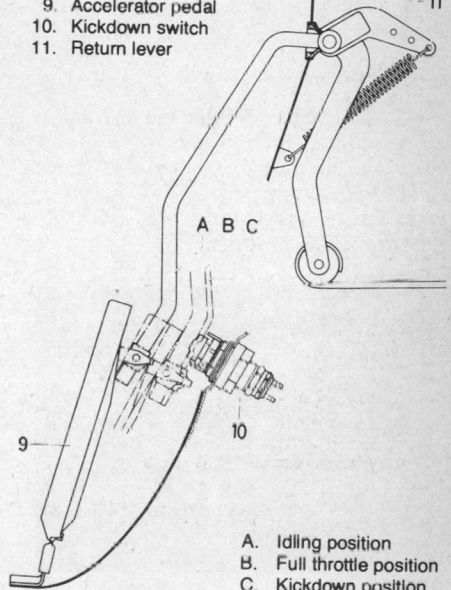

9. Accelerator pedal
10. Kickdown switch
11. Return lever

A. Idling position
B. Full throttle position
C. Kickdown position

Kickdown switch adjustment

1. Selector range lever
2. Washer
3. Adjusting screw
4. Shaft
5. Locating pin
6. Clamping screw

(a)—Column shift for left-hand and right-hand drive vehicles 220/8, 220 D/8, 230/8, 280 S/8, 280 SE/8 and 300 SEL/8.

(b)—Steering wheel shift for left-hand drive vehicles (220/8, 220 D/8, 230/8, 250/8)

(c)—Steering wheel shift for right-hand drive vehicles (220/8, 220 D/8, 230/8, 250/8)

(d)—Steering wheel shift for left-hand drive vehicles (280S/8, 280 SE/8, 300 SEL/8, 280 SE/3.5 and 300 SEL/3.5)

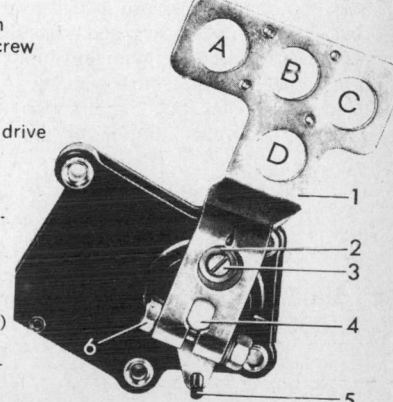

Starter lockout and backup light switch adjustment

57. Control pressure rod
58. Ball socket
59. Counternut
120. Angle lever
144. Connecting rod

Control pressure rod adjustment—6-cylinder engine

4. Tighten the counternut after adjustment.

V8 Engines

1. Remove the air filter and disconnect the control pressure linkage.
2. The throttle valve should rest against the idle speed stop.
3. Push the regulating lever and angle lever to the idle position.

7. Roller
11. Connecting rod
12. Bearing bracket
13. Control pressure rod
17. Regulating lever
18. Stop pin
19. Gate lever
20. Angle lever
31. Connecting rod

Control pressure rod adjustment—1978–80 V8 engines

4. Push the control pressure rod completely rearward against the stop and adjust the length of the rod so there is no tension.
5. When checking the rod for length, hold it to the left of the socket, not above to compensate for rotary motion of the linkage.

CONTROL PRESSURE CABLE—1981 AND LATER

380SE, 380SEC, 380SEL, 380SL, 380SLC, 500SEC and 500SEL

1. Remove the air cleaner.
2. Loosen the clamping screw.
3. Push the ball socket back, then carefully forward until a slight resistance is felt.

At this point, tighten the clamp screw.
4. Install the air cleaner.

Turbodiesels

1. Pry off the ball socket.
2. Push the ball socket back, then pull carefully forward until a slight resistance is felt.
3. Hold the ball socket above the ball head. The drag lever should rest against the stop.
4. Adjust the cable at the adjusting screw so that the ball socket can be attached with no strain.

190D

1. Remove the ball socket (19) and extend the telescoping rod (8) to its full length.

Control pressure cable adjustment—190D

2. Pull the control cable forward until a slight resistance is felt. Hold the ball socket over the ball head and engage tension free.
3. Adjust by using the telescoping rod if so required.

190E

1. Turn the adjusting screw (15) inward until the compression nipple on the spacing sleeve (17) has approximately 1mm of play left.
2. Unscrew the adjusting screw until the tip of the pointer rests directly above the groove on the adjusting screw.

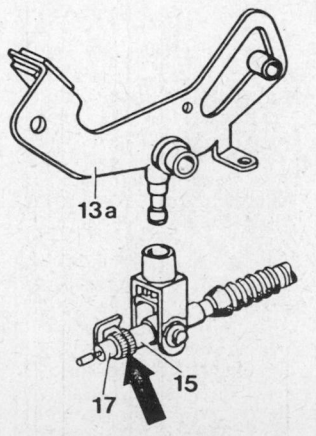

Control pressure cable adjustment—190E

DRIVE AXLE

Mercedes-Benz automobiles use either two or three piece driveshafts to connect the transmission to a hypoid independent rear axle. All models covered in this book use independent rear suspension with open or enclosed driveshafts to the rear wheels.

Driveshaft and U-Joints

REMOVAL & INSTALLATION

230, 240D, 300D, 300CD, 300TD, 230, 280E and 280CE

Matchmark all driveshaft connections prior to removal.

1. Remove the equalizer and disconnect the parking brake cables.
2. Remove the bolts which secure the two brackets to the chassis at the front and rear and remove the brackets. It may be necessary to lower the exhaust system slightly to allow access to the left hand bolts on the rear bracket.
3. Loosen the nut on the driveshaft about 2 turns without pushing the rubber sleeve back (it slides along). On a two-piece shaft, only loosen the front clamp nut.
4. Remove the nuts which secure the attaching plate to the transmission flange and rear axle.

NOTE: A new coupling flange is used on 1981 and later, 280E and 280CE models. The new coupling flange uses a thinner washer in place of the previous self-locking hex nut and thicker washers. Do not mix the two types.

5. Remove the bolts which secure the intermediate bearing(s) to the chassis. Push the driveshaft together and slightly down, and remove the driveshaft from the vehicle.

NOTE: If possible, do not separate the parts of the driveshaft since each driveshaft is balanced at the factory. If separation is necessary, all parts must be marked and reassembled in the same relative positions to assure that the driveshafts will remain reasonably well balanced.

6. Installation is the reverse of removal.
7. Pack the cavities of the two centering sleeves with special Mercedes-Benz grease.
8. Install the driveshaft and attach the intermediate bearing(s) to the chassis.
9. Rock the car backward and forward several times to be sure that the driveshaft is properly centered without forcing.
10. Prior to tightening the clamp nuts on a three piece driveshaft, be sure that the intermediate shaft does not contact either the front or rear intermediate bearing. The clearance between the intermediate shaft and the bearing should be the same at both ends.

All Other Models

NOTE: Steps 1–3 apply to 4 cylinder and V8 models. Matchmark all driveshaft connections prior to removal.

1. Fold the torsion bar down after disconnecting the level control linkage (if equipped).
2. Remove the exhaust system.
3. Remove the heat shield from the frame.
4. Support the transmission with a jack and completely remove the rear engine mount crossmember.
5. Without sliding the rubber sleeve back, loosen the clamp nut approximately two turns (the rubber sleeve will slide along).

1981 driveshafts use a new design coupling flange with thinner washers

NOTE: On 3 piece driveshafts, only the front clamp nut need be loosened.

6. Unscrew the U-joint mounting flange from the U-joint plate.

NOTE: The 1981 and later 380SEL and 380SEC uses a new design coupling flange with thinner washers under a new hex nut. The previous design used thicker washers. Do not mix the two types.

7. Bend back the locktabs and remove the bolts that attach the driveshaft to the rear axle pinion yoke.
8. Remove the bolts which attach the intermediate bearing(s) to the frame. Push the driveshaft together slightly and remove it from the vehicle.
9. Try not to separate the driveshafts. If it is absolutely necessary, matchmark all components so that they can be reassembled in the same order.
10. Installation is the reverse of removal. Always use new self-locking nuts. After the driveshaft is installed, rock the car back and forth several times to settle the driveshaft. Make sure that neither intermediate shaft is binding against either intermediate bearing, and that the clearance between the intermediate bearing and the driveshaft is the same at both ends.

U–JOINT OVERHAUL

For all U–Joint overhaul procedures, please refer to "U–Joint/CV–Joint Overhaul" in the Unit Repair section.

Axle Shaft

NOTE: The rubber covered joints are filled with special oil. If they are disassembled for any reason, they must be refilled with special oil.

REMOVAL & INSTALLATION

All Except 190D, 190E, 380SEC and 500SEC

MODELS WITHOUT TORQUE COMPENSATOR (TORSION BAR)

NOTE: On the 280E only, axle shafts identified with a yellow paint dot or part No. 107 350 07 10 (left) or Part No. 107 350 0810 (right) can be installed.

Most models do not use a torque compensator (torsion bar) which is actually a steel bar used to locate the rear axle under acceleration. In general, only the large sedans use a torque compensator, but it is wise to check for one prior to servicing the axle shaft. The illustrations apply to either type.

1. Jack up the rear of the car and remove the wheel and center axle hold-down bolt (in hub).
2. Remove the brake caliper and suspend it from a hook.

Removing the lock-ring (26) from the axle shaft with pliers (1) or a screwdriver

Axle shaft markings (r)

3. Drain the differential oil and place a jack under the differential housing.
4. Unbolt the rubber mount from the chassis and the differential housing, then remove the differential housing cover to expose the ring and pinion gears.
5. Press the shaft from the axle flange. If necessary, loosen the shock absorber.
6. Using a pry bar, remove the axle lock ring inside the differential case.
7. Pull the axle from the housing by pulling the splined end from the side gears, with the spacer.

NOTE: Axle shafts are stamped R and L for right and left units. Always use new lockrings.

8. Installation is the reverse of removal. Fill the rear axle. New radial seal rings are used on 1980 and later models. Lubricate the outside diameter of rubber covered radial sealing rings with hypoid gear lubricant prior to installation.

— CAUTION —

Check end-play of the lockring in the groove. If necessary, install a thicker lockring or spacer to eliminate all end-play, while still allowing the lockring to rotate. Do not allow the joints in the axle shaft to hang free or the joint bearing may be damaged and leak.

MODELS WITH TORQUE COMPENSATOR (TORSION BAR)

1. Drain the oil from the rear axle.
2. Disconnect and plug the brake lines.
3. Loosen the connecting rod and unscrew the torsion bar bearing bracket. Lower the exhaust system slightly and remove the torsion bar.
4. Loosen the shock absorber.
5. Remove the bolt which attaches the rear axle shaft to the rear axle shaft flange.
6. Disconnect the brake cable control. Remove the bracket from the wheel carrier, remove the rubber sleeve, and push back the cover.
7. Force the rear axle shaft out of the flange with a suitable tool.
8. Support the rear axle with a jack.
9. Remove the rubber mount.
10. Clean the axle housing and remove the cover fan from the housing.

NOTE: The axle shafts are the floating type and can be compressed in the constant velocity joints.

11. Remove the locking ring from the end of the axle shafts which engage the side gears in the differential.
12. Disengage the axle shaft from the side gear and remove the axle shaft together with the spacer.

— CAUTION —

Do not hang the outer constant velocity joint in a free position (without any support) as the shaft may be damaged and the constant velocity joint housing may leak.

13. Installation is the reverse of removal.

14. If either axle shaft is replaced, be sure that the proper replacement shaft is installed. Axle shafts are marked L and R for left and right.

15. Check the end-play between the lock-ring on the axle shaft and the side gear. There should be no noticeable end-play, but the lock-ring should be able to turn in the groove.

16. Be sure to bleed the brakes and fill the rear axle with the proper quantity and type of lubricant. New radial seal rings are used on 1980 and later models. Lubricate the outside diameter of rubber covered radial seal rings with hypoid gear lubricant prior to installation.

190D, 190E, 380SEC and 500SEC

1. Loosen, but do not remove, the axle shaft collar nut.

2. Raise the rear of the vehicle and support it on jackstands.

3. Disconnect the axle shaft from the hub assembly. On the 190, make sure that while loosening the locking screws, the bit is seated properly in the multi-tooth profile of the screws.

4. Remove the self-locking screws that attach the inner CV-joint to the connecting flange on the differential. Always loosen the screws in a crosswise manner.

Lock the collar nut on the 190 at the crush flange (arrow)

NOTE: Make sure that the end cover on the inner CV-joint is not damaged when separated from the connecting flange.

5. While supporting the axle shaft, use a slide hammer or the like and press the axle shaft out of the hub assembly.

6. Tilt the axle shaft down and remove it.

——————— CAUTION ———————
Make sure that the CV-joint boots are not damaged during the removal process.
—————————————————————

7. Installation is in the reverse order of removal. Please note the following:

a. Always clean the connecting flanges before installation.

b. Always use new self-locking screws. On the 190, lubricate the screw threads and contact faces with oil before installing. Tighten the screws to 51 ft. lbs. (70 Nm) on the 190 and 90–105 ft. lbs. (125–145 Nm) on the others. Always tighten the screws in a crosswise pattern.

c. Tighten the axle shaft collar nut to 203–230 ft. lbs. (280–320 Nm) on the 190 and 22 ft. lbs. (30 Nm) on the others. On the 190, lock the collar nut at the crush flange (see illustration).

Differential

REMOVAL & INSTALLATION

All Models Except 190D and 190E

1. Drain the oil from the rear axle.

2. On cars without torque compensation, remove the brake caliper and suspend it on a hook.

3. On cars with torque compensation, disconnect the brake cable control, unbolt the holding bracket on the wheel carrier, remove the rubber sleeve and push the cover back.

4. Remove the bolt from both sides that holds the rear axle shaft to the flange.

5. Press the rear axle shaft out of the flange.

6. If required, loosen the right hand rear shock absorber and lower it to the stop.

7. Remove the exhaust system, if necessary.

8. On sedans remove the heat shield, if equipped.

9. Loosen the clamp nut and remove the intermediate bearing from the floor pan. On 3 piece driveshafts, only remove the front nut.

10. Unbolt the driveshaft and remove it.

11. Support the rear axle housing.

12. Unbolt the rear rubber mount from the frame floor.

13. On the 500, 450 and 380 series the 280SE and the 300SD, lower the jack until the self-locking nuts are accessible.

14. Unbolt the rear axle center housing from the rear axle carrier.

15. On all other models, remove the bolt from the rubber mount on the cover of the rear axle housing. Fold back the rubber mat in the trunk and remove the rubber plugs; unbolt the rear axle center housing from the rear axle carrier.

16. Lower the rear axle center housing and remove it with the axle shaft. Do not allow the axle shafts to hang free, or the seals will be damaged, resulting in leaks.

17. Installation is the reverse of removal. Install new self-locking nuts, adjust the parking brake and fill the rear axle with the correct fluid.

190D and 190E

1. Drain the oil from the differential.

2. Remove the exhaust shielding plate.

3. Loosen the clamp nut on the driveshaft. Unscrew the intermediate bearing screws at the floor pan and remove.

4. Disconnect the driveshaft from the universal flange of the drive pinion and push it forward to remove. Position the drive-shaft out of the way and support it with wire.

5. Disconnect the inner CV-joints from the differential connecting flange and wire them out of the way.

6. Support the differential with a floor jack.

7. Remove the four bolts and two locking plates at the rear differential mount.

8. Loosen and remove the screw from the front mount where it connects to the rear axle carrier.

9. Lower the jack and remove the differential.

To install:

1. Raise the differential into position.

2. Position the screw in the front mount but do not tighten it.

3. Install the rear mount screws and plates. Tighten to 29–33 ft. lbs. (40–45 Nm). Now tighten the front mount screw to 33 ft. lbs. (45 Nm).

NOTE: Always use new self-locking screws and plates.

4. Position the driveshaft and install the intermediate bearing. Do not tighten it yet.

5. Tighten the driveshaft clamp nut to 25–29 ft. lbs. (35–40 Nm). Now tighten the intermediate bearing screws to 19 ft. lbs. (25 Nm).

6. Installation of the remaining components is in the reverse order of removal.

OVERHAUL

For differential overhaul procedures, please refer to ''Drive Axles'' in the Unit Repair section.

REAR SUSPENSION

Springs

REMOVAL & INSTALLATION

190D and 190E

1. Raise the rear of the vehicle and support it with jackstands. Remove the wheel.

2. Disconnect the holding clamps for the spring link cover and then remove the cover.

3. Install a spring compressor and compress the spring until the spring link is free of all load.

4. Disconnect the lower end of the shock absorber.

5. Increase the tension on the spring compressor and remove the spring.

6. Installation is in the reverse order of removal. Please note the following:

a. Position the spring so that the end of the lower coil is seated in the impression of the spring seat and the upper coil

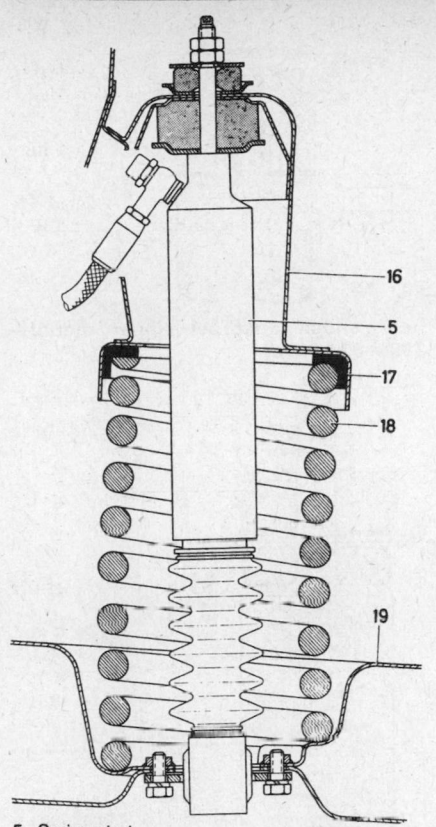

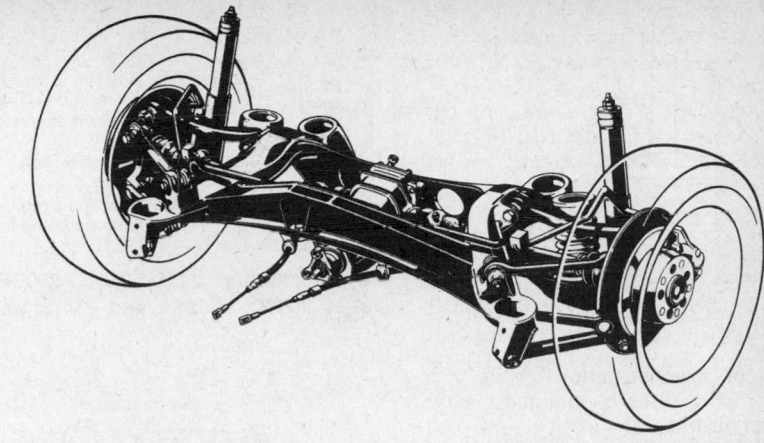

Rear suspension on the 190D and 190E. Five separate links keep the wheels in alignment under all conditions.

5. Spring strut
16. Dome on frame floor
17. Rubber mount
18. Rear spring
19. Semi-trailing arm

Rear spring—380SL, 380SLC, 450SL and 450SLC

seats properly in the rubber mount in the frame floor.

b. Do not release tension on the spring compressor until the lower end of the shock absorber is connected and tightened to 47 ft. lbs. (65 Nm).

380SL, 380SLC, 450SL and 450SLC

1. Jack up the rear of the car.
2. Remove the rear shock absorber.
3. With a floor jack, raise the control arm to approximately a horizontal position. Install a spring compressor to aid in this operation.
4. Carefully lower the jack until the control arm contacts the stop on the rear axle support.
5. Remove the spring and spring compressor with great care.
6. Installation is the reverse of removal. For ease of installation, attach the rubber seats to the springs with masking tape.

All Others

1. Raise and support the rear of the car and the trailing arm.
2. Remove the rear shock absorber.
3. Be sure that the upper shock absorber attachment is released first.
4. Compress the spring with a spring compressor.

5. Remove the rear spring with the rubber mount.
6. Installation is the reverse of removal. When installing the shock absorber, tighten the lower mount first.

Shock Absorber
REMOVAL & INSTALLATION
190D, 190E, 380SL, 380SLC, 450SL and 450SLC

1. Jack up the rear of the car and support the control arm.

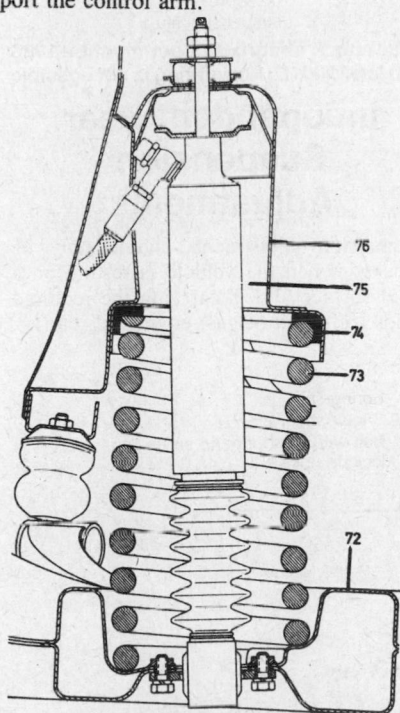

72. Semi-trailing arm
73. Rear spring
74. Rubber mounting
75. Shock absorber or spring strut
76. Dome on frame floor

Rear spring—all models except 190D, 190E, 380SL, 380SLC, 450SL and 450SLC

2. From inside the trunk (sedans), remove the rubber cap, locknut, and hex nut from the upper mount of the shock absorber. On 380SL and 450SL, the upper mount of the rear shock absorber is accessible after removing the top, top flap, rear seat, backrest and lining. On the 380SLC and 450SLC, remove the rear seat, backrest and cover plate.

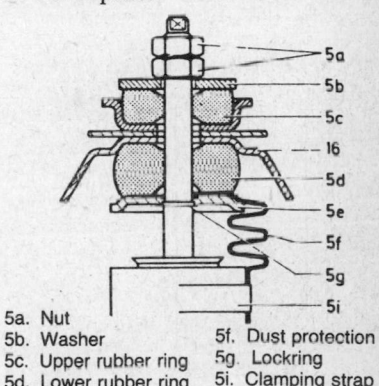

5a. Nut
5b. Washer
5c. Upper rubber ring
5d. Lower rubber ring
5e. Plate
5f. Dust protection
5g. Lockring
5i. Clamping strap
16. Dome on frame floor

Rear shock absorber upper mount—1981 and later 300SD, 380SE, 380SEC, 380SEL, 380SL, 380SLC, 450SL, 450SLC, 500SEC and 500SEL (5f not used in U.S.)

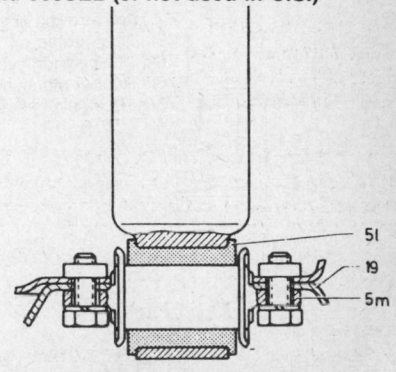

5l. Rubber mounting
5m. Fastening clip
19. Semi-trailing arm

Rear shock absorber lower mount—all 380 models, 450SL, 450SLC, 500SEC and 500SEL

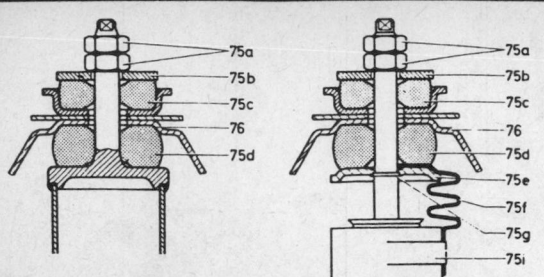

75a. Nuts
75b. Washer
75c. Upper rubber ring
75d. Lower rubber ring
75e. Plate
75f. Dust protection
75g. Locking ring
75i. Clamping strap
76. Dome on frame floor

Rear shock absorber upper mount—1978–83 230 and 240D, 280E, 280CE, 280SE, 1978–80 300SD, 300D, 300CD, 1979–80 300TD, 450SEL and 6.9 (5f not used in U.S.)

3. Unbolt the mounting for the rear shock absorber at the bottom and remove the shock absorber.
4. Installation is the reverse of removal.

All Other Models

1. Remove the rear seat and backrest.
2. Remove the cover from the rear wall.
3. Raise and support the car and the trailing arm.
4. Loosen the nuts on the upper mount. Remove the washer and rubber ring.
5. Loosen the lower mount and remove the shock absorber downward.
6. Installation is the reverse of removal. Tighten the upper mounting nut to the end of the threads.

Bilstein

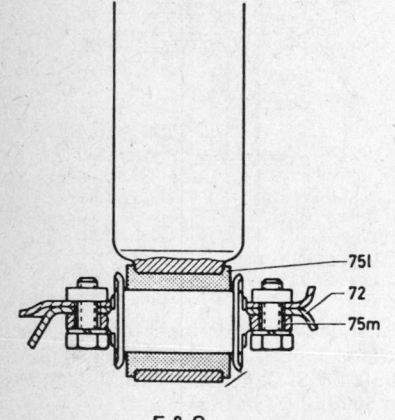

F & S

72. Semi-trailing arm
75f. Dust protection
75k. Suspension eye
75l. Rubber mounting
75m. Fastening stirrup

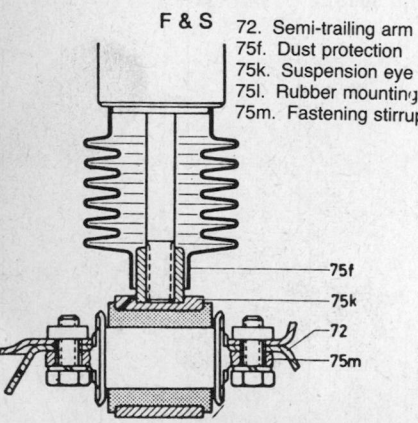

Rear shock absorber lower mount—1978–83 230 and 240D, 280E, 280CE, 280SE, 1978–80 300SD, 300D, 300CD, 1979–80 300TD, 450SEL and 6.9

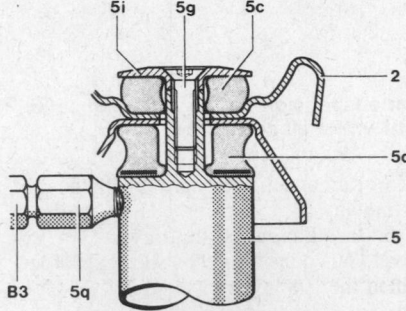

2. Frame—transverse member
5. Suspension strut
5c. Upper rubber mount
5d. Lower rubber mount
5g. Special screw
5i. Plate
5q. Stud
B3. Pressure line (pressure hose), pressure reservoir—suspension strut

Rear shock absorber upper mount—1983 and later 300TD. Retrofitting is not possible

Independent Rear Suspension Adjustments

Suspension adjustments should only be checked when the vehicle is resting on a level surface and is carrying the required fluids (full tank of gas, engine oil, etc.).

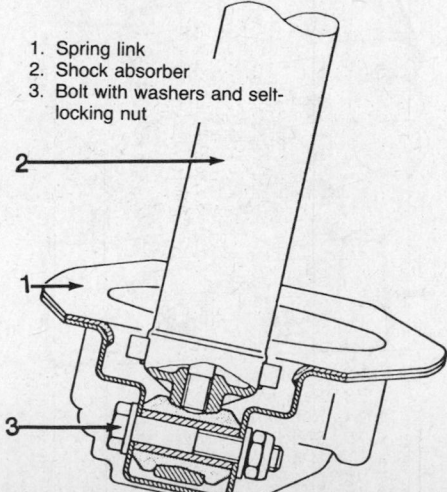

1. Spring link
2. Shock absorber
3. Bolt with washers and selt-locking nut

Rear shock absorber lower mount—190D and 190E

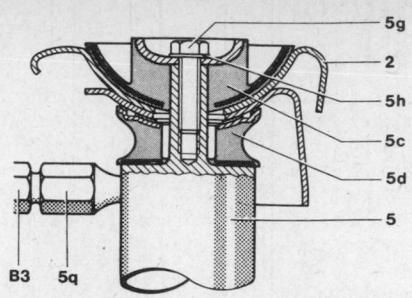

Rear shock absorber upper mount—1981–82 300TD

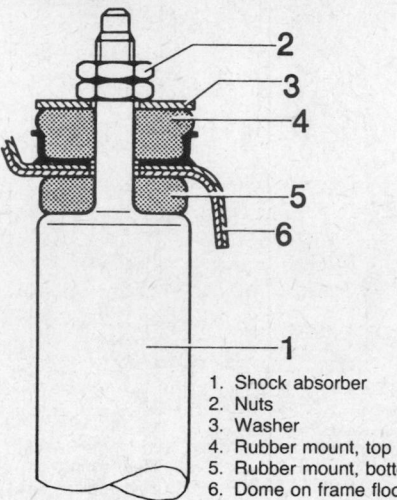

1. Shock absorber
2. Nuts
3. Washer
4. Rubber mount, top
5. Rubber mount, bottom
6. Dome on frame floor

Rear shock absorber upper mount—190D and 190E

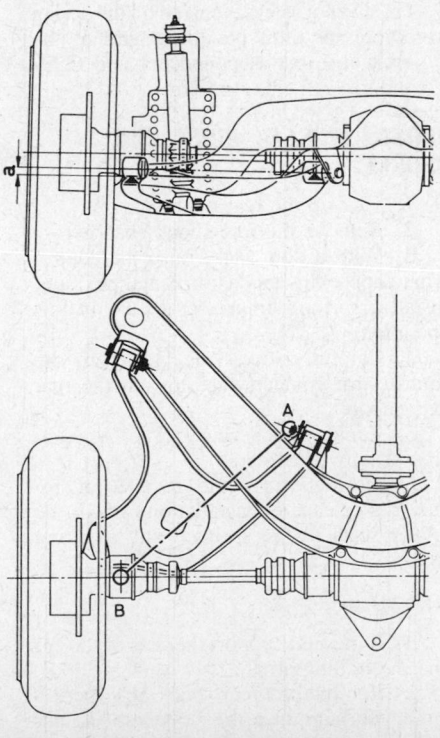

Rear wheel camber measurement on all models except the 190D, 190E, 380SL, 380SLC, 450SL and 450SLC

CAMBER

All Models

Rear wheel camber is determined by the position of the control arm. The difference in height (a) between the axis of the control arm mounting point on the rear axle subframe and lower edge of the cup on the constant velocity joint is directly translated in degrees of camber.

TOE-IN

Toe-in, on the rear wheels, is dependent on the camber of the rear wheels.

Hydropneumatic Suspension

The hydropneumatic suspension is ued on the 380SEL, 500SEL and the 6.9. Service of this system should be left to a Mercedes-Benz dealer or other qualified service establishment.

OPERATION

The system is a gas pressure system with a hydraulic level control. The car is supported by 4 suspension struts that also serve as shock absorbers. The suspension consists of a strut and pressure reservoir, connected by a line. The load is transmitted to the pressure reservoirs via the struts, resulting in an adjustment of the gas cushion in each pressure reservoir.

To regulate the level of the car, the oil level in the struts is increased or reduced by the hydraulic system, composed of an oil pump, pressure regulator, main pressure reservoir, and oil reservoir. The pressure regulator also contains a level selector valve as part of the unit.

The oil volume is controlled by a levelling valve at the front and rear axle and by the level selector valve. This allows adjustment of the vehicle level by using the level selector switch on the dashboard. When the engine is not running, the main pressure reservoir supplies the system.

A hydraulic oil pump, driven by the engine, pumps oil from the oil reservoir to the main pressure reservoir. When the maximum oil pressure in the main reservoir is reached, the pressure regulator in the reservoir valve unit reverses the flow of oil. If the pressure in the reservoir drops to a pre-set minimum (as a result of operation of the system) the pressure regulator again reverses the flow of oil, pumping oil into the pressure reservoir until maximum pressure is reached, when the flow will be reversed once more.

The oil in the pressure reservoir is connected to the level selector valve and to the individual levelling valves by pressure lines. If the car level drops, due to an increased load, the levelling valve opens the passage to the suspension struts, allowing the pas-

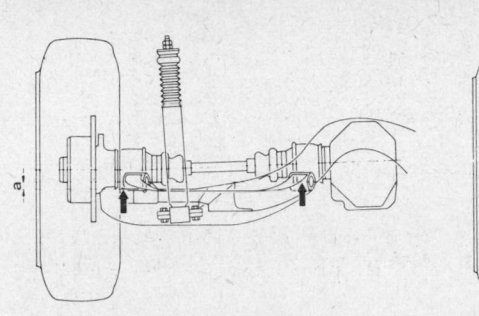

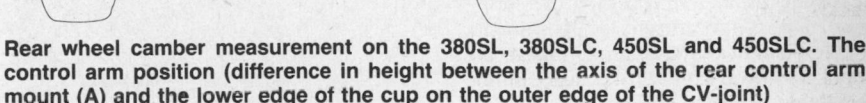

Rear wheel camber measurement on the 380SL, 380SLC, 450SL and 450SLC. The control arm position (difference in height between the axis of the rear control arm mount (A) and the lower edge of the cup on the outer edge of the CV-joint)

sage of oil until normal vehicle attitude is reached. If the level rises, due to a decreased load, the levelling valve opens and allows oil to flow from the suspension struts back to the oil reservoir, until the car resumes its normal level.

FRONT SUSPENSION

Springs

REMOVAL & INSTALLATION

190D and 190E

1. Raise the front of the vehicle and support it with jackstands. Remove the wheel.

2. Remove the engine compartment lining underneath the vehicle (if so equipped).

3. Install a spring compressor so that at least 7½ coils are engaged.

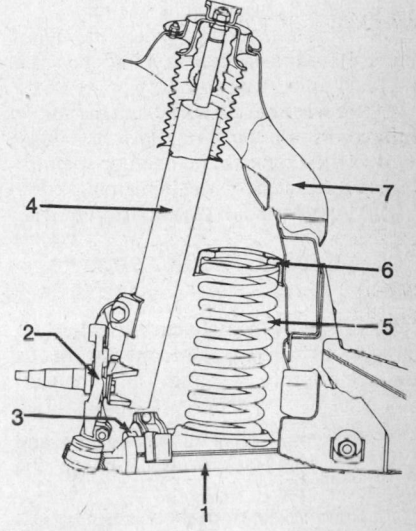

1. Wishbone (control arm)
2. Steering knuckle
3. Torsion bar
4. Damper strut
5. Front spring
6. Spring-rubber mount
7. Front end

Front spring—190D and 190E

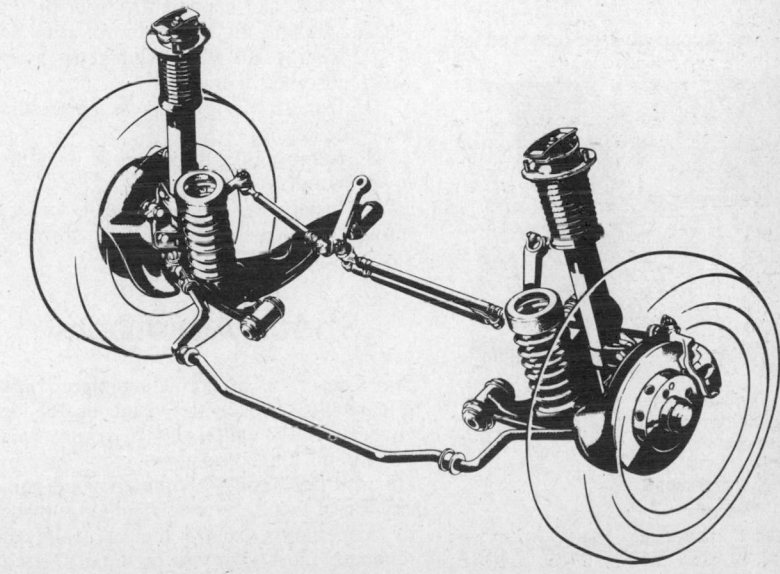

Front suspension—190D and 190E

4. Support the lower control arm with a floor jack and then loosen the retaining nut at the upper end of the damper strut.

— CAUTION —

NEVER loosen the damper strut retaining nut unless the wheels are on the ground, the control arm is supported or the springs have been removed.

5. Lower the jack under the control arm slightly and then remove the spring toward the front.

6. On installation, position the spring between the control arm and the upper mount so that when the control arm is raised, the end of the lower coil will be seated in the impression in the control arm.

7. Use the jack and raise the control arm until the spring is held securely.

8. Using a new nut, tighten the upper end of the damper strut to 44 ft. lbs. (60 Nm).

9. Slowly ease the tension on the spring compressor until the spring is seated properly and then remove the compressor.

10. Installation of the remaining components is in the reverse order of removal.

380SL, 380SLC, 450SL and 450SLC

NOTE: Be extremely careful when attempting to remove the front springs as they are compressed and under considerable load.

1. Raise the front of the vehicle and support it with jackstands. Remove the wheels.

2. Remove the front shock absorber and disconnect the sway bar.

3. First punchmark the position of the eccentric adjusters, then loosen the hex bolts.

4. Support the lower control arm with a jack.

5. Knock out the eccentric pins and gradually lower the arm until spring tension is relieved.

6. The spring can now be removed.

1. Front axle carrier
3. Lower control arm
4. Upper control arm
10. Front spring
11. Front shock absorber
12. Torsion bar
29. Rubber mounting
31. Rubber mounting for front spring

Front spring removal—450SL, 450SLC, 380SL and 380SLC

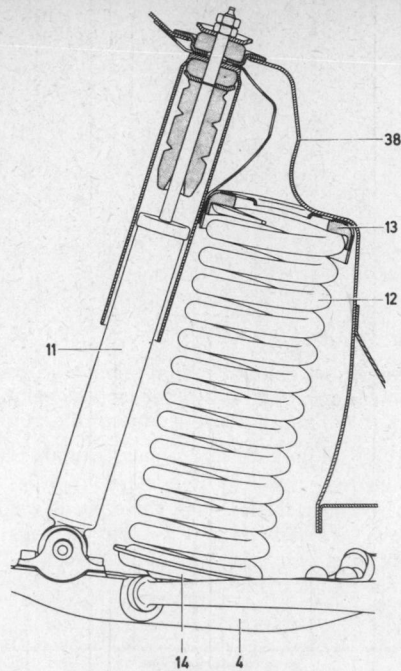

4. Lower control arm
11. Front shock absorber
12. Front spring
13. Rubber mount for front spring
14. Retainer for front spring
38. Front end

Front spring—all models except 190D, 190E, 380SL, 380SLC, 450SL and 450SLC

NOTE: Check caster and camber after installing a new spring.

7. Installation is the reverse of removal.

8. For ease of installation, tape the rubber mounts to the springs.

9. If the eccentric adjusters were not matchmarked, install the eccentric bolts as illustrated under ''Front End Alignment''.

All Other Models

1. Raise and support the front of the car and support the lower control arm.

2. Remove the wheel. Unbolt the upper shock absorber mount.

3. Install a spring compressor and compress the spring.

4. Remove the front spring with the lower mount.

5. Installation is the reverse of removal. Tighten the upper shock absorber suspension.

Shock Absorbers

Shock absorbers are normally replaced only if leaking excessively (oil visible on outside cover) or if worn internally to a point where the car no longer rides smoothly and rebounds after hitting a bump. A good general test of shock absorber condition is made by bouncing the front of the car. If the car rebounds more than two or three times it can be assumed that the shock absorbers need replacement.

REMOVAL & INSTALLATION

380SL, 380SLC, 450SL, and 450SLC

1. For removal and installation of shock absorbers, it is best to jack up the front of the car until the weight is off of the wheels and support the car securely on jack stands.

2. When removing the shock absorbers, it is also wise to draw a simple diagram of the location of parts such as lockrings, rubber stops, locknuts and steel plates, since many shock absorbers require their own peculiar installation of these parts.

3. Raise the hood and locate the upper shock absorber mount.

4. Support the lower control arm with a jack.

5. Unbolt the mount for the shock absorber at the top. Remove the coolant expansion tank to allow access to the right front shock absorber.

6. Remove the nuts which secure the shock absorber to the lower control arm.

7. Push the shock absorber piston rod in, install the stirrup, and remove the shock absorber.

8. Remove the stirrup, since this must be installed on replacement shock absorbers.

9. Installation is the reverse of removal. Always use new bushings when installing replacement shock absorbers.

All Other Models (Except 190D and 190E)

1. Jack and support the car. Support the lower control arm.

2. Loosen the nuts on the upper shock absorber mount. Remove the plate and ring.

3. Place the shock absorber vertical to the lower control arm and remove the lower mounting bolts.

4. Remove the shock absorber.

5. Installation is the reverse of removal. On Bilstein shocks, do not confuse the upper and lower plates.

NOTE: The 1981 and later 380SEL shock absorber uses a protective plastic sleeve that must be installed between the lower retainer and lower rubber ring. Also, a slot is provided for holding the piston rod, in place of the 2 flats used previously.

NOTE: 380SEC shock absorbers have the same part number regardless of manufacturer. However, the shock absorbers on these cars have a larger diameter and narrower lower mounting eye than other models.

Damper Strut

REMOVAL & INSTALLATION

190D and 190E

1. Raise the front of the vehicle and support it with jackstands. Remove the wheel.

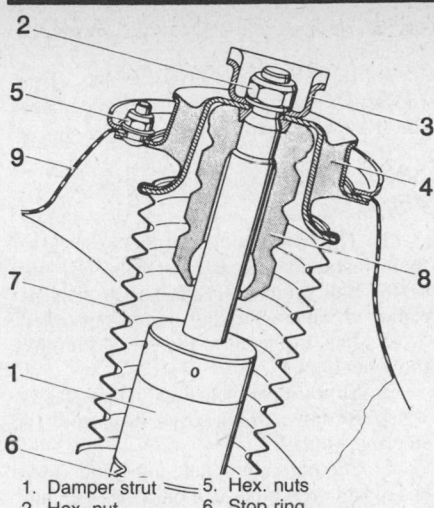

1. Damper strut
2. Hex. nut
3. Rebound stop
4. Rubber mount
5. Hex. nuts
6. Stop ring
7. Sleeve
8. Additional PU spring
9. Front end

Upper damper strut mounting—190D and 190E

2. Using a spring compressor, compress the spring until any load is removed from the lower control arm.

NOTE: When using a spring compressor, be sure that at least 7½ coils are engaged before applying tension.

3. Support the lower control arm with a floor jack. Loosen the retaining bolt for the upper end of the damper strut by holding the inner piston rod with an Allen wrench and then unscrewing the nut. *NEVER use an impact wrench on the retaining nut.*

—————— **CAUTION** ——————
Never unscrew the nut with the axle half at full rebound—the spring may fly out with considerable force, causing personal injury.

4. Unbolt the two screws and one nut and then disconnect the lower damper strut from the steering knuckle.

5. Remove the strut down and forward. Secure the steering knuckle in position so that it won't tilt.

6. Installation is in the reverse order of removal. Please note the following:
   a. When attaching the lower end of the damper strut to the steering knuckle, first position all three screws; next tighten the two lower screws to 72 ft. lbs. (100 Nm); finally, tighten the nut on the upper clamping connection screw to 54 ft. lbs. (75 Nm).
   b. Tighten the retaining nut on the upper end of the damper strut to 44 ft. lbs. (60 Nm).

Steering Knuckle and Ball Joints

CHECKING BALL JOINTS

1. To check the steering knuckles or ball joints, jack up the car, placing a jack

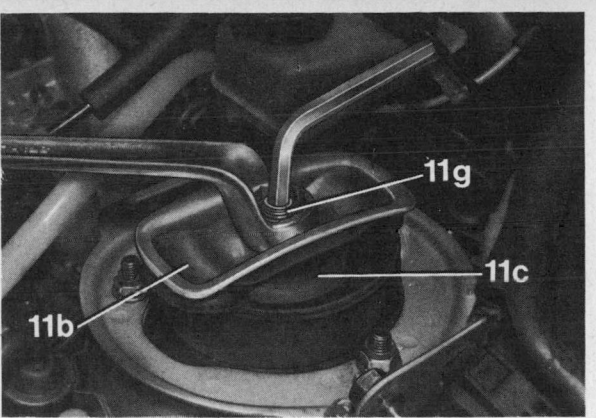

11b Rebound limiter
11c Rubber mount
11g Piston rod

Remove the upper damper strut retaining nut by locking the piston rod with an Allen wrench—190D and 190E

directly under the front spring plate. This unloads the front suspension to allow the maximum play to be observed.

2. Late model ball joints need to be replaced only if dried out with plainly visible wear and/or play.

REMOVAL & INSTALLATION

190D and 190E

1. Raise the front of the vehicle and support it with jackstands. Remove the wheel.

2. Install a spring compressor on the spring.

3. Remove the brake caliper and then wire it out of the way. Be careful not to damage the brake line.

4. Remove the brake disc and wheel hub.

5. Unscrew the three socket-head bolts and then remove the brake backing plate from the steering knuckle.

6. Tighten the spring compressor until

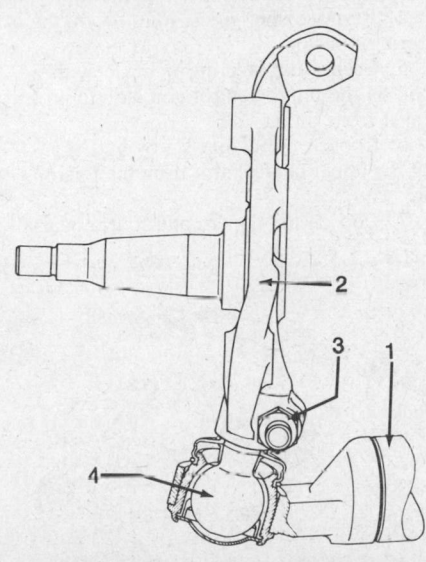

1. Wishbone
2. Steering knuckle
3. Bolt with nut
4. Ball joint

Steering knuckle/ball joint—190D and 190E

all tension and/or load has been removed from the lower control arm.

7. Disconnect the steering knuckle arm from the steering knuckle (this is the arm attached to the tie rod).

—————— **CAUTION** ——————
There must be no tension on the lower control arm.

8. Unscrew the three bolts and disconnect the lower end of the damper strut from the steering knuckle.

9. Remove the hex-head clamp nut at the supporting joint (lower ball joint).

10. Remove the steering knuckle.

11. Installation is in the reverse order of removal. Please note the following:
   a. Tighten the supporting joint clamp nut to 70 ft lbs. (125 Nm).
   b. Refer to the "Damper Strut Removal and Installation" procedure when connecting the lower end of the damper strut to the steering knuckle.

380SL, 380SLC, 450SL and 450SLC

1. This should only be done with the front shock absorber installed. If, however, the front shock absorber has been removed, the lower control arm should be supported with a jack and the spring should be clamped with a spring tensioner. In this case, the hex nut on the guide joint should not be loosened without the spring tensioner installed.

2. Jack up the front of the car and support it on jack stands.

3. Remove the wheel.

4. Remove the brake caliper.

5. Unbolt the steering relay lever from the steering knuckle. For safety, install spring clamps on the front springs.

6. Remove the hex nuts from the upper and lower ball joints.

7. Remove the ball joints from the steering knuckle with the aid of a puller.

8. Remove the steering knuckle.

9. Installation is the reverse of removal. Be sure that the seats for the pins of the ball joints are free of grease.

10. Bleed the brakes.

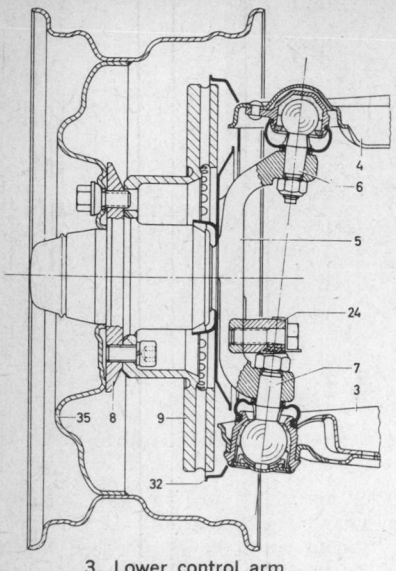

3. Lower control arm
4. Upper control arm
5. Steering knuckle
6. Guide joint
7. Supporting joint
8. Front wheel hub
9. Brake disc
24. Steering knuckle arm
32. Cover plate
35. Wheel

Steering knuckle/ball joint—380SL, 380SLC, 450SL and 450SLC

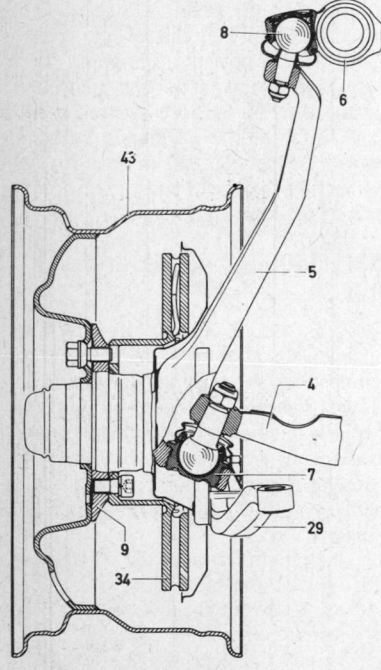

4. Lower control arm
5. Steering knuckle
6. Upper control arm
7. Support joint
8. Guide joint
9. Front wheel hub
29. Steering knuckle arm
34. Brake disc
43. Wheel

Steering knuckle/ball joint—all models except 190D, 190E, 380SL, 380SLC, 450SL and 450SLC

All Other Models

1. Raise and support the car. For safety, it's a good idea to install some type of clamp on the front spring. Position jack stands at the outside front against the lower control arms.
2. Remove the wheel.
3. Remove the steering knuckle arm from the steering knuckle.
4. Remove and suspend the brake caliper.
5. Remove the front wheel hub.
6. Loosen the brake hose holder on the cover plate.
7. Loosen the nut on the guide joint and remove the joint from the steering knuckle.
8. Loosen the nut on the support joint.
9. Swivel the steering knuckle outward and force the ball joint from the lower control arm.
10. Remove the steering knuckle.
11. If necessary, remove the cover plate from the steering knuckle.
12. Installation is the reverse of removal. Use self-locking nuts and adjust the wheel bearings.

Upper Control Arm

NOTE: The 190D and 190E models have no upper control arm.

REMOVAL & INSTALLATION

All Models Except 380SL, 380SLC, 450SC and 450SLC

1. Raise and support the car. Position jack stands at the outside front against the lower control arms.
2. Remove the wheel.
3. Loosen the nut on the guide joint.
4. Remove the guide joint from the steering knuckle.
5. Secure the steering knuckle with a hook on the upper control arm stop to prevent it from tilting.
6. Loosen the clamp screw and separate the upper control arm from the torsion bar.
7. Loosen the upper control arm bear-

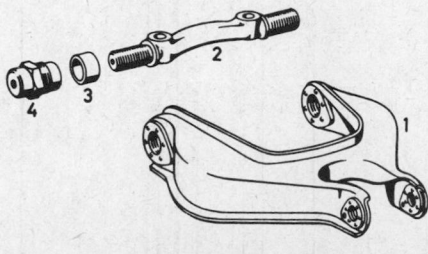

1. Upper control arm
2. Pivot pin
3. Rubber sealing ring
4. Threaded bushing

Upper control arm and pivot shaft

ing at the front and remove the upper control arm.
8. Installation is the reverse of removal. Use new self-locking nuts and check the front wheel alignment.

380SL, 380SLC, 450SL and 450SLC

1. The front shock absorbers should remain installed. Never loosen the hex nuts of the ball joints with the shock absorber removed, unless a spring clamp is installed.
2. Jack the front of the car and remove the wheel.
3. Support the front end on jack stands.
4. Remove the steering arm from the steering knuckle.
5. Separate the brake line and brake hose from each other and plug the openings.
6. Support the lower control arm and unscrew the nuts from the ball joints.
7. Remove the ball joints from the steering knuckle.
8. Loosen the bolts on the upper control arm and remove the upper control arm.
9. Installation is the reverse of removal.

—————— CAUTION ——————
Mount the front hex bolt from the rear in a forward direction, and the rear hex bolt from the front in a rearward direction.
—————————————————

10. Bleed the brakes.

Lower Control Arm

REMOVAL & INSTALLATION

All Models Except 190D, 190E, 380SL, 380SLC, 450SL and 450SLC

The lower control arm is the same as the front axle half. For safety install a spring compressor on the coil spring.
1. Raise and support the front of the car and remove the wheels.
2. Remove the front shock absorber. Loosen the top mount first.
3. Remove the front springs.
4. Separate and plug the brake lines.
5. Remove the track rod from the steering knuckle arm.
6. Matchmark the position of the eccentric bolts on the bearing of the lower control arm in relation to the crossmember.
7. Remove the shield from the cross yoke.
8. Support the front axle half.
9. Loosen the eccentric bolt on the front and rear bearing of the lower control arm and knock them out.
10. Remove the bolt from the cross yoke bearing.
11. Loosen the screw at the opposite end of the cross yoke bearing.
12. Pull the cross yoke bearing down slightly.
13. Loosen the support of the upper con-

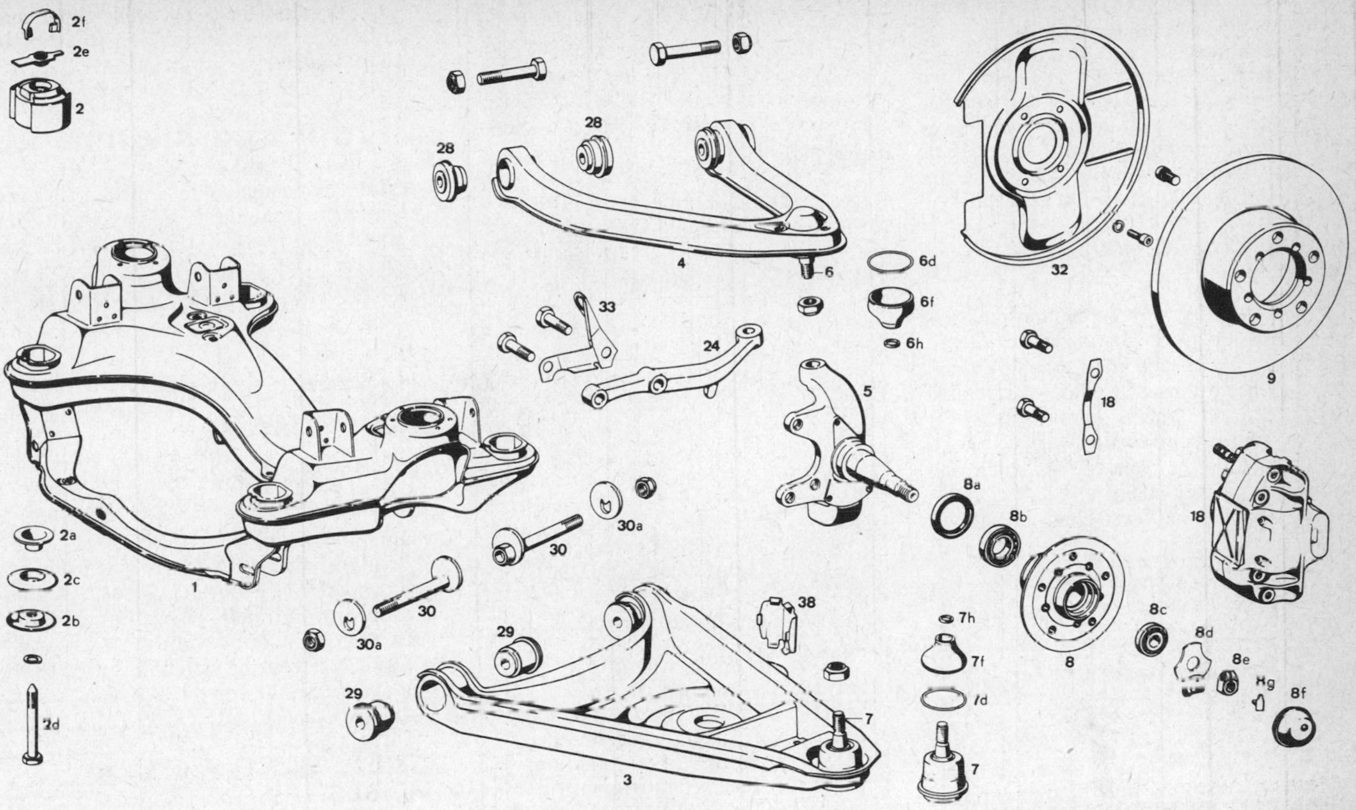

The following is a legend for the exploded diagram:

1.	Front axle carrier
2.	Rubber mount for suspension of front axle
2a.	Stop buffer for inward deflection
2b.	Stop plate
2c.	Stop buffer for outward deflections
2d.	Hex. bolt with snap-ring
2e.	Fastening nut
2f.	Nut holder
3.	Lower control arm
4.	Upper control arm
5.	Steering knuckle
6.	Guide joint
6d.	Circlip
6f.	Sleeve
6h.	Clamping ring
7.	Supporting joint
7d.	Circlip
7f.	Sleeve
7h.	Clamping ring
8.	Front wheel hub
8a.	Radial sealing ring
8b.	Inside tapered roller bearing
8c.	Outside tapered roller bearing
8d.	Washer
8e.	Clamp nut
8f.	Wheel cap
8g.	Contact spring
9.	Brake disc
18.	Brake caliper
18a.	Lockwasher
24.	Steering knuckle arm
28.	Rubber slide bearing
29.	Rubber bearing (torsion bearing)
30.	Cam bolt
30a.	Cam washer
32.	Cover plate
33.	Holder for brake hose
38.	Protective cap for steering lock

Lower control arm and pivot shaft

trol arm on the torsion bar. Remove the clamp screw from the clamp.

14. Remove the upper control arm bearing on the front end.

15. Remove the front axle half.

16. Installation is the reverse of removal. Tighten the eccentric bolts of the lower control arm bearing with the car resting on the wheels. Bleed the brakes and check the front end alignment.

190D and 190E

1. Remove the engine compartment lining at the bottom of the vehicle (if so equipped).

2. Raise the front of the vehicle and support it with jackstands. Remove the wheel.

3. Support the lower control arm with jackstands and then disconnect the torsion bar bearing at the control arm.

4. Remove the spring as detailed earlier in this chapter.

5. Disconnect the tie rod at the steering knuckle and then press out the ball joint with the proper tool.

6. Remove the brake caliper and position it out of the way. Be sure that you do not damage the brake line.

7. Remove the brake disc/wheel hub assembly.

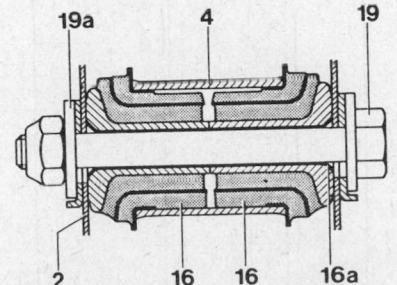

1. Frame cross member
2. Wishbone
3. Torsion rubber bushing
4. Clamping sleeve
5. Eccentric bolt (camber adjustment)
6. Eccentric washer

Cross section of the front lower control arm bushing on 190 models

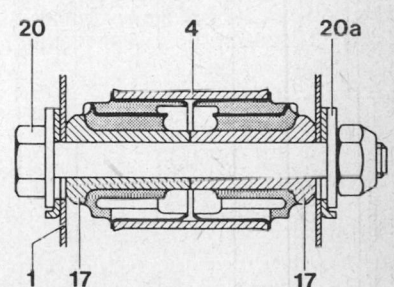

1. Frame side member
2. Wishbone
3. Torsion rubber bushing
4. Eccentric bolt (caster adjustment)
5. Eccentric washer

Cross section of the rear lower control arm bushing on 190 models

8. Disconnect the lower end of the damper strut from the steering knuckle and then remove the knuckle.

9. Mark the position of the inner eccentric pins, relative to the frame, on the bearing of the control arm.

10. Unscrew and remove the pins.

11. Remove the jackstands and remove the lower control arm.

12. Installation is in the reverse order of removal. Please note the following:

a. Tighten the eccentric bolts on the inner arm to 130 ft. lbs. (180 Nm).

b. To facilitate torsion bar installation, raise the opposite side of the lower control arm with a jack.

c. Tighten the clamp nut on the tie rod ball joint to 25 ft. lbs. (35 Nm).

380SL, 380SLC, 450SL and 450SLC

1. Since the front shock absorber acts as a deflection stop for the front wheels, the lower shock absorber attaching point should not be loosened unless the vehicle is resting on the wheels or unless the lower control arm is supported.

2. Jack up the front of the vehicle and support it on jack stands.

3. Support the lower control arm.

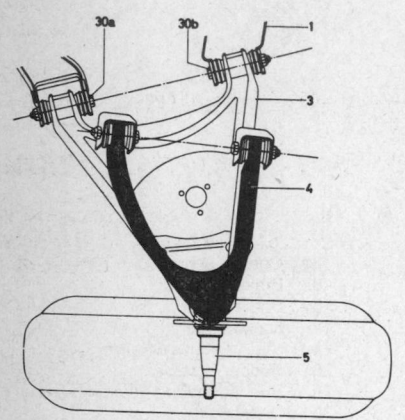

1. Front axle carrier
3. Lower control arm
4. Upper control arm
5. Steering knuckle
30a. Cam bolt front (caster)
30b. Cam bolt rear (camber)

Caster and camber adjustment points on the 380SL, 380SLC, 450SL and 450SLC

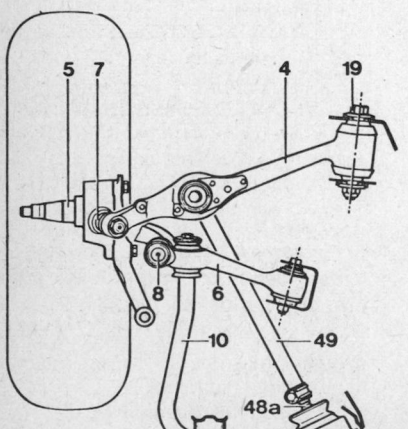

1. Frame side member
2. Frame cross member for front axle
4. Lower control arm
5. Steering knuckle
6. Upper control arm
7. Supporting joint
8. Guide joint
10. Torsion bar
19. Eccentric bolt (camber adjustment)
21. Torsion bar mounting on front end
48. Supporting joint
48a. Ball pin (caster adjustment)
49. Supporting tube

Caster and camber adjustment points on all other models

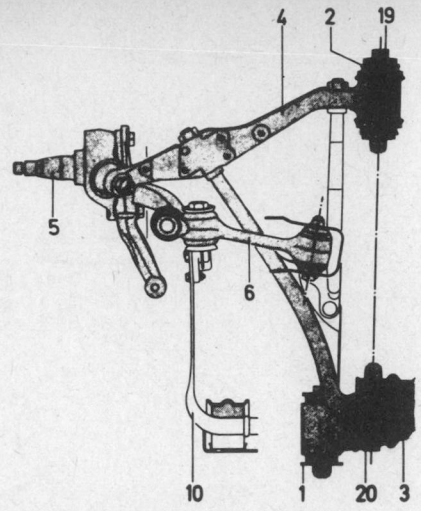

1. Frame side member
2. Frame cross member for front axle
3. Cross yoke
4. Lower control arm
5. Steering knuckle
6. Upper control arm
10. Torsion bar
19. Cam bolt of front bearing (camber adjustment)
20. Cam bolt of rear bearing (caster adjustment)

Caster and camber adjustment points on the 280SE, 1978–80 300SD, 450 SEL and 6.9

4. Loosen the lower shock absorber attachment.

5. Unscrew the steering arm from the steering knuckle.

6. Separate the brake line and brake hose and plug the openings.

7. Remove the front spring.

8. Unscrew the hex nuts on the ball joints.

9. Remove the lower ball joint and remove the lower control arm.

10. Installation is the reverse of removal. Bleed the brakes and check the front end alignment.

Front End Alignment

Caster and camber are critical to proper handling and tire wear. Neither adjustment should be attempted without the specialized equipment to accurately measure the geometry of the front end.

CASTER/CAMBER ADJUSTMENT

All Models Except 380SL, 380SLC, 450SL and 450SLC

The front axle provides for caster and camber adjustment, but both wheel adjustments can only be made together. Adjustments are made with cam bolts on the lower control arm bearings.

The front bearing cam bolt is used to set caster, while the rear bearing cam bolt is used for camber.

380SL, 380SLC, 450SL and 450SLC

Caster and camber are dependent upon each other and cannot be adjusted independently. They can only be adjusted simultaneously.

Caster is adjusted by turning the lower control arm around the front mounting, using the eccentric bolt.

Camber is adjusted by turning the lower control arm about the rear mounting, using the eccentric bolt. Bear in mind that caster will be changed accordingly.

When camber is adjusted in a positive direction, caster is changed in a negative direction, and vice versa. Adjustment of camber by 0°15′ results in a caster change of approximately 0°20′. Adjustment of caster by 1° results in a camber change of approximately 0°7′.

TOE-IN ADJUSTMENT

Toe-in is the difference of the distance between the front edges of the wheel rims and the rear edges of the wheel rims.

To measure toe-in, the steering should be in the straight ahead position and the marks on the pitman arm and pitman shaft should be aligned.

Toe-in is adjusted by changing the length of the two tie rods or track rods with the wheels in the straight ahead position. Some older models have a hex nut locking arrangement rather than the newer clamp, but adjustment is the same.

NOTE: Install new tie rods so that the left-handed thread points toward the left-hand side of the car.

1. Frame side member
2. Frame cross member
3. Wishbone
4. Steering knuckle
5. Supporting ball joint
6. Torsion bar
7. Damper strut
8. Eccentric bolt of front bushing (camber adjustment)
9. Eccentric bolt of rear bushing (caster adjustment)
10. Torsion bar bushing on wishbone
11. Pitman arm
12. Tie rod
13. Steering knuckle arm

Caster and camber adjustment points—190D and 190E

STEERING

Steering Wheel

REMOVAL & INSTALLATION

380SL, 380SLC, 450SL and 450SLC

1. Pry the three-pointed star trademark from the center padding.
2. Unscrew the hex nut from the steering shaft and remove the spring washer and the steering wheel.

NOTE: 1980 and later models use an Allen screw in place of a hex nut. The Allen screw must be renewed if removed.

3. Installation is the reverse of removal. Be sure that the alignment mark on the steering shaft is pointing upward and be sure that the slightly curved spoke of the steering wheel is down.

All Models Except 380SL, 380SLC, 450SL and 450SLC

E: 380SEC uses a bolt and spring hes the power piston into the teeth itman shaft when the steering is nter position. Any backlash (play teering wheel) is taken up.

.cmove the padded plate. Pull at er near the wheel spokes.

Jnscrew the hex nut from the steer-: and remove the spring washer and ing wheel.

E: 1980 and later models use an rew in place of the hex nut. The rew must be replaced if removed.

istallation is the reverse of re-3e sure that the alignment mark on

the steering shaft is pointing upward and be sure that the slightly curved spoke of the steering wheel is down.

Power Steering Gear

REMOVAL & INSTALLATION

1. Suck the oil from the power steering reservoir using a syringe.
2. Detach the high-pressure hose and oil return hose from the steering assembly.
3. Cap both lines to prevent entry of dirt, then remove the clamp screw from the lower part of the coupling flange.
4. Remove the rubber plug from the cover plate and remove the U-joint socket screw. On LS90 power steering units, remove the steering spindle. Pull the steering spindle up only until the coupling is no longer engaged with the worn gear.
5. The tailpipe and left side exhaust pipe may have to be removed for access.
6. Detach the tie rod and center tie rod (or drag link and track rod) from the pitman arm, using pullers or a tie rod splitter.
7. Remove the hex-head bolts that hold the gearbox to the frame, then press the worm shaft stub from the steering coupling and remove the gearbox from underneath the car.
8. To install, first install the pitman arm (if it has been removed) aligning the matchmarks. Tighten the pitman arm nut to 110 ft. lbs. and install the cotter pin. Use new self-locking nuts to attach the gear to the frame.
9. Remove the screw plug from the steering box. Turn the wormshaft until the center of the power piston is directly below the bore in the housing. Check dimension (a) which can be altered by changing the position of the pitman arm on its shaft.

10. Center the steering wheel.
11. Press the worm shaft stub into the steering shaft coupling, making sure not to damage the serrations.

NOTE: Install assembly pin as for manual steering.

12. Install and tighten the hex-head screws that hold the gearbox to the chassis, then install and tighten the coupling clamp screw.
13. Install the plug in the gearbox, using a new gasket; attach the tie rods to the pitman arm and make sure that the steering knuckle arms rest against their stops at full left and right lock.
14. Check toe-in and correct if necessary. Remove the dust covers from the fluid lines, then reconnect the high- and low-pressure lines.
15. Fill the reservoir and connect a hose between the bleed screw on the steering and the reservoir.
16. Open the bleed screw and, with engine running, bleed the system and top up.

Power Steering Pump

REMOVAL & INSTALLATION

Many types of power steering pumps are used on Mercedes-Benz vehicles. Use only the instructions that apply to your vehicle.

All Models

1. Remove the nut from the supply tank.
2. Remove the spring and damping plate.
3. Drain the oil from the tank with a syringe.
4. Loosen and remove the expanding and return hoses from the pump. Plug all connections and pump openings.
5. If necessary for clearance, loosen the radiator shell. Loosen the mounting bolts, and move the pump toward the engine by using the toothed wheel. Remove the belt. Remove the pulley, and then remove the pump.
6. Loosen the nut on the attaching plate and the bolt on the support.
7. Push the pump toward the engine and remove the belts from the pulley.
8. Unscrew the mounting bolts and remove the pump and carrier.
9. Installation is the reverse of removal.

Steering Linkage

REMOVAL & INSTALLATION

All Models
TRACK ROD

1. Remove the cotter pins and castellated nuts from the track rod joints. The 190D and 190E use only a self-locking nut.
2. Remove the track rod from the steering arms with a puller.

3. Check the track rod ends. The rods use 22mm ball joints and should be replaced if either ball joint is defective.

4. Check the rubber sleeves. The ball joint should be replaced if the sleeve is defective.

5. Installation is the reverse of removal. Install the track rods so that the end with the left hand threads is on the left side. Use new locknuts on the 190D and 190E.

DRAG LINK

1. Remove the castle nuts from the drag link joints.

2. Unbolt the steering damper and force it from the bracket.

3. Remove the drag link with a puller.

4. Installation is the reverse of removal.

5. Check the front wheel alignment.

BRAKES

All Mercedes-Benz cars imported into the U.S. are equipped with 4-wheel disc brakes. The disc brakes are basically similar on all models, though there may be slight differences in design from model to model. The caliper bore sizes, for instance, differ depending upon application. The bore size (in mm) is usually stamped on the outside of the caliper, but occasionally, a code is used. For instance, the 14 on a Teves (ATE) caliper is really a 57 mm bore. (Obviously, it isn't a 14mm bore).

Three different manufacturers make calipers for Mercedes-Benz production—Teves (ATE), Bendix or Girling—but calipers of the same manufacturer are installed on the same axle. For service, install calipers of the same manufacturer on the axle; on the rear axle, calipers of any manufacturer can be installed.

Most models are equipped with brake pad wear indicators to indicate when the pad lining requires replacement. A step-type master cylinder is used which eliminates the need for the vacuum pump previously used on 230, 280, 280C and 280S. The front brakes are connected to the primary side of the master cylinder and the rear brakes to the secondary side. A pressure differential warning indicator is also used, which will immediately indicate the total loss of one part of the braking system by lighting the brake warning light on the dash. Once the warning light has come on, it will remain on until the system is repaired and the switch on the master cylinder reset. The warning light will only go out after pushing the reset pin in the switch.

On the models covered in this section, the pressure differential warning indicator has been eliminated from models with the step-type master cylinder. The master cylinder reservoir has 2 chambers with 2 sets of electrical contacts. Loss of brake fluid in either reservoir will light the warning light on the dash.

For all brake system service and repair procedures not detailed below, please refer to "Brakes" in the Unit Repair section.

Adjustment

Since disc brakes are used at all four wheels, no adjustments are necessary. Disc brakes are inherently self-adjusting. The only adjustment possible is to the handbrake, which is covered at the end of this section.

Master Cylinder

The dual master cylinder has a safety feature which the single unit lacks—if a leak develops in one brake circuit (rear wheels, for example), the other circuit will still operate.

Failure of one system is immediately obvious—the pedal travel increases appreciably and a warning light is activated. When the fluid falls below a certain level, a switch activates the circuit.

Reset pin (arrow) on master cylinder with pressure warning differential

—— CAUTION ——
This design was not intended to allow driving the car for any distance with, in effect, a two-wheel brake system. If one brake circuit fails, braking action is correspondingly lower. Front circuit failure is the more serious, however, since the front brakes contribute up to 75% of the braking force required to stop the car.

REMOVAL & INSTALLATION

1. To remove the master cylinder, first open a bleed screw at one front, and one rear wheel.

2. Pump the pedal to empty the reservoir completely. Make sure both reservoirs are completely drained.

3. Disconnect the switch connectors using a small screwdriver. Disconnect the brake lines at the master cylinder. Plug the ends with bleed screw caps or the equivalent.

4. Unbolt the master cylinder from the power brake unit and remove. Be careful you do not lose the O-ring in the flange groove of the master cylinder.

5. Installation is the reverse of removal. Be sure to replace the O-ring between the master cylinder and the power brake unit, since this must be absolutely

tight. Torque the nuts to 12–15 ft. lbs. Be sure that both chambers are completely filled with brake fluid and bleed the brakes.

Wheel Bearings

REMOVAL & INSTALLATION

If the wheel bearing play is being checked for correct setting only, it is not necessary to remove the caliper. It is only necessary to remove the brake pads.

1. Remove the brake caliper.

2. Pull the cap from the hub with a pair of channel-lock pliers. Remove the radio suppression spring, if equipped.

3. Loosen the socket screw of the clamp nut on the wheel spindle. Remove the clamp nut and washer.

4. Remove the front wheel hub and brake disc.

5. Remove the inner race with the roller cage of the outer bearing.

6. Using a brass or aluminum drift, carefully tap the outer race of the inner bearing until it can be removed with the inner race, bearing cage, and seal.

7. In the same manner, tap the outer race of the bearing out of the hub.

8. Separate the front hub from the brake disc.

9. To assemble, press the outer races into the front wheel hub.

10. Pack the bearing cage with bearing

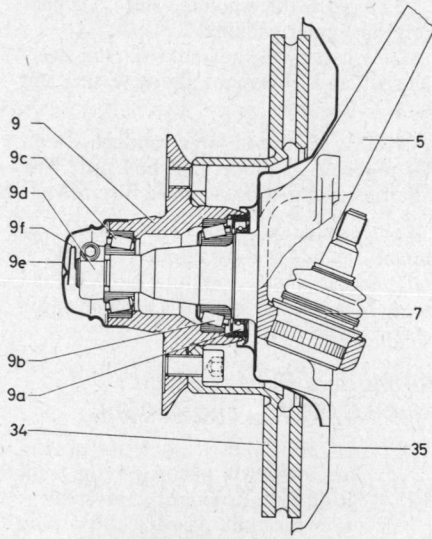

5.	Steering knuckle
7.	Supporting joint
9.	Front wheel hub
9a.	Radial sealing ring
9b.	Tapered roller bearing, inside
9c.	Tapered roller bearing, outside
9d.	Clamping nut
9e.	Wheel cap
9f.	Contact spring
34.	Brake disc
35.	Cover plate

Wheel bearing cutaway—all except 450SL, 450SLC, 380SL and 380SLC

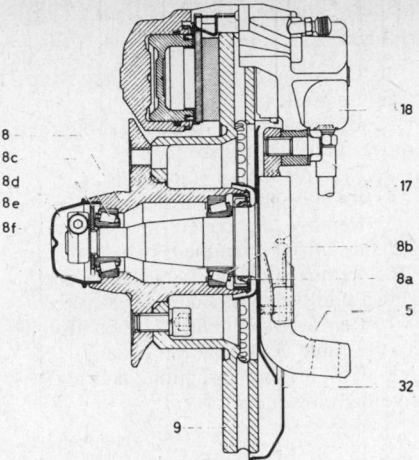

5. Steering knuckle
8. Wheel hub
8a. Radial sealing ring
8b. Tapered roller bearing, outside
8c. Tapered roller bearing, inside
8d. Washer
8e. Clamping nut
8f. Wheel cap
9. Brake disc
17. Brake hose
18. Brake caliper
32. Cover plate

Wheel bearing cutaway—450SL, 450SLC, 380SL and 380SLC

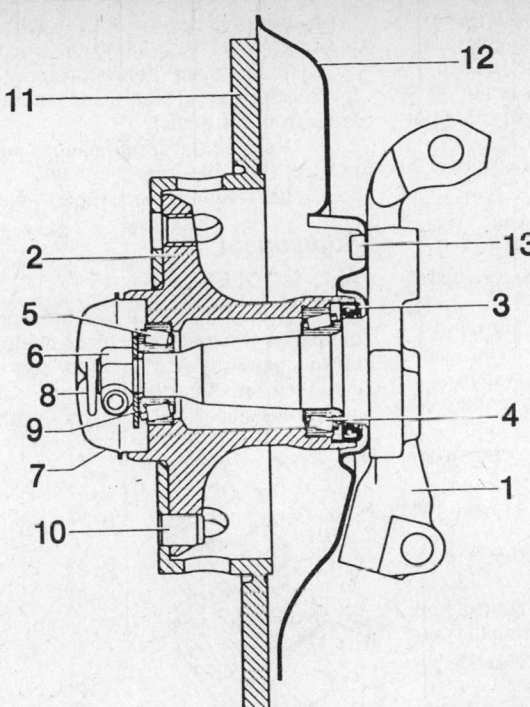

1. Steering knuckle
2. Front wheel hub
3. Radial seal ring
4. Tapered roller bearing, inner
5. Tapered roller bearing, outer
6. Clamping nut
7. Greaso cap
8. Contact spring
9. Washer
10. Clamping sleeve
11. Brake disk
12. Brake backing plate
13. Allen screws

Wheel bearing cutaway—190D and 190E

grease and insert the inner race with the bearing into the wheel hub.

11. Coat the sealing ring with sealant and press it into the hub.

12. Pack the front wheel hub with 45–55 grams of wheel bearing grease. The races of the tapered bearing should be well packed and also apply grease to the front faces of the rollers. Pack the front bearings with the specified amount of grease. Too much grease will cause overheating of the lubricant and it may lose its lubricity. Too little grease will not lubricate properly.

13. Coat the contact surface of the sealing ring on the wheel spindle with Moly-kote® paste.

14. Press the wheel hub onto the wheel spindle.

15. Install the inner race and cage of the outer bearing.

16. Install the steel washer and the clamp nut.

ADJUSTMENT

1. Tighten the clamp nut until the hub can just be turned.

2. Slacken the clamp nut and seat the bearings on the spindle by rapping the spindle sharply with a hammer.

3. Attach a dial indicator, with the pointer indexed, onto the wheel hub.

4. Check the end-play of the hub by pushing and pulling on the flange. The end-play should be approximately 0.0004–0.0008 in.

5. Make an additional check by rotat-ing the washer between the inner race of the outer bearing and the clamp nut. It should be able to be turned by hand.

6. Check the position of the suppressor pin in the wheel spindle and the contact spring in the dust cap.

7. Pack the dust cap with 20–25 grams of wheel bearing grease and install the cap.

8. Install the brake caliper and bleed the brakes.

Handbrake

FRONT CABLE

Removal & Installation

190D and 190E

1. Disconnect the return spring at the cable control compensator.

2. Unbolt the brake cable from the intermediate lever and pull the cable away.

Dial indicator set-up for checking wheel bearing play

3. Remove the parking brake lever.

4. Loosen the brake cable at the lever and then pull it out toward the rear, through the floor.

5. Installation is in the reverse order of removal.

230, 240D, 280CE, 300D, 300CD and 300TD

1. Remove the spring from the equalizer.

2. Back off the adjusting screw completely.

3. Detach the relay lever from the bracket on the frame and from the adjusting shackle.

4. Detach the cable from the relay lever by pulling the cotter pin out of the bolt.

5. Remove the clip from the cable guide. Remove the clips from the chassis.

6. Detach the brake cable from the parking brake link. Remove the clip from the cable guide and detach the brake cable from the parkbrake.

7. Pull the cable downward from the chassis.

8. Installation is the reverse of removal.

380SL, 380SLC, 450SL and 450SLC

1. Remove the exhaust system.

2. Disconnect the return spring.

3. Remove the bolts which attach the guide to the intermediate lever and pull the cotter pin from the flange bolt. Remove the flange bolt.

4. Remove the spring clamp from the cable guide and remove the cable control from the bracket.

5. Remove the tunnel cover.

8. Disconnect the brake control from the parking brake and remove the spring clamp from the cable guide. Remove the cable control from the parking brake.

9. Remove the brake control cable out of the frame toward the rear.

10. Installation is the reverse of removal.

All Other Models

1. Remove the floor mat.
2. Remove the legroom cover (upper and lower).
3. Remove the air duct.
4. Disconnect the 4 rubber rings and lower and support the exhaust system.
5. Remove the shield above the exhaust pipes.
6. Disconnect the return spring from the bracket.
7. Back off the adjusting screw on the bracket.
8. Disconnect the intermediate lever from the adjusting bracket.
9. Loosen the brake cable controls on the intermediate lever while pulling the cotter pin from the flange bolt. Remove the flange bolt.
10. Remove the spring clip from the cable guide on the floor pan.
11. Disconnect the brake cable control from the parking brake bracket.
12. Remove the spring clip from the cable and remove the cable control from the parking brake.
13. Pull the cable away upward.
14. Installation is the reverse of removal. Adjust the parking brake.

REAR BRAKE CABLE

Removal & Installation

230, 240D, 280CE, 280E, 300D, 300CD AND 300TD

1. Remove the parking brake shoes after removing the wheel.
2. Remove the screws from the wheel support and detach the brake cable.
3. Back off the adjusting screw from the adjusting shackle.
4. Remove the spring clips, detach the cable, and remove the equalizer.
5. Installation is the reverse of removal.

All Other Models

1. Remove the parking brake shoes.
2. Remove the bolt from the wheel carrier and remove the cable.
3. Remove the exhaust system. On some models the exhaust system can be lowered and supported after removing the rubber rings. If equipped, remove the heat shield from above the exhaust pipes.
4. Disconnect the draw spring from the holder.
5. Detach the guide from the intermediate lever.
6. Remove the adjusting screw from the bracket.
7. Disconnect the intermediate lever on

the bearing and remove it from the adjusting bracket.

8. Remove the holder, compensating lever, cable control plates, and intermediate lever from the tunnel.

9. Remove the spring clamps and disconnect the cable from the plate.

10. Installation is the reverse of removal.

Adjustment
ALL MODELS

1. If the floor pedal can be depressed more than two notches before actuating the brakes, adjust by jacking up the rear of the car, then removing one lug bolt and adjusting the star wheel with a screwdriver.

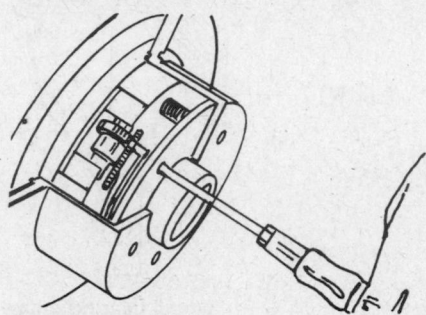

Cut-away view of rear brake shoe adjustment

2. Move the screwdriver upward on the left (driver's) side, downward on the right (passenger's) side to tighten the shoes.

3. When the wheel is locked, back off about 2–4 clicks.

4. With this type system, the adjusting bolt on the cable relay lever only serves to equalize cable length; therefore, do not attempt to adjust the brakes by turning this bolt.

CHASSIS ELECTRICAL

Heater Blower

REMOVAL & INSTALLATION

230, 240D, 280E, 280CE, 300D, 300CD and 300TD

1. Remove the cover from under the right side of the instrument panel.
2. Disconnect the plug from the blower motor.
3. Unscrew the contact plate screw, lift the contact plate and disconnect both wires to the series resistor.
4. Loosen the blower motor flange screws and lift out the blower motor.
5. Installation is in the reverse order of removal.

280SE, 300SD (1978–80), 450SEL and 6.9

1. Disconnect the series resistor plug at the fire wall.
2. Unscrew both mounting bolts and remove the series resistor.
3. Remove the air inlet grille.
4. Remove the glove box.
5. Remove the cover from under the right side of the instrument panel.
6. Remove the hose between the center air duct and the right side ring nozzle.
7. Remove the clamp and then disconnect the cable control at the lever.
8. Unscrew both mounting nuts and remove the blower motor.

NOTE: On installation, make sure that the rubber seal between the blower motor and the firewall is not damaged and that the rubber grommet for the connecting cable is correctly seated.

9. Guide the connecting cable through the air duct on the firewall and into the water box.
10. Insert the blower motor into the housing, position the mounting nuts and then push the blower motor to the left (as far as possible) while tightening.
11. Installation of the remaining components is in the reverse order of installation.

380SL, 380SLC, 450SL and 450SLC

1. Working in the engine compartment, unscrew the eight (8) mounting screws and remove the panel which covers the blower motor.
2. Disconnect the plug from the series resistor at the firewall.
3. Remove the mounting bolts and then remove the series resistor.
4. Unscrew the four (4) blower motor retaining nuts and lift out the motor.
5. Installation is in the reverse order of removal. Be sure that the rubber sealing strip is not damaged.

300SD (1981 and later), 380SE, 380SEL, 380SEC, 500SEL and 500SEC

1. Remove the cover from under the right side of the instrument panel.
2. Remove the cover for the blower motor and disconnect the two-prong plug.
3. Remove the retaining bolts on the blower motor flange and then remove the blower motor.
4. Installation is in the reverse order of removal.

190D and 190E

1. Open the hood to a 90° position and then remove the wiper arms.
2. Disconnect the retaining clips for the air intake cover at the firewall.
3. Remove the rubber sealing strip from the cover and then remove the retaining

screws. Slide the cover out of the lower windshield trim strip and remove it.

4. Disconnect the vacuum line from the heater valve.

5. Remove the heater cover retaining screws.

6. Pull up the rubber sealing strip from the engine side of the defroster plenum (firewall), unscrew the retaining screws and pull up and out on the blower motor cover.

7. Loosen the cable straps on the connecting cable and then disconnect the plug.

8. Unscrew the mounting bolts and then remove the blower motor.

9. Installation is in the reverse order of removal.

Instrument Cluster

REMOVAL & INSTALLATION

280SE, 300SD (1978–80), 380SL, 380SLC, 450SEL, 450SL, 450SLC and 6.9

1. Remove the steering wheel.

NOTE: The instrument cluster is held in the instrument panel by means of a molded rubber strip. When pulling out the cluster, the panel can be slightly raised above the cluster. NEVER force the cluster with a screwdriver or the like.

2. Remove the tachometer shaft from the cable strap underneath the left hand floor mat, near the jacket tube (except 380SL, SLC and 450SL, SLC).

3. Pull the instrument cluster out as much as possible and loosen or remove the tachometer shaft, all electrical connections and the oil pressure line.

4. Remove the instrument cluster to the left.

———— CAUTION ————
Do not bend the oil pressure line.

5. Installation is in the reverse order of removal. Make sure that the speedometer cable is not bent excessively or it will vibrate when running.

190D and 190E

1. Remove the cover under the left side of the instrument panel.

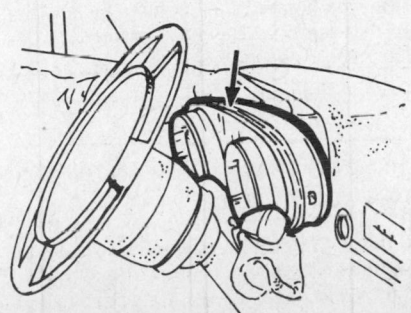

Instrument panel removal showing rubber retaining strip

2. Disconnect the defroster ducting which runs behind the instrument cluster.

3. Unscrew the speedometer cable from below and then push the cluster out far enough to disconnect all connections on the back of the instrument cluster.

4. Remove the five clips which secure the instrument cluster and then remove it.

5. Installation is in the reverse order of removal.

230, 240D, 280E, 280CE, 300D, 300CD, 300SD (1981 and later), 300TD, 380SE, 380SEC, 380SEL, 500SEC and 500SEL

1. Remove the steering wheel (300SD, 380SE, 380SEC, 380SEL, 500SEC and 500SEL only).

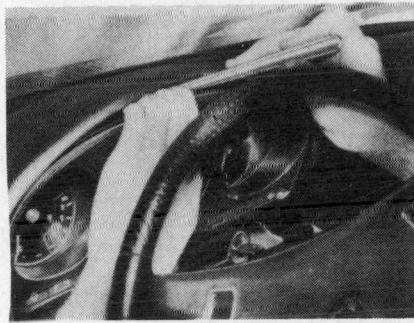

Remove the instrument cluster with a small screwdriver

2. Remove the instrument cluster slightly by hand. Don't pull on the edge of the glass.

3. A removal hook can be fabricated and inserted between the instrument cluster and the dashboard.

4. Guide the removal hook up to the right to the recess (arrow) and pull the instrument cluster out.

NOTE: The 1981 and later 300SD, 380SE, 380SEC, 380SEL, 500SEC and 500SEL models use 5 clips to hold the instrument cluster in place.

Fabricated tool for removing the instrument cluster

Recess slot in the instrument cluster

5. Pull it out as far as possible and disconnect the speedometer cable, electrical connections and oil pressure line.

6. To install, reconnect the electrical connections, oil pressure line and speedometer cable. To avoid speedometer cable noise, guide it into the largest radius possible.

7. Push the instrument cluster firmly into the dashboard.

Combination Switch

REMOVAL & INSTALLATION

190D, 190E, 230, 240D, 280 (all models), 300D, 300CD, 300SD 1978–80), 300TD, 380SL, 380SLC, 450 (all models) and 6.9

1. Remove the rubber sleeve on the switch and then unscrew the retaining screws.

2. Pull the switch out slightly, loosen the screws for the cable connection of the twin carbon contacts and pull out the cable.

3. Remove the cover underneath the left side of the instrument panel.

4. Disconnect the plug and then remove the switch.

5. Installation is in the reverse order of removal.

300SD (1981 and later), 380SE, 380SEC, 380SEL, 500SEC and 500SEL

1. Remove the steering wheel.

2. Remove the cover underneath the left side of the instrument panel.

3. Unscrew the switch retaining screws.

4. Disconnect the 14-prong plug underneath the instrument panel.

5. Remove the switch.

6. Installation is in the reverse order of removal.

Ignition Switch

REMOVAL & INSTALLATION

All Models with Ignition Switch in Dashboard (Except 190D and 190E)

1. Remove the instrument cluster.

2. Remove the right-hand cover plate under the dashboard.

3. Remove the plug connection from the ignition switch.

4. Remove the screws which hold the ignition switch to the rear of the lock cylinder and remove the ignition switch.

5. To install the ignition switch, attach the plug connection, after fastening the switch to the steering lock.

6. Install the instrument cluster.

7. Check the switch for proper function and install the lower cover.

190D AND 190E

1. Remove the cover plate under the left side of the instrument panel.

2. Remove the steering wheel. Remove the instrument cluster.

3. Pry the cylinder rosette (trim ring) upwards and then remove it.

4. Insert the ignition key and turn it to position 1.

5. Disconnect the plug at the rear of the ignition switch.

NOTE: The plug can only be disconnected when the key is in position 1.

6. Loosen the screws and then remove the steering column jacket (upper and lower halves).

7. Release the clamp on the jacket tube. Press in the lock-pin in position 1 and then pull the steering lock out slightly from the jacket tube holder.

8. Pull off the ignition key at the right bottom section, slightly to the rear. Swivel the steering lock so that the lock cylinder clears its hole in the instrument panel.

9. Unscrew the retaining screws and remove the ignition switch from the back of the steering lock.

10. Installation is in the reverse order of removal. Remember to reconnect the switch to the steering lock.

Lock Cylinder (Key Can be Removed in Position 1)

REMOVAL & INSTALLATION

1. Turn the key to position 1 and remove the key.

2. Pry the cover sleeve from the lock cylinder with a small screwdriver.

3. Using a bent paper clip, hook onto the cover sleeve and remove the sleeve. Be sure that you do not remove the rosette in the dashboard also.

4. Insert the paper clip between the rosette and the steering lock and push in the lock pin. Remove the lock cylinder slightly with the key.

5. Insert the paper clip into the locking hole and pull the lock cylinder completely out.

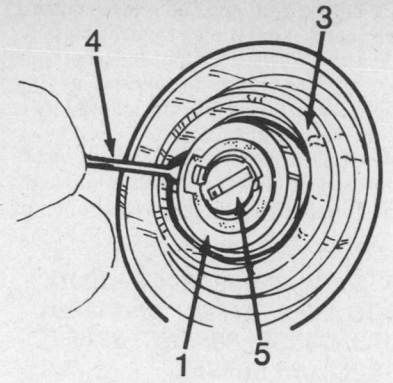

1. Steering lock   4. Steel wire (paper clip)
3. Rosette   5. Locking cylinder

Ignition lock cylinder removal from the instrument panel (both types)

6. Installation is the reverse of removal. Turn the lock cylinder to position 1 and insert it into the steering lock, making sure that the lock pin engages. Push the cover sleeve into position 1.

7. Make sure that the cylinder operates properly.

Lock Cylinder (Key Cannot Be Removed in Position 1)

REMOVAL & INSTALLATION

All Models Except 190D and 1980E

Because of legal requirements, the lock was changed from the previous version, so that the key can only be removed in position 0.

1. Turn the key to position 1.

2. Lift the cover sleeve to the edge of the key and turn the key to position 0.

3. Remove the key and cover sleeve.

4. Insert the key into the lock cylinder and turn to position 1 (90° to the right), push in the lock pin and remove the lock cylinder.

5. To install the lock cylinder, turn the lock cylinder to position 1 and insert the lock cylinder, making sure that the locking pin engages.

6. Turn the key to position 0 and remove the key.

7. Place the cover sleeve on the steering lock, insert and turn the key, and push in the cover sleeve at position 1.

8. Check the locking cylinder for proper function.

190D and 190E

1. Pry the cylinder rosette (trim ring) upwards and then remove it.

2. Insert the ignition key and turn it to position 1.

3. Using a bent paper clip, insert each end into the holes on either side of the lock cylinder. Press the clip ends inward; the pressure will unlock the cylinder from the steering lock.

4. Grasp the key and with pressure still on the paper clip, pull the ignition key/lock cylinder assembly out of the steering lock.

5. Remove the paper clip, turn the key to position 0 and remove it. Slide the lock cylinder out of the cover.
To install:

6. Insert the lock cylinder just enough so that the ridge on the cylinder body engages the groove in the steering lock.

7. Slide the cover onto the lock cylinder so that the detent is on the left side.

8. Insert the ignition key, turn it to position 1 and then push the lock cylinder and its cover into the steering lock.

NOTE: When the ignition key is in position 1 and is aligned with the mark on the cover, the detent on the cover is also aligned with the ridge on the steering lock. This is the only manner in which the lock cylinder/cover can be installed in the steering lock.

9. Check that the lock cylinder functions properly, if so, install the rosette.

Steering Lock

REMOVAL & INSTALLATION

All Models Except 190D and 190E

1. Disconnect the ground cable from the battery.

2. Remove the instrument cluster.

3. Remove the plug connection from the ignition switch behind the dashboard.

4. Pull the ignition key to position 1.

5. Loosen the attaching screw for the steering lock.

6. Remove the cover sleeve from the steering lock.

7. On vehicles with the latest version of the steering lock, pull the connection for the warning buzzer.

8. Push in the lock pin with a small punch.

9. Turn the steering lock and remove it from the holder in the column jacket. Be sure that the rosette is not damaged.

—————— CAUTION ——————
The lock pin can only be pushed in when the cylinder is in position 1.
————————————————————

10. To install the steering lock, connect the warning buzzer if so equipped.

11. Place the steering lock in position 1 and insert the lock into the steering column while pushing the lock pin in. Be sure that the lock pin engages.

12. Tighten the attaching clamp screw.

13. Attach the plug connection to the ignition switch.

14. Push the cover sleeve onto the lock in position 1.

15. Install the instrument cluster.

16. Check to be sure that the steering lock works properly.

190D and 190E

1. Follow Steps 1-8 of "Ignition Switch Removal and Installation."

2. Unplug the switch and remove the steering lock.

3. Installation is in the reverse order of removal.

Headlights

REMOVAL & INSTALLATION

1981 and later 300SD, 380SEL and 380SEC

1. Open the hood and unscrew the 5 plastic knurled nuts.

2. Remove the assembly from the front of the car. Unplug the electrical connector.

3. Remove the headlight attaching screws.

4. Disconnect the electrical connector and remove the headlight.

5. Installation is the reverse of removal.

All Other Models

1. Loosen the attaching screws and remove the cover.

2. Remove the headlight attaching screws and remove the retaining ring and light as a unit.

NOTE: Do not disturb the headlight aiming screws.

3. Pull the retaining ring and light slightly forward and disconnect the plug.

4. Remove the headlight and retaining ring.

5. Installation is the reverse of removal. Be sure that the plug and socket on the rear of the light are tight.

Wiper Arms

REMOVAL & INSTALLATION

NOTE: On the 190D and 190E, the wiper arm is removed by lifting the cover at the bottom of the arm and removing the retaining nut.

1. Lift the wiper arm so that it is at a 90° angle to the windshield.

2. Disengage the lock on the mounting nut covering cap by lifting the cap slightly upward.

3. Continue to hold the cap in a slightly raised position and then lower the wiper arm to the windshield. This should allow the cap to pivot all the way open.

4. Unscrew the mounting nut and remove the wiper arm.

5. Installation is in the reverse order of removal.

Wiper Motor and Linkage

REMOVAL & INSTALLATION

230, 240D, 280E, 280CE, 300D, 300CD, 300SD (1981 and later) and 300TD

1. Remove the wiper arms.

2. Remove the air intake grille on the right side.

3. Remove the covering cap and nut on the left and right side bearing shafts.

4. Remove the four expanding rivets and then remove the left side air intake grille.

5. Remove the center air plenum cover (four expanding rivets and a Phillips screw).

6. Carefully pull the left and right side connecting rods off of the wiper motor crank.

7. Remove the water drain tube from the right side bearing shaft.

8. Disconnect the coupler plug in the engine compartment. Unclip the plug from the firewall and pull it all the way through.

9. Unbolt the wiper motor and remove it toward the right side.

10. Installation is in the reverse order of removal.

300SD (1981 and later), 300SE, 380SEC, 380SEL, 500SEC and 500SEL

1. Remove the wiper arms.

2. Remove the air intake cover. Unscrew the fastening screws and then disconnect the front plug connector.

3. Compress the mounting flange on the rear plug connector. Push the plug out of the firewall toward the front of the car, twist it and then insert it toward the rear of the car.

4. Remove the wiper motor and linkage.

5. Unscrew the nut on the wiper motor shaft.

6. Swivel the wiper linkage and then unscrew the bolts for the wiper motor underneath.

7. Remove the wiper motor.
To install:

8. Mount the wiper motor in the base plate.

9. Push the crank arm on the wiper motor shaft and position the nut. Make sure that the lever on the right hand wiper shaft is pointing down.

10. Align the crank arm so that the upper edge is parallel with the wiper motor shaft.

11. Tighten the nut on the wiper motor shaft.

12. Attach the wiper motor and linkage assembly to the vehicle.

13. Installation of the remaining components is in the reverse order of removal.

280SE, 300SD (1978–80), 450SEL and 6.9

1. Remove the wiper arms.

2. Remove the covering caps and nuts on both wiper shafts.

3. Remove the air intake grille.

4. Unscrew the mounting bolts.

5. Disconnect the wiper motor plug under the left side of the instrument panel and then pull it into the engine compartment along with the rubber grommet in the firewall.

6. Pull off the linkage drive rod and then unscrew the crank on the wiper motor.

7. Unscrew the mounting bolts and remove the wiper motor.

8. Installation is in the reverse order of removal.

NOTE: Remove the rubber seal around the motor housing during installation or leave it off.

190D and 190E

1. Open the hood all the way and disconnect the battery.

2. Remove the wiper arm.

3. Remove the round cover from the wiper shaft.

4. Remove the two clips, the rubber seal and the two screws and then remove the air intake cover.

5. Pull the three-piece air intake pan from the windshield and remove it.

6. Unscrew the wiper motor/linkage assembly.

7. Remove the cover and unscrew the four mounting bolts for the fuse box. Pull the fuse box slightly forward and up and then unplug the wiper motor connection.

8. Remove the wiper motor/linkage assembly.

9. Remove the nut on the wiper motor shaft and then pull off the crank arm and linkage.

10. Unscrew and remove the wiper motor.
To install:

11. Attach the wiper motor to the base plate.

12. Press the crank arm onto the wiper motor shaft. Make sure that the crank arm and the pushrod are parallel.

13. Attach the crank arm to the wiper motor and install the wiper motor/linkage assembly.

14. Installation of the remaining components is in the reverse order of removal.

Fuses

A listing of the protected equipment and the amperage of the fuse is printed in the lid of the fuse box. Spare fuses and a tool for removing and installing fuses are contained in the vehicle tool kit.

Fuses cannot be repaired—they must be replaced. Always determine the cause of the blown fuse before replacing it with a new one.

MERCEDES–BENZ

FUSE BOX LOCATION

230, 240D, 300D, 300TD, 280E, 280CE and 300CD

On early models, the fuse box may be found in the kick panel on the driver's side. On later models the fuse box is located in the engine compartment on the driver's side, next to the brake master cylinder. Some models have separate fuse boxes or inline fuses for additional equipment. The radio is usually fused with a separate inline glass fuse behind the radio and the ignition is unfused.

190D, 190E, 280SE, 300SD, 380SE, 380SEC, 380SEL, 450SEL, 500SEC, 500SEL and 6.9

The fuse box is located in the engine compartment, on the driver's side, next to the brake master cylinder. Some models may have separate fuse boxes or inline fuses in the engine compartment for additional equipment. The radio is usually fused with a separate inline glass fuse behind the radio and the ignition is unfused. The fuse box also contains various relays.

380SL, 380SLC, 450SL and 450SLC

The fuse box is located in the right-hand (passenger's side) kick panel, behind a cover plate. There may also be separate fuse boxes or inline fuses in the engine compartment for additional equipment. The radio is usually fused with a separate inline glass fuse behind the radio and the ignition is unfused. The kick panel area also contains various relays and switches.

Mitsubishi
Cordia, Starion, Tredia

GENERAL ENGINE SPECIFICATIONS

Year	Engine Displacement cu. in. (cc)	Carburetor Type	Horsepower @ rpm	Torque @ rpm (ft. lbs.)	Bore × Stroke (in.)	Compression Ratio	Oil Pressure (psi)
'83	109.5 (1800)	1 × 2bbl	82 @ 5000	93 @ 3000	3.17 × 3.46	8.5:1	63
	155.9 (2600)	Turbo/EFI	145 @ 5000	185 @ 2500	3.59 × 3.86	7.0:1	57–114
'84–'85	109.5 (1800)	Turbo/EFI	120 @ 5500	110 @ 2600	3.17 × 3.46	7.5:1	63
	121.9 (2000)	1 × 2bbl	110 @ 5000	117 @ 3000	3.35 × 3.46	8.5:1	63
	155.9 (2600)	Turbo/EFI	145 @ 5000	185 @ 2500	3.59 × 3.86	7.0:1	57–114

EFI: Electronic Fuel Injection

TUNE-UP SPECIFICATIONS

(When analyzing compression test results, look for uniformity among cylinders, rather than specific pressures.)

Year	Engine Displace. (cc)	Spark Plugs Type	Gap (in.)	Distributor	Ignition Timing (deg) MT	Ignition Timing (deg) AT	Intake Valve Opens (deg) BTDC	Fuel Pump Pressure (psi)	Idle Speed (rpm)	Valve[2] Clear (in.) In.	Valve[2] Clear (in.) Ex.
'83	1800	BUR6EA-11	0.039–0.043	Electronic	5B	5B	19	2.4–3.4	650MT 750AT	0.006	0.010
	2600	BUR6EA-11	0.039–0.043	Electronic	10B	—	25	35–47	850	0.006	0.010
'84–'85	1800	BPR7ES-11	0.039–0.043	Electronic	5B	5B	57	35–47	750	0.006	0.010
	2000	BPR6ES-11	0.039–0.043	Electronic	5B	5B	19	2.4–3.4	700MT[1] 750MT	0.006	0.010
	2600	BUR6EA-11	0.039–0.043	Electronic	10B	10B	25	35–47	750MT 850AT	0.006	0.010

MT Manual Trans.
AT Automatic Trans.

[1] with A/C: 750MT
850AT

[2] Jet Valve: 0.010

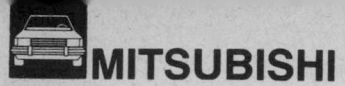

FIRING ORDERS

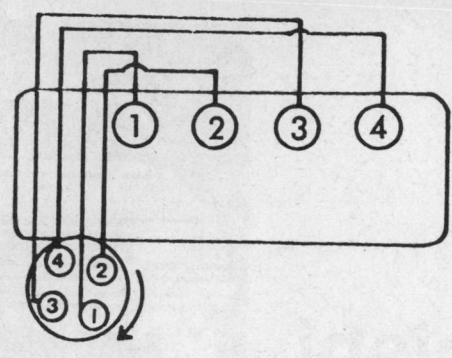

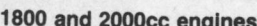

1800 and 2000cc engines

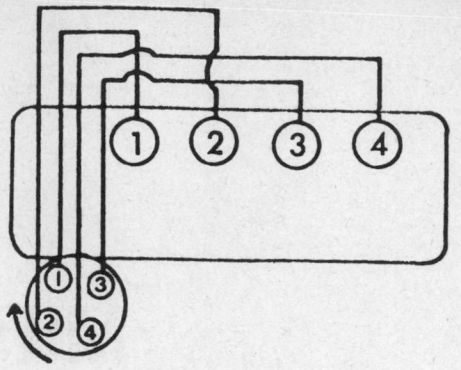

2600cc engines

CAPACITIES
Rear Wheel Drive Cars

Year	Model	Engine Displacement (cc)	Engine Crankcase (qts)		Transmission (qts)		Drive Axle (pts)	Gasoline Tank (gals)	Cooling System (qts)	
			With Filter	Without Filter	Manual	Automatic			W/AC	W/O AC
'83–'85	Starion	2600	4.5	4	2.4	7.4	2.7	19.8	9.7	9.7

CAPACITIES
Front Wheel Drive Cars

Year	Model	Engine Displacement (cc)	Engine Crankcase (qts)		Transaxle (qts)			Gasoline Tank (gals)	Cooling System (qts)	
			With Filter	W/O Filter	Manual		Automatic		W/AC	W/O AC
					4-spd	5-spd				
'83–'85	Cordia Tredia	1800, 2000	4.5	4	2.2	2.2	6.1	13.2	7.4	7.4

CRANKSHAFT AND CONNECTING ROD SPECIFICATIONS
(All measurements are given in inches)

Year	Engine Displace (cc)	Crankshaft				Connecting Rod		
		Main Brg. Journal Dia.	Main Brg. Oil Clearance	Shaft End-Play	Thrust on No.	Journal Diameter	Oil Clearance	Side Clearance
'83–'85	1800, 2000	2.244	0.0008–0.0020	0.0020–0.0071	3	1.772	0.0008–0.0020	0.004–0.010
	2600	2.362	0.0008–0.0020	0.0020–0.0071	3	2.087	0.0008–0.0024	0.004–0.010

VALVE SPECIFICATIONS

Year	Engine Displacement (cc)	Seat Angle (deg)	Face Angle (deg)	Spring Test Pressure (lbs @ in.)	Spring Installed Height (in.)	Stem To Guide Clearance (in.)		Stem Diameter (in.)	
						Intake	Exhaust	Intake	Exhaust
'83–'85	1800, 2000	45	45	62 @ 1.591	1.591	0.001–0.0022	0.002–0.0035	0.315	0.315
	2600	45	45	62 @ 1.591	1.591	0.0012–0.0024	0.002–0.0035	0.315	0.315

PISTON AND RING SPECIFICATIONS
(All measurements in inches)

Year	Engine Displace. (cc)	Piston Clearance	Ring Gap			Ring Side Clearance		
			Top Compression	Bottom Compression	Oil Control	Top Compression	Bottom Compression	Oil Control
'83–'85	1800, 2000	0.0008–0.0016	0.010–0.018	0.008–0.016	0.008–0.020	0.002–0.004	0.001–0.002	—
	2600	0.0008–0.0016	0.012–0.020	0.010–0.016	0.012–0.031	0.002–0.004	0.001–0.002	—

TORQUE SPECIFICATIONS
(All readings in ft. lbs.)

Year	Engine Displace. (cc)	Cylinder Head Bolts	Rod Bearing Bolts	Main Bearing Bolts	Crankshaft Pulley Bolt	Flywheel to Crankshaft Bolts	Manifold	
							Intake	Exhaust
'83–'85	1800, 2000	51–54 (cold)	24–25	37–39	②	94–101M 84–90A	11–14	11–14
	2600	62–72 (cold)①	33–34	55–61	80–94	94–110	11–14	11–14

M Manual Transmission
A Automatic Transmission
① Front bolts (No. 11 in text diagram) 11–15
② 1983: 44–50
   1984–85: 80–94

ALTERNATOR, REGULATOR AND BATTERY SPECIFICATIONS

Year	Alternator			Regulator①				Battery Capacity Ampere-Hour
	Engine	Rated Output	Rotation (Viewed from Pulley)	No Load Adjusted Voltage	Cover Temperature	Charging Light Relay		
						Off Voltage	On Voltage	
'83–'85	1800, 2000	45A @ 12V	Clockwise	14.1 to 14.7V	68°F-20°C	4.0 to 5.8V	0.5 to 3.5	45A
	2600	65A @ 12V	Clockwise	14.1 to 14.7V	68°F-20°C	Ammeter		65A

① All models are equipped with sealed voltage regulators which cannot be adjusted if the readings vary from the specifications.

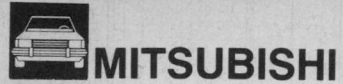

STARTER SPECIFICATIONS

Year	Engine (cc)	No Load Test			Load Test				Stall Test			Brush Spring Tension (lbs.)
		Amp①	Volts	rpm②	Amp①	Volts	Torque②③	rpm②	Amp①	Volts	Torque③	
'83–'85	1800, 2000	55	11.0	6500	150	9.6	2.24	2200	560	6.0	10.85	3.3
	2600	60	11.5	6800	200	9.2	3.83	1600	730	6.0	18.08	3.3

① Less than
② More than
③ Ft. lbs.

BRAKE SPECIFICATIONS
Rear Wheel Drive Cars
(All measurements given are in. unless noted)

Year	Lug Nut Torque ft. lbs.	Master Cylinder Bore	Brake Disc Thickness			Brake Drum			Lining Thickness			
									Front		Rear	
			Max.	Min.	Runout	Diameter	Maximum	Maximum Wear	Max.	Min.①	Max.	Min.①
'83–'85	Steel 50–57 Alu. 57–72	.94 .94	.88	.82	.006	Disc	.650	.590	.39	.04	.33	.04

① Due to variations in state inspection regulations, the minimum allowable lining thickness may be different from that recommended by the manufacturer.

BRAKE SPECIFICATIONS
Front Wheel Drive Cars
(All measurements given are in. unless noted)

Year	Lug Nut Torque ft. lbs.	Master Cylinder Bore	Brake Disc Thickness			Brake Drum			Lining Thickness			
									Front①		Rear①	
			Max.	Min.	Runout	Diameter	Maximum	Maximum Wear	Max.	Min.	Max.	Min.
'83–'85	Steel 50–57 Alu. 57–72	.87	②	②	.006	8.0	8.060	8.10	③	.08	.17	.04

① Due to variations in state inspection regulations, the minimum allowable lining thickness may be different from that recommended by the manufacturer.
② 1983: 0.510 max; 0.450 min.
1984–85: 0.710 max; 0.650 min.
③ 1983: 0.39
1984–85: 0.41

WHEEL ALIGNMENT

Year	Model	Caster (in.)	Camber (in.)	Toe-in (in.)	Steering Angle	
					Inner Wheel (degrees)	Outer Wheel (degrees)
'83–'85	Cordia, Tredia	½	¼	0	—	—
	Starion	5³⁄₁₆	0	0	39	31

SERIAL NUMBER IDENTIFICATION

Vehicle Number

The vehicle identification number (VIN) is mounted on the instrument panel, adjacent to the lower corner of the windshield on the driver's side and is visible through the windshield.

A standard 17 digit VIN code is used, the tenth digit identifies model year (D, 1983; E, 1984; etc.) and the eighth digit identifies the installed engine (4; 1.8 liter; 7; 2.6 liter).

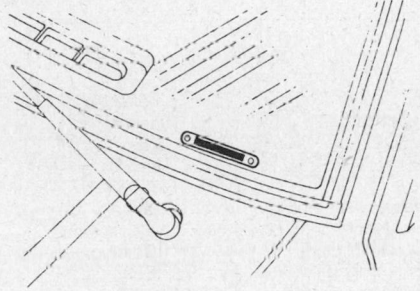

VIN location

A vehicle information code plate is riveted onto the front of the right side wheelhouse or onto the firewall (depending on model). The plate shows model code, engine model, transaxle model and body color code.

A chassis number plate is located on the top center of the firewall in the engine compartment.

Engine Number

The engine number is stamped at the right front side of the engine on the top edge of the block. The 1.8 engine is model G62B, the 2.0 is G63B and the 2.6 engine is G54B.

TUNE-UP PROCEDURES

Spark Plugs

REMOVAL & INSTALLATION

NOTE: Before removing the spark plugs, clean any dirt from the base area of the plugs with compressed air or a stiff brush.

1. Mark or tag the plug wires for correct reinstallation. Grasp the plug wire by the boot end and twist slightly to loosen.

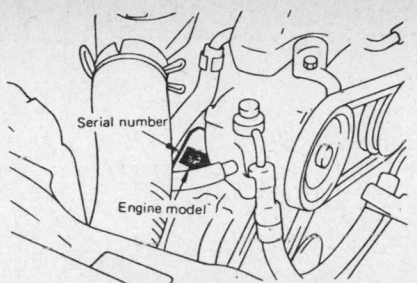

Engine number location

Remove the wire from the spark plug by pulling on the boot. Bending or pulling the plug wire can break the internal conductor.

2. Use a 13/16 in. deep-well spark plug socket and a swivel head rachet type wrench with an extension to remove the spark plugs.

3. Inspect the spark plugs for cracked and damaged insulators or threads, worn electrodes, damaged gasket and carbon or other fouling deposits.

4. If the plugs are to be reused, file the center electrode square.

5. Regap the old spark plugs or check the gap on new spark plugs.

6. Install the spark plugs in the head and torque to 18–21 ft. lbs.

7. Install the spark plug wires after inspecting each for cracks or wear. Clamp the plug wires so they are as far apart from one another as possible to prevent cross firing.

Electronic Ignition

The electronic ignition system consists of the battery, ignition switch, distributor, ignition coil, igniter, spark plug cables and spark plugs. Turbocharged models are also equipped with a detonation and pressure sensor. Any malfunction in the system should be serviced by a mechanic familiar with electronic ignition. The only adjustment necessary is initial ignition timing, dwell is adjusted electronically.

Ignition Timing

— CAUTION —

When checking or adjusting with the engine operating, be careful of contact with the drive belts or fan blades.

1. Locate the timing tab near the engine crankshaft pulley. Mark the appropriate degree line (refer to "Tune-Up Specifications") and the crankshaft pulley notch with chalk or paint.

2. Connect a tachometer and timing light as per the manufacturer's instructions. Start the engine and run at fast idle until normal operating temperature is reached. Shut off engine.

3. On five-speed transmission equipped models, disconnect and plug the vacuum lines at the distributor. Place the transmis-

sion in neutral, set the parking brake and block the wheels.

4. Turn off all lights and accessories. Start the engine and check the curb idle speed. Adjust idle speed to specifications if necessary.

5. On models with an electric cooling fan, the fan must not be operating when checking the timing. Run the engine at fast idle until the fan stops, then proceed with the timing check.

6. Shine the timing light at the timing marks. If the marks do not align, loosen the distributor base retaining nut and rotate the distributor until the marks align. Tighten the base nut.

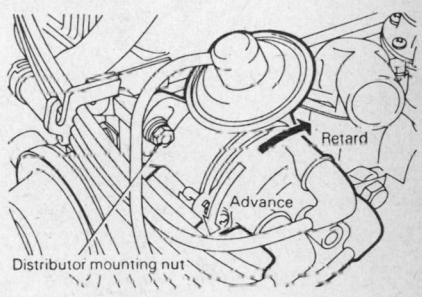

Adjusting ignition timing

7. Shut off the engine, disconnect the tachometer and timing light. Connect the distributor vacuum hoses on five-speed models.

Valve Lash

ADJUSTMENT

NOTE: On models equipped with a jet valve, the jet valve must be adjusted before the intake valve and the intake valve adjuster can be fully loosened.

1. Run the engine until normal operating temperature is reached. Shut off the engine and remove the cylinder head cover.

2. Place the No. 1 piston at top dead center (TDC) of the compression stroke. Valves marked "A" can now be adjusted. They are: No. 1 and 2 intake valves and No. 1 and 3 exhaust valves.

3. Turn the engine until the No. 4 piston is at TDC of the compression stroke. Valves marked "B" can now be adjusted. They are: No. 3 and 4 intake valves and No. 2 and 4 exhaust valves.

4. To adjust the jet valve, back off the intake valve adjusting screw two or more turns. Loosen the locknut on the jet valve adjuster, back off the adjuster screw and place a 0.006 in. feeler gauge between the top of the jet valve and the adjuster screw. Turn the adjuster screw in until slight pressure is felt on the feeler gauge (the jet valve spring is very weak, take care not to force the jet valve in when making adjustment). Hold the adjuster screw in position with a screwdriver and tighten the locknut firmly.

5. Adjust the valves in the "A" and

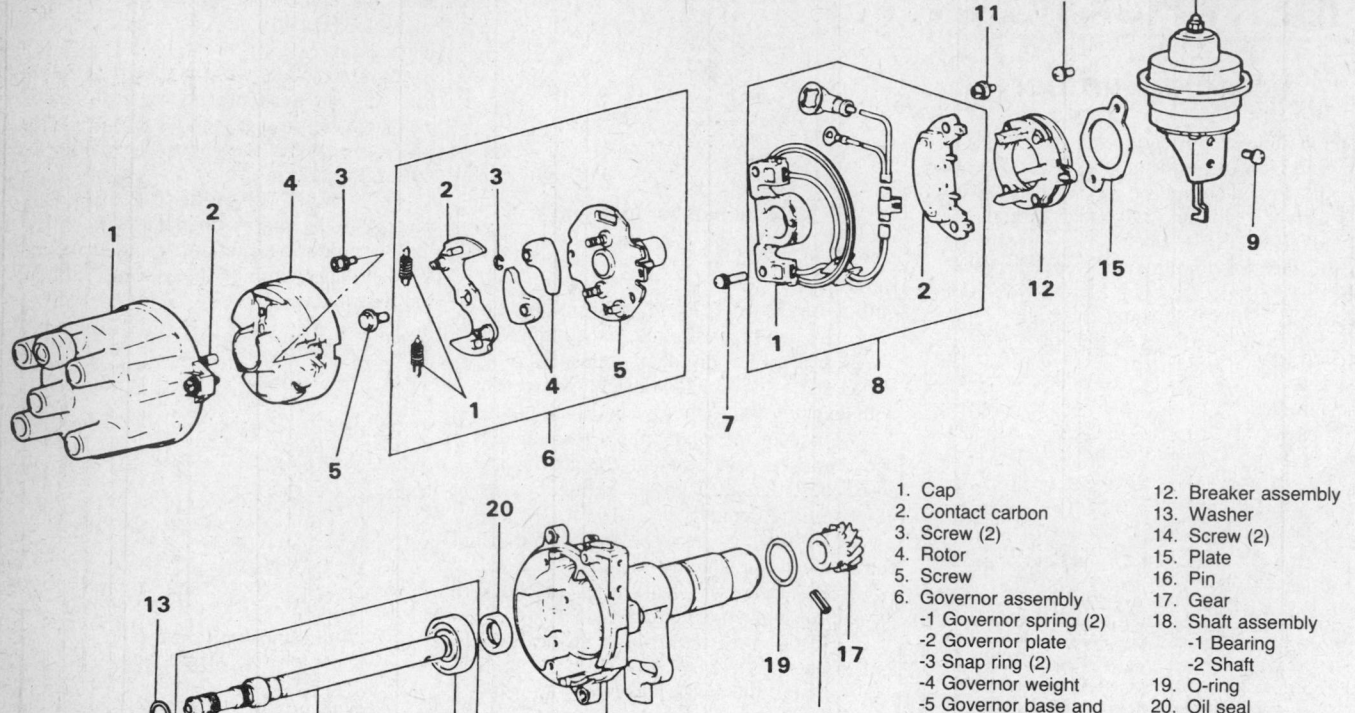

1. Cap
2. Contact carbon
3. Screw (2)
4. Rotor
5. Screw
6. Governor assembly
   -1 Governor spring (2)
   -2 Governor plate
   -3 Snap ring (2)
   -4 Governor weight
   -5 Governor base and signal rotor
7. Screw (2)
8. Pickup coil and igniter
   -1 Pickup coil
   -2 Frame
9. Screw (2)
10. Vacuum controller
11. Screw (2)
12. Breaker assembly
13. Washer
14. Screw (2)
15. Plate
16. Pin
17. Gear
18. Shaft assembly
    -1 Bearing
    -2 Shaft
19. O-ring
20. Oil seal
21. Housing

NOTE
Numbers show order of disassembly.
For reassembly, reverse order of disassembly.

Typical distributor components

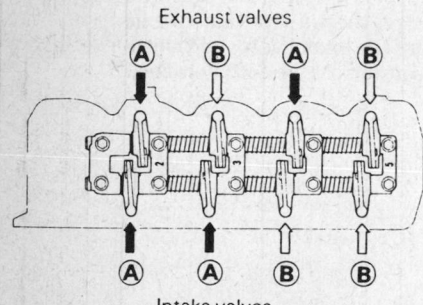

Exhaust valves

Intake valves

"A" and "B" valve adjusting positions

"B" order, using the same adjusting method as on the jet valve. With the engine at normal operating temperature, the intake valve is adjusted to 0.006 in. and the exhaust valve to 0.010 in.

Idle Speed

ADJUSTMENT

Carbureted Engines

1. Run the engine at fast idle until normal operating temperature is reached. Turn off all lights and accessories. The electric cooling fan must not be operating. Set the

Adjusting valve clearance

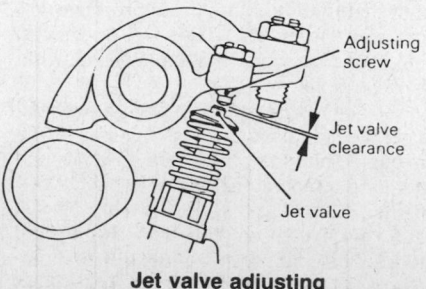

Adjusting screw

Jet valve clearance

Jet valve

Jet valve adjusting

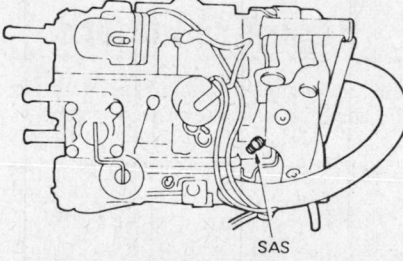

SAS

Idle speed adjusting screw (SAS)

parking brake, block the wheels and place the transmission in neutral.

2. Run the engine between 2000 and 3000 rpm for about five seconds, then allow it to idle for two minutes.

3. Check the idle speed. Adjust (if essary) with th idle speed adjustment screw on the carburetor linkage arm.

Fuel Injected Engines

1. Run the engine until normal operating temperature is reached. Make sure all lights and accessories are turned off.

2. Apply the parking brake and block the wheels. Place the transmission in neutral and stop the engine.

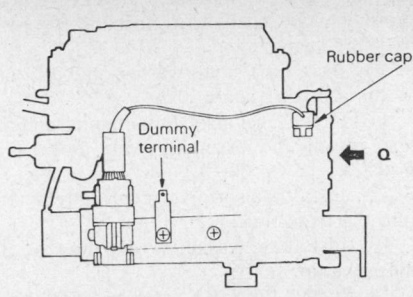 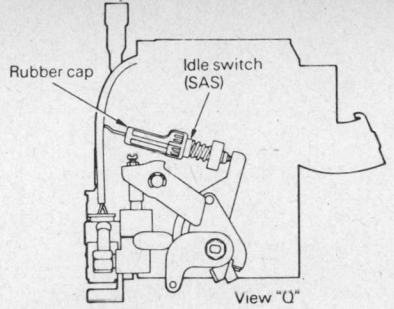

Idle speed adjustment for fuel injection

3. Attach a tachometer and timing light. Start the engine and increase the engine speed to 2000–3000 rpm several times, return to idle and check the ignition timing. Timing should be as noted in the Tune-up Specifications chart at curb idle, adjust if necessary.

4. Remove the rubber cap covering the idle speed adjuster switch, leaving the cable connector connected. The idle adjuster switch is located on the throttle linkage. Adjust the idle speed to the figure noted in the Tune-up Specifications chart.

5. If the idle adjustment screw must be turned more than 1 turn during adjustment, disconnect the connector from the speed adjuster switch and plug it into the dummy terminal on the injector base. Adjust to correct idle speed and reconnect to the idle switch. Remove the tachometer and timing light.

ENGINE ELECTRICAL

Distributor

REMOVAL & INSTALLATION

1. Turn the engine until the No. 1 piston is at top dead center (TDC) of the compression stroke.

2. Remove the distributor cap with the spark plug wires attached and position it out of the way. Disconnect the distributor wiring connector and vacuum hoses.

3. Remove the distributor base retaining nut. Remove the distributor.

4. To install the distributor after checking that the No. 1 piston is at TDC of the compression stroke: align the marks on the bottom of the distributor housing (just above the drive gear) with the punch mark on the distributor drive gear. Install the distributor to the cylinder head while aligning the mark on the base attaching flange with center of the holddown stud. Install the retaining nut, distributor cap and vacuum hoses. Start the engine and adjust the ignition timing.

Alternator

PRECAUTIONS

In order to prevent damage to the alternator observe the following precautions:

1. Reversing the battery connections will result in damage to the diodes.

2. Booster cables should be connected from positive to positive and the negative cable from the booster battery connected to a good ground on the engine of the car with the dead battery.

3. Never use a fast charger as a booster to start the car.

4. When servicing the battery with a fast charger always disconnect the battery cables.

5. Never attempt to polarize an alternator.

6. Avoid long soldering times when replacing diodes or transistors. Prolonged heat is damaging to alternators.

7. Do not use test lamps of more than 12V (volts) for checking diode continuity.

8. Do not short across or ground any of the alternator terminals.

9. The polarity of the battery, alternator and regulator must be matched and considered before making any electrical connections within the system.

10. Never operate the alternator on an open circuit. Make sure all connections within a circuit are clean and tight.

11. Disconnect the negative (or both) battery terminals when performing any service on the electrical system.

12. Disconnect the negative battery cable if arc welding is to be done on any part of the car.

BELT TENSION ADJUSTMENT

1. Check the drive belt(s) for cracking, fraying or any other deterioration. Replace the drive belt if suspect.

2. To replace the drive belt, loosen the fixed point mounting nut and bolt. Loosen the slotted bracket mounting nut and bolt and pivot the driven component to loosen and/or tighten the belt. When adjusting the belt, loosen the mounting bolts (see above) and pull on the driven component to increase tension. When proper tension is present, tighten the slotted bracket nut and bolt and then the fixed point nut and bolt.

3. Belt tension is proper when the belt can be deflected at mid-point 9/32–11/32 in.

REMOVAL & INSTALLATION

1. Disconnect the battery cables and the alternator wires. Note or tag the wires so that you can reinstall them correctly.

2. Loosen and remove the top mounting bolt.

3. Loosen the elongated lower mounting nut. Slide the alternator over in its attaching bracket and remove the fan belt.

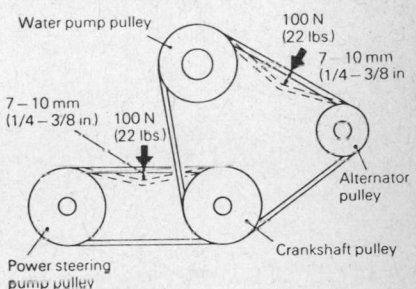

Drive belt adjustment

4. Remove the lower mounting nut and bolt, being sure not to lose any mounting shims.

5. Remove the alternator.

NOTE: Remember when installing the alternator that it is not necessary to polarize the system.

6. Trial fit the alternator on the engine. The shims are installed on the inside of both alternator mounting legs. Add more shims, if necessary, for a tight fit.

7. Install the lower mounting bolt and nut. Do not completely tighten it yet.

8. Fit the fan belt over the alternator and crankshaft pulleys.

9. Loosely install the top mounting bolt and pivot the alternator over until the fan belt is correctly tensioned as outlined above.

10. Finally tighten the top and bottom bolts.

11. Connect the alternator wires and the battery cables.

Regulator

The voltage regulator is of solid-state design and built into the alternator. No normal maintenance is necessary.

Starter

REMOVAL & INSTALLATION

1. Disconnect the negative battery cable and the starter motor wiring.

2. Remove the starter motor-to-engine mounting bolts. Remove the starter motor.

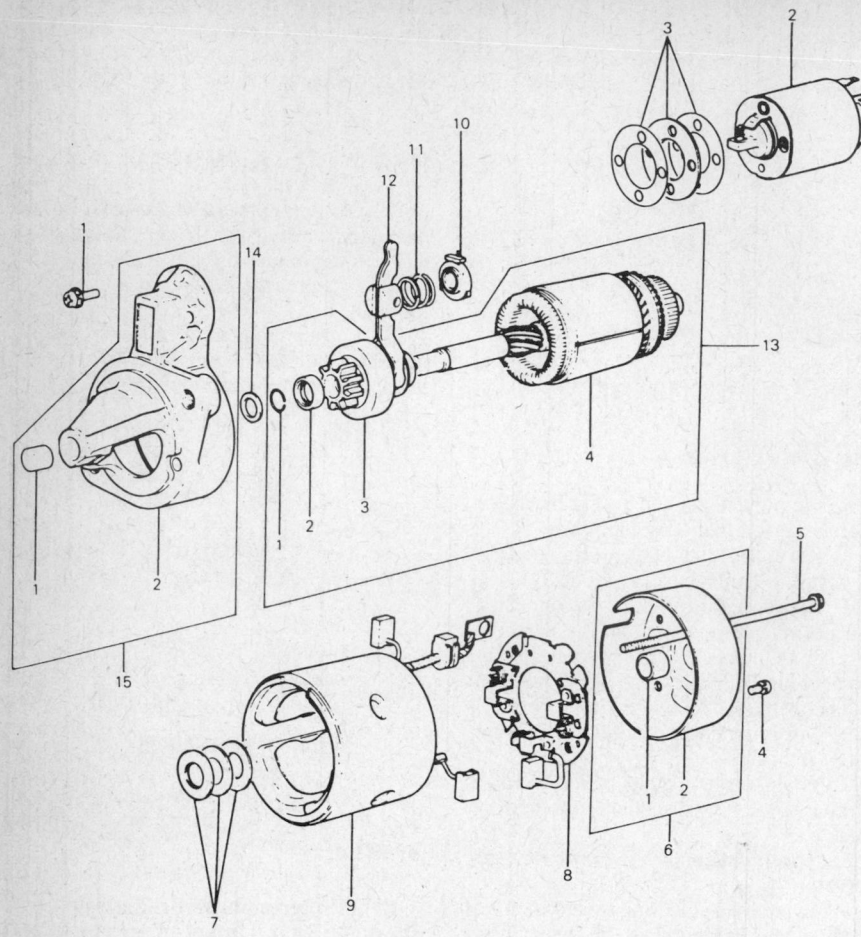

1. Screw (2)
2. Magnetic switch
3. Packing
4. Screw (2)
5. Through bolt (2)
6. Rear bracket
   assembly
   -1 Bushing
   -2 Rear bracket
7. Washer

8. Brush holder
9. Yoke assembly
10. Spring retainer
11. Lever spring
12. Lever
13. Armature assembly
    -1 Snap ring
    -2 Stop ring
    -3 Overrunning clutch
    -4 Armature

14. Washer
15. Front bracket
    assembly
    -1 Bushing
    -2 Front bracket
NOTE
Numbers show order of
disassembly.
For reassembly, reverse
order of disassembly.

Typical starter motor components

3. If various components make starter motor removal difficult from the top of the engine compartment, raise and support the car, then remove the starter from underneath after removing the splash shield.

4. Reinstall the starter motor in the reverse order of removal.

STARTER DRIVE REPLACEMENT

1. Remove the "M" terminal wire and the two solenoid mounting screws. Remove the solenoid.

2. Remove the two long starter through-bolts and separate the armature and yoke assemblies.

3. Carefully remove the armature and lever from the front bracket.

NOTE: Mark or take careful note of the direction of installation on the lever and spring as they are removed, since they must be reinstalled in the proper direction.

4. Using a piece of pipe or the equivalent, tap the stopper toward the starter drive pinion assembly, with a small hammer or mallet. The stopper must clear the snap-ring.

5. Remove the snap-ring, stopper and pinion drive assembly from the armature shaft.

6. Inspect the pinion and spline teeth for wear or damage.

NOTE: If pinion teeth are damaged always inspect the flywheel teeth for possible damage.

7. Rotate the pinion in both directions. It should turn freely in a clockwise direction and lock when turned counterclockwise.

8. Install the over-running clutch and pinion drive onto the armature shaft.

9. Install the stopper and snap-ring on the armature shaft. Push the stopper over the snap-ring. A small gear puller or arbor press may be needed to push the stopper over the snap-ring.

10. Install the small washer on the front of the armature shaft.

11. Fit the lever in the over-running clutch and install the assembly into the front bracket.

12. Install the spring and spring retainer into the front bracket.

13. Install the washer(s) onto the rear of the armature shaft.

14. Install the yoke assembly onto the front bracket and armature assembly.

15. Put the lever in the front end of the solenoid plunger and install and tighten the two solenoid attaching screws.

16. Connect the "M" terminal to the solenoid.

ENGINE MECHANICAL

Engine

REMOVAL & INSTALLATION

—————— CAUTION ——————
If equipped with air conditioning, use EX-TREME CAUTION. Do not disconnect any lines unless you are familiar with safety procedures.

Rear Wheel Drive

NOTE: The engine and transmission are removed together as a unit.

1. See "Caution" above. Drain the cooling system.

2. Disconnect and remove the battery.

3. Disconnect the coil, throttle positioner solenoid, fuel cut-off solenoid, alternator, starter, transmission switch, back-up light switch, temperature and oil pressure gauge sending units, manifold and engine ground straps, brake booster vacuum hose and distributor wiring connector.

4. Remove all air cleaner hoses. Remove the wing nut (and snap clips) and the air cleaner top cover.

5. Remove the two retaining nuts and bracket and remove the air cleaner housing.

6. Disconnect the accelerator cable.

7. Remove and plug the heater hose.

8. Disconnect the exhaust pipe from the manifold or turbocharger.

9. Disconnect the inlet and return fuel lines at the pump on carburetor equipped models. On fuel injected models, disconnect the fuel line clamp and remove the inlet line; remove the two bolts and secondary fuel line from the injector unit. Disconnect the boost sensor hose. Plug them so that foreign matter is kept out of the fuel system.

10. Disconnect the vacuum hose from

the canister purge valve located on the passenger side firewall. Remove the purge hose which runs from the valve, to the intake manifold.

11. Scribe a line around the hood hinges and then remove the hood. Place it away from the work area or it will invariably become scratched or dented.

12. Remove the grille, radiator cross panel, and the radiator. Disconnect and plug the oil cooler lines on automatic transmission equipped cars. Disconnect and plug the engine oil cooler lines (at the engine) on turbo models. Remove and secure the power steering pump (with hoses connected) out of the way.

13. Jack up the front of the car and support it on jackstands. Remove the splash shield. Remove the rear converter and pipe on models so equipped.

14. Drain the engine oil and the transmission oil or fluid. Remove the driveshaft.

15. Disconnect the speedometer cable and back-up switch wire. Remove the neutral switch wire on automatic cars. On manual cars:

NOTE: Disconnect the clutch cable from the clutch lever.

17. Remove the control rod and cross shaft from under the transmission.

18. Untie and open the leather shift boot. Pull the rug back. Remove the four retaining bolts and remove the shift lever.

19. Attach the lifting device to the two engine brackets provided by the factory, one near the water neck at the front and the other on the passenger's side at the rear.

20. Raise the engine a slight amount and remove the retaining nuts on the side mounts and the rear crossmember mount.

21. Lift the engine out of the compartment by tilting it at approximately a 45° angle.

22. Check the condition of the engine mounts. There are three: left front, right front, and rear. If they are at all questionable, now is the time to replace them.

23. Installing the engine is basically a reverse of the removal procedure, noting the following:

  a. Drape heavy rags over the rear of the cylinder head to prevent damaging the firewall when lowering the engine into place.

  b. Tighten the two front mounts first and then the rear crossmember mount. All tightening torques are listed in the chart below.

Front-Wheel Drive

The factory recommends that the engine and transaxle be removed as a unit.

1. Disconnect the battery cables (ground cable first) remove battery hold-down and battery. Remove the battery tray.

2. Remove the air cleaner assembly. Disconnect the purge control vacuum hose from the purge valve. Remove the purge control valve mounting bracket. Remove the windshield washer reservoir, radiator tank and carbon canister.

3. Drain the coolant from the radiator. Remove the radiator assembly with the electric cooling fan attached. Be sure to disconnect the fan wiring harness and the transmission cooler lines (if equipped with automatic trans.).

4. Disconnect the following cables, hoses and wires from the engine and transaxle: clutch, accelerator, speedometer, heater hose, fuel lines, PCV vacuum line, high-altitude compensator vacuum hose (Calif. models), bowl vent valve purge hose (49 states models), inhibitor switch (auto. trans.), control cable (auto. trans.), starter, engine ground cable, alternator, ignition coil, water temperature sensor, back-up light (man. trans.) and oil pressure wires.

5. Remove the ignition coil. The next step will be to jack up the car. Before you do this, look around and make sure all wires and hoses are disconnected.

6. Jack up the front of the car after you block the rear wheels. Support the car on jack stands. Remove the splash shield (if equipped).

7. Drain the lubricant out of the transaxle.

8. Remove the right and left driveshafts from the transaxle and support them with wire. Plug the transaxle case holes so dirt cannot enter.

CAUTION
The driveshaft retainer ring should be replaced whenever the shaft is removed.

9. Disconnect the assist rod and the control rod from the transaxle. If the car is equipped with a range selector, disconnect the selector cable.

10. Remove the mounting bolts/bolt from the front and rear roll control rods.

11. Disconnect the exhaust pipe from the engine and secure it with wire.

12. Loosen the engine and transaxle mounting bracket nuts.

13. Lower the car.

14. Attach a lifting device and a shop crane or chain hoist to the engine. Apply slight lifting pressure to the engine. Remove the engine and transaxle mounting nuts and bolts.

15. Make sure the rear roll control rod is disconnected. Lift the engine and transaxle from the car.

CAUTION
Make sure the transaxle does not hit the battery bracket when the engine and transaxle are lifted.

16. Lower the engine and transaxle carefully into position and loosely install the mounting bolts. Temporarily tighten the front and rear roll control rods mounting bolts. Lower the full weight of the engine and transaxle onto the mounts and tighten the nuts and bolts. Loosen and retighten the roll control rods.

17. The rest of the engine installation is the reverse of the removal. Make sure all cables, hoses and wires are connected. Fill the radiator with coolant, the transaxle with lubricant. Adjust the clutch cable and accelerator cable. Adjust the transaxle control rod. Take another check on everything you have done. Start the engine and check for leaks.

Cylinder Head

REMOVAL & INSTALLATION

CAUTION
Never remove the cylinder head unless the engine is absolutely cold.

1. Turn the engine until the No. 1 pis-

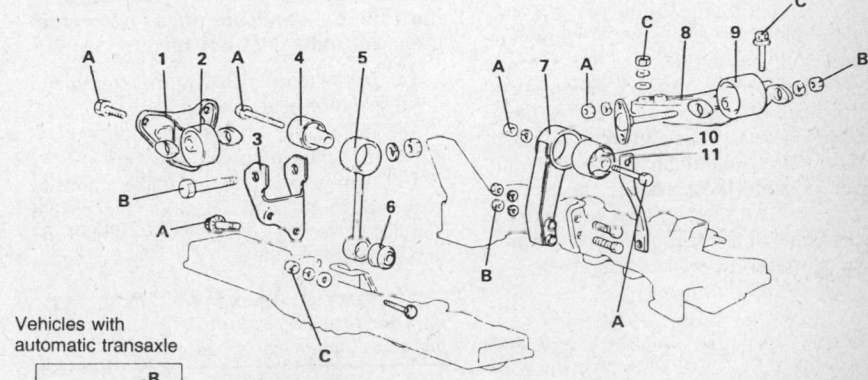

Vehicles with automatic transaxle

1. Transaxle insulator bracket
2. Transaxle mount insulator
3. Transaxle mount bracket
4. Upper roll insulator
5. Front roll rod
6. Lower roll insulator
7. Rear roll stopper bracket
8. Left mount bracket

	Nm	ft.lbs.
A	30–40	22–29
B	60–80	43–58
C	50–65	36–47

9. Left mount insulator
10. Rear roll insulator
11. Rear roll stopper stay

Cordia, Tredia engine/transaxle mounting

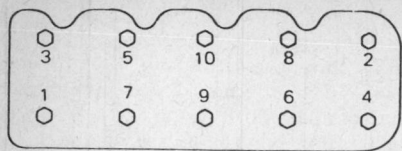

1800 and 2000cc engine head bolt removal sequence

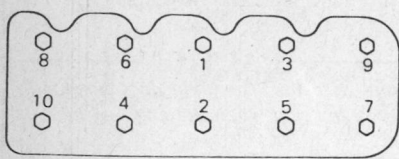

1800 and 2000cc engine head bolt torque sequence

ton is at top dead center on the compression stroke. Disconnect the negative battery cable. Remove the air cleaner assembly, attaching hoses and duct work.

2. Drain the engine coolant. Remove the upper radiator hose and disconnect the heater hoses.

3. Disconnect the fuel lines, wiring harnesses, distributor vacuum lines, spark plug wires (from plugs), purge valves, accelerator linkage and water temperature unit wire.

4. Remove the distributor and the fuel pump from the cylinder head.

5. Remove the nuts connecting the exhaust pipe to the manifold or turbocharger. Lower the exhaust pipe.

6. Remove the turbocharger and/or exhaust manifold.

7. Remove the intake manifold assembly.

8. On 1800cc and 2000cc Engines:

a. Remove the upper, outer front cover. Align the timing mark on the cylinder head with the mark on the camshaft sprocket (engine should already be on the No. 1 piston TDC of the compression stroke).

b. Matchmark the timing belt with the timing mark on the camshaft sprocket using a felt tip marker.

c. Remove the sprocket and insert a 2 in. piece of rubber (old belt) or other material between the camshaft sprocket and sprocket holder on the lower front cover, to hold the sprocket and belt so that the valve timing will not be changed.

d. Remove the timing belt upper under cover and the rocker arm cover.

9. On 2600c Engines:

a. Remove the rocker arm cover.

b. Position the camshaft sprocket dowel pin at the 12 o'clock position with the timing mark (TDC) at the front of the timing case cover (engine should already be on the No. 1 piston TDC of the compression stroke).

c. Match the timing chain with the timing mark on the camshaft sprocket. Take a soft piece of wire and secure the chain and sprocket together at the timing mark and opposite side.

d. Remove the camshaft sprocket bolt, gear and sprocket from the camshaft.

10. Loosen and remove the cylinder head bolts in two or three stages to avoid cylinder head warpage. Start from the outer ends and work toward the middle.

11. Remove the cylinder head from the engine.

12. Clean the cylinder head and block mating surfaces, and install a new cylinder head gasket.

13. Position the cylinder head on the engine block, engage the dowel pins front and rear, and install the cylinder head bolts.

14. Tighten the head bolts in three stages and then torque to specifications.

15. Install the timing belt upper under cover (1800 and 2000cc engines).

16. Locate the camshaft in original position. Pull the camshaft sprocket and belt or chain upward, and install on the camshaft.

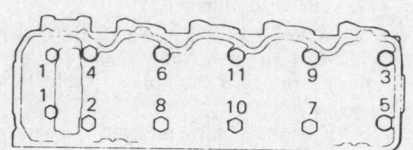

2600cc cylinder head bolt removal sequence

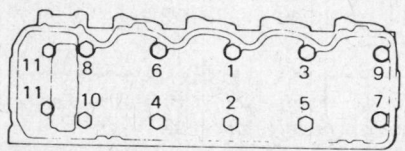

2600cc cylinder head bolt torque sequence

NOTE: If the dowel pin and the dowel pin hole does not line up between the sprocket and the spacer or camshaft, move the camshaft by bumping either of the two projections provided at the rear of No. 2 cylinder exhaust cam of the camshaft, with a light hammer or other tool, until the hole and pin align. Be certain the crankshaft does not turn.

17. Install the camshaft sprocket bolt and the distributor gear, and tighten.

18. Install the timing belt upper front cover and spark plug cable support.

19. Apply sealant to the intake manifold gasket on both sides. Position the gasket and install the intake manifold. Tighten the nuts to specifications.

———— CAUTION ————
Be sure that no sealant enters the jet air passages, when equipped.

20. Install the exhaust manifold gaskets and the manifold assembly. Tighten the nuts to specifications.

21. Connect the exhaust pipe to the exhaust manifold and install the fuel pump. Install the purge valve.

22. Install the water temperature gauge wire, heater hoses and the upper radiator hose.

23. Connect the fuel lines, accelerator linkage, vacuum hoses and the spark plug wires.

24. Fill the cooling system and connect the battery ground cable. Install the distributor.

25. Temporarily adjust the valve clearance to the cold engine specifications.

26. Install the gasket on the rocker arm cover and temporarily install the cover on the engine.

27. Start the engine and bring it to normal operating temperature. Stop the engine and remove the rocker arm cover.

28. Adjust the valves to hot engine specifications.

29. Reinstall the rocker arm cover and tighten securely.

30. Install the air cleaner, hoses, purge valve hose, and any other removed unit.

OVERHAUL

For all cylinder head overhaul procedures, please refer to "Engine Rebuilding" in the Unit Repair section.

Rocker Arms/Camshaft
REMOVAL & INSTALLATION

The camshaft and rocker arms are best removed after the cylinder head has been removed from the engine block.

1. Match-mark the rocker arm bearing caps to the cylinder head.

2. Remove the bearing cap bolts from the cylinder head, but do not remove them from the bearing caps and shafts. Lift the rocker arm assembly from the cylinder head.

3. Remove the camshaft from the bearing saddles.

NOTE: On some engines, a distributor drive gear and spacer are used on the front of the camshaft.

4. The valves, valve springs, and valve guide seals can now be removed from the cylinder head.

NOTE: Refer to the cylinder head overhaul procedures in the "Engine Rebuilding" section. Valve guides are a shrink fit, with oversize guides available. Valve seats are replaceable, with oversize seats available.

5. The rocker arm assembly can be disassembled by the removal of the bolts from the bearing caps and shafts.

NOTE: a. Keep the rocker arms and springs in proper order. The left and right springs have different tension ratings and free lengths.

b. Observe the location of the mating marks of the right and left rocker arm shaft in relation to the front bearing cap mating marks.

6. Observe the mating marks and reassemble the units in the reverse order of the removal.

NOTE: On the 1800 and 2000cc engines, the left rocker shaft is longer than the right.

Jet Valve

REMOVAL & INSTALLATION

The jet valve can be removed from the cylinder head with the rocker arm either in place or removed. Care must be exercised not to twist the socket while removing or replacing the valve, so as not to break it. Torque the valve to 13.5–15.5 ft. lbs.

Intake Manifold

REMOVAL & INSTALLATION

——— CAUTION ———
The intake manifold is cast aluminum.

1. Remove the air cleaner and duct hose assembly.
2. Disconnect the fuel line(s), EGR lines and other vacuum hoses and wire harness connectors.
3. Disconnect the throttle positioner solenoid and fuel cut-off solenoid wires.
4. Disconnect the accelerator linkage and, if equipped with automatic transmission, the shift cables at the carburetor/injector.
5. Drain the coolant.
6. Remove the water hose from carburetor and cylinder head.
7. Remove the heater and water outlet hoses.
8. Disconnect the water temperature sending unit.
9. Remove the manifold and carburetor/injector assembly. Remove mounting nuts/bolts from the ends toward the middle.
10. Clean all mounting surfaces. Before reinstalling the manifold, coat both sides with gasket sealer. Install mounting nuts/bolts starting from the center toward the ends.

Exhaust Manifold

REMOVAL & INSTALLATION

1. Remove the air cleaner and duct hose assembly.
2. Remove the manifold heat stove and hose. Disconnect the EGR lines and reed valve, if equipped.
3. Disconnect the exhaust pipe bracket from the engine block.
4. Remove the exhaust pipe flange bolts from the manifold or turbocharger. (One bolt and nut may have to be removed from under the car.)
5. Remove the manifold flange stud nuts starting from the ends toward the middle and remove the manifold from the cylinder head.
6. Installation is the reverse of re-

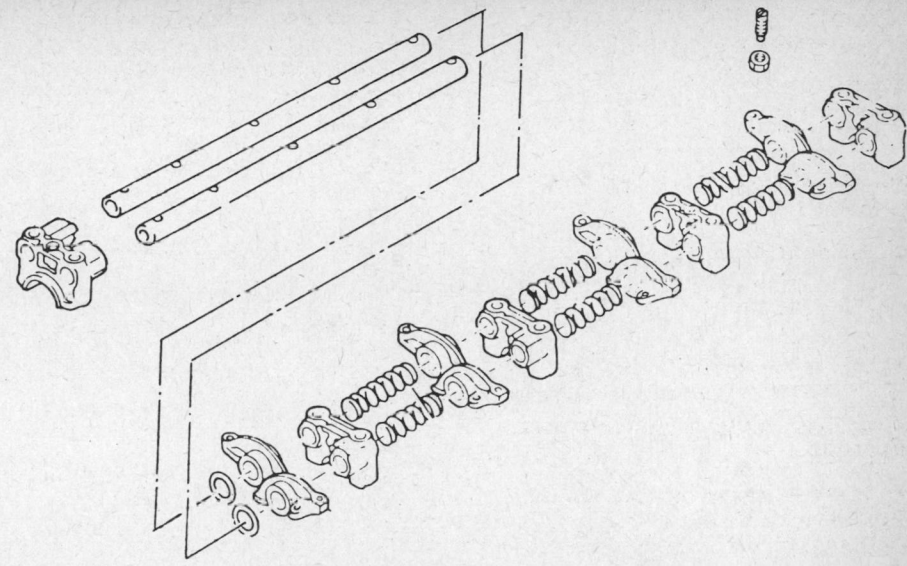

Typical rocker arm and shaft assembly

moval. Install mounting nuts starting from the middle toward the ends.

Turbocharger

For further information on turbocharging, please refer to "Turbocharging" in the Unit Repair section.

REMOVAL & INSTALLATION

NOTE: Before removal, make sure the exhaust system and engine are cool. Take care to protect the oil passages in the turbocharger from dirt. Apply penetrating oil if the mounting nuts and bolts are rusted.

1. Remove the air intake hose between the turbocharger and ECI. Take care of the O-ring at the turbocharger.
2. Remove the heat shield from around the turbocharger.
3. Remove the exhaust pipe from the turbocharger. Disconnect both ends (flare nuts) of the oil feed tube and remove the tube.
4. Remove the two clamps connecting the oil return hose to the pipes. Slide the clamps off the hose. Remove the oil return pipe mounting clip nut. Remove the nuts retaining the oil return line flange to the turbocharger. Remove the line.
5. Remove the lower heat shield, turbocharger mounting bolts and turbocharger.
6. Install in reverse order.

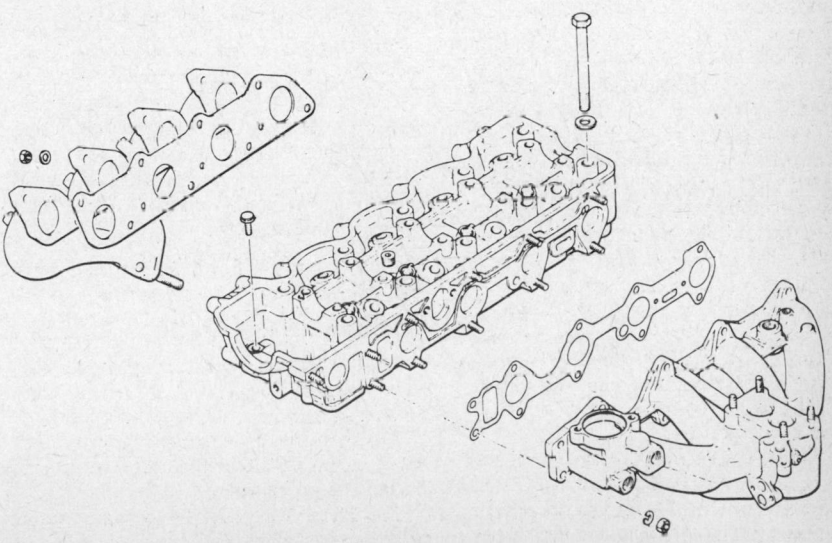

Typical intake and exhaust manifold installation

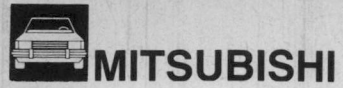

1. Bolt
2. Air intake pipe
3. O-ring
4. Bolt
5. Bolt (2)
6. Heat insulator
7. Nut (3)
8. Washer (3)
9. Heat insulator stay
10. Gasket
11. Bolt
12. Flare nut of oil pipe

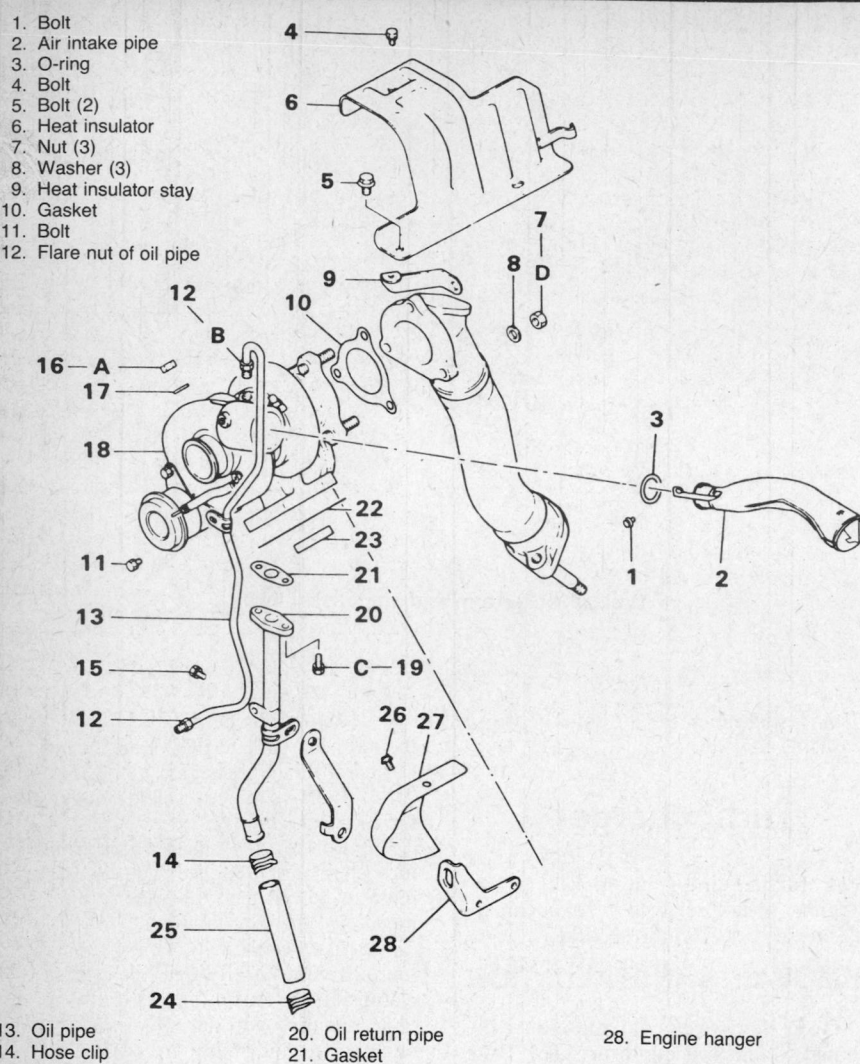

13. Oil pipe
14. Hose clip
15. Bolt
16. Nut (4)
17. Plain washer (4)
18. Turbocharger assembly
19. Bolt (2)
20. Oil return pipe
21. Gasket
22. Gasket
23. Ring
24. Hose clip
25. Oil hose
26. Bolt
27. Heat insulator
28. Engine hanger

	Nm	ft.lbs.
A	49–68	37–50
B	16–23	12–17
C	8–9	6–7
D	49–68	37–50

Turbocharger mounting components

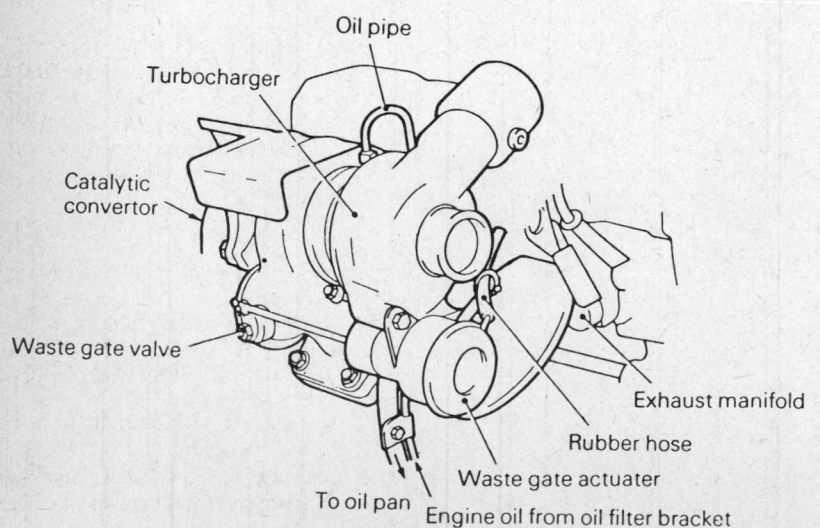

Turbocharger mounting

Timing Cover, Chain/ Belt, Counterbalance Shafts and Tensioner

REMOVAL & INSTALLATION

NOTE: The timing chain case is cast aluminum, so exercise caution when handling this part.

The following outlines are the recommended removal and installation procedures for the timing chain or belt. Some modifications to the procedures may be necessary due to added accessories, sheet-metal parts, or emission control units and connecting hoses.

1800cc and 2000cc Engines

1. Drain the coolant and remove the radiator. Disconnect the battery cable.

2. Remove the alternator and accessory belts.

3. Rotate the crankshaft to bring No. 1 piston to TDC on the compression stroke. Align the notch on the crankshaft pulley with the "T" mark on the timing indicator

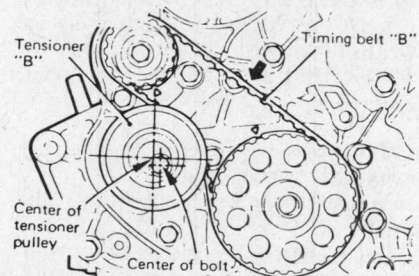

1800 and 2000cc Silent Shaft timing marks

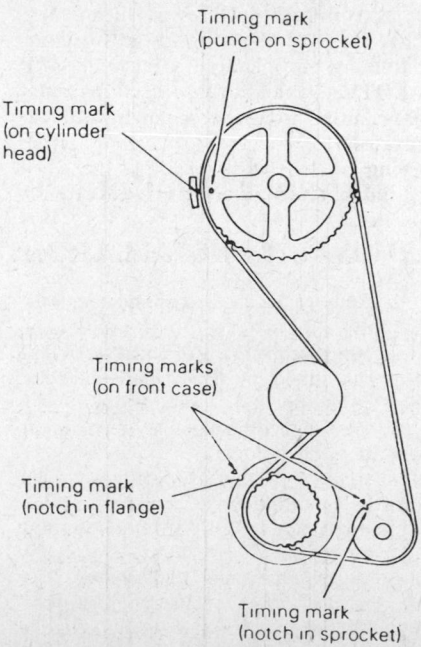

1800 and 2000cc camshaft drive belt timing marks

scale and the timing mark on the upper under cover of the timing belt with the mark on the camshaft sprocket. Mark and remove the distributor.

4. Remove the crankshaft pulley and bolt.

5. Remove the fan and mounting bracket assembly if necessary for working room.

6. Remove the timing belt covers, upper front and lower front.

7. Remove the crankshaft sprocket bolt.

8. Loosen the tensioner mounting nut and bolt. Move the tensioner away from the belt and retighten the nut to keep the tensioner in the off position. Remove the belt.

9. Remove the camshaft sprocket, crankshaft sprocket, flange, and tensioner.

10. a. Loosen the counterbalance shaft sprocket mounting bolt.

b. Remove the belt tensioner and remove the timing belt.

c. Remove the crankshaft sprocket (inner) and counterbalance shaft sprocket.

d. Remove the upper and lower under timing belt covers.

11. The water pump or cylinder head may be removed at this point, depending upon the type of repairs needed.

12. Raise the front of the car and support it safely. Remove any interfering splash pans.

13. Drain the oil pan and remove the pan from the block.

14. Remove the oil pump sprocket and cover.

NOTE: Remove the plug at the bottom of the left side of the cylinder block and insert a screwdriver to keep the left counterbalance shaft in position while removing the sprocket nut.

15. Remove the front cover and oil pump as a unit, with the left counter shaft attached, if equipped.

16. Remove the oil pump gear and left counterbalance shaft.

NOTE: To aid in removal of the front cover, a driver groove is provided on the cover, above the oil pump housing. Avoid prying on the thinner parts of the housing flange or hammering on it to remove the case.

17. Remove the right counterbalance shaft from the engine block.

18. Install a new front seal in the cover. Install the oil pump drive and driven gears in the front case, aligning the timing marks on the pump gears.

19. Install the left counterbalance shaft in the driven gear and temporarily tighten the bolt.

20. Install the right counterbalance shaft into the cylinder block.

21. Install an oil seal guide on the end of the crankshaft, and install a new gasket on the front of the engine block for the front cover.

22. Install a new front case packing, if equipped.

23. Insert the left counterbalance shaft into the engine block and at the same time guide the front cover into place on the front of the engine block.

24. Insert a screwdriver at the bottom of the left side of the block and hold the left counterbalance shaft and tighten the bolt. Install the hole plug.

25. Install an O-ring on the oil pump cover and install it on the front cover.

26. Tighten the oil pump cover bolts and the front cover bolts to 11–13 ft. lbs.

27. Install the oil screen, and using a new gasket, install the oil pan.

28. Install the water pump and/or the cylinder head, if removed previously.

29. Install the upper and lower under covers.

30. Install the spacer on the end of the right counterbalance shaft, with the chamfered edge toward the rear of the engine.

31. Install the counterbalance shaft sprocket and temporarily tighten the bolt.

32. Install the inner crankshaft sprocket and align the timing marks on the sprockets with those on the front case.

33. Install the inner tensioner (B) with the center of the pulley on the left side of the mounting bolt and with the pulley flange toward the front of the engine.

34. Lift the tensioner by hand, clockwise, to apply tension to the belt. Tighten the bolt to secure the tensioner.

35. Check that all alignment marks are in their proper places and the belt deflection is approximately ¼–½ inch on the tension side.

NOTE: When the tensioner bolt is tightened, make sure the shaft of the tensioner does not turn with the bolt. If the belt is too tight there will be noise, and if the belt is too loose, the belt and sprocket may come out of mesh.

36. Tighten the counterbalance shaft sprocket bolt to 22–28.5 ft. lbs.

37. Install the flange and crankshaft sprocket. Tighten the bolt to 43.5–50.5 ft. lbs. on 1983 models and 80–94 ft. lb. on 1984–85 models.

38. Install the camshaft spacer and sprocket. Tighten the bolt to 44–57 ft. lbs.

on 1983 models and 58–72 ft. lb. on 1984–85 models.

39. Align the camshaft sprocket timing mark with the timing mark on the upper inner cover.

40. Install the oil pump sprocket, tightening the nut to 25–28.5 ft. lbs. Align the timing mark on the sprocket with the mark on the case.

CAUTION

To be assured that the phasing of the oil pump sprocket and the left counterbalance shaft is correct, a screwdriver or a metal rod should be inserted in the plugged hole on the left side of the cylinder block. If it can be inserted more than 2⅜ inches, the phasing is correct. If the tool can only be inserted approximately one inch, turn the oil pump sprocket through one turn and realign the timing marks. Keep the screwdriver or metal rod inserted until the installation of the timing belt is completed. Remove the tool from the hole and install the plug, before starting the engine.

---

41. Install the tensioner spring and tensioner. Temporarily tighten the nut. Install the front end of the tensioner spring (bent at right angles) on the projection of the tensioner and the other end (straight) on the water pump body.

42. If the timing belt is correctly tensioned, there should be about 0.5 in. clearance between the outside of the belt and the edge of the belt cover. This is measured about halfway down the side of the belt opposite the tensioner.

43. Complete the assembly by installing the upper and lower front covers.

44. Install the crankshaft pulley, alternator, and accessory belts, and adjust to specifications.

2600cc Engine

1. Drain the coolant and remove the radiator. Disconnect the battery ground cable.

2. Remove the alternator and accessory belts.

3. Rotate the crankshaft to bring No. 1 piston to TDC, on the compression stroke.

4. Mark and remove the distributor.

5. Remove the crankshaft pulley.

6. Remove the water pump assembly.

7. Remove the cylinder head, if necessary.

8. Raise the front of the car and support it safely.

9. Drain the engine oil and remove the oil pan and screen.

10. Remove the timing case cover.

11. Remove the chain guides. Side (A), Top (B), Bottom (C), from the ''B'' chain (outer).

12. Remove the locking bolts from the ''B'' chain sprockets.

13. Remove the crankshaft sprocket, counterbalance shaft sprocket and the outer chain.

14. Remove the crankshaft and cam-

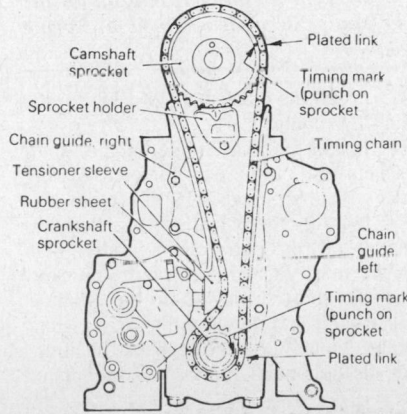

2600cc cam drive chain timing marks

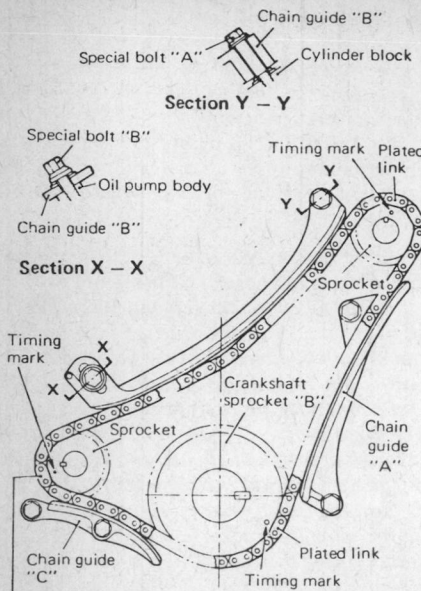

Section Y — Y

Special bolt "A"

Chain guide "B"

Cylinder block

Special bolt "B"

Oil pump body

Chain guide "B"

Timing mark   Plated link

Section X — X

Sprocket

Timing mark

Crankshaft sprocket "B"

Sprocket

Chain guide "A"

Chain guide "C"

Plated link

Timing mark

Plated link

2600cc silent shaft chain timing marks

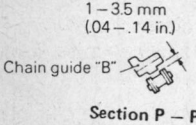

1 — 3.5 mm
(.04 — .14 in.)

Chain guide "B"

Section P — P

Special bolt "A"

Chain guide "B"

Special bolt "B"

2600cc silent shaft timing mark alignment

shaft sprockets and the ''A'' (inner) chain.

15. Remove the camshaft sprocket holder and the chain guides, both left and right. Remove the tensioner spring and sleeve from the oil pump.

16. Remove the oil pump by first removing the bolt locking the oil pump driven gear and the right counterbalance shaft, and then remove the oil pump mounting bolts. Remove the counterbalance shaft from the engine block.

NOTE: If the bolt locking the oil pump driven gear and the counterbalance shaft is hard to loosen, remove the oil pump and the shaft as a unit.

17. Remove the left counterbalance shaft thrust washer and take the shaft from the engine block.

18. Install the right counterbalance shaft into the engine block.

19. Install the oil pump assembly. Do not lose the Woodruff key from the end of the counterbalance shaft. Torque the oil pump mounting bolts to 6–7 ft. lbs.

20. Tighten the counterbalance shaft and the oil pump driven gear mounting bolt.

NOTE: The counterbalance shaft and the oil pump can be installed as a unit, if necessary.

21. Install the left counterbalance shaft into the engine block.

22. Install a new O-ring on the thrust plate and install the unit into the engine block, using a pair of bolts without heads, as alignment guides.

——— CAUTION ———

If the thrust plate is turned to align the bolt holes, the O-ring may be damaged.

23. Remove the guide bolts and install the regular bolts into the thrust plate and tighten securely.

24. Rotate the crankshaft to bring No. 1 piston to TDC.

25. Install the cylinder head, if removed.

26. Install the sprocket holder and the right and left chain guides.

27. Install the tensioner spring and sleeve on the oil pump body.

28. Install the camshaft and crankshaft sprockets on the timing chain, aligning the sprocket punch marks to the plated chain links.

29. While holding the sprocket and chain as a unit, install the crankshaft sprocket over the crankshaft and align it with the keyway.

30. Keeping the dowel pin hole on the camshaft in a vertical position, install the camshaft sprocket and chain on the camshaft.

NOTE: The sprocket timing mark and the plated chain link should be at the 2 to 3 o'clock position when correctly installed.

——— CAUTION ———

The chain must be aligned in the right and left chain guides with the tensioner pushing against the chain. The tension for the inner chain is predetermined by spring tension.

31. Install the crankshaft sprocket for the outer ''B'' chain.

32. Install the two counterbalance shaft sprockets and align the punched mating marks with the plated links of the chain.

33. Holding the two shaft sprockets and chain, install the outer chain in alignment with the mark on the crankshaft sprocket. Install the shaft sprockets on the counterbalance shaft and the oil pump driver gear. Install the lock bolts and recheck the alignment of the punch marks and the plated links.

34. Temporarily install the chain guides, Side (A), Top (B), and Bottom (C).

35. Tighten Side (A) chain guide securely.

36. Tighten Bottom (B) chain guide securely.

37. Adjust the position of the Top (B) chain guide, after shaking the right and left sprockets to collect any chain slack, so that when the chain is moved toward the center, the clearance between the chain guide and the chain links will be approximately 9/64 inch. Tighten the Top (B) chain guide bolts.

38. Install the timing chain cover using a new gasket, being careful not to damage the front seal.

39. Install the oil screen and the oil pan, using a new gasket. Torque the bolts to 4.5–5.5 ft. lbs.

40. Install the crankshaft pulley, alternator and accessory belts, and the distributor.

41. Install the oil pressure switch, if removed, and install the battery ground cable.

42. Install the fan blades, radiator, fill the system with coolant and start the engine.

Piston Installation

In preparation, check the ring gaps for staggered position. The gaps should not align with the piston pin or piston thrust directions. Also, each gap must be as far as possible from its neighboring gap.

NOTE: Installing plastic covers on the cap bolts of the piston rod will avoid damaging the cylinder bore and crank pin surface.

1. Apply engine oil all around the piston, piston rings and cylinder bore.

2. Insert the piston and connecting rod assembly into the cylinder, using a piston ring clamping tool. The cylinder mating

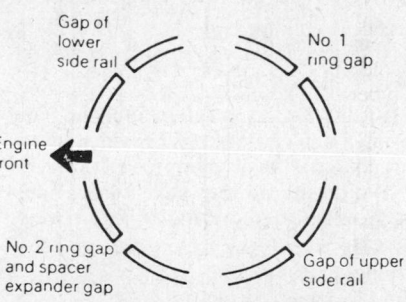

Gap of lower side rail

No 1 ring gap

Engine front

No 2 ring gap and spacer expander gap

Gap of upper side rail

Piston ring positioning

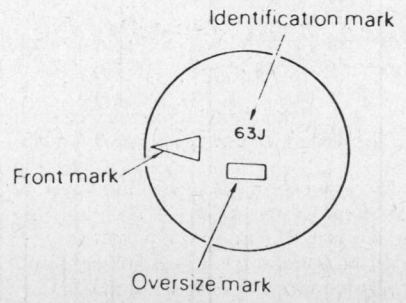

Identification mark

63J

Front mark

Oversize mark

Piston installation

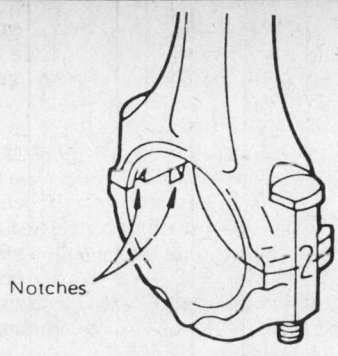

Connecting rod cap installation

mark should agree with the cylinder number and the arrow on the piston head should be directed to the crankshaft pulley end of the engine.

3. Install the connecting rod cap and torque the cap nuts to 24–25 ft. lbs. on 1983 1800cc engines, 37–38 ft. lb. on 1984–85 1800cc and 2000cc engines, and 33–34 ft. lb. on 2600cc engines.

NOTE: Make certain the match mark (cyl. no.) on the connecting rod big end and the match mark (cyl. no.) on the cap are placed in the same direction or the same side.

ENGINE LUBRICATION

Oil Pan

REMOVAL & INSTALLATION

The engine must be raised off its mounts for the pan to clear the suspension crossmember. However, on front wheel drive models there is usually enough room without raising the engine.

1. Remove the underbody splash shield.
2. Unbolt the left and right engine mounts (except front wheel drive).
3. Jack up the engine under the bell housing (except front wheel drive).
4. Remove the oil pan.
5. Installation is the reverse of removal. Torque the pan bolts to 4–6 ft. lb.

Rear Main Bearing Oil Seal

REMOVAL & INSTALLATION

The rear main oil seal is located in a housing on the rear of the block. To replace the seal, remove the transmission and do the work from underneath the car (except front wheel drive models) or remove the engine and do the work on the bench.

1. Remove the housing from the block.
2. Remove the separator from the housing.
3. Pry out the oil seal.
4. Lightly oil the replacement seal. The seal should be installed so that the seal mate fits into the inner contact surface of the seal case. Install the separator with the holes facing down.

Oil Pump

REMOVAL & INSTALLATION

The oil pump is located behind the front timing cover. Refer to the "Timing Cover, Chain/Belt, Counterbalance, and Tensioner" section proceeding.

ENGINE COOLING

Radiator

REMOVAL & INSTALLATION

1. Remove the splash panel from the bottom of the car. Drain the radiator by opening the petcock. Remove the shroud on models so equipped.
2. Disconnect the radiator hoses at the engine. On automatic transmission cars, disconnect and plug the transmission lines to the bottom of the radiator.
3. Remove the two retaining bolts from either side of the radiator. Lift out the radiator. On front wheel drive models, disconnect the electric fan wiring harness. Do not remove the fan motor, blades or bracket—remove as a unit with the radiator.
4. Install the radiator in the reverse order of removal. Tighten the retaining bolts gradually in a criss-cross pattern.

Water Pump

REMOVAL & INSTALLATION

1800cc and 2000cc Engines

1. Drain the cooling system.
2. Remove the belt and water pump pulley.
3. Remove the timing belt covers and tensioner.
4. Remove the water pump bolts and alternator bracket.
5. Lift out the water pump.
6. Installation is the reverse of removal. Coat the O-ring with coolant. Torque the bolts with a 4 on the head to 10 ft. lb.; the bolts with a 7 on the head to 19 ft. lb. Fill the cooling system and check for leaks.

2600cc Engine

1. Drain the cooling system.
2. Remove the fan shroud and radiator if necessary for working room.
3. Remove the alternator belt and accessory belts.
4. Remove the fan blades and/or automatic hub, if equipped.
5. Remove the water pump assembly.
6. Installation is the reverse of removal. Adjust belt tension.
7. Fill the radiator with coolant and test for leaks.

Thermostat

REMOVAL & INSTALLATION

The thermostat is located in the intake manifold under the upper radiator hose.

1. Drain the coolant below the level of the thermostat.
2. Remove the two retaining bolts and lift the thermostat housing off the intake manifold with the hose still attached.

NOTE: If you are careful, it is not necessary to remove the upper radiator hose.

3. Lift the thermostat out of the manifold.
4. Install the thermostat in the reverse order of removal. Use a new gasket and coat the mating surfaces with sealer.

EMISSION CONTROLS

Three potential sources of air pollution exist with a gasoline engine.

1. Engine crankcase emissions
2. Fuel system evaporative emissions
3. Engine exhaust emissions

Components developed to reduce and control the three sources of pollution are:

1. Crankcase Emission Control System
   a. Closed ventilation system
   b. PCV valve
   c. Oil separator (Starion)
2. Evaporative Emission Control System
   a. Canister (dual on some models)
   b. Carbon element
   c. Purge control valve
   d. Bowl vent valve
   e. Fuel filler cap relief valve
   f. Overfill limiter (two-way valve)
   g. Fuel check valve
   h. Thermo valve
3. Exhaust Emission Control System
   a. Jet valve
   b. Catalytic converter(s)
   c. Secondary air supply source
   d. Exhaust gas recirculation via EGR valve(s) and thermo valve (some models)
   e. Jet air control valve (some models)

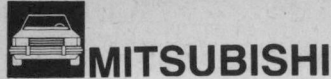

f. Heated air intake
g. Fuel control system (ECI)
h. Deceleration device
i. Coasting air valve (CAV)
j. Air switching valve (ASV)
k. Deceleration spark advance
l. Idle speed control system (A/C models)
m. High altitude compensation system
n. Tamper-proof choke and mixture

Crankcase Ventilation

A closed crankcase ventilation system is used to prevent blow-by gases from escaping into the atmosphere. The system has a positive (one-way) crankcase vent valve (PCV valve) at the rocker arm cover. Blow-by gases are drawn through two passages; one by a rubber vent hose from the rocker arm cover through the PCV valve into the intake manifold, and the other by a rubber hose from the rocker arm cover to the air cleaner.

INSPECTION AND SERVICE

1. Check the PCV valve for operation and the oil separator and oil return pipe (if equipped) for clogging and leaks.
2. Check the PCV valve by removing the valve and hose from the rocker cover while the engine is at idle speed. If the valve is not clogged, a hissing noise will be heard, and strong vacuum will be felt when a finger is placed over the bottom of the valve.
3. Shut off the engine and disconnect the PCV valve from the hose. Blow through the threaded end. If air will not pass through, the valve is clogged and replacement will be required.

Evaporative Control

When the engine is not operating, fuel vapor generated inside the fuel tank is absorbed and stored in the charcoal canister(s). When the engine is running, the fuel vapor absorbed in the canister(s) is drawn into the air intake hose through the purge valve. The purge valve is kept closed at idle, when vacuum reaches a pre-set value the valve opens. On carbureted models, a bowl vent valve controls carburetor vapors. When vacuum reaches a pre-set level, the vapors are allowed to pass into the intake.

INSPECTION AND SERVICE

Canister

1. Replace any hoses that are cracked or broken. Replace any canister that is damaged.
2. When the canister is in service over a long period of time, the interior filter will become clogged requiring canister replacement. Always replace the hoses when renewing the canister.

3. Remove the air cleaner box (Starion). Disconnect all hoses and clamps at both ends of the canister(s) and from the purge valve. Unclamp or remove the canister mounting bands and remove the canister assembly.

Purge Valve

1. Run the engine until normal operating temperature is reached.
2. Disconnect the purge valve from the air cleaner and blow into the purge hose. If air does not pass through the valve, operation is proper. Increase engine speed to 1500–2000 rpm and blow into the hose. Air should pass through if operation is normal.
3. If the valve is not working, check for broken or disconnected vacuum hoses. Replace the valve if necessary.

Exhaust Emission Control

Exhaust emissions are controlled by engine modifications and addition of special control components. Jet air valves, one for each cylinder, are installed in the cylinder head. A jet air passage is provided in the carburetor, intake manifold and cylinder head. Air flows through the passages and when the jet valve opens, into the combustion chambers. Air provided by the jet valve leans out the fuel mixture.

Catalytic Converters are used for the purpose of decreasing harmful emissions. Secondary air systems are used to supply air into the exhaust system for the purpose of promoting oxidation of exhaust emissions in the converter. Exhaust gas recirculation (EGR) is used to reduce oxides of nitrogen in the exhaust by recirculating a portion of the exhaust gases back into the intake manifold below the air/fuel source.

INSPECTION AND SERVICE

Pulse Air Feed (Secondary Air)

1. Remove the hose connected to the air cleaner and check for vacuum. If no vacuum is present, check for cracked or broken hoses.

EGR Control Valve

1. Check the vacuum hose to the EGR valve for cracks or cuts, replace any if necessary.
2. Start the engine and run at idle speed (cold engine). Run the engine to 2500 rpm and check the secondary EGR valve. If the secondary EGR valve is operating the thermo valve is defective.
3. Warm the engine to about 131°F. The secondary EGR valve should operate when the engine is at 2500 rpm. If the valve is not operating, check the EGR control valve and the thermo valve.

4. Disconnect the green stripped hose from the thermo valve. Connect a hand vacuum pump to the thermo valve and apply vacuum. If no vacuum passes, the thermo valve is good.
5. Disconnect the green stripped hose from the carburetor fitting and connect the hose to the hand pump.
6. Open the sub EGR valve by hand and apply approx. 6 in. of vacuum with the hand pump.
7. If the idle speed becomes unstable, the secondary EGR valve is operating properly. If the idle speed remains unchanged, the EGR valve is not working. Replace the EGR valve.

FUEL SYSTEM

Mechanical Fuel Pump

TESTING

Disconnect the fuel line from the carburetor and attach a pressure tester to the end of the line. Crank the engine. The tester should show 3.7–5.1 psi.

REMOVAL & INSTALLATION

1. Remove the fuel lines.
2. Unbolt the pump mounting bolts, and remove the pump, insulator, and gasket. Remove and inspect the fuel pump push rod. Replace if worn.
3. Coat both sides of a new insulator and gasket with sealer, and install the push rod and pump in the reverse order of removal.

NOTE: Installation is alot easier if the engine is rotated so that No. 1 cylinder is at TDC on the compression stroke.

Electric Fuel Pump

REMOVAL & INSTALLATION

Starion Only

1. Fuel pressure must be reduced before the pump is removed. Lift the rear compartment covering and access plate from the floor. Disconnect the electric wiring connector from the pump. Start the engine and allow it to idle until out of gas.

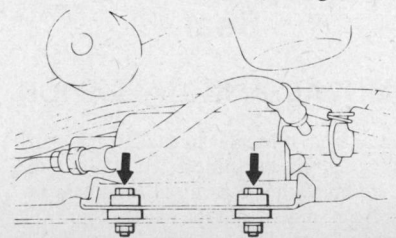

Electric fuel pump. Arrows show mounting bolts

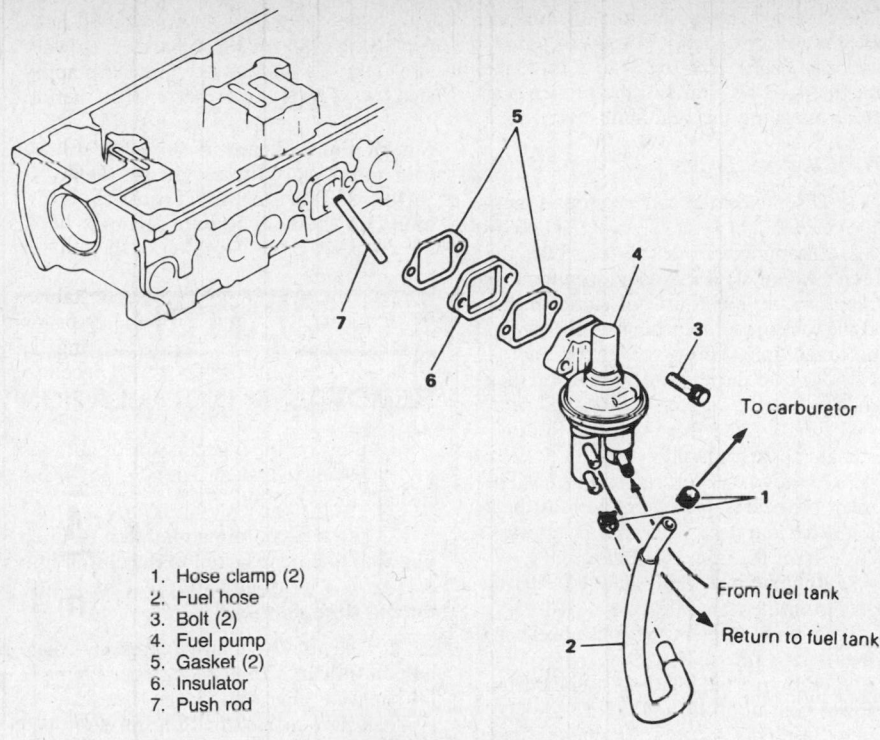

1. Hose clamp (2)
2. Fuel hose
3. Bolt (2)
4. Fuel pump
5. Gasket (2)
6. Insulator
7. Push rod

Mechanical fuel pump

2. Disconnect the negative battery cable. Disconnect the fuel lines and remove the fuel pump from the top of the fuel tank. Lower or remove the fuel tank, if necessary for working room.

3. Install fuel pump in the reverse order of removal.

Fuel Filter

REMOVAL & INSTALLATION

1. On carbureted models, remove the inlet and outlet fuel lines from the filter connections after loosening the fuel line clamps. Remove the old filter. Install the new filter in the reverse order.

2. On fuel injected models, the underhood filter is replaced after first reducing fuel line pressure (see ''Electric Fuel Pump Removal''). Hold the side filter nut securely and remove the mounts. Disconnect the lines and remove the filter. Install the new filter in reverse order.

Fuel filter with fuel injected engines

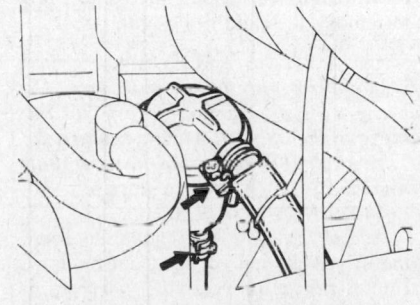

Fuel filter with carbureted engines

Carburetor

REMOVAL & INSTALLATION

1. Remove the solenoid valve wiring.
2. Disconnect the air cleaner breather hose, air duct and vacuum tube.
3. Remove the air cleaner.
4. Remove the air cleaner case.
5. Disconnect the accelerator and shift cables (automatic transmission) at the carburetor.
6. Disconnect the purge valve hose; remove the vacuum compensator, and fuel lines.
7. Drain the coolant.
8. Remove the water hose between the carburetor and the cylinder head.
9. Remove the carburetor.
10. Installation is the reverse of removal.

OVERHAUL

For all carburetor overhaul procedures, please refer to ''Carburetor Service'' in the Unit Repair section.

THROTTLE LINKAGE ADJUSTMENT

1. Apply the parking brake, block the wheels and place the transmission in neutral. Start the engine and allow it to idle.
2. Measure the play at the carburetor linkage end of the cable (should be 0–.08 inches), between the bracket and throttle arm.
3. If adjustment is necessary, loosen the adjusting nuts so that the throttle lever is free. Straighten the cable, if necessary, and position the locknuts to provide the required (0–.08 inches) freeplay.

FLOAT LEVEL ADJUSTMENT

NOTE: Models equipped with a resin-bodied carburetor require a special tool to check the float level. Adjustment should be performed by a qualified service technician.

On all except resin-bodied carburetors, a sight glass is fitted at the float chamber and the fuel level can be checked without disassembling the carburetor. Normal fuel level is within the level mark on the sight glass.

The fuel level adjustment is corrected by increasing or decreasing the number of needle valve packings. The float level may be off 0.160 inch, above or below the level mark and the operation of the engine would not be affected.

AUTOMATIC CHOKE ADJUSTMENT

All carburetors have a tamper-proof choke assembly which is factory adjusted.

THROTTLE OPENER SYSTEM

1. Air conditioned models are equipped with a throttle opener system that increases the idle speed when the air conditioner compressor is operating. Run the engine until normal operating temperature is reached.
2. Turn off all lights and accessories and be sure the electric cooling fan is not running.
3. Check normal idle speed as described earlier.
4. Disconnect the vacuum hose from the throttle opener fitting. Connect a hand vacuum pump to the throttle opener and apply 20 in. Hg. of vacuum.
5. Adjust the idle speed to 1300 rpm, plus or minus 50 rpm with the throttle opener setting screw. Reconnect the vacuum line.

Fuel Injection

For further information on the fuel in-

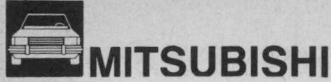

jection, please refer to "Fuel Injection" in the Unit Repair section.

Throttle Body

REMOVAL & INSTALLATION

1. Disconnect the battery ground.
2. Drain the coolant to below manifold level.
3. Disconnect the intake hose from the throttle body.
4. Disconnect the throttle cable and fuel lines.
5. Disconnect the vacuum hoses and remaining electrical connectors.
6. Unbolt and remove the throttle body.
7. Installation is the reverse of removal.

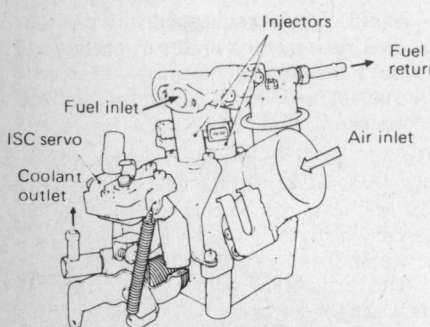

Fuel injection throttle body

MANUAL TRANSMISSION/ TRANSAXLE

REMOVAL & INSTALLATION
Rear Wheel Drive

1. Disconnect the battery ground cable, remove the air cleaner and the starter.
2. Remove the top transmission mounting bolts from the bell housing.
3. From inside the car, raise the console assembly, 1f equipped, or the carpet and remove the dust cover retaining plate at the shift lever.
4. Place the transmission in first gear on 1983 models and neutral on 1984–85 models. Remove the control lever assembly.
5. Raise the car and support it safely. Drain the transmission. Disconnect the speedometer and the back-up light switch.
6. Remove the driveshaft, exhaust pipe, clutch cable or slave cylinder and linkage.
7. Support the transmission and remove the engine rear support bracket.
8. Remove the bell housing cover and bolts, move the transmission rearward, and lower it carefully to the floor. Remove the transmission from under the car.

9. To install the transmission, reverse the removal procedure. Torque the transmission-to-engine bolts to 30–40 ft. lb. Make sure the transmission is in the proper gear before installing the gear shift lever.

Front Wheel Drive

1. Disconnect the battery ground (negative) cable.
2. Disconnect from the transaxle; the clutch cable or slave cylinder, speedometer cable, back-up light harness, starter motor and the four upper bolts connecting the engine to the transaxle.
3. Jack up the car and support on jack stands.
4. Remove the front wheels. Remove the engine splash shield.
5. Remove the shift rod and extension. It may be necessary to remove any heat shields that interfere with your progress.
6. Drain the transaxle fluid.
7. Remove the right and left driveshafts from the transaxle case.
   a. Remove center cap (front wheel hub) and nut.
   b. Remove ball joint and strut bar from lower control arm.
   c. Insert pry bar between transaxle case and double off-set joint; move bar to the right to remove the left driveshaft, left to remove the right driveshaft.

— CAUTION —
Pry on the rib only of the transaxle. Do not insert the pry bar too deeply causing damage to the oil seal. Always replace the DOJ retainer ring each time the driveshaft is removed from the transaxle case.

   d. Use an axle shaft puller to force the driveshaft out of the front hub. Be careful not to prevent the spacer from falling out of place.
8. Disconnect the range selector cable (if equipped). Remove the engine rear cover.
9. Support the weight of the engine from above (chain hoist). Support the transaxle and remove the remaining lower mounting bolts.
10. Remove the transaxle mount insulator bolt.
11. Remove (slide away from the engine) and lower the transaxle.
12. To install reverse the removal procedure. Torque the transaxle-to-engine bolts to 30–40 ft. lb. Be sure to connect all con-

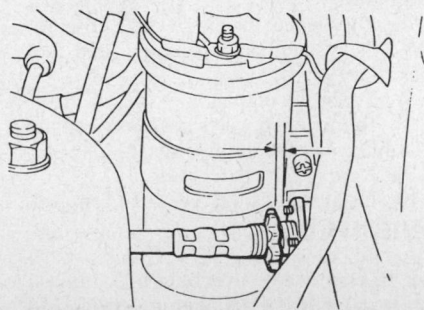

Clutch cable adjustment—front wheel drive

trols and wiring. Use new retaining rings when installing the driveshafts.

OVERHAUL

For all manual transmission or transaxle overhaul procedures, please refer to "Manual Transmission/Transaxle Overhaul" in the Unit Repair section.

CLUTCH

REMOVAL & INSTALLATION

1. Remove the transmission as outlined in the "Manual Transmission Removal and Installation" section.

NOTE: It is recommended that a clutch aligning tool be inserted in the clutch hub to prevent dropping of the clutch disc during disassembly.

2. Diagonally remove pressure plate bolts a little at a time each. Then, remove the pressure plate and driven disc.
3. From inside the transmission bell housing, remove the return spring clip and remove the release bearing assembly. On the Starion, remove the release fork by sliding it in the direction of the arrow to disengage the fulcrum from the clip. Attempting to remove it any other way will damage the clip.
4. If necessary, remove the release control lever and spring pin with a ³⁄₁₆ inch punch. Remove the control lever shaft assembly and clutch shift arm, two felt packings and two return springs.
5. Installation is the reverse of removal. Torque the pressure plate bolts, diagonally, to 11–15 ft. lb.

NOTE: Upon assembly—
a. Apply grease to the inside surface of the bushings and oil seal lips.
b. Apply grease in the clutch hub splines and main drive gear splines.
c. Apply grease to the inside of the release bearing carrier grooves.
d. Apply oil to the two felt packings.

FREE-PLAY ADJUSTMENT
Non-turbocharged Models
1. Depress the clutch pedal by hand, free-play (until tension is felt) should be 0.8–1.2 inches on 1983 models and 0.6–0.8 inch on 1984–85 models.
2. If the free-play is too great or too little, turn the outer cable adjusting nut at the engine compartment firewall for adjustment.
3. After adjustment is made, depress the clutch pedal several times and recheck.

Turbocharged Models
No freeplay adjustment is provided since these models are equipped with an hydraul-

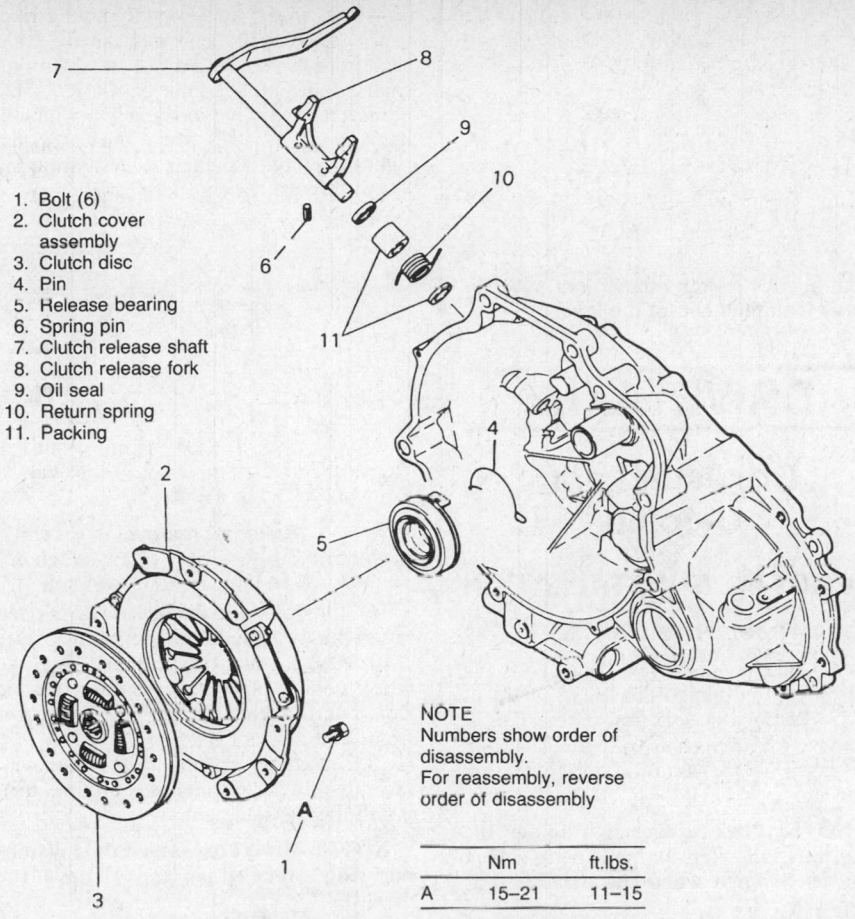

1. Bolt (6)
2. Clutch cover assembly
3. Clutch disc
4. Pin
5. Release bearing
6. Spring pin
7. Clutch release shaft
8. Clutch release fork
9. Oil seal
10. Return spring
11. Packing

NOTE
Numbers show order of disassembly.
For reassembly, reverse order of disassembly

	Nm	ft.lbs.
A	15–21	11–15

Clutch assembly—front wheel drive

ically operated clutch. However, if the clutch has been replaced, or if the clutch pedal feels spongy, bleed the system.

1. Loosen the bleeder screw at the clutch slave cylinder.

2. Push the clutch pedal down slowly while the bleeder screw is opened.

3. Hold the pedal down and tighten the bleeder screw.

4. Check the clutch master cylinder and refill with fluid if necessary. Repeat the bleeding procedure several times until all air is dispelled from the system.

AUTOMATIC TRANSMISSION/ TRANSAXLE

REMOVAL & INSTALLATION

Rear Wheel Drive

The transmission and converter must be removed as an assembly; otherwise, the converter drive plate, pump bushing, or oil seal may be damaged. The drive plate will not support a load; therefore, none of the weight

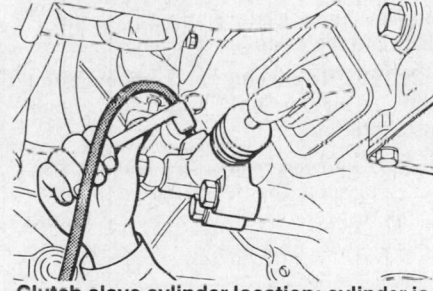

Clutch slave cylinder location; cylinder is being bled

of the transmission should be allowed to rest on the plate during removal.

1. Disconnect battery ground cable, drain the transmission, and remove cooler lines at transmission.

2. Remove starter and cooler line bracket.

3. Rotate crankshaft clockwise and remove bolts attaching torque converter to drive plate.

4. Remove the driveshaft.

5. Disconnect gearshift rod and torque shaft.

6. Disconnect throttle rod from lever at the left side of transmission. Remove linkage bellcrank from transmission if so equipped.

7. Remove the oil filler tube and speedometer cable.

8. Support the rear of the engine with jack.

9. Raise transmission slightly.

10. Remove crossmember.

11. Remove all bell housing bolts.

12. Carefully work transmission converter assembly rearward off engine block dowels and disengage converter hub from end of crankshaft. Attach a small C-clamp to edge of bell housing to hold converter in place during transmission removal.

13. Remove transmission.

14. Installation is the reverse of removal.

Front Wheel Drive

NOTE: The transaxle and converter must be removed and installed as an assembly.

1. Disconnect the battery ground (negative) cable. Remove the shift lever T-handle and floor plate. Disconnect the control cable.

2. Disconnect the throttle control cable at the carburetor and the manual control cable at the transaxle.

3. Disconnect from the transaxle; the inhibitor switch (neutral safety) connector, fluid cooler hose and the four upper bolts connecting the engine to the transaxle.

4. Jack up the car and support on jack stands.

5. Remove the front wheels. Remove the engine splash shield.

6. Drain the transaxle fluid.

7. Remove the right and left driveshafts from the transaxle case. Refer to Step 7 in "Manual Transaxle Removal" for procedure.

8. Disconnect the speedometer cable. Remove the starter motor.

9. Remove the lower cover from the converter housing. Remove the three bolts that connect the converter to the engine drive plate.

NOTE: Never support the full weight of the transaxle on the engine drive plate.

10. Turn and force the converter back and away from the engine drive plate.

11. Support the weight of the engine from above (chain hoist). Support the transaxle and remove the remaining mounting bolts.

12. Remove the transaxle mount insulator bolt.

13. Remove (slide away from the engine) and lower the transaxle and converter as an assembly.

14. To install reverse the removal procedure. Torque the transaxle-to-engine bolts to 30–40 ft. lb. Be sure to connect all controls, wiring and hoses Use new retaining rings when installing the drive axles.

Pan and Filter

REMOVAL & INSTALLATION

1. Raise and support the front of the vehicle.

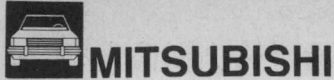
2. Loosen and remove the transmission pan drain plug. Loosen and remove the differential drain plug (lower front).

3. Remove the pan mounting bolts and pan to install a new filter. Clean the oil pan.

4. Reinstall the oil pan using a new gasket. Add the proper amount of Dexron II® fluid after installing the two drain plugs. Start the engine and move the selector lever through all positions. Allow the engine to run until normal operating temperature is reached.

5. Recheck the fluid level with the dipstick, add fluid if necessary.

THROTTLE CABLE ADJUSTMENT

1. Run the engine to normal operating temperature and make sure that the throttle lever on the carburetor is in the curb idle position.

2. Raise the cover on the throttle cable to expose the nipple.

3. Loosen the lower cable mounting bolt.

4. Move the lower cable bracket until the distance between the nipple and the top of the cable end is 0.5mm.

5. Tighten the lower cable bracket mounting bolt and check the adjustment by pulling the cable upward with the throttle plate in the wide open position. The cable should move freely.

KICKDOWN BAND ADJUSTMENT

1. Remove all dirt from the kickdown servo cover. Location is to right of dipstick; the large bump with a round cover.

2. Remove the snap-ring that retains the cover. Use a pair of pliers that fit into the notches of the cover and remove.

3. Loosen the locknut. Hold the kickdown servo piston from turning and tighten the adjusting screw to 7 ft. lbs., then back it off. Repeat the tightening and backing off two times. This will assure the seating of the kickdown band on the drum.

4. Tighten the adjusting screw to 3.5 ft. lbs. and back off 3.5 turns (counterclockwise).

NEUTRAL SAFETY SWITCH ADJUSTMENT

1. Place the control lever in the "N" position.

2. Make sure the short end of the manual control lever covers the switch body flange. Loosen the switch mounting bolts (2) and adjust switch as necessary. Tighten the bolts.

3. Check the switch operation by attempting to start engine in gears other than the P and N positions.

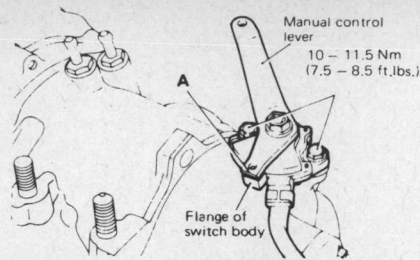

Neutral start switch adjustment. "A" denotes the small end of the lever

DRIVE AXLE

Driveshaft and U-Joints

REMOVAL & INSTALLATION

Rear Wheel Drive Only

1. Matchmark the rear flange yoke and the differential pinion flange.

2. Remove the bolts from the rear flange. Remove the driveshaft by pulling it from the rear of the transmission extension housing.

NOTE: Place a container under the transmission extension housing to collect any oil leakage when the driveshaft is removed.

3. To install the shaft, align the front sleeve yoke with the splines of the transmission output shaft, and push the driveshaft into the extension housing.

NOTE: Be careful not to damage the rear transmission seal lip upon installation.

4. Align the matchmarks on the rear yokes, install the bolts, and tighten securely.

5. Inspect the oil level of the transmission.

U-JOINT OVERHAUL

For all overhaul procedures, please refer to "U-Joint/CV-Joint Overhaul" in the Unit Repair section.

Transaxle Halfshafts

REMOVAL & INSTALLATION

Front Wheel Drive Only

1. Remove the hub center cap and loosen the driveshaft (axle) nut. Loosen tbe wheel lug nuts.

2. Lift the car and support it on jack stands. Remove the front wheels. Remove the engine splash shield.

3. Remove the lower ball joint and strut bar from the lower control arm.

4. Drain the transaxle fluid.

5. Insert a pry bar between the transaxle case (on the raised rib) and the driveshaft double off-set joint case (DOJ). Do not insert the pry bar too deeply or you will damage the oil seal. Move the bar to the right to withdraw the left driveshaft; to the left to remove the right driveshaft.

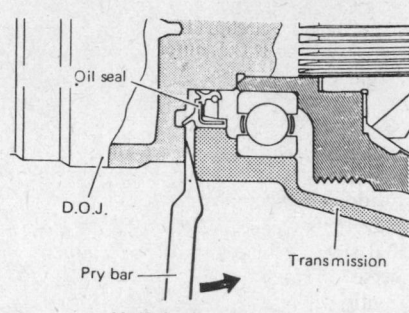

Halfshaft removal

6. Plug the transaxle case with a clean rag to prevent dirt from entering the case.

7. Use a puller-driver mounted on the wheel studs to push the driveshaft from the front hub. Take care to prevent the spacer from falling out of place.

8. Assembly is the reverse of removal. Insert the driveshaft into the hub first, then install the transaxle end.

NOTE: Always use a new DOJ retaining ring every time you remove the driveshaft.

CV-JOINT OVERHAUL

NOTE: The Birfield joint (wheel side) cannot be rebuilt. It must be replaced with the axle, however a boot kit is available.

For all overhaul procedures, please refer to "U-Joint/CV-Joint Overhaul" in the Unit Repair section.

Rear Axle/Axle Shafts

REMOVAL & INSTALLATION

1. Remove the four wheel side flange mounting nuts and bolts.

2. Connect a flanged slide hammer to

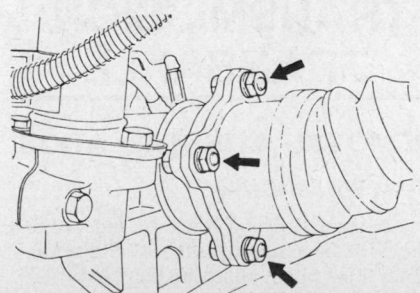

Rear drive axle flange mounting

Rear axle removal with slide hammer

	Nm	ft.lbs.
A	65–80	47–58
B	70–90	51–65
C	80–100	58–72
D	18–25	13–18

1. Suspension arm (R.H.)
2. Dust cover
3. Clamp
4. Bushing A
5. Bushing B
6. Rubber stopper
7. Suspension arm (L.H.)
8. Fixture
9. Rubber bushing

10. Washer
11. Spring upper seat
12. Coil spring
13. Spring lower seat
14. Shock absorber
15. Bump stopper

Rear suspension—front wheel drive models

the axle flange and "pull" the axle from the differential. Take care not to damage the side differential seals.

3. Install a new circlip on the differential side and install the axle shaft in the reverse order of removal. Tighten the mounting nuts and bolts to 36–43 ft. lbs.

Differential

For further information on the differential, please refer to "Drive Axles" in the Unit Repair section.

REMOVAL & INSTALLATION

1. Raise and safely support the rear of the car. Drain the gear oil.
2. Remove the axle shafts. Remove the driveshaft.
3. Remove the bolts attaching the torque tube assembly to the differential and the bolts connecting the front to the support.
4. Attach a flanged slide hammer to the torque tube flange and "pull" to remove the assembly from the differential.
5. Support the differential with a floor jack and remove all mounts. Remove the differential.
6. Reinstall in reverse order. Lubricate the torque tube-to-input shaft cup.

REAR SUSPENSION

Shock Absorbers

REMOVAL & INSTALLATION

Cordia and Tredia

1. Remove the hub cap or wheel cover. Loosen the lug nuts.
2. Raise the rear of the car. Support the car with jack stands.

NOTE: The body sill is marked with two dimples to locate the support position. Never place a stand anywhere but between these marks or you'll damage the body.

3. Position a floor jack under the lower control arm. Remove the upper shock mounting bolt and nut.
4. Compress the shock slightly and remove the lower mounting bolt.
5. Remove the shock absorber.
6. Check the shock for:
   a. Excessive oil leakage, some minor weeping is permissable;
   b. Bent center rod, damaged outer case, or other defects.
   c. Pump the shock absorber several times, if it offers even resistance on full strokes it may be considered serviceable.
7. Install the upper shock mounting nut and bolt. Hand tighten the nut.
8. Install the bottom eye of the shock into the mounting bracket and insert the bolt. Tighten to 47–58 ft. lbs.
9. Finally, tighten the upper nut to 47–58 ft. lbs.

Coil Spring

REMOVAL & INSTALLATION

Cordia and Tredia

1. Raise and support the car safely allowing the rear axle to hang unsupported.
2. Place a jack under the work side control arm and remove the bottom bolts of the shock absorbers.
3. Lower the arm and remove the coil spring.
4. Installation is the reverse of removal.

Strut Assembly

REMOVAL & INSTALLATION

Starion

1. Support the rear of car on jackstands at the frame rails. Position a floor jack under the lower control arm.

2. Remove the rear wheel. Remove the caliper and rotor. Suspend the caliper with wire, do not allow to hang by the brake hose.
3. Disconnect the rear brake hose from the strut assembly.
4. Disconnect the axle shaft from the wheel side flange.
5. Remove the strut assembly-to-axle housing mounting bolts. Separate the strut assembly from the axle housing. Lower the floor jack and push down on the housing while opening the coupling with a small pry bar.
6. Remove the upper strut mounting nuts from under the side trim in rear hatch.
7. Remove the strut assembly.
8. Install in reverse order. Tighten the top mounting nuts to 18–25 ft. lbs. and the lower mountings to 36–51 ft. lbs.

OVERHAUL

For all spring and shock removal and installation procedures and any other strut overhaul procedures please refer to "Strut Overhaul" in the Unit Repair section.

Rear Control Arm

REMOVAL & INSTALLATION

Front Wheel Drive

1. Support the side frame on jack stands and remove the rear wheels. Remove the rear brake assembly.
2. Remove the muffler and jack the control arm just enough to raise it slightly.
3. Remove the shock absorber and lower the jack. Remove the coil spring and temporarily install the shock absorber to the control arm.
4. Disconnect the brake hoses at the rear suspension arms and remove the rear suspension from the body as an assembly.

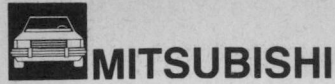

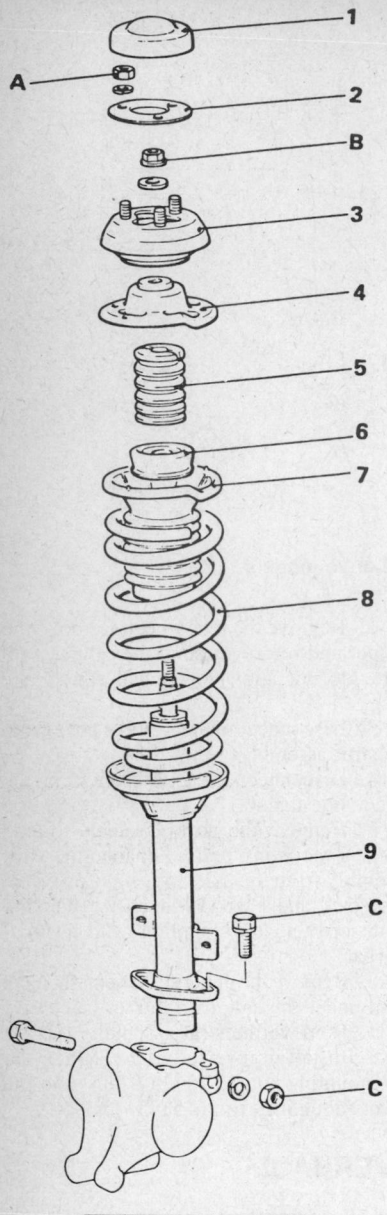

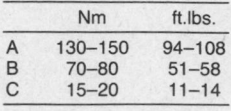

1. Bushing A
2. Bushing B
3. Lower control arm
4. Bushing C
5. Locking pin

	Nm	ft.lbs.
A	130–150	94–108
B	70–80	51–58
C	15–20	11–14

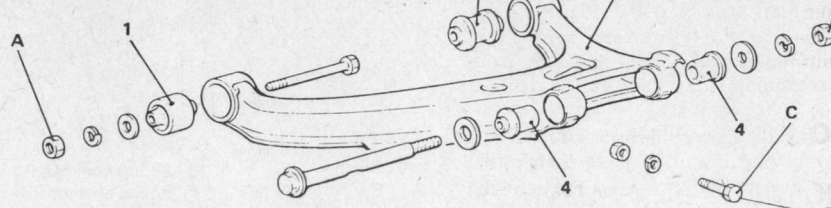

Rear lower control arm on Starion

	Nm	ft.lbs.
A	25–35	18–25
B	70–90	51–65
C	50–70	36–51

1. Strut house cap
2. Gasket
3. Strut insulator
4. Spring seat
5. Rubber helper
6. Rubber helper seat
7. Dust cover
8. Coil spring
9. Strut

Starion rear strut assembly

5. Install the fixture to body bolts and torque to 51–65 ft. lbs.

6. Install the coil springs and loosely install the shock absorbers. Tighten the shock absorber bolts to specification after the vehicle is lowered to the floor.

7. Install the rear brake assembly.

8. Lower the vehicle and tighten the suspension arm end nuts to 58–72 ft. lbs. and the shock bolts to 47.0–58.0 ft. lbs.

9. Install the brake drums and wheels.

10. Bleed the brake system and adjust the rear brake shoe clearance.

Rear Wheel Drive

1. Raise and support the rear of the car on jackstands.

2. Disconnect the parking brake from the control arm brackets. Disconnect the stabilizer bar.

3. Remove the nut and bolt connecting the lower control arm to the front support.

4. Remove the nut and bolt connecting the lower control arm to the crossmember.

5. Remove the lower control arm from the car.

6. Install in reverse order.

FRONT SUSPENSION

Strut

REMOVAL & INSTALLATION

For all spring and shock removal and installation procedures and any other strut overhaul procedures, please refer to "Strut Overhaul" in the Unit Repair section.

Front Wheel Drive

1. Jack up and support the front of the car.

2. Remove the front wheel. Remove the brake line from the strut.

3. Remove the upper and lower mounting nuts/bolts and remove the strut.

NOTE: When installing the strut, apply a non-hardening sealer to the mating surfaces of the strut and knuckle arm.

4. Installation is the reverse of removal. Torque the strut insulator-to-body to 18–25 ft. lb.; strut bar-to-crossmember to 98–115 ft. lb.; strut bar-to-lower arm to 43–50 ft lb. Bleed the front brakes after installation.

Rear Wheel Drive

1. Remove the front wheel and caliper. Remove the front hub with disc and dust cover.

2. Disconnect the stabilizer linkage and the lower arm. Remove the strut assembly, knuckle arm and strut insulator retaining bolts and remove the strut assembly from the wheelhouse.

3. Installation is the reverse of removal. Observe the following torques:
strut bar bracket-to-frame: 25–33 ft. lb.
strut bar-to-lower control arm: 43–51 ft. lb.

NOTE: When installing the strut, apply a non-hardening sealer to the mating surfaces of the strut and knuckle arm.

Ball Joint

REMOVAL & INSTALLATION

Front Wheel Drive

1. Raise and support the front of the car. Remove the wheels.

2. Disconnect the stabilizer bar and strut from the lower arm.

3. Remove the ball joint mounting nut and separate the ball joint from the front knuckle.

4. Remove the lower control arm.

5. Remove the dust cover from the ball joint. Remove the mounting snap ring.

6. Have the ball joint pressed out of the lower control arm.

7. Press a new ball joint into the control arm and install a snap-ring.

8. Install in the reverse order of removal.

Rear Wheel Drive

1. Raise and support the front of the car. Remove the wheels.

2. Remove the strut and tie-rod end from the steering knuckle.

3. Remove the ball joint-to-knuckle arm mounting nut and separate.

4. Remove the ball joint-to-control arm nuts and bolts and remove the ball joint.

5. Install in reverse order. Tighten the ball joint mounting bolts to 43–51 ft. lbs.

Lower Control Arm

REMOVAL & INSTALLATION

Follow the instructions for "Ball Joint" proceeding. After the stabilizer bar and ball joint stud have been disconnected, remove the inner pivot bolt and nut from the crossmember and remove the control arm. Install in the reverse order.

Front Wheel Bearing

ADJUSTMENT

NOTE: Front wheel drive models require no adjustment. The axle washer must be installed, "taper side" facing out. Tighten the axle nut to 144–188 ft. lbs. Align the nearest cotter pin hole and install cotter pin.

1. On rear drive models, remove the wheel and dust cover. Remove the cotter pin and lock cap from the nut.

2. Torque the wheel bearing nut to 14 ft. lbs. and then loosen the nut. Retorque the nut to 4 ft. lbs. and install the lock cap and cotter pin.

3. Install the dust cover and the wheel.

Front Hub and Wheel Bearings

REMOVAL & INSTALLATION

1. Remove the driveshaft and front brake assembly.

2. Disconnect the tie-rod end and strut.

3. Remove the hub and knuckle as an assembly.

4. Remove the front hub from the knuckle. It may be necessary to drive out the hub with a soft (plastic) hammer.

5. Remove the disc rotor from hub.

6. The oil seal and the inner and outer bearings may now be serviced. Refer to the front wheel bearing section.

7. Assembly is the reverse of removal.

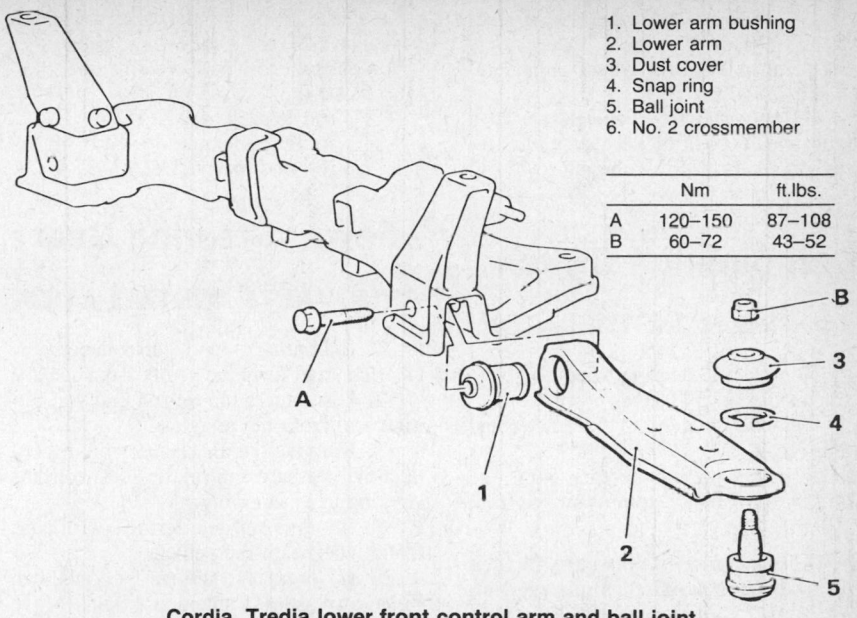

1. Lower arm bushing
2. Lower arm
3. Dust cover
4. Snap ring
5. Ball joint
6. No. 2 crossmember

	Nm	ft.lbs.
A	120–150	87–108
B	60–72	43–52

Cordia, Tredia lower front control arm and ball joint

Front End Alignment

Camber is pre-set at the factory and cannot be adjusted. Caster should not require adjustment, although adjustment (to a certain extent) is possible by adjusting the length of the strut bar. Loosen both nuts and turn in or out as required. Toe adjustment is possible by adjusting both tie-rod end turnbuckles (the same amount) on the Cordia and Tredia, or the left tie-rod end turnbuckle on the Starion.

STEERING

Steering Wheel

REMOVAL & INSTALLATION

1. Pry off the steering wheel center foam pad or remove the mounting screws from the back (depending on model).

2. Remove the steering wheel retaining

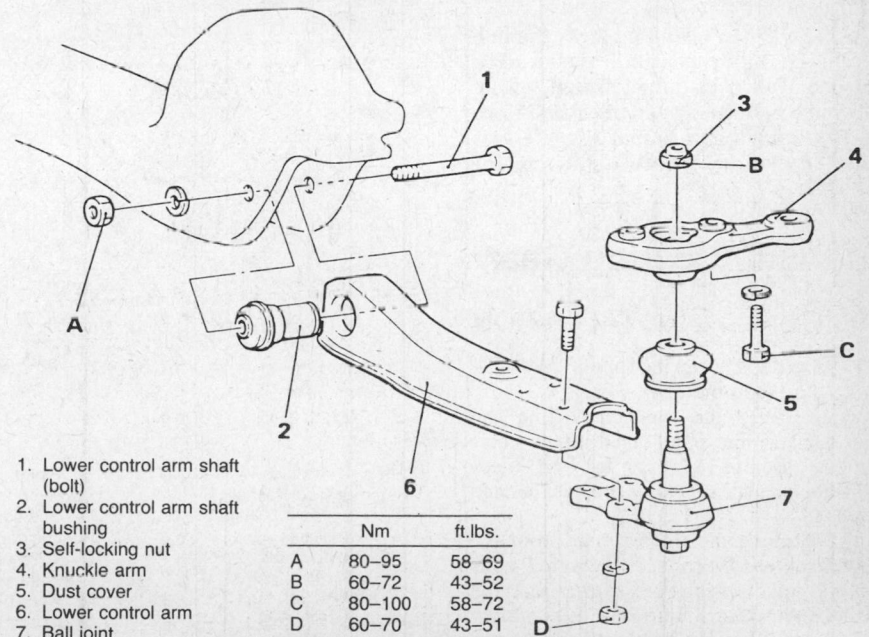

1. Lower control arm shaft (bolt)
2. Lower control arm shaft bushing
3. Self-locking nut
4. Knuckle arm
5. Dust cover
6. Lower control arm
7. Ball joint

	Nm	ft.lbs.
A	80–95	58–69
B	60–72	43–52
C	80–100	58–72
D	60–70	43–51

Starion lower front control arm and ball joint

nut after marking the wheel and shaft position.

3. Using a steering wheel puller, remove the wheel.

4. Be sure the front wheels are in a straight ahead position. Reverse the removal procedure. Torque the nut to 25–32 ft. lb.

Combination Switch

REMOVAL & INSTALLATION

1. Remove the steering wheel and have the tilt handle in the lowest position.

2. Remove the combination meter and column cover.

3. Remove the connectors from the column switch, and the column switch from the column tube.

NOTE: Some models may have the turn signal and hazard switches mounted on a base plate. Removal of the attaching screws will allow these switches to be removed without removal of the remaining switches.

4. Switch installation is the reverse of removal. Be sure that the switch is centered in the column or self-cancelling will be affected.

Ignition Switch

REMOVAL & INSTALLATION

1. Cut a notch in the lock bracket bolt head with a hacksaw.

2. Remove the bolt and lock.

3. Remove the column cover and unbolt and remove the ignition switch.

4. Install both lock and switch in reverse of removal.

NOTE: When installing lock, the bolt should be tightened until the head is crushed. When installing switch, install the switch bolt loosely and insert and work the key a few times to make sure everything checks out before tightening the bolt.

Manual Steering Gear

REMOVAL & INSTALLATION

1. Jack up the car and support it on jack stands. Remove the front wheels.

2. Remove the bolt connecting the steering shaft universal joint with the steering gear. Before removing the bolt, mark its location and be sure the wheels are pointed straight.

3. Remove the tie-rod ends from the hub knuckles. Disconnect mounting bolts (four) located near the inner tie-rods on the crossmember. Remove right side submember from the No. 2 crossmember. Remove the gearbox from the No. 2 crossmember.

4. Installation is the reverse of removal. Observe the following torques:
Gear box-to-No. 2 crossmember: 43–58 ft. lb.
Tie rod-to-rack: 58–72 ft. lb.
Tie rod end locknut: 36–40 ft. lb.
Tie rod end-to-knuckle: 17–25 ft. lb.

Power Steering Gear

REMOVAL & INSTALLATION

1. Matchmark and disconnect the steering shaft from the gearbox main shaft.

2. Disconnect the tie-rod end and pitman arm from the relay rod.

3. Remove the air cleaner and disconnect the pressure and return lines from the steering gear assembly.

4. Remove any interfering splash pans from underneath the vehicle.

5. If necessary, remove the kickdown linkage splash pan shield and bolts. Move the fuel line aside to avoid damage during removal.

6. Remove the frame bolts from the gearbox and lower the unit from the vehicle.

7. Installation is in the reverse order of removal. Observe the following torques:
Gear box mounting bolts:
Starion 40–47 ft. lb.
Cordia, Tredia 48–57 ft. lb.
Pitman Arm: 94–108 ft. lb.

Power Steering Pump

REMOVAL & INSTALLATION

1. Remove the drive belt. If the pulley is to be removed, do so now.

2. Disconnect the pressure and return lines. Catch any leaking fluid.

3. Remove the pump attaching bolts and lift the pump from the brackets.

4. Make sure the bracket bolts are tight and install the pump to the brackets.

5. If pulley had been removed, install it and tighten the nut securely. Bend the lock tab over the nut.

6. Install the drive belt and adjust to a tension of 22 lbs. at a deflection of 0.28–0.39 inches at the top center of the belt. Tighten the pump bolts securely to hold the tension.

7. Connect the pressure and return lines and fill the reservoir with approved fluid.

Steering Linkage

The steering linkage except on cars equipped with rack and pinion steering is of the conventional type, using tie rods, tie rod ends, relay rod, and idler arm assembly. The tie rods and tie rod ends are adjustable for length, and are locked in position by locking nuts. Front wheel drive models have

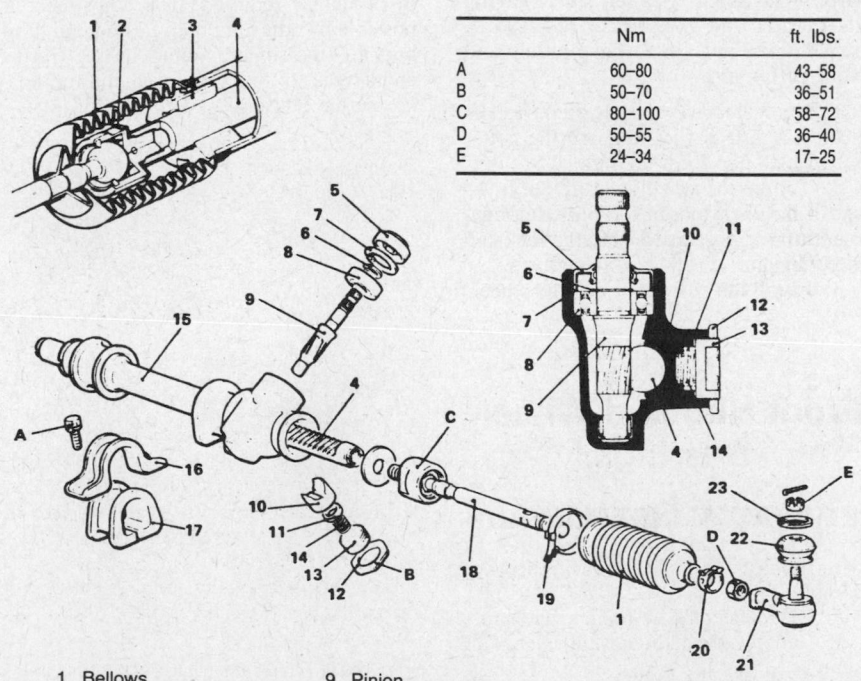

	Nm	ft. lbs.
A	60–80	43–58
B	50–70	36–51
C	80–100	58–72
D	50–55	36–40
E	24–34	17–25

1. Bellows
2. Tab washer
3. Rack bushing
4. Rack
5. Oil seal
6. Snap ring
7. Snap ring
8. Bearing
9. Pinion
10. Support yoke
11. Cushion rubber
12. Locking nut
13. Yoke plug
14. Yoke spring
15. Gear housing
16. Mounting bracket
17. Mounting rubber
18. Tie rod
19. Band
20. Clip
21. Tie rod end
22. Dust cover
23. Clip ring

Manual steering gear assembly

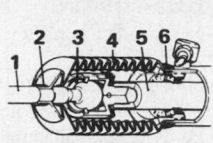

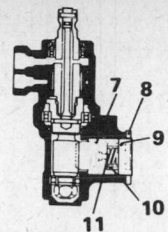

	Nm	ft. lbs.
A	60–80	43–58
B	50–70	36–51
C	80–100	58–72
D	50–55	36–39
E	24–34	17–25

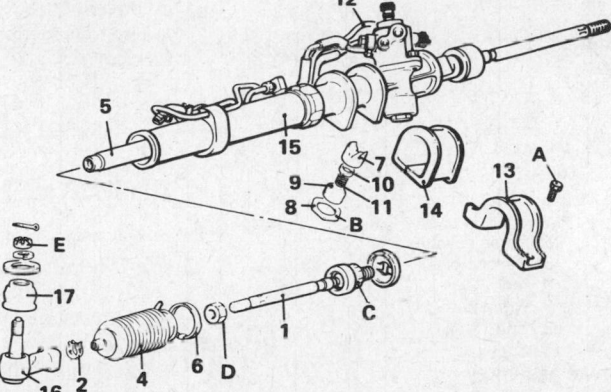

1. Tie rod
2. Clip
3. Tab washer
4. Bellows
5. Rack
6. Band
7. Support yoke
8. Locking nut
9. Yoke plug
10. Cushion rubber
11. Yoke spring
12. Air tube
13. Mounting bracket
14. Mounting rubber
15. Gear box
16. Tie rod end
17. Dust cover

Power steering gear assembly

adjustable outer tie rod ends. Heat shields are used over ball sockets located near the engine to avoid heat loss of lubricating grease.

Lubricating grease is used in the dust cover and the sealer is used to join the cover to the ball socket body.

BRAKES

For all brake system repair and service procedures not detailed below, Please refer to "Brakes" in the Unit Repair section.

Adjustment

Front and/or rear disc brakes require no manual adjustment. Models with rear drum brakes are equipped with self-adjusters.

Master Cylinder

REMOVAL & INSTALLATION

1. Remove all lines connected to the master cylinder. Slowly depress the brake pedal to remove the fluid.
2. Remove the clevis pin from between the master cylinder pushrod and the pedal on non-power brakes.
3. Remove the mounting bolts and then remove the master cylinder from the firewall.
4. Installation is the reverse of removal. Torque the mounting nuts to 36–48 in. lb. Bleed the brakes.

Power Brake Booster

REMOVAL & INSTALLATION

1. Disconnect the vacuum supply line from the brake booster.
2. Remove the master cylinder.
3. Disconnect the pushrod from the brake pedal.
4. Remove the mounting bolts/nuts from the firewall. Remove the booster.
5. Install in reverse order. Torque the mounting nuts to 54–108 in. lb. Bleed the brake system.

Wheel Cylinders

REMOVAL & INSTALLATION

1. Raise and support the rear of the car. Remove the wheel and brake drum. Remove the brake shoes.
2. Place a bucket or some old newspapers under the brake backing plate to catch the brake fluid that will run out of the wheel cylinder. Disconnect the brake line and remove the cylinder mounting bolts. Remove the cylinder from the backing plate.
3. Install a new or rebuilt wheel cylinder. Install brake shoes, etc. Bleed the brake system.

Wheel Bearings

REMOVAL & INSTALLATION

Rear Wheel Drive

1. Raise and support the front of the car. Remove wheel. Remove the caliper.

2. Pry off the dust cap. Tap out and discard the cotter pin. Remove the locknut.
3. Being careful not to drop the outer bearing, pull off the brake disc and wheel hub.
4. Remove the grease inside the wheel hub.
5. Using a brass drift, carefully drive the outer bearing race out of the hub.
6. Remove the inner bearing seal and bearing.
7. Check the bearings for wear or damage and replace them if necessary.
8. Coat the inner surface of the hub with grease.
9. Grease the outer surface of the bearing race and drift it into place in the hub.
10. Pack the inner and outer wheel bearings with grease. (see repacking.)

NOTE: If the brake disc has been removed and/or replaced, tighten the retaining bolts to 25–29 ft. lbs.

11. Install the inner bearing in the hub. Being careful not to distort it, install the oil seal with its lip facing the bearing. Drive the seal on until its outer edge is even with the edge of the hub.
12. Install the hub/disc assembly on the spindle, being careful not to damage the oil seal.
13. Install the outer bearing, washer, and spindle nut. Adjust the bearing.

Front Wheel Drive Models

1. Remove the brake caliper assembly.
2. Remove drive axles.

NOTE: When removing the drive axle from the hub, do not lose the shims or mix them with the opposite side.

3. Use a puller and disconnect the ball joint and tie-rod end from the steering knuckle. Unfasten the two bolts that mount the knuckle to the strut and remove the knuckle, hub and rotor.
4. Remove the hub assembly from the knuckle. If you encounter resistance, mount the knuckle in a vise, support the rotor and hub, and drive out the hub with a soft hammer.
5. Remove the brake disc rotor from the hub.
6. Remove the oil seals and the bearings.
7. Clean and inspect the bearings and races (cups), replace if necessary.
8. If the inner and outer races (cups) need replacing, drive them from the knuckle using a brass drift.
9. Install new races (cups), if necessary, pack the bearings (see repacking) and reinstall in the reverse manner of removal.

BEARING SERVICE

1. Clean the inner and outer bearings and the wheel hub with a suitable solvent. Remove all old grease.
2. Thoroughly dry and wipe clean all components.
3. Clean all old grease from the spindle or steering knuckle.

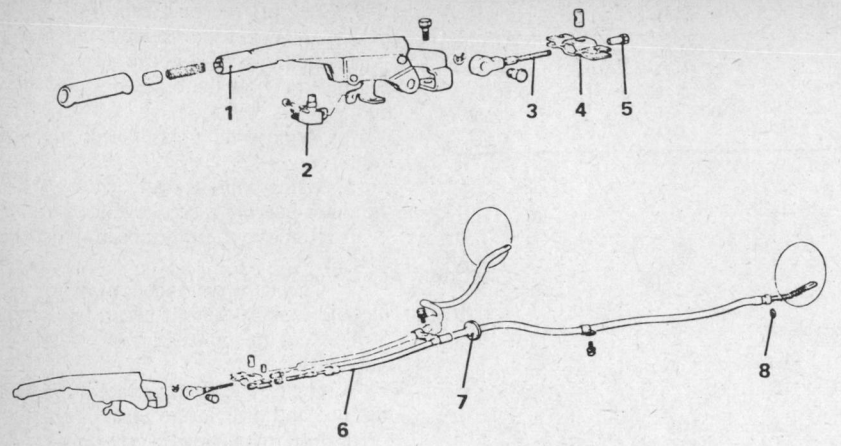

1. Parking brake lever
2. Parking brake switch
3. Parking brake cable, front
4. Equalizer
5. Cable adjuster
6. Parking brake cable, rear
7. Grommet
8. Snap ring

Cordia, Tredia parking brake assembly

4. Carefully check the bearings for any sign of scoring or other damage. If the roller bearings or bearing cages are damaged, the bearing and the corresponding bearing cup in the rotor or knuckle must be replaced. The bearing cups must be driven out of the rotor or knuckle to be removed. The outer bearing cup is driven out of the front of the rotor or knuckle from the rear and vice versa for the inner bearing cup.

5. Whether you are reinstalling the old bearings or installing new ones, the bearings must be packed with wheel bearing grease. To do this, place a glob of grease in your left palm, then, holding one of the bearings in your right hand, drag the edge of the bearing heavily through the grease. This must be done to work as much grease as possible through the roller bearings and cage. Turn the bearing and continue to pull it through the grease until the grease is packed between the bearings and the cage all the way around the circumference of the bearing. Repeat this operation until all of the bearings are packed with grease.

6. Pack the inside of the hub with a moderate amount of grease, between the bearing cups. Do not overload the hub with grease.

7. Apply a small amount of grease to the spindle.

8. Place the knuckle or rotor, face down, on a protected surface and install the inner bearing.

9. Coat the lip of a new grease seal with a small amount of grease and position it on the knuckle.

10. Place a block of wood on top of the grease seal and tap on the block with a hammer to install the seal. Turn the block of wood to different positions to seat it squarely in the hub.

REAR WHEEL BEARINGS

Front Wheel Drive

The rear wheel, on front wheel drive models, rides on bearings contained in the hub of the rear brake drum. The axle is similar to a conventional front wheel spindle. Refer to previous section for bearing removal and service.

Parking Brake

ADJUSTMENT

1. Remove the center console and rear seat if necessary.

2. Apply the parking brake and count the number of clicks (notches) until fully applied.

3. Proper adjustment is 5–7 notches for front wheel drive and 4–5 for rear drive models.

4. Adjust the parking lever stroke by turning the cable adjusting nut after attempting to tighten by applying the brake lever several times to adjust the rear brakes.

5. Raise the rear of the car and safely support. Release the parking brake and turn the rear wheels to confirm that the brakes are not dragging.

REMOVAL & INSTALLATION

Front Wheel Drive

1. Block front wheels, raise rear of car and support on jackstands.

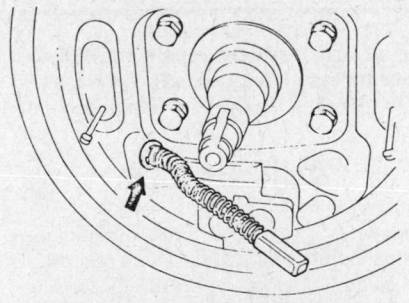

Cable removal—drum brake

2. Disconnect the brake cable at the parking brake lever (brakes released). Remove the cable clamps inside the driver's compartment (two bolts). Disconnect the clamps on the rear suspension arm.

3. Remove the rear brake drums and the brake shoe assemblies. Disconnect the parking brake cable from the lever on the trailing (rear) brake shoe. Remove the brake cables.

4. Installation is the reverse of removal.

Rear Wheel Drive

1. Remove the console and rear seat.

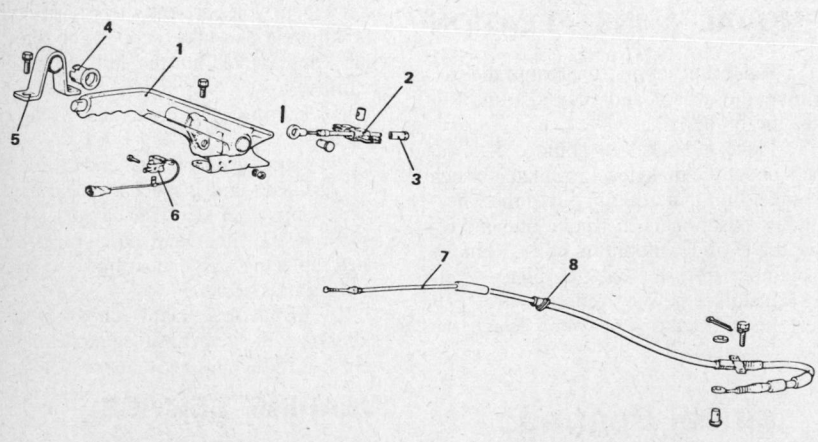

1. Parking brake lever
2. Equalizer
3. Parking brake cable adjuster
4. Bushing
5. Parking brake lever stay
6. Parking brake switch
7. Parking brake cable
8. Grommet

Parking brake assembly—Starion

2. Raise and support the rear of the car.

3. Disconnect all clevis pin connections and the cable ends.

4. Pull the cable through the floor.

5. Install in reverse order.

6. Adjust the cable. Apply sealer to the edge of the grommet at the floor opening. Check the parking brake indicator, the light should come on when the brake is applied one notch.

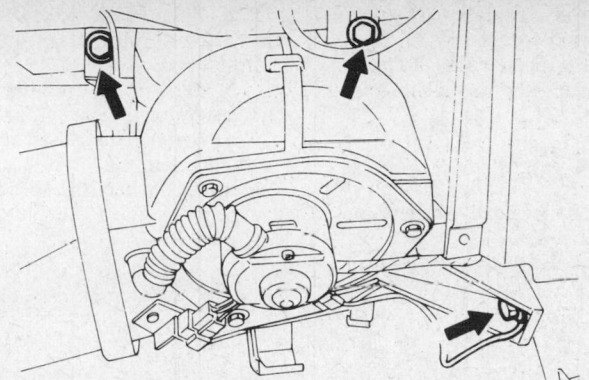

Remove the arrowed bolts and remove the blower motor (Cordia and Tredia)

CHASSIS ELECTRICAL

Heater Blower

REMOVAL & INSTALLATION

Front Wheel Drive

1. Remove the dash panel undercover, the glove box and the side kick panel trim.

2. Disconnect the control wire and duct hose.

3. Remove the blower assembly mounting bolts and the blower assembly.

4. Install in reverse order.

Rear Wheel Drive

1. Remove the dash undercover and the glove box.

2. Disconnect the control wire and duct hose.

3. Remove the duct from the blower assembly. Disconnect the heater fan switch assembly.

4. Remove the blower assembly mounting bolts and the blower assembly.

5. Install in reverse order.

Heater Core

REMOVAL & INSTALLATION

Front Wheel Drive

1. Drain the cooling system and disconnect the negative battery cable.

2. Place the heater control to the ''warm'' position.

3. Remove the instrument panel. Disconnect the center ventilator duct and rear heater duct.

4. Disconnect the heater hose from the heater. Remove the heater mounting bolts and lift out the heater assembly.

5. Remove the heater cover. Disconnect the valve control links and hoses.

6. Remove the heater core from the assembly.

7. Install in reverse order.

Rear Wheel Drive

1. Drain the cooling system and disconnect the negative battery cable.

2. Place the heater control in the ''warm'' position.

3. Disconnect the heater hose at the engine firewall.

4. Remove the instrument panel and the center console.

5. Remove the center ventilator duct, defroster duct and lap duct.

6. Remove the center reinforcement and heater control assembly.

7. Remove the heater assembly mounting bolts and the heater assembly.

8. Remove the heater core.

9. Install in reverse order.

Radio

REMOVAL & INSTALLATION

1. Disconnect the negative battery cable.

2. Remove the radio switch knobs and outer nuts. Remove the panel.

3. On front wheel drive models, remove the glove box. On rear drive models, remove the center panel side cover.

4. Remove the radio mounting screw(s), disconnect the power lead, speaker leads and antenna. Remove the radio.

5. Install in reverse order.

NOTE: The radio fuse is mounted at the rear of the radio. The radio must be removed for fuse replacement.

Windshield Wiper Motor

REMOVAL & INSTALLATION

1. Remove the wiper blade and arm assembly.

2. Remove the cover from the access hole or the deck panel, guide panel and garnish depending on model.

3. Remove the wiper drive mounting bolts at the arm pivots. On the Tredia, remove the washer nozzle.

4. Loosen the wiper motor mounting bolts. Disconnect the wiper motor and linkage and remove. Install in reverse order.

Instrument Cluster

For further information on the instrument cluster, please refer to ''Gauges and Indicators'' in the Unit Repair section.

Front Wheel Drive

1. Disconnect the negative battery cable.

2. Remove the screws at the top of the instrument cluster trim panel. Remove the trim panel.

3. Disconnect the speedometer cable from the back of the speedometer.

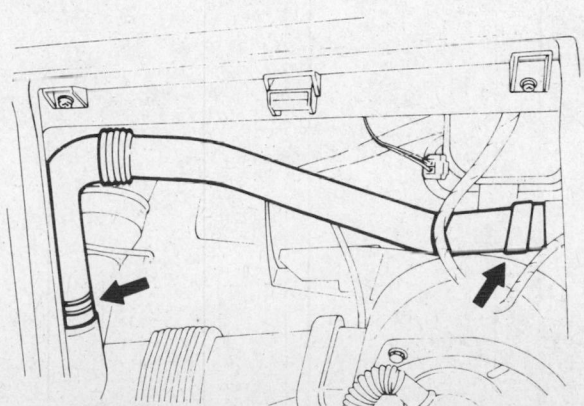

Removing the side defroster hose on the Tredia

4. Remove the cluster mounting screws and pull the cluster forward.

5. Disconnect the electrical connectors and remove the cluster. Install in reverse order.

Rear Wheel Drive

1. Disconnect the negative battery cable.

2. Remove the meter trim hood mounting screws. Pull out and down on the side of the hood.

3. Disconnect the plug connectors on both sides of the cluster.

4. Remove the cluster mounting screws and nuts. Pull the lower sides of the cluster up and disconnect the speedometer cable.

5. Disconnect the plug connectors at the rear of the cluster and remove the cluster. Install in reverse order.

Fuse Box Location

The fuse panel is located under the instrument panel on the driver's side above the cowl side trim.

Peugeot
504, 505, 604

SERIAL NUMBER IDENTIFICATION

Vehicles

504 AND 505

The vehicle serial number is stamped on the left hand engine mounting lug. The same number is stamped on the right front fender well. The manufacturer's identification plate is located on the right fender well. On later models, the VIN may also be located on a plate attached to the driver's side of the dashboard, visible through the windshield.

604

The serial number is stamped on the right front fender well and the manufacturer's plate is located on the right front fender well. On later models, the VIN may also be located on a plate attached to the driver's side of the dashboard, visible through the windshield.

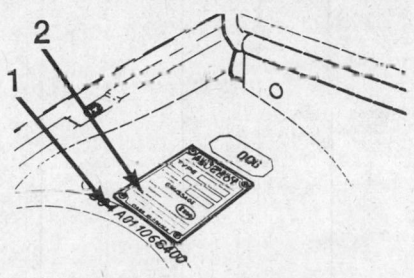

1. Serial number
2. Serial number
3. Engine number

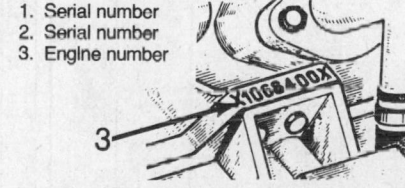

The 504 and 505 serial number is located on the right fender well. The engine number is located on the camshaft tunnel

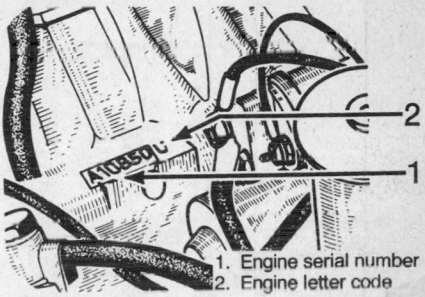

1. Engine serial number
2. Engine letter code

The last digit of the 504 and 505 engine number is a letter code that is keyed to the engine type

Engine

The engine number is stamped on the camshaft tunnel of the engine. The number consists of a letter followed by 5 digits, and a final identification letter.

GENERAL ENGINE SPECIFICATIONS

Year	Model	Engine Displacement cu. in. (cc)	Fuel Delivery	Horsepower @ rpm	Torque @ rpm (ft. lbs.)	Bore × Stroke (in.)	Compression Ratio	Oil Pressure (psi)
'78–'79	504	120.3 (1971)	2–1 bbl	87 @ 5500	119 @ 3000	3.46 × 3.19	7.6:1	27–50
'80–'85	505	120.3 (1971)	F.I.	96 @ 4900	116 @ 3300	3.46 × 3.19	8.35:1	27
'78–'84	504D 505D	140.6 (2304)	D.F.I.	71 @ 4500	99 @ 2500	3.70 × 3.26	23.0:1	27
'81–'85	505TD①	140.6 (2304)	D.F.I.	80 @ 4150	136 @ 2000	3.70 × 3.26	21.0:1	27
'78–'80	604	163 (2664)	1–2 bbl	133 @ 5750	150 @ 3500	3.47 × 2.87	8.2:1	28

GENERAL ENGINE SPECIFICATIONS

Year	Model	Engine Displacement cu. in. (cc)	Fuel Delivery	Horsepower @ rpm	Torque @ rpm (ft. lbs.)	Bore × Stroke (in.)	Compression Ratio	Oil Pressure (psi)
'82–'85	604TD ①	140.6 (2304)	D.F.I.	80 @ 4150	136 @ 2000	3.70 × 3.26	21.0:1	27

F.I. Fuel Injection
D.F.I. Diesel Fuel Injection
① Turbocharged diesel

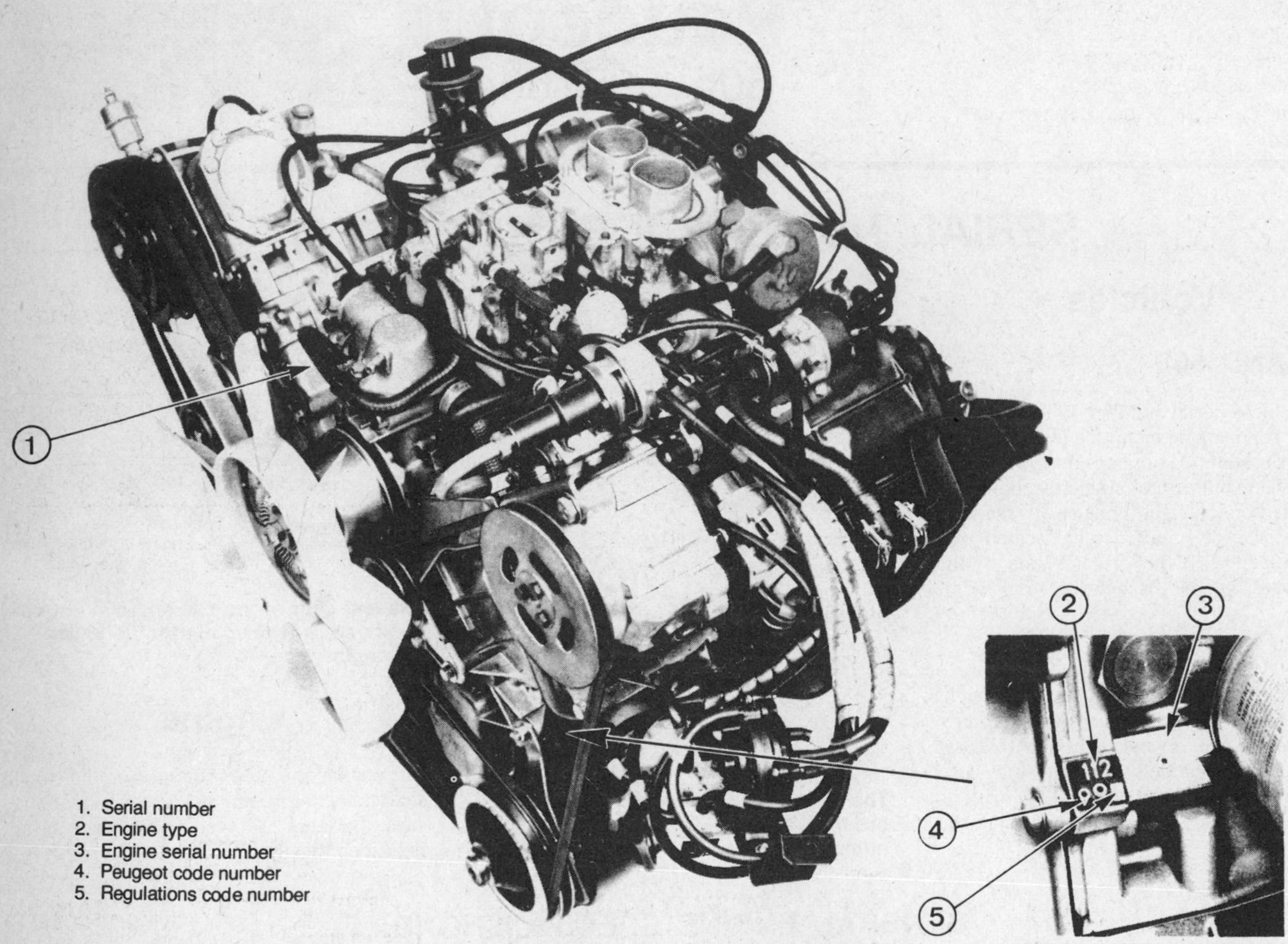

1. Serial number
2. Engine type
3. Engine serial number
4. Peugeot code number
5. Regulations code number

604 model Engine and vehicle serial number location

GASOLINE ENGINE TUNE-UP SPECIFICATIONS

Year	Model	Engine Displacement cu. in. (cc)	Spark Plugs Type	Spark Plugs Gap (in.)	Distributor Point Dwell (deg)	Distributor Point Gap (in.)	Ignition Timing④ MT (deg)	Ignition Timing④ AT (deg)	Idle Speed MT (rpm)	Idle Speed AT (rpm)	Valve Clearance① Intake (in.)	Valve Clearance① Exhaust (in.)
'78–'79	504	120.3 (1971)	44 XL	.024	55–59	.016	5	5	800–850	800–850	.004	.010
'80–'85	505	120.3 (1971)	WR 7 DS	.024	ELECTRONIC		8⑥	8⑥	900–950 ⑦	900–950 ⑦	.004	.010

GASOLINE ENGINE TUNE-UP SPECIFICATIONS

Year	Model	Engine Displacement cu. in. (cc)	Spark Plugs		Distributor		Ignition Timing④		Idle Speed		Valve Clearance①	
			Type	Gap (in.)	Point Dwell (deg)	Point Gap (in.)	MT (deg)	AT (deg)	MT (rpm)	AT (rpm)	Intake (in.)	Exhaust (in.)
'78–'80	604	163 (2664)	BN 9Y	.024	ELECTRONIC②③		12⑤	12⑤	900–950	900–950	.004	.010

NOTE: The underhood specifications sticker often reflects tune-up specification changes made in production. Sticker figures must be used if they disagree with those in this chart.
BTDC Before top dead center
① Valves must be adjusted in proper sequence
② Conventional ignition is used in Canada (.016 in gap or 76° dwell)
③ Air gap on Schlumberger ignition system: .021 in.
④ All timing degrees BTDC
⑤ Schlumberger ignition system: 10°
⑥ 8° ± 2 BTDC @ 900 RPM—1980–81
@ 800 RPM—1982 & Later
⑦ 800–850 in Neutral—1982 and later

DIESEL ENGINE TUNE-UP SPECIFICATIONS

Year	Model	Valve Clearance (cold)		Intake Valve Opens (deg)	Injection Pump Setting (deg)	Injection Nozzle Pressure (psi)		Idle Speed (rpm)	Compression Pressure (psi)
		Intake (in.)	Exhaust (in.)			New	Used		
'78–'85	504D, 505D	.010	.010	12B	13B	1740–1813	1668–1813	780–830①	261④
'81–'85	505TD, 604TD	.006	.010	N.A.	.016②③	1900	NA	830–860	261④

NA Not available at time of publication
① With A/C: 830–860
② Figure is for in. BTDC
③ Canada: .031
④ Maximum variation between cylinders: 72 psi

FIRING ORDERS

NOTE: To avoid confusion, always replace spark plug wires one at a time.

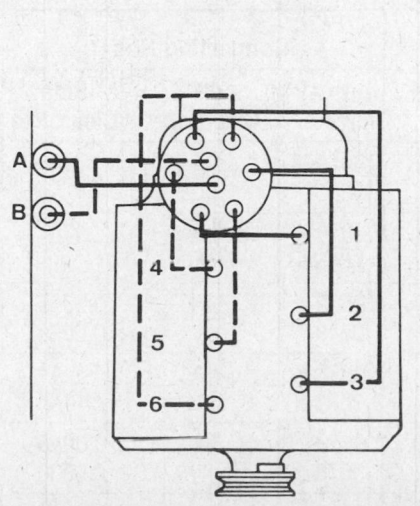

V-6 firing order—conventional ignition

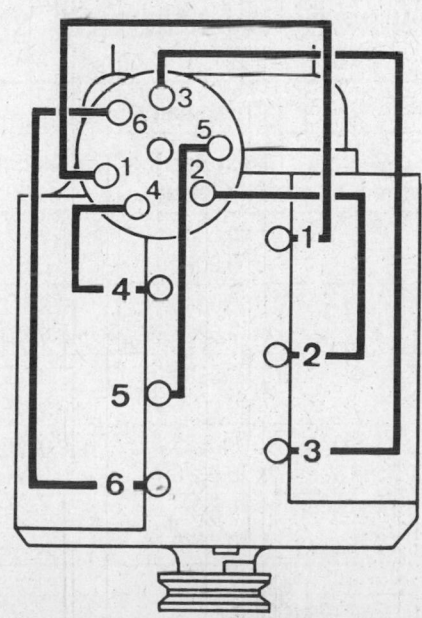

V-6 firing order—electronic ignition

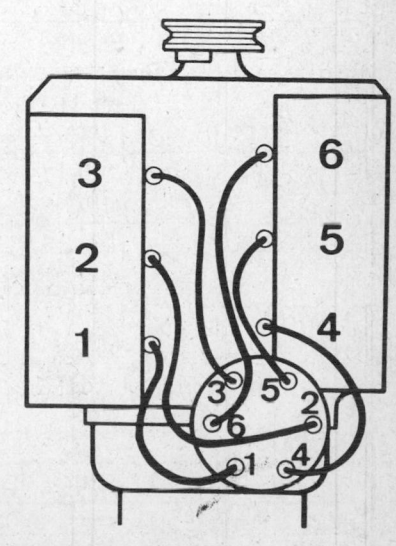

V-6 firing order—Schlumberger electronic ignition

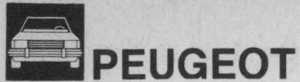
FIRING ORDERS

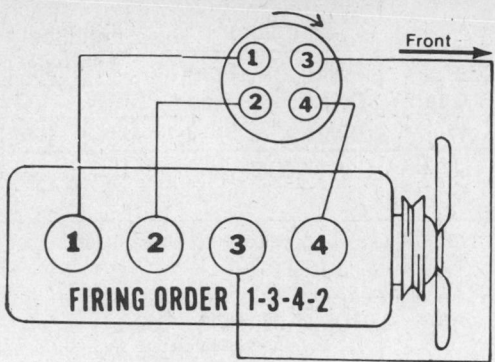

FIRING ORDER 1-3-4-2

4 cylinder firing order

CAPACITIES

Year	Model	Engine Crankcase (qts) With filter	Transmission (pts) Man	Transmission (pts) Auto	Drive Axle (pts)	Gasoline Tank (gals)	Cooling System (qts)
'78–'79	504	4.3	2.1	3.5	2.8	14.8	8.5
	504SW	4.3	2.1	3.5	2.8	15.8	8.5
'80–'85	505	4.3	③	3.4	2.8	18.0	7.5①
'78–'80	604	6.3	2.8	3.2	3.2	18.5	11.0
'78–'83	504D, 505D	5.3	③	3.4	2.8	18.0②	10.6
'81–'83	505TD, 604TD	5.3④	③	3.4	2.8	17.4	10.6
'84–'85	504D Wagon, 505D, TD	5.7	2.4	3.4	3.4⑥	18②	10.6
'84–'85	604 TD	5.3	3.4	3.4	3.2	18	10.1

① 7.7 with AT
② Station wagon: 15.8
③ BA 7: 2.4
   BA 105 and BA 1015: 3.4
④ 1983: 5.7
⑤ 1983: 18
⑥ 504 wagon—3.3
⑦ 1984 and later—5.7

CRANKSHAFT AND CONNECTING ROD SPECIFICATIONS

(All measurements in inches)

Year	Model	Engine Displacement cu. in. (cc)	Crankshaft Main Bearing Journal Dia.	Crankshaft Main Bearing Oil Clearance	Crankshaft End-Play	Connecting Rod Journal Diameter	Connecting Rod Oil Clearance	Connecting Rod Side Clearance
'78–'79	504	120.3 (1971)	①	0.0045–0.0065	0.0031–0.0079	1.9079–1.9685	NA	NA
'80–'85	505	120.3 (1971)	①	0.0045–0.0065	0.0031–0.0079	1.9079–1.9685	NA	NA
'78–'85	504D, 505D	140.6 (2304)	2.3606–2.3602	0.0030–0.0070	0.0031–0.0114	1.9689–1.9678	NA	0.0015–0.0036
'78–'80	604	163 (2664)	2.7576–2.7583	0.0035–0.0075	0.0028–0.0106	2.0578–2.0585	NA	NA
'81–'85	505TD, 604TD	140.6 (2304)	2.1661–2.1651	0.0030–0.0070	0.0031–0.0114	1.9689–1.9678	NA	0.0015–0.0036

NA Not available at time of publication
① Rear journal: 2.1616–2.1646   Front interm.: 2.3050–2.3060
   Rear interm.: 2.2102–2.2073   Front journal: 2.3386–2.3392
   Center: 2.2509–2.2515

VALVE SPECIFICATIONS

Year	Model	Seat Angle (deg)	Spring Test Pressure (lbs. @ in.)	Stem-to-Guide Clearance (in.)		Stem Diameter (in.)	
				Intake	Exhaust	Intake	Exhaust
'78-'85	504, 505	44.5③	181.5 @ 1.18	0.0012-0.0024	0.0024-0.0035	0.3132-0.3135	0.3120-0.3126
'78-'85	504D, 505D	①	②	NA		0.3344-0.3338	0.3336-0.3331
'78-'80	604	44.5	170 @ 1.06	NA		.3096	.3475
'81-'85	505TD, 604TD	45	②	NA		0.3344-0.3338	0.3336-0.3331

NA Not available at time of publication
① Intake: 60
  Exhaust: 45
② Inner: 34.8 @ 0.866
  Outer: 101.4 @ 1.02
③ 1980 and later engines, intake seat
  angle—60°

PISTON AND RING SPECIFICATIONS
(All measurements in inches)

Year	Model	Piston Clearance	Ring Gap			Ring Side Clearance		
			Top Compression	Bottom Compression	Oil Control	Top Compression	Bottom Compression	Oil Control
'78-'85	504, 505 604		PART OF PISTON/LINER KIT					
'78-'85	504D, 505D, TD 604TD	0.0010	0.0137-0.0236	0.0137-0.0236	0.0059-0.0118	0.0012-0.0035	0.0019-0.0032	0.0011-0.0024

TORQUE SPECIFICATIONS
(All readings in ft. lbs.)

Year	Vehicle Model	Cylinder Head Bolts	Rod Bearing Bolts	Main Bearing Bolts	Crankshaft Pulley Bolt	Flywheel to Crankshaft Bolts
'78-'85	504, 505	①	29	55	123.5	49
'78-'80	604	②	34	NA	119.0	31.5
'78-'85	504D, 505D, TD 604TD	③	42④	80	39.9⑤	56

NA Not available at time of publication
① Torque the head bolts in sequence to 36.0 ft. lbs. (51.4 Nm). Loosen the head bolts and retorque to 15 ft. lbs. (20.3 Nm). Match-mark the bolt head to the cylinder head and tighten ¼ of a turn more on the head bolts (90 degrees).
② Torque the head bolts in sequence to 43.2 ft. lbs. (58.8 Nm). Fully loosen the head bolts and then retorque them in sequence to 14.4 ft. lbs. (19.6 Nm). Match-mark the head bolts to the cylinder head and tighten ¼ of a turn more on the head bolts (90 degrees).

③ Torque the head bolts in sequence to 22 ft. lbs. Retorque all bolts in the same sequence to 47 ft. lbs. (51 ft. lbs. on Turbo-Diesels). Loosen the head bolts ¼ turn in the same sequence and then retorque them to 47 ft. lbs. again (51 ft. lbs. on Turbo-Diesels)
④ Turbo-Diesels: 44 ft. lbs.
⑤ Torque to this figure; then turn exactly 60 degrees (one bolt flat) farther.

BRAKE SPECIFICATIONS

(All measurements in inches)

Year	Vehicle Model	Lug Nut Torque (ft. lbs.)	Master Cyl. Bore (in.)	Front Disc		Rear Disc ③		Minimum Lining Thickness	
				Minimum Thickness	Maximum Run-Out	Minimum Thickness	Maximum Run-Out	Front	Rear
'78–'85	504	43.5	①	0.43	0.0028	0.42②	0.0028	0.10	0.10
'78–'85	604	61.2	0.86	N.A.	N.A.	N.A.	N.A.	0.10	0.10
'80–'85	505	43.5	N.A.	0.44	0.0028	0.43	0.0028	0.10	0.10

N.A. Not available at time of publication

① There are seven different type master cylinders on 504 models. The bore could be 0.824 in. or 0.76 in. depending on the type master cylinder in the vehicle.

② Some earlier type rear discs have minimum thickness of 0.34 in. (Girling type AH12MK1)

③ Models equipped with rear drum brakes have a maximum drum oversize of 11.3 in. except Saloon L models which have a maximum oversize of 10.3 inches.

N.A. Not available at time of publication.

WHEEL ALIGNMENT SPECIFICATIONS

Year	Model	Caster		Camber		Toe-In (in.)	King Pin Inclination (deg)
		Range (deg)	Pref. Setting (deg)	Range (deg)	Pref. Setting (deg)		
'78–'83	504	5/64–3 5/64	2 21/32	1/8–1 1/8	5/8	7/32	8 29/32
'78–'83	604①	3–4	3 1/2	− 1/4–1 1/4	1/2	7/32	10
'80–'83	505②	3–4	3 1/2	0–1 1/2	3/4	5/16	9 1/16
'84–'85	604①	3–4	3 1/2	− 1 1/4–1/4	− 1/2	1/8	—
'84–'85	605 Sedan②	3–4	3 1/2	− 1/16–1 7/16	11/16	5/32	9 5/16
'84–'85	505 Wagon②	3–4	3 1/2	5/16–11/16	1/2	1/8	9 5/16

① Rear Wheels: Camber Range − 2– − 1
Preferred − 1 1/2
Toe-in 5/32

② Rear Wheels: Camber Range − 15/16– − 1/16
Preferred − 7/16
Toe-in 9/32

TUNE-UP PROCEDURES

Spark Plugs

The average life of a spark plug is approximately 12,000–20,000 miles. With electronic ignition, this is typically extended to 30,000 miles (the recommended replacement interval on these models. This is, however, dependent on the mechanical condition of the engine, the type of fuel that is used, and the type of driving conditions under which the car is used.

The electrode end of the spark plug is also a very good indicator of the mechanical condition of your engine. If a spark plug should foul and begin to misfire, you will have to find the condition that caused the plug to foul and correct it. It is a good idea to occasionally inspect all the plugs. A small amount of deposit on a spark plug, after it has been in use for any period of time, should be considered normal. But a black liquid deposit on the plugs indicates oil fouling.

REMOVAL

1. Place a piece of masking tape around each plug wire and number it according to its corresponding cylinder.
2. Pull the wires from the spark plugs, grasping the wire by the end of the rubber boot and twisting it off.
3. Loosen each spark plug with a spark plug socket. On the 504 you will need a socket extension attached to the socket in order to reach the plug through the plug tube. It is helpful to use a special type of socket equipped with a soft insert which holds the plug in the socket as you pull it out. When the plug has been loosened a few turns, stop to clean any material from around the spark plug holes. Compressed air is preferable.

NOTE: In no case should foreign matter be allowed to enter the cylinders. Severe damage could result.

4. Finish unscrewing the plugs and remove them from the engine.

INSPECTION

It should be remembered that any type of deposit will decrease the efficiency of the plug. If the plugs are not to be replaced, they should be thoroughly cleaned before installation. If the electrode ends of the plugs are not worn or damaged and if they are to be reused, wipe off the porcelain insulator on each plug and check for cracks or breaks. If either condition exists, the plug must be replaced.

If the plugs are judged reusable, clean on a plug cleaning machine or remove the deposits with a stiff wire brush. Check the plug gap on both new and used plugs before installing them in the engine. The ground electrode must be parallel to the center electrode and the specified size wire gauge should pass through the opening with a slight drag. If the air gap between the two electrodes is not correct, open or close the ground electrode, with the proper tool, to bring it to specifications.

INSTALLATION

1. Lightly oil the spark plug threads and hand-tighten them into the engine. Spark plug threads are self-starting, but be careful to allow the plug to seek its own angle— if you force it, you could cross-thread it into the head.

2. Tighten the plugs securely with a spark plug wrench (only about 10 ft. lbs. of torque is necessary). In any case, avoid overtightening the plugs.

3. Reconnect the wires to the plugs making sure that each is securely fitted.

Breaker Points and Condenser

REMOVAL & INSTALLATION

Early 504 models and certain 604 models sold in Canada are equipped with conventional ignition systems. To replace the points and condenser, follow the procedure outlined below:

1. Remove the distributor cap, and inspect it for carbon tracks and cracks.

NOTE: The procedure for the 604 dual point is the same as outlined below, the only difference is that it must be performed for both sets of points.

2. Disconnect the condenser, primary and breaker point ground wires from the terminal located in the side of the distributor housing.

3. Remove the screw which attaches the condenser to the outside of the distributor housing and remove the condenser.

4. Remove the breaker point set screw using a magnetic or locking screwdriver. Remove the breaker points from the distributor.

5. Wipe all dirt and grease from the distributor plate and cam with a lint-free cloth. Apply a small amount of heat-resistant lubricant to the distributor cam On those distributors with a felt lubricating pad, simply add a small amount of lubricant to the pad.

6. Properly position the new points on the breaker plate and secure with the set screw. Do not allow the screw to fall into the hole in the breaker plate in the distributor.

7. Fit the terminal back into the housing in the distributor body and attach the breaker point ground wire, the condenser wire and primary wire.

8. Adjust the breaker point gap with a feeler gauge or dwell meter, as outlined below.

ADJUSTMENT

1. If the two contact points of the breaker point assembly are not parallel, bend the stationary contact slightly to correct.

NOTE: Bend only the bracket portion of the points, do not bend the other side.

2. Turn the engine until the point gap is at its greatest (where the rubbing block is on one of the four high points or corners of the distributor cam). This can be acccomplished either by having an assistant quickly turn the ignition switch to the "start" position and release it, or by placing the proper size wrench on the bolt in the center of the lower pulley. If you choose the wrench method, *be sure to always turn the engine in the direction of normal rotation.*

3. Insert the correct size feeler gauge between the points. To determine the correct feeler gauge size, see the point gap column in the "Tune-Up Specifications" chart in the front of this section. The gauge should fit between the contacts with just a slight amount of drag. Always insert the gauge so that it is parallel with the contacts on the points.

4. If the point gap is too large or too small, slightly loosen the point set screw and insert a screwdriver blade into the notch in the points. Twist the screwdriver to open or close the points as required. Tighten the breaker point attaching screw when the correct gap is obtained.

5. Recheck the point gap to make sure that it did not change when the breaker point set screw was tightened.

6. Align the rotor with the distributor shaft and push the rotor onto the shaft until it is fully seated.

7. Reinstall the distributor cap and the coil high tension wire.

Dwell Angle

ADJUSTMENT

1. Adjust the points with a feeler gauge as described above.

2. Connect a dwell meter to the engine in accordance with the manufacturer's instructions, between the distributor primary lead and a ground.

3. With the engine warmed up and running at the specified idle speed, observe the reading on the dwell meter.

─────── CAUTION ───────
When working on a vehicle with the engine running, the following precautions must be observed. Work only in a well-ventilated area. Be certain that the transmission is in Neutral and that the parking brake is firmly applied. Always keep your hands, clothing and tools clear of the moving radiator fan.

If your dwell meter does not have a scale for four cylinder engines, multiply the eight

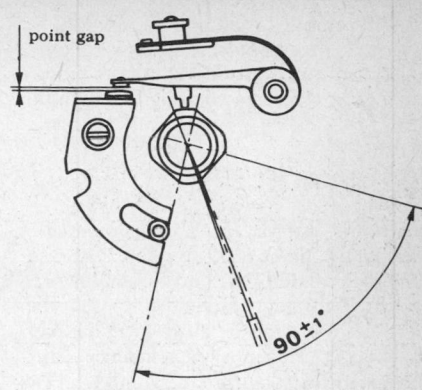

Breaker point gap—typical

cylinder reading by two. If the reading is within the specified range, turn the engine off and disconnect the meter.

4. If the reading is above the specified range, the breaker point gap is too small. If the reading is below the specified range, the gap is too large. In either case, turn off the engine and close or open the point gap as required. Start the engine and recheck the dwell reading. When correct, turn off the engine and disconnect the meter.

5. Check and adjust the ignition timing as required.

NOTE: On vehicles equipped with electronic ignition, this setting is made at the factory, and no adjustment is required.

Electronic Ignition

Electronic ignition is used on all 504, USA models, starting in 1978. In the United States, 604 models use electronic ignition. All 505 models use the electronic ignition.

Electronic ignition uses transistorized switching triggered by magnetic pulse signals to eliminate breaker points.

The type of electronic ignition used in most Peugeot ignition systems has no provision for setting the air gap (with the exception of the Schlumberger ignition system and the Ducellier distributor found in the 505). The reluctor is a stationary piece. The only serviceable part in the distributor is the pick-up coil. To remove the coil, take out the two pick-up piece retaining screws and noting their position, remove the two wires leading from the coil.

MAJOR COMPONENTS

1. Magnetic pulse generator:
   a. Polarity wheel (reluctor): Timer teeth that rotate with the distributor shaft. The system has one tooth for each cylinder.
   b. Electro-magnet coil (pick-up coil): generates the pulse signal to the amplifier module as each timing tooth passes by the core of the pick-up coil.

2. Ignition coil: A special high energy coil is used and cannot be interchanged with conventional coils.

3. Amplifier module: The module receives pick-up impulses, amplifies them to signal the transistor and shuts off the primary current flowing through the ignition coil.

OPERATION

When the polarity wheel teeth come in alignment with the pick–up coil magnet core, a magnetic field is built up around the pick-up coil. This magnetic field collapses when the timer tooth moves away from the pick-up coil core. This movement induces a small current in the pick-up coil windings. This current is amplified in the amplifier module and triggers a transistor to stop the primary current to the ignition coil. The resulting collapse of the primary coil field through the secondary coil windings induces the secondary current to fire the spark plug.

TESTING

By following a certain sequence of tests the correct diagnosis can be made.

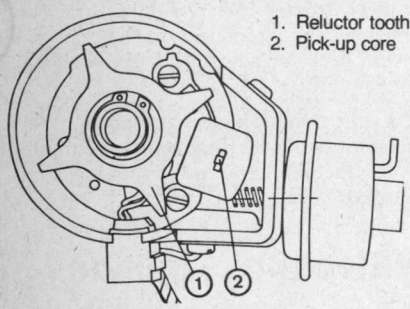

1. Reluctor tooth
2. Pick-up core

To test for spark, position the timing teeth on either side of the pick-up core

Test For Spark

1. Remove the distributor cap.
2. Position the polarity wheel (reluctor) so that two teeth are on either side of the pick-up core (teeth not aligned with the core).
3. Remove the high tension lead from the distributor cap.
4. Turn the ignition key on.
5. Position the high tension lead ½ in. away from ground.

NOTE: Choose a ground point as far away from the coil and module as possible.

6. Pass a screwdriver over the pick-up

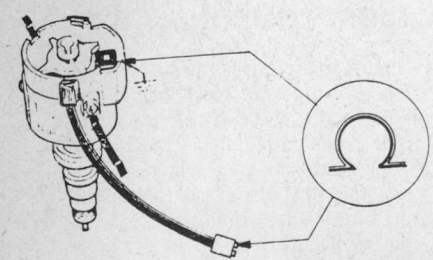

Check the pick-up coil for insulation to ground

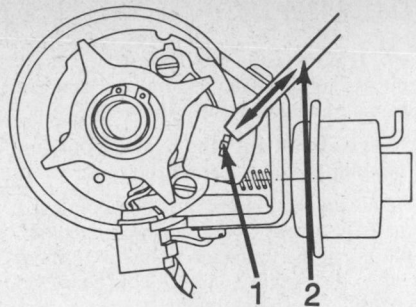

1. Pick-up core
2. Screwdriver

Pass a screwdriver over the pick-up core and a spark should occur

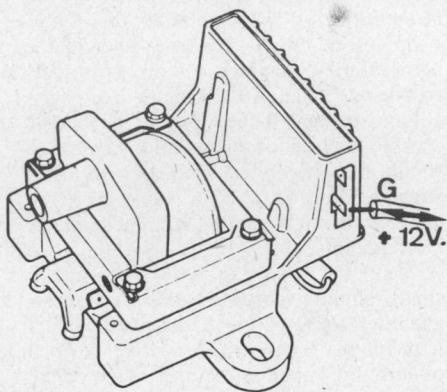

Check for voltage at the electronic control module

coil core. A spark should occur with each pass of the screwdriver.

7. If there is no spark:
  a. Check the primary voltage at the ignition coil.
  b. Check the pick-up coil.
  c. Test the ignition coil.
  d. Test the amplifier module.

Primary Voltage Test at the Ignition Coil

1. Connect a test lamp from the coil positive terminal to ground. If the test lamp lights, continue with the electronic ignition test procedures. If the test lamp does not light, check for a primary ignition wiring problem or faulty ignition switch.

Test the Pick-Up Coil

1. Turn the ignition off and disconnect the pick-up coil connector from the module.
2. Attach an ohmmeter between the pick-up coil terminals.
3. Check the pick-up coil resistance for 900–110 ohms.
4. Remove the vacuum line from the vacuum advance unit and attach an outside vacuum source to the advance unit.
5. While observing the ohmmeter, apply slowly and steadily, up to 20 inches of vacuum to the advance unit.
6. If the ohm values move out of the 900–1100 range by more than 50 ohms, replace the pick-up coil.

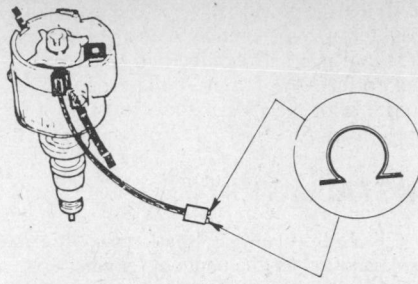

Check the pick-up coil for resistance

7. Check pick-up coil insulation by attaching the ohmmeter between one of the coil terminals and ground.
8. If a less than infinite reading is obtained, replace the pick-up coil.

Testing the Ignition Coil

1. Remove the coil connector from the coil terminals and using an ohmmeter, check:
  a. The primary coil windings for 0.48–0.61 ohms.
  b. The secondary coil windings for 9000–11,000 ohms.
  c. Check the leads connecting the control module to the ignition coil for continuity (0) ohms.
2. Replace the ignition coil if not within specifications.

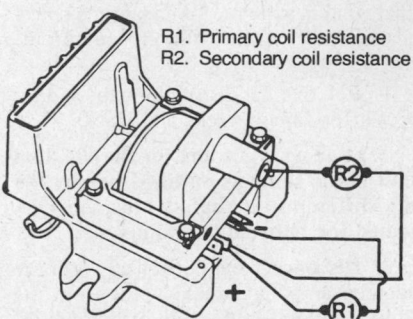

R1. Primary coil resistance
R2. Secondary coil resistance

Checking the electronic ignition coil

Testing the Amplifier Module

1. Remove the distributor connector from the module and the high tension wire from the distributor cap.
2. Position the high tension wire ½ inch from ground and as far from the module and coil as possible.
3. Turn on the ignition.
4. Using a jumper wire from the positive battery terminal, make and break contact with the G terminal of the module.
5. At each impulse, a spark should occur. If there is no spark, repeat the test using a new amplifier module.

AIR GAP ADJUSTMENT— SCHULMBERGER IGNITION

1. Position the engine so the mark on the timing sprocket is opposite the sensor port, and the notch in the pulley is approximately 30° in front of the 0 graduation on the timing plate.

The mark on the timing sprocket (1) should be opposite the sensor port before tightening the screw (2)

2. Fit the sensor holder in place using new seals, and lightly tighten the screw.

3. Pivot the holder as far as it will go in a clockwise direction (maximum retard).

4. Position the sensor towards the slot in its holder.

5. Insert an 0.022 in. (0.55mm) thick feeler gauge between the end of the sensor and the sprocket web.

6. Tighten the sensor into the holder until a slight drag is felt on the feeler gauge.

7. Find the No. 1 cylinder advance point.

8. The mark on the distributor arm should be located between the marks on the casing and the pulley notch opposite the 10° graduation in the timing plate.

9. Pivot the sensor holder in a counterclockwise direction (maximum advance).

10. Repeat Steps 4–6 above.

REPLACING THE PICKUP COIL

505 (Ducellier Distributor)

1. Remove the distributor coil, rotor, and plastic protector.

2. Remove the attaching screw (1) from the side of the distributor.

3. Pull the connector (2) upward and remove it from the side of the distributor. Disconnect the wiring, noting how the connections go.

Numbers indicate attaching screws and connectors for the pickup coil used in the 505 (for identification, see text)

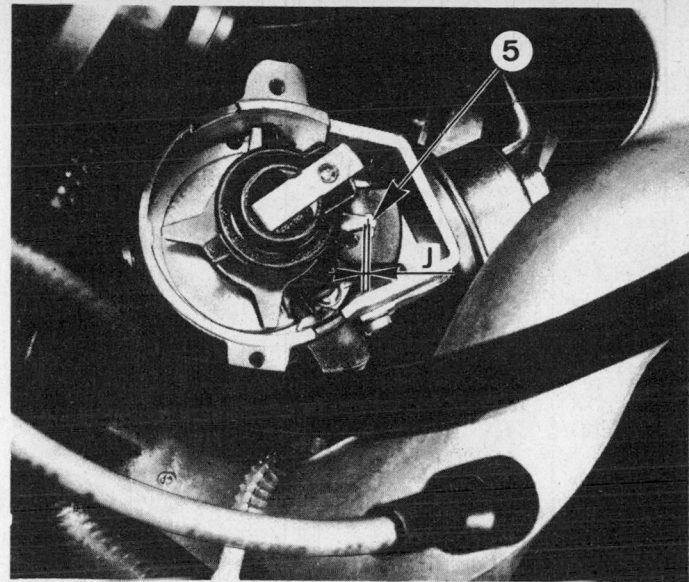

Measuring pickup coil air gap (5)—505

4. Remove the coil mounting screws (3a and 3b) and remove the coil.

5. To install, reverse the above procedures, tightening the mounting screws (3a and 3b) only lightly.

6. Turn the engine over until a wheel vane is positioned directly opposite the core (5).

7. Using a non-magnetic (brass or paper) feeler gauge, rotate the coil around screw 3b until the gap is .012–.020 in. Tighten the mounting screws and recheck the gap. Then, replace the protector, rotor, and coil.

REPLACING AMPLIFIER MODULE

All Electronic Ignition Systems

The aluminum base to which the amplified module is mounted serves as a cooling system for the heat created in electronic switching. Silicone grease, packed with the module, conducts heat from the module to the metal base. Make sure to coat the new module with grease, or heat will destroy it. Also, make sure the mounting bolts are snug to provide a proper ground connection.

Ignition Timing

504 AND 505

1. Loosen the distributor clamp bolt.

2. Disconnect the vacuum line from the advance unit and plug the line.

3. Connect a timing light to the No. 1 spark plug wire and a tachometer to the negative coil terminal. Ground the tachometer.

4. While checking and adjusting initial

Fit the sensor (3) into the holder. Set the gap by tightening the screw (4)

timing, do not exceed an idle of 850 rpm except on 1980–81 505 models. These are set at 900 rpm, while 1982–84 505s are set at 800 rpm.

5. Loosen the distributor clamp bolt.

6. On most models adjust the distributor so that the timing mark is at 5° BTDC on the timing plate. On the 1980–84 505, the 8 degree reference notch should be aligned with the notch in the pulley. Check the ''Tune-Up Specifications'' chart. Adjustment is made by turning the distributor until the timing marks are properly aligned.

7. Tighten the distributor clamp and recheck the timing with the timing light.

604 WITH CONVENTIONAL IGNITION

The 604 conventional type ignition has dual points and dual coils. The distributor cam has three lobes and each set of ignition points fires just three cylinders. For this reason, the timing light must be attached to the No. 1 spark plug wire and then to the No. 6 spark plug wire, when adjusting the timing.

The factory high tension coil leads are color coded. The color code on the front coil (4, 5, and 6 cylinders) is grey and the back coil (1, 2, and 3 cylinders) is black.

1. To adjust the timing, loosen the distributor clamp bolt.

2. Disconnect and plug the vacuum advance line.

3. Connect a timing light to the No. 1 spark plug wire.

4. Attach a tachometer to the negative post of the rear coil and ground the other tachometer lead.

5. Check the timing on the No. 1 cylinder and adjust it to 0° BTDC. To adjust

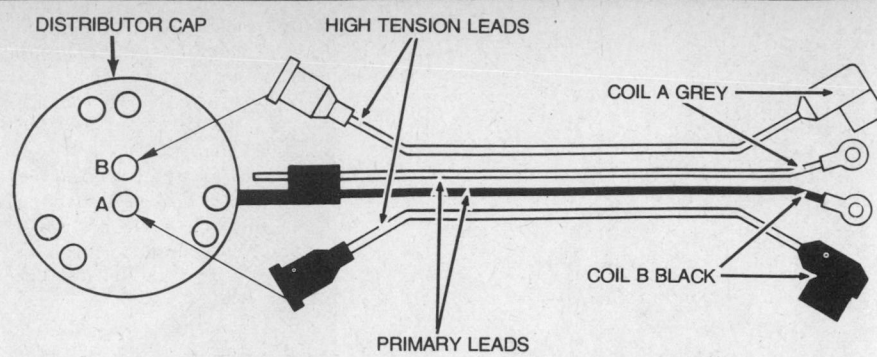

DISTRIBUTOR CAP   HIGH TENSION LEADS   COIL A GREY   COIL B BLACK   B   A   PRIMARY LEADS

Color codes on the distributor-to-coil high tension wires

the No. 1 cylinder timing; rotate the distributor.

6. Check the timing on the No. 6 spark plug wire and adjust it to 0° BTDC. To adjust the No. 6 cylinder timing; turn the screw located on the outside of the distributor body.

604 WITH SCHLUMBERGER® ELECTRONIC IGNITION

1. Remove the vacuum advance line and plug it.

2. Attach a tachometer to the negative coil post and ground the other tachometer lead.

3. Connect a timing light to the No. 1 spark plug wire.

4. Start the engine and idle it at a maximum of 950 rpm.

5. If the timing is out of specifications, loosen the timing sensor (at the front of the left cylinder head) and rotate the sensor counterclockwise to increase advance and clockwise to decrease advance.

6. Tighten the sensor and recheck the timing.

604 WITH BOSCH® ELECTRONIC IGNITION

1. Remove the vacuum advance line and plug it.

2. Attach the timing light to the No. 6 spark plug wire. Connect a tachometer to the negative coil post and ground.

3. Start the engine and idle it a maximum of 900 rpm.

4. Set the timing to a specification of 12° BTDC. If the timing is out of specification, adjust it by rotating the distributor until the timing light shows the pulley mark lining up with 12° BTDC on the timing plate.

5. Stop the engine, reconnect the vacuum advance hose and remove the tachometer and timing light.

6. If necessary, adjust the idle speed to 900 rpm.

Valve Lash

ADJUSTMENT

504 and 505

1. Remove the air cleaner (carburetor models), the spark plug wires, the spark plugs and any hoses, vacuum lines or wires in the way of the valve cover. Remove the valve cover.

2. Adjust the valves with the engine cold. It must have been off at least 6 hours.

3. Place a wrench on the lower crankshaft pulley bolt and turn the wrench in the direction of engine rotation until the No. 1 exhaust valve is fully open (all the exhaust valves are on the exhaust manifold side).

4. Using a feeler gauge, check the clearance between the rocker arm and the camshaft lobe of the No. 3 intake and the

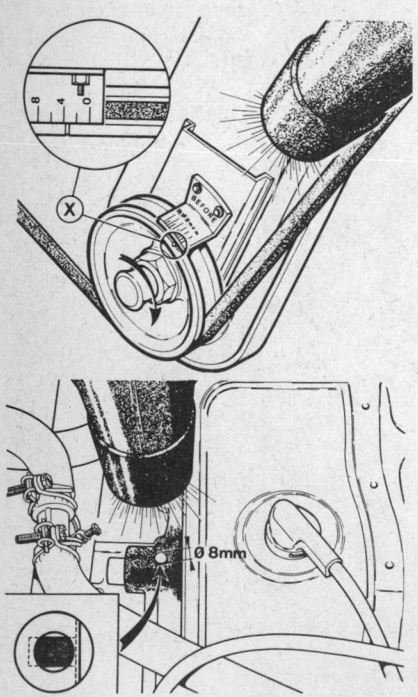

504 timing mark and hole location

604 timing mark location

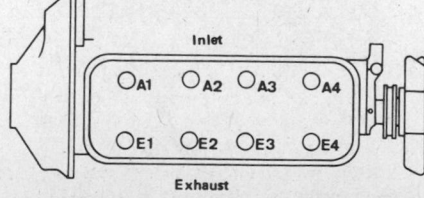

Set fully open	to adjust	
E1	A3	E4
E3	A4	E2
E4	A2	E1
E2	A1	E3

E = Exhaust – A = Inlet

Inlet: A1 A2 A3 A4

Exhaust: E1 E2 E3 E4

504 and 505 valve clearance adjusting sequence

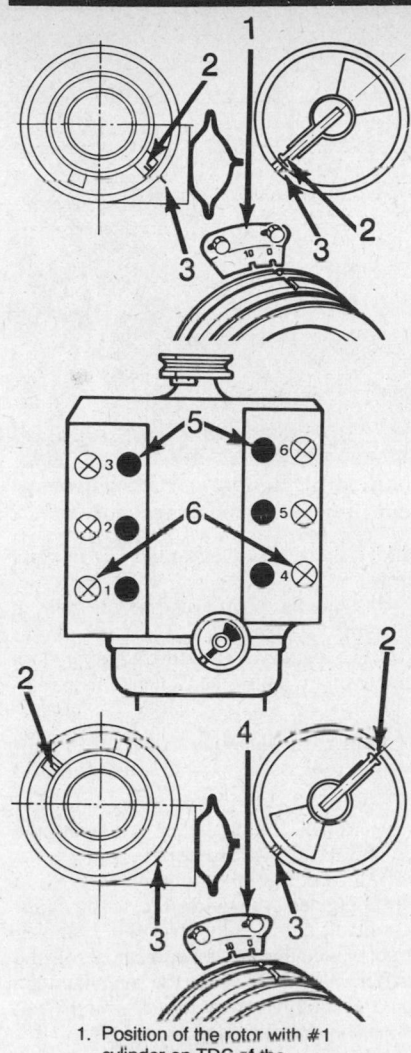

1. Position of the rotor with #1 cylinder on TDC of the compression stroke
2. Mark on rotor
3. Mark on distributor
4. Position of the rotor with #1 cylinder on the end of the exhaust stroke and the beginning of the intake stroke
5. Intake valve
6. Exhaust valve

Valve lash sequence for V6 engines

No. 4 exhaust valves. If the clearance does not correspond to the value given in the chart, loosen the locknut with an open-end wrench and turn the adjusting stud with a screwdriver to increase or decrease the clearance. When the setting is correct, tighten the locknut, making sure that you do not disturb the setting.

5. Repeat Steps 3–4 for the rest of the valves in sequence.

604

1. Using a remote starter switch, bring the No. 1 piston to TOP DEAD CENTER (TDC) on the compression stroke.

2. Remove the distributor cap and check the position of the rotor. The arm should be directly in line with the marks on the distributor housing.

3. Check the location of the notch on the belt pulley, it should be aligned with the "O" notch on the timing plate.

4. With the engine in this position, adjust the No. 1, 2, and 4 intake valves and the No. 1, 3, and 6 exhaust valves.

5. Again using the starter switch, bring the piston to the end of the exhaust stroke and to the beginning of the intake stroke.

6. The rotor arm should be pointing 180° away from the markings on the distributor housing.

7. The notch of the belt pulley should again be aligned with the "O" notch on the timing plate.

8. With the engine in this position, adjust the No. 3, 5, and 6 intake valves and the No. 2, 4, and 6 exhaust valves.

9. Using new gaskets, install the valve covers, distributor cap and vacuum lines.

604 ROCKER ARM ADJUSTMENT SEQUENCE

No. 1 Piston on TDC	Rocker Arms To Be Adjusted	
Firing stroke	A1①	F1②
	A2①	E3②
	A4①	E6②
End of exhaust	A3①	E2②
Commencement of inlet stroke	A5①	E4①
	A6①	E5②

① Inlet: 0.10mm
② Exhaust: 0.25mm

Carburetors

IDLE SPEED AND MIXTURE

General

1. Select Park on an automatic transmission or Neutral on a manual transmission.
2. Set the parking brake.
3. Turn off the air conditioning and all electrical accessories.
4. Route the pressure from the air injector pump, away from the manifolds by connecting a jumper wire across the electrovalve control switch terminals.

Without CO Analyzer

1. Adjust the engine idle speed to 950–100 rpm.
2. Adjust the idle mixture screw to obtain the highest rpm.
3. Adjust the idle speed back to 950–1000 rpm.
4. Repeat these procedures until the 950–1000 rpm is obtained as the highest idle mixture rpm.
5. Adjust the idle speed to 900–950 rpm.
6. Remove the jumper wire from the electro-valve and adjust the idle to 900–950 rpm.

With a CO Analyzer

1. Connect the CO analyzer according to the manufacturer's instructions.

1. Primary carburetor
2. Secondary carburetor
3. Idle speed screw
4. Idle mixture screw

Adjusting the 604 carburetors

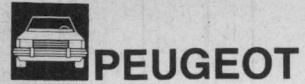
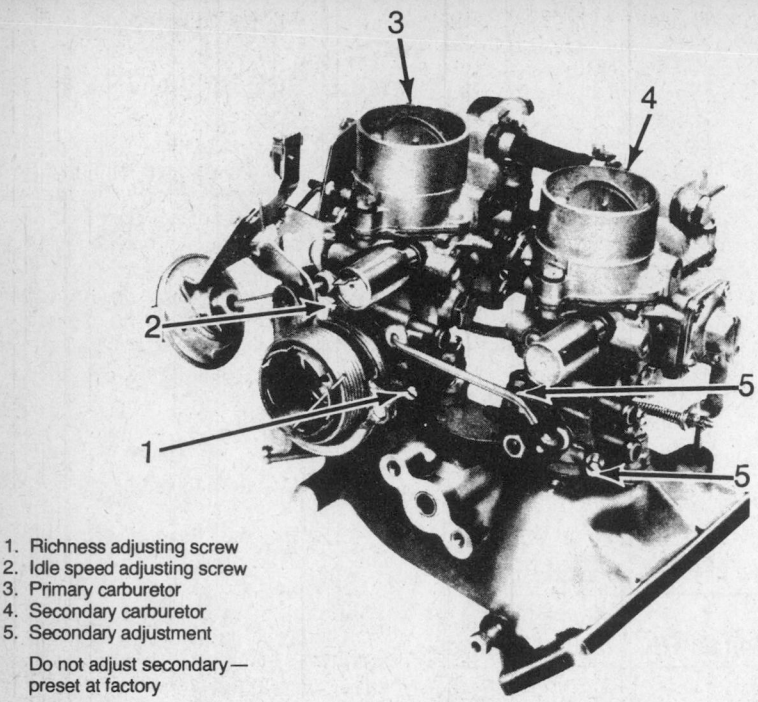

1. Richness adjusting screw
2. Idle speed adjusting screw
3. Primary carburetor
4. Secondary carburetor
5. Secondary adjustment

Do not adjust secondary—
preset at factory

Adjusting the 504 twin single barrel carburetors

NOTE: The exhaust system and test equipment must be free of leaks to prevent erroneous readings.

2. Turn the mixture screw to obtain a CO level of 1.5–2.5%.

3. Adjust the idle speed to 900–950 rpm again.

4. Repeat the procedures until a 1.5–2.5% CO reading is obtained at 900–950 rpm. The 604 models, should be adjusted to 800–850 rpm and 3.0–4.0% CO.

5. Remove the electro-valve jumper wire and adjust the engine idle to 900–950 rpm.

———— **CAUTION** ————
Never adjust the secondary carburetor (the side that does not have the deceleration valve attached) on 504 models.

NOTE: During adjustments if the engine idles for more than three minutes at a time, increase the engine speed to 2000 rpm for one minute to clear the engine of a rich idle mixture.

Fuel Injection

IDLE SPEED AND MIXTURE

1978–81

Several Peugeot special tools or their equivalent will be needed to adjust the idle speed and fuel mixture on Peugeot K-Jetronic® fuel injection. The tools are: a mixture adjusting tool, an idle speed adjusting tool and a CO sampling connecting tube.

In addition, a good tachometer and an infra-red HC/CO analyzer will be needed.

1. Connect the tachometer and using the idle adjustment tool, adjust the air bleed to obtain an idle speed of 900–950 rpm.

2. Disconnect the wire 47c from the air slide valve thermo-contact and connect it to ground three near the vacuum switches.

3. Disconnect and plug the vacuum supply hose at the canister purge valve.

4. Remove the air injection hose at the intake port of the diverter valve and plug it with a 0.9 in. (23mm) plug.

5. Attach the CO sampling tube to the front of the catalytic converter. Connect the CO analyzer.

6. Locate the CO mixture regulator and

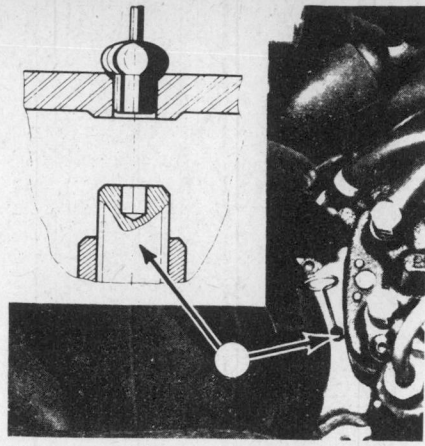

Location of the fuel mixture adjusting screw on the mixture regulator

remove the access plug to the CO mixture screw.

7. Start the engine and set the idle at 900 rpm.

8. Using the CO mixture adjusting tool or equivalent, adjust the CO reading to 0.5–1.5%.

NOTE: Do not push down on the adjusting tool as it will change the CO reading.

9. Repeat the procedure until both the idle and the CO % are correct.

10. Install the mixture plug.

11. Connect the wire 47c to the thermocontact, the vacuum hose to the canister purge valve, the air injection hose on the diverter valve and remove the sampling tube from the catalytic converter. Install the cap nut on the converter tap.

1982 and Later

To adjust or check the fuel richness at idle, two methods can be used. A Bosch KDJE/7457, a Sun tach–dwell meter, type TDT–

1. Wire (47C)
2. Air slide valve thermo-contact
3. Vacuum supply hose to canister purge valve
4. Air injection hose
5. Diverter valve intake port
6. Fire wall
7. Right side shock tower

The location of wires and hoses to be altered and disconnected during fuel injection adjustment

12 or their equivalents is the first method, used to find the Open Cycle Ratio (OCR), which will register on the meter's dial. A test lead is connected to the engine's wiring as a source of meter to engine connection.

With the meters calibrated as per the manufacturer's recommendations and connected to the engine test lead (No. 153 on 505), the engine operating at an idle speed of 800 rpm, the OCR value on the Bosch meter must be equal to $65\% \pm 3\%$ or with a dwell meter having a scale from $0°$ to $90°$, the correction figure would be $58,5° \pm 3°$.

The second method is with the use of a CO meter, measuring the CO percentage from the front top of the catalytic converter. This sampling should be $0.8\% \pm 0.5\%$.

Should any adjustments be necessary, the locations of the adjusters are as follows;

    a. Air bleed screw on the air by–pass assembly.

    b. CO mixture screw on the mixture regulator, accessible by the removal of the "no tampering" plug.

    c. The CO sampling plug on the front top of the catalytic converter.

Removing the "No-Tamper" Plug

1. Disconnect the air intake boot, air pump supply hose, and PCV hose.

To remove the "Do Not Tamper" plug, first disconnect the air intake boot (1), air pump supply hose (2), and PCV hose (3).

2. Disconnect the fuel delivery and return connectors for both the circuit to the fuel tank and the control pressure regulator.

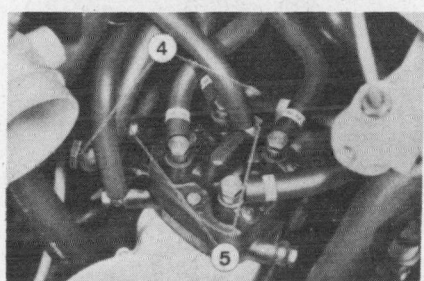

Fuel lines that must be disconnected include delivery and return lines from/to the fuel tank (4) and control pressure regulator (5)

3. Unscrew the four large attaching screws (springs underneath), and pull the fuel metering distributor off. Turn it upside down.

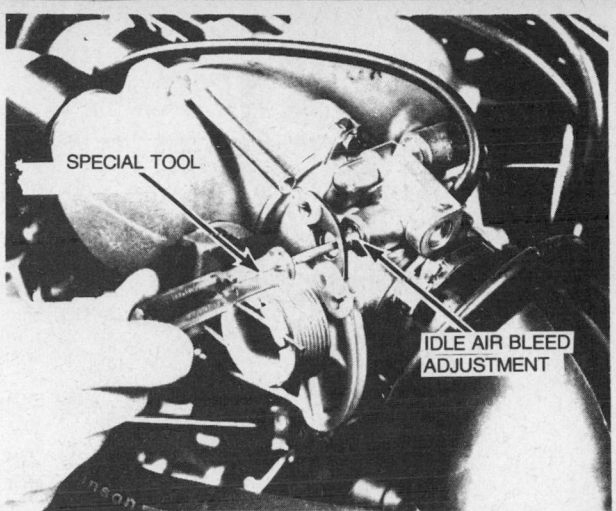

Adjusting the idle speed on Peugeot K-Jetronic® fuel injection system

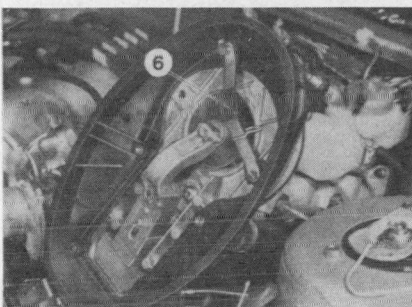

Removing the anti-stall stop (6)

4. Unscrew and remove the anti-stall stop.

5. Then, using a small (0.118 in. diameter) drift, tap the "No-Tamper" plug out.

6. Reinstall the anti-stall stop and then the fuel metering distributor. Remake all connections in reverse of Steps 1 and 2.

7. After adjusting the idle mixture via a dwell meter or exhaust analyzer, gently tap in a new "No-Tamper" plug, Peugeot part No. 1923.10 or equivalent.

ENGINE ELECTRICAL

Distributor

REMOVAL & INSTALLATION

1. Remove the common intake manifold on 505 models only.

2. Bring the No. 1 piston to TDC of the compression stroke. Match mark the position of the rotor to the distributor body.

3. Disconnect the vacuum advance line at the advance unit. Disconnect the harness connector at the module. Loosen the distributor clamp bolt all the way (until there

Driving out the "Do Not Tamper" plug

is no tension on it). Lift out the distributor. Do not rotate the engine crankshaft.

4. Install the distributor in the same position it was when it was removed.

5. Install the common intake manifold on the 505 models.

6. Check and adjust the timing.

INSTALLATION WITH ENGINE DISTURBED

Except 505

If the engine was cranked with the distributor removed, it will be necessary to re–time the engine. If you have installed the distributor incorrectly and the engine will not start, remove the distributor from the engine and proceed with the following steps:

1. Hold the distributor close to the engine and install the cap on the distributor in its normal position.

2. Locate the No. 1 spark plug wire tower on the distributor cap.

3. Scribe a mark on the body of the distributor directly below the No. 1 spark plug wire tower on the distributor cap.

4. Remove the distributor cap from the distributor and move the distributor and cap out of the way.

5. Remove the No. 1 spark plug and crank the engine over until the No. 1 cylinder is on the compression stroke. To accomplish this, place a wrench on the lower

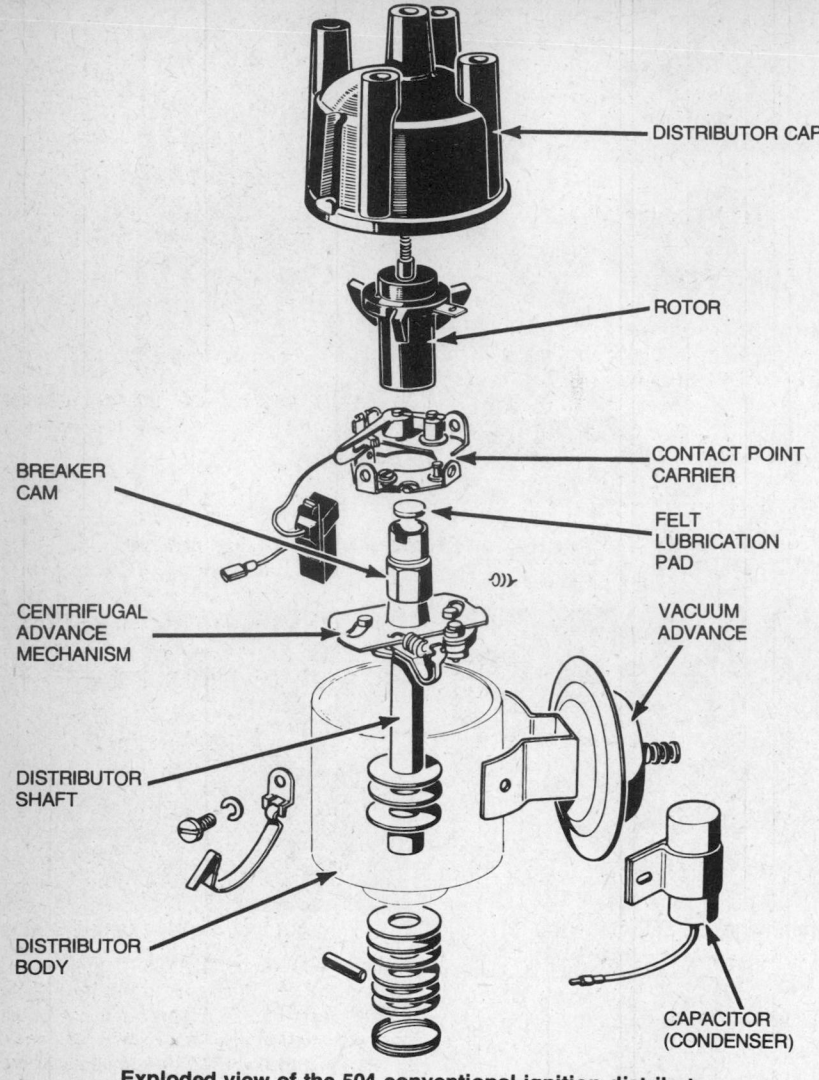

DISTRIBUTOR CAP

ROTOR

CONTACT POINT CARRIER

BREAKER CAM

FELT LUBRICATION PAD

CENTRIFUGAL ADVANCE MECHANISM

VACUUM ADVANCE

DISTRIBUTOR SHAFT

DISTRIBUTOR BODY

CAPACITOR (CONDENSER)

Exploded view of the 504 conventional ignition distributor

engine pulley and turn the engine slowly in the direction of normal engine rotation.

CAUTION
Never turn the engine against its normal rotational direction.

When the No. 1 piston is on the compression stroke, air will be forced out of the No. 1 spark plug hole. When the No. 1 cylinder is on the compression stroke, continue to turn the engine over until the ignition timing marks are properly aligned on the scale and pulley. The proper timing mark is the ignition timing figure given in the "Tune-Up Specifications" chart.

6. With the timing mark aligned, align the distributor rotor with the mark which was scribed on the distributor housing in Step 3.

7. Install the distributor in the engine keeping the rotor aligned with the mark.

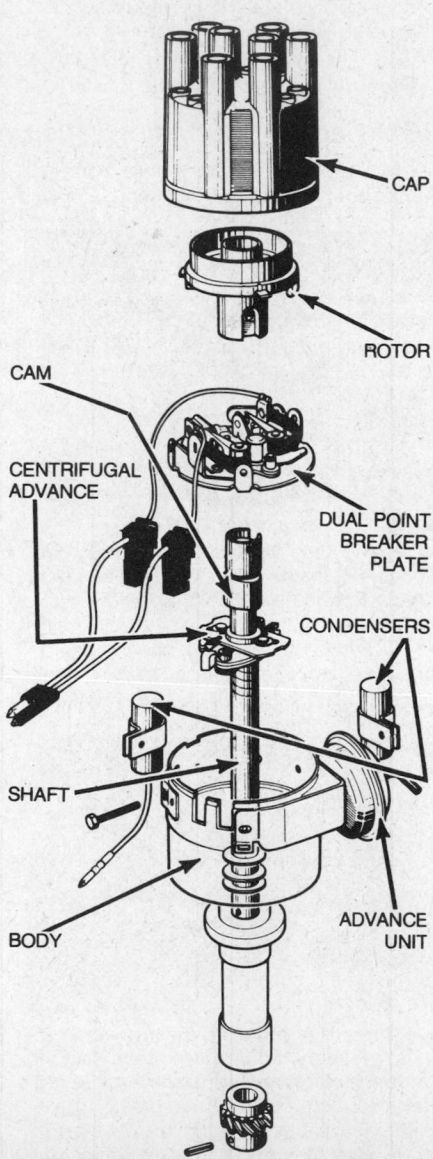

CAP

ROTOR

CAM

CENTRIFUGAL ADVANCE

DUAL POINT BREAKER PLATE

CONDENSERS

SHAFT

BODY

ADVANCE UNIT

Exploded view of the 604 conventional ignition distributor

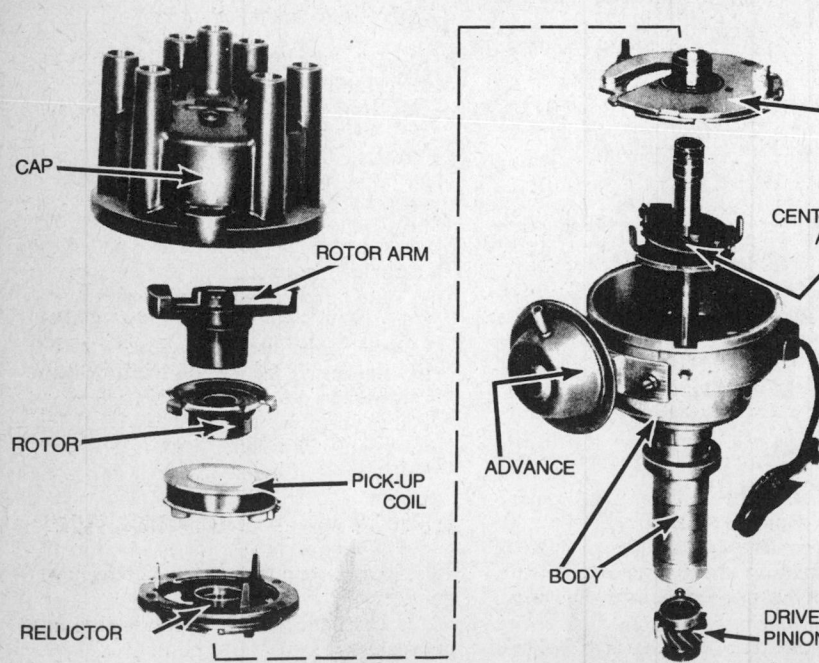

CAP

ROTOR ARM

ROTOR

PICK-UP COIL

RELUCTOR

PLATE

CENTRIFUGAL ADVANCE

ADVANCE

BODY

DRIVE PINION

Exploded view of the Bosch® electronic ignition distributor used on 604 models

While inserting the distributor into the collar, be sure to properly engage the end of the distributor driveshaft into the oil pump drive slot. Install and hand-tighten the collar nut.

8. Turn the distributor in the engine until the points just start to open. Tighten the distributor collar nut.

9. Install the distributor cap and wires. Plug the vacuum line(s) to the distributor.

10. Attach a timing light and check and adjust the ignition timing.

11. After checking and correcting the timing, reconnect the distributor vacuum line(s).

505

1. Rotate the engine crankshaft with a pulley, in the normal direction of rotation, until the notch on the crankshaft pulley is aligned with the 8 degree BTDC notch on

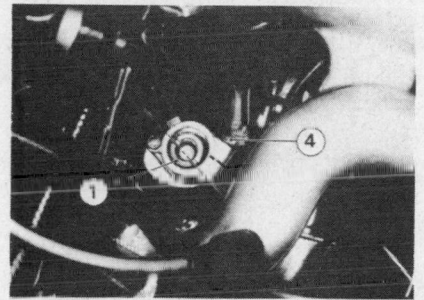

Installing the 505 distributor. If the engine is at No. 1 firing position, the distributor drive coupling's smaller half (1) will face the block. The bolt that clamps the distributor into position is at (4).

the timing plate. Check the appearance of the distributor drive. The smaller half of the notched coupling should be toward the engine block. If not, rotate the engine one more full turn, again aligning the 8 degree mark. If both these conditions are met, that means the engine is at firing position for No. 1 cylinder.

2. Slide the distributor part way into its mounting sleeve. Turn the rotor until one

The No. 1 vane of the polarity wheel (2) must align with the pickup coil (3) with the rotor in the position shown

of the vanes on the polarity wheel is aligned with the pickup coil *and* the rotor is in the position shown. Then, force the distributor on down into the mounting sleeve until the drive engages. It may help to turn the rotor back and forth very slightly as you push downward to get the drive to engage.

3. Tighten the mounting bolt just slightly. Plug the harness connector back in at the module. Install the distributor cap.

4. Set the ignition timing as described above. Tighten the mounting bolt and reconnect the vacuum advance hose.

Alternator

PRECAUTIONS

1. Observe the proper polarity of the battery connections by making sure that the positive (+) and negative (−) terminal connections are not reversed. Misconnection will allow current to flow in the reverse direction, resulting in damaged diodes and an overheated wire harness.

2. Never ground or short out any alternator or regulator terminals.

3. Never operate the alternator with any of its or the battery's leads disconnected.

4. Always remove the battery or disconnect its output lead while charging it.

5. Always disconnect the ground cable when replacing any electrical components.

6. Never subject the alternator to excessive heat or dampness if the engine is being steam cleaned.

7. Never use arc welding equipment with the alternator connected.

REMOVAL & INSTALLATION

Except 505 Gasoline Engine

1. Disconnect the negative battery cable.

2. Tag and disconnect the wires leading from the alternator.

3. Loosen the alternator mounting bolts and remove the belt. On the Diesel, this requires that you first loosen the vacuum pump mounting bolts and remove the vacuum pump belt. Then, loosen the bolt positioning the tensioner for the alternator and fan belt and remove that belt.

4. Remove the alternator mounting bolts and remove the alternator. On the Diesel, remove the lug support on the cylinder block.

5. On the Diesel, to install, first check the clearance between the support lug and the two fastening bosses on the cylinder block. Should the clearance be in excess of 0.004 in., insert adjusting washers to bring the clearance within proper specifications.

6. On all models, be sure to adjust the alternator belt tension and to complete all installation procedures (in the reverse order of removal) before connecting the negative battery cable.

505 Gasoline Engine

1. Disconnect the battery negative connector. Loosen the two bolts (2) which hold the idler pulley for the alternator/air pump belt in position. Loosen the idler and then remove the belt.

2. Tag and then disconnect all alternator wiring connectors.

3. Remove the mounting bolts from the

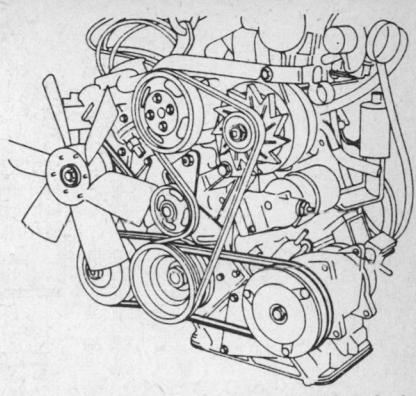

The layout of alternator mounting bolts and belt. The alternator is at top/right.

top and bottom of the alternator and remove it.

4. To install, put the alternator in position and install the mounting bolts. Make sure you reconnect the hose clamp to the top bolt before reinstalling the nut.

5. Reposition the belt, and then use a torque wrench to turn bolt (3) counterclockwise with a torque of just over 36 ft. lb

The air pump/alternator belt is tensioned by tensioner (1). Bolt (3) is torqued to produce tension and bolts (2) maintain tension adjustment.

Tighten the mounting bolts for the tensioner with the torque maintained.

6. Reconnect all wiring and then the battery negative terminal.

Regulator

ADJUSTMENT

The regulator should be set to produce between 13.6 and 14.8 volts at 3000 rpm. There is a switch on the regulator that can be set to heavy or light electrical load. Position number one (1) is for high electrical load and position number two (2) is for light electrical load.

REMOVAL & INSTALLATION

1. Disconnect the negative cable from the battery.

2. Disconnect the wiring harness from the regulator.

3. Remove the regulator attaching screws and the regulator.

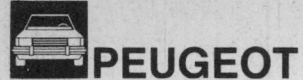

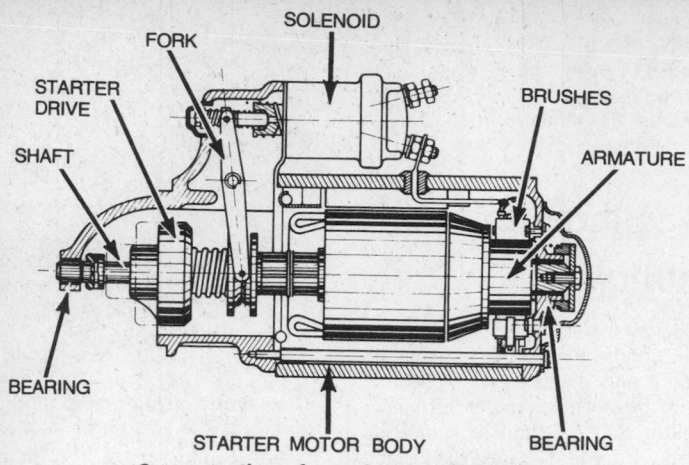

Cross section of a typical starter motor

4. To install, reverse the removal procedures

Starter

The positive engagement starter is connected to the battery (when the ignition key is turned to the "start" position) by a starter relay. When current is received from the battery, the starter drive engages the starter with the flywheel and turns the engine.

REMOVAL & INSTALLATION

1. Disconnect the starter cable from the starter. On the 504 and Diesel, this may be facilitated by first removing the battery and battery support.

2. Remove the starter attaching bolts (including the fastening screw on the Diesel cylinder block and, if necessary, the angle iron support), and the starter.

3. To install, reverse the removal procedures. Tighten the clutch housing bolts to 14.5 ft. lbs.

STARTER DRIVE DISASSEMBLY

1. Remove the starter from the engine.
2. Remove the brush cover band.
3. Remove the thru-bolts and solenoid cover housing bolts just enough to allow removal of the rear drive end housing and the plunger lever.
4. Remove the pivot pin which attaches the starter drive plunger lever to the starter end housing frame.
5. Remove the stop ring retainer and stop ring from the armature shaft.
6. Remove the starter drive from the armature shaft.
7. Inspect the teeth on the starter drive. If they are excessively worn, inspect the teeth on the ring gear of the flywheel. If the teeth on the flywheel are excessively worn, the flywheel should be replaced.
8. To install, first apply a thin coat of white grease to the armature shaft in the area in which the starter drive operates.

9. Install the starter drive on the armature shaft and install a new stop ring.
10. Fill the drive end housing bearing bore ¼ full with grease.
11. Position the plunger lever in the end housing and install the pivot pin with a new stop ring.
12. Fit the drive end housing, with plunger lever attached, to the starter frame.

NOTE: Make sure that the plunger lever is properly engaged with the starter drive.

13. Tighten the starter thru-bolts and install the brush cover band on the starter.
14. Install the starter.

ENGINE MECHANICAL

Engine

REMOVAL & INSTALLATION

504

1. On vehicles with automatic transmissions, drain the fluid from the transmission assembly, remove the battery and the tray.
2. Remove the hood and the radiator.
3. Remove the ignition coil and the starter.
4. Disconnect the heater hoses and the carburetor fuel line.
5. Noting their exact position, remove the carburetor linkages.
6. Remove the air filter bracket and the air filter.
7. Turn the steering wheel to the left and lower the steering rack.
8. Remove the exhaust pipe from the exhaust manifold.
9. Remove the flywheel protector plates and the clutch housing bolts.
10. Noting their positions, remove the main vacuum line and all electrical wires that interfere with the removal of the engine.

11. Using Peugeot engine hoist or equivalent, attach the hoist hooks to the holes marked "404" and raise the engine until it is under a slight load.
12. Remove the four securing bolts from the crossmember.
13. Raise the engine until the transmission touches the tunnel.

NOTE: Make sure that the left brake line is tight against the crossmember.

14. On vehicles with automatic transmissions, remove the torque converter–to–flywheel bolts and disconnect the converter.
15. Separate the engine from the transmission without changing the position of the engine hoist.
16. Installation is the reverse of removal. Torque the automatic transmission converter bolts to 16 ft.lbs. (22.1 Nm). Other installation torques are:
Clutch housing–to–engine—40 ft.lbs. (53.9 Nm)
Starter bolts—14.5 ft.lbs.(19.6 Nm)
Crossmember bolts—7.2 ft.lbs.(9.8 Nm)

—— **CAUTION** ——
Make sure to check the engine oil and water levels before attempting to start.

505

1. Remove the hood. Disconnect both connectors and remove the battery.
2. Remove the two mounting bolts from

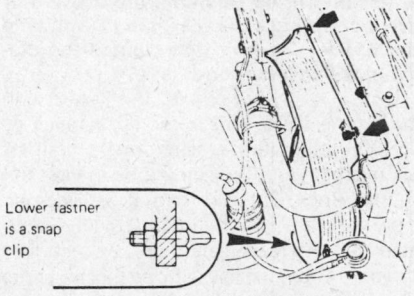

Lower fastener is a snap clip

505 fan shroud removal. Remove two arrowed bolts, and disconnect lower fastener by simply pulling it out.

the top of the fan shroud, unsnap the lower connection, and remove the shroud.
3. Disconnect the evaporative emissions canister hoses, remove the canister mounting nut from the fender, and remove the canister.
4. Drain the radiator and block. Disconnect the upper and lower radiator hoses at the engine block. Also, disconnect the harness connecting the canister hose to the upper radiator hose.
5. Disconnect the wiring connectors 57 and 58 at the radiator mounted thermostatic switch.
6. Remove the two bolts attaching the radiator at the top. Remove the four cushioned bolts locating the bottom of the unit from underneath.
7. Loosen both hose clamps and then remove the air intake boot from the mixture regulator and throttle plate housing. Dis-

connect and remove the two hoses blocking removal of the throttle plate housing.

8. Disconnect fuel supply and return hoses, cold start and PCV hoses, and the two wiring connectors (numbered 1–6) involved with the mixture regulator.

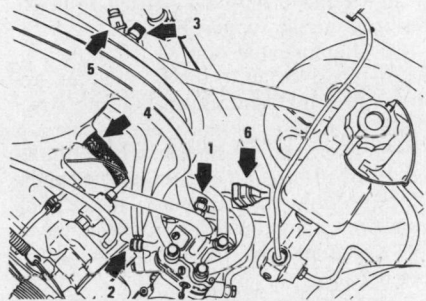

Disconnect fuel supply and return hoses (1 and 2), cold start injector hose (3), PCV hose (4) and electrical connectors (5 and 6)

9. Disconnect the wiring connector and two fuel hoses connected to the fuel pressure regulator, located under the throttle plate housing.

10. Label the fuel lines and then gently pull all four injectors out of the intake manifold.

11. Unscrew the four attaching screws and remove the mixture regulator unit.

12. Remove the attaching nuts and remove the air filter.

13. Remove the freon hose clamp from the alternator bracket. Then, loosen arrowed bolts and lift the air conditioner compressor off the engine. Support it out of the way to prevent putting stress on the refrigerant hoses.

14. Disconnect the accelerator cable at the throttle plate housing. Disconnect the engine electrical harness at the TDC diagnostic plug near the coil. Disconnect the coil high tension lead.

15. Disconnect the heater hose at the front of the block. Disconnect the two mounting bolts and remove the power steering reservoir from the front of the block. Support it nearby.

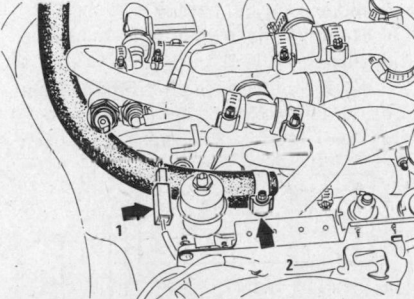

Disconnect Lambda sensor wire (1) and air injection line to the catalytic converter (2)

16. Disconnect the Lambda sensor electrical wire (1) and air injection hose leading to the catalytic converter (2).

17. Label and the disconnect the three vacuum hoses leading to the vacuum

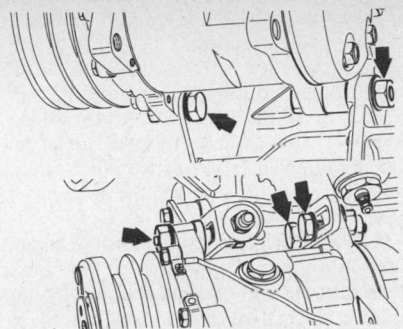

Remove arrowed bolts to remove 505 air conditioner compressor

switches near the coil. Then, remove the mounting nuts and remove the support for the vacuum switches. Disconnect the connector nearby.

18. Label and disconnect starter wiring. From the driver's side of the engine, remove the two starter mounting bolts and the starter. Remove the bell housing bolt located right near the starter. Remove the two lower engine mounting bolts.

19. Remove the two lower mounting bolts from the right side engine mount.

20. Remove the one upper power steering pump mounting bolt. Remove the two lower pump mounting bolts and nuts.

21. Disconnect the exhaust header pipe at either end and remove it.

22. On manual transmission vehicles, remove the mounting bolts and remove the inspection plates from the front of the bell housing (underneath).

23. Remove the two allen screws from the right side of the bell housing.

24. On automatic transmission equipped vehicles, turn the engine over to position the torque converter support plate as shown.

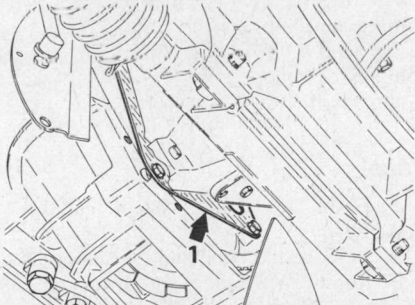

Position the automatic transmission's torque converter support plate as shown

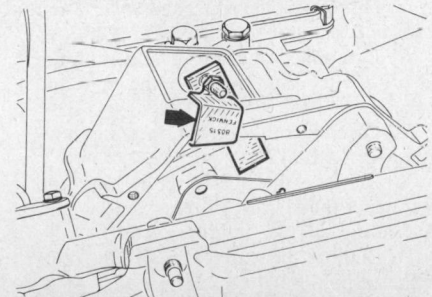

Utilize a clip such as that pictured to keep the torque converter in place

Then, mark the relationship between the TDC notch on the flywheel and support plate. This will maintain the TDC sensor adjustment for reinstallation. Then, buy or fashion a clamp similar to that shown to keep the torque converter in place.

24. If the vehicle has air conditioning, remove the two mounting nuts for the receiver drier and the two (from underneath) for the condenser. Also, remove the four condenser bolts from up top. Then, carefully lift the condenser-receiver-drier assembly out of the way to the left. Leave the hoses connected.

25. Install a lifting sling to both front and rear hooks on the engine. Lift it until the bell housing just touches the bottom of the firewall.

26. Securely support the transmission in this position at the front of the bell housing.

27. Pull the engine forward lightly to disengage it from the clutch or converter and then pull it out of the top of the engine compartment.

Install in reverse order, noting these points:

1. Generously grease the torque converter centering nipple.

2. When reconnecting the automatic transmission converter and support plate first make sure the reference marks you made are in alignment. Install the bolts coated with Normal Holding Loctite® or equivalent and torque to 22 ft. lbs.

3. On vehicles with manual transmissions, lightly lubricate the front of the mainshaft, its splines, and the pilot bushing with a grease such as Molykote® 321. Put the transmission in gear.

4. Torque engine mounts on both sides to 22 ft.-lbs. Bellhousing allen screws are torque to 40 ft. lbs.

5. On manual transmission vehicles, adjust a new sensor so the three nipples are in contact. If reusing an old sensor, first remove any burrs and then check to make sure the gap between sensor and ring gear is .026 in. or less. Otherwise, the sensor must be replaced.

6. To adjust the throttle, first have someone hold the pedal down with a .020 in. gauge between the pedal and stop. Then, with the throttle cable connected to the throttle drum, rotate the drum to full throttle position. Lightly pull on the throttle cable housing stop to place the control under light load. Install the cable clip in the groove on the cable housing that's closest to the common manifold.

7. Adjust the automatic transmission cable as described in the "Transmission Cable Adjustment" procedure later in this section.

8. Replenish all fluids, then check for leaks with the engine operating.

604

1. Remove the hood. Drain the automatic transmission if equipped.

2. Remove the air mixer and air filter.

3. Drain the cooling system.

4. Disconnect the electrical connectors

at the electric fan, the oil pressure switch, the air conditioning compressor and the thermostat.

5. Remove the electric fan.

6. Remove the radiator supports and battery on air conditioned cars.

7. Remove the top and bottom radiator hoses and transmission cooler lines if equipped.

8. Separate the condenser and receiver dryer from the radiator.

9. Remove the fan shroud and the radiator.

10. Remove the air conditioning compressor and set it on the right fender, leaving the freon lines attached.

11. Disconnect the battery ground cable, the temperature sending unit, the vacuum line to the brake booster and the fuel pump lines.

12. Remove the carburetor controls and the primary and secondary coil leads.

13. On air conditioned vehicles, disconnect the electro-valve wire and the lead to the carburetor idle cut out switch.

14. Remove the heater hoses and plug the ends.

15. Disconnect the starter and alternator harness connectors.

16. Remove the top bolts from the clutch housing or the torque converter if automatic transmission.

17. Disconnect the filter tube on automatic transmission vehicles.

18. Remove the exhaust pipe clamp bolts and the engine mounting bolts.

19. Remove the exhaust pipes, heat deflector and brackets.

20. Remove the starter and the clutch/converter cover.

21. Remove the power steering pump, support and power steering belt.

22. Support the weight of the engine on the hoist. When the gearbox makes contact with the transmission tunnel, then lower it .04 in. (1 cm).

23. Remove the power steering pump and set it to one side without disconnecting the lines.

24. Retract the front seats and remove the inner securing bolts.

25. Raise and safely support the vehicle. Using the threaded rods supplied with Peugeot tool number 8.1511 or equivalent, install the tool (driveshaft support bar) under the floor of the vehicle. Use the threaded rods in the seat bolt holes under the floor.

26. Remove the upper flex coupling bolt from the steering shaft.

27. Temporarily install the two rear main crossmember bolts in place.

28. Remove the front crossmember securing bolts and loosen the rear crossmember bolts enought to lower the crossmember ⅛ in. (3mm).

29. On automatic transmissions, remove the torque converter-to-ring gear bolts.

30. Remove the two lower clutch housing or torque converter housing bolts.

31. Move the engine forward in order to separate from transmission. Hold the torque converter in place on automatic transmission equipped vehicles.

32. Installation is the reverse of removal except for the following adjustments.

33. Adjust the automatic transmission kickdown cable. Set the accelerator pedal stop at 2 in. (51mm). Place a 0.3 in. (7mm) spacer between the stop and the accelerator pedal.

34. Hold the carburetor control quadrant in the fully open position. Unclip the linkage return springs. Secure the accelerator cable in place, pull on the cable lightly to tension it, but do not compress the compensator spring. The accelerator cable goes through a hole in the quadrant and is secured ⅞ of the way around the quadrant at the accelerator holding tab.

35. Clip the kickdown cable into the control quadrant. Put tension on the kickdown cable by pulling on it lightly.

36. Set the cable stop into the cable bracket and tighten the nuts on both sides of the bracket.

37. One nut will tighten against the lug. Adjust the other nut to obtain 0.04 in. (1mm) clearance between the nut and the bracket.

38. Remove the spacer at the accelerator pedal and check for proper carburetor operation.

39. When the engine is hot, the clearance on the accelerator cable should be 0.08 in. (2 mm).

Use the following torque specifications when installing the 604 engine:
Flywheel–to–starter ring
  34.2 ft. lbs. (46.6 Nm)
Crossmember–to–frame
  30.6 ft. lbs. (41.6 Nm)
Steering column clamp
  10.8 ft. lbs. (14.7 Nm)
Gearbox–to–engine
  28.8 ft. lbs. (39.2 Nm)
Compressor mounting
  12.6 ft. lbs. (17.2 Nm)
Compressor pulley
  9.0 ft. lbs. (12.3 Nm)

Diesel

1. Drain the cooling system and the crankcase.

2. Remove the hood and its supports.

3. Remove the battery and its tray, the coolant expansion tank, and the air filter.

4. Disconnect the intake pipe on the vacuum pump.

5. Disconnect the upper and lower water hoses and radiator mounts.

6. Disconnect the self-disengaging fan cut-off switch and remove the fan and radiator.

7. Disconnect the injection pump controls and the fuel lines.

8. Remove the heater return line and disconnect the starter, oil pressure switch, pre-heating circuit, and thermistor.

9. Remove the wastegate attaching bolts on the turbodiesel.

10. Disconnect the alternator and cooling hose from the cylinder head.

11. Disconnect the exhaust pipe from the manifold.

12. Remove the retaining nut from the righthand engine support block.

13. Remove the clutch housing sealing plates and the upper housing bolts.

14. Remove the retaining nut from the lefthand engine support block.

15. Remove the bolt securing the exhaust pipe bracket to the gearbox and remove the righthand clutch housing cover plate.

16. Insert lifting hooks into the holes provided at the front and rear of the engine block and raise the engine until the gearbox comes into contact with the driveshaft tunnel.

17. Remove the two lower clutch housing bolts.

18. Pull the engine forward to release the transmission input shaft and hoist the engine from the compartment.

19. Installation is the reverse of the removal procedure. However, be sure to pay attention to the following points:

a. When the engine comes in contact with the clutch housing, first insert the upper housing bolt and then the two lower bolts. Tighten the three bolts to 43.5 ft lbs.

b. Bleed the fuel system after replacing all fluids and completing all connections.

c. Adjust the injection delay mechanism on the injection pump.

Cylinder Head

REMOVAL & INSTALLATION

504

1. Drain the coolant from the block.

2. Remove the air cleaner, carburetor, ignition distributor, spark plugs, upper radiator hose and water pump belt.

3. Remove the spark plug tube seals and cups.

4. Separate the exhaust pipe from the manifold.

5. Remove the head bolts and install the cylinder head guide pins.

6. Remove the rocker shaft assembly and pushrods.

7. Remove the guide pin from the front end of the engine.

8. Pivot the head to separate it from

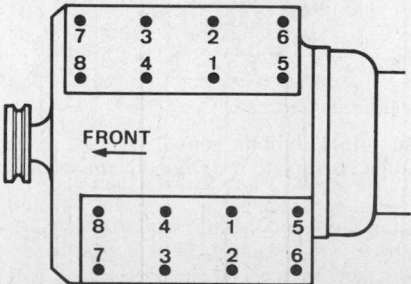

V-6 cylinder head torque sequence

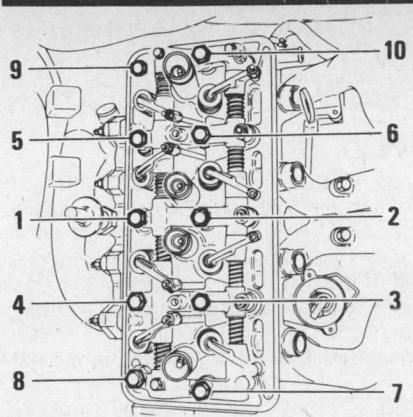

504 and 505 cylinder head torque sequence

the block and lift off the head. Remove the gasket and second cylinder head guide.

9. Lock the cylinder liners with the Peugeot tool 8.0104D or equivalent retaining screws.

10. Installation is the reverse of removal.

11. Torque the head bolts in sequence to 36 ft. lbs. (49 Nm). Loosen the head bolts, and retorque to 15 ft. lbs. (20.3 Nm). Then match mark the bolt head to the cylinder head. Then tighten exactly 90° (¼ turn) more. Do this to all head bolts, in sequence.

505

1. Drain the cooling system and remove the Lambda® sensor (if equipped) from the exhaust header pipe.

2. Remove the header pipe from the exhaust manifold connector.

3. Remove the mounting brackets from the intake/exhaust manifold.

4. Disconnect the battery ground cable.

5. Separate the intake manifold.

6. Remove the distributor cap.

7. Remove the fuel injectors. Remove the diagnostic plug bracket.

8. Tag and remove the following electrical wires:

   a. Primary ignition at the coil.

   b. Secondary ignition at the coil.

   c. Temperature sending unit at the engine.

   d. Thermo-time switch at the engine.

   e. Thermocontact sender unit in the heater hose.

   f. Temperature sending units at the water pump.

   g. Spark plug wires at the spark plugs.

9. Remove and tag the following air and vacuum hoses:

   a. All injection pump hoses and the auxiliary air device.

   b. Two vacuum hoses on the fuel distributor.

   c. Vacuum hoses at the three vacuum regulators on the fender well (manifold side of engine). All other vacuum lines on the manifold side.

10. Remove the upper radiator hose and the water pump ends of the lower radiator hose and heater hose.

11. Remove the power steering pump reservoir bracket from the head.

12. Remove the radiator fan shroud.

13. Remove the fan blades. Remove only the 3 nuts that are lined up with the recesses in the fan hub.

14. Remove the water pump belt.

15. Remove the vacuum hoses, electrical wire and coolant hoses from the air slide valve. Remove the air slide valve bracket.

16. Remove the remaining air injection hoses and the air injection assembly.

17. Remove the rocker arm oil feed pipe (sometimes referred to as "banjo fittings").

18. Remove the valve cover, declutchable fan brush holder and spark plug tube sealing rings.

19. Remove the rocker arm assembly, pushrods and cylinder head bolts.

20. Using Peugeot tools number 0.0149 or equivalent, break the cylinder head loose.

21. Install Peugeot tools 8.0132A1Z or equivalent retainers to keep the cylinder sleeves from moving in the engine block.

Check cylinder sleeve protrusion above the block deck at the engine centerline. Protrusion must be .00275–.0055 in. Protrusion between two adjoining sleeves must not differ by more than .0015 in. Replace the sleeve seals if both conditions are not met. Cylinder head warpage must not exceed .004 in. If the head must be machined, thickness must be at least 3.616 in. Install the head gasket with "DESSUS", "ALTO" or "TOP" facing the head.

22. Installation of the head is the reverse of removal. It's best to use guidestuds in the two end bolt holes on the exhaust side. Install bolts lightly oiled and with flat washers in place. Follow the specified torque sequence, going first to 36 ft. lbs. (49 Nm). Torque the rocker arm nuts to 10.9 ft. lbs. (14.7 Nm) at this point. Now, loosen No. 1 head bolt fully and retorque to 15 ft. lbs. (20.3 Nm). Matchmark its position on the head, and then turn it further exactly 90 degrees (¼ turn). Repeat the entire sequence on each of the remaining head bolts, in numbered sequence.

23. Adjust the valve clearances. Use the clearances listed below, NOT those in the "Tune-Up Specifications" chart! Adjust

intake valves to: .006 in. and exhaust to: .012 in. After 1000–1500 miles of driving, retorque the head bolts and adjust valves in the normal way to standard settings.

604

1. Drain the cooling system.

2. Remove the hood, air mixer chamber casing, air filter and battery.

3. Remove the intake manifold.

4. Remove the plate fitted under the intake manifold.

5. Remove the clips between the cylinder head and the water pump.

6. When removing the head from under the power brake booster, the engine crossmember must be lowered.

7. The accessories on the head opposite the brake booster do not have to be removed.

8. Remove all hoses and vacuum lines.

9. On the left hand cylinder head:

   a. Remove the fuel pump leaving the line connected.

   b. Remove the hot air duct.

   c. Loosen the positive battery lead and remove the negative battery lead.

10. On the right hand cylinder head:

   a. Remove the distributor and the front ignition coil.

   b. Remove the automatic transmission fill tube if equipped.

11. Remove the front exhaust silencer mounting bracket.

12. Remove the exhaust pipe from the exhaust manifold.

13. On the left side, remove the bolt from the steering flex coupling upper end.

14. Using Peugeot tool 8.1511C or equivalent; lower the crossmember 0.12 in or (3mm).

15. Remove the rocker arm cover and camshaft rear cover plate.

16. Remove the camshaft sprocket bolt access plug from both heads.

17. Position both sprockets with the drive studs (timing marks) at the top.

18. Hold the crankshaft from turning with a 35mm box wrench. Loosen the camshaft sprocket with Peugeot tool ST 10 or equivalent Allen type socket wrench tool.

19. Place the Peugeot tool 8.0134M or equivalent camshaft sprocket supports on the timing gear casing. Secure the support finger tight with two bolts. Torque the bolts to 10.8 ft. lbs. (14.7 Nm).

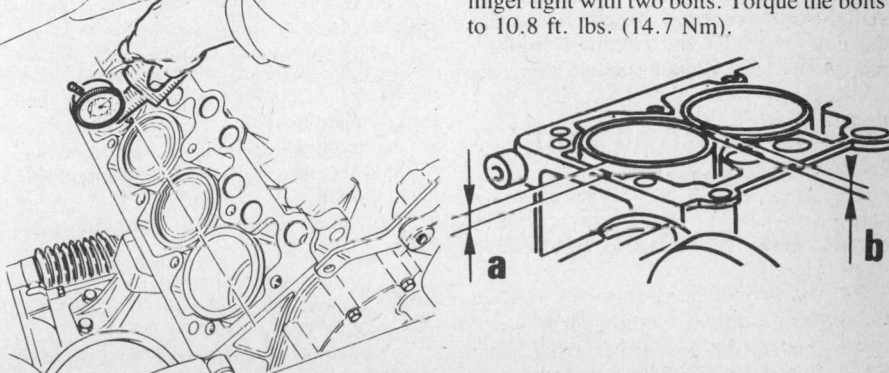

Checking cylinder liner protrusion on the 505 gasoline engine. "a" is liner protrusion above the block, while "b" is variation in protrusion between cylinders.

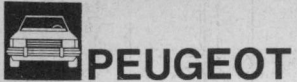
20. Unscrew 8 bolts on each cylinder head and remove all but the two bolts under the power brake booster. Raise the two bolts as far as they will go and secure them with a rubber band.

21. Loosen the camshaft thrust flange bolt and remove the thrust flange.

22. Remove the camshaft. Make sure the cams do not mark the rocker arm pads while unscrewing the sprocket bolt.

23. On the left hand cylinder, lift the rocker arm to clear the camshaft.

24. Remove the timing gear case-to-cylinder head bolts from both the left and right heads.

25. Insert the two levers into two head bolts holes. Break the cylinder head loose by prying on the levers.

26. Remove the rocker arm assembly.

27. Clean the head gasket surface and retain the cylinder liners with special retainers, Peugeot tool 8.0132A or equivalent.

28. Remove the cylinder head locating dowels using Peugeot tool 8.0134L (extractor) or equivalent.

29. Install the Peugeot temporary camshaft bearing tools 8.0134N or equivalent on both heads.

30. Shims may be required under the bearing bracket, on the head surface.

31. Installation is the reverse of removal.

— CAUTION —

Do not release the timing chain tension or disturb the chain position while removing and installing heads.

32. Torque the camshaft flange bolts to 9.4 ft. lbs. (12.7 Nm). Torque the camshaft sprocket bolts to 54.0 ft. lbs. (73.5 Nm).

33. Torque the head in sequence and to 36 ft. lbs. (49 Nm). Loosen the head bolts, and retorque to 15 ft. lbs. (20.3 Nm). Then match mark the head bolt to the cylinder head. Then tighten exactly 90° (¼ turn) more. Do this to all head bolts, in sequence.

34. Adjust the valve clearances.

35. Install the rocker covers and follow the reverse of Steps 1–13 for completing the re-installation. Install coolant and check the system by running the engine.

OVERHAUL

For all cylinder head overhaul procedures, please refer to "Engine Rebuilding" in the Unit Repair section.

Rocker Arms and Shafts

REMOVAL & INSTALLATION

504 and 505

1. Remove the rocker arm cover.

2. Remove the five rocker stand nuts and ten head bolts. Lift off the rocker shaft.

3. Install in the reverse order of removal. Torque the head bolts in sequence

to 36 ft. lbs. (12.7 Nm). Loosen the head bolts, and retorque to 15 ft. lbs. (20.3 Nm). Then match mark the head bolt to cylinder head. Then tighten exactly 90° (¼ turn) more. Do this to all head bolts, in sequence.

4. Adjust the valve clearances.

— CAUTION —

With the head bolts removed, the cylinder head can be broken loose from the block. Do not jar the cylinder head or rotate the crankshaft.

604

1. Remove the air filter, heater air inlet, battery ground cable and rocker arm covers.

2. Remove the rocker shaft retaining bolts from the left rear and right front support bosses.

3. Remove all head bolts from both banks. The two left rear head bolts under the brake booster may be hard to remove. If necessary, move the engine slightly so they will clear the brake booster.

— CAUTION —

With the head bolts removed, the cylinder head can be broken loose from the block. Do not jar the cylinder head or rotate the crankshaft.

4. Installation is the reverse of removal.

5. Torque the head bolts in sequence to 36 ft. lbs. (12.7 Nm). Loosen the head bolts, and retorque to 15 ft. lbs. (20.3 Nm). Then match mark the head bolt to cylinder head. Then tighten exactly 90° (¼ turn) more. Do this to all head bolts, in sequence.

Intake Manifold

REMOVAL & INSTALLATION

504

1. Remove the air intake tubing and any wires or vacuum lines in the way of manifold removal.

2. Remove the air cleaner and carburetor.

3. Remove the intake manifold bolts. Lift out the manifold.

505

1. Remove the air intake boot and electrical and vacuum connections from the throttle plate housing.

2. Remove the intake manifold mounting brackets and slide the intake manifold back and out.

604

1. Drain the cooling system.

2. Remove the air mixer casing and intake tube.

3. Remove the air filter and disconnect the negative battery cable.

4. Remove the intake manifold.

5. Installation is the reverse of removal.

Exhaust Manifold

REMOVAL & INSTALLATION

504

1. Remove the nuts and the clamp holding the exhaust pipe to the exhaust manifold.

2. Using caution, move the exhaust pipe out of the way.

3. Remove the eight retaining bolts and remove the manifold.

4. Installation is the reverse of removal.

505

1. Remove the Lambda® sensor wire and the three nuts holding the header pipe to the exhaust manifold.

2. Remove the exhaust manifold retaining nuts and lift out the manifold.

3. Installation is the reverse of removal.

604

1. Remove the right and left side exhaust pipes from the manifolds.

2. Remove six manifold-to-head bolts on the right and left sides of the engine.

3. Lift out the manifolds.

4. Installation is the reverse of removal.

Turbocharger

REMOVAL & INSTALLATION

1. Remove the air filter.

2. Disconnect the electrical connection from the temperature switch.

3. Loosen the lower hose on the air duct that connects the air filter with the compressor housing.

4. Remove the vacuum line and the crankcase breather pipe.

5. Remove the air filter and the air intake duct.

6. Disconnect the oil supply and drain line at the turbocharger.

7. Remove the air filter mounting bracket.

8. Disconnect the turbocharger at the exhaust flange.

9. Disconnect and remove the pipe bracket on automatic transmission models.

10. Push the exhaust pipe toward the rear.

11. Remove the mounting bracket at the intermediate flange.

12. Unbolt and remove the turbocharger.

13. Remove the intermediate flange and the oil line at the turbocharger.

14. Installation is the reverse of removal. Before installing the turbocharger, install the oil return line and the intermediate flange. Use new copper gaskets to seal the oil lines.

OVERHAUL

For further information on turbochargers, please refer to "Turbocharging" in the Unit Repair Section.

Timing Chain Cover

REMOVAL & INSTALLATION

504 and 505

1. Drain the coolant.
2. Remove the radiator, fan belt, spark plugs and the crankshaft pulley.

NOTE: To hold the crankshaft from turning in manual transmission equipped vehicles, apply the handbrake and engage 4th gear. On vehicles with automatic transmissions, remove the torque converter cover and hold the flywheel.

3. Remove the timing housing.
4. Installation is the reverse of removal. On the XN6 engine (505), torque the pulley bolt to 123 ft. lbs.

604

1. Drain the engine oil.
2. Disconnect the negative battery cable.
3. Remove the air filter and the air mixer casing and the hot air duct.
4. Drain the cooling system.
5. Remove the radiator struts, radiator hoses and separate the fan casing from the radiator.
6. Remove the fan and the fan casing.
7. Remove the power steering belt and the alternator belt.
8. Remove the power steering pump and hang it to the fender well with wire.
9. Remove the clutch or converter housing cover plate.
10. Use Peugeot tool 8.01234 or equivalent to lock the flywheel in place.
11. Remove the crankshaft pulley.
12. Remove the power steering pump bracket, the hot air duct and the rocker arm covers.
13. Remove the timing gear casing bolts and lift the timing gear casing from the engine.
14. Installation is the reverse of removal. Torque the crankshaft pulley nut to 123 ft.lbs. (166 Nm).

Diesel

1. Remove the radiator from the engine compartment and unbolt the fan from the injection pump pulley.
2. Remove the fan belt and crankshaft pulley belt.
3. Remove the injection pump pulley nut and crankshaft pulley nut. Then remove both pulleys.

NOTE: Be sure that the handbrake is applied and the transmission is in 4th gear while the pulleys are being removed.

4. Remove the timing gear housing bolts, the housing, and the oil slinger.
5. Before installing the cover, refit the oil slinger cup and a new timing housing gasket.
6. Refit the cover and tighten the cover bolts to 8 ft.lbs.
7. Refit the woodruff key(s) and the pulley(s). Tighten the crankshaft pulley bolt to 123 ft.lbs.

Timing Chain Cover Oil Seal

REPLACEMENT

504 Gasoline Engine Models

The 504 (XN1 engine) uses an oil slinger on the front end of the crankshaft. This means that some leakage can occur when parking on steep grades. There is no oil seal to be replaced.

505 Gasoline Engine

1. Remove the crankshaft pulley with a puller, if necessary. Remove all the timing cover mounting bolts. Break the cover loose from the gasket gently. Pull the seal with a seal puller. Replace the gasket. Install the cover with bolts just started.
2. Using a tool such as Peugeot tool .0128, install the tool on the crankshaft to center the timing cover around the crankshaft. Then, torque the timing cover bolts.
3. Lightly lubricate the outside diameter of the seal. Then, using a tool such as

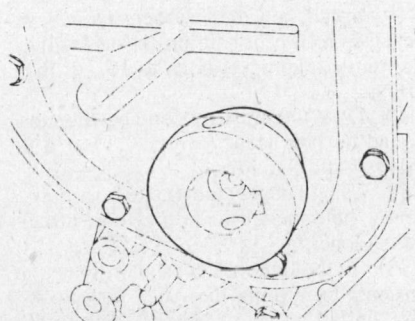
Timing cover centering tool for the 505 gas engine

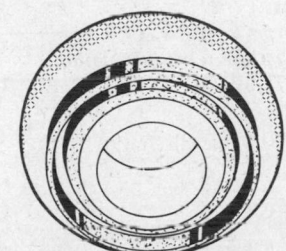
Timing cover oil seal—505 gas engine

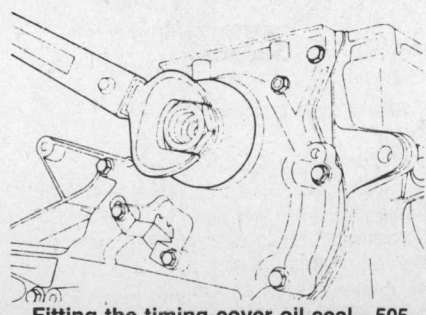
Fitting the timing cover oil seal—505

Peugeot 8.0141 BD, and a metric bolt which screws into the threads in the center of the crankshaft, press the seal into place.

V6 and Diesel Engine Models

1. Remove the crankshaft pulley and the oil seal.
2. Install the seal and the woodruff key.
3. Install the crankshaft pulley. Torque the nut to 123 ft.lbs. (166 Nm) on the V6. On the diesel, torque to 40 ft. lbs. and then turn it farther exactly 60 degrees (one flat on the bolt).

Timing Chain and Tensioner

REMOVAL & INSTALLATION

504 and 505

1. Remove the timing chain cover.
2. Loosen the tensioner spring.

RENOLD® TENSIONER

a. Remove the tensioner adjuster plug.
b. Using a .12 inch (3mm) Allen wrench, turn the adjuster key clockwise to release the tension on the timing chain.

SEDIS® TENSIONER

a. Turn the ratchet clockwise with a screwdriver to release the tension on the timing chain.

3. Remove the tensioner and tension plate.
4. Remove the filter from the block.
5. Before removing the timing chain, position the crankshaft Woodruff key slot to the left and the two white timing chain links to the right, while facing the front of the engine. An imaginary line through the Woodruff key slot and the middle of the two white links should be parallel to the leading edge of the oil pan. Now, remove the camshaft sprocket bolts, pull the sprocket off the camshaft, and remove the chain from both sprockets.

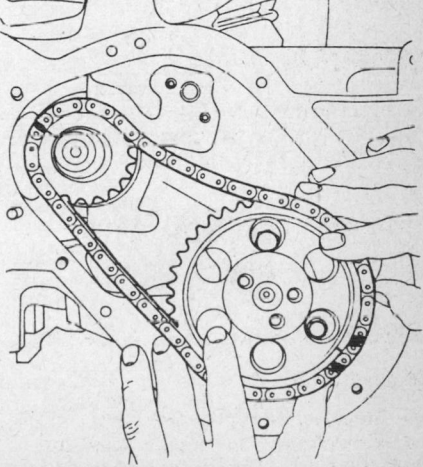
This shows how the sprocket and chain marks coincide when the chain is properly timed

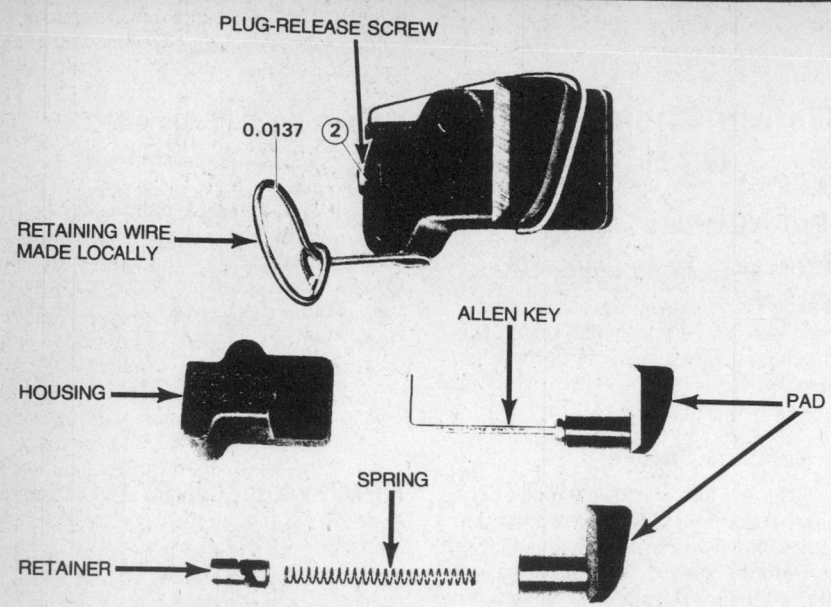

PLUG-RELEASE SCREW

0.0137 ②

RETAINING WIRE MADE LOCALLY

HOUSING

ALLEN KEY

PAD

SPRING

RETAINER

Reynholds® timing chain tensioner used in some 504 models

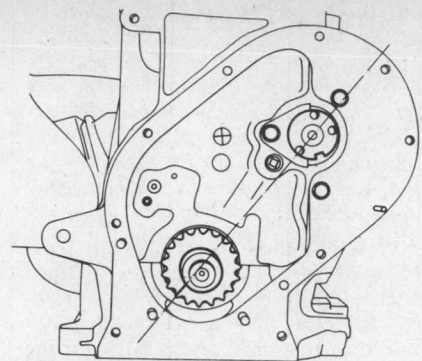

This is the position crankshaft and camshaft should be in before installing the camshaft sprocket and chain (505)

CAUTION

If either the crankshaft or camshaft are rotated with the timing chain removed, valve damage might occur. Never rotate the crankshaft and always position the crankshaft as described in Step 5 before rotating the camshaft, when the timing chain is removed.

6. Take the tensioner apart and clean it.

CAUTION

On the Sedis® tensioner, do not remove the ratchet screw (tension adjusting screw). Once removed it is impossible to put it back.

7. Without altering the position of the crankshaft, install the Woodruff key and the crankshaft sprocket, if it has been removed.

8. Keep the two white timing chain links at the camshaft sprocket mark and the one

white link at the crankshaft sprocket mark with the centers of the crankshaft and camshaft, forming a straight line through the white chain links and the reference marks on the sprockets.

9. Install new tab washers or a new lockplate on the camshaft sprocket and torque the camshaft sprocket bolts to 16.3 ft.lbs. (20 Nm).

10. Lock the bolts by bending the tabs around the bolt heads.

11. Install the filter.

12. Using Peugeot tool 0.0137 or equivalent to hold the tensioner together, install the tensioner.

13. On the Renold® tensioner, load the tensioner by turning the Allen key clockwise. Install a new tab washer and install the plug. Bend the tab to lock the plug.

14. Remove the retaining tool.

CAUTION

Never assist the tensioner action.

---

15. Load the Sedis® tensioner by turning the screw clockwise.

NOTE: The Sedis® and Renold® tensioners are interchangeable as a unit.

16. Install the thrust washer if needed and the oil thrower cup.

NOTE: The 505 uses an oil seal. Always install a new seal during reassembly.

17. Use a new housing gasket and center the timing housing with Peugeot tool 0.0128 or equivalent. Tighten the housing bolts. Then, install a new seal as described above.

18. Install the Woodruff key and the crankshaft pulley. Torque the pulley nut to 123 ft.lbs. (166 Nm).

19. Bend the tab around the nut.

20. Install remaining components in the reverse order of removal.

21. Fill the engine with oil and the radiator with coolant.

22. Check the timing.

XD, XDP Diesel

1. Remove the timing gear cover.

2. Unload the chain tensioner by first removing the sealing plug from the tensioner body and then engaging a 3mm allen wrench through the hole in the tensioner piston recess. Turn the allen wrench clockwise to release the tensioner shoe.

3. Loosen the eccentric rod gear fastening nut. Then move the pinion to its slackest position.

4. Remove the following:

  a. The injection pump pinion and the chain;

  b. The injection pump pinion hub and bearing;

  c. The rod gear with its eccentric;

  d. The guide shoe and the chain;

  e. The crankshaft pinion;

  f. The chain tensioner;

  g. The housing gasket.

5. To install, reassemble the components in the reverse order of removal, paying attention to the following points:

  a. To facilitate installation of the chain, adjust the eccentric in the position for maximum slack.

  b. With the crankshaft pinion reference mark facing down, simultaneously

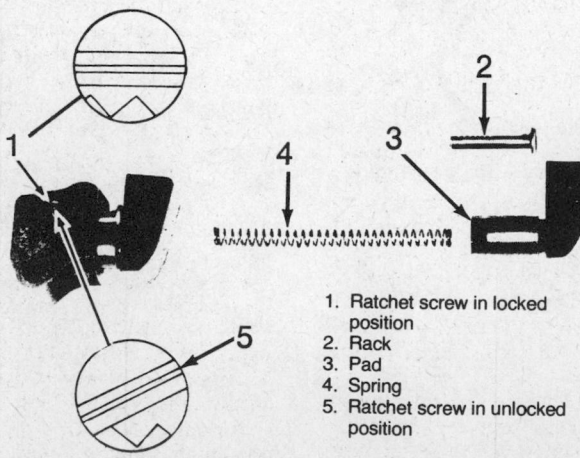

1. Ratchet screw in locked position
2. Rack
3. Pad
4. Spring
5. Ratchet screw in unlocked position

Sedis timing chain tensioner used in some 504 models

install the injection pump pinion and the chain, conforming to the reference marks. The copper link should be opposite the crankshaft pinion mark; the links marked by a line should be opposite the camshaft pinion mark and the injection pump bearing mark. Then install the pump bearing pinion and the pin;

c. After installing the chain, adjust the idler pinion eccentric, rotating it in the direction opposite to that of engine rotation so that the play between the tensioner pad and its support is from 0.02–0.04 in. Then tighten the eccentric fastening nut to 36 ft.lbs. Load the tensioner by turning the allen wrench to the right and stop turning when the pad is pushed onto the chain. Be sure to screw in and lock the tensioner plug bolt;

d. Place a straightedge on the chain connecting the camshaft pinions and the injection pump. Be sure that the guide shoe is flush against the chain, readjusting if necessary;

e. Be sure to recheck the timing.

XD2, XD2C, and XD2S Diesel

1. Remove the radiator, belts, alternator, cooling fan blades, water pump, and crankshaft pulley. Protect the A/C condenser.

2. Remove the timing chain cover. Turn the crankshaft to bring the crankshaft keyway to a vertical position.

3. Unload the timing chain tensioner, depending on its type, as follows:

a. Both the normally aspirated and turbocharged engines may use a Sedis® tensioner (B), which has a locking pawl visible through a small hole on the left side, below the left mounting bolt hole. First, make sure the groove in the head

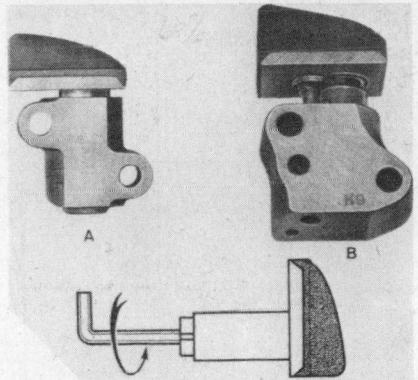

To unload the Sedis® type tensioner, first place the lock in position (1), then push the pad all the way in, and finally hold the pad and turn the lock to position (2) with a screwdriver

of the pawl is vertical. Then, depress the pad all the way toward the tensioner. Hold it there and turn the locking pawl counterclockwise until it locks.

The Brampton® type tensioner is at left (A) while the Sedis® is at the right (B). Lock the Brampton® pad, spring, and piston together by turning the piston with an al Allen wrench as shown.

b. On the Brampton® type tensioner (A), (also used on both engines) you must securely wire the tensioner parts together with the pad fully depressed.

4. Unbolt and remove the eccentric idler

Reinstall the eccentric idler with the reference mark (2) facing the block, and assembled as shown. Timing chain reference links and pinion references must be aligned as shown.

pinion. Remove the chain without disturbing the position of any sprocket.

5. If the engine uses the Brampton® type tensioner, carefully remove the bailing wire while holding the tensioner depressed. Then slowly release the tension and remove the pad, spring and piston. Assemble them together and lock them together by inserting an Allen wrench into the bottom of the piston and turning clockwise. Once they are locked together, reinstall them into the tensioner. Install a wire or spacer of .079 in. diameter/thickness betwen the pad and body of this type tensioner only.

6. Install the new timing chain with all reference links aligned with their respective pinion references.

7. Reinstall the eccentric idler pinion and route the chain toward the inside. Do not tighten the mounting bolt all the way. Insert an Allen wrench into the hole in the lever on the front of the pinion assembly.

Rotate the wrench and pinion counterclockwise and measure the play between the chain and tensioner pad. Adjust the eccentric pinion so there is .039–.079 in. of play between the two. Then, hold the position of the Allen wrench and torque the eccentric pinion mounting bolt to 20 ft. lbs.

8. On the Sedis® type tensioner, rotate the locking pawl clockwise until the screwdriver groove is vertical. Allow the tensioner to freely take up slack. On the Brampton® tensioner, remove the spacer or wire, push the pad toward the tensioner body all the way, and release the pad suddenly (don't try to control its motion).

9. Rotate the crankshaft slowly one full turn in normal direction of rotation and make sure there is no valve-to-piston contact.

10. Install the timing cover and other parts in reverse of the above. Make sure to torque the crankshaft pulley to specification. Adjust injection timing.

604

TIMING CHAIN

1. Remove the timing chain cover.

2. Check the timing chain tensioner projection. If the projection is greater than 0.38 in. (9.5 mm) replace the timing chains.

3. Rotate both the tensioner adjusters counterclockwise to release the timing chain tension.

4. Remove the oil pump drive chain and sprockets. Also remove the oil pump crankshaft spacer and Woodruff key.

5. Remove the oil pump.

6. Bring the No. 1 piston up to TDC on the compression stroke and mark the position of the crankshaft sprocket reference line. Also, mark the position of both of the camshaft sprocket reference lines.

7. Secure the crankshaft from rotating by installing Peugeot tool 8.01311 or equivalent on the flywheel.

8. Remove the camshaft sprocket bolts.

9. Remove the right hand camshaft sprocket and timing chain and then the left side camshaft sprocket and timing chain.

10. Remove both tensioners and the small oil filter in the block behind each tensioner.

11. Install the left bank chain and sprocket along with the crankshaft sprocket and Woodruff key. The camshaft sprocket reference mark should be centered between the two white marks on the timing chain. The crankshaft sprocket reference should be directly in line with the single white mark on the timing chain. This means that there is no slack in the lower half of the chain and all of the slack is on the upper side (tensioner side). The match marks should be exactly where they were marked before the chain was removed.

12. Install the right bank chain and camshaft sprocket. Position the camshaft sprocket reference mark between the two white marks on the timing chain. The single white mark on the chain should be directly opposite the crankshaft sprocket reference mark. This means that all of the slack is on the tensioner side of the timing chain. The match

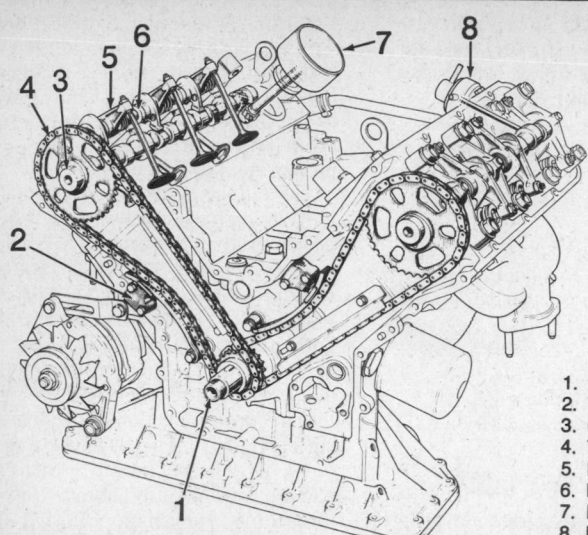

1. Crankshaft
2. Timing chain tensioner
3. Camshaft
4. Timing chain
5. Rocker arm
6. Rocker arm shaft
7. Distributor
8. Fuel pump

Cutaway view of the 604 engine timing and valve train

marks should be exactly where they were before the timing chain was removed.

13. Install the tensioners and filters. Torque the tensioner bolts to 5.5 ft.lbs. (7.8 Nm).

14. Place the two chains under tension by turning the tensioner adjusters clockwise.

CAUTION
Never attempt to assist the tensioning action of the tensioners.

15. Install the spacer, Woodruff key and sprocket for the oil pump chain drive.

16. Install the oil pump, using new lock washers on the four bolts. Torque the oil pump bolts to 9 ft.lbs. (13 Nm).

17. Place the chain over both sprockets and install the three sprocket–to–oil pump bolts. Use new lock washers on the bolts and torque them to 4.0 ft.lbs. (5.9 Nm).

18. Install new timing chain cover gaskets and secure the cover with twenty five bolts. Torque the bolts to 9 ft.lbs. (13 Nm).

19. Lubricate and install a new crankshaft pulley seal. Use Peugeot special tool 8.0134 or equivalent and tap the seal in with a mallet.

20. Install the crankshaft pulley and bolt. Coat the bolt threads with a medium duty locking compound. Torque the bolts to 123 ft.lbs. (166 Nm).

21. Reinstall all components removed during the removal procedure of the timing chain cover.

22. Install engine oil and coolant.

23. Remove the special tool holding the flywheel in place and install the clutch or converter housing cover plate.

VALVE TIMING

If the timing is not marked while the piston of the No. 1 cylinder is on the compression stroke or the marks are lost, then use the following valve timing procedure.

1. Rotate the crankshaft clockwise so that the Woodruff key slot is straight up in a vertical position.

2. On the left hand cylinder head, place the camshaft so that the rocker arms on the No. 1 cylinder are in balance. The camshaft slot will be aligned with the edge of the camshaft thrust flange. The slot and sprocket reference mark will be in a vertical position with the head installed on the block.

3. Rotate the crankshaft clockwise until the crankshaft Woodruff key slot is aimed at the center line of the left bank camshaft.

4. Install the timing chain over the left camshaft sprocket with the reference mark centered between the two white marks on the timing chain.

5. Install the timing chain over the crankshaft sprocket with the reference mark lined up with the single white mark on the timing chain.

6. Fasten the camshaft sprocket with the sprocket bolt and torque the bolt to 51 ft.lbs. (73 Nm).

7. Rotate the right side camshaft to a position where the No. 4 cylinder rocker arms are balanced. The slot in the camshaft will be pointing to an imaginary line through the center of the camshaft and parallel to the lower surface of the head.

8. Turn the crankshaft clockwise until the crankshaft sprocket reference mark lines up with the center of the lowest oil pump bolt hole.

9. Install the timing chain over the right side camshaft sprocket with the reference mark between the two white marks on the timing chain.

10. Install the timing chain on the outer crankshaft sprocket with the single white mark on the chain lined up with the reference mark on the crankshaft sprocket.

11. Install the bolt and the camshaft sprocket on the camshaft and torque the bolt to 51 ft.lbs. (73 Nm).

12. Install the timing chain tensioners and filters. Torque the tensioner bolts to 5.5 ft.lbs. (7.8 Nm).

13. Place the timing chains under tension by turning the tensioner adjusters clockwise.

CAUTION
Never attempt to assist the tensioning action of the tensioners.

14. Install the timing gear cover, using new gaskets.

15. Install a new timing cover oil seal.

16. Install the crankshaft pulley and install the bolt to a torque of 123 ft.lbs. (166 Nm).

17. Install the power steering pump brackets and the power steering pump.

18. Install the rocker arm covers and the hot air duct.

19. Install the power steering and water pump belts.

20. Install the fan casing and fan.

21. Install the radiator hoses and radiator struts.

22. Install the engine coolant and engine oil.

23. Install the air mixer, hot air duct and air filter. Connect the negative battery cable.

Camshaft
REMOVAL & INSTALLATION
504 and 505

1. Drain the engine oil, the coolant and disconnect the battery ground cable.

2. Remove the air cleaner assembly, spark plugs, distributor, carburetor, rocker arm cover, fan belt, radiator and various wire and hose connections. On the XN6 engine, remove the distributor support and distributor driveshaft.

NOTE: On 505 fuel injected vehicles, remove the Lambda® sensor wire at the exhaust pipe, fuel injectors at the intake manifold, all electrical wires, air hoses, water hoses, power steering, thermoslide valve connections, air induction hoses and rocker arm oil feed line.

3. Remove the spark plug tubes from the head and the exhaust pipe from the exhaust manifold.

4. Remove the head bolts and install Peugeot head guide tools 8.0115Y or equivalent.

5. Remove the rocker shaft assembly and the push rods. Mark the pushrods for installation in the same positions.

6. Remove the front head guide and pivot the head on the back head guide to break it loose from the block and lift off the head.

7. Lock the cylinder liners with special retainer tools, Peugeot number 8.0104D or equivalent.

8. Remove the valve lifters (cam followers). Mark the lifters for installation in the same positions.

9. Remove the crankshaft pulley nut.

NOTE: On vehicles with manual transmissions, apply the parking brake and engage 4th gear to hold the crankshaft from rotating while removing the crankshaft pulley and camshaft sprocket.

To remove the crankshaft pulley and camshaft sprocket on automatic transmission vehicles, remove the converter cover and use a flywheel tool to hold the engine.

10. Remove the timing chain cover.

11. If the engine is equipped with a Ren-old® tensioner, remove the plug and turn the adjuster clockwise with an Allen wrench to release the timing chain tension.

12. If the engine is equipped with a Sedis® tensioner, turn the ratchet adjuster counterclockwise with a screwdriver to release the timing chain tension.

13. Remove the chain tensioner and the filter behind it.

14. Remove the camshaft sprocket, crankshaft sprocket, Woodruff key and the timing chain.

15. Remove the camshaft thrust flange and withdraw the camshaft.

16. Installation is the reverse of removal.

17. Install a new filter behind the tensioner and use Peugeot special tool 0.0137 or equivalent to hold the tensioner together while installing it. See the timing chain installation procedure above for proper timing and chain retensioning information. Set the crankshaft at TDC No. 1 firing position and engage the distributor driveshaft with the camshaft gear so it lines up as shown on the XN6 engine. Make sure the driveshaft is in proper position and engages the oil pump drive, as well.

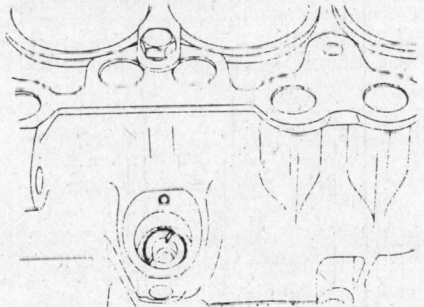

Position of the distributor driveshaft on XN6 engines with No. 1 cylinder at firing position

604

1. Drain the engine oil and coolant.

2. Disconnect the ground cable from the battery.

3. Remove the air filter, the air mixer casing and the hot air duct.

4. Remove the radiator struts, disconnect the hoses and separate the fan casing from the radiator.

5. Remove the fan and the fan casing.

6. Remove the power steering belt and the alternator drive belt.

7. Remove the power steering pump and hang it to the side, without removing the hoses.

8. Remove the clutch/converter housing cover plate.

9. Install the flywheel locking tool Peugeot number 0.0134C or equivalent.

10. Remove the crankshaft pulley.

11. Remove the hot air duct from the exhaust manifold and the rocker arm covers.

12. Remove the power steering pump support bracket.

13. Remove the timing chain cover.

14. Remove both oil pump drive sprockets, the oil pump chain, the spacer and the Woodruff key.

15. Remove the oil pump.

16. Release the two tensioners.

17. Match mark the camshaft drive sprockets to the head.

18. Remove the right camshaft sprocket and timing chain and then remove the left camshaft sprocket and timing chain.

19. Remove both chain tensioners and the filters behind them.

20. Remove the camshaft sprocket and Woodruff key.

21. Remove the right and the left side rocker arm assemblies. Mark the rocker arms right and left for reinstallation.

22. Remove the camshaft thrust flange from the front of the head, the bearing cover plate and gasket.

23. Remove the camshaft from the rear of the head.

24. Installation is the reverse of removal.

NOTE: The left hand camshaft has the fuel pump cam on it and the right hand camshaft has the distributor drive pinion on it.

25. Torque the rear cover plates to 4.3 ft.lbs. (5.8 Nm).

26. Torque the thrust flange bolts to 9.4 ft.lbs. (12.7 Nm).

XD and XDP Diesel

1. Remove the engine and follow Steps 1–4 of the 504 timing gear section.

2. After removing the timing housing gasket, remove the valve cover, rocker arm shaft, tappet inspection holes, pushrods and tappets.

3. Using a two-jawed puller, remove the camshaft pinion, its thrust plate and woodruff key.

4. Gently withdraw the camshaft from the engine being careful to avoid scoring the bearings.

5. To reassemble, first heat the camshaft pinion in well heated oil.

6. Install the thrust plate, woodruff key and pinion onto the camshaft, pressing the pinion onto the shaft until there is a clearance of 0.002–0.006 in. between the sprocket hub and the shaft flange.

7. Lubricate the cam lobes and journals and insert the camshaft, with the pinion attached, into the block.

8. Reassemble the remaining components in the reverse order of removal.

Pistons and Connecting Rods

REMOVAL & INSTALLATION

504 and 505

1. Remove the cylinder head.

2. Remove the lifters, the distributor support and the distributor driveshaft.

3. Remove the oil pan and oil pump. Reinstall engine mounting bolts for safety.

4. Mark the pistons and rods, 1–4, rear to front. The No. 1 cylinder is at the clutch end of the engine.

5. Remove the end caps from the connecting rods. On the XN6 engine, fasten the liners in place (using head bolts and a retaining strap such as Peugeot 8.0132 A 1Z). Ream ridges out of the tops of the liners (see the Engine Rebuilding section). Then, push the pistons and rods upward and out of the engine from underneath. On other engines, push the piston and liner assembly from the block. Keep the end caps with the proper piston and liner as it is removed. On the XN6 engine, now remove the liners by forcing them out from underneath.

6. Set the liners in position in the block without the seals and check them for distortion with a flat surface and a dial indicator.

7. Take a dial indicator reading at the four points around the liner shown in the illustration. The difference between the four measurements should be less than 0.0028 in. (0.07 mm).

NOTE: The 505 procedure is the same except that the protrusion specification is 0.0055 in. (0.14mm) and the maximum

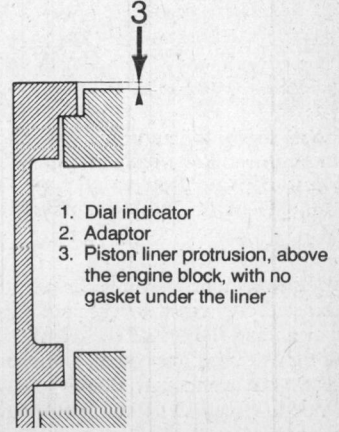

1. Dial indicator
2. Adaptor
3. Piston liner protrusion, above the engine block, with no gasket under the liner

Checking the liner protrusion above the block on the 504 and 505

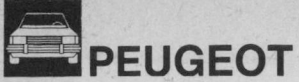
difference between liners is 0.0016 in. (0.04mm). On the XN6 engine used in 505 only, the maximum difference between liners is 0.0028 in.

NOTE: The distance being measured is the amount of protrusion of the cylinder liners above the cylinder block.

8. Select the proper size liner seal by subtracting the measured distance with no seal from the maximum allowable liner protrusion. Pick the seal size nearest to and not exceeding the subtracted difference.

9. Install the liners in the same positions as match marked before removal.

10. Install special Peugeot tools 8.0128 or equivalent to compress the cylinder liner gaskets, on the XN1 and XN6 engines. You'll have to measure the liners on one end of the engine and then reverse the tool and measure the other two. Remember to record the reading for the center liner so as to compare it to its opposite member.

11. Check the dial indicator readings on each liner and if they are from zero to 0.0055 in. (0.14 mm), install the liner retainer bolts, Peugeot number 8.0104D or equivalent. Remove the Peugeot liner compressor tool number 8.0128 or equivalent.

12. Using a ring expander tool, install the rings on the pistons. Install the pistons into the liners from the top side, follow the match marks made on removal. On the XN6 engine, align pistons and connecting rods with each other and with the block as shown in the illustration.

13. Install the rod bearing caps and nuts. Torque the rod bearing cap nuts to 29 ft.lbs. (39 Nm).

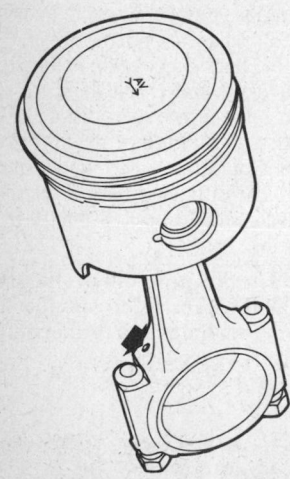

When assembling rods and pistons, align the connecting rod oil hole with the arrow on the top of the piston as shown. The arrow on top of the piston must point forward.

14. Remove liner clamps. Install the cylinder head, the wires, the vacuum lines and air cleaner assembly. Reinstall the oil pump and pan. Replenish fluids and check for leaks. Retorque the head and adjust valves as specified in "Cylinder Head Removal & Installation".

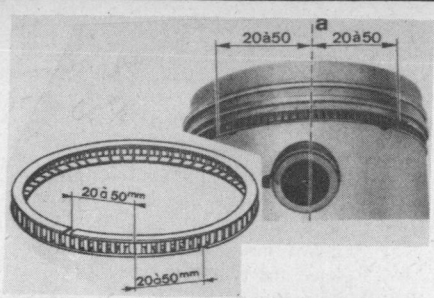

Position the gaps at top and bottom of the oil scraper ring as shown—each .78–.9 inches from the center of the piston pin. Position the gaps for the two compression rings each 120 degrees away from the center point between the two oil scraper ring gaps ("a").

PISTON AND LINER MATCHING CHART② XD2, XDP Engines

Mark On Piston	Matching Mark On The Liner①
A	1 mark
B	2 marks
C	3 marks

①Machined lines mark the upper edge of the liner.

②Piston ring gap and clearance specifications are not given. It is recommended by the manufacturer that pistons, rings and liners be replaced as complete new set for all cylinders.

604

1. Remove the air cleaner, wires, vacuum lines and the cylinder heads.

2. Use Peugeot tool 8.0134N and M or equivalents on both head surfaces to secure the camshaft sprockets. Shims are available in selected thicknesses to install under the camshaft sprocket holding tools. The shims may be needed to ensure the tightness of the timing chains while working on the pistons.

--- **CAUTION** ---

If slack is allowed in the timing chains or the special tools are not available the timing chains will have to be removed and the valve timing reset.

3. Use the special tools, cylinder liner retainers, Peugeot number 8.0132A or equivalent, to secure the cylinder liners in the block.

4. Remove the lower oil pan, the oil strainer, the anti-emulsion baffle, the sump securing bolts, the main bearing securing nuts and remove the oil sump.

5. Remove the connecting rod cap nuts.

6. Matchmark the cylinder liners to the block and the connecting rod caps to the connecting rods. Normally, the pistons have arrows on them to mark the direction of

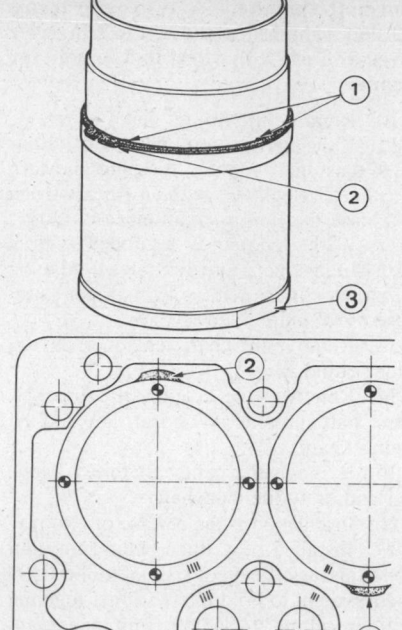

1. Inner tabs fit into grooves in the liner
2. Reference tab position at right angle to the flat spot
3. Flat spot

Installing the piston liner seals with the tab in the proper position in the 504 and 505 models

installation. If the pistons have the arrows, note the direction before removal and reinstall in the same direction. If no arrows are on the pistons, mark them with a felt tip pen for future reference.

7. Remove the pistons, piston rods and cylinder liners at the same time. Keep matching parts together.

8. If the liner is distorted beyond specification, install a new liner set.

NOTE: Pistons, rings, and liners are available in sets only. This helps retain engine balance.

9. The piston liners must project above the cylinder block gasket face between 0.0064 in. (0.16mm) and 0.0092 in. (0.23mm).

10. Cylinder liner seals are to be installed between the liner and the lower flange of the block.

11. Cylinder liner seals are available in the following thicknesses.:

604 MODEL SELECTIVE CYLINDER LINER SEALS

Color	Thickness
Blue	0.0034 in. (0.087mm)
White	0.0040 in. (0.102mm)

604 MODEL SELECTIVE CYLINDER LINER SEALS

Color	Thickness
Red	0.0048 in. (0.122mm)
Yellow	0.0058 in. (0.147mm)

12. Measure the cylinder liner projection above the engine block with no seal under it. Subtract this measurement from 0.0092 in. (0.23mm) and select a seal that will provide a maximum cylinder liner projection of 0.0092 in. (0.23mm), or as close to it as possible without exceeding the maximum. For example:

Maximum allowable
projection   0.0092 in.
Largest measurement—
no seal   0.0040 in.

Difference to be taken up
by the selected seal   0.0052 in.
The seal selected will be red 0.0488 in. (0.122mm).

13. Install the seals with their color code facing the top of the engine.

14. Install the liners and seals in a position so that the color tabs are visible and will not be squeezed under the adjacent liner.

15. Check the final liner projection above the block for each cylinder liner. Mark the position of the liners on the straight edge of the block.

16. Install a piston ring tool around the piston crown and compress the rings. Oil the liner and install the piston. Match the marks on the liner and the piston.

17. When installing pistons and liners, always match the letter on the piston crown to the number of machine marks on the liner.

18. Install the piston and liner assemblies into the block.

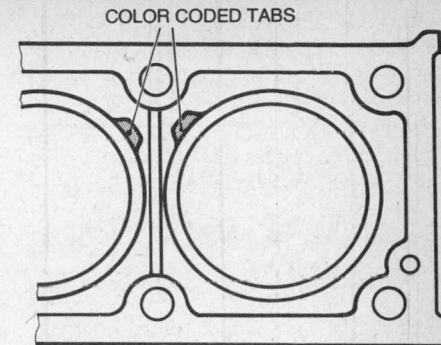

Correct position of the tabs on the 604 model piston liners, when correctly installed

19. Install the rod bearings and rod caps. Torque the rod bearing cap nuts to 34 ft.lbs. (46 Nm).

20. Install the cylinder heads and all related wires, vacuum lines and the air cleaner assembly.

GASKET TO BE FITTED

Highest Point on the Liner (Without Gasket)	Reference	Thickness
0.0015 to 0.0018 in. (0.039 to 0.045 mm)		0.0028 to 0.0041 in. (0.070 to 0.105 mm)
0.0007 to 0.0015 in. (0.019 to 0.038 mm)		0.0033 to 0.0047 in. (0.085 to 0.120 mm)
−0.0002 to +0.0007 in. (−0.006 to +0.018 mm)		0.0041 to 0.0055 in. (0.105 to 0.140 mm)
−0.0037 to −0.0003 in. (−0.095 to −0.007 mm)		0.0051 to 0.0065 in. (0.130 to 0.165 mm)

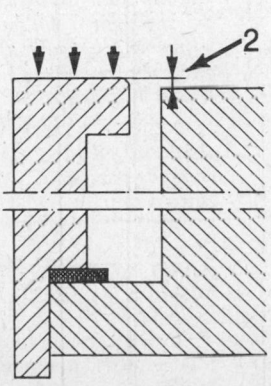
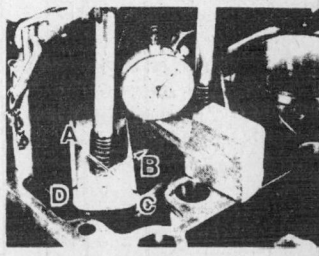

1. Liner compressing tool
2. Piston liner protrusion

Measuring liner protrusion with the gasket installed on 504 models with compressed type liners

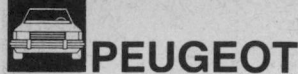

ENGINE LUBRICATION

Oil Pan

REMOVAL & INSTALLATION

504 and 505

The Peugeot four cylinder engines have a separate oil sump pan on the bottom of the crankcase pan.

1. To remove the oil sump, remove the bolts and the sump pan.

2. To remove the entire crankcase pan, the engine will have to be raised for working clearances.

3. Installation is the reverse of removal. Torque gas engine sump and pan bolts to 7 ft. lbs.

4. On the diesel, be sure to position the pump so that the feed tube is engaged in the hole in the strainer and that the thrust washer is under a light spring tension.

604

The 6 cylinder engines have a front lower oil sump that is removable with the engine in the vehicle. If the entire crankcase must be removed, the engine must be removed from the vehicle.

NOTE: If the entire crankcase must be removed, refer to the "Engine Removal and Installation" section.

1. Drain the engine oil.

2. Remove the sump pan bolts and take off the sump pan.

3. Clean off the gasket surfaces and install a new gasket.

4. Install the sump pan and torque the bolts to 9.4 ft.lbs. (12.7 Nm).

5. Torque the drain plug to 27 ft.lbs. (36 Nm).

6. Fill the engine with 6.3 quarts (6.0 liters) of engine oil.

Rear Main Oil Seal

REMOVAL & INSTALLATION

504 and 505

Seals are not used on the rear of the crankshaft. An oil slinger arrangement is used to direct the oil back into the reservoir. The crankshaft may need new thrust washers, if end play is excessive. Side seals are used on the rear main bearing cap.

1. Check the end float of the crankshaft. The end float (end-play) must be between 0.003 in. (0.08mm) and 0.008 in. (0.20mm).

2. If there is too much end float (end-play), oversize thrust washers are available in thicknesses of: 0.096 in. (2.4mm), 0.098 in. (2.45mm), and 0.10 in. (2.5mm).

3. Install the new rear bearing cap side seals and torque the bearing cap bolts to 55 ft.lbs. (73.5 Nm).

604

The transmission and the flywheel must be removed on 604 models in order to work on the rear main seal. See "Transmission Removal and Installation" for procedures.

1. Check the crankshaft end play for between 0.0028 in. (0.07mm) and 0.0108 in. (0.27mm).

2. If needed, install oversized thrust washers selected from available sizes of: 0.092 in. (2.3mm), 0.096 in. (2.4mm), 0.098 in. (2.45mm) and 0.10 in. (2.5mm).

3. Remove the seal and fit a new seal by hand.

4. Install the flywheel and transmission.

Oil Pump

REMOVAL & INSTALLATION

504 and 505

NOTE: The oil pump procedures for the XD and XDP diesel are the same. The only difference in the pumps is that the diesel pump is larger and has a greater volume.

1. Drain the oil.

2. Remove the oil sump and oil pump. Do not lose the two oil pump locating dowels.

3. Install a new O-ring on the bottom of the oil pump.

4. Be certain that the locating dowels are in place.

5. Be certain that the oil pump drive blade engages the oil pump drive rod.

6. Torque the bolts to 7 ft.lbs. (9.8 Nm).

7. Use a new gasket and install the oil sump.

8. Torque the sump bolts to 7 ft.lbs. (9.8 Nm).

9. Install the drain plug and fill the engine with oil.

— CAUTION —
Oil sumps made of either pressed steel or aluminum which do not have an oil return passage, must not be installed on XM engines with a rear main bearing cap which incorporates an oil return hole.

— CAUTION —
A special oil pan gasket of rubber/asbestos must be used on USA models with a metal alloy sump.

505D, 604D, XD2, XD2C and XD2S Engines

1. Drain and remove the oil pan. Fashion a removal tool out of a bolt or nut that's 19mm across the flats—for example a wheel lug nut with the chamfer ground off. Insert the bolt or nut into the recess in the top of the capnut located on the side of the block.

Turn the top of the bolt or nut with a 19mm box wrench.

2. Remove the blind cap nut from the side of the block. Hold the oil pump up as you remove the positioning screw. Lower the pump. You may have to turn the crankshaft just lightly to get the pump free.

3. To install, reinsert the pump up into the block until the drive gear engages. Align the tapered hole in the pump body with the threaded hole in the block. Install the pump shaft positioning screw and locking cap.

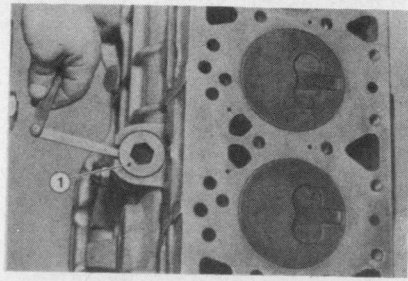
Measuring the clearance between the oil pump cap nut and block

Install the shaft cap so it just touches the top of the pump shaft.

4. With feeler gauge, measure the clearance between the top of the cap nut and block ("e").

5. Remove the cap nuts, and insert a shim .0039 in. (.1mm) thicker than the play. Shims are available in thicknesses of .1, .2, .5, and 1.0mm (.0039, .0078, .0197, and .039 in.).

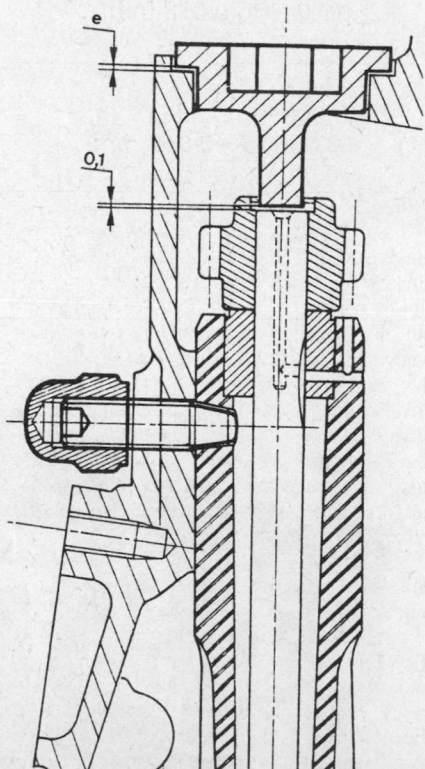
When the proper shim is installed, the clearance between the base of the cap nut and the top of the shaft will be 1mm

6. Remove the cap nut, install the shim, and reinstall the cap nut, torquing it to 65.25 ft. lbs.

7. Install the oil pan with a new gasket, and refill it.

604

1. Drain the engine oil and remove the timing chain cover.
2. Remove the oil pump drive sprockets, drive chain and Woodruff key.
3. Remove the oil pump.
4. Installation is the reverse of removal.
5. Torque the oil pump sprocket bolts to 4 ft.lbs. (5.0 Nm).
6. Torque the oil pump bolts to 9 ft.lbs. (12.7 Nm).

ENGINE COOLING

Radiator

REMOVAL & INSTALLATION

504

1. Drain the coolant.
2. Remove the fan shroud retaining bolts.
3. Remove the upper and lower radiator hose.
4. Remove the lower radiator bolts.
5. Remove the radiator.
6. Installation is the reverse of removal.

505

1. With the engine cool, remove the radiator cap and then open the drain cock at the bottom of the radiator to drain the coolant.
2. Remove the two bolts at top/rear of the radiator that hold the fan shroud on. Unsnap the lower snap on either side by simply pulling to the rear. Pull the fan shroud out of the engine compartment. On models where the fan blades will not clear, remove the four bolts attaching the blade to the electric fan clutch, and then remove the fan blades and shroud simultaneously.
3. Disconnect upper and lower radiator hoses at the radiator. Disconnect wire connectors 57 and 58 at the thermostatic switch screwed into the radiator.
4. Remove the four nuts and rubber cusions holding the radiator to the body at the bottom from underneath the car.
5. Remove the two bolts fastening the top of the radiator at the top, and pull it up and out of the engine compartment.
6. Install in reverse order. Replenish the coolant with the proper anti-freeze/water mix. Run the engine at about 1,000 rpm until after the thermostat opens and air is expelled from the system, and add more coolant, if necessary. Install the cap, and check for leaks.

604

1. Drain the cooling system.
2. On air conditioned vehicles:
   a. Remove the electric fan lead,
   b. Remove the oil pressure switch wires,
   c. Remove the compressor wire,
   d. Remove the temperature sending wire,
   e. Remove the three electric fan bolts,
   f. Remove the radiator stays,
   g. Remove the battery.
3. Remove the overflow hose from the left side of the radiator.
4. Remove the top and the bottom radiator hoses.
5. On vehicles with an automatic transmission, remove the transmission cooler lines.
6. On air conditioned vehicles, disconnect the condenser receiver/dryer assembly from the radiator.
7. Remove the fan cowl and the radiator.
8. Installation is the reverse of removal.
9. Refill the cooling system.

Water Pump

REMOVAL & INSTALLATION

504 and 505

1. Drain the coolant.
2. Remove the top radiator hose and the heater hose from the water pump.
3. Remove the fan belt. Unbolt the fan shroud (see the Radiator Removal & Installation procedure above) and the cooling fan. Remove the shroud and fan together.
4. Remove the water pump bolts and remove the water pump.
5. Clean the gasket surfaces.
6. Replace the gasket, coat it on both sides with sealer, and install the pump in the reverse order or removal.
7. Install coolant in the engine.

604

1. Drain the cooling system.
2. Remove the air mixer casing and duct, the hot air duct and the air filter.
3. Remove the intake manifold and the insulating plate under the manifold.
4. Remove the water pump belt and the alternator drive belt.
5. Separate the fan casing from radiator.
6. Remove the heater and radiator hoses at the water pump.
7. Remove the wire lead from the temperature sending unit.
8. Loosen the hose clamps on the two rubber hoses at the heads.
9. Remove the bolts securing the water casings to the block.
10. Remove the two heater hoses from the back of the water pump.
11. Remove the water pump bolts.
12. Remove the water pump and casing as an assembly.

13. Installation is the reverse of removal.

NOTE: Install new O-rings where the casing fits to the block.

14. Torque the water casing bolts to 9.4 ft.lbs. (12.7 Nm).
15. Torque the water pump bolts to 14.6 ft.lbs. (17.2 Nm).

Diesel

1. Drain the radiator.
2. On the 505D with automatic transmission only, remove the center portion of the front grille. Then, unscrew the two connections and disconnect the two transmission cooler lines, raising them to prevent loss of fluid. Remove the radiator, the top hose, and then the fan belt.
3. Disconnect the heater hose from the pump.
4. Disconnect the self-disengaging fan brush holder.
5. Remove the pump attaching bolts and the pump.
6. Clean the mating surfaces of the pump and cylinder head.
7. Apply Permatex® No. 2 on both sides of a new gasket and install the pump in the reverse order of removal.
8. Adjust the fan belt, install the radiator, connect the hoses and refill the cooling system. On the 505D with automatic, reconnect cooler lines and install the grille. Check transmission Fluid level.

Radiator Fan

REMOVAL & INSTALLATION

504

1. Remove the water pump.
2. Using a pulley holder tool mounted in a vise, remove the pump hub nut.
3. Tap on the end of the shaft to disengage the pump body from the pulley. Remove the Woodruff key from the slot in the shaft.
4. Installation is the reverse of removal.
5. Torque the pump hub nut to 25 ft.lbs. (34.2 Nm).

505 and 604

1. Remove the fan casing from the radiator.
2. Remove the four fan-to-thermostatic fan clutch bolts.
3. Lift off the fan.
4. Installation is the reverse of removal.

Belt Tension Adjustment

Peugeot recommends that all of their belts be adjusted by measuring reference marks on the belts, except on the model 505 air pump-alternator belt the adjustment is made by loosening the idler pulley bolts and

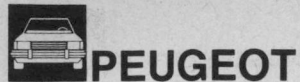

torqueing the idler bracket nut to 58.0 ft.lbs. (78.4 Nm). For all other belts:

1. Loosen the belt adjusting bracket bolts.

2. With no tension on it, mark two reference lines on the belt, 4 inches (100mm) apart.

3. Stretch the belt when tightening it so that the reference marks will be 4.12 inches (103mm) apart.

EMISSION CONTROLS

The Peugeot emission controls are composed of three major systems on gasoline engines: crankcase emissions control, evaporative emissions control and exhaust emissions control. Diesel engines contain primarily a rather sophisticated EGR system that may affect engine operation if it requires service.

Differences may occur between California and Federal vehicles. Therefore, the emission control information label on the vehicle should be consulted before repairs are made.

Crankcase Emission Control System

The system is considered a closed system with the crankcase breathing from the air cleaner air intake. The PCV valve vents measured amounts of crankcase gases and vapors into the intake manifold to be burned with the air/fuel mixture.

Evaporative Emission Control System

In order to control the evaporation of fuel into the atmosphere from the fuel tank and

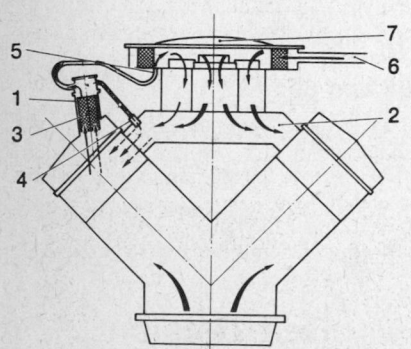

1. PCV recirculating tube
2. Intake manifold
3. Filter
4. Calibrated jet
5. Calibrated hole in air cleaner
6. Air intake
7. Air cleaner assembly

604 crankcase emission system

the carburetor when the engine is shut off, both are vented into a charcoal canister. A calibrated valve in the fuel tank line meters the flow of vapors into the charcoal canister to an amount that the canister can handle. The station wagons have an additional vapor-liquid separator located near the fuel tank. When the engine is started, the system pulls the vapors out of the charcoal canister and into the intake manifold, thereby purging the canister of fuel vapors.

Exhaust Emission Control Systems

AIR INJECTION

The air injection system adds oxygen into the exhaust manifold, allowing unburned hydrocarbons (HC) in the hot exhaust gases to be burned more completely. The system

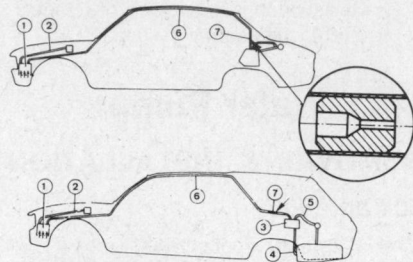

1. Charcoal canister
2. Canister to carburetor vapor hose
3. Vapor-liquid separator (wagon only)
4. Separator return hose (wagon only)
5. Filler neck to separator hose (wagon only)
6. Fuel tank to canister hose
7. Calibrated jet

Evaporative emission system used on all models

consists of a belt driven rotary vane air pump, a diverter valve, an electro-valve, an intake manifold injection valve and non-return valves.

Air Pump

Some precautions should be taken when working on the air pump.

1. Do not operate the engine with the pump removed or drive belt disconnected.

2. Do not lubricate the pump.

3. If the filter is contaminated, replace it. Do not attempt to clean it.

4. When adjusting the drive belt, never pry on the pump body.

5. Never clamp the pump body in a vise.

6. The internal parts of the air pump are not serviceable. Replace the pump as an assembly.

7. The following external parts may be replaced on the pump: drive pulley, filter and pressure relief valve.

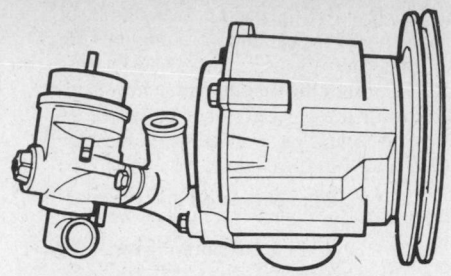

504 air injection pump

8. Do not hand rotate the pulley on a new pump and never rotate the pulley in the direction opposite to the normal direction.

EGR VALVE

In order to reduce the nitrogen oxide (NO_x) in the exhaust, a controlled amount of exhaust gas is recirculated into the intake manifold. The main component of the system is the valve, which opens between the exhaust and intake manifolds. The valve opening is controlled by vacuum, according to engine conditions, by a vacuum control electro-valve and a vacuum amplifier. California engines have an additional vacuum switch.

ELECTRO-VALVE

During engine start up and warm up, the electro-valve stops the flow of vacuum to the EGR valve, to prevent the EGR valve from opening when the choke is operating.

VACUUM AMPLIFIER

This valve controls the amount of vacuum to the EGR valve according to engine conditions.

VACUUM SWITCH

This switch reacts to close the EGR valve during high intake manifold vacuum situations. The valve is only used on California vehicles.

CATALYTIC CONVERTER

The catalytic converter reduces hydrocarbons (HC) and carbon monoxide (C) by converting them to carbon dioxide and water.

Lambda® Sensor

The 505 fuel injected models use the Lambda® oxygen sensor system to check the exhaust gases for unburned hydrocarbons. The sensor sends signals from the exhaust pipe to the control unit. Under certain conditions, the signals will cause the control unit to alter the fuel ratio to bring it into specifications. If the engine has not reached operating temperature, the signals will be overridden and the enrichment system will operate.

DIESEL EGR

This system is used on the XD2C and XD2S engines to recirculate a small percentage of exhaust gas into the engine's intake to reduce peak combustion temperatures and therefore nitrogen oxide emissions. Because of the relative absence of intake manifold vacuum in the normally unthrottled diesel, the system is more complex than that which is used on most gasoline engines.

XD2C Engines

The EGR valve itself contains two vacuum diaphragms and, therefore, has two stages of operation. The system incorporates a vacuum operated air throttle which operates in the first stage of operation to ensure enough intake vacuum exists so that exhaust will be drawn effectively into the intake manifold. Electrically operated vacuum valves coordinate the staged operation of the EGR valve and the medium-throttle operation of the air throttle with the travel of the injection pump throttle lever and the engine rpm, as measured by a flywheel mounted speed sensor.

XD2S Engines

This system is generally similar to the one on the XD2C. Instead of a staged EGR valve and associated solenoid operated vacuum valves, it uses an injection pump mounted vacuum converter—a regulator that uses vacuum produced by the engine's accessory vacuum pump. The converter converts the injection pump throttle rod's position to a vacuum signal which then operates the EGR valve according to engine load. An electric valve also cuts EGR off when the engine is cold, is below 1,500 rpm, or is above 3,100 rpm.

Diesel engines are not as sensitive as gasoline engines to a small excess of EGR—that is, they usually don't misfire if the EGR system is providing a little too much exhaust. But, if the system is providing full EGR under the wrong conditions the engine will show black smoke in the exhaust and will lack full power.

Checking Out the XD2C EGR

1. A quick check for incorrect control of the EGR valve can be made by disconnecting the connector (C3) for the speed sensor. If the engine now runs without black smoke and with full power, the EGR system is at fault. You should make the next test to at least ensure that the EGR valve stem moves before suspecting a problem with the engine's injection system or basic mechanical parts.

2. Next, with the engine warm, watch the EGR valve stem and the throttle flap stem. Accelerate the engine using the link-rod going to the injection pump. At about 1,300–1,500 rpm, the throttle flap stem should open and the EGR valve should open all the way. The vacuum tubes to both EGR

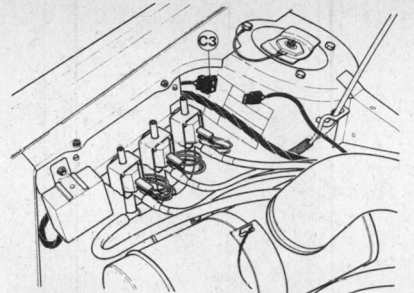

Disconnect the C3 connector on XD2C engines to make the EGR system inoperative

chambers should have vacuum at this point; so should the vacuum line to the throttle flap diaphragm.

As you accelerate further, the throttle flap will first close, then the EGR valve lower chamber will lose its vacuum and, finally at near-maximum engine speeds, the EGR valve will lose all actuating vacuum and will close.

3. If there is any doubt about the response of the EGR valve, you should remove it, labeling vacuum hoses first. Clean it with a safe solvent, and reinstall it with a new gasket. Make sure the stem moves freely. If the valve still does not respond and you're getting proper vacuum supply, it probably has one or two perforated diaphragms and should be replaced.

4. If you're not getting the vacuum supply in the proper sequence, check the speed sensor. It's located on the top of the flywheel housing. Check to see if the sensor is tightly mounted, and if it is, proceed to the next test. If not, adjust it by first pushing it against the flywheel, then pulling it back about .020 in. Tighten the mounting clamp.

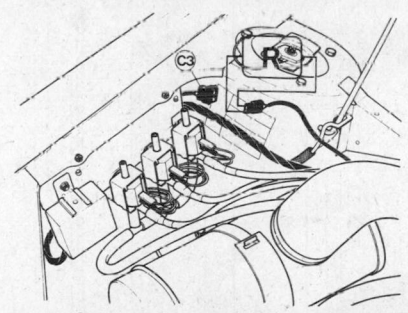

The speed sensor connector (C3) for the SD2C EGR system. Measure resistance as shown. The solenoid operated vacuum valves are nearby.

You can check the sensor's resistance with an ohmmeter. Pull the connector shown in the illustration and measure the resistance as shown. It must be 40–60 ohms, or the sensor requires replacement.

5. You can also check the resistance of any or all of the solenoid operated vacuum valves, located under the EGR computer, near the air cleaner. Simply disconnect both wiring connectors (noting how they connect) and measure resistance with an ohmmeter. It should be 40 ohms. Otherwise, replace the valve.

Checking the XD2S EGR

1. Start with the engine cold (well under 120 degrees F.). Unplug the vacuum line to the EGR valve. Start the engine and accelerate it up to about 2,000 rpm with the injection pump rod while checking for vacuum in the vacuum line. You can plug a vacuum gauge into the line to test for vacuum, if you have one. There should be no vacuum while the engine is cold.

2. Run the engine until it is warm. As the engine passes 120 degrees F. (well below normal operating temperature), you should begin to get vacuum at the EGR vacuum line when the engine is accelerated. With the line plugged in, the EGR valve should open as the engine passes 1,500 rpm with manual transmission, and 1,300 rpm with automatics. If the EGR valve does not open with the line connected, disconnect the line and measure for vacuum with a gauge or check with your finger. If there is vacuum even when the engine is cold, check the wiring to the thermosensor. If the wiring is OK, replace the thermosensor. If you have found that vacuum is getting to the EGR valve (under the proper conditions), and the valve stem still did not move, remove the valve and clean it with a safe

The EGR thermosensor on XD2S engines is located as shown (2)

solvent. If you do not find that the valve responds to cleaning, test for adequate vacuum to the valve by measuring the vacuum as the engine is accelerated warm. The valve must respond to a little over 4 in. Hg. of vacuum, or it must be replaced.

3. Disconnect the ground wire from the vacuum solenoid valve (wire No. 146). Connect a jumper wire from the ground wire connector on the valve to a good ground. Then, disconnect the link-rod from the converter lever, removing just a little of the shrink tubing, if necessary (leave as much

Jumper (F) the vacuum solenoid valve to ground, as shown (XD2S engines)

of the tubing on as possible). With the engine idling, move the lever on the vacuum converter steadily in the direction of acceleration and carefully observe the movement of the EGR valve stem. If the EGR valve moves smoothly, the vacuum converter is ok. If it moves in spurts, and you're sure it is clean and the stem is free to move, the vacuum converter is probably faulty. It can only be tested with specially designed equipment.

Disconnect the link-rod (10) from the vacuum converter lever (3a)

4. Reconnect the link-rod and wiring. Accelerate the engine and watch the response of the EGR valve. The valve should begin opening at a moderate rpm (1,500 with manual transmission, 1,300 with automatic) and then close again past 3,100 rpm. If the valve does not respond this way there is a problem in the speed sensor, electronic control box, or the wiring. If the valve never responds, and it worked in doing the above test, check the electrical connection between the solenoid valve and the control box, and between the control box and the thermosensor. You can test the thermosensor for failing off by grounding the wire leading to it and repeating the test in

Checking speed sensor resistance—XD2S EGR system

this step. If the valve now works, replace the thermosensor. Check the speed sensor as described in Step 6. If that is OK and the wiring is OK but there is still no vacuum to the EGR valve (the solenoid valve does not open), the electronic control box or its wiring is defective.

If the solenoid valve comes on as the engine is accelerated, but never goes off above 3,100 rpm, or if its response is inconsistent (coming on and going off at varying rpm) first check associated wiring and then replace the electronic control box.

5. If the solenoid valve does not re-

spond, you can check its resistance with an ohmmeter. Disconnect both wires (noting routing). Connect the ohmmeter between the two connectors. Resistance is normally about 40 ohms. If it's much higher than this or infinite, replace the valve.

6. Check the speed sensor as in Step 4 of the EGR troubleshooting procedure for the XD2C engine above. They are identical. The location and appearance of the electrical connector for this sensor on the XD2S is shown in the illustration.

FUEL SYSTEM

Fuel Filter

REMOVAL & INSTALLATION

6 Cylinder Engines

1. Unscrew the fuel return valve and plug it at the carburetor.
2. Remove the fuel filter.
3. Replace the gasket at the seal plug.
4. Install the new filter and check for leaks.

6 Cylinder Engines (Fuel Injected)

1. Unscrew the cover box.
2. Remove the pressure hoses.
3. Loosen the attaching screws and remove the filter. Remove the connecting plug from the old filter and install it on the new filter with a new gasket.
4. Install the new filter.
5. Replace the attaching screws.

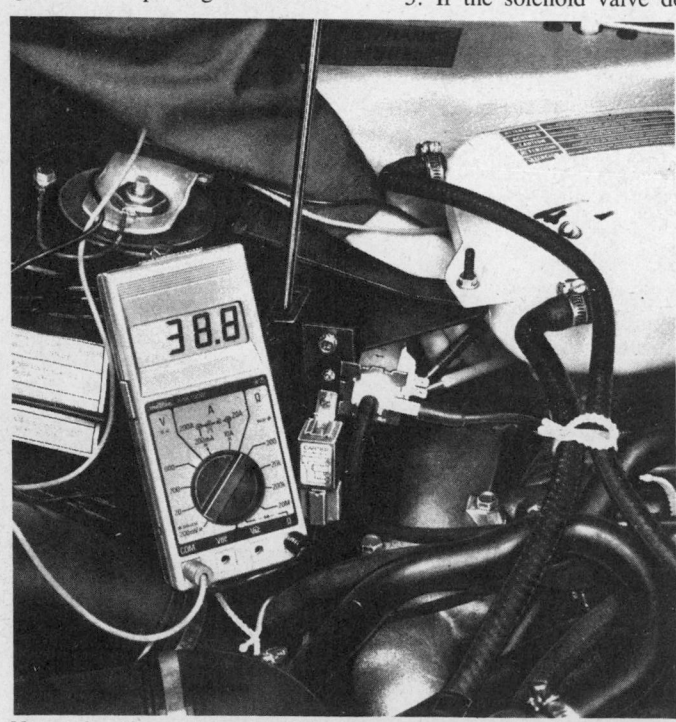

Measuring the resistance of the vacuum solenoid valve (XD2S)

6. Install the pressure hoses.

7. Replace the cover box and check for leaks.

4 Cylinder Engines

1. Loosen the hose clips.
2. Remove the fuel filter.
3. Install a new filter along with new hoses.
4. Replace the hose clips.
5. Check for leaks.

Diesel Engines (XD2, XD2C)

1. The diesel filter is changed at 12,500 miles on SD2 engines and at 30,000 miles on XD2C engines. To change the filter, open the drain cock (operated by a thumbscrew on the bottom and drain the unit completely. Close the drain cock.

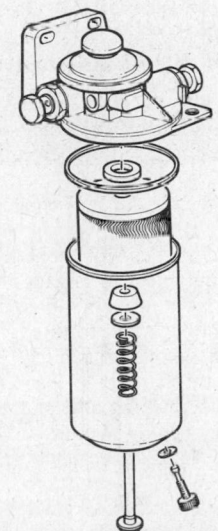

Diesel fuel filter (XD2, XD2C)

2. Remove the through-bolt from the bottom, and pull the bolt, housing, and cartridge out. Remove internal parts and clean the bowl with clean diesel fuel.

3. Remove the gaskets from the filter mounting pad and install new ones. Insert the through-bolt and install the spring, washer, and filter mount.

4. Position the bowl up against the mounting pad and then install and tighten the through-bolt. Open the bleed screw located on the top/right, and pump air out of the system by repeatedly depressing the pump actuator on top. When air-free fuel is discharged, close the bleed screw.

Fuel Pump

REMOVAL & INSTALLATION

All Models

The fuel pump is located on the driver's side of the engine. Disconnect the fuel inlet and outlet lines. Remove the attaching bolts and the pump.

When installing, make sure the fuel pump rocker arm is positioned correctly on the cam.

Adjusting the throttle cable at the retaining bracket on 504 and 604 models

Carburetors

REMOVAL & INSTALLATION

1. Remove the accelerator cable.
2. Remove the downshift cable on vehicles equipped with automatic transmissions.
3. Remove all fuel and vacuum lines.
4. Remove the carburetor mounting bolts and lift off the carburetor.
5. Installation is the reverse of removal.

OVERHAUL

For all carburetor overhaul procedures, please refer to "Carburetor Service" in the Unit Repair section.

THROTTLE LINKAGE ADJUSTMENT

504

Adjust the throttle linkage to 0.08 in. (2mm) of clearance, with the engine warm.

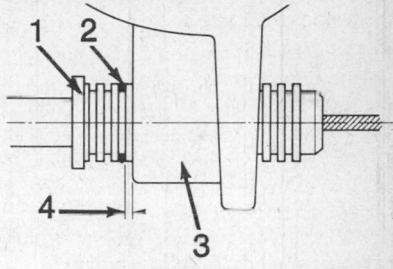

1. Throttle cable
2. Snap ring
3. Common intake manifold
4. 0.08 in. (2 mm)

504 throttle cable adjustment

604

1. Check the height of the accelerator pedal stop. The pedal stop height should be 2.04 in. (51mm).
2. Place a 0.28 in. (7mm) spacer between the accelerator pedal and the pedal stop.
3. Hold the accelerator pedal and the spacer in a fully depressed position.

1. Throttle drum
2. Stop washer
3. Throttle rod
4. Fixed stop
5. Moveable stop

VIEW A

VIEW B

604 throttle linkage adjustment

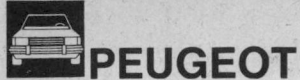
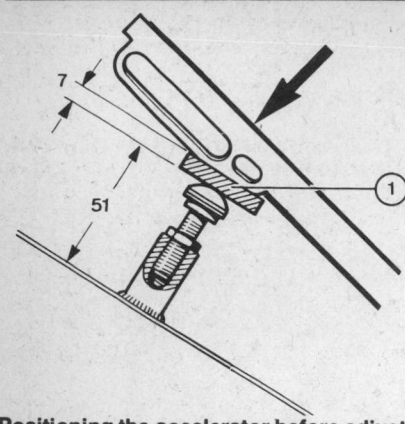

Positioning the accelerator before adjusting the throttle cable on 604 models

4. Remove the two linkage return springs.

5. Hold the carburetor control quadrant in the fully open position.

6. Secure the accelerator cable in place on the control quadrant, pulling on the cable just enough to tension it. Do not compress the compensator spring on the cable when tensioning it.

7. Install the two linkage return springs.

8. Remove the spacer from under the accelerator pedal.

9. When the engine is hot, the clearance on the accelerator cable–to–holding bracket should be 0.08 in. (2mm).

FLOAT LEVEL ADJUSTMENT

504

1. Remove the air cleaner, connecting linkages and fuel lines from the float bowl cover of the carburetor.

2. Remove the float bowl cover from the carburetor.

3. With the needle valve completely closed, check the float level by measuring the distance from the float bowl cover mat-ing surface to the small diameter of the float.

4. If the float level does not measure 1.4 in. (35.5mm) adjust it by bending the pivot arm on the float.

604

1. Remove the air cleaner, linkages and fuel line.

2. Remove the float chamber cover.

3. Drain the fuel and clean out the float chamber.

4. Hold the float chamber cover in a vertical position with the fuel inlet pointing up.

5. With float chamber gasket in position, check the float level from the mating surface of the cover to the bottom of the float.

6. If the float level does not check to 1.6 in. (40mm), adjust the float level by bending the tab on the float.

7. Invert the air horn so that the float is at its lowest point. Check the float for 0.5 in. (12.5mm) of drop. Adjust by bending the float drop tab.

AUTOMATIC CHOKE ADJUSTMENT

504

1. Pull out the manual choke control.

2. Push in the vacuum pull-off rod to obtain the initial choke opening.

3. Measure the opening between the venturi and the choke butterfly at the notch in the lower end of the butterfly.

4. If the gap is not between 0.08 in. (2mm) and 0.12 in. (3mm), adjust by bending the tab on the linkage.

604

1. Start the engine and bring it up to operating temperature.

— **CAUTION** —
Make sure the gearshift is in Neutral or Park and the handbrake is set.

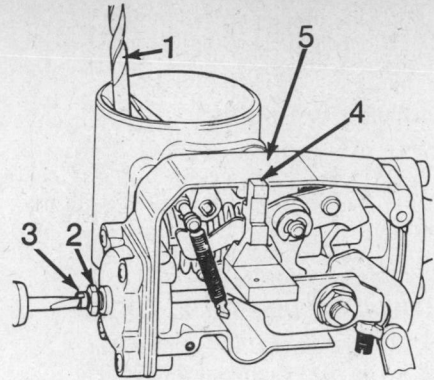

1. 0.295 in. (7 mm) drill or gauge rod
2. Locknut
3. Adjusting screw
4. Choke gauge tool (8.0143)
5. Choke housing

604 choke adjustment

2. Always check the idle speed and mixture for correct setting before adjusting the choke.

3. Remove the air and choke housing cover plate.

4. Install the Peugeot choke gauge tool 8.0143 or equivalent to engage the choke mechanism pivoting roller onto the tool. Rock the tool back and forth slightly until it contacts the choke housing.

5. Increase the engine speed to obtain the total choke opening after start (COAS). The pull-off opening should be 0.295 in. (7.5mm) from the choke plate to the wall of the choke bore.

6. If the choke plate clearance is incorrect, loosen the adjusting locknut and turn the screw to obtain the proper clearance. Tighten the locknut.

7. Remove the gauge tool.

8. Install the choke housing cover and the air cleaner assembly.

Fuel Injection

For all fuel injection system service and repair procedures not detailed below, please refer to ''Fuel Injection'' in the Unit Repair section.

CHECKING FOR AIR LEAKS

K-Jetronic System (XN6 engine)

The system determines fuel requirements by measuring the air flowing through an air flow sensor. Any vacuum leaks in the system will increase airflow without affecting the operation of the airflow sensor and increasing fuel flow. Thus, the engine will run lean, causing hesitation and possible misfire or poor gas mileage.

Check for leaks between hoses and the

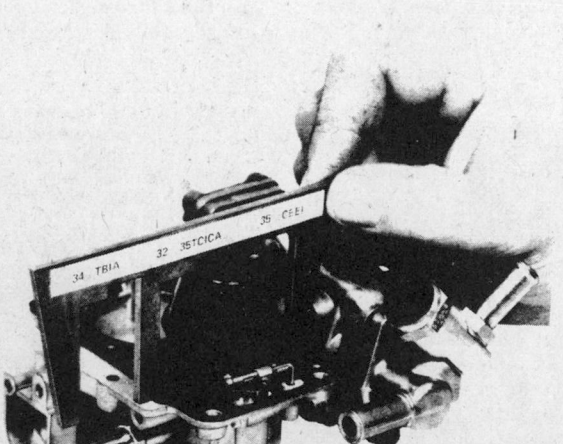

Checking the float level on 34TBIA Solex® carburetors used on 604 models

Checking for leaks in the K-Jetronic fuel injection system (XN6 engine)

parts they connect to as shown in the illustration:

1. rubber duct hose and mixture regulator

Checking for leaks in the K-Jetronic fuel injection system (XN6 engine), continued. See text for number references.

2. throttle flap housing and duct hose
3. cold start injector and common manifold (check that the O-ring is there and in proper position)
4. intake manifold and cylinder head (check bolt torque and, if necessary, gaskets)
5. injectors and their seals
6. duct hoses connecting the common manifold to the intake manifold
7. auxiliary air device hoses
8. throttle flap housing/common manifold connections.

INJECTOR

Removal & Installation

1. Remove the fuel line from the injector.
2. Pull the injector out of the rubber seal.

———————— CAUTION ————————
Do not pull on the fuel line when removing the injector. Pull directly on the injector body.
————————————————————————

3. Always use a new rubber seal when reinstalling an injector.

NOTE: Moisten the new rubber seal with fuel before installing the injector.

4. Press in the injector until it is fully seated.

Testing

1. Use injector test stand, Peugeot

number 8.0141A and adaptors 8.0141B, 8.0141C and 8.0141H or equivalents.
2. Close the test stand valve.
3. Install adaptors 8.0141B and 8.0141C or equivalents on the test stand.
4. Install test adaptor 8.0141H or equivalent on the injector and install the assembly onto the test stand. Do not tighten the assembly.
5. Before tightening the nut on the test stand pipe, activiate the tester several times to bleed the pipe.
6. Tighten the nut on the pipe-to-adaptor fitting.
7. Activate the tester several times until the injector is bled.
8. Open the test stand valve one turn.
9. Pump the test stand lever one stroke every two seconds until the injector sprays.
10. The injector opening pressure should be from 43.6–59.5 psi (3–4.1 bar).
11. If the opening pressure is not within specifications, replace the injector.

NOTE: The injectors can be replaced individually.

12. Loosen the test stand valve and increase the pressure to 7.0 lbs (0.5 bar) below the opening injector pressure. Maintain this pressure for 15 seconds. No leakage should occur. If an injector leaks, replace it.
13. During spray testing, the injector should make a groaning noise and have a spray span of 35°. If an injector is not operating properly, replace it.

FUEL FILTER

Removal & Installation

1. Remove the negative cable from the battery.
2. Remove the fuel filter mounting screw.
3. Remove the fuel filter from its mounting.
4. Loosen the fuel lines to relieve the pressure, then remove the fuel lines. Remove the filter.
5. Install new sealing rings on the filter fittings and torque the inlet and outlet nuts to 24.5 ft.lbs. (32.3 Nm). Torque the outlet banjo bolt to 18.0 ft.lbs. (23.8 Nm.)

Diesel Injection Pump

REMOVAL & INSTALLATION

XD and XDP Engines

1. Disconnect the battery.
2. Disconnect the stop, fast idle and acceleration linkages from the pump.
3. Disconnect the injector return hose and the fuel inlet and outlet couplings.
4. Remove the injector pipe assembly and leave the couplings on the pump and the injector holder.
5. Plug all couplings.
6. Remove the pump rear support from the cylinder head.

7. Remove the injection pump.
8. Installation is the reverse of removal.

XD2 and XD2C Engines

NOTE: Injection pump work is a highly specialized field, and the procedures used in timing this pump are intended only for use with specialized tools.

1. Remove the battery. Disconnect the fuel supply and return lines and control cables at the pump. Cap the open fuel connections. Disconnect the fuel shutoff wire and, on the XD2C the load sensor harness for the EGR system.
2. Disconnect the injector pipes at both ends and remove them. Cap all openings.
3. Remove the two front mounting bolts

Remove the two arrowed bolts to remove the XD2, XD2C injection pump

(arrowed). Support the pump, remove the rear support, and then carefully remove the pump.
4. Now, remove the valve cover and bring the valves of No. 1 (flywheel end) cylinder to the rocking (overlap) position—i.e., exhaust valve closing, intake opening. Turn the engine backward 90 degrees.
5. Compress the No. 4 (front) cylinder's exhaust valve spring very slightly, slide its rocker arm over against spring pressure, and tilt it away from its normal position (away from the valve on the valve side).
6. Rotate the engine back to the rocking position of No. 1 valves.
7. Compress the No. 4 valve spring again and remove the half cones, washer, and valve spring. Install a dial indicator calibrated in mm onto the top of the stud that holds the valve cover (you can use support 8.0117ZZ). The indicator's stem must rest against the valve stem. Read the indicator and use the readings as you rock the engine to bring the engine to TDC (highest point). The valve will be supported by the top of the piston and will move with it.
8. Zero the dial indicator. Then, rotate the engine backwards until the indicator needle has traveled 7mm backwards (it will read 3 on the inner scale).
9. Make sure the dial indicator for the pump, and the hydraulic head (rear connections) are all extremely clean. Remove the inspection plug from the rear of the pump, in the center of the injection line

Installing a dial indicator to read the motion of the exhaust valve

connections. Turn the pump shaft so the double tooth of the pinion is in line with the double groove of the engine pump hub pinion. Coat a new gasket with grease and install it on the flange of the pump.

10. Position the pump onto the engine engaging the pump pinion and engine hub by rotating the engine slightly, if necessary. Install the pump mounting bolts loosely enough so that the pump can be turned.

11. Rotate the pump body away from the engine (full retard). Install the dial indicator 8.0117 F or equivalent to read the pump motion through the inspection plug hole. Extension 8.0117 T, support 8.0117 P and reducer 8.0117 S or equivalent are needed.

12. Turn the engine back and forth and locate the BDC and TDC points on the pump's dial indicator, reflecting total travel of 2.2mm. At BDC there should be some preload on the indicator. Zero the indicator at pump BDC.

13. Bring piston No. 4 to TDC compression stroke. Check the zero point of the engine dial indicator. Then, turn the engine 90 degrees in reverse of normal rotation and recheck the pump dial indicator.

14. Turn the engine in the normal direction of rotation and bring piston No. 4 (XD2 engine) to 1.35mm (13 degrees) BTDC; or (XD2C engine) to 0.97mm (11 degrees) BTDC.

15. Now rotate the pump toward the engine, advancing the timing, until the pump dial indicator shows a pump lift of 0.5mm (see illustration).

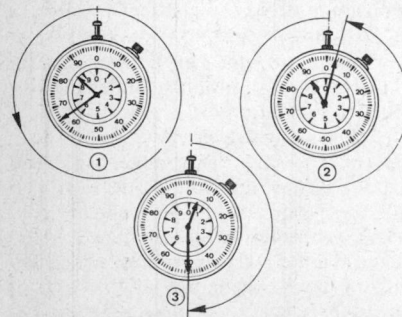

Appearance of the engine dial indicator at injection pump timing point for the XD2 engine (1); and XD2C engine (2). The pump timing indicator should appear as shown in (3).

16. Now tighten both front and rear pump mounting bolts.

17. Rotate the engine two turns in the normal direction of rotation. Turn it backward 90 degrees. Now, rotate it foward very slowly while watching the pump dial indicator. Stop rotating right when the pump indicator shows a lift of 0.5mm.

18. The engine indicator should now show that the No. 4 piston is at 0.97mm plug or minus .03mm BTDC on the XD2C engine, or 1.35mm plus or minus .03mm BTDC for the XD2 engine. If necessary, loosen and rotate the pump slightly, and retighten bolts to change the adjustment. Recheck the adjustment.

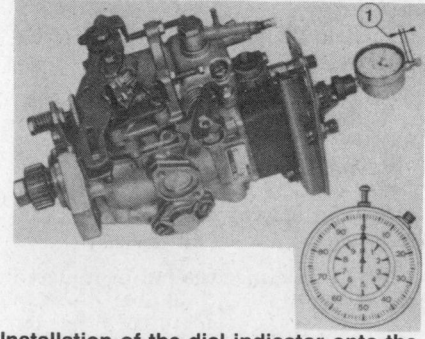

Installation of the dial indicator onto the injection pump of XD2 and XD2C engines. (1) indicates indicator preload (see text).

19. Once the adjustment checks out, remove the dial indicators and supports, and reinstall: the inspection plug for the pump with a new gasket; the springs, washer, and half cones for No. 4 exhaust valve (reposition the rocker arm and adjust the valve lash); replace the valve cover; install the fuel injection pump piping and fuel inlet and outlet hoses; install and adjust the throttle cables; install electrical connector and on engines with EGR the harness; bleed the fuel injection system.

XD2S Engine

1. Follow Steps 1-8 of the procedure above.

2. Position the double tooth on the pump pinion as shown. It should correspond with

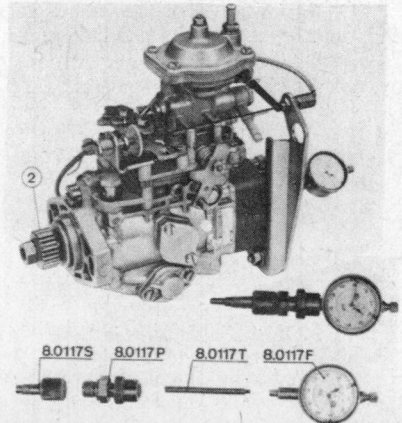

On the XD2S engine, position the double tooth of the pinion as shown before installing the injection pump. Use the dial indicator and fittings numbered or their equivalent.

the position of the corresponding spline in the engine pinion.

3. Remove the pump's timing plug (make sure the area around the plug is clean). Install the dial indicator and accesories specified in the illustration or their equivalent. Install in the order shown.

4. Install a new pump gasket onto the pump flange, using a small amount of grease to hold it in position. Position the pump on the engine and install the mounting bolts just tight enough to retain the pump without preventing it from turning. Rotate the pump away from the engine as far as it will go (full retard).

5. Turn the crankshaft and look for the BDC position of pump rotation (lowest indicator reading). Zero the indicator at BDC position.

6. Now, turn the engine in the normal direction of rotation until it reaches 0.40 mm BTDC as measured on the engine dial indicator. For Canadian models, use 0.8mm BTDC.

7. Turn the pump body toward the engine slowly to get a pump piston (indicator) position of 0.50mm (Canada: 0.30mm). Tighten all pump bolts.

8. Check the timing. First rotate the crankshaft in the direction of rotation to find the zero point of the dial indicator on the engine. Then, turn the crankshaft backwards until the indicator on the engine has turned backward exactly 7 turns. The pump dial indicator should now be back at zero.

9. Turn the engine in the normal direction of rotation to again get the pump piston lift of 0.50mm (USA) or 0.40mm (Canada). At this point, the engine indicator should show the piston at 0.40mm plus or minus 0.02mm (USA) or 0.80mm plus or minus 0.03mm (Canada). If the readings are not correct, readjust pump timing and recheck it.

10. Remove the dial indicators and supports. Torque the pump front mounting bolts to 14.5 ft. lbs.

11. Reinstall the pump timing plug. Reinstall the valve springs, retaining cup, and keepers on the No. 4 exhaust valve.

12. Turn the engine backwards until No. 1 cylinder is again at valve overlap. Reposition the rocker arm, by slightly compressing the valve spring and adjust the valve to .010 in. clearance.

13. Reinstall the valve cover and all injection piping and fuel supply and return lines. Bleed the injection system.

MANUAL TRANSMISSION

REMOVAL & INSTALLATION

504

1. Disconnect the negative battery cable.
2. Drain the gear oil.

3. Remove the ignition coil, the upper radiator mounting and both bolts from the lower radiator mounting on the front crossmember.

NOTE: Draining the cooling system will not be necessary.

4. Remove the starter motor and starter motor dust cover plate.

5. Remove the air cleaner.

6. Remove the nuts securing the exhaust pipe to the exhaust manifold.

7. Remove the nut on the hanger holding the exhaust pipe at the front silencer.

8. Remove the hanger on the exhaust pipe near the rear end of the transmission extension housing.

9. Remove the rear tail pipe hanger.

10. Turn the steering wheel to a clockwise position, so that the front exhaust pipe can be disengaged.

11. Allow the exhaust system to rest on the rear crossmember.

12. Remove the heat dissipation plate.

13. Install the gearbox support tool, Peugeot number 8.0125 or equivalent. Line the slot in the bolt adaptor with the notch in the forward flange of the clutch housing.

14. If the special gearbox support tool is not available, use a jack stand to support the clutch housing.

15. Using an 8mm Allen type socket, remove the three bolts from the differential-to-gearbox connecting tube (at the gearbox). Loosen the fourth bolt with an 8mm shouldered Allen key.

16. Remove the two differential-to-cross-member Allen bolts.

17. Separate the connecting tube and the driveshaft from the gearbox. Install the driveshaft holding plate, Peugeot number 8.0403S or equivalent.

18. Remove the clutch slave cylinder without disconnecting the hydraulic line.

19. Remove the shift lever and shift rods.

20. Remove the back-up light switch leads, gearbox ground strap and speedometer cable.

21. Remove the lower steering shaft pinch bolt, (remove 2 steering knuckle bolts on 505 models).

22. Remove the steering gear housing bolts.

23. Lower the steering gear housing without removing any more bolts.

24. Remove the clutch housing cover plates.

25. Remove the clutch housing support, Peugeot number 8.0125 or the jack stand.

26. Remove the three Allen bolts holding the clutch housing to the engine.

27. Install the engine hoisting brackets on the engine.

28. Using an engine lift or equivalent, lift the engine to rotate it on its rubber mounting blocks in order to remove the gearbox from the engine.

29. Install a block of wood between the radiator and the hoisting bracket to avoid damage to the radiator hoses.

30. Rotate the gearbox a quarter turn counterclockwise and remove the gearbox by pulling it back.

31. Remove the clutch release ball bearing.

32. Installation is the reverse of removal.

33. Torque the bolts as follows:

Item	Ft.lbs. (Nm)
Connecting tube to gearbox	43.5 ft.lbs. (58.8 Nm)
Gearbox drain plug	20.0 ft.lbs. (22.0 Nm)
Starter motor bolts	14.5 ft.lbs. (19.6 Nm)

NOTE: Use grease on the release bearing guide and the engine driveshaft before installing them.

34. Adjust the gear shift linkage and check the clutch pedal for proper operation.

505

1. Remove the gearshift knob and handbrake cover. Remove the front and rear sections of the console, heater duct, and cover underneath. Remove the bolt securing the rear engine mount from the top of the driveshaft tunnel. Disconnect the handbrake cables.

2. Remove the hood. Disconnect the battery. Remove the radiator mounts and fan shroud (hoses need not be disconnected). Protect the rear of the radiator with cardboard. Remove the starter motor and air filter. Remove the air filter hose connecting it with the engine.

3. On the diesel: remove the battery-protector. On all cars: remove the bolts holding the exhaust downpipe; remove the TDC sensor and bracket; remove the clutch

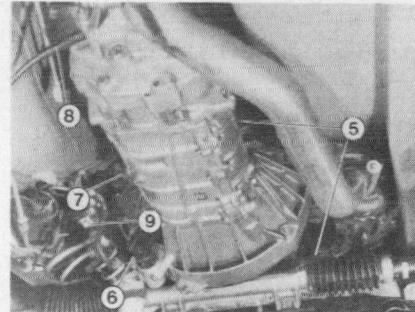

505 transmission removal. Disconnect the TDC sensor (5), clutch slave cylinder (6), reverse light wiring (7), speedometer cable (8). Mark the location of the Septor coupling flange (9).

housing covers. Disconnect and set aside the clutch slave cylinder reverse light switch wiring and speedometer drive cable.

4. Unclip the brake pipes from the body. Without disconnecting anything, remove the handbrake compensator and spring. Remove the screw mounting the three-way connector nearby.

5. Support the transmission securely. Remove the four rear engine mounting bolts. Remove the reinforcement for the front seat.

6. Remove the pivot bolt from either side of the rear anti-roll bar. Disconnect both lower rear shock mounts.

7. Raise the rear of the vehicle as high as possible without dislocating the rear springs, and support it securely.

8. Lower the transmission jack as far as possible without permitting the engine to hit the steering rack. Remove the four mounting screws from the ball cover at the front of the torque tube.

9. Pull the rear axle back and support the torque tube on a support that will prevent stressing either the Panhard rod or brake lines. Pull off the rear engine mount.

10. The crossmember must now be lowered 50mm (just under two inches). Peugeot supplies special bolts 8.1511C, or you may be able to purchase an equivalent elsewhere. Remove two of the original bolts and install the long bolts, as shown. Remove the two other original bolts. Now,

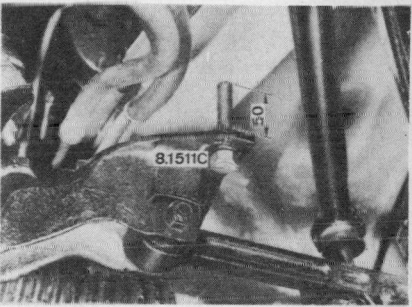

Lowering the 505 crossmember with special bolts

lower the crossmember the required distance by unscrewing the two bolts. Do not allow the power steering pump pulley to hit the anti-roll bar at the front. Support the engine securely in this position.

11. Remove the three screws securing the clutch housing with a large hex head wrench. Separate the gearbox from the engine and remove it.

12. Install the gearbox in reverse order, noting the following points:

a. Coat the input shaft splines with MOLYKOTE® 321 or equivalent. Make sure the thrust bearing is in the proper position.

b. Use new lockwashers, washers, and NYLSTOP nuts.

c. Before lowering the body, make sure both rear springs are properly located in support cups at top and bottom.

d. Lubricate the unthreaded portion of both lower shock mounting bolts. The shocks and rear axle must be separate by washers to ensure the body of the shock and rear axle will not contact each other. Torque the bolts to 41.5 ft. lbs.

e. Observe the following torque figures:

Rear antiroll bar bolts and exhaust pipe bolts—25.5 ft. lbs.
Steering coupling bolts—12.7 ft. lbs.
Clutch housing screws—39.8 ft. lbs.
Torque tube to ball cover on the transmission—30.8 ft. lbs.

Rear engine crossmember-to-body bolts—52.5 ft. lbs. and rear engine upper mounting bolts—72.5

f. Make sure to resecure all brake pipes and lines and adjust the handbrake and compensator. Refill the gearbox with the required lubricant.

604

On the 604 models, the engine and transmission must be removed as a unit.

1. Drain the gearbox oil.
2. Remove the hood, the air mixer housing and the air filter.
3. Drain the cooling system.
4. Remove the radiator support struts and the battery.
5. Disconnect the radiator hoses at the radiator.
6. Remove the radiator and the fan casing.
7. Remove the ground cable at the engine, the temperature sending unit, the power brake booster vacuum hose and the fuel pump hoses.
8. Remove the carburetor controls, primary coil leads and high tension coil-to-distributor wire.
9. Remove and plug the heater hoses.
10. Remove the starter and alternator harness connection.
11. Remove the exhaust pipe-to-manifold flange bolts and separate the pipe from the manifold.
12. Remove the engine mounting bolts.
13. Remove the exhaust mounting brackets at the silencers, the center exhaust mounting and the heat baffle.
14. Remove the clutch housing lower cover plate.
15. Remove the starter harness retaining clip.
16. Remove the power steering pump and the power steering belt.
17. Raise the engine with engine lift tool Peugeot number 8.0135Z or equivalent, until the gearbox contacts the floor tunnel. Lower the engine until the gearbox clears the tunnel by 0.4 in. (10.16mm).
18. Push back the front seats and remove the front seat securing bolts.
19. Install studs Peugeot number 8.1511B or equivalent, under the vehicle in the seat bolts holes.
20. Install flat washers and nuts on the studs on the inside of the vehicle. Tighten the nuts.
21. Install the driveshaft support tool Peugeot number 8.1511A or equivalent and adjust the support tool to contact the driveshaft tube.
22. Remove the bolt from the steering shaft pinch clamp at the flexible coupling flange.
23. Remove the two rear main crossmember bolts and replace them with longer bolts, Peugeot number 8.1511C or equivalent.
24. Remove the two front crossmember bolts and lower the longer bolts so that the crossmember drops 1.2 in. (30.5mm).

25. Remove the clutch cylinder snap-ring and push the cylinder back 0.12 in. (3mm).
26. Remove the clutch cylinder bolts and wire the cylinder to the side of the vehicle.
27. Remove the back-up light switch leads, the gearshift control and the speedometer drive fitting.
28. Remove the driveshaft tube-to-gearbox bolts.
29. Separate the driveshaft and driveshaft tube from the gearbox and install the driveshaft retaining plate Peugeot number 8.0403SZ or equivalent on the driveshaft.
30. Remove the engine and gearbox together by tilting them up in the front and raising the assembly out of the vehicle.

───────── CAUTION ─────────
Do not damage the power steering hoses.

31. Lower the assembly onto an engine stand.
32. Remove the clutch housing cover plate, the starter casing and the clutch housing-to-engine bolts.
33. Separate the gearbox from the engine.
34. Installation is the reverse of removal.
35. Follow these torque sepcifications:

Item	ft. lbs. (Nm)
Clutch housing to engine	12.6 (17.1)
Driveshaft tube to gearbox	39.6 (53.9)
Steering shaft pinch-clamp	12.8 (17.1)

NOTE: The clearance between the steering wheel and the steering column casing should be 0.08 in. (2mm).

LINKAGE ADJUSTMENT

1. To adjust the linkage, first raise the front of the car and support it with safety stands.
2. Remove the return spring and the two control links. Clean the plastic ball joint sockets and make sure they have not been damaged during dismantling. Replace any defective parts and grease the ball joints prior to installation.
3. Check and adjust the socket center-to-socket center distances of the two link rods before refitting. Their lengths are 287 and 89mm respectively.
4. Place the bottom selector lever in the Neutral position. Fit the lower link rod on its gear shifter and bottom lever socket balls, positioning the ball sockets for fit. Then tighten the locknut on the link rod shaft.
5. Make sure that the gear selector lever is in Neutral and connect the fixed ball socket on the selector link to the selector jack lever.
6. Push the link upward as far as possible and check the alignment of the ball joint with the lever on the gearbox.
7. Correctly position the link bottom

ball joint socket on the gear selector lever and tighten the locknut on the link shaft.

8. Install the return spring.

OVERHAUL

For all manual transmission overhaul procedures, please refer to "Manual Transmission Overhaul" in the Unit Repair section.

CLUTCH

REMOVAL & INSTALLATION

504 and 505

1. Remove the transmission.
2. Matchmark the clutch assembly in relation to the flywheel, if the unit is to be reused.
3. Remove the clutch assembly retaining bolts and separate the assembly from the flywheel.
4. Check the bearing surface of the disc on the flywheel. If needed, remove the flywheel and true-up the surface on a lathe.

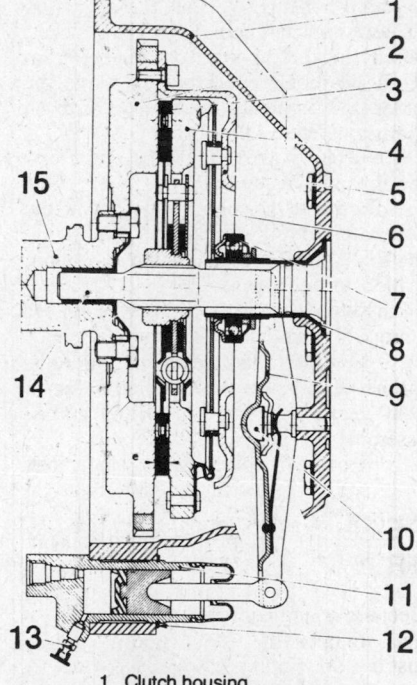

1. Clutch housing
2. Flywheel
3. Clutch disc
4. Clutch pressure plate
5. Cover
6. Diaphragm
7. Guided thrust bearing
8. Bushing
9. Clutch fork
10. Pivot
11. Release cylinder
12. Release cylinder housing
13. Bleed screw
14. Driveshaft
15. Crankshaft

Cross section of the 504 clutch assembly

Always take the same cut from the disc surface and the bolt attaching surface in order to maintain the same clutch diaphragm tension and height.

5. Place the clutch disc correctly with the flexible hub facing the gearbox. Center the disc on the flywheel using a centering tool.

6. Align the matchmarks (on a reinstalled unit), and install the clutch assembly to the flywheel with the attaching bolts. Torque the bolts to 10 ft. lbs. (15 Nm).

7. Reinstall the transmission and complete the assembly.

604

1. Remove the engine and transmission as a unit before separating the transmission.
2. Remove the clutch housing cover plate.
3. Remove the two starter-to-clutch housing bolts. Remove the four clutch housing-to-engine bolts.
4. Matchmark the clutch assembly in relation to the flywheel, (if the unit is to be re-used).
5. Remove the clutch assembly retaining bolts and separate the assembly from the flywheel.
6. Check the bearing surface of the disc on the flywheel. If needed, remove the flywheel and true up the surface on a lathe. Always take the same cut from the disc surface and the bolt attaching surface in order to maintain the same clutch diaphragm tension and height.
7. Place the clutch disc correctly with the flexible hub facing the gearbox. Center the disc on the flywheel using a centering tool.
8. Align the matchmarks (on a reinstalled unit), and install the clutch assembly to the flywheel with the attaching bolts. Torque the bolts to 15 ft. lbs. (20 Nm).
9. Install the gearbox on the engine and torque the bolts to 12 ft. lbs. (17 Nm).
10. Install the engine and transmission assembly into the vehicle.

PEDAL ADJUSTMENT AND FREE-PLAY

Because of the hydraulic operation of Peugeot clutches, the clutch is largely self-adjusting. Should excessive play or slackness become evident at the clutch pedal, then fluid is somehow draining out of the clutch hydraulic system and must be investigated and corrected at once.

A minimal adjustment can be made on the linkage by adjusting the screw locknut on the slave cylinder pushrod. The free travel at the clutch fork stop should be 0.10 in. (2mm). This should correspond to a free pedal travel of 1.2–1.4 in. If you are unable to obtain the correct free travel after adjusting the screw to the above specifications, check, and if necessary, bleed the hydraulic system.

Clutch Slave Cylinder

REMOVAL & INSTALLATION

1. Remove and plug the hydraulic line.
2. Remove the cylinder.
3. Install the cylinder and the hydraulic line.
4. Fill the clutch master cylinder reservoir and bleed the system.

BLEED THE SYSTEM

Peugeot recommends using a pressure bleed tank to bleed the clutch slave cylinder. However, if a pressure tank is not available, the system can be bled manually by depressing the clutch and opening the bleeder screw momentarily, to allow air to escape.

1. Attach a pressure bleeding tank to the bleed screw on the slave cylinder.
2. Adjust the pressure to approximately 25 psi.
3. Open the bleed screw one full turn.
4. Check the rise of fluid in the reservoir.
5. Stop the bleeding when the level in the reservoir is correct.
6. Check the hydraulic control operation.

AUTOMATIC TRANSMISSION

REMOVAL & INSTALLATION

504 and 505

1. Remove the exhaust hanger at the intermediate exhaust pipe, the middle exhaust hanger and the exhaust hanger near the front end of the differential.
2. Remove the two differential side mounting bolts.
3. Place the driveshaft connecting tube on the rear crossmember.
4. Remove the two steering shaft flange bolts on 505 models.
   a. Conventional Steering Gearbox—Remove the two steering box bolts and lower the steering gearbox without disconnecting the steering links.
   b. Power Steering Gearbox—Replace the rear bolts on the front crossmember with Peugeot tool number 8.1511C or equivalent and remove the two forward crossmember bolts. Lower the crossmember 2.0 in. (50.8mm) by turning the special tool bolts.
5. Remove the steering shaft pinch bolt on 504 models and the steering gear housing bolts. Lower the steering, without disconnecting the steering linkage.
6. Drain the transmission fluid.
7. Remove the oil cooler lines at the transmission and plug them.
8. Remove the two starter-to-torque converter housing bolts.
9. Remove the transmission fill tube.

10. Remove the passenger side converter housing cover plate.
11. Remove the sensor plate cover and the sensor from the front driver's side of the transmission converter housing on 505 models, if so equipped.

NOTE: Take care not to alter the adjustment of the sensor.

12. Remove the converter-to-flexplate bolts and lock the ring gear with Peugeot tool number 8.0144B, 8.0110J or equivalents.
13. Secure the torque converter with Peugeot tool number 8.0135A or equivalent.
14. Place a transmission jack under the transmission and raise the jack to support the weight of the transmission.
15. Remove the four driveshaft connecting tube-to-extension housing bolts. Separate the connecting tube and driveshaft from the extension housing.
16. Install Peugeot tool 8.0403SZ or equivalent, driveshaft retaining plate on the driveshaft.
17. Remove the gearshift linkage, transmission wiring harness and speedometer drive fitting.
18. Drop the transmission as far down as it will go by lowering the transmission jack. Remove the converter/flexplate bolts.
19. Install engine lifting bracket, Peugeot number 8.0102X or equivalent.
20. Move the engine as far as it will go with the engine mounts still in place, to clear the transmission under the floor tunnel.
21. Remove the torque converter housing-to-engine bolts and separate the converter from the flexplate.
22. Lower the transmission on the transmission jack.
23. Installation is the reverse of removal.
24. Use the following torque specifications:

Item	ft. lbs. (Nm)
Starter	18.0 (24.5)
Torque converter	39.6 (53.9)
Flywheel	21.6 (29.4)
Driveshaft tube	39.6 (53.9)
505 steering coupling	12.6 (17.1)
504 steering pinch bolt	12.6 (17.1)

604

1. Remove the hood.
2. Remove the air filter and assembly.
3. Drain the cooling system.
4. Remove the radiator hoses and upper radiator struts.
5. Remove the battery, the fan motor wires and the transmission cooler lines.
6. Remove the radiator and the fan casing.
7. Remove the ground cable at the engine and the temperature sending unit.
8. Remove the brake booster vacuum hose and the fuel pump lines.

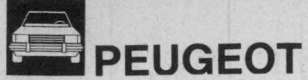
9. Remove the carburetor controls and the primary coil leads. Remove the high tension coil wire.

10. Remove the heater hoses and plug the ends.

11. Remove the starter and alternator harness connectors.

12. Remove the exhaust pipe-to-exhaust manifold bolts and the engine mounting bolts.

13. Remove the front and center exhaust hangers.

14. Remove the heat baffle.

15. Remove the lower torque converter housing cover plate.

16. Remove the starter harness retainer clip.

17. Remove the power assisted steering pump and power steering belt.

18. Secure the power steering pump assembly to the fender well.

19. Lift the engine with a hoist until the transmission makes contact with the tunnel, then lower it approximately 0.4 in. (10.16 mm).

20. Push back the front seats and remove the seat securing bolts.

21. Raise the vehicle. Install threaded rods, Peugeot number 8.1511B or equivalent, into the seat bolts holes.

22. Lower the vehicle. Install flat washers and nuts on the ends of the threaded rods and tighten them.

23. Install the driveshaft support tool, Peugeot number 8.1511 or equivalent, onto the threaded rods. Adjust the tool to support the driveshaft tube.

24. Remove the bolt from the pinch clamp on the steering shaft.

25. Remove the two rear main crossmember bolts and install tool, Peugeot number 8.1511C or equivalent. Remove the two front main crossmember bolts. Lower the main crossmember 1.2 in. (30.5mm), by turning the special bolts.

26. Remove the cooler lines and the electrical connector at the transmission.

27. Remove the driveshaft tube-to-extension housing bolts.

28. Separate the driveshaft and driveshaft tube from the extension housing.

29. Install the driveshaft retaining plate tool, Peugeot number 8.0403SZ or equivalent, onto the driveshaft.

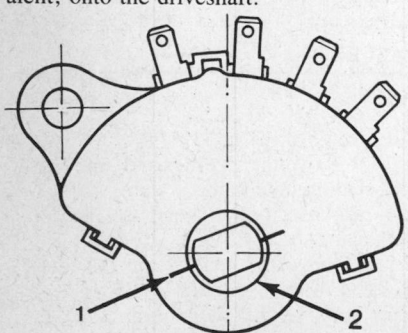

1. Mark on the switch body
2. Pivot housing

Adjusting alignment marks on the GM transmission neutral safety switch

30. Move the back of the engine/transmission assembly out of the vehicle.

── **CAUTION** ──
Do not damage the power steering hoses or the transmission cooler lines.

31. Separate the transmission from the engine. Leave the converter with the transmission. Installation is the reverse of removal.

32. Use the following torque specifications during reassembly and installation.

Item	ft. lbs. (Nm)
Driveshaft tube	43.5 (58.8)
Starter motor	14.5 (19.6)
Converter to ring gear	34.7 (46.6)
Converter housing	28.8 (39.2)
Steering flange	10.8 (14.9)

33. Adjust the kickdown cable.

34. Fill the transmission with fluid.

NEUTRAL SAFETY SWITCH ADJUSTMENTS

ZF Transmissions

Two types of neutral start switches are used on the ZF automatic transmissions.

TYPE 1

The Type 1 switch is attached to the side of the transmission case and is operated by a connecting rod attached to the transmission manual lever. The adjustment of the switch must be checked after the manual linkage has been adjusted.

1. Locate the selector lever in the Neutral position.

2. Loosen the switch retaining screw and the switch lever nut. Adjust the switch so that the engine will start only in the Neutral or Park positions.

3. Tighten the switch retaining screw and the lever nut.

TYPE 2

The Type 2 switch is located with the selector lever assembly and cannot be adjusted. To replace the switch assembly, the console assembly must be removed. Remove the shift lever assembly from the floor. Remove the switch retaining screw and install the new switch. The switch pins must be engaged in the holes in the shift gate.

GM Transmission

1. Place the gear shift selector lever in Neutral.

2. Loosen the retaining nuts on the switch retaining bracket.

3. Align the mark on the switch body with the mark on the pivot housing.

4. Tighten the retaining nuts.

5. Check for starting in Neutral and Park. Check for not starting in Reverse, 3, 2, and 1. In the reverse position, the back-up lights should operate.

SHIFT LINKAGE ADJUSTMENT

1. Disconnect the rod at the transmission lever.

2. Set the gear shift selector lever in the Neutral position.

3. Set the transmission lever in Neutral. The position is provided by the ball lock inside the transmission.

4. If the rod will not fit into the transmission lever without moving the lever, ad-

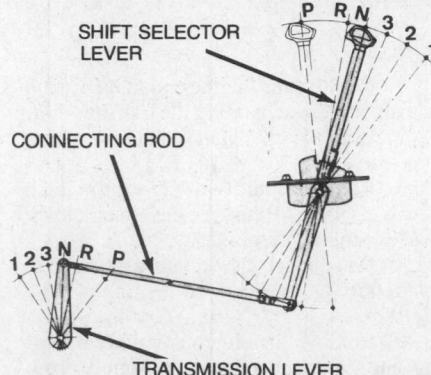

SHIFT SELECTOR LEVER

CONNECTING ROD

TRANSMISSION LEVER

Adjusting the shift linkage on automatic transmissions for all models

just the rod length so that it will fit into the transmission lever.

5. Install the rod on the transmission lever.

BAND ADJUSTMENT

GM Transmission Only

The GM transmissions have no external band adjustment. The servo apply pins are available in different lengths. Selecting the proper length pin is equivalent to adjusting the bands. This can only be done with the transmission disassembled.

DRIVE AXLES

Driveshaft

REMOVAL & INSTALLATION

504 and 505

1. Remove the exhaust system from the exhaust manifold and remove all exhaust hangers. Let the system rest on the front and rear crossmembers.

2. Remove the heat dissipation plate.

3. Remove the two differential bolts. Let the rear part of the driveshaft tube rest on the rear crossmember.

4. Place a jack under the left side crossmember support.

5. Remove the rear seat cushion. Loosen all three left side crossmember nuts. Raise the tab lock and remove the plastic plug from the guide hole. Screw the threaded end of the guide rod, Peugeot No. 8.0906K1

or equivalent, through the guide hole and into the crossmember. Insert a pin into the guide rod.

6. Remove the crossmember securing nuts.

7. Lower the jack until the pin rests on the floor. Repeat these operations on the right hand crossmember support.

8. Remove the driveshaft tube from the differential.

9. Move the differential back and support it on a wooden block.

10. Remove the small spring from the end of the driveshaft.

NOTE: If the vehicle is to be moved from one work area to another, secure the differential to the rear crossmember with two Peugeot No. 204 cylinder head bolts or equivalent.

11. Remove the driveshaft tube at the transmission.

12. Install driveshaft holding plate, Peugeot tool number 8.0403S or equivalent.

13. Lower the exhaust pipe at the front end.

14. Angle the driveshaft and driveshaft tube and remove them toward the front of the vehicle.

15. Installation is the reverse of removal.

16. Use the following torque specifications:

Item	ft. lbs. (Nm)
Driveshaft tube bolts	43.5 (58.8)
Differential attaching bolts	27.0 (36.8)

17. Install the rear seat cushion and lubricate the driveshaft center bearing.

604

1. Remove the console shifter trim.

2. Pull back the bellows and remove the two shift lever bolts.

3. Remove the heat baffle and the center exhaust pipe hanger.

4. From under the vehicle, remove the front gearshift lever nut.

5. Using a jack stand or other safe method, take the weight off the extension housing of the transmission.

6. Remove the four driveshaft tube-to-extension housing bolts.

7. Remove the four driveshaft tube-to-differential bolts.

8. Remove the driveshaft and driveshaft tube toward the rear of the vehicle.

9. Install the driveshaft and tube onto the differential and transmission. Torque the bolts to 43.2 ft. lbs. (58.8 Nm).

10. Install the front nut on the shift lever, from under the vehicle.

11. Set the exhaust baffles over the muffler.

12. Install the exhaust pipe hangers on the exhaust pipe.

13. Bolt on the heat baffles.

14. Install the two gear shift lever bolts, the bellows and the trim.

Axleshafts

REMOVAL & INSTALLATION

504 and 604

1. Raise the rear of the vehicle and place jack stands under the suspension arms.

2. Remove the wheel and install holding tool, Peugeot number 8.0521 A or equivalent, on the hub.

3. Loosen the hub nut without removing it and remove the holding tool.

4. Remove the brake thrust spring, pad returning fork and brake pads.

5. Loosen the brake line retaining clamp on the rear control arm.

6. Remove the caliper and hang it on the body without distorting the brake line.

7. Remove the hub-to-disc retaining screw. Mark the location of the retaining screw on the disc.

8. Remove the disc.

9. Remove the bolts holding the spindle hub to the suspension arm.

10. Install special bolts, Peugeot Nos. 8.0521 B1 and B2 or equivalents, into the back of the hub assembly. Install the thrust plate, Peugeot number 8.0521 B3 or equivalent onto the hub.

11. To remove the hub assembly, alternately tighten bolts B1 and B2 against plate B3.

12. Remove the disc brake backing plate, if equipped.

13. Remove the hub nut washer.

14. Remove the final driveshaft from the hub knuckle. Use an arbor press, if necessary.

15. Installation is the reverse of removal.

—— **CAUTION** ——
Use a new final driveshaft nut on every re-installation. Stake the new nut to hold it.

16. Use the following torque specifications:

Brake pad holding fork	31.0 (40.9 Nm)
Final driveshaft nut	181.0 (245 Nm)
Wheel lug nuts	43.5 (58.8 Nm)

NOTE: The station wagon has axle housings attached to the differential and the axle shafts are enclosed.

505

1. Raise the car and support it securely under the rear suspension arm. Unclip the brake hose at the arm.

2. Remove the mounts which secure the hose to the suspension arm.

3. You'll need Peugeot special tool 8.0521 AZ or equivalent, or you'll need to fabricate a tool that will securely keep the axle shaft from turning while you remove the hub nut. Install the tool, install the lug nuts, and then remove the hub nut.

4. Remove the rear brake caliper (see the Brake section). Remove the four bolts that attach the stub axle to the rear suspension arm.

5. Remove the hub-stub axle-half shaft assembly.

Remove the nut (1) and washer (2) and press out the half shaft

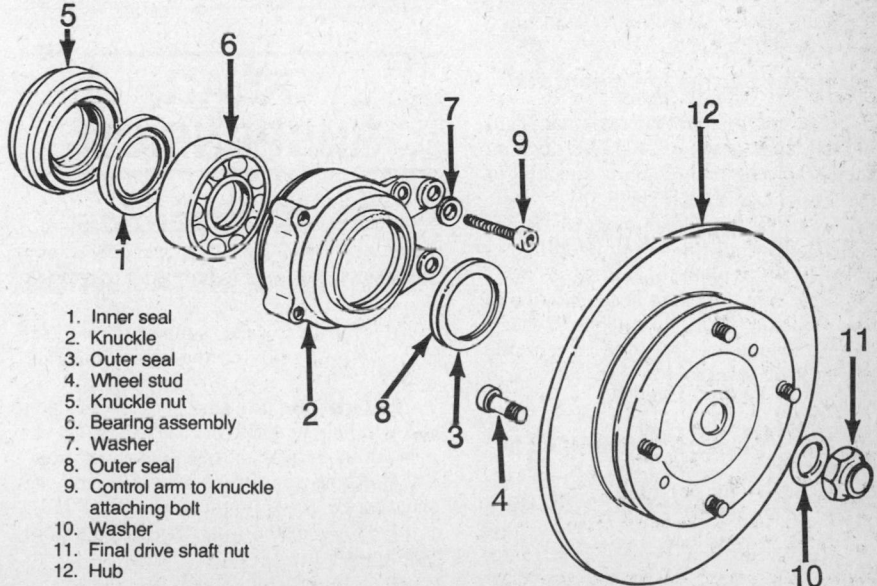

1. Inner seal
2. Knuckle
3. Outer seal
4. Wheel stud
5. Knuckle nut
6. Bearing assembly
7. Washer
8. Outer seal
9. Control arm to knuckle attaching bolt
10. Washer
11. Final drive shaft nut
12. Hub

Exploded view of rear wheel bearing assembly—typical

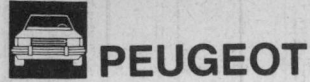

NOTE: Some axles are of a type that does not require the press to remove the disc.

6. Remove the nut and washer, and place the assembly in a large press. Press the half shaft out of the disc.

7. Before reinstalling, coat the splines at the hub end with Molykote® 321 or the equivalent lubricant spray. Grease the splines at the differential end. Fill the space between the lips on seals at either end with grease (see the illustration).

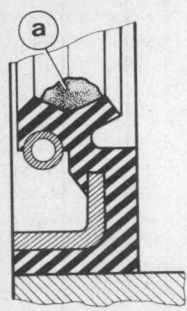

Fill the lips of the seals at either end of the stub axle with grease as shown

8. Put the stub axle in a vise. Start the disc onto the axle. Install the spacing washer and a nut with a height of 0.767 in. (19.5mm). Install the special tool which keeps the disc from turning and lug nuts. Now, torque the hub nut to 44 ft. lbs. Now, support the bottom of the nut against a solid surface and use a center punch to lock it in place, as shown.

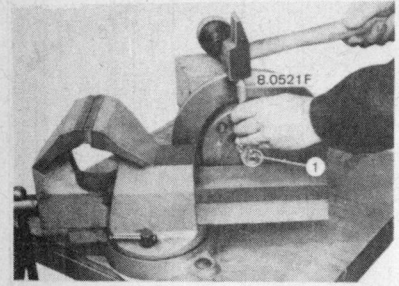

Locking the hub nut to the stub axle

9. Reinstall the hub-stub axle-half shaft assembly and new BLOCFOR locking washers. Torque the four bolts attaching it to the suspension arm to 36 ft. lbs.

10. Reinstall the caliper (refer to the Brake section) and install the mounting bolts behind the backing plate to 31 ft. lbs.

11. Resecure the brake hose and pipe to the suspension arm. Install the wheel, torquing lug nuts to 44 ft. lbs. Check the differential oil level and refill if necessary.

Rear Wheel Bearings

REMOVAL & INSTALLATION

1. Remove the final drive axleshaft from the vehicle.

2. Separate the hub and knuckle assem-

1. Rear axle knuckle assembly
2. Rear axle retaining washer
3. Rear axle retaining nut

Rear axle hub assembly

bly from the final drive axleshaft. Use an arbor press if necessary.

3. Clamp the hub assembly in a soft jawed vise.

4. Remove the hub assembly nut.

5. Press the hub from the knuckle assembly.

6. Press out the bearing assembly from the knuckle.

7. Turn the knuckle over in the vise and remove the outer oil seal.

8. Install a new outer oil seal.

9. Install a new inner oil seal.

10. Press in a new bearing assembly.

11. Install the knuckle nut and torque it to 181 ft. lbs. (245 Nm).

12. Install the hub onto the knuckle assembly.

13. Install the final drive axleshaft into the hub and knuckle assembly.

14. Complete the installation on the vehicle.

15. Torque the final drive axleshaft nut to 181 ft. lbs. (245 Nm).

─── **CAUTION** ───

Use a new final drive axleshaft nut on every reinstallation. Stake the new nut to hold it.

REAR SUSPENSION

Shock Absorbers

REMOVAL & INSTALLATION

1. If a lift is used, support the control arms before removing the shock absorber bolts.

2. Open the trunk lid and use an open end wrench to hold the shock while removing the shock nut from the shock bolt.

3. Remove the rubber washer and the sheet metal cup from the upper shock bolt.

4. Remove the lower shock bolt from the control arm.

5. Remove the shock by pulling it through the hole in the control arm.

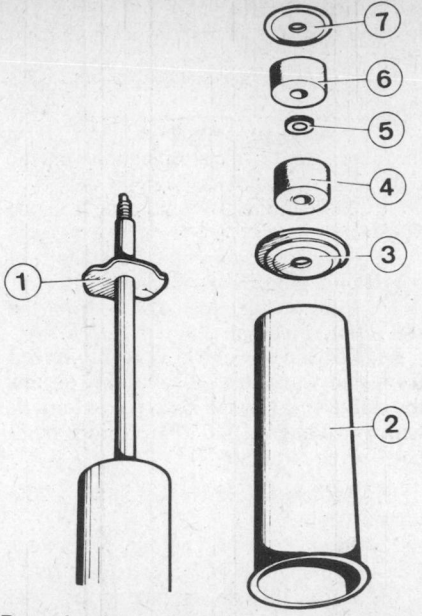

Rear shocks on the 505 include the thrust cup (1), protective cover (2), locating cup (3), lower rubber bush (4), nylon spacer (5), upper rubber bush (6), and upper steel cup (7)

6. Always replace the rubber washer, upper sheet metal cup and upper self locking nut, when the shock is installed.

7. Fully extend the shock absorber rod and install the thrust cup, rod protector, centering cup, rubber washer and nylon spacer.

8. Use new lock washers and install the lower shock bolt on the control arm. Torque it to 33 ft. lbs.

9. Place the new rubber washer and metal cup on the shock and secure it with a new locknut. Torque the nut to 9 ft. lbs.

Rear Control Arm and Coil Springs

REMOVAL & INSTALLATION

1. Remove the final driveshafts from both sides.

2. Support the rear control arms and remove the rear shocks.

3. Remove the stabilizer bar links at the control arms.

4. Slowly lower the rear control arms to release the tension on the coil springs. Remove the coil springs.

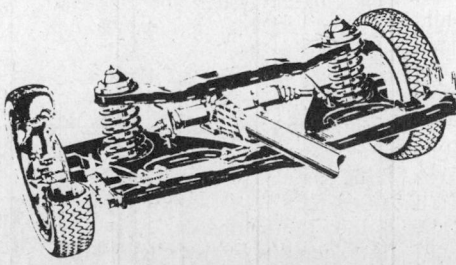

504 rear suspension

5. Remove the four control arm-to-crossmember bolts and lower the control arms.

6. Installation is the reverse of removal.

FRONT SUSPENSION

MacPherson Strut

For all spring and shock absorber removal and installation procedures and any other strut overhaul procedures, please refer to "Strut Overhaul" in the Unit Repair section.

REMOVAL & INSTALLATION

504 and 604

1. Raise the vehicle and support both sides of the front crossmember.

2. Remove the front wheel.

3. Remove the brake caliper and suspend it from the frame.

4. Remove the steering rod end from the knuckle.

5. Remove the connecting link from the rear bar of the triangular suspension arm.

6. Remove the strut from the knuckle.

7. Remove the locking nut securing the front arm to the rear arm.

8. Place a jack under the wheel hub.

9. Remove the three bolts securing the upper spring holder to the inner fender well.

10. Lower the jack and remove the strut assembly from the vehicle.

505

1. Support the front of the vehicle on axle stands. Remove the wheels.

2. Remove and support the brake caliper without disconnecting the hose.

3. Remove the ball joint nut and press the ball joint out of the track rod.

4. Remove the hinge pin from the inner portion of the rear suspension arm. Tap it to free the splined section. Remove the anti-roll bar hinge bolt from the rear suspension arm. Remove the nut that secures the outer end of the rear arm to the front arm. Pull the rear arm free at both ends.

5. Support the weight of the strut assembly from underneath. Remove the three bolts securing the upper end of the strut to the body from the engine compartment.

6. Hold the upper portion of the strut while lowering the jack. Free the unit and remove it.

7. To reinstall the strut, position the safety cup at the top so it is parallel with the centerline of the vehicle. Using a jack, position the strut assembly in the vehicle. Install the ground lead onto the outer bolt, and install all three bolts, torquing to 8 ft. lbs.

8. Make sure that the thrust washer is installed onto the front suspension arm with

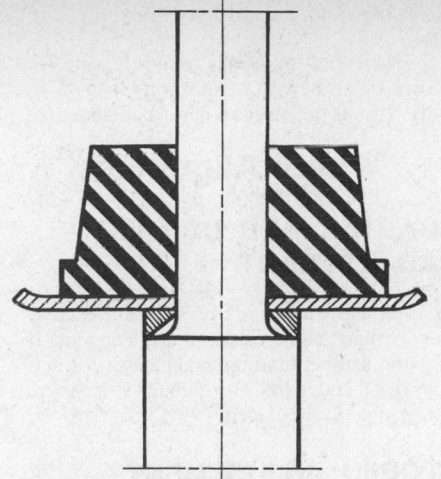

Install the thrust washer, cup, and first rubber cone to the front suspension arm as shown

the chamfer towards the bar, and that the cup and first rubber cone are installed as shown.

9. Install the front arm into the rear arm. Then install the second rubber cone, cup, and a new Nylstop nut (loosely).

10. Reconnect the anti-roll bar link, using a new Nylstop nut.

11. Install the rear arm hinge pin, with its head toward the rear of the car, until it is flush with the splines. Loosely install a new Nylstop nut.

12. Insert the ball joint stud into the track rod. Install a new skirted nut and torque to 25 ft. lbs.

13. Clean all brake caliper parts and the disc. Install the caliper, tightening the bolts to 64 ft. lbs. on the Teves caliper. Fold over the lockwasher. On the DBA caliper, install the bolts without washers and coated with Loctite® or equivalent and torque to 94 ft. lbs.

14. Install the front wheel and torque the lugs. Lower the vehicle onto its wheels. Roll it back and forth slightly.

15. Drive in the rear suspension arm hinge pin with a drift. Torque all of the following to 33 ft. lbs.:

• the hinge pin nut on the crossmember

• the anti-roll bar link securing nut on the rear suspension arm

• the nut attaching the front arm to the rear arm.

Ball Joint

INSPECTION

Check ball joint play as follows:

a. Raise the front of the car and support it with safety stands.

b. Clamp a dial indicator onto the lower control arm and place the indicator tip on the knuckle, near the ball joint.

c. Place a pry bar between the lower control arm and the knuckle. Replace the ball joint if the play exceeds 0.1 in. vertical motion or 0.25 in. horizontal motion.

REMOVAL & INSTALLATION

504, 604

1. Raise the front of the car and support with safety stands.

2. Unlock the lower ball joint locknut using special socket No. 8.0906 C or D.

3. Remove the ball joint retaining nut with the castled socket No. 8.0906 F.

4. Use the extractor No. 8.0906 B to remove the arm from the steering knuckle. Remove the extractor, the rubber dust cover and its spring clip, the lower cup, ball joint, and upper cup.

5. Before reassembling, the following parts must be replaced:

a. Rubber dust cover;
b. Cover spring clip;
c. Upper ball joint cup;
d. Ball joint head (if necessary);
e. Lower cup;
f. Locknut (with grease nipple).

6. Grease the ball joint housing and then place the arm on the steering knuckle ball joint cone.

7. Position the ball head and tighten the securing nut to 33 ft. lbs. using socket No. 8.0906 F.

8. Lock the securing nut using drift No. 8.0906 P.

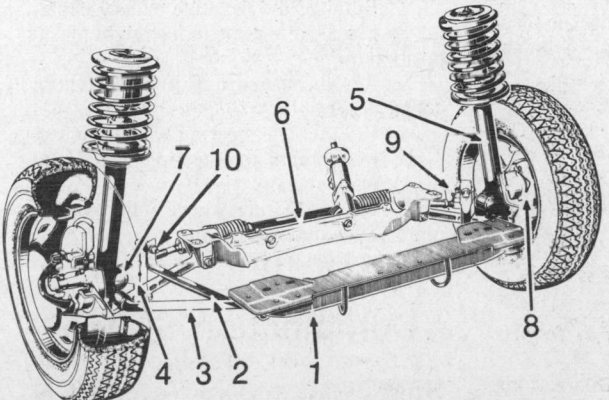

1. Front crossmember
2. Stabilizer bar
3. A-frame front arm
4. A-frame rear arm
5. Strut
6. Main crossmember
7. Knuckle
8. Brake caliper
9. Steering rod end (tie rod)
10. Connecting link

504 and 505 front suspension

9. Position the lower cup (10mm thick) on the ball head and fit a *new* locknut. Tighten the locknut using socket No. 8.0906 C or D to 5.5 ft. lbs. Move the arm and retighten the nut to the specified torque until the two half cups are correctly positioned.

10. Lock the nut using a standard flat pointed punch into both grooves provided on the ball joint housing.

11. Reinstall the wheel and lower the car. Work on the front of the car to settle it to its correct road height position.

505

1. Remove the front strut as described above. Remove its attaching nut and, with a puller, remove the track control arm from the strut.

2. Raise up and break the two locking tangs on the lockwasher.

Removing the ball joint—505. Raise and break the two locking tangs (1).

3. You'll need a tool (Peugeot No. 8.0616 F or equivalent) that will go over the ballstud and engage with the ball joint, as shown. Install the tool, engage it with the ball joint, and install the knurled nut or similar to hold it in place. The strut will have to be mounted in a vise in a manner that will prevent direct pressure on the strut body, which contains hydraulic parts and can be easily distorted. Note the band type clamp in the illustration. Use a wrench on the flats of the special tool and unscrew the housing.

4. Lubricate the threads of a new ball joint housing where they screw into the strut. Install a new lockwasher. Make sure the lockwasher is in position so that its tangs will bend over to lock the assembly in place the way it was. Engage the tool with the

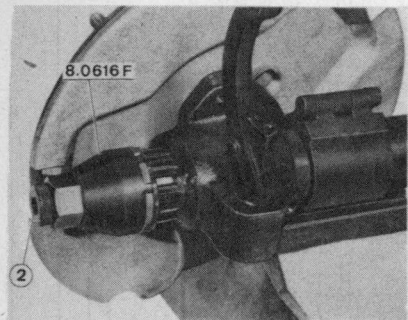

The special tool is held onto the ballstud with a knurled nut (2)

housing and tighten the assembly to 123 ft. lbs.

5. Install the track control arm followed by a new nut and torque it to 33 ft. lbs. Install the strut as described above.

Wheel Alignment

CASTER AND CAMBER ADJUSTMENT

Caster and camber are preset at the factory and cannot be adjusted on any Peugeot. If caster, camber or kingpin angle is incorrect, or front end parts are damaged or worn, they must be replaced.

TOE-IN ADJUSTMENT

Toe-in (or toe-out) is the difference of the distance the forward extremes of the front tires and the distance between the rearward extremes of the front tires. Toe-in is adjustable on all Peugeots.

1. Make sure that the car is in its correct riding position and that the front wheels are pointed straight ahead.

2. Slacken the two clamp nuts on the adjustable tie-rod.

3. Hold the tie-rod ball joint with its two flats *horizontally* using a 14mm open end wrench.

4. Screw or unscrew the tie-rod to obtain the specified toe-in.

NOTE: One turn of the tie-rod is equivalent to 0.177 in. at the wheel rim.

5. Hold the tie-rod in the newly corrected position and tighten the two clamp bolts to 9 ft. lbs. (32.6 ft. lbs. on 505) while ensuring that the ball joint remains on a horizontal plane.

STEERING

Steering Wheel

REMOVAL & INSTALLATION

1. Remove the negative battery cable.
2. Place the wheels in a straight ahead position.
3. Remove the horn cover pad and horn contact assembly.
4. Remove the steering wheel nut.
5. Matchmark the steering wheel and the steering shaft.
6. Use a steering wheel puller tool to remove the steering wheel.
7. Installation is the reverse of removal.

Combination Switch

REMOVAL & INSTALLATION

1. Remove the steering wheel.

2. Remove the horn assembly and column cover.
3. Disconnect all wiring to the switch.
4. Remove the switch.
5. Installation is the reverse of removal.

Ignition Switch

REMOVAL & INSTALLATION

The steering wheel does not have to be removed.

1. Remove the negative battery cable.
2. Remove the steering column and ignition switch cover to expose the ignition switch.
3. Remove the wiring from the switch connections.
4. Remove the switch-to-column attaching bolts and remove the switch. Installation is the reverse of the removal procedure.

Manual Steering Gear

REMOVAL & INSTALLATION

504 and 604

1. Remove the tie-rod ends from the steering arm knuckles.
2. Remove the steering gear bolts and the lower shaft flange bolt.
3. Insert a 0.24 in. (6mm) diameter punch in the flange bolt hole.
4. Disengage the gearbox by rocking it with the punch. Remove the gearbox assembly.
5. When installing, position the steering wheel bars vertically.
6. Place the passenger side front wheel in the straight ahead position.
7. Place the driver's side wheel to a turned-in position.
8. Center the rack in relation to the rack housing.
9. Temporarily connect the tie-rod end on the passenger side.
10. Rotate the flange ¼ turn to align the flange collar with the splined end of the steering shaft.
11. Rock the flange slightly to install it on the splined shaft.
12. Install the steering gear to crossmember bolts. Torque the bolts to 22.7 ft. lbs. (31.8 Nm).
13. Install the bolt and a new locknut on the flange-to-column collar. Torque the nut to 10.8 ft. lbs. (14.7 Nm).
14. Install the tie-rod ends on the steering arm knuckles.
15. If the tie-rod end has a cotter pin hole in the stud, position the hole parallel to the length of the tie-rod, tighten the nut and install the cotter pin.
16. Without the cotter pin, use a new locking nut and torque the nut to 30.6 ft. lbs. (41.7 Nm).
17. Adjust the front wheel toe-in.

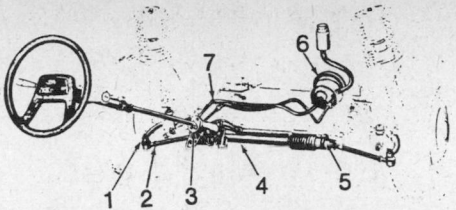
Power Steering Gear

REMOVAL & INSTALLATION

504 and 604

The removal and installation of the power type gearbox is basically the same procedure as the manual type gearbox. The system must be drained of hydraulic fluid and the hydraulic lines disconnected from the pump.

505

1. Raise the car and support it well above the ground in a secure manner. Remove the rear two fluid connections from the steering unit and allow the unit to drain. Turn the wheel slowly from lock to lock to force the remaining fluid out. Then, plug all openings.

2. Press both tie rod ends out. Remove the nut securing the hydraulic ram to the crossmember.

3. Remove the steering coupling bolts. Unlock and remove the bolts securing the steering box to the crossmember. Then, pull the box rearward and out. Make sure you don't distort the rigid pipes connecting the valve to the rack.

4. Turn the steering wheel to the straight ahead position, and do the same for the rack by finding the midpoint in its travel. Install the stud and spacer where the hydraulic ram connects to the crossmember while the unit is off the car.

5. Install the assembly, being sure to push the stud for the hydraulic ram as far as it will going into the crossmember. Install the steering box mounting bolts, torque to 24 ft. lbs. and fold over the lockwashers. Install a new Nylstop nut onto the ram stud and torque it to 40 ft. lbs.

6. Install the steering coupling bolts with new nuts and torque to 18 ft. lbs.

7. Reconnect low and high pressure lines and torque to 18 ft. lbs.

8. Reconnect the ball joints, using new Nylstop nuts torque to 25 ft. lbs. Set the wheel alignment as described above. Torque the locknuts to 33 ft. lbs. You can adjust the tie-rods so the dimension from the center of the tie-rod end to the unthreaded portion of the rod is 2.16 in. Align the front end.

9. Refill the power steering reservoir and keep it full as you bleed the system as described in the "Power Steering Pump Removal and Installation" procedure, below.

Power Steering Pump

REMOVAL & INSTALLATION

1. Remove the high pressure hose and drain the system. Move the steering wheel back and forth to insure complete drainage. Do not start engine.

2. Remove the belt adjusting nut, remove the belt and the pump attaching bolts.

3. Remove the pump.

4. Installation is the reverse of removal.

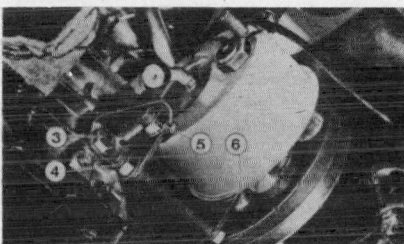

1. Tie rod end
2. Tie rod
3. Steering column knuckle
4. Crossmember
5. Housing
6. Power steering pump
7. Power steering hoses

504 and 505 power steering assembly

505

1. Turn off the ignition switch and disconnect the battery. Remove the cap from the reservoir and remove the union nut from the high pressure line (further away from the engine) on the back of the pump. Allow all the oil to drain. Then, slowly force the rest of the fluid out of the system by turning the steering wheel gradually from lock to lock several times. Remove the low pressure line's union nut and disconnect it at the pump.

2. From under the pump on the mounting bracket, remove the bolt (3) from the block and the nut (4) at the rear of the bracket. Loosen the pivot nut (5) and bolt (6).

Removing the 505 power steering pump. See the text

3. Remove the air filter and block the air intake. Loosen the bolt on the side of the tensioner.

4. Remove the four pulley bolts from the front of the pulley. Pull the pulley off and put the belt to one side.

5. Disconnect the pipe leading to the pump reservoir and pull the two remaining bolts out. Remove the pump.

6. Install the pump in reverse order, first tightening all bolts and nuts only finger tight. Then tighten the rear/lower bracket bolt and nut before tightening the bolt going into the engine block. Torque both to 25 ft. lbs.

7. Clean the face of the hub on the pump, and install the pulley, torquing bolts to 5 ft. lbs.

8. Make sure there is a spacer between the pump and adjusting slide. Tension the belt and then torque that nut and the nut and bolt on which the pump pivots at the bottom to 25 ft. lbs. Install the two hydraulic connections and torque the high pressure connection to 18 ft. lbs.

9. Fill the reservoir, and then bleed the system by turning the wheel from lock to lock with the engine idling. Keep the reservoir full to the "COLD" mark as you do this.

BELT ADJUSTMENT

1. Make two marks on the belt to be installed 4 in. (100mm) apart.

2. On a used belt tighten the belt so that the marks are 4.06 in. (101.5mm) apart.

3. On a new belt, tighten the belt so that the marks are 4.1 in. (102.5mm) apart.

SYSTEM BLEEDING

The power steering system is automatically bled by turning the steering gear to its full stop in both directions, several times.

BRAKE SYSTEM

All Peugeot models are equipped with disc brakes on the front. The 504 models are equipped with drum brakes on the rear, while the remaining models are equipped with rear disc brakes.

For all brake system repair and service procedures not detailed below, please refer to "Brakes" in the Unit Repair section.

Drum Brake Adjustment

1. Remove the plug on the adjustment hole located in the rear of the drum brake housing.

2. Using a brake spoon, turn the drum slowly while adjusting the brakes until the drum cannot be turned.

3. Back the adjustment wheel off until a slight drag is felt when the drum is turned.

Master Cylinder

REMOVAL & INSTALLATION

─── CAUTION ───
Care should be taken to insure that the correct parts are used for replacement.

1. Drain the reservoir.
2. Remove the brake lines.
3. Remove the master cylinder retaining bolts and carefully remove the master cylinder.

─── CAUTION ───
Do not pull the thrust rod from the booster unit.

4. Installation is the reverse of removal.

Power Brake Unit

REMOVAL & INSTALLATION

Remove the brake pedal linkage. Drain the brake fluid. Remove the brake lines from the master cylinder and remove the bolts at the firewall. Remove the power brake unit.

Front Wheel Bearings

Both tapered and angular type front wheel bearings are used on the 504 models, and tapered wheel bearings used on the 604 models.

The removal and installation procedure is in the conventional manner, by the removal of the locking nut and washer. The hub can be removed with the help of a hub puller or may be removed by hand pressure from the spindle.

The inner and outer bearing races must be removed and installed by a press or a special race remover or installer tool from the hub assembly. The bearings and races are in matched sets and must remain as such when put in use.

ADJUSTMENT

Torque the hub nut to 28 ft. lbs. (39 Nm), then loosen the nut and retorque it to 7 ft. lbs. (9.8 Nm). Lock the hub nut in place.

Rear Wheel Cylinders

REMOVAL & INSTALLATION
504

1. Remove the wheels and drums.
2. Remove the brake lining return spring and release the shoes from the wheel cylinder.
3. Remove the brake fluid line from the back of the wheel cylinder.
4. Remove the wheel cylinder bolts and the wheel cylinder.
5. Installation is the reverse of removal.

Parking Brake Adjustment

FLOOR MOUNTED LEVER

504 and 604

1. Raise the vehicle and remove the rear wheels.
2. Loosen the cable adjusting nuts so that no tension exists on the cable.
3. If the vehicle is equipped with drum brakes adjust them.
4. Apply the parking brake four clicks and adjust the cable.
5. Release the handbrake and make sure the rotors or drums can rotate freely.
6. Install the wheels and lower the vehicle.

505

1. Raise the car and support it securely. Release the handbrake.
2. Make sure the brake system is properly bled. Run the engine at idle and depress the brake pedal hard several times. Turn the engine off.

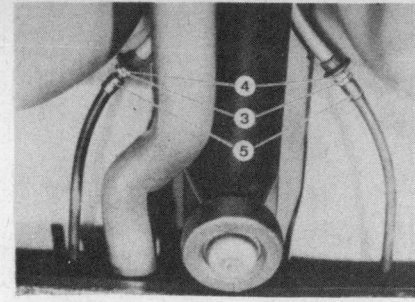

Adjusting the 505 rear disc brake handbrake. See the text.

3. Loosen the locknuts (3) at the front of the brake cable tubes simultaneously until the actuating levers on the rear calipers just lift off the nylon pads. Then, unscrew each locknut one half turn and tighten the locknut.
4. Check that the handbrake engages after moving upward 7–13 notches. Check also that the threaded ends of the cables (5) project an identical amount so the hand brake equalizer is perpendicular to the handle.

CHASSIS ELECTRICAL

Heater Blower/Core

REMOVAL & INSTALLATION
504

The heater blower unit is located underneath the dashboard. To remove the unit, first drain the cooling system and then remove the center console. Remove the radio and, on cars so equipped, the air conditioning vent unit screwed on underneath the dash. Pull the knobs off the heating control levers. Loosen and remove the two screws which hold the subdash unit containing the heater controls. Loosen the clamps and pull the two water hoses off the heater unit, being careful to catch any spilling coolant. Three screws on each side at the top hold the blower unit to the car. Remove the six screws and pull the unit out of the car. The heater core is housed within the blower unit and can be reached by disengaging the assembling clips or, on older models, by pulling out the pop-rivets (be sure that you know how to reinstall these before disassembling). Reassembly and installation of the heater unit is the reverse of the removal procedure. Be sure that all lines are properly secured and that the correct amount of coolant is added.

505 and 604

The blower motor for these models is located on the passenger side firewall.

1. Remove the box which contains the heater blower.
2. Loosen the blower retaining nuts.
3. Pull the plug from the series resistance cable that is located on the firewall.
4. Remove the cable.
5. Remove the blower.
6. Installation is the reverse of removal. Make sure that the sealing frame is not damaged.

Radio

REMOVAL & INSTALLATION

To remove the radio, first disconnect the antenna lead and then pull off the front knobs. Remove the front control shaft nuts and template and disconnect the power and speaker leads to the rear of the radio. Disconnect the rear support and pull the radio out from under the dash. To install, reverse the removal procedure, making sure that all wires are properly connected or damage to the radio and/or speaker could result.

Windshield Wiper/ Washer Motor

REMOVAL & INSTALLATION

1. Disconnect the battery ground cable.
2. Remove the air grill from the area under and in front of the windshield.
3. Disconnect the wires to the motor.
4. Remove the instrument cluster from the dash.
5. Reach into the dash area and remove the spindle drive nut and the three nuts securing the wiper motor to the firewall.
6. Remove the motor from the grill area.
7. Installation is the reverse of the removal procedure.

Instrument Cluster

REMOVAL & INSTALLATION

1. Remove all screws retaining the instrument cluster panel to the main dash.
2. Lift the panel out and disconnect all wiring from the back of the instrument cluster.
3. Remove the speedometer cable.
4. Lift out the instrument panel.
5. Installation is the reverse of removal.

Fuse Box Location

504 and 604

The fuse box is located under the driver's side of the dash, to the left of the steering column.

505

The fuse box is located on the top of the left inner front fender.

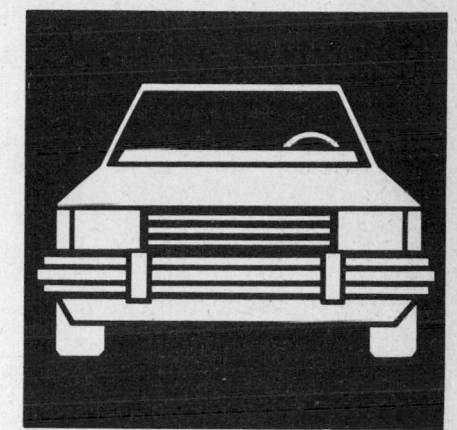

Porsche
911, 930 Turbo

SERIAL NUMBER IDENTIFICATION

Chassis

The chassis number on all models is located on the driver's side windshield post and is visible from the outside of the car. The chassis number is also found in the luggage compartment under the rug and on the identification plate near the front hood lock catch.

The chassis identification number breaks down in the following manner:

Serial Number Example—
911-6-2-1-0001

Series Type	911, 911S, 911SC or 930 (Turbo)

Model Year	8 = 1978
	9 = 1979
	0 = 1980
	1 = 1981
	2 = 1982
	3 = 1983
	4 = 1984
	5 = 1985
Engine Type	1 = T
	2 = E or 2.7S
	3 = S
	4 = Carrera
	8 = Turbo
Body Type	0 = Coupe
	1 = Targa

Four Digit Serial Number—Sequential.

Engine Type 6 = cylinder	
Engine Model	1 = T—Japan—3.01 ltr.
	2 = E—USA—3.01 ltr.
	3 = S—Rest of World—3.01 ltr.
	4 = Carrera
	5 = Calif.—3.01 ltr.
	8 = Turbo—3.31 ltr.
Model Year	8 = 1978
	9 = 1979
	0 = 1980
	1 = 1981
	C = 1982
	D = 1983
	E = 1984

Four digit sequential number—0001

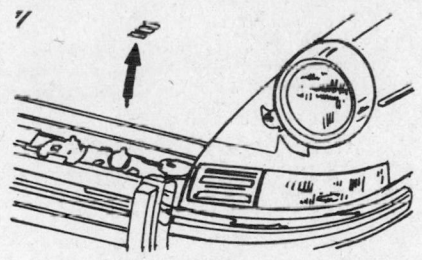

Chassis serial number location

Engine

The engine number is located on the right side of the crankcase adjacent to the blower. Engine numbers are divided as follows:

Engine Number Example—
6-3-6-0001

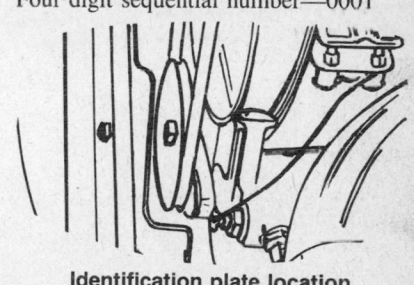

Identification plate location

GENERAL ENGINE SPECIFICATIONS

Year	Model	Engine Displacement cc	(cu. in.)	Carburetor Type	Horsepower @ rpm	Torque @ rpm	Bore × Stroke (in.)	Compression Ratio
'78–'79	930 Turbo	3299	(201.3)	Fuel inj. ④	261 @ 5500	291 @ 4000	3.82 × 2.93	7.0:1
'78–'83	911, SC	2994	(182.7)	Fuel inj. ④	172 @ 5500	175 @ 4200 ②	3.74 × 2.77	8.5:1 ①
'84–'85	911 Carrera	3164	(193)	Fuel inj. ③	200 @ 5900	185 @ 4800	3.74 × 2.93	9.5:1

NOTE: The underhood specifications sticker often reflects tune-up specification changes made in production. Sticker information must be used if it disagrees with the information in this chart.

① 1980–83: 9.3:1
② 1978–79: 180 @ 4200

③ Bosch Motronic injection/engine control system

④ CIS (K-Jetronic) fuel injection with oxygen sensor

TUNE-UP SPECIFICATIONS

Year	Model	Engine Displacement cc (cu. in.)	Spark Plugs		Distributor		Ignition Timing (deg)	Intake Valve Opens (deg)	Compres. Press (psi)	Idle Speed (rpm)	Valve Clearance (in.)	
			Type ①	Gap (in.)	Point Dwell (deg)	Point Gap (in.)	@ idle rpm				In	Ex
'78–'79	Turbo (930)	3299 (201.3)	W280–P21	0.024	Electronic		7A @ 950	1B ⑤	③	900–1000	0.004	0.004
'78–'83	911,SC	2994 (183)	④	0.028	Electronic		5B @ 950 ②	6A ⑤	③	900–1000	0.004	0.004
'84–'85	911 Carrera	3164 (193)	W7DC	0.028	Electronic		3A @ 800	9 ⑤	③	800	0.004	0.004

NOTE: The underhood specifications sticker often reflects tune-up specification changes made in production. Sticker figures should always be used if they differ from those in this chart.

B Before Top Dead Center
A After Top Dead Center
① Bosch spark plugs
② 1978–79 California models: 15 ATDC

③ All cylinders should be within 22 psi of the highest reading. Compression test to be performed with the engine above 140°F
④ 1978–79: W145T30 (W8D)
   1980–83: W225T30 (W5D)
⑤ With valve clearance of 0.1 mm

FIRING ORDERS

The position of No. 1 tower on the distributor cap may vary. To avoid confusion when replacing wires, always replace wires one at a time. The notch cut into the rim of the distributor body always indicates No. 1 cylinder.

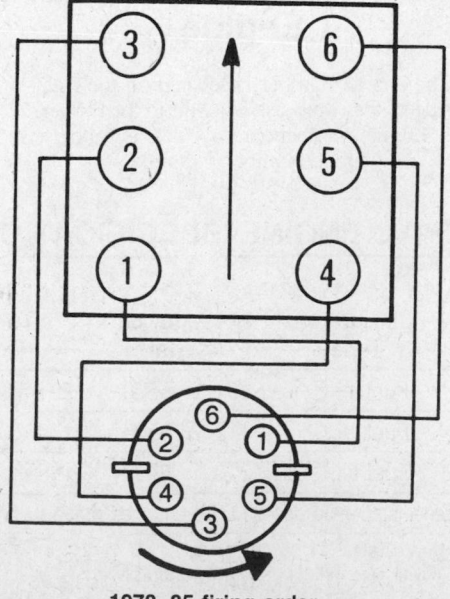

FIRING ORDER: 1-6-2-4-3-5

1978–85 firing order

CAPACITIES

Year	Model	Engine Displacement cc (cu. in.)	Engine Crankcase (qts)	Transaxle (qts)	Gasoline Tank① (gals)
'78–'85	911,SC	2994 (182.7)	⑤	3.2	21③
	Turbo (930)	3299 (201.3)	⑤	4.0	21④

① Including 1.6 gal reserve
② 15 qts with Sportomatic
③ 1978–85—2.1 reserve
④ 1978–79—2.0 reserve
⑤ Initial filling including oil cooler is 13.7 qts
   10.6 qts for refill

CRANKSHAFT AND CONNECTING ROD SPECIFICATIONS
(All measurements in inches)

Model	Engine Displacement cc	(cu. in.)	Crankshaft Main Brg. Journal Dia.①	Main Brg. Oil Clearance	Shaft End-Play	Thrust on No.	Connecting Rod Journal Diameter①	Oil Clearance	Side Clearance
911, Turbo (930)	All except 3164 cc②		2.2429–2.2437	0.0004–0.0028	0.0004–0.0077	1	2.0461–2.0468	0.0012–0.0035	0.0079–0.0158

① Undersize bearings available in 0.0098, 0.0197, 0.0295 inch sizes
② Information on the 3164cc engine not available at time of publication

VALVE SPECIFICATIONS

Model	Engine Displacement cc (cu. in.)	Face Angle (deg)	Spring Test Pressure (lbs. @ in.)	Spring Installed Height (in.)	Stem to Guide Clearance (in.) Intake	Exhaust	Stem Diameter (in.) Intake	Exhaust
911	All except 3164cc④	45	176.4 @ 1.21①	1.3779②③	0.030–0.057	0.050–0.077	0.3531	0.3523

① Intake: 165.3 @ 1.25 for exhaust
② 1.3976 in. for exhaust
③ 1.5197 in. for exhaust (911SE)
④ Information on the 3164cc engine not available at time of publication

PISTON AND RING SPECIFICATIONS
(All measurements in inches)

Model	Engine Displacement cc	(cu. in.)	Piston Clearance	Ring Gap Top Compression	Bottom Compression	Oil Control	Ring Side Clearance Top Compression	Bottom Compression	Oil Control
911 Turbo (930)	2994	(182.7)	0.006	0.004–0.008	0.004–0.008	0.006–0.012	0.003–0.004	0.002–0.003	0.001–0.002
Turbo (930)	3299	(201.3)	0.006	0.004–0.008	0.004–0.008	0.006–0.012	0.003–0.004	0.002–0.003	0.001–0.002

TORQUE SPECIFICATIONS
(All readings in ft. lbs.)

Model	Engine Displacement cc (cu. in.)	Cylinder Head Bolts	Rod Bearing Bolts	Main Bearing Bolts	Crankshaft Pulley Bolt	Flywheel To Crankshaft Bolts
911, Turbo (930)	All①	24	36	25	58	109

①Except 1984 and later 3164cc; information not available at time of publication

ALTERNATOR AND REGULATOR SPECIFICATIONS

Model	Alternator Part No. or Manufacturer	Output (amps.)	Regulator Part No. or Manufacturer	Field Relay Air Gap (in.)	Field Relay Point Gap (in.)	Field Relay Volts to Close	Regulator Air Gap (in.)	Regulator Point Gap (in.)	Volts @ 75°
911	Bosch	55①	Bosch		Not adjustable				13.5–14.5

① 1978–'81: 70
  1982–'83: 75

BRAKE SPECIFICATIONS
(All measurements given are in inches unless noted)

Year	Model	Lug Nut Torque (ft. lbs.)	Master Cylinder Bore	Brake Disc Minimum Thickness	Brake Disc Maximum Run-Out	Minimum Lining Thickness Front	Minimum Lining Thickness Rear
'78–'84	911	94	0.75	0.70	0.008	0.08	0.08

NOTE: Minimum lining thickness is as recommended by the manufacturer. Due to variations in state inspection regulations, the minimum allowable thickness may be different than recommended by the manufacturer.

WHEEL ALIGNMENT

Year	Model	Caster Range (deg)	Caster Pref Setting (deg)	Camber Range (deg)	Camber Pref Setting (deg)	Toe-In (deg)
'78–'84	911	6¹⁄₁₆ ± ¼	6¹⁄₁₆	+½ − (±)³⁄₁₆	+½	0

NOTE: These specifications eliminate the need to laterally preload the front wheels when checking/adjusting toe-in.
①Rear wheels: +10′ ± 10′

TUNE-UP

Spark Plugs

NOTE: It is necessary to completely remove the engine in order to remove the spark plugs on Turbo 930 models.

Before removing the spark plug leads, number the towers on the distributor cap with tape. Grasp each spark plug boot and pull it straight out. Check the condition of the rubber boot and/or shroud seals and replace them if necessary. Install the spark plug socket on the plug's hex and remove it. If removal is difficult, loosen the plug only slightly and drip some light oil onto the threads. Allow the oil to penetrate and then unscrew the spark plug. Proceeding this way will prevent damaging the threads in the cylinder head. Be sure to keep the socket straight to avoid breaking the ceramic insulator. Most spark plug sockets are lined with rubber for this reason. Inspect the plugs using the "Troubleshooting" section illustrations and then clean or discard them according to their condition. Recommended spark plug gap is given in the "Tune-Up Specifications" chart. Use a spark plug wire gauge for checking the gap. The wire should pass through the electrodes with just a slight drag. Using the electrode bending tool on the end of the gauge, bend the side electrode to adjust the gap. Never attempt to adjust the center electrode. Lightly oil the threads of the replacement plug and install it hand-tight. The spark plugs in all engines should be tightened to a torque of 18–21 ft. lbs. Install the ignition wire boots firmly on the spark plugs.

Electronic Ignition

All Porsche 911 models covered in this section are equipped with an inductive pickup-type electronic ignition system. This system replaces the breaker points with an inductive signal. When the timing teeth of the rotor come in alignment with the triggering projections on the pick-up coil, a magnetic field builds around the pick-up coil. When the timing teeth leave the area of the triggering projection, the magnetic field collapses around the pick-up coil and generates a small current pulse.

Using a transistor in the control unit, this small current pulse switches the primary voltage to the ignition coil on and off. The secondary voltage produced by the coil fires the spark plug. Dwell is controlled by the electronic system. However, timing is set in the normal way.

NOTE: Inspection or adjustment of the dwell angle on electronic ignition-equipped models is neither possible nor necessary.

MAJOR COMPONENTS

1. Rotor (reluctor)—timing teeth build a magnetic field at each pick-up coil triggering projection.
2. Pick-up coil—sends a small induced current signal to the control unit each time a tooth in the rotor passes a pick-up coil triggering projection.
3. Control unit—receives signals from the pick-up coil. These signals switch the primary current at the ignition coil off and on. This collapses the primary field and generates the secondary voltage necessary to fire the spark plug.
4. Ignition coil—electronic coils cannot be interchanged with standard ignition coils.
5. Spark advance and retard—conventional type operation.

TESTING

Always check for spark. If no spark is available, then check for primary voltage at the ignition coil. If no voltage is available at the coil, check the primary resistors and electrical connectors for looseness or corrosion.

If voltage is available at the coil, check all of the components of the electronic ignition system as listed in the "Testing Specifications" chart. If voltage is available at the control unit and all other components check out good, replace the control unit.

If the engine is missing or breaking down under load, check the secondary ignition and wires. Check the pick-up coil ohms while applying vacuum to the vacuum advance from an outside source. Check for dwell variation at 1500 r.p.m. and 5000 r.p.m.

Electronic Ignition Testing Specifications

Component Tested	Specification (ohms)
Rotor resistance	5000
Pick-up coil	890–1285
Ignition coil (primary)	0.95–1.40
Ignition coil (secondary)	5500–8000
High tension coil lead	Less than 5000

Ignition Timing

—CAUTION—
When performing this or any other adjustment with the engine running, be very careful of the fan belt and pulley.

Ignition timing should always be checked as part of any tune up. An inductive, stroboscopic timing light is a necessity for timing any Porsche and, in addition, a static 12 V timing light is necessary. On all models, the Z1 notch on the crankshaft pulley is the TDC mark, and a 5° ATDC mark is directly to the left of the Z1 on some models. Other pulley timing marks include 30, 35, 29 and 25° marks, depending on model.

ADJUSTMENT

1978–79 911

NOTE: Ignition timing is checked at idle (950 rpm) and at 6000 rpm. To measure engine speed, use a tester/tachometer with an inductive pick-up.

1. Start the engine and let it warm up to normal operating temperature. A 20 minute drive should accomplish this. Normal operating temperature is approximately 176°F/80°C.
2. Stop the engine and connect an inductive timing light according to the manufacturer's instructions.
3. Restart the engine. Make sure that the idle speed is 950 rpm. The vacuum hose to the distributor remains connected for this procedure.
4. When the timing light flashes, the 5° BTDC mark on the crankshaft pulley

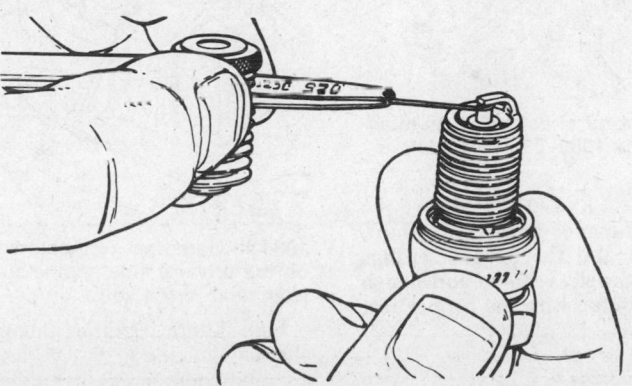

Checking the spark plug gap

should be aligned with the reference notch on the fan (blower) housing at 950 rpm.

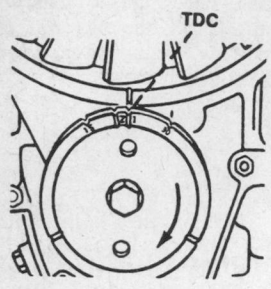

Timing marks

5. If the notches do not align, loosen the retaining nut at the bottom of the distributor mounting flange and slowly rotate the distributor as necessary until the notch and pulley mark are aligned. Ignition timing is now correct at idle.

6. Dynamic timing is now checked. Total ignition advance at 6000 rpm should be 26° with the vacuum hose disconnected. Have an assistant accelerate the engine to 6000 rpm for an instant while you check the timing marks. If the timing is incorrect, loosen the distributor nut and slowly rotate the distributor to adjust.

NOTE: If either the idle or full throttle timing cannot be properly adjusted by rotating the distributor, the distributor should be removed and bench tested for possible problems.

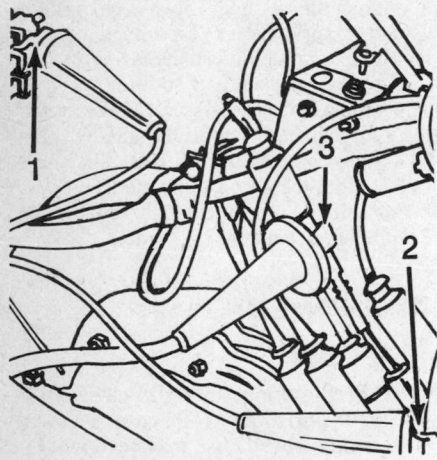

1. Positive connection
2. Ground connection
3. No. 1 terminal

Timing light hook–up

1980–83 911

1. Run the engine up to operating temperature, approximately 194°F/90°C.

2. Stop the engine and connect an inductive timing light according to the manufacturer's instructions. Connect an inductive tester/tachometer.

3. Remove the red and blue distributor vacuum hoses. Adjust the engine idle speed to 950 rpm.

4. When the timing light flashes, the 5°BTDC mark on the crankshaft pulley should be aligned with the reference notch on the fan (blower) housing at 950 rpm. If the notches do not align, loosen the retaining nut at the bottom of the distributor mounting flange and slowly rotate the distributor as necessary until the notch and pulley mark are aligned.

5. Ignition timing is now correct at idle. Reconnect the vacuum hoses and recheck idle speed. Adjust if necessary.

6. To check the centrifugal advance mechanism, make sure the ignition timing is properly adjusted for idle rpm (950). Disconnect the distributor vacuum hoses. Check the timing in the normal manner as described in the above procedures. Timing must be between 15 and 20° BTDC at 3000 rpm, and between 19 and 25° BTDC at 6000 rpm.

7. To check the vacuum retard, run the engine at idle speed. Connect the blue (retard) hose at connection 1 of the double vacuum box on the distributor and disconnect the red (advance) hose at connection 2. See the accompanying illustration for details of the connections and hoses. Check the ignition timing with the timing light; timing should be between 3 and 7° ATDC.

8. To check the vacuum advance, connect the blue (retard) hose on connection 2 (following the same illustration as Step 7). Adjust engine speed to 950 rpm. Ignition timing must be between 8 and 12° BTDC. Connect vacuum hoses and check that engine idle speed is 950 rpm. Adjust if necessary.

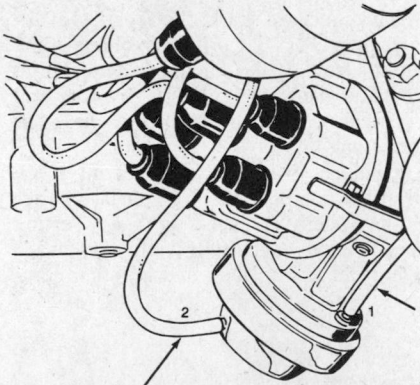

Hose locations for checking vacuum advance/retard on 1980–83 911 models

NOTE: If the above procedures have been followed and the proper settings cannot be achieved, remove and bench test the distributor with the proper test equipment.

1978–83 911S, SC and Turbo

Timing adjustment procedures are similar

to those given above for 911 models. Timing for the 49 states 911S is TDC at normal idle (Z1 notch on the crank pulley). California 911S models get 15° ATDC at idle speed (15° notch to the left of Z1). The centrifugal advance timing check is no longer performed on these models. Basic timing for the Turbo is 7° ATDC at idle. Full centrifugal advance should be 29° BTDC and it should begin at 4000 rpm.

1984 911 Carrera

To check idle speed on these models, a Porsche special tool (VAG 1367 tester) is required. Terminals B and C of the test jack (see illustration; location is on the driver's side of the engine compartment, next to the coil) must be bridged with a jumper in order to stop operation of the idle regulator. Timing is then checked in the normal manner. At 800 rpm, ignition timing should be 3° ATDC.

Ignition timing test connector—1984 and later

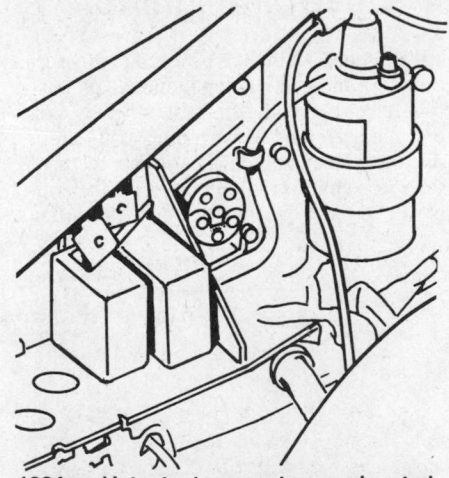

1984 and later test connectors are located on the driver's side engine compartment wall, next to the coil

Full throttle ignition timing is again checked with the VAG 1367 tester, or with a stroboscopic timing light directed at the 25° timing mark on the crankshaft pulley. Make sure the engine is at normal operating temperature (approximately 194°F/90°C), and that all electrical accessories are OFF. Also, be certain that the distributor rotor is correctly installed in relation to the mark on the distributor housing.

Bridge terminals B and C of the test jack; this stimulates full throttle on the control unit and stops operation of the idle regulator. Full throttle timing should be 25° BTDC at 3800 rpm.

Valve Lash

ADJUSTMENT

1. The engine must be cold when adjusting the valves on any Porsche. Remove the rocker arm covers, two per head in the case of the 911.

2. The valves of each cylinder are adjusted with that piston at the top of its compression stroke. Both the intake and exhaust valves will be closed at this point. Turn the engine to align the TDC mark ("Z1") with the reference mark.

3. Using a feeler gauge (thickness equal to a figure given in the "Tune-Up Specifications" chart), check the clearance between the valve stem and the rocker arm. The feeler gauge should just slip through, if it has to be forced, the clearance will be incorrect.

4. If the clearance is not within specifications, loosen the locknut with a box wrench and, using a screwdriver, turn the rocker arm adjusting screw while holding the locknut. A tool to simplify this procedure is available from automotive suppliers. It has a screwdriver bit which can be turned while the locknut is held with a socket.

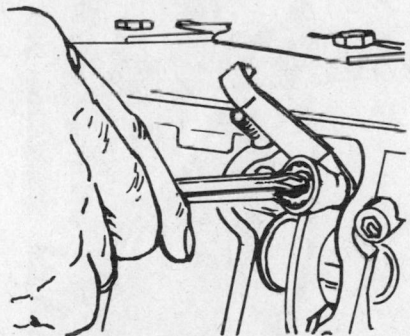

Valve clearance adjustment

5. Tighten the locknut while holding the adjusting screw. Recheck the valve clearance to ensure that it wasn't changed when the locknut was tightened. Repeat this procedure on the other valve of No. 1 cylinder.

6. Proceed to adjust the valves of the remaining cylinders in an order of 1-6-2-4-3-5. The piston of the cylinder on which the valves are being adjusted must be at TDC. Turn the engine until both valves of

the cylinder being adjusted are closed. Six-cylinder engines have TDC marks for each cylinder on the crankshaft pulley. Adjust the valves in the same manner as detailed for the No. 1 cylinder.

7. Install the rocker arm or camshaft housing covers with new gaskets. Start the engine and check for leaks.

Fuel Injection

IDLE SPEED ADJUSTMENT

The idle speed adjustment on the CIS system used on all later models is done with the bypass screw on the throttle valve housing. The engine should be at normal operating temperature.

NOTE: For all repair and maintenance information on the CIS injection system, please turn to "Fuel Injection" in the Unit Repair section.

1984 and later 911

NOTE: Idle adjustment on these models can only be performed using a CO analyzer. For accurate adjustments, the procedure must be closely followed.

1. Run the engine up to normal operating temperature. Engine oil temperature must be approximately 194°F (90°C). Intake air temperature must be between 59 and 95°F.

2. Disconnect the oxygen sensor.

3. Connect the CO analyzer in front of the catalytic converter. Check the CO content percentage at idle. Content in the exhaust gas should be 0.6–1.0%.

4. Reconnect the oxygen sensor.

5. Bridge terminals B and C on the test connection jack (located to the rear of the coil on the driver's side engine compartment wall). This makes the idle stabilizer inoperative.

6. Check the idle speed (rpm), and adjust if necessary. Idle speed should be 800 rpm. Adjustments are made with the throttle housing adjustment screw.

7. Remove the bridge from the test jack. Recheck the CO% content and idle rpm. Remove the CO analyzer probe, and close the catalytic converter connection.

ENGINE PERFORMANCE DIAGNOSIS

1984 and later 911 (Motronic fuel injection system)

Poor engine performance can result from problems in the following areas/components. Each component should be checked if the noted peformance symptoms arise.

NOTE: Please refer to the "Fuel Injection" Unit Repair section for more information on the Bosch Motronic injection system.

● **Check temperature sensor,** located in the left cylinder head by No. 3 cylinder. Using an ohmmeter, check resistance sensor at the following temperatures:

Temperature	Resistance values
50°F (10°C)	3.3 to 4.1K ohms
68°F (20°C)	2.2 to 2.8K ohms
104°F (40°C)	1.0 to 1.3K ohms
176°F (80°C)	290 to 350 ohms
212°F (100°C)	160 to 210 ohms

The sensor is responsible for correct warmup enrichment in the injection system. If the sensor is disconnected (resistance = ∞), the engine will run too rich and stall at idle. If the sensor is shorted to ground (resistance = 0 ohms), the engine may be difficult to start from cold, or when warmed-up.

● **Check the engine speed sensor and reference mark.** Porsche specifies that the distance between the engine speed sensor and the flywheel must be 0.8 ± 0.3mm. If the distance approaches 2mm, a longer cranking time will result, and the engine may not start at lower temperatures. The engine will run normally during warm-up, but may idle higher than normal at operating temperature. If the distance approaches 3mm, the engine will hesitate during acceleration, and will "miss". Due to heat expansion, the engine may stop running for short periods.

● **Check the fuel return hose.** If the fuel return hose is kinked or blocked, fuel pressure will rise, causing rich running and stalling at idle.

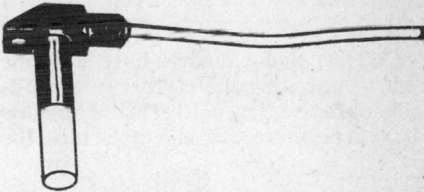

Engine speed sensor, located in the engine cases above the flywheel.

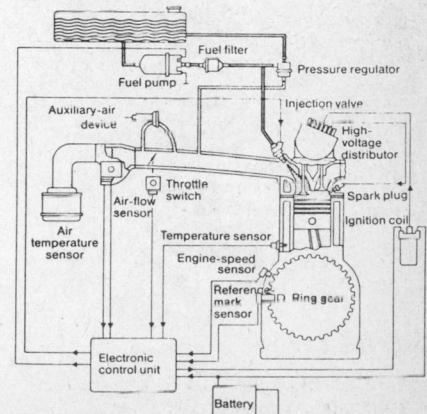

Basic diagrams of the Motronic system which combines control of both fuel injection and ignition. Note engine speed sensor location

NOTE: If the CO% cannot be adjusted to specifications or the engine surges at idle or when cold or under partial load, test the fuel pressure. With the vacuum hose connected, pressure should be 2 bar at idle.

- **Check spark plugs.** The wear limit on the spark plug electrode gap is 1.3mm. Replace the plugs if wear exceeds this limit.
- **Check the acceleration linkage adjustment.** The long rod on the transmission relay lever must have a clearance of 0.5–1.0mm, for proper operation of the idle microswitch.
- **Check the idle microswitch.** An inoperative (open) switch will produce an increased idle, approximately 1100 rpm, and the ignition timing will be advanced. Also, when decelerating from over 5000 to under 4000 rpm, the engine will hesitate when you next accelerate. Acceleration may also be delayed by 1° of throttle opening with a cold engine, while the engine surges.

ENGINE ELECTRICAL

Distributor

REMOVAL & INSTALLATION

1. Remove the heated air intake duct.
2. Unsnap and remove the distributor cap. Position it out of the way.
3. Mark the direction in which the rotor is pointing on the body of the distributor.

NOTE: Some models have a scribe mark indicating the correct rotor positioning for No. 1 cylinder. On these models it will be more convenient to turn the

engine so that the rotor points to this mark before removing the distributor.

4. Detach the distributor leads. Remove the vacuum line.
5. Loosen and remove the retaining nut from the base of the distributor. Pull the distributor straight out of the engine. Check and, if necessary, replace the sealing ring on the distributor housing.
6. Insert the distributor into the engine. Swivel the rotor back and forth to engage the distributor and crankshaft gears. If the engine has been turned while the distributor was out, bring the No. 1 cylinder to TDC as described before under ''Ignition Timing.''
7. Adjust the timing.

Alternator

PRECAUTIONS

A few precautions should be observed when servicing an electrical system that uses an alternator. Failure to do so can result in serious damage to the charging system. The negative terminal(s) of the battery(ies) is (are) always grounded. Always connect the correct battery terminals when attaching a battery charger or replacing a battery. Never operate the alternator on an open, uncontrolled circuit. Never ground or short across any regulator or alternator terminals. Never attempt to polarize the alternator. Remove

Alternator pulley nut removal

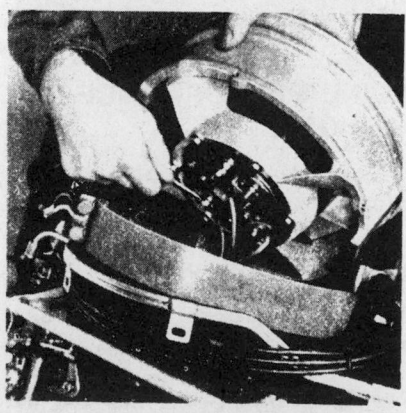

Alternator removal

1. Rotor
2. Stator

Electronic distributor disassembled in major components

the battery cables from the terminals when charging the battery in the car.

REMOVAL & INSTALLATION

The alternator is located in the blower housing.

1. Disconnect the battery ground straps.
2. Remove the air cleaner assembly.
3. Remove the upper shroud retaining bolts.
4. Hold the alternator pulley and remove the pulley nut.
5. Remove the drive belt.
6. Remove the blower housing strap retaining bolts.
7. Pull the blower housing/alternator towards the rear until there is enough clearance to disconnect the wiring.
8. Remove the alternator.
9. Install the alternator in the reverse order of removal. Be sure that the blower housing is seated on the dowel in the crankcase.
10. Tighten the pulley nut to 29 ft. lbs.

BELT TENSION ADJUSTMENT

A correctly tensioned belt can be deflected ½–¾ in. by light hand pressure. If the tension is not within specifications, follow the steps below to adjust or replace the belt.

1. Remove the pulley nut as outlined above in ''Alternator Removal and Installation.''
2. Remove the outside half of the pulley.
3. Remove the adjustment spacers to increase belt tension. Add spacers to decrease belt tension.

Fan belt pulley adjustment spacers

4. When the correct spacer grouping is achieved, install the belt, pulley half, spacers, and nut.
5. Tighten the nut to 29 ft. lbs.

NOTE: If you have removed spacers, install the extra spacers on the outside of the pulley so they won't become lost or misplaced.

6. Recheck the belt tension after about 60 miles of driving.

Regulator

REMOVAL & INSTALLATION

1. Disconnect the ground cable from the battery.
2. Disconnect the wiring from the regulator.
3. Remove the mounting screws and remove the regulator.
4. Install the regulator. Do not over-tighten the screws. An alternator system requires no polarization.

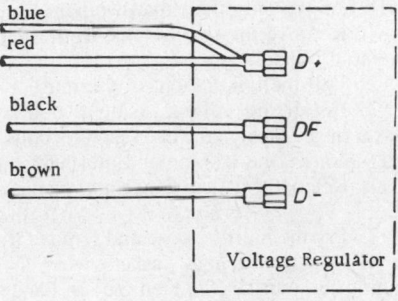

Voltage regulator wiring schematic

Starter

REMOVAL & INSTALLATION

1. Disconnect the battery ground strap.
2. Jack up the rear of the car and support it with jack stands.
3. Note their locations (tag to be sure) and then remove the starter electrical connections.
4. Loosen the retaining bolts, support the starter, remove the bolts, and then pull out the starter.
5. Install the starter using the reverse order of the removal procedure. Ensure that the terminal connections are correctly installed and tight.
6. Lower the car and connect the battery ground strap.

OVERRUN CLUTCH AND DRIVE

Replacement

1. Remove the starter
2. Press clutch operating shaft by turning slightly.
3. Pull both off the shaft by turning slightly.
4. Hold the armature in a vise and push the pinion and sleeve onto the shaft until the detent locks.

ENGINE MECHANICAL

Engine

REMOVAL & INSTALLATION

All Porsche engines are removed and installed with the transaxle attached. The recommended method for removal is to raise the rear of the car high enough for working clearance and then support it on jack stands. A hydraulic transmission/differential jack or service jack of at least 800 lbs. capacity is required for lowering the engine/transaxle and raising it back into the chassis. Have an assistant steady the engine/transaxle during removal. Strap the engine to the jack so that it doesn't slide off. Proceed slowly and carefully as the engine/transaxle combination is both heavy and delicate.

1. Disconnect the battery. Drain the engine and transaxle oil.
2. Open the engine compartment lid and detach the hot air ducts from the air gates and exhaust manifold heat exchangers.
3. Detach the two heater control cables.

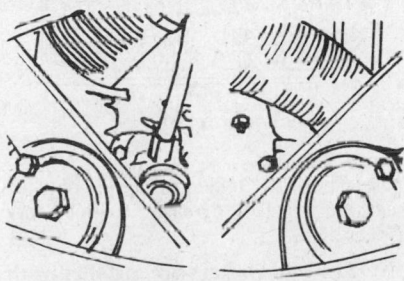

Rear engine–to–body mounts

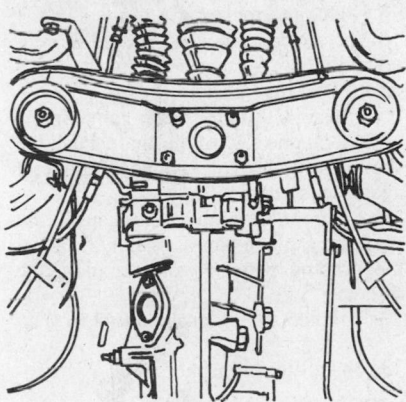

Transaxle crossmember mounting

4. Remove the hot air ducts from the the T-union between the air cleaners and then remove the T-union from the blower housing.
5. Remove the tops of the air cleaners.
6. Tag for installation and then remove the electrical cables from the generator and blower housing.

7. Tag for installation and remove the wires from the coil.
8. Remove the connections from the oil temperature and pressure sending units.
9. Remove the fuel line from the fuel pump and detach its clip from the engine shield.
10. Remove the Allen bolts retaining the axle shaft flange to the transaxle. Free the axle shafts from the transaxle and drop them out of the way.
11. Remove the starter electrical leads.
12. Disconnect the clutch cable from the control lever.
13. Remove the ground strap.
14. Detach the back-up light lead.
15. Disconnect the throttle linkage from the cross-shaft at the transaxle.
16. Remove the cover in the center of the rear floor.
17. Detach the rubber shift lever cover from the flange on the body and pull it forward on the control lever.
18. Remove the safety wire from the square-headed joint. Loosen the screw and slide the shift rod off its base.
19. Position the jack, including the flat support plate, under the engine/transaxle. The jack should be under the point of balance of the powertrain.
20. Raise the jack a slight amount.
21. Remove the body mounting bolts on either side of the engine compartment.
22. Remove the body mounting bolts from the short transaxle crossmember. The engine is removed with this crossmember attached.
23. Very carefully lower the engine while your assistants help balance it.
24. Roll the engine/transaxle out from under the car.

Follow Steps 25–30 for engine and transaxle separation.

Releasing throwout bearing tension

Remove the starter. Release the throwout fork tension by disconnecting the return spring if one is used.

After releasing throwout bearing tension, it is necessary to slide the throwout fork past the bearing. To do this, insert a screwdriver in the opening in the transaxle and turn the bearing 90°. Slide the fork past the bearing. The transaxle may now be separated from the engine.

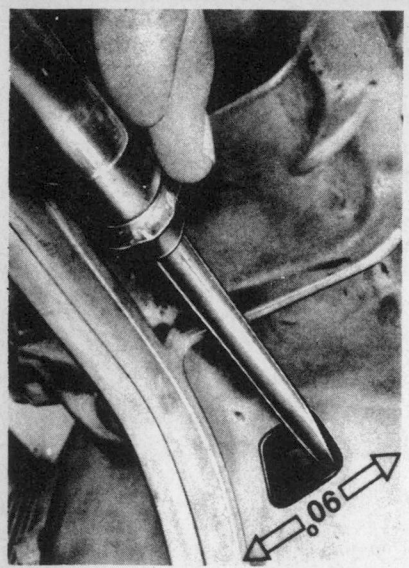

Sliding the fork past the throwout bearing

25. Remove the engine-to-transaxle bolts and nuts. Carefully pull the transaxle away from the engine. Be sure that the full weight of the transaxle is supported, so as not to damage the pilot bushing, throwout bearing, clutch disc, or pressure plate.

26. Whichever component you are repairing, rebuilding, or replacing may now be moved to a suitable workbench, dolly or engine stand.

27. Before reinstalling the transaxle, fill the pilot bushing in the gland nut with a small amount of graphite grease (no more than 3 cc, or 1/10 oz.).

28. Lightly grease the transmission input shaft splines, starter shaft bushing, and the starter and flywheel gear teeth.

29. Carefully attach the transaxle to the engine. Remember the transmission input shaft will be passing through the throwout bearing, pressure plate, clutch disc, and pilot bushing, so give it ample support during the attachment procedure.

NOTE: If the clutch disc splines and the input shaft splines don't line up, as they so often won't, have an assistant turn the crankshaft pulley until they do.

30. Push the transaxle home so that the mounting flanges are flush. Align the bottom holes and install the bolts. Install the top bolts, and then tighten all of the retaining bolts evenly.

31. The engine/transaxle is installed by following the removal steps in reverse order.

32. After the engine is installed, check the clutch adjustment.

33. Refill the engine and transaxle with the correct lubricant. Lower the car.

34. Start the engine and check for leaks.

Cylinder Head

For removal and installation, see the "Engine Disassembly and Assembly" section.

Rocker Shafts

REMOVAL & INSTALLATION

Each rocker arm has an individual shaft on this single overhead camshaft engine. One or all of the shafts and rocker arms may be removed with the engine in the chassis.

1. Remove the camshaft housing cover nuts and spring washers. Remove the covers.

2. Scribe the rocker arms being removed so that they can be returned to the same position.

3. Unscrew the Allen bolt in the rocker shaft. Push the shaft out of its bore and remove it along with the rocker arm.

NOTE: If the rocker is under pressure, you won't be able to push the shaft out. Turn the crankshaft until the rocker rests on the heel of the cam lobe.

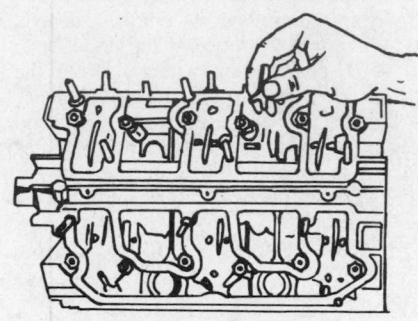

Rocker arm removal

4. Check the rocker arm and shaft for excessive wear or damage. Replace any suspect piece.

NOTE: End rockers are installed with the Allen screw heads facing towards cylinders No. 2 and 5 respectively.

5. Place the rocker arm on its shaft.

6. The rocker arm shaft should be centered in its bore so that each groove is recessed 0.059 in. (1.15mm).

   a. Insert a 0.06 in. feeler gauge in the groove on one side of the shaft. Push the shaft in until the feeler gauge is held tight against the edge.

   b. Carefully remove the gauge and push the shaft in approximately 0.06 in. more, using the feeler gauge to judge the distance.

7. Tighten the Allen bolt to 156 inch lbs.

8. Install the camshaft cover.

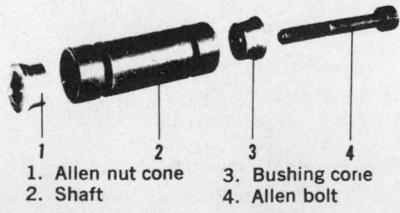

1. Allen nut cone   3. Bushing cone
2. Shaft   4. Allen bolt

Rocker arm shaft assembly

Exhaust Pipe and Muffler

REMOVAL & INSTALLATION

1. Remove the flange nuts and bolts.
2. Loosen the retaining clamps and detach the muffler from its support.
3. Position the muffler on its support and then fit the clamps.
4. Install new gaskets between the muffler and exhaust manifold/heat exchanger.
5. Install and alternately tighten the flange nuts and bolts.

To remove only the exhaust pipe:
1. Remove the two tailpipe-to-muffler retaining bolts.
2. Pull the tailpipe out of the muffler.
3. Install the tailpipe using two new gasket rings. Tighten the two retaining bolts.

To remove the tailpipe and muffler:
1. Remove the three flange nuts on each side.
2. Pry the muffler loose and remove it.
3. Use new flange gaskets when installing the muffler. Tighten the six flange retaining nuts alternately.

Exhaust Manifold/Heat Exchanger

REMOVAL & INSTALLATION

1. Remove the muffler as previously outlined. Detach and remove the connecting hose from the heat exchanger to the heater valve chamber.

2. Detach the heater hose from the heat exchanger.

3. Remove the three sunken bolts from the bottom of the heat exchanger.

4. Remove the six cylinder head-to-heat exchanger nuts using a universal socket setup.

5. Remove the heat exchanger.

6. Examine the heat exchanger for damaged flanges or cracks. Replace it, if necessary.

7. Install the heat exchanger in the reverse order of removal. Use new flange gaskets and tighten the retaining nuts and bolts alternately.

Engine Disassembly and Assembly

NOTE: Further component removal and installation requires engine removal and disassembly. Follow the steps of engine disassembly and then assembly for the part being replaced. A general engine rebuilding section is included at the end of the book.

Mount the engine on a stand. Drain the

engine oil and remove the muffler and heat exchanger. Remove the rear engine cover plate. Remove the intake distributor and intake pipe with the injection valves.

Remove the ignition distributor and the front engine cover plate. Remove the cooling blower impeller. Remove the cooling blower housing with the alternator attached. Remove the engine mount. Remove the front and rear cylinder jackets with the warm air guides. Remove the oil cooler, oil filter and oil pump. Remove the rocker arm shafts with the protective tubes, pushrods, and tappets. Removal of the cylinder heads on the 911 involves removing the overhead camshafts. All three cylinder heads on each bank can be removed as a unit complete with the camshaft and rockers or each cylinder head can be removed individually. For access to the cylinder heads and valves, the camshaft housing must be disassembled and removed.

Rockers: Scribe a mark on the rockers for later installation. Remove the 5mm Allen retaining screws in the rocker shafts, holding the cone-nut that is released on the other end of the shaft. Push out the shafts and lift away the rockers. *Position the camshaft so that the cam lobe does not press against the rocker being removed.*

Camshaft: Remove the timing chain cover at each camshaft. Unbolt the chain tensioner and the intermediate wheel, using tools P 202 and P 203. Withdraw the dowel pin from the camshaft wheel with tool P212. Remove the sliding wedges and withdraw the wheel and flange. Take the key from the camshaft, unscrew the three sealing ring screws, and remove the sealing ring together with the O-ring and the gasket. Withdraw the camshaft toward the rear. Note that both camshafts turn in the same direction and therefore require that the cam lobes be positioned differently.

Cam housing: Unscrew the hex nuts and the three Allen screws to lift off the camshaft housing. Each housing fits either cylinder bank.

Cylinder head: Loosen the cylinder head securing nuts (using tool P 119) and remove the cylinder head. Cylinders are numbered from the crankshaft pulley on the left bank as 1, 2 and 3 (left when facing the front of the car), and on the right bank as 4, 5 and 6.

The upper and lower sealing surfaces of the cylinder head (between the head and the camshaft and between the head and the cylinder) should not be machined. Permitted distortion at the cylinder seating surface must not exceed 0.15mm (0.0059 in.). Examine the mating surfaces to ensure that they are in good condition.

NOTE: If a cylinder head stud is broken above the threads in 911 and Turbo crankcases, a new Dilavar cylinder head stud should be installed. Grind the broken stud flat, then center punch it in the center. Using a ¼ in. carbide-tipped drill bit chucked into a drill press, drill approximately 15mm into the stud. Drive a No. 3 screw extractor approximately 10mm into the bore. Heat the case evenly in an oven or with a torch to 200°C to loosen the grip of the Loctite.® Turn out the broken stud, re-tap the threads in the crankcase and install a new Dilavar stud (part No. 928 101 921 00).

When installing the cylinder heads, use new cylinder head gaskets with the perforations set toward the cylinder. Carefully position each head, insert the washers and tighten the hex nuts lightly.

The camshaft housing is sealed to the cylinder heads only with sealing compound. Assemble the camshaft housing and oil return pipes on the cylinder heads, but only hand-tighten.

Porsche suggests that at this point in reassembly, the cylinder head be torqued down first and then the camshaft housing. Some mechanics prefer to torque the camshaft housing first for more accurate tensioning. Either way, the camshaft must be checked frequently for free turning. If tightening one side binds the crankshaft, tightening the opposite side must free it again. If not, the housing must be loosened, and tightening steps must be made in a different sequence.

Tighten the cylinder head to 21.6–23.8 ft. lbs. (3.0–3.3 mkg). Tighten the camshaft housing to 15.9–18.1 ft. lbs. (2.2–2.5 mkg).

Valve timing adjustment for the 911: Turn the crankshaft until the mark "Z1" on the crankshaft pulley lines up exactly with the crankcase joint. Taking care that the valves and pistons do not collide with each other, turn both camshafts (tool P 202) to bring the punch marks, stamped on the face of the camshafts, exactly above the shaft vertical center. Back off a little if the slightest resistance is felt during the turn. Then turn the free shaft to bring the valves and pistons into proper harmony before continuing with the first shaft.

With the crankshaft timing marks aligned and the camshaft punch marks exactly on the top, the engine is timed at the firing point in cylinder No. 1 with overlapping in cylinder No. 4. Find which hole in the camshaft sprocket lines up with a corresponding hole in the sprocket flange and insert the aligning dowel pin.

Slip on the washer and tighten the retaining nut to 101 ft. lbs. (14.7 mkg).

Adjust cylinder No. 1 intake valve clearance to 0.10mm (0.004 in.) and attach a dial gauge. The gauge sensor must be positioned exactly on the edge of the valve spring retaining collar. Adjust the gauge to a preload of 10mm (0.39 in.) to provide for sensor travel when the cam lobe depresses the valve. Depress the chain tensioner with

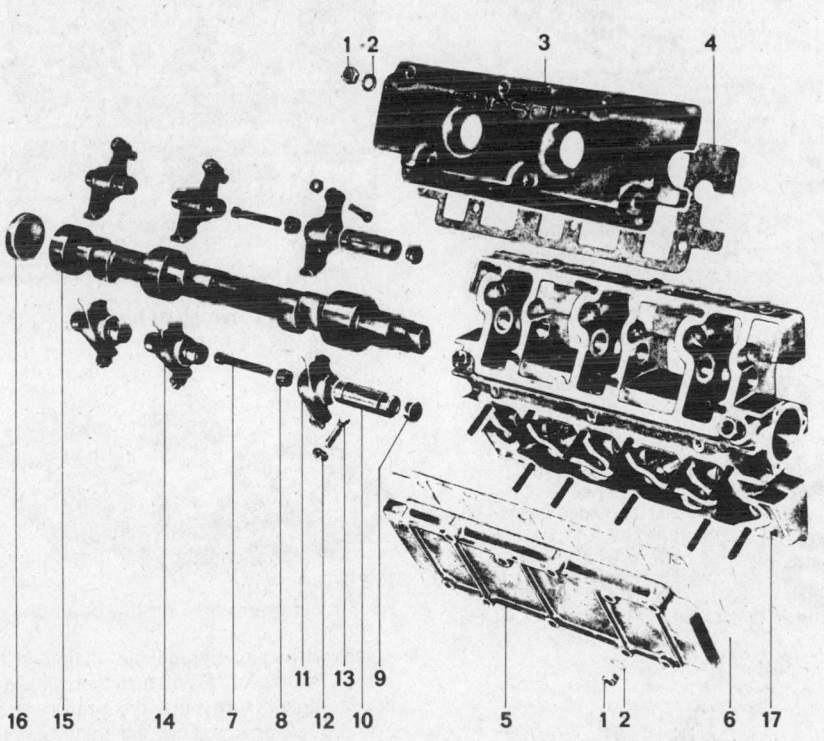

1. Nut
2. Aluminum washer
3. Cover
4. Gasket
5. Cover
6. Gasket
7. Bolt
8. Bushing
9. Nut
10. Rocker arm shaft
11. Rocker arm
12. Nut
13. Adjusting screw
14. Rocker arm assembly
15. Camshaft
16. Cover
17. Housing

Camshaft housing assembly

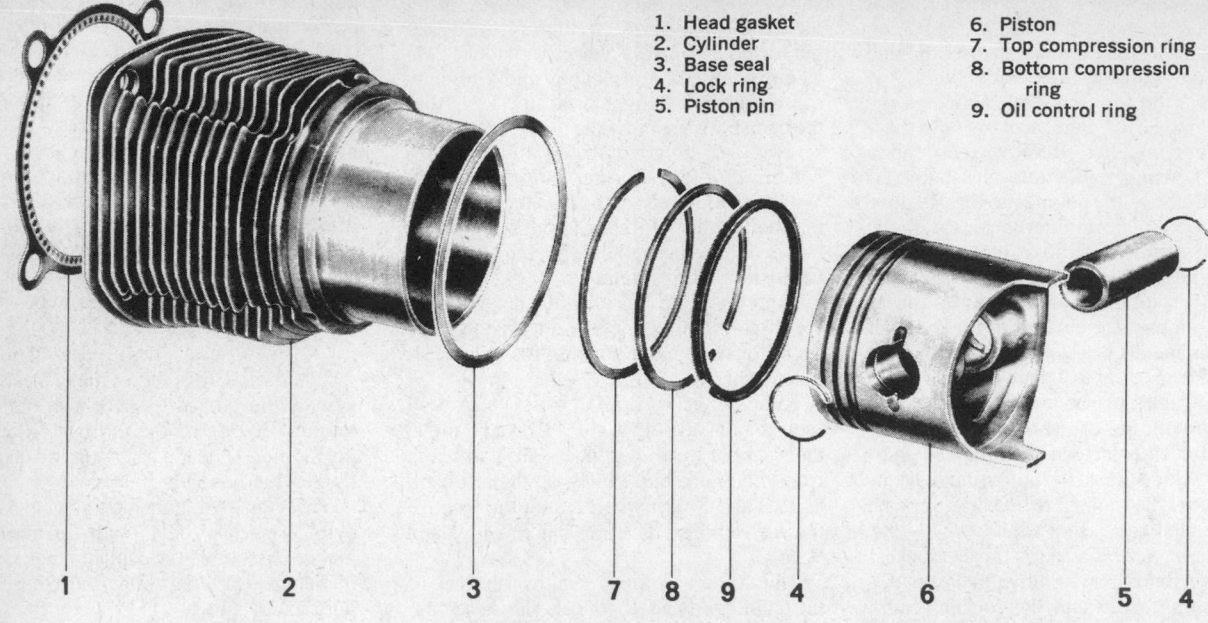

1. Head gasket
2. Cylinder
3. Base seal
4. Lock ring
5. Piston pin

6. Piston
7. Top compression ring
8. Bottom compression ring
9. Oil control ring

Cylinder and piston assembly

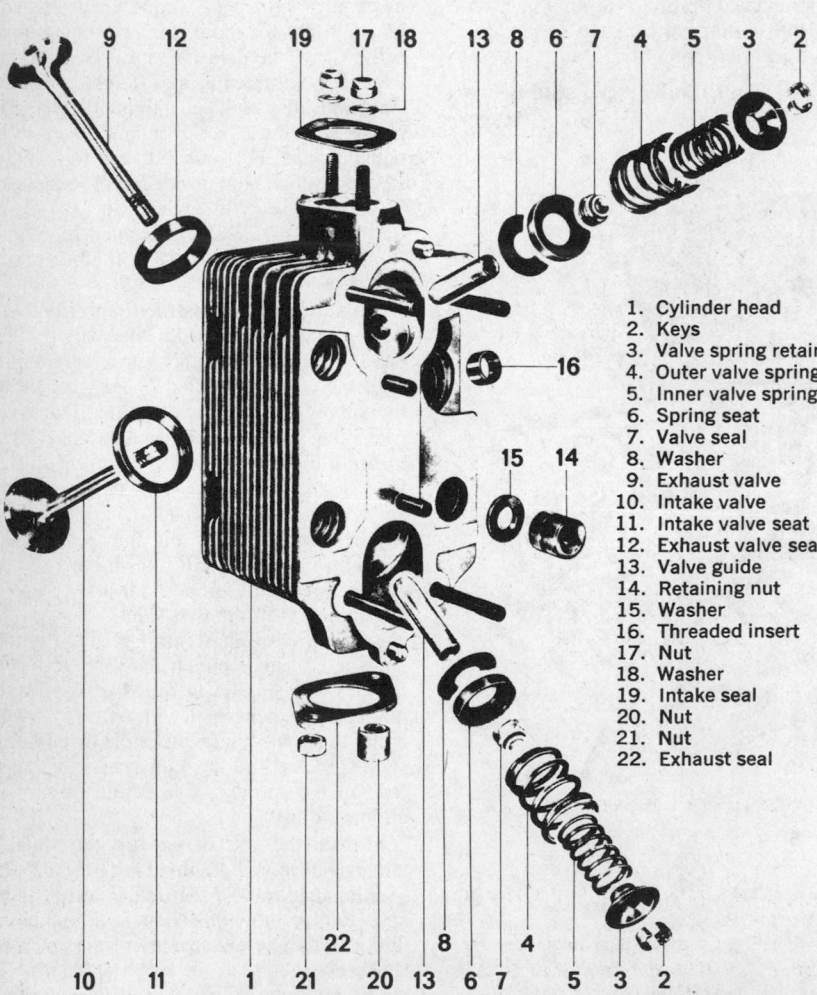

1. Cylinder head
2. Keys
3. Valve spring retainer
4. Outer valve spring
5. Inner valve spring
6. Spring seat
7. Valve seal
8. Washer
9. Exhaust valve
10. Intake valve
11. Intake valve seat
12. Exhaust valve seat
13. Valve guide
14. Retaining nut
15. Washer
16. Threaded insert
17. Nut
18. Washer
19. Intake seal
20. Nut
21. Nut
22. Exhaust seal

Cylinder head components

Removing the camshaft housing and cylinder heads as a unit

Six cylinder valve timing position

a screwdriver to tighten the chain (on the side to be measured) and turn the crankshaft one complete turn until the timing marks are aligned again. The dial gauge should read between 4.2 and 4.6mm (0.165–0.181 in.). A preferred range is 4.25 to 4.45mm.

If the gauge shows a lower or higher reading, the camshaft has to be readjusted as follows:

1. Remove the sprocket retaining nut, spring washer and aligning dowel pin.

2. Make sure that the crankshaft pulley mark is still aligned with the crankcase joint.

1 ⟶

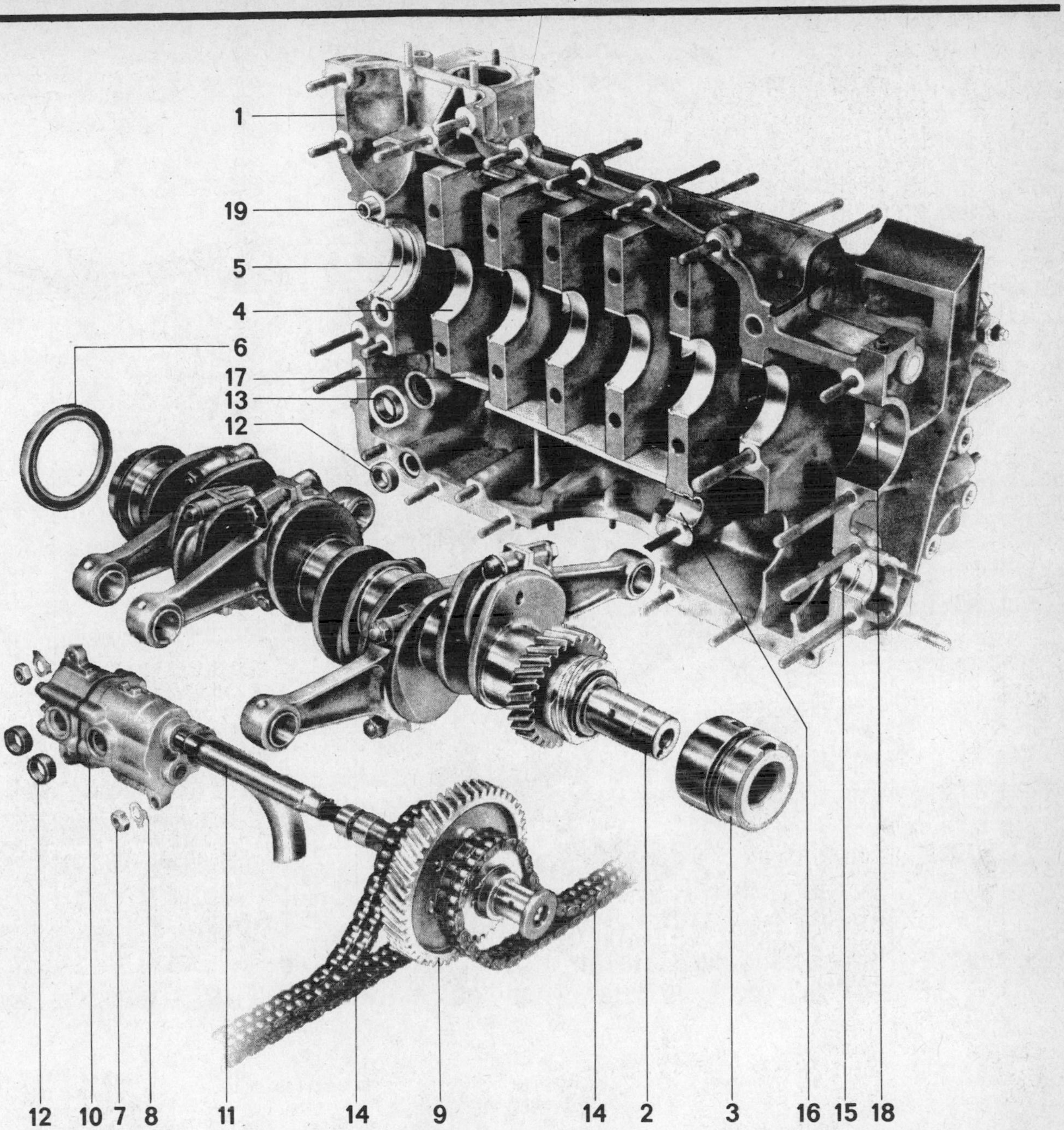

19 ⟶

5 ⟶

4 ⟶

6 ⟶

17 ⟶
13 ⟶
12 ⟶

12   10   7   8   11   14   9   14   2   3   16   15   18

1. Crankcase half	8. Lock washer	15. Intermediate shaft thrust bearing
2. Crankshaft assembly	9. Intermediate shaft	16. Intermediate shaft bearing
3. No. 8 bearing	10. Oil pump assembly	17. Oil strainer
4. Bearing shell	11. Connecting shaft	18. pin
5. Thrust bearing shell	12. Seal	19. bushing
6. Seal	13. Seal	
7. Nut	14. Camshaft chain	

Crankcase assembly

3. Depress the tensioner to tighten the chain and turn the camshaft until the dial gauge indicates 4.4 to 4.45mm (0.173–0.175 in.).

4. Find the hole in the camshaft sprocket which lines up with the sprocket flange and insert the dowel pin. Replace the spring washer and nut and tighten.

5. Turn the crankshaft two complete turns to the right and read the dial gauge. If the specified value is still not obtained, repeat the steps above.

When the valves overlap in cylinder No. 1, cylinder No. 4 is at firing point (TDC). Repeat the procedure for cylinder No. 4 valve timing adjustment.

Remove the cylinder heads, cylinders and pistons. Remove the clutch and flywheel.

Disassemble the crankcase, being careful not to score any of the mating surfaces by trying to pry the halves apart. Remove the camshaft and crankshaft with the connecting rods.

Assembly is the reverse of disassembly, noting the following procedures. Check the riveting of the camshaft gear and the camshaft. Check the camshaft for out-of-true

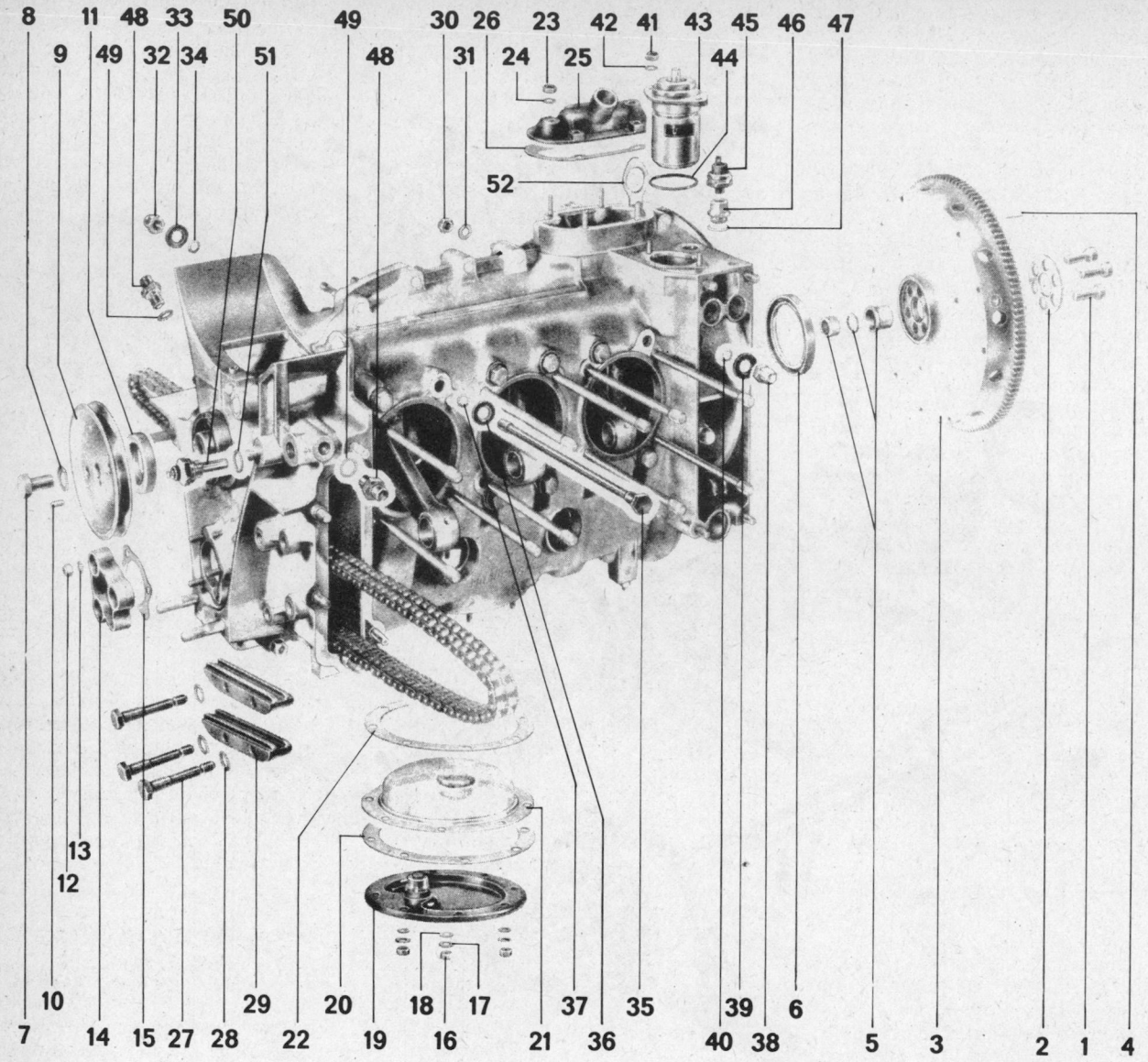

Crankcase assembly

1. Bolt	12. Nut	23. Nut	34. Seal
2. Washer	13. Washer	24. Washer	35. Crankcase bolt
3. Flywheel	14. Cover	25. Breather cover	36. Washer
4. Pin	15. Seal	26. Seal	37. Seal
5. Bushing	16. Nut	27. Slide rail bolt	38. Nut
6. Seal	17. Spring washer	28. Seal	39. Washer
7. Bolt	18. Washer	29. Slide rail	40. Nut
8. Spring washer	19. Cover	30. Nut	41. Nut
9. Pulley	20. Seal	31. Washer	42. Spring washer
10. Pin	21. Oil strainer	32. Nut	43. Thermostat
11. Seal	22. Seal	33. Washer	44. Seal

45. Oil pressure switch
46. Nut
47. Washer
48. Plug
49. Washer
50. Oil temperature switch
51. Washer
52. Hook

using V-blocks. The maximum allowable wear is 0.0016 in. Check the end-play of the guide bearing which should be 0.0016–0.0051 in. The oil holes in the crankshaft bearing journals and bearings should have no sharp edges. Carefully remove any metallic, foreign substances. Install the crankshaft and connecting rods. Install the camshaft and gear so that the tooth marked with a 0 is located between the two teeth of the crankshaft gear which are identified with a

punch mark. Coat the mating surfaces of the housing halves with a thin coat of sealing compound. Be sure that no sealing compound enters the oil ducts. Assemble the crankcase halves and lightly tighten the screw for the oil intake pipe. Screw on the sealing nuts with the sealing ring on the outside and tighten to the specified torque. Rotate the crankshaft to ensure free rotation. Grease the needle bearing in the flywheel with a small amount of multipurpose grease.

Moisten the felt ring with engine oil, wiping off any excess. Install the flywheel and adjust the axial play of the crankshaft. Measure the axial play by installing the flywheel with two spacing washers but without the sealing rings. Using a dial gauge, measure the play by rotating the flywheel. The thickness of the third spacer can be computed by subtracting 0.0039 in. from the measured result. Remove the flywheel and install the sealing ring, felt ring and three spacers. Three spacers must always be installed for the required thickness. Spacers are available in the following sizes: 0.0094, 0.0118, 0.0126, 0.0134, 0.0142 and 0.0150 in. Each spacer is marked for proper identification. The axial play of the crankshaft, measured with the engine assembled and the flywheel screwed on, should be 0.0028–0.0051 in. Clean the contact surface of the clutch disc and flywheel. Check the splining of the input shaft and coat lightly with molybdenum disulphide powder, applied with a brush. The clutch disc should slide easily. Check the throwout bearing. Do not wash in any solvent, but wipe it clean. Replace bearings which are contaminated or noisy. Grease the guide bushing lightly with molybdenum disulphide paste. Center the clutch disc and clutch on the flywheel using an input shaft. When a new clutch is installed, the balancing marks should be 180° apart. A white paint stripe on the outside edge of the flywheel indicates the heavy end, and a white paint stripe indicates the heavy end of the clutch. Tighten the bolts to 14.5 ft. lbs. Clean all pistons and check for wear. Check the marking of the pistons according to the following designations:

The letter next to the arrow is the index of the spare parts number.

The punched-in arrow indicates that the piston must be installed with the arrow facing the flywheel.

The color dot (blue, pink or green) indicates the paired size of the piston.

A statement of weight class (+ or −) is punched in or printed.

The weight class is indicated by a color dot (brown equals (−) weight and grey equals (+) weight).

Number indicates the piston size in mm.

Fit the compression and oil scraper rings. The designation TOP should face up. Insert the locking rings of pistons 1 and 2 on the side facing the flywheel. The locking rings of pistons 3 and 4 should be fitted on the impeller side. Fit the piston pin. The piston pin may slide in easily by hand, which is normal. Should the pin not fit easily, heat the piston to approximately 176°F and slide in the piston pin without bottoming the pin on the locking ring. Seat the second locking

ring. Lubricate the piston and piston pin. Compress the piston rings. Lubricate the cylinder bore and fit the cylinder bore. The sealing ring must also be fitted. The studs of the crankcase may not touch the cooling fins of the cylinder. Check the cylinder head for cracks and the spark plug threads for damage. Replace the sealing ring and the cylinder head. Pre-tighten the cylinder head nuts slightly and finally tighten according to sequence. Replace the baffle plate. Insert the tappets with engine oil. Slide the protective tubes with new sealing rings up to the stop, taking care not to damage the sealing rings. Slide the bearing pieces on the rocker arm shafts so that the slots face downward and the broken edges outward when settling on the studs. The clip which secures the protective tubes should enter the slots of the bearing pieces and rest against the bottom edges of the protective tubes. Lubricate the gear wheel and driveshaft and insert into the oil pump housing. Install the oil pump cover with the lubricated rubber sealing ring. Check the gear wheels for proper running. Install the oil pump, with a new seal, into the crankcase. The journal of the driveshaft should be in alignment with the slot in the camshaft gear. Center the oil pump by two crankshaft revolutions and tighten the nuts. Clean the sealing surface on the flange for the oil filter. Lubricate the rubber seal slightly and screw the filter in until the filter is seated. Tighten the oil filter. Replace the oil cooler after checking for leaks and tightening all welded seats. Replace the front and rear cylinder jackets and warm air guides. Replace the engine mount. Replace the cooling blower housing with the alternator and adjust the V-belt tension. Replace the cooling blower impeller and the front engine cover plate. Replace the ignition distributor. Bring cylinder No. 1 to the firing point. The black notch should be in alignment with the reference mark. The center offset slot in the head of the ignition distributor driveshaft should be at an angle of approximately 12° in relation to the longitudinal axis of the

engine. Turn the distributor rotor to the mark for cylinder No. 1 on the distributor housing. Insert the ignition distributor. Replace the oil filler neck with the oil vent. Replace the intake distributor with the intake pipes and injection valves. Mount the rear engine cover plate. Replace the exhaust muffler and heat exchanger. Fill the engine with oil and replace the engine in the car. Adjust the ignition timing.

EMISSION CONTROLS

Crankcase Ventilation System

All models are equipped with a crankcase ventilation systems. The purpose of the crankcase ventilation system is two-fold. It keeps harmful vapors from escaping into the atmosphere and prevents the build-up of pressures within the crankcase which could cause oil leaks.

The system carries vapors from the crankcase to the oil tank and then to the air cleaner. The crankcase emissions are then burned along with the air/fuel mixture. The only maintenance required on the crankcase ventilation system is a periodic check. At every tune-up, examine the hoses for clogging or deterioration. Clean or replace the hoses as required.

Evaporative Emission Control System

The system used on the 911 consists of an expansion chamber, evaporation chamber and an activated charcoal filter. Fuel vapors which reach the filter deposit hydrocarbons on the surface of the charcoal element. The

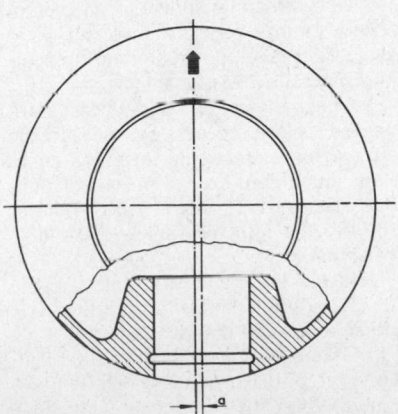

Piston positioning

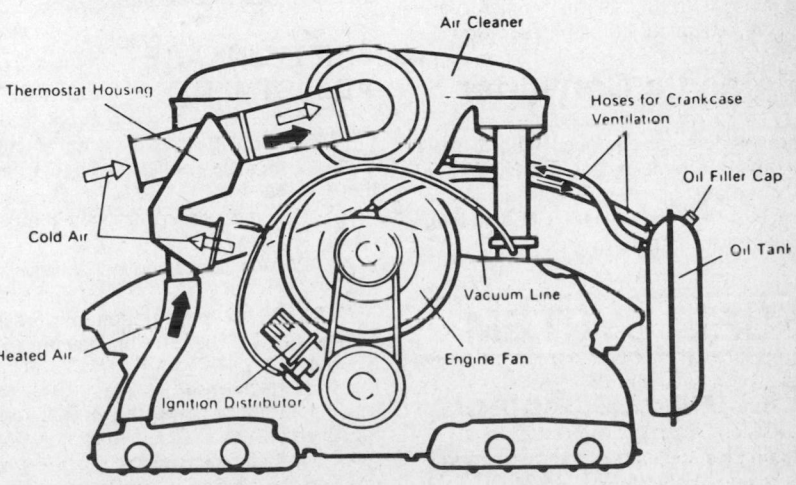

Crankcase ventilation schematic

engine fan forces fresh air into the charcoal filter when the engine is running. The air purges the filter and the hydrocarbons are sent into the air cleaner, where they become part of the air/fuel mixture and are burned.

Maintenance on this system consists of checking the condition of the various connecting lines and the charcoal filter at 10,000 mile intervals. The charcoal filter, which is located in the front luggage compartment, should be replaced at 50,000 mile intervals.

Dual Diaphragm Distributors

The purpose of the dual diaphragm distributor is to improve exhaust emissions during idling. The distributor has a vacuum retard diaphragm, in addition to a vacuum advance diaphragm.

TESTING

1. Connect a timing light to the engine. Check the ignition timing.
2. Remove the retard hose from the distributor and plug it. Increase the engine speed. The ignition timing should advance. If it doesn't, then the vacuum unit is faulty and must be replaced.

Exhaust Gas Recirculation

This system directs a portion of the exhaust gases back into the intake where they combine with the incoming mixture. This diluting of the mixture lowers peak combustion temperatures and reduces NO_x.

Thermal Reactor

A thermal reactor is used on certain 911 models. The thermal reactor is used to reduce HC and CO emissions by supplying an improved location for exhaust combustion. 911s with the thermal reactor are equipped with an additional heater blower.

Catalytic Converter

Certain models are equipped with a catalytic converter in the exhaust system. When the hot exhaust gases mix with air in the presence of the catalyst, HC, CO, and NO_x are reduced to harmless gases.

FUEL SYSTEM

Electric Fuel Pump

REMOVAL & INSTALLATION

The Turbo is equipped with two electric

pumps. One is mounted at the front cross-member, near the fuel tank; the second at the rear, near the engine. All 911 fuel pumps are located at the front near the tank.

1. Remove the cap nuts.
2. Withdraw the pump with its mounting bracket.
3. Loosen the hose clamp and remove the pump from the bracket.
4. Loosen the hose clamps and remove the three fuel lines from the pump.
5. Install the pump using a reverse of the removal procedure. Coat both electrical terminals with grease and make sure that the rubber boot is firmly seated.

Fuel pump removal

Fuel Injection

For all fuel injection system repair and service procedures, please refer to "Fuel Injection" in the Unit Repair section.

TRANSAXLE

REMOVAL & INSTALLATION

Transaxle separation is covered in the "Engine Removal" procedure.

SHIFT LINKAGE ADJUSTMENT

1. Position the shift lever in Neutral. Remove the rear tunnel cover in front of the rear seat.
2. Pull the rubber dust cover forward on the shift rod.
3. Loosen the clamp bolt on the shift rod.
4. Move the transmission selector shaft all the way to its left stop, keeping it in Neutral.
5. With the transmission still in Neutral, move the gearshift rod to the right to its stop.
6. Tighten the clamp bolt to 18 ft. lbs.
7. Test the shift lever. Play should be the same in all gears in all directions.

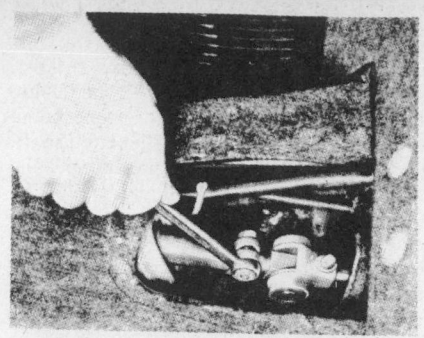

Linkage adjustment

OVERHAUL

For all transaxle overhaul procedures, please refer to "Manual Transaxle Overhaul" in the Unit Repair section.

CLUTCH

REMOVAL & INSTALLATION

1. Separate the engine/transaxle.
2. Gradually loosen the pressure plate bolts one or two turns at a time in a criss-cross pattern to prevent distortion.
3. Remove the pressure plate and clutch disc.

Clutch disc centering

4. Check the clutch disc for uneven or excessive lining wear. Examine the pressure plate for cracking, scorching, or scoring. Replace any questionable components.
5. Check the clutch release bearing for wear, and replace if necessary. Measure the clutch disc for wear; new thickness is 8.1mm, and the maximum wear limit is 6.3mm. Clutch disc run-out (maximum) is 0.6mm.
6. Fill the pilot bearing with about 2 cc of grease.
7. Install the clutch disc and pressure plate. Use a pilot shaft or an old transaxle input shaft to keep the disc centered.
8. Gradually tighten the pressure plate-to-flywheel bolts in a criss-cross pattern. Torque the bolts to 18 ft. lbs.
9. Install the throwout bearing.
10. Install the transaxle on the engine.

FREE PLAY ADJUSTMENT

These models are equipped with an auxiliary spring to reduce pedal effort. Free-play is no longer checked at the pedal. Play is checked by measuring the distance between the adjusting belt and the positioning lever. The distance should be 1mm (0.04 in.).

1. Release the cable.
2. Adjust clutch play to 1.2mm (0.047 in.).
3. Tighten the cable at the holder until play is reduced to 1mm. (0.04 in.).
4. Adjust the stop on the pedal floor plate so that the release travel is 25mm (0.984 in.) for the S or 27mm (1.063 in.) when the clutch pedal is depressed.

Pedal travel adjustment

PEDAL TRAVEL ADJUSTMENT

1. Pull the front carpeting back.
2. Loosen the two retaining bolts on the pedal stop.
3. Move the pedal up or down until reverse can be engaged with only a slight amount of gear clash.
4. Tighten the pedal stop bolts.
5. Double check the adjustment by shifting into reverse several times. Reinstall the floor carpeting.

DRIVE AXLES

Axle Driveshaft

REMOVAL & INSTALLATION

1. Jack up the rear of the car and support it on stands.
2. Remove the wheels. Remove the brake caliper and disc.
3. Raise the trailing arm with a hydraulic jack.
4. Remove the lower shock absorber mounting.
5. Install a fixture similar to Porsche tool P36b to hold the hub.
6. Remove the cotter pin and, using a long ratchet handle extension, remove the hub nut.

7. Remove the Allen bolts at the axle driveshaft/transaxle flange.
8. Use a flat chisel to pry the flanges apart.

Hub nut removal (Porsche tool P36b shown)

------ CAUTION ------
Don't damage the flanges when separating them.

9. Check the axle driveshaft joints for excessive play and replace them if necessary.
10. Use a new gasket on the transaxle flange. Ensure that the flanges are clean and free from burrs.
11. Pack the joints with a moly grease.
12. Install the axle driveshaft using a reverse of the removal procedure.
13. Tighten the flange bolts to 60 ft. lbs. The hollow side of the lock washer should face the spacer slate.
14. Using a long extension handle wrench, tighten the castellated nut to 217–253 ft. lbs. and install a new cotter pin.

NOTE: Be prepared to apply considerable force on this unit.

15. Tighten the shock absorber bolt to 54 ft. lbs.
16. Install the brake caliper and disc.
17. Install the wheels and lower the car.

CV–Joints

For information on CV–Joints, please refer to "U–Joint/CV–Joint Overhaul" in the Unit Repair Section.

REAR SUSPENSION

All models covered in this section have independent rear suspension. The rear suspension is a semi-trailing arm design. Springing is provided by transverse torsion bars located forward of each trailing arm. Telescopic shock absorbers at each wheel provide dampening. A rear stabilizer bar is standard equipment on the 911S Turbo and Carrera and optional on the other 911 models.

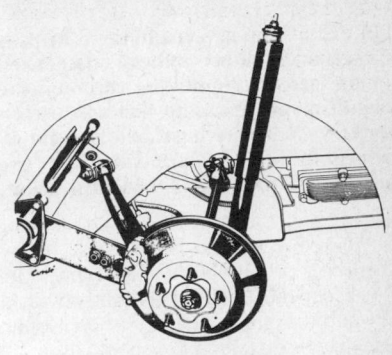

Rear suspension

Torsion Bars

REMOVAL & INSTALLATION

1. Jack up the rear of the car and support it safely with stands.
2. Remove the wheel on the side where the torsion bar is being removed.
3. Fabricate a fixture similar to the one shown. The fixture is necessary to hold the trailing arm while it is raised and lowered. The special Porsche tool for this purpose is number P 289.
4. Using a hydraulic jack under the holding fixture, raise the trailing arm.
5. Remove the lower shock absorber bolt.
6. Remove the trailing arm retaining bolts. Remove the toe and chamber adjusting bolts.
7. Remove the four retaining bolts from the trailing arm cover. Withdraw the spacer.
8. Using two small prybars, pry off the trailing arm cover.
9. Remove the holding fixture.
10. Knock out the round body plug and remove the trailing arm.
11. Paint a reference mark on the torsion bar support, matching the location of the "L" or "R" side identification letter, so that the torsion bar may be installed in the same position.

NOTE: The torsion bars are splined to allow adjustment of the rear riding height.

Raising the trailing arm

12. Remove the torsion bar. Do not scratch the protective paint on the torsion bar, or it will corrode and possibly develop fatigue cracks.

NOTE: If you are removing a broken torsion bar, the inner end can be knocked from its seat by removing the opposite torsion bar and tapping through with a steel rod. Torsion bars are not interchangeable from side-to-side and are marked "L" and "R" for identification.

13. Check the torsion bar splines for damage and replace it if necessary. If any corrosion is present on the bar, replace it.

14. Coat the torsion bar lightly with a multi-purpose grease. Carefully grease the splines.

15. Apply glycerine or another rubber preservative to the torsion bar support.

16. Install the torsion bar, matching the "L" or "R" with the paint mark you made before removal.

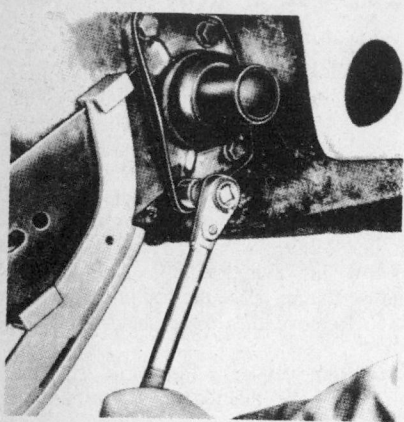

Installing the trailing arm cover

17. Install the trailing arm cover into position and start the three accessible bolts.

18. Raise the trailing arm into place with the holding fixture (or special tool P 289) until the spacer and the fourth bolt can be installed.

19. Assemble the remaining components in a reverse order of their removal.

20. Tighten the trailing arm cover bolts to 34 ft. lbs. Tighten the trailing arm retaining bolts to 65 ft. lbs.

21. Tighten the camber adjusting bolt to 43 ft. lbs. and the toe-in adjusting bolt to 36 ft. lbs. Tighten the shock absorber bolt to 45 ft. lbs.

22. Adjust the rear wheel camber and toe-in.

Shock Absorbers

REMOVAL & INSTALLATION

1. Leave the car standing on the ground so that the shock absorber is not tensioned.

2. Open the engine compartment lid and remove the rubber cover from the top of the shock absorber.

Bottom shock absorber mounting

3. Hold the shock absorber shaft and remove the nut.

4. On the bottom, remove the retaining nut and bolt.

5. Remove the shock absorber.

6. If the shock exhibits excessive free travel or is leaking, replace it.

7. Install the shock up through the body and screw the nut on hand-tight.

8. Align the shock absorber eye with the hole in the trailing arm and install the nut and bolt.

9. Tighten the top nut and install the rubber cover.

10. Tighten the bottom retaining bolt to 54 ft. lbs.

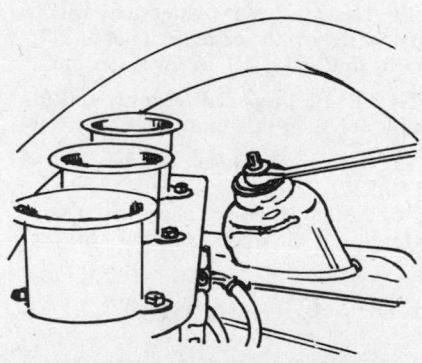

Top shock absorber mounting

Stabilizer

REMOVAL & INSTALLATION

1. Raise the rear of the car and safely support it with stands.

2. Using a large prybar, pry the upper eyes of the stabilizer bar off the studs in the trailing arm.

3. Remove the body mounting brackets.

4. Remove the stabilizer.

5. Check the rubber bushings for wear or damage and, if necessary, replace them.

6. Install the stabilizer bar using a reverse of the removal steps.

Adjustments

CAMBER

The rearmost of the two Allen bolts on the trailing arm provides camber adjustment. Tighten the bolt to 43 ft. lbs. after the camber is adjusted to specifications.

TOE-IN

The front Allen bolt on the trailing arm adjusts the toe-in. Tighten the bolt to 36 ft. lbs. after toe-in is adjusted to specification.

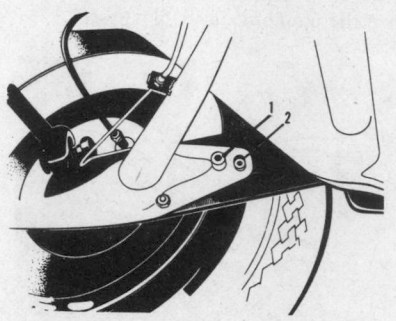

1. Camber
2. Toe-in

Rear wheel alignment adjustment points

FRONT SUSPENSION

Springing is provided by a longitudinal torsion bar at each wheel. A triangular lower arm links the torsion bar to the shock absorber strut and steering knuckle. A permanently lubricated ball joint is located at the bottom of the strut.

Torsion Bars

REMOVAL & INSTALLATION

1. Jack up the front of the car and support it safely with stands.

2. Remove the torsion bar adjusting screw.

3. Take the adjusting lever off the torsion bar and withdraw the seal.

4. Unscrew the retaining bolts from the front mount cover bracket and remove the bracket.

5. Using a drift, carefully drive the torsion bar out of the front of the arm.

6. Check the torsion bar for spline damage and rust. If necessary, replace the bar.

7. Give the torsion bar a light coating of grease before installing it.

NOTE: Torsion bars are marked "L" or "R" to identify them and are not interchangeable.

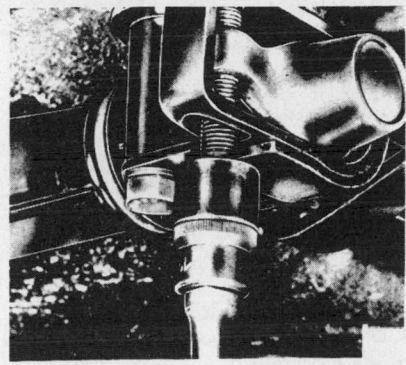

Loosening torsion bar adjusting screw

8. Insert the end cap of the torsion bar, protruding side out, into the control arm. Drive the torsion bar into position with a drift. Carefully.

9. Tighten the retaining bolts on the front mount to 34 ft. lbs.

10. Slide the seal onto the torsion bar from the open side of the crossmember.

11. Using a tire iron, or other suitable lever, pry the control arm down as far as possible. While holding the control arm, slide the adjusting lever onto the splines of the torsion bar. There should only be a slight amount of clearance at the lever adjusting point.

12. Grease the adjusting screw threads with a moly grease and hand tighten the screw.

13. Check that the end cap is properly seated in the control arm.

14. Install the rubber mount cover

bracket. Tighten the retaining bolts to 34 ft. lbs.

15. Lower the car.

16. Check the front wheel alignment.

Shock Absorbers

REMOVAL & INSTALLATION

1. Jack up the front of the car and support it safely on stands. Remove the wheels.

2. Remove the brake line from the clip on the suspension strut. A small amount of brake fluid will run out of the line, plug it so that dirt cannot enter the system.

3. Unscrew the retaining bolts and remove the caliper.

4. Using a soft mallet, tap the hub cap to loosen it.

5. Pry the hub cap off with a small prybar.

6. Loosen the Allen screw in the wheel bearing clamp. Unscrew the clamp nut and remove the nut and washer.

7. Remove the wheel hub along with the brake disc and wheel bearing.

8. Remove the backing plate retaining bolts and remove the plate.

9. Withdraw the cotter pin from the castellated nut on the tie-rod end and remove the nut. Using a suitable puller, remove the tie-rod joint from the strut.

10. Remove the control arm-to-strut ball joint retaining bolt and pull the ball joint out of the strut by pulling down on the lower control arm.

NOTE: The torsion bar adjusting screw will have to be loosened and the adjusting arm removed.

11. Remove the keeper for the nut on the top of the strut. Unscrew the nut and remove it, the keeper plate, and washer.

12. Remove the strut from the bottom. It will be necessary to loosen and pull the side of the luggage compartment out for clearance.

13. Check the shock absorber strut for excessive free travel and leaking. Replace the shock absorber if it is at all suspect.

14. Install the strut in a reverse order of the removal.

15. Tighten the top nut to 58 ft. lbs. Use

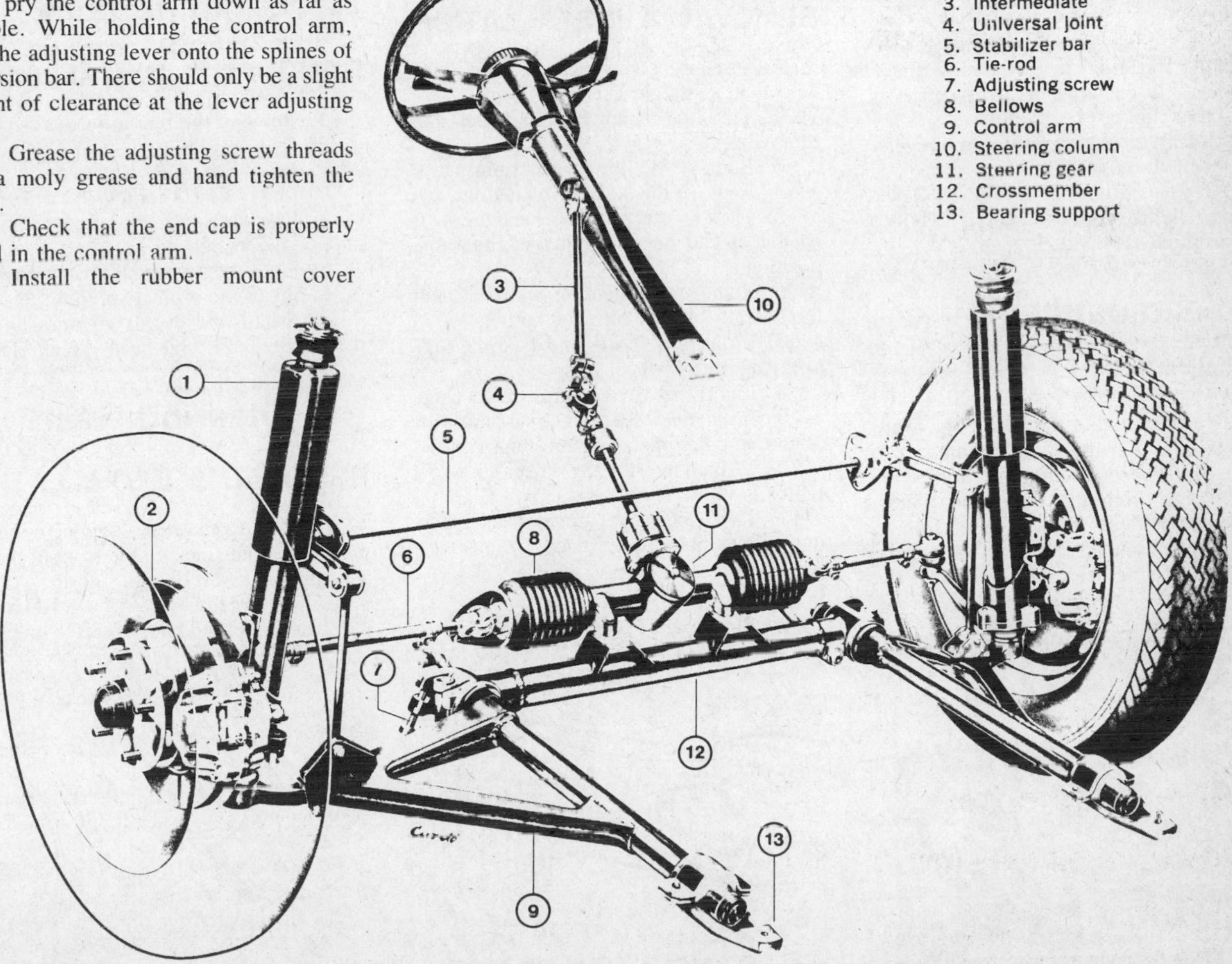

1. Strut
2. Brake disc
3. Intermediate
4. Universal joint
5. Stabilizer bar
6. Tie-rod
7. Adjusting screw
8. Bellows
9. Control arm
10. Steering column
11. Steering gear
12. Crossmember
13. Bearing support

Front suspension and steering

a new keeper plate and ensure that the peg on the plate is pointing up.

16. Tighten the ball joint bolt to 47 ft. lbs.

NOTE: Remember to install the washer between the ball joint seal and strut.

17. Install the torsion bar adjusting lever as described in ''Torsion Bar Removal and Installation.''

18. Tighten the tie-rod nut to 33 ft. lbs. and install a new cotter pin.

19. Torque the backing plate bolts to 18 ft. lbs.

20. Install and adjust the wheel bearings.

21. Tighten the caliper retaining bolts to 50 ft. lbs.

22. Bleed the brakes.

23. Install the wheels and lower the car.

24. Check the wheel alignment.

Stabilizer Bar

REMOVAL & INSTALLATION

1. Jack up the front of the car and safely support it on stands.

2. Loosen the stabilizer clamp bolts and pry the lever ends off their mounts.

3. Remove the stabilizer bar along with the levers.

4. Check the rubber bushings for deterioration and, if necessary, replace them. Lubricate the bushings with glycerine or some other rubber preservative.

5. Install the stabilizer bar in a reverse order of the removal.

6. The square end of the stabilizer should protrude slightly above the clamp. Tighten the clamp nuts to 18 ft. lbs.

Adjustments

CAMBER

Camber is adjusted at the top of the strut. Pull back the luggage compartment rug to expose the three mounting bolts. Scrape the undercoating from the bolts and plates. Scribe the positions of the two plates under the bolts. Loosen the bolts and move the strut in or out as necessary to correct the camber angle.

Caster and camber adjustment location

CASTER

Caster is adjusted in the same manner as camber, except that the strut is moved forward or backward to change the caster angle.

TOE-IN

Toe-in is set with the front wheels straight ahead. Tie-rod length is adjusted by loosening the tie-rod clamps and moving them an equal amount in or out to obtain the correct toe-in.

STEERING

All models are equipped with rack and pinion type steering gear. No maintenance is required on the steering system. It is filled with a special lubricant at the time of manufacture and does not require checking or filling.

Steering Wheel

REMOVAL & INSTALLATION

1. Disconnect the battery(ies). Place the wheels in a straight ahead position.

2. Twist the center cover to the left and remove it.

3. Remove the horn contact pin.

4. Remove the steering wheel nut.

5. Mark the steering wheel and the shaft so that it can be reinstalled in the same position.

6. Remove the steering wheel. Catch the bearing support ring and spring.

7. Install the spring and bearing support ring on the wheel hub.

8. Lightly grease the horn contact ring.

9. Install the wheel. Make sure that you align the match marks before removal.

10. Tighten the steering wheel nut to 58 ft. lbs.

11. Twist the center cover back on to the right to snap it into place.

Steering wheel center cover removal

Turn Signal/Headlight Flasher Switch

REMOVAL & INSTALLATION

The combination turn signal, headlight dimmer, and flasher switch is located in the steering column housing. The wiper/washer switch removal and installation procedure is identical.

1. Remove the steering wheel as outlined above.

2. Reach under the instrument panel and disconnect all wiring to the switch.

3. Remove the two horn contact ring screws, disconnect the wire, and remove the ring.

4. Remove the two upper housing retaining nuts. Pull the entire assembly off the column, leading the switch wires through the hole in the housing.

5. Remove the three retaining screws and remove the switch.

6. Reverse the removal steps to reinstall the switch.

Ignition Switch/ Steering Lock

REMOVAL & INSTALLATION

1. Remove the ignition switch cover.

2. Drill out the two shear bolts which retain the switch.

3. Remove the steering lock and spacer.

4. Disconnect the electrical wiring and remove the switch.

5. Place the steering lock into position.

6. Insert the protective plate.

7. Install and evenly tighten the new shear bolts until their heads break off.

Steering Gear

REMOVAL & INSTALLATION

1. Remove the front luggage compartment carpeting. Jack up the front of the car and support it safely with stands.

2. Remove the auxiliary heater duct from the steering post and position it to one side.

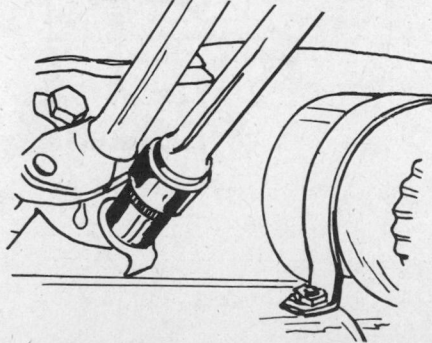

Disconnecting steering coupling

3. Open the access door and the intermediate steering shaft cover by prying the spring clips off with a small prybar.

4. Remove the three heater fuel pump retaining bolts and position the pump to one side.

5. Remove the cotter pin from the lower universal joint bolt and loosen the castellated nut. Pull the universal joint off the steering shaft.

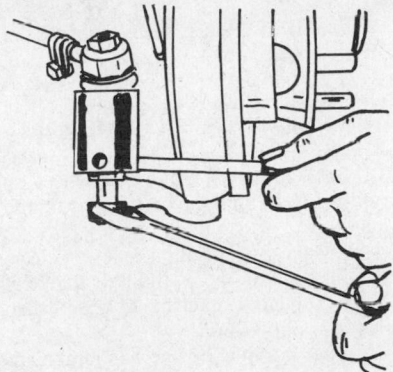

Removing the tie—rod ends

6. Remove the Allen bolts from the steering shaft bushing bracket. Remove the bracket and pull the bushing and dust cover.

7. Loosen and remove the steering coupling bolts.

8. Remove the retaining bolts and remove the bottom shield.

9. Remove the cotter pins and nuts, and then pull the tie-rod ends out of the suspension struts with a suitable puller.

10. Remove the two rack and pinion housing retaining bolts.

11. Remove the right side crossmember brace.

12. Pull the steering assembly out the right side of the car.

13. Remove the retaining bolts from the tie rod yokes.

14. Installation is the reverse of the removal procedure.

15. Tighten the yoke bolts to 34 ft. lbs.

16. Make sure that the crossmember brace mounts without binding. Tighten the nuts to 47 ft. lbs. and the bolts to 34 ft. lbs.

17. Install the steering housing bolts with new lockwashers and tighten to 34 ft. lbs.

18. Tighten the tie-rod end nuts to 33 ft. lbs. and install new cotter pins.

19. Tighten the steering bushing bracket Allen bolts to 18 ft. lbs.

20. Install new washers on the steering coupling bolts and tighten them to 18 ft. lbs.

21. Lower the car.

BRAKE SYSTEM

All models are equipped with four wheel disc brakes. Fixed, two-piston calipers are utilized on each system. 911s are equipped with internally vented discs at each wheel. Disc brakes on all of these models are self-adjusting and require no periodic adjustment.

Each car has a tandem master cylinder, remote reservoir (mounted in the front luggage compartment for convenience), and separate hydraulic circuits for the front and rear brakes. All models are equipped with power brakes. A vacuum booster is mounted in tandem with the master cylinder. It is located under the luggage compartment carpet.

For all brake system repair and service procedures not detailed below, please refer to "Brakes" in the Unit Repair section.

Master Cylinder

REMOVAL & INSTALLATION

1. Pull the accelerator back and out of its pushrod. Pull back the driver's side carpeting.

2. Unscrew the floorboard retainer(s) under the brake and clutch pedals.

3. Remove the master cylinder dust cover.

4. Jack the front of the car up and support it with stands.

5. Siphon the brake fluid out of the reservoir. Discard the fluid, don't save it for reuse.

6. Unbolt the front splash shield.

7. Remove the brake lines from the master cylinder. Disconnect the brake failure warning light sending unit wire.

8. Remove the two master cylinder mounting nuts.

9. Disconnect the reservoir lines and remove the master cylinder.

10. Before installing the master cylinder, apply body sealer around the mounting flange.

11. Install the cylinder, making sure that the piston pushrod is correctly positioned. Torque the mounting nuts to 18 ft. lbs.

12. The piston pushrod should have 0.04 in. (1mm) clearance between it and the piston. Loosen the piston rod nut and turn the rod to adjust the clearance.

13. Refill the system with new brake fluid. Bleed the brakes as detailed in "Brakes" in the Unit Repair section.

14. Tighten the splash shield bolts to 34 ft. lbs. (larger bolt) and 18 ft. lbs. (smaller bolt).

15. Test the brake failure warning light.

a. Switch on the ignition. The handbrake warning light will go on. If it doesn't, replace the bulb.

b. Start the engine. While you depress the brake pedal, have an assistant open a bleeder valve on one of the wheels to simulate a brake failure. The light should go on.

c. When your assistant closes the valve, the light should go out.

d. Repeat the test on the other brake circuit.

If the light fails to light during one of the tests, check the circuit failure sender which screws into the master cylinder.

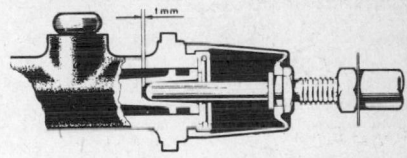

Correct piston pushrod clearance

Wheel Bearings

REMOVAL & INSTALLATION

NOTE: The inner bearing, seal, and outer bearing may be removed and lubricated once the hub/disc assembly is off the car. If after cleaning, the bearings are noticeably worn or damaged they should be replaced along with their races. If the bearings are satisfactory, skip the race removal steps.

1. Remove the brake disc/hub assembly.

2. Match mark the hub and disc for correct reassembly, remove the five assembly bolts, and separate the hub and disc.

3. Pry the inner seal out of the hub. Remove the inner bearing and outer bearing.

4. Wash the bearings in solvent and blow them dry. Examine the bearings for pitting, scoring, or other damage. Replace

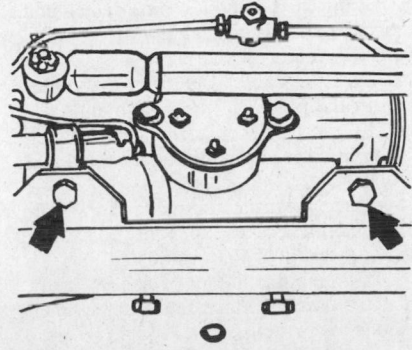

Rack and pinion retaining bolts

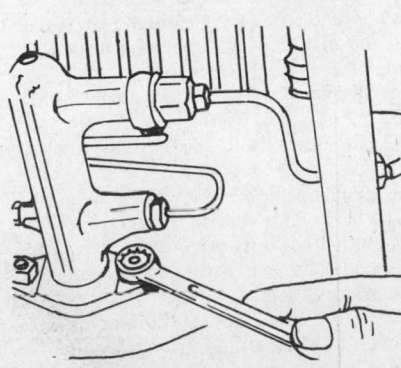

Master cylinder removal

the bearing and race as a unit if there is any question as to their condition.

5. Heat the wheel hub to 250°–300°F.

6. Press the inner bearing race out of the hub on a press table, using suitable spacers to prevent damaging the hub.

7. Press out the outer bearing race, using suitable spacers and a support fabricated from the accompanying drawing.

8. Press a new inner bearing race into the hub and then press in a new outer bearing race.

9. Pack the bearings with a lithium multipurpose grease.

10. Align the match marks and install the hub on the disc. Insert the assembly bolts from the inside out and tighten them to 17 ft. lbs.

11. Lightly coat the spindle with grease. Fill the hub with about 2 oz of grease. Lubricate and install the bearings.

12. Grease the sealing edges of a new inner oil seal and carefully tap it into place. The oil seal must be flush with the hub.

13. Install the hub/disc assembly on the car.

14. Adjust the wheel bearings.

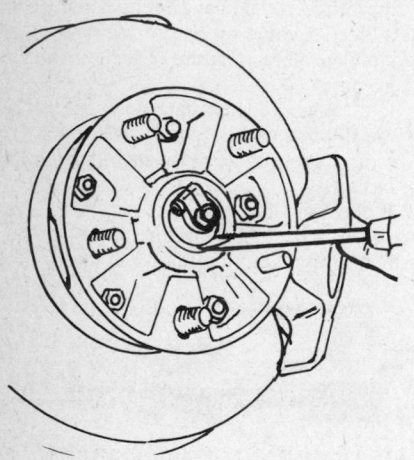

Checking wheel bearing play

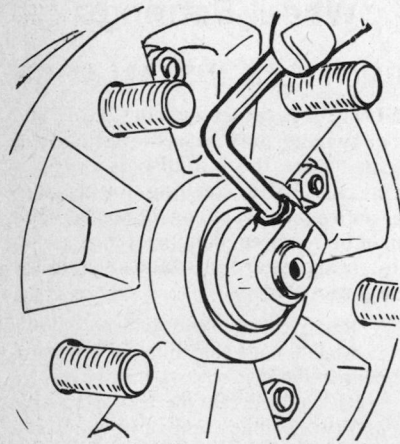

Final tightening of the wheel clamp nut—check play again before installing hub cap

ADJUSTMENT

Check and adjust the front wheel bearings after the car has not been run for a few hours. The bearings will be cold then.

1. The front wheel bearings are correctly adjusted when the thrust washer can be moved slightly sideways under light pressure from a small prybar, but no bearing play is evident when the wheel hub is shaken axially.

2. Jack up the front of the car, support it on stands, and remove the wheels. Turn the hub several times to seat the bearings.

3. Pry the hub cap off and perform the check described in Step 1.

NOTE: Don't press the prybar against the hub. Hold it lightly in your hand so you get a better feel.

4. If the bearings require an adjustment, loosen the Allen screw and turn the clamp nut in or out as necessary.

5. Tighten the clamp nut Allen screw to 11 ft. lbs. without altering the adjusted position of the clamp nut.

6. Double check the adjustment and readjust, if necessary.

7. Give the clamp nut and thrust washer a light coating of lithium grease. Tap the hub cap into place with a plastic or rubber mallet.

8. Install the wheels and lower the car.

Handbrake

The 911 models are equipped with a separate handbrake system. The center, pull-up lever mechanically operates a pair of brake shoes inside each rear disc, which act as drums through a pot-shaped center section.

CABLE

Adjustment

1. Jack up the rear of the car and support it on stands. Remove the wheels.

2. Release the handbrake lever.

3. Push the brake pads away from the disc so that it can be turned by hand.

4. Loosen the cable adjusting nuts to release tension.

5. Insert a screwdriver into the disc access hole and rotate the handbrake star wheel until the disc can no longer be turned by hand.

6. Repeat this operation on the other side.

7. Readjust the cable nuts to take up the slack.

8. Pull up the center tunnel cover and handbrake lever boot at the rear. By looking through the two inspection holes, see if the cable equalizer is exactly perpendicular to the car's centerline.

9. If the equalizer positioning is off, correct it by loosening or tightening the cable adjusting nuts. Tighten the locknuts after the adjustment is correct.

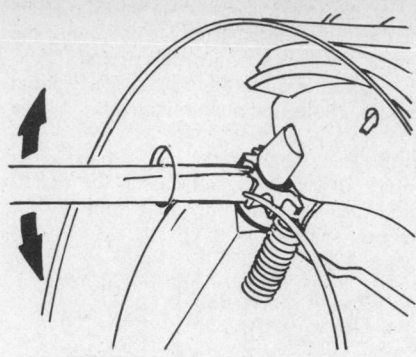

Hand brake star wheel adjustment

10. Back off each brake star wheel by four or five teeth until the disc can be turned by hand.

11. Check the handbrake lever clearance. There should be a slight clearance at the lever. The handbrake should be set when the lever is pulled up.

12. After completing the handbrake adjustment, depress the brake pedal several times to reposition the rear caliper pistons. Check the fluid level in the reservoir and top it up, if necessary.

Removal & Installation

1. Jack up the rear of the car and support it on stands. Remove the wheels.

2. Remove the center tunnel cover and handbrake lever boot.

3. Remove the heater control knob.

4. Undo the handbrake support housing bolts.

5. Unscrew the heater control lever nut. Remove the cup spring, discs, and the lever.

6. Slightly raise the handbrake support housing. Snap off the retaining clip and pull out the cable equalizing stud.

7. Disconnect the handbrake light switch wire.

8. Remove the handbrake support housing.

9. Detach the cables from the cable equalizer.

10. Remove the rear brake calipers.

11. Remove the rear brake discs and spacer rings.

12. Remove the cotter pin, castellated nut, and disc from each cable. Pull the cable toward the center of the car.

13. Pull the cables out from the center tunnel in the passenger compartment.

14. Lubricate the replacement cables with multipurpose grease and then feed them into the tube.

15. Place a washer between the spacer sleeve and the brake expander. Place another washer under the castellated nut.

16. Tighten the nut until a new cotter pin can be inserted. Make sure that the brake expander is correctly seated.

17. Install the brake disc and calipers.

18. Connect the handbrake light wire to the switch.

19. Insert the heater control lever into the handbrake support housing.

20. Install and clip the equalizer stud. Ensure that the handbrake cables are correctly seated.

21. Torque the handbrake support housing bolts to 18 ft. lbs.

22. Install a friction disc, the heater control lever, another friction disc, pressure disc, cup spring, and the nut.

23. Tighten the nut so that the lever doesn't slip back when the heater is on full, and yet isn't too tight to operate.

24. Bleed the brakes.

25. Check the handbrake adjustment.

26. Install the wheels and lower the car.

HANDBRAKE SHOES

Removal & Installation

1. Jack up the rear of the car and support it on stands. Remove the wheels.

2. Remove the brake calipers.

3. Detach the brake discs.

4. Remove the cotter pin, castellated nut, and washer from the brake cable.

5. Pull the cable out toward the center of the car.

6. Remove the expander and spring.

7. Depress the upper spring and twist the holddown cup to remove it and the spring.

8. Pull the brake shoe outward and remove the pin through the rear.

9. Using a small prybar, raise the upper brake shoe and remove the star wheel assembly. Unhook the spring.

10. Repeat Steps 7 and 8 for the bottom shoe.

11. Unhook the front return spring and remove both shoes.

NOTE: Complete the brake shoe removal and installation one side at a time, so the opposite side can be used as a reference.

12. Clean all metal parts in alcohol. Contaminated or worn brake shoes should be replaced.

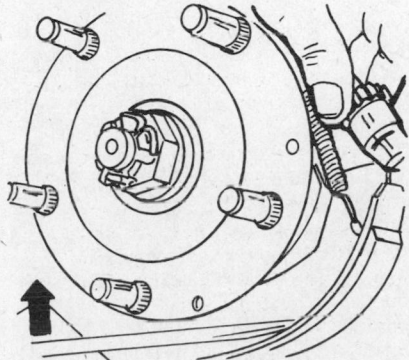

Star wheel assembly removal

13. Insert the brake cable from the back and slide the inner part of the expander onto the cable. Don't forget to install a washer between the spacer tube and the expander.

14. Install the front return spring (two coils) so that the coils point towards the center of the axle.

15. Install the upper and lower brake shoes.

16. Install the pins, springs, and holddown cups.

17. Insert the inner expander into the seats in the brake shoes.

18. Raise the upper brake shoe with a small prybar and install the star wheel assembly so that the adjusting sprocket is on both brake shoes.

19. Install the outer brake return spring.

20. Turn the cable adjusting nut in the tube all the way back.

21. Install the spring, second expander half, washer, and castellated nut. Tighten the nut until a new cotter pin can be installed.

22. Install the brake discs and calipers.

23. Bleed the hydraulic system.

24. Adjust the handbrake.

25. Install the wheels and lower the car.

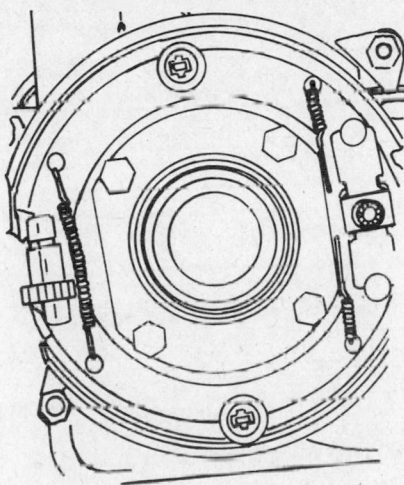

Correct handbrake lining and spring installation

CHASSIS ELECTRICAL

Heater

The primary heating system in all models uses fresh air drawn in by the engine cooling fan, directs it to heat exchangers around the exhaust pipes, through a muffler, and distributes warm air into the passenger compartment via a system of ducts. A variable speed blower, located in the front luggage compartment on all models, speeds the circulation of heated and/or fresh air. An auxiliary, gasfired heater is an option on some models.

Blower

REMOVAL & INSTALLATION

1. Disconnect the battery cables.

2. Remove the front luggage compartment carpeting.

3. Open the blower compartment lid. Remove the steering shaft cover.

4. Disconnect the electrical wiring.

5. Loosen the hose clamps and disconnect the hoses from the blower.

6. Pull the blower off the air intake stack and remove it from the car.

7. Install the blower on the intake stack. Make sure that the sealing ring is correctly seated.

8. Fasten the hoses on the blower and tighten the hose clamps.

9. Connect the electrical wiring.

10. Install the steering shaft cover and close the blower compartment lid.

11. Cement the carpeting to the right front side panel.

12. Connect the battery cables.

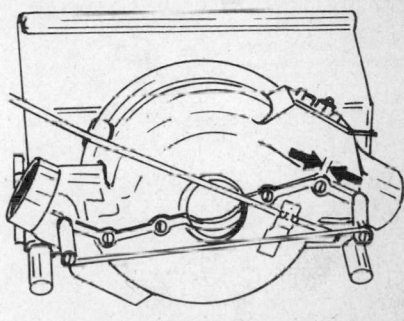

Correct blower cable installation

Auxiliary Heater

The 911 auxiliary heater assembly is mounted in the front luggage compartment in the place of the standard blower.

REMOVAL & INSTALLATION

1. Jack up the front of the car and support it on stands.

2. Disconnect the battery cables.

3. Remove the luggage compartment lid.

4. Open the heater compartment lid.

5. Loosen the clamp on the hot air hose and pull the hose off the heater unit.

6. Remove the three mixture pump retaining bolts and remove them from the bracket.

7. Disconnect the fuel lines and wiring from the pump.

8. Working under the car, loosen the front muffler clamp. Disconnect the exhaust pipe and bend it down and out of the way.

9. Remove the muffler clamp and slide the white collar onto the heater unit.

10. Disconnect all wiring to the heater and carefully lift it out of the car.

11. Installation is the reverse of the removal procedure. Ensure that the wiring is correctly reinstalled.

Windshield Wiper Motor and Linkage

REMOVAL & INSTALLATION

The windshield wiper motor and linkage are located in front of the instrument panel.

1. Pull back the front luggage compartment carpeting. Disconnect the battery cables.

2. Remove the retaining clip and air duct. Remove the fresh air box.

3. Disconnect the blower motor wires.

4. Remove the wiper arms. Remove the rubber bushings under the arms and unscrew the shaft retaining nuts.

5. Pull the motor and linkage down as a unit. Separate the motor and linkage.

6. Installation is the reverse of the removal procedure.

Rear Window Wiper

1. Pull the wiper arm from the rear window.

2. Open the engine compartment lid.

3. Disconnect the wiper motor electrical wiring.

4. Disconnect the wiper arm linkage at the bellcrank.

5. Remove the three wiper motor bracket bolts and remove the motor/linkage assembly.

6. Install the wiper motor/linkage assembly in a reverse order of removal.

7. Adjust the linkage at the bellcrank for correct wiper operation.

Instrument Panel

REMOVAL & INSTALLATION

The gauges are mounted in individual rubber rings.

1. Pry the gauge out until you can grip it firmly, and then pull it out of the instrument panel.

2. Disconnect the wiring and/or cable and remove the gauge.

3. Connect the wiring or cable and position the gauge in its opening.

4. Align the gauge and then push it into place.

Fuse Box Location

The fuse box is located in the left front of the luggage compartment.

Porsche
924, 928, 944

SERIAL NUMBER IDENTIFICATION

Vehicle

The chassis serial number is located on the left windshield post and can be viewed from the outside. The vehicle identification plate is in the engine compartment near the battery.

Engine

The engine serial number is stamped on the left of the crankcase near the clutch housing.

WPO AAO 94 O E N 45 0001–9999

USA/Canada

Serial number
Code for body and engine
Vehicle type together with 7th and 8th digits
Manufacturing site
Model year (E = 1984)
Test code or fill-in letter
Vehicle type together with 12th digit
Fill-in letters or code for USA and Canada cars
World manufacturing code

944 serial number

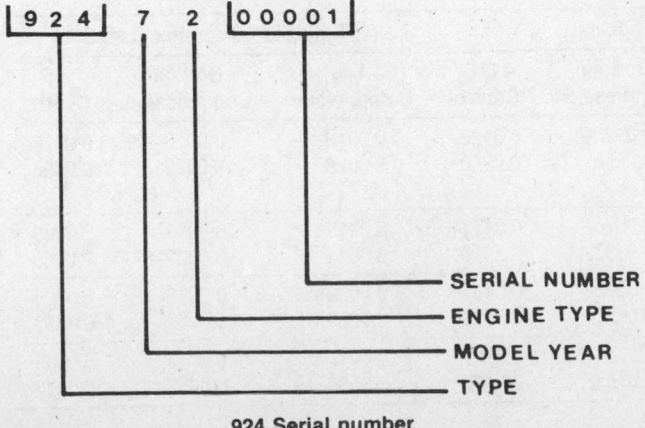

924 | 7 | 2 | 00001

SERIAL NUMBER
ENGINE TYPE
MODEL YEAR
TYPE

924 Serial number

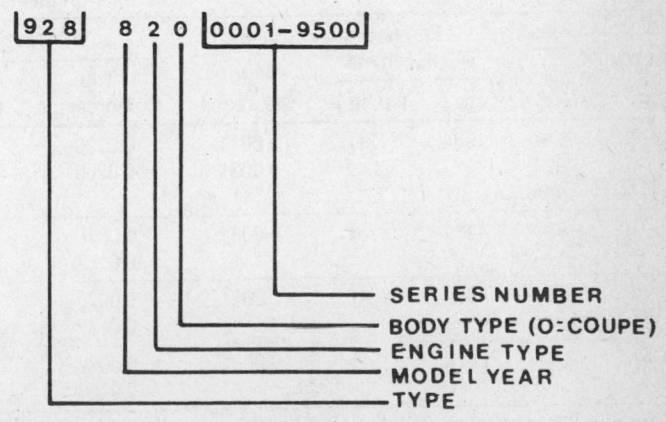

928 | 8 | 2 | 0 | 0001–9500

SERIES NUMBER
BODY TYPE (0=COUPE)
ENGINE TYPE
MODEL YEAR
TYPE

928 Serial number

CAPACITIES

Year	Model	Engine Displacement		Engine Crankcase (qts)		Transaxle (qts.)		Gasoline Tank (gal.)	Cooling System (qts.)
		cc	(cu. in.)	With Filter	Without Filter	Manual	Auto.		
'78–'82	924	1984	(121)	5.30	4.75	2.75①	3.17②	16.4④	8.5
'79–'82	924 Turbo.	1984	(121)	5.30	4.75	2.6	5.5	18.6④	8.5
'78–'79	928	4474	(273)	7.90	6.40	4.0③	5.8	22.7	16
'80–'82	928	4474	(273)	8.50	8.00	4.0⑤	5.8	23	17
'83–'85	928S	4664	(284)	8.50	8.00	4.0	6.0	23	17
'83–'85	944	2479	(151)	5.80	—	2.75	3.0⑦	17.4	8.5

NA—Not available.
① SAE 80 or 80W gear oil
② At oil change ATF Dexron®, differential 1.06 qt. SAE 90 gear oil
③ Mid-1978 model year—change manual gear oil usage to Dexron® ATF
④ 1982 and later—17.4
⑤ Use SAE 75w-90 oil, meeting API/GL5 specifications.
⑥ Use SAE 80 oil, meeting API/GL4 specifications.
⑦ Dry refill capacity—6.9 qts. Use Dexron® transmission fluid.

VALVE SPECIFICATIONS

Year	Model	Engine Displacement		Seat Angle (deg)	Face Angle (deg)	Stem-to-Guide Clearance (Maximum)		Stem Diameter (Minimum)	
		cc	(cu. in.)			Intake (in.)	Exhaust (in.)	Intake (in.)	Exhaust (in.)
'78–'82	924, 924 Turbo.	1984	(121)	45	45¼	0.0196	0.0196	0.352	0.352
'78–'82	928	4474	(273)	45	45	0.0196	0.0196	0.352	0.352
'83–'85	928S	4664	(284)	45	45	0.0196	0.0196	0.352	0.352
'83–'85	944	2479	(151)	45	45	0.0196	0.0196	0.352	0.352

PISTON AND RING SPECIFICATIONS
(All measurements given in inches)

Year	Model	Engine Displacement		Piston Clearance	Ring Gap (Limit)			Ring Side Clearance (Limit)		
		cc	(cu. in.)		Top Compression	Bottom Compression	Oil Control	Top Compression	Bottom Compression	Oil Control
'78–'82	924, 924 Turbo.	1984	(121)	0.0011–0.0031	0.0120–0.0200	0.0120–0.0200	0.0120–0.0200	0.0016–0.0028	0.0016–0.0028	0.0016–0.0028
'78–'82	928	4474	(273)	0.0031①	0.0078–0.0157	0.0078–0.0157	0.0157–0.5510	0.0019–0.0032	0.0019–0.0032	0.0009–0.0053
'83–'85	928S	4664	(284)	0.0031①	0.0078–0.0157	0.0078–0.0157	0.0157–0.5510	0.0019–0.0032	0.0019–0.0032	0.0009–0.0053
'83–'85	944	2479	(151)	0.0031①	0.0078–0.0157	0.0078–0.0157	0.0157–0.5510	0.0019–0.0032	0.0019–0.0032	0.0009–0.0053

① Maximum clearance

TORQUE SPECIFICATIONS
(All readings in ft. lbs.)

Year	Model	Engine Displacement cc	Engine Displacement (cu. in.)	Cylinder Head Bolts	Rod Bearing Bolts	Main Bearing Bolts	Crankshaft Pulley Bolt	Flywheel to Crankshaft Bolts	Manifold Intake	Manifold Exhaust
'78–'81	924	1984	(121)	56①	34–42	58②	181	65	15	15
	924 Turbo.	1984	(121)	72	47	58②	181	65	15	15
	928	4474	(273)	58③	42	29④	181	69	N.A.	N.A.
'82	924	1984	(121)	47⑤	34–42	58②	181	65	15	15
	924 Turbo.	1984	(121)	⑥	47	58②	181	72	15	15
	928	4474	(273)	⑦	44.5	⑧	181	69	N.A.	15
'83–'85	928S	4664	(284)	⑦	44.5	⑧	181	69	N.A.	15
	944	2479	(151)	⑦	44.5	⑧	181	65	N.A.	15

N.A.—Not available at time of publication
① 63 ft. lbs. warm
② Allen head bolts on cap #5 are torqued to 47 ft. lbs.
③ Tighten in three steps: 1st—14 ft. lbs.; 2nd—36 ft. lbs.; 3rd—61 ft. lbs. Thirty minutes later, loosen each bolt ¼ turn, then retorque each bolt (in order) to 58 ft. lbs.
④ Tighten in two steps: 1st—14 ft. lbs.; 2nd—29 ft. lbs.
⑤ Tighten all head bolts in order to 47 ft. lbs., then (in order) tighten each bolt ½ turn further.
⑥ Tighten in three steps (in order each time): 1st—29 ft. lbs.; 2nd—58 ft. lbs; 3rd—80 ft. lbs. (engine warm). One hour later, loosen each bolt 30° then repeat tightening sequence. Run the engine to 176°F. (coolant temp.), loosen each bolt 30°, then repeat the tightening sequence again.
⑦ Tighten in three steps (in order each time): 1st—14 ft. lbs.; 2nd—36 ft. lbs.; 3rd—65 ft. lbs. Thirty minutes later, loosen each bolt ¼ turn then repeat the tightening sequence.
⑧ M10 bolts: 1st step—14.5 ft. lbs.; 2nd step—33.5 ft. lbs.
M12 bolts: 1st step—14.5 ft. lbs.; 2nd step—30.0 ft. lbs.; 3rd step—48 ft. lbs.

ALTERNATOR AND REGULATOR SPECIFICATIONS

Year	Model	Alternator Manufacturer	Alternator Output (amps)	Regulator Manufacturer	Field Relay Air Gap (in.)	Field Relay Point Gap (in.)	Field Relay Volts to Close	Regulator Air Gap (in.)	Regulator Point Gap (in.)	Regulator Volts @ 75 degrees
'78–'82	924	Bosch	75	Bosch	—Sealed unit not adjustable—					13.5–14.5
'79–'82	924 Turbo.	Bosch	68	Bosch	—Sealed unit not adjustable—					13.5–14.5
'78–'85	928, 928S 944	Bosch	90	Bosch	—Sealed unit not adjustable—					13.5–14.8

C645

GENERAL ENGINE SPECIFICATIONS

Year	Model	Engine Displacement		Fuel System	Horsepower @ rpm	Torque @ rpm	Bore × Stroke (in.)	Compression Ratio	Oil Pressure @ rpm (psi)
		cc	(cu. in.)						
'78–'82	924	1984	(121)	Fuel inj.	110 @ 5750	111.3 @ 3500	3.41 × 3.32	8.5:1	71–100 @ 5000
'79–'80	924 Turbo	1984	(121)	Fuel inj.	143 @ 5500	147 @ 3000	3.41 × 3.32	7.5:1	70 @ 5500
'81–'82	924 Turbo	1984	(121)	Fuel inj.	154 @ 5750	154.8 @ 3500	3.41 × 3.32	8.0:1	70 @ 5500
'78–'79	928	4474	(273)	Fuel inj.	219 @ 5250	245 @ 3600	3.74 × 3.11	8.5:1	70 @ 5500
'80–'82	928	4474	(273)	Fuel inj.	220 @ 5500	265 @ 4000	3.74 × 3.11	9.0:1	70 @ 5500
'83–'85	928S	4664	(284)	Fuel inj.	234 @ 5250	263 @ 4000	3.82 × 3.11	9.3:1	70 @ 5500
'83–'85	944	2479	(151)	Fuel inj.	143 @ 5500	137 @ 3000	3.94 × 3.11	9.5:1	50–70 @ 5500

TUNE-UP SPECIFICATIONS

Year	Model	Engine Displacement		Spark Plugs		Ignition Timing① (rpm)	Intake Valve Opens (deg)	Idle Speed (rpm)	Valve Clearance (cold) (in.)	
		cc	(cu. in.)	Type	Gap (in.)				Intake	Exhaust
'78–'81	924	1984	(121)	W200-T30	.028–.032	10°A @ 925	5°BTDC	850–1000	0.004	0.016
'79–'81	924 Turbo.	1984	(121)	WR7DS	.024	20°B @ 2000	—	900–1000	0.004	0.016
'82	924	1984	(121)	WR6DS	.028	0° ± 1° @ 750–800③	—	850–1000	0.006	0.016
'82	924 Turbo	1984	(121)	WR6DS	.028④	6°–10°B @ 900⑤	—	900–1000	0.006	0.016
'78–'79	928	4474	(273)	W145-T30	.028–.032	31°B @ 3000	8°ATDC②	800	Hyd.	Hyd.
'80–'81	928	4474	(273)	WR8DS	.028	23°B @ 3000	12°ATDC	700–800	Hyd.	Hyd.
'82	928	4474	(273)	WR8DS	.028–.032	23°B @ 3000	—	700–800	Hyd.	Hyd.
'83–'85	928S	4664	(284)	WR8DS	.028–.032	20°B @ 3000	11°ATDC	700–800⑥	Hyd.	Hyd.
'83–'85	944	2479	(151)	WR8DS	.028–.032	3°–7°B @ 900⑤	1°ATDC	850–950	Hyd.	Hyd.

NA—Not Available at time of publication
A—After Top Dead Center
B—Before Top Dead Center
① With vacuum hose disconnected, if so equipped.
② .0393 in., zero valve clearance
③ With connector above idle stabilizer in front of the left wheel arch disconnected.
④ If Champion N7GY is used, gap should be .024 in.
⑤ Checking specification only; timing is self-adjusting.
⑥ Not adjustable—electronically controlled

FIRING ORDER

NOTE: To avoid confusion, always replace spark plug wires one at a time.

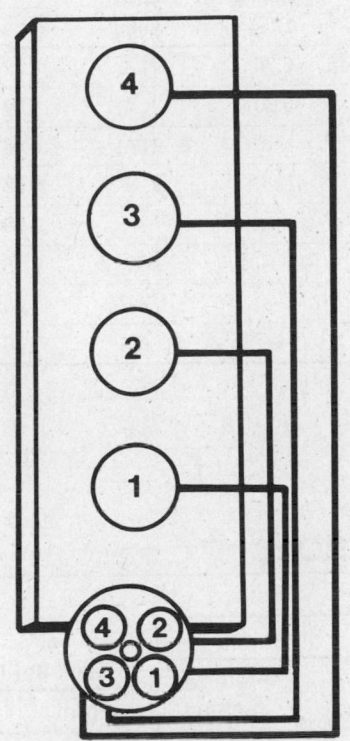

Firing order—944 engine
Distributor rotation—clockwise

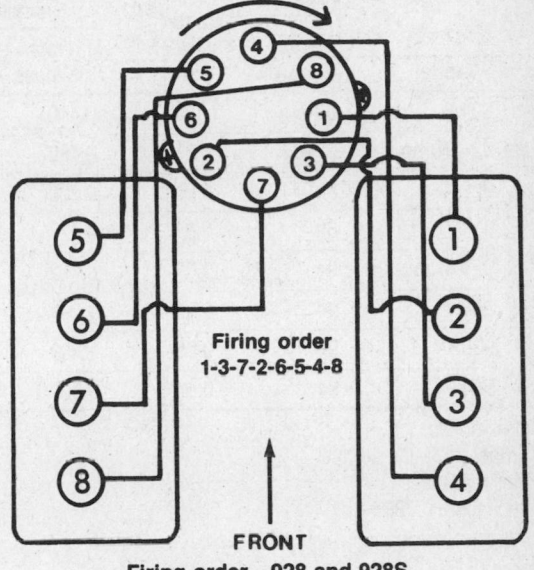

Firing order
1-3-7-2-6-5-4-8

FRONT
Firing order—928 and 928S

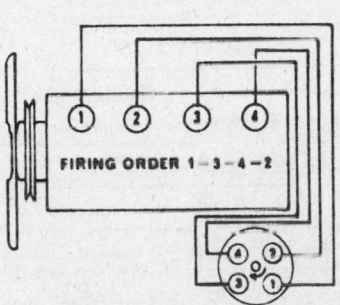

FIRING ORDER 1 - 3 - 4 - 2

Firing order—924 engines

CRANKSHAFT AND CONNECTING ROD SPECIFICATIONS

(All measurements given in inches)

| Year | Model | Engine Displacement | | Crankshaft | | | | Connecting Rod | | |
		(cc)	(cu. in.)	Main Brg. Journal Diameter	Main Brg. Oil Clearance	Shaft End-Play	Thrust on No.	Journal Diameter	Oil Clearance	Side Clearance
'78–'82	924	1984	(121)	2.40	0.0020–0.0040	0.0040	3	1.90	0.0008–0.0032	0.0040–0.0092
'79–'82	924 Turbo.	1984	(121)	2.50	0.0008–0.0030	0.0040	3	1.89–1.97	0.0008–0.0030	0.0020–0.0120
'78–'82	928	4474	(273)	2.80	0.0008–0.0039	0.0044–0.0124	3	2.08	0.0008–0.0028	—
'83–'85	928S	4664	(284)	2.80	0.0008–0.0039	0.0044–0.0124	3	2.08	0.0008–0.0028	—
'83–'85	944	2479	(151)	2.80	0.0008–0.0039	0.0044–0.0124	3	2.08	0.0008–0.0028	—

BRAKE SPECIFICATIONS
(All specifications given in inches, unless noted)

Year	Model	Lug Nut Torque (ft. lbs.)	Master Cylinder Bore	Brake Disc		Brake Drum			Minimum Lining Thickness	
				Minimum Thickness	Maximum Run-Out	Diameter	Maximum Machine (O/S)	Maximum Wear Limit	Front	Rear
'78–'81	924	80①	0.81	0.410	N.A.	9.06	0.30	N.A.	0.07	0.09
	924 Turbo.	80①	0.83	0.480	N.A.	9.20	0.30	N.A.	0.07	0.09
	928	80①	0.95	0.720	N.A.	N.A.	N.A.	N.A.	0.08	0.08
'82	924	80①	0.81	0.472	N.A.	N.A.	N.A.	9.094	0.08	0.09
	924 Turbo.	94	0.83	0.752②	N.A.	—	—	—	0.08	0.08
	928	94	0.95	1.228②	N.A.	—	—	—	0.08	0.08
'83–'85	928S	94	0.95	1.228	N.A.	—	—	—	0.08	0.08
	944	94	0.94	0.807③	N.A.	—	—	—	0.08	0.08

N.A.—Not available
① Alloy wheel 94 ft. lbs. torque
② 0.756 for rear discs.
③ New thickness; 0.788 rear

WHEEL ALIGNMENT SPECIFICATIONS

Year	Model	Caster (Degrees)		Camber (Degrees)				Toe In (Inches)	
				Front		Rear			
		Range	Preferred Setting	Range	Preferred Setting	Range	Preferred Setting	Front	Rear
'78–'82	924	2¼P–3P	2½P	9⁄16N–1⁄16N	5⁄16N	1½N–½N	1N	3⁄32 ± 1⁄32	0 ± 1⁄32
	928	3P–3½P	3P	11⁄16N–5⁄16N	½N	7⁄8N–½N	11⁄16N	3⁄32 ± 1⁄32	3⁄32 ± 1⁄32
'83–'85	928S	3¼P–3¾P	3½P	11⁄16N–5⁄16N	½N	7⁄8N–½N	11⁄16N	1⁄8 ± 1⁄32	3⁄32 ± 1⁄32
	944	2¼P–3P	2½P	1⁄16P–9⁄16P	5⁄16P	1⁄16P–15⁄16N	3⁄8N	3⁄32 ± 1⁄32	0 ± 3⁄32

N—Negative
P—Positive

TUNE-UP PROCEDURES

Spark Plugs

Because Porsche engines use aluminum cylinder heads, always apply a small amount of graphite or anti-seize compound to the threads of the plug prior to installation. Be very careful when threading the plug into the head. NEVER use a wrench to "start" the plug. Finally tighten the plugs to 18–22 ft. lbs.

Electronic Ignition

—— CAUTION ——
The engine should be turned off or the battery cable disconnected when ignition system parts are replaced or engine test equipment is connected to the ignition system, because of the dangerous current that can be present in the primary and secondary circuits. Personal injury could occur.

Three fully electronic ignition systems have been used. All 928 models and 1978–80 924s have used a Bosch transistorized ignition coil system. 1981 and later non-turbocharged 924 models use a Hall Effect electronic system, while the 1981–82 924 Turbo and 944 use a Digital Ignition Timing Control (DITC) ignition system.

The 1983–85 944 uses a self-adjusting DME (Digital Motor Electronic) ignition system.

Tune-up maintenance is limited to checking the ignition wires, distributor cap and rotor condition. Except for ignition timing (where applicable), adjustments to any of the electronic ignition systems is not necessary.

Ignition Timing

ADJUSTMENT

924, and 924 Turbo Through 1980

—— CAUTION ——
The engine should be turned off or the battery cable disconnected when ignition system parts are replaced or engine test equipment is connected to the ignition system, because of the dangerous current that can be present in the primary and secondary circuits.

1. Run the engine to normal operating temperature.

2. Leave the vacuum hoses on the distributor and connect a timing light according to the light manufacturer's instructions.

3. The timing marks are not on the crankshaft pulley, but are on the flywheel,

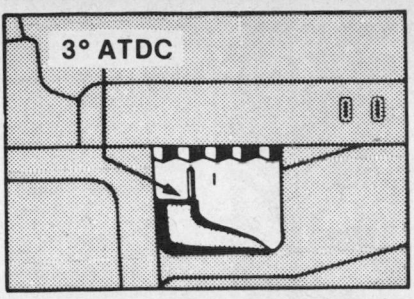

Timing mark—1978–80 924 and 924 Turbo models

visible through a small access hole in the clutch housing.

4. With the engine at the correct idle speed, focus the timing light on the timing slot.

5. If the timing is not correct, loosen the distributor hold-down bolt and turn the distributor as necessary. Retighten the bolt when the timing is correct.

924—1981–82

1. Run the engine to normal operating temperature.

2. By pass the idle stabilizer by disconnecting the connector plugs from each other. The plugs are located on the wiring harness on the driver's front wheel well inside the engine compartment.

3. Set the engine idle speed to 800 rpm.

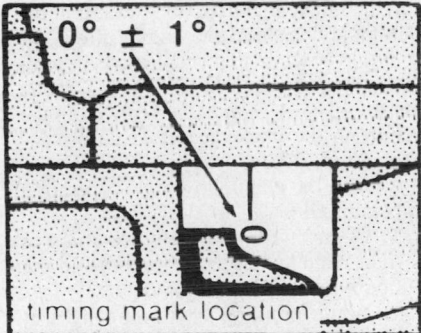

Timing mark—1981 and later 924 models

4. Connect a timing light to number one cylinder spark plug lead according to the timing light manufacturer's instructions.

5. With the engine idling, focus the timing light on the timing port. The timing marks are located on the flywheel.

6. If timing is off, loosen the distributor holddown clamp and turn the distributor until the timing is correct. Retighten the holddown bolt.

7. After adjusting, reconnect the idle stabilizer leads and rev the engine a few times.

8. Check the idle speed.

924 Turbo—1981–82

Due to the DITC fully electronic transistor ignition system, ignition timing adjustments are not necessary.

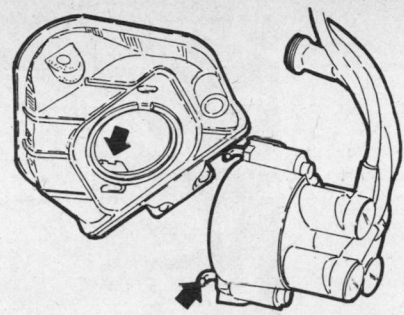

Distributor cap and distributor cap mount of the 944. Note how the distributor cap screw clips are to engage (arrows)

1983–85 944

The Digital Motor Electronic ignition system is a self-adjusting system. No adjustment is possible.

928 and 928S

— CAUTION —
See "CAUTION" under "924 through 1980", above.

1. Run the engine to normal operating temperature.

2. Connect a timing light to the engine. A positive terminal for connecting the timing light is located in the engine compartment. Connect a tachometer.

Timing marks on the 928 and 928S are located on the vibration damper at the front of the engine.

3. With the timing light connected to the ignition cable for cylinder No. 1, detach both vacuum hoses at the distributor.

— CAUTION —
When connecting test equipment to the ignition system, the ignition key must be off or the battery disconnected.

4. The timing marks are located on the crankshaft pulley and are colored for identification. With the engine at 3000 rpm, focus the timing light on the timing marks. Timing should be as specified. See the specifications charts.

5. To adjust, loosen the distributor holddown bolt and turn the distributor as necessary. Tighten the holddown bolt when the timing is correct.

Valve Lash

ADJUSTMENT

924 (Including Turbo)

— CAUTION —
When turning the engine for valve adjustment, do not turn it with the camshaft pulley. Use the crankshaft pulley or "bump" the starter. The timing belt can be damaged by turning the camshaft pulley.

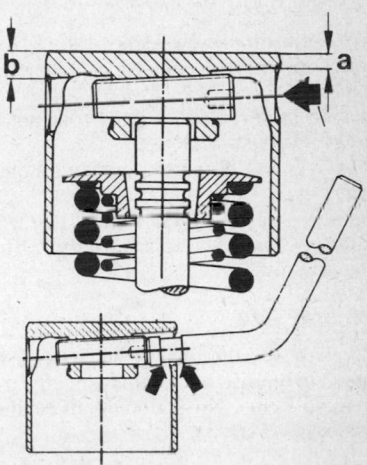

924 and 924 Turbo valve lash adjustment. One full turn of the wedge screw changes the valve clearance 0.002 in.

Adjustment is made by means of a wedge type adjustment screw which is flat on one side. The flat side rides directly on the valve stem. Five different diameter adjustment screws are available to compensate for wear. Adjustment is made by inserting an Allen wrench through the hole in the cam follower. Adjustment is made in full turns. If more than several turns are necessary to correct the clearance, the adjustment screw will probably have to be replaced with the next larger size. Always start with the smallest adjustment screws (white) after a valve job.

NOTE: One turn of the screw changes the valve clearance 0.002 in.

1. Remove the camshaft cover.

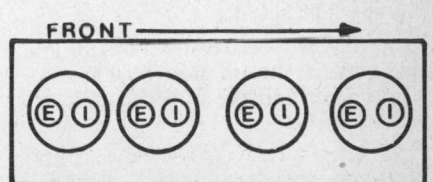

Intake (I) and exhaust (E) valve arrangement of the 924 and 924 Turbo

2. Turn the crankshaft pulley until No. 1 cylinder is at TDC of the compression stroke (both cam lobes pointing up).

3. Insert the correct feeler gauge between the cam follower and the camshaft heel.

4. If adjustment is necessary, insert an Allen wrench and turn the adjustment screw until clearance is correct.

5. Proceed to adjust the valve clearance for each cylinder in the same way.

NOTE: Early engine models had paint colors as identifying marks on the adjusting screws. Later engine models use notches, ground on the screw end, opposite the adjusting tool hole, as the identity marks. The higher number of notches indicates the increased thickness of the adjusting screw.

Valve adjusting screw identification No. 2
White—6.6mm—Replaced by ''no notch'' screw
Blue—6.9mm—Replaced by ''one notch'' screw
Red—7.2mm—Replaced by ''two notch'' screw
No color—new—''three notch'' screw
Yellow—7.5mm—Replaced by ''four notch'' screw

928 and 944

The overhead cams operate bucket-type hydraulic valve lifters, located directly over the valve stems. No periodic valve adjustment is necessary.

Idle Speed and Mixture Adjustments

The idle speed can be adjusted on 1978–81 models without the use of emissions testing equipment. Idle mixture on all models, and idle speed on 1982 and later models cannot be properly adjusted without the use of a CO meter.

IDLE SPEED

924 and 924 Turbo Through 1980

The engine must be in perfect running condition and the ignition timing must be set correctly before adjusting the idle speed.

1. Run the engine to normal operating temperature.

2. Idle speed is adjusted at the bypass screw located on the throttle housing. Turn the screw in or out as necessary to obtain the proper idle speed.

NOTE: Any special instructions for idle speed adjustments on individual engines may be found on the underhood specifications sticker.

1981 924

Idle speed adjustments are performed in the same manner as on the 924 through 1980,

Idle adjustment screw location on the 924 (arrow)

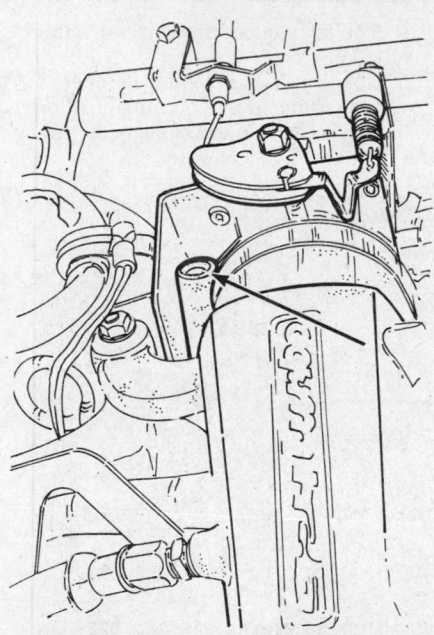

Idle adjustment screw location on the 924 Turbo (arrow)

except for one procedure. The idle stabilizer must be disconnected and bridged before the idle can be adjusted or the stabilizer will attempt to offset any adjustment by advancing or retarding the ignition timing. To by-pass the oxygen stabilizer, disconnect its connector, located on the wiring harness on the driver's side front fender well inside the engine compartment.

1981 924 Turbo

The timing control unit stabilizes the idle speed by varying the ignition timing at idle.

As a result, basic idle speed adjustment must be made using a timing light.

To eliminate the influence of the intake air temperature sensor, it must be removed during the idle adjustment procedure.

1. Unscrew the temperature air sensor from the intake manifold and place it in the fresh air tray behind the engine fire wall, leaving the wire connected (sensor temperature must be below 120°F). A suitable plug (M 14 × 1.5) must be screwed in the opening in the intake manifold during adjustment procedures.

2. Run the engine to normal operating temperature.

3. Connect a timing light according to the light manufacturer's instructions to the ignition wire for No. 1 cylinder.

4. While pointing the timing light at the timing marks, turn the idle control screw (by-pass air screw) until the ignition timing mark (dot) is fully visible at the reference edge and jumps partially below the mark.

5. The idle speed should not be below 900 rpm (timing will vary slightly because the ignition timing is being regulated).

928 Through 1981

Idle speed is adjusted at the idle speed screw on the throttle housing. The engine must be at normal operating temperature and in perfect running order. In addition, a separate tachometer must be used; do not adjust the idle speed using the tachometer in the instrument panel. Consult the underhood specifications sticker for any special information concerning individual engines.

1982 and Later Models

Idle speed is electronically controlled on these models.

Before adjusting the idle speed on the 1981 924 Turbo, the fresh air sensor (arrow) must be removed and its hole plugged

Idle adjustment screw location on the 928 (arrow)

ENGINE ELECTRICAL

Distributor

REMOVAL & INSTALLATION

All Models Except 1981–82 924 Turbo and 944

1. Disconnect the negative battery cable.
2. Unsnap the two retaining clips and remove the distributor cap.
3. Set the No. 1 cylinder at top dead dead center when the TDC mark on the flywheel or crank pulley aligns with the timing pointer and the distributor rotor points toward the distributor cap tower for the No.

one cylinder spark plug wire. Turn the engine over by hand until these signs are evident.

4. Disconnect the vacuum hose(s) from the distributor, then disconnect the electrical connections at the distributor.

On 1983 and later cars with Hall Effect ignition, a more positive hold–down clip secures the electrical connector. If earlier cars develop an ignition miss, install clip (Part No. 071 905 252).

5. Loosen and remove the distributor holddown bolt and clamp, then remove the distributor.

6. If the engine has not been turned over since the distributor was removed, align the rotor on the distributor with the No. 1 cylinder distributor cap tower. There is a notch in the distributor body which the rotor will point to when in this position. Install the distributor.

7. If the engine was turned while the distributor was removed, it will be necessary to relocate No. 1 cylinder TDC. To do this, remove No. 1 cylinder spark plug, then turn the engine over in the normal direction of rotation while holding your thumb over the No. 1 cylinder spark plug hole. When the piston starts blowing air out of the hole, the No. 1 cylinder is on its compression stroke. When this happens, continue turning the engine until the timing mark for TDC on the flywheel or crank

924 and 924 Turbo distributor holddown bolt location (arrow)

pulley aligns with the timing pointer. Install the distributor (see Step 6).

8. Install the vacuum hoses, electrical connections and distributor cap. Adjust the ignition timing.

1981–82 924 Turbo

1. Disconnect the negative battery cable.
2. Remove the distributor cap and place it out of the way. Do not disconnect the spark plug leads from the cap.
3. Set the No. 1 cylinder on TDC. In this position, the Z1 mark on the flywheel will align with the timing pointer edge and the mark on the camshaft will be opposite the notch at the top rear of the timing belt cover.
4. Remove the primary wiring from the distributor.
5. Loosen and remove the holddown bolt and clamp, then remove the distributor.
6. If the engine was not turned while the distributor was removed, install the distributor so that the tab for the distributor cap faces the flywheel and the distributor cap mounting clips face in the direction of the car's longitudinal axis. In addition, the distributor rotor must be mounted so that it faces the notch on the distributor body for cylinder No. 1 and aligns with the No. 1 cylinder distributor cap tower.
7. If the engine was moved while the distributor was removed, set the No. 1 cylinder at TDC as described in Step 2 of this procedure, then install the distributor as described in Step 5.
8. When the distributor is installed, reconnect the electrical connections and install the distributor cap.

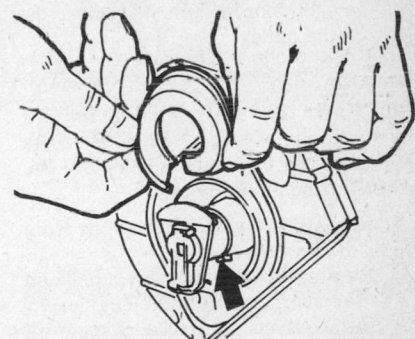

On the 944, the distributor rotor is held to the shaft by a screw (arrow).

944

The 944 distributor is not removable. Only the cap is removable. Noise appearing to originate in the vicinity of the distributor is usually due to a worn Woodruff key on the camshaft sprocket.

NOTE: The distributor rotor is retained by a hex head screw accessible after removing the dust cover. If the rotor is removed, a new retaining screw must be installed, or the old one coated with non-hardening sealant.

Alternator

REMOVAL & INSTALLATION

924 and 924 Turbo

The alternator and voltage regulator are combined in one housing. No voltage adjustment can be made with this unit. The regulator can be replaced without removing and disassembling the alternator, just unbolt it from the rear.

1. Disconnect the battery cables.
2. Remove the cooling shroud and scoop from the alternator. The scoop is retained by a snap clip.
3. Remove the oil filter.
4. Disconnect the multi-connector from the rear of the alternator.
5. Loosen and remove the two Allen head retaining bolts.
6. Remove the fan belt. Remove the alternator.
7. Installation is the reverse of removal. Properly tension the fan belt. Deflection of the belt midway between the pulleys should be about 3/8 in.

928, 928S and 944

The voltage regulator is bolted to the rear of the alternator. Remove the alternator before attempting to remove the voltage regulator.

The alternator is removed from the bottom of the vehicle.

1. Remove the battery ground cable.
2. Raise the vehicle and support safely.
3. Remove the engine splash shield and the alternator cooling vent cover and tube.
4. Loosen the belt tension lock bolt, move the alternator inward and remove the belt from the pulley.

NOTE: On the 944, first loosen the end bolts of the tensioner, then loosen the locknuts of the tensioner and rotate the tensioner tube as necessary.

5. Remove the wire connections from the rear of the alternator.
6. Remove the alternator pivot bolt and remove the alternator from the engine.
7. Installation is the reverse of removal.

Starter

REMOVAL & INSTALLATION

1. Disconnect the battery ground cable.
2. Jack and support the right front corner of the car.
3. Disconnect the two small wires from the starter solenoid. One wire connects to the ignition coil and the second to the ignition switch through the wiring harness.
4. Disconnect the large cable, which is the positive battery cable, from the solenoid.
5. Remove the two starter retaining bolts.

The alternator on the 924 and 924 Turbo (black arrow) is located on the passenger side of the engine. The air intake hose (white arrow) supplies fresh air to the alternator to keep it cool

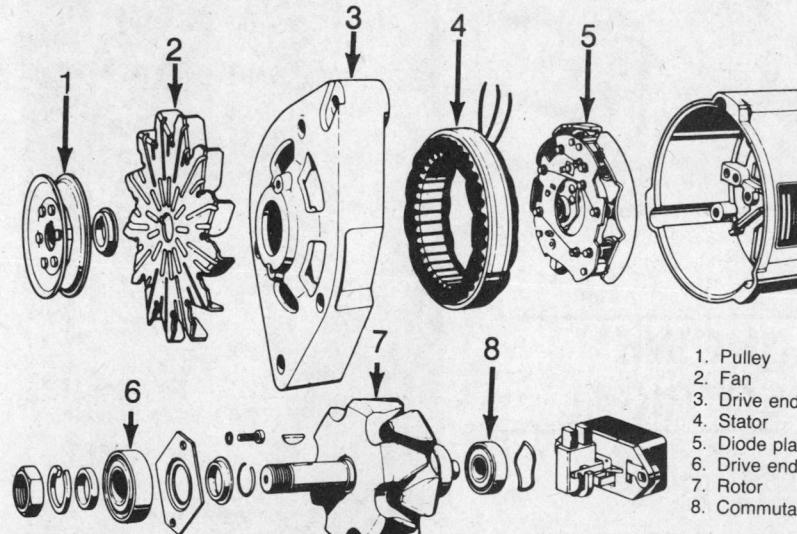

1. Pulley
2. Fan
3. Drive end housing
4. Stator
5. Diode plate
6. Drive end bearing
7. Rotor
8. Commutator bearing

Exploded view of a typical alternator

6. Pull the starter straight out and to the front, then lower it out of the car.
7. Installation is the reverse of removal.

OVERHAUL

To replace brushes or starter drive:
1. Remove the solenoid.
2. Remove the end bearing cap.

3. Loosen both of the long housing screws.
4. Remove the lockwasher and spacer washers.
5. Remove the long housing screws and remove the end cover.
6. Pull the two field coil brushes out of the brush housing.
7. Remove the brush housing assembly.

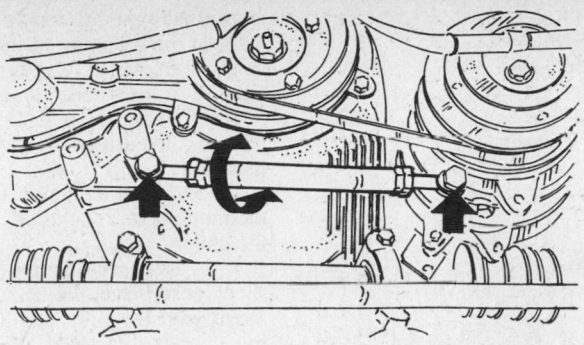

To loosen the alternator and air conditioning compressor drive belt of the 944: Loosen the tensioner end bolts (outer arrow); loosen the locknuts; then turn the tensioner tube (circular arrow) as required. When tightening the belt, the end bolts are to be tightened last

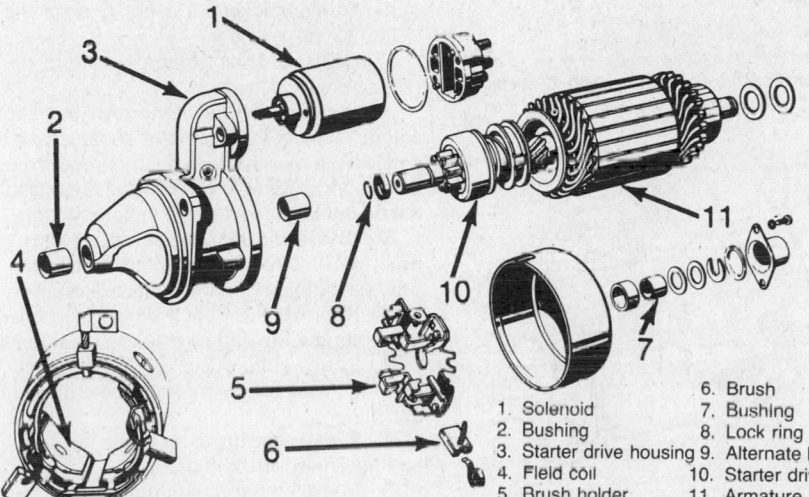

1. Solenoid	6. Brush
2. Bushing	7. Bushing
3. Starter drive housing	8. Lock ring
4. Field coil	9. Alternate bushing
5. Brush holder	10. Starter drive
	11. Armature

Exploded view of the starter

8. Loosen the nut on the solenoid housing, remove the sealing disc, and remove the solenoid operating lever.

9. Loosen the large screws on the side of the starter body and remove the field coil along with the brushes.

NOTE: If the brushes require replacement, the field coil and brushes and/or the brush housing and its brushes must be replaced as a unit. The armature should be "turned" on a lathe if it is out-of-round, scored, or grooved.

10. If the starter drive is being replaced, push the stop-ring down and remove the circlip on the end of the shaft. Remove the stop-ring and remove the drive.

11. Assembly is the reverse of disassembly. Use a gear puller to install the stop-ring in its groove. Use a new circlip on the shaft.

SOLENOID REPLACEMENT

1. Remove the starter.

2. Remove the nut which secures the connector strip on the end of the solenoid.

3. Take out the two retaining screws on the mounting bracket and withdraw the solenoid after it has been unhooked from the operating lever.

4. Installation is the reverse of removal. In order to facilitate engagement of the lever, the pinion should be pulled as far as possible when inserting the solenoid.

ENGINE MECHANICAL

The 924 engine is based on an Audi cylinder block. It is a watercooled, inline four with a belt driven overhead cam. The engine is inclined 40° to the right.

A V8 engine with an overhead cam mounted on each head and driven by a toothed belt from the crankshaft, is used in the 928 and 928S models. The two piece

engine block and cylinder heads are of cast aluminum. The cylinder walls are impregnated with a silicone compound, making cylinder liners unnecessary.

The 944 inline four cylinder engine, derived from the 928 V-8, is an overhead camshaft (belt-driven) water cooled design. The engine employs twin, belt driven balance shafts which cancel the vibration inherent with most large-displacement four cylinder engines. Both the cylinder head and engine block are aluminum, with the block having linerless, silicone-impregnated cylinder walls.

Engine

REMOVAL & INSTALLATION

924, 924 Turbo and 944

NOTE: On the 924 Turbo, some turbocharger components may have to be removed during engine removal. Wastegate and turbocharger services can be found following "Exhaust Manifold Removal and Installation."

1. Disconnect the battery cables. Raise the car and support it on jack stands.

2. Support the engine. Use an overhead hoist. If using a jack under the engine be careful not to damage the aluminum oil pan. Use a wooden block between the jack and pan.

3. Remove the splash panel. Remove the windshield washer tank and bracket and place it behind the right headlight.

4. On models so equipped, disconnect the clutch cable. Remove the bottom clutch adjustment locknut and detach the cable from the lever.

5. Remove the access plate from the bottom of the clutch housing.

6. Have an assistant turn the engine with the crankshaft pulley. Remove the pressure plate bolts gradually until all pressure is released.

7. Remove the exhaust pipe flange bolts.

8. Remove the bracket at the rear of the transaxle.

9. Remove the entire exhaust system.

10. Remove the back up light switch from the transaxle.

11. Disconnect the axle driveshafts at the transaxle and let them hang down out of the way.

NOTE: If the car is going to be moved around with the engine out of the car, wire the driveshafts up so that they don't become damaged.

12. Remove the clutch housing-to-engine bolts.

13. Place a wooden block under the front tunnel reinforcement to support the transaxle tube.

14. Remove the transaxle mounting bolts and slide the transaxle toward the rear.

15. Remove the air cleaner. Disconnect the brake booster vacuum line.

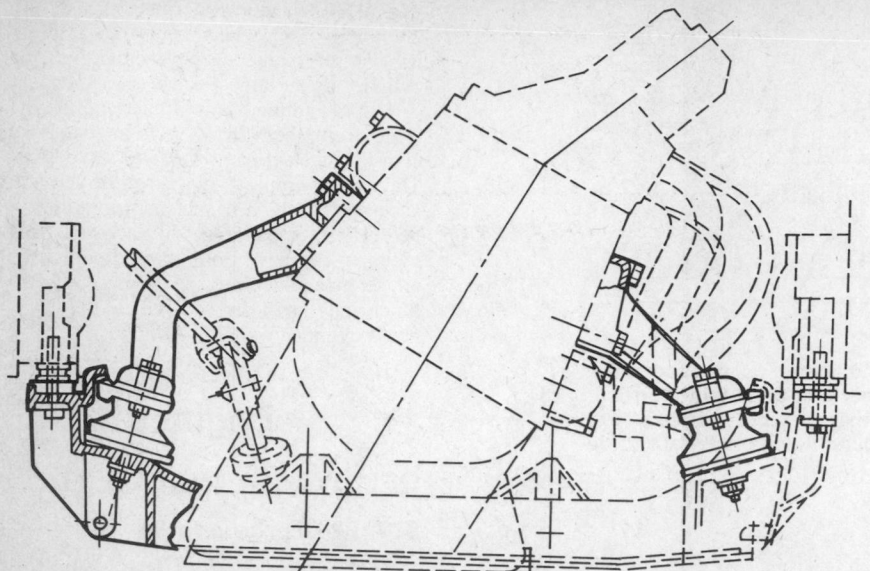

The 944 engine mounts are hydraulically damped. Antifreeze flows through a small hole in a plate between 2 chambers when the mount is under stress, not unlike the action of a hydraulic shock absorber.

16. Disconnect and plug the fuel line.
17. Disconnect the accelerator cable.
18. Drain the cooling system.
19. Disconnect the radiator hoses. Remove the electric cooling fan.
20. Remove the hood. Detach the air conditioning compressor and place it out of the way. Do not disconnect the lines.
21. Remove the radiator and expansion tank. Disconnect the heater hoses from the engine.
22. Disconnect the starter wiring.
23. Attach the engine lift chains to the hoist points on the engine. Disconnect the steering at the rack universal joint.
24. Disconnect the two side mounts on the engine block. Remove the left side mount from the car.

NOTE: 944 models use hydraulically damped engine mounts.

25. Lift the engine from the car.
26. Installation is basically the reverse of removal. Tighten the pressure plate bolts to 24 ft. lbs., the clutch housing bolts to 60 ft. lbs. (12mm bolt), 36 ft. lbs. (10mm bolt) and 20 ft. lbs. (8mm bolt).

NOTE: Be sure the engine–to–frame ground wire on 944 models is securely connected. Starting the engine with the ground wire disconnected or loose can damage the DME electronic control unit.

928

1. Disconnect the battery ground cable.
2. Remove the engine compartment cross brace.

NOTE: The vehicle must be on its wheels when the cross brace is removed or replaced.

3. Disconnect wiring and hoses to the

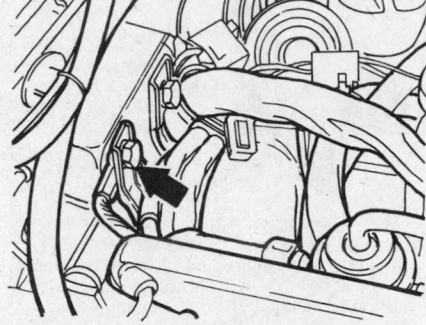

A loose or disconnected engine ground strap on the 944 could cause damage to the DME electronic control unit.

under side of the hood, loosen hood bolts and supports, and remove the hood.
4. Remove the air intake hoses and the air cleaner assembly.
5. Raise and support the vehicle.
6. Remove the bottom splash pan and drain the coolant from the radiator.
7. Drain the engine block of coolant by removing the drain plugs on the right and left sides of the crankcase.
8. Drain the engine oil.
9. Remove the lower body brace.
10. Disconnect the exhaust pipes at the exhaust manifolds and the right and left side heat shields.
11. Disconnect the body ground cable from the engine.
12. Remove the clutch slave cylinder at the clutch housing. Do not disconnect the hydraulic line.
13. Disconnect the starter wires and remove the starter along with the clutch housing cover.
14. Disconnect the clutch release lever

at the ball pin by depressing the release lever in the direction of the clutch.
15. Remove the starter wires from the clamps on the steering crossmember.
16. Remove the bolts from the clamping sleeve on the driveshaft and slide the sleeve rearward.
17. Unscrew the throwout bearing sleeve mounting bolts and push the sleeve towards the clutch.
18. Disconnect the left and right engine shock absorber at the control arms and remove with the right and left upper shock mounts.
19. On vehicles with air conditioning:
   a. Disconnect the temperature switch wires on the radiator.
   b. Disconnect the power lead to the compressor.
   c. Loosen the compressor, remove the belt and remove the compressor from the mounting brackets. Do not remove the hoses.
   d. Suspend the compressor from the frame with a wire.
20. Remove the air pump filter housing and disconnect the alternator cooling hose.
21. Remove the lower fan shroud from the radiator, remove the cooling hoses and the oil cooler line from the radiator bottom.
22. By lifting the engine one side at a time, remove the engine mounts and carefully set the engine on the front crossmember.
23. Remove the clutch housing to engine bolts and lower the vehicle to the floor.
24. Remove the upper coolant hose and the vent from the radiator and thermostat housing.
25. Remove the upper oil cooler line from the upper part of the radiator.
26. Loosen the top mountings of the radiator and remove the assembly carefully.
27. Remove the heater hoses and electrical connections from the engine.
28. Remove the electronic control unit and loosen the ignition coil and set aside.
29. Disconnect the feed and return fuel lines.
30. Disconnect the lines at the power steering pump.
31. Disconnect the vacuum line to the power brake cylinder at the manifold.
32. Disconnect the accelerator cable by removing the holder and clamp.

NOTE: On air conditioned vehicles, cover the condenser with a wood board to prevent damage during the engine removal.

33. Attach a lifting cable to lifting device and to the engine.
34. Raise the assembly slightly and remove the engine block-to-clutch housing upper mounting bolts.
35. Pull the engine forward and remove the short driveshaft with the guide tube.
36. Lift the engine carefully from the engine compartment.
37. Installation is the reverse of removal.

Cylinder Head

REMOVAL & INSTALLATION

924 and 924 Turbo

1. Disconnect the battery cables.
2. Drain the cooling system.
3. Remove the air cleaner.
4. Disconnect the radiator and heater hoses.
5. Disconnect all electrical wires from the cylinder head.
6. Detach the spark plug wires. Remove the distributor.
7. Disconnect the exhaust manifold from the exhaust pipe.
8. Disconnect the EGR line. Remove the exhaust manifold.
9. Remove the fuel injection lines from the cylinder head.
10. Remove the throttle valve housing and intake manifold as a unit.
11. Disconnect the air pump lines on models so equipped.
12. Remove the timing belt cover. Loosen the tensioner and remove the belt.
13. Loosen the cylinder head bolts in the reverse of the tightening sequence and remove the bolts.
14. Carefully lift off the cylinder head.
15. Installation is the reverse of removal. Be sure to correctly position the new cylinder head gasket. Align the timing marks and install the timing belt and properly tension it. This procedure is under Timing Belt. Tighten the cylinder head bolts in the proper order and to the correct value. Refer to the Torque Specifications at the beginning of this section. Follow the information with the chart EXACTLY.

928

NOTE: The cylinder heads can be removed with the engine in the vehicle.

1. Drain the cooling system; both radiator and engine block.

─────── **CAUTION** ───────
Because of the use of aluminum, do not allow the anti-freeze coolant mixture to enter the cylinders. Severe engine damage could result after engine start-up.

2. Remove the upper timing belt cover assembly.
3. Remove the upper coolant hoses and heater hoses from the thermostat housing area.
4. Remove the air intake tube and the air cleaner assembly.
5. Remove all connecting linkages, wires and hoses from the intake manifold and injector system.
6. Rotate the engine to bring the crankshaft pulley mark to TDC, and, if working with the left cylinder head, mark and remove the distributor assembly.
7. Remove the intake manifold and injector system from the cylinder head and engine block.

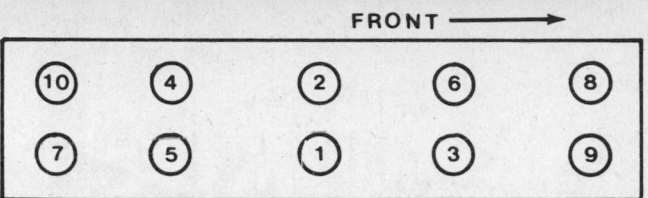

Cylinder head bolt torque sequence—924 engine

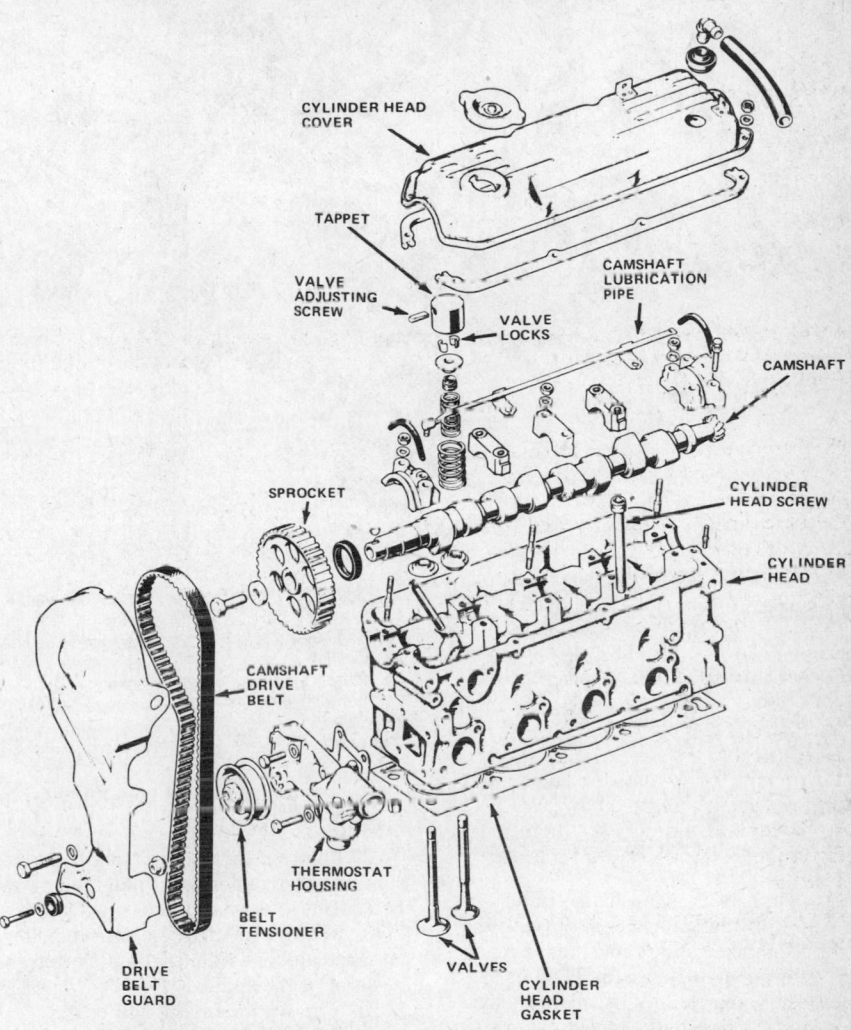

924 cylinder head and related components (924 Turbo similar)

8. From the lower right side of the engine block, loosen the timing belt tensioner bolt and remove the timing belt from the sprockets.

NOTE: Accessory drive belts may have to be either loosened or removed.

9. Remove the rubber plugs from the upper portion of the camshaft housing and remove the Allen head screws from the holes.
10. Remove the exposed Allen head screws from the lower portion of the camshaft housing and remove the housing from the cylinder head.

NOTE: The camshaft housing must be removed and replaced as an assembly.

11. Remove the exhaust manifold from the cylinder head. Remove the inner right and left belt housing, as necessary.
12. Remove the cylinder head nuts and washers by starting from the center and alternating toward each end.
13. Remove the cylinder head from the engine block studs, being careful not to mark or scratch the cylinder head sealing surface.
14. Remove the head gasket from the studs and clean both the head and the block.
15. Installation is the reverse of removal.
16. During the installation, attention should be given to the following:
   a. Left and right cylinder head gaskets

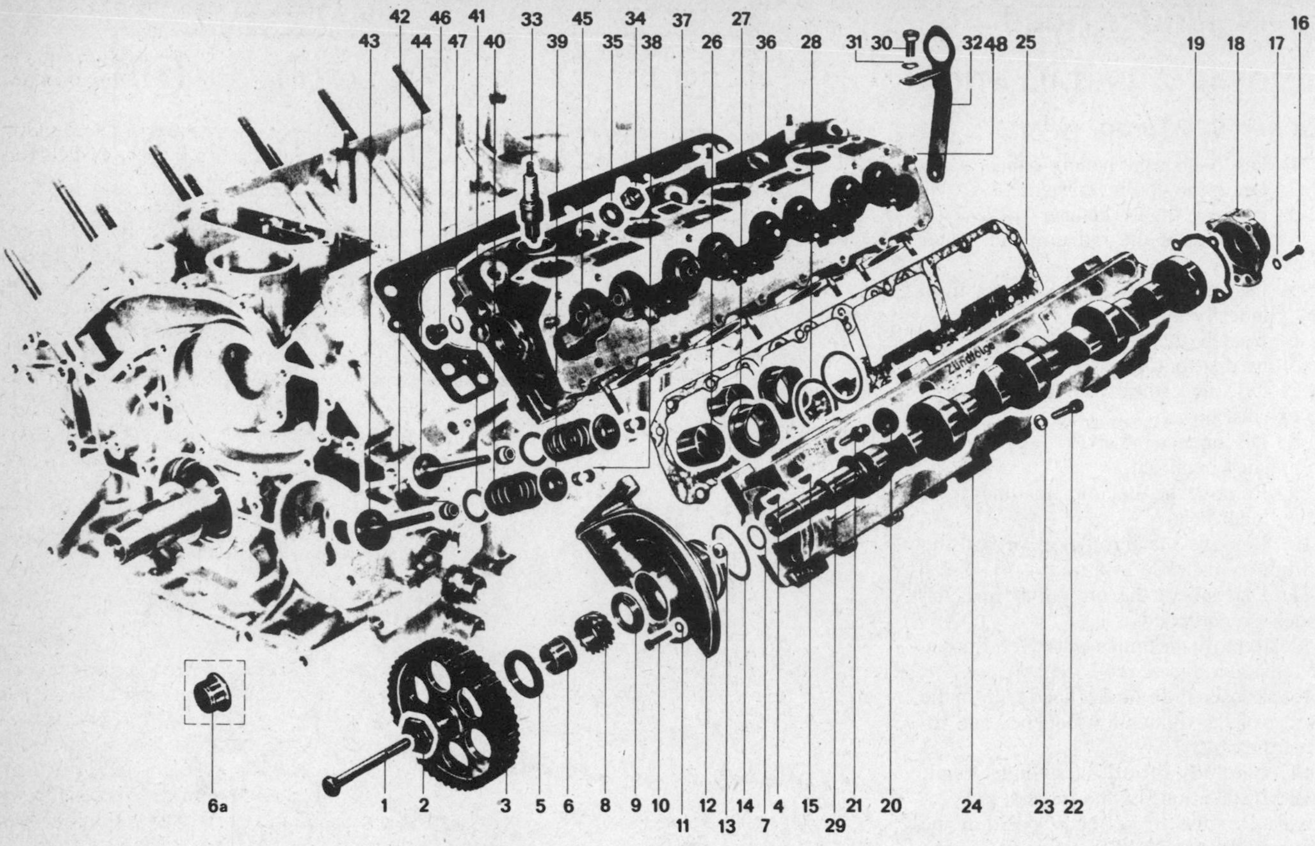

Component legend:

1. Bolt	8. Distributor drive gear	16. Bolt	24. Camshaft housing	32. Lifting eye	40. Valve spring
2. Washer	9. Spacer	17. Washer	25. Gasket	33. Spark plug	41. Shim
3. Camshaft sprocket	10. Bolt	18. End cover	26. Hydraulic valve lifter	34. Nut	42. Valve stem seal
4. Woodruff key	11. Washer	19. Gasket	27. Lifter sleeve	35. Washer	43. Intake valve
5. Camshaft oil seal	12. Bearing carrier	20. Plug	28. Gasket	36. Cylinder head	44. Exhaust valve
6. Spacer	13. Seal	21. Bolt with washers	29. Left camshaft	37. Left gasket	45. Valve guide
6a. Spacer	14. O-ring	22. Bolt	30. Bolt	38. Valve keeper	46. Plug
7. O-ring	15. Woodruff key	23. Washer	31. Washer	39. Spring retainer	47. Seal
					48. Dowel pin

928 and 928S cylinder head and related components; the 944 is similar.

are different. TOP/OBEN faces up and the arrow faces forward.

b. Turn both camshafts until the notches on the sprockets align with the marks on the camshaft housings. Be sure the crankshaft pulley is at TDC (No. 1 piston on compression). Install the toothed belt and the belt tensioner.

c. If leaks occur between the cylinder head and block, install a new cylinder head gasket, Part No. 928 104 371/372 09. This gasket is original equipment on cars built after 6/15/82.

Tighten the cylinder head bolts in the proper order and to the correct specification. Refer to the Torque Specifications at the beginning of this section. Follow the information with the chart EXACTLY.

944

NOTE: It is not necessary to remove the engine in order to remove the cylinder head.

1. Disconnect the negative (ground) battery cable and remove the cap from the coolant expansion tank.

2. Remove the engine splash guard. Remove the radiator drain plug and allow the coolant to drain into a clean container.

3. Remove the drive belt for the alternator and air conditioning compressor from the front of the engine.

4. Remove the timing belt cover.

5. Rotate the engine as necessary to position the No. 1 piston on TDC—compression. Align the marks of both the camshaft sprocket and the flywheel according to the accompanying illustrations.

6. Remove the distributor cap. Unscrew the distributor arm and remove the plastic cap.

7. Remove the distributor cap mount.

8. Release the tension of the camshaft drive belt and pull the belt off of the camshaft sprocket.

9. Remove the two rear drive belt cover mounting bolts.

10. Detach the fuel lines from the locations shown in the accompanying illustration.

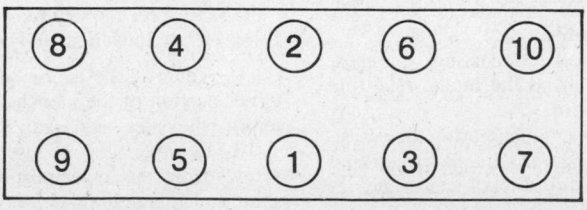

Cylinder head bolt torque sequence—944 engine

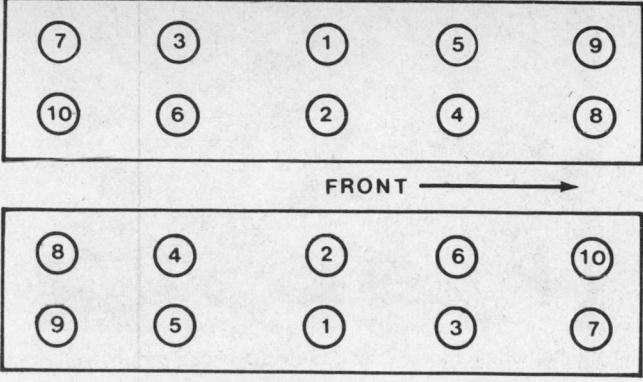

Cylinder head bolt torque sequence—928 and 928S

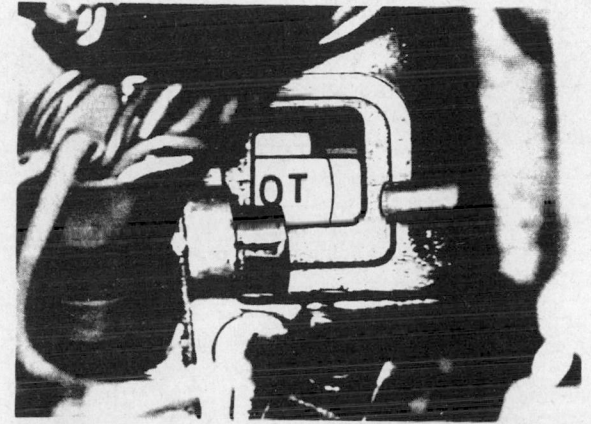

Alignment of the flywheel and clutch housing timing marks—944

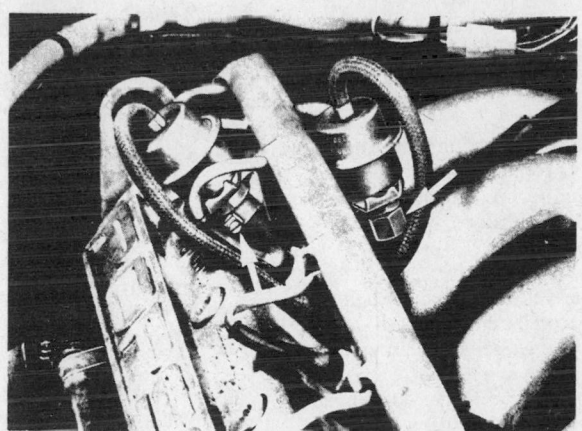

During removal of the 944 cylinder head, disconnect the fuel lines where indicated (arrows).

11. Remove the plastic cover from the fuel collection tube. Detach the wiring from the fuel injectors and lay the wiring harness aside.

12. Remove the aluminum plugs from the camshaft housing and detach the coolant line from the camshaft housing. Remove the camshaft housing from the cylinder head.

NOTE: Use care to keep the hydraulic valve tappets in place.

13. Remove the air cleaner assembly. Remove the bolt of the air intake brace.

14. Remove the intake manifold by disconnecting the following items:
   a. Oil dipstick tube bracket
   b. Brake booster hose
   c. Intake manifold hose
   d. Accelerator cable retaining clamp

15. Remove the intake manifold mounting bolts then remove the manifold.

16. Remove the bolts from the exhaust manifold/converter pipe flange.

17. Remove the hose clamp from the heater regulating valve and the two screws from the valve neck.

18. Remove the cylinder head mounting bolts in the reverse order of the installation torque sequence.

19. Remove the cylinder head.

20. Installation is performed in the reverse order of the previous steps. After installing the head, tighten the bolts to the correct specification, and in the proper order. Refer to the Torque Specifications at the beginning of this section. Torque the camshaft housing mounting bolts to 14 ft. lbs. and the aluminum plugs to 29 ft. lbs. Install and adjust the camshaft drive (timing) belt as outlined later in the Engine section ("Timing Belt Removal and Installation" procedure). Adjust the alternator and air conditioning compressor drive belt tension.

OVERHAUL

If partial loss of oil pressure is encountered, it may be due to oil seepage through the crankcase mounting nuts. New sealing nuts are used since 5/17/82 production and these can be installed on earlier vehicles.

For all cylinder head overhaul procedures, please refer to "Engine Rebuilding" in the Unit Repair section.

Intake Manifold

REMOVAL & INSTALLATION

924 and 924 Turbo

The intake manifold and throttle valve housing are removed as one unit.

1. Remove the air cleaner on the 924.

2. Disconnect the accelerator cable.

3. Disconnect the EGR connections.

4. Detach all electrical leads.

5. On the 924 Turbo, remove the pressure duct, being careful not to drop anything into the turbocharger housing. Cap the turbocharger opening after removing the duct.

6. Disconnect the auxiliary air regulator hose.

7. Remove all vacuum hoses attached to the intake manifold.

8. Remove the eight retaining nuts and remove the throttle valve housing and intake manifold as a unit.

9. Installation is the reverse of removal. Tighten the nuts to 15 ft. lbs.

Exhaust Manifold

REMOVAL & INSTALLATION

NOTE: Always purchase new gaskets before removing the exhaust manifold.

1. On the 924 Turbo, remove the turbocharger and wastegate as outlined later.

2. Disconnect the EGR line from the manifold.

3. On models so equipped, remove the air pump connections.

4. Disconnect the exhaust pipe(s) from the manifold(s).

5. Remove the retaining nuts and remove the manifold(s).

6. Clean the cylinder head(s) and manifold mating surfaces.

7. Using new gaskets, install the exhaust manifold(s).

8. Tighten the nuts to 15 ft. lbs. Work from the inside out.

9. Install the remaining components in the reverse order of removal. Use a new manifold flange gasket if the old one is deteriorated.

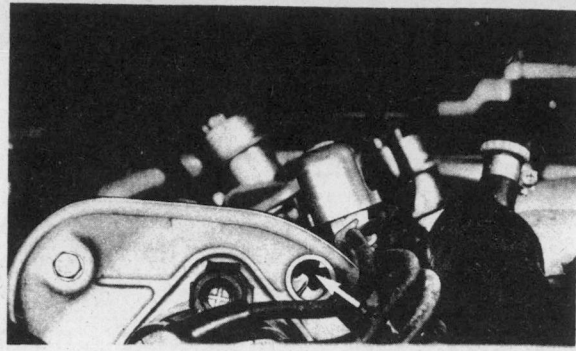

Alignment of the camshaft sprocket and distributor cap mount timing marks—944

Turbocharging System

The exhaust gas turbocharger is mounted at the right side of the engine under the exhaust manifold. The turbocharger wastegate is located near the right side of the bell housing. A boost pressure safety switch is located in the pressure duct between the turbocharger and the throttle valve housing. When the boost pressure increases to about 1.1–1.4 bar, the safety switch will turn off the two fuel pumps until pressure recedes. In operation, the exhaust gases flow into the turbocharger, and from there through the 3-way catalyst and rear muffler. The connection for the wastegate is integrated in the manifold. The pipe from the wastegate is attached to the catalytic converter housing.

For additional information on turbocharger maintenance, please refer to "Turbocharging" in the Unit Repair Section.

WASTEGATE REMOVAL AND INSTALLATION

1. Jack up the vehicle and support it on stands.

2. Pull off the rubber cap from plug terminal for oxygen sensor and plug.

3. Remove the starter. Remove the bypass line between the exhaust manifold and wastegate.

4. Remove the nuts between the turbine housing and the exhaust pipe.

5. Unscrew the mounting bolts on the flange of the primary muffler/final muffler.

6. Loosen the final muffler bracket and strap, then remove the final muffler.

7. Loosen the heat shields over bypass line II, then loosen the pipe clamp at bypass line II.

8. Detach the holder and control line at the wastegate, then remove the entire line with the wastegate.

——— CAUTION ———
Do not damage the oxygen sensor.

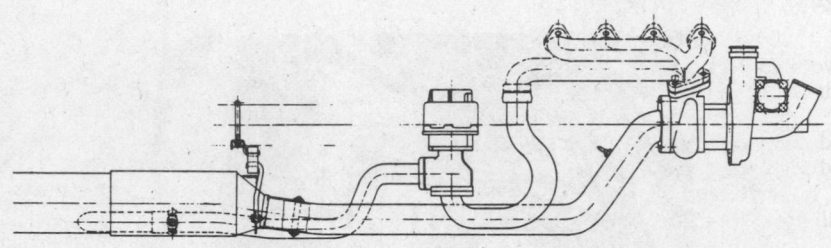

Turbocharger component configuration

NOTE: Some of the early production 924 Turbos have a vent line for the wastegate. The vent line connector will be accessible only after lowering the exhaust pipe.

9. Installation is the reverse of removal. Use new gaskets where applicable.

TURBOCHARGER REMOVAL AND INSTALLATION

NOTE: When replacing the turbocharger, always replace the oil filter and change the engine oil. Premature turbocharger bearing failure will result if this is not done.

1. Disconnect the negative battery cable.

2. Raise the vehicle and support it on jack stands. Remove the engine splash shield.

3. Remove the wastegate as previously outlined.

4. Disconnect the oil lines leading to the engine oil cooler, then disconnect the oil feed line for the turbocharger at the oil filter flange. Plug all oil lines.

NOTE: 1981–82 924 Turbos use a metal pipe connecting the oil return hose and turbocharger in place of a breather hose.

5. Disconnect and remove the oil filter flange. Have a pan ready to catch escaping oil.

6. Loosen oil line clamps and pull out the oil lines toward the front.

7. Disconnect the oil return line.

8. Disconnect the pressure duct and remove.

9. Take off the air cleaner duct and remove.

10. Take off the air cleaner upper and lower sections.

11. Remove the three mounting nuts from the bottom of the fuel distributor.

12. Loosen the hose clamps on the dust cover and move the fuel distributor to one side.

13. Unscrew the mounting bolt on the pressure duct and take off the pressure duct.

14. Remove the nuts holding the exhaust manifold/turbocharger. Unscrew the allen head bolts at the base of the unit, then loosen the hose clamp at the bottom of the turbocharger.

15. Disconnect both sides of the stabilizer, then disconnect the steering gear from the control arm.

16. Disconnect the turbocharger base and remove the turbocharger with console toward the front.

17. Pull off the hose for the wastegate connection.

Installation is the reverse of removal with the following notes:

a. When placing the turbocharger on the engine, the allen bolts loosened in Step 13 must still be loose.

b. Push the hose on at the bottom of the turbocharger while installing the unit. There is not enough clearance to install the hose after the turbocharger is installed.

c. First tighten the mounting nuts of the exhaust manifold/turbocharger, then tighten the turbocharger base bolts.

d. Always use new seals on oil lines.

e. Make sure that the round seal fits properly on the pressure duct.

f. First install both pressure ducts, then tighten the bolt(s).

g. Tighten the steering gear bolts to 14 ft. lbs.

h. Before starting the engine for the first time, lubricating oil for the turbocharger has to be primed for 15 seconds. To do this, pull off the plugs from the manifold pressure limiting switch and operate the starter.

Timing Belt Cover

REMOVAL & INSTALLATION

924 and 924 Turbo

1. Loosen the alternator mounting bolts, pivot the alternator over, and slip the drive belt off the pulleys.

2. Unscrew the cover retaining bolts and remove the cover. Keep the washers and spacers together.

3. Reposition the spacers and then install the washers and bolts.

4. Install the alternator belt and adjust the tension.

928

The timing cover consists of an outer right upper, an outer left upper and an outer bottom cover. Left and right inner belt guide covers are also used. The outer upper covers can be removed without the removal of the drive belts.

944

1. Disconnect the negative (ground) battery cable.

2. Loosen the alternator and compressor drive belt tensioner and remove the belt.

3. Remove the timing belt cover.

4. Installation is performed in the reverse of the previous steps.

Timing Belts

CHECKING TENSION

928 and 928S

A special tool is recommended to check the tension of the drive belt.

1. Remove the upper section of the drive belt guard.

2. Rotate the engine in the normal direction of rotation and set the engine to TDC on the compression stroke of No. 1 cylinder. The marks of the camshaft sprockets should be aligned with the marks on the flange bearings.

3. Turn the engine 2 additional turns until the TDC mark is reached again. While the engine is being turned, check the condition of the drive belt.

4. Special tool #9201 is recommended to check the tension. Pull the lockpin and gauge pin completely out and zero the gauge.

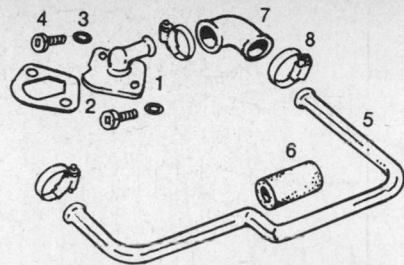

1 & 3. Washer
2 & 4. Bolt
5. Breather pipe
6. Rubber hose
7. Rubber elbow
8. Clamp

On 1981–82 924 Turbos, a metal pipe replaces the breather hose between the turbocharger and crankcase.

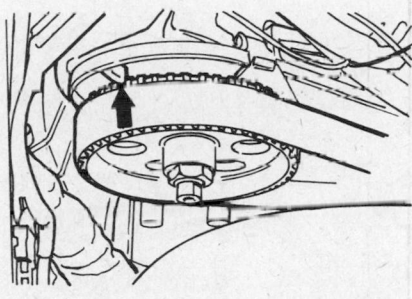

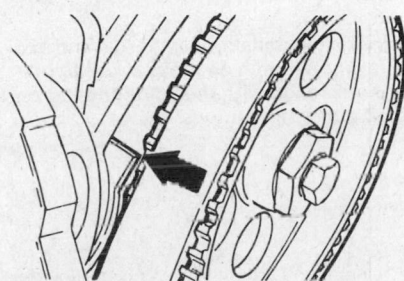

When the 928, 928S engine is at TDC on No. 1 cylinder, the camshaft sprocket marks (arrow) will align with the marks on the housing.

Slide the tool onto the belt between the tensioning roller and the lower camshaft sprocket. The measuring pin must rest in the groove of the belt. Push the tester down slowly until the gauge needle engages the belt. Keep the tester horizontal and out of contact with the surrounding objects. Read the value on the gauge. Repeat the process to be sure of an accurate reading.

5. See "Removal, Installation and Tensioning" to tension the drive belt. The gauge should read 9.2 on the scale for a new belt or 7.6–9.0 for a used belt.

944

BALANCE SHAFTS DRIVE BELT

1. Remove the splash guard under the engine.

2. Remove the alternator compressor belt.

3. Remove the upper and lower belt covers.

4. Release the tension from the belt. There are two methods to release the tension. On older models equipped with guide rollers without a slot, turn the eccentric to release the tension from the belt. On newer models with a locking nut on the guide roller (with slot), loosen the locknut and slide the roller away from the belt.

5. Remove the plug from the distributor cap mount.

6. Turn the crankshaft in the direction of normal rotation until the TDC mark on the camshaft sprocket aligns with the cast mark.

7. Check to be sure the scribe mark on the flywheel is visible through the clutch housing and opposite the TDC mark.

8. Check that the balance shaft marks are aligned with the marks on the rear belt cover.

9. Special tool #9201 is recommended to check the belt tension. Pull out the lockpin and let the gauge slide drop. Zero the gauge and slide it onto the belt. Push up on the measuring slide until you can hear the lockpin engage. Pull out the lockpin and remove the gauge. Read the measured value. If the guide rollers have no slot, the gauge should read 4.0–4.6 for a new belt, or 3.7–4.3 for a used belt. If the guide roller has a slot, the gauge should read 2.4–3.0 for new and used belts. If necessary, adjust the tension. See "Removal, Installation and Tensioning."

CAMSHAFT BELT

The engine must be cold. A special tool is recommended to check the drive belt tension.

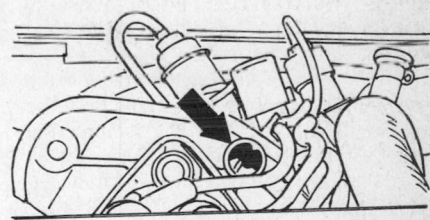

On 944 models, the TDC mark of the camshaft sprocket will align with the cast mark as shown (arrow).

On the 944, check that the scribe mark on the flywheel is aligned with the TDC mark on the clutch housing.

1. Remove the splash guard, belt covers and alternator compressor belt.

2. Turn the crankshaft in the direction of normal rotation and check the condition of the drive belt. If damaged or worn, it should be replaced.

3. Remove the plug from the distributor cap mount.

4. Turn the crankshaft in the direction of normal rotation until the TDC mark on the camshaft sprocket is aligned with the cast mark on the mounting for the distributor cap.

5. Be sure the TDC mark on the flywheel and clutch housing are aligned.

6. Turn the crankshaft counterclockwise approximately 10° (1½ teeth on the camshaft sprocket). *This step is mandatory. If it is not performed, the tension measurement may be incorrect and engine damage could result.*

7. Prepare the gauge to take the reading. Pull the lockpin from Tool #9201 and listen for the gauge slide to drop. Zero the gauge and slide it onto the belt. Push up on the measuring slide until you can hear the lockpin engage. Pull the lockpin out and read the gauge. It should read 2.4–3.0 for both new and used belts. If the tension needs adjusting, see "Removal, Installation and Tensioning."

REMOVAL, INSTALLATION & TENSIONING

924 and 924 Turbo

1. Remove the timing belt cover.

2. While holding the larger hex on the tensioner pulley, loosen the pulley locknut.

3. Release the tensioner from the timing belt.

4. Slide the belt off the two toothed pulleys and remove it.

5. Using the large center bolt on the crankshaft pulley, turn the engine until the No. 1 cylinder is at TDC of the compression stroke. At this point, both valves will be closed and the timing marks at the flywheel will be aligned.

6. Check that the timing dot on the rear face of the camshaft pulley is aligned with the camshaft cover as shown in the illustration. If not, turn the pulley so that it does.

7. Check that the V-notch in the crankshaft pulley aligns with the adjusting lug on the oil pump housing as shown. If they don't align, turn the crankshaft until they do.

─────── **CAUTION** ───────

If the timing marks are not correctly aligned with the No. 1 piston at TDC of the compression stroke and the belt is installed, valve timing will be incorrect. Poor performance and possible engine damage can result from improper valve timing.

8. Install the belt on the pulleys.

9. Adjust the tensioner by turning the large hex on the pulley to the left until the

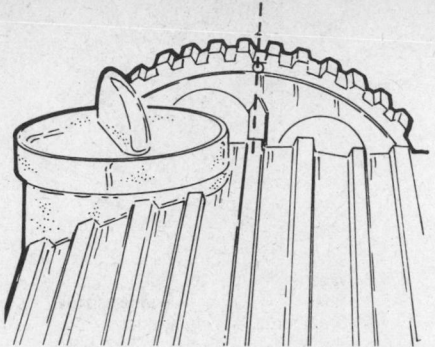

Timing belt installation on the 924 and 924 Turbo: The dot on the camshaft sprocket should align as shown

Timing belt installation on the 924 and 924 Turbo: The V-notch on the crankshaft pulley should align with the adjusting lug on the oil pump housing as shown

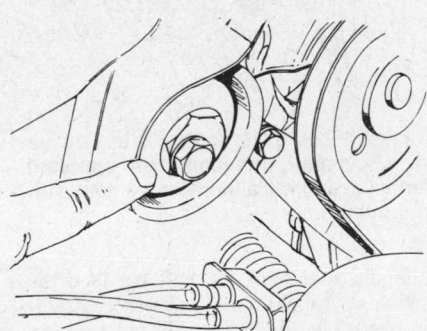

Timing belt tensioner bolt of the 924 and 924 Turbo

belt can be twisted 90° with the thumb and forefinger at the midpoint between the camshaft pulley and the crankshaft pulley. Tighten the locknut to 30 ft. lbs.

10. Install the timing belt cover and check the ignition timing.

928

1. Loosen and remove the drive belts for the power steering pump, fan and air pump, alternator and air conditioning compressor.

2. Remove the fan assembly and bracket for clearance.

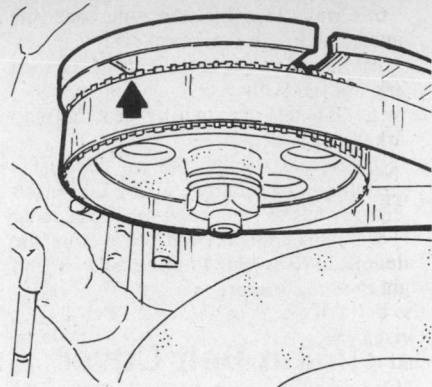

Right-hand camshaft alignment on 928 and 928S

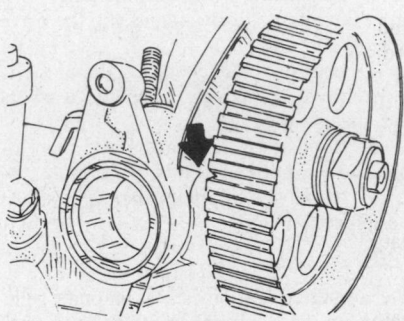

Left hand camshaft alignment of the 928

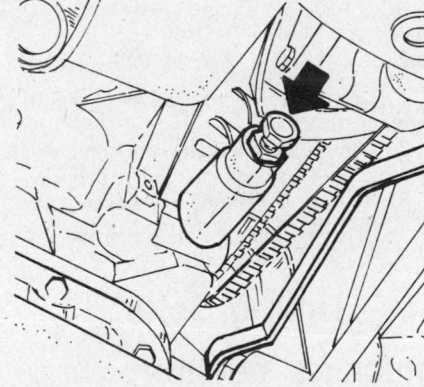

Timing belt tensioner on the 928 and 928S viewed from beneath the car.

NOTE: Do not lay the fan assembly flat. The silicone oil filler will leak out and the fan will become inoperative.

3. Remove any hoses or lines that may interfere with the cover or belt removal.

4. Remove the upper right, upper left and the bottom cover from the front of the engine.

5. Rotate the engine to TDC with the No. 1 piston on the compression stroke and the distributor rotor pointing to the No. 1 cylinder spark plug wire terminal of distributor cap.

6. Loosen the belt tensioner bolt and remove the belt from the sprockets.

7. Align the camshaft notches with the marks on the cam housings and install a new toothed belt, being sure the crankshaft marks remain aligned at TDC.

NOTE: The water pump pulley is turned by the back of the toothed belt.

8. The drive belt adjusting screw is located on the bottom of the engine at the right front. On models prior to 1982, tighten the belt tensioner bolt until the belt can be twisted only 90° between the tension roller and the right camshaft sprocket.

On 1982 and later models, loosen the locknut on the adjusting screw and turn it until the correct tension is achieved. Tighten the locknut and turn the engine 2 additional turns. Recheck the tension.

9. Install the covers, hoses or lines, fan and bracket assembly, and the drive belts. Adjust the drive belts to have a deflection of ½ inch between pulleys.

10. Check and adjust the ignition timing as necessary.

944

1. Disconnect the negative (ground) battery cable.

2. Remove the engine splash guard.

3. Remove the drive belt for the alternator and air conditioning compressor from the front of the engine.

4. Remove the upper and lower timing belt cover.

5. Rotate the engine as necessary to position the No. 1 piston on TDC—compression. Align the marks of both the camshaft pulley and the flywheel according to the illustrations given with "Cylinder Head Removal and Installation".

6. Remove the distributor cap. Unscrew the distributor arm and remove the plastic cap.

7. Remove the distributor cap mount.

8. Release the tension of the camshaft drive (timing) belt and carefully remove the belt from the sprockets.

— **CAUTION** —

DO NOT rotate any of the sprockets while the belt is removed.

9. After making sure that all timing marks are still properly aligned, the new belt may be installed in the following manner:

a. Install the belt on the crankshaft sprocket first, then to the tensioning roller, water pump pulley, and the camshaft sprocket. Preload the belt slightly by hand each time it is routed around the components, so that it can be pushed onto the camshaft sprocket.

b. Again, make sure all timing marks have remained aligned.

c. Carefully turn the crankshaft about 10 crankshaft degrees counterclockwise, which is equal to 1½ teeth to the mark on the camshaft sprocket.

Prior to installation of the 944 timing belt, the camshaft sprocket and the rear timing belt cover should be aligned as shown

1. Crankshaft sprocket
2. Tensioning roller
3. Water pump pulley
4. Camshaft sprocket

The 944 timing belt should be installed on each sprocket/pulley in the numerical order shown

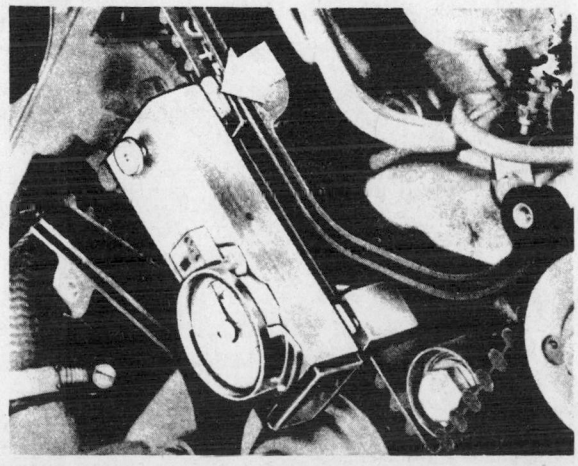

Special timing belt tension tool shown installed on the 944 timing belt. Note that the tool is installed in the same manner on the balance shaft drive belt. Measuring needle (arrow) to be pushed in when "setting-up" the tool

Timing belt tensioner of the 944—turn the large hex as required to tighten or loosen the belt

NOTE: Porsche special tool #9201 is needed to complete the remainder of the procedure.

d. Pull the lockpin out of the special tool. Completely push out the gauge pin which is opposite the lock pin.

e. Zero the telltale needle of the special tool and slide the special tool onto the belt.

NOTE: The slides of the special tool must rest flat with the full surface of the belt.

——— CAUTION ———
DO NOT turn or move the belt while testing the belt tension.

f. Push the measuring needle of the tool inward slowly until you hear the lockpin engage. Read the value on the dial gauge of the special tool. The value should read as follows:
New belt—2.0 ± 0.3
Old belt—1.6 ± 0.3

g. If necessary, adjust the belt tension according to the above specifications.

h. Remove the special tool from the belt and install /attach remaining components in the reverse of Steps 1–8.

Balance Shaft Drive Belt

REMOVAL & INSTALLATION
944

1. Disconnect the negative (ground) battery cable.
2. Remove the engine splash guard.
3. Remove the alternator and air conditioning drive belt.
4. Remove the camshaft drive (timing) belt cover.
5. Loosen the balance shaft idler pulley

so that the pulley does not touch the balance shaft drive belt.

6. Rotate the crankshaft clockwise as necessary to position the No. 1 cylinder at TDC—compression.

NOTE: At this point, the marks on the balance shaft sprockets should be aligned with the marks on the rear belt cover.

7. Turn the tensioner nut counterclockwise to loosen the balance shaft drive belt. Carefully remove the old belt from the sprockets.

NOTE: There are 2 types of tensioners used. The older type (without a slot) is an eccentric that is turned to adjust tension. The newer type (with a slot) is held in place by a locknut and slides away from the belt to release tension.

——— CAUTION ———
DO NOT move any sprocket while the belt is removed, or while installing the new belt.

8. Carefully route the new belt around the sprockets, making sure that the color coded tooth of the belt faces away from the sprockets.

9. Adjust the belt tension in the same manner as the camshaft drive (timing) belt, according to the appropriate steps of the ''Timing Belt Removal and Installation'' procedure. Turn the tensioner nut (same one used during Step 7) to tighten the belt to the proper value (2.4–3.0 dial reading).

On guide rollers with no slot, loosen the locknut and turn the eccentric clockwise to tighten or counterclockwise to loosen. Tighten the locknut to 33 ft. lbs.

10. On rollers with a slot, adjust the idler pulley so that there is 0.5mm clearance between the pulley and the portion of the belt below the pulley. Tighten the pulley nut in this position.

NOTE: If the correct clearance cannot be obtained, rotate the pulley 180° and repeat Step 10.

11. The remaining components are installed in the reverse order of removal.

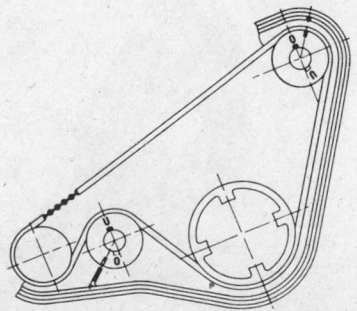

Prior to removing or installing the balance shaft drive belt, the balance shaft sprocket marks should be aligned with the marks on the rear cover as shown

Timing Sprockets

REMOVAL & INSTALLATION

The camshaft and crankshaft sprockets are located by keys on their respective shafts and each is retained by a bolt. To remove either or both of the sprockets, first remove the timing belt cover and belt and then use the following procedure.

NOTE: When removing the crankshaft sprocket on the 924, don't remove the four bolts which retain the outer belt pulley to the timing belt sprocket.

1. Remove the center bolt.
2. Gently pry the sprocket off the shaft. If the sprocket is stubborn, use a gear puller. Don't hammer on the sprocket.
3. Remove the sprocket and the key.
4. Install the sprocket in the reverse order of removal.
5. Tighten the center bolt on the crankshaft sprocket to 58 ft. lbs. Tighten the camshaft sprocket retaining bolt to 33 ft. lbs.

NOTE: 944 models equipped with polygon-head bolts instead of the Allen head bolts should be torqued to 48 ft. lbs.

6. Install the timing belt, check valve timing, belt tension, and install the cover.

Camshaft

REMOVAL & INSTALLATION
924 and 924 Turbo

1. Remove the timing belt.
2. Remove the camshaft sprocket.
3. Remove the air cleaner.
4. Remove the camshaft cover.
5. Remove the distributor and mounting housing.
6. Remove the oil injection tube and then reinstall the retaining nuts hand tight.
7. Unscrew and remove the Nos. 1, 3 and 5 bearing caps (No. 1 is at the front of the engine).
8. Unscrew the Nos. 2 and 4 bearing caps, diagonally and in increments.
9. Lift the camshaft out of the cylinder head.
10. Lubricate the camshaft journals and lobes with assembly lube or gear oil before installing it in the cylinder head. Bolts are tightened to 8 ft. lbs. and nuts to 20 ft. lbs.
11. Tighten bearing caps Nos. 2 and 4 carefully in a diagonal pattern.
12. Install bearing caps Nos. 1, 3 and 5.
13. Install the oil injection tube. You will have to loosen the nuts on Nos. 2 and 4 again.
14. Install the camshaft cover using new gaskets and seals.
15. Install the camshaft pulley and the timing belt.

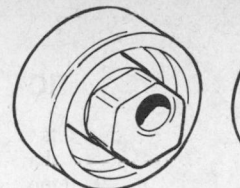 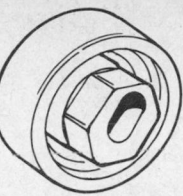

Old style eccentric tensioner (with no slot) is on the left. Newer style with slot is on the right.

16. Check the valve clearance.

928, 928S and 944

Refer to the "Cylinder Head Removal and Installation" section for the removal of the cam housing as a unit.

1. Remove the hydraulic lifters, lifter sleeves and gaskets from the cam housing.

2. Remove the rear housing end plate and gasket.

3. On the 928, remove the camshaft sprocket, the front bearing carrier on the right head and the distributor and bearing carrier on the left cam housing. On the 944, remove the camshaft sprocket and the bearing carriers.

4. Pull the camshaft to the rear and out of the cam housing.

5. The distributor gear and spacer can be removed from the camshaft at this time.

6. Installation is the reverse of removal.

NOTE: The front camshaft seals can be replaced while the front bearing carriers are off the cam housings or when the timing sprocket is removed from the camshaft.

Pistons and Connecting Rods

REMOVAL & INSTALLATION

924 and 924 Turbo

Pistons and connecting rods are removed after the cylinder head and oil pan have been removed. Connecting rod and piston assemblies must be marked on disassembly. The projections on the connecting rods must face toward the front of the engine when installed. The arrow or notch in the piston crown must face toward the front of the engine.

928, 928S and 944

The pistons and connecting rods may be removed after the cylinder head and the pan have been removed. The connecting rod ends are offset. On the 928, make sure that the narrow side with the small chamfer faces the neighboring connecting rod, while the wide side with the large chamfer faces the crankshaft web. The pistons must be installed with the valve pockets facing toward

Balance shaft idler pulley of the 944. During removal of the balance shaft drive belt, the pulley should be adjusted so that it does not touch the belt

The balance shaft tensioner nut of the 944. Turn the nut counterclockwise to loosen the belt; clockwise to tighten

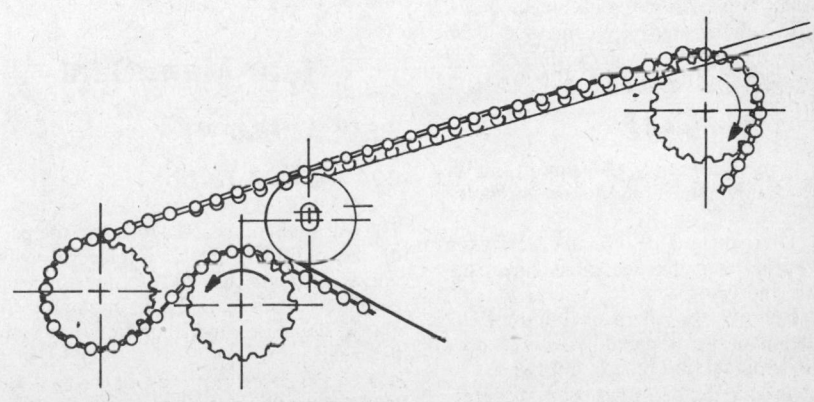

Maintain 0.002-0.004 in. clearance between the guide roller and the lower balance shaft on the 944.

the exhaust manifold. The wrist pin is pressed out of the piston after the snap-rings are removed.

ENGINE LUBRICATION

The 924 full pressure lubrication system consists of a wet sump, crankshaft driven oil pump, oil temperature gauge with sender in the oil pan, and a disposable type oil filter on the passenger side of the block.

The 928, 928S and 944 oil sump lower section is divided into four chambers to maintain a constant oil supply for the suction pipe during periods of high speed driving and sharp turns. A thermostatically controlled oil cooler is located in the radiator and the oil pump is mounted on the front of the engine and is driven by the toothed belt. The oil filler tube and oil level sending unit are threaded into the top of the oil pan front. A full pressure lubrication system is used.

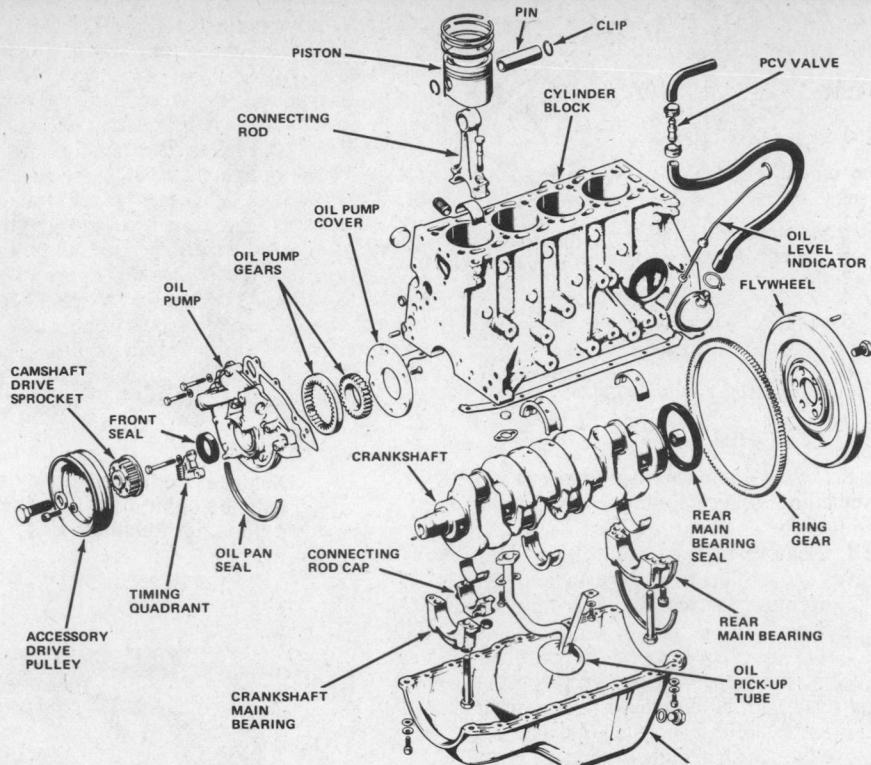

Cylinder block and related components of the 924 and 924 Turbo

Oil Pan

REMOVAL & INSTALLATION

924 and 924 Turbo

1. Drain the oil. Remove the engine splash shield.

2. Disconnect the temperature sending unit wire.

3. Disconnect the side engine mounts and raise the engine for pan removal clearance.

4. Remove the pan retaining bolts and lower the pan from the car.

5. Install the pan using the reverse of the removal procedure. Use new gaskets and seals. Remove the oil dipstick for additional venting when refilling the engine with oil. This will prevent blue exhaust smoke following any oil change due to oil entering the intake system through the breather.

928, 928S and 944

1. Raise the vehicle and support safely.

2. Remove the bottom protective engine plate.

3. Drain the engine oil and unscrew the oil fill pipe from the pan. Disconnect the oil level indicator wire.

4. Remove the oil pan retaining bolts and maneuver the oil pan downward so that the oil pump suction tube is not twisted or damaged.

5. Using a new gasket, install the oil pan in the reverse order of removal.

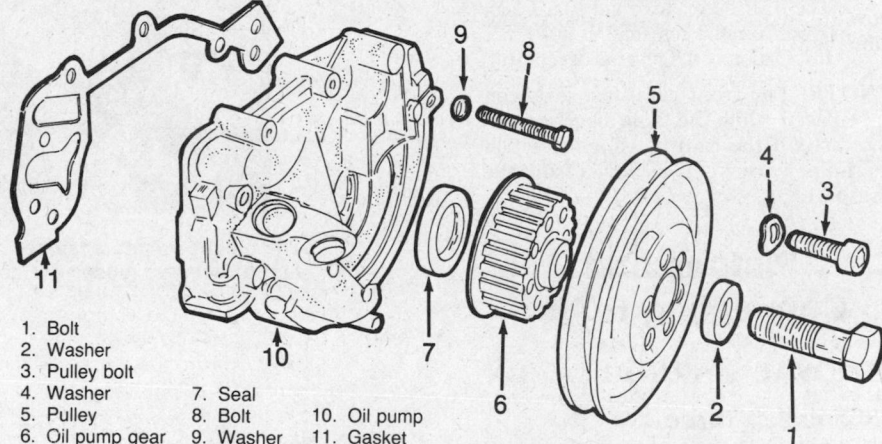

1. Bolt
2. Washer
3. Pulley bolt
4. Washer
5. Pulley
6. Oil pump gear
7. Seal
8. Bolt
9. Washer
10. Oil pump
11. Gasket

Exploded view of the 924 and 924 Turbo oil pump

Rear Main Seal

REPLACEMENT

924 and 924 Turbo

The rear main oil seal is located in the back of the cylinder block. Replacement involves disconnecting the torque tube and pulling the transaxle back, removing the clutch housing, and then removing the flywheel.

1. Carefully pry the seal out.

2. Lightly oil the replacement seal with engine oil and carefully tap it into place.

Do not damage the seal or score the flywheel.

3. Install the flywheel, clutch housing and torque tube and transaxle. Tighten the flywheel-to-crankshaft bolts to 65 ft. lbs.

928, 928S and 944

The rear main oil seal can be replaced by separating the clutch housing from the engine and removing the flywheel. Remove the seal from the engine block with a sharp edged tool, being careful not to mark the crankshaft surface. Using a special centering tool, install the seal into the engine block with the lubricated lip towards the crankshaft. Reassemble in the reverse order of disassembly.

Oil Pump

REMOVAL & INSTALLATION

924 and 924 Turbo

The oil pump is driven directly from the crankshaft.

1. Remove the oil pan.
2. Remove the timing belt cover.
3. Remove the timing belt.
4. Remove the crankshaft pulley.
5. Unbolt and remove the oil pump. Remove the oil pickup.
6. Clean and then install the oil pickup to the replacement oil pump.
7. Install the oil pump. Tighten the pump-to-crankcase bolts to 8 ft. lbs.
8. Install the remaining components in reverse order of removal.

928, 928S and 944

The oil pump is located on the front of the engine block and is driven by the toothed timing belt.

1. Remove the toothed timing belt (refer to the "Timing Belt Removal and Installation" section.)
2. Remove the oil pump sprocket and the oil pump retaining bolts.
3. Remove the oil pump from the engine block.
4. Installation is the reverse of removal. Install a new O-ring seal on the pump body.

NOTE: An oil pump shaft seal is used and can be replaced after removal of the sprocket and woodruff key.

ENGINE COOLING

The 924 and 944 cooling system consists of a radiator, belt driven water pump, expansion tank, electric thermostatically controlled fan, and a conventional thermostat.

The 928 and 928S cooling system includes a radiator, belt driven water pump located on the upper front of the engine block, thermostat and a temperature controlled fan assembly. An expansion tank and coolant level sending unit is located in the right rear of the engine compartment.

NOTE: Porsche recommends using only a phosphate-free coolant/antifreeze in the cooling system. Use of other types of coolant/antifreeze may cause corrosion of the cooling system, causing overheating and damage.

Radiator

REMOVAL & INSTALLATION

1. Drain the cooling system.
2. Remove the fan and radiator shroud.

3. Remove the radiator hoses.
4. Disconnect the expansion tank (924 and 944) and move it out of the way.
5. Unbolt the radiator and remove it.
6. Installation is the reverse of removal. Refill the cooling system as follows: set the heater on the hot position, remove the vent plug on the radiator hose, fill the cooling system, start the engine and run it for one minute at fast idle, replace the vent plug when no more air bubbles appear at the plug opening. The coolant hose on 944 models, from radiator to expansion tank, has been known to rub the headlight linkage. Tie the hose away from the linkage and secure the front hood cable to the coolant hose. A new preformed top coolant hose is installed on newer models.

Water Pump

REMOVAL & INSTALLATION

924 and 924 Turbo

1. Drain the cooling system.
2. Remove the timing belt cover.
3. Remove the fan belt.
4. Disconnect the radiator hoses from the pump.
5. Unbolt and remove the water pump.
6. Clean the crankcase and pump mating surfaces.
7. Install the water pump using a new gasket.
8. Install the remaining components in the reverse order of removal. Refill the cooling system. See "Radiator Removal and Installation."

928, 928S and 944

1. Drain the cooling system.
2. Rotate the engine to TDC, with the Number one piston on the firing stroke and the distributor rotor pointing to Number one terminal of the distributor cap.
3. On the 944, remove the timing belt cover assembly as previously outlined. On the 928, remove the upper right and left timing belt covers and remove the fan and bracket.

NOTE: Maintain upright position of the fan assembly so that the silicone fluid does not drain out (928).

4. Loosen and remove the toothed belt from the water pump pulley (refer to the "Timing Belt Removal and Installation" section).
5. Remove the bolts and water pump from the engine block.
6. Using a new gasket, install the water pump in the reverse order of removal.

Thermostat

REMOVAL & INSTALLATION

The thermostat is located in the upper radiator hose neck on the engine.

1. Drain the cooling system.
2. Don't disconnect the radiator hose, unbolt the neck and lift out the thermostat.
3. Clean the mating surfaces and install the new thermostat (spring down) using a new gasket.
4. Refill the cooling system. See "Radiator Removal and Installation."

EMISSION CONTROLS

Positive Crankcase Ventilation (PCV)

The 924 uses a conventional crankcase ventilation system. A PCV valve, located on the driver's side of the engine, meters blow-by gases into the air intake.

The 928, 928S and 944 crankcase ventilation system utilizes an oil separator, which is also used as an oil filler tube. The crankcase fumes are routed through the separator pipe, where the liquid oil can settle and flow back into the crankcase. The fumes continue through a hose to the lower section of the air cleaner, where a flame arrestor is located. A coolant preheat line is placed

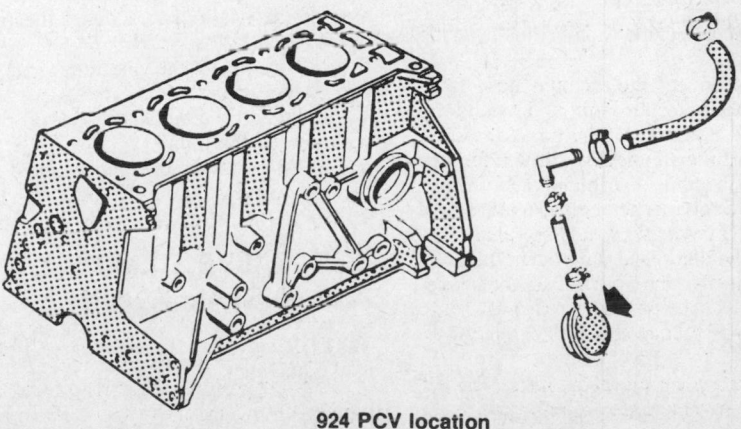

924 PCV location

along a portion of the vent hose to warm the crankcase fumes before entering the air cleaner.

SERVICE

The PCV valve should be replaced at the recommended intervals. Check hoses for plugging and cracking and replace as necessary.

Exhaust Gas Recirculation (EGR)

All models are equipped with this system which lowers NOx emissions. Metered amounts of cooling exhaust gases are added to the air/fuel mixture. The recirculated gas lowers the peak flame temperature during combustion to cut the output of oxides of nitrogen. Exhaust gas from the exhaust pipe passes through a filter where it is cleaned. The vacuum operated EGR valve controls the amount of exhaust gas which enters the intake.

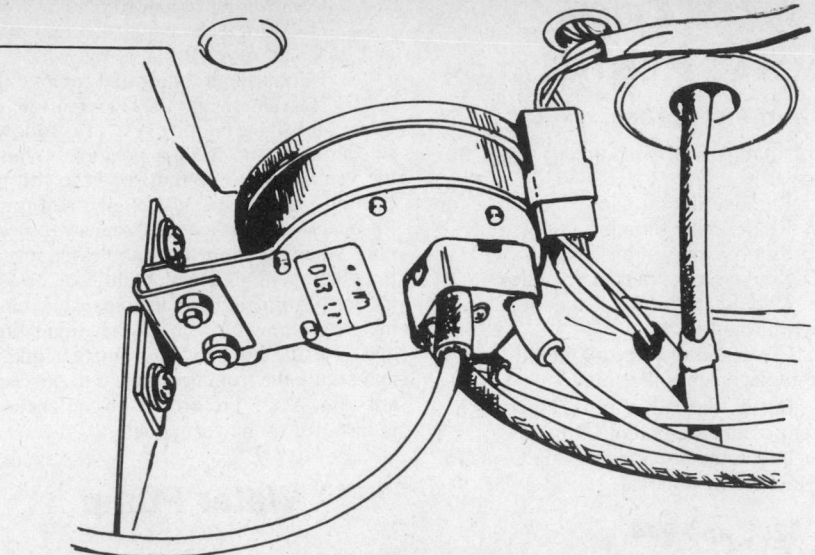

The EGR vacuum amplifier is located on the right side inner fender panel—model 924

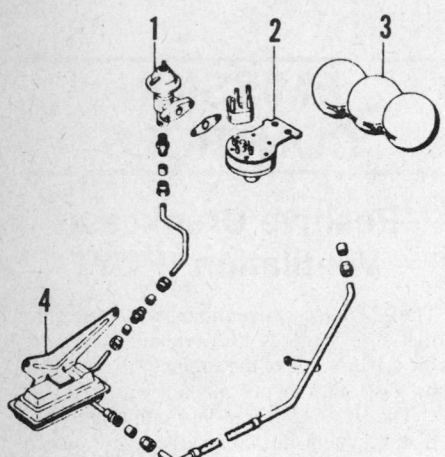

1. EGR valve
2. Vacuum amplifier
3. Vacuum reservoir
4. EGR filter

EGR system—typical

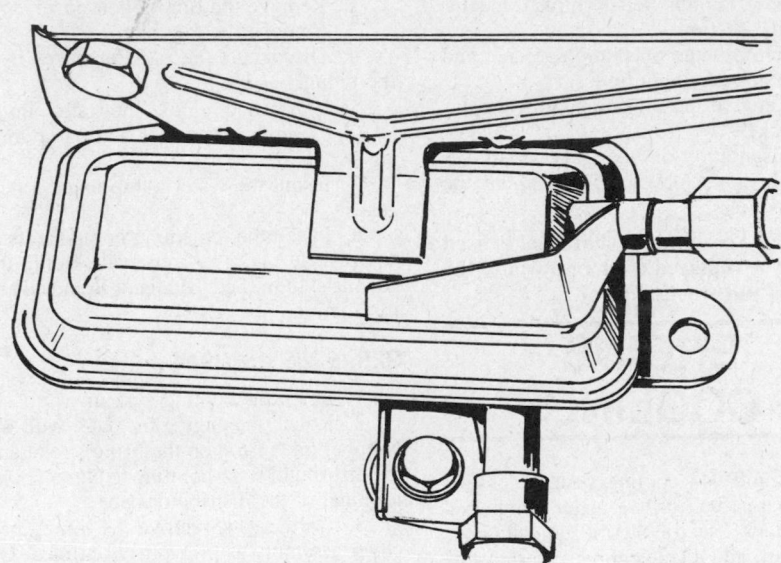

The 924 EGR filter is located on the driver's side of the engine

TESTING

1. Disconnect the vacuum line from the EGR valve.
2. Disconnect the vacuum hose from the distributor vacuum unit and extend the hose.
3. Start the engine and allow it to idle.
4. Connect the distributor vacuum hose to the EGR valve. The engine should stumble or stall.
5. If the idle speed stays even, the EGR line is clogged or the EGR valve is defective.

SERVICE

The only required maintenance is that the EGR filter be replaced at the recommended

intervals. The filter is located on the right side of the engine block under the intake housing.

1. Disconnect the line fittings at each end of the filter.
2. Unbolt the bracket retaining screws and remove the filter.
3. Install the bracket replacement filter using the reverse order of removal.

EGR VALVE REMOVAL AND INSTALLATION

The EGR valve is located on the rear of the intake housing.

1. Disconnect the vacuum line from the EGR valve.

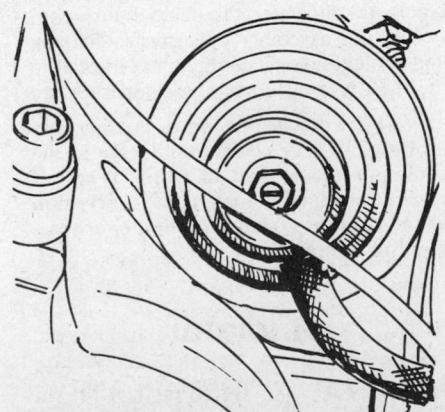

The 924 EGR valve is located on the rear of the intake housing

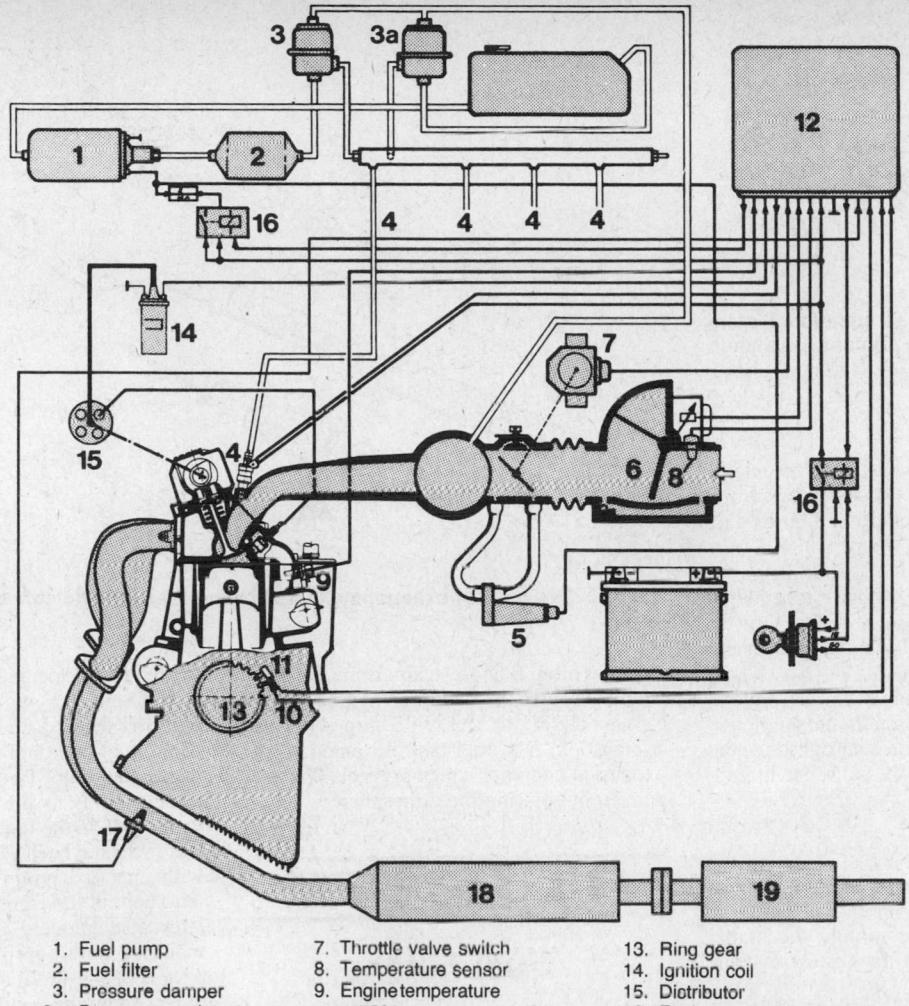

1. Fuel pump
2. Fuel filter
3. Pressure damper
3a. Pressure regulator
4. Injector
5. Auxilliary air valve
6. Air flow meter
7. Throttle valve switch
8. Temperature sensor
9. Engine temperature sensor
10. Speed sensor
11. Reference mark sensor
12. Control unit
13. Ring gear
14. Ignition coil
15. Distributor
16. Fuel pump/control unit relay
17. Oxygen sensor
18. Catalytic converter
19. Muffler

1983 944 emission control schematic

2. Unbolt the EGR line fitting on the opposite side of the valve.

3. Remove the two retaining bolts and lift the EGR valve from the intake housing.

4. Install the EGR valve in the reverse order of removal. Use a new gasket.

Air Injection

This system is used on 1978–79 924 models in California only. All 928 models are equipped with the air injection system.

This system reduces exhaust emissions by pumping fresh air into the exhaust port. There it combines with the hot exhaust gas to burn away excess hydrocarbons and reduce carbon monoxide. The system consists of a belt driven pump, air filter, diverter valve and check valve.

1. Air pump
2. Check valve
3. Air filter

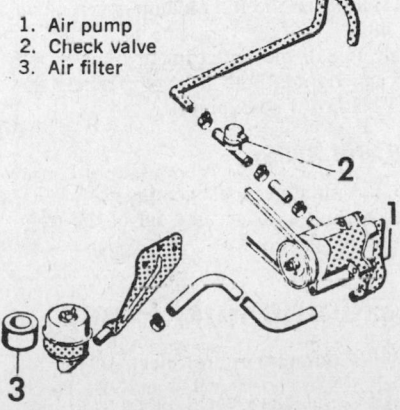

Air injection system—typical

TESTING

Diverter Valve

The diverter valve is located between the air pump and the check valve on the intake housing. The diverter valve also houses a relief valve, so that it serves two functions. The valve diverts air during deceleration to prevent backfiring and relieves excess pressure during high rpm to prevent damage to the hoses and air pump.

To test the valve:

1. Pinch the vacuum line closed and wait a few seconds for the vacuum to stabilize on either side of the diaphragm.

2. When the line is released, the sudden surge of vacuum will make the valve work. If it's operating properly, you should be able to hear it open and exhaust air.

The filter for the 924 air injection system is located under the coolant expansion tank

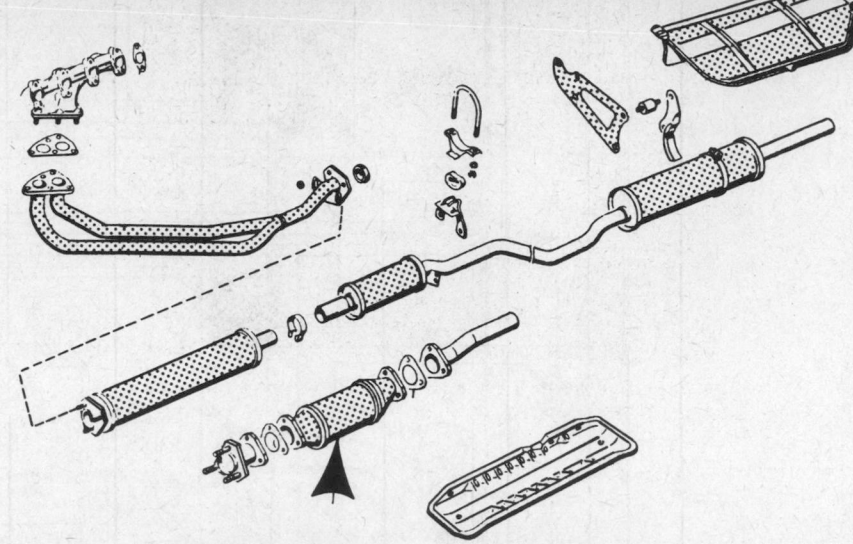

Typical 924 exhaust system showing the catalytic convertor (arrow)

Check Valve

The check valve is located on the intake housing. It keeps hot exhaust gases from flowing back into the pump and hoses and destroying them.

To test the valve:

1. With the engine off and cool enough so that there is no danger of being burned, disconnect the hose and use mouth pressure to blow through it.

2. You should be able to easily blow through the valve towards the intake housing but the valves should seal tightly when you draw back. Replace the valve if it doesn't seal.

Air Pump

1. Disconnect a hose at the diverter valve.

2. With the engine idling, check the flow of air by feeling at the hose with your hand.

3. Increase the engine speed to about 1500 rpm and again check the air flow. If it increases as the engine is accelerated, the pump output is sufficient.

4. Inspect the filter element in the air cleaner for blockage and replace it if necessary before assuming the pump to be deficient.

Catalytic Converter

Catalytic converters were made standard on all 1978 and later 924, 928 and 944 models. This device contains noble metals which act as catalysts to cause a reaction to convert hydrocarbons and carbon monoxide into harmless water and carbon dioxide. Service on the converter consists of replacing it when it malfunctions.

Evaporative Emission Control System

This system prevents the escape of raw fuel vapors into the atmosphere. The system consists of a charcoal canister and an expansion chamber. Vapors from the fuel tank are trapped in the canister. When the engine is running, fresh air is drawn in through the charcoal filter. The fresh air cleans the canister and routes the unburned hydrocarbons through the air cleaner to be burned during combustion. The fuel tank is vented to an expansion chamber which prevents fuel vapors from entering the atmosphere.

FUEL SYSTEM

Fuel Filter

REPLACEMENT

924, 924 Turbo and 944

On all models except the 944, the fuel filter is located in the fuel line on the driver's side of the engine compartment. The fuel filter of the 944 is at the right rear of the vehicle above the axle halfshaft.

1. Place a shop rag under the filter.

2. Using a line wrench, unscrew both line connections from the filter.

3. Loosen the filter clamp and remove the filter.

4. Install the replacement filter in the line and tighten both fittings. Tighten the filter clamp, if so equipped.

928 and 928S

The fuel filter and fuel accumulator are located behind a cover, in front of the right rear wheel well.

Electric Fuel Pump

The fuel pump(s) is(are) electrical on all models. 1980 and later 924 and 924 Turbo models and 1978–79 928 models are equipped with dual fuel pumps, the feed pump is located in the fuel tank, while the main pump is located in the right rear wheel well. On the 928 with dual pumps, one fuel pump is located under a plate on the rear of the fuel tank and the second is mounted inside the tank. Two pumps were used on these models to prevent the occurence of vapor lock in the fuel system. 1978–79 924 and 1983 and later 944 models are equipped with one fuel pump located near the fuel tank behind the right rear wheel. 1980 and later 928 models have one fuel pump mounted on a console with the fuel filter, on top of the fuel tank.

Cars equipped with C.I.S. fuel injection require a fuel pressure accumulator (some models have two) which improves warm engine start-ups by trapping a pressurized amount of fuel in the system when the engine is stopped. This trapped fuel is released when the engine is first turned over and is the initial fuel charge used to start the car. Because of the fuel accumulator, the warm engine may be started instantly, with no time wasted waiting for the fuel pump to build up pressure. The fuel pressure accumulator also helps smooth out pressure pulses in the fuel system and helps prevent vapor lock. The accumulator(s) is(are) usually located side by side with the main fuel pump or the fuel filter.

REMOVAL & INSTALLATION

1978–79 924 and 944

The fuel pump is located near the fuel tank behind the right rear wheel.

1. Raise the rear of the car and support it on jack stands. Disconnect the negative battery cable.

2. Locate the fuel pump. There will be pressurized fuel in the lines. Allow the engine to cool, then wrap a rag around one of the fuel pump fittings and crack it open with a wrench to bleed off the fuel.

Fuel filter on the 944. Loosen the line fittings first (outer arrows) then the filter mounting clamp (inner arrow) to remove the filter

— CAUTION —

Do not allow fuel to splash on hot exhaust components.

3. Unplug the electrical connections at the pump, taking note of their positions.
4. Disconnect the fuel lines and plug them.
5. Unscrew the retaining clamp and remove the pump.
6. Install the new pump. Clean the electrical connections to ensure continuity.

1980 and Later 924, 924 Turbo

Two fuel pumps are used. One is located in the fuel tank and the second is located in the right rear wheel well.

IN-TANK PUMP

1. Disconnect the negative battery cable.
2. Raise the rear of the vehicle.
3. Drain the fuel tank.
4. Disconnect the electrical connections from the fuel pump.
5. Disconnect the fuel line. Have a container ready to catch any residual fuel left in the system.
6. Unscrew the pump from the bottom of the fuel tank.
7. When installing a new pump, make sure the gasket for the pump is in place. After installation, fill the tank with a few gallons of fuel and check for leaks.

EXTERNAL PUMP

1. Disconnect the negative battery cable. Drain the fuel tank.
2. Raise the rear of the vehicle and support it with jack stands.
3. Locate the fuel pump. Quickly remove and plug the fuel lines from the pump. Have a container ready to catch the fuel.
4. Loosen the strap and remove the fuel pump.
5. Install a new pump in the reverse order of the removal procedure.

928 Through 1979

Two fuel pumps are used, one located under a plate on the rear of the fuel tank and

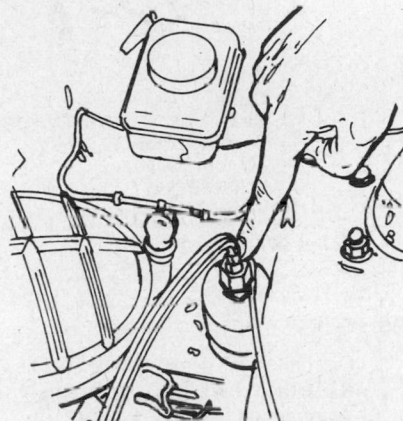

Fuel filter location—model 924

the second mounted in the fuel tank. See the in-tank fuel pump removal procedure for the 1980 and later 924, 924 Turbo for removal and installation procedures for the in-tank fuel pump. To remove the external pump, remove the guard plate on the rear of the fuel tank, pinch shut the hose running from the pump to the fuel tank with a suitable clamp, then disconnect and remove the pump. Have a container ready to catch the fuel that will be present in the fuel lines. Installation is the reverse of removal.

1980 and later 928 and 928S

A single fuel pump is located with the fuel filter on a mutual console underneath a plastic hood on the fuel tank.
1. Disconnect the negative battery cable.
2. Raise the rear of the vehicle and support it on jack stands. Expose the fuel pump.
3. Pinch shut the hose running from the fuel tank to the fuel pump with a suitable clamp.
4. Disconnect the pump wiring, disconnect both fittings from the pump, loosen its retaining strap and remove the pump. Some fuel will be present in the lines. Have a container ready to catch it.
5. Install a new pump in the reverse order of pump removal.

TESTING & ADJUSTMENT

No adjustments may be made to the fuel pump. If the pump is not functioning properly, it must be discarded and replaced. To check the function of the fuel pump, the pump should be connected to a pressure gauge. Be careful not to switch the electrical leads. If the pump fails to pump its normal capacity, or if it cannot pump that capacity at its specified rate of current consumption, it must be replaced.

Fuel Injection

924 and 924 Turbo models are equipped with the Bosch continuous flow injection system (CIS). Prior to 1980, the 928 also used CIS, but changed to the Bosch L-Jetronic in 1980. The 928 L-Jetronic system is used up to and including the current model year. The 944 uses a new Bosch Digital Motor Electronic (DME) fuel injection system.

For all fuel injection system repair and service procedures, please refer to "Fuel Injection" in the Unit Repair section.

CLUTCH

REMOVAL & INSTALLATION

924 (All) and 924 Turbo (79–80)

To gain access to the clutch disc and pressure plate assembly, the transaxle, torque tube and clutch housing must be unbolted and pulled back out of the way.
1. Disconnect the battery ground cable. Raise and support the car.
2. Support the engine with an overhead hoist or a jack and cradle under the engine.
3. Remove the engine splash shield.
4. Disconnect the clutch cable.
5. Remove the bottom clutch adjustment lock nut and detach the cable from the lever.
6. On the four speed, remove the access plate from the bottom of the clutch housing. Have an assistant turn the engine with the crankshaft pulley. Remove the pressure plate bolts gradually until all pressure is released.
7. Remove the exhaust pipe flange bolts.
8. Remove the bracket at the rear of the transaxle and any other attachment which will hinder the transaxle's rearward movement.
9. Remove the entire exhaust system.
10. Remove the back-up light switch from the transaxle.
11. Disconnect the axle driveshafts at the transaxle and let them hang down out of the way.
12. On the 4 speed, remove the clutch housing-to-engine bolts. On the 5 speed, disconnect the center tube from the clutch housing.

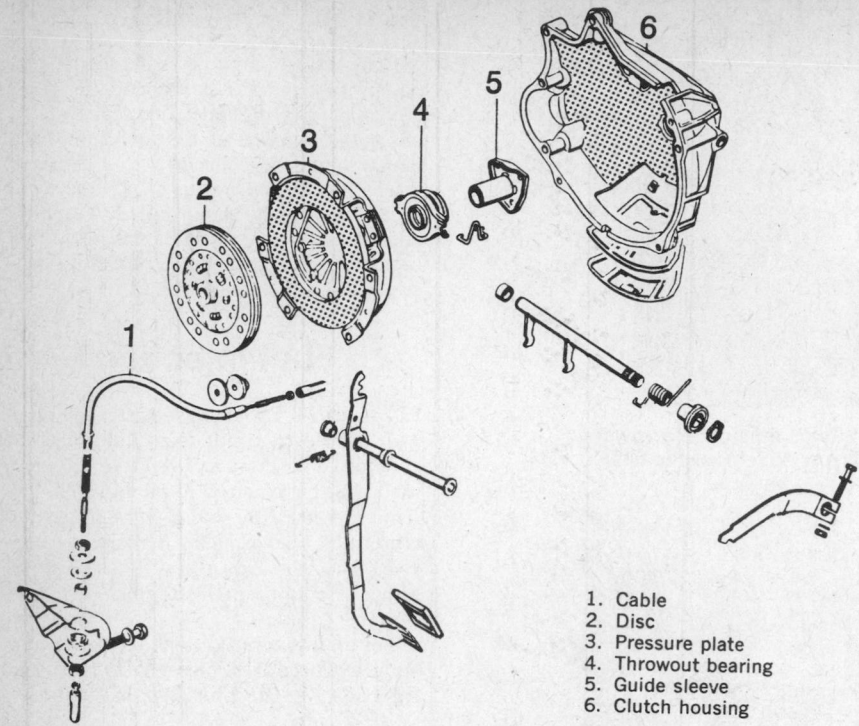

1. Cable
2. Disc
3. Pressure plate
4. Throwout bearing
5. Guide sleeve
6. Clutch housing

Clutch components of the 924 (except 924 Turbo)

7. Remove the release bearing sleeve bolts and move the sleeve towards the flywheel.

8. Matchmark the clutch components and loosen all pressure plate mounting bolts evenly until all the pressure is removed from the plate.

9. Remove the mounting bolts and press down on the release lever (towards the fly-wheel) and disconnect the release lever at the ball stud.

10. Push the complete clutch assembly rearward and move the assembly downward and out of the clutch housing.

NOTE: The clutch assembly consists of the pressure plate, front and rear clutch discs, release lever, release bearing sleeve and short driveshaft.

Installation is the reverse of removal.

NOTE: The clutch discs are different.
a. The clutch disc with the rigid center is installed between the flywheel and the intermediate plate.
b. The clutch disc with the spring center is installed between the intermediate plate and the pressure plate.

——————— **CAUTION** ———————
To prevent clutch drag, move the three stop brackets towards the pressure plate until a gap of 0.0275–0.0394 in. exists between the intermediate plate and the stop bracket.

FREE-PLAY ADJUSTMENT

924

Clutch pedal free-play should be ¾–1 in. (20–25mm).

Adjust the clutch pedal free-play by loosening the two nuts on the cable near the intake housing. After obtaining the correct free-play at the pedal, tighten the adjusting nuts.

13. Place a wooden block under the front tunnel reinforcement to support the transaxle tube.

14. Remove the transaxle mounting bolts and slide the transaxle toward the rear. Support the transaxle on a jack.

15. On the five speed, remove the clutch housing bolts, the clutch housing and the clutch assembly.

16. On the 4 speed, remove the pressure plate and clutch disc.

17. On the 4 speed install the pressure plate and clutch disc onto the driveshaft in the clutch housing. On the 5 speed install the clutch using a centering pilot. The word "Schwungradseite" on the clutch disc faces the flywheel.

18. Push the transaxle, torque tube, and clutch housing assembly forward to the engine.

19. Install the clutch housing-to-engine bolts. Tighten the 12mm bolts to 60 ft. lbs., the 10mm bolts to 36 ft. lbs. and the 8mm bolts to 24 ft. lbs. in a gradual diagonal pattern.

20. Install the remaining components in the reverse order of removal. Adjust the clutch.

928

1. Disconnect the negative battery cable.
2. Raise the vehicle and support safely.
3. Remove the lower body brace.
4. Remove the clutch slave cylinder and keep hydraulic lines attached.
5. Remove the starter and clutch housing cover as a unit and attach to the stabilizer bar with a wire. If applicable, remove the catalytic converter.
6. Remove the coupling screws and push the coupler rearward on the driveshaft.

924 Turbo (1981–82) and 944

The flywheel sensing components used in these models for the digital ignition system are very delicate and easily damaged. Removal and installation procedures are not available at time of publication.

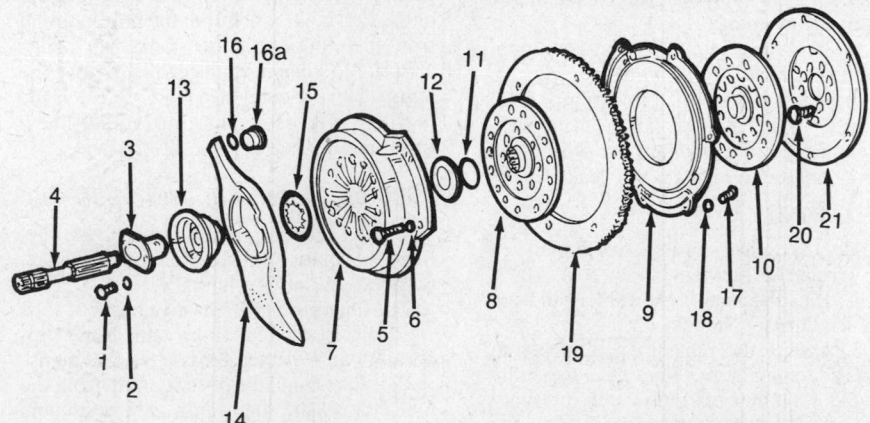

1. Bolt
2. Washer
3. Guide sleeve
4. Driveshaft
5. Bolt
6. Washer
7. Pressure plate
8. Clutch disc (spring loaded)
9. Intermediate plate
10. Clutch disc (not spring loaded)
11. Snap-ring
12. Thrust washer
13. Release bearing
14. Release lever
15. Preload washer
16. Snap-ring
16A. Ball socket bushing
17. Bolt
18. Washer
19. Starter ring
20. Bolt
21. Flywheel with centering collar

Diameter centered clutch assembly on 928 and 928S

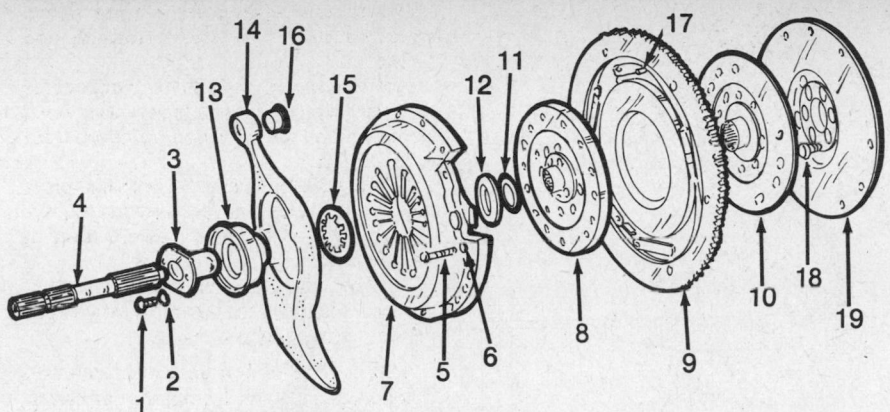

1. Bolt
2. Washer
3. Guide sleeve
4. Driveshaft
5. Bolt
6. Washer
7. Pressure plate
8. Clutch disc (spring loaded)
9. Starter ring
10. Clutch disc (not spring loaded)
11. Snap-ring
12. Thrust washer
13. Release bearing
14. Release lever
15. Preload washer
16. Ball socket bushing
17. Intermediate plate

Dowel pin centered clutch assembly on 928 and 928S

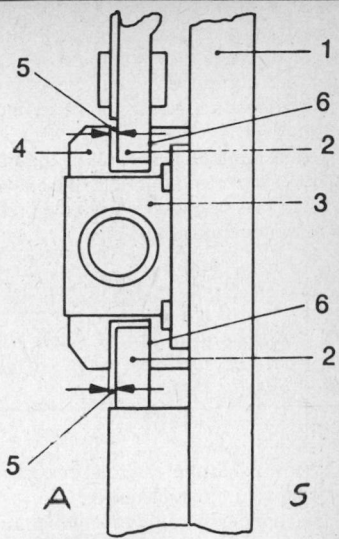

1. Intermediate ring
2. Intermediate plate
3. Stop bracket
4. Stop
5. Distance 0.7 to 1.0 mm
6. Position of intermediate plate
A. Release bearing side
S. Flywheel side

To prevent clutch drag on the 928, move the three clutch stop brackets toward the pressure plate until the correct gap (5) exists

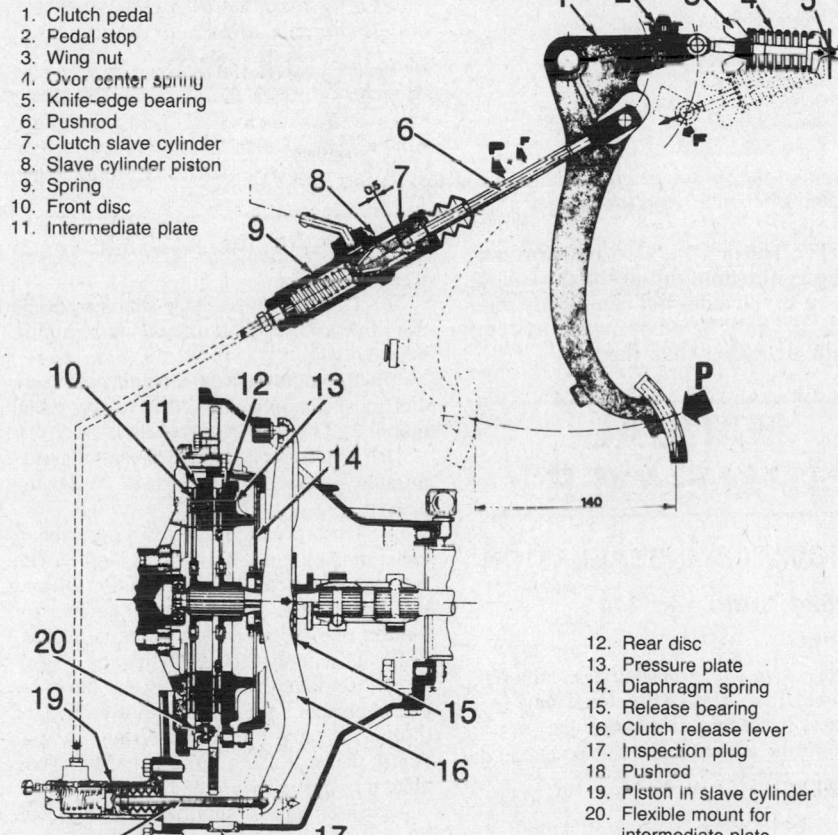

1. Clutch pedal
2. Pedal stop
3. Wing nut
4. Over center spring
5. Knife-edge bearing
6. Pushrod
7. Clutch slave cylinder
8. Slave cylinder piston
9. Spring
10. Front disc
11. Intermediate plate

12. Rear disc
13. Pressure plate
14. Diaphragm spring
15. Release bearing
16. Clutch release lever
17. Inspection plug
18. Pushrod
19. Piston in slave cylinder
20. Flexible mount for intermediate plate

Hydraulic clutch actuation system on the 928 and 928S. Clutch wear can be checked after removing the rubber plug (17).

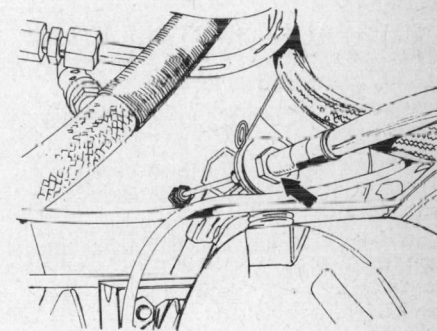

Clutch cable adjusting nut location of the 924 (except 924 Turbo)

924 Turbo and 944

The clutch linkage is self-adjusting. Clutch wear can be checked by removing the rubber plug located on the starter side of the bell housing. The throwout lever gradually moves backwards as the clutch wears. On a new clutch, there should be 18mm clearance between the lever and the front of the hole. On a worn clutch the replace distance is 34mm.

928 and 928S

Clutch adjustment is not necessary because of the automatic adjustment of the slave cylinder. The only clearance check should

be a $3/32$ inch free play between the push rod and the clutch master cylinder piston, which should give a $3/16$ inch pedal free play.

The clutch wear limit is reached when, upon removal of a rubber plug on the slave cylinder side of the clutch housing, the front edge of the release lever can just be seen.

Clutch Master Cylinder

REMOVAL & INSTALLATION

924 Turbo, 928 and 944

The clutch master cylinder is located beside the brake master cylinder in the engine compartment and shares the brake master cylinder's fluid reservoir. Access is limited, and, depending on model year and options, several other components may have to be relocated before the clutch master cylinder can be removed.

1. Drain the clutch section of the fluid reservoir. Remove and plug the line leading to the clutch master cylinder from the brakes master cylinder fluid reservoir.

CAUTION

Be very careful not to let any brake fluid drip onto painted surfaces, as it will permanently discolor them.

---

2. From inside the car, disconnect the clutch master cylinder pushrod.

3. Disconnect the fluid tube which runs to the clutch slave cylinder from the master cylinder and plug it. Before loosening the tube's fitting, wrap a rag around it so that brake fluid is not spilled.

4. Disconnect and remove the master cylinder from the vehicle.

5. Installation is the reverse of removal. Bleed the system at the slave cylinder. For information, see the slave cylinder removal procedure.

Clutch Slave Cylinder

REMOVAL & INSTALLATION

924 Turbo, 928 and 944

1. Drain the clutch section of the brake fluid reservoir.

2. Jack up the vehicle and support it on stands. Locate the slave cylinder—it is at the bottom of the bell housing.

3. Disconnect the clutch fluid line from the slave cylinder.

4. Remove the retaining bolts and remove the slave cylinder.

5. Installation is the reverse of removal. Prime the cylinder with clean brake fluid before installing.

When the slave cylinder is installed, the system must be bled. To bleed the system, fill the clutch portion of the fluid reservoir with clean brake fluid, then attach a hose to the bleed nipple on the slave cylinder and position the other end of the hose so that it is submerged in a partially filled container of brake fluid. Have an assistant pump up the clutch pedal several times, then open the bleed nipple with a wrench. Air bubbles will appear at the side of the hose submerged in the brake fluid. When the bubbles stop (with your assistant's foot still pressing on the clutch pedal), close the bleed nipple. Have your assistant pump up the pedal again and repeat the process until no bubbles appear in the container, then close the bleed nipple and test the pedal. If the pedal feels spongy or "not right," there is probably still some air in the system. Repeat the bleeding procedure.

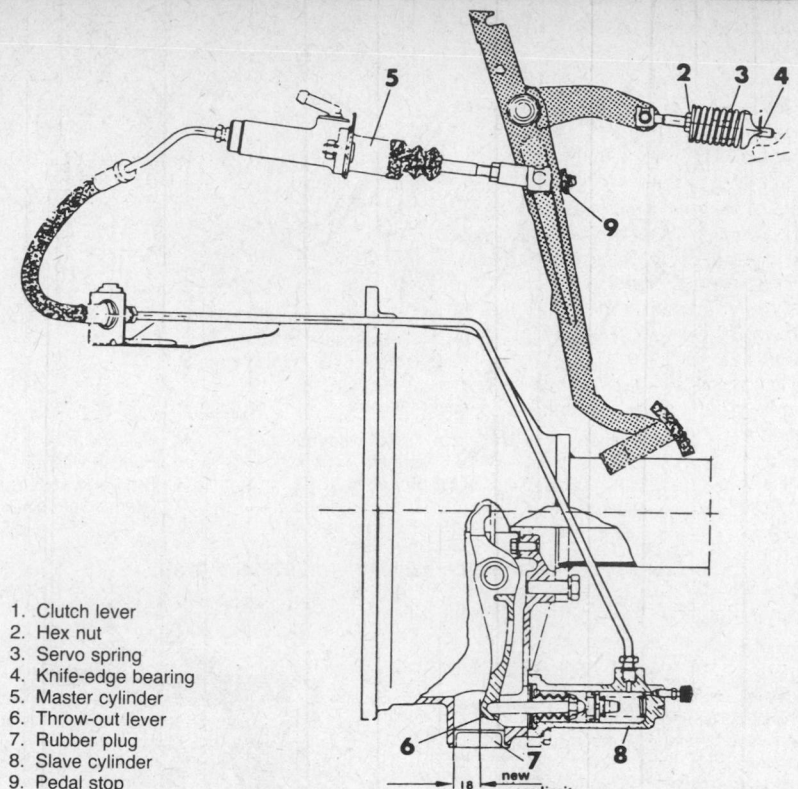

1. Clutch lever
2. Hex nut
3. Servo spring
4. Knife-edge bearing
5. Master cylinder
6. Throw-out lever
7. Rubber plug
8. Slave cylinder
9. Pedal stop

Hydraulic clutch actuation system of the 924 Turbo and 944. Clutch wear may be checked after removing the rubber plug (7)

NOTE: During the bleeding process, make sure the fluid in the clutch section of the reservoir does not completely disappear or you'll be pumping the system up with air rather than fluid.

MANUAL TRANSAXLE

REMOVAL & INSTALLATION

924, 924 Turbo and 944
4 SPEED

Transaxle removal and installation are outlined with the "Clutch Removal and Installation" procedure. Disconnect the torque tube from the transaxle for servicing.

5 SPEED

1. Jack up the vehicle and support it on stands.

2. Remove the entire exhaust system from behind the catalytic converter.

3. Disconnect the wires from the backup light switch.

4. Remove the reinforcement strut at the front of the transaxle to facilitate work procedures.

5. Engage 5th gear. Remove the rubber cap from the front transmission cover. Position the socket head screw for removal by turning a rear wheel (hold the other wheel). Unscrew the screw from the coupling using

a long reach extension and a 6mm socket. Keep the transaxle in 5th gear.

6. Detach the axle half-shafts from the transaxle and suspend them on wire to prevent damage.

7. Remove the self-locking nuts from the transmission mounts (the rubber/metal mounts).

8. Position a jack underneath the transmission and secure the transaxle to it using a strap.

9. Unscrew the bolts from the rubber/metal mounts, lift the transaxle slightly with the jack and remove the mounts. Do not lift the unit too far, as the brake line for the left rear wheel may become damaged.

10. Disconnect the shift linkage.

11. Remove the bolts between the drive shaft tube and the transaxle. Remove or disconnect any other interfering components, then carefully remove the transaxle unit, moving rearward and down.

12. Installation is the reverse of removal.

928 and 928S

1. Remove the nuts from the spring struts bolts, extending into the trunk compartment.

2. Remove the battery and loosen the rear wheels.

3. Place the transmission in fifth gear.

4. Raise the vehicle and remove the rubber plug from underneath the front of the transmission. Looking into the hole, position the coupling bolt head between the

drive and input shafts, so that it can be removed.

NOTE: During removal of the bolt, do not allow the shaft to turn and jam the socket or bolt in the transmission housing.

5. Place the transmission in neutral, remove the rear wheels and remove the brake calipers, wire them to the frame.
6. Remove the exhaust system, from the catalytic converter rearward.
7. Remove the exhaust heat shield and the battery box.
8. Disconnect the back-up light switch wires and loosen the pulse transmitter for the speedometer. Remove the wires from the clip.
9. Move the dust cover from the shift rod coupling and remove the locking set screw. Remove the shift rod from the main rod.
10. Disconnect the axle shafts at the transmission end. Suspend the axles from the cross member.
11. Disconnect the stabilizer bar at the lower control arm.
12. With the use of a strap, chain or heavy wire, support the transaxle assembly from the stabilizer bar.
13. Remove the transmission-to-rear axle cross member bolts and the bolts between the rear axle cross member and frame.
14. Mark the position of the rear axle cross member and place a jack under member. Remove the bolts and tilt the rear axle so that the spring struts and control arms do not twist. Support the rear axle in the tilted position to keep the weight off the lower control arm link pins.
15. Place jack under the transmission assembly and remove the bolts between the drive shaft tube and the transmission. Remove the holding strap, pull the unit rearward and lower.
16. Installation is the reverse of removal.

LINKAGE ADJUSTMENT

Linkage adjustments are not normally required and should be attempted only if the mechanic is familiar with direct-distant shift mechanisms.

924 4 Speed

1. Place the transaxle in neutral.
2. Raise the rear of the vehicle, support it on stands and block the front wheels.
3. Make sure the intermediate lever on the selector shaft leans toward the back of the car approximately 5°. If not, loosen the lever's pinch bolt and adjust it to this position.
4. Move the intermediate lever to the middle of the neutral travel.
5. Loosen the link piece retaining bolt at the rear of the selector shaft and move the bolt in its slot until the link piece is vertical. Tighten the bolt.
6. Adjust the shift plate at the bottom

of the shift lever in the passenger compartment until the lever is at an 82° angle (rearward) with the propeller shaft tunnel.

All 5 Speeds

These transaxles usually require adjustment only when the unit has been overhauled.

OVERHAUL

For all transaxle overhaul procedures, please refer to "Manual Transaxle Overhaul" in the Unit Repair section.

Axle Halfshafts

Power is transferred to the rear wheels by independent axle halfshafts. Each shaft is equipped with both an inner and an outer constant velocity joint.

REMOVAL & INSTALLATION

1. Jack and support the rear of the car.
2. Remove the six star bolts on the inside joint at the transaxle.
3. Remove the six star bolts at the stub axle. Use a wide, flat bladed prybar to pry the flanges apart.
4. Drop the axle driveshaft down and out of the 924 and 924 Turbo. On the 928 and 928S, remove the axle from the upper left side of the hub assembly.
5. Pack the constant velocity joints with grease before installation.
6. Installation is the reverse of removal. Tighten the bolts to 30 ft. lbs.

AUTOMATIC TRANSAXLE

REMOVAL & INSTALLATION

Removal and installation of the automatic transaxle is performed in the same manner as the previous "Manual Transmission Removal and Installation." Be sure to mark all linkage, etc. to facilitate the installation of the unit.

Shift Linkage

ADJUSTMENT

924

1. Raise the vehicle and support it on jack stands.
2. Move the selector lever into the Park position.
3. Loosen the clamping bolt at the transmission lever.
4. Pull the transmission lever against the stop.

5. Tighten the clamping bolt with the lever in this position.

NOTE: When tightening the clamping bolt, make sure that the cable does not twist and that the transmission lever does not bend. The in-car selector lever must not touch the selector gate in either the "P" or the "1" positions.

6. Run the engine at idle and move the selector lever from "P" to "R", from "N" to "R" and from "N" to "D". In each case the gear should engage within one second after the selector is moved. The clearance between the selector and the front of the selector gate in position "P" should be the same as the clearance between the selector and the back of the gate in position "1".

Neutral Safety Switch

ADJUSTMENT

924

The neutral safety switch prevents the engine from being started in any position except "P" and "N". To test it, position the selector lever in every position of its quadrant and attempt to start the engine. If the engine starts in any position besides "P" or "N", the neutral safety switch is out of adjustment. To adjust it, remove the selector gate for the selector lever, loosen the neutral safety switch mounting bolts and adjust its position, then retighten the bolts.

Throttle Cable and Transmission Cable

ADJUSTMENTS

1978—924 models

1. With the accelerator pedal against its idle stop and the throttle valve lever closed, make sure the transmission lever is in the rest position. Also make sure that the safety yoke is flat against the bracket on the upper accelerator pedal.
2. At the safety yoke, adjust both cables so that they can be attached without tension. Adjust the cable to the throttle housing at its mount on the intake manifold. Adjust the transmission lever cable at the mounting bracket on the side of the transmission.
3. To test the kickdown position adjustment, make sure no obstructions, such as optional floor mats, are under the accelerator pedal kickdown stop. Just before the accelerator pedal is fully depressed, there should be a slight movement (about 2mm) of the transmission lever. If not, or if the movement is too great, readjust the cable at the transmission bracket.
4. To test the full throttle adjustment, depress the accelerator pedal to the first

noticeable pressure point (beginning of the kickdown detent). In this position the throttle valve lever should be fully open. If not, adjust at the cable.

924—1979–82

1. Screw in the cable sleeve mounting nut on the transmission bracket completely and tighten.

2. Loosen the bolts on the roller holder bracket, push the roller holder in its slot forward (as seen from the driving direction) as far as possible and tighten the bolts.

3. Completely loosen the short cable at the firewall and the long cable on the roller holder.

4. Turn the roller so that the operating lever faces forward at an angle of 29° (in this position the opening for the cable locator will face the reinforcement rib of the holder).

5. Hold the roller in this position and mount the throttle valve push rod without tension on the rod.

6. Place the cable around the roller in the correct position and adjust the long cable sleeve until the cable locator just rests in the opening without tension.

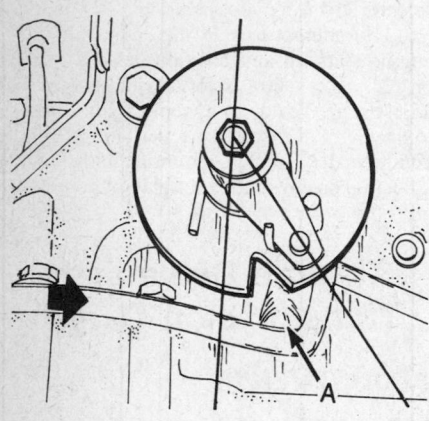

A. Reinforcement rib

On the 1979 and later 924, turn the roller so that the operating lever faces forward at an angle of 29°

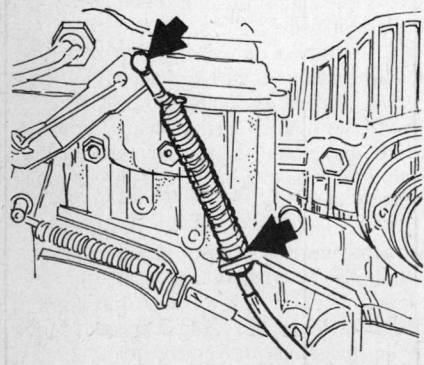

To adjust the throttle cable of the 1979 and later 924, screw in the cable sleeve mounting nut as far as possible on the bracket then tighten (lower arrow)

7. Adjust the cable going to the accelerator pedal so that it does not have tension at the adjuster.

When the cable has been adjusted correctly, the accelerator pedal will be in its neutral position (11°30′ inclination from the pedal stop), the throttle valve will be closed and the lever on the transmission will be on its bottom stop.

8. To check the full throttle position adjustment, depress the accelerator pedal to the first noticeable pressure point and check whether the throttle valve is fully open.

9. To check the kickdown adjustment, depress the pedal past the full throttle pressure point until it comes against its stop and check to make sure the roller stop has lifted off the operating lever by about ¼ in. In this position the lever on the transmission should be resting on the final stop or at most about 1° away.

BAND ADJUSTMENTS

924

Only the second gear band is adjustable.

NOTE: Only adjust the band with the transmission positioned horizontally, or the band could jam.

1. Locate the second gear band adjuster. It is on the driver's side of the case next to the selector levers.

2. Loosen the locknut and tighten the adjusting screw to 7 ft. lbs.

3. Loosen the screw and tighten it to 4 ft. lbs.

4. From this position, loosen the screw exactly 2½ turns and secure with the locknut.

928

Band adjustments are not normally required on the 928 automatic transmission.

REAR SUSPENSION

Torsion Bars

REMOVAL & INSTALLATION

924, 924 Turbo and 944

NOTE: This procedure requires that the rear wheel camber and toe-in be checked and adjusted as the final step.

1. Jack up the rear of the car and support it on stands.

2. Remove the wheel on the side where the torsion bar is being removed.

3. Using a hydraulic jack and a block of wood with a slot cut in it, raise the trailing arm.

4. Remove the lower shock absorber bolt.

5. Remove the trailing arm retaining bolts. Remove the toe and camber adjusting bolts.

6. Remove the four retaining bolts from the trailing arm cover.

7. Pry off the trailing arm cover.

8. Lower the jack.

9. Remove the round body plug and remove the trailing arm.

10. Paint a reference mark on the torsion bar support, matching the location of the L or R side identification letter, so that the torsion bar may be installed in the same position.

NOTE: The torsion bars are splined to allow adjustment of the rear riding height.

11. Remove the torsion bar. Do not scratch the protective paint on the torsion bar, or it will corrode and possibly develop fatigue cracks.

NOTE: If you are removing a broken torsion bar, the inner end can be knocked from its seat by removing the opposite torsion bar and tapping it through with a steel bar. Torsion bars are not interchangeable from side to side and are marked "L" and "R" for identification.

12. Check the torsion bar splines for damage and replace the bar if necessary. If there is any corrosion on the bar, replace it.

13. Coat the torsion bar lightly with grease. Carefully grease the splines.

14. Apply glycerine or another rubber preservative to the torsion bar support.

15. Install the torsion bar, matching the L or R with the paint mark you made before removal.

16. Install the trailing arm cover into position and start the three accessible bolts.

17. Raise the trailing arm into place with a jack and wooden block until the spacer and the fourth bolt can be installed.

18. Assemble the remaining components in the reverse order of their removal.

19. Tighten the trailing arm cover bolts to 25 ft. lbs. Tighten the shock absorber bolt to 50 ft. lbs.

20. Adjust rear wheel camber and toe-in.

Upper Control Arm

REMOVAL & INSTALLATION

928 and 928S

1. Raise the vehicle and support it safely. Remove the rear wheels and support the lower arm assembly with a jack.

2. Loosen and remove the inner and outer bolts from the upper arm ends.

3. Remove the upper arm from the rear crossmember and from the rear flexible mount.

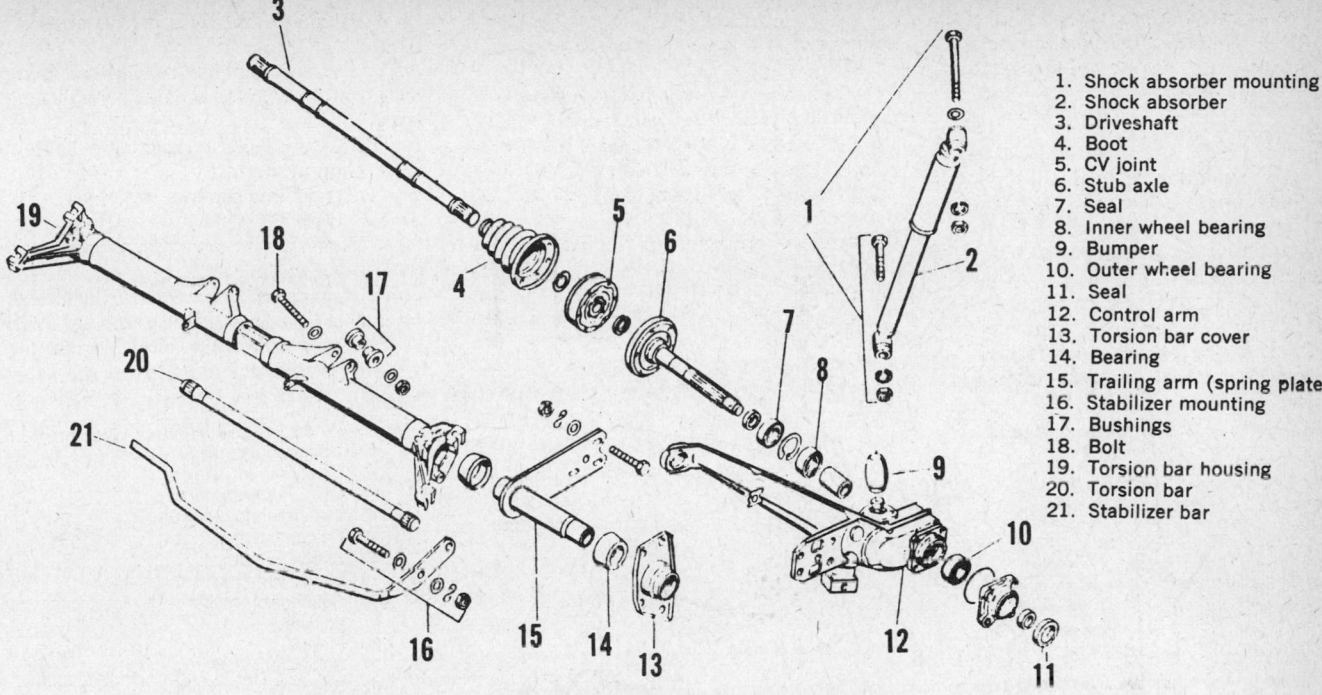

1. Shock absorber mounting
2. Shock absorber
3. Driveshaft
4. Boot
5. CV joint
6. Stub axle
7. Seal
8. Inner wheel bearing
9. Bumper
10. Outer wheel bearing
11. Seal
12. Control arm
13. Torsion bar cover
14. Bearing
15. Trailing arm (spring plate)
16. Stabilizer mounting
17. Bushings
18. Bolt
19. Torsion bar housing
20. Torsion bar
21. Stabilizer bar

Rear control arm and related components of the 924 and 924 Turbo (944 similar)

NOTE: The bushings are replaceable. Installation is the reverse of removal.

Lower Control Arm

REMOVAL & INSTALLATION

928 and 928S

1. Raise and support the vehicle. Re move the rear wheels.

2. Support the hub assembly and the spring strut with a jack.

3. Remove the outer pivot pin nuts and washers. Disconnect the stabilizer bar link.

4. Remove the inner pivot bolts from the arm and pull the front pivot pin from the hub assembly and the spring strut.

NOTE: The bushings are replaceable.

5. Installation is the reverse of removal.

Shock Absorbers

REMOVAL & INSTALLATION

924, 924 Turbo and 944

1. Raise the car on a drive-on hoist or support the wheels on stands for this procedure.

2. Remove the bottom retaining bolt and nut.

3. Remove the top bolt.

4. Remove the shock absorber.

5. Install the replacement shock in the reverse order of removal. Tighten the re taining bolts to 50 ft. lbs.

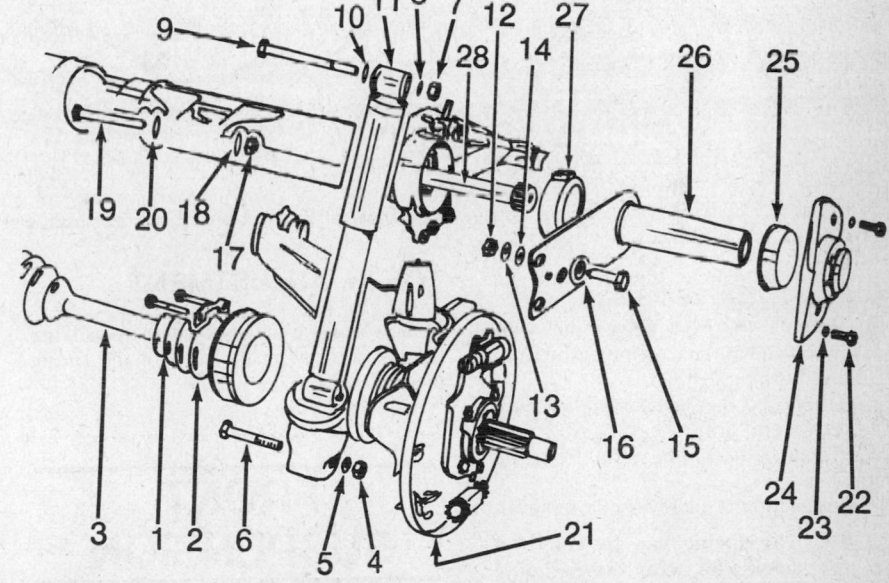

1. Allen head bolt	8. Lockwasher	15. Bolt	22. Bolt
2. Plate	9. Bolt	16. Plain washer	23. Lockwasher
3. Axle shaft	10. Washer	17. Nut, self-locking	24. Cover
4. Nut	11. Shock absorber	18. Plain washer	25. Rubber mount, outer
5. Lockwasher	12. Nut	19. Bolt	26. Torsion plate
6. Bolt	13. Washer	20. Plain washer	27. Rubber mount, inner
7. Nut	14. Plain washer	21. Trailing arm	28. Torsion bar

Rear suspension of the 924 and 924 Turbo (944 similar)

Struts

For all spring and shock removal and installation procedures and any other strut overhaul procedures, please refer to "Strut Overhaul" in the Unit Repair section.

REMOVAL & INSTALLATION

928 and 928S

1. Remove the locking nuts from the spring strut, located within the trunk area.

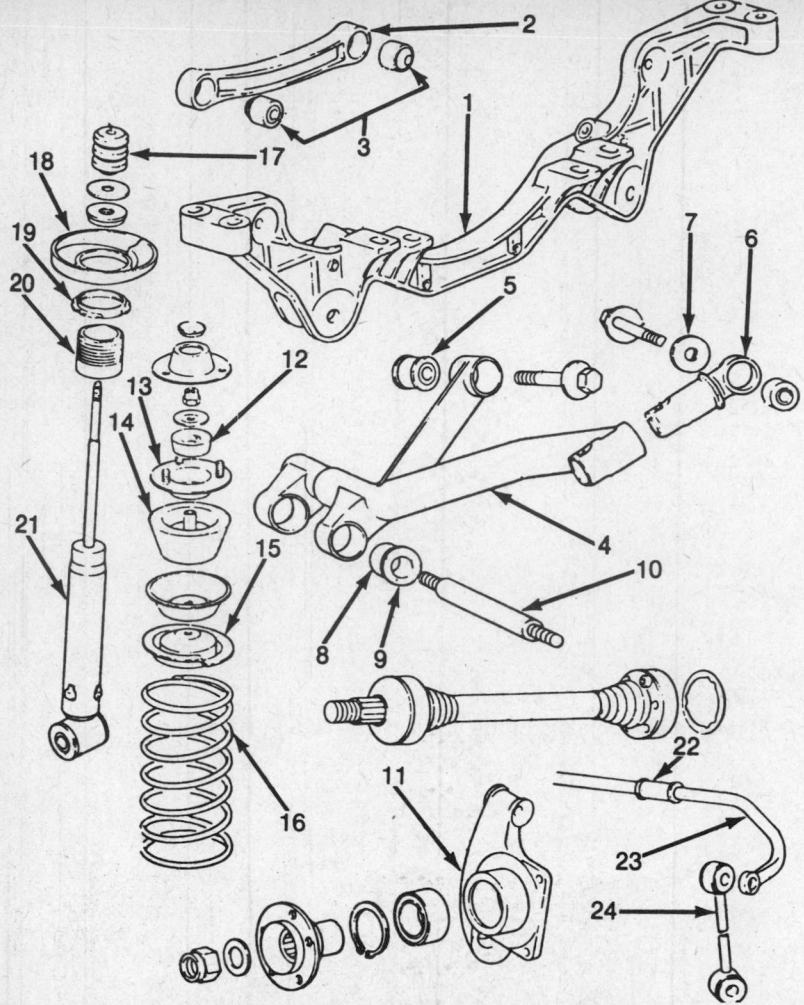

1. Rear axle crossmember
2. Upper strut
3. Upper strut bushings
4. Lower control arm
5. Lower control arm inner bushing
6. Lower control arm rocker mount
7. Lower control eccentric
8. Lower control arm outer bushing
9. Cone washer
10. Pivot pin
11. Wheel bearing carrier
12. Upper shock mount
13. Shock mount retainer
14. Lower shock mount
15. Upper spring mount
16. Coil spring
17. Shock bumper
18. Lower spring seat
19. Suspension height adjuster
20. Flange
21. Shock absorber
22. Stablizer bar mount
23. Stabilizer bar
24. Link

Exploded view of the 928 and 928S rear suspension

2. Raise the vehicle, support safely and remove the wheel.

3. Remove the front nut on the outer pivot pin rod and remove the pivot rod from the rubber bushings.

4. Disconnect the stablizer bar link from the lower control arm.

5. Remove the spring strut from the vehicle.

6. Installation is the reverse of removal.

NOTE: The spring can be removed from the shock unit with the use of a spring clamping tool. An adjusting nut and sleeve is used to control the vehicle rear height.

Rear Wheel Alignment

CAMBER ADJUSTMENT

Rear wheel camber is adjusted by changing the trailing arm spring plate setting. To increase positive camber, loosen the spring plate-to-trailing arm bolts (with the wheels on the ground). To increase negative camber, do so with car on hoist. Tighten bolts after adjustment.

TOE-IN ADJUSTMENT

Rear wheel toe-in is adjusted by moving the control arm in the slots of the spring plates.

FRONT SUSPENSION

924, 924 Turbo and 944

The 924 front suspension is a MacPherson strut design. The strut consists of the strut housing, a shock absorber insert in the housing, and a concentric coil spring. The steering knuckle is bolted to the strut assembly. A lower control arm locates the strut at the bottom. A ball joint is riveted to the control arm and bolted to the steering knuckle.

928 and 928S

The 928 front suspension is an independent type with upper and lower control arms, coil springs mounted on the shock absorbers and upper and lower ball joints. Provisions for front end alignment are provided by eccentrics located at the bottom of the lower ball joint mounting plate.

MacPherson Strut

REMOVAL & INSTALLATION

For all strut overhaul procedures, please refer to "Strut Overhaul" in the Unit Repair section.

924, 924 Turbo and 944

Front wheel alignment must be reset after a strut is removed.

1. Jack up the front of the car and support it on stands.

2. Remove the brake line from the bracket on the strut.

3. Remove the two through bolts that retain the strut to the steering knuckle.

4. Remove the four retaining nuts from the inner fender in the engine compartment.

5. Pry the lower control arm down and remove the strut from the car.

6. To replace either the spring or shock absorber, place the strut in a spring compressor and remove the large retaining nut at the top.

7. Installation is the reverse of removal.

928 and 928S

1. Remove the self-locking nuts on the upper strut mount, located on the inner fender panel.

2. Remove the front wheel. Remove the flange locknut and press the upper ball joint from the spindle carrier.

3. Remove the inner pivot shaft nuts from the upper control arm.

4. Remove the shock absorber mounting bolts and remove the shock and upper arm as an assembly.

Lower Control Arm

REMOVAL & INSTALLATION

924, 924 Turbo and 944

1. Jack up the front of the car and support it on stands.

2. Remove the thru-bolt at the front that retains the control arm to the suspension crossmember.

3. Detach the stabilizer bar from the control arm.

4. Remove the two bolts that retain the control arm bracket at the rear.

5. Remove the ball joint pinch bolt at the steering knuckle.

6. Pry the control arm down and remove it from the car.

7. Installation is the reverse of removal. Caster must be reset after the control arm has been removed.

928 and 928S

NOTE: The front end must be aligned upon completion of the installation.

1. Raise and support the vehicle then remove the wheel.

2. Mark the alignment eccentrics on the lower arm for approximate installation location, if the ball joint is to be removed.

3. Remove the strut bottom link bracket and stabilizer link bolt.

4. Remove the lower ball joint stud nut and press the stud from the spindle. Move the spindle and upper arm upward and block it to gain working clearance.

Rear wheel alignment points of the 924 and 924 Turbo. Loosen the fasteners (arrows) to alter the camber and toe-in

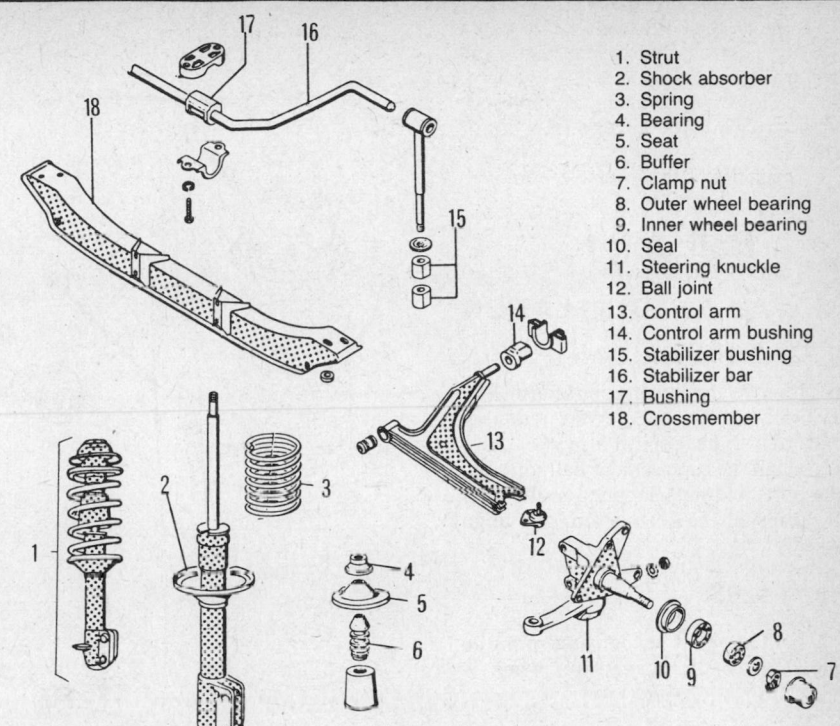

1.	Strut
2.	Shock absorber
3.	Spring
4.	Bearing
5.	Seat
6.	Buffer
7.	Clamp nut
8.	Outer wheel bearing
9.	Inner wheel bearing
10.	Seal
11.	Steering knuckle
12.	Ball joint
13.	Control arm
14.	Control arm bushing
15.	Stabilizer bushing
16.	Stabilizer bar
17.	Bushing
18.	Crossmember

Front suspension of the 924, 924 Turbo, and 944

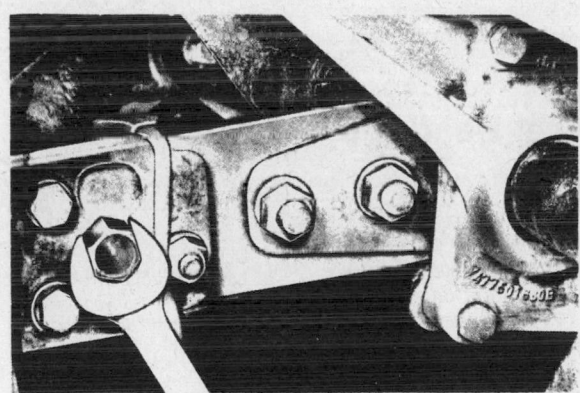

Rear toe-in adjustment on the 944

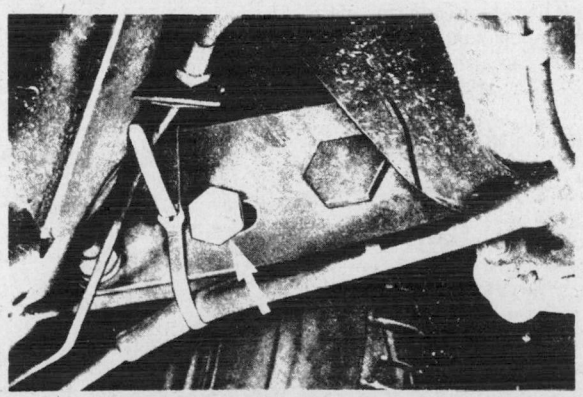

Rear camber adjustment on the 944

5. Remove the bolts from the tie-down bracket and control arm bracket. Lower the control arm from the vehicle.

6. The lower ball joint can be replaced, if necessary, while the lower arm is out of the vehicle.

7. Installation is the reverse of removal.

Ball Joint

REMOVAL & INSTALLATION

924, 924 Turbo and 944

1. Remove the lower control arm.
2. Drill out the three rivets retaining the ball joint to the control arm.
3. Install the replacement ball joint using the bolts and nuts supplied in the kit.
4. Reinstall the control arm and align the wheels.

928 and 928S

NOTE: The front suspension must be realigned after the suspension work is done.

The upper ball joint is replaced as a unit with the upper arm assembly. Refer to the "Strut Removal and Installation" section.

The lower ball joint may be replaced by removing the nut from the ball joint stud and pressing the stud from the spindle. The alignment eccentric bolts are removable and the ball joint can be removed from the lower arm assembly.

Front Wheel Bearings

ADJUSTMENT

The front wheel bearings are correctly adjusted when the thrust washer can be moved slightly sideways under light pressure, but no bearing play is evident when the wheel hub is shaken axially.

1. Remove the wheels.
2. Pry the hub cap off and perform the check as described above. Don't press against the hub.
3. If the bearings require an adjustment, loosen the Allen screw and turn the clamp nut. Proper adjustment is achieved when the flat washer can just be moved by finger pressure on a screwdriver.
4. Tighten the clamp nut Allen screw to 11 ft. lbs. without altering the adjusted position of the clamp nut.

Front End Alignment

CAMBER ADJUSTMENT

924, 924 Turbo and 944

Camber is adjusted at the upper strut-to-steering knuckle retaining bolt.

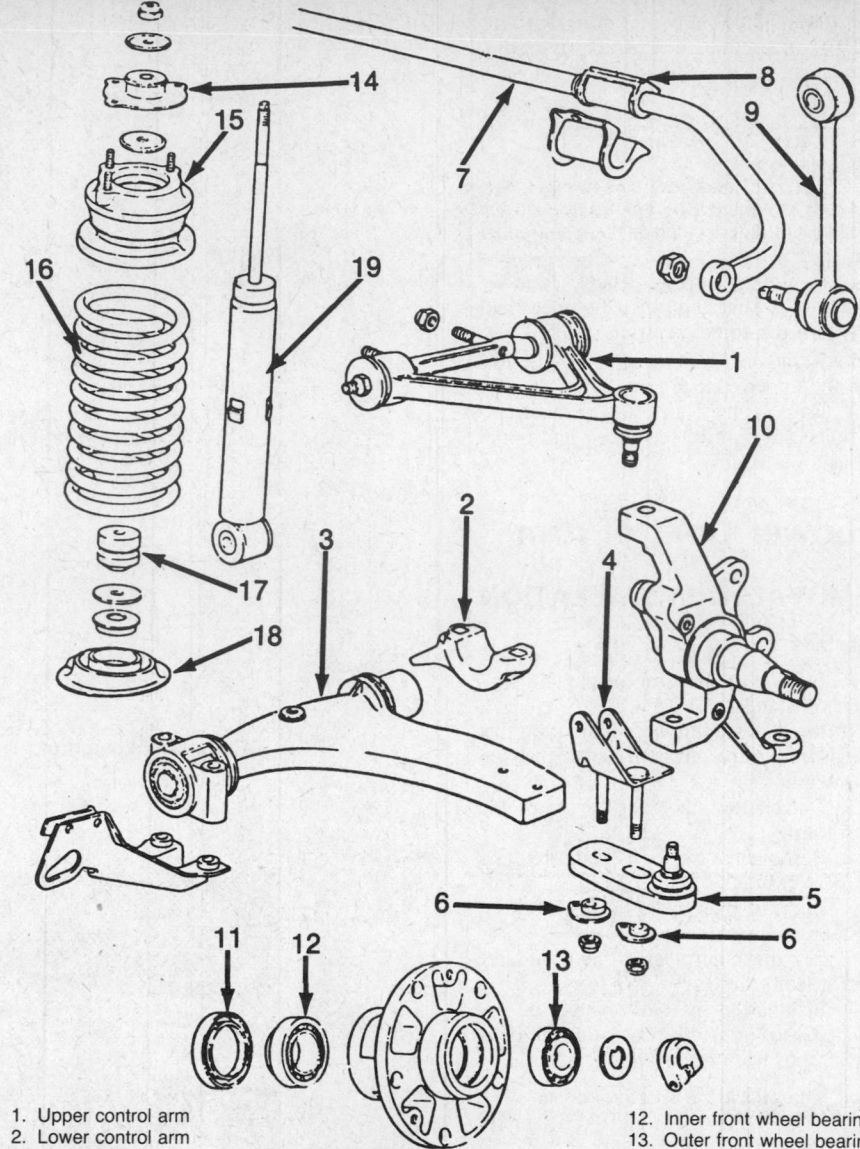

1. Upper control arm	12. Inner front wheel bearing
2. Lower control arm support	13. Outer front wheel bearing
3. Lower control arm	14. Upper shock mount
4. Lower shock mount	15. Upper spring seat
5. Lower ball joint	16. Spring
6. Caster eccentric (outer), camber eccentric (inner)	17. Suspension stop
7. Stabilizer bar	18. Lower spring seat
8. Bushing	19. Shock absorber
9. Link	
10. Steering knuckle	
11. Inner front wheel seal	

Exploded view of the 928 and 928S front suspension

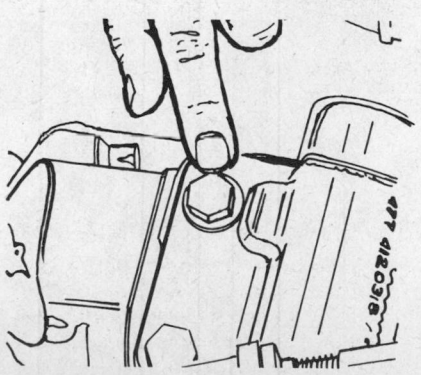

Camber is adjusted at the upper strut eccentric on the 924, 924 Turbo, and 944

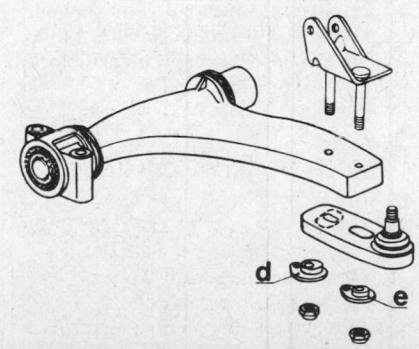

Front suspension caster (e) and camber (d) adjustment eccentrics on the 928 and 928S

928 and 928S

Camber is adjusted by turning the cam bolts on the inner arm bushings.

CASTER ADJUSTMENT

NOTE: 1983 and later 928 models have the slots for adjusting the caster eccentrics sealed with an elastic sealing compound. This compound must be removed to make camber adjustments, then replaced after adjustment to prevent the entry of dirt which could make adjusting difficult.

Caster is adjusted by loosening the two control arms-to-crossmember bolts and moving the control arm laterally.

TOE-IN ADJUSTMENT

924, 924 Turbo and 944

Toe-in is set by loosening the locknuts on the tie rod ends and turning them in or out as necessary.

928 and 928S

Toe-in adjustments are made by turning cam bolts, located at the front of the rear control arms.

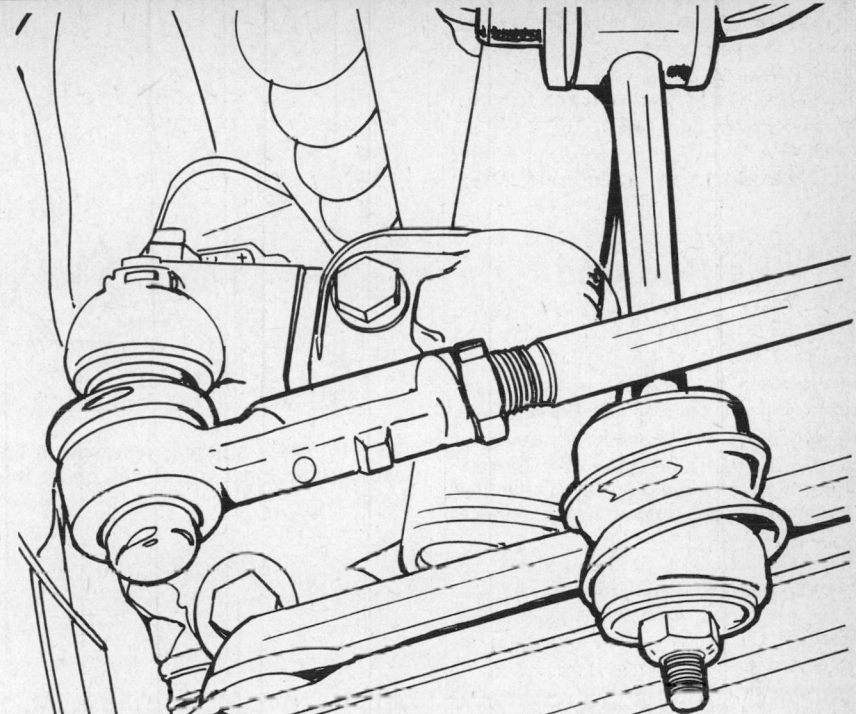

Tie-rod ends are adjustable for toe (924 shown)

STEERING

Steering Wheel

REMOVAL & INSTALLATION

1. Disconnect the negative battery cable.
2. Remove horn pad and straighten the front wheels.
3. If necessary, disconnect the horn wiring. Matchmark the steering wheel to the steering shaft.
4. Remove retaining nut and washer.
5. Using a steering wheel puller, remove the wheel.

— **CAUTION** —
Do NOT strike the steering wheel!

6. Installation is the reverse of above. Make sure the wheels are straight ahead and steering wheel is centered. Torque steering wheel nut to 33 ft. lbs.

Turn Signal Switch

REMOVAL & INSTALLATION

1. Disconnect the negative battery cable.
2. Remove steering wheel.
3. Disconnect electrical connector at switch.
4. Remove four screws holding switch.
5. To install, reverse the above.

Caster is adjusted at the lower control arm mounting on the 924, 924 Turbo, and 944

Ignition Lock and Switch

REMOVAL & INSTALLATION

1. Disconnect the negative battery cable.
2. Remove steering wheel.
3. Drill out casing tube shear bolts, disconnect electrical connectors, and pull column and casing out of car.
4. Remove the casing from steering column.

5. Remove pinch bolt holding switch housing to column.
6. Remove retaining screw and pull ignition switch from rear of casing.
7. Depress lock cylinder retainer with an ice pick or similar tool and remove lock cylinder.
8. Installation is the reverse of removal. Make sure the wheels are straight ahead and steering wheel is centered when installing. Torque steering wheel nut to 33 ft. lbs. Torque shear bolts to 23 ft. lbs.

Steering Gear

REMOVAL & INSTALLATION

1. Remove bolt connecting gear box to steering column driveshaft.
2. Press out tie rod ends.
3. Remove steering gear and tie rods from car.
4. Remove tie rods from steering gear.
5. To install, reverse the above. Center steering gear with Porsche special tool 9116 or its equivalent. Be sure that both tie rod lengths are equal (68–68.5mm). Tighten tie rod counter nuts to 29 ft. lbs. and gear box to driveshaft bolt to 23 ft. lbs.

ADJUSTMENT

1. Tighten adjusting screw (on front of gear box) until it just touches the washer.
2. Hold adjusting screw tightly and tighten locknut.

Power Steering Pump

The power steering pump is mounted in the right balance shaft bearing housing. It is belt driven from the engine.

The power steering reservoir is under the hood, attached to the right hand wheel housing.

Tie Rod End

REPLACEMENT

1. Loosen the jam nut which connects the tie rod end to the knuckle. Mark the tie rod position on the threads of the rod.

2. Using a ball joint separator, remove the tie rod end from the knuckle, counting how many complete turns it takes to remove it.

3. Install a new tie rod end in reverse order of removal. Install the new tie rod end the same number of turns as counted in Step 2. Check the wheel alignment as soon as possible.

BRAKES

All 924 models including the Turbo use front disc brakes and rear drum brakes. The 928 and the 944 both use disc brakes all around.

A vacuum brake booster is used on all models to decrease brake pedal apply effort. The hydraulic system of all models is of the split/diagonal design, which allows one front brake and one rear brake (opposite sides) to stop the car in the event of hydraulic failure in the other half of the system.

The cable-operated parking brake acts on the rear drum brakes, expanding the brake shoes against the drums (924 & 924 Turbo), or expanding small brake shoes within drums cut into the rear brake discs (928 & 944).

For all brake system repair and service procedures not detailed below, please refer to "Brakes" in the Unit Repair section.

Adjustment

The front disc brakes require no adjustment, as disc brakes automatically adjust themselves to compensate for pad wear. The rear drum brakes must be periodically adjusted, or whenever free travel is one third or more of the total pedal travel.

1. Raise the car.

2. Block the front wheels and release the parking brake. Step on the brake pedal hard to center the linings.

3. Remove the rubber plugs from the rear of the backing plate on each wheel.

4. Insert a brake adjusting tool or wide-blade screwdriver and turn the adjuster wheel until the brakes drag as you turn the tire/wheel.

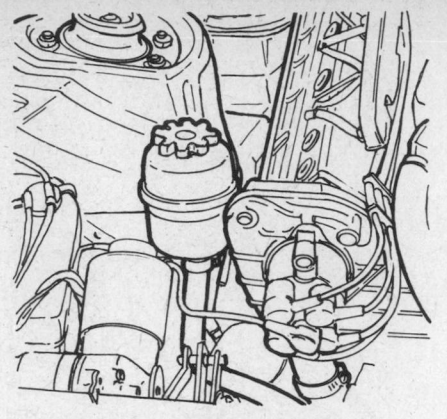

The 944 power steering reservoir is located on the inner wheel well under the hood.

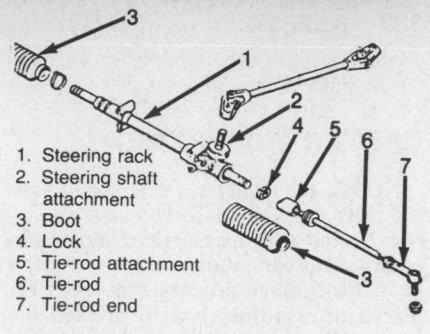

1. Steering rack
2. Steering shaft attachment
3. Boot
4. Lock
5. Tie-rod attachment
6. Tie-rod
7. Tie-rod end

Steering rack of the 924, 924 Turbo, and 944

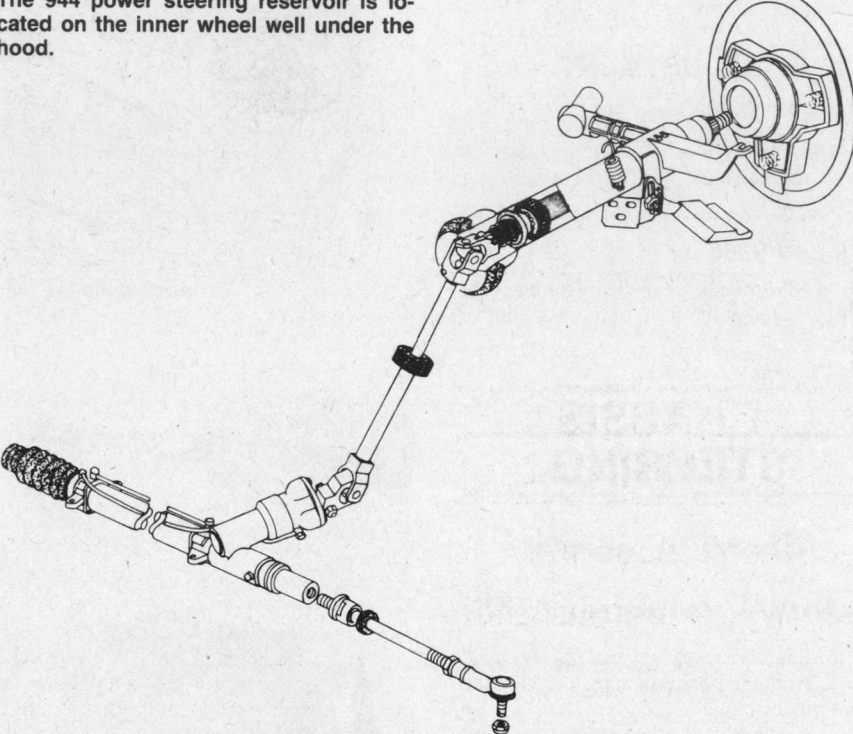

Steering column and gear used on the 928 and 928S

5. Turn the adjuster in the opposite direction until you just pass the point of drag.

6. Repeat on the other wheel.

7. Lower the car and road test. Readjust, if necessary.

Master Cylinder

REMOVAL & INSTALLATION

1. To prevent brake fluid from spilling out and damaging the paint, place a protective cover over the fender.

2. Disconnect and plug the brake lines.

3. Disconnect the electrical plug from the sending unit for the brake failure switch.

4. Remove the two master cylinder mounting nuts.

5. Lift the master cylinder and reservoir out of the engine compartment being careful not to spill any fluid on the fender. Empty out and discard the brake fluid.

─── **CAUTION** ───
Do not depress the brake pedal while the master cylinder is removed.

6. Position the master cylinder and reservoir assembly onto the studs for the booster and install the washers and nuts. Tighten the nuts to no more than 10 ft. lbs.

7. Remove the plugs and connect the brake lines.

8. Bleed the brake system.

Parking Brake

ADJUSTMENT

924 and 924 Turbo

1. Raise the rear wheels and support on stands. Adjust the rear brakes.

2. Remove the parking brake handle boot.

3. Pull the lever up two teeth.

4. Tighten the parking brake adjusting nut until both wheels can just barely be turned by hand.

928, 928S and 944

1. Raise the vehicle and remove the rear wheels.

2. Release the parking brake lever and move the disc brake pads so that the rotor can be easily moved.

3. Loosen the cable adjusting nuts so that no tension exists on the cable.

4. Insert a screwdriver through the hole in the brake rotor and turn the brake adjuster until the rotor cannot be moved.

5. Turn the adjuster in the opposite direction just until the rotor is free to rotate.

6. Pull the brake lever up two notches and adjust the cable so that the rotors can just be turned.

NOTE: At four notches of the lever, the rotors should be tight and unable to turn.

7. Release the handbrake and make sure the rotors turn freely. Install the wheels and lower the vehicle.

924 and 924 Turbo rear drum brakes—remove the rubber plugs (arrows) in order to gain access to the brake adjusters

CHASSIS ELECTRICAL

Heater Assembly

REMOVAL & INSTALLATION

The heater core and blower are contained in the heater assembly which is removed and disassembled to service either component. The heater assembly is located under the center of the instrument panel.

1. Disconnect the battery ground cable.
2. Drain the cooling system.
3. Disconnect the two hoses from the heater core connections at the firewall.
4. Unplug the heater electrical connector.

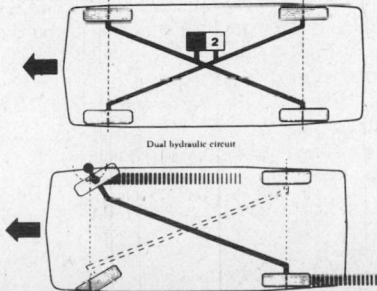

Split/diagonal hydraulic brake system. If half of the hydraulic circuit fails, one front and one rear brake will remain operational to stop the vehicle

5. Detach the center console and the right side of the instrument panel.

6. Remove the heater control knobs from the instrument panel.

7. Remove the two retaining screws and remove the controls from the instrument panel.

8. Disconnect the heater control cables.

9. Using a screwdriver, pry the retaining clip off the heater housing. Detach the left and right hoses.

10. Remove the heater-to-instrument panel mounting screws and lower the heater.

11. Pull out the two pins and remove the heater top cover. Pry the retaining clips off and separate the two heater halves.

12. Remove the heater core and/or blower.

13. Installation is the reverse of removal. Refill the cooling system. See "Radiator Removal and Installation."

Radio

REMOVAL & INSTALLATION

NOTE: Many radios are dealer installed options, therefore this procedure may differ from unit to unit. The following is a general removal and installation procedure.

1. Disconnect the battery ground cable.
2. Remove the radio knobs.
3. Release the radio bezel by pressing the springs in the shaft openings outward to their stops.
4. Remove the bezel.

5. Remove the nuts on the shafts.
6. Loosen the brackets and pull the radio out.
7. Disconnect the fuse, ground, speaker, and antenna wires. Remove the radio.
8. Installation is performed in the reverse of the previous steps.

Windshield Wiper Motor

REMOVAL & INSTALLATION

The windshield wiper motor is located on the driver's side of the cowl under a plastic cover.

1. Remove the cover.
2. Disconnect the battery ground cable.
3. Unscrew the wiper linkage, disconnect the electrical plugs, unscrew the motor, remove the mounting screw on the frame, lift frame slightly, and remove motor.
4. Installation is the reverse of removal. Note the following during installation:

a. Connect the plug and turn on the ignition before fastening the linkage.

b. Move the wiper arms to the off position and mount the linkage.

Instrument Cluster

REMOVAL & INSTALLATION

928 and 928S

1. Disconnect the negative battery cable.

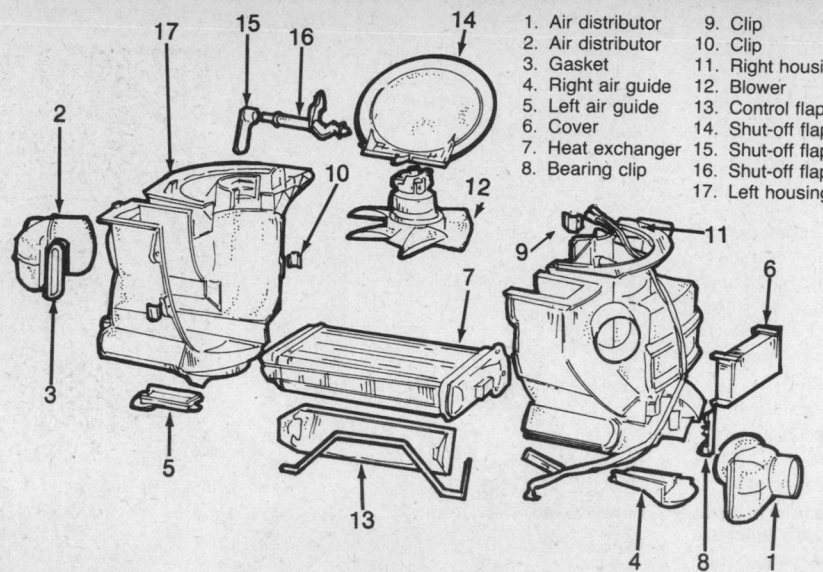

1. Air distributor	9. Clip
2. Air distributor	10. Clip
3. Gasket	11. Right housing half
4. Right air guide	12. Blower
5. Left air guide	13. Control flap
6. Cover	14. Shut-off flap
7. Heat exchanger	15. Shut-off flap lever
8. Bearing clip	16. Shut-off flap shaft
	17. Left housing half

Heater unit of the 924, 924 Turbo, and 944

2. Remove the steering wheel.

3. Remove the steering column switch.

4. Remove the instrument cover mounting screws.

5. Remove the rear window wiper and defogger switch.

6. Disconnect the two 12-pin multi-plugs at the instrument cluster.

7. Lift the instrument cluster carefully and tilt it to the rear. Unscrew the mounting bolt and remove the instrument cluster.

Center Console Instruments

REMOVAL & INSTALLATION

924, 924 Turbo and 944

1. Disconnect the negative battery cable.

2. Remove the two screws at the top of the instrument panel and pull out the panel while lifting the bottom slightly.

3. Remove the knurled knobs and brackets to remove individual instruments. Disconnect wiring.

Installation is the reverse of removal.

Speedometer, Tachometer, Combination Meter

For additional information on instruments, please refer to "Gauges and Indicators" in the Unit Repair section.

REMOVAL & INSTALLATION

924, 924 Turbo and 944

1. Disconnect the negative battery cable.

2. The individual instruments are pressed out of the instrument panel toward the driver's seat from behind the instrument panel. Remove the tachometer and combination meter first.

3. To remove the speedometer, it is better to remove the other two instruments first, then press out the speedometer. It may be necessary to insert an appropriate tool (angled flat iron bar, large socket wrench, etc.) behind the speedometer housing to press out the speedometer.

4. Press in the instruments to install. Do not apply force to the instrument glass when installing.

Fuse and Relay Panel Location

The fuse panel on the 924, 924 Turbo, and 944 is located underneath the dashboard on the driver's side of the vehicle. The relays are arranged above the fuses. On some models, an additional line of fuses is located above the main fuse/relay panel.

The fuse panel on the 928 is located beneath a hinged wooden panel at the front of the passenger's floor area. Pull back the carpet to expose the cover. The relays are arranged below the fuse line.

On all models, fuse amperage ratings and applications are given in the owner's manual.

Renault

Alliance, Encore, Fuego, LeCar, 18i

SERIAL NUMBER IDENTIFICATION

Vehicle

Renault vehicles are identified by two plates in the engine compartment. One plate, diamond shaped through 1979 and rectangular beginning in 1980, shows the model number, serial number, maximum gross vehicle weight (GVW), maximum gross axle weight rating, date of manufacture and vehicle class.

The other plate, oval in shape, as indicated by the accompanying illustration, shows:
- the model number
- the transmission type
- basic equipment code
- optional equipment code
- manufacturer's number.

Engine

The engine identification plate is attached to the engine block on the left side at the rear, just below the head. On earlier models, all plates were uniformly rectangular on all engines. On later models, however, the size and shape of the plate was determined by available space. Through 1979 the plate showed the engine type, index and manufacturing sequence number. Beginning in 1980, the plate shows, as illustrated:

A. The engine type
B. The French Ministry of Mines homologation number
C. Engine equipment
D. Manufacturer's identification number
E. Engine index number
F. The manufacturing sequence number.

Transaxle

The transaxle identification tag is located under a bolt on the transaxle at the end opposite the engine. The plate shows the type and the manufacturing sequence number.

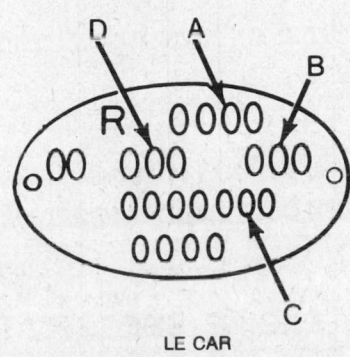

LE CAR

A. Vehicle type
B. Equipment number
C. Manufacturing number
D. Version number

Oval identification plate

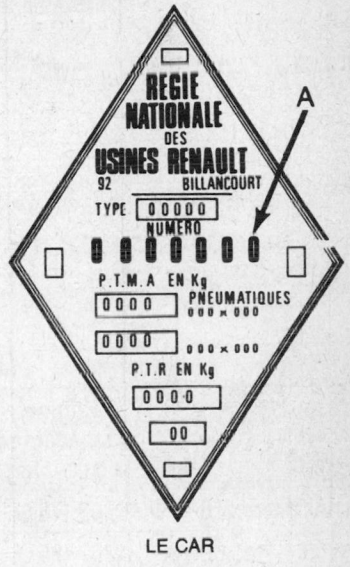

LE CAR

Diamond shaped identification plates

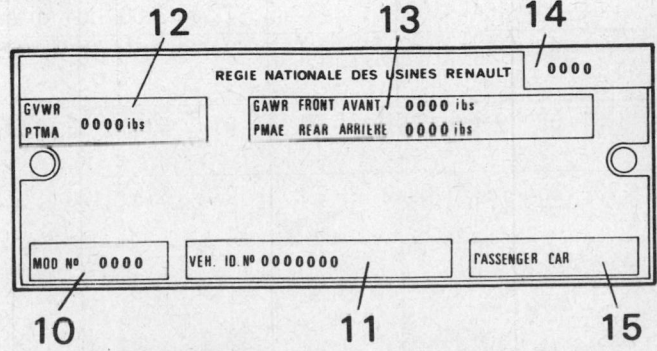

10. The model number
11. The serial number
12. The maximum allowable load for the vehicle
13. The maximum allowable load for the front and rear axles
14. The date of manufacture (month-year)
15. The vehicle class

Rectangular identification plate

C683

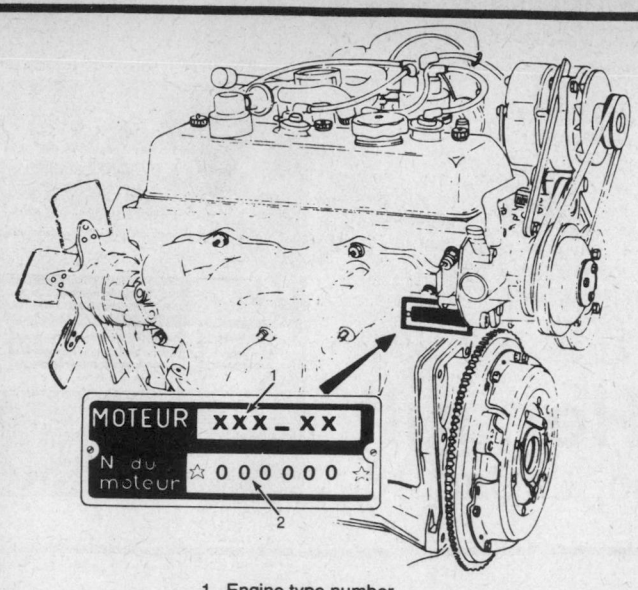

1. Engine type number
2. Engine fabrication number

Engine identification plate

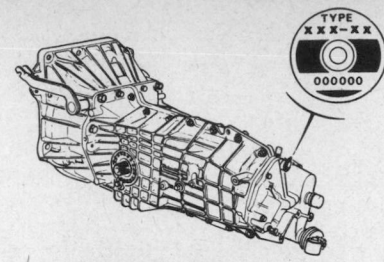

Transaxle identification plate

GENERAL ENGINE SPECIFICATIONS

Model	Year	Engine Displacement cc (cu. in.)	Fuel System Type	Horsepower @ rpm	Torque @ rpm (ft. lbs.)	Bore and Stroke (in.)	Compression Ratio	Oil Pressure psi @ 4000 rpm
LeCar, Alliance	'78–'79	1289 (78.6)	2-bbl	60 @ 6000	66 @ 3000	2.874 × 3.031	9.5:1	50
	'80–'83	1397 (85.2)	2-bbl/F.I.	①	67 @ 2500	2.992 × 3.031	8.8:1 ④	50
Alliance, Encore	'84–'85	1397 (85.2)	F.I.	⑥	67 @ 2500	2.992 × 3.031	9.0:1	50
18 ⑤	'81–'84	1647 (100.5)	2-bbl	72 @ 5500	84 @ 2500	3.110 × 3.307	8.0:1	50
18i, Fuego, Sport Wagon	'81–'83	1647 (100.5)	F.I.	②	86 @ 2500	3.110 × 3.307	③	50
Sport Wagon, Fuego	'84–'85	2165 (132.1)	F.I.	91 @ 5000	98 @ 2500	3.464 × 3.897	8.7:1	50
Fuego	'82–'85	1647 (100.5)	F.I. Turbo	107 @ 5500	120 @ 2500	3.110 × 3.307	8.0:1	50

① LeCar Calif.: 53 @ 500
   U.S.: 51 @ 5000
  Alliance Calif.: 72 @ 5500
         U.S.: 65 @ 5000
② 18i and Fuego: 81.5 @ 5500
③ 18i and Fuego: 8.6:1
④ Alliance: 9.0:1
⑤ Canada
⑥ Calif.: 75 @ 5500
  49s.: 70 @ 5000

TUNE-UP SPECIFICATIONS

Model	Year	Engine Displacement cu in. (cc)	Spark Plug Type	Spark Plug Gap (in.)	Distributor Point Dwell (deg)	Distributor Point Gap (in.)	Ignition Timing (deg) MT	Ignition Timing (deg) AT	Intake Valve Opens (deg)	Fuel Pump Pressure (psi)	Idle Speed (rpm) MT	Idle Speed (rpm) AT	Valve Clearance (in.) In	Valve Clearance (in.) Ex
LeCar, Alliance, Encore	'78–'79	78.6 (1289)	①	②	57	.016–.020	0	—	22B	2.5–3.5	775③	—	.006	.008
	'80–'81	85.2 (1397)	WD9DS	.022–.026	Electronic		3B⑤	—	12B	2.5–3.5	700④	—	.006	.008
	'82–'85	85.2 (1397)	RN-12Y	.032	Electronic		8B	8B	12B	28–36	700	700	.006	.008
18i, Fuego, Sport Wagon	'81–'84	100.5 (1647)	WR7DS	.024–.028	Electronic		10B	10B	22B	28–36	800	650	.008	.010
Fuego	'84–'85	132.0 (2165)	see underhood sticker											

NOTE: The underhood sticker often reflects tune-up specification changes made in production. Sticker figures must be used if they disagree with those in this chart.
B: Before Top Dead Center
① 1978 exc. Calif.: L-874
   1979 exc. Calif.: L-92Y
② 1978 exc. Calif.: .026–.029
   All others: .022–.026
③ W/air pump: 850
④ W/air pump: 750
⑤ Canada: 0

FIRING ORDERS

NOTE: To avoid confusion, always replace spark plug wires one at a time.

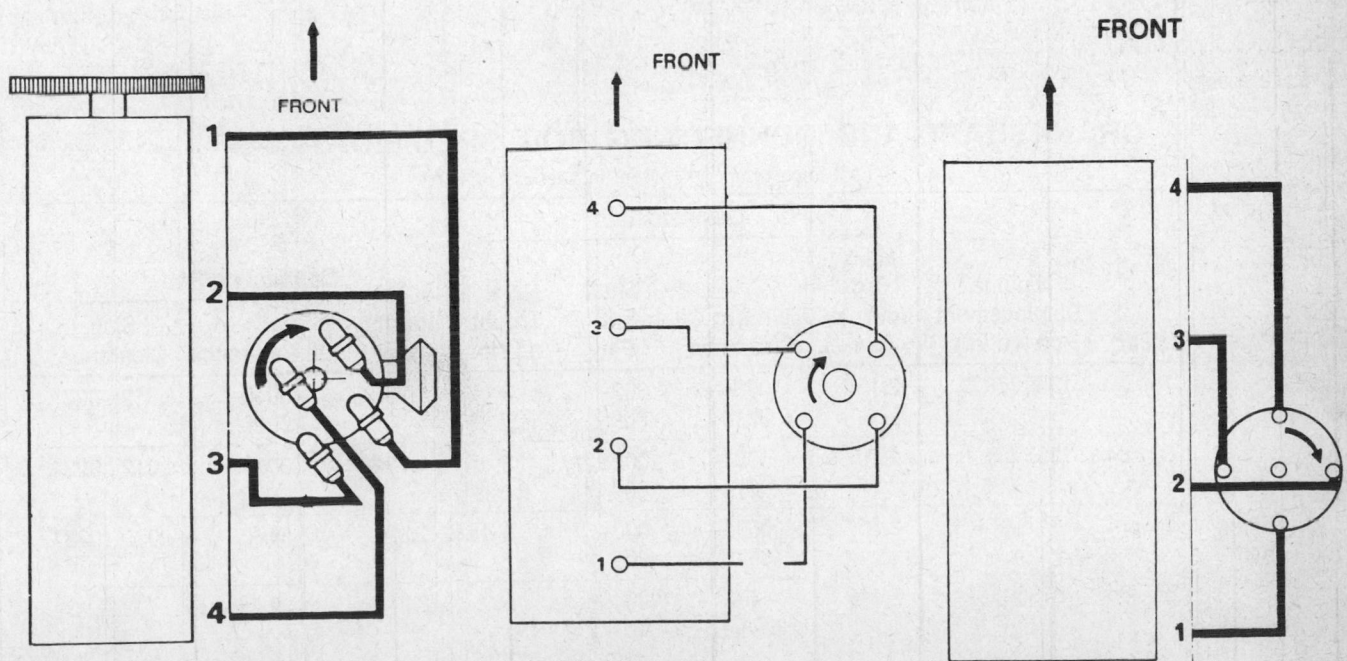

LeCar, Alliance and Encore spark plug wiring diagram

Spark plug wiring diagram for 18i and Fuego engines

Spark plug wiring diagram for R–18 carbureted engines

CAPACITIES

Model	Year	Crankcase Incl. Filter (qts.)	Transmission Pints to Refill After Draining		Fuel Tank (gal.)	Cooling System (qts.)	
			Manual	Automatic●		With Heater	With A/C
LeCar	All	3.5	4.0	—	10.0	6.5	6.5
18,18i, Sport Wagon	'81–'83	4.5	4.5	10.5	①	6.5	6.75
Fuego	'82–'83	4.5	4.5	10.5	15.0	6.4	6.75
Alliance	'82–'83	3.5	7.0	9.0	12.5	4.4	4.8
Alliance, Encore	'84–'85	4.0	②	7.5	12.5	4.4	4.8
Sport Wagon, Fuego	'84–'85	NA	NA	NA	15.0	NA	NA
Fuego Turbo	'84–'85	4.5	4.5	10.5	15.0	6.4	6.75

NA Not Available
● Includes converter
① Sedan: 14
  Sta. Wgn.: 15
② 4sp: 6.4
  5sp: 6.8

VALVE SPECIFICATIONS

Model	Year	Engine Displacement cc (cu in.)	Seat Angle (deg)	Face Angle (deg)	Spring Test Pressure (lbs. @ in.)		Stem-to-Guide Clearance (in.)		Stem Diameter (in.)	
					Outer	Inner	Intake	Exhaust	Intake	Exhaust
LeCar, Alliance, Encore	'78–'79	1289 (78.6)	45	45	80 @ 1.00	—	.0010	.0010	.276	.276
	'80–'85	1397 (85.2)	①	①	81 @ .984	—	.0010	.0010	.276	.276
18,18i, Fuego, Sport Wagon	'81–'85	1647 (100.5)	45	45	99 @ 1.140②	20 @ .750	.0010③	.0010③	.315	.315
Fuego	'84–'85	2165 (132)	④	④	N.A.	—	.0040	.0040	.315	.315

① Intake: 60
  Exhaust: 45
② 18i and Fuego: 47 @ 1.173
③ 18i and Fuego: .0016
④ Int.: 60
  Exh.: 45
N.A.: Not available

CRANKSHAFT AND CONNECTING ROD SPECIFICATIONS

(All measurements given in inches)

Model	Year	Engine Displacement cc (cu in.)	Crankshaft				Connecting Rod		
			Main Brg Journal Dia	Main Brg Oil Clearance	Shaft End-Play	Thrust on No.	Journal Dia	Oil Clearance	Side Clearance
LeCar, Alliance, Encore	'78–'79	1289 (78.6)	2.157	.0004– .0014	.002– .009	3	1.732	.0010– .0026	.012–.023
	'80–'84	1397 (85.2)	2.157	.0004– .0014	.002–① .009	3	1.732	.0010– .0026	.012–.023
18,18i, Fuego, Sport Wagon	'81–'84	1647 (100.5)	2.157	.0006– .0015	.002– .009	3	1.890	N.A.	.012–.023
Fuego	'84–'85	2165 (132)	2.476	N.A.	.0005– .0011	3	2.215	N.A.	N.A.

N.A.: Information not available at time of publication
① 1981–83: .004–.009

PISTON AND LINER SPECIFICATIONS
(Measurement in inches)

	Year	Engine cc (cu. in)	Bore	Base Locating Diameter	Liner Protrusion	Base Seal Thickness	Piston Pin Length	Piston Pin Diameter
ice, Encore	'78–'79	1289 (78.6)	2.874	3.091	.0016–.005	①	2.385	.787
	'80–'84	1397 (85.2)	2.992	3.173	.001–.004②	.045–.053	2.520	.790
, Sport Wagon	'81–'84	1647 (100.5)	3.110	3.307	.004–.007②	.045–.053	2.717	.827
	'84–'85	2165 (132)	3.460	3.685	.003–.006	.029–.049	2.952	.905

003
04
: .005
hout O-ring

TORQUE SPECIFICATIONS
(All readings in ft. lbs. unless noted)

Year	Engine Displacement cc (cu. in)	Cylinder Head Bolts	Rod Bearing Bolts	Main Bearing Bolts	Crankshaft Pulley Bolts	Flywheel to Crankshaft Bolts	Manifolds Intake	Manifolds Exhaust
'78–'79	1289 (78.6)	40①	35	50	65	40	25	25
'80–'84	1397 (85.2)	40①	35	50	81	40	25	25
'81–'84	1647 (100.5)	60②	30	45	67	35	20	20
'84–'85	2165 (132)	72	46	69	96	44	20	20

e until hot, let cool for 50 minutes, then retorque to 45 ft. lb.
ne until hot, let cool for 50 minutes, then retorque to 65 ft. lb.

ALTERNATOR AND REGULATOR SPECIFICATIONS

Alternator Output Amps @ Generator rpm	Charge Indicator Relay Back Gap (in.)	Charge Indicator Relay Point Gap (in.)	Voltage Regulator Back Gap (in.)	Voltage Regulator Air Gap (in.)	Voltage Regulator Point Gap (in.)	Regulated Voltage
50 @ 3500	integral—not adjustable					13.8–14.8
30 @ 3000	integral—not adjustable					13.3–14.8
30 @ 3000	integral—not adjustable					13.3–14.8

154
4-30
1228312/
1227702

BRAKE SPECIFICATIONS
(All measurements are given in inches)

Model	Master Cylinder Bore (in.)	Wheel Cylinder or Caliper Bore Front	Wheel Cylinder or Caliper Bore Rear	Brake rotor or Drum Diameter Front	Brake rotor or Drum Diameter Rear	Minimum Lining Thickness	Brake Disc Minimum Thickness	Brake Disc Maximum Run-out	Brake Drum Max. Diam.
eCar	.811	1.772	.866	9.000	7.096	9/32	.354	.004	7.136
uego, 18, 18i, ort Wagon	.748	1.890	.866	9.370	9.000	9/32	.354	.004	9.040
liance, ncore	.811	1.772	.866	9.000	8.000	9/32	.433	.003	8.060

WHEEL ALIGNMENT SPECIFICATIONS

Model	Toe-out Range in.	Toe-out Preferred in.	Camber Range (deg)	Camber Preferred (deg)	Caster Range (deg)	Caster Preferred (deg)	
'78 LeCar	3/16 to 3/64	1/8	0 to 1P	1/2P	12P to 13P	12 1/2P	
'79-'84 LeCar	0 to 3/64	1/64	0 to 1P	1/2P	3P to 6P	4 1/2P	
18,18i	0 to 3/64	1/64	1/2N to 1/2P	0	①	②	
Alliance, Encore	1/64 to 3/64	1/32	1/16N to 3/16N	1/8N	1/2P to 2P	1°30'P	
Fuego	0 to 3/64	1/64	1/2N to 1/2P	0	①	②	

① Pwr. Str.: 1 1/2P to 3 1/2P
  Non-Pwr. Str.: 1/2P to 2 1/2P
② Pwr. Str.: 2 1/2P
  Non-Pwr. Str.: 1 1/2P

TUNE-UP

Spark Plugs

When replacing spark plugs, mark or tag the ignition cables to avoid placing them on the wrong spark plug during reassembly. When replacing the spark plug cables, remove and replace one at a time to avoid cross-firing when the engine is started.

Breaker Points and Condenser

REMOVAL & INSTALLATION

NOTE: Some 1980 and all 1981 and later models are equipped with a breakerless, solid state ignition system. This system eliminates the points and condenser.

1. Remove the coil wire from the top of the distributor cap. Remove the cap from the distributor and place it out of the way. Remove the rotor from the distributor shaft.
2. Loosen the screw which holds the condenser lead to the body of the breaker points and remove the condenser lead from the points.
3. Remove the screw which holds the condenser to the distributor body. Remove the condenser and discard it.
4. Remove the points assembly attaching screws and adjustment lockscrews. A screwdriver with a holding mechanism will come in handy here so that you don't drop a screw into the distributor and have to remove the entire distributor to retrieve it.
5. Remove the points by lifing them straight up and off the locating dowel on the plate. Wipe off the cam and apply new cam lubricant. Discard the old set of points.

6. Slip the new set of points onto the locating dowel and install the screws that hold the assembly onto the plate. Do not tighten them all the way.
7. Attach the new condenser to the plate with the ground screw.
8. Attach the condenser lead to the points at the proper place.
9. Apply a small amount of cam lubricant to the shaft where the rubbing block of the points touches.

ADJUSTMENT

With A Feeler Gauge

1. If the contact points of the assembly are not parallel, bend the stationary contact so that they make contact across the entire surface of the contacts. Bend only the stationary bracket part of the point assembly; *not the moveable contact*.
2. Turn the engine until the rubbing block of the points is on one of the high points of the distributor cam. You can do this by either turning the ignition switch to the start position and releasing it quickly ("bumping" the engine) or by using a wrench on the bolt which holds the crankshaft pulley to the crankshaft.
3. Place the correct size feeler gauge between the contacts. Make sure that it is parallel with the contact surfaces.
4. With your free hand, insert a screwdriver into the notch provided for adjustment or into the eccentric adjusting screw, then twist the screwdriver to either increase or decrease the gap to the proper setting.
5. Tighten the adjustment lockscrew and recheck the gap to make sure that it didn't change when the lockscrew was tightened.
6. Replace the rotor and distributor cap, and the wire that connects the top of the distributor and the coil. Make sure that the rotor is firmly seated all the way onto the distributor shaft and that the tab of the rotor is aligned with the notch in the shaft. Align

the tab in the base of the dis with the notch in the distributor sure that the cap is firmly sea distributor and that the retainer place. Make sure that the end of tension wire is firmly placed the distributor and the coil.

With A Dwell Meter

1. Adjust the points with a as described earlier.
2. Connect the dwell meter nition circuit according to the m er's instructions. One lead of th connected to a ground and the connected to the distributor pos An adapter is usually provi purpose.
3. If the dwell meter has a it, adjust the meter to zero the i
4. Start the engine.

NOTE: Be careful when workin any vehicle while the engine is runn Make sure that the transmission is i Neutral or Park and that the parking brake is applied. Keep hands, clothing, tools, and the wires of the test instruments clear of the rotating fan blades.

5. Observe the reading on the dwell meter. If the reading is within the specified range, turn off the engine and remove the dwell meter.
6. If the reading is above the specified range, the breaker point gap is too small. If the reading is below the specified range, the gap is too large. In either case, the engine must be stopped and the gap adjusted in the manner previously covered. After making the adjustment, start the engine and check the reading on the dwell meter. When the correct reading is obtained, disconnect the dwell meter.
7. Check the adjustment of the ignition timing.

Electronic Ignition

ADJUSTMENTS

Although it is possible to adjust certain components of the distributor, these adjustments are not normally required at each tune-up.

Trigger Plate Gap

1. Loosen the impulse sender retaining screws slightly.

2. Measure the distance between an impulse sender stud and one of the arms of the trigger plate. The gap must be 0.012–0.24 in. (0.3–0.6mm).

3. Move the impulse sender(s) as required and tighten the retaining screws. Check the gap for all four arms of the trigger wheel and adjust as necessary.

NOTE: If the trigger wheel gap for certain arms of the trigger wheel cannot be correctly adjusted, replace the distributor.

Secondary Impulse Sender Timing

NOTE: This adjustment must be performed after every trigger plate gap adjustment.

1. Loosen the screw (6 & 7) as illustrated in the accompanying diagram.

2. Align one arm of the trigger plate with the primary impulse sender stud (10).

3. Move the secondary impulse sender so that the center of the secondary impulse sender stud (9) is located opposite the edge of the trigger plate arm which is aligned with the primary impulse sender stud.

4. Tighten the screws which were loosened in Step 1.

Offset Adjustment

This adjustment is made after the trigger plate adjustment.

1. Loosen the screws 6 & 7.

2. Line up the rotor cam 11, opposite the pickup tip 10.

3. For coil offset more than 3°, move the coil B1 so that the center of tip 9, is opposite rotor tip 8.

4. For coils offset more than 5°, move the coil B, so that point 12 on tip 9, is opposite point 8 of the rotor tip opposite tip 11.

5. Tighten screws 6 & 7.

Ignition Timing

ADJUSTMENT

1. Locate the timing marks on the flywheel and the flywheel housing.

2. Clean the timing marks so that you can see them.

3. Mark the timing marks with a piece of chalk or with paint. Color the mark on

the scale that will indicate the correct timing when it is aligned with the mark on the flywheel. It is also helpful to mark the notch in the flywheel with a small dab of color.

4. Attach a tachometer to the engine.

5. Attach a timing light according to the manufacturer's instructions. If the timing light has three wires, one is attached to the No. 1 spark plug with an adapter. The other wires are connected to the battery. The red wire goes to the positive side of the battery and the black wire is connected to the negative terminal of the battery.

6. Disconnect the vacuum line at the distributor and plug it. A golf tee does a fine job.

7. Check to make sure that all of the wires clear the fan and then start the engine.

8. Adjust the idle to the correct setting.

9. Aim the timing light at the timing marks. If the marks that you put on the

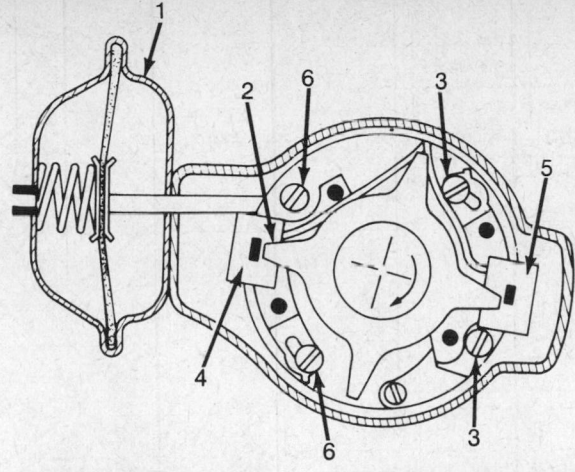

1. Vacuum advance capsule
2. Trigger plate
3. Adjustment screws for the secondary impulse sender-to-trigger plate clearance
4. Main impulse sender
5. Secondary impulse sender
6. Adjustment screws for the main impulse sender-to-trigger plate clearance

Electronic distributor ignition parts identification

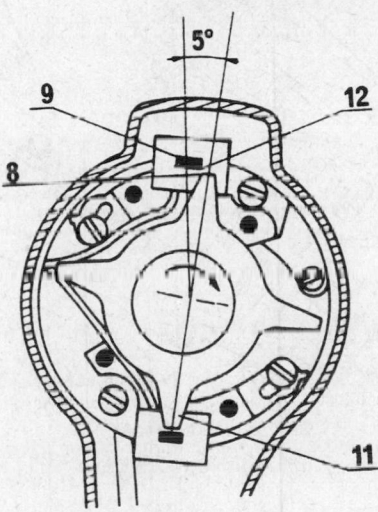

Adjustment for coils offset 5 degrees

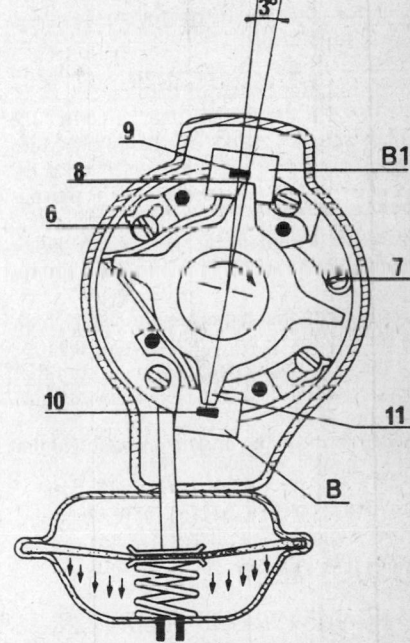

Adjustment for coils offset 3 degrees

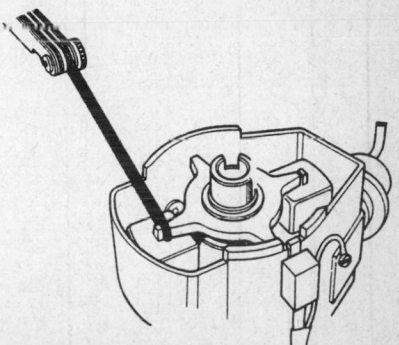

Measuring the trigger plate gap adjustment with a non-magnetic feeler gauge (plastic or brass)

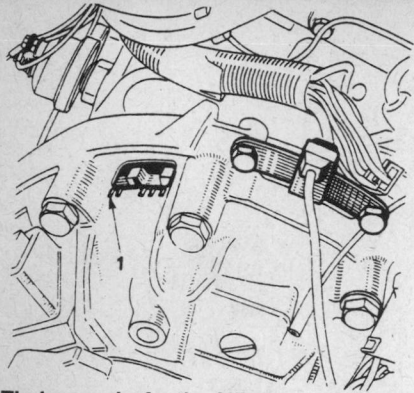

Timing marks for the Alliance and Encore. Point 1 is TDC; each graduation is 2 degrees

flywheel and the flywheel housing are aligned when the light flashes, the timing is correct. Turn off the engine and remove the tachometer and the timing light. If the marks are not in alignment, proceed with the following steps.

10. Turn off the engine.

11. Loosen the distributor lockbolt just enough so that the distributor can be turned with a little effort.

12. Start the engine. Keep the wires of the timing light clear of the fan.

13. With the timing light aimed at the pulley and the marks on the engine, turn the distributor in the direction of rotor rotation to retard the spark, and in the opposite direction of rotor rotation to advance the spark. Align the marks on the pulley and the engine with the flashes of the timing light.

14. When the marks are aligned, tighten the distributor lockbolt and recheck the timing with the timing light to make sure that the distributor did not move when you tightened the lockbolt.

15. Turn off the engine and remove the timing light.

Valve Clearance

ADJUSTMENT

All except 1984–85 Fuego 2.2L

1. Rotate the engine in correct rotation until the exhaust valve for the No. 1 cylinder is fully open.

2. Adjust the rocker arms of the intake valve for the No. 3 cylinder and the exhaust valve for the No. 4 cylinder.

3. Rotate the engine in correct rotation until the No. 3 cylinder exhaust valve is fully open. Adjust the rocker arms of the intake valve for No. 4 cylinder and the exhaust valve for No. 2 cylinder.

4. Rotate the engine in correct rotation until the No. 4 cylinder exhaust valve is fully open. Adjust the rocker arms of the intake valve for No. 2 cylinder and the exhaust valve for No. 1 cylinder.

5. Rotate the engine in correct rotation until the No. 2 cylinder exhaust valve is fully open. Adjust the rocker arms of the

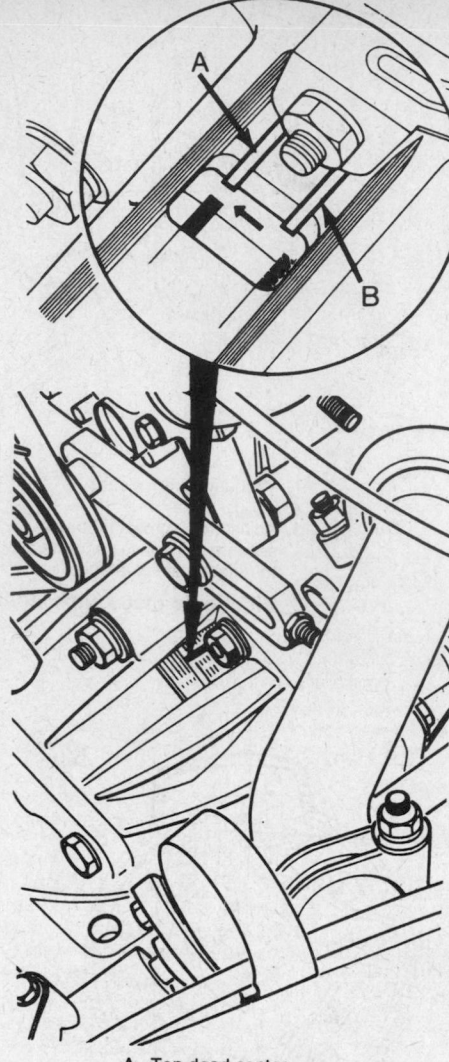

A. Top dead center
B. 4 degrees advanced

Ignition timing —Le Car

intake valve for the No. 1 cylinder and the exhaust valve for the No. 3 cylinder.

6. Rotate the engine in the correct rotation, and recheck the rocker arm adjustments for proper specifications clearances.

1984–85 Fuego 2.2L OHC Engine

NOTE: If the engine is equipped with a rear window in the timing belt cover, use Procedure A. If there is no rear window in the cover, use Procedure B.

PROCEDURE A

1. Rotate the crankshaft clockwise and align the No. 1 piston TDC mark with the notch in the FRONT cover window. Remember, No. 1 piston is at the flywheel end.

2. Rotate the crankshaft clockwise until the first mark appears in the REAR cover window. Align that mark with the cover notch. Loosen the locknut and adjust the No. 2 intake and No. 4 exhaust valves to

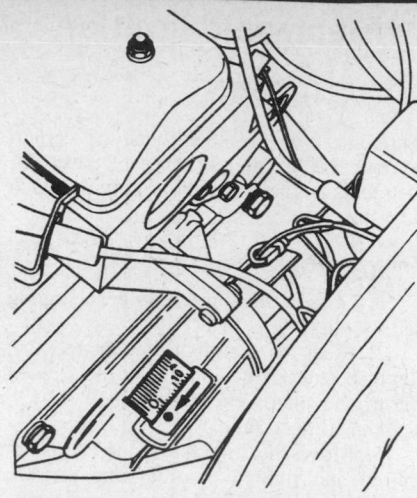

Timing marks for 18i and Fuego with automatic transaxle

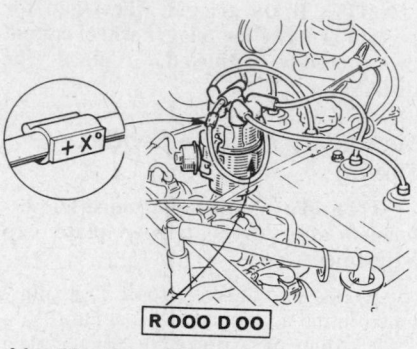

R OOO D OO

Identification of initial timing—typical

give a clearance of 0.004–0.008 in. for intakes and 0.008–0.010 in. for exhaust. Repeat the procedure as follows:

2nd mark: No. 1 intake & No. 2 exhaust
3rd mark: No. 3 intake & No. 1 exhaust
4th mark: No. 4 intake & No. 3 exhaust

PROCEDURE B

NOTE: A special tool is needed for this procedure.

1. Remove the distributor cap and rotor.

2. Rotate the crankshaft clockwise and align the No. 1 piston TDC mark with the notch in the timing cover window.

3. Position Alignment Rotor Ms.1774 on the distributor shaft. Position flexible pointer Mot.591 on the #10 head bolt (nearest the distributor on the left).

4. Align the pointer with the TDC index (hole) on the alignment rotor.

5. Rotate the crankshaft clockwise two complete turns and re-align the pointer with the TDC index.

6. Rotate the crankshaft, slowly, until the #1 index on the alignment rotor is aligned with the pointer. Loosen the locknut and adjust the No. 2 intake and No. 4 exhaust valves to provide a clearance of 0.004–0.006 in. for intakes and 0.008–0.010 in. for exhausts. Tighten the locknuts. Rotate the

crankshaft to each cylinder number in turn
and adjust the valves as follows:

mark #2: No. 1 intake & No. 2 exhaust
    #3: No. 3 intake & No. 1 exhaust
    #4: No. 4 intake & No. 3 exhaust

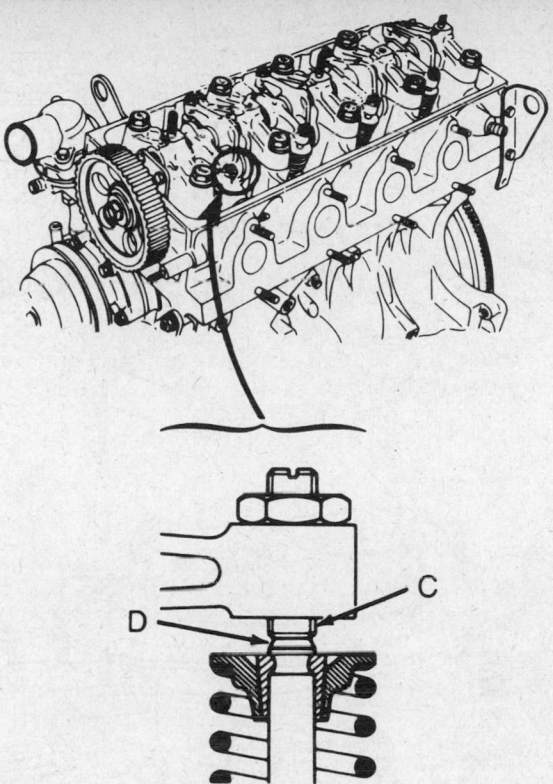

Carburetor

IDLE SPEED AND MIXTURE ADJUSTMENT

NOTE: 1978–85 models must be adjusted with the use of a CO meter to obtain the correct emissions reading and idle speed. If a CO meter is not available, and the idle speed and mixture *must* be adjusted, use the following procedure.

Without a CO Meter (Except California)

1. Clamp off the air injection hose between the diverter valve and the engine, using the appropriate special tool.

2. Turn the throttle plate screw so that the engine speed is 775 rpm.

3. Turn the idle mixture screw to obtain the highest possible idle speed.

4. Lower the engine speed 20–25 rpm by turning the idle mixture screw clockwise. Remove the air injection hose block-off clamp and check the idle speed which should be 850 ± 50 rpm. If the idle speed is incorrect, turn the throttle plate screw to adjust.

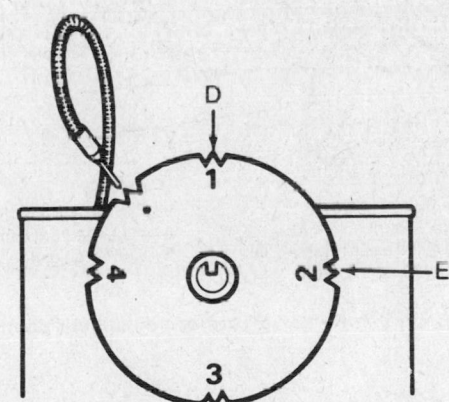

Valve adjustment point. C is the adjustment screw; D is the valve stem

Fuel Injection

IDLE SPEED ADJUSTMENT

18i, Fuego, Sport Wagon and California Alliance and Encore

1. Start the engine and allow it to come to operating temperature.

2. Connect a tachometer to leads D1–1 and D1–3 of the diagnostic connector.

3. Turn all accessories off: Wait for the electric fan to shut off.

4. Turn the throttle plate bypass screw to obtain the correct idle speed.

Alliance and Encore, except California

These cars use Throttle Body Injection. Idle speed adjustment is necessary only if the Idle Speed Control motor (ISC) has been replaced.

1. Remove the air cleaner.

2. Start the engine and allow it to reach normal operating temperature. Make sure that the A/C control is off.

3. Connect a tachometer to terminals D1–1 and D1–3 of the diagnostic connector.

4. Turn the engine off. The ISC plunger should move to the fully extended position.

5. Disconnect the ISC motor wire connector and start the engine.

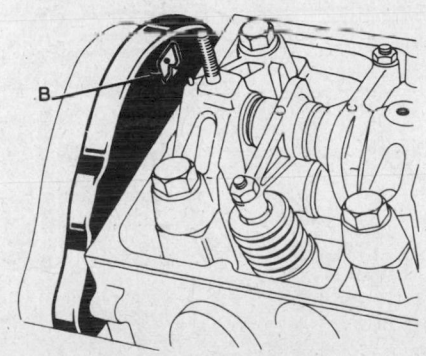

Alignment rotor Ms.1774 and flexible pointer Mot.591. D & E are piston location points

Timing cover rear window

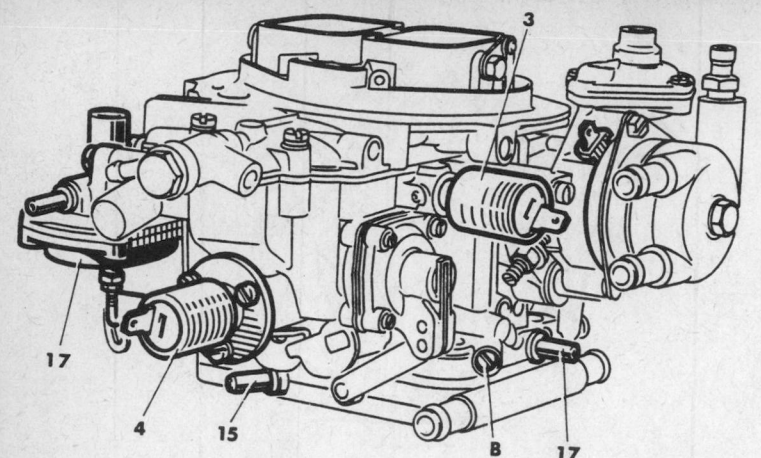

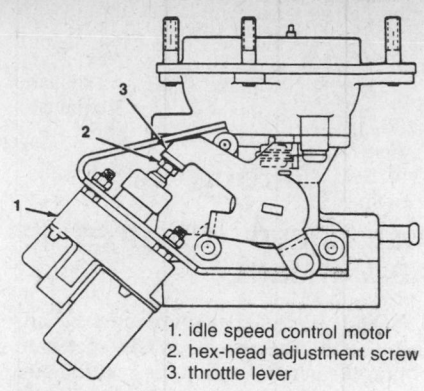

1. idle speed control motor
2. hex-head adjustment screw
3. throttle lever

Idle speed adjustment points on non–California Alliance

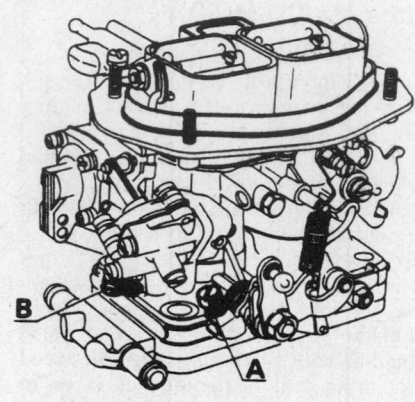

LeCar idle speed and mixture adjustment points

3. anti-dieseling solenoid
4. mixture control solenoid
15. 3-way thermovalve tube
17. fast idle throttle control

V. fast idle adjustment screw
A. idle speed adjustment screw
B. mixture adjustment screw

Canadian R–18 carburetor adjustment points

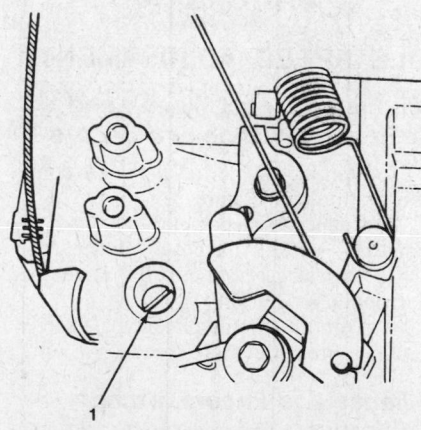

Idle speed adjustment on the 18i, Fuego and California Alliance. Point 1 is the idle speed screw located on top of the throttle plate housing

6. Engine speed should be 3300–3700 rpm. If not, turn the hex head bolt on the end of the plunger to obtain 3500 rpm.

7. Fully retract the ISC motor plunger by holding the closed throttle switch plunger with the throttle open. The closed throttle switch plunger should not be touching the throttle lever when the throttle is returned to the closed position. If contact is noted,

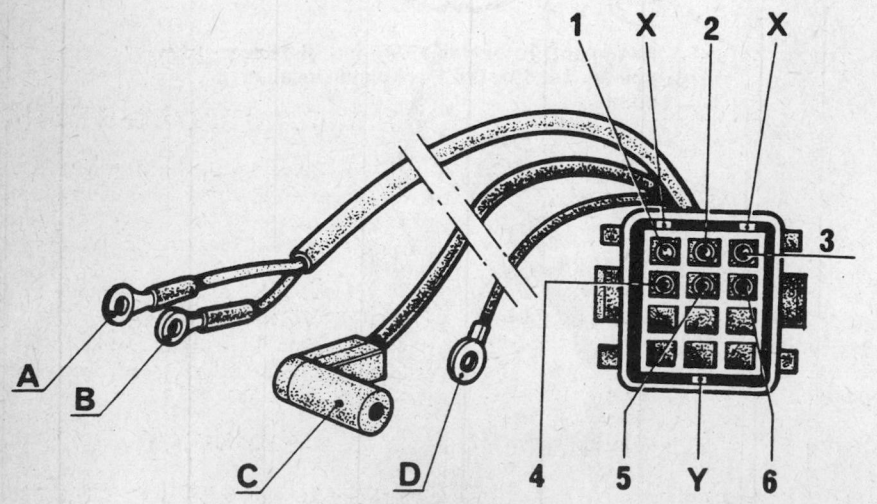

Typical diagnostic connector

check the throttle linkage and/or cable for binding.

8. Connect the ISC wire.

9. Turn the engine off for 10 seconds. The ISC motor plunger should move to the fully extended position.

10. Start the engine. The engine should speed up to 3500 rpm, stay there for a brief time, then drop off to normal idle speed as shown on the underhood sticker, and in the Tune-Up chart.

11. Shut off the engine, disconnect the tachometer and apply a penetrating thread sealant to the adjustment screw threads.

ENGINE ELECTRICAL

Distributor

REMOVAL & INSTALLATION

LeCar, Alliance and Encore

1. Rotate the engine in order to position the No. 1 cylinder at top dead center. Remove the distributor cap.

2. Mark the relationship between the distributor body and the engine, and the firing point of the rotor and the distributor body (point one).

3. Remove the hold-down clamp and remove the distributor. Mark the position of the rotor on the distributor body after removal (point two).

4. Installation is the reverse of the removal procedure. Do not turn the engine while the distributor is removed. Position the rotor at the mark made during Step 3 (point two). The distributor drive (camshaft) and driven gears are helical cut, causing the rotor to rotate towards the removal marking (point one) during installation.

5. Adjust the ignition timing.

18i, Sport Wagon and Fuego

1. Remove distributor cap and wire assembly.

2. Rotate the engine until the No. 1 cylinder is in its firing position, with the rotor end tab pointing to the No. 1 spark plug wire terminal in the distributor cap.

3. The hole in the converter should line up with the "O" mark on the graduated plate of the converter housing, if equipped with an automatic transmission, or if equipped with a standard transmission, the slot in the flywheel should line up with the "O" mark on the bell housing graduated section.

4. With the flywheel or converter marks lined up and the distributor rotor end tab pointing towards the No. 1 spark plug wire terminal in the distributor cap, the firing position of No. 1 cylinder is verified.

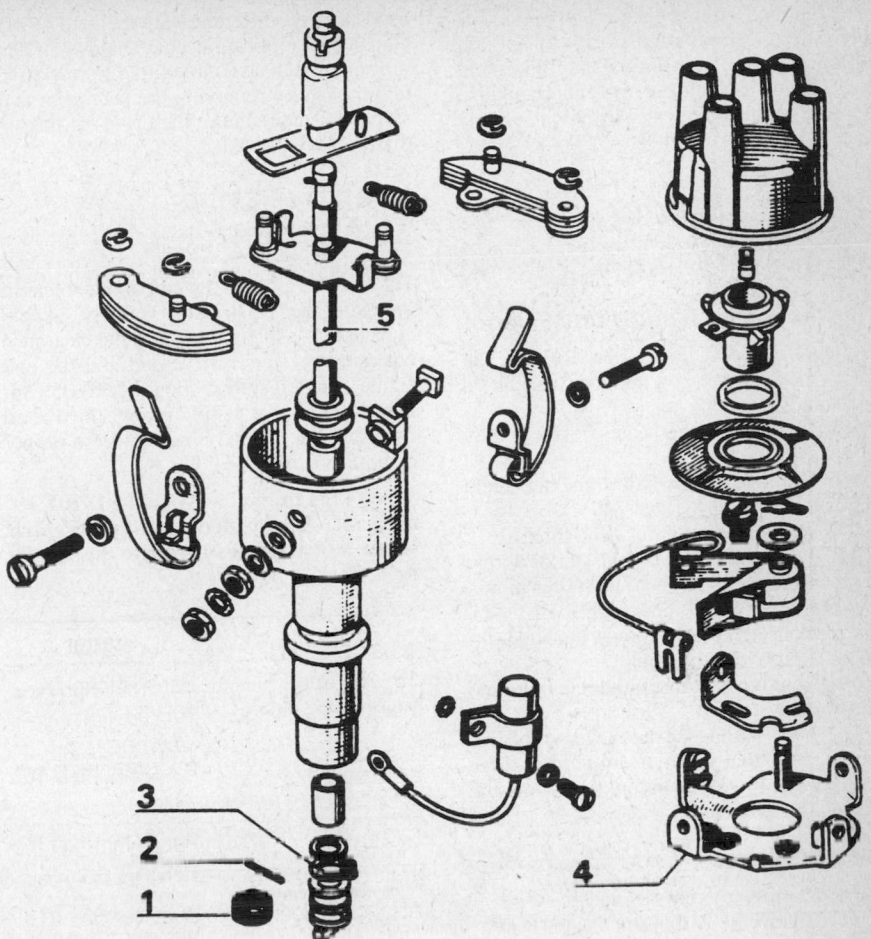

Point type distributor. LeCar uses a distributor cap with horizontal terminals

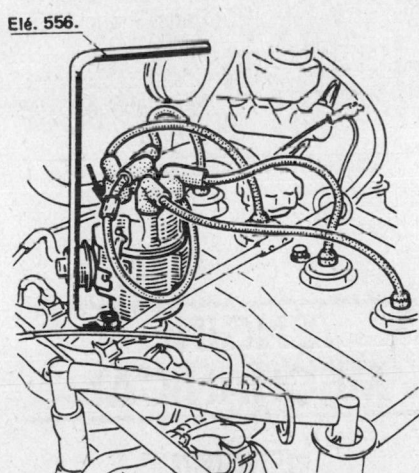

Elé. 556.

Removing the distributor holddown bolt

5. Remove the distributor hold down clamp, the vacuum hose to the vacuum advance and the electrical wire connectors. Remove the distributor from the engine.

6. Observe the position of the off-set lug at the bottom of the distributor shaft and the location of the matching lug in the distributor drive gear bore.

7. Do not rotate the engine crankshaft while the distributor is out of the engine.

8. Installation of the distributor is the reverse of the removal procedure. Be sure the distributor bore drive lug is in the same position as it was when the distributor was removed.

9. Connect the electrical and vacuum connections and reinstall the distributor cap and wire assembly.

10. Time the distributor to the engine as required.

Alternator

REMOVAL & INSTALLATION

1. Disconnect the negative battery cable.

2. Tag and disconnect the alternator wiring.

3. Remove the belt tension adjusting bolt and the drive belt.

4. Remove the remaining alternator attaching bolt and remove the alternator. Installation is the reverse of the removal procedure. Adjust the belt to a maximum of ½ in. total deflection.

Regulator

REMOVAL & INSTALLATION

All Renault models covered in this manual

are equipped with regulators built into the alternators. These regulators are not adjustable. Repairs are limited to replacement only. When replacing an external regulator, be sure to tag the wires to aid in correct installation.

Starter

REMOVAL & INSTALLATION

18, 18i, Sport Wagon and Fuego

1. Disconnect the battery. Remove the air cleaner. Raise and support the car on jackstands.
2. Disconnect the heater hoses, if they interfere.
3. Remove the catalytic converter shield and the converter.
4. Remove the starter heat shield.
5. Disconnect and tag the starter wires.
6. Remove the upper left starter mount bolt and loosen the upper right bolt.
7. Loosen the rear support bracket bolt.
8. Remove the spacer.
9. Remove the three mounting bolts and remove the starter.
10. Installation is the reverse of removal. Note that you must tighten the three starter mounting bolts before tightening the rear support bolt.

LeCar

1. Remove the air cleaner.
2. Clamp the carburetor heater hoses.
3. Disconnect the battery.
4. Disconnect the accelerator linkage.
5. Remove the exhaust manifold.
6. Disconnect and tag the starter wires.
7. Remove the lower starter bolt using a ⅜ in. drive ratchet and 13mm socket, holding the nut with a 13mm box wrench. Remove the upper bolt with special tool Ele. 565 or its equivalent.
8. Remove the starter.
9. Installation is the reverse of removal.

Alliance and Encore

1. Disconnect the battery.
2. Disconnect and tag the starter wires.
3. Remove the starter support bracket.
4. Remove the three starter mount bolts and remove the starter.
5. Installation is the reverse of removal. Note that the three mounting bolts must be tightened before tightening the support bolt.

--- CAUTION ---

To avoid cross-threading the bolts, make certain that the starter motor locating dowel is centered in its hole.

STARTER DRIVE REPLACEMENT

To replace the starter drive, the starter body must be disassembled. Renault cars have used thirteen different starters since 1977. Check the application chart below. When the starter is disassembled, the starter drive is removed by removing the snap-ring and stop ring, then sliding the drive off the armature shaft.

STARTER DRIVE ADJUSTMENT

Take out the plug at the end of the solenoid opposite the electrical terminals. Apply current to the solenoid. Check the clearance between the starter drive end and the end frame. The clearance should be 0.059 in. If not, turn the adjusting screw, uncovered by removing the end plug, until the proper clearance is obtained.

NOTE: On the Paris-Rhone D 10E 79, clearance is adjusted with an eccentric screw which passes through the starter drive fork.

Car Line	Starter
18, 18i, Sport Wagon and Fuego	Paris-Rhone D 10E 63
	Paris-Rhone D 10E 79
LeCar	Paris-Rhone D 8E 121
Alliance, Encore	Ducellier 534 019
	Ducellier 534 031
	Paris-Rhone D 9E 39
	Paris-Rhone D 9E 62

ENGINE MECHANICAL

Engine

REMOVAL & INSTALLATION

18, 18i, Sport Wagon and Fuego

1. Disconnect the battery.
2. Remove the engine under-pan.
3. Drain the cooling system.
4. Drain the engine oil.
5. Remove the grille.
6. Remove the grille upper crossmember.
7. Remove the radiator and cooling fan. Vehicles with air conditioning have two fans. Both must be removed. On these vehicles, the air conditioning system should not be discharged. The condenser can be set aside without disconnecting any lines.
8. Remove the battery.
9. Remove the starter.
10. Remove the exhaust heat shields.
11. Remove the air cleaner.
12. Disconnect the exhaust pipe at the manifold.
13. Remove the catalytic converter.
14. Remove the clutch cable and its bracket on cars with manual transmission.
15. Disconnect and remove the alternator.
16. Remove the power steering pump from its bracket without disconnecting the hoses. Position it out of the way.
17. Remove the air conditioning compressor from its bracket without disconnecting the refrigerant lines. Position it out of the way.
18. Disconnect and tag all hoses, wire and cables connected to the engine.
19. Attach a shop crane or hoist to the engine and just barely take up the engine weight.
20. Remove the upper engine-transmission bolts.
21. Remove the flywheel cover plate.
22. Remove the lower engine-transmission bolts.
23. Remove the side engine-transmission bolts.
24. Unbolt the automatic transmission torque converter from the flywheel. The flywheel will have to be turned by hand to reach all the bolts.
25. Raise the engine until the transmission just touches the steering crossmember.
26. Support the transmission with a jack or jackstand.
27. Pull the engine forward to clear the transmission and raise it clear of the car. Be careful not to pull the converter off of the transmission.
28. Installation is the reverse of removal. Note the following points:
   a. On cars with a manual transmission, coat the input shaft splines with chassis lube.
   b. Adjust the clutch cable.
   c. On cars with automatic transmission, coat the crankshaft recess with chassis lube.
   d. The painted mark on the torque converter (automatic transmission) must be aligned with the sharp-edged spoke on the flywheel. New bolts of equal grade must be used to attach the torque converter to the flywheel.
   e. Adjust the automatic speed control cable, the accelerator cable and adjust the upper grille crossmember as shown.

LeCar

NOTE: The engine must be removed together with the transaxle.

1. Raise the front of the car and support it on jackstands under the frame rails.

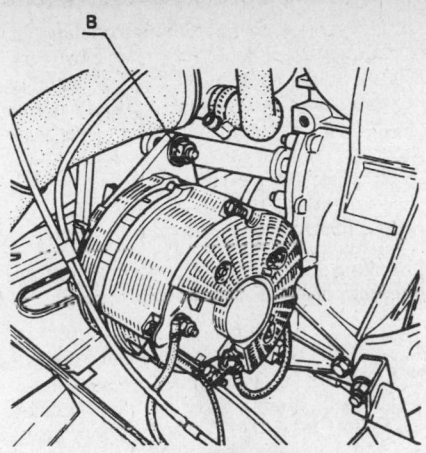

Typical alternator adjusting bolt

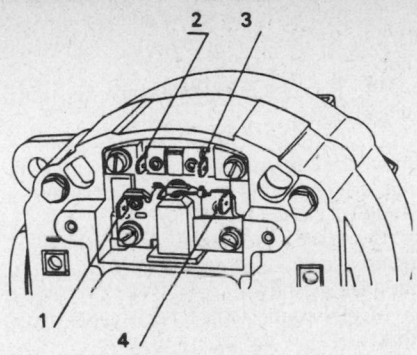

Typical alternator mounted regulator. The wiring colors are (1) black, (2) orange, (3) violet and (4) green

2. Disconnect and remove the battery.
3. Drain the cooling system at the radiator and block.
4. Drain the transaxle.
5. Remove the grille, the hood and the two cowl-to-inner fender support braces.
6. Remove the air cleaner.
7. Disconnect and tag all hoses, wires and cables attached to the engine, except for air conditioning and power steering hoses.
8. Remove the windshield washer bottle.
9. Remove the transaxle cover.
10. Remove the air cleaner support rod.
11. Disconnect the exhaust pipe at the manifold.
12. Remove the radiator, cooling fan and expansion tank.
13. Remove the steering column flexible coupling bolts.
14. Remove the front wheels.
15. Remove the brake calipers, but do not disconnect the brake lines. Support the calipers out of the way.
16. Disconnect the steering arms at the rack ends.
17. Disconnect the ball joints and tilt the spindles out of the way.
18. Unbolt and remove the steering gear box. Mark the right and left shims so that they can be installed properly to maintain steering box height.
19. Remove the air pump, filter and bracket.
20. An engine lifting frame is available which bolts under the two top engine-to-transaxle bolts. If one cannot be obtained, attach a shop crane or hoist in a manner which will maintain engine-transaxle balance while lifting. If the lifting frame (part # Mot. 498) is used, the bolts must be replaced with 1⅜ in. long bolts to adequately support the weight.
21. Take up the weight of the engine with the hoist or lifting device. Remove the engine mount bolts.
22. Unbolt the transaxle shift rod support.
23. Disconnect the clutch cable at the fork.
24. Remove the front transaxle mount.
25. Push the transaxle left and right to free the driveshaft ends.

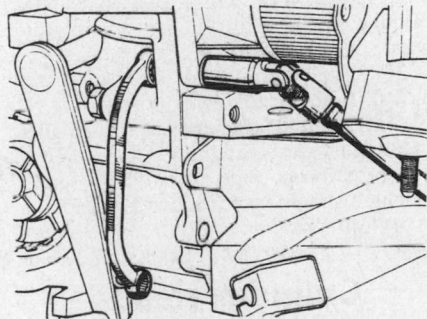

LeCar starter bolt removal

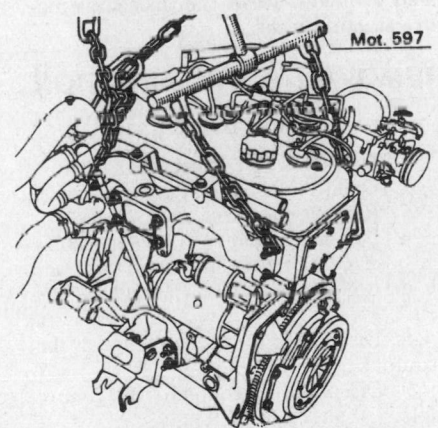

Engine lifting sling in position on the 18i or Fuego

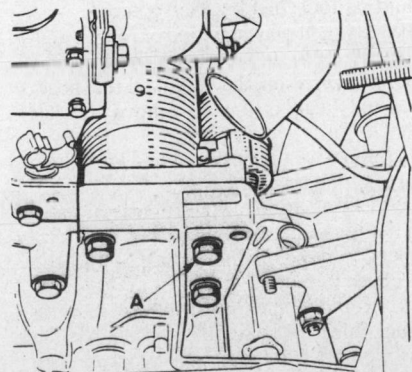

Alliance and Encore starter mounting bolts. (A) is the bolt that's easy to crossthread

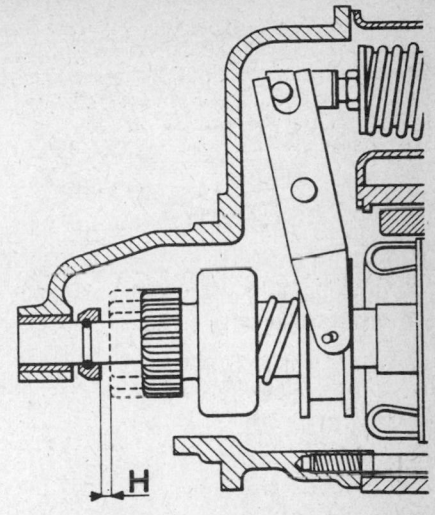

Starter drive adjustment. The gap is measured at (H)

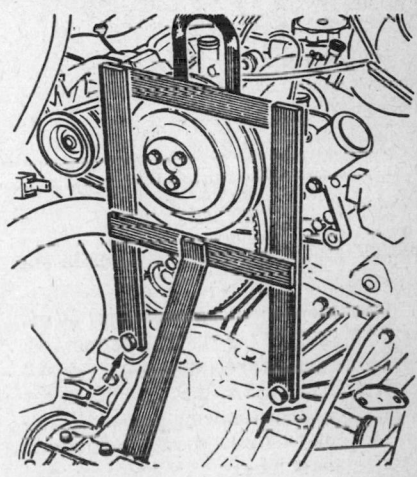

LeCar engine lifting fixture

Typical starter drive disassembly

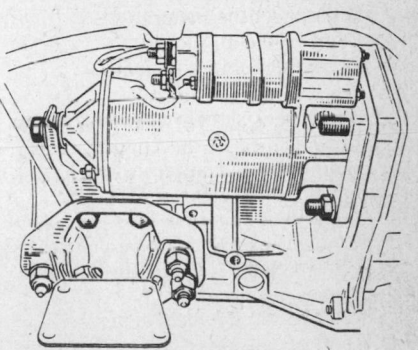

18i and Fuego starter mounting

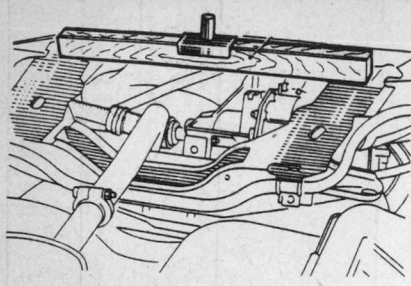

4 × 4 attached to the jack cradle for support on the Alliance

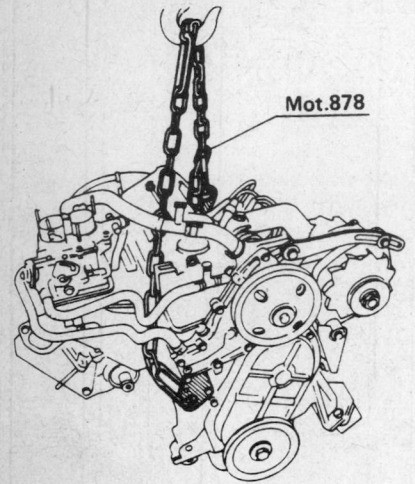

Engine lifting sling for the Alliance and Encore

26. Gradually lift the engine/transaxle assembly clear of the car.

27. Installation is the reverse of removal. Note the following points:

a. Lightly grease the driveshaft ends with chassis lube.

b. When installing the driveshaft ends, take care not to damage the seal lips. Make certain that the driveshaft ends fully engage the differential side gears.

c. Adjust the clutch.

d. Make sure to replace the rubber bushing at the steering flexible coupling.

e. Adjust the accelerator and choke cable.

Alliance and Encore

1. Remove the hood.
2. Disconnect the battery.
3. Remove the air cleaner.
4. Drain the cooling system.
5. Remove the radiator.
6. Disconnect and tag all wires, hoses and cables attached to the engine, except for air conditioning and power steering hoses. Raise and support the car on jackstands.
7. Drain the engine oil.
8. Remove the exhaust pipe clamp.
9. Remove the engine-to-transaxle support rod.
10. Remove the flywheel cover.
11. Remove all drive belts from the engine.

12. Remove the water pump.
13. Remove the crankshaft pulley and hub.
14. Remove the torque converter-to-flywheel bolts.
15. On cars with air conditioning, remove the compressor from its mounts without disconnecting the hoses, and position it out of the way.
16. Place a jack under the engine cradle, using a length of 4 × 4 lumber attached to the jack as shown.
17. Disconnect the clutch cable at the fork.
18. Remove the 5 engine-to-transaxle bolts.
19. Attach a shop crane or hoist to the engine and take up the weight.
20. Position a jack or jackstand under the transaxle and lift the engine, first forward, then up and out.
21. Installation is the reverse of removal. Note the following points:

a. Bleed the cooling system of air after filling.

b. Exhaust pipe clamp bolt spring length should be 1.7 in. at a bolt torque of 33 ft. lbs.

Cylinder Head

NOTE: A special tool is needed for head removal. Read the procedure before starting work.

REMOVAL & INSTALLATION

LeCar, Alliance and Encore

1. Disconnect the battery.
2. Drain the cooling system.
3. Remove the air cleaner.
4. Disconnect and tag all wires, cables and hoses connected to any part of the head.
5. Loosen the air pump and remove the belt.
6. Disconnect the exhaust pipe at the manifold.
7. Disconnect the hood lock control cable.
8. Remove the valve cover.
9. Remove all the cylinder head bolts, except the one next to the distributor, which should be loosened one half a turn.
10. Using a plastic, wood or rubber mallet, break the head loose from the liners by tapping *lightly* on the sides of the head. Once the head is loose, remove the last bolts.
11. Remove the pushrods and keep them in order for replacement.
12. Lift the head off the engine. Be careful, it's heavy.
13. Clean the mating surface of the head and block thoroughly.
14. Remove the manifolds, carburetor or fuel injection assemblies. Remove the spark plugs. Remove the rocker arm assembly.
15. Clean the threaded holes in the head with compressed air.

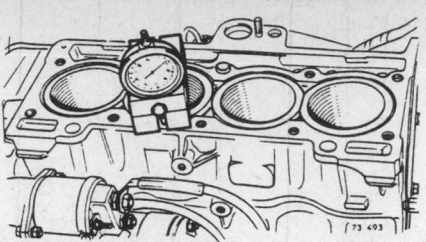

Checking liner protrusion on the LeCar, Alliance, and Encore

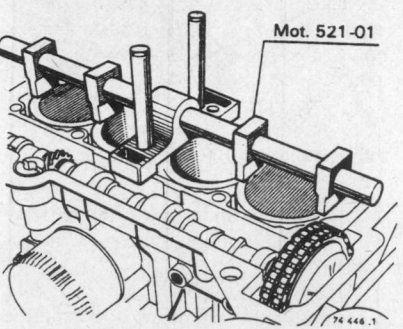

Liner retaining clamp installed

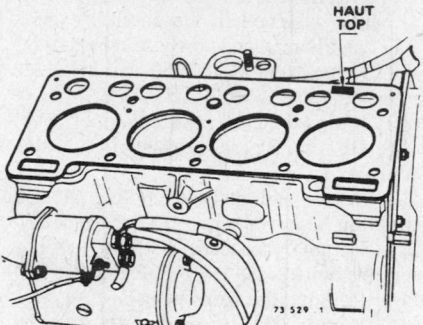

Head gasket installation on the LeCar, Alliance and Encore

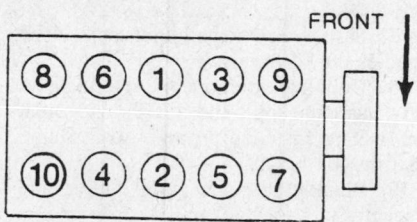

LeCar, Alliance and Encore head bolt torque sequence

16. Check the liner protrusion. Liner protrusion should be 0.0016—0.0050 in. If not, the liner bottom seals must be replaced.

17. Remove all other parts from the head except for the valves.

18. Using a stiff wire brush made for the purpose, mounted in an electric drill, clean the carbon from the cylinder head combustion chambers.

19. Lay a straight-edge across the head mating surface. Measure at different points between the head and the straight-edge with feeler gauges. The maximum gap should be 0.002 in. If deformation exceeds this,

the head must be milled flat. The minimum head height should be 1.870 in. If milling cuts below this, the head must be replaced.

20. If the valves are to be replaced, go on to "Valve Removal & Installation", later in the text.

21. If you'd like to decarbon the tops of the pistons at this time, or do anything which will result in the turning of the crankshaft, you'll need a special tool (Mot. 521) to hold the liners in place.

22. When you're ready to install the head, make sure you use a new gasket. Do not use sealer on the head gasket or on the water pump or end plate gaskets. The head gasket is positioned with the stamped word HAUTE-Top up. Place the gasket on the block and place the head in position. Make sure the gasket is still in alignment. Install the head bolts and hand tighten all of them. Torque the bolts to 40 ft. lb. in a circular pattern beginning at the middle and working towards the ends. All other parts should be installed in reverse order of removal.

18, 18i, Sport Wagon and Fuego through 1983, and Fuego Turbo through 1985

1. Disconnect the battery.
2. Drain the cooling system.
3. Remove the air cleaner.
4. Remove the grille and the grille upper crossmember.
5. Disconnect all wires, cables and hoses connected to any part on the head. Tag these for easy installation. On fuel injected cars, clamp off the injection hoses after removal to prevent fuel spillage.
6. Remove the valve cover.
7. Remove the water pump and alternator drive belts.
8. Remove the distributor.
9. Disconnect the exhaust pipe at the manifold. On cars with catalytic converters, remove the converter.
10. Remove the diagnostic connector.
11. Remove the alternator.
12. Remove the rocker arm shaft assembly.
13. Remove the pushrods, keeping them in order for replacement in their original positions.
14. Remove the rubber washers and cups in the spark plug recesses.
15. Remove the head bolts in the reverse order of the tightening sequence.
16. The head will stick to the cylinder liners. DO NOT ATTEMPT TO LIFT OFF THE HEAD BEFORE IT IS BROKEN LOOSE FROM THE LINERS! To break the head loose, tap around the head with a plastic, wood or rubber mallet, *gently*, and rotate the head using the built-in locating dowel in the block, near the distributor, as a pivot point.
17. Lift the head slightly, and remove the valve lifters, keeping them in order for replacement in their original locations.
18. Remove the head.

19. Remove the valve lifter housing gasket.

20. Using a special tool Mot. 521-01, secure the cylinder liners in place. Keep this tool in place the whole time the head is off. This tool prevents dislodgment of, or damage to, the liner seals.

21. Clean the mating surfaces of the head and block thoroughly. There must be no trace of old gasket material or other debris. Do not scrape the surfaces! If necessary, use a gasket dissolver, available in most auto parts stores.

22. Take care that no debris enters the oil, coolant or bolt holes. Clean these holes thoroughly.

23. All bolt holes must be free of any oil. Use a kitchen baster for this operation.

24. Decarbon the combustion chambers using brushes made for this purpose mounted in an electric drill. Remove all traces of carbon from the chambers and valve faces.

25. If the valves are being removed, skip on to "Valve Removal & Installation".

26. Lay a straight-edge across the face of the head. Using feeler gauges, check between the straight-edge and the head's gasket surface. There should be no gap ideally, but a gap of up to .002 in. is acceptable. Resurface the head if necessary. Most automotive machine shops perform this operation.

27. Check the head for any sign of cracks. Auto machine shops have ultraviolet crack detectors for this purpose.

28. Check the liner protrusion above the block surface. Protrusion should be 0.004–0.007 in. If not, the liner seals must be replaced.

29. Head installation is the reverse of removal. Note the following points:

   a. Never reuse a gasket.

   b. Cylinder head positioning is vitally important since it can effect alignment of the distributor shaft with its drive pinion. Renault recommends using an alignment gauge. Mot. 446 and aligning tool, Mot. 451, when installing the head.

   c. Once the head has been positioned on the block, the head gasket cannot be reused, if it is necessary to lift the head for any reason.

   d. When installing the head, be careful not to move the valve lifter chamber gasket.

   e. Make sure that the lifters are firmly seated in the head so they won't drop out during head installation.

   f. Lubricate the head bolts with a light coating of clean engine oil prior to insertion. Hand tighten all the bolts, then torque them to the value shown in the "Torque Specifications" chart, in the sequence shown.

   g. When assembly is complete, start the engine, allow it to reach normal operating temperature. Shut it off and allow it to cool for 50 minutes, then back off the bolts ½ turn in sequence and tighten each, in sequence to 60–65 ft. lb. Check rocker arm adjustment.

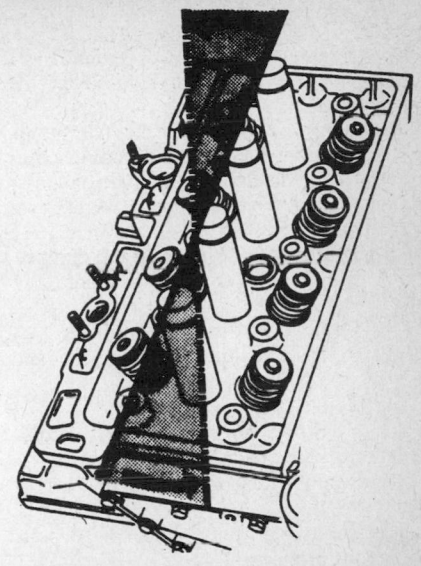

Breaking loose the 18i and Fuego cylinder head using the locating dowel, near the distributor, as a pivot point

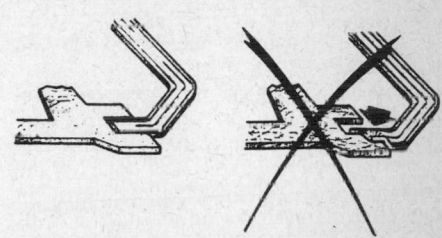

Correct gasket tab mating—18i and Fuego

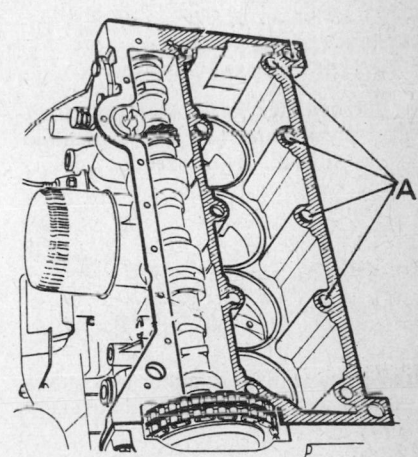

The four longest head bolts go in the holes marked R—18i and Fuego

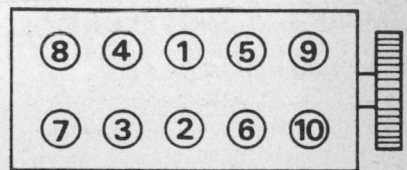

Cylinder head bolt torque sequence for 18i and Fuego, 1.6 & 2.2L engines

1984–85 Fuego 2.2L

1. Disconnect the battery ground.
2. Remove the drive belts from the accessories.
3. Remove the alternator and AIR pump.
4. Remove the air conditioning compressor from its mounts, but do not disconnect the refrigerant lines. Wire it securely out of the way.
5. Drain the coolant from the engine.
6. Remove the crankshaft balancer.
7. Remove the manifolds.
8. Remove the timing belt cover.
9. Release the timing belt tensioner and remove the belt.
10. Remove the rocker cover.
11. Hold the camshaft sprocket firmly. There are tools made for this purpose.
12. Remove the sprocket nut and lift off the sprocket.
13. Remove all the cylinder head bolts except the front right one.
14. Loosen the remaining bolt and pivot the head on it to break the head loose from the liners. It may be necessary to get the head moving by tapping it with a wood mallet.
15. Install cylinder liner clamp #588 on the block.
16. Installation is the reverse of removal. Make sure that all gasket material is removed from the mating surfaces. Always use a new gasket. The dowel at the right front of the head will help you in aligning the head during installation. Follow the sequence illustrated when tightening the head bolts. Tighten the bolts first to 37 ft. lb., then 59 ft. lb., then back them off ½ turn and retorque them to 64–72 ft. lb.

Overhaul

For all cylinder head overhaul procedures, please refer to "Engine Rebuilding" in the Unit Repair section.

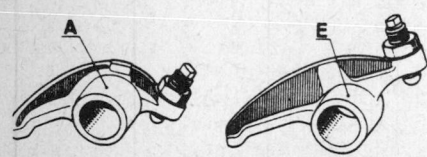

On engines with dual rocker arm shafts, the intake arms (A), and the exhaust arms (E), are different

Rocker Arms and/or Rocker Shaft

REMOVAL & INSTALLATION

LeCar, Alliance and Encore

1. Remove the rocker arm cover.
2. Loosen the rocker arm shaft retaining bolts a little at a time each, working alternately from the ends towards the center. When the bolts are loose, remove them and the rocker shaft.

3. Place the shaft on a clean work surface.
4. Remove the retaining clips from the shaft ends.
5. Remove the spring, rocker arm, pedestal, etc., in turn. Keep all parts in the same order of which they were removed! Make sure you know which side of the shaft is up! The oil holes must face downward!

NOTE: If some of the pedestals are stuck, do not hammer them off. Use a penetrating oil to free them.

6. Clean the shaft of deposits. Clean the inside surfaces of the rocker arms and make certain that all oil passages are clear. Check the bearing surface of each rocker arm for wear, scratches or other damage.
7. Freely lubricate the parts with clean engine oil.
8. Install the parts in reverse order of disassembly so that all parts are in their original places.
9. Place the shaft on the head, install the bolts and tighten them a little at a time, in turn, from the center toward the ends, to 10–15 ft. lb.

18, 18i, Sport Wagon and Fuego through 1983 and Fuego Turbo through 1985

1. Remove the rocker arm cover.
2. Remove the rocker shaft attaching bolts from the pedestals and lift off the rocker arm assembly.
3. Using a thin punch, drive the roll pins from opposite ends of the shaft assemblies.
4. Slide the parts off of the shafts, keeping them in the same order in which they were on the shafts.
5. Clean all the parts in a safe solvent.
6. Check the bearing surfaces of the rocker arms for wear, scratches or other damage. Replace them if they are badly damaged. Check the rocker arms for signs of cracking. Check the shafts, at the point where the rocker arms ride, for wear or scratches. Check that the springs are in good condition.
7. Coat all parts liberally with clean engine oil.
8. Assemble all parts in exactly the same place that they originally were.

NOTE: The oil holes in the shafts must face downward.

9. Place the rocker arm shaft assembly on the head. Install the bolts and tighten them a little at a time each, starting at the center and working toward the ends. Final tightening torque should be 25 ft. lb.

1984–85 Fuego 2.2L

NOTE: The rocker shaft assembly retaining bolts are also the head bolts.

1. Remove the rocker cover.
2. Remove the head bolts and lift off the rocker shaft assembly.

3. Remove the end plug and filter from one end and the roll pin from the other.
4. Slide the components from the shaft, keeping them in order.

NOTE: Never hammer the components from the shaft. If they won't come off, use liberal amounts of gum-dissolving compound on the shaft.

5. Installation is the reverse of removal. See the Cylinder Head bolt torque illustration and read the last step of the "Cylinder Head" procedure.

Valves

REMOVAL

All Engines

1. Remove the cylinder head.
2. Remove the rocker arm shaft assembly.
3. Using a valve spring compressor, available in most auto parts stores, compress the valve springs, remove the keepers (they are also called keys or locks), remove the spring retaining collars and release the springs. Remove the springs and the base collars.
4. Some engines have rubber valve stem seals. If so remove these and discard them. Slide the valve from the valve guide.

INSPECTION, CLEANING AND REFACING

1. Using a stiff wire, drill-mounted brush, remove all traces of carbon and other deposits from the valve.

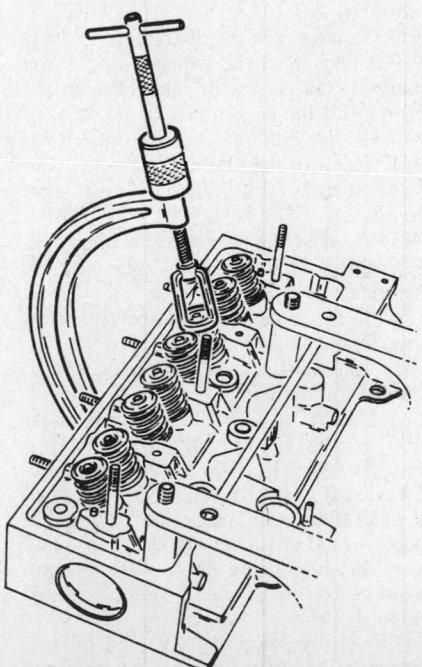

Typical valve spring compressor tool for valve removal

2. Check the valves for cracks, excessive scoring or pitting and other damage. If cracked or excessively damaged, especially in the face area, replace them.

3. Check the valve stems for bending. If at all bent, replace the valve. Check the stem for wear; if the stem is worm beyond the diameter shown in the "Valve Specifications" chart, replace it.

4. Using a valve grinding tool, reface the valves to the degree shown in the "Valve Specifications" chart.

5. Coat the valve face with a dye such as Prussian Blue and insert it into the head. Holding the stem, turn the valve in its seat and carefully remove it. The dye should be distributed evenly on the valve face and seat. If not, check the angle ground on the seat. It may need regrinding. If no good contact can be established by grinding, replace the valve.

INSTALLATION

1. Coat the face of each valve with lapping compound and insert them into the head. Using a lapping tool, turn the valves in the seat to establish a finely honed and polished fit. Remove any left-over lapping compound.

2. Assembly is the reverse of removal.

NOTE: Make sure that the keepers are firmly seated. Make sure that the closer coils of the springs are at the bottom.

Valve Guides

ALL ENGINES

The guides are replaceable. However, a press is needed for this job.

1. Press the old guide out from the top side of the head.

2. Check the guide to see if it is original equipment or an oversize replacement. The outside diameter of the replacement guide must be one size larger than the one it is replacing. Oversize guides are available in two sizes and are identified by grooves cut in the outside diameter. Use the chart below to determine the oversize guide that you need:

Engine	Original OD	One Groove	Two Grooves
1289cc	.433 (11mm)	.437 (11.1mm)	.443 (11.25mm)
1397cc	.433 (11mm)	.437 (11.1mm)	.443 (11.25mm)
1647cc	.512 (13mm)	.516 (13.1mm)	.522 (13.25)
2165cc	.512 (13mm)	.521 (13.25mm)	—

3. Ream the valve guide hole in the head to accept the new guide.

4. Press the new guide into place. Check the distance between the valve seat and the end of the guide.

Engine	Intake	Exhaust
1289, 1397cc	1.043 in.	1.032 in.
1647cc	1.437 in.	1.161 in.
2165cc	1.220 in.	1.290 in.

5. Ream the guide bore to the proper ID as shown in the "Valve Specifications" chart.

Intake/Exhaust Manifold

REMOVAL & INSTALLATION

Canadian R–18

1. Disconnect the battery ground.
2. Remove the air cleaner.
3. Drain the cooling system to a level below the manifold.
4. Disconnect the linkage at the carburetor.
5. Disconnect the manifold coolant hoses.
6. Remove the carburetor.
7. Unbolt and remove the manifold.
8. Clean the old gasket material from the mating surfaces. Always use a new gasket.
9. Installation is the reverse of removal. Torque the bolts to the value shown in the torque chart.

18i, Sport Wagon and Fuego

The intake manifold is designed as an integral part of the fuel injection system, and is disassembled with that system's components.

LeCar, Alliance (Exc. Calif.) and Encore

1. Disconnect the battery ground.
2. Remove the air cleaner.
3. Drain the cooling system to a point just below the manifold.
4. Disconnect the linkage from the carburetor or Throttle Body Injection (TBI) unit.
5. Disconnect the manifold coolant hoses.
6. Remove the carburetor or TBI unit.
7. Unbolt and remove the manifolds.
8. Installation is the reverse of removal. Make sure that the mating surfaces are clean and that a new gasket is used. Torque the bolts to the value shown in the "Torque Specifications" chart.

Alliance Built for Sale in California

The intake manifold and exhaust manifold are integral with the fuel injection system and may be disassembled with that system's components.

Exhaust Manifold

REMOVAL & INSTALLATION

18i, Sport Wagon and Fuego

1. Remove the air cleaner.
2. Unbolt the exhaust pipe from the manifold.
3. Unbolt the manifold from its bracket and the head. Lift off the manifold.
4. Installation is the reverse of removal.

Turbocharger

For information on the turbocharger, please refer to "Turbocharging" in the Unit Repair section.

Timing Chain Cover, Chain and Seal

REMOVAL & INSTALLATION

LeCar

1. Remove the engine/transaxle assembly from the vehicle according to the "Engine Removal and Installation" procedure in the beginning of this section.
2. Remove the timing cover and clean all of the gasket surfaces.
3. If the timing chain is to be replaced, secure the shoe of the tensioner (component that actually contacts the chain) to the body of the tensioner with a piece of wire.
4. Remove the chain tensioner assembly.
5. Remove the camshaft sprocket bolt and install a suitable puller. Tighten the puller to draw the camshaft sprocket and chain off of the camshaft.
6. If the crankshaft gear is to be replaced, draw the gear off of the crankshaft with a suitable puller.
7. Press the crankshaft sprocket onto the crankshaft using a suitable tool.
8. Temporarily install the camshaft sprocket (marking facing outward) without the timing chain and align the timing marks.

— CAUTION —

Do not rotate either the camshaft or the crankshaft once the timing marks are aligned.

9. Remove the camshaft sprocket.
10. Position the timing chain onto the camshaft sprocket and reinstall the camshaft sprocket/timing chain assembly, making sure that the timing marks are aligned properly.
11. Install the camshaft sprocket retaining bolt and torque the bolt to 20 ft. lbs.
12. Install the timing chain tensioner.
13. Using a new gasket and cover-to-oil pan seal, install the timing cover.

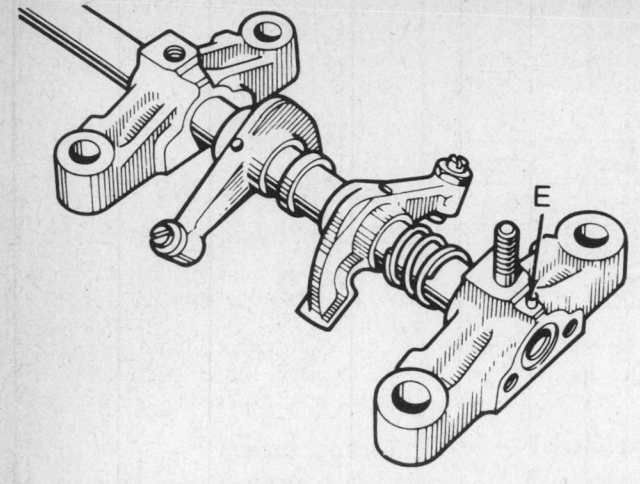

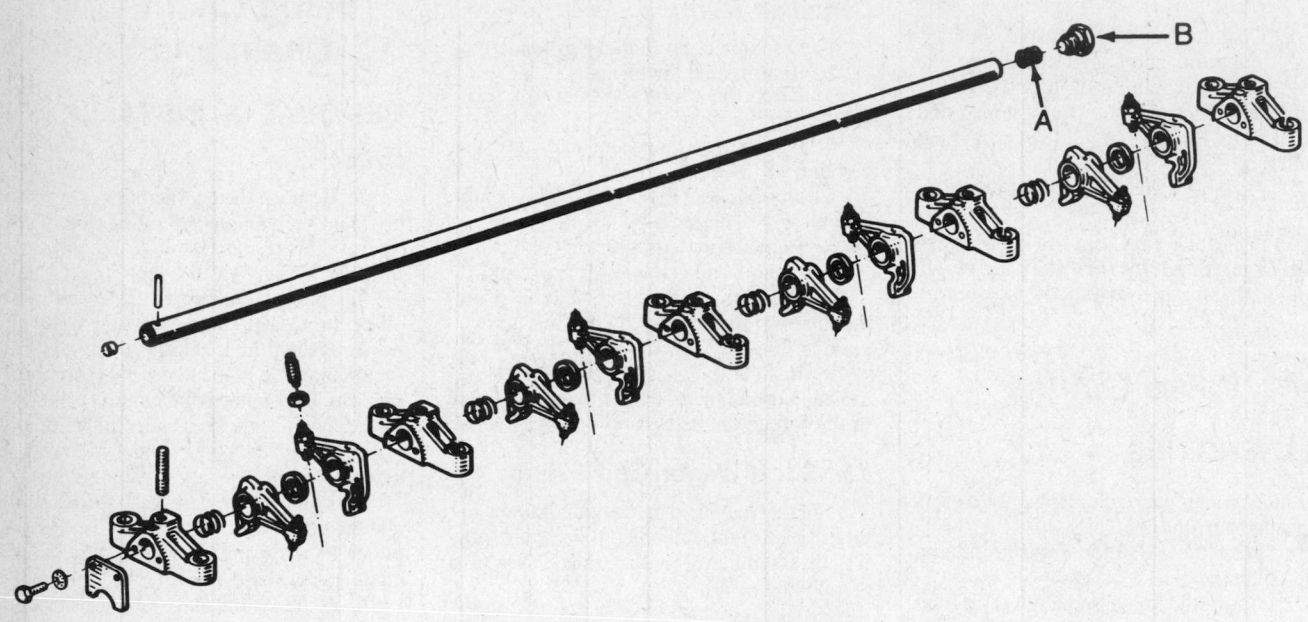

2.2L Fuego Engine rocker arm shaft assembly. E is the retaining pin, B is the end cap and A is the filter

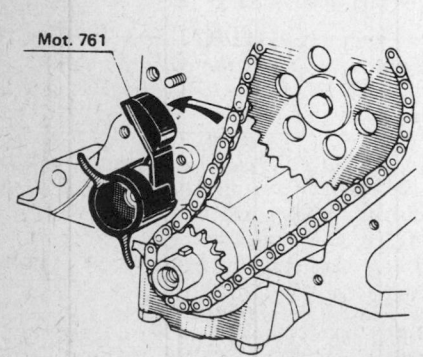

Using a special tool to remove the Alliance chain tensioner

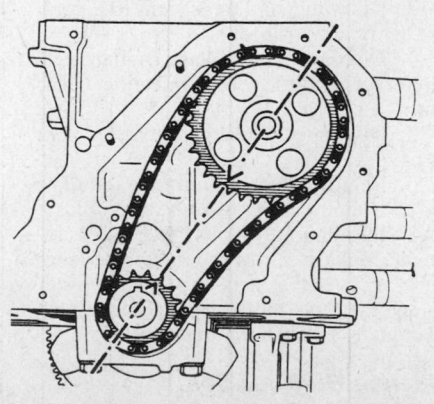

Timing chain alignment on the 1289 and 1397cc engines

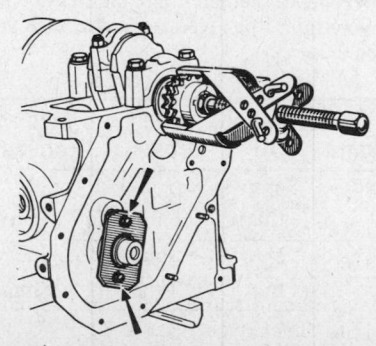

Removing the crankshaft sprocket and arrows showing the location of the camshaft flange screws on 1289 and 1397cc engines

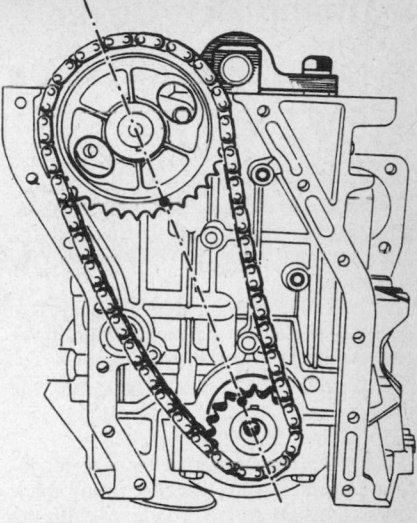

14. Install the engine/transaxle assembly according to the "Engine Removal and Installation" procedure in the beginning of this section.

Alliance and Encore

1. Disconnect the battery ground.
2. Drain the engine oil.
3. Remove the engine support rod and spacer.
4. Remove the oil pan.
5. Remove the air conditioning compressor belt.
6. Remove the water pump belt, pulley and hub.
7. On cars with air conditioning, place a jack under the engine cradle, remove the two bolts on the right side of the cradle and lower the jack until the pulley clears the crossmember.
8. Remove the timing chain cover. Crank the engine until the V shaped timing marks on the sprockets are aligned.
9. Move the chain tensioner as far as possible from the chain and secure it out of the way.
10. Remove the tensioner.
11. Remove the camshaft sprocket bolt, pull the sprocket loose with a three-jawed puller and remove the sprocket and chain.
12. To pull the crankshaft sprocket, you must machine a large depression into the head of a bolt that will fit into the nose of the crankshaft. Use this bolt as a center point for a puller.
13. Installation is the reverse of removal. Some later models have a timing cover assembled with RTV silicone gasket material in place of a paper gasket. Use only this material when assembling. The camshaft sprocket bolt is torqued to 22 ft. lb. Make sure that the timing marks are aligned.

18, 18i, Sport Wagon and Fuego

1. Disconnect the battery cables.
2. Remove the cylinder head, distributor and distributor drive gear.
3. Remove the radiator.
4. Remove the crankshaft pulley retaining bolt. Using a suitable puller, remove the crankshaft pulley.
5. Remove the timing cover; raise the engine if necessary to gain working clearance.
6. Remove the timing chain guide shoes and chain tensioner.
7. Remove the two camshaft retaining bolts.
8. Using a suitable puller, remove the crankshaft sprocket and key along with the timing chain.
9. Position the timing chain onto the camshaft sprocket. Position the camshaft sprocket timing mark so that the mark points toward the crankshaft centerline.
10. Install the crankshaft key and rotate the crankshaft so that the key faces up.
11. Place the crankshaft sprocket inside the timing chain to simulate installation.

Make sure that the timing marks align properly.
12. After the marks have been aligned as necessary, install the crankshaft sprocket and timing chain.
13. Install the following items:
   a. Camshaft retaining bolts
   b. Timing chain tensioner
   c. Timing chain guide shoes—push the chain guides against Renault gauge Mot. 420 (or its equivalent) and tighten the guide bolts.
   d. Timing cover, using a new gasket and seal
   e. Radiator
   f. Crankshaft pulley
   g. Cylinder head, distributor drive gear and distributor. Time engine.
14. Reconnect the battery cables.

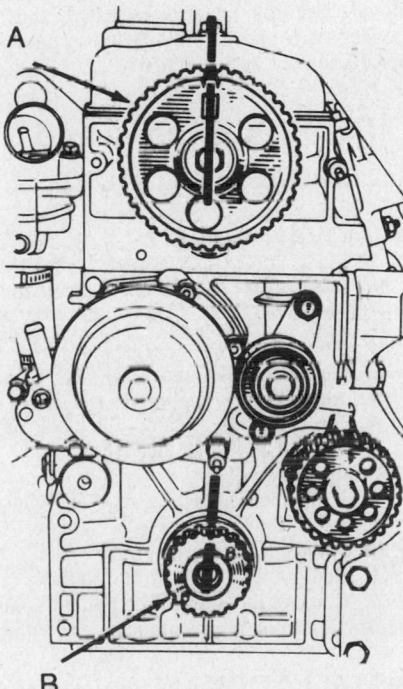

2.2L timing belt installation. A is the camshaft sprocket; B is the crankshaft sprocket

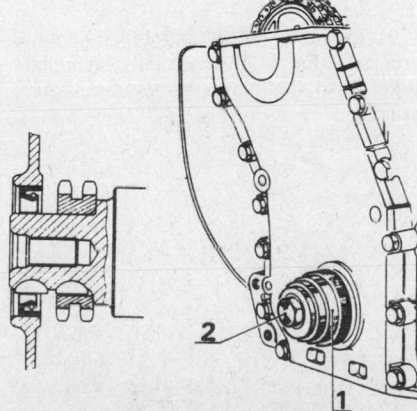

18i and Fuego timing cover seal installation. (1) is the seal sleeve; (2) is the installing bolt used to press the seal into place

18i and Fuego timing gear alignment

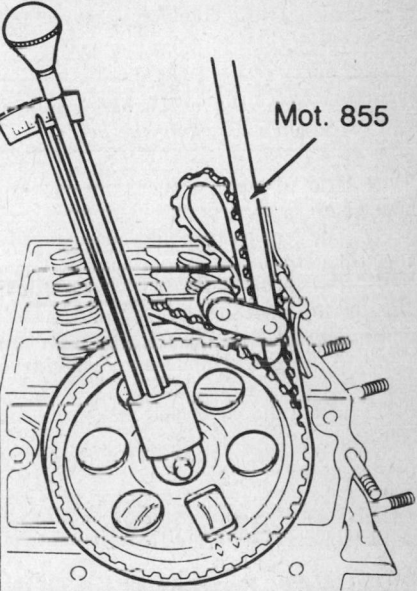

A camshaft holding tool in place on the 2.2L engine

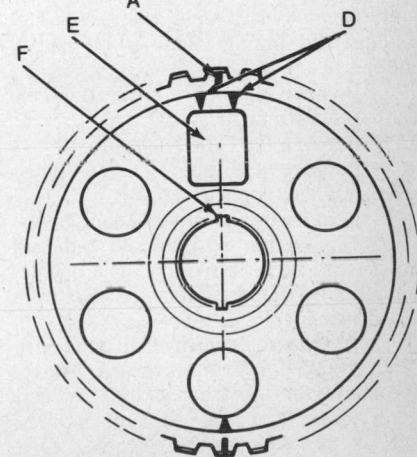

The camshaft sprocket on the 2.2L engine has a timing index (A), two bosses (D), a rectangular hole (E) and a keyway (F) all of which are used for valve adjustments

Timing Belt Cover

REMOVAL & INSTALLATION

2.2L OHC Engines

1. Follow Steps 1–9 of "Cylinder Head Removal & Installation", omitting Step 5.

2. For installation, position the camshaft sprocket timing mark in line with the static timing mark as shown in the illustration.

3. Position the crankshaft so that No. 1 piston is at TDC on the compression stroke as shown in the illustration.

4. Install the timing belt on the sprockets.

5. Tighten the tensioner.

6. Place the timing belt cover in position and make sure that the timing mark on the camshaft sprocket indexes with the cover notch.

7. Remove the cover and rotate the crankshaft two complete revolutions clockwise.

——— CAUTION ———
NEVER rotate the crankshaft counterclockwise when adjusting the belt.

8. Loosen the tensioner bolts ¼ turn, maximum.

9. The tensioner should automatically adjust the belt to the proper tension.

10. Tighten the bottom tensioner bolt first, then the top, to 18 ft. lb.

11. Timing belt deflection, mid-point along its longest straight run, should be 7mm.

12. Install the cover and make sure the belt doesn't rub.

Camshaft

REMOVAL & INSTALLATION

OHV Engines

1. Remove the timing cover, camshaft sprocket and timing chain as previously outlined.

2. Remove the valve cover (and the pushrods where applicable).

3. Remove the cylinder head.

4. Remove the air injection pump sprocket where applicable.

5. Remove the camshaft flange screws.

6. Temporarily reinstall the camshaft sprocket (to assist in removal as a handle) and carefully withdraw the camshaft from the engine.

7. Remove the camshaft oil seal.

8. Installation is the reverse of the removal procedure. Take note of the following:

a. On LeCar and Alliance models, check the clearance between the camshaft and the flange with a feeler gauge. The clearance should be between 0.002–0.005 in. If the clearance is excessive, the flange should be replaced.

b. On 18i and Fuego engines, make sure there is .012–.020 in. clearance between the chain and the tensioner pads.

c. Use the proper seal installation tool to install a new camshaft oil seal.

d. Install the camshaft from the timing chain end of the engine.

OHC Engines

1. Remove the rocker cover.

2. Remove the rocker shaft assembly.

3. Remove the camshaft thrust plate.

4. Remove the timing belt and camshaft sprocket as described earlier.

5. Remove the camshaft oil seal, taking great care to avoid scratching the seal bore.

6. Slide the camshaft from the head.

7. Installation is the reverse of removal. See the procedures listed under Rocker Arm and Timing Belt for proper installations of components.

Pistons, Liners and Connecting Rods

REMOVAL

NOTE: Special tools are required for this procedure.

1. Remove the cylinder head.

2. Remove the oil pan.

3. Remove the oil pump.

4. Place the liner clamp, in place on the block (see "Cylinder Head" section for illustration).

5. Mark the connecting rods and caps for reassembly. Note that No. 1 cylinder is at the flywheel end.

6. Remove the connecting rod caps.

7. Remove the liner clamp and pull out the liner and piston assemblies.

INSTALLATION

NOTE: Special tools are required for this procedure.

1. Clean the head and block mating surfaces using a commercially available gasket dissolver. Never scrape the mating surfaces.

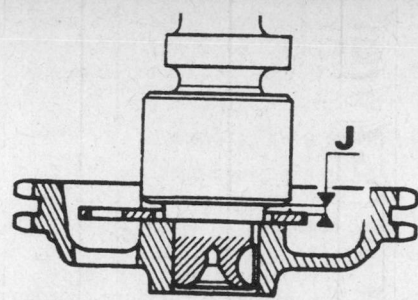

Checking the camshaft flange clearance on 18i and Fuego engines

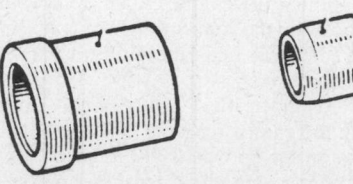

Camshaft oil seal installation tool

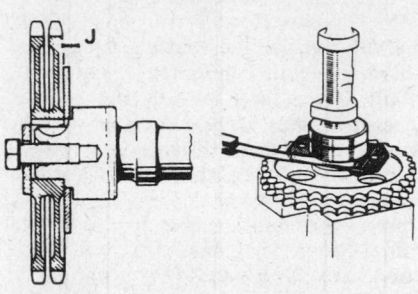

Checking the camshaft flange clearance on LeCar, Alliance and Encore

2. Thoroughly clean the block bores, the liner seal locations and the crankshaft.

NOTE: Liners, pistons, rings and piston pins are sold in matched sets. No honing of the liners is necessary. No adjustments to the rings are possible.

3. Obtain a new, matched set of liner-piston assemblies. Mark each in order, one through four to assure easy installation.

4. All of the new parts are coated with an anti-rust film. Remove this film with a safe solvent.

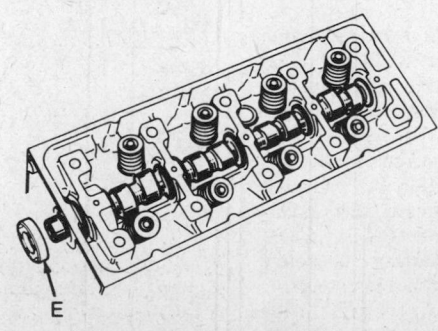

2.2L camshaft oil seal (E)

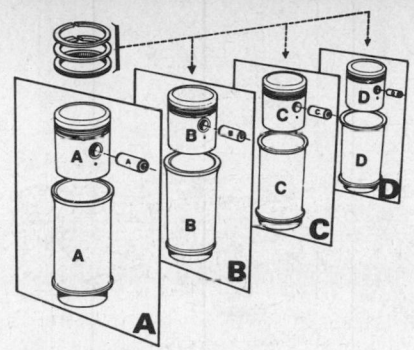

Liner, piston and ring assembly in kit form. Note markings

5. Drive the piston pins from the old piston and rod assemblies and assemble the new pistons to the rods using the new pins. If there is any difficulty inserting the new pins into the rods, the rods must be heated to 482°F (250°C). A special hot plate tool is available for this purpose. Since only the affected end of the rod should be heated to this degree, this tool, rather than an oven, is recommended. The tool number is Mot.574.

NOTE: When assembling the piston and rod, make sure that the arrow on the piston top faces the flywheel end of the engine and the mark made on the connecting rod faces the side away from the camshaft. The piston and rod must be assembled quickly to avoid heat loss. A press and mandrel are essential for rapid assembly. If one cannot be obtained, this job is best left to a machine shop. The pin must not protrude beyond the piston skirt on either side.

6. The piston rings are pregapped. There is no adjustment possible. Use a ring compressor/expander to install the rings. The rings gaps should be staggered 90° apart, so that no two gaps line up. When installing the compression rings, make sure that the side stamped with an O faces up.

7. With the rings installed, lubricate the piston assembly with clean engine oil. Using a ring compressor, slide the piston/rod assembly into the liner. The machined sides of the connecting rod big end must be parallel with the flat edge on top of the liner.

8. Place the upper bearing half into the rod.

NOTE: When installing the liners, it is necessary to determine what thickness seals to use. To do this you must measure the liner protrusion above the block surface. Check the protrusion at two opposite points as shown and subtract the greater figure from 0.005 in. Choose a seal equal to or just above the result obtained by subtraction. Seals are identified by a color spot to indicate thickness: Blue is 0.033 in., Red is 0.004 in., and Green is 0.005 in. thick. Place the new seals on the liners, insert the liners, press them down by hand, and recheck their protrusion according to the "Piston and

Liner" chart. The difference between liners should not exceed 0.0016 in.

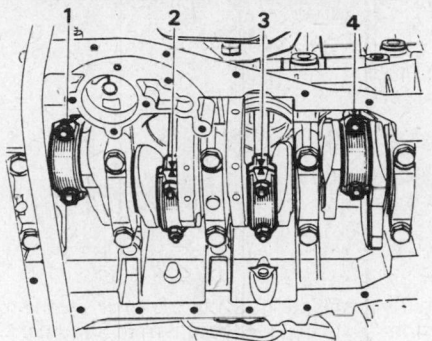

Marking the connecting rod caps

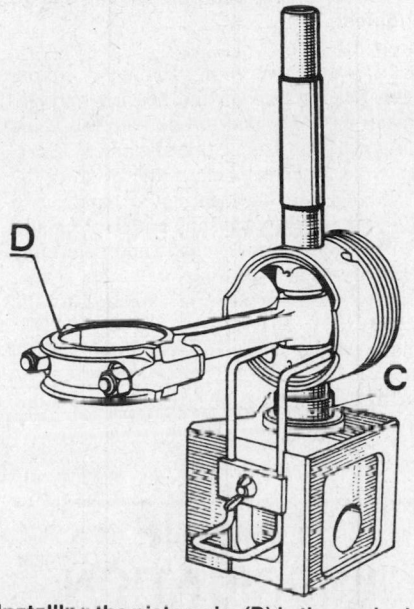

Installing the piston pin. (D) is the marked side of the rod; (C) is the thrust collar

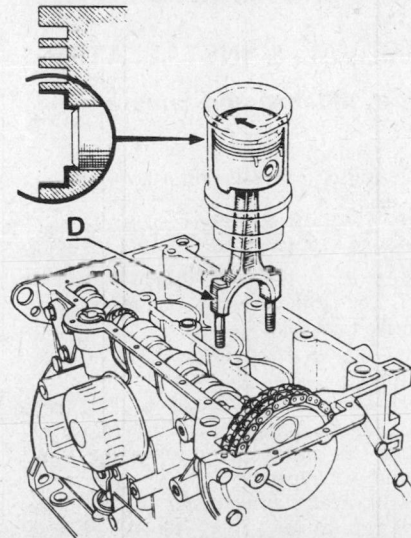

Proper pin installation should have the pin recess showing on the same side of the piston as the arrow denoting forward, which is stamped on top of the piston. (D) is the marked side of the rod

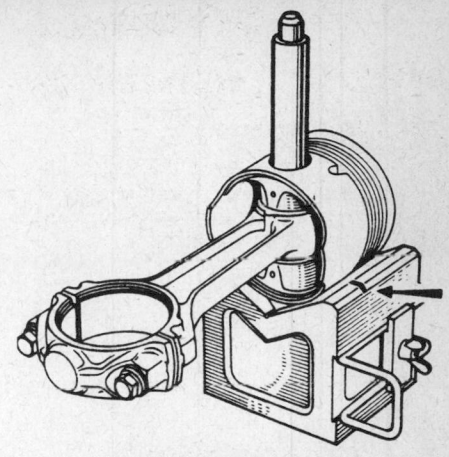

Removing the piston pin

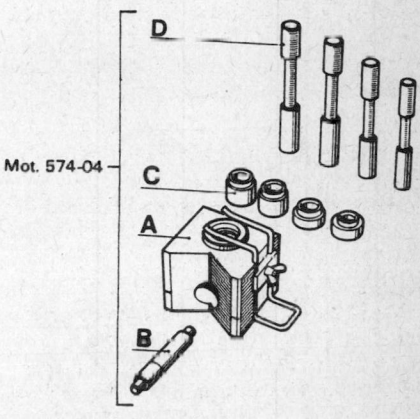

Mot. 574-04

Piston pin removal and installation tool

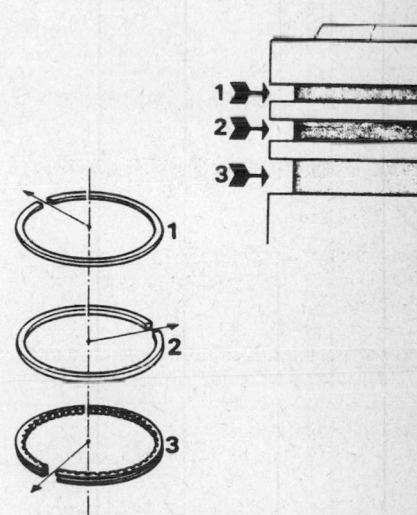

Proper piston ring installation

9. Slide the liner assemblies, in order, into the block. Don't forget that No. 1 is at the flywheel end of the block. The arrows on the pistons must face the flywheel.

10. Position the liner clamp on the block.

11. Lubricate the crankshaft journals and pull each rod down into contact with the journals.

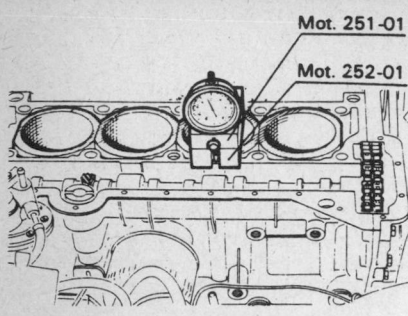
Measuring liner protrusion

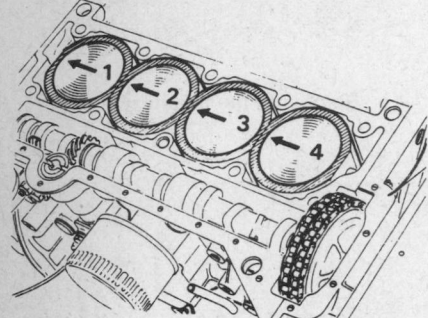
Piston and liner assemblies installed

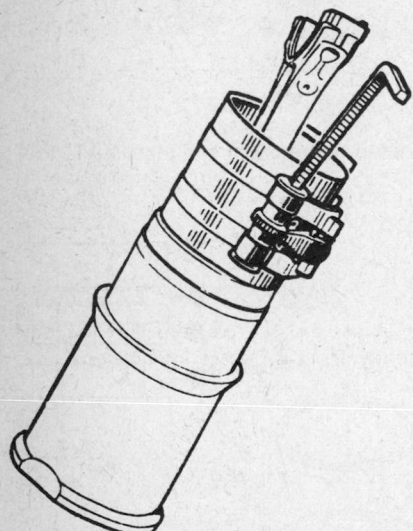
Installing the piston and rod assembly into the liner with a ring compressor

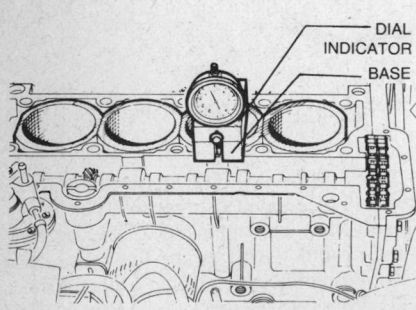
Checking liner protrusion with dial indicator

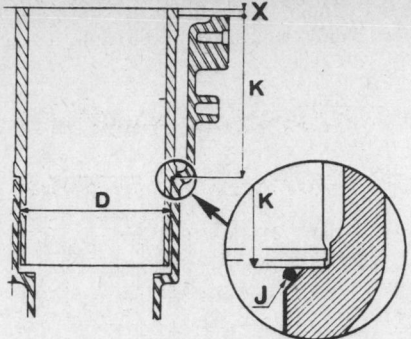
Liner installation. (X) is the liner protrusion; (K) is the liner height from shoulder to top; (D) is the liner width and (J) is the base seal O-ring used on 18i and Fuego engines

12. Lay a piece of Plastigage® across each bearing cap on the bearing surface. Install each cap and torque it to the value shown in the "Torque Specifications" chart. Remove the cap and check the width of the Plastigage® on the bearing, compare it to the bearing clearance shown in the "Crankshaft Specifications" chart, and determine if you need new bearings.

13. Install the bearing caps and torque them.

14. Make sure that everything moves freely.

15. Assembly is the reverse of disassembly from here on.

ENGINE LUBRICATION

Oil Pan

REMOVAL & INSTALLATION

LeCar, Alliance and Encore

1. Drain the oil.
2. Raise and support the car on jackstands.
3. Remove the front anti-sway bar bushings.
4. Remove the lower transaxle shield.
5. Unbolt the gearshift control bracket from the transaxle.
6. Remove the right, lateral reinforcement piece.
7. Remove the clutch shield.
8. Place a floor jack under the nose of the transaxle and support it so that the front pad can be removed.
9. Raise the front of the transaxle as much as possible.
10. Remove the oil pan bolts. Tilt down the front of the pan and turn the crankshaft so that the crankshaft throws do not interfere with pan removal. Remove the pan and gaskets.

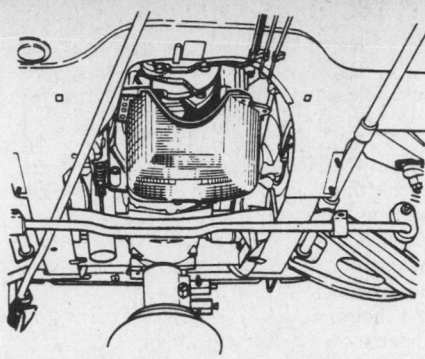
Oil pan removal on LeCar, Alliance and Encore. Note position of the crankshaft

11. Installation is the reverse of removal. Make sure that the mating surfaces are clean. Coat the new gasket and seals with sealer.

18, 18i, Sport Wagon and Fuego

1. Raise and support the car on jackstands.
2. Drain the oil.
3. Remove the oil pan bolts and lower the pan.
4. Installation is the reverse of removal. Make sure that the mating surfaces are free of old gasket material and dirt. Never reuse a gasket. Coat the gasket surfaces with sealer, position the gasket and seals on the pan, install the pan and tighten the bolts to 5–7 ft. lb. (60–84 inch lb.).

Oil Pump

REMOVAL & INSTALLATION

All Engines

1. Remove the oil pan.
2. Unbolt and remove the pump and pick-up.
3. Installation is the reverse of removal.

OVERHAUL

LeCar, Alliance and Encore

1. Remove the four pump cover bolts.

NOTE: Don't let the ball seat, ball and pressure limiter valve jump out!

2. Remove the driven gear, drive gear and drive gear shaft.
3. Clean all the parts in solvent. Check each part for signs of wear or damage. Replace parts as needed.
4. Check the pump seal surface. If the surface is at all marked, it must be polished or reground to remove the marks.
5. Check the clearance between the gears and pump body. Maximum clearance is 0.008 in. If the clearance exceeds that figure, the gears must be replaced.
6. Assembly is the reverse of disassembly.

18, 18i, Sport Wagon and Fuego

1. Remove the pick-up tube bolts.
2. Remove the cotter pin from the pressure release valve and take out the spring cup, spring and piston.
3. Remove the rotors.
4. Clean all parts in a safe solvent and check them for wear or damage. Replace parts as necessary.
5. Check the rotor clearance as shown. In position 1, the clearance (A) should be 0.002–0.011 in. In position 2, clearance (B) should be 0.001–0.006 in. If the clearance exceeds these figures, replace the rotors.

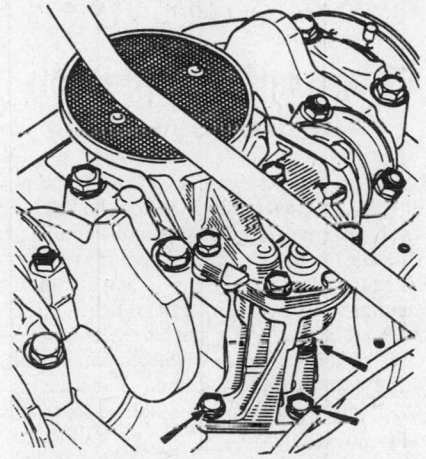

LeCar, Alliance and Encore oil pump

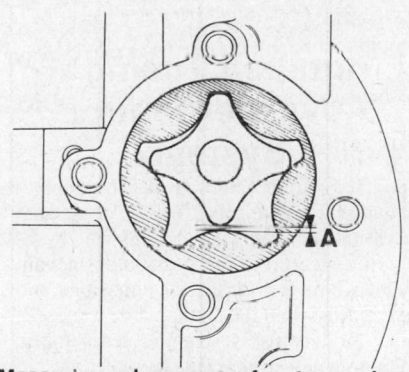

Measuring clearance of rotors—clearance from 0.002 to 0.011 inch (A clearance)

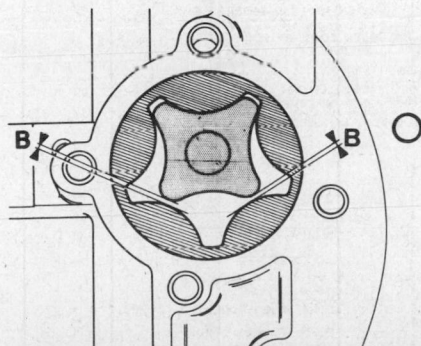

Measuring clearance of rotors—clearance from 0.001 to 0.006 inch (B clearance)

6. Assembly is the reverse of disassembly.

Rear Main Seal

REMOVAL & INSTALLATION

OHV Engines

1. Remove the transmission.
2. Remove the clutch, or torque converter.
3. Remove the flywheel.
4. Pry out the old seal.
5. Coat the new seal with clean engine oil and, using a seal driver, install the new seal in its bore until firmly seated.
6. Install the other parts in reverse order of removal.

OHC Engines

NOTE: There are main seals at each end of the crankshaft. Each seal is replaced in the same manner. If the rear seal is replaced, the engine must be removed.

1. Raise and support the car on jackstands.
2. Remove the oil pan.

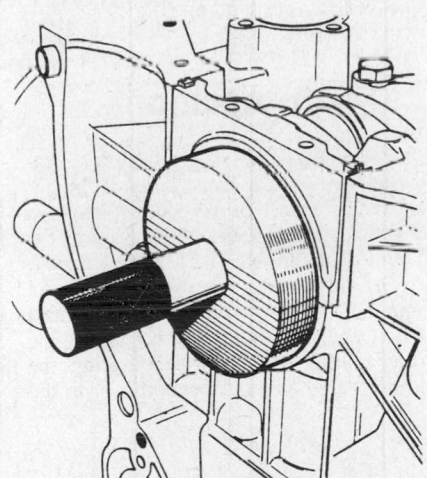

Rear main oil seal installation

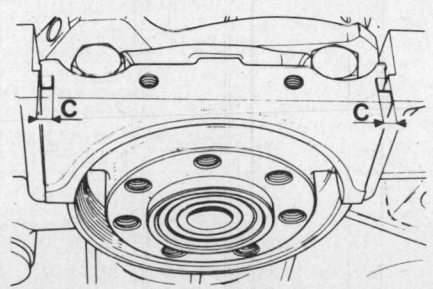

Measure the distance (C) between the bearing cap and the block on the 2.2L

3. Replacement seals are available in two sizes: 5.4mm and 5.1mm thick. Measure the distance between the bearing cap and the block (C in the illustration). If the distance is 5mm or less, use a 5.1mm seal. If the distance is greater, use the larger seal.
4. Remove the cap and pull out the old seal.
5. Insert the side seals in the cap with the groove facing outward. Each side seal should protrude about 0.2mm outward from the cap.

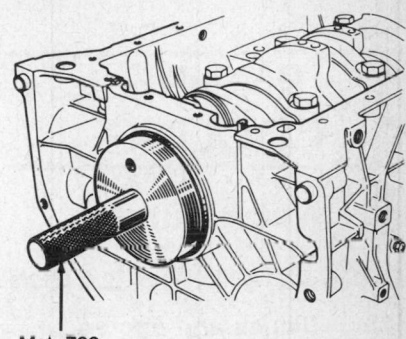

Mot. 788

Installing rear circular seal on the 2.2L crankshaft

Position a strip of foil (B) on each side of the bearing cap before installation

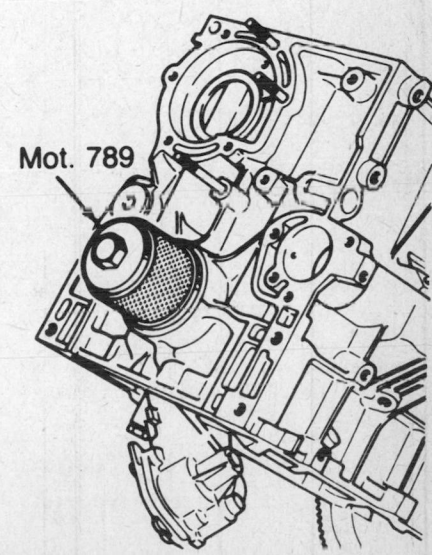

Mot. 789

Installing the front circular seal on the 2.2L crankshaft

6. Lubricate the contact surfaces of the side seals with clean engine oil.

7. Position a strip of foil on each side of the main bearing cap and install the cap. Make sure that each seal protrudes outwardly. Torque the cap bolts to 65–72 ft. lb.

8. Cut the seal ends so that a protrusion of 0.5–0.7mm remains.

9. Install the front and rear circular seals with a seal driver as shown.

ENGINE COOLING

Water Pump

REMOVAL & INSTALLATION

LeCar, Alliance and Encore

NOTE: The water pump cannot be repaired. It is a sealed unit.

1. Disconnect the battery.
2. Drain the cooling system.
3. Loosen the alternator and move it out of the way.
4. Remove the water pump tensioner, the drive belt, the air pump, the water pump pulley and toothed belt and the temperature sending unit.
5. Unbolt and remove the pump. It may be necessary to tap the pump free with a wood mallet.

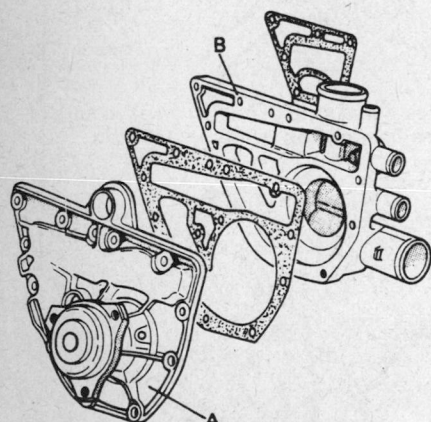

18i and Fuego water pump. (A) is the pump cover; (B) is the pump body

6. Clean the gasket mating surfaces thoroughly. Install the pump using a new gasket. Do not use sealer.

18, 18i, Sport Wagon and Fuego

NOTE: The pump cannot be repaired, just replaced.

1. Disconnect the battery.
2. Drain the cooling system.

3. Disconnect the hoses at the pump.
4. Remove the upper grille crossmember.
5. Remove the grille.
6. Remove the radiator and fan.
7. Remove the pump drive belt.
8. Remove the pump bolts and tap the pump loose with a wood or rubber mallet.
9. Clean the gasket surfaces thoroughly. Always use a new gasket. Do not use sealer on the gasket. Installation is the reverse of removal.

Thermostat

REMOVAL & INSTALLATION

All Engines

The thermostat is located in the water outlet hose at the pump. This is the large hose that runs from the pump to the top of the radiator. To replace the thermostat, simply disconnect the hose at the pump and remove the thermostat. On models so equipped, make sure that the ball check valve faces upward.

EMISSION CONTROLS

Most vehicles are equipped with the following systems:

Air Injection

A belt-driven pump delivers fresh, compressed air to the exhaust ports of the engine. The presence of oxygen will lengthen the combustion process, which reduces the amount of unburned gases in the exhaust. A relief valve and a diverter valve control the amount of air delivered to the exhaust ports. Depending upon whether the engine is accelerating/cruising or decelerating, the diverter valve either delivers the air to the

exhaust ports, or closes off the air passage to the exhaust ports, respectively. A check valve is provided in the system which will prevent damage to the air injection pump should the engine backfire.

Accelerated Idle System

This system is intended to reduce the amount of hydrocarbon emissions during deceleration. The primary throttle plate is opened slightly during deceleration, between speeds of 15–20 miles per hour.

Evaporative Emission Control System

The main component is a canister containing charcoal and a filter. When the engine is off, gasoline vapor settles in the charcoal instead of being vented to the atmosphere. When the engine is started, intake manifold vacuum pulls fresh air in from beneath the charcoal (filtered) and carries the unburned gases to the intake manifold to be burned in the combustion chambers. The vacuum will continue to draw a small amount of vapor from the tank (through a calibrated orifice) even while the engine is running. The process will cycle in this manner, beginning at the time the engine is turned off.

Ignition Timing Advance Control System

A contact switch which works in conjunction with the choke cable (on LeCar models) closes and activates a solenoid which admits full vacuum to the distributor vacuum advance unit for improved emissions and driveability when the choke valve is closed. Some models use a coolant temperature sensing switch to activate the solenoid.

VEHICLE EMISSION CONTROL INFORMATION			
ENGINE FAMILY: DRE 1.0V5FZ9 ENGINE CID: 100.5 EXHAUST EMISSION CONTROL TYPE: EFI CL CAT. EVAPORATIVE FAMILY: ECS 4			THIS VEHICLE CONFORMS TO U.S. E.P.A. AND STATE OF CALIFORNIA REGULATIONS APPLICABLE TO 1981 NEW MOTOR VEHICLES PROVIDED THAT THIS VEHICLE IS ONLY INTRODUCED INTO COMMERCE FOR SALE IN THE STATE OF CALIFORNIA

CATALYST	COMPLIANCE DEMONSTRATED ALTITUDE: ☐ OVER 4000 ft ☒ UNDER 4000 ft		

ENGINE TUNE UP SPECIFICATIONS AND ADJUSTMENTS: AT NORMAL OPERATING AND IN NEUTRAL OR DRIVE POSITION. ALL ACCESSORIES OFF.			
ITEM	SPECIFICATION		INSTRUCTIONS
	MANUAL TRANS.	AUTO. TRANS.	
1 TIMING SETTING (DEGREES AT RPM)	10°±1° BTDC AT 800±50 RPM	10°±1° BTDC AT 650±50 RPM	VACUUM ADVANCE DISCONNECTED
2 IDLE SPEED (RPM)	800±50 RPM	650±50 RPM	SET BY TURNING AIR BY PASS THROTTLE PLATE HOUSING
3 IDLE MIXTURE	NOT ADJUSTABLE	NOT ADJUSTABLE	IDLE MIXTURE IS PRESET AT FACTORY AND NOT ADJUSTED DURING SCHEDULED MAINTENANCE.
RECONNECT ALL CONNECTIONS: DISTRIBUTOR AND VACUUM HOSES. SEE SERVICE MANUAL AND SCHEDULE MAINTENANCE FOR ADDITIONAL INFORMATION.			
CHOKE SETTING COLD START INJECTOR	VALVE LASH INTAKE : 0.008 in EXHAUST: 0.010 in		SPARK PLUG TYPE: BOSCHWR 7DS SPARK PLUG GAP: 0.024 TO 0.028 in
REGIE NATIONALE DES USINES RENAULT			7700692724

Emission control label—typical (18i shown)

Carburetor Air Intake Pre-Heating System

A thermostatically controlled air cleaner mixes heated and ambient incoming air to the carburetor, thereby improving fuel vaporization which assists in improving emissions and driveability during cold engine operation.

P.C.V. (Positive Crankcase Ventilation) System

Crankcase vapors are routed to the induction system to be burned in the combustion chambers instead of merely being vented to the atmosphere.

Catalytic Converter

The catalytic converter chemically alters the exhaust gases before the gases reach the atmosphere. A "two-way" catalyst uses either pellets or screens coated with platinum and palladium. The chemical content of the precious metals oxidizes (neutralizes) controlled amounts of carbon monoxide and hydrocarbons. A "three-way" catalyst uses platinum, palladium, and rhodium, which acts on oxides of nitrogen emissions. Some "three-way" converters also are ported to accept fresh air (from an injection pump) which further reduces oxides of nitrogen emissions.

E.G.R. (Exhaust Gas Recirculation) System

The E.G.R. valve admits varying amounts of exhaust gases into the combustion chambers, thereby diluting the incoming air/fuel mixture to reduce oxides of nitrogen. The introduction of "pre-burned" gases into the combustion chambers also lowers combustion chamber temperature. If detonation is a problem, check the E.G.R. system for proper operation.

FUEL SYSTEM CARBURETED ENGINES

Fuel Pump

NOTE: All carbureted engines use a mechanical fuel pump located on the engine block, on the distributor side.

REMOVAL & INSTALLATION

1. Disconnect and plug the hoses at the pump.

Three way catalytic converter—typical

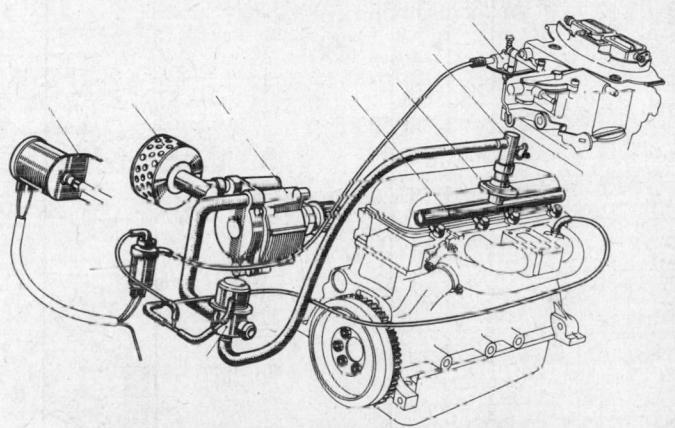
Air Injection Reactor system (A.I.R.)—typical

Oxygen sensor—typical

2. Remove the pump mounting bolts and lift off the pump.

3. Thoroughly clean the mounting surfaces of dirt and old gasket material. Discard the old gasket.

4. Using a new gasket, coated with sealer, position the pump on the block making sure that the drive surface of the pump actuating arm contacts the camshaft drive lobe. The engine may have to be rotated to ease installation. Install the mounting bolts.

5. Unplug and reconnect the hoses.

TESTING

To test the pump, connect a pressure gauge in-line on the output side of the pump. The pressure should be equal to that listed in the Tune-Up chart in this book.

Carburetor

Carburetors used on Renault cars are as follows:

LeCar 1978 exc. Calif.	Weber 32DIR56
Calif.	Weber 32DIR53
LeCar 1979 exc. Calif.	Weber 32DIR55
Calif.	Weber 32DIR53
LeCar 1980 exc. Calif.	Weber 32DIR55
Calif.	Weber 32DIR80
LeCar 1981–82 All	Weber 32DIR80
R-18 Canada	Weber 32DARA27 (MT)
	Weber 32DARA28 (AT)

As you will note in the above chart, all the carburetors used are basically similar, being the Weber 32 model. This is the base model. All carburetors are variations on this base model. Adjustments and repair procedures for all models are, therefore, similar. Differences will be noted below.

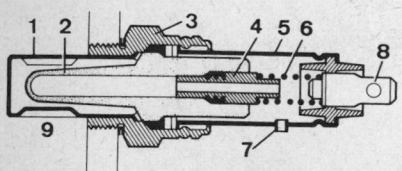

1. Protective sleeve
2. Ceramic sensor
3. Base
4. Contact cover
5. Protective cover
6. Contact spring
7. Air opening
8. Electrical connection
9. Exhaust gas

Cross section of oxygen sensor—typical

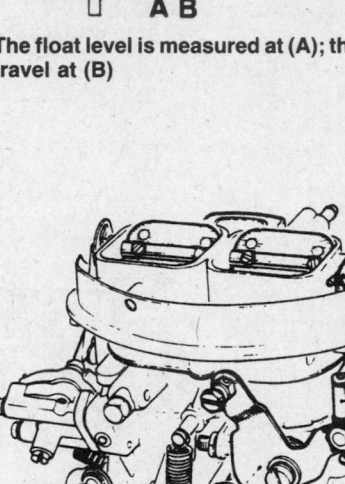

1. needle valve
2. check ball
3. float arm
4. float tab
5. float travel tab

The float level is measured at (A); the float travel at (B)

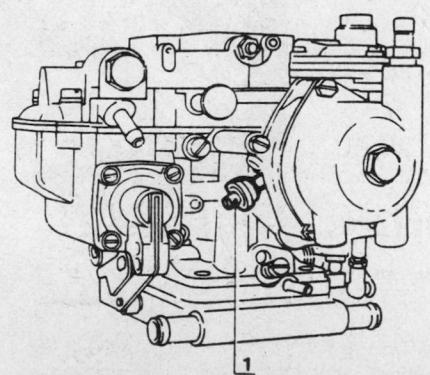

LeCar mechanical choke linkage adjustment. (2) is the sleeve; (3) is the cam and (4) is the link which is bent to make the adjustment

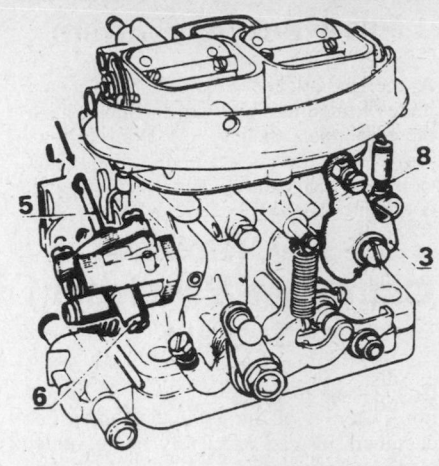

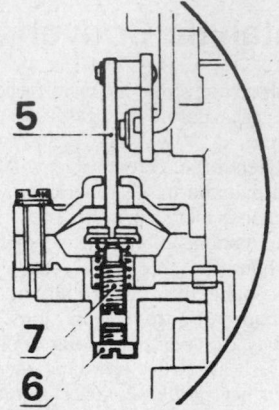

Choke vacuum break adjustment typical of all except the R-18. (3) is the choke arm; (5) is the push link; (6) is the screw plug; (7) is the adjusting screw and (8) is the spring

REMOVAL & INSTALLATION

1. Remove the air cleaner.
2. Disconnect the battery ground. Disconnect the carburetor linkage.
3. Disconnect and tag all wires and hoses attached to the carburetor. On those models with water heated choke, drain a little coolant from the radiator to avoid spillage.
4. Unbolt and remove the carburetor.
5. Install the carburetor using a new gasket. Do not reuse the old gasket. Do not use sealer on the gasket. Connect all wires and hoses. Connect the linkage.

THROTTLE LINKAGE ADJUSTMENT

1. Remove the carburetor.
2. Close the choke plate completely.
3. Check the gap between the throttle plate edge and the air horn wall. The gap should be ³⁄₆₄ in. If not, turn the adjusting screw on the throttle linkage where it bears on the choke cam, until the proper gap is reached.
4. Install the carburetor.

R-18 throttle linkage adjustment. (1) is the adjusting screw

FLOAT ADJUSTMENT

1. Remove the top of the carburetor (float bowl cover).

2. Hold the top in a vertical position with the float end up, so that the weight of the float closes the needle valve without the check ball entering the valve.

3. Check the gap between the float chamber gasket and the float. The gap should be 9/32 in.

4. To adjust the gap, bend the float arm making sure that the tab resting on the needle valve remains perpendicular to the needle valve centerline.

5. To adjust the float travel, measure the distance the float travels between the position above and its maximum point of travel. The distance should be 5/16 in.

6. To adjust the travel, bend the tongue (the bent portion of the float arm).

MECHANICAL CHOKE LINKAGE ADJUSTMENT

1. Close the choke plates fully and bring the sleeve on the choke linkage into contact with the cam by pushing on the choke plate.

2. Measure the choke plate initial opening, between the bottom of the plate and the air horn wall. The gap should be as noted below.

3. If not, bend the choke cam link until it is.

Model	Year	Gap
LeCar	1978	13/64
	1979 Calif.	5/32
	1979 49s	3/16
	1980 49s	3/16
	1980 Calif.	17/64
	1981–82 Calif.	17/64
R-18 Canada	1981–82 49s	15/64
	All	5/32

CHOKE VACUUM BREAK ADJUSTMENT

All except R-18

1. Push the vacuum break link in as far as possible, then close the choke plates using the choke cam link until the pull-down spring is slightly compressed.

2. Measure the choke plate initial opening between the bottom of the plates and the air horn wall. The gap should be as below.

3. To adjust the gap, remove the threaded plug from the vacuum break housing and turn the adjustment screw, located inside, until the gap is correct.

Model	Year	Gap
LeCar	1978	1/4
	1979 Calif.	9/32
	1979–80 49s	17/64
	1980–82 Calif.	13/32
	1981–82 49s	23/64

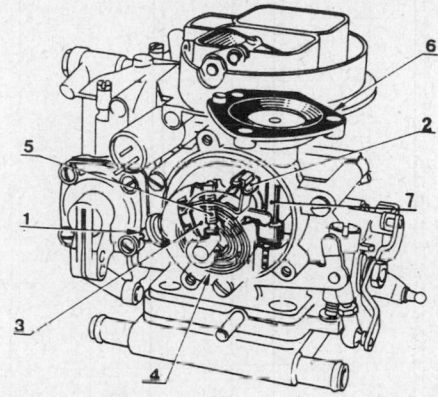

1. adjusting screw
2. lever
3. fast idle cam
4. thermostatic spring
5. spring
6. vacuum diaphragm
7. rod

R-18 vacuum break adjustment

R-18

1. Push on the throttle plate linkage to close the choke plate.

2. Remove the choke thermostatic cover and push the vacuum break rod all the way into the vacuum break diaphragm.

3. Hold the lever, which engages the choke coil spring, against the vacuum break rod.

4. Measure the gap between the bottom of the choke plate and the air horn wall. The gap should be 5/16 in.

5. Adjust the gap using the adjusting screw inside the vacuum break housing cover.

OVERHAUL

For complete overhaul procedures, please refer to "Carburetor Service" in the Unit Repair section.

FUEL SYSTEM FUEL INJECTED ENGINES

All fuel injected engines are equipped with the Bosch L-Jetronic direct injection system, except for the Alliance models built for sale outside of California. These 49 state models use a Throttle Body Injection system (TBI) regulated by an Electronic Control Unit (ECU).

Fuel Pump

All injected engines use an electric fuel pump. On the LeCar and 18i and Fuego, the pump is located on the right rear frame member. On the Alliance and Encore, the pump is located in the fuel tank.

REMOVAL & INSTALLATION

All except Alliance, LeCar and Encore

1. Disconnect the battery ground.
2. Disconnect and plug the fuel lines at the pump.
3. Remove the pump.
4. Installation is the reverse of removal.

Alliance, LeCar, and Encore

1. Disconnect the battery. Drain the fuel tank.

2. Remove the fuel cap and remove the screws holding the filler neck pipe to the sheet metal.

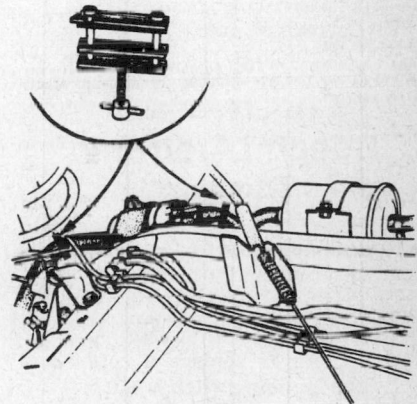

Typical fuel filter location for all except LeCar, Alliance and Encore. Clamp the hoses where shown prior to removal

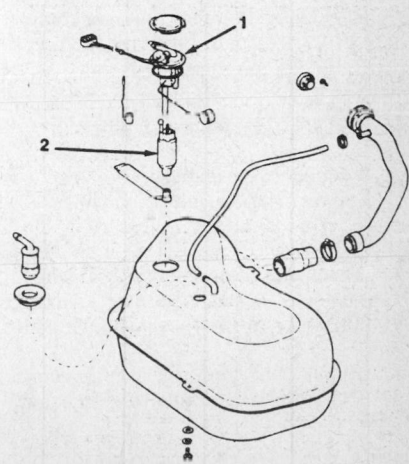

Alliance and Encore fuel pump removal and installation

RENAULT

3. Clean the areas surrounding the rubber connecting pipe between the filler neck and the tank. Unclamp and remove the pipe.

4. Some tanks are secured directly to the floor by bolts; others are secured by straps. Place a floor jack under the tank to support it and remove the bolts and/or straps. Lower the tank slightly and disconnect the wiring and remaining hoses. Lower the tank completely and remove it from the car.

--- CAUTION ---

When working around the gas tank, be extremely careful. Even if empty, the vapors in the tank are highly explosive. DO NOT SMOKE ANYWHERE NEAR THE FUEL TANK! DO NOT CAUSE ANY SPARKS WHEN WORKING ON THE FUEL TANK!

5. The locking ring around the pump can be turned with a screwdriver. If it is stuck, tap it off using a hammer and brass drift. Do not use a hammer and steel or iron drift as sparks could occur. After removing the locking ring, check the rubber O-ring or gasket. Discard it if damaged or squashed.

6. Remove the fuel pump and sending unit.

7. Disconnect and tag the wires. One terminal is marked +, the other is marked −.

8. Unbolt the pump.

9. Installation is the reverse of removal. Use a new gasket or O-ring under the locking ring, if necessary.

Bosch L-Jetronic System

For all fuel injection system service and repair procedures not detailed below, please refer to ''Fuel Injection'' in the Unit Repair section.

NOTE: Never replace a component unless the ignition switch is off!

FUEL FILTER REPLACEMENT

The filter is located on the right rear frame rail on all cars. It is an in-line type, replaced simply by unclamping and replacing.

INJECTOR REPLACEMENT

1. Disconnect the battery.
2. Remove the air intake chamber, if necessary. This is usually necessary on the Alliance.
3. Disconnect the fuel hoses and wires at the injectors. On the 18i the hoses have to be cut away from the injectors and replaced.
4. Unbolt and remove the injector ramps. Clean the area around the injector thoroughly.
5. Pull the injectors from the head. Check the O-ring on the injector. It's best to replace it if at all questionable.

6. Installation is the reverse of removal.

COLD START INJECTOR REPLACEMENT

1. Disconnect the battery.
2. Remove the wiring from the cold start injector.
3. Unbolt and remove the injector.
4. Installation is the reverse of removal.

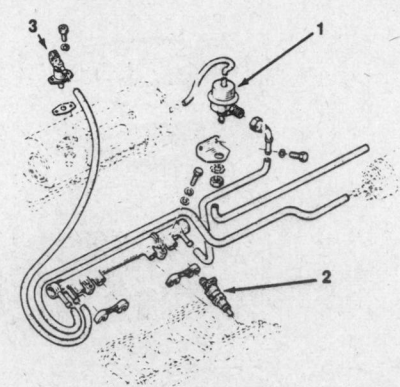

Injector replacement. (1) is the pressure regulator; (2) is the injector; (3) is the cold start injector

Throttle Body Fuel Injection

All Alliance and Encore models, except those built for sale in California, use this system. The throttle body system injects fuel into a throttle body (visually resembling a carburetor). Fuel is metered through a throttle blade by an electronically controlled fuel injector. The Electronic Control Unit (ECU controls injectors through input sent by sensors that detect exhaust gas oxygen content, coolant temperature, manifold pressure, crankshaft position and throttle position.

For all fuel injection system service and repair procedures not detailed below, please refer to ''Fuel Injection'' in the Unit Repair section.

FUEL FILTER REPLACEMENT

The filter is located in-line, under the right rear floorpan. It is replaced by unclamping from the rubber connectors and replacing the filter, clamps and rubber connecting hoses.

FUEL INJECTOR REPLACEMENT

1. Remove the air cleaner.
2. Disconnect the battery.
3. Remove the wire at the injector.
4. Remove the injector retaining ring screws.

5. Remove the injector retaining ring.

6. Using small pliers, carefully grasp the center collar of the injector (between the two terminals) and pull it out with a twisting motion.

7. Discard the upper and lower rubber O-rings. Note that the back-up ring at the bottom, fits over the O-ring.

8. Coat the new O-rings with light oil and install them. Install the back-up ring over the lower O-ring.

9. Insert the injector in the throttle body with a pushing, twisting motion, making certain that it seats fully. Make sure that the wire terminals are parallel with the retaining ring screws.

10. Install the retaining ring and screws.

THROTTLE BODY REPLACEMENT

1. Remove the throttle cable and return spring.
2. Disconnect the injector wiring.
3. Disconnect the wide open throttle switch wire.
4. Disconnect the Idle Speed Control motor wiring.
5. Disconnect the fuel pipe at the throttle body.
6. Disconnect the fuel return pipe at the throttle body.
7. Disconnect and tag the vacuum hoses at the throttle body.
8. Unbolt and remove the throttle body from the manifold.
9. Installation is the reverse of removal.

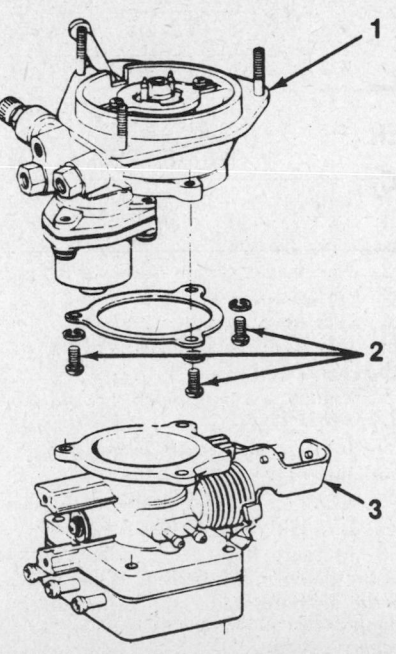

Fuel body replacement. (1) is the fuel body; (2) are the Torx–head screws; (3) is the throttle body

C710

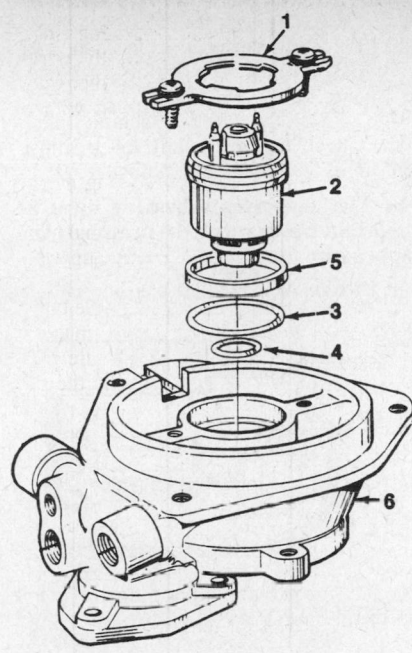

Throttle body injector replacement

FUEL BODY ASSEMBLY REPLACEMENT

1. Remove the throttle body.
2. Remove the three Torx screws retaining the fuel body from the throttle body.
3. Lift off the fuel body.
4. Installation is the reverse of removal.

MANUAL TRANSAXLE

REMOVAL & INSTALLATION

LeCar

1. Disconnect the battery leads and the transaxle ground wire.
2. Disconnect the speedometer cable.
3. Remove the water pump drive belt.
4. Remove the crankshaft pulley, the air pump filter, the air pump and the mounting bracket.
5. Remove the two upper bolts on the starter.
6. Remove the clutch housing bolts which are on the engine.
7. Remove the wheels and the brake calipers without disconnecting the brake hoses.
8. Disconnect the steering arms at the steering rack end.
9. Disconnect the upper ball joints from the upper suspension.
10. Remove the drive shafts from the side gears by tilting the stub axle carriers downward.

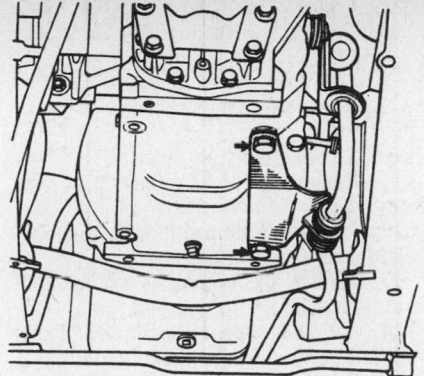

Support plate mounting bolts on the LeCar transmission

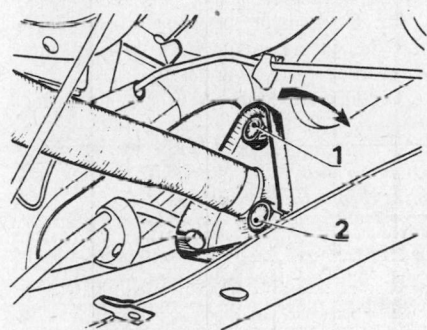

Remove the tubular crossmember in the direction of the arrow.

— CAUTION —

Do not damage the oil seal lips on the differential adjusting nuts while removing the drive shafts.

11. Remove the two mounting bolts from the support on the transaxle.
12. Disconnect the clutch cable at the lever and push the sleeve retainer to free it from the supporting tab.
13. Remove the top bolt and then the tubular crossmember, in the direction of the arrow.
14. Replace the top bolt in the frame hole and then remove the bottom bolts from the crossmember.
15. Tap the crossmember towards the rear of the vehicle and remove it.
16. Replace the bottom bolt in the frame hole.
17. Support the front end of the transaxle with a jack and remove the front mounting pad with its bracket.
18. Remove the starter bottom bolt and then the starter.
19. Remove the side reinforcement mounting bolts and the clutch cover.
20. Special holding tools should be used to hold the engine while the transaxle is removed from the vehicle body. Remove the transaxle assembly.
21. The installation of the transaxle is the reverse of the removal procedure. The clutch free-play at the end of the clutch lever should be adjusted to within 1/8–5/32 inch.

Alliance and Encore

NOTE: This procedure covers both the JB-O 4-speed and the JB-1 5-speed transmissions.

1. Place the vehicle on jack stands.
2. Remove the filler and drain plugs and drain the transaxle.
3. Remove the front wheels and disconnect the drive shafts.
4. Disconnect the gearshift lever linkage and the engine/transaxle support rod.
5. Remove the clutch shield and all mounting pad nuts.
6. Remove the air filter.
7. Disconnect the back–up lamp switch wire connector and remove the TDC sensor.
8. Disconnect the clutch cable, speedometer cable and ground wire.
9. Remove the radiator and lay it on the engine without disconnecting the hoses.
10. Using a suitable lifting device, raise the engine slightly to free the rear mounts.
11. Attach a second lifting device to the clutch cable bracket and bolt on the transaxle.
12. Remove the starter motor mounting bolts.
13. Remove the transaxle retaining bolts, separate the transaxle from the engine and lift it free of the chassis.

NOTE: For the JB 1 transaxle, slide the 5th speed casing between the sidemembers.

14. Raise the engine and slide the transaxle into the clutch splines.
15. Install the transaxle retaining nuts and remove the lifting device from the transaxle.
16. Install the starter motor mounting bolts.
17. Lower the engine onto the mounting pads, install the nuts and tighten them to 40–50 ft. lb.
18. Install the radiator and the clutch shield.
19. Connect the clutch cable, the speedometer cable and the ground wire. Secure the speedometer cable with the clip.
20. Connect the back-up lamp wire connector switch and install the TDC sensor.
21. Install the air filter.
22. Connect the gearshift lever linkage and the engine-transaxle support rod.
23. Connect the driveshafts.
24. Install the front wheels and tighten the nuts to the specified torque.
25. Refill the transaxle and install the filler plug.

NOTE: Remove the breather plug before attempting to refill the transaxle to allow for air displacement.

18, 18i, Sport Wagon and Fuego

The transmissions may be removed with the engine from the top of the vehicle or separately from the bottom of the vehicle. The procedure given is the removal of the transmission separately from the bottom of the vehicle.

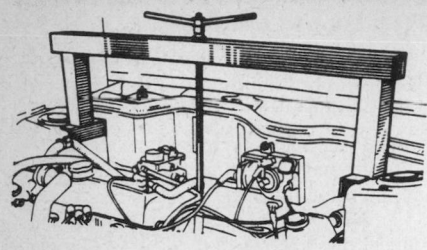

Engine support device used on Alliance and Encore

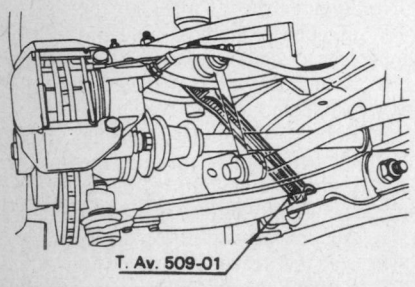

T. Av. 509-01

Installing the support arm tools between the lower shock mounts and the lower suspension arms

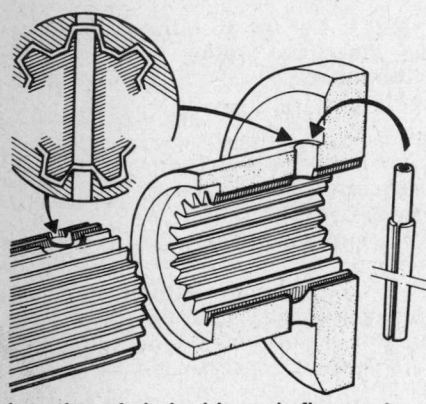

Location of pin in drive axle flange—typical

NOTE: It is not necessary to drain the lubrication from the transmission since the side gears are sealed.

1. Disconnect the battery, the positive cable to the starter and the power lead to the solenoid.
2. Remove the three starter attaching bolts from the bell housing.
3. Remove the rear attaching bolt of the starter.
4. Loosen the bolt of the engine mount on the starter side and swing the rear fixing bracket into a horizontal position.
5. Pull the starter back the length of its nose. On the 352 model transmissions, turn the starter 90 degrees and remove the starter (both transmission models).
6. Disconnect the clutch cable at the fork lever.
7. Place the special transmission removal tool support plates (T. Av. 509-01)

between the lower shock absorber fixing pins and the lower suspension arm shafts, if using the tool.
8. Loosen the front wheel bolts.
9. Raise the vehicle on a hoist or by other means.
10. Remove the front wheels.
11. Remove the brake calipers from both front wheel assemblies.
12. Punch out the roll pins on the sides of the gear/axle shafts.
13. Remove the steering tie-rod ball joint nut and loosen the tie-rod ball joint.
14. Loosen the upper suspension ball joint stud after removing the retaining nut.
15. Tilt the stub axle carrier, disengaging the drive axle shaft from the side gear shaft. Remove the opposite axle shaft in the same manner.
16. Disconnect the speedometer cable and the wiring to the back-up lights and emission control switches.
17. Disconnect the gear shift linkage.

—————— CAUTION ——————
Do not remove the gear shift linkage ball joints from their housings.

18. Remove the clutch protective shield.
19. If using the transmission remover jack assembly, place it under the transmission and lift the transmission slightly. Remove the left and right transmission mounts.
20. Remove the transmission attaching bolts and pull the assembly to the rear, being careful not to damage the pressure plate. Lower the transmission to the floor.
To Install:
1. Lightly lubricate the splines of the clutch shaft and raise the transmission in line with the engine/flywheel assembly.
2. Push the transmission assembly forward into position with the engine, while engaging the clutch shaft into the clutch plate.
3. Install the left and right transmission supports and remove the installing jack.
4. Install the clutch protective cover and be sure the top dead center sensor is positioned 1.0mm (0.039 in.) from the engine flywheel.
5. Reconnect the speedometer cable, the back-up light wires, the emission control switch wires and the gear shift linkage.
6. Lightly lubricate the splines of the differential side gears and position the drive axle shaft next to the side gear (either side).
7. Tilt the stub axle while engaging the drive axle shaft in the side gear. Line the holes in the driveshaft and stub axle and install the roll pin. Do the same procedure on the opposite side. Be sure the roll pin is installed.
8. Engage the stub axle carrier in the upper suspension ball joint and lock the cone. Tighten the nut to the proper torque.
9. Engage the tie-rod ball joints. Tighten the nuts to the proper torque.
10. Install the front calipers.
11. Install the front wheels and lower the vehicle. Tighten the wheel lugs.

12. Connect the clutch cable to the fork.
13. Place the starter in its housing, pull the support bracket into position and tighten the bracket bolt.
14. Tighten the starter attaching bolts.
15. Check the gear shift lever adjustment and the clutch cable adjustment.

NOTE: The release bearing must be in constant contact with the pressure plate diaphragm.

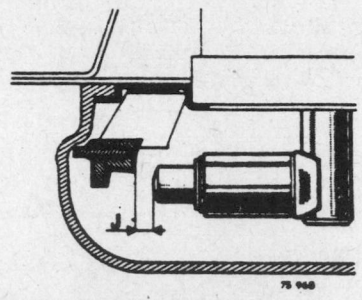

Lever–to–stop plate adjustment. (J) is the gap to be measured—LeCar

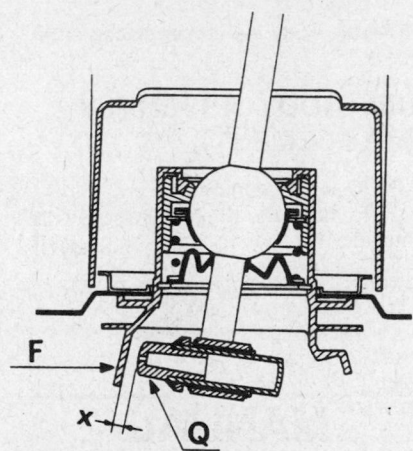

Shift linkage adjustment point on the 18i and Fuego. The gap should be measured between the link (F) and the end piece (Q)

16. Complete the assembly of disconnected components.
17. Connect the battery and road test the vehicle.

SHIFT LINKAGE ADJUSTMENT

LeCar

1. Remove the shift lever boot.
2. Place the transaxle in 3rd gear.
3. Press the lever over towards the 1st-2nd gear position.
4. Using the slots cut in the stop plate, visually check the clearance between the end of the lever and the stop plate. Clearance should be ⅛ in. Adjustment is made by placing washers between the stop plate and floor panel.

18, 18i, Sport Wagon and Fuego

1. Place the transaxle in neutral.

2. Unlock the shift linkage yoke nut so that the linkage can turn freely.

3. Place the case shift lever against the 3–4 shift point.

4. Place a shim (2mm for the 4-speed and 10mm for the 5-speed) between the endpiece of the linkage and the surface of the case. Tighten the yoke nut.

OVERHAUL

For all transaxle overhaul procedures, please refer to "Manual Transaxle Overhaul" in the Unit Repair section.

CLUTCH

REMOVAL & INSTALLATION

NOTE: A clutch aligning tool is needed for this job.

1. Remove the transaxle.

2. Remove the pressure plate bolts evenly and in a cross-wise pattern to avoid distortion. Remove the pressure plate and driven plate.

3. Check the flywheel surface for cracks or scoring. If the flywheel surface is excessively cracked or scored, it must be resurfaced at a machine shop. Before taking the flywheel for resurfacing, remove the dowels. The minimum thickness for the flywheel for LeCar and Alliance is 1.531 in. If resurfacing would take it below this figure, it must be replaced. When you get the resurfaced flywheel back, install the dowels making sure that they protrude 0.276 in. above the flywheel surface.

4. Make sure that the flywheel is free of grease and position the new driven plate against the flywheel with the protruding hub facing the engine.

5. Install the aligning tool and position the pressure plate against the flywheel. Tighten the bolts cross-wise to 20–30 ft. lb. Remove the aligning tool.

6. Install the transaxle.

7. Adjust the clutch.

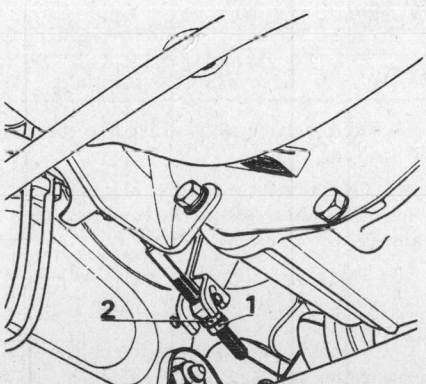

Typical clutch adjustment point

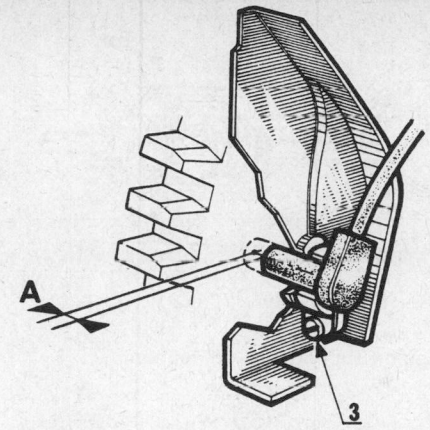

TDC sensor alignment. (A) is the gap; (3) is the attaching screw

ADJUSTMENT

All except Alliance and Encore

1. From under the car, unscrew the locknut on the clutch lever link.

2. Screw the adjusting nut in or out to obtain a clearance of ⅛–5/32 in. for the LeCar, and 3/32 in. for the R-18 and Fuego at the end of the lever.

Alliance and Encore

An automatic adjuster is used with no manual adjustment possible.

AUTOMATIC TRANSMISSION

REMOVAL & INSTALLATION

18, 18i, Sport Wagon and Fuego

1. Disconnect the battery and drain the transmission assembly.

2. Disconnect the vacuum control hose and the wiring connectors. Remove the support.

3. Special spacers (tool T.Av. 509) should be placed between the lower shock absorber base and the lower suspension arm pivot shaft.

4. Place the vehicle on jack stands and drive out the roll pins from the driveshafts.

5. Separate the steering ball joints and the upper suspension ball joints.

6. Tilt the stub axle carriers to free the driveshafts from the side gears.

7. Disconnect the selector linkage while the lever is in the neutral position.

8. Remove the transmission dipstick and the converter protector plate.

9. Remove the three converter bolts and the exhaust pipe bracket nut which is attached to the transmission.

10. Place a jack assembly under the vehicle and remove the two transmission supports.

11. Lower the transmission enough to disconnect the speedometer and the governor cables.

12. Remove the engine/transmission bolts and lower the transmission from the vehicle.

NOTE: Do not allow the converter to slip out of bell housing.
Installation is the reverse of the removal procedure. Note the following steps:

1. When installing the converter, place the boss that is located opposite the timing hole in line with the sharp cornered edge on the converter drive plate, which is marked by a dab of paint.

2. Lightly lubricate the side gear splines and position the driveshafts in line with the side gears.

3. If the vehicle is equipped with a TDC sensor, the sensor must be positioned approximately 0.039 in. (1.0mm) from the engine flywheel.

4. Adjust the gear selector lever and the governor cable.

5. Be sure the computer and governor connections are made and the transmission ground wire is connected.

Alliance and Encore

1. Disconnect the battery.

2. Drain the transaxle fluid.

3. Drain the engine oil.

4. Drain the cooling system.

5. Remove the air cleaner.

6. Remove the radiator.

7. Disconnect and tag all wires, hoses and cables from the engine and transaxle.

8. Disconnect the exhaust pipe at the manifold.

9. Disconnect the transaxle linkage.

10. Remove the front wheels.

11. Disconnect the tie-rod ends using a ball joint separator.

12. Unbolt the brake calipers and hang them out of the way without disconnecting the brake hoses.

13. Disconnect the driveshafts at the transaxle.

14. Place a jack under the engine-transaxle unit and unbolt the mounts. Attach a lifting device to the engine and lift it from the car.

NOTE: When separating the engine from the transaxle, first unbolt the torque converter. Take care not to drop the converter.

15. Installation is the reverse of removal.

NOTE: When attaching the exhaust pipe, tighten the bolts until each spring on each bolt is 1.71 in. (43.5mm) long. Tighten the torque converter bolts in alternating order to 20–25 ft. lb.

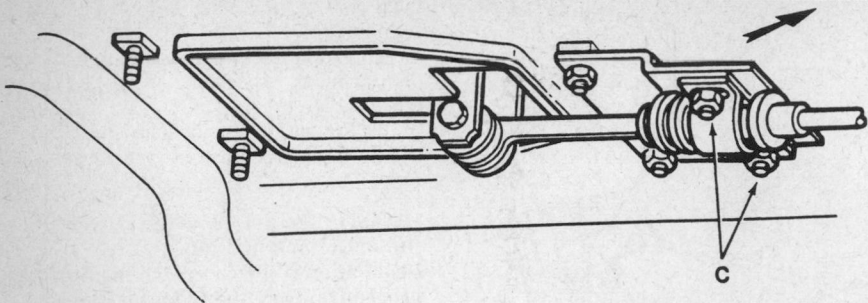

Alliance and Encore automatic transmission shift linkage adjustment

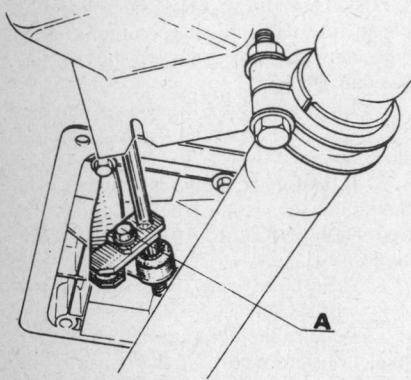

18i and Fuego shift linkage adjustment

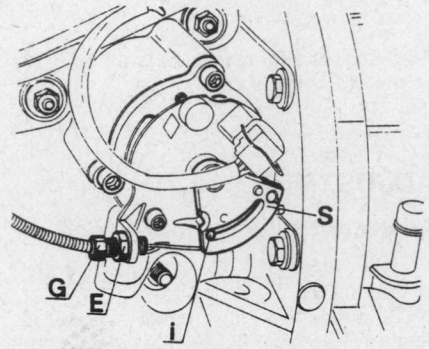

Governor cable adjustment location. (G) is the locknut; (E) is the adjusting nut; (I) is the cable end; (S) is the quadrant

SHIFT LINKAGE ADJUSTMENT

Alliance and Encore

1. Place the selector in Park.
2. Raise and support the car on jackstands.
3. Loosen the adjustment yoke nuts and slide the yoke and cable forward to take up all slack.
4. Tighten the yoke nuts and lower the car.

18, 18i, Sport Wagon and Fuego

1. Raise and support the car on jackstands.
2. Place the shifter in neutral.
3. Unbolt the shift linkage rod at the shifter end, make sure that the transmission case shift lever is in the neutral position.
4. Reconnect the linkage rod and torque the bolt to 13 ft. lb.

KICK-DOWN SWITCH ADJUSTMENT

This adjustment is closely related to the governor cable adjustment and should be made in conjunction with that adjustment. Kickdown adjustment is made at the accelerator pedal.

With the accelerator pedal completely depressed, make sure that the cable stop sleeve can still move about 1/16 in.

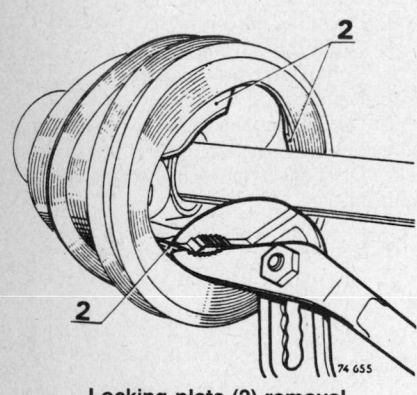

Locking plate (2) removal

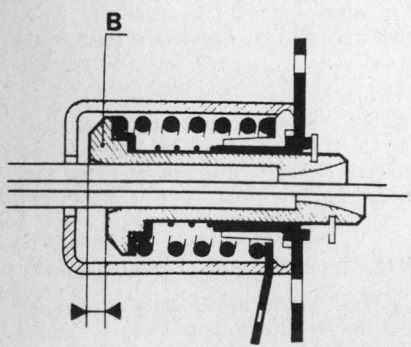

Kickdown switch adjustment. (B) is the gap measurement point

GOVERNOR CONTROL CABLE ADJUSTMENT

1. Back off the locknut on the governor cable at the governor control lever. Remove the cable end from the control lever.
2. Turn the threaded cable end so that it is about one half way into the control lever.
3. Place the cable end ball into its slot in the control lever.
4. Make sure that the outer end of the cable is in place at the carburetor.
5. Depress the accelerator all the way, and remove all play from the cable by adjusting the sleeve stop on the cable at the carburetor end.

HALFSHAFTS

REMOVAL

1. Lift the vehicle on the side to be repaired, by a hoist or jack. Remove the wheel assembly.
2. Remove the stub axle nut.
3. Loosen the upper ball joint nut and the steering arm nut, but do not remove them.
4. Loosen the ball joint cones with special tools.
5. Remove the two caliper retaining bolts and lift the caliper assembly from the rotor. Do not disconnect the brake hose.
6. Remove the ball joint and steering arm nuts and tilt the stub axle carrier in order to disengage the halfshaft.
7. Drive the roll pins from the halfshaft coupling on the gear box side of the drive shaft.
8. Remove the halfshaft.
9. Installation is the reverse of removal.

Boot Replacement

1. Remove the collar from the stub axle.
2. Remove as much grease as possible from the assembly.
3. Remove the bell-shaped stub axle from the halfshaft by raising the arms of the retaining starplate, one by one.

——— **CAUTION** ———
Do not twist the arms of the starplate.

4. Remove the boot. Save the thrust ball and the spring.

NOTE: A special boot replacing tool should be used to install the boot to avoid damage.

5. Place the halfshaft in a vise with the shaft yoke up. Fully engage the installing tool on the shaft yoke.
6. Lubricate the inside of the boot with clean engine oil.
7. Pull the boot over the end of the special tool with the small end first.

Plastic collar installed over the spider

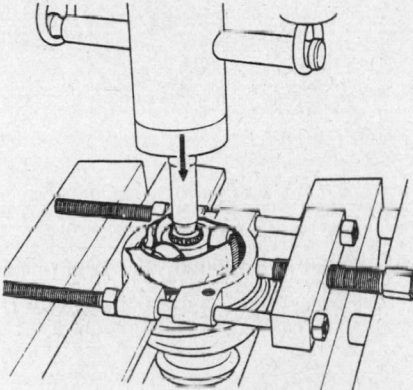

Pressing out the spider assembly

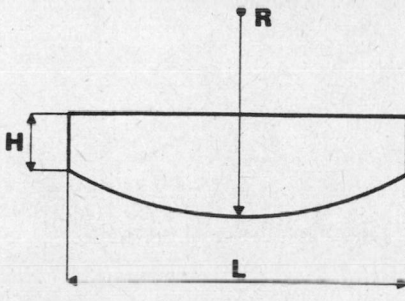

L=40mm
H=6mm
R=45mm
Shim thickness=2.5mm

Fabricating the shim

8. Bring the boot as close as possible to the cylindrical part of the tool and let it return halfway back. Do this several times in order to soften the rubber of the boot. Relubricate the arms of the tool and the boot as required during the installation.

9. Place the spring and the thrust ball joint in the spider.

10. Move the roller cages towards the center and position the retaining star plate. Each arm should be the bisector of the angles formed by the spider.

11. Install the collar and secure.

Axle Spider or Yoke Replacement

1. Place a piece of adhesive tape or a protective end piece on the seal surface of the differential adjuster nuts.

2. Cut the retaining collar and the boot along their whole length. Remove as much of the grease as possible.

3. Remove the three tabs of the locking plate and remove the yoke.

NOTE: Do not remove the rollers from their respective journals. The roller cages and needle bearings are matched and must never be separated. To prevent the separating of the unit during this operation, mount the plastic collar that is furnished with new spiders. Tape the collar as a safeguard to prevent the collar from coming off.

4. Using a press, remove the spider assembly.

5. To replace the spider or a boot:

   a. Lubricate the driveshaft and slide on the new retaining collar and boot.

   b. Push the spider back on the splined shaft.

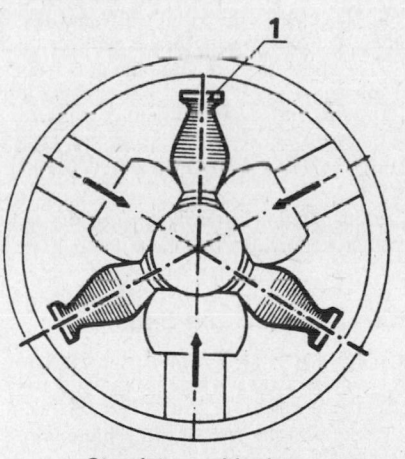

Starplate positioning

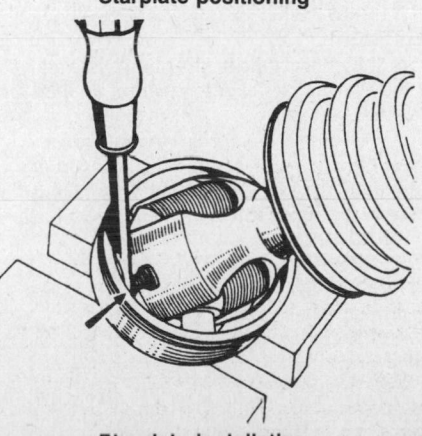

Starplate installation

c. Make three crimps with 120° spacing by stamping the metal splines on the driveshaft.

d. Take off the plastic collar and/or tape. Engage the spider in the yoke and insert a shim (special tool) between the locking plate and the yoke.

e. Carefully put the locking tabs of the plate back into their original positions and then remove the special tool shim.

f. Put approximately 5¼ oz. of grease into the boot and yoke. Position the lips of the boot in the grooves of the drive shaft and on the metal housing.

g. Install the retaining spring on the boot. Insert a smooth round-ended rod between the boot and the yoke to relieve the air trapped in the boot.

h. Lengthen or shorten the joint until a measurement of 6.378 ± 0.039 in. (162.0 ± 1.0mm) is obtained between the end of the boot and the largest diameter machined face of the yoke. When the joint has been adjusted correctly, remove the air release rod.

i. Place the retaining spring on the boot with a flexible wire.

CAUTION
The spring must not be stretched and the coils must still be touching after assembly.

---

6. If the yoke must be replaced:

   a. Lubricate the halfshaft and slide on the retaining collar and the new boot.

   b. Engage the yoke's metal housing on the shaft and the spider on the splines of the shaft.

   c. Make three crimps with 120° spacing by stamping the metal splines on the driveshaft.

   d. Fit the two bosses of the metal housing facing a perforation on the yoke, supplied with its new O-ring and fit the parts one inside the other.

   e. The crimping of the housing is on the yoke and is done on a press, by a hammer and a crimping tool.

INSTALLATION

1. Coat the splines of the shaft with lubricant and engage the halfshaft into the side gear. Check the positioning of the halfshaft retaining pin holes.

2. Install the retaining roll pins.

3. Engage the halfshaft into the hub. Install the washer and stub axle nut on the axle.

4. Reconnect the upper ball joint and steering arm joint and install the nuts. Tighten as required.

5. Torque the stub axle nut to 185 ft. lbs.

6. Reinstall the brake caliper and the wheel assembly. Operate the brakes several times to re-seat the disc pads to the rotor.

REAR SUSPENSION

Rear Axle Assembly

REMOVAL & INSTALLATION

18, 18i, Sport Wagon and Fuego

1. Position the vehicle on a hoist or on jack stands.

2. Remove the wheels and the lower mountings on the shock absorbers. Push the shock absorbers upward as far as possible.

3. Remove the flexible brake lines from the limiter.

4. Pull downward on the rear axle to remove the springs.

5. Remove the two side arm nuts on the chassis side and remove the two bolts.

6. Disconnect the parking brake cables at the adjusters, and remove them from the retaining bracket.

7. Place a jack under the rear axle assembly.

8. Disconnect the brake limiter valve.

9. Remove the two center arm bolts and remove the rear axle assembly.

Installation is the reverse of the removal procedure. With the components in place and tightened correctly, place the vehicle back on its wheels.

1. Check the brake limiter valve adjustment.

2. Bleed the brake system.

3. Adjust the parking brake.

4. With the weight of the vehicle on the rear suspension, retighten all bolts as required. Torque the center arm bolts to 59 ft. lb. and the side arm bolts to 25-30 ft. lb.

Center Arm

REMOVAL & INSTALLATION

18, 18i, Sport Wagon and Fuego

1. Place the vehicle on a lift and disconnect the brake limiter control rod.

2. Remove the nuts from the front and rear attaching bolts.

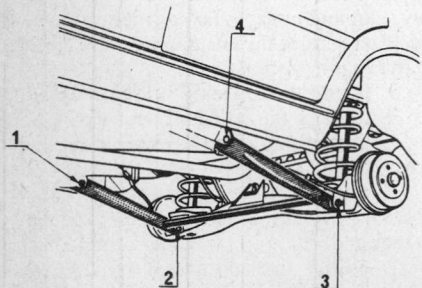

Side arm attaching bolts. The bolts must be removed and installed in the order shown

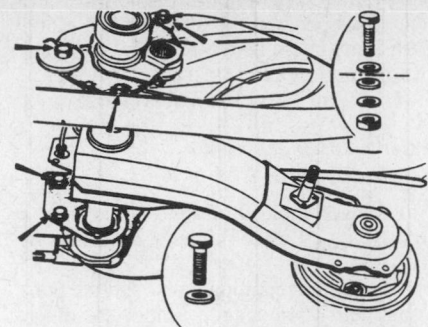

LeCar, Alliance and Encore sidearm attaching points

3. Remove the clamp and the center arm retaining bolts.

4. Remove the center arm. The bushings must be pressed in and out of the arm.

5. Installation is in the reverse of the removal procedure. Torque the rubber bushing bolt to 30 ft. lb.; the clamp nuts to 10 ft. lb.; the left and right bolts to 60 ft. lb.

Side Arms/Stabilizer Assembly

REMOVAL & INSTALLATION

18, 18i, Sport Wagon and Fuego

1. Place the vehicle on a lift and disconnect the two parking brake cables.

2. Remove the arm retaining nuts front and rear.

3. Drive the bolts from the arms and remove the arm stabilizer assembly. The bushings must be pressed from and into the arm.

4. Installation is the reverse of the removal procedure. Torque the bolts to 30 ft. lb.

LeCar, Alliance and Encore

The rear suspension is an individual torque arm type unit and each side is removed and replaced separately.

1. Support the rear of the vehicle with jack stands.

2. Remove the sway bar and the shock absorber.

3. Disconnect the flexible brake line and set the torsion bars to zero position by their adjusting cams.

4. Assemble the special torsion bar removal tool in place of the shock absorber and tighten the tool until the adjusting lever lifts off the cam. Remove the torsion bar from both sides.

5. Remove the two other mounting bolts and the three inner mounting bolts. Remove the arm.

6. Installation is the reverse of the removal procedure. Torque the suspension–to–body bolts to 55 ft. lb.; the sway bar bolts to 37 ft. lb.; the shock absorber lower nut to 60 ft. lb. Be sure to bleed the brake

system, check the limiter cut-off pressure and check the rear wheels for proper tracking.

BUSHING REPLACEMENT

LeCar, Alliance and Encore

1. Both the inner and outer arm bushings are pressed into the arm tube. Bend back the crimped lugs with a chisel and remove the outer case.

2. Remove the rubber bushing outer sleeve using a three jawed puller. This operation will tear the rubber.

3. Saw through the rubber bushing inner sleeve, being careful not to mar the tube.

4. Press the new bushings in place with a press, crimping the lugs while the arms are in the press.

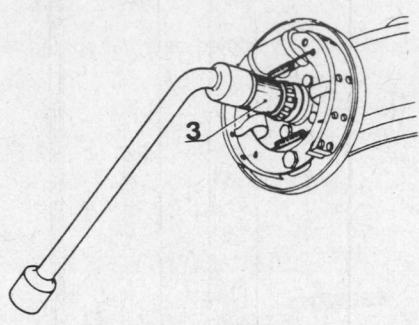

Cold method of installing the LeCar rear axle bearing

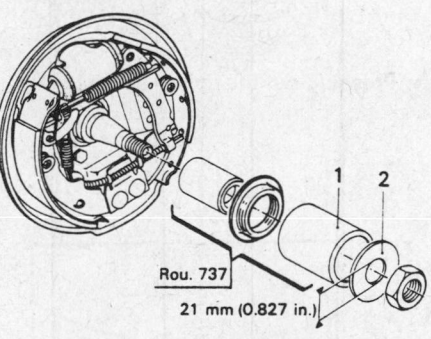

Installing the inner deflector

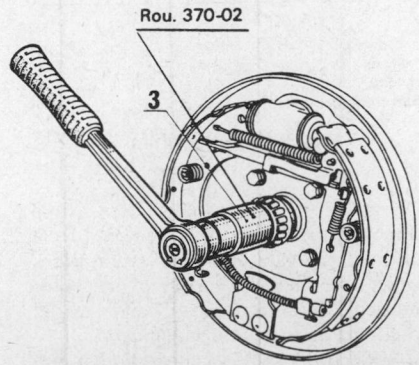

Installing the inner bearing

Rear Axle Bearings

REMOVAL & INSTALLATION

18, 18i, Sport Wagon and Fuego

1. Raise the rear of the vehicle and remove the wheels.

2. Remove the rear brake drum;

   a. Release the parking brake.

   b. Slacken the secondary cables of the parking brake so that the lever may be pulled back.

   c. Remove the dust plug in the backing plate so that the automatic adjusting system may be disengaged.

   d. Insert a screwdriver-type tool (tool no. Rou. 370-02) into the hole in the backing plate, through a companion hole in the brake shoe, to the parking brake lever.

   e. Push in with the tool to disengage the catch from the brake shoe. Push the lever to the rear with the tool.

   f. Remove the dust cover, the retaining lock nut/cotter pin, the stub axle nut and washer.

   g. Remove the drum, the outer bearing and seal as an assembly.

3. With the use of special pulling tools (No. Rou. 15-01 and B. Vi. 28-01), the inner bearing is removed from the stub axle, along with the deflector.

4. Install the inner deflector, making sure it is mounted correctly.

5. Install the inner bearing on the stub axle by carefully driving it to its seat.

6. Install any of the bearing cups as required. Add lubricant to the bearings and cups.

7. Install the drum assembly in the reverse of its removal procedure.

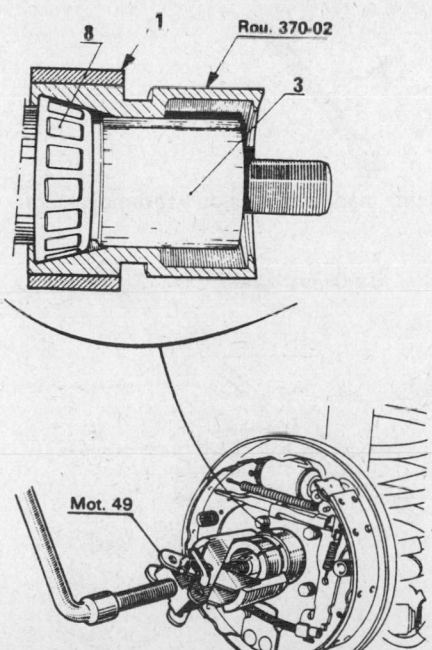

Inner bearing removal—18i and Fuego

8. Check the bearing end play, which should be between 0.000 and 0.001 in. (0.00 and 0.03mm).

9. Adjust the foot brake by repeatedly pushing down on the brake pedal.

10. Adjust the parking brake. Install the plug in the rear of the backing plate.

LeCar

1. Raise the vehicle and support safely.

2. Remove the rear wheel(s) and the brake drum.

3. Remove the outer bearing and the oil seal.

4. Remove the bearing races as required.

5. With a special puller, remove the inner bearing from the rear axle spindle.

NOTE: Some inner bearings will have a thrust washer that must be removed with the bearing assembly. A different type bearing puller is then used.

There are two methods of bearing replacement, hot or cold. The hot method is preferred and consists of pre-heating the washer so that it can be assembled to the stub axle without the use of tools. The cold method utilizes the special tools to press the components in place. The components should be heated to approximately 200–250 degrees F.

—————— CAUTION ——————
Do not use an open flame to pre-heat the components.

Alliance and Encore

NOTE: This procedure requires the use of special tools.

1. Raise and support the car on jackstands.

2. Remove the wheel.

3. Loosen the handbrake cable.

4. Remove the grease cap from the end of the axle shaft. Remove the shaft end nut and washer.

5. Remove the brake drum. It may be necessary to back off the brake shoe adjustment to free the drum. If the drum still won't slide off, it will be necessary to mount a combination slide hammer/hub puller and remove the drum.

6. From the drum, remove the bearing retaining clip and drive the bearing out with a length of 49mm diameter pipe.

7. Installation is the reverse of removal. Drive the new bearing in with a length of 51mm pipe. Torque the shaft end nut to 118 ft. lb. Adjust the handbrake. Pump the brake pedal several times to adjust the brakes.

ADJUSTMENT

LeCar

An end play of 0.004–0.002 in. (0.01–0.05mm) should exist between the brake drum and the stub axle. Rotate the stub axle

nut in or out to obtain this required adjustment. Install the lockplate, nut and cotter pin. Add ⅓ oz. of grease in the dust cover and install.

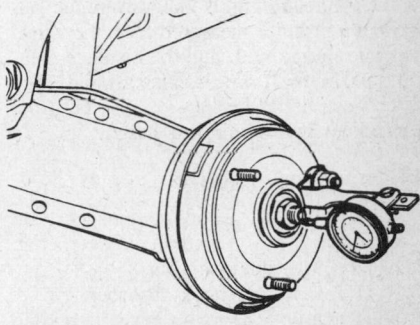

Adjusting the LeCar rear axle bearing; others similar

Alliance and Encore

No adjustment is necessary.

18, 18i, Sport Wagon and Fuego

NOTE: A special tool is needed for this procedure.

1. Raise and support the car on jackstands.

2. Remove the wheel.

3. While turning the drum by hand, tighten the axle shaft nut to 22 ft. lb.

4. Tap the drum lightly to make sure the bearing is seated.

5. Back off the shaft nut about ¼ turn.

6. Attach a dial indicator under one of the lug nuts and mount the pointer on the end of the axle shaft.

7. Push and pull on the drum and check the endplay on the indicator. Endplay should be 0–.001 in. Use the shaft end nut to obtain this figure.

8. Assemble all remaining parts.

Torsion Bars

REMOVAL & INSTALLATION

LeCar

A special tool, which can be made at home, will aid in the removal of the torsion bar.

1. Raise and support the car on jackstands.

2. Loosen the cam locking nut and zero the cam.

3. Remove the shock absorber.

4. Assemble the torsion bar tool in place of the shock absorber.

5. Tighten nut A until the adjusting lever lifts off of cam D.

6. Remove the torsion bar.

7. Move the adjusting lever until it touches the cam.

8. Apply chassis lube to the torsion bar splines and insert it into the lever and arm.

NOTE: Adjust nut A on the torsion bar remover 23¼ in. for the right arm, or 23⅝ in. for the left arm, prior to torsion bar installation.

9. Tighten the cam locknut. Remove the tool.

10. Install the shock absorber.

11. Lower the vehicle and check the ride height. Ride height is the difference between the distance measured from the wheel center to the ground, and the distance measured from the frame to the ground. The difference should be $1/16$–$13/16$ in. Turn the cam adjuster to obtain this height.

Alliance and Encore

1. Raise and support the car on jackstands.

2. Remove the sway bar.

3. Remove the shock absorber.

4. Remove the torsion bar with a slide hammer.

5. For installation, make a tool identical to that described in the LeCar procedure, above. Install this tool in place of the shock absorber. Turn the nut to obtain a tool length of 24.04 in. for either side.

6. Coat the torsion bar splines with chassis lube and install it. Search around until the easiest point of entry, at each end, is found.

7. Remove the tool. Install the shock and sway bar.

8. Check and adjust the ride height, if necessary. To adjust the ride height, see the LeCar section above. Ride height should be 2.048 in.

Springs

REMOVAL & INSTALLATION

18, 18i, Sport Wagon and Fuego

1. Raise and support the car on jackstands placed under the frame.

2. Disconnect the shock absorber lower end.

3. Compress the shock as far as it will go.

4. Remove the brake hose clips from the rear axle.

5. Jack up the rear of the car to allow the axle to drop and the spring to be pulled out and down.

6. Installation is the reverse of removal. Make certain that the lower open coil end is against the stop on the spring pad.

Shock Absorbers

REMOVAL & INSTALLATION

LeCar, Alliance and Encore

1. Working through the trunk, remove the upper nut.

2. Raise and support the car on jackstands.

3. Remove the lower nut and remove the shock absorber.

4. Installation is the reverse of removal. It's best to attach the upper end first.

Torque the upper nut to 18 ft. lb.; the bottom nut to 60 ft. lb.

18, 18i, Sport Wagon and Fuego

1. Open the trunk and remove the gas tank protection shield.

2. Remove the upper fastener (nut).

3. Raise the vehicle and remove the wheel(s).

4. Remove the lower fastening nut and compress the shock absorber by hand.

5. Remove the retaining clips of the brake hoses from the rear axle.

6. Push the axle assembly downward and remove the shock absorber with the spring. Remove the spacers and the rubber bushings.

Before installing a new shock absorber, pump it up and down manually several times while in an upright position.

1. Place the rubber insulators on the shock absorbers as required on both the top and bottom.

2. Push down on the rear axle assembly and engage the shock absorber with the spring, positioning the spring so that its lower end is placed in the stop of the lower cup.

3. Attach the upper half of the shock absorber with the retaining nut. Be sure to replace the bushings and cups as they were removed.

4. Extend the shock absorber and install its lower retaining nut. Again, be sure to replace the bushings and cups as they were removed.

5. Install the retaining clips of the brake hose to the rear axle.

6. Install the wheels and lower the vehicle to the ground.

FRONT SUSPENSION

Upper Control Arm

NOTE: Alliance and Encore have no upper control arm.

REMOVAL & INSTALLATION

LeCar

1. Remove the cooling system expansion bottle and the ignition coil. Raise the front end.

2. Disconnect the upper ball joint using the removal tool.

3. Screw on and tighten a lock nut on the front end of the arm hinge pin (bolt). Remove the rear lock nut.

4. Drive the pin and lock nut assembly towards the front.

5. Remove the upper arm from the chassis.

6. To install the upper arm, reverse the removal procedure. Tighten the nuts to 70 ft. lb.

18, 18i, Sport Wagon and Fuego

1. Raise and support the car on jackstands.

2. Disconnect the castor tie-rod.

3. Remove the sway bar.

4. Using a ball joint separator, disconnect the ball joint.

5. Disconnect the tie-rod ball joint.

6. Unbolt and remove the upper arm hinge pin.

7. Disconnect the shock absorber lower end.

8. Tilt the arm upward to free the ball joint and free the other end from the shock absorber.

9. Installation is the reverse of removal. Install the arm on the shock absorber first, then the upper ball joint followed by the tie-rod ball joint. Hand tighten the nuts. Install the hinge pin, liberally coated with chassis lube and hand tighten the nuts. Install the sway bar; hand tighten the nuts. Attach the castor tie-rod. NOW, tighten all nuts.

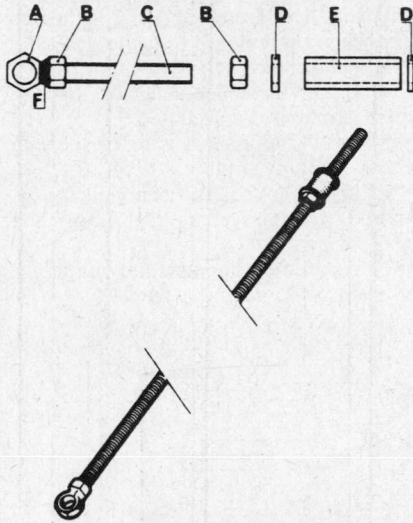

Home made rear torsion bar removal tool

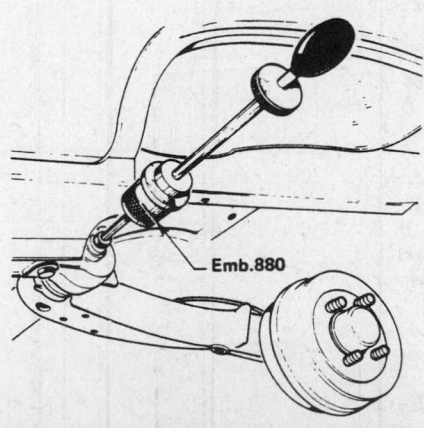

Use a slide hammer to remove the torsion bar on the Alliance and Encore

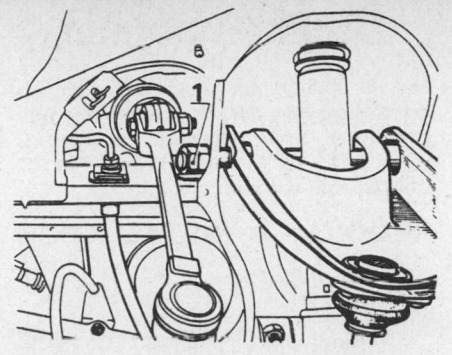

Installing a locknut on the arm hinge pin (bolt)

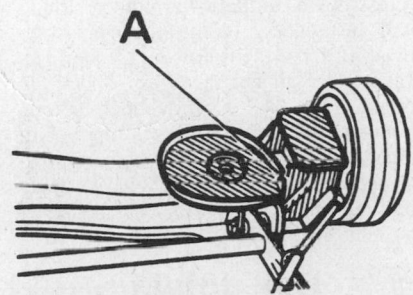

When installing the spring, make sure that the spring end is against the stop (A)

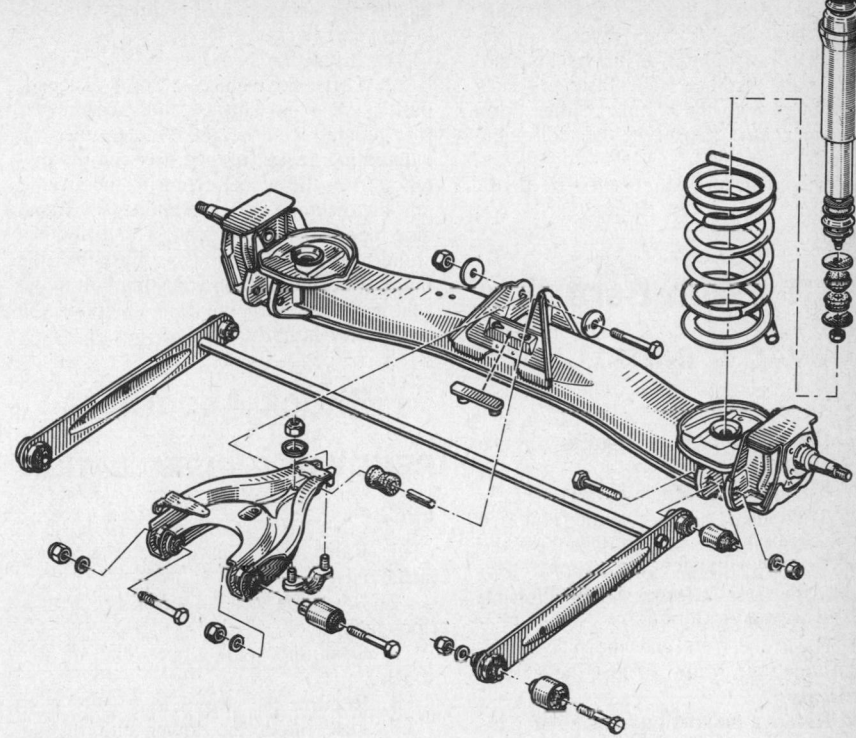

Exploded view of rear suspension—18i and Fuego

- Upper ball joint—48 ft. lb.
- Control arm hinge pin nuts—70 ft. lb.
- Lower shock absorber nuts—55 ft. lb.
- Tie-rod ball joint—48 ft. lb.
- Sway bar—20 ft. lb.
- Caster link nut—60 ft. lb.

Lower Control Arm

REMOVAL & INSTALLATION

LeCar

1. Remove the torsion bar.
2. Remove the halfshaft.
3. Remove the sway bar.
4. Disconnect the shock absorber lower end and remove the bolt.
5. Disconnect the steering arm ball joint and lower control arm ball joint with a ball joint separator.
6. Unbolt and remove the lower control arm hinge pin.
7. Install a hub puller on the hub end and tighten the puller until the ball joint pulls free of the axle shaft carrier.
8. Installation is the reverse of removal. Observe the following torques:
- Lower control arm hinge pin nuts—75 ft. lb.
- Lower shock absorber nut—25 ft.lb.
- Lower ball joint nut—40 ft. lb.

Alliance and Encore

1. Raise and support the car on jackstands.

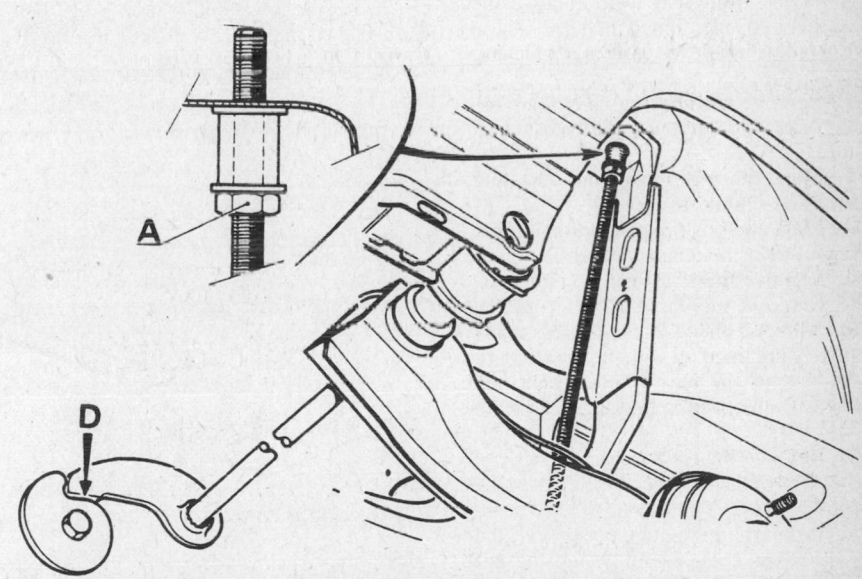

Tool Installation adjustment

2. Remove the sway bar.
3. Remove the wheels.
4. Using a ball joint separator, disconnect the lower control arm ball joint.
5. Remove the control arm hinge pins.
6. Remove the control arm.
7. Installation is the reverse of removal. Don't tighten any nuts completely, until all parts are installed. The nuts are tightened with the car's weight on the suspension. Note the following torques:

- Lower arm hinge pins—55 ft. lb.
- Lower ball joint nut—40 ft. lb.
- Sway bar bolts—16 ft. lb.

18i and Fuego

1. Raise and support the car on jackstands.
2. Using a ball joint separator, disconnect the lower ball joint.
3. Unbolt and remove the control arm hinge pin.

4. Free the lower ball joint from the spindle and remove the arm from the car.

5. Installation is the reverse of removal. Do not tighten any fasteners until all parts are installed. The fasteners must be tightened with the weight of the car on the suspension. Observe the following torques:
• Lower control arm hinge pin—67 ft. lb.
• Ball joint nut—35 ft. lb.

Torsion Bars

REMOVAL & INSTALLATION

LeCar

The following procedure requires the use of a special tool.

1. Tilt the front seat forward.

2. There are four bolts on the front face of the seat well. The largest of these is the torsion bar cam bolt. Loosen (but do not remove) the bolt and turn the cam left all the way to zero it.

3. Raise the front end and place jackstands under the frame so that the wheels hang freely.

4. Remove the torsion bar adjusting lever cover.

5. Insert tool Sus.545 in the adjusting lever.

6. In the front seat well, remove the three other bolts mentioned in Step 2. These are the adjusting lever housing attaching bolts.

7. Remove the housing cover cam assembly and gradually ease the pressure on the tool.

8. Mark the position of the adjusting lever on the floor pan.

9. Mark the position of the torsion bar on the lower arm anchor sleeve.

10. Remove the sway bar bushings.

11. Remove the torsion bar from the control arm and check that the marks made previously are lined up with the punch mark on the end of the bar. If not, count and record the number of splines the marks are off.

12. Remove the torsion bar.

13. Apply chassis lube to the ends of the torsion bar.

14. Install the protective cover seal, the housing cover cam assembly and the adjusting lever on the torsion bar.

15. Pass the housing cover cam assembly and the adjusting lever inside the crossmember. Slide the torsion bar into position above the sway bar.

16. Insert the torsion bar into the lower control arm aligning the marks.

17. Position the adjusting lever on the splines, aligning the marks made earlier on the floor crossmember.

18. Position the adjusting lever ⅜–¾ in. to the left of its travel.

19. With the tool Sus.545 inserted in the adjusting lever, take up the tension on the bar. Center the cover by resetting the cam.

20. Hold the torsion bar assembly against its bushing with a pair of locking pliers and bolt it together.

21. Install the sway bar.

22. Drive the vehicle a short distance, park it on a flat surface and measure the ride height. Ride height is determined by calculating the difference between the distance from the wheel center to the ground and the distance from the underbody frame side member to the ground. The difference should be 1⅞–2⅝ in. To adjust the ride height, loosen the cam adjusting bolt in the seat well and turn the cam to obtain the proper ride height.

Shock Absorber

REMOVAL & INSTALLATION

LeCar

1. Raise and support the car on jackstands.

2. Raise the lower control arm with a floor jack.

3. Disconnect the upper end of the shock.

4. Remove the sway bar.

5. Disconnect the lower end of the shock.

6. Install the shock absorber and sway bar, and tighten the bolts finger tight.

7. Let the lower control arm hang, then raise it 1¾ in., or, about half its travel. Tighten all fasteners.

MacPherson Strut

For all spring and shock absorber removal and installation procedures, and any other strut overhaul procedures, please refer to "Strut Overhaul" in the Unit Repair section.

REMOVAL & INSTALLATION

All except LeCar

Special tools are needed for this job.

1. Raise and support the car on jackstands placed under the frame. Remove the wheel.

2. Unbolt the strut at the top and bottom. Pull the strut out. It may be necessary to press down on the lower control arm.

3. Installation is the reverse of removal. Observe the following torque specifications for all but the R-18: Shock top mounting nut, 44 ft. lb.; shock bottom mounting nut, 55 ft. lb.; Shock top mounting pad nuts, 17 ft. lb. Observe the following specifications for the R-18: Shock upper mounting nut, 11 ft. lb.; shock lower mounting nut, 30 ft. lb.

Ball Joints

REMOVAL & INSTALLATION

All Models

NOTE: The Alliance and Encore have no upper ball joint or control arm.

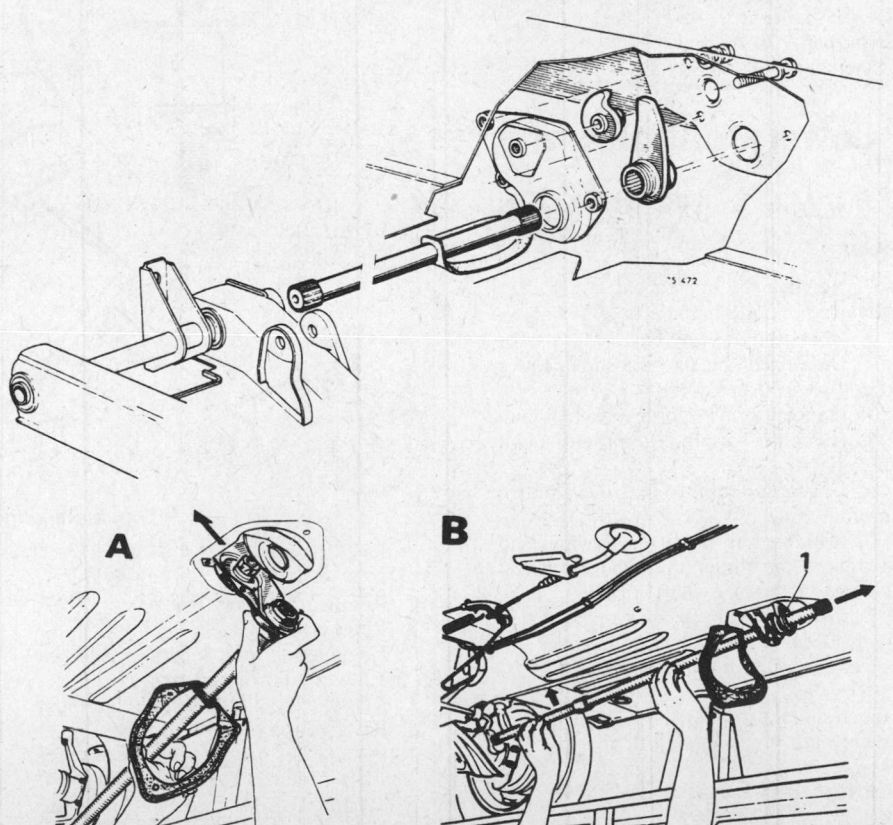

A   B

Installing the LeCar torsion bar

1. Raise and support the car on jackstands.

2. Remove the ball joint nut. Using a ball joint separator, disconnect the ball joint.

3. Drill out the rivets securing the ball joint to the upper arm and remove the ball joint.

4. The new ball joint kit will come with bolts and nuts to replace the rivets and the upper ball joint has a shim which should go on top of the control arm. Install the ball joint and shim. The bolt heads go on the dust cover side. Torque the ball joint large nut to 49 ft. lb.

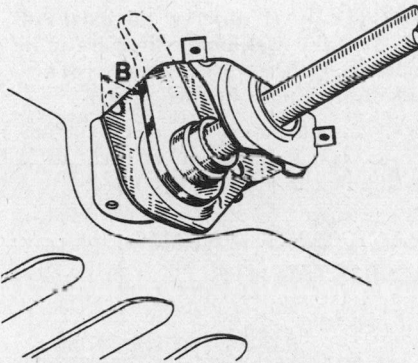

Positioning the LeCar torsion bar adjusting lever

LeCar torsion bar mounting and adjusting bolts

STEERING

Steering Wheel

REMOVAL & INSTALLATION

Remove the snap cap and the steering wheel retaining nut from the steering shaft. Use a protective puller and remove the steering wheel from the steering shaft.

NOTE: Depending upon the type puller used, the steering column top and bottom bezel may have to be removed to gain access.

Combination Lighting– Directional Signal Switch

REMOVAL & INSTALLATION

LeCar

1. Disconnect the battery.
2. Remove the instrument panel housing screws.
3. Remove the switch bottom shell.
4. Remove the switch screws and disconnect the junction blocks.
5. Remove the switch.
6. The installation is the reverse of the removal procedure.

All Except LeCar

1. Disconnect the battery.
2. Remove the steering wheel and the two half housings.
3. Remove the retaining bolt and the retaining screw. Remove the junction block.
4. Remove the switch assembly by pulling it upward.
5. The installation is the reverse of the removal procedure.

Ignition Switch

REMOVAL & INSTALLATION

LeCar

1. Disconnect the battery and remove the combination switch shell assembly.
2. Disconnect the ignition switch connector.
3. Turn the key to the "garage" position and remove the key.
4. Remove the retaining screw from the side of the switch housing.
5. Press the retaining catch with the top of a scriber and push the switch out from behind to withdraw it.
6. To install the switch, reverse the removal procedure, using a new switch assembly.

All Except LeCar

1. Disconnect the battery.
2. Remove the steering wheel and the two half housings around the steering column.
3. Disconnect the ignition switch connector.
4. Place the key in the park position and remove the key.
5. Remove the retaining screw and push in on the retaining pin and push behind the switch to remove it from the housing.
6. Installation is the reverse of the removal procedure.

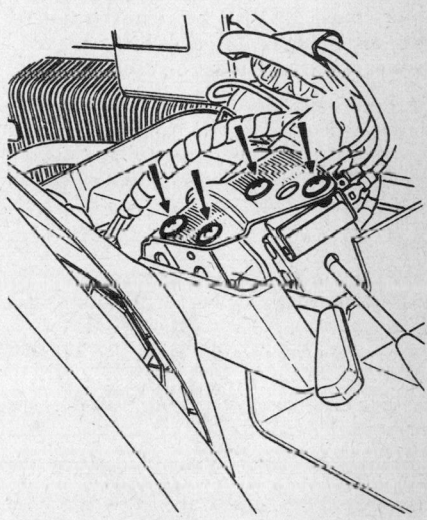

LeCar combination switch removal

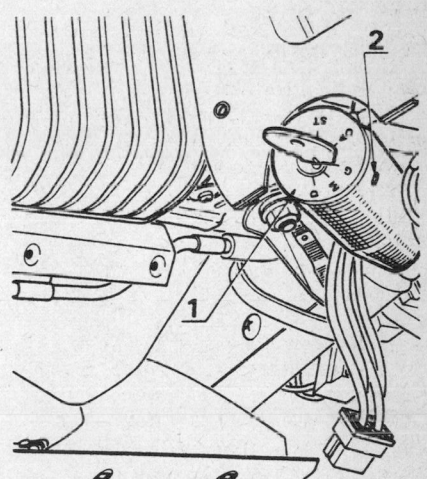

LeCar ignition switch removal

Steering Linkage

REMOVAL & INSTALLATION

Alliance and Encore

NOTE: This procedure requires the use of special tools.

1. Raise and support the front of the car on jackstands.

2. Remove the steering arm ball joint nuts.

3. Using a ball joint separator, disconnect the ball joints.

4. Remove the steering shaft universal bolt.

5. Mark the postion of the steering shaft, steering wheel, universal joint and steering rack and pinion in relation to one another.

6. Remove the two steering rack and pinion mounting bolts. On models with power steering, disconnect the hoses.

7. Lift out the rack and pinion, along with the steering arms.

NOTE: The steering rack axial ball joints must NEVER be removed unless they are being replaced. When replaced, new lockwashers must be used.

8. Installation is the reverse of removal. The steering arm ball joint nuts are torqued to 26 ft. lb.; the rack and pinion mounting bolts are torqued to 40 ft. lb.

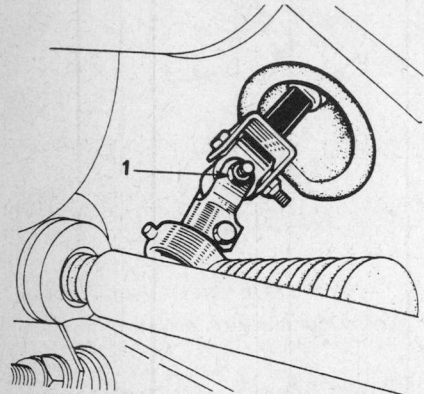

Removing the Alliance and Encore steering shaft bolt

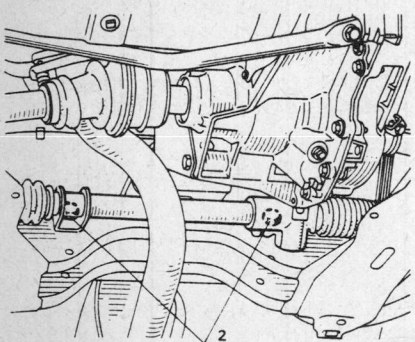

Steering rack bolts (2) on the Alliance and Encore

LeCar

1. Disconnect the battery.
2. Remove the spare tire.
3. Remove the air cleaner.
4. Remove, but do not disconnect the cooling fan motor relay.
5. Disconnect the governor, connector and valve.
6. Disconnect the outlet pipe from the air pump.

7. Disconnect and place aside, the air pump and air pump filter.

8. Disconnect the steering shaft flexible coupling, but retain the rubber spacer.

9. Remove the rack and pinion attaching bolts.

10. Take note of the number and position of the adjusting shims and lift out the steering gear assembly.

11. Installation is the reverse of removal. Torque the steering shaft flexible coupling nuts to 10 ft. lb.; the rack and pinion mounting nuts to 25 ft. lb.

18, 18i, Sport Wagon and Fuego

NOTE: This procedure requires the use of special tools.

1. Raise and support the front end on jackstands.

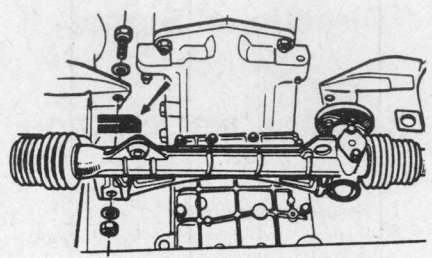

LeCar steering gear

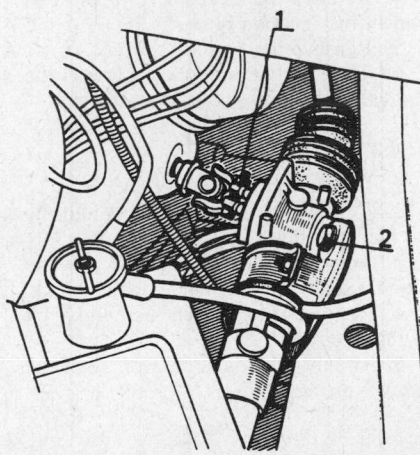

R-18 and Fuego steering U-joint. (1) is the key bolt; (2) is one of the 4 attaching bolts

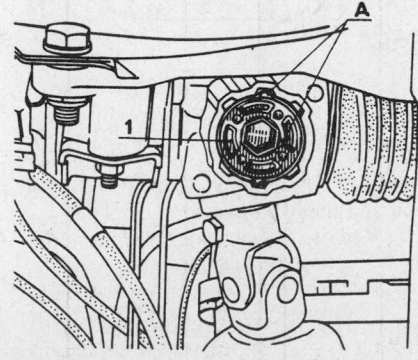

Steering gear adjustment points. (A) is the lock collar; (1) is the adjusting nut

2. Remove the tie-rod end nuts.

3. Using a tool such as Renault No. T.Av. 476, remove the stub axle carrier ball joint cones.

4. Remove the steering shaft U-joint key bolt. Mark the position of the U-joint with respect to the shaft splines, and disconnect the U-joint.

5. Remove the four rack housing-to-crossmember bolts. On cars with power steering, clamp the hoses at the reservoir. Disconnect the pipes at the reservoir and the pump.

6. Remove the rack assembly through the hole on the cowl side.

NOTE: Never unscrew the axial ball joints on the rack unless they are to be replaced. If they are being replaced, new lockwashers must be used.

7. Installation is the reverse of removal. Torque the tie-rod end nuts to 25 ft. lb.; the ball joint nut to 30 ft. lb.

RACK AND PINION ADJUSTMENTS

All Models

1. Raise and support the front end under the frame with jackstands, so that the steering is free to move.

2. Remove the front wheels.

3. Unlock the steering rack adjusting nut by bending away the tabs.

4. Using a 10mm hex key, tighten the adjusting nut to 7½–8 ft. lb., then back it off ¼ turn. The steering should move freely and smoothly from lock to lock. Bend back the tabs to lock the adjusting nut.

Power Steering Pump

REMOVAL & INSTALLATION

1. Clamp the pump input hose.
2. Place a drip pan under the car.
3. Disconnect the hoses from the pump.
4. Loosen the pump and remove the drive belt.
5. Unbolt and remove the pump.
6. Installation is the reverse of removal. Adjust the drive belt so that it has a ½ in. deflection when pressed at the midpoint of its longest straight run. Bleed the system.

BLEEDING THE POWER STEERING SYSTEM

NOTE: System capacity is 1.33 qts.

1. Completely fill the reservoir.
2. Start the engine and slowly turn the steering wheel from lock to lock and back to the midpoint.
3. Fill the reservoir to the FULL HOT mark.
4. Turn the steering wheel from lock to lock again.
5. Add fluid as necessary.

BRAKES

For all brake system repair and service procedures not detailed below, please refer to "Brakes" in the Unit Repair section.

Adjustment

FRONT BRAKES

The front brakes are of the disc brake design and require no adjustments.

REAR BRAKES

LeCar

NOTE: **Always start with the leading shoe.**

The rear brakes are of the conventional shoe design and require adjustments at regular intervals. To adjust, raise the wheels and turn the adjuster lug of the front shoe, in a downward movement to the front. Lock the drum and then release the adjuster until the wheel turns freely. Adjust the rear lug in the same manner, only to the rear in a downward movement.

— CAUTION —

Be certain the rear drums are not dragging as the wheels are rotated in checking for freeness of the brakes.

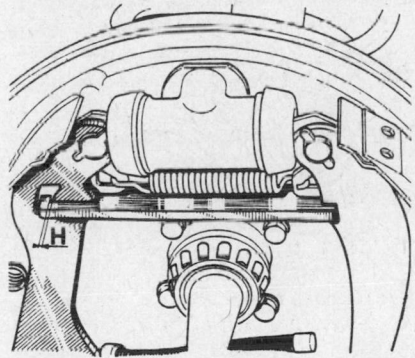

18i and Fuego rear brake shoe adjustment. Measurement should be made at (H)

All except LeCar

1. Raise and support the rear of the car on jackstands.
2. Remove the wheels.
3. Remove the brake drums.
4. Look at the front shoe. The brake shoe cross link has a hooked end which enters the shoe webbing. Measure the gap (H in the illustration) between the inner face of the hooked end and the shoe webbing. The gap should be 0.039 in. (1mm). This measurement should be taken with all tension released from the parking brake. If this dimension is not correct, it will be necessary to replace cross link tension spring as well as the two brake shoe holddown springs.
5. Install the brake drum and adjust the bearing end play.
6. Press down on the brake pedal several times.
7. Adjust the parking brake.

Master Cylinder

REMOVAL & INSTALLATION

LeCar

NOTE: **The master cylinder is not repairable.**

1. Drain the brake fluid reservoir with a turkey baster.

— CAUTION —

Brake fluid is a terrific paint remover! Take great care to keep it off of your car's painted surfaces.

2. Disconnect the brake lines and disconnect the warning light switch wire.
3. Withdraw the master cylinder pushrod.
4. Remove the two retaining bolts and remove the master cylinder.
5. Installation is in the reverse of removal. Be sure to do the following during the installation:
   a. Seal the master cylinder sealing surface to firewall with RTV silicon sealant.
   b. Adjust the pedal clearance to $^{13}/_{64}$ in. at the pedal pad (free play).
   c. Bleed the main brake system and then the by-pass system.

All except LeCar

1. Empty the brake fluid reservoir with a turkey baster.
2. Remove the reservoir with the seals.
3. Unscrew the four brake lines and mark them for reinstallation.
4. Remove the two retaining nuts and then the master cylinder.
5. The installation is the reverse of the removal procedure. Torque the mounting nuts to 15 ft. lb. The brake lines must be in their correct positions when reattached to the master cylinder.
6. Bleed the brake system.

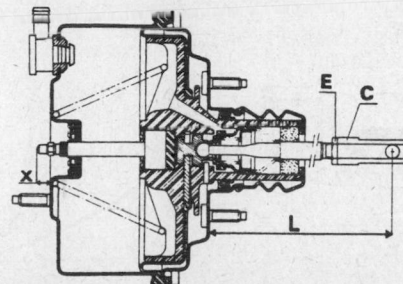

Adjusting the master cylinder operating clearance. (X) is the pushrod protrusion; (E) is the locknut; (C) is the clevis; (L) is the link length (4.961 in.)

NOTE: **The piston rod projection from the power unit should be 0.354 in. from the mating surface of the power unit, to the end of the piston rod.**

MASTER CYLINDER OPERATING CLEARANCE ADJUSTMENT

All except LeCar

Operating clearance is determined by the length of the booster pushrod that protrudes past the face of the booster. Protrusion should be 0.354 in. ($^{23}/_{64}$ in. or 9mm). Adjustment is made at the pushrod clevis, in at the brake pedal. Loosen the clevis locknut and turn the clevis until the proper protrusion is reached.

LeCar

1. Loosen the master cylinder pushrod locknut.
2. Turn the pushrod until pedal free travel, at the pedal surface is $^{13}/_{64}$ in.
3. Tighten the locknut.

Power Brake Booster

REMOVAL & INSTALLATION

All Models

1. Disconnect the power booster pushrod at the pedal.
2. Disconnect the vacuum hose from the booster.
3. Unbolt the master cylinder from the booster and carefully move it forward without disconnecting the brake lines.
4. Unbolt and remove the booster.
5. Installation is the reverse of removal. Torque the booster-to-firewall nuts to 18 ft. lb. and the master cylinder-to-booster nuts to 15 ft. lb.

Front Hub Bearings

REMOVAL & INSTALLATION

NOTE: **Special tools are required for this procedure.**

Alliance and Encore

1. Raise and support the front end on jackstands.
2. Remove the wheels.
3. Remove the caliper and suspend it out of the way, without disconnecting the brake hose.
4. Remove the rotor.
5. Place the hub in a vise. Using Renault tool number T.Ar.65 and the bolts from Renault tool number B.Tr.02, or equivalent tools, remove the inner bushing from the hub.
6. Remove the thrust washer.

7. Using a ball joint separator, disconnect the steering arm from the stub axle carrier.

8. Remove the shock absorber lower bolt and remove the lower ball joint and nut.

9. Remove the snap ring from inside the hub.

10. Press out the outer track ring using one of the two original inner track rings. Leave the ball cage and seals in position.

11. The new bearing should have covers protecting the seals. Remove these.

12. Press in the complete bearing assembly, with the plastic sleeve holding the two inner track rings using a piece of tubing having an outside diameter of 63mm and an inside diameter of 59mm.

13. Place the assembly in a press with the press load on the outer track ring.

NOTE: Bearings must always be replaced as a complete assembly. Once a bearing is removed, for any reason, it is damaged and must not be reused.

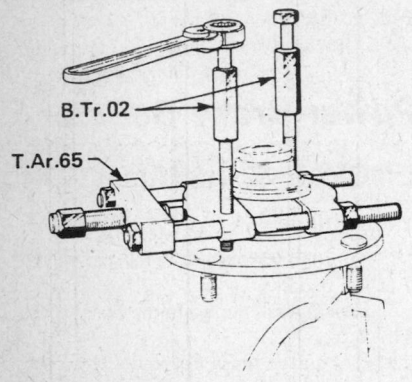

Removing the inner bushing from the Alliance front hub

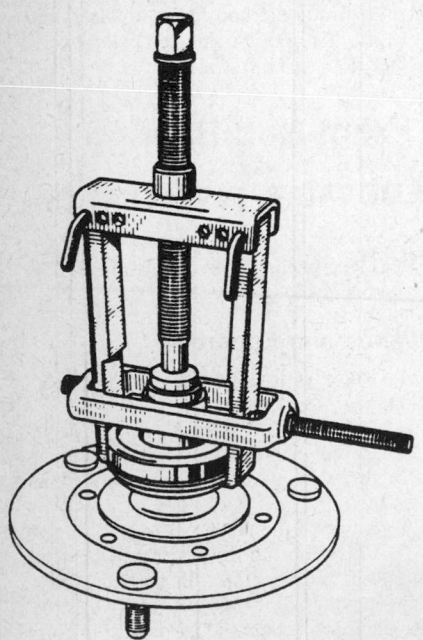

Removing the outer bearing from the LeCar

14. Remove the plastic sleeve after the bearing is installed.

15. Install the snap ring against the face of the bearing outer track ring.

16. Coat the seal lips with chassis lube.

17. Slip the thrust washer onto the hub and press into position using a piece of tubing with an outside diameter of 45mm and an inner diameter of 39mm. Apply the press load to the inner bearing track ring.

18. Install all other parts. Observe the following torques:
- Shock absorber lower end: 40 ft. lb.
- Lower ball joint key nut: 40 ft. lb.
- Steering arm ball joint nut: 25 ft. lb.
- Caliper bolts: 26 ft. lb.
- Stub axle shaft nut: 157 ft. lb.

LeCar

1. Remove the rotor/hub assembly as described above.

2. Mount protective fitting, Renault tool number Rou. 15-01 on the hub.

3. Remove the outer bearing using Renault tool number B.V.28-01, or its equivalent.

NOTE: If only the outer bearing is being installed, press it in at this time using a 1⅜ in. diameter pipe. Install the parts in reverse order of removal. If the inner bearing is being replaced, go on to Step 4.

4. Remove the stub axle carrier.

5. Remove the bearing closure plate.

6. Press out the inner bearing. Make sure that the press load is taken by a ring with a 2⁹⁄₁₆ in. inside diameter.

7. Check the condition of the stub axle bore. If it is excessively damaged, replace it.

8. Press in a new bearing using a ring with a 2⅜ in. outside diameter.

9. Pack the stub axle carrier center section with about 1 ounce of chassis lube or wheel bearing grease having a lithium base.

10. Mount the deflector and install the attaching bolts.

11. Press in the stub axle carrier/hub/rotor assembly using a 1⅜ in. diameter pipe. Don't forget the spacer.

12. Apply RTV sealer on the cover plate and install it.

13. Install all other parts. Torque the stub axle shaft nut to 90 ft. lb.

18, 18i, Sport Wagon and Fuego

1. Remove the rotor.

2. Remove the stub axle nut.

3. Remove the hub. You can do this by inserting a metal bar behind the hub housing and running two wheel lugs in through their holes and against the bar. Gradually tighten each lug until the hub comes off.

4. Remove the six bearing retaining bolts. They are Torx-head type.

5. Remove the bearing and inner race.

6. Remove the outer bearing race from the hub with a puller.

7. Place the inner bearing race on the stub axle and install the bearing.

8. Drive the outer bearing race in the hub using a 40mm ID pipe.

9. Pack the bearing and races with multi-purpose chassis lube.

10. Place the hub on the stub axle. It may be necessary to drive it into position with a mallet, until the stub axle nut can be threaded on. Don't forget the positioning cup behind the nut.

11. Drive the hub all the way on with the shaft nut and torque the nut to 185 ft. lb.

12. Install all other parts as previously described. Torque the bearing retaining bolts to 11 ft. lb.; the caliper bolts to 74 ft. lb.

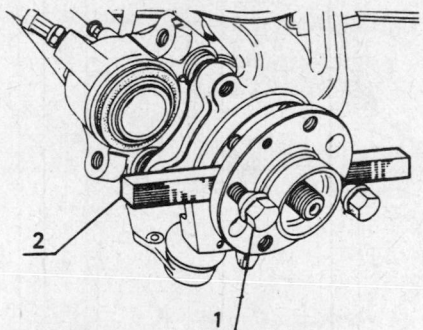

Removing the hub from the 18i or Fuego. (1) is a lug nut; (2) is a metal bar

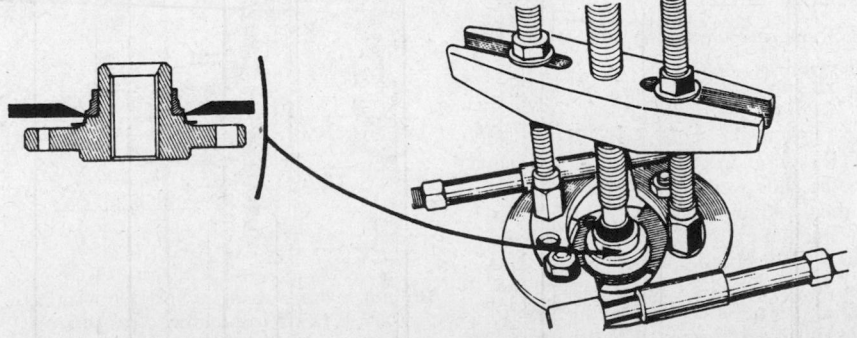

Removing the inner bearing race from the hub on the 18i or Fuego

Wheel Cylinders

REMOVAL & INSTALLATION

All Models

1. Raise and support the car on jackstands.
2. Remove the wheels, brake drums and brake shoes.
3. Disconnect the brake pipe from the wheel cylinder.
4. Unbolt and remove the wheel cylinder.
5. Installation is the reverse of removal. Torque the wheel cylinder bolts to 10-13 ft. lb.

Parking Brake

ADJUSTMENT

LeCar

NOTE: The brake shoes must be properly adjusted before adjusting the handbrake.

1. Release the handbrake completely.
2. Raise and support the car on jackstands.
3. Loosen the locknut on the handbrake rod.
4. The wheels should be turning freely by hand with no drag.
5. Turn the adjusting nut until a slight drag is felt at each rear wheel.
6. Lift the handbrake noting the number of notches in the complete travel. Six notches should be felt or heard.
7. Tighten the locknut.

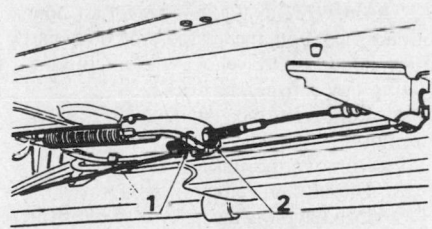

LeCar parking brake adjustment point

Alliance and Encore

NOTE: The only time that the handbrake should be adjusted is when replacing the brake shoes, parking brake cables or lever.

1. Release the handbrake completely.
2. Raise and support the rear end on jackstands.
3. Loosen the locknut on the handbrake rod.
4. Turn the adjusting nut until the brake shoes make light contact with the drums.

Back off the adjusting nut until all drag is released.
5. Check the lever travel. 7–8 notches is the correct travel. If not, readjust the cable travel with the adjusting nut. When the adjustment is complete, tighten the locknut.

18i and Fuego with Drum Brakes

NOTE: The only time that the parking brake is adjusted should be when the brake shoes, cable or lever is replaced. During adjustment, the car should be resting on its wheels.

1. Fully release the lever.
2. Loosen the locknut at the adjusting clevis.
3. Turn the adjusting nut until all slack is removed from the cables, but the cables are not pulled taut.
4. Measure the distance from the midpoint of each cable to the floor pan. The distance should be ¾ in. for the 18i and Fuego. If not, turn the adjusting nut until it is. Lever travel should be 12 or 13 notches total.

Cars with Rear Disc Brakes

1. Raise and support the rear end on jackstands.
2. Completly release the handbrake lever.
3. Loosen the locknut on the adjusting clevis.
4. Tighten the adjusting nut until the pads just touch the disc. Check the lever travel. Total travel should be 6 notches.

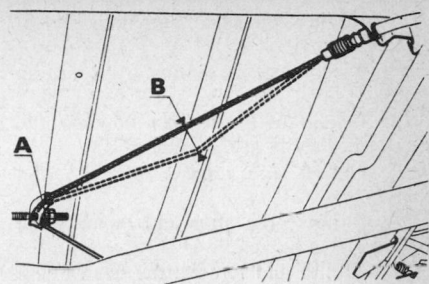

Parking brake cable adjustment on the 18i and Fuego. (A) is the adusting nut; (B) is the deflection measurement

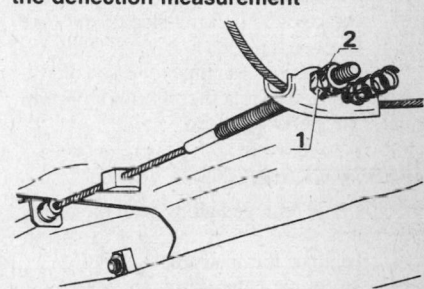

Handbrake adjustment on cars with rear disc brakes. (1) is the adjusting nut; (2) is the locknut

CHASSIS ELECTRICAL

Blower Motor

REMOVAL & INSTALLATION
LeCar

1. Disconnect the battery.

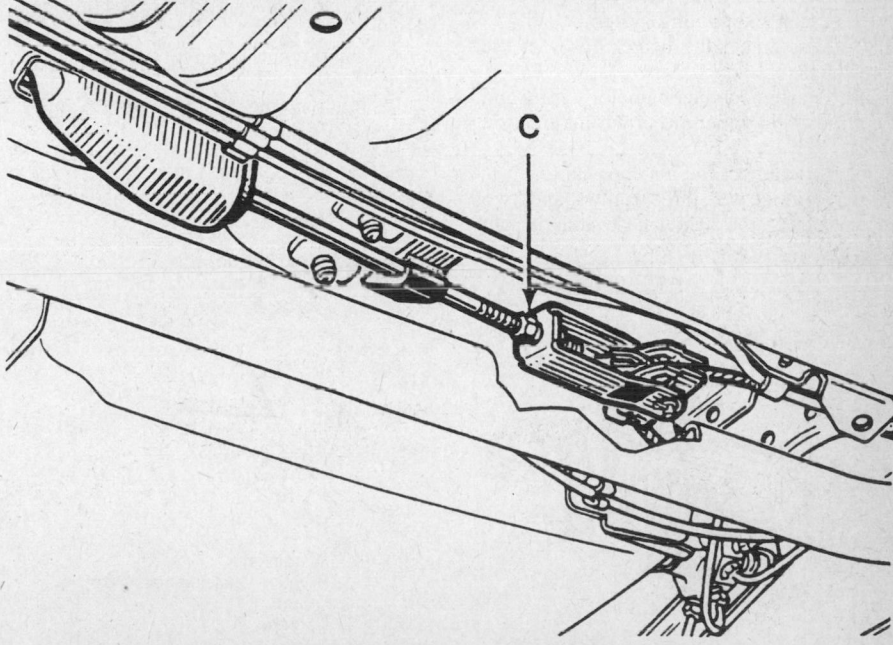

Alliance and Encore parking brake cable adjusting point; (C) is the locknut

2. Remove the heater case door control cable.

3. Disconnect the wiring from the fan motor.

4. Unclip the bleed screw hose and the accelerator cable at the case.

5. Unbolt and remove the air inlet chamber.

6. Remove the clips and separate the air duct case halves.

7. Unclip and remove the heater case door support panel.

8. Remove the three motor mount screws on the air inlet fan housing top case. Save the rubber anti–vibration washers.

9. Remove the locking sleeve and take out the blower fan.

10. Installation is the reverse of removal. Make sure that the case door control cable is properly adjusted.

Alliance and Encore

The blower is removed along with the heater core.

1. Remove the instrument panel.

2. Disconnect the wires and cables at the case.

3. Drain the cooling system. Disconnect the heater hoses at the core tubes.

4. Remove the 4 screws retaining the heater assembly and lift it out of the car.

5. Bend out the 4 tabs holding the core and remove the core from the case.

6. Remove the retaining clips from the motor and the case halve clips and open the case. Lift out the blower motor.

7. Installation is the reverse of removal.

18, 18i, Sport Wagon and Fuego

The blower is removed along with the heater core.

1. Disconnect the battery.

2. Drain the cooling system.

3. Disconnect the heater hoses at the core tubes.

4. Disconnect the fan motor wiring and the windshield wiper motor wiring junction block.

5. Disconnect the air door cable.

6. Remove the three screws and two nuts securing the heater case and lift out the case.

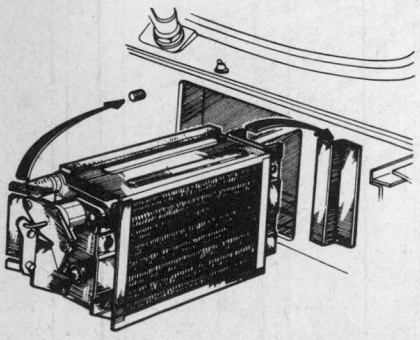

Heater core removal and installation—Le Car

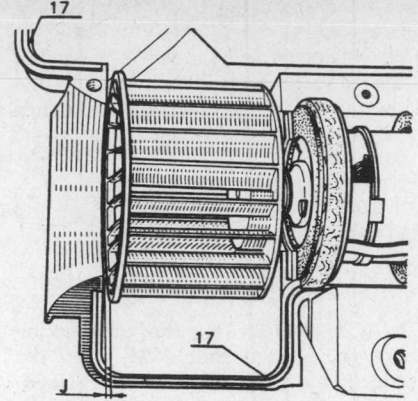

Installing the blower motor on the R-18 or Fuego. Smear the seal surface (17) with RTV sealant and make sure the blower end–play (J) is the same on both sides

7. Remove the heater case seal.

8. Unclip the case halves, separate the halves and lift out the blower motor.

9. Installation is the reverse of removal. Use RTV sealer on the housing seal and make sure that the blowers turn freely with equal play at each end.

Heater Core

REMOVAL & INSTALLATION

All except LeCar

See the blower motor removal and installation procedure.

LeCar

1. Disconnect the battery.

2. Drain the cooling system.

3. Disconnect the hoses at the core tube.

4. Remove the blower fan.

5. Remove the cable from the hot water valve.

6. Unbolt and remove the hot water valve.

7. Remove the heater core mounting bolts and lift out the core.

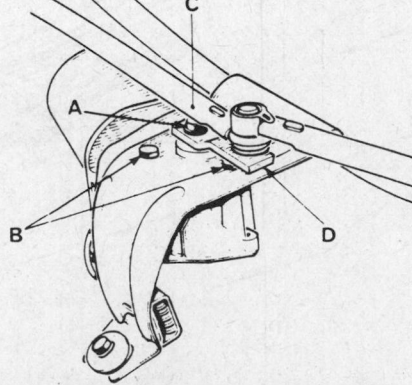

A. crank nut
B. motor retaining bolts
C. arm
D. crank

Wiper motor linkage connection on Alliance and Encore

Radio

REMOVAL & INSTALLATION

Because of the many types of radio assemblies that are available for the vehicles, no procedure is recommended, but must rely upon the radio manufacturer for specific instructions. Above all, before attempting any removal or installation of electrical components, disconnect the battery cables to avoid damage to the unit.

Windshield Wiper Motor

REMOVAL & INSTALLATION

LeCar

FRONT WIPER MOTOR

1. Remove the driving arm nut from the motor shaft.

2. Remove the motor mounting screws and lift out the motor. Disconnect the wiring connector.

3. Installation is the reverse of removal.

REAR WIPER MOTOR

1. Disconnect the wiring from the motor.

2. Remove the wiper arm.

3. Remove the outside nut and the inside bolts which hold the motor in place.

4. Installation is the reverse of removal.

Alliance and Encore

1. Disconnect the battery.

2. Remove the wiper arms.

3. Remove the wiper driveshaft nuts on the cowl.

4. Remove the linkage junction block.

5. On vehicles equipped with air conditioning, unbolt the evaporator core and move it out of the way, without disconnecting any refrigerant lines.

6. Remove the windshield wiper assembly.

7. Remove the linkage crank nut.

8. Unbolt and remove the motor.

9. Installation is the reverse of removal.

18, 18i, Sport Wagon

1. Remove the wiper arms.

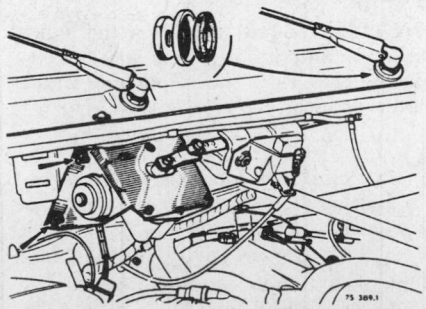

Wiper motor removal from LeCar

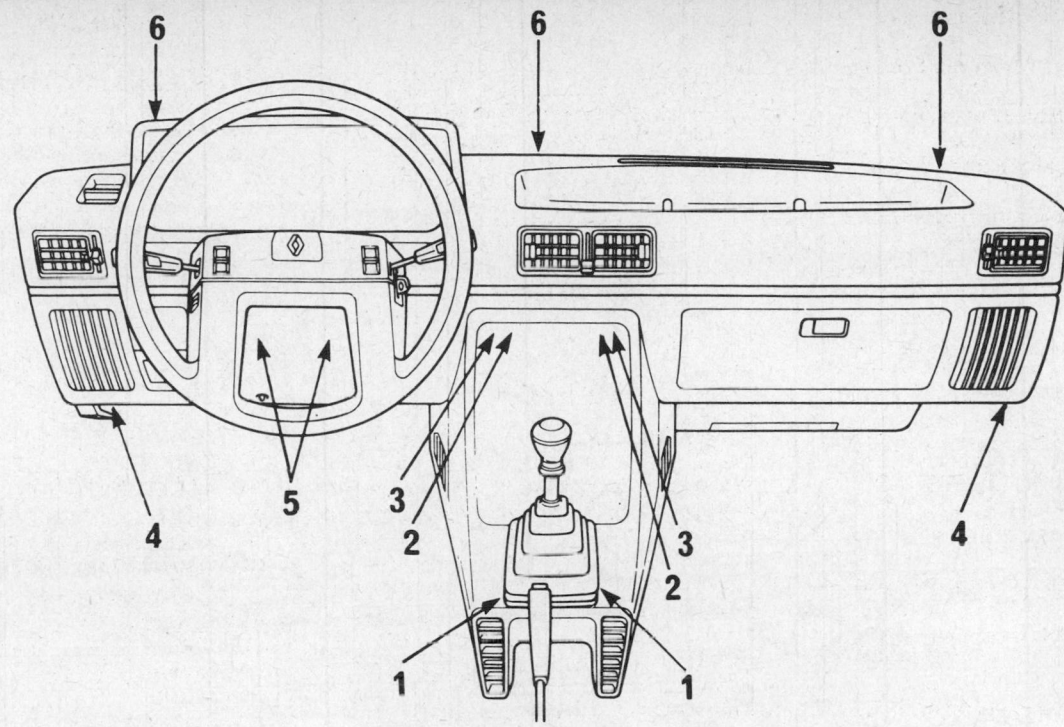

Dashboard removal points—Alliance

2. Remove the wiper arm driveshaft nuts on the cowl.

3. Remove the electrical junction block.

4. Disconnect the ground wire at the wiper mechanism plate.

5. Remove the wiper mechanism mounting plate bolt.

6. Push inward to free the two spindles, then pull the assembly toward the driver's side and out of the car.

7. Remove the crank nut and unbolt the motor.

8. Installation is the reverse of removal.

Instrument Cluster

REMOVAL & INSTALLATION

LeCar

1. Disonnect the battery.

2. Unclip the speedometer cable in the engine compartment.

3. Unclip and remove the instrument cluster trim panel.

4. The cluster is secured by one clip on each side. Press inward on the side clips until they clear the support plate, then pull the cluster out.

5. Unscrew the speedometer cable.

6. For access to any gauge, remove the cluster cover glass.

7. Installation is the reverse of removal.

Alliance and Encore

1. Disconnect the battery.

2. Remove the cluster retaining bolts (2) at the bottom of the cluster housing.

3. Grasp the sides of the cluster housing and press inwards to detach the housing. Depress the two top retaining clips, pull the housing out far enough to disconnect the wiring and speedometer cable.

4. Installation is the reverse of removal.

18, 18i, Sport Wagon and Fuego
CUSTOM MODELS

1. Disconnect the battery.

2. Remove the upper and lower steering column covers.

3. Remove the two screws securing the instrument panel to the dash. The screws are at the bottom.

4. Reach behind the panel and disconnect the wiring and speedometer cable.

5. Tilt the panel forward, and using a small screwdriver, pry out on the top of the panel, while pushing the bottom in by hand.

6. Installation is the reverse of removal. Make sure that the panel hinges on the two pins when installing.

DELUXE MODELS

1. Disconnect the battery.

2. On either side of the panel there are three button or switch positions. On all models the bottom ones are blank. These are covers over the cluster retaining screws. Pry these covers off and remove the screws. Lift off the cluster bezel.

3. Disconnect the switches and remove the switch panel.

4. Squeeze the instrument panel retaining clips and pull the panel out far enough to disconnect the speedometer and wiring. Lift the panel out of the car.

5. Installation is the reverse of removal.

Fuses

On all models, except the Alliance and Encore, the fuse panel is located on the left side, under the dash, next to the steering column. On the Alliance and Encore, the fuse panel is located under the glove compartment. To remove the fuse panel, on all except Alliance and Encore, remove the attaching screws and/or clips. To remove the Alliance and Encore fuse panel, first depress the clips and swing the fuse panel cover out of the way, then unscrew the fuse panel.

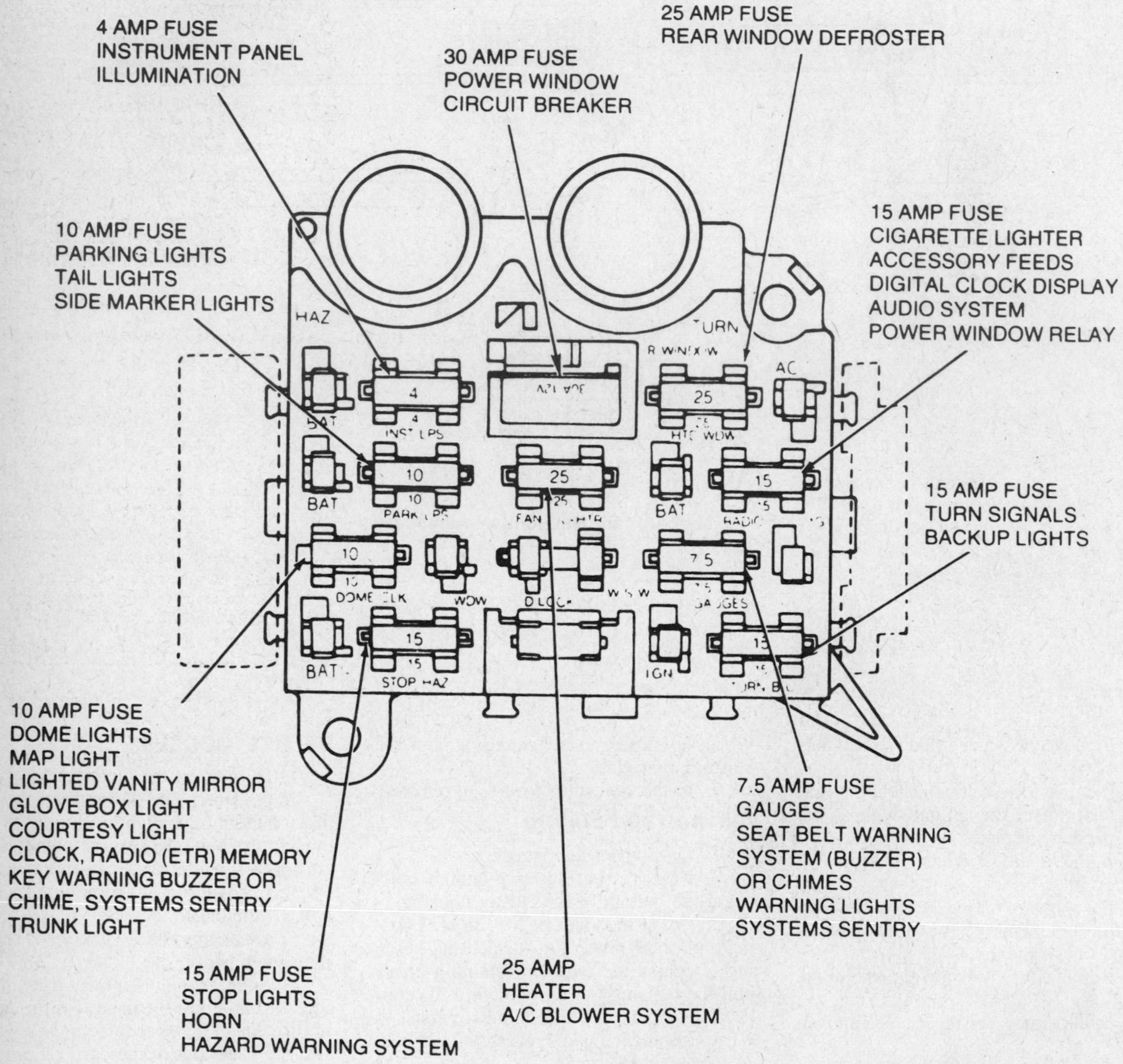

4 AMP FUSE
INSTRUMENT PANEL
ILLUMINATION

30 AMP FUSE
POWER WINDOW
CIRCUIT BREAKER

25 AMP FUSE
REAR WINDOW DEFROSTER

10 AMP FUSE
PARKING LIGHTS
TAIL LIGHTS
SIDE MARKER LIGHTS

15 AMP FUSE
CIGARETTE LIGHTER
ACCESSORY FEEDS
DIGITAL CLOCK DISPLAY
AUDIO SYSTEM
POWER WINDOW RELAY

15 AMP FUSE
TURN SIGNALS
BACKUP LIGHTS

10 AMP FUSE
DOME LIGHTS
MAP LIGHT
LIGHTED VANITY MIRROR
GLOVE BOX LIGHT
COURTESY LIGHT
CLOCK, RADIO (ETR) MEMORY
KEY WARNING BUZZER OR
CHIME, SYSTEMS SENTRY
TRUNK LIGHT

7.5 AMP FUSE
GAUGES
SEAT BELT WARNING
SYSTEM (BUZZER)
OR CHIMES
WARNING LIGHTS
SYSTEMS SENTRY

15 AMP FUSE
STOP LIGHTS
HORN
HAZARD WARNING SYSTEM

25 AMP
HEATER
A/C BLOWER SYSTEM

Alliance/Encore Fuse Panel

SAAB
99, 900

SERIAL NUMBER IDENTIFICATION

Vehicle

The vehicle serial number is located in two places on all SAAB models: the serial number is stamped on a plate at the lower left hand corner of the windshield, and the serial number is punched in the car body under the left side of the rear seat cushion.

Beginning with the 1981 and later models, the vehicle serial number is located on the right side of the rear cross beam in the luggage compartment.

CHASSIS NUMBER
Up To and Including 1980 (11 Digits)

Example—

$$\underset{(1)}{90}\ \underset{(2)}{79}\ \underset{(3)}{2}\ \underset{(4)}{000001}$$

(1) Model:
   90 = 900
   99 = 99
(2) Year:
   78 = 1978
   79 = 1979
   80 = 1980
(3) Assembly Plant:
   1 = Trollhättan
   2 = Trollhättan
   3 = Nystäd (Finland)
(4) Serial number:
   000001

CHASSIS NUMBER
Beginning With 1981 and Later (17 Digits)

Example—

$$\underset{(1)}{YS3}\ \underset{(2)}{A}\ \underset{(3)}{G}\ \underset{(4)}{3}\ \underset{(5)}{1}\ \underset{(6)}{S}\ \underset{(7)}{X}\ \underset{(8)}{B}\ \underset{(9)}{1}\ \underset{(10)}{000001}$$

(1) Manufacturer:
   YS3 = Sweden
   YK1 = Finland
(2) Production line:
   A = 900

(3) Series:
   G = 900
   S = 900S
   E = 900S
   T = Turbo 900
(4) Body Type:
   3 = Two side doors and one tailgate
   4 = Four side doors
   5 = Four side doors and one tailgate
(5) Engine:
   1 = B20C
   2 = B20T
   3 = B20I
   4 = B20S
(6) Safety equipment:
   A = Air bags
   P = Passive safety belts
   S = Active safety belts
(7) Check digit:
   0–9 or X
(8) Model Year:
   B = 1981
   C = 1982
   D = 1983
   E = 1984
   F = 1985
(9) Assembly Plant:
   1 = Trollhättan—Line one
   2 = Trollhättan—Line two
   3 = Arlov
   4 = Nystäd (Finland)
(10) Serial Number:
   000001

ENGINE NUMBER
Up To and Including 1980

Example—

$$\underset{(1)}{BT}\ \underset{(2)}{20}\ \underset{(3)}{P01}\ \underset{(4)}{000001}$$

(1) BT = Gasoline engine, twin carburetor
   BI = Gasoline engine, mechanical injection

BSI = Gasoline engine, Turbo and mechanical injection
(2) Cylinder volume in deciliter (dl). (deciliter equals ¹⁄₁₀ of liter)
(3) Variant designation, such as engine/transmission combination and geographic location
(4) Serial number in six digits

ENGINE NUMBER
From 1981 and Later

Example—

$$\underset{(1)}{B}\ \underset{(2)}{20}\ \underset{(3)}{S}\ \underset{(4)}{M}\ \underset{(5)}{UC}\ \underset{(6)}{01}\ \underset{(7)}{B}\ \underset{(8)}{000001}$$

(1) B = Gasoline engine
(2) Cylinder volume in deciliter (dl) (deciliter equal ¹⁄₁₀ of liter)
(3) Model:
   C = Single carburetor
   T = Twin carburetor
   I = Fuel injection
   S = Turbo
(4) Transmission type:
   M = Manual
   A = Automatic
(5) Exhaust emission control level:
   UC = USA
   SW = Sweden
   EU = Europe
(6) Equipment variants, such as engine/transmission combinations and geographic locations
(7) Year designations:
   B = 1981
   C = 1982
   D = 1983
   E = 1984
   F = 1985
(8) Serial number in six digits

Engine

On the 1985 cc engine the number is stamped on a plate which is secured to the upper portion of the engine directly forward of the fuel injection unit.

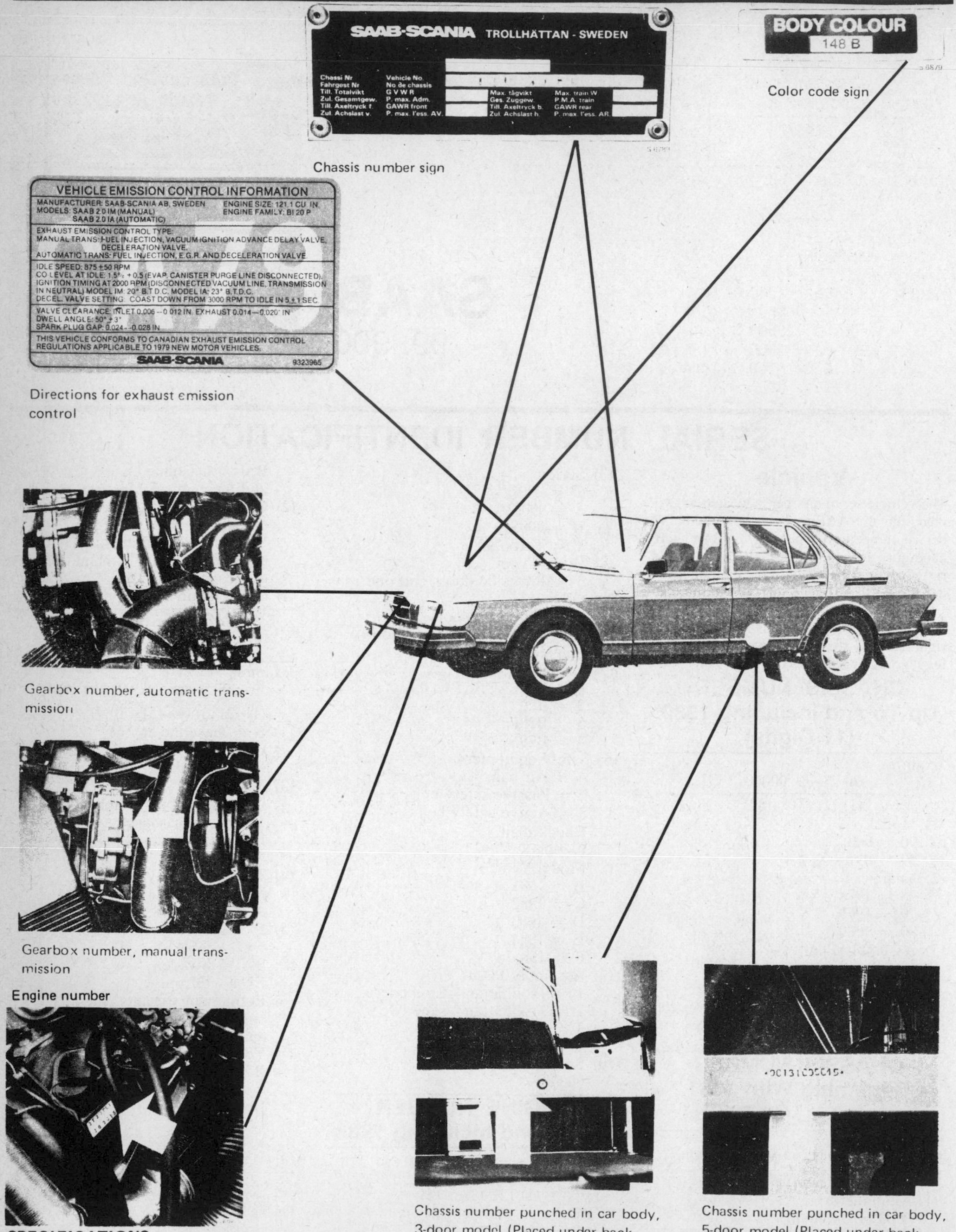

SAAB-SCANIA TROLLHÄTTAN - SWEDEN

Chassi Nr	Vehicle No.		
Fahrgest Nr	No de chassis		
Till. Totalvikt	G V W R	Max. tägvikt	Max. train W
Zul. Gesamtgew.	P. max. Adm.	Ges. Zuggew.	P. M.A. train
Till. Axeltryck f.	GAWR front	Till. Axeltryck b.	GAWR rear
Zul. Achslast v.	P. max. l'ess. AV.	Zul. Achslast h.	P. max. l'ess. AR.

Chassis number sign

BODY COLOUR
148 B

Color code sign

VEHICLE EMISSION CONTROL INFORMATION
MANUFACTURER: SAAB-SCANIA AB, SWEDEN   ENGINE SIZE: 121.1 CU IN.
MODELS: SAAB 2.0 IM (MANUAL)   ENGINE FAMILY: BI 20 P
        SAAB 2.0 IA (AUTOMATIC)
EXHAUST EMISSION CONTROL TYPE:
MANUAL TRANS: FUEL INJECTION, VACUUM IGNITION ADVANCE DELAY VALVE,
        DECELERATION VALVE.
AUTOMATIC TRANS: FUEL INJECTION, E.G.R. AND DECELERATION VALVE.
IDLE SPEED: 875 ±50 RPM
CO LEVEL AT IDLE: 1.5% + 0.5 (EVAP. CANISTER PURGE LINE DISCONNECTED).
IGNITION TIMING AT 2000 RPM (DISCONNECTED VACUUM LINE, TRANSMISSION
IN NEUTRAL) MODEL IM: 20° B.T.D.C. MODEL IA: 23° B.T.D.C.
DECEL. VALVE SETTING : COAST DOWN FROM 3000 RPM TO IDLE IN 5.±1 SEC.
VALVE CLEARANCE: INLET 0.006—0.012 IN. EXHAUST 0.014—0.020 IN.
DWELL ANGLE: 50° + 3°
SPARK PLUG GAP: 0.024—0.028 IN.
THIS VEHICLE CONFORMS TO CANADIAN EXHAUST EMISSION CONTROL
REGULATIONS APPLICABLE TO 1979 NEW MOTOR VEHICLES.
SAAB-SCANIA   9323965

Directions for exhaust emission
control

Gearbox number, automatic transmission

Gearbox number, manual transmission

Engine number

SPECIFICATIONS

Chassis number punched in car body,
3-door model (Placed under back
seat cushion)

Chassis number punched in car body,
5-door model (Placed under back
seat cushion)

Component identification number locations

GENERAL ENGINE SPECIFICATIONS

Year	Engine Displacement cc (cu. in.)	Fuel Delivery Type	Horsepower @ rpm	Torque @ rpm	Bore × Stroke (in.)	Compression Ratio	Maximum Oil Pressure (psi)
'78–'85	1985 (121.0)	Bosch C.I.S. Fuel injection	②	③	3.543 × 3.071	①	57–71

① Federal Model—1978–85   9.25:1
    California—1978–79   8.7:1
                1980–85   9.25:1
    Canada—1978–84   9.25:1
    Turbo—1979–85   7.2:1
    Turbo APC 1982–85   8.5
② 1978—   115 @ 5500 Federal
           110 @ 5500 California
           118 @ 5500 Canada
   1979–80—100 @ 5200 w/single carburetor
           108 @ 5200 w/twin carburetor
           118 @ 5500 w/fuel injection
           145 @ 5000 Turbo
   1981–85—110 @ 5500 w/catalyst equipped, except Turbo

           115 @ 5500 non-catalyst
           135 @ 4800 Turbo
           118 @ 4800 Canada
③ 1978—123 @ 3500 Federal and Canada
           119 @ 3500 California
   1979–80—115 @ 3500 w/single carburetor
           127 @ 3300 w/twin carburetor
           123 @ 3700 w/fuel injection
           174 @ 3000 Turbo
   1981–85—119 @ 3500 w/catalyst equipped engine except Turbo
           160 @ 3500 Turbo
           123 @ 3500 Canada and non-catalyst Federal engine

TUNE-UP SPECIFICATIONS

Year	Engine Displacement (cc)	Spark Plugs Type	Spark Plugs Gap	Distributor Point Dwell (deg)	Distributor Reluctor Gap (in.)⑧	Basic Ignition Timing (deg)	Intake Valve Opens (deg)	Fuel Pump Pressure (psi)	Idle Speed (rpm)	Valve Clearance (in.) Intake	Valve Clearance (in.) Exhaust
'78–'85	1985	③	0.024–0.028	Electronic ⑦	0.010 ⑧	②⑥	10 BTDC⑤	①	875	0.008–0.010	0.016–④ 0.018

NOTE: If these specifications differ from those on the engine compartment stickers, use the sticker specifications.

① Fuel injected engines (all models): Fuel line pressure before the control pressure regulator is 66.9–69.7 (setting valve), and 48.5–54.0 psi (warm engine) after the control pressure regulator (located in fuel distributor).

② '78–'85—20° @ 2000 rpm
'78–'85 Canada, manual transmission—20° BTDC @ 2000 rpm
'78–'85 Canada, automatic transmission—23° BTDC @ 2000 rpm

③ Turbo—NGK-BP7ES, Champion N7Y or N7YC; non-Turbo NGK BP6ES, Bosch W70 or Champion N9Y, N9YC

④ Turbo—.018–.020

⑤ Turbo—12° BTDC

⑥ With vacuum hose disconnected

⑦ Canadian models with points ignition, 47–53°

⑧ Point gap (Canadian models) 0.016 in. (0.4mm)

FIRING ORDERS

NOTE: To avoid confusion, always replace spark plug wires one at a time.

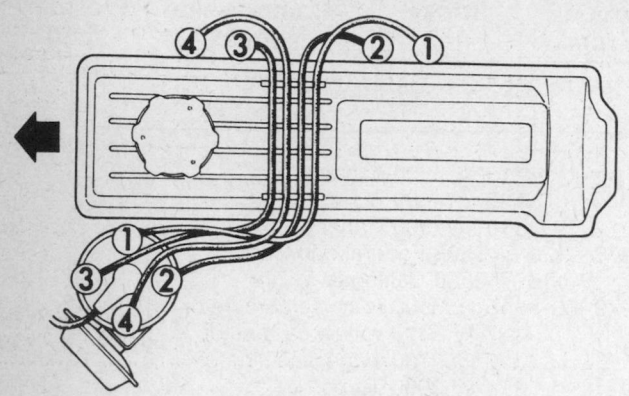

Firing order and ignition cable positioning to 1980

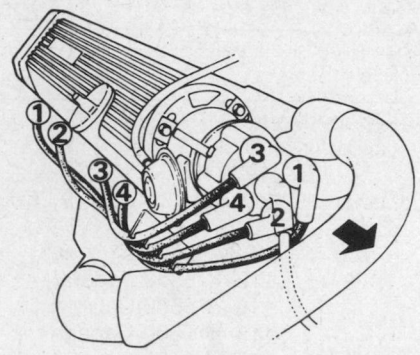

Firing order and ignition cable positioning—1981 and later

CAPACITIES

Year	Engine Displacement (cc)	Engine Crankcase (qts.) With Filter	Engine Crankcase (qts.) Without Filter	Transmission (pts.) Manual	Transmission (pts.) Automatic	Drive Axle (pts.)	Fuel Tank (gals.)	Cooling System (qts.) w/o AC
'78–'85	1985	3.7	3.2	5.2①	17	1.3	14.5③	8.5②

① 6.4—5 speed trans. & 4 speed w/o dipstick
② '79–'80—10.5, '81–'83—10.8 qts
③ '80–'85—16.6 U.S. gals.

CRANKSHAFT AND CONNECTING ROD SPECIFICATIONS

Year	Engine Displacement (cc)	Crankshaft Main Bearing Journal Diameter (in.)	Crankshaft Main Bearing Oil Clearance (in.)	Crankshaft Shaft End-Play (in.)	Crankshaft Thrust on No.	Connecting Rod Journal Diameter (in.)	Connecting Rod Oil Clearance (in.)
'78–'85	1985	2.283–2.284	0.0008–0.0025	0.003–0.011	3	2.0465–2.0472	0.0010–0.0025

VALVE SPECIFICATIONS

Year	Engine Displacement (cc)	Valve Seat Angle (deg)	Valve Face Angle (deg)	Spring Test Pressure (lbs. @ in.)	Installed Spring Height (in.)	Stem-To-Guide Clearance (in.) Intake	Stem-To-Guide Clearance (in.) Exhaust	Stem Diameter (in.) Intake	Stem Diameter (in.) Exhaust
'78–'85	1985	45	44.5	178–198 @ 1.16	1.56	0.020①	0.020①	0.3134–0.3139	0.3132–0.3142

① Maximum clearance measured with valve face pulled 3 mm (0.12 in.) from valve seat

PISTON AND RING SPECIFICATIONS

Year	Engine Displacement (cc)	Piston Diameter (in.)	Ring Gap (in.) Top Compression	Ring Gap (in.) Bottom Compression	Ring Gap (in.) Oil Control	Ring Side Clearance (in groove) (in.) Top Compression	Ring Side Clearance (in groove) (in.) Bottom Compression
'78–'85	1985	3.5425–3.5428	0.014–0.022	0.012–0.018	0.015–0.055	0.002–0.003	0.002–0.003

BRAKE SPECIFICATIONS

Year	Wheel Lug Nut Torque (ft. lbs.)	Master Cylinder Bore	Brake Disc (in.)		Pad Thickness (in.)	
			Minimum Thickness	Maximum Axial Run-Out	Front	Rear
'78–'85	65–80	7/8	0.461 Front 0.374 Rear	0.004	0.425	0.335

TORQUE SPECIFICATIONS
(ft. lbs.)

Year	Engine Displacement (cc)	Cylinder Head Bolts	Rod Bearing Bolts	Main Bearing Bolts	Crankshaft Pulley or Gear Bolt	Flywheel to Crankshaft Bolts	Camshaft Gear Bolt	Intake Manifold	Exhaust Manifold
'78–'85	1985	① ②	40	79	137	43	14	13	18

① 1978–81—with 17mm screw head: 69 ft. lbs.
    with 15mm screw head: 1st stage—44 ft. lbs.
        2nd stage—65 ft. lbs.—Run engine to warm.
        Allow 30 minutes cool time—Retighten to 65 ft. lbs.
② 1982 and later—1st stage—43 ft. lbs.
    2nd stage—72 ft. lbs.—Run engine to warm.
    Allow 30 minutes cool time—Retighten to 72 ft. lbs.
    1984–85: Tighten each bolt another 1¾ (90°) of a turn.

BATTERY AND STARTER SPECIFICATIONS

Year	Engine Displacement (cc)	Battery			Starter						Brush Spring Tension (oz.)
		Ampere Hour Capacity	Volts	Terminal Ground	Load Test			No Load Test			
					Amps.	Volts	@ rpm	Amps.	Volts	@ rpm	
'78–'85	1985	60	12	Neg.	205–235	9	1000–1300	35–55	11.5	6500–8500	41–46

ALTERNATOR AND REGULATOR SPECIFICATIONS

Year	Engine Displacement (cc)	Model	Alternator					
			Rated Voltage (volts @ rpm)	Maximum Continuous Load (amps. @ rpm)	Minimum Brush Length (in.)	Brush Spring Pressure (oz.)	Regulating Voltage	
'78–'80	1985	99	14 @ 2000	55 @ 5000	0.34	10.5–14	13.5–14.2	
'78–'85	1985	900	14 @ 2000	55 @ 5000	①	10.5–14	13.5–14.2	
'78–'85	1985	900	14 @ 2100	65 @ 5000	①	10.5–14	13.5–14.2	
'78–'85	1985	900	14 @ 2100	70 @ 5000	①	10.5–14	13.5–14.2	

① 0.020 inch protruding from opening of brushnut assembly

WHEEL ALIGNMENT

Year	Caster	Camber	Toe-In (in.)①	King Pin Angle	Wheel Angle During Turns (deg)	
					Inner Wheel	Outer Wheel
'78–'85	1 ± ½ ②	½ ± ½	0.08 ± 0.04	1½ ± 1	20¾ ± ½ ③	20

① Measured at the rims
② 2° ± ½°—vehicles equipped with
    power steering
③ 20½° ± 1°—SAAB 99 series

SAAB

TUNE UP

Spark Plugs

The spark plugs are replaced in the conventional manner. Anyone unfamiliar with the spark plug firing order, should remove and replace only one spark plug wire and spark plug at a time or tag each wire and number them, starting at the rear of the engine at number one cylinder and working towards the front, to avoid mismatching the spark plug wires to the proper spark plugs.

Breaker Points—Canadian Models

Some Canadian model SAABs are available with conventional breaker points-type ignition systems.

REMOVAL, ADJUSTMENT AND INSTALLATION

1. Remove the distributor cap, rotor and dust shield.

NOTE: All models except 1979 and 1980 have a bearing holder that is removed along with the dust shield.

2. Position the gearshift in neutral and apply the handbrake.

3. Disconnect the electrical lead from the points assembly. Remove the securing screw for the breaker points and remove the contacts.

4. Apply a dab of grease to the distributor cam lobe.

5. Install the new breaker assembly, and snug, but do not fully tighten, the securing screw. Reconnect the electrical lead. Using a socket wrench on the crankshaft pulley sprocket, rotate the crankshaft until the breaker points rubbing block is in direct contact with the tip of the distributor cam lobe. Insert a screwdriver between the two pins, into the slot at the side of the fixed contact plate. Insert a 0.016 in. (0.4mm) feeler gauge between the contacts, and adjust the securing screw until there is just a slight drag on the feeler gauge as you slide it between the contacts. Tighten the screw

Adjusting the breaker points on Canadian models

and recheck the point gap after turning the crankshaft through one complete revolution.

6. Connect a dwell meter to the engine according to the manufacturer's instructions. Turn the engine over using the starter motor. The dwell angle should be between 47 and 53. Set the angle to the lower number, as dwell will increase with wear. Recheck the point gap after checking/setting the dwell.

7. Refit the dust shield and rotor, and distributor cap. Check the ignition timing and set to specifications by loosening the distributor mounting bolts and rotating the distributor to either advance or retard the timing.

Check the distributor rotor resistance at these two points

CHECKING THE ROTOR, DISTRIBUTOR CAP AND SPARK PLUG WIRES

1. Connect an ohmmeter between the center of the rotor and the brass contact on the side. Resistance should be 5000 ohms.

Replace the rotor if it is out of specification. Connect the ohmmeter between the end cap (spark plug contact) on each plug wire and on that wire's brass contact inside the distributor, to check plug wire resistance. Resistance should be between 2000 and 4000 ohms.

Electronic Ignition

1978–80

All vehicles that are sold in the United States are equipped with a breakerless ignition system with an electromagnetic pulse generator in the distributor and an electronic control unit which performs the task of the conventional point system.

1981 and later

An electronic ignition system using a semiconductor impulse transmitter (Hall transmitter) in the distributor with a control unit incorporating an electronic breaker, is used on all models destined for the United States and is also used on all Turbo engines. The ignition coil used with this system is capable of producing approximately 15% more voltage than the earlier breakerless ignition system and should not be interchanged. The ignition coil is provided with a safety fuse, should the coil become overheated.

Ignition Timing

Ignition timing is set in the conventional manner, using the marks that are located on the flywheel.

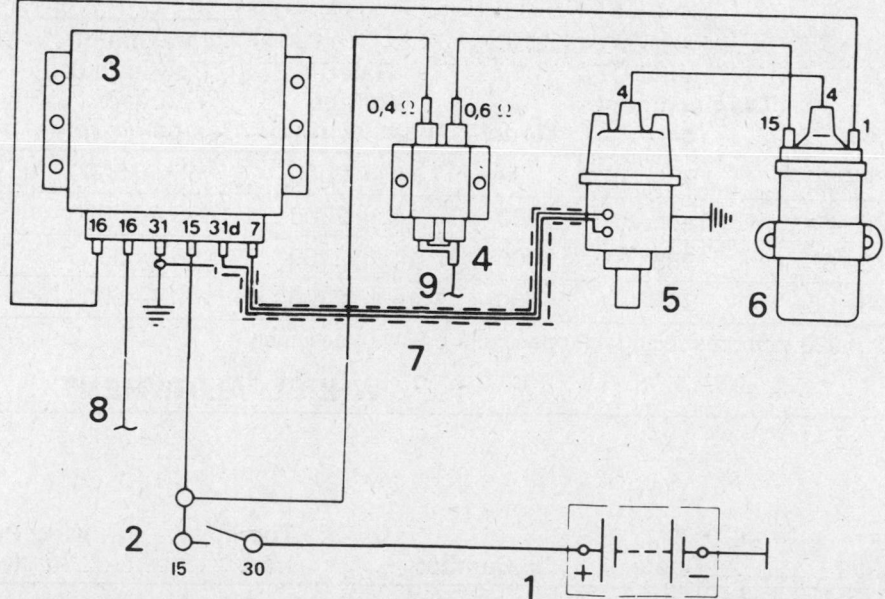

1. Battery
2. Ignition switch
3. Electronic control unit
4. Compensating resistor
5. Distributor
6. Ignition coil
7. Screened cable
8. To fuel pump relay, tachometer and TSI socket
9. To relay terminal 87a (connected at start)

Electronic ignition system schematic—1978–80

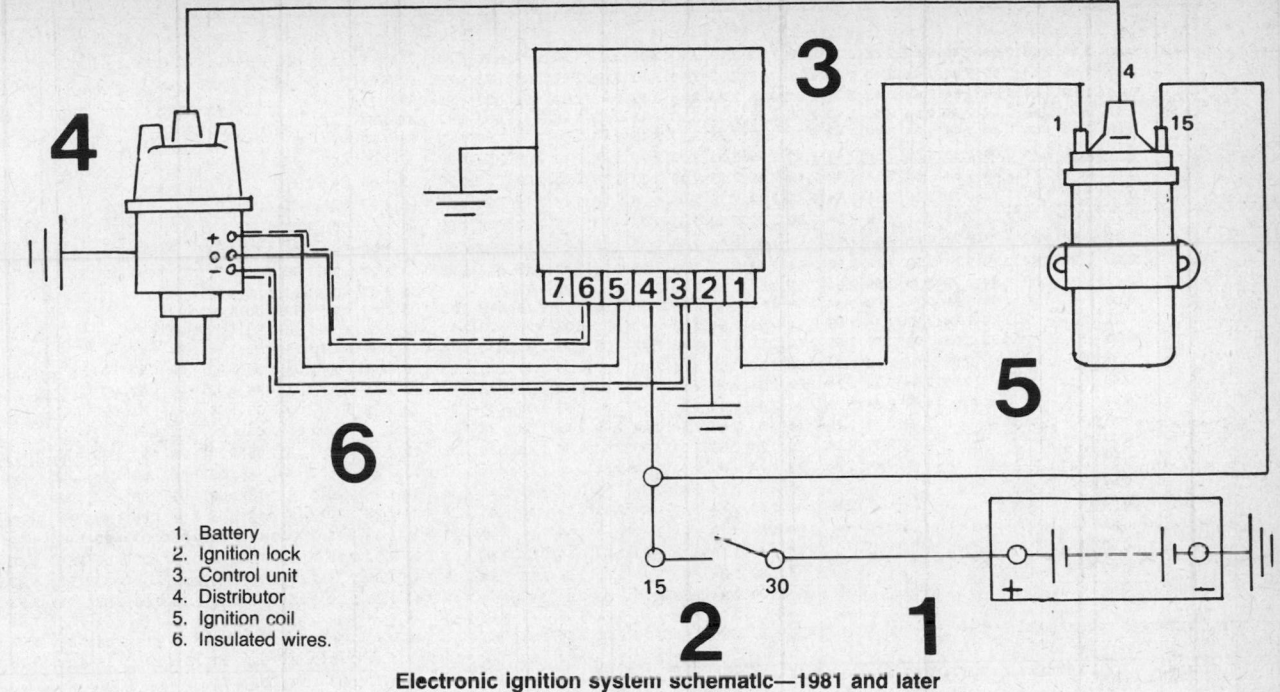

1. Battery
2. Ignition lock
3. Control unit
4. Distributor
5. Ignition coil
6. Insulated wires.

Electronic ignition system schematic—1981 and later

ELECTRONIC IGNITION DIAGNOSIS—EXCEPT HALL EFFECT
Engine Completely Dead, Fires Without Starting or Is Difficult to Start

Check	Reading	Condition of the system Probable fault	Check and remedy as necessary
1. Turn the engine over on the starter and check the length of the spark between the high tension lead from the coil and ground	More than 12 mm	Starter circuit and starter relay probably working	Check 0.4 mm compensating resistor by means of ohmmeter. Check the ignition setting. Check for flashover in coil isolator, distributor cap, rotor, ignition leads and plugs. Check the fuel system.
	Less than 12 mm or no spark		Check that current flows from the starter relay circuit to the connection on the compensating resistor. When the starter is running, the voltage between the common connection and the + on the battery should be 0. If not, check the relay and wiring. Proceed to step 2.
2. Switch on the ignition. Before proceeding, check that the battery charge is at least 11 V	Less than 11 V		Charge the battery; readings taken with insufficient battery voltage will give faulty values.
	More than 11 V		Proceed to step 3.

SAAB

Valve clearance measured with dial indicator (mm)																								
0,00	2,64	2,59	2,54	2,48	2,43	2,38	2,33	2,28	2,23	2,18	2,13	2,08	2,03	1,98	1,93	1,88	1,82	1,77					
0,02	2,69	2,64	2,59	2,54	2,48	2,43	2,38	2,33	2,28	2,23	2,18	2,13	2,08	2,03	1,98	1,93	1,88	1,82	1,77				
0,05	2,69	2,64	2,59	2,54	2,48	2,43	2,38	2,33	2,28	2,23	2,18	2,13	2,08	2,03	1,98	1,93	1,88	1,82	1,77				
0,07	2,74	2,69	2,64	2,59	2,54	2,48	2,43	2,38	2,33	2,28	2,23	2,18	2,13	2,08	2,03	1,98	1,93	1,88	1,82	1,77			
0,10	2,74	2,69	2,64	2,59	2,54	2,48	2,43	2,38	2,33	2,28	2,23	2,18	2,13	2,08	2,03	1,98	1,93	1,88	1,82	1,77			
0,12	2,79	2,74	2,69	2,64	2,59	2,54	2,48	2,43	2,38	2,33	2,28	2,23	2,18	2,13	2,08	2,03	1,98	1,93	1,88	1,82	1,77		
0,15	2,79	2,74	2,69	2,64	2,59	2,54	2,48	2,43	2,38	2,33	2,28	2,23	2,18	2,13	2,08	2,03	1,98	1,93	1,88	1,82	1,77		
0,17	2,84	2,79	2,74	2,69	2,64	2,59	2,54	2,48	2,43	2,38	2,33	2,28	2,23	2,18	2,13	2,08	2,03	1,98	1,93	1,88	1,82	1,77	
0,20	2,84	2,79	2,74	2,69	2,64	2,59	2,54	2,48	2,43	2,38	2,33	2,28	2,23	2,18	2,13	2,08	2,03	1,98	1,93	1,88	1,82	1,77	
0,22	2,89	2,84	2,79	2,74	2,69	2,64	2,59	2,54	2,48	2,43	2,38	2,33	2,28	2,23	2,18	2,13	2,08	2,03	1,98	1,93	1,88	1,82	1,77
0,25	2,89	2,84	2,79	2,74	2,69	2,64	2,59	2,54	2,48	2,43	2,38	2,33	2,28	2,23	2,18	2,13	2,08	2,03	1,98	1,93	1,88	1,82	1,77
0,27		2,89	2,84	2,79	2,74	2,69	2,64	2,59	2,54	2,48	2,43	2,38	2,33	2,28	2,23	2,18	2,13	2,08	2,03	1,98	1,93	1,88	1,82	1,77
0,30		2,89	2,84	2,79	2,74	2,69	2,64	2,59	2,54	2,48	2,43	2,38	2,33	2,28	2,23	2,18	2,13	2,08	2,03	1,98	1,93	1,88	1,82	1,77
0,32			2,89	2,84	2,79	2,74	2,69	2,64	2,59	2,54	2,48	2,43	2,38	2,33	2,28	2,23	2,18	2,13	2,08	2,03	1,98	1,93	1,88	1,82	1,77
0,35			2,89	2,84	2,79	2,74	2,69	2,64	2,59	2,54	2,48	2,43	2,38	2,33	2,28	2,23	2,18	2,13	2,08	2,03	1,98	1,93	1,88	1,82	1,77
0,37				2,89	2,84	2,79	2,74	2,69	2,64	2,59	2,54	2,48	2,43	2,38	2,33	2,28	2,23	2,18	2,13	2,08	2,03	1,98	1,93	1,88	1,82	1,77
0,40				2,89	2,84	2,79	2,74	2,69	2,64	2,59	2,54	2,48	2,43	2,38	2,33	2,28	2,23	2,18	2,13	2,08	2,03	1,98	1,93	1,88	1,82	1,77
0,42					2,89	2,84	2,79	2,74	2,69	2,64	2,59	2,54	2,48	2,43	2,38	2,33	2,28	2,23	2,18	2,13	2,08	2,03	1,98	1,93	1,88	1,82	1,77
0,45					2,89	2,84	2,79	2,74	2,69	2,64	2,59	2,54	2,48	2,43	2,38	2,33	2,28	2,23	2,18	2,13	2,08	2,03	1,98	1,93	1,88	1,82	1,77
0,47						2,89	2,84	2,79	2,74	2,69	2,64	2,59	2,54	2,48	2,43	2,38	2,33	2,28	2,23	2,18	2,13	2,08	2,03	1,98	1,93	1,88	1,82
0,50						2,89	2,84	2,79	2,74	2,69	2,64	2,59	2,54	2,48	2,43	2,38	2,33	2,28	2,23	2,18	2,13	2,08	2,03	1,98	1,93	1,88	1,82	1,77
0,52							2,89	2,84	2,79	2,74	2,69	2,64	2,59	2,54	2,48	2,43	2,38	2,33	2,28	2,23	2,18	2,13	2,08	2,03	1,98	1,93	1,88	1,77
0,55							2,89	2,84	2,79	2,74	2,69	2,64	2,59	2,54	2,48	2,43	2,38	2,33	2,28	2,23	2,18	2,13	2,08	2,03	1,98	1,93	1,88	1,82
0,57								2,89	2,84	2,79	2,74	2,69	2,64	2,59	2,54	2,48	2,43	2,38	2,33	2,28	2,23	2,18	2,13	2,08	2,03	1,98	1,93	1,88	1,82
0,60								2,89	2,84	2,79	2,74	2,69	2,64	2,59	2,54	2,48	2,43	2,38	2,33	2,28	2,23	2,18	2,13	2,08	2,03	1,98	1,93	1,88
0,62									2,89	2,84	2,79	2,74	2,69	2,64	2,59	2,54	2,48	2,43	2,38	2,33	2,28	2,23	2,18	2,13	2,08	2,03	1,98	1,93
0,65									2,89	2,84	2,79	2,74	2,69	2,64	2,59	2,54	2,48	2,43	2,38	2,33	2,28	2,23	2,18	2,13	2,08	2,03	1,98	1,93
0,68										2,89	2,84	2,79	2,74	2,69	2,64	2,59	2,54	2,48	2,43	2,38	2,33	2,28	2,23	2,18	2,13	2,08	2,03	1,98
0,70										2,89	2,84	2,79	2,74	2,69	2,64	2,59	2,54	2,48	2,43	2,38	2,33	2,28	2,23	2,18	2,13	2,08	2,03	1,92
0,72											2,89	2,84	2,79	2,74	2,69	2,64	2,59	2,54	2,48	2,43	2,38	2,33	2,28	2,23	2,18	2,13	2,08	2,03

Pallet thickness measured																								
Inlet, mm	2,89	2,84	2,79	2,74	2,69	2,64	2,59	2,54	2,48	2,43	2,38	2,33	2,28	2,23	2,18	2,13	2,08	2,03	1,98	1,93	1,88	1,82	1,77
Exhaust (standard) mm	2,89	2,84	2,79	2,74	2,69	2,64	2,59	2,54	2,48	2,43	2,38	2,33	2,28	2,23	2,18	2,13	2,08	2,03	1,98	1,93	1,88	1,82	1,77
Exhaust (Turbo) mm				2,89	2,84	2,79	2,74	2,69	2,64	2,59	2,54	2,48	2,43	2,38	2,33	2,28	2,23	2,18	2,13	2,08	2,03	1,98	1,93	1,88	1,82	1,77

6. Using a micrometer, measure and record the thickness of the pallet (shim). This thickness plus the valve clearance adds up to the total distance between the valve and the cam.

7. The choice of the adjusting pallet (shim) is determined by the measured total distance between the valve depressor (tappet) and the cam, less the specified valve clearance for an intake or exhaust valve as the case may be.

8. Insert the new adjusting pallet (shim) and the valve depressor (tappet) and reinstall the camshaft.

9. Repeat the measurement procedure to insure that the clearances are correct.

10. Install the valve cover using a new valve cover gasket.

Fuel Injection

IDLE SPEED AND MIXTURE

NOTE: This procedure requires the use of a CO meter for proper mixture adjustment.

1. Run the engine until it reaches operating temperature.

2. Adjust the idle speed to 875 ± 50 rpm.

3. If the vehicle is not equipped with a catalytic converter, remove the pulse-air hose and plug the air intake to the non-return valves. On 1979 vehicles sold in the United States and Canada, remove the large bore hose from the charcoal canister. Connect the CO meter sensor to the exhaust pipe.

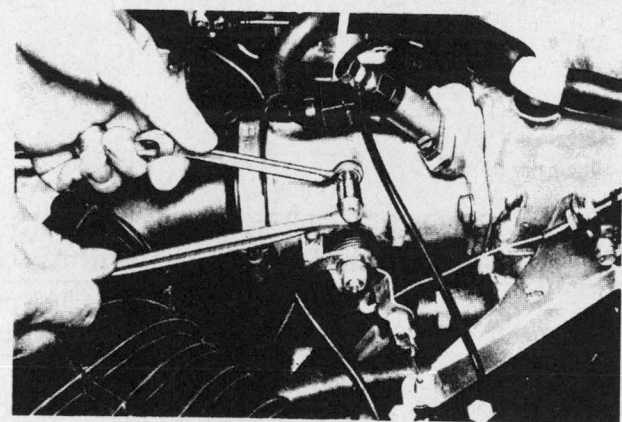

Adjusting the idle speed

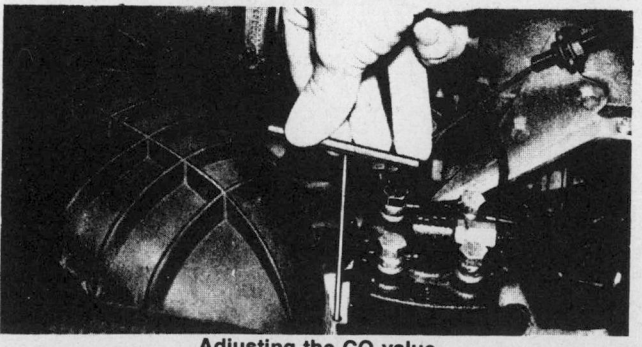

Adjusting the CO value

PERMISSIBLE CO CONTENT OF EXHAUST GASES

Non-catalyst equipped, 1978 models① ②	1.25 ± 0.75%
Non-catalyst equipped, from 1980 models① ②	0.75 ± 0.25%
Catalyst equipped, up to and including 1979 models② ③	0.75 + 0.25 or −0.5%⑤
Catalyst equipped, from 1980 models③ ④	1.0 ± 0.25%⑥
Canada, except Turbo②	1.5 ± 0.5%

① Pulse air disconnected and plugged
② Charcoal canister disconnected
③ Check value with sensor connected, after catalyst. Maximum 0.4 to 1981 models. Maximum 0.3% 1982 and later.

④ 1982 models and later, probe in front of catalyst—0.5 to 1.2% CO. Probe behind catalyst—less than 0.3% CO.
⑤ Sensor disconnected, test probe after catalyst.
⑥ Sensor disconnected, test probe before catalyst.

4. On 1979 vehicles equipped with a catalytic converter, remove the large bore hose at the charcoal canister. Connect the CO meter sensor to the exhaust pipe. Remove the oxygen sensor wire.

5. On 1980 and later vehicles equipped with a catalytic converter, remove and plug the front exhaust pipe and connect the CO meter sensor to the pipe with the aid of a connecting piece. Remove the oxygen sensor wire.

6. Read and adjust the idle speed and CO valve as required. Before each reading, increase the engine speed and allow it to return to idle. Wait 30 seconds before taking the next CO reading.

7. Adjust the idle speed by turning the idle adjusting screw on the throttle valve housing.

8. Adjust the CO by turning the adjusting screw located on the fuel distributor (clockwise—richer mixture; counterclockwise—leaner mixture).

NOTE: These adjustments affect each other, therefore the adjustments should be carried out in steps.

9. On 1980 and later catalyst equipped vehicles: Connect the oxygen sensor wire and remove the CO meter probe from the front exhaust pipe connection. Install the plug in the front exhaust pipe. Insert the probe at the rear of the tailpipe. The CO meter reading should be less than 0.4% (less than 0.3%, 1982 and later) with the engine at idle, and the engine and converter at normal operating temperature.

ENGINE ELECTRICAL

Distributor

REMOVAL & INSTALLATION

1978–80

1. Release the distributor cap hold-down clips, and lift the cap off of the distributor

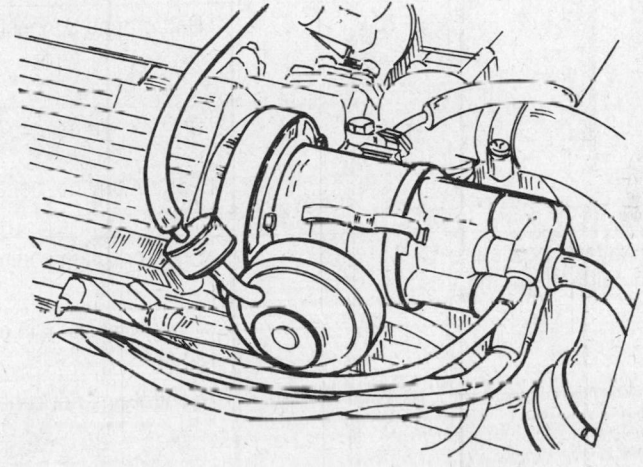

Distributor location—1981 and later

and out of the way. On some models, it may be necessary to remove the cap from the vehicle completely due to space limitations.

2. Disconnect the low voltage wire from the ignition coil. Pull off the vacuum hose.

3. Crank the engine until the flywheel marking is at the ignition position on No. 1 cylinder.

4. Remove the distributor retaining screw and remove the distributor from the engine.

5. Installation is the reverse of removal.

1981 and Later

1. Remove the distributor cap after marking the location of the No. 1 spark plug wire on the distributor housing.

NOTE: Number one cylinder is at the rear of the engine.

2. Disconnect the primary wire connector from the distributor and hose from the vacuum advance unit.

3. Crank the engine until the flywheel marking is at TDC (0°) and the distributor rotor is pointing to the indicating or reference mark on the distributor housing for the number one cylinder.

4. Match mark the distributor housing

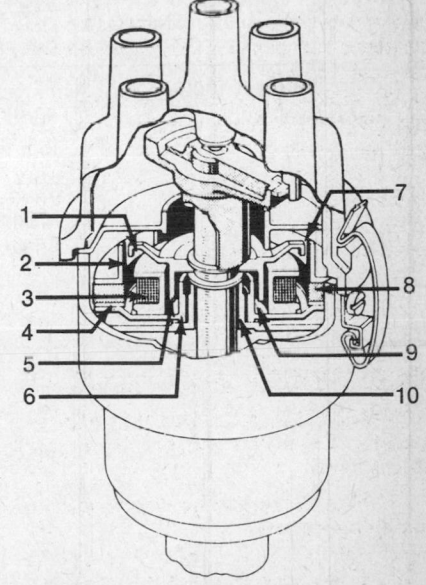

1. Rotor	6. Stator sleeve
2. Stator	7. Outer gap
3. Induction coil	8. Magnet
4. Stator plate	9. Inner gap
5. Rotor sleeve	10. Retaining plate and sleeve

Cross section of electronic distributor—to 1981

ELECTRONIC IGNITION DIAGNOSIS—EXCEPT HALL EFFECT
Engine Completely Dead, Fires Without Starting or Is Difficult to Start

Check	Reading	Condition of the system Probable fault	Check and remedy as necessary
3. Measure the voltage between terminal 15 on the coil and ground	0 V	Break in compensating resistor or leakage from terminal 15 on ignition switch	Check compensating resistor by means of ohmmeter. Check that voltage from the ignition switch is present at the single terminal on the 0.4 ohm resistor. If not, check ignition switch and wiring.
	Less than 6 V	Short-circuit in primary winding of coil	Check resistance of primary winding (0.95–1.4 ohm)
	6–8 V	Primary coil winding and compensating resistor sound.	Proceed to step 4.
	8–12 V	Bad ground connection	Check using ohmmeter that contact pin 31 on the control unit connector has good ground connection.
	12 V	Break in primary coil winding	Check using ohmmeter (0.95–1.4 ohm)
		Control unit not conducting	Check for battery voltage at contact pin 15, using voltmeter
4. Measure the voltage between terminal 1 on coil and ground	0 V	Short-circuit in control unit	Exchange control unit
	0.5–2 V	Power transistor in control unit sound	Proceed to step 5.
	12 V	Control unit not conducing	Change control unit. Check for faulty insulation on cables to terminal 16 on the control unit.
5. Measure resistance in the coil winding	Should be 5, 5–8 k ohm		
	Appreciable deviation	Defective secondary winding in coil	Change the coil Proceed to step 6
6. Connect a dwell meter Check dwell angle	60–80° (65–90%)	Control unit and impluse transmitter probably without fault.	
	Maximum reading on scale	Dwell meter range insufficient (many dwell meters have maximum reading of 70°) and consequently no information is obtained	Connect a voltmeter across pins 7 and 31d of control unit cable connector. At starting speed (100 rev/min), a minimum reading of 1 V a.c. should be obtained. This indicates that impulses of sufficient strength are being generated. If there is no voltage or the voltage is too low, check the screened impulse cable. Thereafter, check the impulse transmitter in the distributor using an ohmmeter (895–1285 ohm). Check the air gap between the rotor and the stator and, if necessary, adjust to 0.25 mm using a non-magnetic feeler gauge. If the fault persists, change the impulse transmitter.

ELECTRONIC IGNITION DIAGNOSIS—EXCEPT HALL EFFECT
Engine Completely Dead, Fires Without Starting or Is Difficult to Start

Check	Reading	Condition of the system Probable fault	Check and remedy as necessary
6. Connect a dwell meter Check dwell angle		The control unit does not react to impulses from the impulse transmitter	Change the control unit

NOTE: Poor running of the engine is unlikely to be caused by faulty electronics. Check the following items first:
1. Good connections throughout ignition system.
2. Ignition setting and centrifugal and vacuum advance.
3. General condition of spark plugs.

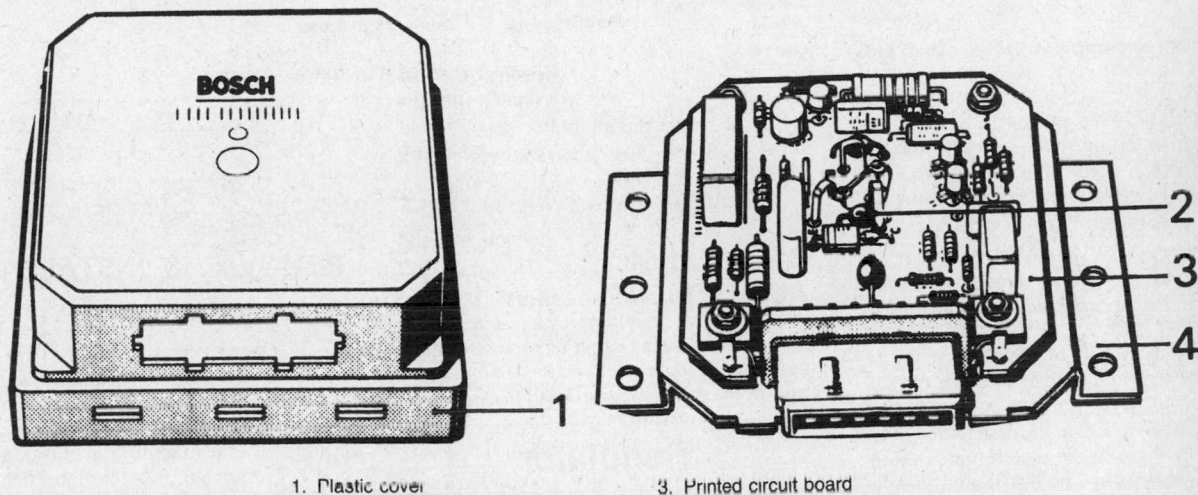

1. Plastic cover
2. Power transistor
3. Printed circuit board
4. Base plate

Electronic Control Unit (ECU) for the electronic ignition system

However, the engine is also equipped for checking the timing using an ignition service instrument.

The equipment in the vehicle comprises a pin in the engine flywheel and a service socket in the clutch cover. The ignition service instrument is connected to the clutch cover by means of a special connector and to the plug lead No. 1 cylinder by means of a terminal. The ignition service instrument is also connected to the ignition service socket at the fuse box and by means of an impulse transmitter at the plug lead for No. 1 cylinder.

NOTE: The SAAB ignition service instrument consists of a tachometer, cam angle meter, stroboscope lamp and switch for operating the starter.

Valve Lash

1. Remove the valve cover (1981 and later models, the pistons of cylinders numbers one and four must be at TDC before distributor and valve cover can be removed).
2. Using an appropriate special tool (Saab No. 8392185 or its equivalent), rotate the crankshaft as necessary to position the high point of the camshaft lobe 180° away from the valve depressor face (base circle of the cam lobe must contact the valve depressor) on the valve which the clearance is to be checked.

NOTE: The special crankshaft turning wrench fits the center screw of the crankshaft belt pulley at the dash panel.

3. Try the maximum and minimum clearances with a feeler gauge. The minimum feeler should slip in, but the maximum feeler should not.
4. Measure and record the clearance of all the valves in the same manner. Adjust the clearance of any valves that do not lie within the following limits.
Intake valves: 0.008–0.010 in.
Exhaust valves (except turbo.): 0.016–0.018 in.
Exhaust valves (turbo):0.018–0.020 in.
5. To adjust the valves, remove the camshaft, tappets and adjusting pallets (shims) of any valves that need to be adjusted.

NOTE: See the proper procedure for camshaft removal and installation which is located in this section of this manual.

Checking valve clearance with feeler gauge

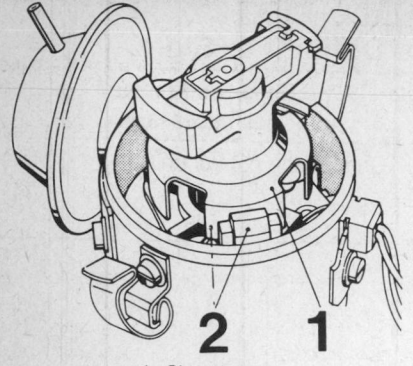

1. Slotted rotor
2. Hall transmitter

Distributor assembly with Hall effect pick-up

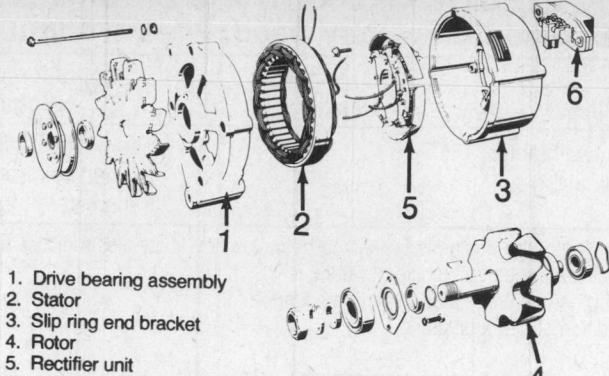

1. Drive bearing assembly
2. Stator
3. Slip ring end bracket
4. Rotor
5. Rectifier unit
6. Voltage regulator and carbon brush holder

Exploded view of alternator—typical

to the valve cover housing. Remove the distributor retaining bolts and pull the distributor forward from the end of the valve cover housing. Note the position of the distributor drive lugs.

— CAUTION —

Do not rotate the engine crankshaft when the distributor is removed from the engine.

5. Installation is the reverse of the removal procedure. Be sure to align the distributor rotor to the number one spark plug wire reference mark on the distributor housing, while aligning the match marks on the valve cover housing and distributor housing.

Alternator

REMOVAL & INSTALLATION

1. Disconnect the negative battery cable.
2. Remove the alternator wiring connections, retaining screw and the adjusting screw.

3. Remove the alternator belt.
4. Remove the alternator from the vehicle.
5. Installation is the reverse of removal.

BELT TENSION ADJUSTMENT

Adjust the alternator belt tension so that the belt can be depressed about ½ in. at the mid-point of its longest straight run.

Regulator

REMOVAL & INSTALLATION

NOTE: On 900 series, the voltage regulator is incorporated into the back of the alternator.

1. Disconnect the negative battery cable.
2. Remove the voltage regulator connecting wires.
3. Remove the hold-down screws and remove the unit from the vehicle.

4. Installation is the reverse of removal.

Starter

REMOVAL & INSTALLATION

All Except Turbo

1. Disconnect the battery. On the 99 series, disconnect the pre-heater hose.
2. Remove the flywheel cover. Remove the gearbox dipstick if the vehicle is equipped with manual transmission.
3. Remove the starter motor heat shield and the rear mounting bolts.
4. Disconnect the starter motor wires. Remove the front mounting bolts.
5. Carefully remove the starter from the vehicle.
6. Installation is the reverse of removal.

Turbo

1. Disconnect the battery. On the 99 series, remove the battery and the battery tray.

1. Screws, bearing housing
2. Solenoid
3. Drive housing
4. Bushing, drive side
5. Capsule bracket
6. U-washer
7. Shim
8. Rubber gasket
9. Bushing, commutator side
10. Commutator bearing housing
11. Brush plate
12. Field winding
13. Starter housing
14. Rotor
15. Rubber washer
16. Steel washer
17. Engaging lever arm
18. Pinon
19. Bushing, pinion
20. Stop ring
21. Lock ring

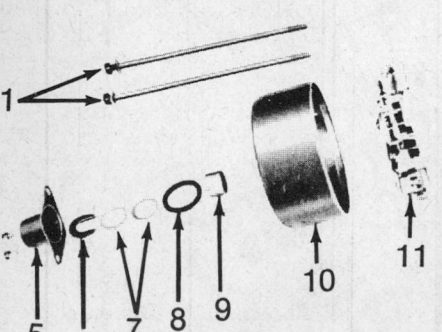

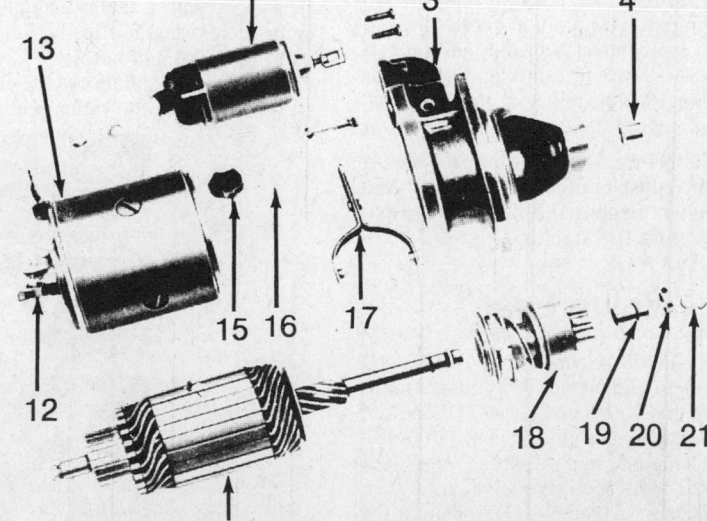

Exploded view of starter assembly—typical

2. Remove the turbocharger suction pipe, pre-heater hose and the flywheel cover.

3. On the 900 series, remove the gearbox dipstick (manual transmission only). Remove the bracket and bolts between the turbocharger and the gearbox.

4. Disconnect the starter motor wires. On the 99 series, remove the front starter mounting bolts.

5. Loosen the oil return pipe on the turbocharger enough to allow it to be bent outwards somewhat. On the 99 series, remove the oil return pipe.

6. Remove the starter motor heat shield and the rear mounting bolts.

7. On the 900 series, remove the front starter mounting bolts.

8. Carefully remove the starter from the vehicle.

9. To install, reverse the removal procedure. Be careful to fit a new gasket on the oil return pipe connecting flange on the turbocharger.

ENGINE MECHANICAL

Engine

REMOVAL & INSTALLATION

99 Series

NOTE: The engine and transmission should be removed from the vehicle as a unit.

1. Remove the hood.

2. Disconnect the battery cables. Remove the battery.

3. Remove the servo cylinder vacuum hose from the inlet manifold and remove the rubber bellows from between the air flow sensor and the inlet manifold.

4. Remove the connections on the fuel distributor and detach the lines. Disconnect the electrical connection on the air flow sensor.

5. On vehicles sold in California, detach the EGR system vacuum hoses from the venturi tap at the air cleaner and from the EGR valve at the throttle valve housing. Remove the clamps at the rubber bellows.

6. Remove the air cleaner and the mixture control unit.

7. Remove the cable connections from the ignition coil, temperature transmitter, radiator fan, thermostat contact, headlights and the switch on the transmission (automatic transmission only).

8. Disconnect the cables from the injection system at the warm-up regulator, auxiliary air valve, cold start valve and the thermo-time switch.

9. Detach the throttle control cable from the bracket on the throttle valve housing.

10. Detach the hoses at the connections to the thermostat housing, radiator, inlet manifold and water pump.

11. Remove the grille. Remove the hood lock operating cable from its position at the dash panel and wheel housing. Remove the two front sheet metal screws and nuts, and the four sheet metal screws holding the headlights to the body. Remove the complete front assembly by lifting forward and upward.

12. If the vehicle is equipped with manual transmission, disconnect the clutch hose from the slave cylinder. Plug the hose and the hole in the slave cylinder.

13. If the vehicle is equipped with automatic transmission, remove the protective cover from the exhaust manifold.

14. Disconnect the exhaust pipe at the exhaust manifold.

15. Disconnect the ground cable from the transmission. On some vehicles it may be necessary to remove the alternator, depending on the type of engine lifting crane that is being used for the removal procedure.

16. On California vehicles, remove the air pump.

17. Raise the vehicle on a hoist and support it safely.

18. If the vehicle is equipped with manual transmission, put the gear lever in Neutral. Tap out the front taper pin from the gear shift rod joint and pull the rubber bellows free of the groove in the gear selector rod. Separate the gear selector rod from the gear selector joint.

19. If the vehicle is equipped with automatic transmission, remove the gear selector cable retaining screw from the transmission and position the gear selector lever in "P".

NOTE: On early models, detach the spring which holds the cable to the gear selector by inserting a pliers in the end of the spring. Rotate it slightly and then pull out the cable. On later models, push back the spring-loaded sleeve on the gear selector lever and release the end of the cable.

20. Remove the speedometer cable from the transmission. Remove the engine brackets.

21. Remove the large clips from around the rubber bellows on the inner universal joints.

22. Install the engine lifting hoist to the two engine lifting lugs.

23. Remove the lower end piece from the control arm on the right side and turn the steering wheel to the left.

24. Raise the engine and transmission from the rear engine cushions and withdraw the left universal joint, by moving the assembly to the right. Move the assembly to the left and withdraw the right universal joint.

25. Lift the unit and disconnect the starter wires and cables.

26. Carefully remove the unit from the vehicle. Install protective caps over the inner drivers and rubber bellows.

27. Installation is the reverse of removal.

900 Series

NOTE: The engine and transmission should be removed as a unit.

1. Disconnect the positive battery cable. Drain the radiator.

2. Disconnect the windshield washer hose, unbolt the hood hinge links and remove the hood from the vehicle.

3. If the vehicle is equipped with power steering, disconnect the lines at the servo pump.

4. Disconnect the positive battery lead at the starter. Remove the radiator hoses. Remove the engine ground wire. Disconnect the temperature transmitter cable. Remove the coil.

5. Disconnect the cable harness from the clutch cover. If the vehicle is equipped with manual transmission, disconnect the hydraulic line from the clutch slave cylinder and plug the lines.

6. Disconnect the CI system electrical connections from the warm-up regulator, thermo-time switch cold start valve and the auxiliary air valve. On catalytic converter equipped vehicles, also disconnect the oxygen sensor and the throttle switch cables.

7. Disconnect the oil pressure transmitter cable. Loosen the fuel line connections at the fuel distributor. Remove the air filter along with the mixture control unit.

8. Disconnect the throttle cable. Disconnect the hose at the expansion tank. Disconnect the heater hoses at the heater. Disconnect the brake vacuum hose.

9. Remove the clips and remove the bellows from the inner drivers.

10. Place the spacer (Saab tool No. 83-93-209) or equivalent between the upper control arm underside and the car body.

NOTE: Insert the tool from the engine compartment side. The spacer makes the front suspension unloaded when the vehicle is raised.

11. Lift the front end of the vehicle and support it safely.

12. Remove the lower end piece from the control arm. Pull out the steering knuckle assembly and support the end piece against the control arm outer end.

13. If the vehicle is equipped with manual transmission put the gear lever in Neutral. Remove the nut and tap out the taper pin in the gear shift rod joint. Separate the joint from the gear shift rod.

14. If the vehicle is equipped with automatic transmission, remove the retaining screw from the gear selector cable at the transmission. Withdraw the cable with the gear selector rod in its extreme forward position "P". Slide back the spring-loaded sleeve on the gear shift rod and unhook the end of the cable.

15. Separate the exhaust pipe from the exhaust manifold. Disconnect the speedometer cable from the transmission.

16. Remove the rear engine mounting bolts. Slacken the front engine mounting

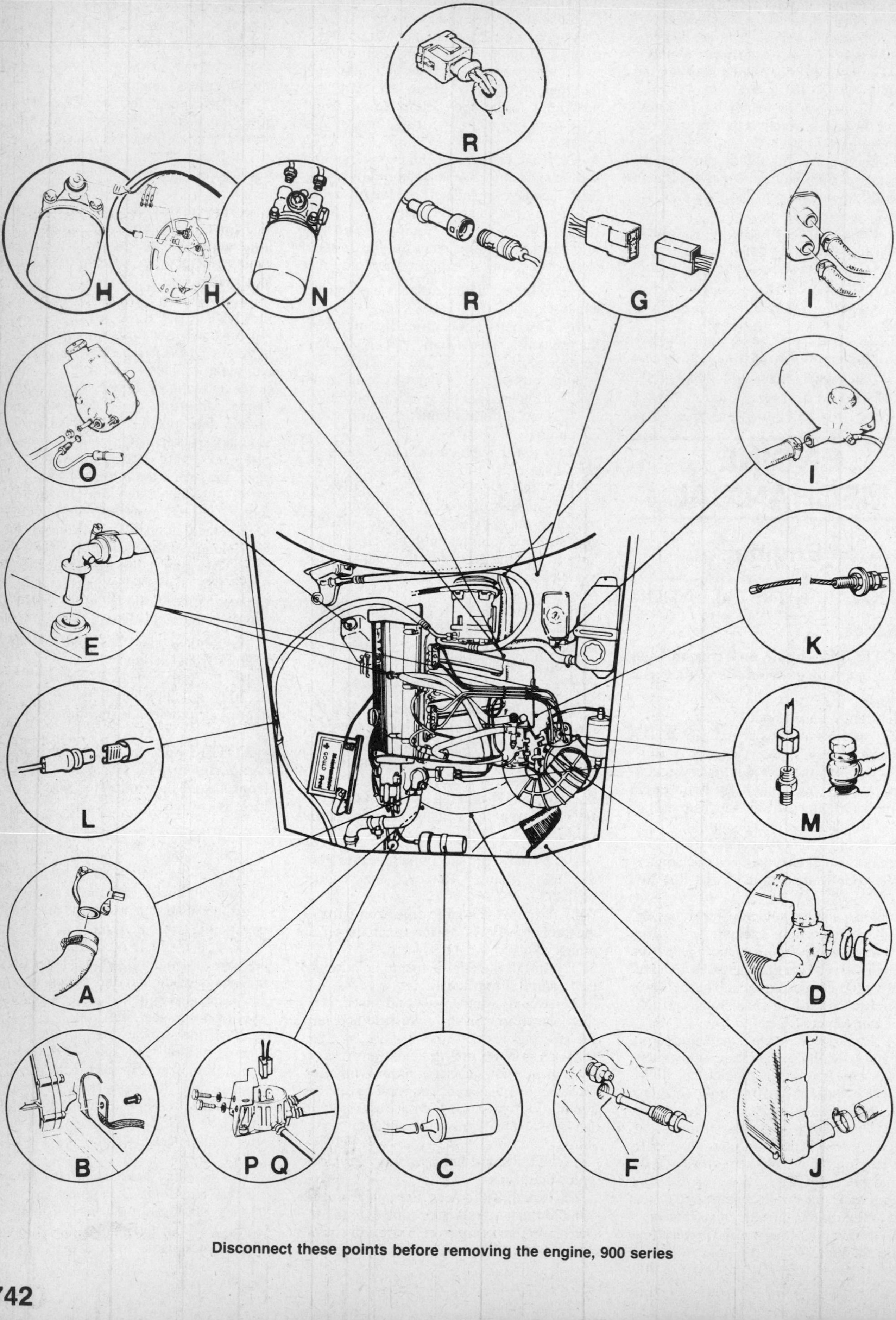

R

H H N R G I

O I

E K

L M

A D

B P Q C F J

Disconnect these points before removing the engine, 900 series

nut so that the mounting can be lifted out of the bracket.

17. Attach the hoist to the two lugs on the engine and raise the assembly slightly. Move the assembly to one side and free the two universal joints.

18. Carefully remove the unit from the vehicle.

19. Installation is the reverse of removal.

NOTE: 1984 and later models beginning with VIN Nos. E1004580 and E2001945 utilize a new-type steel gasket between the engine and transaxle. Because of changes made to the timing cover to accomodate this new gasket, it may only be used after the above VIN numbers.

The steel gasket must only be used once. To install, thoroughly clean both mating surfaces and position the new gasket on one surface. Apply a high temperature (minimum 500°F) silicone sealer to the grooves at each end of the gasket; additional sealant around the entire gasket is not necessary. Assemble the engine and transaxle immediately.

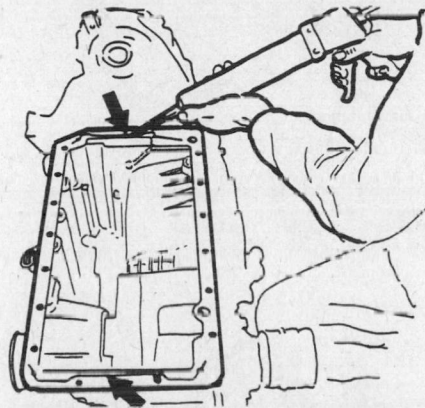

Sealer should only be applied to the grooves at each end of the steel engine-to-transaxle gasket on 1984 and later models

Cylinder Head

REMOVAL & INSTALLATION

1. Disconnect the battery cables. Drain the radiator.

2. Remove the rubber bellows from between the air flow sensor and the throttle valve housing and disconnect the throttle cable from the throttle valve housing.

3. Disconnect the cable from the temperature transmitter. Remove the vacuum hose of the power brake booster from the intake manifold.

4. Disconnect the fuel lines from the fuel distributor to the injection valves. Tape the ends of the lines to prevent dirt from entering the system. Remove the bracket from the throttle valve housing mounting.

5. Remove the hose clamps at the connections to the thermostat housing, water pump and intake manifold.

6. Unbolt the exhaust pipe from the exhaust manifold.

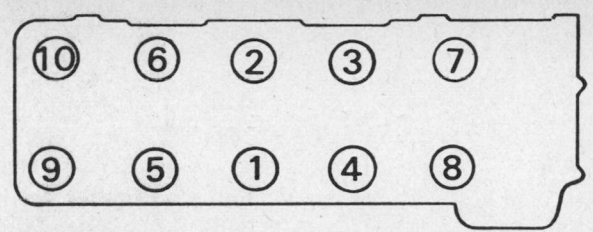

Cylinder head bolt torque sequence to 1980

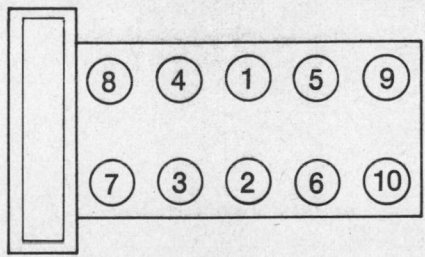

Cylinder head bolt torque sequence, 1981 and later

7. Remove the distributor cap and ignition wires. Remove the valve cover. 1981 and later, rotate the engine until cylinders one or four are at TDC, before lifting the valve cover from the engine. The design of the distributor driving dog only allows the valve cover/distributor assembly to be removed with the engine in this position.

8. Remove the camshaft sprocket as follows: 1978–1980 models—bolt the mounting plate to the center of the camshaft sprocket, using one of the camshaft sprocket retaining screws. Tighten the nut (screw) securely to immobilize the center stud. Otherwise the chain tensioner will tighten the chain and lock in a new position so that the sprocket cannot be refitted. The chain tensioner cannot be reset without lifting the engine out of the car.

1981 and later, remove the sprocket bolts. Keep chain on sprocket and place sprocket/chain assembly between chain guide and tensioner. A center bolt is not used on the sprocket.

9. 1978–1980 models—Remove the retaining screws from the camshaft sprocket. Separate the wheel from the camshaft plate until it hangs free in the mounting plate by the center stud. 1981 and later—Remove the two bolts from the timing cover under the front of the head.

10. Remove the cylinder head bolts. Mount two guide pins in two of the cylinder head bolt holes (1978–1981 models).

11. Raise the vehicle on the hoist and support it safely. Place a support under the rear end of the engine. Remove the engine mounting bolt in the cylinder head.

12. Remove the screws in the transmission cover. Remove the cylinder head from the vehicle.

13. Installation is the reverse of removal with the following additions: Be sure to use a new cylinder head gasket. Torque the bolts first to 44 ft. lbs. and then to 70 ft. lbs.

NOTE: A new type cylinder head bolt was introduced on 1984 models beginning with VIN No. E53614. This is a TORX® type bolt, size E16, ½ in. drive and requires a socket of the same type. The new bolt will also be found on engine Nos. E42621 to E46906. Follow the torque procedure listed under the "Torque Specifications" chart in the front of this section.

14. Make sure that the markings on the camshaft and the bearing cap are in line with one another.

15. Check that the flywheel mark is in line with the mark on the cylinder block and that the engine is set on No. 1 cylinder.

16. 1978–80 models—When mounting the camshaft sprocket, the nut (screw) on the camshaft sprocket center must not be unscrewed before the sprocket is tightly screwed to the camshaft.

17. 1981 and later—Refit the two screws in the timing cover on the front of the cylinder head. Refit the timing chain and sprocket as follows:

a. Remove the tension from the chain tensioner with special tool No. 83 93 357 or equivalent. Hook the tool into the catch of the tensioner and pull upwards.

b. Place the timing sprocket on the camshaft so that the mark on the sprocket and the screw holes coincide. If necessary, move the chain to position.

c. Install the three retaining bolts in the sprocket and cam shaft.

d. If the distributor is mounted to the valve cover, the rotor should be facing the line on the edge of the distributor housing.

OVERHAUL

For all cylinder head overhaul procedures not listed below, please refer to "Engine Rebuilding" in the Unit Repair section.

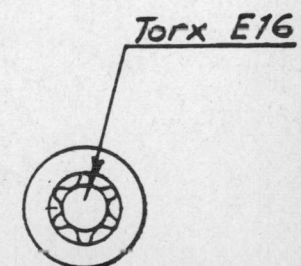

Top view of the 1984 and later Torx cylinder head bolts

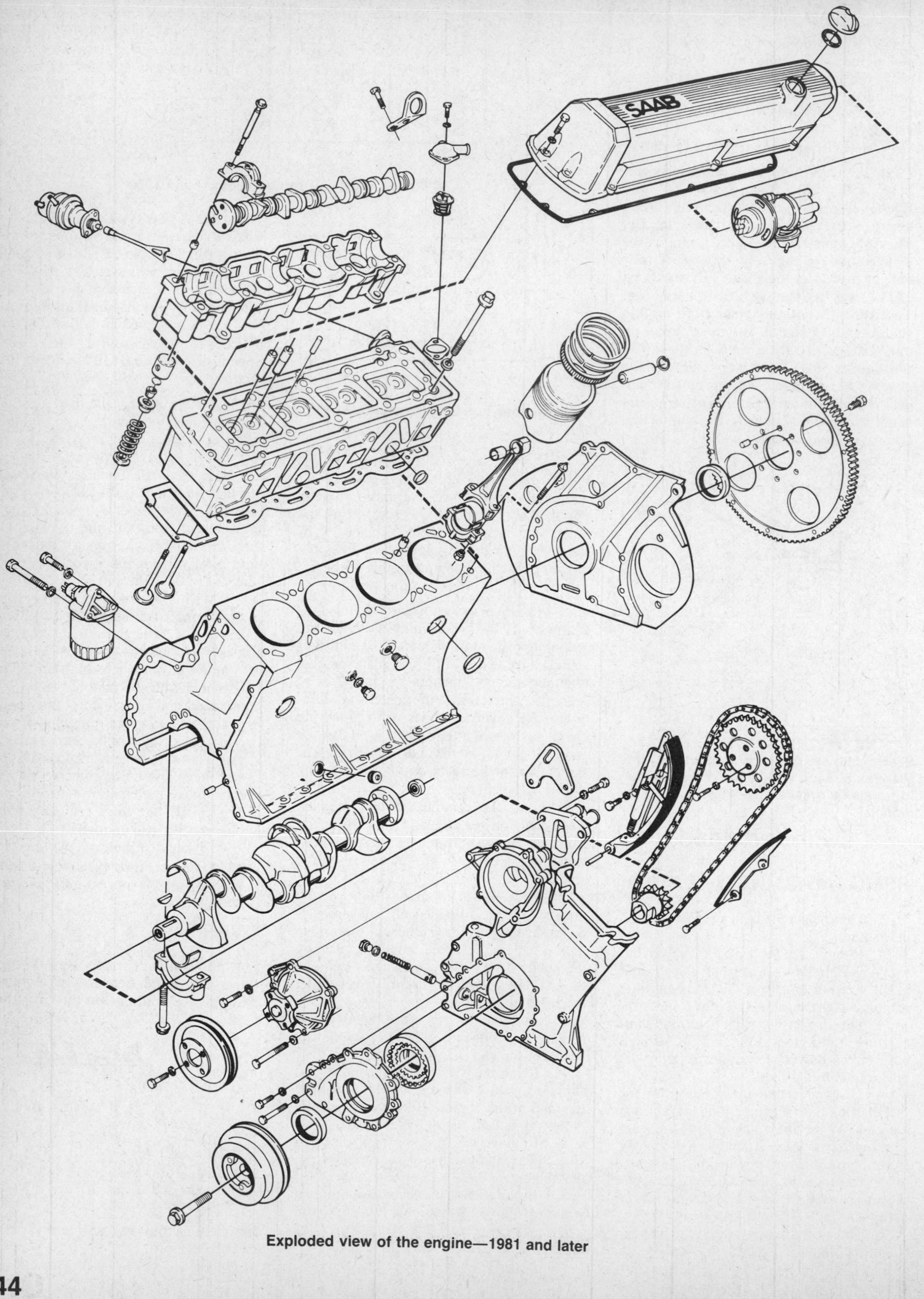

Exploded view of the engine—1981 and later

Valves

REMOVAL
(Cylinder head removed from the block)

1. Remove the camshaft bearing caps.
2. Lift the camshaft from the cylinder head.
3. Using a magnetic probe, remove the valve depressers.
4. Remove the adjusting pallets, keeping them in their proper order.
5. Remove the camshaft bearing assembly. Install a valve spring depressing tool.
6. Depress the valve spring and remove the valve lock clips. Release the spring tension and remove the valve spring tool.
7. Remove the top valve retainer, valve spring and guide sleeve. Withdraw the valve from the guide.

INSTALLATION

1. Oil the valve stem and install the valve into the valve guide.
2. Install the valve guide sleeve, the spring and the spring retainer.

3. Using a valve spring depressing tool, depress the valve spring and install the valve lock clips.
4. Mount the camshaft bearing assembly to the cylinder head.
5. Install the adjusting pallets by replacing them in their original position.
6. Install the valve depressers and lubricate the bearing surface with oil.
7. Install the camshaft and the bearing caps.

— CAUTION —
Do not turn or tip the cylinder head after inserting the valve depressers. The depressers and the adjusting pallets will fall out of position and be randomized.

NOTE: Never discard sodium filled valves before they have been properly treated by drilling into the center of the valve head to the sodium content. Drill or cut the stem approximately one inch from the bottom. Throw the valve in a bucket of water to neutralize the sodium. A safe distance from the bucket is no closer than three feet.

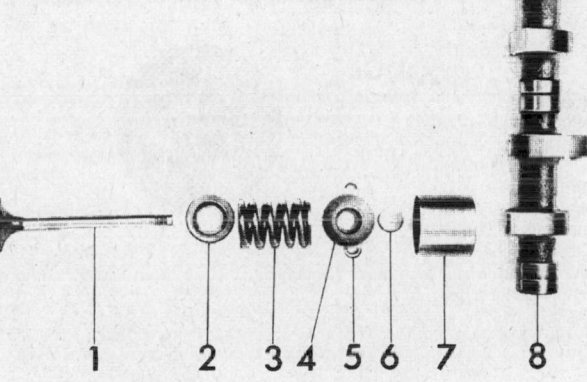

1. Valve
2. Valve spring seat
3. Valve spring
4. Retainer
5. Lock
6. Adjusting pallet
7. Valve depressor
8. Camshaft

Valve mechanism components

— CAUTION —
Keep the valve and sodium compound well away from the water when drilling or cutting the valve. Exposing the sodium to water or other compounds will cause an explosion.

Valve Guides
CHECKING

1. Pull the valve out from its seat approximately 0.120 in. and check the radial play by rocking the valve head. If radial play exceeds 0.020 in., the valve guide must be replaced.

REPLACING THE VALVE GUIDE

1. Heat the cylinder head and withdraw the valve guide from the camshaft side, using a special pull rod and washers.
2. To replace the guide, heat the cylinder head and press the valve guide into place with SAAB special installing tool or equivalent.
3. After the guide is pressed into position, the valve seat must be reground to 45 degrees.

Intake Manifold

REMOVAL & INSTALLATION

1. Disconnect all hoses, wires and connectors that would inhibit the intake manifold from being removed.

NOTE: It may be necessary to remove the distributor cap and the ignition wires to gain clearance.

2. Remove the throttle valve housing.
3. Remove the manifold bolts and remove the manifold from the vehicle together with the engine lifting lug.
4. Installation is the reverse of removal.

NOTE: Be sure the proper gasket is used. A coolant leakage could occur if the wrong one is used.

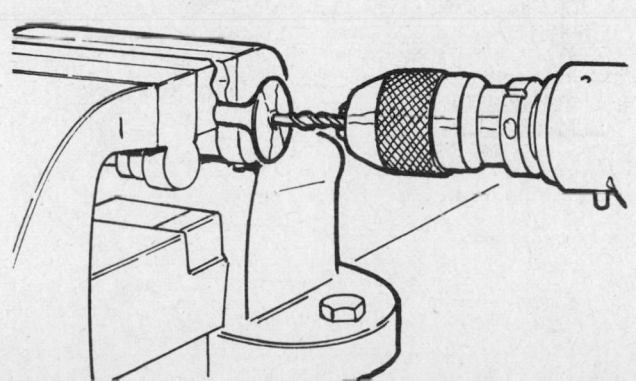 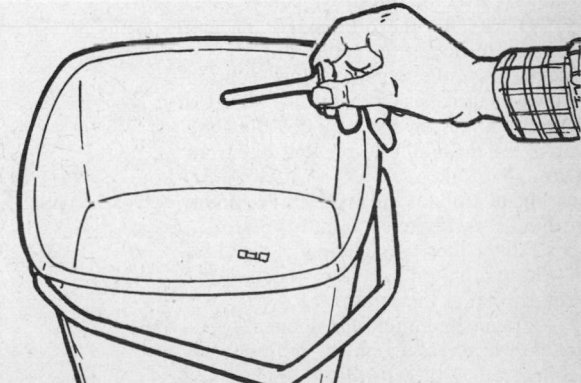

Preparing sodium filled valves for discard

Exhaust Manifold

REMOVAL & INSTALLATION

1. Disconnect all necessary hoses, wires, and connectors that would inhibit the exhaust manifold from being removed.

2. Unbolt the exhaust pipe at the connecting flange.

3. If the vehicle is equipped with a heat shield, remove it.

4. Remove the manifold bolts and remove the exhaust manifold from the vehicle.

5. Installation is the reverse of removal.

Turbocharger

Turbocharging is achieved by means of a turbo-compressor which utilizes the exhaust gases from the engine to drive the turbine. The exhaust gases are routed to an exhaust gas turbine, causing the wheel to rotate. The turbine wheel is mounted on the same shaft as a compressor impeller which rotates at the same speed. The compressor is located in the induction system where it effects an increase in the charging pressure in the combustion chamber.

The Saab Turbo has been designed to start operating at relatively low engine speeds, in order to provide increased torque at engine speeds typical of normal driving conditions.

To prevent engine overspeeding, the pump relay cuts off the fuel pump at engine rpm above 6000. While at excessive charging pressures, an overpressure switch cuts off the current to the fuel pump.

For further information on the turbocharger, please refer to "Turbocharging" in the Unit Repair section.

REMOVAL & INSTALLATION

1. Remove the charge pressure regulator and block off the exhaust pipe. Remove the battery as required.

2. Disconnect the hose between the compressor and the throttle housing.

3. Disconnect the oil supply line and the oil return line at the turbo unit.

4. Remove the retaining bolts securing the turbo to the exhaust manifold. Remove the turbo unit from the vehicle. Plug the holes in the turbo unit to prevent dirt from entering.

5. Installation is the reverse of removal with the following exceptions.

6. Fill the lubricating inflow of the turbo unit with engine oil before connecting the oil return line at the turbo.

7. Crank the engine for about 30 seconds with terminal 15 on the ignition coil disconnected. This will fill the lubricating system of the turbo before the engine is started.

1. Turbo-compressor
2. Charge pressure regulator
3. Pressure switch
4. Turbo instrument
5. Suction pipe
6. Pressure pipe
7. Bellows pipe
8. Exhaust pipe
9. Oil supply line
10. Oil return line
11. Cooling air pipe
12. Exhaust pressure line

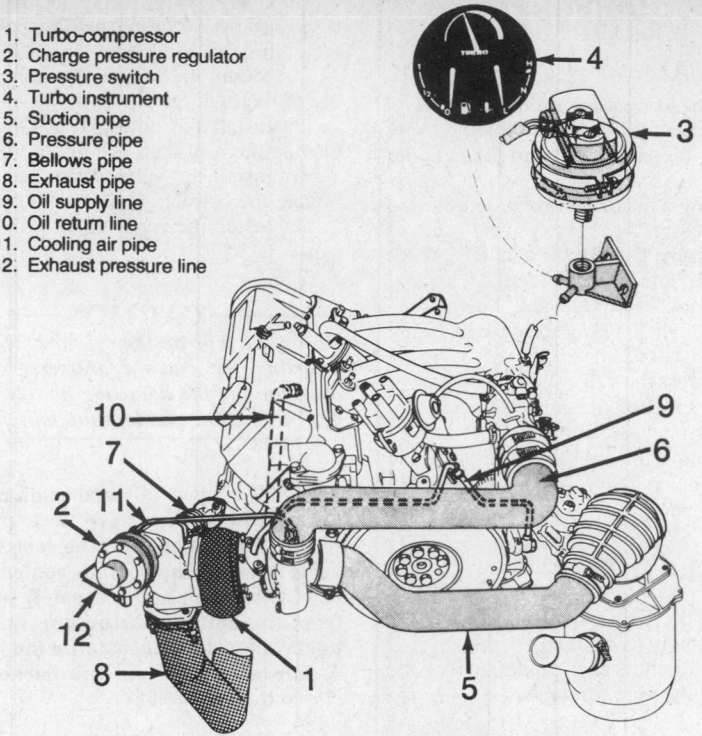

Typical turbocharger system—to 1980

1. Turbocharger
2. Wastegate boost control
3. Diaphragm capsule
4. Over-pressure guard
5. Turbo gauge
6. Hose, air cleaner to turbocharger
7. Hose, turbocharger to inlet manifold
8. Exhaust outlet pipe
9. Oil supply line
10. Oil return line

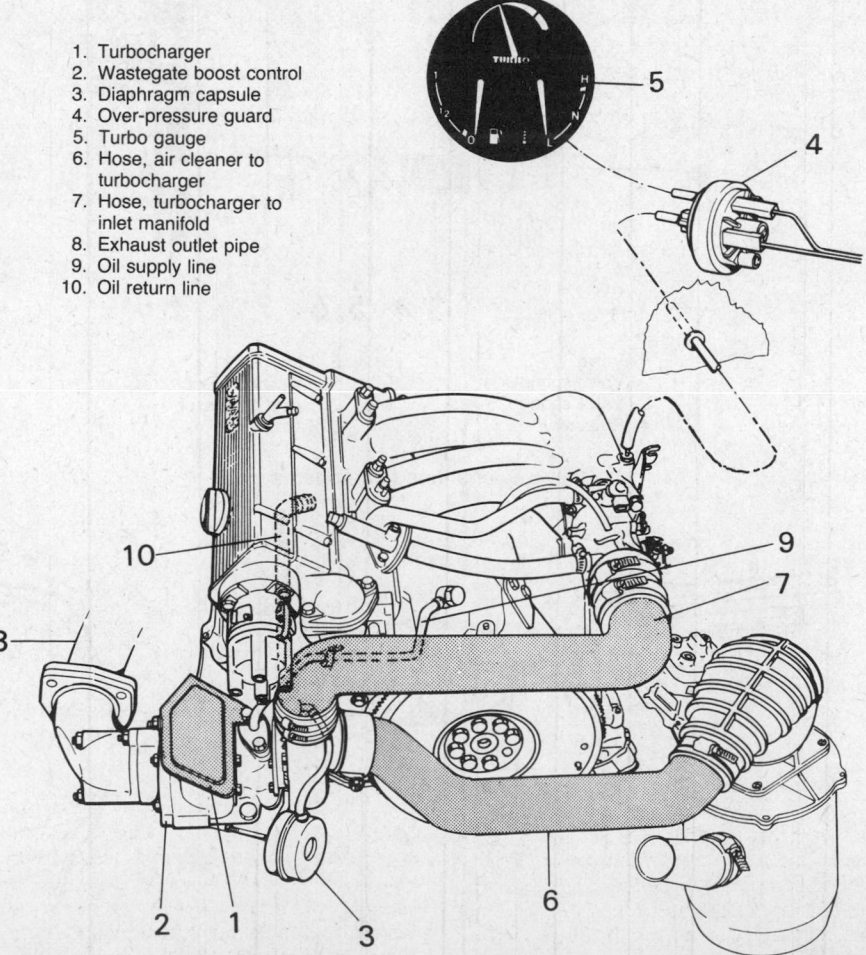

Turbocharger system—1981 and later

Timing Chain

REMOVAL & INSTALLATION

1978–1980

NOTE: In order to accomplish the following procedure the engine will have to be removed from the vehicle.

1. Remove the engine from the vehicle.
2. Remove the cylinder head. See the proper procedure in this section of the repair manual.
3. Remove the belt pulley bolt and the pulley, using the necessary puller.
4. Remove the timing chain cover. Remove the timing chain tensioner.
5. Remove the chain guides and the mounting plate with the camshaft sprocket and the timing chain.
6. Remove the crankshaft sprocket using a suitable gear puller, if necessary.
7. Remove the idler shaft sprocket, if it is going to be replaced.
8. Installation is the reverse of removal. Note the following.
9. If it was removed, install the idler shaft. The marking (the bulge in the hold on the idler shaft chainwheel) should line up with the small hole in the keeper plate.
10. Assemble the camshaft sprocket and mounting plate if they have been disassembled. Fit the chain over the camshaft sprocket. Lower the timing chain and mounting plate past the camshaft flange until the center stud of the sprocket is lined up with the camshaft.
11. Rotate the camshaft sprocket until the screw holes match the threaded holes in the camshaft flange.
12. Install the timing chain over the other sprockets so that it hangs straight from the camshaft to the crankshaft.

NOTE: The shaft settings must not be altered.

13. Guide the center stud of the camshaft sprocket into the camshaft. Install the retaining bolts.
14. Mount the curved chain guide plate together with the mounting plate (the chain guide plate nearest the block) with its mounting bolts and stretch the chain as required.
15. Check the camshaft-crankshaft-idler shaft setting.
16. Install the timing chain tensioner.

NOTE: Different versions of the chain tensioner exist and the assembly procedures are different.

REYNHOLDS VERSION

Before installation, remove the tensioner neck. Tension the spring, by turning the ratchet sleeve (actuated by the spring) clockwise and at the same time pushing it until it locks in its innermost position. Fit the tensioner neck and a spacer piece, so that the tensioner neck will not bottom in the chain tensioner housing and release the self-adjuster.

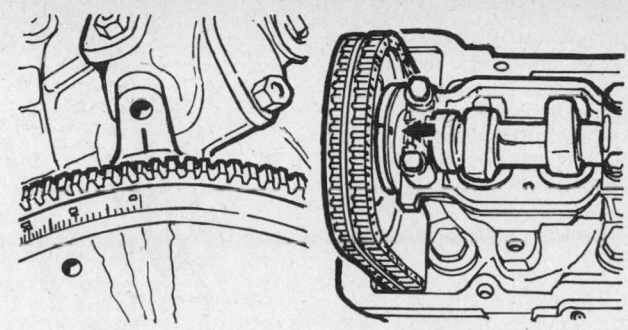

Timing mark locations on cam gear and flywheel—1981 and later (1980 and earlier similar)

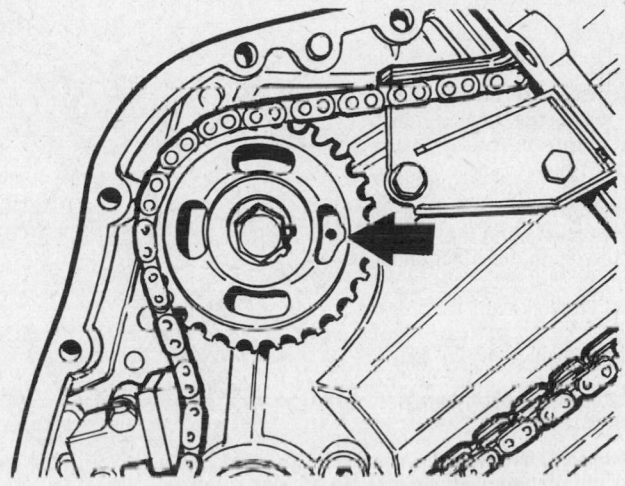

idler shaft timing marks—1980 and earlier models

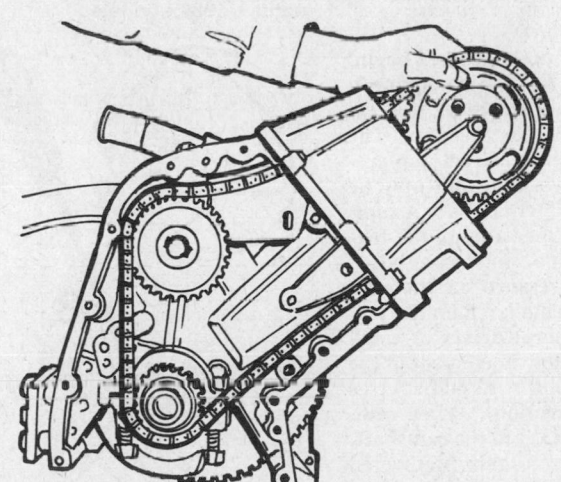

Timing chain assembly—1980 and earlier models

JWIS VERSION

Place the lock washer with the spiral rod in the chain tensioner housing. Install the spring with the small diameter against the lock washer. Fit the tensioner neck into the housing by simultaneously pressing and turning it into its inner position. The tensioner neck must be held depressed while the chain tensioner is being fitted, right until the chain has been tensioned.

17. Mount the chain tensioner with the guide plate on the engine block.
18. Press the curved chain guide against the chain to stretch it and push the tensioner neck against the spacer piece. Remove the spacer piece while the chain is kept tensioned. Then adjust to leave a clearance of 0.02 in. between the housing and the tensioner neck.

Tighten the chain guides.

19. Rotate the crankshaft one full turn in its normal sense and check the chain tension. The movement of the tensioner neck from its butted position must be at least 0.02 in. and not more than 0.06 in.

20. Remove the bolt from the camshaft sprocket center. Install the timing chain cover using a new gasket.

1981 and Later

1. Remove the engine from the vehicle, following the prescribed outline.

2. Support the engine safely and rotate the crankshaft until the number one cylinder is on its firing stroke and the "0" mark on the flywheel lines up with the line on the rear engine plate.

3. The mark on the rotor should line up with the line on the distributor housing.

NOTE: If no line is found on the distributor housing, mark the housing in line with the rotor point.

4. Remove the valve cover assembly as previously outlined.

5. Remove the sprocket from the camshaft and rest it on the chain tensioner and the chain guide.

6. Remove the cylinder head as previously outlined.

7. Remove the crankshaft pulley and oil pump assembly.

8. Remove the water pump and pulley assembly.

9. Remove the timing chain cover.

10. Remove the timing chain and chain wheel (sprocket) from the engine.

11. Remove the chain tensioner, if required.

NOTE: 1984 and later engines beginning with engine No. E57340 are equipped with a new cam chain tensioner that requires a different release procedure. The new tensioner is also a direct replacement for the old style unit and may be used in all 1981 and later engines. A complete tensioner kit, consisting of the tensioner body and guide, must be used.

To release the pressure on the cam chain, pivot the reverse latch on the tensioner body with a screwdriver or small pry bar. This will allow movement of the chain guide from point A to point B (see accompanying illustration). When reinstalling the camsprocket to the camshaft, the reverse latch must again be pivoted to release pressure on the chain guide.

12. To install the chain assembly, have the No. 1 piston at TDC and the camshaft in position for No. 1 cylinder firing position

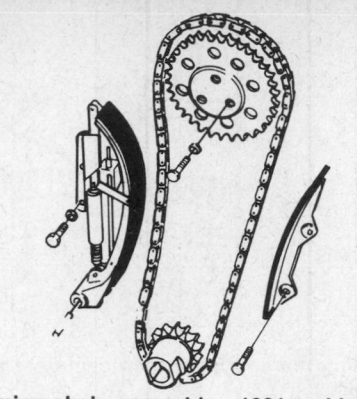

Timing chain assembly—1981 and later

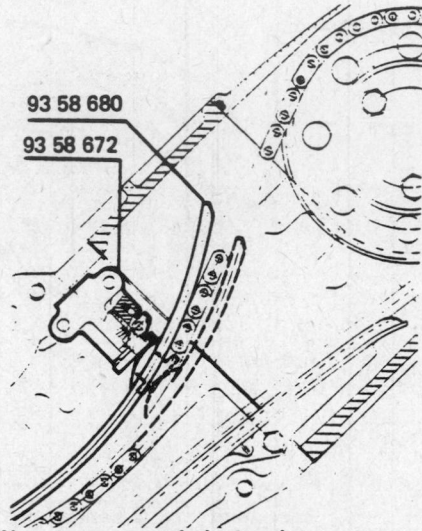

93 58 680

93 58 672

New type cam chain tensioner components—1984 and later

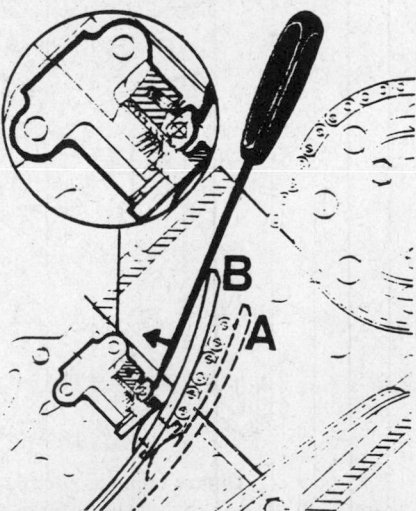

B

A

Releasing the cam chain tensioner—1984 and later models

to be in its firing mode, before the cylinder head is installed.

NOTE: Do not rotate either the camshaft or the crankshaft without the chain in place. Damage to the valves or pistons can occur, after the cylinder head is installed.

13. Replace the chain tensioner, if removed.

14. Place the camshaft sprocket to the chain and suspend it from the crankshaft sprocket. Position the chain between the chain guide and the tensioner.

15. Install the timing chain cover assembly while pulling up the chain to avoid being caught under the cover.

16. Install the water pump assembly and install the cylinder head. Torque the head bolts to specifications.

17. Using the tensioner release tool, disengage the tensioner and refit the cam sprocket and chain to the camshaft. Align the marks on the sprocket and the camshaft bearing.

18. Install the sprocket retaining bolts. Release the tensioner assembly.

19. Install the oil pump assembly, seal and pulley.

20. Complete the assembly as required.

——— **CAUTION** ———
Do not use an early type inlet manifold gasket. Coolant leakage could occur within the engine.

Timing Chain Oil Seal

The timing chain oil seal can be removed without removing the engine from the vehicle.

1. Disconnect the negative battery cable. Remove the alternator belt. If the vehicle is equipped with power steering or air conditioning, remove the required belts.

2. Remove the clutch cover (torque converter cover) and lock the crankshaft using Saab tool No. 83-92-987 or equivalent by locking the tool to the ring gear.

3. From beneath the vehicle, remove the pulley retaining bolt using Saab tool No. 83-92-961 or equivalent. Remove the pulley from the vehicle.

4. Pull off the old seal ring using a suitable tool.

5. Installation is the reverse of removal. Torque the retaining bolt to 137 ft. lbs.

Jwis timing chain tensioner

Reynholds timing chain tensioner

Crankshaft locking procedure

CHECKING TIMING CHAIN TENSION

1978–80

In order to prevent damage caused by the chain tensioner running out too far, the position of the chain tensioner can be checked with the engine mounted in the car.

1. Remove the valve cover.
2. Insert a steel ruler down against the rubber neck on the chain tensioner and measure the distance to the level of the cylinder head cover.
3. The distance should be more than 11.8 in. If the distance is less than 11.8 in., the engine should be removed as soon as possible for correction. For completely tight chain tensioners (newly adjusted chains), the distance should be about 12.3 in.

Camshaft

REMOVAL & INSTALLATION

1978–80

1. Remove the valve cover.
2. Remove the camshaft sprocket as follows. Bolt the mounting plate to the center of the camshaft sprocket using one of the camshaft sprocket retaining screws.

NOTE: Tighten the nut (screw) securely to immobilize the center stud. Otherwise the chain tensioner will tighten the chain and lock in a new position so that the sprocket cannot be refitted. The chain tensioner cannot be reset without lifting the engine out of the car.

3. Undo the retaining screws from the camshaft sprocket. Separate the wheel from the camshaft plate until it hangs free in the mounting plate by the center stud.
4. Remove the camshaft bearing cups.
5. Remove the camshaft from the vehicle.
6. Installation is the reverse of removal with the following notations.
7. Make sure that the markings on the camshaft and the bearing caps are in line with one another.

8. Check that the flywheel mark is in line with the mark on the No. 1 cylinder block and that the ignition is set on No. 1 cylinder.
9. The screw on the camshaft sprocket center must not be unscrewed before the sprocket is tightly screwed to the camshaft.

1981 and Later

1. Rotate the flywheel until the "0" mark indexes with the line on the bell housing. The No. 1 cylinder should be on its firing mode.
2. Remove the valve cover assembly as previously outlined.
3. Be sure both the crankshaft and camshaft are at the No. 1 cylinder firing mode and the indexing lines still are aligned.
4. Remove the camshaft sprocket, keeping the chain on the sprocket. Place the sprocket between the chain guide and tensioner.
5. Remove the camshaft bearing caps and lift the camshaft from the bearing assembly housing. The bearing assembly housing can then be removed, if necessary.
6. To install, reverse the removal procedure. Be certain the timing marks are properly aligned.

Pistons and Connecting Rods

REMOVAL & INSTALLATION

1. Remove the engine from the vehicle and separate the unit from the transmission.
2. Inspect the connecting rods to make sure that all rods have been numbered correctly.
3. Remove the ring ridge at the top of the cylinder bore, if present, to avoid ring and piston damage, upon removal of the pistons.
4. Loosen the connecting rod cap bolts and lightly tap the caps to loosen. Remove the caps and push the connecting rod and piston assembly upward and out of the cylinder bore.

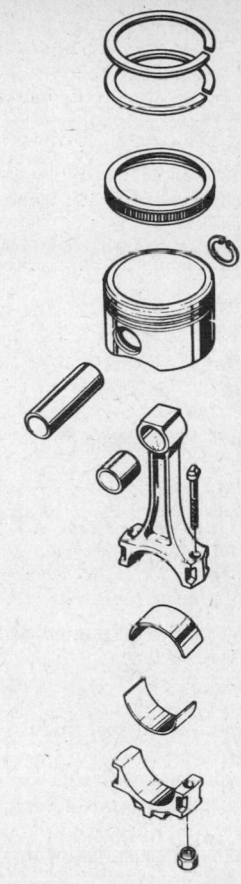

Piston and connecting rod assembly

5. Upon installation of the piston rings, place the lower compression ring with the side marked "TOP" uppermost.
6. Rotate the compression rings so that the gaps in alternate rings will be at 180 degrees to each other, positioned alternately over the two ends of the piston pins.
7. Make sure that the spring gaps of the top and bottom rings in the three-piece scraper ring are staggered.

NOTE: Oil the piston rings before assembly.

8. Continue the installation in the reverse of the removal procedure.

ENGINE LUBRICATION

Rear Main Oil Seal

REMOVAL & INSTALLATION

This seal is otherwise known as the crankshaft seal at the flywheel end. The seal can be changed with the engine in the vehicle, but the clutch and flywheel must first be removed.

1. Remove the clutch and the flywheel from the vehicle.

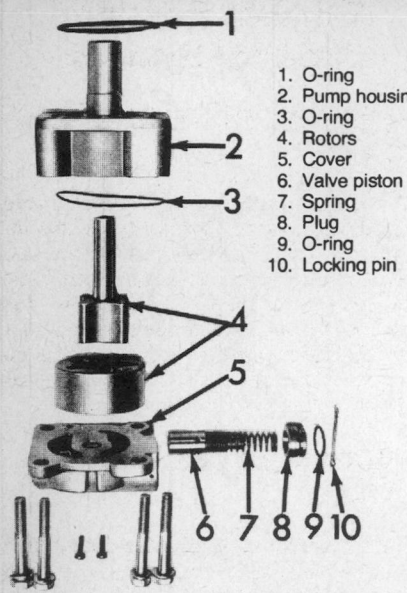

1. O-ring
2. Pump housing
3. O-ring
4. Rotors
5. Cover
6. Valve piston
7. Spring
8. Plug
9. O-ring
10. Locking pin

Exploded view of the oil pump—1978–80

2. Remove the old seal ring using the proper tool.

3. Install the new seal with the spring ring turned inwards toward the crankshaft using the proper seal installation tool.

4. Continue the installation in the reverse order of the removal.

Oil Pump

REMOVAL & INSTALLATION

1978–80

1. Remove the four retaining screws from the oil pump body.

2. Remove the oil pump and the sealing ring between the pump and the intermediate plate from the vehicle.

3. Installation is the reverse of removal.

1981 and Later

The oil pump is a gear-type pump and is driven by the crankshaft. It is positioned between the timing cover and crankshaft pulley. The pump assembly can be removed with the engine in the vehicle.

1. Remove the crankshaft pulley.

2. Lock the crankshaft in place by using a flywheel locking bracket.

3. Remove the oil pump retaining bolts. Remove the oil pump from the timing cover.

4. Before installation, prime the pump assembly and be sure the mark on the outer gear is visible.

5. Install a new gasket and refit the pump and the timing cover. Complete the assembly as required.

6. Before starting the engine, remove the oil filter base and fill the passageway on the pressure side with oil. Replace the filter base.

CHECKING CLEARANCES

1978–80

1. Remove the screws holding the pump cover and the pump housing together and separate the two.

2. Remove the rotors and the O-ring from the pump housing.

3. Remove the pressure reducing valve located in the cover by pulling out the locking pin and then removing the plug, the O-ring, the spring and the valve piston.

4. Check the axial clearance of the inner and outer rotors to the rotor housing with a rule and feeler gauge. The clearance should be 0.00197–0.00354 in.

5. If the clearance must be adjusted, grind the sealing surface of the housing or the sides of the rotor with fine emery cloth on a flat surface.

6. Check the evenness to the cover with a ruler. All deformities, scratches and pits should be removed by grinding.

7. Assemble the pump in the reverse order of the removal.

NOTE: The chamfered edge of the outer rotor faces inwards in the pump housing (toward the driveshaft).

NOTE: Published data on oil pump clearance for 1981 and later engines is not available.

ENGINE COOLING

Radiator

REMOVAL & INSTALLATION

99 Series

1. Drain the radiator.

2. Remove the hose clamps at the radiator and disconnect the hoses.

3. Disconnect the wiring terminals for the radiator fan and the thermoswitch.

4. Remove the grill. Remove the hood lock operating cable from its fastenings at the dash panel and wheel housing.

5. Remove the two front sheet retaining screws and nuts, and the four screws holding the headlights to the body.

6. Remove the front sheet metal complete with the radiator assembly, lifting forward and upward.

7. Installation is the reverse of removal.

900 Series

1. Drain the radiator.

2. Remove the hose clamps on the radiator hoses and disconnect the hoses from the radiator.

3. Disconnect the leads to the radiator fan and the auxiliary fan, if equipped.

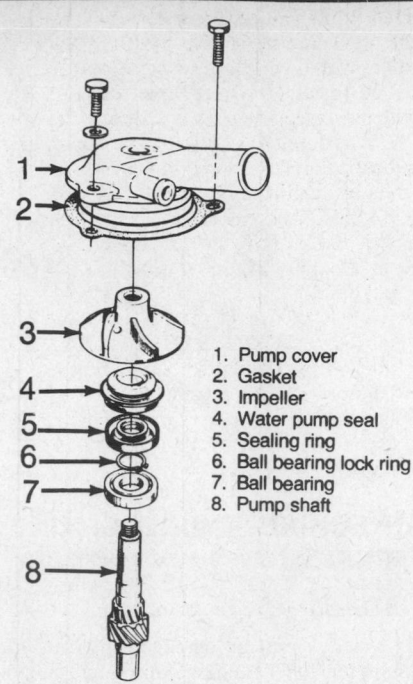

1. Pump cover
2. Gasket
3. Impeller
4. Water pump seal
5. Sealing ring
6. Ball bearing lock ring
7. Ball bearing
8. Pump shaft

Exploded view of the water pump— 1978–80

4. Disconnect the lead to the thermal switch. Remove the ignition coil.

5. Remove the two bolts in the upper radiator support, and lift the radiator out of the vehicle, pulling the top of the radiator slightly backwards.

6. Installation is the reverse of removal.

Water Pump

REMOVAL & INSTALLATION

1978–80

1. Drain the radiator. Remove the battery ground cable. Disconnect the intake manifold.

2. Remove the alternator and the alternator bracket.

3. On 99 series vehicles, unbolt both rear engine mounts. Place a jack under the rear of the engine and raise the engine high enough to remove the upper bolt holding the alternator bracket to the transmission cover. Slacken the lower retaining screw and turn the bracket so that it is as far from the engine as possible.

4. Remove the retaining bolts from the water pump cover and remove the cover.

NOTE: Tapping-out hammers or equivalent must not be used during the removal or installation process.

5. Remove the water pump using Saab tool No. 83-92-649 or 83-92-490 or equivalent. The tool fits into the threaded end of the shaft.

NOTE: With regard to water pump removal, if the impeller is not immobi-

lized while the center bolt is unscrewed, the gear teeth on the pump shaft and idler shaft are liable to be damaged.

6. Installation is the reverse of removal with the exception of the following notations.

a. Mount the pump shaft with the bearing and the circlip in the engine block using Saab tool No. 83-90-551 and No. 82-92-490 or equivalent. Check to insure that the pump gear engages to the gear on the idler shaft before pressing into position.

b. Install the lower and upper seal using Saab tool No. 83-0551 and No. 83-90-536 or equivalent. Press on the impeller shaft. Turn the tightening bolt ¼ turn at a time, unscrew it and then tighten down ¼ turn again until the impeller is finally in position.

1981 and Later

The water pump is located on the engine front and is driven by a "V" belt from the crankshaft pulley. The pump removal is accomplished by removing the "V" belt, pulley and pump retaining bolt. Installation is the reverse of the removal procedure.

Radiator Fan

REMOVAL & INSTALLATION

1. Disconnect the negative battery cable.
2. On some models, it may be necessary to remove the battery.
3. Disconnect the wires and cables from the ignition coil and the fan motor.
4. Disconnect the cable harness from the fan housing.
5. Remove the fan housing and remove the fan motor from the vehicle.
6. Installation is the reverse of removal.

EMISSION CONTROLS

Crankcase Emission Controls

The crankcase ventilation system is completely enclosed. The system is comprised of a three-way nipple in the valve cover, from which a small hose is routed to the inlet manifold, and a thicker hose routed to the air cleaner assembly. The sizes of the hoses are designed to efficiently regulate the removal of the crankcase gases and to route them into the engine to be mixed with the air/fuel mixture for combustion. The normal routing of the gases are to the inlet manifold, but at times of full acceleration, the gases are routed directly to the air cleaner assembly and mixed with the air as it is drawn into the inlet manifold.

Exhaust Emission Control System

ELECTRIC DECELERATION DEVICE

This device consists of an electronic speed transmitter which is located below the instrument panel. This transmitter is actuated by electric pulses from the speedometer and the solenoid at the throttle housing. The solenoid serves as a variable idling stop. During engine overrun the idle speed is increased if the speed of the vehicle exceeds 10 mph.

VACUUM DECELERATION DEVICE

This system consists of a vacuum controlled spring-loaded valve cone which is actuated by the vacuum in the intake manifold.

DASHPOT DECELERATION DEVICE

This device is installed on the throttle housing and acts to mechanically dampen the throttle valve when it shuts. The retardation time can be altered by loosening the locknut and screwing it in away from the throttle stop, which causes shorter deceleration time

EMISSION CONTROL EQUIPMENT

System	'78–'79 with Catalytic Converter	'78–'79 w/o Catalytic Converter	'80 and Later with Catalytic Converter	Turbo. '79	Turbo. '80 and Later
Deceleration device electric				X	
Deceleration device vacuum	X	X	X		X
Deceleration device dashpot			X		X
Delay valve		X			
EGR on-off					X
EGR proportional					
EGR two port		X	X		
Air injection					
Pulse air		X			
Oxygen sensor & catalytic converter	X		X	X	X
Compression 7.2:1				X	X
Compression 8.7:1	X				
Compression 9.25:1		X	X		
ELCD system	X	X	X	X	X

① Automatic transmission only

The colored end of the delay valve should be towards the vacuum advance on the distributor

or toward the throttle stop, which causes longer deceleration time.

DELAY VALVE

Canadian Models Only

A delay valve is mounted in the vacuum passage between the throttle valve housing and the vacuum control unit of the distributor. The valve delays the formation of a vacuum by around 6 seconds. The ignition advance is therefore also delayed during acceleration and the emission of nitric oxide (NO_x) is reduced.

The colored end of the delay valve should be towards the vacuum control unit of the distributor. It is also important that the valve is fitted with the shorter hose running between the valve and the vacuum control unit of the distributor.

When the suction line is to be disconnected (e.g. in conjunction with checking of ignition timing), always disconnect the hose at the throttle housing. Otherwise there will be a risk of dirt entering and clogging the delay valve.

ON-OFF EGR

When this type of EGR valve opens, a small quantity of exhaust gases flows via the metering orifice from the exhaust manifold, through the EGR crosspipe and the EGR valve to the inlet manifold. The EGR valve is controlled by means of a vacuum from the throttle valve housing. The vacuum hole is located relative to the throttle valve so that a vacuum signal is obtained when the engine speed is about 1.900 rev/min. or somewhat higher. Even during conditions of small loads, a sufficiently strong vacuum is obtained to open the valve completely. At full throttle and slightly below, the vacuum is so weak that the valve does not open.

The PVS valve senses the temperature of the coolant and cuts out the vacuum at temperatures lower than approximately 100° F (38°C) which means that improved driveability is obtained immediately after starting with a cold engine.

PROPORTIONAL EGR

The EGR valve is controlled by means of a vacuum regulator. When the valve opens, a small quantity of the exhaust gases is recirculated through the EGR crosspipe and the EGR valve to the inlet manifold. When the induction air passes through the venturi, a venturi signal which is proportional to the total air flow is obtained. The signal is transmitted to the EGR vacuum amplifier which amplifies the signal 14 times by means of the manifold vacuum reservoir.

The manifold vacuum reservoir is connected to the amplifier. The amplified signal then goes via the vacuum signal switch and the PVS valve to the EGR valve. The vacuum signal switch cuts out the EGR signal at engine speed below 2,500 ± 500 rev/min. This has been arranged by means of a hole drilled through the throttle valve housing (during the running-in of the engine, the cut-off speed can be somewhat lower). The PVS valve senses the temperature of the coolant and cuts off the EGR signal at temperatures lower than approx. 100°F, which results in improved driveability immediately after cold engine starting. At wide open throttle, the vacuum in the manifold reservoir disappears after a few seconds and the EGR valve closes.

TWO-PORT EGR

In the two-port EGR system, the opening of the EGR valve is regulated by two adjacent vacuum ports in the throttle valve housing, a holding valve, a release valve and a PVS valve. When the EGR valve opens, a small proportion of the exhaust gases are recirculated to the inlet manifold.

As the throttle valve is opened slightly and the valve passes the two vacuum ports, a gradual increase in the vacuum is obtained and, consequently, a gradual opening of the EGR valve.

When the throttle valve is opened wide and the vacuum in the ports diminishes, the earlier vacuum at the EGR valve is maintained for about six seconds by means of the holding valve.

When the throttle valve is closed, the EGR valve must also be closed to prevent rough idling of the engine. A release valve is fitted for this purpose and the valve is regulated by an additional port located inside the throttle valve housing. Thus, the vacuum maintained by the holding valve is released.

When the temperature of the engine is below approx. 104°F (40°C), the PVS valve shuts off the vacuum between the throttle valve and the EGR valve to improve the running of the engine during the warming-up period.

AIR INJECTION SYSTEM

The function of the air injection system is to create afterburning in the exhaust pipes and the exhaust manifold. The air pump is driven by a belt from the crankshaft pulley. The air is drawn into the pump via a labyrinth seal at the pulley and is pumped out to the air hose and the distributor pipe. A

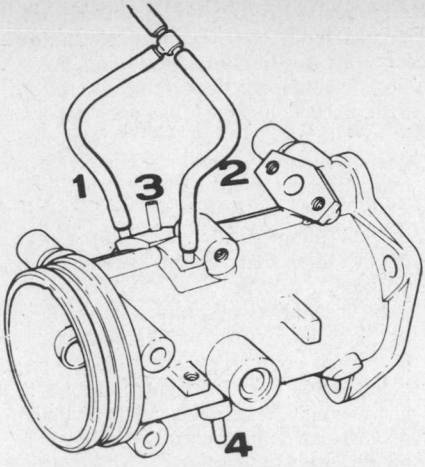

Throttle body, 2-port EGR. 1 and 2 are EGR outlets; 3 is the vacuum distribution outlet, and 4 is a plugged outlet

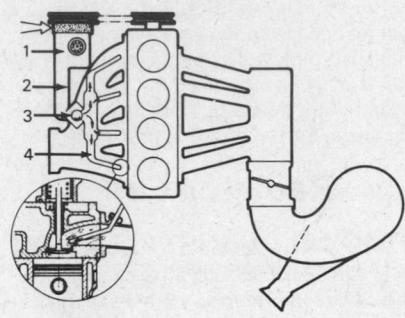

1. Air pump
2. Air inlet hose
3. Check valve
4. Air distribution pipe with injection tubes

Air injection system—typical

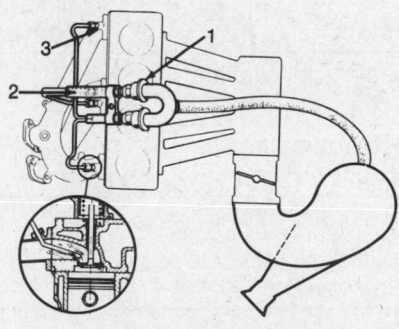

1. Check valves
2. Distribution pipes
3. Inlet pipes

Pulse air system—typical

relief valve opens if the pressure in the distributor becomes too great.

The function of the check valve is to prevent exhaust gases from entering the air pump if the belt should break. The air distribution pipe connects the check valve with the four injection tubes. The ends of injection tubes are located at the hottest part of the exhaust passage in order to achieve a maximum afterburning effect.

The pump noise is partly absorbed by the labyrinth seal and partly by a small silencer located above the relief valve. In addition, insulation is glued to the dash panel behind the pump.

PULSE AIR SYSTEM

Federal cars are equipped with a pulse air system. In common with the air injection system, the purpose of the pulse air system is to supply air to the exhaust gases from the engine to bring about continued oxidation of the hydrocarbons and carbon monoxide in the exhaust system.

The system is composed of two check valves which are connected to the exhaust manifold by means of dual inlet pipes. The pipes open into the exhaust valves where the exhaust gases are hot, which is important in achieving efficient oxidation in the exhaust system.

The check valves are grouped so that one goes to No. 1 and No. 4 cylinders, and the other to no. 2 and no. 3 cylinders. Air is supplied to the valves by means of a hose from the air cleaner.

The function of the pulse air system is based on the vacuum occurring in the exhaust system during the pulses. For a brief moment immediately prior to the closing of the exhaust valve (at the start of the suction stroke), a vacuum is produced in the exhaust manifold whereupon the check valve opens and a small amount of air is drawn into the exhaust manifold.

Inspection Service

Remove the hose between the air cleaner and the check valve and check that it is free from dents or cracks. Run the engine at idling speed and check that air is drawn through the check valves. Suction should be felt with the thumbs placed over the openings.

CATALYTIC CONVERTER

The catalytic converter is located in the exhaust system between the engine and muffler. The unit is composed of a ceramic material insert of honeycomb design. Prior to the use of the Lambda oxygen sensor in conjunction with the special continuous injection system, the cars were equipped with a dual-type catalytic converter, but with the use of the oxygen sensor and CIS system, a new three-way converter is now employed. This new three-way converter is capable of reducing the content of the exhaust gases of hydrocarbons, carbon monoxide and oxides of nitrogen, down to the prescribed Federal and State emission levels, on the conditions that the accurate regulation of the air/fuel ratio is maintained under all driving conditions.

Platinum and palladium are used in the dual type converter, while platinum, palladium and rhodium are used as the catalyst in the three-way converters.

Evaporative Emission Control System

EVAPORATIVE LOSS CONTROL DEVICE (ELCD)

The ELCD device is a charcoal filter, which absorbs the vapor from the fuel tank. The charcoal canister is placed in the engine compartment. It is connected to the vent hose of the fuel tank and with a hose to the air cleaner. When the engine is running, fresh air is drawn through the charcoal filter and to the engine inlet system. The filter will then be cleaned of vapors. The vehicles are equipped with a roll-over valve. The valve is connected to the ventilation hose between the filler tube and the charcoal canister. In the event of the car rolling over or ending up on its side, a pendulum will actuate the valve which will shut off the ventilation hose thereby preventing the escape of fuel.

OXYGEN SENSOR REGULATED CI-SYSTEM

All 1980 and later vehicles are equipped with a special continuous injection system combined with an electronic control system which is regulated by an oxygen sensor that is located in the exhaust manifold. These vehicles are also equipped with a three-way catalytic converter which is located between the exhaust manifold and the muffler in the exhaust system. The sensor-regulated injection system ensures that the air/fuel mixture is continually kept within the required limits for vehicle operation and emission controls.

NOTE: For more information on the oxygen sensor-equipped CIS injection system, please refer to "Fuel Injection" in the Unit Repair section.

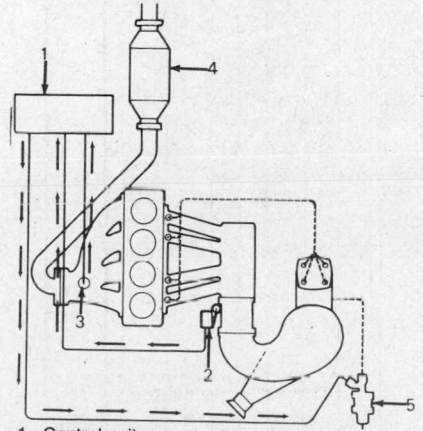

1. Control unit
2. Throttle valve switch, full-load enrichment
3. Oxygen sensor
4. Catalytic converter
5. Modulating valve

Oxygen-sensor regulated CI system

FUEL SYSTEM

Fuel Pump

REMOVAL & INSTALLATION
1978–79

1. Disconnect the negative battery cable.
2. On all vehicles except SAAB 900 series and the 99 Combi Coupe, roll back the carpet in the trunk.
3. On the 900 series and the 99 Combi Coupe, remove the rear floor cover and the floor panel in the luggage compartment.
4. Remove the circular cover plate on top of the pump mounting.
5. Remove the rubber cover from the fuel pump, if equipped. Disconnect the electric terminals at the fuel pump.
6. Disconnect the fuel line from the fuel pump.

NOTE: Hold the fuel pump with an open-end spanner wrench when loosening the connection.

7. Using the proper tool, turn the fuel pump mounting counterclockwise to the nearest groove to unlock the bayonet socket.
8. Lift the fuel pump out carefully. Save the O-ring for installation.

NOTE: The fuel pump can only be removed in one position, as one of the bayonet tongues is wider than the others.

9. Installation is the reverse of removal.

1980 and later

NOTE: Beginning in 1980, all models are equipped with a plastic gas tank. Care should be exercised when removing the fuel pump from the plastic gas tank.

1. Disconnect the negative battery cable.
2. Remove the rear floor panel in the luggage compartment. Remove the valve cover from above the fuel pump.
3. Disconnect the electrical connections from the fuel pump.
4. Disconnect the fuel pipes from the pump.

NOTE: Use an open-ended spanner wrench to hold the pump steady while loosening the connections.

5. Remove the fuel pump mounting clamp. Lift the fuel pump from the vehicle.
6. Installation is the reverse order of removal.

FUEL PUMP DELIVERY CHECK

Voltage Check

1. Remove the round cover plate from the top of the fuel pump.
2. Measure the voltage between the positive and negative terminals when the fuel pump is operating.

3. The lowest permissible voltage is 11.5 volts.

Capacity Check

NOTE: Be sure that the fuel filter is not clogged and that the battery is fully charged.

1. Disconnect the return fuel pipe from the fuel distributor.

2. Connect the test pipe to the fuel distributor and place the other end in a suitable container.

3. On vehicles with the safety switch on the air flow sensor, remove the switch connector from the air flow sensor.

4. On vehicles with the fuel pump relay and the pulse sensor, remove the pump relay. Connect a jumper lead between terminals 15 and 87 on 99 series and terminals 30 and 87 on 900 series vehicles.

5. Switch on the ignition and allow the pump to run for 30 seconds. Measure the quantity of fuel. The proper specification should be 750 cc/30 sec. up to and including 1979 models and 900 cc/30 sec. for 1980 and later models, measured in the return line.

Fuel Injection

All Saab vehicles sold in the U.S. are equipped with a Bosch CIS (continuous injection; also known as K-Jetronic) injection system.

An electric fuel pump which is mounted inside the gas tank provides fuel at a constant pressure to the mixture control unit. The latter consists of an air flow sensor which measures the flow of air to the engine and which acts mechanically on the fuel distributor. The fuel distributor provides the injection valves with the correct amount of fuel. The fuel is injected continuously into the intake manifold immediately upstream of the inlet valve. 1980 and later vehicles are equipped with a special CIS system which is composed of an electronic control unit that is regulated by an oxygen sensor located in the exhaust manifold.

For all repair and adjustment procedures not detailed below, please refer to "Fuel Injection" in the Unit Repair section.

Injector
REMOVAL & INSTALLATION

1. Thoroughly clean the area around the injection nozzle and its connection.

2. Disconnect the fuel line from the injector. Hold the injector with an open end

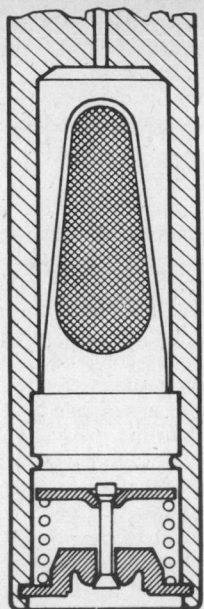

Injection valve cross section

wrench to prevent it from turning.

3. Loosen the bolt and remove the injector retaining plate.

4. Lift out the injector and remove the rubber seal.

5. Installation is in the reverse order of removal.

TESTING

1. Remove the rubber bellows from the air flow sensor.

2. Remove the injection valves from the intake manifold. Place the valves in a suitable container.

NOTE: The fuel lines should be left connected.

3. Turn on the ignition and remove the safety circuit plug from the air flow sensor. On 1978 and later 99 series vehicles, connect a jumper lead between the terminals 15 and 87 and between terminals 30 and 87 on 1979 and later 900 series in the relay holder. This will enable the fuel pump to operate.

4. For fuel atomization, lift the lever in the air flow sensor and check the spray pattern that is being emitted at the injection valves. If atomization is poor, correct as necessary.

5. For valve tightness, turn off the ignition to obtain the rest pressure. Wipe the area dry around the injection nozzles. Lift the lever and check for leakage. It should not take less than 15 seconds for a drop to form. Correct as required.

Fuel Distributor
REMOVAL & INSTALLATION

1. Clean and remove fuel lines at distributor.

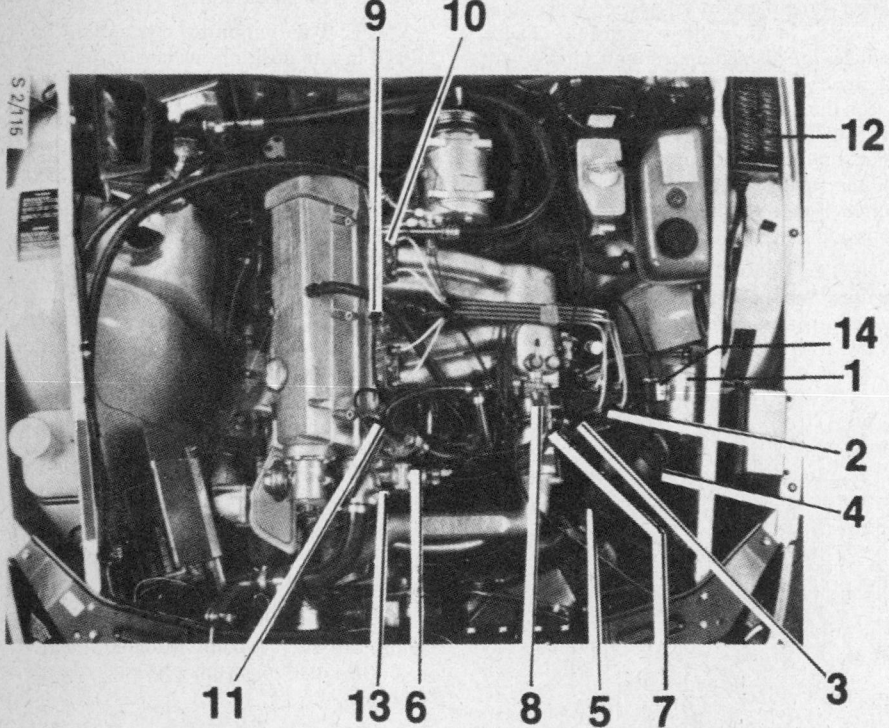

1. Fuel filter
2. Fuel distributor
3. Air flow sensor
4. Air cleaner
5. Rubber bellows
6. Warm-up regulator
7. Throttle valve housing
8. Cold start valve
9. Thermo-time switch
10. Injection valve
11. Auxiliary air valve
12. Fuses and relay box
13. Thermo switch
14. Pressure impulse contact

CIS (K-Jetronic) fuel injection components location—900 series

2. Remove retaining bolts and carefully lift out distributor. Take care not to drop control piston.

3. If control plunger has been removed, moisten with fuel before installing and insert small shoulder first.

4. Reinstall distributor using new O-rings.

NOTE: The fuel distributor must not be disassembled, but should be replaced when faulty.

Fuel Filter

REMOVAL & INSTALLATION

The fuel filter is bolted in-line and must be uncoupled for replacement. Filter is installed with arrows pointing in direction of flow.

Fuel Accumulator

REMOVAL & INSTALLATION

1. Clean the area around the fuel accumulator connections.

2. Disconnect the connections and remove the fuel accumulator from the vehicle.

3. Installation is the reverse of removal.

Air Cleaner Element

REPLACEMENT

1. Remove the rubber bellows from between the air flow sensor and the throttle valve housing.

2. Remove the retaining bolts holding the lower section of the air flow meter to the air cleaner.

3. Raise the mixture control slightly and remove the cleaner element. Do not damage the fuel line.

4. Remove the element holder from the bottom of the cleaner assembly and clean the air cleaner casing.

5. Install the new air cleaner element and reassemble in the reverse order of the removal procedure.

MANUAL TRANSAXLE

REMOVAL & INSTALLATION

1. Remove the engine and transmission as a unit from the vehicle.

2. Drain the engine oil. Remove the clutch cover. Remove the starter.

3. Withdraw the clutch shaft using a drift or equivalent.

4. Remove the three bolts for the slave cylinder.

5. Remove the screws in the mating flanges of the engine and transmission.

6. Carefully separate the engine from the transmission. At the same time, remove the release bearing guide sleeve.

7. Installation is the reverse of removal.

NOTE: When fitting the engine and transmission together, make sure that the mating surfaces are clean. Check that the two guide sleeves are fitted in the transmission. Install a new gasket on the transmission flange.

NOTE: 1984 and later models beginning with VIN Nos. E1004580 and E2001945 utilize a new-type steel gasket between the engine and transaxle. Because of changes made to the timing cover to accommodate this new gasket, it may only be used after the above VIN numbers.

The steel gasket must only be used once. To install, thoroughly clean both mating surfaces and position the new gasket on one surface. Apply a high-temperature (minimum 500°F) silicone sealer to the grooves at each end of the gasket; additional sealant around the entire gasket is not necessary. Assemble the engine and transaxle immediately.

OVERHAUL

For all transaxle overhaul procedures, please refer to "Manual Transaxle Overhaul" in the Unit Repair section.

CLUTCH

REMOVAL & INSTALLATION
99 Series

1. Drain the radiator. Remove the hood. Disconnect the negative battery cable.

2. Disconnect the cable harness from the fan housing. Disconnect the cables to the ignition coil, oil pressure switch, temperature transmitter, headlamp wiper motor and the fan thermal switch on the radiator.

3. Disconnect the hoses from the radiator. Remove the grille. Remove the radiator assembly.

4. Remove the clutch cover bolts, then remove the clutch cover.

5. Mount spacer (Saab part No. 8390023) between the clutch cover and the diaphragm spring. When installing the spacer, make sure that the clutch pedal is fully depressed.

6. Remove the retaining clip and the seal cap from the clutch shaft. Remove plastic propeller from the clutch shaft.

7. Remove the clutch shaft using a tapping-out hammer or equivalent.

8. Remove the retaining bolts that secure the slave cylinder (guide sleeve) to the primary gear housing.

Pressure plate and related components

9. Remove the clutch retaining screws, the clutch, clutch disc, slave cylinder (guide sleeve) and the release bearing. It is not necessary to disconnect the hydraulic hose on the slave cylinder (guide sleeve).

NOTE: Be sure that the diaphragm spring does not damage the slave cylinder.

10. Installation is the reverse of removal.

900 Series

1. Remove the clutch housing cover.

2. Install the spacer (Saab part No. 8390023) between the clutch fork and the diaphragm spring. Keep the clutch pedal depressed when the ring is being installed.

3. Unhook the spring clip and remove the cover located in front of the clutch shaft. Remove the clutch shaft plastic propeller.

4. Remove the clutch shaft by means of an M8 bolt installed in the shaft end and Saab tool No. 83-93-175. Withdraw the shaft as far as possible.

5. Remove the clutch slave cylinder retaining bolts.

6. Remove the clutch retaining bolts and remove the clutch, clutch disc and the slave cylinder complete with the clutch release bearing.

NOTE: Make sure that the slave cylinder sleeve is not damaged by the clutch during the removal procedure.

7. Installation is the reverse of removal.

CHECKING CLUTCH WEAR
Early Design Slave Cylinder

1. Remove the inspection hole cover on the clutch housing.

2. Disengage the clutch and then release the pedal. The release bearing will then be in contact with the fingers on the pressure plate.

3. Looking through the inspection hole, check that the sliding lock ring on the piston in the slave cylinder is in contact with the cylinder walls.

4. Check the distance between the sliding lock ring and the lock ring behind the release bearing.

5. If distance is 0–1.0mm, the clutch must be replaced. The distance on a new clutch disc would be 6.0mm.

Later Design Slave Cylinder

1. Remove the inspection hole cover and look through the inspection hole.

2. When the distance between the plastic sleeve front edge and the front edge of the turned surface is less than 2.0mm the clutch disc must be replaced.

Clutch Master Cylinder

REMOVAL & INSTALLATION

1. Remove the clamp holding the pipe from the cylinder at the body and remove the pipe at the cylinder.

2. Remove the left hand screen under the instrument panel.

3. Remove the pin holding the push rod to the clutch pedal.

4. Remove the bolts inside the dash panel. Remove the clutch cylinder from inside the engine compartment.

5. Remove the hose from the fluid container and hang it out of the way so that the fluid does not come out.

6. Installation is the reverse of removal.

BLEEDING

1. Connect a hose to the slave cylinder bleeder valve. Place the other end of the hose in a suitable jar partially filled with brake fluid.

2. Fill the master cylinder with brake fluid.

3. Open the bleeder valve on the slave cylinder a half turn.

4. Place a cooling system tester gauge over the opening of the master cylinder.

5. Pump the tester until all air has been expelled from the system.

6. Close the slave cylinder bleeder valve.

7. Check that all air has been removed

from the system by depressing the clutch pedal.

Clutch Slave Cylinder

In order to remove the clutch slave cylinder, the clutch must first be removed. Refer to the clutch removal procedure in this section for the proper information.

AUTOMATIC TRANSAXLE

REMOVAL & INSTALLATION

1. Remove the engine and transmission as a unit from the vehicle.

2. Drain the engine oil. Remove the flywheel cover. Remove the starter.

3. Disconnect the throttle wire from the throttle valve housing.

4. Remove all bolts from the mating surfaces of the engine and transmission.

5. Remove the four bolts securing the flywheel ring gear to the torque converter.

NOTE: These bolts can be reached from above the oil pump mounting.

6. Turn the flywheel so that the two plate angles will be horizontal. Carefully lift the engine off of the transmission.

7. Installation is the reverse of removal.

NOTE: When fitting the engine and transmission together, make sure that the mating surfaces are clean. Check that the two guide sleeves are fitted into the transmission.

NEUTRAL SAFETY SWITCH ADJUSTMENT

1. Disconnect the wires from the switch.

NOTE: The wide terminals are for back–up lights and the narrow ones are for the starter motor.

2. Loosen the locknut using an $^{11}/_{16}$ in. crows foot and unscrew the switch two turns.

3. With the selector in Drive, connect a test light between the narrow terminals. The light should light up.

4. Screw in the switch until the light goes out. Mark that position on both the transmission and the switch.

5. Move the test lamp, the wide terminals and screw switch in until the light goes out again. Count the number between the two lights going out.

6. Turn the switch to a point halfway between the two lights–out points.

7. Secure the locknut to 4–6 ft. lbs. torque.

NOTE: If the safety switch is locked too tight, it may be damaged.

SHIFT LINKAGE

Checking

1. Move the selector lever to "N". Check the clearance from the selection lever pin to the neutral detent.

2. Move the selector lever to "D". Check the clearance from the selector lever pin to the drive detent. The clearance at the "N" and the "D" position should be equal. If they are not equal adjust the cable.

3. Check for proper selector lever pin position in the "P", "R", "2" and "1" ranges.

Adjusting

1. Remove the gear selector lever cover.

2. Slack off the gear selector lever housing nuts with tool no. 839123 or equivalent.

3. Lift the gear selector lever housing and turn it so that the adjustment nuts of the cable will be reachable.

4. Adjust the cable longer or shorter to bring the "N" and "D" clearance into equality.

5. Assemble the gear selector housing and check the clearance in "N" and "D".

6. A fine setting of the selector cable can be accomplished by adding or removing shims at the transmission case end of the cable. A maximum of three shims may be used.

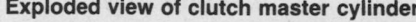

1. Housing
2. Spring with seat
3. Sealing
4. Washer
5. Piston and rear seal
6. Push rod assembly

Exploded view of clutch master cylinder

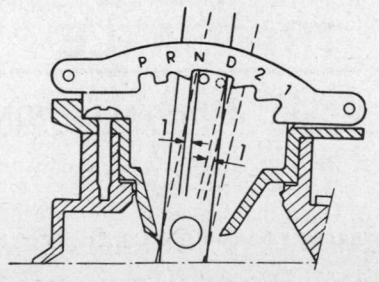

Manual linkage clearance, equal in "N" and "D"

BAND ADJUSTMENT

Type 35 Transmission

FRONT BAND (INSIDE TRANSMISSION)

1. Place tool No. 8790073 or equivalent, ¼ inch thickness gauge between the adjusting screw and the boss on the piston.
2. Loosen the lock nut.
3. Tighten the adjusting screw to 10 in. lbs. of torque and tighten the lock nut.

NOTE: On transmissions with self-adjusting mechanism, check the gap between the self-adjusting spring and the lever. It should be 1.5 to 2.0 thread flights.

REAR BAND

The rear band adjusting screw is located outside the transmission case on the driver's side.

1. Loosen the lock nut a few turns.
2. Tighten the adjusting screw to 10 ft lbs. and then back off ¾ turn.
3. Hold the adjusting screw and torque the lock nut to 30–40 ft. lbs.

Type 37 Transmission

FRONT BAND (INSIDE TRANSMISSION)

Up to serial numbers 001-1700, 002-2800

1. Loosen the locknut and position tool number 87-90-073 or equivalent ¼ inch thick, between the adjusting screw and the piston pin.
2. Tighten the adjusting screw to 9 ft. lbs. and then loosen one turn.
3. Hold the adjusting screw and tighten the locknut to 24–28 ft. lbs.

After serial numbers 001-1710, 002-2801

1. Loosen the locknut and position tool number 87-90-030 or equivalent, ¹¹⁄₃₂ in. thick, between the screw and the piston pin.
2. Tighten the adjusting screw to 9 ft. lbs. *Do not* loosen the adjusting screw.
3. Hold the adjusting screw and tighten the locknut to 24–28 ft. lbs.

REAR BAND

The rear band adjusting screw is located on the outside of the transmission on the left side.

1. Loosen the locknut a few turns.
2. Tighten the adjusting screw to 10 ft. lbs. with tool number 87-90-115 or equivalent. Back off the adjusting screw ¾ turn.
3. Hold the adjusting screw and tighten the locknut to 24–28 ft. lbs.

DRIVE AXLES

Driveshaft

REMOVAL & INSTALLATION

NOTE: The entire front axle assembly must be removed in order to remove the driveshaft from the vehicle.

1. On 900 series vehicles, remove the upper bolt of the shock absorber before jacking up the vehicle.
2. Raise the vehicle on a hoist and support it safely. Remove the wheel.
3. Remove the brake housing and hang it on the wheel housing to avoid damage to the brake hose. Remove the brake disc and parking brake assembly with the cable.
4. Remove the large clamp from the rubber bellows on the inner universal joint.

NOTE: To separate the inner universal joint, install the cover (Saab part No. 7323736) in the rubber bellows to stop the needle bearings from falling out and to keep dirt from entering. Install the protective cap (Saab part No. 7838469) on the inner driver.

5. Disconnect the tie-rod from the steering arm using the proper tool. Remove the nut on the upper ball joint. Remove the bolts from the lower control arm bracket.
6. Remove the driveshaft through the wheel housing and remove the entire front axle assembly.
7. If the differential bearing cap is to be removed, remove the retaining bolts and remove the cap and the inner drive using the proper removal tools.
8. Installation is the reverse of removal.

OVERHAUL

1. Mount the steering knuckle housing in a press and press out the outer driveshaft.
2. Remove the intermediate driveshaft from the outer universal joint by loosening the rubber bellows on the outer universal joint and sliding it along the shaft.
3. Mount the shaft in a press and press together the two conical washers so that the circlip inside the hub can move in its groove.
4. Open the circlip using pliers to remove the pressure.
5. Withdraw the intermediate shaft from the hub together with the spherical shaped washer, the two conical washers and the shaft locking ring. The circlip on the hub remains in the groove.
6. Installation is the reverse of removal.

REAR AXLE

REMOVAL & INSTALLATION

1. Jack up the rear of the vehicle and support it safely.

CAUTION
Do not place jack under rear axle to lift vehicle. Damage to the rear axle could occur.

---

2. Disconnect the brake hoses in front of the rear axle. Disconnect the lower shock absorber bolts and the cross bar.
3. Lower the axle and remove the rear springs.

4. Remove the bolts of the spring link rear bushings and lift away the rear axle assembly.
5. Installation is the reverse of removal. Bleed the hydraulic brake system.

NOTE: The rubber bearings must be mounted in such a way that no strain occurs when the weight of the vehicle is supported by the wheels. They must be drawn tight only when the vehicle is standing empty on its four wheels.

Rear Wheel Bearings

REMOVAL & INSTALLATION

NOTE: Each rear wheel hub has two tapered roller bearings. On 1978 models, these two bearings were the same size. Beginning with the 1979 models, the inner bearing has a larger diameter than the outer bearing.

1. Raise the vehicle on a hoist and support it safely.

NOTE: Do not place the jack under the rear axle, as this is likely to deform the axle.

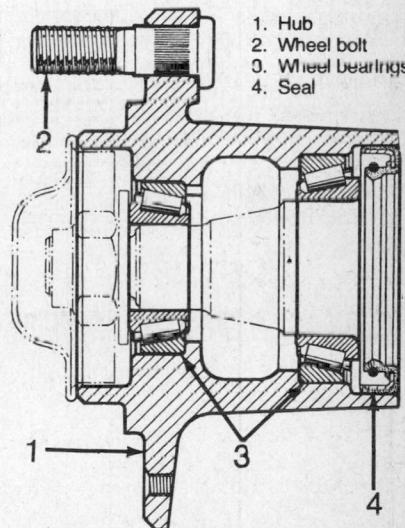

1. Hub
2. Wheel bolt
3. Wheel bearings
4. Seal

Rear wheel hub and bearings—typical

2. Remove the wheel. Remove the brake housing and the brake disc. Support the brake housing to avoid damage to the brake pipe.
3. Remove the dust cap. Remove the locknut and the washer. Pull off the hub. If necessary, use a suitable puller.
4. Break out the seal ring with a suitable tool (it cannot be removed intact). Remove the inner rings of both bearings.
5. Place a suitable drift in the milled recesses of the hub and drive out the outer bearing rings.

NOTE: It is advisable to place a wooden board under the hub to avoid deforming the end faces.

6. Installation is the reverse of removal. Torque the locknut to 36 ft. lbs., than slacken the nut completely and torque it to 2.9 ft. lbs.

REAR SUSPENSION

Shock Absorbers

REMOVAL & INSTALLATION

Pneumatic Shock

NOTE: Pneumatic shock absorbers are gas filled which can cause injury if not handled properly. In order to avoid the risk of injury the shock absorbers should be emptied of the gas before being scrapped. This is accomplished by drilling a 2mm hole in the pressure chamber 10–15mm from the edge of the shock housing.

1. Raise the vehicle on a hoist and support it safely.
2. Place an additional jack stand under the rear axle to prevent it from dropping and stretching the brake lines.
3. Insert a jack at the rear of the spring-link. Remove the shock absorber retaining nuts.
4. Remove the bolts in the spring-link mounting on the rear axle.
5. Using the jack, lower the spring-link so that the shock absorber can be removed from the vehicle.
6. Installation is the reverse of removal.

Springs

REMOVAL & INSTALLATION

1. Raise the vehicle on a hoist and support it safely.

1. Rear axle	7. Spring seat
2. End piece	8. Coil spring
3. Stub axle	9. Spring insulator
4. Spring links	10. Rubber buffer
5. Rear links	11. Stop
6. Cross bar	12. Shock absorber

Rear suspension assembly

2. Remove the hub cap, tire wheel assembly. Install a jack under the spring-link and disconnect the lower end of the shock absorber.
3. From underneath of the vehicle, remove the two locknuts that secure the front spring-link bearing to the body of the vehicle.
4. Place a jack stand under the rear axle to prevent the brake lines from being damaged by the weight of the rear axle.
5. Lower the spring-link so that the spring can be removed from the vehicle together with the upper spring support and the rubber spacer at the lower spring seating which is retained by the spring tension.
6. Installation is the reverse of removal.

FRONT SUSPENSION

Shock Absorbers

Some vehicles are equipped with pneumatic shocks.

NOTE: Pneumatic shock absorbers are gas-filled which can cause injury if not handled properly. In order to avoid the risk of injury, the shock abosrbers should be emptied of the gas before being scrapped. This is accomplished by drilling a 2mm hole in the pressure chamber 10–15mm from the edge of the shock housing.

REMOVAL & INSTALLATION

1. On 900 series vehicles, remove the upper shock absorber nut before raising the vehicle.
2. Raise the vehicle and support it safely. Remove the wheels.

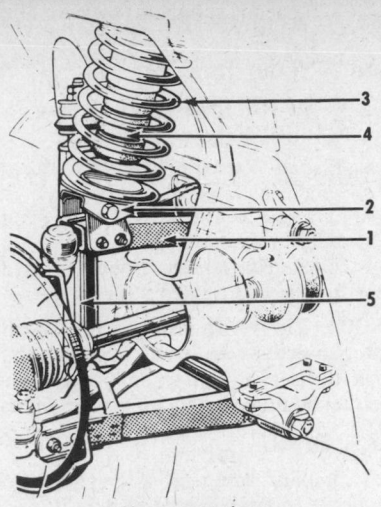

1. Upper control arm
2. Lower spring support
3. Coil spring
4. Rubber buffer
5. Shock absorber

Front suspension assembly

3. Remove the shock absorber retaining bolts and remove the shock from the vehicle. Save all washers and rubber parts.
4. Installation is the reverse of removal.

Ball Joints

REMOVAL & INSTALLATION

1. Raise the vehicle and support it safely. Remove the wheel.
2. Remove the brake housing and hang it out of the way so that the brake hose will not be damaged.
3. Remove the nut that holds the ball joint ball bolt to the steering knuckle housing. Remove the bolt using the proper removal tool.
4. Remove the ball joint from the control arm assembly.
5. Installation is the reverse of removal.

Springs

REMOVAL & INSTALLATION

1. On 900 series remove the upper shock absorber nuts before raising the vehicle.
2. Raise the vehicle on a hoist and support it safely. Remove the wheel.
3. Install a spring compression tool or equivalent, engaging the upper shanks directly in the spring at the second free turn from the top of the lower shanks around the spring cups.

NOTE: These are located on the last turn of the spring with the color-coded cup right beside the end of the coil.

4. Compress the spring at the top end, approximately 1½ in. If the upper spring attachment of the steel cone is left behind in the wheel housing, remove it.

5. Remove the spring and the steel cone from the vehicle.

6. Installation is the reverse of removal.

Upper Control Arm

REMOVAL & INSTALLATION

NOTE: To remove the left upper control arm, the engine must first be removed from the vehicle. See the engine removal procedure in this section of this manual.

1. Raise the vehicle on a hoist and support it safely.

2. Remove the wheel. Remove the shock absorber. Compress the coil spring, using a spring compression tool.

3. Back-off and remove the two bolts attaching the upper ball joint and lower spring seat to the upper control arm.

4. Remove the bolts from both upper control arm bearing brackets.

5. Remove the coil spring from the vehicle.

6. Remove the control arm and bearings from the vehicle.

NOTE: Save the spacers under the bearings and record the number of spacers used under each bearing.

7. Remove both of the bearing nuts. Now the bearings and bushings can be removed from the control arm.

8. Installation is the reverse of removal.

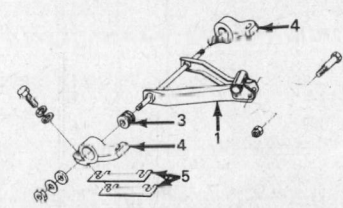

1. Upper control arm 4. Bearing
3. Rubber bushing 5. Spacers

Upper control arm assembly

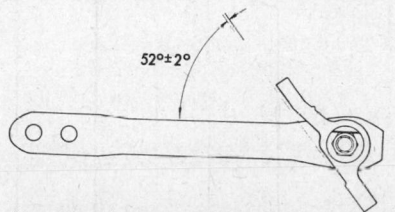

Checking the angle between the upper control arm and bearing

NOTE: When mounting the bearings to the control arm, the angle between the control arm and the bearing should be 52 ± 2° when both nuts are tightened.

Lower Control Arm
REMOVAL & INSTALLATION

1. Raise the vehicle on the hoist and support it safely. Remove the wheel.

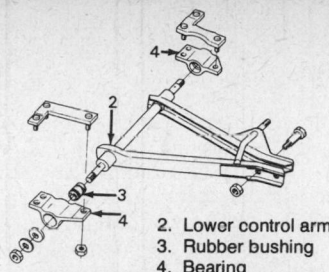

2. Lower control arm
3. Rubber bushing
4. Bearing

Lower control arm assembly

Checking the angle between the lower control arm and bearing

2. Disconnect the lower end of the shock absorber.

3. Back-off and remove the two bolts that attach the ball joint to the control arm.

4. Remove the lower control arm attaching bolts from under the engine compartment floor.

5. Remove the control arm and its attaching brackets from the vehicle.

6. Remove the control arm bearing nuts and remove the bearings from the control arm.

7. Installation is the reverse of removal.

NOTE: When mounting the bearings to the control arm, the angle between the control arm and the bearing should be 18 ± 2° when both nuts are tightened.

Front End Alignment

TOE-IN

1. Roll the car straight forward on a level floor and stop it without using brakes. It must not be moved backward after this.

2. Take a reading of measurement A with the toe-in gauge between the front wheel rims level with the axles. Mark the measurement points with chalk. Roll the car forward until the chalk marks are level with but behind the axles, and take a reading of B. Any necessary adjustment is made by altering the length of the tie-rod.

3. Remove the nut on the outer end of the tie-rod and the outer clip on the steering gear rubber bellows.

4. Use a suitable pair of grippers to twist the tie-rod right or left; adjust until the toe-in is right. Hold the bellows during the twisting.

CASTER

The caster is the angle by which the steering knuckle axis departs from the vertical when viewed from the side and the measurement is generally expressed in degrees. If the caster needs adjusting, spacers are inserted under the bearing brackets of the upper control arms.

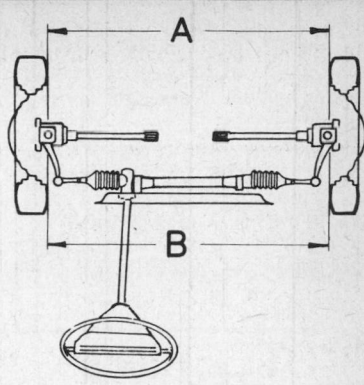

Toe-in adjustment

To increase the caster, transfer spacers from the front bracket to the rear bracket. To reduce the caster, transfer spacers from the rear bracket to the front bracket. In either case, the total spacer thickness removed from one bracket must be added to the other one.

CAMBER

Camber is the angle by which the centerlines of the wheels lean from the vertical. The camber is positive (+) if the wheels lean outward, and negative (−) if they lean inward.

The camber, and with it the "king pin" angle, can be adjusted with spacers placed under the two bearing brackets of the upper control arms. The desired result can thus be obtained by increasing or reducing the number of spacers used. To increase or reduce camber, use the same number of spacers under both brackets.

Front Wheel Bearings

REMOVAL & INSTALLATION

NOTE: The entire front axle assembly must be removed from the vehicle when removing the wheel bearings.

1. On 900 series vehicles, remove the upper bolt of the shock absorber before jacking up the vehicle.

2. Raise the vehicle on a hoist and support it safely. Remove the wheel.

3. Remove the brake housing and hang it by the wheel housing to avoid damage to the brake hose. Remove the brake disc and parking brake assembly with the cable.

4. Remove the large clamp from the rubber bellows on the inner universal joint.

NOTE: To separate the inner universal joint, install the cover (Saab part No. 7323736) in the rubber bellows to stop the needle bearings from falling out and to keep dirt from entering. Install the protective cap (Saab part No. 7838469) on the inner drive.

5. Disconnect the tie-rod from the steering arm using the proper tool. Remove

the nut on the upper ball joint. Remove the bolts from the lower control arm bracket.

6. Remove the driveshaft through the wheel housing and remove the entire front axle assembly.

7. Place the steering knuckle housing in a press and press out the driveshaft.

8. Remove the lock-ring and press out the bearing using a suitable drift.

9. Installation is the reverse of removal.

STEERING

Steering Wheel

REMOVAL & INSTALLATION

1. Disconnect the negative battery cable.

2. On early models, remove the bottom cover of the steering wheel bearing.

3. Remove the steering wheel safety pad. 1981 models, remove the steering wheel emblem by lifting with a small screwdriver. Remove the horn contact. Remove the steering wheel holding nut and washer.

4. Remove the steering wheel using the proper steering wheel removal tool.

5. Installation is the reverse of removal.

Combination Switch

REMOVAL & INSTALLATION

NOTE: From 1981 models, the turn-signal arm return actuator is removable.

1. Disconnect the negative battery cable.

2. Remove the steering wheel.

3. Remove the cover beneath the bearing support.

4. Remove the combination switch retaining bolts and electrical connections.

5. Remove the switch from the vehicle.

6. Installation is the reverse of removal.

Manual Steering Gear

REMOVAL & INSTALLATION

1. Remove the left screen under the instrument panel and loosen the rubber bellows at the body lead-through for the steering gear intermediate shaft, if required.

2. Raise the vehicle and remove the bolt holding the joint to the steering gear pinion or intermediate shaft.

3. Loosen the steering column tube from the body and separate the steering column joint from the pinion.

NOTE: Hang up the steering column so that the wiring harness is not damaged.

4. Remove the front wheels from the vehicle.

5. Remove the tie-rod ends at the steering arms with the proper removal tool.

6. Remove the two steering gear clamps.

7. Move the rack to the right as far as possible.

8. Lift the steering gear to the right so that the tie-rod can be bent down in the opening of the engine compartment floor.

9. Pull the rack (maximal stroke) to the left and lift the steering gear down through the opening in the engine compartment floor.

10. Installation is the reverse of removal.

ADJUSTMENT

Radial Play

1. Fit the plunger without the spring and screw on the cap without the gasket by hand until it butts against the plunger. Do not use a wrench, as you will damage the cap.

2. Measure the clearance between the cap and the housing with a feeler gauge.

3. Add 0.002–0.006 in. to the measured clearance to allow for the play to be left between the plunger and cap after assembly. Measure the thickness of the gasket and shims with a micrometer. Shims are available in thickness of 0.005 in., 0.0075 in., 0.010 in., 0.015 in. and 0.020 in.

Power Steering Gear

REMOVAL & INSTALLATION

99 Series

1. Drain the fluid from the power steering reservoir.

2. Loosen the power steering pump and remove it from its mounting so that the double joint and the servo valve are accessible.

3. Raise the vehicle and remove the left engine mounting.

4. Turn the steering wheel to the full left position and remove the clamp screw which holds the double joint on the intermediate shaft to the steering gear.

5. Remove the pipe clamps at the front suspension panel.

6. Raise the vehicle on a hoist and support it safely. Remove the wheels.

7. Remove the tie-rod ends at the steering arm using the proper removal tool. Unscrew the left tie-rod end.

8. Disconnect the speedometer cable from the gear box. Disconnect the left handbrake cable at the brake yoke and wheel housing. Remove the right handbrake cable clamp on the steering gear.

9. Remove the steering gear mountings from the body. On the left side, remove the two retaining bolts and remove the intermediate piece. On the right side, remove the yoke and the intermediate piece.

10. Disconnect the hoses from the servo valve.

11. Release the intermediate shaft by pulling the steering gear downward and slightly to the right.

12. Move the steering gear to the right

until the left tie-rod can be bent down through the opening in the body. At the same time, twist the valve housing backwards.

13. Remove the steering gear from the vehicle by guiding it down and to the left.

14. Installation is the reverse of removal.

900 Series

Other than the removal and installation of the fluid lines, the power steering unit is removed and re-installed in the vehicle following the procedures for the manual steering gear removal and installation.

ADJUSTMENT

Radial Play

1. Screw in the adjusting screw all the way until the resistance of the twisting steering gear is felt.

2. Back off the adjusting screw ½ turn.

3. Check that the steering gear can be turned from lock to lock in both directions without jamming.

4. Tighten the lock nut with a torque of 50–60 ft. lbs.

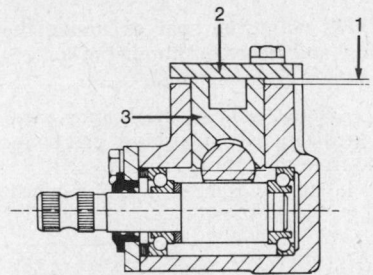

1. Clearance to be measured with feeler gauge
2. Cap
3. Plunger

Radial-play adjustment

Power Steering Pump

REMOVAL & INSTALLATION

1. Drain the fluid from the power steering pump.

2. Drain the coolant from the drain cock on the engine block and disconnect the hose from between the expansion tank and the water pump.

3. Disconnect the power steering pump hoses.

NOTE: Grip the heaxagonal nipple on the pump when removing the delivery line.

4. Unbolt the pump unit from the bracket and the engine mounting. Lift off the power steering belt and remove the pump unit complete with its mounting.

5. Installation is the reverse of removal.

BELT ADJUSTMENT

Tighten the belt so that when pressure is applied to the belt at a given point the distance between both belt pulleys is 5–10 mm.

SYSTEM BLEEDING

1. Fill the power steering pump with the proper fluid.

2. Start the engine and top-off the level of fluid to .4 inch above the bottom of the filter.

3. Turn the steering wheel from left to right several times to expel air from the system.

4. Refill the pump as needed.

Steering Linkage

REMOVAL & INSTALLATION

Tie-Rod Ends

1. Raise the vehicle on the hoist and support it safely.

2. Remove the wheel. Remove the nut.

3. Disconnect the ball bolt from the steering arm using the proper removal tool.

NOTE: Do not knock the ball bolt out, as this could cause damage to the ball bolt and other related parts.

4. Back off the nut that locks the end assembly to the tie-rod.

5. Unscrew the end assembly from the tie-rod.

6. Installation is the reverse of removal. Check and adjust the toe-in as required.

BRAKE SYSTEM

For all service and adjustment procedures not detailed below, please refer to "Brakes" in the Unit Repair section.

Master Cylinder

REMOVAL & INSTALLATION

1. Disconnect the electrical connection to the brake warning switch.

2. Disconnect the hose from the clutch master cylinder to the fluid reservoir. Insert a plastic stopper in the nipple of the reservoir.

3. Disconnect the brake lines to the master cylinder.

4. Remove the nuts that hold the master cylinder to the power brake booster. Remove the master cylinder from the vehicle.

5. Installation is the reverse of removal. Bleed the system as required.

Vacuum Booster

REMOVAL & INSTALLATION

1. Remove the steering column bearing cover, ash tray and safety padding screw Remove the upper circlip on the brake pedal push rod, if equipped.

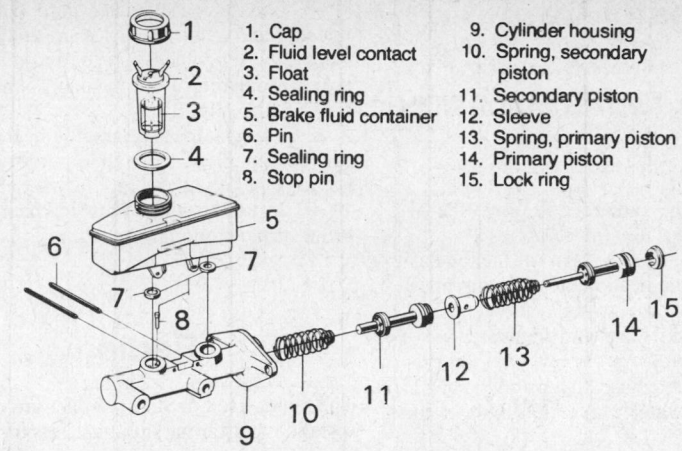

1. Cap
2. Fluid level contact
3. Float
4. Sealing ring
5. Brake fluid container
6. Pin
7. Sealing ring
8. Stop pin
9. Cylinder housing
10. Spring, secondary piston
11. Secondary piston
12. Sleeve
13. Spring, primary piston
14. Primary piston
15. Lock ring

Typical brake master cylinder

2. Remove the two electrical connections on the brake light switch. Remove the safety padding screws in the engine compartment.

3. Remove the vacuum hose from the non-return valve which is located on the vacuum booster.

4. Disconnect the brake lines and the electrical connections for the brake warning switch from the master cylinder. Disconnect the line to the clutch master cylinder from the fluid reservoir. Insert stoppers in the lines to prevent loss of the brake fluid.

5. Remove the cotter pin from the servo unit push rod at the brake pedal.

6. Remove the vacuum booster together with the master cylinder and the bracket.

NOTE: The bracket is mounted on the dash panel with four bolts and nuts. Three of these bolts are accessible from underneath in the passenger compartment after removal of the screen section and parts of the dash panel insulation felt below the instrument panel. The fourth nut is accessible from the engine compartment by the bracket.

7. Separate the master cylinder and the bracket from the vacuum booster.

8. Installation is the reverse of removal. Bleed the system as required.

Parking Brake

ADJUSTMENT

Check the adjustment of the handbrake cable. Check the distance between the handbrake lever and the yoke: the clearance should be a maximum 0.019 in. (0.50mm) and should be equal on both sides. Adjust as necessary using the adjustment nut on the handbrake lever.

Note that the cables cross over; therefore, the right-hand adjustment nut should be used to adjust the left-hand brake mechanism and vice versa.

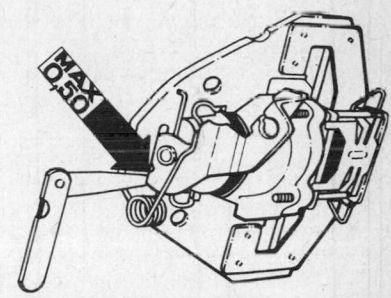

Parking brake adjustment procedure

CHASSIS ELECTRICAL

Heater Blower Motor

REMOVAL & INSTALLATION

99 Series

1. Remove the windshield wiper motor assembly.

2. Disconnect the blower motor cables.

3. Remove the three blower motor retaining screws and pull the motor along with the impeller out of the housing carefully.

4. Separate the motor from the impeller at the rubber coupling. Remove the motor first, then the impeller.

5. Remove the plate with the fan bearing on the opposite side of the fan casing.

6. Installation is the reverse of removal.

900 Series

1. Disconnect the positive battery cable.

2. Remove the switch panel and the upper section of the instrument panel.

3. Disconnect the electrical leads to the fan motor.

4. Remove the retaining screws for the right hand defroster valve housing.

5. Remove the fan retaining screws and lift the fan from its housing.

6. The installation is in the reverse of the removal procedure.

Heater Core

REMOVAL & INSTALLATION

99 Series

1. Drain the radiator. Remove the alternator and radiator fan relay.
2. Remove the front part of the fan casing. Unscrew the heater core retaining plate.
3. Remove the water valve cap, remove the control wire and the water valve retaining screws.
4. Loosen the hose clamps on the heater core and the water valve. Disconnect the hoses.
5. Disconnect the thermostat coil from the heater core and remove the water valve with its coil.
6. Remove the heater core from the thermostat housing.
7. Installation is the reverse of removal.

900 Series

When removing the heater core and/or the coolant shut off valve, remove as a unit.

1. Remove the cover under the switches on the steering column and the lower section of the instrument panel.
2. Remove the air diffuser and retaining screws.
3. Remove the left defroster and speaker grill.
4. Remove the control rod from between the coolant shut off valve and the control rod by sliding the rod as far forward as it will go to free it from the knob, then pull it rearward to free it from the shut off valve.

NOTE: The plastic joint at the control knob is accessible from underneath once the switches below the heater controls have been pressed backwards.

5. Remove the lower section of the heater housing.
6. Drain the coolant and disconnect the hoses. Plug the ends of the hoses to prevent coolant from leaking into the compartment.

7. Separate the heater core from the housing and guide it backward and downward. It will be necessary to disconnect the brake pedal return spring and depress the brake pedal slightly.
8. The water valve and the heater core can be separated after their removal. Do not kink or break the capillary tube.
9. Install the assembly in the reverse order of the removal procedure.

Radio

The radios used in Saab vehicles are dealer-installed or aftermarket units. It is therefore impossible to give specific procedures for removal and installation of these units. Care should be exercised when servicing a vehicle that has a radio problem.

Windshield Wiper Motor

REMOVAL & INSTALLATION

99 Series

1. Remove the wiper arms from the wiper spindles.
2. Remove the nut that holds the steel tube to the wiper motor.
3. Release the wiper motor and remove the motor and the flexible cable (pull the cable out of the tube).
4. Installation is the reverse of removal.

900 Series

1. Remove the wiper arms from the vehicle. Remove the rubber grommets.
2. Remove the four screws and disconnect the lead. Remove the wiper unit from the vehicle.
3. Separate the wiper motor from the wiper assembly.
4. Installation is the reverse of removal.

Instrument Cluster

REMOVAL & INSTALLATION

99 Series

1. Disconnect the negative battery cable. Remove the safety padding.
2. Remove the four screws that secure the panel.
3. Disconnect the speedometer wire and the electric wiring to the clock and combination instrument panel. Remove the instrument panel illumination bulb holder.
4. Carefully lift the instrument panel from the vehicle.
5. Installation is the reverse of removal.

900 Series

1. Disconnect the positive battery cable. Remove the steering wheel.
2. Remove the four screws in the switch panel and tilt the panel back. Watch the length of the screws as they are not interchangeable.
3. Remove the left speaker/defroster grille. Pull apart the instrument panel connectors. Disconnect the speedometer cable.
4. Remove the instrument panel retaining screws. Carefully remove the unit from the vehicle.
5. Installation is the reverse of removal.

Ignition Switch

REMOVAL & INSTALLATION

1. Disconnect the negative battery cable.
2. Remove the center console.
3. Disconnect the electrical connections from the switch.
4. Remove the assembly from the vehicle.
5. Installation is the reverse of removal.

Fuse Box Location

The fuse panel is located under the hood of the vehicle. It is on the left hand side for the 900 series and on the right hand side for the 99 series.

Subaru
1600, 1800—All Models

SERIAL NUMBER IDENTIFICATION

The Vehicle Identification Number is stamped on a tab located on the top of the dashboard on the driver's side, visible through the windshield. The vehicle identification plate is on the bulkhead in the engine compartment. The engine number is stamped on the crankcase, behind the distributor.

GENERAL ENGINE SPECIFICATIONS

Year	Type	Displacement cu. in. (cc)	Carburetor	Horsepower @ rpm	Torque @ rpm	Bore and Stroke (in.)	Comp. Ratio	Normal Oil Pressure (psi)
'78–'85	4 cylinder horizontally opposed	97 (1595)	2 bbl	67 @ 5200	81 @ 2400	3.62 × 2.36	8.5:1 ③	36–57
'80–'85	4 cylinder horizontally opposed	109 (1781)	2 bbl②	72 @ 4800①	92 @ 2400	3.62 × 2.64	8.7:1	50–57
'83–'85	4 cylinder horizontally opposed	109 (1781)	④	95 @ 4800	123 @ 2000	3.62 × 2.64	7.7:1	NA

N.A.—Not available
① 4WD: 71 @ 4200
② Feedback control of mixture on California and 49-state non-4WD cars
③ 1983 and later: 9.0:1
④ Electronic Fuel Injection (Turbocharged)

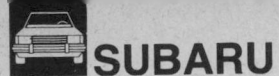

TUNE-UP SPECIFICATIONS

(When analyzing compression test results, look for uniformity among cylinders, rather than specific pressures)

Year	Engine Displacement (cu. in.)	Spark Plugs ⑤ Type	Gap (in.)	Distributor Point Dwell (deg)	Distributor Point Gap (in.)	Ignition Timing (deg)	Intake Valve Opens (deg)	Fuel Pump Pressure (psi)	Idle Speed (rpm)	Valve Clearance (in.) In	Valve Clearance (in.) Ex
'78–'79	(1600)	BP6ES	.032	49–55②	0.018②	8B @ 850	24B	2.6	850①	0.010	0.014
'80	(1600)	BP6ES	.032	Electronic		8B @ 850	24B	2.6	850①	0.009	0.013
	(1800)	BP6ES	.032	Electronic		8B @ 850	24B	2.6	850①	0.009	0.013
'81–'82	(1600)	BPES-11	.040	Electronic		8B @ 700	20B	1.3–2.0	700	0.010	0.014
	(1800)	BPES-11	.040	Electronic		8B @ 700③	20B	1.3–2.0	700④	0.010	0.014
'83	(1600)	BPR6ES-11	.040	Electronic		8B @ 700	20B	1.3–2.0	700④	0.010	0.014
	(1800)	BPR6ES-11	.040	Electronic		8B @ 700③	20B	1.3–2.0	700④	0.010⑥	0.014⑥
	(1800 Turbo)	BPR6ES-11	.040	Electronic		15B @ 800	16B	43.4	800	0	0
'84–'85	(1600)	BPR6ES-11	.040	Electronic		8B @ 650⑦	20B	1.3–2.0	650⑦	.010	.014
	(1800)	BPR6ES-11	.040	Electronic		8B @ 700④	20B	1.3–2.0	700④	.010⑥	.014⑥
	(1800 Turbo)	BPR6ES-11	.040	Electronic		15 @ 800	16B	43.4	800	0	0

NOTE: The underhood specifications sticker often reflects tune-up specification changes made in production. Sticker figures must be used if they disagree with those in this chart.
B—Before top dead center
M—Manual transmission
A—Automatic transmission
① California 900

② California—Electronic ignition
③ Auto trans and 4WD; 8B @ 800
④ 800 rpm w/Auto trans.

⑤ OEM spark plugs or NGK.
⑥ with automatic—O (hydraulic lifters)
⑦ with 5–speed—700

FIRING ORDER

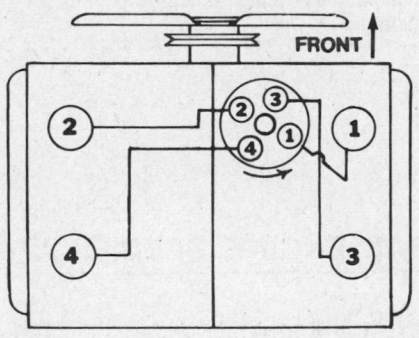

FRONT

Counter Clock wise

Firing order is 1-3-2-4

CAPACITIES

Year	Model	Engine Displacement (CC)	Engine Crankcase (Qts) With Filter	Engine Crankcase (Qts) Without Filter	Transmission (Pts) 4-spd	Transmission (Pts) 5-spd	Auto	4WD	Gasoline Tank (Gals)	Cooling System (Qts)
'78–'79	1600 series	1600	3.8	3.5	5.2	5.8	12.5	6.34	13.2	6.3
'80–'82	1600 series	1600	3.8	3.5	5.8	5.8	12.5③	6.34①	13.2②	5.6
'80–'82	1800 series	1800	3.8	3.5	5.8	5.8	12.5③	6.34①	13.2②	5.8
'83–'85	1600 Series	1600	4.2	—	5.8	5.8	10.8–12.6⑤	⑥	15.9⑦	5.6

CAPACITIES

Year	Model	Engine Displacement (CC)	Engine Crankcase (Qts) With Filter	Engine Crankcase (Qts) Without Filter	Transmission (Pts) 4-spd	Transmission (Pts) 5-spd	Auto	4WD	Gasoline Tank (Gals)	Cooling System (Qts)
'83–'85	1800 Series	1800	4.2	—	5.8	5.8	10.8–12.6⑤	⑥	15.9⑦	5.8

①4WD rear differential; 1.7 pts
②4WD vehicles; 11.9 gal
③Automatic transmission differential: 2.5 pts
④Station wagon w/4WD: 14.5 gal.,
 2 dr. hatchback (2WD): 13.2 gal.,
 2 dr: hatchback (4WD): 11.9 gal.

⑤4WD Automatic: 12.6–13.6
 Automatic differential: 2.6
 4WD Rear differential: 1.6
⑥4WD Manual 4 and 5 spd.: 6.4
 4WD rear differential: 1.6

⑦4WD: 14.5
 Regular Hatchback: 13.2
 4WD Hatchback: 11.9

CRANKSHAFT AND CONNECTING ROD SPECIFICATIONS

(All measurements are given in inches)

Year	Engine	Crankshaft Main Brg. Journal Dia.	Crankshaft Main Brg. Oil Clearance	Crankshaft Shaft End-Play	Crankshaft Thrust On. No.	Connecting Rod Journal Diameter	Connecting Rod Oil Clearance	Connecting Rod Side Clearance
'78–'82	1600	1.9667–① 1.9673	0.0004–② 0.0016	0.0016– 0.0054	2	1.7715– 1.7720	0.0008– 0.0028	0.0028– 0.0130
'80–'82	1800	2.1636– 2.1642	0.0004–③ 0.0012	0.0016–④ 0.0054	2	1.7715– 1.7720	0.0008– 0.0028	0.0028– 0.0130
'83–'85	1600	2.1636– 2.1642	0.0004– 0.0014⑤	0.0004– 0.0037	2	1.7715 1.7720	0.0008– 0.0028	0.0028– 0.0130
'83–'85	1800	1.9668– 1.9673	0.0004– 0.0012	0.0004– 0.0037	2	1.7715– 1.7720	0.0008– 0.0028	0.0028– 0.0130

① Center: 1.9673–1.9677 inch
② 1978–79 center: 0–0.0018
  1980–84: 0.0004–0.0014 with the center:
  0.0004–0.0010
③ Center: 0.0004–0.0010
④ 1982–84: 0.0004 0.0037
⑤ Center: 0.0004–0.0012

VALVE SPECIFICATIONS

Year	Engine Year	Seat Angle (deg)	Face Angle (deg)	Spring Test Pressure (lbs.) Inner	Spring Test Pressure (lbs.) Outer	Spring Compressed Height (in.) Inner	Spring Compressed Height (in.) Outer	Stem-to-Guide Clearance (in.) ▲ Intake	Stem-to-Guide Clearance (in.) ▲ Exhaust	Stem Diameter (in.) Intake	Stem Diameter (in.) Exhaust
'78–'79	1600	45	45	43–50 @ 1.10	91–105 @ 1.22	1.008	1.16	0.0015– 0.0026	0.0016– 0.0028	0.3130– 0.3136	0.3128– 0.3134
'80–'82	1600	45	45	42–48 @ 1.22	112–127 @ 1.201	1.18	1.20	0.0014– 0.0026	0.0016– 0.0028	0.3130– 0.3136	0.3128– 0.3134
'80–'81	1800	45	45	42–48 @ 1.22	112–127 @ 1.201	1.18	1.20	0.0014– 0.0026	0.0016– 0.0028	0.3130– 0.3136	0.3128– 0.3134
'83–'85	1600,1800 Man.	45	45–45.5	41.7–48.3 @ 1.122	112.5–127.9 @ 1.201	—	—	0.0014– 0.0026	0.0016– 0.0028	0.3130– 0.3136	0.3128– 0.3134
'83–'85	1800 Auto.	45	45–45.5	45.2–51.8 @ 1.181	116.6–134.7 @ 1.260	—	—	0.0014– 0.0026	0.0016– 0.0028	0.3130– 0.3136	0.3128– 0.3134

▲ Valve guides are removable

C765

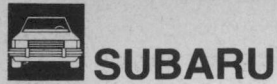

SUBARU

PISTON AND RING SPECIFICATIONS

Year	Engine	Piston Clearance	Ring Gap			Ring Side Clearance		
			Top Compression	Bottom Compression	Oil Control	Top Compression	Bottom Compression	Oil Control
'78–'79	1600	.001–.002	.012–.020	.012–.020	.012–.035	.001–.003	.001–.003	None
'80–'82	1600	.001–.002	.008–.013	.008–.013	.008–.035	.001–.003	.001–.003	None
'80–'82	1800	.001–.002	.008–.013	.008–.013	.008–.035	.001–.003	.001–.003	None
'83–'85	1600,1800	0.0004–0.0016	0.0079–0.0138	0.0079–0.0138	0.0079–0.0354	0.0016–0.0031	0.0012–0.0028	None

TORQUE SPECIFICATIONS

(All readings in ft. lbs.)

Year	Engine	Cylinder Head Bolts	Rod Bearing Bolts	Crankcase Halves	Crankshaft Pulley Bolt	Flywheel To Crankshaft Bolt	Manifold	
							Intake	Exhaust
'78–'85	1600, 1800	37–43①	29–31	10 mm bolts 29–35 8 mm bolts 17–19 6 mm bolts 3–4	39–42②	30–33③	13–16	12-15④

① 1978; 1600 cc (1st step) 14 ft. lbs.
   (2nd step) 25–29 ft. lbs.
   (3rd step) 37–43 ft. lbs.

1979–84; 1600 cc (1st step) 22 ft. lbs.
1980–84; 1800 cc (2nd step) 43 ft. lbs.
   (3rd step) 47 ft. lbs.

② 1983–84: 47–54
③ Driveplate (A.T.): 36–39
④ 1983–84: 19–22

ALTERNATOR AND REGULATOR SPECIFICATIONS

Year	Model	Alternator Output (amps) @ 12 Volts	Regulator							
			Charge Relay				Voltage Regulator			
			Yoke Gap (in.)	Core Gap (in.)	Point Gap (in.)	Volts to Open	Yoke Gap (in.)	Core Gap (in.)	Point Gap (in.)	Volts @ 1200 & 75°
'78–'79	all models	50	.035	.032–.039	.016–.024	8–10	.035	.024–.039	.014–.018	14.0
'80–'81	all models	50①	.035	.032–.039	.016–.024	8–10	.035	.024–.039	.014–.018	14.0
'82–'85	all models	55	—	—	—	—	Solid State Internally Mounted			14.2–14.8②

① 1980 station wagon 4WD GL: 55A
② at 68° F.

BATTERY AND STARTER SPECIFICATIONS

Year	Model	Battery		Terminal Grounded	Lock Test			No Load Test			Brush Spring Tension (oz.)
		Amp-Hour Capacity	Volts		Amps	Volts	Torque (ft. lbs.)	Amps	Volts	rpm	
'78–'79	all models	50	12	Neg	600	7.7①	9.4②	50③	11	5000	37–47.6
'80–'82	all models	60④	12	Neg	600⑤	7.7⑥	9–13⑦	50⑧	11	5000⑨	37–47.6
'83–'85	1600	55	12	Neg	600⑫	7.7	50	—	11	5000	37–47
'83–'85	1800	65	12	Neg	300⑬	2.5	90	—	11.5	3000	—
'83–'85	1800AT⑩	75⑪	12	Neg	400⑭	2.4	90	—	11.5	4100	—

① Automatic transmission vehicles except California—7.0
② Automatic transmission vehicles except California—13.0
③ Automatic transmission vehicles except California—60
④ Optional—65A
⑤ Gear reduction—400A

⑥ Gear reduction—2.4V
⑦ Gear reduction—8 ft. lbs. (5 ft. lbs. if manual transmission)
⑧ Gear reduction—90A
⑨ Gear reduction—4100 rpm (3000 rpm if manual transmission)
⑩ Automatic transmission
⑪ Figure applies to '84; '83—65

⑫ at 1,200 rpm
⑬ at 1,800 rpm
⑭ at 1,000 rpm

BRAKE SPECIFICATIONS

(All measurements given are (in.) unless noted)

Year	Model	Lug Nut Torque (ft. lbs.)	Master Cylinder Bore	Brake Disc		Brake Drum			Minimum Lining Thickness	
				Minimum Thickness	Maximum Run-Out	Diameter	Maximum Machine O/S	Maximum Wear Limit	Front	Rear
'78–'79	all models	58–72	.75	.33	.006	7.09	7.17	7.17	.06	.06
'80–'81	all models	58–72	.8125	.394	.0039	7.09	7.17	7.17	.295 ①	.06
'82–'83	all models	58–72	.8125	.394	.0039	7.24	7.17	7.17	.295 ①	.059
'84–'85	all models	58–72	.8125	.610 ②	.0039	7.24	7.17	7.17	.295 ①	.059

NOTE: Minimum lining thickness is as recommended by the manufacturer. Because of variations in state inspection regulations, the minimum allowable thickness may be different than recommended by the manufacturer.

① Includes back metal

② On unventilated 1983 discs, minimum thickness

FRONT WHEEL ALIGNMENT

Year	Model	Caster ① Range (deg)	Caster ① Pref. Setting (deg)	Camber ① Range (deg)	Camber ① Pref. Setting (deg)	Toe-In Range (in.)
'78–'79	2WD exc. Station Wagon	−1 19/32– −3/32	−27/32	1–2 1/2	1 3/4	3/32–21/64
	2WD Wagon	−29/32–19/32	−5/32	1–2 1/2	1 3/4	3/32–21/64
	4WD	−1 19/32–3/32	−27/32	1/2–2	1 1/4	15/64–15/32
'80–'81	2WD exc. Station Wagon	−1 3/16–5/16	−7/16	3/4–2 1/4	1 1/2	1/16–5/16
	2WD Wagon	−13/16–11/16	−1/16	1–2 1/2	1 3/4	1/16–5/16
	4WD exc. Wagon	−1 1/4–1/4	−1/2	1 13/16–3 5/16	2 9/16	1/4–15/32
	4WD Wagon	−1 7/16–1/16	−11/16	1 13/16–3 5/16	2 9/16	1/4–15/32
'82	4WD exc. Wagon	−1 1/4–1/4	−1/2	1 13/16–3 5/16	2 9/16	3/64–1/8
	4WD Wagon	−1 7/16–1/16	−11/16	1 13/16–3 5/16	2 9/16	3/64–1/8
	2WD exc. Station Wagon	−1 3/16–5/16	−7/16	3/4–2 1/4	1 1/2	0–5/64
	2WD Wagon	−13/16–11/16	−1/16	1–2 1/2	1 3/4	0–5/64
'83–'85	2WD exc. Station Wagon	−1 1/4–1/4	−1/2	1 7/16–2 15/16	2 3/16	1/4–5/32
	2WD Wagon	−13/16–11/16	−1/16	1–2 1/2	1 3/4	0–5/64
	4WD exc. Station Wagon	−1 1/4–1/4	−1/2	1 11/16–3 3/16	2 7/16	15/64–5/32 ②
	4WD Wagon	−1 7/16–1/16	−11/16	1 11/16–3 3/16 11/16	2 7/16	15/64–5/32 ②

① Not Adjustable—MacPherson struts

② Toe out

REAR END ALIGNMENT

Year	Model	Body Type	Ride Height ① (in.)	Camber Range (in.)	Toe-In Range (in.)	Tracking (in.) ②
'78–'79	DL, GL, GF	Sedan, Coupe, H.T.	11.2–12.0	−13/32–1 3/32	3/64–13/64	−1/8–1/8
	DL	Wagon	12.2–13.0	−13/32–1 3/32	5/64–15/64	1/8–1/8
	4WD	Wagon	13.6–14.4	19/32–2 3/32	5/64–15/64	0–5/32

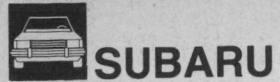
REAR END ALIGNMENT

Year	Model	Body Type	Ride Height① (in.)	Camber Range (in.)	Toe-In Range (in.)	Tracking (in.)②
'80–'81	exc. 4WD	Sedan, H.T.	10.2–11.0	−³/₄–³/₄	¹/₈–¹/₈	−¹³/₆₄–¹³/₆₄
	exc. 4WD	Station Wagon	11.0–11.8	−³/₄–³/₄	¹/₈–¹/₈	−¹³/₆₄–¹³/₆₄
	4WD	Sedan	12.6–13.4	−³/₄–³/₄	¹/₈–¹/₈	−¹³/₆₄–¹³/₆₄
	4WD	exc. Sedan	13.1–13.9	−⁷/₁₆–1¹/₁₆	¹/₈–¹/₈	−¹³/₆₄–¹³/₆₄
'82	exc. 4WD	Hatchback, Sedan and Hardtop	10.3–11.1	−³/₄–³/₄	−¹/₈–¹/₈	−¹³/₆₄–¹³/₆₄
	exc. 4WD	Station Wagon	11.1–11.9	−³/₄–³/₄	−¹/₈–¹/₈	−¹³/₆₄–¹³/₆₄
	4WD	Hatchback	12.6–13.4	−³/₄–³/₄	−¹/₈–¹/₈	−¹³/₆₄–¹³/₆₄
	4WD	Exc. Hatchback	13.2–14.0	−⁷/₁₆–1¹/₁₆	−¹/₈–¹/₈	−¹³/₆₄–¹³/₆₄
'83–'85	exc. 4WD	Hatchback, Sedan Hardtop	10.24–11.02③	−³/₄–³/₄	−¹/₈–¹/₈	−¹³/₆₄–¹³/₆₄
	exc. 4WD	Station Wagon	11.02–11.81③	−³/₄–³/₄	−¹/₈–¹/₈	−¹³/₆₄–¹³/₆₄
	4WD	Hatchback and Sedan	12.80–13.58③	−³/₄–³/₄	−¹/₈–¹/₈	−¹³/₆₄–¹³/₆₄
	4WD	Station Wagon, BRAT	13.39–14.17③④	−⁷/₁₆–1¹/₁₆	−¹/₈–¹/₈	−¹³/₆₄–¹³/₆₄
	4WD	TURBO	12.80–13.58③⑤	−1³/₃₂–1⁹/₃₂	−¹/₈–¹/₈	−¹³/₆₄–¹³/₆₄

①Measured from outer center of torsion bar
②Measured with one passenger aboard
③Measured at center of front end (face of transverse link attaching bolt)

④Applies to 1984; 1983—12.60–13.39
⑤Applies to 1984; 1983—13.19–13.98

TUNE-UP PROCEDURES

Spark Plugs

NOTE: Number the spark plug wires before removing them.

1. Using a spark plug wrench, remove all of the spark plugs.
2. Check for damage or wear and clean or replace them.
3. Set the gap between the two electrodes, using a spark plug gap gauge.
4. Install the spark plugs in the engine, tightening to 13–17 ft. lbs. on models up to 1982, and 14–22 ft. lbs. on later models.

Breaker Points and Condenser

1. To replace the points, remove the hold-down screws, the ground lead and the condenser lead.
2. Lift out the point assembly and insert the new assembly.

NOTE: Always replace the condenser when replacing the points.

3. Install the hold-down screws and the leads in their proper positions. Do not tighten the attaching screws, just leave them snug so the point gap can be adjusted.
4. Adjust the gap by placing the proper size feeler gauge between the contacts and turning the adjusting eccentric with a screwdriver.
5. The breaker point arm must be on a high point of the cam. Turn the eccentric screw until there is a slight drag when the gauge is drawn through the gap.
6. Lubricate the cam surface with cam lube.
7. Replace the distributor cap, making sure that the spark plug wires are installed tightly in the top of the cap.

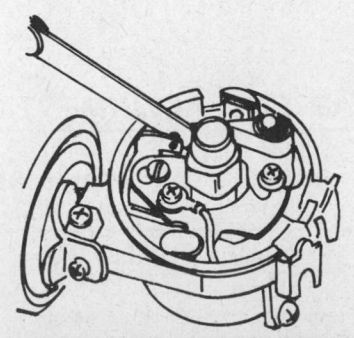

Checking the breaker point gap

Dwell Angle

1. Hook up a dwell meter according to the manufacturer's instructions. Start the engine and read the meter. If the dwell is correct, shut off the engine and remove the dwell meter.
2. If the dwell must be adjusted, shut off the engine, remove the distributor cap and adjust the point gap.
3. Open the points to decrease the dwell, close them to increase the dwell.
4. Replace the cap and start the engine. Check the dwell. If it is correct, shut off the engine and remove the dwell meter. If the dwell is not correct, repeat the above steps.

Breakerless Distributor

1978–1979, California engines and all engines from 1980 have a breakerless distributor. The centrifugal advance, vacuum advance, and retard units are the same as with the conventional distributor.

AIR GAP ADJUSTMENT

1. The distributor cap is held on by two clips. Release them with a screwdriver and lift the cap straight up and off, with the

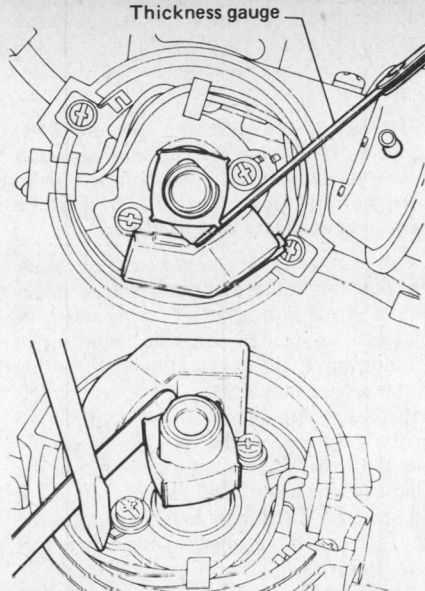

Adjusting air gap on a typical breakerless ignition

wires attached. Inspect the cap for cracks, carbon tracks, or a worn center contact. Replace it if necessary, transferring the wires one at a time from the old cap to the new.

2. Pull the ignition rotor straight up to remove. Replace it if its contacts are worn, burned, or pitted. Do not file the contacts. To replace, press it firmly onto the shaft.

3. Before replacing the ignition rotor, check the reluctor air gap. *Use a non-magnetic feeler gauge.* Rotate the engine until a reluctor spoke is aligned with the pickup coil (either bump the engine around with the starter, or turn it with a wrench on the crankshaft pulley bolt).

Air Gap Adjustment

1978–79	
Calif; Manual Trans.	.008–.016
Calif; Auto Trans.	.012–.016
1980	
Exc. 4-WD;	.008–.016
4-WD;	.012–.016
1981–83	
Exc. 4-WD;	.008–.016
4-WD;	.012–.020
1984'	
Except Below;	.012–.020
49 State Manual Trans. w/2WD and all Calif. Man. Trans.	.008–.016

Adjustment, if necessary, is made by loosening the pick-up coil mounting screws and shifting its position on the "breaker plate" either closer to, or farther from, the reluctor. Tighten the screws and recheck the gap.

4. Inspect the ignition wires for cracks or brittleness. Replace them one at a time to prevent cross-wiring, carefully pressing

the replacement wires into place. The cores of wires used with electronic ignition are more susceptible to breakage than those of standard wires, so treat them gently.

Ignition Timing

On normally aspirated engines, the ignition timing marks are located on the edge of the flywheel at the rear of the engine. On the turbocharged engine, they are located right near the crankshaft pulley which drives the alternator. The marks mounted on the flywheel are graduated in increments of 2° from 0° to 16° and are visible through a port in the flywheel housing located just behind the dipstick. A plastic cover protects the port through which the flywheel-mounted marks are visible.

NOTE: If your vehicle is equipped with electronic ignition, an inductive timing light is recommended because it is not susceptible to cross-firing or false triggering due to the greater voltage.

1. After cleaning the timing marks, connect a timing light to the ignition following the manufacturer's instruction. Disconnect and plug the distributor vacuum line(s).

2. Start the engine and aim the timing light at the timing marks on the flywheel.

3. Adjust the ignition timing by loosening the bolt on the distributor retaining plate, and rotating the distributor clockwise to advance or counterclockwise to retard the timing.

Non-TURBO

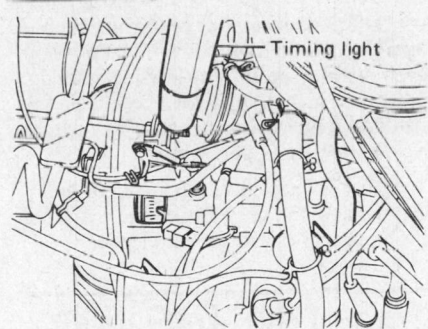

TURBO

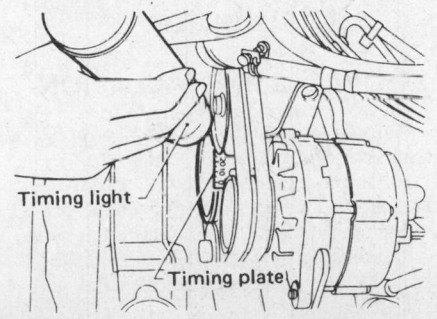

Ignition timing marks for 1983–84 normally aspirated and turbo engines

Valve Lash

ADJUSTMENT

Before adjusting the valves, make sure the cylinder head nuts/bolts are torqued (tightened) to the proper specifications. To torque the head and intake manifold nuts/bolts, use the following procedure.

1. Make sure the engine is cold.

2. Remove the valve covers from both sides of the engine.

3. Loosen the three bolts holding the intake manifold on the right (No. 1–No. 3) side cylinder head (as viewed from the driver's seat). These bolts should be loosened no more than 60°. Do not loosen the left side (No. 2–No. 4) intake manifold bolts.

4. Refer to the "Cylinder Head" section for the correct pattern to use while checking and retorquing the cylinder head.

NOTE: It is important to follow the proper tightening sequence when checking the head nuts/bolts. Warpage of the cylinder or water leaks could occur if the proper tightening pattern is not followed.

5. Loosen the center cylinder head nut/bolt no more than 60°. If loosened too much, coolant leaks may occur. Lubricate the nut/bolt with engine oil, tighten and loosen it several times. Retighten the nut/bolt to the specified torque.

6. Move on to the next nut/bolt and perform the same steps as before, proceed until all of the nuts/bolts have been tightened.

7. Go back to No. 1 nut/bolt and recheck the torque, tighten if necessary. Recheck the rest of the nuts/bolts following the specified order.

8. After rechecking all the head nuts/bolts tighten the intake manifold bolts on the right side (No. 1–No. 3) cylinder head.

9. Rotate the engine so that the No. 1 piston is at top dead center (TDC) of its compression stroke. To determine TDC, remove the distributor cap and the plastic flywheel housing dust cover (normally aspirated engines only). The No. 1 piston is at top dead center when the distributor rotor is pointing to the No. 1 spark plug lead terminal (as though the distributor cap were in place) and the "O" mark on the flywheel or front pulley is opposite the pointer on the housing or front cover.

10. Check the clearance of both the intake and exhaust valves of the No. 1 cylinder by inserting a feeler gauge between each valve stem and rocker arm. See the "Tune-Up Specifications" chart for the proper stem-to-rocker arm clearance.

11. If the clearance is not within specifications, loosen the locknut with the proper size metric box wrench and turn the adjusting stud either in or out until the valve clearance is correct. The stud should just touch the gauge. Don't clamp the gauge tightly between the stud and head of the valve.

12. Tighten the locknut and recheck the valve stem-to-rocker clearance.

13. The rest of the valves are adjusted in the same way; bring each piston to TDC of its compression stroke, then check and adjust the valves for that cylinder. The proper valve adjustment sequence is 1-3-2-4, which is the firing order.

14. To bring the No. 3 piston to TDC of its compression stroke, rotate the crankshaft 180° and make sure that the distributor rotor is pointing to the No. 3 spark plug terminal. Rotate the crankshaft 180° after each valve adjustment before going on to the next adjustment.

15. When the valve adjustment is complete, install the distributor cap, the valve covers, and the dust cover on the flywheel housing port.

Carburetor

IDLE SPEED AND MIXTURE ADJUSTMENT

1. Run the engine and allow it to reach normal operating temperature.

2. Stop the engine and connect a tachometer in accordance with the manufacturer's instructions.

3. Then, do one of the following:

a. On models which have air injection (air pump), disconnect the air hoses from the air distribution manifolds. Plug the hoses and the manifold openings.

b. On other models, disconnect and plug the hose that runs to the distributor vacuum retard unit, if equipped.

c. Models that have a secondary air

Idle speed adjustment

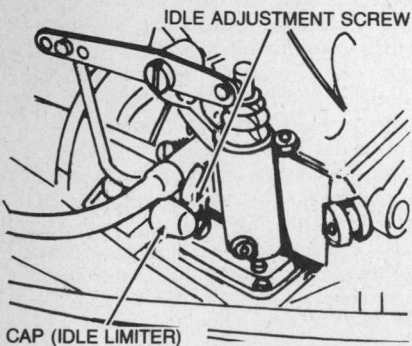

CAP (IDLE LIMITER)
Idle mixture adjustment

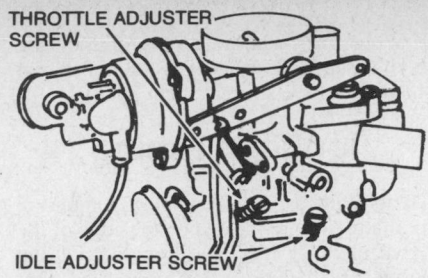

THROTTLE ADJUSTER SCREW

IDLE ADJUSTER SCREW

Throttle adjuster and idle adjuster screw locations

cleaner, or purge valve and hose: Remove and plug the hose that connects to the engine.

4. Remove the air cleaner.

5. Check proper idle speed in the "Tune-Up Specifications" chart and adjust to that setting by turning the throttle adjusting screw.

NOTE: On 1980 and later cars, idle mixture can be adjusted with a CO meter only. Steps 6 and 7 apply only to 1979 and earlier cars.

6. Continue adjusting the idle, this time by means of the throttle adjusting screw and the idle mixture adjusting screw, until a reading of 50 rpm above the proper idle setting is attained.

NOTE: The idle mixture adjusting screw should have a plastic limiter cap on it; adjustments must be made within the range of this cap or exhaust emissions will be increased. Do not remove the cap.

7. Turn the idle mixture adjusting screw *clockwise* until the idle speed drops to the figure given in the "Tune-Up Specifications" chart.

NOTE: Following this procedure should keep the carbon monoxide (CO) emission level within pollution law standards. However, it is a good idea to check the CO level with an exhaust analyzer whenever a tune-up is performed.

8. Disconnect the tachometer. Reconnect the hoses to the air injection manifold (if equipped). Install the air cleaner.

ENGINE ELECTRICAL

Distributor

REMOVAL & INSTALLATION

1. Remove the air cleaner assembly, taking note of the hose locations.

2. On models equipped with a conventional ignition system, disconnect the primary wire at the coil. On models equipped with a breakerless ignition, disconnect the distributor wiring connector from the vehicle wiring harness.

3. Note the positions of the vacuum line(s) on the distributor diaphragm, dis-

connect the lines at the diaphragm. Unsnap the two distributor cap retaining clamps and remove the cap. Position the cap and ignition wires to one side.

NOTE: If it is necessary to remove the ignition wires from the cap to get enough room to remove the distributor, make sure to label each wire and the cap for easy and accurate reinstallation.

4. Use chalk or paint to carefully mark the position of the distributor rotor in relationship to the distributor housing and mark the position of the distributor housing in relationship to the engine block. When this is done, you should have a line on the distributor housing directly in line with the tip of the rotor and another line on the engine block directly in line with the mark on the distributor housing. This is very important because the distributor must be reinstalled in the exact same position from which it was removed, if correct ignition timing is to be maintained.

5. Remove the distributor hold-down bolt.

6. Remove the distributor from the engine, taking care not to damage or lose the O-ring.

NOTE: Do not disturb the engine while the distributor is removed. If you crank or rotate the engine while the distributor is removed you will have to retime the engine.

7. If the engine was not disturbed while the distributor was removed, position the distributor in the block (make sure the O-ring is in place) have the rotor aligned with the mark previously scribed on the distributor body and the marks on the distributor body and engine in alignment. Install the octane selector, if so equipped, and tighten the hold-down bolt finger tight.

8. Reinstall the distributor rotor, cap and wires, if removed. Reconnect the primary wire to the coil or reconnect the wiring harness. Install the air cleaner.

9. Plug the vacuum line(s) to the distributor and recheck the timing using a timing light.

INSTALLATION—TIMING LOST

If the engine has been cranked, disassembled or the timing otherwise lost, proceed as follows.

1. Remove the plastic dust cover from the timing port on the flywheel housing.

2. Remove the No. 1 spark plug. Use a wrench on the crankshaft pulley bolt (on manual transmission cars, place the transmission in Neutral) and slowly rotate the engine until the TDC "O" mark on the flywheel aligns with the pointer.

2a. If Step 2 is impractical for any reason, the following method can be used to get the No. 1 piston on TDC. Remove the two bolts that hold the right valve cover and remove the cover to expose the valves on No. 1 cylinder. Rotate the engine so that the valves in No. 1 cylinder are closed and the TDC ''O'' mark on the flywheel lines up with the pointer.

3. Align the small depression on the distributor drive pinion with the mark on the distributor body; this will align the rotor with the No. 1 spark plug terminal on the distributor cap. On models with the octane selector, set the pointer midway between the ''A'' and ''R''. Make sure the O-ring is located in the proper position.

4. Align the matchmarks on the distributor body with those on the engine block and install the distributor in the engine. Make sure the drive is engaged. Install the hold-down bolt fingertight. Time the engine with a timing light.

Alternator

REMOVAL & INSTALLATION

1. To remove the alternator from the vehicle, first disconnect the negative battery terminal.

2. Tag and disconnect the wiring to the alternator.

3. Remove the alternator attaching bolts and nuts.

4. Remove the drive belt and take out the alternator.

5. Install in the reverse order of removal.

BELT TENSION ADJUSTMENT

1. To adjust the belt tension, first loosen the adjusting bolt on the right of the alternator (looking from the rear).

2. Lift up on the alternator to increase the tension on the belt. When it takes moderate thumb pressure to move the longest span of belt ½ in., the tension adjustment is correct.

3. Tighten the adjusting bolt so that the alternator will not move in the adjusting bracket.

Regulator

NOTE: Late models have a solid state regulator built into the alternator. This regulator is non-adjustable and is serviced, when necessary, by replacement.

REMOVAL & INSTALLATION

1. Disconnect the cable from the negative (−) battery terminal.

2. Disconnect the multi-wire connector and automatic choke lead from the regulator.

3. Remove the two regulator mounting screws and remove the regulator from the fender panel.

4. Installation is the reverse of the removal procedures.

VOLTAGE ADJUSTMENTS— ON THE CAR

This test should be made after the engine compartment and the regulator have had a chance to cool down. The test should never be done on a ''hot'' engine.

1. Make sure all electrical equipment on the car is turned off or disconnected.

2. Using an ammeter rated at 10 amps, a 30-volt voltmeter, and a resistor rated at .25 ohms, connect up a test circuit as shown in the illustration.

3. BEFORE STARTING THE ENGINE, connect a jumper wire from the far terminal of the .25 ohm resister to the negative (−) terminal of the ammeter. After the engine is started, disconnect the jumper but be sure to reconnect it each time the engine is restarted.

1. Pulley nut set
2. Alternator pulley set
3. Alternator front cover
4. Pan head screw
5. Packing
6. Packing retainer
7. Ball bearing
8. Alternator bearing retainer

4. Start the engine and gradually increase the speed from idle to about 2000 rpm. 2000 engine rpm is equal to about 1200 alternator rpm.

5. The voltage reading shown should compare with that on the spec chart, allowing for the temperature around the regulator.

NOTE: The ammeter reading should be below 5 amps. Recharge or substitute the battery with a charged one if the reading is not below 5 amps.

6. If the voltage is not within the specified range, adjust as follows;

a. Remove the screws and take off the regulator cover. Loosen the locknut and turn the adjusting screw until the voltage falls within specifications.

b. If the voltage cannot be brought within specs, proceed with a mechanical adjustment.

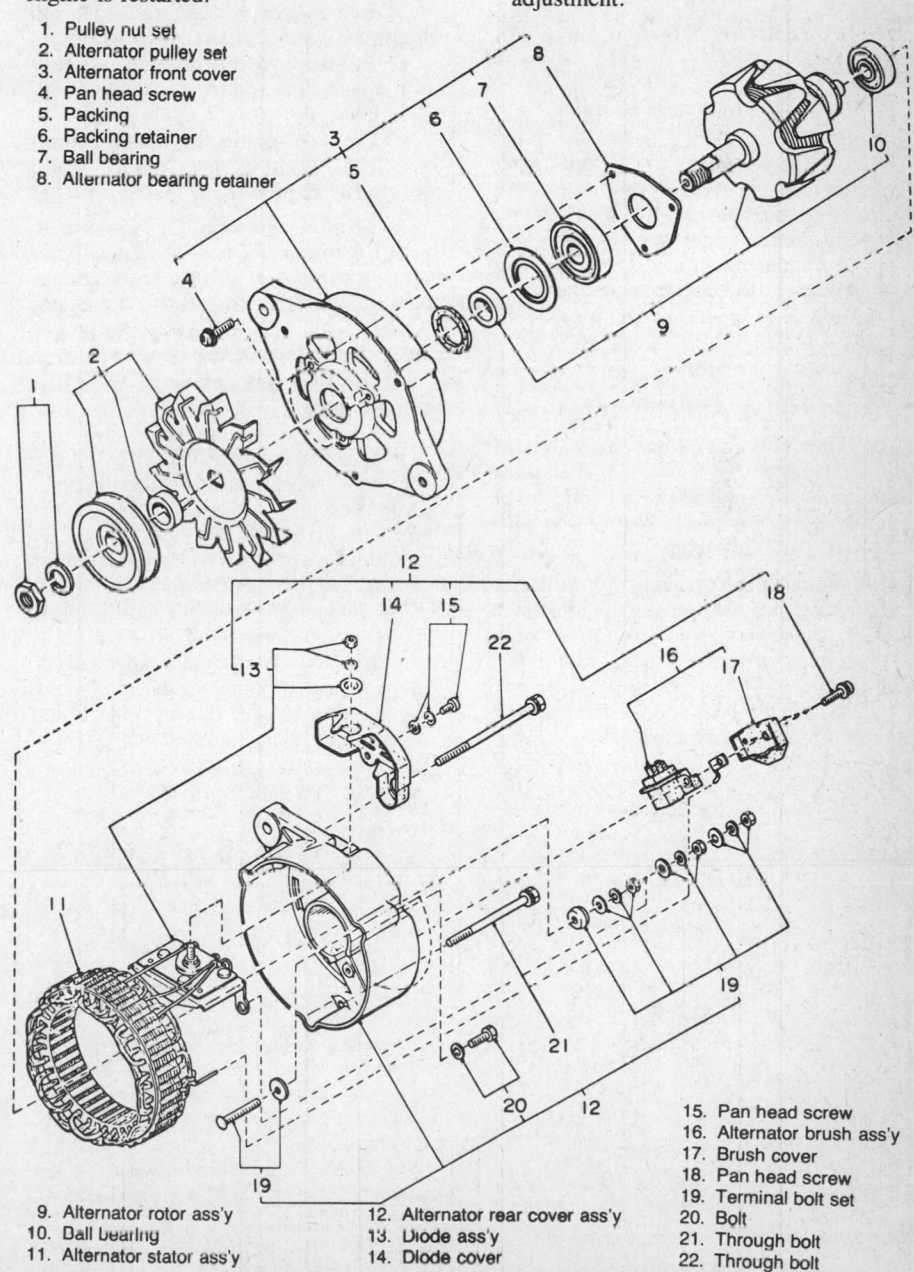

9. Alternator rotor ass'y
10. Ball bearing
11. Alternator stator ass'y
12. Alternator rear cover ass'y
13. Diode ass'y
14. Diode cover
15. Pan head screw
16. Alternator brush ass'y
17. Brush cover
18. Pan head screw
19. Terminal bolt set
20. Bolt
21. Through bolt
22. Through bolt

Exploded view of a typical alternator

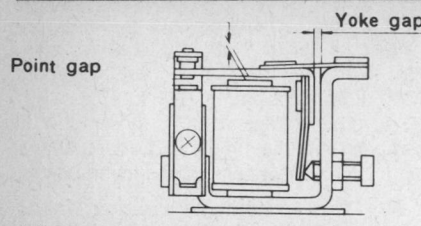

Adjustment points of the voltage regulator

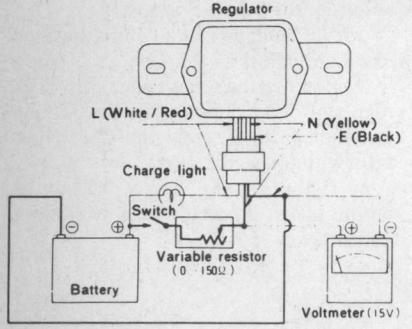

Charge relay test circuit

c. If the voltage is now within the required specs: shut off the engine, remove the test equipment, replace the regulator cover and reconnect any electrical system components or accessories you disconnected at the beginning of the test.

VOLTAGE ADJUSTMENTS—OFF THE CAR

Charge Relay Adjustment

NOTE: The opening voltage of the charge relay is 8–10 volts at alternator terminal "A". However, the coil on the charge relay operates at half of this voltage (i.e., 4–5 volts).

1. Remove the regulator from the car.
2. Hook up the test circuit illustrated with a car battery, 0–150 ohm rheostat, voltmeter, heavy-duty switch, and a test light.
3. Close the switch with the rheostat set at 150 ohms (maximum).
4. Gradually decrease the resistance.
5. When the test light goes out, the voltmeter should read 4–5 volts.

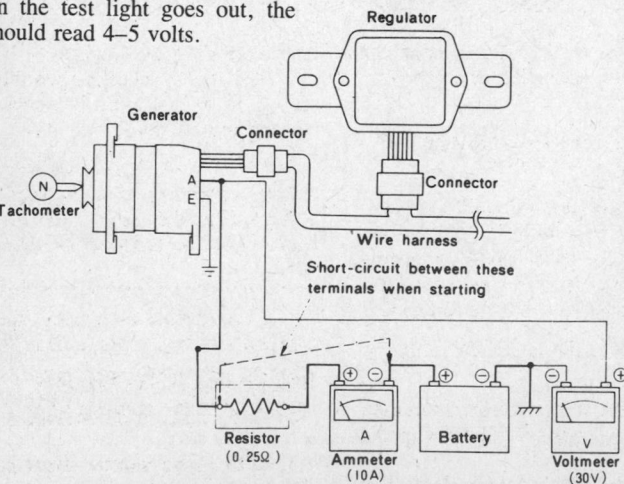

Voltage adjustment test schematic

6. If the light doesn't go out at the specified setting, remove the regulator cover and make the following adjustments. Loosen the locknut on the charge relay, and turn the adjusting screw until the voltage is within specifications. Tighten the locknut.
7. If the charge relay voltage cannot be brought within specifications, perform the "Mechanical Adjustments" outlined next.
8. If the charge relay is working properly, put the cover on the regulator and install it in the car.

Mechanical Adjustments

——— **CAUTION** ———

All mechanical adjustments must be performed with the regulator removed from the car to prevent battery and charging system damage.

1. Remove the voltage regulator from the car and remove the regulator cover.
2. Inspect both sets of points. If they are rough or dirty, polish them with an ignition point file.

NOTE: If the points are so badly damaged that polishing them doesn't help, replace the regulator.

3. Measure and adjust the gaps of both the voltage regulator and the charge relay in the same manner. Use the specifications given in the "Alternator and Regulator Specifications" chart, Adjust both sets of gaps in the following sequence:

NOTE: It is not necessary to adjust the yoke gap.

a. Core gap—measure the clearance for both the regulator and charge relay between their armatures and coil cores. Adjust each, as necessary, by loosening the 4mm screw which secures the contact set to the yoke and moving the set up or down. Tighten the screw.

b. Point gap—measure the distances between the points for both the voltage regulator and charge relay. Adjust each, as necessary, by loosening the 3mm screw which secures the upper contact and moving the contact up or down. Tighten the screw.

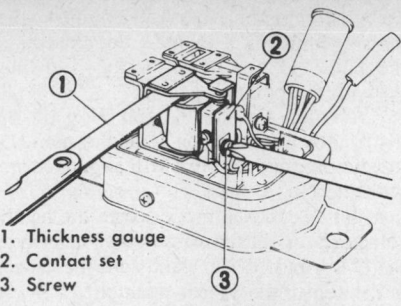

1. Thickness gauge
2. Contact set
3. Screw

Adjusting the core gap

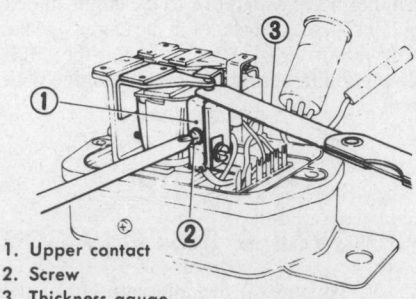

1. Upper contact
2. Screw
3. Thickness gauge

Adjusting the point gap

4. Reinstall the regulator and test its operation as outlined above. If the voltage still cannot be brought within specifications, replace the regulator. If the voltage is still incorrect, the fault probably lies in the alternator.

Starter

Two types of starter motor are used, the direct drive motor and the reduction gear motor.

The direct drive motor uses a drive mounted on the end of the armature to engage the engine flywheel.

The reduction gear motor uses an idler gear driven by the end of the armature to turn the starter drive. The rotation speed of the starter drive is reduced to approximately ⅓ of the armature speed.

REMOVAL & INSTALLATION

1. Remove the spare tire from the engine compartment.
2. Disconnect the cable from the negative (ground) battery terminal.
3. Disconnect the wiring harness at the starter located on top of the transaxle at the rear of the engine.
4. Remove the two nuts which secure the starter to the transaxle and pull the starter out.
5. Starter installation is the reverse of removal.

SOLENOID REPLACEMENT—DIRECT DRIVE STARTER

1. With the starter removed from the car, remove the nut underneath the solenoid terminal and disconnect the wires from the starter.

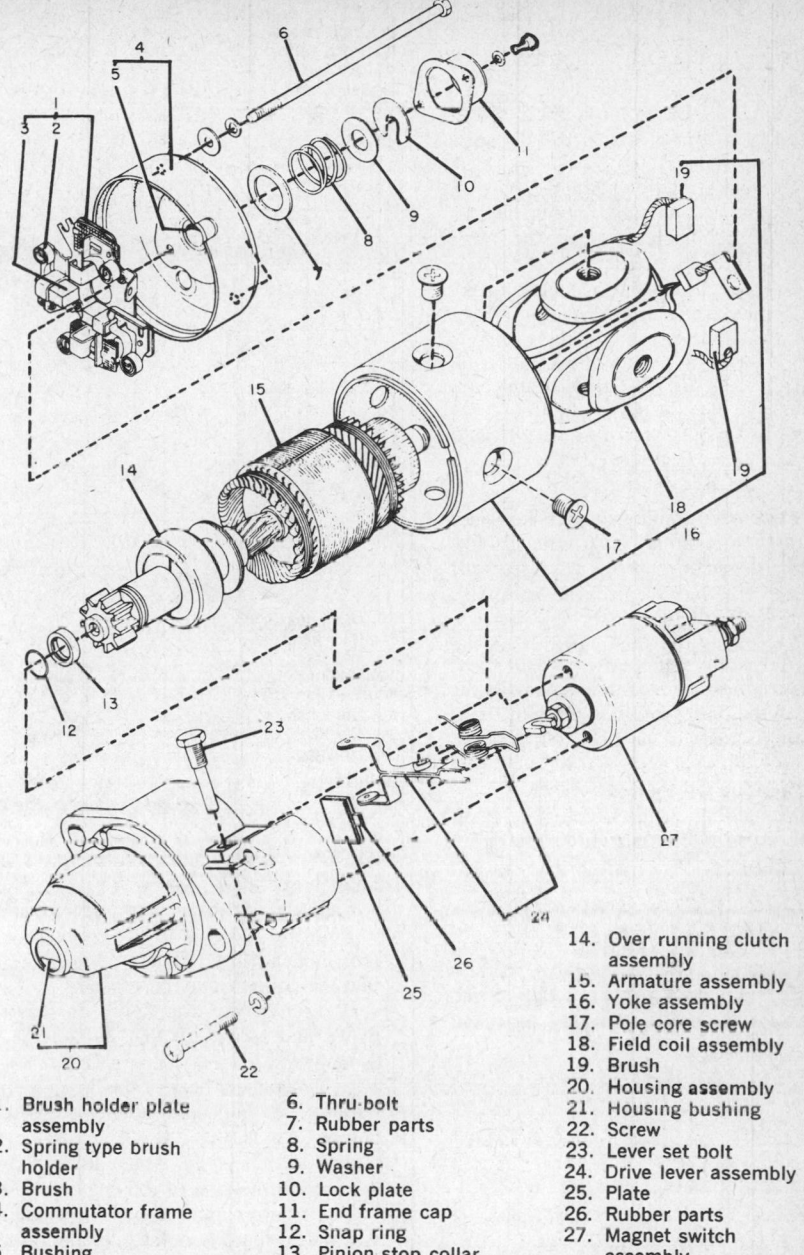

2. Remove the two screws which hold the solenoid to the starter.

NOTE: It may be necessary to use an impact driver to remove the two screws.

3. Lift the solenoid up and then pull it toward the rear in order to separate it from the starter.

4. Installation is performed in the reverse order of removal. Be sure to engage the hook on the end of the solenoid with the starter drive lever before installing the solenoid securing screws.

STARTER OVERHAUL— DIRECT DRIVE STARTER
Starter Drive Replacement

1. Remove the attaching nut and disconnect the terminal (labeled "M") that feeds power to the starter windings. Then, remove the solenoid as described in the procedure above.

2. Remove the end frame cap, lock plate, spring, and rubber seal.

3. Remove the two through-bolts and then pull the end frame toward the rear to remove it. Remove the brushes from their holders by first pushing the holder spring aside.

4. Remove the brush holder plate. Then, pull the yoke off the main housing (which surrounds the stator coils). Remove the plate and seal from the rear of the yoke.

5. Unscrew and remove the solenoid lever set bolt. Then, pull the armature, overrunning clutch, and lever out of the yoke.

6. Using a length of pipe the same diameter as the armature shaft, tap the pinion stop collar down toward the starter drive so that it is off the snap-ring. Use a pair of snap-ring pliers to remove the snap-ring from the armature shaft. Slide off the pinion stop collar.

7. Remove the starter drive from the threaded spline, taking care not to damage the spline.

8. To install the starter drive, slip the starter drive onto the armature shaft and drive the pinion stop collar down past the snap-ring groove. Gently push the snap ring over the end of the armature shaft. Work it down until it slips in to the snap-ring groove.

9. Supporting the stop collar as shown (the armature must hang below, unsupported) press the end of the armature shaft downward until the collar rests against the ring and the ring is in the groove of the collar.

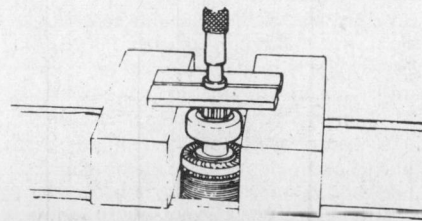

Pressing snap ring collar back into position

1. Brush holder plate assembly	6. Thru-bolt
2. Spring type brush holder	7. Rubber parts
3. Brush	8. Spring
4. Commutator frame assembly	9. Washer
5. Bushing	10. Lock plate
	11. End frame cap
	12. Snap ring
	13. Pinion stop collar

14. Over running clutch assembly
15. Armature assembly
16. Yoke assembly
17. Pole core screw
18. Field coil assembly
19. Brush
20. Housing assembly
21. Housing bushing
22. Screw
23. Lever set bolt
24. Drive lever assembly
25. Plate
26. Rubber parts
27. Magnet switch assembly

Exploded view of the direct drive starter motor

10. Simply follow the remainder of the disassembly steps in reverse order to reassemble the starter.

Brush Replacement—Direct Drive Starter

1. Remove the starter from the engine. Remove the two thru-bolts.

2. Remove the two small mounting screws which hold the end frame cap. Remove the cap, lock plate, spring and rubber seal.

3. Slide the end frame off the starter assembly.

4. Remove the starter brushes from their holders by moving each brush holder spring aside.

5. Lift off the brush holder plate. The yoke may now be separated from the housing by sliding them apart.

6. If the brushes are worn to less than 0.043 in. they should be replaced by soldering in new ones.

— **CAUTION** —
When soldering in new positive brushes (those attached to the field coil) be careful not to get excess solder or dirt on the field coil.

7. Assemble and install the starter in reverse order of removal and disassembly.

REDUCTION GEAR STARTER REPAIRS

NOTE: The starter must be removed from the car to perform any of these operations.

1. Disconnect the lead wire between the solenoid and the starter body by removing the attaching nut. Never loosen the terminal bolt.

2. Remove the two through bolts. Remove the two screws that secure the solenoid to the housing.

3. On gear reduction starters used with manual transmissions only, remove the two screws that attach the rear frame to the starter and remove the rear frame.

4. Separate the housing and the solenoid.

5. Remove the starter drive unit. Take care not to lose the spring or the ball.

6. Remove the two field brushes from the brush holder and remove the holder. Be careful not to scratch the armature.

7. Remove the idler gear and starter drive from the solenoid. Be careful not to lose the five rollers.

8. Inspect the component parts for wear. If the solenoid is faulty, replace it as a unit. Check the gears for chips or worn teeth. If the brushes are worn, replace the assembly. Take care when soldering in the field brushes, do not get excessive solder or dirt on the field coils.

9. Assembly of the starter motor is the reverse of the disassembly. Grease the ball, rollers and gears with high temperature grease. If you have removed the armature be sure to reinstall the felt washer.

10. Reinstall the starter motor in the engine. Make sure all connections are tight.

ENGINE MECHANICAL

Engine

REMOVAL & INSTALLATION

All Models Except Turbo

NOTE: On all models, the engine is removed separately from the transaxle.

1. Open the hood as far as possible and secure it with the stay.

2. Disconnect the ground cable from the negative (−) battery terminal.

3. Remove the 8mm bolt which secures the ground cable at the intake man-ifold and disconnect the cable. It is unnecessary to remove the cable fully; leave it routed along the side of the body.

4. Remove the spare tire from the engine compartment.

5. Remove the emission control system hoses from the air cleaner. Remove the air cleaner brackets, remove the wing nut, and lift the air cleaner assembly off the carburetor.

6. Place a suitable container under the fuel line union to catch the gasoline. Disconnect the hoses at the union by removing the clip and pulling the hose off. Drain the engine oil.

1. Through bolt
2. Brush holder
3. Brush spring
4. Felt washer
5. Ball bearing
6. Armature
7. Yoke
8. Rubber packing
9. Magnet switch

10. Drive gear
11. Idler gear
12. Roller
13. Retainer
14. Coil spring
15. Steel ball
16. Clutch
17. Housing

Exploded view of the gear reduction starter motor

7. Drain the coolant and disconnect the radiator hoses.

a. Place a clean container, large enough to hold the contents of the cooling system, beneath the radiator drain plug so that the coolant may be reused.

b. Loosen the drain plug on the radiator and turn it so that its slot faces downward.

c. Disconnect both of the hoses at the radiator, leaving them connected to the engine.

d. Disconnect the heater hoses from the pipe at the side of the engine.

e. On automatic transmission models, disconnect the oil cooler inlet and outlet hoses at the radiator.

8. Disconnect the following electrical wiring.

a. Alternator multi-connector
b. Oil pressure sender connection
c. Three engine cooling fan connectors
d. Temperature sender connection
e. Primary distributor lead
f. Secondary ignition leads (ignition side)
g. Starter wiring harness
h. Anti-dieseling solenoid lead
i. Automatic choke lead
j. EGR vacuum solenoid
k. EGR coolant temperature switch
l. On automatic transmission models, disconnect the neutral safety switch harness and downshift solenoid harness.

9. Loosen the two radiator securing bolts, remove the ground lead from the upper side of the radiator, and lift the radiator out.

NOTE: On 4WD models, remove the engine fan from the pulley.

10. Remove the horizontal damper in the following order.

a. Remove the front nut from the damper.

b. Remove the nut on the body bracket and withdraw the damper.

c. Pull the damper rearward away from the engine lifting hook. Be careful not to lose any of the damper parts.

11. Remove the starter.

12. Disconnect the following cables, hoses and linkages.

a. Loosen the screw in the carburetor throttle lever. Remove the outer end of the accelerator cable and withdraw it.

b. Remove vacuum hose and purge hose from vapor canister.

c. On standard transmission models, remove the clutch return spring from the release lever and intake manifold, and remove the clutch cable from the lever.

d. On automatic transmission models, disconnect the vacuum hose attached to the transmission.

e. Disconnect the vacuum hose from the power brake unit (if so equipped).

13. On 4WD models, remove the under guard by unscrewing the attaching bolts.

14. Remove the Y-shaped exhaust pipe.

a. Loosen the clamp fastening the air intake hose to the air stove on the exhaust pipe, and remove the hose.

b. Remove the air stove and remove the four nuts attaching the exhaust pipe to the cylinder heads.

c. Remove the two bolts and nuts connecting the exhaust pipe to the pre-muffler.

d. While supporting the exhaust pipe by hand, remove the two bolts attaching the exhaust pipe to the transmission bracket. Lower the exhaust pipe.

15. On automatic transmission models, remove the torque converter bolts.

a. Remove the timing hole cover from the torque converter housing.

b. Remove the four bolts connecting the torque converter to the drive plate through the timing hole.

NOTE: Be careful that the bolts do not fall into the torque converter housing.

16. Set up a chain hoist on the engine, with hooks at the front and rear engine hangers. Adjust the hoist so that the weight of the engine is supported, but do not raise the engine.

17. Position a suitable jack under the transaxle to support its weight when the engine is removed.

18. Remove the four nuts (four each on top and bottom) connecting the engine and transmission.

19. Remove the nuts holding the front engine mounts (rubber) to the crossmember.

20. Before going on to the next step, be sure that all of the above steps have been completed.

21. Using the hoist, raise the engine slightly (about 1 in.). Keeping it level, move the engine forward, off the transaxle input shaft.

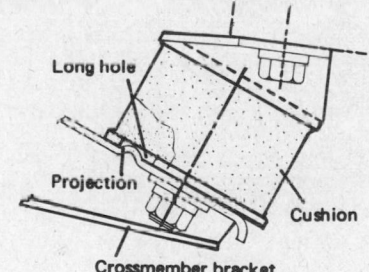

Engine mount alignment

Long hole
Projection
Cushion
Crossmember bracket

—————— CAUTION ——————

Do not raise the engine more than one inch prior to removing it from the input shaft or damage may occur to the driveshaft double offset joints. On standard transmission models, be sure that the input shaft does not interfere with the clutch spring assembly. On automatic transmission models, leave the torque converter on the transaxle input shaft.

22. Hoist the engine carefully until it is completely out of the car, and place it on a suitable stand or workbench.

Engine installation is performed in the reverse order of removal. However, be sure to observe the following:

1. Use the following torque specifications when installing the engine.

Transmission-to-engine: 34–40 ft. lbs.
Torque converter-to-drive plate: 17–20 ft. lbs.

Engine mount-to-cross member: 14–24 ft. lbs.
Horizontal damper nut: 7–10 ft. lbs.
Exhaust pipe-to-engine:
   19–22 ft. lbs.
Exhaust pipe to pre-muffler: 31–38 ft. lbs.
Radiator mounting bolt: 6–10 ft. lbs.

2. Use care not to damage the input shaft splines or the clutch spring while lowering the engine in place.

3. When installing the exhaust pipe and/or converter always use new gaskets.

4. Perform the following adjustment to the horizontal damper:

a. Tighten the body bracket nut.

b. Turn the front nut until the clearance between the front washer and rubber cushion is zero.

c. Insert the bushing and tighten the front nut to specifications (Step 1).

5. Make all of the clutch and accelator linkage adjustments, as detailed elsewhere in the book.

6. Replenish the engine oil and coolant supplies.

1800 Turbo

1. Open the hood and prop it securely. Remove the spare tire. Remove the spare tire bracket.

2. Decrease fuel pressure in the injection system by disconnecting the fuel pump connector and then cranking the engine for at least 5 seconds. If the engine starts, allow it to run until it stalls. Then, reconnect the fuel pump connector.

3. Remove the battery ground cable entirely.

4. Disconnect the air temperature sensor plug in the engine compartment.

5. Remove the fuel system hoses and evaporative emissions system hoses.

6. Disconnect the vacuum hoses from the cruise control, Master-Vac, air intake shutter, and heater air intake door.

7. Disconnect the wiring and remove the harness from the alternator, EGI, thermoswitch, electric fan, A/C condenser, and ignition coil. Disconnect the main engine harness.

8. Disconnect ignition high tension wires, and engine ground wire.

9. Disconnect the fusible link assembly.

10. Disconnect the accelerator linkage. Remove the washer fluid tank and store it behind the right side strut tower.

11. Remove the power steering pump as follows:

a. Loosen the alternator adjusting and lock bolts, shift the alternator to loosen the belt and then remove the belt.

b. Remove the pump pulley.

c. Remove the pump mounting bolts and clamp.

d. Remove the engine oil filler pipe brace.

e. Then, remove the power steering pump and place it on the bulkhead without disturbing lines.

12. Loosen hose clamps and remove

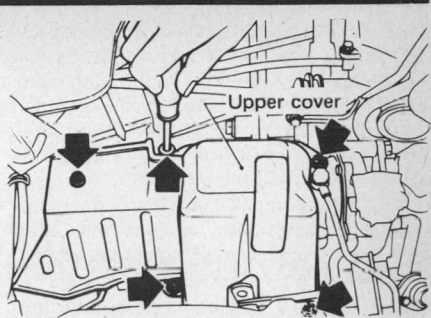

Removing the upper cover—turbo vehicles

Upper cover

the air intake duct. Seal openings to keep dirt out of air intake passages. Remove the upper cover.

13. Remove the air intake line running to the flowmeter. Cover the openings.

14. Remove the horizontal damper and clip.

15. Remove the center section of the exhaust pipe as follows:

a. Disconnect the temperature sensor connector.

b. Disconnect the exhaust pipe at the turbocharger body.

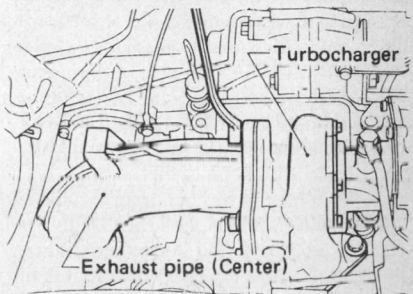

Turbocharger
Exhaust pipe (Center)

Disconnecting the exhaust pipe at the turbocharger

c. Remove the rear cover.

d. Remove the bolt attaching the center exhaust section to the transmission.

e. Remove the bolts from the hangers, and carefully remove the pipe (clearance is tight) so as to avoid damage.

Slightly loosen the attaching bolts and remove the converter cover.

16. Disconnect the turbocharger oil supply and drain lines. Then, remove the three bolts attaching the turbo to the exhaust system, and remove the turbo assembly, lower cover, and gasket.

17. Disconnect the O_2 sensor connector.

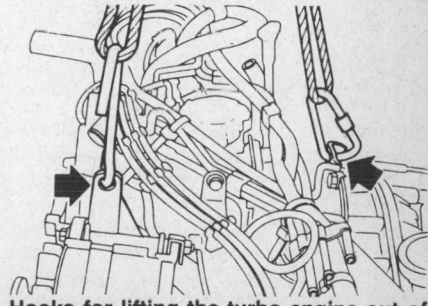

Hooks for lifting the turbo engine out of the vehicle

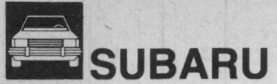
Remove the bolts connecting the torque converter to the drive plate.

18. Hook a chain hoist to the horizontal damper bracket and support the engine. Then, remove the upper engine-to-transmission bolts. Leave the starter in place.

19. Drain the engine coolant, using a hose to lead coolant to a clean container. Then, disconnect upper and lower radiator coolant hoses and oil cooler lines, and ground wire, and remove the radiator.

20. Disconnect oil cooler lines at the engine. Drain oil into a clean container. Disconnect the heater hoses from the side of the engine.

21. Remove the front engine mount. Then, remove the lower nuts joining the engine to the transmission.

22. Locate a jack under the transmission. Raise both engine and transmission slightly. Then, pull the engine forward until the transmission shaft clears the clutch. Carefully raise the engine out of the engine compartment.

23. To install, reverse the removal procedure, keeping the following points in mind:

   a. After installing all major mounting nuts and bolts finger tight, tighten upper transmission-to-engine bolts just snug. Then, remove support from the engine and transmission. Then, tighten lower transmission-to-engine bolts. Next, tighten engine mount nuts. Finally, fully tighten upper transmission-to-engine bolts. Torque all to 14–17 ft. lbs.

   b. In torquing turbocharger mounting and exhaust system mounting bolts, be sure to go back and forth and tighten bolts evenly. Use new gaskets throughout.

   c. Observe the following torque figures:

      Torque converter-drive plate—17–20 ft. lb.

      Turbo to exhaust system—31–38 ft. lb.

      Exhaust system-to transmission bolt—18–25 ft. lb.

      Exhaust system hanger bolts—7–13 ft. lb.

      Rear exhaust pipe joint—7–13 ft. lb.

      Power steering pump pulley—25–30 ft. lb.

      Power steering pump mounting bolts—18–25 ft. lb.

   d. Adjust the horizontal damper by

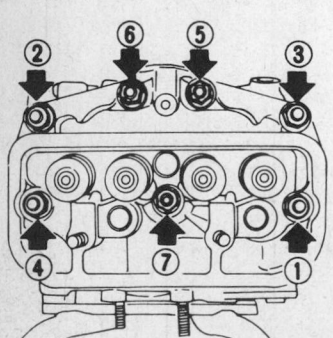

Loosening sequence for cylinder head nuts of models up to 1979

tightening the nuts on the body side of the damper until the clearance is 0.08 in. Torque the locknuts to 6.5–9.4 ft. lb.

   e. Adjust the accelerator pedal so there is .04–1.2 in. between the pin and stop. Adjust the cable for an end play of 0–.08 in. on the actuator side.

   f. Install radiator hoses onto radiator connections before installing it.

   g. Replenish all fluids. Warm the engine and then run at 4000 rpm to check for leaks in oil cooler and lines.

Cylinder Head

REMOVAL & INSTALLATION

The engine must be removed from the vehicle to remove the cylinder heads. Although it is physically possible (on some models) to remove the cylinder heads with the engine installed, head gasket failure will result upon installation, due to misalignment of the cylinders. The cylinder heads should be removed with the engine cold to prevent warpage.

1. Remove the engine from the vehicle and mount it on a workstand.

2. Unbolt and remove the intake manifold together with the carburetor and the various pollution control devices. (The pipe attached to the exhaust manifold port in the cylinder head should have been removed before the engine was taken out.) On 1977 and later models, remove the EGR pipe from the intake manifold and cylinder head.

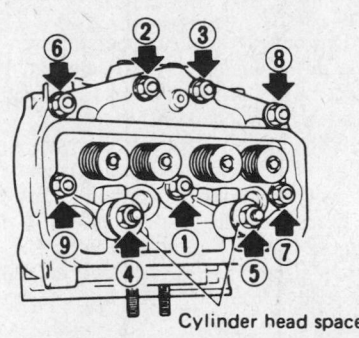

Tightening sequence of cylinder head bolts on models up to 1979

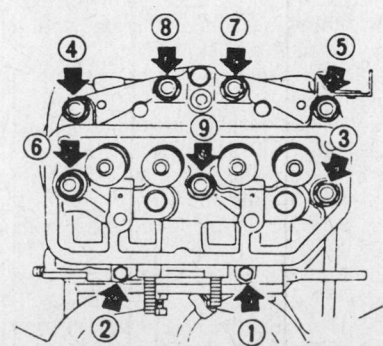

Loosening sequence for cylinder head bolts—1980

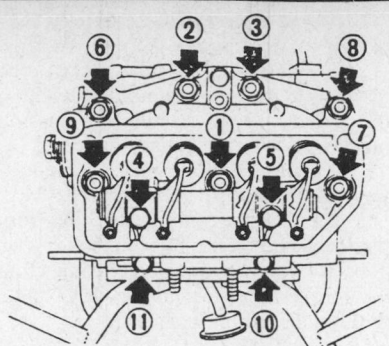

Tightening sequence for cylinder head bolts—1980

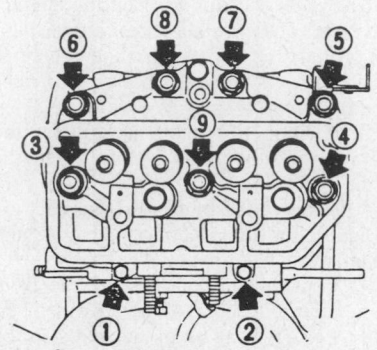

Loosening sequence for cylinder head bolts—1981

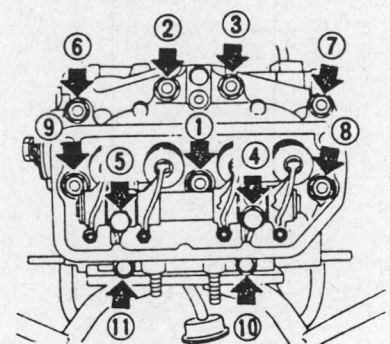

Tightening sequence for cylinder head bolts—1981

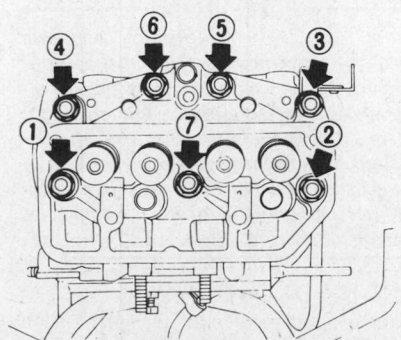

Loosening sequence for cylinder head bolts—1982–84

On 1982–84 models, this includes removing the thermostatic water valve and hose and the oil filler pipe brackets. On the turbo, remove the turbocharger and exhaust manifold, and disconnect the fuel injection lines.

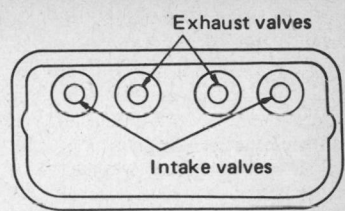

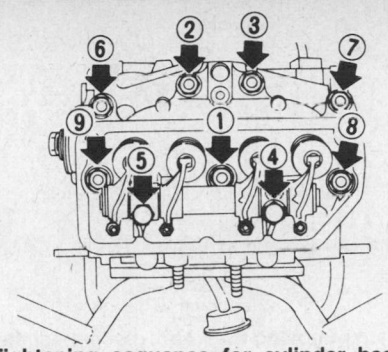

Tightening sequence for cylinder head bolts—1982–84

NOTE: Move or disconnect any engine wiring that might impair intake manifold removal.

3. Remove the spark plugs.

4. Disconnect the crankcase ventilation hose(s) and remove the valve covers.

5. Loosen the alternator adjusting bolts, and unbolt the alternator bracket from the cylinder head.

6. Remove the air injection distributor tubes from the cylinder heads by unscrewing the fittings on models so equipped.

NOTE: Do not distort the injection tubes.

NOTE: In the next step, in removal of the rocker shaft assemblies, it is necessary to loosen the valve rocker locknuts and adjusting screws. This applies to solid lifter engines only. 1983–85 engines with automatic transmission have hydraulic lifters. On hydraulic lifter-equipped engines, the adjustment of these screws and locknuts must not be disturbed!

On the 1800 Turbo, remove the knock sensor with a 27mm deep well socket only! (A standard socket will damage electrical terminals). Then, remove the fuel injectors with a Phillips screwdriver.

7. Loosen the valve rocker locknuts and adjusting screws (solid lifter engines only). Loosen the rocker shaft mounting nuts, and remove the rocker arm assembly and pushrods.

NOTE: If the pushrods are to be reused, keep them in order so that they are installed in the original positions. The pushrods for all engines are identified by knurling (or the absence of knurling). If you are replacing pushrods, make sure knurled patterns are similar or that unmarked pushrods are replaced by unmarked rods. Markings vary from year to year. For example, for 1981 and 1982, 1800 cc engines used pushrods with two knurled marks, while 1983–84 engines have 2 knurled marks for 1600cc engines, a single mark for solid lifter, 1800 engines, and no markings for hydraulic lifter engines.

8. Loosen the head nuts as illustrated. Remove the cylinder heads and gaskets.

9. Install the heads in the reverse order of removal.

The cylinder heads must be installed with the cylinders vertical to avoid misalignment and to permit the head gasket to settle evenly around the cylinder. Torque in specified sequence, in stages, using a spacer (see illustration) in the place of the rocker shaft support on 1978–79 models. After the head is torqued to specifications (see "Torque Specifications" chart), remove the rocker shaft bolts (or nuts) and the spacers, and install the rocker shafts on these models. On later models, torque the head with the rocker shaft in place, in the sequence shown for the model year. Recheck the torque of the No. 1 bolt after torque is correct on the others.

Use liquid sealer on both sides of a new head gasket.

On models which use studs and nuts, lightly oil the threads before installing nuts.

SERVICE

Using a straightedge, check the cylinder heads for warpage. Should warpage exceed 0.002 in., the cylinder head must be resurfaced (grinding limit 0.016 in.). Should the valve sink exceed approximately 0.040

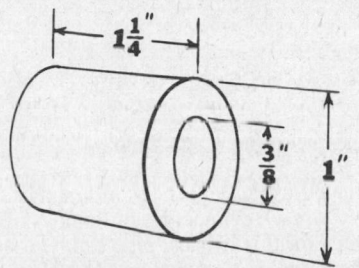

Cylinder head installation spacer

in., the seats must be replaced. The valve guides are pressed in, and should be replaced if clearance exceeds specifications. The intake valve guide should extend 0.71 and the exhaust 0.91 in. from the spring seat.

For further information on cylinder head overhaul procedures, please refer to "Engine Rebuilding" in the Unit Repair section.

Rocker Shafts

1. Remove the engine from the vehicle and mount it in a workstand.

2. Remove the valve covers and their gaskets from the heads.

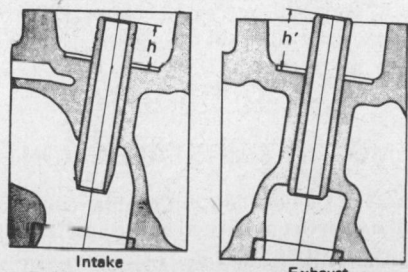

Valve guide installed height

Exhaust valves

Intake valves

Valve arrangement in cylinder head

3. Remove the nuts which secure the rocker assemblies to the cylinder heads.

4. Withdraw the pushrods from their bores, being sure to keep them in the same sequence in which they were removed.

NOTE: It is a good idea to tag each pushrod as it is removed from its bore, to aid in correct installation.

Installation is performed in the reverse order of removal. Tighten the valve rocker assembly mounting bolts to 37–43 ft. lb. on models thru 1979 and 47 ft. lb. on 1980 and later models.

Intake Manifold

REMOVAL & INSTALLATION

——— CAUTION ———
Do not perform this operation on a warm engine; wait until the engine is cold.

1. Remove the spare tire from the engine compartment.

2. Disconnect the emission control system hoses, remove the mounting bracket screws, and withdraw the air cleaner assembly. On 1800 Turbo models, loosen hose clamps, disconnect hoses, and remove the air intake duct.

3. Drain the cooling system and detach all of the water hoses from the thermostat housing.

4. Disconnect the thermoswitch connector.

5. On models having a distributor vacuum control valve, disconnect the hoses and leads from it. Disconnect the anti-dieseling solenoid leads, as well.

6. On models, which have an air injection system, perform the following:

   a. Disconnect the lines from the anti-afterburn valve.

   b. Unbolt the air injection manifold mounting brackets from the intake manifold.

   c. Remove the by-pass valve (if so equipped).

7. On 1978 and later models, disconnect the following:

   a. Automatic choke-to-voltage regulator wire at the connector.

   b. EGR solenoid wiring (if so equipped).

   c. The EGR pipe by removing the nuts which secure it to the intake manifold and the cylinder head (if so equipped).

8. Disconnect the throttle cable and manual choke cable (if so equipped) from their brackets. Disconnect the fuel line from the carburetor. On 1800 Turbo models, dis-

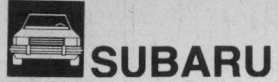
1. Nut
2. Spring washer
3. Carburetor gasket
4. Washer
5. Bolt (8 x 26 x 23)
6. Bolt
7. Thermostat case cover
8. Thermostat case cover gasket
9. Thermostat
10. Thermometer
11. Bolt
12. Bolt
13. Spring washer

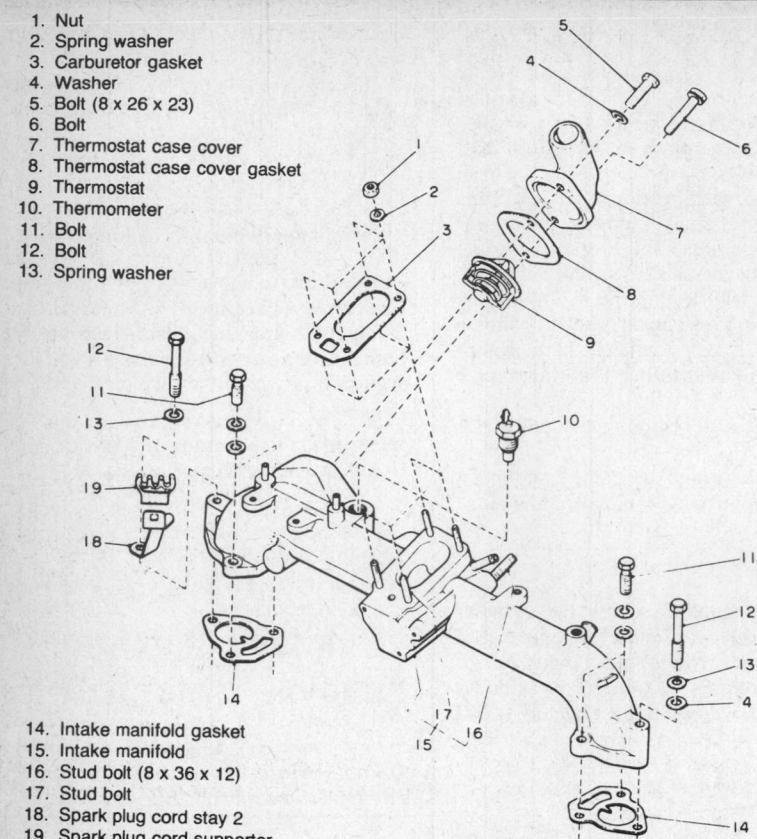

14. Intake manifold gasket
15. Intake manifold
16. Stud bolt (8 x 36 x 12)
17. Stud bolt
18. Spark plug cord stay 2
19. Spark plug cord supporter

Exploded view of a typical 1600 intake manifold (1800 similar)

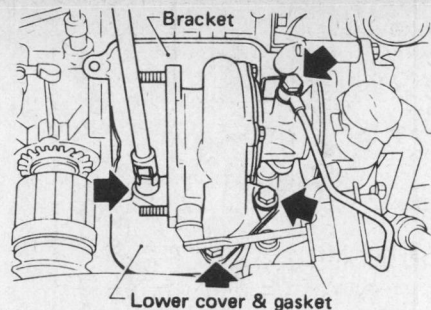

Lower cover & gasket

When removing the turbo, disconnect the oil supply line at upper right, and then remove the three bolts from the lower flange, the turbo assembly, and, finally, the gasket

connect the hose clamps, pull off hoses, and remove the fuel pressure regulator assembly. Also, unbolt and remove the vacuum pipe assembly.

9. Unbolt the intake manifold from the cylinder heads and remove the manifold assembly. On 1982–85 models, air cleaner brackets will come off as the unit is unbolted. Make sure to note locations of these brackets and remove them. Be careful not to lose any of the gaskets.

NOTE: Cover the intake ports in the cylinder head while the manifold is removed to prevent anything from being dropped in them.

10. The manifold may be disassembled further by removing the carburetor or throttle body and the applicable emission control system components from it.

Installation is performed in the reverse order of removal. Be sure to use new gaskets. Tighten the bolts evenly, in stages, to the specifications given in the "Torque Specifications" chart. Adjust the choke and throttle linkages.

Exhaust Manifolds

REMOVAL & INSTALLATION

Except Turbo

An exhaust manifold, as a separate item, is not found on these models. Instead, the Y-shaped exhaust pipe bolts directly to a flange on each cylinder head. Removal procedures for this exhaust pipe can be found in the "Engine Removal and Installation" section.

1800 Turbo

This model is unique in having a crossover pipe that links both exhaust ports at the cylinder heads and the exhaust inlet at the turbocharger so as to feed all the exhaust through the turbo.

1. Disconnect the connection at the turbocharger by removing the two nuts and accompaning washers from the top of the turbo exhaust inlet flange.

2. From under the car, remove the two nuts at either cylinder head exhaust port and then pull the crossover pipe off the cylinder head studs while guiding the studs integral with the pipe out of the base of the turbocharger. Be careful to pull all three gaskets off.

3. To install, reverse the removal procedure, using new gaskets.

Turbocharger

REMOVAL & INSTALLATION

NOTE: Do not allow dirt to enter either intake or outlet openings, or the unit may be destroyed at startup.

1. Remove the air cleaner.

2. Disconnect hose clamps at the airflow meter and turbocharger inlet, and remove the air intake boot. Cover the airflow meter opening and turbocharger opening.

3. Loosen clamps at the turbocharger air outlet and throttle body inlet hose. Loosen the clamp on the hose coming from the thermostat housing and pull the hose off the air intake duct. Now, pull the duct out of its connecting hoses and remove it. Plug all openings.

4. Unscrew the two bolts and disconnect the center exhaust pipe at the turbocharger exhaust outlet.

5. Disconnect the oil line at the top of the turbo-unit by removing the bolt. Disconnect the hose clamp on the oil drain line. Finally, remove the three exhaust inlet mounting bolts, and pull the turbo and gasket off the exhaust manifold, disconnecting the oil drain line as the turbo is removed.

6. To install, clean gasket surfaces and install a new gasket on top of the exhaust manifold. Put the turbo in position as you slide the nipple on the bottom of the unit over the oil drain line.

7. Install the three mounting bolts that fasten the unit to the exhaust manifold. Install the oil drain line clamp. Then, install the oil supply line by putting it into position and installing the bolt. Torque to 31–38 ft. lb.

8. Connect the center exhaust pipe to the turbocharger exhaust outlet by installing the two bolts and torquing to 31–38 ft. lb.

9. Install the air intake duct and boot and auxiliary hoses in reverse order. Install the air cleaner.

10. Operate the engine and check for oil leaks.

Timing Gear Cover

REMOVAL & INSTALLATION

The flywheel housing covers the timing gears. In order to remove it, the engine has to be removed from the vehicle.

1. Separate the engine from the transmission. Remove the torque converter with the automatic transmission.

2. Remove the clutch cover and the

clutch disc from the flywheel. Remove the flywheel or automatic transmission converter drive plate.

3. Remove the flywheel housing bolts and work the housing from the two aligning dowels.

4. Install the cover in the reverse of removal.

TIMING GEAR COVER (FLYWHEEL HOUSING) OIL SEAL REPLACEMENT

The housing cover oil seal is pressed in.

1. Remove the engine from the vehicle, separating the transmission from the engine.

2. Remove the flywheel and clutch assembly or converter drive plate from the engine.

3. Remove the housing from the engine and remove the oil seal from the housing.

4. Install the new oil seal, pressing it into place.

5. Reassemble the engine and install it in the reverse order of disassembly and removal.

Camshaft

REMOVAL & INSTALLATION

The camshaft turns on journals that are machined directly into the crankcase. To remove the camshaft, the engine must be removed from the vehicle, disassembled and the crankcase separated.

1. Remove the engine from the vehicle, separating the transmission from the engine.

2. Remove the clutch and flywheel assembly or converter drive plate.

3. Remove the flywheel housing.

4. Straighten the lockwashers and remove the bolts that hold the camshaft retaining plate to the crankcase. The lockwashers are straightened and the bolts removed through the access holes in the camshaft gear.

5. Remove the intake manifold as described above. See Steps 4–7 below to separate the crankcase halves.

6. Before installing the camshaft, measure the end-play of the camshaft, using a feeler gauge. The end-play should be 0.012 in. or less. Install the camshaft in the reverse order of removal.

USE THIS SHAPE
OF WRENCH

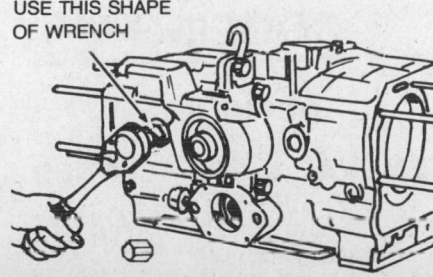

Removing or installing crankcase plugs

7. Assemble the engine and reinstall it in the vehicle in the reverse order of disassembly and removal.

NOTE: One of the bolt holes in the crankshaft gear has a larger chamber than the others.

Position the crankshaft so that the punch mark on the cam gear tooth can be seen through this bolt hole.

Pistons and Connecting Rods

REMOVAL & INSTALLATION

To remove the pistons and connecting rods, it is necessary that the engine be removed from the vehicle.

1. Separate the engine and the transmission.

2. Remove the intake manifold, oil pan, flywheel and clutch assembly, flywheel housing, cylinder heads and gaskets.

3. Unscrew and remove the two bolts and lockwashers that hold the camshaft retaining plate in place. The bolts and lockwashers are removed through two access holes in the camshaft gear.

4. Remove the crankcase plugs from the crankcase by using an Allen wrench.

5. Remove the circlips that hold the wrist pins in the pistons by inserting the piston circlip pliers through the crankcase plug holes.

6. Remove the wrist pins by inserting the wrist pin remover through the crankcase plug holes. Keep the pistons and the wrist pins together for each cylinder so that they do not become mixed. Make marks on the pistons and the liners so as not to change the direction in which they are installed.

On solid lifter engines, install valve lifter retaining clips (Subaru part No. 899804700 or equivalent) to keep the lifters from dropping out of the upper crankcase. On hydraulic lifter engines, tilt the crankcase and take out the lifters. Mark them for replacement in the same positions. Remove the nuts, bolts, and/or stud nuts securing the halves of the crankcase.

7. Separate the crankcase halves. Remove the oil seal. Be sure to replace it with a new one when reassembling the engine.

8. Remove the crankshaft together with the connecting rod and the distributor gear as an assembly.

9. Mark the connecting rods for identification purposes so they can be installed in the same position from which they were removed.

It is necessary to remove the ridge at the top of the cylinder (unworn area) to facilitate the removal of the pistons.

--- CAUTION ---
If the ridge is not removed, and new rings are installed, damage to the new rings will result!

a. Place the piston at the bottom of its bore and cover it with a rag.

b. Cut the ridge away using a ridge reamer, exercising extreme care to avoid cutting too deeply.

c. Remove the rag and remove the cuttings that remain on the piston.

10. If the piston rings are to be replaced, remove them with a ring expander. Keep the rings in removal sequence and with the piston from which they were removed. Check all clearances. See the Engine Rebuilding Unit Repair section and the appropriate specification charts. Install pistons with a ring compressor.

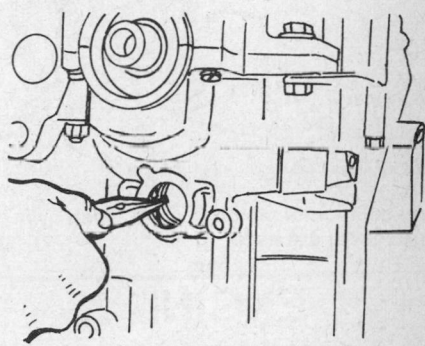

Removing or installing the piston pin circlip through the crankcase holes

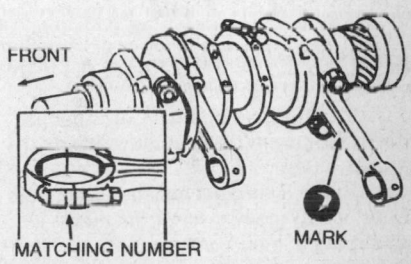

Position each connecting rod with the side mark facing forward. Each connecting rod has its own mating cap with a matching number

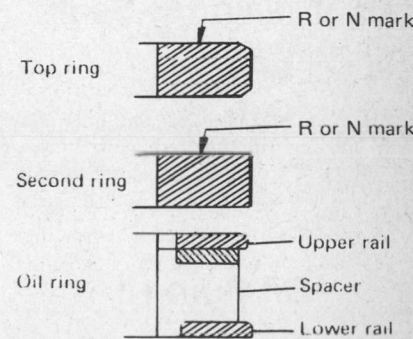

Installation of the piston rings. The top and second rings are provided with an "R" or "N" mark. Install the rings with the mark facing upward.

11. Assemble the engine in reverse order, paying particular attention to all torque figures and sequences.

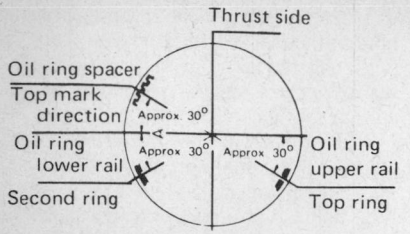

Piston ring gap position

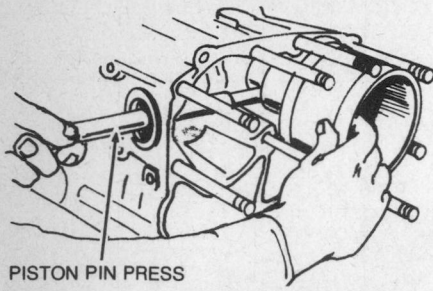

PISTON PIN PRESS

Installation of piston and pin when cylinder liners are used

1. Oil filter
2. Oil pump body
3. Bolt (6X54 mm)
4. Bolt (6X32 mm)
5. Spring washer
6. Washer
7. Oil relief valve

8. Relief valve spring
9. Washer (6 mm)
10. Washer

11. Plug
12. O ring
13. Rotor
14. Gear

15. Oil pump holder
16. Screw
17. O ring
18. Bypass valve spring
19. Ball
20. O ring
21. Gasket

Exploded view of the oil pump

ENGINE LUBRICATION

Oil Pan

REMOVAL & INSTALLATION

1. To remove the oil pan, it is not necessary that the engine be removed from the vehicle.

2. Remove the attaching bolts that hold the oil pan to the bottom of the crankcase, and remove the oil pan.

3. Remove the oil pan gasket and clean the mating surfaces of the oil pan and the crankcase.

4. Install in the reverse order of removal.

Rear Main Oil Seal

REPLACEMENT

The rear main oil seal is located in the flywheel housing (timing gear cover). See "Timing Gear Cover Removal and Installation" for the rear main oil seal replacement procedures.

Oil Pump

REMOVAL & INSTALLATION

Except 1800 Turbo

The oil pump can be removed with the engine in the vehicle. The oil pump and the oil filter can be removed as a unit. Remove the four attaching bolts, and remove the oil pump from the engine along with the gasket. The oil pump is driven directly by the

camshaft. The oil pump shaft fits into a slot in the end of the camshaft. When the oil pump is reinstalled, make sure that the oil pump shaft fits into the slot in the end of the camshaft and that the mating surfaces are flush. Install in the reverse order of removal.

1800 Turbo

1. Place a pan underneath oil filter and pump assembly to collect oil, and, using a strap wrench, remove the filter.

2. Next, remove the three bolts which fasten the two oil cooler lines (at bottom) and the turbocharger supply line (at the side) of the attachment. Remove the bolt fastening the brace for the two oil cooler pipes to the block.

3. Support the attachment with one hand while you unscrew the connector which retains it with the other. Now, gently pull the

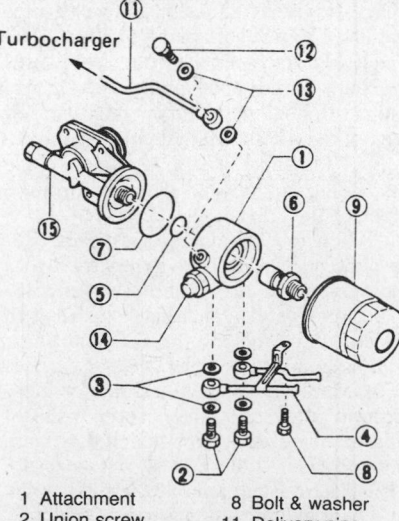

1 Attachment
2 Union screw
3 Gasket
4 Pipe
5 O-ring
6 Connector
7 O-ring

8 Bolt & washer
11 Delivery pipe
12 Union screw
13 Gasket
14 Thermo valve
15 Oil pump

Modified oil pump as used with turbo engine

attachment free of the O-rings which seal it. Remove the oil pump attaching bolts, and remove the pump.

4. Replace the washers which go over the bolts, as well as the oil pump-to-block O-ring, and the two attachment O-rings. Oil all O-rings. Then, install in reverse order, using the following torques:
   Piping to attachment—25 ft. lb.
   Attachment connector—22 ft. lb.
   Piping brace-to-block bolt—20 ft. lb.

Oil Cooler

REMOVAL & INSTALLATION

1800 Turbo

1. Put an oil drain pan nearby. Remove the two bolts connecting the oil cooler lines to the bottom of the attachment. Drain oil into the pan.

2. Remove the bolt connecting the bracket for these two oil lines to the block. Pull the oil lines away from the block and drain them into the pan.

3. Remove the three oil cooler mounting bolts and remove it.

4. To install, reverse the above procedure, using new sealing gaskets on the cooler lines. Torque the piping brace-to-block bolt to 20 ft. lb., and the piping-to-attachment bolts to 25 ft. lb.

ENGINE COOLING

Radiators

REMOVAL & INSTALLATION

1. On 1982–85 models, remove the cover from underneath, on the right side of the vehicle. You may want to connect a hose to the drain cock to carry coolant away

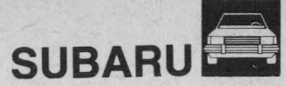

on these models. Drain the cooling system by removing the drain plug in the bottom of the radiator. After loosening the drain plug, remove the radiator cap, which will allow the coolant to drain faster.

2. Loosen the hose clamps and remove the inlet (upper) and outlet (lower) hoses from the radiator. Disconnect the inlet and outlet oil cooler lines on vehicles with automatic transmissions.

3. Remove the two radiator mounting bolts.

4. Before removing the radiator from the vehicle, disconnect the wiring harness of the following items: thermostat and thermoswitch wiring, oil pressure switch wiring, fan motor wiring, and secondary terminal of the distributor.

5. Remove the fan and motor assembly from the radiator by removing the four bolts which hold the assembly to the radiator. 4WD models also have an engine driven fan.

6. Install the radiator in the reverse order of removal.

Water Pump

REMOVAL & INSTALLATION

─────── CAUTION ───────
Do not perform this operation on a hot engine. Depress the button on the radiator cap to relieve the pressure in the cooling system.

1. Drain the cooling system by loosening the plugs on the radiator and cylinder block.

NOTE: Place a large, clean container of adequate capacity underneath the drains to catch the coolant for reuse.

2. Loosen the bolts on the alternator bracket and remove the drive belt.

3. Remove the hoses connected to the pump, which is located on the driver's side at the front of the engine, by unfastening the hose clamps.

4. Remove the bolts which secure the water pump and remove the pump assembly. On the 1800 Turbo, the timing scale plate will come off along with the top/left bolts. Note the location of the scale and then remove it with those two bolts.

Installation is performed in the reverse order of removal. Adjust the drive belt tension and replenish the cooling system to the proper level, as detailed elsewhere in this book. Run the engine and check for leaks or abnormal noise.

Thermostat

REMOVAL & INSTALLATION

─────── CAUTION ───────
Do not perform this operation on a hot engine. Depress the button on the radiator cap to relieve the pressure in the cooling system.

1. Remove the spare tire to gain working clearance. Drain about half a gallon of coolant through the radiator drain cock.

2. Remove the air cleaner assembly, by unfastening its hoses, brackets, and wing nut. On the 1800 Turbo, disconnect the air line to the turbocharger duct, and the coolant bypass hose.

3. Unfasten the bolts which secure the thermostat housing to the intake manifold. Lift the cover up, and remove the gasket.

4. Withdraw the thermostat; be sure to note its mounting position.

Installation is performed in the reverse order of removal. Use a new gasket on the thermostat housing.

─────── CAUTION ───────
Be sure that the thermostat is installed in the position observed in Step 4. The wax pellet must face downward.

EMISSION CONTROLS

Crankcase Emission Control System

1600cc Engines—1978

The closed crankcase ventilation system used on these engines is a closed system consisting of a sealed oil filler cap, hoses and an oil separator integral with the air cleaner. Blow-by gases from the crankcase are routed to the air cleaner via the two hoses, where they are pulled into the carburetor and burned with the air/fuel mixture.

The oil, which is trapped by the oil separator in the air cleaner, returns through the crankcase ventilation system hoses to the valve covers, where it is mixed with the oil used to lubricate the valve train.

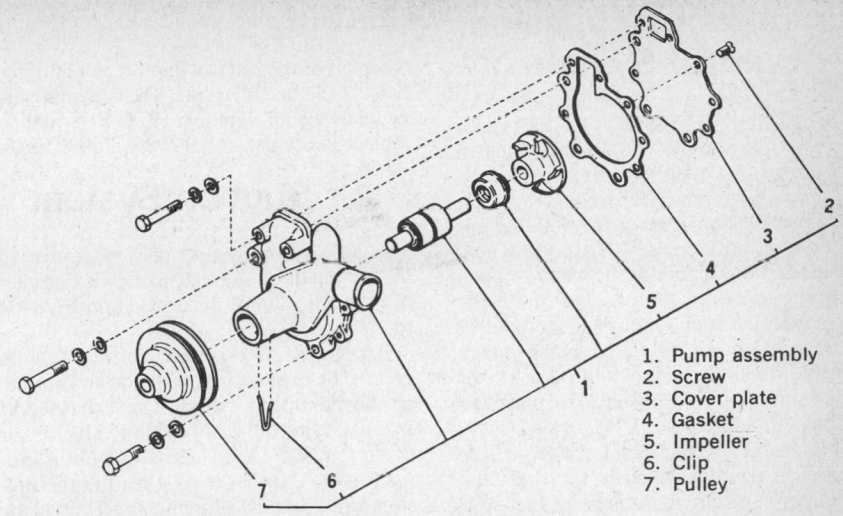

1. Pump assembly
2. Screw
3. Cover plate
4. Gasket
5. Impeller
6. Clip
7. Pulley

Exploded view of the water pump

1600cc and 1800cc Engines— 1979 and Later

These engines use a sealed crankcase emission system, which prevents blow-by gases from being emitted to the air. The system consists of a sealed oil filler cap, valve covers with an emission outlet and a fresh air inlet, connecting hoses, a PCV (positive crankcase ventilation) valve and an air cleaner.

Strong intake vacuum at part throttle sucks blow-by gases from the crankcase, through a connecting hose (from No. 2 and No. 4 valve cover) and into the intake manifold via the PCV valve. However, at wide open throttle, the increase in volume of blow-by and the decrease in manifold vacuum make the flow through the PCV valve inadequate. Under these conditions excess vapors are drawn into the air cleaner (via a connecting hose from No. 1 and No. 3 valve cover) and pass through the carburetor into the engine.

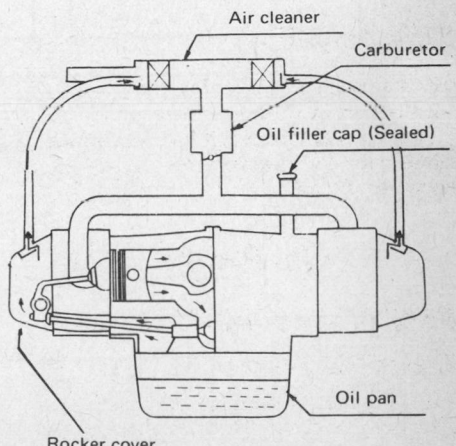

Diagram of the crankcase emission control system

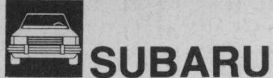

Evaporative Emission Control System

The EEC system was revised to include a vapor canister which collects the fuel vapor before it reaches the carburetor. Once in the canister, the fuel vapor is absorbed on a supply of activated charcoal particles. These particles hold the vapor until the engine idle speed increases to a point where the carburetor vacuum is sufficient to open the purge valve on the canister. With the valve open the fuel vapor is sucked out of the charcoal particles and into the intake manifold; fresh air is drawn through a filter at the bottom of the canister to displace the escaping fuel vapor.

The system also incorporates two orifices located on the line between the fuel tank and vapor canister, these prevent fuel spillage in the event of impact. On station wagons (1978–79), two small reserve tanks on both sides of the fuel tank are employed to prevent liquid fuel from flowing into the air cleaner in case of an abrupt stop, etc. California models (1978–79) have a check valve on the line between the canister and the intake manifold to prevent a build-up of vapor in the manifold when the engine is stopped. 1980 and later California models have a carburetor vapor line connecting the float chamber and canister, as well as a tank vapor line. The (1978–79) 49 state (high altitude) models employ a two-way valve between the fuel tank and canister. It functions to control the flow of fuel vapor to the canister according to pressure in the fuel tank.

SERVICE

Keep all of the lines in good repair and free from cracks and blockage. The system should be relatively air tight. On 1978–1979 models replace the canister filter every 25,000 miles.

Air Suction System

The air suction system is very similar to the air injection system, except it does not use an air pump. It is used on 1978–84 models.

To operate, the system utilizes vacuum created by exhaust gas pulsation and normal intake manifold vacuum. Each exhaust port is connected to the air suction valve by air suction manifolds. When a vacuum is created in the exhaust ports a reed in the suction valve opens allowing fresh air to be sucked through the air cleaner and silencer (pre-1980 models) or the secondary air cleaner (1980 models) and into the exhaust ports. When there is pressure rather than vacuum in the exhaust ports, the reed in the air suction valve closes, preventing the flow of exhaust gases.

The fresh air sucked through the air suction valve is used for oxidation of HC and CO in the exhaust passages and partly for combustion in the cylinders.

1982–85 models incorporate an electronically controlled solenoid that either deactivates this system entirely, or partially a short time after the engine is started cold. The only way to determine that there is a problem with this system is to remove the solenoid and test it electrically. See the test procedure below.

These models also incorporate an Air Suction Valve which can be disassembled and serviced. See the procedure below for service.

Port Liner—from 1980

Various models have an exhaust port liner made from stainless steel plate built into the cylinder head as one unit.

The port liner has a built in air layer which decreases heat transfer to the cylinder head while keeping the exhaust port at a higher temperature. The insulation of the exhaust port helps oxidation of residual HC and CO with the help of the remaining air in the exhaust gases.

Anti-afterburning Valve—from 1980

The anti-afterburning valve prevents afterburning that occurs on cold starts. Below about 50 degrees centigrade the temperature valve has an open passage connecting the afterburning valve with the intake manifold via a vacuum line. The vacuum line remains opened and the afterburning valve in operation until the coolant temperature becomes hot enough to shut off the vacuum and override the afterburning system.

REMOVAL & INSTALLATION

Silencer—Early Models

1. Loosen the sleeve nut which mounts the silencer to the top of the air suction valve.

2. Pull the silencer from the hose connecting it to the air cleaner.

NOTE: Be careful not to lose the small tapered sleeve below the sleeve nut when lifting off the silencer.

Installation is the reverse of removal.

Secondary Air Cleaner—Late Models

On late model EA71 and EA81 engines, the air flowing to the air suction valve passes through a secondary air cleaner instead of the carburetor air cleaner and silencer. Do not attempt to clean the filter element. Replace the cleaner element every 30 months or 30,000 miles, whichever occurs first.

Air Suction Valve

1. Remove the air silencer or secondary air cleaner.

2. Remove the four bolts which run through the air suction valve, mounting it between the two air suction manifolds.

3. Pull the suction valve from between the manifolds. Take care not to damage the reeds.

NOTE: If the gaskets on the sides of the air suction valve are worn or damaged, replace them.

Installation is the reverse of removal.

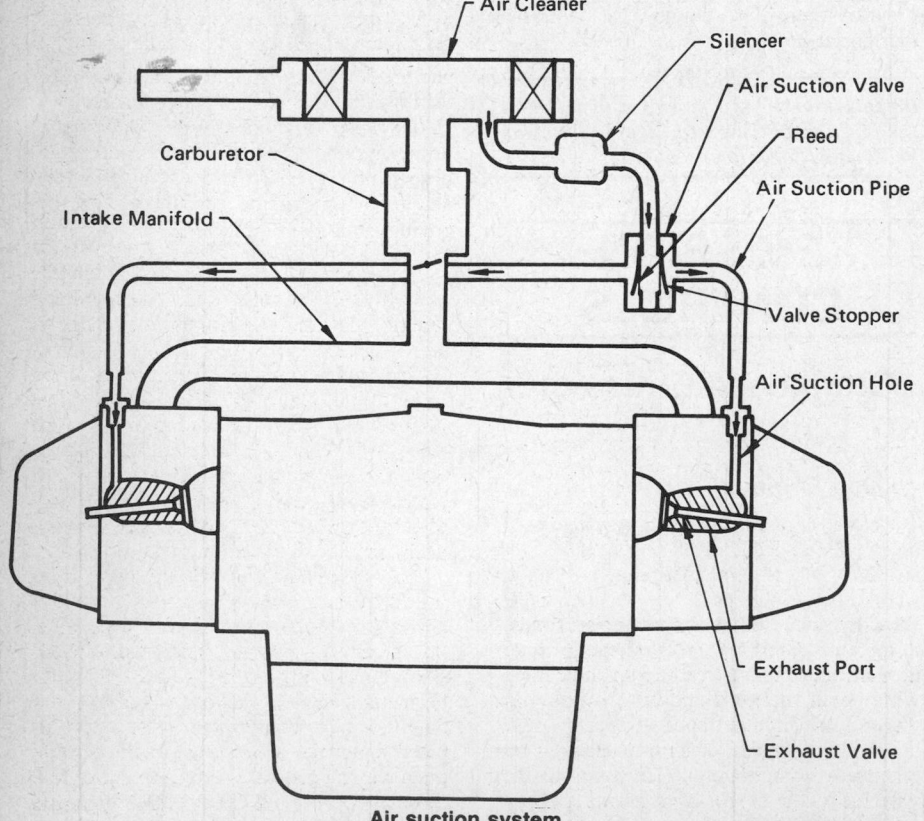

Air suction system

Air Suction Manifolds

1. Remove the air silencer or secondary air cleaner and the air suction valve.

2. Remove the clamp which supports the right side suction manifold by loosening the mounting bolt.

3. Loosen the threaded sleeves (two on each manifold) which mount the suction manifolds to the engine. Lift off the manifolds.

Installation is the reverse of removal. Remember to lightly oil the threaded sleeves before mounting the suction manifold to the engine.

TESTING

Solenoid Valve (1982–84 Only)

1. Remove the valve from the engine. Using an ohmmeter, test the resistance between the electrical terminals. It must be 32.7–39.9 ohms. If not, replace it.

2. If resistance is o.k., check the resistance between each terminal and the solenoid body. It must be 1,000 ohms or more in both places, or the valve should be replaced.

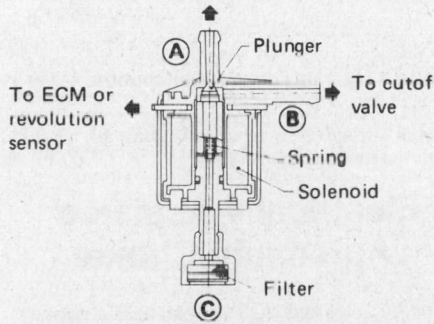

The air suction solenoid for 1984 models—1982–83 models work similarly

3. Apply 12 volts between the plus and minus terminals (positive battery terminal to positive solenoid terminal). When current is on, you should be able to blow through the solenoid from A to B. When it is off, it must seal off tight from A to B and open from B to C. Otherwise, replace the solenoid.

DISASSEMBLY

Air Suction Valve (1982–85 only)

1. Remove the three screws, and separate the control valve assembly, seat, and reed valve cover.

2. Separate the reed valve assembly by pulling it and its gasket from the inside of the valve cover.

3. Remove the O-ring from the control valve assembly.

4. Now, inspect the valve parts as follows:

    A. Apply vacuum to the vacuum inlet. The valve should retract fully. Release the vacuum. The valve should extend fully.

    B. Check the O-ring for cracks or other damage.

    C. Inspect the reed valve gasket for damage. Then, clean the reed valve in a safe, non-volatile solvent and inspect it for any damage such as waviness, cracks or dents, or rust.

5. Replace parts that are damaged, reassemble the valve in reverse order, and reinstall it.

MAINTENANCE

1. Check the air suction hose and manifolds for cracks, damage, looseness or leakage.

2. Check the reed valve for cracks or abnormal projections. Check the rubber seat for cracks.

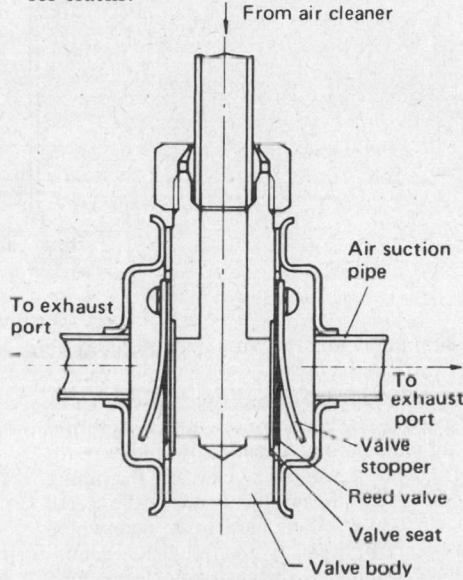

Cross section of reed valve assembly

Anti-Afterburning Valve

The anti-afterburning valve prevents afterburning that occurs on cold starts. Below about 50°C, the temperature valve has an open passage connecting the afterburning valve with the intake manifold via a vacuum line. The vacuum line remains opened and the afterburning valve in operation until the coolant temperature becomes hot enough to shut off the vacuum and override the afterburning system.

Coasting Bypass System

To control the HC emissions while the vehicle is in the coasting or decelerating mode, a controlled amount of air/fuel mixture is channelled through the coasting bypass passage in the carburetor.

The high engine vacuum reacts on a bypass valve diaphragm, opening a vacuum passage to the servo valve on the carburetor, which in turn opens a metered passage from the carburetor air horn to the section of the throttle bore below the secondary throttle plate.

As engine vacuum drops on acceleration, the bypass valve closes the passage to the servo valve and the carburetor returns to its normal function.

Engine Modification System

The principle of this system is not only to obtain correct air/fuel mixture while the vehicle is decelerating, but also to promote complete combustion by retarding the ignition timing, thus reducing the amount of emissions released into the atmosphere.

While the vehicle is decelerating, the primary throttle valve is closed, causing a high vacuum in the intake manifold. This vacuum is conducted through a vacuum control valve and on to the carburetor where a bypass jet is opened and extra mixture is allowed to enter the venturi below the throttle plates. This enriches the mixture and promotes cleaner combustion.

The vacuum is also routed to the distributor vacuum retard unit.

There is an anti-dieseling solenoid mounted opposite the float bowl on the carburetor. This switch prevents the engine from dieseling when the ignition switch is turned off. When the ignition switch is turned off, an electromagnet in the switch is also cut off. A spring inside the housing forces a plunger into position, blocking the fuel passages leading to the opening below the throttle plates. When the ignition switch is turned on, it energizes the electromagnet in the switch and pulls the plunger out of the fuel passage, allowing fuel to reach the opening below the throttle plates.

On 1982–85 models, this system operates the vacuum advance diaphragm of the distributor via a thermal-vacuum valve. The valve opens the entire vacuum advance circuit to atmospheric pressure in a certain temperature range. This range (measured at the intake manifold cooling water circuit) is 59°F. to 95°F. on all but the turbo-charged engine. On the 1800 Turbo, this range is 113°F. to 131°F.

The valve simultaneously activates the EGR valve so that when vacuum advance is turned off the EGR valve does not work either. If this system is operating improperly, the car would exhibit very poor operation when cold. Symptoms such as very poor fuel mileage and performance with the engine hot, or slow warmup may also occur.

The system draws its vacuum supply from a port in the carburetor (or throttle body) above the throttle, so vacuum advance is not present at normal hot-engine idle speed, but begins as the throttle is opened past idle. On certain models, advance is also desirable at idle. These incorporate a port located under the lower edge of the throttle plate which becomes ineffective above idle throttle opening. A check valve connects this port to the rest of the system. These

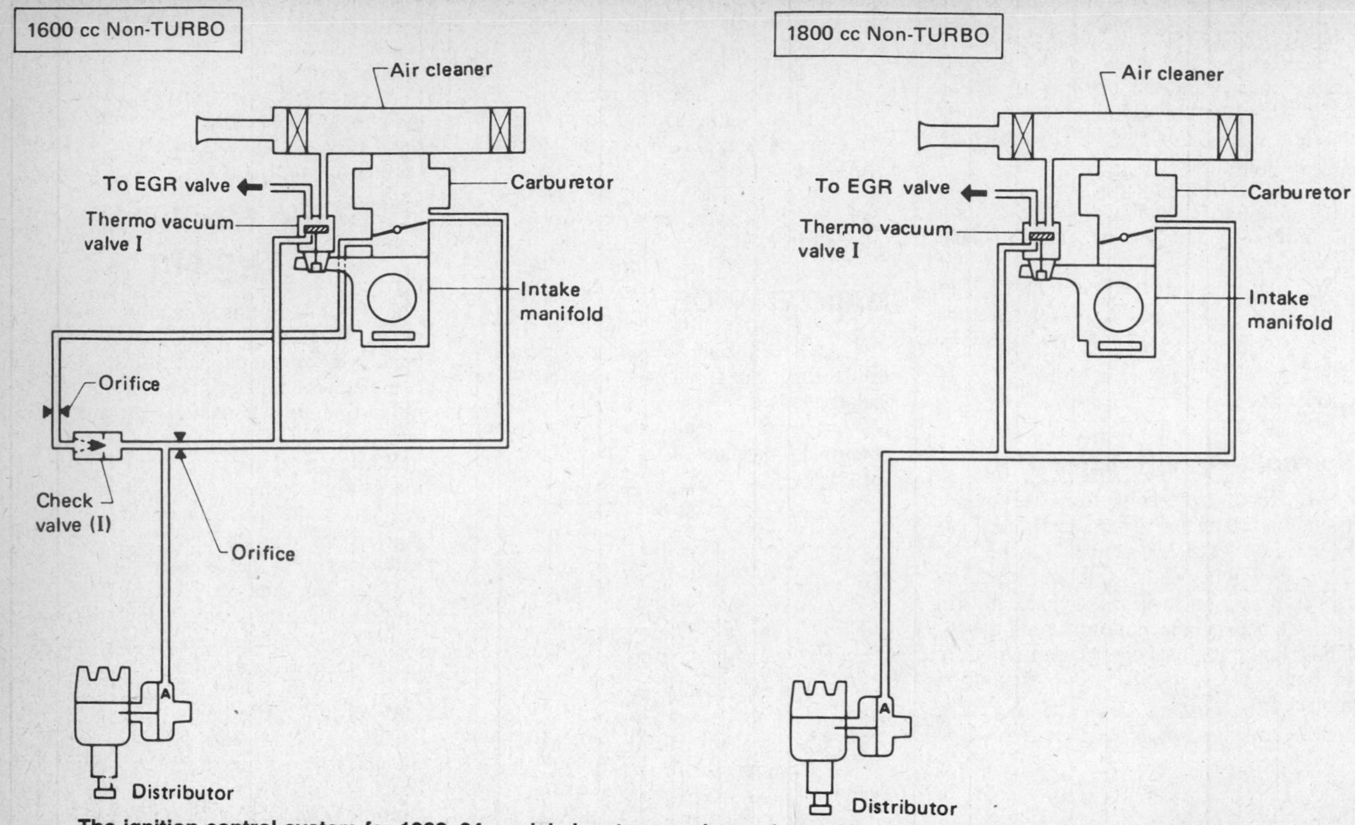

1600 cc Non-TURBO

- Air cleaner
- Carburetor
- To EGR valve
- Thermo vacuum valve I
- Intake manifold
- Orifice
- Check valve (I)
- Orifice
- Distributor

1800 cc Non-TURBO

- Air cleaner
- Carburetor
- To EGR valve
- Thermo vacuum valve I
- Intake manifold
- Distributor

The ignition control system for 1982–84 models has two versions, pictured here. See text for exact model delineation.

models are: 1800 Turbo, 1982 1600 2-door Hatchback GL (5MT), 4-door GL (5MT) and Hardtop GLF (5MT); and all 1983–85 1600 cc models. If the check valve fails, symptoms would include slow or erratic idle and, possibly, a slight hesitation.

To check the function of the thermal vacuum valve, drain a little coolant, remove the air cleaner, disconnect hoses, and remove the valve from the intake manifold. Cap off the center (EGR) port and connect hoses to the upper and lower ports. These hoses must seal tightly so no water will get into the top part of the valve. The tops of the hoses must also stay dry.

Immerse the valve in a pan of water that also contains a 200°F. thermometer. If necessary, use ice to cool the water below 59° F. unless your car is an 1800 Turbo. Heat the water while blowing into the air cleaner hose connection. The valve should seal at first as the temperature passes the 59°F. mark, or as it passes the 113°F. mark on the Turbo, the valve should open and you should be able to blow air through it freely. Again, at 104°F (or 131°F. on the Turbo), the valve should seal tightly. If it fails any of these tests, replace the valve. Coat the valve with sealer before screwing it back into the intake manifold.

To check for proper functioning of the check valve, install a timing light and idle the engine after it is fully warmed up. Accelerate the engine up to about 2,000 rpm and then slowly return the throttle to normal idle position while watching the point at which the ignition fires. The timing should

remain fully advanced right down to idle speed. If the check valve is stuck shut, timing will retard fairly suddenly at idle speed. If the check valve is stuck open, the timing will abruptly retard slightly above idle speed.

If the valve fails these tests, note which end of the valve is connected to vacuum lines leading to the distributor, and then pull off the vacuum lines on either end of the valve. To confirm your test results, blow through the valve in the direction of flow from the carburetor lower port toward the distributor. Air should flow freely. Then, turn the valve around and blow through it in the other direction. The valve should seal tightly. Replace the valve if *either* test is failed.

REMOVAL & INSTALLATION

NOTE: Remove the spare tire and the air cleaner assembly from the engine compartment to gain access to the various components of the engine modifications system.

Vacuum Control Valve

1. Detach the vacuum hoses from the distributor retard unit, carburetor by-pass servo diaphragm, automatic choke main diaphragm (if so equipped), and the intake manifold.

2. Remove the bolts which secure the vacuum control valve to the intake manifold.

3. Lift the valve assembly off the manifold.

Valve installation is performed in the re-

verse order of removal. Be sure to route the vacuum hoses correctly.

Electrically Assisted Automatic Choke

The vacuum automatic choke uses a choke cap containing a heating element to speed up choke valve opening and reduce CO emissions during warm-up. The heating element gets its power from a special tap on the voltage regulator, when the ignition is on and the engine running.

TESTING

1. Disconnect the choke lead from the voltage regulator.

2. Connect an ohmmeter between the lead that you just disconnected and a good ground. The ohmmeter should read about 9 ohms.

3. Replace the choke cap if the reading shows an opened (no resistance) or shorted (infinite resistance) heating coil.

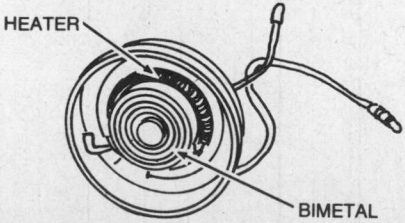

HEATER

BIMETAL

Choke cap with bi-metal spring and heating element

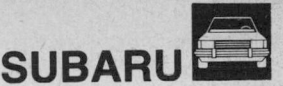

Carburetor Dashpot

ADJUSTMENT

1. Be sure that the throttle valve is in the idle (closed) position.

2. The dashpot stem should be able to move about 0.16 in. beyond the throttle lever's idle position.

3. If the stem does not move the correct distance, adjust the dashpot, by loosening its locknut and rotating the dashpot until the correct amount of movement is obtained.

4. Tighten the locknut and recheck dashpot stem movement.

Exhaust Gas Recirculation (EGR) System

An exhaust gas recirculation (EGR) system is used to reduce NO_x (oxides of nitrogen) emissions by lowering peak flame temperature during combustion. A small portion of the exhaust gases are routed into the intake manifold via a vacuum-operated EGR control valve.

TESTING

EGR System

1. Start the engine and allow it to reach normal operating temperature.

2. Increase the engine speed to 3000–3500 rpm (no load). The valve shaft should move upward. Note that on 1983 and later California cars, the EGR system does not function for the first eight minutes of engine operation.

3. Decrease the engine speed to idle, the valve shaft should go down.

4. If the valve shaft fails to raise in Step 2, check the vacuum lines, connections, and the carburetor throttle vacuum port. Replace any clogged or damaged hoses, and clean the throttle port if it is clogged.

5. Connect the EGR valve vacuum hose directly to the throttle port on th carburetor. Speed the engine up and return it to idle as in Step 2 and 3. If the valve works, the fault lies in the vacuum solenoid valve or the temperature switch.

6. If the EGR valve doesn't work, perform the following EGR valve checks:

a. Remove the EGR valve from the intake manifold.

b. Plug the vacuum inlet on the top of the valve diaphragm.

c. Depress and release the pintle (valve plunger) several times.

d. The pintle should remain depressed as long as the vacuum inlet is plugged. If it doesn't, the diaphragm is leaking and the valve assembly must be replaced.

e. If the valve stem appears to be stuck, clean the pintle with a wire brush or spark plug cleaning machine.

f. Install the valve and retest it.

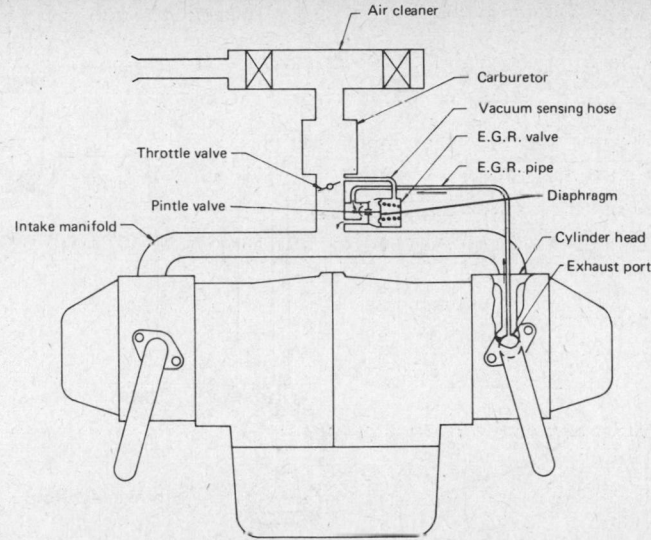

Exhaust gas recirculation system

Vacuum Solenoid Valve and Coolant Temperature Switch

1. Disconnect the vacuum solenoid leads.

2. Connect the solenoid directly to a 12-volt power source. The solenoid should click.

3. If the solenoid is working properly and everything else in the system is in proper operating order, replace the coolant temperature switch.

Thermal-Vacuum Valve (1982 and later)

This valve actuates both vacuum spark advance and the EGR valve. It turns the EGR valve off until the engine is warmed up to help ensure smooth cold-engine performance.

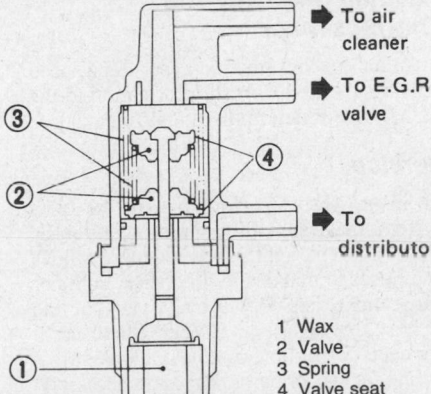

1 Wax
2 Valve
3 Spring
4 Valve seat

The thermal-vacuum valve as used on 1982–84 EGR systems

Drain some coolant out of the system, disconnect the vacuum hoses, and remove the valve from the intake manifold.

Cap off the top (air cleaner) port and install hoses onto the other two ports to keep the top of the valve dry. Then, immerse the valve in cool water. Use a thermometer to measure water temperature. The valve must be open when water passes 68°F. Blow into either hose and warm the water (for example, on a stove). Now, remove the water from heat and chill with ice cubes. The valve must close as the temperature drops below 50°F. If both tests are not passed, replace the valve.

Hot Air Control System

The hot air control system consists of the air cleaner, the air stove on the exhaust pipe and the air intake hose connecting the air cleaner and air stove. The air cleaner is equipped with an air control valve which maintains the temperature of the air being drawn into the carburetor at 100°–127° F to reduce HC emission when the underhood temperature is below 100° F. This system should be inspected every 12,000 miles.

TEMPERATURE SENSOR

Removal and Installation

1. Using pliers, flatten the clip securing the vacuum hose to the sensor vacuum pipe.

2. Disconnect the hose from the sensor.

3. Remove the clip from the sensor vacuum pipe and remove the sensor body from the air cleaner.

NOTE: The gasket is glued to the air cleaner and should not be removed.

4. To install reverse the removal procedure.

VACUUM MOTOR

Removal and Installation

1. Remove the screws securing the vacuum motor to the air cleaner.

2. Disconnect the valve shaft, attached to the vacuum motor diaphragm, at the air control valve, and remove the vacuum motor from the air cleaner.

3. To install reverse the removal procedure.

C785

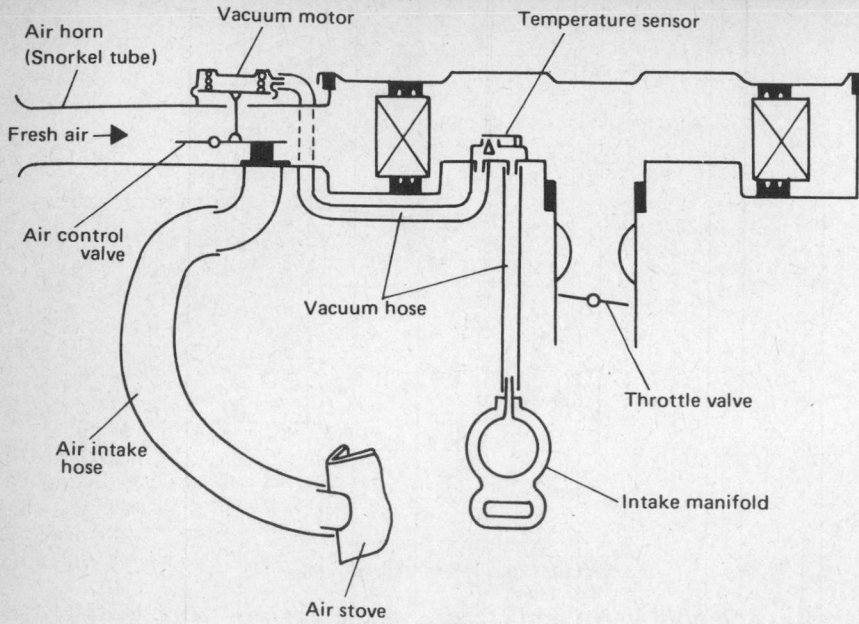

Hot air control system

ECC System

An electronically controlled carburetor (ECC) is used on late models in conjunction with a three–way catalyst, exhaust gas recirculation, air injection, an ignition control system and (in some cases) a high altitude kit.

The three-way catalyst reduces HC, CO and NOx in exhaust gases and permits simultaneous oxidation. The concentration of exhaust gas pollutants varies with the air/fuel mixture (ratio).

The air/fuel ratio needs to be controlled to a value within a very narrow range to purify the exhaust gas components. The ECC system is employed to control the air/fuel ratio.

The system includes: an oxygen sensor, an electronic control module (ECM), a duty solenoid and a carburetor. The components provide a feedback system to control the air/fuel ratio during operation by supplying a measured amount of air into the carburetor air bleeders. To avoid feedback during certain driving conditions, vacuum switches, a thermosensor and an engine speed sensing circuit are provided.

ECC COMPONENT FUNCTIONS

Oxygen (O₂) Sensor

The oxygen sensor is installed on the exhaust manifold and provides information to the Electronic Control Module (ECM) that pertains to the amount of pollutants in the exhaust gases caused by an over-rich or lean air/fuel ratio.

Electronic Control Module (ECM)

Upon receiving information from the O_2 sensor (value of the air/fuel mixture) the ECM signals the duty solenoid to allow either more or less air into the carburetor to maintain the correct air/fuel mixture.

Duty Solenoid

The duty solenoid(s) is (are) controlled by the ECM. At a given signal, the duty solenoid will admit more or less air to the carburetor; maintaining the proper air/fuel ratio.

NOTE: On late models equipped with an Hitachi carburetor, two duty solenoids are installed on the exhaust manifold. Models equipped with a C-W (Carter-Weber) carburetor have the duty solenoid mounted on the carburetor.

Vacuum Switches and Thermosensor

Vacuum switches, thermosensors (and speed sensing circuits) furnish information to the ECM to help determine the air/fuel ratio.

Service

To insure proper performance of the ECC system, make sure all vacuum and air hoses are connected tightly. Check the air lines and hoses to make sure no cracks, splits or hardening exists. Replace any vacuum line or hose that is suspect. Check all electrical connects for tightness. Check all electrical wiring for cuts or burns. Repair as necessary.

FUEL SYSTEM

Fuel Filter

All Subarus use a cartridge fuel filter, located in the fuel pump-to-carburetor fuel line. The filter is the disposable type which cannot be cleaned.

To replace the filter cartridge:
1. Loosen, but do not remove, the nuts which secure the two hose clamps located at either end of the filter.
2. Work the hoses off the filter necks.
3. Snap the filter out of its mounting bracket, if so equipped.
4. Throw the old filter away.

NOTE: When removing the old filter, be careful not to allow any fuel to drip onto hot engine components. Installation is the reverse of removal. Be sure that the hose clamps are tightened securely.

Fuel Pump

The electric fuel pump is located in the engine compartment, mounted on the right side. It is to be replaced as an assembly if defective.

REMOVAL & INSTALLATION

Normally Aspirated Engines

1. Remove the fuel delivery hoses from the fuel pump.
2. Tag and disconnect the fuel pump wiring.
3. Loosen the fuel pump mounting nuts and remove the fuel pump from the vehicle. Be careful not to lose any washers or cushions.
4. Install in the reverse order of removal. Be sure the ground wire does not contact the pump body, or the unit may vibrate. Push-fit the fuel lines at least ¾ in. over the fittings and secure tightly with hose clamps.

1800 Turbo

1. Disconnect the wiring connector to the fuel pump. Then, crank the engine for at least five seconds. If the engine starts, let it run until it stalls. Then, turn off the ignition.

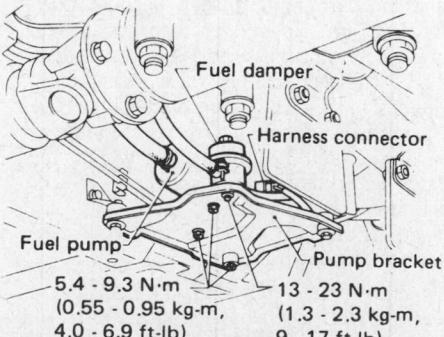

Fuel pump and damper on the 1800 Turbo wagon

2. Raise the car and support it securely. Devise a clamp for the thicker hose leading to the pump and clamp it off a few inches from the nipple on the pump. This will prevent the fuel from running out of the tank while the pump is disconnected.
3. Being careful not to bend the hose sharply, loosen the hose clamp and discon-

nect the large hose leading into the pump. Do the same with the outlet from the damper.

4. Then, remove the three pump bracket mounting bolts and remove the pump and damper.

5. If you want to check whether or not the pump operates, you can connect a 12-volt power supply via the harness connector. But, be sure to make the connections that actually start the pump well away from the pump in case spilled fuel is present or fuel comes out when the pump starts up. Don't run the pump for more than a few seconds.

6. If it is necessary to replace the pump, disconnect the clamp and hose, unbolt it, and remove.

7. Install in reverse order. Make sure all hoses are in good condition (no cracks), or replace them. If the connector for the hose between the tank and pump has a thicker portion to limit the position of the hose, make sure to install the hose until it rests against the limit. Otherwise, make sure the hose is at least 1 in. past the end of the connector. Make sure the clamp is installed behind the end of the hose but well past the first bulge on the connector. Be careful not to lose the rubber mount.

TESTING

Check all hoses for leaks and tightness. Make sure all wiring connections are tight. Disconnect the fuel line (filter to pump) from the filter and place a finger over the hose to check for suction.

Carburetor
REMOVAL & INSTALLATION

1978–81

1. Remove the air cleaner emission control system hoses, mounting bracket screws, wing nut, and lift the air cleaner assembly off the carburetor.

2. Disconnect the fuel lines from the carburetor.

3. Unfasten the vacuum hoses from the servo diaphragm, automatic choke diaphragms, distributor, and the EGR port (if so equipped).

4. Disconnect the anti-dieseling switch and automatic choke heater electrical leads.

5. Remove the accelerator cable from the throttle lever.

6. Unfasten the 4 nuts which secure the carburetor and take it off the intake manifold. Cover the hole in the intake manifold, to prevent anything from falling in.

Installation is the reverse of removal.

1982 and later

1. Remove the air cleaner.

2. Disconnect fuel supply and return lines at the carburetor.

3. Disconnect the carburetor vent hose for the ECC system.

4. Disconnect remaining vacuum hoses to distributor, etc.

---

5. Disconnect the EGR tube.

On the Hitachi carburetor

A. disconnect the ignition retard, if applicable.

B. Disconnect vacuum hoses for solenoid valves, the main diaphragm, and, on high-altitude carburetors, the secondary main air bleed.

C. Disconnect the duty solenoid valve connector on those models so equipped.

6. On both types of carburetor, disconnect the harness connectors and then disconnect the accelerator cable from the throttle lever.

7. Drain some coolant out of the radiator so as to drain water out of the water-heated throttle bore.

8. Remove the four mounting nuts on the Hitachi or two nuts on the C-W, and remove the carburetor. On the C-W, disconnect the vent hose and remove its connector with the spacer and gasket. Cover the intake manifold opening.

9. Installation is the reverse of removal. Make sure to adjust the throttle linkage.

OVERHAUL

For all carburetor overhaul procedures, please refer to "Carburetor Overhaul" in the Unit Repair section.

PRIMARY/SECONDARY THROTTLE LINKAGE ADJUSTMENT

Hitachi

1. With the carburetor removed from the engine, operate the linkage so that the

---

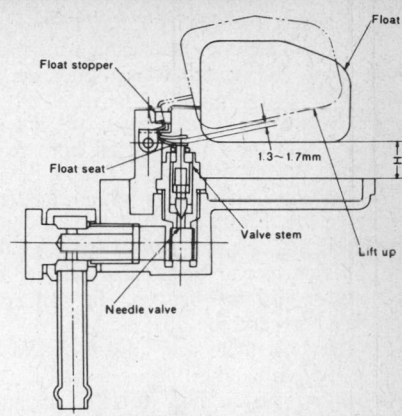

Float adjustment—Hitachi

connecting rod contacts the groove on the end of the secondary actuating lever.

2. Measure the clearance between the lower end of the primary throttle valve and its bore. It should be about 0.24 in. for all models.

3. Adjust the clearance by bending the connecting rod.

4. Check that the linkage operates smoothly.

FLOAT AND FUEL LEVEL ADJUSTMENT

Hitachi

On models with a sight glass on the carburetor float bowl, the fuel should be level (within $\frac{1}{16}$ in.) with the dot on the glass when the engine is running.

The float level may be adjusted with the carburetor installed on the engine:

1. Disconnect the accelerator pump actuating rod from the pump lever.

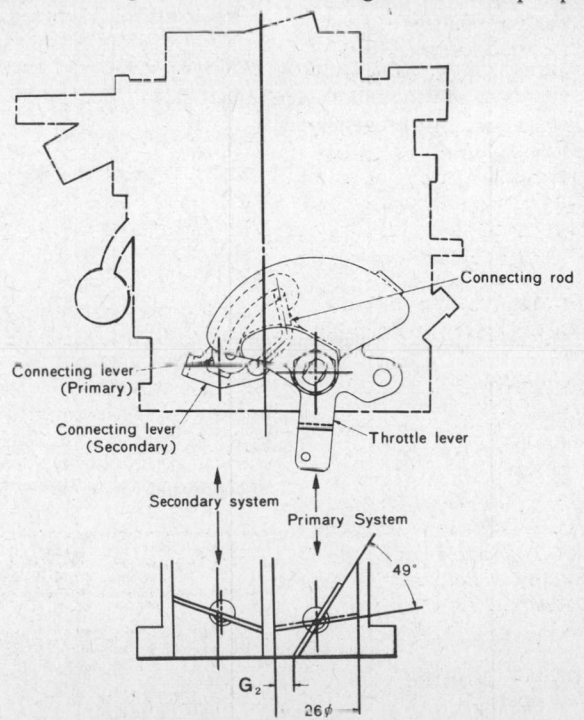

$G_2 = 6.0$mm when primary throttle valve opening is 49° from full close.
(EA63A)

Throttle linkage adjustment—Hitachi

2. Remove the throttle return spring.

3. Disconnect the choke cable from the choke lever, and remove it from the spring hanger.

4. Remove the spring hanger, the choke bellcrank, and the remaining air horn retaining screws.

5. Lift the air horn slightly, disconnect the choke connecting rod, and remove the air horn.

6. Invert the air horn (float up), and measure the distance between the surface of the air horn and the float.

7. Bend the float arm until the clearance is approximately 0.41 in.

8. Invert the air horn to its installed position and measure the distance between the float arm and the needle valve stem. This dimension should be 0.050–0.065 in., and is adjusted by bending the float stops.

Carter–Weber

1. Remove the air horn gasket, then position the float at the air horn.

2. Turn the air horn upside down to free the float.

3. Measure the distance between the surface of the air horn and the float. Bend portion (A) to adjust.

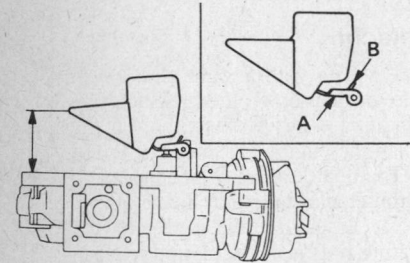

Float setting—Carter/Weber

4. Turn the air horn right side up to lower the float. Measure the distance from the lower surface of the air horn to the tip end of the float and make sure it is not less than 1.50 in. Bend portion (B) to adjust.

NOTE: The needle must be free while adjusting the distance.

FAST IDLE ADJUSTMENT

Hitachi

1. With the carburetor removed from the engine, set the fast idle cam adjusting lever on the fourth step of the fast idle cam.

2. Check to be sure that the choke valve is fully closed.

3. Measure the clearance between the lower edge of the primary throttle valve and its bore. The clearance should be as specified in the "Fast Idle" chart, below.

4. If the clearance is incorrect, turn the fast idle adjusting screw to bring it within specifications. Turning the screw *in* increases the throttle clearance and vice versa.

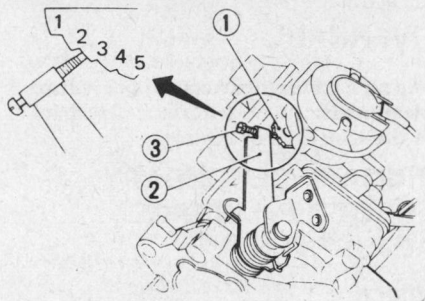

1. Cam
2. Fast idle lever
3. Fast idle adjusting screw

Fast idle adjustment—Carter/Weber

FAST IDLE

Model	Primary Throttle-to-Bore Clearance
1978–79	0.047 in. ①
1980–82 all auto. trans.	0.060 in.
manual trans. (exc. C-W)	0.050 in. ②
1983–84	
DCP 306-17	.0386 in.
DCP 306-18	
DCP 306-21	.0480 in.
DCP 306-19	
DCP 306-22	

① California models and 49 state high altitude models—0.060 in.
② HB-STD, HB-DL, SD-DL, and HT-DL use 0.041 in.

Carter–Weber

NOTE: Before adjusting the fast idle make sure the idle speed and mixture have been adjusted properly.

1. With the engine at operating temperature and the choke fully open, place the fast idle lever on the 3rd step of the cam.

2. Turn the fast idle adjusting screw until the speed is 2000 rpm.

AUTOMATIC CHOKE ADJUSTMENT

Hitachi

1. Adjust the fast idle as detailed above, and perform the adjustments which follow, in the sequence given.

2. Pull the main choke diaphragm lever as far as it will go to the left and measure the clearance between the upper end of the choke valve and its bore with a wire gauge. The clearance should be 0.046–0.055 in. Adjust, as necessary, by bending the diaphragm-to-choke connecting rod.

3. Apply 8–9 in. Hg of vacuum to the main diaphragm, it should operate the choke valve. If it does not, replace the diaphragm with a new one.

4. Place the fast idle cam adjusting lever on the highest step of the fast idle cam. Measure the clearance between the upper end of the choke valve and its bore. The clearance should be 0.026–0.037 in. for 1978–80 cars and 0.039–0.054 for later models. On earlier models, carefully bend (turn) the fast idle cam to obtain the correct clearance, as necessary. To obtain the clearance, bend the cam clockwise; to decrease it, bend the cam counterclockwise. On later models turn the adjusting screw.

5. On models with an adjustable choke cover, loosen the 3 choke cap securing screws, and match the line on it up with the longest line on the choke coil housing. Tighten the retaining screws.

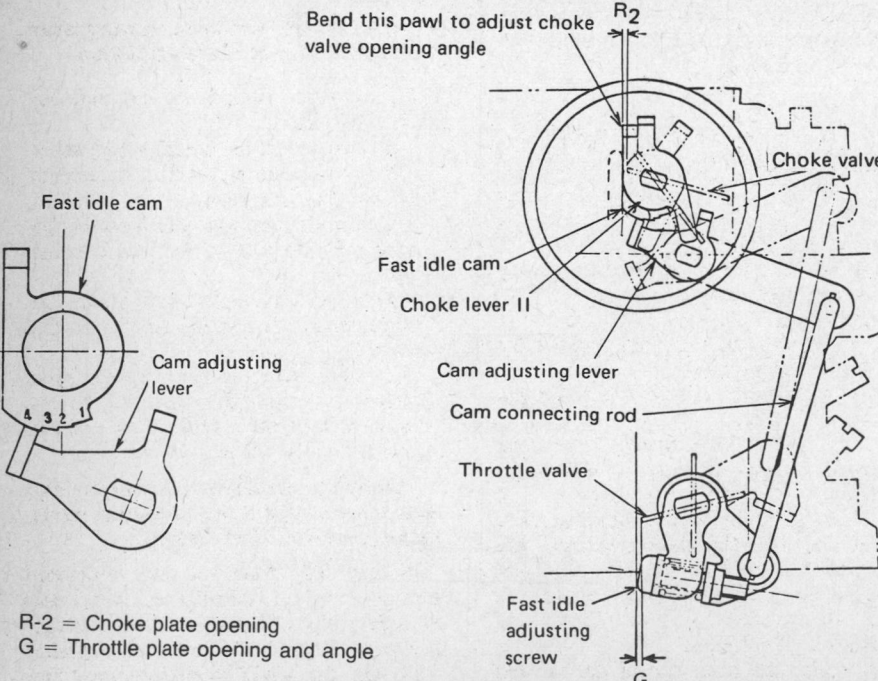

R-2 = Choke plate opening
G = Throttle plate opening and angle

Fast idle adjustment—Hitachi

Do not loosen the screw which secures the choke lever.

6. Fit the tang on the bi-metal lever, which is connected to the auxiliary diaphragm, against the stop in the choke coil housing. Pull the setting piston of the auxiliary diaphragm back and, with the piston in this position, tighten the compensator adjusting screw so that it contacts the tang on the bi-metal lever; the gap should be 0.34 in.

7. Apply vacuum from an outside source to the auxiliary diaphragm. It should take 6.9–9.2 in. Hg of vacuum to operate the diaphragm. To adjust the vacuum setting, bend the diaphragm rod. Vacuum is reduced when the rod is bent to shorten it and increased when the rod is bent to lengthen it.

NOTE: When the setting piston is released, there should be no clearance between the tang on the bi-metal lever and the stop on the coil housing. If they don't contact, the bi-metal lever has been bent too much.

Fuel Injectors

For further information on the fuel injection system, please refer to "Fuel Injection" in the Unit Repair section.

REMOVAL & INSTALLATION

1. Disconnect fuel lines. Remove the injector by screwing it out of the manifold with a Phillips screwdriver.
2. Install in reverse order.

TRANSAXLE

REMOVAL & INSTALLATION

All Models Except 1800 Turbo

NOTE: The transaxle can be removed separately from the car.

1. Open the hood and secure it.
2. Remove the spare wheel from engine compartment, if installed.
3. Disconnect the battery cable from the negative terminal.
4. Remove the spare wheel supporter.
5. On MT (manual transaxle), disengage the clutch cable as follows:
   a. Remove the clutch cable return spring.
   b. Remove both the lock nut and adjusting nut from the clutch cable.
   c. Unfasten the clip which retains the outer cable.
   d. Detach the rubber boot.
6. On AT (automatic transaxle), disconnect the diaphragm vacuum hose.
7. Disconnect the speedometer cable from the transmission. Unfasten the clip on the speedometer cable.

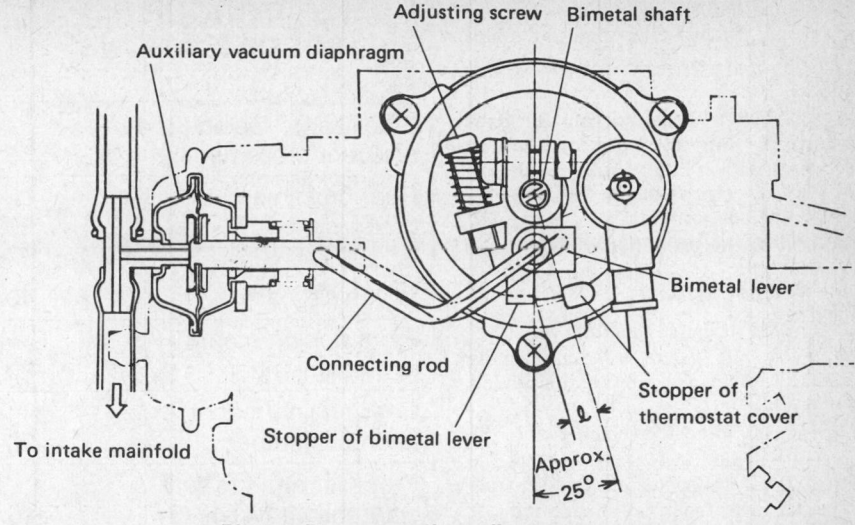

Bi-metal compensation adjustment—Hitachi

8. Disconnect the following wiring connections.
   a. Back-up lamp switch connector
   b. Ground cable (on the car body)
   c. Starter harness (black and white)
9. On AT, remove the four bolts connecting the torque converter to the drive plate through the timing hole.

NOTE: Be careful that the bolts do not fall into the converter housing.

10. On AT, disconnect the oil cooler hose from the transmission. Plug the lines.
11. Remove the starter with the battery cable, and put the starter on the bulkhead.
12. Remove the upper bolts which secure the engine to the transmission; loosen the lower nuts.
13. Loosen the nut which retains the pitching stopper to the transmission side, and tighten the nut by an equal amount on the engine side. Slightly tilt the engine backward in order to facilitate removal of the transmission.

NOTE: Do not loosen or tighten the nut more than 10mm.

14. On the 4WD model, separate both the 4WD selector system and gearshift system from the transmission as follows:
   a. Remove the hand brake tray cover, and then the hand brake cover.
   b. Remove the rod cover.
   c. Set the drive selector lever at the "4WD" position.
   d. Remove the nut connecting the two rods.
   e. Remove the two nuts to separate the rod and drive selector lever from the plate.
   f. Remove the boot installing screws.
   g. Remove the nut connecting the gearshift lever with the lever, and pull up the gearshift lever with the boot.
15. Disconnect O_2 sensor harness and unclamp it, if equipped.
16. Raise the front end of the car and support with jackstands.

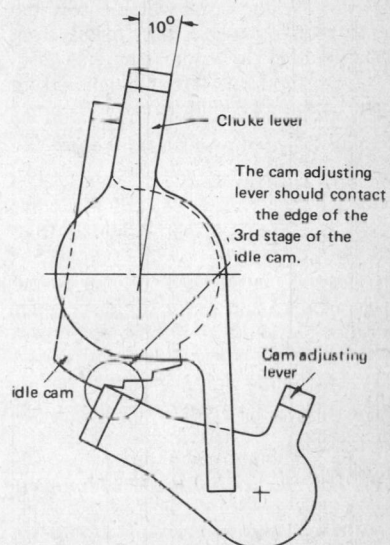

Automatic choke fast idle adjusting lever on the third step of the fast idle cam

17. Remove the front exhaust pipe assembly as follows:
   a. Disconnect the hot air intake hose.
   b. Loosen the nuts which secure the exhaust pipe assembly.
   c. Remove the bolts which secure the front exhaust pipe to the rear exhaust pipe.
   d. Remove the bolts which secure the front exhaust pipe to the bracket on the car body.
   e. Supporting the front exhaust pipe assembly, remove the nuts from the exhaust port of the engine. The exhaust pipe assembly can now be removed.

NOTE: Be careful not to strike the oxygen sensor against any adjacent parts during removal, if equipped.

18. On AT, drain out the automatic transmission fluid and then disconnect the oil supply pipe. Take care not to damage the O-ring. Drain the MT transmission fluid.
19. On the 4WD models remove the transmission shield.

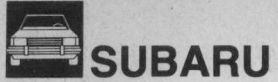

20. On the 4WD model, remove the bolts which secure the propeller shaft to the rear differential gear, and detach the propeller shaft.

NOTE: When disconnecting the propeller shaft, plug the open end of the drive shaft with a cap to prevent the oil from running out of the drive shaft. Be careful not to damage the oil seal located at the end of the propeller shaft.

21. Remove the exhaust cover, if so equipped.

22. On MT, remove the bolts which secure the gearshift system to free it from the transmission (all manual transmission models except 4WD).

23. On AT, move the select lever to the ''P'' position, and at this point, mark the location of the connector nut and separate the manual lever from the linkage rod.

24. Remove the stabilizer.

25. Remove the bolts which secure the left and right transverse links to the front crossmember, and lower the transverse links.

26. Drive both the left and right spring pins out of the axle shaft.

NOTE: Discard and do not re-use the spring pins.

27. Push the wheels toward the outer side, separate the axle shaft from the drive shaft.

28. On MT, unfasten the clamp on the left side of the hand brake cable, in order to facilitate the removal of the center crossmember. On the automatic transmission model, remove the right hand brake cover, in order to facilitate the removal of the rear crossmember.

29. On MT, remove the nuts which secure the left and right transmission mount rubber cushions.

30. On AT, remove the mount retaining nut from the rear crossmember.

31. Securely support the transmission by placing a jack under it.

32. Remove the crossmember.

33. Remove the two nuts which secure the engine to the tranmission, and move the transmission away from the engine just enough so that the transmission mainshaft does not interfere with the engine. Lower the jack and remove the transmission.

34. Installation is in the reverse order of removal.

NOTE: Apply a slight coat of grease on the transmission mainshaft before installation. If the mainshaft is hard to align, turn the left and right shafts until the mainshaft engages.

TORQUE SPECIFICATIONS
(ft. lbs.)

Transverse link to front crossmember	50

TORQUE SPECIFICATIONS
(ft. lbs.)

Stabilizer to leading rod and rear crossmember	15
Rear crossmember to vehicle body	60
Front crossmember to vehicle body	40
Front engine mount to crossmember	20
Rear engine mount to crossmember	20
Propeller shaft to rear differential (4WD)	15

OVERHAUL

For all overhaul procedures, please refer to ''Manual Transaxle Overhaul'' in the Unit Repair section.

1800 Turbo

1. Open the front hood and support it securely. Remove the spare tire.

2. Disconnect the battery ground cable.

3. Remove the spare tire mounting bracket. Remove the thermosensor.

4. Disconnect vacuum hoses from the air intake shutter, transmission breather, and vacuum control diaphragm.

5. Disconnect the accelerator cable and link and move them out of the way.

6. Disconnect the speedometer cable at the transmission and move it out of the way.

7. Disconnect wiring harnesses at the transfer solenoid connector, transmission kickdown solenoid connector, body ground, O_2 sensor connector, and starter connector.

8. Remove the upper cover from the turbocharger.

9. Remove the center exhaust pipe by: detaching it at the turbocharger body; removing the rear cover; removing the bolt supporting the pipe at the transmission; disconnecting it from the rear exhaust pipe; and removing the hanger bolt from the bottom of the transmission. Then, disengage the pipe from the attaching studs and remove it.

10. Loosen (do not remove) the attaching bolts and remove the front exhaust pipe cover.

11. Remove the turbocharger as follows: remove the intake duct; remove the air flow meter boot; disconnect the inlet oil pipe; remove the mounting bolts and remove the turbocharger together with the outlet oil hose, lower cover and gasket (you may want to refer to the ''Turbocharger Removal & Installation'' procedure in the engine section for more detail).

12. Raise the car and support it on jackstands. Remove the bolts attaching the torque converter to the drive plate. Remove the bolts joining the engine and transmission to one another and the starter to the transmission. The starter-to-battery cable may be lift connected.

13. Disconnect both oil cooler lines at the transmission.

14. Loosen the retaining bolt on the transmission side of the pitching stopper about .4 in, and tighten the nut on the opposite side a corresponding amount. This will tilt the engine backward to aid in transmission removal. Do not loosen/tighten the nuts more than the specified amount!

15. Drain the torque converter.

16. Remove the oil supply pipe, being careful not to damage the O-ring.

17. Mark the position of the transmission shift rod nut. Remove the nut for the transmission shift rod and disconnect the rod. Set the selector lever on the transmission to Park position if it is not already there.

18. Remove the stabilizer by removing the two bolts and nut.

19. Remove the right and left side hand brake clamps.

20. Remove the inner transverse link by removing the nut and bolt on both sides that fastens it to the front suspension crossmember. Lower the link and remove it.

21. Separate the right and left side axle shafts from the transmission drive shaft. On each side, remove the spring pin, and then separate the axle shaft from the driveshaft by pushing the rear of either front wheel outward.

22. Remove the lower engine-to-transmission nuts. Do *not* loosen upper nuts yet.

23. Remove the rear transmission mount nuts. Disconnect the driveshaft, and cap off the opening to retain transmission fluid.

24. Support the transmission securely with a jack. Remove the rear crossmember. Now, remove the upper transmission-to-engine mounting nuts. Move the jack rearward until the front of the transmission is no longer in contact with the front crossmember. Lower the transmission and pull it out.

25. Install in reverse of the removal procedure. Use new spring pins in the axle shafts. When installing the rear crossmember, make sure it's positioned properly on the rubber bushings. There are guides on the crossmember and bushings. Torque the 8mm nuts to 7–13 ft. lb., and the 12mm nuts to 65–87 ft. lb.

Additional torque figures in ft. lb. are:
Lower transmission-to-engie nuts: 34–40
Driveshaft bolts/nuts: 13–18
Rear mount nuts: 14–25
Transverse link bolts (use new self-locking nuts): 13–16
Stabilizer (make sure slits on bushings face inward: 13–16
Linkage rod nut: 5.8–8.7
Pitching stopper (adjusted to .08 in. clearance): 6.5–9.4
Starter-to-transmission and engine: 34–40
Torque converter to drive-plate: 17–20

Make sure the transmission fluid level is correct with the engine idling.

CLUTCH

REMOVAL & INSTALLATION

1. To remove the clutch, the transaxle must be removed from the vehicle.

2. Gradually unscrew the six bolts which hold the pressure plate assembly on the flywheel. Loosen the bolts only one turn at a time, working around the pressure plate. Do not unscrew all the bolts on one side at one time.

3. When all of the bolts have been removed, remove the clutch plate and disc.

CAUTION
Do not get oil or grease on the clutch facing.

4. Unfasten the two retaining springs and remove the throw-out bearing and the release fork.

Do not disassemble either the clutch cover or disc. Inspect the parts for wear or damage and replace any parts as necessary. Replace the clutch disc if there is any oil or grease on the facing.

Do not wash or attempt to lubricate the throw-out bearing. If it requires replacement, the bearing may be pressed out and a new one pressed into the holder.

Installation is as follows:

1. Fit the release fork boot on the front of the transmission housing; Install the release fork.

2. Insert the throw-out bearing assembly and secure it with the two springs. Coat the inside diameter of the bearing holder and the fork-to-holder contact points with grease.

3. Insert a pilot shaft through the clutch cover and disc, then insert the end of the pilot into the needle bearing.

4. Gradually tighten the pressure plate retaining bolts one turn at a time, working around the cover. Torque to 12 ft. lbs.

NOTE: When installing the clutch pressure plate assembly, make sure that the "O" marks on the flywheel and the clutch pressure plate assembly are at least 120° apart. This is for purposes of balance. Also, make sure that the clutch disc is installed properly, noting the FRONT and REAR markings.

5. After installation, adjust the pedal free-play and height.

Clutch Cable

REMOVAL & INSTALLATION

The clutch cable is connected to the clutch pedal at one end and to the clutch release lever on the other end.

The cable conduit is retained by a bolt and clamp on the clutch pedal bracket and by a clip type clamp on a bracket mounted on the flywheel housing.

To replace the cable assembly, disconnect both the cable and conduit and remove the assembly from under the vehicle.

Install the replacement cable assembly and secure both the cable and conduit.

CABLE ADJUSTMENT

The clutch cable can be adjusted at the cable bracket where the cable is attached to the side of the transmission housing. To adjust the length of the cable, remove the circlip and clamp, slide the cable end in the direction desired and then replace the circlip and clamp into the nearest gutters on the cable end. The cable should not be stretched out straight nor should it have right angle kinks in it. Any curves should be gradual.

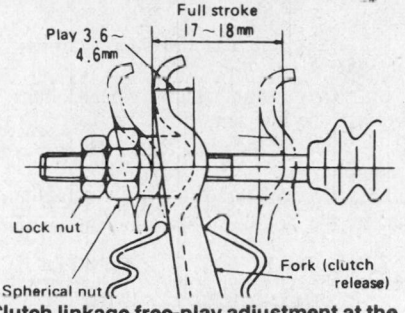
Clutch linkage free-play adjustment at the release fork

FREE-PLAY ADJUSTMENT

Remove the clutch release fork return spring, loosen the cable locknut, and adjust the spherical nut so that there is 0.142–0.181 in. play between the spherical nut and the release fork seat. Tighten the locknut and reconnect the release spring.

The pedal free-play should be 0.94–1.18 in. with a full stroke of 5.12 in. The pedal stroke is adjustable at the pedal bracket.

Automatic Transmission

BRAKE BAND ADJUSTMENT

This adjustment can be performed on the outside of the transmission.

1. Park the car on a level surface or support it on jackstands, engine off.

2. Locate the adjusting screw above the pan on the left side of the transmission.

3. Loosen the locknut.

4. **1978–81:** Torque the adjusting screw to 6.5 ft. lbs., then turn it back exactly two full turns.

From 1981: Torque the adjusting screw to 18 ft. lbs., then turn it back exactly ¾ turn.

5. Tighten the lock nut.

Following the above procedure will adjust the transmission brake band to the factory specified setting. However, if any of the following conditions are detected the adjusting screw can be moved ¼ turn in either direction after Step 4:

Turn ¼ turn clockwise if transmission:
—jolts when shifting from 1st to 2nd;
—engine speed abruptly rises from 2nd to 3rd; or,
—shift delays in kickdown from 3rd to 2nd.

Turn ¼ turn counterclockwise if
—car slips from 1st to 2nd; or
—there is braking action at shift from 2nd to 3rd.

NEUTRAL SAFETY SWITCH ADJUSTMENT

This switch is mounted on the transmission shift lever shaft, bolted to the transmission. It also operates the back-up lights.

1. Remove the shift lever shaft nut.

2. Remove the shift lever from the shaft.

3. Make sure that the slot in the shaft is vertical (Neutral position).

4. Remove the switch mounting bolts, but leave the switch in place.

5. Remove the setscrew from the lower face of the switch.

6. Insert a 0.059 in. drill bit through the set screw hole. Turn the switch slightly so that the bit passes through into the back part of the switch.

7. Bolt the switch down.

8. Remove the bit and replace the set screw.

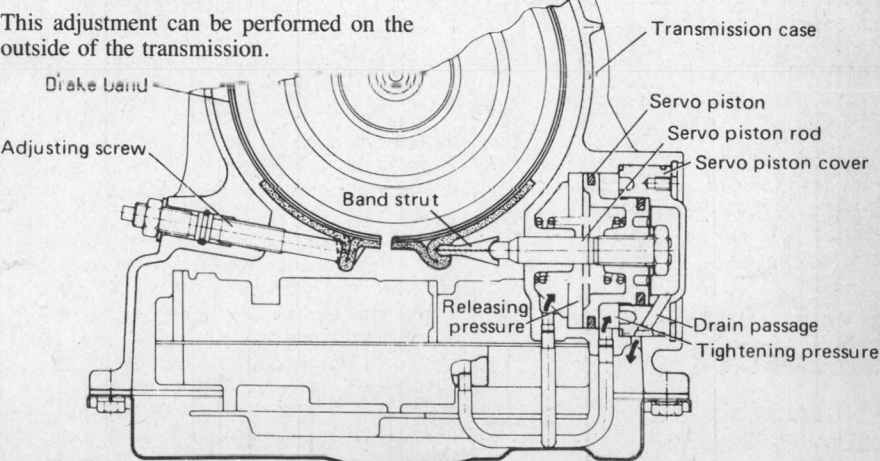
Second gear band adjustment mechanism

SHIFT LINKAGE ADJUSTMENT

1. Loosen the clamp nuts on the shifting rod at the bottom of the shift lever on the transmission.
2. Put the selector lever in Neutral and hold it forward against the detent.
3. Check that the transmission shift lever is in the Neutral position (pull it all the way back into Park and push it forward two positions).
4. Tighten the clamp nuts.

KICKDOWN SOLENOID

An audible click should be heard from the solenoid on the right side of the transmission, when the accelerator pedal is pushed down all the way with the engine off and the ignition switch on. The switch is operated by the upper part of the accelerator lever inside the car. The position of the switch can be varied to give quicker or slower kickdown response.

DRIVE AXLE

The drive axle consists of a double-offset joint (DOJ) at the inner end, an axle shaft, a constant velocity joint at the outer end, and a stub axle.

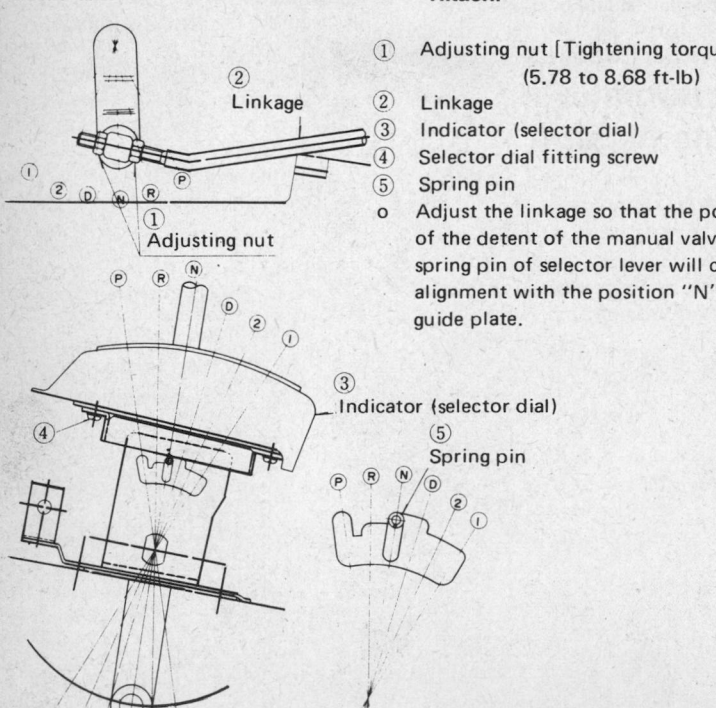

Details for automatic shift linkage adjustment

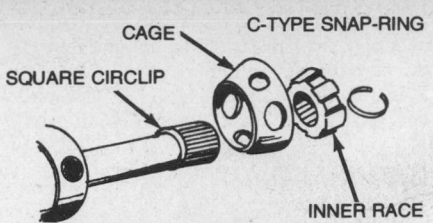

Disassembled double-offset joint

Axle Shaft
REMOVAL & INSTALLATION

1. Engage the parking brake. Remove the wheel cover (sedans and wagon), and loosen the lug nuts. Loosen the hub nut. Later models have the hub nut staked in place; unstake it with a thin chisel or a punch.
2. Raise the car the support it with jackstands.
3. Remove the lug nuts, wheel and tire. Remove the hub nut.
4. Remove the drum brake or disc brake assembly.
5. Drive out the spring (roll) pin, which fastens the double-offset joint end of the

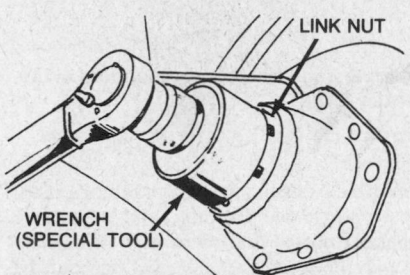

Automatic choke fast idle adjusting lever on the third step of the fast idle cam—Hitachi

① Adjusting nut [Tightening torque: (5.78 to 8.68 ft-lb)
② Linkage
③ Indicator (selector dial)
④ Selector dial fitting screw
⑤ Spring pin
o Adjust the linkage so that the position "N" of the detent of the manual valve and the spring pin of selector lever will come in alignment with the position "N" of the guide plate.

axle shaft to the driveshaft, by lightly tapping with a hammer. Throw the old pin away; do not reuse it.
6. Remove the self-locking nuts which attach the ends of the control arm to the stabilizer bar and the crossmember inner pivot.
7. Separate the control arm from the crossmember pivot by prying it rearward with a suitable lever.
8. To disconnect the control arm from the stabilizer bar, swing the link forward.
9. Pull the axle shaft out of the driveshaft (double-offset joint side) by pushing outward on the front suspension assembly.

NOTE: Be careful not to damage the boots on the double-offset and constant velocity joints.

10. Pull the other end of the drive axle out of the housing, while holding the shaft so that it doesn't drop.

—————— CAUTION ——————
Do not hammer on the end of the drive axle to remove it; damage to both the bearing and the splines will result.

Installation is as follows:
1. Thread a metric bolt which is long enough to fit through the axle housing, into the end of the stub axle.
2. Fit the bolt through the axle housing, using care not to damage the oil seal, splines, or bearing. Draw the drive axle assembly into place by grasping the end of the bolt with a puller.
3. Install the brake disc and hub.

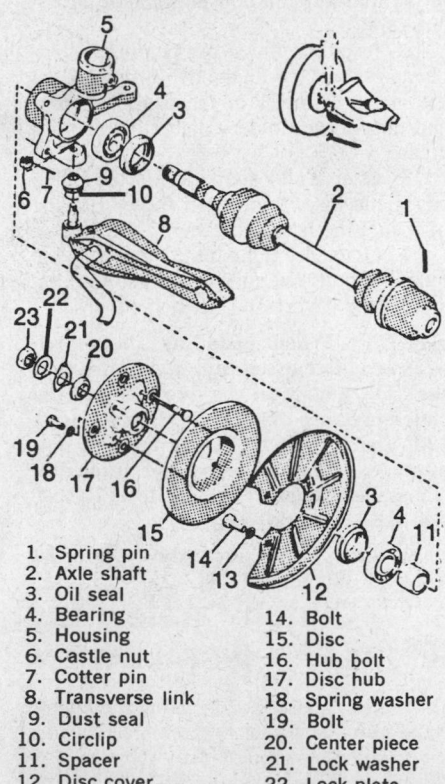

1. Spring pin
2. Axle shaft
3. Oil seal
4. Bearing
5. Housing
6. Castle nut
7. Cotter pin
8. Transverse link
9. Dust seal
10. Circlip
11. Spacer
12. Disc cover
13. Spring washer
14. Bolt
15. Disc
16. Hub bolt
17. Disc hub
18. Spring washer
19. Bolt
20. Center piece
21. Lock washer
22. Lock plate
23. Nut

Exploded view of a typical front axle assembly

4. Install the spacer, conical spring washer and the hub nut. Tighten the nut to 160–180 ft. lbs. (174 ft. lbs. preferred). Secure the hub nut to the axle shaft by using a punch to stake the flange on the nut to the groove in the end of the axle shaft.

5. Connect the double-offset joint side of the axle shaft to the driveshaft and secure them with a new spring pin.

6. Fit the washer and bushing over the end of the stabilizer bar and then connect the transverse link to the end of the stabilizer.

Install the remaining washer and bushing and temporarily secure them with a new self-locking nut.

7. Install the control arm to the cross-member pivot. Temporarily secure them with another new self-locking nut.

8. Install the dust cover, caliper, and parking brake cable.

9. Install the wheel and remove the jackstands.

10. Tighten the new self-locking nuts used at each end of the transverse link to 72–87 ft. lbs. with the car resting on its wheels.

CV-JOINT OVERHAUL
For all overhaul procedures, please refer to "U-Joint/CV-Joint Overhaul" in the Unit Repair section.

Rear Axle Shaft—Four Wheel Drive
REMOVAL & INSTALLATION

Early Models
1. Jack up the rear of the body and support with jack stands.
2. Turn the rear wheel to position the driveshaft and remove the driveshaft retaining bolts on the wheel side and the differential gear side.
3. Remove the driveshaft assembly.
4. To disassemble the ball spline hold the driveshaft in a vise and remove the rubber band, snap-ring and stopper.
5. To disassemble the U-joint remove the snap-ring and needle bearing.
6. To reassemble and install, reverse the above procedure.
7. Selective snap-rings are used to obtain a clearance of 0.0008 in. between the bearing cap and driveshaft yoke.
8. Snap-ring thicknesses are as follow:

0.0587 in.	
0.0598 in.	0.0457 in.
0.0610 in.	0.0646 in.
0.0622 in.	0.0657 in.

Late Models
1. Drain the differential oil.
2. Raise the rear wheels and support the car on jackstands.
3. Remove the rear wheels. Drive out the spring pins from the inner and outer DOJs (double offset joints)
4. Detach the outer DOJ from the spindle, lower it and disconnect from the differential spindle.

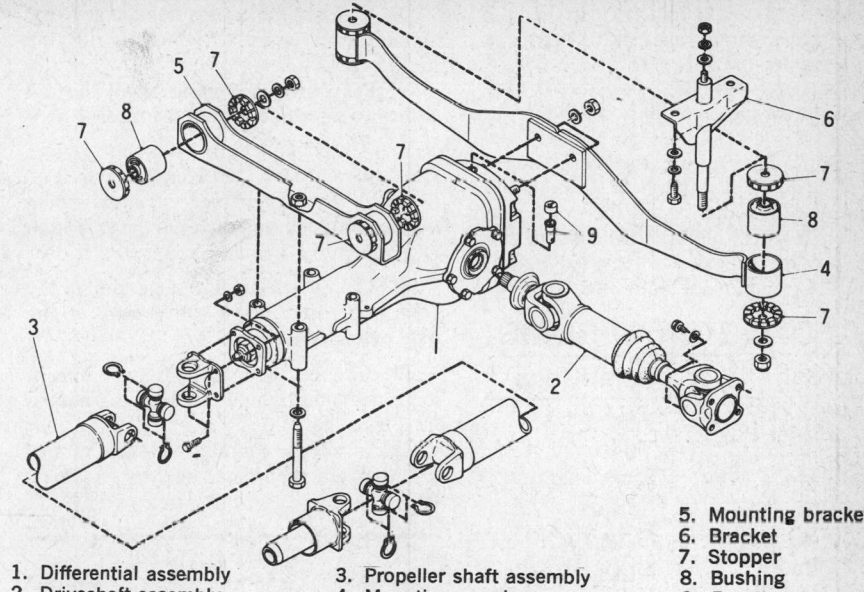

1. Differential assembly
2. Driveshaft assembly
3. Propeller shaft assembly
4. Mounting member
5. Mounting bracket
6. Bracket
7. Stopper
8. Bushing
9. Breather cap

Rear drive assembly—4WD vehicles

5. Installation is in the reverse order of removal. Use new spring pins on installation.

Driveshaft (Four Wheel Drive)

REMOVAL & INSTALLATION

1. Drain the transmission oil.
2. Jack up the rear of the body, and support with jack stands.

3. Remove the bolts connecting the driveshaft yoke to the rear differential companion flange.
4. Gently pull the driveshaft rearward to remove.
5. To install reverse the removal procedure.

OVERHAUL

Selective snap-rings are used to provide proper clearance of the bearing cap to yoke.

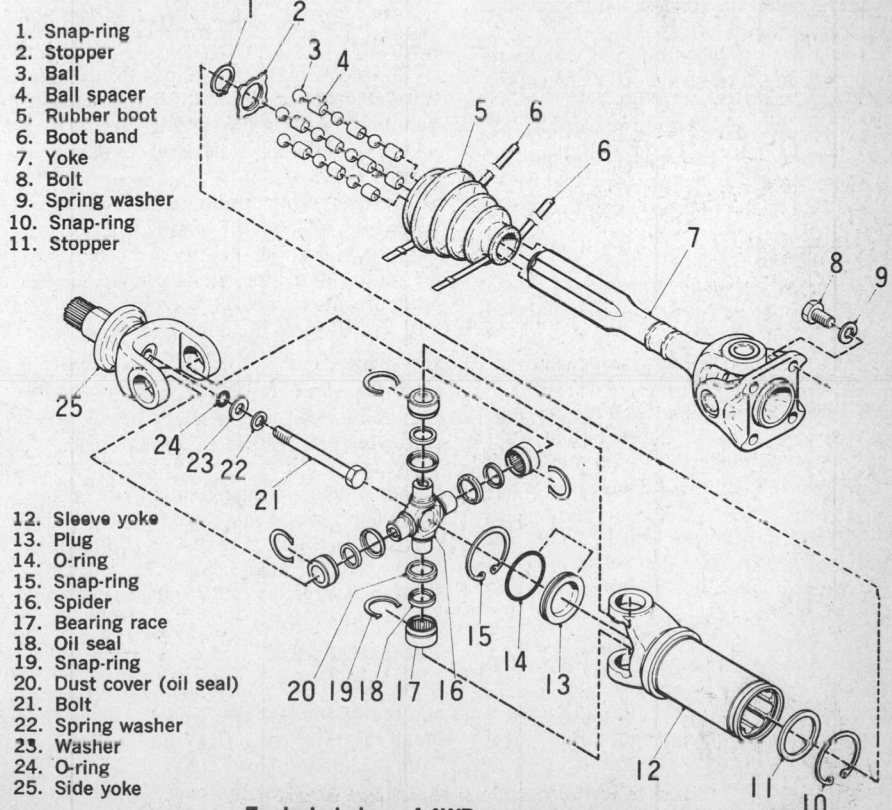

1. Snap-ring
2. Stopper
3. Ball
4. Ball spacer
5. Rubber boot
6. Boot band
7. Yoke
8. Bolt
9. Spring washer
10. Snap-ring
11. Stopper
12. Sleeve yoke
13. Plug
14. O-ring
15. Snap-ring
16. Spider
17. Bearing race
18. Oil seal
19. Snap-ring
20. Dust cover (oil seal)
21. Bolt
22. Spring washer
23. Washer
24. O-ring
25. Side yoke

Exploded view of 4WD rear axle shaft

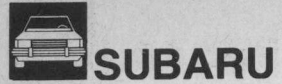
The clearance should be 0.0008 in. and the opposing snap-rings must be of the same thickness.

Matchmark the flange yoke, sleeve yoke and U-joint so parts can be reassembled in the exact same relationship. You can remove snap rings retaining the bearing races with a flat-blade screwdriver. Remove the bearing race by tapping on the other side of the yoke with a hammer. Make sure you don't lose any rollers. Use new grease approved for this purpose before reassembly.

SELECTIVE SNAP-RINGS

Thickness	Paint Color
0.0787 in.	White
0.0795 in.	Yellow
0.0803 in.	Red
0.0811 in.	Green
0.0819 in.	Blue
0.0827 in.	Light Brown
0.0835 in.	No paint
0.0843 in.	Pink

Rear Axle Spindle, Bearing and Seals (Four Wheel Drive)

REMOVAL & INSTALLATION

1. Jack up the car and remove the wheel.
2. Loosen the axle nut.
3. Disconnect the axle shaft from the rear axle companion flange.
4. Remove the nut retaining the companion flange to the spindle and remove the companion flange.
5. Pull the brake drum and spindle to the outer side and take the outer oil seal off with the spindle.
6. Remove the axle nut from the spindle, disconnect the brake drum and pull out the outer oil seal.
7. Unlock the link nut and remove the nut with a wrench (special tool).
8. Remove the inner seal.
9. New seals may be pressed into place at this time or if the bearing is to be replaced proceed as follows:
10. Dismount the rear suspension including the rear brake back plate.
11. Use a press and remove the bearing.
12. When replacing the inner and outer seals place the inner and outer side of the housing on a V-block and press the seals into place.
13. Hold the trailing arm in a vise and lightly tighten the link nut in the housing with the special wrench. Torque the nut to 130–166 ft. lbs.
14. Lock the link nut.
15. Install the rear trailing arm to the body.
16. Fit the back plate (22–35 ft. lbs.) and connect the brake pipe (11–14 ft. lbs.).
17. Temporarily fit the brake drum to the spindle.
18. Bleed brake system.

19. Position the companion flange to the spindle inner end and tighten the locknut to 145–181 ft. lbs.

NOTE: When tightening, apply the foot brake to produce reaction force.

20. Make sure the bearing rotates smoothly and stake the locknut.
21. Fit the center piece, conical spring washer and retaining nut onto the axle shaft and tighten the retaining nut to 174 ft. lbs.

NOTE: Punch the flange portion of the retaining nut toward the groove of the axle after tightening.

22. Connect the axle shaft and companion flange and tighten the retaining nuts to 29–36 ft. lbs.
23. Install the spindle and wheel assembly. Tighten the wheel nuts to 58–72 ft. lbs.

REAR SUSPENSION

Semi-trailing arms mounted to torque tubes, which act on an internal torsion bar are used. Shock absorbers are mounted to the trailing arm, close to the stub axle.

Torsion Bars

REMOVAL & INSTALLATION

1978–79

1. Remove the shock absorber lower retaining nut, and separate the shock absorber from the trailing arm.
2. Raise the vehicle, support it, and rewheel.
3. Index mark the splines on the outside and inside of the torsion bar, to indicate mounting position for installation.
4. Remove the lockbolt from the outer torsion bar bushing.
5. Position the trailing arm so as to remove all load from the torsion bar, and tap the torsion bar out.
6. Install the torsion bars in the reverse order of removal. Each torsion bar is marked "R" or "L," on the outer end, to indicate on which side it is installed.

——— CAUTION ———
Installation on the incorrect side will result in premature failure of the bars.

Index the splines according to the marks made during removal, install the wheel and check ride height. If necessary, adjust ride height as indicated below. Remount the shock absorber after the vehicle has been lowered.

1980 and later

1. Raise the vehicle and support it securely. Remove the rear wheel. Support the brake drum in a position eliminating load from the torsion bar.
2. Remove the lockbolt for the outer bush and the three outer arm to inner arm

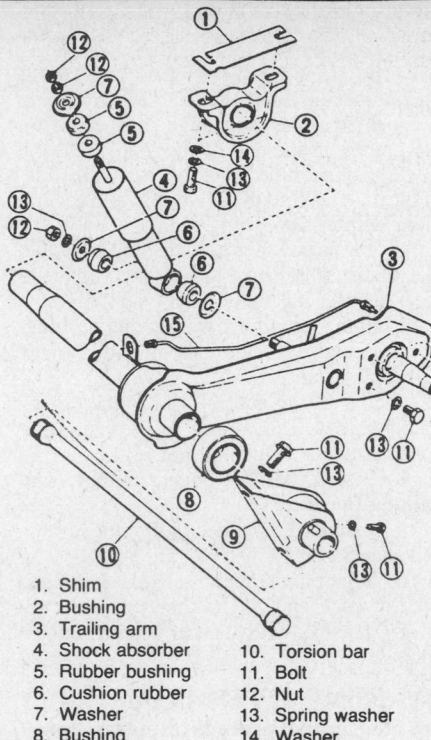

1. Shim
2. Bushing
3. Trailing arm
4. Shock absorber
5. Rubber bushing
6. Cushion rubber
7. Washer
8. Bushing
9. Bracket
10. Torsion bar
11. Bolt
12. Nut
13. Spring washer
14. Washer
15. Brake pipe

Exploded view of the typical rear suspension

connecting bolts. Pull the outer arm and torsion bar out of the crossmember. The torsion bar may not be removed from the outer arm.

3. To install, reverse the removal procedure, keeping the following points in mind:
   a. The torsion bar's splines must be aligned with those in the outer arm and crossmember so that the outer arm lines up with the inner arm as it did during removal, or ride height will be effected.

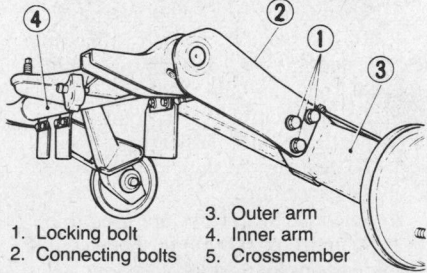

1. Locking bolt
2. Connecting bolts
3. Outer arm
4. Inner arm
5. Crossmember

Torsion bar removal—1980 and later models

   b. If you are removing both torsion bars, make sure the markings ("R" or "L") correspond with the side of the car you're installing the bar on.
   c. Use the following torques, in ft. lb.:
inner arm to outer arm—87–101 ft. lb.
outer bush lockbolt—23–29 ft. lb.

Shock Absorbers

REMOVAL & INSTALLATION

1. Remove the wheel cover and loosen

the lug nuts. Raise the rear of the car and support it with jackstands, after setting the parking brake and blocking the front wheels.

2. Remove the lug nuts and the rear wheels.

3. Loosen the two upper shock absorber mounting nuts. Remove the washer and the bushing, being sure to note their correct assembly sequence for installation.

4. Unfasten the nut on the trailing arm pin (nut and bolt on later models) and remove the shock absorber. Note the installing positions of the washers.

Installation is the reverse of removal. Do not fully tighten the upper mounting nuts until the lower shock nut has been installed with the washer and the pin shoulder contacting each other. Tighten the upper nuts to 22–32 ft. lbs. Adjust the ride height bolts, if so equipped.

Ride Height

Vehicle height can be adjusted by turning the outer and inner end of the torsion bar by the same number of serration teeth in the opposite direction to the arrow mark on the outer end surface of the torsion bar.

Turning the torsion bar in the direction of the arrow lowers the vehicle height, and changes the height 0.20 in. per tooth shifted.

The torsion bar must be removed from the inner and outer brackets to make the adjustment. 4-wheel drive vehicles have a unique adjusting device that will alter the ride height (in addition to adjusting the torsion bars). See the following procedure.

ADJUSTMENT OF REAR ROAD CLEARANCE

1980 and Later 4 Wheel Drive Vehicles

1. Measure the height of the vehicle from the lowest point of the rear axle crossmember to the ground.

2. To adjust the rear height, remove the access cover from the service hole in the vehicle's floor above the rear axle. Turn the adjusting bolt clockwise to increase the height, counterclockwise to lower it.

FRONT SUSPENSION

MacPherson Strut Assembly

REMOVAL & INSTALLATION

For all shock absorber and spring removal and installation procedures, and any other strut overhaul procedures, please refer to "Strut Overhaul" in the Unit Repair section.

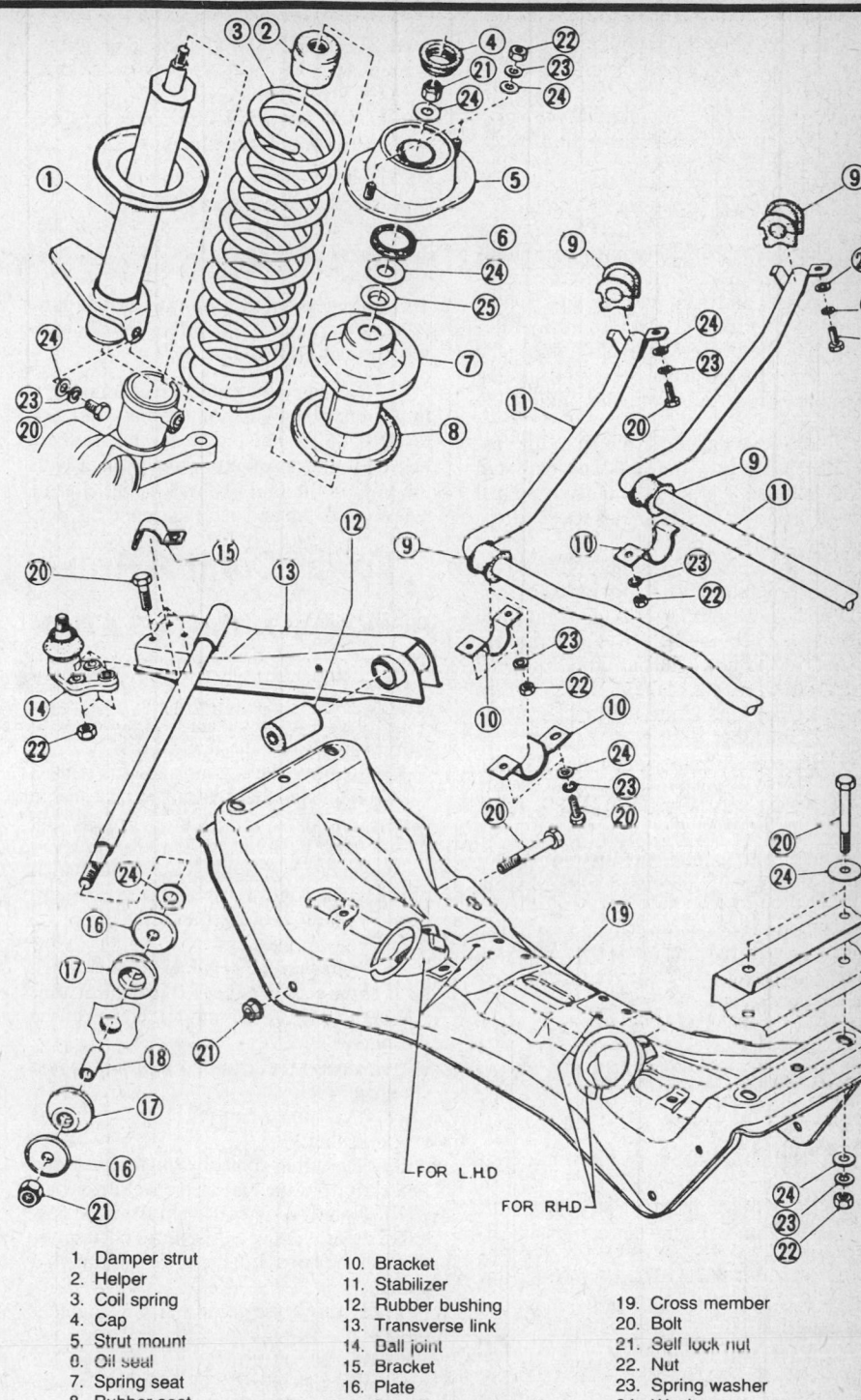

1. Damper strut	10. Bracket
2. Helper	11. Stabilizer
3. Coil spring	12. Rubber bushing
4. Cap	13. Transverse link
5. Strut mount	14. Ball joint
6. Oil seal	15. Bracket
7. Spring seat	16. Plate
8. Rubber seat	17. Bushing
9. Stabilizer bushing	18. Pipe

19. Cross member
20. Bolt
21. Self lock nut
22. Nut
23. Spring washer
24. Washer
25. Thrust washer

Exploded view of the typical front suspension

1. Raise and support the vehicle. Remove the battery cable from the negative terminal of the battery.

2. Remove the hub caps, loosen the lug nuts, jack up the vehicle until the tire clears the ground and remove the lug nuts and the wheel/tire assembly. Place the jackstands under the vehicle and remove the jack. Perform this operation on the opposite side if the suspension is to be removed from both sides of the vehicle.

3. Remove the handbrake cable bracket and the handbrake cable hanger from the transverse link and the tie-rod end. Remove the handbrake cable end.

4. Remove the axle nut, lockplate, washer, and center piece and remove the front brake drums by using a puller.

5. Disconnect the brake hoses from the brake fluid pipes.

6. With front disc brakes, remove the handbrake cable end from the caliper lever.

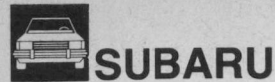

Remove the outer cable clip from the cable-end support bracket at the caliper. Remove the handbrake cable bracket from the housing mount by loosening the nuts.

7. Drive out the spring pins of the double offset joint by using a drift pin and a hammer. The double offset side of the axle is the side closest to the transaxle.

8. Remove the lower control arm by loosening the self-locking nut which holds it to the inner pivot shaft of the crossmember. Loosen and remove the nuts which clamp the control arm to the stabilizer. Remove the stabilizer rearward from the crossmember by using a lever and pulling the control arm out from the end of the stabilizer.

9. Remove the cotter pin from the castle nut and remove the nuts and ball stud from the knuckle arm of the tie-rod end ball joint housing. Take care not to bend the housing.

10. Disconnect the leading rod from the rear crossmember by removing the self-locking nut, washers, plates, bushings and pipe. Disconnect the stabilizer by removing the bolt at the bracket connecting one end of the stabilizer to the leading rod, and then removing the nuts fixing the bracket to the rear crossmember.

11. Remove the nuts which hold the strut mount to the body (suspension assembly upper mounting nut-top of the shock absorber tower).

12. Pull the double offset joint out of the driveshaft and then remove the suspension assembly from the body.

Install the suspension assembly in the reverse order of removal. Bleed the brakes after installation.

Ball Joints

REMOVAL & INSTALLATION

1978–79

1. Jack up the front of the car and remove the wheel.

2. Disconnect the ball stud from the housing by removing the cotter pin and castle nut.

3. Remove the bolt attaching the ball nut to the transverse link and remove the ball joint.

4. To install reverse the removal procedure. Torque the castle nut to 35–40 ft. lbs., ball joint to transverse link nut to 80–94 ft. lbs.

1980 and Later Models

1. Raise the front of the car and install axle stands. Remove the wheels.

2. Remove the cotter pin and remove the castellated nut. Remove the bolt on the steering knuckle, and remove the ball joint.

3. Inspect the joint, if you're considering reusing it, for damage to the boot that retains grease or stress cracks.

4. To install, insert the ball stud, ungreased, into the steering knuckle, install the bolt, and torque it to 22–29 ft. lb.

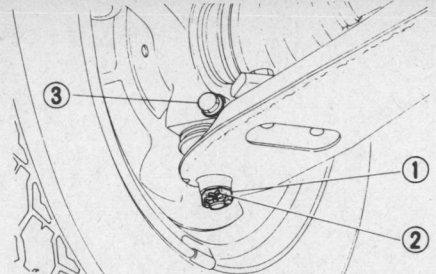

To remove ball joints on late model cars (1980–84), remove the cotter pin (2), castellated nut (1) and bolt (3)

5. Connect the joint to the transverse link and install the castellated nut, torquing to 29 ft. lb. Then, torque the nut further, just until the castellations are aligned with the hole in the end of the ballstud. Install a new cotter pin and bend it around the nut.

Lower Control Arm

REMOVAL & INSTALLATION

1. Remove the wheel cover and loosen the lug nuts.

2. Jack up the car and support it with jackstands. Block the rear wheels.

3. Remove the lug nuts and the wheel.

4. Remove the parking brake cable clamp from the control arm by unfastening its nut.

5. Unfasten the self-locking nut which attaches the control arm to the crossmember. Be sure to note the installation sequence of the washers.

6. Unfasten the self-locking nut which secures the stabilizer bar to the control arm. Again, note the installation sequence of the washers.

7. Unbolt the leading rod from the rear crossmember.

8. Pry the control arm off the crossmember.

9. Push the control arm forward and detach it from the end of the stabilizer bar.

10. Remove the cotter pin from the castellated nut. Unfasten the nut and remove the ball joint from the axle housing with a puller.

11. Remove the control arm from under the car.

Installation is the reverse of removal. Do not grease the upper ball joint stud which fits into the axle housing. Tighten the castellated nut to 30–40 ft. lbs. Use new self-locking nuts on the crossmember and stabilizer bar mounts. Tighten the new self-locking nuts to 73–87 ft. lbs. with the vehicle resting on the wheels.

Front End Alignment

CASTER AND CAMBER

Caster and camber are not adjustable on these models. If either of these specifications is not within the factory recommended range, this would indicate bent or damaged parts that must be replaced.

TOE-IN

Toe-in is adjusted by loosening the locknuts on the tie-rods, and turning the tie-rods.

NOTE: Before performing the toe-in adjustment, be sure that the steering gear is centered by aligning the marks on it, and that the wheels are straightahead.

Tighten the locknuts after the toe-in adjustment is completed.

STEERING

Steering Wheel

REMOVAL & INSTALLATION

1. Disconnect the negative battery cable.

2. Unfasten the horn lead from the wiring harness beneath the instrument panel.

3. Working from behind the steering wheel remove the horn assembly retaining screws. It may be necessary to lower the column from the dash by removing the mounting screws.

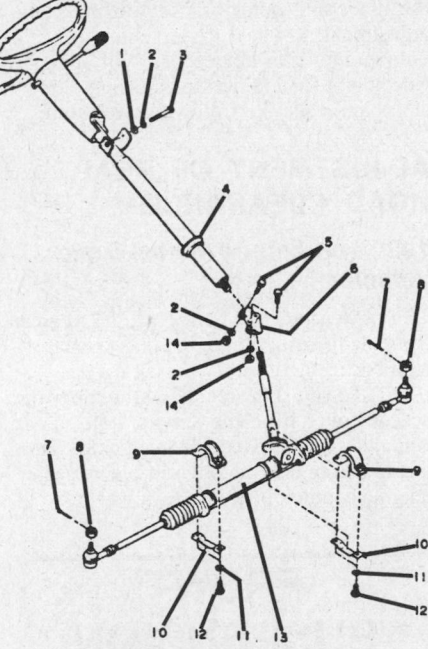

1. Washer
2. Spring washer
3. Bolt
4. Bushing (steering column)
5. Bolt
6. Universal joint
7. Cotter pin
8. Castle nut
9. Gearbox bracket
10. Lock plate
11. Washer
12. Bolt
13. Steering gearbox
14. Nut

Typical steering system

4. Lift the crash pad assembly off the front of the wheel.

5. Matchmark the steering wheel and the column for installation.

6. Remove the steering wheel retaining nut and pull the wheel from the column with a puller.

Installation is the reverse of removal. Index the matchmarks and tighten the retaining nut to 20–29 ft. lbs.

CAUTION

Do not hammer on the steering wheel or the steering column; damage to the collapsible column could result.

Turn Signal Switch
REMOVAL & INSTALLATION

1. Remove the steering wheel.

2. Separate the steering column wiring connectors underneath the instrument panel.

3. Remove the turn signal switch securing screws and unscrew the hazard warning switch knob.

4. Remove the contact plate, cancelling cam, and switch assembly from the steering column housing.

5. Installation is the reverse of removal.

Ignition Switch
REMOVAL & INSTALLATION

The ignition switch is mounted to the steering column using shear bolts. These bolts are constructed so that the head is sheared off when the bolt is tightened. For this reason removal of the ignition switch is rather complicated.

1. Remove the steering wheel as outlined above.

2. Disconnect the steering shaft from the universal joint (located near the steering gear box) by loosening the locking bolt.

3. Remove the steering shaft installing bolt from the instrument panel.

4. Pull the steering shaft assembly from the hole in the floor board and remove the assembly from the car.

5. Loosen the screws holding the column cover to the steering column and hazard knob, and pull the steering shaft out of the column cover.

6. Drill into the shaft of the shear bolts and extract them with a screw extractor. Remove the switch.

7. Installation is the reverse of removal. Be sure to use new shear bolts to install the ignition switch.

Manual Steering Gear

All Subaru models are equipped with rack and pinion steering. No maintenance is required.

REMOVAL & INSTALLATION

1. Jack up the front of the vehicle and remove the front wheels.

2. Remove the cotter pin and loosen

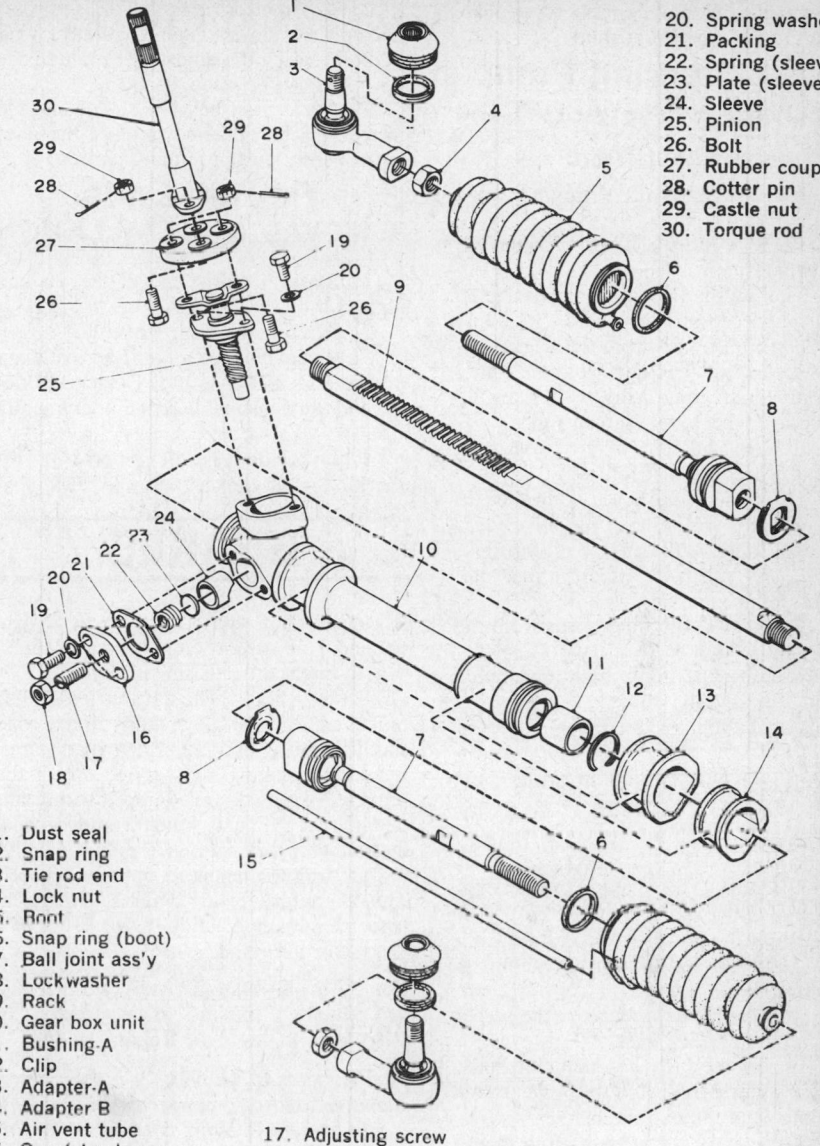

1. Dust seal
2. Snap ring
3. Tie rod end
4. Lock nut
5. Boot
6. Snap ring (boot)
7. Ball joint ass'y
8. Lockwasher
9. Rack
10. Gear box unit
11. Bushing-A
12. Clip
13. Adapter-A
14. Adapter B
15. Air vent tube
16. Cap (steering gear box)
17. Adjusting screw
18. Lock nut
19. Bolt
20. Spring washer
21. Packing
22. Spring (sleeve)
23. Plate (sleeve)
24. Sleeve
25. Pinion
26. Bolt
27. Rubber coupling
28. Cotter pin
29. Castle nut
30. Torque rod

Exploded view of the steering gear

the castle nut. Remove the tie-rod end from the knuckle arm of the housing.

3. Remove the handbrake cable hanger from the tie-rod.

4. Pull out the cotter pins and remove the rubber coupling connecting bolts and disconnect the pinion with the gearbox from the steering shaft.

5. Straighten the lockplate and remove the bolts which hold the gearbox bracket to the crossmember.

6. On DL, GF, and GL models, loosen the front engine mounting bolts and lift up the engine by about 0.2 in. to avoid touching the gearbox with the engine. Remove the gearbox from the vehicle.

NOTE: On 4WD models remove the fan protector on top of the radiator and remove the pitching stopper before lifting the engine.

Installation is the reverse of removal. Tighten the rack and pinion assembly se-

curing bolts to 33–40 ft. lbs. Tighten the rubber coupling castellated nut to 4–5 ft. lbs. Tighten the tie-rod end castellated nuts to 18–22 ft. lbs. Adjust the toe-in after completing installation.

NOTE: Check the collapsible steering shaft for straightness or looseness and always replace with a new one if found damaged.

ADJUSTMENT

Tighten the backlash adjuster fully to bottom, back off the screw ⅛ turn, and lock the locknut. A clearance of 0.006 in. is provided between the screw tip and the sleeve plate.

Power Steering

The power steering gearbox is a rack and pinion type integral system. The power cylinder is built in the gearbox, using the rack

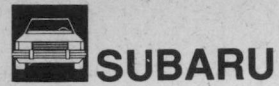
shaft as a piston. The control valve is arranged around the pinion shaft.

Power Steering Pump
REMOVAL & INSTALLATION

All Models Except Turbo

1. Remove the battery ground cable from the battery.
2. Remove the spare tire from the engine compartment.
3. Jack up the front of the vehicle and safely support it on jackstands.
4. Drain the fluid from the system by removing the line flare nuts from the center of the power steering gearbox and turning the steering wheel from left to right.
5. Loosen and remove the drive belt. See belt procedure that follows.
6. Disconnect the hoses connected to the air cleaner and remove the air cleaner assembly. Remove the engine oil dipstick. Remove any other interference that will prevent pump removal.
7. Disconnect the fluid hoses from the back of the pump.
8. Remove the pump mounting bolts/nuts and remove the pump.
9. Installation is in the reverse order of removal.
10. Fill the pump with fluid before starting the engine.

Turbo

1. Disconnect the battery ground cable. Remove the spare tire.
2. Drain the power steering fluid from the oil reservoir located on the pump by syphoning the oil out.
3. Loosen but do not remove the power steering pump pulley nut.
4. Loosen the alternator mounting bolts, move the alternator toward the power steering pump, and remove the belts.
5. Remove the nut and pull off the pump pulley.
6. Disconnect the oil pump line at the pipe using two wrenches. Loosen the clamp and disconnect the line where it connects to the tank. Keep oil off belts.
7. Remove the three bolts attaching the front of the pump to the mount and remove it.
8. To install reverse the removal procedure, but keep these points in mind:
   a. Do not twist hoses.
   b. It's easier to final tighten the power steering pulley bolt after the belts are installed and adjusted.
   c. Fill the fluid reservoir with the specified fluid and have someone keep it filled (use new fluid only). Idle the engine and turn the steering wheel from lock to lock to force air out of the system.

DRIVE BELT ADJUSTMENT

1. Remove the idler cover cap by turning and pulling. Adjustable jawed pliers with a piece of rag between the jaws can be used.

2. Turn the adjusting bolt until the correct belt tension is obtained. If removing the belt, loosen the adjusting bolt until the drive belt can be removed.
3. After a new belt is installed and the correct tension obtained, replace the idler cap cover by pushing in and turning.

Tie-Rod Ends
REMOVAL & INSTALLATION

1. Raise the front end of the car and support it on jack stands.
2. Remove the front wheels.
3. Remove the cotter pin and castle nut from the tie-rod end stud. Detach the tie-rod end using a suitable puller or extracting tool.
4. Installation is the reverse of removal. Torque the castle nut to 20 ft. lbs.

BRAKES

All models are equipped with front disc brakes. This system employs piston pressure to force two pads against both surfaces of a disc, or rotor. The advantages of disc brakes are in over all braking effect, road stability during braking effect, road stability during braking and service life of the brakes. All models are equipped with a tandem master cylinder, which employs a dual hydraulic circuit with each circuit supplying pressure to diagonally opposed wheels. This is a safety feature which allows for at least 50% braking action on the event of a fluid leak at any one wheel.

For all brake system repair and service not detailed below, please refer to "Brakes" in the Unit Repair section.

— CAUTION —
Asbestos, a known cancer-causing agent, is still present in many types of brake lining. Do not use compressed air to clean accumulated dust from your brake system. A safer method is to use rags soaked with a safe solvent so that dust will not be able to enter your throat and lungs.

Adjustment
FRONT DISC BRAKES

The front disc brakes require no adjustment, as hydraulic pressure maintains the proper brake pad-to-disc contact at all times.

NOTE: The brake fluid level in the master cylinder should be checked regularly.

REAR BRAKES— ALL MODELS

Perform rear brake adjustment every 6 months/6,000 miles, whichever occurs first. Adjust the rear brakes by turning the wedge, which is located on the bottom of the backing plate.
1. Chock the front wheels and set the parking brake.

2. Raise the rear of the car and support it with jackstands.
3. Loosen the locknut on the wedge.
4. While rotating the wheel, turn the wedge clockwise until the brakes lock.
5. Turn the wedge back 180° (½-turn) from the locked position.
6. Tighten the locknut and perform the adjustment on the other rear drum.

Wheel Cylinder
REMOVAL & INSTALLATION

1. Remove the brake drum and the brake shoes from the backing plate.
2. Remove the wheel cylinder from the backing plate by unscrewing the attaching bolts.
3. Remove the rubber boots from both ends of the wheel cylinder and push out the inner pistons and spring together with the rubber cups.
4. Inspect the inside of the wheel cylinder bore. If it is worn or scratched in any way, it should be honed with a wheel cylinder hone or a piece or crocus cloth until the scratches are removed.
5. Replace the rubber cups with new ones. The internal replacement parts are usually supplied in a wheel cylinder rebuilding kit.
6. Reassemble the wheel cylinder and replace it on the backing plate in the reverse order of removal.
7. After reinstalling the brake line and the brake assembly together with the brake drum, bleed the brake system.

Master Cylinder
REMOVAL & INSTALLATION

— CAUTION —
Avoid spilling brake fluid on painted surfaces.

1. Remove the brake lines from the master cylinder.
2. Remove the nuts which connect the master cylinder to the pedal bracket or power booster.
3. Pull the master cylinder assembly forward and out.
4. Install in the reverse order of removal.

Power Brake Booster

The power brake booster uses engine manifold vacuum against a diaphragm to assist in the application of the brakes. The vacuum is regulated to be proportional to the pressure placed on the pedal.

REMOVAL & INSTALLATION

1. Remove the master cylinder.
2. Disconnect the vacuum hose.
3. Disconnect the brake pedal from the power booster push rod by removing the spring pin and clevis pin.
4. Remove the four nuts that mount the booster to the firewall.

5. Remove the booster.

6. Installation is the reverse of removal.

Parking Brake Cable

REMOVAL & INSTALLATION

1978–79 Models

1. Jack up the vehicle and remove the wheel and tire.

2. Remove the brake drum (drum brake type).

3. Remove the hand brake cover and console.

4. Loosen the cable adjusting nut.

5. Remove the cable end from the equalizer.

6. Remove the cable end tightening clip.

7. Remove the service hole cover on the tunnel.

8. Remove the cable clamp from the crossmember.

9. Remove the cable installing bracket from the control arm.

10. Remove the handbrake cable hanger from the tie-rod end.

11. Remove the handbrake cable end from the handbrake lever by removing the secondary shoe.

12. Remove the cable end nut, washer, and spring washer from the inside of the backing plate and pull the handbrake cable out from the backing plate (drum brakes).

13. Pull the brake hose clamp out and remove the handbrake cable end from the lever and spindle assembly (disc brakes).

14. Pull the handbrake cable assembly from the engine compartment and remove it from the body together with the grommet.

15. Installation is the reverse order of removal.

1980 and Later

1. Loosen the wheel nuts, and then jack up and support the front of the vehicle securely. Remove the front wheels.

2. Remove the parking brake cover. Loosen the locknut and then loosen the parking brake adjuster until tension is almost gone. Then, disconnect the inner cable ends from the equalizer.

3. Remove the clips that fasten the cable grommets in place where the cable passes through the body.

4. Pull the parking brake cable clamp out of the caliper and disconnect the end of the cable.

5. On 1980 cars, disconnect the front exhaust pipe and remove it. On 1980 and '81 cars, remove the front-most exhaust system cover.

6. Remove the attaching bolt and remove the bracket holding the cable to the transverse link.

7. Remove the bolt and remove the bracket attaching the cable to the crossmember bracket.

8. Detach the cable from the guide the rear crossmember. Then, pull the cable out of the passenger compartment.

9. To install, reverse this procedure,

making sure the cable passes through the guide inside the driveshaft tunnel. Adjust the brake as described below.

ADJUSTMENT

1. Pull the parking brake lever up forcefully. Release it and repeat several times.

2. It should take the specified number of notches to apply the parking brake:
   * 1978–82—6–9 notches
   * 1983–85—3–4 notches

3. Loosen the locknut on the turnbuckle and adjust the length of the cable, so that the parking brake is applied within specifications.

4. Tighten the locknut and recheck operation of the parking brake lever.

Hill-Holder

The hill-holder was introduced on late model cars. It is a device that prevents the car from drifting backwards when starting up an incline from a stop. The hill-holder holds the brake on temporarily until the clutch pedal is released and the car is in forward motion.

CHASSIS ELECTRICAL

Heater Unit

Most Subaru models (until '81) use dealer-installed air conditioning units which work separately from the car's heating system. Therefore, heater service should be unaffected by the addition of air conditioning, save only that some of the A/C components may get in the way during heater removal and installation. In this case do not attempt to service any of the A/C system components; if accidentally discharged, refrigerant could cause severe burns or damage could result to the air conditioning system.

REMOVAL & INSTALLATION

1978–79 Without Air Conditioning

The heater unit contains the core and blower. The entire assembly must be removed from the car before either the blower or core can be serviced. To remove the heater unit:

1. Disconnect the ground cable from the battery.

2. Remove the console, luggage shelf, meter and visor assembly, and center ventilation grill.

3. Drain the coolant and disconnect the two heater hoses in the engine compartment.

4. Disconnect the heater control cable, fan motor harness, and the control rod connecting the air flow fan switch control lever

on the instrument panel to the heater unit, on the right side.

Remove the two mounting bolts and remove the heater unit.

5. To install reverse the removal procedure.

6. To reconnect the control rod, push up the link provided at the side of the heater unit to its full stroke, set the air/fan switch control lever to vent and then connect the rod to the link.

7. To reconnect the heater control cable, set the temperature control lever to cold, the heater control lever on the heater unit to off, then connect the cock cable.

1980 and later–Without Air Conditioning

On various models the heater unit contains the core and blower. The entire assembly must be removed from the car before either the blower or core can be serviced. To remove the heater unit, use the following procedure. If, however, the blower motor is exposed on the passenger's kickpanel, refer to next section.

1. Disconnect the ground cable (–) from the negative terminal of the battery.

2. Drain the engine coolant through the radiator drain plug.

3. Disconnect the heater hoses in the engine compartment.

4. Remove the rubber grommet that the heater hoses run through on the kick panel inside the car. The location is slightly above and to the right of the accelerator pedal.

5. Remove the radio box or console.

6. Remove the instrument panel.

7. If the car has a luggage shelf, remove it.

8. Disconnect the heater control cables and fan motor harness.

9. Disconnect the duct between the heater unit and blower assembly. Remove the right and left defroster nozzles.

10. Remove the two mounting bolts at the top sides of the heater unit.

11. Lift up and out on the heater unit.

12. Installation is the reverse of removal.

Blower Motor and Heater Core

REMOVAL & INSTALLATION

Without Air Conditioning
1978–79

After the heater unit has been removed the case is separated by removing the retaining springs and any necessary service can be carried out.

HEATER CORE—1980 AND LATER

If the car has an exposed blower,

1. Disconnect the ground cable from the battery.

2. Remove the luggage shelf and glove box.

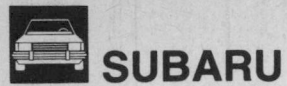

3. Detach the heater duct from the blower assembly.

4. Set the mode control to the CIRC position and disconnect the vacuum hose.

5. Disconnect the wiring harness to the blower motor.

6. Remove the actuator from the blower assembly.

7. Remove the blower motor assembly from the heater body.

8. Separate the blower case.

9. Installation is in the reverse order of removal.

BLOWER MOTOR—1980 AND LATER

1. Disconnect the battery ground cable.

2. Remove the luggage shelf and glovebox.

3. Detach the heater duct at the blower case.

4. Set the mode lever to CIRC for access and then disconnect the vacuum hose at the actuator.

5. Disconnect the blower electrical connector. Remove the actuator from the blower case by removing two screws and a clip.

6. Remove the blower case assembly from the body of the heater unit. Remove the two bolts, and remove the blower and motor assembly and seal from the case.

7. If you're replacing the motor, remove the attaching nut and washers, and pull the blower off the motor shaft. Transfer these parts to the new motor.

8. Installation is the reverse of removal. Make sure the seal is in good condition or, if necessary, replace it.

NOTE: Some Subaru owners report that the blower may sometimes rub the case in which it is mounted as it warms up. If this seems to be the case (you hear a rubbing noise after the blower has run for a while), ascertain that the blower is properly mounted to the shaft. If so, replace the motor assembly.

Radio

REMOVAL & INSTALLATION

1. Disconnect the cable from the negative terminal of the battery.

2. Remove the center console assembly by removing the mounting screws and disconnecting the wire harness and antenna cable.

3. Pull off the radio control knobs.

4. Remove the radio mounting nuts from the control stems.

5. Remove the radio mounting screw from the back of the radio.

6. Lift out the radio.

Windshield Wiper Motor

REMOVAL & INSTALLATION

1978–79

1. Disconnect the negative battery cable.

2. Remove the windshield washer reservoir.

3. Unfasten the 3 screws which secure the motor to the firewall.

4. Remove the wiper arms and cowl by unfastening their respective securing nuts (2) and screws (6).

5. Disconnect the wiper motor wiring.

6. Unfasten the clip which attaches the motor to the link, and remove the motor.

7. Installation is the reverse of removal.

1980 and Later

1. Disconnect the negative (−) battery cable.

2. Remove the wiper blades from the wiper arms by pulling the retaining lever up and sliding the blade away from the arm.

3. Slide the covering boot up the wiper arm.

4. Remove the retaining nuts that hold the wiper arms to the linkage and remove the arms.

5. Disconnect the electric wires to the wiper motor.

6. Remove the screws holding the cowl to the body. Remove the cowl.

7. Find or fabricate a ring which has the same diameter as the outer diameter of the plastic joint that retains the linkage to the wiper motor. Force the ring down over the joint to force the four plastic retaining jaws inward, and then disconnect and remove the linkage.

8. Remove the bolts that mount the wiper motor to the firewall. Remove the motor.

9. Installation is the reverse of removal. Install the arms after the ignition switch has been on for a few seconds to put the linkage in park position. Install the wiper unit with the red marking on the driver's side.

Instrument Cluster

REMOVAL & INSTALLATION

1978

1. Disconnect the cable from the negative terminal of the battery.

2. Remove the instrument cluster bezel, with rear window defogger switch, by removing the mounting screws.

3. Remove the four screws mounting the instrument cluster.

4. Disconnect the speedometer cable and wiring harness from the back of the instrument cluster.

5. Remove the instrument cluster. Installation is the reverse of removal.

1979 and Later

1. Disconnect the negative cable.

2. Remove the bolts securing the steering column and pull it down.

3. Disconnect the electrical wiring connectors then remove the screws securing the meter visor and remove the visor except on GL and GLF models.

4. On the GL and GLF models remove the center ventilator control lever by pulling it. Then, remove the three screws accessible through the ventilator grill to the right of the cluster and the one screw accessible through the grill on the left. Then, remove the visor.

5. On the station wagon 4WD GL, remove the passing lamp switch.

6. Remove the screws securing the combination meter then pull the meter out far enough to disconnect the speedometer cable and electrical connectors from behind and remove the combination meter.

7. Installation is the reverse of removal.

Toyota

Camry, Celica, Corolla, Corona
Cressida, Starlet, Supra, Tercel, Van

SERIAL NUMBER IDENTIFICATION

Vehicle

All models have the vehicle identification number (VIN) stamped on a plate which is attached to the left side of the instrument panel. This plate is visible through the windshield.

The serial number consists of a series identification number followed by a six-digit production number.

Engine

Bascially, 1978–85 Toyota vehicles have used eight types of engines: The "A" series (1A-C, 3A, 3A-C, 4A-C); "K" series (3K-C, 4K-C, 4K-E); "M" series (4M, 4M-E, 5M-E, 5M-GE); "R" series (20R, 22R, 22R-E); "S" series (2S-E), "T" series (2T-C, 3T-C); "C" series diesel (1C-L, 1C-L) and the "Y" series (3Y-EC). Engines within each series are similar, as the cylinder block designs are the same. Variances within each series may be due to ignition types (point or electronic), displacements (bore × stroke), cylinder head design (single or double-overhead camshafts) and fuel system type (carburetor or fuel injection). Refer to the accompanying engine I.D. chart.

When ordering engine parts, it may be necessary to obtain the engine serial number. Serial numbers of the engines may be found on the following locations:

"A" series engines—stamped vertically on the left side rear of the engine block.
"K" series engine—stamped on the right side of the engine, below the spark plugs.
"M" series engines—stamped horizontally on the passenger side of the engine block, behind the alternator.
"R" series engine—stamped horizontally on the driver's side of the engine block, behind the alternator.
"T" series engines—stamped horizontally on the driver's side of the engine block, just above the alternator.
"S" and "C" engines—stamped horizontally on the front side of the block.
"Y" series engines—stamped horizontally on the right side of the block.

CHASSIS IDENTIFICATION

Model	Year	Chassis Designation
Corolla 1200	'78–'79	KE
Corolla 1600	'78–'79	TE
Corolla 1800	'80–'82	TE
Corolla (Gasoline Engine)	'83–'85	AE
Corolla (Diesel Engine)	'84–'85	CE
Corona	'78–'82	RT
Celica (exc. Supra)	'78–'85	RA
Celica Supra	'79–'85	MA
Cressida	'78–'84	MX
Starlet	'81–'85	KP

CHASSIS IDENTIFICATION

Model	Year	Chassis Designation
Tercel	'80–'85	AL
Camry (Gasoline Engine)	'83–'85	SV
Camry (Diesel Engine)	'84–'85	CV
Van	'84–85	YR

ENGINE IDENTIFICATION

Model	Year	Engine Displacement Cu. in.(cc)	Engine Series Identification	No. of Cylinders	Engine Type
Camry	'83–'85	121.7 (1995)	2S-E	4	SOHC
	'84–'85	112.2 (1839)	1C-TL	4	SOHC
Celica	'78–'80	133.6 (2189)	20R	4	SOHC
	'81–'85	144.4 (2367)	22R, 22R-E	4	SOHC
Supra	'79½–'80	156.4 (2563)	4M-E	6	SOHC
	'81	168.4 (2759)	5M-E	6	SOHC
	'82–'85	168.4 (2759)	5M-GE	6	DOHC
Corolla	'78–'79	71.2 (1116)	3K-C	4	OHV
	'78–'79	96.9 (1588)	2T-C	4	OHV
	'80–'82	108.0 (1800)	3T-C	4	OHV
	'83–'85	97 (1587)	4A-C	4	SOHC
	'84–'85	112.2 (1839)	1C-L	4	SOHC
Tercel	'80–'85	88.6 (1452)	1A-C, 3A, 3A-C	4	SOHC
Corona	'78–'80	133.6 (2189)	20R	4	SOHC
	'81–'82	144.4 (2367)	22R	4	SOHC
Cressida	'78–'79	156.4 (2563)	4M	6	SOHC
	'80	156.4 (2563)	4M-E	6	SOHC
	'81–'82	168.4 (2759)	5M-E	6	SOHC
	'83–'85	168.4 (2759)	5M-GE	6	DOHC
Starlet	'81–'82	78.7 (1290)	4K-C	4	OHV
	'83–'85	79 (1290)	4K-E	4	OHV
Van	'84–'85	122 (1998)	3Y-EC	4	OHV

DOHC—Double-overhead camshaft   SOHC—Single-overhead camshaft
OHV—Pushrod-actuated Overhead valves

GENERAL ENGINE SPECIFICATIONS

Engine Type	Year	Engine Displacement cu. in. (cc)	Fuel System Type	Horsepower @ rpm①	Torque @ rpm (ft. lbs.)①	Bore × Stroke (in.)	Compression Ratio
1A-C, 3A	'80–'82	88.6 (1452)	2 bbl.	60 @ 4800	72 @ 2800	3.05 × 3.03	8.7:1
2T-C	'78–'79	96.9 (1588)	2 bbl.	75 @ 5800	83 @ 3800	3.35 × 2.76	9.0:1

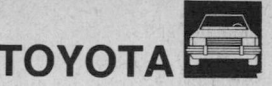
GENERAL ENGINE SPECIFICATIONS

Engine Type	Year	Engine Displacement cu. in. (cc)	Fuel System Type	Horsepower @ rpm[1]	Torque @ rpm (ft. lbs.)[1]	Bore × Stroke (in.)	Compression Ratio
3K-C	'78–'79	71.8 (1166)	2 bbl.	58 @ 5800	63 @ 3800	2.95 × 2.60	9.0:1
3A-C	'81	88.6 (1452)	2 bbl.	62 @ 4800	75 @ 2800	3.05 × 3.03	9.0:1
	'82–'85	88.6 (1452)	2 bbl.	62 @ 5200	75 @ 2800	3.05 × 3.03	9.0:1
4A-C	'83–'85	97 (1587)	2 bbl.	70 @ 4800	85 @ 2800	3.94 × 3.03	9.0:1
3T-C	'80–'81	108.0 (1770)	2 bbl.	75 @ 5000[2]	95 @ 2600[2]	3.35 × 3.07	9.0:1
	'82	108.0 (1770)	2 bbl.	70 @ 4600	93 @ 2400	3.35 × 3.07	9.0:1
4K-C	'81–'82	78.7 (1290)	2 bbl.	58 @ 5200	67 @ 3600	2.95 × 2.87	9.0:1
4K-E	'83–'85	79 (1290)	EFI	58 @ 4200	74 @ 3400	2.95 × 2.87	9.5:1
4M	'78–'79	156.4 (2563)	2 bbl.	108 @ 5000	134 @ 2800	3.15 × 3.35	8.5:1
4M-E	'79–'80	156.4 (2563)	EFI	110 @ 4800	136 @ 2400	3.15 × 3.35	8.5:1
5M-E	'81–'83	168.4 (2759)	EFI	116 @ 4800	145 @ 3600	3.27 × 3.35	8.8:1
5M-GE	'82	168.4 (2759)	EFI	145 @ 5200	155 @ 4800	3.27 × 3.35	8.8:1
	'83–'85	168.4 (2759)	EFI	150 @ 5200[5]	159 @ 4400[6]	3.27 × 3.35	8.8:1
20R	'78	133.6 (2189)	2 bbl.	96 @ 4800[3]	120 @ 2800[4]	3.48 × 3.50	8.4:1
	'79–'80	133.6 (2189)	2 bbl.	90 @ 4800	122 @ 2400	3.48 × 3.50	8.4:1
22R	'81–'83	144.4 (2367)	2 bbl.	96 @ 4800	129 @ 2800	3.62 × 3.50	9.0:1
22R-E	'83–'85	144.4 (2367)	EFI	105 @ 4800	137 @ 2800	3.62 × 3.50	9.0:1
2S-E	'83–'85	121.7 (1995)	EFI	92 @ 4200	113 @ 2400	3.31 × 3.54	8.7:1
3Y-EC	'84–'85	122 (1998)	EFI	90 @ 4400	120 @ 3000	3.39 × 3.39	8.8:1
1C-TL	'84–'85	112.2 (1830)	Diesel	72 @ 4500	104 @ 3000	3.27 × 3.35	22.5:1
1C-L	'84–'85	112.2 (1839)	Diesel	56 @ 4500	76 @ 3000	3.27 × 3.35	22.5:1

EFI Electronic Fuel Injection
[1] Horsepower and torque ratings are given in SAE net figures
[2] Calif. — 73 hp @ 5000 rpm; 90 ft. lbs. @ 2600 rpm
[3] '78 Calif.: 90 @ 4800
[4] '78 Calif.: 122 @ 2400
[5] Cressida: 143 @ 5200
[6] Cressida: 154 @ 4400

GASOLINE ENGINE TUNE-UP SPECIFICATIONS

Year	Engine Type	Spark Plugs Type (NGK)	Spark Plugs Gap (in.)	Distributor Point Dwell (deg)	Distributor Point Gap (in.)	Ignition Timing (deg)[5] MT	Ignition Timing (deg)[5] AT	Compression Press.	Fuel Pump Press.	Idle Speed (rpm) MT	Idle Speed (rpm) AT	Valve Clearance (in.) (hot) Intake	Valve Clearance (in.) (hot) Exhaust
'78–'79	3K-C	BPR5EA-L	0.031	Electronic		8B	8B	156	3.0–4.5	750	750	0.008	0.012
	2T-C	BP5EA-L	0.031	Electronic[4]		10B[10]	10B[10]	171	3.0–4.5	850	850	0.008	0.013
	4M	BPR5EA-L	0.031	Electronic[4]		10B[10]	10B[10]	156	4.2–5.4	750	750	0.011	0.014
	20R	BP5EA-L[11]	0.031	Electronic[4]		8B	8B	156	2.2–4.2	800	850	0.008	0.012
'80–'81	1A-C	BP6EK-A	0.039	Electronic[4]		5B	—	177	—	650	800	0.008	0.012
	3A	BPR5EA-L	0.031	52	0.018	5B	5B	177	—	650	800[13]	0.008	0.012
	3A-C	BPR5EA-11[14]	0.043	Electronic[4]		5B	5B[5]	177	—	550[13][15]	800[13]	0.008	0.012
	3T-C	BPR5EA	0.043	Electronic[4]		10B[23]	10B[23]	163	—	850[6]	850[6]	0.008	0.013
	4K-C	BPR5EA-11[19]	0.043[19]	Electronic[4]		8B	—	156	2.8–4.2	650[13][20]	—	0.008	0.012
	4M-E	BPR5EA-L	0.031	Electronic[4]		12B	12B	156	33–38	800	800	0.011	0.014

TUNE-UP SPECIFICATIONS

Year	Engine Type	Spark Plugs Type (NGK)	Spark Plugs Gap (in.)	Distributor Point Dwell (deg)	Distributor Point Gap (in.)	Ignition Timing (deg)⑤ MT	Ignition Timing (deg)⑤ AT	Compression Press.	Fuel Pump Press.	Idle Speed (rpm) MT	Idle Speed (rpm) AT	Valve Clearance (in.) (hot) Intake	Valve Clearance (in.) (hot) Exhaust
'80–'81	5M-E	BPR5EA-L	0.031	Electronic④		8B	8B	156	33–38	800	800	0.011	0.014
	20R, 22R	BPR5EA-L	0.031	Electronic④		8B	8B	156㉔	2.2–4.3	800⑫	850	0.008	0.012
'82	3A	BPR5EA-L	0.031	52	0.018	5B	5B	177	—	650	800⑬	0.008	0.012
	3A-C	BPR5EA-11⑭	0.043	Electronic④		5B⑤	5B⑤	177	—	550⑬⑮	800⑬	0.008	0.012
	3T-C	BPR5EA-11⑯	0.043⑯	Electronic④		7B⑤⑰	7B⑤⑰	163	—	⑱	⑱	0.008	0.013
	4K-C	BPR5EA-11⑲	0.043⑲	Electronic④		8B	—	156	2.8–4.2	650⑬⑳	—	0.008	0.012
	5M-E	BPR5EA-L	0.031	Electronic④		—	8B	156	33–38	—	800	0.011	0.014
	5M-GE	BPR5EY	0.031	Electronic④		8B⑬	8B⑬	164	35–38	650	650	㉑	㉑
	22R	BPR5EA-L	0.031	Electronic④		8B⑬	8B⑬	171	—	700㉒	750㉒	0.008	0.012
'83	3A	BPR5EA-L	0.031	Electronic④		5B	5B	178	—	㉕	㉕	.008	.012
	3A-C	BPR5EA-11⑭	0.043	Electronic④		5B	5B	178	—	㉖	㉖	.008	.012
	4A-C	BPR5EA-L11㉗	0.043	Electronic④		5B	5B	163	2.5–3.5	㉘	㉘	.008	.012
	4K-E	㉙	0.043	Electronic④		5B	—	185	36–38	700	—	㉑	㉑
	5M-GE	BPR5EP-11	0.043	Electronic④		10B	10B	164	35–38	650	650	㉑	㉑
	22R-E	BPR5EY	0.031	Electronic④		5B	5B	171	35–38	750	750	.008	.012
	22R	BPR5EY	0.031	Electronic④		8B	8B	171	2.5–3.8	700	700	.008	.012
	2S-E	BPR5EA-L11	0.043	Electronic④		5B	5B	156	28–36	㉚	㉚	㉑	㉑
'84	2S-E	BPR5EA-L11	0.043	Electronic④		5B	5B	156	28–36	700	700	Hyd.	Hyd.
	3A-C	BPR5EA-11	0.043	Electronic④		5B	5B	177	2.6–3.5	㉖	㉖	.008	.012
	3Y-EC	BPR5EP-11	0.043	Electronic④		8B	8B	171	33–38	950	950	Hyd.	Hyd.
	4A-C	BPR5EZ-L11③	0.043	Electronic④		5B	5B	163	2.5–3.5	700	700	.008	.012
	4K-E	BPR5EP-11⑦	0.043	Electronic④		5B	—	185	36–38	700	—	Hyd.	Hyd.
	5M-GE	BPR5EP-11	0.043	Electronic④		10B	10B	156	35–38	650	650	㉑	㉑
	22R-E	BPR5EY	0.031	Electronic④		5B	5B	171	35–38	950	950	.008	.012
'85	All				Refer to Underhood Specifications Sticker									

NOTE: If the information given in this chart disagrees with the information on the emission control specification decal, use the specifications on the decal.

MT Manual transmission
AT Automatic transmission
TDC Top dead center
B Before top dead center
Hyd. Hydraulic valve lash adjusters
① Except California
② California only
③ Calif.: BPR5EA-L11
④ Air gap 0.008–0.016 inch
⑤ With vacuum advance disconnected
⑥ M/T without power steering—700 rpm
A/T without power steering—750 rpm
⑦ 5 sp.: BRE529Y-11
⑧ Electric pump (California)—2.4 to 3.8 psi
⑨ California model Celica GT equipped with transistorized ignition
⑩ California—8B
⑪ Celica—BPR5EA-L
⑫ Four-speed manual—700 rpm
⑬ With cooling fan OFF; trans. in Neutral

⑭ California models use BPR5EA-L11
⑮ For 4-speed transmission. 5-speed—650 rpm
⑯ Canada models use BPR5ES, gapped at 0.031 in.
⑰ Canada models—10°BTDC
⑱ Without power steering:
U.S., M.T.—650 rpm
U.S., A.T.—750 rpm
Canada, M.T.—700 rpm
Canada, A.T.—750 rpm
With power steering: 850 rpm
⑲ California models use BPR5EA-L, gapped at 0.031
⑳ California models—700 rpm w/cooling fan OFF, trans. in Neutral
㉑ Self-adjusting lash adjusters are used—no adjustment necessary
㉒ Canadian models—850 rpm

㉓ '81 USA models: 7B
㉔ 22R: 171
㉕ W/PS: MT—800
AT—900
W/OPS: MT—650
AT—800
㉖ W/PS: MT—800
AT—900
W/OPS: 4 spd—550
5 spd—650
AT—700
㉗ Canada: BPR5EA-L; gap—0.031
㉘ W/PS: MT—650
AT—800
W/OPS: MT—800
AT—900
㉙ 4 Spd: BPR5EP-11
5 Spd: BRE529-Y11
㉚ Refer to underhood specifications sticker

FIRING ORDERS

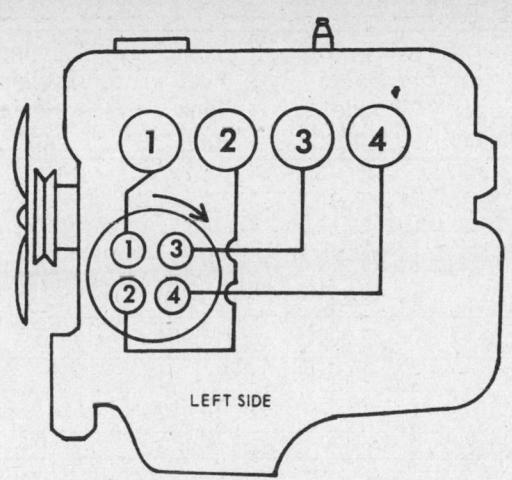

Firing order—R-series engines

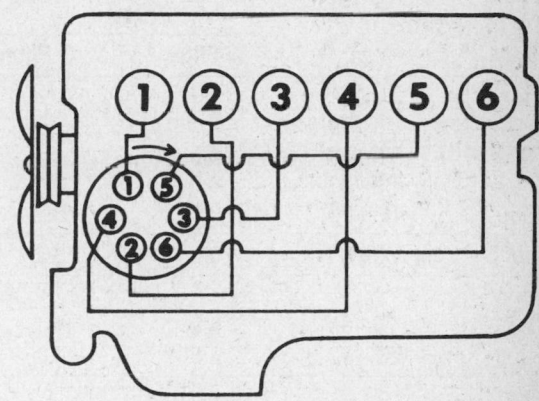

Firing order—5M-GE engines

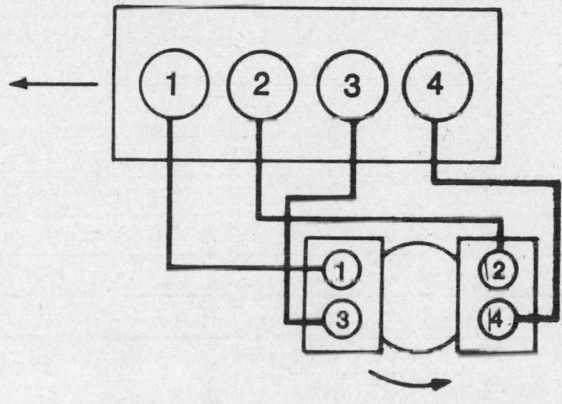

Firing order—A-series engines (1983 shown; others similar)

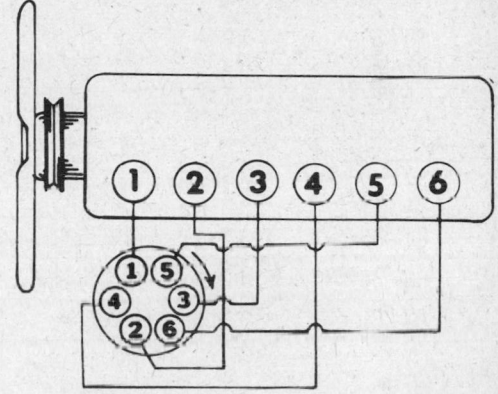

Firing order—4M, 4M-E and 5M-E engines

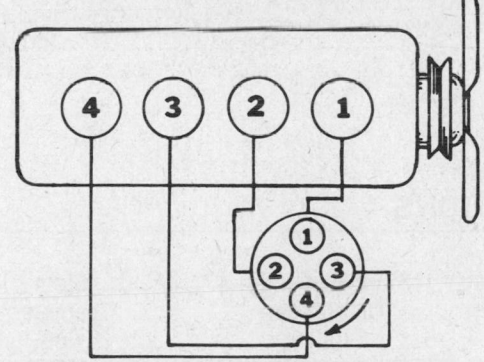

Firing order—all T– and K-series engines

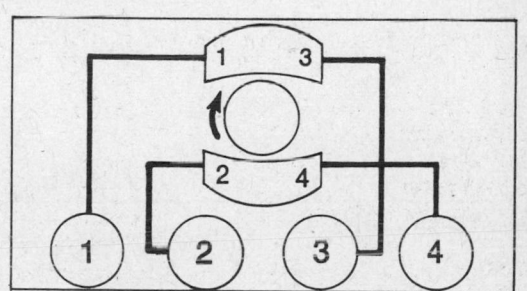

Firing order—2-SE engine

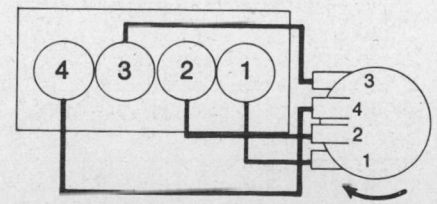

Firing order—3Y-EC engine

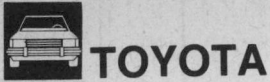

CAPACITIES

Model	Year	Crankcase (qt) W/Filter	Crankcase (qt) W/O Filter	Transmission (qt) Manual	Transmission (qt) Automatic	Drive Axle (pt)	Fuel Tank (gal)	Cooling System w/Heater (qt)
Corolla								
1200	'78–'79	3.7	2.9	①	—	2.2	12.0	5.1
1600	'78–'79	4.6	3.7	1.6	2.5	2.4	13.2	8.8
1800	'80–'82	4.0	3.5	1.8	2.5	2.2	13.2	8.8
1600	'83–'85	3.5㉒	3.2	1.8	2.5	2.2㉓	13.2⑨	⑭㉑
Tercel	'80–'85	3.5	3.2	3.4⑮	2.3	2.0⑯	11.9⑳	5.4
Corona								
2200	'78–'80	4.8	4.1	2.9②	2.3③	⑤	14.5④	7.4⑥
2400	'81–'82	4.8	4.1	2.9②	2.3③	⑤	16.1	8.5
Celica								
2200	'78–'80	4.9	4.0	2.9②	2.3③	⑤	13.0⑦	8.9
2400	'81–'85	4.9	4.0	2.5	2.5	⑤	16.1	8.9
Cressida								
2600	'78–'80	4.9⑩	4.3⑩	—	2.5⑪	3.0	17.2⑫	11.6
2800	'81–'85	5.4	4.9	2.5	2.5	⑬	17.2⑫	8.8⑲
Supra								
2600	'79½–'80	4.9	4.3	2.8	2.5	3.2	16.1	9.5
2800	'81	4.9	4.3	2.7	2.5	3.2	16.1	9.5
2800	'82–'85	5.4	4.9	2.7	2.5	2.6	16.1	8.5
Starlet	'81–'85	3.7	3.2	2.6	—	2.2	10.6	5.5
Camry	'83–'85	4.2⑱	3.7⑱	2.7	2.5	⑰	13.8	7.4⑧
Van	'84–'85	3.7	3.2	2.3	2.3	2.6	15.9	7.5

① 4 sp: 1.8
   5 sp: 2.6
② 5 speed: 2.8
③ '78–'80: 2.5
④ 1978–79: 15.5; '80: 16.1
⑤ Unitized type: 2.6
   Banjo type: 2.8
⑥ '79–'80: 8.5
⑦ '78–'79: 15.5; '80: 16.1
⑧ Diesel: 8.0

⑨ Sta. Wag.: 12.4
⑩ 1978: 5.7, 4.7
⑪ 1978: 2.3
⑫ Sta. wag.: 16.2
⑬ With 7.5 in. ring gear—1.3; With 8.0 in. ring gear—1.9
⑭ M/T: 5.7
   A/T: 6.6
⑮ W/Transaxle 4 × 4: 4.1
⑯ 4 × 4: 2.2

⑰ M/T: 2.7
   A/T: 2.1
⑱ Diesel: 4.5 w/filter
     4.0 wo/filter
⑲ 1984–85: 9.5
⑳ 1984–85: 13.2
㉑ Diesel: 7.9
㉒ Diesel: 4.5 U.S. & Canada
     4.9 Calif.
㉓ Diesel: 2.1

VALVE SPECIFICATIONS

Engine Type	Seat Angle (deg)	Face Angle (deg)	Spring Test Pressure (lbs) Inner	Spring Test Pressure (lbs) Outer	Spring Installed Height (in.) Inner	Spring Installed Height (in.) Outer	Stem-To-Guide Clearance (in.) Intake	Stem-To-Guide Clearance (in.) Exhaust	Stem Diameter (in.) Intake	Stem Diameter (in.) Exhaust
3K-C	45	44.5	—	70.1	—	1.512	0.0012–0.0026	0.0014–0.0028	0.3140	0.3140
2T-C	45	44.5	—	57.9	—	1.484	0.0012–0.0020	0.0012–0.0024	0.3140	0.3140
20R	45	44.5	—	55.1	—	1.594	0.0006–0.0024	0.0012–0.0026	0.3141	0.3140
4M	45	44.5	15.5	63.1①	1.504	1.642②	0.0006–0.0018	0.0010–0.0024	0.3146	0.3140

VALVE SPECIFICATIONS

Engine Type	Seat Angle (deg)	Face Angle (deg)	Spring Test Pressure (lbs)		Spring Installed Height (in.)		Stem-To-Guide Clearance (in.)		Stem Diameter (in.)	
			Inner	Outer	Inner	Outer	Intake	Exhaust	Intake	Exhaust
1A-C, 3A, 3A-C, 4A-C	45	45.5	—	52.0	—	1.520	0.0010–0.0024	0.0012–0.0026	0.2744–0.2750	0.2742–0.2748
4M-E	45	44.5	15.6	41.6	1.49	1.630	0.0010–0.0024	0.0014–0.0028	0.3141	0.3137
3T-C	45	44.5	—	57.9	—	1.484	0.0010–0.0024	0.0012–0.0026	0.3139	0.3139
4K-C, 4K-E	45	44.5	—	70.1⑧	—	1.512	0.0012–0.0026③	0.0014–0.0028④	0.3136–0.3142	0.3134–0.3140
22R, 22R-E	45	44.5	—	55.1	—	1.594	0.0008–0.0024③	0.0012–0.0028④	0.3188–0.3145	0.3136–0.3142
5M-E	45	44.5	14.1–17.2	37.3–46.5	1.492	1.630	0.0010–0.0024④	0.0014–0.0028⑦	0.3138–0.3144	0.3134–0.3140
5M-GE	45	44.5		⑤		⑥	0.0010–0.0024③	0.0012–0.0026④	0.3138–0.3144	0.3136–0.3142
2S-E	45.5	45.5	—	68.0	—	1.555	0.0010–0.0024	0.0012–0.0026	0.3138–0.3144	0.3136–0.3142
1C-L, 1C-TL	45	44.5	—	53.0	—	1.587	0.0008–0.0022	0.0014–0.0028	0.3140–0.3146	0.3134–0.3140
3Y-EC	45	45.5	—	63.0	—	1.589	0.0010–0.0024	0.0012–0.0026	0.3138–0.3144	0.3136–0.3142

① Exhaust valve spring test pressure: inner—21.6 lbs; outer—59.4 lbs, intake and exhaust: 41.9
② Exhaust valve installed height: inner—1.520 in.; outer—1.657 in.
③ 0.0031 maximum
④ 0.0039 maximum
⑤ Intake: 76.5–84.4; Exhaust: 73.4–80.9
⑥ Intake: 1.575; Exhaust: 1.693
⑦ 0.0051 maximum
⑧ 4K-E: 77.2

CRANKSHAFT AND CONNECTING ROD SPECIFICATIONS

(All measurements in inches)

Engine Type	Crankshaft				Connecting Rod		
	Main Brg. Journal Dia.	Main Brg. Oil Clearance	Shaft End-Play	Thrust on No.	Journal Diameter	Oil Clearance	Side Clearance
3K-C	1.9675–1.9685	0.0005–0.0015	0.0016–0.0087	3	1.6525–1.6535	0.0009–0.0019	0.0043–0.0084
2-TC	2.2827–2.2834	0.0012–0.0024②	0.0010–0.0090	3	1.8889–1.8897	0.0008–0.0020	0.0063–0.0102
20R	2.3614–2.3622	0.0010–0.0022	0.0010–0.0080	3	2.0862–2.0866	0.0010–0.0022	0.0063–0.0102
4M	2.3617–2.3627	0.0012–0.0021	0.0020–0.0100	4	2.0463–2.0472	0.0008–0.0021	0.0063–0.0117

CRANKSHAFT AND CONNECTING ROD SPECIFICATIONS

(All measurements in inches)

Engine Type	Crankshaft				Connecting Rod		
	Main Brg. Journal Dia.	Main Brg. Oil Clearance	Shaft End-Play	Thrust on No.	Journal Diameter	Oil Clearance	Side Clearance
1A-C, 3A, 3A-C, 4A-C	1.8892–1.8898	0.0005–0.0019	0.0008–0.0073	3	1.5742–1.5748	0.0008–0.0020	0.0059–0.0098
4M-E	2.3617–2.3627	0.0013–0.0023	0.0020–0.0098	4	2.0463–2.0472	0.0008–0.0021	0.0063–0.0117
3T-C	2.2825–2.2835	0.0009–0.0019	0.0008–0.0087	3	1.8889–1.8897	0.0009–0.0019	0.0063–0.0012
4K-C, 4K-E	1.9676–1.9685	0.0006–0.0016	0.0016–0.0095	3	1.6526–1.6535	0.0006–0.0016	0.0079–0.0150
22R, 22R-E	2.3614–2.3622	0.0006–0.0020	0.0008–0.0087	3	2.0862–2.0866	0.0010–0.0022	0.0063–0.0102
5M-E, 5M-GE	2.3617–2.3627	0.0013–0.0023	0.0020–0.0098	4	2.0463–2.0472	0.0008–0.0021	0.0063–0.0117
2S-E	2.1648–2.1654	0.0008–0.0019	0.0008–0.0087	3	1.8892–1.8898	0.0009–0.0022	0.0063–0.0083
3Y-EC	2.2829–2.2835	0.0008–0.0020	0.0008–0.0087	③	1.8892–1.8898	0.0008–0.0020	0.0008–0.0087
1C-L, 1C-TL	2.2435–2.2441	0.0013–0.0026	0.0016–0.0094	③	1.9877–1.9882	0.0014–0.0025	0.0031–0.0118

PISTON AND RING SPECIFICATIONS

(All measurements in inches)

Engine Type	Piston Clearance	Ring Gap			Ring Side Clearance		
		Top Compression	Bottom Compression	Oil Control	Top Compression	Bottom Compression	Oil Control
3K-C	0.0010–0.0020	0.0004–0.0011	0.0004–0.0011	0.0008–0.0035	0.0011–0.0027	0.0010–0.0030	0.0006–0.0023
2T-C	0.0024–0.0031	0.0006–0.0011	0.0008–0.0013	0.0008–0.0028	0.0008–0.0024	0.0006–0.0022	0.0008–0.0035
20R	0.0012–0.0020	0.0004–0.0012	0.0004–0.0012	snug	0.0008	0.0008	snug
4M	0.0020–0.0030	0.0039–0.0110	0.0059–0.0110	0.0008–0.0020	0.0010–0.0030	0.0008–0.0035	snug
1A-C, 3A, 3A-C, 4A-C	0.0039–0.0047	0.0079–0.0157①	0.0059–0.0138②	0.0039–0.0236③	0.0016–0.0031	0.0012–0.0028	snug
4M-E	0.0020–0.0028	0.0039–0.0110	0.0039–0.0110	0.0079–0.0200	0.0012–0.0028	0.0008–0.0024	snug
3T-C	0.0020–0.0028	0.0039–0.0098	0.0059–0.0118	0.0079–0.0276	0.0008–0.0024	0.0006–0.0022	snug
4K-C, 4K-E	0.0012–0.0020	0.0039–0.0110④	0.0039–0.0118⑤	0.0080–0.0350⑥	0.0012–0.0028	0.0008–0.0024	snug
22R, 22R-E	0.0020–0.0028	0.0094–0.0142	0.0071–0.0154	snug	0.0080 max.	0.0080 max.	snug
5M-E	0.0020–0.0028	0.0039–0.0110	0.0039–0.0110	0.0079–0.0200	0.0012–0.0028	0.0008–0.0024	snug

PISTON AND RING SPECIFICATIONS

(All measurements in inches)

Engine Type	Piston Clearance	Ring Gap			Ring Side Clearance		
		Top Compression	Bottom Compression	Oil Control	Top Compression	Bottom Compression	Oil Control
5M-GE	0.0020–0.0028	0.0083–0.0146	0.0067–0.0209	0.0079–0.0276	0.0012–0.0028	0.0008–0.0024	snug
2S-E	0.0006–0.0014	0.0110–0.0197	0.0079–0.0177	0.0079–0.0311	0.0012–0.0028	0.0012–0.0028	snug
3Y-EC	0.0030–0.0037	0.0087–0.0138	0.0059–0.0118	0.0079–0.0311	0.0012–0.0028	0.0012–0.0028	snug
1C-L, 1C-TL	0.0016–0.0024	0.0098–0.0193	0.0079–0.0173	0.0079–0.0193	0.0079–0.0081	0.0079–0.0081	snug

① 4A-C: TP—0.0098–0.0138
   Riken—0.0079–0.0138
② 4A-C: 0.0059–0.0118
③ 4A-C: TP—0.0079–0.0276
   Riken—0.0118–0.0354
④ 4K-E: 0.0063–0.0118
⑤ 4K-E: 0.0059–0.0118
⑥ 4K-E: T—0.008–0.028
   R—0.012–0.035

CAMSHAFT SPECIFICATIONS

(All measurements in inches)

Engine	Journal Diameter							Bearing Clearance	Camshaft End Play
	1	2	3	4	5	6	7		
2T-C, 3T-C	1.8291–1.8297	1.8292–1.8199	1.8094–1.8100	1.7996–1.8002	1.7897–1.7904	—	—	0.0010–0.0026	0.003–0.006
3K-C, 4K-C, 4K-E	1.7011–1.7018	1.6911–1.6917	1.6813–1.6819	1.6716–1.6722	—	—	—	①	0.003–0.006
1A-C, 3A, 3A-C, 4A-C	1.1015–1.1022	1.1015–1.1022	1.1015–1.1022	1.1015–1.1022	—	—	—	0.0015–0.0029	0.0031–0.0071
20R, 22R, 22R-E	1.2984–1.2992	1.2984–1.2992	1.2984–1.2992	1.2984–1.2992	—	—	—	0.0004–0.0020	0.0031–0.0071
2S-E	1.8291–1.8297	1.8192–1.8199	1.8094–1.8160	1.7996–1.8002	1.7897–1.7904	1.7799–1.7805	—	0.0010–0.0026	0.0031–0.0091
4M, 4M-E, 5M-E	1.3378–1.3384	1.3378–1.3384	1.3378–1.3384	1.3378–1.3384	1.3378–1.3384	1.3378–1.3384	1.3378–1.3384	0.0007–0.0022	0.0031–0.0071
5M-GE	1.4944–1.4951	1.6913–1.6919	1.7110–1.7116	1.7307–1.7313	1.7504–1.7510	1.7700–1.7707	1.7897–1.7904	0.0010–0.0026	0.0020–0.0098
3Y-EC	1.8291–1.8297	1.8192–1.8199	1.8094–1.8100	1.7996–1.8002	1.7897–1.7904	—	—	0.0010–0.0032	0.0028–0.0087
1C-L, 1C-TL	1.1014–1.1022	1.1014–1.1022	1.1014–1.1022	1.1014–1.1022	1.1014–1.1022	—	—	0.0015–0.0029	0.0031–0.0071

① 3K-C, 4K-C: Nos. 1 & 4—0.0010–0.0026
        Nos. 2 & 3—0.0014–0.0028
 4K-E: Nos. 1 & 4—0.0010–0.0026
     Nos. 2 & 3—0.0016–0.0030

TOYOTA

TORQUE SPECIFICATIONS
(All readings in ft. lbs.)

Engine Type	Cylinder Head Bolts	Rod Bearing Bolts	Main Bearing Bolts	Crankshaft Pulley Bolt	Flywheel to Crankshaft Bolts	Manifold Intake	Manifold Exhaust
3K-C	39.0–47.7	28.9–37.6	39.0–47.7	29–43	39–48	14–22 ①	
2T-C	61–68	28.9–36.1	52.0–63.5	28.9–43.3	41.9–47.7	14–18	22–32
4M	55–61 ⑥	30–36	72–78	98–119	51–57 ⑦	17–21 ④	10–15 ⑤
20R	52–64	39–48	69–83	102–130	73–79	11–15	29–36
1A-C, 3A, 3A-C, 4A-C	40–47	26–32 ⑪	40–47	55–61 ⑨	55–61	15–21	15–21
3T-C	62–68	29–36	53–63	47–61 ⑧	42–47	14–18	22–32
4M-E	55–61 ⑥	31–34	72–78	98–119	51–57	10–15	13–16
4K-C, 4K-E	40–47	29–37	40–47	55–75	40–47	15–21 ①	
22R, 22R-E	53–63	40–47	69–83	102–130	73–86	13–19	29–36
5M-E	55–61	31–34	72–78	98–119	51–57	10–15	13–16
5M-GE	55–61	31–34	72–78	98–119	51–57	15–17	26–32
1C-L, 1C-TL	60–65	45–50	75–78	70–75	63–68	10–15	32–36
3Y-EC	⑩	33–38	55–60	78–82	60–63	7–11	33–38
2S-E	45–50	33–38	40–45	78–82	70–75	30–33	30–33

① Intake and exhaust manifolds combined
② 8 mm bolts: 11–14 ft. lbs.
   13 mm bolts: 54–61 ft. lbs.
③ Flex-plate (automatic): 14–22 ft. lbs.
④ Intake manifold stud bolt: 14–18 ft. lbs.
⑤ Exhaust manifold stud bolt: 6–7 ft. lbs.
⑥ 8 mm bolts: 7–12 ft. lbs.
⑦ 10 mm bolts: 54–61 ft. lbs.
⑧ 1981 and later: 55–75
⑨ 1981 and later: 80–94
⑩ 12 mm bolt: 12–16
   14 mm bolt: 63–68
⑪ For installation of connecting rods
   purchased on or after 2/15/84: 34–39 ft.lb.

ALTERNATOR AND REGULATOR SPECIFICATIONS

Engine Type	Alternator Manufacturer	Alternator Output (amps)	Regulator Manufacturer	Field Relay Contact Spring Deflection (in.)	Field Relay Point Gap (in.)	Field Relay Volts to Close	Regulator Air Gap (in.)	Regulator Point Gap (in.)	Regulator Volts
3K-C, 4K-C ⑧, 4K-E	Nippon Denso	25 ①	Nippon Denso	0.008–0.024	0.016–0.047	4.5–5.8	0.012	0.010–0.018	3.8–14.8 ② ⑨
2TC, 20R, 22R ⑤, 22R-E	Nippon Denso	40 ③	Nippon Denso	0.008–0.024	0.016–0.047 ④	4.5–5.8	0.012	0.010–0.018	13.8–14.8 ②
3T-C	Nippon Denso	50	Nippon Denso	Not adjustable					13.4–14.8 ⑦
4M	Nippon Denso	55	Nippon Denso	0.008–0.024	0.016–0.047	4.5–5.8	0.012	0.008–0.024	3.8–14.8
4M-E, 5M-E, 5M-GE	Nippon Denso	55	Nippon Denso	Not adjustable					14.0–14.7 ⑥

ALTERNATOR AND REGULATOR SPECIFICATIONS

| Engine Type | Alternator | | Regulator | | | | | | |
| | Manufacturer | Output (amps) | Manufacturer | Field Relay | | | Regulator | | |
				Contact Spring Deflection (in.)	Point Gap (in.)	Volts to Close	Air Gap (in.)	Point Gap (in.)	Volts
1A-C & 3A, 3A-C, 4A-C	Nippon Denso	30, 40 50 & 55	Nippon Denso	Not adjustable					13.8– 14.8⑦
2S-E	Nippon Denso	70	Nippon Denso	Not adjustable					13.5– 15.1
1C-L, 1C-TL	Nippon Denso	55, 60	Nippon Denso	Not adjustable					13.8– 14.4
3Y-EC	Nippon Denso	60	Nippon Denso	Not adjustable					13.5– 15.1

① 1978–79: 50 and 55; 1980 and later 4K-C: 45 amp
② W/55 amp alt.: 14.0–14.7
③ Optional: 55 & 60 on 20R and 22R engines
④ 1978–79: 0.0118–0.0177
⑤ 1980 and later has non-adjustable regulator
⑥ 1980 and later: 14.3–14.9
⑦ W/55 amp: 14.0–14.7
⑧ Some models use non-adjustable regulator, see text
⑨ 4K-C with non-adjustable regulator—13.8–14.4V

BRAKE SPECIFICATIONS
(All measurements in inches, unless noted)

| Model | Lug Nut Torque (ft. lbs.) | Master Cylinder Bore | Brake Disc | | Maximum Brake Drum Diameter | Minimum Lining Thickness | |
			Minimum Thickness	Maximum Runout		Front	Rear
Corolla							
1200	65–86	0.626	0.350	0.006	7.953	0.040	0.040
1600	65–86	0.813	0.350	0.006	9.079	0.040	0.040
1800, 1600 ('83–'85)	65–86	②	0.453	0.006	9.079	0.040	0.040
Celica (exc. Supra)							
'78–'79	65–86	0.813	0.450	0.006	9.079	0.040	0.040
'80	65–86	0.813	0.453	0.006	9.079	0.040	0.040
'81	65–86	0.813	0.453	0.006	9.079	0.118	0.040
'82–'85	65–86	②	0.750	0.006	9.079	0.118	0.040
Celica Supra							
'79–'80	65–86	0.813	0.453①	0.006	—	0.040	0.040
'81	65–86	0.813	0.453①	0.006	—	0.118	0.040
'82–'85	65–86	②	0.750③	0.006	—	0.118	0.118
Corona							
'70–'82	65–86	0.876	0.453	0.006	9.079	0.040	0.040

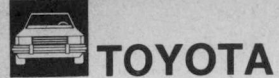

BRAKE SPECIFICATIONS

(All measurements in inches, unless noted)

Model	Lug Nut Torque (ft. lbs.)	Master Cylinder Bore	Brake Disc Minimum Thickness	Brake Disc Maximum Runout	Maximum Brake Drum Diameter	Minimum Lining Thickness Front	Minimum Lining Thickness Rear
Cressida '78–'80	65–86	②	0.453	0.006	9.079	0.040	0.040
'81–'85	65–86	②	0.669	0.006	9.079	0.040	0.040
Starlet	65–86	0.813	0.350	0.006	7.950	0.040	0.040
Tercel	65–86	②	0.354④	0.006	7.126⑤	0.040	0.040
Camry	65–86	②	0.827	0.006	7.913	0.040	0.040
Van	65–86	②	0.748	0.006	10.079	0.040	0.040

①0.354 for the rear disc
②Not specified by the manufacturer
③0.669 for the rear disc
④1983 and later: 0.394
⑤4 × 4: 7.913
⑥Figure is for front disc

WHEEL ALIGNMENT SPECIFICATIONS

Model	Year	Caster Range (deg.)	Caster Pref. (deg.)	Camber Range (deg.)	Camber Pref. (deg.)	Toe-In (in.)	Steering Axis Inclination (deg.)	Wheel Pivot Ratio (deg.) Inner	Wheel Pivot Ratio (deg.) Outer
Corolla	'78–79	1⅓P–2⅓P	1⅚P	½P–1½P	1P	0.08–0.16	7¾P	37–39	29½–33½
	'80–'83 exc. wgn.	¾P–2¼P	1¾P	½P–1½P	1P	0.04–0.16	8½P	38–40	29–33
	'80–'83 wgn.	1 1/15P–2¼P	1 17/30P	½P–1½P	1P	0.04–0.16	8⅓P	38–40	29–33
	'84–'85 exc. SR5	⅓P–1⅓P	⅚P	1N–0	½N	0–0.04	—	—	—
	'84–'84 SR5 models	①	②	¼N–¾P	¼P	0–0.08	—	—	—
Celica	'78–'81	1⅙P–2⅙P	1⅔P	½P–1½P	1P	③	7½P	36–38	28–32
	'82–'85	2⅚P–3⅚P	3⅓P	½P–1½P	1P	④	9⅓P	33–37	30–34
Supra	'79–'81	1¼P–2¼P	1¾P	⅓P–1⅓P	⅚P	0.04 out–0.04 in	7⅔P	35–37	28–32
	'82–'85	3⅔P–4⅔P	4⅙P	⅓P–1⅓P	⅚P	0.08–0.16	10½P	35–39	30–32
Corona	'78–'79	⅓P–1⅓P	⅘P	1/12P–1 1/16P	⅗P	0.04–0.12	7P	36–38	30–32
	'80–'82	1¼P–2¼P	1¾P	½P–1½P	1P	0–0.08	7⅔P	36–38	28–32
Cressida	'78–'80	½P–1½P	1P	⅓P–1⅓P	⅚P	0.08–0.16	7½P	36–39	30–34
	'81–'83	1P–2P	1½P	⅓P–1⅓P	⅚P	0.08–0.16	9P	35–39	30–32
	'84–'85 sedan	2P–3P	2½P	¼P–1¼P	¾P	0.08–0.16	9P	35–39	30–32
	'84–'85 sta. wgn.	1⅔P–2⅔P	2⅙P	⅔P–1⅓P	⅚P	0.08–0.16	9P	35–39	30–32
Tercel	'80–'82	1⅔P–2⅔P	2⅙P	0–1P	½P	0.04–0.12	11⅓P	34–36	32–34
	'83 exc. 4 × 4	⑤	⑥	⅙N–⅚P	⅓P	0.06 out–0.04 in	12½P	35–37	31–34
	'83 4 × 4	1⅚P–2⅚P	2½P	⅓P–1⅓P	⅚P	0	11⅔P	35–38	32–35
	'84–'85 sedan	⑤	⑥	⅙N–⅚P	⅓P	0.06 out–0.04 in	12½P	35–37	31–34
	'84–'85 wgn.	⑦	⑧	¼N–¾P	¼P	0.04 out–0.04 in	13P	35–37	31–34
	'84–'85 4 × 4	2P–3P	2½P	⅓P–2⅓P	⅚P	0.04 out–0.04 in	11⅔P	35–38	32–35

WHEEL ALIGNMENT SPECIFICATIONS

Model	Year	Caster Range (deg.)	Caster Pref. (deg.)	Camber Range (deg.)	Camber Pref. (deg.)	Toe-In (in.)	Steering Axis Inclination (deg.)	Wheel Pivot Ratio (deg.) Inner	Wheel Pivot Ratio (deg.) Outer
Starlet	'81–82 sedan	1⅔P–2⅓P	2P	⅓P–1P	⅔P	0.04–0.12	9¾P	36–38	33–35
	'81–'82 wgn.	1⅓P–2 1/12P	1¾P	¼P–1P	½P	0.04–0.12	9⅚P	36–38	33–35
	'83–'85	1⅓P–2⅓P	1⅚P	⅙P–1⅙P	⅔P	0.04–0.12	9¾P	36–38	32–35
Camry	'83–'85	⑨	⑩	0–1P	½P	⑪	—	—	—
Van	'84–'85	1½P–2½P	2P	0–1P	½P	0.04 out–0.04 in	—	—	—

① Man. Str.: 2¼P–3¼P
Pwr. Str.: 3⅙P–4⅙P
② Man. Str.: 2¾P
Pwr. Str.: 3⅔P
③ Man. Str.: 0–0.08
Pwr. Str.: 0.12–0.20
④ Man. Str.: 0.12–0.20
Pwr. Str.: 0.16–0.24
⑥ Man. Str.: ⅔P–1⅔P
Pwr. Str.: 2⅙P–3⅙P
⑥ Man. Str.: 1⅙P
Pwr. Str. 2⅔P
⑦ Man. Str.: ⅙N–1⅓P
Pwr. Str.: 1¼P–3P
⑧ Man. Str.: ⅔P
Pwr. Str.: 2¼P
⑨ Man. Str.: ½P–1½P
Pwr. Str.: 2P 3P
⑩ Man. Str.: 1P
Pwr. Str.: 2½P
⑪ Man. Str.: 0
Pwr. Str.: 0.08

TUNE-UP PROCEDURES

Spark Plugs

Check, clean, and adjust the spark plugs every 6000 miles. Replace them every 12,000 miles. 1980 and later vehicles require plug changes at 15,000 miles.

Clean any foreign material from around the spark plugs before removing them. Use the spark plug wrench supplied in the tool kit.

Clean any plugs which appear to be dirty and file their electrodes flat. Adjust the gap to the figure given in the "Tune-up Specifications" chart, above, using a wire feeler gauge.

NOTE: Do not use a flat gauge; an inaccurate reading will result.

Inspect the spark plug hole threads for rust and, if necessary, use a 14mm plug tap to clean them.

Examine the condition of the spark plugs and check them against the diagnosis guide at the end of the manual.

Lightly oil the threads and torque the plugs to 11–14 ft. lbs. *Use caution when tightening the plugs, as most Toyota models use aluminum heads.*

Breaker Points and Condenser

NOTE: All but the Tercel with the 3A engine are equipped with transistorized, electronic ignition systems; no breaker point adjustment is necessary or possible.

Loosen the clips which attach the distributor cap to the distributor body and lift the cap straight up. Leave the leads connected to the cap. Remove the rotor and dust cover.

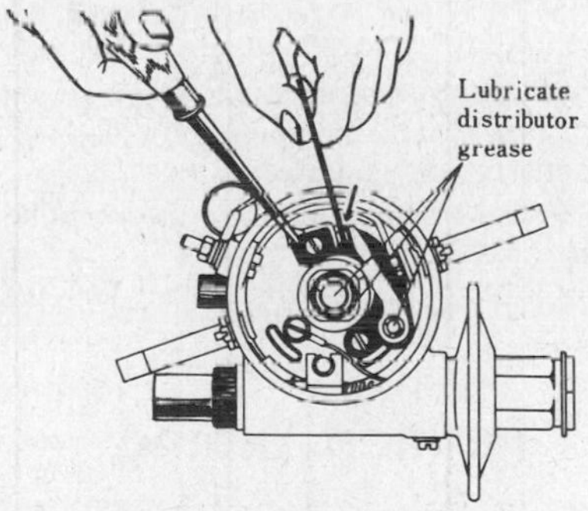

Point gap : 0.018 inch

Adjusting breaker point gap

Clean the distributor cap and rotor with alcohol. Inspect them for cracks and other signs of wear or damage. Polish the points with a point file.

NOTE: Do not use emery cloth or sandpaper; these may leave particles on the points, causing them to arc.

If the points are badly pitted or worn, replace them as follows:

1. Unfasten the point lead connector.
2. Remove the point retaining clip and remove the point hold-down screw.
3. Remove the point set.
4. Installation is the reverse of removal.

After replacing the points, or as routine maintenance, adjust the points to the specifications given in the tune-up chart at the beginning of this section as follows:

1. Rotate the engine by hand or by using a remote starter switch, so that the rubbing block is on the high point of the cam lobe.
2. Insert a feeler gauge of the proper thickness between the points; a slight drag should be felt.
3. If no drag is felt or if the feeler gauge cannot be inserted at all, loosen, but do not remove, the point hold-down screw.
4. Insert a screwdriver into the adjustment slot. Rotate the screwdriver until the proper point gap is attained.
5. Tighten the point hold-down screw. Lubricate the cam lobes, breaker arm, rubbing block, arm pivot, and distributor shaft with a small amount of special high-temperature distributor grease.

Check the operation of the centrifugal advance mechanism by moving the rotor clockwise. Release the rotor; it should return to its original position. If it does not, check it for binding.

Check the vacuum advance unit by removing the cap and pressing in on the octane selector. Release the octane selector. It should snap back to its original position. Check for binding if it fails to do so.

Replace the condenser if it is suspect or as routine maintenance during the point replacement operation, in the following manner:

1. Remove the nut and washer from the condenser lead terminal.
2. Remove the condenser mounting screw and withdraw the condenser.
3. Installation is the reverse of removal.

NOTE: The condenser is mounted on the outside of the distributor body on all models.

Install the dust cover, rotor, and the distributor cap on the distributor. Adjust the dwell and timing, as outlined below.

Dwell Angle

Connect a dwell/tachometer, in accordance with its manufacturer's instructions, between the distributor primary lead and a ground.

—— CAUTION ——

On models with electronic ignition, hook the dwell meter or tachometer to the negative (−) side of the coil, not to the distributor primary lead; damage to the ignition control unit will result.

With the engine warmed up and running at the specified idle speed (see the tune-up chart), take a dwell reading.

If the point dwell is not within specifications, shut the engine off and adjust the point gap, as outlined above.

NOTE: Increasing the point gap decreases the dwell angle and vice versa.

Install the dust cover, rotor, and cap. Check the dwell reading again.

Electronic Ignition

All gasoline engine models are equipped with fully transistorized electronic ignition except the Tercel with the 3A engine. The 3A engine uses a breaker point-type ignition.

The electronic ignition system uses an ignition signal generating system in place of the breaker points. It consists of a rotor, a magnetic element and a pickup coil all mounted inside the distributor. The system needs no routine maintenance. Repair is limited to replacement of defective parts and adjustment of the air gap.

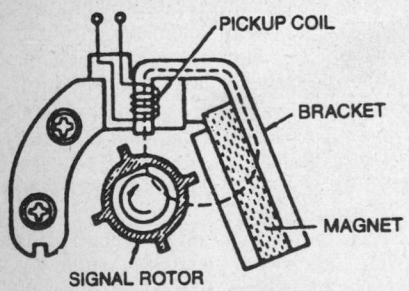

Components of the electronic ignition signal generator

AIR GAP ADJUSTMENT

1. Remove the distributor cap, rotor, and the dust shield.
2. Turn the crankshaft until a tooth of the signal rotor aligns with the projection of the pick-up coil.
3. Using a non-magnetic feeler gauge, measure the distance between the signal rotor tooth and the pick-up coil projection. The gap should be 0.008–0.016 in.

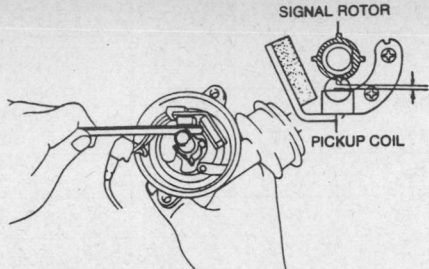

Checking the air gap on the electronic ignition system—all engines except 1983 and later 3A-C and 4A-C

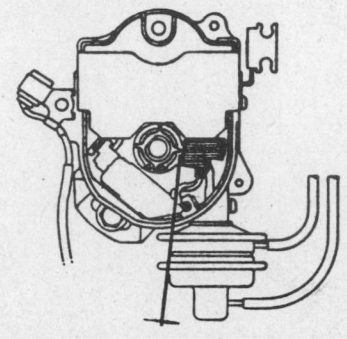

Checking the air gap on the electronic ignition system—1983 and later 3A-C and 4A-C

—— CAUTION ——
Do not use an ordinary metal feeler gauge.

4. If the gap is incorrect, loosen the two pick-up coil-to-distributor mounting screws. Using a screwdriver in the notch of the pick-up coil mounting, turn the pick-up until the gap is correct.
5. Tighten the pick-up coil mounting screws and recheck the gap.
6. Install the distributor cap and the rotor.

Ignition Timing

EXCEPT DUAL POINT SYSTEMS

1. Warm up the engine and set the parking brake. Connect a tachometer and check the engine idle speed to see that it is within specifications. Adjust it as outlined below if it is not.

—— CAUTION ——

On models with electronic ignition, hook the dwell meter or tachometer to the negative (−) side of the coil, not to the distributor primary lead; damage to the ignition control unit will result.

NOTE: 1983 and later A-series engines and all 1984–85 engines require a special type of tachometer which hooks up to the service connector wire coming out of the distributor. As many tachometers are not compatible with this hook-up, we recommend that you consult with the manufacturer before purchasing a certain type.

If the timing mark is difficult to see, use chalk or a dab of paint to make it more visible.

2. Connect a timing light to the engine, as outlined in the instructions supplied by the manufacturer of the light.
3. Disconnect the vacuum line from the distributor vacuum unit and plug the line. If a vacuum advance/retard distributor is used, disconnect and plug both vacuum lines from the distributor.

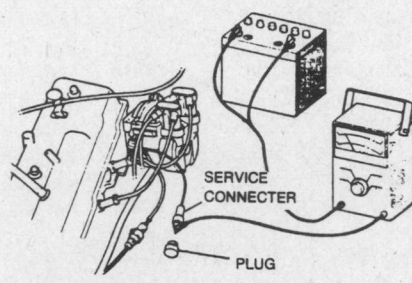

1983 and later A-series engines require a special tachometer hook-up

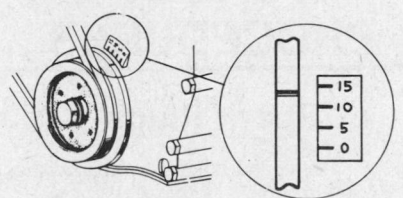

Timing marks—4M, 4M–E and 5M–E engines

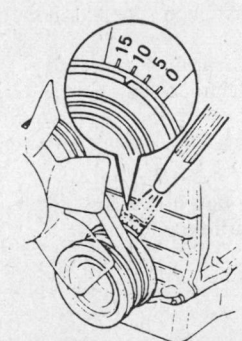

Timing marks for the 5M-GE and 2SE

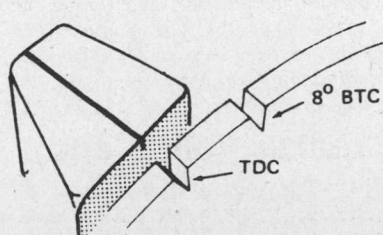

Timing marks—20R engines

Timing marks—22R and 22R-E engines

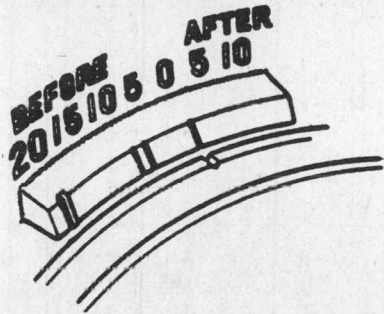

Timing marks—1A-C, 3A and 1980–82 3A-C engines

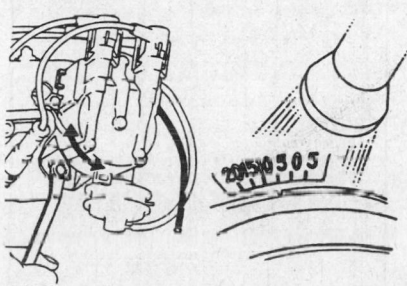

Timing marks—4A-C and 1983 and later 3A-C engines (note disconnected vacuum hose)

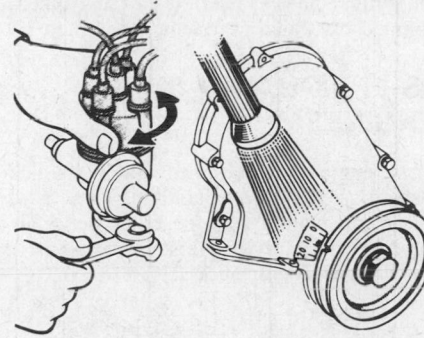

Timing marks—4K–C and 4K–E engines

4. Allow the engine to run at the specified idle speed with the gear shift in Neutral for cars with manual transmissions, and in Drive (D) for cars with automatic transmissions.

—— **CAUTION** ——

Be sure that the parking brake is firmly set and that the wheels are chocked.

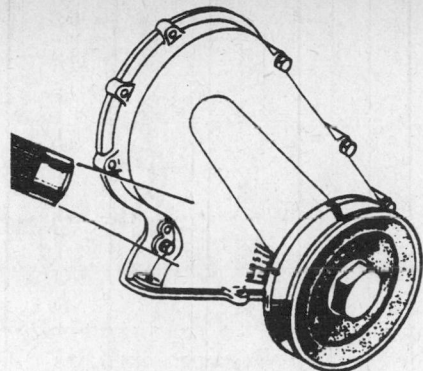

Timing marks—3K-C and 2T-C engines

Timing marks—3T-C engines

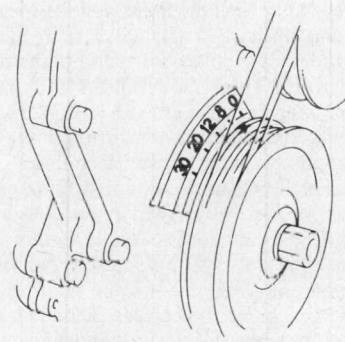

3Y-EC timing marks

5. Point the timing light at the timing marks as indicated in the accompanying illustrations. With the engine at idle, timing should be at the specification given in the tune-up chart at the beginning of this section. If it is not, loosen the pinch bolt at the base and rotate the distributor to advance or retard the timing, as required.

6. Stop the engine and tighten the pinch bolt. Start the engine and recheck the timing.

7. Stop the engine and disconnect the timing light and the tachometer. Connect the vacuum line(s) to the vacuum advance unit.

Octane Selector

The octane selector is used as a fine adjustment to match the vehicle's ignition timing to the grade of gasoline being used. It is located near the distributor vacuum

unit, beneath a plastic dust cover. The octane selector system is used mainly on point-type ignition systems. Normally the octane selector should not require adjustment, however, if necessary, adjustment is as follows:

1. Align the setting line with the threaded end of the housing and then align the center line with the setting mark on the housing.

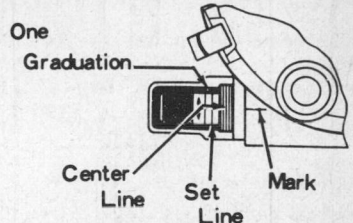

Octane selector

2. Drive the car to the speed specified on the chart below, in high gear, on a level road.

3. Depress the accelerator pedal all the way to the floor. A slight "pinging" sound should be heard. As the car accelerates, the sound should gradually go away.

4. If the pinging sound is loud or if it fails to disappear as the vehicle speed increases, retard the timing by turning the knurled knob on the selector toward "R" (Retard).

5. If there is no pinging sound at all, advance the timing by turning the knob toward "A" (Advance).

6. When the adjustment is completed, replace the plastic dust cover.

NOTE: One graduation of the octane selector is equal to about ten degrees of crankshaft angle.

OCTANE SELECTOR TEST SPEEDS

Engine Type	Test Speed (mph)
3K-C	19–21
2T-C, 20 R	16–22
4M	25

Valve Lash

ADJUSTMENT

All Engines Except 2S-E, 4K-E and 5M-GE

NOTE: Although Toyota recommends that the valve lash on certain models be set while the engine is running, we feel that for the average owner-mechanic it is more convenient to adjust the valves statically (engine off). Thus, running valve lash adjustment procedures have been omitted from this manual.

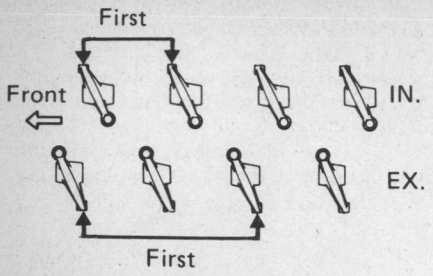

Adjust these valves 1st on T–series engines

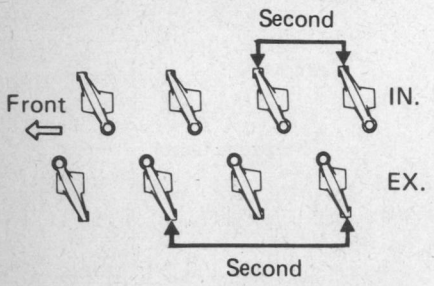

Adjust these valves 2nd on T–series engines

1. Start the engine and run it until it reaches normal operating temperature.

2. Stop the engine. Remove the air cleaner assembly. Remove any other hoses, cables, etc. which are attached to, or in the way of the cylinder head cover. Remove the cylinder head cover.

— CAUTION —
Be careful when removing components as the engine will be hot.

3. Turn the crankshaft until the point or notch on the pulley aligns with the 'O' or 'T' mark on the timing scale. This will insure that the engine is at TDC.

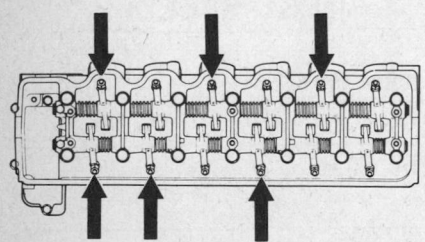

Adjust these valves 1st on M–series engines (except 5M–GE)

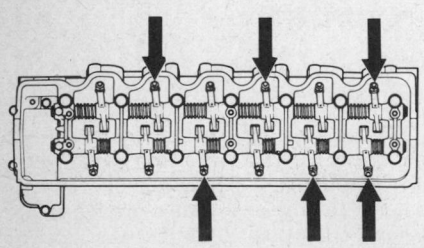

Adjust these valves 2nd on M-series engines (except 5M–GE)

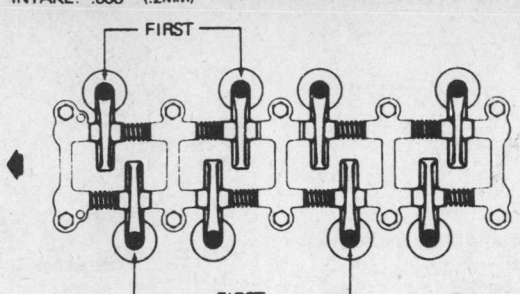

Adjust these valves 1st on R–series engines

NOTE: **Check that the rocker arms on the No. 1 cylinder are loose. If not, turn the crankshaft one complete revolution (360°).**

4. Retighten the cylinder head bolts on all engines to the proper torque specifications (see ''Torque Specifications''). Also, retighten the valve rocker support bolts to the proper specifications.

— CAUTION —
Tighten all of the bolts in Step 4 in the proper sequence and stages (see ''Cylinder Head Removal and Installation'').

5. Using a flat feeler gauge, check the clearance between the bottom of the rocker arm and the top of the valve stem. This measurement should correspond to the one given in the ''Tune-Up Specifications'' chart. Check only the valves listed under ''First' in the accompanying valve arrangement illustrations for your particular engine.

6. If the clearance is not within specifications, the valves will require adjustment. Loosen the locknut on the end of the rocker arm and, still holding the nut with an open end wrench, turn the adjustment screw to achieve the correct clearance.

7. Once the correct valve clearance is achieved, keep the adjustment screw from turning with your screwdriver and then tighten the locknut. Recheck the valve clearances.

8. Turn the engine one complete revolution (360°) and adjust the remaining valves. Follow Steps 5–7 and use the valve arrangement illustration marked 'Second'.

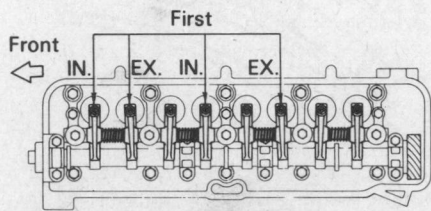

Adjust these valves 1st on A–series engines

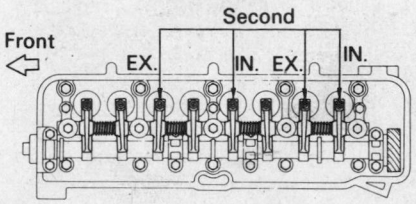

Adjust these valves 2nd on A–series engines

9. Use a new gasket and then install the cylinder head cover. Install any other components which were removed in Step 2.

2S-E, 4K-E AND 5M-GE ENGINES

These engines are equipped with hydraulic lash adjusters in the valve train. These adjusters maintain a zero clearance between the rocker arm and valve stem; no adjustment is possible or necessary.

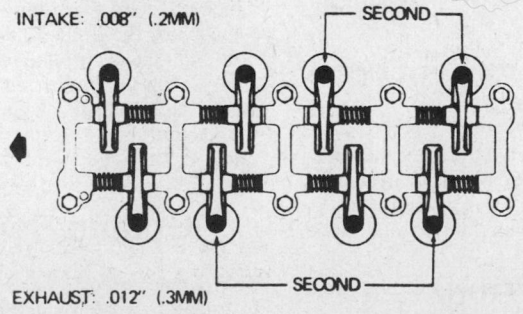

Adjust these valves 2nd on R–series engines

Idle Speed and Mixture

ADJUSTMENT

All Except 2S-E, 3Y-EC, 22R-E, 4M-E, 5M-E and 5M-GE, and Diesel

The idle speed and mixture should be adjusted under the following conditions: the air cleaner must be installed, the choke fully opened, the transmission should be in Neutral (N), all accessories (incl. the electric engine cooling fan, if so equipped) should be turned off, all vacuum lines should be connected, and the ignition timing should be set to specification.

1. Start the engine and allow it to reach normal operating temperature.

2. Check the float setting; the fuel level should be just about even with the spot on the sight glass. If the fuel level is too high or low, adjust the float level as outlined in the "Fuel System" section.

3. Connect a tachometer in accordance with its manufacturer's instructions. However, connect the tachometer positive (+) lead to the coil Negative (−) terminal. DO NOT hook it up to the distributor side; damage to the transistorized ignition could result.

NOTE: 1983 and later A–series and all 1984–85 engines require a special type of tachometer which hooks up to the service connector wire coming out of the distributor. As many tachometers are not compatible with this hook-up, we recommend that you consult with the manufacturer before purchasing a certain type.

NOTE: On 1980 and later models, all of which have tamper-proof idle mixture screws, merely turn the idle speed adjusting screw until the proper idle speed is obtained. Disregard the following steps.

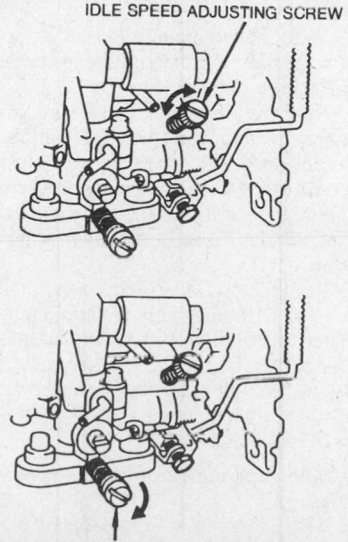

Carburetor adjustment points for the 4K-C engine

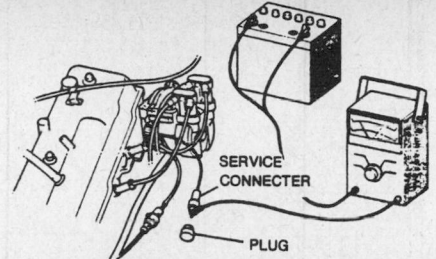

1983 and later A-series engines require a special tachometer hook-up

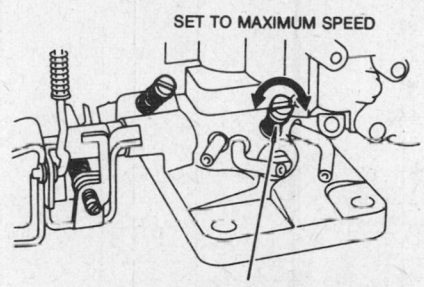

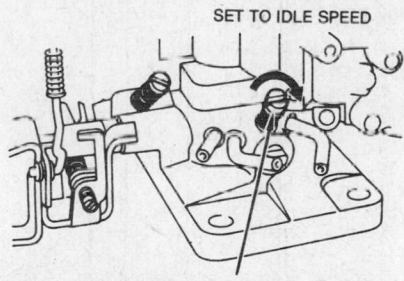

Carburetor adjustment points for the "A" series engines—typical

Disconnect the tachometer after the adjustment is complete.

4. Turn the idle speed adjusting screw to obtain one of the following initial idle speeds:

    3K-C, 2T-C—930 rpm
    20R—900 rpm
    4M—820 rpm
    1A-C, 2A-3A—750 rpm

NOTE: On the 1983 Starlet, race the engine at 2500 rpm for 2 min. before adjusting the idle speed.

5. Turn the idle mixture adjusting screw to increase the idle speed as much as is possible.

6. Next, turn the idle speed screw to again obtain the same idle speed figure given in Step 4.

7. If possible, turn the idle mixture screw to increase the idle speed again.

8. Keep repeating Steps 6 and 7 until the idle mixture adjusting screw will no longer increase the idle speed above the figure specified in Step 4.

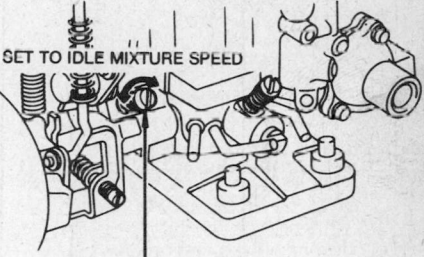

Carburetor adjustment points for the 3T-C engine

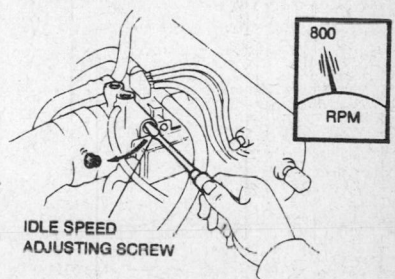

Idle speed adjustment—5M-GE engines

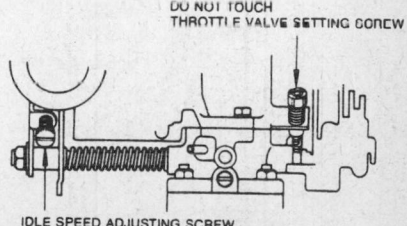

Carburetor adjustment for the 3K-C engines

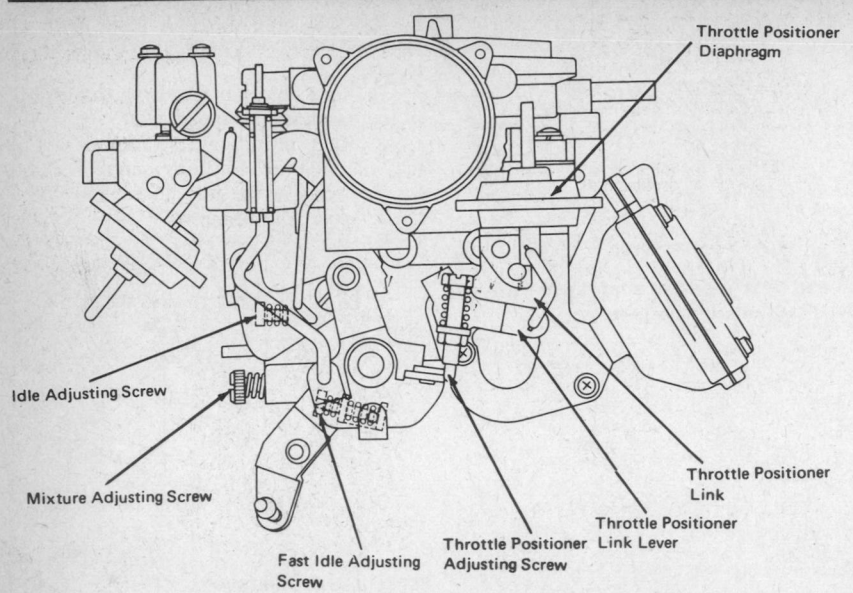

Idle Adjusting Screw

Mixture Adjusting Screw

Fast Idle Adjusting Screw

Throttle Positioner Adjusting Screw

Throttle Positioner Link Lever

Throttle Positioner Link

Throttle Positioner Diaphragm

Carburetor adjustment points for the 4M engine

9. Slowly turn the idle mixture screw *clockwise*, until the idle speed specified in the "Tune-Up Specifications" chart is reached (this makes the mixture leaner).

10. Disconnect the tachometer.

22R-E, 4M-E, 5M-E and 5M-GE

NOTE: In order to complete this procedure you will need a voltmeter and an EFI idle adjusting wire harness (Special Service Tool 09842-14010) which is available at your Toyota dealer.

1. Behind the battery on the left front fender apron is a service connector. Remove the rubber caps from the connector and connect the EFI idle adjusting wire harness.

2. Connect the positive lead of the voltmeter to the red wire of the wiring harness and then connect the negative lead to the black wire.

3. Hook up a tachometer as per the manufacturer's instructions.

4. Warm up the oxygen sensor by run-

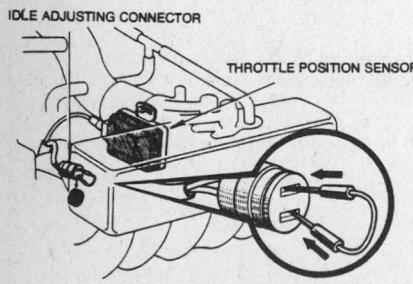

Short the idle adjustment connector

Idle adjusting harness Special Service Tool

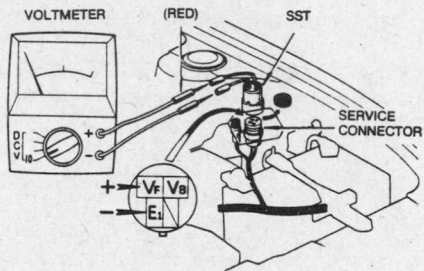

The service connector is found on the left front fender apron; right front apron on 1982 and later Supra

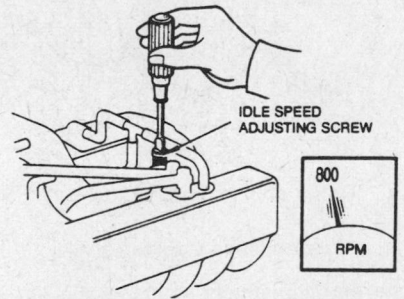

Idle speed adjustment—22R-E, 4M-E and 5M-E engines

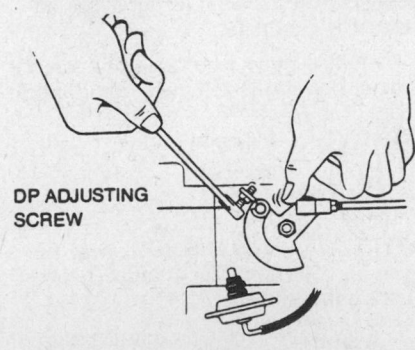

Loosen the locknut and turn the adjusting screw to set the dashpot

ning the engine at 2,500 rpm for about two minutes. The needle of the voltmeter should be fluctuating at this time, if not, turn the idle mixture adjusting screw until it does.

5. Set the idle speed to specifications (see "Tune-Up Specifications" chart) by turning the idle speed adjusting screw.

NOTE: The idle speed should be set immediately after warm-up while the needle of the voltmeter is fluctuating.

6. The idle adjustment procedure for the 22R-E and 5M-GE engines is now complete. Follow the remaining steps for the 4M-E and 5M-E engines.

7. Remove the rubber cap from the idle adjusting connector and short both terminals of the connector with a wire.

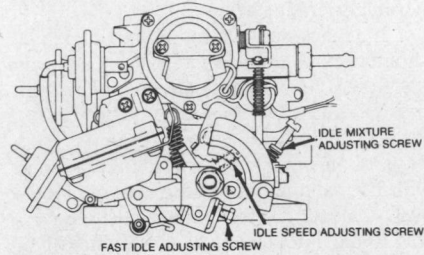

Carburetor adjustment points for the 2T-C engine

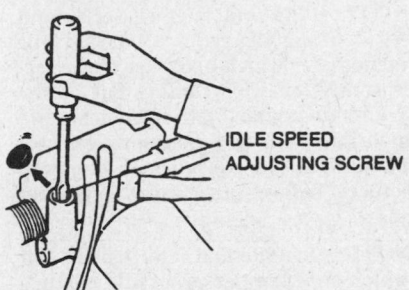

Idle speed adjustment on the 4K-E engines

8. While the connector is still shorted, run the engine at 2,500 rpm for two more minutes.

9. With the engine at idle and the connector still shorted, read and remember the voltage shown on the voltmeter.

10. Remove the short circuit wire from the connector and then race the engine to 2,500 rpm once.

11. Adjust the idle mixture adjusting screw until the median of the indicated voltage range is the same as the reading taken in Step 8.

12. Replug the idle mixture adjusting screw hole. Disconnect the tachometer, the voltmeter and the special wiring harness. Replace the rubber cap to the service connector and the idle adjusting connector.

2S-E and 3Y-EC

1. Run the engine to normal operating temperature.

2. The air cleaner should be in place and all wires and vacuum hoses connected. All accessories should be off and the transmission in neutral.

3. Connect a tachometer to the engine.

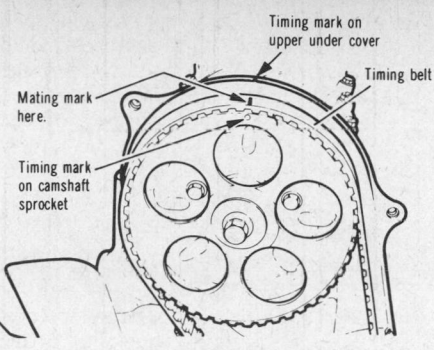

2S-E idle speed adjustment

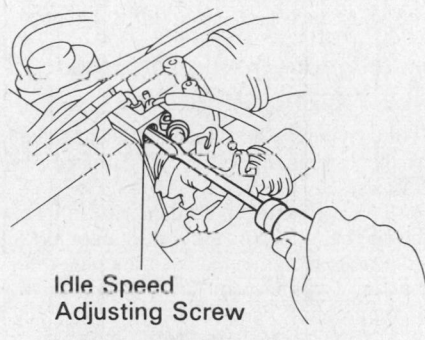

Idle Speed Adjusting Screw

3Y-EC idle speed adjustment

On the 3Y-EC the positive lead to the tach should be connected to the − side of the coil. On the 2S-E, it should be connected to the coil connector marked IIA.

—————— **CAUTION** ——————

Never allow the tachometer or coil terminals to be grounded. This will damage the injection system.

4. Run the engine at 2500 rpm for 2 minutes.

5. Let the engine return to idle and set the idle speed by turning the idle adjusting screw to obtain 700 rpm for MT or 750 rpm for AT.

6. Remove the tachometer.

Diesels

1. Run the engine to normal operating temperature.

2. The air cleaner should be in place and all accessories off.

3. The transmission should be in neutral.

4. Install a tachometer compatible with diesels.

5. Turn the idle adjusting screw to obtain 700 rpm.

6. Remove the tachometer.

Idle Speed Adjusting Screw

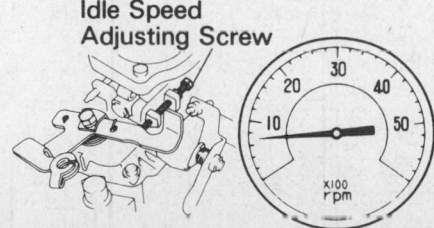

Diesel idle speed adjustment

ENGINE ELECTRICAL

Distributor

1978–83 ALL MODELS AND 1984 STARLET

Removal

1. Unfasten the cables from the spark plugs, after marking the wiring order. Remove the high tension cable from the coil.

2. Remove the primary wire and the vacuum line from the distributor. Remove the distributor cap.

3. Matchmark the distributor housing and the engine block; mark the rotor position in the distributor as well. This will aid in correct positioning of the distributor during installation.

4. Remove the clamp from the distributor. Withdraw the distributor from the block.

NOTE: It is easier to install the distributor if the engine timing is not disturbed while it is removed. If the timing has been lost, see "Installation—Timing Disturbed" below.

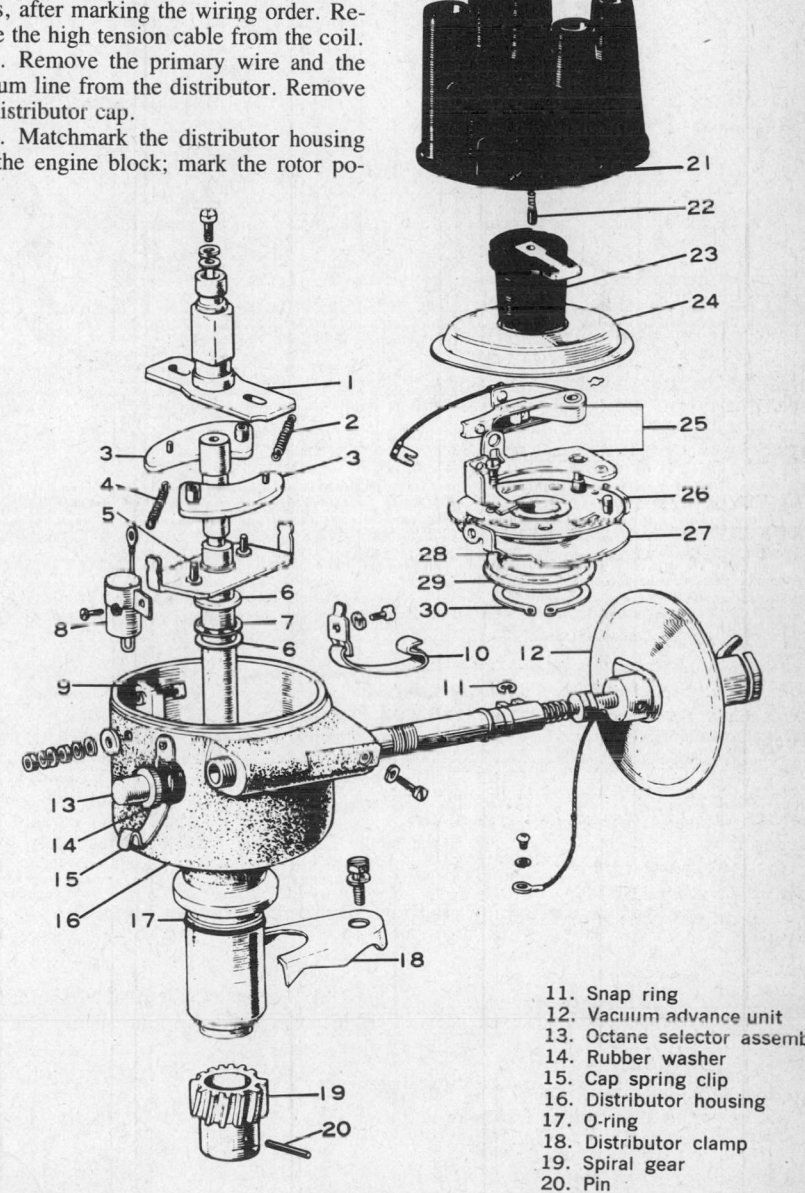

1. Cam
2. Governor spring
3. Governor weight
4. Governor spring
5. Distributor shaft
6. Metal washer
7. Bakelite washer
8. Condenser
9. Insulator
10. Cap spring clip
11. Snap ring
12. Vacuum advance unit
13. Octane selector assembly
14. Rubber washer
15. Cap spring clip
16. Distributor housing
17. O-ring
18. Distributor clamp
19. Spiral gear
20. Pin
21. Distributor cap
22. Spring
23. Rotor
24. Dust cover
25. Breaker point assembly
26. Movable plate
27. Stationary plate
28. Adjusting washer
29. Wave washer
30. Snap ring

An exploded view of the breaker point-type distributor—typical

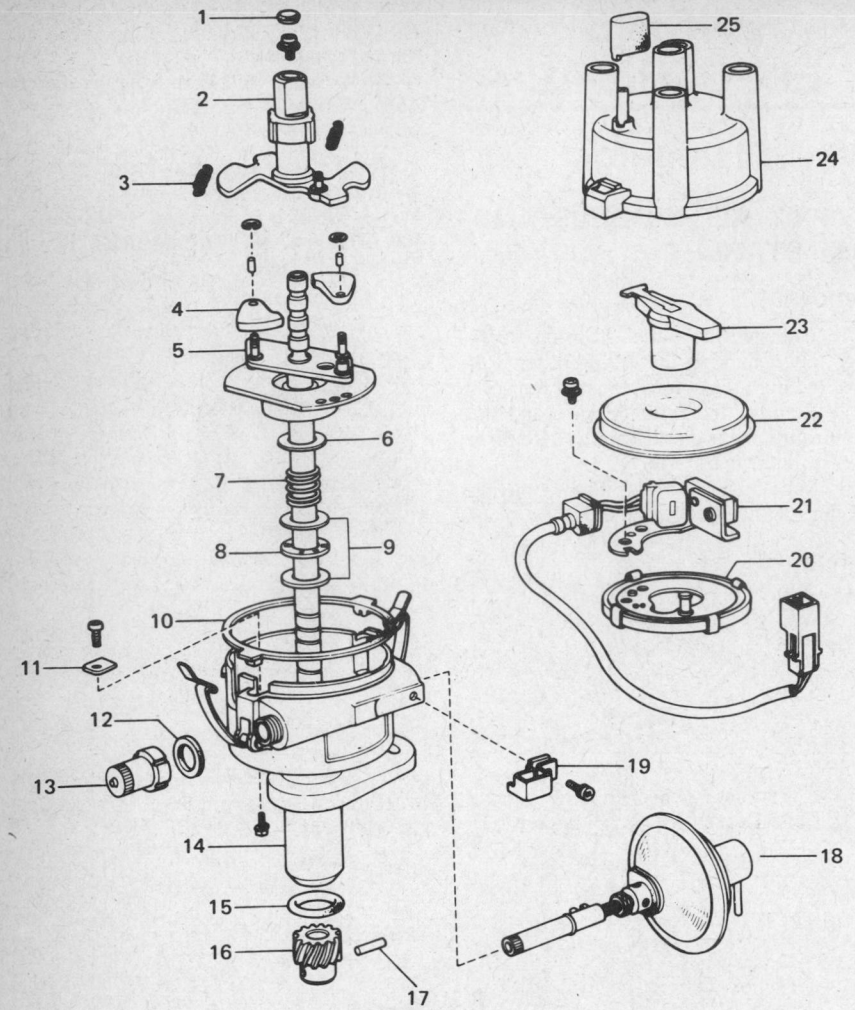

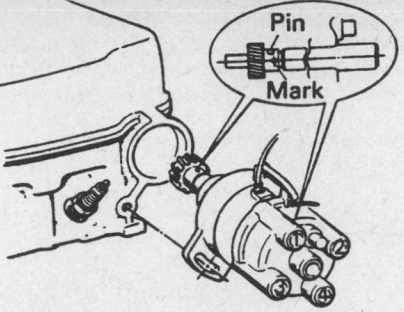

1980–82 A-series distributor alignment

1. Cam grease stopper
2. Signal rotor
3. Governor spring
4. Governor weight
5. Governor shaft
6. Plate washer
7. Compression coil spring
8. Thrust bearing
9. Washer
10. Dustproof packing
11. Steel plate washer
12. Rubber washer
13. Octane selector cap
14. Housing
15. O-ring
16. Sprial gear
17. Pin
18. Vacuum advance
19. Cord clamp
20. Breaker plate
21. Signal generator
22. Dustproof cover
23. Distributor rotor
24. Distributor cap
25. Rubber cap

Exploded view of a fully electronic ignition distributor—typical

Installation—Timing Not Disturbed

1. Insert the distributor in the block and align the matchmarks made during removal.

2. Engage the distributor drive with the oil pump driveshaft.

NOTE: Before installing the distributor on A–series engines, there is one further step. On 1980–82 models: Align the drilled mark on the driven gear (not the driven gear straight pin) with the center of the No. 1 terminal on the distributor cap and then align the stationary flange center with the bolt hole center. On 1983 models: Align the protrusion on the housing center of the flange with that of the bolt hole on the cylinder head.

3. Install the distributor clamp, cap, high tension wire, primary wire, and vacuum line.

4. Install the wires on the spark plugs.

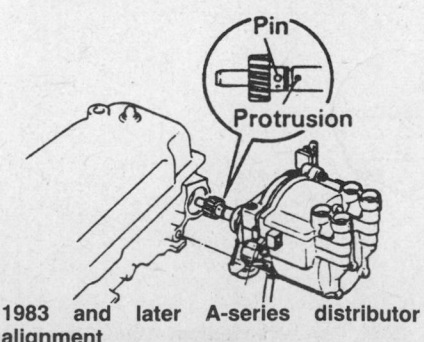

1983 and later A-series distributor alignment

5. Start the engine. Check the timing and adjust the octane selector, if so equipped.

Installation—Timing Disturbed
ALL EXCEPT 5M-GE

If the engine has been cranked, dismantled, or the timing otherwise lost, proceed as follows:

1. Determine top dead center (TDC) of the number one (No. 1) cylinder's compression stroke by removing the spark plug from the No. 1 cylinder and placing a finger or a compression gauge over the spark plug hole. Crank the engine until compression pressure starts to build up. Continue cranking the engine until the timing marks indicate TDC (or 0°).

2. Next, align the timing marks to the specifications given in the "Ignition Timing" column of the tune-up chart at the beginning of this section.

3. Temporarily install the rotor in the distributor shaft so that the rotor is pointing toward the No. 1 terminal in the distributor cap. The points should just be about to open.

4. Use a small screwdriver to align the slot on the distributor drive (oil pump driveshaft) with the key on the bottom of the distributor shaft.

5. Install the distributor in the block by rotating it slightly (no more than one gear tooth in either direction) until the driven gear meshes with the drive.

NOTE: Oil the distributor spiral gear and the oil pump driveshaft end before distributor installation.

6. Rotate the distributor, once it is installed, so that the points are just about to open. Temporarily tighten the pinch bolt.

7. Remove the rotor and install the dust cover. Replace the rotor and the distributor cap.

8. Install the primary wire and the vacuum line.

9. Install the No. 1 cylinder spark plug. Connect the cables to the spark plugs in the proper order by using the marks made during removal. Install the high tension wire on the coil.

10. Start the engine. Adjust the ignition timing and the octane selector (if so equipped), as outlined above.

5M-GE

1. Follow Step 1 of the above procedure.

2. Remove the oil filler cap. Looking into the camshaft housing with the aid of a flashlight, check to make sure that the match hole on the second (No. 2) journal of the camshaft housing is aligned with the hole in the No. 2 journal of the camshaft. If the holes are not aligned, rotate the camshaft one full turn.

3. Install a new O-ring on the distributor shaft. Make sure the distributor cap is still removed at this time.

4. Align the matchmark on the distributor spiral gear with that of the distributor housing as shown.

5. Insert the distributor into the camshaft housing, aligning the center of the mounting flange with that of the bolt hole in the side of the housing.

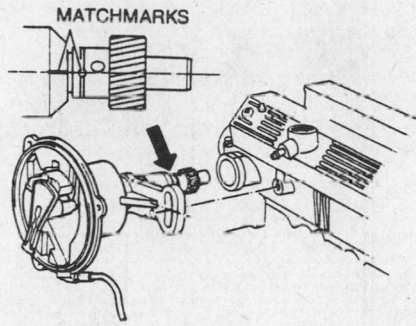

Align the matchmarks on the distributor gear and housing

6. Align the rotor tooth in the distributor with the pickup coil. Temporarily install the distributor pinch bolt.

7. Install the distributor cap, and install the oil filler cap.

8. Follow Steps 9 and 10 of the above procedure.

1984–85 MODELS, EXC. STARLET

Removal

1. On the Van, remove the right front seat and engine service hole cover.

2. On all engines, disconnect the battery ground, disconnect the electrical leads, vacuum hoses and spark plug wires from the distributor.

3. Remove the hold down bolts, and pull the distributor from the engine.

Installation

1. Set the engine at TDC of #1 cylinder's firing stroke. This can be accomplished by removing #1 spark plug and turn the engine by hand with your thumb over the spark plug hole. As #1 is coming up on its firing stroke, you'll feel pressure against your thumb. Make sure the timing marks are set at 0.

2. On all except the Van and Camry, coat the spiral gear and governor shaft tip with clean engine oil. Align the protrusion on the distributor housing with the pin on the spiral gear drill mark side. Insert the distributor, aligning the center of the flange with the bolt hole on the cylinder head. Tighten the bolts.

3. On the Van, align the drilled mark on the driven gear with the groove on the distributor housing. Insert the distributor, aligning the stationary flange center with the bolt hole in the head. Tighten the bolts.

4. On the Camry, remove the right front wheel and fender apron seal, remove the hole plug of the #2 timing belt cover, and, using a mirror, align the mark on the oil seal retainer with the center of the small hole on the camshaft timing pulley by turning the crankshaft pulley clockwise. Install the plug, fender apron and seal, and the wheel. Coat the spiral gear with clean engine oil, align the protrusion on the housing with the mark on the spiral gear and insert the distributor, aligning the center of the flange with the bolt hole on the head. Tighten the bolts.

Alternator

PRECAUTIONS

1. Always observe proper polarity of the battery connections; be especially careful when jump-starting the car.

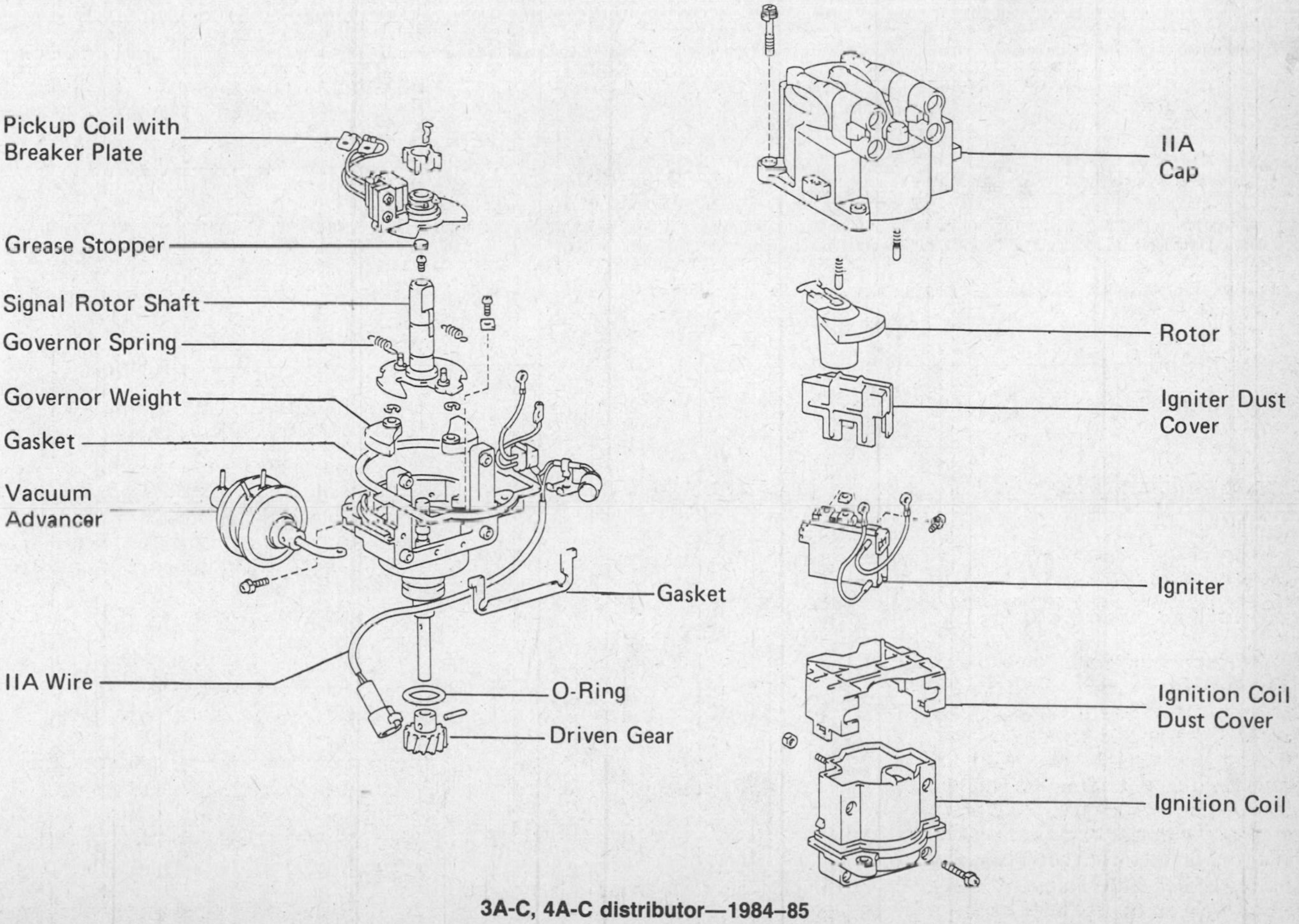

Pickup Coil with Breaker Plate

Grease Stopper

Signal Rotor Shaft

Governor Spring

Governor Weight

Gasket

Vacuum Advancer

IIA Wire

Gasket

O-Ring

Driven Gear

IIA Cap

Rotor

Igniter Dust Cover

Igniter

Ignition Coil Dust Cover

Ignition Coil

3A-C, 4A-C distributor—1984–85

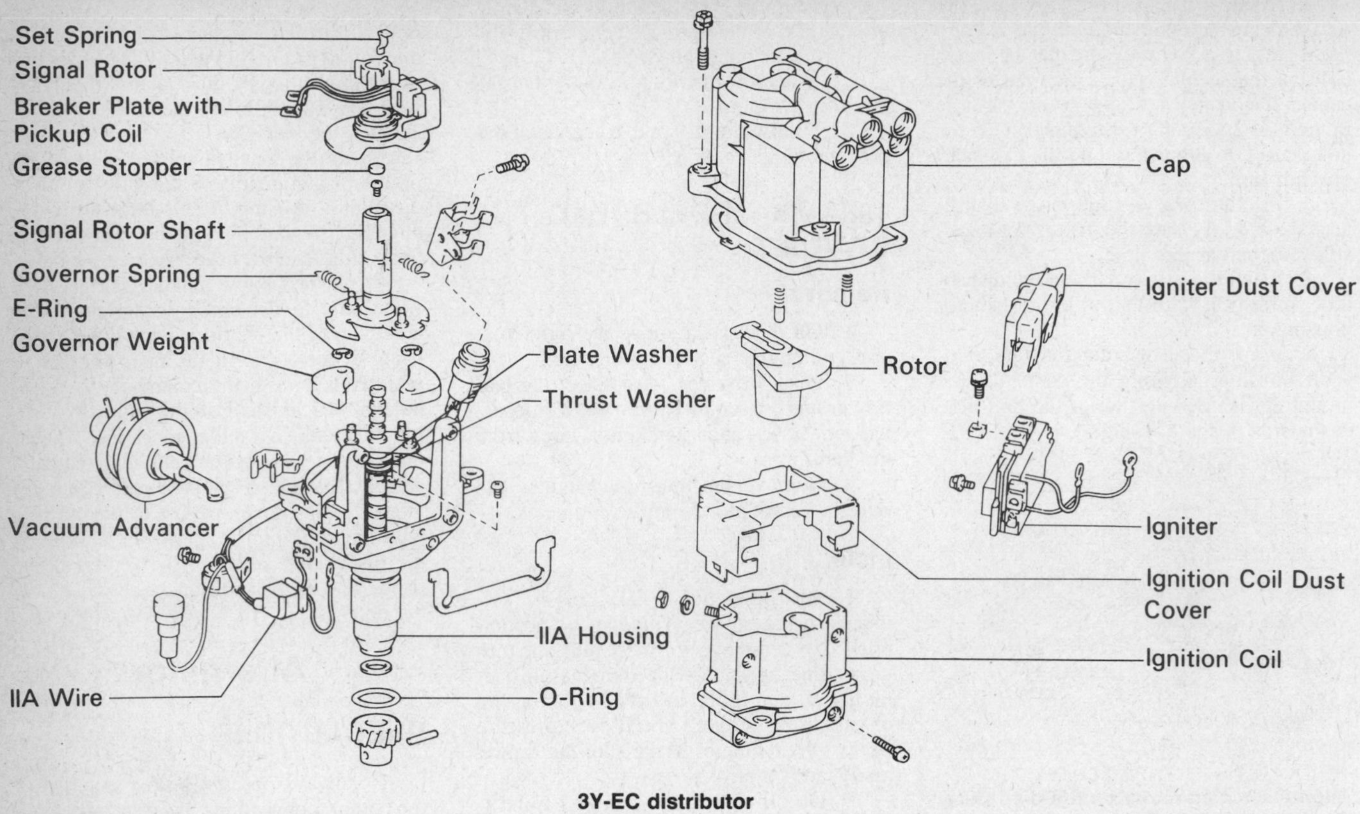

Set Spring
Signal Rotor
Breaker Plate with Pickup Coil
Grease Stopper

Signal Rotor Shaft
Governor Spring
E-Ring
Governor Weight

Plate Washer
Thrust Washer

Vacuum Advancer

IIA Wire

IIA Housing

O-Ring

Cap

Rotor

Igniter Dust Cover

Igniter

Ignition Coil Dust Cover

Ignition Coil

3Y-EC distributor

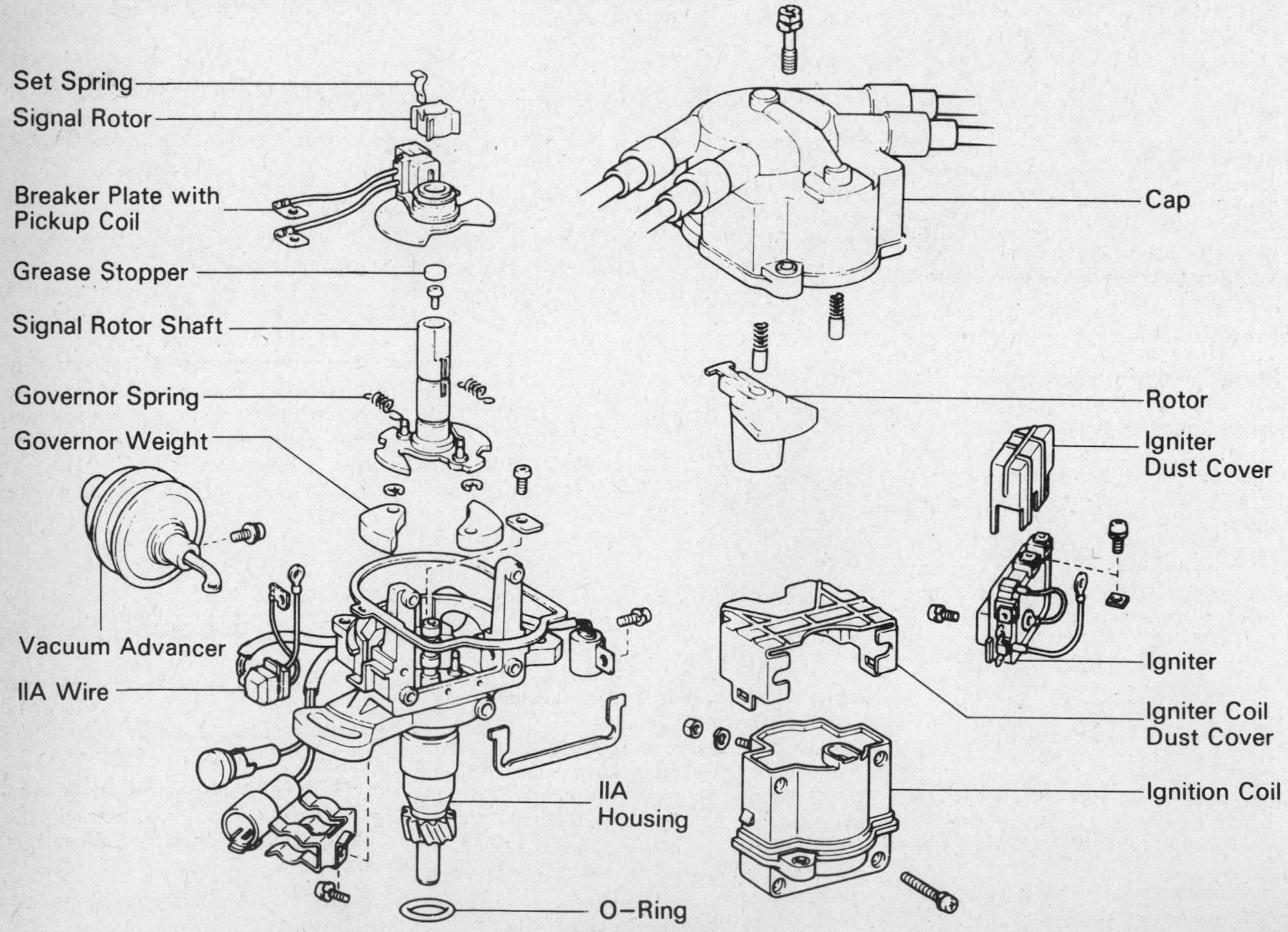

Set Spring
Signal Rotor

Breaker Plate with Pickup Coil

Grease Stopper

Signal Rotor Shaft

Governor Spring

Governor Weight

Vacuum Advancer

IIA Wire

IIA Housing

O-Ring

Cap

Rotor

Igniter Dust Cover

Igniter

Igniter Coil Dust Cover

Ignition Coil

2SE distributor

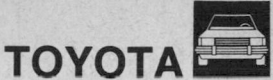

2. Never ground or short out any alternator or alternator regulator terminals.

3. Never operate the alternator with any of its or the battery's leads disconnected.

4. Always remove the battery or disconnect its output lead while charging it.

5. Always disconnect the ground cable when replacing any electrical components.

6. Never subject the alternator to excessive heat or dampness if the engine is being steam-cleaned.

7. Never use arc-welding equipment with the alternator connected.

REMOVAL & INSTALLATION

NOTE: On some models, the alternator is mounted very low on the engine. On these models it may be necessary to remove the gravel shield and work from underneath the car in order to gain access to the alternator.

1. Disconnect the battery cables at the battery.

2. Remove the air cleaner, if necessary, to gain access to the alternator.

3. Unfasten the bolts which attach the adjusting link to the alternator. Remove the alternator drive belt.

4. Unfasten and tag the alternator attaching bolt and then withdraw the alternator from its bracket.

5. Installation is the reverse order of removal. After installing the alternator, adjust the belt tension.

BELT TENSION ADJUSTMENT

Inspection and adjustment to the alternator drive belt should be performed every 3,000 miles or if the alternator has been removed.

1. Inspect the drive belt to see that it is not cracked or worn. Be sure that its surfaces are free of grease or oil.

2. Push down on the belt halfway between the fan and the alternator pulleys (or crankshaft pulley) with thumb pressure. Belt deflection should be ⅜–½ in.

3. If the belt tension requires adjustment, loosen the adjusting link bolt and move the alternator until the proper belt tension is obtained.

─────── CAUTION ───────
Do not overtighten the belt; damage to the alternator bearings could result.

4. Tighten the adjusting link bolt.

External Regulator

REMOVAL & INSTALLATION

1. Disconnect the battery cables at the battery.

2. Disconnect the wiring harness connector from the regulator.

3. Remove the regulator securing bolts.

Remove the regulator, complete with its condenser.

4. Installation is the reverse order of removal.

VOLTAGE ADJUSTMENT

1. Connect a voltmeter to the battery terminals.

2. Start the engine and gradually increase its speed to about 1500 rpm.

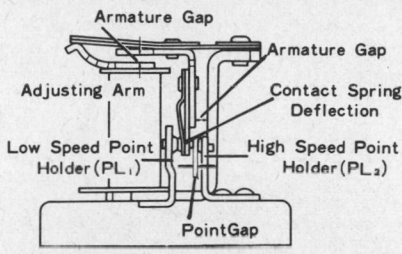

Voltage regulator components

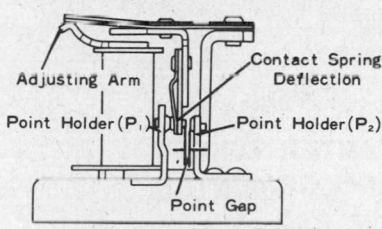

Field relay components

3. At this speed, the voltage reading should fall within the range specified in the chart above.

4. If the voltage does not fall within the specifications, remove the cover from the regulator and adjust it by bending the adjusting arm.

5. Repeat Steps 2 and 3; if the voltage cannot be brought to specifications, proceed with the mechanical adjustments, outlined below.

MECHANICAL ADJUSTMENTS

NOTE: Perform the preceding voltage adjustment before beginning the mechanical adjustments.

Field Relay

1. Remove the cover from the regulator assembly.

2. Use a feeler gauge to check the amount that the contact spring is deflected while the armature is being depressed.

3. If the measurement is not within specifications, adjust the regulator by bending point holder P (see illustration).

4. Check the point gap with a feeler gauge against the specifications in the chart.

5. Adjust the point gap, as required, by bending the point holder P_1 (see the illustration).

6. Clean off the points with emery cloth if they are dirty and wash them with solvent.

Voltage Regulator

1. Use a feeler gauge to measure the air (armature) gap. If it is not within the specifications, adjust it by bending the *low*-speed point holder.

2. Check the point gap with a feeler gauge. If it is not within specifications, adjust it by bending the *high*-speed point holder. Clean the points with emery cloth and wash them off with solvent.

3. Check the amount of contact spring deflection while depressing the armature. The specification should be the same as that for the contact spring on the field relay. If the amount of deflection is not within specification, replace, do not adjust, the voltage regulator.

Go back and perform the steps outlined under "Voltage Adjustment," above. If the voltage cannot be brought within specifications after regulator replacement, the alternator is probably defective and should be replaced.

NOTE: On all vehicles with the "IC" type regulator there are no adjustments necessary. If found to be defective, it must be replaced.

Internal (IC) Regulator

The IC regulator is mounted on the alternator housing, is transistorized, and is non-adjustable.

REMOVAL & INSTALLATION

1. Disconnect the battery cables at the battery.

2. Remove the end cover of the regulator.

3. Remove the three screws that go through the terminals.

4. Remove the (two) top mounting screws that mount the regulator to the alternator. Remove the regulator.

5. To install the new IC regulator. Place the regulator in position on the alternator. Install and secure the (two) top mounting screws. Install the (three) terminal screws. Install the end cover.

6. Reconnect the battery ground cable.

Starter

REMOVAL & INSTALLATION

1. Disconnect the cable which runs from the starter to the battery, at the battery end.

2. Remove the air cleaner assembly, if necessary, to gain access to the starter.

NOTE: On some models with automatic transmissions, it may be necessary to disconnect the throttle linkage connecting rod.

3. On Corolla 1200 models, perform the following:

a. Disconnect the manual choke cable

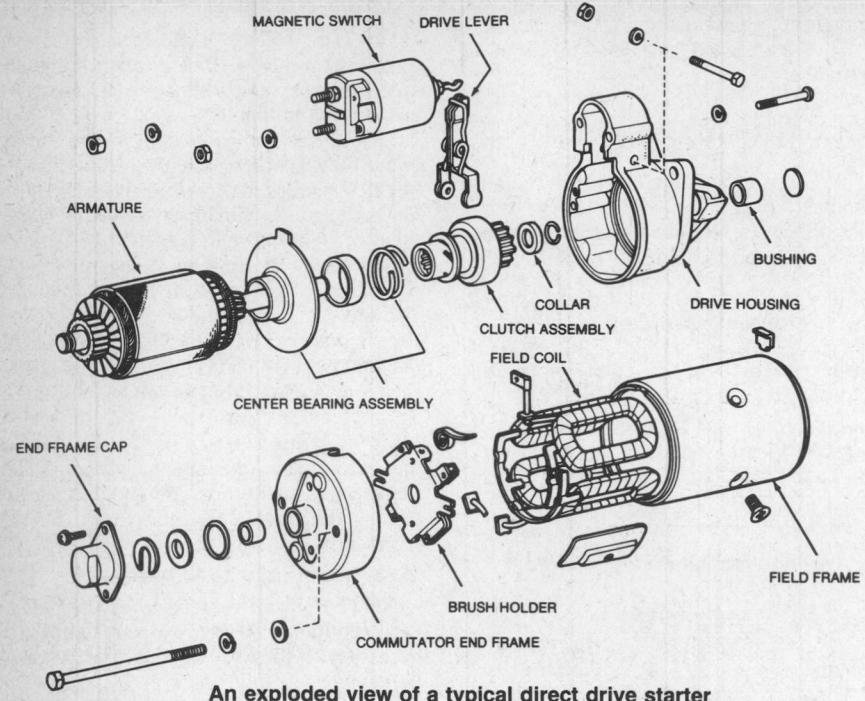

An exploded view of a typical direct drive starter

and the accelerator cable from the carburetor.

b. Unbolt the front exhaust pipe flange from the manifold and then remove the complete manifold assembly.

4. Disconnect all of the wiring at the starter.

5. Remove the starter toward the front of the car.

6. Installation is in the reverse order of removal.

FIELD FRAME ASSEMBLY

ARMATURE

FELT SEAL

BRUSH SPRING

BRUSH HOLDER

IDLER GEAR

PINION GEAR

O-RING

MAGNETIC SWITCH ASSEMBLY

STEEL BALL   CLUTCH ASSEMBLY   STARTER HOUSING

An exploded view of a typical reduction gear starter

STARTER DRIVE REPLACEMENT

Direct Drive Starter

1. Disconnect the wiring and remove the starter from the engine.

2. Remove the solenoid from the starter.

3. Remove the through bolts and take off the end plate.

4. Slide the armature shaft far enough out to disengage the clutch forks.

5. Remove the retaining clip and washer from the shaft.

6. Slide the starter drive assembly from the shaft.

7. Install in reverse of removal. Always use a new retaining clip.

Reduction Gear Starter

Remove the starter as previously outlined, then follow Steps 1–4 of the starter solenoid procedure for the reduction gear starter which follows. Also note the assembly information at the end of the same procedure.

STARTER SOLENOID & BRUSH REPLACEMENT

Direct Drive Starter

NOTE: The starter must be removed from the car in order to perform this operation.

1. Remove the field coil lead from the solenoid terminal.

2. Unfasten the solenoid retaining screws. Remove the solenoid by tilting it upward and withdrawing it.

3. Remove the end frame bearing cover screws and remove the cover.

4. Remove the thru-bolts. Remove the commutator end-frame.

5. Withdraw the brushes from their holder if they are to be replaced.

6. Minimum brush length should be 0.40 in. Replace the brushes with new ones if required.

7. Dress the new brushes with emery cloth so that they will make proper contact.

8. Use a spring scale to check the brush spring tension. Replace the springs if they do not meet specification.

9. Assembly is the reverse of disassembly. Pack the end bearing cover with multipurpose grease before installing it.

Reduction Gear Starter

NOTE: The starter must be removed from the car in order to perform this operation.

1. Disconnect the solenoid lead.

2. Loosen the two bolts on the starter housing and separate the field frame from the solenoid. Remove the O-ring and felt dust seal.

3. Remove the two screws and separate the starter drive from the solenoid.

4. Withdraw the clutch and gears. Remove the ball from the clutch shaft bore or solenoid.

5. Using a screwdriver, separate the brush and brush spring and remove the brush from the brush holder.

6. Minimum brush length should be 0.40 in. Replace the brushes if they are too short.

7. Check the gears for wear or damage. Replace as required.

8. Assembly is the reverse of disassembly. Lubricate all bearings and gears with high temperature grease. Grease the ball

before inserting in the clutch shaft bore. Align the tab on the brush holder with the notch on the field frame. Check the positive (+) brush leads to see that they aren't grounded. Align the mark on the solenoid with the bolt anchors on the field frame.

ENGINE MECHANICAL

Engine

REMOVAL & INSTALLATION

——— **CAUTION** ———
Be sure that the car is supported securely, during engine removal.

3K-C, 4K-C and 4K-E

1. Drain the entire cooling system.
2. Unfasten the cable which runs from the battery to the starter at the battery terminal.
3. Scribe marks on the hood and hinges to aid in hood alignment during assembly. Remove the hood.
4. Unfasten the headlight bezel retaining screws and remove the bezels. Remove the five radiator grille attachment screws and remove the grille.
5. Remove the hood lock assembly after detaching the release cable.
6. Unfasten the nuts from the horn retainers and disconnect the wiring. Remove the horn assembly.
7. Remove the air cleaner from its bracket.
8. Remove the windshield washer tank from its bracket.
9. Remove both the upper and lower radiator hoses from the engine.

NOTE: On models with automatic transmissions, disconnect the oil lines from the oil cooler.

10. Detach the radiator mounting bolts and remove the radiator.
11. Remove the accelerator cable from its support on the cylinder head cover. Unfasten the cable at the carburetor throttle arm. (Except 4K-E). Disconnect the choke cable from the carburetor. (Except 4K-E).
12. Detach the water hose retainer from the cylinder head.
13. Disconnect the bypass and heater hoses at the water pump. Disconnect the other end of the heater hose from the water valve. Remove the heater control cable from the water valve.
14. Disconnect the wiring harness multiconnectors.
15. Detach the downpipe from the exhaust manifold.
16. Detach the wires from the water temperature and oil pressure sending units.

17. Remove the nut from the front left-hand engine mount.
18. Remove the fuel line from the fuel pump.
19. Detach the battery ground cable from the cylinder block.
20. Remove the nut from the front right-hand engine mount.
21. Remove the clip and detach the cable from the clutch release lever.
22. Remove the primary and high-tension wires from the coil.
23. Detach the back-up light switch wire at its connector on the right side of the extension housing.
The following steps apply to Corolla models with manual transmissions and Starlet:
24. Remove the carpet from the transmission tunnel. Remove the boots from the shift lever.
25. Remove the snap ring from the gearshift selector lever base. Withdraw the selector lever assembly.
The following steps apply to Corolla models with automatic transmissions:
26. Disconnect the accelerator linkage torque rod at the carburetor.
27. Disconnect the throttle linkage connecting rod from the bellcrank lever.
28. Drain the oil from the transmission oil pan.
29. Detach the transmission gear selector shift rod from the control shaft.
The following steps apply to Corollas with both manual and automatic transmissions and Starlet:
30. Raise the rear wheels of the car. Support the car with jack stands.
31. Disconnect the driveshaft from the transmission.

NOTE: Drain the oil from the manual transmission.

32. Detach the exhaust pipe support bracket from the extension housing.
33. Remove the insulator bolt from the rear engine mount.
34. Place a jack under the transmission and remove the four bolts from the rear (engine support) crossmember.
35. Install lifting hooks on the engine lifting brackets. Attach a suitable hoist.
36. Lift the engine slightly; then move it toward the front of the car. Bring the engine the rest of the way out at an angle.
37. Engine installation is the reverse of removal. Adjust all transmission and carburetor linkages. Install and adjust the hood. Refill the engine, radiator, and transmission to capacity.

2T-C, 3T-C and 4A-C

1. Drain the radiator, cooling system, transmission, and engine oil.
2. Disconnect the battery-to-starter cable at the positive battery terminal.
3. Scribe marks on the hood and its hinges to aid in alignment during installation.
4. Remove the hood supports from the body. Remove the hood.

NOTE: Do not remove the supports from the hood.

5. On Corolla models, perform Steps 4–6 as detailed in the 3K-C "Engine Removal" section above.
6. Detach both the upper and lower hoses from the radiator. On cars with an automatic transmission, disconnect the lines from the oil cooler. Remove the radiator.
7. Unfasten the clamps and remove the heater and bypass hoses from the engine. Remove the heater control cable from the water valve.
8. Remove the wiring from the coolant temperature and oil pressure sending units.
9. Remove the air cleaner from its bracket, complete with its attendant hoses.
10. Unfasten the accelerator torque rod from the carburetor. On models equipped with automatic transmissions, remove the transmission linkage as well.
11. Remove the emission control system hoses and wiring, as necessary.
12. Remove the clutch hydraulic line support bracket.
13. Unfasten the high-tension and primary wires from the coil.
14. Mark the spark plug cables and remove them from the distributor.
15. Detach the right-hand front engine mount.
16. Remove the fuel line at the pump.
17. Detach the downpipe from the exhaust manifold.
18. Detach the left-hand front engine mount.
19. Disconnect all of the wiring harness multiconnectors.
20. On cars equipped with manual transmissions, remove the shift lever boot and the shift lever cap boot.
21. Unfasten the four gear selector lever cap retaining screws, remove the gasket and withdraw the gear selector lever assembly from the top of the transmission.

NOTE: On Corolla five-speed models, the floor console must be removed first.

22. Lift the rear wheels of the car off the ground and support the car with jack stands.
23. On cars equipped with automatic transmissions, disconnect the gear selector control rod.
24. Detach the exhaust pipe support bracket.
25. Disconnect the driveshaft from the rear of the transmission.
26. Unfasten the speedometer cable from the transmission. Disconnect the wiring from the back-up light switch and the neutral safety switch (automatic only).
27. Detach the clutch release cylinder assembly, complete with hydraulic lines. Do not disconnect the lines.
28. Unbolt the rear support member mounting insulators.
29. Support the transmission and detach the rear support member retaining bolts. Withdraw the support member from under the car.

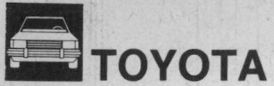
30. Install lifting hooks on the engine lifting brackets. Attach a suitable hoist to the engine.

31. Remove the jack from under the transmission.

32. Raise the engine and move it toward the front of the car. Use care to avoid damaging the components which remain on the car.

33. Support the engine on a workstand. Install the engine in the reverse order of removal. Adjust all of the linkages as detailed in the appropriate section. Install the hood and adjust it. Replenish the fluid levels in the engine, radiator, and transmission.

20R and 22R
EXCEPT 1982–83

1. Perform Steps 1–4 of the 2T-C and 3T-C ''Engine Removal'' procedure.

2. Remove the headlight bezel and the radiator grille.

3. Remove the fan shroud, the hood lock base and the base support.

4. Perform Steps 8–19 of the 2T-C and 3T-C ''Engine Removal'' procedure.

Perform the following steps on models with manual transmissions:

5. Remove the center console if so equipped.

6. Remove the shift lever boot(s).

7. Unfasten the four shift lever cap retaining screws. Remove the cap and withdraw the shift lever assembly.

Perform the following steps on models equipped with automatic transmissions:

8. Remove the transmission selector linkages:

a. On models equipped with a floor-mounted selector, disconnect the control rod from the transmission.

b. On column-mounted gear selector models, remove the shifter rod.

9. Disconnect the neutral safety switch wiring connector.

Perform the following steps on all models:

10. Raise the rear of the vehicle.

11. Remove the retaining screws and remove the parking brake equalizer support bracket. Disconnect the cable which runs between the lever and the equalizer.

12. Remove the speedometer cable from the transmission. Disconnect the back-up light wiring.

13. Detach the driveshaft from the rear of the transmission.

NOTE: If oil runs out of the transmission, an old U-joint yoke sleeve makes an excellent plug.

14. Perform Steps 27–33 of the 2T-C and 3T-C ''Engine Removal'' procedure.

15. Installation of the engine is the reverse order of removal. Refer to the appropriate chapters for transmission and carburetor adjustments. Refill the engine oil, coolant, and transmission oil to the proper levels.

1982–83

1. Disconnect the battery cables at the battery.

2. Mark the hood to indicate the relationship beween the hood and the hood hinges. Unbolt and remove the hood.

3. Drain the coolant from both the radiator and the engine block.

4. Remove the air cleaner assembly (mark any disconnected hoses for reassembly purposes).

5. Disconnect the accelerator linkage from the carburetor.

6. Disconnect the transmission cable from the carburetor on automatic transmission equipped models.

7. Mark and disconnect all wiring and hoses from the engine. Label each item so that it may be reattached correctly during assembly.

8. Remove the radiator grille.

9. Remove the hood lock brace, radiator upper baffle, and the hood lock.

10. Remove the radiator and the fan shroud.

11. If the vehicle is equipped with air conditioning, have the refrigerant discharged from the system by a professional service technician. Remove the air conditioning condenser from the vehicle.

12. If equipped with air conditioning, loosen the air conditioning compressor mounting bolts, remove the drive belt, remove the mounting bolts, and lay the compressor aside.

NOTE: It is not necessary to disconnect the refrigerant hoses from the compressor.

13. If the vehicle is equipped with power steering:

a. Loosen the idler pulley bolts.

b. Remove the power steering pump drive belt.

c. Remove the power steering pump mounting bolts.

d. Move the pump out of the way. It is not necessary to disconnect the hydraulic lines from the pump.

14. Disconnect the upper side of the engine shock absorber from the left engine mount.

15. Remove the engine mount bolts from each side of the engine.

16. Remove the console box to gain access to the shift lever on vehicles with manual transmissions. Also, remove the shift lever on these models.

17. Raise the vehicle and support it safely with jackstands.

18. Remove the engine undercover and drain the engine oil.

19. Remove the exhaust pipe clamp from the transmission housing, disconnect the exhaust pipe from the manifold, and allow the pipe to hang downward.

20. On vehicles with manual transmissions, remove the clutch release cylinder.

21. Disconnect the speedometer cable from the transmission and tie the cable out of the way.

22. On vehicles with automatic transmissions, disconnect the shift linkage from the shift lever.

23. Disconnect the wiring from the following items:

a. Back-up light switch

b. Neutral start switch (auto. trans. only)

c. Overdrive solenoid (auto. trans. only)

d. Oil pressure sending unit

e. Starter motor

24. Place a jack under the transmission, with a block of wood between the jack and the transmission. Raise the jack just enough to support the transmission and remove the transmission crossmember.

25. Detach the driveshaft from the rear of the transmission and plug the transmission.

26. Attach the engine lifting equipment to the engine. CAREFULLY lift the engine and transmission assembly out of the vehicle.

27. Installation of the engine is performed in the reverse of the previous steps. Refer to the appropriate sections for linkage adjustments. Replenish all fluid levels and check for leaks after the engine has been started.

22R-E

1. Follow Steps 1–10 of the above procedure.

2. Disconnect the automatic transmission actuator cable, accelerator cable and throttle cable from the bracket on the side of the EFI intake chamber.

3. Tag and disconnect the PCV hoses, the brake booster hose, the actuator hose (if equipped with cruise control), the air control valve hose and the air control valve.

4. Remove the EGR vacuum modulator and bracket after tagging and disconnecting the EGR modulator hoses.

5. Tag and disconnect the remaining emission control hoses as necessary, including the air valve hoses from the intake chamber and throttle body, the water bypass hoses from the throttle body, the air control valve hose to the actuator and the pressure regulator hose from the intake chamber.

6. Tag and disconnect the cold start injector pipe and cold start injector.

7. Tag and disconnect the throttle position sensor wire and the air valve wire.

8. Remove the bolt holding the EGR valve to the intake chamber. Disconnect the chamber from the stay, then remove the chamber from the intake manifold with the throttle body attached.

9. Tag and disconnect the water temperature sender, overdrive (with A/T) thermo switch, start injection time, temperature sensor and injection wires.

10. Remove the two set bolts from the top and bottom of the steering universal, and remover the sliding yoke.

11. Disconnect the tie-rod ends. Disconnect the pressure line mounting bolts from the front crossmember.

12. Without disconnecting the oil pipe,

remove the mounting bolts to the rack-and-pinion assembly and carefully suspend it from the front crossmember without stretching the fluid hoses.

13. Follow Steps 13–27 of the above procedure.

4M, 4M-E and 5M-E

1. Disconnect the battery cables and remove the battery.

2. Scribe aligning marks on the hood and hinges to aid in their assembly. Remove the hood.

3. Remove the fan shroud and drain the cooling system.

4. Disconnect both the upper and lower radiator hoses. Disconnect and plug the oil lines from the oil cooler on cars with automatic transmissions.

5. Detach the hose which runs to the thermal expansion tank and remove the expansion tank from its mounting bracket.

6. Remove the radiator.

7. Disconnect the heater and bypass hoses from the engine.

8. Disconnect the oil pressure light sender wiring, the alternator multiconnector, and the back-up light switch wiring.

9. Disconnect the power brake unit vacuum lines.

10. Disconnect the engine oil cooler hoses at the oil filter, if so equipped.

11. Disconnect the power steering fluid cooler hose, if so equipped.

12. Remove the air cleaner assembly from its bracket, complete with hoses.

13. Detach the emission control system wires and hoses, as required.

14. Unfasten the distributor primary wire and the high tension wire from the coil.

15. Disconnect the wiring from the starter and temperature gauge sender.

16. Remove the fuel line from the fuel pump.

17. Disconnect the heater control cable from the water valve. Unfasten the heater control vacuum hose.

18. Remove the accelerator linkage from the carburetor. On fuel injected models, disconnect the accelerator linkage from the throttle body. Tag and disconnect any remaining hoses, lines, or wires which may still be attached to the engine.

19. Detach the clutch hydraulic line from its master cylinder connections (manual transmission only). Install a cap on the master cylinder fitting to keep the hydraulic fluid from running out.

20. Detach the pressure-feed lines from the steering gear housing on models equipped with power steering.

21. Raise both the front and the rear of the car with jacks. Support the car with jack stands.

22. Detach the exhaust pipe from the downpipe and remove the exhaust pipe hangers.

23. Disconnect the speedometer cable from the right side of the transmission.

24. On models with manual transmissions:

a. Remove the center console securing screws, the gearshift knob, the gearshift boot, and then unfasten the console wiring multiconnector. Lift the console over the gearshift lever.

b. Remove the four screws which attach the shift lever retainer to the shift tower and withdraw the shift lever assembly.

25. On models equipped with an automatic transmission, unfasten the connecting rod swivel nut and detach the control rod from the gear selector lever.

26. Disconnect the parking brake lever rod, return spring, intermediate rod, and the cable from the equalizer.

27. Disconnect the driveshaft from the end of the transmission.

NOTE: If oil runs out from the transmission, an old U-joint yoke makes a good plug.

28. Remove the left-hand gravel shield and then the front engine mounts.

29. Support the transmission with a jack.

30. Remove the rear engine mounts and the rear crossmember.

31. Attach a hoist to the engine and lift it up and forward, so that it clears the car.

32. Installation is in the reverse order of removal. Adjust the transmission and carburetor linkages, as detailed in the appropriate sections. Bleed the clutch. Install the hood and adjust it. Replenish the fluid levels.

5M-GE

1. Follow Steps 1—6 of the "4M, 4M-E, 5M-E".

2. Remove the air cleaner assembly, including the air flow meter and air intake connector pipe.

3. On cars equipped with automatic transmissions, remove the throttle cable bracket from the cylinder head. On all models, remove the accelerator and actuator cable bracket from the cylinder head.

4. Tag and disconnect the cylinder head ground cable, the oxygen sensor wire, oil pressure sending unit and alternator wires, the high tension coil wire, the water temperature sending and thermo switch (A/T) wires, and the starter wires.

5. Tag and disconnect the ECT connectors and the solenoid resistor wire connector.

6. Tag and disconnect the brake booster vacuum hose from the air intake chamber, along with the EGR valve vacuum hose and the actuator vacuum hose from the air intake chamber (if equipped with cruise control).

7. Disconnect the heater and by-pass hoses from the engine.

8. Remove the glove box, and remove the ECU computer module. Disconnect the three connectors, and pull out the EFI (fuel injection) wiring harness from the engine compartment side of the firewall.

9. Remove the four shroud and four

fluid coupling screws, and the shroud and coupling as a unit.

10. Remove the engine undercover protector.

11. Disconnect the coolant reservoir hose and remove the radiator. Remove the coolant expansion tank.

12. Remove the A/C compressor drive belt, and remove the compressor mounting bolts. Without disconnecting the refrigerant hoses, lay the compressor to one side and secure it.

CAUTION
The A/C system is charged with the refrigerant R-12, which is dangerous when released. DO NOT disconnect the A/C hoses when removing the engine, unless absolutely necessary.

13. Disconnect the power steering pump drive belt and remove the pump stay. Unbolt the pump and lay it aside without disconnecting the fluid hoses.

14. Remove the engine mounting bolts from each side of the engine. Remove the engine ground cable.

15. On manual transmission cars, remove the shift lever from inside the car.

16. Jack up the car and safely support it with jackstands. Drain the engine oil.

17. Disconnect the exhaust pipe from the exhaust manifold. Remove the exhaust pipe clamp from the transmission housing.

18. On manual transmission cars, remove the clutch slave cylinder.

19. Disconnect the speedometer cable at the transmission.

20. On automatic transmission cars, disconnect the shift linkage from the shift lever. On manual transmission cars, disconnect the wire from the back-up light switch.

21. Remove the stiffener plate from the ground cable.

22. Disconnect the fuel line from the fuel filter and the return hose from the fuel hose support. Be sure to catch any leaking fuel. Plug the fuel line.

23. Follow Steps 10–12 of the 22R-E engine removal procedure.

24. Remove the intermediate shaft from the driveshaft.

25. Position a hydraulic jack under the transmission, with a wooden block between the two to prevent damage to the transmission case. Place a wooden block between the cowl panel and cylinder head rear end to prevent damage to the heater hoses.

26. Unbolt the engine rear support member from the frame, along with the ground cable.

27. Make sure all wiring is disconnected (and tagged for later assembly), all hoses disconnected, and everything clear of the engine and transmission. Attach an engine lift hoist chain to the lift brackets on the engine, and carefully lift the engine and transmission up and out of the car. *It is very helpful to have two or three helpers on this job.* Place the engine on a work stand, and remove the transmission at this time.

28. Installation is the reverse of removal.

1A-C, 3A, and 3A-C

1. Disconnect the negative battery terminal.
2. Remove the hood.
3. Remove the air cleaner and all necessary lines attached to it.
4. Drain the radiator.
5. Cover both driveshaft boots with a shop towel.
6. Remove the solenoid valve connector, water temperature switch connector, and the electric fan connector.
7. Remove the exhaust support plate bolts, and the exhaust pipe.
8. Remove the top radiator support.
9. Remove the top and bottom radiator hoses and remove the radiator with the fan.

NOTE: On cars equipped with automatic transmissions remove the cooling lines before removing the radiator.

10. Remove the windshield washer tank.
11. Remove the heater hoses and the lines to the fuel pump.

NOTE: Plug the gas line to prevent gas from leaking out.

12. Remove the accelerator cable, choke cable, and the ground strap.
13. Remove the brake booster vacuum line.
14. Remove the coil wire and unplug the alternator.
15. Remove the clutch release cable.
16. Remove the wires on the starter.
17. Remove the temperature sending and oil pressure switch connectors.
18. Remove the battery ground strap from the block.
19. Jack up your vehicle and support it with jack stands.
20. Remove the engine mounting bolts and the engine shock absorbers.
21. Support the differential with a jack.
22. Remove the transaxle mounting bolts.

NOTE: It is probably easier to remove these bolts from underneath the car.

23. Remove the engine.
24. Tie the bell housing to the cowl to keep support on the transaxle.

NOTE: The grill may be removed if necessary to give better leverage when removing the engine.

25. Installation is the reverse of removal. Adjust all linkages as covered in the appropriate section. Refill all fluids to the proper levels. Tighten the transaxle bolts to 37–57 ft. lbs.
On cars with automatic transmissions, the following procedures are necessary.
1. Remove the starter.
2. Remove the cooling lines from the transmission.
3. Support the transmission with a jack.
4. Remove the transaxle mounting bolts.
5. Remove the torque converter bolts (4).

NOTE: In order to turn the converter, place a wrench on the crankshaft pulley and turn it until you see a bolt appear in the area where the starter was.

6. While the engine is suspended from the hoist, pull it forward about 2 in.
7. Insert a pry bar in this opening and gently separate the torque converter from the engine.
8. Installation is the reverse of removal.
The following are necessary before the cylinder head can be installed. Confirm that the converter contact surface is 1.02 in. from the housing. Install a guide bolt in one of the mounting bolt holes. Remove the engine mounting insulator (left side) and the mounting bracket (right side). To secure the transaxle to the engine temporarily install the top two mounting bolts. This will facilitate easier engine installation.

2S-E, 1C-L, 1C-TL

1. Drain the engine coolant.
2. Remove the hood.
3. Remove the battery.
4. Disconnect and tag all cables attached to various engine parts.
5. Disconnect and tag all electrical wires attached to various engine parts.
6. Disconnect and tag all vacuum lines connected to various engine parts.
7. Remove the cruise control actuator and bracket.
8. Disconnect the radiator and heater hoses.
9. Disconnect the automatic transmission cooler lines.
10. Unbolt the two radiator supports and lift out the radiator.
11. Remove the air cleaner assembly and air flow meter.
12. Disconnect all wiring and linkage at the transmission.
13. Pull out the fuel injection system wiring harness and secure to the right side fender apron.
14. Disconnect the fuel lines at the fuel filter and return pipes.
15. Disconnect the spedometer cable at the transmission.
16. Remove the clutch release cylinder without disconnecting the fluid line.
17. Unbolt the air conditioning compressor and secure it out of the way.
18. Raise and support the car on jackstands.
19. Drain the transaxle fluid.
20. While someone holds the brake pedal depressed, unbolt both axle shafts. It's a good idea to wrap the boots with shop towels to prevent grease loss.
21. Unbolt the power steering pump and secure it out of the way.
22. Disconnect the exhaust pipe from the manifold.
23. Disconnect the front and rear engine mounts at the frame member.
24. Lower the vehicle.
25. Attach an engine crane at the lifting eyes.

26. Take up the engine weight with the crane and remove the right and left side engine mounts.
27. Slowly and carefully, remove the engine and transaxle assembly.
28. Installation is the reverse of removal. Torque the engine mount bolts to 29 ft. lb. Torque the axle shaft bolts to 27 ft. lb. Torque the fuel line connectors to 22 ft. lb.

3Y-EC

1. Disconnect the battery.
2. Remove the right front seat.
3. Remove the engine cover.
4. Drain the coolant.
5. Disconnect the radiator and heater hoses.
6. Disconnect and tag all vacuum hoses attached to various engine parts.
7. Disconnect and tag all wires attached to various engines parts.
8. Disconnect and tag all cables attached to various engine parts.
9. Remove the air cleaner.
10. Unbolt the power steering pump and secure it out of the way.
11. Remove the fan shroud.
12. Remove the fan and fan clutch. Do not lay the fan on its side. If you do, the fluid will leak out and the fan clutch will be permanently ruined.
13. Unbolt the air conditioning compressor and secure it out of the way.
14. Raise the vehicle about 40 inches off the floor and support it securely.
15. Drain the engine oil.
16. Disconnect the driveshaft.
17. Disconnect and remove the exhaust system.
18. Remove the transmission control cable.
19. Remove the clutch release cylinder.
20. Remove the starter.
21. Remove the speedometer cable.
22. Disconnect all remaining hoses and cables from the transmission.
23. Remove the engine tensioner cable.
24. Remove the engine underpan.
25. Remove the strut bar.
26. Place an engine jack under the engine and take up the weight. Unbolt and remove the engine mounts and lower the engine from the vehicle.
27. Installation is the reverse of removal. Torque the engine mount bolts to 58 ft. lb.

Cylinder Head

CAUTION

Do not perform this operation on a warm engine. Remove the head bolts in sequence and in several steps. Loosen the head bolts evenly. Keep the pushrods in their original order. Do not attempt to slide the cylinder head off of the block, as it is located with dowel pins. Lift the head straight up and off the block.

REMOVAL & INSTALLATION

3K-C and 4K-C

1. Disconnect the battery and drain the cooling system.

2. Remove the air cleaner assembly from its bracket, complete with its attendant hoses.

3. Disconnect the hoses from the air injection system or the vacuum switching valve lines.

4. Detach the accelerator cable from its support on the cylinder head cover and also from the carburetor throttle arm.

5. Remove the choke cable and fuel lines from the carburetor.

6. Remove the water hose bracket from the cylinder head cover.

7. Unfasten the water hose clamps and remove the hoses from the water pump and the water valve. Detach the heater temperature control cable from the water valve.

8. Disconnect the PCV line from the cylinder head cover.

9. Unbolt and remove the valve cover.

10. Remove the valve rocker support securing bolts and nuts. Lift out the valve rocker assembly.

11. Withdraw the pushrods from their bores.

12. Unfasten the hose clamps and remove the upper radiator hose from the water outlet.

13. Remove the wires from the spark plugs.

14. Disconnect the wiring and the fluid line from the windshield washer assembly. Remove the assembly.

NOTE: Use a clean container to catch the fluid from the windshield washer reservoir when disconnecting its fluid line.

15. Unfasten the exhaust pipe flange from the exhaust manifold.

16. Remove the head assembly retaining bolts and remove the head from the engine.

17. Place the cylinder head on *wooden* blocks to prevent damage to it.

18. Installation is essentially the reverse order of removal. Clean both the cylinder head and block gasket mounting surfaces. Always use a new head gasket.

NOTE: Be sure that the top side of the gasket is facing upward.

When installing the head on the block, be sure to tighten the bolts in the sequence shown, in several stages, to the specified torque.

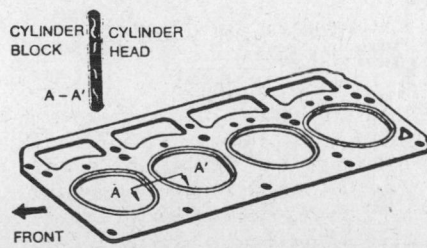

Gasket installation—4K-E

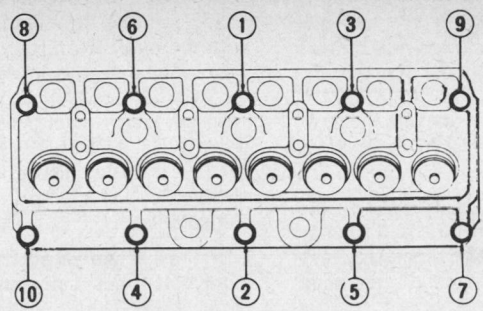

Cylinder head tightening sequence—K–series engines

The valve rocker assembly nuts and bolts should be tightened to 13–16 ft. lbs.

NOTE: The valve clearance should be adjusted to specification with each piston at top dead center (TDC) of its compression stroke.

4K-E

1. Disconnect the negative battery cable.

2. Drain the engine coolant into a suitable container.

3. Loosen the two hose clamps and remove the air cleaner hose.

4. Disconnect the throttle cable from the two places it attaches to the air intake chamber and the throttle body.

5. Tag and disconnect the four vacuum hoses connected to the air intake chamber.

Do the same for the spark plug wires, the temperature detect switch wire and the water temperature sender gauge wire.

6. Tag and disconnect all remaining wires, hoses and leads attached to the cylinder head or which might interfere with its removal.

7. Remove the spark plugs and tube.

8. Remove the intake and exhaust manifolds as detailed in the appropriate section.

9. Remove the cylinder head cover and then remove the rocker shaft assembly as detailed in the appropriate section.

10. Lift out the pushrods.

NOTE: Make sure that the pushrods remain in the correct order.

11. Little-by-little, in the proper sequence, loosen the cylinder head bolts (see illustration under "4K-C" procedure).

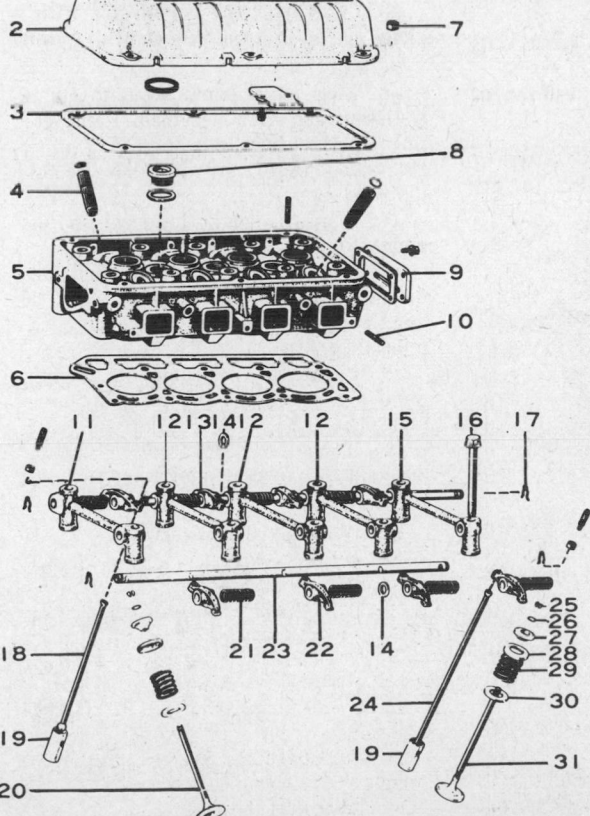

1. Oil filler cap
2. Valve cover
3. Valve cover gasket
4. Valve guide (intake)
5. Cylinder head
6. Cylinder head gasket
7. Nut
8. Screw plug
9. Cylinder head rear cover
10. Stud
11. Valve rocker support
12. Valve rocker support
13. Valve rocker arm
14. Washer
15. Valve rocker support
16. Bolt
17. Retainer spring
18. Pushrod
19. Valve lifter
20. Intake valve
21. Compression spring
22. Valve rocker arm
23. Valve rocker shaft
24. Pushrod
25. Lock spring
26. O-ring
27. Valve spring retainer
28. Oil splash shield
29. Compression spring
30. Plate washer
31. Exhaust valve

"T" series engine—cylinder head and related components

―――― **CAUTION** ――――
*Head warpage or cracking could result
from removing the bolts in the wrong order.*

12. Lift the cylinder head from the dowels on the block and place it on wooden blocks.

NOTE: If the head is difficult to remove, carefully pry with a small prybar between the head and the block. Be very careful not to damage the cylinder head and/or block surfaces.

13. Installation is in the reverse order of removal. Clean the cylinder head and block gasket mounting surfaces.

NOTE: Install the cylinder head gasket as illustrated.

The cylinder head bolts should be torqued in the proper sequence (see ''4K-C'' procedure) to the proper specifications. Adjust the valves.

2T-C and 3T-C

1. Perform Steps 1–2 of ''3K-C and 4K-C'' head removal procedure.
2. Disconnect the vacuum lines which run from the vacuum switching valve to the various emission control devices mounted on the cylinder head.
3. Disconnect the mixture control valve hose which runs to the intake manifold and remove the valve from its mounting bracket.
4. Perform Step 7 of the ''3K-C and 4K-C'' head removal procedure.
5. Detach the water temperature sender wiring.
6. Remove the choke stove pipe and its intake pipe.
7. Remove the PCV hose from the intake manifold.

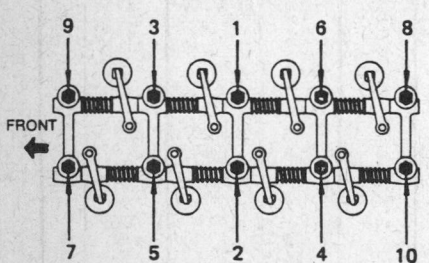

Cylinder head tightening sequence—T-series engines

8. Disconnect the fuel and vacuum lines from the carburetor.
9. Remove the clutch hydraulic line bracket from the cylinder head.
10. Raise the car and support it with jack stands. Unfasten the exhaust pipe clamp. Remove the exhaust manifold from the cylinder head.
11. Remove the valve cover.
12. Remove the cylinder head bolts in the reverse of the tightening sequence.
13. Perform Steps 10–11 of the 3K-C and 4K-C ''Cylinder Head Removal'' procedure.

14. Remove the cylinder head, complete with the intake manifold.
15. Separate the intake manifold from the cylinder head.
Install the cylinder head in the following order:
1. Clean the gasket mounting surfaces of the cylinder head and the block completely.

NOTE: Remove oil from the cylinder head bolt holes if present.

2. Place a *new* gasket on the block and install the head assembly.
3. Install the pushrods and the valve rocker assembly.
4. Tighten the cylinder head bolts *evenly*, in stages, as illustrated. See the ''Torque Specifications'' chart for the proper tightening torque.
5. Install the intake manifold, using a new gasket and tighten it to specifications.
6. The rest of the installation procedure is the reverse of removal. Adjust the valve clearances.

20R and 22R

1. Disconnect the battery.
2. Remove the three exhaust pipe flange nuts and separate the pipe from the manifold.
3. Drain the engine oil.
4. Drain the cooling system (both radiator and block). Save the coolant to be reused.
5. Remove the air cleaner, complete with hoses, from the carburetor.

NOTE: Cover the carburetor with a clean rag so that nothing can fall into it.

6. Mark all vacuum hoses to aid installation, and disconnect them. Remove all linkages, fuel lines, etc. from the carburetor, cylinder head, and manifolds. Remove the wire supports.
7. Mark the spark plug leads and disconnect them from the plugs.
8. If so equipped, disconnect and move the air injection system hoses. Mark the hose locations so that they may be properly reinstalled.
9. If equipped with air conditioning, remove the upper compressor mounting bracket.
10. If equipped with power steering, dismount the power steering pump and move

it out of the way, WITHOUT disconnecting the hydraulic lines.
11. Matchmark the distributor housing and block. Disconnect the primary lead and remove the distributor. Installation will be easier if you leave the cap leads in place.
12. Remove the valve cover.
13. Using a wrench on the crankshaft pulley, rotate the crankshaft until the No. 1 cylinder is at TDC on its compression stroke (both valves of the No. 1 cylinder—closed).
14. Place matchmarks on both the camshaft sprocket and the timing chain to indicate the relationship between these items.
15. Remove the rubber camshaft seals. Use a 19 mm wrench to remove the cam sprocket bolt. Slide the distributor drive gear off of the cam and wire the cam sprocket in place.
16. Remove the timing chain cover 14 mm bolt at the front of the head. *This must be done before the head bolts are removed.*
17. Remove the cylinder head bolts in the proper order. Improper removal could cause head damage.
18. Using pry bars applied evenly at the front and the rear of the valve rocker assembly, pry the assembly off of its mounting dowels.
19. Lift the head off of its dowels. DO NOT pry it off. Support the head on a workbench.
20. Drain the engine oil from the crankcase *after* the head has been removed, because the oil will become contaminated with coolant while the head is being removed.
Installation is in the following order:
1. Apply liquid sealer to the front corners of the block and install the head gasket.
2. Lower the head over the locating dowels. Do not attempt to slide it into place.
3. Install the rocker arm assembly over its positioning dowels.
4. Tighten the cylinder head bolts evenly, in three stages, and in order to 52–63 ft. lbs.
5. Install the timing chain cover bolt and tighten it to 7–11 ft. lbs.
6. Remove the wire and install the sprocket over the camshaft dowel. If the chain won't allow the sprocket to reach, rotate the crankshaft bolt to 51–65 ft. lbs.
7. Set the No. 1 piston at TDC of its compression stroke and adjust the valves.
8. After completing valve adjustment,

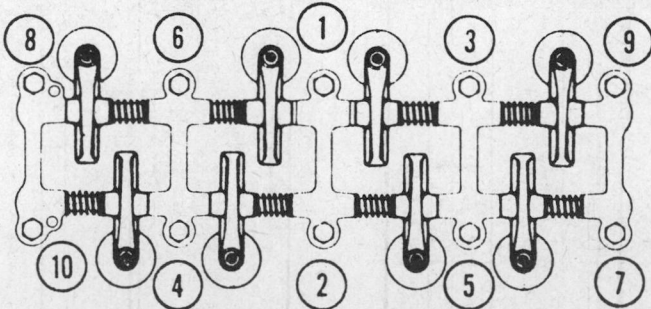

Cylinder head tightening sequence—R–series engines

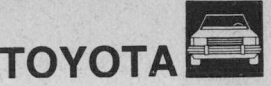
rotate the crankshaft one turn, so that the 8°-BTDC mark on the pulley aligns with the pointer.

9. Install the distributor, as previously outlined.

10. Install the spark plugs and leads.

11. Fill the engine with oil after installing the rubber cam seals. Pour the oil over the distributor drive gear and the valve rockers.

12. Install the rocker cover and tighten the bolts to 8–11 ft. lbs.

13. Connect all the vacuum hoses and electrical leads that were removed during disassembly. Install the spark plug lead supports. Fill the cooling system. Install the air cleaner.

14. Tighten the exhaust pipe-to-manifold flange bolts to 25–33 ft. lbs.

15. Mount and/or reattach the air injection, air conditioning, and power steering items, as equipped.

16. Reconnect the battery. Start the engine and allow it to reach normal operating temperature. Check and adjust the timing and valve clearance. Adjust the idle speed and mixture. Road test the vehicle.

22R-E

1. Disconnect the negative battery cable.

2. Drain the coolant from the radiator and then drain the engine oil. Remove the air cleaner hose.

3. Disconnect the oxygen sensor wire and then disconnect the exhaust pipe from the manifold.

4. Disconnect the upper radiator hose and the heater hose.

5. Disconnect the actuator, accelerator and throttle (for A/T) cables from the bracket on the side of the cylinder head.

6. Tag and disconnect all hoses from the head.

7. Remove the EGR vacuum modulator and its bracket.

8. Tag and disconnect the throttle position sensor wire, the cold start injector pipe and wire.

9. Remove the EGR valve. Disconnect the air intake chamber and its stay, unscrew the mounting bolts and remove the chamber along with the throttle body.

10. Tag and disconnect all remaining wires.

11. Remove the fuel line, the pulsation damper and the air valve.

12. Remove the distributor and the spark plugs.

13. Remove the power steering pump (if so equipped) and position it to one side with the hoses still attached.

14. Remove the cylinder head cover.

CAUTION

After removing the cylinder head cover, cover the oil return hole in the head with a rag to prevent objects from falling in.

15. Remaining removal and installation procedures are detailed in the "20R and 22R" section beginning with Step 11.

4M, 4M-E, and 5M-E

NOTE: The engine must be cold before performing this operation.

CARBURETED ENGINES

1. Disconnect the battery cables from the battery.

2. Remove the air cleaner assembly and mounting brackets, complete with attached hoses. Mark the hoses so that they may be correctly attached during installation.

3. Mark and disconnect the hoses from the air injection system and the vacuum switching valve, if so equipped.

4. Disconnect the following items:

   a. Accelerator cable—from both the support on the cylinder head and the throttle arm. If so equipped, also disconnect the automatic transmission linkage connected to the carburetor and the intake manifold.

   b. Water hoses—upper and lower from the engine, and from the heater control valve.

   c. Control cable—heater valve control.

   d. PCV valve—hose to the cylinder head cover.

   e. Fuel lines—to the carburetor.

   f. Choke lines—lines and/or hoses to the choke.

   g. Other—disconnect all other vacuum lines, hoses, and electrical connec-

tors that are attached to the intake manifold. Mark the items for proper reconnection during assembly.

5. Loosen the intake manifold mounting fasteners, working from the outer fasteners, towards the center. Remove the intake manifold and carburetor as an assembly.

FUEL INJECTED ENGINES

1. Disconnect the negative battery cable.

2. Drain the cooling system.

3. Remove the water hose bracket from the cylinder head cover.

4. Unfasten the hose clamps and remove the hoses from the water pump and the water valve.

5. Disconnect the heater temperature control cable from the water valve.

6. Disconnect the PCV hoses from the cylinder head cover and the intake air connector.

7. Disconnect the air valve and the air control valve hoses from the intake air connector.

8. Disconnect the intake air connector from the air intake chamber and the air flow meter and remove it.

9. Tag and disconnect all hoses, lines and wires leading from the air intake chamber and the throttle body (it is a good idea to follow the numerical removal sequence shown in the illustration).

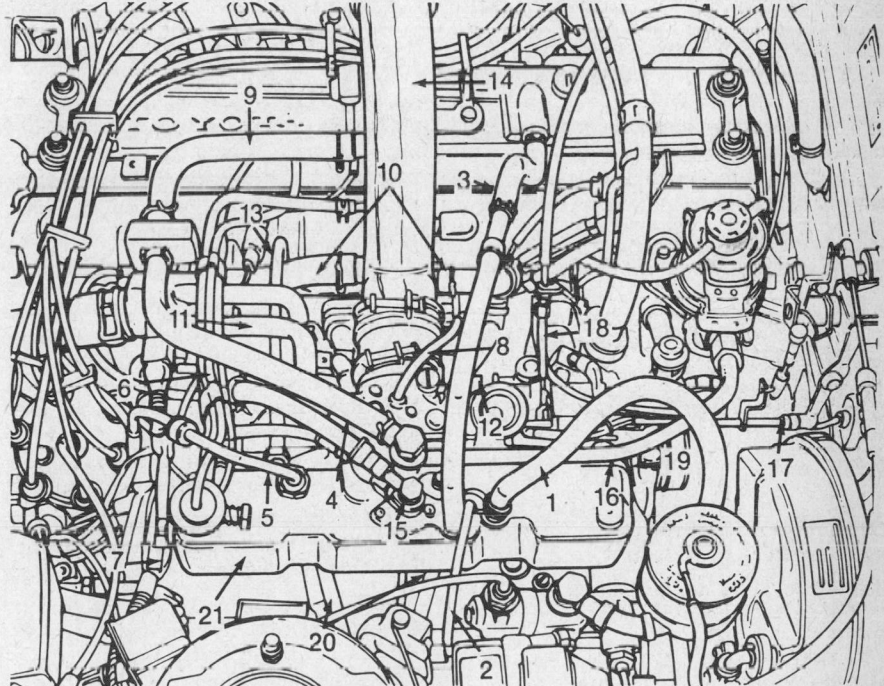

1. Hose	9. Hose	16. EGR pipe
2. Hose	10. Hose	17. Throttle link
3. Hose (for PCV)	11. Water hose	18. Throttle wire for A/T
4. Hose	12. Water hose	19. Ground wire
5. Hose	13. Hose	20. Hose
6. Hose (for Idle-up)	14. Intake air connector	21. Air intake chamber
7. Wiring	15. Cold start injector w/ gasket	
8. Hose		

Before removing the cylinder head from 4M-E and 5M-E engines, remove the hoses in the order indicated

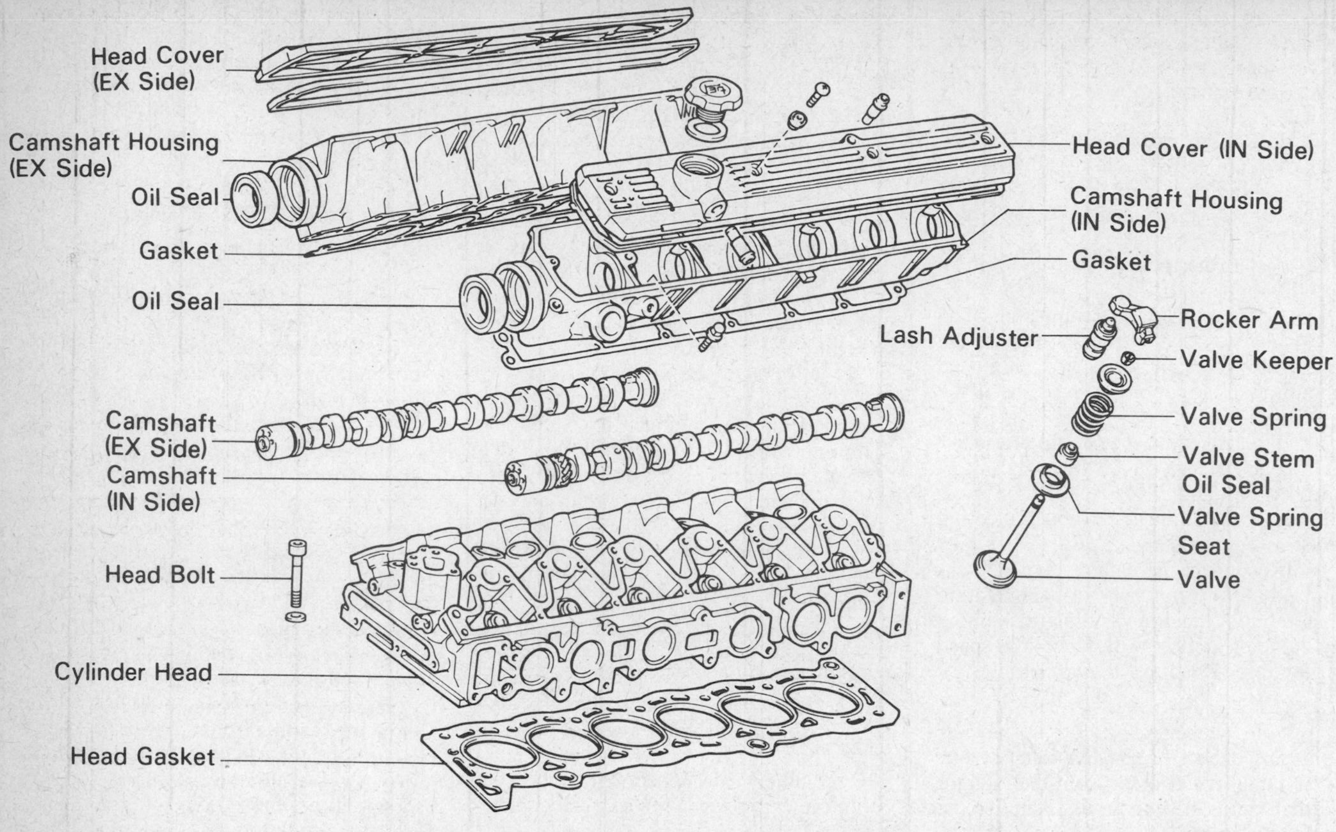

Head Cover (EX Side)

Camshaft Housing (EX Side)

Oil Seal

Gasket

Oil Seal

Camshaft (EX Side)

Camshaft (IN Side)

Head Bolt

Cylinder Head

Head Gasket

Head Cover (IN Side)

Camshaft Housing (IN Side)

Gasket

Lash Adjuster

Rocker Arm

Valve Keeper

Valve Spring

Valve Stem Oil Seal

Valve Spring Seat

Valve

Cylinder head and related components—5M-GE engine

10. Unscrew the seven mounting bolts and remove the air intake chamber and the throttle body as one unit.

11. Tag and disconnect the wiring connectors at the fuel injectors.

12. Unscrew the four mounting bolts and remove the fuel delivery pipe with the injectors.

CAUTION

When removing the injectors and the delivery pipe, be sure to have a container underneath, to catch the large quantity of fuel.

13. Unscrew the eight mounting bolts and remove the intake manifold.

ALL ENGINES

1. Remove the spark plug wires from their supports on the cylinder head cover and from the spark plugs themselves.

2. Remove the distributor assembly.

3. Remove the exhaust manifold and the oil pressure light sender.

4. Unfasten the retaining bolts and remove the valve cover assembly.

NOTE: Place a cloth over the timing gear to prevent anything from falling into the timing gear cover.

5. Turn the engine so that the No. 1 piston is at TDC on its compression stroke (both valves closed).

6. Remove the timing chain tensioner.

NOTE: The matchmarks on the timing chain and gear should now be aligned.

7. Straighten out the lockplate and unfasten the timing gear retaining bolt (left-hand thread). Withdraw the timing gear from the camshaft.

8. Loosen and remove the rocker arm shaft mounting bolts. Loosen the bolt in two or three stages. Remove the rocker arm shaft assembly.

9. Remove the camshaft bearing caps (keep them in order) and lift the camshaft off of the head.

10. In two or three stages, loosen then remove the cylinder head bolts in the reverse order of the installation torque sequence. Lift the cylinder head off of the engine block.

Installation is performed in the following manner: Prior to installation, thoroughly clean the cylinder block and head mating surfaces. Refer to the Unit Repair section for details on checking the head and block for flatness, and other services which may be necessary.

1. Use compressed air to blow out the cylinder head mounting bolt holes. Make sure that the holes are clean and free of water.

2. Use a liquid sealer around the oil and water holes of both the head and the block, and on the timing cover upper surfaces. *Be careful not to get sealer in the passages or in the mounting holes.*

3. Place a new head gasket on the engine block and lower the cylinder head into position.

4. Using the proper sequence, tighten the cylinder head bolts in two or three stages to specifications.

5. Install the lower camshaft bearing halves, if previously removed. Install the camshaft and the bearing caps. Tighten the bearing cap fasteners to 12–17 ft. lbs.

NOTE: Camshaft bearing oil clearance may be checked in the same manner

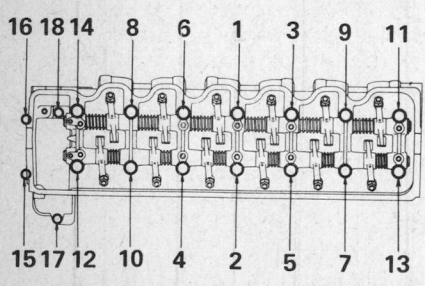

Cylinder head tightening sequence—4M and 4M–E engines

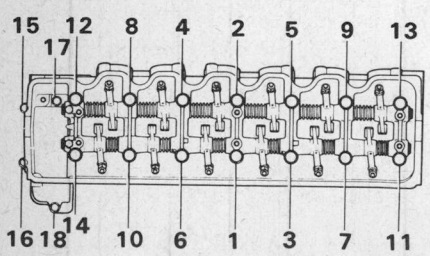

Cylinder head tightening sequence—5M–E engines

as the crankshaft and connecting rod oil clearance. Refer to the Unit Repair section for information concerning the use of Plastigage®.

6. Install the rocker arm shaft assembly. Tighten the mounting bolts to 12–17 ft. lbs., in sequence and in two or three stages.

7. Make sure the engine has not been turned from no. 1 (cylinder) TDC. The crankshaft pulley should have its "V" notch aligned with the zero mark on the timing cover scale.

8. Align the "V" notch on the camshaft pulley with the 5/32 in. hole on the No. 1 camshaft bearing cap; or align the pin on the camshaft flange with the embossed pointer on the No. 1 rocker shaft support.

9. Install the timing chain (marked link UP) on the camshaft gear (mark on gear aligned with marked link). Then attach the gear and chain unit to the front of the camshaft.

10. Install the timing gear-to-camshaft bolt (left hand thread) with the locking tab. Tighten the bolt to 47–54 ft. lbs.

11. Install the timing chain tensioner. Tighten to 22–29 ft. lbs.

12. Turn the crankshaft two complete revolutions. If, at the end of the two revolutions, the timing marks do not align, repeat Steps 7—11. If they still will not align, see Step 14.

13. Adjust the timing chain tensioner. Turn the crankshaft in the regular direction until there is a maximum amount of slack in the chain. Loosen the locknut on the tensioner and turn the screw clockwise until resistance is felt. Loosen the screw two turns and tighten the locknut.

NOTE: If the timing marks do not align after once again turning the engine two complete revolutions the chain could be stretched. Toyota has provided other pin holes in the cam gear to correct this problem.

14. If the crankshaft pulley notch will not align with the zero mark while the cam gear and chain are aligned with the rocker arm support. Remove and reposition the cam gear to the second pin hole position. Recheck crankshaft timing marks.

15. Adjust the valve clearance to the following cold specifications:

Intake—0.006 in.

Exhaust—0.008 in.

16. The rest of the cylinder head installation is in the reverse order of removal.

NOTE: Before starting the engine, change the motor oil. The old oil could be contaminated from coolant.

5M-GE

1. Disconnect the battery cables.
2. Drain the cooling system.
3. Disconnect the the exhaust pipe from the exhaust manifold.
4. Remove the throttle cable bracket from the cylinder head if equipped with automatic transmission, and remove the accelerator and actuator cable bracket.

5. Tag and disconnect the ground cable, oxygen sensor wire, high tension coil wire, distributor connector, solenoid resistor wire connector and thermo switch wire (A/T).

6. Tag and disconnect the brake booster vacuum hose, EGR valve vacuum hose, fuel hose from the intake manifold and actuator vacuum hose (if equipped with cruise control).

7. Disconnect the radiator upper hose from the thermostat housing, and disconnect the two heater hoses.

8. Disconnect the No. 1 air hose from the air intake connector. Remove the two clamp bolts, loosen the throttle body hose clamp and remove the air intake connector and the connector pipe.

9. Tag and disconnect all emission control hoses from the throttle body and airintake chamber, the two PCV hoses from the cam cover and the fuel hose from the fuel hose support.

10. Remove the air intake chamber stay and the vacuum pipe and ground cable.

11. Remove the bolt that attaches the spark plug wire clip, leaving the wires attached to the clip. Remove the distributor from the cylinder head with the cap and wires attached, by removing the distributor holding bolt.

12. Tag and disconnect the cold start injector wire and disconnect the cold start injector fuel hose from the delivery pipe.

13. Loosen the nut of the EGR pipe, remove the five bolts and two nuts and remove the air intake chamber and gasket.

14. Remove the glove box and remove the ECU module. Disconnect the three connectors and pull the EFI (fuel injection) wire harness out through the engine side of the firewall.

15. Remove the pulsation damper and the No. 1 fuel pipe.

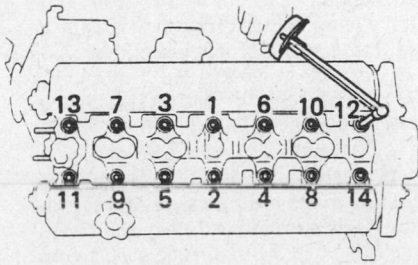

Cylinder head tightening sequence—5M-GE engines

16. Remove the water outlet housing by first loosening the clamp and disconnecting the water by-pass hose.

17. Remove the intake manifold.

18. Disconnect the power steering pump drive belt and remove the power steering pump without disconnecting the fluid hoses. Temporarily see pump out of the way.

19. Disconnect the oxygen sensor connector and remove the exhaust manifold.

20. Remove the timing belt and camshaft timing gears.

21. Remove the timing belt cover stay, and remove the oil pressure regulator and gasket.

22. Remove the No. 2 timing belt cover and gasket.

23. Tag and disconnect any other wires, linkage and/or hoses still attached to the cylinder head.

24. Using a long extension on your ratchet handle (thin enough to get inside the head bolt recesses), remove the fourteen head bolts gradually in two or three passes in the numerical order shown.

—— **CAUTION** ——

Head warpage or cracking could result from removing the head bolts in incorrect order.

25. Carefully life the cylinder head from the dowels on the cylinder block, resting the mating surface on wooden blocks on the work bench. If the head is difficult to remove, tap around the mating surface gently with a rubber hammer. *Keep in mind the head is aluminum and is easily damaged.*

26. Installation is performed by first following Steps 1–4 of the "4M-E/5M-E" cylinder head installation procedure, then reversing the above installation procedures. Use new gaskets everywhere. Fill the radiator with coolant and set the timing. Road test the car and check for leaks.

1A-C, 3A, 3A-C and 4A-C

1. Disconnect the negative battery terminal.
2. Remove the exhaust pipe from the manifold.
3. Drain the cooling system. Save the coolant as it can be reused.
4. Remove the air cleaner and all necessary hoses.
5. Mark all vacuum lines for easy installation and then remove them.
6. Remove all linkage from the carburetor, fuel lines, etc. from the head and manifold.
7. Remove the fuel pump.

NOTE: Before removing the carburetor cover it with a clean rag to prevent dirt from entering it.

8. Remove the carburetor.
9. Remove the manifold.
10. Remove the valve cover.
11. Note the position of the spark plug wires and remove them.
12. Remove the spark plugs.
13. Set the engine on No. 1 cylinder—top dead center. This is accomplished by removing the No. 1 spark plug, placing your finger over the hole and then turning the crankshaft pulley until you feel pressure exerted against your finger.

—— **CAUTION** ——

Do not put your finger into the spark plug hole.

14. Remove the crankshaft pulley with an appropriate puller.

15. Remove the water pump pulley.

16. Remove the top and bottom timing chain cover.

17. Matchmark the camshaft pulley and timing belt for reassembly.

18. Loosen the belt tensioner.

19. Remove the water pump.

20. Remove the timing belt. Do not bend, twist, or turn the belt inside out.

NOTE: Check the belt for wear, cracks, or glazing. Once the belt is removed it is a good idea to replace it with a new one even though it is not necessary.

21. Remove the rocker arm bolts and remove the rocker arms.

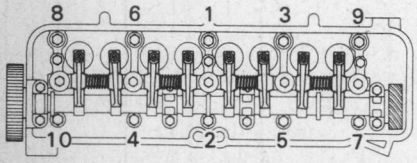

Cylinder head tightening sequence—A–series engines

22. Remove the camshaft pulley by holding the camshaft with a pair of channel lock pliers and removing the belt in the pulley end of the shaft.

NOTE: Do not hold the cam on the lobes, as damage will result.

23. Remove the camshaft seal.

24. Remove the camshaft bearing caps and set them down in the order they appear on the engine.

25. Remove the camshaft.

26. Loosen the head bolts in the reverse of the torque sequence.

27. Lift the head directly up. Do not attempt to slide it off.

28. Installation is the reverse of removal.

NOTE: When replacing the head always use a new gasket. Also replace the camshaft seal, making sure to grease the lip before installation.

The following torques are needed for installation: cam bearing caps 8–10 ft. lbs., cam sprocket 29–39 ft. lbs., crankshaft pulley 55–61 ft. lbs., manifold bolts 15–21 ft. lbs., rocker arm bolts 17–19 ft. lbs., timing gear idler bolt 22–32 ft. lbs., belt tension 0.24–0.28 in. Adjust the valves to the proper clearances.

2S-E

1. Disconnect the battery ground.

2. Drain the coolant.

3. Disconnect the throttle cable.

4. Remove the air cleaner assembly.

5. Disconnect and tag all wires connected to or running across the head.

6. Disconnect and tag all vacuum hoses connected to or running across the head.

7. Remove the vacuum pipe from the head cover.

8. Disconnect and tag any remaining cables.

9. Remove the alternator.

10. Remove the distributor.

11. Remove the upper radiator hose and bypass hose.

12. Unbolt and remove the water outlet housing.

13. Disconnect the heater hoses.

14. Disconnect the two air hoses from the fuel injection air valve.

15. Unbolt and remove the rear end housing.

16. Remove the heater pipe.

17. Disconnect the fuel line at the filter and the fuel return line at the return pipe.

18. Raise and support the car on jackstands.

19. Drain the oil.

20. Disconnect the exhaust pipe at the manifold.

21. Disconnect the power steering pump hoses.

22. Remove the intake manifold stay.

23. Lower the car.

24. Remove the timing belt.

25. Remove the #1 idler pulley and tension spring.

26. Remove the throttle body.

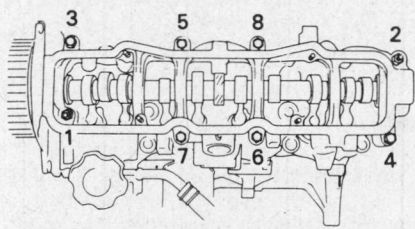

2SE cam housing removal sequence

27. Remove the valve cover.

28. Unbolt and remove the camshaft housing. Loosen the bolts gradually in the order shown.

29. Remove the rocker arms and lash adjusters.

30. Loosen and remove the head bolts, in three passes in the order shown. Lift the head from the engine and place it on wood blocks in a clean work area.

31. Installation is the reverse of removal. Note the following points:

   a. Always use a new head gasket.

   b. Tighten the head bolts, in three passes, in the order shown, to 47 ft. lb.

   c. When installing the camshaft housing, note that RTV silicone gasket compound is used in place of a gasket. Run a 2 mm bead of compound around the sealing surface of the housing. Torque the housing bolts, in three passes, in the order shown, to 11 ft. lb.

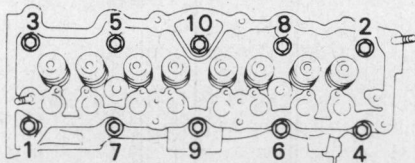

2SE head bolt loosening sequence

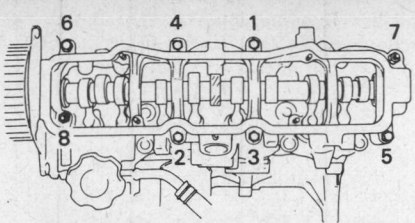

2SE cam housing torque sequence

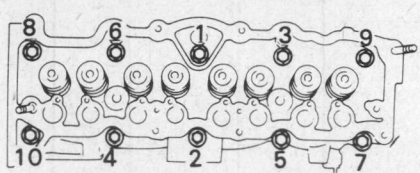

2SE head bolt torque sequence

   d. Torque the fuel line connections to 22 ft. lb.

   e. Road test the car.

1C-L and 1C-TL

1. Disconnect the battery ground.

2. Drain the coolant.

3. Remove the cruise control actuator.

4. Disconnect and tag all wires connected to or running across the head.

5. Disconnect and tag all vacuum hoses connected to or running across the head.

6. Disconnect and tag all cables and linkage rods connected to or running across the head.

7. Raise and support the car on jackstands.

8. Drain the oil.

9. Disconnect the exhaust pipe from the turbocharger or manifold.

10. Lower the car.

11. Remove the turbocharger.

12. Remove the water outlet and pipe.

13. Remove the heater hoses.

14. Remove the heater pipe.

15. Remove the bypass hoses.

16. Remove the glow plugs.

17. Remove the injector nozzles.

18. Remove the level gauge guide support mounting bolt.

19. Remove the number 2 timing cover.

20. Turn the engine so that #1 cylinder is at TDC of the firing stroke. Make sure that the line mark on the camshaft pulley is aligned with the top surface of the head.

21. Remove the timing belt and camshaft pulley.

22. Remove the belt tension spring.

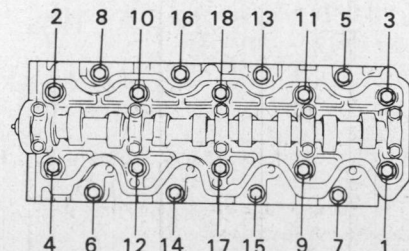

Diesel engine head bolt removal sequence

23. Remove the #1 idler pulley. Remove the camshaft #3 cover.

24. Remove the valve cover.

25. Remove the front head lifting eye.

26. Loosen the head bolts gradually, in three passes, in the order shown. Lift off the head. If the head is difficult to break loose, there is a recess at the front end in which you may pry with a suitable tool.

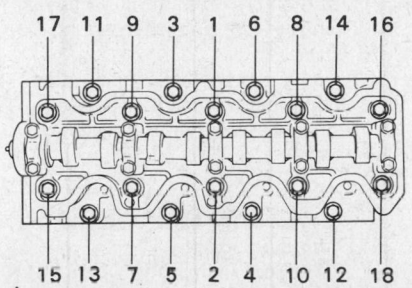

Diesel engine head bolt torque sequence

27. Installation is the reverse of removal. Note the following points:

a. Always use a new head gasket.

b. Make sure that all sealing surfaces are absolutely clean.

c. Coat all bolt threads with clean engine oil, lightly.

d. Tighten the head bolts, in three passes, in the order shown, to 62 ft. lb.

e. When installing the valve cover, note that RTV silicone gasket compound is used in place of a gasket.

f. Torque the valve cover bolts to 65 in. lb.

g. Torque the camshaft pulley bolt to 72 ft. lb.

h. Make sure that the timing marks align by rotating the engine 2 full revolutions and rechecking the alignment.

i. Torque the #1 idler pulley bolt to 27 ft. lb.

j. Road test the car.

3Y-EC

1. Disconnect the battery ground.

2. Remove the right front seat.

3. Remove the engine cover.

4. Drain the coolant.

5. Drain the oil.

6. Remove the power steering pump.

7. Disconnect the exhaust pipe at the manifold.

8. Disconnect and tag all wires, vacuum hoses and cables attached to or running acrose the head.

9. Remove the throttle body.

10. Remove the EGR valve.

11. Disconnect the coolant bypass hoses.

12. Remove the air intake chamber.

13. Remove the fuel lines from the injectors.

14. Disconnect the fuel line and fuel return line.

15. Remove the spark plugs and tubes.

16. Remove the valve cover.

17. Remove the rocker arm shaft assembly, loosening the bolts in the order shown.

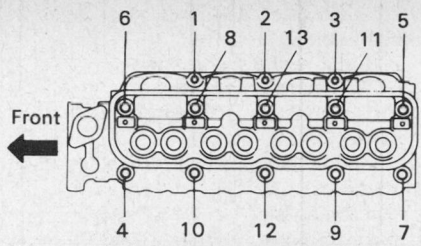

3Y-EC head bolt loosening sequence

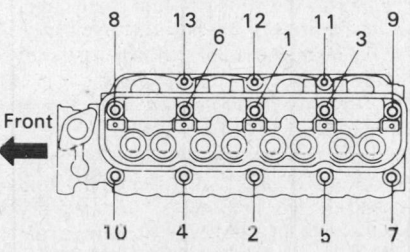

3Y-EC head bolt torque sequence

18. Remove the pushrods. Keep them in order for installation.

19. Loosen the head bolts, in three passes, in the order shown. Lift off the head. If the head is difficult to break loose, there is a recess at the front of the head in which you may pry with a suitable tool.

20. Installation is the reverse of removal. Note the following points:

a. Always use a new head gasket. Make sure that all sealing surfaces are clean.

b. Tighten the head bolts gradually, in three passes, in the order shown, to 65 ft. lb. for 14mm bolts and 14 ft. lb. for 12mm bolts.

c. Tighten the rocker shaft bolts, in the order shown, to 17 ft. lb.

d. Torque the spark plugs to 13 ft. lb.

e. Torque the air intake chamber bolts to 9 ft. lb.

f. Torque the throttle body bolts to 9 ft. lb.

g. Road test the car.

OVERHAUL

For all cylinder head overhual procedures, please refer to "Engine Rebuilding" in the Unit Repair section.

Turbocharger

REMOVAL & INSTALLATION

1. Remove the air cleaner.

2. Disconnect and tag all wiring and hoses in the way of turbocharger removal.

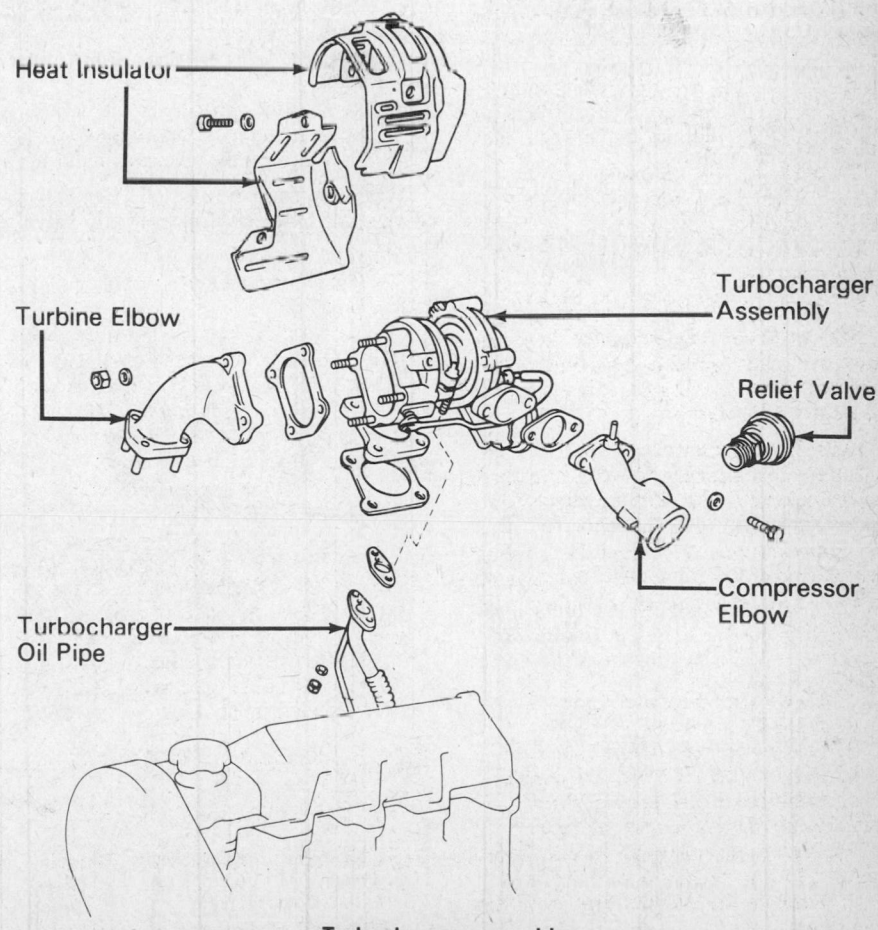

Turbocharger assembly

3. Remove the compressor elbow and relief hose.

4. Remove the heat shields.

5. Disconnect the exhaust pipe from the turbine elbow.

6. Disconnect the turbocharger oil pipes.

7. Unbolt and remove the turbocharger.

8. Installation is the reverse of removal. Torque the turbocharger mounting nuts to 38 ft. lb.

Rocker Arm Shafts

REMOVAL & INSTALLATION

3K-C, 4K-C and 4K-E

1. Remove the air cleaner.
2. Remove the PCV valve.
3. Remove the spark plug wires.
4. Remove the valve cover.
5. Loosen the rocker shaft bolts, alternating front to rear.
6. Remove the shaft assembly and oil tube.
7. Install in reverse of removal. Torque bolts in alternating, front to rear sequence, to 14–16 ft. lbs. Torque the oil pipe bolts to 14 ft. lbs. Check the valve clearance.

4M, 4M-E, and 5M-E

1. Remove the air cleaner assembly.
2. Remove the choke stove outlet and inlet hose.
3. Remove the valve cover.
4. Remove the two front clamp bolts.
5. Loosen the rocker arm shaft bolts in a rotating order starting at the ends and working toward the center.
6. Remove the bolts and lift off the rocker shaft assemblies.
7. Install in reverse of removal. Tighten the rocker shaft bolts, in a rotating order from the center to the ends, to 25 ft. lbs. Torque the front end clamp bolts to 9 ft. lbs. Check the valve clearance.

2T-C and 3T-C

1. Remove the air cleaner.
2. Remove the PCV valve.
3. Remove the spark plug wires.
4. Disconnect the fuel inlet from the carburetor.
5. Remove the valve cover.

NOTE: The cylinder head bolts also serve as the rocker arm shaft bolts. Remove in circular rotation from the ends toward the center.

6. Lift off the shaft assemblies.
7. Install the reverse of removal. Install and tighten the cylinder head bolts in a circular rotation from the center toward the ends. Torque to 63 ft. lbs. Check valve clearance.

20R, 22R and 22R-E

1. Remove the air cleaner.

---

2. Disconnect all hoses and linkage clipped to the valve cover.
3. Remove the spark plug wires.
4. Remove the carburetor.
5. Remove the valve cover.
6. Remove the distributor.
7. Set the No. 1 piston at TDC of the compression stroke.
8. Paint mating marks on the timing chain and sprocket, and drive gear.
9. Remove the distributor drive gear, leaving the chain and sprocket in position.
10. Remove the one 14 mm chain cover bolt in the front of the head. This must be done before the head bolts, which also serve as rocker shaft bolts, are removed.
11. Remove the head bolts in a diagonal pattern. Start at the front carburetor side. This must be done to prevent head warpage.
12. Remove the shaft assemblies from the head. It may be necessary to use a pry bar to evenly lift the assemblies from the dowels.
13. Install in reverse of removal. Torque the head bolts in a diagonal pattern, starting at the center. Tighten in three equal stages to 64 ft. lbs. Torque the chain cover bolt to 12 ft. lbs. Torque the drive gear bolt to 65 ft. lbs.

1A-C, 3A, 3A-C, 4A-C, and 3Y-EC

1. Disconnect the negative battery terminal.
2. Remove the air cleaner and all necessary hoses.
3. Remove all linkage from the carburetor.
4. Remove the valve cover and gasket.
5. Remove the rocker arm bolts.
6. Installation is the reverse of removal.

NOTE: Remember to install a new valve cover gasket before replacing the valve cover.

7. Tighten the rocker arm bolt 17–19 ft. lbs.

Intake Manifold

REMOVAL & INSTALLATION

1C-L and 1C-TL

1. Disconnect the battery ground.
2. Drain the coolant.
3. Remove the air cleaner.
4. Disconnect and tag any wire, hose or cable in the way of manifold removal.
5. Remove the turbocharger as described later.
6. Remove the coolant by-pass pipe.
7. Unbolt and remove the manifold.
8. Installation is the reverse of removal.

2S-E

1. Disconnect the battery ground.
2. Drain the coolant.
3. Disconnect and tag any wires, hoses or cable in the way of manifold removal.
4. Remove the throttle body.
5. Unbolt and remove the manifold.
6. Installation is the reverse of removal.

3Y-EC

1. Disconnect the battery ground.
2. Remove the right front seat.
3. Remove the engine cover.
4. Drain the coolant.
5. Disconnect and tag any wires, hoses or cables in the way of manifold removal.
6. Remove the air intake chamber and manifold.
7. Installation is the reverse of removal.

2T-C and 3T-C

1. Drain the cooling system.
2. Remove the air cleaner assembly, complete with hoses, from its bracket.
3. Remove the choke stove hoses, fuel lines, and vacuum lines from the carburetor. Unfasten the emission control system hoses and the accelerator linkage from it.

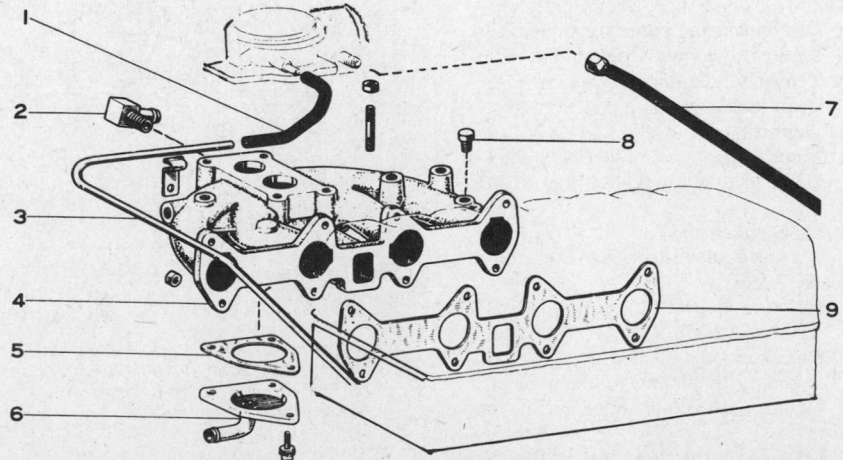

1. Choke stove intake hose
2. Elbow
3. Choke stove intake
4. Intake manifold
5. Gasket
6. Water by-pass outlet
7. Choke stove outlet
8. Plug
9. Intake manifold gasket

Intake manifold of the "T" series engine—typical

4. Unfasten the four nuts which secure the carburetor to the manifold and remove the carburetor.

5. Disconnect the PCV hose.

6. Disconnect the water bypass hose from the intake manifold.

7. Unbolt and remove the manifold.

Installation is performed in the reverse order of removal. Remember to use *new* gaskets. Tighten the intake manifold bolts to specifications.

NOTE: Tighten the bolts, in several stages, working from the inside out.

20R and 22R

1. Disconnect the battery.

2. Drain the cooling system.

3. Remove the air cleaner, complete with hoses, from the carburetor.

4. Disconnect the vacuum lines from the EGR valve and carburetor. Mark them first, to aid in installation.

5. Remove the fuel lines, electrical leads, accelerator linkage, and water hose from the carburetor.

6. Remove the water by-pass hose from the manifold.

7. Unbolt and remove the intake manifold, complete with carburetor and EGR valve.

8. Cover the cylinder head ports with clean rags to keep anything from falling into the cylinder head or block.

Installation is the reverse of removal. Replace the gasket with a new one. Torque the mounting bolts to specifications. Tighten the bolts in several stages working from the inside bolts outward. Refill the cooling system.

22R-E

1. Disconnect the battery.

2. Drain the cooling system.

3. Disconnect the air intake hose from both the air cleaner assembly on one end and the air intake chamber on the other.

4. Tag and disconnect all vacuum lines attached to the intake chamber and manifold.

5. Tag and disconnect the wires to the cold start injector, throttle position sensor, and the water hoses from the throttle body.

6. Remove the EGR valve from the intake chamber.

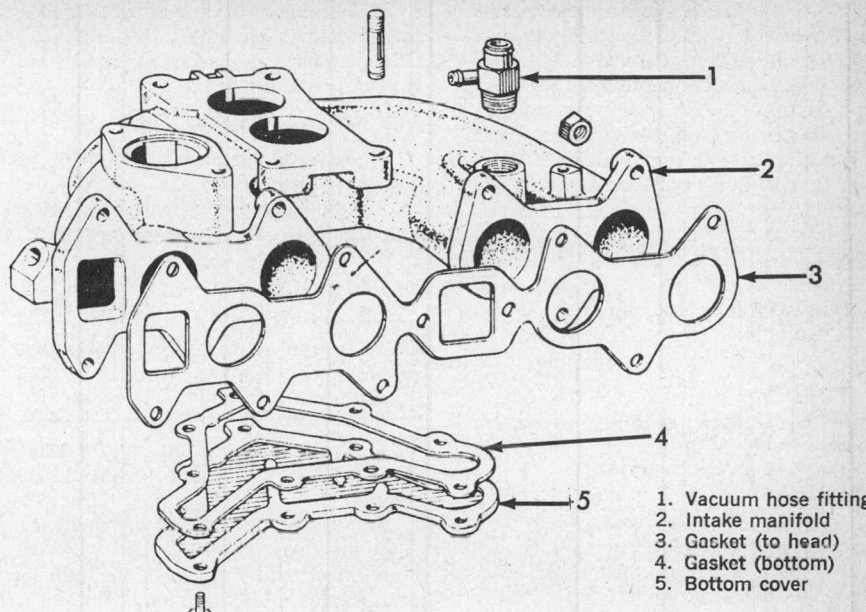

1. Vacuum hose fitting
2. Intake manifold
3. Gasket (to head)
4. Gasket (bottom)
5. Bottom cover

Intake manifold assembly—20R and 22R

7. Tag and disconnect the actuator cable, accelerator cable and A/T throttle cable (if equipped) from the cable bracket on the intake chamber.

8. Unbolt the air intake chamber from the intake manifold and remove the chamber with the throttle body attached.

9. Disconnect the fuel hose from the fuel delivery pipe.

10. Tag and disconnect the air valve hose from the intake manifold.

11. Make sure all hoses, lines and wires are tagged for later installation and disconnected from the intake manifold. Unbolt the manifold from the cylinder head, removing the delivery pipe and injection nozzle in unit with the manifold.

4M

1. Drain the cooling system.

2. Remove the air cleaner assembly, complete with hoses, from its mounting bracket.

3. Remove the distributor cap.

4. Remove the upper radiator hose from the elbow.

5. Remove the wiring from the temperature gauge sending unit.

6. Remove the following from the car-

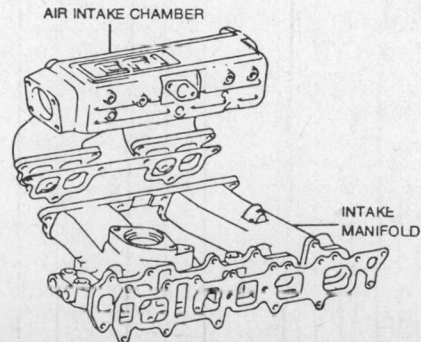

AIR INTAKE CHAMBER

INTAKE MANIFOLD

Intake manifold assembly—22R-E

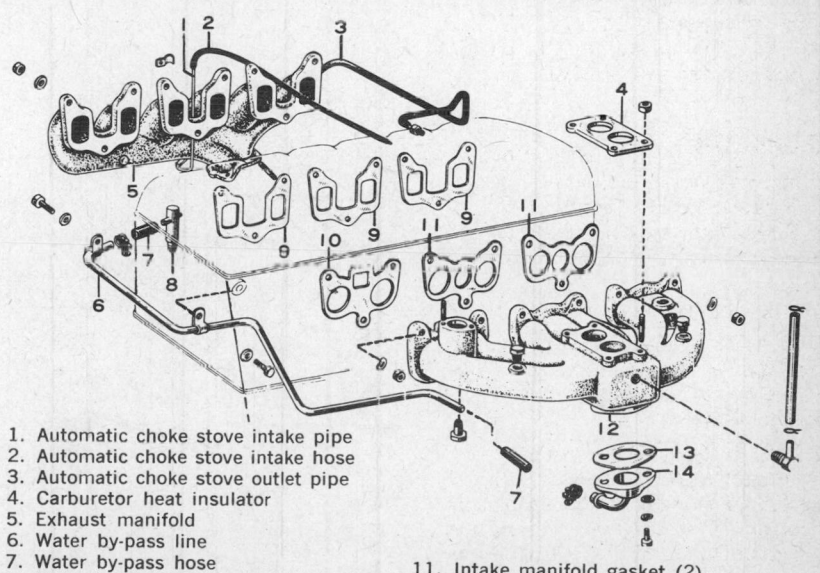

1. Automatic choke stove intake pipe
2. Automatic choke stove intake hose
3. Automatic choke stove outlet pipe
4. Carburetor heat insulator
5. Exhaust manifold
6. Water by-pass line
7. Water by-pass hose
8. Water hose joint
9. Exhaust manifold gasket
10. Intake manifold gasket (1)
11. Intake manifold gasket (2)
12. Intake manifold
13. Gasket
14. Water by-pass outlet

Intake and exhaust manifolds of the 4M engine

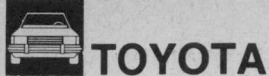

buretor; fuel lines; vacuum line; choke stove hoses; emission control system hoses; accelerator torque rod; and automatic transmission linkage (if so equipped).

7. Remove the emission control system lines and wiring from the manifold when equipped with a vacuum switching valve. Remove the EGR pipe from the intake manifold.

8. Remove the water bypass hose from the manifold.

9. Unbolt and remove the manifold, complete with the carburetor.

10. Installation is in the reverse order of removal. Torque the mounting bolts to specifications.

NOTE: Tighten the bolts, in stages, working from the inside out.

4M-E, 5M-E and 5M-GE
AIR INTAKE CHAMBER

1. Disconnect the battery cables at the battery.

2. Drain the engine coolant from the radiator.

3. Refer to the numbered illustration with the "Cylinder Head Removal and Installation" procedure (for these engines) and remove/disconnect parts in the same order. Mark the items so that they may be properly reinstalled.

4. Unbolt and remove the air intake chamber.

5. Installation is performed in the reverse of the previous steps. During installation, torque the air intake chamber fasteners to 16–20 ft. lbs.

AIR INTAKE MANIFOLD

1. Remove the air intake chamber as previously outlined.

2. Disconnect and move the wiring away from the fuel delivery and injector pipe.

3. Remove the fuel injector and delivery pipe.

— CAUTION —

Place a container under the pipe—a large amount of fuel will be released as the pipe is removed.

4. Remove the fuel pressure regulator (mounted on the center of the intake manifold).

5. Remove the EGR valve from the rear of the manifold.

6. Mark and disconnect the radiator hoses, heater hoses, and vacuum lines from the intake manifold.

7. Unlatch the distributor cap and move it out of the way.

8. Unbolt and remove the intake manifold and gasket.

9. Installation is performed in the reverse of removal. Torque the manifold fasteners to 10–15 ft. lbs.

NOTE: Use a new gasket when installing the manifold assembly.

Exhaust Manifold

REMOVAL & INSTALLATION

— CAUTION —

Do not perform this operation on a warm or hot engine.

2T-C and 3T-C

1. Detach the manifold heat stove intake pipe.

2. Unfasten the nut on the stove outlet pipe union.

3. Remove the wiring from the emission control system thermosensor.

4. Unfasten the U-bolt from the downpipe bracket.

5. Unfasten the downpipe flange from the manifold.

6. In order to remove the manifold, unfasten the manifold retaining bolts.

— CAUTION —

Remove the bolts in two or three stages, working from the inside out.

7. Installation of the manifold is performed in the reverse order of removal. Use a *new* gasket.

20R, 22R and 22R-E

1. Remove the three exhaust pipe flange bolts and disconnect the exhaust pipe from the manifold.

2. Disconnect the spark plug leads.

3. Matchmark the distributor rotor, housing and the engine block. Remove the distributor.

4. Remove the air cleaner tube from the heat stove. Remove the outer part of the heat stove.

5. Remove the manifold complete with air injection tubes and the inner portion of the heat stove.

6. Separate the inner portion of the heat stove from the manifold.

7. Installation is the reverse of removal. Tighten the retaining nuts to 29–36 ft. lbs. working from the inside out. Install the distributor and set the timing. Tighten the exhaust pipe flange nuts to 25–32 ft. lbs.

4M, 4M-E, 5M-E, 3Y-EC, 2SE, 1C-L and 1C-TL

1. Raise the front and the rear of the car and support it with jack stands.

2. Remove the right-hand gravel shield from beneath the engine.

3. Remove the downpipe support bracket.

4. Unfasten the bolts from the flange and detach the downpipe from the manifold.

5. Remove the automatic choke and air cleaner stove hoses from the exhaust manifold, if so equipped. Remove the EGR valve, if so equipped.

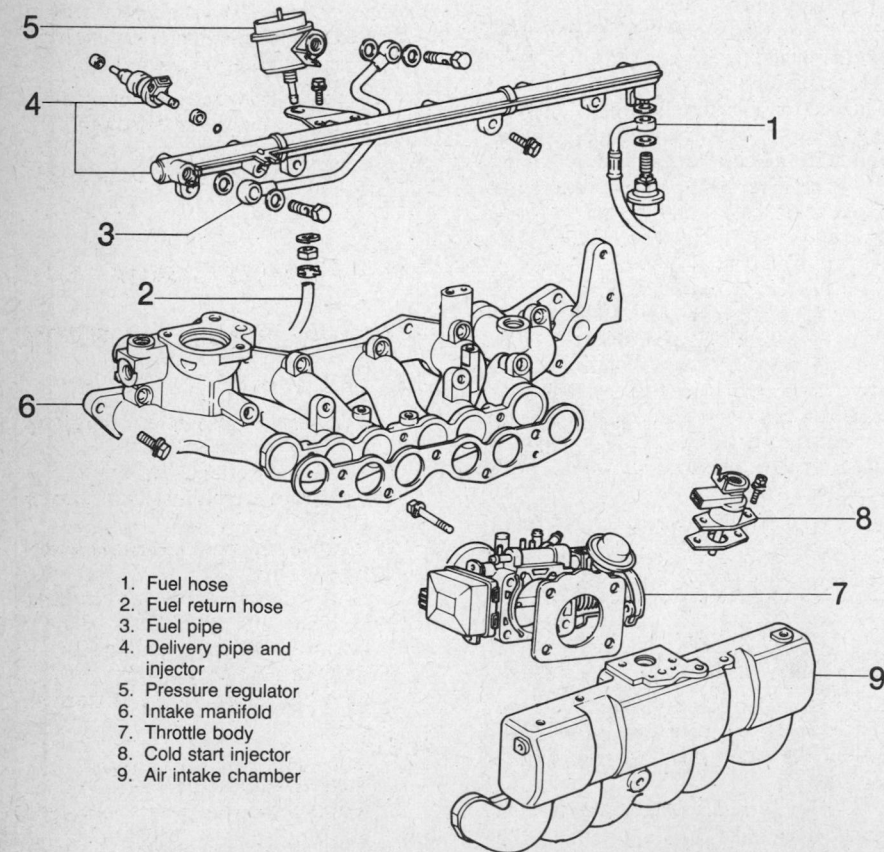

1. Fuel hose
2. Fuel return hose
3. Fuel pipe
4. Delivery pipe and injector
5. Pressure regulator
6. Intake manifold
7. Throttle body
8. Cold start injector
9. Air intake chamber

Intake manifold assembly—4M–E, 5M–E and 5M–GE

6. Remove, or move aside, any of the air injection system components which may be in the way when removing the manifold.

7. In order to remove the manifold, unfasten the manifold retaining bolts.

--- CAUTION ---
Remove and tighten the bolts in two or three stages, starting from the inside, working out.

8. Installation is performed in the reverse order of removal. Use a new gasket. Tighten the retaining bolts to specifications.

5M-GE

NOTE: **The air intake hose may have to be removed to give access to all the manifold nuts.**

1. Jack up the front end of the car and safely support it with jackstands.
2. Remove the right-hand gravel shield from underneath the car.
3. Remove the exhaust pipe support stay.
4. Unbolt the exhaust pipe from the exhaust manifold flange.
5. Disconnect the oxygen sensor connector.
6. Remove the seven nuts and remove the exhaust manifold.
7. Installation is the reverse of removal. Use a new manifold gasket and torque all nuts evenly to 25–33 ft. lbs.

Combination Manifold

REMOVAL & INSTALLATION

--- CAUTION ---
Do not perform this procedure on a warm engine.

3K-C and 4K-C

1. Remove the air cleaner assembly, complete with hoses.
2. Disconnect the accelerator and choke linkages from the carburetor, as well as the fuel and vacuum lines.
3. Remove, or move aside, any of the emission control system components which are in the way.

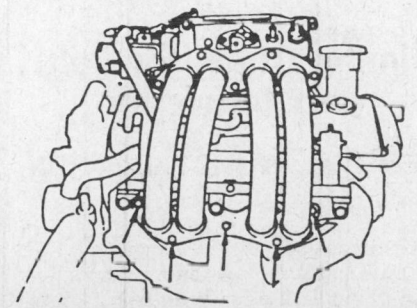

Remove the air intake chamber and pipes as an assembly—4K-E

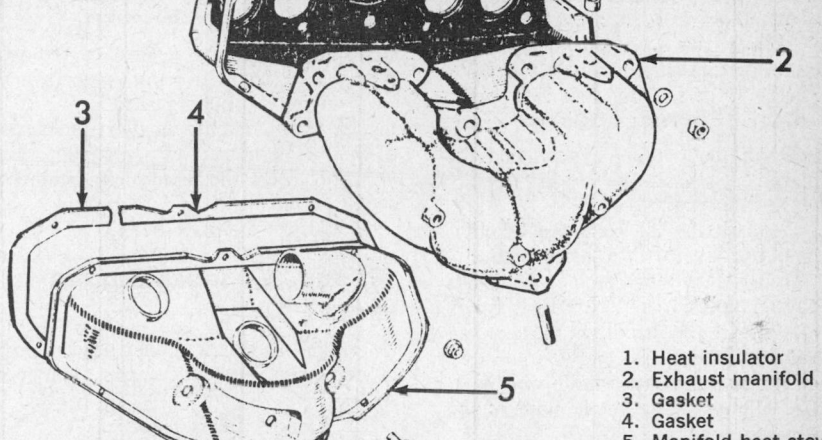

1. Heat insulator
2. Exhaust manifold
3. Gasket
4. Gasket
5. Manifold heat stove

Exhaust manifold of the "R" series engine—typical

4. Unfasten the retaining bolts and remove the carburetor from the manifold.
5. Loosen the manifold retaining nuts, working from the inside out.
6. Remove the intake/exhaust manifold assembly from the cylinder head as a complete unit.
7. Installation is performed in the reverse order of removal. Use *new* gaskets. Tighten the bolts, working from the inside out.

NOTE: **Tighten the bolts in two or three stages.**

4K-E

1. Loosen the two hose clamps and remove the air cleaner hose.
2. Disconnect the throttle cable from its two attachment points on the air intake chamber and the throttle body. Position the cable out of the way.
3. Tag and disconnect all vacuum hoses leading from the air intake chamber.
4. Tag and disconnect the three electrical leads attached to the air intake chamber.
5. Unscrew and remove the two air intake chamber support brackets. Remove the air intake pipe–to—manifold retaining bolts and lift off the air intake chamber and pipes as an assembly.

--- CAUTION ---
The air intake assembly must be supported while removing the pipe retaining bolts.

6. Tag and disconnect the four injector wires. Remove the two wire harness clamps and then remove the EFI solenoid wiring harness from the delivery pipe.
7. Disconnect the heater outlet hoses. Remove the two bracket set bolts and remove the pipe.
8. Disconnect the exhaust pipe from the exhaust manifold.
9. Remove the six mounting bolts and then remove the combination manifold.

10. Installation is in the reverse order of removal.

1A-C, 3A, 3A-C and 4A-C

1. Disconnect the negative battery terminal.
2. Remove the air cleaner and all necessary hoses.
3. Remove all the carburetor linkages.
4. Remove the carburetor.

NOTE: **Cover the carburetor with a clean towel to prevent dirt from entering it.**

5. Remove the exhaust manifold pipe.
6. Remove the exhaust manifold.
7. Installation is the reverse of removal. Tighten the manifold bolts to 15–21 ft. lbs.

Timing Cover

REMOVAL & INSTALLATION

2SE, 1C-L and 1C-TL

1. Remove the right front wheel.
2. Remove the fender liner.
3. Remove the alternator belt.
4. Remove the cruise control actuator and bracket.
5. Remove the power steering reservoir and belt.
6. Using a wood block on the jack, raise the engine slightly.
7. Remove the right engine mount.
8. Remove the timing covers.
9. Installation is the reverse of removal.

3Y-EC

1. Remove the radiator.
2. Remove the water pump pulley and belt.
3. Remove the distributor.
4. Remove the cold start injector.

5. Remove the crankshaft pulley. A puller must be used.

6. Unbolt and remove the cover.

7. Installation is the reverse of removal. Always use a new gasket and clean the gasket mating surfaces.

"K" and "T" Series Engines

1. Drain the cooling system and the crankcase.

2. Disconnect the battery.

3. Remove the air cleaner assembly, complete with hoses, from its bracket.

4. Remove the hood latch as well as its brace and support.

5. Remove the headlight bezels and grille assembly.

6. Unfasten the upper and lower radiator hose clamps and remove both of the hoses from the engine.

7. Unfasten the radiator securing bolts and remove the radiator.

NOTE: Take off the shroud first, if so equipped.

8. Loosen the drive belt adjusting link and remove the drive belt. Unfasten the alternator multiconnector, withdraw the retaining bolts, and remove the alternator.

9. Remove the air injection pump, if so equipped. Disconnect the hoses from the pump before removing it.

10. Remove the fan and water pump as an assembly.

11. Unfasten the crankshaft pulley retaining bolt. Remove the crankshaft pulley with a gear puller.

12. Remove the gravel shield from underneath the engine.

13. The following steps apply to "K" engines only:

   a. Remove the nuts and washers from both the right and left front engine mounts.

   b. Detach the exhaust pipe flange from the exhaust manifold.

   c. Slightly raise the front of the engine.

14. On "T" engines, remove the right-hand brace plate.

15. Remove the front oil pan bolts, to gain access to the bottom of the timing chain cover.

NOTE: It may be necessary to insert a thin knife between the pan and the gasket in order to break the pan loose. Use care not to damage the gasket.

Installation is the reverse of removal. Apply sealer to the two front corners of the "T" engine's oil pan gasket.

1. Apply sealer to the two front corners of the "T" engine's oil pan gaket.

2. Tighten the crankshaft pulley to specifications.

3. Adjust the drive belts.

"R" and "M" Series Engines
EXCEPT 5M-GE

1. Perform the cylinder head removal procedure as detailed in the appropriate section.

2. Remove the radiator.

3. Remove the alternator.

4. On engines equipped with air pumps, remove the pump and bracket from the engine.

NOTE: If the car is equipped with power steering, remove the pump.

5. Remove the fan and water pump as a complete assembly.

———— CAUTION ————
To prevent the fluid from running out from the fan coupling, do not tip the assembly over on its side.

6. Unfasten the crankshaft pulley securing bolts and remove the pulley with a gear puller.

———— CAUTION ————
Do not remove the 10 mm bolt from its hole, if installed, as it is used for balancing.

7. Loosen the bolts which secure the front of the oil pan, after draining the engine oil. Lower the front of the oil pan.

8. Remove the bolts which secure the timing chain cover. Withdraw the cover.

Installation is the reverse of removal. Apply sealer to the gaskets for both the timing chain cover and the oil pan.

NOTE: "M" engines use two gaskets on the timing chain cover.

Tighten the timing chain cover bolts to the specifications below:
"R" series engines:
All bolts—8–11 ft. lbs.
"M" series engines:
8 mm bolts—7–12 ft. lbs.
10 mm bolts—14–22 ft. lbs.

5M-GE

The 5M-GE engine uses three timing belt covers: front upper, front lower, and rear upper. To gain access to the timing belt, only the front covers need to be removed. Refer to the "Timing Belt Removal and Installation" procedure to remove these covers.

1A-C, 3A, 3A-C and 4A-C

1. Disconnect the negative battery terminal.

2. Remove all the drive belts.

3. Bring the No. 1 cylinder to TDC on the compression stroke.

4. Remove the crankshaft pulley with a suitable puller.

5. Remove the water pump pulley.

6. Remove the upper and lower timing case covers.

7. Installation is the reverse of removal. Tighten the timing belt cover to 61–99 in. lbs.

Timing Cover Oil Seal Replacement

1. Remove the timing cover, as detailed in the appropriate section above.

2. Inspect the oil seal for signs of wear, leakage, or damage.

3. If worn, pry the old oil seal out. Remove it toward the *front* of the cover.

NOTE: Once the oil seal has been removed, it must be replaced.

4. Use a socket, pipe, or block of wood and a hammer to drive the oil seal into place. Work from the *front* of the cover.

———— CAUTION ————
Be extremely careful not to damage the seal.

5. Install the timing cover as outlined above.

Timing Chain (or Belt) and Tensioner

REMOVAL & INSTALLATION
IC-L and 1C-TL

1. Disconnect the battery ground.

2. Remove the right front wheel.

3. Remove the fender liner.

4. Remove the washer bottle and radiator overflow.

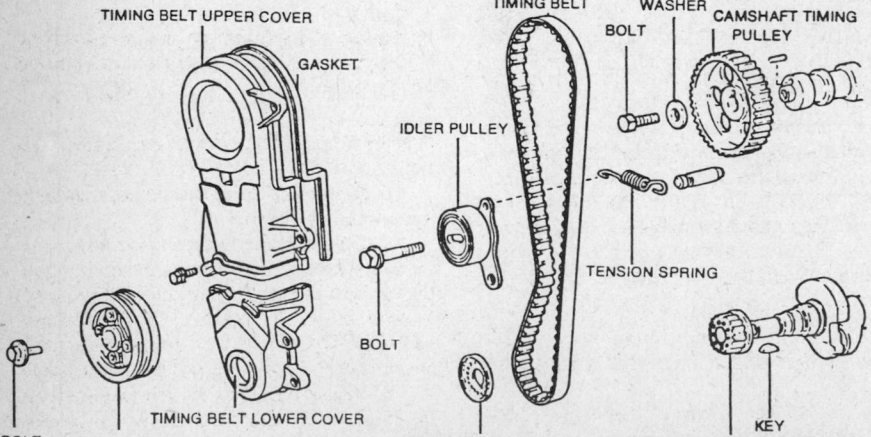
Front cover and related components—A-series engines

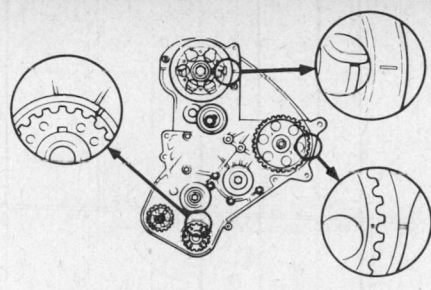

Diesel engine valve timing marks

5. Remove the cruise control acuator.
6. Remove the power steering pump and bracket.
7. Remove the AC idler pulleys and bracket.
8. Remove the alternator.
9. Remove the lower belt cover.
10. Turn the engine to No. 1 cylinder at TDC compression.
11. Using a puller, remove the crankshaft pulley.
12. Remove the upper belt cover.
13. Remove the belt guide.
14. Jack up the engine slightly.
15. Remove the right side engine mount.
16. If the belt is to be reused, matchmark the belt and the pulleys with paint.
17. Remove the belt tensioner spring.
18. Loosen the idler pulley bolt and remove the belt.
19. Installation is the reverse of removal.

2SE

1. Follow Steps 1–9 of the ''1C-L'' procedure.
2. Remove the spark plugs.
3. Align the oil seal retainer mark with the center of the small hole on the camshaft timing pulley by turning the crankshaft pul-

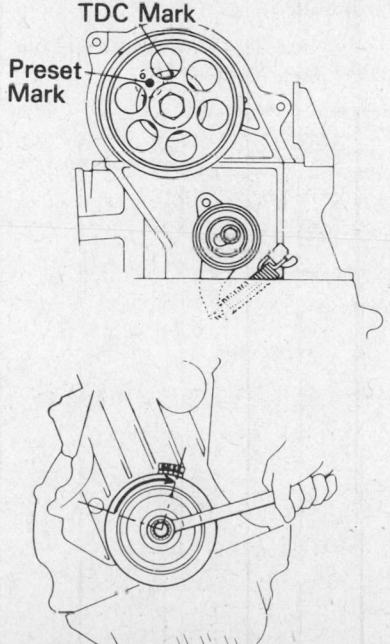

2SE valve timing marks

ley clockwise. This will set No. 1 piston at BDC.
4. If reusing the belt, matchmark it and the pulleys with paint.
5. Loosen the idler pulley and remove the belt.
6. Installation is the reverse of removal.

3Y-EC

1. Remove the radiator.
2. Remove the water pump drive belt and pulley.
3. Remove the distributor.
4. Remove the cold start injector.
5. Remove the crankshaft pulley with a puller.
6. Remove the chain cover.
7. Check the chain slack at the center point of the left side. Free play should not exceed ½ inch. If it does, replace the chain.
8. Set the engine to No. 1 piston TDC.
9. Remove the crankshaft and camshaft pulleys and chain.
10. Installation is the reverse of removal.
11. If the engine was turned while the chain was off, make sure that the camshaft and crankshaft keys are in the upper side position and aligned with the marks on their thrust plates.

1A-C, 3A, 3A-C and 4A-C

1. Remove the timing belt upper and lower dust covers and gaskets as previously detailed.
2. If the timing belt is to be re-used, mark an arrow in the direction of engine revolution on its surface. Matchmark the belt to the pulleys as shown in the illustration.
3. Loosen the idler pulley bolt, push it to the left as far as it will go and then temporarily tighten it.
4. Remove the timing belt, idler pulley bolt, idler pulley and the return spring.

NOTE: Do not bend, twist, or turn the belt inside out. Do not allow grease or water to come in contact with it.

5. Inspect the timing belt for cracks, missing teeth or overall wear. Replace as necessary.
6. Install the return spring and idler pulley.
7. Install the timing belt. Align the marks made earlier if re–using the old belt.
8. Adjust the idler pulley so that the belt deflection is 0.24–0.28 in. at 4.5 lbs.
9. Check the valve timing.
10. Installation of the remaining components is in the reverse order of removal.

K-Series and T-Series

1. Remove the drive belts.
2. Remove the crankshaft set bolt and then, using a puller, remove the crankshaft pulley.
3. Remove the front cover as previously detailed.
4. Using a spring scale, measure the timing chain slack. If the slack is more than

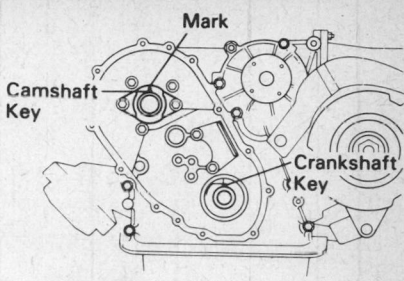

3Y-EC valve timing marks

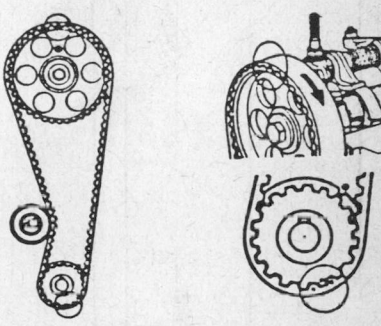

Mark the timing belt before removal

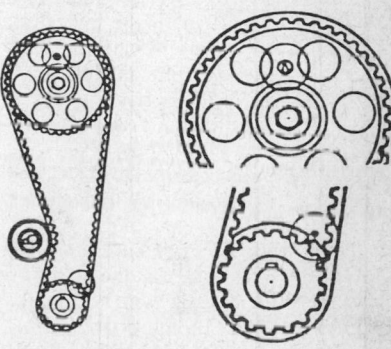

When checking the valve timing, turn the crankshaft two (2) complete revolutions clockwise from TDC to TDC and make sure that each pulley aligns with the marks shown

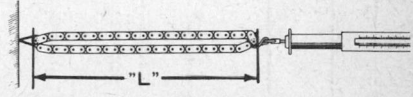

"K" and "T" series engines—measure the timing chain stretch between the arrows as indicated

0.531 in. at 22 lbs. of tension, replace the chain and sprockets (K–series only).
5. Remove the timing chain tensioner and vibration damper.
6. On K–series engines, remove the camshaft sprocket set bolt and then remove the timing chain and sprocket together. Use a gear puller to remove the crankshaft sprocket. On T–series engines remove the chain and both sprockets at the same time.
7. Measure the timing chain length with the chain fully stretched. It should be no more than 10.7 in. for K–series engines or 11.472 in. for T–series engines in any three positions. Wrap the chain around a sprocket.

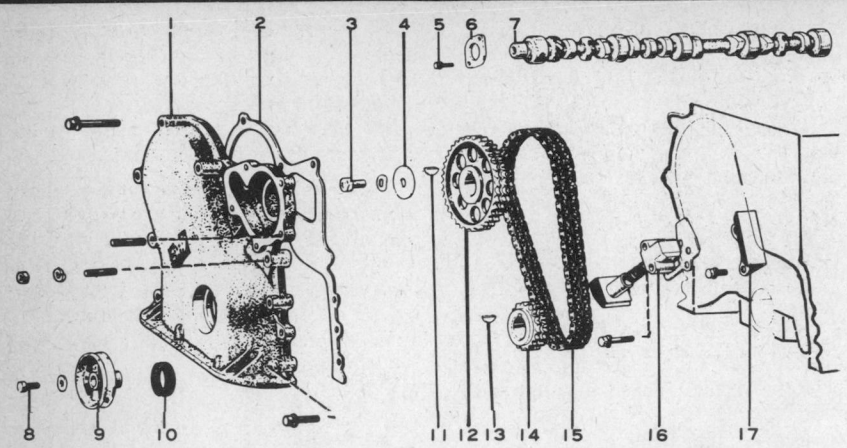

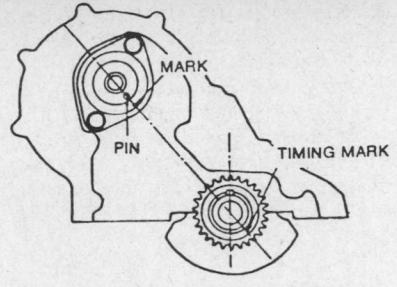

Align the camshaft dowel pin and mark on the thrust plate

1. Timing chain cover
2. Timing chain cover gasket
3. Bolt
4. Plate washer
5. Bolt
6. Plate
7. Camshaft
8. Bolt
9. Crankshaft pulley
10. Front oil seal
11. Woodruff key
12. Camshaft sprocket
13. Woodruff key
14. Crankshaft sprocket
15. Timing chain
16. Chain tensioner
17. Chain vibration damper

Timing chain and related components—"T" series engines

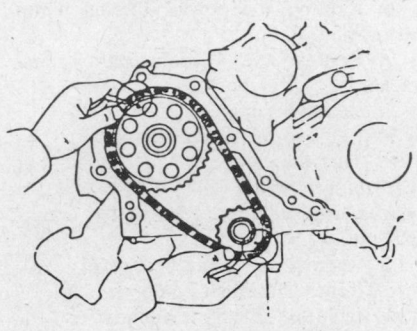

Align the marks on the two sprockets with the bright links on the timing chain

Using a vernier caliper, measure the outer sides of the chain rollers. If the measurement is less than 2.339 in. on the crankshaft sprocket or 4.480 in. around the camshaft sprocket, replace the chain and sprocket.

Installation for the K–series engines is performed in the following order:

1. Install the crankshaft sprocket.

2. Set the No. 1 piston to TDC and align the camshaft dowel pin with the mark on the thrust plate.

3. Install the timing chain around the two sprockets. make sure that the marks on the sprockets are aligned with the marks (usually bright links) on the timing chain.

4. Install the timing chain and the two sprockets on to the shafts. Make sure the timing marks are aligned with the camshaft dowel pin and the mark on the thrust plate.

5. Install the timing chain tensioner and the vibration damper.

6. Installation of the remaining components is in the reverse order of removal.

Installation for the T–series engines is performed in the following order:

1. Align the key in the camshaft with the mark on the thrust plate. Face the key in the crankshaft straight up.

2. Install the timing chain around the two sprockets so that the bright links line up with the timing marks on the sprockets.

3. Install the chain and gears on to the shafts.

4. Squirt oil into the cylinder in the chain tensioner and then install it to the cylinder block.

5. Install the chain damper parallel to the chain so that there is a 0.020 in. space in between.

6. Installation of the remaining components is in the reverse order of removal.

20R, 22R and 22R-E

1. Remove the cylinder head and timing cover as outlined above.

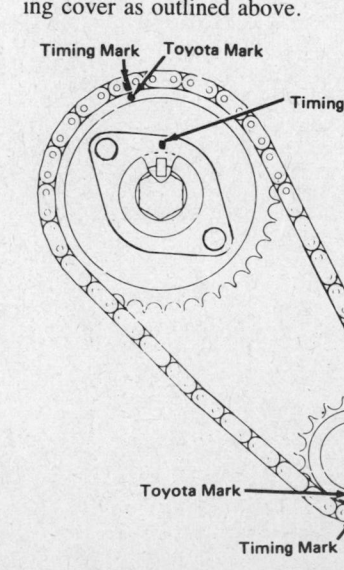

Proper alignment of the "T" series engine timing marks

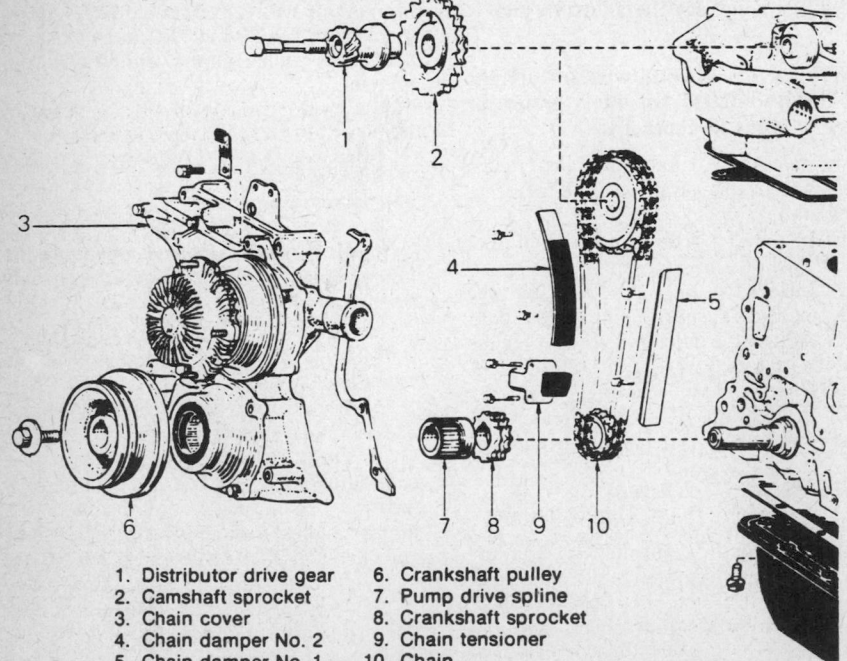

1. Distributor drive gear
2. Camshaft sprocket
3. Chain cover
4. Chain damper No. 2
5. Chain damper No. 1
6. Crankshaft pulley
7. Pump drive spline
8. Crankshaft sprocket
9. Chain tensioner
10. Chain

Front cover and timing chain components—R-series engines

2. Separate the chain from the damper, and remove the chain, complete with the camshaft sprocket.

3. Remove the crankshaft sprocket and the oil pump drive with a puller.

4. Inspect the chain for wear or damage. Replace it, if necessary.

5. Inspect the chain tensioner for wear. If it measures less than 0.43 in., replace it.

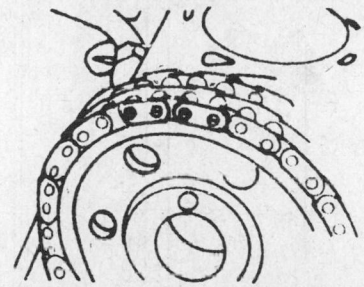

"R" series engines—align the timing marks between the two bright links of the timing chain

6. Check the dampers for wear. If they are below specification replace them:
Upper damper—0.20 in.
Lower damper—0.18 in.
Installation is performed in the following order:

1. Rotate the crankshaft until its key is at TDC. Slide the sprocket in place over the key.

2. Place the chain over the sprocket so that its *single* bright link aligns with the mark on the crank sprocket.

3. Install the cam sprocket so that the timing mark falls between the *two* bright links on the chain.

4. Fit the oil pump drive spline over the crankshaft key.

5. Install the timing cover gasket on the front of the block.

6. Rotate the camshaft sprocket counterclockwise to remove the slack from the chain.

7. Install the timing chain cover and cylinder head, as outlined above.

4M, 4M-E, and 5M-E

1. Remove the cylinder head and timing cover, as outlined above.

2. Remove the chain tensioner assembly (arm and gear).

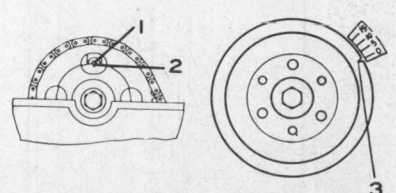

1. Valve timing mark (5/32 in. hole)
2. V-notch—camshaft flange
3. V-notch—crankshaft pulley

"M" series engines (except 5M-GE)—correct alignment of the crankshaft and camshaft timing marks

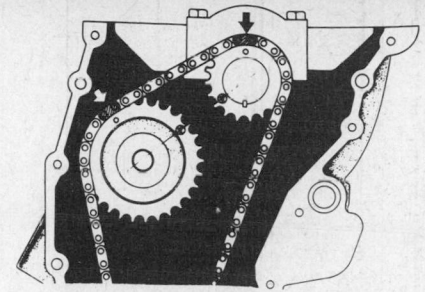

4M and 4M-E timing mark alignment (except the camshaft sprocket)

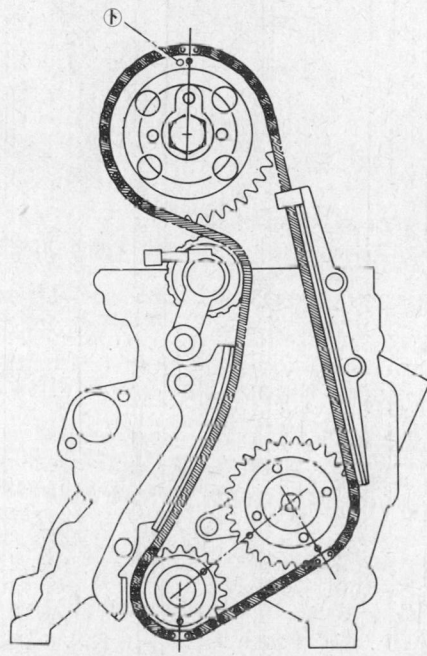

5M-E engines—proper alignment of the timing chain and gear markings

3. Unfasten the bolts which retain the chain damper and damper guide and withdraw the damper and guide.

4. Remove the oil slinger from the crankshaft.

5. Withdraw the timing chain.

6. Inspect the chain for wear or damage. Replace it if necessary.

Installation is performed in the following manner:

1. Position the No. 1 cylinder at TDC.

2. Position the crankshaft sprocket 0-mark downward, facing the oil pan.

3. Align the "Toyota" trademarks on the sprockets as illustrated.

4. Fit the tensioner gear assembly on the block.

NOTE: Its dowel pin should be positioned 1.5 in. from the surface of the block.

5. Install the chain over the two gears while maintaining tension.

6. Install both of the vibration dampers and the damper guide.

7. Fit the oil slinger to the crankshaft.

8. Tie the chain to the upper vibration damper, to keep it from falling into the chain cover, once the cover is installed.

9. Install the timing cover.

10. Perform the cylinder head installation procedure as detailed above.

NOTE: If proper valve timing cannot be obtained, it is possible to adjust it by placing the camshaft slotted pin in the second or third hole on the camshaft timing gear, as required. If the timing is out by more than 15°, replace the chain and both sprockets.

5M-GE

1. Disconnect the battery cables at the battery.

2. Loosen the mounting bolts of each of the crankshaft-driven components at the front of the engine and remove the drive belts.

3. Rotate the crankshaft in order to set the no. 1 cylinder to TDC of its compression stroke (both valves of the no. 1 cylinder closed, and TDC marks aligned).

4. Remove the upper, front (No. 3) timing belt cover and gasket (five bolts).

5. Loosen the idler pulley bolt and lever the idler pulley toward the alternator side of the engine in order to relieve the tension on the timing belt. Hand-tighten the idler pulley bolt.

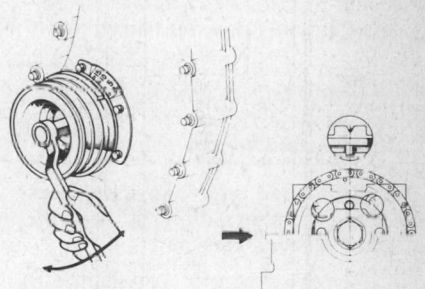

4M and 4M-E timing mark alignment—timing chain and camshaft sprocket

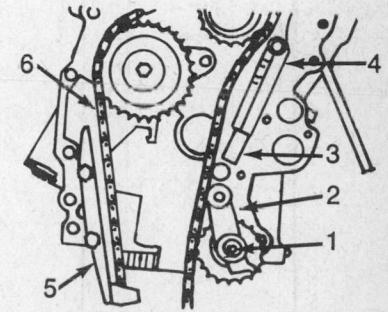

1. Timing chain tensioner gear
2. Timing chain tensioner arm
3. Damper guide
4. Vibration damper
5. Vibration damper
6. Crankshaft oil slinger

Removing the timing chain from "M" series engines (except 5M-GE)

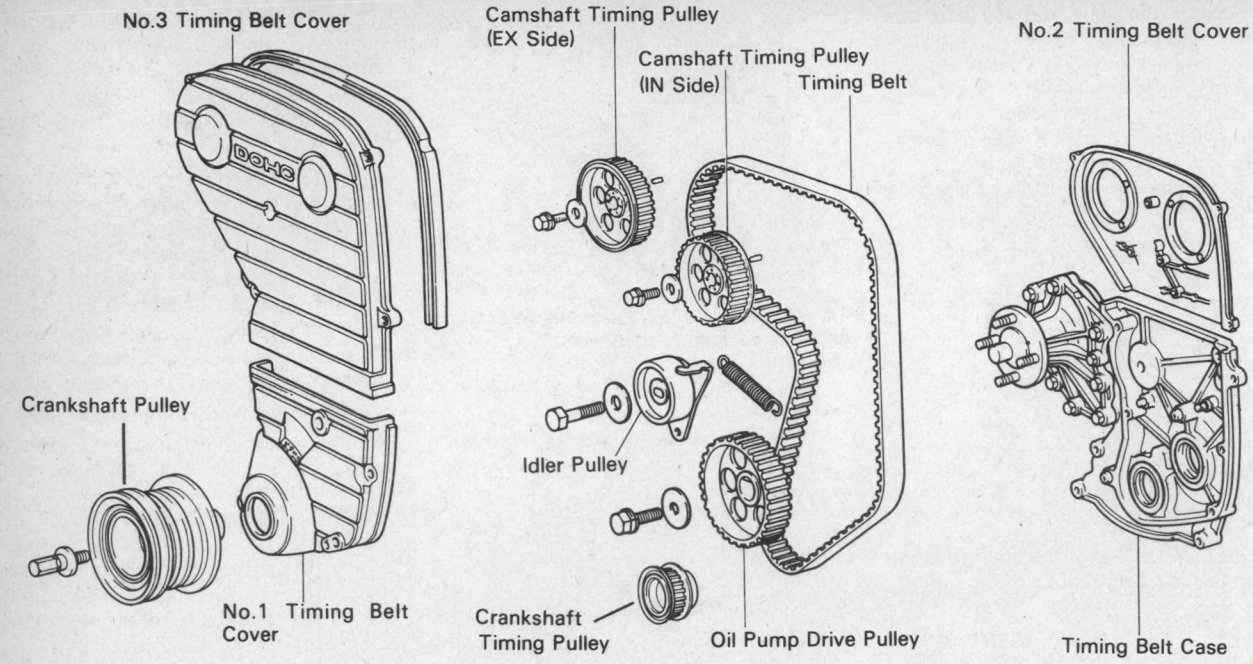

No.3 Timing Belt Cover   Camshaft Timing Pulley (EX Side)   Camshaft Timing Pulley (IN Side)   Timing Belt   No.2 Timing Belt Cover

Crankshaft Pulley

No.1 Timing Belt Cover   Idler Pulley   Crankshaft Timing Pulley   Oil Pump Drive Pulley   Timing Belt Case

Timing chain, covers and related components—5M-GE engines

6. Remove the timing belt from the camshaft pulleys.

7. Remove the camshaft timing pulleys as follows:

   a. Hold the pulleys stationary with a spanner wrench.

   b. Remove the center pulley bolt.

CAUTION

DO NOT attempt to use timing belt tension as a tool to remove the center pulley bolts, as the belt could become damaged.

NOTE: Do not interchange the intake and exhaust timing pulleys, as they differ for use with each camshaft.

8. Remove the center crankshaft pulley bolt. Using a puller, remove the crankshaft pulley.

9. Using chalk or a crayon, mark the timing belt to indicate its direction of rotation. This mark must face the same direction during installation of the belt.

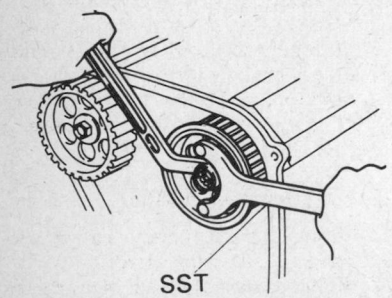

SST

5M-GE engines—Use a spanner wrench (SST) as shown, to hold the camshaft sprocket while loosening the camshaft sprocket bolt. DO NOT attempt to use belt tension to hold the sprocket in place while removing the camshaft sprocket bolt

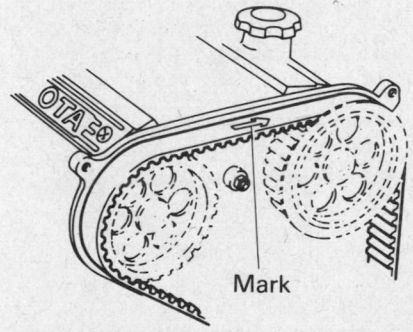

Mark

5M-GE engines—Paint a mark on the timing belt prior to belt removal to indicate the belts direction of normal rotation. Point the mark in the same direction if the belt is to be reinstalled

10. Remove the lower timing belt cover, then the belt.

11. If damaged, the crankshaft pulley can be removed using a puller; the oil pump drive shaft pulley can be removed in the same manner as the camshaft pulleys.

12. Inspect the timing belt for damage, such as cuts, cracks, missing teeth, abrasions, nicks, etc.

   a. If the belt teeth are damaged, check that the camshafts rotate freely and correct as necessary.

   b. Should damage be evident on the belt face, check the idler pulley belt surface for damage.

   c. If damage is present on one side of the belt only, check the belt guide and the alignment of each pulley.

   d. If the belt teeth are excessively worn, check the timing belt cover gasket for damage and/or proper installation.

13. Check the idler pulley for damage and smoothness of rotation. Also check the

free length of the tension spring, which should be 2.776 in., measured between the inside of each end "clip". Replace the spring if the length exceeds this limit.

Install the timing belt as follows:

1. Install the crankshaft and oil pump drive shaft if these items were removed previously. Torque the oil pump drive shaft pulley center bolt to 14–18 ft. lbs. The crankshaft pulley must be evenly driven into place.

2. Install the idler pulley and the tension spring. Lever the pulley towards the alternator side of the engine and tighten bolt.

3. Check the mark made during Step 9 of removal and temporarily install the timing belt on the crankshaft pulley. The mark must face in the same direction as it did originally.

4. Install the lower timing belt cover.

5. Install the crankshaft pulley and torque the center pulley bolt to 98–119 ft. lbs.

6. Remove the oil filler cap of the in-

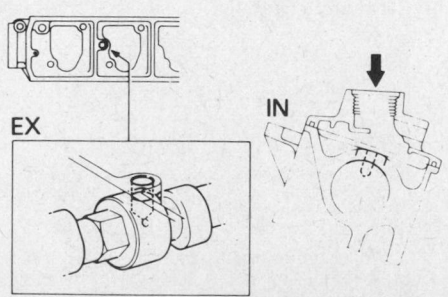

EX   IN

5M-GE engines—Proper alignment of the camshaft matchmarks with the match holes of the camshaft housings (IN—intake; EX—exhaust)

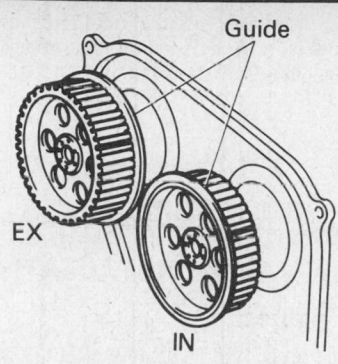

5M-GE engines—When installing the camshaft sprockets, be sure that the guides are positioned as shown. (IN—intake camshaft sprocket; EX—exhaust camshaft sprocket)

take camshaft cover, and the complete camshaft cover on the exhaust side.

7. Check that the match holes of both No. 2 camshaft journals are visible through the camshaft housing match holes. If necessary, temporarily install the camshaft pulley and guide pin, and rotate the camshaft(s) until the holes are aligned.

8. Install the timing pulleys. Note that the belt guide of the exhaust camshaft pulley should be positioned towards the engine; the belt guide of the intake camshaft pulley should be positioned away from the engine. DO NOT yet install the pulley retaining bolts.

9. Align the following marks:
a. Each camshaft pulley mark must be

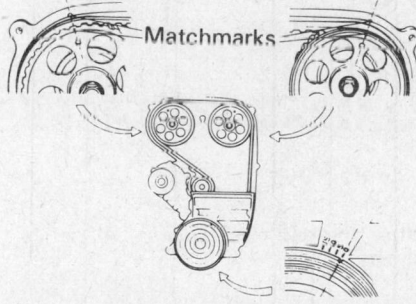

5M-GE engines—Alignment of the camshaft sprocket marks with the no. 2 timing cover marks. Note the position of the crankshaft pulley (TDC)

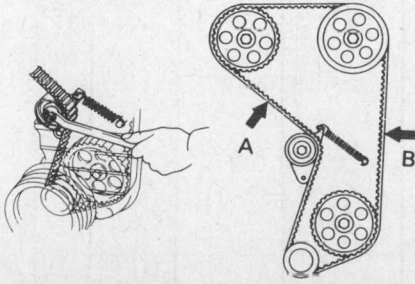

5M-GE engines—When adjusting the timing belt tension, be sure the tension at "A" is the same as that at "B"

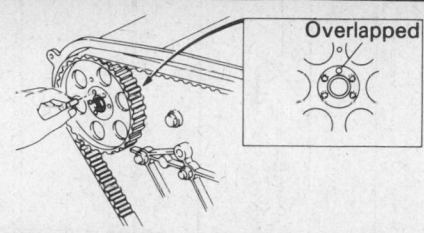

5M-GE engines—Locating the overlapped holes of the camshaft and the camshaft sprocket. Install the match pin into the aligned set of holes (typical of either the intake or exhaust camshaft)

aligned with its respective mark on the rear, upper (No. 2) timing belt cover.
b. Align the crankshaft pulley notch with the TDC (0) mark of the timing tab.

NOTE: The No. 1 cylinder MUST be positioned at TDC on its compression stroke.

10. Install the timing belt.
11. Loosen the idler pulley bolt and tension the timing belt. The timing belt tension must be the same between the exhaust camshaft pulley and the crankshaft pulley, as it is between the intake camshaft pulley and the oil pump driveshaft pulley.
12. There are five pin holes on each camshaft and each timing pulley. On the exhaust side: Install the match pin into the one hole of the pulley which is aligned with one of the camshaft pin holes. Repeat this on the intake side. Only one of the holes of each side should be aligned to allow insertion of the match pins.
13. Using a spanner wrench to hold the camshaft pulleys, install and tighten the camshaft pulley bolts. These bolts should be torqued to 48–54 ft. lbs.
14. Install the exhaust camshaft cover, using a new gasket. Install the oil filler cap.
15. Install the timing belt cover and gasket.
16. Install and adjust the drive belts at the front of the engine. Reconnect the battery cables.

Timing Gears

REMOVAL & INSTALLATION
1A-C, 3A, 3A-C, 4A-C, and 3Y-EC

1. Remove the air cleaner.

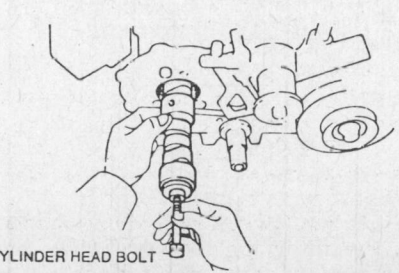

CYLINDER HEAD BOLT

Use a cylinder head bolt to remove and install the camshaft

2. Remove the throttle linkage.
3. Remove the valve cover.
4. Remove the crankshaft and water pump pulleys.
5. Remove the top and bottom timing belt cover.
6. Remove the belt tensioner.
7. Matchmark the belt and camshaft gear for easy installation.
8. Remove the timing belt.
9. Remove the bolt from the camshaft gear and remove the gear.

NOTE: In order to remove this gear use a pair of locking pliers to hold the cam from turning. Do not hold the cam by the lobes as damage may result.

10. Installation is the reverse of removal.

Camshaft

REMOVAL & INSTALLATION
2SE

1. Remove the timing belt as previously detailed.
2. Remove the camshaft housing as described in "Cylinder Head Removal".
3. Remove the camshaft pulley.
4. Remove the camshaft bearing caps.
5. Turning the camshaft slowly, slide it from the housing.
6. Installation is the reverse of removal. Always use new oil seals.
7. Installation is the reverse of removal. See the "Cylinder Head Installation" procedure.

1C-L and 1C-TL

1. Remove the cylinder head.
2. Remove the camshaft pulley.
3. Remove the thrust plate.
4. Unbolt and remove the camshaft bearing caps.
5. Turning the camshaft slowly, slide the camshaft from the head.
6. Installation is the reverse of removal.

3Y-EC

1. Remove the timing chain as previously detailed.
2. Remove the camshaft thrust plate.
3. Turning the camshaft slowly, slide it from the block.
4. Installation is the reverse of removal. Coat the camshaft with clean engine oil prior to insertion.

K–Series and T–Series

1. Remove the cylinder head as detailed previously in this chapter.
2. Remove the distributor. Remove the radiator.
3. Remove the timing chain as detailed previously.
4. Remove the valve lifters in the proper sequence. Be sure to keep them in order.
5. Remove the fuel pump on carbureted engines.

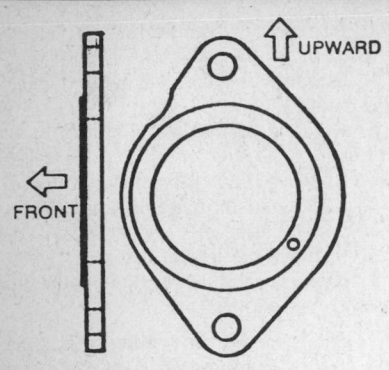

Proper positioning of the thrust plate—K-series engines

6. Remove the two thrust plate set bolts and pull off the thrust plate.

7. Screw a cylinder head bolt into the end of the camshaft. Slowly turn the camshaft and pull it out being careful not to damage the bearing.

8. Inspect the camshaft and bearings.

9. Coat the camshaft bearings and journals lightly with oil and then carefully install it into the cylinder block.

10. Install the thrust plate in the proper position and torque the two bolts to 4–6 ft. lbs. on the K–series engines and 7–11 ft. lbs. on the T–series engines.

11. Installation of the remaining components is in the reverse order of removal.

All Other Engines
EXCEPT 5M-GE

All of these engines utilize an overhead camshaft (OHC). Therefore, the procedure for removing the camshaft is given as part of the cylinder head removal procedure.

NOTE: It will not be necessary to completely remove the cylinder head in order

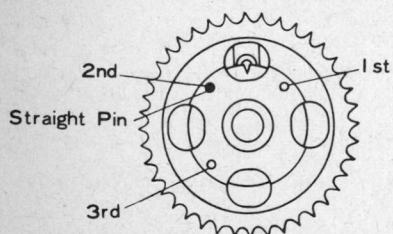

"M" series engines (except 5M-GE)—camshaft sprocket installation for 3–9° valve timing retard

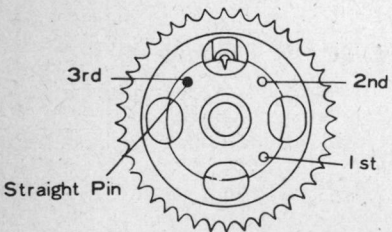

"M" series engines (except 5M-GE)—camshaft sprocket installation for 9–15° valve timing retard

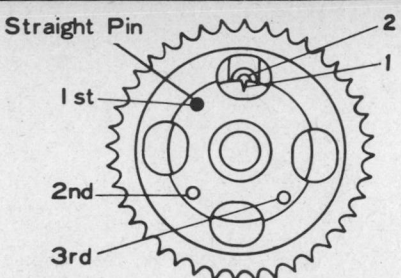

"M" series engines (except 5M-GE)—camshaft sprocket installation for normal valve timing

to remove the camshaft. Therefore, proceed only as far as is necessary, to remove the camshaft, with the cylinder head removal procedure.

5M-GE

1. Remove the two camshaft covers.

2. Remove the timing belt assembly and gears as previously detailed.

3. Following the sequence shown, loosen the camshaft housing nuts and bolts in three passes. Remove the housings (with camshafts) from the cylinder head.

4. Remove the camshaft housing rear covers. Squirt clean oil down around the cam journals in the housing, to lubricate the lobes, oil seals and bearings as the cam is removed. Begin to pull the camshaft out of the back of the housing slowly, turning it as you pull. Remove the cam completely.

5. To install, lubricate the entire camshaft with clean oil. Insert the cam into the housing from the back, and slowly turn it as you push it into the housing. Install new O-rings and the housing end covers.

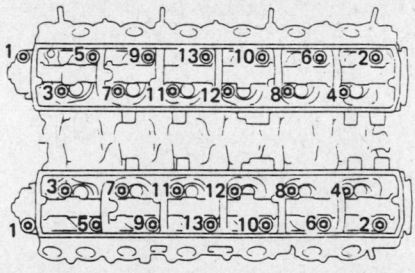

5M-GE camshaft housing bolt removal sequence. Loosen bolts gradually on three passes

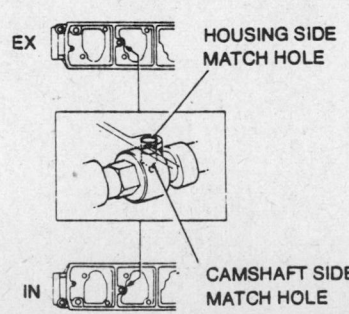

5M-GE camshaft housing torque sequence

6. Installation of the remaining components is in the reverse order of removal. Tighten camshaft housing bolts to 15–17 ft. lbs. in the proper sequence.

Pistons and Connecting Rods

REMOVAL & INSTALLATION

All Engines

See the procedure in "Engine Rebuilding" in the Unit Repair section.

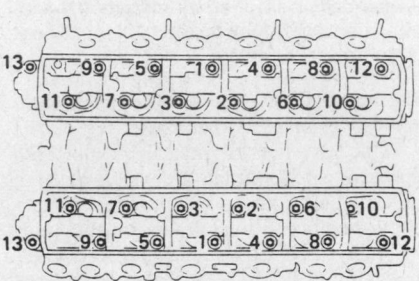

Before installing the camshaft housings, align the match hole on each No. 2 cam journal with the hole in the housing

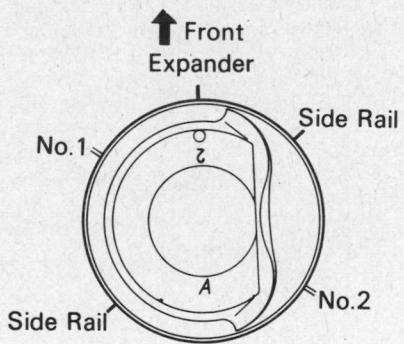

Piston ring gap positioning—"A" series engines

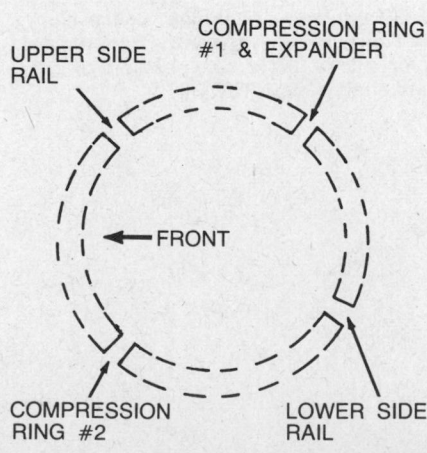

Piston ring installation on the 3Y-EC, 2SE and M series

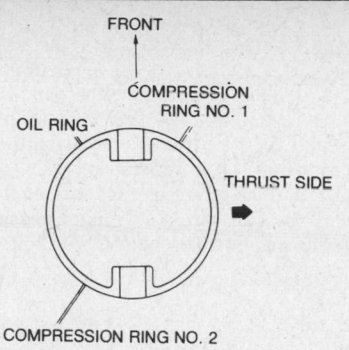

Piston ring gap positioning—"K" series engines

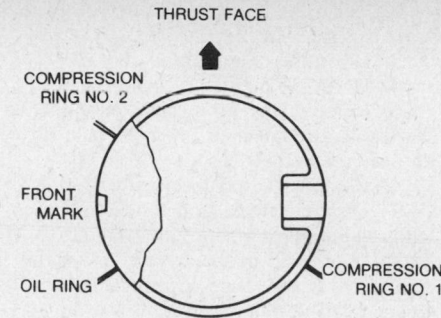

Piston ring gap positioning—"R" series engines

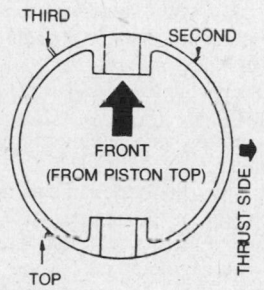

Piston ring installation on the Diesel and T series engines

ENGINE LUBRICATION

Oil Pan

REMOVAL & INSTALLATION

Corolla, Corona, and Starlet

1. Open the engine compartment hood.
2. Raise the front end of the car and support it with jack stands.
3. Remove the splash shield from underneath the engine.
4. Place a jack under the transmission to support it.
5. Unfasten the bolts which secure the engine rear supporting crossmember to the chassis.
6. Raise the jack under the transmission, *slightly*.
7. Unbolt the oil pan and work it out from underneath the engine.

NOTE: If the oil pan does not come out easily, it may be necessary to unbolt the rear engine mounts from the crossmember.

Installation is performed in the reverse order of removal. On Corolla models equipped with the 2T-C and 3T-C engines and Corona models, apply liquid sealer to the four corners of the oil pan. Tighten the oil pan securing bolts to the following specifications:

3K-C, 4K-C and 4K-E engine: 2–3 ft. lbs.

2T-C and 3T-C engines: 4–6 ft. lbs.

20R and 22R engines: 3–6 ft. lbs.

Camry
GASOLINE ENGINE

1. Raise and support the front of the car on jackstands.
2. Drain the oil.
3. Remove the engine undercover.
4. Remove the dipstick.
5. Unbolt and remove the oil pan.
6. Installation is the reverse of removal. Clean the gasket mating surfaces. Always use a new pan gasket. Some engines were assembled using RTV gasket material in place of a conventional gasket. In that case, apply a thin (5mm) bead of RTV material to the groove around the pan mating surface. Assemble the pan within 15 minutes. Torque pan bolts to 48 in. lb.

DIESEL ENGINE

1. Raise and support the front of the car on jackstands.
2. Drain the oil.
3. Remove the engine undercovers.
4. Remove the timing belt.
5. Remove the lower idler pulley and crankshaft pulley.
6. With the engine supported by a hoist or jack, remove the center crossmember.
7. Unbolt and remove the oil pan.
8. Installation is the reverse of removal. Clean the mating surface of the pan and block. Apply a 5mm bead of RTV silicone gasket material to the groove around the pan mating surface. Install the pan within

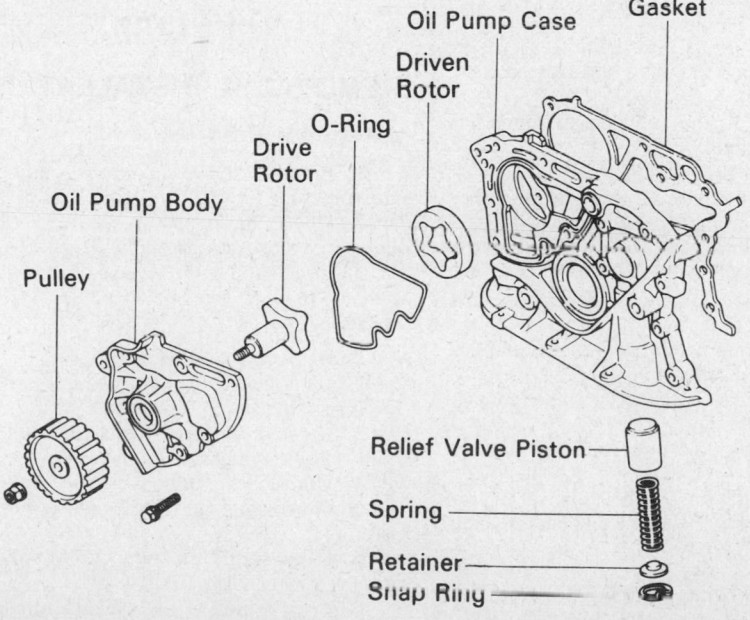

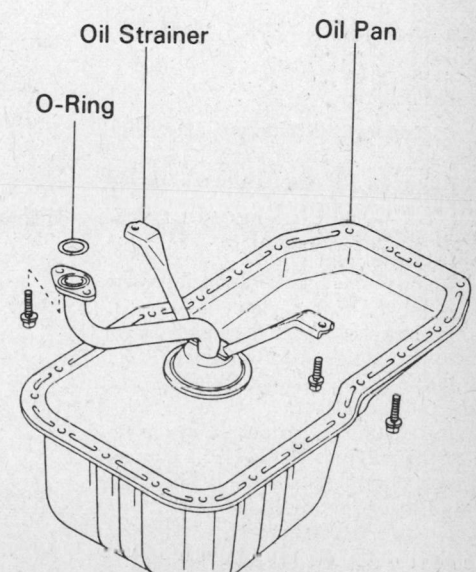

2SE oil pan and pump

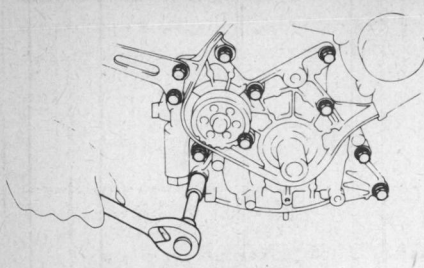

Diesel oil pump removal

15 minutes of applying the sealant. Torque the pan bolts to 48 in. lb.

Celica and Supra (1978–81) and Cressida

1. Drain the oil.
2. Raise the front end of the car with jacks and support it with jack stands.

━━━━━━━━ **CAUTION** ━━━━━━━━

Be sure that the car is supported securely. Remember, you will be working underneath it.

3. Detach the steering relay rod and the tie rods from the idler arm, pitman arm, and steering knuckles, as detailed below.
4. Remove the engine stiffening plates.
5. Remove the splash shields from underneath the engine.
6. Support the front of the engine with a jack and remove the front engine mount attaching bolts.
7. Raise the front of the engine *slightly* with the jack.
8. Unbolt and withdraw the oil pan.

Installation is performed in the reverse order of removal. Apply liquid sealer to the four corners of the oil pan gasket used on 2T-C and 3T-C engines. Torque the oil pan securing bolts to 4–6 ft. lbs.

Celica and Supra (1982 and Later)

22R and 22R-E

1. Disconnect the battery cables at the battery.
2. Raise the front of the vehicle and support it with jackstands.
3. Remove the engine undercover.
4. Drain the engine oil.
5. Remove the engine shock absorber.
6. Remove the motor mount bolts.
7. Place a jack under the transmission and raise the engine about one inch.
8. Remove the oil pan fasteners, the oil pan, and the gasket.
9. Installation is performed in the reverse of the previous steps. Use a new oil pan gasket during installation. Torque the oil pan fasteners to 35–69 in. lbs.

5M-GE

1. Disconnect the battery cables at the battery.

2. Raise the front of the vehicle and support it safely with jacstands.
3. Drain the engine oil.
4. Drain the cooling system.
5. Remove the air cleaner assembly. Mark any disconnected lines and/or hoses for easy reassembly.
6. Remove the oil level gauge.
7. Disconnect the upper radiator hose at the radiator.
8. Loosen all of the drive belts for the crankshaft-driven accessories (alternator, power steering pump, etc.).
9. Remove the four fan shroud bolts.
10. Remove the four fluid coupling flange attaching nuts, then remove the fluid coupling along with the fan and the fan shroud.
11. Remove the engine undercover.
12. Remove the exhaust pipe clamp bolt from the exhaust pipe stay.
13. Remove the two stiffener plates from the exhaust pipe.
14. Remove the clutch housing undercover.
15. Remove the four engine mount bolts from each side of the engine.
16. Place a jack under the transmission and raise the engine about 1¾ in.
17. Remove the oil pan mounting bolts and remove the oil pan from the engine.

NOTE: If difficulty is encountered while removing the pan, rotate the crankshaft a small amount to gain extra clearance.

18. Installation is the reverse of the previous steps. Use a new oil pan gasket during installation. Apply a small amount of sealer to the oil pan gasket at each of the four corners of the oil pan. Torque the oil pan fasteners to 57–82 in. lbs. Adjust the drive belts and replenish the engine with oil and the cooling system with the proper type and quantity of coolant. Check for leaks after the engine is started.

Tercel

1. Disconnect the negative battery terminal.
2. Jack up the vehicle and support it with jack stands.
3. Drain the oil.
4. Remove the sway bar and any other necessary steering linkage parts.
5. Disconnect the exhaust pipe from the manifold.
6. Jack up the engine enough to take the weight off it.
7. Remove the engine mounts and engine shock absorber.
8. Continue to jack up the engine enough to remove the pan.
9. Remove the pan bolts and remove the pan.
10. Installation is the reverse of removal. Always use a new pan gasket when reinstalling the pan.

Van

1. Raise and support the front of the car on jackstands.

2. Drain the oil.
3. Remove the left and right stiffener plates.
4. Unbolt and remove the pan.
5. Installation is the reverse of removal. Clean the pan and block mating surfaces. Apply a 5mm bead of RTV gasket material to the groove around the pan flange. Install the pan within 15 minutes of applying the sealant. Torque the pan bolts to 9 ft. lb.

Rear Main Oil Seal

REPLACEMENT

All Engines

NOTE: On the 1A-C, 3A, and 3A-C engines, they must be removed before this procedure can be attempted.

1. Remove the transmission.
2. Remove the clutch cover assembly and flywheel.
3. Remove the oil seal retaining plate, complete with the oil seal.
4. Use a screwdriver to pry the old seal from the retaining plate. Be careful not to damage the plate.
5. Install the new seal, carefully, by using a block of wood to drift it into place.

━━━━━━━━ **CAUTION** ━━━━━━━━
Do not damage the seal; a leak will result.

6. Lubricate the lips of the seal with multipurpose grease.

Installation is the reverse of removal.

Oil Pump

REMOVAL & INSTALLATION

All Except R-Series

1. Remove the oil pan, as outlined previously.
2. Unbolt the oil pump securing bolts and remove it as an assembly.
3. Installation is the reverse of removal.

R-Series

1. Remove the oil pan.
2. Remove the three bolts which secure the oil strainer.
3. Remove the drive belts, the pulley bolt, and the crankshaft pulley.
4. Unfasten the bolts which secure the oil pump housing and remove the pump assembly.
5. Remove the oil pump drive spline and the rubber O-ring.
6. Installation is the reverse of removal. Apply sealer to the top oil pump housing bolt. Use a new oil strainer gasket.

ENGINE COOLING

Radiator

REMOVAL & INSTALLATION

All Models

1. Drain the cooling system.
2. Unfasten the clamps and remove the radiator upper and lower hoses. If equipped with an automatic transmission, remove the oil cooler lines.
3. Detach the hood lock cable and remove the hood lock from the radiator upper support.

NOTE: It may be necessary to remove the grille in order to gain access to the hood lock/radiator support assembly.

4. Remove the fan shroud, if so equipped.
5. On models equipped with the closed cooling system, disconnect the hose from the thermal expansion tank and remove the tank from its bracket.
6. Unbolt and remove the radiator upper support.
7. Unfasten the bolts and remove the radiator.

— CAUTION —
Use care not to damage the radiator fins on the cooling fan.

8. Installation is performed in the reverse order of removal. Remember to check the transmission fluid level on cars with automatic transmissions.

Certain models are equipped with an electric, rather than a belt-driven, cooling fan. Using a radiator-mounted thermo-switch, the fan operates when the coolant temperatures reach 203°F and stops when it lowers to 190°F. It is attached to the radiator by the four radiator retaining bolts. Radiator removal is the same for this engine as all others, except for disconnecting the wiring harness and thermo switch connector.

Water Pump

REMOVAL & INSTALLATION

All Except A-Series

1. Drain the cooling system.
2. Unfasten the fan shroud securing bolts and remove the fan shroud, if so equipped.
3. Loosen the alternator adjusting link bolt and remove the drive belt. On the Camry with the 2SE engine, remove the timing covers. On the diesel Camry, remove the timing covers and injection pump pulley.
4. Repeat Step 3 for the air pump, air conditioning compressor, or power steering pump drive belts, if so equipped.

NOTE: On some models, it may be necessary to remove the air cleaner assembly. On all 5M-GE engines, remove the air cleaner case.

5. Detach the bypass and radiator hoses from the water pump.
6. Unfasten the water pump retaining bolts and remove the water pump and fan assembly, using care not to damage the radiator with the fan.

— CAUTION —
If the fan is equipped with a fluid coupling, do not tip the fan/pump assembly on its side, as the fluid will run out.

7. Installation is the reverse of removal. Always use a new gasket between the pump body and its mounting. Check for leaks after installation is completed.

A-Series

1. Drain the radiator. Save the coolant as it can be reused.
2. Loosen all necessary drive belts.
3. Remove the top timing belt cover.
4. Remove the bottom radiator hose from the water pump.
5. Remove the pump bolts and remove the pump.

NOTE: Always use a new gasket when replacing the pump.

6. Installation is the reverse of removal.

Thermostat

REMOVAL & INSTALLATION

All Engines

1. Drain the cooling system.
2. Unfasten the clamp and remove the upper radiator hose from the water outlet elbow.
3. Unbolt and remove the water outlet (thermostat housing).
4. Withdraw the thermostat.
5. Installation is performed in the reverse order of removal procedure. Use a new gasket on the water outlet.

— CAUTION —
Be sure that the thermostat is installed with the spring pointing down.

EMISSION CONTROLS

NOTE: Due to the complexity of most late models, only the major systems and basic services will be covered. Detailed servicing of any emission system should be referred to a professional technician having the proper testing equipment.

Positive Crankcase Ventilation (PCV) System

A positive crankcase ventilation (PCV) system is used on all Toyotas sold in the United States. Blow-by gases are routed from the crankcase to the carburetor, where they are combined with the fuel/air mixture and burned during combustion.

A (PCV) valve is used in the line to prevent the gases in the crankcase from being ignited in case of a backfire. The amount of blow-by gases entering the mixture is also regulated by the PCV valve, which is spring-loaded and has a variable orifice.

The valve is either mounted on the valve cover or in the line which runs from the intake manifold to the crankcase.

REMOVAL & INSTALLATION

Remove the PCV valve from the cylinder head cover on "K" and "A" series engines. Remove the hose from the valve.

On the remainder of the engines, remove the valve from the manifold-to-crankcase hose.

Installation is the reverse of removal.

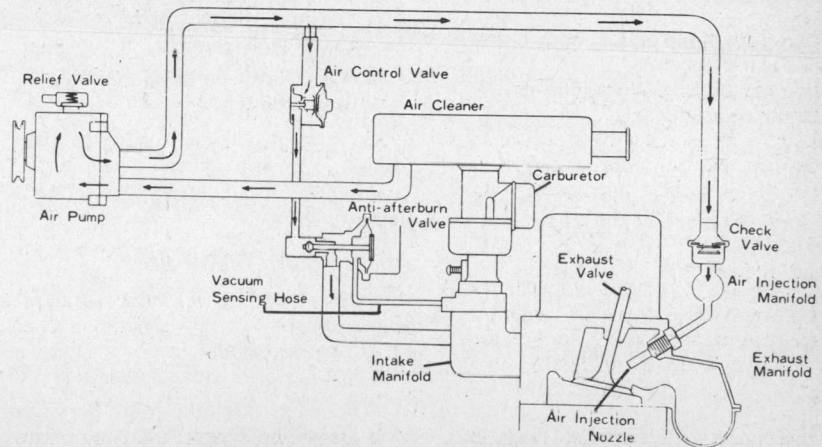

Schematic of a typical air injection system

TESTING

Check the PCV system hoses and connections, to see that there are no leaks; then replace or tighten, as necessary.

To check the valve, remove it and blow through both ends. When blowing from the side which goes toward the intake manifold, very little air should pass through. When blowing from the crankcase (valve cover) side, air should pass through freely.

Replace the valve if it fails to function as outlined.

NOTE: Do not attempt to clean or adjust the valve; replace it with a new one.

Air Injection System

A belt-driven air pump supplies air to an injection manifold which has nozzles in each exhaust port. Injection of air at this point causes combustion of unburned hydrocarbons in the exhaust manifold rather than allowing them to escape into the atmosphere. An antibackfire valve controls the flow of air from the pump to prevent backfiring which results from an overly rich mixture under closed throttle conditions.

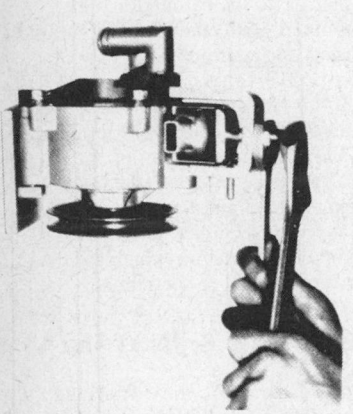

Removing the relief valve from the air pump

A check valve prevents hot exhaust gas backflow into the pump and hoses, in case of a pump failure, or when the antibackfire valve is working.

In addition newer engines have an air switching valve (ASV). On engines without catalytic converters, the ASV is used to stop air injection under a constant heavy engine load.

On engines with catalytic converters the ASV is used to protect the catalyst from overheating, by blocking the air necessary for the reaction.

On all engines, the relief valve is built into the ASV.

REMOVAL & INSTALLATION

Air Pump

1. Disconnect the air hoses from the pump.

2. Loosen the bolt on the adjusting link and remove the drive belt.
3. Remove the pump.

——— CAUTION ———
Do not pry on the pump housing; it may be distorted.

4. Installation is in the reverse order of removal. Adjust the drive belt tension to ½–¾ in. under thumb pressure.

Antibackfire Valve and Air Switching Valve.

1. Detach the air hoses from the valve.
2. Remove the valve securing bolt.
3. Withdraw the valve.
4. Installation is performed in the reverse order of removal.

Check Valve

1. Detach the intake hose from the valve.
2. Use an open-end wrench to remove the valve from its mounting.
3. Installation is the reverse of removal.

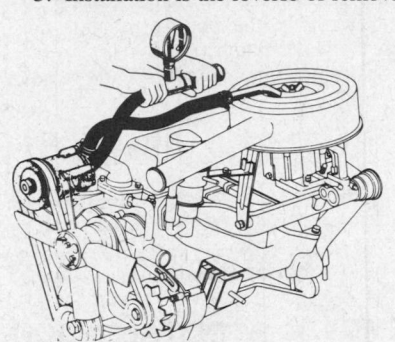

Checking the air pump output

Relief Valve

1. Remove the air pump from the car.
2. Support the pump so that it cannot rotate.

——— CAUTION ———
Never clamp the pump in a vise; the aluminum case will become distorted.

3. Use a jaw-type puller to remove the relief valve from the top of the pump.
4. Position the new relief valve over the opening in the pump.

NOTE: The air outlet should be pointing toward the left.

5. Gently tap the relief valve into place, using a block of wood and a hammer.
6. Install the pump on the engine, as outlined above.

Air Injection Manifold

1. Remove the check valve, as outlined above.
2. Loosen the air injection manifold attachment nuts and withdraw the manifold.

NOTE: On "R" and "M" series engines, it will first be necessary to remove the exhaust manifold.

3. Installation is in the reverse of removal.

Air Injection Nozzles

1. Remove the air injection manifold as outlined above.
2. Remove the cylinder head, as detailed in the appropriate section, above.
3. Place a new nozzle on the cylinder head.
4. Install the air injection manifold over it.
5. Install the cylinder head on the engine block.

TESTING

Air Pump

——— CAUTION ———
Do not hammer, pry, or bend the pump housing while tightening the drive belt or testing the pump.

BELT TENSION AND AIR LEAKS

1. Before proceeding with the tests, check the pump drive belt tension to see if it is within specifications.
2. Turn the pump by hand. If it has seized, the belt will slip, making a noise. Disregard any chirping, squealing, or rolling sounds from inside the pump; these are normal when it is turned by hand.
3. Check the hoses and connections for leaks. Hissing or a blast of air is indicative of a leak. Soapy water, applied lightly around the area in question, is a good method for detecting leaks.

AIR OUTPUT

1. Disconnect the air supply hose at the antibackfire valve.
2. Connect a pressure gauge, using a suitable adaptor, to the air supply hose.

NOTE: If there are two hoses, plug the second one.

3. With the engine at normal operating temperature, increase the idle speed to 1000–1500 rpm (1950 rpm-2T-C and 3T-C) and watch the gauge.
4. The air flow from the pump should be steady and fall between 2 and 6 psi. If it is unsteady or falls below this, the pump is defective and must be replaced.

PUMP NOISE DIAGNOSIS

The air pump is normally noisy; as engine speed increases, the noise of the pump will rise in pitch. The rolling sound the pump bearings make is normal. But if this sound becomes objectionable at certain speeds, the pump is defective and will have to be replaced.

A continual hissing sound from the air pump pressure relief valve at idle, indicates a defective valve. Replace the relief valve.

If the pump rear bearing fails, a continual knocking sound will be heard.

Antibackfire Valve Testing

1. Detach the hose, which runs from the bypass valve to the check valve, at the bypass valve hose connection.

2. Connect a tachometer to the engine. With the engine running at normal idle speed, check to see that air is flowing from the bypass valve hose connection.

3. Speed up the engine so it is running at 1500–2000 rpm. Allow the throttle to snap shut. The flow of air from the bypass valve at the check valve hose connection should stop momentarily and air should then flow from the exhaust port on the valve body or the silencer assembly.

4. Repeat Step 3 several times. If the flow of air is not diverted into the atmosphere from the valve exhaust port or if it fails to stop flowing from the hose connection, check the vacuum lines and connections. If these are tight, the valve is defective and requires replacement.

5. A leaking diaphragm will cause the air to flow out both the hose connection and the exhaust port at the same time. If this happens, replace the valve.

Air Switching Valve (ASV) Tests
"T" AND "R" SERIES ENGINES

1. Start the engine and allow it to reach normal operating temperature.

2. At curb idle, the air from the bypass valve should be discharged through the hose which runs to the ASV.

3. When the vacuum line to the ASV is disconnected, the air from the bypass valve should be diverted out through the ASV-to-air cleaner hose. Reconnect the vacuum line.

4. Disconnect the ASV-to-check valve hose and connect a pressure gauge to it.

5. Increase the engine speed. The relief valve should open when the pressure gauge registers 2.7–6.5 psi.

6. If the ASV fails any of the above tests, replace it. Reconnect all hoses.

"M" SERIES ENGINES

1. Start the engine and allow it to reach normal operating temperature.

2. At curb idle, air from the pump should be discharged through the hose which runs to the check valve.

3. Race the engine and allow the throttle valve to snap shut. The air from the pump should be discharged into the air cleaner.

4. Disconnect the ASV-to-check valve hose and connect a pressure gauge to it.

5. Increase the engine speed gradually. The relief valve should open when the gauge registers 3.7–7.7 psi. Reconnect the check valve hose.

6. Unfasten the wiring connector and the hoses from the solenoid valve, which is attached to the ASV. Air should pass through the solenoid valve when either the top or bottom port is blown into.

7. Connect a 12V power source to the terminals on the valve. No air should flow through the valve when either port is blown into.

8. If the solenoid valve or the ASV fail any of the above tests, replace either or both of them, as necessary.

Vacuum Delay Valve Test
"T" AND "R" SERIES ENGINES

The vacuum delay valve is located in the line which runs from the intake manifold to either the vacuum surge tank ("R" engines) or to the ASV ("T" engines). To check it, proceed as follows:

1. Remove the vacuum delay valve from the vacuum line. Be sure to note which end points toward the intake manifold.

2. When air is blown in from the ASV (surge tank) side, it should pass through the valve freely.

3. When air is blown in from the intake manifold side, a resistance should be felt.

4. Replace the valve if it fails either of the above tests.

5. Install the valve in the vacuum line, being careful not to install it backwards.

Check Valve Test

1. Before starting the test, check all of the hoses and connections for leaks.

2. Detach the air supply hose from the check valve.

3. Insert a suitable probe into the check valve and depress the plate. Release it; the plate should return to its original position against the valve seat. If binding is evident, replace the valve.

4. With the engine running at normal operating temperature, gradually increase its speed to 1500 rpm. Check for exhaust gas leakage. If any is present, replace the valve assembly.

NOTE: Vibration and flutter of the check valve at idle speed is a normal condition and does not mean that the valve should be replaced.

Evaporative Emission Control System

To prevent hydrocarbon emissions from entering the atmosphere, Toyota vehicles use evaporative emission control (EEC) systems. All models use a "charcoal canister" storage system.

The charcoal canister storage system stores fuel vapors in a canister filled with activated charcoal. All models use a vacuum switching valve to purge the system. The air filter is an integral part of the charcoal canister.

REMOVAL & INSTALLATION

Removal and installation of the various evaporative emission control system components consists of disconnecting hoses, loosening securing screws, and removing the part which is to be replaced from its mounting bracket. Installation is the reverse of removal.

NOTE: When replacing any EEC system hoses, always use hoses that are fuel-resistant or are marked "EVAP."

TESTING

EEC System Troubleshooting

There are several things which may be checked if a malfunction of the evaporative emission control system is suspected.

1. Leaks may be traced by using a hydrocarbon tester. Run the test probe along the lines and connections. The meter will indicate the presence of a leak by a high hydrocarbon (HC) reading. This method is much more accurate than visual inspection which would only indicate the presence of leaks large enough to pass liquid.

2. Leaks may be caused by any of the following:

  a. Defective or worn hoses;

  b. Disconnected or pinched hoses;

  c. Improperly routed hoses;

  d. A defective filler cap or safety valve (sealed cap system).

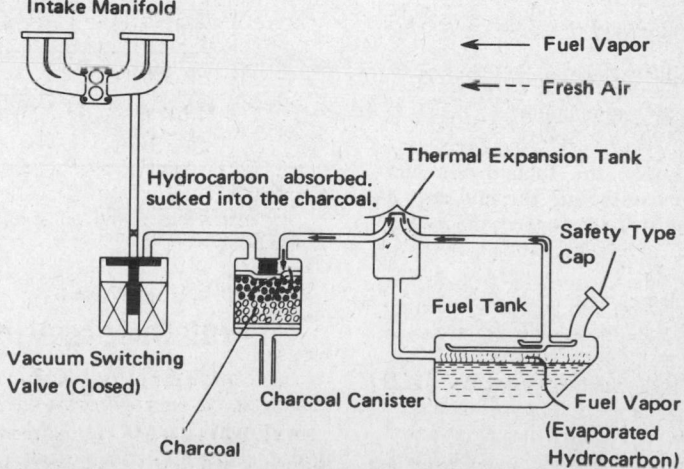

Schematic of a typical evaporative emission control system

NOTE: If it becomes necessary to replace any of the hoses used in the evaporative emission control system, use only hoses which are fuel-resistant or are marked "EVAP."

3. If the fuel tank, storage case, or thermal expansion tank collapse, it may be the fault of clogged or pinched vent lines, a defective vapor separator, or a plugged or incorrect filler cap.

4. To test the filler cap (if it is the safety valve type), blow into the relief valve housing. If the cap passes pressure with light blowing or if it fails to release with hard blowing, it is defective and must be replaced.

NOTE: Use the proper cap for the type of system used; either a sealed cap or safety valve cap, as required.

Check Valve

Rough idling when the gas tank is full is probably caused by a defective check valve. To test it, proceed as follows:

1. Run the engine at idle.
2. Clamp the hose between the vacuum switching valve or carburetor (4M-Calif) and the charcoal canister.
3. If the engine idle becomes smooth, replace the check valve.

Throttle Positioner

On Toyotas with an engine modification system, a throttle positioner is included to reduce exhaust emissions during deceleration. The positioner prevents the throttle from closing completely. Vacuum is reduced under the throttle valve which, in turn, acts on the retard chamber of the distributor vacuum unit (if so equipped). This compensates for the loss of engine braking caused by the partially open throttle.

Once the vehicle drops below a predetermined speed, the vacuum switching valve provides vacuum to the throttle positioner diaphragm; the throttle positioner retracts allowing the throttle valve to close completely. The distributor also is returned to normal operation.

ADJUSTMENT

1. Start the engine and allow it to reach normal operating temperature.
2. Adjust the idle speed.

NOTE: Leave the tachometer connected after completing the idle adjustments, as it will be needed in Step 5, below.

3. Detach the vacuum line from the positioner diaphragm unit and plug the line.
4. Accelerate the engine slightly to set the throttle positioner.
5. Check the engine speed with a tachometer when the throttle positioner is set.
6. If necessary, adjust the engine speed, with the throttle positioner adjusting screw, to the specifications.

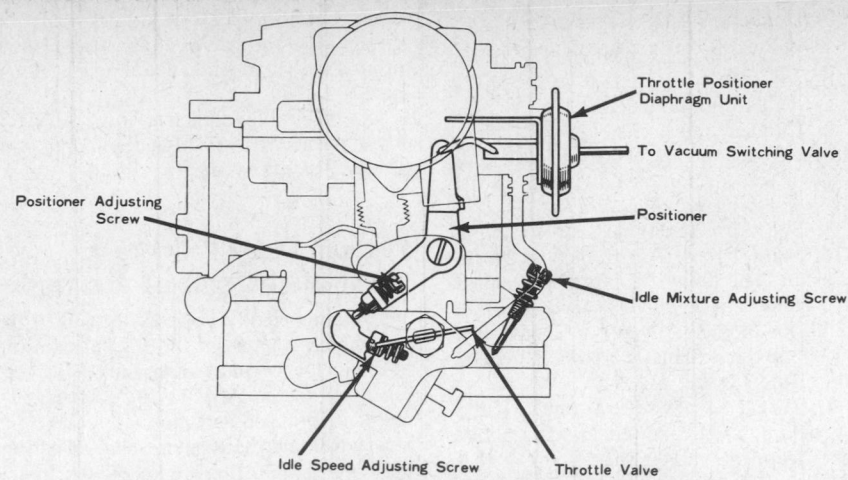

Components of a typical throttle positioner system

7. Connect the vacuum hose to the positioner diaphragm.
8. The throttle lever should be freed from the positioner as soon as the vacuum hose is connected. Engine idle should return to normal.
9. If the throttle positioner fails to function properly, check its linkage, and vacuum diaphragm. If there are no defects in either of these, the fault probably lies in the vacuum switching valve or the speed marker unit.

NOTE: Due to the complexity of these two components they require special test equipment.

THROTTLE POSITIONER SETTINGS
(rpm)

Year	Engine	Engine rpm (Positioner Set)
'78–'85	2T-C	1400 MT 1200 AT
	3T-C	1600 MT 1300 AT②
	20R, 22R	1050
	4M	950
	1A-C, 3A, 3A-C	N.A.

② Calif: 1400
AT Automatic transmission
MT Manual transmission

Dual-Diaphragm Distributor

Some Toyota models are equipped with a dual-diaphragm distributor unit. This distributor has a retard diaphragm, as well as a diaphragm for advance. Retarding the timing helps to reduce exhaust emissions, as well as making up for the lack of engine braking on models equipped with a throttle positioner.

TESTING

1. Connect a timing light to the engine. Check the ignition timing.

NOTE: Before proceeding with the tests, disconnect any spark control devices, distributor vacuum valves, etc. If these are left connected, inaccurate results may be obtained.

2. Remove the retard hose from the distributor and plug it. Increase the engine speed. The timing should advance. If it fails to do so, then the vacuum unit is faulty and must be replaced.

3. Check the timing with the engine at normal idle speed. Unplug the retard hose and connect it to the vacuum unit. The timing should instantly be retarded from 4 to 10 degrees. I; this does not occur, the retard diaphragm has a leak and the vacuum unit must be replaced.

Engine Modifications System

Toyota uses an assortment of engine modifications to regulate exhaust emissions. Most of these devices fall into the category of engine vacuum controls. There are three principal components used on the engine modifications system, as well as a number of smaller parts. The three major components are: a speed sensor; a computer (speed marker); and a vacuum switching valve.

The vacuum switching valve and computer circuit operates most of the emission control components. Depending upon year and engine usage, the vacuum switching valve and computer may operate the purge control for the evaporative emission control system; the transmission controlled spark

(TCS) or speed controlled spark (SCS); the dual-diaphragm distributor; and the throttle positioner systems.

The functions of the evaporative emission control system, the throttle positioner, and the dual-diaphragm distributor are described in detail in the sections above. However, a word is necessary about the functions of the TCS and SCS systems before discussing the operation of the vacuum switching valve/computer circuit.

The major difference between the transmission controlled spark and speed controlled spark systems is in the manner in which systems operation is determined.

Below a predetermined speed, or any gear other than fourth, the vacuum advance unit on the distributor is rendered inoperative. By changing the distributor advance curve in this manner, it is possible to reduce emissions of oxides of nitrogen (NOx).

NOTE: Some engines are equipped with a thermo-sensor so that the TDS or SCS system only operates when the coolant temperature is 140°–212°F.

Aside from determining the conditions outlined above, the vacuum switching valve computer circuit operates other devices in the emission control system.

The computer acts as a speed marker; at certain speeds it sends a signal to the vacuum switching valve which acts as a gate, opening and closing the emission control system vacuum circuits.

SYSTEM CHECKS

Due to the complexity of the components involved, about the only engine modification system checks which can be made without the use of special test equipment, are the following:

1. Examine the vacuum lines to see that they are not clogged, pinched, or loose.

2. Check the electrical connections for tightness and corrosion.

3. Be sure that the vacuum sources for the vacuum switching valve are not plugged.

4. On models equipped with speed controlled spark, a broken speedometer cable could also render the system inoperative.

5. Test the thermo-sensor in the following manner:

a. Remove the lead from its center terminal.

b. Touch one test prod of an ohmmeter to the sensor housing.

c. Connect the other test prod in series with a 10 ohm resistor to the center terminal of the sensor.

d. If the engine temperature is between about 140°–212°F, the meter should show no continuity.

e. If the engine is above or below these temperatures, the meter should show continuity.

f. Replace the thermo-sensor if it isn't working properly.

6. If everything else is in good working order, the fault probably lies in the vacuum

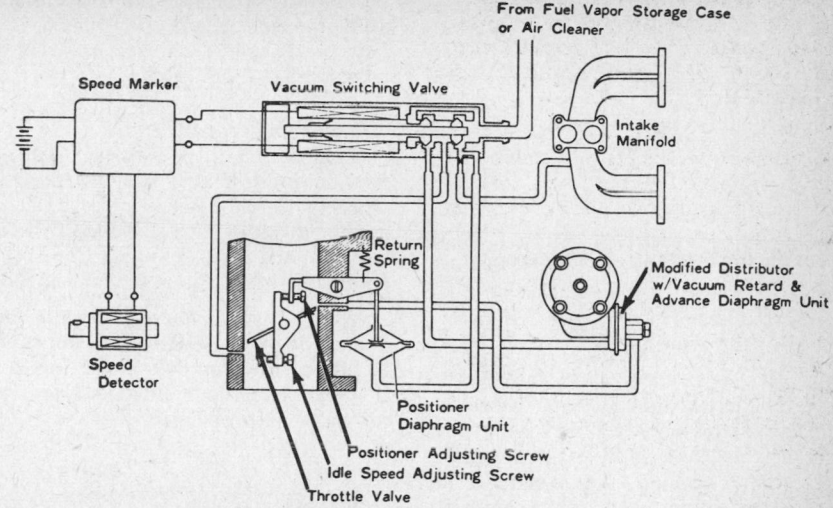

Engine modification system

switching valve or the computer (speed marker). About the only way to test these, without using special equipment, is by substitution of new units.

NOTE: A faulty vacuum switching valve or computer could cause more than one of the emission control systems to fail. Therefore, if several systems are out, these two units (and the speedometer cable) would be the first things to check.

Exhaust Gas Recirculation (EGR)

In all cases, the EGR valve is controlled by the same computer and vacuum switching valve which is used to operate other emission control system components.

Vacuum from the carburetor vacuum advance port flows through the vacuum switching valve to an EGR vacuum control valve. The vacuum from the advance port opens the vacuum control valve which then allows venturi vacuum to act on the chamber *above* the EGR valve diaphragm, causing the EGR valve to open. When exhaust gas recirculation is not required, the vacuum switching valve stops sending the advance port vacuum signal to the EGR vacuum control valve which closes, sending intake manifold vacuum to the chamber *below* the EGR valve diaphragm. This closes the EGR valve, blocking the flow of exhaust gases to the intake manifold.

On all engines there are several conditions, determined by the computer and vacuum switching valve, which permit exhaust gas recirculation to take place:
1. Vehicle speed
2. Engine coolant temperature

EGR VALVE CHECKS

All Except "M" Series Engines

1. Allow the engine to warm up and remove the top from the air cleaner.

NOTE: Do not remove the entire air cleaner assembly.

2. Disconnect the hose (white tape coded), which runs from the vacuum switching valve to the EGR valve, at its EGR valve end.

3. Remove the intake manifold hose (red coded) from the vacuum switching valve and connect it to the EGR valve. When the engine is at idle, a "hollow" sound should be heard coming from the air cleaner.

4. Disconnect the hose from the EGR valve; the hollow sound should disappear.

5. If the sound doesn't vary, the EGR valve is defective and must be replaced.

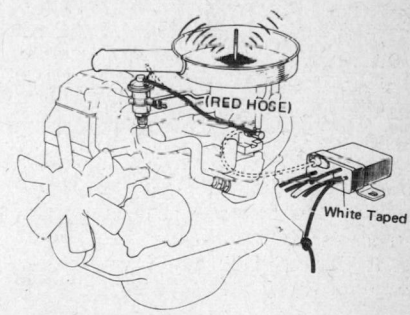

Typical EGR valve testing—except "M" series engines

6. Reconnect the vacuum hoses as they were originally found. Install the top on the air cleaner.

"M" Series Engines

1. Warm up the engine and allow it to idle.

2. Disconnect the vacuum sensing line from the *upper* vacuum chamber of the EGR valve.

3. Disconnect the sensing line from the *lower* chamber of the EGR valve.

4. Now, take the hose which was disconnected from the *lower* chamber and connect it to the upper EGR valve chamber.

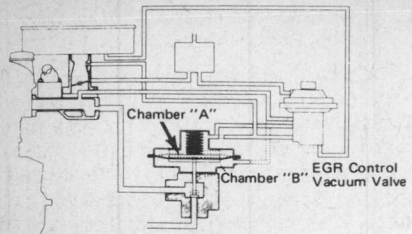

Checking the EGR valve on the 4M engine

NOTE: Leave the lower chamber vented to the atmosphere.

5. The engine idle should become rough or the engine should stall with the hoses connected in this manner. If the engine runs normally, check the EGR vacuum control valve. If the vacuum control valve is in good working order, then replace the EGR valve.

6. Reconnect the vacuum sensing lines as they were originally found.

EGR VACUUM CONTROL VALVE TESTING

1. Connect the EGR vacuum control valve hoses up, so that carburetor advance port vacuum operates directly on its diaphragm (top hose connection).

2. Disconnect the two hoses from the EGR vacuum control valve which run to the upper and lower diaphragm chambers of the EGR valve.

3. Take two vacuum gauges and connect one to each of the ports.

4. Race the engine; the vacuum gauges should indicate the following:

Upper chamber port—Venturi vacuum
Lower chamber port—Atmospheric pressure

5. Disconnect the sensing hose from the carburetor advance port.

6. The vacuum gauges should now show the following:

Upper chamber port—Atmospheric pressure
Lower chamber port—Intake manifold vacuum

NOTE: The atmospheric pressure reading should be nearly equal to that obtained in Step 4.

7. Replace the EGR vacuum control valve if the readings on the vacuum gauges are incorrect.

8. Hook up the vacuum lines as they were originally found.

SYSTEM CHECKS

If, after having completed the above tests, the EGR system still doesn't work right and everything else checks out OK, the fault probably lies in the computer or the vacuum switching valve systems. Proceed with the tests outlined under "System Checks" in the Engine Modification section above.

NOTE: A good indication that the fault doesn't lie in the EGR system, but rather in the vacuum supply system, would be if several emission control systems were not working properly.

Catalytic Converters

All Toyota vehicles sold in this country were equipped with converters. The converters are used to oxidize hydrocarbons (HC) and carbon monoxide (CO). The converters are necessary because of the stricter emission level standards for the post-1975 models.

The catalysts are made of noble metals (platinum and palladium) which are bonded to individual pellets. These catalysts cause the HC and CO to break down into water and carbon dioxide (CO_2) without taking part in the reaction; hence, a catalyst life of 50,000 miles may be expected under normal conditions.

On the 4M-E engines, there are two catalytic converters. The first one is designed to reduce the NOx to dinitrogen. The second one operates the same as the vehicles equipped with only one converter. Most late model (1980 and later) engines use a single, three-way catalytic converter which reduces HC, CO, AND NOx emission levels.

An air pump is used to supply air to the exhaust system to aid in the reaction. A thermosensor, inserted into the converter, shuts off the air supply if the catalyst temperature becomes excessive.

The same sensor circuit also causes a dash warning light labeled "EXH TEMP" to come on when the catalyst temperature gets too high.

NOTE: It is normal for the light to come on temporarily if the car is being driven downhill for long periods of time (such as descending a mountain).

The light will come on and stay on if the air injection system is malfunctioning or if the engine is misfiring.

Precautions:
1. Use only unleaded fuel.
2. Avoid prolonged idling; the engine should run no longer than 20 minutes at curb idle, nor longer than 10 minutes at fast idle.
3. Reduce the fast idle speed, by quickly depressing and releasing the accelerator pedal, as soon as the coolant temperature reaches 120°F.
4. Do not disconnect any spark plug leads while the engine is running.
5. Make engine compression checks as quickly as possible.
6. Do not dispose of the catalyst in a place where anything coated with grease, gas, or oil is present; spontaneous combustion could result.

WARNING LIGHT CHECKS

NOTE: The warning light comes on while the engine is being cranked, to test its operation, just like any of the other warning lights.

1. If the warning light comes on and stays on, check the components of the air injection system, as outlined above. If these are not defective, check the ignition system for faulty leads, plugs, points, or control box.

2. If no problems can be found in Step 1, check the wiring for the light for shorts or opened circuits.

3. If nothing else can be found wrong in Steps 1 and 2 above, check the operation of the emission control system computer, either by substitution of a new unit, or by taking it to a service facility which has Toyota's special emission control system checker.

CONVERTER REMOVAL AND INSTALLATION

——————— CAUTION ———————
Do not perform the operation on a hot (or even warm) engine. Catalyst temperatures may go as high as 1700°F, so that any contact with the catalyst could cause severe burns.

1. Disconnect the lead from the converter thermosensor.
2. Remove the wiring shield.
3. Unfasten the pipe clamp securing bolts at either end of the converter. Remove the clamps.
4. Push the tailpipe rearward and remove the converter, complete with thermosensor.
5. Carry the converter with the thermosensor upward to prevent the catalyst from falling out.
6. Unfasten the screws and withdraw the thermosensor and gasket.

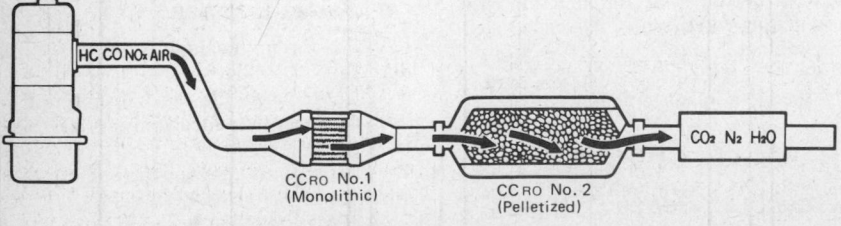

Typical catalytic converter system

Installation is performed in the following order:

1. Place a new gasket on the thermosensor. Push the thermosensor into the converter and secure it with its two bolts. Be careful not to drop the thermosensor.

NOTE: Service replacement converters are provided with a plastic thermosensor guide. Slide the sensor into the guide to install it. Do not remove the guide.

2. Install new gaskets on the converter mounting flanges.
3. Secure the converter with its mounting clamps.
4. If the converter is attached to the body with rubber O-rings, install the O-rings over the body and converter mounting hooks.
5. Install the wire protector and connect the lead to the thermosensor.

Oxygen Sensor System

The three way catalytic converter, which is capable of reducing HC, CO and NO_x into CO_2, H_2O, O_2 and N_2, can only function as long as the fuel/air mixture is kept within a critically precise range. The oxygen sensor system is what keeps the oxygen range in control.

Basically, the oxygen sensor system works like this: As soon as the engine warms up, the EFI computer begins to work. The oxygen sensor, located in the exhaust manifold, senses the oxygen content of the exhaust gases. The amount of oxygen in the exhaust varies according to the fuel/air mixture. The O_2 sensor produces a small voltage that varies depending on the amount of oxygen in the exhaust at the time. This voltage is picked up by the EFI computer. The EFI computer works together with the fuel distributor and together they will vary the amount of fuel which is delivered to the engine at any given time.

If the amount of oxygen in the exhaust system is low, which indicates a rich mixture, the sensor voltage signal sent to the EFI computer, the more it will reduce the amount of fuel supplied to the engine. The amount of fuel is reduced until the amount of oxygen in the exhaust system increases, indicating a lean mixture. When the mixture is lean, the sensor will send a low voltage signal to the EFI computer. The computer will then increase the quantity of fuel until the sensor voltage increases again and then the cycle will start all over.

OXYGEN SENSOR REPLACEMENT

1. Disconnect the negative battery cable.
2. Unplug the wiring connector leading from the O_2 sensor.

NOTE: Be careful not to bend the waterproof hose as the oxygen sensor will not function properly if the air passage is blocked.

3. Unscrew the two nuts and carefully pull out the sensor.
4. Installation is in the reverse order of removal. Please note the following:
—Always use a new gasket.
—Tighten the nuts to 13–16 ft. lbs.

OXYGEN SENSOR WARNING LIGHT

Many models are equipped with an oxygen sensor warning light on the instrument panel. The light may go on when the car is started, then it should go out. If the light stays on, check your odometer. The light is hooked up to an elapsed mileage counter which goes off every 30,000 miles. This is your signal that it is time to replace the oxygen sensor and have the entire system checked out. After replacement of the sensor, the elapsed mileage counter must be reset. To reset:

1. Locate the counter. It can be found under the left side of the instrument panel, on the brake pedal bracket.
2. Unscrew the mounting bolt, disconnect the wiring connector and remove the counter.
3. Remove the bolt on top of the counter.
4. Lift off the counter cover and push the reset switch.

NOTE. The warning light on the instrument panel must go out at this time.

5. Installation is in the reverse order of removal.

GASOLINE ENGINE FUEL SYSTEM

Fuel Filter

REPLACEMENT

Carbureted Engines

All engines employ a disposable, inline filter; when dirty, or at recommended intervals, remove from line and replace.

Fuel Injected Engines

1. Unbolt the retaining screws and remove the protective shield for the fuel filter.
2. Place a pan under the delivery pipe (large connection) to catch the dripping fuel and SLOWLY loosen the union bolt to bleed off the fuel pressure.
3. Remove the union bolt and drain the remaining fuel.

4. Disconnect and plug the inlet line.
5. Unbolt and remove the fuel filter.

NOTE: When tightening the fuel line bolts to the fuel filter, you must use a torque wrench. The tightening torque is very important, as under or over tightening may cause fuel leakage. Insure that there is no fuel line interference and that there is sufficient clearance between it and any other parts.

6. Coat the flare nut, union nut and bolt threads with engine oil.
7. Hand tighten the inlet line to the fuel filter.
8. Install the fuel filter and then tighten the inlet bolt to 23–33 ft. lbs.
9. Reconnect the delivery pipe using new gaskets and then tighten the union bolt to 18–25 ft. lbs.
10. Run the engine for a few minutes and check for any fuel leaks.
11. Install the protective shield.

Mechanical Fuel Pump

All 1A-C, 3A, 3A-C and 4A-C engines use a mechanical type fuel pump. It is located on the right rear of the cylinder head. 1980 and later 20R and 22R engines also use a mechanical type fuel pump. It is located on the right front of the cylinder head.

REMOVAL & INSTALLATION

1. Disconnect and plug the fuel lines to the pump.
2. Remove the bolts which hold the pump to the cylinder head.
3. Remove the pump assembly.
4. Installation is the reverse of removal. Always use a new gasket when installing a fuel pump.

TESTING

1. Remove the line which runs from the fuel pump to the carburetor.
2. Attach a pressure gauge to the outlet side of the pump.
3. Run the engine and check the pressure.
4. Check the pressure against the specifications.
5. If the pressure is below the specifications replace the pump.
6. Reconnect the carburetor line.

Electric Fuel Pump

All models (except those mentioned previously) use an electric fuel pump.

On models with carbureted engines, and the Van, the electric fuel pump is located inside of the fuel tank. On fuel injected engines, the fuel pump is mounted at the rear of the vehicle, outside of the fuel tank.

Either type of fuel pump cannot be repaired if defective—it must be replaced.

TYPE I

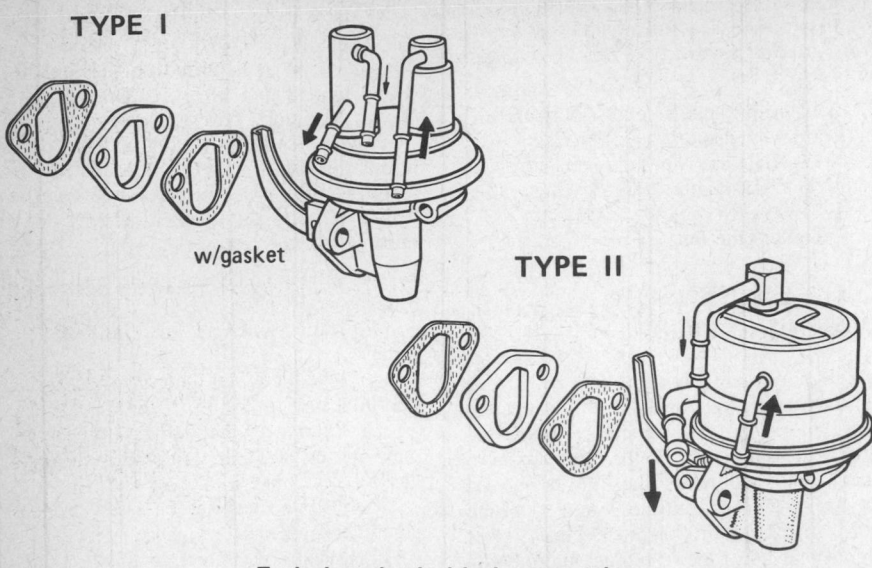

w/gasket

TYPE II

Typical mechanical fuel pump styles

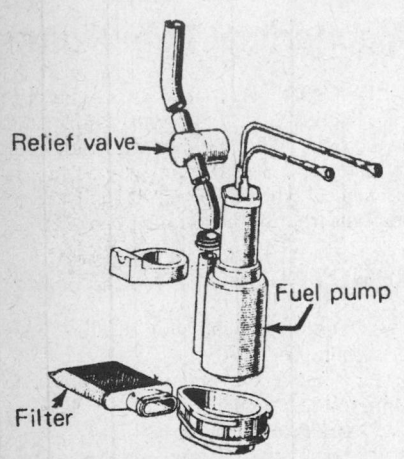

Relief valve

Fuel pump

Filter

Typical electric fuel pump

REMOVAL & INSTALLATION

Carbureted Engines and Van

1. Disconnect the negative (−) cable from the battery.

2a. On sedans and hardtops, remove the trim panel from inside the trunk.

  b. On station wagons, raise the rear of the vehicle, in order to gain access to the pump.

3. Remove the screws which secure the pump access plate to the tank. Withdraw the plate, gasket, and pump assembly.

4. Disconnect the leads and hoses from the pump.

5. Installation is performed in the reverse order of removal. Use a new gasket on the pump access plate.

Fuel Injected Engines—except Van

The pump used on these models is removed by simply disconnecting the fuel lines and electrical connector from the pump and dismounting the pump.

TESTING

----- CAUTION -----
Do not operate the fuel pump unless it is immersed in gasoline and connected to its resistor.

Carbureted Engines

1. Disconnect the lead from the oil pressure warning light sender.

2. Unfasten the line from the outlet side of the fuel filter.

3. Connect a pressure gauge to the filter outlet with a length of rubber hose.

4. Turn the ignition switch to the "ON" position, but do not start the engine.

5. Check the pressure gauge reading against the figure given in the "Tune-Up Specifications" chart.

6. Check for a clogged filter or pinched lines if the pressure is not up to specification.

7. If there is nothing wrong with the filter or lines, replace the fuel pump.

8. Turn the ignition off and reconnect the fuel line to the filter. Connect the lead to the oil pressure sender.

Fuel Injected Engines
1978–79 CELICA

----- CAUTION -----
Do not operate the fuel pump unless it is immersed in gasoline and connected to its resistor.

1. Disconnect the lead from the oil pressure warning light sender.

2. Unfasten the line from the outlet side of the fuel filter.

3. Connect a pressure gauge to the filter outlet with a length of rubber hose.

4. Turn the ignition switch on the "ON" position, but do not start the engine.

5. Check the pressure gauge reading against the figure given in the "Tune-Up Specifications" chart.

6. Check for a clogged filter on pinched lines if the pressure is not up to specification.

7. If there is nothing wrong with the filter or lines, replace the fuel pump.

8. Turn the ignition off and reconnect the fuel line to the filter. Connect the lead to the oil pressure sender also.

ALL OTHERS

1. Turn the ignition switch to the "ON" position, but don't start the engine.

2. Remove the rubber cap from the fuel pump check connector and short both terminals.

3. Check that there is pressure in the hose to the cold start injector.

NOTE: At this time you should be able to hear the fuel return noise from the pressure regulator.

4. If no pressure can be felt in the line, check the fuses and all other related electrical connections. If everything is alright, the fuel pump will probably require replacement.

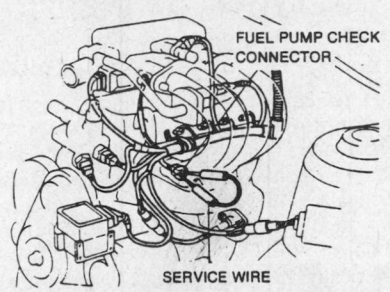

FUEL PUMP CHECK CONNECTOR

SERVICE WIRE

Shorting the fuel pump check connector—typical

5. Remove the service wire, reinstall the rubber cap and turn off the ignition switch.

Fuel Return Cut Valve

Carbureted Engines Only

The fuel return cut valve controls the amount of fuel returned to the gas tank according to engine load. This prevents percolation when the engine is hot and the load light.

INSPECTION

Attach a long tube to the return pipe of the valve. Put a container under it to catch the fuel. With the engine at idle, fuel should go into the container.

Pinch-off the vacuum line. If valve is operating correctly, the fuel flow should stop.

Carburetors

The carburetors used on Toyota models are conventional two-barrel, down-draft types similar to domestic carburetors.

The main circuits are: *primary*, for normal operational requirements; *secondary*, to supply high-speed fuel needs; *float*, to supply fuel to the primary and secondary circuits; *accelerator*, to supply fuel for quick and safe acceleration; *choke*, for reliable starting in cold weather; and *power valve*, for fuel economy and increased high rpm/high load performance. Although slight differences in appearance may be noted, these carburetors arc basically alike. Of course, different jets and settings are demanded by the different engines to which they are fitted.

REMOVAL & INSTALLATION

NOTE: During carburetor removal, be sure to mark all hoses, lines, electrical connectors, etc., so that these items may be properly reconnected during installation.

1. Remove the air cleaner housing, disconnect all air hoses from the air cleaner base, and disconnect the battery ground cable.

NOTE: On 20R and 22R engines, drain the coolant to prevent it from running into the intake manifold when the carburetor is removed.

2. Disconnect the fuel line, choke pipe, and distributor vacuum line. On 20R and 22R engines disconnect the choke coolant hose.

3. Remove the accelerator linkage. (With an automatic transmission, also remove the throttle rod to the transmission.)

4. Disconnect any remaining hoses, etc., from the carburetor.

5. Remove the four nuts that secure the carburetor to the manifold and lift off the carburetor and gasket.

6. Cover the open manifold with a clean rag to prevent small objects from dropping into the engine.

7. Installation is performed in the reverse order of removal. After the engine is started, check for fuel leaks and float level settings.

OVERHAUL

For all carburetor overhaul procedures, please refer to "Carburetor Service" in the Unit Repair section.

FLOAT LEVEL ADJUSTMENT

Float level adjustments are unnecessary on models equipped with a carburetor sight glass, if the fuel level falls within the lines or aligns with the dot when the engine is running.

There are two float level adjustments which may be made on Toyota carburetors. One is with the air horn inverted, so that the float is in a fully *raised* position; the other is with the air horn in an upright position, so that the float falls to the bottom of its travel.

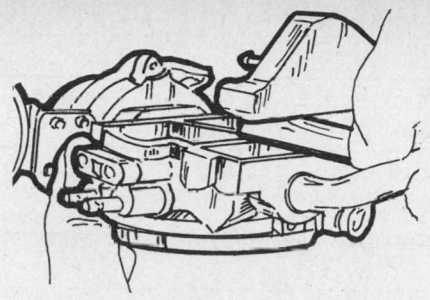

"A" and "T" series engines—measure the raised float level as shown

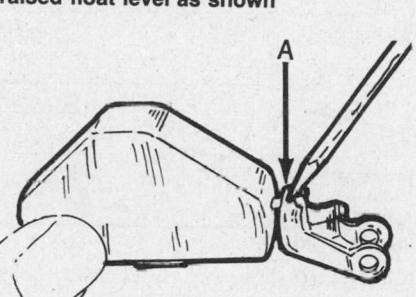

"A" and "T" series engines—adjust the raised float level at (A)

"A" and "T" series engines—measure the lowered float level as shown

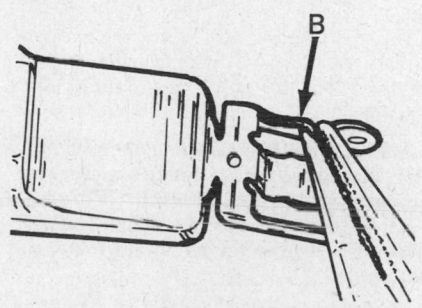

"A" and "T" series engines—adjust the lowered float level at (B)

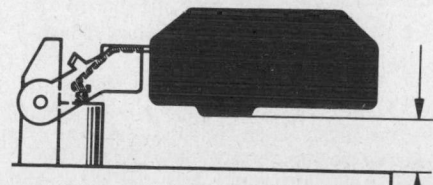

"K" series engines—measure the raised float level as indicated

"K" series engines—adjust the raised float level at (A)

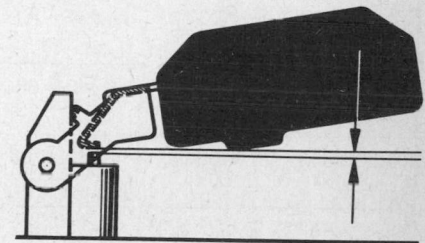

"K" series engines—measure the lowered float level as indicated

"K" series engines—adjust the lowered float level at (B)

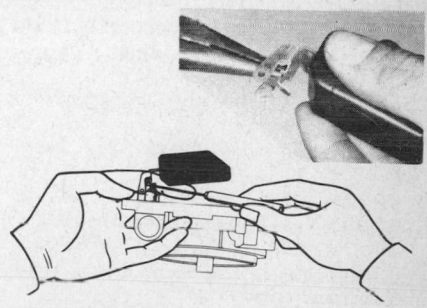

4M engines—adjusting the lowered float level. Measure as indicated and bend to adjust as shown in the inset

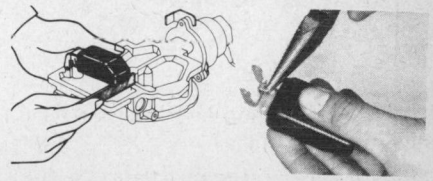

4M engines—adjusting the raised float level. Measure as indicated and bend to adjust as shown in the inset

FLOAT LEVEL ADJUSTMENTS

Engine	Float Raised			Float Lowered		
	Gauge Type	Measure Distance Between	Gap (in.)	Gauge Type	Measure Distance Between	Gap (in.)
3K-C	Special	Float end and air horn	0.056②	Special	Lowest point of float and upper side of gauge	1.89①
2T-C, 3T-C	Block	Float tip and air horn	0.138③	Wire	Needle valve bushing pin and float lip	0.047
1A-C, 3A, 3A-C, 4A-C	Special	Float tip and air horn	0.158	Special	Needle valve plunger and float tab	0.047
4K-C	Special	Float tip and air horn	0.030	Special	Needle valve plunger and float tip	0.02
20R '78–'80	Special	Float end and air horn	0.197④	Special	Needle valve bushing pin and float tab	0.039
22R '81–'83	Special	Float top and air horn	0.386	Special	Needle valve plunger and float lip	1.890

① 1978–79—float lip gap .024
  1980–81—float tip gap 0.020
② 1978–81—0.30
③ 1978–81—0.236
④ 1978–79—0.276

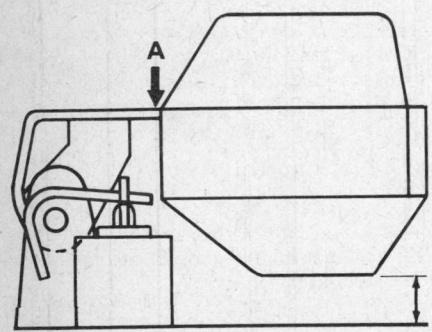

"R" series engines—measure as indicated and bend at (A) to adjust

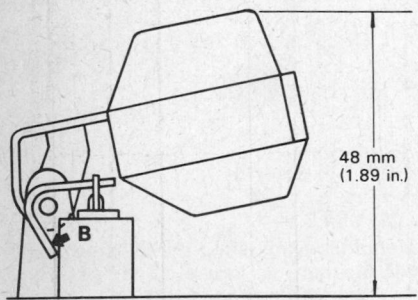

48 mm (1.89 in.)

"R" series engines—measure as indicated and bend at (B) to adjust

The float level is either measured with a special carburetor float level gauge, which comes with a rebuilding kit, or with a standard wire gauge.

NOTE: Gap specifications are also given so that a float level gauge may be fabricated.

Adjust the float level by bending the tabs on the float levers, either upper or lower, as required.

FAST IDLE ADJUSTMENT

Off Vehicle

The fast idle adjustment is performed with the choke valve fully *closed*, except on the 2T-C and 3T-C engines which should have the choke valve fully *opened*.

Adjust the gap between the throttle valve edge and bore to the specifications, where given, in the "Fast Idle Specifications" chart. Use a wire gauge to determine the gap.

The chart below also gives the proper primary throttle valve opening angle, where necessary, and the proper means of fast idle adjustment.

NOTE: The throttle valve opening angle is measured with a gauge supplied in the carburetor rebuilding kit. It is also possible to make one out of cardboard by using a protractor to obtain the correct angle.

On Vehicle

NOTE: Disconnect the EGR valve vacuum line on 20R and 22R engines.

1. Adjust the idle speed/mixture. Leave the tachometer connected.
2. Remove the top of the air cleaner.
3. Open the throttle valve slightly and close the choke valve. Hold the choke valve and close the throttle valve. The choke valve is now fully closed.
4. Without depressing the accelerator pedal, start the engine.

5. Check the engine fast idle speed against the chart below.
6. If the reading on the tachometer is not within specifications, adjust the fast idle speed by turning the fast idle screw.
7. Disconnect the tachometer, install the air cleaner cover, and connect the EGR valve vacuum line if it was disconnected.

FAST IDLE SPEED

2T-C (US)—3000 rpm (1978–79—3400)
2T-C (Calif.)—2700 rpm (1978–79—3000)
3T-C (man. trans.)—3200 rpm
3T-C (auto. trans.)—3000 rpm
20R, 22R—2400 rpm (1981–83—2600)
4M (US)—2600 rpm
4M (Calif.)—2400 rpm
1A-C and 3A-C—3600 rpm (1981–85—3000)
3A—3000 rpm
4K-C—3500 rpm

AUTOMATIC CHOKE ADJUSTMENT

NOTE: The automatic choke should be adjusted with the carburetor installed and the engine running. On 20R and 22R engines, do not loosen the center bolt; the coolant will leak out.

1. Check to see that the choke valve will close from fully opened when the coil housing is turned counterclockwise (4M engines—clockwise).
2. Align the mark on the coil housing with the center line on the thermostat case. In this position, the choke valve should be fully closed when the ambient temperature is 77°F.

FAST IDLE ADJUSTMENT

Engine	Throttle Valve to Bore Clearance (in.)	Primary Throttle Angle (deg)	To Adjust Fast Idle
3K-C, 4K-C	0.040①	9②	Bend the fast idle lever
2T-C, 3T-C	0.032③	7	Turn the fast idle adjusting screw
20R, 22R	0.047	24	Turn the fast idle screw
4M	—	16—from closed④	Turn the fast idle adjusting screw
1A-C	—	22	Turn the fast idle screw
3A	—	21	Turn the fast idle screw
3A-C, 4A-C	—	⑤	Turn the fast idle screw

—Not applicable
①0.037 in 1978–83
②20° open
③1978–79: 0.043
④1978–79: 9°

⑤1980–82: 22°
1983–84 (exc. Canada wag. w/ 4 × 4): 20°
(Canada wag. w/4 × 4): 21°

3. If necessary, adjust the mixture by turning the coil housing. If the mixture is too *rich*, rotate the housing *clockwise*; if too *lean*, rotate the housing *counterclockwise*. On models equipped with the 4M engine, rotate the housing in exactly the reverse direction of the above.

NOTE: Each graduation on the thermostat case is equivalent to 9°F.

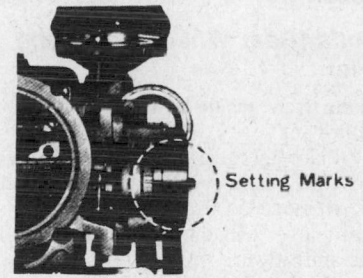

Align the marks on the choke housing

MANUAL CHOKE ADJUSTMENT

1. Close the choke by turning the choke shaft lever.
2. Check the 1st throttle valve opening angle with the tool supplied in the rebuild kit.
3. Adjust by turning the fast idle adjusting screw.

CHOKE BREAK ADJUSTMENT

20R and 22R

1. Push the rod which comes out of the upper (choke break) diaphragm so that the choke valve opens.
2. Measure the choke valve opening angle. It should be 38°.
3. Adjust the angle, if necessary, by bending the relief lever link.

INITIAL IDLE MIXTURE SCREW ADJUSTMENT

When assembling the carburetor, turn the idle mixture screw the number of turns specified below. After the carburetor is installed, perform the appropriate idle speed/ mixture adjustment as outlined above.

- 3K-C, 4K-C—1½ turns from seating
- 1A-C—2¼ turns from seating
- 3A, 3A-C, 4A-C—2¾ turns from seating
- 20R, 22R—1¾ turns from seating
- 4M—1½ turns from seating

— CAUTION —
Seat the idle mixture screw lightly; overtightening will damage its tip.

UNLOADER ADJUSTMENT

Make the unloader adjustment with the primary valve fully opened. The total angle of choke valve opening, in the chart, is

CHOKE UNLOADER ADJUSTMENT

Engine	Choke Valve Angle (deg)			Bend to Adjust
	Throttle Valve Fully Closed (deg)	From Closed to Fully Open (deg)	Throttle Valve Open (Total) (deg)	
3K-C, 4K-C	9	20	90	Fast idle cam follower or choke shaft tab
2T-C	7	38	90	Fast idle lever, follower or choke shaft tab
20R, 22R	—	50①	90	Fast idle lever, follower or choke shaft tab
3T-C, 1A, 3A, 3A-C, 4A-C	20	—	47	Fast idle lever
4M	20	15	90	Fast idle lever

—Not applicable
①45° for 22R engines

measured with either a special gauge, supplied in the carburetor rebuilding kit, or a guage of the proper angle fabricated from cardboard.

Electronic Fuel Injection

For all fuel injection system repair and adjustments not detailed below, please refer to "Fuel Injection" in the Unit Repair section.

FUEL SYSTEM

An electronic fuel pump supplies sufficient fuel, under constant pressure, to the injectors. These injectors meter the fuel into the intake manifold in accordance with signals from the EFI computer. Each injector injects, at the same time, one half of the fuel required for ideal combustion with each engine revolution.

Fuel Injector Replacement

1. Disconnect the negative battery cable.
2. Place a suitable container under the intake manifold to catch any dripping fuel.
3. Remove the air intake chamber as previously described.
4. Unplug the wiring connectors from the tops of the fuel injectors and remove the two plastic clamps that hold the wiring harness to the fuel delivery pipe.
5. Unscrew the mounting bolts and remove the delivery pipe with the injectors attached.
6. Pull the injectors out of the delivery pipe. To install:
7. Insert new insulators into the injector holes on the intake manifold.
8. Install the grommet and a new O-ring to the delivery pipe end of each injector.
9. Apply a thin coat of gasoline to the O-ring on each injector and then press them into the delivery pipe.
10. Install the injectors together with the delivery pipe to the intake manifold. Tighten the mounting bolts to 11–15 ft. lbs.
11. Installation of the remaining components is in the reverse order of removal.
12. Start the engine and check for any fuel leaks.

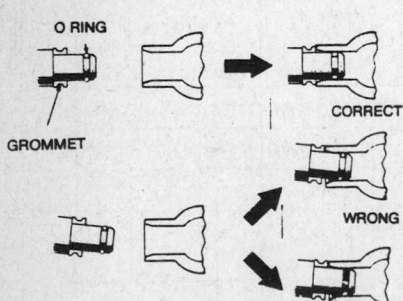

Make sure that you insert the injector into the fuel delivery pipe properly

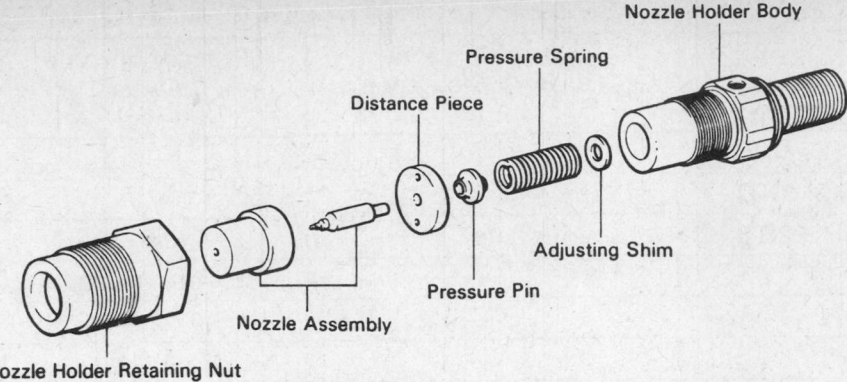

Diesel injection nozzle

DIESEL ENGINE FUEL SYSTEM

NOTE: For all service procedures not listed below, please refer to "Diesel Service" in the Unit Repair section.

Injection Nozzle

REMOVAL & INSTALLATION

1. Loosen the clamps and remove the injection hoses from between the injection pump and pipe.
2. Disconnect both ends of the injection pipes from the pump and nozzle holders.
3. Disconnect the fuel cut off wire from the connector clamp.
4. Remove the nut, connector clamp and bond cable.
5. Unbolt and remove the injector pipes.
6. Disconnect the fuel hoses from the leakage pipes.
7. Remove the four nuts, leakage pipe and four washers.
8. Unscrew and remove the nozzles.
9. Installation is the reverse of removal. Torque the nozzles to 47 ft. lb. Always use new nozzle seat gaskets and seats. Bleed the system by loosening the pipes at the nozzles and cranking the engine until all air is expelled and fuel sprays.

Injection Pump

REMOVAL & INSTALLATION

1. Drain the cooling system.
2. Disconnect the accelerator and cruise control cables from the pump.
3. Disconnect the fuel cut off wire at the pump.
4. Disconnect the fuel inlet and outlet hoses, the water by-pass hoses, the boost compensator hoses, the A/C or heater idle-up vacuum hoses and the heater hose.
5. Remove the injector pipes at the pump.

6. Remove the pump pulley.
7. Matchmark the raised timing mark on the pump flange with the block. Unbolt and remove the pump.
8. Installattion is the reverse of removal. *There must be no clearance between the pump bracket and stay.*

MANUAL TRANSMISSION

REMOVAL & INSTALLATION

Corolla (Rear Wheel Drive) and Starlet

Working from inside of the car, perform the following:
1. Place the gear selector in Neutral. Remove the center console, if so equipped.
2. Remove the trim boot at the base of the shift lever and the boot underneath it on the shift tower.
3. On Corolla 1200 and Starlet models only:
   a. Unfasten the snap-ring from the base of the shift lever.
   b. Withdraw the conical spring and the shift lever itself.
4. On Corolla 1600 models only:
   a. Remove the four shift lever plate retaining screws.
   b. Remove the shift lever assembly.
   c. Remove the gasket.

NOTE: Cover the hole with a clean cloth to prevent anything from falling into the transmission case.

Working from inside of the car, perform the following:
5. Drain the cooling system and disconnect the cable from the positive side of the battery.
6. Remove the radiator hoses.
7. On Corolla 1200 models only:
   a. Disconnect the backup lamp switch connector.
   b. Remove the engine fan.

8. On Corolla 1600 models only:

a. Remove the air cleaner, complete with hoses.

b. Unfasten the accelerator torque rod at the carburetor.

c. Remove the clutch hydraulic line support bracket.

d. Remove the starter assembly from the left side of the engine.

e. Remove the upper left-hand clutch housing bolt, from the flat at the top of the clutch housing.

9. On Starlet models:

a. Remove the upper radiator hose.

b. Remove the air cleaner assembly.

c. Disconnect the accelerator pump lever.

d. Disconnect the wiring harness connector.

e. Wrap the steering rack boot with a rag.

f. Remove the starter assembly as previously outlined.

10. Raise the vehicle and support it safely with jackstands.

11. Drain the transmission oil.

12. Detach the exhaust pipe from the manifold and remove the exhaust pipe support bracket.

13. Remove the driveshaft.

NOTE: It will be necessary to plug the opening in the end of the transmission with an old yoke or, if none is available, cover it with a plastic bag secured by a rubber band.

14. Unfasten the speedometer cable from the right side of the transmission.

15. On Corolla 1600 models, only:

a. Remove the clutch release cylinder assembly from the transmission and tie it aside, so that it is out of the way.

b. Unplug the back-up lamp switch connector.

16. Support the front of the transmission with a jack.

17. Unbolt the engine rear mounts. Remove the rear crossmember.

18. Remove the jack from under the transmission.

19. On Corolla 1600 models, unbolt the clutch housing from the engine and withdraw the transmission assembly.

NOTE: Remove the brace, if so equipped.

20. Perform the following on Corolla 1200 and Starlet models, before removing the transmission:

a. Remove the cotter pin from the clutch release linkage.

b. Remove the clutch release cable.

c. Remove the stiffener plate, if so equipped.

d. Unbolt the clutch housing from the engine by removing the bolts in the order illustrated.

Installation is the reverse of removal, but observe the following:

Apply a light coating of multipurpose grease to the input shaft end, input shaft spline, clutch release bearing, and driveshaft end. On Corolla 1200 and Starlet models, apply multipurpose grease to the ball on the end of the gearshift lever assembly; and to the clutch release cable end.

On Corolla 1200 and Starlet models, install the clutch housing-to-engine bolts in two or three stages, and in the order shown.

After installation:

1. Fill the transmission and cooling system.

2. Adjust the clutch as detailed below.

3. Check to see that the back-up lamps function when Reverse is selected.

Corolla (Front Wheel Drive)

1. Disconnect the negative battery cable.

2. Drain the coolant.

3. Remove the air cleaner.

4. Disconnect the back-up light switch.

5. Remove the speedometer cable.

6. Disconnect the control cable at the transaxle.

7. Unbolt the coolant inlet line from the transaxle.

8. Remove the clutch release cylinder.

9. Remove the undercover.

10. Remove the front and rear support members.

11. Remove the engine center support member.

12. Unbolt the right driveshaft from the transaxle.

13. Disconnect the steering knuckle from the lower arm.

14. Pull the steering knuckle outward and remove the left driveshaft.

15. Remove the starter.

16. Remove the flywheel cover plate.

17. Place a wood block on a floor jack and take up the weight of the engine with the jack.

18. Disconnect the left engine mount.

19. Remove the transaxle-to-engine attaching bolts. Lower the left side of the engine and pull the transaxle free.

20. Installation is the reverse of removal. Coat the input shaft splines with chassis lube prior to installation. Torque the transaxle attaching bolts to:

12mm bolts: 47 ft. lb.
10mm bolts: 30 ft. lb.

Torque the left engine mount bolt to 38 ft. lb.; the starter bolts to 29 ft. lb.; the steering knuckle and left driveshaft bolts to 47 ft. lb.; the right driveshaft bolts to 27 ft. lb.; the engine center support bolts to 29 ft. lb.; the transaxle support bolts to 29 ft. lb.

Camry

The transaxle must be removed along with the engine. See "Engine Removal and Installation" earlier in this section. Once the whole unit is out of the car, unbolt the transaxle from the engine.

Corona

1. Disconnect the negative battery cable and then the positive battery-to-starter cable, complete with fusible link.

2. Drain the coolant from the radiator into a suitable clean container for re-use. Unfasten the upper radiator hose.

3. Detach the accelerator rod and link at the firewall side.

4. Raise both ends of the car and support them with jack stands.

5. Working underneath the car, remove the exhaust pipe clamp and clutch release cylinder (don't disconnect its hydraulic line; set the cylinder out of the way). Next, disconnect the back-up light switch lead and speedometer cable.

6. Remove the driveshaft from the transmission, after matchmarking it and the companion flange for assembly.

NOTE: To prevent oil from draining out of the transmission, install a spare U-joint or if none is available, cover the opening with a plastic bag secured with a rubber band.

7. Place a block of wood on the lift pad of a jack to protect the transmission, and support the transmission with it.

8. Cover the back end of the valve cover with cloths, remove the rear crossmember (see "Engine Removal"), and lower the jack.

9. Unfasten the bolts which secure the shift lever, and remove the shift lever.

10. Remove the starter motor from the clutch housing.

11. Remove the bolts which secure the clutch housing to the engine block.

12. Move the transmission and jack rearward, until the input shaft has cleared the clutch cover. Remove the transmission from underneath the car.

13. Installation is the reverse of removal. Be sure to apply a thin coating of grease to the input shaft splines. The clutch housing-to-cylinder block bolts should be tightened to 37–58 ft. lbs. Adjust the clutch and fill the transmission with API GL-4 SAE 90 gear oil. Grease the shift lever spring seat and shift lever tip. Use the matchmarks to install the driveshaft.

Celica and Supra (1978–81) and Cressida

Perform the removal procedures as outlined for the Corolla 1600. In addition, perform the following:

1. Remove the accelerator connecting rod from the linkage.

2. With the car jacked up and supported:

a. Remove the left-hand, rear stone shield before removing the clutch release cylinder.

b. Remove the flywheel housing lower cover and its braces.

Installation is the reverse of removal.

NOTE: Use a clutch guide tool, during installation, to locate the clutch disc.

Celica and Supra (1982 and later)

1. Disconnect the battery cables at the battery.

C861

2. Drain the coolant from the radiator and engine.

3. Remove the upper radiator hose.

4. Remove the console box and the shift lever from inside the vehicle.

5. Raise the vehicle and support it safely with jackstands.

6. Drain the transmission fluid.

7. Remove the driveshaft assembly from the vehicle. Mark the driveshaft and flange so that the assembly may be installed in its original position.

8. Remove the bolt from the exhaust pipe stiffener plate.

9. Disconnect the speedometer cable and the back-up lamp switch connector from the transmission.

10. Unbolt the clutch release cylinder and tie it out of the way. It is NOT necessary to disconnect the hydraulic line from the cylinder.

11. Remove the starter assembly as previously outlined.

12. Using a jack, raise the transmission just enough to take the weight of the transmission off of the support crossmember.

13. Remove the transmission support crossmember.

NOTE: It may be wise to enlist the aid of an assistant to remove the transmission.

14. Remove the transmission mounting bolts. Carefully, pull the transmission rearward, down, and out of the vehicle.

15. Installation is the reverse of the previous steps. Note the following points during installation:

a. Observe the following bolt torques:
Transmission mounting bolts—37–57 ft. lbs.
Transmission crossmember bolts—14–22 ft. lbs.
Exhaust pipe stiffener plate bolt—22–32 ft. lbs.
Starter mounting bolts—37–57 ft. lbs.
U-joint strap bolts—22–32 ft. lbs.

b. Use 2.5 quarts of API service GL-4 or GL-5 SAE 70W-90 or 80W-90 to refill the transmission.

Tercel

1. Disconnect the negative battery cable.

2. Drain the coolant from the radiator tank and remove the top radiator hose.

3. Remove the air cleaner intake duct.

4. Remove the intermediate steering shaft.

5. Drain the gear oil from the transmission. Remove both half shafts.

NOTE: Remove all three drain plugs.

6. Remove the exhaust pipe. On 4 × 4 models, remove the center console and shift lever.

7. Remove the No. 1 gear shift rod and shift lever housing rod.

8. Remove the speedometer cable and back-up light switch connector.

9. Remove the rear engine support crossmember. On 4 × 4 models, remove the driveshaft, 4 × 4 link and 4 × 4 indicator wire.

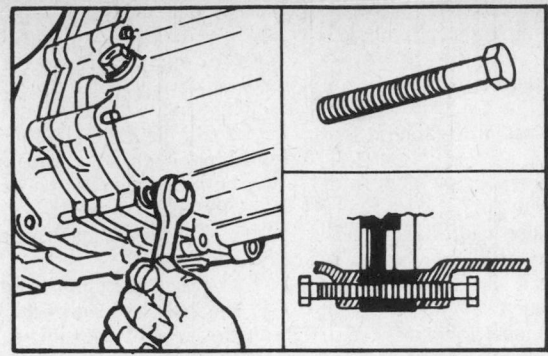

Split the transmission from the transaxle like this on the Tercel

NOTE: Support the transaxle with a jack and a block of wood.

10. Remove the nine transmission bolts.

11. Install 4 bolts on the transaxle side to an equal depth.

NOTE: Install the bolts into holes which still contain a bolt on the transmission side.

12. Separate the transmission by tightening the bolts a little at a time on the transmission side.

13. Remove the transmission.

14. Installation is the reverse of removal. Tighten the transmission bolts 8–11 ft. lbs. Fill the transmission with 6.5 pints of gear oil.

Van

1. Disconnect the negative battery cable.

2. Raise and support the vehicle on jackstands.

3. Drain the transmission.

4. Matchmark the driveshaft and remove it from the vehicle.

5. Remove the transmission control cables.

6. Remove the clutch release cylinder.

7. Remove the starter.

8. Disconnect the speedometer cable.

9. Disconnect the back-up light switch.

10. Remove the exhaust clamp and bracket from the case.

11. Remove the stiffener plate.

12. Take up the weight of the tranmission with a floor jack.

13. Remove the rear engine mount and bracket.

14. Remove the engine-to-transmission attaching bolts and slide the transmission from the engine.

15. Installation is the reverse of removal. Coat the input shaft splines with chassis lube prior to installation. Observe the following torques:

Transmission attaching bolts: 53 ft. lb.
Engine rear mount bolts: 20 ft. lb.
Fill the unit with 80W-90 gear oil.

OVERHAUL

For all overhaul procedures, please refer to "Manual Transmission Overhaul" in the Unit Repair section.

Floor Shifter Adjustment

All Toyota models equipped with a floor shifter have internally-mounted shift linkages. On older models, the linkage is contained in the side cover which is bolted on the transmission case. Newer cars have the shift linkage mounted in the top of the transmission case itself.

No external adjustment is needed or possible.

Shift Cable Adjustment

Models equipped with a shift cable have a cable stroke adjustment.

1. Remove the shift console.

2. Loosen the cable locknut.

3. Place the shifter in Neutral.

4. Insert a No. 2 Phillips screwdriver into the neutral adjustment hole on the cable bracket.

5. Adjust the cable stroke as necessary to allow insertion of the screwdriver.

6. Tighten the locknut and replace the console.

CLUTCH

The clutch is a single-plate, dry disc type. Later models use a diaphragm-spring pressure plate. Clutch release bearings are sealed ball bearing units which need no lubrication and should never be washed in any kind of solvent. All clutches, except those on the Tercel Starlet and Corolla 1200 are hydraulically operated.

REMOVAL & INSTALLATION

— CAUTION —
Do not allow grease or oil to get on any of the disc, pressure plate, or flywheel surfaces.

All Models Except Tercel

1. Remove the transmission from the car as detailed above.

2. Remove the clutch cover and disc from the bellhousing.

3. Unfasten the release fork bearing clips. Withdraw the release bearing hub, complete with the release bearing.

4. Remove the tension spring from the clutch linkage.

5. Remove the release fork and support.

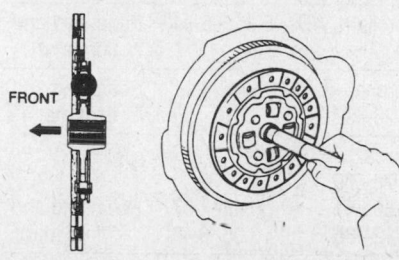

Use a clutch pilot tool to center the clutch disc on the flywheel

6. Punch matchmarks on the clutch cover and the pressure plate so the pressure plate can be returned to its original position during installation.

7. Slowly unfasten the screws which attach the retracting springs.

NOTE: If the screws are released too fast, the clutch assembly will fly apart, causing possible injury or loss of parts.

8. Separate the pressure plate from the clutch cover/spring assembly.

Inspect the parts for wear or deterioration. Replace parts as required.

Installation is performed in the reverse order of removal. Several points should be noted, however:

1. Be sure to align the matchmarks on the clutch cover and pressure plate which were made during disassembly.

2. Apply a thin coating of multipurpose grease to the release bearing hub and release fork contact points. Also, pack the groove inside the clutch hub with multipurpose grease.

3. Center the clutch disc by using a clutch pilot tool or an old input shaft. Insert the pilot into the end of the input shaft front bearing and bolt the clutch to the flywheel.

NOTE: Bolt the clutch assembly to the flywheel in two or three stages.

4. Adjust the clutch as outlined following.

Tercel

In order to replace the clutch, the engine must be removed. See the engine removal section.

1. After the engine has been removed tie the bell housing to the cowl.

2. Place matchmarks on the clutch cover and flywheel.

3. Remove the clutch cover.

NOTE: Loosen each bolt gradually to prevent distortion of the cover.

4. Remove the disc.

5. Installation is the reverse of removal.

NOTE: Do not allow grease to get on the disc lining, flywheel, or cover. When reinstalling the clutch be sure to use a spline alignment tool or an old input shaft to properly align the clutch. Tighten the cover bolts to 11–15 ft. lbs.

FREE-PLAY ADJUSTMENT

All Except Tercel, Starlet and Corolla 1200

1. Adjust the clearance between the master cylinder piston and the pushrod to the specifications given in the chart below. Loosen the pushrod locknut and rotate the pushrod while depressing the clutch pedal lightly with your finger.

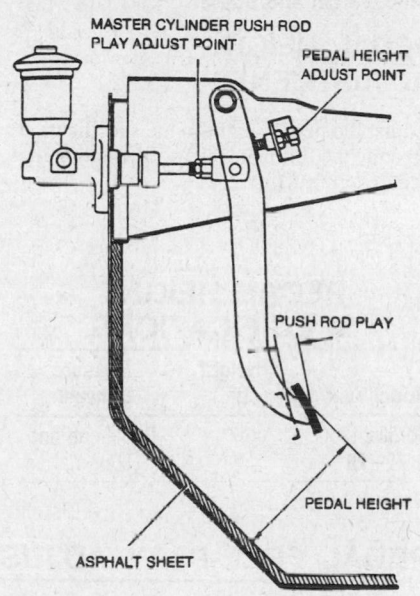

Clutch pedal adjusting points—all except the Tercel, Starlet and Corolla 1200

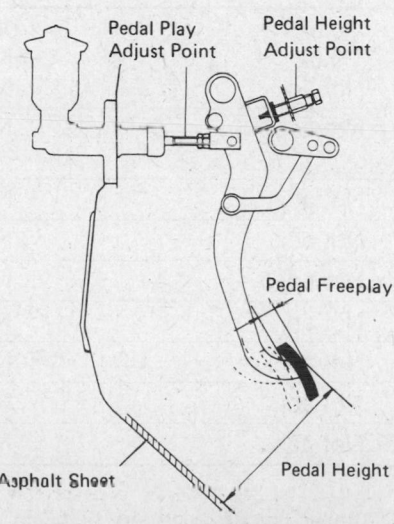

Camry clutch pedal adjustment

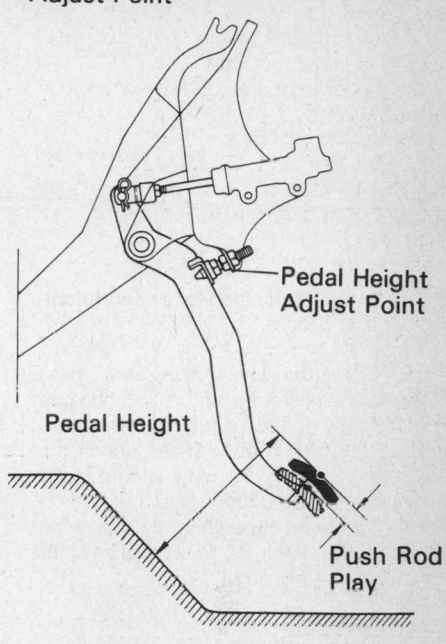

Van clutch pedal adjustment

2. Tighten the locknut when finished the adjustment.

3. Adjust the release cylinder free-play by loosening the release cylinder pushrod locknut and rotating the pushrod until the specification in the chart is obtained.

4. Measure the clutch pedal free play after performing the above adjustments. If it fails to fall within specifications, repeat Steps 1–3 until it does.

Tercel and Starlet

1. Depress the pedal several times.

2. Depress the pedal by hand until resistance is felt. Free play should be as specified in the chart.

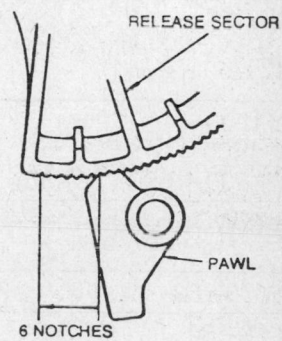

Minimum pawl and sector position for a used clutch—Tercel and Starlet

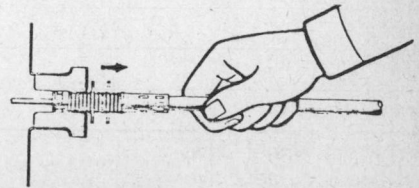

E-ring adjustment—1981–82 Starlet

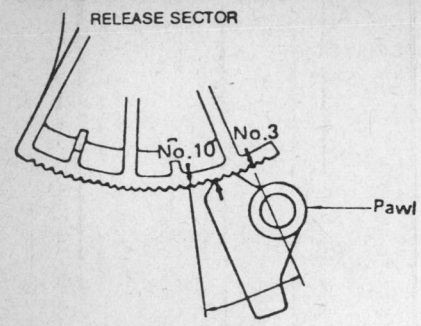

Pawl and sector position for a new clutch—Tercel and Starlet

3. Check the clutch release sector pawl. Six notches should remain between the pawl and the end of the sector. If less than 6, replace the clutch disc. If the clutch disc has been replaced, the pawl should be between the 3rd and 10th notch.

4. To obtain either the used or new position on the 1981–82 Starlet, change the position of the E-ring.

Corolla 1200

1. Pull on the clutch release cable at the clutch support flange until a resistance is felt when the release bearing contacts the clutch diaphragm spring.

2. Holding the cable in this position, measure the distance between the E-ring and the end of the wire support flange. The distance should be 5–6 threads.

3. If adjustment is required, change the position of the E-ring.

4. After completing the adjustment, check the clutch pedal free-play which should be 0.8–1.4 in. after the pedal is depressed several times.

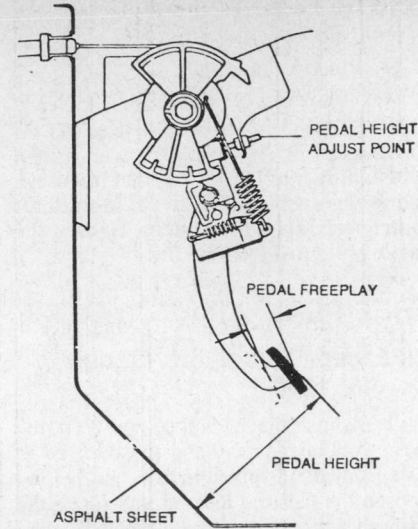

Clutch pedal adjusting points—Corolla 1200, Tercel and Starlet

PEDAL HEIGHT ADJUSTMENT

Adjust the pedal height to the specification given in the following chart, by rotating the pedal stop (nut).

PEDAL HEIGHT SPECIFICATIONS

Model/Year	Height (in.)	Measure Between
Corolla 1200 '78–'79	6.7	Pedal pad and floor mat

PEDAL HEIGHT SPECIFICATIONS

Model/Year	Height (in.)	Measure Between
Tercel '80–'83	6.65	Pedal pad and floor mat
Corolla 1600 '78–'83	6.5	Pedal pad and floormat
Corolla 1800	6.89–7.28	
Corolla (FWD)	5.650–6.043	Pedal pad and floor mat
Corona '78–'82	6.5–6.9	Pedal pad and floor mat
Celica '78–'79 '80–'81 '82–'85	6.67 6.48–4.87 6.06–6.46	Pedal pad and floor mat
Celica Supra '80–'85	6.48–6.87	Pedal and floor mat
Cressida '78–'85	6.1–6.5	From floor mat
Station Wagon (all)	9.6	Pedal pad and firewall
Starlet	6.93	Pedal pad and floor mat
Camry	7.539–7.933	Pedal pad and kick panel
Van	6.57–7.97	Pedal pad and floor mat

① Pedal depressed

CLUTCH PEDAL FREE-PLAY ADJUSTMENTS

Model	Master Cylinder piston-to-pushrod clearance (in.)	Release cylinder-to-release fork free-play (in.)	Pedal free-play (in.)
Corolla 1200	0.02	1.00–1.40	0.8–1.4
(RWD) 1600	0.02	Not adj.	0.79–1.58
1800, 1600 ('83–'85)	Not adj.	Not adj.	0.51–0.91
Corolla (FWD)	Not adj.	Not adj.	0.51–0.91 (gas) 0.20–0.59 (diesel)
Corona '78–'82	Not adj.	Not adj.	0.51–0.91
Celica '78–'84	Not adj.	Not adj.	0.51–0.91
Supra	Not adj.	Not adj.	0.20–0.59
Starlet	Not adj.	Not adj.	0.08–1.18①
Tercel	Not adj.	Not adj.	0.08–1.10
Van	Not adj.	Not adj.	0.20–0.59
Camry	Not adj.	Not adj.	0.20–0.59

FWD Front Wheel Drive
RWD Rear Wheel Drive
① '83–'85: 0.08–1.38

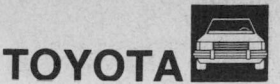

Clutch Master Cylinder

REMOVAL & INSTALLATION

1. Remove the clevis pin.
2. Detach the hydraulic line from the tube.
3. Unfasten the bolts which secure the master cylinder to the firewall. Withdraw the assembly.
4. Installation is performed in the reverse order of removal. Bleed the system. Adjust the clutch pedal height and free-play.

Clutch Release Cylinder

REMOVAL & INSTALLATION

1. Plug the master cylinder cap to prevent fluid leakage.
2. Raise the front of the vehicle and support it with jack stands.
3. Remove the gravel shield, if necessary, to gain access to the release cylinder.
4. Unfasten the clutch fork return spring at the fork.
5. Detach the hydraulic line from the release cylinder.
6. Screw the release cylinder pushrod in.
7. Loosen and remove the securing nuts from the release cylinder. Remove the cylinder.
8. Installation is performed in the reverse order of removal. Adjust the release fork-to-release cylinder free-play and bleed the hydraulic system, after installation is completed.

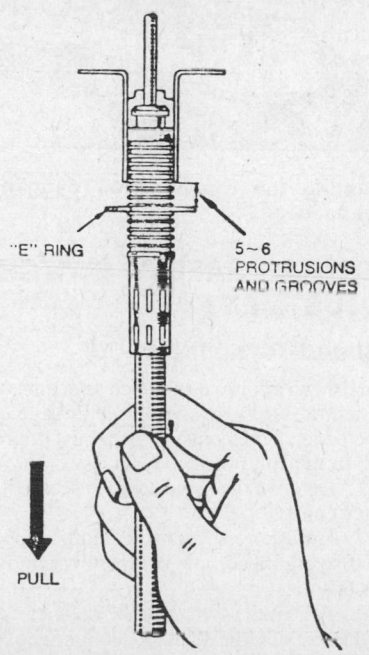

"E" RING

5~6 PROTRUSIONS AND GROOVES

PULL

Adjusting the clutch release cable on the Corolla 1200

AUTOMATIC TRANSMISSION

REMOVAL & INSTALLATION

Tercel

1. Disconnect the negative battery cable.
2. Drain the coolant from the radiator tank and remove the top hose.
3. Remove the air cleaner inlet duct.
4. Remove the intermediate steering shaft.
5. Drain the fluid from the transmission.
6. Remove the exhaust pipe.
7. Remove the shift lever rod.
8. Remove the speedometer cable, back-up light connector and any throttle linkage.
9. Remove the cooling lines from the transmission.
10. Support the transaxle with a jack.
11. Remove the rear crossmember.
12. Separate the transmission from the transaxle.
13. Remove the transmission.
14. Installation is the reverse of removal.

Corolla with Front Wheel Drive

1. Disconnect the negative battery cable.
2. Remove the air cleaner.
3. Disconnect the neutral start switch.
4. Disconnect the speedometer cable.
5. Remove the shift control cable.
6. Disconnect the oil cooler hose.
7. Remove the water inlet pipe.
8. Raise and support the vehicle on jackstands.
9. Drain the fluid.
10. Remove the engine undercover.
11. Remove the front and rear transaxle mounts.
12. Support the transaxle with a jack.
13. Remove the engine center support member.
14. Remove the halfshafts.
15. Remove the steering knuckles.
16. Remove the starter motor.
17. Remove the flywheel cover plate.
18. Remove the 6 torque converter bolts, through the opening covered by the cover plate.
19. Remove the left engine mount.
20. Remove the transaxle-to-engine bolts and slowly and carefully back the transaxle away from the engine.
21. Installation is the reverse of removal. Observe the following torques.
    Transaxle-to-engine bolts:
    12mm 47 ft. lb.
    10mm 25 ft. lb.
    Left engine mount: 38 ft. lb.
    Torque converter bolts: 13 ft. lb.
    Support bolts: 28 ft. lb.
Fill the unit with Dexron® II ATF.

Camry

The engine must be removed with the transaxle. See "Engine Removal and Instal-

lation." Once the assembly is out, unbolt and separate the transaxle from the engine. When assembling note the following torques:
    Transaxle-to-engine: 12mm 47 ft. lb.
    10mm 25 ft. lb.
    Torque converter: 13 ft. lb.

Van

1. Disconnect the negative battery cable.
2. Disconnect the throttle cable.
3. Disconnect all wires attached to the transmission.
4. Raise and support the vehicle on jackstands.
5. Drain the fluid.
6. Matchmark and remove the driveshaft.
7. Disconnect the exhaust pipe from the case.
8. Disconnect the shift cable.
9. Disconnect the speedometer cable.
10. Disconnect the oil cooler lines.
11. Remove the starter.
12. Support the transmission with a floor jack.
13. Support the fuel tank on jackstands, remove the fuel tank mounting bolts, and remove the rear transmission support bolt.
14. Remove the two stiffener plates from the transmission.
15. Pry out the service hole cover at the torque converter housing and remove the six torque converter bolts.
16. Remove the transmission-to-engine bolts and slowly and carefully guide the transmission away from the engine.
17. Installation is the reverse order of removal. Observe the following torques:
    Transmission-to-engine: 47 ft. lb.
    Torque converter: 14 ft. lb.
    Stiffener plates: 27 ft. lb.
    Starter: 27 ft. lb.
    Rear support bolt: 36 ft. lb.
Fill the unit with Dexron® II ATF.

3-Speed Toyoglide (A-30)

1. Disconnect the battery.
2. Remove the air cleaner and disconnect the accelerator torque link or the cable.
3. Disconnect the throttle link rod at the carburetor side, then disconnect the backup light wiring at the firewall (on early models).
4. Jack up the car and support it on stands, then drain the transmission (use a clean receptacle so that the fluid can be checked for color, smell and foreign matter).
5. Disconnect all shift linkage.
6. On early models, remove the cross shaft from the frame.
7. Disconnect the throttle link rod at the transmission side and remove the speedometer cable, cooler lines and parking brake equalizer bracket.
8. Loosen the exhaust flange nuts and remove the exhaust pipe clamp and bracket.
9. Remove the driveshaft and the rear mounting bracket, then lower the rear end of the transmission carefully.
10. Unbolt the torque converter from the drive plate. Support the engine with a suit-

C865

able jack stand and remove the seven bolts that hold the transmission to the engine.

Reverse the order of the removal procedures with the following precautions.

1. Install the drive plate and ring gear, tighten the attaching bolts to 37–43 ft. lbs.

2. After assembling the torque converter to the transmission, check the clearance, it should be about 0.59 in.

3. Before installing the transmission, install the oil pump locator pin on the torque converter to facilitate installation.

4. While rotating the crankshaft, tighten the converter attaching bolts, a little at a time.

5. After installing the throttle connecting second rod, make sure the throttle valve lever indicator aligns with the mark on the transmission with the carburetor throttle valve fully opened. If required, adjust the rod.

6. To install the transmission control rod correctly, move the transmission lever to N (Neutral), and the selector lever to Neutral. Fill the transmission with automatic transmission fluid (Type F only), then start the engine. Run the engine at idle speed and apply the brakes while moving the selector lever through all positions, then return it to Neutral.

7. After warming the engine, move the selector lever through all positions, then back to Neutral, and check the fluid level. Fill as necessary.

8. Adjust the engine idle to 550–650 rpm with the selector lever at Drive. Road test the vehicle.

9. With the selector lever at 2 or Drive, check the point at which the transmission shifts. Check for shock, noise and slipping with the selector lever in all positions. Check for leaks from the transmission.

A-40, A-40D, and A-43D

To remove and install the transmission, proceed in the following manner:

1. Perform Steps 1–3 of the three-speed Toyoglide removal procedure.

2. Remove the upper starter mounting nuts.

3. Raise the car and support it securely with jack stands. Drain the transmission.

4. Remove the lower starter mounting bolt and lay the starter along side of the engine. Don't let it hang by the wires.

5. Unbolt the parking brake equalizer support.

6. Matchmark the driveshaft and the companion flange, to ensure correct installation. Remove the bolts securing the driveshaft to the companion flange.

7. Slide the driveshaft straight back and out of the transmission. Use a spare U-joint yoke or tie a plastic bag over the end of the transmission to keep any fluid from dripping out.

8. Remove the bolts from the cross-shaft body bracket, the cotter pin from the manual lever, and the cross-shaft socket from the transmission.

9. Remove the exhaust pipe bracket from the torque converter bell housing.

10. Disconnect the oil cooler lines from the transmission and remove the line bracket from the bell housing.

11. Disconnect the speedometer cable from the transmission.

12. Unbolt both support braces from the bell housing.

13. Use a transmission jack to raise the transmission slightly.

14. Unbolt the rear crossmember and lower the transmission about 3 in.

15. Pry the two rubber torque converter access plugs out of their holes at the back of the engine.

16. Remove the six torque converter mounting bolts through the access hole. Rotate the engine with the crankshaft pulley.

17. Cut the head off a bolt to make a guide pin for the torque converter. Install the pin on the converter.

18. Remove the converter bell housing-to-engine bolts.

19. Push on the end of the guide pin in order to remove the converter with the transmission. Remove the transmission rearward and then bring it out from under the car.

CAUTION
Don't catch the throttle cable during removal.

Installation is the reverse of removal. Be sure to note the following, however:

1. Install the two long bolts on the upper converter housing and tighten them to 36–58 ft. lbs.

2. Tighten the converter-to-flex-plate bolts finger-tight, and then tighten them with a torque wrench to 11–16 ft. lbs.

3. When installing the speedometer cable, make sure that the felt dust protector and washer are on the cable end.

4. Tighten the cooling line and exhaust pipe bracket mounting bolts to 37–58 ft. lbs. Tighten the cooling lines to 14–22 ft. lbs.

5. Align the matchmarks made on the driveshaft and the companion flange during removal. Tighten the driveshaft mounting bolts to 11–16 ft. lbs.

6. Be sure to install the oil pan drain plug. Tighten it to 11–14 ft. lbs.

7. Adjust the throttle cable.

8. Fill the transmission to the proper capacity. Use only type "F" (ATF) fluid. Start the engine, run the selector through all gear ranges and place it in Park (P). Check the level on the dipstick and add type F fluid, as necessary.

9. Road test the car and check for leaks.

PAN REMOVAL

1. Remove the plug and drain the fluid from the transmission.

2. Unfasten the pan securing bolts.

3. Remove the pan.

4. Installation is the reverse of re-

moval. Torque the pan securing bolts to 4–6 ft. lbs. Refill the transmission with fluid.

FRONT BAND ADJUSTMENTS

NOTE: Band adjustments are not possible on A-40, A-40D, or A-43D transmissions.

3–Speed Toyoglide (A-30)

1. Remove the pan as outlined above.

2. Pry the band engagement lever toward the band with a small prybar.

3. The gap between the end of the piston rod and the engagement bolt should be 0.138 in.

4. If the gap does not meet the specifications, adjust it by turning the engagement bolt.

5. Install the pan and refill the transmission as outlined above.

Rear Band Adjustment
3-SPEED TOYOGLIDE (A-30)

The rear band adjusting bolt is located on the outside of the case, so it is not necessary to remove the pan in order to adjust the band.

1. Loosen the adjusting bolt locknut and fully screw in the adjusting bolt.

2. Loosen the adjusting bolt one turn.

3. Tighten the locknut while holding the bolt so that it cannot turn.

Adjusting the three-speed Toyoglide front band

NEUTRAL SAFETY SWITCH ADJUSTMENT

3-Speed Toyoglide (A-30)

Models with a console-mounted selector have the neutral safety switch on the linkage located beneath the console. To adjust it, proceed in the following manner:

1. Remove the screws which secure the center console.

2. Unfasten the console multiconnector, if so equipped, and completely remove the console.

3. Adjust the switch in the manner outlined in the column selector section, above.

4. Install the console in the reverse order of removal after completion of the switch adjustment.

The neutral safety switch/reverse lamp switch on the Toyoglide transmission with a column-mounted selector is located under the hood on the shift linkage. If the switch is not functioning properly, adjust as follows:

1. Loosen the switch securing bolt.
2. Move the switch so that its arm just contacts the control shaft lever when the gear selector is in Drive position.
3. Tighten the switch securing bolt.
4. Check the operation of the switch; the car should start only in Park or Neutral and the back-up lamps should come on only when Reverse is selected.
5. If the switch cannot be adjusted so that it functions properly, replace it. Perform the adjustment as outlined.

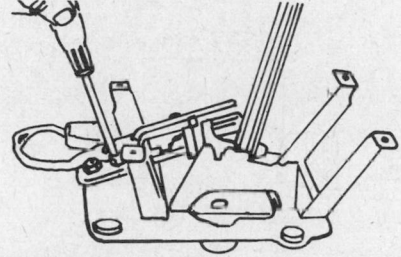

Adjusting the neutral safety switch on models with the three speed Toyoglide and floor mounted shift

All Others

If the engine will start in any range except Neutral or Park, the neutral safety switch will require adjustment.

1. Locate the neutral safety switch on the side of the transmission and loosen the switch bolt.
2. Move the gear selector to the Neutral position.

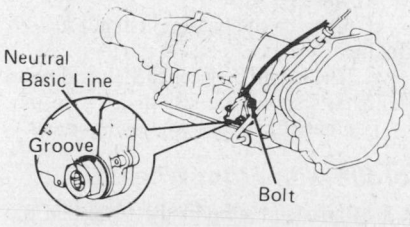

Neutral safety switch adjustment

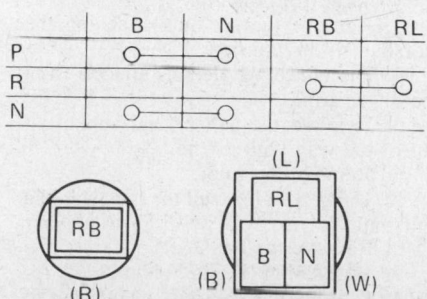

	B	N	RB	RL
P	○—	—○		
R			○—	—○
N	○—	—○		

Checking the neutral safety switch for continuity between the connectors

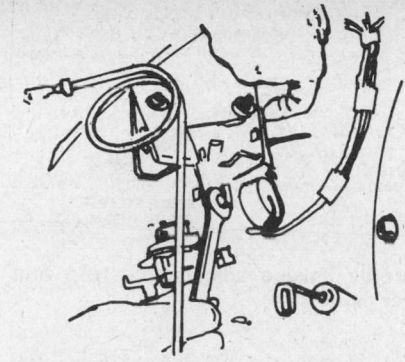

Adjusting the neutral safety switch on models with the three speed Toyoglide and a column-mounted shift

3. Align the groove on the safety switch shaft with the basic line which is scribed on the housing.
4. Tighten the switch bolt.
5. Using an ohmmeter, check the continuity between the switch terminals as shown in the accompanying illustration. If a continuity problem is found, replace the switch.

SHIFT LINKAGE ADJUSTMENT

3-Speed Toyoglide (A-30)

1. Check all of the shift linkage bushings for wear. Replace any worn bushings.
2. Loosen the connecting rod swivel locknut.
3. Move the selector lever and check movement of the pointer in the shift quadrant.
4. When the control shaft is set in the neutral position the quadrant pointer should indicate "N" (Neutral), as well.

Steps 5-7 apply only to cars equipped with column-mounted shift levers.

5. If the pointer does not indicate Neutral, then check the drive cord adjustment.
6. Remove the steering column shroud.
7. Turn the drive cord adjuster with a Phillips screwdriver until the pointer indicates Neutral.

Steps 8–10 apply to both column-mounted and floor-mounted selectors:

8. Position the manual valve lever on the transmission so that it is in the Neutral position.

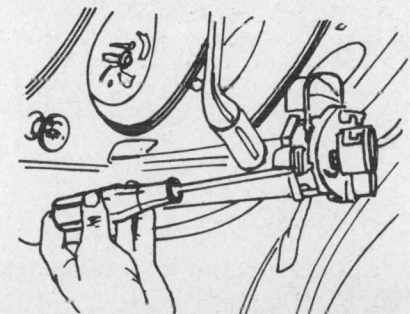

Adjusting the column shift indicator drive cord

9. Lock the connecting rod swivel with the locknut so that the pointer, selector, and manual valve lever are all positioned in Neutral.
10. Check the operation of the gear selector by moving it through all ranges.

All Others Except Cable Controls

1. Check the linkage for freedom of movement.
2. Push the manual valve lever toward the front of the car, as far as it will go.
3. Bring the lever back to its third notch (Neutral).
4. Have someone hold the shift lever in Neutral, while you tighten the linkage so that it can't slip.

Models with Cable Control

1. Loosen the swivel nut on the lever.
2. Push the lever toward the engine as far as it will go.
3. Bring the lever back two notches to Neutral.
4. Place the shifter in Neutral.
5. While holding the lever lightly toward the engine, tighten the nut.

THROTTLE LINKAGE ADJUSTMENT

3-Speed Toyoglide (A-30)

1. Loosen the locknut at each end of the linkage adjusting turnbuckle.
2. Detach the throttle linkage connecting rod from the carburetor.
3. Align the pointer on the throttle valve lever with the mark stamped on the transmission case.
4. Rotate the turnbuckle so that the end of the throttle linkage rod and the carburetor throttle lever are aligned.

NOTE: The carburetor throttle valve must be fully opened during this adjustment.

5. Tighten the turnbuckle locknuts and reconnect the throttle rod to the carburetor.
6. Open the throttle valve and check the pointer alignment with the mark on the transmission case.
7. Road test the car. If the transmission "hunts," i.e., keeps shifting rapidly back and forth between gears at certain speeds

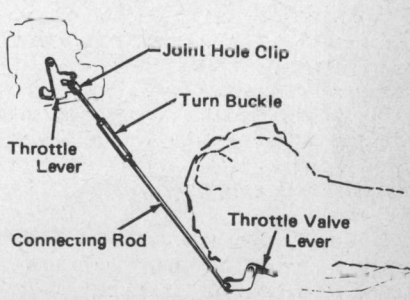

Toyoglide throttle linkage components

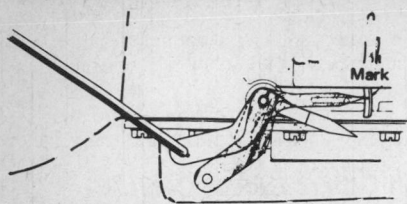

Toyoglide throttle linkage aligning marks

or if it fails to downshift properly when going up hills, repeat the throttle linkage adjustment.

All Others

1. Remove the air cleaner.
2. Confirm that the accelerator linkage opens the throttle fully. Adjust the link as necessary.
3. Peel the rubber dust book back from the throttle cable.
4. Loosen the adjustment nuts on the throttle cable bracket (rocker cover) just enough to allow cable housing movement.
5. Have someone depress the accelerator pedal fully.

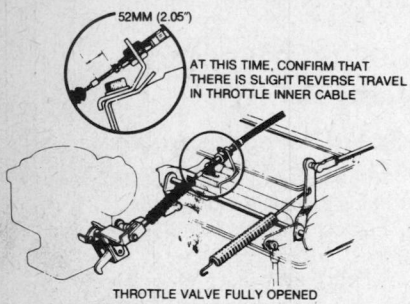

Throttle linkage adjustment—1979 and earlier models

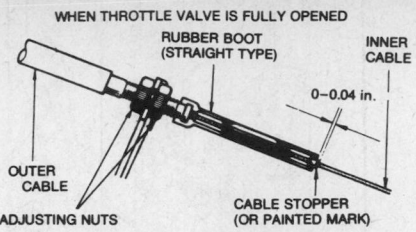

Throttle linkage adjustment—1980 and later models

6. Adjust the cable housing so that the distance between its end and the cable stop collar is 2.05 in. (0.04 in.—1980 and later).
7. Tighten the adjustment nuts. Make sure that the adjustment hasn't changed. Install the dust boot and the air cleaner.

DRIVE AXLE

Halfshafts

REMOVAL & INSTALLATION

Tercel

1. Raise the front of the vehicle and support it with jackstands. Remove the tires.
2. Remove the cotter pin and locknut cap.
3. Have an assistant step on the brake pedal and at the same time, loosen the bearing locknut.
4. Remove the brake caliper and then position it out of the way. Remove the brake disc.

1. Wheel
2. Bearing locknut
3. Disc brake caliper
4. Stablizer bar end
5. Bolt
6. Stiffener plate
7. Driveshaft

5. Remove the cotter pin and nut from the tie rod end and then, using a tie rod end puller, disconnect the tie rod end from the steering knuckle.
6. Matchmark the lower strut mounting bracket where it attaches to the steering knuckle, remove the mounting bolts and then disconnect the steering knuckle from the strut bracket.
7. Pull the axle hub off of the outer half-shaft end.
8. Remove the stiffener plate from the left side of the transaxle assembly.
9. Using a special tool available from Toyota, tap the halfshaft out of the transaxle casing.

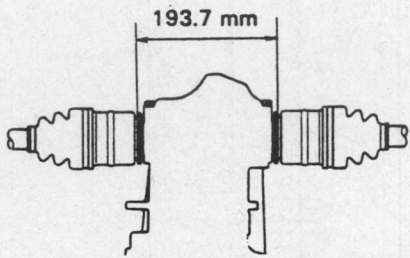

The left and right halfshafts should be 7.626 in. apart

NOTE: Be sure to cover the halfshaft input hole.

10. Installation is in the reverse order at removal. Please note the following.
  a. Coat the oil seal in the transaxle input hole with MP grease before inserting the halfshaft.
  b. Tighten the steering knuckle–to–strut bolts to 105 ft. lbs.
  c. Tighten the tie rod end nut to 29–43 ft. lbs.
  d. Tighten the bearing locknut to 137 ft. lbs.
  e. The length between the left and right halfshafts should be less than 7.626 in.
  f. Check the front wheel alignment.

Corolla with Front Wheel Drive

1. Raise and support the front end on jackstands.
2. Remove the cotter pin, locknut cap and locknut from the hub.
3. Remove the six nuts attaching the halfshaft to the transaxle.
4. Disconnect the steering knuckle from the lower arm.
5. Remove the caliper and support it out of the way with a wire.
6. Remove the rotor.
7. Using a puller, pull the hub from the halfshaft.
8. Remove the halfshaft.
9. Installation is the reverse of removal. Torque thē steering knuckle nut to 47 ft. lb.; the caliper bolts to 65 ft. lb.; the bearing nut to 137 ft. lb. and the halfshaft nuts to 27 ft. lb.

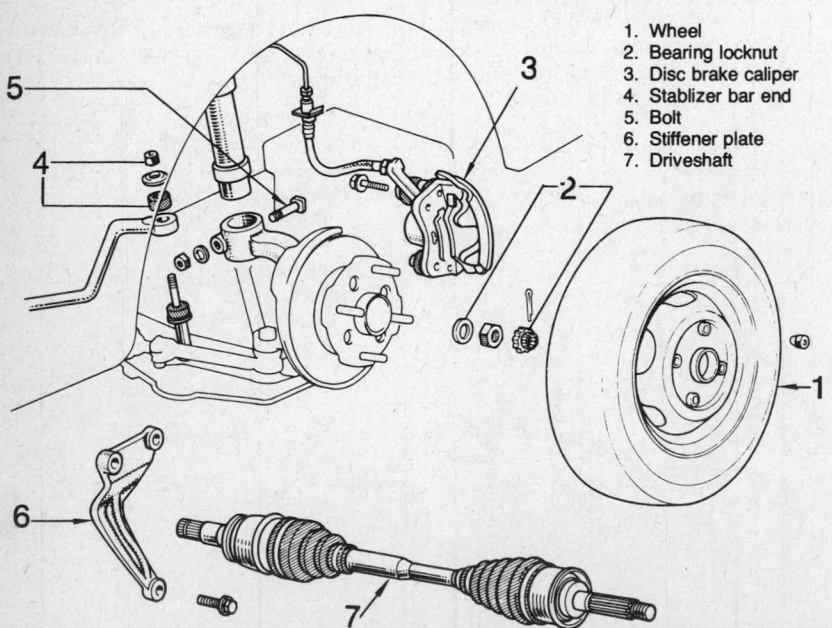

Halfshaft and related components—Tercel

Camry

1. Follow Steps 1–3 of the "Corolla" procedure above.

2. Remove the caliper and support it out of the way with a wire.

3. Remove the rotor.

4. Remove the left side case shield.

5. Remove the axle hub from the shaft with a puller.

6. Unbolt the right side intermediate shaft from the block bracket. Remove the intermediate shaft from the U-joint.

7. With a slide hammer, pull the U-joint from the case.

8. Installation is the reverse of removal. Torque the intermediate shaft bracket bolts to 40 ft. lb.; the caliper bolts to 65 ft. lb.; the hub bearing nut to 137 ft. lb. and the driveshaft-to-intermediate shaft nuts to 27 ft. lb.

Overhaul

For all CV-Joint overhaul procedures, please refer to "U-Joint/CV-Joint Overhaul" in the Unit Repair section.

Driveshaft and U-Joints

REMOVAL & INSTALLATION

Rear Wheel Drive and 4X4 Only

1. Raise the rear of the car with jacks and support the rear axle housing with jack stands.

2. Matchmark the driveshaft and companion flange. Unfasten the bolts which attach the driveshaft universal joint yoke flange to the mounting flange on the differential drive pinion.

3. On models equipped with three universal joints, perform the following:

   a. Remove the driveshaft subassembly from the U-joint sleeve yoke.

   b. Remove the center support bearing from its bracket.

4. Remove the driveshaft end from the transmission.

5. Install an old U-joint yoke in the transmission or, if none is available, use a plastic bag secured with a rubber band over the hole to keep the transmission oil from running out.

NOTE: On 1982 and later Supra models, the exhaust pipe assembly must be removed in order to remove the driveshaft assembly.

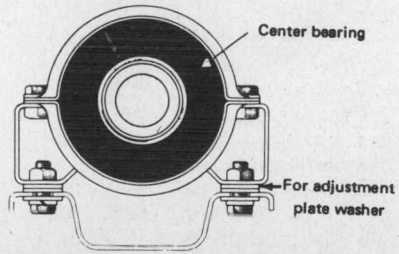

Center bearing adjustment

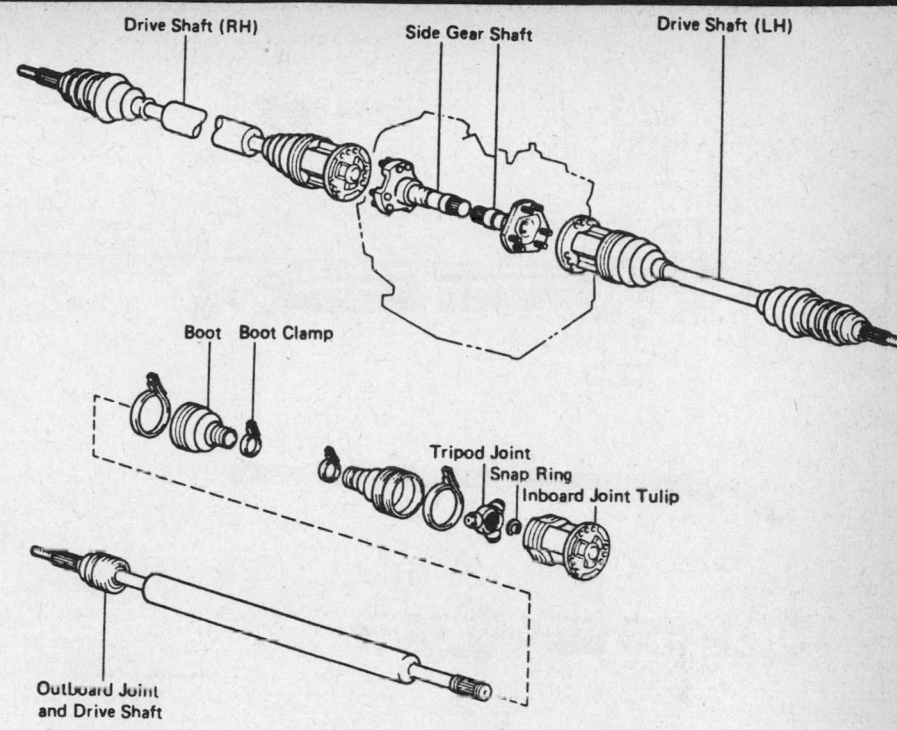

Drive Shaft (RH)   Side Gear Shaft   Drive Shaft (LH)

Boot   Boot Clamp

Tripod Joint
Snap Ring
Inboard Joint Tulip

Outboard Joint and Drive Shaft

Front wheel drive Corolla front axle

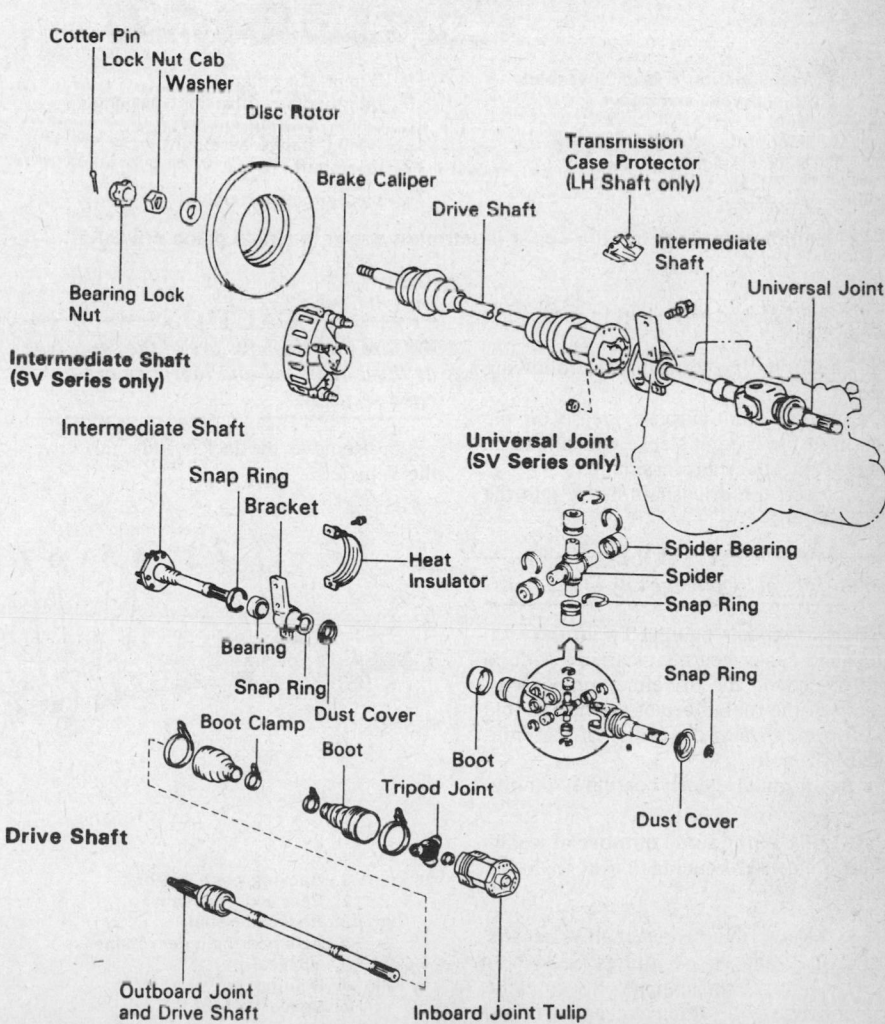

Cotter Pin
Lock Nut Cab
Washer
Disc Rotor

Bearing Lock Nut

Brake Caliper

Drive Shaft

Transmission Case Protector (LH Shaft only)

Intermediate Shaft

Universal Joint

Intermediate Shaft (SV Series only)

Intermediate Shaft

Snap Ring

Bracket

Heat Insulator

Universal Joint (SV Series only)

Spider Bearing
Spider
Snap Ring

Bearing

Snap Ring
Dust Cover

Snap Ring

Boot Clamp

Boot

Boot

Tripod Joint

Dust Cover

Drive Shaft

Outboard Joint and Drive Shaft

Inboard Joint Tulip

Camry front axle

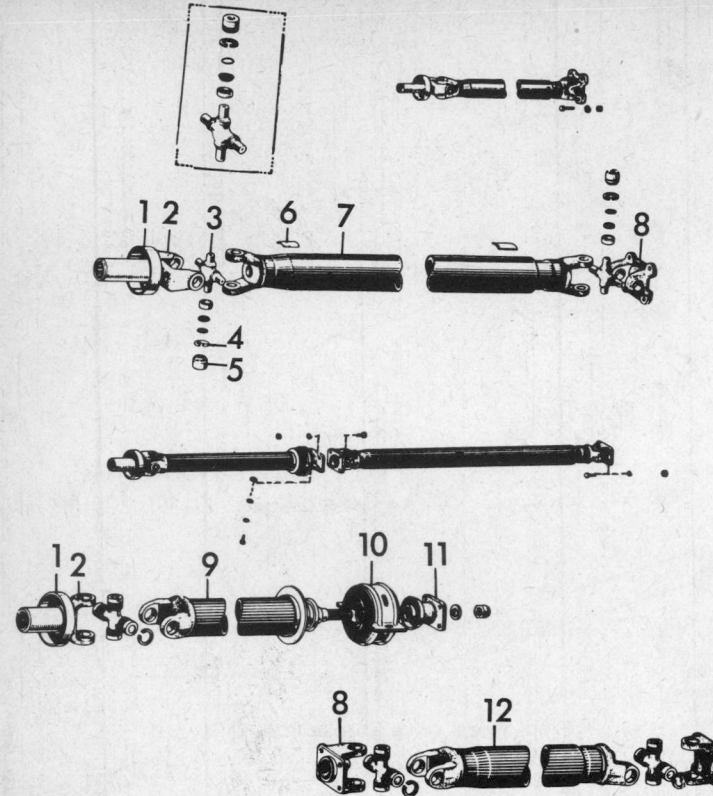

1. Transmission end of driveshaft
2. U-joint yoke and sleeve
3. U-joint spider
4. Snap ring
5. U-joint spider bearing
6. Balancing weight
7. Driveshaft
8. U-joint yoke flange
9. Intermediate driveshaft assembly
10. Center bearing support
11. U-joint flange assembly
12. Driveshaft

Two-piece driveshaft only

Driveshaft components—the upper illustration shows a single piece driveshaft

U-JOINT OVERHAUL

For all overhaul procedures, please refer to "U-Joint/CV-Joint Overhaul" in the Unit Repair section.

NOTE: As the U-joints on many late model vehicles are non-serviceable, the entire driveshaft must be replaced in the vent of U-joint problems.

Rear Axle Shafts

REMOVAL & INSTALLATION

Rear Wheel Drive Models, except 1982 and Later Supra and 1983 and Later Celica GTS

1. Raise the rear of the car and support it securely by using jack stands.
2. Drain the oil from the axle housing.
3. Remove the wheel disc, unfasten the lug nuts, and remove the wheel.
4. Punch matchmarks on the brake drum and the axle shaft to maintain rotational balance.
5. Remove the brake drum and related components, as detailed below.
6. Remove the rear bearing retaining nut.
7. Remove the backing plate attachment nuts through the access holes in the rear axle shaft flange.
8. Use a slide hammer with a suitable adapter to withdraw the axle shaft from its housing.

— CAUTION —

Use care not to damage the oil seal when removing the axle shaft.

9. Repeat the procedure for the axle shaft on the opposite side.

— CAUTION —

Be careful not to mix the components of the two sides.

6. Remove the driveshaft from beneath the vehicle.

Installation is performed in the following order:

1. Apply multipurpose grease on the section of the U-joint sleeve which is to be inserted into the transmission.
2. Insert the driveshaft sleeve into the transmission.

— CAUTION —

Be careful not to damage any of the seals.

3. For models equipped with three U-joints and center bearing clearance with no load placed on the driveline components; the top of the rubber center cushion should be 0.04 in. *behind* the center of the elongated bolt hole.

b. Install the center bearing assembly.

NOTE: Use the same number of washers on the center bearing bracket as were removed.

c. Match the arrow marks on the driveshaft and grease fittings.
4. Align the matchmarks. Secure the U-joint flange to the differential pinion flange with the mounting bolts.

— CAUTION —

Be sure that the bolts are of the same type as those removed and that they are tightened securely.

5. Remove the jack stands and lower the vehicle.

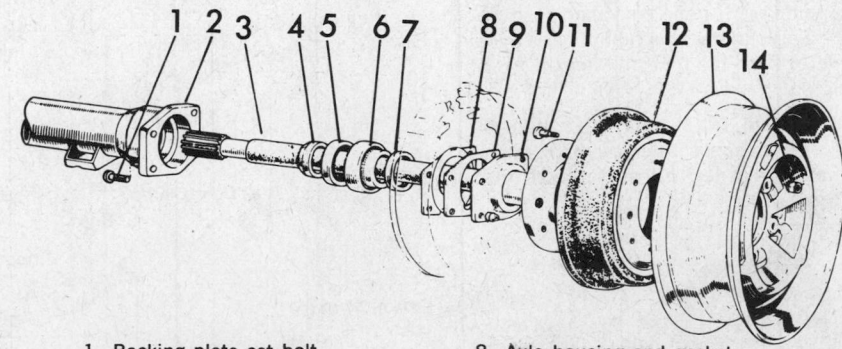

1. Backing plate set bolt
2. Rear axle housing
3. Rear axle shaft
4. Axle bearing inner retainer
5. Oil seal
6. Bearing
7. Spacer
8. Axle housing end gasket
9. Bearing retainer gasket
10. Axle bearing inner retainer
11. Hub bolt
12. Brake drum assembly
13. Wheel
14. Hub nut

Typical solid rear axle components exc. 1982 and Later Supra

10. Installation is performed in the reverse order of removal. Coat the lips of the rear housing oil seal with multipurpose grease prior to installation of the rear axle shaft. Torque the bearing retaining nut to specifications.

NOTE: Always use new nuts, as they are the self-locking type.

AXLE BEARING RETAINING NUT SPECIFICATIONS

Model	Torque range (ft. lbs.)
Corolla 1200	15–22
Corolla 1600	26–38
Corolla 1800	19–23
Corona	29–36
Tercel	22
Celica②	19–23
Supra①	19–23
Cressida	22
Van	48

①Except 1982 and later—See text
②Except 1983 and later GTS—See text.

Supra (1982 and Later) and Celica GTS (1983 and Later)

Remove the axle shaft in the following manner:

1. Raise the rear of the vehicle and support it safely with jackstands.

2. Disconnect the axle drive shaft from the axle flange and lower the axle drive shaft out of the way.

3. Apply the parking brake completely (pulled up as far as possible).

4. Remove the axle flange nut.

NOTE: The axle flange nut is staked in place. It will be necessary to loosen the staked part of the nut with a hammer and chisel, prior to loosening the nut.

5. Using Toyota special service tool #SST 09557-22022 (or its equivalent), disconnect the axle flange from the axle shaft. Be careful not to lose the plate washer from the bearing side of the flange.

6. Remove the parking brake shoes.

7. Using Toyota special service tool #SST 09520-00031 (or its equivalent), pull out the rear axle shaft, along with the oil seal and outer bearing.

Inspect the components:

8. Clean and inspect the bearings, races, and seal. If these parts are in good condition, repack the bearings with MP grease No. 2 and proceed to Step 15 to install the axle shaft.

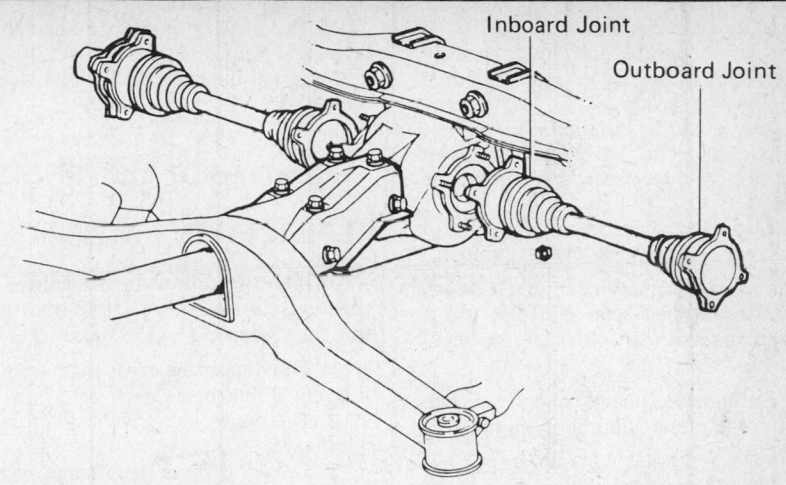

Rear axle halfshafts—Supra (1982 and later) and Celica GTS (1983 and later)

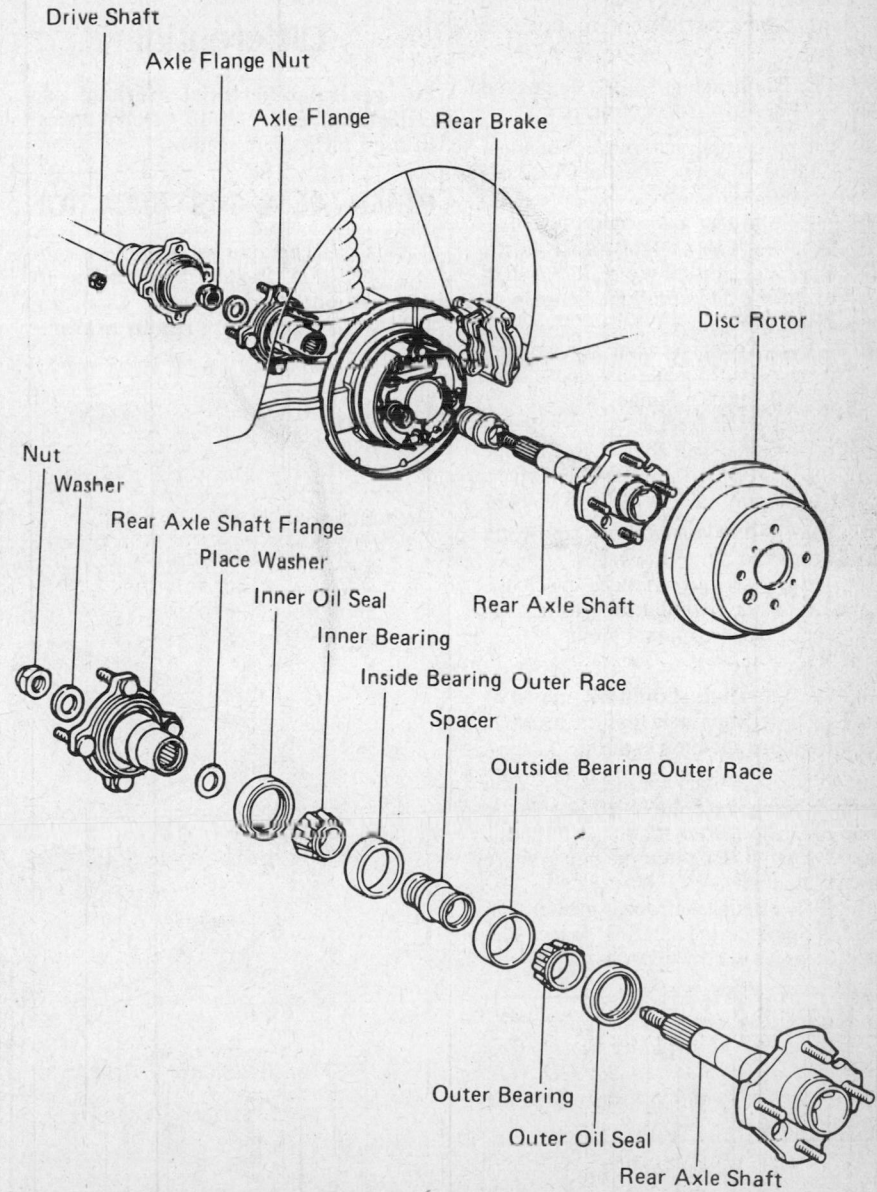

Rear axle shaft—Supra (1982 and later) and Celica GTS (1983 and later)

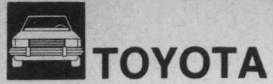
To replace the bearings and seals:

9. Using a hammer and chisel, increase the clearance between the axle shaft hub and the outer bearing.

10. Using a puller installed with the jaws in the gap made in Step 9, pull the outer bearing from the axle shaft and remove the oil seal.

11. Drive the outer bearing race out of the hub with a brass drift and a hammer.

NOTE: Bearing and races must be replaced in matched sets. NEVER use a new bearing with an old race, or vice-versa.

12. Drive the new outer bearing race into the axle shaft hub until it is completely seated.

NOTE: The inner bearing race is replaced in the same manner as Steps 11 and 12.

13. Repack and install both bearings into the hub, being careful not to mix the bearings.

NOTE: The bearings should be packed with No. 2 multipurpose grease.

14. Drive the seals into place. The inner seal should be driven to a depth of 1.22 in.; the outer to 0.217 in.

To install the rear axle shaft:

15. Apply a thin coat of grease to the axle shaft flange. Install the rear axle shaft into the housing and install the flange with the plate washer.

16. Using Toyota special service tool #SST 09557-22022 (or its equivalent), draw the axle shaft into the flange.

17. Remove the special service tool and install a new axle shaft flange nut. Torque the nut to 22–36 ft. lbs. There should be no horizontal play evident at the axle shaft.

18. Turn the axle shaft back and forth and retorque the nut to 58 ft. lbs.

19. Using a torque wrench, check the amount of torque required to turn the axle shaft. The correct rotational torque is 0.9–3.5 in lbs.

NOTE: The shaft should be turned at a rate of 6 seconds per turn to attain a true rotational torque reading.

20. If the rotational torque is less than specified, tighten the nut 5–10 degrees at a time until the proper rotational torque is reached. DO NOT tighten the nut to more than 145 ft. lbs.

21. If the rotational torque is greater than specified, replace the bearing spacer and repeat Steps 18–20 (if necessary).

--- **CAUTION** ---

If the maximum torque is exceeded while retightening the nut, replace the bearing spacer and repeat Steps 18–20. DO NOT back off the axle shaft nut to reduce the rotational torque.

22. After the proper rotational torque is reached, restake the nut into position.

23. Install the parking brake shoes.

24. Connect the axle drive shaft to the flange and torque the nuts to 44–57 ft. lbs.

25. Install the rear wheel and lower the vehicle.

Rear Axle Halfshaft

REPLACEMENT

NOTE: The following procedure applies only to the Supra (1982 and later) and the Celica GTS (1983 and later).

1. Disconnect the drive shaft from the differential flange.

2. Disconnect the drive shaft from the axle flange.

3. Lift either drive shaft flange over the flange studs and remove the drive shaft.

4. Installation is performed in the reverse of the previous steps.

Differential

For general differential overhaul procedures, please refer to "Drive Axles" in the Unit Repair section.

REMOVAL & INSTALLATION

NOTE: Rear axle servicing is a complex operation. Repair should not be attempted unless the special tools and knowledge required are readily available.

Removable Rear Carrier

ALL MODELS EXCEPT SUPRA (1982 AND LATER) AND CELICA GTS (1983 AND LATER)

1. Remove the axle shaft.

2. Disconnect the driveshaft from the pinion shaft flange.

3. Unfasten the carrier securing nuts and remove the carrier assembly.

4. Installation is performed in the reverse order of removal. Be sure to apply liquid sealer to both the carrier gasket and the lower carrier securing nuts.

SUPRA (1982 AND LATER) AND CELICA GTS (1983 AND LATER)

1. Raise the rear of the vehicle and support it safely with jackstands.

2. Remove the differential drain plug and allow the differential oil to drain.

3. Disconnect the axle drive shafts from the differential flanges.

4. Disconnect the propeller shaft flange from the differential companion flange.

5. Remove the NO. 1 differential support member mounting bolt.

6. Place a jack under the differential and raise the jack in order to support the differential.

7. Remove the eight differential-to-carrier mounting bolts.

8. CAREFULLY lower the differential from the vehicle.

9. Installation is performed in the re-

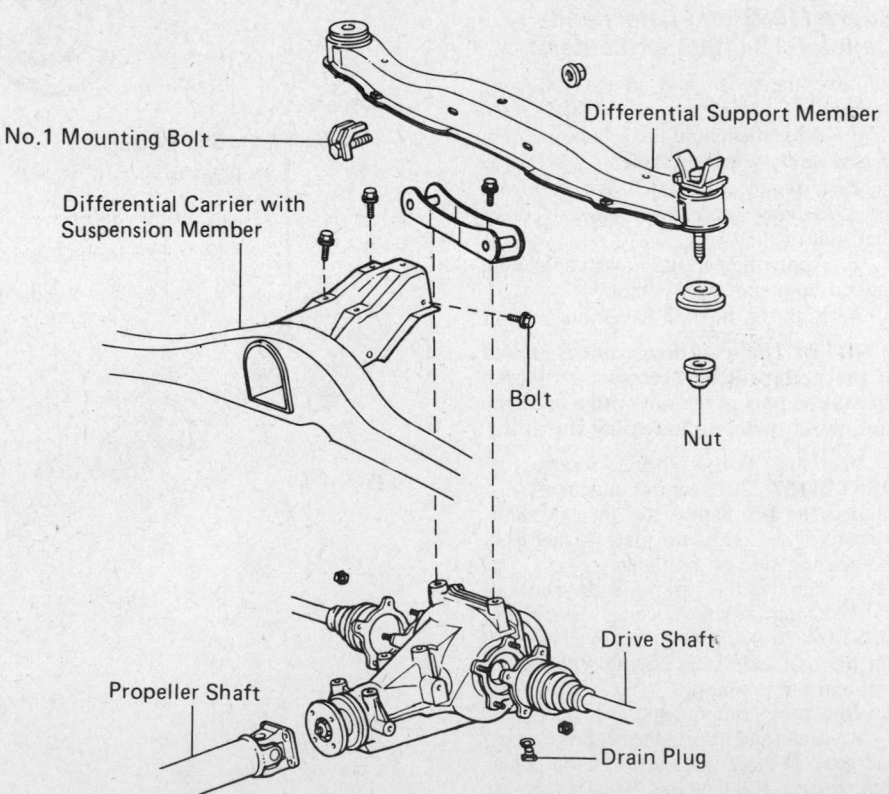

Differential mounting—Supra (1982 and later) and Celica GTS (1983 and later)

verse of the previous steps. Observe the following fastener torques during installation:

Differential-to-carrier mounting bolts—51–72 ft. lbs.

No. 1 support member mounting bolt—51–72 ft. lbs.

Rear axle drive shaft fasteners—44–57 ft. lbs.

NOTE: The differential oil capacity is 1.3 qts. Use SAE 90 oil if ambient temperature is above 0°F; SAE 80W or 80W-90 if temperature is below 0°F. In limited-slip differentials, use oil which is specified only for this purpose.

REAR SUSPENSION

Springs

REMOVAL & INSTALLATION

Leaf Springs

1. Loosen the rear wheel lug nuts.
2. Raise the rear of the vehicle. Support the frame and rear axle housing with stands.
3. Remove the lug nuts and the wheel.
4. Remove the cotter pin, nut, and washer from the lower end of the shock absorber.
5. Detach the shock absorber from the spring seat pivot pin.
6. Remove the parking brake cable clamp.

NOTE: Remove the parking brake equalizer, if necessary.

7. Unfasten the U-bolt nuts and remove the spring seat assemblies.
8. Adjust the height of the rear axle housing so that the weight of the rear axle is removed from the rear springs.

9. Unfasten the spring shackle retaining nuts. Withdraw the spring shackle inner plate. Carefully pry out the spring shackle with a bar.
10. Remove the spring bracket pin from the front end of the spring hanger and remove the rubber bushings.
11. Remove the spring.

— **CAUTION** —
Use care not to damage the hydraulic brake line or the parking brake cable.

Installation is performed in the following order:

1. Install the rubber bushings in the eye of the spring.
2. Align the eye of the spring with the spring hanger bracket and drive the pin through the bracket holes and rubber bushings.

NOTE: Use soapy water as lubricant, if necessary, to aid in pin installation. Never use oil or grease.

3. Finger-tighten the spring hanger nuts and/or bolts.
4. Install the rubber bushings in the spring eye at the opposite end of the spring.

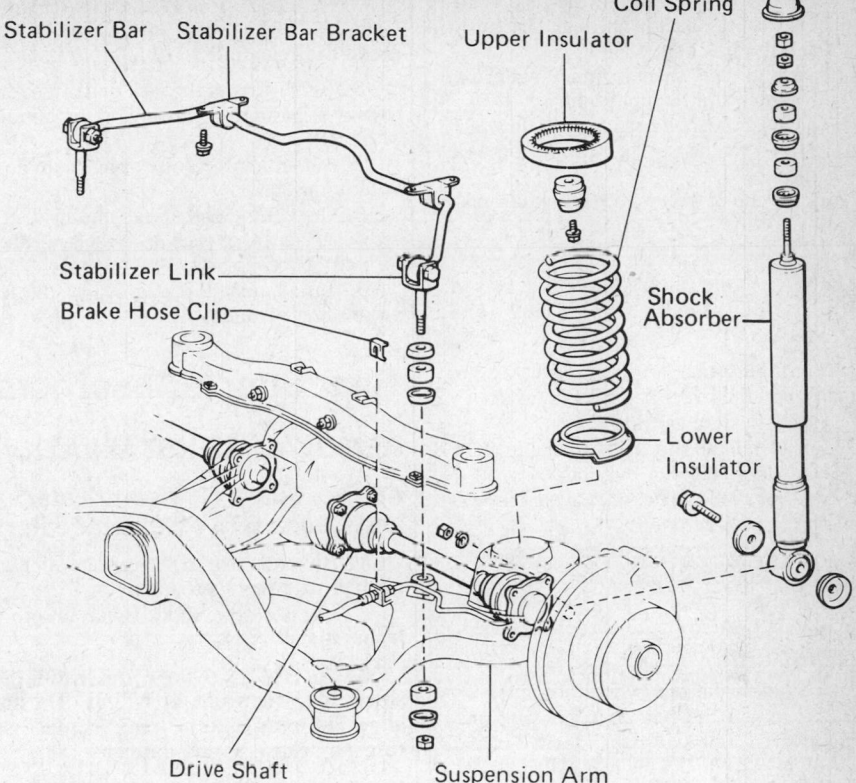

Rear suspension—1982 and later Supra

1. Rear spring
2. Rear shock absorber
3. Cotter pin
4. Castle nut
5. Shock absorber cushion washer
6. Bushing
7. Shock absorber cushion washer
8. Spring bracket
9. Rear spring bumper
10. Spring washer
11. Bolt
12. Rear spring shackle
13. Nut
14. Spring washer
15. Bushing
16. Spring bracket
17. Rear spring hanger pin
18. Spring washer
19. Bolt
20. Rear spring leaf
21. Nut
22. Nut
23. Rear spring clip bolt
24. Clip bolt
25. Rear spring clip
26. Round rivet
27. Rear spring leaf
28. Rear spring leaf
29. Rear spring center bolt
30. U-bolt seat
31. U-bolt
32. Spring washer
33. Nut
34. Rear spring leaf
35. Rear spring clip
36. Round rivet
37. Rear spring leaf
38. Rear spring leaf

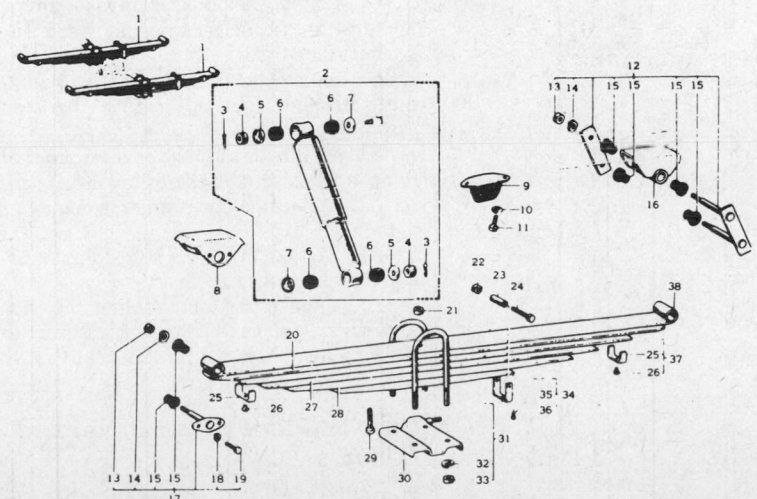

Typical leaf spring rear suspension

5. Raise the free end of the spring. Install the spring shackle through the bushings and the bracket.

6. Install the shackle inner plate and finger-tighten the retaining nuts.

7. Center the bolt head in the hole which is provided in the spring seat on the axle housing.

8. Fit the U-bolts over the axle housing. Install the lower spring seat.

9. Tighten the U-bolt nuts.

NOTE: Some models have two sets of nuts, while others have a nut and lockwasher.

10. Install the parking brake cable clamp. Install the equalizer, if it was removed.

11. On passenger cars:

a. Install the shock absorber end at the spring seat. Tighten the nuts.

b. Install the wheel and lug nuts. Lower the car to the ground.

c. Bounce the car several times.

d. Tighten the spring bracket pins and shackles.

Coil Springs

1. Loosen the rear wheel lug nuts.

2. Jack up the rear axle housing and support the frame with jack stands. Leave the jack in place under the rear axle housing.

3. Remove the lug nuts and wheel.

4. If so equipped, disconnect the rear stabilizer bar from the axle housing (or suspension arm, on Supra (1982 and later) and Celica GTS (1983 and later) models.

5. Unfasten the lower shock absorber end. On the Van, disconnect the lateral control rod from the axle.

NOTE: On Supra (1982 and later) and Celica GTS (1983 and later) models, remove the rear halfshafts.

6. Slowly lower the jack under the rear axle housing until the axle is at the bottom of its travel.

7. Withdraw the coil spring, complete with its insulator.

8. Inspect the coil spring and insulator for wear, cracks, or weakness; replace either or both, as necessary.

9. Installation is performed in the reverse order of removal.

Rear Shock Absorbers

REMOVAL & INSTALLATION

All Exc. Supra (1982 and Later) and Celica GTS (1983 and Later)

1. Raise the rear of the car and support the rear axle with jackstands.

2. Unfasten the upper shock absorber retaining nuts.

NOTE: Always remove and install the shock absorbers one at a time. Do not allow the rear axle to hang in place as this may cause undue damage.

3. Remove the lower shock retaining nut where it attaches to the rear axle housing.

4. Remove the shock absorber.

5. Inspect the shock for wear, leaks or other signs of damage.

6. Installation is in the reverse order of removal. Please note the following:

—tighten the upper retaining nuts to 16–24 ft. lbs.

—tighten the lower retaining nuts to 22–32 ft.lbs.

Supra (1983 and Later) and Celica GTS (1983 and Later)

1. Jack up the rear end of the car, keeping the pad of the hydraulic floor jack underneath the differential housing. Support the suspension control arms with safety stands.

2. Remove the brake hose clips. Disconnect the stabilizer bar end.

3. Disconnect the drive halfshaft at the CV joint on the wheel side.

4. With a jackstand underneath the suspension control arm, unbolt the shock absorber at its lower end. Using a screwdriver to keep the shaft from turning, remove the nut holding the shock absorber to its upper mounting. Remove the shock.

5. Installation is in the reverse order of removal. Torque the halfshaft nuts to 44–57 ft. lbs.; torque the upper shock mounting nut to 14–22 ft. lbs., and the lower shock mounting nut to 22–32 ft. lbs.

MacPherson Struts

REMOVAL & INSTALLATION

Tercel

1. Working inside the car, remove the shock absorber cover and package tray bracket.

2. Raise the rear of the vehicle and support it with jackstands. Remove the wheel.

3. Disconnect the brake line from the wheel cylinder. Disconnect the brake line from the flexible hose at the mounting bracket on the strut tube. Disconnect the flexible hose from the strut.

4. Loosen the nut holding the suspension support to the shock absorber.

—— **CAUTION** ——
Do not remove the nut.

5. Remove the bolts and nuts mounting the strut on the axle carrier and then disconnect the strut.

6. Remove the three upper strut mounting nuts and carefully remove the strut assembly.

7. Installation is in the reverse order of removal. Please note the following:

a. Tighten the upper strut retaining nuts to 17 ft. lbs.

b. Tighten the lower strut-to-axle carrier bolts to 105 ft. lbs.

c. Tighten the nut holding the suspension support to the shock absorber to 36 ft. lbs.

d. Bleed the brakes.

Corolla (Front Wheel Drive) and Camry

For all spring and shock absorber removal and installation procedures, and all strut overhaul procedures, please re-

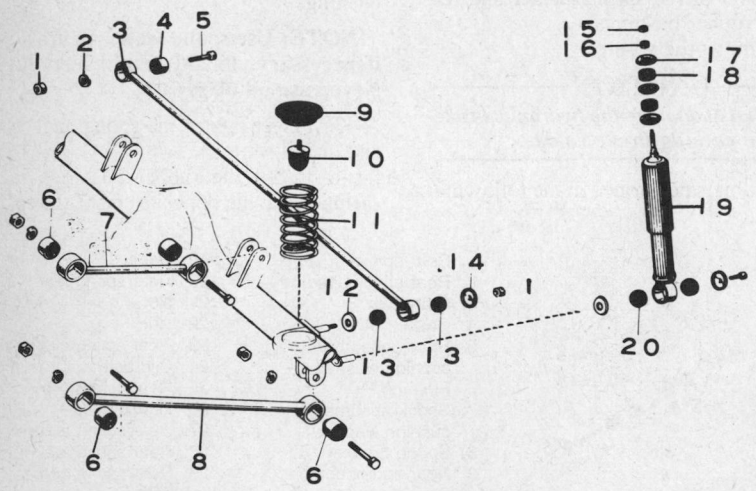

1. Nut
2. Washer
3. Lateral control rod
4. Bushing
5. Bolt
6. Bushing
7. Upper control arm
8. Lower control arm
9. Spring insulator
10. Spring bumper
11. Coil spring
12. Washer
13. Bushing
14. Washer
15. Nut
16. Nut
17. Washer
18. Bushing
19. Shock absorber
20. Bushing

Solid, coil-sprung rear suspension—typical of all models which use rear coil springs (except the Mark II and the 1982 and later Supra)

fer to "Strut Overhaul" in the Unit Repair section.

1. On the 4-dr sedan, remove the package tray and vent duct.

2. On the hatchback, remove the speaker grilles.

3. Disconnect the brake line from the wheel cylinder.

4. Remove the brake line from the brake hose.

5. Disconnect the brake hose from its bracket on the strut.

6. Loosen, but do not remove, the nut holding the suspension support to the strut.

7. Unbolt the strut from the rear arm.

8. Unbolt the strut from the body.

9. Installation is the reverse of removal. Torque the strut-to-body bolts to 17 ft. lb.; the strut-to-rear arm bolts to 150 ft. lb. and the suspension support-to-strut nut to 36 ft. lb.

FRONT SUSPENSION

MacPherson Struts

REMOVAL & INSTALLATION

All except Van

For all spring and shock absorber removal and installation procedures, and all strut overhaul procedures, please refer to "Strut Overhaul" in the Unit Repair section.

1. Remove the hubcap and loosen the lug nuts.

2. Raise the front of the car and support it on the chassis jacking plates provided, with jack stands.

— CAUTION —

Do not support the weight of the car on the suspension arm; the arm will deform under its weight.

3. Unfasten the lug nuts and remove the wheel.

4. Detach the front brake line from its clamp.

5. Remove the caliper and wire it out of the way.

6. Unfasten the three nuts which secure the upper shock absorber mounting plate to the top of the wheel arch.

7. Remove the two bolts which attach the shock absorber lower end to the steering knuckle lower arm.

NOTE: Press down on the suspension lower arm, in order to remove the strut assembly. This must be done to clear the collars on the steering knuckle arm bolt holes when removing the shock/spring assembly.

Installation is performed in the reverse

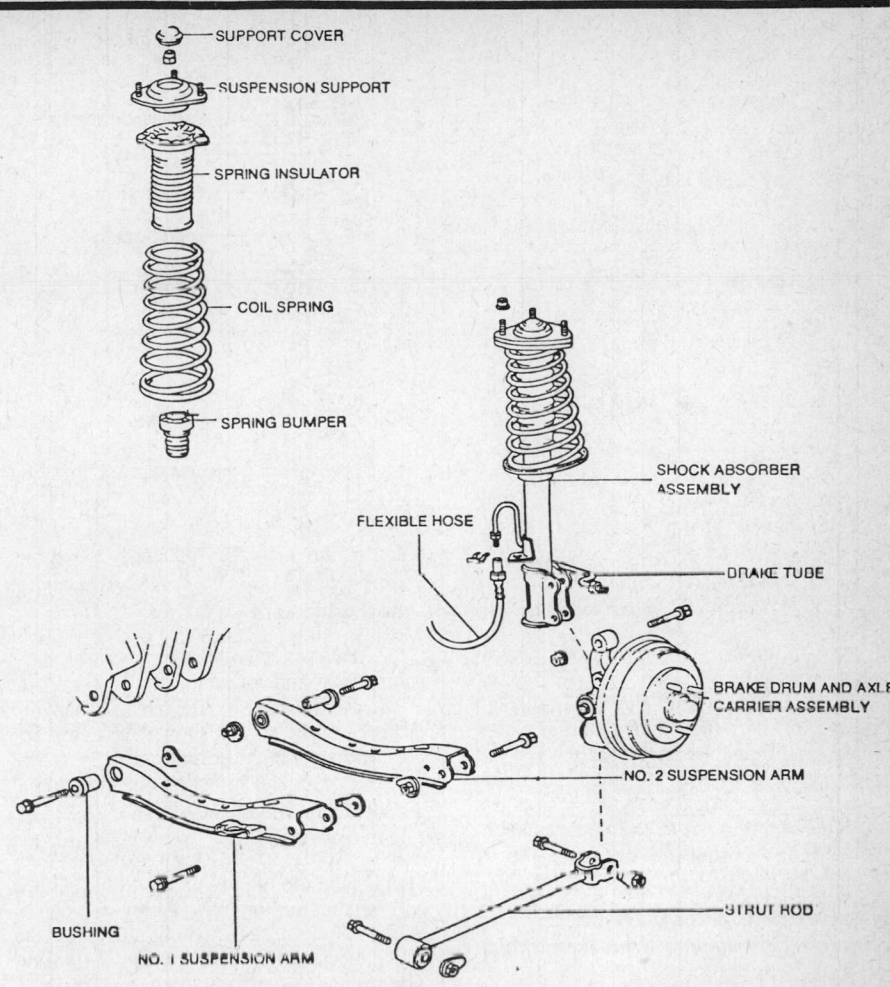

Rear suspension components—1983 and later Tercel (exc 4 × 4), Camry and front wheel drive Corolla

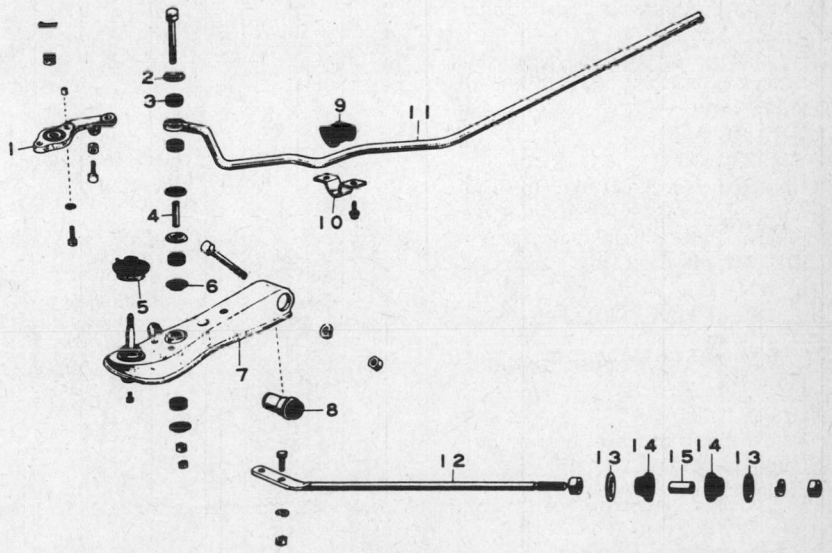

1. Steering knuckle arm	6. Retainer	11. Stabilizer bar
2. Retainer	7. Lower control arm	12. Strut
3. Cushion	8. Bushing	13. Retainer
4. Collar	9. Bushing	14. Cushion
5. Dust cover	10. Bracket	15. Collar

Components of a typical MacPherson strut front suspension

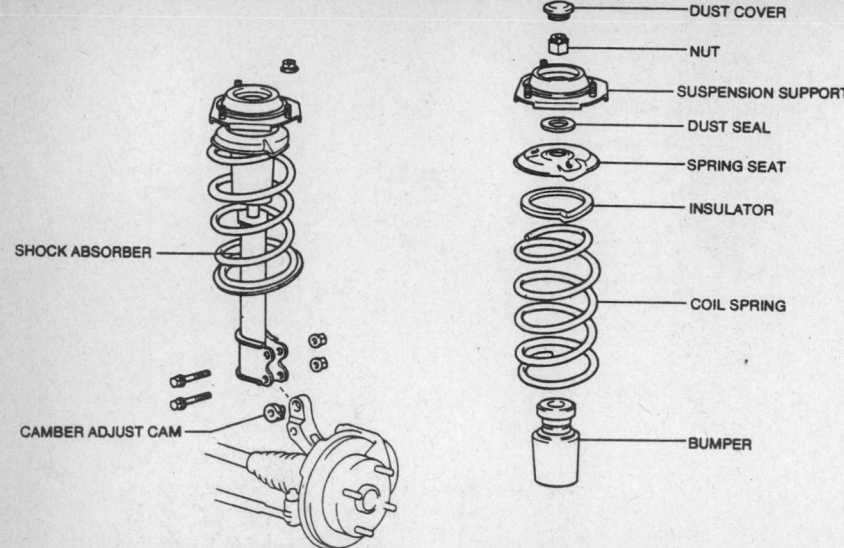

Strut used on all front wheel drive cars

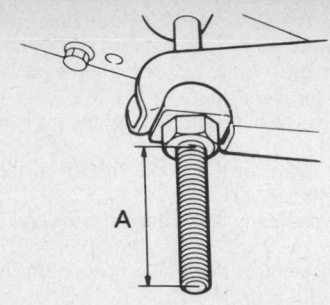

Measuring the threaded end of the torsion bar

order of removal. Be sure to note the following, however:

1. Align the hole in the upper suspension support with the shock absorber piston rod end, so that they fit properly.

2. Always use a *new* nut and nylon washer on the shock absorber piston rod end when securing it to the upper suspension support. Torque the nut to 29–40 ft. lbs.

— CAUTION —

Do not use an impact wrench to tighten the nut.

3. Coat the suspension support bearing with multipurpose grease prior to installation. Pack the space in the upper support with multipurpose grease, also, after installation.

4. Tighten the suspension support-to-wheel arch bolts to the following specification:
Corolla—11–16 ft. lb.
Celica—14–23 ft. lb.

5. Tighten the shock absorber-to-steering knuckle arm bolts to the following specifications:
Corolla (RWD): 50–65 ft. lbs.
Corolla (FWD): Gas 105 ft. lb.
Diesel 152 ft. lb.
Camry: 152 ft. lb.
Tercel: 105 ft. lb.
Celica and Supra: 72 ft. lb.
All others: 65 ft. lb.

6. Adjust the front wheel bearing preload as outlined below.

7. Bleed the brake system.

Torsion Bars

REMOVAL & INSTALLATION

Van

1. Raise and support the front end on jackstands under the frame.

2. Paint match marks on the torsion bar, anchor arm and torque arm.

3. Remove the locknut and measure the threaded end "A" as shown. Use this figure for an installation reference.

4. Loosen the adjusting nut and remove the anchor arm and torsion bar.

5. Installation is the reverse of removal. Apply a light coating of molybdenum disulphide lithium grease to the splined end of the torsion bar. Align all matchmarks. Tighten the adjusting nut so that the exact length of thread appears as before. The proper length should be 2.76 in.

Lower Ball Joints

INSPECTION

Corolla (RWD), Cressida, Corona, 1978–81 Celica, Starlet

Jack up the lower suspension arm (except Corolla, Celica and Cressida). Check the front wheel play. Replace the lower ball joint if the play at the wheel rim exceeds 0.1 in. vertical motion or 0.25 in. horizontal motion. Be sure that the dust covers are not torn and that they are securely glued to the ball joints.

— CAUTION —

Do not jack up the control arm on Corolla, Celica or Cressida models; damage to the arm will result.

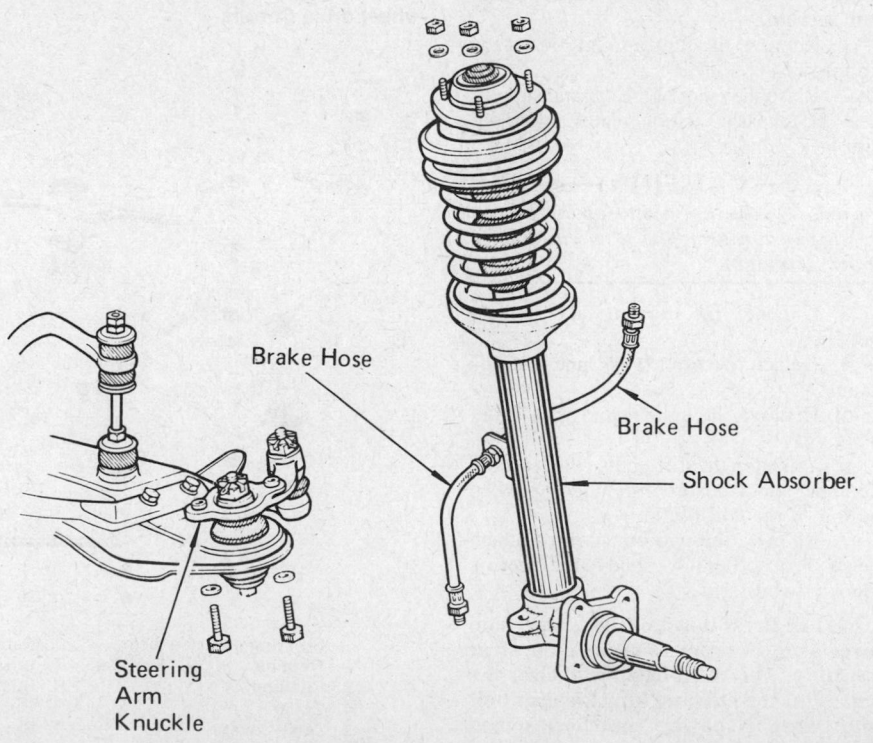

Strut used on all rear wheel drive cars exc. Van

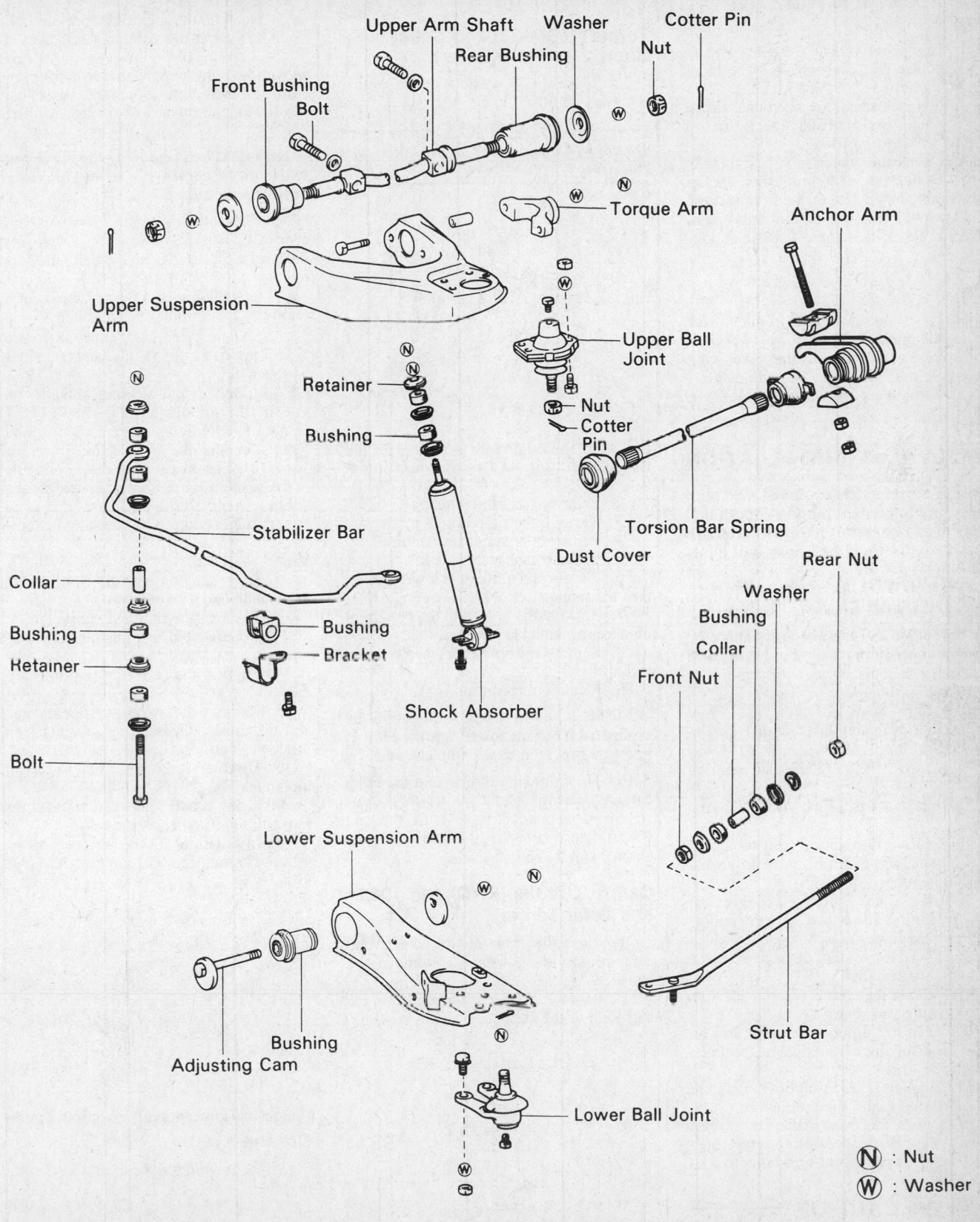

Van front suspension

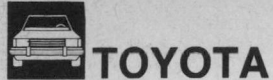

Tercel, Camry, Corolla (FWD) and Celica/Supra (1982 and Later)

1. Jack up the vehicle and place wooden blocks under the front wheels. The block height should be 7.09–7.87 inches.
2. Use jack stands for additional safety.
3. Make sure the front wheels are in a straight forward position.
4. Chock the wheels.
5. Lower the jack until there is approximately half a load on the front springs.
6. Move the lower control arm up and down to check that there is no ball joint play.

Van

1. Raise and support the front end with jackstands under the frame.
2. Have someone apply the brakes while you move the lower arm up and down.
3. Vertical play should not exceed 0.09 in.

REMOVAL & INSTALLATION

NOTE: On models equipped with both upper and lower ball joints—if both ball joints are to be removed, always remove the lower and then the upper ball joint.

Corolla (RWD), Cressida, 1978–81 Celica and Starlet

The ball joint and control arm cannot be separated from each other. If one fails, then both must be replaced as an assembly, in the following manner:
1. Perform Steps 1–7 of the first "Front Spring Removal and Installation" procedure. Skip Step 6.
2. Remove the stabilizer bar securing bolts.
3. Unfasten the torque strut mounting bolts.
4. Remove the control arm mounting bolt and detach the arm from the front suspension member.
5. Remove the steering knuckle arm from the control arm with a ball joint puller.

Inspect the suspension components, which were removed for wear or damage. Replace any parts, as required.

Installation is the reverse of removal. Note the following, however:
1. When installing the control arm on the suspension member, tighten the bolts partially at first.
2. Complete the assembly procedure and lower the car to the ground.
3. Bounce the front of the car several times. Allow the suspension to settle, then tighten the lower control arm bolts to 51–65 ft. lbs.

——— CAUTION ———
Use only the bolt which was designed to fit the lower control arm. If a replacement is necessary, see an authorized dealer for the proper part.

4. Remember to lubricate the ball joint. Check front-end alignment.

Tercel (1980–82) and Celica/Supra (1982 and Later)

1. Jack up your vehicle and support it with jack stands.

——— CAUTION ———
Do not jack up your car on the lower control arms.

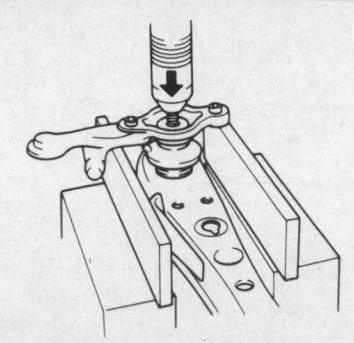

Ball joint removal, with a press, on the Celica, RWD Corolla, Cressida and Starlet

2. Remove the front wheels.
3. Remove the tie-rod end.
4. Remove the stabilizer bar end.
5. Remove the strut bar end.
6. Place a jack under the lower control arm for support.
7. Remove the bolt from the bottom of the steering knuckle.
8. Remove the bolt from the lower control arm.
9. Remove the control arm.

NOTE: The lower ball joint cannot be separated from the lower control arm. It must be replaced as a complete unit.

10. The following torques are required: Bottom steering knuckle nut 40–52 ft. lbs.; stabilizer bar 11–15 ft. lbs.; tie rod end 37–50 ft. lbs.; strut bar 29–39 ft. lbs.; lower control arm 51–65 ft. lbs.

Camry, Corolla (FWD) and 1983 and Later Tercel

1. Raise the front of the vehicle and support it with jackstands. Remove the wheel.
2. Remove the two bolts attaching the ball joint to the steering knuckle.

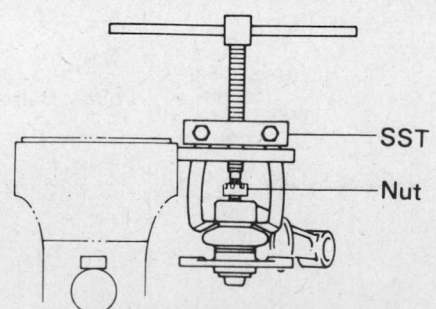

1983–85 Tercel Ball joint removal

3. Remove the stabilizer bar nut, retainer and cushion.
4. Jack up the opposite wheel until the body of the car just lifts off the jackstand.
5. Loosen the lower control arm mounting bolt, wiggle the arm back and forth and then remove the bolt. Disconnect the lower control arm from the stabilizer bar.

NOTE: When removing the lower control arm, be careful not to lose the caster adjustment spacer.

6. Carefully mount the lower control arm in a vise and then, using a ball joint removal tool, disconnect the ball joint from the arm.
7. Installation is in the reverse order of removal. Please note the following:
   a. Tighten the ball joint–to–control arm nut to 51–65 ft. lbs. and use a new cotter pin.
   b. Tighten the steering knuckle–to–control arm bolts to 59 ft. lbs.
   c. Before tightening the stabilizer bar nuts, mount the wheels and lower the car. Bounce the car several times to settle the suspension and then tighten the stabilizer bolts to 66–90 ft. lbs.
   d. Check the front–end alignment.

Van

1. Raise and support the front end on jackstands under the frame.
2. Remove the hub and caliper.
3. Remove the steering knuckle dust cover.
4. Support the lower arm with a floor jack.
5. Remove the two cotter pins and nuts and disconnect the steering knuckle from the lower ball joint.
6. Disconnect the upper ball joint from the knuckle.
7. Using a ball joint removal tool, remove the ball joint from the arm.
8. Installation is the reverse of removal. Torque the ball joint nut to 50 ft. lb.

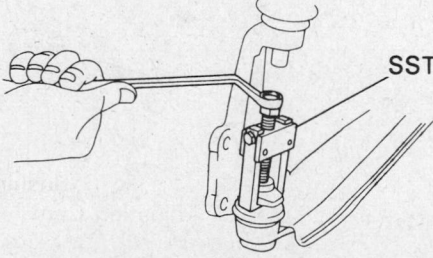

Typical ball joint separation without a press

Corona

1. Remove the hubcap and loosen the lug nuts.
2. Jack up your vehicle and support it with jack stands.
3. Remove the lug nuts and the wheel.
4. Compress the coil spring by placing a jack underneath the control arm and raising it.

5. Remove the cotter pin and the castelated nut from the ball joint.

6. Use a ball joint puller to detach the lower ball joint from the steering knuckle.

7. Wire the steering knuckle out of the way.

8. Remove the bolt and remove the ball joint.

Installation is the reverse of removal. Tighten the stud nut 51–65 ft. lbs.

Upper Ball Joint

INSPECTION

Disconnect the ball joint from the steering knuckle and check free-play by hand. Replace the ball joint, if it is noticeably loose.

REMOVAL & INSTALLATION

NOTE: On models equipped with both upper and lower ball joints—if both are to be removed, always remove the lower one first.

Corona and Van

1. Remove the steering knuckle as detailed in "Lower Ball Joint Removal & Installation".

2. Suspend the steering knuckle with a wire.

3. Use an open-end wrench to remove the upper ball joint.

Installation is performed in the reverse order from removal. Note the following:

1. Install the upper ball joint dust cover with the escape valve toward the rear.

2. Use sealer on the dust cover before installing it.

3. Tighten the upper ball joint-to-steering knuckle bolt to 40–50 ft. lbs. on the Corona, and 22 ft. lb. on the Van.

Lower Control Arm

REMOVAL & INSTALLATION

Corolla (RWD), 1978–81 Celica, Cressida, Starlet

1. Raise and support the front end.

2. Remove the wheel.

3. Disconnect the steering knuckle from the control arm.

4. Disconnect the tie-rod, stabilizer bar and strut bar from the control arm.

5. Remove the control arm mounting bolts, and remove the arm.

6. Install in reverse of above. Tighten, but do not torque fasteners until car is on ground.

7. Lower car to ground, rock it from side-to-side several times and torque control arm mounting bolts to 51–65 ft. lbs., stabilizer bar to 16 ft. lbs., strut bar to 40 ft. lbs., and shock absorber to 65 ft. lbs.

Corona

1. Raise and support the vehicle.

2. Remove the front wheel.

3. Remove the shock absorber and disconnect the stabilizer from the lower arm.

4. Install a spring compressor and fully tighten it.

5. Place a jack under the lower arm seat.

6. Disconnect the lower ball joint from the knuckle and lower the jack.

7. Remove the ball joint from the arm, remove the cam plates and bolts and take off the arm.

8. Install in reverse of above. Tighten all fasteners, but do not torque them to specification until vehicle is on ground.

9. Lower vehicle and rock it from side-to-side several times.

10. With no load in vehicle, torque the lower arm mounting bolts to 94–130 ft. lbs.

Tercel and Celica/Supra (1982 and Later)

See the lower ball joint removal section.

Camry and Corolla (FWD)

1. Raise and support the front end with jackstands under the frame.

2. Remove the two bolts holding the ball joint to the knuckle. Disconnect the lower arm from the knuckle.

3. Disconnect the stabilizer bar from the arm.

4. Unbolt and remove the arm.

5. Installation is the reverse of removal. Observe the following torques:

Ball joint nut: 67 ft. lb.
Steering knuckle-to-arm: 83 ft. lb.
Stabilizer bar nut: 86 ft. lb.
Lower arm-to-body: 83 ft. lb.

Van

1. Raise and support the front end on jackstands under the frame.

2. Remove the shock absorber.

3. Disconnect the stabilizer bar from the arm.

4. Disconnect the strut bar from the arm.

5. Remove the ball joint nut and disconnect the ball joint from the knuckle. A ball joint separator is necessary.

6. Place a matchmark on the adjusting cam.

7. Remove the adjusting cam and nut and remove the lower arm.

8. Installation is the reverse of removal. Observe the following torques:

Ball joint nut: 50 ft. lb.
Ball joint-to-knuckle: 76 ft. lb.
Shock absorber upper nut: 19 ft. lb.

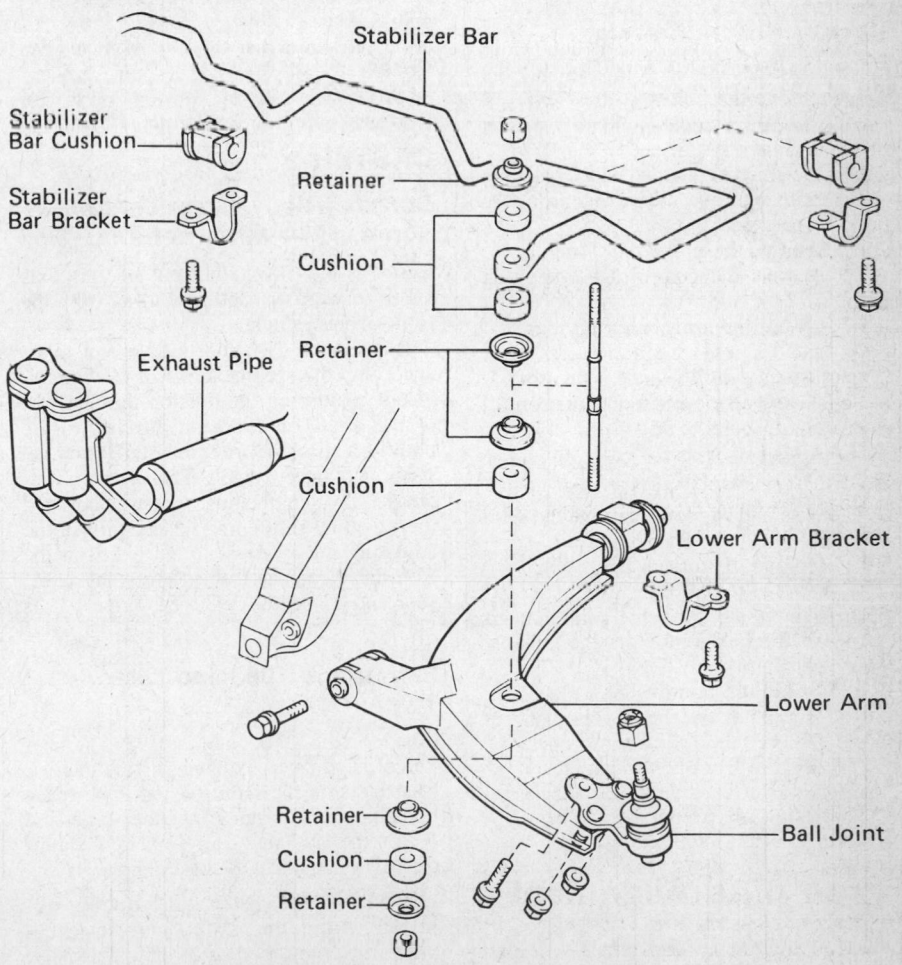

Front wheel drive Corolla front suspension

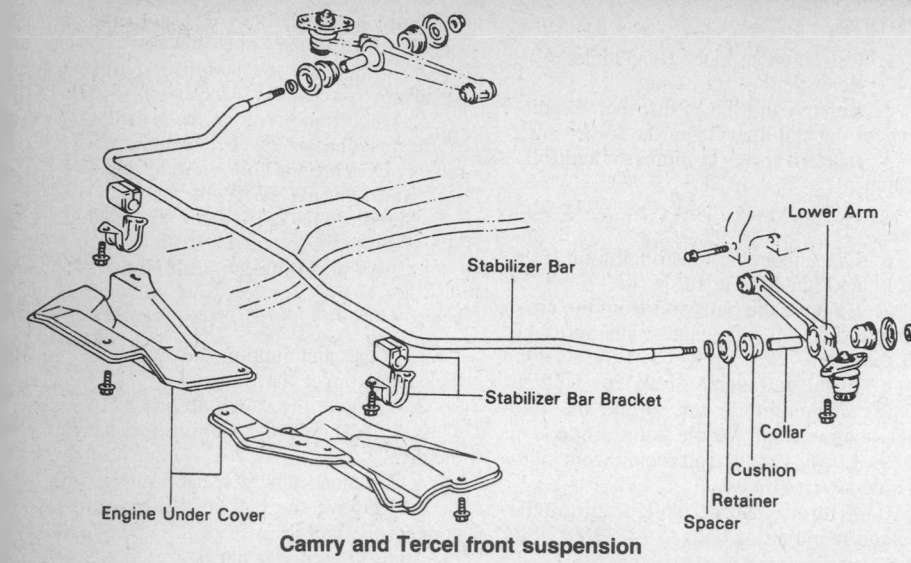

Camry and Tercel front suspension

Shock absorber lower bolts: 13 ft. lb.
Strut bar-to-arm: 50 ft. lb.
Adjusting cam nut: 112 ft. lb.

Upper Control Arm

REMOVAL & INSTALLATION

Corona

1. Remove the upper arm mounting nuts from inside the engine compartment, but do not remove the bolts.
2. Raise the vehicle, support the lower arm and remove the wheel.
3. On vehicles equipped with a ball joint wear sensor, remove the wiring from the clamp on the arm.
4. Remove the upper ball joint.
5. Remove the control arm mounting bolts.
6. Pry out the arm with a pry bar.
7. Install in reverse of removal. Do not tighten fasteners until vehicle is on ground.
8. Lower vehicle and torque the control arm mounting bolts to 95–130 ft. lbs.

Van

1. Raise and support the front end with jackstands under the frame.
2. Remove the torsion bar.
3. Remove the air duct.
4. Remove the upper ball joint nut and disconnect the ball joint from the knuckle using a separator.
5. Unbolt and remove the arm.
6. Installation is the reverse of removal. Observe the following torques:
   Upper arm front bolt: 65 ft. lb.
   Upper arm rear bolt: 112 ft. lb.
   Ball joint-to-arm nut: 22 ft. lb.
   Ball join-to-knuckle: 58 ft. lb.

Front-End Alignment

Front-end alignment measurements require the use of special equipment. Before mea-suring alignment or attempting to adjust it, always check the following points:

1. Be sure that the tires are properly inflated.
2. See that the wheels are properly balanced.
3. Check the ball joints to determine worn or loose.
4. Check front wheel bearing adjustment.
5. Be sure that the car is on a level surface.
6. Check all suspension parts for tightness.

CASTER

Corolla (RWD), Cressida, Celica, Supra, 1980–82 Tercel

Caster is the tilt of the front steering axis either forward or backward away from the front of the vehicle.

If the caster is found to be out of toler-ance with the specifications, it may be ad-justed by turning the nuts on the rear end of the strut bar (where it attaches to the body) on all models but the Starlet and the 1983 and later Tercel. The caster is de-creased by lengthening the strut bar and increased by shortening it. One turn of the adjusting nut is equal to 8' of tilt on the Corolla, 9' on the Celica/Supra and Cres-sida and 7' on the 1980–82 Tercel. 1' is ⅟₆₀ of a degree.

Starlet and 1983 and Later Tercel

Caster on the Starlet and the 1983 and later Tercel is adjusted by changing the number of spacers on the stabilizer bar. One space will change the caster 24' on the Starlet and 13' on the 1983 and later Tercel. One min-ute (1') is equal to ⅟₆₀ of a degree.

NOTE: If the caster still cannot be ad-justed within the limits, inspect or re-place any damaged or worn suspension parts.

Camry

Increase or decrease the number of spacers on the stabilizer bar. Each spacer changes caster by 30'.

Van

Caster is changed by turning the adjusting cam or strut bar nut. Each graduation of the cam gives 12' of change; each turn of the nut gives 25' change.

Corolla (FWD)

Caster is not adjustable.

CAMBER

Except Corona

Camber is the slope of the front wheels from the vertical when viewed from the front of the vehicle. When the wheels tilt outward at the top, the camber is positive (+). When the wheels tilt inward at the top, the camber is negative (−). The amount of positive and negative camber is mea-sured in degrees from the vertical and the measurement is called camber angle. Cam-ber is preset at the factory, therefore it it is not adjustable on any model but the 1983 and later Tercel, Camry, Van and FWD

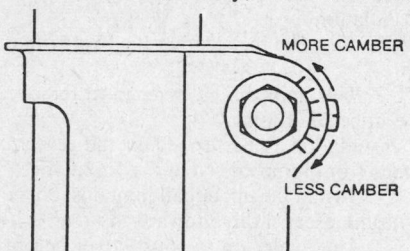

Camber adjusting bolt on the 1983 and later Tercel, front wheel drive Corolla and Camry

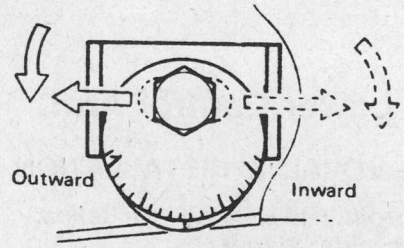

Left side

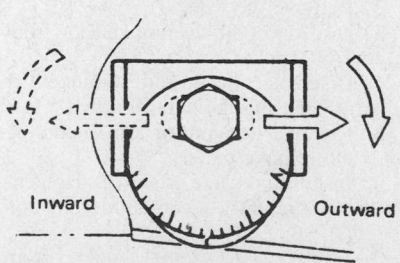

Right side

Corona front end alignment adjusting cams

Corolla. If the camber angle is out of tolerance, inspect or replace worn or damaged suspension parts.

Camber on these models is adjustable by means of a camber adjustment bolt on the lower strut mounting bracket. Loosen the shock absorber set nut and then turn the adjusting bolt until the camber is within specifications. Camber will change about 20' for each gradation on the cam. One minute (1') is equal to 1/60 of a degree.

CASTER AND CAMBER

Corona

Caster and camber angles are measured in the same way and with the same equipment as all the other models above.

However, the method of adjustment is different:
1. Measure the camber and adjust it with the *rear* adjusting cam.
2. Measure the caster and adjust it with the *front* adjusting cam.
3. Check the caster and camber again.
4. Tighten the lower control arm mounting bolts to 94–132 ft. lbs.

NOTE: There should be no more than six graduations difference between the front and rear cams; inspect for damaged suspension parts if there is.

Toe

Toe is the amount, measured in a fraction of an inch, that the front wheels are closer together at one end than the other. Toe-in means that the front wheels are closer together at the front of the tire than at the rear; toe-out means that the rear of the tires are closer together than the front.

The wheels must be dead straight ahead. The car must have a full tank of gas, all fluids must be at their proper levels, all other suspension and steering adjustments must be correct and the tires must be properly inflated to their cold specification.
1. Toe can be determined by measuring the distance between the centers of the tire treads, at the front of the tire and the rear. If the tread pattern of your car's tires makes this impossible, you can measure between the edges of the wheel rims, but be sure to move the car and measure in a few places to avoid errors caused by bent rims or wheel run-out.
2. If the measurement is not within specifications, loosen the four retaining clamp locknuts on the adjustable tie-rods.

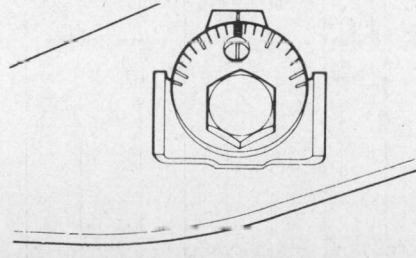

Van caster and camber adjustment cam

3. Turn the left and right tie-rods EQUAL amounts until the measurements are within specifications.
4. Tighten the lock bolts and then recheck the measurements. Check to see that the steering wheel is still in the proper position. If not, remove it and reposition it.

STEERING

Steering Wheel

REMOVAL & INSTALLATION

Three-Spoke

———— CAUTION ————

Do not attempt to remove or install the steering wheel by hammering on it. Damage to the energy-absorbing steering column could result.

1. Unfasten the horn and turn signal multiconnector(s) at the base of the steering column shroud.
2. Loosen the trim pad retaining screws from the back side of the steering wheel.
3. Lift the trim pad and horn button assembly(ies) from the wheel.
4. Remove the steering wheel hub retaining nut.
5. Scratch matchmarks on the hub and shaft to aid in correct installation.
6. Use a steering wheel puller to remove the steering wheel.

Installation is the reverse of removal. Tighten the wheel retaining nut to 15–22 ft. lbs., on 1978–82 models; 25 ft. lb on 1983 and later models.

Two-Spoke

The two-spoke steering wheel is removed in the same manner as the three-spoke, except that the trim pad should be pried off with a small prybar. Remove the pad by lifting it toward the top of the wheel.

Four-Spoke

———— CAUTION ————

Do not attempt to remove or install the steering wheel by hammering on it. Damage to the energy absorbing steering column could result.

1. Unfasten the horn and turn signal connectors at the base of the steering column shroud, underneath the instrument panel.
2. Gently pry the center emblem off the front of the steering wheel.
3. Insert a wrench through the hole and remove the steering wheel retaining nut.
4. Scratch matchmarks on the hub and shaft to aid installation.
5. Use a steering wheel puller to remove the steering wheel.

Installation is the reverse of removal. Tighten the steering wheel retaining nut to 15–22 ft. lbs., except on the Celica/Supra which is tightened to 22–28 ft. lbs.

Combination Switch

REMOVAL & INSTALLATION

1. Disconnect the negative battery cable.
2. Unscrew the two retaining bolts and remove the steering column garnish.
3. Remove the upper and lower steering column covers.
4. Remove the steering wheel as detailed previously.
5. Trace the switch wiring harness to the multiconnector. Push in the lock levers and pull apart the connector.
6. Unscrew the four mounting screws and remove the switch.
7. Installation is in the reverse order of removal.

Ignition Lock/Switch

REMOVAL & INSTALLATION

1. Disconnect the negative (−) battery cable.
2. Unfasten the ignition switch connector underneath the instrument panel.
3. Remove the screws which secure the upper and lower halves of the steering column cover. Remove the lower instrument panel garnish on Corona models first.
4. Turn the lock cylinder to the "ACC" position with the ignition key.
5. Push the lock cylinder stop in with a small, round object (cotter pin, punch, etc.).

NOTE: On some models it may be necessary to remove the steering wheel and turn signal switch first.

6. Withdraw the lock cylinder from the lock housing while depressing the stop tab.
7. To remove the ignition switch, unfasten its securing screws and withdraw the switch from the lock housing.

Installation is performed in the following order:
1. Align the locking cam with the hole in the ignition switch and insert the switch in the lock housing.
2. Secure the switch with its screw(s).
3. Make sure that both the lock cylinder and the column lock are in the "ACC" position. Slide the cylinder into the lock housing until the stop tab engages the hole in the lock.
4. The rest of installation is performed in the reverse order of removal.

Manual Steering Gear

REMOVAL & INSTALLATION

Corolla (RWD) and Corona

1. Remove the bolt attaching the coupling yoke to the steering worm.
2. Disconnect the relay rod from the pitman arm.
3. Remove the steering gear housing down and to the left.

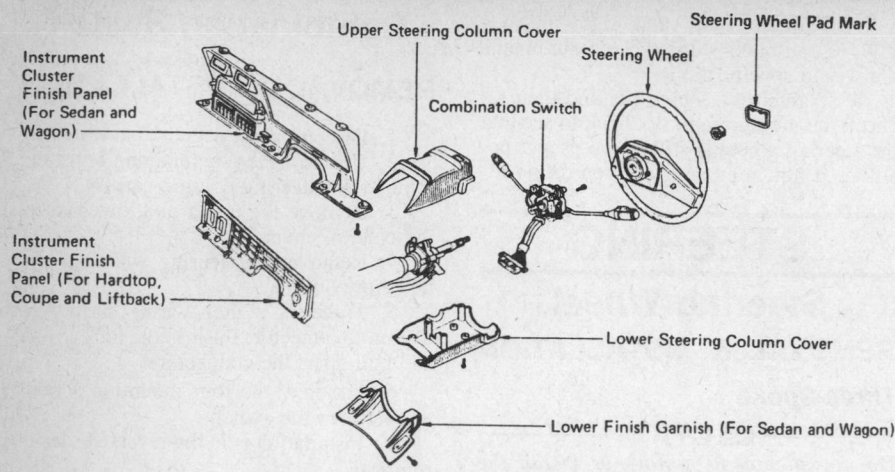

Typical combination switch mounting

4. Install in reverse of removal. Torque the housing-to-frame bolts to 25–36 ft. lbs.; the coupling yoke bolt to 15–20 ft. lbs.; the relay rod to 36–50 ft. lbs.

Cressida and 1978–81 Celica/Supra

1. Open the hood, and find the steering gearbox. Place matchmarks on the coupling and steering column shaft.

2. Disconnect the Pitman arm from the relay rod using a tie rod puller on the Pitman arm set nut.

3. Disconnect the steering gearbox at the coupling. Unbolt the gearbox from the chassis and remove.

4. Installation is in the reverse order of removal, with the exception of first aligning the matchmarks and connecting the steering shaft to the coupling before you bolt the gearbox into the car permanently.

Corolla (FWD), Camry and 1982 and Later Celica/Supra

1. Open the hood. Remove the two set bolts, and remove the sliding yoke from between the steering rack housing and the steering column shaft. On Supras, unbolt and remove the intermediate shaft (rack housing side first).

2. Remove the cotter pin and nut holding the knuckle arm to the tie-rod end. Using a tie-rod puller, disconnect the tie-rod end from the knuckle arm.

3. Tag and disconnect the power steering lines if equipped. Remove the steering housing brackets and remove the housing.

4. Installation is the reverse of removal. Torque the rack housing mounting bolts to 29–39 ft. lbs., on the Celica and Supra; 43 ft. lb. on the Corolla and Camry, and the tie-rod set nuts to 37–50 ft. lbs. on the Celica and Supra; 36 ft. lb. on the Corolla and Camry. *Use a new cotter pin.* On Supras, install the intermediate shaft column side first, then rack side. On power steering-equipped cars, bleed the power steering system and check for fluid leaks. Adjust toe-in on all models.

Tercel and Starlet

1. Jack up the vehicle and support it with jack stands.

2. Remove both front wheels.

3. Remove the intermediate shaft from the worm gear shaft.

4. Remove both tie-rod ends.

5. Remove the lower suspension crossmember.

6. Remove the rack housing bracket mounting bolts and brackets.

NOTE: Be careful not to damage the rubber boots.

7. Remove the steering linkage.

8. Installation is the reverse of removal.

Van

1. Raise and support the front and on jackstands.

2. Remove the steering shaft coupling bolt. Disconnect the fluid lines.

3. Remove the Pitman arm nut; loosen the drag link set nut.

4. Using a puller, remove the Pitman arm.

5. Unbolt and remove the gear housing.

6. Installation is the reverse of removal. Torque the gear housing bolts to 70 ft. lb.; the Pitman arm nut to 90 ft. lb. and the coupling bolt to 18 ft. lb.

ADJUSTMENTS

Adjustments to the manual steering gear are not necessary during normal service. Adjustments are performed only as part of overhaul.

Power Steering Pump

REMOVAL & INSTALLATION

1. Remove the fan shroud.
2. Unfasten the nut from the center of the pump pulley.

NOTE: Use the drive belt as a brake to keep the pulley from rotating.

3. Withdraw the drive belt.
4. Remove the pulley and the Woodruff key from the pump shaft.
5. Detach the intake and outlet hoses from the pump reservoir.

NOTE: Tie the hose ends up high so the fluid cannot flow out of them. Drain or plug the pump to prevent fluid leakage.

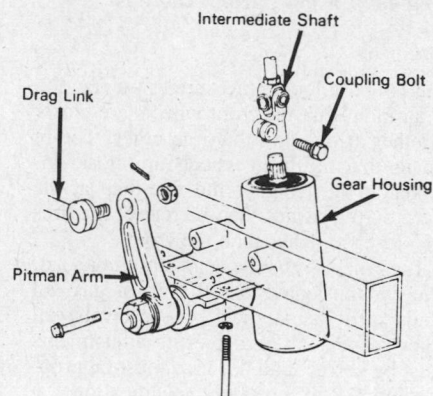

Van steering gear

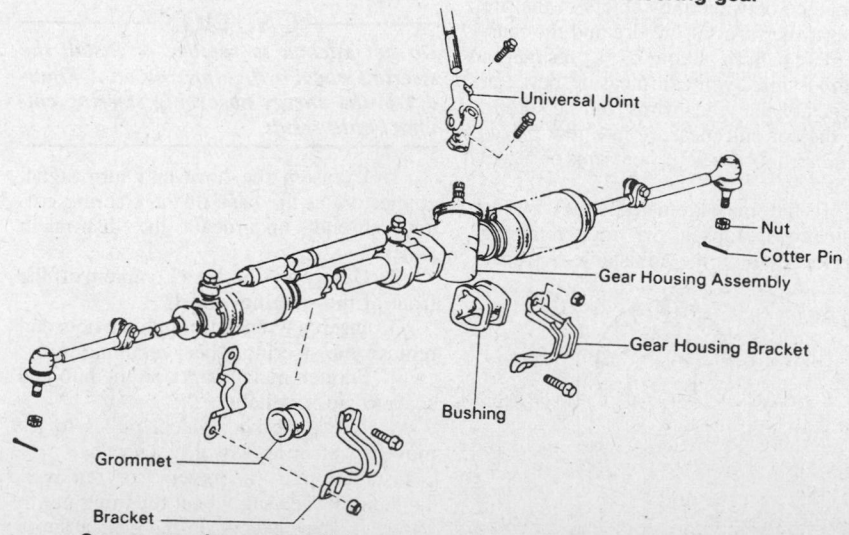

Camry steering gear. Other rack-and-pinion systems mount similarly

8. Center the wheel at the midpoint of its travel. Stop the engine.

9. The fluid level should not have risen more than 0.2 in. If it does, repeat Step 7.

10. Check for fluid leakage.

Tie Rod

REMOVAL & INSTALLATION

1. Scribe alignment marks on the tie rod and rack end (rack and pinion cars only).

2. Working at the steering knuckle arm, pull out the cotter pin and then remove the castellated nut.

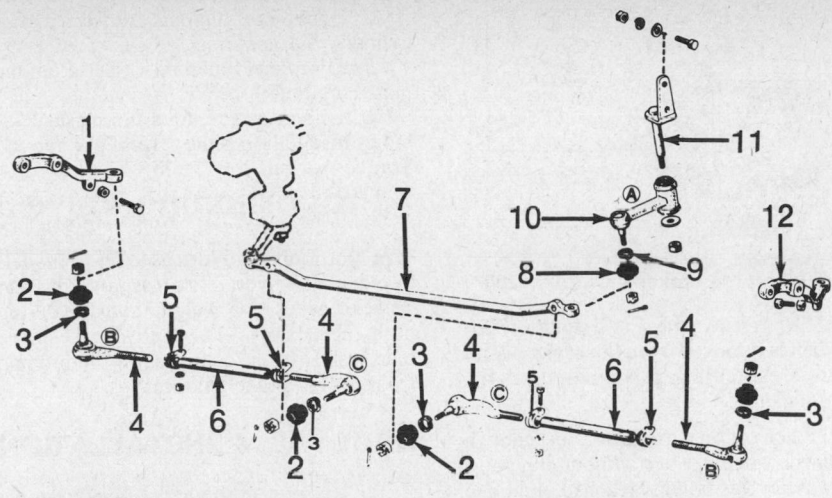

1. Steering knuckle arm—right-hand
2. Dust seal
3. Clip
4. Tie rod end
5. Tie rod end clamp
6. Tie rod adjusting tube
7. Steering relay rod
8. Dust seal
9. Lock ring
10. Steering idler arm
11. Idler arm support
12. Steering knuckle arm—left-hand

(a)—Idler arm assembly
(b)—Tie rod end assembly
(c)—Tie rod adjusting tube

Steering linkage components—except those models with rack-and-pinion steering

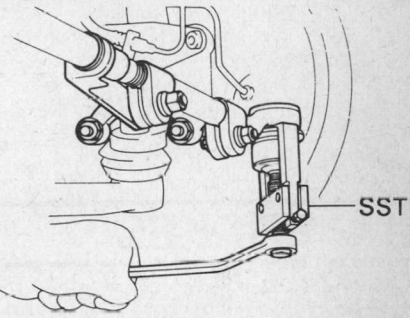

Typical tie rod end removal

6. Remove the bolt from the rear mounting brace.

7. Remove the front bracket bolts and withdraw the pump.

Installation is performed in the reverse order of removal. Note the following, however:

1. Tighten the pump pulley mounting bolt to 25–39 ft. lbs.

2. Adjust the pump drive belt tension. The belt should deflect 0.13–0.93 in. under thumb pressure applied midway between the air pump and the power steering pump.

3. Fill the reservoir with Dexron® automatic transmission fluid. Bleed the air from the system.

BLEEDING

1. Raise the front of the car and support it securely with jack stands.

2. Fill the pump reservoir with Dextron® automatic transmission fluid.

3. Rotate the steering wheel from lock to lock several times. Add fluid as necessary.

4. With the steering wheel turned fully to one lock, crank the starter while watching the fluid level in the reservoir.

NOTE: Do not start the engine. Operate the starter with a remote starter switch or have an assistant do it from inside of the car. Do not run the starter for prolonged periods.

5. Repeat Step 4 with the steering wheel turned to the opposite lock.

6. Start the engine. With the engine idling, turn the steering wheel from lock to lock two or three times.

7. Lower the front of the car and repeat Step 6.

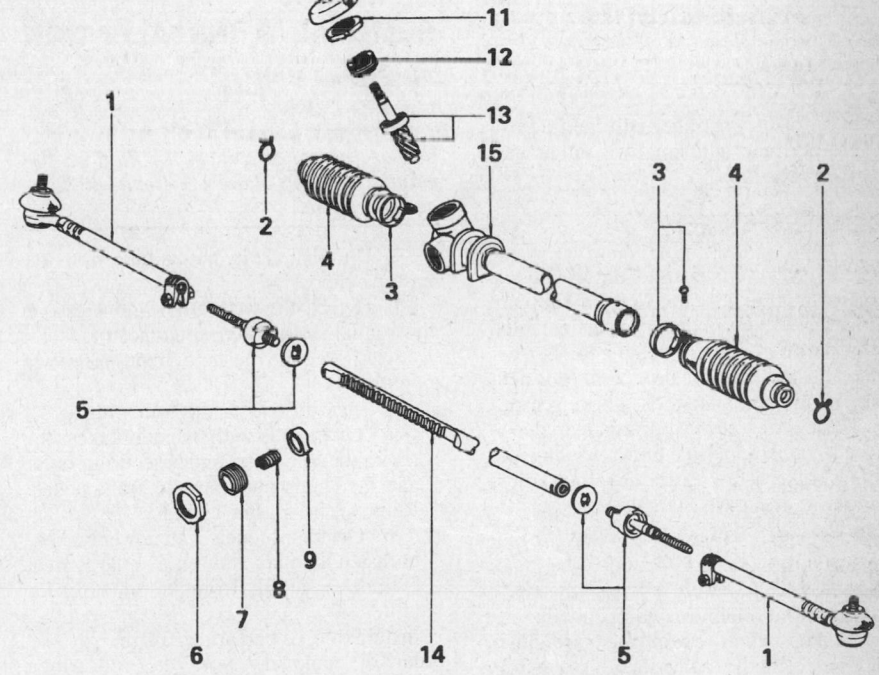

1. Tie rod end
2. Clip
3. Clamp
4. Rack boot
5. Rack end & claw washer
6. Lock nut
7. Rack guide spring cap
8. Spring
9. Rack guide
10. Dust cover
11. Lock nut
12. Pinion bearing adjusting screw
13. Pinion & Bearing
14. Rack
15. Rack housing

Tercel rack-and-pinion steering gear. Other rack-and-pinion models similar

3. Using a tie rod end puller, disconnect the tie rod from the steering knuckle arm.

4. Repeat the first two steps on the other end of the tie rod (where it attaches to the relay rod).

To install (non-rack and pinion cars):

1. Turn the tie rods in their adjusting tubes until they are of equal lengths.

2. Turn the tie rods so that they cross at 90°. Tighten the adjusting tube clamps so that they lock the ends in position.

3. Connect the tie rods and tighten the nuts to 37–50 ft. lbs.

4. Check the toe. Adjust if necessary.

Rack and pinion cars:

1. Align the alignment marks on the tie-rod and rack end.

2. Install the tie rod end.

3. Tighten the nuts to 11–14 ft. lbs. on 1978–83 models; 19 ft. lb. on 1984 and later models.

BRAKES

For all brake system repair and service procedures not detailed below, please refer to "Brakes" in the Unit Repair section.

Adjustments

DISC BRAKES

All disc brakes are inherently self-adjusting. No periodic adjustment is either necessary or possible.

DRUM BRAKES

The rear drum brakes used on all models in this manual except the Corolla 1200 are equipped with automatic adjusters actuated by the parking brake mechanism. No periodic adjustment of the drum brakes is necessary if this mechanism is working properly. If the brake shoe to drum clearance is incorrect, and applying and releasing the parking brake a few times does not adjust it properly, the parts will have to be disassembled for repair.

Corolla 1200

Corolla 1200 models are equipped with rear drum brakes which require manual adjustment. Perform the adjustment in the following order:

1. Chock the front wheels and fully release the parking brake.

2. Raise the rear of the car and support it with jackstands.

3. Remove the adjusting hole plug from the backing plate.

4. Expand the brake shoes by turning the adjusting wheel with a starwheel adjuster or a thin-bladed screwdriver.

5. Pump the brake pedal several times, while expanding the shoes, so that the shoe contacts the drum evenly.

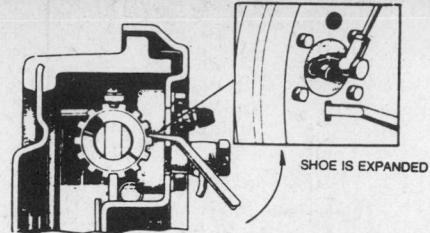

Adjusting the brakes—Corolla 1200

NOTE: If the wheel still turns when your foot is removed from the brake pedal, continue expanding the shoes until the wheel locks.

6. Back off on the adjuster, just enough so that the wheel rotates without dragging.

7. After this point is reached, continue backing off for *five* additional notches.

8. If the wheel still does not turn freely, back off one or two more notches. If after this, it still drags, check for worn or defective parts.

9. Pump the brake pedal again, and check wheel rotation.

10. Reverse Steps 1–3.

Master Cylinder

REMOVAL & INSTALLATION

All Except Van

— CAUTION —

Be careful not to spill brake fluid on the painted surfaces of the vehicle; it will damage the paint.

1. Unfasten the hydraulic lines from the master cylinder.

2. Detach the hydraulic fluid pressure differential switch wiring connectors.

3. Loosen the master cylinder reservoir mounting bolt.

4. Then do one of the following:

a. On models with manual brakes, remove the master cylinder securing bolts and the clevis pin from the brake pedal. Remove the master cylinder.

b. On other models with power brakes, unfasten the nuts and remove the master cylinder assembly from the power brake unit.

Installation is performed in the reverse order of removal. Note the following, however:

1. Before tightening the master cylinder mounting nuts or bolts, screw the hydraulic line into the cylinder body a few turns.

2. After installation is completed, bleed the master cylinder and the brake system.

Van

1. Disconnect the negative battery cable.

2. Remove the instrument cluster face panel, cluster and lower cluster panel.

3. Remove the defroster ducts.

4. Syphon off the fluid from the master cylinder with a syringe.

5. Disconnect the brake lines from the master cylinder.

6. Unbolt and remove the master cylinder. Installation is the reverse of removal. Torque the nuts to 9 ft. lb.

Proportioning Valve

A proportioning valve is used on all models to reduce the hydraulic pressure to the rear brakes because of weight transfer during high speed stops. This helps to keep the rear brakes from locking up by improving front to rear brake balance.

REMOVAL & INSTALLATION

1. Disconnect the brake lines from the valve unions.

2. Remove the valve mounting bolt, if used, and remove the valve.

NOTE: If the proportioning valve is defective, it must be replaced as an assembly; it cannot be rebuilt.

3. Installation is the reverse of removal. Bleed the brake system after it is completed.

Front Wheel Bearings

NOTE: For information concerning rear wheel bearings/adjustment on 1982 and later Supra and 1983 and later Celica GTS models, refer to the "Axle Shaft Removal and Installation" procedure for that model.

REMOVAL & INSTALLATION

Rear Wheel Drive

1. Remove the disc/hub assembly, as detailed above.

2. If either the disc or the entire hub assembly is to be replaced, unbolt the hub from the disc.

NOTE: If only the bearings are to be replaced, do not separate the disc and hub.

3. Using a brass rod as a drift, tap the inner bearings cone out. Remove the oil seal and the inner bearing.

NOTE: Throw the old oil seal away.

4. Drive out the inner bearing cup.

5. Drive out the outer bearing cup.

Inspect the bearings and the hub for signs of wear or damage. Replace components, as necessary.

Installation is performed in the following order:

1. Install the inner bearing cup and then the outer bearing cup, by driving them into place.

— CAUTION —

Use care not to cock the bearing cups in the hub.

2. Pack the bearings, hub inner well and grease cap with multipurpose grease.

3. Install the inner bearing into the hub.

4. Carefully install a new oil seal with a soft drift.

5. Install the hub on the spindle. Be sure to install all of the washers and nuts which were removed.

6. Adjust the bearing preload.

7. Install the caliper assembly.

PRELOAD ADJUSTMENT

1. With the front hub/disc assembly installed, tighten the castellated nut to the torque figure specified.

2. Rotate the disc back and forth, two or three times, to allow the bearing to seat properly.

3. Loosen the castellated nut until it is only finger-tight.

4. Tighten the nut firmly, using a box wrench.

5. Measure the bearing preload with a spring scale attached to a wheel mounting stud. Check it against the specifications.

6. Install the cotter pin.

NOTE: If the hole does not align with the nut (or cap) holes, tighten the nut slightly until it does.

7. Finish installing the brake components and the wheel.

Front Wheel Drive

1. Raise and support the front end.

2. Remove the caliper and wire it out of the way.

3. Remove the bearing cap, cotter pin, locknut and nut.

4. Remove the hub, rotor and outer bearing.

PRELOAD SPECIFICATIONS

Model/Year	Initial Torque Setting (ft. lbs.)	Preload (oz.)
Tercel '80–'83	22	13–30
Corolla	19–23	11–25
Celica	19–26	11–25
Corona	19–26	12–31
Supra ①	19–23	11–24
Cressida	22	37–56
Starlet		
'81–'82	22	1–1.5
'83–'85	22	0.8–1.9

① Except 1982 and later—see text

5. Installation is the reverse of removal. Torque the caliper bolts to 65 ft. lb. and the bearing locknut to 137 ft. lb.

Measuring wheel bearing pre-load with a spring scale

Wheel Cylinders

REMOVAL & INSTALLATION

1. Plug the master cylinder inlet to prevent hydraulic fluid from leaking.

2. Remove the brake drums and shoes.

3. Working from behind the backing plate, disconnect the hydraulic line from the wheel cylinder.

4. Unfasten the screws retaining the wheel cylinder and withdraw the cylinder.

Installation is performed in the reverse order of removal. However, once the hydraulic line has been disconnected from the wheel cylinder, the union seat must be replaced. To replace the seat, proceed in the following manner:

1. Use a screw extractor with a diameter of 0.1 in. and having reverse threads, to remove the union seat from the wheel cylinder.

2. Drive in the new union seat with a 5/16 in. bar, used as a drift.

Remember to bleed the brake system after completing wheel cylinder, brake shoe and drum installation.

Parking Brake

ADJUSTMENTS

NOTE: The rear brake components should be in good condition and be properly adjusted before performing this adjustment.

NOTE: On Corolla 1200 models, the rear brake shoes must be adjusted before performing this procedure.

1. Slowly pull the parking brake lever upward, without depressing the button on the end of it, and while counting the number

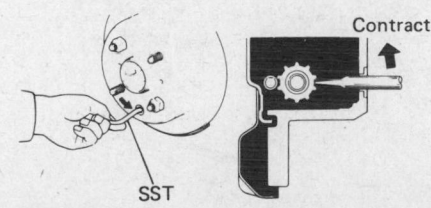

1982 and later Supra parking brake adjustment—the arrow indicates the direction for loosening the parking brake shoes

of notches required until the parking brake is applied.

NOTE: Two "clicks" are equal to one notch.

2. Check the number of notches against specifications.

3. If the brake requires adjustment, loosen the cable adjusting nut cap which is located at the rear of the parking brake lever.

NOTE: On some models, the adjustment and lock nuts are located under the vehicle, beneath the lever assembly.

4. Take up the slack in the parking brake cable by rotating the adjusting nut with another open-end wrench.

a. If the number of notches is *less* than specified, turn the nut *counterclockwise*.

b. If the number of notches is *more* than specified, turn the nut *clockwise*.

5. Tighten the adjusting cap, using care not to disturb the setting of the adjusting nut.

6. Check the rotation of the rear wheels to be sure that the brakes are not dragging.

PARKING BRAKE AdJUSTMENT

Model/Year	Range of Adjustment (notches)
Corolla 1200	4–12
Corolla 1600 ('78–'79)	4–12
Corolla 1800, Camry and Starlet	4–7
Tercel	2–5 ②
Celica ②	3–7
Corona	3–6
Corona	
Console	3–6
Pedal	4–8
Cressida, Supra ①	5–8
Van	7–9

① 1982 and later Celica/Supra: 4–7
② 1983 and later 4 × 2: 5–8
4 × 4: 6-8

PARKING BRAKE SHOE REPLACEMENT

Supra (1982 and Later) and Celica GTS (1983 and Later)

1. Raise and safely support the rear of the vehicle.

2. Remove the rear wheels.

3. Disconnect the brake line from the brake cylinder (caliper).

4. Remove the brake cylinder attaching bolts and remove the brake cylinder assembly.

5. Remove the torque plate.

6. With the parking brake lever fully

released, remove the brake disc attaching screw(s) and remove the brake disc.

NOTE: If the brake disc sticks, preventing removal, it will be necessary to back-off the self adjusters. This is done through the access hole in the brake disc as shown in the accompanying illustration.

7. Remove the brake shoe return springs. Conventional return spring removal tools may be used, though Toyota special service tool #SST 09717-20010 is recommended for this purpose.

8. Remove the brake shoe hold-down springs. Again, conventional tools may be used, but #SST 09718-00010 is recommended.

9. Remove the front brake shoe, strut, and self-adjuster assembly.

10. Disconnect the parking brake cable from the parking brake shoe lever and remove the rear parking brake shoe.

11. Inspect all parts for excessive wear and/or damage.

Note the following for inspection purposes:

Minimum brake shoe lining thickness—0.039 in.

Maximum brake disc inner diameter—6.61 in.

If out of round or scored, the parking brake surface of the disc may be machined, as long as the maximum diameter is not greater than the above specification.

12. If the shoes are to be replaced, remove the lever from the rear brake shoe by prying the C-washer apart and removing the washer. When installing the lever on the new shoe, first install the shim over the pin, then close the C-washer into the pin slot. A new C-washer should be used. Check the clearance between the shim and the lever; the clearance should not exceed 0.013 in. If the clearance is excessive, thicker shims are available through Toyota.

13. Apply a small amount of high-temperature grease to each of the backing plate contact pads.

14. Disassemble and clean the self-adjusters. During assembly of the adjusters, apply high-temperature to the parts as shown in the accompanying illustration.

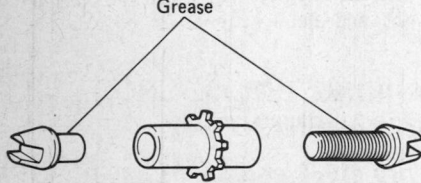

Grease

1982 and later Supra parking brake—before assembly, lubricate the adjuster parts as indicated

15. Further installation of the shoes is performed in the reverse order of the removal steps.

16. Adjust the parking brake shoe clearance as follows:

a. Temporarily install the disc assembly, with two of the lug nuts hand-tight-

ened on the studs. The lug nuts should be installed with the flat sides towards the disc.

b. Using a star wheel adjusting tool, turn the star wheel until the disc locks.

c. Return the adjuster (star wheel) 8 notches.

17. Install the torque plate, brake cylinder, and brake line. Bleed the brake system as previously outlined. Install the wheels, lower the vehicle, and adjust the parking brake lever travel as previously outlined.

CHASSIS ELECTRICAL

Heater Blower

NOTE: On some models the air conditioner, if so equipped, is integral with the heater, and therefore, heater removal may differ from the procedures detailed below.

REMOVAL & INSTALLATION

Tercel and Corolla (FWD)

1. Disconnect the negative battery terminal.

2. Remove the under tray (if so equipped).

3. Remove the blower duct and air duct.

NOTE: Before removing the air duct remember to remove the two attaching clamps.

4. Remove the glove box.

5. Remove the control cable.

6. Disconnect the electrical connector on the blower motor.

7. Remove the blower motor bolts and remove the motor.

8. Installation is the reverse of removal.

Corolla (RWD) and Starlet

1. Disconnect the blower wiring harness.

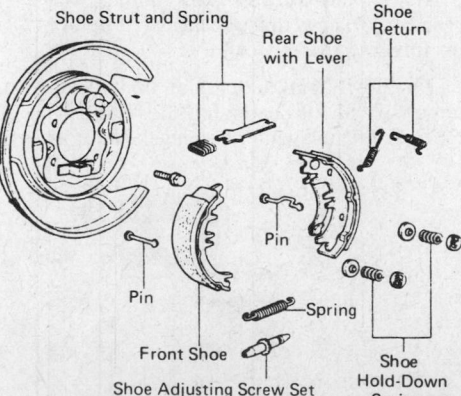

Shoe Strut and Spring
Rear Shoe with Lever
Shoe Return
Pin
Pin
Spring
Front Shoe
Shoe Adjusting Screw Set
Shoe Hold-Down Spring

Exploded view of the 1982 and later Supra rear parking brake

2. Remove the right-hand defroster hose.

3. Remove the three screws which secure the blower motor and lift out the motor.

4. Separate the fan from the motor. Installation is the reverse of removal.

Celica, Supra, Camry and Cressida

1. Working from under the instrument panel, unfasten the defroster hoses from the heater box.

2. Unplug the multiconnector.

3. Loosen the mounting screws and withdraw the blower assembly.

4. Installation is the reverse of removal.

Corona

1. Remove the package tray.

2. Remove the trim panel.

3. Disconnect the heater blower motor wiring harness.

4. Loosen the three screws which secure the motor to the housing and remove the motor/blower assembly.

5. Installation is the reverse of removal.

Heater Core

REMOVAL & INSTALLATION

Tercel and Corolla (FWD)

1. Disconnect the negative battery terminal.

2. Drain the radiator.

3. Remove the ash tray and retainer.

4. Remove the rear heater duct (optional).

5. Remove the left and right side defroster ducts.

6. Remove the under tray (optional).

7. Remove the glove box.

8. Remove the main air duct.

9. Disconnect the radio and remove it.

10. Disconnect the heater control cables and remove them.

11. Disconnect the heater hoses.

12. Remove the front and rear air ducts.

13. Remove the electrical connector.

14. Remove the heater bolts and remove the heater.

NOTE: Slide the heater to the right side of car to remove it.

15. Remove the heater core.

16. Installation is the reverse of removal.

Corolla (RWD) and Starlet

1. Disconnect the negative battery cable and drain the cooling system.

2. Disconnect the heater hose from the engine compartment side.

3. Remove the knobs from the heater and fan controls.

4. Remove the two securing screws, and take the heater control panel off.

5. Remove the heater control, complete with cables.

6. Disconnect the wiring harness.

7. Remove the three heater assembly securing bolts and remove the assembly.

8. Separate the core from the heater assembly.

9. Installation is the reverse of removal.

Celica, Supra, Camry and Cressida

1. Drain the cooling system.

2. Remove the console, if so equipped, by removing the shift knob (manual), wiring connector, and console attaching screws.

3. Remove the carpeting from the tunnel.

4. If necessary, remove the cigarette lighter and ash tray.

5. Remove the package tray, if it makes access to the heater core difficult.

6. Remove the securing screws and remove the center air outlet on the Mark II/6.

7. Remove the bottom cover/intake assembly screws and withdraw the assembly.

8. Remove the cover from the water valve.

9. Remove the water valve.

10. Remove the hose clamps and remove the hoses from the core.

11. Remove the core.

12. Installation is the reverse of removal.

Corona

1. Disconnect the negative battery cable.

2. Drain the cooling system.

3. Disconnect the heater hoses from the engine.

4. Remove the center console, if so equipped.

5. Remove the package tray and disconnect the heater air duct.

6. Unfasten the screws and take the glove compartment out of the dash.

7. Working through the glove compartment opening, remove the rear duct.

8. Detach the ventilation duct.

9. Remove the instrument cluster, as detailed below.

10. Remove the radio, if installed.

11. Remove the heater control assembly.

12. Take the defroster duct assembly out.

13. Tilt the heater assembly to the right and withdraw it from the package tray side.

14. Remove the water valve and outlet hose from the heater assembly.

15. Take off the retaining band and remove the bolt.

16. Take out the core.

17. Installation is the reverse of removal.

Radio

───────── CAUTION ─────────

Never operate the radio without a speaker; severe damage to the output transistors will result. If the speaker must be replaced, use a speaker of the correct im-

pedance (ohms) or else the output transistors will be damaged and require replacement.

REMOVAL & INSTALLATION

Celica, Supra, Camry and Cressida

1. Remove the knobs from the radio.

2. Remove the nuts from the radio control shafts.

3. Detach the antenna lead from the jack on the radio case.

4. Remove the cowl air intake duct.

5. Detach the power and speaker leads.

6. Remove the radio support nuts and bolts.

7. Remove the radio from beneath the dashboard.

8. Remove the nuts which secure the speaker through the service hole in the top of the glove box.

9. Remove remainder of the speaker securing nuts from above the radio mounting location.

10. Remove the speaker.

11. Installation is the reverse of removal.

Corolla Tercel and Starlet

1. Remove the two screws from the top of the dashboard center trim panel.

2. Lift the center panel out far enough to gain access to the cigarette lighter wiring and disconnect the wiring. Remove the trim panel.

3. Unfasten the screws which secure the radio to the instrument panel braces.

4. Lift out the radio and disconnect the leads from it. Remove the radio.

5. Installation is the reverse of removal.

Corona
INSTRUMENT PANEL–MOUNTED

1. Remove the two screws securing the instrument cluster surround and remove the surround.

2. Remove the knobs from the heater controls and remove the heater control face.

3. Remove the four screws which secure the center trim panel (two are behind the heater control opening).

4. Remove the radio knobs and remove the center trim panel.

5. Remove the four screws which secure the radio bracket.

6. Pull the radio far enough out to remove the antenna, power, and speaker leads.

7. Remove the radio.

8. Installation is the reverse of removal.

CONSOLE–MOUNTED

1. Remove the screws which secure the console and remove the console, by lowering the armrest rearward and lifting up on the center of the console.

2. Unplug the radio and disconnect the antenna lead.

3. Remove the radio knobs.

4. Remove the radio bracket and then remove the radio.

5. Installation is the reverse of removal.

Windshield Wiper Motor

REMOVAL & INSTALLATION

Tercel and Corolla (FWD)

1. Disconnect the negative battery terminal.

2. Insert a small prybar between the linkage and the motor.

3. Pry up to separate the linkage from the motor.

4. Disconnect the electrical connector from the motor.

5. Remove the mounting bolts and remove the motor.

6. Installation is the reverse of removal.

Corolla (RWD), Corona, and Starlet

1. Disconnect the wiper motor connector.

2. Remove the service cover and loosen the wiper motor bolts.

3. Use a small prybar to separate the wiper link-to-motor connection.

───────── CAUTION ─────────

Be careful not to bend the linkage.

4. Withdraw the wiper motor assembly.

5. Installation is the reverse of removal.

Celica, Supra, Camry and Cressida

1. Remove the access hole cover.

2. Separate the wiper and motor by prying gently with a small prybar.

3. Remove the left and right cowl ventilators.

4. Remove the wiper arms and the linkage mounting nuts. Push the linkage pivot ports into the ventilators.

5. Loosen the wiper link connectors at their ends and with the linkage from the cowl ventilator.

6. Start the wiper motor and turn the ignition key off when the crank is at the position illustrated.

NOTE: The wiper motor is difficult to remove when it is in the parked position. If the motor is turned off at the wiper switch, it will automatically return to this position.

7. Unplug the connector.

8. Loosen the motor bolts and withdraw the motor.

9. Installation is the reverse of removal. Be sure to install the wiper motor with it in the park position by connecting the multiconnector and operating the wiper control switch. Assemble the crank.

Instrument Cluster

For further information on the instruments, please refer to "Gauges and Indicators" in the Unit Repair section.

REMOVAL & INSTALLATION

Corolla (RWD) and Starlet

1. Disconnect the negative battery cable.
2. Remove the instrument cluster surround.
3. Remove the center trim panel. Disconnect the cigarette lighter wiring before completely removing the panel.
4. Remove the speedometer cable and disconnect it.
5. Pull the instrument cluster out just far enough so that its wiring harness may be disconnected.
6. Remove the cluster.
7. Installation is the reverse of removal.

Corona

1. Disconnect the negative (−) battery cable.
2. Remove the two instrument cluster surround.
3. Remove the side air outlet control knob and the clock setting knob.
4. Lift off the panel.
5. Unfasten the five screws which secure the cluster to the instrument panel support.
6. Disconnect the speedometer cable and the instrument cluster wiring harness.
7. Lift out the cluster assembly.
8. Installation is the reverse of removal.

Cressida

1. Disconnect the battery.

2. Detach the heater control cables at the heater box.
3. Loosen the steering column clamping nuts and lower the column.

—————— CAUTION ——————

Be careful when handling the column; it is the collapsible type. Cover the column shroud with a cloth to protect it.

———————————————————

4. Loosen the instrument panel screws and tilt the panel forward.
5. Detach the speedometer cable and wiring connectors. Remove the entire panel assembly.
6. Remove the instruments from the panel as required.
7. Installation is the reverse of removal.

Tercel and Corolla (FWD)

1. Disconnect the negative battery terminal.
2. Remove the steering column cover.

NOTE: Be careful not to damage the collapsible steering column mechanism.

3. Remove the screws from the instrument panel.
4. Gently pull the panel out approximately half way.
5. Disconnect the speedometer and any other electrical connections that are necessary.
6. Remove the panel at this time.
7. Installation is the reverse of removal.

Camry, Celica and Supra

1. Disconnect the negative battery cable at the battery.
2. Remove the fuse box cover from under the left side of the instrument panel.
3. Remove the heater control knobs.
4. Using a screwdriver, carefully pry off the heater control panel.

5. Unscrew the cluster finish panel retaining screws and pull out the bottom of the panel.
6. Unplug the two electrical connectors and unhook the speedometer cable.
7. Remove the instrument cluster.
8. Installation is performed in the reverse of the previous steps.

Fuses and Fusible Links

Except Celica, Supra and Van

The fuse box is located on the left-hand side, underneath the dashboard, on all models. All models are equipped with fusible links on the battery cables running from the positive (+) battery terminal.

Van

The fuse box is located on the right side of the dash, behind the glove box.

Celica and Supra
1978–79

The fuse block is located behind a panel on the far left side of the instrument panel. The cover panel is next to the steering column and below the warning light display.

1980–81

These models have two fuse blocks; one is located behind a panel in the dash (same as 1978–79), while the other can be found on the left front fender apron.

1982–85

A single fuse block unit is located under the hood (driver's side) on these models.

Volkswagen
Dasher, Jetta, Rabbit, Quantum, Scirocco

SERIAL NUMBER IDENTIFICATION

Vehicle Identification Plate

On the Rabbit, Jetta, Scirocco and Quantum, the vehicle identification plate is on top of the body crossmember above the grille. The same plate on the Dasher is riveted to the inner right fender. The date of manufacture and the chassis number are stamped on the plate.

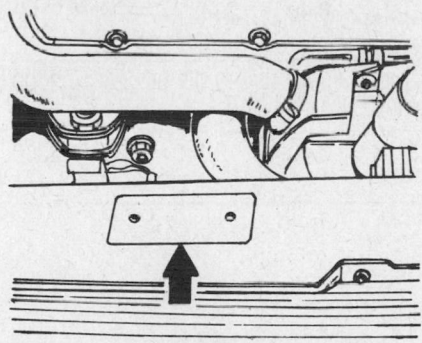

Identification plate

Chassis/VIN Number

The chassis number plate is located on the driver's side windshield pillar on the Scirocco and Dasher, and on the left front corner of the dashboard on the Rabbit, Jetta and Quantum (visible through the wind-

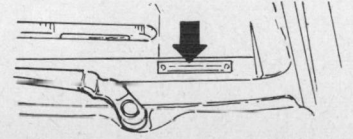

Rabbit, Jetta, Quantum chassis number

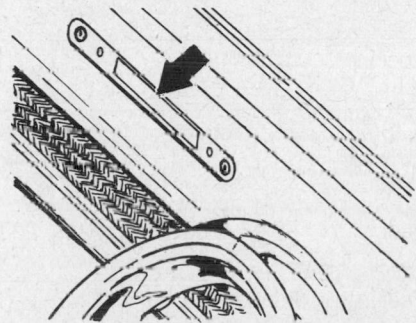

Dasher and Scirocco chassis number

shield). The Dasher and Quantum chassis numbers are also stamped on the firewall over the windshield washer reservoir. The Rabbit, Jetta and Scirocco chassis number is also found on top of the right front suspension strut pillar. It also appears on the vehicle identification plate.

1981 and later models use a seventeen digit code. On seventeen digit codes, the fifth position indicates engine and the tenth, the year. The year code will be a letter. "B"—1981; "C"—1982; etc.

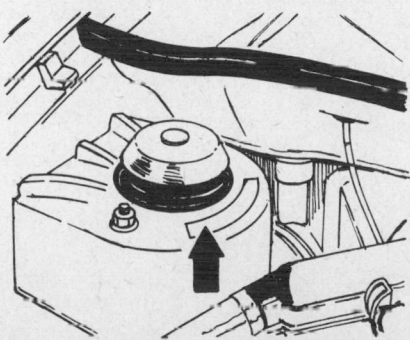

Rabbit, Jetta chassis number

Engine Number

The engine number is stamped on a flat boss on the left side (front on the Rabbit, Jetta,

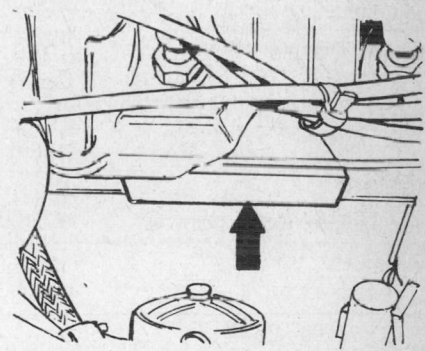

Engine number location

Scirocco and Quantum) of the engine block, just below the cylinder head between the fuel pump and distributor.

Vehicle Identification Label

This label is located in the luggage compartment beside the spare wheel on the Rabbit, Jetta and Scirocco, under the floor covering on the Quantum, and on the left side of the cross panel behind the rear bench seat on the Rabbit Convertible. The label is marked with the Vehicle Identification Number, Vehicle Code, Engine and Transmission Code, Paint and Interior code (needed for matching paint colors) and Option codes.

GENERAL ENGINE SPECIFICATIONS

Year/Model	Engine Displacement cu. in. (cc)	Fuel Delivery	Horsepower @ rpm	Torque @ rpm ft. lbs.	Bore × Stroke (in.)	Compression Ratio	Oil Pressure @ rpm (psi)
'78–'80 Rabbit (Diesel)	89.7 (1471)	Fuel inj.	48 @ 5000	56.5 @ 3000	3.01 × 3.15	23.5:1	27 @ 2000
'78–'80 Dasher	97.0 (1588)	Fuel inj.	78 @ 5500①	84 @ 3200②	3.13 × 3.15	8.0:1	28 @ 2000
'79–'80 Dasher (Diesel)	89.7 (1471)	Fuel inj.	48 @ 5000	56.5 @ 3000	3.01 × 3.15	23.5:1	28 @ 2000
'78–'80 Rabbit	88.9 (1457)	Fuel⑤ inj.	71 @ 5800③	73 @ 3500④	3.13 × 2.89	8.0:1	28 @ 2000
'80–'81 Jetta	97.0 (1588)	Fuel inj.	78 @ 5500	84 @ 3200	3.13 × 3.15	8.0:1	28 @ 2000
'78 Scirocco	88.9 (1457)	Fuel inj.	73 @ 5800	73 @ 3500④	3.13 × 2.89	8.0:1	28 @ 2000
'79–'80 Scirocco	97.0 (1588)	Fuel inj.	78 @ 5500①	84 @ 3200②	3.13 × 3.15	8.0:1	28 @ 2000
'81 Jetta, Scirocco, Rabbit	105.0 (1715)	Fuel inj.	74 @ 5000⑥	90 @ 3000⑦	3.13 × 3.40	8.2:1	28 @ 2000
'81 Dasher Rabbit (Diesel)	97.0 (1588)	Fuel inj.	52 @ 4800	72 @ 3000	3.01 × 3.40	23.0:1	28 @ 2000
'82–'85 Jetta, Rabbit, Scirocco, Quantum	105.0 (1715)	CIS⑤ Fuel inj.	74 @ 5000⑥	90 @ 3000⑦	3.13 × 3.40	8.2:1	28 @ 2000
'82–'85 Diesels	97.0 (1588)	Fuel inj.	52 @ 4800	72 @ 2000	3.01 × 3.40	23.0:1	28 @ 2000
'83–'85 Turbo-diesel	97.0 (1588)	Fuel inj.	68 @ 4500	98 @ 2800	3.01 × 3.40	23.0:1	⑧
'83–'85 GTI, GLI, Scirocco, Conv. ⑨	109.0 (1780)	CIS Fuel inj.	90 @ 5500	100 @ 3000	3.19 × 3.40	8.5:1	28 @ 2000
'83–'85 Quantum	130.8 (2144)	CIS Fuel inj.	100 @ 5100	112 @ 3000	3.12 × 3.40	8.2:1	28 @ 2000

① 76 @ 5000—Calif.
② 83 @ 3200—Calif.
③ 70 @ 5800—Calif.
④ 72 @ 3500—Calif.
⑤ Some '78, '80 and '82 and later Rabbits
   are equipped with a 1 bbl. carburetor; '82
   and later w/oxygen sensor
⑥ Canada: 76 hp
⑦ Canada: 92 ft. lbs.
⑧ 7 psi @ idle; 74 psi @ 5000 rpm
⑨ 1.8 liter engine

DIESEL TUNE-UP SPECIFICATIONS

Model	Valve Clearance (cold) ①		Intake Valve Opens (deg)	Injection Pump Setting (deg)	Injection Nozzle Pressure (psi)		Idle Speed (rpm)	Cranking Compression Pressure (psi)
	Intake (in.)	Exhaust (in.)			New	Used		
Diesel (All models)	0.008–0.012	0.016–0.020	N.A.	Align marks	1885③	1706③	800–850② ④	406 minimum

N.A. Not Available

① Warm clearance given—Cold clearance:
   Intake   0.006–0.010
   Exhaust   0.014–0.018
② Volkswagen has lowered the idle speed on
   early models to this specification.
Valve clearance need not be adjusted unless
il varies more than 0.002 in. from
specification.
③ Turbo diesel: New–2306; Used–2139
④ Turbo diesel: 900–1000

GASOLINE ENGINE TUNE-UP SPECIFICATIONS

Year Model	Spark Plugs		Distributor		Ignition Timing (deg)	Intake Valve Opens (deg)	Compression Pressure (psi)	Idle Speed (rpm)	Valve Clearance (In.)	
	Type	Gap (in.)	Point Dwell (deg)	Point Gap (in.)					In⑤	Ex⑤
'78–'79 Dasher	W215 T30 N7Y	0.024–0.028	44–50	0.016	3 ATDC @ Idle	4 BTDC	142–184	850–1000	0.008–0.012	0.016–0.020
'78 Rabbit, Scirocco	W175 T30 N8Y	0.024–0.028	44–50	0.016	②	4 BTDC	142–184	850–1000	0.008–0.012	0.016–0.020
'79 Rabbit	W175 T30 N8Y	0.024–0.032	44–50	0.016	3 ATDC @ Idle	4 BTDC	142–184	850–1000	0.008–0.012	0.016–0.020
'79 Scirocco	W175 T30 N8Y	0.024–0.032	44–50	0.016	3 ATDC @ Idle	4 BTDC	142–184	850–1000	0.008–0.012	0.016–0.020
'80–'81 Dasher (49 states)	W175 T30 N8Y	0.024–0.032	44–50⑥	0.016⑥	3 ATDC @ Idle	4 BTDC	142–184	850–1000④	0.008–0.012	0.016–0.020
'80–'81 Dasher (California)	WR7DS N8GY	0.024–0.028	Electronic		3 ATDC @ Idle	4 BTDC	142–184	880–1000	0.008–0.012	0.016–0.020
'80–'85 Rabbit, Jetta, Scirocco, Quantum (49 states)⑧	W175 T30 N8Y	0.024–0.032	44–50⑥	0.016⑥	3 ATDC @ Idle③ ⑫	4 BTDC	142–184⑦	850–1000④	0.008–0.012	0.016–0.020
'80–'85 Rabbit, Jetta, Scirocco, Quantum (California)⑧	WR7DS N8GY	0.024–0.028	Electronic		3 ATDC @ Idle ⑫	4 BTDC	142–184⑦	880–1000	0.008–0.012	0.016–0.020
'83–'85 GTI, GLI, Scirocco⑨, Conv.⑨	WR7DS N8YGY	0.024–0.028	Electronic		6 BTDC @ Idle	—	131–174	880–1000	0.008–0.012	0.016–0.020

GASOLINE ENGINE TUNE-UP SPECIFICATIONS

| Year Model | Spark Plugs | | Distributor | | Ignition Timing (deg) | Intake Valve Opens (deg) | Compression Pressure (psi) | Idle Speed (rpm) | Valve Clearance (in.) | |
	Type	Gap (in.)	Point Dwell (deg)	Point Gap (in.)					In ⑤	Ex ⑤
'83–'85 Quantum ⑩	W7D N8Y ⑬	0.024– 0.028	Electronic		6 BTDC @ Idle⑪	6 BTDC	142– 184	850– 1000	0.008– 0.012	0.016– 0.020

NOTE: The underhood specifications sticker often reflects tune-up specification changes made in production. Sticker figures must be used if they disagree with those in this chart.

① 47°–53° California

② 3 ATDC @ Idle with CIS fuel injection: 7½ BTDC @ Idle with 34 PICT-5 Carburetor

③ Non-California Rabbit w/1 barrel carburetor; timing 7½ BTDC @ Idle

④ W/o Idle stabilizer

⑤ Valve clearance need not be adjusted unless it varies more than 0.002 in. from specifications.

⑥ 1981 and later have electronic ignition

⑦ '82 and later compression pressure 131– 174 psi.

⑧ Except 1.8 and 5 cylinder engines

⑨ 1.8 liter engine

⑩ 5 cylinder

⑪ 1983: M/T: 6° BTDC; A/T: 3° ATDC

⑫ 1984 and later: M/T: 6° BTDC; A/T: 3° ATDC

⑬ California: WR7DS: N8GY

FIRING ORDERS

NOTE: To avoid confusion, always replace spark plug wires one at a time.

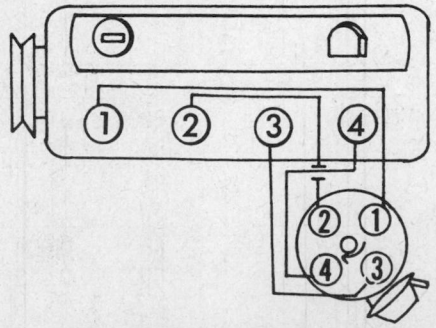

Firing order: 4 cylinder engines; 1–3–4–2

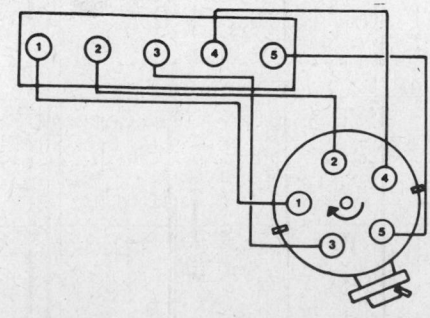

Firing order: 5 cylinder engine: 1–2–4–5–3

CAPACITIES

Year	Model	Engine Crankcase (qts) With Filter	Engine Crankcase (qts) Without Filter	ansmission (pts) Manual	ansmission (pts) Automatic	Drive Axle (pts)	Gasoline Tank (gals)	Cooling stem (pts)
'78–'80	Dasher	3.2	2.6	3.4	12.4②	1.6	12.1	12.6
'78–'80	Rabbit (Diesel)	3.7	3.2	2.6	—	1.6	10.9	12.6
'78–'80	Rabbit	3.7	3.2	2.6②	12.8①	1.6	10.6	9.8
'78	Scirocco	3.7	3.2	3.2②	12.8①	1.6	10.6	9.8
'79–'80	Scirocco	3.7	3.2	3.2②	12.8①	1.6	10.6	9.8
	Dasher (Diesel)	3.7	3.2	3.2②	—	1.6	11.9	9.8
'80	Jetta	3.7	3.2	3.2②	12.8①	1.6	10.5	10.2
'81	Scirocco, Rabbit, Jetta	4.5	4.0	3.2②	12.8①	1.6	10.0③	9.8
'81	Dasher, Rabbit Jetta (Diesel)	3.7	3.2	3.2②	—	1.6	10.0③	14.3④
'82–'85	Rabbit, Jetta, Scirocco, Quantum	4.7	4.2	3.2②	12.8①	1.6	⑤	14.3⑥
	Rabbit, Jetta Quantum (Diesel)	3.7	3.2	3.2②	12.8①	1.6	⑤	14.3

—Not applicable
① Dry refill; normal refill is 6.4 pts
② 5-speed—4.2
③ Dasher: 12.0
④ Dasher: 12.2
⑤ 10.0 Rabbit; 10.6 Jetta, Convertible, Scirocco; 15.8 Quantum
⑥ Except 1.8 and 5 cylinder engine; 1.8 engine: 13.8; 5 cylinder: 14.3.

TORQUE SPECIFICATIONS
(All readings in ft. lbs.)

Year/Model	Cylinder Head Bolts	Rod Bearing Bolts④	Main Bearing Bolts	Crankshaft Pulley Bolt	Flywheel To Crankshaft Bolts	Manifold Intake	Manifold Exhaust
'78–'81 Dasher	65①	33	47	58	54	18	18
'78–'85 Rabbit, Scirocco, Jetta, Quantum	③	33⑥	47	58⑦	54②	18	18

TORQUE SPECIFICATIONS
(All readings in ft. lbs.)

Year/Model	Cylinder Head Bolts	Rod Bearing Bolts④	Main Bearing Bolts	Crankshaft Pulley Bolt	Flywheel To Crankshaft Bolts	Manifold	
						Intake	Exhaust
'78–'85 Diesel Rabbit, Dasher, Jetta, Quantum	⑤	33⑧	47	56⑦	54②	18	18

①Torque in 5 steps:
  1st step - 36 ft/lbs.
  2nd step - 51 ft/lbs.
  3rd step - 65 ft/lbs.
  4th step - run engine until fan starts to run.
  5th step - retorque to 65 ft/lbs.
  After 1,000 miles, head bolts must be loosen 30° and retorqued to 65 ft/lbs.
②Pressure plate to crankshaft bolts
③With 12 point (polygon) head bolts
Torque in 4 steps:
  1st step - 29 ft/lbs.
  2nd step - 43 ft/lbs.
  3rd step - additional ½ turn (180°) further in one movement (two 90° turns are permissible)
  Note tightening sequence
  Do not retorque at 1,000 miles

With 6 point (hex) head bolts
  Torque in steps to 54 ft/lbs. with engine cold, when engine is warmed up, torque to 61 ft/lbs.
  Head bolts must be retorqued after 1,000 miles.

④Always use new bolts
⑤Rabbit/Jetta/Quantum
  1979–85 **after** engine number CR700693
Torque in 6 steps
  1st step - 29 ft/lbs.
  2nd step - 43 ft/lbs.
  3rd step - additional ½ turn (180°) further in one movement (two 90° turns are permissible)
  Note tightening sequence
  4th step - run engine until oil temp is 50°C.
  5th step - tighten bolts ¼ turn more.
Head bolts must be retorqued after 1,000 miles.
1978–79 **before** engine number CR 700693
Torque in steps to 61 ft/lbs. with engine cold, when engine is warmed up, torque to 69 ft/lbs. After 1,000 miles, loosen head bolts 30° and retorque to 69 ft/lbs.
⑥5 cylinder—36 ft. lbs.
⑦'83–'85 w/14mm bolt; 145 ft. lbs. 5 cylinder—250

⑧1983–'85 Turbo diesel and 1.8L gas engines torque in two steps:
  1st step—22 ft/lbs
  2nd step—¼ turn (90°) additional

BRAKE SPECIFICATIONS
(All measurements in inches unless noted)

Year	Model	Lug Nut Torque (ft. lbs.)	Master Cylinder Bore	Brake Disc		Brake Drum			Minimum Brake Lining Thickness	
				Minimum Thickness	Maximum Run-Out	Diameter	Maximum Machine o/s	Maximum Wear Limit	Front	Rear
'78–'81	Dasher	80	0.82	0.41	0.004	7.87	7.90	7.97	0.250	0.098
'78–'85	Rabbit, Jetta, Scirocco Quantum	80	0.82	0.41	0.004	7.08①	7.10②	7.12③⑤	0.250④	0.098

*NOTE: Minimum lining thickness is as recommended by manufacturer. Due to variations in state inspection regulations, the minimum thickness may be different than that recommended by the manufacturer.
①Rabbit front brake drums—9.05–9.06 in.
②Rabbit front brake drums—9.087 in.
③Rabbit front brake drums—9.106 in.
④Rabbit front brake drums—0.039 in.
⑤7.91 in Quantum

BATTERY AND STARTER SPECIFICATIONS

(All models use 12 volt, negative ground system)

| Year | Model | Battery Amp Hour Capacity | Lock Test | | | No Load Test | | | Brush Spring Tension (oz.) | Minimum Brush Length (in.) |
			Amps	Volts	Torque (ft. lbs.)	Amps	Volts	rpm		
'78–'85	All	45/54①②	280–370	7.5	2.42	33–55	11.5	6000–8000	35.5	0.5

①With air conditioning and '81 and later
②63 Ah with diesel, and Canadian gasoline engines

CRANKSHAFT AND CONNECTING ROD SPECIFICATIONS

(All measurements are given in inches)

| Year/Model | Crankshaft | | | | Connecting Rod | | |
	Main Brg. Journal Dia.	Main Brg. Oil Clearance	Shaft End/Play	Thrust on No.	Journal Diameter	Oil Clearance	Side Clearance (max.)
'78–'85 All 4 cyl.	2.126	0.001–0.003	0.003–0.007	3	1.811①	0.001–0.003	0.015
'83–'85 All 5 cyl.	2.2822	0.0006–0.003	0.003–0.007	4	1.811	0.0006–0.002	0.016

NOTE: Main and connecting rod bearings are available in three undersizes
①1.8L engine: 1.881

VALVE SPECIFICATIONS

| Year/Model | Seat Angle (deg) | Face Angle (deg) | Stem-to-Guide Clearance (in.) | | Stem Diameter (in.) | |
			Intake	Exhaust	Intake	Exhaust
'78–'85 All	45	45	0.039 MAX①	0.051 MAX.	0.3140	0.3130

NOTE: Exhaust valves must be ground by hand.
①Diesels: 0.051 max.

PISTON AND RING SPECIFICATIONS

(All measurements in inches)

| Year/Model | Piston Clearance | Ring Gap | | | Ring Side Clearance | | |
		Top Compression	Bottom Compression	Oil Control	Top Compression	Bottom Compression	Oil Control
'78–'85 All Gasoline Engines	0.001–0.003	0.012–②0.018	0.012–②0.018	0.010–②④0.016	0.0008–③0.002	0.0008–③0.002	0.0008–③0.002
'78–'85 All Diesel Engines	0.001–0.003	0.012–0.020	0.012–0.020	0.010–0.016	0.002–0.004	0.002–0.003	0.001–0.002

NOTE: Three piston sizes are available to accommodate over-bores up to 0.040 in.
①5 cylinder: 0.0011
②5 cylinder: 0.010–0.020
③5 cylinder: 0.0008–0.003
④1981 and later: 0.012–0.018

WHEEL ALIGNMENT

Year	Model	Caster ① Range (deg)	Caster ① Pref Setting (deg)	Camber ② Range (deg)	Camber ② Pref Setting (deg)	Toe-In ③ (in.)	Steering Axis Inclination ① (deg)
All	Dasher	0–1	½	0–1	½	³⁄₃₂	10½
All	Rabbit, Scirocco Jetta	1⁵⁄₁₆–2⁵⁄₁₆	1¹³⁄₁₆	−³⁄₁₆–1³⁄₁₆	⁵⁄₁₆	⅛	10½
'82–'85	Quantum	0–1	½	−1⁵⁄₃₂– −⁵⁄₃₂	−²¹⁄₃₂	⁵⁄₆₄	NA

① Not adjustable
② Rear wheel camber (not adjustable)
  Rabbit (to Ch. No. 176 3 241 690): −1⁹⁄₁₆ to −⁷⁄₁₆
  Rabbit (from Ch. No. 176 3 261 691): −1¹³⁄₁₆ to −1¹⁄₁₆
  Scirocco (all): −1¹³⁄₁₆ to −1¹¹⁄₁₆
  Dasher (all): −1⅜–0
  Quantum: −2 to −1¹¹⁄₃₂
  Jetta: −1¹³⁄₁₆ to −1¹¹⁄₁₆

③ Rear wheel toe-in (not adjustable)
  Rabbit: 0–⁵⁄₁₆
  Scirocco (to Ch. No. 536 2 031 722): ⁵⁄₃₂ to ¹¹⁄₃₂
  Scirocco (from Ch. No. 536 2 031 723): ³⁄₃₂ to ¹³⁄₃₂
  Quantum: ⁵⁄₆₄ to ²¹⁄₆₄
  Jetta: 0 to ⁵⁄₁₆

ELECTRONIC IGNITION TESTING SPECIFICATIONS ①

Component Tested	Specification
Rotor resistance ②	1000 ohm; rotor must be marked R1
Ignition Timing: CIS Carburetor Vacuum hoses during testing	3° ± 2° ATDC when checking ③ 3° ± 1° ATDC when adjusting ③ 7½° BTDC Connected (CIS) Except TYF carb: disconnect and plug retard line. TYF carb: disconnect and plug both lines.
Ignition coil primary resistance: ② Resistance between positive and negative terminals	0.52–0.76 ohms
Ignition coil secondary resistance: ② Resistance between negative terminal and coil tower	2400–3500 ohms

① All USA, California, and Canada models with electronic ignition
② See illustration
③ '83–'84 with manual trans: 6° BTDC

TUNE-UP PROCEDURES

VW recommends a tune-up, including new points and plugs, at 12,000 mile intervals for all gasoline engines. The only procedure required for diesel engines in this section is the valve lash adjustment and minimum/maximum engine speed checking and adjustment.

Spark Plugs

The firing order is 1-3-4-2, or 1,2,4,5,3 (for five cylinder models) with No. 1 cylinder at the front (right on the Rabbit, Jetta and Scirocco) of the engine.

1. Grasp the spark plug boot and pull it straight out. Don't pull on the wire. Either number the wires or remove them one at a time to avoid mix–ups.

2. Place the spark plug socket squarely on the plug and screw the spark plug out.

NOTE: The cylinder head is aluminum alloy, which is easily stripped of threads. Remove the plugs only when the engine is cold.

If removal is difficult, loosen the plug only slightly and drip penetrating oil onto the threads.

3. For the price of a set of new spark plugs, it usually isn't worth cleaning the old plugs. Purchase a new set of plugs, and set the gaps as they come out of the box(es). The recommended spark plug gap is listed in the "Tune Up Specifications" chart. Use a round wire feeler gauge to check the gap between the plug electrodes. If the gap is incorrect, gently bend the side electrode to correct. *Do not bend the center electrode.*

4. Torque the new spark plugs to 22 ft. lbs. Install the ignition wire boots firmly.

Breaker Points and Condenser

Snap off the two retaining clips on the distributor cap. Unfasten the ground strap at the suppressor leads on 1979 and 1980 distributors. Remove the cap and examine it for cracks, deterioration, or carbon tracking. Replace the cap, if necessary, by transferring one wire at a time from the old cap to the new one. Replace the rotor at every other tune-up. Remove the dust shield. Check the points for pitting and burning.

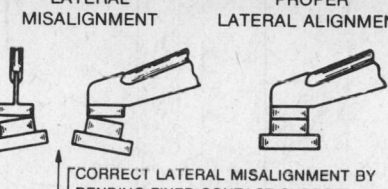

LATERAL MISALIGNMENT	PROPER LATERAL ALIGNMENT

CORRECT LATERAL MISALIGNMENT BY BENDING FIXED CONTACT SUPPORT *NEVER BEND BREAKER LEVER*

Points must be correctly aligned

Slight imperfections on the contact surface may be filed off with a point file. It is best to replace the breaker point set. Always replace the condenser when you replace the point set.

To replace the breaker points:

1. Remove the distributor cap.
2. Remove the rotor.
3. Unsnap the point connector from the terminal at the side of the distributor. Remove the retaining screw, and lift out the point set.
4. Install the new point set, making sure that the pin on the bottom engages the hole in the breaker plate.
5. Install the wire connector and the retaining screws (hand-tight).
6. Turn the engine with a wrench on the crankshaft pulley until the breaker arm rubbing block on the points set is on the high point of one of the cam lobes. Turn the engine only in the direction of normal rotation to avoid damage to the timing belt.
7. A 0.016 in. feeler gauge should just slip through the points with a slight drag. If the gap is incorrect, pivot a screwdriver in the point set notch and the two projections on the breaker plate to bring it within specifications.
8. When the gap is correct, tighten the retaining screw. Recheck the adjustment.
9. Lubricate the distributor cam with silicone grease (some points sets come with a grease capsule).
10. Install the dust cover, rotor and distributor cap.
11. Check the dwell angle and the ignition timing.
12. The condenser is mounted on the outside of the distributor. Undo the mounting screw and the terminal block to replace.

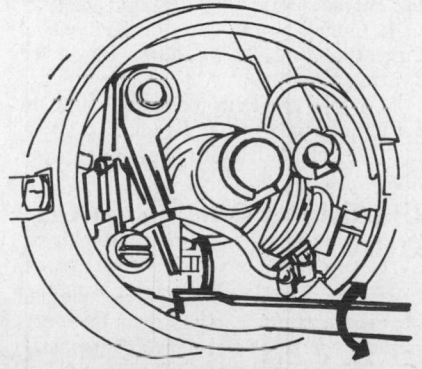

Adjusting point gap

Dwell Angle

The dwell angle or cam angle is the number of degrees that the distributor cam rotates while the points are closed. There is an inverse relationship between dwell angle and point gap. Increasing the point gap will decrease the dwell angle and vice versa. Checking the dwell angle with a meter is a far more accurate method of measuring point opening than the feeler gauge method.

After setting the point gap to specification with a feeler gauge, check the dwell angle. Attach the dwell meter. The negative lead is grounded and the positive lead is connected to the primary wire, Terminal No. 1 that runs from the coil to the distributor. Start the engine, let it idle and reach operating temperature, and observe the dwell on the meter. The reading should fall within the allowable range. If it does not, the gap will have to be reset. Dwell can also be checked with the engine cranking. In this case, dwell will vary between 0° and the dwell figure for that setting.

Electronic Ignition

The 1980–81 Dasher, Jetta and Scirocco destined for California, the 1980 Rabbit 1.6 liter (California) and 1.5 liter (49 states) and all 1981 and later Rabbits, Sciroccos, Jettas and Quantums are equipped with the Hall effect electronic ignition system.

The distributor contains the Hall Effect pick-up assembly which replaces the breaker points assembly in conventional systems.

The "Hall Effect" is a shift in magnetic field caused when one of the rotors on the distributor shaft passes the sensors mounted in the distributor. This shift performs the same function as breaker points, which is to allow the current (coil field) stored in the coil to collapse, causing a spark to run from the coil to the distributor and down to the spark plugs, which make the current jump a gap between the two spark plug electrodes, causing a spark which ignites the air/fuel mixture in the combustion chamber. Since there are no breaker points and condenser to replace, the system should be maintenance free, except for rotor replacement at regular intervals.

ELECTRONIC IGNITION PRECAUTIONS

When working on the Hall ignition, observe the following precautions to prevent damage to the ignition system.

1. Connect and disconnect test equipment only when the ignition switch is OFF.
2. On the carbureted Rabbit, if you use a conventional tachometer, you will have to rig up an adapter. See the following paragraph for instructions.
3. Do not crank the engine with the starter for compression tests, etc., until the high tension coil wire (terminal 4) is grounded.

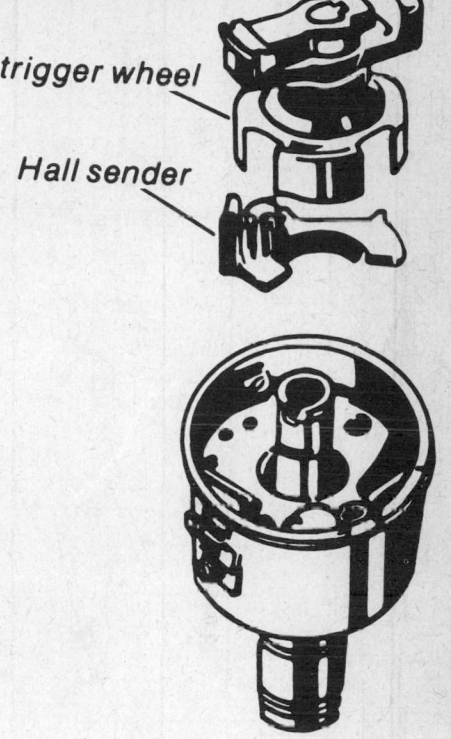

trigger wheel

Hall sender

Hall effect electronic ignition distributor

4. Do not replace the original equipment coil with a conventional coil.
5. Do not install any kind of condenser to coil terminal 1.
6. Do not use a battery booster for longer than 1 (one) minute.
7. On the fuel injected models, do not tow cars with defective ignition systems without disconnecting the plugs on the idle stabilizer at the ignition control unit.

TACHOMETER ADAPTATION (CARBURETED RABBITS)

An adapter must be used when connecting a conventional tachometer to the Hall Effect ignition system to prevent damage to the ignition components. Use the illustration as a guide. All components will be available to you locally. Connect the positive wire of the tachometer to the adapter and the negative wire to the ground.

IGNITION COIL TEST

A defective Hall ignition coil cannot be checked with standard coil testing equipment. If there is no high tension current and all other components of the ignition system check out, see if you're getting a spark from the coil wire to the distributor cap by unplugging the coil wire at the distributor, holding the end of it with insulated pliers about ½ in. from ground (engine block, etc.) and turning over the engine. If a weak or no spark is obtained, replace the coil.

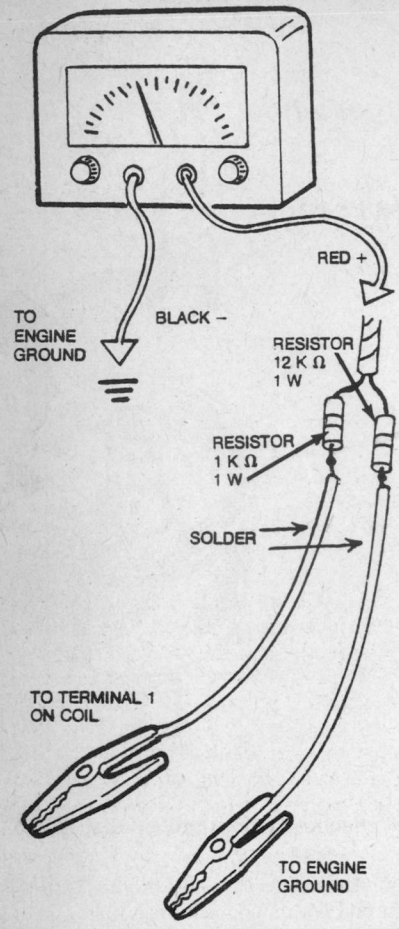

Adapter for attaching a tachometer to 1980 and later carbureted Rabbit with electronic ignition

HALL PICK-UP UNIT TEST

1. Check for voltage on terminal 15 (+) of the ignition coil. There should be voltage with the ignition ON.

2. Ground a high tension coil wire.

3. Connect a test light (4 to 24 volts) between terminal 15 (+) and terminal 1 (−).

4. Crank the engine with the starter for approximately 5 seconds. The test light should flicker. If not, replace the ignition distributor.

IGNITION CONTROL UNIT TEST

1. On fuel injected models, disconnect the plugs at the control unit and connect the plugs to each other. Ground the high tension coil wire on carbureted Rabbit.

2. Turn the ignition switch on and make sure there is current at terminal 15 (+) of the ignition coil. Turn the ignition OFF.

3. Disconnect the high tension wire between the ignition coil and the distributor at the distributor on fuel injected models.

4. Disconnect the wire (plug) between the control unit and the distributor at the distributor.

5. Connect the positive (+) terminal of the voltmeter 1 of the ignition coil and the negative (−) terminal to ground.

6. Turn the ignition ON. There must be a voltage reading of at least 12 volts. If voltage drops below 12 volts in one second, turn off the ignition. The control unit is defective and will have to be replaced.

7. Disconnect the green wire where it connects to the distributor and ground the wire. Turn the ignition switch ON. The voltmeter should read about 12 volts. Disconnect the ground wire. The voltage should drop to 6 volts. If not, replace the control unit. Turn off the ignition.

8. On fuel injected models, connect the terminals of the voltmeter to the outer connector of the control unit. Connect the positive (+) lead to the red wire and the negative (−) lead to the brown wire. Switch on the ignition. The voltmeter should read about 10 volts. If not, replace the control unit.

IDLE STABILIZER

The idle stabilizer is located on top of the ignition control unit. The idle stabilizer controls idle speed by either advancing or retarding the distributor timing in accordance with engine load (air conditioner on, lights on, etc.) If idle speed is erratic or if the engine fails to start, try bypassing the idle stabilizer by disconnecting the two plugs at the idle stabilizer and plugging them together. If idle improves, the idle stabilizer should probably be replaced.

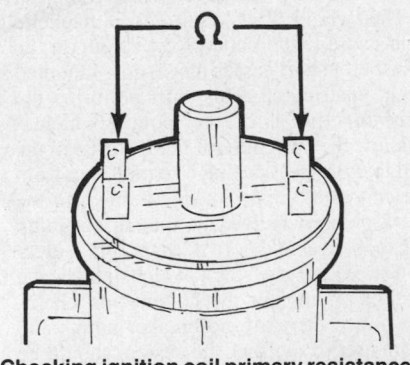

Checking ignition coil primary resistance

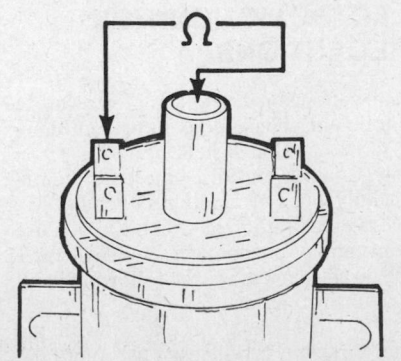

Checking ignition coil secondary resistance

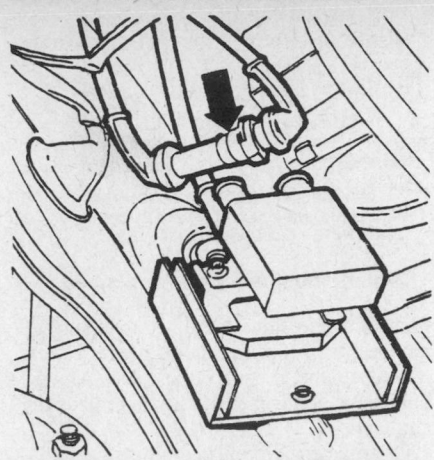

Disconnect the plugs on the idle stabilizer at the control unit and plug them together

Ignition Timing

NOTE: On 1984 and later Rabbit models with 5-speed trans. and fuel injection, the flywheel must be marked at 6° BTDC to allow the use of a standard (strobe) timing light. The 3° ATDC timing mark does not apply to these models.

The following procedure should be used to locate and mark the flywheel:

1. Unscrew the plastic plug in the timing hole. This can be found on top of the transaxle, near the engine block.

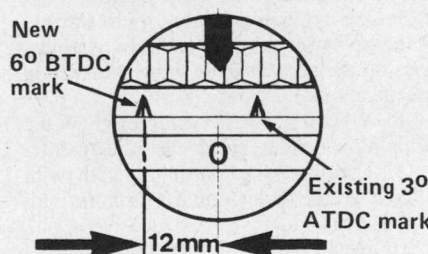

Timing mark conversion—1.7 liter Rabbit with 5-speed transmission and fuel injection

2. Turn the engine to TDC on the No. 1 cylinder.

3. Spray the flywheel in this area with blue engineering dye or the equivalent.

4. Use a compass to scribe the flywheel 12mm (0.47 in.) to the left of the "O" TDC mark.

5. Use a chisel to mark the measured spot permanently on the flywheel.

6. Check and adjust the timing, and reinstall the plastic plug.

BREAKER POINT IGNITION SYSTEMS

1. Attach the timing light as outlined above or according to the manufacturer's instructions. Hook-up a dwell/tachometer since you'll need an rpm indication for correct timing.

2. Locate the timing mark opening in the clutch or torque converter housing at the rear of the engine directly behind the distributor. The OT mark stands for TDC or 0° advance. The other mark designates the correct timing position. Mark them with chalk so that they will be more visible. Don't disconnect the vacuum line.

NOTE: Some models do not have an OT mark.

3. Start the engine and allow it to reach the normal operating temperature. The engine should be running at normal idle speed.

4. Shine the timing light at the marks.

5. The light should now be flashing when the timing mark and the V-shaped pointer are aligned.

6. If not, loosen the distributor hold-down bolt and rotate the distributor very slowly to align the marks.

7. Tighten the mounting nut when the ignition timing is correct.

8. Recheck the timing when the distributor is secured.

With ignition timing correctly adjusted, the spark plugs will fire just before the piston hits the top of the compression stroke, thus providing maximum power and economy.

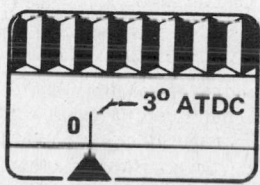

Timing mark—Quantum with A/T and Dasher. Early Dashers had two marks on the flywheel, when timing early models use the 3° mark to the right of the OT mark

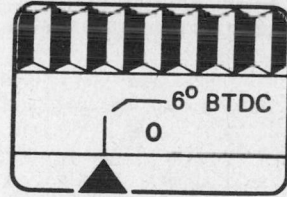

Timing mark—Quantum with M/T

ELECTRONIC IGNITION

1. Run the engine to normal operating temperature. Connect tachometer. See "Electronic Ignition Precautions," above.

2. Stop the engine. Disconnect the plugs on the idle stabilizer at the control unit and plug them together (see illustration). On the carbureted Rabbit except models with the Carter TYF feedback model, disconnect the vacuum retard hose and plug it. Disconnect and plug both vacuum lines on models with the Carter TYF carburetor.

3. Check the idle speed. It should be between 800 and 1000 rpm.

4. With your timing light attached according to manufacturer's instructions, shine the light on the timing hole. The pointer in

the hole must line up with the notch in the flywheel. To adjust the timing, loosen the distribution at its base and turn it until the timing marks line up.

5. On the carbureted Rabbit, reinstall the vacuum hoses. Idle speed should drop to 600–750 rpm.

6. Stop the engine and reconnect the plugs at the control unit. On the carbureted Rabbit, start the engine and rev it a few times to activate the idle stabilizer. On the carbureted Rabbit, the idle speed should now be 850–950 rpm.

Valve Lash

ADJUSTMENT

The overhead cam acts directly on the valves through bucket-type cam followers which fit over the springs and valves. Adjustment is made with an adjusting disc (shim) which fits into the cam follower. Different thickness discs result in changes in valve clearance.

NOTE: VW recommends that two special tools be used to remove and install the adjustment discs. One is a pry bar to compress the valve springs and the

Tach. Conv. Chart.

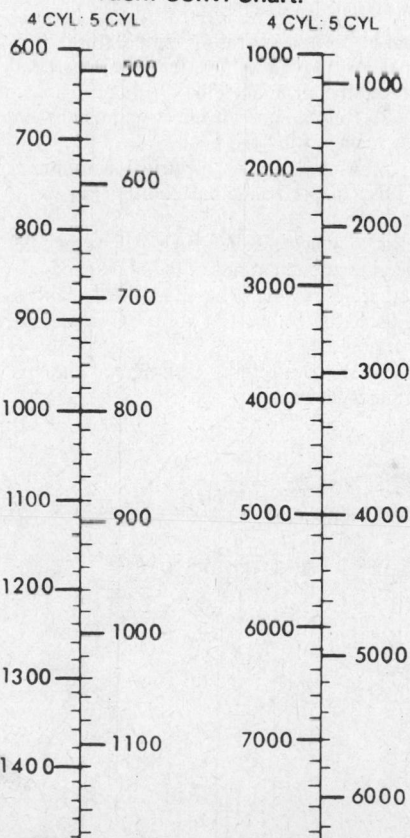

Conversion chart—to convert 4 cylinder tachometer reading to 5 cylinder applications

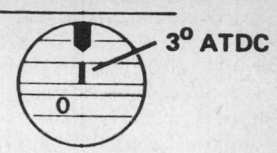

Timing mark—Rabbit, Jetta and Scirocco models with CIS, except 1.8 liter and carbureted engines

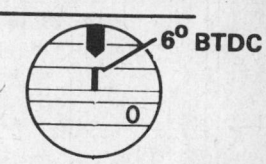

1.8 liter, manual transmission timing mark. Carbureted engines are also timed at BTDC. The mark, in this case, represents 7½°

other a pair of special pliers to remove the disc. If the purchase of these tools is not possible, a flat metal plate can be used to compress the valve springs if you are careful not to gouge the camshaft lobes. The cam follower has two slots which permit the disc to be lifted out. Again, you can improvise with a thin bladed screwdriver. An assistant to pry the spring down while you remove the disc would be the ideal way to perform the operation if you must improvise your own tools.

Valve clearance is checked with the engine moderately warm (coolant temperature should be about 95°F(35°C).

1. Remove the accelerator linkage (if necessary), the upper drive belt cover (if necessary), the air cleaner and any hoses or lines which may be in the way.

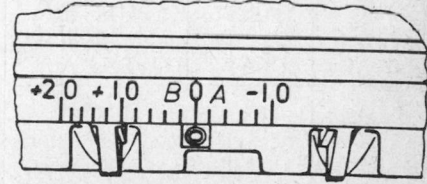

Westmoreland Rabbits with a 200mm clutch may have a "universal" flywheel installed. Each timing mark is equal to 2°. Marks to the left of the O are BTDC, to the right ATDC

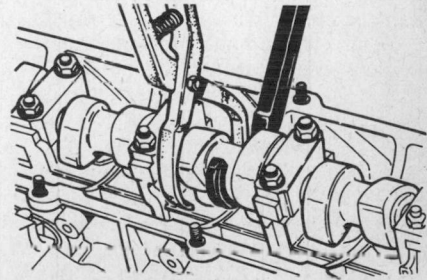

Tools used for valve adjustment

2. Remove the cylinder head cover.

Valve clearance is checked in the firing order 1-3-4-2 for the 4 cylinder and 1-2-4-5-3 for the 5 cylinder engines, with the piston of the cylinder being checked at TDC of the compression stroke. Both valves will be closed at this position and the cam lobes will be pointing straight up.

NOTE: When adjusting the clearances on the diesel engine, the pistons must not be at TDC. Turn the crankshaft ¼ turn past TDC so that the valves do not contact the pistons when the tappets are depressed.

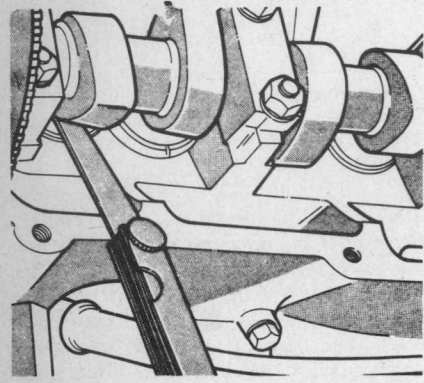

Check the valve clearance with a feeler gauge. The camshaft lobe should not be putting pressure on the valve shim

3. Turn the crankshaft pulley bolt with a socket wrench to position the camshaft for checking.

NOTE: There is a hole behind the front license plate, on Dasher models, through which a wrench can be inserted.

— CAUTION —

Do not turn the camshaft by the camshaft mounting bolt, this will stretch the drive belt. When turning the crankshaft pulley bolt, turn it CLOCKWISE ONLY.

4. With the No. 1 piston at TDC (¼ turn past for the diesel) of the compression stroke, determine the clearance with a feeler gauge. Intake clearance should be 0.008–0.012 in; exhaust clearance should be 0.016–0.020 in. (0.006–0.010 and 0.014–0.018 for the Diesel).

5. Continue on to check the other cylinders in the firing order, turning the crankshaft to bring each particular piston to the top of the compression stroke (¼ turn for the diesel). Record the individual clearances as you go along.

6. If measured clearance is within tolerance levels (0.002 in.), it is not necessary to replace the adjusting discs.

7. If adjustment is necessary, the discs will have to be removed and replaced with thicker or thinner ones which will yield the correct clearance. Discs are available in 0.002 in. increments from 0.12 in. to 0.17 in.

NOTE: The thickness of the adjusting discs are etched on one side. When installing, the marks must face the cam followers. Discs can be reused if they are not worn or damaged.

8. To remove the discs, turn the cam followers so that the grooves are accessible when the pry bar is depressed.

9. Press the cam follower down with the pry bar and remove the adjusting discs with the special pliers or the screwdriver.

10. Replace the adjustment discs as necessary to bring the clearance within the 0.002 in. tolerance level. If the measured clearance is larger than the given tolerance, remove the existing disc and insert a thicker one to bring the clearance up to specification. If it is smaller, insert a thinner one.

11. Recheck all valve clearances after adjustment.

12. Install the cylinder head cover with a new gasket.

13. Install the accelerator linkage, the upper drive belt cover and any wires or lines which were removed.

Carburetor

IDLE SPEED ADJUSTMENT

Solex 34 PICT-5 Carburetor
1978 RABBIT

The choke must be fully open and the engine at normal operating temperature.

1. Remove the hose from the charcoal filter at the air intake elbow. Plug the hose.

2. Remove the air injection hose at the air cleaner. Plug the hose.

3. Make sure no electrical equipment is ON. In particular the cooling fan must be OFF.

4. Connect a tachometer. Adjust the idle speed to specifications at the idle speed adjusting screw (A). The CO content can be adjusted at screw (B) if a CO meter is available.

5. Disconnect the tachometer and reconnect the hoses.

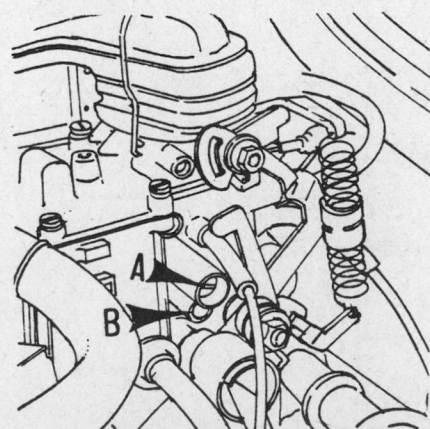

Idle speed screw (A) and idle mixture screw (B)—1978 and 1980 carbureted Rabbit

1980 RABBIT

1. The engine must be at operating temperature and the choke must be fully open.

2. Remove the two hoses from the carburetor air intake elbow and plug the two hose inlets in the elbow. The air intake elbow sits right on top of the carburetor.

3. Remove both of the air injection hoses at the air injection valves, located side by side in the front middle of the engine. Plug the air injection valves.

4. Shut off all electrical equipment, including the air conditioner (if so equipped).

5. Connect a tachometer, timing light and CO meter (if available) to the engine.

— CAUTION —

See "Tachometer Adaptation (Carbureted Rabbits)," under the electronic ignition section, above, for method of connecting tachometer. If you do not follow these instructions, you will damage your ignition system. Also refer to the conversion chart if working on a 5 cylinder engine.

6. Start the engine. Rev the engine a few times to start the idle stabilizer.

7. Check the idle; it should be 850–950 rpm. If the idle is not correct, disconnect the plugs at the control unit and plug them together (see "Electronic Ignition System", above).

8. Remove the vacuum advance and retard hoses, then plug the hoses.

9. Adjust the idle speed to 800–1000 rpm at the idle adjustment screw. Check the timing.

10. If the timing was off, recheck the idle speed.

11. Reconnect the advance and retard hoses. Adjust the CO lever at the CO adjusting screw to 0.5–1.1%.

12. Reconnect the plugs at the control unit.

13. Rev the engine to re-activate the idle stabilizer and check the idle speed and CO. Idle speed should be 850–950 rpm, CO should be 0.5–1.5%.

14. If the idle speed is still not correct, replace the control unit or the idle stabilizer.

Carter TYF

1982 AND LATER RABBIT

NOTE: This procedure requires a special duty cycle meter which is not commonly available to the owner mechanic. Do not perform this procedure without the proper equipment.

1. Run engine up to operating temperature. Make sure the choke is fully open and not sticking. Remove the PCV valve from the side of the valve cover. Shut off all electrical equipment including the air conditioner (if so equipped). Radiator fan must not be running for idle adjustment. Check the timing with a timing light and adjust to 7½° BTDC ± 1° if necessary (set pointer to mark on flywheel by turning distributor).

2. Connect a tachometer to the engine according to the manufacturer's instructions.

3. Connect a duty cycle meter to the test connector on the left strut tower.

4. Start the engine, and run at 2000 rpm for 5 seconds. Check the idle speed—it should be 850–1000 rpm. Duty cycle should be fluctuating between 20% and 50%.

5. To adjust the idle speed, disconnect both plugs at the idle stabilizer and connect the plugs together.

6. Remove the vacuum advance and retard hoses at the distributor. Plug the hoses with golf tees or pencils.

7. Adjust the idle speed to 820–900 rpm by turning the idle screw ("A" in illustration). Duty cycle should still be fluctuating between 20% and 50%. If the duty cycle reading is incorrect, the car should be adjusted to correct the reading by a professional, as a tamper-proof plug must be removed from the carburetor body to make this adjustment.

NOTE: On air conditioned cars, turn the air conditioner "On" and set the control to max. "cold" and "fast" fan speed before setting the idle speed to 820–900 rpm.

IDLE MIXTURE ADJUSTMENT

This adjustment should only be performed with a CO meter.

Rabbit, Scirocco and Dasher

1. Run the engine until it reaches normal operating temperature.

2. Check the ignition timing and idle speed as specified.

3. Adjust the CO level with the idle mixture screw.

1978, 1980 And Later Rabbit

Mixture adjustment is contained in the idle speed adjustment procedure, above.

Fuel Injection

IDLE AND CO ADJUSTMENT

All Except 1980 California And 1981 and Later Models

4 CYLINDER ENGINE

The following adjustments can be made *only* with a CO meter and the CO adjusting tool (VW-P377).

1. Run the engine until it reaches normal operating temperature.

2. Adjust the ignition timing to specification with the vacuum hoses connected and the engine at idle.

3. Adjust the idle speed to specification.

4. Remove the charcoal filter hose from the air cleaner except on Canadian models.

5. Turn on the headlight high beams.

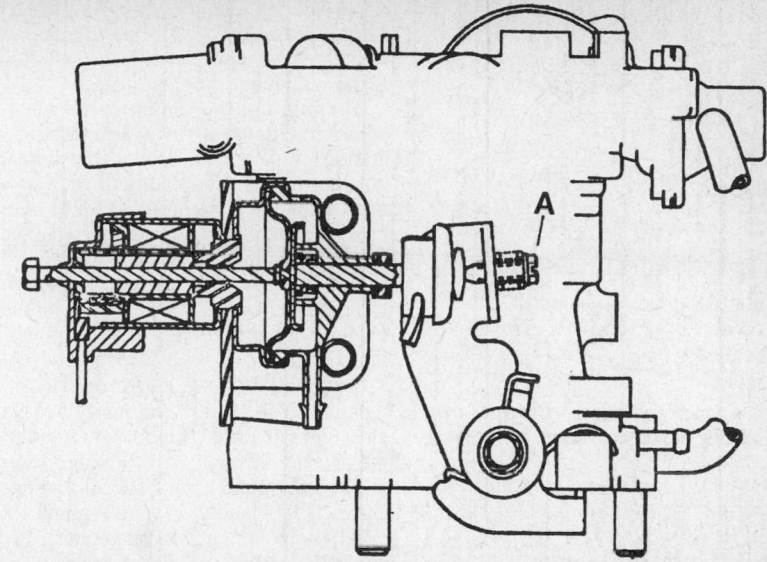

Idle speed adjustment screw (A)—Carter TYF carburetor

6. Remove the plug from the CO adjusting hole and insert adjustment tool VW-P377. Turn the adjustment screw clockwise to raise the percentage of CO and counterclockwise to lower the percentage of CO.

------ CAUTION ------
Do not push the adjustment tool down or accelerate the engine with the tool in place.

7. Remove the tool after each adjustment and accelerate the engine briefly before reading the percentage of CO. The correct CO values are as follows:
49 States:1978: 1.5% M/T;
   1978: 1.0% A/T
   1979–80 0.6 + 0.4%
California:1978: 0.3%
   1979: 0.5 + 0.4%

1980 California, 1981 and Later Models

NOTE: 1.8 CIS engines are equipped with a manual preheat valve on the air cleaner housing. The valve is marked S (summer) and W (winter). When servicing, position the valve to S (unless working area is below freezing). After servicing, return valve to the position that matches climate conditions.

1. The engine must be at operating temperature.

2. Disconnect the crankcase breather hose at the cylinder head cover and plug the hose on models through 1982. On 1983 and later models, except the 5 cylinder, leave the hose open. Plug the hose on 5 cylinder models.

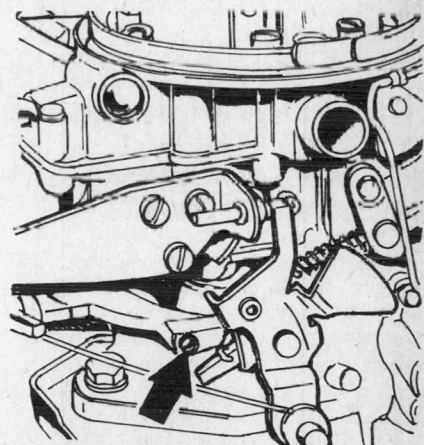

Idle mixture adjustment screw—all except 1978, 1980 and later carbureted Rabbit

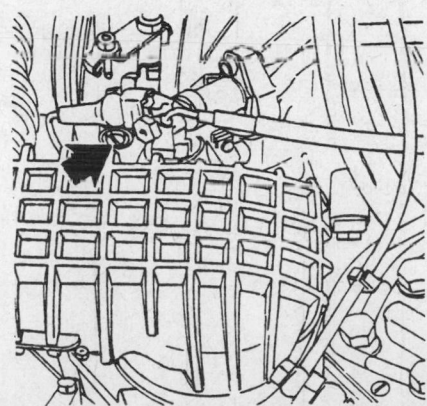

Idle speed adjustment screw—fuel injected Dasher

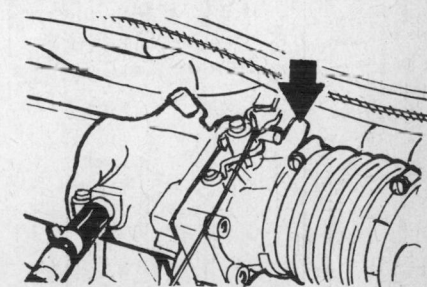

Idle speed adjustment screw—fuel injected Rabbit, Jetta, Scirocco

CO adjusting tool installed—CIS fuel injection (Rabbit, Jetta, Scirocco shown)

3. Disconnect the two plugs on the idle stabilizer at the control unit and plug them together.

4. Do not have any electrical accessories (air conditioner, lights, etc.) on.

5. Connect a tachometer and timing light. Check the timing. Adjust if necessary.

6. Check the idle speed against the specifications chart or your underhood sticker. Adjust the idle at the idle adjustment screw on the throttle chamber (880–1000 rpm).

NOTE: Only adjust the idle when the radiator fan is not on.

The CO adjustment on these engines is sealed to prevent unauthorized adjustment. The only way CO levels can be adjusted on these models is with special dealer tools (frequency counter, CO tester, etc.) which are usually not available to the general public.

Diesel Fuel Injection

IDLE SPEED/MAXIMUM SPEED ADJUSTMENTS

Volkswagen diesel engines have both an idle speed and a maximum speed adjustment. The maximum engine speed adjustment prevents the engine from over-revving and self-destructing. The adjusters are lo-

Special adapter VW 1324 is necessary to use an external tachometer on diesel engines

cated side by side on top of the injection pump. The screw closest to the engine is the idle speed adjuster, while the outer screw is the maximum speed adjuster.

The idle and maximum speed must be adjusted with the engine warm (normal operating temperature). Because the diesel engine has no conventional ignition, you will need a special adaptor (VW 1324) to connect your tachometer, or use the tachometer in the instrument panel, if equipped. You should check with the manufacturer of your tachometer to see if it will work with diesel engines. Adjust all engines to the specified idle speed.

When adjustment is correct, lock the locknut on the screw and apply non-hardening thread sealer (Loctite® or similar) to prevent the screw from vibrating loose.

The maximum speed for all engines is between 5500 and 5600 rpm (through 1980) or 5300–5400 rpm (1981 and later). If it is not in this range, loosen the screw and correct the speed (turning the screw clockwise decreases rpm). Lock the nut on the adjusting screw and apply a dab of thread sealer in the same manner as you did on the idle screw.

--- **CAUTION** ---
Do not attempt to squeeze more power out of your engine by raising the maximum speed (rpm). If you do, you'll probably be in for a major overhaul in the not too distant future.

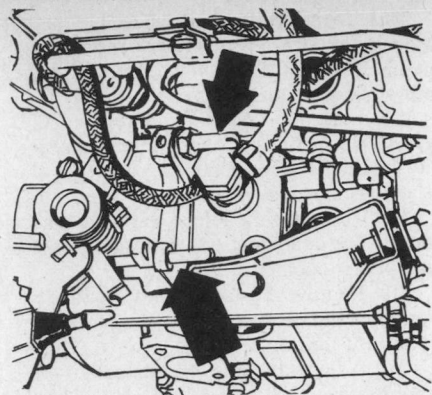

Diesel engine idle speed (upper) and maximum speed (lower) adjustment screws

ENGINE ELECTRICAL

Distributor

The distributor is a single breaker point unit on all 1978–79 models, and some 1980 models. Electronic ignition is used on all 1981 and later models and some 1980 models. It has both centrifugal and vacuum advance mechanisms. A vacuum retard system works only at idle.

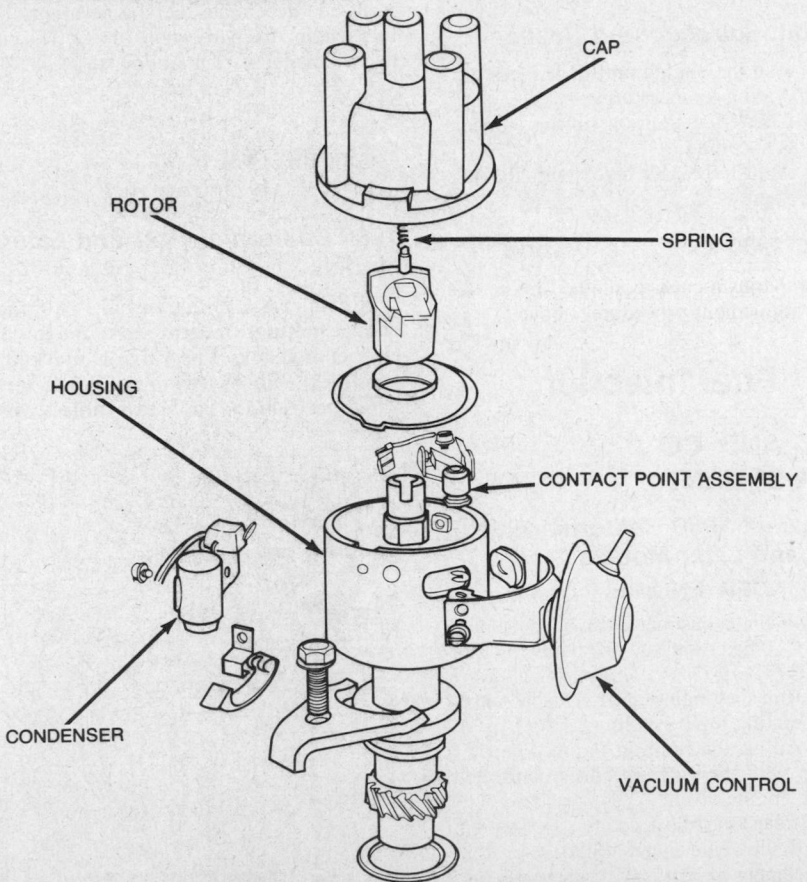

Exploded view of the points-type distributor

The distributor is gear driven by an intermediate shaft which also drives the fuel pump. The distributor shaft also turns the oil pump.

REMOVAL & INSTALLATION

1. Disconnect the coil high tension wire.
2. Detach the primary wire. Late models use a connector plug retained by a spring clip. Unfasten the clip and disconnect the plug. Remove the distributor cap and shield (if so equipped).
3. Turn the engine until the rotor aligns with the index mark on the outer edge of the distributor and the 0°T timing mark is aligned with the V–shaped pointer at the flywheel. This is the No. 1 position. Mark the bottom of the distributor housing and its mounting flange on the engine.
4. Remove the bolt and lift off the retaining flange. Lift the distributor straight out of the engine.

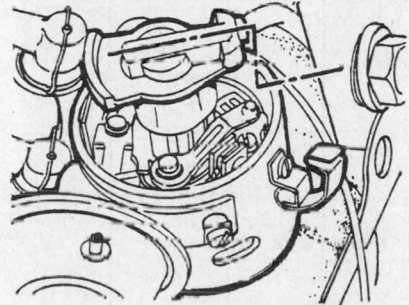

Rotor alignment with the notch for No. 1 cylinder

If the engine has not been disturbed while the distributor was out i.e., the crankshaft was not turned, then reinstall the distributor in the reverse order of removal. Carefully align the marks.

If the engine has been rotated while the distributor was out, then proceed as follows:

1. Turn the crankshaft so that No. 1 piston is on its compression stroke and the 0°T timing mark is aligned with the V-shaped pointer.
2. Turn the distributor so that the rotor points approximately 15° before the No. 1 cylinder position on the distributor.
3. Insert the distributor into the engine block. If the oil pump drive doesn't engage, remove the distributor and, using a long screwdriver, turn the pump shaft so that it is parallel to the centerline of the crankshaft.
4. Install the distributor, aligning the marks. Tighten the retaining nut.
5. Install the cap. Adjust the ignition timing.

Alternator

PRECAUTIONS

An alternating current (AC) generator (alternator) is used. Unlike the direct current

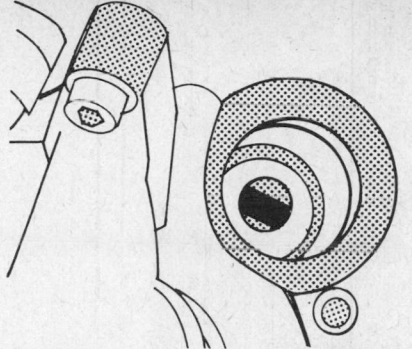

The oil pump drive should be parallel to the crankshaft

(DC) generators used in many older cars, there are several precautions which must be strictly observed in order to avoid damaging the unit.

1. Reversing the battery connections will result in damage to the diodes.
2. Booster batteries should be connected from *negative to negative, and positive to positive.*
3. Never use a fast charger as a booster to start cars with AC circuits; use a "trickle charger."
4. When servicing the battery with a charger, always disconnect the car battery cables.
5. Never attempt to polarize an AC generator.
6. Avoid long soldering times when replacing diodes or transistors. Prolonged heat is damaging to AC generators.
7. Do not use test lamps of more than 12 volts (V) for checking diode continuity.
8. Do not short across or ground any of the terminals on the AC generator.
9. The polarity of the battery, generator, and regulator must be matched and considered before making any electrical connections within the system.
10. Never operate the AC generator on an open circuit. Make sure that all connections within the circuit are clean and tight.
11. Disconnect the battery terminals when performing any service on the electrical system. This will eliminate the possibility of accidental reversal of polarity.
12. Disconnect the battery ground cable if arc welding is to be done on any part of the car.

REMOVAL & INSTALLATION

The alternator and voltage regulator are combined in one housing. No voltage adjustment can be made with this unit. The regulator can be replaced without removing the alternator. Unbolt the regulator and remove from the rear.

1. Disconnect the battery cables.
2. Remove the multi-connector retaining bracket and unplug the connector from the rear of the alternator.
3. Loosen and remove the top mounting nut and bolt.
4. Using a socket inserted through the

timing belt cover (it is not necessary to remove the cover), loosen the lower mounting bolt.
5. Swing the alternator over and remove the alternator belt.
6. Remove the lower nut and bolt.
7. Remove the alternator.
8. Install the alternator with the lower bolt. *Do not* tighten it at this point.
9. Install the alternator belt over the pulleys.
10. Loosely install the top mounting bolt and pivot the alternator until the belt is correctly tensioned.
11. Tighten the top and bottom bolts to 14 ft. lbs.
12. Connect the alternator and battery wires.

Removing the lower alternator bolt through the timing cover

BELT REPLACEMENT AND TENSIONING

1. Loosen the top alternator mounting bolt.
2. Using a socket inserted through the timing belt cover, loosen the lower mounting bolt.
3. Lever the alternator over and remove the belt.
4. Slip the new belt over the pulleys.
5. Pull the alternator over until the belt deflection midway between the crankshaft pulley and the alternator pulley is ⅜–⁹⁄₁₆ in. (10–15mm).
6. Securely tighten the mounting bolts.

Starter

REMOVAL & INSTALLATION

All Models Except Dasher and Quantum Diesel

1. Disconnect the battery ground cable.
2. Raise the front of the car.
3. Mark with tape and then disconnect the wires from the starter solenoid.
4. Disconnect the large cable.
5. Remove the starter retaining nuts.
6. Unscrew the bolt. Remove the starter.
7. Installation of the starter is carried out in reverse order of removal.

Dasher and Quantum Diesel

1. Disconnect the battery ground cable.

Alternator V-belt tension measurement

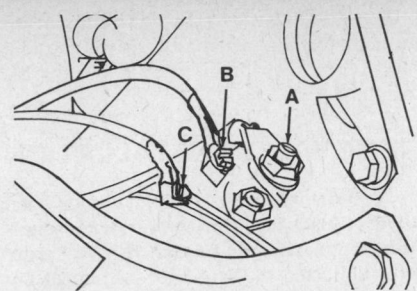

Dasher starter electrical connections: (A) solenoid, (B) coil, (C) positive battery cable

Quantum and Dasher starter removal—remove the engine mount and carrier on the starter side (arrows)

2. Support the weight of the engine with either Volkswagen Special Tool 10-222 or use a jack with a block of wood under the oil pan. Don't jack the engine too high, just take the weight off the motor mounts. *Be careful not to bend the oil pan.*

3. Remove the engine/transmission cover plate.

4. Unbolt and remove the starter side motor mount and carrier.

5. Disconnect and mark the starter wiring.

6. Remove the bolts holding the starter and remove the starter.

7. Install the starter and tighten the nuts and bolts to 14 ft. lbs.

8. Install the engine mount and carrier.

9. Install and attach remaining components. Don't forget to reconnect the battery cable.

OVERHAUL

Use the following procedure to replace brushes or starter drive.

1. Remove the solenoid.

2. Remove the end bearing cap.

3. Loosen both of the long housing screws.

4. Remove the lockwasher and spacer washers.

5. Remove the long housing screws and remove the end cover.

6. Pull the two field coil brushes out of the brush housing.

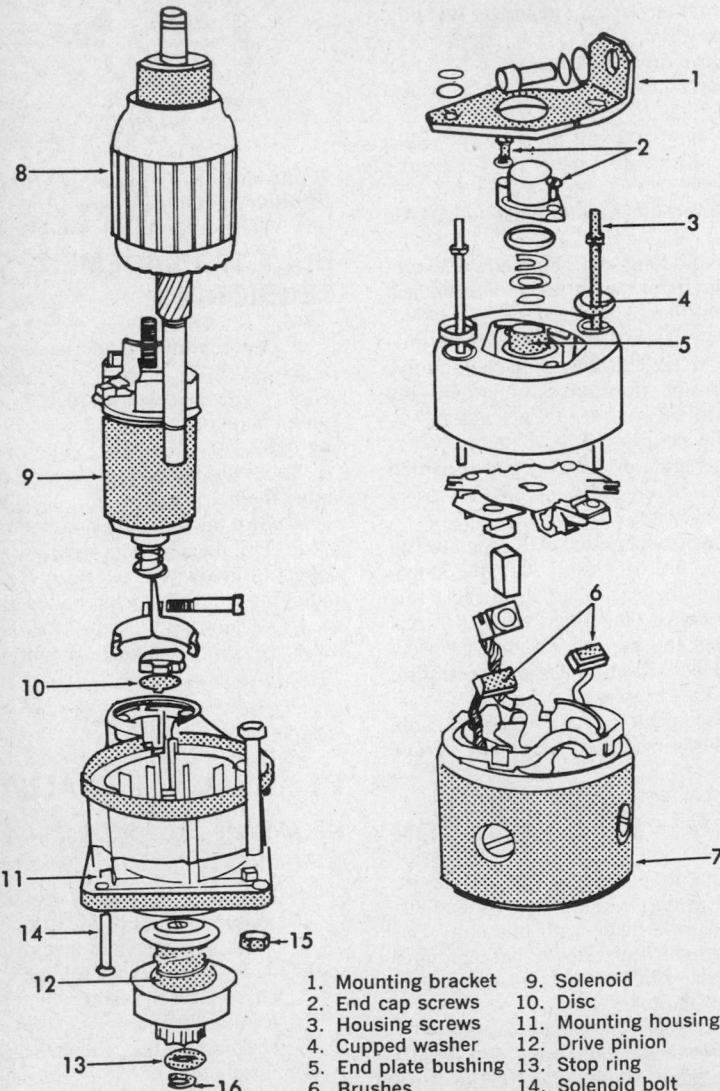

1. Mounting bracket	9. Solenoid
2. End cap screws	10. Disc
3. Housing screws	11. Mounting housing
4. Cupped washer	12. Drive pinion
5. End plate bushing	13. Stop ring
6. Brushes	14. Solenoid bolt
7. Field coil housing	15. Starter bolt and nut
8. Armature	16. Circlip

Exploded view of typical starter

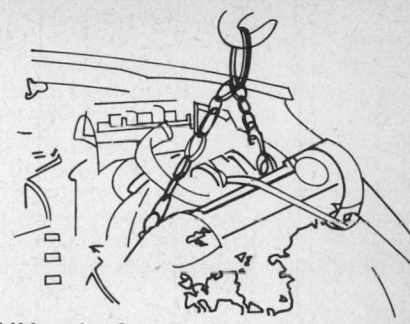

Lifting the Quantum and Dasher engine out of the car. Note that it must be turned for removal

7. Remove the brush housing assembly.

8. Loosen the nut on the solenoid housing, remove the sealing disc, and remove the solenoid operating lever.

9. Loosen the large screws on the side of the starter body and remove the field coil along with the brushes.

NOTE: If the brushes require replacement, the field coil and brushes and/or the brush housing and its brushes must be replaced as a unit.

10. If the starter drive is being replaced, push the stop-ring down and remove the circlip on the end of the shaft. Remove the stop-ring and remove the drive.

11. Assembly of the starter is carried out in the reverse order of disassembly. Use a gear puller to install the stop-ring in its groove (on models so equipped). Use a new circlip on the shaft.

SOLENOID REPLACEMENT

1. Remove the starter.

2. Remove the nut which secures the connector strip on the end of the solenoid.

3. Take out the two retaining screws on the mounting bracket and pull out the solenoid after it has been unhooked from the operating lever.

4. Installation is the reverse of removal. In order to facilitate engagement of the lever, the pinion should be pulled out as far as possible when inserting the solenoid.

Diesel Engine

GLOW PLUG SYSTEM CHECK

NOTE: The 1982 and later diesels, except turbocharged models, have a new type quick-glow system. Nominal glow time is seven seconds. Although the wiring for this system is the same as the earlier system, the glow plugs and relay cannot be paired or interchanged with earlier parts or vice versa.

1. Connect a test light between, No. 4 cylinder (rear cylinder on Dasher and Quantum and the cylinder closest to the driver's side on the Rabbit and Jetta) glow plug and ground. The glow plugs are connected by a flat, coated busbar (located near the bottom of the cylinder head).

2. Turn the ignition key to the heating (pre-glow) position. The test light should light.

3. If not, possible problems include the glow plug relay, the ignition switch and the fuse box relay plate and the glow plug fuse or a break in the wire to the relay terminal.

INDIVIDUAL GLOW PLUG TEST

1. Remove the wire and busbar from the glow plugs.

2. Connect a test light to the battery positive terminal.

3. Touch the test light probe to each glow plug in turn.

If the test light lights, the plug is good. If the light does not light, replace the glow plug(s).

ENGINE MECHANICAL

Engine

REMOVAL & INSTALLATION

NOTE: A good rule to follow when removing engines from all models is to label all hoses, electrical wires, and linkages and their connections with tape. Number each tape tag and the place it connects; this should help eliminate the hassles of "Where does this go?" during installation.

Dasher and Quantum
GASOLINE ENGINES

1. Disconnect the battery cables.

2. Remove the exhaust manifold heater hose and breather hose from the air cleaner.

3. Remove the air cleaner assembly.

4. On carbureted models, pull the clip off the accelerator cable and detach the cable. On fuel injected models, disconnect the electrical connector for the fuel injection, cold start valve, oxygen sensor and frequency valve (if equipped), and detach the control pressure regulator lines.

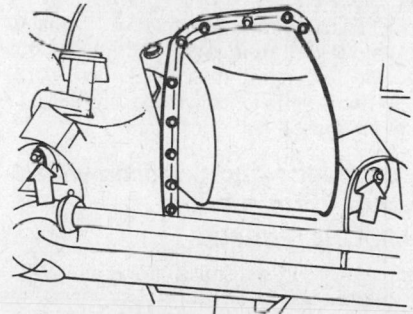

Quantum, Dasher engine side mounts

5. Loosen the upper adjustment nut on the clutch cable and detach it (on the Quantum, remove the clip on the clutch cable and unhook the cable).

6. On carbureted models only, disconnect the fuel line from the fuel pump, plug it, and place it out of the way. On fuel injected models, disconnect the air duct. Remove the cold start valve. Remove the fuel injectors from the head (protect the ends with caps) and the accelerator cable. Remove the air flow sensor with the fuel distributor and place out of the way.

7. Detach emission control hoses. Re-

move the power steering pump and V-belts, if so equipped.

8. Disconnect the wiring from the alternator.

9. Detach the clip and remove the heater cable.

— **CAUTION** —
Do not disconnect refrigerant lines on cars equipped with air conditioning.

10. On cars with air conditioning:
  a. Remove the horn, compressor and condenser assemblies.
  b. Move the compressor and condensers out of the way, without disconnecting the refrigerant lines.
  c. Disconnect the vacuum hoses and brake booster hose, if so equipped.

11. Disconnect the front engine mount and remove the mount bracket.

12. Drain the coolant from the radiator. The plug is located near the lower hose, or remove the hose on models without the drain plug. Drain the cylinder block at the plug near the starter.

13. Disconnect the electrical wire from the coil and distributor, oil pressure and temperature sending units, fan and the thermal switch on the radiator.

14. Disconnect the radiator and heater hoses from the engine. Detach the heater valve cable.

15. Loosen the radiator shroud retainers. Remove the mounting bolts and nuts and lift out the radiator and fan.

16. Raise the front of the car and safely support it.

17. Remove the starter.

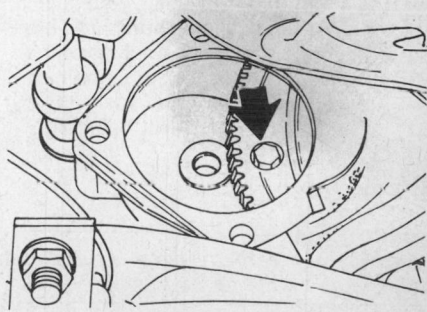

On automatic transmissions, remove three torque converter-to-flywheel bolts through the starter hole (Quantum and Dasher)

18. Disconnect the exhaust pipe from the manifold.

19. Detach the engine side mounts.

20. Loosen the upper engine-to-transmission bolts. Remove the lower bolts. If the car is equipped with an automatic transmission, remove the three torque converter-to-flywheel bolts by working through the starter hole. Use a bar to hold the flywheel. Also disconnect the automatic transmission vacuum hose.

21. Support the transmission with a floor jack.

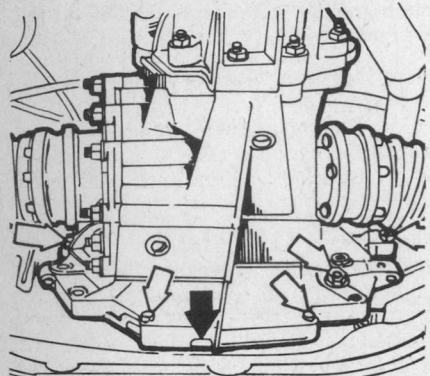

Remove the lower engine/transmission bolts and flywheel cover (arrows)

22. Lower the car until the wheels are on the ground.

23. Attach the hoist to the engine lift points.

24. Raise the engine/transmission until the transmission touches the steering rack.

25. Adjust your jack or support so that the transmission is held firmly.

26. Remove the upper engine-to-transmission bolts.

27. Pry the engine and transmission apart and remove the intermediate plate. Install a bar or cable to the torque converter housing on automatic cars to prevent the converter from falling out.

28. Remove the engine by slowly lifting and turning simultaneously.

CAUTION

Do this very carefully to avoid damaging the halfshafts or transmission.

29. Installation is the reverse of removal. Be careful not to damage the input shaft of the transmission during installation. Install new torque converter mounting bolts. Tighten the torque converter bolts to 25 ft. lbs.; engine–to–transaxle bolts to 40 ft. lbs., and the engine mount bolts to 32 ft. lbs.

DIESEL ENGINES

CAUTION

Do not disconnect the refrigerant lines on cars equipped with air conditioning.

1. Remove the negative battery cable.

2. Set the heat control to hot. Remove the lower radiator hose and remove the thermostat to drain the coolant. Remove the thermoswitch electrical connector and the radiator brace at the bottom of the radiator, remove the top radiator shroud, upper hose, radiator mounting bolts, and remove the radiator and fan.

3. Remove the supply and return lines from the injection pump. Disconnect the throttle cable from the pump and remove the cable mounting bracket. Disconnect the cold start cable at the pin, and remove the electrical connector from the fuel shut-off solenoid.

4. Disconnect the electrical connectors from the oil pressure switch, coolant temperature sensor and glow plugs. Remove the radiator hose from the head and the vacuum hose from the vacuum pump.

5. Loosen the adjusting nuts and unhook the clutch cable from the lever.

6. Remove the hose from the water pump.

7. On the Quantum, unbolt the rear of the turbocharger (if equipped) from the exhaust system.

8. Loosen the right engine mount.

9. Remove the alternator after tagging the wires for installation.

10. Remove the front engine mounts.

11. Disconnect the exhaust pipe from the manifold, and the pipe bracket from the transmission.

12. Loosen the left engine mount.

13. Remove the starter.

14. Remove the engine-to-transmission bolts, and the flywheel cover bolts.

15. Attach a lifting chain to the engine and raise the engine until the transmission touches the steering rack. Remove the left engine mount.

16. Support the transmission with a jack and raise and turn the engine at the same time to remove.

17. Installation is the reverse. Tighten the engine-to-transmission bolts to 40 ft. lbs. and the engine mount bolts to 29 ft. lbs. After installation adjust the throttle and cold starting cables.

Rabbit, Jetta and Scirocco with Manual Transmission
GASOLINE ENGINES

The engine and transmission are removed as an assembly.

1. Disconnect the battery ground cable.

2. Drain the coolant by unbolting the lower water pump flange or by removing the hoses.

CAUTION

Do not disconnect or loosen any refrigerant hose connections during engine removal on cars equipped with air conditioning.

3. On cars equipped with air conditioning:

   a. Loosen the compressor support bolts and remove the compressor.

   b. Remove the radiator cooling fan, air ducts and radiator.

   c. Remove the condenser.

   d. Place the air conditioning compressor and condenser out of the way without disconnecting any refrigerant lines.

4. Remove the radiator with the air ducts and fan.

5. Detach and label all the electrical wires connecting the engine to the body.

6. Disconnect and plug the fuel line at the fuel pump. Detach the coolant hoses at the left end of the engine. Disconnect the accelerator cable and remove the air cleaner.

7. Disconnect the speedometer cable from the transmission. Detach the clutch cable.

8. Remove the engine support to the right of the starter.

9. Remove the headlight caps inside the engine compartment.

10. Unbolt the halfshafts from the transmission and wire them up.

11. Unbolt the exhaust pipe from the manifold and unbolt the exhaust pipe brace.

12. Unbolt the transmission rear mount from the body (alongside the tunnel).

13. Detach the ground strap from the transmission and body.

14. Remove the shift linkage.

15. Attach a chain sling to the alternator bracket and the lifting eye at the left end of the engine. Lift the engine and transmission slightly.

16. Detach the engine carrier from the body and remove the left transmission carrier.

17. Lift the engine/transmission assembly carefully out of the car.

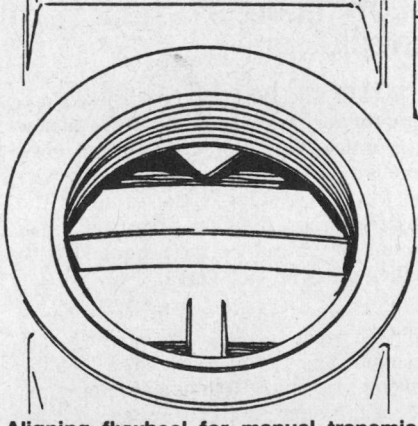

Aligning flywheel for manual transmission and engine separation—Rabbit, Jetta, Scirocco

18. To separate the engine and transmission, turn the flywheel to align the lug on the flywheel (to the left of TDC) with the pointer in the opening. The engine and transmission can only be separated in this position. Remove the cover plate over the driveshaft flange and remove the engine–to–transmission bolts and the transmission housing cover plate.

To install the engine:

19. To attach the transmission to the engine, the recess in the flywheel edge must be at 3:00 o'clock (facing the left end of

the engine). Torque the engine–to–transmission bolts to 40 ft. lbs. Lift the engine/transmission assembly into place. Loosen the bolts for the engine and transmission mounts. Move the engine assembly from side to side until the rear transmission mount is straight. Center the left and right transmission mounts and tighten all transmission bolts. Push the front mount upward to center the rubber cone, then tighten the mount. Loosen the exhaust pipe clamps, release any strain, then tighten the clamps. Torque the 10mm bolts to 29 ft. lbs. Torque the driveshaft flange bolts to 32 ft. lbs. Refill the cooling system.

Rabbit, Jetta and Scirocco with Automatic Transmission
GASOLINE ENGINES

The engine and transmission are removed as an assembly.

1. Shift the transmission into "Park." Disconnect both battery cables.
2. Drain the coolant by unbolting the lower water pump flange or by removing the hoses.

----- **CAUTION** -----
Do not disconnect or loosen any refrigerant hose connections during engine removal on cars equipped with air conditioning.

3. On cars equipped with air conditioning proceed as follows:
 a. Loosen the compressor support bolts and remove the compressor.
 b. Remove the radiator cooling fan, air ducts, and radiator.
 c. Remove the condenser.
 d. Place the air conditioning components out of the way without disconnecting any refrigerant lines.
4. Remove the radiator with the air ducts and fan.
5. Remove the air cleaner.
6. Detach the speedometer cable from the transmission.
7. Detach and label all electrical wires connecting the engine to the body. Detach and label all heater and coolant hoses.
8. Remove the screws holding the accelerator cable bracket to the carburetor float bowl (do not disassemble linkage), detach the end of the gearshift selector cable from the transmission, detach the accelerator cable and pedal cable at the transmission, and remove the two bracket bolts behind this linkage on the transmission.
9. Unbolt the exhaust pipe from the manifold.
10. Remove the rear transmission mount. Unbolt the halfshafts and wire them up and out of the way.
11. Remove the converter cover plate and remove the three torque converter–to–drive plate bolts.
12. Attach a chain sling to the alternator bracket and the lifting eye at the left end of the engine. It may be necessary to re-

move the alternator. Lift the engine and transmission slightly.
13. Detach the engine front mounting support; remove the left transmission carrier and the right engine carrier.
14. Lift the engine/transmission assembly carefully out of the car.
15. The transmission can now be detached from the engine.

To install the engine:

16. The engine–to–transmission bolts should be torqued to 40 ft. lbs. Lift the engine/transmission assembly into place and install the left transmission carrier, tightening first the body, then the transmission bolts. Lower the assembly to attach the engine carrier to the body, tightening the bolts to 40 ft. lbs. Install the engine mounting support. Check that all mounts and clamps are free of strain. Torque converter bolts should be torqued to 21 ft. lbs. and half–shaft bolts to 32 ft. lbs. Refill the cooling system. Check the adjustment of transmission and carburetor linkages.

DIESEL ENGINES

----- **CAUTION** -----
Do not disconnect or loosen any refrigerant hose connections during engine removal on cars equipped with air conditioning.

The diesel engine is removed with the transmission attached.

1. Disconnect the battery.
2. Disconnect the radiator hoses and drain the coolant. It can be saved for reuse, if it's not too old.
3. Remove the radiator complete with fan.
4. Remove the alternator.
5. Disconnect the fuel filter and set it aside near the windshield washer reservoir.
6. Detach the supply and return lines from the injection pump.
7. Disconnect the accelerator cable from the lever on the injection pump and remove the injection pump complete with bracket.
8. Disconnect the cold start cable from the pump.
9. Disconnect and label all electrical wires and leads.
10. Remove the front transmission mount.
11. Disconnect the clutch cable.
12. Remove the relay rod and connecting rod from the transmission and turn the relay lever shaft to the rear.
13. Disconnect the selector rod.
14. Unbolt the halfshafts and wire them up out of the way. Remove the rear support.
15. Disconnect the exhaust pipe at the manifold, or unbolt the rear of the turbocharger (if so equipped) from the exhaust system, and remove the rear transmission mount.
16. Attach a lifting sling to the engine and take the weight from the engine mounts. Remove the left and right transmission mounts.

17. Carefully guide the engine out of the car while turning it slightly.
18. To separate the engine from the transmission, unscrew the plug from the TDC sensor opening and turn the flywheel to align the mark on the flywheel with the pointer. The engine/transmission can only be separated in this position.
19. Remove the cover plate over the halfshaft flange and remove the engine-to-transmission bolts.
20. Press the engine off the transmission.
21. Installation is the reverse of removal. Turn the flywheel so that the recess in the flywheel is level with the driveshaft flange. Lower the engine into the car and attach the left transmission mount to the transmission first. Align the rear transmission mount, center the engine/transmission and center the front transmission mount. Adjust the accelerator and cold start cables and bleed the injection system.

Cylinder Head

REMOVAL & INSTALLATION

The engine should be cold before the cylinder head can be removed. The four-cylinder head is retained by 10 head bolts and the five-cylinder head uses 12 head bolts. It can be removed without removing the intake and exhaust manifolds.

----- **CAUTION** -----
Do not disconnect or loosen any refrigerant hose connections during cylinder head removal.

Carbureted Engines

1. Disconnect the battery ground cable.
2. Drain the cooling system.
3. Remove the air cleaner. Disconnect the fuel line.
4. Disconnect the radiator, heater, and choke hoses.
5. Disconnect all electrical wires. Remove the spark plug wires.
6. Separate the exhaust manifold from the exhaust pipe.
7. Disconnect the EGR line from the exhaust manifold. Remove the EGR valve and filter from the intake manifold.
8. Remove the carburetor.
9. Disconnect the air pump fittings.
10. Remove the timing belt cover and belt.
11. Loosen the cylinder head bolts in the reverse of the tightening sequence.
12. Remove the bolts and lift the head straight off.
13. Install the *new* cylinder head gasket with the word TOP or OBEN up.
14. Install bolts No. 10 and 8 first; these holes are smaller and will properly locate the gasket and cylinder head.
15. Install the remaining bolts. Tighten them in stages in the sequence shown in

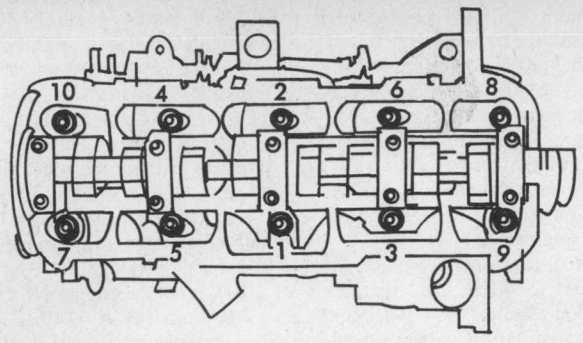

Cylinder head tightening sequence—4 cylinder engines

the illustration. Refer to the "Torque Specifications" chart for specific tightening instructions.

16. Install the remaining components in the reverse order of removal.

Fuel Injected Engines

1. Disconnect the battery ground cable.
2. Drain the cooling system.
3. Disconnect the air duct from the throttle valve assembly.
4. Disconnect the throttle valve assembly.
5. Remove the injectors and disconnect the line from the cold start valve.

6. Disconnect the radiator and heater hoses.
7. Disconnect the vacuum and PCV lines (label lines for installation).
8. Remove the auxiliary air regulator from the intake manifold.
9. Disconnect all electrical lines and remove the spark plugs (label all lines and wires for installation).
10. Separate the exhaust manifold from the exhaust pipe.
11. Remove the EGR line from the exhaust manifold.
12. Remove the intake manifold.
13. Remove the timing belt cover and belt.

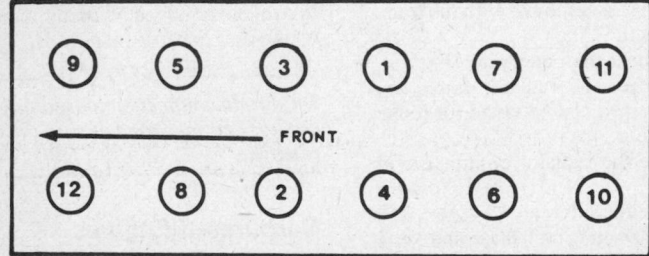

Cylinder head tightening sequence—5 cylinder engines

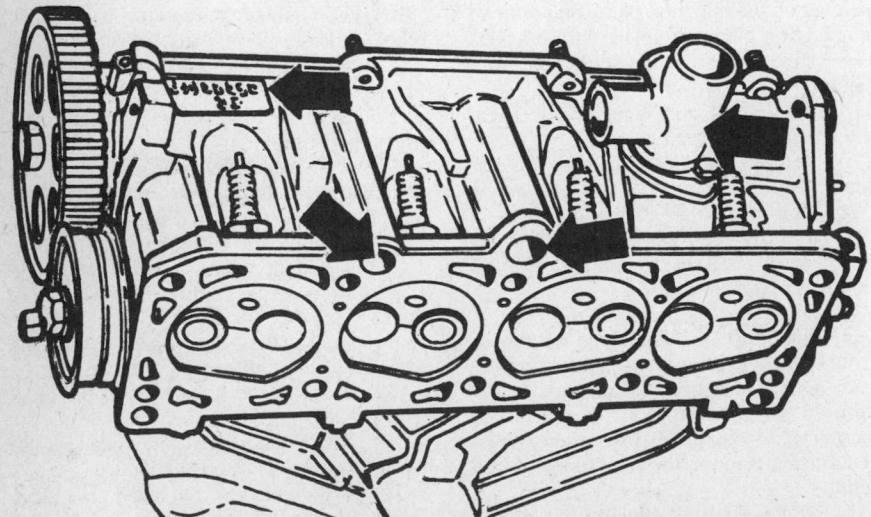

Cylinder heads for 1.8 liter engines can be identified by two breather holes on the gasket surface, the hose connection between Nos. 3 and 4 cylinder and a casting number above No. 1 plug location

Cylinder head gaskets for the 1.8 liter engine have two breather holes and larger bore dimension

14. Loosen the cylinder head bolts in the reverse of the tightening sequence.
15. Remove the bolts and lift the head straight off.
16. Check the flatness of the cylinder block in both width and length, then diagonally from each corner.
17. Install the *new* cylinder head gasket with the word TOP or OBEN facing upward.
18. Install bolts No. 10 and 8 first on 4 cylinder engines; these holes are smaller and will properly locate the gasket and cylinder head.
19. Install the remaining bolts. Tighten them in stages, using the sequence shown in the illustration. Refer to the "Torque Specifications" chart for specific tightening instructions.
20. Install the remaining components in the reverse order of removal.

Diesel and Turbo Diesel

NOTE: Cylinder head removal should not be attempted unless the engine is cold.

1. Disconnect the negative battery cable.
2. Drain the cooling system.
3. Remove the air cleaner.
4. Clean and disconnect the fuel (injector) lines.
5. Tag and disconnect all electrical wires and leads.
6. Disconnect and plug all lines coming from the brake booster vacuum pump and remove the pump.
7. Disconnect the air supply tubes (Turbo Diesels only) and then unbolt and remove the intake manifold.
8. Disconnect and plug all lines coming from the power steering pump and remove the pump and V-belt (if so equipped).
9. Disconnect and remove the oil supply and return lines from the Turbocharger (if applicable).
10. Remove the exhaust manifold heat shields (if so equipped).
11. Separate the exhaust pipe from the exhaust manifold or turbocharger and then remove the manifold.

NOTE: On turbo diesels, the exhaust manifold is removed with the turbocharger and wastegate still attached.

12. Disconnect all radiator and heater hoses where they are attached to the cylinder head and position them out of the way.
13. Remove the drive belt cover and the drive belt.
14. Remove the PCV hose.

15. Remove the cylinder head cover.

16. Loosen the cylinder head bolts in the reverse order of the tightening sequence shown in the illustration.

17. Remove the bolts and lift the cylinder head straight off.

— **CAUTION** —

If the head sticks, loosen it by compression or rap it upward with a soft rubber mallet. Do not force anything between the head and the engine block to pry it upward; this may result in serious damage.

18. Clean the cylinder head and engine block mating surfaces thoroughly and then install the new gasket without any sealing compound. Make sure the words TOP or OBEN are facing up when the gasket is installed.

NOTE: Depending upon piston height above the top surface of the engine block, there are three gaskets of different thicknesses which can be used. Be sure that the new gasket has the same identifying number as the one being replaced.

19. Place the cylinder head on the engine block and install bolts No. 8 and 10 first. These holes are smaller and will properly locate the gasket and the head on the engine block.

20. Install the remaining bolts. Tighten them in stages (see "Torque Specifications"), using the sequence shown in the illustration.

21. Installation of all other components is in the reverse order of removal.

22. After reassembly, start the engine and let it run until it reaches normal operating temperature (when the radiator fan switches on). Stop the engine, remove the cylinder head cover and check to see that all bolts are still at the proper tightness.

23. After about 1000 miles, remove the cylinder head cover and retighten the cylinder head bolts, turning the bolts in sequence ¼ turn (90°) WITHOUT loosening them first. This is done one bolt at a time, in the proper sequence, without interruption.

OVERHAUL/VALVE GUIDES

Valve guides are a shrink fit. Always install new valve seals when doing a valve job. Valve seats are not replaceable; the cylinder head should be replaced if the seat width and face angle cannot be maintained.

For all other cylinder head overhaul procedures, please refer to "Engine Rebuilding" in the Unit Repair section.

Intake Manifold

REMOVAL & INSTALLATION

Carbureted Models

1. Remove the air cleaner. Drain the cooling system.

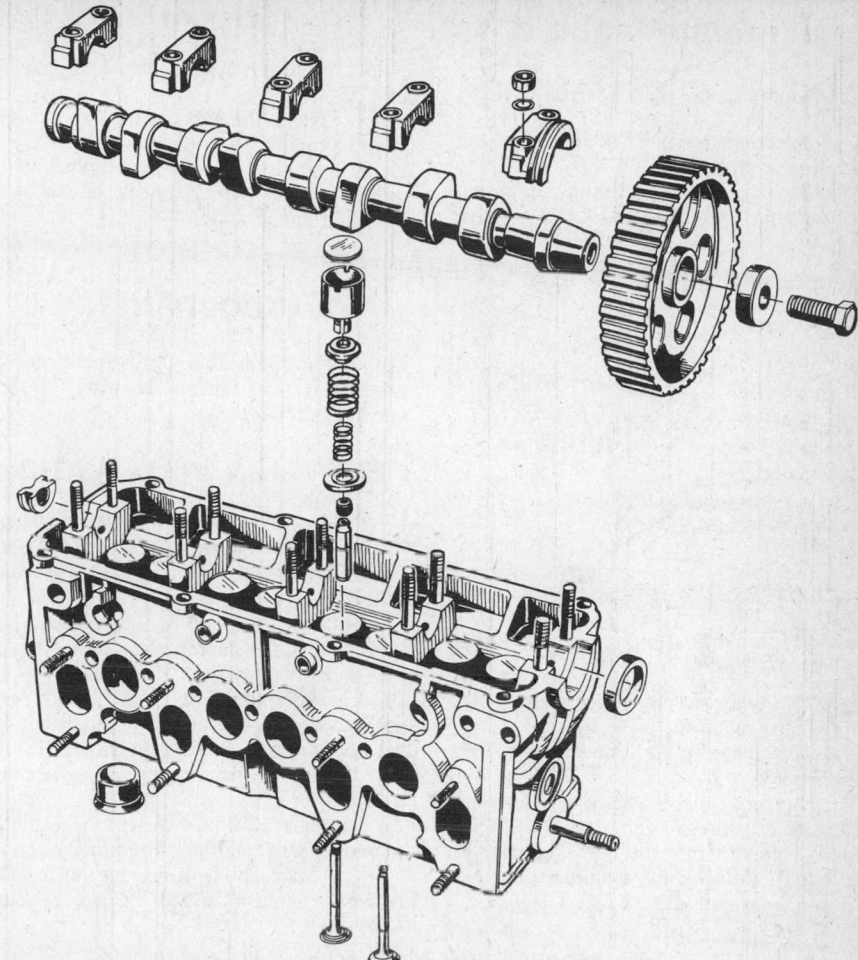

Exploded view of the diesel engine cylinder head. Note tapered camshaft nose. Gasoline engine has a blunt camshaft nose and key–located drive sprocket

2. Disconnect the accelerator cable.

3. Disconnect the EGR valve connections.

4. Detach all electrical leads.

5. Disconnect the coolant hoses.

6. Disconnect the fuel line from the carburetor.

7. Remove the vacuum hoses from the carburetor.

8. Loosen and remove the retaining bolts and lift off the manifold.

9. Install a new gasket. Install the manifold and tighten the bolts from the inside out. Tightening torque is 18 ft. lbs.

10. Install the remaining components in the reverse order of removal. Refill the cooling system.

Fuel Injected Models

1. Disconnect the air duct from the throttle valve body. Drain the cooling system.

2. Disconnect the accelerator cable.

3. Remove the injectors and disconnect the line from the cold start valve.

4. Disconnect all coolant hoses.

5. Disconnect all vacuum and emission control hoses (label all hoses for installation).

6. Remove the auxiliary air regulator.

7. Disconnect all electrical lines (label all wires for installation).

8. Disconnect the EGR line from the exhaust manifold.

9. Loosen and remove the retaining bolts and lift off the manifold.

10. Install a new gasket. Install the manifold and tighten the bolts to 18 ft. lbs.

11. Install the remaining components in the reverse order of removal.

Diesel and Turbo Diesel

1. Disconnect the negative battery cable.

2. Drain the cooling system.

3. Disconnect the hose that runs between the air duct and the turbocharger (turbo diesel only).

4. Remove the air cleaner.

5. Disconnect and plug all lines coming from the brake booster vacuum pump and remove the pump.

6. Disconnect the PCV line.

7. Disconnect and remove the blow-off valve and then disconnect the hose which runs from the intake manifold to the turbocharger (turbo diesel only).

8. Remove the manifold.

9. Installation is in the reverse order of removal.

Exhaust Manifold

REMOVAL & INSTALLATION

1. Disconnect the EGR tube from the exhaust manifold.

2. Remove the interfering air pump components if so equipped.

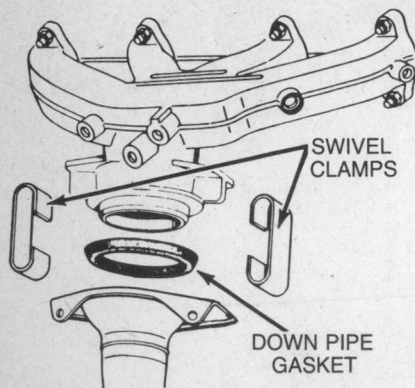

Swivel type exhaust pipe mounting used on various models from 1983

3. Remove the air cleaner hose from the exhaust manifold.

4. Disconnect the intake manifold support.

5. Separate the exhaust pipe from the manifold or turbocharger.

6. Remove the turbocharger (if so equipped). Remove the retaining nuts and remove the manifold.

7. Clean the cylinder head and manifold mating surfaces.

8. Install the exhaust manifold using a new gasket.

9. Tighten the nuts to 18 ft. lbs. Work from the inside out.

10. Install the remaining components in the reverse order of removal. Use a new manifold flange gasket.

Turbocharger

For more information on turbochargers, please refer to "Turbo-Charging" in the Unit Repair section.

REMOVAL & INSTALLATION

1. Disconnect the negative battery cable.

2. Remove the engine and transmission cover shield to gain access to the turbocharger.

3. Loosen the stabilizer bar clamps on both sides of the stabilizer and push the bar down out of the way.

4. Loosen the oil return connector bolt at the bottom of the turbocharger. Remove the side support bolt. Have a container ready to catch the oil when disconnecting the bottom adapter.

5. Remove the turbocharger heat shield mounting nuts and the oil return line.

6. Remove both hoses, turbocharger–to–intake manifold and air cleaner. Loosen and remove the oil supply line to the turbocharger.

7. Remove the exhaust pipe–to–turbocharger mounting bolts and the turbocharger exhaust manifold mounting bolts. Remove the turbocharger.

8. To install: position the turbocharger on the exhaust manifold and hand tighten the two mounting bolts. Install the lower vertical oil return connector mounting bolt and the lower side support bolt, tighten hand tight. Torque the mounting bolts in the following sequence: Manifold–to–turbocharger; 50 ft. lbs. Lower oil connection; 18 ft. lbs. Lower side mount; 18 ft. lbs.

9. Fill the upper oil supply connection on the turbocharger with oil. Install the remaining turbocharger connections, shields, etc. in the reverse order of removal.

10. When installation is complete, start the engine and allow to idle for several minutes. Do not increase engine speed above idle until the turbocharger oil supply system has had a chance to fill.

Timing Belt Cover

REMOVAL & INSTALLATION

1. Loosen the alternator mounting bolts and if equipped, the power steering pump and air conditioner compressor bolts, if their drive belts will interfere with cover removal.

2. Pivot the alternator or driven component and slip the drive belt from the pulleys.

3. Unscrew the belt cover retaining nuts and remove the cover. On some models with two piece covers, it may be necessary to remove the crankshaft pulley.

4. Reposition the spacers and nuts on the mounting studs so they will not get lost.

5. Service vehicle as necessary and reinstall the belt cover in the reverse order of removal.

Timing Belt

NOTE: The timing belt is designed to last for more than 60,000 miles and normally does not require tension adjustment. If the belt is removed, breaks or is replaced, the basic valve timing must be checked and the belt retensioned.

REMOVAL & INSTALLATION

Gasoline Engines

NOTE: Timing belt installation will be less confusing if the engine is set for No. 1 cylinder at TDC (top dead center) prior to belt removal or replacement.

1. Remove the front belt cover(s).

2. Turn the engine until the 0° mark on the flywheel is aligned with the stationary pointer on the bell housing. Turn the camshaft or make sure the camshaft sprocket is

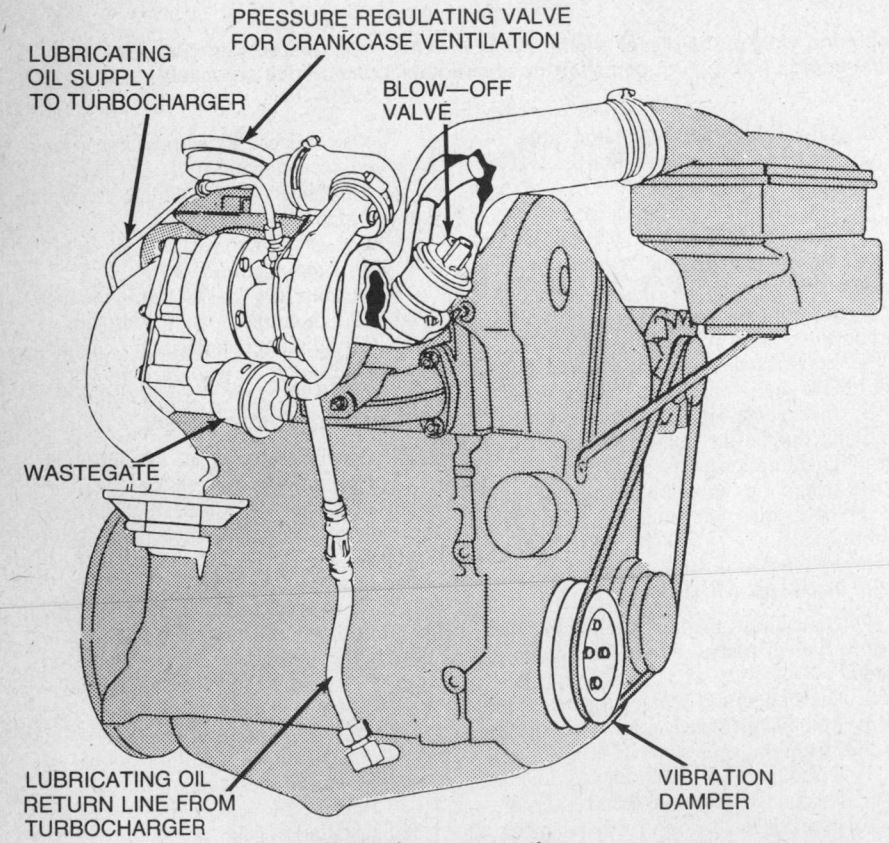

Turbocharger mounting

turned until the mark on the rear of the sprocket is aligned (4 cylinder engines) with the upper edge of the rear drive belt cover (or valve (cam) cover edge, depending on year) on the left side (spark plug side) of the engine or (5 cylinder engines) the left side edge of the camshaft housing. The notch on the crankshaft pulley should align with the dot on the intermediate shaft sprocket and the distributor rotor (remove distributor cap) should be pointing toward the mark on the rim of the distributor housing.

3. Remove the crankshaft accessories drive pulley(s).

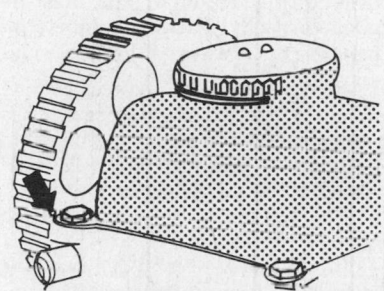

Camshaft sprocket timing marks aligned with cover flange (shown) or inner-upper timing cover bracket

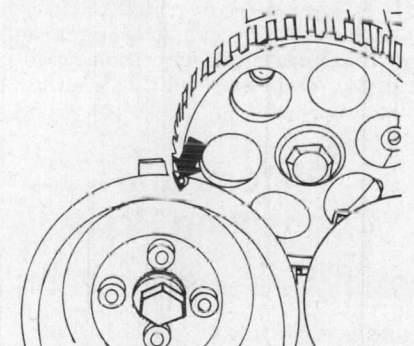

Crankshaft pulley and intermediate shaft sprocket alignment

4. On 4 cylinder engines, hold the large nut on the tensioner pulley and loosen the smaller pulley lock nut. Turn the tensioner counterclockwise to relieve the tension on the timing belt.

5. On 5 cylinder engines; loosen the water pump bolts and turn the pump clockwise to relieve timing belt tension.

6. Slide the timing belt from the pulleys.

7. Install the timing belt and re-tension with pulley or water pump. Reinstall the crankshaft pulley(s). Recheck alignment of timing marks.

— **CAUTION** —

If the timing marks are not correctly aligned with the No. 1 piston at TDC of the compression stroke and the belt is installed, valve timing will be incorrect. Poor performance and possible engine damage can result from improper valve timing.

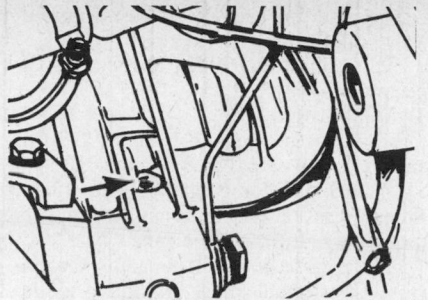

0° T or TDC mark on the flywheel

8. Check the timing belt tension. The tension is correct when the belt can be twisted 90° with the thumb and index finger along the straight run between the camshaft sprocket and the water pump.

9. Turn the engine two complete revolutions (clockwise rotation) and align the flywheel mark at TDC. Recheck belt tension and timing marks. Readjust as required.

10. Reinstall the timing belt cover and drive belts in the reverse order of removal.

1. Alternator belt
2. Belt pulleys
3. Timing gear cover
4. Crankshaft sprocket
5. Intermediate sprocket
6. Drive belt
7. Tensioner
8. Camshaft sprocket

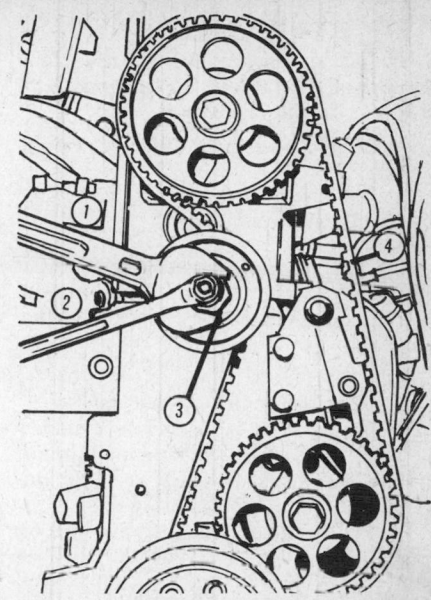

Turn the tensioner (3) toward (1) to tighten belt and toward (2) to loosen. Check tension at (4)

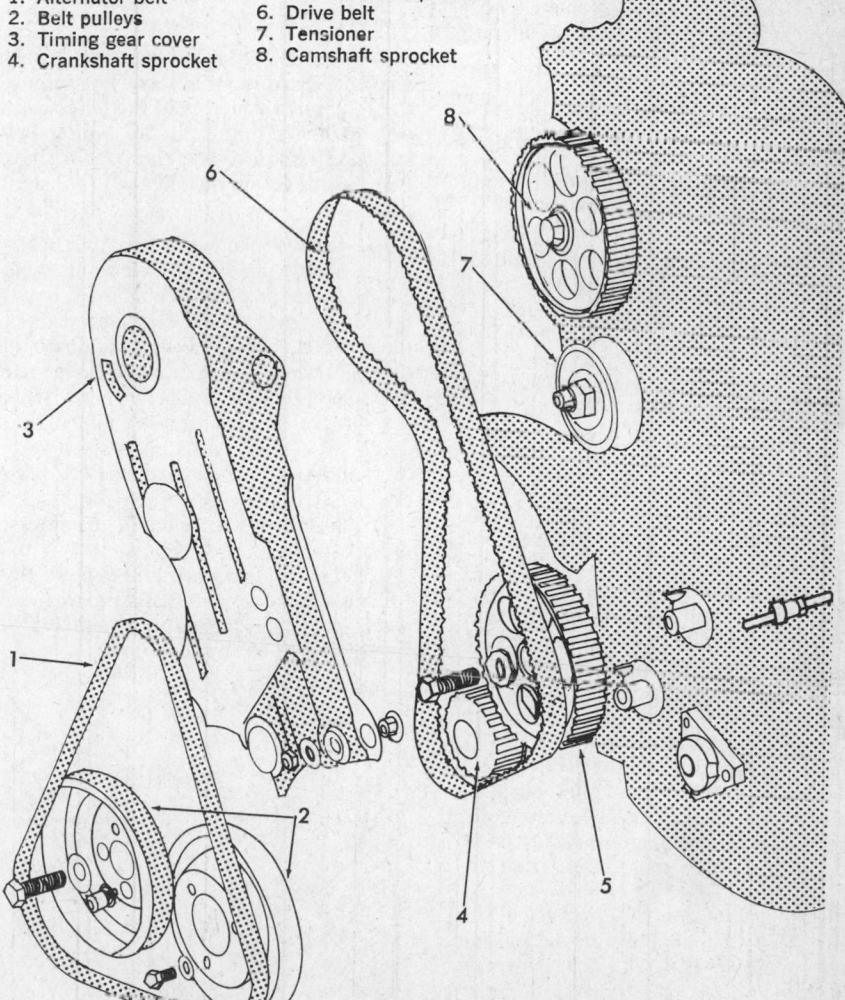

Exploded view of camshaft drive arrangement

Diesel Engine

NOTE: This procedure will require a number of special tools and a certain expertise with diesel engines.

To Check Valve and Injector Pump Timing:

1. Remove the cylinder head cover and the timing belt cover(s).

NOTE: The drive belt must be checked for proper tension and must be centered in the sprockets before checking the timing.

2. Turn the engine so that the No. 1 cylinder is at TDC. The No. 1 cylinder camshaft lobes should be pointing upward and the TDC mark on the flywheel should be aligned with the bellhousing mark.

3. Fix the camshaft in position with tool VW 2065 or 2065A. Align the tool as follows:
—turn the camshaft until one end of the tool touches the cylinder head
—measure the gap at the other end of the tool with a feeler gauge
—take half of the measurement and insert a feeler gauge of that thickness between the tool and the cylinder head; turn the camshaft so the tool rests on the feeler gauge
—insert a second feeler gauge of the same thickness on the other side, between the tool and the cylinder head.

4. Lock the injector pump sprocket in position with pin 2064.

5. Check that the marks on the sprocket, pump and mounting plate are approximately aligned. Check that the TDC mark on the flywheel is aligned with the bellhousing mark.

To Adjust

1. Refer to Steps 1–4 of the above procedure.

2. After the camshaft is set in position and the timing is at TDC, loosen the camshaft sprocket mounting bolt 1 turn.

3. Tap the back of sprocket with a rubber hammer to loosen. Hand tighten the bolt to remove endplay.

4. Loosen the belt adjuster and remove the belt from the injector pump sprocket.

5. Turn the injector pump sprocket until the marks on the sprocket, pump and mounting bracket align. Insert pin 2064 through the hole in the sprocket and mounting bracket to lock in position.

6. Reinstall the camshaft drive belt. Tighten the camshaft mounting bolt to 33 ft. lbs. Remove the camshaft setting bar and the lock pin from the injector pump sprocket. Install VW tool VW210 (Belt tension gauge).

7. Adjust tension by turning the tensioner clockwise, reading on the tension gauge should be 12-13. Lock tensioner in position.

8. Turn the crankshaft 2 complete turns (clockwise rotation) and recheck belt tension. Strike the drive belt once with a rub-

ber hammer between the camshaft and injector pump sprockets to eliminate play.

9. Recheck the timing and re-adjust if necessary.

To Install Belt:

1. Refer to Steps 1–5 of the "Valve and Injector Pump Timing" procedure.

2. Align all timing marks as described. Release tension on the timing belt and remove the belt from the engine.

3. Install a new belt and adjust the tension. Check and adjust the timing as described in the previous section. Reinstall the belt cover(s) and driven component belts.

Timing Sprockets

REMOVAL & INSTALLATION

All Engines

Depending on the year and model, the timing sprockets are located on the shaft by a key, a self-contained drive lug, or in the case of the diesel engine camshaft—a tapered fit. All sprockets are retained by a bolt. To remove any or all sprockets, removal of the timing belt cover(s) and belt is required.

NOTE: When removing the crankshaft pulley, it is not necessary to remove the four bolts which hold the outer component drive pulley to the timing belt sprocket. Remove the component drive belt, center retaining bolt and crankshaft pulley.

1. Remove the center retaining bolt.

2. Gently pry the sprocket off the shaft.

3. If the sprocket is stubborn in coming off, use a gear puller. Don't hammer on the sprocket. On diesel engines, loosen the camshaft center bolt 1 turn and tap the rear of the sprocket with a rubber hammer. When the sprocket loosens, remove the bolt and gear.

4. Remove the sprocket and key (if so equipped).

5. Install the sprocket in the reverse order of removal.

6. Tighten the center bolt to 58 ft. lbs. Models having a crankshaft sprocket with a self-contained index lug require 145 ft. lbs. of torque on the center bolt.

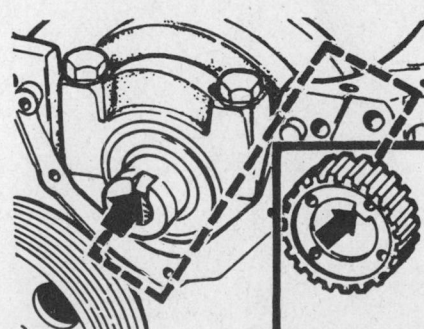

Late models have a locating lug contained by the crankshaft sprocket

7. Install the timing belt, check valve timing, tension belt, and install the cover.

Camshaft

REMOVAL & INSTALLATION

1. Remove the timing belt cover(s), the timing belt, camshaft sprocket and camshaft (valve) cover.

NOTE: Number the bearing caps from front to back. Scribe an arrow facing front. The caps are offset and must be installed correctly. Factory numbers on the caps are not always on the same side.

2. Remove the front and rear bearing caps. Loosen the remaining bearing cap nuts diagonally in several steps, starting from the outside caps near the ends of the head and working toward the center.

3. Remove the bearing caps and the camshaft.

4. Install a new oil seal and end plug in the cylinder head. Lightly coat the camshaft bearing journals and lobes with a film of assembly lube or heavy engine oil. Install the bearing caps in the reverse order of removal. Tighten the cap nuts diagonally and in several steps until they are torqued to 14 ft. lbs.

5. Install the drive sprocket and timing belt. Check valve clearance and adjust if necessary. Install remaining parts in reverse order of removal.

Pistons and Connecting Rods

REMOVAL & INSTALLATION

Gasoline Engines

1. Follow the instructions under "Timing Belt" and "Cylinder Head" removal.

2. Remove the oil pan.

3. Turn the crankshaft until the piston to be removed is at the bottom of its travel.

4. Make sure the connecting rod and cap are marked for reference as to cylinder location and position match (scribe across the rod end and cap so that the cap will be installed in mating position). Mark the piston heads from front to back, in order, for reinstallation identification.

5. Place a rag down the cylinder bore on the head of the piston to be removed. Remove the cylinder ridge and carbon deposits with a ridge reamer; following the instructions of the reamer's manufacturer.

— **CAUTION** —

Do not cut too deeply or remove more than 1/32 in. from the ring travel area when removing the ridge.

6. Remove the rag and metal cuttings from the cylinder bore. Remove the connecting rod cap and bearing insert.

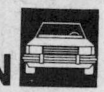

The arrow on the piston must face the camshaft drive belt

7. Push the connecting rod up the bore slightly and remove the upper bearing insert.

8. Push the connecting rod and piston assembly up and out of the cylinder with a wooden hammer handle.

9. Wipe any dirt or oil from the connecting rod bearing saddle and rod cap. Install the bearing inserts (if to be reused) in the connecting rod and cap. Install the cap and secure with rod bolts.

10. Remove the rest of the rod and piston assemblies in a like manner.

CAUTION

When removing the pistons, take care not to score the crankshaft journals or cylinder walls.

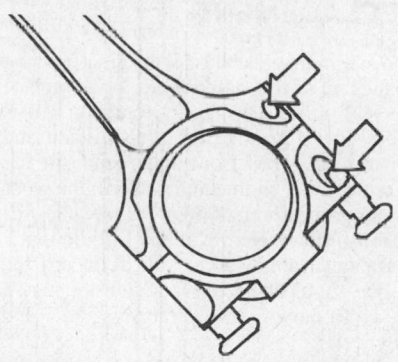

The connecting rod and cap alignment casting grooves must face the intermediate shaft

11. Lubricate the piston, rings and cylinder wall. Install and lubricate the upper bearing insert. Install a piston ring compressor over the rings and top of the piston; be sure the piston ring ends are staggered. Lower the piston and rod assembly into the cylinder bore with the arrow on the piston head facing the front of the engine. When the ring compressor contacts the top of the engine block, use a wooden hammer handle to tap the piston into the bore.

NOTE: If unusual resistance is encountered when starting the piston into the cylinder bore, it is possible that a ring slipped out of the compressor and is caught at the top of the cylinder. Remove the piston and reinstall compressor.

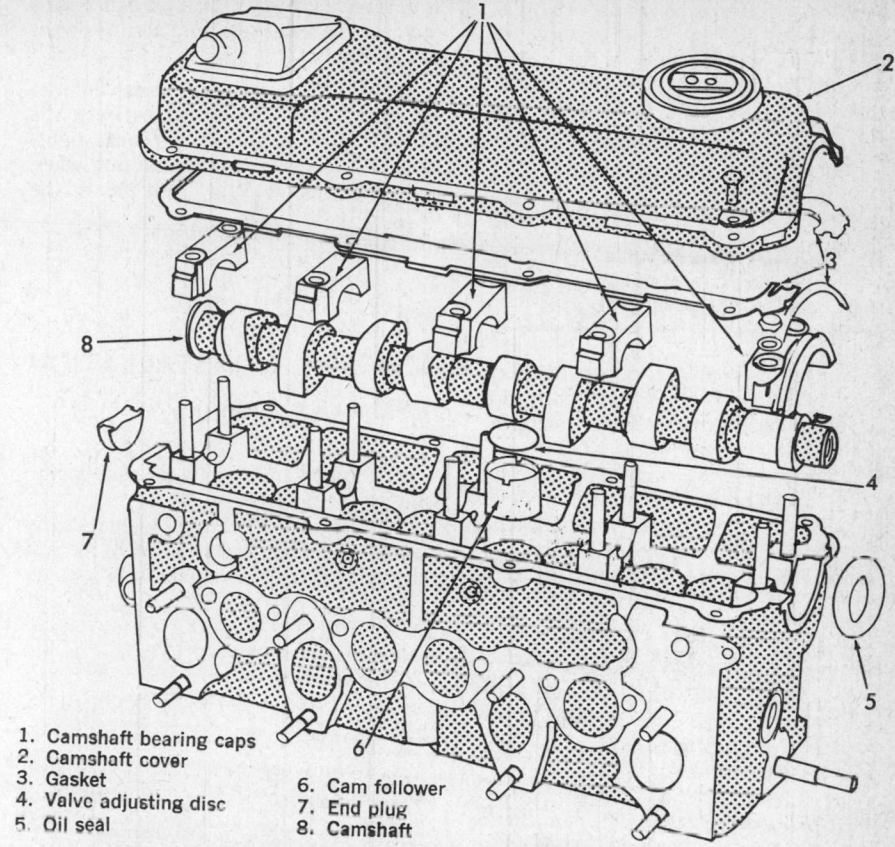

1. Camshaft bearing caps
2. Camshaft cover
3. Gasket
4. Valve adjusting disc
5. Oil seal
6. Cam follower
7. End plug
8. Camshaft

Exploded view of the camshaft assembly—gasoline engines (diesel similar)

Guide the connecting rod down the cylinder bore and over the crankshaft journal taking care not to score the wall or shaft. Install the lower bearing insert into the connecting rod cap. Lubricate the insert and mount the cap on the rod with match marks aligned. Install the rod bolts and tighten to specifications.

NOTE: Engines (1.8L) using rod bolts with a smooth surface between threads and short knurled shank and having a round head containing six notches are stretch type bolts and cannot be reused. Always use new bolts when servicing.

12. Install the remaining piston and rod assemblies in a like manner, turning the crankshaft each time so the crank journal of the piston being installed is at the bottom of travel.

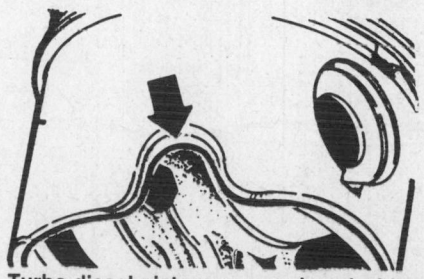

Turbo diesel pistons are equipped with a cut-out to provide clearance for a block mounted oil spray valve

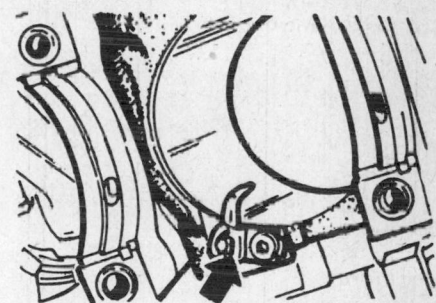

Oil jet used in turbo diesel engine to provide a spray of oil to the piston which helps cooling and lubrication

Diesel Engines

The same installation procedures apply to the diesel as to the gas engine. However, whenever new pistons or a short block are installed, the piston projection must be checked.

A spacer (VW 385/17) and bar with a micrometer are necessary, and must be set up to measure the maximum amount of piston projection above the deck height. A head gasket of suitable thickness must be used. Head gasket thickness is coded by the number of notches located on the edge. Always install a gasket with the same number of notches as the one removed. Consult your VW dealer if new pistons are installed.

NOTE: 1978 and later models (beginning with engine CK 024 944) have pis-

tons with a new piston height and a thicker cylinder head gasket. These pistons are marked with a "9" next to the installation direction arrow. New pistons can be used in earlier cars, but only in sets of 4.

ENGINE LUBRICATION

The lubrication system is a conventional wet-sump design. The gear–type oil pump is driven by the intermediate shaft. A pressure relief valve limits pressure and prevents extreme pressure from developing in the system. All oil is filtered by a full flow replaceable filter. A bypass valve assures lubrication in the event the filter becomes plugged. The oil pressure switch is located at the end of the cylinder head gallery (the end of the system) to assure accurate pressure readings.

NOTE: Turbocharged diesel engines use an oil cooler mounted between the oil filter and engine. Always check tightness of the cooler retaining nut when changing the oil filter. Nut should be torqued to 18 ft. lbs.

Oil Pan

REMOVAL & INSTALLATION

Dasher and Quantum

1. Drain the oil pan.
2. Support and slightly raise the engine with an overhead hoist.
3. Gradually loosen the engine crossmember mounting bolts. Remove the left and right side engine mounts.

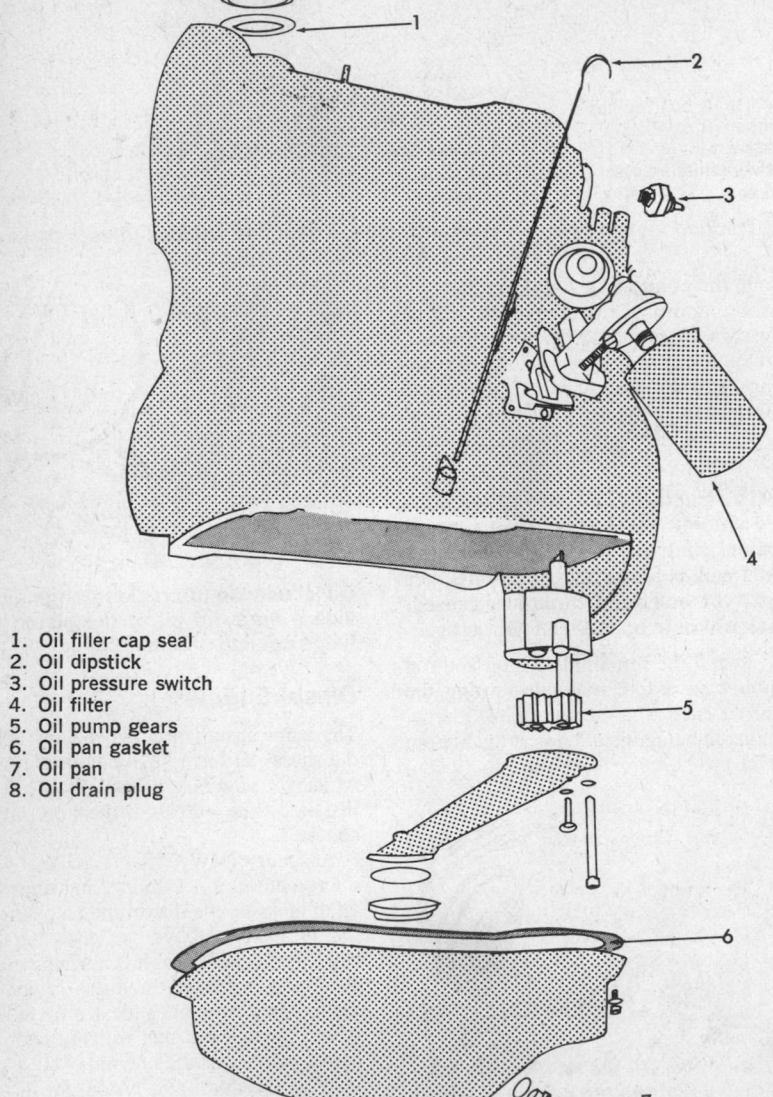

1. Oil filler cap seal
2. Oil dipstick
3. Oil pressure switch
4. Oil filter
5. Oil pump gears
6. Oil pan gasket
7. Oil pan
8. Oil drain plug

Lubrication system components

4. Lower the crossmember very carefully.
5. Loosen and remove the oil pan retaining bolts.
6. Lower the pan from the car.
7. Install the pan using a new gasket and sealer.
8. Tighten the retaining bolts in a crosswise pattern. Tighten hex head bolts to 14 ft. lbs., or Allen head bolts to 7 ft. lbs.
9. Raise the crossmember. Tighten the crossmember bolts to 42 ft. lbs. and the engine mounting bolts to 32 ft. lbs.
10. Refill the engine with oil. Start the engine and check for leaks.

Rabbit, Jetta and Scirocco

1. Drain the engine oil.
2. Loosen and remove the bolts retaining the oil pan.
3. Lower the pan from the car.
4. Install the pan using a new oil pan gasket.
5. Tighten the retaining bolts in a crisscross pattern. Tighten hex head bolts to 14 ft. lbs., or Allen head bolts to 7 ft. lbs.
6. Refill the engine with oil. Start the engine and examine the pan for leaks.

Rear Main Oil Seal

REPLACEMENT

The rear main oil seal is located in a housing on the rear of the cylinder block. To replace the seal on the Dasher and Quantum, it is necessary to remove the transmission and perform the work from underneath the car or remove the engine and perform the work on an engine stand or work bench. See "Transmission Removal and Installation."

On the Rabbit, Jetta and Scirocco, the engine should be removed from the car.

1. Remove the transmission and flywheel.
2. Using a small pry bar, very carefully pry the old seal out of the support ring.
3. Remove the seal.
4. Lightly oil the replacement seal and then press it into place using a circular piece of flat metal. Be careful not to damage the seal or score the crankshaft.
5. Install the flywheel and transmission. Flywheel-to-engine bolts are tightened to 36 ft. lbs.

Oil Pump

REMOVAL & INSTALLATION

1. Remove the oil pan.
2. Remove the two mounting bolts.
3. Pull the oil pump down and out of the engine.
4. Unscrew the two bolts and separate the pump halves.
5. Remove the driveshaft and gear from the upper body.

1. Oil seal
2. Flywheel

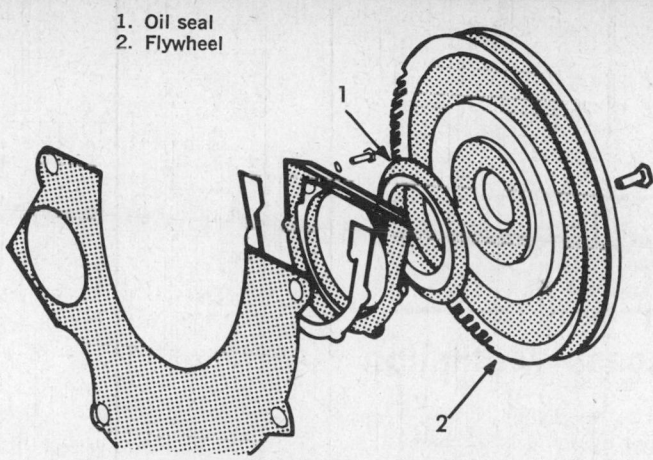

Rear main oil seal assembly

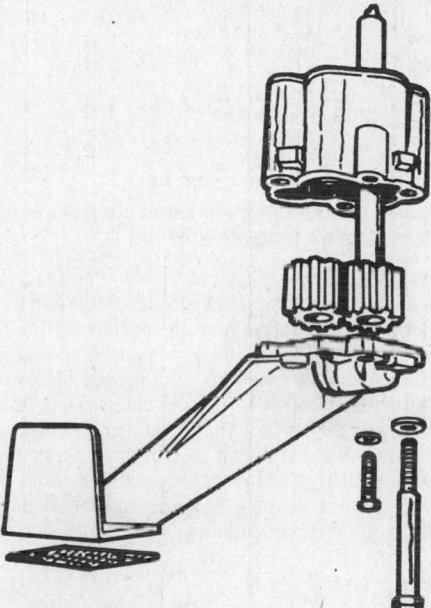

Turbo diesel oil pump—most models similar

6. Clean the bottom half in solvent. Pry up the metal edges to remove the filter screen for cleaning.

7. Examine the gears and driveshaft for wear or damage. Replace them if necessary.

8. Reassemble the pump halves.

9. Prime the pump with oil and install in the reverse order of removal.

ENGINE COOLING

The cooling system consists of a belt driven, external water pump, thermostat, radiator, and thermostatically controlled electric cooling fan. When the engine is cold the thermostat is closed and blocks the water from the radiator so the coolant is circulated only through the engine. When the engine warms up, the thermostat opens and the radiator is included in the coolant circuit. The thermostatic switch is in the bottom of the radiator and turns the electrical fan(s) on at 199°F, off at 186°F. This reduces power loss and engine noise.

NOTE: When replacing coolant/antifreeze in all models, only a phosphate-free product must be used to help prevent damage to the water jacket sealing surfaces of the cylinder head. Other types of coolant may cause corrosion of the cooling system thus leading to engine overheating and damage.

Radiator and Fan

REMOVAL & INSTALLATION

4 Cylinder

1. Drain the cooling system.

NOTE: Various late models have the radiator retained by locating tabs at the bottom and two mounting brackets at the top. Disconnect hoses, wiring connectors and top brackets. Remove the radiator and fan assembly.

2. Remove the inner shroud mounting bolts.

3. Disconnect the lower radiator hose.

4. Disconnect the thermostatic switch lead.

5. Remove the lower radiator shroud.

6. Remove the lower radiator mounting units.

7. Disconnect the upper radiator hose.

8. Detach the upper radiator shroud.

9. Disconnect the heater and intake manifold hoses.

10. Remove the side mounting bolts and top clip and lift the radiator and fan out as an assembly.

11. Installation is the reverse of removal.

5 Cylinder

1. Drain the cooling system.

2. Remove the three pieces of the radiator cowl and the fan motor assembly. Take care in removing the fan motor connectors to avoid bending them.

3. Remove the upper and lower radiator hoses and the coolant tank supply hose.

4. Disconnect the coolant temperature switch located on the lower right side of the radiator.

5. Remove the radiator mounting bolts and lift out the radiator.

6. Installation is the reverse of removal. Torque radiator mounting bolts to 14 ft. lbs. and cowl bolts to 7 ft. lbs.

Thermostat

REMOVAL & INSTALLATION

4 Cylinder

The thermostat is located in the bottom radiator hose neck on the water pump.

1. Drain the cooling system.

2. Remove the two retaining bolts from the lower water pump neck.

NOTE: It's not necessary to disconnect the hose.

3. Move the neck, with the hoses attached, out of the way.

4. Remove the thermostat.

5. Install a new seal on the water pump neck.

6. Install the thermostat with the spring end up.

7. Replace the water pump neck and tighten the two retaining bolts.

5 Cylinder

The thermostat is located in the lower radiator hose neck, on the left side of the engine block, behind the water pump housing.

Follow Steps 1–3 of the "4 Cylinder" procedure.

1. Carefully pry the thermostat out of the engine block.

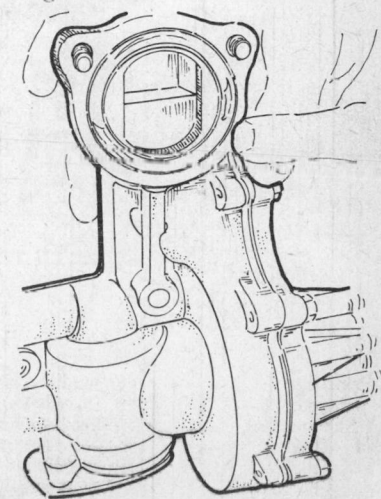

Check the condition of the O-ring before installing the water pump

2. Install a new O-ring on the water pump neck.

3. Install the thermostat.

NOTE: When installing the thermostat, the spring end should be pointing toward the engine block.

4. Reposition the water pump neck and tighten the retaining bolts.

Water Pump

REMOVAL & INSTALLATION

4 Cylinder

1. Drain the cooling system.
2. Remove the alternator and drive belt.
3. Remove the timing belt cover.
4. Disconnect the lower radiator hose, engine hose, and heater hose from the water pump.
5. Remove the four pump retaining bolts. Notice where the different length bolts are located.
6. Turn the pump slightly and lift it out of the engine block.
7. Installation is the reverse of removal. Use a new seal on the mating surface of the engine.

5 Cylinder

1. Drain the cooling system.
2. Remove the V-belts, timing belt covers and timing belts as outlined earlier in this section.
3. Unscrew the water pump pulley retaining bolts (3) and remove the pulley.
4. Unscrew the intermediate shaft drive sprocket retaining bolt and remove the sprocket.
5. Unscrew the water pump retaining bolts and remove the pump from its housing.

6. Always replace the old gasket with a new one.

7. Installation is in the reverse order of removal.

EMISSION CONTROLS

Crankcase Ventilation

The crankcase ventilation system keeps harmful vapor by-products of combustion from escaping into the atmosphere and prevents the building of crankcase pressure which can lead to oil leaking. Crankcase vapors are recirculated from the camshaft cover through a hose to the air cleaner. Here they are mixed with the air/fuel mixture and burned in the combustion chamber.

SERVICE

The only maintenance required on the crankcase ventilation system is a periodic check. At every tune-up, examine the hoses for clogging or deterioration. Clean or replace the hoses as necessary.

Evaporation Emission Control System

This system prevents the escape of raw fuel vapors (unburned hydrocarbons or HC) into the atmosphere. The system consists of a sealed carburetor, unvented fuel tank filler cap, fuel tank expansion chamber, an ac-

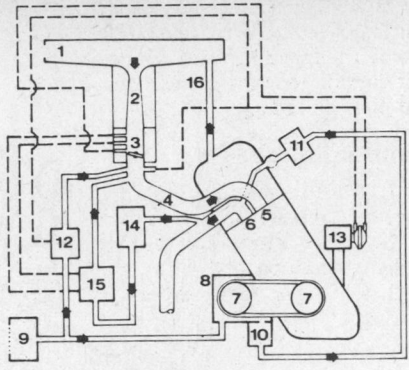

1. Air cleaner
2. Carburetor venturi
3. Throttle valve
4. Intake manifold
5. Cylinder head intake port
6. Cylinder head exhaust port
7. Belt drive for air pump
8. Air pump
9. Air pump filter
10. Pressure relief valve
11. Check valve
12. Diverter valve
13. Distributor
14. EGR filter
15. EGR valve
16. Crankcase ventilation

Carbureted Dasher emission control system. Arrows indicate flow

tivated charcoal filter canister and connector hoses. Fuel vapors which reach the filter deposit hydrocarbons on the surface of the charcoal filter element. Fresh air enters the filter when the engine is running and forces the hydrocarbons to the air cleaner where they join the air/fuel mixture and are burned.

Many 1979 and later models are equipped with a charcoal filter valve which prevents vapors from escaping from the canister when the engine is not running.

SERVICE

Maintenance of the system requires checking the condition of the various connector hoses and the charcoal filter at 10,000 mile intervals. The charcoal filter should be replaced at 50,000 mile intervals.

Dual Diaphragm Distributors

The purpose of the dual diaphragm distributor is to improve exhaust emissions during one of the engine's dirtier operating modes—idling. The distributor has a vacuum retard diaphragm, in addition to a vacuum advance diaphragm. A temperature valve shuts off vacuum from the carburetor when coolant temperatures are below 130°F.

TESTING

Advance Diaphragm

1. Connect a timing light to the engine. Check the ignition timing.

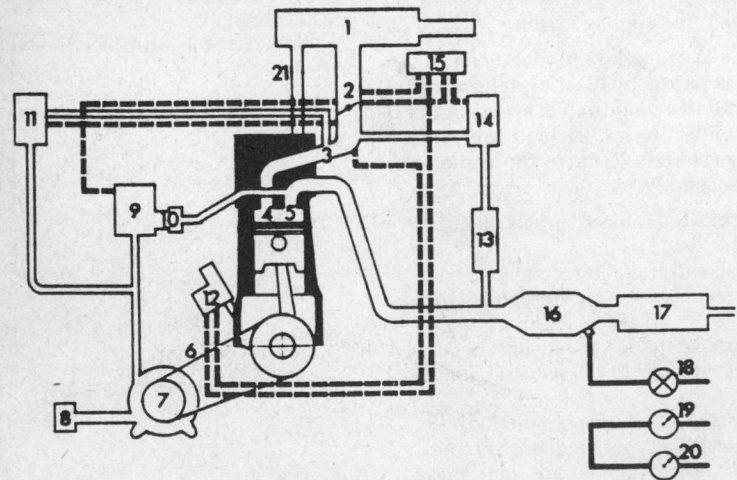

1. Air cleaner
2. Carburetor
3. Intake manifold
4. Intake port
5. Exhaust port
6. Air pump belt
7. Air pump
8. Air pump air filter
9. Diverter valve
10. Pressure valve
11. Anti-backfire valve
12. Distributor
13. EGR filter
14. EGR valve
15. Temperature valve
16. Catalytic converter
17. Muffler
18. Converter temperature light
19. EGR system indicator light
20. Converter indicator light
21. Crankcase ventilation line

Typical carbureted Rabbit, Scirocco emission control system

2. Remove the retard hose from the distributor and plug it. Increase the engine speed. The ignition timing should advance. If it doesn't, then the vacuum unit is faulty and must be replaced.

Temperature Valve

1. Remove the temperature valve and place the threaded portion in hot water.
2. Create a vacuum by sucking on the angled connection.
3. The valve must be open above approximately 130°F.

Exhaust Gas Recirculation (EGR)

To reduce NOx (oxides of nitrogen) emissions, metered amounts of exhaust gases are added to the air/fuel mixture. The recirculated exhaust gas lowers the peak flame temperature during combustion. Exhaust gas from the manifold passes through a filter where it is cleaned. The vacuum operated EGR valve controls the volume of this exhaust gas which is allowed into the intake manifold. There is no EGR at idle, partial at slight throttle and full EGR at mid-throttle.

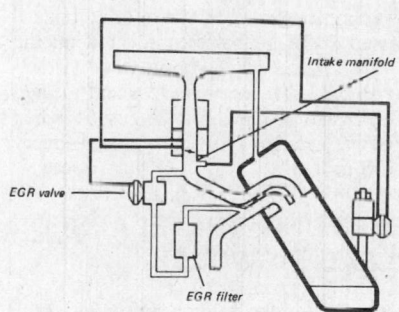

EGR system schematic

The EGR valve on fuel injected models is controlled by a temperature valve and a vacuum amplifier. The valve is located at the front of the intake manifold.

TESTING

EGR Valve

Be sure the vacuum lines are not leaking. Replace any that are leaking or cracked.
1. Warm the engine to normal operating temperature.
2. Run the engine at idle.
3. Remove the vacuum hose from the EGR valve.
4. Connect the line from the brake booster to the EGR valve (this can be done by installing a Tee in the vacuum line to the retard side of the distributor diaphragm and running a separate hose from there to the EGR valve).
5. If the engine speed does not change, the EGR valve is clogged or damaged.

EGR Temperature Valve

Warm the engine to normal operating temperature.
1. With the engine at idle, attach a vacuum gauge between the EGR temperature control valve and the EGR valve. The valve should be replaced if the gauge shows less than 2 in. Hg.

EGR Deceleration Valve

1. Remove the hose from the deceleration valve. Plug the hose.
2. Run the engine for a few seconds at 3000 rpm.
3. Snap the throttle valve closed.
4. With your finger, check for suction at the hose connection.
5. Remove the hose from the connector.
6. Run the engine at about 3000 rpm. No suction should be felt.

EGR Vacuum Amplifier

1. Run the engine at idle.
2. Connect a vacuum gauge between the vacuum amplifier and the throttle valve port.
3. The gauge should read 0.2–0.3 in. Hg. If not, check the throttle plate for correct position or check the port for obstruction.
4. Connect a vacuum gauge between the vacuum amplifier and the temperature valve.
5. Replace the vacuum amplifier if the gauge reads less than 2 in. Hg.

MAINTENANCE

The only maintenance is to reset the EGR elapsed mileage switch.

Resetting the Elapsed Mileage Switch

The EGR reminder light in the speedometer should light up every 15,000 miles as a reminder for maintenance.

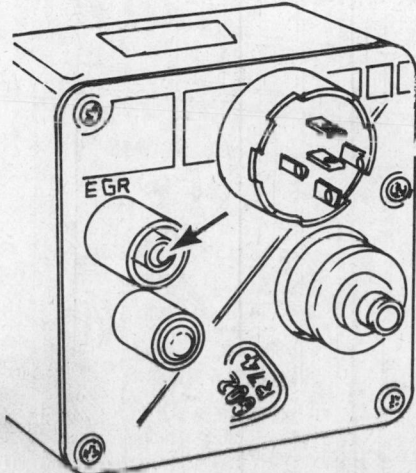

Resetting the EGR elapsed mileage odometer

To reset the light switch, press the white button. The speedometer light should go out.

Filter Replacement

1. Disconnect the filter EGR line fittings.
2. Remove the filter and discard.
3. Install the new filter into the EGR lines and securely tighten the fittings.

REMOVAL & INSTALLATION
EGR Valve

1. Disconnect the vacuum hose from the EGR valve.
2. Unbolt the EGR line fitting on the opposite side of the valve.
3. Remove the two remaining bolts and lift the EGR valve from the intake manifold.
4. Install the EGR valve in the reverse order of removal. Use a new gasket at the intake manifold.

Air Injection

The air injection system used on most carbureted engines, except the 1978 and 1980 Rabbit with 34 PICT-5 carburetor and the 1982 and later Rabbit with the TYF carburetor, includes a belt driven air pump, filter, check valve, anti-backfire valve or gulp valve, and connecting hoses and air lines. The system reduces exhaust emissions by pumping fresh air to the exhaust manifold or directly behind the exhaust valves where it combines with the hot exhaust gas to burn away excess hydrocarbons and reduce carbon monoxide.

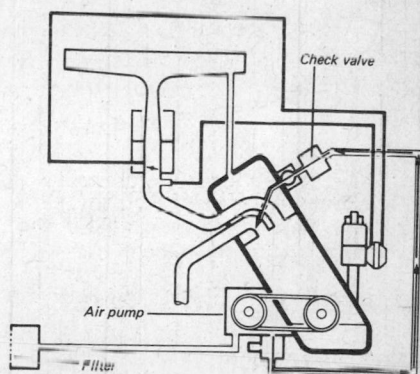

Air injection system schematic. The arrows indicate air flow

The air injection systems on the 1978, 1980 and later Rabbits with carburetors do not have air pumps. Instead, air is drawn from the air cleaner through a silencer to two check valves. The valves turn blue when overheated. If the valves are blue, replace them.

MAINTENANCE

Required maintenance on the air pump involves visually checking the pump, control valves, hoses and lines every 10,000 miles.

Clean the air pump filter element at this interval. The filter element should be replaced every 20,000 miles or two years.

TESTING AND SERVICE

Air Pump System

1. Remove and clean the air manifold.
2. Blow compressed air into the anti-backfire valve in the direction of the air flow.
3. Clean or replace the air pump filter.
4. Start the engine.
5. Exhaust gas should flow equally from each air inlet.
6. With the engine idling, block the relief valve air outlet—only a slight pressure should be felt if the system is operating properly.

Anti-Backfire Valve

1. Disconnect the air pump filter line from the anti-backfire valve.
2. Briefly disconnect the anti-backfire valve vacuum line with the engine running. There should be a noticeable vacuum.
3. Replace the anti-backfire valve if the engine backfires.

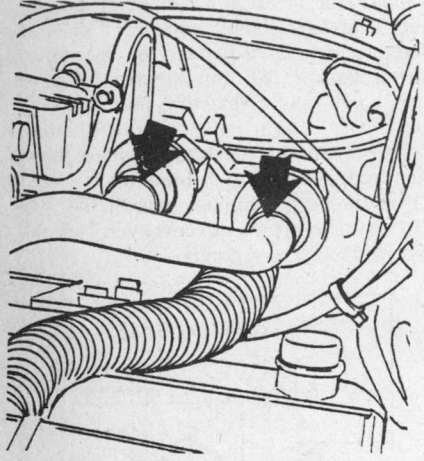

Air injection check valves on the 1978 and 1980 Rabbit (carbureted). If the valves turn blue, replace them

Catalytic Converter

MAINTENANCE

Required maintenance on the catalytic converter involves checking the condition of the ceramic insert every 30,000 miles. As this interval is reached, an indicator light on the dash will glow. Once service to the converter is performed, the odometer must be reset.

TESTING AND SERVICE

— CAUTION —

Do not drop or strike the converter assembly or damage to the ceramic insert will result.

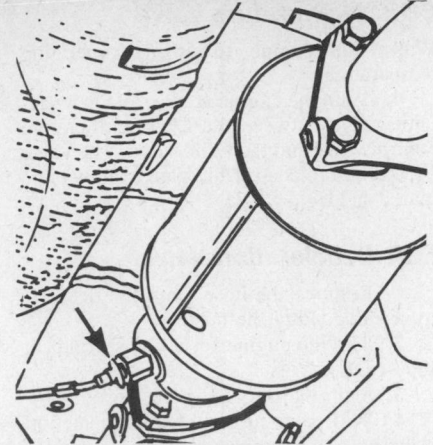

Checking catalytic converter arrow indicates the temperature sensor

Damage and overheating of the catalytic converter, indicated by the flickering of the "CAT" warning light, can be caused by the following:

1. Engine misfire caused by faulty spark plug, ignition wires and so on.
2. Improper ignition timing.
3. CO valve set too high.
4. Faulty air pump diverter valve.
5. Faulty temperature sensor.
6. Engine under strain caused by trailer hauling, high speed driving in hot weather, etc.

A faulty converter is indicated by one of the following symptoms:

1. Poor engine performance.
2. The engine stalls.
3. Rattling in the exhaust system.
4. A CO reading greater than 0.4% at the tail pipe.

Check or replace the converter as follows:

1. Disconnect the temperature sensor.
2. Loosen and remove the bolts holding the converter to the exhaust system and the chassis.
3. Remove the converter.
4. Hold the converter up to a strong light and look through both ends, checking

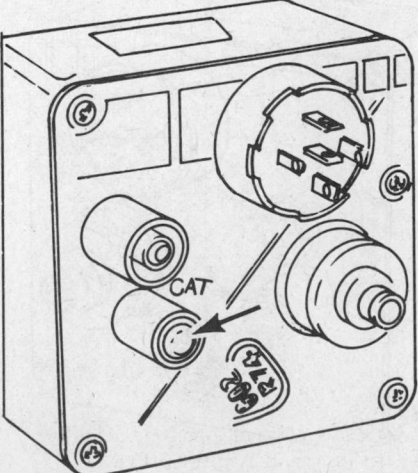

Oxygen sensor/catalytic converter reset button

for blockages. If the converter is blocked, replace it.
5. Install the converter in the reverse order of removal.
6. Reset the elapsed mileage odometer by pushing the white button marked "CAT".

Oxygen Sensor System

Many 1980 fuel injected California and all 1981 and later models are equipped with an oxygen sensor system which lowers toxic exhaust emissions while increasing fuel economy. In effect, the sensor system monitors the oxygen content in the exhaust system and, through a control unit and frequency valve, makes adjustments to the air/fuel mixture to achieve maximum fuel efficiency over a wide range of operating conditions. The system consists of the following:

Oxygen Sensor: located in the exhaust manifold. Unscrew to replace.
Control Unit: located behind the glove compartment cover.
Frequency Valve: located next to the fuel distributor .
Thermoswitch: located in the coolant system.
Oxygen Sensor System Relay: white colored relay located in the fuse/relay panel.
Elapsed Mileage Switch: located on the firewall.
Warning Light: marked OXS and located in the instrument panel. Comes on when the oxygen sensor must be replaced (every 30,000 miles).

RESETTING THE ELAPSED MILEAGE SWITCH

After replacing the oxygen sensor, reset the elapsed mileage switch by pushing the white button on the front of the switch.

FUEL SYSTEM

Mechanical Fuel Pump

CLEANING

NOTE: The mechanical fuel pump found on carbureted Rabbits is mounted on the side of the engine block.

The filter screen can be removed from the pump and cleaned.

1. Remove the center cover screw.
2. Remove the screen and gasket. Clean the screen in solvent.
3. Replace the screen.
4. Install a new gasket and replace the cover.

NOTE: Make sure the depression in the pump cover engages the projection on the body of the pump.

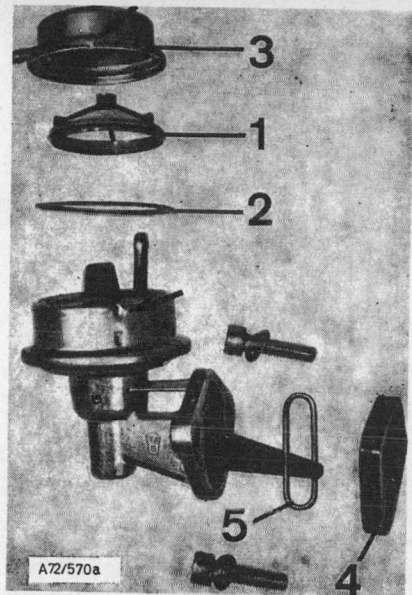

1. Screen
2. Gasket
3. Cover
4. Plastic flange
5. Flange seal

Exploded view of mechanical fuel pump

REMOVAL & INSTALLATION

The pump cannot be repaired and must be replaced when defective.

1. Disconnect and plug both fuel lines.
2. Remove the two Allen head retaining bolts.
3. Remove the fuel pump and its plastic flange.
4. Replace the pump in the reverse order of removal. Use a new flange seal.

Electric Fuel Pump

TESTING—ELECTRICAL

NOTE: Volkswagen uses a continuous injection system (CIS) in its fuel injected gasoline engines. The system includes an electric fuel pump mounted in front of the right rear axle on Rabbits and Sciroccos, and mounted below the fuel accumulator near the rear wheel on Dashers. The Jetta fuel pump is on the passenger's side in front of the rear wheel (accessible through a cover plate). The Quantum fuel pump is mounted inside the top of the car's plastic fuel tank (accessible through the rear cargo area, underneath the carpet).

1. Have an assistant operate the starter. Listen at the rear wheel to determine if the pump is running.
2. If the pump is not running, check the fuse on the front of the fuel pump relay.
3. If the fuse is good, replace the fuel pump relay.
4. If the fuel pump still does not operate, the fuel pump is faulty and must be replaced.

TESTING—FUEL PUMP DELIVERY

1. Check the condition of the fuel filter, make sure it is clean.
2. Connect a jumper wire between the No. 1 terminal on the ignition coil and ground.
3. Disconnect the return fuel line and hold it in a measuring container with a capacity of 1 quart or 1000cc.
4. Have an assistant run the starter for 30 seconds while watching the quantity of fuel delivered.

The minimum allowable flow for the 1978 Rabbit and Scirocco is 750cc ¾ of a quart) in 30 seconds; 900cc (⁹/₁₀ of a quart) in 30 seconds for 1979 and later Rabbits, Jettas and Sciroccos.

For Dashers with the type A fuel pump, identified by the fuel inlet and outlet ports being at opposite ends of the pump, the pump must deliver 1000cc (1 quart) of fuel in 32 seconds. For Dashers with the type B fuel pump, identified by the inlet and outlet ports forming a 90° angle through the center of the pump, the pump must deliver 1000cc (1 quart) of fuel in 40 seconds. Quantum fuel pump must deliver 700cc of fuel in 30 seconds.

NOTE: For the above test, the battery must be fully charged. Also, make sure you have plenty of fuel in the tank.

If the pump fails its specific test, check for a dirty fuel filter, blocked lines or blocked fuel tank strainer (if so equipped). If all of these are in good condition, replace the pump.

REMOVAL & INSTALLATION

All Models Except Quantum

1. Raise the vehicle and support it on jack stands. Disconnect the battery ground cable.
2. Remove the right rear wheel on all cars.
3. Remove the gas tank filler cap to release the fuel pressure.

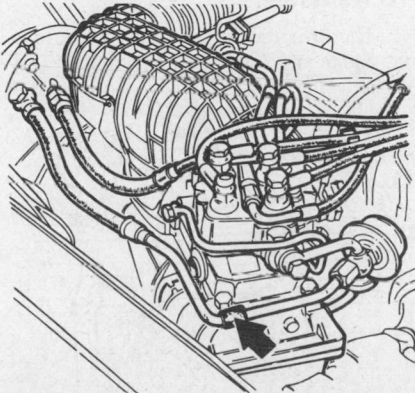

Excessive fuel pump noise on Quantum models can be eliminated with the installation of a fuel damper. Consult the dealer for necessary parts

4. Clamp off the line between the fuel pump and the fuel tank with a pair of soft jawed vise grips or other suitable lock pliers. Don't clamp the line too tightly or you may damage it.
5. Disconnect the clamped line from the fuel pump. There's bound to be a little gas in the line, so be careful.
6. If your vehicle has an accumulator mounted next to the fuel pump, disconnect the fuel lines from the accumulator. Disconnect the wiring from the fuel pump and remove all other lines after marking them for assembly.
7. Loosen and remove the retaining nuts and remove the fuel pump on Dashers and pre-79 Rabbits and Sciroccos. On 1979 and later Rabbits, Jettas and Sciroccos, remove the nuts on the lower bracket, loosen the nut on the upper slotted bracket where it connects to the body and slide the pump out.
8. Install the new fuel pump in the reverse order of removal. Make sure that the new seal washers are installed on the fuel discharge line.

Quantum

1. Pull up the carpet under the rear cargo area, revealing fuel pump access.
2. Remove the cover over the sending unit.
3. Detach the fuel return hose, fuel supply hose, and vent hose from the top of the fuel pump.
4. Disconnect the electrical wire from the sending unit and fuel pump.
5. Loosen the fuel pump attaching screws and pull the fuel pump out in one motion.
6. Installation is the reverse of removal.

Carburetor

REMOVAL & INSTALLATION

1. Remove the air cleaner.
2. Disconnect the fuel line.
3. Drain some of the coolant and then disconnect the choke hoses.
4. Disconnect the distributor and EGR valve vacuum lines.
5. Disconnect the electrical lead for the idle cut-off valve. For 1982 and later models, also disconnect the feedback solenoid, anti diesel connector and the bowl vent connector.
6. Remove the clip which secures the throttle linkage to the carburetor. Detach the linkage, being careful not to lose any washers or bushings.
7. Unbolt the carburetor from the manifold and remove it.
8. Use a new gasket when replacing the carburetor. Don't overtighten the nuts.

AUTOMATIC CHOKE ADJUSTMENT

The standard adjustment on all versions of the automatic choke is with the two notches aligned with the notch on the housing. To adjust, loosen the three clamping screws and move the outer part of the choke unit.

THROTTLE GAP ADJUSTMENT

1978 Rabbit

A vacuum gauge is required to set the throttle valve. The stop screw (1) is set at the factory, and should not be moved. If the screw is accidentally turned, proceed as follows. Make no adjustment at screw (2).

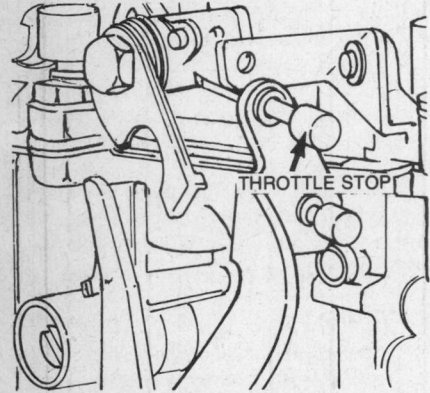

1978 Rabbit throttle gap adjustment (basic)

1. Run the engine at idle.
2. Remove the vacuum advance hose at the carburetor and connect a vacuum gauge.
3. Remove the plastic screw cap and turn the stop screw in until the gauge indicates vacuum.
4. Turn the stop screw out until the gauge indicates no vacuum. Turn the screw an additional ¼ turn and install the plastic cap.
5. Adjust the idle and CO.

1980 and 1982 and Later Rabbit

Throttle gap is set at the factory and should not be tampered with.

FAST IDLE ADJUSTMENT

1978 and 1980 Rabbit

1. Run the engine up to operating temperature and make sure the ignition setting and the idle adjustment are correct.
2. Run the engine at idle and set the adjusting screw on its third notch on the choke valve lever.
3. Open the choke valve fully by hand using the choke valve lever.
4. Connect a tachometer and check the rpm, or use the tachometer in the car, if equipped.

— CAUTION —

See "Electronic Ignition Precaution," above, for warning about connecting tachometers to electronic ignition systems.

5. The fast idle speed should be between 2350–2450 rpm. If not, adjust with fast idle adjustment screw. Lock the screw with a safety cap after adjustment.
6. On 1978 models, stop the engine, open the choke valve fully and check the gap between the adjusting screw and fast idle cam. It should be 0.008 in.

1982 and Later Rabbit

1. Run the engine until it reaches normal operating temperature. Make sure that the timing and idle speed are set to specifications.
2. Run the engine at idle and set the fast idle adjustment screw to the second step of the fast idle cam.
3. Disconnect the purge valve. Disconnect and plug the vacuum hose at the EGR valve.

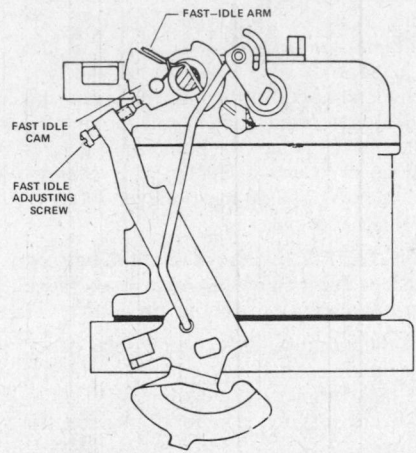

Adjusting the fast idle—1982 Rabbit

4. Connect a tachometer as per the manufacturer's instructions and check that the engine speed is 2800–3200 rpm. If not, turn the fast idle screw until it is.
5. Reconnect the purge valve and the vacuum hose at the EGR valve.

CHOKE GAP ADJUSTMENT

1978 Rabbit

1. Remove the cover from the automatic choke and fully close the choke.

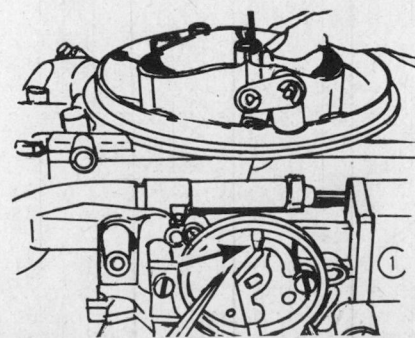

Adjusting the choke gap. (1) indicates vacuum unit which houses the choke valve gap adjusting screw (not shown)

2. Push the choke rod in the direction of the arrow and check the gap between the choke valve and the air horn wall. It should be 0.11–0.13 in.
3. Adjust the gap with the adjusting screw in the end of the vacuum unit at the side of the choke unit.
4. Reassemble the choke cover. There is an index mark on the choke housing and another on the choke cover.

1980, 1982 and Later Rabbit

1. Set the cold idle speed adjuster screw in its upper notch.
2. Connect a manually operated vacuum pump to the connection on the pulldown unit and build up vacuum.
3. Close the choke valve by hand with the lever and check the choke valve gap with a drill. The gap should be 3.3–3.7 mm. (3.9mm for 1982 and later).
4. Adjust the gap using the adjusting screw in the end of the vacuum unit at the side of the choke unit. After adjusting, lock the screw with sealant.

THROTTLE LINKAGE ADJUSTMENT

All Models (Carburetor Equipped)

Throttle linkage adjustments are not normally required. However, it is a good idea to make sure that the throttle valve(s) in the carburetor open all the way when the accelerator pedal is held in the wide-open position. Only the primary (first stage) throttle valve will open when the pedal is pushed with the engine off: the secondary throttle on Volkswagen two-barrel carburetors is vacuum-operated.

Make note of the following:
a. Always be careful not to kink or twist the cables during installation or adjustment—this can cause rapid wear and binding.
b. The accelerator cable will only bend one way—make sure you install it with the bends in the right positions.

NOTE: When installing new cables, all bends should be as wide as possible, and fittings between which the inner cable is exposed must be aligned.

OVERHAUL

For all carburetor overhaul procedures, please refer to "Carburetor Service" in the Unit Repair section.

Fuel Injection

For all fuel injection repair and service procedures not detailed below, please refer to "Fuel Injection" in the Unit Repair section.

THROTTLE CABLE ADJUSTMENT

Adjustment is made at the two locknuts where the cable is mounted on the valve (cam) cover.

1. Check that the throttle valve is closed (idle position).
2. If adjustment is necessary, loosen the locknut and turn the adjusting nut until the throttle cable is free of slack or tension.
3. Check for full throttle throw, and recheck idle position. Tighten the locknut.

Fuel Injectors

REMOVAL & INSTALLATION

1. Grasp the injector body (see illustration). DO NOT grasp and pull on the fuel line. Pull the injector straight out of the manifold.
2. Protect the injector tip—it is a precision instrument and is easily damaged. Proceed to the next injector and so on.
3. Moisten a *new* rubber seal with gasoline before reinstalling the injectors.
4. Press each injector in fully until seated.

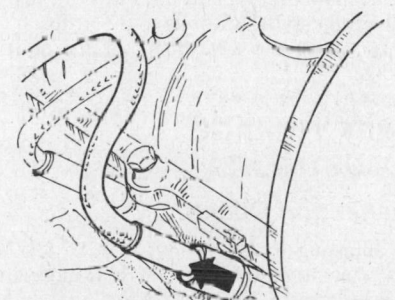

Removing fuel injector (gasoline engine). Pull on metal area near arrow, NOT on fuel line

TESTING

1. Remove the injector but leave it connected to the fuel line.
2. Point the injector into a measuring container.
3. Remove the fuel pump relay and bridge the relay plate terminals L13 and L14 with a fused (8 amp) jumper wire.
4. Remove the air duct from the air flow sensor.
5. Have an assistant turn the ignition switch on.
6. Lift the air flow sensor plate with a magnet and observe the injector nozzle spray pattern. The spray pattern must be cone shaped and even; if not, replace the injector.
7. Turn the ignition off and hold the injector horizontally. It should not drip.

NOTE: One or more injectors may be checked at the same time.

8. Moisten the rubber seals on the injectors with fuel before installing.

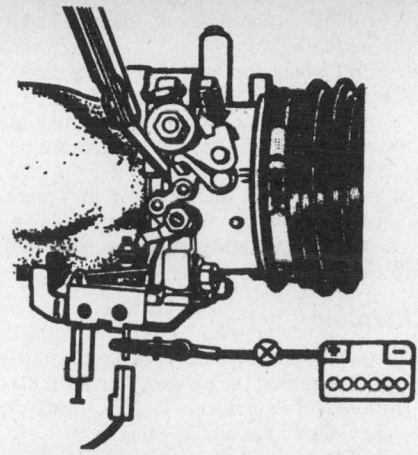

Full load enrichment switch adjustment (1.8 CIS engines). To adjust—disconnect wire on throttle valve switch and connect a test light between switch and battery. Open throttle until test light comes on. Check gap with feeler gauge. Adjust, if necessary, to .047 inches

9. Press the injectors firmly into place.

Diesel Fuel Injection

The diesel fuel system is an extremely complex and sensitive system. Very few repairs or adjustments are possible unless the owner/mechanic or professional is equipped with the proper knolwedge and tools. The injection pump itself is not repairable; it can only be replaced.

Any work done to the diesel fuel injection should be done with absolute cleanliness. Even the smallest specks of dirt will have a disastrous effect on the injection system.

Do not attempt to remove the fuel injectors. They are very delicate and must be removed with a special tool to prevent damage. The fuel in the system is also under tremendous pressure (1700–1850 psi), so it's not wise to loosen any lines with the engine running. Exposing your skin to the spray from the injector at working pressure can cause fuel to penetrate the skin.

CHECKING INJECTION PUMP TIMING

Checking the injection pump timing also involves checking the valve timing. To alter the injection pump timing, the camshaft gear must be removed and repositioned. This also changes the valve timing. Special tool (VW 210) is necessary to properly tension the injection pump drive belt on the diesel engine.

1. Set the engine at TDC on No. 1 cylinder. In this position, the TDC mark on the flywheel should be aligned with the boss on the bell housing and both valves of No. 1 cylinder should be closed.
2. The marks on the pump and mounting plate should also be aligned.

3. If the valve timing is incorrect, set the valve timing as detailed in the engine section.

ACCELERATOR CABLE ADJUSTMENT

The ball pin on the pump lever should be pointing up and be aligned with the mark in the slot. The accelerator cable should be attached at the upper hole in the bracket. With the pedal in the full throttle position, adjust the cable so that the pump lever contacts the stop with no binding or strain.

COLD START CABLE ADJUSTMENT

When the cold start knob on the dash is pulled out, the fuel injection pump timing is advanced 2.5°. This improves cold starting and running until the engine warms up.

1. Insert the washer on the cable.
2. Insert the cable in the bracket with the rubber housing. Install the cable in the pin.
3. Install the lockwasher.
4. Move the lever to the zero position (direction of arrow). Pull the inner cable tight and tighten the clamp screw.

BLOW-OFF VALVE

A blow-off valve is provided as a safety device should a turbocharger system malfunction occur. If boost pressure is too low, or a sudden loss of power occurs, a defective blow-off valve could be the cause.

To check the blow-off valve:
Disconnect the blow-off valve hose from the intake air duct. Plug the air hose with a one inch plug secured with a hose clamp. Perform a boost pressure test. If the boost pressure test is OK, replace the blow-off valve. If boost pressure test is still not OK, replace the turbocharger.

Boost Pressure Test

A special test gauge (VW1397) reading "Bar" and "PSI" is required. The VW gauge is an "overpressure" type gauge.

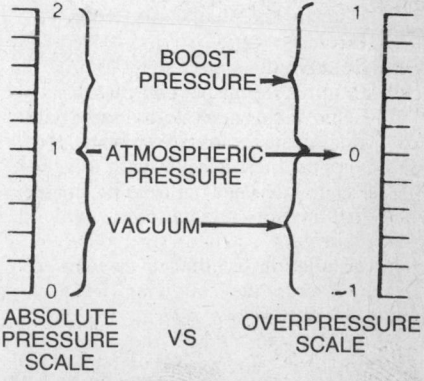

Conversion chart comparing an absolute pressure gauge and a overpressure gauge

Other test gauge manufacturer's produce "absolute pressure", a reading of 0.6 Bar is six-tenths of a bar over atmospheric pressure. On an "absolute pressure" gauge, a reading on 1 Bar indicates normal atmospheric pressure. A reading of over "1 bar" indicates boost pressure. A reading below "1 bar" on an absolute gauge indicates intake manifold pressure.

To install gauge: Connect gauge tee fitting to the boost pressure line at the injection pump. Route the hose and gauge out of the corner of the hood and in through the passenger's window. Test drive the car with the engine at normal operating temperature. Open the valve to the pressure gauge. Accelerate in 3rd gear, or number 2 drive position, and hold the vehicle speed constant at 35 mph (4000 rpm). Close the gauge valve after operating the car for about two seconds at required rpm. The boost pressure should be 0.64–0.70 Bar (9.3–10.2 psi).

If boost pressure is too high, possible causes are a leak in the control line to the wastegate or a defective wastegate. If the boost reading is too low, possible causes are a defective blow–off valve, wastegate or turbocharger. A dirty air cleaner or leaks in the turbo system will also cause low pressure readings. If tests indicate problems in the turbocharger or wastegate, a replacement unit is required since no repairs are possible.

MANUAL TRANSMISSION

REMOVAL & INSTALLATION

Dasher

1. Disconnect the battery ground cable.
2. Disconnect the exhaust pipe from the manifold and its bracket on the transaxle.
3. Remove the square-headed bolt on the shift linkage. Later models have a hex head bolt.
4. Press the shift linkage coupling off.
5. Disconnect the clutch cable.
6. Disconnect the speedometer cable.
7. Detach the halfshafts from the transaxle.
8. Remove the starter.
9. Remove the inspection plate.
10. Remove the engine-to-transaxle bolts.
11. Remove the transaxle crossmember.
12. Support the transaxle with a jack.
13. Pry the transaxle out from the engine.
14. Lift the transaxle out of the car with an assistant.
15. Installation is the reverse of removal. Observe the following when installing the transaxle.
    a. When installing the transaxle crossmember, do not fully tighten the bolts until the transaxle is aligned and fully installed in the vehicle.

b. Tighten the engine-to-transaxle bolts to 40 ft. lbs.
c. Tighten the axle shaft bolts to 33 ft. lbs.
d. On models with the rubber core rear transaxle mount, the rubber core must be centered in its housing.
e. Make sure there is a ⅜ in. clearance between the header pipe and the floor of the vehicle.
f. Adjust the clutch (see below).

Quantum

1. Disconnect the battery ground strap.
2. Disconnect the exhaust pipe from the manifold and its bracket.
3. Unhook the clutch cable.
4. Detach the speedometer cable.
5. Remove the upper engine/transmission bolts.
6. Remove the engine support bolts on both sides of the engine block (front).
7. Remove the front muffler and exhaust pipe.
8. Unbolt both driveshafts (halfshafts) at the transmission.
9. Disconnect the back-up light wiring.
10. Remove the inspection plate on the bottom of transmission case.
11. Remove the starter bolt.
12. Remove the shift rod coupling bolt; pry off the shift rod coupling ball with a prybar.
13. Pull off the shift rod coupling from the shift rod.
14. Place a jack under the transmission and lift slightly.
15. Remove the transmission support bolts, and transmission rubber mounts.
16. Remove the front transmission support bolts, and lower the transmission/engine support bolts.
17. Slowly pry the transmission from the engine.
18. Lower the transmission out of the car.

When installing the transmission in the reverse order of removal, make sure the main-shaft splines are clean and lubricated with a molybdenum-disulfide grease. Make sure the inspection plate is properly seated, and that all engine/transmission mounting bolts are aligned and free of tension (holes lined up) before tightening everything. Readjust the shift mechanism if necessary.
    a. Tighten the transmission/engine bolts to 40 ft. lbs.
    b. Tighten the driveshaft/drive flange bolts to 33 ft. lbs.
    c. Front transmission support-to-transmission is tightened to 18 ft. lbs.
    d. Transmission-to-body bolts are tightened to 80 ft. lbs.

Rabbit, Scirocco, Jetta

The engine and transaxle may be removed together as explained under "Engine Removal and Installation" or the transaxle may be removed alone, as explained here.
1. Disconnect the battery ground cable.

2. Support the left end of the engine at the lifting eye.
3. Remove the left transmission mount (between the transmission and the firewall).
4. Turn the engine until the lug on the flywheel (to the left of the TDC mark) aligns with the flywheel timing pointer.
5. Detach the speedometer drive cable, back–up light wire, and clutch cable.
6. Remove the engine–to–transmission bolts.
7. Disconnect the shift linkage.
8. Detach the transmission ground strap.
9. Remove the starter.
10. Remove the engine mounting support near the starter.
11. Remove the rear transmission mount.
12. Unbolt and wire up the halfshafts.
13. From underneath, remove the bolts for the large cover plate, but don't remove it. Unbolt the small cover plate on the firewall side of the engine. Remove the engine–to–transmission nut immediately below the small plate.
14. Press the transmission off the dowels and remove it from below the car.
To install the transaxle:
15. The recess in the flywheel edge must be at 3:00 o'clock. Tighten the engine–to–transmission bolts to 47 ft. lbs. Tighten the engine mounting support bolts to 47 ft. lbs. Tighten the halfshaft bolts to 32 ft. lbs.
16. Check the adjustment of the shift linkage.

SHIFT LINKAGE ADJUSTMENT

Dasher and Quantum

An adjusting tool, VW 3014, (VW 3057 for Quantum) must be used on these models.
1. Place the lever in Neutral.
2. Working under the car, loosen the clamp nut.
3. Inside the car, remove the gear lever knob and the shift boot. It is not necessary to remove the console. Align the centering holes of the lever housing and the lever bearing housing.
4. Install the tool with the locating pin toward the front. Push the lever to the left side of the tool cut-out. Tighten the lower knurled knob to secure the tool.

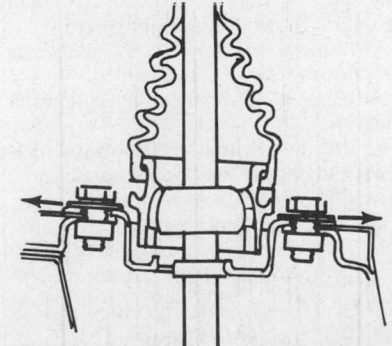

Quantum and Dasher manual transmission second gear shift lever adjustment

5. Move the top slide of the tool to the left stop and tighten the upper knurled knob.

6. Push the shift lever to the right side of the cutout. Align the shift rod and shift finger under the car, and tighten the clamp nut. Remove the tool.

7. Place the lever in first. Press the lever to the left side against the stop. Release the lever; it should spring back ¼–½ in. If not, move the lever housing slightly sideways to correct. Check that all gears can be engaged easily, particularly reverse.

Rabbit, Scirocco, Jetta

1. Align the holes of the lever housing plate with the holes of the lever bearing plate.

2. Loosen the shift rod clamp. Pull the boot off the lever housing and push it out of the way. It may be necessary to loosen the screws in the cover plate to free the boot.

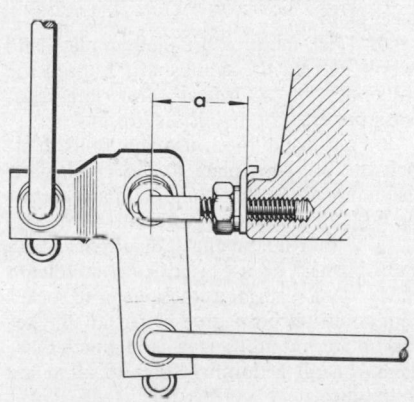

The short angled rod on the Rabbit and Scirocco shift linkage is to be adjusted to a length (a) of 1.18—1.25 in.

3. Check that the shift finger is in the center of the stopping plate.

4. Adjust the shift rod end so that it is ¾ in. (⁹⁄₃₂ in. for five speed transmissions) from the right side of the lever housing. Tighten the shift rod clamp and check the shifter operation.

SELECTOR SHAFT LOCKBOLT ADJUSTMENT

Make this adjustment on Rabbits, Jettas and Sciroccos after linkage adjustment, if the linkage still feels spongy or jams.

1. Disconnect the shift linkage and put the transmission in Neutral.

2. Loosen the locknut and turn the adjusting sleeve in until the lockring lifts off the sleeve.

3. Turn the adjusting sleeve back until the lockring just contacts the sleeve. Tighten the locknut.

4. Turn the shaft slightly. The lockring should lift as soon as the shaft is turned.

5. Reconnect the linkage.

FIFTH GEAR LOCKBOLT ADJUSTMENT

Rabbit, Scirocco, Jetta Only

This adjustment is made with the transmission in neutral. The fifth gear lockbolt is located on top of the transmission next to the selector shaft lockbolt. It has a large protective cap over it.

1. Remove the protective cap.

2. Loosen the locknut and tighten the adjusting sleeve until the detent plunger in the center of the sleeve just begins to move up.

3. Loosen the adjusting sleeve ⅓ of a turn and tighten the locknut. Make sure the transmission shifts in and out of fifth gear easily. Replace the protective cap.

OVERHAUL

For all overhaul procedures, please refer to "Manual Transxale Overhaul" in the Unit Repair section.

CLUTCH

PEDAL FREE PLAY ADJUSTMENT

Clutch pedal free–play should be ⅝ in. for all Dashers and pre-1979 Rabbits and Sciroccos. 1979 and later models should have ²⁷⁄₃₂ to 1 in. free–play.

Clutch pedal free–play is the distance the pedal can be depressed before the linkage starts to act on the throwout bearing. Clutch free–play insures that the clutch plate is fully engaged and not slipping. Clutches with no, or insufficient, free–play often wear

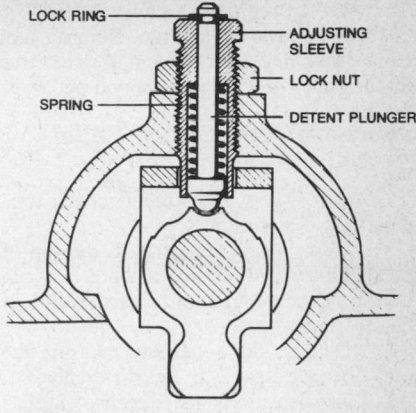

On Rabbit, Jetta and Scirocco, loosen the locknut and turn the adjusting sleeve

out quickly and give marginal power performance.

1. Adjust the clutch pedal free–play by loosening or tightening the two nuts (or locknut and threaded sleeve) on the cable near the oil filter on Dasher and Quantum. On the Rabbit, Jetta and Scirocco, the left side (driver's) at the front of the transaxle.

NOTE: Correct free–play cannot be measured correctly if the floor covering interferes with clutch pedal travel. See the following section for instructions on late model adjustment.

2. Loosen the locknut and loosen or tighten the adjusting nut or sleeve until desired play is present. Depress the clutch pedal several times and recheck free–play. Readjust if necessary. Tighten the locknut.

3. On late models, VW recommends that a special tool (US5043) be used to determine proper adjustment. The procedure for adjustment follows; depress the clutch pedal several times. Loosen the locknut and insert the tool. Adjust the sleeve until zero

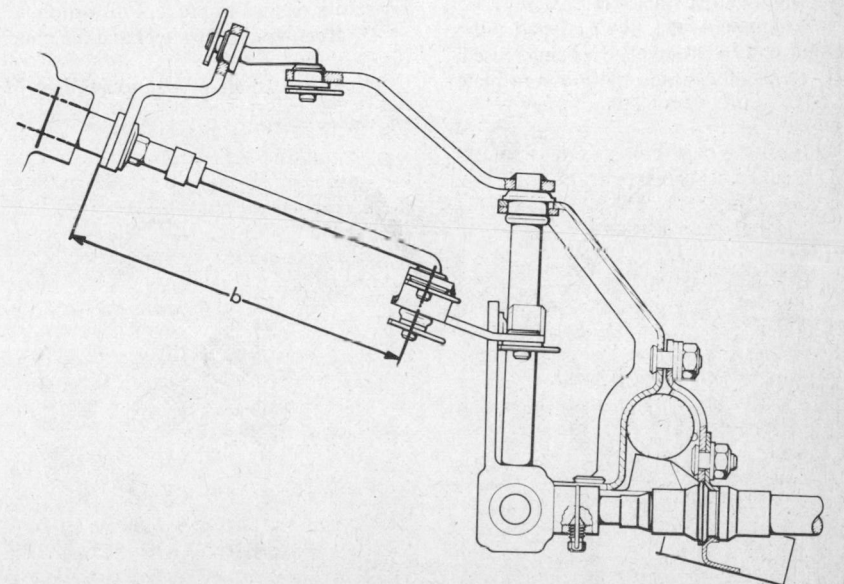

The long rod on the Rabbit and Scirocco shift linkage is to be adjusted to a length (b) of 6.42-6.50 in.

clearance between the sleeve and tool is reached. Tighten the locknut. Remove tool and depress the clutch pedal at least five times. Check free–play at clutch pedal.

Checking Total Clutch Pedal Travel

Prior to free–play adjustment, check total pedal travel as follows;

1. Hook a tape measure to the top of the clutch pedal. Measure distance between the top of the pedal and the center–line of the steering wheel.

2. Depress the pedal and measure the total distance again. If the difference between the measurements exceeds 4.68 in., the floor covering may be interfering with pedal travel.

CABLE REMOVAL & INSTALLATION

1. Loosen the adjustment.
2. Disengage the cable from the clutch arm.
3. Unhook the cable from the pedal. Remove the threaded eye from the end of the cable. Remove the adjustment nut(s).
4. Remove the C-clip which holds the outer cable at the adjustment point. Remove all the washers and bushings, first noting their locations.
5. Pull the cable out of the firewall toward the engine compartment side.
6. Install and connect the new cable. Adjust the pedal free-play.

Clutch Assembly

REMOVAL & INSTALLATION

Dasher and Quantum

1. Remove the transaxle.
2. Matchmark the flywheel and pressure plate if the pressure plate is being reused.
3. Gradually loosen the pressure plate

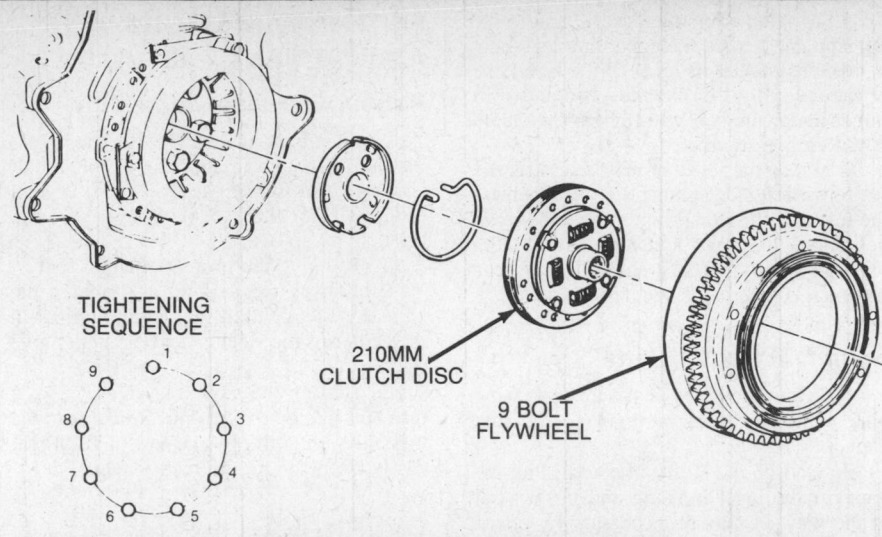

TIGHTENING SEQUENCE

210MM CLUTCH DISC

9 BOLT FLYWHEEL

Clutch assembly on transverse mounted engines. 210mm late model shown

bolts one or two turns at a time in a criss-cross pattern to prevent distortion.

4. Remove the pressure plate and disc.
5. Check the clutch disc for uneven or excessive lining wear. Examine the pressure plate for cracking, scorching, or scoring. Replace any questionable components.
6. Install the clutch disc and pressure plate. Use a dummy shaft to keep the disc centered.
7. Gradually tighten the pressure plate-to-flywheel bolts in a crisscross pattern. Tighten the bolts to 18 ft. lbs.
8. Install the throwout bearing.
9. Install the transaxle on the engine.
10. Replace the transaxle.

Rabbit, Scirocco, Jetta

1. Remove the transmission.
2. Attach a toothed flywheel holder and gradually loosen the flywheel–to–pressure plate bolts one or two turns at a time in a crisscross pattern to prevent distortion.
3. Remove the flywheel and the clutch disc.
4. Use a small prybar to remove the

release plate retaining ring. Remove the release plate.

5. Lock the pressure plate in place and unbolt it from the crankshaft. Loosen the bolts one or two turns at a time in a crisscross pattern to prevent distortion.
6. On installation, use new bolts to attach the pressure plate to the crankshaft. Use a thread locking compound and torque the bolts in a diagonal pattern to 54 ft. lbs.
7. Lubricate the clutch disc splines with multi-purpose grease. Lubricate the release plate contact surface and pushrod socket with multi-purpose grease. Install the release plate, retaining ring, and clutch disc.
8. Install a dummy shaft to align the clutch disc.
9. Install the flywheel, tightening the bolts one or two turns at a time in a crisscross pattern to prevent distortion. Torque the bolts to 14 ft. lbs.
10. Replace the transmission.

AUTOMATIC TRANSMISSION

REMOVAL & INSTALLATION

Dasher and Quantum

The following procedures are for both types of Dasher automatic transmissions, the 003 and the 089. The type numbers are visible on the top of the automatic transmission unit (as opposed to the differential unit) of the transaxle. Another way to tell the type 003 transmission from the 089 is the type 003 has a vacuum modulator hose coming from the driver's side front of the transmission above the pan. The type 089 does not. Don't confuse the ATF filler pipe with the above mentioned hose. Quantum transmission is the 089 model.

1. Disconnect the battery ground strap.

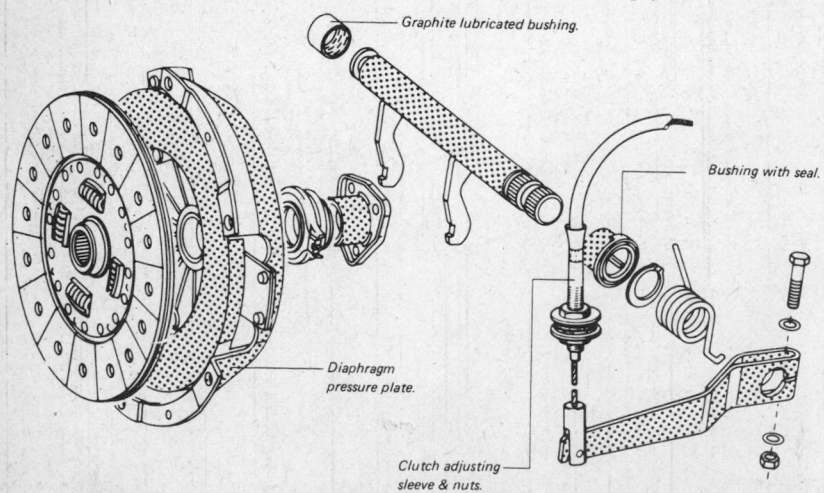

Graphite lubricated bushing.

Bushing with seal.

Diaphragm pressure plate.

Clutch adjusting sleeve & nuts.

Quantum and Dasher clutch components; the adjusting sleeve and nuts are adjacent to the oil filter in the engine compartment

2. Raise the car and place the support stands so that you will have free access to the transaxle and axle shafts.

3. Disconnect the speedometer cable.

4. On the 089, remove the accelerator cable from the throttle valve housing.

5. Remove two of the upper engine/transaxle bolts. On the 089 transmission, support the engine with either special tool 10-222 or an appropriate jack.

6. Disconnect the exhaust pipe.

7. Remove the torque converter cover plate. On the 003 transmission, remove the vacuum modulator hose.

8. Remove the circlip holding the selector lever cable to the lever and remove the cable.

9. Remove the starter.

10. On the 003, disconnect the kickdown switch wires.

11. The torque converter is mounted to the flywheel by three bolts. The bolts are accesible through the starter hole. You'll have to turn the engine over by hand to remove all three.

12. Remove the axle shaft-to-transaxle socket head bolts.

13. Matchmark the position of the ball joint on the left control arm and remove the ball joint from the arm. Hold the wheel assembly out away from the arm to provide clearance between the axle shaft and the transmission.

14. Remove the exhaust pipe from the transaxle bracket.

15. Disconnect the remaining transmission controls. Those you cannot reach can be removed when the transaxle is lowered a little.

16. Unbolt the transaxle crossmember and remove it from the transaxle.

17. Support the transaxle on a jack and loosen the lower engine/transaxle bolts.

18. On the 089 transmission, remove all engine/transaxle bolts. Have an assistant pull the left wheel out as far as it will go and slowly lower the transmission, making sure the torque converter does not fall off.

19. On the 003 transmission, loosen the union nut on the ATF filler pipe so that the pipe can be swivelled. Remove the engine/transaxle bolts and lower the unit. You may have to pull the left wheel out a little so that the axle shaft clears the transaxle case. Make sure the torque converter does not fall off.

20. Installation is the reverse of removal with the following notes.

   a. On both transaxles, the torque converter nipple must be about $^{13}/_{16}$ in. from the bell housing face surface. If it sticks out further than this, the oil pump shaft has probably pulled out. You'll have to manipulate the converter and shaft until it goes in again.

   b. Tighten the engine/transaxle bolts to 40 ft. lbs. and the torque converter bolts to 20–23 ft. lbs. New torque converter bolts should be used. Torque the axleshaft bolts to 33 ft. lbs., and the ball joint-to-control arm bolts to 45 ft. lbs.

Check the shift linkage adjustment.

Rabbit, Scirocco, Jetta

The engine and transaxle may be removed together as explained under "Engine Removal and Installation" or the transaxle may be removed alone, as explained here.

1. Disconnect both battery cables.

2. Disconnect the speedometer cable at the transmission.

3. Support the left end of the engine at the lifting eye. Attach a hoist to the transaxle.

4. Unbolt the rear transmission carrier from the body then from the transaxle. Unbolt the left side carrier from the body.

5. Unbolt the halfshafts and wire them up.

6. Remove the starter.

7. Remove the three converter-to-drive plate bolts.

8. Shift into P and disconnect the floorshift linkage at the transmission.

9. Remove the accelerator and carburetor cable bracket at the transmission.

10. Unbolt the left side transmission carrier from the transmission.

11. Unbolt the front transmission mount from the transmission.

12. Unbolt the bottom of the engine from the transmission. Lift the transaxle slightly, remove the rest of the bolts, pull the transmission off the mounting dowels, and lower the transaxle out of the car. Secure the converter so it doesn't fall out.

— CAUTION —
Don't tilt the torque converter.

To install:

13. Be sure the torque converter is fully seated on the one-way clutch support. Push the transmission onto the mounting dowels and install two bolts. Lift the unit until the left driveshaft can be installed and install the rest of the bolts. Torque them to 39 ft. lbs.

14. Tighten the front transmission mount bolts to 39 ft. lbs. Install the left side transmission carrier to the transmission.

15. Connect the accelerator and carburetor cable bracket. Connect the floorshift linkage.

16. Tighten the torque converter–to–drive plate bolts to 22 ft. lbs. Torque the driveshaft bolts to 32 ft. lbs.

17. Install the rear transmission carrier and make sure that the left side carrier is aligned in the center of the body mount. Bolt the left side carrier to the body.

18. Connect the speedometer cable and the battery cables.

PAN & STRAINER SERVICE

Dasher and Quantum

VW recommends that the automatic transmission fluid be replaced every 30,000 miles, or 20,000 miles if used for trailer towing, mountain driving, or other severe service.

1. Four (4) quarts of automatic trans-

mission fluid (Dexron®) and a pan gasket are required.

2. Slide a drain pan under the transmission. Jack up the front of the car and support it.

3. Remove the drain plug and allow all the fluid to drain.

NOTE: Some models are not equipped with pan drain plugs. In this case, empty the pan by loosening the pan bolts and allowing the fluid to drain out.

4. Remove the pan retaining bolts and drop the pan.

5. Discard the old gasket and clean the pan with solvent.

6. Unscrew and clean the circular strainer. If it is dirty, it should be replaced.

7. Install the strainer, but don't tighten the bolt too much—specified torque is only 4 ft. lbs.

8. Refill the transmission with about 2¾ qts. of fluid. Check the level with the dipstick. Run the car for a few minutes and check again.

Rabbit, Scirocco, Jetta

NOTE: As of transmission No. 09096 a new, cleanable oil filter is used which

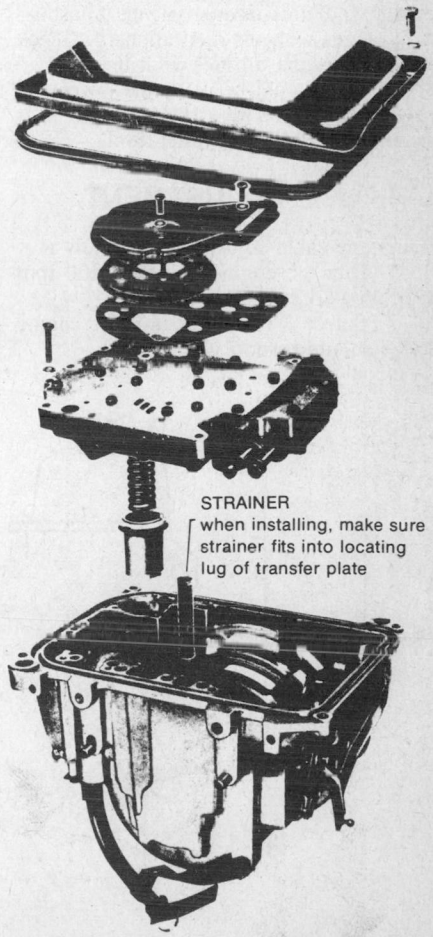

STRAINER
when installing, make sure strainer fits into locating lug of transfer plate

Beginning with transaxle 13 03 8, an additional strainer is used beneath the valve body. It cannot be installed on earlier models

requires a deeper oil pan. Also beginning with transmission number EQ-15 106, the drain plug was no longer installed in the oil pan.

1. Remove the drain plug and let the fluid drain into a pan. If the pan has no drain plug, loosen the pan bolts until a corner of the pan can be lowered to drain the fluid.

2. Remove the pan bolts and take off the pan.

3. Discard the old gasket and clean the pan out. Be very careful not to get any threads or lint from rags into the pan.

4. The filter needn't be replaced unless the fluid is dirty or smells burnt. The specified torque for the strainer screws is 2 ft. lbs.

NOTE: Beginning with Transmission number 13 03 8, there is an additional strainer under the valve body. When installing it, be sure it fits into the locating lug of the transfer plate.

5. Replace the pan with a new gasket and tighten the bolts, in a crisscross pattern, to 14 ft. lbs.

6. Using a long-necked funnel, pour in 2½ qts. of Dexron® automatic transmission fluid through the dipstick tube. Start the engine and shift through all the transmission ranges with the car stationary. Check the level on the dipstick with the lever in Neutral. It should be up to the lower end of the dipstick. Drive the car until it is warmed up and recheck the level.

LINKAGE ADJUSTMENT

Check the cable adjustment as follows:

1. Run the engine at 1000–1200 rpm with the parking brake on.

2. Select Reverse—a drop in engine speed should be noticed.

3. Select Park—engine speed should increase. Pull the shift lever against Reverse, the engine speed shouldn't drop (because reverse gear has not been engaged).

4. Move the shift lever to engage Reverse—engine speed should drop as the gear engages.

5. Move the shift lever to Neutral—an increase in engine speed should be noticed.

6. Shift the lever into Drive—a noticeable drop in engine speed should result.

7. Shift into 1—the lever must engage without having to overcome any resistance.

8. To adjust the cable—shift into Park. On Dashers (from chassis no. 3-5 2 044 957 and later) and Quantum, the shift cable clamp is loosened from inside the passenger's compartment. Have an assistant under the car press the transmission lever toward the Park position and tighten the clamp.

On the Rabbit, Jetta and Scirocco, shift into Park, loosen the cable clamp at the transmission end of the cable, press the transmission lever all the way to the left and tighten the cable clamp.

TRANSMISSION CABLE ADJUSTMENT

NOTE: Early Dashers with the type 003 automatic transmission (identified by the modulator hose attached to the driver's side front of the transmission above the pan) have a kickdown switch rather than a throttle cable. See below for switch test.

Make sure the throttle is closed, and the choke and fast idle cam are off (carbureted models).

1. Detach the cable end at the transmission.

2. Press the lever at the transmission into its closed throttle position.

3. You should be able to attach the cable end onto the transmission lever without moving the lever.

4. Adjust the cable length to the correct setting.

KICKDOWN SWITCH CHECK

Dasher

NOTE: Early Dashers with the type 003 automatic transmission (identified by the modulator hose attached to the driver's side front of the transmission above the pan) are the only VWs equipped with kickdown switches. All other models have throttle cable kickdowns (see above).

1. Turn the ignition switch ON.

2. Floor the accelerator—you should hear a click from the solenoid on the transmission.

3. Replace the solenoid if no sound is heard. The solenoid is housed in the valve body and is accessible only be removing this unit from the transmission: a job you should depend on a qualified mechanic to perform.

FIRST AND SECOND GEAR (FRONT AND REAR) BAND ADJUSTMENTS

Dasher W/Type 003 Transmission Only

The type 003 transmission is identified by the modulator hose attached to the driver's side front of the transmission above the pan.

NOTE: The transmission must be horizontal when the band adjustments are performed.

The adjustment screws are located at the top of the transmission housing with the first gear band being closest to the front of the unit on the passenger's side of the car. The second gear band adjustment screw is located toward the rear of the unit on the driver's side of the vehicle.

1. To adjust the first gear band, loosen

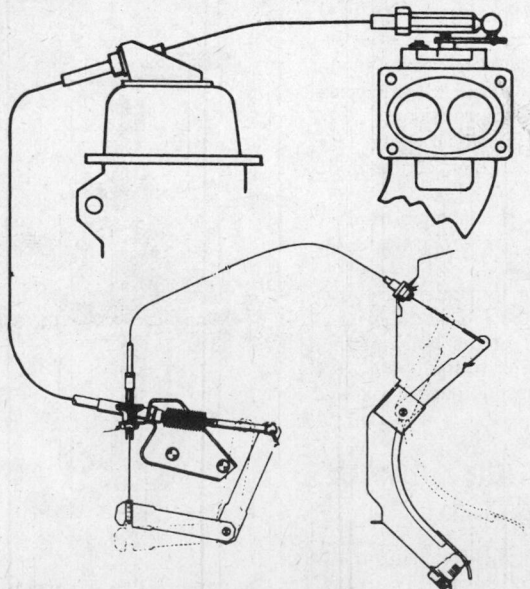

Rabbit, Jetta, Scirocco automatic transmission cable arrangement—fuel injected

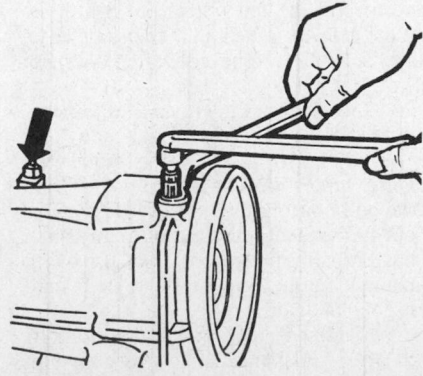

Dasher type 003 transaxle band adjustment—front band (first gear) being adjusted, arrow locates second gear band adjustment screw

the locknut and tighten the adjusting screw to 7 ft. lbs.

2. Loosen the screw and retighten it to 3.5 ft. lbs.

3. Turn the screw out 3¼–3½ turns and then tighten the locknut.

4. To adjust the second gear band, repeat Steps 1 and 2 on the second gear band adjusting screw, then turn the screw out exactly 2½ turns and tighten the locknut.

SECOND GEAR (REAR) BAND ADJUSTMENT

Dasher and Quantum W/Type 089 Transmission, Rabbit, Jetta, Scirocco

NOTE: The transmission must be horizontal when band adjustments are performed.

1. Loosen the locknut on the adjusting screw, which is located on the front of the Rabbit and Scirocco transmission and the driver's side on the Dasher.

2. Tighten the adjusting screw to 7 ft. lbs.

3. Loosen the screw and tighten it again to 4 ft. lbs.

4. Turn the screw out exactly 2½ turns and then tighten the locknut.

NEUTRAL START/BACK–UP LIGHT SWITCH

The combination neutral start and back-up light switch is mounted inside the shifter housing. The starter should operate in Park or Neutral only. Adjust the switch by moving it on its mounts. The back-up lights should only come on when the shift selector is in the Reverse position.

DRIVE AXLES

Halfshafts

REMOVAL & INSTALLATION

Dasher and Quantum

NOTE: When removing the right side halfshaft, you must detach the exhaust pipe from the manifold and the transaxle bracket. Be sure to buy a new exhaust flange gasket.

1. With the car on the ground, remove the front axle nut.

NOTE: Use a longer breaker bar with an extension (length of pipe).

2. Raise and support the front of the vehicle.

3. Remove the socket head bolts retaining the halfshaft to the transaxle.

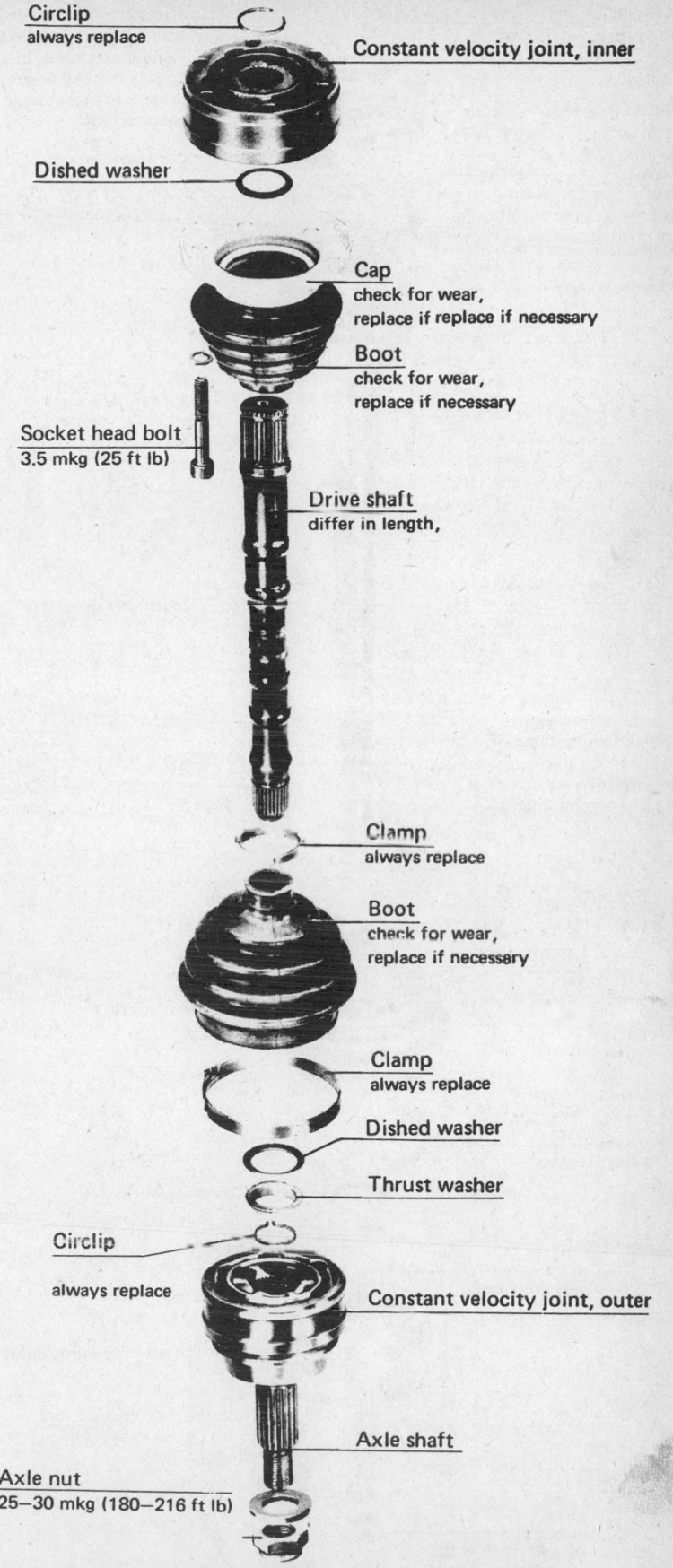

Circlip
always replace

Constant velocity joint, inner

Dished washer

Cap
check for wear,
replace if replace if necessary

Boot
check for wear,
replace if necessary

Socket head bolt
3.5 mkg (25 ft lb)

Drive shaft
differ in length,

Clamp
always replace

Boot
check for wear,
replace if necessary

Clamp
always replace

Dished washer

Thrust washer

Circlip
always replace

Constant velocity joint, outer

Axle shaft

Axle nut
25–30 mkg (180–216 ft lb)

Exploded view of the Dasher halfshaft—Quantum similar

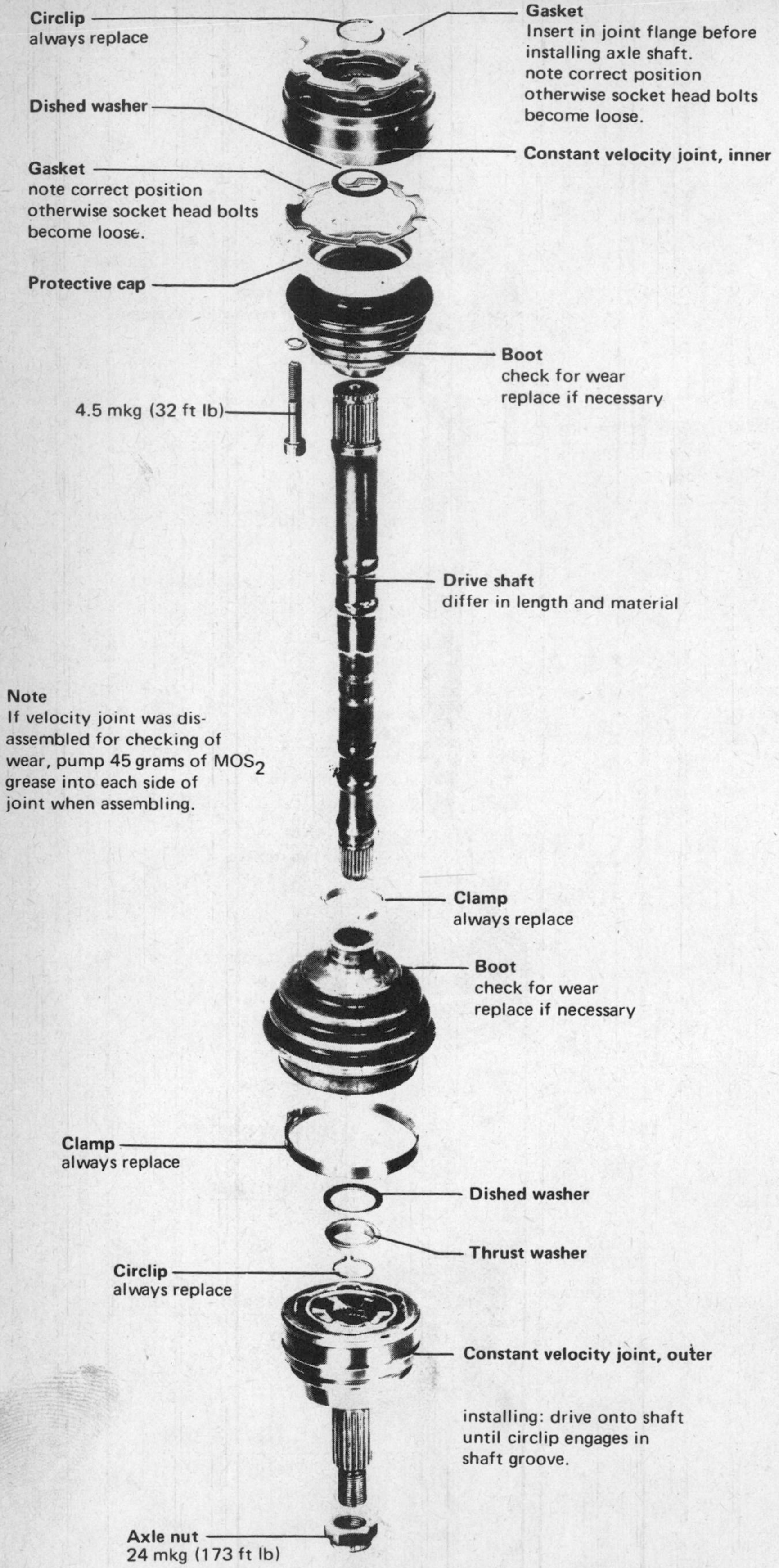

Circlip
always replace

Gasket
Insert in joint flange before
installing axle shaft.
note correct position
otherwise socket head bolts
become loose.

Dished washer

Constant velocity joint, inner

Gasket
note correct position
otherwise socket head bolts
become loose.

Protective cap

Boot
check for wear
replace if necessary

4.5 mkg (32 ft lb)

Drive shaft
differ in length and material

Note
If velocity joint was disassembled for checking of
wear, pump 45 grams of MOS_2
grease into each side of
joint when assembling.

Clamp
always replace

Boot
check for wear
replace if necessary

Clamp
always replace

Dished washer

Thrust washer

Circlip
always replace

Constant velocity joint, outer

installing: drive onto shaft
until circlip engages in
shaft groove.

Axle nut
24 mkg (173 ft lb)

Exploded view of the Rabbit, Jetta and Scirocco halfshaft

NOTE: When removing the left side halfshaft on automatic transmission models, matchmark the ball joint (left side) mounting position in relation to the lower control arm. Remove the two ball joint retaining nuts and remove the ball joint from the control arm to create room to remove the halfshaft.

4. Pull the transaxle side of the half-shaft out and up and place it on top of the transaxle.

5. Pull the axle shaft from the steering knuckle.

6. Installation is the reverse of removal. Tighten the transaxle bolts to 25–33 ft. lbs. The axle nut should be tightened to 145 ft. lbs. (M 18 nut), or 175 ft. lbs. (M 20 nut).

NOTE: Be aware that the halfshafts are two different lengths on automatic transmission models, with the left side shaft being slightly longer than the right. Manual transmission and automatic transmission shafts are of different lengths and should not be interchanged.

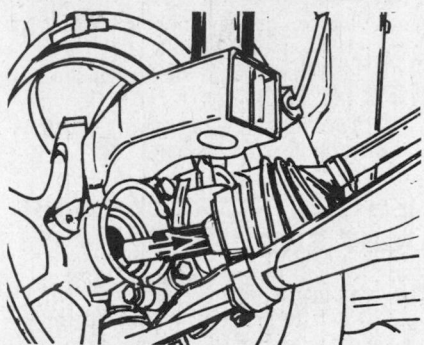

Pulling the Dasher halfshaft from the steering knuckle—Quantum similar

Rabbit, Scirocco, Jetta

1. Complete Steps 1–3 under "Dasher and Quantum". Disregard the first NOTE.

2. Remove the bolt holding the ball joint to the steering knuckle and separate the knuckle from the ball joint.

3. Removing the ball joint from the knuckle should give enough clearance to

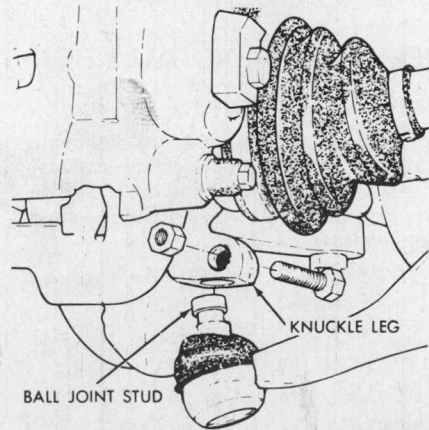

KNUCKLE LEG

BALL JOINT STUD

Remove ball joint from knuckle to remove axle shaft—Rabbit, Jetta, Scirocco

remove the shaft. It pulls right out of the steering hub.

4. Installation is the reverse of removal. Tighten the axle shaft–to–transaxle bolts to 32 ft. lbs., the ball joint bolt to 21 ft. lbs. and the axle nut to 173 ft. lbs. Be sure to check the alignment after work is completed.

CV–Joints

OVERHAUL

The constant velocity joints (CV) can be disassembled. However, VW states that the components are machined to a matched tolerance and that the entire CV–joint must be replaced.

For further information on CV–joints, please refer to "U–Joint/CV–Joint Overhaul" in the Unit Repair section.

REAR SUSPENSION

Coil Springs

REMOVAL & INSTALLATION

Dasher Only

1. Raise the car on a lift.
2. Support the axle.
3. Install a spring compressor on the coil spring, and remove.
4. Installation is the reverse of removal.

NOTE: It is not necessary to replace both springs if only one is damaged.

Shock Absorbers

REMOVAL & INSTALLATION

Dasher Only

NOTE: Only remove one shock absorber at a time. Do not allow the rear axle to hang by its body mounts only, as it may damage the brake lines.

This operation requires the use of either special tool VW 655/3 or a suitable spring compressor and floor jack.

1. Raise the car and support it on jack stands. Do not place the jack stands under the axle beam.
2. Remove the wheel.
3. Attach special tool VW 655/3 between the axle beam and a prefabricated hook hung on the body frame above the beam. Jack the tool until you can see the shock absorber compressing. If you are using a spring compressor and a floor jack, compress the spring a little and, placing the

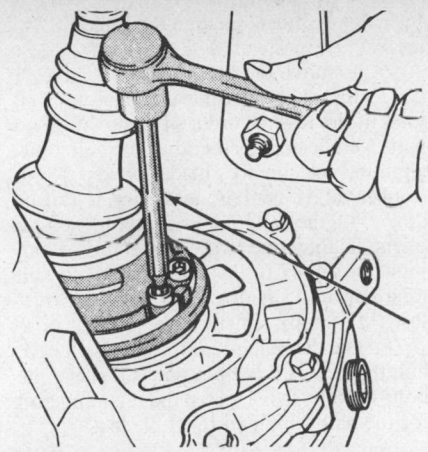

Remove the socket head (Allen) bolts holding the axle shaft to the transaxle

floor jack under the beam below the spring, jack it up until you see the shock absorber compress.

4. Unbolt and remove the shock absorber.
5. Installation is the reverse of removal. Tighten the shock absorber bolts to 43 ft. lbs.

NOTE: **There are two types of shock absorbers for the Dasher and they have different mounts. Make sure you get the correct type for your vehicle.**

Strut Assembly

REMOVAL & INSTALLATION

Rabbit, Jetta, Scirocco

1. Raise the car on a lift.
2. Support the axle, but do not put any load on the springs.
3. Remove the rubber guard from inside the car.
4. Remove the nut, washer and mounting disc.
5. Unbolt the strut assembly from the rear axle and remove it.
6. Installation is the reverse of removal.

Quantum

1. Remove the shock strut cover inside car.
2. Unscrew the strut from the body.
3. Slowly lift the vehicle until the wheels are slightly off the ground.
4. Unscrew the strut from the axle.
5. Take the strut out of the lower mounting. Press the wheel down slightly when removing the strut.

—— CAUTION ——
Do not remove both suspension struts at the same time as this will overload the axle beam bushings.

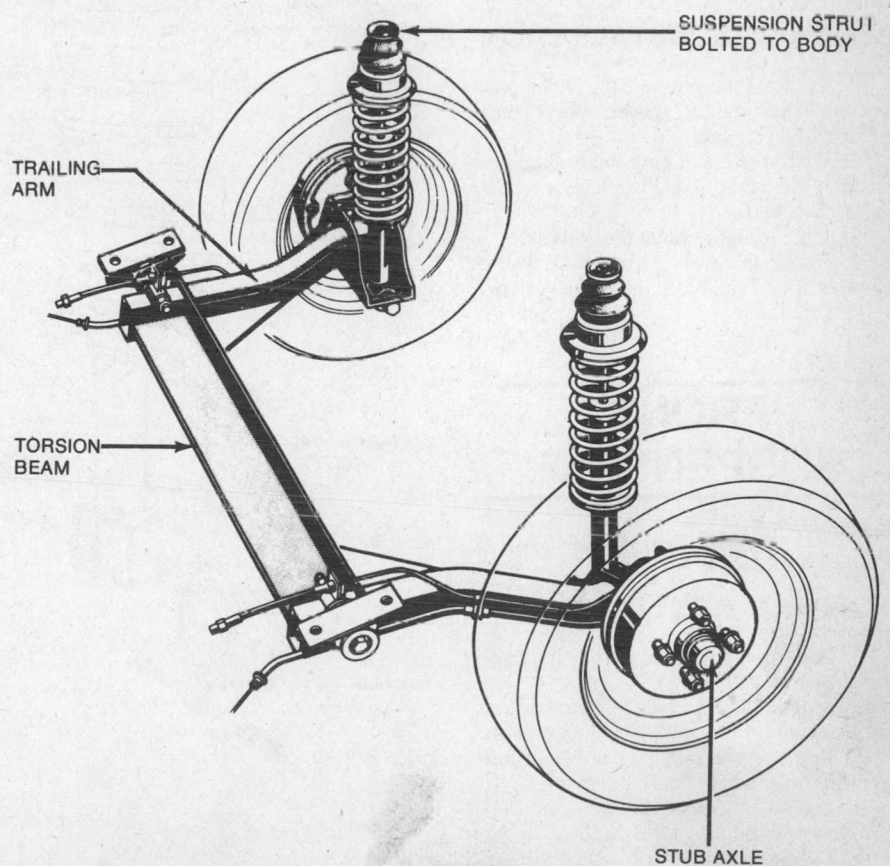

Typical rear suspension (except Dasher). Various models are equipped with a rear stabilizer (not shown)

SUSPENSION STRUT BOLTED TO BODY

TRAILING ARM

TORSION BEAM

STUB AXLE

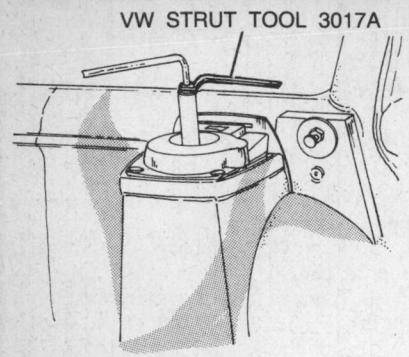

VW STRUT TOOL 3017A

Strut self-locking nut, removal/installation

6. Guide the strut out carefully between the wheel and the wheel housing. Do not damage the paint on the spring and wheel housing.

7. Installation is the reverse of removal.

OVERHAUL

For all spring and shock absorber removal and installation procedures, and all overhaul procedures, please refer to "Strut Overhaul" in the Unit Repair section.

Stub Axle

REMOVAL & INSTALLATION

1. Remove the grease cap, cotter pin, locknut, adjusting nut, spacer, wheel bearing and brake drum.

2. Disconnect and plug the brake line. Remove the brake backing plate with the brakes attached.

3. Unbolt and remove the stub axle.

4. Install in reverse order, repack the wheel bearings and bleed the brake system.

FRONT SUSPENSION

Ball Joint

REMOVAL & INSTALLATION

1. Jack up the front of the car and support it on stands.

2. Matchmark the ball joint-to-control arm position on the Dasher and Quantum.

3. Remove the retaining bolt and nut from the hub (wheel bearing housing).

4. Pry the lower control arm and ball joint down and out of the strut.

5. Remove the two ball joint-to-lower control arm retaining nuts and bolts on the Dasher. Drill out the rivets on the Rabbit,

Jetta and Scirocco; enlarge the holes to $2\frac{1}{64}$ in.

6. Remove the ball joint assembly.

7. Install the Dasher or Quantum ball joint in the reverse order of removal. If no parts were installed other than the ball joint, align the matchmarks made in Step 2. No camber adjustment is necessary if this is done. Pull the ball joint into alignment with pliers. Tighten the two control arm-to-ball joint bolts to 47 ft. lbs. and the strut-to-ball joint bolt to 25 ft. lbs. (M8 bolt) or 36 ft. lbs. (M10 bolt).

8. On the Rabbit, Jetta and Scirocco, bolt the new ball joint in place. Torque the bolts to 18 ft. lbs. Tighten the retaining bolt for the ball joint stud to 21 ft. lbs.

MacPherson Strut

REMOVAL & INSTALLATION

Dasher and Quantum

1. With the car on the ground, remove the front axle nut. Loosen the wheel bolts.

2. Raise and support the front of the car. Remove the wheels.

3. Remove the brake caliper from the strut and hang it with wire. Detach the brake line clips from the strut.

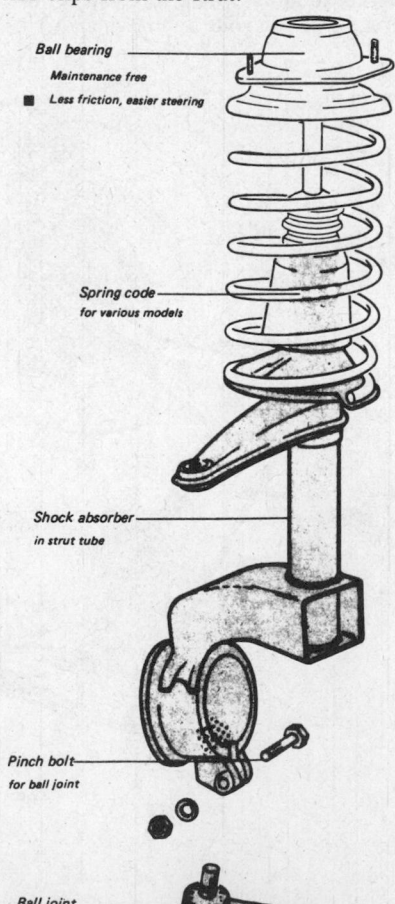

Ball bearing
Maintenance free
■ Less friction, easier steering
Spring code
for various models
Shock absorber
in strut tube
Pinch bolt
for ball joint
Ball joint
Maintenance free

A pinch bolt holds the ball joint to the combination strut and steering knuckle

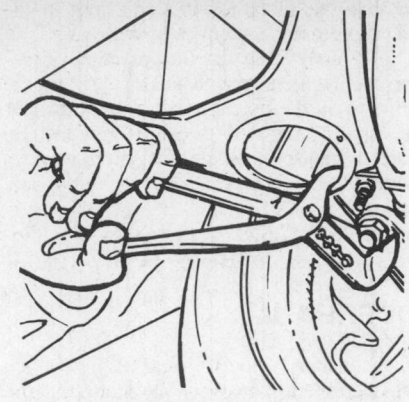

Pulling the Dasher ball joint into alignment on installation

4. At the tie-rod end, remove the cotter pin, back off the castellated nut, and pull the end off the strut with a puller.

5. Loosen the stabilizer bar bushings and detach the end from the strut being removed.

6. Remove the ball joint from the strut.

7. Pull the axle driveshaft from the strut.

8. Remove the upper strut-to-fender retaining nuts.

9. Pull the strut assembly down and out of the car.

10. Installation is the reverse of removal. The axle nut is tightened to 145 ft. lbs. (M 18 nut) or 175 ft. lbs. (M 20 nut). Tighten the ball joint-to-strut nut to 25 ft. lbs. (M8 nut) or 36 ft. lbs. (M10 nut), the caliper-to-strut bolts to 44 ft. lbs. and the stabilizer-to-control arm bolts to 7 ft. lbs.

Rabbit, Jetta and Scirocco

1. Remove the brake hose from the strut clip.

2. Mark the position of the camber adjustment bolts before removing them from

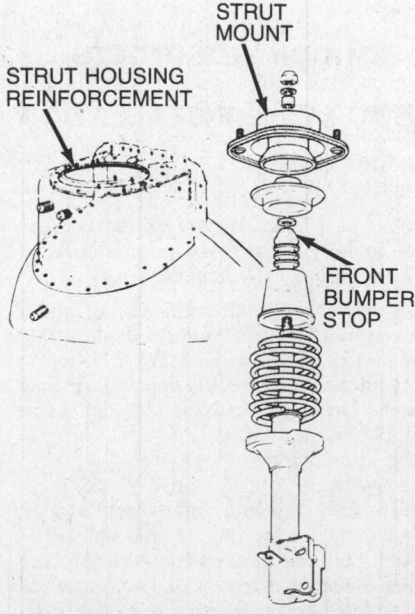

STRUT MOUNT
STRUT HOUSING REINFORCEMENT
FRONT BUMPER STOP

Front strut and mounting—GTI

the hub (wheel bearing housing). These bolts also serve as the lower strut mounting bolts.

3. Remove the upper mounting nuts and remove the strut from the car.

4. Installation is the reverse of removal. The upper nuts are tightened to 14 ft. lbs. and the adjusting bolt (upper) to hub to 58 ft. lbs. Tighten the lower adjusting bolt-to-hub to 43 ft. lbs. Use new washers on the lower bolts. If the shock absorber was replaced, camber will have to be adjusted.

OVERHAUL

For all spring and shock absorber removal and installation procedures, and all overhaul procedures, please refer to "Strut Overhaul" in the Unit Repair section.

Lower Control Arm (Wishbone)
REMOVAL & INSTALLATION

Volkswagen refers to the lower control arm as the wishbone.

NOTE: When removing the left side (driver's side) control arm on the Rabbit, Jetta and Scirocco equipped with an automatic transmission, remove the front left engine mounting, remove the nut for the rear mounting, remove the engine mounting support and raise the engine to expose the front control arm bolt.

1. Raise the vehicle and support it on jack stands. Remove the wheel.

2. Remove the nut and bolt attaching the ball joint to the hub (wheel bearing housing) and pry the joint down and out of the hub.

3. Unfasten the stabilizer bar on models so equipped.

4. Unbolt and remove the control arm-to-subframe (crossmember) mounting bolts on the Dasher or Quantum. On the Rabbit, Jetta and Scirocco, remove the control arm mounting bolts from the frame.

5. Remove the control arm. See procedures above for ball joint removal and installation.

6. Installation is the reverse of removal. Tighten the Dasher or Quantum control arm-to-subframe bolts to 50 ft. lbs., and the Rabbit, Jetta and Scirocco control arm-to-frame front bolt to 43 ft. lbs., rear bolts to 32 ft. lbs. Tighten the ball joint to hub bolt to 21 ft. lbs. on the Rabbit, Jetta and Scirocco, and to 25 ft. lbs. (M 8 nut) or 36 ft. lbs. (M 10 nut).

Front Wheel Bearings

The front wheel bearings are non-adjustable on all models and are sealed, so they should be maintenance-free. Removing the front wheel bearings requires a stand press and

1. Cotter pin
2. Tie–rod
3. Axle driveshaft
4. Circlip
5. Retainer nut
6. Brake caliper
7. Wheel bearing
8. Hub
9. Brake disc
10. Axle nut

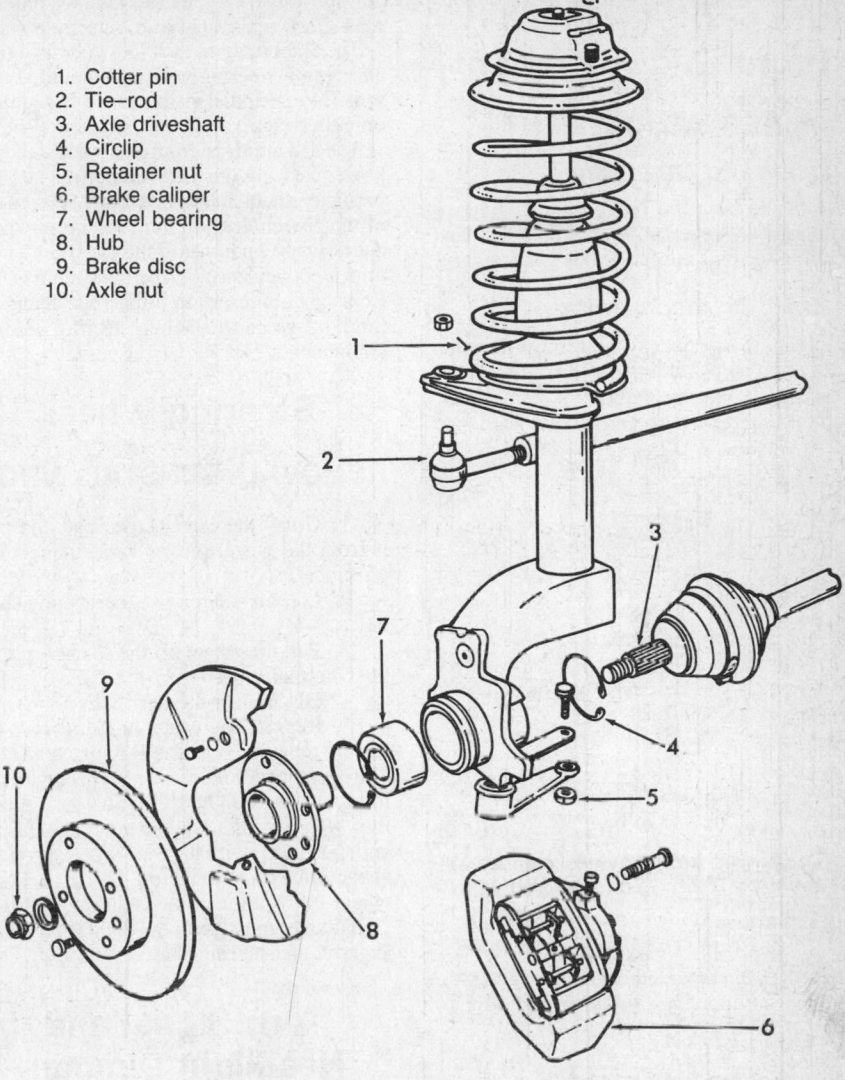

Dasher front suspension components—Quantum similar

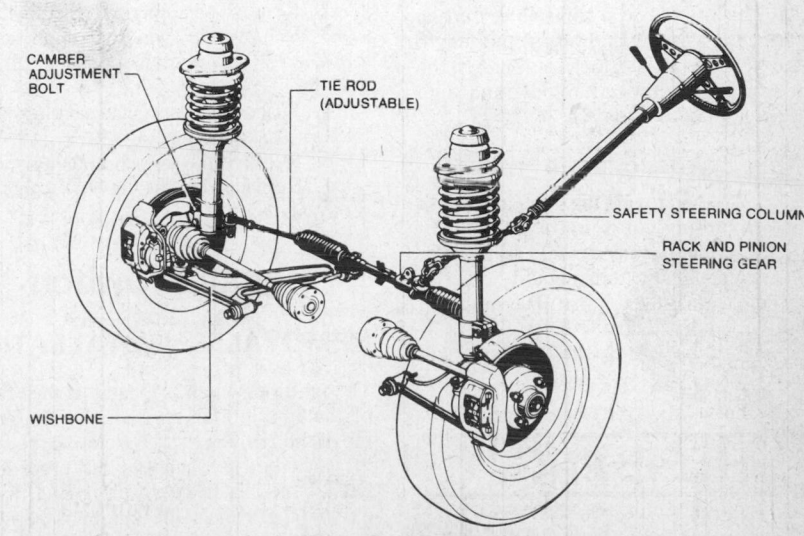

CAMBER ADJUSTMENT BOLT

TIE ROD (ADJUSTABLE)

SAFETY STEERING COLUMN

RACK AND PINION STEERING GEAR

WISHBONE

Typical Rabbit, Jetta, Scirocco steering and front suspension components

a myriad of special Volkswagen tools, so the procedure is not given here.

Front End Alignment

CAMBER ADJUSTMENT

Dasher and Quantum

Camber is adjusted by loosening the two ball joint-to-lower control arm bolts, and moving the ball joint in or out as necessary.

Rabbit, Scirocco, Jetta

Camber is adjusted by loosening the nuts of the two bolts holding the top of the wheel bearing housing to the bottom of the strut, and turning the top eccentric bolt. The range of adjustment is 2°.

Top eccentric bolt provides camber adjustment on Rabbit, Scirocco and Jetta

CASTER

Other than the replacement of damaged suspension components, caster is not adjustable on any model.

TOE-IN ADJUSTMENT

Dasher and Quantum

Toe-in is checked with the wheels straight ahead. The left tie-rod is adjustable. Loosen the nuts and clamps and adjust the length of the tie-rod for correct toe-out. If the steering wheel is crooked, remove and align it.

Rabbit, Scirocco, Jetta

Toe-in is checked with the wheels straight ahead. Only the right tie-rod is adjustable, but replacement left tie-rods are adjustable. Replacement left tie-rods should be set to the same length as the original. Toe-in should be adjusted only with the right tie-rod. If the steering wheel is crooked, remove and align it.

STEERING

The Dasher has rack and pinion steering gear with center-mounted tie-rods. This al-lows very little toe-in change during suspension travel. A steering damper reduces road shock transmittal to the steering wheel.

The Rabbit, Jetta and Scirocco have rack and pinion steering with end-mounted tie-rods. No periodic maintenance is required on either rack and pinion steering system.

The Quantum is equipped with standard power steering (rack and pinion). The only periodic maintenance required is a check of the power steering fluid reservoir, and a check when underneath the car (oil change time is convenient) for steering system leaks. Replace fluid reservoir filter when changing fluid or when replacing steering system components.

Steering Wheel

REMOVAL & INSTALLATION

1. Grasp the center cover pad and pull it from the wheel (cover varies depending on model).
2. Loosen and remove the steering shaft nut.
3. Pull the wheel off the shaft. A puller isn't normally needed.
4. Disconnect the horn wire.
5. Replace the wheel in the reverse order of removal. On the Rabbit, Jetta and Scirocco, install the steering wheel with the road wheels straight ahead and the cancelling lug pointing to the left. On the Dasher and Quantum, with the road wheels straight ahead, the cancelling lug on the steering wheel must point to the right and the turn signal lever must be in the neutral position. Tighten the steering shaft nut to 36 ft. lbs.

Turn Signal and Headlight Dimmer Switch Replacement

1. Disconnect the battery ground cable.
2. Remove the steering wheel.
3. Remove the switch retaining screws.
4. Pry the switch housing off the column.
5. Disconnect the electrical plugs at the back of the switch.
6. Remove the switch housing.
7. Replace in the reverse order of removal.

Ignition Switch

REMOVAL & INSTALLATION

The ignition switch is located at the bottom of the ignition key cylinder body. To remove the ignition switch, remove the steering lock body, see below for procedures. On all models, remove the switch by removing the screw at the bottom of the switch and pulling the switch out.

Installation is the reverse of removal.

Steering Lock

REMOVAL & INSTALLATION

On some models, the hole in the lock body for removing the steering lock cylinder was not drilled by Volkswagen. To make the hole, use the following measurements in conjunction with the illustrations. Drill the hole where "a" and "b" intersect on the lock body. The hole should be drilled ⅛ in. deep.

1978 and later Rabbit, Jetta, Scirocco, 1978 and later Dasher, Quantum
a = 12mm (0.472 in.)
b = 10mm (0.393 in.)

NOTE: Measurements are given in metric form first because this unit of measurement will be easier to make.

Remove the lock cylinder by pushing a small drill bit or piece of wire into the hole and pulling the cylinder out. It might be easier to insert the ignition key, turn it to the right a little and pull on it.

To remove the lock body, proceed as follows:
1. Remove the steering wheel and turn signal switch. See above for procedures. Remove the steering column shaft covers.
2. The lock is clamped to the steering column with special bolts whose heads shear off on installation. These must be drilled out in order to remove the switch.

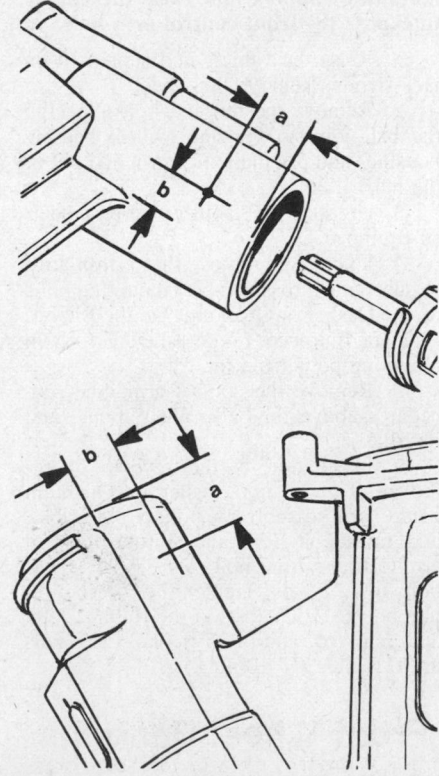

Dimensions for drilling ignition lock cylinder hole (if not equipped)—1977 and later Rabbit, Jetta, Scirocco and 1978 and later Dasher and Quantum

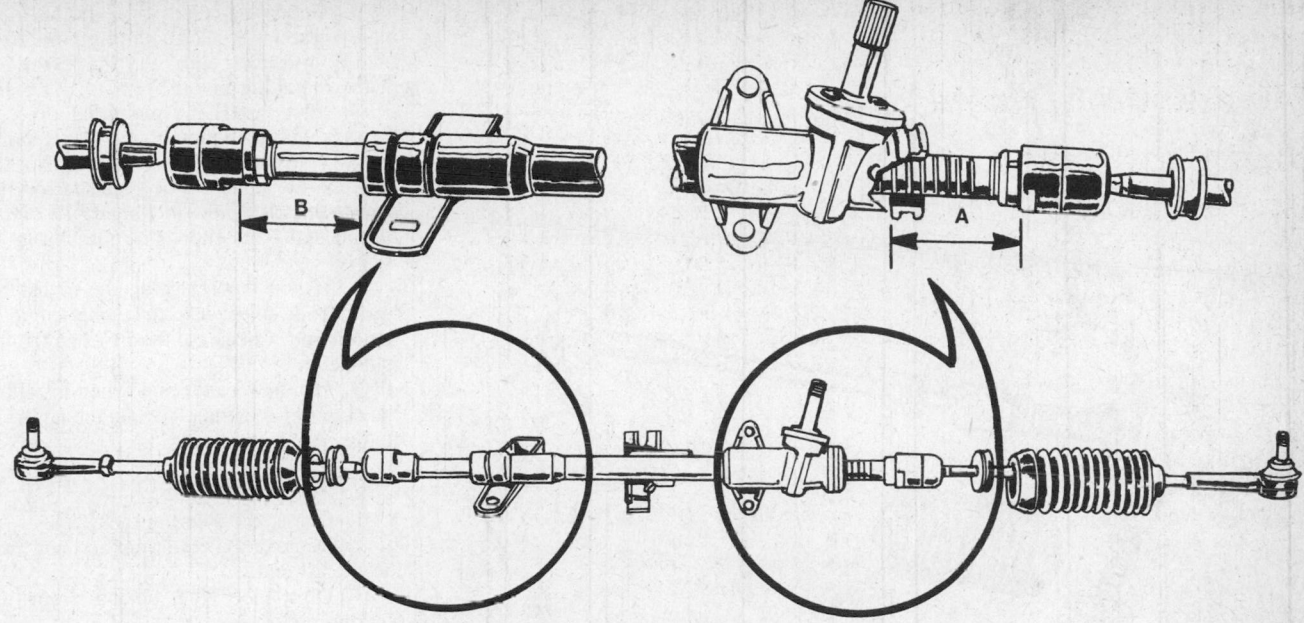

Adjusting Rabbit and Scirocco tie-rod position. b=2.64 in.

3. On replacement, make sure that the lock tang is aligned with the slot in the steering column.

Steering Gear

REMOVAL & INSTALLATION

Dasher and Quantum

1. Pry off the lock plate and remove both tie-rod mounting bolts from the steering rack, inside the engine compartment. Pry the tie-rods out of the mounting pivot.

2. Remove the lower instrument panel trim.

3. Remove the shaft clamp bolt, pry off the clip, and drive the shaft toward the inside of the car with a brass drift.

4. Disconnect the power steering lines (if so equipped). Remove the steering gear mounting bolts.

5. Turn the wheels all the way to the right and remove the steering gear through the opening in the right wheelhousing.

6. For installation, temporarily install the tie-rod mounting pivot to the rack with both mounting bolts. Remove one bolt, install the tie-rod, and replace the bolt. Do the same on the other tie-rod. Make sure to install a new lockplate. Torque the tie-rod bolts to 39 ft. lbs., the mounting pivot bolt to 15 ft. lbs., and the steering gear to body mounting bolts to 15 ft. lbs.

Rabbit, Jetta and Scirocco

1. Disconnect the steering shaft universal joint and wire up out of the way.

2. Disconnect the tie-rods at the steering rack and wire up and out of the way.

3. Remove the steering rack and drive.

4. Install the steering rack and drive and torque the attaching hardware to 14 ft. lbs.

5. Set the steering rack with equal distances between the housing on the right side and left side.

6. Install the tie-rods and screw both sides to the measurements shown in the illustration.

7. Tighten the steering gear adjusting screw until it touches the thrust washer. Tighten the locknut.

8. Install the steering shaft.

9. Check the front end alignment.

Steering Linkage

TIE—ROD REMOVAL & INSTALLATION

Dasher and Quantum

1. Raise the car and remove the front wheels.

2. Disconnect the outer end of the steering tie-rod from the steering knuckle by removing the cotter pin and nut and pressing out the tie-rod end. A small puller or press is required to free the tie-rod end.

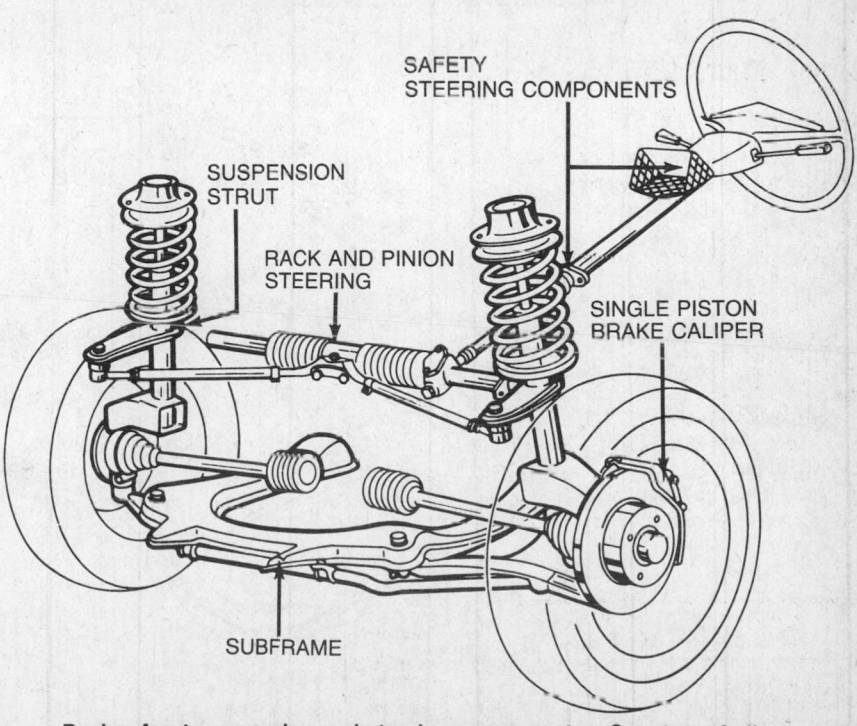

SAFETY STEERING COMPONENTS

SUSPENSION STRUT

RACK AND PINION STEERING

SINGLE PISTON BRAKE CALIPER

SUBFRAME

Dasher front suspension and steering components—Quantum similar

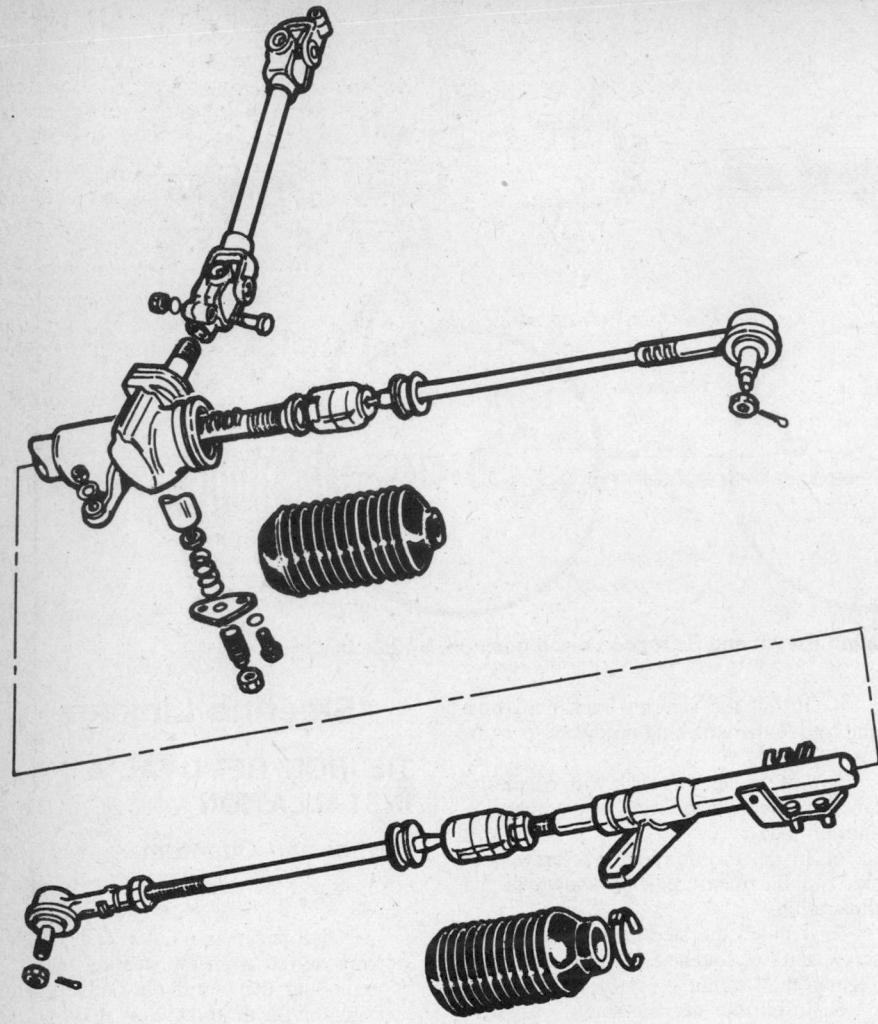

Rabbit, Jetta, Scirocco steering gear

3. Under the hood, pry off the lockplate and remove the mounting bolts from both tie-rod inner ends. Pry the tie-rod out of the mounting pivot.

4. First install the mounting pivot to the rack with both mounting bolts. Remove one bolt, install the tie-rod, and replace the bolt. Do the same on the other tie-rod. Be sure to install a new lockplate. The inner tie-rod end bolts should be torqued to 40 ft. lbs.

5. If you are replacing the adjustable left tie-rod, adjust it to the same length as the old one. Check the toe-in when the job is done.

6. Use new cotter pins when installing the outer tie-rod ends. Torque the nut to 22 ft. lbs.

Rabbit, Jetta and Scirocco

1. Center the steering rack.

2. Remove the cotter pin and nut from the tie-rod end.

3. Disconnect the tie-rod from the steering rack.

4. If the left side tie-rod is being replaced, adjust it to 14.92 in. (379mm).

5. Adjust the steering rack and tie-rods as outlined in Steps 5 and 6 of the Rabbit and Scirocco "Steering Gear Removal and Installation."

6. Tighten the tie-rod end retaining nut to 21 ft. lbs. and install a new cotter pin.

BRAKES

NOTE: During the 1984 model year VW introduced DOT 4 brake fluid in all production vehicles. The DOT 4 fluid is recommended for all Volkswagen brake

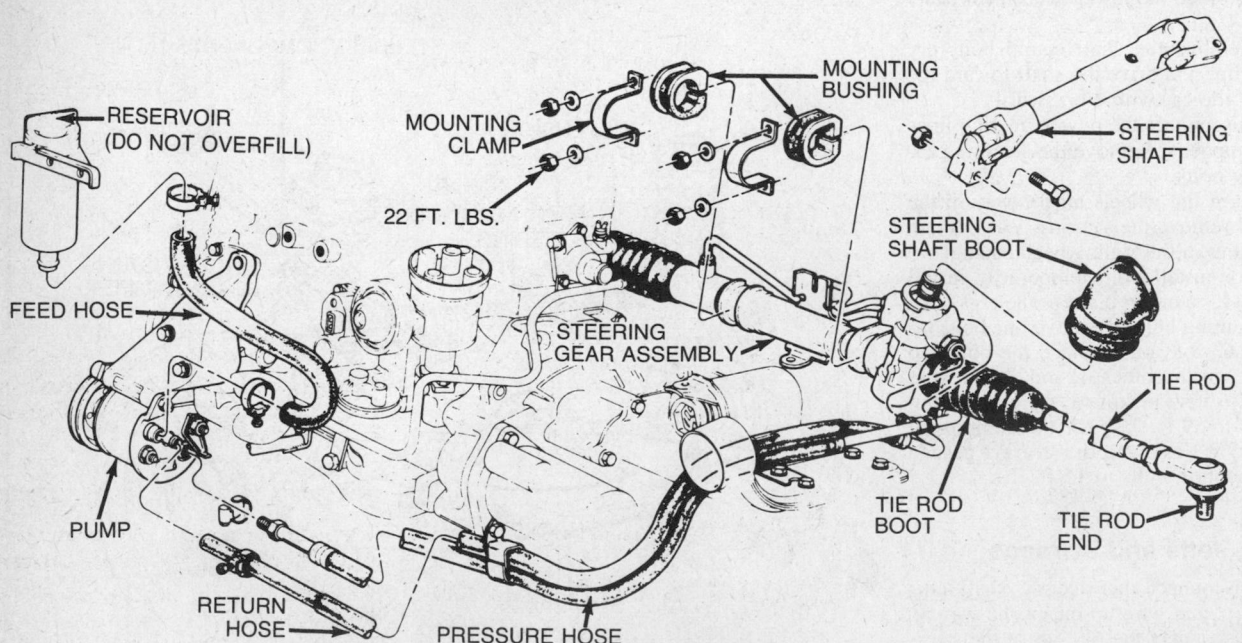

Typical rack and pinion power steering

systems and is completely compatible with the previous DOT 3 fluid.

All models, except some base model 1978 Rabbits are equipped with front disc and rear drum brakes. On some base model 1978 Rabbits drum brakes are used on all four wheels.

The hydraulic system is a dual circuit type that has the advantage of retaining 50% braking effectiveness in the event of failure in one system. The circuits are arranged so that you always have one front and one rear brake for a more controlled emergency stop. The right front and left rear are in one circuit; the left front and right rear are in the second circuit.

There is also a brake failure switch and a proportioning valve.

The brake failure unit is a hydraulic valve/electrical switch which warns of brake problems by the warning light on the instrument panel. A piston inside the switch is kept centered by one brake system pressure on one side and the other system pressure on the opposite side. Should a failure occur in one system, the piston would go to the "failed" side and complete an electrical circuit to the warning lamp. This switch also functions as a parking brake reminder light and will go out when the parking brake is released. The proportioning valve, actually two separate valves on manual transmission Dasher sedans, provides balanced front-to-rear braking during hard stops.

Extreme brake line pressure will overcome the spring pressure on the piston within the valve causing it to proportionately restrict pressure to the rear brakes. In this manner, the rear brakes are kept from locking. The proportioner doesn't operate under normal braking conditions.

For all brake system repair and service procedures not detailed below, please refer to "Brakes" in the Unit Repair section.

Adjustment

The front disc brakes require no adjustment, as disc brakes automatically adjust themselves to compensate for pad wear. The drum brakes must be adjusted whenever free travel is one third or more of the total pedal travel. All 1979 and later Dashers, Jettas, Quantums, and many 1979 and later Rabbits and Sciroccos have self-adjusting rear brakes.

FRONT DRUM BRAKES

Rabbit Only

1. Raise and support the front of the car. Block the rear wheels.
2. Remove the rubber plugs covering the adjusters.
3. Insert a screwdriver through the hole and turn the adjuster clockwise until the brake locks.
4. Back off the adjuster until the wheel can be turned. The shoes should drag lightly.

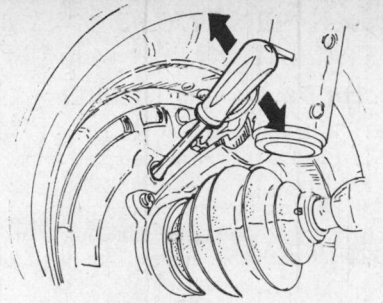

Typical drum brake adjustment

5. Back off the adjuster two notches. The wheel should spin without brake drag. Replace the rubber plugs.

REAR DRUM BRAKES

All Models

NOTE: On all models except manual transmission Dasher sedans, it is necessary to push the brake proportioning lever toward the rear axle to relieve the pressure in the right rear brake line.

1. Raise the rear of the car and support on jackstands. Place the jack under the center of the Dasher torsion bar/axle. The jack pad should be at least 4 in. square, otherwise you may damage the axle.

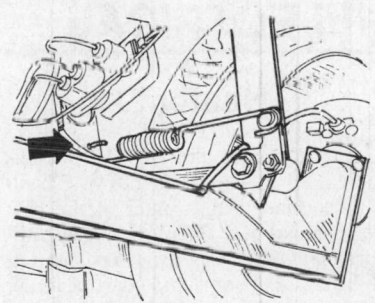

Relieving pressure at the proportioning valve. Push lever (arrow) toward rear axle

2. Block the front wheels and release the parking brake. Step on the brake pedal hard to center the linings.
3. Remove the rubber plug from the rear of the backing plate on each wheel.
4. Insert a brake adjusting tool or wide-bladed screwdriver and turn the adjuster wheel clockwise until the brakes drag as you turn the wheel in the forward direction.
5. Turn the adjuster in the opposite direction until you just pass the point of drag.
6. Repeat on the other wheel.
7. Lower the car and road test. Readjust, if necessary.

Master Cylinder

REMOVAL & INSTALLATION

1. Disconnect and plug the brake lines.
2. Disconnect the electrical plug from the sending unit for the brake failure switch.

3. Remove the two master cylinder mounting nuts.
4. Lift the master cylinder and reservoir out of the engine compartment being careful not to spill any fluid on the fender. Empty out and discard the brake fluid.

————— **CAUTION** —————

Do not depress the brake pedal while the master cylinder, front brake discs, or drum brake shoes are removed.

5. Position the master cylinder and reservoir assembly onto the studs for the booster and install the washers and nuts. Tighten the nuts to no more than 9 ft. lbs.
6. Remove the plugs and connect the brake lines.
7. Bleed the entire brake system.

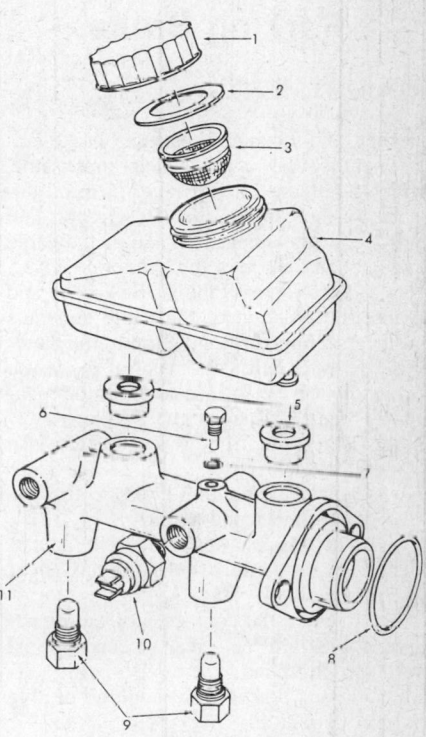

1. Reservoir cap
2. Washer
3. Filter screen
4. Reservoir
5. Master cylinder plugs
6. Stop screw
7. Stop screw seal
8. Master cylinder seal
9. Residual pressure valves
10. Warning light sender unit
11. Brake master cylinder housing

Master cylinder assembly for Rabbit, Jetta and Scirocco (typical)—Dasher and Quantum similar

Front Wheel Bearings

NOTE: For rear wheel bearing service see the previous "Stub Axle" section.

There is no front wheel bearing adjustment. The bearing is pressed into the steering knuckle. Axle nut torque is 175 ft. lbs. The axle nut should be tightened only with the wheels resting on the ground.

Wheel Cylinders

REMOVAL & INSTALLATION

1. Remove the brake shoes.
2. Loosen the brake line on the rear of the cylinder, but do not pull the line away from the cylinder or it may bend.
3. Remove the bolts and lockwashers that attach the wheel cylinder to the backing plate and remove the cylinder.
4. Position the new wheel cylinder on the backing plate and install the cylinder attaching bolts and lockwashers.
5. Attach the brake line.
6. Install the brakes and bleed the system.

Parking Brake

ADJUSTMENT

Dasher and Quantum parking brake adjustment is made at the cable compensator, which is attached to the lever pushrod underneath the car. On the 1978 Rabbit and Scirocco, adjustment is made at the cable end nuts on the top of the handbrake lever. On 1979 and later Rabbits, Sciroccos and Jettas, the position of the cable end nuts has been changed from the top of the handbrake lever to below the front of the lever. Adjustment is performed in the same manner as on 1978 Rabbits and Sciroccos.

1. Block the front wheels. Raise the rear of the car.
2. Apply the parking brake so that the lever is on the second notch.
3. The Dasher and Quantum adjustment is made directly under the passenger compartment.
4. Tighten the compensator nut or adjusting nuts until both rear wheels can just be turned by hand. On models with self-adjusting rear brakes, you shouldn't be able to turn them at all.
5. Release the parking brake lever and check that both wheels can be easily turned.
6. Lubricate the Dasher and Quantum compensator with chassis grease.

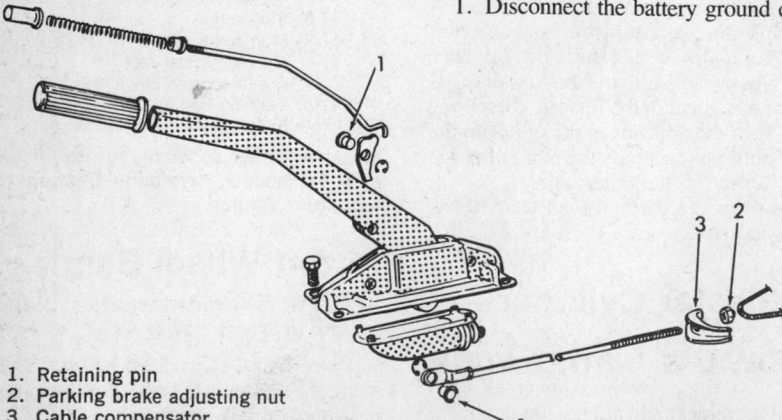

1. Retaining pin
2. Parking brake adjusting nut
3. Cable compensator

Dasher parking brake linkage and adjusting point (Quantum similar)

CABLE REMOVAL & INSTALLATION

Except Dasher and Quantum

1. Jack up the rear of the car.
2. Block the front wheels and release the handbrake.
3. Remove the rear brake shoes.
4. Remove the cable adjusting nut(s) and detach the cable guides from the floor pan.
5. Replace the cable and brake shoes. Check the parking brake adjustment.

Dasher and Quantum

1. Raise and support the rear of the car. Release the parking brake.
2. Remove the rear brake drums.
3. Disconnect the cable from the shoe assembly by pushing the spring forward and removing the cable from the adjusting arm.
4. Remove the cable compensating spring.
5. Back off the equalizer nut and guide the cable through the trailing arms and supports.
6. Installation is the reverse of removal.
7. Adjust if necessary.

CHASSIS ELECTRICAL

Heater

The heater core and blower on all models are contained in the heater box (fresh air housing located in the center of the passenger compartment under the dashboard. On air conditioned Rabbits, Jettas and Sciroccos, the evaporator is located in the heater box. On air conditioned Dashers and Quantums, the evaporator is located under the hood separate from the heater box.

REMOVAL & INSTALLATION

Without Console

1. Disconnect the battery ground cable.

2. Drain the cooling system.
3. Remove the windshield washer container from its mounts and remove the ignition coil only if they restrict your access to the heater components under the hood.
4. Disconnect the two hoses from the heater core connections at the firewall.
5. Unplug the blower fan electrical connections. Some models are equipped with an external series resistor mounted on the heater box. Do not try to remove the wires from the resistor.
6. Remove the heater control knobs on the dash.
7. Remove the two retaining screws and remove the controls from the dash complete with brackets.
8. Some models have a cable attached to a lever which is operated by a round knob on the dashboard. Remove the cable from the lever.
9. Remove either the clips or the screws holding the heater box in place and remove the heater box with the heater controls.

Installation is the reverse of removal. Be sure to refill the cooling system.

With Center Console

1. Disconnect the negative battery cable.
2. Drain the engine coolant.

NOTE: Save the coolant for reuse.

3. Trace the heater hoses coming from the firewall and disconnect them. One leads to the back of the cylinder head and the other leads to the heater valve located above and behind the oil filter.
4. Detach the cable for the heater valve.
5. Remove the center console.
6. Remove the left and right covers below the instrument panel.
7. Pull off the fresh air/heater control knobs.
8. Pull off the trim plate.
9. Remove the screws for the controls.
10. Remove the center cover mounting screws and remove the cover.
11. Detach the right, left and center air ducts.
12. Remove the heater housing retaining spring.
13. Remove the cowl for the air plenum which is located under the hood and in front of the windshield.
14. Remove the heater housing mounting screws and remove the heater housing. The mounting screws are under the hood where the air plenum was.
15. Installation is in the reverse order of removal. Be sure to replace all sealing material.

Heater Blower

REMOVAL & INSTALLATION

1. Remove the heater unit from the vehicle. See above for procedures.
2. Remove the screws holding the cover on the heater box and remove the cover.

Remove the blower motor cover, if so equipped.

3. Remove the electrical connections from the blower motor after matchmarking them to insure that you assemble them in the correct order.

4. Remove the clamp or screws holding the motor in place and remove the motor.

5. Installation is the reverse of removal.

Heater Core

REMOVAL & INSTALLATION

NOTE: On some models, it is possible to remove the heater core without removing the heater box. Proceed as follows:

   a. Drain the cooling system.

   b. Locate and remove the heater core cover in the side of the heater box.

   c. Disconnect the heater hoses from the core and pull the core out.

1. Remove the heater box from the vehicle.

2. If the unit has a core cover in its side, remove the screws or unclip the cover and remove it. The core should pull out.

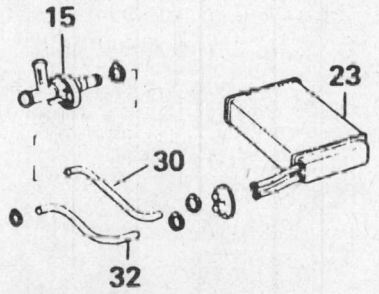

Rabbit, Scirocco and Jetta heater core (23), hoses (30 and 32), and heater control valve (15)

3. On other models, remove the heater box clips that hold the two halves of the heater box together, separate the halves after removing any components that are in the way, and remove the heater core.

Windshield Wiper Motor

REMOVAL & INSTALLATION

Dasher and Quantum

1. Unplug the multi-connector from the wiper motor.

2. Remove the three motor-to-linkage bracket retaining screws.

3. Carefully pry the motor crank out of the two linkage arms.

4. Remove the motor from the car.

5. Install the motor in the reverse order of removal. The crank arm should be at a right angle to the motor.

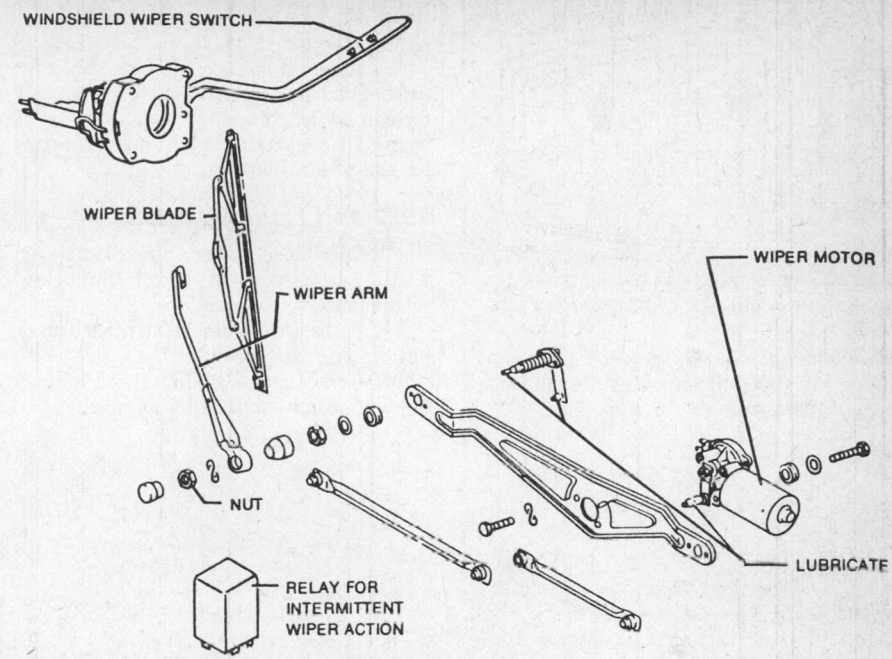

Rabbit, Jetta, Scirocco front wiper motor and linkage

Rabbit, Scirocco, Jetta

When removing the wiper motor, leave the mounting frame in place. On all models with two front wiper arms, do not remove the wiper drive crank from the motor shaft.

On Sciroccos with one front wiper arm, matchmark the drive crank and motor arm and then remove the arm.

NOTE: If, for any reason you must remove the wiper drive crank from the motor shaft on two wiper arm models, matchmark both parts for reassembly.

1. Access is with the hood open. Disconnect the battery ground cable.

2. Detach the connecting rods from the motor crank arm.

3. Pull off the wiring plug.

4. Remove the 4 mounting bolts. You may have to energize the motor for access to the top bolt.

5. Remove the motor. Reverse the procedure for installation.

Instrument Cluster

For additional information on the instrument cluster, please refer to "Gauges and Indicators" in the Unit Repair section.

REMOVAL & INSTALLATION

1978 and Later Dasher

1. Remove the radio or shelf.

2. Pull the knobs off the fresh air control and fan switch.

3. Remove the six instrument cluster to dashboard retaining screws.

4. Snap out the light, emergency flasher and rear window defogger switches.

5. Disconnect the air fan switch electrical connector.

6. Remove the instrument cluster and disconnect the speedometer cable and the multi-point connector from the back of the cluster.

Scirocco 1978–81, Rabbit and Jetta

1. Disconnect the battery ground cable.

2. Remove the fresh air controls trim plate.

3. Remove the radio or glove box.

4. Unscrew the speedometer drive cable from the back of the speedometer. Detach the electrical plug.

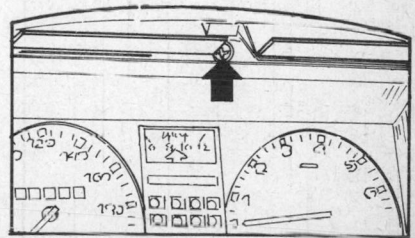

Tip down cluster panel, revealing inside Phillips screw

5. Remove the attaching screw inside the radio/glove box opening.

6. Remove the instrument cluster. Reverse the procedure for installation.

1982 and Later Scirocco

1. Disconnect battery ground cab[le]

2. Remove the two Phillips hea[ds] on the inner top surface of the i[nstrument] compartment (see illustration).

3. Start to pull down on th[e] compartment. Inside the top [of]

Instrument cluster removal—Scirocco (Quantum similar)

compartment you will see another Phillips screw (as you pull the compartment out). Remove the screws.

4. Tip out the top of the instrument cluster.

5. Remove the speedometer cable by twisting the tabs of the plastic fixture around the end of the cable.

6. Disconnect the multi-point connector and remove instrument cluster.

1982 and Later Quantum

1. Disconnect battery ground strap.

2. Carefully pry off switch trim below instruments.

3. Pull heater control knobs off and press out heater control trim.

4. Remove two Phillips head screws holding heater control trim to panel.

5. Remove 7 Phillips screws around perimeter of instrument cluster.

6. Disconnect all wiring to switches and warning lamps. Remove all trim panels.

7. The remainder of the procedure can be completed by following the Scirocco procedure beginning at Step 3.

Fuses and Relays

The fuse/relay panel on all models is located in the lower left side of the dashboard. VW recommends that relays be replaced by your dealer.

Volkswagen

Beetle, Bus, Camper, Kombi, Vanagon

SERIAL NUMBER IDENTIFICATION

Vehicle (Chassis) Number

The first two numbers are the first two digits of the car's model number and the third digit stands for the car's model year. For example a 0 as the third digit means that the car was produced during the 1980 model year, a 1 would signify 1981, and so forth.

The chassis number is on the frame tunnel under the back seat in the Type 1. In the Type 2, the chassis number is on the right engine cover plate in the engine compartment and behind the front passenger's seat. All models also have an identification plate bearing the chassis number on the top of the instrument panel at the driver's side. This plate is easily visible through the windshield and aids in rapid identification.

Another identification plate bearing the vehicle's serial number and paint, body, and assembly codes, is found in the luggage compartment of the Type 1.

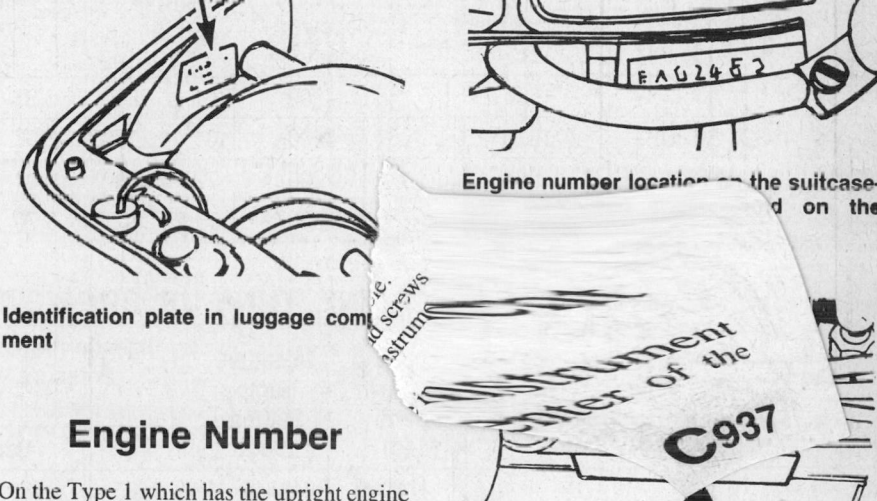

Identification plate in luggage compartment

Engine Number

On the Type 1 which has the upright engine cooling fan housing, the engine number is on the crankcase flange for the generator support. The number can readily be seen by looking through the center of the fan belt.

On Type 2 models with both the suitcase air-cooled engine and the Waterboxer (1984

Engine number location on the suitcase-air-cooled engine and on the Waterboxer engine [partially obscured]

Engine number location—Type 2 with diesel

and later) engine, the number is stamped on the crankcase near the ignition coil and below the crankcase breather. The engine can be identified by the letter or pair of letters preceding the serial number. Engine specifications are listed according to the letters and model year.

Transmission Identification

Transmission identification marks are stamped into the bell housing or on the final drive housing.

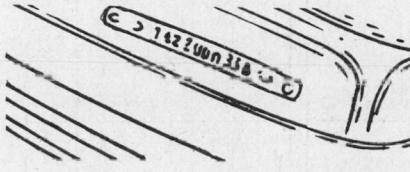

Chassis number location on dashboard

Chassis number location under rear seat

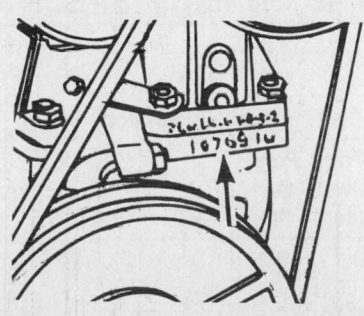

Engine number location on upright fan engine

VOLKSWAGEN REAR WHEEL DRIVE

ENGINE IDENTIFICATION CHART

Engine Code Letter	Vehicle Type	First Production Year	Last Production Year	Engine Type	Common Designation
AJ	1	1975	1979	Air cooled flat four, fan driven by generator	1600
GD	2	1976	1978	Air cooled flat four, fan driven by crankshaft	2000
GE	2	1979	1980	Air cooled flat four, fan driven by crankshaft	2000
CV	2	1980	1983	Air cooled flat four, fan driven by crankshaft	2000
CS	2	1982	—	Water cooled inline diesel	1600
DH	2	1984	—	Water cooled flat four	Waterboxer

GENERAL ENGINE SPECIFICATIONS

Year	Engine Code	Displacement cc	Horsepower @ rpm	Torque @ rpm (ft. lbs.)	Bore × Stroke (in.)	Compression Ratio	Oil Pressure @ rpm (psi)
'78–'79	AJ	1584	48 @ 4200	73.1 @ 2800	3.37 × 2.72	7.3:1	42
'78–'83	GD, GE, CV	1970	67 @ 4200	101 @ 3000	3.70 × 2.80	7.3:1	42
'82–'85	CS	1588	49 @ 4200	72 @ 2000	3.01 × 3.40	23.0:1	28 @ 2000
'83–'85	DH	1915	82 @ 4800	106 @ 2600	3.70 × 2.72	8.6:1	29 @ 2000

DIESEL ENGINE TUNE-UP SPECIFICATIONS

Model	Valve Clearance ① Intake (in.)	Exhaust (in.)	Intake Valve Opens (deg)	Injection Pump Setting (deg)	Injection Nozzle Pressure (psi) New	Used	Idle Speed (rpm)	Cranking Compression Pressure (psi)
Diesel	.008–.012	.016–.020	NA	Align marks	1885–2001	1740–1885	770–870	406–493

NA Not available at time of publication
① Valve clearance need not be adjusted unless it varies more than .002 in. from specification

GASOLINE ENGINE TUNE-UP SPECIFICATIONS

Year	Code	Type	Common Designation	Spark Plugs Type ①	Gap (in.)	Distributor Point Dwell (deg)	Point Gap (in.)	Ignition Timing (deg) MT	AT	Fuel Pump Pressure (psi) @ 4000 rpm	Compression Pressure (psi)	Idle Speed (rpm) MT	AT	Valve Clearance (in. cold) In	Ex
'78	AJ	1	1600	Bosch W145M1 Champ. L288	.028	44–50	.016	5A	5A	28	85–135	800–950	800–950	.006	.006
	GE	2	2000	Bosch W145M2 Champ. N288	.028	44–50	.016	7½B	7½B	28	85–135	800–950	900–1000	Hyd.	Hyd. ⑨

GASOLINE ENGINE TUNE-UP SPECIFICATIONS

Year	Code	Type	Common Designation	Spark Plugs Type ①	Gap (in.)	Distributor Point Dwell (deg)	Point Gap (in.)	Ignition Timing (deg) MT	AT	Fuel Pump Pressure (psi) @ 4000 rpm	Compression Pressure (psi)	Idle Speed (rpm) MT	AT	Valve Clearance (in. cold) In	Ex
'79	AJ	1	1600	Bosch W145M1 Champ. L288	.028	44–50	.016	5A	5A	28	85–135	800–950	800–950	.006	.006
'79–'83	GE, CV	2	2000	Bosch W145M2 Champ. N288	.028	44–50⑤	.016⑤	7½B②	7½B②	28	85–135	800–950③	850–1000④	Hyd.	Hyd.⑨
'84–'85	DH	2	Water-boxer (1900)	Bosch W7CO Champ. N288 Beru 14L-7C	.028	⑥	⑥	5A	5A	⑧	116–189	800–900⑦	800–900⑦	Hyd.	Hyd.⑨

A After Top Dead Center
B Before Top Dead Center
MT Manual trans.
AT Automatic trans.
① Recommended by manufacturer
② 5ATDC, Calif.—idle stabilizer must be bypassed (plugs connected together)
③ Calif.: 850–950

④ Calif.: 850–950
⑤ 1980–83 Vanagon (Calif.)— electronic ignition; point gap and dwell preset and non-adjustable
⑥ 1984 and later: electronic ignition; point gap and dwell preset and non-adjustable

⑦ With vacuum hoses connected
⑧ 29 psi @ idle speed @ approx. 2.0 bar with vacuum hose connected
⑨ Valves must still be adjusted when cylinder heads have been removed; see "Valve Lash" in text.

FIRING ORDERS

NOTE: To avoid confusion, always replace spark plug wires one at a time. The Type 2 Diesel engine's cylinders are numbered 1-2-3-4, starting from the crankshaft pulley and working back. Firing order is 1-3-4-2. Water boxer cylinder numbering and firing order is the same as the air-cooled engine shown below.

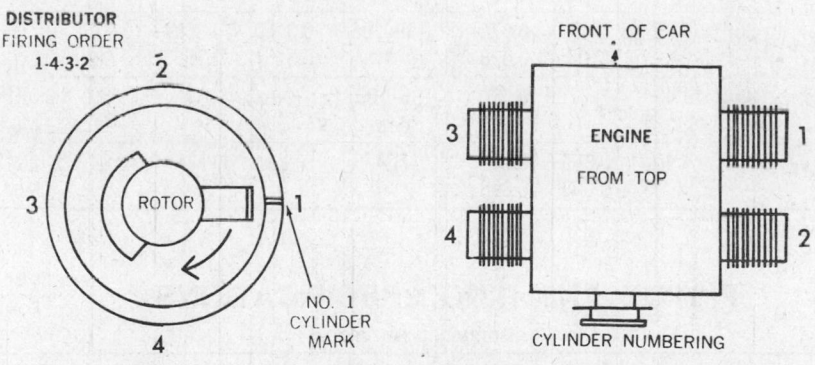

CAPACITIES

Year	Type	Engine Displacement (cc)	Engine Crankcase (qts.) With Filter	Without Filter	Transaxle (pts.) Manual	Automatic Conv.	Final Drive	Gasoline Tank (gal.)
'78–'79	1	1600	—	2.5	6.3	7.6	6.3①	10.6③
'78–'85	2	1600, 1800, 2000	3.7④	3.2⑤	7.4	②	①	15.9
'84–'85	2	1915	4.7	3.7	⑥	②	①	15.9

Conv. = torque converter
① 5.3 when changed
② 6.4 refill; 12.8 when changed
③ Convertible (11.1)
④ Diesel: 4.2
⑤ Diesel: 3.7

⑥ Type 091: 3.7 qt.
Type 091/1: 3.2 qt. w/gasoline engine; 4.2 qt. with diesel
Type 094: 4.0 qt.

CRANKSHAFT AND CONNECTING ROD SPECIFICATIONS

(All measurements are given in inches)

		Crankshaft										
		Main Bearing Journal Diameter		Main Bearing Oil Clearance				Connecting Rods			
Year	Engine	No. 1, 2, 3	No. 4	No. 1, 3	No. 2	No. 4	Crankshaft End-Play	Thrust on No.	Journal Diameter	Oil Clearance	End-Play
'78–'79	1600	2.1640–2.1648	1.5739–1.5748	.0016–.004	.001–.003	.002–.004	.0027–.005	1 at flywheel	2.1644–2.1653	.0008–.0027	.004–.016
'78–'83	1800, 2000	2.3609–2.3617	1.5739–1.5748	.002–.004	.0012–.0035	.002–.004	.0027–.005	1 at flywheel	2.1644–2.1653①	.0008–.0027	.004–.016
'82–'85	Diesel	2.1244–2.1252	2.1244–2.1252	.001–.003	.001–.003	.001–.003	.003–.007	3	1.8803–1.8811	.0011–.0034	.014②
'84–'85	Waterboxer 1900	2.3992–2.3996③	1.5993–1.6000	N.A.	N.A.	N.A.	.003–.005	1 at flywheel	2.1993–2.1998	N.A.	.028②

N.A. Not Available at time of publication
① On 1978–79 2000 models, connecting rod journal diameter is 1.968 in.
② Wear limit
③ Bearings marked with blue dot. Bearings marked with red dot 2.3988–2.3991. Both specs for journals 1 and 3 only. No. 2 journal diamater 2.1988–2.1996 in.

VALVE SPECIFICATIONS

		Seat Angle (deg)		Face Angle (deg)		Valve Seat Width (in.)		Spring Test Pressure (lbs. @ in.)	Valve Guide Inside Dia (in.)		Stem to Guide Clearance (in.)		Stem Diameter (in.)	
Year	Type	Intake	Exhaust	Intake	Exhaust	Intake	Exhaust		Intake	Exhaust	Intake	Exhaust	Intake	Exhaust
'78–'79	1	45	45	45	45	0.05–0.10	0.05–0.10	117.7–134.8 @ 1.22	0.3150–0.3157	0.353–0.354	0.009–0.010	0.009–0.010	0.3125–0.3129	0.350–0.351
'78–'83	2	30	45	30	45	0.07–0.08	0.078–0.098	168–186 @ 1.14	0.3150–0.3157	0.3534–0.3538	0.018	0.014	0.3125–0.3129	0.3507–0.3511
'82–'85	2 (diesel)	45	45	45	45	0.078	0.096	96–106 @ 0.92	NA	NA	0.039 Max	0.051 Max	0.314	0.313
'84–'85	2 (Waterboxer)	45	45	45	45	0.055–0.098	0.055–0.098	N.A.	N.A.	N.A.	0.047 Max.	0.047 Max.	0.313–0.314	0.3508–0.3512

N.A. Not Available at time of publication

PISTON AND RING SPECIFICATIONS

(All measurements in inches)

			Ring Gap			Ring Side Clearance		
Year	Engine Displacement	Piston Clearance	Top Compression	Bottom Compression	Oil Control	Top Compression	Bottom Compression	Oil Control
'78–'79	1600	0.0016–0.0023	0.012–0.018	0.012–0.018	0.010–0.016	0.0027–0.0039	0.002–0.0027	0.0011–0.0019
'78–'80	1800, 2000	0.0016–0.0023	0.014–0.021	0.012–0.022	0.010–0.016	0.0023–0.0035	0.0016–0.0027	0.0008–0.0019
'80–'83	2000	0.0016–0.0023	0.016–0.021	0.016–0.021	0.010–0.016	0.002–0.003	0.002–0.003	0.001–0.002
'82–'85	Diesel	0.001–0.003	0.012–0.020	0.012–0.020	0.010–0.016	0.002–0.004	0.002–0.003	0.001–0.002
'84–'85	1900 Waterboxer	0.001–0.002①	0.012–0.018	0.012–0.020	0.010–0.016	0.002–0.003	0.002–0.003	0.001–0.002

① New clearance; max. wear limit 0.008 in.

GASOLINE ENGINE TORQUE SPECIFICATIONS

(All readings in ft. lbs.)

Year	Type Vehicle	Cylinder Head Nuts	Rod Bearing Bolts	Generator Pulley	Crankshaft Pulley Bolt	Flywheel to Crankshaft Bolts	Fan to Hub	Hub to Crankshaft	Crankcase Half Nuts Sealing Nuts	Crankcase Half Nuts Non-Sealing Nuts	Drive Plate to Crankshaft④	Spark Plugs	Oil Strainer Cover
'78–'79	1	23	22–25	40–47	29–36	253	—	—	18	14	—	25	5
'78–'83	2	23	24	—	—	80①	14	23	23	14	61	22	7–9
'84–'85	2	②	33	—	253③	80	—	—	⑤	⑤	65	14	—

①Automatic transmission drive plate—65 ft. lbs. (1980 and later Vanagon)
②Coat surface of cap nuts with D3 sealing compound, torque all bolts in sequence to 7 ft. lbs., then torque all bolts in sequence to 25 ft. lbs.

③Triple V-belt pulley on cars with air conditioning or power steering only. Single V-belt pulley bolt 43 ft. lbs.
④Torque converter plate

⑤Crankcase top (small) nuts 14 ft. lbs. after coating both sides of washer with D3 compound; lower nuts (large) 25 ft. lbs. after coating with D3.

DIESEL ENGINE TORQUE SPECIFICATIONS

(All readings in ft. lbs.)

Year	Model	Cylinder Head Bolts	Rod Bearing Bolts②	Main Bearing Bolts	Crankshaft Pulley Bolt	Flywheel To Crankshaft Bolts	Manifold Intake	Manifold Exhaust
'82–'85	Diesel	65②④	33	47	56⑤	54①	18	18

①Pressure plate to crankshaft bolts
②Cold, 69 ft. lbs. warm
③Always use new bolts
④'82 uses 12mm, 12-pt. cyl. head bolts. Bolts must always be replaced during repairs to head.

⑤Replacement bolt and washer: 108 ft. lbs.
Models with built-in lug: 145 ft. lbs.

ALTERNATOR AND REGULATOR SPECIFICATIONS

Year	Type	Alternator Maximum Output (amps)	Alternator Stator Winding Resistance (ohms)	Alternator Exciter Winding Resistance (ohms)	Regulator Load Current (amps)	Regulator Regulating Voltage Under Load (volts)
'78–'79	1	50	.13 ± .13	4.0 ± .4	25–30	13.8–14.9①
'78–'85	2	55②	.13 ± .13	4.0 ± .4	25–30	13.8–14.9①

①@ 2000 engine rpm's
②1982 and later: 65

STARTER SPECIFICATIONS

Starter Number	Lock Test Amps	Lock Test Volts	No Load Test Amps	No Load Test Volts	No Load Test rpm	Brush Spring Tension (oz)
111 911 023A	270–290	6	25–40	12	6700–7800	42
311 911 023B	250–300	6	35–45	12	7400–8100	42
003 911 023A	250–300	6	35–50	12	6400–7900	42

BRAKE SPECIFICATIONS
(All measurements are given in inches)

Year	Type	Lug Nut Torque (ft. lbs.)	Master Cylinder Bore	Brake Disc Minimum Thickness	Brake Disc Maximum Run-Out	Brake Drum Diameter	Brake Drum Max. Machine O/S	Brake Drum Max. Wear Limit	Minimum Lining Thickness Front	Minimum Lining Thickness Rear
'78–'79	Type 1 (Super Beetle)	87–94	0.750	—	—	9.768 (fr) 9.059 (rr)	9.80 (fr) 9.10 (rr)	9.823 (fr) 9.114 (rr)	0.100	0.100
'78–'85	Type 2 (Bus)	87–94	0.938	0.472①	0.0008②	9.920	9.97③	9.98	0.079	0.100④

NOTE: Minimum lining thickness is as recommended by the manufacturer. Due to variations in state inspection regulations, the minimum allowable thickness may be different than recommended by the manufacturer.
(fr)—front
(rr)—rear
—not applicable
① 1980 and later: 0.453
② 1980 and later: 0.004
③ 1980 and later: 9.96
④ 0.098 in. 1984 and later

WHEEL ALIGNMENT SPECIFICATIONS

Year	Model	Front Axle Caster Range (deg)	Front Axle Caster Pref Setting (deg)	Front Axle Camber Range (deg)	Front Axle Camber Pref Setting (deg)	Front Axle Toe-In (in.)	Rear Axle Camber Range (deg)	Rear Axle Camber Pref Setting (deg)	Rear Axle Toe-In (in.)
'78–'79	Type 1①	1⁷⁄₁₆–2⁹⁄₁₆	2	⁵⁄₁₆–1⁵⁄₁₆	1	¼	−1¹¹⁄₁₆––⁵⁄₁₆	−1	0
'78–'79	Type 2	2⁵⁄₁₆–3¹¹⁄₁₆	3	⅜–1	¹¹⁄₁₆	⅛	−1⁵⁄₁₆––⁵⁄₁₆	−1³⁄₁₆	³⁄₃₂
'80	Type 2	7–7½	7¼	³⁄₁₆–1³⁄₁₆	¹¹⁄₁₆	¹¹⁄₃₂	−1⁵⁄₁₆––⁵⁄₁₆	−1³⁄₁₆	0
'81–'85	Type 2	7–7½	7¼	−½–½	0	⁵⁄₆₄	−1⁵⁄₁₆––⁵⁄₁₆	−1³⁄₁₆	0

① Super Beetle

TUNE-UP PROCEDURES

---CAUTION---

When working with a running engine, make sure that the transmission is in Neutral (unless otherwise specified) and the parking brake is fully applied. When the ignition is turned on and the engine running, do not grasp the ignition wires, distributor cap, or coil wire, as a shock in excess of 20,000 volts may result. Whenever working near the distributor, even if the engine is not running, make sure that the ignition is switched off. Always keep clear of the cooling fan and pulleys. Also, stay clear of the hot exhaust manifolds and catalytic converter (if so equipped).

Spark Plugs

Before attempting any work on the cylinder head, it is very important to note that the cylinder head is cast aluminum alloy. It is extremely easy to damage threads in the cylinder head. Care must be taken not to cross-thread the spark plugs or any bolts or studs. *Never overtighten the spark plugs, bolts, or studs.*

---CAUTION---

Always lubricate the spark plug threads with anti-seize compound prior to installation.

To avoid cross-threading the spark plugs, always start the plugs in their threads with your fingers. Never force the plugs into the cylinder head. Do not use a wrench until you are certain that the plug is correctly threaded.

VW spark plugs should be cleaned and regapped every 6000 miles and replaced every 12,000.

REMOVAL & INSTALLATION

To install the spark plugs, remove the spark plug wire from the plug. Grasp the plug connector and, while removing, do not pull on the wire. Using a ¹³⁄₁₆ in. spark plug socket, remove the old spark plugs. Examine the threads of the old plugs; if one or more of the plugs have aluminum clogged threads, it will be necessary to rethread the spark plug hole. See the following section for the necessary information.

Obtain the proper heat range and type of new plug. Set the gap by bending the side electrode only. Do not bend the center electrode to adjust the gap. The proper gap is listed in the "Tune-Up Specifications" chart. Lubricate the plug threads.

Start each new plug in its hole using your fingers. Tighten the plug several turns by hand to assure that the plug is not cross-threaded. Using a wrench, tighten the plug just enough to compress the gasket. *Do not overtighten the plug.*

RETHREADING SPARK PLUG HOLE

It is possible to repair light damage to spark plug hole threads by using a spark plug hole tap of the proper diameter and thread. Plenty of grease should be used on the tap to catch any metal chips. Exercise caution when using the tap as it is possible to cut a second set of threads instead of straightening the old ones.

If the old threads are beyond repair, then the hole must be drilled and tapped to accept a steel bushing of Heli-Coil®. It is not always necessary to remove the cylinder head to re-thread the spark plug holes. Bushing kits, Heli-Coil® kits, and spark plug hole taps are available at most auto parts stores. Heli-Coil® information is contained in the "Engine Rebuilding" section of this book.

Breaker Points and Condenser

REMOVAL & INSTALLATION

NOTE: 1979–83 California Type 2 vehicles, and all 1984 and later Type 2s are equipped with an electronic ignition system.

1. Release the spring clips which secure the distributor cap and lift the cap from the distributor. Pull the rotor from the distributor shaft.

NOTE: Vehicles with a radio may be equipped with a static shield. Unscrew the ground strap and remove the shield before removing the cap.

2. Disconnect the points wire from the condenser snap connection inside the distributor.

3. Remove the locking screw from the stationary breaker point.

4. To remove the condenser which is located on the outside of the distributor, remove the screw which secures the condenser bracket and condenser connection to the distributor.

5. Disconnect the condenser wire from the coil.

6. With a clean rag, wipe the excess oil from the breaker plate.

NOTE: Make sure that the new point contacts are clean and oil free.

7. Installation of the points and condenser is the reverse of the above; however, it will be necessary to adjust the point gap, (or dwell), and check the timing. Lubricate the point cam with a small amount of lithium or white grease. Set the dwell, or gap, before the ignition timing.

Breaker point removal is accomplished by disconnecting the snap connection (1) and removing the attaching screw (2)

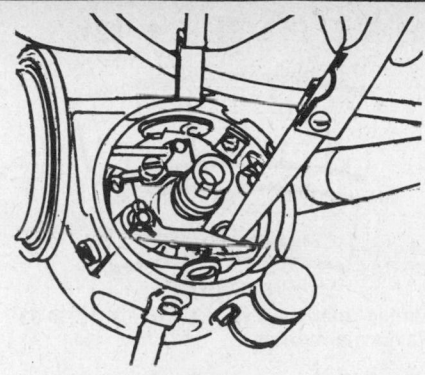

Checking the point gap with a feeler gauge

ADJUSTMENT

1. Remove the distributor cap and rotor.

2. Turn the engine by hand until the fiber rubbing block on the movable breaker point rests on a high point of the cam lobe. The point gap is the maximum distance between the points and must be set at the top of a cam lobe.

3. Using a screwdriver, loosen the locking screw of the stationary breaker point.

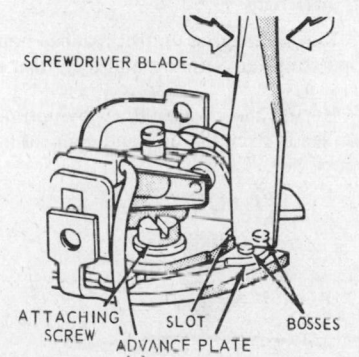

Adjusting point gap by moving stationary arm with a screwdriver

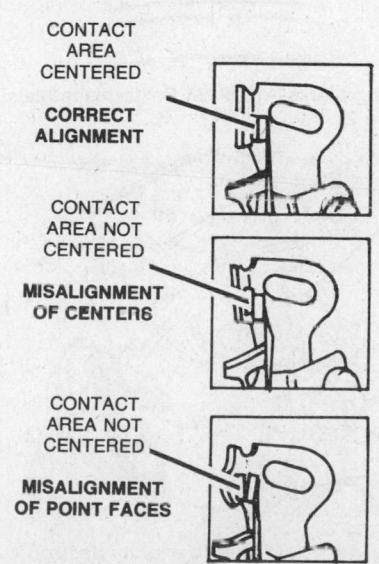

Breaker point alignment guide

4. Move the stationary point plate so that the gap is set as specified and then tighten the screw. Make sure that the feeler gauge is clean. After tightening the screw, recheck the gap.

Dwell Angle

ADJUSTMENT

NOTE: The dwell angle on all cars with the electronic ignition system is set at the factory and not adjustable.

1. Setting the dwell angle with a dwell meter achieves the same effect as setting the point gap but offers better accuracy.

NOTE: The dwell must be set before setting the timing. Setting the dwell will alter the timing, but when the timing is set, the dwell will not change.

2. Attach the positive lead of the dwell meter to the coil terminal which has a wire leading to the distributor. The negative lead should be attached to a good ground.

3. Remove the distributor cap and rotor. Turn the ignition ON and turn the engine over using a starter or a starter button. Read the dwell from the meter and open or close the points to adjust the dwell.

NOTE: Increasing the gap decreases the dwell and decreasing the gap increases the dwell.

Dwell specifications are listed in the "Tune-Up Specifications" chart.

4. Reinstall the cap and rotor and start the engine. Check the dwell and reset it if necessary.

Electronic Ignition

All 1979–83 Type 2 vehicles which were made for use in California, and all 1984 and later Type 2s are equipped with a breakerless, transistorized ignition system. This system consists of a distributor with a "Hall" sender unit, an idle stabilizer, a stronger ignition coil and an electronic control unit to monitor the whole system.

The factory states that there are no adjustments or services to be performed on this system. Any problems which are believed to be originating in the electronic ignition system should only be handled if the proper workshop test equipment is available.

PRECAUTIONS

1. DO NOT disconnect or connect any wires with the ignition switched "ON".

2. When cranking the engine, without wanting it to start (such as when performing a compression test), always disconnect the high tension wire on the distributor and then connect it to ground.

3. DO NOT install any standard ignition coil (always note the part number of the old one).

4. DO NOT connect a condenser to the negative terminal of the ignition coil.

5. DO NOT connect a quick charger (for boost starting) for any longer than 1 minute.

6. Only connect/disconnect test instrument when ignition is switched OFF.

7. DO NOT connect any condenser to terminal 1.

8. DO NOT crank engine before high tension wire of distributor cap (terminal 4) is connected to ground with jumper wire (example: compression check, etc.)

9. DO NOT leave battery connected when electric welding on car.

10. DO NOT substitute rotor of ignition distributor with one of different type.

11. When installing suppressor, use ONLY 1000 ohms for high tension wires and 1000–5000 ohms for spark plug connectors.

12. DO NOT wash engine when it is running.

13. DO NOT use battery booster longer than 1 minute nor exceed 16.5 volts with booster.

Ignition Timing

ADJUSTMENT

Type 1 and 2 (Except 1979–83 Type 2 Calif. and all 1984 and later Models)

Dwell or point gap must be set before the timing is set. Also, the idle speed must be set to specifications.

NOTE: The engine must be warmed up before the timing is set (oil temperature of 122–158°F).

1. Remove the No. 1 spark plug wire from the distributor cap and attach the tim-

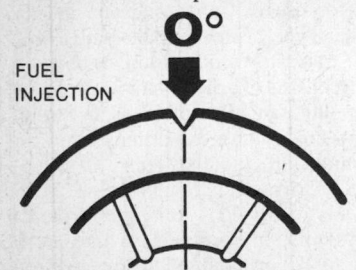

Timing marks—fuel injected Type 1 with Automatic Stick Shift and all 1984 and later Waterboxers

ing light lead. Disconnect the vacuum hose if so advised by the "Tune-Up Specifications" chart (and readjust the idle speed if necessary).

2. Start the engine and run it at the specified rpm. Aim the timing light at the crankshaft pulley on upright fan engines and at the engine cooling fan on the suitcase engines. The rubber plug in the fan housing will have to be removed before the timing marks on the suitcase engine can be seen.

3. Read the timing and rotate the distributor accordingly.

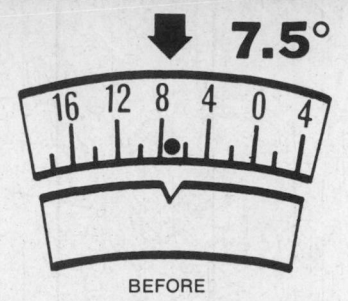

Timing marks—Type 2 except 1979–83 California models

NOTE: Rotate the distributor in the opposite direction of normal rotor rotation to advance the timing. Retard the timing by turning the distributor in the normal direction of rotor rotation.

4. It is necessary to loosen the clamp at the base of the distributor before the distributor can be rotated. It may also be necessary to put a small amount of white paint or chalk on the timing marks to make them more visible.

1979–83 Type 2 Calif. Models and All 1984 and Later Models

1. Run the engine until it reaches normal operating temperature and then turn it off.

2. Bypass the idle stabilizer by pulling the two leads from the unit and connecting them together.

Timing marks—1979–83 California models (Type 2)

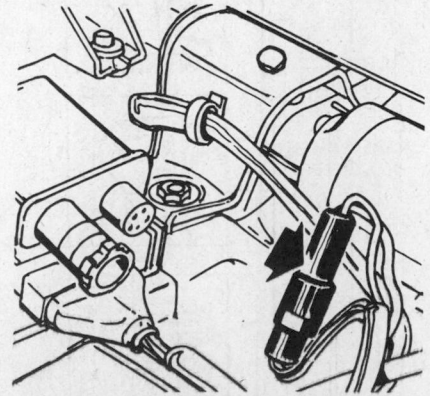

Bypass the idle stabilizer unit (electronic ignition only) by unplugging the two leads and connecting them together

3. Hook up a dwell/tachometer as per the manufacturer's instructions, start the engine and check that the idle is between 850 and 950 rpm, or 800 and 900 rpm on 1984 and later models.

4. Turn off the engine and follow Steps 1–3 of the previous procedure.

5. Be sure to reconnect the idle stabilizer after the timing has been set. Squeeze the plugs together to release them.

Valve Lash

ADJUSTMENT

Gasoline Engines

1978 and later Type 2s are equipped with hydraulic valve lifters. No routine valve adjustment is necessary, as the lifter constantly adjusts to take up clearance in the valve train. However, the valves must still be adjusted whenever the cylinder heads have been removed.

The rocker arms in these engines are equipped with conventional locknut-type adjusters. The rockers must be adjusted only when the head(s) have been removed. Remove the rocker arm covers first.

1. Back out the adjusting screws on the rocker arms so that the ball-shaped end is flush with the surface of the rocker arm.

2. Turn the crankshaft until No. 1 cylinder is at TDC on compression. Both valves should be closed, and the mark on the distributor rotor should be in line with the mark on the distributor housing.

3. Turn the adjusting screws in so that they just touch the valve stems.

4. Turn the adjusting screws 2 turns clockwise and tighten the locknuts.

5. Rotate the crankshaft 180° and adjust cylinder No. 2. Repeat the procedure on cylinders 3 and 4 until all valves are adjusted.

Diesel Engines

Check the valve clearance every 20,000 miles in firing order, with the engine at normal operating temperature.

1. Remove the camshaft cover.

2. Set the engine at TDC on No. 1 cylinder by aligning the 0°T mark on the flywheel with the pointer.

NOTE: When adjusting clearances on a diesel, the pistons must not be at TDC. Turn the crankshaft ¼ turn past TDC, so that the valves do not contact the pistons when the tappets are depressed.

3. The valve clearances of cylinder No. 1 should be checked when the valves of No. 4 cylinder overlap, i.e., when both No. 4 cylinder valves move in opposite directions simultaneously. It may be necessary to turn the crankshaft slightly to find this position. When this happens, the exhaust valve is closing and the intake opening. Check and note the clearance of both the intake and exhaust valves for No. 1 cylinder.

4. Turn the crankshaft 180° in the nor-

mal direction of rotation. Check and note the valve clearances of cylinder No. 3 at the overlap position of cylinder No. 2.

5. Turn the crankshaft 180°. Check and note the valve clearances of cylinder No. 4 at the overlap position of cylinder No. 1.

6. Turn the crankshaft 180°. Check and note the valve clearances of cylinder No. 2 at the overlap position of cylinder No. 3.

7. Compare the noted clearances with those listed in the "Tune-Up Specifications" chart. Adjustment is made by replacing the tappet clearance shim in the top of each tappet. These are available in 26 sizes ranging from 3.0mm (0.119 in.) to 4.25mm (0.166 in.) in increments of 0.05mm (0.002 in.). The thickness of each shim is marked on the bottom (these shims are available from VW dealers).

NOTE: If a valve clearance deviates 0.002 in. or less from the specified clearance, it need not be adjusted.

8. To remove a tappet clearance shim, turn the cylinder to TDC and press down the tappet so that the shim can be lifted out.

A special tool is available from VW for this operation. Once the shim is removed, check its size and determine what size will be needed to produce the required adjustment.

9. Install the required shim. When all the clearances have been corrected, recheck valve clearances.

Fuel System Adjustments

IDLE SPEED AND MIXTURE

Gasoline Engines

IDLE MIXTURE

Volkswagen states that the idle mixture should not require adjustment during a tune-up or routine maintenance. The only time that it will require an adjustment is after replacement of the intake air sensor or after extensive engine rebuilding. An infrared exhaust gas analyzer (CO meter) is required to properly perform this adjustment.

IDLE SPEED

1979–83

1. Thoroughly warm up the engine so that the oil will be hot and the auxiliary air regulator will be fully closed.

NOTE: On 1979–83 Type 2 Calif. models the idle stabilizer must be bypassed. Pull the two leads from the stabilizer and connect them together.

2. Turn off the engine and hook up a dwell/tachometer as per the manufacturer's instructions.

NOTE: Don't forget to set the meter to the four cylinder scale.

3. Start the engine, speed it up and then allow it to return to idle. The idle speed for cars with manual transmissions should be

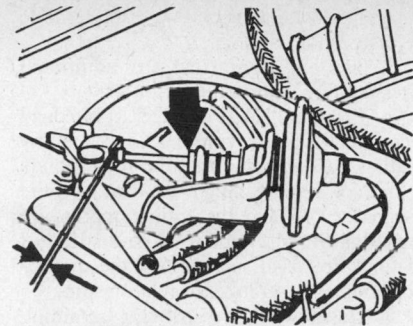

Idle speed regulator adjustment—Type 2 with automatic transmission

850–950 rpm. The idle speed for cars with automatic transmissions should be 900–1000 rpm. If the idle speed is not within the limits, it will require adjustment.

4. To adjust the idle, use a screwdriver to turn the bypass screw in the throttle valve housing. Turn the screw clockwise to decrease the idle and counterclockwise to increase it.

NOTE: Make sure you reconnect the idle stabilizer if your car is so equipped.

All Type 2 vehicles with an automatic transmission require one further adjustment. When the idle speed has been set properly, set the parking brake, block the front wheels and then put the car in "Drive." The idle should drop between 150–200 rpm. If it drops more than this you will have to adjust the idle speed regulator. To adjust:

1. With the engine idling, place the transmission in "Park" and use a feeler gauge to check the clearance between the end of the plunger and the lever on the throttle valve shaft. It should be between 0.020–0.040 in.

2. If the gap is not within specifications, loosen the locknut on the plunger and screw the plunger in or out until the clearance is correct.

1984 and later

1. Make sure the engine has been run

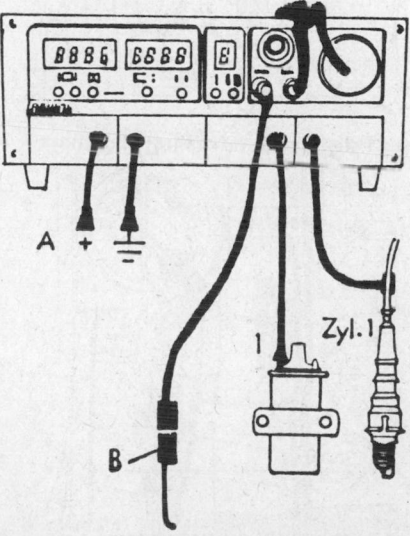

Ignition testing—showing VW tester

up to operating temperature, all electrical accessories are OFF (including the radiator fan), and the throttle valve switch is ON at idle. Always make sure the ignition switch is OFF when the tester is connected.

2. Connect the tester (VW part No. VAG 1367 or equivalent) as shown in the accompanying illustration: "A" to the alternator or terminal box, and "B" to the TDC sender.

3. Connect the CO meter to the recepticle in the left exhaust pipe.

4. Check the ignition timing, and adjust if necessary.

5. Disconnect the idle stabilizer electrical plugs, and connect them together. Start the engine and again check ignition timing. Timing should be 5° ATDC with rpm below 1000. Adjust if necessary.

6. Run the engine at idle speed. Check engine speed after two minutes and adjust if necessary. Adjust by turning the screw on the throttle valve housing.

7. Stop the engine. Check the CO and adjust if necessary. Connect the idle stabilizer. Disconnect the electrical connection at the oxygen sensor. Start the engine and check the CO content—it should be 0.3–1.1%.

8. If the CO value is above 1.1%, pinch the crankcase hose. The CO should drop below 1.1%. If it does, a CO adjustment is not necessary. If it does NOT, continue.

9. Stop the engine. To adjust the CO, first remove the intake air sensor. Center punch the plug in the CO adjusting hole. Drill a ³⁄₃₂ in. hole in the center of the plug,

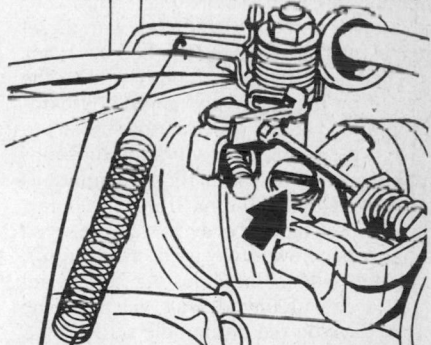

Fuel injection idle speed (by-pass screw) adjustment—Type 1

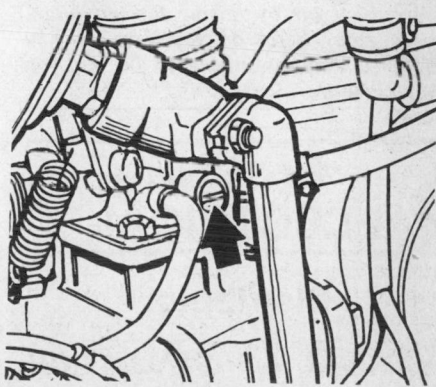

Fuel injection idle speed (by-pass screw) adjustment—Type 2

⁹⁄₆₄ to ⁵⁄₃₂ in. deep, NO MORE. Keep the area clean of metal shavings.

10. Screw a ⅛ in. sheet metal screw into the plug and remove the plug, using pliers.

11. Reinstall the air intake sensor, and with the oxygen sensor disconnected, start the engine.

12. Adjust the CO content to 0.7% using the CO adjusting screw (underneath the plug).

13. Stop the engine. Drive in a new plug until it is flush with the intake air sensor. Reconnect the electrical connection at the oxygen sensor. CO content should be 0.3–1.1% with both the oxygen sensor and the idle stabilizer connected.

Diesel Engines

IDLE SPEED/MAXIMUM SPEED ADJUSTMENTS

Volkswagen diesel engines have both an idle speed and a maximum speed adjustment. The maximum engine speed adjustment prevents the engine from over-revving and self-destructing. The adjusters are located side by side on top of the injection pump. The screw closest to the engine is the idle speed adjuster, while the outer screw is the maximum speed adjuster.

The idle and maximum speed must be adjusted with the engine warm (normal operating temperature). Because the diesel engine has no conventional ignition, you will need a special adaptor (VW 1324) to connect your tachometer, or use the tachometer in the instrument panel, if equipped. You should check with the manufacturer of your tachometer to see if it will work with diesel engines. Adjust all engines to 800–850 rpm.

When adjustment is correct, lock the locknut on the screw and apply non-hardening thread sealer (Loctite® or similar) to prevent the screw from vibrating loose.

The maximum speed for all engines is between 5300–5400 rpm. If it is not in this range, loosen the screw and correct the speed (turning the screw clockwise decreases rpm). Lock the nut on the adjusting screw and apply a dab of thread sealer in the same manner as you did on the idle screw.

CAUTION

Do not attempt to squeeze more power out of your engine by raising the maximum speed (rpm). If you do, you'll probably be in for a major overhaul in the not too distant future.

ENGINE ELECTRICAL

Distributor

REMOVAL & INSTALLATION

1. Take off the vacuum hose(s) at the distributor.

2. Disconnect the coil wire and remove the distributor cap.

3. Tag and disconnect any additional wires leading from the distributor.

4. Bring the No. 1 cylinder to top dead center (TDC) on the compression stroke by rotating the engine so that the rotor points to the No. 1 spark plug wire tower on the distributor cap and the timing marks are aligned at 0°. Mark the rotor-to-distributor relationship. Also, matchmark the distributor housing-to-crankcase relationship.

5. Unscrew the distributor retaining screw on the crankcase and lift the distributor out.

6. If the engine has been rotated since the distributor was removed, bring the No. 1 cylinder to TDC on the compression stroke and align the timing marks on 0°. Align the matchmarks and insert the distributor into the crankcase. If the matchmarks are gone, have the rotor pointing to the No. 1 spark plug wire tower upon insertion.

7. Replace the distributor retaining screw and reconnect the condenser and coil wires. Reinstall the distributor cap.

8. Retime the engine.

Distributor Driveshaft

REMOVAL & INSTALLATION

1. Bring the engine to TDC on the compression stroke of No. 1 cylinder. Align the timing marks at 0°.

2. Remove the distributor.

3. Remove the spacer spring from the driveshaft.

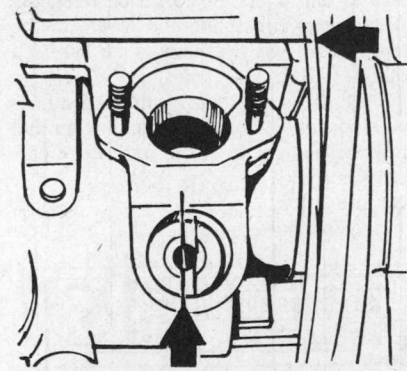

Type 1 distributor driveshaft alignment

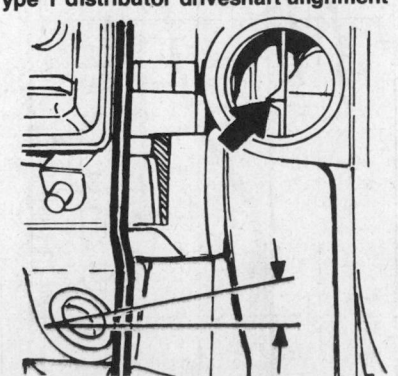

Type 2 distributor driveshaft alignment— air-cooled engine shown

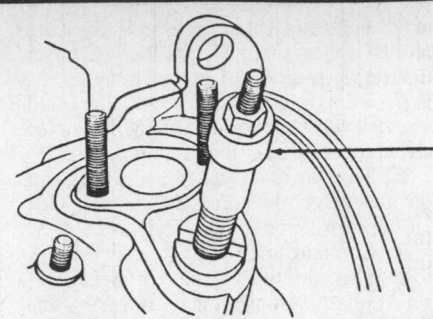

Removing the distributor driveshaft using VW special puller (arrow)—Waterboxer

4. Grasp the shaft and turn it slowly to the left while withdrawing it from its bore.

On the 1984 and later Waterboxer, an extractor with a 0.583–0.782 in. diameter must be screwed into the driveshaft, in order to remove the shaft.

5. Remove the washer found under the shaft.

CAUTION

Make sure that this washer does not fall down into the engine.

---

6. To install, make sure that the engine is at TDC on the compression stroke for No. 1 cylinder with the timing marks aligned

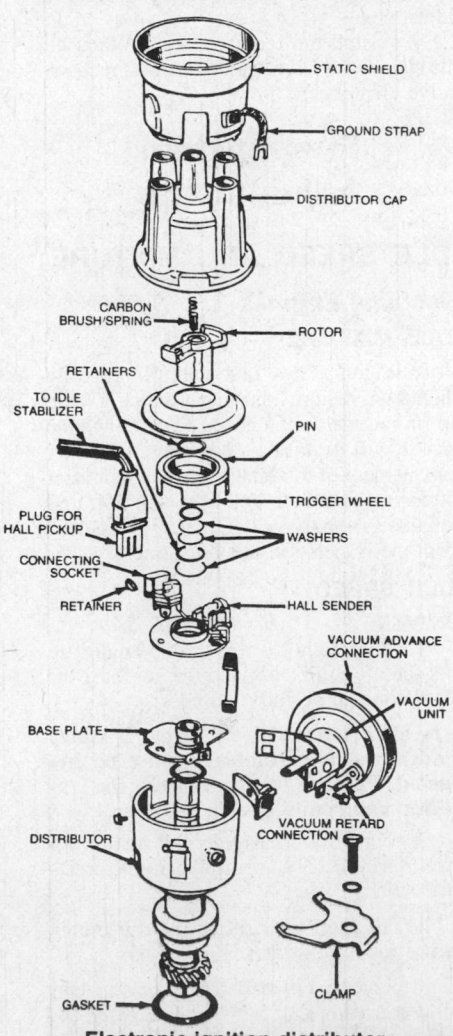

Electronic ignition distributor

at 0°. Make sure the rotor is pointing to the No. 1 cylinder mark on the edge of the distributor housing. If not, turn it until it is.

7. Replace the washer and insert the shaft into its bore.

NOTE: Due to the slant of the teeth on the drive gears, the shaft must be rotated slightly to the left when it is inserted into the crankcase.

8. When the shaft is properly inserted, the offset slot in the driveshaft of Type 1 engines will be perpendicular to the crankcase joint and the slot offset will be facing the crankshaft pulley. On Type 2/1800 and 2/2000 engines, the slot should be about 12° out of parallel with the center line of the engine and the slot offset should be facing outside the engine.

On the 1984 and later Waterboxer, insert the shaft so that the offset slot in the top of the driveshaft is pointing toward the tapped hole in the crankcase. The small-segment points toward the water pump.

9. Reinstall the spacer spring.
10. Reinstall the distributor and fuel pump, if removed.
11. Retime the engine.

Alternator

PRECAUTIONS

1. Battery polarity should be checked before any connections, such as jumper cables or battery charge leads, are made. Reversing the battery connections will damage the diodes in the alternator. It is recommended that the battery cables be disconnected before connecting a battery charger.

2. The battery must never be disconnected while the alternator is running.

3. Always disconnect the battery ground lead before working on the charging system, especially when replacing an alternator.

4. Do not short across or ground any alternator or regulator terminals.

5. If electric arc welding has to be done to the car, first disconnect the battery and alternator cables. Never start the car with the welding unit attached.

REMOVAL & INSTALLATION

Type 1

1. Disconnect the battery.
2. Remove the fan belt.
3. Remove the air cleaner and the intake air sensor.
4. Pull out the accelerator cable guide tube.
5. Remove the alternator retaining strap.
6. Disconnect the ignition cables and any hoses, air ducts and wires that might prevent the fan housing from being lifted upward.
7. Loosen and remove the mounting screws at each end of the fan housing.
8. Unbolt and remove the thermostat.
9. Raise the fan housing slightly and unscrew the four alternator mounting bolts.

10. Remove the alternator and the fan from the fan housing.

11. Remove the fan from the alternator by unscrewing the special nut and pulling the fan off the keyed alternator shaft. Note the position of any shims, as these are used to maintain a gap of 0.08 in. between the fan and the fan cover.

12. Installation is in the reverse order of removal.

Type 2/1800, 2/2000, 2/Waterboxer (Fuel Injected)

1. Disconnect the negative battery cable.
2. Disconnect the alternator wiring harness at the voltage regulator (non-integral voltage regulator models) and starter.
3. Pull out the dipstick and remove the oil filler neck.
4. Loosen the alternator adjusting bolt and remove the drive belt.
5. Remove the right rear engine cover plate and the alternator cover plate.
6. Disconnect the warm air duct at the right side, and remove the heat exchanger bracket and connecting pipe from the blower.
7. Disconnect the cool air intake elbow at the alternator. Remove the attaching bolt and lift out the alternator from above.
8. Reverse the above procedure to install, taking care to ensure that the rubber grommet on the intake cover for the wiring harness is installed correctly. After installation, adjust the drive belt so that moderate thumb pressure midway on the belt depresses the belt about ½ in.

ALTERNATOR BELT ADJUSTMENT

1. Remove the insert in the cover plate and loosen the bolt in the slotted hole.
2. Move the alternator left or right to adjust the tension and then tighten the bolt. Tension is correct if the bolt can be deflected no more than ½ in. at the midpoint of the pulleys.

Voltage Regulator

REMOVAL & INSTALLATION

Type 1

The regulator is located under the rear seat on the left side. It is secured to the frame by two screws. Take careful note of the wiring connections before removing the wiring from the regulator. Disconnect the battery before removing the regulator.

— CAUTION —
Interchanging the connections on the regulator will destroy the regulator and generator.

Type 2 (with Separate Regulator)

Disconnect the battery. The regulator is lo-

Alternator belt tension adjustment

cated in the engine compartment and is secured in place by two screws. Take careful note of the wiring connections before removing the wiring from the regulator.

Type 2 (with Integral Regulator)

Later Type 2 models, both air and water-cooled, are equipped with voltage regulators which are built into the alternator. These regulators can be replaced without removing the alternator. To replace the regulator, remove the alternator drive belt and remove the front half of the alternator case. The regulator is the six-sided black component inside.

NOTE: If the voltage regulator is replaced, a suppressor condenser must be added (if not already installed) in the alternator. This condenser is noticeable as a rectangular black component mounted above the voltage regulator in the alternator.

VOLTAGE ADJUSTMENT

Volkswagen voltage regulators are sealed and cannot be adjusted. A malfunctioning regulator must be replaced as a unit.

Starter

REMOVAL & INSTALLATION

1. Disconnect the battery.
2. Disconnect the wiring from the starter.
3. The starter is held in place by two bolts. Remove the upper bolt through the engine compartment. Remove the lower bolt from underneath the car.
4. Remove the starter from the car.
5. Before installing the starter, lubricate the outboard bushing with grease. Apply sealing compound to the mating surfaces between the starter and the transmission.
6. Place the long starter bolt in its hole in the starter and locate the starter on the transmission housing. Install the other bolt.
7. Connect the starter wiring and battery cables.

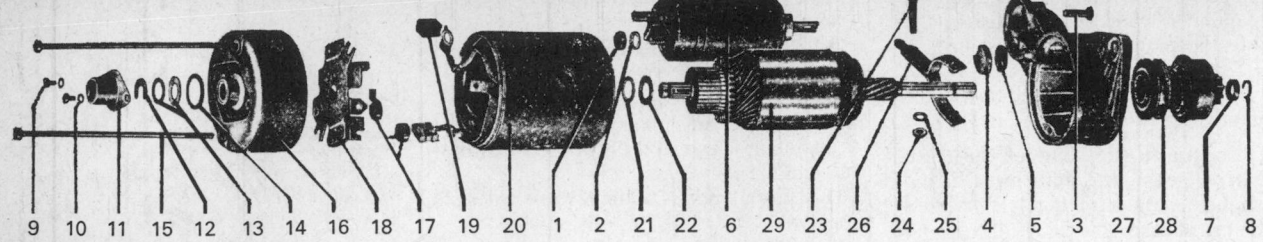

1. Nut
2. Lockwasher
3. Screw
4. Rubber seal
5. Disc
6. Solenoid switch
7. Stop-ring
8. Circlip
9. Screw
10. Washer
11. End cap
12. C-washer
13. Shim
14. Sealing ring
15. Housing screw
16. End plate
17. Spring
18. Brush holder
19. Rubber grommet
20. Housing
21. Insulating washer
22. Thrust washer
23. Pin
24. Nut
25. Lockwasher
26. Operating lever
27. Drive end plate
28. Drive pinion
29. Armature

Exploded view of Bosch 311 911 023B starter

SOLENOID REPLACEMENT

1. Remove the starter.
2. Remove the nut which secures the connector strip at the end of the solenoid.
3. Take out the two retaining screws on the mounting bracket and withdraw the solenoid after it has been unhooked from its actuating lever.
4. When replacing a defective solenoid with a new one, care should be taken to see that the distance (a) in the accompanying diagram is 19 mm when the magnet is drawn inside the solenoid.
5. Installation is the reverse of removal. In order to facilitate engagement of the actuating rod, the pinion should be pulled out as far as possible when inserting the solenoid.

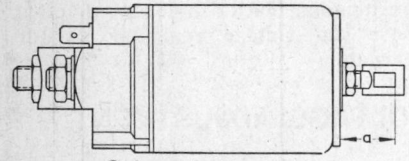

Solenoid adjustment

Diesel Engine

GLOW PLUG SYSTEM CHECK

NOTE: The 1982 and later diesels have a new type quick-glow system. Nominal glow time is seven seconds. Although the wiring for this system is the same as the earlier system, the glow plugs and relay cannot be paired or interchanged with earlier parts or vice versa.

1. Connect a test light between the No. 4 cylinder glow plug and ground. The glow plugs are connected by a flat, coated busbar (located near the bottom of the cylinder head).
2. Turn the ignition key to the heating (pre-glow) position. The test light should light.
3. If not, possible problems include the glow plug relay, the ignition switch and fuse box relay plate and the glow plug fuse or a break in the wire to the relay terminal.

INDIVIDUAL GLOW PLUG TEST

1. Remove the wire and busbar from the glow plugs.
2. Connect a test light to the battery positive terminal.
3. Touch the test light probe to each glow plug in turn.
If the test light lights, the plug is good. If the light does not light, replace the glow plug(s).

ENGINE MECHANICAL

NOTE: For all Vanagon diesel engine mechanical procedures not described here, please refer to "Engine Mechanical" in the Volkswagen Front Wheel Drive section of this manual.

Engine

REMOVAL & INSTALLATION

All Air-Cooled Models

The Volkswagen engine is mounted on the transmission, which in turn is attached to the frame. In the Type 1 and 2 models, there are two bolts and two studs attaching the engine to the transmission.

When removing the engine from the car, it is recommended that the rear of the car be about 3 ft. off the ground. Remove the engine by bringing it out from underneath the car. Proceed with the following steps to remove the engine.

1. Disconnect the battery ground cable.
2. Disconnect the generator wiring.
3. Remove the air cleaner. On Type 1 engines, remove the rear engine cover plate.
4. Disconnect the throttle cable and remove the electrical connections to the automatic choke, coil, electromagnetic cutoff jet, and the oil pressure sending unit.
5. Disconnect the fuel hose at the front engine cover plate and seal it to prevent leakage.

6. Raise the car and support it with jack stands.
7. Remove the flexible air hoses between the engine and heat exchangers, disconnect the heater flap cables, unscrew the two lower engine mounting nuts, and slide a jack under the engine. On Type 2 engines, remove the two bolts from the rubber engine mounts located next to the muffler.

Removing the upper engine mounting bolts

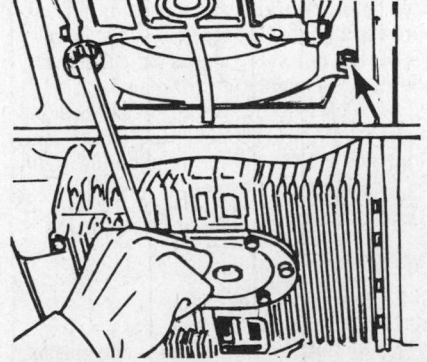

Removing the lower engine mounting bolts

8. On Type 1 Automatic Stick Shift models, disconnect the control valve cable and the manifold vacuum hoses. Disconnect the ATF suction line and plug it.
9. On all Automatic Stick Shift and fully automatic models, remove the four bolts from the converter drive plate through the holes in the transmission case. After the engine is removed, hold the torque converter on the transmission input shaft by using a strap bolted to the bellhousing.

10. Raise the jack until it just contacts the engine and have an assistant hold the two upper mounting bolts so that the nuts can be removed from the bottom.

11. When the engine mounts are disconnected and there are no remaining cables or wires left to be disconnected, move the engine toward the back of the car so that the clutch or converter plate disengages from the transmission.

12. Lower the engine out of the car.

13. Installation is the reverse of the above. When the engine is lifted into position, it should be rotated using the generator pulley so that the clutch plate hub will engage the transmission shaft splines. Tighten the upper mounting bolts first. Check the clutch, pressure plate, throwout bearing, and pilot bearing for wear.

1984 and later Type 2 Waterboxer

1. Disconnect the battery ground cable.
2. Remove the air cleaner from the air flow sensor and the air intake duct.
3. Tag and disconnect the alternator wire at the alternator.
4. Tag and disconnect the plugs at the fuel injectors, the plug at the throttle valve switch, and the plug at the auxiliary air regulator.
5. Disconnect the hoses at the charcoal filter valve.
6. Tag and disconnect the fuel hoses near the distributor. Remove the accelerator cable from the throttle valve lever. On automatic transmission models, remove the circlip and spring from the accelerator rod.
7. Tag and disconnect the plug at the oxygen sensor, the plugs at the distributor, oil pressure switch, temperature sensor, temperature sender, and coolant level warning switch (located at the coolant expansion tank).
8. Block the coolant hoses with clamps and open the coolant expansion tank cap. Remove the drain plugs at the cylinder heads and drain the coolant.

NOTE: Always replace the sealing rings underneath the drain plugs during installation.

9. Disconnect the brake booster line, and disconnect all coolant hoses. Remove the coolant expansion tank.
10. Remove the engine-to-transaxle bolts and nuts on the left and right sides.
11. On automatic transmission models, remove the three bolts which attach the torque converter to the drive plate through the hole on the top of the transaxle housing.
12. Disconnect the starter wiring.
13. On automatic transmission models, disconnect the accelerator rod.
14. Jack up the vehicle (if not already done) and safely support it with jackstands, raising the vehicle high enough that the engine can be lowered out from underneath.

CAUTION

The safe support of the rear end of the vehicle in this procedure is crucial.

---

15. Remove the engine plates from underneath.
16. Loosen the transmission mounting bolt.
17. Support the underside of the engine with a transmission jack, making sure there is a wooden block or pad between the jack and engine.
18. Remove the engine carrier bolts. Carefully lower the engine/transaxle assembly slightly. Keep the wiring harness aside so that it can pass the oil filler tube. Lower the assembly more so that you have access to the lower engine mounting bolts. Remove the engine from the transaxle and lower it out of the vehicle. Mount the engine on an engine stand for service.
19. To install, reverse the above procedure and note the following:
  a. Replace all self-locking nuts on the engine mounts during reassembly.
  b. Check the clutch release bearing for wear and replace if necessary.
  c. Lube the clutch release bearing and main shaft splines lightly with a molybdenum disulfide grease. DO NOT lube the guide sleeve for the release bearing.
  d. Check and adjust the accelerator cable and throttle controls.
  e. Use the following torque specifications for installation: Engine-to-transmission, 22 ft. lbs.; engine carrier-to-body, 18 ft. lbs., transmission mounts 22 ft. lbs.; torque converter-to-drive plate 14 ft. lbs.
  f. Refill the cooling system, following "Cooling System Refill" later in this section.

Cylinder Head

REMOVAL & INSTALLATION

All Air-Cooled Models

In order to remove the cylinder head from either pair of cylinders, it is necessary to lower the engine.

1. Remove the valve cover and gasket. Remove the rocker arm assembly. Unbolt the intake manifold from the cylinder head. The cylinder head is held in place by eight studs. Since the cylinder head also holds the cylinders in place in the VW engine, and the cylinders are not going to be removed it will be necessary to hold the cylinders in place after the head is removed.

2. After the rocker arm cover, rocker arm retaining nuts, and rocker arm assembly have been removed, the cylinder head nuts can be removed and the cylinder head lifted off.

3. When reinstalling the cylinder head, the head should be checked for cracks both in the combustion chamber and in the intake and exhaust ports. Cracked heads must be replaced.

4. Spark plug threads should be checked. New seals should be used on the pushrod tube ends and they should be checked for proper seating.

5. The pushrod tubes should be turned so that the seam faces upward. In order to ensure perfect sealing, used tubes should be stretched slightly before they are reinstalled.

6. Install the cylinder head. Using new rocker shaft stud seals, install the pushrods and rocker shaft assembly.

NOTE: Pay careful attention to the orientation of the shaft as described in the "Rocker Shaft" section.

7. Torque the cylinder head in three stages. Adjust the valve clearance. Using a new gasket, install the rocker cover. It may be necessary to readjust the valves after the engine has been run a few minutes and allowed to cool.

Waterboxer

On the Waterboxer, it is not necessary to remove or lower the engine to remove the cylinder heads. Either head can be removed and installed while the engine is in place in the vehicle.

1. Drain the coolant from the cooling system using the coolant drain plugs on the bottom of each cylinder head.

NOTE: When installing the drain plugs, always use new sealing rings underneath the plugs.

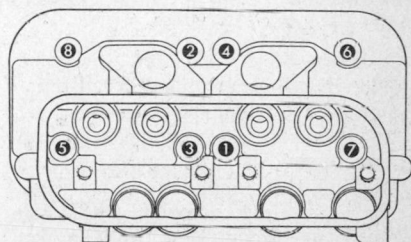

Cylinder head torque sequence—air-cooled Type 2

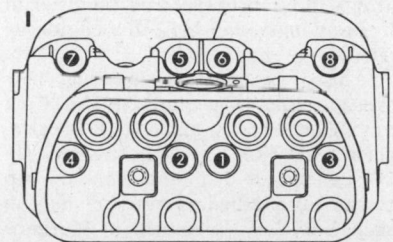

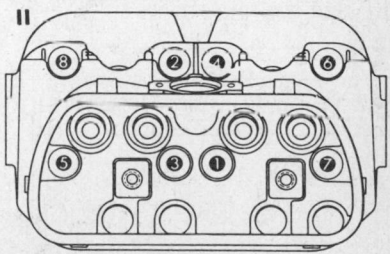

For 1600 cc engines, the cylinder head nuts should initially be tightened to 7 ft. lbs. in order I, then tightened to the recommended torque in order II.

1. Cylinder head cover
2. Gasket
3. Nut
4. Spring washer
5. Rocker shaft
6. Clip
7. Thrust washer
8. Spring washer
9. Rocker arm
10. Adjusting screw
11. Nut
12. Support
13. Stud seal
14. Nut
15. Washer

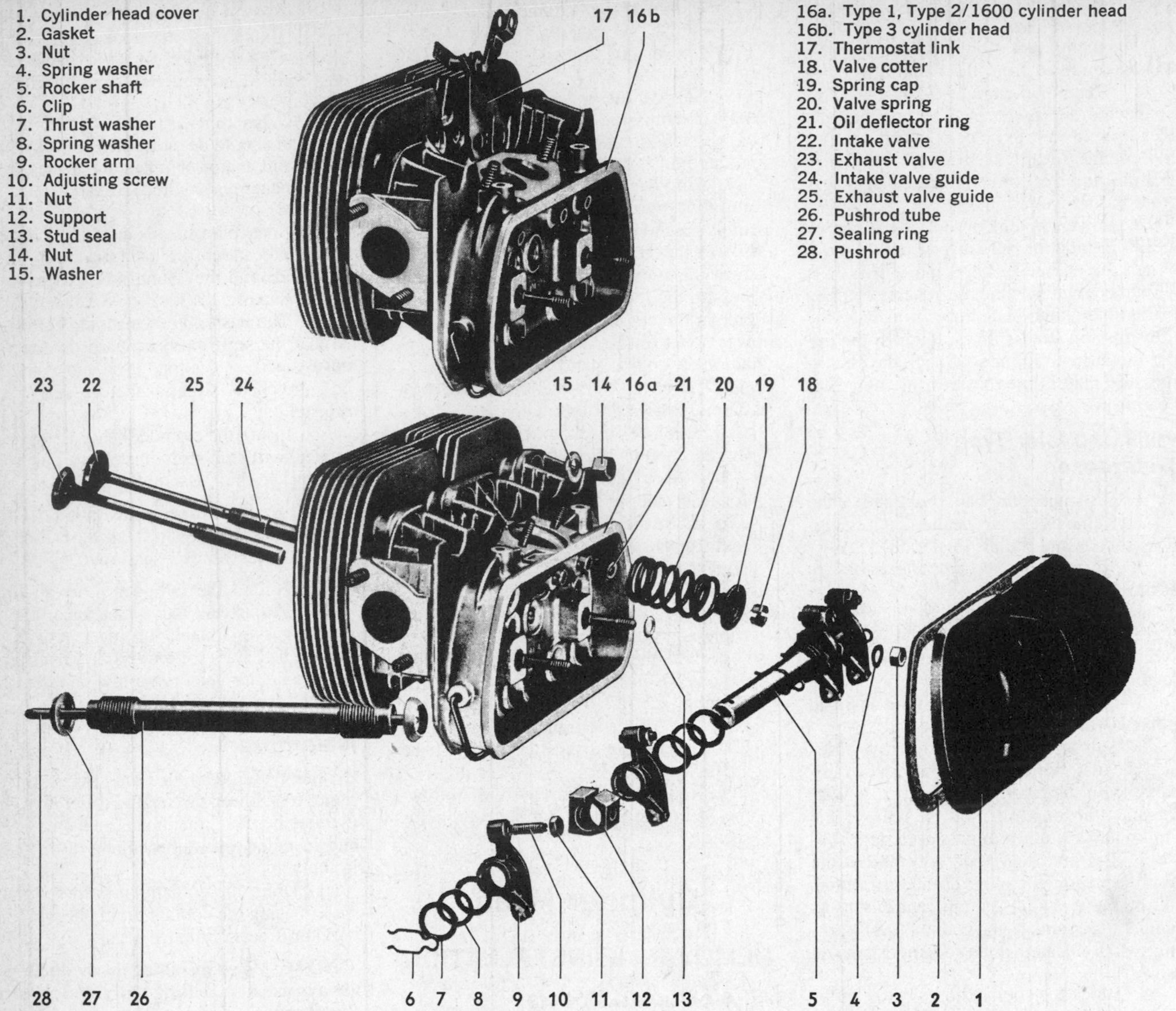

16a. Type 1, Type 2/1600 cylinder head
16b. Type 3 cylinder head
17. Thermostat link
18. Valve cotter
19. Spring cap
20. Valve spring
21. Oil deflector ring
22. Intake valve
23. Exhaust valve
24. Intake valve guide
25. Exhaust valve guide
26. Pushrod tube
27. Sealing ring
28. Pushrod

Exploded view of the air-cooled Type 1 cylinder head showing valve train. Except for lack of cooling fins, Waterboxer head is very similar

2. Follow Steps 1 and 2 of "Air Cooled Cylinder Head" removal and installation.

3. Before installing the head, make sure all gasket contact areas are completely clean and free of any damage. *Always replace the head gasket,* applying a thin bead (1–2mm) of sealing compound D 000 400 (VW part No. or equivalent) to the gasket surface facing the cylinder head. Do not use too much, as excess sealant could plug cylinder head coolant passages.

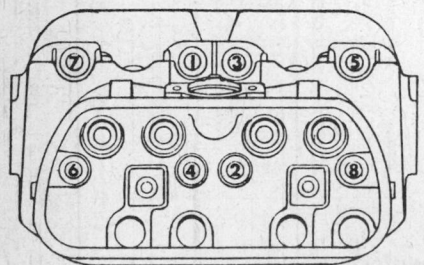

Waterboxer cylinder head torque sequence

4. The pushrod tubes should be installed so that the small end faces the cylinder head, and so that the seam on the tube is facing upward. Guide the tubes into the hydraulic lifter holes carefully. Always replace the sealing rings.

NOTE: If the pushrod tube rests on the edge of the valve lifter, the basic valve setting will be incorrect and the lifter(s) will be damaged when the engine is started.

5. Install the cylinder head, using a new gasket and sealer as mentioned above. Coat the cylinder head cap nuts with D3 sealer. Tighten Stud No. 1 (see illustration) cap nut just enough so that the remaining 7 cap nuts can be installed. Torque all nuts in sequence to 7 ft. lbs., then in sequence again to the final torque of 25 ft. lbs. Install the remaining parts in the reverse order of removal. Torque the rocker shaft nuts to 18 ft. lbs. Use new rocker cover gaskets. Fill

the cooling system, following "Cooling System Filling" later in this section.

VALVE SEATS

On all air-cooled VW engines, the valve seats are shrunk-fit into the cylinder head. This usually involves freezing the seat with liquid nitrogen or some other refrigerant to about 200°F below zero, and heating up the cylinder head to approximately 400°F. Due to the extreme temperatures required to shrink-fit these items, and because of the extra care needed when working with metals at these extreme temperatures, it is advised that this operation be handled by a machine shop.

OVERHAUL

For all cylinder head overhaul procedures, please refer to "Engine Rebuilding" in the Unit Repair section.

Rocker Shafts

REMOVAL & INSTALLATION

1. Before the valve rocker assembly can be reached, it is necessary to lever off the clip that retains the valve cover and then remove the valve cover.

2. Remove the rocker arm retaining nuts, the rocker arm shaft, and the rocker arms. Remove the stud seals.

3. Before installing the rocker arm mechanism, be sure that the parts are as clean as possible.

On Type 1 models, install the rocker shaft with the chamfer out and the slot up

On Type 2/1800 models, install the rocker shaft with the chamfer out and the slots down

4. Install new stud seals. On the Type 1, install the rocker shaft assembly with the chamfered edges of the rocker shaft supports pointing outward and the slots pointing upward. On the Type 2/1800, 2/2000 models, the chamfered edges must point outward and the slots must face downward and the pushrod tube retaining wire must engage the slots in the rocker arm shaft supports as well as the grooves in the pushrod tubes. On the Type 2 Waterboxer, the slot on the rocker shaft support faces upward.

5. Tighten the retaining nuts to the proper torque. Use only the copper colored nuts that were supplied with the engine.

6. Make sure that the ball ends of the pushrods are centered in the sockets of the rocker arms.

7. Adjust the valve clearance. Install the valve cover using a new gasket.

Intake Manifold

REMOVAL & INSTALLATION

1. Remove the air cleaner.

2. Remove the pressure switch which is mounted under the right pair of intake manifold pipes. Disconnect the injector wiring.

3. Remove the fuel injectors by removing the two nuts which secure them in place. See Step 7 for proper injector installation.

4. After removing the intake manifold outer cover plate, remove the two screws which secure the manifold inner cover plate.

5. The manifold may be removed by removing the two nuts and washers which hold the manifold flange to the cylinder head.

6. Installation is the reverse of the above. The inner manifold cover should be installed first, but leave the cover loose until the outer cover and manifold are in place. Always use new gaskets.

7. Connect the fuel hoses to the injectors, if removed, after assembling the injector retainer plate in place. Make sure that the sleeves are in place on the injector securing studs. Carefully slip the injectors into the manifold and install the securing nuts. Never force the injectors in or out of the manifold. Reconnect the injector wiring.

Intake Air Distributor

REMOVAL & INSTALLATION

The intake air distributor is located at the center of the engine at the junction of the intake manifold pipes.

NOTE: It is not necessary to remove the distributor if only the manifold pipes are to be removed.

1. Remove the air cleaner and pressure switch which are located under the right pair of manifold pipes.

2. Push the four rubber hoses onto the intake manifold pipes.

3. Remove the accelerator cable and the throttle valve switch.

4. Disconnect the accelerator cable.

5. Disconnect the vacuum hoses leading to the ignition distributor and the pressure sensor and disconnect the hose running to the auxiliary air regulator.

6. Remove those bolts under the air distributor which secure the air distributor to the crankcase and remove the air distributor.

7. Installation is the reverse of removal.

Mufflers, Tailpipes, Heat Exchangers

REMOVAL & INSTALLATION

Muffler
TYPE 1

1. Working under the hood, disconnect the pre-heater hoses.

2. Remove the pre-heater pipe protection plate on each side of the engine. The plates are secured by three screws.

3. Remove the crankshaft pulley cover plate.

4. Remove the rear engine cover plate from the engine compartment. It is held in place by screws at the center, right, and left sides.

5. Remove the four intake manifold preheat pipe bolts. There are two bolts on each side of the engine.

6. Disconnect the warm air channel clamps at the left and right side of the engine.

7. Disconnect the heat exchanger clamps at the left and right side of the engine.

8. Remove the muffler from the engine.

9. Installation is the reverse of above. Always use new gaskets to install the muffler.

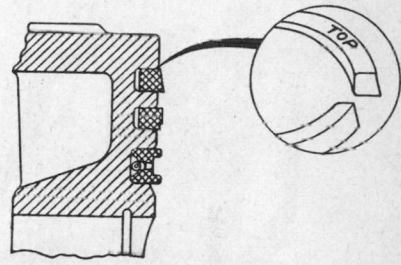

Piston ring positioning—Waterboxer

TYPE 2/1800, 2/2000

The muffler is secured to the left and right heat exchangers by three bolts. There is a bracket at the left end of the muffler. Always use new gaskets when installing a new muffler.

TYPE 2/WATERBOXER

Use the accompanying illustration to remove and install the Waterboxer muffler and exhaust system.

Heat Exchangers
TYPE 1

1. Disconnect the air tube at the outlet end of the exchanger.

2. Remove the clamp which secures the muffler to the exchanger.

3. Loosen the clamp which secures the exchanger to the heater hose connection at the muffler.

4. Remove the two nuts which secure the exchanger to the forward end of the cylinder head.

5. Remove the heater flap control wire.

6. Reverse the above to install. Always use new gaskets.

TYPE 2/1800, 2/2000

1. Disconnect the air hose at the outlet of each exchanger.

2. Disconnect the warm air tube at the outside end of the exchanger.

3. Disconnect the three bolts which secure each exchanger to the muffler.

4. Remove the four nuts, two at each exhaust port, which secure the exchanger to the cylinder head.

Installation is the reverse of the above. Always use new gaskets.

1. Tail pipe
2. Retaining ring
3. Seal
4. Nut
5. Clapm
6. Bolt
7. Muffler
8. Seal
9. Heater hose
10. Hose clamp
11. Rubber grommet
12. Connecting pipe
13. Gasket
14. Gasket
15. Gasket
16. Self-locking nut
17. Clamp
18. Heat exchanger
19. Bolt
20. Pin
21. Circlip
22. Link
23. Pin
24. Pin
25. Heater flap lever
26. Return spring
27. Damper pipe
28. Bolt
29. Washer
30. Lockwasher
31. Bolt
32. Damper pipe bracket
33. Bracket clamp
34. Bolt
35. Clamp
36. Tailpipe

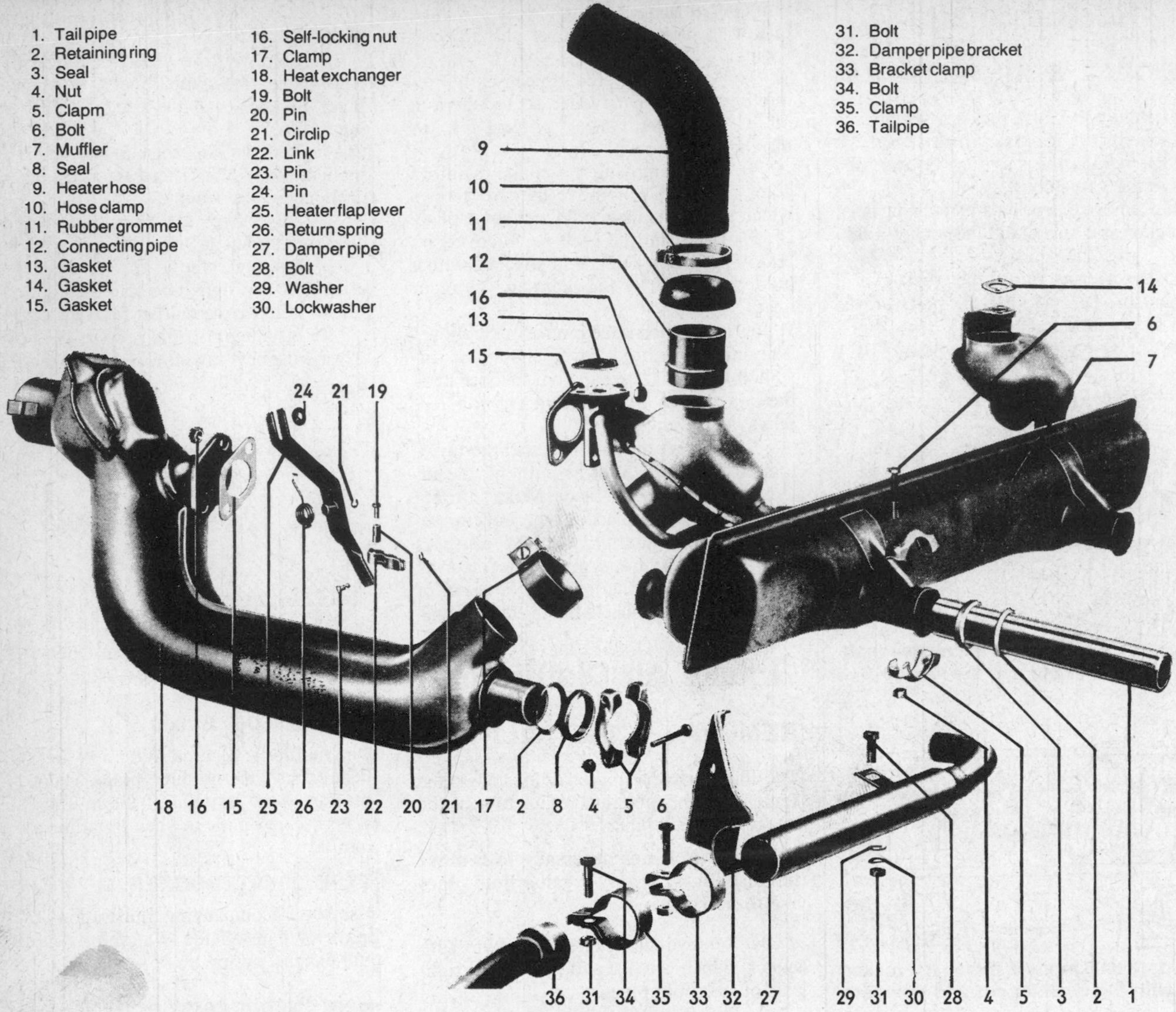

Exhaust system—Type 1

TYPE 2/WATERBOXER

Use the accompanying illustration when removing and installing the exhaust pipes on the 1984 and later models. Always use new gaskets.

Tailpipes
TYPE 1

Loosen the clamps on the tailpipes and apply penetrating oil. Work the pipe side-to-side while trying to pull the tailpipe out of the muffler.

NOTE: It is often difficult to remove the tailpipes without damaging them.

TYPE 2/1800, 2/2000

Remove the bolt which secures the pipe to the muffler. Remove the bolt which secures the pipe to the body and remove the pipe.

TYPE 2/WATERBOXER

Use the accompanying illustration when removing and installing the tailpipe on the 1984 and later models.

Pistons and Cylinders

Pistons and cylinders are matched according to their size. When replacing pistons and cylinders, make sure that they are properly sized.

NOTE: See the "Engine Rebuilding" section for cylinder refinishing.

CYLINDER REMOVAL & INSTALLATION

All Air-Cooled Engines

1. Remove the engine. Remove the cylinder head, pushrod tubes, and the deflector plate.
2. Slide the cylinder out of its groove in the crankcase and off the piston. Matchmark the cylinders for reassembly. The cylinders must be returned to their original bore in the crankcase. If a cylinder is to be replaced, it must be replaced with a matching piston.

3. Cylinders should be checked for wear and, if necessary, replaced with another matched cylinder and piston assembly of the same size.
4. Check the cylinder seating surface on the crankcase, cylinder shoulder, and gasket, for cleanliness and deep scores. When reinstalling the cylinders, a new gas-

Installing a cylinder—air-cooled engines

After burner pipe

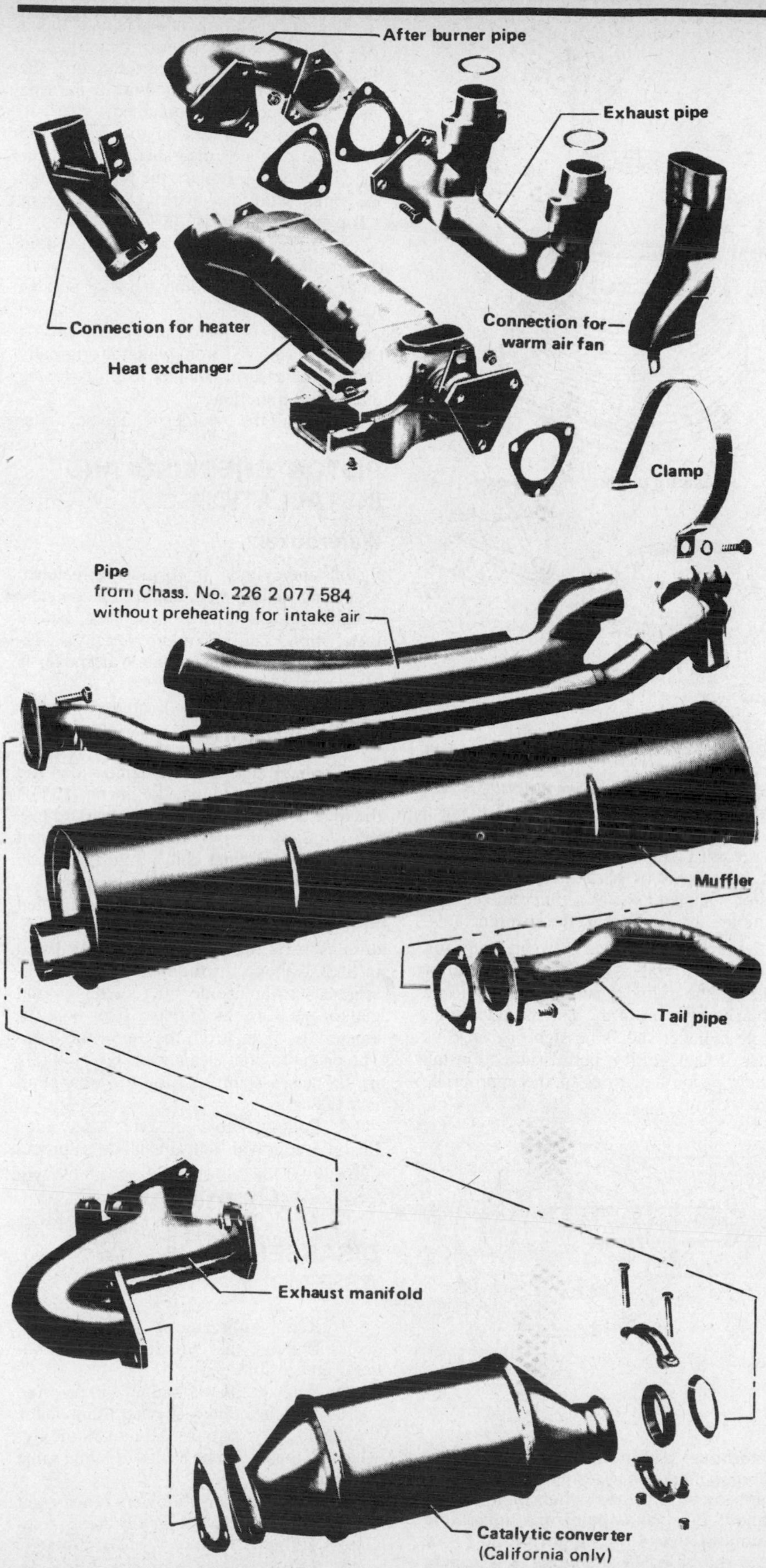

Exhaust pipe

Connection for heater

Heat exchanger

Connection for warm air fan

Clamp

Pipe
from Chass. No. 226 2 077 584
without preheating for intake air

Muffler

Tail pipe

Exhaust manifold

Catalytic converter
(California only)

Exhaust system—Type 2 gasoline engine

ket, if required, should be used between each cylinder and the crankcase.

5. The piston, as well as the piston rings and pin must be oiled before reassembly.

6. Be sure that the ring gaps are of the correct dimension. Stagger the ring gaps around the piston, but make sure that the oil ring gap is positioned up when the pistons are in position on the connecting rods.

7. Compress the rings with a ring compressor, oil the cylinder wall, and slide the cylinder onto the piston. Make sure that the cylinder base gasket is in place.

8. Install the deflector plates.

9. Install the pushrod tubes using new gaskets. Install the pushrods. Make sure that the seam in the pushrod tube is facing upward.

10. Install the cylinder head.

Waterboxer

The cylinders of this engine are actually removable liners (sleeves) which fit into removable, cast aluminum cylinder blocs (which actually function as just a water jacket). Each cylinder bloc accepts two liners. Pistons and liners must be removed first before the cylinder bloc can be removed.

1. Remove the engine from the vehicle.

2. Remove the cylinder head(s) and pushrod tubes.

3. Match mark the tops of each piston to its respective cylinder liner. Pistons and liners must be installed in the same locations. Note the boss on the inner side of each liner.

4. Set the piston to be removed at TDC. Using puller No. 3092 or an equivalent sleeve puller, pull out the cylinder until the piston pin circlip is visible through the coolant passage on the V-belt side of the engine. Remove the circlip with circlip pliers. Remove the sleeve, then remove the circlip on the flywheel side. Remove the wrist pin through the same coolant passage using wrist pin puller No. 3091 or equivalent.

5. The cylinder bloc can be removed after the second piston on each side of the crankcase is removed. The block simply slides off of the cylinder bloc/cylinder head studs which protrude from the crankcases.

6. To install, first see "Piston Checking and Installation, Waterboxer" below. Make sure the cylinder bloc-to-crankcase mating surfaces are clean. Install the cylinder bloc onto the crankcase.

7. The sealing rings on the top and bottom sides of the cylinder liners must always be replaced. The cylinder head end ring is

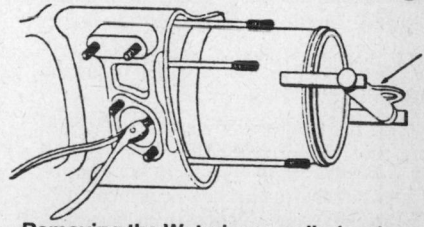

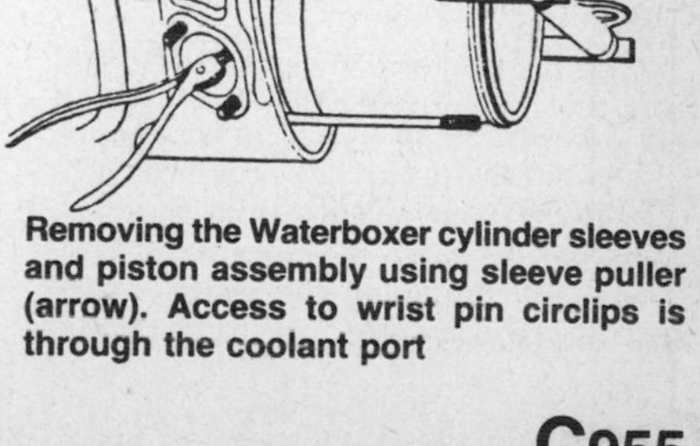

Removing the Waterboxer cylinder sleeves and piston assembly using sleeve puller (arrow). Access to wrist pin circlips is through the coolant port

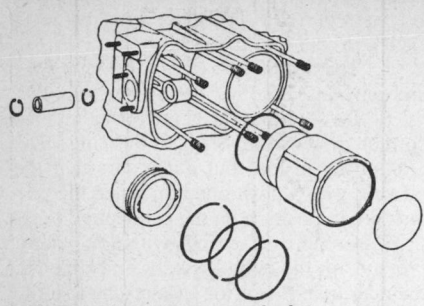

Cylinder bloc, sleeve and piston assemblies—Waterboxer

a thin green ring, and the crankcase end ring is thick and black in color.

8. Lube the piston and liner bore with clean engine oil. Install the piston into the cylinder sleeve. The arrow on the piston faces the flywheel side of the engine. The gap on the oil scraper ring must be to the top, and the piston ring gaps must be offset by 180°. See the accompanying illustration. Install the flywheel-side wrist pin circlip into the piston.

9. Obtain a connecting rod support tool No. 3090. Note the markings on the tool; R is the right side of the engine, L is the left side. Push the connecting rod support onto the center stud so that the finger of the tool supports the connecting rod, then secure it with a rubber band to prevent it from slipping. Align the connecting rod so that the piston wrist pin can be installed through the same coolant passage from which it was removed. The crankshaft must be at TDC, and the lug on the rod faces UP.

10. Install the piston/sleeve assembly. The piston should be protruding from the bottom of the sleeve just enough that the entire wrist pin area diameter is exposed. Using tool No. 3091 or equivalent, install the wrist pin through the coolant passage. Install the other wrist pin clip, and slide the liner (sleeve) down into seated position.

11. Repeat this procedure for all cylinders. Install the cylinder head and remaining components in the reverse order of removal.

PISTON REMOVAL & INSTALLATION

All Air-Cooled Engines

1. Remove the engine. Remove the cylinder head and, after matchmarking the cylinders, remove the cylinders.

2. Matchmark the pistons to indicate the cylinder number and which side points toward the clutch.

3. Remove the circlips which retain the piston pin.

4. Heat the piston to 176° F. To heat the piston, boil a clean rag in water and wrap it around the piston. Remove the piston pin after the piston has been heated.

5. Remove the piston from the connecting rod.

6. Before installing the pistons, they should first be cleaned and checked for wear.

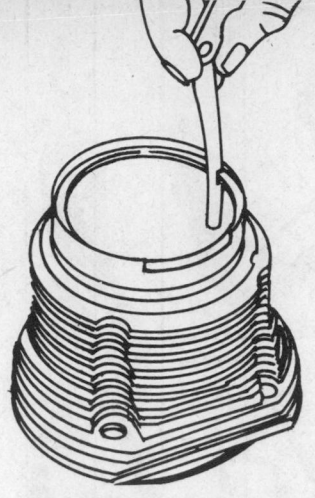

Checking piston ring end gap

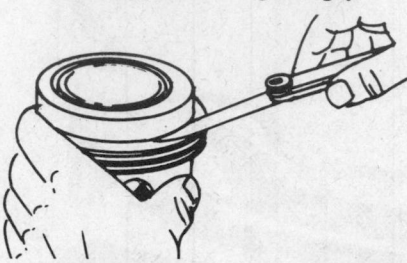

Checking piston ring side clearance

Remove the old rings. Clean the ring grooves using a groove cleaner or a broken piece of ring. Clean the piston with solvent but do not use a wire brush or sandpaper. Check for any cracks or scuff marks. Check the piston diameter with a micrometer and compare the readings to the specifications.

If the running clearance between the piston and cylinder wall is 0.008 in. (0.2mm) or greater, the cylinder and piston should be replaced by a set of the same size grading. If the cylinder shows no sign of excessive wear or damage, it is permissable to install a new piston and rings of the appropriate size.

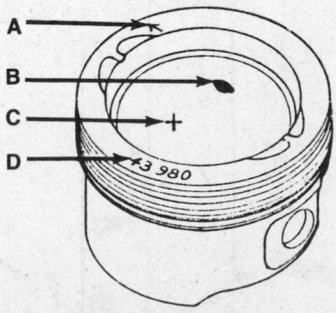

Waterboxer piston identification and positioning marks: A = stamped arrow, must point toward flywheel when piston is installed; B = blue paint dot, indicating matching size; C = weight group (+ or −)—weight is 448-456 gms., + weight is 457-464 gms.; D = piston size in mm

7. Place each ring in turn in its cylinder bore and check the piston ring end-gap. If the gap is too large, replace the ring. If the gap is too narrow, file the end of the ring until the proper gap is obtained.

8. Insert the rings on the piston and check the ring side clearance. If the clearance is too large, replace the piston. Install the rings with the marking "Open" or "Top" pointing upward.

9. If new rings are installed in a used piston, the ring ridge at the top of the cylinder bore must be removed with a ridge reamer.

10. Install the piston and piston pin on the connecting rod from which it originally came. Make sure that the piston is facing the proper direction.

11. Install the cylinders and the cylinder heads.

PISTON CHECKING AND INSTALLATION

Waterboxer

Pistons and cylinder liners must be matched according to their size, and pistons must be weighed in relation to each other, before installation. The maximum weight difference between pistons in the Waterboxer is 10 grams.

1. Using the accompanying illustration, check the markings on the piston top. "A" is the arrow which must point towards the flywheel side of the engine when the pistons are installed into the liners. "B" is the blue dot which indicates a standard piston of 3.759 in. (93.98mm), which must be matched to a liner with a 3.7602–3.7606 in. (94.005–94.016mm) bore diameter.

2. Follow Step 6 of the "Air-Cooled Piston" removal and installation procedure, substituting the specifications listed in Step 1 above for the piston-to-liner figures. Using an inside micrometer or dial gauge, measure the cylinder liner bore diameter, $\frac{3}{8}$–$\frac{5}{8}$ in. from the top of the bore. The piston-to-bore clearance is 0.001–0.002 in. on new assemblies, and the wear limit is 0.008 in.

3. Follow Step 7 of the "Air-Cooled Piston" removal and installation procedure, to check ring gap.

Crankcase

DISASSEMBLY & ASSEMBLY

1. Remove the engine.

2. Remove the cylinder heads, cylinders, and pistons.

3. Remove the oil strainer, oil pressure switch, and the crankcase nuts. Remove the flywheel and oil pump. Matchmark the flywheel so that it can be replaced in the same position.

4. Keep the cam followers in the right crankcase half in position by using a retaining spring.

5. Use a rubber hammer to break the seal between the crankcase halves.

Check the dowel pins for tightness

— CAUTION —

Never insert sharp metal tools, wedges, or any prying device between the crankcase halves. This will ruin the gasket surface and cause serious oil leakage.

6. After the seal between the crankcase halves is broken, remove the right-hand crankcase half, the crankshaft oil seal and the camshaft can now be lifted out of the crankcase half.

7. Remove the cam followers, bearing shells, and the oil pressure relief valve.

8. Before starting reassembly, check the crankcase for any damage or cracks.

9. Flush and blow out all ducts and oil passages. Check the studs for tightness. If the tapped holes are worn install a Heli-Coil.

10. Install the crankshaft bearing dowel pins and bearing shells for the crankshaft and camshaft. Make sure that the bearing shells with thrust flanges are installed in the proper journal.

Tighten the 8 mm nut located next to the 12 mm stud of the No. 1 crankcase bearing first on the Type 1

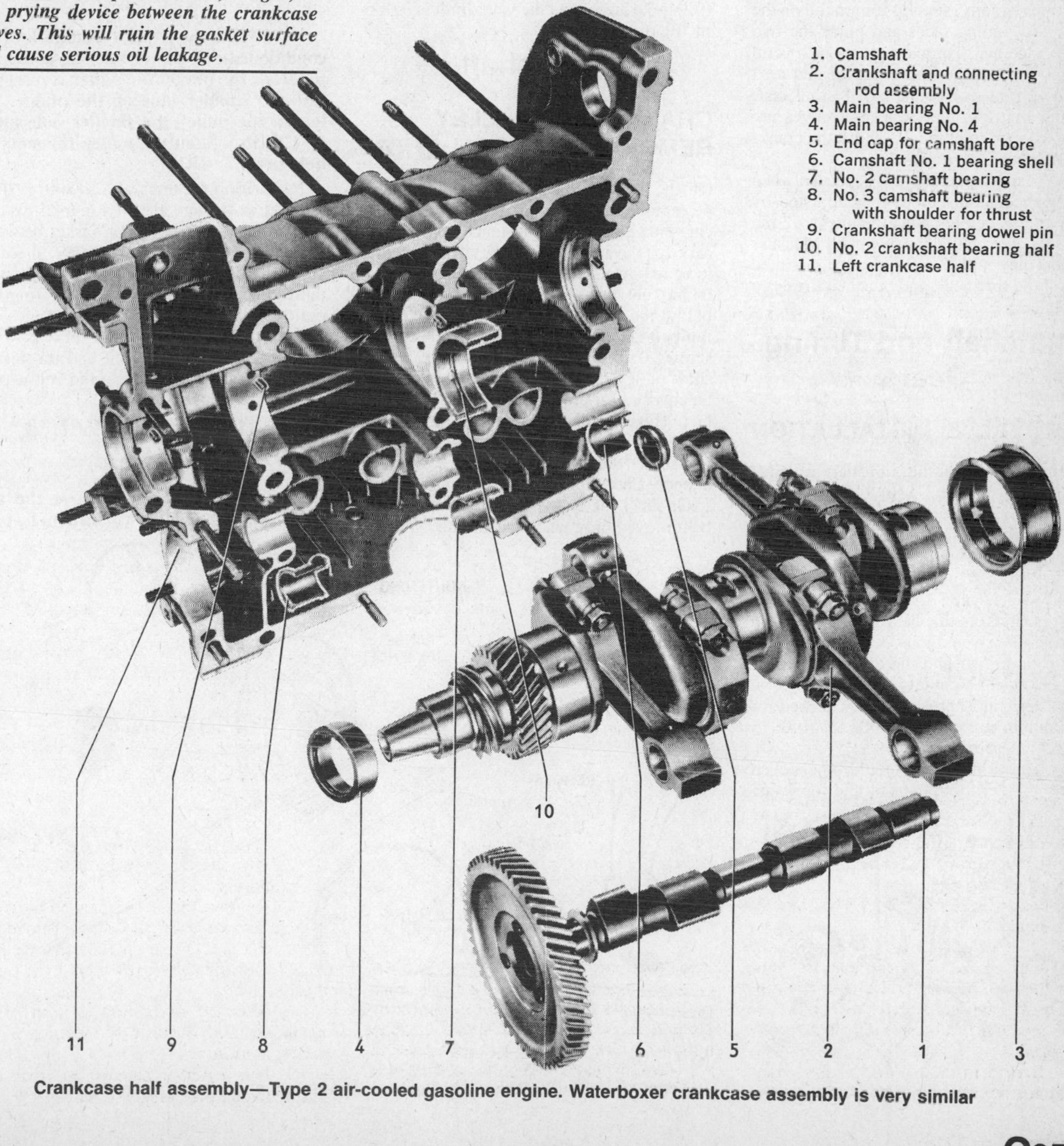

1. Camshaft
2. Crankshaft and connecting rod assembly
3. Main bearing No. 1
4. Main bearing No. 4
5. End cap for camshaft bore
6. Camshaft No. 1 bearing shell
7. No. 2 camshaft bearing
8. No. 3 camshaft bearing with shoulder for thrust
9. Crankshaft bearing dowel pin
10. No. 2 crankshaft bearing half
11. Left crankcase half

Crankcase half assembly—Type 2 air-cooled gasoline engine. Waterboxer crankcase assembly is very similar

11. Install the crankshaft and camshaft after the bearings have been well lubricated. When installing the camshaft and crankshaft, make sure that the timing marks on the timing gears are aligned.

12. Install the oil pressure relief valve.

13. Oil and install the cam followers.

14. Install the camshaft end plug using sealing compound.

15. Install the thrust washers and crankshaft oil seal. The oil seal must rest squarely on the bottom of its recess in the crankcase. The thrust washers at the flywheel end of the crankshaft are shims used to set the crankshaft end-play.

16. Spread a thin film of AMV 188 000 02 (VW part No.) or Waterboxer cases, or Dow-Corning Silastic 730RTV®, Fluorosilicone (following the manufacturer's instructions exactly) sealing compound on the crankcase joining faces and place the two halves together. Torque the nuts in several stages. Tighten the 8 mm nut located next to the 12 mm stud of the No. 1 crankshaft bearing first. As the crankcase halves are being torqued, continually check the crankshaft for ease of rotation.

17. Crankshaft end-play is checked when the flywheel is installed. It is adjusted by varying the number and thickness of the shims located behind the flywheel. Measure the end-play with a dial indicator mounted against the flywheel, and attached firmly to the crankcase.

Camshaft and Timing Gears

REMOVAL & INSTALLATION

1. Removal of the camshaft requires splitting the crankcase. See "Crankcase Disassembly". The camshaft and its bearing shells are then removed from the crankcase halves.

2. Before reinstalling the camshaft, it should be checked for wear on the lobe surfaces and on the bearing surfaces. In addition, the riveted joint between the camshaft timing gear and the camshaft should be checked for tightness.

3. The camshaft should be checked for a maximum run-out of 0.0008 in. (0.0015 in. on Waterboxer).

4. The timing gear should be checked for the correct tooth contact and for wear.

Aligning valve timing marks on gears

5. If the camshaft bearing shells are worn or damaged, new shells should be fitted. The camshaft bearing shells should be installed with the tabs engaging the notches in the crankcase. It is usually a good idea to replace the bearing shells under any circumstances. Before installing the camshaft, the bearing journals and cam lobes should be generously coated with oil.

6. When the camshaft is installed, care should be taken to ensure that the timing gear tooth marked (0) is located between the two teeth of the crankshaft timing gear marked with a center punch. Coat the camshaft end cap with sealant, and make sure it is installed in its original position.

7. The camshaft end-play is measured at the No. 3 bearing on all engines including Waterboxer. End-play is 0.0015–0.005 in. (0.04–0.12mm) and the wear limit is 0.006 in. (0.16mm).

Crankshaft

CRANKSHAFT PULLEY REMOVAL & INSTALLATION

On the Type 1, the crankshaft pulley can be removed while the engine is still in the car. However, in this instance it is necessary for the rear cover plate of the engine to be removed. Remove the cover plate after taking out the screws in the cover plate below the crankshaft pulley. Remove the fan belt and the crankshaft pulley securing screw. Using a puller, remove the crankshaft pulley. The crankshaft pulley should be checked for proper seating and belt contact. The oil return thread should be cleaned and lubricated with oil. The crankshaft pulley should be installed in the reverse sequence. Check for oil leaks after installation.

On the Type 2, the crankshaft pulley can be removed only when the engine is out of

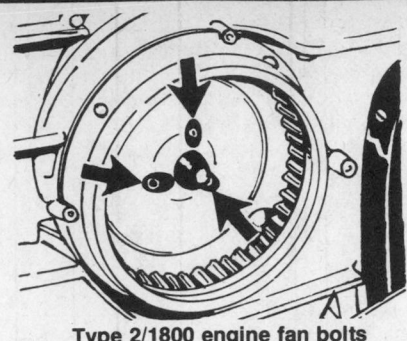

Type 2/1800 engine fan bolts

the car and the muffler, alternator and cooling air intake housing are removed. After these parts have been removed, take out the plastic cap in the pulley. Unscrew the three socket head screws and the self-locking nut and then remove the pulley.

NOTE: On the triple V-belt pulley (air conditioned and power steering-equipped models), the pin on the puller is inserted into the smaller hole on the pulley. To loosen the pulley the smaller hole must be UP; to tighten the pulley the smaller hole must be DOWN.

Installation for the Type 2/1800, 2/2000 engines is the reverse of removal. When installing, use a new paper gasket between the fan and the crankshaft pulley. If shims are used, do not forget them. Don't use more than two shims. When inserting the pulley, make sure that the pin engages the hole in the fan. Ensure that the clearance between the generator belt and the intake housing is at least 4mm and the belt is parallel to the housing.

FLYWHEEL REMOVAL & INSTALLATION

NOTE: In order to remove the flywheel, the crankshaft will have to be pre-

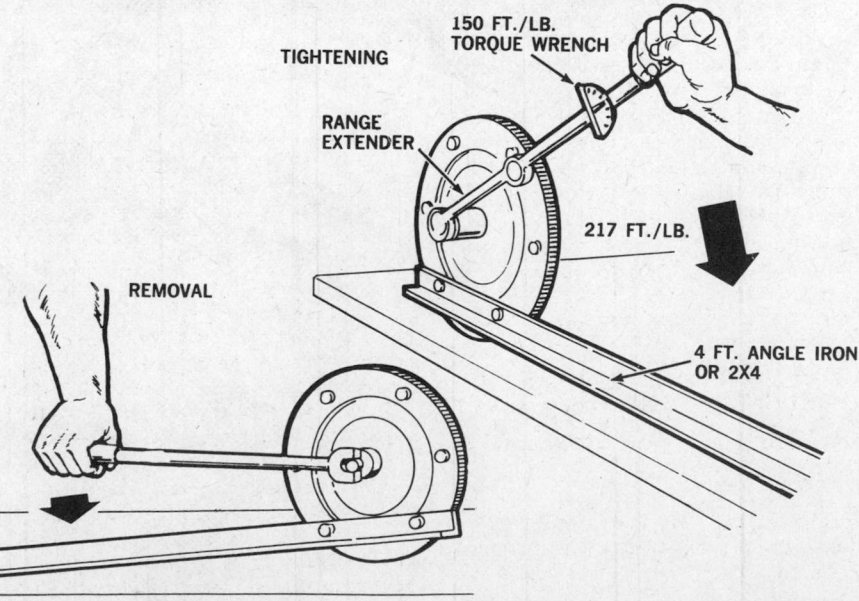

Removing or installing the flywheel on 1600 cc engines using the special bar

vented from turning. This may be accomplished on Type 1 models by using a 3 or 4 foot length of angle iron or thick stock sheet steel, such as an old fence post. Drill out two holes in the metal bar that correspond to two of the pressure plate retaining bolt holes. The metal bar is installed as per the accompanying illustration.

Type 1

1. The flywheel is attached to the crankshaft with a gland nut and is located by four dowel pins. An oil seal is recessed in the crankcase casting at No. 1 main bearing. A needle bearing, which supports the main driveshaft, is located in the gland nut. Prior to removing the flywheel, it is necessary to remove the clutch pressure plate and the clutch disc.

2. Loosen the gland nut and remove it, using a 36 mm wrench.

3. Before removing the flywheel, matchmark the flywheel and the crankshaft.

4. Installation is the reverse of removal. Before installing the flywheel, check the flywheel teeth for any wear or damage. Check the dowel pins for correct fit in the crankshaft and in the flywheel.

5. Adjust the crankshaft end-play and check the needle bearing in the gland nut for wear.

Type 2

Removal and installation is similar to the Type 1 except that the flywheel is secured to the crankshaft by five socket head screws.

CRANKSHAFT OIL SEAL (FLYWHEEL END)

Replacement

The seal is removed after removing the flywheel. After the flywheel is removed, inspect the surface on the flywheel joining flange where the seal makes contact. If there is a deep groove or any other damage, the flywheel must be replaced. Remove the oil seal by prying it out of its bore. Before installing a new seal, clean the crankcase oil seal recess and coat it thinly with a sealing compound. Be sure that the seal rests squarely on the bottom of its recess. Make sure that the correct side of the seal is facing outward, that is, the lip of the seal should be facing the inside of the crankcase. Reinstall the flywheel after coating the oil seal contact surface with oil.

NOTE: Be careful not to damage the seal when sliding the flywheel into place.

CRANKSHAFT REMOVAL & INSTALLATION

NOTE: See the "Engine Rebuilding" section for crankshaft refinishing procedures.

1. Removal of the crankshaft requires splitting the crankcase. See "Crankcase Disassembly."

2. After the crankcase is opened, the crankshaft can then be lifted out.

3. The crankshaft bearings are held in place by dowel pins. These pins must be checked for tightness.

4. When installing the bearings, make sure that the oil holes in the shells are properly aligned. Be sure that the bearing shells are properly aligned. Be sure that the bearing shells are seated properly on their dowel pins. Bearing shells are available in three undersizes. Measure the crankshaft bearing journals to determine the proper bearing size. Place one half of the No. 2 crankshaft bearing in the crankcase. Slide the No. 1 bearing on the crankshaft so that the dowel pin hole is toward the flywheel and the oil groove faces toward the flywheel and the oil groove faces toward the fan. The No. 3 bearing is installed with the dowel pin hole facing toward the crankshaft web.

5. To remove the No. 3 main bearing, remove the distributor gear circlip and the distributor drive gear. Mild heat (176° F) must be applied to remove the gear. Next slide the spacer off the crankshaft.

6. The crankshaft timing gear should now be pressed off the crankshaft after mild heating.

7. When the timing gear is reinstalled, the chamfer must face towards the No. 3 bearing. The No. 3 bearing can then be replaced. When removing and installing the gears on the crankshaft, be careful not to damage the No. 4 bearing journal.

8. When all of the crankshaft bearings are in place, lift the crankshaft and the connecting rod assembly into the crankcase and align the valve timing marks.

9. Install the crankcase half and reassemble the engine.

Connecting Rods

REMOVAL & INSTALLATION

NOTE: See the "Engine Rebuilding" section for additional information.

1. After splitting the crankcase (See "Crankcase Disassembly"), remove the crankshaft and the connecting rod assembly.

2. Remove the connecting rods, clamping bolts, and the connecting rod caps.

3. Inspect the piston pin bushing. With a new bushing, the correct clearance is indicated by a light finger push fit of the pin at room temperature.

4. Reinsert the new connecting rod bearings after all parts have been thoroughly cleaned.

5. Assemble the connecting rods on the crankshaft, making sure that the rods are oriented properly on the crankshaft. The identification numbers stamped on the connecting rods and connecting rod caps must be on the same side. Note that the marks on the connecting rods are pointing upward, while the rods are pointing toward their respective cylinders. Lubricate the bearing shells before installing.

6. Tighten the connecting rod bolts to

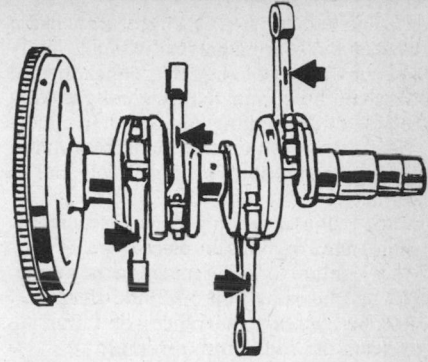

Forge marks on connecting rods must face up

Measuring the connecting rod side clearance

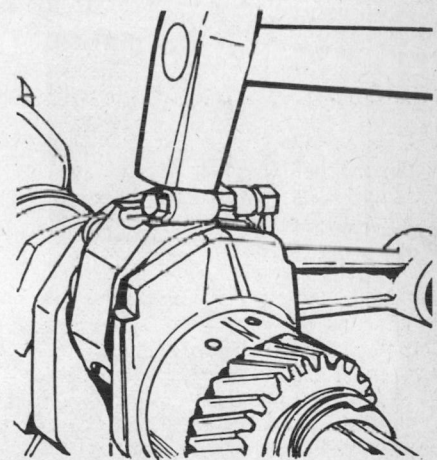

Rapping the connecting rod to relieve pre-tension

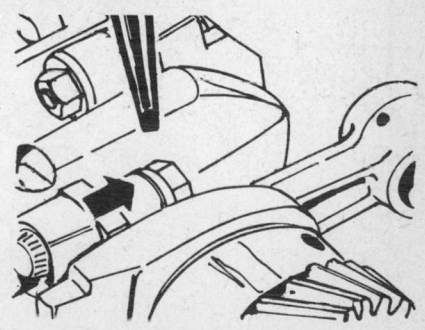

Staking the connecting rod bolt

the specified torque. A slight pre-tension between the bearing halves, which is likely to occur when tightening the connecting rod bolts, can be eliminated by gently striking the side of the bearing cap with a hammer.

7. Do not install the connecting rod in the engine unless it swings freely on its journal.

8. Using a peening chisel, secure the connecting rod bolts in place.

9. Failure to swing freely on the journal may be caused by improper side clearance, improper bearing clearance, or failure to lubricate the rod before assembly.

ENGINE LUBRICATION— GASOLINE ENGINE

Oil Strainer

REMOVAL & INSTALLATION

All Models Except Waterboxer

The oil strainer can be easily removed by removing the retaining nuts, washers, oil strainer plate, strainer, and gaskets. The Type 2/1800 and 2/2000 strainer is secured by a single bolt at the center of the strainer. Once taken out, the strainer must be thoroughly cleaned and all traces of oil gaskets removed prior to installing new ones. The suction pipe should be checked for tightness and proper position. When the strainer is installed, be sure that the suction pipe is correctly seated in the strainer. If necessary, the strainer may be bent slightly. The measurement from the strainer flange to the tip of the suction pipe should be 10 mm. The measurement from the flange to the bottom of the strainer should be 6 mm. The cap nuts on Type 1 engines must not be overtightened. The Type 2/1800 and 2/2000 have a spin-off replaceable oil filter as well as the strainer in the crankcase. The oil filter is located at the left rear corner of the engine.

Waterboxer

The water-cooled engine does not employ an oil strainer. Instead, it relies solely on a spin-on oil filter.

Oil Cooler

REMOVAL & INSTALLATION

> NOTE: The Waterboxer does not employ an oil cooler.

The Type 1 oil cooler is located under the engine cooling fan housing at the left side of the engine. The Type 2/1800 and 2/2000

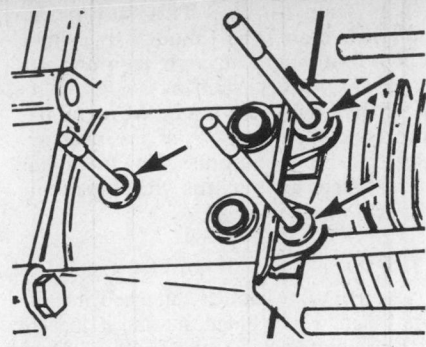

Oil cooler spacers on suitcase engines

coolers are mounted near the oil filter, at the left corner of the engine.

The oil cooler may be removed without taking the engine out of the car. On Type 1 models, the engine fan housing must be removed. The Type 2/1800 and 2/2000 cooler is accessible through the left side engine cowling, working either in the engine compartment or from underneath the car.

The oil cooler can be removed after the three retaining nuts have been taken off. The gaskets should be removed along with the cooler and replaced with new gaskets. If the cooler is leaking, check the oil pressure relief valve. The studs and bracket on the cooler should be checked for tightness. Make certain that the hollow ribs of the cooler do not touch one another. The cooler must not be clogged with dirt. Clean the

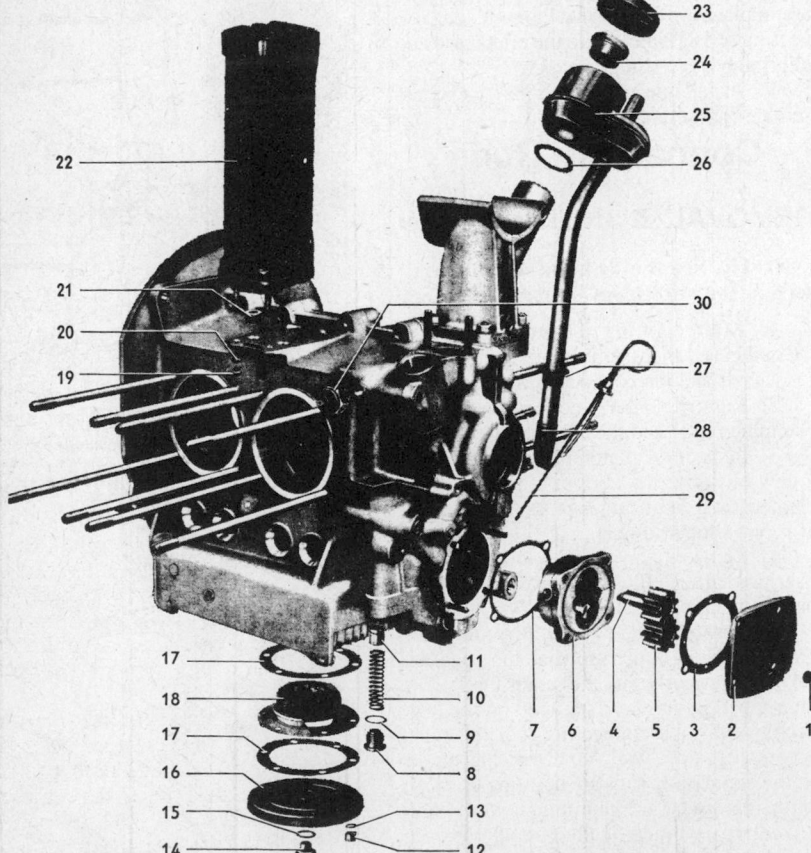

1. Sealing nut
2. Oil pump cover
3. Pump cover gasket
4. Driveshaft
5. Oil pump gear
6. Oil pump housing
7. Housing gasket
8. Plug
9. Seal
10. Spring
11. Relief valve piston
12. Cap nut
13. Seal
14. Oil drain plug
15. Seal
16. Oil strainer cover
17. Gasket
18. Oil strainer
19. Nut
20. Lockwasher
21. Oil cooler seal
22. Oil cooler
23. Oil filler neck cap
24. Breather gland nut
25. Oil filler and breather assembly
26. Seal
27. Grommet
28. Breather rubber valve
29. Dipstick
30. Oil pressure switch

Type 1 lubrication system

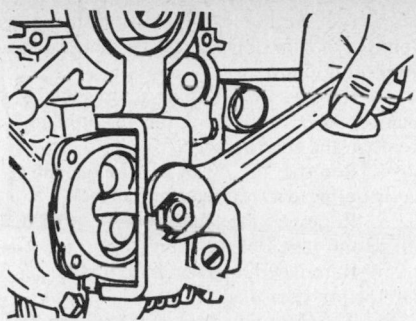

Removing the oil pump housing—Type 1

contact surfaces on the crankcase, install new gaskets, and attach the oil cooler. Types 2/1800 and 2/2000 have a spacer ring between the crankcase and the cooler at each securing screw. If these rings are omitted, the seals may be squeezed too tightly, resulting in oil stoppage and resultant engine damage. Use double retaining nuts and locking compound on the cooler studs.

Oil Pump

REMOVAL & INSTALLATION

1. On the Type 1, the pump can be removed while the engine is in the car, but it is first necessary to remove the cover plate, the crankshaft pulley, and the cover plate under the pulley.

2. On Types 2/1800 and 2/2000 and Waterboxer, the oil pump can be taken out only after the engine is removed from the car and the air intake housing, the belt pul-

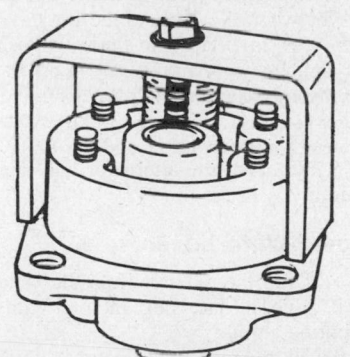

Disassembling the Type 2 air-cooled gasoline engine oil pump. Waterboxer pump similar

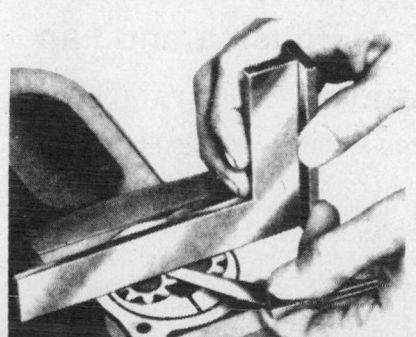

Checking oil pump end play

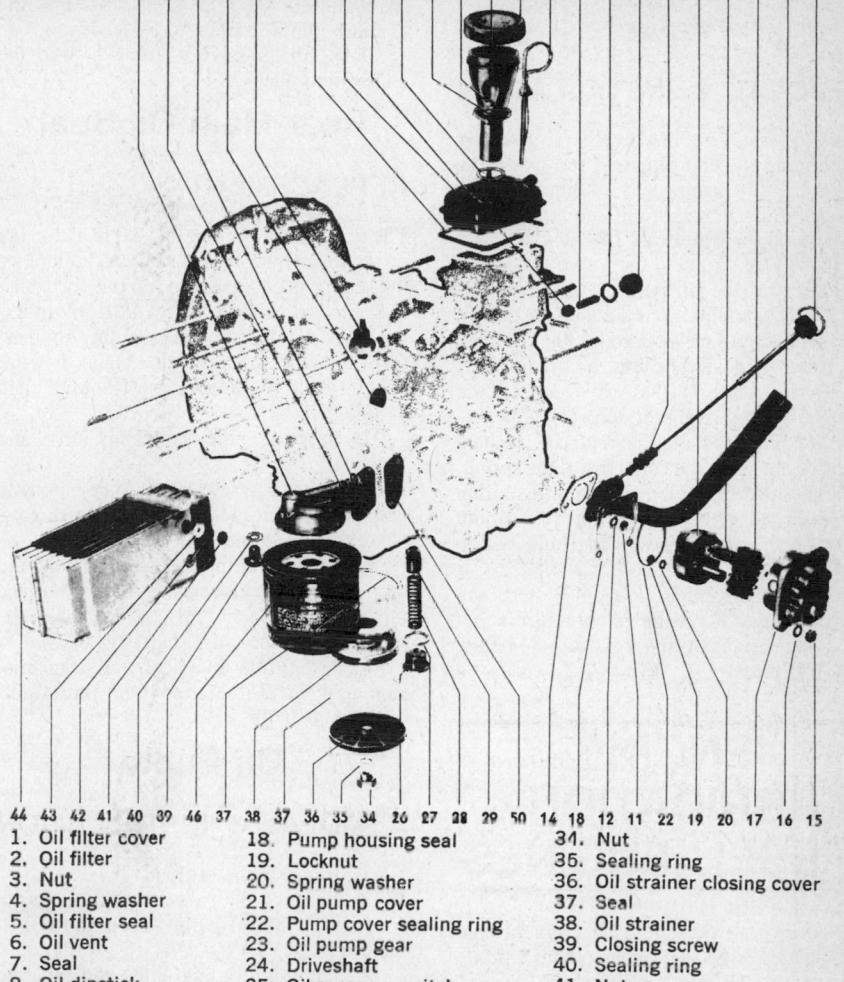

1. Oil filter cover	18. Pump housing seal
2. Oil filter	19. Locknut
3. Nut	20. Spring washer
4. Spring washer	21. Oil pump cover
5. Oil filter seal	22. Pump cover sealing ring
6. Oil vent	23. Oil pump gear
7. Seal	24. Driveshaft
8. Oil dipstick	25. Oil pressure switch
9. Dipstick	26. Screw
10. Bellows	27. Sealing ring
11. Nut	28. Spring
12. Spring washer	29. Piston for oil relief valve
13. Oil filler	30. Screw
14. Gasket	31. Sealing ring
15. Nut	32. Spring
16. Spring washer	33. Piston for oil pressure
17. Oil pump housing	control valve

34. Nut	
35. Sealing ring	
36. Oil strainer closing cover	
37. Seal	
38. Oil strainer	
39. Closing screw	
40. Sealing ring	
41. Nut	
42. Spring washer	
43. Washer	
44. Oil cooler	
45. Oil cooler sealing ring	
46. Oil filter	
47. Nut	
48. Spring washer	
49. Oil filter intermediate flange	
50. Seal	

Type 2 air-cooled gasoline engine lubrication system

ley fan housing, and fan are dismantled.

3. On the Automatic Stick Shift models, the torque converter oil pump is driven by the engine oil pump.

4. On the Type 1, remove the nuts from the oil pump cover and then remove the cover and its gasket. Remove the gears and take out the pump with a special extractor that pulls the body out of the crankcase. Care should be taken so as not to damage the inside of the pump housing.

5. On Type 2/1800 and 2/2000 and Waterboxer engines, remove the four pump securing nuts and, prying on either side of the pump, pry the pump assembly out of the crankcase.

6. To disassemble the pump, the pump cover must be pressed apart.

7. Prior to assembly, check the oil pump body for wear, especially the gear seating surface. If the pump body is worn, the re-

sult will be loss of oil pressure. Check the driven gear shaft for tightness and, if necessary, peen it tightly into place or replace the pump housing. The gears should be checked for excessive wear, backlash, and end-play. Maximum end-play without a gasket is 1mm (0.004 in.). The end-play can be checked using a T-square and a feeler gauge. Check the mating surface of the pump body and the crankcase for damage and cleanliness. Install the pump into the crankcase with a new gasket. Do not use any sealing compound.

8. Turn the camshaft several revolutions in order to center the pump body opposite the slot in the camshaft.

9. On the Type 1, the cover may now be installed.

10. On Type 2/1800 and 2/2000 models, the pump was installed complete.

11. Tighten the securing nuts.

Oil Pressure Relief Valve

REMOVAL & INSTALLATION

The oil pressure relief valve is removed by unscrewing the end plug and removing the gasket ring, spring, and plunger. If the plunger sticks in its bore, it can be removed by screwing a 10mm tap into it.

On 1600cc engines, the valve is located to the left of the oil pump. On Automatic Stick Shift models, it is located in the oil pump housing. On 1800 and 2000 engines, the valve is located beside the oil filter.

Before installing the valve, check the plunger for any signs of seizure. If necessary, the plunger should be replaced. If there is any doubt about the condition of the spring, it should also be replaced. When installing the relief valve, be careful that you do not scratch the bore. Reinstall the plug with a new gasket.

Type 2/1800 and 2/2000 and Waterboxer engines, have a second oil pressure relief valve located just to the right of, and below the oil filter.

ENGINE LUBRICATION— DIESEL ENGINES

The lubrication system is a conventional wet-sump design. The gear-type oil pump is driven by the intermediate shaft. A pressure relief valve limits pressure and prevents extreme pressure from developing in the system. All oil is filtered by a full flow replaceable filter. A bypass valve assures lubrication in the event the filter becomes plugged. The oil pressure switch is located at the end of the cylinder head gallery (the end of the system) to assure accurate pressure readings.

Oil Pan

REMOVAL & INSTALLATION

1. Drain the oil pan.
2. Support and slightly raise the engine with an overhead hoist.
3. Gradually loosen the engine crossmember mounting bolts. Remove the front and rear side engine mounts.
4. Lower the crossmember very carefully.
5. Loosen and remove the oil pan retaining bolts.
6. Lower the pan from the car.
7. Install the pan using a new gasket and sealer.
8. Tighten the retaining bolts in a crosswise pattern. Tighten hex head bolts to 14 ft. lbs., or Allen head bolts to 7 ft. lbs.

9. Raise the crossmember. Tighten the crossmember bolts to 42 ft. lbs. and the engine mounting bolts to 32 ft. lbs.
10. Refill the engine with oil. Start the engine and check for leaks.

Rear Main Oil Seal

REPLACEMENT

The rear main oil seal is located in a housing on the rear of the cylinder block. To replace the seal, it is necessary to remove the transmission and perform the work from underneath the car or remove the engine and perform the work on an engine stand or work bench. See "Transmission Removal and Installation."

1. Remove the transmission and flywheel.
2. Using a screwdriver, very carefully pry the old seal out of the support ring.
3. Remove the seal.
4. Lightly oil the replacement seal and then press it into place using a circular piece of flat metal. Be careful not to damage the seal or score the crankshaft.
5. Install the flywheel and transmission. Flywheel-to-engine bolts are tightened to 36 ft. lb.s

Oil Pump

REMOVAL & INSTALLATION

1. Remove the oil pan.
2. Remove the two mounting bolts.
3. Pull the oil pump down and out of the engine.
4. Unscrew the two bolts and separate the pump halves.
5. Remove the drivehshaft and gear from the upper body.
6. Clean the bottom half in solvent. Pry up the metal edges to remove the filter screen for cleaning.
7. Examine the gear and driveshaft for wear or damage. Replace them if necessary.
8. Reassemble the pump halves.
9. Prime the pump with oil and install in the reverse order of removal.

ENGINE COOLING— GASOLINE ENGINES

Fan Housing

REMOVAL & INSTALLATION

Type 1

1. Remove the two heater hoses and the generator strap.

2. Pull out the lead wire from the coil. Remove the distributor cap and take off the spark plug connectors.
3. Remove the retaining screws that are located on both sides of the fan housing. Remove the rear hood.
4. Remove the outer half of the alternator pulley and remove the fan belt.
5. Remove the thermostat securing screw and take out the thermostat.
6. Remove the lower part of the carburetor pre-heat duct.
7. The fan housing can now be removed with the alternator. After removal, check the fan housing for damage and for loose air deflector plates.
8. Installation is the reverse of the above.
9. Make sure that the thermostat connecting rod is inserted into its hole in the cylinder head. The fan housing should be fitted properly on the cylinder cover plates so that there is no loss of cooling air.

Fan

REMOVAL & INSTALLATION

Type 1

1. Remove the alternator and fan assembly as described in the "Alternator Removal and Installation" section.
2. While holding the fan, unscrew the fan retaining nut and take off the fan, spacer washers, and the hub.
3. To install, place the hub on the alternator shaft, making sure that the woodruff key is securely positioned.
4. Insert the spacer washers. The clearance between the fan and the fan cover is 0.06–0.07 in. Place the fan into position and tighten its retaining nut. Correct the spacing by inserting the proper number of spacer washers. Place any extra washers between the lockwasher and the fan.
5. Reinstall the alternator and the fan assembly.

Type 2/Waterboxer

1. Drop the radiator from the vehicle.
2. Unbolt the fan motor from its mounting shroud.
3. Disconnect the electrical connection. Remove the fan/motor assembly.
4. Reverse the procedure to install.

Fan Housing and Fan

REMOVAL & INSTALLATION

Type 2/1800 and 2/2000

1. Pry out the alternator cover insert, and, using a 12 point Allen wrench, loosen the alternator adjusting bolt. Remove the alternator drive belt, the ignition timing scale and the grille over the fan. Remove the three socket head screws attaching the fan and crankshaft assembly to the crankshaft and remove the fan and pulley.

1. Cover plate insert	19. Screw	37. Washer
2. Socket head capscrew	20. Spring washer	38. Nut
3. Spring washer	21. Alternator cover plate	39. Screw
4. Nut	22. Alternator	40. Spring washer
5. Belt	23. Alternator sealing ring	41. Shaft retaining spring
6. Socket head capscrew	24. Alternator elbow	42. Right flap and shaft
7. Spring washer	25. Nut	43. Bearing
8. Flat washer	26. Spring washer	44. Flap link
9. Cap	27. Fan housing—rear half	45. Left flap
10. Crankshaft pulley	28. Fan housing—front half	46. Plug
11. Fan	29. Bolt	47. Bolt
12. Nut	30. Spring washer	48. Cooling air control cable roller
13. Spring nut	31. Screw	49. Sealing washer
14. Socket head capscrew	32. Spring washer	50. Cooling air control cable
15. Spacer	33. Air non-return flap	51. Bolt
16. Bolt	34. Inspection hole cover	52. Washer
17. Spring washer	35. Plug	53. Thermostat washer
18. Nut	36. Bolt	54. Thermostat
		55. Thermostat bracket

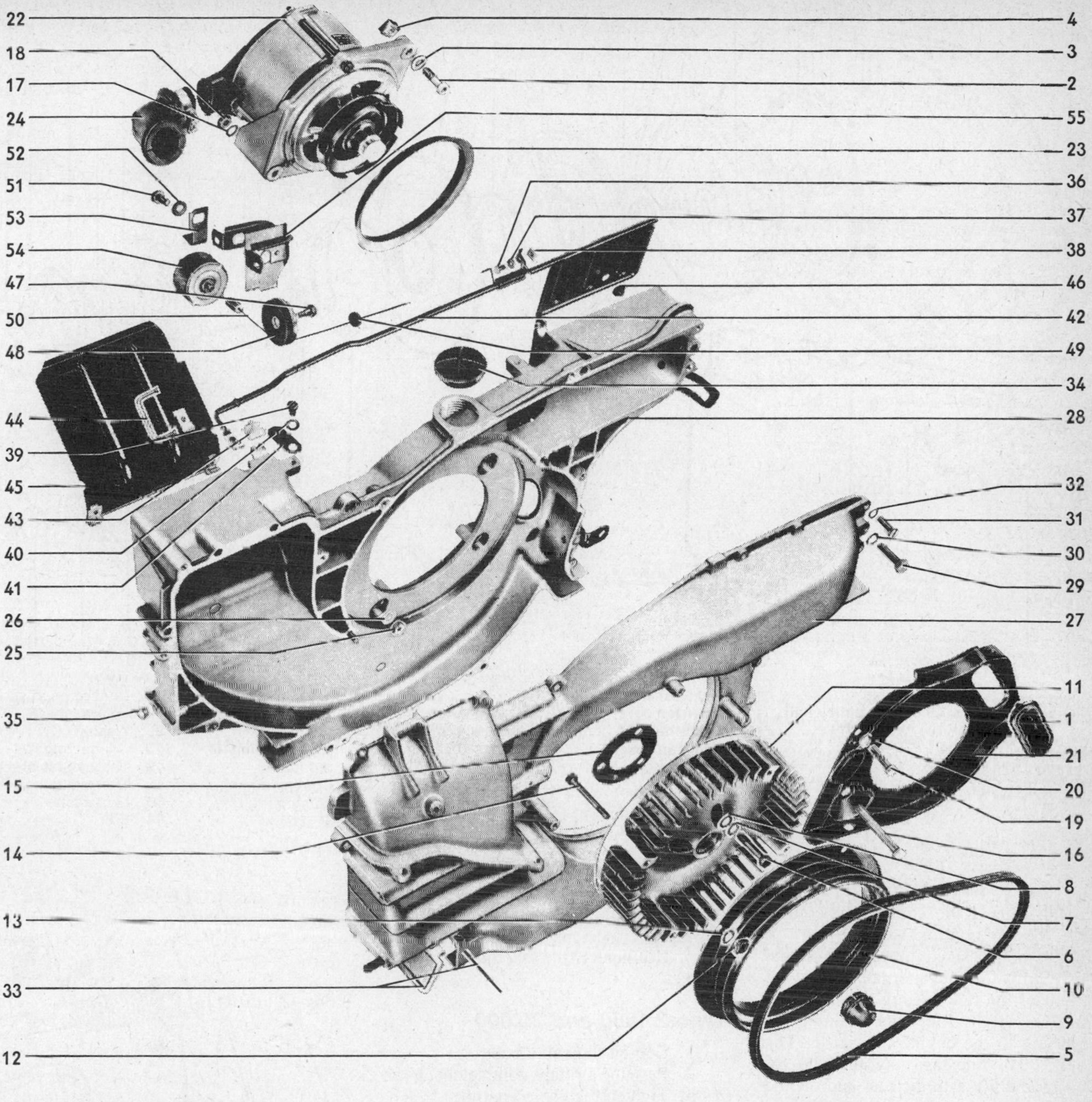

Type 2 air-cooled gasoline engine cooling system

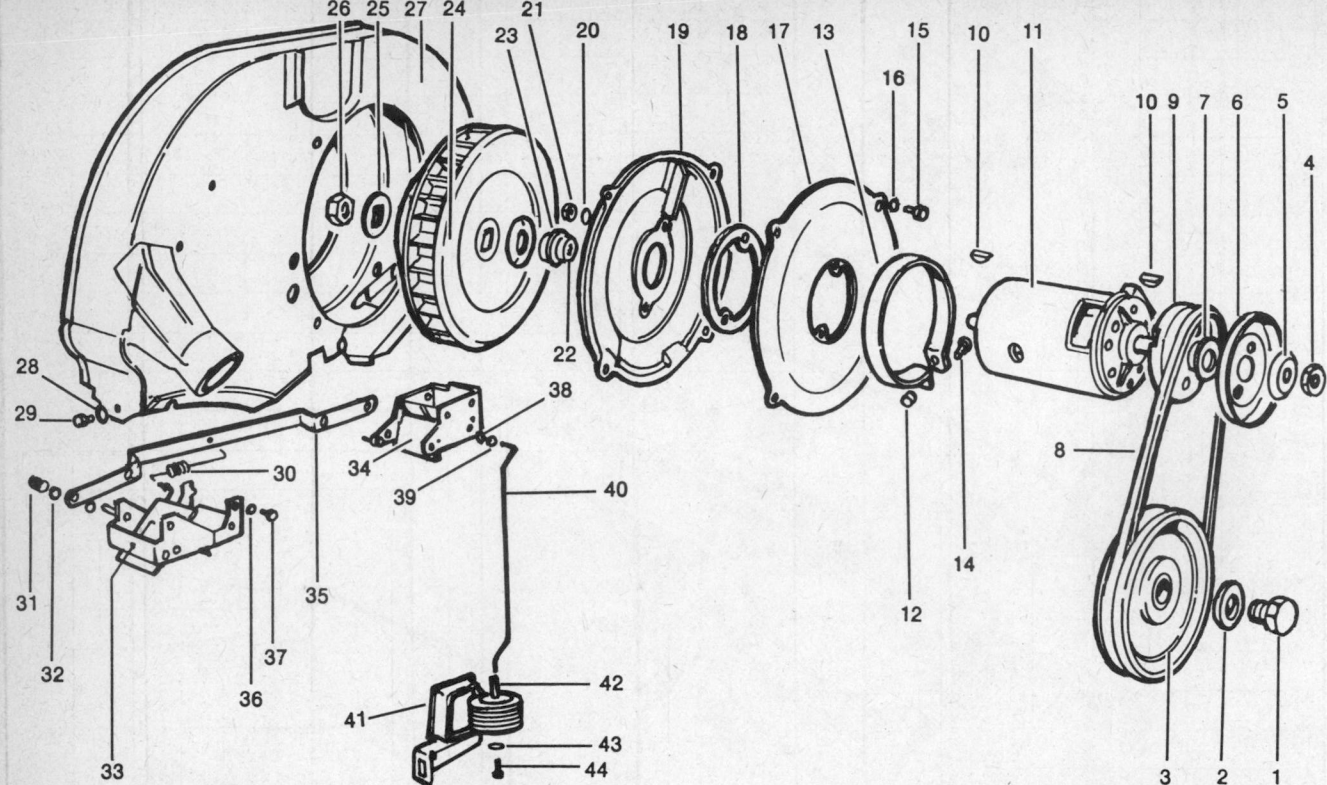

1. Pulley bolt
2. Dished washer
3. Crankshaft pulley
4. Pulley nut
5. Special washer
6. Rear pulley half
7. Spacer washer
8. V-belt
9. Front pulley half
10. Woodruff key
11. Generator
12. Nut
13. Strap
14. Bolt
15. Bolt
16. Lockwasher
17. Outer fan cover
18. Reinforcement flange
19. Inner fan cover
20. Lockwasher
21. Nut
22. Fan hub
23. Shim
24. Fan
25. Lockwasher
26. Special nut
27. Cheese head screw
28. Washer
29. Cheese head screw
30. Return spring
31. Spring
32. Washer
33. Left cooling air regulator
34. Right cooling air regulator
35. Cooling air regulator connecting rod
36. Washer
37. Cheese head screw
38. Lockwasher
39. Washer
40. Connecting rod
41. Thermostat bracket
42. Thermostat
43. Lockwasher
44. Bolt

Type 1 cooling system

2. Disconnect the cooling air control cable at the flap control shaft.

3. On models so equipped, pull out the rubber elbow for the alternator from the front half of the fan housing.

4. Remove the four nuts retaining the fan housing to the engine crankcase. The assembled fan housing may then be removed by pulling it to the rear and off the engine. It is not necessary to separate the fan housing halves or remove the alternator to remove the fan housing.

5. Reverse the above procedure to install.

Air Flap and Thermostat

ADJUSTMENT

Type 1

1. Loosen the thermostat bracket securing nut and disconnect the thermostat from the bracket.

2. Push the thermostat upwards to fully open the air flaps.

3. Reposition the thermostat bracket so that the thermostat contacts the bracket at the upper stop, and then tighten the bracket nut.

4. Reconnect the thermostat to the bracket.

Type 2/1800 and 2/2000

1. Loosen the cable control.
2. Push the air flaps completely closed.
3. Tighten the cable control.

Thermostat

REMOVAL & INSTALLATION

Waterboxer

The thermostat is mounted inside a coolant elbow on the driver's side cylinder head (the left side, as you face the rear of the vehicle). Unbolt the elbow and remove the thermostat. Make sure the O-ring is in good condition and properly seated during installation.

CHECKING

Heat the thermostat in water. It should begin to open at 185°F (85°C), and stop open-

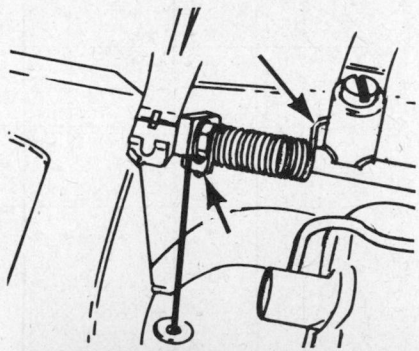

Air-cooled Type 2 gasoline engine air flap cable control

Engine cooling air thermostat

ing at 221°F (105°C). Replace the thermostat if opening rates do not agree with these rates.

Thermoswitch

REMOVAL & INSTALLATION

Waterboxer

The thermoswitch is located at the lower left of the radiator. To remove, remove the radiator grille and move the left cardboard air deflector to the side. Install in the reverse order.

Radiator

REMOVAL & INSTALLATION

Type 2/Waterboxer

Remove the spare tire, the spare tire bracket and the radiator grille. Drain the cooling system. Disconnect the coolant hoses. Unbolt and remove the radiator. Reverse the above procedure to install. Follow the procedure below for filling the cooling system.

FILLING THE COOLING SYSTEM

Type 2 Waterboxer

NOTE: Volkswagen specifies the use of a specially-formulated coolant, part No. ZVW 237 102 in the Waterboxer engine. Anti-freeze other than this may cause corrosion of the cooling system, leading to engine damage.

1. Set the heater control to maximum heat.
2. Open the control valve for the auxiliary heater under the rear seat.
3. Remove the radiator grille.
4. Jack up the vehicle approximately 15¾ in. at the front, under the crossmember using a floor jack. Support the front end with jackstands.
5. Open the bleeder screw on the radiator.
6. Open the bleeder valve in the engine compartment.
7. Fill the coolant expansion tank until the tank is full (approximately 4.25–5.3 qts.).
8. Start the engine. Run it up to 2000 rpm, and top up the tank until coolant flows from the bleeder screw on the radiator. Wait until the coolant flowing is free of bubbles.
9. Add more coolant until the tank is full. Close the tank cap.
10. Shut off the engine. Restart the engine after 20 seconds.
11. At 2000 rpm, open the expansion tank cap.
12. Close the bleeder screw on the radiator when coolant flows out. Add coolant if necessary and close the tank cap.
13. Close the bleeder screw in the engine compartment, and switch off the engine. If necessary, top up the expansion tank.

ENGINE COOLING— DIESEL ENGINES

The cooling system consists of a belt driven, external water pump, thermostat, radiator, and thermostatically controlled electric cooling fan. When the engine is cold the thermostat is closed and blocks the water from the radiator so the coolant is circulated only through the engine. When the engine warms up, the thermostat opens and the radiator is included in the coolant circuit. The thermostatic switch is in the bottom of the radiator and turns the electrical fan on at 199°F, off at 186°F. This reduced power loss and engine noise.

Radiator and Fan

REMOVAL & INSTALLATION

1. Drain the cooling system.
2. Remove the inner shroud mounting bolts.
3. Disconnet the lower radiator hose.
4. Disconnet the thermostatic switch lead.
5. Remove the lower radiator shroud.
6. Remove the lower radiator mounting units.
7. Disconnect the upper radiator hose.
8. Detach the upper radiator shroud.
9. Remove the side mounting bolts and lift the radiator and fan out as an assembly.
10. Installation is the reverse of removal.

Thermostat

REMOVAL & INSTALLATION

The thermostat is located in the bottom radiator hose neck on the water pump.
1. Drain the cooling system.
2. Remove the two retaining bolts from the lower water pump neck.

NOTE: It isn't necessary to disconnect the hose.

3. Move the neck, with the hoses attached, out of the way.
4. Remove the thermostat.
5. Install a new seal on the water pump neck.
6. Install the thermostat with the spring end up.
7. Replace the water pump neck and tighten the two retaining bolts.

Water Pump

REMOVAL & INSTALLATION

1. Drain the cooling system.
2. Remove the alternator and drive belt.
3. Remove the timing belt cover.

4. Disconnect the lower radiator hoses, engine hose, and heater hose from the water pump.
5. Remove the pump retaining bolts. Notice where the different length bolts are located.
6. Turn the pump slightly and lift it out of the engine block.
7. Installation is the reverse of removal. Use a new seal on the mating surface with the engine. Check O-ring condition and replace if necessary.

EMISSION CONTROLS

Crankcase Ventilation System

All models are equipped with a crankcase ventilation system. The purpose of the crankcase ventilation system is two-fold. It keeps harmful vapors from escaping into the atmosphere and prevents the buildup of crankcase pressure. Prior to the 1960s, most cars employed a vented oil filler cap and road draft tube to dispose of crankcase vapor. The crankcase ventilation systems now in use are improvements over the old method and, when functioning properly, will not reduce engine efficiency.

Type 1 and 2 crankcase vapors are recirculated from the oil breather through a rubber hose to the air cleaner. The vapors then join the air/fuel mixture and are burned in the engine. Fuel injected cars mix crankcase vapors into the air/fuel mixture to be burned in the combustion chambers. Fresh air is forced through the engine to evacuate vapors and recirculate them into the oil breather, intake air distributor, and then to be burned.

The only maintenance required on the crankcase ventilation system is a periodic check. At every tune-up, examine the hoses for clogging or deterioration. Clean or replace the hoses as required.

Evaporative Emission Control System

This system prevents raw fuel vapors from entering the atmosphere. The various systems for different models are similar. They consist of an expansion chamber, activated charcoal filter, and connecting lines. Fuel vapors are vented to the charcoal filter where hydrocarbons are deposited on the element. The engine fan forces fresh air into the filter when the engine is running. The air purges the filter and the hydrocarbons are forced into the air cleaner to become part of the air/fuel mixture and burned.

Maintenance of this system consists of checking the condition of the various con-

C965

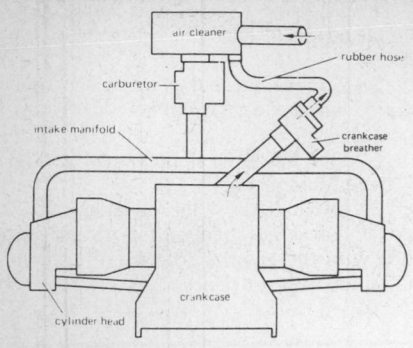

Crankcase ventilation system—Type 1

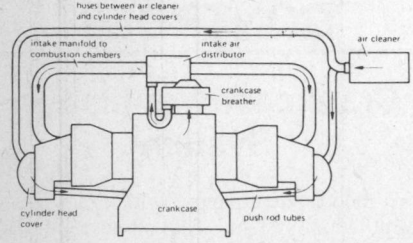

Crankcase ventilation system—air-cooled Type 2. Waterboxer system similar

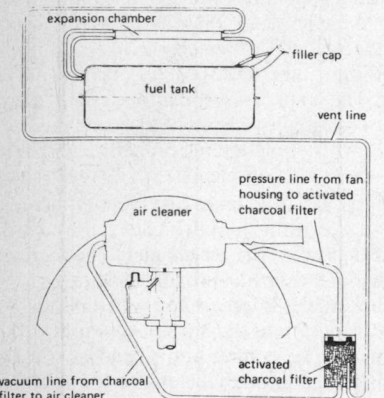

Typical evaporative emission control system

necting lines and the charcoal filter at 10,000 mile intervals. The charcoal filter, which is located under the engine compartment, should be replaced at 48,000 mile intervals.

Exhaust Gas Recirculation System

In order to control exhaust emissions of oxides of nitrogen (NO_x), an exhaust gas recirculation (EGR) system is employed on all models. The system lowers peak flame temperature during combustion by introducing a small (about 10%) percentage of relatively inert exhaust gas into the intake charge. Since the exhaust gas contains little or no oxygen, it cannot react with nor influence the air/fuel mixture. However, the exhaust gas does (by volume) take up space in the combustion chambers (space that would otherwise be occupied by a heat-producing, explosive air/fuel mixture), and does serve to lower peak combustion cham-

ber temperature. The amount of exhaust gas directed to the combustion chambers is infinitely variable by means of a vacuum operated EGR valve. For system specifics, see the vehicle type breakdown under "General Description."

GENERAL DESCRIPTION

Type 1

EGR is installed on all models. All applications use the element type filter and single stage EGR valve. Recirculations occurs during part throttle applications as before. The system is controlled by a throttle valve switch which measures throttle position, and an intake air sensor which reacts to engine vacuum. An odometer actuated EGR reminder light (on the dashboard) is used to inform the driver that it is time to service the EGR system. The reminder light measures elapsed mileage and lights at 15,000 mile intervals. A reset button is located behind the switch.

NOTE: On 1978 and later Calif. models, the EGR valve is operated mechanically by a rod attached to the throttle valve lever.

Type 2

All models utilize an EGR system. A single stage EGR valve and element type filter are used on all applications. Recirculation occurs during part throttle openings, and is controlled by throttle position, engine vacuum, and engine compartment temperature. When the ambient temperature exceeds 54° F, a sensor switch (located above the battery) opens, permitting EGR during part throttle applications. At 15,000 mile intervals, a dash mounted EGR service reminder light is activated to warn the driver that EGR service is now due. A reset button is located behind the switch.

EGR VALVE CHECKING

Type 1 and 2 (except Type 1 Calif. cars)

1. With the engine idling, pull the plug off the EGR valve's vacuum unit. The engine should slow down noticeably or stall,

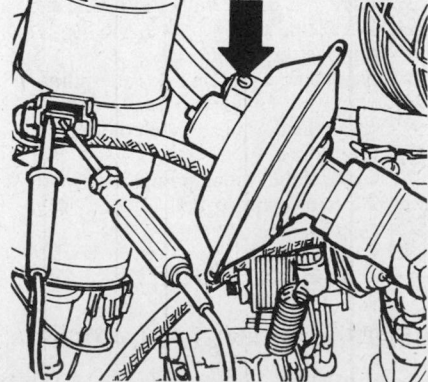

Testing the EGR valve; arrow indicates the location of the plug on the vacuum unit

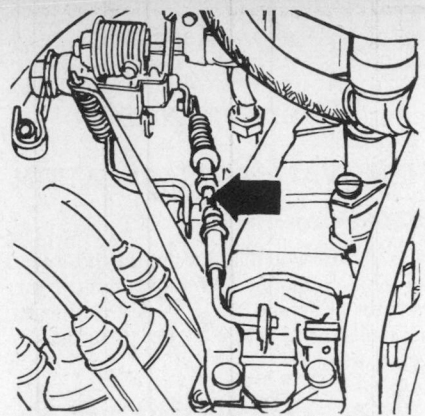

1978 and later Type 1 (Calif.) EGR linkage; arrow indicates hex-with-pin that is turned to adjust the valve

indicating that the EGR gases are being recirculated.

2. If there is no change when the plug is pulled, stop the engine. Turn the ignition key to the running (2) position without starting the engine.

3. Connect a test lamp as shown in the illustration. Now operate the throttle valve by hand, moving the throttle valve shaft from the idle position into the mid-speed range.

4. If the test light goes off when the throttle is moved off the idle position and lights at idle and at or near full throttle, the EGR valve is faulty and should be replaced.

Type 1 Calif. Cars

1. Remove the E-clip that holds the operating rod to the EGR valve.

2. With the engine idling, hand open the EGR valve.

3. The engine should slow down or stall, indicating that the exhaust gases are being recirculated. If not, the EGR valve or the EGR pipe is clogged and will require replacement or cleaning.

Catalytic Converter System

All Type 1 and 2 models are equipped with a catalytic converter. The converter is installed in the exhaust system, upstream and adjacent to the muffler.

Catalytic converters change noxious emissions of hydrocarbons (HC) and carbon monoxide (CO) into harmless carbon dioxide and water vapor. The reaction takes place inside the converter at great heat using platinum and palladium metals as the catalyst. If the engine is operated on lead-free fuel, they are designed to last 50,000 miles before replacement.

Starting in 1980, all Type 2 models made for Calif. utilize a three-way catalytic converter. The three-way converter not only reduces HC and CO emissions but it can also reduce oxides of nitrogen (NO).

However, the three-way converter can only achieve this reduction of harmful pollutants with the aid of the Lambda Control

Temperature switch
checking: opens at temperature
above 12°C (54° F)

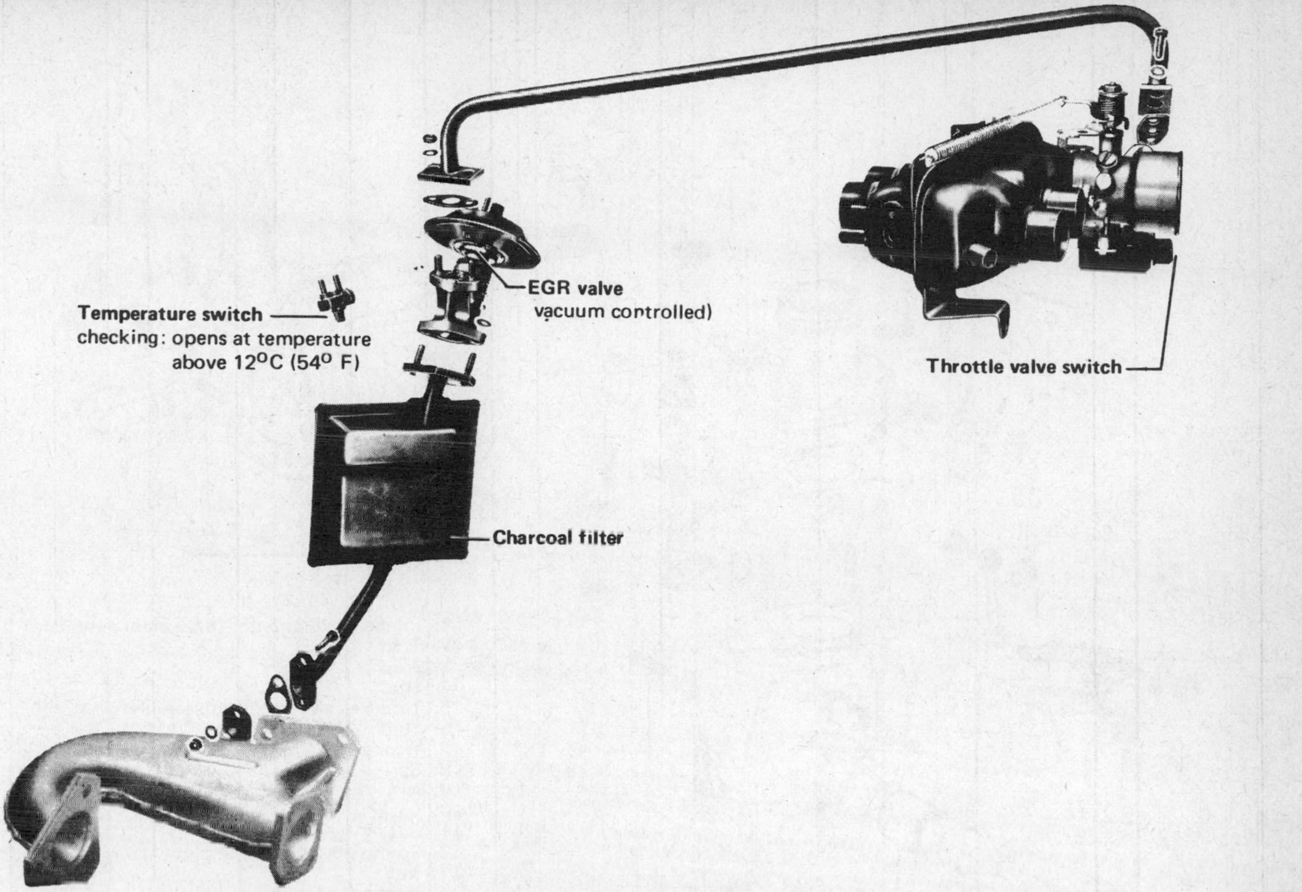

EGR valve
vacuum controlled)

Throttle valve switch

Charcoal filter

Type 2 EGR system. Air-cooled engine system shown, Waterboxer similar

System. This system is designed to maintain close control of the air/fuel mixture under all operating conditions.

Lambda Control System

All 1980–83 Type 2 models made for use in Calif. and all 1984 and later models are equipped with the Lambda Control System. Basically, the Lambda Control System is an oxygen sensor which is installed in the exhaust manifold. This oxygen sensor makes it possible to maintain the precise air/fuel mixture required by the three-way catalytic converter. The oxygen sensor continuously senses the oxygen content of the exhaust and signals the information to an electronic control unit. The control unit corrects the fuel injector operating time, so that the engine always receives an accurately metered air/fuel mixture.

The oxygen sensor system is monitored by an indicator light in the instrument panel which will light up every 30,000 miles, signalling a need for system service.

Deceleration Control

All Type 2 models, as well as those Type 1 models equipped with manual transmission, are equipped with deceleration control to prevent an overly rich fuel mixture from

reaching the exhaust. During deceleration, a vacuum valve (manual transmission) or electrical transmission switch (automatic transmission) opens, bypassing the closed throttle plate and allowing air to enter the combustion chambers.

FUEL SYSTEM

Electric Fuel Pump

All gasoline engine models have an electric pump. The fuel pump is located near the front axle.

REMOVAL & INSTALLATION

1. Disconnect the fuel pump wiring. Pull the plug from the pump but do not pull on the wiring.
2. Disconnect the fuel hoses and plug them to prevent any leakage.
3. Remove the two nuts which secure the pump and then remove the pump.
4. Reconnect the fuel pump hoses and wiring and install the pump on the vehicle.

ADJUSTMENTS

Electric fuel pump pressure is 28 psi (29 psi on the Waterboxer). Fuel pump pressure is determined by a pressure regulator which diverts part of the fuel pump output to the

gas tank when 28 psi is reached. The regulator, located on the engine firewall, has a screw and locknut on its end. Loosen the locknut and adjust the screw to adjust the pressure. Do not force the screw in or out if it does not turn.

Fuel Injection— Gasoline Engines

All gasoline engined models are equipped with an improved system known as the Air Flow Controlled Electronic Fuel Injection

Air-cooled Type 2 fuel pump location (1) and filter (2)

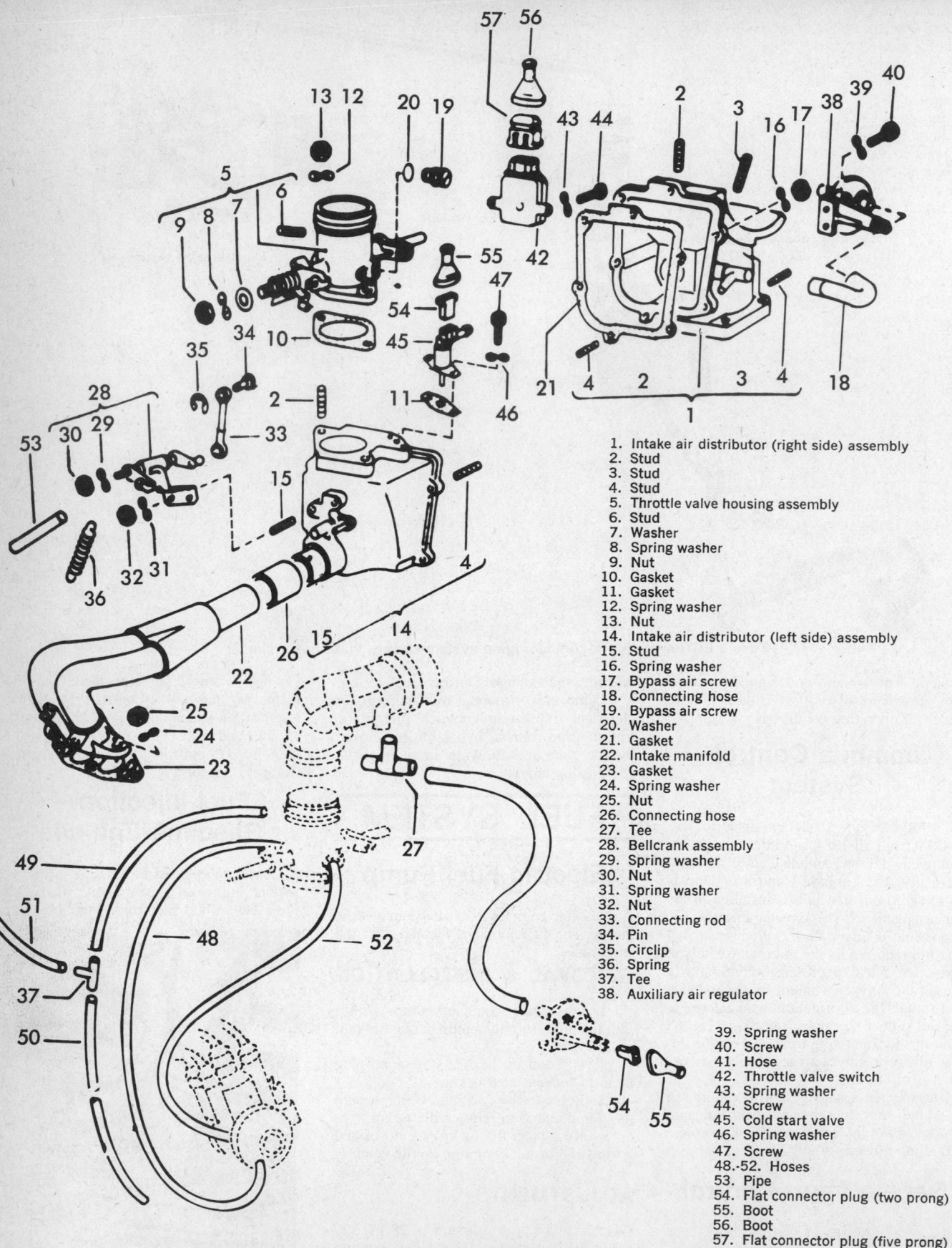

1. Intake air distributor (right side) assembly
2. Stud
3. Stud
4. Stud
5. Throttle valve housing assembly
6. Stud
7. Washer
8. Spring washer
9. Nut
10. Gasket
11. Gasket
12. Spring washer
13. Nut
14. Intake air distributor (left side) assembly
15. Stud
16. Spring washer
17. Bypass air screw
18. Connecting hose
19. Bypass air screw
20. Washer
21. Gasket
22. Intake manifold
23. Gasket
24. Spring washer
25. Nut
26. Connecting hose
27. Tee
28. Bellcrank assembly
29. Spring washer
30. Nut
31. Spring washer
32. Nut
33. Connecting rod
34. Pin
35. Circlip
36. Spring
37. Tee
38. Auxiliary air regulator

39. Spring washer
40. Screw
41. Hose
42. Throttle valve switch
43. Spring washer
44. Screw
45. Cold start valve
46. Spring washer
47. Screw
48.-52. Hoses
53. Pipe
54. Flat connector plug (two prong)
55. Boot
56. Boot
57. Flat connector plug (five prong)

Exploded view of the Type 1 airflow controlled electronic fuel injection system

System. With this system, some of the electronic sensors and wiring are eliminated, and the control box is smaller. Fuel is metered according to intake air flow.

The system consists of the following components;

Intake air sensor—measures intake air volume and temperature and sends voltage signals to the control unit (brain box). It also controls the electric fuel pump by shutting it off when intake air stops. It is located between the air cleaner and the intake air distributor.

Ignition contact breaker points—these are the regular points inside the distributor. When the points open, all four injectors are triggered. The points also send engine speed signals to the control unit. No separate triggering contacts are used.

Throttle valve switch—provides only for full load enrichment. This switch is not adjustable.

Temperature sensor I—senses intake temperature as before. It is now located in the intake air sensor.

Temperature sensor II—senses cylinder head temperature as before.

Control unit (brain box)—contains only 80 components compared to the old system's 300.

Pressure regulator—is connected by a vacuum hose to the intake air distributor and is no longer adjustable. It adjusts fuel pressure according to manifold vacuum.

Auxiliary air regulator—provides more air during cold warmup.

NOTE: For all fuel injection system service and repair procedures not de-tailed below, please refer to "Fuel Injection" in the Unit Repair section.**

FUEL INJECTORS

There are two types of injectors. One type is secured in place by a ring that holds a single injector. The second type of injector is secured to the intake manifold in pairs by a common bracket.

Removal & Installation

SINGLE INJECTORS

1. Remove the nut which secures the injector bracket to the manifold.

2. If the injector is not going to be replaced, do not disconnect the fuel line. Disconnect the injector wiring.

3. Gently slide the injector bracket up the injector and pull the injector from the intake manifold. Be careful not to damage the inner and outer rubber sealing rings. These sealing rings are used to seal the injector to the manifold and must be replaced if they show any sign of deterioration.

4. Installation is the reverse of removal. Be careful not to damage the injector tip or contaminate the injector with dirt.

PAIRED INJECTORS

1. Disconnect the injector wiring.

2. Remove the two nuts which secure the injector bracket to the manifold. Slide the bracket up the injector. Do not disconnect the fuel lines if the injector is not going to be replaced.

3. Gently slide the pair of injectors out of their bores along with the rubber sealing

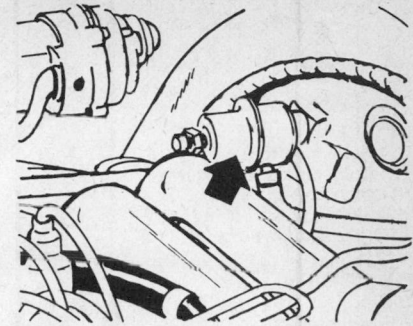

Fuel pressure regulator with locknut and adjusting screw at left end

rings, injector plate, and the inner and outer injector locating bushings. It may be necessary to remove the inner bushings from the intake manifold after the injectors are removed since they sometimes lodge within the manifold.

NOTE: There are two sleeves that fit over the injector bracket studs. Be careful not lose them.

4. Upon installation, place the injector bracket, the outer bushings, the injector plate, and the inner locating bushings on the pair of injectors in that order.

5. Gently slip the injector assembly into the manifold and install the bracket nuts. Be careful not to damage the injector tips or contaminate the injectors with dirt.

6. Reconnect the injector wiring

THROTTLE VALVE SWITCH

Removal & Installation

1. Remove the air filter.

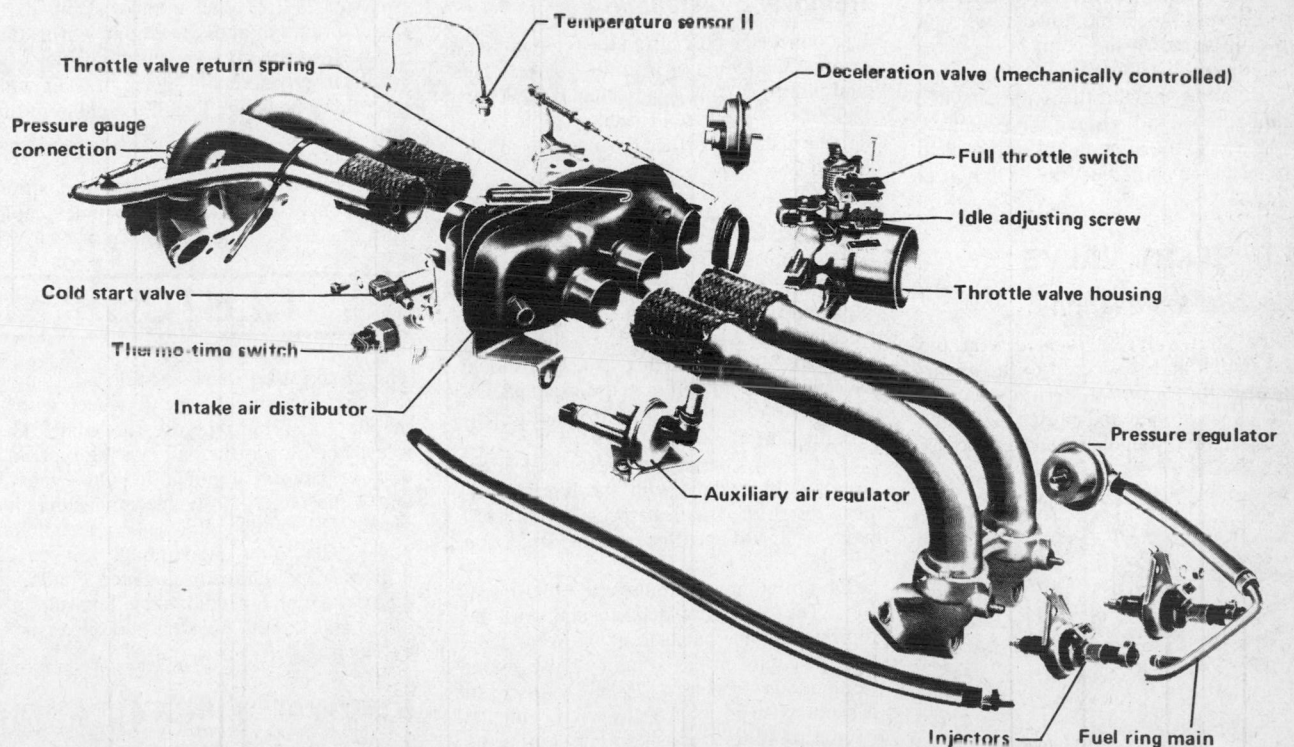

Exploded view of the Type 2 (air-cooled engine) airflow controlled (AFC) electronic fuel injection system.

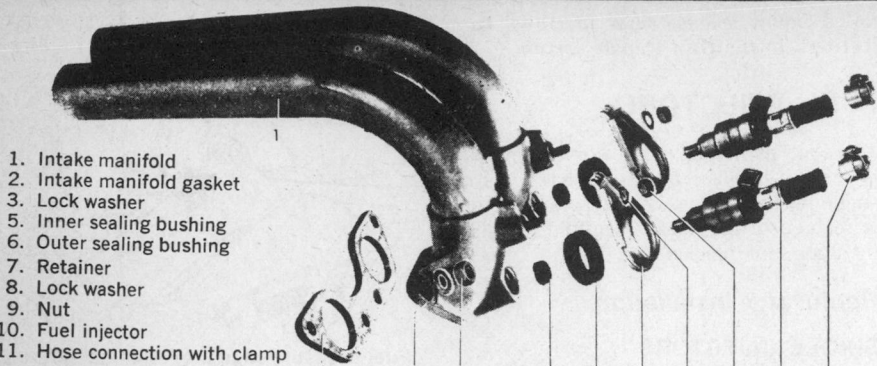

1. Intake manifold
2. Intake manifold gasket
3. Lock washer
5. Inner sealing bushing
6. Outer sealing bushing
7. Retainer
8. Lock washer
9. Nut
10. Fuel injector
11. Hose connection with clamp

Individually mounted fuel injectors

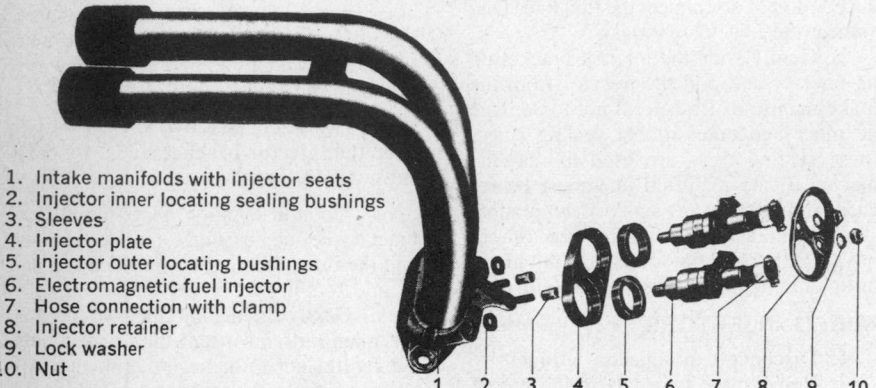

1. Intake manifolds with injector seats
2. Injector inner locating sealing bushings
3. Sleeves
4. Injector plate
5. Injector outer locating bushings
6. Electromagnetic fuel injector
7. Hose connection with clamp
8. Injector retainer
9. Lock washer
10. Nut

Paired fuel injectors

2. The switch is located on the throttle valve housing. Disconnect the throttle valve return spring.

3. Remove the throttle valve assembly but do not disconnect the bowden wire for the throttle valve or the connecting hoses to the ignition distributor.

4. Remove the throttle valve, switch securing screws and remove the switch.

5. Reverse the above steps to install. It will be necessary to adjust the switch after installation.

COLD START VALVE

Removal & Installation

The cold start valve is located near the thermo-switch and is secured to the air intake distributor by two screws. This valve sometimes jams open and causes excessive fuel consumption, rough idle, and low power output.

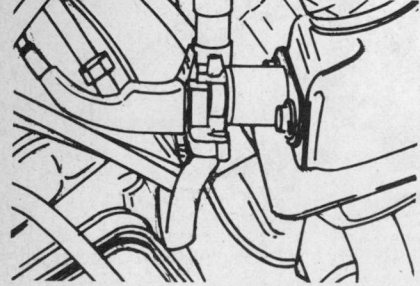

Cold start valve location

FUEL PRESSURE REGULATOR

Removal & Installation

Disconnect the hoses from the regulator and remove the regulator from its bracket. The fuel pump pressure is adjustable; however, lack of fuel pressure is usually due to other defects in the system and the regulator should be adjusted only as a last resort.

Diesel Fuel Injection

The diesel fuel system is an extremely complex and sensitive system. Very few repairs or adjustments are possible by the owner. Any service other than that listed here should be referred to an authorized diesel specialist. The injection pump itself is not repairable; it can only be replaced.

Any work done to the diesel fuel injection should be done with absolute cleanliness. Even the smallest specks of dirt will have a disatrous effect on the injection system.

Do not attempt to remove the fuel injectors. They are very delicate and must be removed with a special tool to prevent damage. The fuel in the system is also under tremendous pressure (1700–1850 psi), so it's not wise to loosen any lines with the engine running. Exposing your skin to the spray from the injector at working pressure can cause fuel to penetrate the skin.

CHECKING INJECTION PUMP TIMING

Checking the injection pump timing also involves checking the valve timing. To alter the injection pump timing, the camshaft gear must be removed and repositioned. This also changes the valve timing. Special tool (VW 210) is necessary to properly tension the injection pump drive belt on the diesel engine.

1. Set the engine at TDC on No. 1 cylinder. In this position, the TDC mark on the flywheel should be aligned with boss on the bell housing and both valves of No. 1 cylinder should be closed.

2. The marks on the pump and mounting plate should also be aligned.

3. If the valve timing is incorrect, set the valve timing as detailed in the engine section.

ACCELERATOR CABLE ADJUSTMENT

The ball pin on the pump lever should be pointing up and be aligned with the mark in the slot. The accelerator cable should be attached at the upper hole in the bracket. With the pedal in the full throttle position, adjust the cable so that the pump lever contacts the stop with no binding or strain.

COLD START CABLE ADJUSTMENT

When the cold start knob on the dash is pulled out, the fuel injection pump timing is advanced 2.5°. This improves cold starting and running until the engine warms up.

1. Insert the washer on the cable.

2. Insert the cable in the bracket with the rubber housing. Install the cable in the pin.

3. Install the lockwasher.

4. Move the lever to the zero position (direction of arrow). Pull the inner cable tight and tighten the clamp screw.

CLUTCH

The clutch used in all models is a single dry disc mounted on the flywheel with a diaphragm spring type pressure plate. The release bearing is the ball bearing type and does not require lubrication. On Types 1 and 2 the clutch is engaged mechanically via a cable which attaches to the clutch pedal. The Vanagon, although a Type 2, utilizes a hydraulically engaged clutch. It features a clutch pedal operated master cylinder and a bell housing mounted slave cylinder.

REMOVAL & INSTALLATION

Manual Transmission

1. Remove the engine.

2. Remove the pressure plate securing bolts one turn at a time until all spring pressure is released.

3. Remove the bolts and remove the clutch assembly.

NOTE: Notice which side of the clutch disc faces the flywheel and install the new disc in the same direction.

4. Before installing the new clutch, check the condition of the flywheel. It should not have excessive heat cracks and the friction surface should not be scored or warped. Check the condition of the throw out bearing. If the bearing is worn, replace it.

5. Lubricate the pilot bearing in the end of the crankshaft with grease.

6. Insert a pilot shaft, used for centering the clutch disc, through the clutch disc and place the disc against the flywheel. The pilot shaft will hold the disc in place.

7. Place the pressure plate over the disc and loosely install the bolts.

NOTE: Make sure the correct side of the clutch disc is facing outward. The disc will rub the flywheel if it is incorrectly positioned.

8. After making sure that the pressure plate aligning dowels will fit into the pressure plate, gradually tighten the bolts.

9. Remove the pilot shaft and reinstall the engine.

10. Adjust the clutch pedal free-play.

11. Bleed the clutch (Vanagon only).

Automatic Stick Shift

1. Disconnect the negative battery cable.
2. Remove the engine.
3. Remove the transaxle.
4. Remove the torque converter by sliding it off the input shaft. Seal off the hub opening.
5. Mount the transaxle in a repair stand or on a suitable bench.
6. Loosen the clamp screw and pull off clutch operating lever. Remove the transmission cover.
7. Remove the hex nuts between the clutch housing and the transmission case.

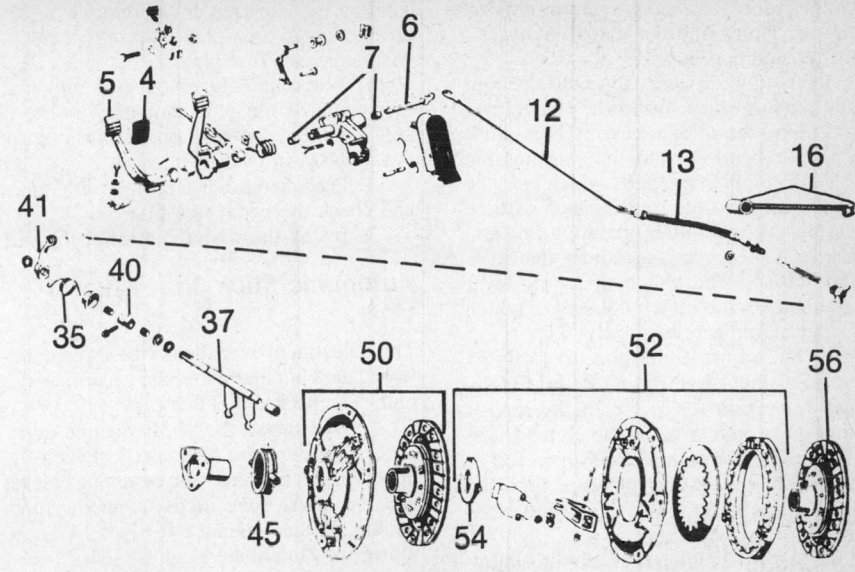

4. Clutch pedal pad	16. Angle plate for clutch cable	45. Clutch release bearing
5. Clutch pedal	35. Clutch return spring	50. Clutch
6. Clutch pedal shaft	37. Clutch cross shaft	52. Pressure plate
7. Bushings for pedal cluster	40. Bushing—operating shaft	54. Clutch release plate
12. Clutch cable	41. Clutch operating lever	56. Clutch disc
13. Clutch cable sleeve		

Type 1 clutch components

NOTE: Two nuts are located inside the differential housing.

8. The oil need not be drained if the clutch is removed with the cover opening up and the gearshift housing breather blocked.

9. Pull the transmission from the clutch housing studs.

10. Turn the clutch lever shaft to disengage the release bearing.

11. Remove both lower engine mounting bolts.

12. Loosen the clutch retaining bolts gradually and alternately to prevent distortion. Remove the bolts, pressure plate, clutch plate, and release bearing.

13. Do not wash the release bearing. Wipe it dry only.

14. Check the clutch plate, pressure plate, and release bearing for wear and damage.

Check the clutch carrier plate, needle bearing, and seat for wear. Replace the necessary parts.

15. If the clutch is wet with ATF, replace the clutch carrier plate seal and the clutch disc. If the clutch is wet with transmission oil, replace the transmission case seal and clutch disc.

16. Coat the release bearing guide on the transmission case neck and both lugs on the release bearing with grease. Insert the bearing into the clutch.

17. Grease the carrier plate needle bearing. Install the clutch disc and pressure plate using a pilot shaft to center the disc on the flywheel.

18. Tighten the pressure plate retaining bolts evenly and alternately. Make sure that the release bearing is correctly located in the diaphragm spring.

19. Insert the lower engine mounting bolts

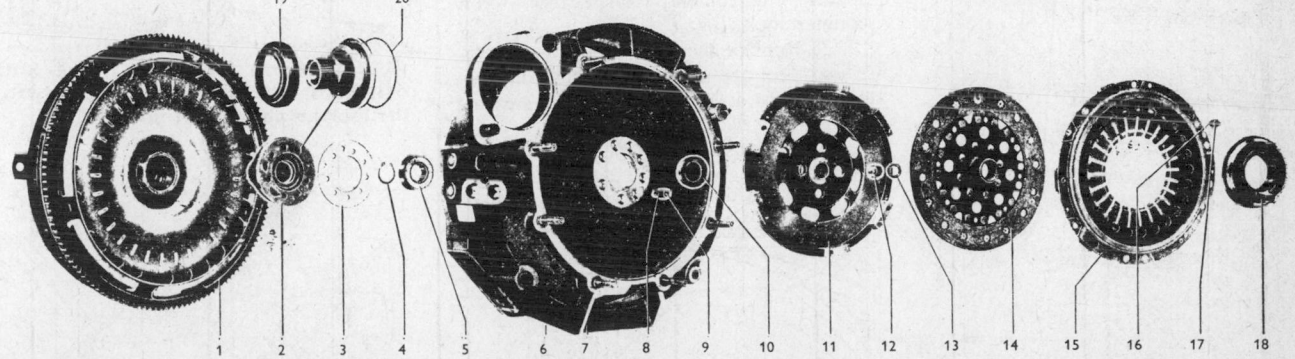

1. Torque converter	5. Ball bearing	9. Socket head screw	13. Seal/carrier plate	17. Socket head screw
2. One-way clutch support	6. O-ring for stud	10. Seal	14. Clutch plate	18. Release bearing
3. Gasket	7. Converter housing	11. Clutch carrier plate	15. Diaphragm clutch pressure plate	19. Seal/converter
4. Circlip for carrier plate	8. Spring washer	12. Needle bearing	16. Spring washer	20. O-ring/one-way clutch support

Automatic Stick Shift clutch assembly

from the front. Replace the sealing rings if necessary. Some units have aluminum sealing rings and cap nuts.

20. Push the transmission onto the converter housing studs. Insert the clutch lever shaft behind the release bearing lugs. Push the release bearing onto the transmission case neck. Tighten the bolts which hold the clutch housing to the transmission case.

21. Install the clutch operating lever.

22. It is necessary to adjust the basic clutch setting. The clutch operating lever should contact the clutch housing. Tighten the lever clamp screw slightly.

23. First adjust dimension (a) to 0.335 in. Adjust dimension (b) to 3.03 in. Finally adjust dimension (c) to 1.6 in. by repositioning the clutch lever on the clutch shaft. Tighten the lever clamp screw.

24. Push the torque converter onto the support tube. Insert it into the turbine shaft by turning the converter.

25. Check the clutch play after installing the transaxle and engine.

CLUTCH CABLE ADJUSTMENT

Manual Transmission

1. Check the clutch pedal travel by measuring the distance the pedal travels toward the floor until pressure is exerted against the clutch. The distance is 3/8–3/4 in.

2. To adjust the clutch, jack up the rear of the car and support it on jackstands.

3. Remove the left rear wheel.

4. Adjust the cable tension by turning the wing nut on the end of the clutch cable.

Turning the wing nut counterclockwise decreases pedal free-play, turning it clockwise increases free-play.

5. When the adjustment is completed, the wings of the wing nut must be horizontal so that the lugs on the nut engage the recesses in the clutch lever.

6. Push on the clutch pedal several times and check the pedal free-play.

7. Install the wheel and lower the car.

Automatic Stick Shift—Type 1 Only

The adjustment is made on the linkage between the clutch arm and the vacuum servo unit. To check the clutch play:

1. Disconnect the servo vacuum hose.

2. Measure the clearance between the upper edge of the servo unit mounting bracket and the lower edge of the adjusting turnbuckle. If the clearance (e) is 0.16 in. or more, the clutch needs adjustment.

3. Reconnect the vacuum hose.

To adjust the clutch:

1. Disconnect the servo vacuum hose.

2. Loosen the turnbuckle locknut and back it off completely to the lever arm. Then turn the servo turnbuckle against the locknut. Now back off the turnbuckle 5–5½ turns. The distance between the locknut and the turnbuckle should be 0.25 in.

3. Tighten the locknut against the adjusting sleeve.

4. Reconnect the vacuum hose and road test the vehicle. The clutch is properly adjusted when Reverse gear can be engaged silently and the clutch does not slip on acceleration. If the clutch arm contacts the clutch housing, there is no more adjustment possible and the clutch plate must be replaced.

The speed of engagement of the Automatic Stick Shift clutch is regulated by the vacuum operated valve rather than by the driver's foot. The adjusting screw is on top of the valve under a small protective cap. Adjust the valve as follows:

1. Remove the cap.

2. To slow the engagement, turn the adjusting screw ¼–½ turn clockwise. To speed engagement, turn the screw counterclockwise.

3. Replace the cap.

4. Test operation by shifting from Second to First at 44 mph without depressing

the accelerator. The shift should take exactly one second to occur.

CLUTCH CABLE REPLACEMENT

Types 1 and 2

1. Jack up the car and remove the left rear wheel.

2. Disconnect the cable from the clutch operating lever.

3. Remove the rubber boot from the end of the guide tube and off the end of the cable.

4. On the Type 1, unbolt the pedal cluster and remove it from the car. It will also be necessary to disconnect the brake master cylinder push rod and throttle cable from the pedal cluster. On the Type 2, remove the cover under the pedal cluster,

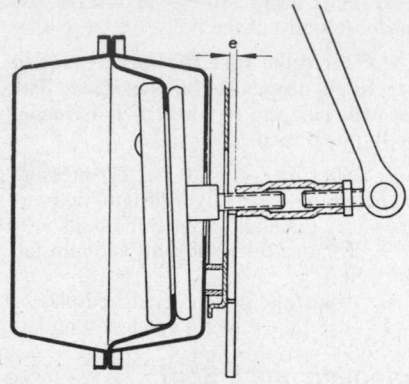

Checking the clutch adjustment on the Automatic Stick Shift

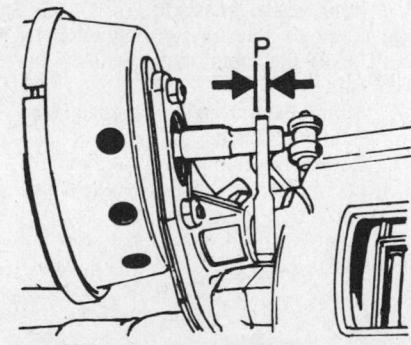

Adjusting the Automatic Stick Shift clutch; (d) is 0.25 in., measured between the locknut and the turnbuckle

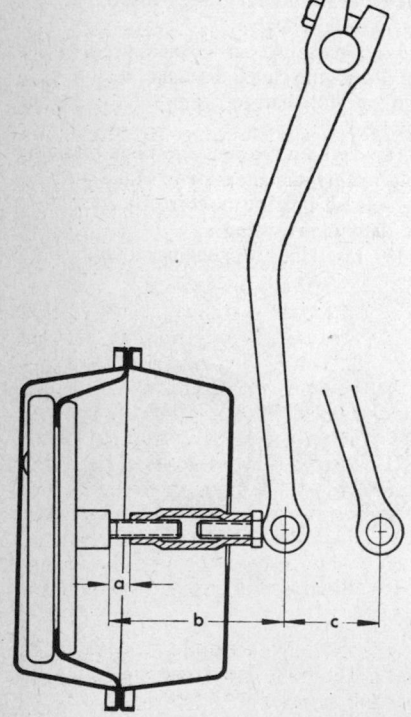

Automatic Stick Shift basic clutch adjusting dimensions

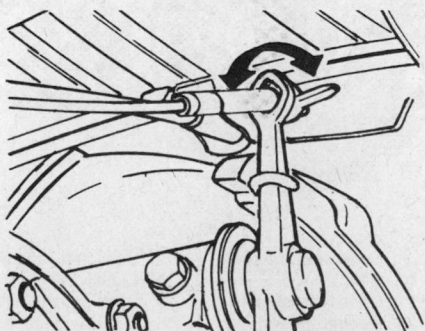

Wing nut for clutch cable adjustment

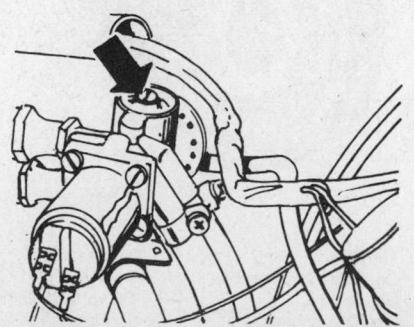

Adjusting screw for speed of engagement

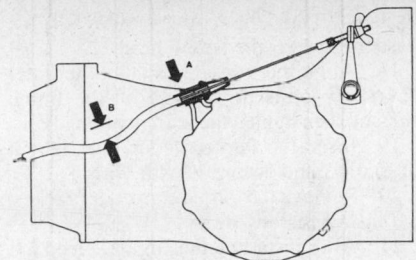

For smooth clutch action, dimension B should be 1.0-1.7 in. Adjust the cable to provide slight sag at point B by installing spacer washers at point A.

then remove the pin from the clevis on the end of the clutch cable.

5. Pull the cable out of its guide tube from the pedal cluster end.

6. Installation is the reverse of the above.

NOTE: Grease the cable before installing it and readjust the clutch pedal freeplay.

Clutch Master Cylinder

REMOVAL & INSTALLATION

Vanagon

1. Siphon the hydraulic fluid from the master cylinder (clutch) reservoir.

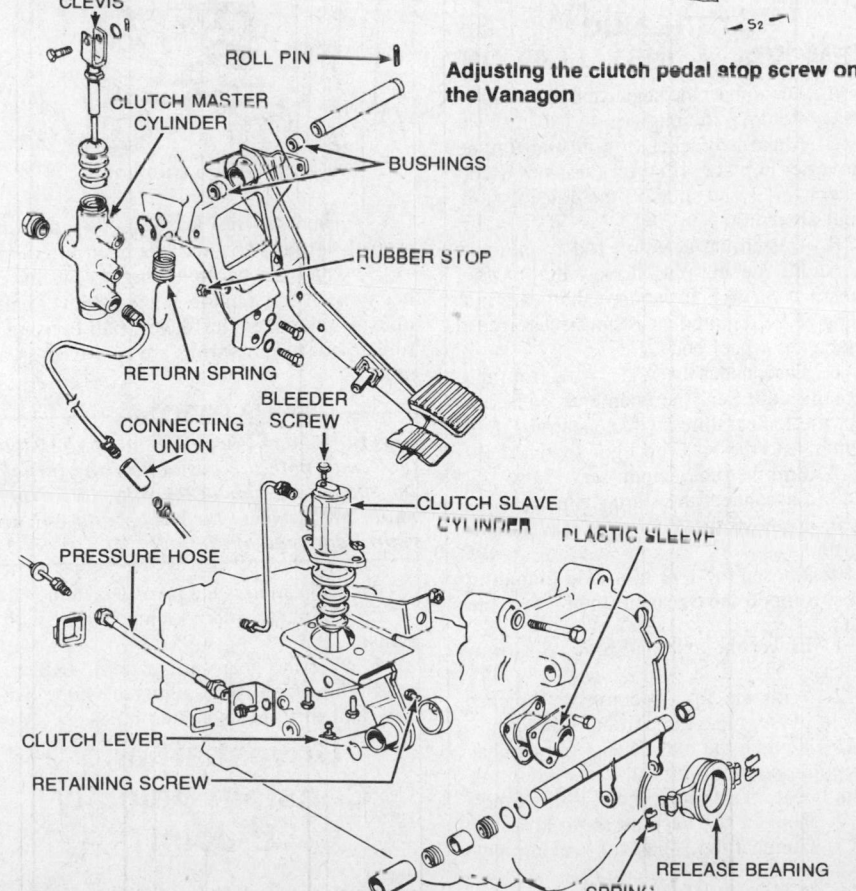

Components of the Vanagon hydraulic clutch system

2. Pull back the carpeting from the pedal area and lay down some absorbent rags.

3. Pull the elbow connection from the top of the master cylinder.

4. Disconnect and plug the pressure line from the rear of the master cylinder.

5. Remove the master cylinder mounting bolts and remove the cylinder to the rear.

6. Reverse the above procedure to install, taking care to bleed the system and adjust pedal free-play.

Clutch Slave Cylinder

REMOVAL & INSTALLATION

Vanagon

1. Locate the slave cylinder on the bell housing.

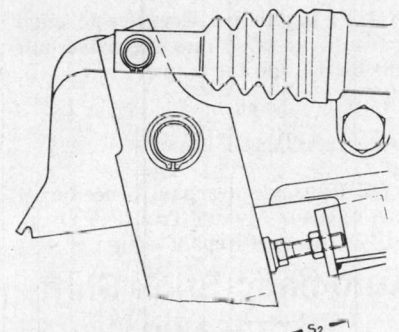

Adjusting the clutch pedal stop screw on the Vanagon

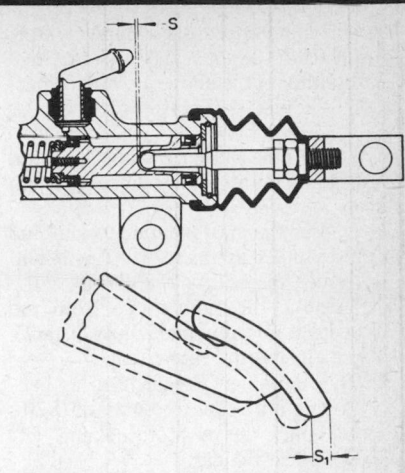

Adjusting the clutch pedal free play on the Vanagon

2. Disconnect and plug the pressure line from the slave cylinder.

3. Disconnect the return spring from the pushrod.

4. Remove the retaining circlip from the boot and remove the boot.

5. Remove the circlip and slide the slave cylinder rearwards from its mount.

6. Remove the spring clip from the mount.

7. Reverse the above procedure to install, taking care to bleed the system and adjust pedal free-play.

CLUTCH SYSTEM BLEEDING AND ADJUSTMENT

Vanagon

Whenever air enters the clutch hydraulic system due to leakage, or if any part of the system is removed for service, the system must be bled. The hydraulic system uses high quality brake fluid meeting SAE J1703 or DOT3 or DOT4 specifications. Brake fluid is highly corrosive to paint finishes and care should be exercised that no spillage occurs. The procedure is as follows:

1. Top up the clutch fluid reservoir and make sure the cap vent is open.

2. Locate the slave cylinder bleed nipple and remove all dirt and grease from the valve. Attach a hose to the nipple and submerge the other end of the hose in a jar containing a few inches of clean brake fluid.

3. Find a friend to operate the clutch pedal. When your friend depresses the clutch pedal slowly to the floor, open the bleeder valve about one turn. Have your friend keep the pedal on the floor until you close the bleeder valve. Repeat this operation several times until no air bubbles are emitted from the tube.

NOTE: Keep a close check on the fluid level in the fluid reservoir. Never let the level fall below the ½ full mark.

4. After bleeding discard the old fluid and top up the reservoir.

5. The clutch pedal should have a free-play of 0.20–0.28 in., and a 7 in. total travel. If either of the above are not to specifications, adjust the master cylinder as follows.

6. Loosen the master cylinder pushrod locknut and shorten the pushrod length slightly.

7. Loosen the master cylinder bolts and push the cylinder as far forward as it will go. Retighten the bolts.

8. Remove the rubber cap from the clutch pedal stop screw and adjust distance to 0.89 in. Install the rubber cap.

9. Then lengthen the pushrod as necessary to obtain a pedal free-play of 0.20–0.28 in. Tighten the pushrod locknut.

10. Road-test the car.

TRANSAXLE

Manual Transaxle
REMOVAL & INSTALLATION

1. Disconnect the negative battery cable.
2. Remove the engine.
3. Remove the socket head screws which secure the driveshafts to the transmission. Remove the bolts from the transmission end first and then remove the shafts.

NOTE: It is not necessary to remove the driveshafts entirely from the car if the car does not have to be moved while the transaxle is out.

4. Disconnect the clutch cable from the clutch lever and remove the clutch cable and its guide tube from the transaxle. Loosen the square head bolt at the shift linkage coupling located near the rear of the transaxle. Slide the coupling off the inner shaft lever. There is an access plate under the rear seat to reach the coupling on Type 1.

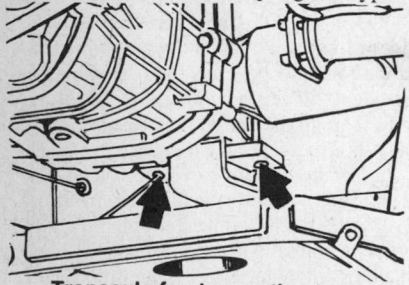

Transaxle front mounting bolts

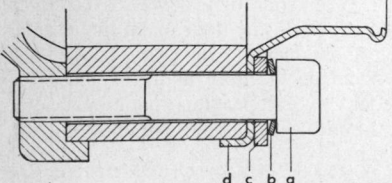

a. Socket head screws
b. Lock washer
c. Spacer
d. Protective cap

Drive axle bolt and washer positioning

It is necessary to work under the car to reach the coupling on Type 2 models.

5. Disconnect the starter wiring.
6. Disconnect the back-up light switch wiring.
7. Remove the front transaxle mounting bolts.
8. Support the transaxle with a jack and remove the transaxle from the car.
9. Carefully lower the jack and remove the transaxle from the car.
10. To install, jack the transaxle into position and loosely install the bolts.
11. Tighten the transmission carrier bolts first, then tighten the front mounting nuts.
12. Install the driveshaft bolts with new lockwashers. The lockwashers should be positioned on the bolt with the convex side toward the screw head.
13. Reconnect the wiring, the clutch cable, and the shift linkage.

NOTE: It may be necessary to align the transmission so that the driveshaft joints do not rub the frame.

14. Install the engine.

OVERHAUL

For all transaxle overhaul procedures, please refer to "Manual Transaxle Overhaul" in the Unit Repair section.

Automatic Stick Shift Transaxle
REMOVAL & INSTALLATION

1. Disconnect the negative battery cable.
2. Remove the engine.
3. Make a bracket to hold the torque converter in place. If a bracket is not used, the converter will slide off the transmission input shaft.
4. Detach the gearshift rod coupling.
5. Disconnect the driveshafts at the transmission end. If the driveshafts are not going to be repaired, it is not necessary to detach the wheel end.
6. Disconnect the ATF hoses from the transmission. Seal the open ends. Disconnect the temperature switch, neutral safety switch, and the back-up light switch.
7. Pull off the vacuum servo hose.
8. Disconnect the starter wiring.
9. Remove the front transaxle mounting nuts.
10. Loosen the rear transaxle mounting bolts. Support the transaxle and remove the bolts.
11. Lower the axle and remove it from the car.
12. With the torque converter bracket still in place, raise the axle into the car.
13. Tighten the nuts for the front transmission mounting. Insert the rear mounting bolts but do not tighten them at this time.
14. Replace the vacuum servo hose.
15. Connect the ATF hoses, using new washers. The washers are seals.
16. Connect the temperature switch and starter cables.
17. Install the driveshafts, using new

washers. Turn the convex sides of the washers toward the screw head.

18. Align the transaxle so that the inner driveshaft joints do not rub on the frame fork and then tighten the rear mounting bolts.
19. Insert the shift rod coupling, tighten the screw, and secure it with wire.
20. Remove the torque converter bracket, and install the engine.
21. After installing the engine, bleed the ATF lines if return flow has not started after 2–3 minutes.

SHIFT LINKAGE ADJUSTMENT

1. The Volkswagen shift linkage is not adjustable. When shifting becomes difficult or there is an excessive amount of play in the linkage, check the shifting mechanism for worn parts. Make sure the shift linkage coupling is tightly connected to the inner shaft lever located at the rear of the transaxle under the rear seat. Worn parts may be found in the shift lever mechanism and the supports for the linkage rod sometimes wear out.

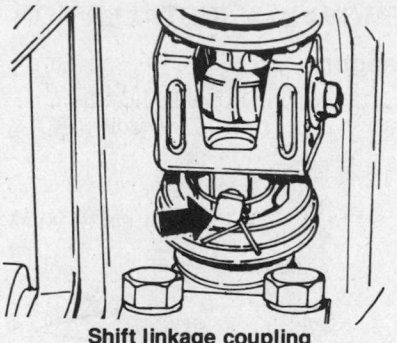

Shift linkage coupling

2. The gear shift lever can be removed after the front floor mat has been lifted.
3. After the two retaining screws have been removed from the gear shift lever ball housing, the gear shift lever, ball housing, rubber boot, and spring are removed as a unit.

─────── CAUTION ───────
Carefully mark the position of the stop plate and note the position of the turned up ramp at the side of the stop plate. Normally the ramp is turned up and on the right hand side of the hole.
───────────────────────

4. Installation is the reverse of removal.
5. Lubricate all moving parts with grease.
6. Test the gear shift pattern. If there is difficulty in shifting, adjust the stop plate back and forth in its slotted holes.

Driveshaft and Constant Velocity U-Joint

REMOVAL & INSTALLATION

1. Remove the bolts which secure the

joints at each end of the shaft, tilt the shaft down, and remove the shaft.

2. Loosen the clamps which secure the rubber boot to the axle and slide the boot back on the axle.

3. Drive the stamped steel cover off the joint with a drift.

NOTE: After the cover is removed, do not tilt the ball hub as the balls will fall out of the hub.

4. Remove the circlip from the end of the axle and press the axle out of the joint.

5. Reverse the above steps to install. The position of the dished washer is dependent on the type of transmission. On automatic transmissions, it is placed between the ball hub and the circlip. On manual transmissions, it is placed between the ball hub and the shoulder on the shaft. Be sure to pack the joint with grease.

NOTE: The chamfer on the splined inside diameter of the ball hub faces the shoulder on the driveshaft.

AUTOMATIC TRANSMISSION

REMOVAL & INSTALLATION

NOTE: The engine and transmission must be removed as an assembly on the Type 2/1800 and 2/2000.

1. Remove the battery ground cable.
2. On the sedan, remove the cooling air intake duct with the heating fan and hoses. Remove the cooling air intake connection and bellows, then detach the hoses to the air cleaner.
3. On the station wagons, remove the warm air hoses and air cleaner. Remove the boot between the dipstick tube and the body and the boot between the oil filler neck and the body. Disconnect the cooling air bellows at the body.
4. Disconnect the wires at the regulator and the alternator wires at the snap connector located by the regulator. Disconnect the auxiliary air regulator and the oil pressure switch at the snap connectors located by the distributor.
5. Disconnect the accelerator cable.
6. Disconnect the right fuel return line.
7. Raise the car.
8. Disconnect the hoses from the heat exchangers.
9. Disconnect the starter wires and push the engine wiring harness through the engine cover plate.
10. Disconnect the fuel supply line and plug it.
11. Remove the heater booster exhaust pipe.
12. Remove the rear axles and cover the ends to protect them from dirt.
13. Remove the selector cable by unscrewing the cable sleeve.

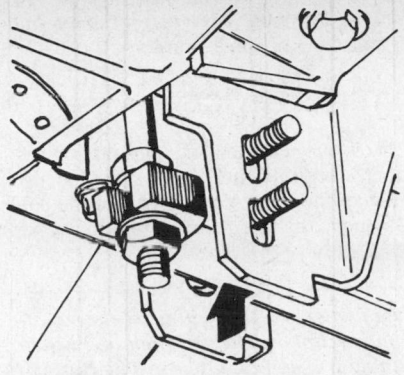

Engine carrier bolts positioned at the top of their elongated holes

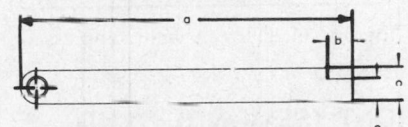

a. 5.095 in. c. 0.590 in.
b. 0.472 in. d. 0.393, 0.433, and 0.472 in.
Buffer alignment gauge

14. Remove the wire from the kickdown switch.
15. Remove the bolts from the rubber transmission mountings, taking careful note of the position, number, and thickness of the spacers that are present.

— CAUTION —
These spacers must be reinstalled exactly as they were removed. Do not detach the transmission carrier from the body.

16. Support the engine and transmission assembly in such a way that it may be lowered and moved rearward at the same time.
17. Remove the engine carrier bolts and the engine and transmission assembly from the car.
18. Matchmark the flywheel and the torque converter and remove the three attaching bolts.
19. Remove the engine-to-transmission bolts and separate the engine and transmission.

— CAUTION —
Exercise care when separating the engine and transmission as the torque converter will easily slip off the input shaft if the transmission is tilted downward.

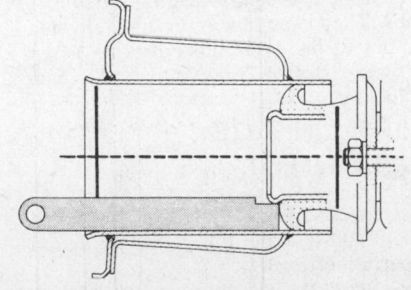

Measuring procedure for centering the buffer

20. Installation is as follows. Install and tighten the engine-to-transmission bolts after aligning the match marks on the flywheel and converter.
21. Making sure the matchmarks are aligned, install the converter-to-flywheel bolts.
22. Make sure the rubber buffer is in place and the two securing studs do not project more than 0.7 in. from the transmission case.
23. Tie a cord to the slot in the engine compartment seal. This will make positioning the seal easier.
24. Lift the assembly far enough to allow the accelerator cable to be pushed through the front engine cover.
25. Continue lifting the assembly into place. Slide the rubber buffer into the locating tube in the rear axle carrier.
26. Insert the engine carrier bolts and raise the engine until the bolts are at the top of their elongated slots. Tighten the bolts.

NOTE: A set of three gauges must be obtained to check the alignment of the rubber buffer in its locating tube. The dimensions are given in the illustration as is the measuring technique. The rubber buffer is centered horizontally where the 11mm gauge can be inserted on both sides. The buffer is located vertically when the 10mm gauge can be inserted on the bottom side and the 12mm gauge can be inserted on the top side. See Steps 27 and 28 for adjustment.

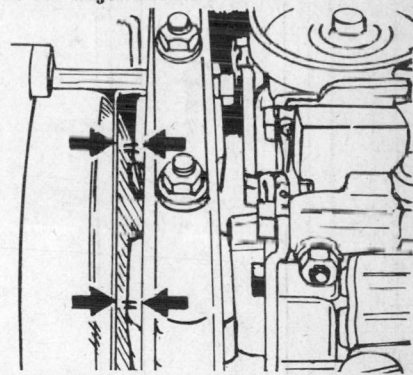

Checking the position of the engine carrier

27. Install the rubber transmission mount bolts with spacers of the correct thickness. The purpose of the spacers is to center the rubber buffer vertically in its support tube. The buffer is not supposed to carry any weight; it absorbs torsional forces only.
28. To locate the buffer horizontally in its locating tube, the engine carrier must be vertical and parallel to the fan housing. It is adjusted by moving the engine carrier bolts in elongated slots. Further travel may be obtained by moving the brackets attached to the body. It may be necessary to adjust the two rear suspension wishbones with the center of the transmission after the rubber buffer is horizontally centered. Take the car to a dealer or alignment specialist to align the rear suspension.

29. Adjust the selector lever cable.

30. Connect the wire to the kickdown switch.

31. Install the rear axles. Make sure the lockwashers are placed with the convex side out.

32. Reconnect the fuel hoses and heat exchanger hoses. Install the pipe for the heater booster.

33. Lower the car and pull the engine compartment seal into place with the cord.

34. Reconnect the fuel injection and engine wiring. Push the starter wires through the engine cover plate and connect the wires to the starter.

35. Install the intake duct with the fan and hoses, also the cooling air intake.

PAN REMOVAL AND INSTALLATION

1. Some models have a drain plug in the pan. Remove the plug and drain the transmission. On models without the plug, loosen the pan bolts 2–3 turns and lower one corner of the pan to drain.

2. Remove the pan bolts and remove the pan from the transmission.

NOTE: It may be necessary to tap the pan with a rubber hammer to loosen it.

3. Use a new gasket and install the pan. Tighten the bolts loosely until the pan is properly in place, then tighten the bolts fully, moving in a diagonal pattern.

NOTE: Do not overtighten the bolts.

4. Refill the transmission with ATF.

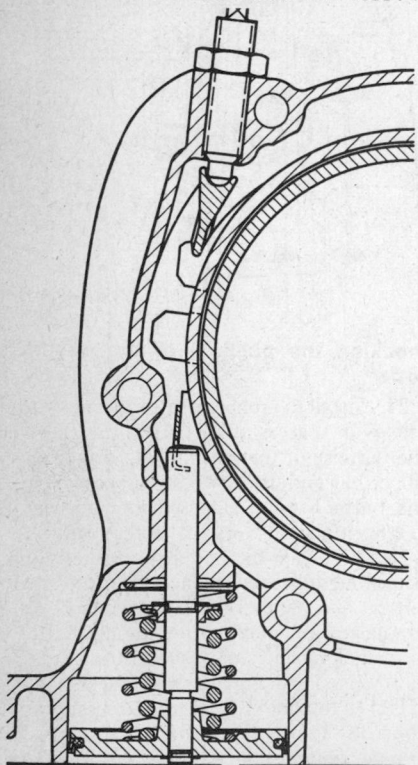

Front band assembly adjustment screw at top

C976

5. At 5 minute intervals, retighten the pan bolts two or three times.

FILTER SERVICE

The Volkswagen automatic transmission has a filter screen secured by a screw to the bottom of the valve body. Remove the pan and remove the filter screen from the valve body.

——— CAUTION ———

Never use a cloth that will leave the slightest bit of lint in the transmission when cleaning transmission parts. The lint will expand when exposed to transmission fluid and clog the valve body and filter.

Clean the filter screen with compressed air.

FRONT (SECOND) BAND ADJUSTMENT

Tighten the front band adjusting screw to 7 ft. lbs. Then loosen the screw and tighten it to 3.5 ft. lbs. From this position, loosen the screw exactly 1¾–2 turns and tighten the locknut.

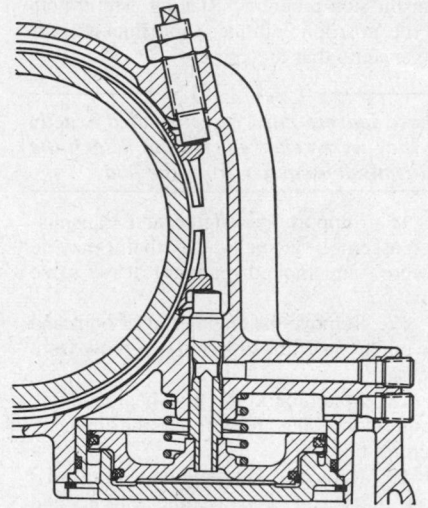

Rear band assembly adjustment screw at top

REAR (FIRST) BAND ADJUSTMENT

Tighten the rear band adjusting screw to 7 ft. lbs. Then loosen the screw and retighten it to 3.5 ft. lbs. From this position, loosen the screw exactly 3¼–3½ turns and tighten the locknut.

SHIFT LINKAGE ADJUSTMENT

Make sure the shifting cable is not kinked or bent and that the linkage and cable are properly lubricated.

1. Move the gear shift lever to the Park position.

2. Loosen the clamp which holds the

front and rear halves of the shifting rod together. Loosen the clamping bolts on the transmission lever.

3. Press the lever on the transmission rearward as far as possible. Spring pressure will be felt. The manual valve must be on the stop in the valve body.

4. Holding the transmission lever against its stop, tighten the clamping bolt.

5. Holding the rear shifting rod half, push the front half forward to take up any clearance and tighten the clamp bolt.

6. Test the shift pattern.

REAR SUSPENSION

Diagonal Arm Suspension—Types 1 and 2 (Except Vanagon)

DIAGONAL ARM REMOVAL AND INSTALLATION

1. Remove the wheel shaft nuts.

——— CAUTION ———

Do not raise the car to remove the nuts. They can be safely removed only if the weight on the car is on its wheels.

2. Disconnect the driveshaft of the side to be removed.

3. Remove the lower shock absorber mount. Raise the car and remove the wheel and tire.

4. Remove the brake drum, disconnect the brake lines and emergency brake cable, and remove the backing plate.

5. Matchmark the torsion bar plate and the diagonal arm with a cold chisel.

6. Remove the four bolts and nuts which secure the plate to the diagonal arm.

7. Remove the pivot bolts for the diagonal arm and remove the arm from the car.

NOTE: Take careful note of the washers at the pivot bolts. These washers are used to determine alignment and they must be put back in the same place.

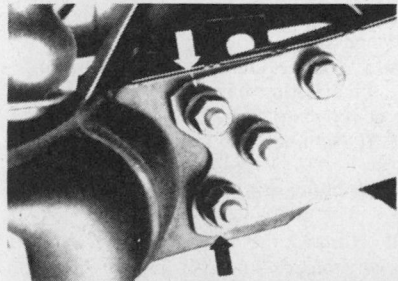

Matchmark the torsion bar and diagonal arm with a cold chisel

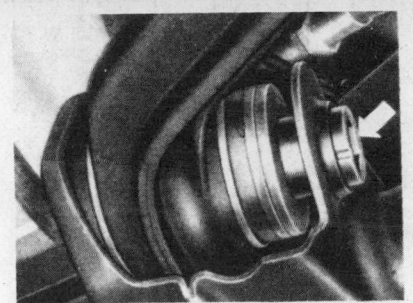

Proper positioning of the diagonal arm pivot bolt with both spacer washers on the outside

8. Remove the spring plate hub cover.

9. Using a steel bar, lift the spring plate off the lower suspension stop.

10. On Type 1, remove the five bolts at the front of the fender. On all others, remove the cover in the side of the fender.

11. Remove the spring plate and pull the torsion bar out of its housing.

NOTE: There are left and right torsion bars designated by an (L) or (R) on the end face. (Coat any rubber bushings with talcum powder upon installation. Do not use graphite, silicon, or grease.)

12. To install, insert the torsion bar, outer bushing, and spring plate. The torsion bar is properly adjusted when the spring plate, with no load, is the specified number of degrees below a horizontal position.

13. Using two bolts, loosely secure the spring plate hub cover. Place a thick nut between the leaves of the spring plate.

14. Lift the spring plate up to the lower suspension stop and install the remaining bolts into the hub cover. Tighten the hub cover bolts.

15. Install the diagonal arm pivot bolt and washers and peen it with a chisel. There must always be at least one washer on the outside end of the bolt.

16. Align the chisel marks and attach the diagonal arm to the spring plate.

17. Install the backing plate, parking brake cable, and brake lines.

18. Reconnect the shock absorber. Install the brake drum and wheel shaft nuts.

19. Reconnect the drive shaft. Bleed the brakes.

20. Install the wheel and tire.

21. Check the suspension alignment.

Trailing Arm Suspension—Vanagon

TRAILING ARM REMOVAL AND INSTALLATION

1. Raise the rear of the car and support it with jack stands.

2. Remove the wheel and then disconnect the brake line from the wheel cylinder.

3. Unbolt the driveshaft at the transaxle side.

4. Unscrew the four wheel hub mounting bolts and remove it along with the driveshaft.

NOTE: Removal of the brake drum may provide better access to the wheel hub mounting bolts.

5. Place a floor jack under the trailing arm to hold its position and then remove the upper and lower shock absorber retaining bolts and remove the shock absorber.

6. Lower the trailing arm until you can remove the coil spring. Note the positioning of the upper spring plate and the lower spring seat.

7. Unscrew the two trailing arm mounting bolts and then remove the trailing arm.

8. Installation is in the reverse order of removal. When installing the coil spring, be sure that the contours for the end of the spring in the seat and the trailing arm are aligned. Also, turn the spring plate so that the end of the spring fits into the depression on the plate.

9. Adjust the camber and toe.

Shock Absorber

REMOVAL & INSTALLATION

Diagonal Arm Suspension

The shock absorber is secured at the top and bottom by a through bolt. Raise the car and remove the bolts. Remove the shock absorber from the car.

Trailing Arm Suspension

Procedures for removing the shock absorbers are detailed in the "Trailing Arm Removal and Installation" section.

Coil Spring

REMOVAL & INSTALLATION

Vanagon Only

Procedures for removing the coil spring are detailed in the "Trailing Arm Removal and Installation" section.

Rear Suspension Adjustments

TYPE 1, DIAGONAL ARM SUSPENSION

The only adjustment is the toe-in adjustment. The adjustment is performed by varying the number of washers at the diagonal arm pivot. There must always be

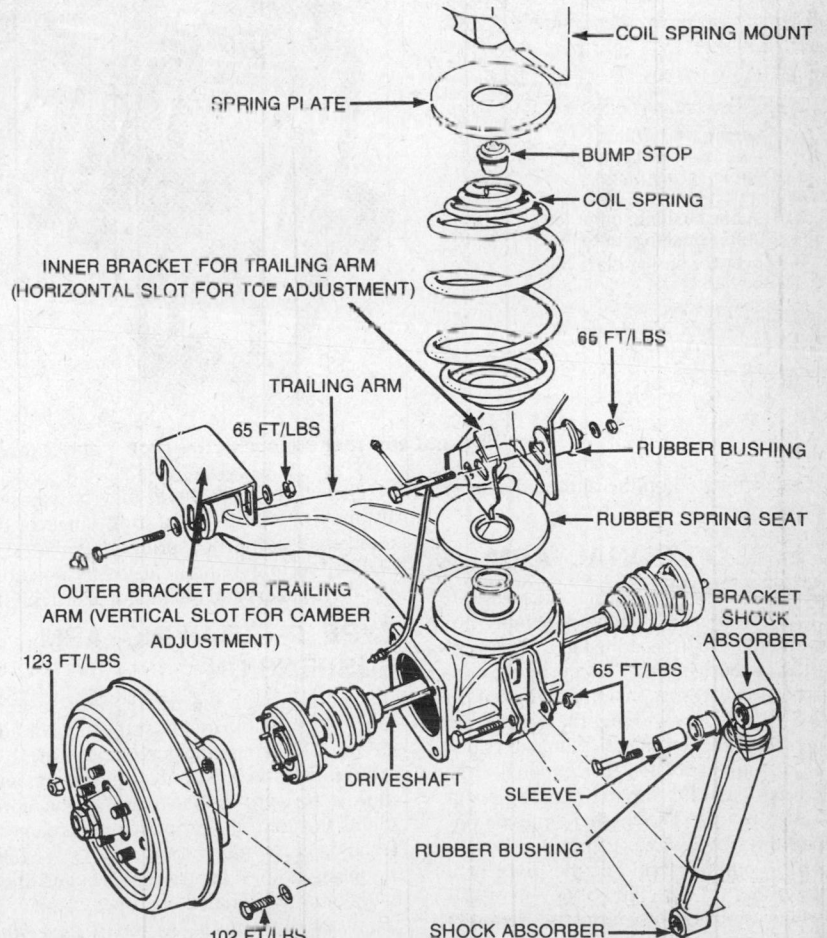

Exploded view of the Vanagon rear suspension

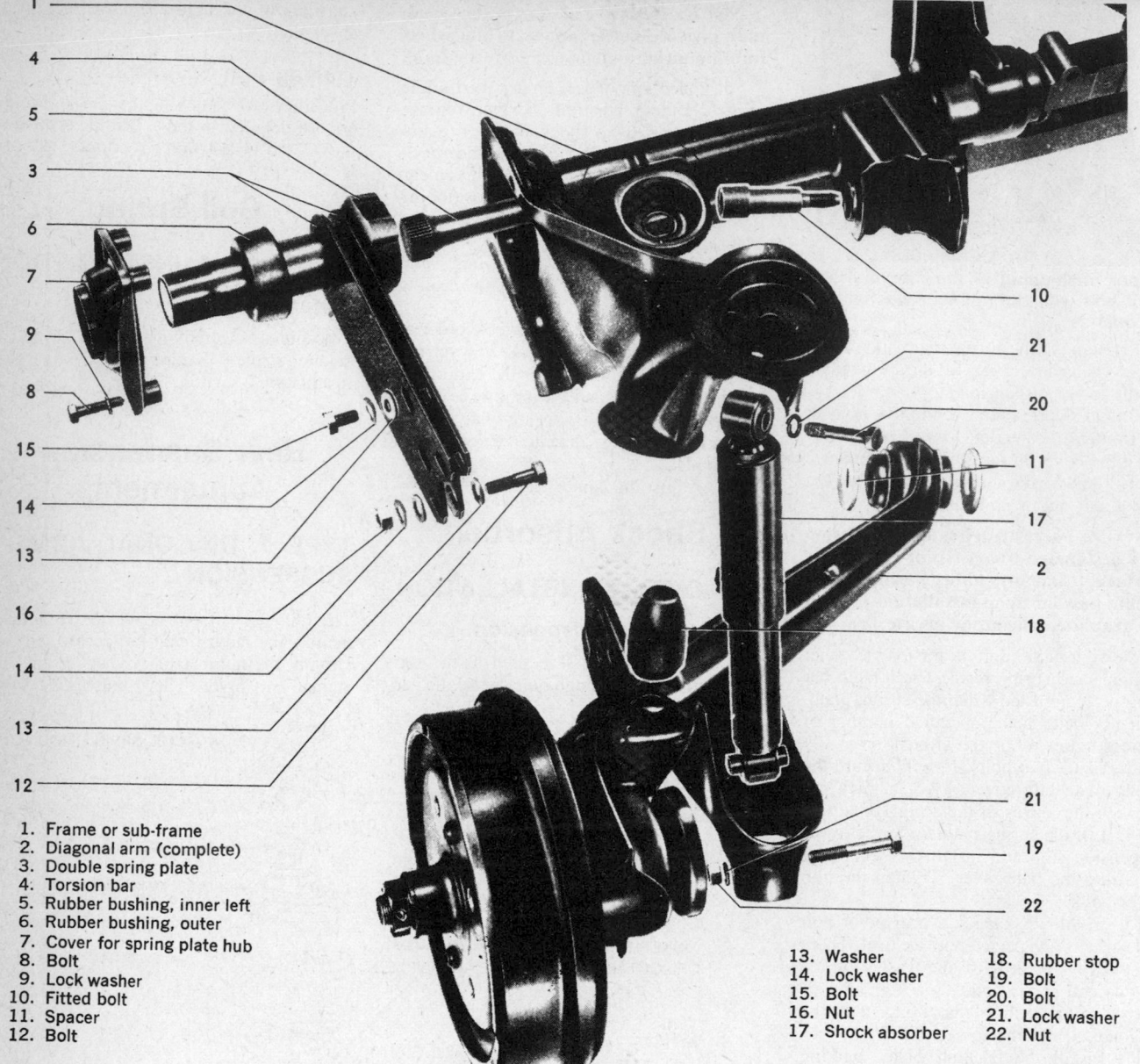

1. Frame or sub-frame
2. Diagonal arm (complete)
3. Double spring plate
4. Torsion bar
5. Rubber bushing, inner left
6. Rubber bushing, outer
7. Cover for spring plate hub
8. Bolt
9. Lock washer
10. Fitted bolt
11. Spacer
12. Bolt
13. Washer
14. Lock washer
15. Bolt
16. Nut
17. Shock absorber
18. Rubber stop
19. Bolt
20. Bolt
21. Lock washer
22. Nut

Diagonal arm rear suspension—Type 1 and 2 (except Vanagon)

one washer located on the outboard side of the pivot.

TYPE 2, DIAGONAL ARM SUSPENSION

The transmission and engine assembly position in the vehicle is adjustable. It is necessary that the assembly be correctly centered before the suspension is aligned. It may be adjusted by moving the engine and transmission brackets in their elongated slots.

The distance between the diagonal arms may be adjusted by moving the washers at the A-arm pivots. The washers may be positioned only two ways. Either both washers on the outboard side of the pivot or a single washer on each side of the pivot. To adjust the distance, position the diagonal arms and move the washers in the same manner at both pivots.

The wheel track angle may be adjusted by moving the diagonal arm flange in the elongated slot in the spring plate.

The toe-in may be adjusted by positioning the washers and the diagonal arm pivot.

TYPE 2—TRAILING ARM SUSPENSION

On vehicles with the trailing arm suspension, it is possible to adjust the camber and the toe. To adjust the toe, loosen the INSIDE mounting bolt on the trailing arm and slide it forward or backward in the horizontal slot until the proper toe is achieved. To adjust the camber, loosen the OUTSIDE mounting bolt on the trailing arm and slide it up or down until the proper camber is achieved. Being careful not to move the bolts, tighten them both to 65 ft. lbs. after adjustment.

FRONT SUSPENSION

Torsion Bar Suspension—Types 1 and 2 (Except Super Beetle and Beetle Convertible)

TORSION BAR REMOVAL AND INSTALLATION

1. Jack up the car and remove both wheels and brake drums.

A notched ball joint on a car with a torsion bar suspension indicates that it is oversized

2. Remove the ball joint nuts and remove the left and right steering knuckles. A forked ball joint removing tool is available at an auto parts store.

─────── **CAUTION** ───────
Never strike the ball joint stud.

3. Remove those arms attached to the torsion bars on one side only. To remove the arms, loosen and remove the arm setscrew and pull the arm off the end of the torsion bar.

4. Loosen and remove the setscrew which secures the torsion bar to the torsion bar housing.

5. Pull the torsion bar out of its housing.

6. To install, carefully note the number of leaves and the position of the countersink marks for the torsion bar and the torsion arm.

7. Align the countersink mark in the center of the bar with the hole for the setscrew and insert the torsion bar into its housing. Install the torsion arm.

8. Reverse Steps 1–3 to complete.

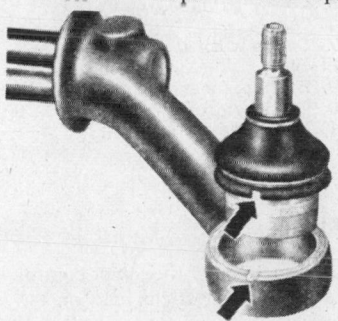

Align the square notch in the ball joint with the notch in the torsion bar upon installation

TORSION ARM REMOVAL AND INSTALLATION

1. Jack up the car and remove the wheel and tire.

2. Remove the brake drum and the steering knuckle.

3. If the lower torsion arm is being removed, disconnect the stabilizer bar. To remove the stabilizer bar clamp, tap the wedge shaped keeper toward the outside of the car or in the direction the narrow end of the keeper is pointing.

4. Back off on the setscrew locknut and remove the setscrew.

5. Slide the torsion arm off the end of the torsion bar.

6. Reverse the above steps to install. Check the camber and toe-in settings.

Strut Suspension— Super Beetle, Beetle Convertible

SUSPENSION STRUT REMOVAL & INSTALLATION

NOTE: For all strut overhaul procedures, please refer to ''Strut Overhaul'' in the Unit Repair section.

1. Jack up the car and remove the wheel and tire.

2. If the left strut is to be removed, remove the speedometer cable from the steering knuckle.

3. Disconnect the brake line from the bracket on the strut.

4. At the base of the strut, bend down the locking tabs for the three bolts and remove the bolts.

5. Push down on the steering knuckle and pull the strut out of the knuckle.

6. Remove the three nuts which secure the top of the strut to the body. Before removing the last nut, support the strut so that it does not fall out of the car.

7. Reverse the above steps to install the strut. Always use new nuts and locking tabs during installation.

TRACK CONTROL ARM REMOVAL & INSTALLATION

1. Remove the ball joint stud nut and remove the stud from the control arm.

2. Disconnect the stabilizer bar from the control arm.

3. Remove the nut and eccentric bolt at the frame. This is the pivot bolt for the control arm and is used to adjust camber.

4. Pull the arm downward and remove it from the vehicle.

5. Reverse the above steps to install. Make sure the groove in the stabilizer bar bushing is horizontal.

6. Realign the front end.

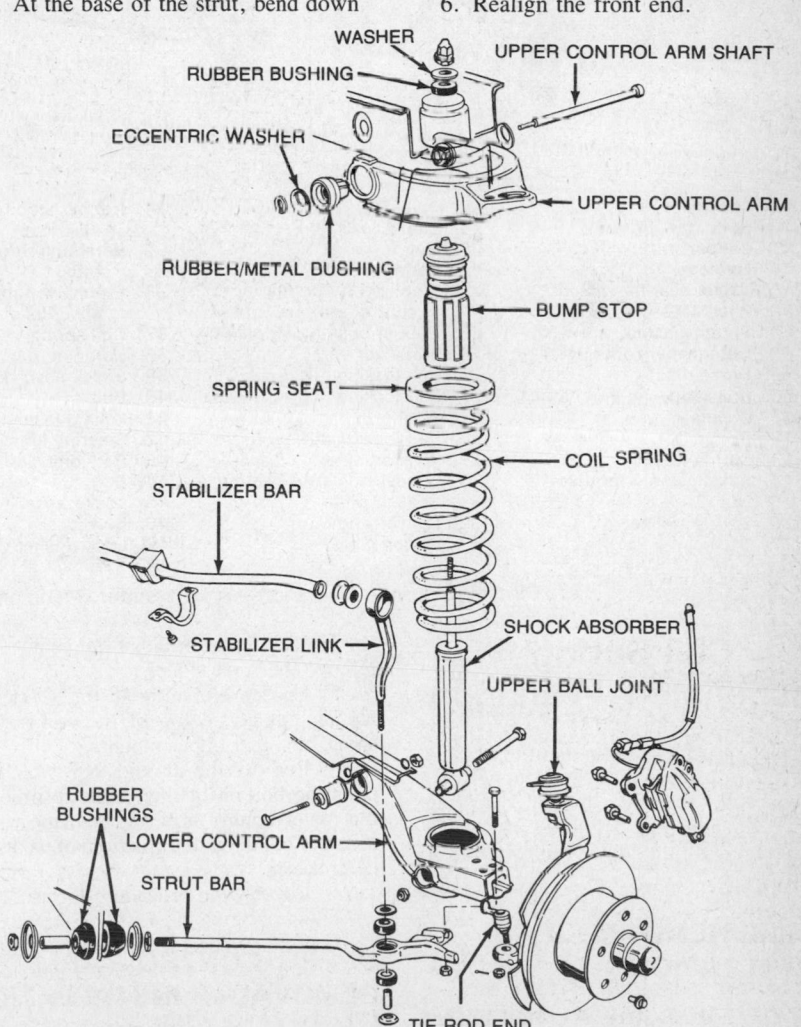

Exploded view of the Vanagon front suspension

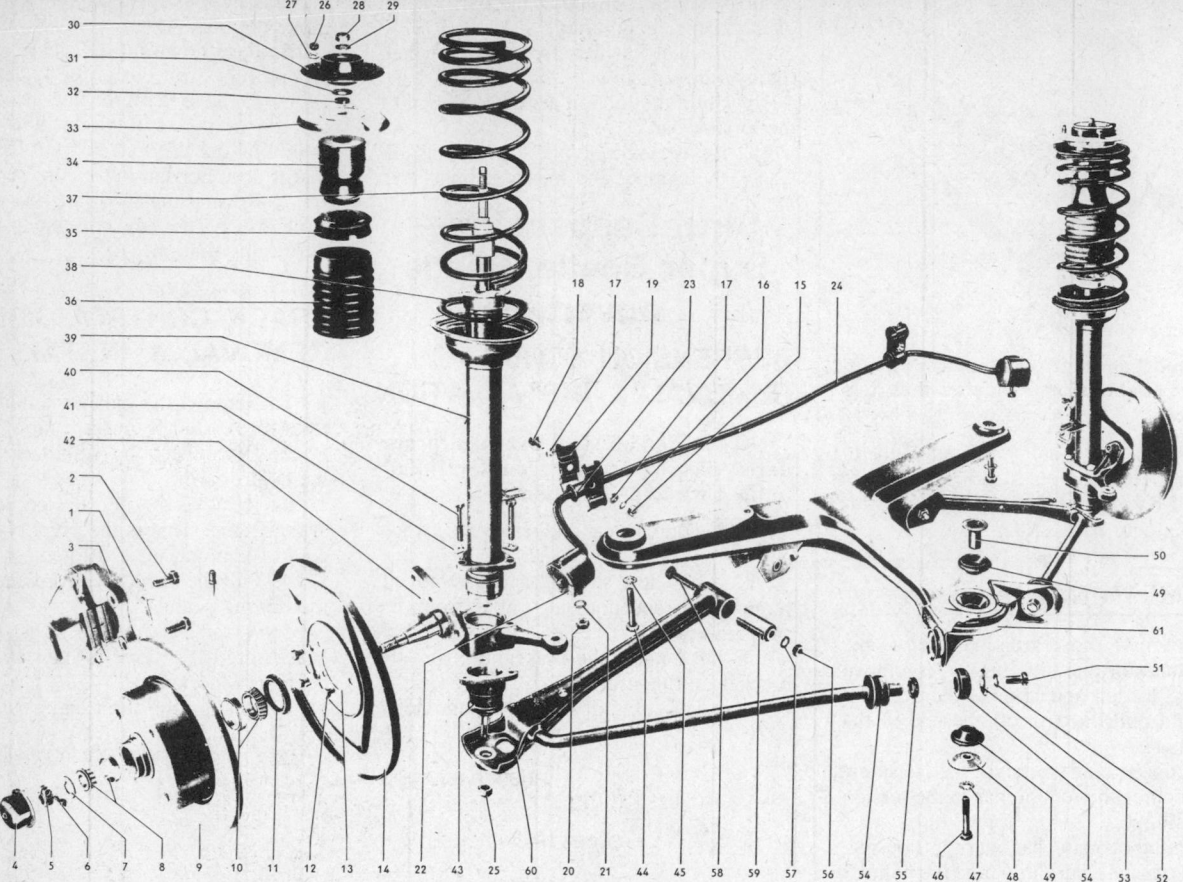

1. Lockplate
2. Bolt
3. Caliper
4. Hub cap
5. Wheel bearing locknut
6. Allen screw for locknut
7. Thrust washer
8. Outer taper roller bearing
9. Brake disc
10. Inner taper roller bearing
11. Oil seal
12. Bolt
13. Spring washer
14. Splash shield for disc
15. Nut
16. Spring washer
17. Washer

18. Bolt
19. Clamp for stabilizer bar
20. Nut
21. Spring washer
22. Stabilizer mounting for control arm
23. Rubber bushing for clamp
24. Stabilizer bar
25. Self-locking nut
26. Self-locking nut
27. Washer
28. Self-locking nut
29. Washer, small
30. Suspension strut bearing
31. Sealing plate
32. Spacer ring
33. Spring plate

34. Rubber stop for shock absorber
35. Retaining ring for protective tube
36. Protective tube for shock absorber
37. Coil spring
38. Damping ring, coil spring
39. Shock absorber
40. Bolt
41. Lock washer
42. Steering knuckle
43. Ball joint
44. Bolt
45. Lock washer
46. Bolt
47. Lock washer

48. Seat for damping ring
49. Damping ring for front axle carrier
50. Spacer sleeve
51. Bolt
52. Spring washer
53. Plate for damping ring
54. Damping ring for radius rod
55. Locating ring for radius rod
56. Nut
57. Spring washer
58. Bolt
59. Bushing for track control arm
60. Track control arm
61. Front axle carrier

Strut type front suspension—Type 1 Super Beetle and Beetle Convertible

Coil Spring Suspension—Vanagon

The front suspension consists of upper and lower control arms, a separate upper coil spring/shock absorber mount, steering knuckle and attaching ball joints and a strut arm mounted on the lower control arm for stability.

STRUT REMOVAL & INSTALLATION

NOTE: For all strut overhaul procedures, please refer to "Strut Overhaul" in the Unit Repair section.

1. Jack up the front of the vehicle and remove the front wheel.
2. Loosen and remove the single retaining nut at the top of the coil spring/shock absorber upper mount.
3. Remove the through bolt which retains the bottom of the shock absorber to the lower control arm and pull the shock absorber out through the bottom of the lower control arm.
4. Reverse the procedure to install.

UPPER CONTROL ARM REMOVAL & INSTALLATION

1. Jack up the vehicle and remove the front wheel.

2. Place a jack under the lower control arm and raise to put a slight load on the coil spring.
3. Free the upper ball joint from the steering knuckle.
4. Remove the upper control arm to frame mounting bolt and remove the control arm.
5. Reverse procedure to install. Check and adjust wheel alignment.

LOWER CONTROL ARM REMOVAL & INSTALLATION

1. Jack up the vehicle and remove the wheel.
2. Remove the coil spring.
3. Remove the lower control arm to

1. Nut
2. Spring washer
3. Washer
4. Bolt
5. Nut
6. Spring washer
7. Bolt
8. Support for axle
9. Bolt
10. Spring washer
11. Plate
12. Rubber packing, upper
13. Rubber packing, lower
14. Bolt
15. Spring washer
16. Lock washer
17. Dust cap
18. Clamp nut for wheel bearing
19. Socket hd. screw for clamp nut
20. Thrust washer
21. Outer tapered roller bearing
22. Brake drum
23. Oil seal
24. Inner tapered roller bearing
25. Bolt
26. Spring washer
27. Front wheel brake and backing plate
28. Steering knuckle
29. Retainer, small
30. Retainer, large
31. Clip, small
32. Clip, large
33. Plate, small
34. Plate, large
35. Rubber mounting, small
36. Rubber mounting, large
37. Stabilizer bar
38. Self-locking nut
39. Washer, small
40. Washer, large
41. Eccentric bushing for camber adjustment
42. Upper ball joint
43. Lower ball joint
44. Ring for rubber boot
45. Boot for lower joint
46. Boot for upper joint
47. Ring for rubber boot
48. Plug
49. Locknut
50. Setscrew for torsion bar
51. Torsion arm, upper
52. Torsion arm, lower
53. Pin
54. Pin for shock absorber
55. Nut
56. Lock washer
57. Lock washer
58. Nut
59. Plate for damper bushing
60. Damper bushing
61. Pin for buffer
62. Buffer
63. Tube
54. Shock absorber
65. Sleeve for rubber bushing
66. Rubber bushing
67. Torsion bar—10 leaf
68. Seal for upper torsion arm
69. Seal for lower torsion arm
70. Needle bearing, upper
71. Needle bearing, lower
72. Grease fitting
74. Axle
75. Bolt

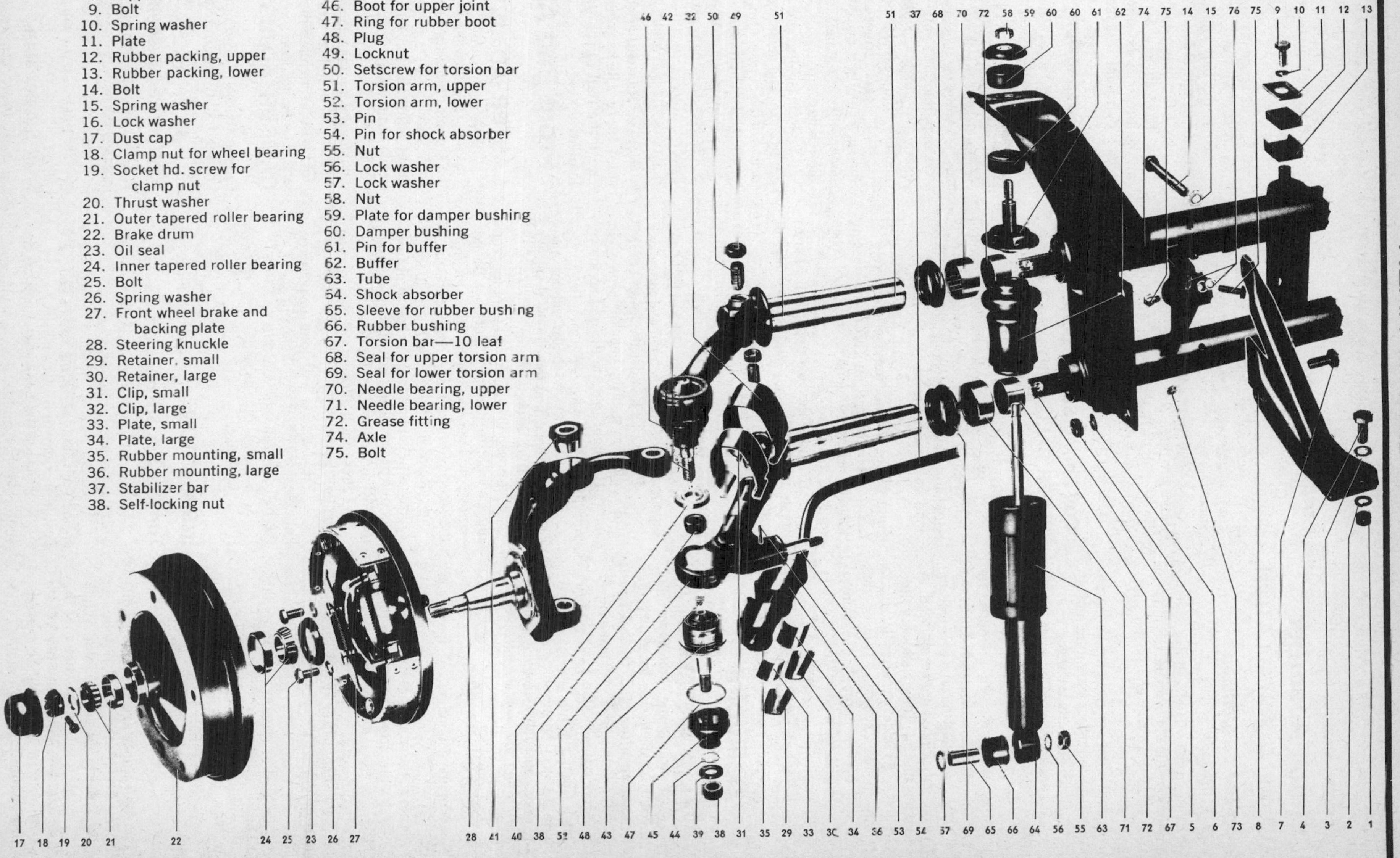

Types 1 and 2 torsion bar front suspension

C981

frame mounting bolt and remove the control arm.

4. Reverse procedure to install.

Shock Absorber

REMOVAL & INSTALLATION

Torsion Bar Suspension (Types 1 and 2)

1. Remove the wheel and tire.

2. Remove the nut from the torsion arm stud and slide the lower end of the shock off the stud.

3. Remove the nut from the shock absorber shaft at the upper mounting and remove the shock from the vehicle.

4. The shock is tested by operating it by hand. As the shock is extended and compressed, it should operate smoothly over its entire stroke with an even pressure. Its damping action should be clearly felt at the end of each stroke. If the shock is leaking slightly, the shock need not be replaced. A shock that has had an excessive loss of fluid will have flat spots in the stroke as the shock is compressed and extended. That is, the pressure will feel as through it has been suddenly released for a short distance during the stroke.

5. Installation is the reverse of Steps 1–3.

Ball Joint

REMOVAL & INSTALLATION

Vehicles with strut suspension have only one ball joint on each side located at the base of the strut in the track control arm. Vehicles with torsion bar suspension have two ball joints on each side located at the end of each torsion arm.

Vehicles with coil spring suspension have two ball joints on each side located at the ends of the upper and lower control arms.

Torsion Bar Suspension

1. Jack up the car and remove the wheel and tire.

2. Remove the brake drum and disconnect the brake line from the backing plate.

3. Remove the nut from each ball joint stud and remove the ball joint stud from the steering knuckle. Remove the steering knuckle from the car. Do not strike the ball joint stud.

4. Remove the torsion arm from the torsion bar.

5. Remove the ball joint from the torsion arm by pressing it out.

6. Press a new ball joint in, making sure that the square notch in the joint is in line with the notch in the torsion arm eye.

NOTE: Ball joints are supplied in different sizes designated by V-notches in the ring around the side of the joint. When replacing a ball joint, make sure that the new part has the same number of V-notches. If it has no notches, the replacement joint should have no notches.

7. Reverse Steps 1–4 to complete the installation.

Strut Suspension

1. Jack up the car and remove the wheel and tire.

2. Remove the nut from the ball joint stud and remove the stud from the track control arm.

3. Bend back the locking tab and remove the three ball joint securing screws.

4. Pull the track control arm downward and remove the ball joint from the strut.

5. Reverse the above steps to install.

Coil Spring Suspension

UPPER BALL JOINT

1. Raise the vehicle and support it on jack stands, then remove the wheel.

2. Place a jack under the lower control arm as close to the steering knuckle as possible and jack up just enough to put a slight load on the coil spring.

3. Loosen the steering knuckle-to-ball joint nut but do not remove completely.

4. Free the ball joint from the steering knuckle using a ball joint removal tool. Then remove the nut.

5. Remove the two upper ball joint to upper control arm bolts and remove the ball joint.

6. Reverse procedure to install. Check wheel alignment.

LOWER BALL JOINT

1. Jack up the front of the vehicle and support it on stands, then remove the wheel.

2. Place a jack under the lower control arm as close to steering knuckle as possible and put a slight load on the coil spring by jacking up the jack.

3. Disconnect the brake caliper hose form the caliper, and remove the brake caliper and rotor if they are in the way.

4. Loosen the upper ball joint to steering knuckle to ball joint nut, but do not remove it. Free the upper ball joint from the steering knuckle and remove the nut.

5. Remove the lower ball joint to lower control arm nut and free the ball joint from the control arm using a ball joint removal tool. Remove the steering knuckle.

6. Press the ball joint off the steering knuckle.

7. Press a new ball joint in place on knuckle, observing any alignment marks on the ball joint and the knuckle.

8. Reverse the procedure to install. Bleed the brakes.

INSPECTION

Torsion Bar Suspension

1. A quick initial inspection can be made with the vehicle on the ground.

2. Grasp the top of the tire and vigorously pull the top of the tire in and out. Test both sides in this manner.

3. If the ball joints are excessively worn, there will be an audible tap as the ball moves

around in its socket. Excess play can sometimes be felt through the tire.

4. A more rigorous test may be performed by jacking the car under the lower torsion arm and inserting a lever under the tire.

5. Lift up gently on the lever so as to pry the tire upward.

6. If the ball joints are worn, the tire will move upward $\frac{1}{8}$–$\frac{1}{4}$ in. or more.

7. If the tire displays excessive movement, have an assistant inspect each joint, as the tire is pried upward, to determine which ball joint is defective.

Strut Suspension

1. Raise the car and support it under the frame. The wheel must be clear of the ground.

2. With a lever, apply upward pressure to the track control arm.

3. Apply the pressure gently and slowly; it is important that only enough pressure be exerted to check the play in the ball joint and not compress the suspension.

4. Using a vernier caliper, measure the distance between the control arm and the lower edge of the ball joint flange. Record the reading.

5. Release the pressure on the track control arm and again measure the distance between the control arm and the lower edge of the ball joint flange.

6. Record the reading.

7. Subtract the higher reading from the lower reading. If the difference is more than 0.10 in., the ball joint should be replaced.

NOTE: Remember that even in a new joint there will be measureable play because the ball in the ball joint is spring loaded.

Front End Alignment

CASTER ADJUSTMENT

Caster is the forward or backward tilt of the spindle. Forward tilt is negative caster and backward tilt is positive caster. Caster is not adjustable on either the torsion bar or the strut suspensions.

Caster on the coil spring suspension is adjusted by moving the strut bar. Loosen the locknut and then turn the adjusting nut clockwise to increase the caster and counterclockwise to decrease the caster.

CAMBER ADJUSTMENT

Camber is the tilt of the top of the wheel, inward or outward, from true vertical. Outward tilt is positive, inward tilt is negative.

Torsion Bar Suspension

The upper ball joint on each side is mounted in an eccentric bushing. The bushing has a hex head and it may be rotated in either direction using a wrench.

Strut Suspension

The track control arm pivots on an eccentric

bolt. Camber is adjusted by loosening the nut and rotating the bolt.

Coil Spring Suspension

The upper control arm pivots on an eccentric bolt. To adjust the camber, loosen the retaining nut and rotate the bolt.

TOE-IN ADJUSTMENT

Toe-in is the adjustment made to make the front wheels point slightly into the front. Toe-in is adjusted on all types of front suspensions by adjusting the length of the tie-rod sleeves.

STEERING

Steering Wheel

REMOVAL & INSTALLATION

1. Disconnect the negative battery cable.
2. Remove the center emblem. This emblem will gently pry off the wheel, or is attached by screws from the back of the steering wheel.
3. Remove the nut from the steering shaft. This is a right hand thread

NOTE: Mark the steering shaft and steering wheel so that the wheel may be installed in the same position on the shaft.

4 Using a steering wheel puller, remove the wheel from the splined steering shaft. Do not strike the end of the steering shaft.
5. Reverse the above steps to install. Make sure to align the matchmarks made on the steering wheel and steering shaft. The gap between the turn signal switch housing and the back of the wheel is 0.08–0.12 in. (0.08–0.159 for Vanagon). Install the switch with the lever on the central position.

Turn Signal Switch

REMOVAL & INSTALLATION

1. Disconnect the negative battery cable.
2. Remove the steering wheel.
3. Remove the four turn signal switch securing screws.
4. Disconnect the turn signal switch wiring plug under the steering column.
5. Pull the switch and wiring guide rail up and out of the steering column.
6. Reverse the above steps to install. Make sure the spacers located behind the switch, if installed originally, are in position. The distance between the steering wheel and the steering column housing is 0.08–0.12 in. (0.08–0.159 for Vanagon). Install the switch with the lever on the central position.

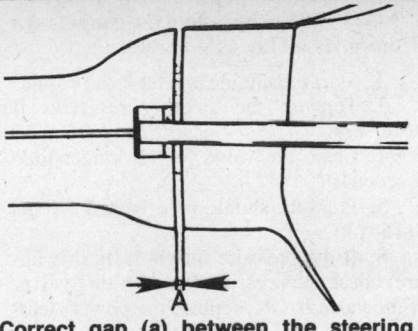

Correct gap (a) between the steering wheel and column

Ignition Switch

REMOVAL & INSTALLATION

Type 1 and 2 (Except Vanagon)

Disconnect the steering column wiring at the block located behind the instrument panel and pull the column wiring harness into the passenger compartment.

1. Remove the steering wheel.
2. Remove the circlip on the steering shaft.
3. Insert the key and turn the switch to the ON position.
4. Remove the three securing screws and slide the switch assembly from the steering column tube.
5. After removing the wiring retainer, press the ignition switch wiring block upward and out of the housing and disconnect the wiring.
6. Remove the lock cylinder and the steering lock mechanism.
7. Remove the ignition switch screw and pull the ignition switch rearward.
8. Reverse the above steps to install.
When reinstalling the turn signal switch, make sure the lever is in the center position.

Vanagon

1. Disconnect the negative battery terminal.
2. Remove the steering wheel.
3. Loosen the mounting screws and then remove the upper and lower steering column trim.
4. Unscrew the four retaining bolts and then pull off the steering column switch.
5. Loosen the steering lock housing clamp bolt and pull the assembly up and out slightly.

Turn signal switch retaining screws

6. Disconnect the wiring and remove the steering lock housing.
7. Unscrew the ignition switch screw and pull out the switch.
8. Installation is in the reverse order of removal.

Ignition Lock Cylinder

REMOVAL & INSTALLATION

1. Remove the ignition switch.
2. With the key in the cylinder and turned to the ON position, pull the lock cylinder out far enough so the securing pin can be depressed through a hole in the side of the lock cylinder housing.

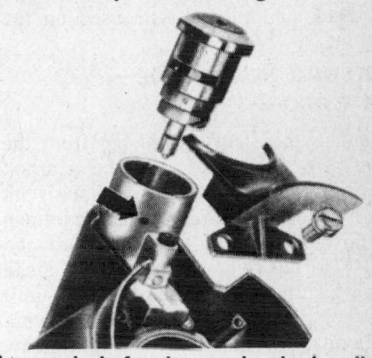

Access hole for depressing lock cylinder retaining pin

3. As the pin is depressed, gently push the cylinder into its housing. Make sure the pin engages correctly and that the retainer fits easily in place. Do not force any parts together; when they are correctly aligned, they will fit easily together.

Steering Linkage

REMOVAL & INSTALLATION

1. All tie-ends are secured by a nut which holds the tapered tie-rod end stud into a matching tapered hole. There are several ways to remove the tapered stud from its hole after the nut has been removed.
2. First, there are several types of removal tools available from auto parts stores. These tools include directions for their use. One of the most commonly available tools is the fork shaped tool which is a wedge that is forced under the tie-rod end. This tool should be used with caution because instead of removing the tie-rod end from its hole it may pull the ball out of its socket, ruining the tie-rod end.
3. It is also possible to remove the tie-rod end by holding a heavy hammer on one side of the tapered hole and striking the opposite side of the hole sharply with another hammer. The stud will pop out of its hole, usually.

— CAUTION —
Never strike the end of the tie-rod stud. It is impossible to remove the tie-rod end in this manner.

4. Once the tie-rod end stud has been removed, turn the tie-rod end out of the adjustment sleeve.

5. On the pieces of the steering linkage that are not used to adjust the toe-in, the tie-rod end is welded in place and it will be necessary to replace the whole assembly.

6. When reassembling the steering linkage, never put lubricant in the tapered hole.

MANUAL STEERING GEAR ADJUSTMENT

There are two types of steering gear boxes. The first type is the roller type, identified by the square housing cover secured by four screws, one at each corner. The second type is the rack and pinion type used on the Vanagon.

Worm and Roller Type—Type 1 and 2

Disconnect the steering linkage from the pitman arm and make sure the gearbox mounting bolts are tight. Have an assistant rotate the steering wheel so that the pitman arm move alternately 10° to the left and then 10° to the right of the straight ahead position. Turn the adjusting screw in until no further play can be felt while moving the pitman arm. Tighten the adjusting screw locknut and recheck the adjustment.

Rack and Pinion Type—Vanagon

The steering gear on the Vanagon is not adjustable. If problems develop, the gear must be replaced.

Power Steering System

CHECKING FOR LEAKS

Vanagon
1984 AND LATER

1. With the engine running, rotate the steering wheel lock-to-lock and hold it in position no longer than 5 seconds.

2. Check all line connections and tighten them if necessary.

3. If the steering pinion is leaking, replace the valve housing seal, the pinion housing seal, and the O-ring between the valve housing and pinion housing.

4. If the steering rack seals are leaking (check by pulling the boot off the steering gear), disassemble the steering gear and replace all sealing components.

5. Check the power steering pump for leaks.

NOTE: Always change the reservoir filter whenever the fluid is changed.

PRESSURE CHECK

1. Connect a pressure gauge between the pressure line and the valve housing, with the gauge valve in the open position.

NOTE: When installing the gauge, turn it upwards as far as possible.

2. Start the engine and let it run at idle.

3. Top up the steering reservoir if necessary.

4. Close the valve for no longer than 5 seconds.

5. Pressure should read 1668-1740 psi (115–120 bar).

6. If the pressure differs from this figure, check the pressure/flow limiting valve. If the valve is OK, replace the power steering pump.

BLEEDING

1. Fill the power steering reservoir to MAX with ATF (automatic transmission fluid).

2. Jack up the front of the vehicle so the wheels clear the ground. Safely support the vehicle with jackstands.

3. With the engine off, rotate the steering wheel from lock to lock.

4. Top up the reservoir with ATF to the MAX mark.

5. Start the engine briefly several times, switching OFF immediately after the engine starts. Add ATF as necessary, maintaining the level at the MAX mark.

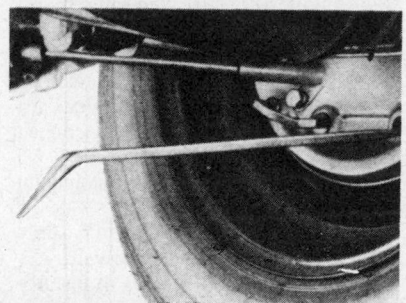

Adjusting drum brakes through the access hole in the backing plate; rear brakes shown

---
— CAUTION —
Never let the reservoir to be pumped dry.

---

6. When the ATF level no longer drops, start and run the engine. Rotate the steering wheel lock to lock several times. Check that no bubbles appear in the reservoir, and that the level remains steady.

BRAKES

NOTE: For all brake system repair and service procedures not detailed below, please refer to "Brakes" in the Unit Repair section.

Brake Adjustment

Disc brakes are self adjusting, and cannot be adjusted by hand. As the pads wear, they will automatically compensate for the wear by moving closer to the disc, maintaining the proper operating clearance.

Drum brakes, however, must be manually adjusted to take up excess clearance as the shoes wear.

1. To adjust drum brakes, both front and rear, it is necessary to raise the car and support it on a jack stand. The wheel must spin freely.

2. On the backing plate there are four inspection holes with a rubber plug in each hole. Two of the holes are for checking the thickness of the brake lining and the other two are used for adjustment.

NOTE: There is an adjustment for each brake shoe. That means that on each wheel it is necessary to make two adjustments, one for each shoe on that wheel.

3. Remove the adjustment hole plugs and, using a screwdriver or brake adjusting tool, insert the tool into the hole.

4. Turn the star wheel until a slight drag is noticed as the wheel is rotated by hand.

5. Back off on the star wheel 3–4 notches so that the wheel turns freely.

6. Perform the same adjustment on the other shoe.

NOTE: One of the star wheels in each wheel has left-hand threads and the other star wheel has right-hand threads.

7. Repeat the above procedure on each wheel with drum brakes.

Master Cylinder

NOTE: The master cylinder fluid reservoirs on Volkswagens are found in a number of different places. The reservoirs on all Type 1 models can be found in the front luggage compartment. On Type 2 models (except the Vanagon), the reservoir is located underneath the driver's seat, while on the Vanagon, it is underneath the raised portion of the instrument panel.

With the exception of the Vanagon, all Type 2 models, in addition to the refill reservoir mentioned above, also have a twin-chamber reservoir attached directly to the master cylinder.

The notched adjusters must be positioned as shown

REMOVAL & INSTALLATION

Type 1 and 2 (except Vanagon)

1. Drain the brake fluid from the master cylinder reservoir.

——————— **CAUTION** ———————
Do not get any brake fluid on the paint, as it will dissolve the paint.

2. Pull the plastic elbows out of the rubber sealing rings on the top of the master cylinder.

3. Remove the two bolts which secure the master cylinder to the frame and remove the cylinder. Note the spacers on the Type 1 between the frame and the master cylinder.

4. To install, bolt the master cylinder to the frame. Do not forget the spacers on the Type 1.

5. Lubricate the elbows with brake fluid and insert them into the rubber seals.

6. If necessary, adjust the brake pedal free travel. On Type 1, adjust the length of the master cylinder pushrod so that there is 5–7 mm of brake pedal free-play before the pushrod contacts the master cylinder piston. On Type 2, the free-play is properly adjusted when the length of the pushrod, measured between the ball end and the center of the clevis pin hole, is 4.17 in.

7. Refill the master cylinder reservoir and bleed the brakes.

Vanagon

1. Grasp the two recesses provided on the back of the instrument cluster frame and pull it forward.

2. Tag and disconnect any wiring leading to the back of the instrument cluster and then remove it.

Front Wheel Bearings

REMOVAL & INSTALLATION

1. Jack up the car and remove the wheel and tire.

2. Remove the caliper and disc (if equipped with disc brakes) or brake drum.

3. To remove the inside wheel bearing, pry the dust seal out of the hub with a screwdriver. Lift out the bearing and its inner race.

4. To remove the outer race for either the inner or outer wheel bearing, insert a long punch into the hub opposite the end from which the race is to be removed. The race rests against a shoulder in the hub. The shoulder has two notches cut into it so that it is possible to place the end of the punch directly against the back side of the race and drive it out of the hub.

5. Carefully clean the hub.

6. Install new races in the hub. Drive them in with a soft faced hammer or a large piece of pipe of the proper diameter. Lubricate the races with a light coating of wheel bearing grease.

7. Force wheel bearing grease into the sides of the tapered roller bearings so that all the spaces are filled.

8. Place a small amount of grease inside the hub.

9. Place the inner wheel bearing into its race in the hub and tap a new seal into the hub. Lubricate the sealing surface of the seal with grease.

10. Install the hub on the spindle and install the outer wheel bearing.

11. Adjust the wheel bearing and install the dust cover.

12. Install the caliper (if equipped with disc brakes).

ADJUSTMENT

The bearing may be adjusted by feel or by a dial indicator.

To adjust the bearing by feel, tighten the adjusting nut so that all the play is taken up in the bearing. There will be a slight amount of drag on the wheel if it is hand spun. Back off fully on the adjusting nut and retighten very lightly. There should be no drag when the wheel is hand spun and there should be no perceptible play in the bearing when the wheel is grasped and wiggled from side to side.

To use a dial indicator, remove the dust cover and mount a dial indicator against the hub. Grasp the wheel at the side and pull the wheel in and out along the axis of the spindle. Read the axial play on the dial indicator. Screw the adjusting nut in or out to obtain 0.001–0.005 in. of axial play. Secure the adjusting nut and recheck the axial play.

Wheel Cylinder—Front Drum Brakes

REMOVAL & INSTALLATION

1. Remove the brake shoes.

2. Disconnect the brake line from the rear of the cylinder.

3. Remove the bolts which secure the cylinder to the backing plate and remove the cylinder from the vehicle.

4. Reverse the above steps to install and bleed the brakes.

Wheel Cylinder—Rear Drum Brakes

REMOVAL & INSTALLATION

Remove the brake drum and brake shoes. Disconnect the brake line from the cylinder and remove the bolts which secure the cylinder to the backing plate. Remove the cylinder from the vehicle.

Parking Brake
CABLE ADJUSTMENT

Brake cable adjustment is performed at the handbrake lever in the passenger compartment. There is a cable for each rear wheel and there are two adjusting nuts at the lever.

To adjust the cable, loosen the locknut. Jack up the rear wheel to be adjusted so that it can be hand spun. Turn the adjusting nut until a very slight drag is felt as the wheel is spun. Then back off on the adjusting nut until the lever can be pulled up three notches.

——————— **CAUTION** ———————
Never pull up on the handbrake lever with the cables disconnected.

CABLE

Removal & Installation

1. Disconnect the cables at the handbrake lever by removing the two nuts which secure the cables to the lever. Pull the cables rearward to remove that end from the lever bracket.

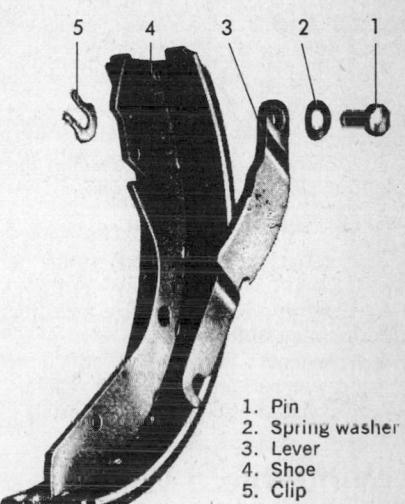

1. Pin
2. Spring washer
3. Lever
4. Shoe
5. Clip

Parking brake hand lever and cable end assembly

2. Remove the brake drum and detach the cable end from the lever attached to the rear brake shoe.

3. Remove the brake cable bracket from the backing plate and remove the cable from the vehicle.

4. Reverse the above steps to install and adjust the cable.

Parking brake cable adjusting nuts

CHASSIS ELECTRICAL

Heater

The Volkswagen heating system has no electrical blower. The engine cooling fan blows air over the engine and out through the cooling ducts. If the heater flaps are opened, then a portion of the heated air from the engine is diverted to the passenger compartment. An auxiliary gas heater is optional on Types 1 and 2, and standard on the Vanagon.

Cable for Heater Outlet

REMOVAL & INSTALLATION

Types 1 and 2

1. Remove the rear air outlet, hose, and heater pipe as an assembly.
2. Remove the hose from the outlet and from the pipe.
3. Remove the pin which attaches the cable to the flap in the heater pipe.

NOTE: The pin is push-fit.

4. Remove the heater pipe from the outlet.
5. Bend up the tabs which secure the cable shielding to the outlet.
6. Disconnect the opposite end from the heater controls and remove the cable.
7. Reverse the above steps to install.

Windshield Wipers

MOTOR REMOVAL AND INSTALLATION

Type 1

1. Disconnect the battery ground cable.
2. Loosen the clamp screws and remove the wiper arms.
3. Remove the wiper bearing nuts as well as the washers. Take off the outer bearing seals.
4. Remove the back of the instrument panel from the luggage compartment.
5. Disconnect the cable from the wiper motor.
6. Remove the glove compartment box.
7. Remove the screw which secures the wiper frame to the body.
8. Remove the frame and motor with the linkage.

NOTE: The ball joints at the ends of the linkage may be slipped apart by gently popping the ball and socket apart with a screwdriver. Always lubricate the joints upon reassembly.

9. Remove the lock and spring washers from the motor driveshaft and remove the

connecting rod. Matchmark the motor and frame to ensure proper realignment when the motor is reinstalled.

10. Remove the nut located at the base of the motor driveshaft, and the nut at the side of the driveshaft, and remove the motor from the frame.
11. To install, reverse the above steps and heed the following reminders.
12. The pressed lug on the wiper frame must engage the groove in the wiper bearing. Make sure that the wiper spindles are perpendicular to the plane of the windshield.
13. Check the linkage bushings for wear.
14. The hollow side of the links must face toward the frame with the angled end of the driving link toward the right bearing.
15. The inner bearing seal should be placed so that the shoulder of the rubber molding faces the wiper arm.

Type 2

1. Disconnect the ground wire from the battery.
2. Remove both wiper arms.
3. Remove the bearing cover and nut.
4. Remove the heater branch connections under the instrument panel.
5. Disconnect the wiper motor wiring.
6. Remove the wiper motor securing screw and remove the motor.
7. Reverse the above steps to install.

LINKAGE REMOVAL AND INSTALLATION

The windshield wiper linkage is secured at the ends by a ball and socket type joint. The ball and joint may be gently pryed apart with the aid of a screwdriver. Always lubricate the joints with grease before reassembly.

Wiper Arm Shaft

1. Remove the wiper arm.
2. Remove the bearing cover or the shaft seal depending on the type.
3. Remove the large wiper shaft bearing securing nut and remove the accompanying washer and rubber seal.
4. Disconnect the wiper linkage from the wiper arm shaft.
5. Working from inside the car, slide the shaft out of its bearing.

NOTE: It may be necessary to lightly tap the shaft out of its bearing. Use a soft face hammer.

6. Reverse the above steps to install.

Instrument Cluster

NOTE: To remove the instrument cluster on the Vanagon, grasp the two recesses provided at the back of the cluster and pull it forward.

All instruments (speedometer, clock, fuel gauge, etc.) are removed from the

back. Unhook any wiring leading from the particular gauge and then remove the retaining screws. Pull the gauge out from the rear of the cluster. Installation is in the reverse order of removal.

SPEEDOMETER

Removal & Installation

1. Disconnect the negative battery cable.
2. Disconnect the speedometer light bulb wires.
3. Unscrew the knurled nut which secures the speedometer cable to the back of the speedometer. Pull the cable from the back of the speedometer.
4. Using a 4 mm Allen wrench, remove the two knurled nuts which secure the speedometer brackets. Remove the brackets.
5. Remove the speedometer from the dashboard by sliding it out toward the steering wheel.
6. Reverse the above steps to install. Before fully tightening the nuts for the speedometer brackets, make sure the speedometer is correctly positioned in the dash.

FUEL GAUGE AND CLOCK ASSEMBLY

Removal & Installation

1. Disconnect the negative battery cable.
2. Disconnect the wiring from the back of the assembly.
3. Remove the knurled nuts and brackets which secure the assembly in the dash. Use a 4 mm Allen wrench.
4. Remove the assembly by gently sliding it toward the steering wheel and out of the dash.
5. The fuel gauge is secured into the base of the clock by two screws. Remove the screws and slip the fuel gauge out of the clock.
6. Reverse the above steps to install. Make sure the clock and fuel gauge assembly is properly centered in the dash before fully tightening the nuts.

Fuse Box Location

All major circuits are protected from overloading or short circuiting by fuses. A 12 position fusebox is located beneath the dashboard near the steering column, or located in the luggage compartment on some air conditioned models.

When a fuse blows, the cause should be investigated. Never install a fuse of a larger capacity than specified and never use foil or a bolt or nail in place of a fuse. However, always carry a few spares in case of emergency. There are 10 8 amp (white) fuses and two 16 amp (red) fuses in the VW fusebox. Circuits number 9 and 10 use the 16 amp fuses. To replace a fuse, pry off the clear plastic cover at either end of the subject fuse.

Volvo
242, 244, 245, 262, 265, 760, DL, GL, GT, GLE, GLT, Coupe

SERIAL NUMBER IDENTIFICATION

Vehicle Type Designation And Chassis Number

Important identification labels appear at several locations on every Volvo, depending on year and model. On 1978–79 models, the type designation (242, 262, etc.) and the chassis number appear on a metal plate riveted to the engine side of the firewall. They also appear on the VIN plate, located at the foot of the left door post, and are stamped into the sheet metal of the right front door pillar.

For 1980–85, the model designations are DL-GL-GT-GLT and Turbo (formerly 242-244-245), GLE (formerly 264-265, to 1982), Coupe (formerly 262C), Diesel, and 760 GLE (1983 and later). The VIN plate on these cars is located on the top left surface of the dash, and is also stamped on the right hand door pillar. Emission control information is on a label located on the left hand shock tower under the hood. There is also a model plate on the right hand shock tower that includes the VIN number, engine type, emission equipment, vehicle weights and color codes.

Model designation and engine availability are related in the following way: from 1978 until 1979, all four cylinder Volvos are in the 240 series—242, 244 and 245. Six cylinder cars are 260 series—262, 264, 265. Starting in 1980, the 240 series became the DL, GL and GLT series. The 260 series evolved into the GLE cars, through 1982. The 760 series took over the GLE designation when launched in 1983.

Engine, Transmission, And Final Drive Identification

The engine type designation, part number, and serial number are given on the left side of the block (4). The last figures of the part

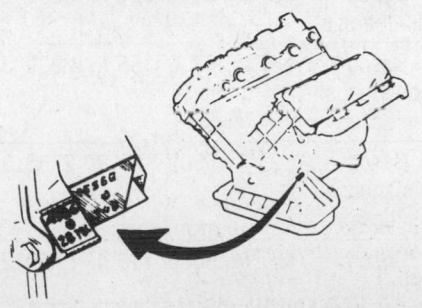

Last three digits of Engine Identification Number printed on label on timing belt cover.

B21 series engine number locations

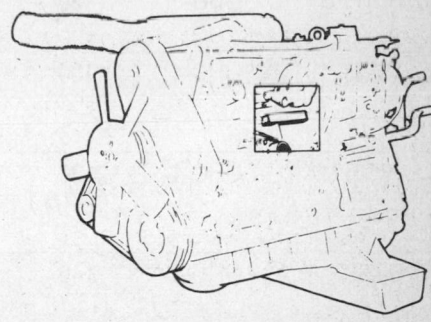

B27F and D20F engine number locations

number are stamped on a tab and are followed by the serial number stamped on the block.

The transmission type designation, serial number, and part number appear on a metal plate (5) riveted to the underside of the transmission. The final drive reduction ratio, part number, and serial number are found on a metal plate (6) riveted to the left-hand side of the differential.

D24 and D24T engine number location

Component Identification

A component data plate is used to specify the manufacturer of major serviceable components such as the brakes, fuel pump, clutch, alternator, and steering gear. The plate is located on the right front door pillar on some models. Each component manufacturer is assigned a code.

VOLVO

CHASSIS NUMBER CHART

Year	Model	Starting Chassis No.
'78	242	122895
	244	274965
	245	163835
	262	2660
	264	46515
	265	10920
'79	242	142125
	244	364650
	245	211325
	262	4330
	264	62105
	265	15735

CHASSIS NUMBER CHART

Year	Model	Starting Chassis No.
'80	DL, GT (2 dr.)	165570
	DL, GL (4 dr.)	482505
	Coupe	6450
	GLE	83055
	4 cyl. wgn.	264755
	6 cyl. wgn.	21755
'81	DL, GL, GLT (2 dr.)	189180
	DL, GL (4 dr.)	592110
	Coupe	8375
	GLE	107610
	4 cyl. wgn.	317940
	6 cyl. wgn.	28320

CHASSIS NUMBER CHART

Year	Model	Starting Chassis No.
'82	DL, GL, GLT (2 dr.)	306780
	DL, GL (4 dr.)	686100
	GLE	125110
	4 cyl. wgn.	368310
'83	760 GLE	3800
	DL, GL (2 dr.)	223940
	DL, GL (4 dr.)	812610
	4 cyl. wagon	434460
'84	760 GLE	33720
	DL, Turbo (2 dr.)	237370
	DL, GL (4 dr.)	939340
	4 cyl. wagon	506270

GENERAL ENGINE SPECIFICATIONS

Year and Engine Model	Engine Type	Engine Displacement cu. in. (cc)	Fuel Delivery Type	Horsepower @ rpm	Torque @ rpm (ft. lbs.)	Bore × Stroke (in.)	Compression Ratio	Oil Pressure @ rpm (psi)
'78 B21F	OHC-4	130 (2127)	Bosch continuous injection	102 @ 5200 ①	114 @ 2500 ②	3.62 × 3.15	8.5:1	35–85 @ 2000
'79–'82 B21F	OHC-4	130 (2127)	Bosch continuous injection	107 @ 5500 ③	114 @ 2500	3.62 × 3.15	9.3:1	35–85 @ 2000
'82 B21FLH	OHC-4	130 (2127)	Bosch LH-Jetronic	105 @ 5400	119 @ 3000	3.62 × 3.15	9.3:1	35–85 @ 2000
'81–'85 B21FT④	OHC-4	130 (2127)	Bosch continuous injection	127 @ 5400	150 @ 3750	3.62 × 3.15	7.5:1	35–85 @ 2000
'81–'85 B21A⑦	OHC-4	130 (2127)	Zenith or SU 1-bbl carburetor	100 @ 5250 ⑧	122 @ 2500 ⑨	3.62 × 3.15	9.3:1	35–85 @ 2000
'83 B23E⑦	OHC-4	140 (2320)	Bosch continuous injection	115 @ 5000	133 @ 3000	3.78 × 3.15	10.3:1	35–85 @ 2000
'83–'85 B23F	OHC-4	140 (2320)	Bosch LH-Jetronic	107 @ 5400	127 @ 3500	3.78 × 3.15	10.3:1	35–85 @ 2000
'84–'85 B23FT④	OHC-4	140 (2320)	Bosch continuous injection	157 @ 5300	185 @ 2900	3.78 × 3.15	8.7:1	N.A.
'78 B27F	OHC-V6	162 (2660)	Bosch continuous injection	125 @ 5500 ⑤	150 @ 2750 ⑥	3.46 × 2.87	8.2:1	58 @ 3000
'79–'80 B27F	OHC-V6	162 (2660)	Bosch continuous injection	127 @ 5500	146 @ 2750	3.46 × 2.87	8.8:1	58 @ 3000

GENERAL ENGINE SPECIFICATIONS

Year and Engine Model	Engine Type	Engine Displacement cu. in. (cc)	Fuel Delivery Type	Horsepower @ rpm	Torque @ rpm (ft. lbs.)	Bore × Stroke (in.)	Compression Ratio	Oil Pressure @ rpm (psi)
'80–'85 B28F	OHC-V6	174 (2849)	Bosch continuous injection	130 @ 5500	153 @ 2750	3.58 × 2.86	8.8:1	60 @ 3000
'80–'85 D24	OHC-6	145 (2383)	Diesel	78 @ 4800	102 @ 3000	3.01 × 3.40	23.0:1	28 @ 2000
'83–'85 D24T	OHC-6	145 (2383)	Turbo Diesel	103 @ 4800	139 @ 2400	3.01 × 3.40	23.0:1	28 @ 2000

NOTE: OHC is Overhead Camshaft
① 99 @ 5200 in Calif.
② 114 @ 2500 in Calif.
③ 98 @ 5000, '82 and later
④ Turbocharged
⑤ 121 @ 5500 in Calif.
⑥ 148 @ 2750 in Calif.
⑦ Canada only
⑧ 96 @ 5250 in 1981
⑨ 121 @ 2500 in 1981
N.A.—Not Available

GASOLINE ENGINE TUNE-UP SPECIFICATIONS

(When analyzing compression test results, look for uniformity among cylinders, rather than specific pressures)

Year	Engine Model and Displacement cu. in.	Spark Plugs Type	Gap (in.)	Point Dwell (deg)	Point Gap (in.)	Ignition Timing (deg) MT	Ignition Timing (deg) AT	Intake Valve Opens (deg)	Fuel Pump Pressure (psi)	Idle Speed (rpm) MT	Idle Speed (rpm) AT	Valve Clearance (cold) (in.) In	Valve Clearance (cold) (in.) Ex
'78	B 21 F 130	Bosch WA175T30	0.030	Electronic		12B ①	12B ①	—	64–75	900	900	0.014–0.016	0.014–0.016
'78–'79	B 27 F 162	Bosch WA200T30	0.030	Electronic		10B ①	10B ①	—	64–75	900	900	0.004–0.006	0.010–0.012
'79	B 21 F 130	Bosch W6DC	0.030	Electronic		10B ①③	10B ①③	—	64–75	900	900	0.014–0.016	0.014–0.016
'80–'83	B 21 F⑤ 130	Bosch WR7DS	0.030	Electronic		8B ⑥⑨④	8B ⑥⑨④	—	64–75	900	900	0.014–0.016	0.014–0.016
'81–'85	B 21 FT⑫ 130	Bosch WR7DS	0.030	Electronic		12B ⑦④	12B ⑦④	—	64–75	900	900	0.014–0.016	0.014–0.016
'81–'85	B 21 A 130	Bosch W7DC	0.030	62	0.016–0.018	12B ⑥⑧④	12B ⑥⑧④	—	64–75	900	900	0.014–0.016	0.014–0.016
'83–'85	B 23 E 140	Bosch W6DC	0.030	Electronic		10B ⑥④	10B ⑥④	—	64–75	900	900	0.014–0.016	0.014–0.016
'83–'85	B 23 F⑩ 140	Bosch WR7DS	0.030	Electronic		12B ⑥④	12B ⑥④	—	64–75	750	750	0.014–0.016	0.014–0.016
'80–'82	B 28 F 174	Bosch WR6DS	0.030	Electronic		10B ⑦④	10B ⑦④	—	64–75	900	900	0.008–0.010	0.012–0.014

VOLVO

GASOLINE ENGINE TUNE-UP SPECIFICATIONS

(When analyzing compression test results, look for uniformity among cylinders, rather than specific pressures)

Year	Engine Model and Displacement cu. in.	Spark Plugs Type	Spark Plugs Gap (in.)	Distributor Point Dwell (deg)	Distributor Point Gap (in.)	Ignition Timing (deg) MT	Ignition Timing (deg) AT	Intake Valve Opens (deg)	Fuel Pump Pressure (psi)	Idle Speed (rpm) MT	Idle Speed (rpm) AT	Valve Clearance (cold) (in.) In	Valve Clearance (cold) (in.) Ex
'83	B 28 F 174	Bosch WR6DS	0.026	Electronic		10B ④⑪	10B ④⑪	—	64–75	900	900	0.008–0.010	0.012–0.016
'84–'85	B 28 F 174	Bosch WR6DS	0.024	Electronic		10B ④⑪	10B ④⑪	—	64–75	750	750	0.004–0.006	0.010–0.012

NOTE: Some models are equipped with the Constant Idle Speed system (CIS) and cannot be adjusted
① @ 700 rpm
② 9B—left side; 7B—right side
③ Calif: 8B
④ Vacuum advance disconnected, A/C turned off
⑤ Includes Calif. and L-Jetronic models
⑥ @ 750 rpm
⑦ @ 900 rpm
⑧ 7° '82 and later
⑨ 12° '82 and later
⑩ LH-Jetronic injection with Constant Idle Speed and Knock Sensor
⑪ @ 800 rpm
⑫ Turbo
⑬ LH-Jetronic injection (electronic)

DIESEL ENGINE TUNE-UP SPECIFICATIONS

Year	Model	Valve Clearance① Intake (in.)	Valve Clearance① Exhaust (in.)	Injection Pump Setting⑧ (in.)	Injector Nozzle Opening Pressure (psi)	Idle Speed (rpm)	Compression Pressure (psi)
'80–'85	D24	0.006–0.010	0.014–0.018	0.0265–② 0.0295	1700–1845③	720–④ 880	340 (min.)– 455 (max.)⑤
'83–'85	D24T⑥	0.006–0.010	0.014–0.018	0.0315⑨	2062–2318⑦	750	313 (min.)– 455 (max.)⑤

NOTE: When setting injection timing, distributor plunger stroke must be at Top Dead Center
① Cold
② See text. Acceptable range when checking 0.0287–0.0315 in.
③ Acceptable range. When servicing set to 1775–1920 psi
④ Maximum safe speed: 5100–5200 rpm (high idle)
⑤ Maximum difference between cylinders 115 lbs. psi
⑥ Turbo-Diesel
⑦ Acceptable range. When servicing set to 2205–2318 psi.
⑧ Plunger stroke
⑨ See text. Acceptable range when checking 0.0307–0.0334 in.

FIRING ORDERS

NOTE: To avoid confusion, always replace spark plug wires one at a time.

FIRING ORDER
1-6-3-5-2-4

FIRING ORDER
1-3-4-2

FIRING ORDER
1-5-3-6-4-2

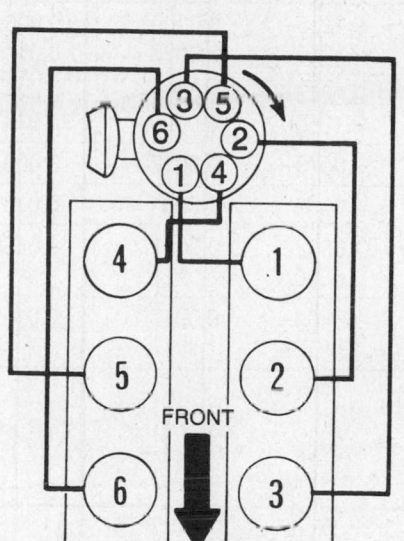

B27F, B28

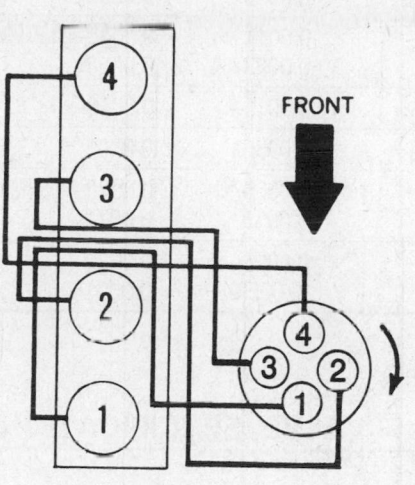

FRONT

B21F and B23 series

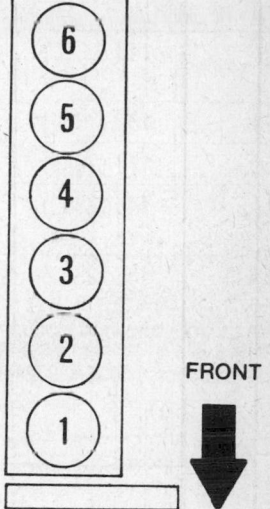

FRONT

D24 Diesel

CAPACITIES

Year	Model	Engine Displacement cu. in. (cc)	Engine Crankcase (qt)		Transmission (pts)		Drive Axle (pt)	Gasoline Tank (gal)	Cooling System (qt)
			With Filter	Without Filter	Manual 4-Spd	Automatic			
'78	242, 244, 245	130 (2127)	4.0	3.5	3.8	14.0	3.4	15.8	10.0
	262, 264, 265	162 (2660)	6.8	6.3	4.8	14.0	3.4	15.8	11.5
'79	242, 244, 245	130 (2127)	4.0	3.5	3.8	14.0②	3.4	15.8	10.0
	262, 264, 265	162 (2660)	6.8	6.3	4.8	14.0②	3.4	15.8	11.5
'80–'83	DL, GL, GT④	130 2127)	4.0⑤	3.5⑤	4.8	14.6③	3.4	15.8	10.0
'80–'82	GLE, Coupe	174 (2849)	6.8	6.3	4.8	14.6③	3.4	15.8	11.5
'80–'85	DL, GL Diesel	145 (2383)	7.4	6.6	4.8	14.6③	3.4	15.8	10.0
'83–'85	DL, GL	140 (2320)	3.5	4.0	4.8	14.6③	3.4	15.8	10.0
'82–'85	GLT Wagon, DL Turbo	130 (2127)	4.0⑤	3.5⑤	4.8	14.6③	3.4	15.8	10.0
'83–'85	760 GLE	174 (2849)	6.8	6.3	4.8	14.6③	3.4	15.8⑥	10.5
'83–'85	760 GLE Turbo Diesel	145 (2383)	7.0	6.2	4.8	14.6③	3.4	15.8⑥	11.5⑦

① With extra capacity fluid pan: 14.6
② Fluid capacity for AW70 and AW71 (1982 and later 4-speed) automatics is 15.6 pts.
③ Includes station wagons
④ Cars w/turbo: if oil cooler drained, add 0.7 qt.
⑤ With increased capacity tank 21.6 gal.
⑥ With automatic trans. 10.5 qt.

CRANKSHAFT AND CONNECTING ROD SPECIFICATIONS

(All measurements are given in inches)

Engine① Model	Engine Displacement cu. in. (cc)	Crankshaft			Thrust on No.	Connecting Rod		
		Main Brg. Journal Dia.	Main Brg. Oil Clearance	Shaft End-Play		Journal Diameter	Oil Clearance	Side Clearance
B 21, B 21 T	130 (2127)	2.4981– 2.4986	0.0011– 0.0033	0.0015– 0.0058	5	2.1255– 2.1260	0.0009– 0.0028	0.006– 0.014
B 23	140 (2320)	2.4981– 2.4986	0.0011– 0.0033	0.0015– 0.0058	5	2.1255– 2.1260	0.0009– 0.0028	0.006– 0.014
B 27 F	162 (2660)	2.7576–	0.0015–	0.0028–	4	2.0578–	0.0012–	0.008–
B 28 F	174 (2849)	2.7583	0.0035	0.0106	4	2.0585	0.0031	0.015
D 24	145 (2383)	2.2833– 2.2825	0.0006– 0.0030	0.0028– 0.0071	4	1.8802– 1.8810	0.0047②	0.0158
D 24 T	145 (2383)	2.2816– 2.2824	0.0006– 0.0029	0.0027– 0.0071	4	1.8802– 1.8810	0.0047②	0.0157

① Includes all variations of each model
② New clearance 0.0005–0.0024 in.

VALVE SPECIFICATIONS

Year	Engine and Displacement cu. in. (cc)	Cylinder Head Seat Angle (deg)	Valve Face Angle (deg)	Seat Width (in.)	Spring Test Pressure (lbs. @ in.)	Spring Installed Height (in.)	Stem-To-Guide Clearance (in.)		Stem Diameter (in.)	
							Intake	Exhaust	Intake	Exhaust
'78–'84	B 21 130 (2127)	44.75	45.5	0.08	170 @ 1.06	1.77	0.0012– 0.0024	0.0024– 0.0035	0.3132– 0.3135	0.3128– 0.3126
'83–'85	B 23 140 (2320)	45	44.5	③	165 @ 1.06	1.77	0.0012– 0.0024	0.0024– 0.0035	0.3132– 0.3138	0.3128– 0.3124
'78–'79	B 27 F 162 (2660) B 28 F 174 (2849)	29.5 int 30 exh	29.5 int 30 exh	①	124.3 @ 1.27	1.86	②	②	0.3136– 0.3142 to 0.3140– 0.3146	0.3128– 0.3134 to 0.3136– 0.3142
'80–'85	B 28 F	29.5 int 30 exh	29.5 int 30 exh	①	143 @ 1.181	1.85	②	②	0.3136– 0.3142 to 0.3140– 0.3146	0.3128– 0.3134 to 0.3136– 0.3142
'80–'85	D 24, D 24 T	45	④	⑤	⑥	⑦	⑧	⑧	0.314	0.313

NOTE: Exhaust valves for turbo engines (including turbo diesel) are stellite coated and must not be machined. They may be ground against the valve seat.

① 0.067–0.083 intake; 0.079–0.094 exhaust
② Tapered; valve guide ID is 0.3150–0.3158
③ 0.051–0.075 intake; 0.066–0.091 exhaust
④ 44.5° intake; 45° exhaust
⑤ 0.08 intake; 0.094 exhaust
⑥ Two springs per valve; inner spring 49 lbs. @ 0.72 in.; outer spring 100 lbs. @ 0.878 in.
⑦ Inner 1.335 in.; outer 1.583 in.
⑧ Clearance measured w/new valve guide and w/valve stem edge to edge w/valve guide upper end. Max. clearance 0.051 in.; new clearance 0.012 in.

PISTON AND RING SPECIFICATIONS

Year	Engine Displacement cu. in. (cc)	Piston Clearance	Ring Gap			Ring Side Clearance		
			Top Compression	Bottom Compression	Oil Control	Top Compression	Bottom Compression	Oil Control
'78–'85	B 21 130 (2127)	0.0004–0.0012①④	0.0138–0.0217②	0.0138–0.0217②	0.010–0.016②	0.0016–0.0028	0.0016–0.0028	0.0016–0.0028③
'83–'85	B 23 140 (2320)	0.0020–0.0028⑤	0.014–0.026	0.014–0.022	0.0010–0.0024	0.0015–0.0028	0.0015–0.0028	0.0012–0.0024
'78–'79 and '80–'85	B 27 F 162 (2660) B 28 F 174 (2849)	0.008–0.0016	0.016–0.022	0.016–0.022	0.015–0.055	0.0018–0.0029	0.0010–0.0021	0.0004–0.0092
'80–'85	D 24 145 (2383)	0.0012–0.0020⑥	0.012–0.020⑦	0.012–0.020⑦	0.010–0.016⑦	0.0024–0.0035⑧	0.0020–0.0032⑧	0.0012–0.0024⑨
'83–'85	D 24 T 145 (2383)	0.0012–0.0020	0.012–0.020	0.012–0.020	0.010–0.019	0.0043–0.0055	0.0028–0.0039	0.0012–0.0028

①0.004–0.0016 in. 1983–84
②0.014–0.026 in. 1983–84 top compression; 0.014–0.022 in. 1983–84 bottom compression; 0.010–0.024 in. 1983–84 oil control
③0.0012–0.0024 in. 1983–84

④0.0008–0.0016 in. 1983–84 Turbo
⑤Pistons with two different heights have been fitted to B23E engines. Piston clearance on version 1 (3.1654 in. piston height) listed above; clearance on version 2 pistons (3.0079 in.) is 0.004–0.0016 in.

⑥Clearance when new; max. wear compared with normal diameter 0.0016 in.
⑦Gap when new; maximum is 0.04 in.
⑧Clearance when new; maximum 0.0079 in.
⑨Clearance when new; maximum is 0.0059 in.

ALTERNATOR AND REGULATOR SPECIFICATIONS

Year	Vehicle Model	Alternator			Regulator	
		Part No. and Manufacturer	Output (amps.)	Min. Brush Length (in.)	Part No. and Manufacturer	Volts @ Alternator rpm (cold)
'78–'85	240 series; DL, GL, GT, 760	14V 55A20 Bosch	55③	0.20	Bosch	13.5–14.1 @ 4000①
'78–'82	260 series; GLE Coupe	S.E.V. Marchal A 14/55A 7160410	55②③	0.20	S.E.V. Marchal 72710502	13.5–14.1 @ 4000①
'83–'85	DL, GL, 760 GLE, GLT, DL Turbo	N114V 70A20 Bosch	70	0.20	0197311008 Bosch	14.4–14.8V @ 6000①
'83 '85	760 GLE	N114V 90A20 Bosch	90	0.20	0192052027 Bosch④	14.1–14.8V @ 3000①

NOTE: GLT is Turbo Wagon
①After driving 10 minutes

②1979 and later—70
③1982 B21F Turbo rated output

770W; max. current 55A
④Early type; late type Bosch 1197311008

BATTERY AND STARTER SPECIFICATIONS
(All cars use 12 volts, negative ground electrical systems)

Model	Battery Amp Hour Capacity	Starter						Brush Spring Tension (lbs.)	Min. Brush Length (in.)
		Lock Test			No Load Test				
		Amps	Volts	Torque (ft. lbs.)	Amps	Volts	rpm		
All	60①②	400–490④	7	—	30–50③	11.5	5800–7800⑤	3.10–3.50⑥	0.52⑦

①260 series: 70 amp hour battery
②Diesel: 88 or 90 ah
③Diesel: 65–95A

④Diesel: 700–880A
⑤Diesel: 6500–8500
⑥Diesel: 5.1–5.5 lbs.
⑦Diesel: 0.35 in.

VOLVO

TORQUE SPECIFICATIONS
(All readings in ft. lbs.)

Year	Engine	Cyl. Head Bolts	Rod Bearing Bolts	Main Bearing Bolts	Crank-shaft Pulley Bolt	Flywheel-To-Crank-shaft Bolts	Manifold Bolts		Cam-shaft Nut	Camshaft Bearing Cap Bolts	Spark Plug	Oil Pan
							Intake	Exhaust				
'78–'83	B 21 F	76–83①	43–48	85–91	107–128	47–54	15	15	32–38		25–29	8
'81–'85	B 21 A, B 21 FT, B23	⑩	43–48	85–91	107–128	47–54	15	15	—		15–18	8
'78–'79 '80–'85	B 27 F B28F	②	33–37	③	118–132④	33–37	7–11	7–11	51–59	—	8–11	7–11
'80–'85	D 24	65⑤⑥	33	48	330⑦	55	18	18	⑨	15	⑧	N.A.
'83–'85	D 24 T	⑥	33	48	258	55	18	18	⑨	15	⑧	—

N.A.—Not Available

①Torque head bolts in two stages; first, tighten in sequence to 43 ft. lbs., then to 76–83 ft. lbs.

②Torque heads bolts in sequence to 7 ft. lbs., then 22 ft. lbs., then 44 ft. lbs. Wait 10–15 minutes and slacken the bolts ½ turn. Then torque to 11–14 ft. lbs. and then protractor torque to 116–120° (⅓ of a turn). Finally run to operating temperature, shut off and allow to cool for 30 min. Following the sequence, slacken, torque to 11–14 ft. lbs., and protractor torque to 113–117° each bolt.

③Torque main bearing nuts to 22 ft. lbs., in sequence. Then slacken 1st nut ½ turn, tighten to 22–26 ft. lbs., and protractor torque to 73–77°. Repeat for remaining nuts following the sequence.

④1978–81: 175–200.

⑤Torque in two stages: 30 ft. lbs. then 65 ft. lbs. After 1000 miles torque to 62 ft. lbs. (warm).

⑥From late 1980 new type cylinder head bolts are used on the diesel. They are longer and 1 mm wider. Torquing these bolts is a six-step procedure:
A. Torque to 30 ft. lbs.
B. Torque to 44 ft. lbs.
C. Torque to 55 ft. lbs.
D. Tighten 180°, in one movement, without stopping.
E. Run engine until oil temperature is minimum 50°C–120°F.
F. Tighten 90°, in one movement, without stopping. After driving 600–1,000 miles, retorque bolts w/engine cold. DO NOT slacken first.

⑦Using regular torque wrench. If Volvo tool 5188 is used, torque to 255 ft. lbs.

⑧Injector: 50 ft. lbs.

⑨Front camshaft bolt: 33; Rear: 73

⑩Torque head bolts in three stages; first, tighten in sequence to 15 ft. lbs., then to 44 ft. lbs. Protractor (angle) tighten 90° more.

BRAKE SPECIFICATIONS
(All measurements given are in. unless noted)

Year	Model	Lug Nut Torque (ft. lbs.)	Master Cylinder Bore	Brake Disc		Minimum Lining Thickness (in.)	
				Minimum Thickness (in.)	Maximum Run-Out (in.)	Front	Rear
'78–'85	240 series, DL, GL, GT, GLT, Turbo	88	0.878	0.557 front 0.331 rear	0.004 front 0.006 rear	0.125	0.125
	260 series, GLE Coupe, Diesel	88	0.878	0.900 front 0.331 rear	0.004 front 0.006 rear	0.125	0.125
'83–'85	760 GLE	63	0.878	0.551 front 0.378 rear	0.003 front 0.0039 rear	0.118	0.078

NOTE: Use only DOT-4 specification brake fluid

WHEEL ALIGNMENT

Year	Model	Caster Range (deg)	Camber Range (deg)	Toe-in (in.)	Steering Axis Inclination (at 0° camber)	Wheel Pivot Ratio (deg) Inner Wheel	Wheel Pivot Ratio (deg) Outer Wheel
'78	240, 260 series	2P–3P	1P–1½P	⅛–¼②	12	20	20.8
'79–'81	All Models	2P–3P③	0–1N	⅛–¼②	12	20	20.8
'82–'85	All Models except GLT, Turbo, 760 GLE	2P–3P③	1P to 1½P	⅛–¼④	12	20	20.8
'82–'85	GLT, Turbo	2P–3P③	¼P to ¾P	⅛–¼④	12	20	20.8
'83–'85	760GLE	3P–6P	13/32	3/32–11/64	N.A.	N.A.	N.A.

NOTE: Toe-in specifications measured from tire outer diameter. Vehicle should not be loaded for these measurements.
N.A. Not Available
① W/manual steering: ⅛ in. to ¼ in.
  w/power steering: 1/16 in. to 3/16 in.
② Power steering: 1/16–3/16
③ Power steering: 3P–4P
④ Power steering: 1/16–3/16

TUNE-UP PROCEDURES

--- CAUTION ---
When working with a running engine, make sure that there is proper ventilation. Also make sure that the transmission is in neutral, and the parking brake is firmly applied. Always keep hands, clothing, and tools well clear of the radiator fan.

Spark Plug

REMOVAL & INSTALLATION

Every six months or 6000 miles, the spark plugs should be removed for inspection. At this time they should be cleaned and re-gapped. At 12-month or 15,000 mile intervals the plugs should be replaced.

Clean the area around each spark plug prior to plug removal, to avoid getting dirt into the engine once the plug is removed. Compressed air is excellent, if available.

Remove each spark plug wire by grasping its rubber boot on the end and twisting slightly to free the wire from the plug. Using a 13/16 in. spark plug socket, turn the plugs counterclockwise to remove them. Do not allow any foreign matter to enter the cylinders through the spark plug holes.

The gap must be checked with a feeler gauge before installing the plug in the engine. With the ground electrode positioned parallel to the center electrode, the specified wire gauge must pass through the opening with a slight drag. If the air gap between the two electrodes is not correct, the ground electrode must be bent to bring it to specifications.

After the plugs are gapped correctly, they may be inserted into their holes and hand-tightened. Be careful not to crossthread the plugs. Install each spark plug wire on its respective plug, making sure that each spark plug end is making good metal-to-metal contact in its wire socket.

Breaker Points

ADJUSTING BREAKER POINTS WITH A DWELL METER

Adjusting the B21A breaker points with a dwell meter (if available) is a more precise method of adjustment than the feeler gauge method. Calibrate the dwell meter to the four-cylinder position, and connect it between the distributor primary terminal and a ground. Remove the distributor cap and rotor. Loosen the breaker point set screw about ⅛ of a turn. Observing the dwell meter, reset the screw of the stationary contact to obtain the proper (62°) dwell angle. Tighten the set screw and recheck the dwell. Install the rotor and cap, start the engine, and make a final dwell check.

ADJUSTING BREAKER POINTS WITH A FEELER GAUGE

The Canadian B21A models (carburetor-equipped) are also equipped with a conventional breaker points type ignition system. We recommend that for the cost of a new set of breaker points and condenser, it really isn't worth readjusting an old set of points. Replace old points with a new set and condenser.

To replace and adjust a new set of points, remove the distributor cap and rotor. Disconnect the wire leads from both points and condenser. Remove the points hold-down screw, condenser attaching screw, and remove the points assembly and condenser. Lightly grease the distributor cam lobe on the surface that makes contact with the points set. Install the new points assembly and condenser, attach the wire leads of both and tighten the condenser attaching screw. *Do not fully tighten the points hold-down screw.*

Turn the crankshaft bottom pulley (by placing a socket on the pulley bolt) until the cam lobe on the distributor shaft has fully raised the breaker arm. The points should now be up on the peak of the shaft eccentric, and should be at their most wide open point. Insert a 0.017 in. feeler gauge in between both contacts, and loosen the breaker plate hold-down screw. There will be a slight drag on the feeler gauge when the gap is properly set. Tighten the hold-down screw when you are satisfied, rotate the engine once and recheck the gap. Make

C995

sure all leads are securely attached, replace the rotor and distributor cap.

Electronic Ignition

There are two major differences from the point type systems: First the points and condenser are replaced by an induction type impulse sender. Second, an electronic module has been added to amplify the electrical impulses between the distributor and coil. The impulse sender is located inside the distributor where the points are normally located on a points-type system. Instead of opening and closing an electrical circuit, the sender opens and closes a magnetic circuit. This induces impulses in a magnetic pick-up. The sender consists of a stator, pickup, rotor, and permanent magnet. The stator and armature each have the same number of teeth as there are cylinders. The permanent magnet creates a magnetic field which goes through the stator. The circuit is closed when the teeth are opposite each other. This means that the rotor opens and closes the magnetic field while rotating. This generates current pulses in the magnetic pick-up.

The electronic module is a solid state design which is fully transistorized. It amplifies the impulses from the sender and controls the dwell angle.

REPLACING THE IMPULSE SENDER

1. Unsnap the lock clasps on the distributor.
2. Remove the cap, rotor and dust cover.

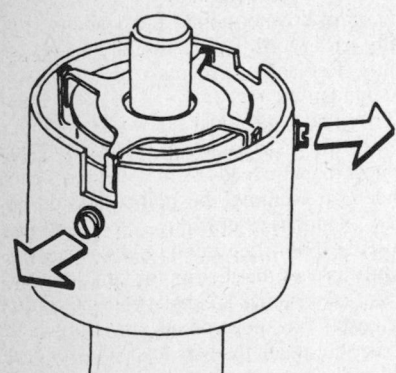

Impulse sender plate removal

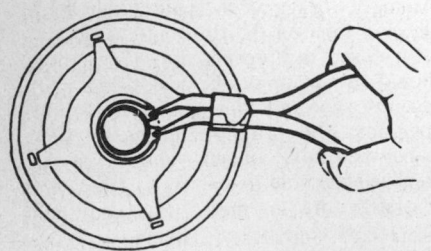

Snap ring and shim removal

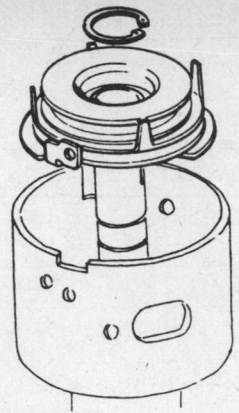

Impulse sender removal

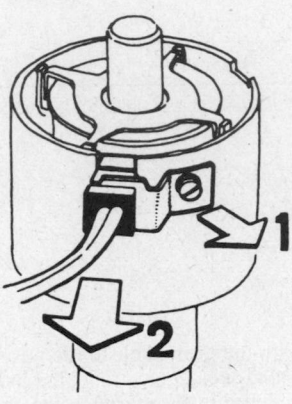

Contact screw removal

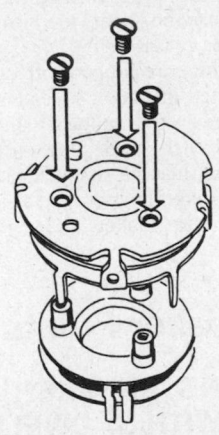

Impulse sender-to-plate installation

3. Remove the vacuum advance unit and the cap hold-down clips.
4. Remove the screw securing the contact and pull the contact straight out.
5. Remove the impulse sender plate screws.
6. Remove the snap-ring and shims and pull the rotor straight off along with the small lock pin.
7. Remove the snap-ring retaining the sender and lift off the sender and plate.
8. Installation is the reverse of removal. Note that the screws for the vacuum

unit and the hold-down clips are different lengths. When attaching the new sender to the plate, the connector pins should be directly opposite and above the attachment ear on the plate. When installation is completed, rotate the shaft several times to make sure there is no noise or binding.

Ignition Timing

ADJUSTMENT

Volvo recommends that the ignition timing be checked at 15,000 mile intervals on 1978–84 models.

Clean the crankshaft damper and pointer on the water pump housing with a solvent-soaked rag so that the marks can be seen. Connect a timing light according to the manufacturer's instructions. Scribe a mark on the crankshaft damper and on the marker with chalk or luminescent (day-glo) paint to highlight the correct timing setting. Disconnect and plug the distributor vacuum line and also disconnect the hose between the air cleaner and the inlet duct at the duct. Disconnect and plug the vacuum hose at the EGR valve.

Attach a tachometer to the engine and set the idle speed to specifications. With the engine running, aim the timing light at

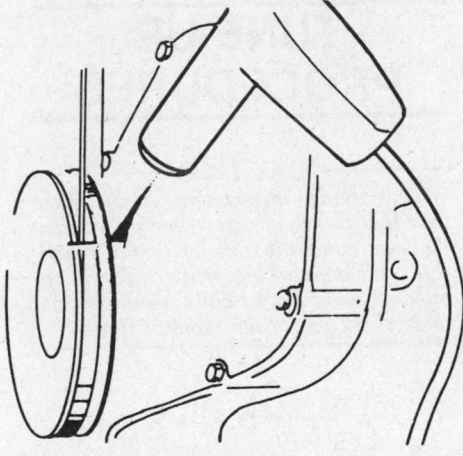

Aim timing light at the pointer and marks on the damper

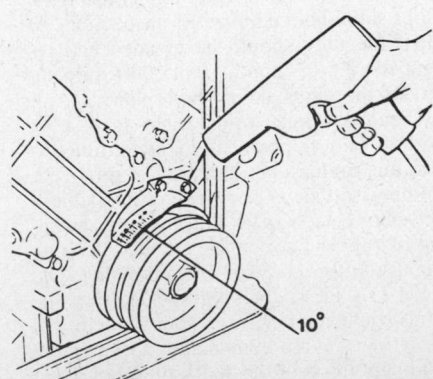

Engine timing marks—B27F and B28F engines

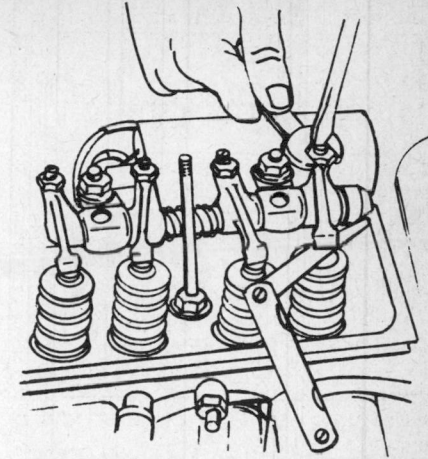

the pointer and the marks on the damper. If the marks do not coincide, stop the engine, loosen the distributor pinch bolt, and start the engine again. While observing the timing light flashes on the markers, grasp the distributor vacuum regulator and rotate the distributor until the marks do coincide. Stop the engine and tighten the distributor pinch bolt, taking care not to disturb the setting.

Reconnect all disconnected hoses and remove the timing light and tachometer from the engine.

NOTE: Refer to the fuel pump section for timing of the D-24 Diesel engine.

Valve Lash

ADJUSTMENT

B21 and B23

Valve clearance is checked every 15,000 miles. If it is necessary to adjust valve clearance, you will need three special tools: first, a valve tappet depressor tool used to push down the tappet sufficiently to remove the adjusting disc (shim) (Volvo tool #999 5022); second, a specially shaped pliers to actually remove and install the valve adjusting disc (Volvo tool #999 5026); and third, a set of varying thickness valve adjusting discs to make the necessary adjustments.

The procedure for checking, and, if necessary, adjusting the valves is as follows.

1. Remove the valve cover. Scribe chalkmarks on the distributor body indicating each of the four spark plug wire leads in the cap. Remove the distributor cap.

2. Crank over the engine with a remote starter switch, or with a wrench on the crankshaft pulley center bolt (22 mm hex) until the engine is in the firing position for No. 1 cylinder. At this point, the 0 degree or TDC mark on the crankshaft pulley is aligned with the timing pointer, the rotor is pointing at the No. 1 spark plug wire cap position, and the camshaft lobes for No. 1 cylinder are pointing at the 10 o'clock and 2 o'clock positions. At this point, the clearance between the cam lobe and valve de-

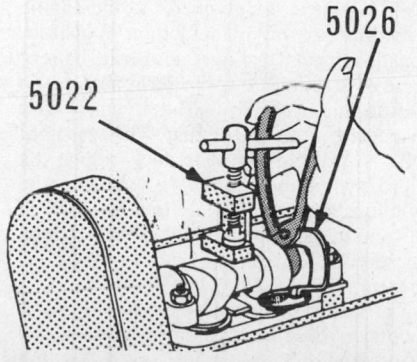

B21 and B23 series valve adjustment tools—tappet depressor is on left, shim pliers on right

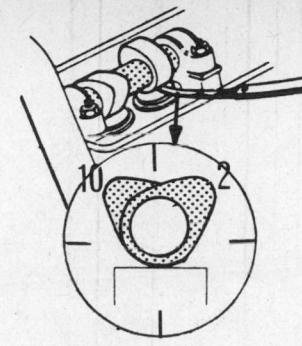

B21 and B23 series camshaft lobes at "10 and 2 o'clock" positions indicating that subject cylinder is in firing position and the valves can be adjusted

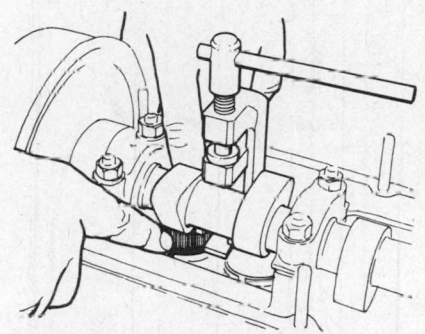

Positioning a new valve adjustment shim in the head. Shim must be oiled

pressor (tappet) may be checked for the intake and exhaust valves of cylinder No. 1, using a feeler gauge. When checking clearance, the wear limit is 0.012–0.018 in. for a cold engine, and 0.012–0.020 in. for a hot one (176°F).

3. Repeat Step 2 for cylinders 3, 4, and 2 (in that order). Each time, rotate the crankshaft pulley 180° so that the rotor is pointing to the spark plug wire cap position for that cylinder, and the cam lobes are pointing at the 10 and 2 o'clock positions for the valves of that cylinder.

4. If any of the valve clearance measurements are outside the wear limit, you will have to remove the old valve adjusting disc and install a new one to bring the clearance within specifications. First, rotate the valve depressors (tappets) until their notches are at a right angle to the engine center line. Attach valve depressor tool 999 5022 or equivalent to the camshaft and screw down the tool spindle until the depressor (tappet) groove is just above the edge of its bore and still accessible with the special pliers (tool No. 999 5026).

5. Remove the valve adjusting disc and measure with a micrometer. The valve clearance should be set to these tolerances; 0.014–0.016 in. for a cold engine, and 0.016–0.018 for a hot one. So, if the measured clearance had been 0.019 in. and the desired clearance 0.016 in. (for a net difference of 0.003 in.), then the new valve

Adjusting valve clearance on the B27 and B28 V6

adjusting disc should be 0.003 in. thicker than the old one to take up the clearance. Valve adjusting discs are available from Volvo in sizes from 0.130 to 0.180 in. (in 0.002 in. increments). Always oil the new disc and install it with the marks facing down.

6. Remove the valve tappet depressor tool. Rotate the engine a few times and recheck clearance. Install the valve cover with a new gasket.

B27 and B28F

Valve clearance is checked every 15,000 miles. No special tools are required.

1. In order to gain access to the valve covers, disconnect or remove the following:
   a. Air conditioning compressor from bracket (do not disconnect refrigerant hoses)
   b. EGR valve and hoses
   c. A/C compressor bracket
   d. Fuel injection control pressure regulator
   e. Air pump
   f. Vacuum pump
   g. Hoses and wires from solenoid valve (Calif. only)

2. Using a 36mm hex socket on the crankshaft pulley bolt, rotate the crankshaft to the No. 1 cylinder TDC position. At this point the "O" mark on the timing plate aligns with the crankshaft pulley notch, the distributor rotor is pointing to the No. 1 cylinder spark plug wire cap position, and both valves for No. 1 cylinder have clearance. At this position, adjust the intake valves of cylinders No. 1, 2 and 4, and the exhaust valves of cylinders No. 1, 3, and 6. Insert a feeler gauge between the rocker arm and valve stem. Loosen the locknut and turn the adjusting screw in the required direction. Tighten the locknut and recheck clearance. Clearance is 0.004–0.006 in. intake and 0.010–0.012 in. exhaust for a cold engine and 0.006–0.008 in. intake and 0.012–0.014 in. exhaust for a hot engine. The B28F cold intake valve adjustment 0.008–0.010 in.; cold exhaust valve adjustment 0.012–0.014 in.

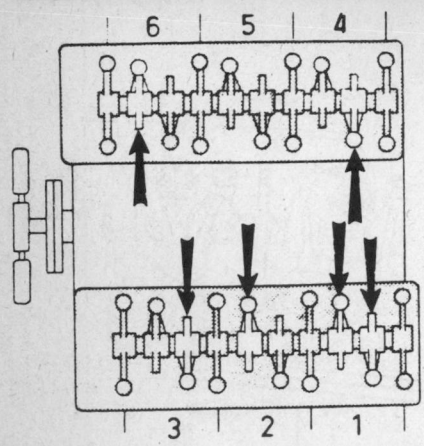

On B27 and 28 with no. 1 cylinder at TDC, adjust these valves (arrows)

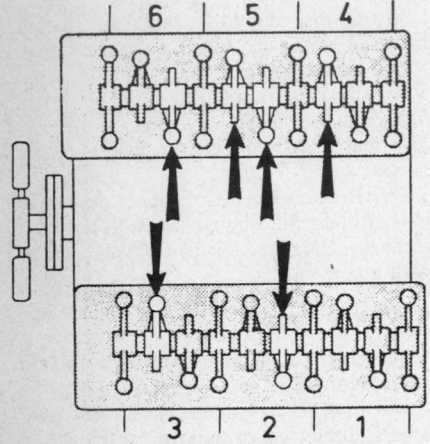

On B27 and 28, rotate the crankshaft 360 degrees and adjust the remaining valves (arrow)

3. Rotate the crankshaft pulley one full 360° turn to adjust the remaining valves. At this point, the "O" mark will again align with the pulley notch, the rotor is pointing 180° opposite its former position, and the No. 1 cylinder rockers contact the ramps of the camshaft. At this position (see illustration), adjust the intake valves of cylinders No. 3, 5, and 6, and the exhaust valves of cylinders No. 2, 4, and 5.

4. Install the valve covers with new gaskets. Connect all disconnected equipment.

D-24 Diesel Engine

NOTE: Always check valve clearances with the cylinder at TDC; turn the engine ¼ turn past TDC to set valves.

1. Remove the valve cover.
2. Use a ¹¹⁄₁₆ in. socket on the crankshaft pulley. Turn the pulley until the engine is ready to fire on the No. 1 cylinder. The flywheel timing mark should be at zero.

NOTE: The piston should be at ¼ turn past top dead center when setting the valve clearance.

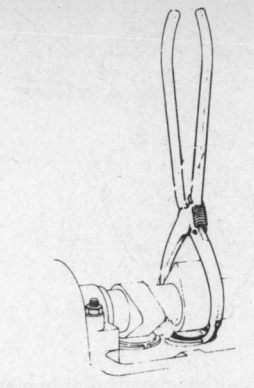

Removing valve adjusting disc (shim)—D24 engines

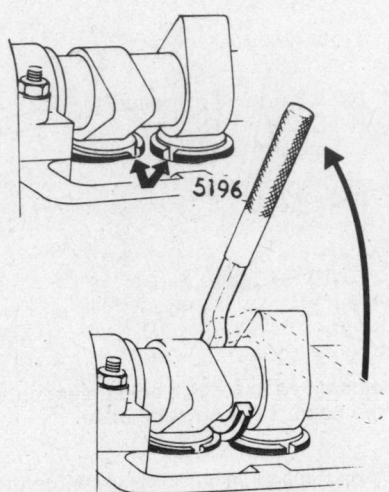

Cam disc removal D24 engine

3. Line up the valve depressors.
4. Turn them so that the notches point slightly upward.

NOTE: Use tool No. 5196 or equivalent to depress the valve depressors. This tool is available from your Volvo dealer.

5. The depressor grooves must be above the face so that the disc can be gripped with pliers. These pliers are available from your Volvo dealer under part No. 5195.
6. Remove the disc.
7. Calculate the disc thickness, using a micrometer. The discs are available in thicknesses of 0.1299–0.1673 in. with increments of 0.002 in.
8. Cold engine 0.008—intake, 0.016—exhaust. Warm engine 0.010—intake, 0.018—exhaust.

NOTE: Always use new discs when performing this procedure.

9. Oil the new disc and install it with the marked side down.
10. Check the remaining valve clearances.
11. Use the following sequence 1, 5, 3, 6, 2, 4.
12. Recheck the valve clearance for all cylinders.

13. Rotate the engine several times, and recheck the clearance.
14. Install the valve cover with a new gasket.

Fuel Injection

IDLE SPEED AND MIXTURE ADJUSTMENT

adjustment of idle mixture on both of these systems requires a CO meter and special training. However, the idle speed adjustment may be set using a tachometer (follow the manufacturer's instructions for hookup).

For all fuel injection system service information not covered here, please turn to "Fuel Injection" in the Unit Repair section.

Mechanical Injection (K-Jetronic)

B21F (INC. TURBO) 1978–80

1. Disconnect and plug the air injection pump output hose and the EGR vacuum hose.
2. With the engine warmed to operating temperature (176°F), check that the idle speed is 900 rpm (Manual trans) or 800 rpm (automatic) with the car idling in nuetral. Adjust as necessary by rotating the air adjusting screw (knob) located beneath the air intake box, (Note different knob location on Turbo).

1981 B21F

1. Run the engine to normal operating temperature. Disconnect the throttle control rod at the lever. Make sure the cable and pulley run smoothly and do not bind in any position.
2. Remove the ECU cover panel. Deactivate the ECU by disconnecting the white-red wire from terminal 12 of the blue connector plug at the ECU. Reinstall the connector plug.

NOTE: The same wire ends at the ignition coil but cannot be disconnected there.

3. Connect a tachometer to the engine according to the manufacturer's instructions. Connect a test light across the battery positive terminal and the terminal on the throttle micro switch with the yellow wire connected. Start the engine. The test light must NOT light up. If it does, adjust the micro switch position by slackening the switch retaining screws. Move the switch down until the light goes out, then retighten the screws. *This adjustment is temporary; final adjustment will follow later on.*

4. Idle speed should be 850–900 rpm. If outside these limits, adjust idle speed by proceeding to Step 5. If idle speed is within these limits, continue to Step 6.

5. If the idle speed is outside the stated limits, use the throttle position adjustment

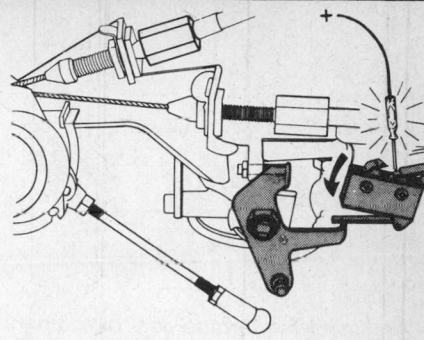

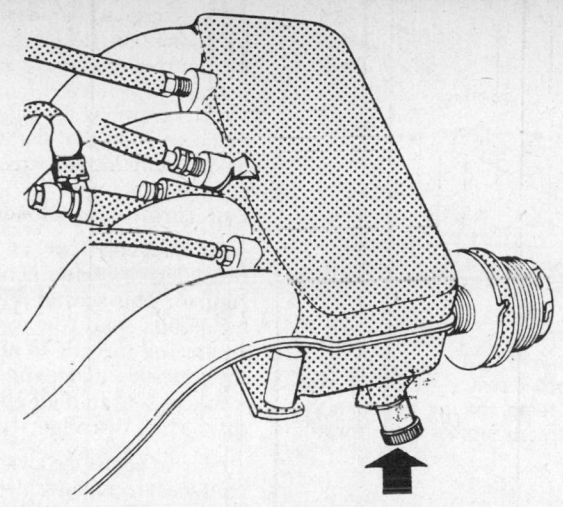

Mechanical (K-Jetronic) injection idle speed adjustment

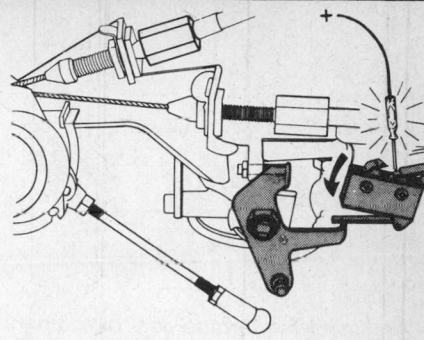

Adjusting throttle micro switch—B21F with K-Jetronic injection. Adjust idle if test light lights up at idle speed

screw to adjust the speed to 850–900 rpm. The test light must NOT light up; if it does, readjust the micro switch position. Reconnect the white-red wire in terminal 12 of the blue connector plug at the ECU to reactivate the ECU. The idle speed should have changed to 900 rpm (850–950 rpm is permitted). Stop the engine.

6. Reconnect the throttle control rod at the lever, making sure the cable pulley is completely retracted. If the control rod length must be adjusted, disconnect the throttle cable and automatic transmission kickdown cable (if equipped). Loosen the locknuts on either end of the rod and adjust the rod as necessary by turning it, then tighten the locknuts. Attach the throttle cable and adjust it if necessary by turning the nut on the end of the cable as shown. Automatic transmission kickdown cable length should be checked at closed and open throttle with the engine OFF. Open throttle cable measurement should be checked with the throttle pedal in the car depressed, NOT by actuating the linkage by hand. The cable should be pulled out 50mm, or 1.9 in.

7. Adjust the micro switch by moving the switch UP, with the engine not running and the throttle closed. Slacken the switch retaining screws, and move the switch UP until the test light lights up. Set the switch position by moving the switch DOWN 2–5.5mm or 0.08–0.10 in. The test light must not light up, or the adjustment will have to be performed again.

8. Remove the test light, reinstall the ECU panel.

1981 B21F MPG, 1982–85 B21F and B23E

The procedures for these engine models are the same as those for the 1981 B21F above, EXCEPT that the ECU from the 1982 on has two extra terminals, 7 and 10. To de-activate the ECU, ground terminal 10 with the connector in place by inserting a copper wire along the terminal wire. Also, the idle speed should be 700 rpm with the ECU de-activated, and 750 rpm, (700–800 rpm permitted) with the ECU activated. On step 2,

NO NOT reinstall the connector plug.

1981–85 B21F Turbo

1. Follow the procedures in Steps 1 and 2 of the 1981 B21F procedure EXCEPT do not reinstall the connector plug. Note the procedure above for de-activating 1982 and later ECUs.

2. Connect a test light across the battery positive terminal and the orange wire terminal on the micro (throttle) switch. The test light must NOT light up while adjusting the idle speed (the electric circuit through the micro switch is open). If the test light illuminates, adjust the micro switch position by slackening the switch retaining screws and moving the switch down until the test light goes out. Tighten the screws. *This is*

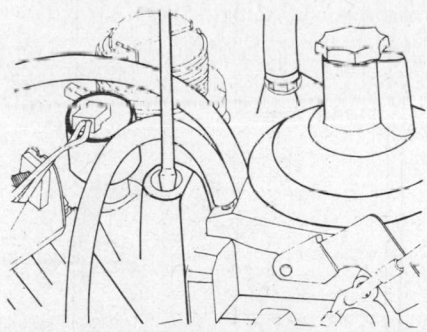

Adjusting idle speed (900 rpm)—Canadian B21A with carburetor

Turbo

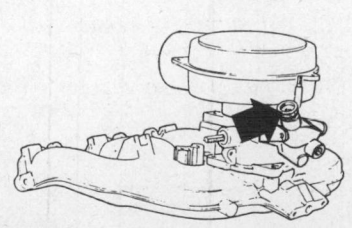

B21F Turbo idle adjustment screw

a temporary adjustment; the final adjustment will follow later on.

3. Run the engine to normal operating temperature if not already done. Connect a tachometer to the engine and check idle speed; idle speed should be 850 rpm. If idle speed is outside these limits, follow the procedure below.

4. Using the throttle position adjustment screw, adjust throttle position until the idle speed reaches 850 rpm. The test light must NOT light up. If necessary, adjust the micro switch position DOWN.

5. Activate the ECU by reconnecting the white-red wire in terminal 12 of the blue connector on 1981 models, and by disconnecting the ground wire that was inserted at terminal 10 of the blue connector on 1982 and later models.

6. After activating the ECU, the idle speed should change to 900 rpm on (850–900 permitted) on 1981 models, and to 900 rpm (880–920 rpm permitted) on 1982 and later models. Stop the engine and install the ECU panel.

7. Reconnect and adjust the throttle control rod and cable, and the automatic transmission kickdown cable (if equipped) by following Step 6 of the "1981 B21F" procedure.

8. Adjust the B21F Turbo throttle switch by inserting a 0.3mm feeler gauge between the throttle adjustment screw and the throttle control lever. Move the switch UP until the test light lights up. Set the switch by moving it DOWN until the test light just goes out. Disconnect all test instruments, install the ECU panel.

B27F and B28F
1978–80

1. Remove the air cleaner and housing. Disconnect the air pump outlet hose (large hose on rear of pump) and plug it with a large diameter screwdriver shaft. Disconnect and plug the vacuum hose at the EGR valve.

2. Set the idle balance screws (No. 1 and No. 2 in the illustration) to their basic setting by screwing them in clockwise until they bottom out, and then backing them off counterclockwise 4 full turns each.

3. Start the engine and allow it to reach operating temperature (176°F). Using the

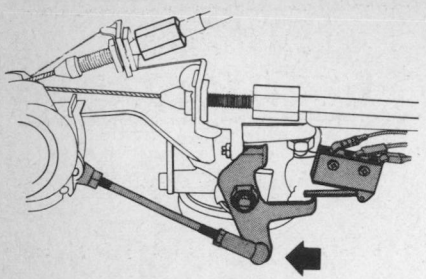

Disconnect the throttle control rod here on B21 engines

idle air adjusting screw (No. 3), set the idle speed to 900 rpm.

1981–1985

1. Disconnect the throttle rod at the cable pulley. Check the cable assembly, making sure the cable and pulley run smoothly and do not bind in any position. Check the throttle; make sure the throttle shaft and plate do not bind during operation.

2. Screw in the idle speed adjustment screw all the way until it just seats.

NOTE: This screw is used to adjust the idle speed on engines without the CIS system.

3. Remove the access panel to the ECU module. (The ECU is located on the passenger's side kick panel on all models except the 760 GLE, on which the ECU is mounted on the driver's side kick panel).

4. On 1981 models, disconnect the white-red wire at terminal 12 of the blue connector plug at the ECU. On 1982 and later models, ground terminal 10 with the connector in place. This can be done by inserting a copper wire along the number 10 terminal wire.

5. Connect a test light across the positive battery terminal and the orange wire terminal on the throttle micro switch. On 1981 models, the test light should light up, while adjusting the switch, indicating the electric circuit through the micro switch is closed. On 1982 and later models, the test light should NOT light up while adjusting the switch, indicating the electric circuit through the micro switch is interrupted.

6. Connect a tachometer to the engine, and run the engine up to normal operating temperature.

7. Adjust the idle speed by adjusting the throttle position adjustment screw. DO NOT adjust the idle speed screw (it should still be screwed in on its seat).

8. Activate the ECU by reconnecting the white-red wire in the blue connector at the ECU. With the ECU activated, the idle speed should change to 900 rpm on 1981 and 1982 models (850–950 permitted on 1981, 880–920 permitted on 1982) and 750 rpm on 1983 and later. Shut off the engine and install the ECU panel.

9. Reconnect the throttle control rod at the cable pulley. Disconnect the throttle cable and automatic transmission kickdown

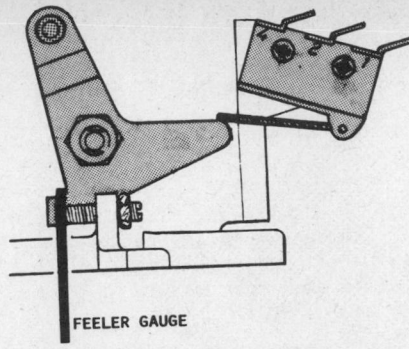

Adjusting throttle switch—B21F Turbo. Insert 0.3 mm feeler gauge between the throttle adjustment screw and throttle control lever

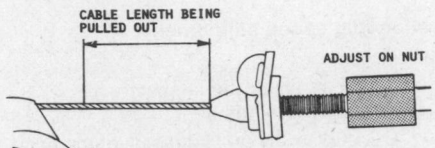

B21F Turbo automatic transmission kickdown cable adjustment

cable. The cable pulley should be completely retracted. Adjust the control rod length as necessary. Attach and adjust the throttle cable.

10. Check automatic transmission kickdown cable length at closed and open throttle with the engine off. Open throttle measurement should be checked with the throttle pedal in the car depressed, NOT by actuating the linkage by hand. Cable movement should be 50mm or about 1.9 in. Cable length with closed throttle should be 1 mm, with open throttle 51mm.

11. To adjust the throttle micro switch, insert 0.12 in. feeler gauge between the throttle position adjustment screw and the throttle stop. On 1981 models, adjust the switch by turning the adjustment screw until the test light goes out. On 1982 and later models, turn the adjustment screw until the test light light up.

Full Throttle Enrichment Switch

NOTE: The B28F V6 is equipped with two micro switches actuated by throttle control. This second micro switch closes a Lambda-sond (the oxygen sensor) circuit at full throttle to provide richer air/fuel mixture at maximum acceleration. Vehicles sold in high-altitude areas have this switch disconnected.

1. To adjust the switch, loosen the micro switch retaining screws. Turn the switch sideways. The test light should come on, then go out 2.5mm (3/32 in.) before the pul-

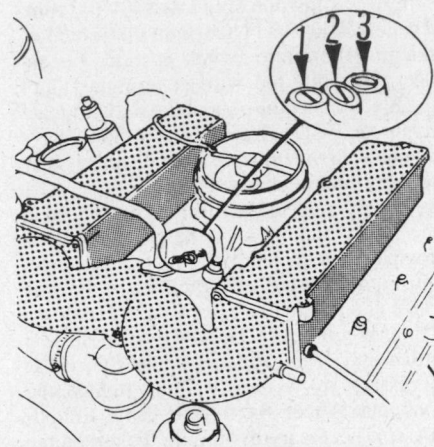

B27, 28 idle balance (nos. 1 and 2), and air adjusting screws (no. 3)

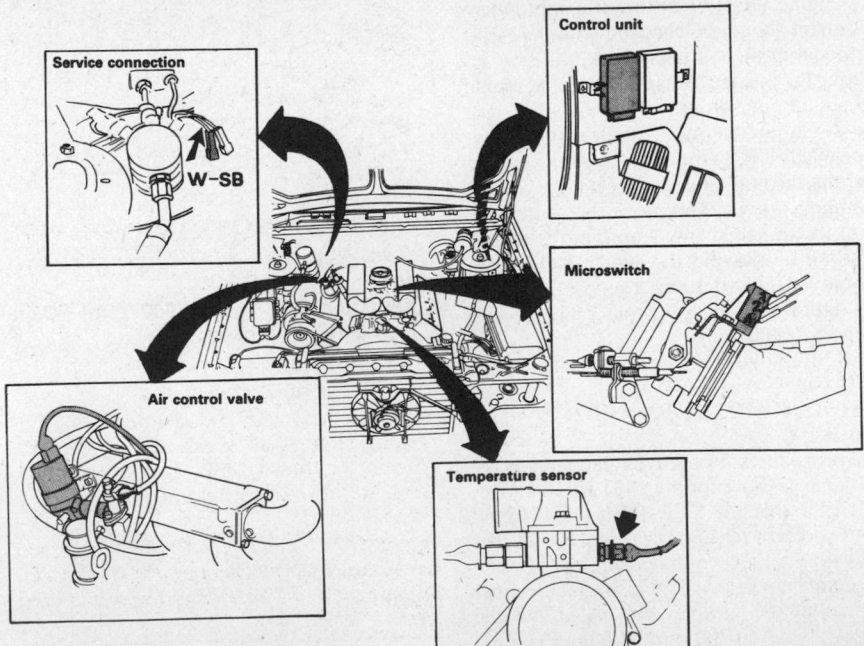

CIS component location—760 B28F

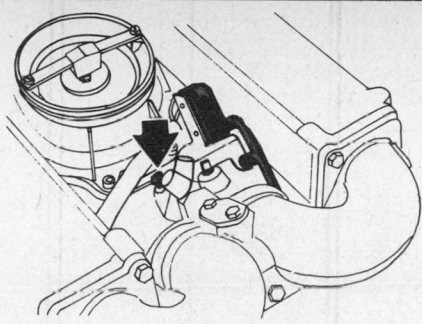

On 1981 and later B28F, make sure the idle speed adjustment screw is bottomed on its seat; this screw is used to adjust idle speed on non-CIS engines

ley touches the full throttle stop. Tighten the retaining screws.

2. To check full throttle enrichment switch operations, disconnect the green wire at the micro switch. Connect a test light between the micro switch terminal and the positive battery terminal.

3. Turn the pulley slowly to the full throttle stop. The test light should light up 1–4mm (1/32 in. 5/32 in.) before the pulley touches the stop. Adjust the switch as necessary, following the switch adjustment procedure above.

Electronic Injection (LH-Jetronic)

1982 B21F and 1983 and later B23F

1. Seat the throttle butterfly valve by loosening the stop nut on the adjuster screw. Unscrew the adjuster a couple of turns. Set the adjuster screw by screwing it in until it just touches the lever, then screw it in an additional 1/4 turn. Tighten the lock nut.

2. Disconnect the CIS connector on the firewall. This is the connector that is directly behind the engine.

3. Connect a test light across the battery positive terminal and the orange wire terminal in the connector. Start the engine. The test light should light up at idle speed. If it does not, readjust the adjuster screw for the throttle butterfly valve position.

4. Open the throttle slightly by hand at the throttle control lever, with the engine running. The test light should go out. If it does not, run through the procedure again and try a new throttle switch.

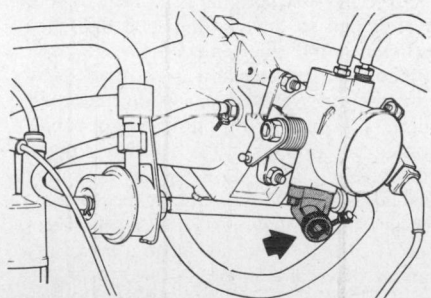

L-Jetronic idle adjustment location

Diesel Fuel Injection

SETTING THE IDLE SPEED

NOTE: To correctly set the idle speed you will need either the Volvo Monotester and adapter 9950 or a suitable photoelectric tachometer, since a gasoline engine tachometer by itself cannot be used on a diesel engine owing to the fact that a diesel engine does not have an electric ignition system.

1. Connect a suitable tachometer to the engine and run the engine to normal operating temperature.

2. Idle speed should be 720–880 rpm.

3. If not, adjust the idle speed by loosening the locknut and turning the idle speed screw on the fuel injection pump.

4. Tighten the locknut and apply a dab of paint or thread sealer to the adjusting screw to prevent it from vibrating loose.

5. After adjusting idle speed and maximum engine speed, adjust the engine throttle likage.

SETTING THE MAXIMUM ENGINE SPEED

The diesel engine is governed by the fuel injection pump so that engine rpm will not exceed 5,100–5,300 rpm. Because of the extremely high compression ratio (23.5:1) and the great stored energy diesel oil contains, the diesel engine cannot be run at the high rpm levels of modern gasoline engines, as it would place a tremendous strain on the pistons, wrist pins, connecting rods and bearings of the engine.

To adjust the maximum idle speed you will need a special tachometer which will work on the diesel engine. See the "NOTE" under "Setting The Idle Speed", above.

1. Connect the tachometer and run the engine to normal operating temperature.

2. Run the engine to maximum speed by turning the cable pulley counterclockwise.

—— CAUTION ——
Do not race the engine longer than absolutely necessary.

3. Maximum speed should be between 5100–5300 rpm.

4. If not, loosen the locknut and adjust using the maximum speed screw.

5. Tighten the locknut and apply a dab of paint or thread sealer to the adjusting screw to prevent it from vibrating loose.

—— CAUTION ——
Do not attempt to squeeze more power out of your diesel by extending the maximum speed.

6. After adjusting the maximum speed, adjust the engine throttle linkage.

Distributor

REMOVAL & INSTALLATION

1. Unsnap the distributor cap clasps and remove the cap.

2. Crank the engine until No. 1 cylinder is at Top Dead Center (TDC). At this point, the rotor should point to the spark plug wire socket for No. 1 cylinder, and the 0° timing mark on the crankshaft damper should be aligned with the pointer. For ease of assembly, scribe a chalkmark on the distributor housing to note the position of the rotor.

3. Disconnect the primary lead from the coil at its terminal on the distributor housing. On electronic fuel-injected models, disconnect the plug for the triggering contacts. On all models except Canadian B21A, remove the retaining screw for the primary voltage wire connector and pull it from the distributor housing.

4. Remove the vacuum hose(s) from the regulator. Take care not to damage the bakelite connection during removal.

5. Remove the distributor attaching screw and lift out the distributor.

6. When ready to install the distributor, if the engine has been disturbed (cranked), find TDC for No. 1 cylinder as outlined under "Valve Lash Adjustment". If the engine has not been disturbed, install the distributor with the rotor pointing to the No. 1 cylinder spark plug wire socket, or the chalkmark made prior to removal. On B21, B27 and B28F engines, the distributor drive gear teeth are bevelled, which will cause the rotor to turn counterclockwise as the distributor is installed. For this reason, it is necessary to back off the rotor clockwise (about 60° and on the B21, and 40° on the B27 and B28F) to compensate for this. What is necessary is that the rotor aligns with the mark made prior to removal after the distributor is bolted down.

7. Connect the primary lead to its terminal on the distributor housing. On electronic fuel-injected models, connect the plug for the triggering contacts. Push the primary voltage wire connector into its slot in the distributor housing and tighten the retaining screw.

8. Connect the vacuum hose(s) to the bakelite connection(s) on the vacuum regulator, (if so equipped).

9. If the distributor was disassembled, or if the contact point setting was disturbed, proceed to set the point gap and/or dwell angle on B21A (Canadian) engines.

10. Install the distributor cap and secure the clasps. Proceed to set the ignition timing. Tighten the distributor attaching screw.

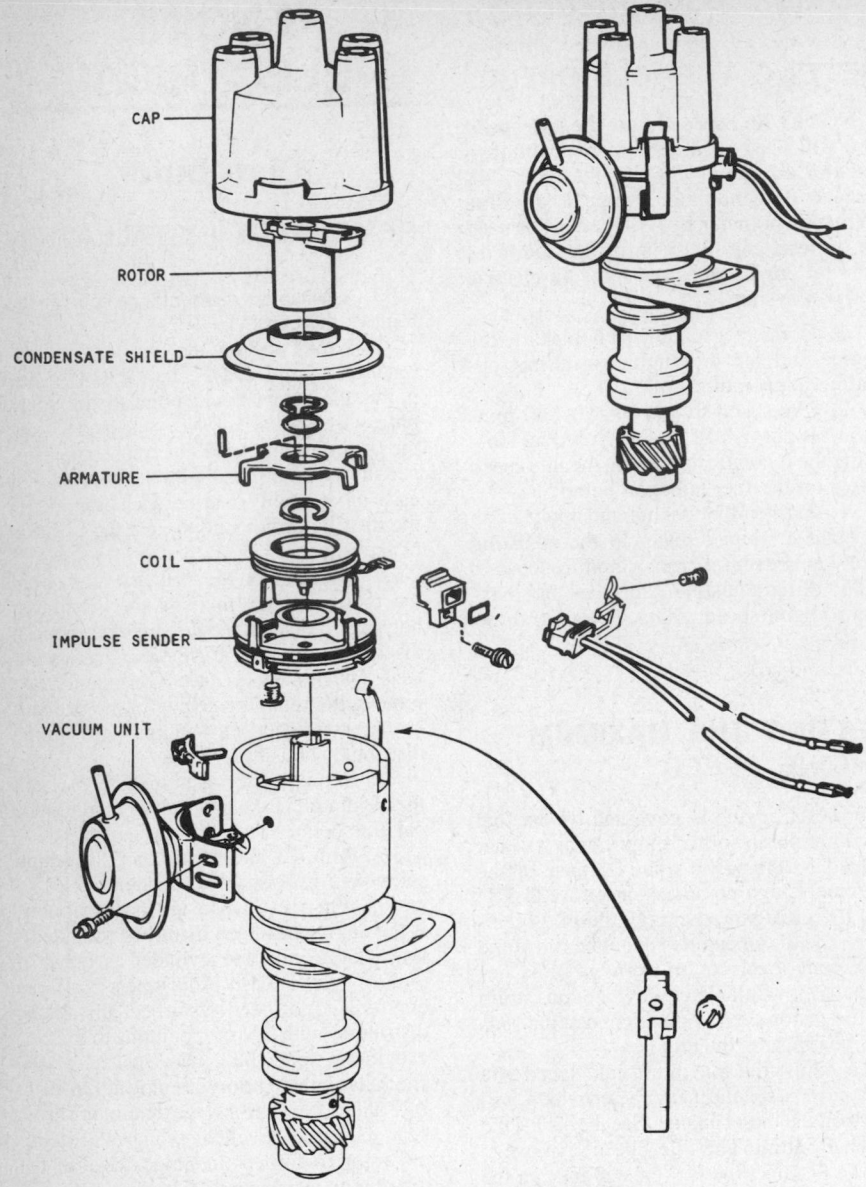

- CAP
- ROTOR
- CONDENSATE SHIELD
- ARMATURE
- COIL
- IMPULSE SENDER
- VACUUM UNIT

Electronic ignition distributor–240 series

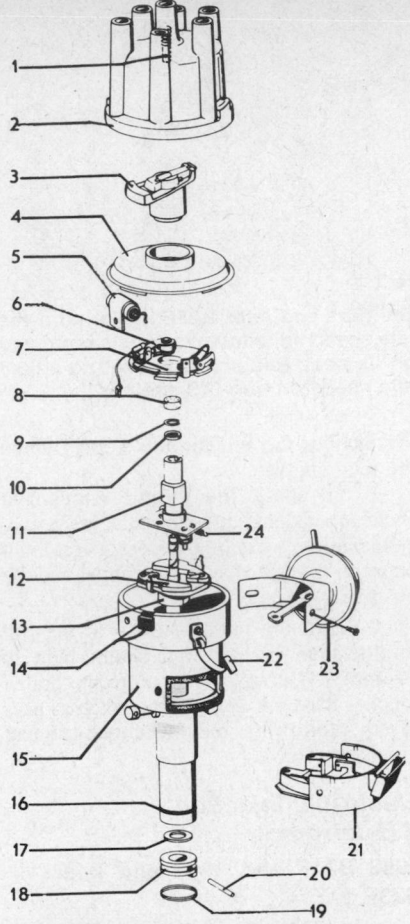

1. Rod brush (carbon)
2. Distributor cap
3. Distributor arm
4. Protective cover
5. Condenser
6. Ignition contact breaker
7. Breaker plate
8. Lubricating felt
9. Circlip
10. Washer
11. Breaker cam
12. Centrifugal weight
13. Cam for triggering contacts
14. Primary terminal
15. Distributor body
16. Rubber seal
17. Washers
18. Driving collar
19. Resilient ring
20. Lock pin
21. Contact device
22. Lock clamp for distr. cap
23. Vacuum regulator
24. Centrifugal governor spring

Distributor assembly—Canadian B21A engines

Accessory drive belt tension is correct when the deflection made with light finger pressure on the belt at a midway point is about ½ in. Any belt that is glazed, frayed, or stretched so that it cannot be tightened sufficiently must be replaced.

Incorrect belt tension is corrected by moving the driven accessory (alternator, air pump, power steering pump or air conditioning compressor) away from or toward the driving pulley. Loosen the mounting and adjusting bolts on the respective accessory and tighten them, once the belt tension is correct. *Never* position a *metal* pry bar on the rear end of the alternator, air pump or power steering pump housing; they can be deformed easily.

Alternator

PRECAUTIONS

Several precautions must be observed when performing work on alternator equipment.

1. If the battery is removed for any reason, make sure that it is reconnected with the correct polarity. Reversing the battery connections may result in damage to the one-way rectifiers.

2. Never operate the alternator with the main circuit broken. Make sure that the battery, alternator, and regulator leads are not disconnected while the engine is running.

3. Never attempt to polarize an alternator.

4. When charging a battery that is installed in the vehicle, disconnect the negative battery cable ᵔ *is very important.*

5. When utilizing a booster battery as a starting aid, always connect it in parallel; negative to negative, and positive to positive.

6. When arc welding is to be performed on any part of the vehicle, disconnect the negative battery cable, disconnect the alternator leads, and unplug the voltage regulator.

DRIVE BELT ADJUSTMENT

Accessory drive belt tension is checked every six months or 6000 miles. On 1980 and later models, no belt adjustment is recommended until 30,000 miles. Loose belts can cause poor engine cooling and diminish alternator output. A belt that is too tight places a severe strain on the water pump, alternator, air injection pumps, or power steering pump bearings.

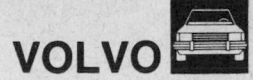
REMOVAL & INSTALLATION

1. Disconnect the negative battery cable.
2. Disconnect the electrical leads to the alternator.
3. Remove the adjusting arm-to-alternator bolt and the adjusting arm-to-engine bolt.
4. Remove the alternator mounting bolt.
5. Remove the fan belt and lift the alternator forward and out.
6. Reverse the above procedure to install, taking care to properly tension the fan (drive) belt.

Voltage Regulator

REMOVAL & INSTALLATION

1. Disconnect the negative battery cable.
2. Disconnect the leads or plug socket from the old regulator taking note of their (its) location.
3. Remove the hold-down screws from the old regulator and install the new one.
4. Connect the leads or plug socket and reconnect the negative battery cable.

VOLTAGE ADJUSTMENT

Motorola (S.E.V. Marchal) Regulator

If the Motorola A.C. regulator is found to be defective, it must be replaced. No adjustments can be made on this unit.

The following test may be performed on the Motorola regulator to see if it is functioning properly. An ammeter, tachometer, and voltmeter are required.

1. Connect the testing equipment to the alternator.
2. Run the engine at 2500 rpm (5000 alternator rpm) for 15 seconds. With no load on the alternator, and the regulator ambient temperature at 77°F, the reading on the voltmeter should be 13.1–14.4 V.

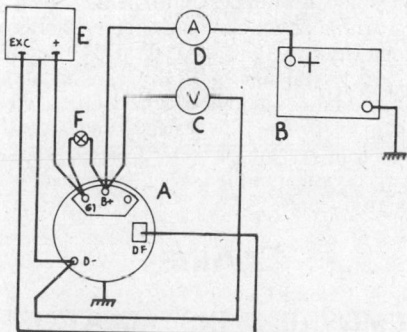

A. Alternator
B. Battery 60 Ah
C. Voltmeter 0—20 amps.
D. Ammeter 0—50 amps.
E. Voltage regulator
F. Warning lamp 12 volts. 2 watts

Wiring diagram for testing Motorola regulator

3. Load the alternator with 10–15 amps (high-beam headlights) while the engine is running at 2500 rpm. The voltmeter reading should again be 13.1–14.4 V. Replace the regulator if it does not fall within these limits.
4. For a more accurate indication of the regulator's performance, drive the vehicle for about 45 minutes at a minimum speed of 30 mph. The regulator will be at the correct working temperature immediately after this drive.
5. With the engine running at 2500 rpm, and the regulator ambient temperature at 77°F, the voltmeter reading should be 13.85–14.25 V.

Bosch A.C. Regulator (35, 55 and 70 Amp)

The Bosch A.C. regulator is fully adjustable. To determine which adjustments are necessary—if any—perform the following test. (An ammeter, 12 V control lamp, tachometer, and voltmeter are required for this test)

NOTE: Where the numerical values differ for the 35 amp voltage regulator and the 55 amp unit, the figures for the 55 amp regulator will be given in parentheses.

1. Connect the alternator and regulator as shown in the illustration.

NOTE: The first reading must be taken within 30 seconds of beginning of test.

2. While running the engine at 2000 rpm, load the alternator with 28–30 amps (44–46 for 55 amp alternator).
3. Rapidly lower the engine to idle speed or 500 rpm, and then return it to 2000 rpm. With a load of 28–30 amps (44–46 for 55 amp alternator), the voltmeter reading should be 14.0–15.0 V (13.9–14.8 V for 55 amp alternator). The regulator should be regulated on the left (lower) contact.
4. Reduce the alternator load to 3–8 amps. The voltmeter reading should not decrease more than 0.3 (0.4 for 44 amp, alternator) V. The regulator should be regulated on the right (upper) contact.
5. Adjustment is made by bending the stop bracket for the bimetal spring. Bending the stop bracket down lowers the regulating voltage; bending it up raises the voltage. If the voltmeter reading for the low amp alternator load decreased more than 0.3 (0.4 for 55 amp alternator), V, compared to the reading for the high amp alternator load, adjust the regulator by bending the holder for the left (lower) contact and simultaneously adjust the gap between the right (upper) contact and the movable contact. The gap should be adjusted to 0.010–0.015 in. (0.25–0.40mm). If the holder is bent toward the right (upper) contact, the regulating voltage under high amp alternator load will be lowered.

To avoid faulty adjustments due to residual magnetism in the regulator core, it may be necessary to rapidly lower the en-

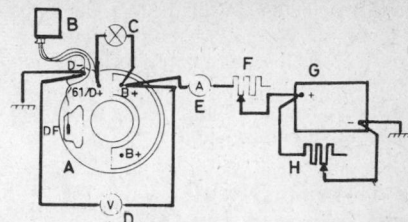

A. Alternator
B. Voltage lamp 12 volts
C. Control lamp 12 volts, 2 watts
D. Voltmeter 0-20 volts
F. Regulator resistance
G. Battery 60 amperehours
H. Load resistance
E. Ammeter 0-50 amps

Wiring diagram for testing Bosch A.C. regulator

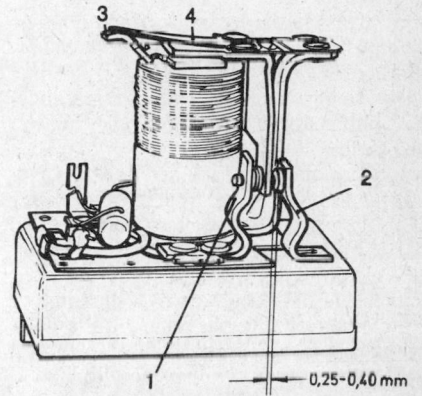

1. Regulator contact for lower control range (lower contact)
2. Regulator contact for upper control range (upper contact)
3. Spring tensioner
4. Spring upper section: Steel spring Lower section: Bimetal spring

Bosch A.C. voltage adjustments

gine rpm to idle after each adjustment, then raise it to 2000 rpm to take a new reading.

NOTE: Warm regulators may be cooled to ambient temperature by directing a stream of compressed air on them. Final readings should be made with the regulator at ambient temperature.

Starter

REMOVAL & INSTALLATION

1. Disconnect the negative battery cable at the battery.
2. Disconnect the leads from the starter motor.
3. Remove the bolts retaining the starter motor brace to the cylinder block (B21 only) and the bolts retaining the starter motor to the flywheel housing and lift it off.
4. Position the starter motor to the fly-

wheel housing and install the retaining bolts finger-tight. Torque the bolts to approximately 25 ft. lbs., and apply locking compound to the threads.

5. Connect the starter motor leads and the negative battery cable.

STARTER DRIVE REPLACEMENT

In order to remove the starter pinion drive, it is necessary to disassemble the starter. The procedure for disassembling the starter is as follows:

1. Remove the starter from the car as outlined in "Starter Removal and Installation."

2. Unscrew the two screws and remove the small cover from the front end of the starter shaft.

3. Unsnap the lockwasher and remove the adjusting washers from the front end of the shaft.

4. Unscrew the two screws retaining the commutator bearing shield and remove the shield.

5. Lift up the brushes and retainers and remove the brush bridge from the rotor shaft. The negative brushes are removed with the bridge while the positive brushes remain in the field winding. Do not remove the steel washer and the fiber washer at this time.

6. Unscrew the nut retaining the field terminal connection to the control solenoid.

7. Unscrew the two solenoid-to-starter housing retaining screws and remove the solenoid.

8. Remove the drive end shield and rotor from the stator.

9. Remove the rubber and metal sealing washers from the housing.

10. Unscrew the nut and remove the screw on which the engaging arm pivots.

11. Remove the rotor, with the pinion and engaging arm attached, from the drive end shield.

12. Push back the stop washer and remove the snap-ring from the rotor shaft.

13. Remove the stop washer and pull off the starter pinion with a gear puller.

While the starter is disassembled, a few quick checks may be performed. Check the rotor shaft, commutator, and windings. If the rotor shaft is bent or worn, it must be replaced. Maximum rotor shaft radial throw is 0.003 in. If the commutator is scored or worn unevenly, it should be turned. Minimum commutator diameter is 1.3 in. Check the end shield which houses the brushes, for excessive wear. Maximum bearing clearance is 0.005 in.

14. Lubricate the starter.

15. Press the starter pinion onto the rotor shaft. Install the stop washer and secure it with a new snap-ring.

16. Position the engaging arm on the pinion. Install the rotor into the drive end frame.

17. Install the screw and nut for the engaging arm pivot.

18. Install the rubber and metal sealing washers into the drive end housing.

19. Install the stator onto the rotor and drive end shield.

20. Position the solenoid so that the eyelet on the end of the solenoid plunger fits onto the engaging arm (shift lever). Tighten the solenoid retaining screws.

21. Place the metal and fiber washers on the rotor shaft.

22. Install the brush bridge on the rotor shaft and replace the brushes.

23. Fit the commutator bearing shield into position and install the retaining screws.

24. Install the adjusting washers and snap a new lockwasher into position on the end of the shaft. Make sure that the rotor axial clearance does not exceed 0.12 in. If necessary, adjust the clearance with washers, maintaining a minimum clearance of 0.002 in.

25. Replace the small cover over the front end of the shaft and install the two retaining screws.

26. Install the starter in the car as outlined in "Starter Removal and Installation."

SOLENOID REPLACEMENT

Before replacing the solenoid when the starter

will not crank, see if the battery has sufficient charge. If the no-crank condition persists when the battery is known to be good, connect a jumper wire between the positive terminal of the battery and the contact screw for the solenoid lead. If the solenoid engages the starter pinion, the starter switch or leads are at fault. If the starter still does not crank, replace the solenoid. To remove the solenoid, remove the starter from the car. The solenoid may be removed from the starter while installed in the car, but then aligning the solenoid is as follows.

1. Remove the starter from the car as outlined in "Starter Removal and Installation."

2. Unscrew the two solenoid-to-starter housing retaining screws and remove the solenoid.

3. As a final test, wipe the solenoid clean and press in the armature. Test its operation by connecting it to a battery. If the solenoid still does not function, replace it with a new unit.

4. Position the new solenoid so that the eyelet on the end of the plunger fits into the engaging arm. Tighten the retaining screws.

5. Replace the starter in the car as outlined in "Starter Removal and Installation."

ENGINE MECHANICAL

Five basic engines are covered here. They are the B21F (2127cc), which is the basic inline four-cylinder, overhead cam engine (the B21FLH and B21FT are variations); the B23 (2320cc), which is very similar to the B21 series, but which has a bigger bore and totally new cylinder block; the B27F (2664cc), an alloy overhead cam V6 with iron liners first introduced in 1976 and phased out in 1980; the B28F (2849cc), which is almost identical in design to the B27F, except with a larger bore and slightly shorter stroke (new in 1980); and the D24 Diesel (2383cc), which is a Volkswagen-manufactured inline six first introduced in Volvo cars in 1980. The D24 is also a single overhead cam design (the D24T is a turbocharged variant of the D24 and shares most design features).

Engine

REMOVAL & INSTALLATION

B21F and B23E Series (Includes B21FLH, B21FT, B23FLH)

1. On cars equipped with manual transmission, remove the four retaining clips and lift up the shifter boot. Then, remove the snap-ring from the shifter.

2. Remove the battery.

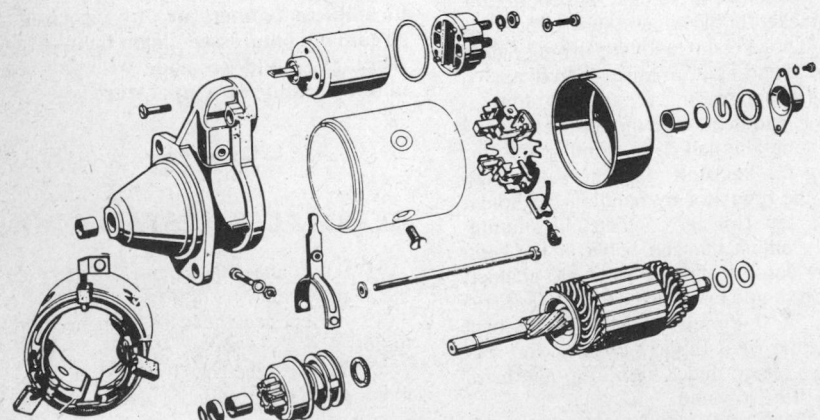

Exploded view of a typical starter motor

3. Disconnect the windshield washer hose and engine compartment light wire. Scribe marks around the hood mount brackets on the underside of the hood for later alignment. Remove the hood.

4. Remove the overflow tank cap. Drain the cooling system by disconnecting the lower radiator hose and opening the engine drain cock (beneath the exhaust manifold).

5. Remove the upper and lower radiator hoses. Disconnect the overflow hoses at the radiator. Disconnect the overflow hoses at the radiator. Disconnect the PCV hose at the cylinder head.

6. On cars equipped with automatic transmission, disconnect the oil cooler lines at the radiator.

7. Remove the radiator and fan shroud.

8. Remove the air cleaner assembly and hoses.

9. Disconnect the hoses at the air pump. Remove the air pump and drive belt, if equipped.

10. Disconnect the vacuum pump hoses and remove the vacuum pump. Disconnect the power brake booster vacuum hose.

11. Remove the power steering pump, drive belt and bracket. Position to one side.

12. On cars equipped with air conditioning, remove the crankshaft pulley (5 mm Allen wrench), and compressor drive belt. Then, install the pulley again for reference. Remove the A/C wire connector and the compressor from its bracket and position to one side. Remove the bracket.

13. Disconnect the vacuum hoses from the engine. Disconnect the carbon canister hoses.

14. Disconnect the distributor wire connector, high tension lead, starter cables, and the clutch cable clamp.

15. Disconnect the wiring harness at the voltage regulator. Disconnect the throttle cable at the pulley, and the wire for the A/C at the intake manifold solenoid.

16. Remove the gas cap. Disconnect the fuel lines at the filter and return pipe.

17. At the firewall, disconnect the electrical connectors for the ballast resistor, and relays. Disconnect the heater hoses.

18. Disconnect the micro switch connectors at the intake manifold, and all remaining harness connectors to the engine.

19. Drain the crankcase.

20. Remove the exhaust manifold flange retaining nuts. Loosen the exhaust pipe clamp bolts and remove the bracket for the front exhaust pipe mount. On B21FT (Turbo) models, disconnect the turbo from the intake hose, disconnect the other hoses from the turbo unit, and disconnect the turbocharger from the exhaust system.

21. From underneath, remove the front motor mount bolts.

22. On cars equipped with automatic transmission, place the gear selector lever in "Park" and disconnect the gear shift control rod from the transmission.

23. On manual transmission cars, disconnect the clutch cable. Then, loosen the set screw, drive out the pivot pin, and re-

move the shifter from the control rod.

24. Disconnect the speedometer and the driveshaft from the transmission.

25. On overdrive equipped models, disconnect the control wire from the shifter.

26. Jack up the front of the car and place jack stands beneath the reinforced box member areas to the rear of each front jacking attachment. Then, using a floor jack and a wooden block, support the weight of the engine beneath the transmission.

27. Remove the bolts for the rear transmission mount. Remove the transmission support crossmember.

28. Lift out the engine.

29. Reverse the above procedure to install. Adjust gear selector linkage, check and adjust throttle linkage.

B27F and B28F

1. On cars equipped with manual transmission, remove the shifter assembly. From underneath, loosen the set screw and drive out the pivot pin. Then, pull up the boot, remove the reverse pawl bracket, and snapring for the shifter, and lift out the shifter.

2. Remove the battery.

3. Disconnect the windshield washer hose and engine compartment light wire. Scribe marks around the hood mount brackets on the underside of the hood for later hood alignment. Remove the hood.

4. Remove the air cleaner assembly.

5. Remove the splash guard under the engine.

6. Drain the cooling system by disconnecting the lower radiator hose and open the drain cocks on both sides of the cylinder block.

7. Remove the overflow tank cap. Remove the upper and lower radiator hoses, and disconnect the overflow hoses at the radiator.

8. On cars equipped with automatic transmission, disconnect the transmission cooler lines at the radiator.

9. Remove the radiator and fan shroud.

10. Disconnect the heater hoses, power brake hose at the intake manifold and the vacuum pump hose at the pump. Remove the vacuum pump and O-ring in the valve cover. Remove the gas cap.

11. At the firewall disconnect the fuel lines (**CAUTION: High pressure**) at the

filter and return pipe, disconnect the relay connectors and all other wire connectors. Disconnect the distributor wires.

12. Disconnect the evaporative control carbon canister hoses and the vacuum hose at the EGR valve.

13. Disconnect the voltage regulator wire connector.

14. Disconnect the throttle cable (and kickdown cable on automatic transmission cars), the vacuum amplifier hose at the T-pipe, and the hoses at the wax thermostat.

15. Disconnect the air pump hose at the backfire valve, the solenoid valve wire, and the micro switch wire.

16. Remove the exhaust manifold flange retaining nuts (both sides).

17. On cars equipped with air conditioning, remove the compressor and drive belt, and place it to one side. Do not disconnect the refrigerant hoses.

18. Drain the crankcase.

19. Remove the power steering pump, drive belt, and bracket. Position to one side.

20. From underneath, remove the retaining nuts for the front motor mounts.

21. On models equipped with a catalytic converter, remove the front exhaust pipe.

22. On 49 states models, remove the front exhaust pipe hangers and clamps and allow the system to hang.

23. On cars equipped with automatic transmission, place the shift lever in "Park". Disconnect the shift control lever at the transmission.

24. On manual transmission cars, disconnect the clutch cylinder from the bell housing. Leave the cylinder connected (secure it to the car).

25. Disconnect the speedometer cable and driveshaft at the transmission.

26. Jack up the front of the car and place jack stands beneath the reinforced box member area to the rear of each front jacking attachment. Then, using a floor jack and a thick, wide wooden block, support the weight of the engine beneath the oil pan.

27. Remove the bolts for the rear transmission mount. Remove the transmission support crossmember.

28. Lift out the engine and transmission as a unit.

29. Reverse the above procedure to install. Adjust gear selector linkage, check and adjust throttle linkage.

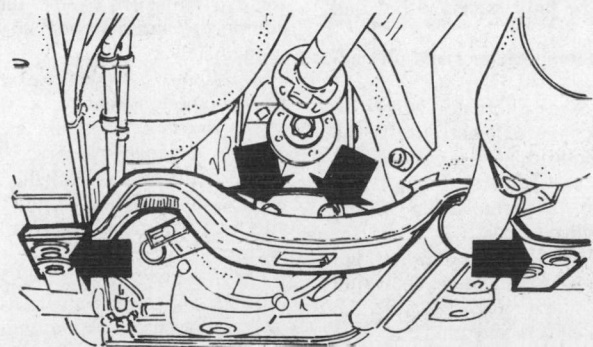

Removing the transmission support member—B21 and B23 series (V6 cars similar)

D24 and D24T

1. Remove the hood.
2. Disconnect the negative battery terminal.
3. Drain the radiator coolant.
4. Remove the four clips and pull up the rubber boot on the shift lever.
5. Disconnect the back-up light and overdrive connector if so equipped.
6. Remove the bracket for the reverse inhibitor.
7. Release the lock ring on the shift lever.
8. Move the lock ring, rubber ring, and plastic journal up on the lever.

NOTE: On cars with automatic transmissions place the shift lever in Park before disconnecting.

9. Disconnect the top and bottom radiator hoses.
10. Disconnect the lower hose at the cold start device, and drain the coolant into a suitable container.
11. On vehicles with automatic transmissions remove the cooling lines from the radiator.
12. Disconnect the expansion tank hose.
13. Unbolt and remove the radiator.
14. Disconnect the electrical connection at the firewall.
15. Remove the heater hoses at the control valve.
16. Disconnect the hose from the vacuum pump.
17. Disconnect the accelerator cable from the pulley and bracket.
18. Disconnect the vacuum line to the brake booster.
19. Disconnect the fuel lines.

NOTE: Thoroughly clean all connections prior to disconnecting them.

20. Plug all fuel lines to prevent dirt from entering them.
21. Disconnect the wires at the main terminal.
22. Disconnect the glow plug relay.
23. Remove the relay retaining screws and hang the relay and the wire bundle on the engine.
24. Remove the steering pump and brackets, and tie it out of the way.
25. Remove the starter wires and the battery ground strap.
26. Remove the fan, spacer, pulley and drive belts.
27. Remove the air cleaner and all necessary hoses.
28. Disconnect the alternator wires.
29. Disconnect the exhaust pipe at the front exhaust manifold.
30. Drain the engine oil.
31. Disconnect the exhaust pipe at the rear exhaust manifold.
32. On D24T models, remove the inlet hose from the turbo pipe, and the snap-ring from the turbo intake pipe. Remove the compressor intake pipe and plug the hole immediately with a clean rag. Disconnect the oil return pipe bolts, and move the re-

turn pipe aside. Plug the holes. Remove the oil delivery pipe from the turbo unit, and plug the holes. Remove the compressor and exhaust pipes from the turbo unit, and remove the turbocharger.
33. Disconnect the clutch cable, return spring, vibration damper, and rubber buffer.
34. Pull out the clutch cable from the clutch lever and housing.
35. Disconnect the speedometer from the transmission.

NOTE: On cars with automatic transmissions disconnect the shift lever.

36. Disconnect the shift lever and push it up into the car.
37. Remove the driveshaft from the transmission.
38. Support the transmission with a jack and remove the rear crossmember.
39. Remove the engine mounts.
   a. Left side: Remove the nuts from the front axle member.
   b. Right side: Remove the lower nut from the rubber pad.
40. Gently put tension on your engine removal hoist.
41. Remove the left engine mount assembly.
42. Remove the engine.
43. Installation is the reverse of removal. Adjust gear selector linkage, and check and adjust throttle linkage. Use new gaskets on the turbocharger if equipped.

Cylinder Head

REMOVAL & INSTALLATION

NOTE: To prevent warpage of the head, removal should be attempted only on a cold engine.

B21F, B21FT, B23 Series

1. Disconnect the battery.
2. Remove the overflow tank cap and drain the coolant. Disconnect the upper radiator hose.
3. Remove the distributor cap and wires.
4. Remove the PCV hoses.
5. Remove the EGR valve and vacuum pump.
6. Remove the air pump, if equipped, and air injection manifold. Disconnect and remove all hoses to the turbocharger if equipped. Plug all open hoses and holes immediately.
7. Remove the exhaust manifold and header pipe bracket.
8. Remove the intake manifold. Disconnect the manifold brace and the hose clamp to the bellows for the fuel injection air/flow unit. Disconnect the throttle cable, and all vacuum hoses and electrical connectors to the fuel injection unit.
9. Remove the fuel injectors.
10. Remove the valve cover.
11. Loosen the fan shroud and remove the fan. Remove the shroud. Remove the upper belts and pulleys.

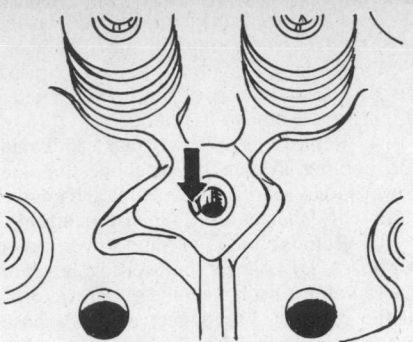
Oil feed hole in head

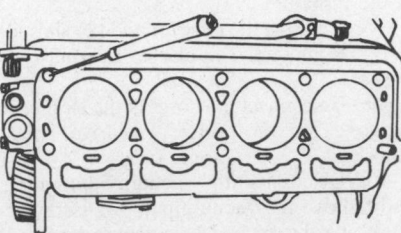
Guide stud installation

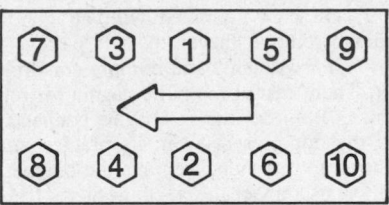
Cylinder head bolt tightening sequence— B21 and B23 series

12. Remove the timing belt cover. Remove the timing belt as described later in this section.
13. Remove the camshaft (if so desired) as outlined later in this section.
14. Remove the cylinder head 10mm Allen head bolts.
15. To install, reverse the removal procedure. Oil the head bolts. Tighten the head bolts in the prescribed torque sequence first to 44 ft. lbs., then to 81 ft. lbs. After the engine has been run 30 minutes, slacken the bolts to relieve any pretension, and then retorque to 81 ft. lbs. To set the valve timing, follow the steps for timing belt installation later in this section.

B27F and B28F

1. Disconnect the battery. Drain the coolant.
2. Remove the air cleaner assembly and all attaching hoses.
3. Disconnect the throttle cable. On automatic transmission equipped cars, disconnect the kick-down cable.
4. Disconnect the EGR vacuum hose and remove the pipe between the EGR valve and manifold.
5. Remove the oil filler cap, and cover the hole with a rag. Disconnect the PCV pipe(s) from the intake manifold.

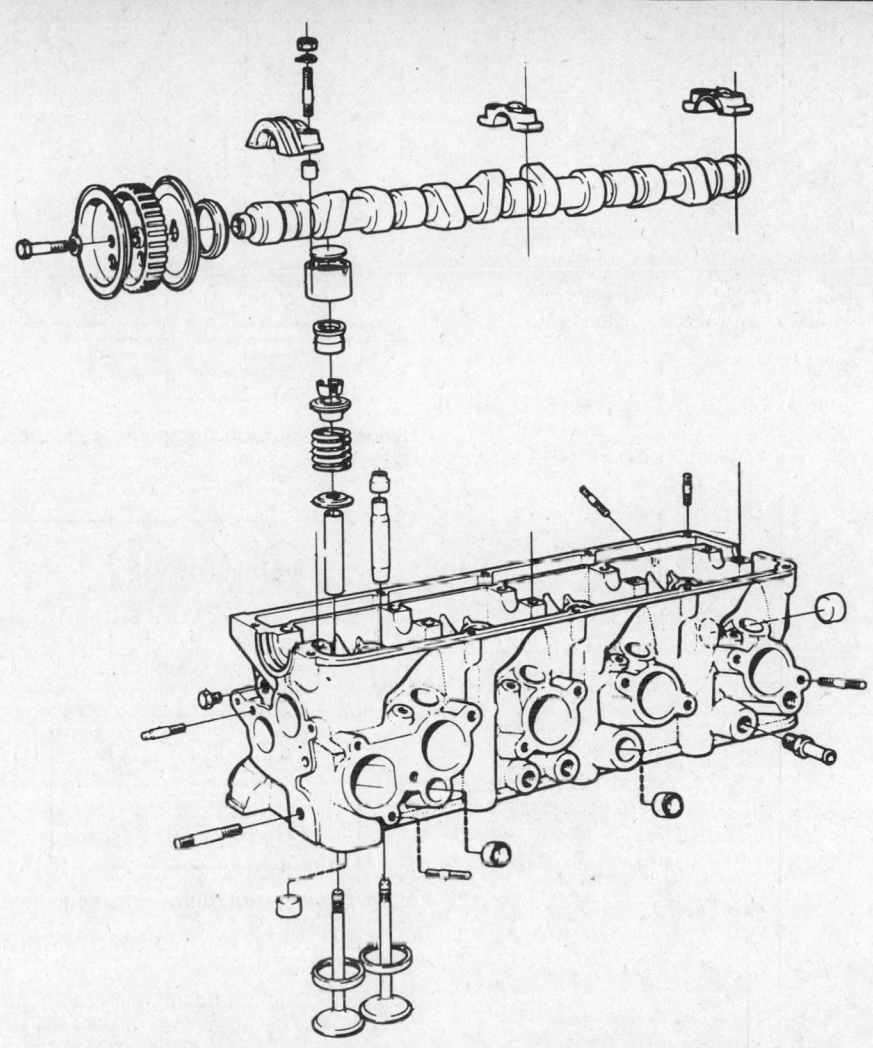

disconnect the electrical connectors at the relays.

25. On air conditioned models, remove the rear compressor bracket.

26. Disconnect the coolant hose(s) from the water pump to the cylinder head(s). If removing the left cylinder head, disconnect the lower radiator hose at the water pump.

27. Disconnect the air injection system supply hose from the applicable cylinder head. Separate the air manifold at the rear of the engine. If removing the left cylinder head, remove the backfire valve and air hose.

28. Remove the valve cover(s).

29. On the left cylinder head, remove the Allen head screw and four upper bolts to the timing gear cover. On the right cylinder head, remove the four upper bolts to the timing gear cover and the front cover plate.

30. From beneath the car, remove the exhaust pipe clamps for both header pipes.

31. If removing the right cylinder head, remove the retainer bracket bolts and pull the dipstick tube out of the crankcase.

32. Remove the applicable exhaust manifold(s).

33. Remove the cover plate at the rear of the cylinder head.

34. Rotate the camshaft sprocket (for the applicable cylinder head) into position so that the large sprocket hole aligns with the rocker arm shaft. With the camshaft in this position, loosen the cylinder head bolts in sequence (same sequence as tightening), and remove the rocker arm and shaft assembly.

35. Loosen the camshaft retaining fork bolt (directly in back of sprocket) and slide the fork away from the camshaft.

36. Next, it is necessary to hold the cam chain stretched during camshaft removal. Otherwise, the chain tensioner will automatically take up the slack, making it impossible to reinstall the sprocket on the cam without removing the timing chain cover to loosen the tensioner device. To accomplish this, a special sprocket retainer tool (Volvo No. 999 5104) is installed over the sprocket with two bolts in the top of the timing chain cover. A bolt is then screwed into the sprocket to hold it in place.

37. Remove the camshaft sprocket center bolt and push the camshaft to the rear, so it clears the sprocket.

38. Remove the cylinder head.

NOTE: Do not remove the cylinder head by pulling straight up. Instead, lever the head off by inserting two spare head bolts into the front and rear inboard cylinder head bolt holes, and pulling toward the applicable wheel housing. Otherwise, the cylinder liners may be pulled up, breaking the lower liner seal and leaking coolant into the crankcase. If any do pull up, new liner seals must be used, and the crankcase completely drained. If the head(s) seem stuck, gently tap around the edges of the head(s) with a rubber mallet, to break the joint.

Cylinder head assembly—all four cylinder engines similar

6. Remove the front section of the intake manifold.

7. Disconnect the electrical connector and fuel line at the cold start injector. Disconnect the vacuum hose, both fuel lines, and the electrical connector from the control pressure regulator.

8. Disconnect the hose, pipe, and electrical connector from the auxiliary air valve. Remove the auxiliary air valve.

9. Disconnect the electrical connector from the fuel distributor. Remove the wire looms from the intake manifolds. Disconnect the spark plug wires.

10. Disconnect the fuel injectors from their holders.

11. Disconnect the distributor vacuum hose, carbon filter hose, and diverter valve hose from the intake manifold. Also, disconnect the power brake hose and heater hose at the intake manifold.

12. Disconnect the throttle control link from its pulley.

13. On cars equipped with an EGR vacuum amplifier, disconnect the wires from the throttle micro switch and solenoid valve.

14. At the firewall, disconnect the fuel

lines from the fuel filter and return line.

15. Remove the two attaching screws and lift out the fuel distributor and throttle housing assembly.

16. On cars not equipped with an EGR vacuum amplifier, disconnect the EGR valve hose from underneath the throttle housing.

17. Remove the cold start injector, rubber ring, and pipe.

18. Remove the four retaining bolts and lift off the intake manifold. Remove the rubber rings.

19. Remove the splash guard beneath the engine.

20. If removing the left cylinder head, remove the air pump from its bracket.

21. Remove the vacuum pump and O-ring in the valve cover. Remove the vacuum hoses from the wax thermostat.

22. If removing the right cylinder head, disconnect the upper radiator hose.

23. On air conditioned models, remove the AC compressor and secure it to one side. *Do not disconnect the refrigerant lines.*

24. Disconnect the distributor leads and remove the distributor. Remove the EGR valve, bracket and pipe. At the firewall,

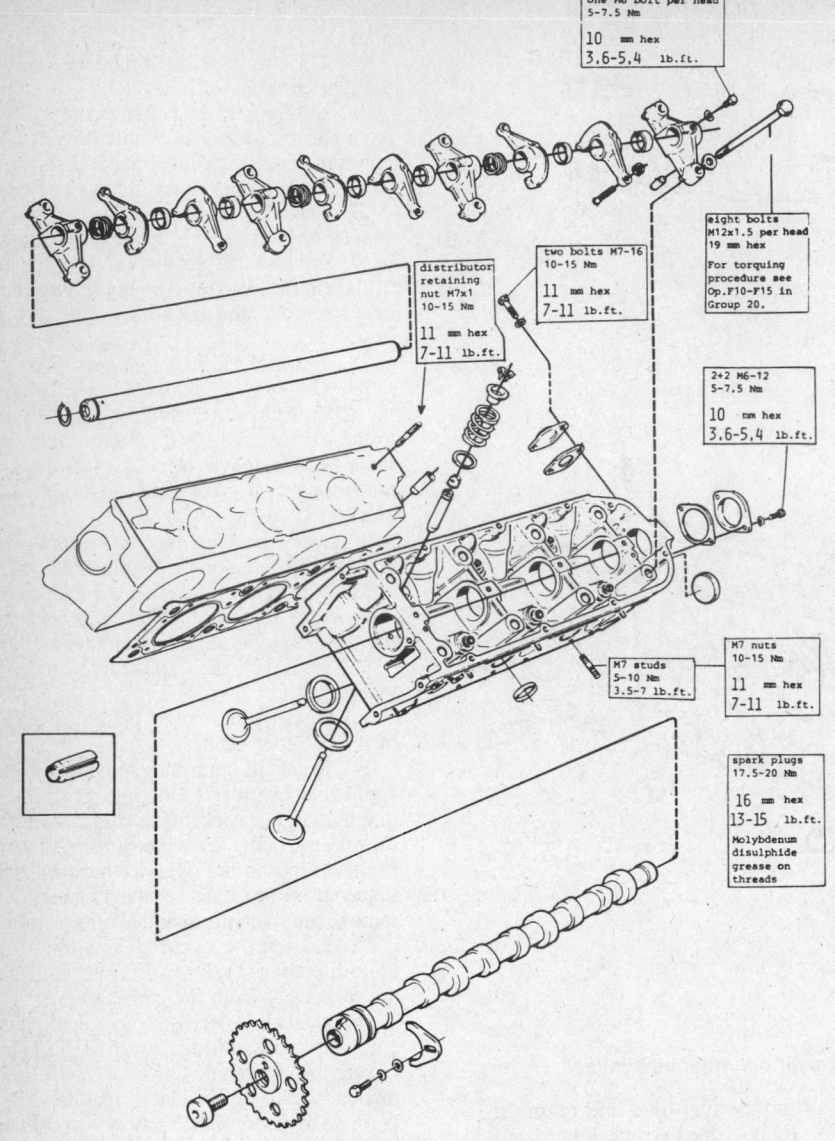

one M6 bolt per head
5-7.5 Nm

10 mm hex
3.6-5.4 lb.ft.

distributor
retaining
nut M7x1
10-15 Nm

11 mm hex
7-11 lb.ft.

two bolts M7-16
10-15 Nm

11 mm hex
7-11 lb.ft.

eight bolts
M12x1.5 per head
19 mm hex

For torquing
procedure see
Op.F10-F15 in
Group 20.

2+2 M6-12
5-7.5 Nm

10 mm hex
3.6-5.4 lb.ft.

M7 studs
5-10 Nm
3.5-7 lb.ft.

M7 nuts
10-15 Nm

11 mm hex
7-11 lb.ft.

spark plugs
17.5-20 Nm

16 mm hex
13-15 lb.ft.

Molybdenum
disulphide
grease on
threads

B27, 28 cylinder head assembly

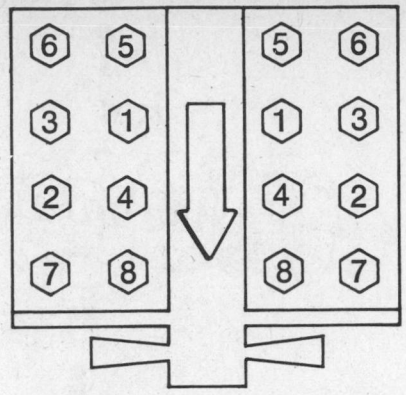

Cylinder head bolt tightening sequence, B27, B28

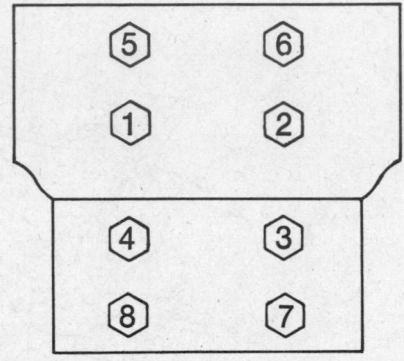

Main bearing nut tightening sequence, B27, B28

39. Remove the head gasket. Clean the contact surfaces with a plastic scraper and lacquer thinner.

40. If the head is going to be off for any length of time, install liner holders (Volvo special tool No. 999 5093) or two strips of thick stock steel with holes for the head bolts, so that the liners stay pressed down against their seals. Install the holders widthwise between the middle four head bolt holes.

41. Reverse the above procedure to install, using the following installation notes:

a. There are a pair of guide dowels at both outboard corners of the head. If they fell down during removal, pull them back out with a puller hammer. They can be propped up with a ⅛ in. drill shank.

b. Remove the liner holders.

c. The right and left head gaskets are different.

d. Check the timing chain cover gasket. If damaged, replace only the upper section.

e. Oil the head bolt threads. Position the head on the dowels and install (hand tight) one center head bolt. Then, slide the camshaft forward into position against the sprocket and install the sprocket center bolts, and remove the retainer tool.

f. Before installing the head bolts, remove the guide dowel shanks, if used.

g. Using the correct tightening sequence, tighten the head bolts to 7 ft. lbs., then 22 ft. lbs., and then 44 ft. lbs. Next slacken the head bolts (in the tightening sequence) to relieve any pre-tension. Now, tighten the bolts to 11–14 ft. lbs. *Finally, tighten the head bolts exactly one-third of a full 360° turn (116–120°) in the tightening sequence. This is critical for proper piston liner O-ring sealing. If necessary, use a protractor to ensure accuracy.*

h. Adjust the valves after completing assembly.

i. After running the engine to operating temperature, allow to cool for 30

minutes, and retorquing the head bolts. Following the tightening sequence slacken the bolts to relieve any pre-tension, then tighten to 11–14 ft. lbs. *and finally protractor torque them to 113–117° (one-third of a full turn).*

D24 and D24T

1. Disconnect the negative battery terminal.

2. Remove the engine splash guard.

3. Disconnect the exhaust pipe from the transmission bracket. On D24T models, disconnect all hoses to the turbocharger, and plug any open holes.

4. Disconnect the exhaust pipe from the rear exhaust manifold.

5. Disconnect the exhaust pipe from the front exhaust manifold.

6. Remove the air cleaner and all necessary hoses.

7. Drain the radiator.

8. Remove the bottom and top radiator hoses.

9. Remove the bottom hose from the cold start device and drain it into a suitable container.

10. Remove the top cold start hose.

11. Remove the vacuum pump and the plunger.

12. Remove all the fuel lines and plug the fuel line connections.

Final step of cylinder head tightening sequence is protractor torquing to 116-120 degrees (1/3 of a full turn)

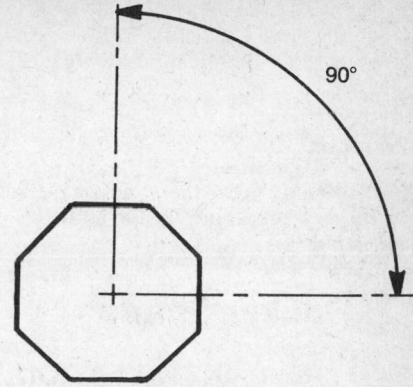

Protractor (angle) torquing, 90° shown. Do not exceed specified degrees

NOTE: Carefully remove all dirt from the fuel line connections to prevent dirt from entering the system.

13. Remove the glow plug wires and temperature sender wire.

14. Remove the rear injector return line hose.

15. Remove the valve cover.

16. Remove the front and rear timing belt covers.

17. Set the engine at top dead center and the fuel pump to the injection position for the Number one cylinder.

18. Remove the timing belt shield from the head.

NOTE: Be careful not to drop the washers or bolts into the lower cover.

19. Loosen the bolts on the water pump and the belt idler pulley.

20. Remove the belt from the camshaft.

21. Use special tool No. 5199 or a suitable replacement to hold the cam gear steady while removing it. This tool is available from your Volvo dealer.

NOTE: Do not allow the camshaft to turn.

22. Loosen the fuel pump bracket retaining screws to loosen the belt tension.

23. Remove the belt.

24. Remove the rear camshaft gear; see Step 21 for this procedure.

25. Remove the head bolts, and remove the head.

26. Installation is the reverse of removal.

NOTE: From late 1980, new type cylinder head bolts are used on the D24 diesel. They are longer and 1mm wide. Torquing these bolts is a six-step procedure:

1. Torque to 30 ft. lbs.
2. Torque to 44 ft. lbs.
3. Torque to 55 ft. lbs.
4. Tighten 180°, in one movement, without stopping.
5. Run engine until oil temperature is minimum 120°F.
6. Tighten 90°, in one movement, without stopping.

NOTE: Always use a new gasket when replacing the head.

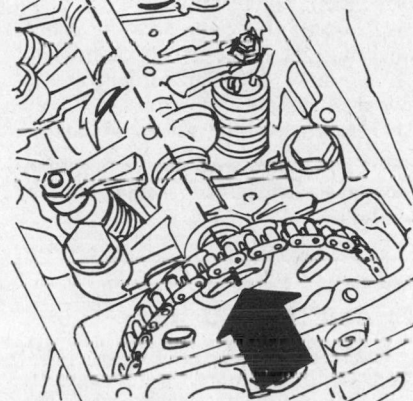

Aligning camshaft for cylinder head removal, B27, 28

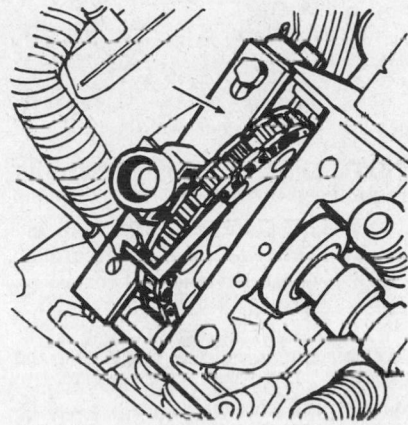

B27, 28 camshaft sprocket retainer tool

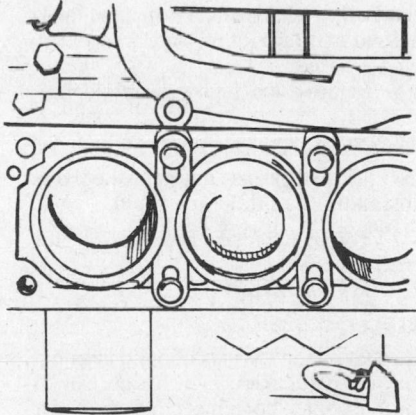

Cylinder liner holders installed

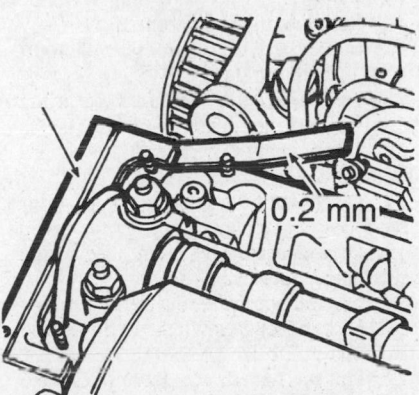

Camshaft position gauge

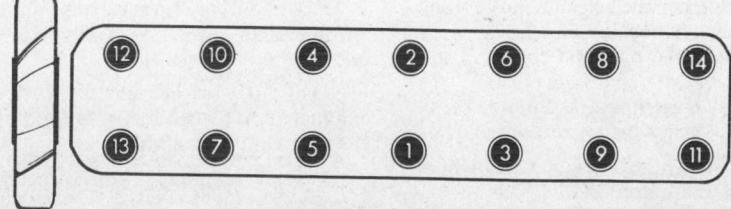

Diesel head bolt torque sequence. Loosen bolts in reverse order starting at 14

The following special tools are needed for reinstallation of the head: Belt tension gauge No. 5197, Camshaft position gauge No. 5190.

OVERHAUL

For all overhaul procedures, please refer to "Engine Rebuilding" in the Unit Repair section.

Rocker Shafts

REMOVAL & INSTALLATION

B27F and B28F

1. Disconnect the battery.
2. Remove the air cleaner assembly.
3. Disconnect the air pump bracket.
4. Remove the left valve cover (if so desired).
5. Tie the upper radiator hose out of the way and remove the oil filler cap and carbon canister hose.
6. On air conditioned models, remove the AC compressor from its bracket. Do not disconnect the hoses.
7. Remove the EGR valve.
8. Remove the AC compressor rear bracket.
9. Remove the control pressure regulator.
10. Disconnect any hoses or wires in the way. Remove the right valve cover (if so desired).
11. The rocker arm bolts double as cylinder head bolts. When loosening, follow the cylinder head bolt tightening sequence diagram. If removing both rocker shafts, mark them left and right.

NOTE: Do not jar or strike head while rockers and bolts are out, as cylinder liner O-ring seals may break, necessitating teardown of engine to clean coolant out of crankcase and installation of new seals.

12. To install, reverse removal procedure. Follow cylinder head installation procedure for proper torque sequence.

Intake and Exhaust Manifolds

REMOVAL & INSTALLATION

Inlet Duct

1. Disconnect the negative battery cable.
2. Disconnect the throttle and downshift linkage. Remove from the inlet duct, the positive crankcase ventilation, distributor advance, pressure sensor (electronic fuel-injection models only) and power brake hoses.
3. On electronic fuel injected models (B21FLH, B23F), disconnect the contact

---

for the throttle valve switch, and remove the ground cable for the inlet duct.

4. Remove the bolts for the inlet duct stay. Remove the inlet duct-to-cylinder head retaining nuts and slide the inlet duct off the studs. Discard the old gasket.
5. To install, reverse the above procedure. Use a new inlet duct gasket. Torque the nuts to 13–16 ft. lbs.

Intake Manifold
B27F and B28F

1. Remove the air cleaner and all necessary hoses.
2. Drain the radiator coolant.
3. Remove the throttle cable from the pulley and bracket.
4. On automatic transmission cars remove the throttle cable that is connected to the transmission.
5. Remove the EGR pipe from the EGR valve to the manifold.
6. Disconnect the EGR vacuum line.
7. Remove the oil filler cap and PCV valve.

NOTE: Cover the oil cap opening with a rag to keep dirt out.

8. Remove the front manifold bolts and remove the front section of the manifold.
9. Disconnect the cold start connector, fuel line, and injector.
10. Disconnect the pressure control regulator vacuum lines, fuel lines, and the connector.
11. Remove the auxiliary valve and its necessary piping.
12. Disconnect the electrical connections at the air fuel control unit.
13. Remove all six spark plug wires.
14. Remove all six injectors.
15. Move the wiring harness to the outside of the manifold.
16. Disconnect the vacuum hose at the distributor and the intake manifold.
17. Disconnect the heater hose at the intake manifold.
18. Disconnect the hose to the diverter valve.
19. Disconnect the vacuum hose to the power brake booster.
20. Disconnect the throttle cable link.
21. Disconnect the wires to the micro switch.
22. Pull the wires away from the intake manifold.
23. Remove the fuel filter line and the return line.
24. Remove the air control unit.
25. Disconnect the vacuum hose from the throttle valve housing.
26. Remove the pipe and cold start injector assembly.
27. Remove the intake assembly.
28. Installation is the reverse of removal.

NOTE: Always use new gaskets when reinstalling the manifold.

29. Torque the manifold bolts to 7–11 ft. lbs.

B21F and B21FT

1. Remove the air cleaner and all necessary hoses.
2. Remove the PCV valve.
3. Remove the connector at the cold start injector.
4. Remove the fuel hose from the cold start injector.
5. Remove the cold start injector.
6. Remove the connector on the auxiliary valve.
7. Disconnect the hoses at the auxiliary valve.
8. Remove the auxiliary valve.
9. On B21FT models, disconnect the turbocharger inlet hose (between turbo unit and intake manifold). Plug the hose immediately.
10. Remove the intake manifold brace.
11. Disconnect the distributor vacuum hose at the intake manifold.
12. Loosen the clamp for the rubber connecting pipe on the air-fuel control unit.
13. Remove the manifold bolts and remove the manifold.
14. Installation is the reverse of removal.

NOTE: Remember to install new manifold gaskets before replacing the manifold.

15. Torque the manifold bolts to 15 ft. lbs.

D24 AND D24T DIESEL

1. Disconnect the negative battery terminal.
2. Remove the air cleaner and all necessary hoses.
3. Remove any other necessary vacuum or electrical lines.
4. On D24T models, disconnect the turbocharger inlet hose (between the intake manifold and turbo unit) and immediately plug the hose.
5. Remove the intake manifold bolts and remove the manifold.
6. Installation is the reverse of removal.

NOTE: Always use a new gasket when reinstalling the intake manifold.

7. Torque the intake bolts to 18 ft. lbs.

Exhaust Manifold
B27F and B28F

Depending upon the type of optional equipment your particular vehicle has the exhaust manifolds may be removed from underneath the car.

1. Jack up your vehicle and support it with jack stands.
2. Unbolt the crossover pipe from the left and right side of your exhaust manifolds, (if so equipped).

NOTE: If your car has the "Y" type exhaust pipe disconnect this pipe at the left and right manifolds.

3. Remove any other necessary hardware.
4. Remove the left and right side manifolds.

5. Installation is the reverse of removal.

NOTE: Always use new gaskets when reinstalling the manifolds.

6. Torque the manifold bolts to 7–11 ft. lbs.

B21F and B21FT

1. Remove the air cleaner and all necessary hoses.

2. Remove the EGR valve pipe from the manifold.

3. Remove the exhaust pipe from the exhaust manifold. On B21FT, remove the exhaust pipe from the turbocharger.

4. Remove the manifold bolts and remove the manifold.

NOTE: Remember to install new manifold gaskets before installing the manifold.

5. Installation is the reverse of removal.

6. Torque the manifold bolts to 10–20 ft. lbs.

D24 AND D24T DIESEL

1. Disconnect the negative battery terminal.

2. Remove the air cleaner and all necessary hoses.

3. Remove the exhaust pipes from the manifolds. On D24T models, remove the exhaust pipe from the turbocharger.

NOTE: The exhaust manifold is made in two separate sections.

4. Remove any other necessary hardware.

5. Remove the intake manifold. See the "Intake Manifold" removal section.

6. Remove the exhaust manifold in two sections.

7. Installation is the reverse of removal.

NOTE: Always use new gaskets when reinstalling the exhaust manifold.

8. Torque the bolts to 18 ft. lbs.

Turbocharger

For further information on turbocharging, please refer to "Turbocharging" in the Unit Repair section.

REMOVAL & INSTALLATION

B21FT and B23FT

1. Disconnect battery ground cable.

2. Disconnect expansion tank from retainer. Remove expansion tank retainer.

3. Remove preheater hose to the air cleaner. Remove the pipe and rubber bellows between the air/fuel control unit and the turbocharger unit. Pull out the crankcase ventilation hose from the pipe.

4. Remove the pipe and pipe connector between the turbocharger unit and the intake manifold.

NOTE: Cover the turbocharger intake and outlet ports to keep dirt out of the system.

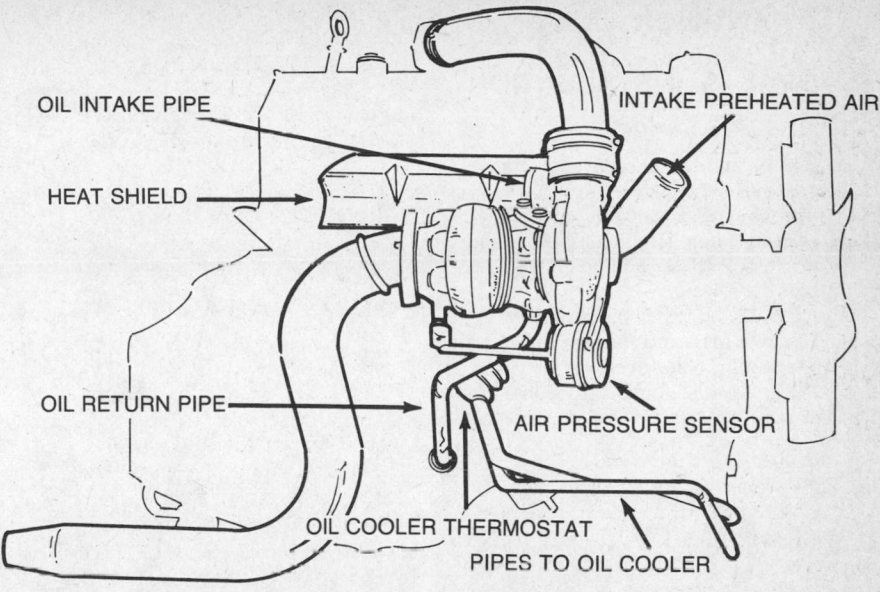

Turbocharger system component location

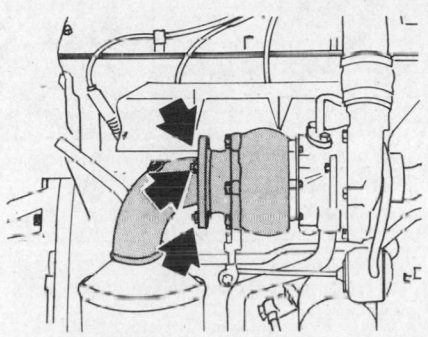

Disconnect the turbocharger unit from the exhaust system

5. Disconnect the exhaust pipe and secure it aside.

6. Disconnect the spark plug wires at the plugs.

7. Remove the upper heat shield. Remove the brace between the turbocharger unit and the manifold.

8. Remove the lower heat shield by removing the one retaining screw underneath the manifold.

9. Remove the oil pipe clamp, retaining screws on the turbo unit and the pipe connection screw in the cylinder block under the manifold. DO NOT allow any dirt to enter the oilways.

10. Remove the manifold retaining screws and washers. Let one nut remain in position to keep the manifold in position.

11. Remove the oil delivery pipe. Cover the opening on the turbo unit.

12. Disconnect the air/fuel control unit by loosening the clamps. Move the unit with the lower section of the air cleaner up to the right side wheel housing. Place a cover over the wheel housing as protection.

13. Remove the air cleaner filter.

14. Remove the remaining nut and washer on the manifold. Lift the assembly forward and up. Remove the manifold gaskets. Disconnect the return oil pipe O-ring from the cylinder block.

15. Disconnect the turbocharger unit from the manifold.

16. Installation is the reverse of removal. Be sure to use a new gasket for the exhaust manifold and a new O-ring to the return oil pipe. Keep everything clean during assembly, and use extreme care in keeping dirt out of the various turbo inlet and outlet pipes and hoses.

D24T

1. Remove the negative battery cable.

2. Remove the inlet hose from the turbo pipe.

3. Remove the complete air cleaner assembly, and the preheater hoses.

4. Remove the snap-ring from the turbocharger intake pipe, and remove the compressor intake pipe. *Plug the hose immediately.*

5. Disconnect the bolts securing the oil return pipe to the turbo unit. Move the pipe aside, and *plug the holes immediately.*

6. Remove the oil delivery pipe from the turbocharger and *plug the holes.*

7. Press the compressor pipe into the intake pipe. Remove the exhaust pipe from the turbocharger.

8. Jack up the car, and place jack stands safely underneath. Remove the exhaust pipe from the transmission support bracket and from the joint. Remove the exhaust pipe.

9. Remove the turbocharger securing nuts, and lower the front end of the turbo unit. Remove the turbocharger. Remove the compressor pipe.

10. If the turbocharger is replaced complete, transfer the necessary parts to the new unit. *Always use new gaskets.*

11. Installation is the reverse of removal. Make sure all hoses are connected without the addition of any dirt into the system. *This is crucial to the life of the turbocharger and the engine.*

VOLVO

Timing Belt Cover

REMOVAL & INSTALLATION

B21F and B23 Series

1. Loosen the fan shroud and remove the fan. Remove the shroud.

2. Loosen the alternator, air pump, power steering pump (if so equipped), and A/C compressor (if so equipped) and remove their drive belts.

3. Remove the water pump pulley.

4. Remove the four retaining bolts and lift off the timing belt cover.

5. Reverse the above procedure to install.

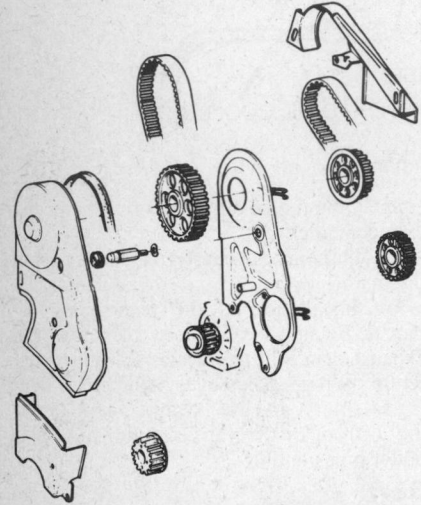

D24 Diesel timing belt cover and assembly

D24 and D24T

1. Drain the engine coolant.

2. Remove the splash guard under the engine. Disconnect the lower hose at the radiator. Remove the expansion tank cap.

3. Remove the radiator.

4. Remove the cooling fan with spacer and pulley.

5. Remove the fan belt. Remove the drive belt for the power steering pump.

6. Remove the valve cover.

7. Remove the front and rear timing gear covers.

8. Installation is the reverse of removal.

Timing Belt

REMOVAL & INSTALLATION

B21F and B23 Series

1. Remove the timing belt cover as outlined previously.

2. To remove the tension from the belt, loosen the nut for the tensioner and press the idler roller back. The tension spring can be locked in this position by inserting the shank end of a 3mm drill through the pusher rod.

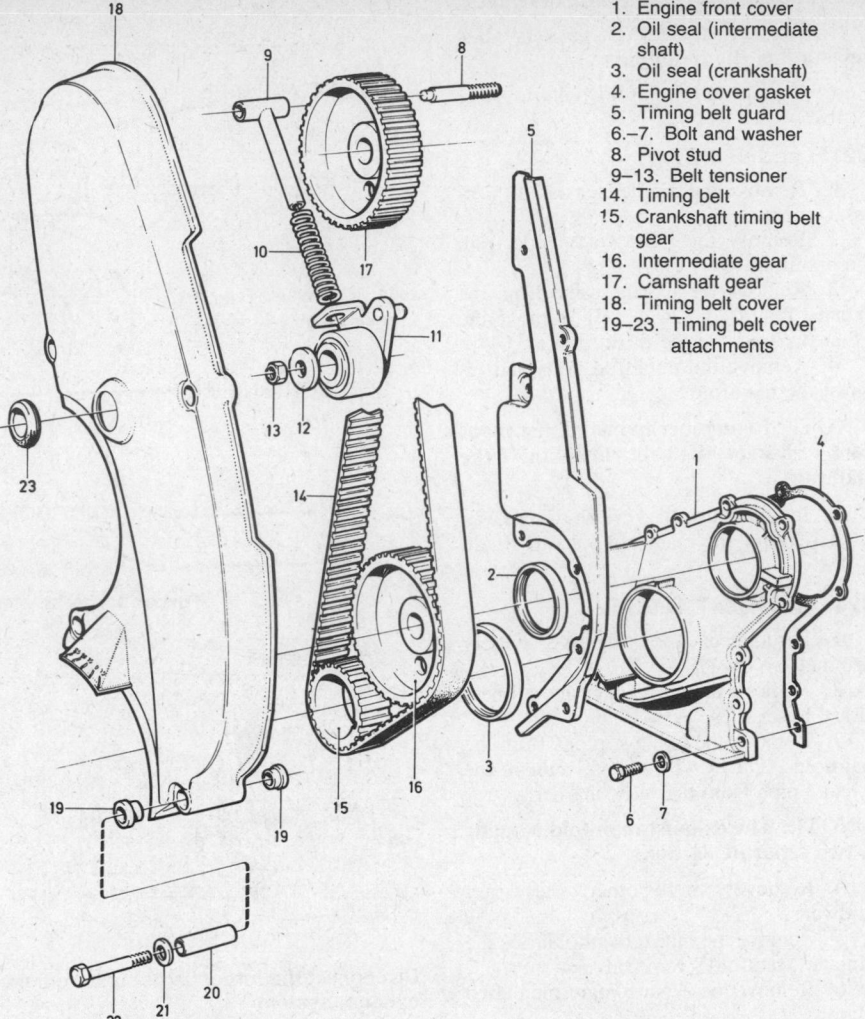

1. Engine front cover
2. Oil seal (intermediate shaft)
3. Oil seal (crankshaft)
4. Engine cover gasket
5. Timing belt guard
6.–7. Bolt and washer
8. Pivot stud
9–13. Belt tensioner
14. Timing belt
15. Crankshaft timing belt gear
16. Intermediate gear
17. Camshaft gear
18. Timing belt cover
19–23. Timing belt cover attachments

Timing belt assembly—all four cylinder engines similar

3. Remove the six retaining bolts and the crankshaft pulley.

4. Remove the belt, taking care not to bend it at any sharp angles. The belt should be replaced at 45,000 mile intervals, if it becomes oil soaked or frayed, or if it is on a car that has been sitting idle for any length of time.

5. If the crankshaft, idler shaft, or camshaft were disturbed while the belt was out, align each shaft with its corresponding index mark to assure proper valve timing and ignition timing, as follows:

  a. Rotate the crankshaft so that the notch in the convex crankshaft gear belt guide aligns with the embossed mark on the front cover (12 o'clock position).

  b. Rotate the idler shaft so that the dot on the idler shaft drive sprocket aligns with the notch on the timing belt rear cover (four o'clock position).

  c. Rotate the camshaft so that the notch in the camshaft sprocket inner belt guide aligns with the notch in the forward edge of the valve cover (12 o'clock position).

6. Install the timing belt (don't use any sharp tools) over the sprockets, and then

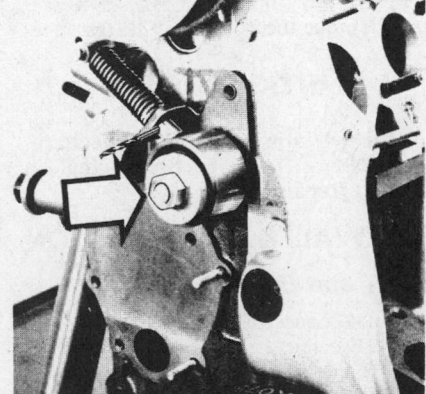

Locking the tensioner spring with drill bit shank

over the tensioner roller. New belts have yellow marks. The two lines on the drive belt should fit toward the crankshaft marks. The next mark should then fit toward the intermediate shaft marks, etc. Loosen the tensioner nut and let the spring tension automatically take up the slack. Tighten the tensioner nut to 37 ft. lbs.

C1012

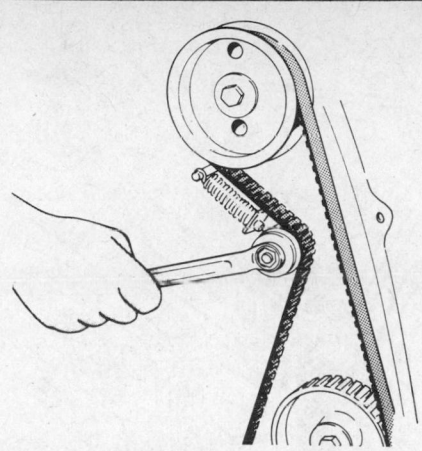

Timing belt tensioner—four cylinder engines

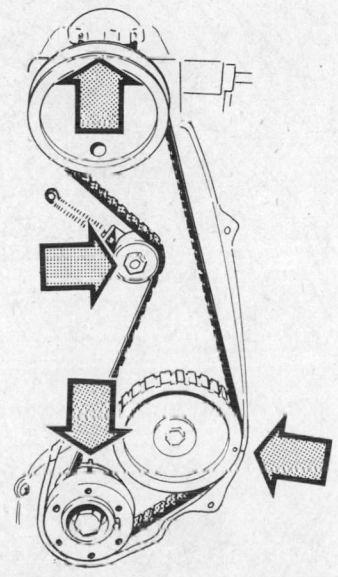

Make sure all marks are lined up including marks on new belt—B21 and B23 series

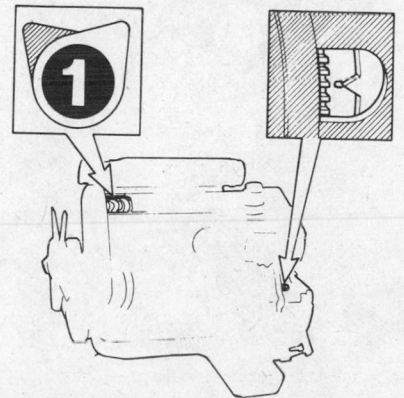

Setting No. 1 cylinder to TDC and injection position—D24. Cam lobes are "up", flywheel on 0

7. Rotate the crankshaft one full revolution clockwise, and make sure the timing marks still align.

8. Reverse Steps 1-3 to install.

D24 and D24T

1. Remove the timing belt cover as previously outlined.

2. Set cylinder No. 1 to TDC and injection, using a 27mm (1 1/16 in.) socket on the vibration damper bolt to turn the engine to position for No. 1 cylinder injection. Both cam lobes should point up at equally large angles. The flywheel timing mark should be set at 0.

3. Remove the vibration damper center bolt. It may be necessary to use Volvo special wrenches 5187 (to hold) and 5188 (to remove). The engine may have to be turned slightly to allow the holding wrench to rest temporarily on the cooling fan.

4. Check to make sure No. 1 cylinder is at TDC. If necessary, adjust the flywheel to the 0 mark.

5. Remove the vibration damper by removing the four 6mm Allen bolts.

NOTE: The vibration damper and the crankshaft gear may be stuck together. You may have to tap them apart.

6. Remove the camshaft gear belt by removing the lower belt shield, and releasing the retaining bolts for coolant pump.

7. Pull the gear belt straight out and off of the gears.

8. Installation is the reverse of removal.

NOTE: The idler pulley MUST be replaced when replacing the timing gear belt. Remove the center bolt using a puller. Tap the new idler pulley into position, and install the center bolt.

Timing Chain Cover

REMOVAL & INSTALLATION

B27F and B28F

1. Remove the air cleaner and valve covers.

2. Loosen the fan shroud and remove the fan. Remove the shroud.

3. Loosen the alternator, air pump, power steering pump, and A/C compressor (if so equipped) and remove their drive belts.

4. Block the flywheel from turning, remove the crankshaft pulley nut (36mm) and the pulley.

NOTE: Do not drop the pulley key into the crankcase.

5. Remove the power steering pump and place to one side. Remove the pump bracket.

6. Remove the timing chain cover retaining bolts (25 11mm hex bolts), tap and remove the cover.

7. Clean the gasket contact surfaces. Place the upper gasket on the cover and the lower gasket on the block. Install the cover and tighten to 7–11 ft. lbs. Trim the gaskets flush with the valve cover.

8. Install a new crankshaft seal.

9. Block the flywheel, install the pul-

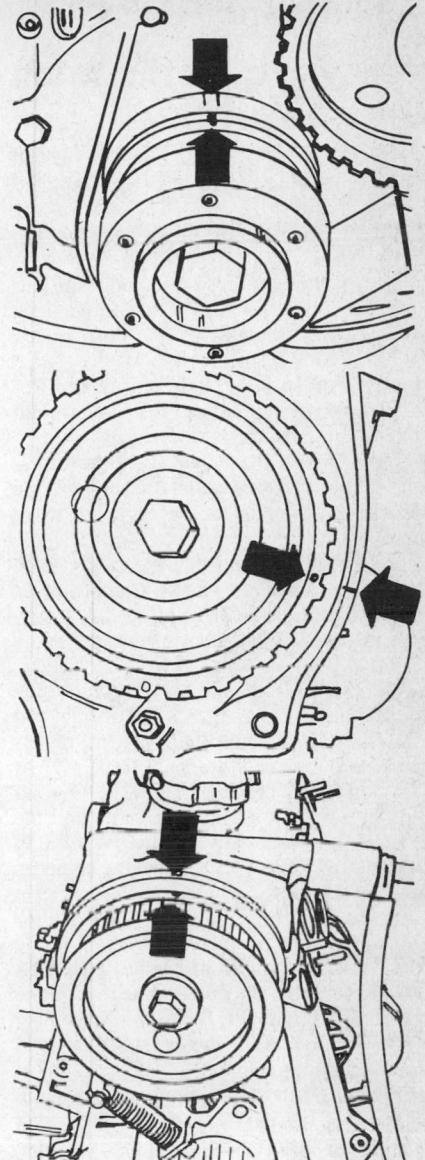

Aligning (top to bottom) crankshaft sprocket, idler shaft sprocket, and camshaft sprocket with their respective timing index marks prior to installing timing belt

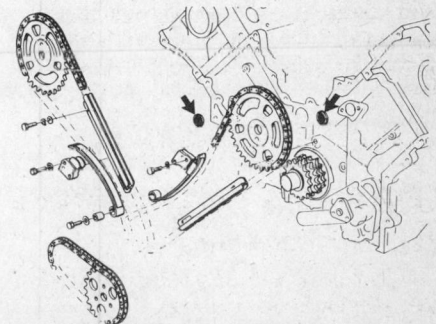

B28 timing chain tensioner and chain assembly

ley, (and key) and tighten the 36mm nut to 118–132 ft. lbs.

10. Reverse Steps 1–5 to install.

Timing Chain

REMOVAL & INSTALLATION

B27F and B28F

1. Remove the timing chain cover and adjacent engine accessories as outlined previously.

2. Remove the oil pump sprocket and drive chain.

3. Slacken the tension in both camshaft timing chains by rotating each tensioner lock ¼ turn counterclockwise and pushing the rubbing block piston.

4. Remove both chain tensioners. Remove the two curved and the two straight chain damper/runners.

5. Remove the camshaft sprocket retaining bolt (10mm Allen head) and the sprocket and chain assembly. Repeat for the other side.

6. Install the chain tensioners and tighten to 5 ft. lbs. Install the curved chain damper/runners and tighten to 7–11 ft. lbs. Install the straight chain damper/runners and torque to 5 ft. lbs.

7. First install the left (driver) side camshaft sprocket and chain. Rotate the crankshaft (use crankshaft nut, if necessary) until No. 1 cylinder is at TDC. At this point, the crankshaft key is pointing directly to the left side camshaft, and the left side camshaft key groove is pointing straight up (12 o'clock). Place the chain on the left side sprocket so that the sprocket notchmark is centered precisely between the two white lines on the chain. Position the chain on the crankshaft sprocket (inner), making sure that the other white line on the chain aligns with the crankshaft sprocket notch. While holding the left side chain and sprockets in this position, install the sprocket and chain on the left side camshaft (chain stretched on tension side) so that the sprocket pin fits into the camshaft recess. Tighten the sprocket center bolt to 51–59 ft. lbs. (use screwdriver to keep cam from turning).

8. To install the right side camshaft sprocket and chain, rotate the crankshaft clockwise until the crankshaft key points straight down (6 o'clock). Align the camshaft key groove so that it is pointing halfway between the 8 and 9 o'clock positions (at this position, the No. 6 cylinder rocker arms will rock). Place the chain on the right

side sprocket so that the sprocket notchmark is centered precisely between the two white lines on the chain. Then, position the chain on the middle crankshaft sprocket, making sure that the other white line aligns with the crankshaft sprocket notch. Install the sprocket and chain on the camshaft so that the sprocket notch fits into the camshaft recess. Tighten the sprocket nut to 51–59 ft. lbs.

9. Rotate the chain tensioners ¼ turn clockwise each. The chains are tensioned by rotating the crankshaft two full turns clockwise. Recheck to make sure the alignment marks coincide.

10. Install the oil pump sprocket and chain.

11. Install the timing chain cover and engine accessories as outlined previously.

Camshaft

REMOVAL & INSTALLATION

B21F and B23 Series

1. Remove the timing belt cover and timing belt as outlined in their appropriate sections.

2. Remove the valve cover.

3. Remove the camshaft center bearing cap. Install special camshaft press tool (Volvo No. 5021) over the center bearing journal to hold the camshaft in place while removing the other bearing caps.

4. Remove the four remaining bearing caps.

5. Remove the seal from the forward edge of the camshaft.

6. Release camshaft press tool, and lift out the camshaft.

7. Reverse the above procedure to install. Make sure the camshaft and followers are well oiled before installation.

B27F and B28F

1. Remove the cylinder head as outlined previously.

2. Remove the camshaft rear cover plate.

3. Remove the camshaft retaining fork at the front of the cylinder head.

4. Pull the camshaft out the rear of the head.

5. Reverse the above to install. Oil the camshaft and followers before installation.

D24 and D24T Diesel
TIMING GEAR

NOTE: This is the timing gear removal procedure. Camshaft removal follows.

1. Disconnect the negative battery terminal.

2. Drain the radiator.

3. Remove the expansion tank hose.

4. Remove the top and bottom radiator hoses.

5. Remove the fan with the spacer and pulley.

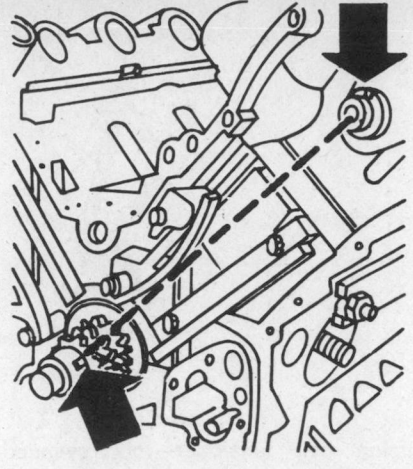

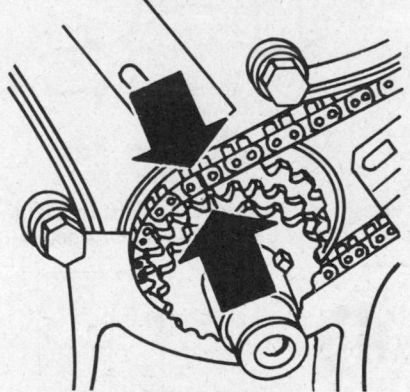

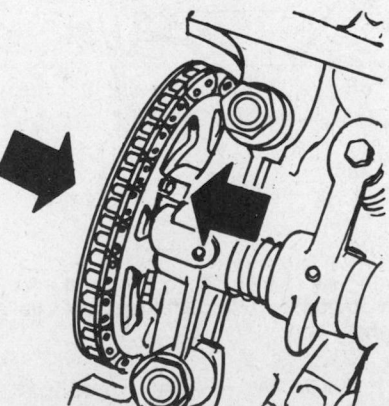

Left side camshaft timing chain installation sequence—V6 engines

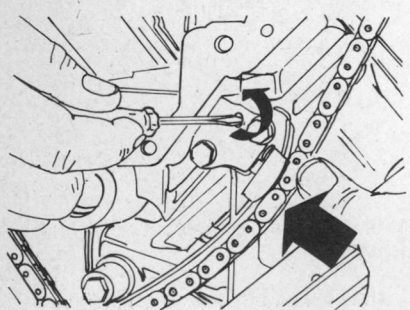

Relieving chain tension

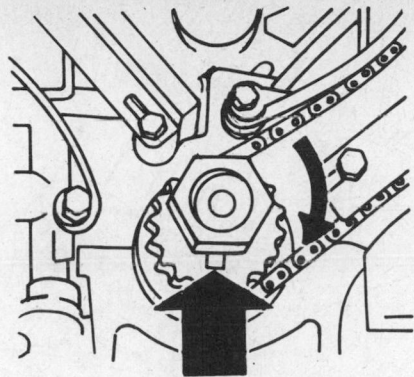

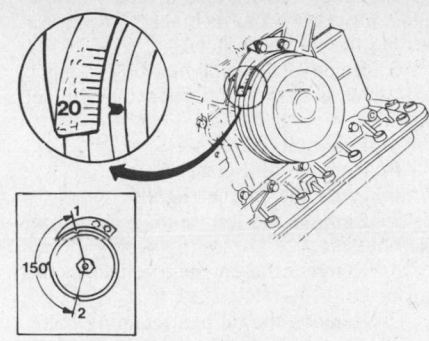

B28F static timing. Rotate the crankshaft until the engine is approximately 20° B.T.D.C. on cylinder 1. The pulley has two marks: "1" is T.D.C. for cylinder No. 1; "2" is T.D.C. for cylinder No. 6. The marks are 150° apart.

Four cylinder camshaft press tool installed

6. Remove all the drive belts.
7. Remove the valve cover.
8. Remove the timing gear belt cover.
9. Set the Number 1 cylinder to top dead center.

NOTE: This is accomplished by turning the crankshaft pulley with an 1¹/₁₆ in. socket. The flywheel timing mark should be set at zero.

10. Remove the crankshaft pulley bolt.
11. Remove the four Allen head bolts in the center of the pulley and remove the pulley.

NOTE: The pulley and the crankshaft gear may be stuck together. Gently tap them apart with a rubber hammer.

12. Remove the lower belt shield.
13. Loosen and remove the timing belt.
14. Remove the front camshaft gear.

NOTE: Use Volvo tool No. 5199 or another suitable tool to prevent the camshaft from turning.

15. Remove the rear timing belt cover.
16. Loosen the injection pump bracket to release tension from the injection pump drive belt.
17. Remove the timing belt.
18. Remove the rear camshaft gear.

NOTE: See Step #14 for this procedure.

19. Installation is the reverse of removal.

Right side camshaft timing chain installation sequence

The following torque specifications are needed: Front camshaft gear 33 ft. lbs., rear camshaft gear 73 ft. lbs., crankshaft pulley 330 ft. lbs., crankshaft pulley Allen bolts 15 ft. lbs.

CAMSHAFT

1. Follow the procedure for the camshaft gear removal.
2. Remove the first and fourth bearing caps.
3. Remove the second and third bearing caps.

NOTE: Loosen the bearing cap nuts on an alternating basis to prevent cam distortion.

4. Remove the camshaft and discard the seals.
5. Installation is the reverse of removal, with the following suggestions.
   a. When reinstalling the cam you must use special tool No. 5190 available from your Volvo dealer.
   b. Place grease on the oil seal lips before installation. The seals must be driven into place with Volvo tool No. 5200 or a suitable substitute.
   c. Torque the cam bearing caps to 15 ft. lbs.
   d. The second and third bearing caps should be installed first.

Pistons and Connecting Rods

PISTON AND CONNECTING ROD POSITIONING

On all engines, the notch or arrow stamped

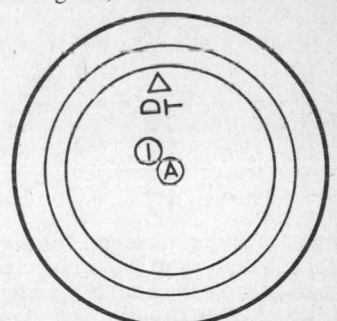

B27, 28 piston positioning. Arrowhead faces forward

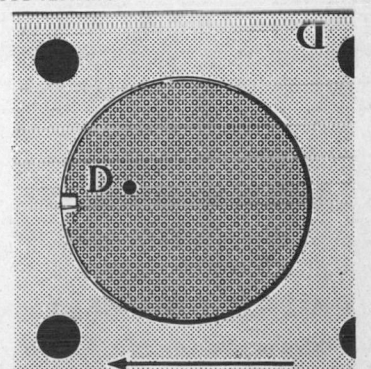

B21F series piston positioning. Notch faces forward

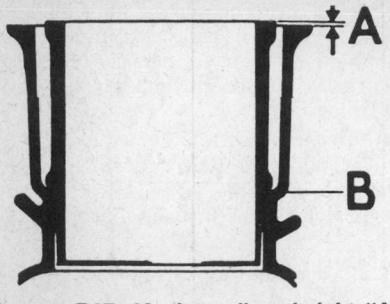

Correct B27, 28 piston liner height "A" above block face is 0.0091 in. Shims are available for installation at point "B" and should be uniform for all cylinders

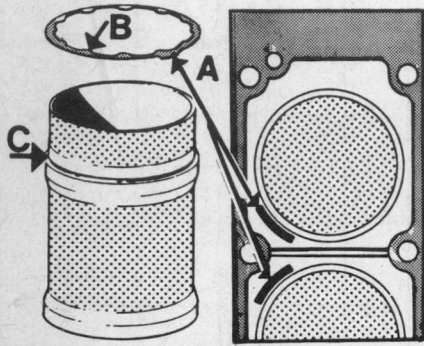

When installing B27 and B28 liner shims, color marking "A" must face up and be positioned where shown. Inside tabs "B" fit into liner groove

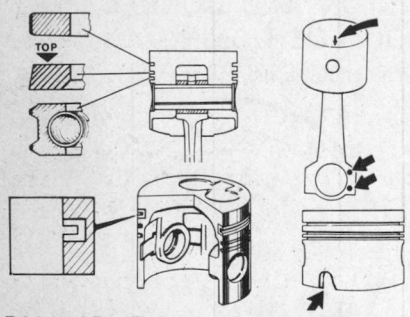

D24 and D24T piston markings. The arrow on the piston crown and marks on the con rod big-end denote the front of the engine (must be facing front). The lower compression ring is marked with the word "TOP" to indicate this side must face up.

on top of the piston must face the front of the engine. On the B21 the connecting rod marking must face the front of the engine.

ENGINE LUBRICATION
Oil Pan

REMOVAL & INSTALLATION
B21F

1. Attach a chain/pulley hoist to the lifting eye on the thermostat housing.

2. On air conditioned models, remove the compressor from its bracket to gain access to the motor mount.

3. Remove the retaining bolts for the left (drive side) motor mount at the cylinder block.

4. Drain the crankcase.

5. Remove the splash guard.

6. Raise the engine slightly.

7. Remove the left motor mount from the chassis.

8. Remove the engine-to-clutch housing brace.

9. Remove the oil pan retaining bolts. Tap the pan loose, swivel and remove.

10. Reverse the removal procedure to install.

B21F (Late '79 and Later) and B23 Series

A new oil pan was introduced in May 1979. It is deeper with a lowered oil baffle, and designed to insure oil supply during rapid acceleration and provide less engine noise.

Pan support bracket—B21 and B23 series engines (view from under car)

1. Jack up your vehicle and support it with jack stands.

2. Drain the engine oil.

3. Remove the splash guard.

4. Remove the engine mount retaining nuts.

5. Remove the lower bolt and loosen the top bolt on the steering column yoke.

6. Slide the yoke assembly up on the steering shaft.

7. Jack up the front of the engine.

8. Remove the retaining bolts for the front axle crossmember.

9. Remove the crossmember.

10. Remove the left engine mount.

11. Remove the pan support bracket.

12. Remove the pan bolts and remove the pan.

13. Installation is the reverse of removal.

NOTE: Always use a new pan gasket when reinstalling the pan.

The following torque specifications are needed: Pan bolts 8 ft. lbs. Steering yoke lower bolt, 18 ft. lbs.

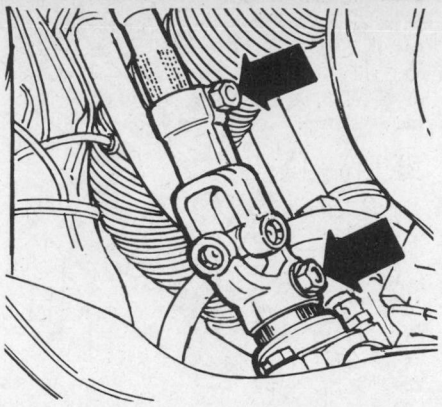

Steering yoke removal; arrows indicate retaining nuts

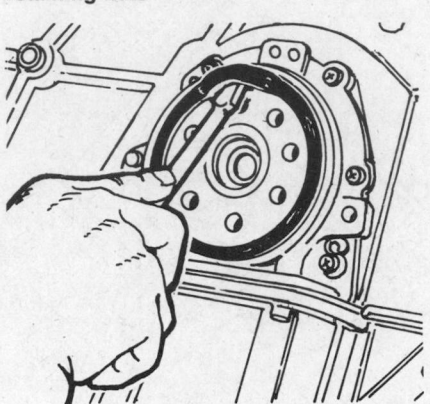

Removing diesel crankshaft rear oil seal

B27F and B28F

1. Remove the splash guard.

2. Drain the crankcase.

3. Remove the oil pan retaining bolts. Swivel the pan past the stabilizer bar and remove.

4. Reverse the above to install.

REAR MAIN OIL SEAL REPLACEMENT

D24 and D24T

1. Disconnect the negative battery terminal.

2. Remove the transmission, (see the transmission removal section).

3. Remove all but one starter bolt to keep it from falling out.

4. Remove the clutch and pressure plate assembly (if so equipped).

5. Remove the pilot bearing.

6. Remove the flywheel.

NOTE: Use special tool No. 5112 or a suitable replacement to keep the flywheel from turning while removing the bolts.

7. Remove the oil seal with a screwdriver.

8. Check the contact surfaces on the seal holder and crankshaft.

9. Installation is the reverse of removal. When reinstalling a new seal use special tool No. 5208 available from Volvo or a

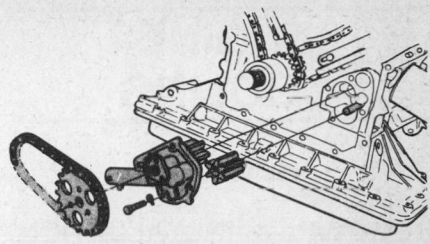

suitable replacement. Coat the seal with oil before installation. Torque the flywheel bolts to 55 ft. lbs. Use a liquid sealer (Loctite® or similar product) on the bolts prior to installing them.

B27F and B28F

1. Disconnect the negative battery terminal.
2. Remove the transmission (see the transmission removal section).
3. Remove the clutch and pressure plate (if so equipped).
4. Remove the flywheel (drive plate on automatic transmissions).

NOTE: On automatic transmissions remove the crankshaft spacer.

5. Remove the two rear pan bolts.
6. Remove the bolts in the seal housing and then the housing.

NOTE: Gently remove the housing so as not to damage the oil pan gasket.

7. Use special tool No. 5107 to remove the old seal and install the new one. This tool is available from Volvo or use a suitable replacement.
8. Installation is the reverse of removal. The following torque specifications are needed; Flywheel 33–37 ft. lbs., Seal housing 7–11 ft. lbs.

B21F and B23 Series

1. Disconnect the negative battery terminal.
2. Remove the transmission (see the transmission removal section).
3. Remove the clutch and pressure plate (if so equipped).
4. Remove the pilot bearing snap-ring and remove the bearing.
5. Remove the flywheel or driveplate which ever is applicable.

NOTE: Be careful not to press in the activator pins for the timing device.

6. Remove the rear oil pan brace.
7. Remove the two center bolts from the pan that bolt into the seal housing.

8. Loosen two bolts on either side of the two in the seal housing.
9. Remove the six seal housing bolts, and remove the seal housing.

NOTE: Be careful not to damage the oil pan gasket when removing the seal housing.

10. Remove the seal using special tool No. 2817 or a suitable replacement.
11. Installation is the reverse of removal.

NOTE: Use a new gasket on the seal housing and coat the seal with oil prior to installation.

Torque the flywheel to 47–54 ft. lbs. When installing the flywheel turn the crankshaft to bring the No. 1 piston to top dead center. The lower flywheel pin should be installed approximately 15° from the horizontal and opposite the starter. Install the bolts.

Oil Pump

REPLACEMENT

B21F and B23 Series

1. Remove the oil pan as described previously.
2. Remove the two oil pump retaining bolts, and pull the delivery tube from the block.
3. When installing, use new sealing rings at either end of the delivery tube. Also, make sure you "prime" the pump (remove all air) by filling it with clean engine oil and operating the pump by hand, before installation.

NOTE: On 1980 and later, the oil pump has been redesigned to position the suction pipe and strainer further forward in the oil pan.

B27F and B28F

The oil pump body is cast integrally with the cylinder block. It is chain driven by a separate sprocket on the crankshaft and is

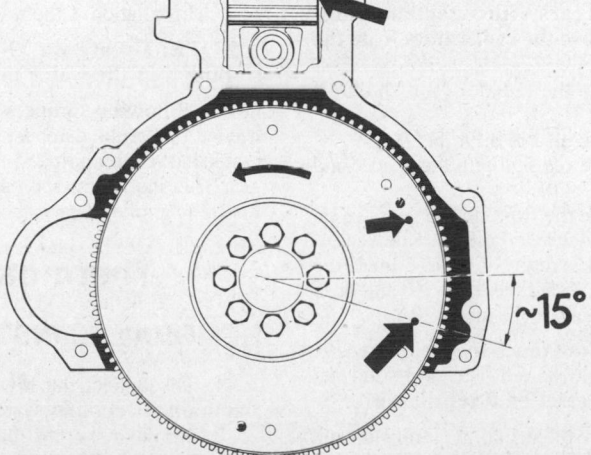

B28F oil pump installation—B27 similar

located behind the timing chain cover. The pick-up screen and tube are serviced by removing the oil pan. To check the pump gears or remove the oil pump cover:

1. Remove the air cleaner and valve covers.
2. Loosen the fan shroud and remove the fan. Remove the shroud.
3. Loosen the alternator, air pump, power steering pump, and AC compressor (if so equipped) and remove their drive belts.
4. Block the flywheel from turning, and remove the 36mm bolt and the crankshaft pulley.

NOTE: Do not drop key into crankcase.

5. Remove the timing gear cover (25 bolts).
6. Remove the oil pump drive sprocket and chain.
7. Remove the oil pump cover, and gears.
8. Reverse the removal procedure to install. Prime the pump (remove all air) by filling it with clean engine oil and operating the pump by hands, before installation.

D24 and D24T

The oil pan can not be removed without removing the engine. Refer to the "Engine Removal" section. This procedure requires quite a few special tools, and cannot be accomplished without them.

1. Remove the engine from the car.
2. Remove the oil pan and the oil suction pipe.
3. Remove the front timing belt cover, timing belt, vibration damper, and lower timing belt cover.

NOTE: Do not allow the crankshaft to turn when disconnected from the camshaft. If this should happen the fuel injection timing must be reset.

4. Remove the crankshaft gear and seal with a puller.
5. Remove the timing belt inner shield.
6. Remove the oil pump bolts and remove the pump.

NOTE: The oil pump can not be repaired. It must be replaced as a unit.

7. When installing the oil pump the triangular mark on the pump outer gear must face the oil pump rear cover.
8. Installation is the reverse of removal. Fill the oil pump with clean engine oil and "prime" the pump by operating it by hand prior to installation.

Flywheel installation—B21 and B23 series engines

ENGINE COOLING

Radiator

REMOVAL & INSTALLATION

1. Remove the radiator and expansion tank caps, disconnect the lower radiator hose, and drain the cooling system.

2. Remove the expansion tank and hose, and drain the coolant. Remove the upper radiator hose. On cars with automatic transmissions, disconnect and plug the transmission oil cooler lines at the radiator.

3. Remove the retaining bolts for the radiator and fan shroud, if so equipped, and lift out the radiator.

4. To install, place the radiator and fan shroud in position and install the retaining bolts.

5. On automatic transmission cars, connect the oil cooler lines.

6. Install the lower and upper radiator hoses.

7. Install the expansion tank with its hose. Make sure that the overflow hose is clear of the fan and is free of any sharp bends.

8. Fill the cooling system with a 50 percent ethylene glycol, 40 percent water solution. Replace the caps.

9. Start the engine and check for leaks. After the engine has reached operating temperature make sure that the coolant level in the expansion tank is between the maximum and minimum marks.

Water Pump

REMOVAL & INSTALLATION

B21F and B23 Series

1. Remove the overflow tank cap. Drain the cooling system by opening the cylinder block drain cock (beneath the exhaust mainfold) and disconnecting the lower radiator hose.

2. Remove the fan and fan shroud.

3. Remove the alternator and air pump drive belts. Remove the water pump pulley.

4. Remove the timing belt cover.

5. Remove the lower radiator hose.

6. Remove the retaining bolt for the coolant pipe (beneath exhaust manifold) and pull the pipe rearward.

7. Remove the six retaining bolts and lift off the water pump.

8. Clean the gasket contact surfaces thoroughly, and use a new gasket and O-rings (especially between the cylinder head and top of water pump).

9. Reverse Steps 1–7 to install.

B27F and B28F

1. Remove the front and main sections

Make sure the O-ring around the lower lip of water pump is in good condition. Replace if there is any damage

of the intake manifold.

2. Remove the overflow tank cap and drain the cooling system.

3. Disconnect both radiator hoses. On automatic transmission cars, disconnect the transmission cooler lines at the radiator. Disconnect the fan shroud. Remove the radiator and fan shroud.

4. Remove the fan.

5. Remove the hoses from the water pump to each cylinder head.

6. Remove the fan belts. Remove the water pump pulley.

7. Loosen the hose clamps at the rear of the water pump.

8. Transfer the thermal time sender and temperature sensor to the new pump.

9. Remove the water pump from the block (three bolts).

10. Transfer the thermostat cover, thermostat, and rear pump cover to the new pump.

11. Reverse the removal procedure to install.

D24 and D24T

1. Drain the radiator.

2. Remove the splash gear under the engine.

3. Remove the expansion tank.

4. Remove the top and bottom radiator hoses.

NOTE: On cars with automatic transmissions remove the cooler lines from the radiator.

5. Remove the radiator (and shroud if so equipped).

6. Remove all the drive belts.

7. Remove the fan with the spacer and pulley.

8. Remove the front timing gear cover.

9. Disconnect the cold start device.

10. Loosen screw No. 1 and push the lever forward, rotate the lever 90° and push it backward against the stop.

NOTE: Do not touch the second screw. If it becomes loosened, the cold start device must be reset on a test bench.

11. Remove the injection pump plug and install a dial indicator gauge with a measuring range of 0–0.118 in.

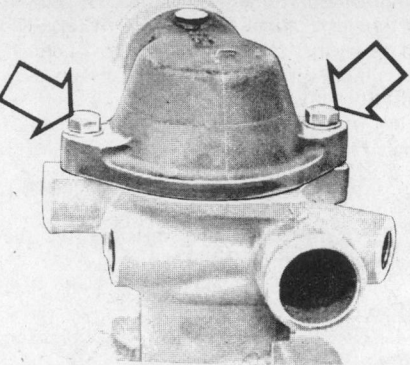

Remove the two top water pump bolts for access to the V6 thermostat

NOTE: This gauge must have adapter No. 5194, (available from Volvo) attached to it.

12. Set the gauge to approximately .078 in.

13. Set the No. 1 cylinder to TDC.

14. The marking on the injection pump gear should coincide with the marking on the injection pump bracket.

15. The flywheel timing mark should be at zero.

16. Turn the engine ¼ turn past zero and then back to zero again. This is done in order to place slack in the timing belt on the drive side. Otherwise the engine setting would be incorrect.

NOTE: The gauge must not move during the remainder of the work. If it does the engine must be completely retimed.

17. Loosen the water pump bolts to release the belt tension.

18. Remove the timing bolt from the camshaft gear.

19. Remove the camshaft gear.

20. Remove the vibration damper.

21. Remove the lower belt guard.

22. Loosen the bracket for the fan and alternator.

23. Remove the lower retaining bolt and move the bracket away from the engine.

24. Remove the inner belt shield and water pump.

25. Installation is the reverse of removal.

NOTE: Grease the O-ring before installing it in the water pump.

The following torque specifications are needed. Vibration damper screws 15 ft. lbs., crankshaft center bolt 255 ft. lbs., camshaft gear 33 ft. lbs., pump setting 0.0256–.0287 in.

Thermostat

REMOVAL & INSTALLATION

1. Disconnect the lower radiator hose and drain the cooling system.

2. Remove the two bolts securing the thermostat housing to the cylinder head and carefully lift the housing free.

3. Remove all old gasket material from the mating surfaces and remove the thermostat.

4. Test the operation of the thermostat by immersing it in a container of heated water. Replace any thermostat that does not open at the correct temperature.

5. Place the thermostat, with a new gasket, in the cylinder head. Fit the thermostat housing to the head and hand-tighten the two bolts until snug. Do not tighten the bolts more than ¼ turn past snug.

6. Connect the lower radiator hose and replace the coolant.

EMISSION CONTROLS

PCV System

Volvos have been equipped with positive crankcase ventilation (PCV) systems to control crankcase vapors since the early 1960s. The present system is a closed one; it is sealed to the atmosphere. A metal filter located inline between the fresh air source and the crankcase prevents engine backfire from reaching the crankcase and oil from being drawn into the induction system.

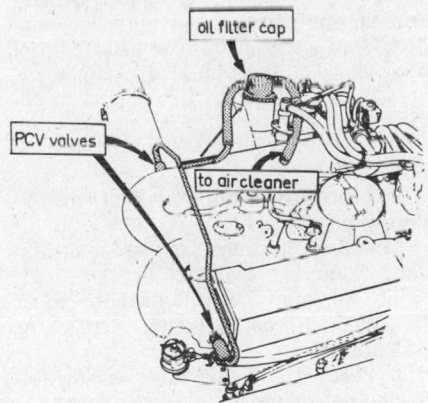

PCV valves and lines—V6

Evaporative Control System

All model Volvos are equipped with an evaporative control system to prevent unburnt fuel vapors in the fuel tank from escaping into the atmosphere. An expansion tank above the fuel tank provides for thermal expansion of fuel vapors in warm weather.

NOTE: All models have the expansion tank inside the fuel tank.

Those vapors which do not condense and return to the fuel tank are displaced and drawn into an activated charcoal canister in the engine compartment. The charcoal canister then absorbs and stores these fuel tank

vapors when the engine is shut off or is idling. Throttling the engine causes the vapors to be drawn out of the canister into the inlet duct and then into the combustion chambers where they are burned.

NOTE: All 1980 and later B21F, B23F, B23FT, B23E and B28F engines are equipped with a rollover valve. It is designed to close at 45° from horizontal. This valve will prevent a fuel spill through the carbon filter, if the car is involved in a rollover.

Exhaust Emission Control

Various measures have been taken to limit exhaust emissions of hydrocarbons, carbon monoxide, and more revently, oxides of nitrogen. Basic modifications include a distributor which retards the timing from its basic setting during idle, and the installation of a "hotter" 190°F thermostat in the cooling system.

PRE-HEATING AIR INTAKE

NOTE: This system is installed on various four cylinder and V6 engines; installation varies according to engine.

This system is designed to improve cold engine performance. Its advantages are as follows:

1. Improved cold engine performance.
2. Ambient temperatures do not influence engine performance.
3. Icing has been eliminated.

The pre-heating device consists of a heater on the left side of the manifold, a thermostat controlled air mixer, and hoses.

The thermostat senses the intake air temperature and controls the air mixture.

Exhaust Gas Recirculation (EGR) System

In order to control emissions of NOx, 1978–79 models are equipped with an exhaust gas recirculation system.

NOTE: Models equipped with the Lambda-Sond oxygen sensor system do not have EGR valves. These include 78–80 California and all 1980 and later vehicles.

The system consists of a metering valve, a tubular pipe running from the exhaust manifold to the valve, another tubular pipe running from the valve to the inlet duct, and a vacuum hose running from the valve's diaphragm to the inlet duct in front of the air regulator shutter. The valve permits a regulated amount of exhaust gases to enter the inlet duct and mix with the incoming intake air when the throttle is partly open. Replace the EGR valve every 30,000 miles with a new one.

The EGR system is modified to improve cold start driveability by the addition of a venturi vacuum amplifier system. The EGR system with vacuum amplifier works as follows: Venturi vacuum at the air intake is used to measure the total air flow. This weak vacuum signal controls the vacuum amplifier which regulates the EGR valve via a solenoid valve. The vacuum amplifier receives inputs both from the strong intake manifold source which is used as a power source, and from the weak air intake source which is to be amplified. The intake vacuum is stored in the vacuum reservoir and is controlled by a check valve in the amplifier. This allows a generous amount of vacuum on tap regardless of variations in engine manifold vacuum. The amplifier then continues to supply adequate vacuum at higher speeds and moderate throttle openings, when manifold vacuum normally would drop to an insufficient amount. The EGR system functions as before, except that the exhaust gases are prevented from recirculation at idle and full throttle by a throttle angle sensing microswitch and an electrically operated solenoid valve, rather than simple vacuum. On 1978 and later models, a wax thermostat blocks exhaust gas recirculation until the engine warns to 140°F.

All Volvos are equipped with an EGR service reminder light which is actuated by the odometer at 15,000 mile intervals. The light may be reset by pressing a white button at the rear of the odometer.

Air Injection Reactor System

All 1978 and later Volvos (except Canadian B21A and B23E engines, which are equipped with a Pulsair system) are equipped with an air injection reactor system except the diesel. Basically, the system injects filtered air into the exhaust manifold in order to reduce emissions of carbon monoxide and hydrocarbons. The oxygen in the air reacts with the exhaust gas and promotes further combustion in the exhaust manifold.

The system consists of an air pump (belt-driven), a diverter valve, a backfiring valve, and an air manifold which is attached to the exhaust manifold. Under normal conditions, air is pumped from the air pump via the diverter valve, the backfiring valve and the air manifold into the exhaust manifold ports. The air pump takes in filtered air which is then compressed and discharged to the diverter valve. The diverter valve sends the air through to the backfiring valve, except during deceleration. The diverter valve also releases some of the air into the atmosphere if the pressure is too great. The backfiring valve is a one-way valve which prevents the exhaust gases from flowing back towards the air injection components, but allows the pump air to pass into the air manifold and exhaust manifold.

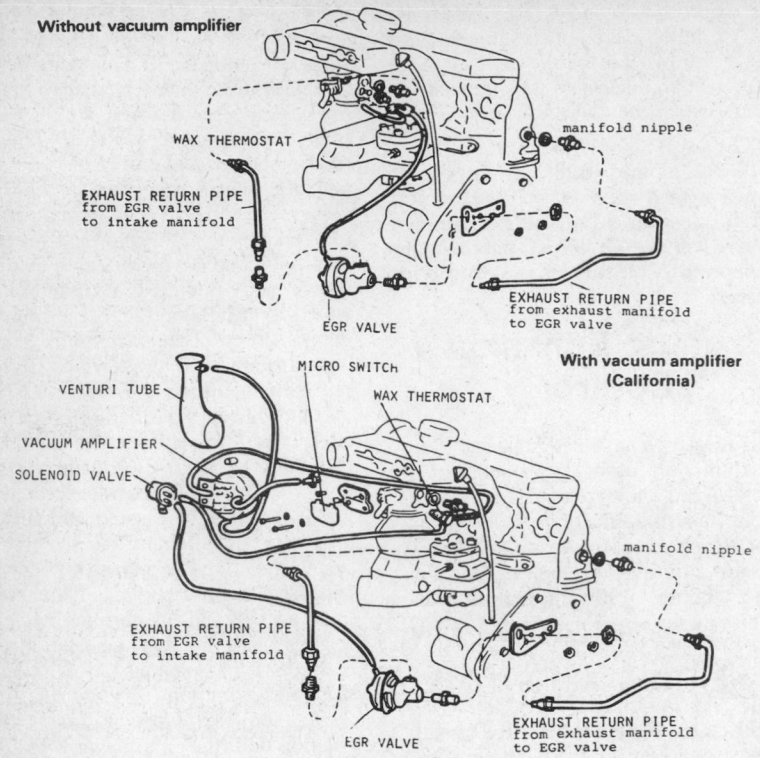

Without vacuum amplifier

WAX THERMOSTAT

manifold nipple

EXHAUST RETURN PIPE
from EGR valve
to intake manifold

EGR VALVE

EXHAUST RETURN PIPE
from exhaust manifold
to EGR valve

With vacuum amplifier
(California)

VENTURI TUBE

MICRO SWITCH

WAX THERMOSTAT

VACUUM AMPLIFIER

SOLENOID VALVE

manifold nipple

EXHAUST RETURN PIPE
from EGR valve
to intake manifold

EGR VALVE

EXHAUST RETURN PIPE
from exhaust manifold
to EGR valve

B21 EGR system

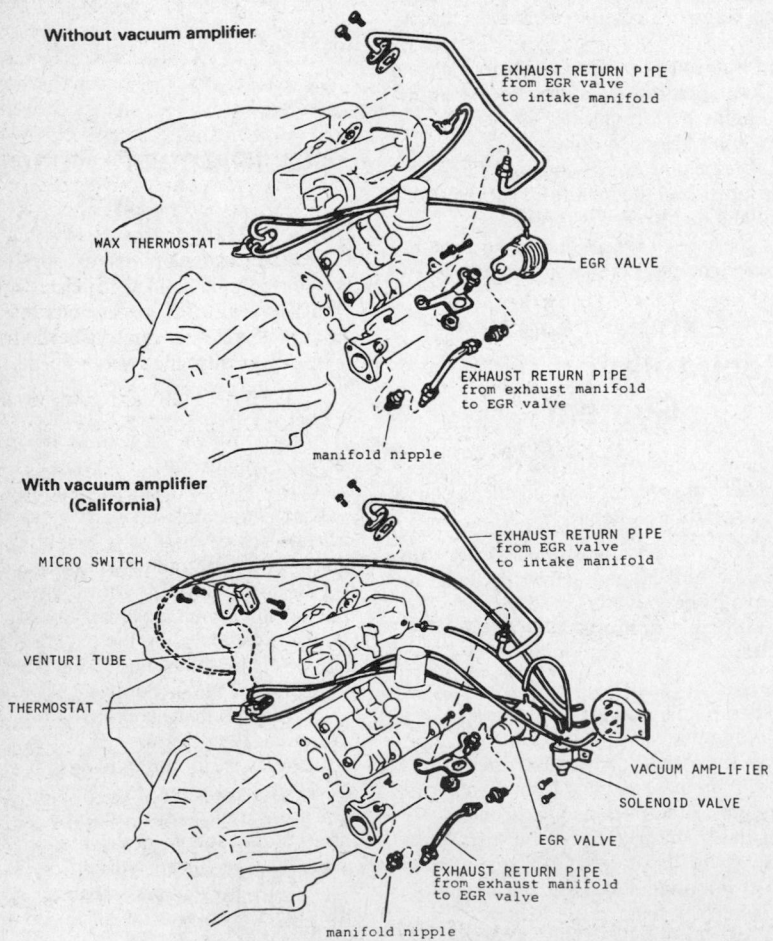

Without vacuum amplifier

EXHAUST RETURN PIPE
from EGR valve
to intake manifold

WAX THERMOSTAT

EGR VALVE

EXHAUST RETURN PIPE
from exhaust manifold
to EGR valve

manifold nipple

With vacuum amplifier
(California)

MICRO SWITCH

EXHAUST RETURN PIPE
from EGR valve
to intake manifold

VENTURI TUBE

WAX THERMOSTAT

VACUUM AMPLIFIER

SOLENOID VALVE

EGR VALVE

EXHAUST RETURN PIPE
from exhaust manifold
to EGR valve

manifold nipple

B27F/B28F EGR system

EGR, catalytic converter service reminder light reset button

CHECKING THE AIR SYSTEM

Service the AIR system every 15,000 miles. Make sure the drive belt is in good condition on the air pump. If the belt breaks, the backfire valve must be checked.

Make sure all attaching nuts and bolts for the air pump and bracket are secure.

To check the air pump, use the following procedure.

Start the engine and listen for excessive noise from the pump. Remember, though, that the air pump is not normally completely noiseless, and it can make a bit of a racket when its cold. Under normal circumstances, the noise rises in pitch as engine speed increases. *Do not attempt to lubricate or repair the pump: it must be replaced*.

To check the backfire valve, use the following procedure.

1. Disconnect the hose from the diverter valve.

2. Apply a vacuum to the hose: no air should come through. If it does, replace the backfire valve.

To check the diverter valve, use the following procedure.

1. Disconnect and plug the hose from the diverter valve.

2. Run the engine at idle. Air should only be coming out of point "A" in the illustration.

3. Increase the engine speed to 3000–3500 rpm, then quickly release the throttle. Air should now flow from points "B" in the illustration. If not, replace the diverter valve.

1978–79 Models Equipped with Vacuum Amplifier

NOTE: Use the illustration to identify the vacuum amplifier. It is located in the engine compartment.

1. With a cold engine (below 130°F coolant temperature), check the operation of the wax thermostat. Disconnect the vacuum hose at the solenoid valve and disconnect the vacuum hose at the vacuum

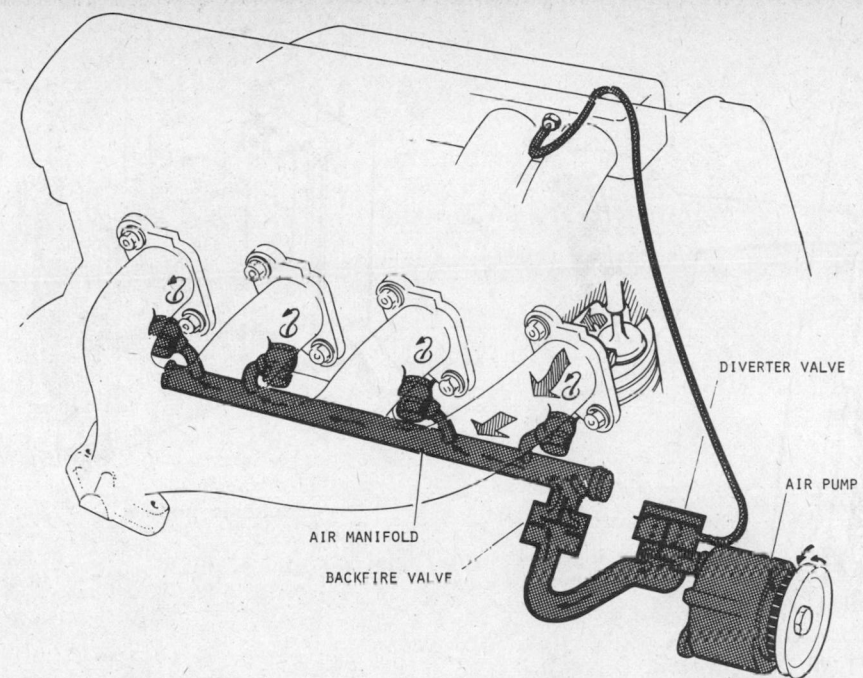

DIVERTER VALVE

AIR PUMP

AIR MANIFOLD

BACKFIRE VALVE

Four cylinder AIR system—V6 engines similar except have an AIR manifold for each cylinder bank.

amplifier connection "S". Suck one of the disconnected hoses. If any air passes, one of the hoses has a vacuum leak or the wax thermostat is faulty. Connect the hoses.

2. Start the engine and warm to operating temperature (176°F). Stop the engine. Disconnect the two hoses again, and apply a vacuum through either of the hoses. This time the thermostat should be open, and air should pass through. If not, replace the wax thermostat.

3. Connect the hoses. Check the throttle position sensing micro-switch next. Connect a 12v test light in series between the upper wire connector and its upper terminal. Switch the ignition to the "on" position. Pull back the throttle lever and insert a 0.006 in. feeler gauge between the screw and the lever stop. When the lever is released and the throttle screw makes contact with the switch plunger, the test light should illuminate. This indicates that current is reaching the solenoid valve, the micro-switch is activating, and the fuse is good. Then, repeat by inserting an 0.008 in. feeler gauge between the screw and lever stop. This time, the test light should not light and the throttle screw should not make contact with the switch plunger. Adjust as necessary by loosening the locknut on the stopscrew and adjusting for 0.006 in. clearance.

4. Check the solenoid valve next. Start the engine and idle. Disconnect the hose from connection "1", and create a vacuum. With the engine idling, the EGR valve should remain closed (no change in rpm). If not, the solenoid valve is defective.

5. With the vacuum pump still connected, and engine idling, check that the vacuum reading does not change for 10 seconds. If the reading changes, this indicates

a bad amplifier or leaking hoses.

6. Finally, with the engine idling, increase the rpm while observing the EGR valve. If the EGR valve rod does not open, check for a clogged venturi or leaking venturi vacuum hose. Then, suddenly release the throttle and check that the EGR valve rod closes. If not, the solenoid valve is faulty.

Pulsair System
SYSTEM CHECK

Canadian 240 (DL) with B21A, B23E and B21F Engines

Beginning in 1979, Canadian B21A and

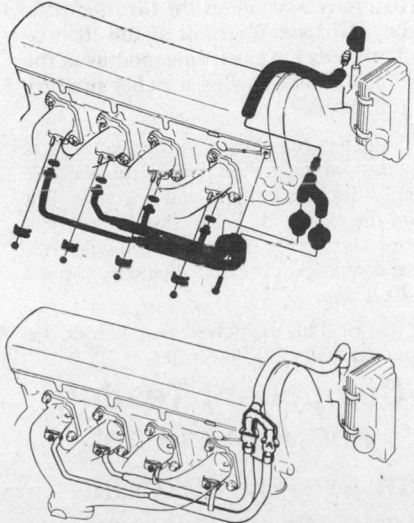

Pulsair system—Canadian B21 A/F and B23E models. Box at right is intake

some B21F engines were fitted with the then then-new "Pulsair" air injection system. The system was also incorporated into Canadian B23E engines in 1983. In the Pulsair, the natural pressure pulses in the engine's exhaust system help to draw air into the exhaust system. The air is then injected into the end of the exhaust port, as in the air pump system, and the oxygen in the injected air aids in the further burning of emissions. The air pump is eliminated in the Pulsair system. Check valves in the system exhaust gases from entering the air cleaner during the pressure pulses.

To check the operation of the system, disconnect the air hose at the air cleaner. With the engine idling, check that air is being drawn in with the palm of your hand and that no back pressure exists.

Catalytic Converter System

All 1978 and later Volvos are equipped with a catalytic converter. The converters are installed to further control emissions of carbon monoxide and hydrocarbons which have resisted the treatment of the air injection system.

The converter is installed in the exhaust system ahead of the muffler. The catalytic converter on 1980 and later B28F engines is located closer to the engine compartment. This design allows quicker warm-up and reduced emissions. The converter uses platinum and palladium metals in a substrate or beaded form as the catalyst. The catalyst and the oxygen supplied by the air pump then react with the exhaust gases producing harmless carbon dioxide and water vapor, as well as a minute amount of sulphur dioxide or sulphuric acid.

All 1978–80 260 California series, all 1979 49 states 260 series and the 1979 49 states 242 GT are equipped with three way catalytic converters.

NOTE: All 1980 and later models use the three way catalytic converter.

The purpose of the three way catalytic converter is to neutralize carbon monoxide, hydrocarbons and oxides of nitrogen in the exhaust gases. The main difference between this catalytic converter and the oxidation converter is that the three way converter is able to process large amounts of oxides of nitrogen (NO_x), while the oxidation catalyst cannot.

The operating range of the three way catalyst is limited to a narrow band around the ideal air/fuel mixture for the engine. To keep the mixture within this narrow band, an oxygen sensor is used to monitor the amount of oxygen in the exhaust gases and fine tune the air/fuel mixture. See "Oxygen Sensor Feedback System (Lambda Sond)" for more information on the oxygen sensor system.

The converter is designed, if properly

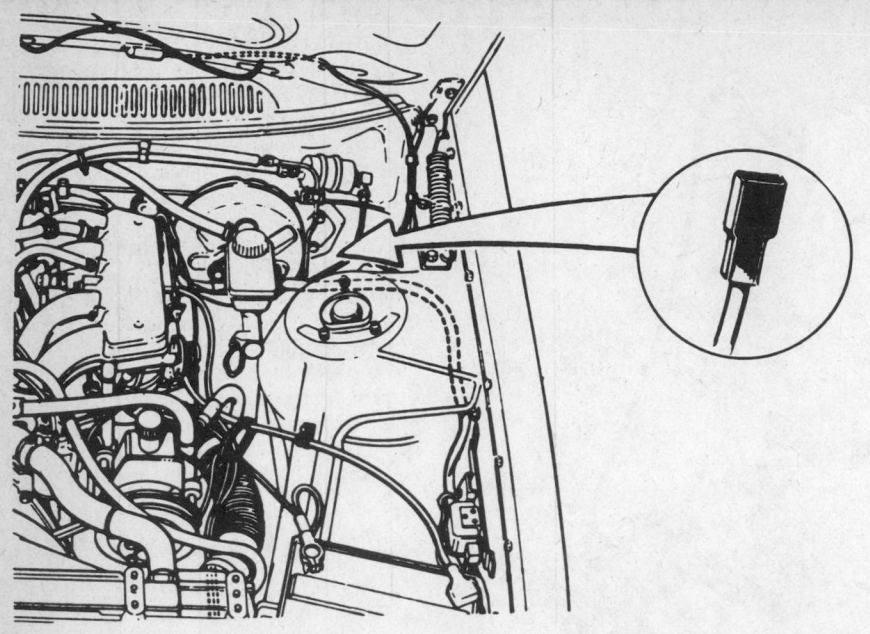

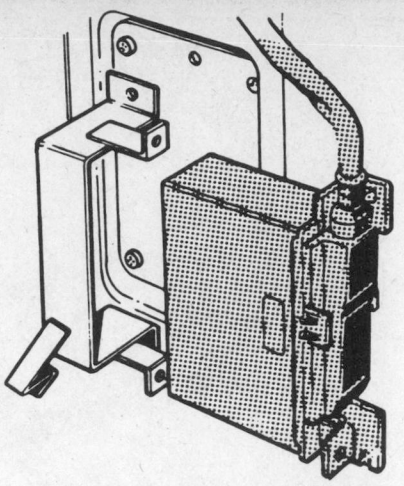

Electronic module

Instrument pick–up

maintained, to last 50,000 miles as long as leaded gasoline is not used. The lead in gasoline will coat the catalytic substrate or beads, thereby preventing the reaction process, rendering the converter ineffective.

At 15,000 mile intervals the retaining bolts for the converter must be checked for tightness. A service reminder light on the dashboard lights at 15,000 mile intervals. To extinguish the light, press the white reset button at the rear of the odometer.

NOTE: The 1980 and later diesel engine is not equipped with a catalytic converter.

Oxygen Sensor Feedback System (Lambda-Sond)

This is a self-tuning engine controlled system, designed to reduce emissions and improve fuel economy. An exhaust gas sensor (oxygen sensor or lambda sensor) located in the exhaust manifold, monitors the composition of the exhaust gases leaving the engine. This analysis is fed into a closed loop feedback system. This continuously adjusts the air-fuel mixture to provide optimum conditions for combustion and efficient breakdown of all three major pollutants by a three-way catalytic converter.

The major components of the system are: the oxygen sensor, the electronic module and the frequency valve. The oxygen sensor is a platinum coated ceramic tube. It is located in the exhaust manifold. The inside is vented to the atmosphere while the outside is connected to the exhaust gas flow. The output from the sensor is fed to the electronic module. This device supplies a control current to the frequency valve. The frequency valve alters the flow of fuel in

the injection system by activating a diaphragm in the fuel pressure regulating valve. The frequency valve, so called because it operates on a set frequency, functions during what is called its duty cycle. This duty cycle corresponds to the ratio of closed-to-open circuit impulses from the electronic module. The cycle can be measured in terms of degrees by using an ordinary ignition system dwell meter. The dwell meter is connected to an instrument pick-up connector located on a wire coming from the electronic module. The pick-up connector is located on the firewall, in the engine compartment to the left of the master cylinder. The duty cycle of the B21F system is 54° while that of the B27F system is 40–50°. The B28F (1980 and later) cycle is 49–59°.

NOTE: 1980 and later B28F engines have a micro-switch at the throttle cable pulley. It closes a circuit at full throttle and grounds the electronic module of the Lambda Sond allowing a richer mixture at full throttle.

If the oxygen sensor in the manifold is obviously damaged, it can be replaced by simply disconnecting it and unscrewing it from the manifold. When installing a new sensor, the threads must be coated with anti-seize compound. The unit should be torqued to 40 ft. lbs.

NOTE: The oxygen sensor should be replaced every 30,000 miles.

Component Testing and Adjustment

EGR SYSTEM CHECKING
49 States Models—B21, B27

1. With a cold engine, check the op-

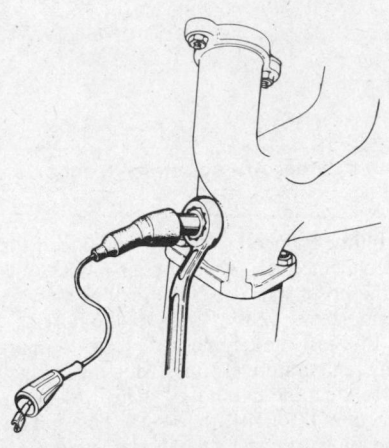

Replace oxygen sensor (Lambda-sond) every 15,000 miles. Apply an anti-locking compound before installation

eration of the wax thermostat. Start the engine and idle. Manipulate the throttle by hand and check that the EGR valve rod does not move in and out. If it does, the thermostat is faulty. It should not operate the EGR valve until the the coolant reaches 130–140°F.

2. With the engine warmed up (176°F), check that the EGR valve rod does move in and out when the throttle is opened and closed. If not, the wax thermostat, hoses or EGR valve may be at fault.

3. Stop the engine. Disconnect the vacuum hose from the EGR valve. Blow through the hose. If no air passes, the wax thermostat is faulty. If air does pass, either the hose is incorrectly installed or the EGR valve is defective.

4. Finally, connect the EGR vacuum hose and start the engine. Open the throttle to 3000–4000rpm and then quickly release. The EGR valve rod should close. If not, replace the EGR valve.

California Models—B21, B27 and B28F

1. With a cold engine (below 130°F coolant temperature), check the operation

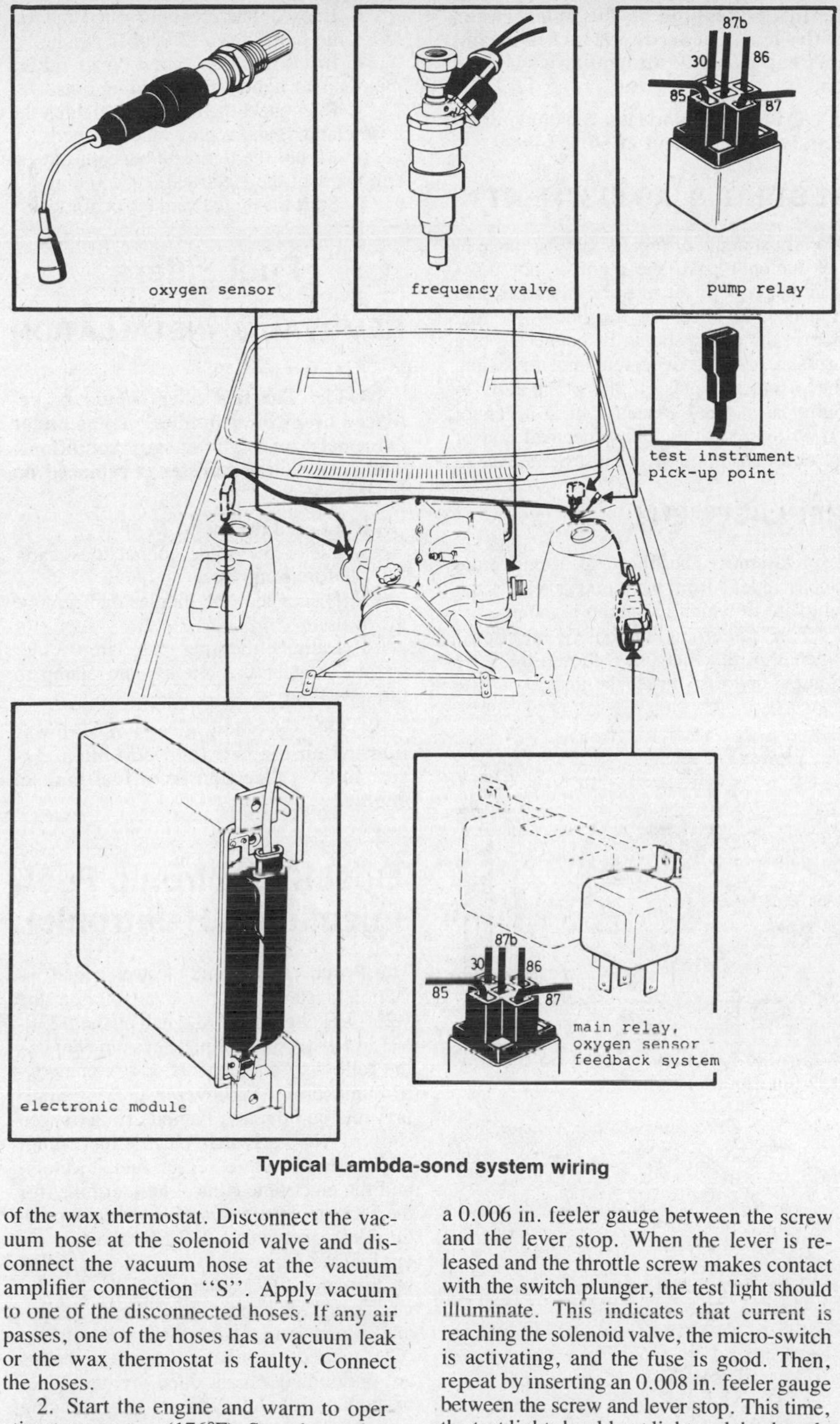

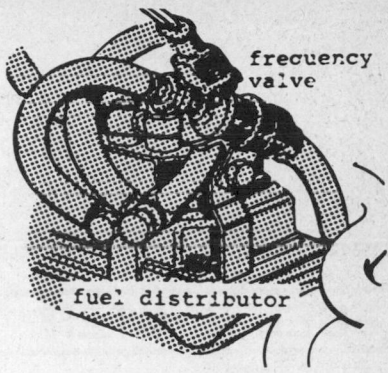

Frequency valve

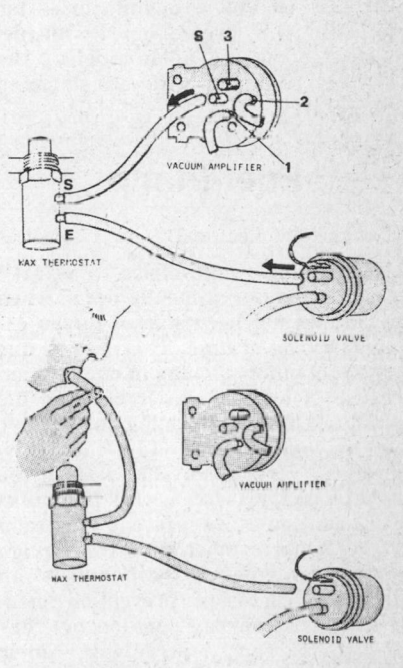

Checking wax thermostat

oxygen sensor

frequency valve

pump relay

test instrument pick-up point

electronic module

main relay, oxygen sensor feedback system

Typical Lambda-sond system wiring

of the wax thermostat. Disconnect the vacuum hose at the solenoid valve and disconnect the vacuum hose at the vacuum amplifier connection "S". Apply vacuum to one of the disconnected hoses. If any air passes, one of the hoses has a vacuum leak or the wax thermostat is faulty. Connect the hoses.

2. Start the engine and warm to operating temperature (176°F). Stop the engine. Disconnect the two hoses again, and apply vacuum through either of the hoses. This time the thermostat should be open, and air should pass through. If not, replace the wax thermostat.

3. Connect the hoses. Check the throttle position sensing micro-switch next. Connect a 12v test light in series between the upper wire connector and its upper terminal. Switch the ignition to the "on" position. Pull back the throttle lever and insert a 0.006 in. feeler gauge between the screw and the lever stop. When the lever is released and the throttle screw makes contact with the switch plunger, the test light should illuminate. This indicates that current is reaching the solenoid valve, the micro-switch is activating, and the fuse is good. Then, repeat by inserting an 0.008 in. feeler gauge between the screw and lever stop. This time, the test light should not light and the throttle screw should not make contact with the switch plunger. Adjust as necessary by loosening the locknut on the stopscrew and adjusting for 0.006 in. clearance.

4. Check the solenoid valve next. Start the engine and idle. Disconnect the hose from connection "1", and create a vacuum. With the engine idling, the EGR valve should remain closed (no change in rpm). If not, the solenoid valve is defective.

5. With the vacuum pump still connected, and engine idling, check that the vacuum reading does not change for 10 seconds. If the reading changes, this indicates a bad amplifier or leaking hoses.

6. Finally, with the engine idling, increase the rpm while observing the EGR valve. If the EGR valve rod does not open, check for a clogged venturi or leaking venturi vacuum hose. Then, suddenly release the throttle and check that the EGR valve rod closes. If not, the solenoid valve is faulty.

Component Service

POSITIVE CRANKCASE VENTILATION SYSTEM

The only service required for the PCV system is the cleaning of the hoses, nipples, and metal filter every 15,000 miles (1978–79), 60,000 miles 1980 and later gasoline engines; 15,000 miles 1980 and later diesel engines.

FUEL EVAPORATIVE CONTROL SYSTEM

The only items requiring service in the evaporative control system are the foam plastic filter in the bottom of the charcoal canister. The canister filter is replaced every 45,000 miles (all models and years).

FUEL SYSTEM

NOTE: All Volvos manufactured for sale in the U.S. are equipped with fuel injection. One Canadian engine, the B21A, is equipped with a one-barrel carburetor.

Fuel Pump

All pumps are electrical.

NOTE: Volvo states that a "no-start" condition may occasionally occur when the car has not been started for an extended period of time. This may be due to the fuel pump sticking in one position because of foreign matter entering the pump, or corrosion forming on the rotor shaft or commutator and brushes. It is, therefore, very important to clean the fuel tank pick-up screen every 12 months or 12,000 miles to prevent corrosion causing water condensation and foreign matter from entering the pump. As an additional corrosion prevention measure, add an alcohol solution or "dry gas" to the fuel, especially in winter months. If, however, the pump does become "stuck" in one position for any of the above reasons, it may be "unstuck"

by lightly rapping on the pump casing with a length of hardwood such as a hammer handle, while the ignition is switched on.

NOTE: 1980–and later fuel tank filters require replacement at 60,000 miles.

TESTING & ADJUSTMENT

No adjustments or repairs may be made to the fuel pump. If the pump is not functioning properly, it must be discarded and replaced. To check the function of the fuel pump, the pump should be connected to a pressure gauge. Be careful not to switch the electrical leads. If the pump fails to pump its normal capacity, or if it cannot pump that capacity at its specified rate of current consumption, it must be replaced.

REPLACEMENT

1. Remove the filler cap. Remove the electrical lead from the pump as well as the template to which the pump is mounted.
2. Clean around the hose connections. Pinch shut the fuel lines, loosen the hose clamps, and disconnect the lines.

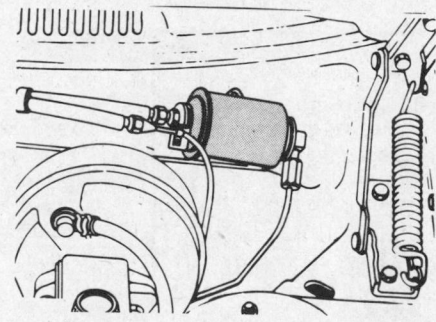

K-Jetronic fuel filter located on the firewall (all models)

3. Loosen the retaining nuts and remove the pump from its rubber mounts.
4. Install the new pump on its rubber mounts and tighten the retaining nuts.
5. Reconnect the fuel lines, tighten the hose clamps, and remove the pinchers.
6. Mount the template beneath the car and connect the electrical lead.
7. Start the engine and check for leaks.

Fuel Filters

REMOVAL & INSTALLATION

NOTE: The fuel filter should be replaced every 30,000 miles, or less under extremely dusty or smoggy conditions. The entire filter canister is replaced on both systems.

1. Loosen the fuel cap.
2. Clean the filter connections carefully before removing.
3. Disconnect the nipples and remove the seals.
4. Remove the filter and clamp.
5. Transfer the nipples and clamp to the new filter.

NOTE: Fuel flow direction arrow is marked on the new (and old) filter. Arrow follows direction from fuel tank to engine.

Bosch Electronic Fuel Injection (LH-Jetronic)

The Bosch LH-Jetronic electronic fuel injection system became available on the B21F-LH engine in 1982, and on the B23F-LH in 1983. The complete system contains the following components: L-Jetronic control unit (brain), airflow sensor, system relay, fuel pump relay, Lambda-sond oxygen sensor, vacuum switch, electric fuel pump, coolant temperature sensor fuel injectors, and the electronic control unit terminal for the Constant Idle System (CIS) (if equipped). On 1983 and later B23F-LH, the fuel injection and CIS system are both controlled by the same ECU mounted on the passenger's side kick panel. The LH-Jetronic system differs from the mechanical K-Jetronic (CI) injection system in that the injectors are individually controlled by the Electronic Control Unit, and are only spraying when told to do so (versus continually spraying in the mechanical injection system). The control unit is supplied information from the various sensors, which constantly respond to changes in the engine's operating environment (such as coolant temperature, ambient air temperature, etc.).

For all fuel injection system repair and service procedures not detailed below, please refer to "Fuel Injection" in the Unit Repair section.

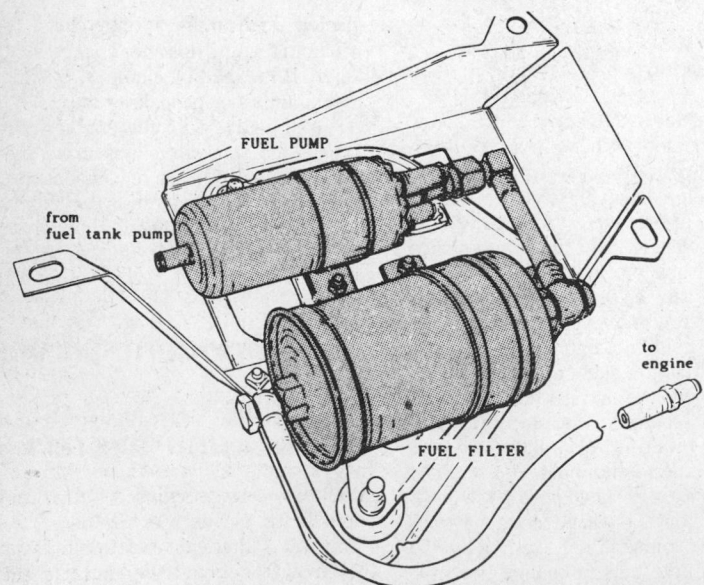

FUEL PUMP

from fuel tank pump

to engine

FUEL FILTER

L-Jetronic fuel pump and filter location on bracket under left side of car

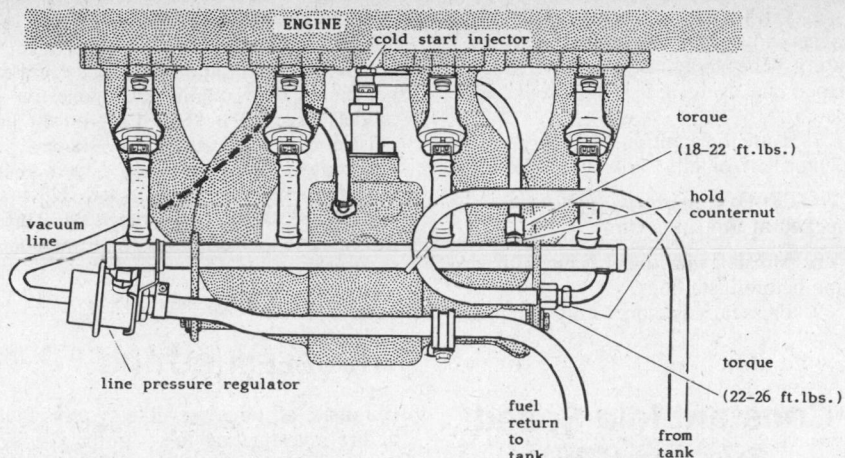

B21 and B23F-LH L-Jetronic injection manifold—1982 and later

FUEL INJECTION SYSTEM PRECAUTIONS

Due to the highly sensitive nature of the Bosch electronic fuel injection system, the following special precautions must be strictly adhered to in order to avoid damage to the system.

1. Do not operate the engine with the battery disconnected.

2. Do not utilize a high-speed battery charger as a starting aid.

3. When using a high-speed battery charger to charge the battery while it is installed in the vehicle, at least one battery cable must be disconnected.

4. Do not allow the control unit to be subjected to temperatures exceeding 185°F, such as when the vehicle is being baked after painting. If there is a risk of the temperature exceeding 185°F, the control unit must be removed.

5. The engine must not be started when the ambient temperature exceeds 158°F, or damage to the control unit will result.

6. The ignition must be in the off position when disconnecting or connecting the control unit.

7. When working on the fuel system, take care not to allow dirt to enter the system. Small dust particles may jam fuel injectors.

COMPONENT REPLACEMENT

The fuel injection system is repaired simply by replacing the defective component. There are some adjustments that can be made to some components. To make resistance checks, use an ohmmeter, and for continuity checks, a 12V test light. If the control unit is defective, install a new unit.

Control Unit

1. Disconnect the defroster hose, remove the control unit bracket retaining screws, and lower the unit to the floor, move the passenger's front seat all the way back,

unscrew the bolt securing the seat's front, move the seat forward while folding the seat bottom to the rear, remove the control unit retaining screws, and draw out the unit.

2. Remove the screw for the cap holding the cable harness to the unit. Pull out the plastic cover strip.

3. Construct a puller out of 5/64 in. welding wire to disconnect the main plug contact. Insert the puller in the rear of the control unit and pull out the plug carefully.

4. Press the plug contact firmly into the new or reconditioned control unit. Fit the plastic cover strip, retaining cap, and screw.

5. Fit the control unit into place and install its retaining screws.

Fuel Injectors

1. Remove the air cleaner hoses.
2. Pinch shut the fuel hose to the header pipe.

L-Jetronic injector—pre-1983 models

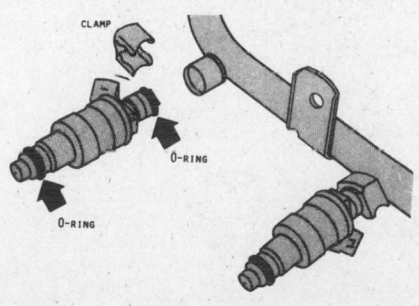

1983 and later L-Jetronic injector installation with clamp

3. Loosen the hose clamps for the injectors and lift up the head pipe.

4. Remove the plug contacts from the injectors. Disconnect the cable harness from the distributing pipe.

5. Turn the lock rings on the 1982 injectors counterclockwise so that they loosen from their bayonet fittings. Lift out the injectors. On 1983 and later injectors, carefully remove the snap clamp from around the injector and remove the injector.

6. Place the new injectors, with *new* washers and rubber sealing rings, in position. Grease the rubber O-rings with petroleum jelly before installing the injectors. Secure them by turning the lock-rings clockwise.

7. Connect the cable harness at the distributing pipe. Connect the plug contacts to the injectors.

8. Place the header pipe in position, and tighten the hose clamps. Remove the pinch clamps.

9. Install the air cleaner hoses.

Cold-Start Valve

NOTE: On the 1983 and later LH-Jetronic system, there is no cold-start valve per se. The injectors inject twice during an engine revolution at cold starts.

1. Remove the air cleaner assembly.
2. Pinch shut the fuel line to the valve.
3. Remove the plug contact and the fuel hose from the valve.
4. Remove the two retaining screws and the cold-start valve from the inlet duct.
5. Place the new cold-start valve in position with packing and install the retaining screws.
6. Connect the plug contact and fuel hose to the valve. Remove the pinch clamp.
7. Install the air cleaner assembly.

Mechanical (K-Jetronic) Fuel Injection (CI)

Continuous (mechanical, or sometimes known as K-Jetronic) fuel injection is standard on all 240 and 260 models (DL and GL) with both the 4 and V6 engines (except B21FLH and B23F). It differs from electronic fuel injection in that injection takes place continuously; controlled through a variation of the fuel flow rate through the injectors, rather than variation of the fuel injection duration. This system has no electronic computer. It is an electro-mechanical system that will provide suitable air/fuel mixtures to accommodate differing driving conditions.

For all K-Jetronic mechanical fuel injection system repair and service not detailed here, please refer to "Fuel Injection" in the Unit Repair section.

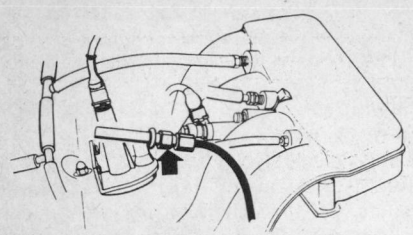

Remove fuel injectors (K-Jetronic shown) by pulling on the injector body, not on the fuel line

COMPONENT TESTING AND ADJUSTING

Fuel Injectors
REMOVAL & INSTALLATION

The fuel injectors on all Volvo CI systems are very close fit in the intake manifold. They are a ''plug in'' fit—they do not screw into the manifold by threads.

1. Grasp the injector body (see arrow in illustration). DO NOT grasp and pull on the fuel line. Pull injector straight out of manifold.

2. Protect injector tip—it is a precision instrument and is easily damaged. Proceed to next injector and so on.

3. Moisten a new rubber seal with gasoline before reinstalling injectors.

4. Press each injector in fully until seated.

TESTING

1. Remove the injector but leave it connected to the fuel line.

2. Point the injector into a container.

3. Remove the fuel pump relay and bridge the relay with a fused (8 amp) jumper wire.

4. Remove the air duct from the air flow sensor.

5. Have an assistant turn the ignition switch on.

6. Lift the air flow sensor plate with a magnet and observe the injector nozzle spray pattern. The spray pattern must be cone shaped and even; if it is not, replace the injector.

7. Turn the ignition off and hold the injector horizontally. It should not drip.

NOTE: One or more injectors may be checked at the same time.

8. Moisten the rubber seals with gasoline before installings.

9. Press the injectors firmly into place.

Constant Idle Speed System (CIS)

This system, introduced in 1981, controls engine idle speed by regulating air flow around (bypassing) the throttle valve in the intake manifold. It is used on gasoline engines with both K- and LH-Jetronic fuel injection systems.

There are five main components in the CIS systems: the Electronic Control Unit (ECU), which processes information from the sensors on engine speed, engine temperature and throttle position and accordingly signals the Air Control Valve to regulate air flow; the Air Control Valve, which is actually a small electric motor that rotates open or closed depending on the signal from the ECU; a micro switch at the throttle which signals the ECU when the throttle goes back to idle; the ignition coil, which provides information to the ECU on engine speed; and a coolant temperature sensor, which signals the ECU to increase the idle speed when the engine is cold, or decrease idle speed when the engine warms up. On 1982 and later CIS systems, a micro switch in the air conditioning control unit signals the ECU to set a higher idle speed when the A/C is turned on (improving A/C operation

and cooling due to the coolant pump and fan running faster).

The ECU is mounted inside the passenger's side door on the kick panel on all models except the 760 GLE—on the 760 it is located inside the driver's side door. Air contol valves are located next to the intake chamber on the B21 and B23 fours and on the B28 V6; on the B21F Turbo, the valve is located under the front side of the intake manifold.

TROUBLESHOOTING

Eliminate all other possible systems faults before investigating faults in the CIS system. Consult the accompanying chart for possible reasons for an incorrect idle speed.

A common source of problems in the CIS system may be the wires and/or connectors. There are two connectors, blue at top and black on bottom, at the ECU, and two other ECU connectors at the center and right-hand side of the firewall. The air control valve also has a connector, right at the valve.

If engine idle speed is considerably lower than specified, check the engine vacuum hoses for possible obstructions. The air control valve can be stuck or obstructed by deposits from the PCV valve and system.

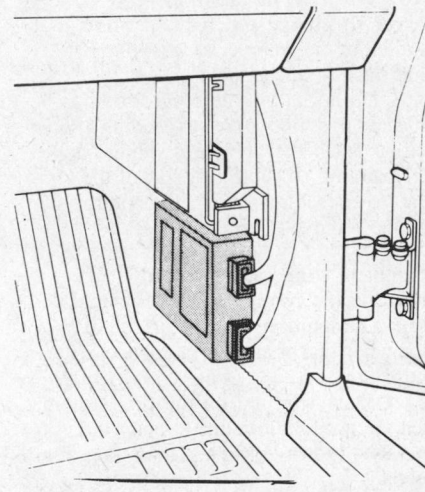

ECU location, CIS system. Location on 760 is on driver's side kick panel

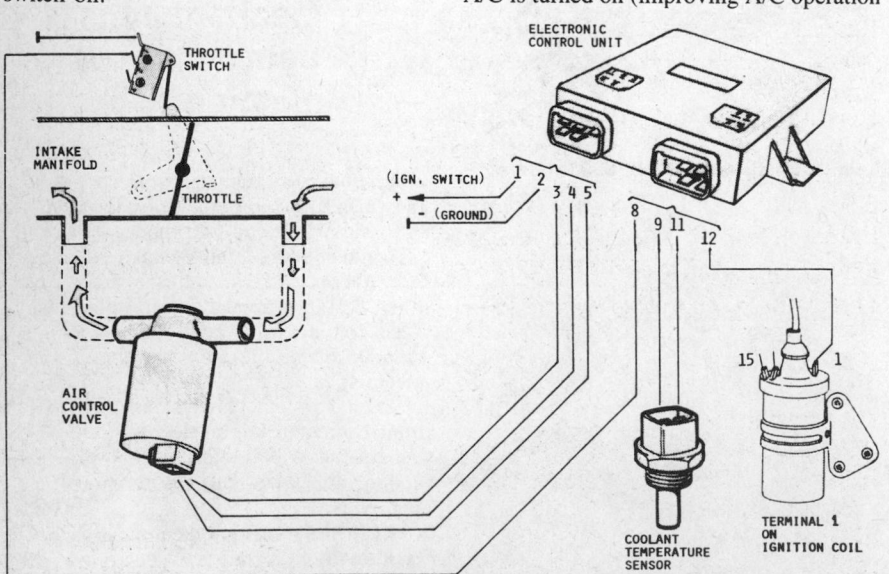

Constant Idle Speed (CIS) components

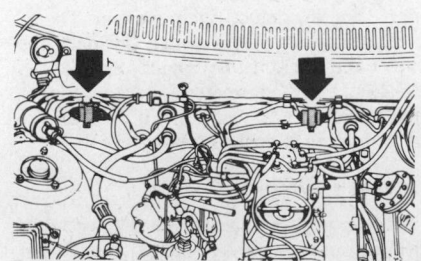

Firewall connectors—CIS system

CIS TROUBLESHOOTING

Symptom	Possible Reasons
Idle varies up and down, more than ± 50 rpm for 1981 models, more than ± 20 rpm for 1982 and later models.	• CO adjustment incorrect. • Ignition timing incorrect. • Throttle butterfly valve incorrectly adjusted. • Electronic Control Unit faulty. • Air control valve faulty.
Idle speed too high.	• Air control valve sticks. • Bad contact in connector. • Throttle switch incorrectly adjusted. • Temperature sensor faulty or not connected.
No speed control.	• Air control valve sticks. • Bad contact in connector. • Throttle switch incorrectly adjusted. • Electronic Control Unit faulty. • Air control valve faulty.
Engine stalls when braking to stop.	• CO adjustment incorrect. • Ignition timing incorrect. • Throttle butterfly valve incorrectly adjusted. • Bad contact in connector. • Electronic Control Unit faulty. • Low basic rpm.
No rapid idle speed when cold.	• Air control valve sticks. • Electronic Control Unit faulty. • Air control valve faulty. • Coolant temperature sensor faulty.

Test Equipment

A good quality volt-ohmmeter, with a range of 0 to approximately 20 volts is necessary to test the CIS system on all models. It is also helpful to have a test light (the type with a pointed contact on the bulb side and an alligator clamp on the other) as this uses more current than a volt-ohmmeter and might is some cases reveal a bad connection better. A tachometer is also necessary.

CAUTION

Although the CIS system voltage and currents are low DO NOT press the test point between the terminal contacts, just TOUCH the test point to them. Otherwise, the terminal contacts may be damaged.

Most common faults of the CIS system are bad connections in the multi-pin connectors on the firewall, at the ECU module and at the Coolant Temperature Sensor.

TESTING

NOTE: To prepare for the test, remove the panel that covers the ECU on the kickpanel, and disconnect both connectors at the ECU. Switch the ignition ON, except where noted.

Current Supply Check

With the ignition ON, terminal 1 is positive (+) and energized from the ignition switch. Terminal 2 is negative (−) and ground. Connect the voltmeter or test lamp across

terminals 1 and 2 in the connector (see the side of the ECU for terminal numbers). The voltmeter should read battery voltage, and the test lamp should be fully illuminated. If there is no reading, first check an alternate ground, then check fuse No. 13 in the fusebox.

Throttle Switch (Micro Switch) Check

Switch the ignition off. Connect the ohmmeter test leads across terminal 8 (blue connector) and terminal 1 (black connector). Check the chart below for ohmmeter

TROUBLESHOOTING

Throttle pedal NOT depressed (idle position)

1981 models:		
B21F, all	infinite resistance	test lamp NOT illuminated
B28F	zero resistance	test lamp illuminated
1982 models:		
B21F, all	infinite resistance	test lamp NOT illuminated
B28F	infinite resistance	test lamp NOT illuminated
1983 models:		
B21F, all	infinite resistance	test lamp NOT illuminated
B23E	infinite resistance	test lamp NOT illuminated
B23F	infinite resistance	test lamp NOT illuminated

Throttle pedal depressed (above idle position)

1981 models:		
B21F, all	zero resistance	test lamp illuminated
B28F	infinite resistance	test lamp NOT illuminated
1982 models:		
B21F, all	zero resistance	test lamp illuminated
B28F	zero resistance	test lamp illuminated
1983 models:		
B21F, all	zero resistance	test lamp illuminated
B23E	zero resistance	test lamp illuminated
B28F	zero resistance	test lamp illuminated

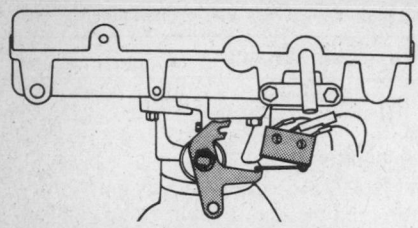

CIS throttle micro switch is located on the throttle linkage

and test lamp results. If the readings are incorrect, adjust the system according to the instructions below for your particular model.

Coolant Temperature Sensor Check

Use the ohmmeter to test coolant temperature sensor resistance. Connect the meter across terminals 9 and 11 of the connectors. See the graphs showing the proper relations of resistance versus temperature.

Ignition Signal Check

Connect a tachometer across terminal 12 and a ground. Start the engine. The tach should show engine speed; if the reading is incorrect or there is no reading at all, check

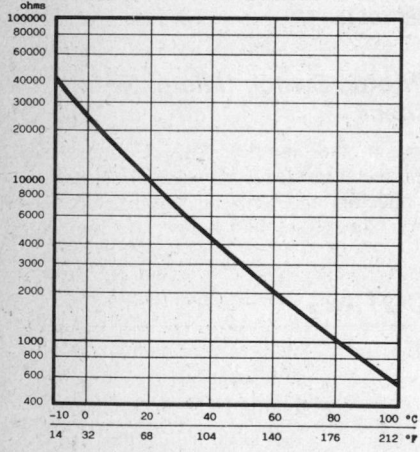

Resistance versus temperature specs, 1981 B21F and 1981 and '82 B28F coolant temperature sensor

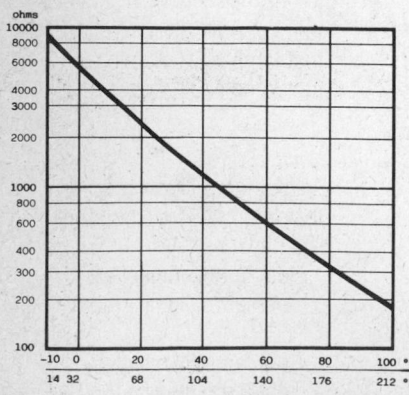

Resistance versus temperature specs—1982 B21F coolant temperature sensor

the connectors on the firewall for good contacts and connection.

Air Control Valve Check

Connect a jumper wire across terminals 4 and 1, and another jumper across terminals 5 and 2. Start the engine. A high idle speed of 1600 to 2400 rpm should be obtained—this indicates that the valve is working properly. If the engine does not obtain that high idle speed, the air control valve is defective. If no fault is found with the air control valve, try a new ECU. Also, check all connectors.

Reconnect all connectors and check the overall operations of the CIS systems.

Diesel Fuel System

The Volvo diesel engine has indirect fuel injection, which means that the fuel is not injected directly into the combustion chamber (as is common diesel practice), but rather is fed into a small pre-combustion chamber in the head. During the compression stroke, air is forced up into the swirl chamber, which is connected to the combustion chamber by a narrow channel in the head. The shape of the swirl chamber causes the air to rotate rapidly. This air speed in the swirl chamber promotes even combustion and is the reason the engine can reach fairly high engine speeds.

Fuel is injected into the swirl chamber just before the piston reaches top dead center and the fuel mixes with the turbulent air. As the piston reaches TDC, it compresses the air/fuel mixture to a ratio of 23.0:1. This ratio is over twice that of a

gasoline engine. The mere act of compressing air to this level generates tremendous heat (1400°F), and it is this heat which ignites the air/fuel mixture.

For further details on diesel engines, please refer to "Diesel Service" in the Unit Repair section.

FUEL FILTER

The fuel filter must be drained every 7,500 miles. Place a drain pan under the drain screw to collect the condensate. Loosen the bleeder screw several turns. Loosen the drain screw and drain until clean fuel flows out. Tighten the drain screw and the bleeder screw.

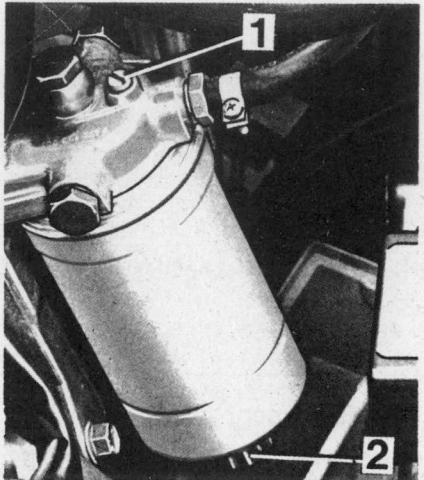

Diesel fuel filter service location. #1 is bleeder screw, #2 is drain

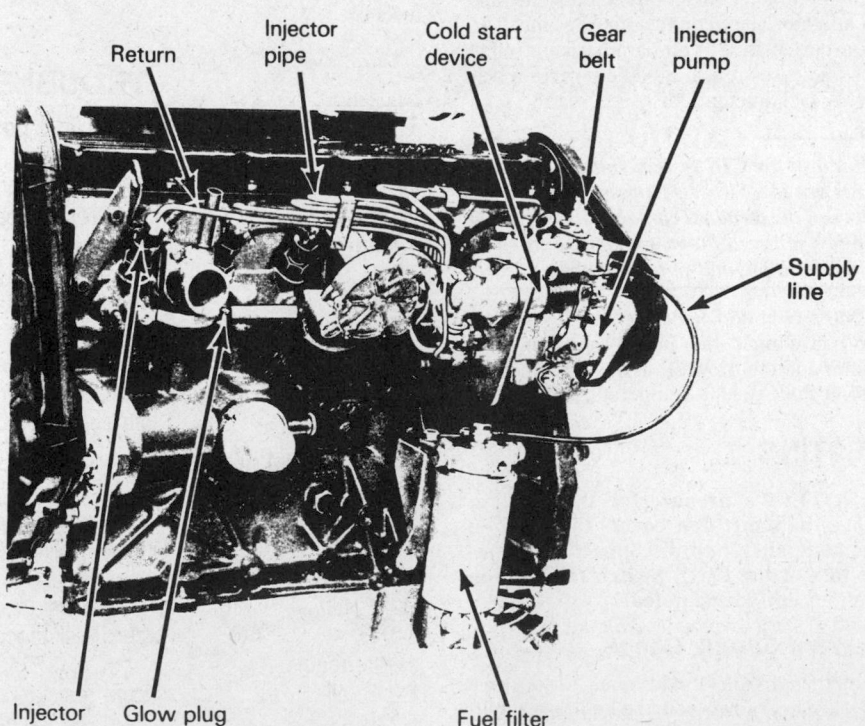

D24 Diesel showing injection system component location—D24T similar

FUEL PUMP/INJECTION PUMP

The fuel pump is also the injection pump and is located on the left rear side of the engine and is driven by a belt running off the rear of the camshaft. The pump supplies the engine with more fuel than it can use, the excess fuel being returned to the fuel tank through suction-return lines. The system constantly bleeds itself of air. Because the pump constantly moves such large amounts of fuel, it tends to stay cool and this reduces the chances of vapor lock. The pump is lubricated by the fuel passing through it. *Do not use fuel additives unless specifically recommended by Volvo for fear of damaging the pump.*

The pump contains a single piston which rotates and distributes fuel to each injector in the correct sequence, much in the same way the distributor on a gasoline engine distributes the spark to the spark plugs.

Removal & Installation

NOTE: Several special tools are needed to remove and install the pump and to set its timing. If these tools are not available, do not attempt to remove the pump. The tool numbers (Volvo part numbers) are given in the procedure.

1. Pinch off and remove the two coolant hoses running to the cold-start device on the fuel pump.

2. Disconnect the accelerator linkage at the pump and disconnect the wire from the stop valve on the top of the pump.

3. Remove the rear timing belt cover and thoroughly clean the fuel lines, and their connections at the injection pump.

4. Disconnect the fuel lines at the pump and plug the open connections to prevent dirt from entering the fuel system.

5. Remove the vacuum pump and its plunger.

6. Clean and remove the delivery lines at the fuel injectors. Plug all connections.

7. Set cylinder No. 1 to TDC on the injection stroke. At this position, the 0 mark on the flywheel aligns with the pointer and the notch on the injection pump pulley aligns with the notch on the pump housing. Both valves on No. 1 cylinder are closed and their camshaft lobes are pointing up at equally large angles.

8. Loosen the retaining bolts for the injection pump and push the pump up, then remove the pump drive belt. Tighten one bolt to hold the pump in the upper position.

9. Loosen the center bolt in the rear camshaft gear while using wrench 5199 to hold the gear. The bolts will be easily accessible if wrench 5201 is used.

NOTE: The camshaft must not rotate. Loosen the bolt only enough to rotate the gear on the camshaft.

10. Insert pin No. 5193 into the injection pump gear to lock it in position and remove the injection pump gear nut.

11. With the pin still in position, use a puller to remove the pump gear.

12. Remove the bolts retaining the front injection pump bracket to the engine, then remove the hex screws retaining the pump and remove the pump from the engine.

13. Install the pump on the engine and tighten the bolts only fingertight so that pump position can be adjusted.

14. Set the injection pump so that the mark on pump and the pump bracket align, then tighten the retaining bolts.

15. Make sure the shaft key is correctly installed and install the injection pump gear, washer and nut. Use pin 5193 to hold the gear while tightening the nut.

16. Proceed to "Setting the Injection Pump Timing," below.

17. After the injection pump timing is set, fill the pump with clean diesel fuel through the fuel line connection *only* if a new fuel pump is being installed or if the old pump was drained and rebuilt.

18. Install the rear timing gear cover. Connect the fuel lines and fuel delivery pipes. Tighten the fuel delivery line cap nuts and the fuel line banjo bolts to 18 ft. lbs.

When installing the fuel line on the pump, do not mix the banjo bolts: the bolt for the fuel return line has a small hole in it and is marked OUT.

19. Install the vacuum pump and all remaining components in the reverse order of removal. Adjust the accelerator linkage.

Setting the Injection Pump Timing

This procedure requires many special tools and gauges. We recommend the procedure be handled by a professional fuel injection technician.

FUEL INJECTORS

Removal & Installation

1. Thoroughly clean the fuel delivery line connections around each fitting before removing.

2. Unscrew each fitting from its injector. Plug or tape the end of each fitting to

prevent any dirt or grit from entering the fuel system.

3. Using a box-end wrench, unscrew the injector from the cylinder head. Remove the small heat shield and discard. Use care not to damage any part of the injector (especially the nozzle tip) while it is out of the engine. Plug each injector hole in the head with a piece of clean rag to prevent dirt from entering.

4. Installation is the reverse of removal. Be sure to use *new* heat shields with each injector. Note the proper way to install the heat shields as in the illustration.

MANUAL TRANSMISSION

REMOVAL & INSTALLATION

The transmission or the transmission-overdrive assembly may be removed with the engine installed in the vehicle.

240 and 260 (DL amd GL)

1. Disconnect the battery. At the firewall, disconnect the back-up light connector.

2. Jack up the front of the car and install jack stands. Loosen the set screw and drive out the pin for the shifter rod. Disconnect the shift lever from the rod.

3. Inside the car, pull up the shift boot. Remove the fork for the reverse gear detent. Remove the snap-ring and lift up the shifter. If overdrive-equipped, disconnect the engaging switch wire.

4. On 240 series models, disconnect the clutch cable and return spring at the throw out fork and flywheel housing. On 260 series models, remove the bolts retaining the slave cylinder to the flywheel housing and tie the cylinder back out of the way (do not disconnect).

5. Disconnect the exhaust pipe bracket(s) from the flywheel cover. Remove the oil pan splash guard.

6. Using a floor jack and a block of wood, support the engine beneath the oil pan. Remove the transmission support crossmember.

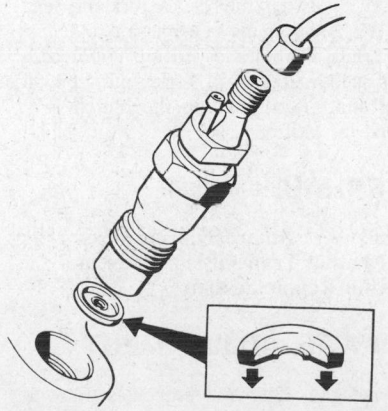

Diesel injector. Make sure you install new heat shields in the manner shown

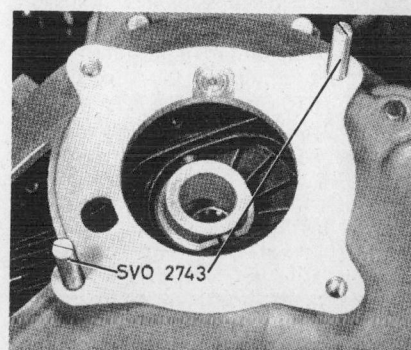

Transmission guide pins installed

7. Disconnect the driveshaft. Disconnect the speedometer cable. If so equipped, disconnect the overdrive wire.

8. Remove the starter retaining bolts and pull free of the flywheel housing.

9. Support beneath the transmission using another floor jack. Remove the flywheel (bell) housing-to-engine bolts and remove the transmission.

10. Reverse Steps 1–9 to install. Tighten the flywheel housing-to-engine bolts to 25–35 ft. lbs.

760 GLE

1. Disconnect the battery ground cable.

2. Remove the ash tray and holder assembly. Remove the trim box around the gear shift lever.

3. Disconnect the shift lever cover from the floor. Remove the snap-ring at the base of the shift lever.

4. Jack up the car and safely support it with jackstands. From underneath the car, disconnect the gear shift rod at the gear shift lever. Remove the lock screw, and press out the pivot pin. Push up on the shift lever, and pull it up and out of the car.

5. Matchmark the driveshaft and transmission flanges for later assembly. Disconnect the driveshaft from the transmission.

6. Separate the exhaust pipe at the joint under the car. Detach the bracket from the front end of the exhaust pipe (near the bend).

7. Unbolt the transmission crossmember; at the same time, detach it from the rear support (rubber bushing).

8. Remove the rear support from the transmission.

9. Tag and disconnect the electrical connectors from the overdrive, back-up light connector and the solenoid.

10. Cut the plastic clamp at the gear shift assembly for the wiring harness.

11. Remove the starter motor retaining bolts. On models with the B28F V6, remove the cover plate under the bellhousing and the cover plate for the other starter motor opening.

12. On B28F models (hydraulic clutch), remove the slave cylinder from the bellhousing and upper bolts holding the bellhousing. On D24T models, (mechanical clutch), detach the clutch cable from the release fork and the belhousing.

13. Place a transmission jack or a standard hydraulic floor jack underneath the gearbox (center section) of the transmission so that the transmission is resting on the jack pad. *It is very helpful here to have another person steadying and guiding the transmission on the jack as it is lowered.* Remove the lower bolts holding the bellhousing, and carefully lower the transmission a few inches as you roll it back so the input shaft will clear. Stop the jack and make sure all wires and linkage are disconnected, then lower the transmission the rest of the way.

14. Reverse the above procedure for removal, making note of the following: use

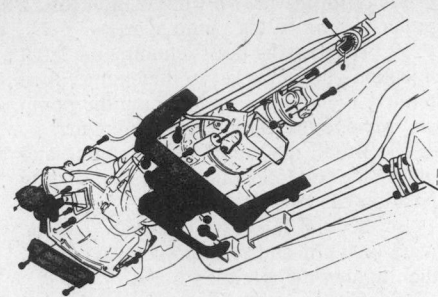

760 GLE manual transmission mounting

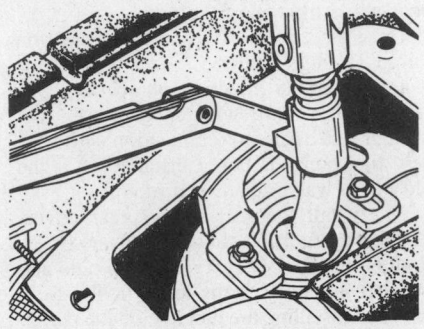

Reverse gear detent clearance adjustment—manual transmission models

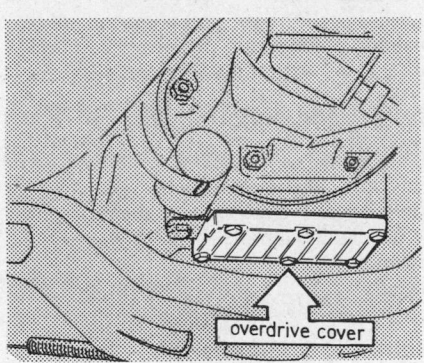

M46 overdrive bottom cover

a plastic cable tie to secure the wiring harness to the gear shift assembly where the original plastic clamp was cut. Adjust clutch clearance on D24T models to 1–3mm (0.04–0.12 in.) between the release fork and bearing. When sliding the transmission into place make sure the release bearing is correctly positioned in the shift fork, and that the input shaft is aligned in the clutch disc. Adjust the shifter.

OVERHAUL

For all overhaul procedures, please refer to ''Manual Transmission Overhaul'' in the Unit Repair Section.

LINKAGE ADJUSTMENT

Reverse gear detent clearance is the only adjustment that can be made to the shift linkage. Remove the shift lever cover, trim frame and ash tray assembly. Engage first

gear and adjust the clearance between the detent plate and the gear shift lever. Also check clearance should be 0.004–0.06 in.

TRANSMISSION LUBRICATION

The Volvo manual transmissions use Automatic Transmission Fluid type F or G. The oil level should be up to the filler plug hole.

OVERDRIVE

The overdrive unit for the M46 transmission is a planetary gear type and is mounted on the rear of the transmission. When the overdrive is in the direct drive position (overdrive switched off) and the car is driven forward, power from the transmission mainshaft is transmitted through the freewheel rollers and uni-directional clutch to the overdrive output shaft. When the car is backing up or during periods of engine braking, torque is transmitted through the clutch sliding member which is held by spring pressure against the tapered portion of the output shaft. When the overdrive is actuated, the clutch sliding member is pressed by hydraulic pressure against the brake disc (ring), which locks the sun wheel. As a result, the output shaft of the overdrive rotates at a higher speed than the mainshaft thereby accomplishing a 20° reduction in engine speed in relation to vehicle speed.

REMOVAL & INSTALLATION

To facilitate removal, the vehicle should first be driven in 4th gear with the overdrive engaged, and then coasted for a few seconds with the overdrive disengaged and the clutch pedal depressed.

1. Remove the transmission from the vehicle as outlined in the applicable ''Transmission Removal and Installation'' section.

2. Disconnect the solenoid cables.

3. If the overdrive unit has not already been drained, remove the six bolts and the overdrive oil pan.

4. Remove the bolts which retain the overdrive unit to the transmission intermediate flange. Pull the unit straight to the rear until it clears the transmission mainshaft.

5. Reverse the above procedure to install. Install the overdrive oil pan with a new gasket. After installation of the transmission (which automatically fills the overdrive) to the proper level with Automatic Transmission Fluid type F or G. Check the lubricant level in the transmission after driving 6–9 miles. The oil level should be up to the filter plug hole.

Overdrive Solenoid
REMOVAL & INSTALLATION

NOTE: The solenoid and operating

valve are one unit, and are replaced together.

1. Disconnect the wire clips from the solenoid unit.

2. Unscrew the solenoid from the side of the overdrive unit.

3. When installing, use a new seal and new O-rings. Immerse the O-rings in ATF (automatic transmission fluid) prior to installation. Screw the solenoid unit into the overdrive by hand until snug. Using a "crow's-foot" open-end wrench attachment on a torque wrench, torque the solenoid unit to 37 ft. lbs. Attach the wire clips, check overdrive oil level and check operations.

CLUTCH

All Volvos are equipped with Borg and Beck or Fichtel and Sachs diaphragm spring clutches. The 240, DL, GL and GT Diesel series use an 8½ in. disc. The 260 uses a 9 in. disc. The 760 GLE with B28 V6, 260 series, pre-'83 GLE and Coupe use a hydraulically-operated clutch, incorporating a clutch master cylinder and slave cylinder. There is no effective adjustment in this type of system. The 760 GLE equipped with the D24T turbodiesel uses a cable-operated (mechanical) clutch. It can be adjusted.

CLUTCH ADJUSTMENT

240, DL, GL, GLT and 760 GLE with D24T Turbodiesel

The play in the manually-operated clutches in these four cylinder Volvos can be adjusted. Clutch play is adjusted underneath the car at the clutch fork. Loosen the lock nut on the fork side of the cable bracket, then turn the adjusting nut until the proper play is achieved. Tighten the lock nut. Clutch play for all 4 cylinder engines except Turbo is 3–5mm (⅛ in.–³⁄₁₆ in.). Turbo clutch play (free movement rearward) is 1–3mm (about ⁵⁄₆₄ in. or 0.04–0.12 in.). D24T clutch play is the same as the gasoline turbo above.

Clutch Master Cylinder

REMOVAL & INSTALLATION

260, GLE and Coupe

1. Drain the clutch reservoir with a bulb syringe. Be careful not to drip brake fluid (used in the clutch cylinders) on any painted surfaces.

2. Remove the fluid pipe from the master cylinder.

3. Remove the two retaining bolts and remove the master cylinder.

4. Install in the reverse order. Fill the reservoir with fluid and bleed the system at the slave cylinder on the flywheel housing.

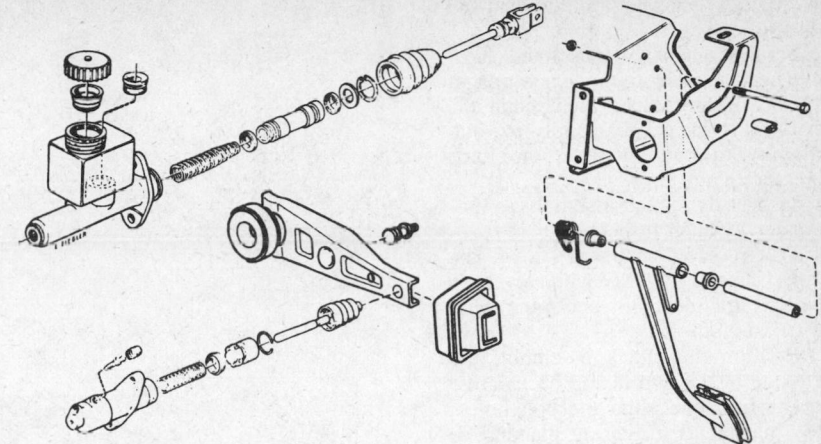

260 series clutch linkage—GLE and Coupe (all V6) similar

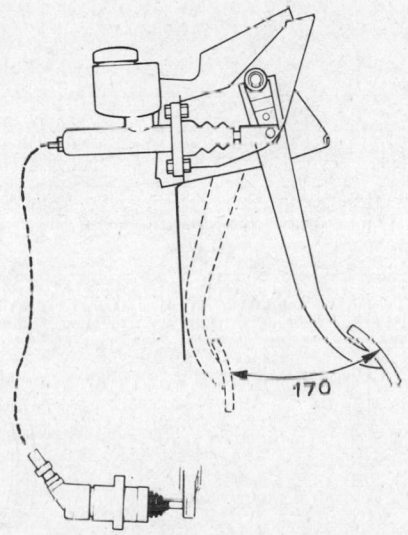

Clutch master cylinder and slave cylinder location—V6 models. Clutch travel is about 6.7 in. (170 mm)

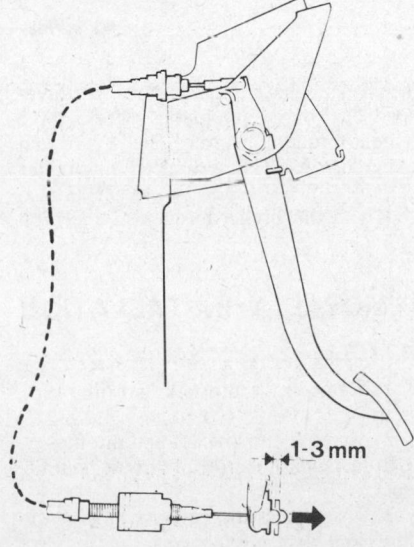

Clutch free-play clearance—B21F Turbo

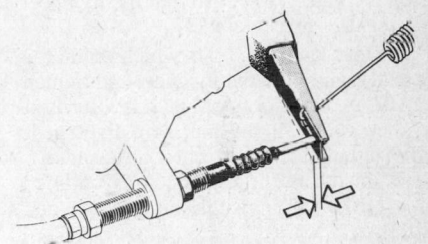

Clutch fork play adjustment, manual (non-hydraulic) clutches. Locknut at center, adjusting nut at left.

760 GLE with B28F V6

1. Remove the panel under the instrument panel. Remove the locking spring and pin from the clutch pedal assembly.

2. Disconnect the hose from the clutch fluid reservoir. *Do not let the brake fluid come in contact with any painted surfaces.*

3. Unscrew the nipple from the cylinder housing. Place a container underneath the cylinder to catch the fluid that will spill out. Unbolt and remove the cylinder housing.

4. Reverse the above procedure to install. Make sure there is 1mm (0.04 in.) clearance between the pushrod and the pistons, and adjust if necessary. Fill the reservoir with DOT 4 brake fluid and bleed the system.

Clutch Slave Cylinder

REMOVAL & INSTALLATION

260, GLE to 1982, Coupe and 760 GLE with V6

The slave cylinder is unbolted from the flywheel housing after its fluid tube is disconnected and plugged. Be sure to bleed the system after installation.

Clutch

REMOVAL & INSTALLATION

1. Remove the transmission as outlined

under "Manual Transmission Removal and Installation".

2. Scribe alignment marks on the clutch and flywheel. In order to prevent warpage, slowly loosen the bolts which retain the clutch to the flywheel diagonally in rotation. Remove the bolts and lift off the clutch and pressure plate.

3. Inspect the clutch assembly as outlined under "Clutch Inspection."

4. When ready to install, wash the pressure plate and flywheel with solvent to remove any traces of oil, and wipe them clean with a cloth.

5. Position the clutch assembly (the longest side of the hub facing backwards) to the flywheel and align the bolt holes. Insert a pilot shaft (centering mandrel or drift), or an input shaft from an old transmission of the same type, through the clutch assembly and flywheel so that the flywheel pilot bearing is centered.

6. Install the six bolts which retain the clutch assembly to the flywheel and tighten them diagonally in rotation, a few turns at a time. After all the bolts are tightened, remove the pilot shaft (centering mandrel).

7. Install the transmission as outlined under "Manual Transmission Removal and Installation".

8. On the 260 (GLE, 760 GLE etc.), bleed the clutch hydraulic system, if necessary.

CLUTCH INSPECTION

Check the pressure plate for heat damage, cracks, scoring, or other damage to the friction surface. Check the curvature of the pressure plate with a steel ruler. Place the ruler diagonally over the pressure plate friction surface and measure the distance between the straight edge of the ruler and the inner diameter of the pressure plate. The measurement must not be greater than 0.0012 in. In addition, there must be no clearance between the straight edge of the ruler and the outer diameter of the pressure points. Replace the clutch as a unit if it proves faulty.

Check the throwout bearing by rotating it several times while applying finger pressure, so that the ball bearings roll against the inside of the races. If the bearing does not turn easily or if it binds at any point, replace it as a unit. Also make sure that the bearing slides easily on the guide sleeve from the transmission.

AUTOMATIC TRANSMISSION

Volvos are available with four different automatic transmissions. The Borg-Warner BW55 (and its Japanese made counterpart the Aisin-Warner AW55) have been used

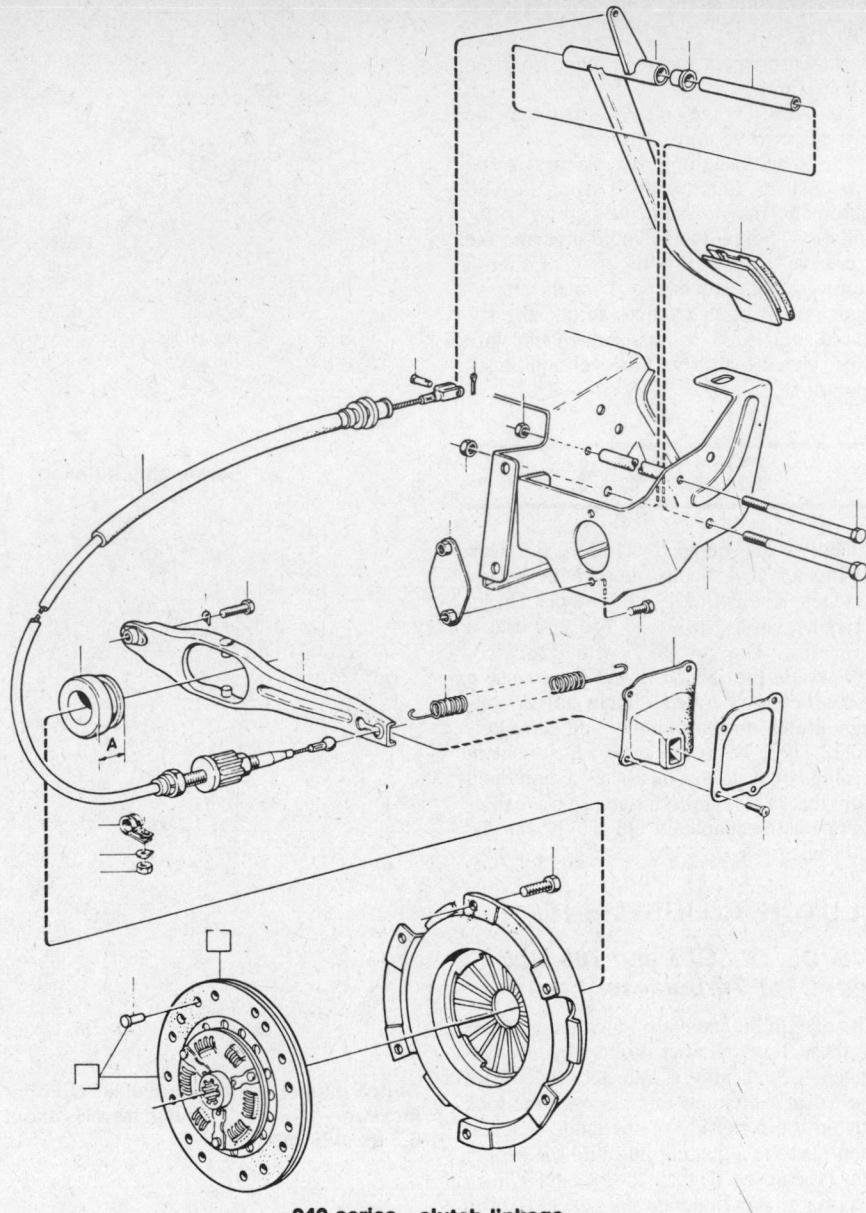

240 series—clutch linkage

since 1976. These transmissions are three-speed dual-range automatics with a three element torque converter. The AW70 and heavy-duty AW71 are 4-speed automatics available since 1982. The AW71 is also used with the higher-torque B21F Turbo engine.

REMOVAL & INSTALLATION
240 (DL)

1. Remove the dipstick and filler pipe clamp.

2. Remove the bracket and throttle cable from the dashboard and throttle control, respectively.

3. Disconnect the exhaust pipe at the manifold.

4. Raise the car and support it on jack stands at the front and rear axles.

5. Drain the fluid into a clean container.

6. Disconnect the driveshaft from the transmission flange.

7. Disconnect the selector lever controls and remove the reinforcing bracket from the pan.

8. Remove the torque converter attaching bolts.

9. Support the transmission with a jack equipped with a holding fixture.

10. Remove the car crossmember.

11. Disconnect the exhaust pipe brackets and remove the speedometer cable from the case.

12. Remove the filler pipe.

13. Place a wooden block between the engine and firewall and lower the jack until the engine is against the block.

NOTE: If the battery cable appears to stretch too much, remove it.

20. Position jack, with holding fixture, under transmission.

21. Remove the two lower converter housing bolts.

22. Pull the transmission back and down to clear the guide pins.

23. Installation is the reverse of removal. Torque the converter housing bolts to 35 ft. lbs. Torque filler pipe nut to 70 ft. lbs. Torque converter-to-drive plate bolts to 35 ft. lbs. Adjust control rod so that 1⅛ in. of thread is visible. Torque crossmember bolts to 35 ft. lbs.

760 GLE

1. Place the gear selector in the "P" position.

2. Disconnect the kickdown cable at the throttle pulley on the engine. Disconnect the battery ground cable.

3. Disconnect the oil filler tube at the oil pan, and drain the transmission oil.

—— CAUTION ——
The oil will be scalding hot if the car was recently driven.

4. Disconnect the control rod at the transmission lever, and disconnect the reaction rod at the transmission housing.

5. On AW 71 transmissions, disconnect the wire at the solenoid (slightly to the rear of the transmission-to-driveshaft flange).

6. Matchmark the transmission-to-driveshaft flange and unbolt the driveshaft.

7. Remove the transmission crossmember assembly.

8. Disconnect the exhaust pipe at the joint and remove the exhaust pipe bracket from the exhaust pipe. Remove the rear engine mount with the exhaust pipe bracket.

9. On D24T models, remove the starter motor. On B28F V6 models, remove the bolts retaining the starter motor.

10. Remove the cover for the alternate starter motor location on B28F models. Remove the cover plate at the torque converter housing bottom on B28F models.

11. Disconnect the oil cooler lines at the transmission.

12. Remove the two upper screws at the torque converter cover. Remove the oil filler tube.

13. Place a transmission jack or a standard hydraulic floor jack underneath the transmission. *It is helpful to have another person steadying and guiding the transmission during this procedure.*

14. Remove the screws retaining the torque converter to the drive plate. Pry the torque converter back from the drive plate with a small pry bar.

15. Slowly lower the transmission as you pull it back to clear the input shaft. *Do not tilt the transmission forward or the torque converter may slide off.*

16. Reverse the above procedure for installation. Move the gear selector to the "P" position before attaching the control rod. Adjust the gear shift linkage and connect and adjust the kickdown cable accord-

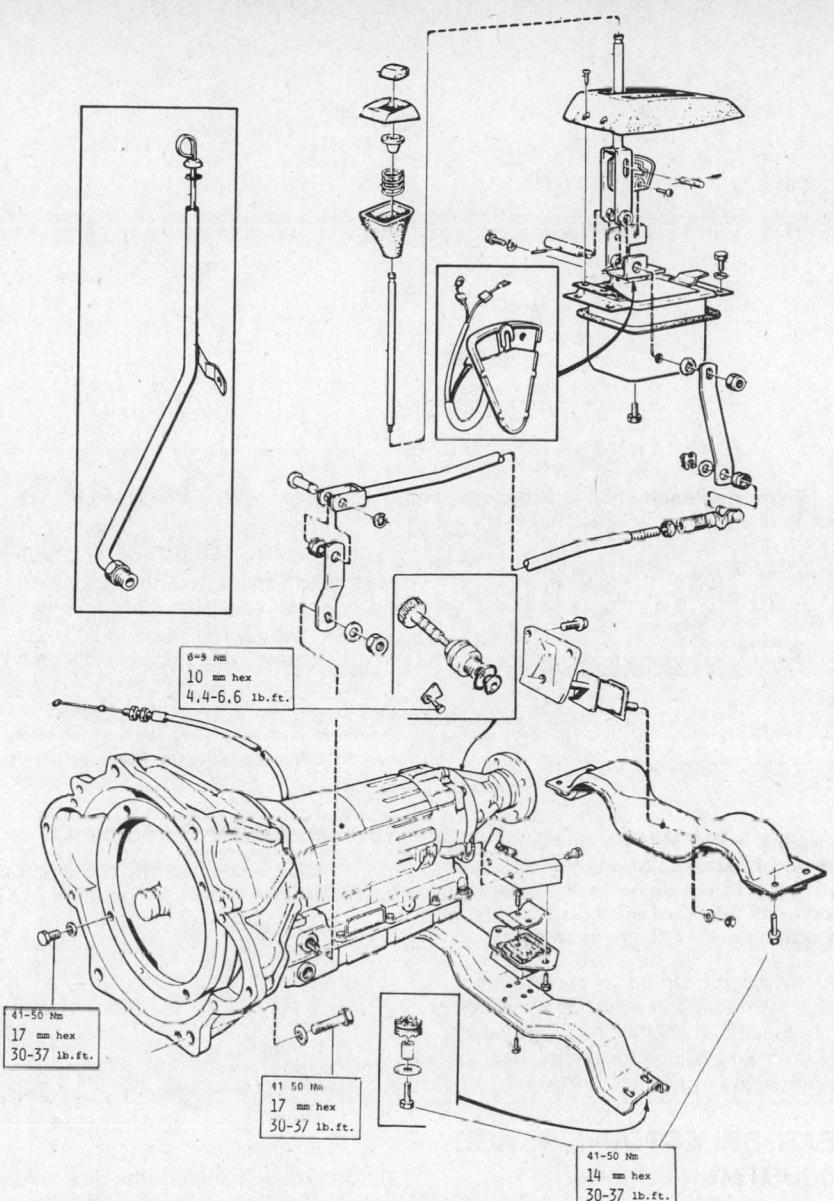

6=5 Nm
10 mm hex
4,4-6,6 lb.ft.

41-50 Nm
17 mm hex
30-37 lb.ft.

41-50 Nm
17 mm hex
30-37 lb.ft.

41-50 Nm
14 mm hex
30-37 lb.ft.

BW55, AW55 mountings and controls—AW70 and AW71 similar

14. Disconnect the starter wires, remove the converter housing bolts and pull the transmission backwards to clear the guide pins.

15. Install in the reverse of removal. Torque all 14mm bolts to 35 ft. lbs.

260 (GL)

1. Remove air cleaner.

2. Disconnect throttle cable.

3. Remove the two upper converter housing bolts.

4. Remove the filler pipe.

5. Raise the vehicle, support it front and rear with jack stands and drain the transmission into a clean container.

6. Remove the splash shield (8 bolts).

7. Disconnect the front muffler from the rubber suspensor.

8. Disconnect the driveshaft from the transmission flange.

9. Remove the exhaust pipe brackets at the rear of the transmission.

10. Remove the rear crossmember.

11. Remove the rear engine support and exhaust pipe bracket.

12. Remove the speedometer cable.

13. Disconnect the cooler lines at the transmission.

14. Remove the electrical connections from transmission.

15. Remove neutral start switch.

16. Remove shift control rod.

17. Remove the engine-to-transmission cover plate.

18. Remove starter motor and cover.

19. Remove converter-to-drive plate bolts.

ing to the "Gear Selector Linkage Adjustment" procedures later in this section.

Fluid Pan

REMOVAL & INSTALLATION

1. Raise the car and place jack stands underneath.

2. The dipstick tube doubles as the filler tube, and when removed, the drain plug. Disconnect the tube from the side of the pan, and drain the transmission.

3. Remove the 14 pan bolts, and lower the pan and gasket (some fluid will remain in the pan).

4. Inspect the magnet (located adjacent to the filter screen) for metal particles. Check the filter screen for the pump. Remove any gum or sludge from the bottom of the pan. Clean and dry the pan and install a new gasket.

5. Position the pan and install the bolts fingertight. Then, stop torque, diagonally in rotation, to 4.4–7.4 ft. lbs.

6. Connect the dipstick tube and tighten to 59–74 ft. lbs.

7. Remove the jack stands and lower the car. Refer to the capacities chart and fill the transmission to the proper level with ATF Type F.

PUMP STRAINER SERVICE

1. Remove the pan as outlined in the "Pan Removal and Installation" section.

2. Remove the bolts which retain the front pump wire-mesh strainer to the valve body, and lower the strainer.

3. Clean the strainers in an alcohol based solvent solution.

4. Position the strainers to the valve body and install the retaining screws and bolts. Torque the bolts to 3.7–4.4 ft. lbs.

5. Install the pan with a new gasket as outlined in the "Pan Removal and Installation" section.

BAND ADJUSTMENTS— ALL TRANSMISSIONS

The BW55 and AW55, AW70 and AW71 transmissions are equipped with a multi-disc brake (band) system which does not require any adjustment. No provision is made for band adjustment, even at overhaul.

NEUTRAL START SWITCH ADJUSTMENT

All models have an adjustable switch, located beneath the shifter quadrant on the tunnel. To adjust:

1. Remove the shifter quadrant cover.

2. Place the shifter lever in Park. Check that the round switch contact centers over the indicating line for "P" (park). If not, loosen the two switch mounting screws and align the switch.

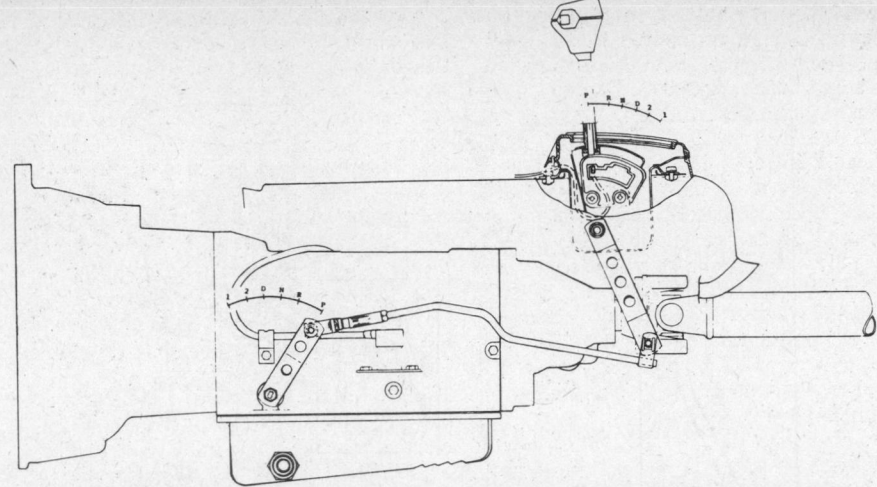

Shortened shaft linkage and closer control console—AW70/AW71 automatics

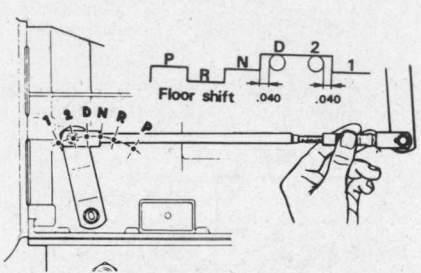

Adjusting automatic transmission gear selector. Clearance in position D toward position N is the same as the clearance in position 2 toward position 1. Adjust at the bottom end of the gear selector.

3. Place the shifter lever in Neutral. Repeat the check and adjust as necessary.

4. Finally, check that the engine starts only in Park or Neutral, and check that the back-up lights work only in Reverse.

GEAR SELECTOR LINKAGE ADJUSTMENT

240, 260 (DL, GL)

NOTE: The gear selector shift console has been moved forward on cars equipped with the AW70/AW71 transmissions. The shift linkage is also shortened on these cars.

1. Disconnect the shift rod from the transmission lever. Place both the transmission lever and the gear selector lever in the "2" position.

2. Adjust the length of the shift control rod so that a small clearance of 0.04 in. is obtained between the gear selector lever inhibitor and the inhibitor plate, when the shift control rod is connected to the transmission lever.

3. Position the gear selector lever in Drive and make sure that a similar small clearance of 0.04 in. exists between the lever inhibitor and the inhibitor plate. Disconnect the shift control rod from the transmission lever and adjust, if necessary.

4. Lock the control rod bolt with its safety clasp and tighten the locknut. Make sure that the control rod lug follows with the transmission lever.

5. After moving the transmission lever to the Park and "1" positions, make sure that the clearances remain the same. In addition, make sure that the output shaft is locked with the selector lever in the Park position.

1978 and Later BW55

1. With the engine off, check that the distance between the "D" position and its

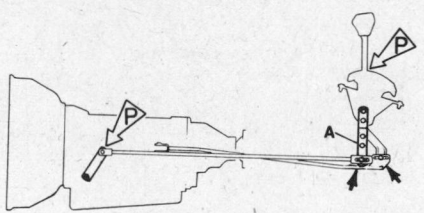

760 automatic transmission gear linkage. "A" is adjusting rod arm; arrows point to locknuts on adjustmnet (left) and reaction rod (right) arms.

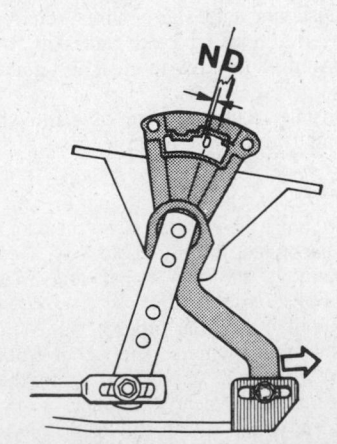

Checking clearance between D and N, and 1 and 2

forward stop is equal to the distance between the "2" position and its rearward stop, when the gear selector is moved. If you are not sure, remove the gear quadrant cover, and measure.

2. If adjustment is necessary, a rough setting is made by loosening the locknut and rotating the clevis on the control rod to the transmission. A fine adjustment can be made by rotating the knurled sleeve between the control rod locknut and the pivot for the gear selector lever. Increasing the rod length will decrease clearance between the "D" position and its forward stop, and vice versa. Maximum permissable length of exposed thread between the locknut and the control rod is 1.1 in.

760 GLE

NOTE: Before adjusting the shift linkage, make sure the starter motor operates only in "P" or "N" positions; that the back-up lights light up only in "R"; that the shift lever is vertical in "P" with the car level; that the clearance between "D" and "N" is the same or less than the clearance between 2 and 1.

BASIC ADJUSTMENT

1. Place the shift lever in "P".
2. Loosen the locknuts on the adjustment and reaction rods (on the linkage under the car).
3. Make sure the shift lever is in "P". Turn the driveshaft until it enters a locked position.
4. Position the adjusting rod arm (A) vertically and tighten the locknut. The gear shift lever may contact the dashboard if the adjusting rod arm is positioned too far backwards.
5. Press the reaction rod arm backwards until a slight resistance is felt. Tighten the locknut to 3.5 ft. lbs.

ADJUSTING CLEARANCE

1. Check that the clearance between "D" and "N" is the same or less than the clearance between 2 and 1 on the shift lever. If clearance is correct, tighten the locknut to 12–17 ft. lbs. If clearance is not correct, adjust as follows:
2. If no clearance is felt in "D", move the reaction rod arm rearwards about 2mm or 0.08 in.
3. If no clearance is felt in position 2, move the reaction rod arm forwards about 3mm or 0.12 in. Tighten the locknut.
4. After adjustment, check that the car starts only in "P" or "N", and that the back-up light does NOT light up in "R", reduce clearance in "D" by moving the rod arm forward slightly.

THROTTLE AND DOWNSHIFT CABLE ADJUSTMENT

1. First, adjust the throttle plate angle

and throttle cable. Disconnect the cable at the control pulley and the linkage rod at the throttle shaft. Set the throttle plate angle by loosening the adjusting screw locknut and backing off the screw. Then, turn in the screw until it just makes contact and then one additional turn. Tighten the locknut. Adjust the linkage rod so that it fits onto the throttle shaft pulley ball without moving the cable pulley. Attach the throttle cable to the pulley and adjust the cable sheath so that the cable is stretched but does not move the cable pulley. Finally, fully depress the gas pedal and check that the pulley contacts the full throttle abutment.

2. With the transmission cable hooked up, check that there is 0.010–0.040 in. clearance between the cable clip and the adjusting sheath. The cable should be stretched at idle. Pull out the cable about ½ in. and release. A distinct click should be heard from the transmission as the throttle can returns to its initial position. Depress the gas pedal again to wide open throttle. Check that the transmission cable moves about 2 in. Adjust as necessary at the adjusting sheath.

DRIVELINE

Driveshaft and U-Joints

The driveshaft is a two-piece, tubular unit, connected by an intermediate universal joint. The rear end of the front section of the driveshaft forms a splined sleeve. A splined shaft forming one of the yokes for the intermediate U-joints fits into this sleeve. The front section is supported by a ball bearing contained in an insulated rubber housing which is attached to the bottom of the driveshaft tunnel. The front section is connected to the transmission flange, and the rear section is connected to the differential housing flange by universal joints. Each joint consists of a spider with four ground trunnions carried in the flange yokes by needle bearings.

REMOVAL & INSTALLATION

1. Jack up the vehicle and install safety stands.
2. Mark the relative positions of the driveshaft yokes and transmission and differential housing flanges for purposes of assembly. Remove the nuts and bolts which retain the front and rear driveshaft sections to the transmission and differential housing flanges, respectively. Remove the support bearing housing from the driveshaft tunnel, and lower the driveshaft and universal joint assembly as a unit.
3. Pry up the lock washer and remove the support bearing retaining nut. Pull off

the rear section of the driveshaft with the intermediate universal joint and splined shaft of the front section. The support bearing may now be pressed off the driveshaft.

4. Remove the support from its housing.
5. For removal of the universal joints from the driveshaft, consult "Universal Joint Overhaul."
6. Inspect the driveshaft sections for straightness. Using a dial indicator, or rolling the shafts along a flat surface, make sure that the driveshaft out-of-round does not exceed 0.010 in. Do not attempt to straighten a damaged shaft. Any shaft exceeding 0.010 in. out-of-round will cause substantial vibration, and must be replaced. Also, inspect the support bearing by pressing the races against each other by hand, and turning them in opposite directions. If the bearing binds at any point, it must be discarded and replaced.
7. Install the support bearing into its housing.
8. Press the support bearing and housing onto the front driveshaft section. Push the splined shaft of the front section, with the intermediate universal joint and rear driveshaft section, into the splined sleeve of the front section. Install the retaining nut and lock washer for the support bearing.
9. Taking note of the alignment marks made prior to removal, position the driveshaft and universal joint assembly to its flange connections and install but do not tighten its retaining nuts and bolts. Position the support bearing housing to the driveshaft tunnel and install the retaining nut. Tighten the nuts which retain the driveshaft sections to the transmission and differential housing flanges to a torque of 25–30 ft. lbs.
10. Remove the safety stands and lower the vehicle. Road test the car and check for driveline vibrations and noise.

UNIVERSAL JOINT OVERHAUL

NOTE: For all universal joint overhaul procedures, please refer to "U-Joint/CV-Joint Overhaul" in the Unit Repair Section.

REAR AXLE

All Volvos utilize a solid rear axle housing carried in two support arms. Two torque rods, connected between the axle shaft tubes and the body, limit the rear axle wind-up. A track bar (Panhard rod) controls lateral movement of the axle housing. The 760 GLE also incorporates a triangulated dual-ladder sub-frame that connects the axle unit to the unibody. Final drive is of the hypoid design, with the drive pinion lying below the ring gear. Each axle shaft is indexed

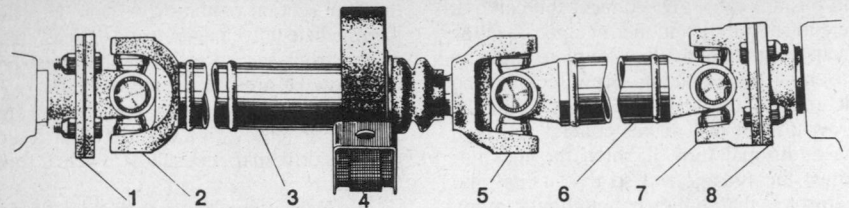

1. Flange on transmission
2. Front universal joint
3. Front section of driveshaft
4. Support bearing
5. Intermediate universal joint
6. Rear section of driveshaft
7. Rear universal joint
8. Flange on rear axle

Driveshaft with support bearing

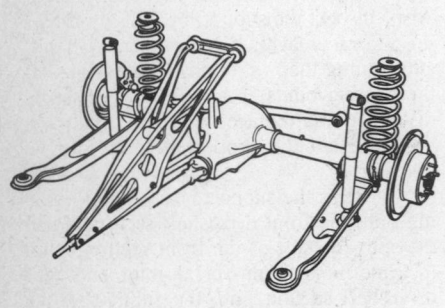

760 series rear axle. Sub-frame is ladder-like assembly above differential

into a splined sleeve for the different side gears, and supported at its outer end in a tapered roller bearing. Bearing clearance is not adjustable by use of shims as on earlier model Volvos, but instead is determined by bearing thickness. Both sides of the axle bearings are protected by oil seals.

Limited Slip Differential

Except for the differential assembly the design is the same as the standard differential.

Two shafts make up the spider for the differential pinion gears. On the side where it is against the differential carrier, each shaft has a V-shaped bevel. The differential carrier is similarly designed. When power from the engine starts to drive the vehicle, the shafts (A) glide up the beveled recess in the differential carrier. This compresses the friction plates behind the differential side gears so that the differential assembly brakes. The bevel angle on the differential carrier is designed and chosen in such a way that the differential gears are not entirely locked, but a maximum of 75% of engine torque can be transmitted to a driveshaft.

NOTE: Never attempt to run the vehicle with only one wheel jacked up. Both rear wheels must be off the ground before running the vehicle or serious damage could result.

Axle Shaft

REMOVAL & INSTALLATION BEARING AND OIL SEAL REPLACEMENT

1. Raise the vehicle and install safety stands.

2. Remove the applicable wheel and tire assembly.

3. Place a wooden block beneath the brake pedal, plug the master cylinder reservoir vent hole, and remove and plug the brake line from the caliper. *Be careful not to allow any brake fluid to spill onto the disc or pads*. Remove the two bolts which retain brake caliper to the axle housing, and lift off the caliper. Lift off the brake disc.

4. Remove the thrust washer bolts through the holes in the axle shaft flange. Using a slide hammer, remove the axle shaft, bearing and oil seal assembly. You may be able to pull out the shaft by temporarily reinstalling the brake disc and using this to grab on to while pulling out the axle shaft.

5. Using an arbor press, remove the axle shaft bearing and its locking ring from the axle shaft. Remove and discard the old oil seal.

6. Fill the space between the lips of the new oil seal with wheel bearing grease. Position the new seal on the axle shaft. Using an arbor press, install the bearing with a new locking ring, onto the axle shaft.

7. Thoroughly pack the bearing with wheel bearing grease. Install the axle shaft into the housing, rotating it so that it indexes with the differential. Install the bolts for the thrust washer and tighten to 36 ft. lbs.

8. Install the brake disc. Position the brake caliper to its retainer on the axle housing and install the two retaining bolts. Torque the caliper retaining bolts to 45–50 ft. lbs.

9. Unplug the brake line and connect it to the caliper. Bleed the caliper of all air trapped in the system.

10. Position the wheel and tire assembly on its lugs and hand-tighten the lug nuts. Remove the jack stands and lower the vehicle. Torque the lug nuts to 70–100 ft. lbs.

Differential

REMOVAL & INSTALLATION
All Models Except 760 GLE

1. Block the front wheels. Unscrew the rear wheel nuts. Jack up the rear of the vehicle. Place blocks in front of the rear jack attachments and lower the jack slightly. Remove the rear wheels.

2. Unscrew the upper bolts for the shock absorbers. Disconnect the handbrake cables from the lever arms and brackets on the brake backing plates.

3. Disconnect the driveshaft from the flange (yoke) on the pinion. Remove the brake line union from the differential carrier.

4. Loosen the front attaching bolt for the support arms about 1 turn. Remove the rear screws for the torque rods. Disconnect the track rod from the bracket on the differential carrier. Remove the lower attaching bolts for the springs.

5. Lower the jack until the support arms release from the springs. Remove the bolts which secure the differential carrier to the support arms. Lower the jack and pull the rear axle forward.

To install:

1. Place the rear axle on a garage jack. Move the axle in under the car and install the bolts for the support arms and torque rods.

2. Raise the jack until the track rod attachment on the shaft is at the level with the attachment on the body. Install the track rod.

3. Install the attaching bolts for the springs. Tighten the nuts for the torque rods and support arms.

4. Install the bracket, union, and brake hoses. Connect the universal joint to the flange.

5. Install the upper bolts for the shock absorbers. Install the handbrake cable in the brackets and at the levers. Adjust the handbrake and bleed the brake system. Fill with oil.

6. Install the wheels and nuts. Lower the car. Tighten the wheel nuts to 70–100 ft. lbs. Fill with oil. Use only hypoid oil, 80w/90.

760 GLE

1. Jack up the rear of the car and support jackstands, at the points recommended in the owner's manual. *Careful, solid placement of the jackstands is very important to the safety in this procedure.*

2. Remove the rear wheels.

3. Remove the brake calipers, keeping the hoses connected. Hang the calipers from the coil springs with wire.

4. Disconnect the parking brake cable from the equalizer and clamps on the rear axle (this is found up above the axle between the axle and the underside of the body.

5. Disconnect the lower torque rod from the axle. Loosen, but do not remove the

torque rod from the subframe.

6. Place a hydraulic floor jack underneath the center of the differential, and pump the jack up slightly.

7. Disconnect the Panhard rod (the track rod which runs parallel to the axle) at the axle.

8. Disconnect the connector at the speedometer sender and the turn clamp on the axle housing.

9. Matchmark the driveshaft-to-axle flanges and disconnect the driveshaft from the axle.

10. Disconnect the upper torque rod at the rear axle.

11. Unbolt the shock absorbers from their lower attaching points.

12. If the car is equipped with an anti-roll bar, disconnect it. Remove the front triangular brackets from the right and left trailing arms. Pry loose the trailing arms from the front attachments.

13. Disconnect the rear axle breather hose (found on the upper right-hand side of the axle).

14. Make one last check to see that the axle is fully disconnected at all points. *It is helpful to have another person stabilizing and guiding the axle as it is lowered.* Slowly lower the axle with the jack, and roll the jack with axle out from under the car.

15. To install, raise the axle so that the trailing arms and shocks can be reconnected, and reverse the order of removal. Torque the trailing arm brackets to 35 ft. lbs., and the nuts to 63 ft. lbs. Torque the shock bolts, panhard rod bolts, and subframe attachment bolts to 63 ft. lbs. Torque the torque rods to 103 ft. lbs. with the axle loaded; if the axle is unloaded, the bushings may turn when the springs become compressed. Torque the brake caliper bolts to 43 ft. lbs.

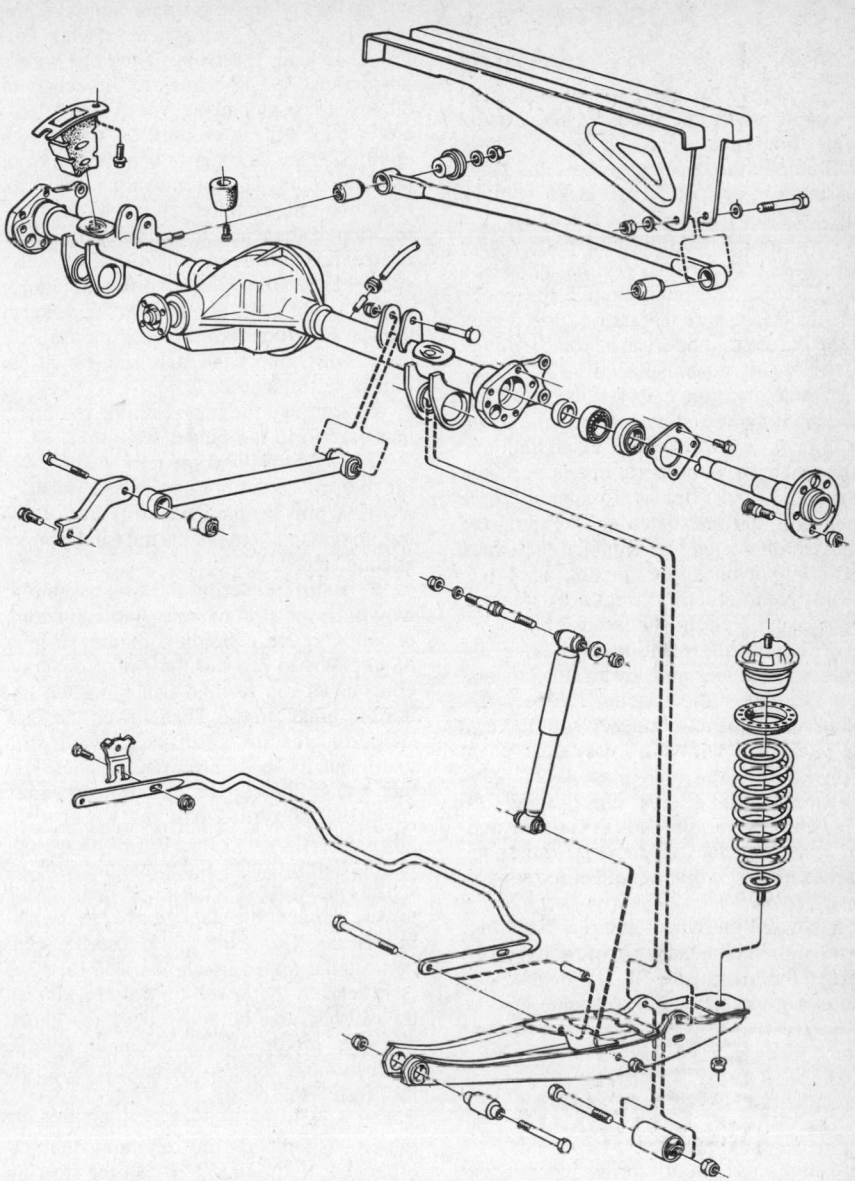

Rear suspension—240, 260 (DL, GL) series

REAR SUSPENSION

All Volvos use a coil spring rear suspension. The solid rear axle is suspended from the rigid frame member by a pair of support arms and damped by a pair of double-acting telescopic shock absorbers. A pair of torque rods control rear axle wind-up and a track rod limits the lateral movement of the rear axle in relation to the car. A rear stabilizer bar, attached to both rear support (trailing) arms, is installed on certain models.

Springs

REMOVAL & INSTALLATION

1. Remove the hub cap and loosen the lug nuts a few turns. Jack up the car and place jack stands in front of the rear jacking points. Remove the wheel and tire assembly.

2. Place a hydraulic jack beneath the rear axle housing and raise the housing sufficiently to compress the spring. Loosen the nuts for the upper and lower spring attachments.

— CAUTION —

Due to the fact that the spring is compressed under several hundred pounds of pressure, when it is freed from its lower attachment, it will attempt to suddenly spring back to its extended position. It is therefore imperative that the axle housing be lowered with extreme care until the spring is fully extended. As an added safety measure, a chain may be attached to the lower spring coil and secured to the axle housing.

3. Disconnect the shock absorber at its upper attachment. Carefully lower the jack and axle housing until the spring is fully extended. Remove the spring.

4. To install, position the retaining bolt and inner washer, for the upper attachment, inside the spring and then, while holding the outer washer and rubber spacer to the upper body attachment, install the spring and inner washer to the upper attachment (sandwiching the rubber spacer), and tighten the retaining bolt.

5. Raise the jack and secure the bottom of the spring to its lower attachment with the washer and retaining bolt.

6. Connect the shock absorber to its upper attachment. Install the wheel and tire assembly.

7. Remove the jack stands and lower the car. Tighten the lug nuts to 70–100 ft. lbs. and install the hub cap.

Shock Absorbers
REMOVAL & INSTALLATION

1. Remove the hub cap and loosen the lug nuts a few turns. Place blocks in front of the front wheels. Jack up the rear of the car to unload the shock absorbers and place jack stands in front of the rear jacking points. Remove the wheel and tire assembly.

2. Remove the nuts and bolts which retain the shock absorber to its upper and lower attachments and remove the shock absorber. Make sure that the spacing sleeve, inside the axle support arm for the lower attachment, is not misplaced.

3. The damping effect of the shock absorber may be tested by securing the lower attachment in a vise and extending and compressing it. A properly operating shock absorber should offer approximately three times as much resistance to extending the unit as compressing it. Replace the shock absorber if it does not function as above, or if its fixed rubber bushings are damaged. Replace any leaking shock absorber.

4. To install, position the shock absorber to its upper and lower attachments. Make sure that the spacing sleeve is installed inside the axle support (trailing) arm and is aligned with the lower attachment bolt hole. Install the retaining nuts and bolts, and torque to 63 ft. lbs. On 240 and 760 series models, the shock fits *inside* the support arm. On all 260 models, the shock attaches on the *outboard* side of the support arm.

5. Install the wheel and tire assembly. Remove the jack stands and lower the car. Tighten the lug nuts to 70–100 ft. lbs., and install the hub cap.

FRONT SUSPENSION

All Volvos use a coil spring independent front suspension utilizing a pair of Mac-Pherson-type struts located between a sheet metal tower at the top and a lower control arm at the bottom. The MacPherson strut design incorporates the coil spring, shock absorber and wheel spindle into a single assembly, eliminating the need for an upper suspension control arm. The MacPherson strut design provides for generous vertical suspension travel allowing the use of softer springs. The strut design is extremely sensitive to front wheel imbalance; the slightest imbalance often leading to front end wobble. Finally, the caster angle of the front suspension is preset and cannot be adjusted. If the caster angle is not up to specifications, the damaged components must be replaced as a unit.

Strut
REMOVAL & INSTALLATION

1. Remove the hub cap and loosen the lug nuts a few turns.

2. Firmly apply the parking brake and place blocks in back of the rear wheels.

3. Jack up the front of the car with a hoist or using a floor jack at the center of the front crossmember. When the wheels are 2–3 in. off the ground, the car is high enough. Place jack stands beneath the front jacking points. Then, remove the floor jack from the crossmember (if used), and reposition it beneath the applicable lower control arm to provide support at the outer end. Remove the wheel and tire assembly.

4. Using a ball joint puller, disconnect the steering rod from the steering arm.

5. Disconnect the stabilizer bar at the link upper attachment.

6. Remove the bolt retaining the brake line bracket to the fender well.

7. Open the hood and remove the cover for the strut assembly upper attachment.

8. While keeping the strut from turning, loosen and remove the nut for the upper attachment.

9. Before lowering the strut assembly, wire or tie the strut to some stationary component, or use a holding fixture such as SVO 5045, to prevent the strut from traveling down too far and damaging the hydraulic brake lines. Then lower the jack supporting the lower arm and allow the strut to tilt out to about a 60 degree angle. At this angle, the top of the strut assembly should just protrude past the wheel well, allowing removal of the strut from the top.

10. Carefully lift and guide the strut assembly into its upper attachment in the spring tower. Connect the stabilizer bar to the stabilizer link. Guide the shock absorber spindle into the upper attachment and raise the jack beneath the lower control arm. Install the washer and nut on top of the shock absorber spindle. While holding the spindle from turning, tighten the nut to 15–25 ft. lbs. Install the cover.

11. Attach the brake line bracket to its mount. Tighten the nut retaining the stabilizer bar to the link. Connect the steering rod at the steering arm.

12. Install the wheel and tire assembly. Remove the jack stands and lower the car. Jounce the suspension a few times and then road test.

OVERHAUL

For all spring and shock absorber removal and installation procedures and any other strut overhaul procedures, please refer to "Strut Overhaul" in the Unit Repair section.

Lower Control Arm
REPLACEMENT

1. Jack up car, support on stands and remove wheels.

2. Remove stabilizer bar.

3. Remove ball joint from control arm.

4. Remove control arm front retaining bolt.

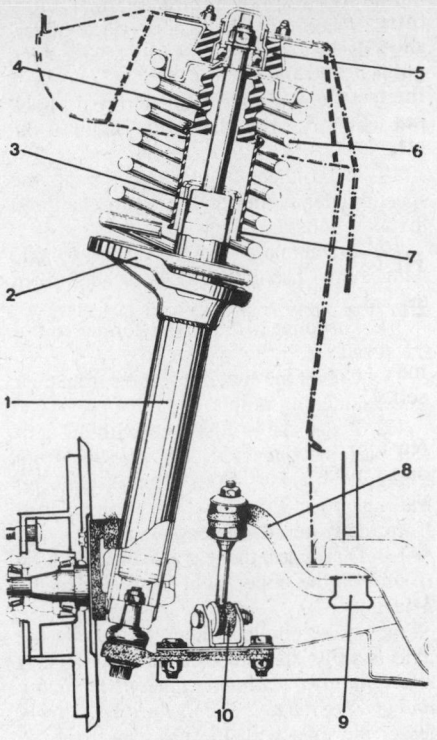

1. Strut assembly
2. Lower spring support
3. Shock absorber
4. Rubber bumper
5. Upper attachment
6. Coil spring
7. Ruber sleeve, protecting the shock absorber
8. Stabilizer bar
9. Stabilizer bar attachment
10. Stabilizer link

Front suspension—240, 260 (DL, GL) series

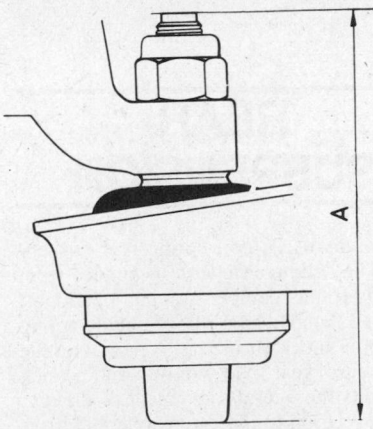

Spring–type lower ball joint maximum allowable length

5. Remove control arm rear attachment plate.

6. Remove attachment plate from control arm.

7. Remove stabilizer link from control arm.

8. Install in reverse of removal.

NOTE: Right and left bushings are not interchangeable. The right side bushing should be turned so that the small slots point horizontally when installed. Torque the front retaining bolt to 55 ft. lbs., the rear bushing to 4 ft. lbs. and the rear attachment bolts to 30 ft. lbs.

Lower Ball Joint

REMOVAL & INSTALLATION

Early Production 240 and 260

1. Follow Steps 1–9 under "Strut Removal and Installation" for the 240, 260 series.

2. While grasping the strut outer tube (casing) with a pair of locking pliers, loosen and remove the shock absorber retaining nut.

3. Pull the shock absorber unit out of the outer tube.

4. Loosen the ball joint retaining nut. Grasp the outer tube at the weld with a pair of channel-lock pliers and loosen the nut with a 19 mm socket and a long extension, until the joint bracket comes loose.

5. Using a drift and hammer, loosen the conical part of the ball joint from the strut assembly.

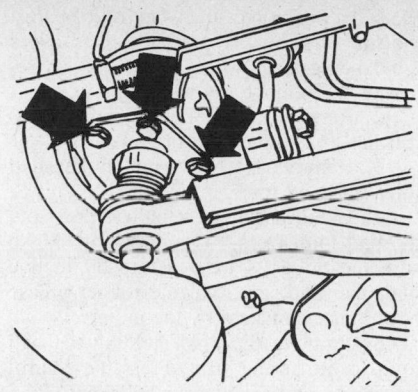

Late type lower ball joint-to-strut retaining bolts

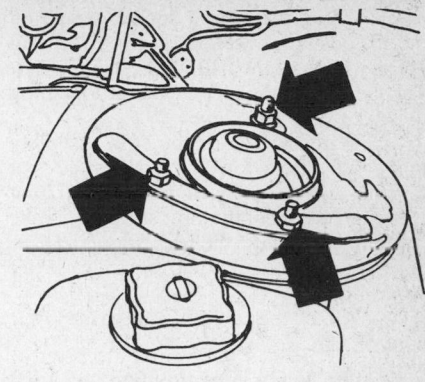

Loosen the upper strut nuts to adjust the camber on 240, 260 (DL, GL) series

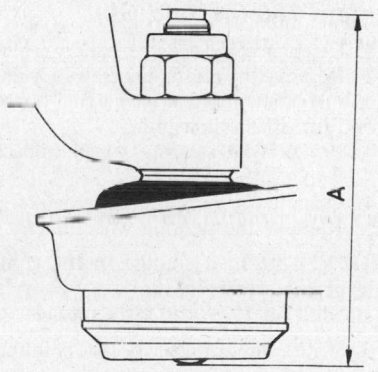

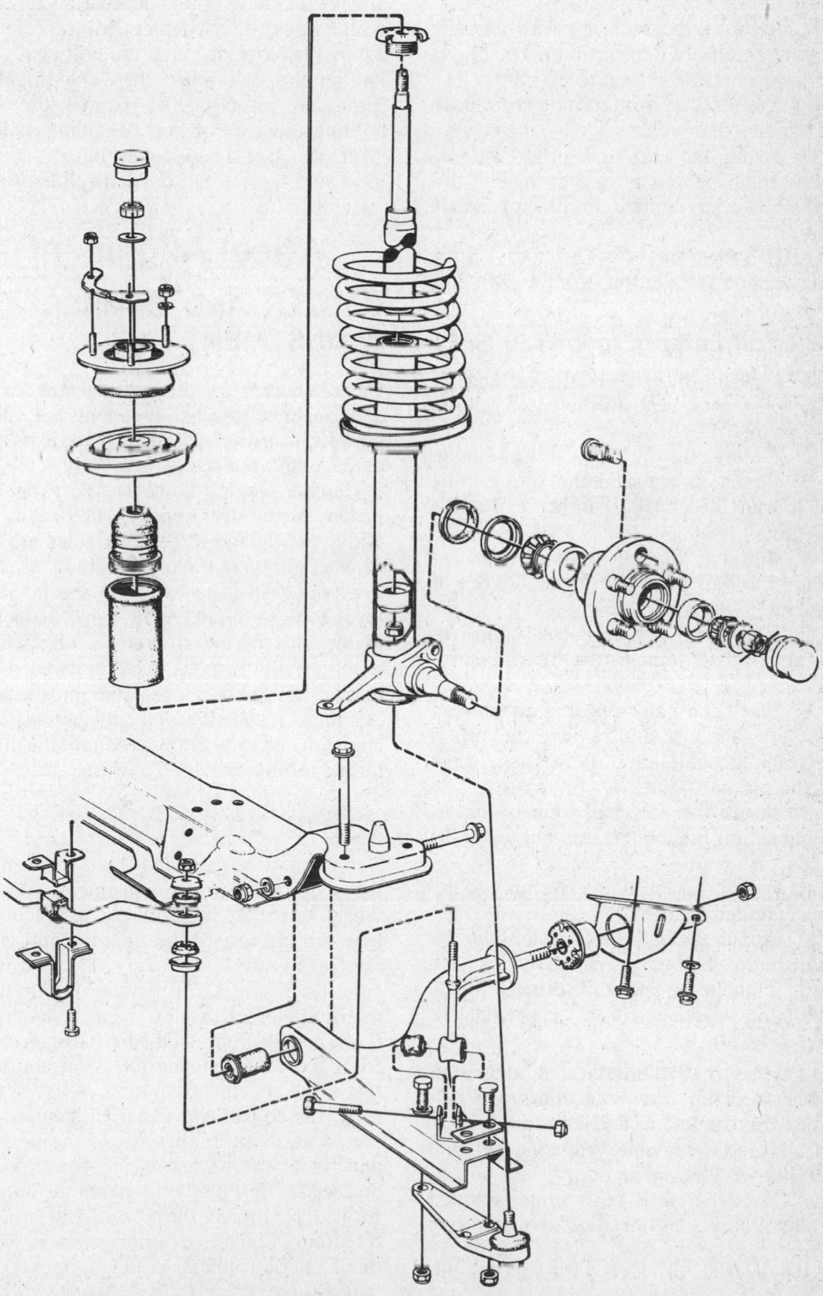

Non-spring type lower ball joint maximum allowable length

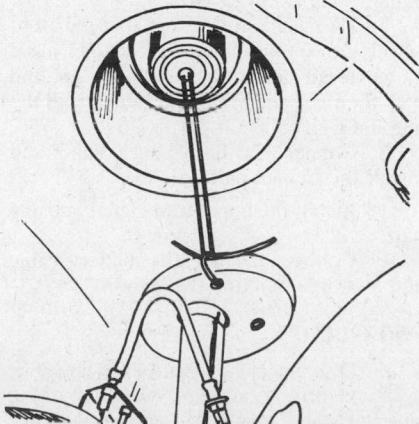

Suspending the top of the strut from the body with a wire while removing the lower ball joint

Front suspension strut—240, 260 (DL, GL) series; 760 similar

6. Using the 19mm socket coated on the inside with vaseline or wheel bearing grease, remove the ball joint retaining nut. The grease should keep the nut from falling down into the strut tube.

7. Wire the top of the strut assembly to the sheet metal tower, and allow the strut to hang vertically. Disconnect the ball joint from the bottom of the strut assembly. Take care not to damage the brake hoses. Then, disconnect the ball joint from the lower control arm.

8. Attach the new ball joint to the lower control arm.

NOTE: Make sure the new ball joint stud is free of grease, or the stud could be tightened too far into the cone making the rubber bellows stick to the strut.

9. Remove the securing wire and lift the strut assembly into position. Install the ball joint nut, and torque to 30–50 ft. lbs. Stop the outer tube from turning with locking pliers at the weld.

10. Install the shock absorber and retaining nut. Tighten as in Step 8. Pull the shock absorber spindle to its uppermost position.

11. Follow Steps 10–12 under "Strut Removal and Installation" for the 240, 260 series.

1979 and Later (Except 760 GLE)

1. Jack up the front of the car and install jack stands beneath the front jacking attachments.

2. Remove the tire and wheel assembly.

3. Reach in between the spring coils and loosen the shock absorber cap nut a few turns.

4. Remove the four bolts (12mm) retaining the ball joint seat to the bottom of the strut.

5. Remove the three nuts (19mm) retaining the ball joint to the lower control arm.

6. Place the ball joint and attachment assembly in a vise and remove the 19mm nut from the ball joint stud. Then, drive out the old ball joint.

7. Install the new ball joint in the attachment and tighten the stud nut to 35–50 ft. lbs.

8. Attach the ball joint assembly to the strut. Tighten to 15–20 ft. lbs.

9. Attach the ball joint assembly to the control arm. Tighten to 70–95 ft. lbs.

10. Tighten the shock absorber cap nut. Install the wheel and tire. Lower the car and road-test.

NOTE: On 1979 and later models with power steering, the ball joints are different for the left and right side.

Compared to previous years, the ball joint is 0.393 in. forward in control rod attachment. It is therefore most important that these ball joints are installed on the correct side.

760 GLE

1. Jack up the front end of the car.

Mark the position of the wheel stud nearest the tire valve on the fender well to avoid rebalancing the wheel when it is remounted. Remove the wheel.

2. Remove the bolt connecting the anti-roll bar link to the control arm.

3. Remove the cotter pin for the ball joint stud and remove the nut.

4. Using a ball joint puller, press out the ball joint from the control arm. Make sure the puller is located directly in line with the stud, and that the rubber grease boot is not damaged by the puller.

5. Remove the bolts holding the ball joint to the spring strut. Press the control arm down and remove the ball joint.

6. Reverse the above procedure for installation. When installing the new ball joint, always use new bolts and coat all threads with a liquid thread sealer. Torque bolts to 22 ft. lbs, checking that the bolt heads sit flat on the ball joint, then angle-tighten (protractor-torque) 90°. Torque the nut holding the control arm ball joint stud to 44 ft. lbs. Use a new cotter pin on the ball joint stud, and install the anti-roll bar link.

Wheel Alignment

CASTER AND CAMBER ADJUSTMENT

Caster angle is fixed by suspension design and cannot be adjusted. If caster is not within specifications, check front end parts for damage and replace as necessary.

Camber angle, however, may be adjusted. At the strut upper attachment to the body, two of the three bolts holes are eccentric, allowing the upper end of the strut to tilt out or in as necessary. A special pivot lever tool SVO No. 5038, which attaches to the tops of the strut upper attachment retaining bolt threads is recommended for this job. To adjust, loosen the three retaining nuts, install the pivot lever tool, and adjust to specifications. After adjusting, torque the nuts to 15–25 ft. lbs.

TOE-IN ADJUSTMENT

Toe-in may be adjusted after performing the caster and camber adjustments. With a wheel spreader, measure the distance (X) between the rear of the right and left front tires, at spindle (hub) height, and then measure the distance (Y) between the front of the right and left front tires, also at spindle (hub) height. Subtract the front distance (Y) from the rear distance (X), and compare that to the specifications table. X−Y = toe-in. If the adjustment is not correct, loosen the locknuts on both sides of the tie rod, and rotate the tie rod itself. Toe-in is increased by turning the tie rod in the normal forward rotation of the wheels, and reduced by turning it in the opposite direction. After the final adjustment is made, torque the locknuts to 55–65 ft. lbs., being careful not to disturb the adjustment.

STEERING

All Volvos use divided steering columns that protect the driver during front end collisions. The manual steering gear used on the 240 (DL) series is a rack and pinion type of either Cam or ZF manufacture. Both units are fully enclosed, with the steering rods attached directly to the rack piston and protected by rubber bellows. However, the Cam unit is filled with steering gear oil while the ZF unit is grease-filled. Power steering is available on all 240 series models and standard equipment on the 260 (GL). Power assist is integral with the steering rear unit, and is supplied by an engine driven pump of ZF or Saginaw manufacture. The Saginaw pump is used in the 260 series, while the ZF pump is used in the 240.

Steering Wheel

REMOVAL & INSTALLATION

NOTE: The use of a knock-off type steering wheel puller, or the use of a hammer may damage the collapsible column and is not recommended.

240 and 260 (DL and GL)

1. Disconnect the negative battery cable.

2. Remove the retaining screws for the upper half of the molded turn signal housing and lift off the housing.

3. Pry off the steering wheel impact pad.

4. Disconnect the horn plug contact.

5. Remove the steering wheel nut.

NOTE: Due to a change in the cone angle of this steering shaft, a puller is not needed on 1979 and later models.

6. With the front wheels pointing straight ahead, and the steering wheel centered, install a steering wheel puller. On 240 and 260 models, use a universal type puller, such as SVO 2263.

7. To install, make sure that the front wheels are pointing straight ahead, then place the centered steering wheel on the column with the plug contact to the left. Install the nut and tighten to 20–30 ft. lbs.

8. Connect the horn plug contact and install the impact pad.

9. Install the upper turn signal housing half.

10. Connect the negative battery cable and test the operation of the horn.

760 GLE

1. Disconnect the negative battery cable.

2. Gently pry up the lower edge of the steering wheel center pad and remove it.

3. Unscrew the steering wheel center nut, and pull off the wheel.

4. When installing, torque the center nut to 26 ft. lbs.

TURN SIGNAL SWITCH REPLACEMENT

See "Steering Wheel Removal and Installation." Remove the upper and lower steering column casings. Unscrew the turn signal switch/lever assembly, and disconnect the wires from the switch.

Ignition Lock and Switch

REPLACEMENT

All Models Except 760 GLE

1. Remove noise insulation panel and center side panel.
2. Disconnect the wires from the switch.
3. Pry out the switch with a short screwdriver.
4. Install in reverse of removal.

760 GLE

1. Remove the sound proofing under the instrument panel.
2. Disconnect the connector from the ignition switch.
3. Remove the upper steering column casing and the panel around the ignition switch.
4. Loosen the mounting screw for the switch.
5. Insert the key and turn it to the start position. Through the hole beneath the holder, press in the catch and remove the ignition switch.
6. To install, insert the key and turn and depress the locking tab. Remove the key. Position the switch and release the locking tab by inserting the key. Tighten the mounting screw and reverse the rest of the removal procedure. Test the switch.

Manual Steering Gear

REMOVAL & INSTALLATION

1. Remove the lock bolt and nut from the column flange (at the steering gear). Bend apart the flange slightly with a screwdriver.
2. Jack up the front end. The stands should be positioned at the jack supports. Remove the front wheels.
3. Disconnect the steering rods from the steering arms, using a ball joint puller.
4. Remove the splash guard.
5. Disconnect the steering gear from the front axle member.
6. Disconnect the steering gear from the steering gear flange. Remove steering gear.
7. Install rubber spacers and plates for the steering gear attachment points.
8. Position the steering gear, and guide the pinion shaft into the steering shaft flange. The recess on the pinion shaft should be

aligned towards the lock bolt opening in the flange.
9. Attach the steering gear to the front axle member. Check that the U-bolts are aligned in the plate slots. Install flat washers and nuts.
10. Install the splash guard.
11. Connect the steering rods to the steering arms.
12. Install the front wheels and lower the vehicle.
13. Install the lock bolt for the steering shaft flange.

PITMAN ARM ADJUSTMENT

On a steering gear with a marked pitman arm and pitman arm shaft (on the steering gear), make sure that the marks align.

On a steering gear without the marks, lift up the front of the vehicle so that the front wheels are free. Turn the steering wheel to its center position (count the number of turns). Lower the vehicle. If the vehicle is correctly loaded, the wheels should now point straight forward. If the wheels do not, remove the pitman arm from the shaft with a puller. Then set the left wheel straight ahead should be in its center position. Tighten the pitman arm nut to 100–120 ft. lbs.

Power Steering Gear

REMOVAL & INSTALLATION

1. Loosen the steering column shaft flange from the pinion shaft. Remove the lock bolt and bend apart the flange slightly.
2. Jack up the front end. Position jack stands at the front jack supports. Remove the front wheels.
3. Disconnect the steering rods from the steering arms, with a ball joint puller.
4. Remove the splash guard.
5. Disconnect the hoses at the steering gear. Install protective plugs in the hose connections.
6. Remove the steering gear from the front axle member.
7. Remove the steering gear by pulling down until it is free from the steering shaft flange. On the 760 GLE, disconnect the lower steering shaft from the steering gear by removing the snap-rings from the clamps. Loosen the upper clamp bolt, remove the lower clamp bolt and slide the joint up on the shaft. Then remove the unit on the left side of the vehicle.
8. Position the steering gear and attach the pinion shaft to the steering shaft flange. Take care to align the recess for the lock bolt. On the 760 GLE, tighten the lower clamp bolt first then the upper. Torque bolts to 15 ft. lbs. Use new snap-rings.
9. Install right side U-bolt and bracket, but do *NOT* tighten the nuts.
10. Install left side retaining bolts, and tighten. Tighten the U-bolt nuts.
11. Connect the steering rods to the steering arms.
12. Install the lock bolt on the steering column flange.

13. Connect the return and pressure hoses to the steering gear.

Power Steering Pump

REMOVAL & INSTALLATION

1. Remove all dirt and grease from around the suction line connections and from around the delivery line on the pump housing.
2. Using a container to catch any power steering fluid that might run out, disconnect the lines, and plug them to prevent dirt from entering the system.
3. Remove the tensioning bolt and the attaching bolts.
4. Clear the pump free of the fan belt and lift it out.
5. If a new pump is to be used, the old brackets, fittings, and pulley must be transferred from the old unit. The pulley may be removed with a puller, and pressed on the pump shaft with a press tool. Under no circumstances should the pulley be hammered on, as this will damage the pump bearings.
6. To install, place the pump in position and loosely fit the attaching bolts. Connect the lines to the pump with new seals.
7. Place the fan belt onto the pulley and adjust the fan belt tension as outlined in Chapter one.
8. Tighten the tensioning bolt and the attaching bolts.
9. Fill the reservoir with Type "A" automatic transmission fluid and bleed the system as outlined under "Power Steering System Bleeding."

POWER STEERING SYSTEM BLEEDING

1. Fill the reservoir up to the edge with Automatic Transmission Fluid Type "A". Raise the front wheels off the ground, and install safety stands. Place the transmission in neutral and apply the parking brake.
2. Keeping a can of ATF Type "A" within easy reach, start the engine and fill the reservoir as the level drops.
3. When the reservoir level has stopped dropping, slowly turn the steering wheel from lock to lock several reservoir if necessary.
4. Locate the bleeder screw on the power steering gear. Open the bleeder screw ½–1 turn, and close it when oil starts flowing out.
5. Continue to turn the steering wheel slowly until the fluid in the reservoir is free of air bubbles.
6. Stop the engine and observe the oil level in the reservoir. If the oil level rises more than ¼ in. past the level mark, air still remains in the system. Continue bleeding until the level rise is correct.
7. Remove the safety stands and lower the car.

STEERING AND TIE-ROD SERVICE

Bent or otherwise damaged steering rods and tie-rods must be replaced, never straightened. All components of the steering linkage, including the pitman arm and idler arm (on worm and roller steering types), are connected by means of ball joints. Ball joints cannot be disassembled or adjusted, so they must be replaced when damaged. They should also be replaced if the rubber seal is broken and the joint contaminated.

The ball joints of the steering rods are made in unit with the rods, therefore the entire rod assembly must be replaced when their ball joints become unserviceable. Maximum permissible axial (vertical) play is .120 in. After removing the cotter pins and ball stud nuts at the rod's connections, press the ball joint out of its connecting socket.

The ball joints of the tie-rod may be replaced individually. After the ball joint is disconnected, the locknut on the tie-rod is loosened and the clamp bolt released. The ball joint is then screwed out of the tie-rod, taking note of the number of turns. The new ball joint is screwed in the same number of turns, and the clamp bolt and locknut tightened. The ball joint is locked to the rod with 55–65 ft. lbs. of torque. The new ball joint is pressed into its connection and the ball stud not tightened to 23–27 ft. lbs.

After reconditioning of the rods and joints, the wheel alignment must be adjusted.

BRAKE SYSTEM

All Volvos are equipped with a four wheel power-assisted disc brake system. The four wheel disc system utilizes a pair of four-piston, fixed calipers at the rear. The calipers are either Girling or ATE manufacture, so when ordering disc pads or caliper rebuilding kits, you must identify which you have. The discs are one-piece castings.

NOTE: All models except DL2/4 door models have ventilated front brake discs.

Whenever adding to or replacing brake fluid, it is imperative that the fluid be of SAE 70 R3 (SAE J 1703) quality or better. Fluid meeting DOT 3 or DOT 4 specifications is also acceptable. Avoid mixing brake fluids from different manufacturersand never reuse old brake fluid.

For all brake system repair and adjustment procedures not detailed below, please refer to "Brakes" in the Unit Repair section.

Disc Brake Adjustment

Disc brakes require no adjustment. They should, however, be checked frequently for wear. Consult the specifications table for new pad thickness. Pads should never be allowed to wear down to less than 0.125 in., or disc damage may occur.

Master Cylinder

REMOVAL & INSTALLATION

1. To prevent brake fluid from spilling onto and damaging the paint, place a protective cover over the fender apron, and rags beneath the master cylinder.
2. Disconnect and plug the brake lines from the master cylinder.
3. Remove the nuts which retain the master cylinder and reservoir assembly to the vacuum booster, and lift the assembly forward, being careful not to spill any fluid on the fender. Empty out and discard the brake fluid.

— CAUTION —
Do not depress the brake pedal while the master cylinder is removed.

4. In order for the master cylinder to function properly when installed to the vacuum booster, the adjusting nut for the thrust rod of the booster must not prevent the primary piston of the master cylinder from returning to its resting position. A clearance (C) of 0.004–0.04 in. is required between the thrust rod and primary piston with the master cylinder installed. The clearance may be adjusted by rotating the adjusting nut for the booster thrust rod in the required direction.

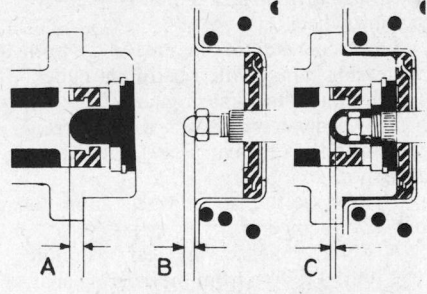

Adjusting thrust rod

To determine what the clearance (C) will be when the master cylinder and booster are connected, first measure the distance (A) between the face of the attaching flange and the center of the primary piston on the master cylinder, then measure the distance (B) that the thrust rod protrudes from the fixed surface of the booster (making sure that the thrust rod is depressed fully with a partial vacuum existing in the booster). When measurement is subtracted from measurement (A), clearance (C) should be obtained. If not, adjust the length of the thrust rod by turning the adjusting screw to suit. After the final adjustment is obtained, apply a few drops of locking compound, such as Loctite®, to the adjusting nut.

5. Position the master cylinder and reservoir assembly onto the studs for the booster, and install the washers and nuts. Tighten the nuts to 17 ft. lbs.
6. Remove the plugs and connect the brake lines.
7. Bleed the entire brake system.

Brake System Warning Valve

The brake system warning valve is located under a bolt on the front axle member. The value is centered by hydraulic pressure from the primary circuit on one side and the secondary circuit on the other. When a hydraulic imbalance exists, such as a leak in one of the calipers, the valve will move off-center toward the system with the leak and, therefore, the lowest pressure. When the valve moves off-center, it closes a circuit to a warning light on the dashboard, warning the driver of the imbalance. Sometimes, the valve will actuate the warning light when one of the systems is bled during normal maintenance. When this happens, the valve has to be reset.

VALVE RESETTING

1. Disconnect the plug contact and screw out the warning switch so that the pistons inside the valve may return to their normal position.
2. Repair and bleed the faulty hydraulic circuit.
3. Screw in the warning switch and tighten it to a torque of 10–14 ft. lbs. Connect the plug contact.

REPLACEMENT

1. Placing a rag beneath the valve to catch the brake fluid, loosen the pipe connections, and disconnect the brake lines. Disconnect the electrical plug contact, and lift out the valve.
2. Connect the new warning valve in the reverse order of removal, and connect the plug contact.
3. Bleed the entire brake system.

Brake System Proportioning Valves

Each of the brake circuits has a proportioning (relief) valve located inline between the rear wheels. The purpose of these valves is to ensure that brake pressure on all four wheels compensates for the change in weight distribution under varied braking conditions. The harder the brakes are applied, the more weight there is on the front wheels. The valves regulate the hydraulic pressure to the rear wheels so that under hard braking conditions, they receive a smaller percentage of the total braking effort. This prevents premature rear wheel lock-up when the brakes are applied in emergency situations.

REPLACEMENT

Sophisticated pressure testing equipment is required to troubleshoot the dual hydraulic system in order to determine if the proportioning valve(s) are in need of replacement. However, if the car is demonstrating signs of rear wheel lock-up under moderate to heavy braking pressure, and other variables such as tire pressure, tread depth, etc., have been ruled out, the valve(s) may be at fault. The valves are not rebuildable, and must be replaced as a unit.

1. Unscrew, disconnect and plug the brake pipe from the master cylinder, at the valve connection.

2. Slacken the connection for the flexible brake hose to the rear wheel a *maximum* of ¼ turn.

3. Remove the bolt(s) which retain the valve to the underbody, and unscrew the valve from the rear brake hose.

4. To install the valve, place a new seal on it, and screw the valve onto the rear brake hose and hand tighten. Secure the valve to the underbody with the retaining bolt(s).

5. Connect the brake pipe and tighten both connections, making sure that there is no tension on the flexible rear hose.

6. Bleed the brake system.

Front Wheel Bearings

REPLACEMENT AND ADJUSTMENT

1. Remove the hub cap, and loosen the lug nuts a few turns.

2. Firmly apply the parking brake. Jack up the front of the car and place jack stands beneath the lower control arms. Remove the wheel and tire assembly.

3. Remove the front caliper.

4. Pry off the grease cap from the hub. Remove the cotter pin and castle nut. Use a hub puller to pull off the hub. On the 760, remove the brake disc. If the inner bearing remains lodged on the stub axle, remove it with a puller.

5. Using a drift, remove the inner and outer bearing rings.

6. Thoroughly clean the hub, brake disc, and grease cap.

7. Press in the new inner and outer bearing rings with a drift.

8. Press grease into both bearings with a bearing packer. If one is not available, pack the bearings with as much wheel bearing grease as possible by hand. Also coat the outsides of the bearings and the outer rings pressed into the hub. Fill the recess in the hub with grease up to the smallest diameter on the outer ring for the outer bearing. Place the inner bearing in position in the hub and press its seal in with a drift. *The felt ring should be thoroughly coated with light engine oil.*

9. Place the hub onto the stub axle.

Install the outer bearing washer, and castle nut.

10. Adjust the front wheel bearings by tightening the castle nut to 45 ft. lbs. to seat the bearings. Then, back off the nut ⅓ of a turn counterclockwise. Torque the nut to 1 ft. lb. If the nut slot does not align with the hole in the stub axle, tighten the nut until the cotter pin may be installed. Make sure that the wheel spins freely without any side play.

11. Fill the grease cap halfway with wheel bearing grease, and install it on the hub.

12. Install the front caliper.

13. Install the wheel and tire assembly. Remove the jack stand and lower the car. Tighten the lug nuts to 70–100 ft. lbs. and install the hub cap.

Parking Brake

The parking brake is mechanically actuated by a cable which is connected, by means of a pull rod and linkage, to a lever mounted on the floor to the left of the driver's seat. The brake consists of two miniature duo-servo drum brakes, one mounted at each end of the rear axle housing inside the hub of the rear brake discs.

ADJUSTMENT

1. Remove the rear ashtray (between the front seat backs) or the rear of the center console on the 760.

2. Tighten the parking brake cable adjusting screw so that the brake is fully applied when pulled up 2–3 notches.

3. If one cable is stretched more than the other, they can be individually adjusted by removing the parking brake cover (2 screws) and turning the individual cable adjusting nut at the front of each yoke pivot.

4. Install the ashtray, and parking brake cover (if equipped).

CABLE REPLACEMENT

All Models Except 760 GLE

1. Apply the parking brake. Remove the hub caps for the rear wheels and loosen the lug nuts a few turns.

2. Place blocks in front of the front wheels. Jack up the rear end and place jackstands beneath the rear axle. Remove the

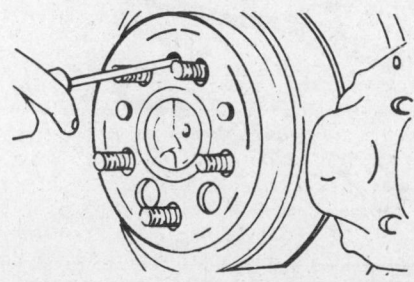

Adjusting the parking brake through the access hole in the rear hub

wheel and tire assembly. Release the parking brake.

3. Remove the bolt and the wheel from the pulley.

4. Remove the rubber cover for the front attachment of the cable sleeve and nut, as well as the attachment for the rubber suspension ring on the frame. Remove the cable from the other side of the attachment in the same manner.

5. Hold the return spring in position. Pry up the lock and remove the lock pin so that the cable releases from the lever.

6. Remove the return spring with washers. Loosen the nut for the rear attachment of the cable sleeve. Lift the cable forward, after loosening both sides of the attachments, and remove it.

7. To install, first adjust the rear brake shoes of the parking brake as outlined in Steps 3, 4 and 5 under "Parking Brake Adjustment."

8. Install new rubber cable guides for the cable suspension. Place the cable in position in the rear attachment and tighten the nut. Install the washers and return spring. Oil the lock pin and install it, together with the cable, on the lever. Install the attachment and rubber cable guide on the frame.

9. Install the cable in the same manner on the side of the vehicle.

10. Place the cable sleeve in position in the front attachments and install the rubber covers.

11. Lubricate and install the pulley on the pull rod. Adjust the pulley so that the parking brake is fully engaged with the lever at the third or fourth notch.

12. Install the wheel and tire assemblies. Remove the jack stands and lower the vehicle. Tighten the lug nut to 70–100 ft. lbs. and install the hub caps.

760 GLE

The 760 parking brake system employs two cables, a short one on the right-hand side and a long one on the left.

SHORT CABLE, RIGHT SIDE

1. Jack up the rear of the car and safely support it with jackstands.

2. Remove the right brake caliper rear wheel. Remove the right brake caliper and hang it from the coil spring with a wire.

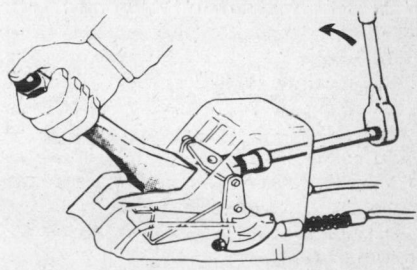

Adjust the 1981 and later parking brake if it is not fully applied after pulling the lever 10–11 notches. After adjusting, good braking power should be obtained after pulling the lever 2–3 notches

Remove the brake disc. Unhook the rear return spring and remove the brake shoes.

3. Push out the pin holding the cable to the brake lever. Remove the rubber bellows (boot) from the backing plate, and remove the bellows from the cable.

4. Remove the spring clip, pin and cable from the back of the differential housing. Remove the cable guide on the differential by removing the top bolt from the housing cover. Remove the cable.

5. Install the cable guide on the new cable. Check the rubber bellows for wear or damage and replace if necessary. Install the bellows and position it through the hole in the backing plate. Make sure the bellows sits correctly on the backing plate.

6. Smear the contact surfaces of the brake levers with a thin layer of heat-resistant graphite grease. Connect the cable to the lever and install the pin.

NOTE: The arrow stamped on the lever should point upwards and outwards.

7. Push the cable through and place the lever in position behind the rear axle flange.

8. Install the cable guide on the axle. Connect the cable to the equalizer using the pin and spring clip.

9. Install the brake shoes and rear return spring. Install the brake disc and caliper. Use new bolts, and torque to 43 ft. lbs. Make sure the disc rotates freely. Adjust the parking brake. Install the wheel and lower the car.

LONG CABLE, LEFT SIDE

1. Remove the center console.
2. Slacken the parking brake adjusting screw. Remove the cable lock ring and remove the cable. Pull out the cable from the spring sleeve.
3. Jack up the rear end of the car and safely support it with jackstands. Remove the left rear wheel.
4. Remove the left rear brake caliper and hang it from the coil spring with a piece of wire. Remove the brake disc and rear return spring. Remove the brake shoes.
5. Push out the pin holding the cable to the lever. Remove the rubber bellows from the backing plate, and remove the bellows from the cable.
6. Pull out the cable from the backing plate and the equalizer on top of the rear axle.

7. Remove the cable clamp on the subframe (above the driveshaft) and the cable.

8. Install the new cable through the grommet in the floor; check that the grommet sits correctly. Clamp the cable to the sub-frame.

9. Follow Steps 6-9 of the "Short Cable" procedure above to finish installation. Adjust the cable and install the console.

PARKING BRAKE SHOE REPLACEMENT

1. Remove the rear ashtray (the cover at the rear of the front console on the 760) and back off the adjusting screw so that the cable goes slack.
2. Jack up and support the rear end.
3. Remove the wheels.
4. Remove the brake line-to-axle clamp.
5. Remove the caliper retaining bolts and suspend the caliper out of the way.
6. Unbolt and remove the brake drum.
7. Unhook the return springs and remove the shoes.
8. Install in reverse of the above. Adjust the parking brake.

CHASSIS ELECTRICAL

Heater

REMOVAL AND INSTALLATION

All Models except 760 GLE STANDARD HEATING SYSTEM

1. Remove the lower radiator hose, open the engine drain plug, and drain the cooling system. Disconnect the negative battery cable.
2. Remove the center panel and the lefthand defroster hose.
3. Lift up the driveshaft tunnel mat, disconnect the front and rear attaching screws of the rear seat heater ducts, and then remove the ducts from the heater.
4. Disconnect the heater control valve and air-mix cables from their shutters.

5. Disconnect and plug the pressure hose at the heater. Also plug the heater pipes to prevent residual coolant from spilling onto the carpet.

6. Remove the attaching screws which secure the left-hand upper bracket to the dashboard and the left-hand lower bracket to the transmission tunnel.

7. Remove the glovebox by unscrewing the four attaching screws, removing the glovebox door stop, and disconnecting the wires from the glovebox courtesy light.

8. Disconnect the defroster and floor heating cables from their levers.

9. Disconnect the fan motor wires at the switch contact plate.

10. Remove the attaching screws which secure the right-hand upper bracket to the dashboard and the right-hand lower bracket to the transmission tunnel.

11. Remove the right-hand defroster hose. Disconnect the hose between the heater and the dashboard circular vents. Lift the heater unit to the right, and then out of the vehicle.

12. Reverse the above procedure to install, taking care to ensure that the air vent rubber seal is properly located, and that the fan motor ground cable is attached to the upper righthand bracket attaching screw.

Combination Heater– Air Conditioner System

——— CAUTION ———
When working on this system, DO NOT disconnect any refrigerant lines. The refrigerant, R-12, is dangerous when released and can burn your skin. Leave all air conditioning repairs to an air conditioning specialist.

1. Remove the lower radiator hose, open the engine drain plug, and drain the cooling system. Disconnect the negative battery cable.
2. Remove the heater hoses from the heater pipes at the engine side of the firewall. Plug the heater pipes.
3. Remove the evaporator hose brackets from their body mounts and disconnect the dryer from its bracket. Position the dryer as close to the firewall as the evaporator hose permits.
4. Remove the instrument cluster by removing the steering column molded casings, removing the bracket retaining screw and lowering it toward the steering column, removing the four instruments cluster retaining screws, disconnecting the speedometer cable, tilting the speedometer out of its snap fitting, moving the electrical plug contacts, then lifting the cluster out of the vehicle.
5. Remove the air hose between the central unit and the left inner air vent. Remove the hose from the vacuum motor for the left defroster nozzle.
6. Remove the left-side panel from the central unit.
7. Lift up the driveshaft tunnel mat and disconnect the rear seat heater duct from the central unit.

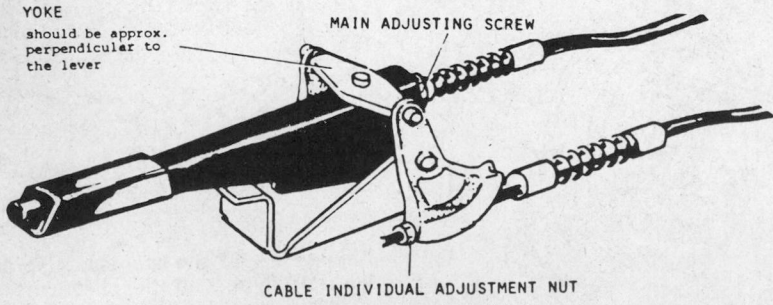

YOKE
should be approx.
perpendicular to
the lever

MAIN ADJUSTING SCREW

CABLE INDIVIDUAL ADJUSTMENT NUT
adjust yoke to correct position

Parking brake cable adjustment—1978–80

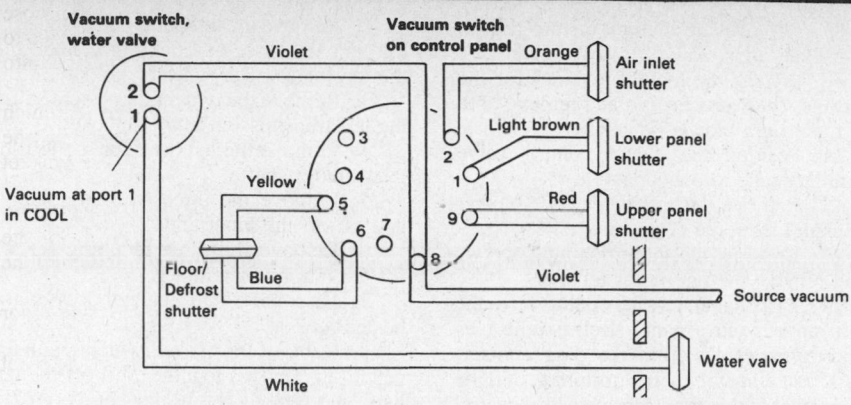

Vacuum switch, water valve

Violet

Vacuum switch on control panel

Orange — Air inlet shutter

2
1

Vacuum at port 1 in COOL

Yellow

3
4
5
6 7
8

Light brown — Lower panel shutter

2
1

Red — Upper panel shutter

9

Floor/Defrost shutter

Blue

Violet — Source vacuum

White — Water valve

Vacuum diagram showing hose colors and connections on 760 GLE climate unit

8. Remove the heater pipes from the passenger side of the firewall.

9. Remove the upper and lower attaching screws for the left support leg. Remove the attaching screws which secure the upper bracket to the dashboard and the lower bracket to the transmission tunnel.

NOTE: If the upper bracket screw holes are slotted, the screws need only be slackened a few turns.

10. Remove the right-side panel from the central unit.

11. Remove the glovebox by unscrewing the four attaching screws, removing the glovebox door stop, and disconnecting the glovebox courtesy light wires.

12. Remove the right defroster nozzle, and also the air hose between the central unit and the right inner air vent.

13. Lift up the driveshaft tunnel mat and disconnect the rear seat heater duct from the central unit.

14. Remove the upper and lower attaching screws for the right support leg. Remove the lower attaching screws for the control panel.

15. Disconnect the fan motor wires and the ground wires from the control panel.

16. Disconnect the yellow lead cable from its plug contact.

17. Separate the halves of the vacuum hose connector and disconnect the vacuum tank hose at the connector.

18. Position the control panel as far back on the transmission tunnel as the cables permit.

19. Remove the screws which attach the upper brackets to the firewall and the lower brackets to the transmission tunnel.

20. Remove the thermostat clamp from the central unit, and the two evaporator cover retaining clamps.

21. Without disconnecting any of the refrigerant lines, remove the evaporator from the central unit, placing it on the right-hand side of the firewall.

22. Remove the molded dashboard padding from beneath the glovebox.

23. Remove the retaining clamps for the right outer vent duct, and remove the duct. Pry off the locking retainer for the blower, and remove the turbine. Remove the clamps which retain the blower housing (inner end) to the central unit and remove the housing.

24. Remove the passenger's front seat cushion and lift the central unit forward and onto the floor of the vehicle. Be careful not to place undue stress on the connected refrigerant lines.

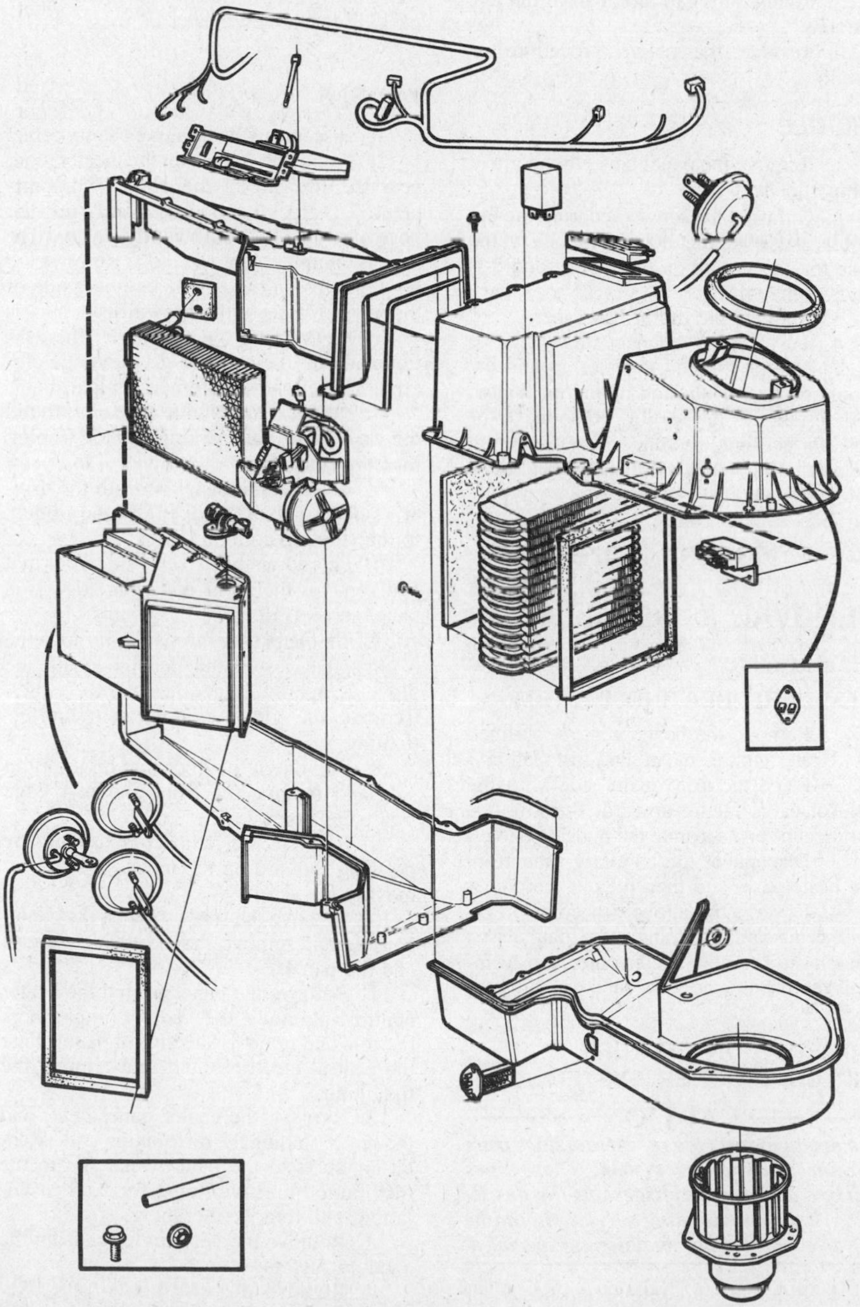

760 climate unit assembly with Automatic Climate Control

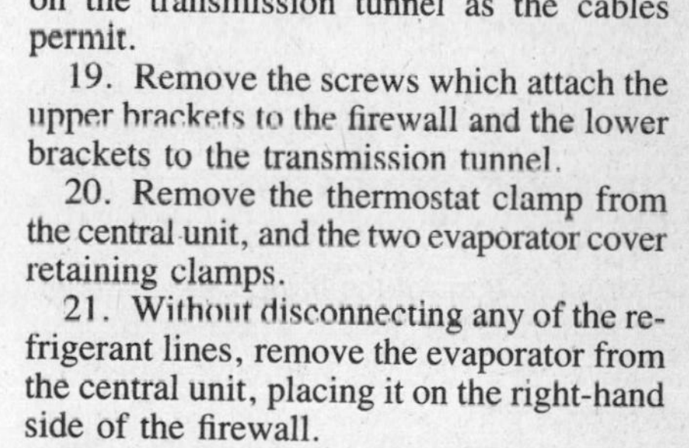

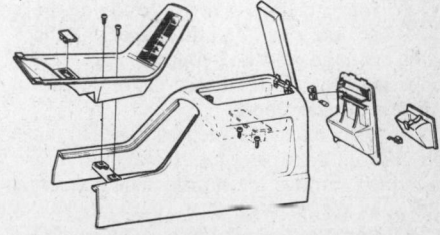

760 center console assembly

25. Reverse the above procedure to install, taking care to ensure that the evaporator pipes and thermostat capillary are enclosed in sealing compound, that the drainage tubes are inserted in the respective transmission tunnel holes, and that the ground cables are connected.

760 GLE

This model is equipped with a climate unit which incorporates a heating and air conditioning system. The steering wheel, passenger's seat and dashboard must be removed entirely for the climate unit to be removed. Heater core and blower motor removal and replacement are covered below.

Blower

REMOVAL & INSTALLATION

DL and GL
STANDARD HEATING SYSTEM

1. Remove the heater unit as outlined in "Heater Unit Removal and Installation."
2. Place the unit on its side with the control valve facing upward. Remove the spring clips and separate the housing halves.
3. Lift out the old fan motor and replace it with a new unit, making sure that the support leg without the "foot" points to the output for the defroster channel.
4. Assemble the heater housing halves with new spring clips, and seal the joint without clips with soft sealing compound.
5. Install the heater unit as outlined in "Heater Unit Removal and Installation."

COMBINATION HEATER–
AIR CONDITIONER SYSTEM

In order to remove the blower motor, both the right and left blower wheels must first be removed. The heater unit does not have to be removed.
1. Disconnect the negative battery cable.
2. Lift the carpet and remove the central unit side panels.
3. Remove the retaining screws for the control panel and move the panel as far back on the transmission tunnel as the electrical cables will permit.
4. Remove the attaching screws for the rear seat heater ducts and disconnect the ducts from the central unit.
5. Remove the instrument cluster as outlined in "Instrument Cluster Removal and Installation."
6. Remove the glovebox by unscrewing the four attaching screws, removing the glovebox door stop, and disconnecting the wires from the glovebox courtesy light. Remove the molded dashboard padding from beheath the glovebox.
7. Disconnect the vacuum hoses to the left and right defroster nozzle vacuum motors, then remove the nozzles and the left and right air ducts.
8. Remove the air hoses between the left and right inside air vents.

9. Remove the clamps on the central unit outer ends, and remove the ends.
10. Pry off the locking retainer for the turbines (blower wheels), and remove both left and right blower wheels.
11. Position the heater control valve capillary tube to one side.
12. Remove the left inner end (blower housing) from the central unit.
13. Unscrew the three retaining screws and remove the fan motor retainer.
14. Disconnect the plug contact from the fan motor control panel. Release the tabs of electric cables from the plug contact, and, removing the rubber grommet, pull the electrical cables down through the central unit right opening.
15. Remove the fan motor from the left opening.
16. Reverse the above procedure to install.

760 GLE

1. Remove the panel beneath the glove compartment.
2. Unfasten the screws securing the fan motor, and lower the motor. Disconnect the hose for air cooling on the motor, and disconnect the wiring.
3. Remove the motor and fan.
4. To install, reconnect the wiring to the fan motor. Spread a sealer around the mounting face of the fan mounting flange, and install the fan motor. Reconnect the hose for cooling, and check fan operation. Reinstall the panel beneath the glove compartment.

Heater Core

REMOVAL & INSTALLATION

DL and GL
STANDARD HEATING SYSTEM

1. Remove the heater unit as outlined in "Heater Unit Removal and Installation."
2. Place the unit on its side with the control valve facing upward. Remove the spring clips and separate the housing halves.
3. Disconnect the capillary tube from the heater core and then lift out the core.
4. Reverse the above procedure to install, being careful to transfer the foam plastic packing to the new heater core, and to install the fragile capillary tube carefully on the core.

COMBINATION HEATER–
AIR CONDITIONER SYSTEM

——————— CAUTION ———————
Do not disconnect the refrigerant lines from the air conditioning system. These lines carry a dangerous refrigerant, the gas R-12. All air conditioning service should be left to a certified air conditioning specialist.

1. Remove the combination heater-air conditioner unit as outlined under "Heater Unit Removal and Installation."

2. Remove the left outer end of the central unit. Remove the locking retainer and the turbine (blower wheel).
3. Remove the two retaining screws for the left transmission tunnel bracket.
4. Remove the lockring for the left intake shutter shaft.
5. Remove the three retaining screws and lift off the inner end.
6. Remove the three retaining screws for the fan motor retainer.
7. Disconnect the heater hoses at the heater core.
8. Remove the clamps which retain the central unit halves together, lift off the left half, and remove the heater core.
9. Reverse the above procedure to install, taking care to transfer the foam plastic packing to the new heater core.

760 GLE

1. Disconnect the negative battery cable.
2. Pinch the hoses to the heater core near the firewall in the engine compartment. Use locking pliers. Make sure the hoses are pinched sufficiently so that the hose is completely blocked off. Remove the hose clamps on the engine compart side of the hoses (close to the firewall).
3. Press down the clip under the ashtray and pull the tray out. Remove the cigarette lighter and the storage compartment.
4. Remove the engine console around the shift lever and parking brake. Unplug the connector.
5. Remove the panel beneath the driver's side dashboard, and remove the air duct to the steering column outlet.
6. Pull down the driver's side floor mat and remove the front and rear edge side panel screws. Remove the panels.
7. On the passenger's side, remove the 3 clips that fasten the panel beneath the glove compartment and remove the panel. Remove the glove compartment and its lighting.
8. Pull down the floor mat on the right side and remove the front and rear edge side panel screws.
9. Remove the radio compartment by pressing forward on the inner wall and removing the screw.
10. Remove the screws inside the center console and remove the side panel screws and the panels.
11. Remove the panel around the heater control. Remove the radio compartment console and remove the control panel. Free the central electrical unit and remove the mounting.
12. Remove the center panel vent, and the screw holding the distribution unit. Mark all air ducts to the panel vents and to the distribution unit with tape for later installation, and remove the ducts.
13. Remove the vacuum hoses from the vacuum motors.
14. Remove the distribution unit. Remove the heater core retaining clips and remove the heater core.

15. To reinstall, reverse the above procedure taking note of the following vacuum hose connections: On climate unit-equipped cars, connect the red hose to the upper shutter for the panel vents, and the light brown hose to the lower shutter. Connect the yellow and blue hoses to the floor/defrost shutter, the yellow to the lower one. On automatic climate control-equipped cars, connect the red hose to the upper shutter for the panel vent, and the blue hose to the defrost vent. Connect the light brown hose to the lower shutter for the panel vent.

Radio

REMOVAL & INSTALLATION

1. Disconnect the negative battery cable.
2. Remove the radio control knobs by pulling them straight out. Remove the control shaft retaining nuts.
3. Disconnect the speaker wires, the power lead (either at the fuse box or the inline fuse connection), and the antenna cable from its jack on the radio.
4. Remove the hardware which attaches the radio to its mounting (support) bracket(s), and slide it back and down from the dash.
5. Reverse the above procedure to install.

Windshield Wiper Motor

REMOVAL & INSTALLATION

All Models Except 760 GLE

1. Disconnect the negative battery cable.

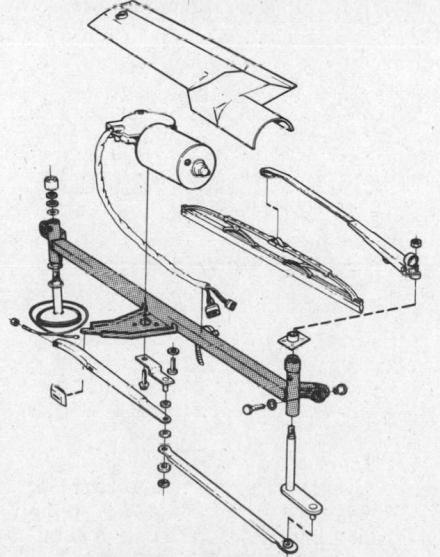

760 series wiper linkage

2. Disconnect the drive link from the wiper motor lever by unsnapping the locking tab underneath the dashboard.
3. Open the hood and disconnect the plug contact from the motor, located on the firewall.
4. Remove the three attaching screws and lift out the motor.
5. Reverse the above procedure to install, taking care to transfer the rubber seal, rubber damper, and spacer sleeves to the new motor.

760 GLE

1. Remove the wiper arms.
2. Lift up the hood to its uppermost position by pushing the catch on the hood hinges.
3. Remove the plastic clips and screw securing the wiper mechanism cover plate. Remove the cover plate by lifting it upwards and forwards. Close the hood.

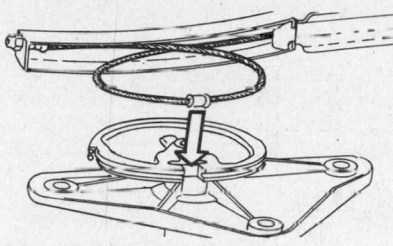

Installing the cable for the drive link and parallel drive link (left side)—240 series and DL, GL, and GLT

4. Remove the cover below the windshield.
5. Unbolt the starter from its mount. Disconnect the starter wires at the connectors.
6. Installation is the reverse of removal.

Tailgate Window Wiper Motor

REMOVAL & INSTALLATION

1. Disconnect the negative battery cable.
2. Remove the upholstered finish panel on the inside of the tailgate.
3. Remove the screws which retain the reinforcing bracket beneath the wiper motor.
4. Disconnect the wiper link arm. Bend the reinforcing bracket to one side and lower the wiper motor until it is clear of the bracket.
5. Disconnect the electrical wires from the motor and remove the motor.
6. Reverse the above procedure to install.

Instrument Cluster

For additional information on the instruments, please refer to "Gauges and Indicators" in the Unit Repair section.

REMOVAL & INSTALLATION

All Models Except 760 GLE

A voltage stabilizer feeds a 10 V current to both the temperature and the fuel gauges. Electrical malfunctions in these gauges must be checked with an ohmmeter, not a 12 V test light. If malfunctions occur simultaneously in all three of the gauges that are fed by the stabilizer, the stabilizer itself is probably malfunctioning. When replacing the voltage stabilizer, the new unit must fit in the same position as the old one. If the stabilizer is not located correctly in the dash, the voltage output may be altered.

1. Disconnect the negative battery cable.
2. Remove the molded plastic casings from the steering column.
3. Remove the bracket retaining screw and lower the bracket toward the steering column.
4. Remove the cluster attaching screws.
5. Disconnect the speedometer cable.
6. Tilt the cluster out of its snap fitting and disconnect the plug contact. On vehicles equipped with a tachometer, disconnect the tachometer sending wire.
7. Lift the cluster out of the dashboard.
8. Reverse the above procedure to install.

760 GLE

1. Remove the soundproofing above the foot pedals.
2. Remove the two catches and screws holding the panel.
3. Press the instrument panel forwards. Remove the panel from the dash.
4. Disconnect the connectors, and remove the instrument panel completely.

Fuses

On 240, 260 series (all DL, GL, GLE, GLT and Coupe models), the fuse box is located beneath a protective cover, below the dashboard, in front of the driver's door. On the 760 GLE, the fuses are located under a plastic panel in the center console, behind the ashtray.

On electronic fuel-injected models, an additional fuse box is located in the engine compartment on the left wheel well. It houses a single fuse protecting the electrical fuel pump.

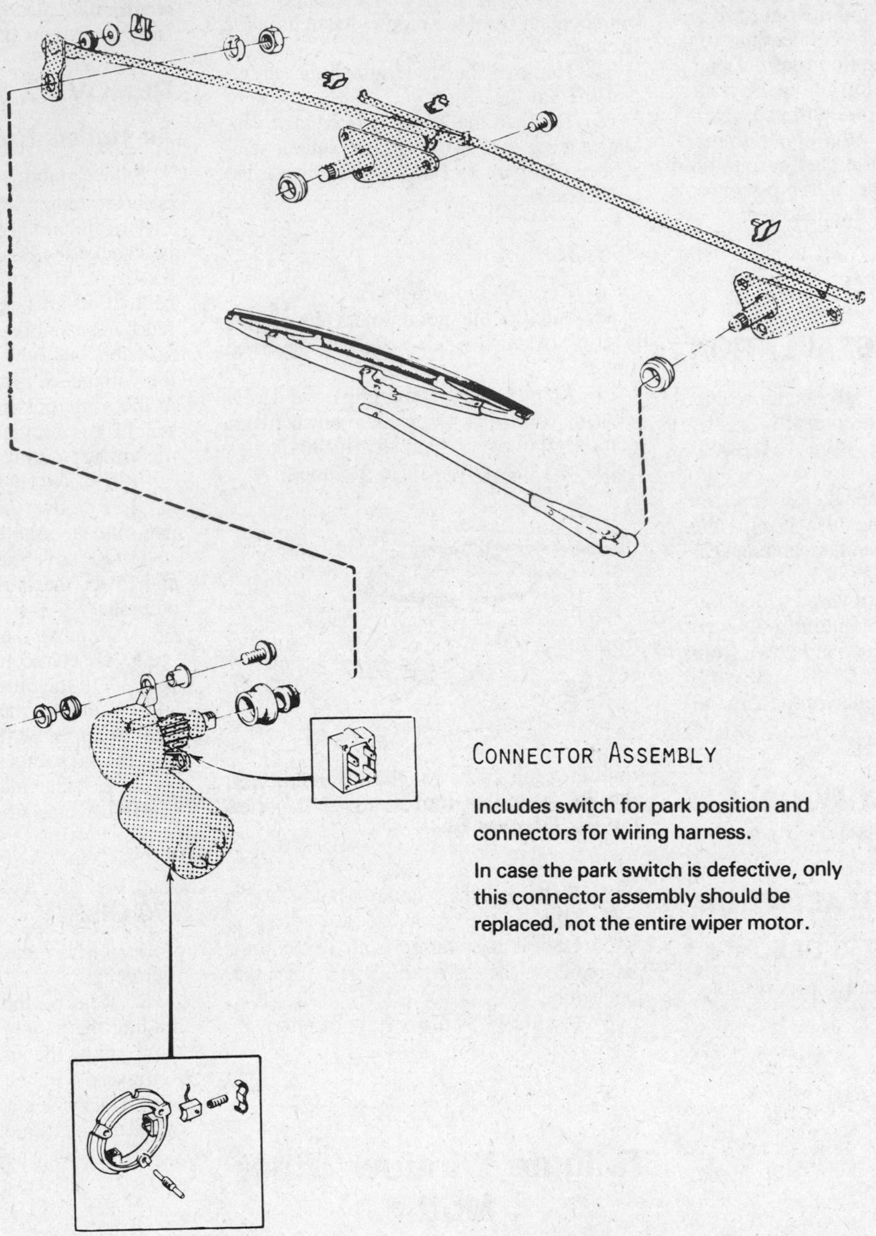

CONNECTOR ASSEMBLY

Includes switch for park position and connectors for wiring harness.

In case the park switch is defective, only this connector assembly should be replaced, not the entire wiper motor.

Typical wiper motor and linkage assembly

Unit Repair Section

Tools and Equipment

The service procedures in this book presuppose a familiarity with hand tools and their proper use. However, it is possible that you may have a limited amount of experience with the sort of equipment needed to work on an automobile. This section is designed to help you assemble a basic set of tools that will handle the majority of jobs you may undertake.

In addition to the normal assortment of screwdrivers and pliers, automotive service work requires an investment in wrenches, sockets and the handles needed to drive them, and various measuring tools such as torque wrenches and feeler gauges.

The best approach to gathering the required equipment is to proceed slowly, buying high-quality tools as they are needed. An initial investment should be made in a set of quality wrenches, ranging in size from ¼ inch to one inch, if your car has standard bolts, or from 5 mm to 19 mm if your car has metric fasteners. High quality forged wrenches are available in three styles: open end, box end, and combination open/box end. The combination tools are generally the most desirable as a starter set; the wrenches shown in the illustration are of the combination type.

The other set of tools inevitably required is a ratchet handle and socket set. This set should have the same size range as your wrench set. The ratchet, extension, and flex drives for the sockets are available in many sizes; it is advisable to choose a ⅜ inch drive set initially. One break in the inch/metric sizing war is that metric-sized sockets sold in the U.S. have inch-sized drive (¼, ⅜, ½, etc.). Sockets are available in six and twelve point versions; six point types are generally cheaper and are a good choice for a first set. The choice of a drive handle for the sockets should be made with some care. If this is your first set, take the plunge and invest in a flex-head ratchet; it will get into many places otherwise accessible only through a long chain of universal joints,

extensions and adapters. An alternative is a flex handle; such a tool is shown in the illustration, below the ratchet handle. In addition to the range of sockets mentioned, a rubber-lined spark plug socket should be purchased. Spark plugs have either a ¹³⁄₁₆ or a ⅝ inch hex; get the correct socket for the plugs in your car.

The most important thing to consider when purchasing hand tools is quality. Don't be misled by the low cost of "bargain" tools. Forged wrenches, tempered screwdriver blades, and fine tooth ratchets are a much better investment than their less expensive counterparts. The skinned knuckles and frustration inflicted by poor quality tools make any job an unhappy chore. Another consideration is that quality tools sold by reputable firms come with an on-the-spot replacement guarantee—if the tool breaks, you get a new one, no questions asked.

The tools needed for basic maintenance jobs, in addition to those just mentioned, include:

1. Jackstands, for support
2. Oil filter wrench
3. Oil filler spout or funnel
4. Grease gun
5. Battery hydrometer
6. Battery post and clamp cleaner
7. Container for draining oil
8. Lots of rags for the inevitable spills

In addition to these items there are several others which are not absolutely necessary, but handy to have around. These include a transmission funnel and filler tube, a drop (trouble) light on a long cord, an adjustable wrench (crescent wrench), and slip joint pliers.

A more extensive list of tools, suitable for tune-up work, can be drawn up easily. While the tools involved are slightly more sophisticated, they need not be outrageously expensive. For example, there are several inexpensive tach/dwell meters on the market that are every bit as good for the average mechanic as a $100.00 profes-

sional model. The key to these purchases is to make them with an eye towards adaptability and wide range. Using the tach/dwell meter example again, if the model you buy runs up to at least 1,500 rpm on the tachometer scale, the dwell meter works on 4, 6, or 8 cylinder engines, and the tachometer unit is adaptable to both conventional and electronic ignitions, it will serve for a long time on a variety of automobiles. A basic list of tune-up tools could include:

1. A tach/dwell meter
2. Spark plug gauge and gapping tool
3. Feeler blades
4. Timing light

In this list, the choice of a timing light should be made carefully. A light which works on the DC current supplied by the car battery is the best choice; it should have a xenon tube for brightness. If your car has electronic ignition, the light should have an inductive pick-up (the timing light illustrated has one of these), and since nearly all cars will have electronic ignition in the future, this feature is a reasonable one to look for.

In addition to these basic tools, there are several other tools and gauges you may find useful. These include:

1. A compression gauge. The screw-in type is slower to use, but eliminates the possibility of a faulty reading due to escaping pressure.
2. A manifold vacuum gauge
3. A test light
4. An induction meter. This is used to determine whether or not there is current flowing in a wire, and thus is extremely helpful in electrical troubleshooting.

Finally, you will probably find a torque wrench necessary for all but the most basic of work. The beam–type models are perfectly adequate, although the newer click (breakaway) type are more precise. Whichever type you choose, plan on having it recalibrated every once in a while.

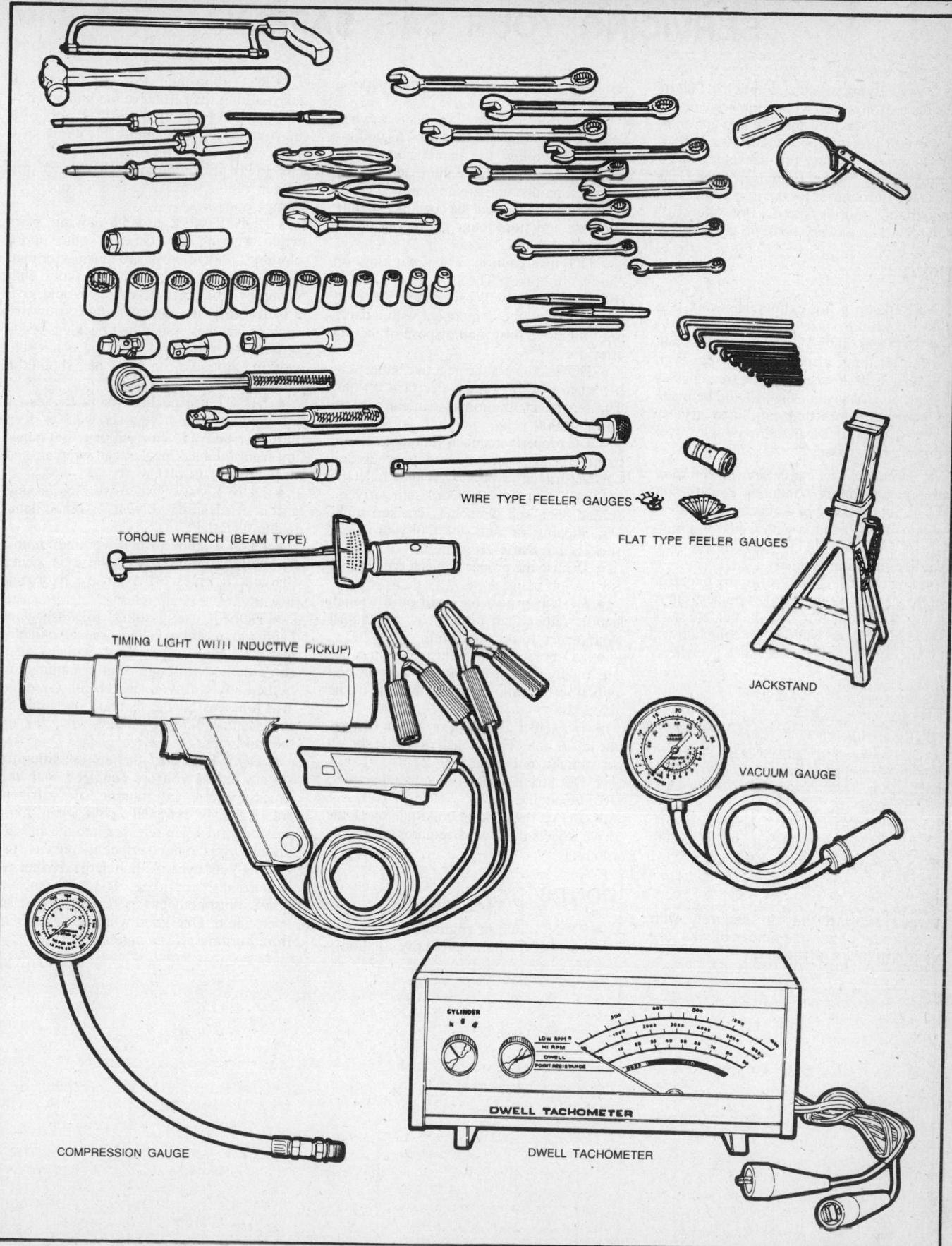

WIRE TYPE FEELER GAUGES

FLAT TYPE FEELER GAUGES

TORQUE WRENCH (BEAM TYPE)

JACKSTAND

TIMING LIGHT (WITH INDUCTIVE PICKUP)

VACUUM GAUGE

CYLINDER

LOW RPM
HI RPM
DWELL
POINT RESISTANCE

DWELL TACHOMETER

COMPRESSION GAUGE

DWELL TACHOMETER

A basic tool collection will handle almost any automotive repair work

SERVICING YOUR CAR SAFELY

It is virtually impossible to anticipate all of the hazards involved with automotive maintenance and service, but care and common sense will prevent most accidents.

The rules of safety for mechanics range from ''don't smoke around gasoline,'' to ''use the proper tool for the job.'' The trick to avoiding injuries is to develop safe work habits and take every possible precaution.

DO'S

• DO keep a fire extinguisher and first aid kit within easy reach.

• DO wear safety glasses or goggles when cutting, drilling, grinding, or prying, even if you have 20-20 vision. If you wear glasses for the sake of vision, they should be made of hardened glass that can serve also as safety glasses, or wear safety goggles over your regular glasses.

• DO shield your eyes whenever you work around the battery. Batteries contain sulphuric acid. In case of contact with the eyes or skin, flush the area with water or a mixture of water and baking soda and get medical attention immediately.

• DO use safety stands for any undercar service. Jacks are for raising vehicles; safety stands are for making sure the vehicle stays raised until you want it to come down. Whenever the car is raised, block the wheels

Always support the car securely with jackstands; never use cinder blocks, tire changing jacks or the like

remaining on the ground and set the parking brake.

• DO use adequate ventilation when working with any chemicals or hazardous materials. Follow the manufacturer's directions for usage. Brake fluid, anti-freeze, solvents, paints, etc. are all deadly poisons if taken internally. Seal the containers tightly after use and store them safely, out of the reach of children.

• DO use caution when working on clutches or brakes. The asbestos used in the friction material will cause lung cancer if inhaled. Wipe the component with a damp rag to remove dust, and dispose of the rag after use.

• DO disconnect the negative battery cable when working on the electrical system. The secondary ignition system can contain up to 40,000 volts.

• DO properly maintain your tools. Loose hammerheads, mushroomed punches and chisels, frayed or poorly grounded electrical cords, excessively worn screwdrivers, spread open-end wrenches, cracked sockets, slipping ratchets, or faulty droplight sockets can cause accidents.

• DO use the proper size and type of tool for the job being done.

• DO when possible, pull on a wrench handle rather than push on it, and adjust your stance to prevent a fall.

• DO be sure that adjustable wrenches are tightly closed on the nut or bolt and pulled so that the face is on the side of the fixed jaw.

• DO select a wrench or socket that fits the nut or bolt. The wrench or socket should sit straight, not cocked.

• DO strike squarely with a hammer; avoid glancing blows.

• DO set the parking brake and block the drive wheels if the work requires the engine running.

DONT'S

• DON'T run an engine in a garage or anywhere else without proper ventilation—

EVER! Carbon monoxide is poisonous; it takes a long time to leave the human body and you can build up a deadly supply of it in your system by simply breathing in a little every day. You may not realize you are slowly poisoning yourself. Always use power vents, windows, fans or open the garage doors.

• DON'T work around moving parts while wearing a necktie or other loose clothing. Short sleeves are much safer than long, loose sleeves; hard-toed shoes with neoprene soles protect your toes and give a better grip on slippery surfaces. Jewelry such as watches, fancy belt buckles, beads or body adornment of any kind is not safe working around a car. Long hair should be hidden under a hat or cap.

• DON'T use pockets for toolboxes. A fall or bump can drive a screwdriver deep into your body. Even a wiping cloth hanging from the back pocket can wrap around a spinning shaft or fan.

• DON'T smoke when working around gasoline, cleaning solvent or other flammable material.

• DON'T smoke when working around the battery. When the battery is being charged, it gives off explosive hydrogen gas.

• DON'T use gasoline to wash your hands; there are excellent soaps available. Gasoline may contain lead, and lead can enter the body through a cut, accumulating in the body until you are very ill. Gasoline also removes all the natural oils from the skin so that bone dry hands will suck up oil and grease.

• DON'T service the air conditioning system unless you are equipped with the necessary tools and training. The refrigerant, R-12, is extremely cold when compressed, and when released into the air will instantly freeze any surface it contacts, including your eyes. Although the refrigerant is normally non-toxic, R-12 becomes a deadly poisonous gas in the presence of an open flame. One good whiff of the vapors from burning refrigerant can be fatal.

Basic Maintenance

INTRODUCTION

Routine maintenance is probably the most important part of automobile care and the easiest to neglect. A regular program aimed at monitoring essential systems ensures that all components are in good and safe working order, and can prevent small problems from developing into major headaches. Routine maintenance also pays big dividends in keeping major repair costs at a minimum and extending the life of the car.

The owner's manual that came with your car includes a maintenance schedule, indicating service intervals in numbers of months or thousand of miles. This schedule should always be followed. We have provided, in each section, a guide to service intervals based on an averaging of manufacturer's recommendations. In most cases, the suggested interval offered here will be close to that given by the manufacturer of your car, but the manufacturer's schedule should always take precedence.

We have divided the maintenance work to be done into three categories: Under Hood, Under Car, and Exterior. The checks in each section require only a few minutes of attention every few weeks; the services to be performed can be easily accomplished in a morning. The most important part of any maintenance program is regularity. The few minutes or occasional morning spent on these seemingly trivial tasks will forestall or eliminate major problems later.

UNDER HOOD
Automatic Transmission, Automatic Transaxle

The fluid level in the automatic transmission or transaxle should be checked every three months or 6000 miles. All automatic transmissions have a dipstick for fluid level checks.

1. Drive the car until it is at normal operating temperature. The level should not be checked immediately after the car has been driven for a long time at high speed, or in city traffic in hot weather; in those cases, the transmission should be given a half hour to cool down.

2. Stop the car, apply the parking brake, then shift slowly through all gear positions, ending in Park. Leave the engine running.

3. Remove the dipstick, wipe it clean, then reinsert it, pushing it fully home.

4. Pull the dipstick again and, holding it horizontally, read the fluid level.

5. Cautiously feel the end of the dipstick to determine the temperature. Most dipsticks are marked with both cool and hot levels. If the fluid is not up to the correct level, more will have to be added.

6. Fluid is added through the dipstick tube. You will probably need the aid of a spout or a long-necked funnel. Be sure that whatever you pour through is perfectly clean and dry. Fluid recommendations can be found in the owner's manual.

Add fluid slowly, and in small amounts, checking the level frequently between additions. Do not overfill, which will cause foaming, fluid loss, slippage, and possible transmission damage.

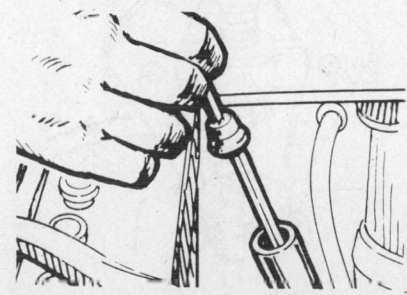
Check the automatic transmission fluid level with the dipstick provided

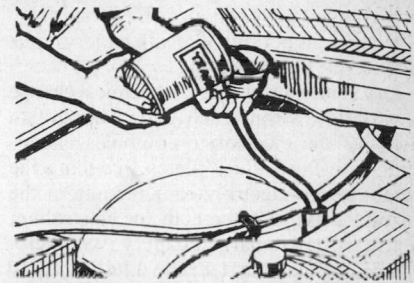
Fill the automatic transmission through the dipstick tube

Battery

FLUID LEVEL (EXCEPT "MAINTENANCE FREE" BATTERIES)

Check the battery electrolyte level at least once a month, or more often in hot weather or during periods of extended car operation. The level can be checked through the case on translucent polypropylene batteries; the cell caps must be removed on other models. The electrolyte level in each cell should be kept filled to the split ring inside, or the line marked on the outside of the case.

If the level is low, add only distilled water, or colorless, odorless drinking water, through

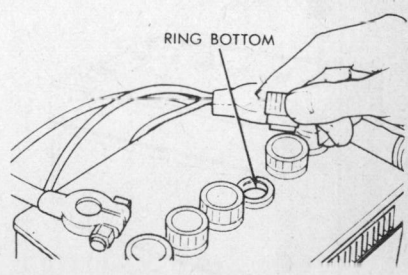
Fill the battery cell to the bottom of the split ring

the opening until the level is correct. Each cell is completely separate from the others, so each must be checked and filled individually.

If water is added in freezing weather, the car should be driven several miles to allow the water to mix with the electrolyte. Otherwise, the battery could freeze.

SPECIFIC GRAVITY (EXCEPT "MAINTENANCE FREE" BATTERIES)

While not technically exact, a practical measurement of the chemical condition of the battery is indicated by measuring the specific gravity of the acid (electrolyte) contained in each cell. The electrolyte in a fully charged battery is usually between 1.260 and 1.280 times as heavy as pure water at the same temperature (80°F). Variations in the specific gravity readings for a fully charged battery may differ. Therefore, it is most important that all battery cells produce an equal reading.

As a battery discharges, a chemical change takes place within each cell. The sulfate factor of the electrolyte combines chemically with the battery plates, reducing the weight of the electrolyte. A reading of the specific gravity of the acid, or electrolyte, of any partially charged battery, will therefore be less than that taken in a fully charged one.

The hydrometer is the instrument used for determining the specific gravity of liquids. The battery hydrometer is readily available from many sources, including local auto replacement parts stores. The following chart gives an indication of specific gravity value, related to battery charge condition. If, after charging, the specific gravity between any two cells varies more than 50 points (.050), the battery is probably bad.

Specific Gravity Reading	Charged Condition
1.260–1.280	Fully charged
1.230–1.250	Three-quarter charged
1.200–1.220	One-half charged
1.170–1.190	One-quarter charged
1.140–1.160	Just about flat
1.110–1.130	All the way down

CABLES AND CLAMPS

Once a year, the battery terminals and the cable clamps should be cleaned. Loosen the clamps and remove the cables, negative cable first. On batteries with posts on top, the use of a puller specially made for the purpose is recommended. These are inexpensive, and available in auto parts stores. Side terminal battery cables are secured with a bolt.

Clean the cable clamps and the battery terminal with a wire brush until all corrosion, grease, etc. is removed and the metal is shiny. It is especially important to clean the inside of the clamp thoroughly, since a small deposit of foreign material or oxidation there will prevent a sound electrical connection and inhibit either starting or charging. Special tools are available for cleaning these parts, one type for conventional batteries and another type for side terminal batteries.

Before installing the cables, loosen the battery hold-down clamp or strap, remove the battery and check the battery tray. Clear it of any debris, and check it for soundness. Rust should be wire brushed away, and the metal given a coat of anti-rust paint. Replace the battery and tighten the hold-down clamp or strap securely, but be careful not to overtighten, which will crack the battery case.

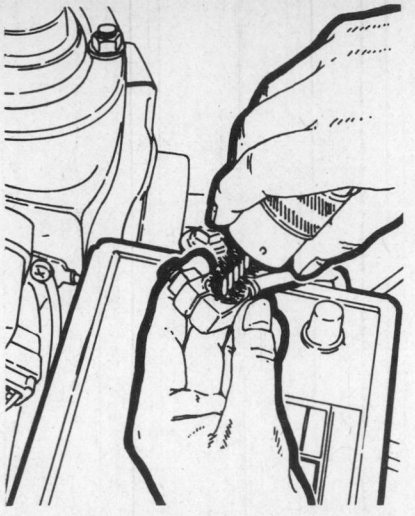

Clean the clamp with a wire brush

After the clamps and terminals are clean, reinstall the cables, negative cable last; do not hammer on the clamps to install. Tighten the clamps securely, but do not distort them. Give the clamps and terminals a thin external coat of grease after installation, to retard corrosion.

Check the cables at the same time that the terminals are cleaned. If the cable insulation is cracked or broken, or if the ends are frayed, the cable should be replaced with a new cable of the same length and gauge.

NOTE: Keep flame or sparks away from the battery; it gives off explosive hydrogen gas. Battery electrolyte contains sulphuric acid. If you should splash any on your skin or in your eyes, flush the affected area with plenty of clear water; if it lands in your eyes, get medical help immediately.

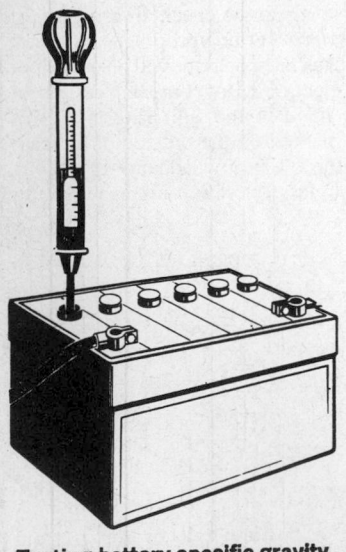

Testing battery specific gravity

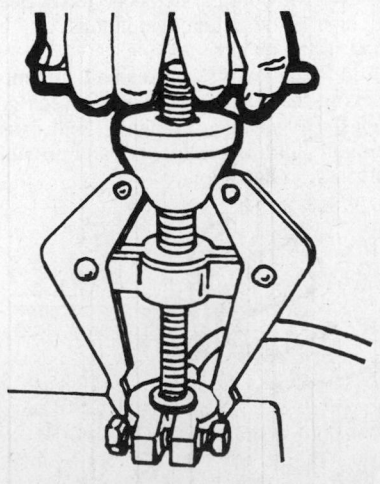

Use a puller to remove the clamp on post-type batteries

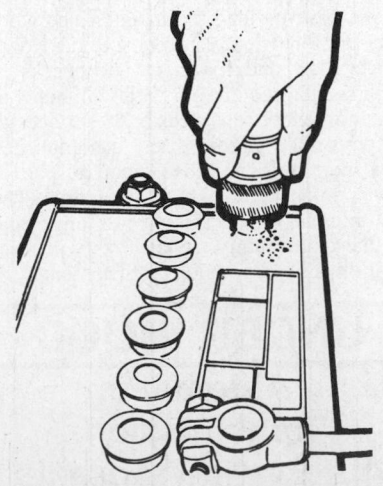

The posts are easily cleaned with a wire brush, or the battery post tool shown

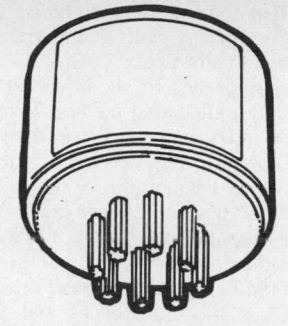

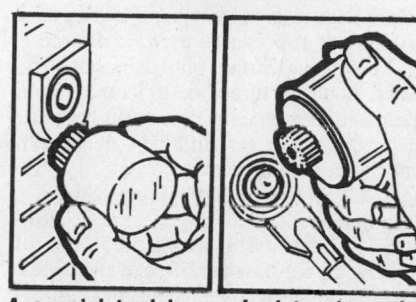

A special tool is required to clean the terminals and clamps on side terminal batteries

Brake Fluid

Once a month, the fluid level in the brake master cylinder should be checked.

1. Park the car on a level surface.

2. Clean off the master cylinder cover before removal. Some covers are retained by a bolt. Some of the newer master cylinders with plastic reservoirs have screw caps. Remove the cover, being careful not to drop or tear the rubber diaphragm which will probably be underneath. Be careful also not to drip any brake fluid on painted surfaces, as it eats paint.

NOTE: Brake fluid absorbs moisture from the air, which reduces effectiveness and will corrode brake parts once in the system. Never leave the master cylinder or the brake fluid container uncovered for any longer than necessary.

3. The fluid level should be about ¼ inch below the lip of the master cylinder well.

4. If fluid addition is necessary, use only extra heavy duty disc brake fluid meeting DOT 3 or DOT 4 specifications. The fluid should be reasonably fresh, because brake fluid deteriorates with age.

5. Replace the cover, making sure that the diaphragm is correctly seated.

If the brake fluid is constantly low, the system should be checked for leaks. However, it is normal for the fluid level to fall gradually as the disc brake pads wear; expect the fluid level to drop about ⅛ inch for every 10,000 miles of wear.

Belt Tension

Every six months or 12,000 miles, check

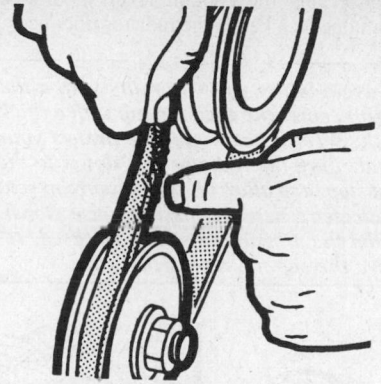

Check the belts for wear

the water pump, alternator, power steering pump, air pump, and air conditioning compressor drive belts for proper tension. Also look for signs of wear, fraying, separation, glazing and so on, and replace the belts as required.

Belt tension should be checked with a gauge made for the purpose. If a gauge is not available, tension can be checked with moderate thumb pressure applied to the belt at its longest span midway between pulleys. If the belt has a free span less than twelve inches, it should deflect approximately ⅛–¼ inch. If the span is longer than twelve inches, deflection can range between ¼ and ⅜ inches.

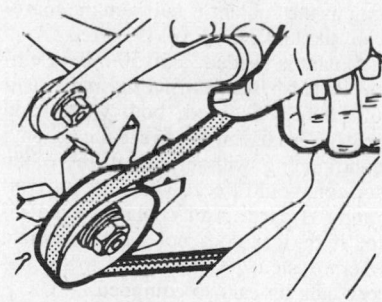

Check the belt tension at the middle of the longest span between pulleys

To adjust or replace belts:

1. Loosen the driven accessory's pivot and mounting bolts. Some air conditioning compressor belts are tensioned by an idler pulley; in this case, loosen the idler pulley and use a ½ in. drive ratchet in the square hole provided to lever the idler pulley up or down.

2. Move the accessory toward or away from the engine until the tension is correct. You can use a wooden hammer handle or broomstick as a lever, but do not use anything metallic.

3. Tighten the bolts and recheck the tension. If new bolts have been installed, run the engine for a few minutes, then recheck and readjust as necessary.

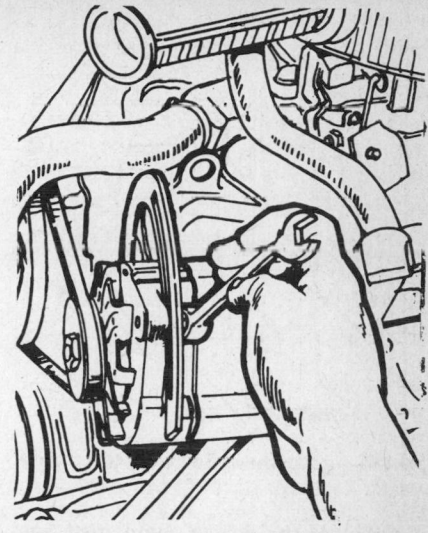

To either adjust or remove a belt, loosen the driven component's adjusting bolt

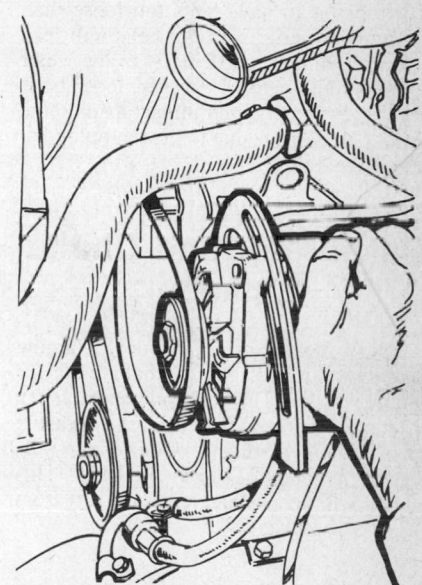

Push the component toward the engine to remove the belt

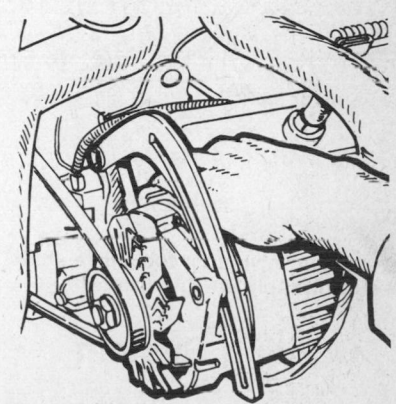

Pull outwards on the component to tension the belt, then tighten the bolts; recheck the belt tension after tightening

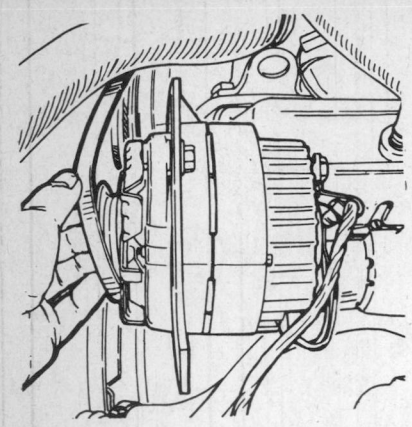

Slip the replacement belt over the pulley

NOTE: If the driven component has two drive belts, the belts should be replaced in pairs to maintain proper tension.

It is better to have belts too loose than too tight, because overtight belts will lead to bearing failure, particularly in the water pump and alternator. However, loose belts place an extremely high impact load on the driven components due to the whipping action of the belt.

Carburetor and Choke Linkage

Every 12 months or 6000 miles, examine the carburetor linkage and choke plate for free movement. The choke plate action can generally be freed, if necessary, with the application of a solvent made for the purpose to the ends of the choke shaft. This solvent will also clean grease and dirt from the throttle linkage.

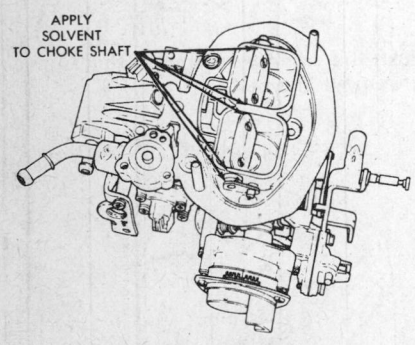

Use a spray solvent on the choke shaft, but do not apply any lubricants

Cooling System

Once a month, the engine coolant level should be checked. On cars without a coolant recovery system, this should only be done when the engine is cold. Remove the radiator cap; the coolant level should be about one inch below the radiator filler neck.

CAUTION

To avoid injury when working with a hot engine, cover the radiator cap with a thick cloth. Wear a heavy glove to protect your hand. Turn the radiator cap slowly to the first stop, and allow all the pressure to vent (indicated when the hissing noise stops). When the pressure has been released, remove the cap the rest of the way.

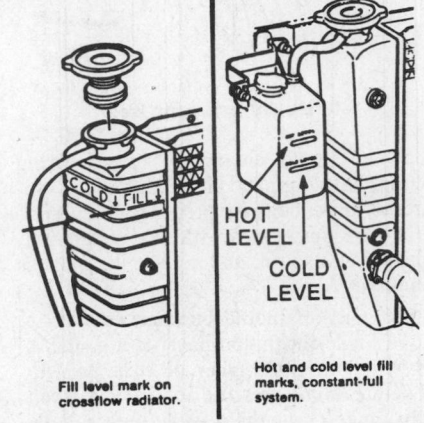

Fill level mark on crossflow radiator.

Hot and cold level fill marks, constant-full system.

Proper coolant level is about one inch below the radiator neck, or between the lines on the recovery tank

On cars with a coolant recovery tank, coolant should be visible within the tank; as long as the coolant is between the markings on the tank, the level is correct.

If coolant is needed, a 50/50 mix of ethylene glycol-based antifreeze and water should always be used, both winter and summer. This is imperative on cars with air conditioning; without the antifreeze, the heater core could freeze when the air conditioning is used. Add coolant to the radiator if the car does not have a coolant recovery system. Add coolant to the recovery tank on cars so equipped.

The radiator hoses and clamps and the radiator cap should be checked at the same time as the coolant level. Hoses which are brittle, cracked, or swollen should be replaced. Clamps should be checked for tightness (screwdriver tight only—do not allow the clamp to cut into the hose or crush the fitting). The radiator cap gasket should

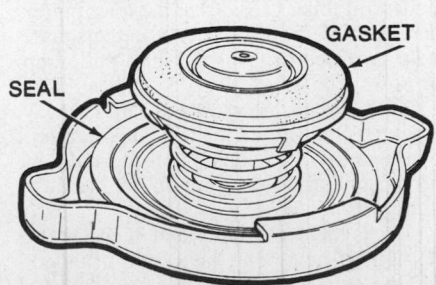

Check the radiator cap gasket and sealing surface

be checked for any obvious tears, cracks or swelling, or any signs of incorrect seating in the radiator neck.

The cooling system should be drained, flushed and refilled after the first 24 months or 24,000 miles, and every year thereafter.

1. Drain the radiator by opening the drain cock at the bottom. Some radiators do not have these; the lower radiator hose must be disconnected at the radiator instead. If the engine block has drain plugs, they should be opened to speed draining.

2. Close the drain cocks and fill the system with clear water. A cooling system flushing additive can be used, if desired.

3. Run the engine until it is hot. The heater should be turned on to its maximum heat position so that the core is flushed out.

4. Drain the system, then flush with water until it runs clear.

5. Clean out the coolant recovery tank, if equipped.

6. Fill the system with a 50/50 mix of ethylene glycol-based antifreeze and water. Fill the coolant recovery tank midway between the marks with this mixture also.

7. Run the engine until it is hot, then let it cool and top up the radiator or coolant recovery tank as necessary with the antifreeze/water mixture.

Heat Riser

The heat riser is a thermostatically or vacuum operated valve in the exhaust manifold (not all cars have one). It closes when the engine is warming up, in order to preheat the incoming fuel/air mixture. If it sticks open, the result will be frequent stalling during warmup, especially in cold and damp weather. If it sticks shut, the result will be a rough idle after the engine is warm.

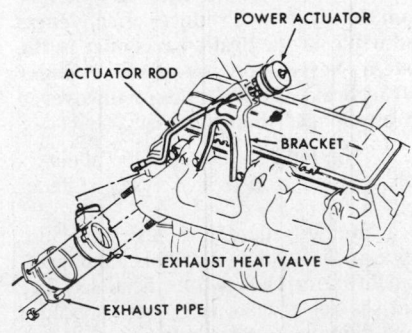

Exploded view of a vacuum-operated heat riser

The heat riser should move freely. It can be checked easily when the engine is cold by giving the counterweight on the valve shaft a twirl, or pulling the vacuum rod to open and shut the valve. If the valve is sticking or binding, a quick shot of solvent made for the purpose will free it up. This solvent should be applied every six months or 6000 miles to keep the valve free. If the valve is still stuck after application of the solvent, sometimes rapping the end of the

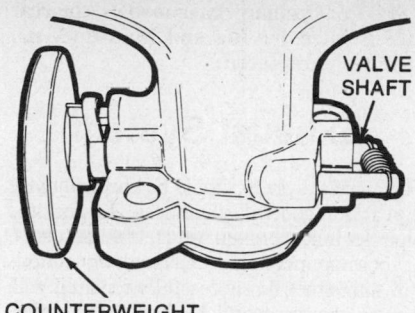

Thermostatically-operated heat control valve

shaft lightly with a hammer will break it loose. Otherwise, the components will have to be removed for further repairs.

Ignition Cables

The ignition system (points, condenser, rotor, spark plugs, etc.) receives regular attention in the form of a tune-up, and thus is not covered here. But one of the most commonly overlooked components is the ignition cable, or spark plug wire.

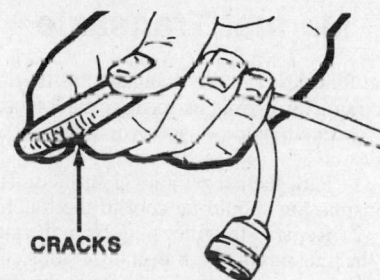

Inspect the ignition cables for cracks or breaks in the insulation

Although they rarely show any visible signs of deterioration, the ignition cables should be checked at every tune-up, and replaced at least every 50,000 miles. Cracking and embrittlement are of course obvious signs of wear, but most newer ca-

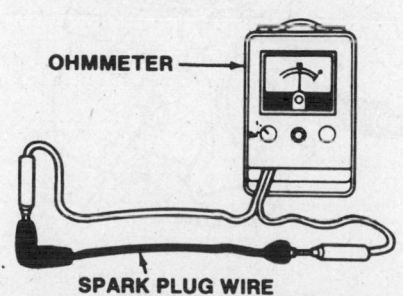

Test the ignition cables with an ohm-meter. Conventional ignition cables should be removed from the distributor cap, but electronic ignition wires should first be tested through the cap

bles have silicone insulation and thus are not prone to display these conditions.

The most reliable way to check the cables is with an ohmmeter. On conventional ignitions, the resistance should be less than 7,000 ohms per foot (wire removed). On cars with electronic ignitions, it is generally recommended to leave the wire attached to the distributor cap; test with one lead from the ohmmeter connected to the corresponding terminal in the distributor cap, the other lead touched to the disconnected end of the cable at the spark plug. Then, if resistance seems close to the limit, remove the wire from the cap and retest. In general, the spark plug wires on electronic ignitions should be replaced if the total resistance is over 36,000 ohms.

Always replace the cables with new ones of the same type. Replace the wires one at a time, working from the longest to the shortest.

Oil Level

The engine oil should be checked on a regular basis, ideally at each fuel stop, or once a week. It is best to check when the engine is at operating temperature, but checking the level immediately after shutting off the engine will give a false reading, because all of the oil will not yet have drained back into the crankcase. The car should be parked on a level surface to obtain an accurate reading.

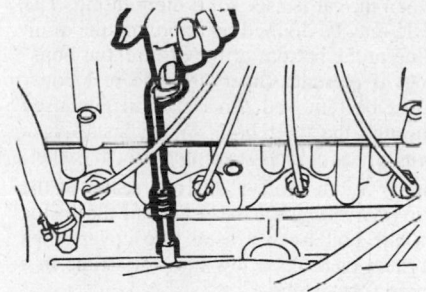

Check the engine oil level with the dipstick

1. Remove the oil dipstick. Wipe it clean, then replace it, seating it firmly.
2. Remove the dipstick again and hold it horizontally to prevent the oil from running. The level should be between the "Add" and "Full" marks on the dipstick. The dipstick may be marked "Add" and "Full," "Add" and "Safe," or may have lines scribed on it; in any case, the oil level should be above the lower marking.
3. If the oil is below the lower mark, enough oil should be added to the engine to raise the level to the upper mark. The markings are usually spaced so that one quart of oil will raise the level from the "Add" mark to the "Full" mark. Oil is added through the capped opening in the valve cover. Only oils labeled SF (gasoline engines) or CC (diesel engines) should be

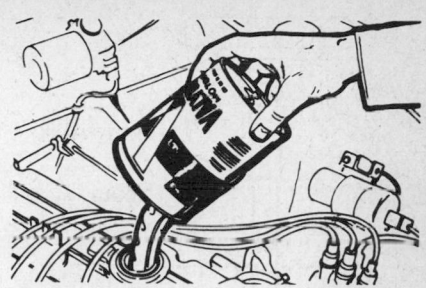

Add oil through the valve cover

used; select a viscosity that will be compatible with the temperatures expected until the next drain interval.
4. Replace the dipstick, then check the level again after any additions of oil. Be careful not to overfill, which will lead to leakage and seal damage.

Power Steering

The power steering fluid level is usually checked with a dipstick inserted into the pump reservoir. The dipstick may be attached to the reservoir cap, or inserted into a tube on the pump body. The level should be checked at every oil change. On some models, the power steering reservoir is translucent, allowing the level to be checked through the sides of the container without removing the cap. On others, the reservoir is a metal canister with a wingnut-attached

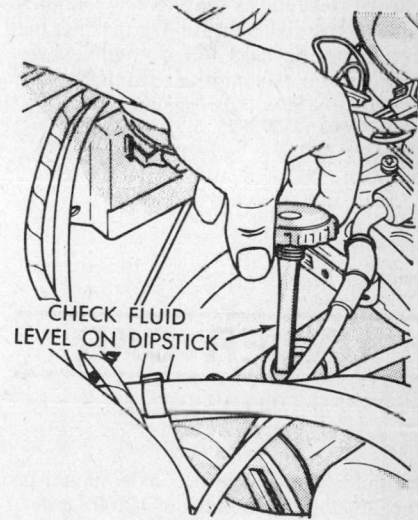

The power steering fluid level on many models is checked by means of a dipstick installed in the reservoir

cap. After the cap is removed, the level is checked with the scribed lines on the inside of the container.

On most models, the fluid level may be checked with the fluid either warm or cold. If checked with the fluid cold, the level will be slightly lower than with the fluid warm. If doubts arise about the specific procedures

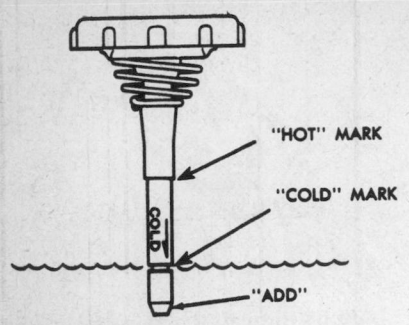

Typical power steering dipstick markings

for the car being checked, consult the owner's manual.

1. On all models, with the engine off, remove the dipstick, remove the cap or check the level through the side of the reservoir. If warm, the level should be between the "Hot" and "Cold" marks or even with the scribed line in the reservoir. If the fluid is cold, the level should be slightly lower.

2. If the level is low, add power steering fluid until the correct level is reached. Do not overfill the reservoir.

Windshield Washer Fluid

Check the fluid level in the windshield washer tank at every oil level check. The fluid can be mixed in a 50% solution with water, if desired, as long as temperatures remain above freezing. Below freezing, the fluid should be used full strength. Never add engine coolant antifreeze to the washer fluid, because it will damage the car's paint.

UNDER CAR

Axle

The fluid level in the rear axle should be checked every 12 months or 12,000 miles.

1. With the car parked on a level surface, remove the filler plug. The plug can be found either in the rear cover of the differential, or on the front of the pinion housing.

2. If lubricant trickles out when the plug is removed, the level is correct. If not, stick your finger in the hole (watch out for sharp threads); the fluid level should be even with edge of the filler hole.

3. If lubricant is needed, use SAE 80W-90 GL-5 gear oil (SAE 80W GL-5 in very cold climates) to fill standard axles. Limited

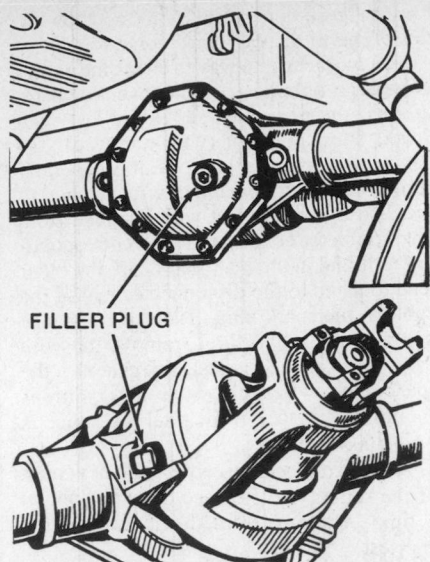

Rear axle filler plug locations

slip axles require a special lubricant, available in auto parts stores.

4. When the level is correct, install the plug and tighten until snug. Do not overtighten.

Standard axles should be drained and refilled with fresh lubricant every 15,000 miles when the car is used to pull a trailer. Limited slip axles should be drained and refilled at the first 7500 miles; the limited slip lubricant should be changed every 7500 miles when the car is used for trailer pulling. The axle may be drained by removing the drain plug at the bottom of the differential housing, if present. Otherwise, the rear cover must be removed, or a suction gun used through the filler hole. When installing a rear cover which does not use a gasket, apply a thin bead of silicone sealer to the cover, running the bead around the inside of the bolt holes. Install the cover, then tighten the bolts a few turns at a time in a crisscross pattern.

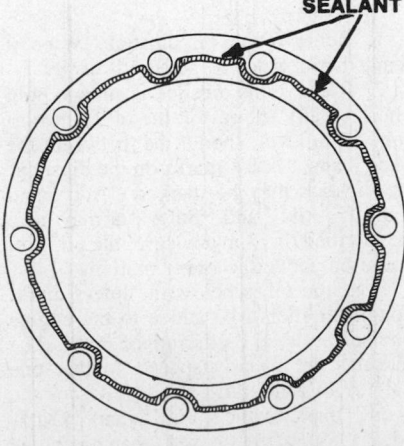

Apply a bead of silicone sealer to the rear cover if no gasket is used

NOTE: On many later models, the rear axle is filled for life and fluid does not have to be replaced.

Exhaust System

The exhaust system should be checked twice a year for general soundness. Inspect the pipes for holes, broken welds, leaking seams, or loose connections. Leaks at connections can sometimes be successfully repaired with the use of a commercial exhaust pipe sealer, but holes or breaks warrant replacement of the part. The exhaust pipe hangers and straps should be examined for any breaks or cracks; replace these as necessary. Some slight cracking of rubber hangers is normal, but deep cracks or cuts are cause for replacement.

———— CAUTION ————
Check the exhaust system only when it is cold. The temperature on an exhaust system using a catalytic converter can reach 1000°F after only a short period of engine operation.

Manual Transmission, Manual Transaxle

The fluid level in the manual transmission (or transaxle on front wheel drive cars) should be checked twice a year, or every 6000 miles.

1. Park the car on a level surface. The transmission should be cool to the touch.

2. Remove the filler plug from the side of the transmission or transaxle. If lubricant trickles out as the plug is removed, the fluid level is correct. If not, stick your finger into the hole (watch out for sharp threads); the lubricant should be right up to the edge of the filler hole.

3. If lubricant is needed, consult the owner's manual for the correct weight and type of fluid.

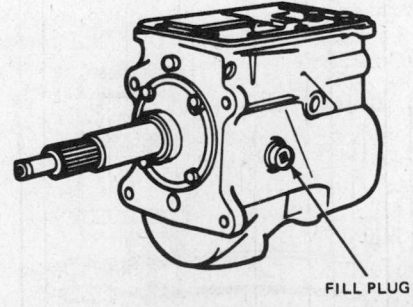

MANUAL TRANSMISSION
FILL TO BOTTOM OF FILLER HOLE WITH VEHICLE ON LEVEL GROUND.

Typical manual transmission filler plug location

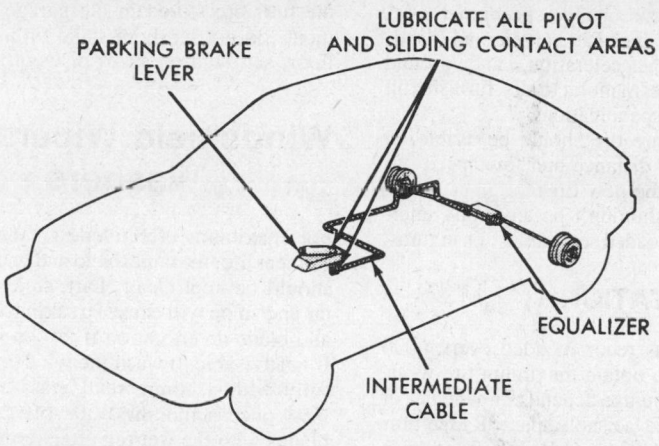

LUBRICATE ALL PIVOT AND SLIDING CONTACT AREAS

PARKING BRAKE LEVER

EQUALIZER

INTERMEDIATE CABLE

Lubricate the parking brake cable with white waterproof grease

NOTE: Some manual transmission/transaxle assemblies are filled with automatic transmission fluid rather than gear oil. Consult the owner's manual for lubricant information.

4. When the level is correct, install the filler plug and tighten until snug.

Parking Brake Linkage

The parking brake cable assembly should be inspected twice a year for fraying, kinks, and binding. A smooth white waterproof lubricant should be applied at the same time to all pivot points and areas in sliding contact.

Suspension Lubrication

Depending on the year of manufacture, there may be as many as twelve grease fittings on the suspension parts, or as few as two. Typical locations for grease nipples are on the ball joints, control arm pivot points, steering linkage, and the tie rod ends.

Lubricate these fittings with a small hand operated grease gun filled with EP chassis lubricant. Pump grease into the fitting slowly, until it begins to ooze out around the joint, or until the grease begins to expand the rubber boot around the fitting. Be extremely careful not to rupture any seals or boots, as this will lead to lubricant loss and contamination of the parts involved.

Occasionally, the grease nipples may become clogged with dirt or hardened grease. If so, unscrew them with a wrench of the proper size and clean them out with solvent. When reinstalled, they may be covered with plastic caps made for the purpose, or a piece of aluminum foil.

The chassis and suspension parts should be lubricated once a year, or every 7500 miles, whichever comes first.

Transfer Case

The transfer case on the four wheel drive Subaru shares a common lubricant supply with the transmission, therefore the transfer case lubricant supply does not have to be checked separately.

EXTERIOR

Drain Holes and Underbody

Most cars have drain holes spaced along the lower edge of the rocker panels and doors. These holes should be cleared of any debris or rust twice a year. A small screwdriver can be used to open plugged drain holes.

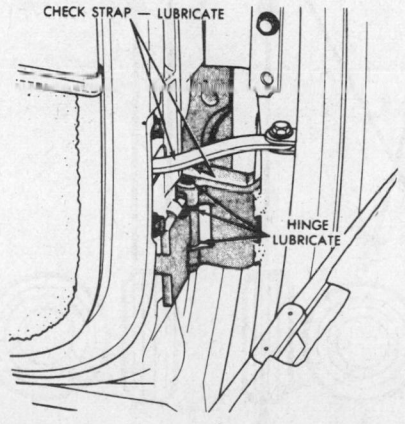

CHECK STRAP — LUBRICATE

HINGE LUBRICATE

Use engine oil to lubricate the door, hood, and trunk hinges

Every spring, the underbody should be flushed with clear water to remove deposits of mud, road salt, and debris. It is advisable to loosen any packed-in sediment before flushing to assure a more thorough cleaning.

Hinges and Locks

Once a year, the door, hood, and trunk hinges, and all locks should be lubricated to ensure smooth operation. The hinge points should be lightly oiled. Lock cylinders may be easily lubricated with a shot of silicone spray directed into the keyhole. Silicone lubricant also works well on the door latch mechanisms, and keeps the door, trunk, and window weatherseals pliable when applied in a light film.

Tires

Tires should be checked weekly for proper air pressure. A chart, located either in the glove compartment or on the driver's or passenger's door, gives the recommended inflation pressures. Maximum fuel economy and tire life will result if the pressure is maintained at the highest figure given on the chart. Pressures should be checked before driving since pressure can increase as

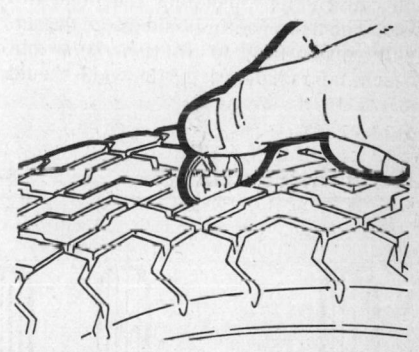

Tire tread depth can be checked with a penny. If the top of Lincoln's head is visible, the tires are due for replacement

much as six pounds per square inch (psi) due to heat buildup. It is a good idea to have your own accurate pressure gauge, because not all gauges on service station air pumps can be trusted. When checking pressures, do not neglect the spare tire. Note that some spare tires require pressures considerably higher than those used in the other tires.

While you are about the task of checking air pressure, inspect the tire treads for cuts, bruises and other damage. Check the air valves to be sure that they are tight. Replace any missing valve caps.

Check the tires for uneven wear that might indicate the need for front end alignment or tire rotation. Tires should be replaced when a tread wear indicator appears as a solid band across the tread.

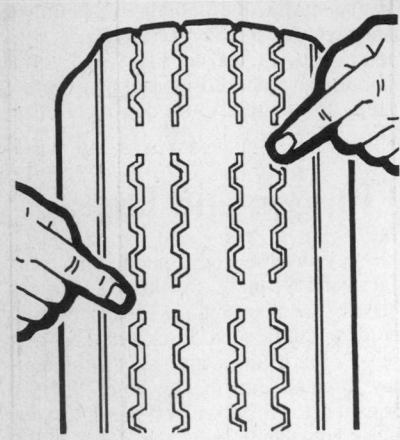

Tread wear indicators will appear as a band across the tire when the tread has worn out.

When buying new tires, give some thought to the following points, especially if you are considering a switch to larger tires or a different profile series:

1. All four tires must be of the same construction type. This rule cannot be violated. Radial, bias, and bias-belted tires must not be mixed.

2. The wheels should be the correct width for the tire. Tire dealers have charts of tire and rim compatibility. A mismatch will cause sloppy handling and rapid tire wear. The tread width should match the rim width (inside bead to inside bead) within an inch. For radial tires, the rim width should

be 80% or less of the tire (not tread) width.

3. The height (mounted diameter) of the new tires can change speedometer accuracy, engine speed at a given road speed, fuel mileage, acceleration, and ground clearance. Tire manufacturers furnish full measurement specifications.

4. The spare tire should be usable, at least for short distance and low speed operation, with the new tires.

5. There shouldn't be any body interference when loaded, on bumps, or in turns.

TIRE ROTATION

Tire rotation is recommended every 6000 miles or so, to obtain maximum tire wear. The pattern you use depends on whether or not your car has a usable spare. Radial tires should not be cross-switched (from one side of the car to the other); they last longer if their direction of rotation is not changed. Snow tires sometimes have directional arrows molded onto the side of their carcass; the arrow shows the direction of rotation. They will wear very rapidly if the rotation is reversed. Studded tires will lose their studs if their rotational direction is reversed.

NOTE: Mark the wheel position or direction of rotation on radial tires or studded snow tires before removing them.

STORAGE

Store the tires at proper inflation pressure

if they are mounted on wheels. Keep them in a cool dry place, laid on their sides. If the tires are stored in the garage or basement, do not let them stand on a concrete floor; set them on strips of wood.

Windshield Wipers and Washers

For maximum effectiveness, and longest element life, the windshield and wiper blades should be kept clean. Dirt, tree sap, road tar and so on will cause streaking, smearing and blade deterioration if left on the glass. It is advisable to wash the windshield carefully with a commercial glass cleaner at least once a month. Wipe off the rubber blades with the wet rag afterwards. For access to the blades on wiper systems which park below the hood line, turn the ignition key to "On" and run the wipers to the center of the windshield. Shut the wipers off with the ignition key, not the wiper switch. Do not attempt to move the wipers by hand; damage to the motor and drive mechanism will result.

If the blades are found to be cracked, broken or torn, they should be replaced immediately. Replacement intervals will vary with usage, although ozone deterioration usually limits blade life to about one year. If the wiper pattern is smeared or streaked, or if the blade chatters across the glass, the elements should be replaced. It is easiest and most sensible to replace the elements

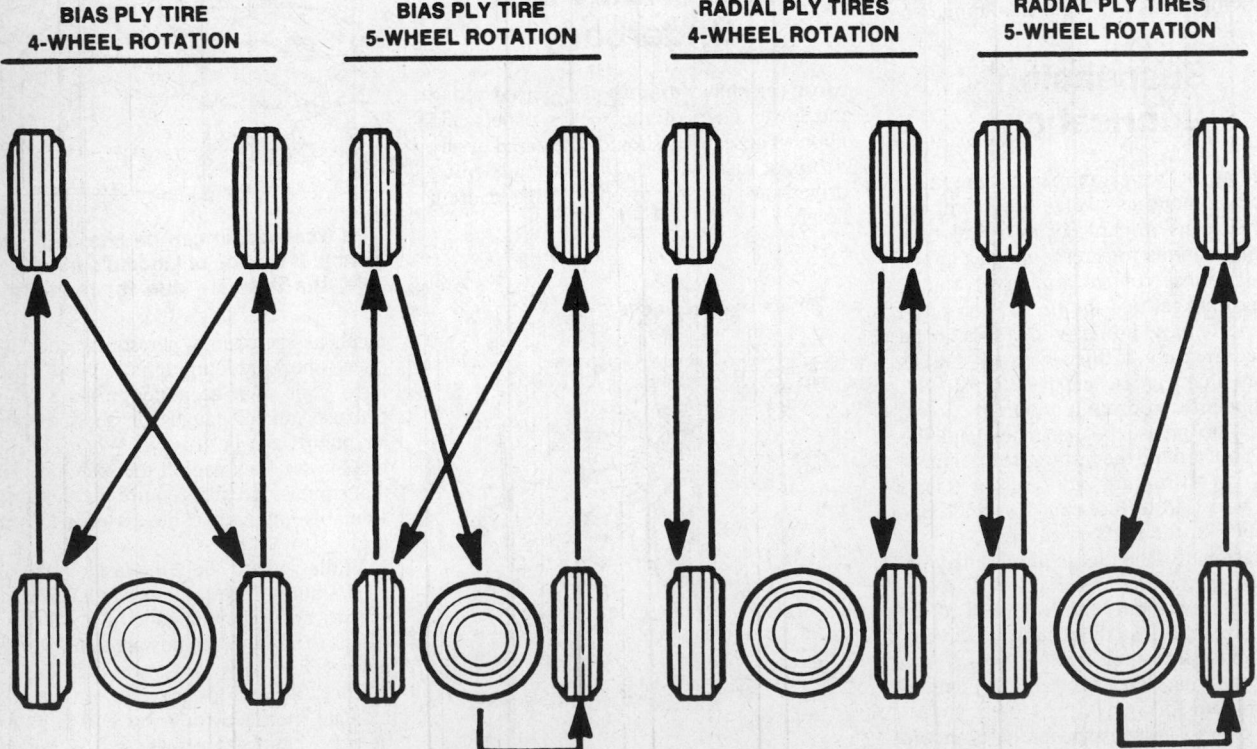

Tire rotation diagrams; note that radials should not be cross-switched

TRICO

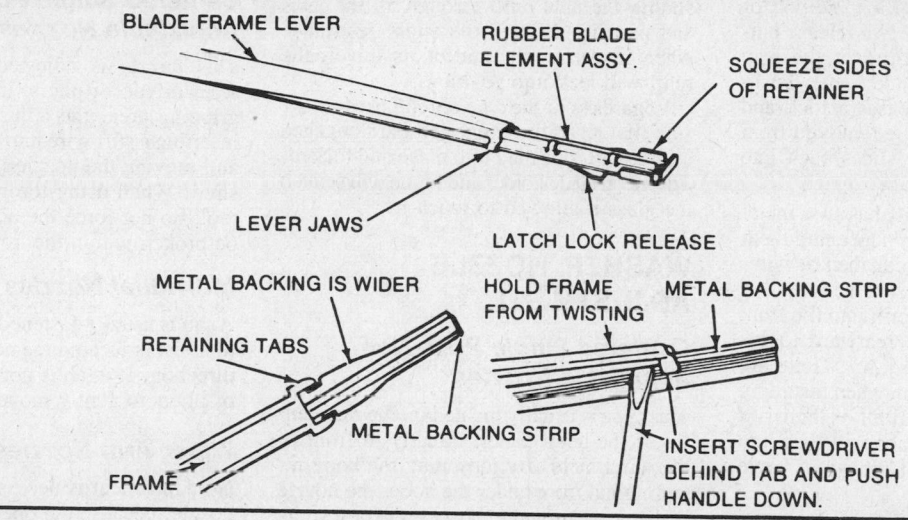

- BLADE FRAME LEVER
- RUBBER BLADE ELEMENT ASSY.
- SQUEEZE SIDES OF RETAINER
- LEVER JAWS
- LATCH LOCK RELEASE
- METAL BACKING IS WIDER
- HOLD FRAME FROM TWISTING
- METAL BACKING STRIP
- RETAINING TABS
- METAL BACKING STRIP
- FRAME
- INSERT SCREWDRIVER BEHIND TAB AND PUSH HANDLE DOWN.

ANCO

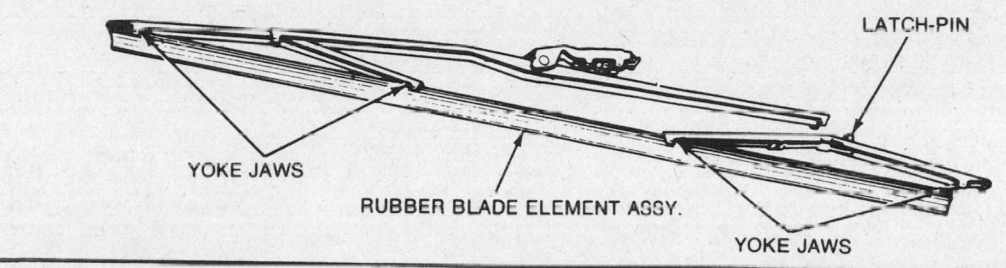

- YOKE JAWS
- RUBBER BLADE ELEMENT ASSY.
- LATCH-PIN
- YOKE JAWS

POLYCARBONATE

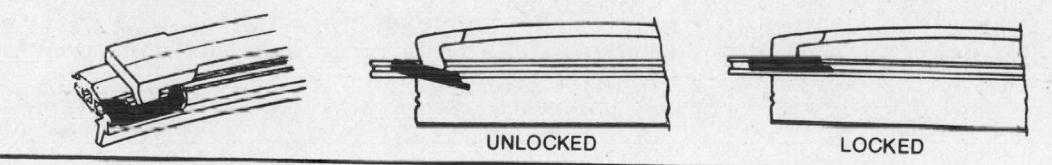

UNLOCKED   LOCKED

TRIDON

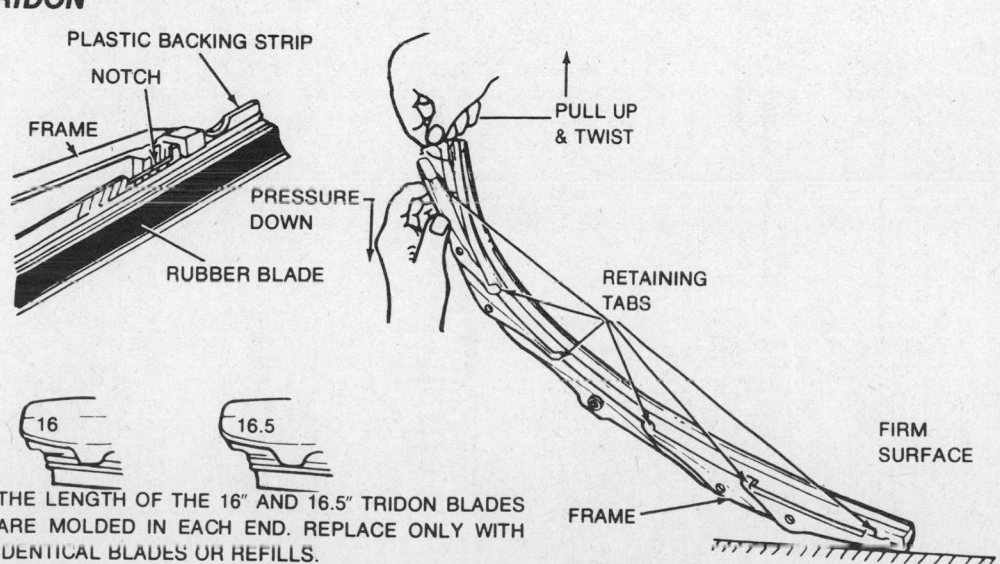

- PLASTIC BACKING STRIP
- NOTCH
- FRAME
- PRESSURE DOWN
- RUBBER BLADE
- PULL UP & TWIST
- RETAINING TABS
- FIRM SURFACE
- FRAME

16   16.5

THE LENGTH OF THE 16" AND 16.5" TRIDON BLADES ARE MOLDED IN EACH END. REPLACE ONLY WITH IDENTICAL BLADES OR REFILLS.

Windshield wiper blade replacement methods

in pairs.

There are basically three different types of refills, which differ in their method of replacement. One type has two release buttons, approximately one-third of the way up from the ends of the blade frame. Pushing the buttons down releases a lock and allows the rubber filler to be removed from the frame. The new filler slides back into the frame and locks in place.

The second type of refill has two metal tabs which are unlocked by squeezing them together. The rubber filler can then be withdrawn from the frame jaws. A new refill is installed by inserting the refill into the front frame jaws and sliding it rearward to engage the remaining frame jaws. There are usually four jaws; be certain when installing that the refill is engaged in all of them. At the end of its travel, the tabs will lock into place on the front jaws of the wiper blade frame.

The third type is a refill made from polycarbonate. The refill has a simple locking device at one end which flexes downward out of the groove into which the jaws of the holder fit, allowing easy release. By sliding the new refill through all the jaws and pushing through the slight resistance when it reaches the end of its travel, the refill will lock into position.

Regardless of the type of refill used, make sure that all of the frame jaws are engaged as the refill is pushed into place and locked. The metal blade holder and frame will scratch the glass if allowed to touch it.

WASHER NOZZLE ADJUSTMENT

Centered Single Post–Non-Adjustable Nozzles

This type is usually located on the rear center of the hood panel, directly in front of the windshield. By loosening the body retaining nut from under the hood, the nozzle body can be turned to provide the best spray discharge to cover the windshield. Tighten the retaining nut while holding the nozzle in position.

Centered Single Post–Adjustable Nozzles

This nozzle is adjusted with a wrench, screwdriver, or pliers. If the nozzle has no gripping area, the adjustment is made by inserting a stiff wire into the nozzle opening and moving the nozzle in the direction desired. When using the wire as an adjuster tool, do not force the nozzle; the wire can be broken within the nozzle opening.

Individual Nozzles

A tab is usually fastened to the nozzle stem to assist in turning the nozzle in the desired direction. If a tab is not present, use a pair of pliers to gently move the nozzle.

Wiper Arm Nozzles

No adjustment is necessary on this type of nozzle, because the opening is centered on the wiper arm and moves along with the arm.

Gauges and Indicators

There are various systems used to indicate values of heat, pressure, vacuum, current flow, and fuel supply. The following are the more popular systems used.

Bourdon Tube

This gauge consists of a flattened tube that is bent to form a curve. The curve tends to straighten under internal pressure caused by engine oil pressure. The curved tube is geared or linked to an indicator needle which may be read on a calibrated scale.

This type of gauge may be easily distinguished from the electrical type by the small copper or nylon tube running from the gauge to the engine.

Bi-Metallic or Thermal

This gauge is activated by the difference in the expansion factors of a bi-metal bar. A sending unit, consisting of a variable resistance conductor, influences current flow to a voltage limiter, or directly to a heating element coiled around a bi-metal bar in the gauge. A bi-metallic gauge pointer will move slowly to its gauging position.

Magnetic

In this system, the indicator needle is moved by changing the balance between the magnetic pull of two coils built in the gauge. When the ignition switch is in the "off" position, the pointer may rest any place on the gauge dial. Balance is controlled by the action of a sending unit or a tank unit containing a rheostat, the value of which varies with temperature, pressure or movement of a float arm. A magnetic gauge will snap to its position when turned on.

Vacuum Gauges

The gauge operates by monitoring engine vacuum. High engine vacuum draws the needle to the high side of the gauge against internal spring tension. As engine vacuum

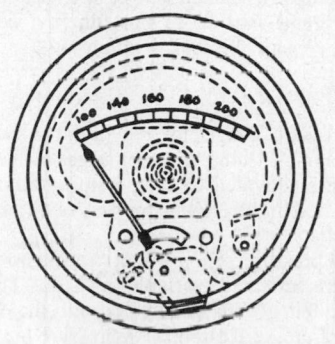

Bourdon tube gauge

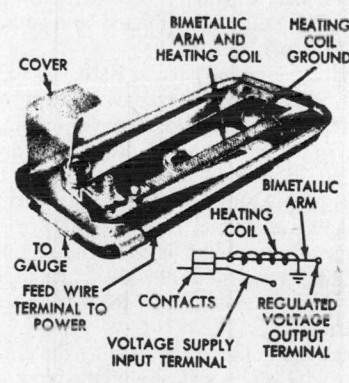

Constant voltage regulator

decreases, the spring tension overcomes the vacuum pull and the needle moves to the low side of the gauge.

Warning Lights

This system is quite popular and may be used to indicate heat, low pressure or as a battery discharge indicator.

Electronic Instruments

These systems use vacuum fluorescent displays to replace the conventional indicator needle type gauge. Typical instrumentation of this type is used for the chronometer, odometer, speedometer, temperature, and fuel gauges. These systems vary, and both digital and graphic displays are used. They are often connected to a microcomputer and used to "call up" additional information. Display information may be shown in English or Metric.

SECTION 1
BOURDON TUBE

Oil Pressure

The gauge is the pressure expansion type and is activated by oil pressure developed by the oil pump, acting directly on the mechanism of the gauge. The gauge is connected by a small tube to the main oil passage in the engine oiling system. This design registers the full pressure of the oil pump.

TESTING

A gauge pointer that flutters is usually an indicator that oil has entered the gauge tube. The tube should contain trapped air to cushion the pulsations of the oil pump and relief valve. Oil can work up into the gauge lines as a result of a gauge or tube leak or improper installation. To correct this condition, renew the unit or correct the leak; then, with the gauge line disconnected at both ends, blow the line clear. Connect line at gauge first and then at the engine.

If the gauge reads too low or reads no pressure, test for a possible obstruction by disconnecting the line at the gauge. Hold the end of the line over an empty container, then start the engine. After a few bubbles, oil should flow steadily.

If oil does not flow satisfactorily, first

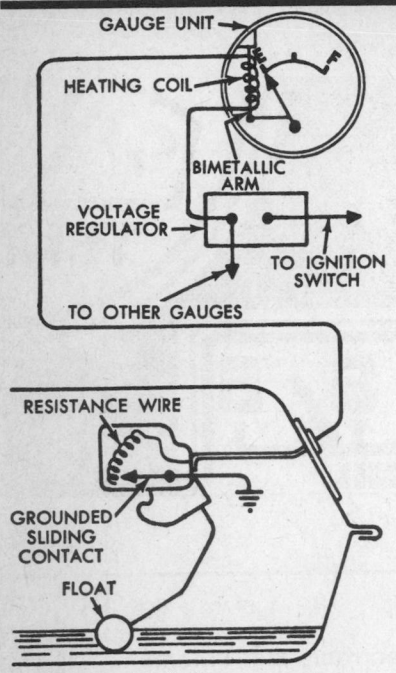

Bi-metallic fuel gauge system

make sure that the oil level is correct and that the oil pump is functioning. Should the engine oil system be operating correctly, the problem is either with the gauge or the line. Check the line for kinks, leaks, or blockage which would prevent oil from reaching the gauge. If the line is unobstructed, remove the gauge unit from the instrument panel. Check to make sure that the hole leading to the Bourdon tube is clear and be sure that the lever linkage and pointer gears operate freely. If none of these points is at fault, the Bourdon tube itself is defective and the gauge must be replaced.

SECTION 2
BI-METAL

Fuel

Bi-metal or thermal type gauges operate on the principle of constant applied voltage and are sensitive only to changes originating at the sending unit.

The fuel gauge system consists of a sending unit, located in the fuel tank, and a registering unit mounted in the instrument cluster. The sending unit is a rheostat that varies its resistance depending on the amount of fuel in the tank.

TESTING THE DASH GAUGE

— CAUTION —

Gauge systems using constant voltage regulators should not be grounded while testing. An excess of 5 volts is likely to burn out the unit.

To safely test this type of voltage regulated system:
1. Have the ignition switch in the ''off'' position.

2. Connect the terminals of four, series-connected. D-type flashlight batteries (total of six volts) to the terminals of the gauge to be tested. Three volts should cause the gauge to read approximately half-scale.

If the gauge reads half-full and was not working properly before, the sending unit in the tank is probably defective.

If the gauge is inaccurate or does not register, replace it.

If both the fuel gauge and temperature gauge are in error, in the same manner, the constant voltage regulator is probably at fault.

While working under the dash, be careful not to ground any of the gauges. A full flow of current through the regulator to ground is likely to burn out the regulator.

TESTING THE SENDING UNIT

If the dash gauge test shows that unit to be satisfactory, the sending unit or gauge system wiring is faulty. Substitute a jumper wire between the gauge and the tank unit. If the gauge now functions, replace the wire. If the gauge still does not function correctly, replace the tank sending unit.

Oil Pressure

Oil pressure gauges of the bi-metal type operate on the same principle as gas gauges. They are activated by temperature and the difference in the expansion factors of a bi-metal bar.

The pressure sending unit consists of a pressure-activated variable resistor. This sealed unit is usually screwed into the engine oil pressure circuit. As pressure is applied to one side of a diaphragm, linkage advances a contact arm across the coils of a resistor. This action reduces resistance in the gauge circuit, thus increasing current flow and heat to the bi-metal arm in the gauge. The gauge is calibrated to read oil pressure in psi.

Run the engine and have an assistant watch the dash gauge. If the gauge reads zero, turn off the engine and remove the sending unit from the engine block. Restart the engine and allow it to idle for a minute. If there is oil pressure, oil should surge from the sending unit hole. If no oil flows from the hole, the problem is with the engine lubricating system. If oil flows, the fault lies with the sending unit, the wiring, or the dash gauge.

Check the gauge by grounding the connecting wire for an instant with the ignition

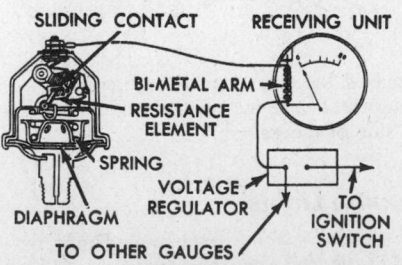

Bi-metallic oil gauge circuit

switch turned on. A good gauge will go to the top of its scale.

— CAUTION —

Grounding the connecting wire for any longer than a moment will damage the dash units.

If the gauge did not move when grounded, check the wiring to the dash unit for continuity. If the wiring is not faulty and the gauge doesn't register when grounded, replace the gauge. If the gauge functions when grounded, replace the sending unit.

Temperature

The temperature gauge consists of a sending unit, mounted in the cylinder head or block, and a remote resistor unit (temperature gauge) mounted on the instrument panel. The principle of operation is essentially the same as the bi-metallic fuel gauge, the exception being that the resistance of the sending unit is influenced by engine temperature instead of tank fuel level, as with the fuel gauge.

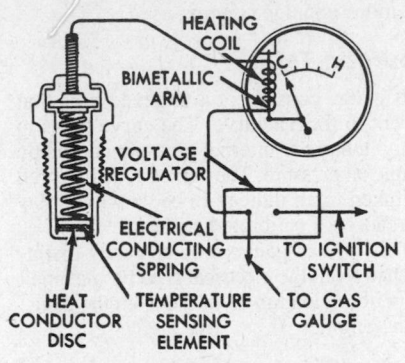

Bi-metallic temperature gauge

The temperature sending unit is constructed with a coil spring and sensing disc. Current passing through this coil encounters increased resistance, proportional to an increase in temperature. The gauge registers this resistance change and is calibrated to indicate the temperature.

TESTING THE DASH GAUGE

Connect four D-cells (total of 6 volts) in series with the dash gauge, with the ignition switched off. A good gauge will register ½ on the scale. Replace the gauge if it does not move.

TESTING THE SENDING UNIT

Bring the engine to normal operating temperature (check with a thermometer). If the gauge doesn't register, disconnect the connecting wire from the engine sending unit and ground the connecting wire for an instant and have an assistant observe the gauge.

— CAUTION —

Grounding the wire for any longer than a moment will damage the dash units.

If the gauge shows no reading, replace the connecting wire. If the gauge registers when grounded, replace the sending unit.

SECTION 3
MAGNETIC

Fuel

The magnetic fuel gauge consists of two units, the dash unit and the sending unit in the fuel tank. One terminal of the dash unit is connected to the ignition switch so that the system is active only when the ignition is on. With the ignition off, the pointer may come to rest at any position on the dial.

The gauge pointer is moved by varying the magnetic pull of two coils in the unit. The magnetic pull is controlled by the action of the tank unit which contains a variable rheostat, the value of which varies with movement of a float and arm.

When the ignition switch is on and the tank unit arm is in the full position, the current flow to ground is through the resistor, battery coil and the ground coil. Because the ground coil has more windings than the battery coil, it builds up a stronger magnetic field and the pointer is pulled to the full position.

When the tank unit arm is in the empty position, the current flow is through the resistor, the battery coil and the wire to ground at the tank unit. The pointer is thus pulled to the empty position. The resistor in series with the battery coil balances resistance between the two coils in the dash unit.

TESTING THE DASH GAUGE

Disconnect the wire from the tank unit. Using a tank unit of known accuracy, clip a test wire from the body of the test unit to ground. Clip another test wire from the connector of the test unit to the tank unit wire. With the ignition on, moving the float arm through its entire range should cause the gauge to respond proportionally. If the dash gauge does not correspond to the movement of the test unit and the wiring to the gauge is OK, the dash unit is bad.

TESTING THE TANK UNIT

If tests indicate that the trouble lies in the tank unit, remove the unit and check for mechanical failure. The unit may have either a ruptured or binding float.

An electrical check for circuit continuity may be made throughout the unit's range.

Temperature

The temperature gauge system consists of a magnetic dash unit and a resistance-type sending unit screwed into the water jacket of the cylinder head or the engine block.

The dash unit has two magnetic poles. One of the windings is connected to the ignition switch and ground. This electromagnet exerts a steady pull to hold the gauge pointer to the left or "cold" position when the ignition is on.

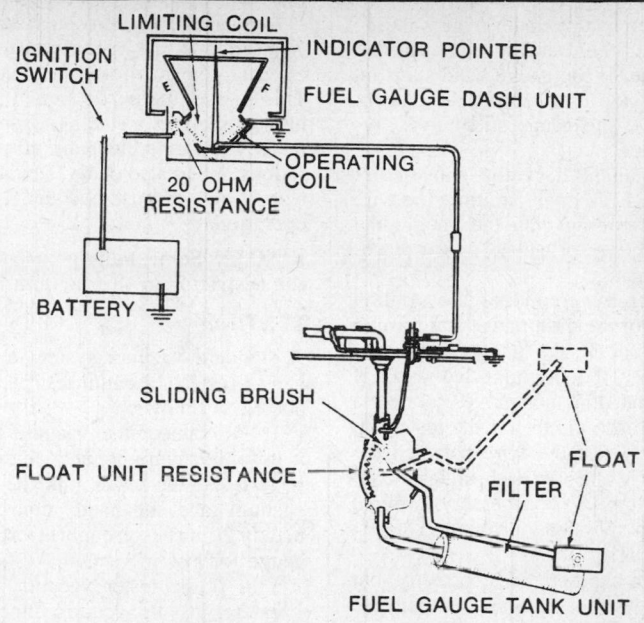

Magnetic fuel gauge circuit

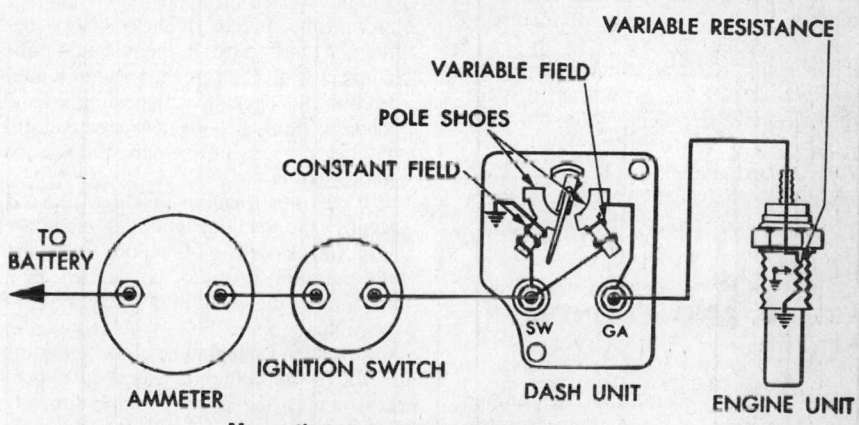

Magnetic temperature gauge circuit

The other winding in the dash unit connects to a ground through the engine sending unit. This electromagnet exerts a steady pull on the gauge pointer toward the right, or "hot" side of the gauge. The strength of this pull is dependent upon the current allowed to pass through the engine unit (sending unit) resistor.

The sending unit, located in the engine cooling system, contains a flat disc (thermistor) that changes resistance as its temperature varies.

NOTE: This sending unit, while similar in appearance, is different and is not interchangeable with the unit used in systems using bi-metal or thermal dash gauges. The resistance of the thermistor disc is maximum when the temperature is cold and minimum when hot. The decrease in resistance allows more current to flow through the electromagnet connected to the engine unit. The resulting increase in magnetic pull causes the gauge pointer to move to the right, or "hot" side.

TESTS

1. Disconnect the wire at the sending unit and turn on the ignition switch. The gauge hand should stay against the cold side stop pin.
2. Ground the wire disconnected from the sending unit. With the ignition switch still on, the gauge hand should swing across the dial to the hot stop pin.

CORRECTIVE MEASURES

If the gauge hand does not stay to the left, either the wire is grounded between the dash unit and the engine unit or the dash unit is defective.

Test further by disconnecting the sending unit wire at the gauge. Turn on the ignition. If the gauge hand stays on the left-hand stop pin, replace the disconnected wire. If the gauge still moves, replace the gauge.

If the gauge hand does not swing across the dial, there is an open circuit in the wire between the sending unit and gauge, the gauge is defective, or current is not reaching the dash gauge.

Test further by grounding the sending unit terminal of the dash gauge and turning on the ignition. If the gauge hand stays on the left-hand stop pin, replace the disconnected wire. If the gauge still moves, replace the gauge.

If the gauge hand does not swing across the dial, there is an open circuit in the wire between the sending unit and gauge, the gauge is defective, or current is not reaching the dash gauge.

Test further by grounding the sending unit terminal of the dash gauge and turning on the ignition. If the gauge hand now moves, replace the disconnected wire. If the gauge hand does not move, connect a test lamp into the circuit. If the test lamp does not light, test the wire between the ignition switch and the dash unit by connecting the lamp to the accessory terminal at the ignition switch and ground. The test lamp should light.

If the gauge hand operates correctly, but the gauge does not indicate temperature correctly, either the sending unit is defective or the dash gauge is out of calibration. Replace sending unit with one of known accuracy. If gauge reading is still incorrect, replace the gauge.

If the gauge hand is at maximum at all times, and tests 1 and 2 indicate that the wiring and the dash unit are good, the sending unit must be replaced.

If the gauge hand will not move, the dash unit is bad, or incorrectly installed. Correct the installation or replace the gauge.

SECTION 4
VACUUM AND ECONOMY GAUGES

The fuel economy gauge indicates engine manifold vacuum, as a function of throttle position and engine load. The face of the gauge dial is divided into three segments; Poor (low vacuum), Good (normal vacuum for cruise), and Decelerate (high vacuum). Although the gauge is not intended as a close tolerance vacuum indicator, it may be assumed that a gauge reading continuously below the Good band (normal cruise or idle) may mean poor engine performance due to improper ignition timing or manifold vacuum leakage.

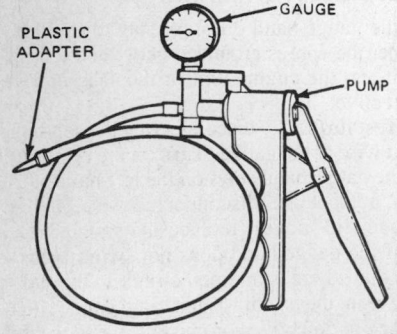

Vacuum hand pump

A manifold vacuum pulsation restrictor is inserted in the vacuum tube at the end closest to the manifold vacuum connection. This enables the inside area of the vacuum hose to serve as a small vacuum reservoir, thereby reducing the manifold vacuum pulsations and to also damp the gauge reading restriction against sudden accelerator operation.

NOTE: Some manufacturers do not use the restrictor in the vacuum line.

TESTING

A standard vacuum system test, using a hand operated vacuum test pump, is conducted as follows:

1. Disconnect the vacuum tube at the manifold vacuum connection.

2. Insert the tester into the end of the vacuum tube and hand pump to approximately 20 inches vacuum. Observe the test gauge for loss in vacuum.

   a. If the tester vacuum gauge indicates a loss in vacuum, remove the vacuum tube connector from the threaded vacuum connector on the back of the gauge. Apply a short length of teflon tape around the threads of the vacuum connection and reinstall the vacuum tube connector on the threaded vacuum connection. Recheck the gauge with the hand vacuum pump. If the tester gauge still indicates a loss in vacuum, replace the gauge assembly.

   b. If the vacuum reading remains steady, the vacuum tube and gauge are OK. Check the end of the tube to be sure the pulsation restrictor is installed; then reconnect the manifold vacuum connection.

Connect the vacuum tube of the test pump directly to the economy gauge tube connector. Pump the tester to approximately 20 inches vacuum and observe the tester gauge for a loss in vacuum.

If the tester gauge indicates a loss in vacuum, replace the economy gauge assembly.

If the tester gauge reading remains steady, the hose to the engine manifold vacuum port must be repaired or replaced.

NOTE: If a hand operated vacuum pump is not available, the engine can be used as a source of vacuum, with a separate vacuum gauge and attaching tee as testing tools.

SECTION 5
WARNING LIGHTS

Oil Pressure

The warning or indicator light system supplies the driver with a visual signal of low engine oil pressure. The light usually lights at pressures below 5 psi.

The low pressure warning light is wired in series with an oil pressure sending unit. The sending unit is tapped into the main oil gallery and is sensitive to oil pressure.

The unit contains a diaphragm, spring linkage and electrical contacts. When the ignition switch is on, the warning light circuit is energized and the circuit is completed through the closed contacts in the sending unit. When the engine starts, oil pressure will compress the diaphragm, opening the contact points and breaking the circuit.

TESTS

The light should light when the engine is not running and the ignition switch is turned on. If the light does not go on, first substitute a new bulb. If there is still no light, check the wire from the light to the switch. If the wire is not at fault, disconnect the wire at the sending unit and ground it. Replace the sending unit if the light now lights.

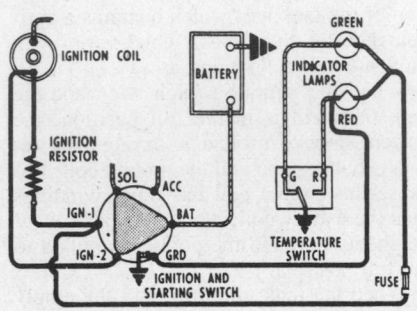

Cold and hot temperature indicator circuit

Temperature

This system employs a heat sending unit with either one or two sets of contacts. Some systems use a green light to indicate subnormal, and a red light to warn of abnormal heat. The more common system, however, uses a simple make-and-break heat-sensitive sending unit screwed into the engine cooling system, and wired in series with the hot indicator light in the instrument panel.

The two-light system uses a bi-metal element mounted between two signal circuits. Normal operating temperature (somewhere between 120°F. and 250°F.) will cause the bi-metal bar to assume a position of no contact between the low and the high temperature circuit. When the ignition switch is turned on, with a cold engine, the cold (green) circuit is complete. If the engine becomes hot enough to move the bi-metal bar so that it touches the contacts of the hot circuit, the hot (red) light comes on. This hot signal indicates that temperatures are in the area of 250°F. in the sealed cooling system.

TESTS

Use the same testing procedure given for oil pressure.

Charge Indicator

A light is used to indicate general charging system operation. When output is below battery potential, a red light is shown. When output is above battery potential, other factors (wiring, voltage regulator, etc.) being normal, the light is out.

The charge indicator bulb is connected to the charging circuit, obtaining its ground through the voltage regulator. When the output rises above battery potential, the current flow causes the light to go out.

When an alternator is used, it is necessary to supply a small amount of excitation current to the alternator field, due to the small amount of residual magnetism. Current can be supplied from the battery, through the indicator light, and to the regulator terminal on the alternator. This current has a value of about 12 volts at .25 amperes and will cause the indicator light to come on. Most systems have a resistor in parallel with the bulb to provide excitation if the bulb burns out and to prevent the light from glowing dimly during normal operation.

When the alternator starts to supply current, an output voltage is developed at the regulator terminal. When this voltage exceeds the battery voltage, current will pass from the alternator to the battery and to the system. This current is flowing in the reverse direction of the voltage supplied by the battery. The current flow coming from the alternator exceeds the battery current by a regulated 1 or 2 volts. This is not enough to light the indicator light, therefore, the light will go out when the alternator is supplying sufficient current.

If the alternator output current should drop below battery voltage, current will begin to flow in the opposite direction. If it exceeds 2 or 3 volts, the light will glow indicating that the alternator is not operating properly.

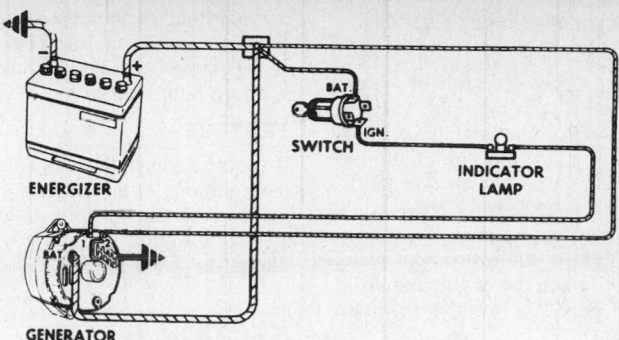

Charging indicator light circuit

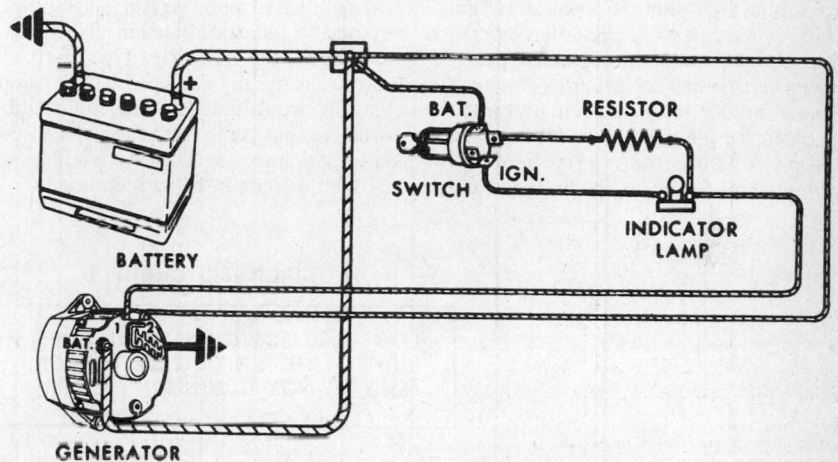

Simplified view of a typical charging system schematic showing the resistor wire in parallel with the charge indicator lamp

Coolant Level Indicator

Some models have a warning light which comes on if the coolant level in the radiator drops below a predetermined level. The coolant level indicator consists of three units; a sending unit which is threaded into the side tank of the radiator, a module which is mounted behind the instrument cluster, and a warning light. As a bulb test, the light is wired so that it comes on when the key is turned to the "START" position.

LIGHT DOESN'T COME ON

Perform the following checks if the warning light won't come on when the key is turned to the "START" position:

1. With the ignition switch in the "ON" position, unfasten the lead from the coolant level sending unit. If the light comes on replace the sending unit.

2. If the light didn't come on in step 1, check the light in the indicator and replace it, if necessary.

3. If the bulb is OK, check the wiring between the sending unit and module, and then between the module and light. If the wiring is not "open," replace the module.

LIGHT WON'T GO OUT

Perform the following checks if the light won't go out when the coolant is at the specified level:

1. Detach the lead from the coolant level

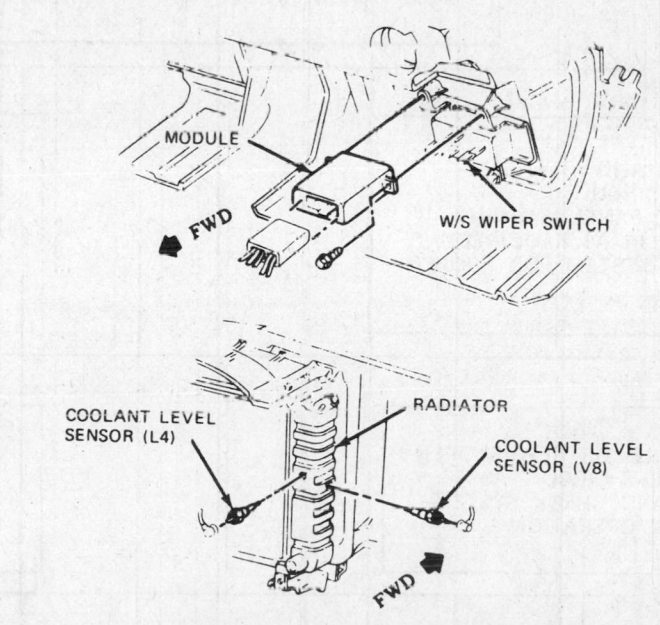

Coolant level sending unit and module

sending unit and ground the lead connector with a jumper wire. Turn the ignition switch to the "ON" position.

2. If the light doesn't come on, replace the sending unit. If the light remains on

disconnect the jumper wire and proceed with the next step.

3. Check for a short in the sending unit-to-module wiring. If there is no short, replace the module.

Fuel Economy Warning Light

The fuel economy warning light system consists of a normally closed vacuum switch, an instrument panel warning light, vacuum hose, wire harness, and attaching hardware. Its operation is similar in function to that of the oil pressure (switch type) indicating system, except the switch opens when vacuum is applied, rather than pressure.

A warning light in the instrument panel warns the driver when the engine manifold vacuum has dropped below the specified limit.

Electrical Circuit

The warning light bulb is powered by the ignition switch accessory circuit through the printed circuit board of the instrument panel. The wire harness and normally closed switch assembly provide the ground circuit for the bulb. With the ignition switch ON and the engine not running, the colored light will be illuminated. As the engine is started and the manifold vacuum reaches the specified limit of about 4 to 6 in. of hg., the vacuum switch opens the ground circuit and the warning light will go out.

TESTING

If the warning light does not operate with the ignition switch on, (engine not running), or if the warning light remains on after the engine has started, refer to the diagnosis charts for repair procedures.

SECTION 6
AMMETERS

The automotive ammeter is a gauge or meter used to indicate direction and relative value of current flow. This type of charge indicator is usually equipped with a dampening device to reduce pointer fluctuation during current surge from the voltage regulator. An ammeter is always wired in series with the circuit being monitored.

The meter will show charge when the battery is being charged and discharge when the battery is being discharged. It merely gives an indication of the state of charge of the battery, since it shows a relatively high charging rate when the battery is low, and a low charging rate when the battery is near full charge. An ammeter does not give a complete report of battery condition, whereas a voltmeter does. Just after cranking the engine, the meter will swing toward the charge side for a short time, if lights and accessories are turned off. As the energy spent in cranking is restored to the battery, the pointer will gradually move back toward center but should stay on the charge side. If the battery charge is low, however, the indicator will show a high charging rate for an indeterminate length of time.

The ammeter does not show the charging rate of the alternator.

At speeds above 30–35 mph, with all lights and accessories on, the indicator should show a reading somewhere on the charge

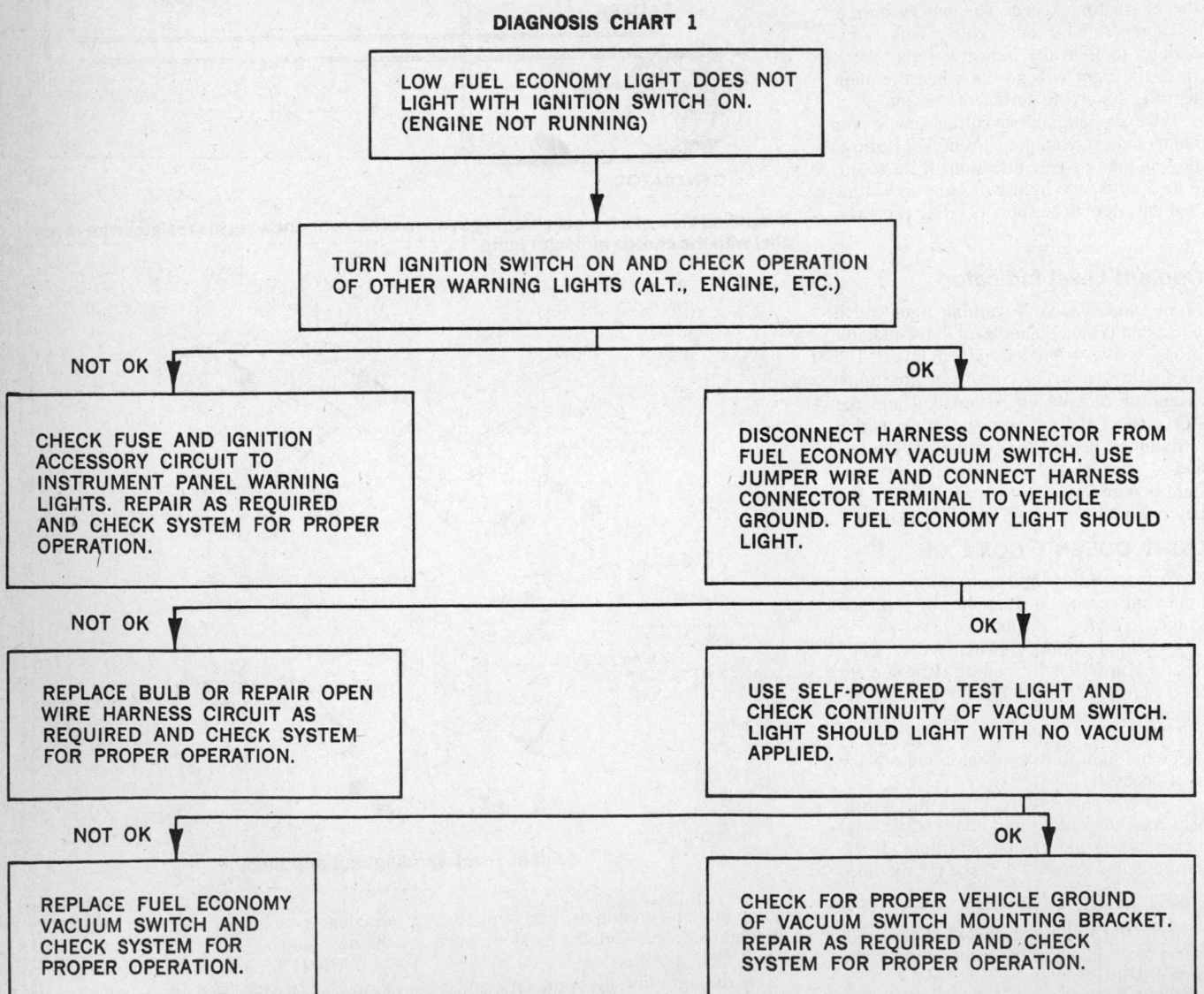

DIAGNOSIS CHART 1

DIAGNOSIS CHART 2

LOW FUEL ECONOMY LIGHT DOES NOT GO OUT WITH ENGINE RUNNING.

↓

START ENGINE. ALLOW TO WARM UP AND RUN AT IDLE. FUEL ECONOMY LIGHT SHOULD BE ON.

↓

IF LOW FUEL ECONOMY LIGHT STAYS ON, DISCONNECT WIRE HARNESS CONNECTOR TO FUEL ECONOMY VACUUM SWITCH. LIGHT SHOULD GO OUT.

NOT OK ↓

CHECK WIRE HARNESS CIRCUIT FOR GROUND OR SHORT. REPAIR AS REQUIRED AND CHECK SYSTEM FOR PROPER OPERATION.

OK ↓

CHECK VACUUM HOSE TO VACUUM SWITCH FOR LEAK. PINCHED OR PLUGGED CONDITION.

NOT OK ↓

REPAIR OR REPLACE VACUUM HOSE AS REQUIRED AND CHECK SYSTEM FOR PROPER OPERATION.

OK ↓

USE HAND VACUUM PUMP AND CHECK VACUUM SWITCH FOR PROPER OPERATION. REPLACE SWITCH, IF REQUIRED, AND CHECK SYSTEM FOR PROPER OPERATION.

side, depending on the state of the battery. Above this speed, the indicator should never show a discharge reading; if it does, the alternator and regulator should be tested.

SECTION 7
VOLTMETERS

A voltmeter is used on some cars, instead of an ammeter. The voltmeter indicates regulated voltage, which shows the charging system's ability to keep the battery charged. A voltmeter is always wired in parallel with the circuit being monitored. Voltmeter readings that are continuously high or low, may indicate a defective regulator, broken or slipping alternator drivebelt, a faulty alternator, or a defective battery.

If a faulty voltmeter is suspected, check the voltage regulator output with a test voltmeter of known accuracy. If the voltage indicated on the test instrument is within specifications, and disagrees with the car's voltmeter reading, replace the car's voltmeter.

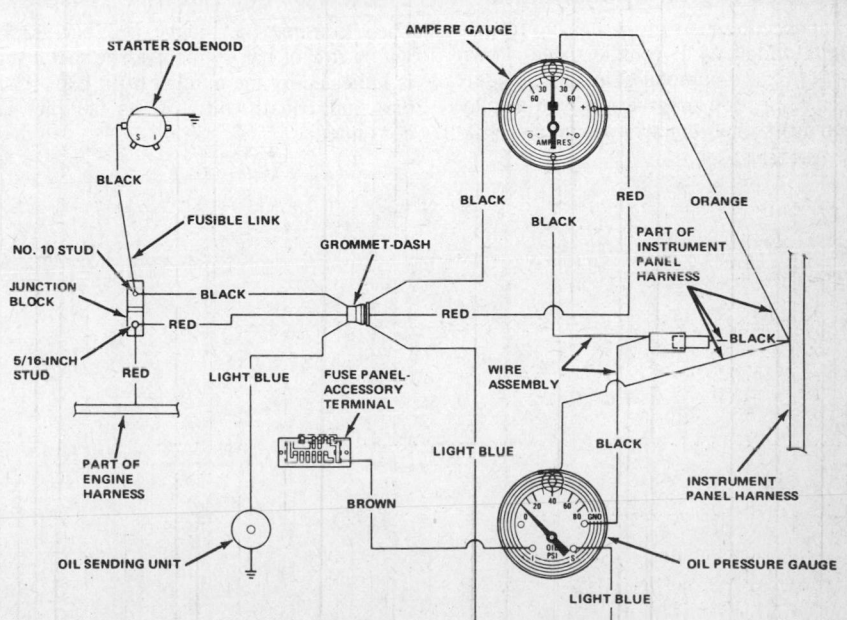

Typical ammeter and oil pressure gauge wiring

AMMETER DIAGNOSIS

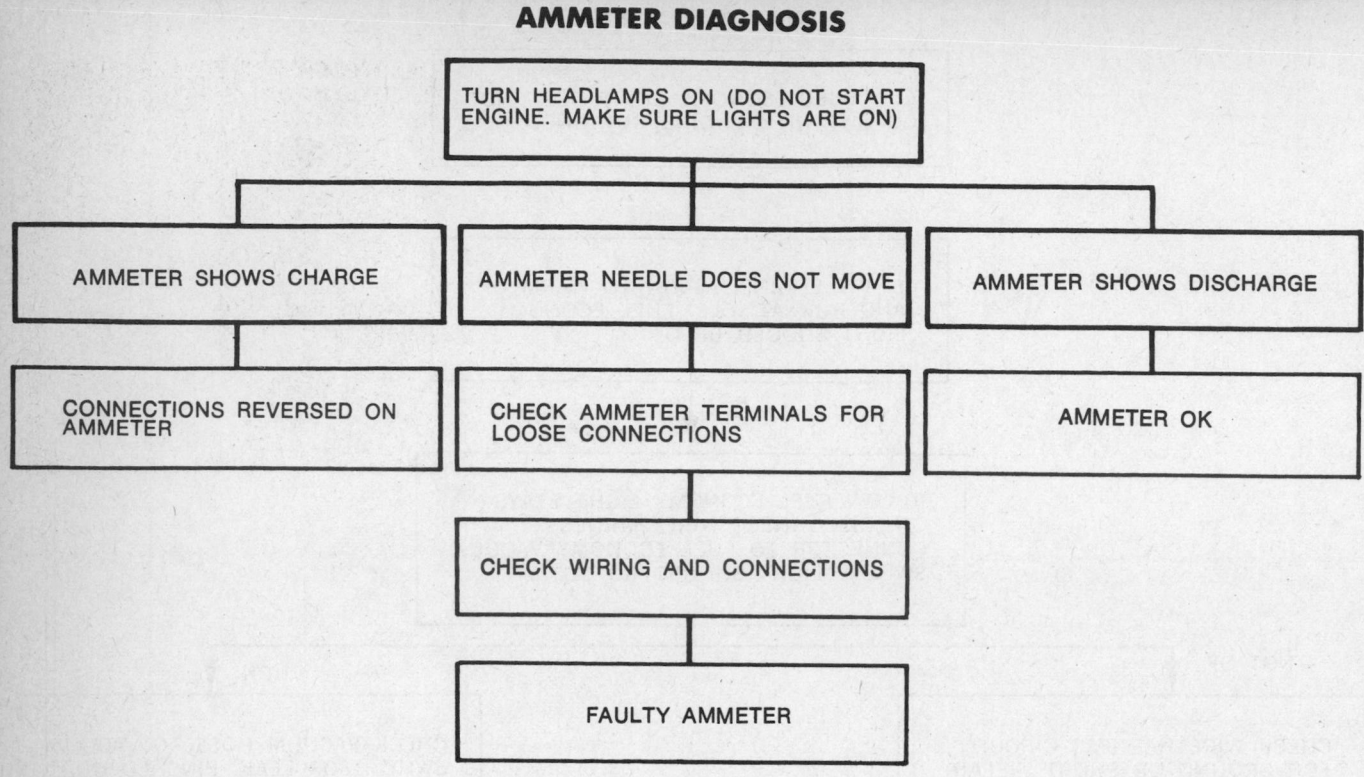

```
          TURN HEADLAMPS ON (DO NOT START
          ENGINE. MAKE SURE LIGHTS ARE ON)
```

| AMMETER SHOWS CHARGE | AMMETER NEEDLE DOES NOT MOVE | AMMETER SHOWS DISCHARGE |

| CONNECTIONS REVERSED ON AMMETER | CHECK AMMETER TERMINALS FOR LOOSE CONNECTIONS | AMMETER OK |

CHECK WIRING AND CONNECTIONS

FAULTY AMMETER

SECTION 8
ELECTRONIC
INSTRUMENTS

Electronic Chronometer

Digital chronometers may be capable of displaying the time of day, month, the day of the month, and on some models an elapsed time function is built-in.

Electronic Digital Speedometer

Digital speedometers are as easy to read as a digital clock, with vehicle speed shown clearly in large numbers. On some models a mode selection may be made to display either miles or kilometers per hour.

Electronic Odometer

Vehicle and trip distance, or kilometers and average speed, are available at the touch of a button from the odometer display on some models. All information is derived from the distance sensor and the internal time base. Accumulated mileage stored in the memory is maintained even if the battery is disconnected.

Electonic Fuel Gauge or Display

The electronic fuel gauge is a bar graph with a row of bar segments. The fuel level is indicated by the number of lit bars. The bars individually turn off as the fuel is consumed.

The electronic fuel display on some models offers multiple functions. In addition to fuel remaining in the tank it may also measure fuel comsumption for range, present fuel efficiency, and trip fuel efficiency. Also a mode selection may be made to display either gallons or liters.

Electronic Temperature Gauge

The electronic temperature gauge is a bar graph with a row of bar segments. The temperature is indicated by the number of lit bars. When the engine coolant rises, causing all the bars to light, an engine over heating warning will be displayed. This over heating symbol continues until the engine temperature is reduced to the normal range.

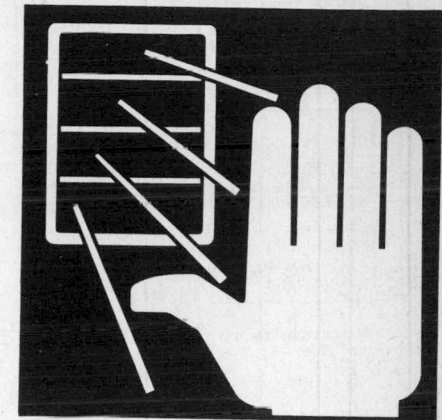

Air Conditioning

AIR CONDITIONING SYSTEMS

Automotive air conditioning systems are basic in design and operation, but many different components are used by the vehicle manufacturers to operate and control the systems to their specifications.

Basic System

The basic air conditioning system utilizes the compressor, condenser, evaporator, receiver-drier, expansion valve and a thermostatic or ambient type switch to control evaporator freeze-up. The controls are manually operated and the unit is basic in design. This system is usually installed as an add-on or after-market unit. A sight glass may be used in the system.

P.O.A. System

The P.O.A. (pilot operated absolute) suction throttling valve system contains the compressor condenser, evaporator, receiver-drier, expansion valve and a suction throttling valve. The suction throttling valve is used to keep the refrigerant gas in the evaporator at a pressure which will not allow the temperature of the evaporator core surface to go below 32 degrees F., thus preventing evaporator freeze-up. For the system to operate effectively, an equalizer line is connected between the suction side of the suction throttling valve and the ex-

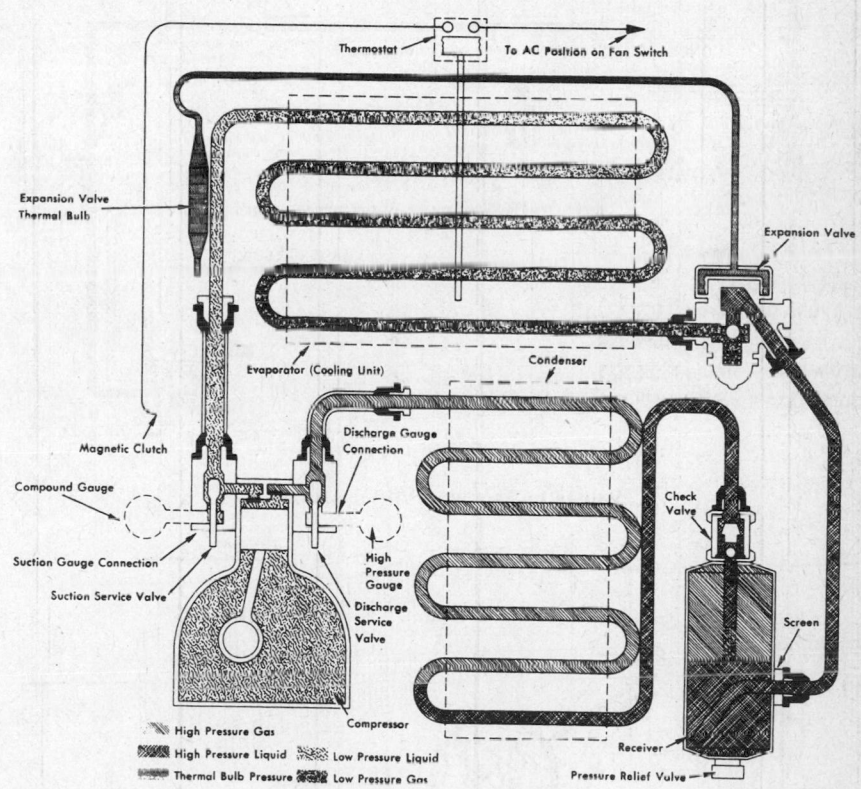

Basic air conditioning system

pansion valve diaphragm. This modifies the operation of the expansion valve which now is controlled by the evaporator outlet temperature and compression suction pressure.

When a crank type compressor is used with the P.O.A. system, an accumulator is placed between the evaporator and the com-

pressor. The accumulator operates as its name implies, accumulating any liquid refrigerant that may have passed from the evaporator and to prevent its moving to the compressor as a liquid, which may, in its form, cause internal compressor damage. A sight glass is normally used in this system.

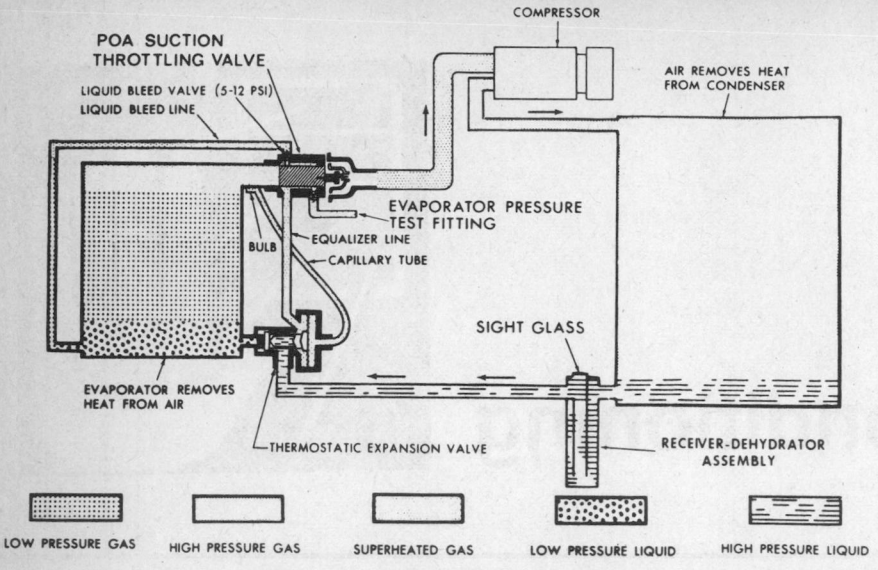

Pilot Operated Absolute (POA) system

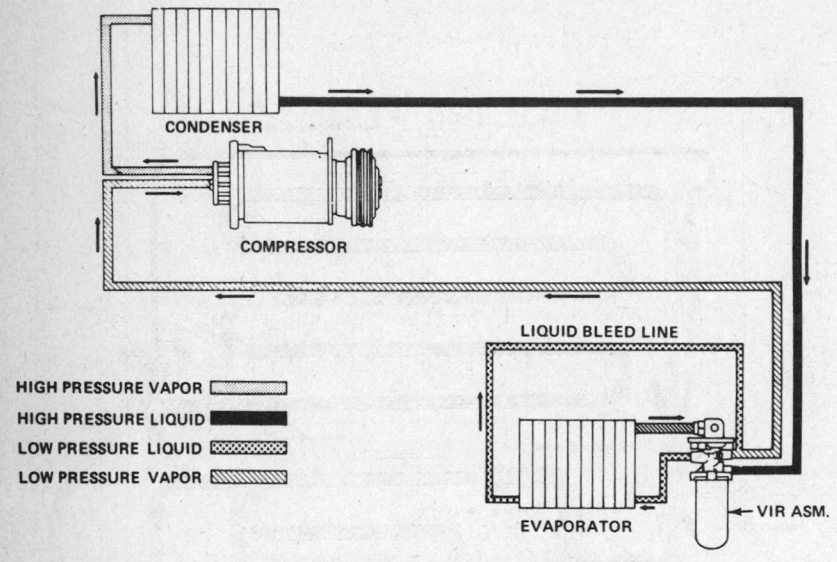

Valves In Receiver (VIR) system

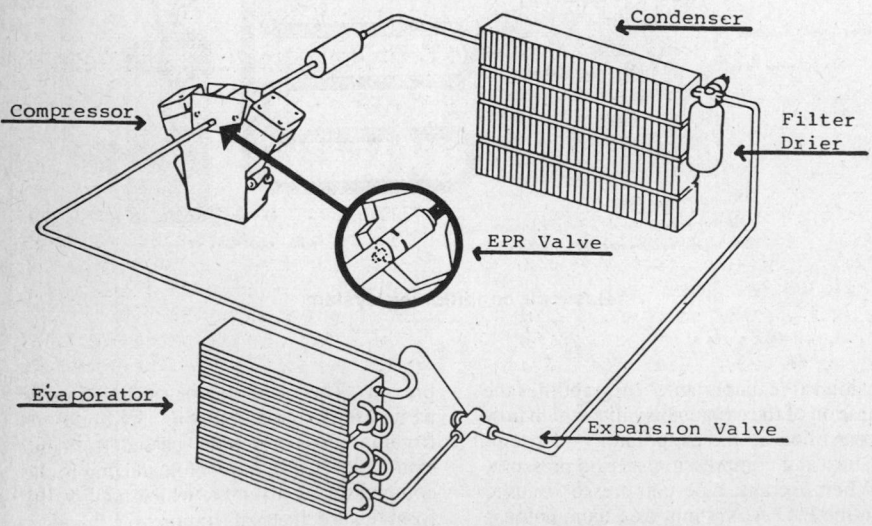

Evaporator Pressure Regulator (EPR) system

V.I.R. System

The V.I.R. system contains the compressor evaporator, condenser, muffler and a unit containing the P.O.A. valve, expansion valve and the receiver-drier. This unit is called the V.I.R. (valves in receiver) assembly. A muffler is normally used with this system and is located between the compressor and the condenser to absorb the compressor pulsations.

The V.I.R. assembly eliminates the outside equalizer line between the outlet of the P.O.A. valve and the expansion valve. The equalizer is now a drilled orfice in the wall between the P.O.A. valve and the expansion valve cavities of the V.I.R. housing. Should the valve prove defective during tests, the unit should be replaced, as it is not repairable or adjustable. A sight glass is normally used with this system.

E.P.R. System

The E.P.R. (evaporator pressure regulator) system includes the condenser, muffler, low pressure shut off valve receiver-drier, expansion valve, evaporator and a V-block, reciprocating crank type compressor. The E.P.R. valve is mounted on the suction side of the compressor and operates in conjunction with the expansion valve assembly, to regulate the flow of refrigerant from the evaporator to the compressor, under light air conditioning loads. By regulating the refrigerant flow, the evaporator temperature is controlled and freezing of the evaporator is prevented.

In contrast to other systems, the E.P.R. system uses the reheat procedure to control the temperature of the air, after it is cooled by passing through the evaporator fins. A manually controlled operating lever is connected to the heater water flow control valve and to a blend air door and the opening of the blend door proportions the amount of air around and through the heater core to control the mix of the cool and hot air for the desired inside temperature. A sight glass is used with this system.

Two types of expansion valves are used with this system. The first type has a capillary tube, mounted in a well on the suction line. The second type has no capillary tube, but senses the need to meter refrigerant into the evaporator by an internal sensing tube. This type of expansion valve is called the "H" type.

"H" Valve System

As was described in the E.P.R. system, the "H" expansion valve can be used with the E.P.R. valve, located in the V-block, reciprocating crank type compressor, to control the amount of refrigerant metered into the evaporator and to control the temperature of the evaporator coils to prevent freeze-up of the condensed moisture. However, when the "H" valve is used with the three piston, axial compressor, a cycling switch is used to control the temperature of the evaporator to prevent freeze-up, rather than the E.P.R. valve, as used with the reciprocating crank type compressor. This can be called the "H" valve system for explanation purposes only and should be recognized as such. The "H" system uses the same components as the other systems, basically the compressor (axial type), condensor, evaporator, expansion valve without a capillary tube ("H" type), receiver-drier, muffler and a low pressure shut off valve. The cycling clutch switch uses a capillary tube, attached to the surface of the suction line, to sense the need for refrigerant movement and compressor operation, therefore causing the electrical clutch pulley and coil to operate the compressor on demand from the cycling switch and to open the circuit to the coil when the demand is not needed. A sight glass is used with this system.

CCOT System

The CCOT (cycling clutch orifice tube) system includes the compressor, condensor, evaporator, an accumulator-drier, a clutch cycling switch with a capillary tube, and a fixed orifice tube, mounted to the evaporator, replacing the expansion valve.

The clutch cycling switch with a temperature probing capillary tube, cycles the compressor clutch off and on as required to maintain a selected comfortable temperature within the vehicle, while preventing evaporator freeze-up. Full control of the system is maintained through the use of a selector control, mounted in the dash assembly. The selector control makes use of a vacuum supply and electrical switches to operate mode doors and the blower motor. A sight glass is not used in this system and one should not be installed. When charging the system, the correct quantity of refrigerant must be installed by measurement.

STV/BPO System

The STV/BPO (suction throttling valve/by-pass orifice) system uses either two types of external expansion valves or a mini combination valve assembly contains an expansion valve, suction throttling valve and a service port. The expansion valve is of the "H" block design and is used to regulate the flow of refrigerant into the evaporator core. It is also the dividing point for the high and low pressure within the system. The suction throttling valve is used to control the evaporator pressure and to prevent coil freeze-up. The suction throttling starts when the compressor suction pressure decreases below the valve setting. The compressor suction pressure can continue to drop, but the evaporator pressure is held steady by the controlling or throttling action

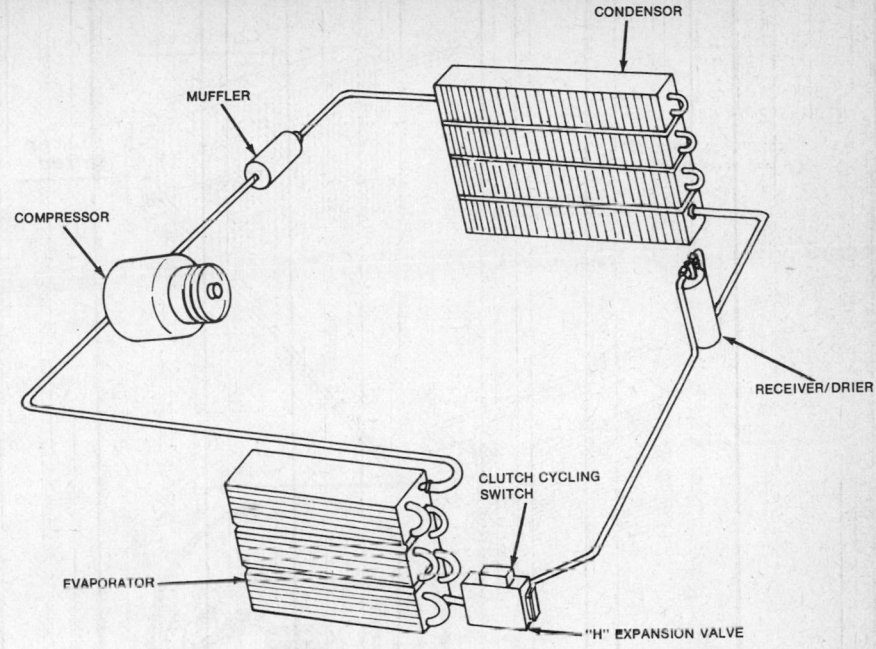

H type expansion valve system

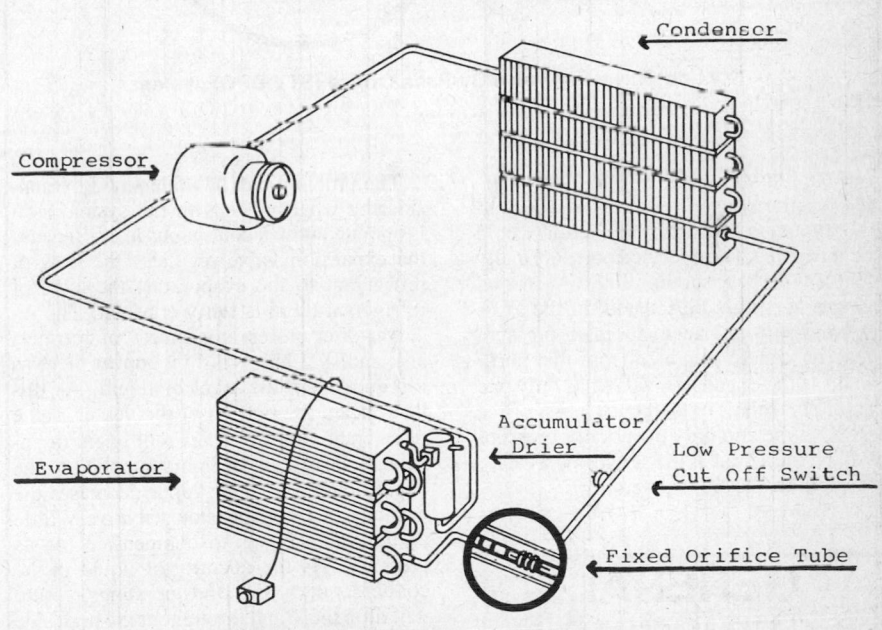

Cycling Clutch Orifice Tube (CCOT) system

of the STV. A pressure differential valve is used within the combination valve assembly, to allow oil-laden refrigerant to by-pass the restriction formed when the STV assembly is closed, to assure oil return to the compressor during times of reduced heat loads on the system. The by-pass valve remains closed under high heat loads since ample oil is moving through the system and compressor.

Evaporator pressure can only be measured on this system and a special type connector must be used to attach the high pressure gauge line to the service gauge port.

When either of the external type expansion valves are used, separate suction throttling valves are used. The operation of each is basically the same as the components of the combination valve assembly.

The type of external expansion valve used with the system will dictate either low suction or evaporator pressure measurements from the gauge service ports. To determine the pressure measurement that may be obtained from the system, examine the external expansion valve for one of the following conditions:

a. Should the expansion valve have

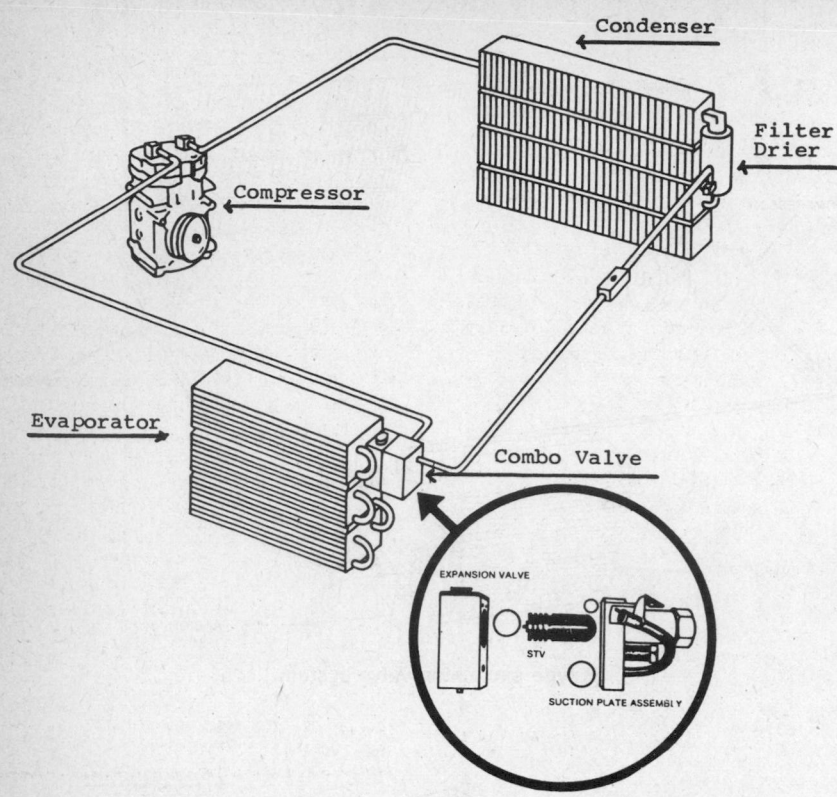

Suction Throttling Valve/By-Pass Orifice (STV/BPO) system

one capillary tube and one equalizer line, it is of the conventional external equalizer type and low pressure suction would be measured at the service port, normally located on the suction line. A second gauge port may be located on the POA valve body and an evaporator pressure reading can be obtained from this port.

b. If the expansion valve has only one capillary tube, it is the by-pass orfice (BPO) type and only evaporator pressure will be measured at the service port valve, located on the STV assembly.

GENERAL SERVICING PROCEDURES

The most important aspect of air conditioning service is the maintenance of a pure and adequate charge of refrigerant in the system. A refrigeration system cannot function properly if a significant percentage of the charge is lost. Leaks are common because the severe vibration encountered in an automobile can easily cause a sufficient cracking or loosening of the air conditioning fittings; as a result, the extreme operating pressures of the system force refrigerant out.

The problem can be understood by considering what happens to the system as it is operated with a continuous leak. Because the expansion valve regulates the flow of refrigerant to the evaporator, the level of refrigerant there is fairly constant. The receiver-drier stores any excess of refrigerant, and so a loss will first appear there as a reduction in the level of liquid. As this level nears the bottom of the vessel, some refrigerant vapor bubbles will begin to appear in the stream of liquid supplied to the expansion valve. This vapor decreases the capacity of the expansion valve very little as the valve opens to compensate for its presence. As the quantity of liquid in the condenser decreases, the operating pressure will drop there and throughout the high side of the system. As the R-12 continues to be expelled, the pressure available to force the liquid through the expansion valve will continue to decrease, and, eventually, the valve's orifice will prove to be too much of a restriction for adquate flow even with the needle fully withdrawn.

At this point, low side pressure will start to drop, and severe reduction in cooling capacity, marked by freeze-up of the evaporator coil, will result. Eventually, the operating pressure of the evaporator will be lower than the pressure of the atmosphere surrounding it, and air will be drawn into the system wherever there are leaks in the low side.

Because all atmospheric air contains at least some moisture, water will enter the system and mix with the R-12 and the oil. Trace amounts of moisture will cause sludging of the oil, and corrosion of the system. Saturation and clogging of the filter-drier, and freezing of the expansion valve orifice will eventually result. As air fills the system to a greater and greater extent, it will interfere more and more with the normal flows of refrigerant and heat.

From this description, it should be obvious that much of the repairman's time will be spent detecting leaks, repairing them, and then restoring the purity and quantity of the refrigerant charge. A list of general precautions that should be observed while doing this follows:

1. Keep all tools as clean and dry as possible.

2. Thoroughly purge the service gauges and hoses of air and moisture before connecting them to the system. Keep them capped when not in use.

3. Thoroughly clean any refrigerant fitting before disconnecting it in order to minimize the entrance of dirt into the system.

4. Plan any operation that requires opening the system beforehand, in order to minimize the length of time it will be exposed to open air. Cap or seal the open ends to minimize the entrance of foreign material.

5. When adding oil, pour it through an extremely clean and dry tube or funnel. Keep the oil capped whenever possible. Do not use oil that has not been kept tightly sealed.

6. Use only refrigerant 12. Purchase refrigerant intended for use in only automatic air conditioning systems. Avoid the use of refrigerant-12 that may be packaged for another use, such as cleaning, or powering a horn, as it is impure.

7. Completely evacuate any system that has been opened to replace a component, or that has leaked sufficiently to draw in moisture and air. This requires evacuating air and moisture with a good vacuum pump for at least one hour.

If a system has been open for a considerable length of time it may be advisable to evacuate the system for up to 12 hours (overnight).

8. Use a wrench on both halves of a fitting that is to be disconnected, so as to avoid placing torque on any of the refrigerant lines.

9. When overhauling a compressor, pour some of the oil into a clean glass and inspect it. If there is evidence of dirt or metal particles, or both, flush all refrigerant components with clean refrigerant before evacuating and recharging the system. In addition, if metal particles are present, the compressor should be replaced.

10. Schrader valves may leak only when under full operating pressure. Therefore, if leakage is suspected but cannot be located, operate the system with a full charge of refrigerant and look for leaks from all Schrader valves. Replace any faulty valves.

Additional Preventive Maintenance Checks

ANTIFREEZE

In order to prevent heater core freeze-up during A/C operation, it is necessary to maintain permanent type antifreeze protection of +15 degrees F. or lower. A reading of −15 degrees F. is ideal since this protection also supplies sufficient corrosion inhibitors for the protection of the engine cooling system.

NOTE: The same antifreeze should not be used longer than the manufacturer specifies.

RADIATOR CAP

For efficient operation of an air conditioned car's cooling system, the radiator cap should have a holding pressure which meets manufacturer's specifications. A cap which fails to hold these pressures should be replaced.

CONDENSER

Any obstruction of, or damage to, the condenser configuration will restrict the air flow which is essential to its efficient operation. It is therefore a good rule to keep this unit clean and in proper physical shape.

NOTE: Bug screens are regarded as obstructions.

CONDENSATION DRAIN TUBE

This single molded drain tube expels the condensation, which accumulates on the bottom of the evaporator housing, into the engine compartment.

If this tube is obstructed, the air conditioning performance can be restricted and condensation buildup can spill over onto the vehicle's floor.

Safety Precautions

Because of the importance of the necessary safety precautions that must be exercised when working with air conditioning systems and R-12 refrigerant, a recap of the safety precautions are outlined.

1. Avoid contact with a charged refrigeration system, even when working on another part of the air conditioning system or vehicle. If a heavy tool comes into contact with a section of copper tubing or a heat exchanger, it can easily cause the relatively soft material to rupture.

2. When it is necessary to apply force to a fitting which contains refrigerant, as when checking that all system couplings are securely tightened, use a wrench on both parts of the fitting involved, if possible. This will avoid putting torque on refrigerant tubing.

(It is advisable, when possible, to use tube or line wrenches when tightening these flare nut fittings

3. Do not attempt to discharge the system by merely loosening a fitting, or removing the service valve caps and cracking these valves. Precise control is possible only when using the service gauges. Place a rag under the open end of the center charging hose while discharging the system to catch any drops of liquid that might escape. Wear protective gloves when connecting or disconnecting service gauge hoses.

4. Discharge the system only in a well ventilated area, as high concentrations of the gas can exclude oxygen and act as an anesthetic. When leak testing or soldering, this is particularly important, as toxic gas is formed when R-12 contacts any flame.

5. Never start a system without first verifying that both service valves are back-seated, if equipped, and that all fittings throughout the system are snugly connected.

6. Avoid applying heat to any refrigerant line or storage vessel. Charging may be aided by using water heated to less than 125° to warm the refrigerant container. Never allow a refrigerant storage container to sit out in the sun, or near any other source of heat, such as a radiator.

7. Always wear goggles when working on a system to protect the eyes. If refrigerant contacts the eyes, it is advisable in all cases to see a physician as soon as possible.

8. Frostbite from liquid refrigerant should be treated by first gradually warming the area with cool water, and then gently applying petroleum jelly. *A physician should be consulted.*

9. Always keep refrigerant drum fittings capped when not in use. Avoid sudden shock to the drum, which might occur from dropping it, or from hanging a heavy tool against it. *Never carry a drum in the passenger compartment of a car.*

10. Always completely discharge the system before painting the vehicle (if the paint is to be baked on), or before welding anywhere near refrigerant lines.

AIR CONDITIONING TOOLS AND GAUGES

Test Gauges

Most of the service work performed on any air conditioning system requires the use of a set of two gauges, one for the high (head) pressure side of the system, the other for the low (suction) side.

The low side gauge records both pressure and vacuum. Vacuum readings are calibrated from 0–30 inches and the pressure graduations read from 0 to no less than 60 psi.

The high side guage measures pressure from 0 to at least 600 psi.

Both gauges are threaded into a manifold that contains two hand shut-off valves. Proper manipulation of these valves and the use of the attached-test hoses allow the user to perform the following services:

1. Test high and low side pressures.
2. Remove air, moisture, and contaminated refrigerant.
3. Purge the system of (refrigerant).
4. Charge the system (with refrigerant).

The manifold valves are designed so they have no direct effect on gauge readings, but serve only to provide for, or cut off, flow of refrigerant through the manifold. During all testing and hook-up operations, the valves are kept in a closed position to

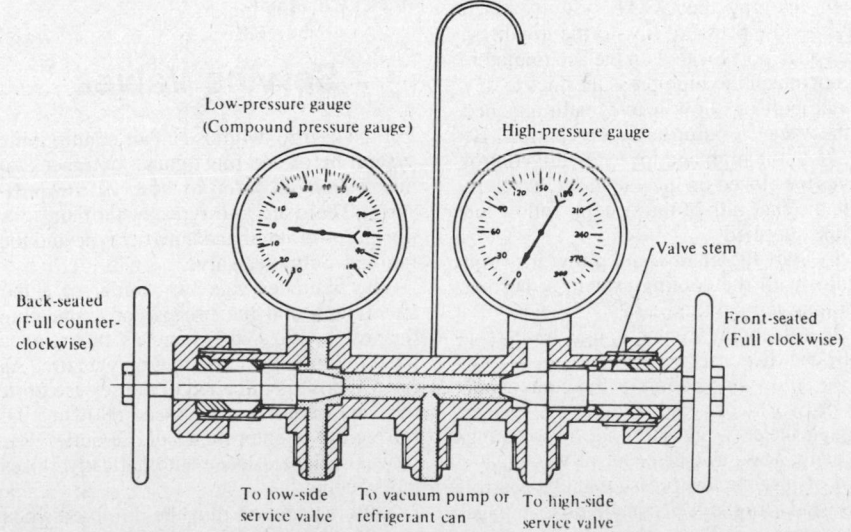

Typical manifold gauge set

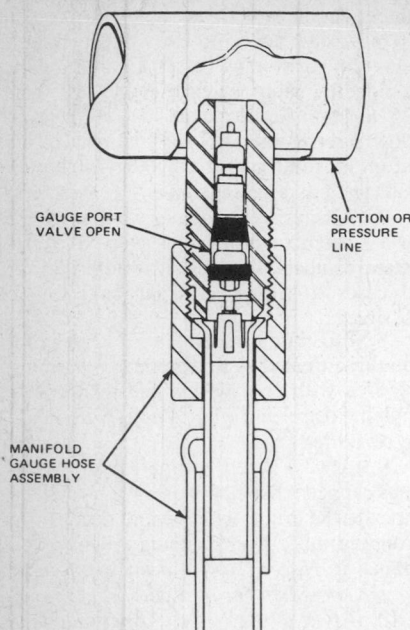

GAUGE PORT VALVE OPEN

SUCTION OR PRESSURE LINE

MANIFOLD GAUGE HOSE ASSEMBLY

Manifold gauge hose connected to a Schraeder type service port

avoid disturbing the refrigeration system. The valves are opened only to purge the system of refrigerant or to charge it.

When purging the system, the center hose is uncapped at the lower end, and both valves are cracked open slightly. This allows refrigerant pressure to force the entire contents of the system out through the center hose. During charging, the valve on the high side of the manifold is closed, and the valve on the low side is cracked open. Under these conditions, the low pressure in the evaporator will draw refrigerant from the relatively warm refrigerant storage container into the system.

SYSTEMS WITH A SIGHT GLASS

Air conditioning systems that use a sight glass as a means to check the refrigerant level should be carefully checked to avoid under or over charging. The gauge set should be attached to the system for verification of pressures.

To check the system with the sight glass, clean the glass and start the vehicle engine. Operate the air conditioning controls on maximum for approximately five minutes to stabilize the system. The room temperature should be above 70 degrees. Check the sight glass for one of the following conditions:

1. If the sight glass is clear, the compressor clutch is engaged, the compressor discharge line is warm and the compressor inlet line is cool, the system has a full charge of refrigerant.

2. If the sight glass is clear, the compressor clutch is engaged and there is no significant temperature difference between

the compressor inlet and discharge lines, the system is empty or nearly empty. By having the gauge set attached to the system, a measurement can be taken. If the gauge reads less than 25 psi, the low pressure cut-off protection switch has failed.

3. If the sight glass is clear and the compressor clutch is disengaged, the clutch is defective, or the clutch circuit is open, or the system is out of refrigerant. Bypass the low pressure cut-off switch momentarily to determine the cause.

4. If the sight glass shows foam or bubbles, the system can be low on refrigerant. Occasional foam or bubbles is normal when the room temperature is above 110 degrees or below 70 degrees. To verify, increase the engine speed to approximately 1500 rpm and block the airflow through the condensor in order to increase the compressor discharge pressure to 225–250 psi. If the sight glass still shows bubbles or foam, the refrigerant level is low.

— CAUTION —

Do not operate the vehicle engine any longer than necessary with the condensor airflow blocked. This blocking action also blocks the cooling system radiator and will cause the system to overheat rapidly.

When the system is low on refrigerant, a leak is present or the system was not properly charged. Use a leak detector and locate the problem area and repair. If no leakage is found, charge the system to its capacity.

— CAUTION —

It is not advisable to add refrigerant to a system utilizing the suction throttling valve and a sight glass, because the amount of refrigerant required to remove the foam or bubbles will result in an overcharge and potentially damage system components.

CCOT SYSTEM

When charging the CCOT system, attach only the low pressure line to the low pressure gauge port located on the accumulator. Do not attach the high pressure lines to any service port or allow it to remain attached to the vacuum pump after evacuation. Be sure both the high and low pressure control valves are closed on the gauge set. To complete the charging of the system, follow the outline supplied.

1. Start the engine and allow it to run at idle, with the cooling system at normal operating temperature.

2. Attach the center gauge hose to a multi-can dispenser.

3. Allow one pound or the contents of one or two 14 oz. cans to enter the system through the low pressure side by opening the gauge low pressure control valve.

4. Close the low pressure gauge control valve and turn the A/C system on to engage the compressor. Place the blower motor in its high mode.

5. Open the low pressure gauge control valve and draw the remaining charge into the system.

6. Close the low pressure gauge control valve and the refrigerant source valve on the multi-can dispenser. Remove the low pressure hose from the accumulator quickly to avoid loss of refrigerant through the Schrader valve.

7. Install the protective cap on the gauge port and check the system for leakage.

8. Test the system for proper operation.

Leak Testing the System

There are several methods of detecting leaks in an air conditioning system; among them, the two most popular are (1) halide leak-detection or the ''open flame method,'' and (2) electronic leak-detection.

The halide leak detection is a torch like device which produces a yellow-green color when refrigerant is introduced into the flame at the burner. A brilliant blue or violet color indicates the presence of large amounts of refrigerant at the burner. A small leak will cause the flame to turn a yellow-green color.

An electronic leak detector is a small portable electronic device with an extended probe. With the unit activated, the probe is passed along those components of the system which contain refrigerant. If a leak is detected, the unit will sound an alarm signal or activate a display signal depending on the manufacturer's design. It is advisable to follow the manufacturer's instructions as the design and function of the detection may vary significantly.

NOTE: Caution should be taken to operate either type of detector in well ventilated areas, so as to reduce the chance of personal injury, which may result from coming in contact with poisonous gases produced when R-12 is exposed to flame or electric spark.

Service Valves

For the user to diagnose an air conditioning system he or she must gain ''entrance'' to the system in order to observe the pressures. There are two types of terminals for this purpose, the hand shut off type and the familiar Schrader valve.

The Schrader valve is similar to a tire valve stem and the process of connecting the test hoses is the same as threading a hand pump outlet hose to a bicycle tire. As the test hose is threaded to the service port, the valve core is depressed, allowing the refrigerant to enter the test hose outlet. Removal of the test hose automatically closes the system.

Extreme caution must be observed when removing test hoses from the Schrader valves as some refrigerant will normally escape,

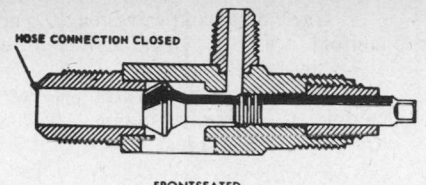

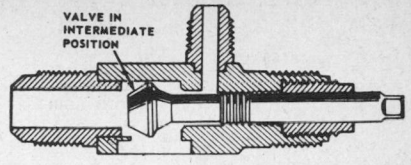

FRONTSEATED   BACKSEATED   MID-POSITION (CRACKED)

Manual service valve positions

usually under high pressure (observe safety precautions).

Some systems have hand shut-off valves (the stem can be rotated with a special racheting box wrench) that can be positioned in the following three ways:

1. FRONT SEATED—Rotated to full clockwise position.

a. Refrigerant will not flow to the compressor, but will reach the test gauge port. COMPRESSOR WILL BE DAMAGED IF SYSTEM IS TURNED ON IN THIS POSITION.

b. The compressor is now isolated and ready for service. However, care must be exercised when removing service valves from the compressor as a residue of refrigerant may still be present within the compressor. Therefore, remove service valves slowly, observing all safety precautions.

2. BACK SEATED—Rotated to full counterclockwise position. Normal position for system while in operation. Refrigerant flows to compressor but not to test gauge.

3. MID-POSITION (CRACKED)—Refrigerant flows to entire system. Gauge port (with hose connected) open for testing.

USING THE MANIFOLD GAUGES

The following are step-by-step procedures to guide the user to correct gauge usage.

1. WEAR GOGGLES OR FACE SHIELD DURING ALL TESTING OPERATIONS. BACKSEAT HAND SHUT-OFF TYPE SERVICE VALVES.

2. Remove caps from the high and low side of the service ports. Make sure both gauge valves are closed.

3. Connect the low side test hose to the service valve that leads to the evaporator (located between the evaporator outlet and the compressor).

4. Attach the high side test hose to the service valve that leads to the condenser.

5. Mid-position hand shutoff type service valves.

6. Start the engine and allow for warm-up. All testing and charging of the system should be done after the engine and system have reached normal operation temperatures (except when using certain charging stations).

7. Adjust the air conditioner controls to maximum cold.

8. Observe the gauge readings. When

BAR GAUGE MANIFOLD AND COMPRESSOR SERVICE VALVE SETTINGS

Condition	Manifold Valves	Compressor Valves
Testing System	Both fully closed	Both cracked off backseat
Depressurizing System	Both cracked open	Both at mid position
Evacuating the system	Both wide open	Both at mid position
Charging in gas form with compressor running	High pressure valve closed Low pressure valve cracked	High pressure valve cracked off backseat Low pressure valve at mid position
Charging in liquid form with compressor off	Low pressure valve closed High pressure valve wide open	Both valves mid positioned

Note: A very small leak, causing system discharge about every two weeks, can be caused by a leaky Schrader type service valve. Check these valves with extra care when testing for a small leak.

the gauges are not being used it is a good idea to:

a. Keep both hand valves in the closed position.

b. Attach both ends of the high and low service hoses to the manifold if extra outlets are present on the manifold, or plug them if not. Also, keep the center charging hose attached to an empty refrigerant can. This extra precaution will reduce the possibility of moisture entering the gauges. If air and moisture have gotten into the gauges, purge the hoses by supplying refrigerant under pressure to the center hose with both gauge valves open and all openings unplugged.

DISCHARGING, EVACUATING AND CHARGING

Discharging the System

——— CAUTION ———
Perform this operation in a well-ventilated area.

When it is necessary to remove (purge)

the refrigerant pressurized in the system, follow this procedure:

1. Operate the air conditioner for at least 10 minutes.

2. Attach the gauges, shut off the engine and air conditioner.

3. Place a container or rag at the outlet of the center charging hose on the gauge. The refrigerant will be discharged there and this precaution will avoid its uncontrolled exposure.

4. Open the low side hand valve on the gauge slightly.

5. Open the high side hand valve slightly.

NOTE: Too rapid a purging process will be identified by the appearance of an oil foam. If this occurs, close the hand valves a little more until this condition stops.

6. Close both hand valves on the gauge set when the pressures read 0 and all the refrigerant has left the system.

Evacuating the System

Before charging any system it is necessary to purge the refrigerant and draw out the trapped moisture with a suitable vacuum pump. Failure to do so will result in ineffective charging and possible damage to the system.

Use this hook-up for the proper evacuation procedure:

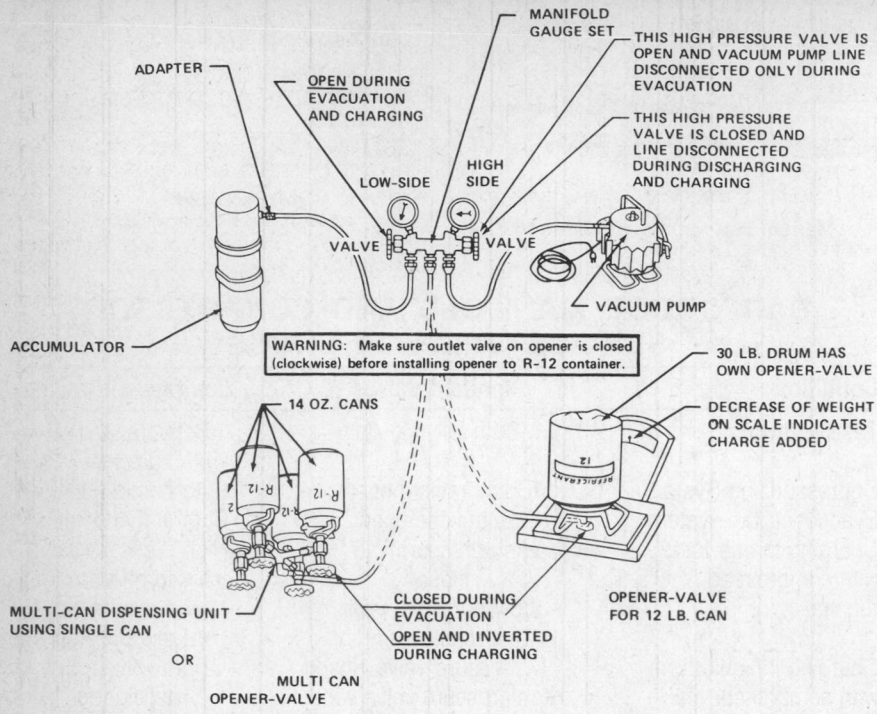

Typical gauge connections for discharge, evacuation and charging the system

1. Connect both service gauge hoses to the high and low service outlets.

2. Open both high and low side hand valves on the gauge manifold.

3. Open both service valves a slight amount (from back seated position), allow the refrigerant to discharge from the system.

4. Install the center charging hose of the gauge set to the vacuum pump.

5. Operate the vacuum pump for at least one hour (if the system has been subjected to open conditions for a prolonged period of time, it may be necessary to "pump the system down" overnight. Refer to the "System Sweep" procedure).

NOTE: If the low pressure gauge does not show at least 28" hg. within 5 minutes, check the system for a leak or loose gauge connectors.

6. Close both hand valves on the gauge manifold.

7. Shut off the pump.

8. Observe the low pressure gauge to determine if vacuum is holding. A vacuum drop may indicate a leak.

System Sweep

An efficient vacuum pump can remove all the air contained in a contaminated air conditioning system very quickly because of its vapor state. Moisture, however, is far more difficult to remove because the vacuum must force the liquid to evaporate before it will be able to remove it from the system. If a system has become severely contaminated, as, for example, it might become after all the charge was lost in conjunction with vehicle accident damage, moisture removal is extremely time consuming. A vacuum pump could remove all of the moisture only if it were operated for 12 hours or more.

Under these conditions, sweeping the system with refrigerant will speed the process of moisture removal considerably. To sweep, follow the following procedure:

1. Connect a vacuum pump to the gauges, operate it until vacuum ceases to increase, then continue operation for ten more minutes.

2. Charge the system with 50% of its rated refrigerant capacity.

3. Operate the system at fast idle for ten minutes.

4. Discharge the system.

5. Repeat twice the process of charging to 50% capacity, running the system for ten minutes, and discharging it, for a total of three sweeps.

6. Replace the drier.

7. Pump the system down as detailed in Step 1.

8. Charge the system.

Charging the System

―――――――― **CAUTION** ――――――――
Never attempt to charge the system by opening the high pressure gauge control while the compressor is operating. The compressor accumulating pressure can burst the refrigerant container, causing severe personal injuries.

BASIC SYSTEM

In this procedure the refrigerant enters the suction side of the system as a vapor while the compressor is running. Before proceeding, the system should be in a partial vacuum after adequate evacuation. Both hand valves on the gauge manifold should be closed.

1. Attach both test hoses to their respective service valve ports. Mid-position manually operated service valves, if present.

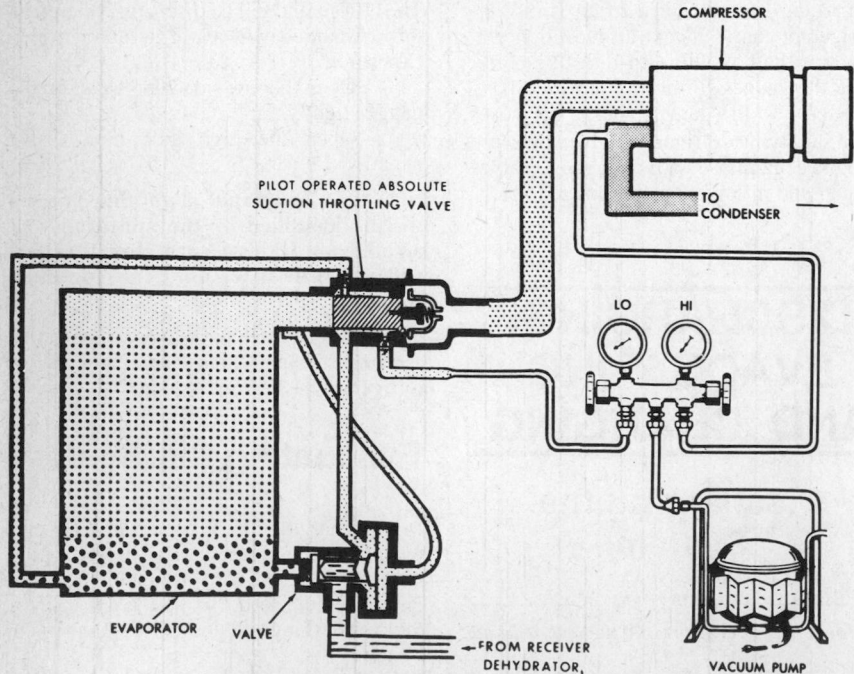

Schematic for evacuating the system

2. Install a dispensing valve (closed position) on the refrigerant container (single and multiple refrigerant manifolds are available to accommodate one to four 15 oz. cans).

3. Attach the center charging hose to the refrigerant container valve.

4. Open the dispensing valve on the refrigerant can.

5. Loosen the center charging hose coupler where it connects to the gauge manifold to allow the escaping refrigerant to purge the hose of contaminants.

6. Tighten the center charging hose connection.

7. Purge the low pressure test hose at the gauge manifold.

8. Start the engine, roll down the windows and adjust the air conditioner to maximum cooling. The engine should be at normal operating temperature before proceeding. The heated environment helps the liquid vaporize more efficiently.

9. Crack open the low side hand valve on the manifold. Manipulate the valve so that the refrigerant that enters the system does not cause the low side pressure to exceed 40 psi. Too sudden a surge may permit the entrance of unwanted liquid to the compressor. Since liquids cannot be compressed, the compressor will suffer damage if compelled to attempt it. If the suction side of the system remains in a vacuum, the system is blocked. Locate and correct the condition before proceeding any further.

NOTE: Placing the refrigerant can in a container of warm water (no hotter than 125° F) will speed the charging process. Slight agitation of the can is helpful too, but be careful not to turn the can upside down.

Some manufacturers allow for a partial charging of the A/C system in the form of a liquid (can inverted and compressor off) by opening the high side gauge valve only, and putting the high side compressor service valve in the middle position (if so equipped). The remainder of the refrigerant is then added in the form of a gas in the normal manner, through the suction side only.

SYSTEMS WITHOUT SIGHT GLASS, EXCEPT CCOT SYSTEM

The following procedure can be used to quickly determine whether or not an air conditioning system has the proper charge of refrigerant (providing ambient temperature is above 70° F. or 21° C.). This check can be made in a manner of minutes, thus facilitating system diagnosis by pinpointing the problem to the amount of charge in the system or by eliminating this possibility from the overall checkout.

1. Engine must be warm (thermostat open).

2. Hood and body doors open.

3. Selector lever set at NORM.
4. Temperature lever at COLD.
5. Blower on HI.
6. Normal engine idle.
7. Hand-feel the temperature of the evaporator inlet and outlet pipes with the compressor engaged.

a. Both same temperature or some degree cooler than ambient—proper condition: check for other problems.

b. Inlet pipe cooler than outlet pipe—low refrigerant charge.

● Add a slight amount of refrigerant until both pipes feel the same.

● Then add 15 oz. (1 can) additional refrigerant.

c. Inlet pipe has front accumulation—outlet pipe warmer: proceed as in Step b above.

If during the charging process the head pressure exceeds 200 psi, place an electric fan in front of the car and direct the turbulent air to the condenser. If no fan is available, repeatedly pour cool water over the top of the condenser. These cooling actions may be necessary on an extremely warm day to help dissipate the heat emitted by the engine during idle.

If this fails and pressure on the discharge side continues to rise, the system may be overcharged or the engine might be overheating. *Never* allow head pressure to go beyond 240 psi. during charging. If this condition occurs, stop the engine, find and correct the problem.

8. Continue dispensing refrigerant until the container is no longer cool to the touch. On a humid day, the outside of the container will frost. When the frost disappears the can is usually empty. To detach the dispensing can:

a. close the low pressure test gauge hand valve.

b. crack open the low pressure test hose at the manifold until the remaining pressure escapes.

c. tighten the hose coupler.

d. loosen the hose coupler connected to the refrigerant can.

e. discard the empty can and repeat Steps 2–8.

9. Continue to add refrigerant to the required capacity of the system. (Usually marked on the compressor).

CAUTION

DO NOT OVERCHARGE. This condition is usually indicated by an abnormally high side pressure reading and a noisy compressor resulting in ineffective cooling and damage to the system.

SYSTEMS WITH A SIGHT GLASS

Air conditioning systems that use a sight glass as a means to check the refrigerant level should be carefully checked to avoid under or over charging. The gauge set should be attached to the system for verification of pressures.

To check the system with the sight glass, clean the glass and start the vehicle engine. Operate the air conditioning controls on maximum for approximately five minutes

Amount of refrigerant \ Check item	Almost no refrigerant	Insufficient	Suitable	Too much refrigerant
Temperature of high pressure and low pressure lines.	Almost no difference between high pressure and low pressure side temperature.	High pressure side is warm and low pressure side is fairly cold.	High pressure side is hot and low pressure side is cold.	High pressure side is abnormally hot.
State in sight glass.	Bubbles flow continuously. **Bubbles will disappear and something like mist will flow when refrigerant is nearly gone.**	The bubbles are seen at intervals of 1 - 2 seconds.	Almost transparent. Bubbles may appear when engine speed is raised and lowered. **No clear difference exists between these two conditions.**	No bubbles can be seen.
Pressure of system.	High pressure side is abnormally low.	Both pressure on high and low pressure sides are slightly low.	Both pressures on high and low pressure sides are normal.	Both pressures on high and low pressure sides are abnormally high.
Repair.	**Stop compressor immediately and conduct an overall check.**	Check for gas leakage, repair as required, replenish and charge system.		Discharge refrigerant from service valve of low pressure side.

Using a sight glass to determine the relative refrigerant charge

to stabilize the system. The room temperature should be above 70 degrees. Check the sight glass for one of the following conditions:

1. If the sight glass is clear, the compressor clutch is engaged, the compressor discharge line is warm and the compressor inlet line is cool, the system has a full charge of refrigerant.

2. If the sight glass is clear, the compressor clutch is engaged and there is no significant temperature difference between the compressor inlet and discharge lines, the system is empty or nearly empty. By having the gauge set attached to the system, a measurement can be taken. If the gauge reads less than 25 psi, the low pressure cut-off protection switch has failed.

3. If the sight glass is clear and the compressor clutch is disengaged, the clutch is defective, or the clutch circuit is open, or the system is out of refrigerant. By-pass the low pressure cut-off switch momentarily to determine the cause.

4. If the sight glass shows foam or bubbles, the system can be low on refrigerant. Occasional foam or bubbles is normal when the room temperature is above 110 degrees or below 70 degrees. To verify, increase the engine speed to approximately 1500 rpm and block the airflow through the condenser in order to increase the compressor discharge pressure to 225–250 psi. If the sight glass still shows bubbles or foam, the refrigerant level is low.

— **CAUTION** —

Do not operate the vehicle engine any longer than necessary with the condenser airflow blocked. This blocking action also blocks the cooling system radiator and will cause the system to overheat rapidly.

When the system is low on refrigerant, a leak is present or the system was not properly charged. Use a leak detector and locate the problem area and repair. If no leakage is found, charge the system to its capacity.

— **CAUTION** —

It is not advisable to add refrigerant to a system utilizing the suction throttling valve and a sight glass, because the amount of refrigerant required to remove the foam or bubbles will result in an overcharge and potentially damaged system components.

CCOT SYSTEM

When charging the CCOT system, attach only the low pressure line to the low pressure gauge port located on the accumulator. Do not attach the high pressure line to any service port or allow it to remain attached to the vacuum pump after evacuation. Be sure both the high and the low pressure control valves are closed on the gauge set. To complete the charging of the system, follow the outline supplied.

1. Start the engine and allow it to run at idle, with the cooling system at normal operating temperature.

2. Attach the center gauge hose to a single or multi-can dispenser.

3. With the multi-can dispenser inverted, allow one pound or the contents of one or two 14 oz. cans to enter the system through the low pressure side by opening the gauge low pressure control valve.

4. Close the low pressure gauge control valve and turn the A/C system on to engage the compressor. Place the blower motor in its high mode.

5. Open the low pressure gauge control valve and draw the remaining charge into the system.

6. Close the low pressure gauge control valve and the refrigerant source valve, on the multi-can dispenser. Remove the low pressure hose from the accumulator quickly to avoid loss of refrigerant through the Schrader valve.

7. Install the protective cap on the gauge port and check the system for leakage.

8. Test the system for proper operation.

Leak Testing the System

There are several methods of detecting leaks in an air conditioning system; among them, the two most popular are (1) halide leak-detection or the ''open flame method,'' and (2) electronic leak-detection.

The halide leak detection is a torch like device which produces a yellow-green color when refrigerant is introduced into the flame at the burner. A purple or violet color indicates the presence of large amounts of refrigerant at the burner.

An electronic leak detector is a small portable electronic device with an extended probe. With the unit activated, the probe is passed along those components of the system which contain refrigerant. If a leak is detected, the unit will sound an alarm signal or activate a display signal depending on the manufacturer's design. It is advisable to follow the manufacturer's instructions as the design and function of the detection may vary significantly.

— **CAUTION** —

Caution should be taken to operate either type of detector in well ventilated areas, so as to reduce the chance of personal injury, which may result from coming in contact with poisonous gases produced when R-12 is exposed to flame or electric spark.

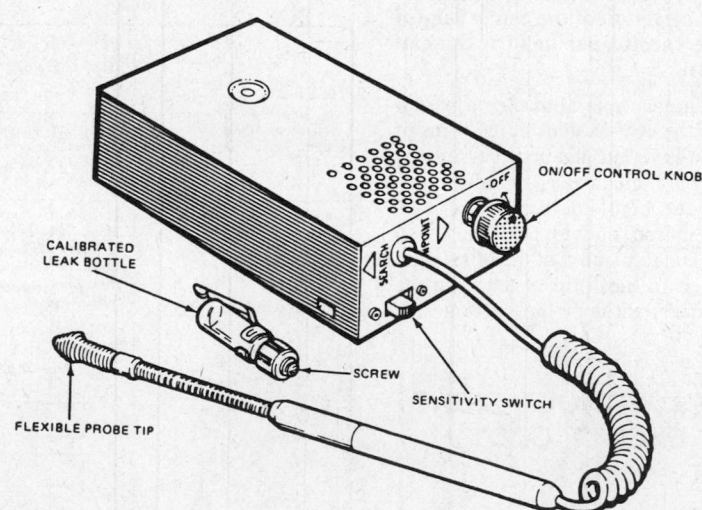

Electronic leak detector

Diesel Service

NOTE: Most procedures associated with diesel engined cars are similar to gas engined cars, although many parts of the diesel engine are unique compared to their gas engine counterparts. Standard maintenance and service procedures are given here while component removal, installation and adjustment procedures unique to diesel engines can be found in the appropriate section.

HOW THE DIESEL ENGINE WORKS

Four-stroke diesels require four piston strokes for the complete cycle of actions, exactly like a gasoline engine. The difference lies in how the fuel mixture is ignited. A diesel engine does not rely on a conventional spark ignition to ignite the fuel mixture for the power stroke. Instead, a diesel relies on the heat produced by compressing air in the combustion chamber to ignite the fuel and produce a power stroke. This is known as a compression-ignition engine. No fuel enters the cylinder on the intake stroke, only air. At the end of the compression stroke, fuel is sprayed into the precombustion chamber (prechamber). The mixture ignites and spreads out into the main combustion chamber, forcing the piston downward (power stroke). The fuel/air mixture ignites because of the very high combustion chamber temperatures generated by the extraordinarily high compression ratios used in diesel engines. Typically, the compression ratios used in automotive diesels run anywhere from 16:1 to 23:1. A typical spark-ignition engine has a ratio of about 8:1. This is why a spark-ignition engine which continues to run after you have shut off the engine is said to be "dieseling". It is running on combustion chamber heat alone.

Designing an engine to ignite on its own combustion chamber heat poses certain problems. For instance, although a diesel engine has no need for a coil, spark plugs, or a distributor, it does need what are known as "glow plugs". These superficially resemble spark plugs, but are only used to warm the combustion chambers when the engine is cold. Without these plugs, cold starting would be impossible, due to the enormously high compression ratios and the characteristics of the diesel fuel itself.

All diesel engines use fuel injection, be-

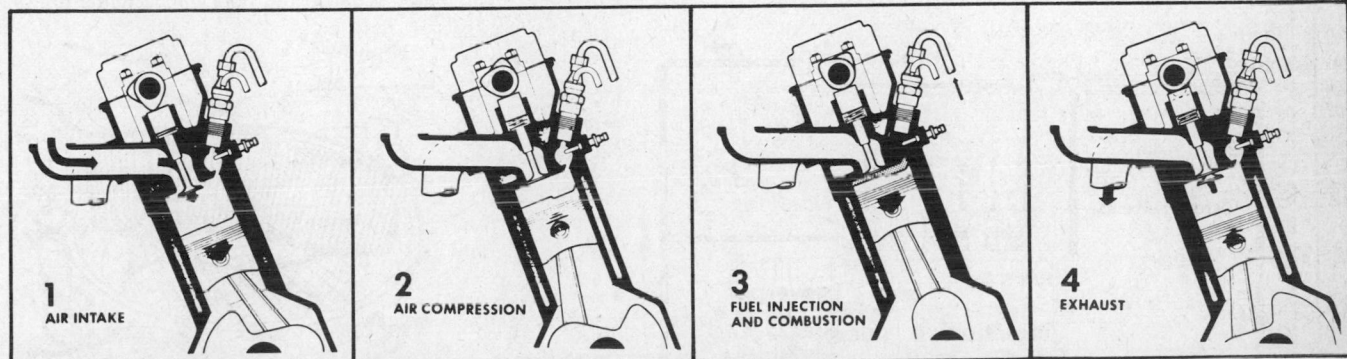

4-stroke diesel engine cycle. At *air intake* (1), rotation of the crankshaft drives a toothed belt that turns the camshaft, opening the intake valve. As the piston moves down, a vacuum is created, sucking fresh air into the cylinder, past the open intake valve. *Air compression* (2): As the piston moves up, both valves are closed, and the air is compressed about 23 times smaller than its original volume. The compressed air reaches a temperature of about 1,650°F., far above the temperature needed to ignite diesel fuel. *Fuel injection and compression* (3): As the piston reaches the top of the stroke, the air temperature is at its maximum. A fine mist of fuel is sprayed into the prechamber, where it ignites, and the flame front spreads rapidly into the combustion chamber. The piston is forced downward by the pressure (about 500 psi) of expanding gases. *Exhaust* (4): As the energy of combustion is spent and the piston begins to move upward again, the exhaust valve opens, and burnt gases are forced out past the open valve. As the piston starts down, the exhaust valve closes, the intake valve opens, and the air intake stroke begins again.

Increasingly, modern diesel engines are being equipped with turbochargers, exhaust gas–driven devices that force more air into the engine to increase power output

Maintenance and Service Procedures

Maintenance procedures for the diesel engine generally fall into three categories:
1. Fuel system
2. Starting system
3. Engine mechanical systems

Of these, the fuel system is usually the most likely source of engine troubles, and should be high on the list for regular maintenance attention.

FUEL SYSTEM

The typical diesel engine fuel system consists of fuel tank, fuel feed and return lines, mechanical fuel injection pump, fuel injectors and lines, and a large capacity fuel filter. On some models, the engine may also be equipped with a small, low pressure fuel pump which feeds the injection pump.

In addition to these, the air intake system (air cleaner, inlet manifold) should be checked over regularly to insure unrestricted air flow into the cylinders.

In operation, fuel is sucked out of the fuel tank by the injection pump (or its feed pump) and fed by the injection pump to the injectors in the cylinder head at a very high pressure. Before the fuel is allowed to enter the main injection pump, it passes through a specially built fuel filter which traps solid particles (and water on some models) in the fuel. Fuel that is not used is pumped back to the fuel tank through the fuel return lines. This recirculated fuel helps cool the injection pump.

Air Cleaner

On a gasoline engine, the volume of air taken in by the engine is controlled by throttle valves. When the throttle valves are closed (engine idling), air intake is restricted. When the throttle valves are wide open (accelerator pedal to the floor), the engine draws

cause unlike spark-ignited engines, the fuel cannot be drawn through the intake tract

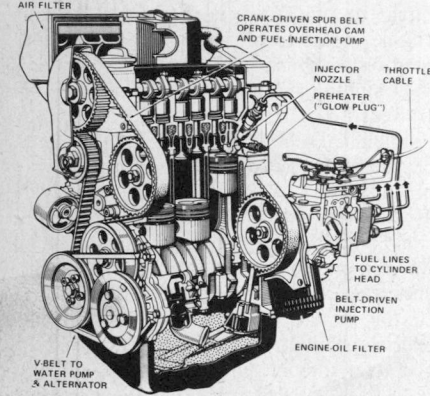

Cutaway view of typical 4-cylinder diesel engine.

and into the cylinders. The introduction of fuel into a diesel engine must be precisely timed so that each cylinder "fires" at the proper moment. Also, the fuel injection pressure (at the cylinder) must be great enough to overcome the high compression pressures, and properly atomize the fuel without the aid of a moving air mass (as in a carbureted gas engine). It is not uncommon for diesel engine fuel injection pressures to be set at 1500–1700 psi.

Diesel engines share many of their basic mechanical components with gasoline engines, though the cylinder block, head(s), crankshaft, connecting rods, pistons, etc., are manufactured to be much stronger for use in diesel engines. The additional strength of the components is necessary due to the very high cylinder pressure generated within the diesel engine.

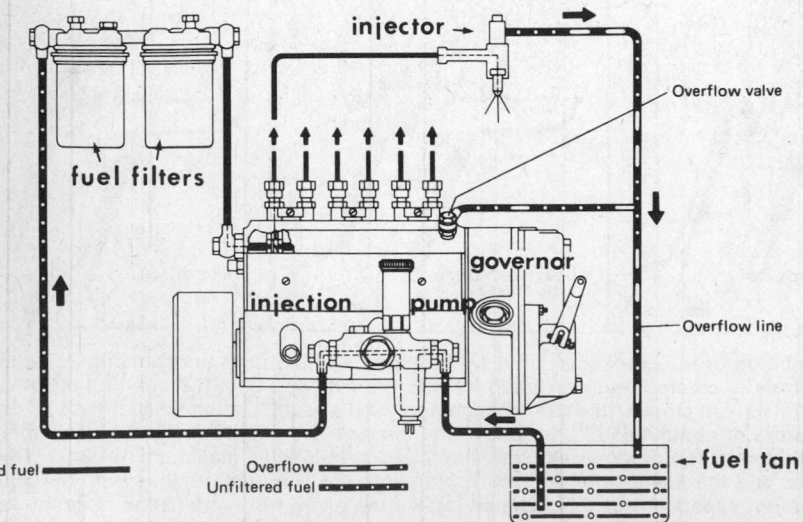

Typical diesel engine fuel system schematic

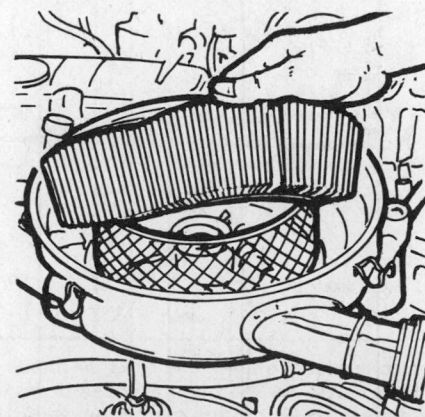

Because a greater quantity of air passes through the diesel engine, air filter maintenance is particularly important. Most diesel air filters on passenger cars are similar to their counterparts on gasoline engines.

in the maximum amount of air it possibly can. This applies to both carbureted and fuel injected gasoline engines.

The speed (rpm) of a diesel engine is controlled by the quantity of fuel which is injected into the engine; no air metering restrictions (throttle valves) are used. Because of this, diesel engines ingest as much air as they possibly can under all conditions. A much greater volume of air passes through the air cleaner of a diesel per mile, therefore, diesel air filters must either be larger or the filter replacement intervals more frequent than those of a similarly sized gasoline engine.

One word of caution: never remove the air cleaner on a diesel with the engine running, and never run the engine with the air cleaner removed. The volume of air drawn through the inlet manifold is very great, and, because the inlet manifold is unobstructed, anything drawn into the inlet manifold (air cleaner wing nut, etc.) goes straight to the combustion chambers, where it can cause major engine damage.

Fuel Filter

The diesel engine fuel filter is usually larger than the filter used on gasoline engines. The extra capacity is needed to trap the suspended particles in diesel fuel, which is generally "dirtier" than gasoline.

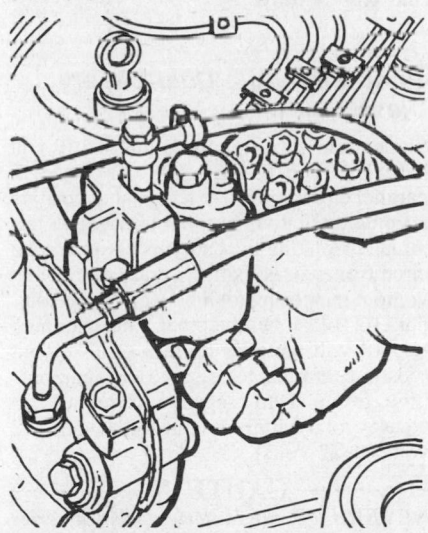

Many diesel engines use a spin-on type primary fuel filter.

On some engines, the fuel filter looks like a second engine oil filter, and is removed and installed in the same manner as the canister-type oil filter.

The fuel filter must be changed according to the manufacturer's suggested interval. See the owner's manual for information.

After installing the fuel filter start the engine and check for leaks. Run the engine for about two minutes, then stop the engine for the same amount of time to allow any air trapped in the injection system to bleed off.

Many diesels also have a small, in-tank filter which is usually maintenance-free.

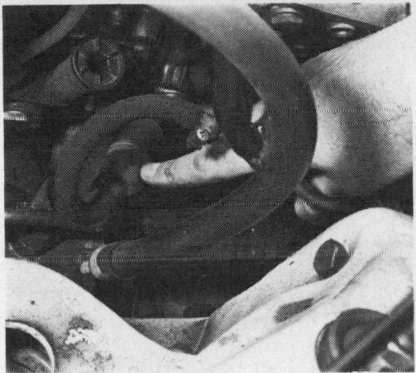

A smaller, in-line secondary filter is used on many engines.

Check the tightness of the clamps securing the injector lines. Note that the injector lines are all the same length.

manual engine stop

Mercedes-Benz diesel engines use this stop switch, which shuts off fuel delivery

Water In Fuel

Diesel fuel is a hydrophilic fluid, that is, it naturally attracts water. Since diesel fuel and water do not mix, the water remains floating beneath the fuel at the bottom of the tank. This water must be removed every now and then, or it will be sucked into the fuel circuit and pass through the injection system, causing corrosion and possible component failure (injection pumps can cost up to $1,000). Water in the fuel system will also cause the engine to run poorly, if at all.

Most diesel fuel tanks are equipped with

a separator which can isolate from 1 to 3 gallons of water from the fuel.

Many diesels are also equipped with "Water in Fuel" lights in the dashboard which warn of the presence of water in the fuel tank. These warning systems can be installed on models not so equipped.

On some diesels, there is a water catcher in the bottom of the fuel filter which can easily be bled off. In addition, there are several bolt-on water filters on the market which attach to the fuel line under the hood and separate water from the fuel. Depending on which kind you buy, draining water from the system is simply a matter of opening the petcock at the bottom of the filter and letting the water drain out, or, if money is no object, a separator is available on which water is drained from the filter simply by activating a switch on the dashboard.

Removing Water from the Fuel Tank

Treat diesel fuel with the same respect you would gasoline, and after the procedure, properly dispose of the fuel.

1. Remove the fuel tank cap.
2. Connect a pump or siphon hose to the ¼ in. fuel return hose (smaller of the two fuel hoses) above the rear axle, or under the hood near the fuel pump (on the passenger's side of the engine, near the front).
3. Siphon until all water is removed from the tank. Do not use your mouth to create siphon vacuum, EVER! The best method is to siphon the water into a large capacity see-through container. The water will collect at the bottom of the container.
4. When all water has been removed from the tank, be sure to reinstall the fuel return hose and fuel cap.

NOTE: If the entire fuel system (not just the tank) is contaminated by water, the vehicle must be stopped immediately and the fuel system must be purged. This includes draining and removing the fuel tank, blowing low pressure compressed air backwards through the fuel feed and return lines, and bleeding the water out of all injection components. This job should be referred to a qualified technician.

Cold Weather Fuel System Maintenance

——— CAUTION ———
NEVER use "starting aids" (e.g.—ether) to help start a diesel engine—serious engine damage will result.

As will be explained later under "Fuel Recommendations", diesel fuel tends to become "cloudy", or thicker, as the temperature drops. The thicker the diesel fuel becomes, the slower it flows through the fuel system, until finally it stops flowing altogether somewhere near the bottom of the thermometer.

One way to fight sluggish fuel flow is to use winterized blends of diesel fuel, straight No. 1 diesel fuel or add cold weather additives to the fuel to improve flow in cold weather.

NOTE: Consult your owners manual for recommendations and be sure to use a fuel conditioner compatible with water separators.

Another way is to install an aftermarket fuel system pre-heater. These are generally canisters which connect into the fuel line and use coolant from the engine cooling system to heat the fuel before it reaches the injection pump. The one drawback with this system is the engine must be started before the pre-heater begins to work. Also available are electric fuel warmers. These preheat the fuel going into the filter and can be used in conjunction with the coolant-type fuel heater.

Cold weather additives and fuel conditioners can help improve cold weather flow of diesel fuel.

Some manufacturers offer an optional electric diesel fuel heater and engine block heaters. The fuel heater is thermostatically controlled to heat the fuel before it enters the fuel filter when fuel temperature is 20°F or lower. The fuel heater works only when the ignition key is in the RUN position. On these models, the fuel tank filter has a bypass valve which allows fuel to flow to the heater when the tank filter is covered with fuel wax. The engine block heater is equipped with an electrical cord wrapped up in the engine compartment. The cord

Some diesel engines come equipped with a built-in heating system to keep the engine warm in cold temperatures.

Most OEM heaters work from 110-volt house current.

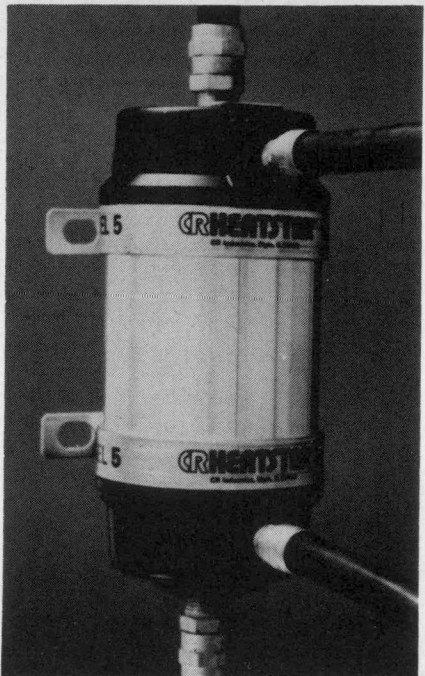

Some aftermarket diesel fuel warmers are thermostatically controlled heat exchangers that use engine coolant to keep diesel fuel above its "cloud point," the temperature at which it gels and forms wax that can clog a fuel system.

plugs into regular 110 volt household current. The block heater can be used, according to the type of oil in the crankcase, up to eight hours or overnight to warm up the block.

STARTING SYSTEM

The diesel starting system includes one (sometimes two) heavy duty batteries, the starter, and the glow plug circuit. In addition to the heavy duty battery(ies), the majority of diesel engines also have starters and battery cables designed specifically as heavy duty items for diesel usage only. Because of the high compression of any diesel, the torque required to turn the engine is much greater than a gasoline engine. The starter must be powerful enough to handle the increased load; the battery cables must be thick enough to withstand the heat generated by the starter load.

For battery maintenance, see the regular "Maintenance" section. Jump starting procedures for a dual battery car are given below. Starter maintenance is included in the appropriate car section.

The glow plug circuit is used on the diesel to initially start the engine. When the ignition switch is turned to the ON position, a light will come on in the instrument panel signalling that the glow plugs are preheating the combustion chambers. After a certain interval (depending on how cold the engine is), the light will go off. This signals that the starter may be engaged and the engine started. If the glow plug circuit mal-functions, especially in cold weather, the engine will be almost impossible to start.

CAUTION

NEVER use "starting aids" (e.g.—ether) to help start a diesel engine—serious engine damage will result.

Glow Plug Testing

To test each individual glow plug, disconnect the busbar and/or wire connector from the glow plug and connect a test light between the glow plug terminal and the positive battery terminal. If the test light lights, the glow plug is working. Replace individual glow plugs which do not work.

NOTE: Some diesel engines are equipped with either "slow glow" or "fast glow" glow plugs. Do not attempt to interchange any parts of these two glow plug systems.

To test the glow plug circuit, connect a test light to the terminal of one of the glow plugs (glow plug wiring still attached) and turn the ignition to the heating position. The test light should light for a short while. If not, the glow plug circuit is malfunctioning and must be diagnosed and repaired.

NOTE: Perform this operation on a cold engine only.

Jump-Starting a Dual Battery Diesel

Some diesels are equipped with two 12 volt batteries. The batteries are connected in parallel circuit (positive terminal to positive terminal, negative terminal to negative terminal). Hooking the batteries up in parallel circuit increases battery cranking power without increasing total battery voltage output (12 volts). On the other hand, hooking two 12 volt batteries up in a series circuit (positive terminal to negative terminal, positive terminal to negative terminal) increases total battery output to 24 volts (12 volts + 12 volts).

CAUTION

NEVER hook the batteries up in a series circuit; SEVERE electrical system damage will result.

In the event that a dual battery diesel must be jumped started, use the following procedure.

1. Open the hood and locate the batteries.

2. Position the donor car so that the jumper cables will reach from its battery (must be 12 volt, negative ground) to the appropriate battery in the diesel. Do not allow the cars to touch.

3. Shut off all electrical equipment on both vehicles. Turn off the engine of the donor car, set the parking brakes on both vehicles and block the wheels. Also, make sure both vehicles are in Neutral (manual

transmission models) or Park (automatic transmission models).

4. Using the jumper cables, connect the positive (+) terminal of the donor car battery to the positive terminal of one (not both) of the diesel batteries.

5. Using the second jumper cable, connect the negative (−) terminal of the donor battery to a solid, stationary, metallic point on the diesel (alternator bracket, engine block, etc.). Be very careful to keep the jumper cables away from moving parts (cooling fan, alternator belt, etc.) on both vehicles.

6. Start the engine of the donor car and run it at moderate speed.

7. Start the engine of the diesel.

8. When the diesel starts, disconnect the battery cables in the reverse order of attachment.

ENGINE MECHANICAL SYSTEMS

Included are engine lubrication and engine compression.

Although diesel engines are very low in carbon monoxide (CO) and hydrocarbon (HC) emissions, "particulate" emission output is very high from diesel engines. This is evident from the black smoke emitted by diesels, which is most noticeable during hard acceleration or high engine loads. The particulates are made up of mostly soot (carbon) and sulpher particles. The majority of these particulates are released into the atmosphere. However, some of the particulate matter, because it is produced within the engines cylinders, is left inside the engine and gradually contaminates the engine oil. This contamination makes the oil corrosive, due to the sulpher, and abrasive, due to the carbon. Serious engine damage will result if these contaminants continue to accumulate in the oil. Engine oil and filters of diesel engines must be changed more frequently than those of gasoline engines, due to the increased rate at which the contaminants form in the diesel. Consult the "Maintenance" section for oil and filter change procedures. The manufacturer's recommended oil change interval will be given in the owner's manual. An explanation of diesel engine oils is given at the end of this section.

As explained earlier, very high cylinder compression is the key to the operation of the diesel engine. The normal compression of most gasoline engines will rarely exceed 180 psi; whereas with diesel engines, compression pressures of 350–400 psi are commonplace.

— CAUTION —

DO NOT attempt to check the compression of a diesel engine with a standard compression gauge—personal injury could result. A special, high pressure compression gauge is needed to safely check the compression of any diesel.

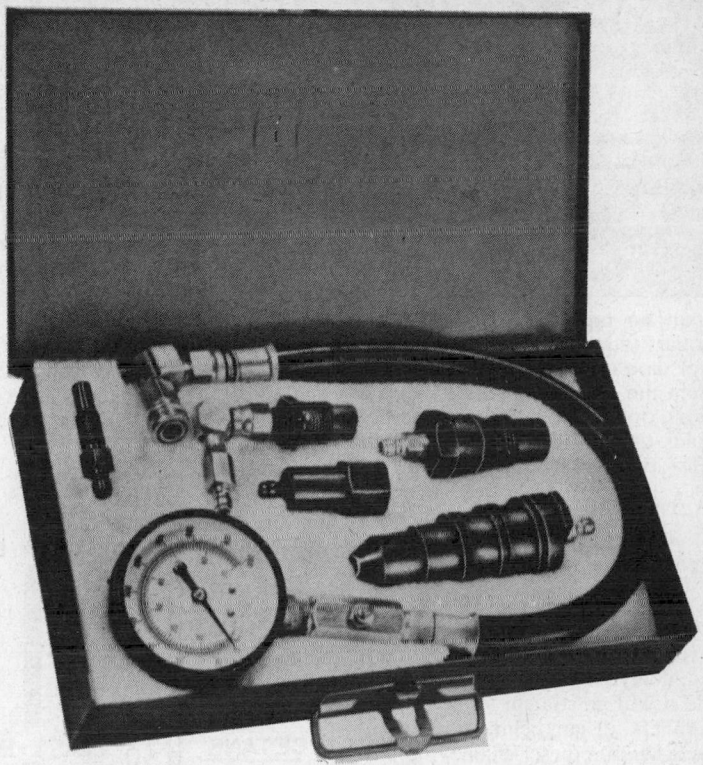

A diesel compression tester kit with adaptors (Courtesy S & G Tools).

Compression Test

1. Remove the air cleaner.

2. Disconnect the wire from the fuel shutoff solenoid terminal of the injection pump.

3. Disconnect the wires from the glow plugs and remove all glow plugs.

4. Screw compression gauge into the glow plug hole in the cylinder being checked.

5. Crank the engine, allowing six "puffs" for each cylinder.

The lowest reading cylinder should not be less than 70% of the highest, and no cylinder should be less than 275 pounds.

Idle Speed Adjustments

Idle speed adjustment procedures for individual diesel engines are given in the car section. Consult the following section for procedures to measure idle speed

Connecting a Tachometer to a Diesel Engine

As mentioned earlier, the diesel engine does not require an electrical ignition system. Because of this, problems arise when attempts are made to connect a tachometer to the engine for the purpose of idle adjustments, etc. The average gasoline engine tachometer senses the ignition spark pulses and converts them into a readable engine rpm signal. This type of tachometer is use-

less on the diesel engine, because of the diesel's compression ignition system.

There are several magnetic and photoelectric tachometers available from various tool manufacturers which were designed specifically for use with the diesel engine. These units can run into a little more money than the average do-it-yourselfer may be willing to spend, in which case any adjustments requiring the monitoring of engine rpm should be performed by a competent service technician.

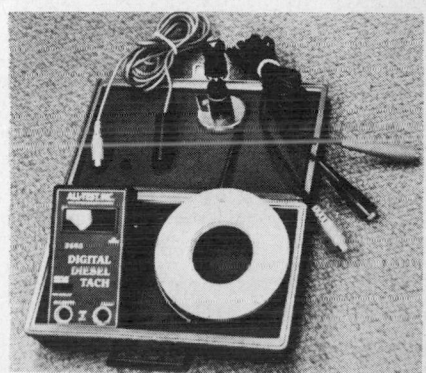

The newest equipment for measuring idle speed on a diesel engine includes (clockwise from lower left) a digital diesel tach display, photomagnetic pick-up with display input, magnetic swivel base (holder), DC power source for the display unit and a roll of magnetic tape.

The magnetic tape is attached to any moving part (such as the balancer). The pieces of tape must be at least 6 inches apart. Aim the photomagnetic pick-up at the moving object and adjust the position of the pick-up until the "on-target" light is lit. Flip the switch to TACH and read the rpm.

Diesel Engine Precautions

- Never run the engine with the air cleaner removed: if anything is sucked into the inlet manifold it will go straight to the combustion chambers, or jam behind a valve.
- Never wash a diesel engine: the reaction of a warm fuel injection pump to cold (or even warm) water can ruin the pump.
- Never operate a diesel engine with one or more fuel injectors removed unless fully familiar with injector testing procedures: some diesel injection pumps spray fuel at up to 1400 psi—enough pressure to allow the fuel to penetrate your skin.
- Do not skip engine oil and filter changes.
- Strictly follow the manufacturer's oil and fuel recommendations as given in the owner's manual.
- Do not use home heating oil as fuel for your diesel.
- Do not use "starting aids" (e.g.—ether) in the automotive diesel engine, as these "aids" can cause severe internal engine damage.
- Do not run a diesel engine with the "Water in Fuel" warning light on in the dashboard.
- If removing water from the fuel tank yourself, use the same caution you would use when working around gasoline engine fuel components.
- Do not allow diesel fuel to come in contact with rubber hoses or components on the engine, as it can damage them.

Fuel and Oil Recommendations

FUEL

Fuel makers produce two grades of diesel fuel, No. 1 and No. 2, for use in automotive diesel engines. Generally speaking, No. 2 fuel is recommended over No. 1 for driving in temperatures above 20°F. In fact, in many areas, No. 2 diesel is the only fuel available. By comparison, No. 2 diesel fuel is less volatile than No. 1 fuel, and gives better fuel economy. No. 2 fuel is also a better injection pump lubricant.

Two important characteristics of diesel fuel are its cetane number and its viscosity.

The cetane number of a diesel fuel refers to the ease with which a diesel fuel ignites. High cetane numbers mean that the fuel will ignite with relative ease or that it ignites well at low temperatures. Naturally, the lower the cetane number, the higher the temperature must be to ignite the fuel. Most commercial fuels have cetane numbers that range from 35 to 65. No. 1 diesel fuel generally has a higher cetane rating than No. 2 fuel.

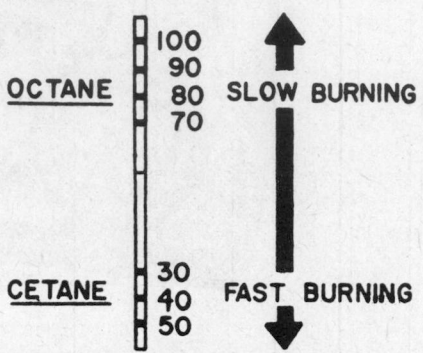

Cetane (diesel engine) versus octane (gasoline engine) ratings. The higher the cetane number, the faster the fuel burns

Viscosity is the ability of a liquid, in this case diesel fuel, to flow. Using straight No. 2 diesel fuel below 20°F can cause problems, because this fuel tends to become cloudy, meaning wax crystals begin forming in the fuel. In extreme cold weather, No. 2 fuel can stop flowing altogether. In either case, fuel flow is restricted, which can result in a "no start" condition or poor engine performance. Fuel manufacturers often "winterize" No. 2 diesel fuel by using various fuel additives and blends (No. 1 diesel fuel, kerosene, etc.) to lower its winter-time viscosity. Generally speaking, though, No. 1 diesel fuel is more satisfactory in extremely cold weather.

NOTE: No. 1 and No. 2 diesel fuels will mix and burn with no ill effects, although the engine manufacturer will undoubtedly recommend one or the other. Consult the owner's manual for information.

Depending on local climate, most fuel manufacturers make winterized No. 2 fuel available seasonally.

Many automobile manufacturers publish pamphlets giving the locations of diesel fuel stations nationwide. Contact the local dealer for information.

Do not substitute home heating oil for automotive diesel fuel. While in some cases, home heating oil refinement levels equal those of diesel fuel, many times they are far below diesel engine requirements. The result of using "dirty" home heating oil will be a clogged fuel system, in which case the entire system may have to be dismantled and cleaned.

One more word on diesel fuels. Don't thin diesel fuel with gasoline in cold weather. The lighter gasoline, which is more explosive, will cause rough running at the very least, and may cause extensive engine damage if enough is used.

OIL

Diesel engines require different engine oil from those used in gasoline engines. Besides doing the things gasoline engine oil does, diesel oil must also deal with increased engine heat and the diesel blow-by gases, which create sulphuric acid, a high corrosive.

Under the American Petroleum Institute (API) classifications, gasoline engine oil codes begin with an "S", and diesel engine oil codes begin with a "C". This first letter designation is followed by a second letter code which explains what type of service (heavy, moderate, light) the oil is meant for. For example, the top of a typical oil can will include: "API SERVICES SC, SD, SE, CA, CB, CC". This means the oil in the can is a good, moderate duty engine oil when used in a diesel engine.

It should be noted here that the further

COMPARISON OF #1 AND #2 DIESEL FUEL

Requirement	1-D	2-D
Flash Point, °F minimum	100	125
Cetane Number, minimum	40	40
Viscosity at 100°F, Centistokes		
Minimum	1.4	2.0
Maximum	2.5	4.3
Water and Sediment, % by volume maximum	Trace	0.05
Sulfur, % by weight maximum	0.5	0.5
Ash, % by weight maximum	0.01	0.01

Flash Point: The temperature at which diesel fuel ignites when exposed to a flame in the open air.
Cetane Number: See text

down the alphabet the second letter of the API classification is, the greater the oil's protective qualities are (CD is the severest duty diesel engine oil, CA is the lightest duty oil, etc.). The same is true for gasoline engine oil classifications (SF is the severest duty gasoline engine oil, SA is the lightest duty oil, etc.).

Many diesel manufacturers recommend an oil with both gasoline and diesel engine API classifications. Consult the owner's manual for specifications.

The top of the oil can will also contain an SAE (Society of Automotive Engineers) designation, which gives the oil's viscosity. A typical designation will be: SAE 10W-30, which means the oil is a "winter" viscosity oil, meaning it will flow and give protection at low temperatures.

On the diesel engine, oil viscosity is critical, because the diesel is much harder to start (due to its higher compression) than a gasoline engine. Obviously, if you fill the crankcase with a very heavy oil during winter (SAE 20W-50, for example), the starter is going to require a lot of current from the battery to turn the engine. And, since batteries don't function well in cold weather in the first place, you may find yourself stranded some morning. Consult the owner's manual for recommended oil specifications for the climate you live in.

LUBE OIL ANALYSIS

From an oil sample a laboratory can diagnose many potential engine problems—from piston wear to impending bearing failure. What's more, the laboratory can spot them quicker, and with greater accuracy. Just as easily, the lab can give the diesel a clean bill of health, saving the car owner unnecessary servicing and other routine preventive maintenance, costly in time and money.

There's nothing new about engine lube oil analysis. Thousands of the nation's trucks and buses regularly have their engine's lube oil analyzed by laboratories specializing in this type of work. What is new is the availability of lube oil analysis to individual vehicle owners rather than, as before, almost exclusively to companies operating fleets of diesel equipment.

Lube oil analysis can be a valuable indicator of internal engine condition.

Here's how lube oil analysis works. You write one of the several laboratories that offer individual diesel vehicle owners lube analysis service. By return mail you'll receive an oil sampling kit. It will probably contain a two-ounce plastic oil sampling container with a screw-on plastic top. Instructions tell you how to take the sample. Usually, a lab-bound sample of diesel lube oil may be taken in any of three ways, but always right after the engine has been shut off, so that the sampled oil is as close as possible to normal engine operating temperature. That's important to assure that the lab's test will be accurate. Oil samples can be taken during normal oil changes, when lube oil is drained anyway. Between oil changes, a sample can be drawn from the engine through the dipstick tube (where you normally check the oil's level). In drawing an oil sample from the dipstick tube, a small suction bulb fitted with a length of disposable tubing is used. The tubing is merely inserted into the dipstick tube, the suction bulb depressed, and the oil sample drawn. The third method of sampling is by loosening the drain plug on the engine's by-pass oil filter (if your diesel has one). A little oil is caught in the lube sampling container. In all cases, extreme cleanliness is a must, so as not to contaminate the sample with dirt, grease, or other substances not actually found inside the engine. For example, using a rag that contains solvents, metal filings, or other impurities can contaminate the oil sample, leading to false and even alarming lab reports. A bit of technique is required: In taking a sample of lube oil during a routine oil drain, about half of the crankcase's lube oil should be allowed to drain out before the sample is taken. The sample taken, the date, make and model of the engine, its mileage, mileage since last oil change, and sometimes oil type are noted on the container's label, and the container is mailed to the laboratory.

Shortly, you'll receive the lab's report, which, based on a number of tests, including spectrochemical analysis (using a spectrometer, which can detect the presence of virtually all basic elements and contaminants), tells what's in the oil in what quantities and analyzes both the probable source of what was found and whether it indicates trouble. For one example, the finding of more than trace amounts of copper in an oil sample may strongly point to excessive bearing wear in a particular diesel whose bearings contain copper. Some analyses report on as many as eighteen basic elements that may be found in a diesel's lube oil sample, and in the report's "recommendation" may pinpoint their probable source—as, "indicates piston ring wear." Also indicated is the presence of such contaminants as water, solids (the products of oxidation and engine blow-by), and fuel dilution. Noted, too, is the lubricity of the sample—whether, or not, in the lab's opinion, it is still doing its internal engine lubricating job.

NOTE: Never use lube analysis and a lab's report of "good oil" to extend, beyond the manufacturer's recommendation, the mileage period between oil changes. Follow the manufacturers recommendations.

The more frequently an engine is lube-sampled, the more accurate and meaningful the lab's reports. Infrequent samplings, although they can spot sudden, unusual changes in internal engine condition, may fail to show the gradual deterioration of engine parts. Ideally, you should have the laboratory analyze a lube sample every other oil change. For most automobile diesels, that's every 6,000 miles. Analysis costs from $7 to $11 per sample. Drive an average 18,000 miles a year and you'd change your diesel's oil three times. In that time, you'd submit three samples to the lab at an annual lube analysis cost of $21 to $33.

Aftermarket Fuel System Accessories

Due to reasons described previously, most diesel engine problems can be attributed to either fuel contamination or cold weather fuel performance characteristics. Diesel-engined vehicle manufacturers have designed and installed various systems to combat these problems, but ultimately, their best efforts are limited by cost.

Inconvenience is a major concern to diesel owners. If water accumulates (in substantial quantities) in the diesel fuel system, the fuel and water must be siphoned from the fuel tank and purged from the remainder of the fuel system. It goes without saying that this operation is a messy, time-consuming process. Even if the vehicle is equipped with a water/fuel separator having a drain valve, the owner must manually open the valve from either under the hood or beneath the vehicle.

Although the fuel filter installed by the manufacturer offers adequate performance when maintained properly, the addition of another, separate diesel fuel filter is a wise improvement.

If you live in an extremely cold climate, you've probably experienced cold starting problems due to fuel "waxing", plugged filters, "gelled" fuel, etc. If your vehicle is not factory-equipped with the optional fuel line or cylinder block heaters, these

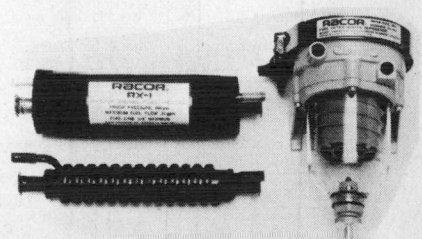

Aftermarket fuel filter/water separator and fuel line heater

heaters can be purchased from the after-market (retail auto parts manufacturers). The installation of either of these items can improve cold-starting dramatically.

WATER/FUEL SEPARATORS

Centrifugal Action

Sometimes referred to as a "cyclonic" water/fuel separator, this device uses baffles which spin the fuel as it comes through the separator inlet. Since water is heavier than diesel fuel, the water will spin away from the fuel, sink to the bottom of the separator, and collect in the sediment bowl.

This type of separator is most efficient in dealing with large water droplets. If the water is in emulsion with the fuel, that is, if the water is equally dispersed through the fuel in very small droplets, some of the water will remain with the fuel to travel through the fuel system.

Coalescing Action

In this type of separator, the fuel must pass through a coalescent filtering media before proceeding through the fuel system. The idea behind the coalescent media is to trap even the smallest droplets of water on the media. As the small droplets combine into larger, heavier droplets, gravity acts on the droplets to pull them downward, off of the media and into the sediment bowl.

FUEL FILTER/SEPARATOR COMBINATION UNITS

Most separators of either the centrifugal or coalescent types are available with disposeable fuel filtering elements which are built into the separator unit. If your car already has a large, disposeable filter, it would probably be more cost-effective to stay with a separator only, and to change the factory-equipped filter at the recommended intervals. Should your vehicle have a fairly small filter, and/or an inconveniently located water drain (or none at all), choose the filter/separator combination. The filter/separator offers both increased fuel filtering ability and efficient water separation.

Convenience Add-Ons

Available with many separators and filter/separators are items such as dash-mounted water-in-fuel indicator lamps, audible water-in-fuel alarms, and dash-controlled water ejection systems. A properly chosen system would warn you of water in the fuel, and allow you to eject the water by simply "flipping" a dash-mounted switch.

Installing a Separator

Clear installation instructions and the necessary installation parts will be provided with the separator kit. Follow those instructions exactly. A general list of suggestions follows:

1. Fuel additives should not be used unless approved by the separator manufacturer.

2. Do not install a separator within 4" of any exhaust system component.

3. If plastic fittings are supplied with the kit, do not replace them with metal fittings. Also, use extreme caution when tightening the fittings, especially those made of plastic.

4. Use a fuel-proof sealer on all fitting threads, only if the threads are not factory-coated with sealer.

5. Use only fuel-proof hoses for the installation.

6. Do not eliminate the original equipment fuel filter, even if a filter/separator is installed.

7. For new car warranty purposes, a filter/separator should be located BEFORE the original equipment filter. The fuel must pass through the original filter last, before entering the fuel injection pump.

8. If any type of fuel line heater is installed, it is best to position the heater between the fuel tank and the separator inlet.

9. To ease the job of the separator, the separator should be installed between the fuel transfer pump and the tank (unless the separator manufacturer specifies otherwise). Fuel and water which have been churned through the fuel transfer pump will be more difficult to separate.

10. Be sure that any wiring (for warning lamps, water ejection, etc.) is routed and connected properly. If the wiring must pass through a drilled hole, be sure to use a rubber grommet between the drilled component(s) and the wire to prevent damage to the wire.

FUEL LINE HEATERS

Two popular types of fuel line heaters are available for diesel passenger cars. Both types raise the temperature of the fuel to prevent "waxing" and "gelling" of the fuel in the lines during cold weather operation. One type uses engine coolant as a heating source. In order for this type to heat the fuel, the engine must first be started and allowed to run until the coolant temperature increases. Though this type of heater will usually increase fuel mileage, it offers no aid in starting ability.

The other type of heater uses a 12V DC electric heating element. This type is recommended, due to its ability to warm the fuel BEFORE the engine is started. This type of heater will also usually increase the overall fuel mileage.

Installation

Follow the manufacturer's instructions exactly. Also, see suggestions 5, 8, and 9 under "Separator Installation".

CYLINDER BLOCK HEATERS

A cylinder block heater electrically (usually 110V house current) heats the engine coolant, which in turn warms the cylinder block, heads, and engine oil. In this case, the warmth is not used to alter the characteristics of the fuel. Block heaters offer two main advantages when starting a diesel in cold weather:

1. The reduced viscosity (thinning) of the engine oil from the warmth allows the engine to be "turned over" easier (and faster) by the starter. Less strain is imposed on the starting system.

2. Because the diesel relies on the heat of compression to ignite the fuel, the increase in the base combustion chamber temperature results in a higher tempeature during compression. This allows the fuel to ignite easier than if just the glow plugs were used.

Installation

Most cylinder block heaters replace one of the existing freeze (or expansion) plugs of the cylinder block. Follow the manufacturers installation instructions exactly. Also, refer to the manufacturers recommendations for usage.

Carburetor Service

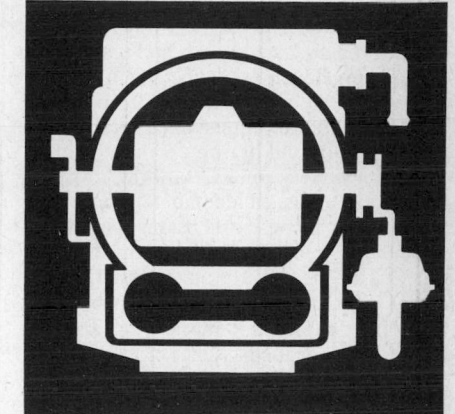

Functions

Gasoline is the source of fuel for power in the automobile engine and the carburetor is the mechanism which automatically mixes liquid fuel with air in the correct proportions to provide the desired power output from the engine. The carburetor performs this function by metering, atomizing, and mixing fuel with air flowing through the engine.

A carburetor also regulates the volume of air-to-fuel mixture which enters the engine. It is the carburetor's regulation of the mixture flow which gives the operator control of the engine speed.

METERING

The automotive internal combustion engine operates efficiently within a relatively small range of air-to-fuel ratios. It is the function of the carburetor to meter the fuel in exact proportions to the air flowing into the engine, so that the optimum ratio of air-to-fuel is maintained under all operating conditions. Regulations governing exhaust gas emissions have made the proper metering of fuel by the carburetor an increasingly important factor. Too rich a mixture will result in poor fuel economy and increased emissions, while too lean a mixture will result in loss of power and generally poor performance.

Carburetors are matched to engines so that metering can be accomplished by using carefully calibrated metering jets which allow fuel to enter the engine at a rate proportional to the engine's ability to draw air.

ATOMIZATION

The liquid fuel must be broken up into small particles so that it will more readily mix with air and vaporize. The more contact the fuel has with the air, the better the vapor-ization. Atomization can be accomplished in two ways: air may be drawn into a stream of fuel which will cause a turbulence and break the solid stream of fuel into smaller particles; or a nozzle can be positioned at the point of highest air velocity in the carburetor and the fuel will be torn into a fine spray as it enters the air stream.

DISTRIBUTION

The carburetor is the primary device involved in the distribution of fuel to the engine. The more efficiently fuel and air are combined in the carburetor, the smoother the flow of vaporized mixture through the intake manifold to each combustion chamber. Hence, the importance of the carburetor in fuel distribution.

Principles

VACUUM

All carburetors operate on the basic principle of pressure difference. Any pressure less than atmospheric pressure is considered vacuum or a low pressure area. In the engine, as the piston moves down on the intake stroke with the intake valve open, a partial vacuum is created in the intake manifold. The farther the piston travels downward, the greater the vacuum created in the manifold. As vacuum increases in the manifold, a difference in pressure occurs between the carburetor and cylinder. The carburetor is positioned in such a way that the high pressure above it, and the vacuum or low pressure beneath it, causes air to be drawn through it. Fuel and air always move from high to low pressure areas.

VENTURI PRINCIPLE

To obtain greater pressure drop at the tip of the fuel nozzle so that fuel will flow, the principle of increasing the air velocity to create a low pressure area is used. The device used to increase the velocity of the air flowing through the carburetor is called a venturi. A venturi is a specially designed restriction placed on the air flow. In order for the air to pass through the restriction, it must accelerate, causing a pressure drop or vacuum as it passes.

Circuits

FLOAT CIRCUIT

The float circuit includes the float, float bowl, and a needle valve and seat. This circuit controls the amount of gas allowed to flow into the carburetor.

As the fuel level rises, it causes the float to rise which pushes the needle valve into its seat. As soon as the valve and seat make contact, the flow of gas is cut off from the fuel inlet. When the level of fuel drops, the float sinks and releases the needle valve from its seat which allows the gas to flow in. In actual operation, the fuel is maintained at practically a constant level. The float tends to hold the needle valve partly closed so that the incoming fuel just balances the fuel being withdrawn.

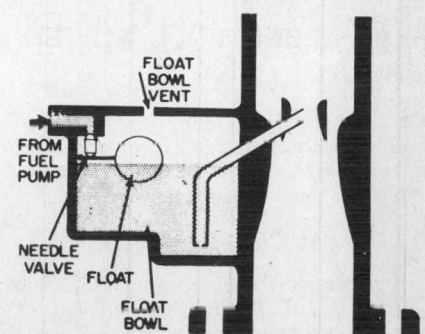

Typical float circuit

IDLE AND LOW SPEED CIRCUIT

When the throttle is closed or only slightly opened, the air speed is low and practically no vacuum develops in the venturi. This means that the fuel nozzle will not feed. Thus, the carburetor must have another circuit to supply fuel during operation with a closed or slightly opened throttle.

This circuit is called the idle and low speed circuit. It consists of passages in which air and gas can flow beneath the throttle plate. With the throttle plate closed, there is high vacuum from the intake manifold. Atmospheric pressure pushes the air/fuel mixture through the passages of the idle and low speed circuit and past the tapered point of the idle adjustment screw, which regulates engine idle mixture volume.

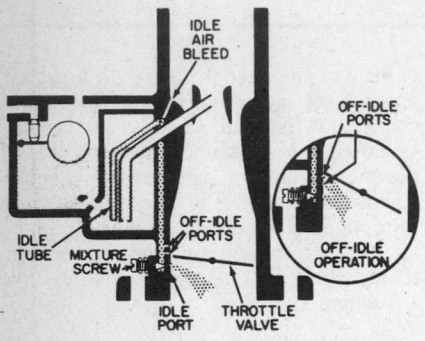

Typical idle and low speed circuit

HIGH SPEED PARTIAL LOAD CIRCUIT

When the throttle plate is opened sufficiently, there is little difference in vacuum between the upper and lower part of the air horn. Thus, little air/fuel mixture will discharge from the low speed and idle circuit. However, under this condition enough air is moving through the air horn to produce vacuum in the venturi to cause the main nozzle or high speed nozzle to discharge fuel. The circuit from the float bowl to the main nozzle is called the high speed partial load circuit. A nearly constant air/fuel ratio is maintained by this circuit from part to full-throttle.

HIGH SPEED FULL POWER CIRCUIT

For high-speed, full-power, wide open throttle operation, the air/fuel mixture must be enriched; this is done either mechanically or by intake manifold vacuum.

Full Power Circuit (Mechanical)

This circuit includes a metering rod jet and a metering rod. The rod has two steps of different diameters and is attached to the throttle linkage.

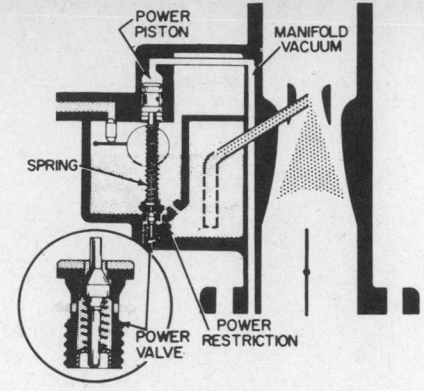

Typical power circuit

When the throttle is wide open, the metering rod is lifted, bringing the smaller diameter of the rod into the jet. When the throttle is partly closed, the larger diameter of the metering rod is in the jet. This restricts fuel flow to the main nozzle but adequate amounts of fuel do flow for part-throttle operation.

Full Power Circuit (Vacuum)

This circuit is operated by intake manifold vacuum. It includes a vacuum diaphragm or piston linked to a valve.

When the throttle is opened so that intake manifold vacuum is reduced, the spring raises the diaphragm or piston. This allows more fuel to flow in, either by lifting a metering rod or by opening a power valve.

ACCELERATOR PUMP CIRCUIT

For acceleration, the carburetor must deliver additional fuel. A sudden inrush of air is caused by rapid acceleration or applying full throttle.

When the throttle is opened, the pump lever pushes the plunger down and this forces fuel to flow through the accelerator pump circuit and out the pump jet. This fuel enters the air passage through the carburetor to supply additional fuel demands.

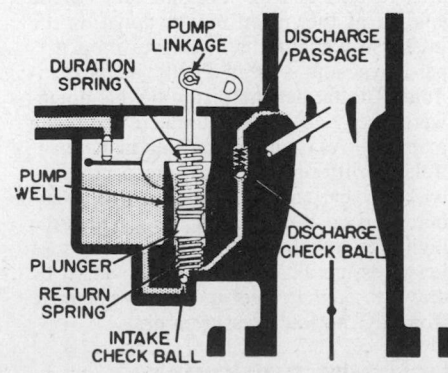

Typical accelerator pump circuit

CHOKE

When starting an engine, it is necessary to increase the amount of fuel delivered to the intake manifold. This increase is controlled by the choke.

The choke consists of a valve in the top of the air horn controlled mechanically by an automatic device. When the choke valve is closed, only a small amount of air can get past it. When the engine is cranked, a fairly high vacuum develops in the air horn. This vacuum causes the main nozzle to discharge a heavy stream of fuel. The quantity delivered is sufficient to produce the correct air/fuel mixture needed for starting the engine. The choke is released either manually or by heat from the engine.

OVERHAUL

Generally, when a carburetor requires major service, a rebuilt one is purchased on an exchange basis, or a kit may be bought for overhauling the carburetor.

The kit contains the necessary parts and some form of instructions for carburetor rebuilding. The instructions may vary between a simple exploded view and detailed step-by-step rebuilding instructions. Unless you are familiar with carburetor overhaul, the latter should be used.

There are some general overhaul procedures which should always be observed:

Efficient carburetion depends greatly on careful cleaning and inspection during overhaul since dirt, gum, water, or varnish in or on the carburetor parts are often responsible for poor performance.

Overhaul your carburetor in a clean, dust-free area. Carefully disassemble the carburetor, referring often to the exploded views. Keep all similar and lookalike parts segregated during disassembly and cleaning to avoid accidental interchange during assembly. Make a note of all jet sizes.

When the carburetor is disassembled, wash all parts except diaphragms, electric choke units, pump plunger, and any other plastic, leather, fiber, or rubber parts in clean carburetor solvent. Do not leave parts in the solvent any longer than is necessary to sufficiently loosen the deposits. Excessive cleaning may remove the special finish from the float bowl and choke valve bodies, leaving these parts unfit for service. Rinse all parts in clean solvent and blow them dry with compressed air or allow them to air dry. Wipe clean all cork, plastic, leather, and fiber parts with a clean, lint-free cloth.

Blow out all passages and jets with compressed air and be sure that there are no restrictions or blockages. Never use wire or similar tools to clean jets, fuel passages, or air bleeds. Clean all jets and valves separately to avoid accidental interchange.

Check all parts for wear or damage. If wear or damage is found, replace the defective parts. Especially check the following:

1. Check the float needle and seat for wear. If wear is found, replace the complete assembly.

2. Check the float hinge pin for wear and the float(s) for dents or distortion. Replace the float if fuel has leaked into it.

3. Check the throttle and choke shaft bores for wear or an out-of-round condition. Damage or wear to the throttle arm, shaft, or shaft bore will often require replacement of the throttle body. These parts require a close tolerance of fit; wear may allow air leakage, which could affect starting and idling.

NOTE: Throttle shafts and bushings are not included in overhaul kits. They can be purchased separately.

4. Inspect the idle mixture adjusting needles for burrs or grooves. Any such condition requires replacement of the needle, since you will not be able to obtain a satisfactory idle.

5. Test the accelerator pump check valves. They should pass air one way but not the other. Test for proper seating by blowing and sucking on the valve. Replace the valve if necessary. If the valve is satisfactory, wash the valve again to remove breath moisture.

6. Check the bowl cover for warped surfaces with a straightedge.

7. Closely inspect the valves and seats for wear and damage, replacing as necessary.

8. After the carburetor is assembled, check the choke valve for freedom of operation.

Carburetor overhaul kits are recommended for each overhaul. These kits contain all gaskets and new parts to replace those that deteriorate most rapidly. Failure to replace all parts supplied with the kit (especially gaskets) can result in poor performance later.

Some carburetor manufacturers supply overhaul kits of three basic types: minor repair; major repair; and gasket kits. Basically, they contain the following:

Minor Repair Kits:
All gaskets
Float needle valve
Volume control screw
All diaphragms
Spring for the pump diaphragm
Major Repair Kits:
All jets and gaskets
All diaphragms
Float needle valve
Volume control screw
Pump ball valve
Main jet carrier
Float
Complete intermediate rod
Intermediate pump lever
Complete injector tube
Some cover hold-down screws and washers
Gasket Kits:
All gaskets

After cleaning and checking all components, reassemble the carburetor, using new parts and referring to the exploded view. When reassembling, make sure that all screws and jets are tight in their seats, but do not overtighten, as the tips will be distorted. Tighten all screws gradually, in rotation. Do not tighten needle valves into their seats; uneven jetting will result. Always use new gaskets. Be sure to adjust the float level when reassembling.

Stromberg Carburetors Only

The preceding information applies to Stromberg carburetors also, but the following, additional suggestions should be followed.

1. Soak the small cork gaskets (jet gland washers) in penetrating oil or hot water for at least a half hour prior to assembly, or they will invariably split.

2. When the jet is fully assembled, the jet tube should be a close fit without any lateral play, but it should be free to move smoothly. A few drops of oil, or polishing of the tube may be necessary to achieve this.

3. If the jet sealing ring washer is made of cork, soak it in hot water for a minute or two prior to installation.

4. Adjust the float height.

5. Center the jet so that the piston will fall freely (when raised) and seat with a distinct click. If the jet is not centered properly, it will hang up in the tube.

TROUBLESHOOTING

NOTE: Carburetor problems cannot be isolated effectively unless all other engine systems are functioning correctly and the engine is properly tuned.

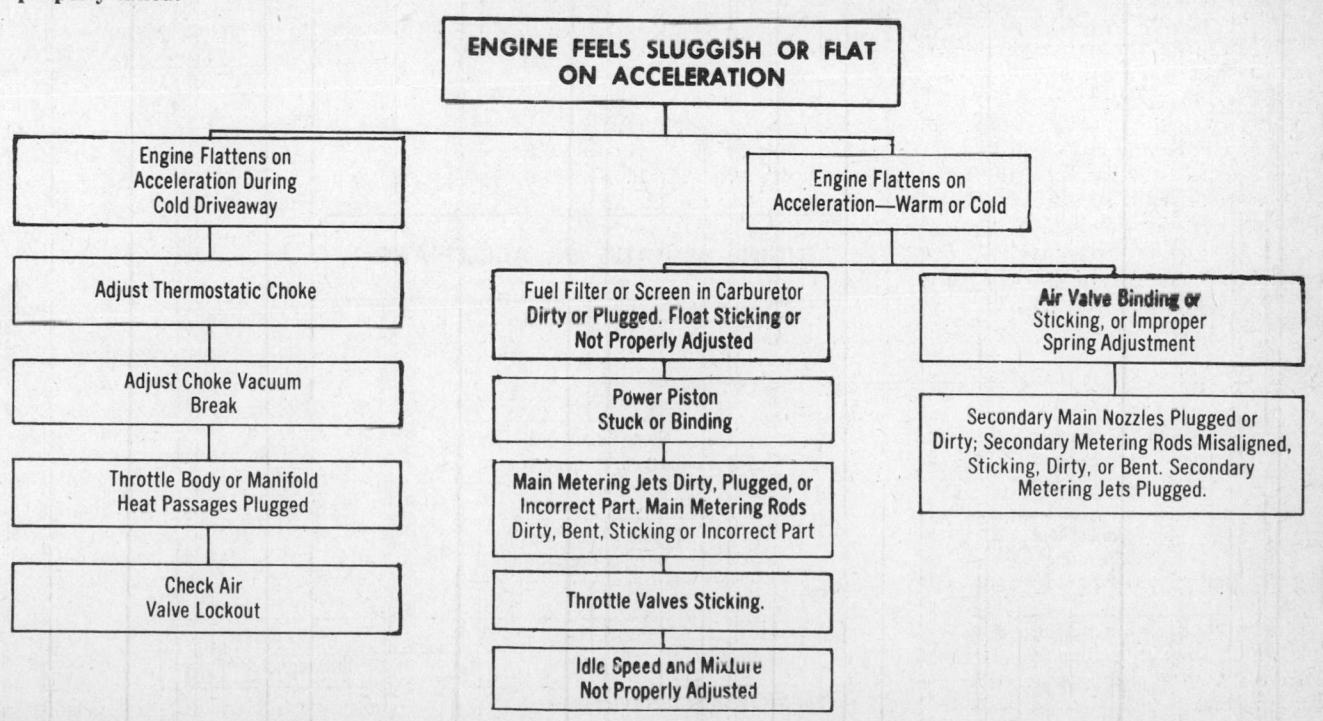

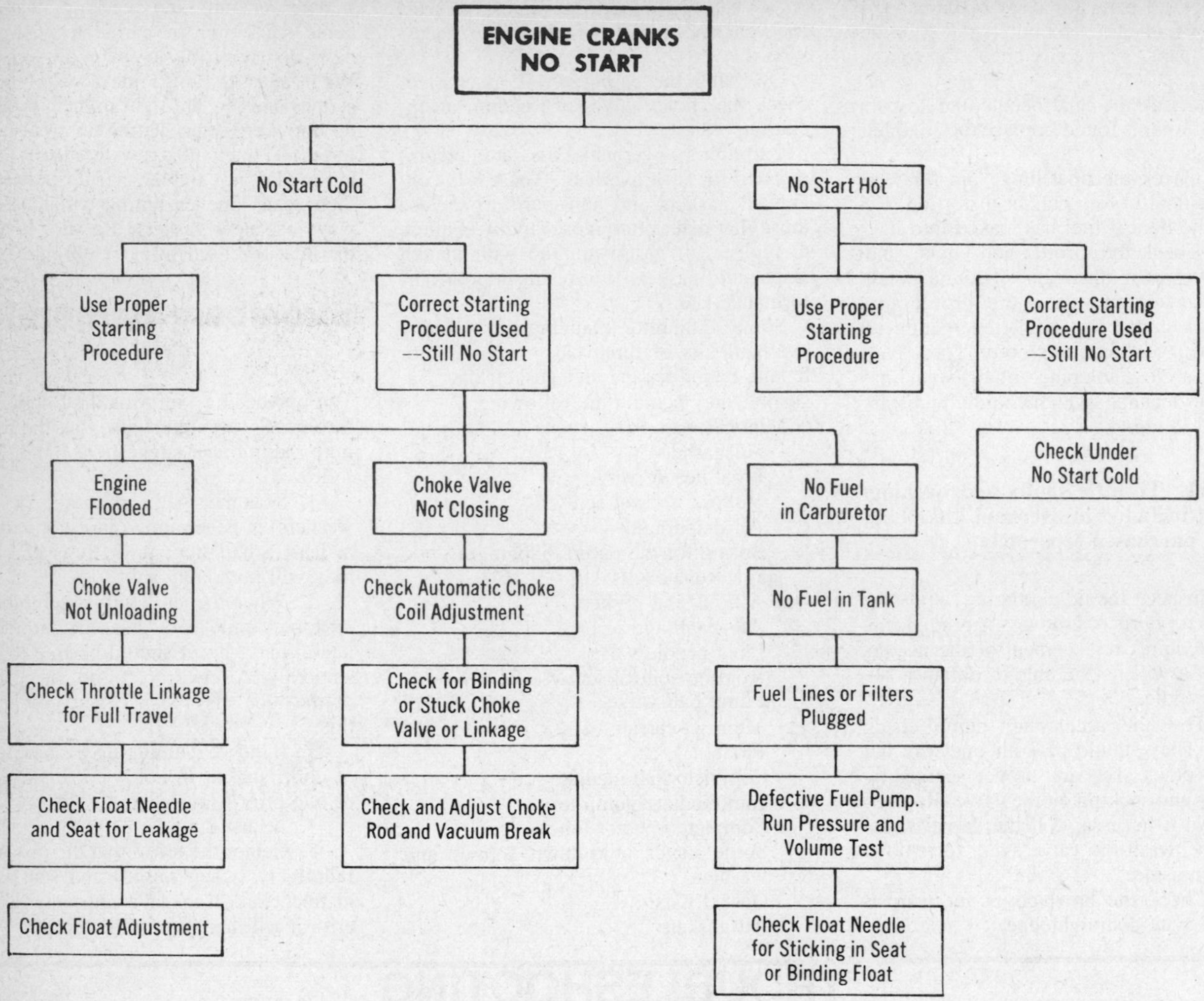

ENGINE CRANKS NO START

- **No Start Cold**
  - Use Proper Starting Procedure
  - Correct Starting Procedure Used —Still No Start
    - Engine Flooded
      - Choke Valve Not Unloading
      - Check Throttle Linkage for Full Travel
      - Check Float Needle and Seat for Leakage
      - Check Float Adjustment
    - Choke Valve Not Closing
      - Check Automatic Choke Coil Adjustment
      - Check for Binding or Stuck Choke Valve or Linkage
      - Check and Adjust Choke Rod and Vacuum Break
    - No Fuel in Carburetor
      - No Fuel in Tank
      - Fuel Lines or Filters Plugged
      - Defective Fuel Pump. Run Pressure and Volume Test
      - Check Float Needle for Sticking in Seat or Binding Float
- **No Start Hot**
  - Use Proper Starting Procedure
  - Correct Starting Procedure Used —Still No Start
    - Check Under No Start Cold

ENGINE HESITATES ON ACCELERATION

- Air Valve Binding or Sticking
  - Air Valve Lockout Not Operating
  - Secondary Throttle Valves Sticking Open Slightly— Check for Damage
- Pump Circuit Dirty, Plugged, or Inoperative
  - Discharge Ball Sticking, Dirty, or Not Seating
  - Low Fuel Level in Float Bowl — Check Fuel Pump Pressure and Volume

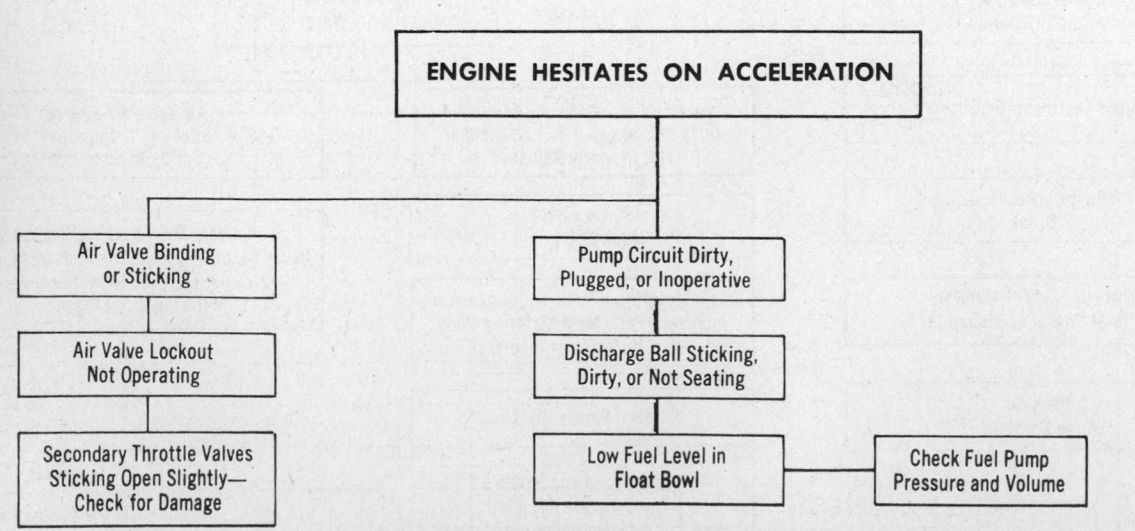

Fuel Injection

GASOLINE FUEL INJECTION APPLICATION CHART

Manufacturer	Model	Throttle Body (TBI)	Air Flow Controlled (AFC)	Constant Injection System (CIS)
Audi	4000 S Quattro			①
	Fox			1978–79
	4000, Coupe			1980 and later
	5000, Turbo, Quattro			1978 and later
BMW	320i			1978–82
	318i		1983 and later	
	325e		⑧	
	528i		1979–81	
	528e		②	
	530i		1978	
	633CSi, 533i		1978 and later ②	
	733i		1978 and later ②	
Chrysler	Colt, Conquest	1984 and later ⑦		
Fiat ③	Spider 2000, Turbo		1980 and later	
	Strada		1980–82	
	X1/9		1980 and later	
	Brava		1980–81	
Isuzu	Impulse		1983 and later ④	
Mercedes–Benz	280E, SE, CE			1978–81
	450SL, 450SLC			1978–80
	450SEL			1978–80
	6.9			1978–79
	380SL, SLC, SEL, SEC, SE			1981 and later

GASOLINE FUEL INJECTION APPLICATION CHART

Manufacturer	Model	Throttle Body (TBI)	Air Flow Controlled (AFC)	Constant Injection System (CIS)
Mercedes–Benz	190E			①
	500SEC, SEL			1984 and later
Mitsubishi	Starion	1983 and later		
	Cordia, Tredia	1984 and later		
Nissan (Datsun)	300ZX, Turbo		1984 and later④	
	200SX		1982 and later	
	280Z, ZX		1978 and later	
	810		1978 and later	
Peugeot	505			1980 and later
Porsche	911SC			1978 and later
	Turbo			1978–79
	924, 924 Turbo			1978–81
	928		1980 and later	1978–79
	944		②	
Renault	Alliance, Encore	1982 and later⑥		
	18i, Sport Wagon		1981 and later	
	Fuego		1982 and later	
SAAB	99			1978
	99 Turbo			1978
	900			1979 and later
	900 Turbo			1979 and later
Toyota	Supra, Celica		1979 and later	
	Cressida		1980 and later	
	Camry, Starlet		1983 and later	
Triumph	TR-8		1980–81	
Volkswagen	Beetle (Type 1)		1978–79	
	Bus (Type 2), Vanagon		1978 and later	
	Dasher			1978–81
	Jetta			1980 and later
	Rabbit			1978 and later①
	Scirocco			1978 and later
	Quantum			1982 and later
Volvo	242, 244, 245			1978–79
	262, 264, 265			1978–79
	DL, GL, GLE, GT, Coupe		⑤	1980–83

Note: See the individual car sections for particular injection system schematic. See text for system variations and modifications on L and K Jetronic.
① 1984 and later—KE Jetronic system
② 1982 and later—Motronic system
③ Pininfarina 2000 and Bertone X1/9 after 1983
④ I-Tec injection system similar to LH Jetronic system
⑤ 1984 and later—LH II Jetronic system
⑥ California models use AFC fuel injection
⑦ Turbocharged engine only
⑧ Motronic system

FUEL INJECTION

General Information

There are three basic types of fuel injection systems currently in production. The Constant Injection System (CIS, or often known by its Bosch designation "K-Jetronic") is a mechanically controlled type of fuel injection that uses an air flow sensor and fuel distributor to regulate the air/fuel mixture. Air Flow Controlled (AFC) and Throttle Body Injection (TBI) systems use an electronic control unit that regulates the fuel mixture by sending electrical impulses to the injector(s) that vary the length of time the nozzle is open. CIS and AFC injection systems are called "port" type because the injectors are mounted in the cylinder head and spray the fuel charge directly behind the intake valve. Throttle body injection (TBI) uses a single injector mounted above the intake manifold much like a conventional carburetor (hence the name) and the fuel charge is drawn into the cylinders in the conventional manner.

Fuel injection combined with electronics and various engine sensors provides a fuel management system that is more capable of meeting the demands for improved fuel economy, increased performance and lower emissions than is possible with a conventional carburetor. An injected engine averages 10% more power and economy with lower emissions than an identical carbureted version. Because of its precise control, fuel injection allows the engine to operate with a stoichiometric or optimum fuel mixture of 14.7 parts air to one part fuel throughout the entire engine rpm range. This 14.7:1 fuel mixture consumes all the carbon and hydrogen in the combustion chamber, producing the lowest combination of unburned hydrocarbons, carbon monoxide and oxides of nitrogen. By using an oxygen sensor to measure the O_2 content of the exhaust gases, the injection system can constantly adjust the fuel mixture in response to changing temperature, load and altitude conditions.

It's important to understand all injection system components and their relationship to one another in operation before attempting any maintenance or repair procedures. All fuel injection systems are delicate and vulnerable to damage from rust, dirt, water and careless handling. Because of the close tolerances (25 millionths of an inch on some injectors) any rust or dirt particles can ruin the fuel pump or injectors and water in the fuel can do more damage than a well-placed grenade. Specifications and test procedures, while similar in many cases, *can vary from one manufacturer to another* so it is very important to identify exactly which type of injection system is being used on a particular engine. In addition, there are modifications within the major groups of CIS, AFC and TBI type systems that although similar in function and appearance

utilize different sensors and electronic control units that are not interchangable. For example, the Bosch L-Jetronic AFC injection system has four modifications that are designated LH, LH II, LU and Motronic. Each individual system has sensors and characteristics unique to its own design, although they all look pretty much the same to the casual observer.

COMPARING CARBURETOR CIRCUITS TO FUEL INJECTION COMPONENTS

It makes fuel injection systems a little easier to understand by comparing the functions of major systems and components in the carburetor to those in a typical injection system. It quickly becomes apparent that fuel injection is merely a more sophisticated way of doing the same thing. One major difference is that the accelerator pedal controls the fuel on a carburetor; on an injection system, the accelerator pedal merely opens or closes a butterfly or throttle plate that allows more air into the system. Fuel quantity is regulated by the fuel distributor (CIS) or the control unit (AFC). In other words, it's impossible to flood a fuel injection system by pumping the accelerator with the engine off-all you're doing is opening and closing an air valve.

Carburetor	EFI
Accelerator pump	Throttle switch
Fast idle cam	Thermo-time switch
Float	Fuel pressure regulator
Power valve metering rod(s)	Manifold pressure sensor (TBI) Airflow sensor (L–Jetronic)
Metering jets & idle fuel system	Injector valves/ electronic control unit

Tools And Equipment

Most of the tools necessary to repair and maintain any fuel injection system are basic items such as line and box wrenches, screwdrivers, a fused jumper wire (called a bridging adapter); in addition, a tach/dwell meter and a volt/ohmmeter should be available when performing tests and routine maintenance. Specialized equipment includes a pressure tester that reads to at least 100 psi and includes connecting lines, tees and a three-way valve to select different fuel pressure tests. If the car is equipped with K-Jetronic fuel injection, a 3 mm allen wrench is required to adjust the fuel mixture. A fuel injection harness repair kit for repairing wires or connectors that are damaged or faulty and a hand vacuum pump are necessary for relieving fuel pressure and testing vacuum boost control switches used on some turbocharged models. An inexpensive multimeter is popular for continuity and volt/ohm testing since modes can be changed at the flip of a switch. OEM test kits are available and occasionally essential for diagnosing control units.

CONSTRUCTION OF BRIDGING ADAPTER

The bridging adapter is simply a fused jumper wire used to connect two terminals of the fuel pump relay socket when energizing the fuel pump during all pressure tests on early K-Jetronic systems. To construct a bridging adapter, attach an 8 amp in-line fuse, two male terminal connectors and an on/off toggle switch together to form a fused jumper wire. Make sure the fuse is 8 amp and use the switch for precise timing of pressure tests. Solder all connections.

NOTE: A bridging adapter is necessary for servicing early K-Jetronic systems safely. Make sure the switch is OFF when making connections at the relay socket.

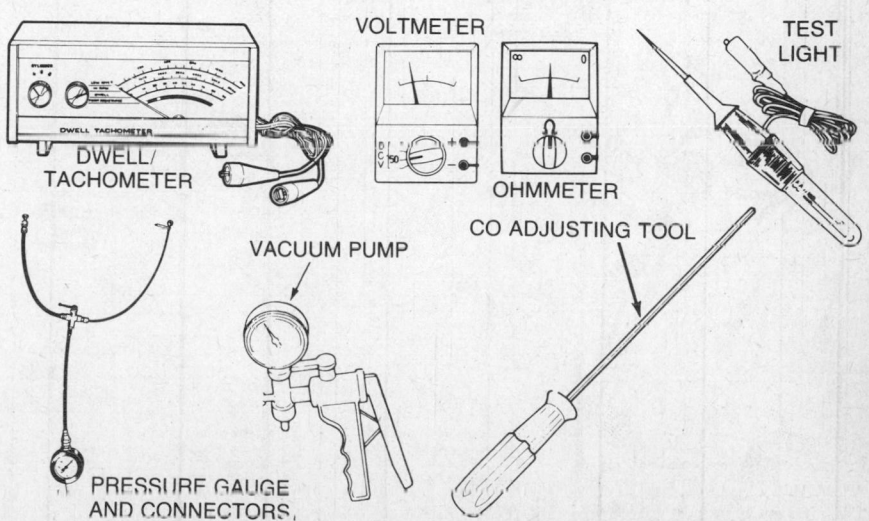

Specialized tools necessary for servicing fuel injection systems

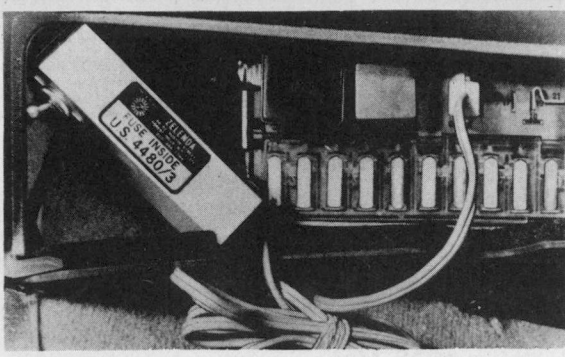

Typical bridging adaptor used for energizing the fuel pump on early K–Jetronic systems

Safety Precautions

CAUTION

Whenever working on or around any fuel injection system, always observe these precautions to prevent the possibility of personal injury or damage to fuel injection components:

- Never start the engine without the battery cable connected.
- Never install or remove battery or jumper cables with the key ON or the engine running.
- Always remove the battery cables before charging the battery. Never use a high-output charger on an installed battery.
- Never remove or attach wiring harness connectors with the ignition ON, especially to the control unit.
- When checking compression on engines with L-Jetronic systems, unplug the cable from the battery to the relays.
- Always depressurize the fuel system before attempting to disconnect any fuel.
- Always use clean rags and tools when working on an open fuel injection system and take great care to prevent any dirt from

entering the system. Wipe all components clean before installation, and prepare a clean area for disassembly and inspection.

- Do not drop any components during service procedures. Never apply 12 volts to a fuel injector directly.
- Remove the control unit if the car is to be placed in a paint spraybooth/oven.

CONTINUOUS INJECTION SYSTEM (CIS)

Bosch K and KE-Jetronic

OPERATION

The Bosch CIS fuel injection system differs from the electronic AFC system in that injection takes place continuously; it is controlled through variation of the fuel flow rate through the injectors, rather than by variation of the fuel injection duration as on the AFC system. Prior to 1983, CIS used no electronic computer, and is an electromechanical system that will provide suitable air/fuel mixtures under all driving conditions.

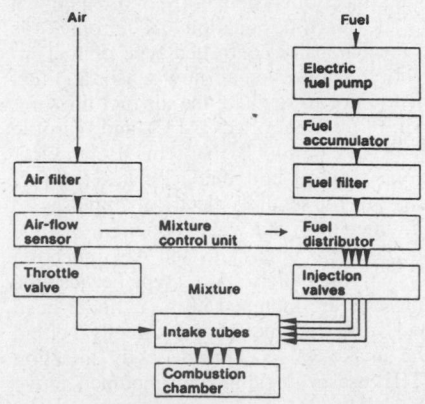

Basic operation schematic—K–Jetronic fuel injection

The complete CIS system consists of the following components: air/fuel control unit (housing both air flow sensor and fuel distributor), electric fuel pump(s) (and fuel pressure accumulator), fuel filter, control pressure regulator, fuel injectors, auxiliary air valve, cold start injector, engine sensors and various switches and relays.

The heart of the early (non-electronic) CIS system is the air/fuel control unit. It consists of an air flow sensor and a fuel distributor. Intake air flows past the air cleaner and through the air venturi raising or lowering the counterbalanced air flow sensor plate. The plate is connected to a pivoting lever which moves the control plunger in the fuel distributor in direct proportion to the intake air flow.

NOTE: The KE type CIS system used on 1984 and later Audi 4000S Quattro Sport Sedans uses a new electronic actuator which replaces several mixture control components, including the push valve, frequency valve and control pressure regulator.

The fuel distributor, which controls the amount of fuel to the injectors, consists of a line pressure regulator, a control plunger, and (4, 6, or 8) pressure regulator valves (one for each injector). The line pressure regulator maintains the fuel distributor inlet pressure at a constant psi., and will recirculate fuel to the tank if pressure exceeds this value. The control plunger, which is connected to the air flow sensor plate, controls the amount of fuel available to each of the pressure regulator valves. The pressure regulator valves maintain a constant fuel pressure differential between the inlet and outlet sides of the control plunger. This is independent of the amount of fuel passing through the valves, which varies according to plunger height.

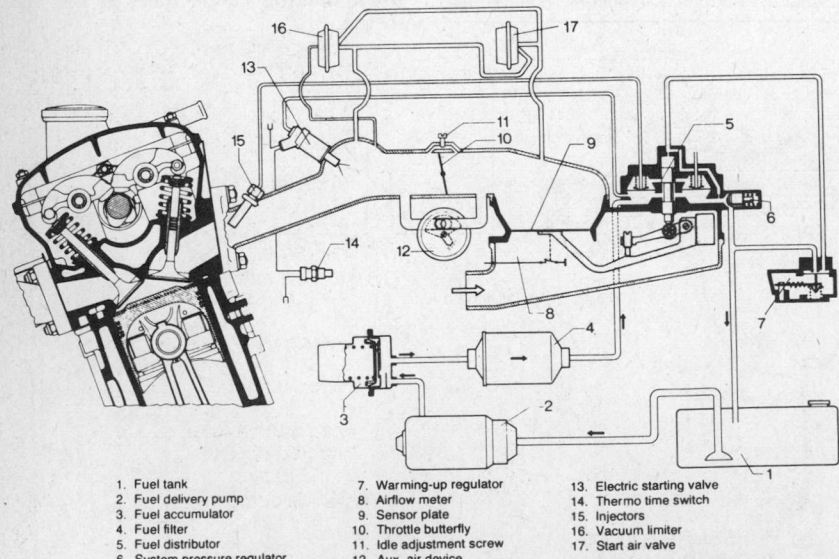

1. Fuel tank
2. Fuel delivery pump
3. Fuel accumulator
4. Fuel filter
5. Fuel distributor
6. System pressure regulator
7. Warming-up regulator
8. Airflow meter
9. Sensor plate
10. Throttle butterfly
11. Idle adjustment screw
12. Aux. air device
13. Electric starting valve
14. Thermo time switch
15. Injectors
16. Vacuum limiter
17. Start air valve

Typical K–Jetronic fuel injection schematic—without push valve

The fuel distributor on the KE-Jetronic is different than the earlier K model. The system pressure regulator piston and pressure compensating valve are no longer installed and the adjusting screws and compression springs are moved to the lower chamber. An additional strainer has been installed in front of the differential pressure valve and a strainer with a permanent magnet is in the supply line to the electrohydraulic actuator to catch any rust particles in the fuel. The pressure on top of the control plunger is now equal to system pressure and there is a pressure measuring connection located in the lower chamber.

The main difference between the K and KE Jetronic is the electrohydraulic actuator used for mixture correction. The actuator is flanged onto the fuel distributor and acts as a pressure regulator which operates as a plate valve. The plate valve position can be varied, causing a differential pressure change in the actuator and lower chamber and thereby correcting the mixture. The signal for actuation comes from an electronic control unit which adjusts the mixture according to the engine operating conditions.

With the ignition ON, the control unit is connected to battery voltage. A voltage correction circuit prevents fluctuations when components are energized and controls the operating voltage to approximately 8 volts. The amount of cranking enrichment depends on coolant temperature. A timing element regulates the enrichment after one second to the warm-up plus the after-starting value. This value remains constant as long as the engine is cranked. The after-start enrichment establishes smooth running characteristics after starting; the amount of after-start enrichment also depends on coolant temperature, as does warm-up enrichment. The lower the temperature, the higher the current rate at the actuator and the greater the fuel enrichment.

NOTE: The KE-Jetronic system also controls altitude enrichment, based on a signal from an altitude correction capsule.

The injectors themselves are spring loaded and calibrated to open at a preset pressure. They are not electrically operated as on the AFC fuel injection system.

The control pressure regulator, located on the intake manifold, acts to regulate the air/fuel mixture according to engine temperature. When the engine is cold, the control pressure regulator enriches the mixture. This is accomplished when a certain amount of fuel is bled off into a separate control pressure system. The control pressure regulator maintains this fuel at a set pressure. The regulator is connected to the upper side of the fuel distributor control plunger. When the engine temperature is below operating parameters, a bi-metal spring in the regulator senses this and reduces the fuel pressure on top of the plunger, allowing the plunger to rise further and channel more fuel to the regulator valves and injectors, thereby enriching the mixture. When the

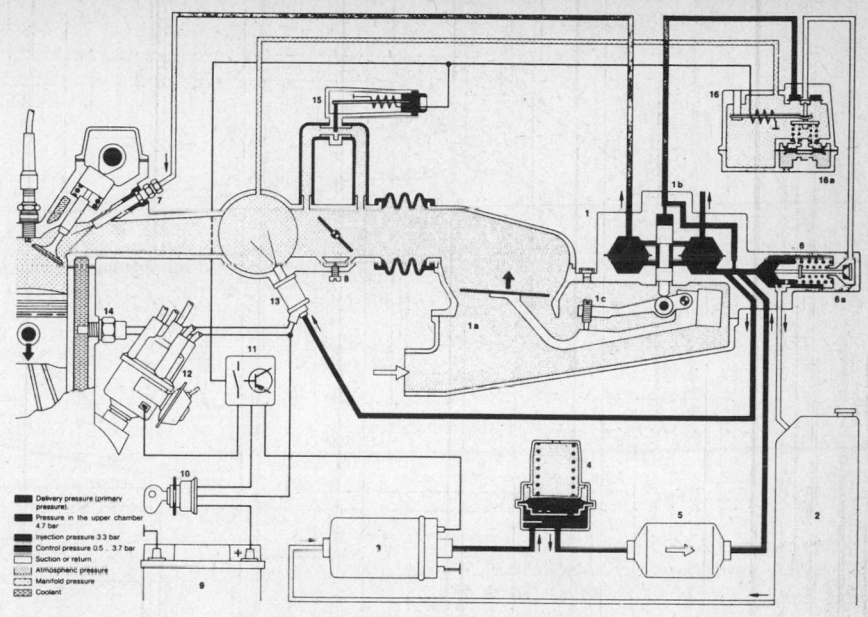

1. Mixture—control unit
1a. Air—flow sensor
1b. Fuel distributor
1c. Idle—mixture adjusting screw
2. Fuel tank
3. Electric fuel pump
4. Fuel accumulator
5. Fuel filter
6. Primary—pressure regulator
6a. Push—up valve
7. Fuel injection valve
8. Idle speed adjusting screw
9. Battery
10. Ignition and starting switch
11. Control relay
12. Ignition distributor
13. Start valve
14. Thermo-time switch
15. Auxiliary air device
16. Warm—up regulator
16a. Full—load diaphragm

Typical K—Jetronic fuel injection schematic—with push valve

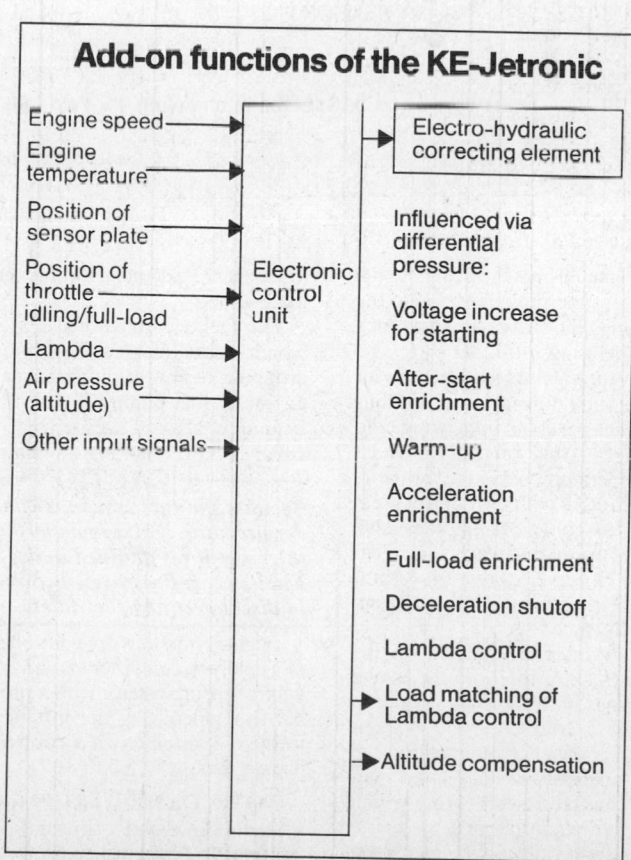

Add-on functions of the KE-Jetronic

Engine speed
Engine temperature
Position of sensor plate
Position of throttle idling/full-load
Lambda
Air pressure (altitude)
Other input signals

Electronic control unit

Electro-hydraulic correcting element

Influenced via differential pressure:

Voltage increase for starting

After-start enrichment

Warm-up

Acceleration enrichment

Full-load enrichment

Deceleration shutoff

Lambda control

Load matching of Lambda control

Altitude compensation

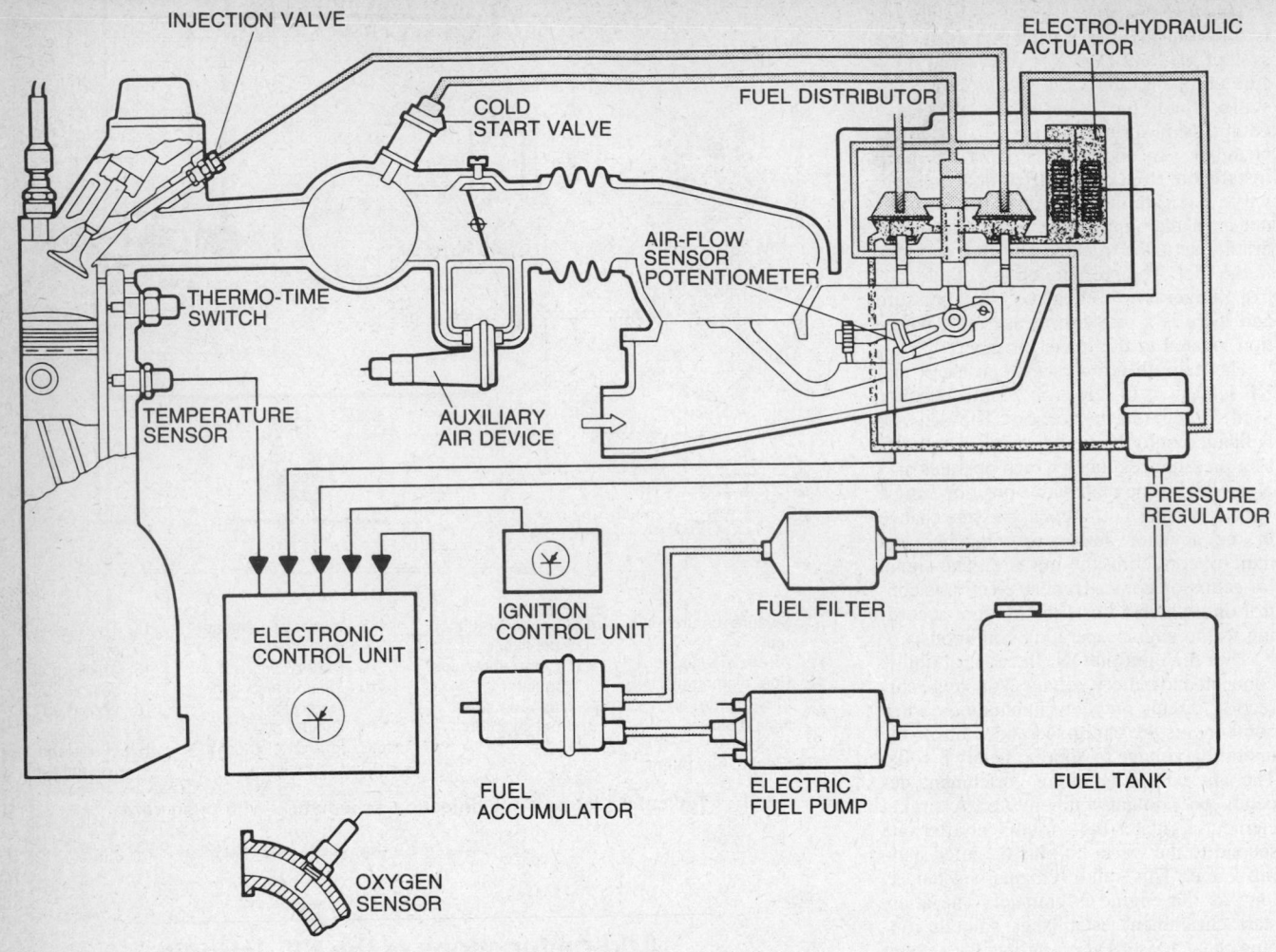

INJECTION VALVE

ELECTRO-HYDRAULIC ACTUATOR

COLD START VALVE

FUEL DISTRIBUTOR

THERMO-TIME SWITCH

AIR-FLOW SENSOR POTENTIOMETER

TEMPERATURE SENSOR

AUXILIARY AIR DEVICE

PRESSURE REGULATOR

ELECTRONIC CONTROL UNIT

IGNITION CONTROL UNIT

FUEL FILTER

FUEL ACCUMULATOR

ELECTRIC FUEL PUMP

FUEL TANK

OXYGEN SENSOR

Schematic of Bosch KE Fuel Injection System

engine warms, the bi-metal spring in the regulator increases the pressure back to the preset value leaning the air/fuel mixture back to its normal operating ratio.

The auxiliary air valve provides extra air for the richer mixture during warm-up, thus raising the engine speed and improving cold driveability. The auxiliary air valve, which also has a temperature sensitive bi-metal spring, works directly with the control pressure regulator. At cold start-up, the valve is fully open. As the engine warms, an electric coil slowly closes the valve (4–8 minutes max.), blocking off the extra air and lowering the idle speed.

The cold start injector, located on the inlet duct, sprays extra fuel into the intake air stream during starter motor operation when the engine is cold.

The thermal time switch, located on the cylinder head, actuates the cold start injector. The switch has a bi-metal spring which senses coolant temperature and an electric coil which limits the cold start injector spray

to about 12 seconds, to prevent flooding the engine.

The fuel accumulator has a check valve which keeps residual fuel pressure from dropping below a minimum psi when the engine or fuel pump are shut off. The fuel system is always pressurized, preventing vapor lock in a hot start situation.

— CAUTION —
Because the fuel system is constantly under pressure, it is very important to follow the procedures outlined under "Relieving Fuel System Pressure" before attempting to disconnect any fuel lines.

Engine emissions are controlled by means of a catalytic converter and/or Lambda (Oxygen) Sensor system, which provides a signal to regulate the fuel mixture according to the measured oxygen content of the exhaust gases.

NOTE: On KE type CIS fuel injection systems the oxygen sensor is electrically heated for faster operation.

Troubleshooting

WATER IN THE FUEL

Water in the fuel, and the resulting rust, are the number one enemies of any fuel injection system, especially CIS. Rust particles inflict more damage more often on K-Jetronic than any other Bosch injection system. Because normal operating pressure on K systems ranges from 65–85 psi, the fuel pump usually pushes any water right through the fuel filter. A small plastic filter in the center of the fuel distributor traps the water, which then rusts out the fuel distributor. Not only will the rust block the tiny metering slits in the fuel distributor, it can also flow into the injectors and warmup compensator. Finding rust in one part usually means there's rust in the other. When rust particles block a metering slit, the cylinder fed by that slit will either die completely or develop an intermittent misfire

TROUBLESHOOTING—K-JETRONIC

Condition → / Cause(s) ↓	Engine does not start or starts poorly when **cold**	Engine does not start or starts poorly when **warm**	Irregular idle (engine shakes) during warm-up	Irregular idle (engine shakes) with engine **warm**	Engine does not draw fuel smoothly with engine **warm**	Engine misfires under full load	Insufficient power	Engine runs on (diesels)	Excessive fuel consumption	Flat spot during acceleration	Idle CO value too **high**	Idle CO value too **low**	Engine speed cannot be adjusted (too high)	Engine stalls immediately after starting
Vacuum system leaking (see *Vacuum Leaks*)	►	►	►	►		►			►		►			
Air flow sensor plate and/or control plunger not moving smoothly (see *Air Flow Sensor Movement*)	►	►		►		►	►		►	►	►			
Air flow sensor plate stop incorrectly set (see *Air Flow Sensor Position*)		►					►							
Auxiliary air valve does not open (see *Auxiliary Air Valve*)	►		►											
Auxiliary air valve does not close (see *Auxiliary Air Valve*)												►		
Electric fuel pump not operating (see *Fuel Pump*)	►	►			►									►
Defective cold start system (see *Cold Start System*)	►													
Leaking cold start valve (see *Cold Start System*)			►	►			►	►		►				
Incorrect cold control pressure (see *Warm-up Regulator*)	►		►											
Warm control pressure too high (see *Warm-up Regulator*)		►		►	►	►	►			►				►
Warm control pressure too low (see *Warm-up Regulator*)				►	►		►		►	►	►			►
Incorrect system pressure (see *System Pressure*)				►	►				►					►
Fuel system pressure leakage (see *Fuel Leaks*)		►												
Injection valve(s) leaking, opening pressure too low (see *Testing Injectors*)		►	►	►		►		►						
Unequal fuel delivery between cylinders (see *Comparative Test*)			►	►			►		►					
Basic idle and/or CO adjustment incorrect (see *Idle and CO Adjustment*)		►	►	►	►		►	►	►	►	►			
Throttle plate does not open completely					►									

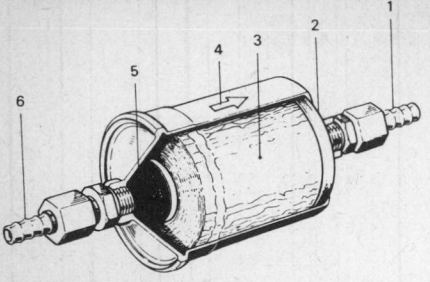

1. Outlet
2. Nylon strainer
3. Paper element
4. Arrow showing direction of flow
5. Rubber cone
6. Inlet

Cross section of a typical fuel filter.

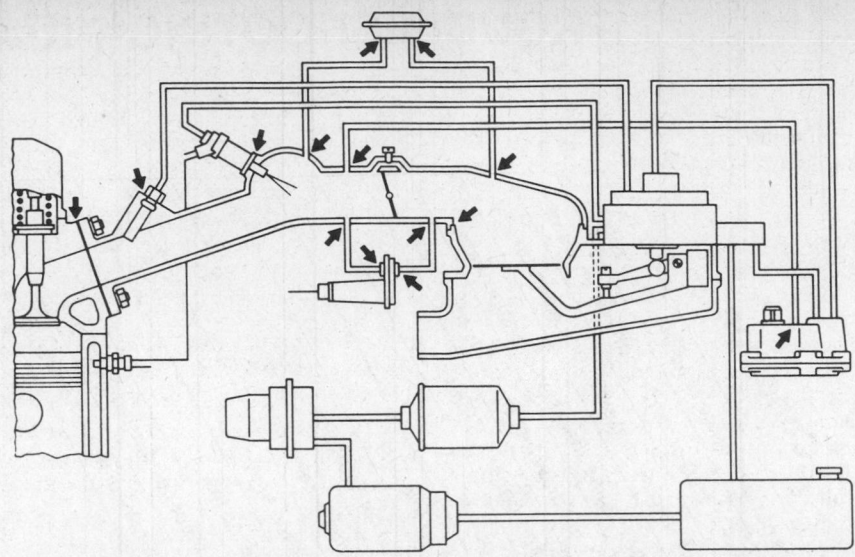

Check K–Jetronic systems for vacuum leaks at the arrows.

closely resembling the conditions created by a bad sparkplug. If the plug is known to be good, look for rust or water in the fuel. Disconnect the injector lines and spread fresh white paper towels on the workbench. Remove the entire fuel distributor and tap it gently against the bench. Shake and tap it again. If rust particles shake out of those injector line openings, replace the fuel distributor and flush the lines.

Water contamination can be prevented with regular fuel filter changes. Filters for these cars are expensive, but a rusty fuel distributor can't be fixed.

PRELIMINARY CHECKS

NOTE: Before doing any injection system testing, first check the three basics; ignition, compression and the fuel gauge.

Always make a complete ignition check first and then perform all the injection pressure tests in sequence.

The cause of many CIS complaints is a minor vacuum leak. Vacuum leaks fool the fuel metering system and affect the mixture. This gives poor gas economy and poor peformance. Look for leaks at:

1. EGR valve
2. Intake manifold
3. Cold start injector
4. Air sensor boot
5. Brake booster vacuum lines
6. Air ducts

Also check vacuum limiter, evaporative canister, and A/C door actuator.

To quick test the system for leaks, disconnect the auxiliary air valve hose, block open the throttle, and apply air pressure to the hose. Use a spray bottle of soapy water to hit all the fittings where leaks could occur.

Fuel Pump

The electric fuel pump is a roller cell type with the electric motor permanently surrounded by fuel. An eccentrically mounted roller disc is fitted with rollers resting in notches around the circumference. These rollers are pressured against the thrust ring

of the pump housing by centrifugal force. The fuel is carried in the cavities between the rollers and the pump delivers more than the maximum requirement to the engine so that fuel pressure is maintained under all operating conditions. During starting, the pump runs as long as the ignition key is turned. The pump continues to run once the engine starts, but has a safety device that will stop the pump if the ignition is turned on but the engine stops moving.

NOTE: Peugeot 505 models utilize a priming fuel pump, mounted in the tank, in addition to the main fuel pump. For all pump removal and installation procedures, see the individual car sections.

RELIEVING FUEL SYSTEM PRESSURE

CAUTION

Fuel pressure must be relieved before attempting to disconnect any fuel lines.

1. Carefully loosen the fuel line on the control pressure regulator (large connection).
2. Wrap a clean rag around the connection while loosening to catch any fuel.

Alternate Method For Relieving Fuel Pressure

1. Disconnect the electrical plug from the cold start valve.
2. Using a jumper wire, apply 12 volts to the cold start valve terminal for 10 seconds.
3. Reconnect the cold start valve.

FUEL PUMP POWER CHECK

Remove the round cover plate from the top of the fuel pump and measure the voltage

between the positive and negative terminals when the pump is operating. The lowest permissible voltage is 11.5 V. Disconnect the terminals connecting the pump to the air flow sensor and the warm-up regulator if these are to be checked later. If the pump is dead, check the fuse, the ground, and try bridging the relay with a jumper wire. During winter months, water in the gas can cause the pump to freeze and then blow a fuse. K-Jetronic type pumps need 12 volts and a good ground. A relay located somewhere in the pump's power wire operates the pumps. And like L-Jetronic systems, the relay may be a hide-and-seek item. All K-Jetronic pumps are fused someplace in the car, usually right in the vehicle's fuse panel.

FUEL PUMP SAFETY CIRCUIT CHECK

The pump will only run if the starter motor is actuated or if the engine is running.

1. Remove the air filter.
2. Turn on the ignition and briefly depress the sensor plate.
3. Remove the coil wire from the distributor.
4. Connect a voltmeter to the positive fuel pump terminal and ground.

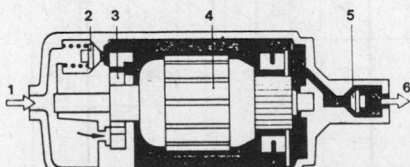

1. Intake side
2. Excess pressure valve
3. Roller cell pump
4. Electric motor armature
5. Non-return check valve
6. Pressure side

Typical roller cell fuel pump

5. Actuate the starter. The voltmeter should indicate 11 volts.

6. If the fuel pump runs only when the sensor plate is depressed or only when the engine is cranked, replace the fuel pump relay. If the pump is already running when the ignition is turned ON, replace the safety switch.

FUEL VOLUME TEST

The test point for fuel pump operation depends on the type of fuel distributor. Fuel distributors WITH push valves (most vehicles covered in this manual) have two fuel lines connecting with the warm-up regulator, the other fuel line connects to a ''T'' and returns to the gas tank. Determine whether the vehicle to be tested is fitted with or without a push valve before proceeding further.

1. Remove the gas cap to vent tank pressure.

2. Disconnect the return fuel line leading to the gas tank at the appropriate test point.

3. Hold the line coming from the fuel distributor in a large container (1500 cc or larger). Inflexible metal fuel lines may require a rubber hose to reach the container.

4. Remove the electric plug from the warm-up regulator and the auxiliary air valve. Bridge the electric safety circuit for 30 seconds. Delivery rate should be about one quart in 30 seconds.

5. If fuel quantity is not within specification, check for sufficient voltage supply to the fuel pump (minimum 11.5 volts) or a dirty fuel filter. If all the above are satisfactory, replace the electric fuel pump.

NOTE: Use a bridging adapter to energize the fuel pump through the relay connector on early models without push valves.

Pressure Tests

Diagnose a K-Jetronic system in this order: check cold control pressure first, hot control pressure next, then primary pressure, and finally rest pressure. The gauge for testing K-Jetronic always tees into the line running between the fuel distributor and the warmup compensator. With the 3-way valve open, the gauge remains teed-in and therefore reads control pressure. Remember that control pressure is derived or fed from the primary circuit pressure so a pressure change in one circuit means a change in the other.

Closing the valve shuts off fuel flow to the warm-up compensator and forces the

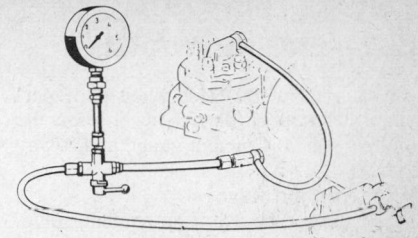

Typical fuel pressure test connection

gauge to read only one circuit—the primary circuit.

When you shut the engine off and leave the 3-way valve open, the teed-in gauge should show the system's holding pressure. This residual pressure is called rest pressure. The valve functions are: *valve open—control pressure; valve closed—primary pressure; valve open and engine off—rest pressure.*

CONTROL PRESSURE TEST-ENGINE COLD

1. Connect a pressure gauge between the fuel distributor and the control pressure regulator.

2. Remove the electrical connector from the regulator.

3. Idle the engine for no more than one minute.

4. Read the control pressure from the chart for cold control. If control pressure is wrong, check the control pressure (warm-up) regulator for proper operation.

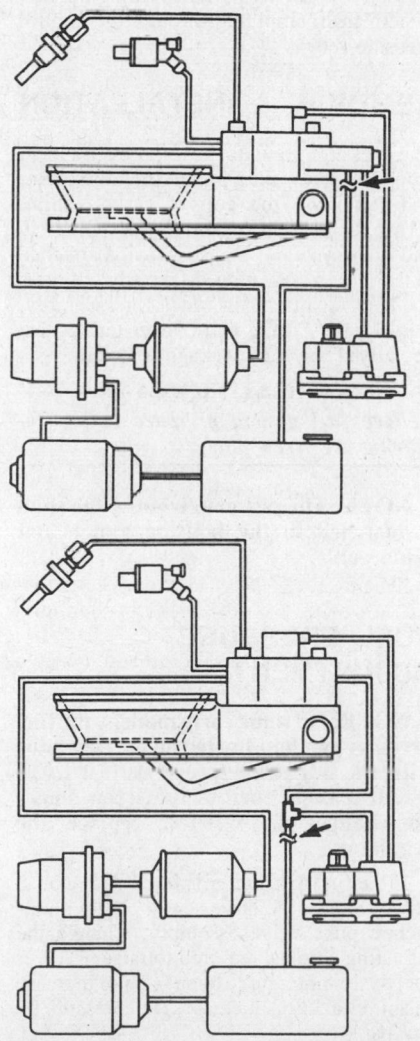

Fuel pressure test points with push valve (top) and without push valve (bottom). Generally, all 1978 and later K-Jetronic systems have push valves

CIS PRESSURE TEST SPECIFICATIONS

(All measurements in PSI)

Model	Normal Fuel Pressure	Injector Opening Pressure	Rest Pressure	System Pressure
Audi (all models)	49–55	36–59	23–35	65–78 ①
BMW 320i	49–55	36–52	23–35	65–75
Mercedes-Benz (all models)	49–55	36–52	41	65–75
Peugeot 505	49–55	44–59	38	65–75
Porsche (all models)	38–55	44–59	14–25	65–75
Saab (all models)	49–55	44–59	14–22	65–75
VW (all models)	49–55	51–59	35	68–78
Volvo (all models)	49–55	37–51	25	65–75 ①

Note: Minimum-maximum test ranges are given. Exact pressures may vary.
① Turbo models: 75–84 psi

CONTROL PRESSURE TEST—ENGINE WARM

1. Carry out this test when poor performance has been experienced when the engine is warm. Connect gauge and 3-way valve.

2. Open the valve.

3. Connect the warm-up regulator plug.

4. Leave the ignition switched on until rest pressure is present.

5. Refer to the test values.

6. If the value should differ, replace the warm-up regulator.

NOTE: Perform primary and rest pressure tests before disconnecting the gauge and 3-way valve.

PRIMARY PRESSURE TEST

Close the 3-way valve. Switch on the ignition. Refer to the test values. If the line pressure should differ from the recommended values this may be due to:

• Insufficient pressure from the fuel pump Blockage of the strainer in the tank

• Leakage in the fuel line

When you close the 3-way valve with the engine idling and the primary pressure reads low, there could be a fuel pump problem or a primary regulator problem. To isolate one from the other, locate the return line leading from the fuel distributor back to the gas tank. Now plug the return line securely at some convenient point. Have an assistant switch on the pump *just long enough* to get a pressure reading. If the pump is good, the pressure will jump almost instantly to 100 psi or higher. Should the primary pressure exceed 116 psi during this momentary test, the check valve in the intake side of the fuel pump will vent the pressure back into the gas tank.

If the fuel pump produces good pressure with the return line plugged, then the primary pressure regulator is causing a low primary pressure reading.

REST PRESSURE TEST

Good rest pressure enables a K–Jetronic-equipped engine to start easily when it's hot. If the K system loses rest pressure for any reason, the injector lines will vapor lock. Then the driver has to crank the engine until the pump can replenish the lines with liquid fuel.

If rest pressure drops off too quickly, start the engine and run it long enough to build the system pressure back up. Stop the engine, pull the electrical connector off the cold start injector and remove the injector from the intake manifold. If the cold start injector is dripping, replace it and re-check the rest pressure.

If the cold start valve is holding pressure, reinstall it and run the engine again to build up pressure. Stop the engine and close the 3-way valve. If the pressure reading remains steady now, the return side of the

system—the warm-up compensator—is leaking. Replace the compensator.

If the rest pressure still drops rapidly after closing the 3-way valve, the leak is in the feed side of the system. This could mean a bad fuel pump, bad accumulator, or a bad primary pressure regulator.

The fuel pump's intake hose is flexible. Clamp this hose shut and recheck rest pressure. If the system holds pressure, then the check ball in the output side of the pump is leaking.

A sharp eye and ear will help isolate a bad accumulator. Watch the pressure gauge as a helper shuts off the engine. If the accumulator is good, the pressure will drop, stop for a second, and then the gauge needle will actually rise—pressure will increase for a moment—before the pressure stabilizes. If you don't see that slight upward needle movement, the accumulator is leaking rest pressure. Furthermore, a bad accumulator will cause a loud, tell-tale groaning noise at the fuel pump. If still in doubt about the accumulator, try blocking off its return line.

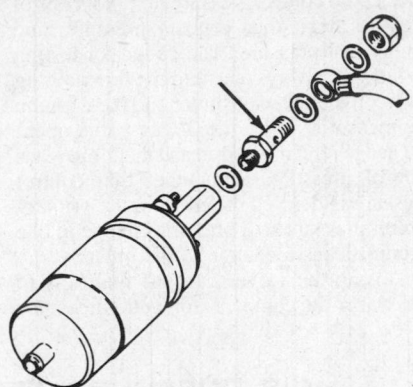

Fuel pressure regulator on fuel pump (arrow)

The same primary pressure regulator that can cause low primary pressure can also leak *rest* pressure. If you've eliminated the fuel pump and the accumulator, install a primary regulator repair kit.

Line Pressure Regulator

The line pressure regulator ensures that the pressure in the circuit remains constant when the fuel pump is in operation and also controls the recirculation of fuel to the tank. When the fuel pump is switched off, the regulator will cause a rapid pressure drop to approximately 2.5 bar (kp/cm², 35 psi), i.e. the rest pressure, which is maintained by means of the O-ring seal and the quantity of fuel contained in the fuel accumulator. The purpose of the rest pressure is to prevent the fuel from vaporizing in the circuit when the engine is warm, which would otherwise make restarting difficult.

The line pressure regulator forms an integral unit with a shut-off valve to which

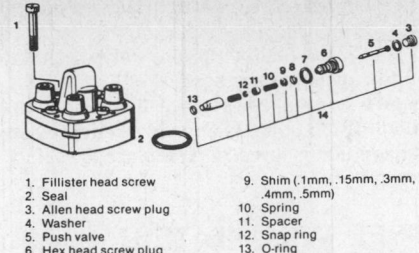

1. Fillister head screw	9. Shim (.1mm, .15mm, .3mm, .4mm, .5mm)
2. Seal	
3. Allen head screw plug	10. Spring
4. Washer	11. Spacer
5. Push valve	12. Snap ring
6. Hex head screw plug	13. O-ring
7. Washer	14. Repair kit including 3-13
8. O-ring	above

Fuel pressure regulator with push valve

the return fuel line from the control pressure regulator is connected. When the fuel pump is operating, the shut-off valve is actuated mechanically by the control pressure regulator, whereupon the return fuel from the control pressure regulator bypasses the shut-off valve to the return line.

When the fuel pump stops running and the line pressure regulator valve is pressed into its seating, the shut-off valve is also pressed into its seating, preventing the fuel system from emptying through the control pressure return.

REMOVAL & INSTALLATION

The pressure regulator is removed by loosening the screw plug on the fuel distributor and removing the copper gasket, shim, spring, control piston and O-ring. On 1979 and later systems, a push valve is attached to the large screw plug. Make sure all parts are kept clean and in order for assembly. Replace the O-ring and copper gasket, especially if any fuel leakage is noted.

— CAUTION —
Relieve fuel system pressure before removing the screw plug.

NOTE: The piston in front of the shim is matched to the housing and is not replaceable.

FUEL PRESSURE ADJUSTMENT

NOTE: On some early models, the fuel pressure can be adjusted on the regulator with the adjusting screw. Adjust to 28 psi. If a slight turn of the screw shows no change of pressure, replace the regulator.

If the fuel distributor is fitted with a push valve, loosen the large screw plug with attached push valve assembly. Change the adjusting shim as required to raise or lower fuel system pressure. Each 0.1mm increase in shim thickness increases fuel pressure by 2.2 psi.

If the fuel distributor doesn't have a push valve, remove the screw plug and change the shim as required. Again, each 0.1mm increase in shim thickness wil increase system pressure by 2.2 psi.

K–JETRONIC INJECTION PRESSURE REGULATOR SHIM CHART

Available Shims	Difference Of Pressure
0.10 mm	2.18 psi (0.15 bar)
0.15 mm	3.34 psi (0.23 bar)
0.30 mm	6.53 psi (0.45 bar)
0.40 mm	8.7 psi (0.60 bar)
0.50 mm	10.88 psi (0.75 bar)

Warm-Up Regulator

When the engine is cold, the warm-up regulator reduces control pressure, causing the metering slits in the fuel distributor to open further. This enrichment process prevents combustion miss during the warm-up phase of engine operation and is continually reduced as temperature rises. The warm-up regulator is a spring controlled flat seat diaphragm-type valve with an electrically heated bi–metal spring. When cold, the bi–metal spring overcomes the valve spring pressure, moving the diaphragm and allowing more fuel to be diverted out of the control pressure circuit thereby lowering the control

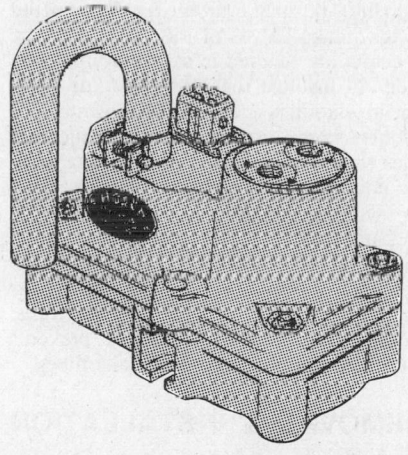

Warm–up regulators typical of California models

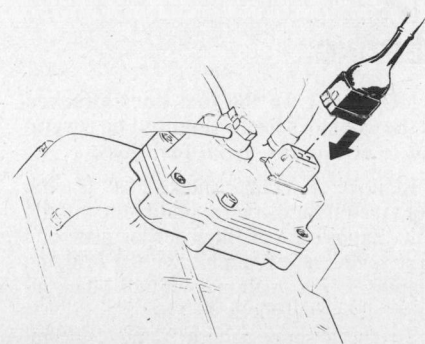

Control pressure regulator showing connector

pressure. When the bi–metal spring is heated electrically or by engine temperature the valve spring pushes the diaphragm up, allowing less fuel to be diverted thereby raising the control pressure. When the bi–metal spring lifts fully off the valve spring the warm-up enrichment is completed and control pressure is maintained at normal level by the valve spring. The warm-up regulator should be checked when testing fuel pressure.

TESTING

1. Disconnect the terminal from the warm-up regulator and connect a voltmeter across the contacts in the connector. Ensure that the ignition is switched on and that the safety circuit connection at the air flow sensor has been bypassed. The lowest permissible voltage is 11.5V.

2. Check that there are no breaks in the heater coil of the regulator by connecting a test lamp in series with the coil. If the coil is found to be damaged, the warm-up regulator should be replaced.

3. Connect an ohmmeter across the terminals in the regulator socket. Resistance must be 16–22 ohms. If the resistance is not within the specifications, the regulator will require replacement.

NOTE: The system is under considerable constant pressure. The only practical test that should be attempted is one using an ohmmeter. Be sure the engine is at normal operating temperature. There should be no loose fuel fittings or other fire hazards when the electrical connections are disengaged.

REMOVAL & INSTALLATION

1. Disconnect the negative battery cable.
2. Unplug the electrical connector.
3. Depressurize the fuel system as previously described.

NOTE: Wrap a cloth around the connection to catch any escaping fuel.

4. Remove both of the fuel lines.
5. Remove the vacuum hose.
6. Unscrew the four mounting bolts and remove the control pressure regulator.
7. Installation is in the reverse order of removal.

Fuel Accumulator

This device maintains the fuel system pressure at a constant level under all operating conditions. The pressure regulator, incorporated into the fuel distributor housing, keeps delivery pressure at approximately 5.0 bar (73 psi). Because the fuel pump delivers more fuel than the engine can use, a plunger shifts in the regulator to open a port which returns excess fuel to the tank. When the engine is switched off and the primary pressure drops, the pressure regulator closes the return port and prevents further pressure reduction in the system.

The fuel accumulator has a check valve which keeps residual fuel pressure from dropping below a pre-determined pressure when the engine or fuel pump are shut off.

REMOVAL & INSTALLATION

The fuel accumulator is usually mounted near or on the fuel pump bracket somewhere near the fuel tank. It may be necessary to remove the fuel pump assembly to gain access to the fuel accumulator. Loosen the hose clamps and the retaining clamp and remove the accumulator. Reverse the procedure to install.

— **CAUTION** —
Relieve fuel system pressure before disconnecting any fuel lines.

TESTING

If the pump fails a volume test, raise the car and trace the fuel feed line back to the pump. Look for crimped fuel lines from a carelessly placed jack. Plug the accumulator return hose and repeat the volume test. If this yields good fuel volume, the accumulator diaphragm is ruptured. Soak a new fuel filter with clean gas and install it. Remember to wet the filter beforehand. When 80 psi of incoming fuel hits a dry filter, it can tear off some of the element and carry the paper debris into the rest of the system.

Fuel Distributor

K-JETRONIC

The fuel distributor meters the correct amount of fuel to the individual cylinders according to the position of the air flow sensor plate. A control plunger opens or closes metering slits in the barrel, allowing more or less fuel to pass into the system. Control pressure assures that the plunger follows the movement of the sensor plate immediately. Control pressure is tapped from primary fuel pressure through a restriction bore. It acts through a damping restriction on the

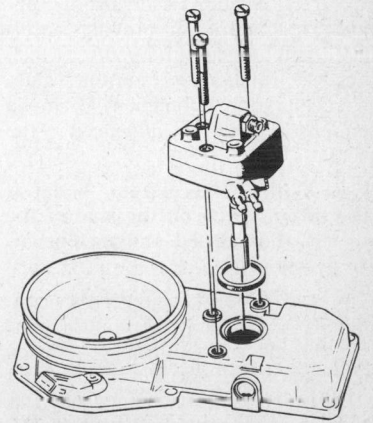

Fuel distributor mounting screws

control plunger, eliminating any oscillations of the sensor plate due to a pulsating air flow. 1978 and later models incorporate a "push valve" in the fuel distributor to maintain pressure when the engine is switched off. The push valve is a one-way device mounted in the primary pressure regulator which is held open in normal operation by the pressure regulator plunger. Differential pressure valves in the fuel distributor hold the drop in pressure at the metering slits at a constant value.

KE-JETRONIC

The internal components and operation of the KE type fuel distributor is slightly different than the K model. With the engine running, a constant system pressure of approximately 79 psi (5.4 bar) is present at the fuel inlet. The plate valve is adjusted depending on current intensity and in this manner determines the flow rate, in combination with a fixed orifice (0.3mm in diameter) at the fuel distributor outlet. The pressure change in the lower chamber causes movement of the diaphragm and regulates the fuel volume flowing to the injectors.

During cold start and warm-up, current at the electrohydraulic actuator (EHA) is approximately 8–120 milliamps. The plate valve is positioned in the direction of the intake port and the differential pressure drop in the lower chamber is approximately 6–22 psi (0.4–1.5 bar). With increasing coolant temperature, the current at the actuator drops to approximately 8 milliamps and the differential pressure drops at the same rate, down to approximately 6 psi (0.4 bar). For acceleration enrichment, the current to the actuator is determined by the coolant temperature and the amount of sensor plate deflection. The plate valve is moved closer to the intake port and the differential pressure decreases by approximately 22 psi (1.5 bar).

NOTE: Acceleration enrichment is cancelled at approximately 176°F (80°C).

The airflow sensor position indicator operates with approximately 8 volts supplied constantly. During acceleration, a voltage signal is transmitted to the control unit, depending on the position of the airflow sensor plate. The control unit provides acceleration enrichment as an impulse which increases the instantaneous current value. During acceleration enrichment, Lambda (oxygen sensor) control is influenced by the control unit.

NOTE: With the accelerator pedal at idle, the microswitch on the side of the airflow sensor is closed and no enrichment is possible.

The throttle valve switch receives a constant 8 volt signal from the control unit. With the throttle valve fully open (switch closed), approximately 8 mA of current flows to the electrohydraulic actuator, independent of engine speed. At full load enrichment, the plate valve moves in the direction

of the intake port and the differential pressure in the lower chamber of the fuel distributor is approximately 6 psi (0.4 bar) below system pressure. Under deceleration, the circuit to the control unit is closed by the microswitch. The speed at which deceleration shutoff occurs depends on coolant temperature. The lower the temperature, the higher the speed at which restart of fuel injection begins. With the microswitch closed, the current at the actuator is approximately 45 mA and the plate valve moves away from the intake port. The pressure difference between the upper and lower chamber is cancelled and system pressure is present in the lower chamber. Operational signals from the control unit will change the direction of the current flow at the actuator plate valve; the plate valve then opens. When the lower chamber pressure changes, pressure and spring force push the diaphragm against the ports to the injectors and cut off the fuel supply.

REMOVAL & INSTALLATION

1. Release the pressure in the system by loosening the fuel line on the control pressure regulator (large connector). Use a clean rag to catch the fuel that escapes.

2. Mark the fuel lines in the top of the distributor in order to put them back in their correct positions.

NOTE: Using different colored paints is usually a good marking device. When marking each line, be sure to mark the spot where it connects to the distributor.

3. Clean the fuel lines, then remove them from the distributor. Remove the little looped wire plug (the CO adjusting screw plug). Remove the two retaining screws in the top of the distributor.

--- CAUTION ---
When removing the fuel distributor be sure the control plunger does not fall out from underneath. Keep all parts clean.

4. If the control plunger has been removed, moisten it with gasoline before installing. The small shoulder on the plunger is inserted first.

NOTE: Always use new gaskets and O-ring when removing and installing fuel distributor. Lock all retaining screws with Loctite® or its equivalent.

Fuel Injectors

The fuel injection valves are mounted in the intake manifold at the cylinder head, and continuously inject atomized fuel upstream of the intake valves.

A spring loaded valve is contained in each injector, calibrated to open at a fuel start pressure of 47–54 psi. The valves also contain a small fuel filter.

The fuel injector (one per cylinder) delivers the fuel allocated by the fuel distrib-

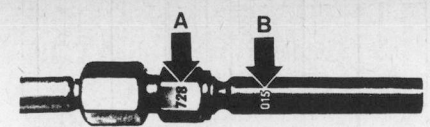

Identification numbers on fuel injector hexagon (A) and shaft (B)

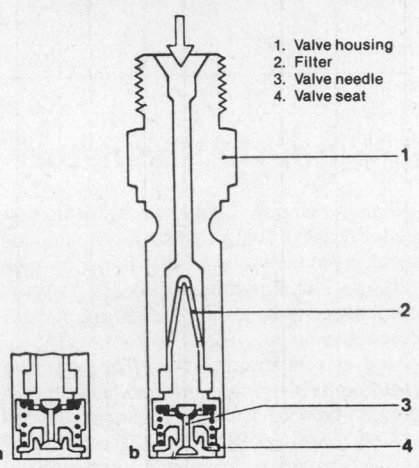

1. Valve housing
2. Filter
3. Valve needle
4. Valve seat

Cross section of typical K–Jetronic fuel injector showing closed (a) and open (b) positions

utor into the intake tubes directly in front of the intake valves of the cylinders. The injectors are secured in a special holder in order to insulate them from engine heat. The insulation is necessary to prevent vapor bubbles from forming in the fuel injection lines which would lead to poor starting when the engine is hot. The fuel injectors have no metering function; they open when the pressure exceeds 47–54 psi and are fitted with a valve needle that "chatters" at high frequency to atomize the fuel. When the engine is switched off, the injection valve closes tightly, forming a seal that prevents fuel from dripping into the intake tubes.

REMOVAL & INSTALLATION

NOTE: See the individual car sections for all removal and installation procedures.

TESTING

NOTE: Leave the fuel lines attached to the injectors for testing, but be careful not to crimp any metal fuel lines.

Remove the rubber intake hose leading from the mixture control unit to the throttle unit. Expose the air flow sensor plate and bypass the safety circuit with a bridging adaptor. Use a small magnet to lift the sensor plate during the test.

To check spray pattern, remove the injectors, one at a time, and hold then over a beaker. Switch the ignition key on and disconnect the electrical connector at the

Uneven spray

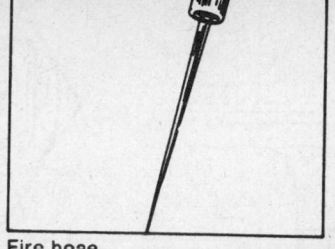

Fire hose

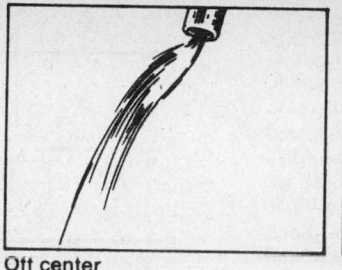

Off center

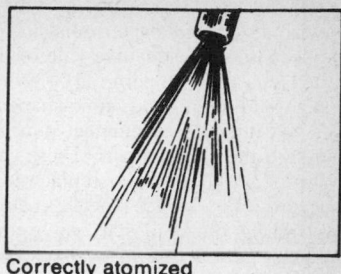

Correctly atomized

Fuel injector spray patterns

air-flow sensor to activate the fuel pump. Move the air flow sensor plate. The injector should provide a dose of uniformly atomized fuel at about a 15–52 degree wide angle.

To check injection quantity, connect the removed injectors via hoses to equal sized beakers. Switch on the ignition. Disconnect the electrical connector at the airflow sensor to activate the fuel pump. Run the pump for approximately 30 seconds to pressurize the system, then connect the air flow sensor to stop the fuel pump. Lift or depress the airflow sensor plate halfway until one of the beakers fills up. Check the beakers. If injection quantity deviates more than 20% between injectors, isolate the problem by swapping the lowest and highest (in fuel quantity) injectors and repeating the test. If the same injector still injects less, clean or replace that injector and fuel supply line. If the other injector is now faulty, the fuel distributor is defective.

The check for injector leak-down (when closed) can now be conducted. Injector leakage (more than slight seepage) may be due to airflow sensor plate set to incorrect height, seizing of fuel distributor plunger, or internal leaks in the fuel distributor. Connect the airflow sensor connector to de-activate the fuel pump and switch off the ignition. Check for injector leakage at rest pressure. Depress the sensor plate to open the fuel distributor slots. Maximum permissible leakage is one drop per 15 seconds. If all injectors leak, the problem may be excessive rest pressure.

NOTE: The injectors can be replaced individually.

Cold Start Valve

The cold start valve is mounted near the throttle valve housing and is connected to the pressure line. The valve, which is operated by a solenoid coil, is actuated by a thermo-time switch which is controlled by the engine temperature.

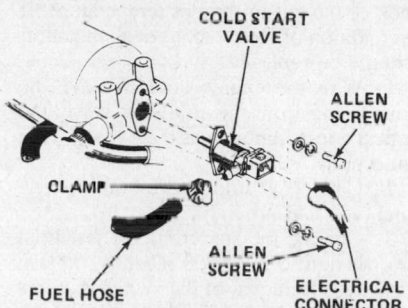

Typical cold start valve installation

During cold starting, part of the fuel mixture is lost due to condensation on the cold cylinder walls. To compensate for this loss, extra fuel is injected by means of a solenoid-operated cold start valve. Fuel is delivered downstream of the throttle valve. A thermo-time switch determines the injection period of the cold start valve according

to either engine temperature or an electrically heated bimetal strip which de-energizes the cold start valve after approximately 8 seconds to prevent flooding. The cold start valve does not funtion when the engine is warm.

REMOVAL & INSTALLATION

The cold start valve is mounted in the intake manifold, downstream from the air flow sensor. The valve is usually retained with two small Allen screws and can be removed for inspection without disconnecting the fuel line. When removing the valve, take care not to damage the valve body which is usually made of plastic. Make sure the valve is clean and the sealing O-ring is seated properly and in good condition when installing. Do not overtighten the mounting screws.

--- **CAUTION** ---
Depressurize the fuel system before attempting to remove any fuel hoses. Use plenty of rags around fuel connections to absorb and deflect any fuel spray.

TESTING

Remove the cold start injector from the intake manifold and hold over a beaker. With a cold engine (95°F or lower coolant temperature, the injector should spray during starter operation (max. 12 seconds). If not, check the voltage between the terminals of the injector when the starter is on. Voltage indicates a bad cold start injector. No volt-

Lift air sensor plate gently with a small magnet

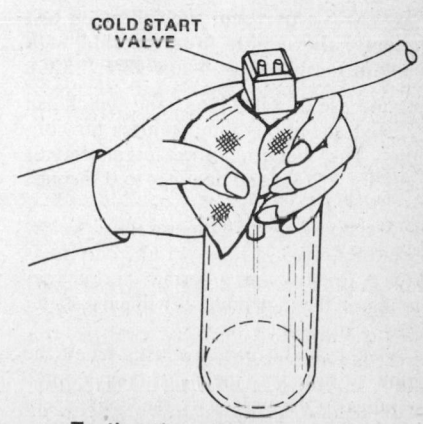

Testing the cold start valve

age indicates a faulty thermo-time switch or wiring. Ground one terminal and connect the second to the positive side of the coil. When you run the pump, 10–30 seconds, you should get a good, cone-shaped spray. Dry the injector, disconnect jumpers, and energize the pump again. There shouldn't be any fuel. If it drips, replace it. Check the thermo-time switch when it's below 95°F. Disconnect the cold start valve and hook up a test light across its connector. Ground the No. 1 coil terminal and run the starter. The light should glow for several seconds and then go out. If not, replace the thermo-time switch.

NOTE: Remove the fuel pump relay and attach a bridging adaptor to energize the fuel pump during testing. See the "Tools" section for specifics on adapter construction.

With the starter off, attach a test relay to operate fuel pump. Check for cold start valve leakage. Maximum allowable leakage is one drop per minute. Any excessive leakage is reason enough to replace the cold start valve. Don't forget to wipe the valve nozzle with a clean towel after every test and before installing.

Thermo-Time Switch

The thermo time switch, located on the cylinder head, actuates the cold start valve. It has a bi-metal spring which senses coolant temperature and an electric coil chich limits the cold start valve spray to 12 seconds. A thermo-time switch also measures water temperature and opens the cold start valve, located on the intake header, a varying amount each time the engine is started, depending on the conditions. With a hot engine (coolant temperature over 95°F), the injector should not operate. If it does, the thermo-time switch is defective. Also, on a cold engine, the cold start valve should not inject fuel for more than 12 seconds (during starter cranking). If it does, the thermo-time switch is defective.

TESTING

NOTE: To perform the following test properly, the engine must be cold with a coolant temperautre below 95°F (35°C).

With the use of a test lamp, the switch can be tested at various temperatures for continuity. The operating time is eight seconds at −4°F (−20C) and declines to 0 seconds at +59°F. (+15C.).

When the engine temperature is below approximately 113°F (+45°C), current is allowed to flow for a certain period (depending on the temperature) while the starter motor is running.

Check that the switch closes when the engine is started by means of connecting a test lamp in series across the contacts of the cold start valve plug.

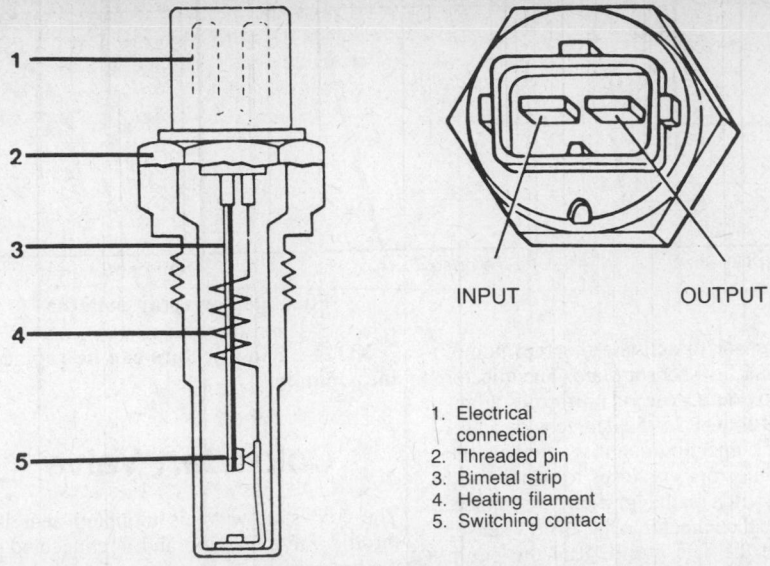

1. Electrical connection
2. Threaded pin
3. Bimetal strip
4. Heating filament
5. Switching contact

Typical thermo–time switch showing construction and terminal location

It is not possible to make a more accurate check of the cut-in time or temperature. If the condition of the switch is at all in doubt, it should be replaced.

1. With the engine cold, remove the harness plug from the cold start valve and connect a test light across the harness plug connections.
2. Connect a jumper wire from coil terminal No. 1 to ground.
3. Operate the starter. If the test light does not light for about 8 seconds, replace the switch. Removal of the switch requires that the engine be cold and the cooling system drained.

REMOVAL & INSTALLATION

1. Disconnect the negative battery cable. Drain the cooling system.
2. Locate the thermo-time switch on the left side of the engine block and disconnect the electrical connection.
3. Unscrew the switch and remove it.
4. Installation is in the reverse order of removal. Refill the cooling system.

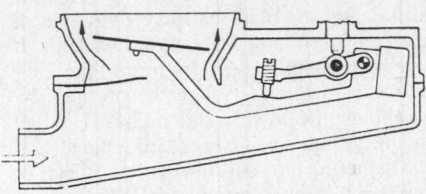

Air flow sensor plate movement

— CAUTION —
The engine must be cold when removing the switch.

Air Flow Sensor

This device measures the amount of air drawn in by the engine. It operates according to the suspended body principle, using a counterbalanced sensor plate that is connected to the fuel distributor control plunger by a lever system. A small leaf spring assures that the sensor plate assumes the correct zero position when the engine is stationary.

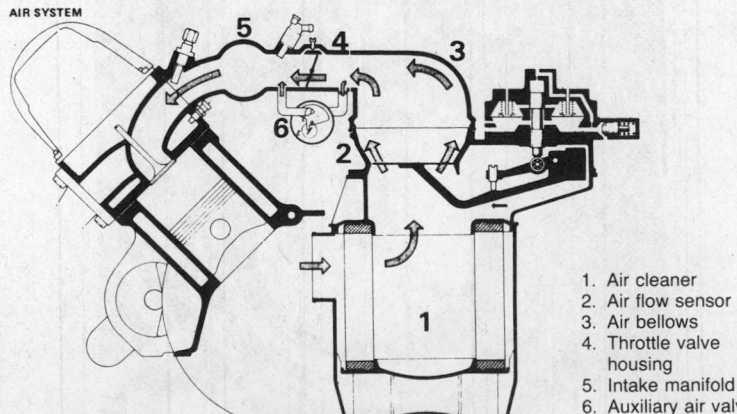

1. Air cleaner
2. Air flow sensor
3. Air bellows
4. Throttle valve housing
5. Intake manifold
6. Auxiliary air valve

Air flow through typical K–Jetronic induction system

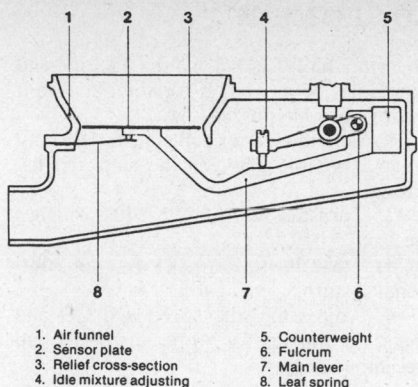

1. Air funnel
2. Sensor plate
3. Relief cross-section
4. Idle mixture adjusting screw
5. Counterweight
6. Fulcrum
7. Main lever
8. Leaf spring

Updraft air flow sensor in zero position

The air flow sensor consists of an air venturi tube in which an air flow sensor plate moves. The air flowing into the venturi from the air cleaner lifts the air flow sensor plate, allowing the air to flow through. The greater the amount of air, the higher the sensor plate will be raised.

The air flow sensor plate is fitted to a lever which is compensated by a counterweight. The lever acts on the control plunger in the fuel distributor which is pressed down by the control pressure, thus counteracting the lifting force of the air flow sensor plate.

The height to which the air flow sensor plate is raised is governed by the magnitude of the air flow.

The air/fuel mixture varies with the engine load. The inclination of the venturi walls therefore varies in stages in order to provide a correct air/fuel mixture at all loads. Thus, the mixture is enriched at full load and leaned at idle.

The lever acts on the control plunger in the fuel distributor by means of an adjustable link with a needle bearing at the contact point. The basic fuel setting, and thus the CO setting, is adjusted by means of the adjustment screw on the link. This adjustment is made with a special tool and access to the screw can be gained through a hole in the air flow sensor between the air venturi and the fuel distributor. The CO adjustment is sealed on later models.

A rubber bellows connects the air flow sensor to the throttle valve housing.

NOTE: On KE systems, the sensor plate rest position is angled upward, not horizontal as is the K system.

TESTING

The air flow sensor plate in the fuel distributor must operate smoothly in order to do a good job of measuring air. Remove the air boot and check the sensor plate movement. When released, the plate should fall freely with one or two bounces. If the plate sticks, loosen the mounting screws and retighten them uniformly. Clean the funnel and sensor plate too, as these can get dirty from PCV fumes.

Check for leakage in the inlet system between the air flow sensor and the engine Air leaking into the system may result in poor engine performance, owing to the fact that it bypasses the air flow sensor, causing a lean mixture.

Leakage can occur in the following places:

a. At the rubber bellows between the air flow sensor and the throttle valve housing.

b. At the gasket on the flange of the cold start valve.

c. At the gasket between the throttle valve housing and the inlet manifold.

d. At the gasket betwen the inlet manifold and the cylinder head.

e. At the hose connections on the throttle valve housing, auxiliary air valve or inlet manifold.

f. Via the crankcase ventilation hose from the oil filler cap, dip stick or valve cover gasket.

NOTE: Move the sensor plate gently with a small magnet.

The plate should not bind, and although the plate will offer some resistance when depressed (due to the control pressure), it should return to its rest position when released. Be careful not to scratch the plate or venturi.

To check the air flow sensor contact switch, depress or lift the sensor plate by hand. The fuel injectors should buzz, and the fuel pump should activate. If the pump operates, but the injectors do not buzz, check the fuel pressure. If the pump does not operate, check for a short in the air flow sensor connector.

SENSOR PLATE POSITION ADJUSTMENT

NOTE: The air flow sensor plate adjustment is critical. The distance between the sensor plate and the plate stop must be 0–0.2 in. The plate must also be centered in the venturi, and must not contact the venturi walls.

1. Remove the air cleaner assembly.

2. Using a 0.004 in. (0.10 mm) feeler gauge, check the clearance around the sensor plate at four opposite points around the plate.

3. If necessary, loosen the bolt in the center of the sensor plate and center the plate. Torque the bolt to 3.6 ft. lbs. (4.9 Nm).

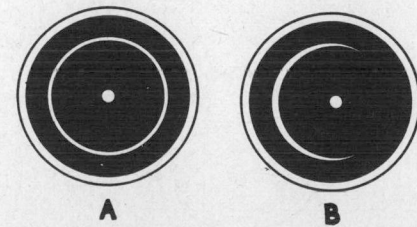

Sensor plate showing correct (A) and incorrect (B) centering in the venturi

SENSOR PLATE HEIGHT ADJUSTMENT

NOTE: The sensor plate height adjustment must be checked under fuel pressure.

1. Install a pressure gauge in the line between the fuel distributor and the control pressure regulator as previously described.

2. Remove the rubber elbow from the air flow sensor assembly.

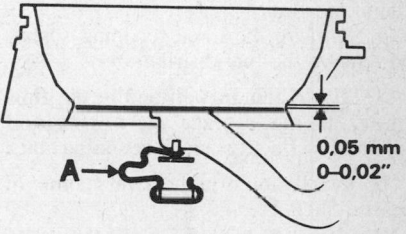

0,05 mm
0–0,02"

Correct sensor plate height in venturi. Adjust by bending spring (A)

3. Remove the fuel pump relay from the fuse panel and install a bridge adapter on pre-1979 models. Check that the fuel pressure is within specifications as previously described.

4. The sensor plate should be flush or 0.02 in. (0.5mm) below the beginning of the venturi taper. If necessary to adjust, remove the mixture control from the intermediate housing and bend the spring accordingly.

NOTE: With the sensor plate too high, the engine will run on and with the sensor plate too low, poor cold and warm engine start-up will result. If the sensor plate movement is erratic, the control piston can be sticking.

5. Recheck the pressure reading after any adjustments.

6. Remove the pressure gauge, reconnect the fuel lines and install the fuel pump relay, if removed.

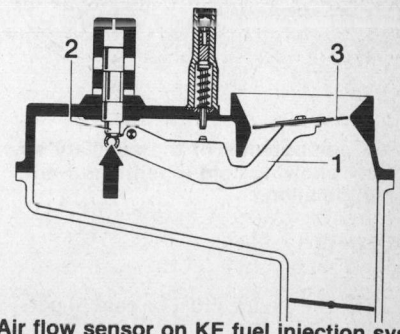

Air flow sensor on KE fuel injection system. The air flow sensor arm (1) moves the fuel metering piston (2) to regulate the mixture. Note the upward angle on the air flow sensor plate (3)

7. Reset the idle speed if necessary. See the individual car sections for details. Anytime an adjustment is made on the fuel system, or if a component is replaced, the idle CO should be reset with a CO meter.

REMOVAL & INSTALLATION

1. Relieve the fuel system pressure as previously described.

NOTE: Wrap a cloth around the connection to catch any escaping fuel.

2. Thoroughly clean all fuel lines on the fuel distributor and then remove them.

3. Remove the rubber air intake duct.

4. Remove the air flow sensor/fuel distributor as a unit.

5. Remove the three retaining screws and remove the fuel distributor.

NOTE: When installing the air flow sensor, always replace the O-ring and gaskets. Use Loctite® on all retaining bolts.

6. Installation is in the reverse order of removal.

Auxiliary Air Regulator

The auxiliary air regulator allows more air/fuel mixture when the engine is cold in order to improve driveability and provide idle stabilization. The increased air volume is measured by the air flow sensor and fuel is metered accordingly. The auxiliary air regulator contains a specially shaped plate attached to a bi-metal spring. The plate changes position according to engine temperature, allowing the moist air to pass when the engine is cold. As the temperature rises, the bi-metal spring slowly closes the air passage. The bi-metal spring is also heated electrically, allowing the opening time to be limited according to engine type. The auxiliary air regulator does not function when the engine is warm.

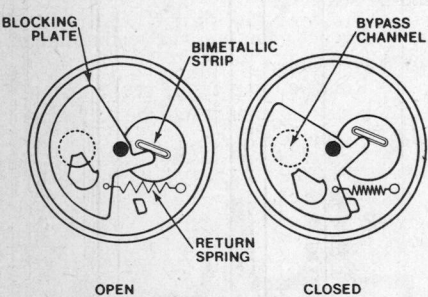

Internal components of the auxiliary air regulator showing cold (open) and warm (closed) positions

TESTING

NOTE: the engine must be cold to perform this test.

1. Disconnect the electrical terminal-plug and the two air hoses at the auxiliary air regulator.

2. Voltage must be present at the terminal plug with the ignition switch ON. Check the continuity of the heater coil by connecting a test light or ohmmeter to the terminals on the regulator.

3. Use a mirror to look through the bore of the regulator. If the air valve is not open, replace the auxiliary air regulator.

4. Connect the terminal plug and the two air hoses to the auxiliary air regulator.

5. Start the engine; the auxiliary air regulator bore should close within five minutes of engine operation by the cut-off valve.

NOTE: A quick check of the auxiliary air regulator can be made by unplugging the electrical connector with the engine cold. Start the engine and pinch the hose between the regulator and the intake manifold—the idle speed should drop. Reconnect the air regulator and allow the engine to warm up. With the engine at operating temperature, pinching the hose to the intake manifold should not affect the idle speed. If it does, replace the auxiliary air regulator.

REMOVAL & INSTALLATION

1. Locate the auxiliary air regulator on the rear of the intake manifold. Disconnect the electrical connection and remove the air hoses.

2. Remove the mounting bolts and remove the regulator.

3. Installation is in the reverse order of removal. Make sure all hose and electrical connections are tight.

Throttle Valve

The throttle valve housing is connected to the intake manifold and, in addition to the throttle valve, it contains the idling air passage and the idling adjustment screw, connections for the hoses to the auxiliary air valve, and the cold start valve and the vacuum outlet for ignition timing.

NOTE: Some later models with electronic engine controls do not use vacuum advance units on the distributor.

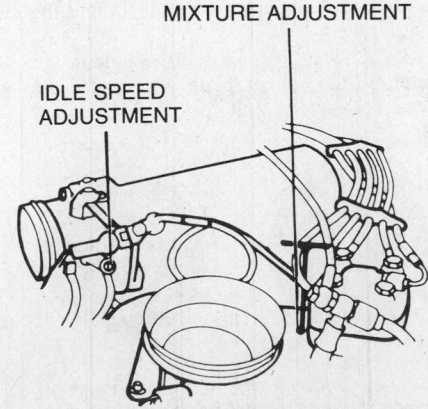

Typical adjustment points on K-Jetronic

ADJUSTMENT

The stop screw is set by the factory and should not be moved. If for some reason it is moved, adjust as follows:

1. Turn the screw counterclockwise until a gap is visible between the stop and the screw.

2. Turn the screw until it just touches the stop.

3. Turn the screw clockwise an additional ½ turn.

4. Adjust the idle speed and CO and check the linkage for proper operation and free movement.

IDLE ADJUSTMENTS

The idle speed screw (called a bypass screw by some manufacturers) on the throttle body housing of a K-Jetronic system bleeds air into the manifold when you increase idle speed—or cuts it off to slow the engine down. When idle speed changes the idle mixture always changes to some degree, and vice-versa. Therefore, you must juggle the speed and mixture adjustments back and forth to get the specified idle speed within the right range of CO. Unlike a carburetor, changing the idle CO changes the mixture throughout the entire rpm range. Never rev the engine with the Allen wrench sitting in the mixture screw or it may damage the air sensor plate.

Engine oil temperature is the most critical factor in getting an accurate CO adjustment on any K-Jetronic system. Don't touch the mixture screw until the oil temperature is between 140–176°F (60–80°C). CO adjustment is sealed on late K and all KE systems.

Lambda (Closed Loop) SYSTEM

K AND KE-JETRONIC

With the advent of the 3-way catalytic converter, the K-Jetronic system has undergone two major modifications; the addition of a Lambda or Oxygen Sensor system (K-Jetronic) and the integration of an elec-

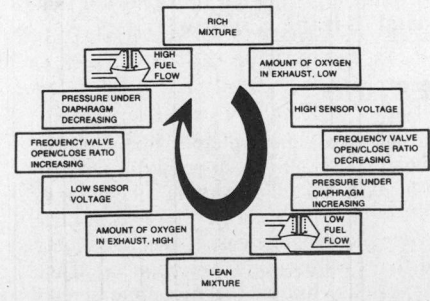

Operational schematic of K-Jetronic Lambda (Oxygen) Sensor system closed loop mode of operation

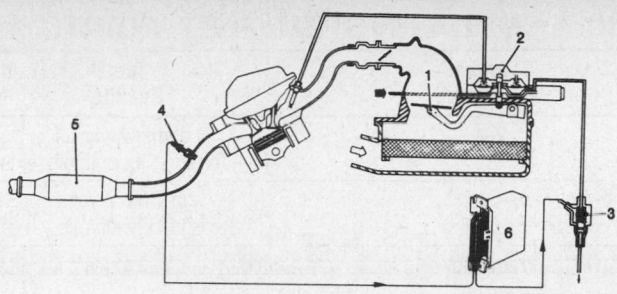

1. Air flow sensor
2. Fuel metering distributor
3. Frequency valve
4. Oxygen sensor
5. Catalytic converter
6. Electronic control unit

Components of K–Jetronic oxygen sensor system

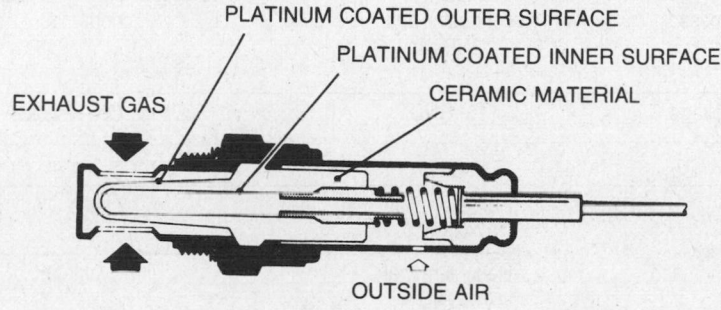

PLATINUM COATED OUTER SURFACE

PLATINUM COATED INNER SURFACE

EXHAUST GAS

CERAMIC MATERIAL

OUTSIDE AIR

Cross section of a typical oxygen sensor

trohydraulic actuator (KE-Jetronic). Both systems use an electronic control unit (ECU) for precise mixture (read emissions) control. Various new components have been integrated, such as an oxygen sensor, an electronic control unit (ECU), and a frequency valve, which convert K-Jet into a closed loop fuel system. In order for the 3-way converter to work effectively, the air/fuel mixture must be kept within a very precise range. Between 15 and 14 parts of air to one part of fuel, there's an ideal ratio called "stoichiometric" where HC, CO, and NO_x emissions are all at a minimum. Bosch calls this ratio (or stoichiometric point) "Lambda". Combined with an oxygen (or Lambda) sensor, mounted in the exhaust manifold, the air/fuel ratio in a fuel injected system can be controlled within a tolerance of 0.02%.

The oxygen sensor in the exhaust system monitors the oxygen content of the exhaust gases. It produces a small amount of voltage that varies depending on the amount of oxygen present in the exhaust. This voltage signal is sent to the ECU. The ECU, in turn, then signals the frequency valve to enrichen or lean the mixture. The voltage signal is approximately one volt. The frequency valve is located between the fuel distributor and the fuel return line. It does not change control pressure in the K-Jet system; it alters system pressure in the lower chamber of the fuel distributor for each cylinder's differential pressure valve.

NOTE: On the KE type CIS injection system, an electronic actuator replaces the frequency valve and control pressure regulator, as described under "Fuel Distributor" earlier. The control units are different for K and KE systems

Operation

When the oxygen sensor signals a rich mixture to the ECU, it will close the frequency valve. This causes pressure in the lower chamber of the fuel distributor to increase and push the diaphragm up to reduce fuel quantity. If the air/fuel mixture is too lean, the frequency valve will be open and reduce pressure in the lower chamber. The diaphragm is then pushed down and the amount of fuel is increased. The valve opens and closes many times per second. The average pressure is determined by the ratio of valve openings and closings. A higher open to closed ratio would provide a richer mixture, a lower open-to-closed ratio would give a leaner mixture. This is called the duty cycle of the frequency valve.

In the KE-Jetronic system, the Lambda control is integrated into the control unit which monitors the input signals from the various engine sensors (including the oxygen sensor), amplifies these signals and then calculates the correct output signal for the electrohydraulic actuator on the fuel distributor to modify the mixture as necessary. There is no frequency valve or control pressure regulator on KE systems. In addition, the oxygen sensor has three wires; one of which supplies current to a heating element that warms the oxygen sensor up to operating temperature faster and doesn't allow it to cool off at idle. The Lambda control system on the KE-Jetronic system is designed to cut out (go to open loop mode) under the following operating conditions:

• Oxygen sensor not warmed up to operating temperature
• During deceleration(fuel shut-off)

• At full load operation (wide open throttle)
• Whenever the engine coolant temperature is below 59°F (15°C) and until engine temperature reaches approximately 104°F (40°C)

The heating element of the oxygen sensor is usually energized from a terminal on the fuel pump relay and is heated as long as the fuel pump is running.

NOTE: Do not interchange different types of oxygen sensors (one, two, or three wire) when servicing. Do not let grease or oil contaminate the sensor tip while it's removed. Replace the oxygen sensor at 30,000 mile intervals.

Testing

Bosch makes a tester for the Lambda system that measures the open-to-closed ratio, or duty cycle. The Bosch KDJE 7453 tester (KDJE-P600 for KE systems) reads out the duty cycle on a percentage meter. A reading of 60, for instance, would be a frequency valve pulse rate of 60%. You can also use a sensitive dwell meter that reads to at least 70° to measure duty cycle on the 4-cyl. scale. Manufacturers using K-Jet with Lambda provide a test socket, so that a duty cycle tester can easily be hooked up. Audi's test connection, for instance, is located behind the throttle valve housing. Saab and most other makers locate the test socket in the wiring harness right near the underhood relay box.

— **CAUTION** —

If connected improperly, an analog meter may damage the oxygen sensor. Read the manufacturer's instructions before any testing

The following is a general procedure for checking the duty cycle with a dwell meter on K-Jetronic systems.

1. Disconnect the thermo switch wiring. Shorting the switch will enrich the mixture to about 60% for a cold engine. The meter needle should stay steady, which indicates an "open loop." This means the system isn't being affected by the oxygen sensor. Reconnect the thermo switch.

2. Disconnect the oxygen sensor with a warm engine. The meter should register a 50% signal.

3. Reconnect the oxygen sensor. You should see a change from open to closed loop. The needle will stay steady in the middle at 50% for about a minute. When the oxygen sensor warms up, it should signal the frequency valve for closed loop operation. That will be shown by a swinging needle on the meter, when the system is working correctly.

NOTE: See the individual car sections for information on resetting the service reminder warning light, if equipped.

The KE-Jetronic system requires the use

of a special tester for diagnosis. Before tracing possible faults in the oxygen sensor regulating system itself, make sure that the symptoms are not caused by mechanical faults in the engine, ignition system or other components in the injection system. For example, an incorrectly adjusted exhaust valve may have a considerable effect on regulation of the system. Aside from the dwell meter test described earlier, extensive testing of the Oxygen Sensor System requires the use of a special Bosch tester or its equivalent equipment.

NOTE: Before testing Lambda system with tester KDJE-P600, or equivalent, unplug the oxygen sensor and run the engine at idle until it reaches normal operating temperature. Read and record the voltage.

1. Connect the oxygen sensor, run the engine at approximately 2000 rpm and check that the readout on the test meter stays around the recorded value (taken with the sensor disconnected) and that the reading never exceeds ± 0.8 volts above or below that value. If these test results are achieved, the Lambda system is operating properly and no further testing is necessary.

2. If the readout is higher than approximately 4.8 volts, or lower than 2.1 volts, then the Lambda control is in need of adjustment. If the readout is constant, replace the oxygen sensor or repair the open circuit between the sensor and the control unit.

3. Test the oxygen sensor with the engine running at operating temperature. Disconnect the sensor electrical lead, run the engine at approximately 2000 rpm, then check the voltage of the sensor to ground. If the voltage does not exceed 450 mV, replace the oxygen sensor. If equipped with a heating element, check the circuit by measuring the voltage at the connector with the fuel pump relay removed and the sockets bridged at the connector. It should read approximately 12 volts and have a current value of 0.5A or greater.

OXYGEN SENSOR

Removal & Installation

Before fitting the oxygen sensor, coat all threads and gaskets with an antiseize compound (e.g. Never Seize® or Molycote 1000®). Do not apply compound to the sensor body.

NOTE: The joint between the oxygen sensor and the exhaust manifold must be gas-tight. Check that the other joints between the cylinder head cover and the muffler are tight.

——————— CAUTION ———————
The oxygen sensor is highly sensitive to knocks and must be handled carefully. Torque the sensor to 15–30 ft. lbs.

K–JETRONIC LAMBDA SYSTEM TEST POINTS

Circuit Tested	Terminal Numbers	Test Results
Check for short circuit	2–4 ①	0 ohms-wiring OK look for short if continuity exists
Ground check	8–GND ②	ign ON-12 volts ign OFF-0 volts
Frequency valve windings	Frequency valve terminals ①	2–3 ohms
Frequency valve harness connector ② valve	harness (+) connector and GND ②	12 volts with ign ON and ECU connected
Battery voltage from ignition switch to ECU	15–GND ②	ign ON-12 volts
Relay operation (ignition ON)	Relay terminal 87-GND②	12 volts-OK
	Relay terminal 87b-GND②	12 volts-OK
	Relay terminal 30-GND②	12 volts
	Relay terminal 86-GND②	12 volts

Note: Turn ignition off between tests and when removing or installing wiring harness connector
GND-Ground
① Ohmmeter connections
② Voltmeter connections

ELECTRONIC CONTROL UNIT (ECU)

Unlike the early K-Jetronic's mechanical control, the later K and KE-Jetronic system control is accomplished by an electronic unit (ECU) that receives and processes signals from various engine sensors to regulate the fuel mixture and accomodate several other functions not present in the early K-Jet system. The control unit is connected to battery voltage and is provided with a voltage correction (safety) circuit to prevent harmful voltage surges. The control unit on the KE-Jetronic system measures:
- Engine speed (tachometer)
- Coolant temperature (sensor in cylinder head)
- Airflow sensor position (position sensor)
- Full load signal (throttle valve switch)
- Idle speed signal (microswitch)
- Oxygen (Lambda) sensor signal
- Signal from altitude compensator

The signals are converted into the appropriate current values and sent to the electrohydraulic actuator and idle speed air valve. The control unit provides an enrichment signal during cranking and establishes smooth running charateristics after starting.

NOTE: The amount of after-start enrichment depends on coolant temperature.

The engine speed is limited by the control unit, which actuates the EHA to shut off fuel to the injectors at a preset rpm. Fuel mixture is also adjusted according to signals from an altitude compensator.

Removal & Installation

Locate the control unit and remove any covers or fastening bolts. The ECU is mounted somewhere in the passenger compartment, usually under the dash or one of the front seats. Carefully pull the unit clear to expose the main connector. Release the clip and remove the connector. Remove the control unit. Reverse the procedure for installation. Make sure all connectors are clean.

NOTE: Some control units are mounted under the passenger seat. Move the seat all the way back to gain access.

MODULATING VALVE

Removal & Installation

NOTE: During removal and fitting of the modulating valve, prevent the rubber valve retainer from coming into contact with gasoline. The rubber is of a special grade to prevent vibrations from the valve

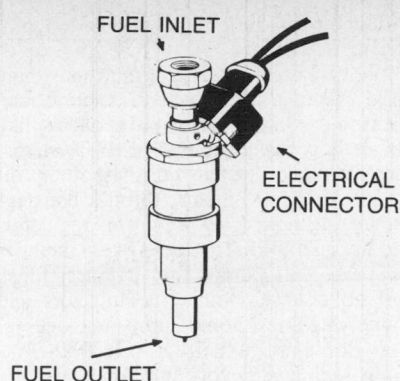

Typical modulating valve assembly

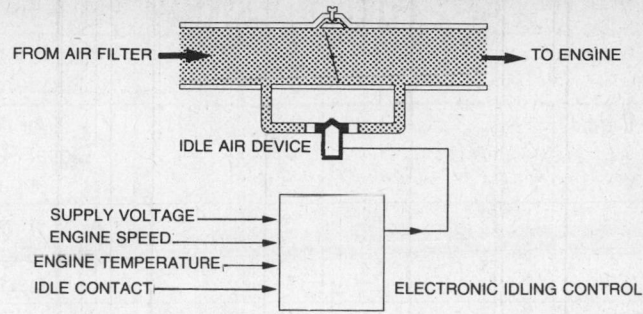

Schematic of Bosch Idle Speed Control System

being transmitted to the body. The rubber swells considerably if allowed to come into contact with gasoline.

1. Disconnect the electric cable.
2. Disconnect the small-bore line to the modulating valve. Grip the hexagonal nut closest to the hose (14 mm) and undo the valve nut (17 mm).
3. Disconnect the modulating valve return line from the warmup regulator, from the fuel distributor and the joint in the return line on the latter.
4. Remove and disconnect the valve and return lines.
5. Installation is the reverse of removal.

Constant Idle Speed (CIS) Control System

General Information

This electronic control system is designed to correct engine idle speed deviations very quickly; holding the idle speed constant even when loads such as power steering, air conditioning or automatic transmission are applied to the engine. Sensors on the engine read the engine speed (rpm), operating temperature and throttle position, then supply a voltage signal to a separate control unit which in turn adjusts the engine speed by feeding more or less air into the injection system by means of an idle air device. The control unit adjusts the idle speed according to pre-set (programmed) "ideal" rpm values contained in its memory.

The constant idle speed system is designed to be maintenance-free and will operate regardless of wear or changes in ignition timing. Under normal circumstances, no adjustment of the idle speed is necessary or possible. The idle air valve is located in a bypass hose which routes air around the throttle valve much the same way as the auxiliary air valve this system replaces. The idle speed control unit processes voltage signals from the various sensors on:

- Engine speed (tachometer)
- Coolant temperature (sensor in cylinder head)
- Throttle position (microswitch)

- Shift lever position (automatic transmission)
- A/C compressor cut-in signal

With the ignition OFF, the idle air valve is opened fully by a set of return springs. With the ignition ON, the idle air valve is controlled by a specific voltage from the control unit, providing an air valve opening dependent on coolant temperature. In this manner, the idle speed is constantly controlled between approximately 1000 rpm @ −4°F (−20°C) to roughly 750 rpm @ 68°F 920°C). The control unit also receives a voltage signal when the transmission shift lever is in PARK or NEUTRAL; this voltage signal usually drops when the transmission is engaged (DRIVE) to maintain the idle speed at the factory-established specification (usually around 650–700 rpm). The same type of voltage signal is produced by the air conditioner compressor, which also drops when the compressor engages, sending another signal to the idle air valve to once again maintain engine idle speed under load.

TESTING

NOTE: Testing the constant idle system (CIS) requires the use of Bosch tester KDJE-P600, or equivalent, along with the proper test cable adapter.

1. Connect test cable to idle air valve and tester. The engine should be idling at normal operating temperature.
2. Press the IR 100% button and note the reading on the tester. It should be 27–29% @ 670–770 rpm. If the reading is correct, the CIS system is operating properly.
3. If the reading on the tester is higher

or lower, adjust to the correct value or test the microswitch for proper operation.

4. If the readout is 0%, test for voltage on the plug for the idle air valve. There should be 12 volts from the feed side of the pin socket to ground. If not, check for an open circuit in the idle air valve harness and repair as necessary.
5. Check the resistance of the idle air valve. It should be approximately 12 ohms between terminals 2 and 3; and the same value between terminals 2 and 1. If not, replace the idle air valve assembly.

NOTE: If the voltage signal to the idle air valve is correct (12 volts), check the ground line to the control unit. Replace the control unit if no ground connection is present. Make sure the ignition switch is OFF before disconnecting or reconnecting any CIS system components.

AIR FLOW CONTROLLED (AFC) FUEL INJECTION

The most common type of AFC fuel injection is the Bosch L-Jetronic system. The L stands for "Luftmengenmessung" which means "air flow management." The L-Jetronic AFC injection system is used, with various modifications, by both European and Asian manufacturers. Different versions of the basic L-Jetronic design include

AFC FUEL INJECTION

Type of System	Primary Control Measurement
L-Jetronic	Air flow
LH II-Jetronic	Air mass
LH-Jetronic	Air mass
LU-Jetronic	Air flow (Utilizes a hybrid ECU that converts analog signals to digital map)

AFC FUEL INJECTION

Type of System	Primary Control Measurement
LU-Jetronic Digital	Air flow Digital ECU with inputs
Motronic	Air flow with digital control of ignition and injection
Mitsubishi ECI	Ultrasonic measurement of Karman vortices ①
Nissan ECCS	Air mass
Isuzu I-TEC	Air flow

① See Mitsubishi ECI system for details

LH, LH II, LU, LU Digital and Motronic. Although similar in design and operation, each separate system uses slightly different components. LH-Jetronic, for example, measures the incoming air mass with a heated wire built into the air flow meter, instead of a flap valve.

Aside from different terminology, most Asian and European AFC systems are similar in both appearance and function. For this reason, it is important to accurately identify the particular type of AFC system being serviced. A small diagram of the fuel injection system is usually found under the hood on a sticker somewhere near the emission control label; it's very important to understand how the different components function and affect one another when troubleshooting any AFC fuel injection system.

L-Jetronic

The Bosch L-Jetronic is an electronically controlled system that injects the fuel charge into the engine intake ports in intermittent pulses by means of electromagnetic, solenoid-type fuel injectors (one per cylinder). The quantity of fuel injected per pulse depends on the length of time the injector is open, which is determined by an electrical impulse signal from the electronic control unit (ECU) that reacts to inputs from various engine sensors. The main control sensor is the air flow meter, which measures the amount of air being inducted into the engine. Sensors for engine temperature, engine speed (rpm), intake air temperature, throttle position, exhaust gas oxygen content and barometric pressure also feed information into the control unit to help determine the fuel injection quantity (mixture) that will produce the best performance with the least emissions. The L-Jetronic control unit is used in both analog and digital versions which are not interchangeable.

Fuel is supplied to the injectors under fairly constant pressure by an electric roller cell pump and a fuel pressure regulator that responds to manifold vacuum and returns excess gasoline to the tank. A set of points in the intake air sensor assures that the pump only gets current when the engine is running or being cranked. This eliminates flooding in the event that an injector springs a leak.

Three components that aren't connected to the computer assist in starting and warm-up. The cold start valve in the intake manifold injects extra fuel while the engine is being cranked. It's controlled by the thermotime switch, a thermostatic device that energizes the cold start valve for 3 to 10 seconds. Its bimetal strip is affected by both engine temperature and an electrical heating coil. The auxiliary air regulator bypasses the throttle plate to provide extra air during warm-up, which prevents stalling. A heating element inside causes it to close gradually.

OPERATION

The L-Jetronic system measures intake air and meters the proper fuel to obtain the correct air/fuel ratio under a wide range of driving conditions.

We can break the L-Jetronic into three basic systems: air intake; fuel supply and electronic control. Some components like the air flow meter are part of two systems. The air intake system consists of the air cleaner, air flow meter, throttle housing, connecting hoses, air valve (air regulator) and the manifold. The fuel system includes the tank, fuel pump, fuel damper, filter, fuel rail, cold start valve, fuel injectors, and connecting lines. Some European L-Jet systems don't use a fuel damper. Both Datsun/Nissan and Toyota employ dampers to reduce pulsation from pump output. Dampers have what looks like an adjusting screw, but *don't attempt any adjustment*. The Datsun 200SX injection system doesn't use a cold start valve.

The electronic control system is made up of the electronic control unit (ECU) and several sensors. Each sensor signals measurements on engine condition to the ECU, which then computes fuel needs. Injectors are then opened and closed by ECU command to feed the needed amount of fuel. Injectors are connected in parallel. All suppply fuel at the same time. They open twice for each rotation of the engine camshaft, injecting ½ the needed fuel each time.

The big sensor, and the one that gives the system its name, is the air flow sensor. This is located in the large airbox. A flap in the box opens and closes in response to air being drawn into the engine. The ECU is then signalled as to the amount of air being taken in. An air temperature sensor in the box sends that information to the ECU. Engine rpm is picked up from the negative side of the coil. A throttle valve switch tells the control unit how much the throttle is open. Engine temperature is transmitted from a coolant temperature sensor. Later model Datsuns/Nissans use a cylinder head temperature sensor instead of a coolant temperature sensor. A signal from the ignition switch tells the ECU when the engine is being started. An O_2 sensor has been added to feed exhaust gas oxygen content to the ECU.

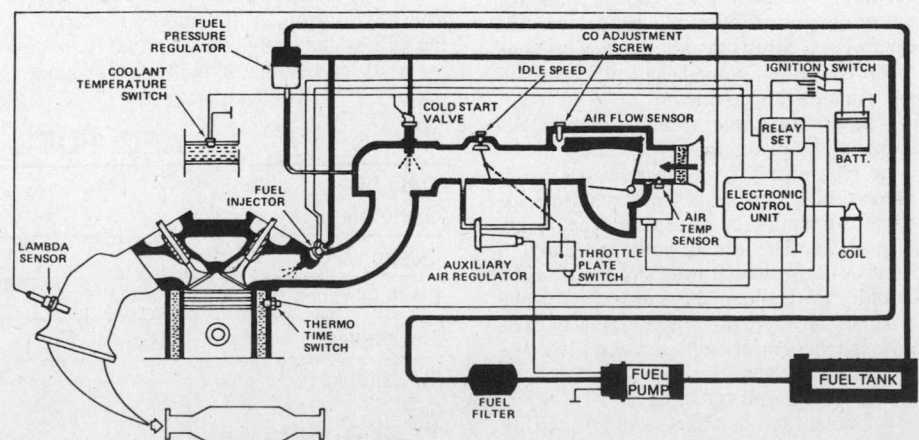

Typical European L–Jetronic injection system schematic

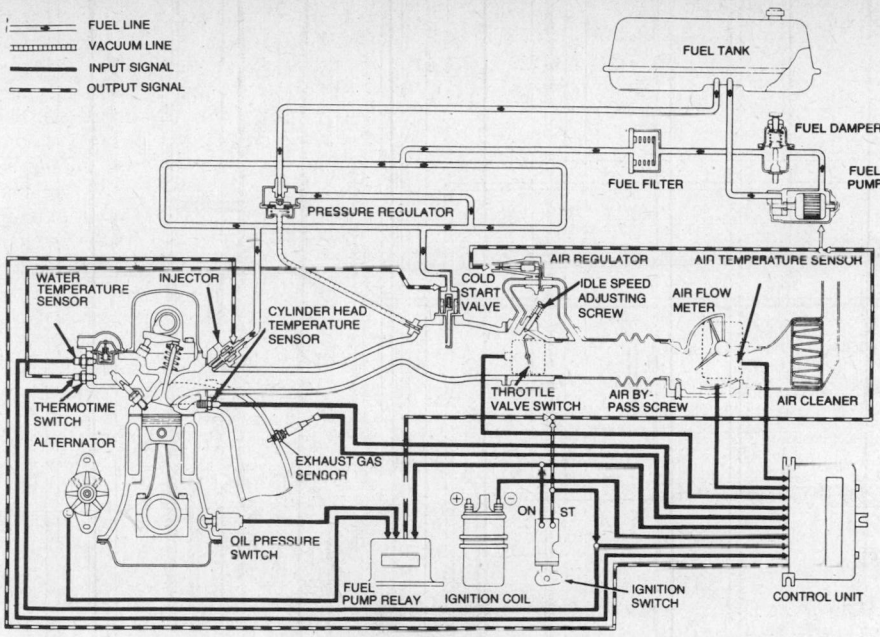

FUEL LINE
VACUUM LINE
INPUT SIGNAL
OUTPUT SIGNAL

Typical Japanese L–Jetronic injection system schematic

LH and LH II-Jetronic

These sytems are further developments of the L-Jetronic. LH is an abbreviation of "Luft-Hitzdracht" which means "hot air wire." Both the LII and LH II work on the same principle as the L system, but instead of an air flow sensor flap to measure intake air quantity, these systems use a heated platinum wire to measure the air mass. In this manner, altitude influences are eliminated from the injection systems input quantities. A very thin platinum wire is stretched across the air intake opening in the air flow meter and forms part of a bridge circuit. Air flowing over the wire draws heat from it, changing the wire's electrical resistance as the temperature changes. An electronic amplifier instantly responds to any such resistance change and regulates the current to the wire so as to maintain it at a virtually constant temperature. The current necessary to maintain the wire temperature is the measure of the air mass flowing into the induction system, and this signal is used by the ECU to determine the injector opening time to adjust the air/fuel mixture.

OPERATION

The LH and LH II-Jetronic fuel injection are electronic systems with the same basic components as the L-Jetronic. The systems consist of a control unit with various engine sensors that measure and monitor engine operating conditions and adjust the fuel mixture for optimum performance with minimum emissions, according to load, throttle position, temperature, etc. The control unit regulates the fuel quantity by varying the length of them the injectors are open and regulates idle speed by varying an air control valve opening. The system measures the air mass entering the engine by means of a heated platinum wire. Because dirt and impurities may accumulate on the wire surface and affect the voltage signal, the system is designed to clean the wire each time the engine is turned off to eliminate impurities and corrosion.

The LH and LH II injection systems operate with a moderate fuel pressure which is held constant by a fuel pressure regulator. Fuel injection is by means of electrically controlled solenoid-type injectors which spray fuel directly behind the engine intake valves. The injection duration is usually measured in milliseconds and is controlled by the electronic control unit (ECU). The ECU receives signals from a set of engine sensors, the most important of which is the air mass meter that continuously measures the mass of air entering the intake manifold. When the engine stops, the wire is heated up to 1050–1920°F for less than one second to burn off any dirt, corrosion or impurities on the filament. If allowed to build up, these impurities would cause false signals to be sent to the control unit and affect the air/fuel mixture. In addition to the air flow meter, the other sensors providing input to the ECU include:

• Throttle valve position sensor (switch)
• Vacuum switch (indicating part and full load/idle conditions)
• Engine speed sensor (tachometer connection)
• Oxygen sensor (Lambda system)
• Coolant temperature sensor
• Cold starting control (enrichment program)

The electronic control unit receives and processes signals from the engine sensors and calculates the correct fuel mixture according to a preprogrammed memory unit contained within the ECU assembly. *The ECU and its connector should be handled with the utmost care during all testing and/or service procedures.*

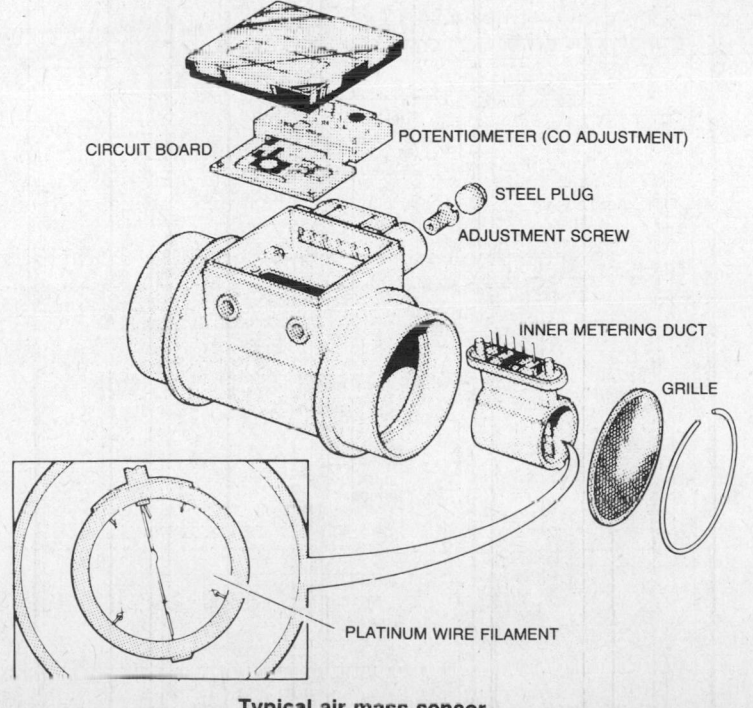

CIRCUIT BOARD
POTENTIOMETER (CO ADJUSTMENT)
STEEL PLUG
ADJUSTMENT SCREW
INNER METERING DUCT
GRILLE
PLATINUM WIRE FILAMENT

Typical air mass sensor

NOTE: Each individual variant of the L-Jetronic injection system use a different control unit. They are not interchangeable.

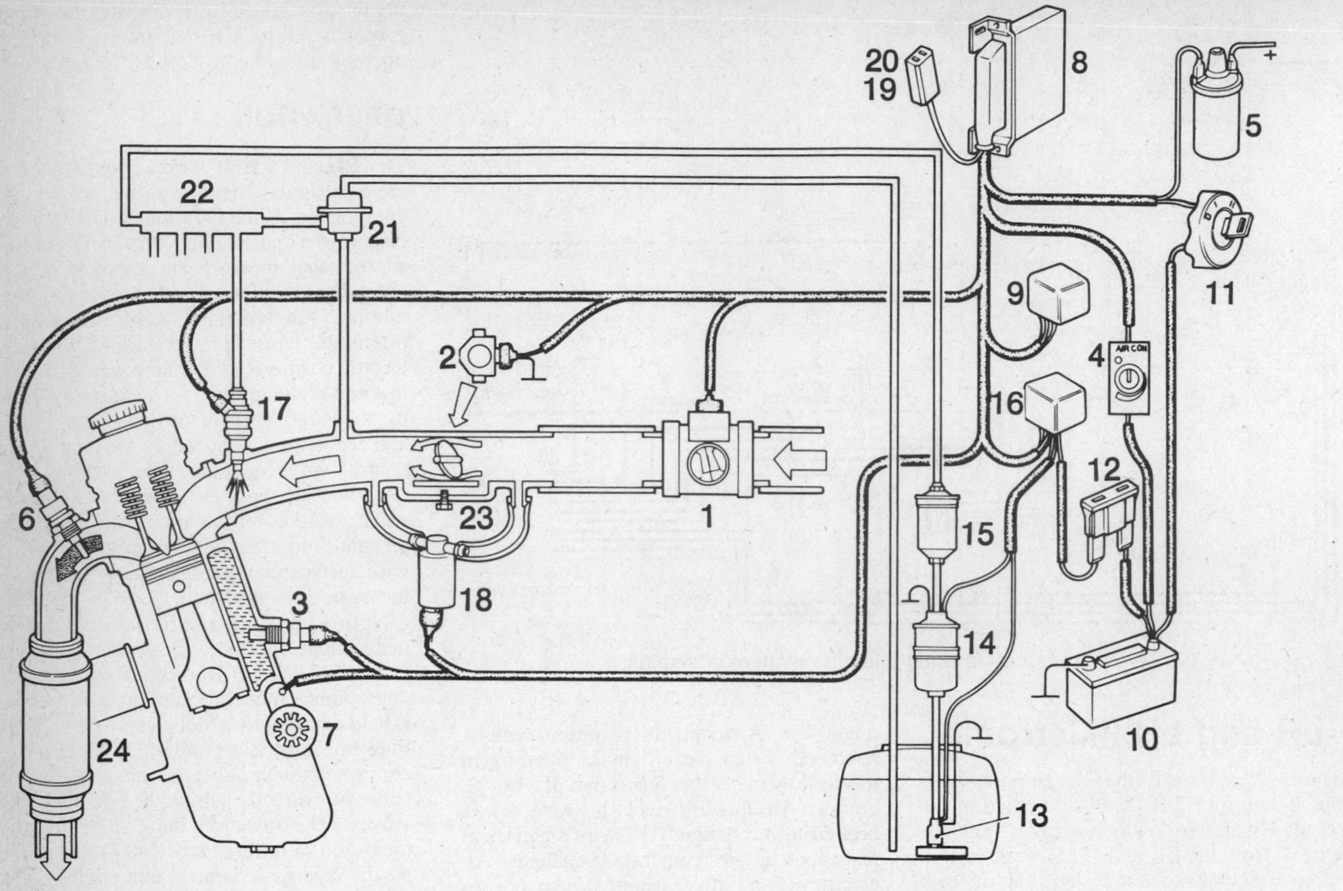

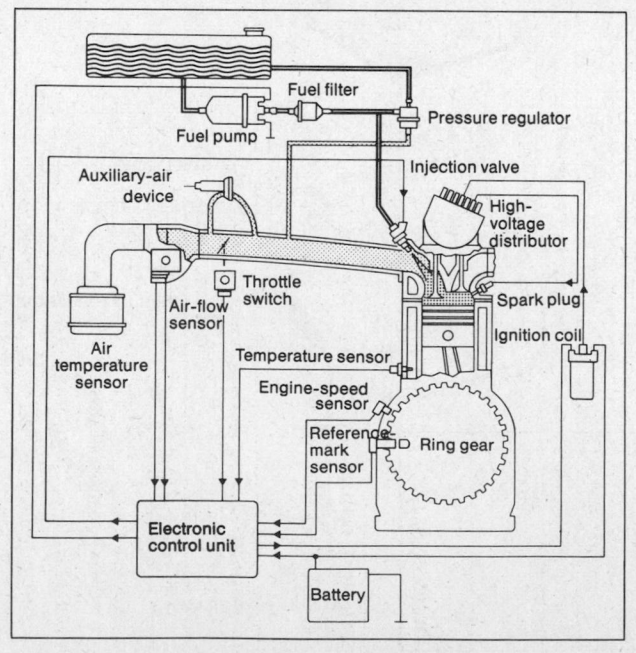

1. Air mass sensor
2. Throttle valve switch
3. Temperature sensor
4. A/C microswitch
5. Ignition coil
6. Oxygen sensor
7. Starter
8. Control unit
9. System relay
10. Battery
11. Ignition switch
12. Fuse
13. Tank pump
14. Fuel pump
15. Fuel filter
16. Fuel pump relay
17. Injectors
18. Air control valve
19. Lambda test point
20. Idle speed test point
21. Line pressure regulator
22. Injection manifold
23. Idle adjustment screw
24. Catalytic converter

Schematic of LH II Fuel Injection System used on Volvo models

Motronic

The Motronic fuel injection system combines the digital control of individual systems such as fuel injection and ignition into a single unit. The heart of the Motronic system is a microcomputer that is programmed according to dynomometer data on a specific engine's characteristics. In operation, various engine sensors deliver data on engine speed (rpm), crankshaft position and temperature (engine and ambient air). From this input, the control unit determines the ideal spark advance and fuel quantity, up to 400 times a second. In this manner, spark advance and fuel quantity is tailored exactly to the engine operating conditions such as idling, part load, full load, warmup, deceleration and transient modes. Optimal fuel injection and ignition settings improve the engine's overall performance while reducing fuel consumption and emissions. Motronic systems can be made to incorporate other features from modified L-Jetronic systems, such as the air mass sensor wire in the intake air meter and electronic control of automatic transmission. Its basic operation is very similar to the previously

Schematic of Motronic Fuel Injection System

TROUBLESHOOTING—L-JETRONIC

Cause	Engine cranks but does not start	Engine starts but then dies	Rough or unstable idle	Idle speed incorrect	CO value incorrect	Erratic running	Engine misses when driving	Fuel consumption too high	No maximum power	Correction
Defect in ignition system	•	•	•			•	•		•	Check battery, distributor, plugs, coil and timing
Mechanical defect in engine	•	•	•				•		•	Check compression, valve adj. and oil pressure
Leaks in air intake system (false air)	•	•	•	•	•	•				Check all hoses and connections; eliminate leaks
Blockage in fuel system	•	•					•		•	Check fuel tank, filter and lines for free flow
Relay defective; wire to injector open	•	•								Test relay; check wiring harness
Fuel pump not operating	•	•								Check pump fuse, pump relay and pump
Fuel system pressure incorrect	•	•	•			•	•	•	•	Check pressure regulator
Cold start valve not operating	•									Test for spray; check wiring and thermo-time switch
Cold start valve leaking	•	•	•		•			•		Check valve for leakage
Thermo-time switch defective	•	•								Test for resistance readings vs. temperature
Auxiliary air valve not operating correctly		•	•	•						Must be open with cold engine; closed with warm
Temperature sensor defective		•	•		•			•		Test for 2–3 kΩ at 68° F.
Air flow meter defective		•	•			•	•		•	Check with ohmmeter and adjust
Throttle butterfly does not completely close or open			•	•					•	Readjust throttle stops
Throttle valve switch defective			•						•	Check pump contacts; test flap for free movement
Idle speed incorrectly adjusted			•	•						Adjust idle speed with bypass screw
Defective injection valve			•			•	•			Check valves individually for spray
CO concentration incorrectly set					•			•		Readjust CO with screw on air flow meter
Loose connection in wiring harness or system ground						•				Check and clean all connections
Control unit defective									•	Use known good unit to confirm defect

described L, LH and LH II injection systems, except for the automatic ignition timing control.

SERVICE PRECAUTIONS

1. Make sure the ignition is switched OFF before removing or installing any component connectors, especially to the control unit.

2. Do not replace any control unit without first checking all wiring and components, otherwise an existing fault could ruin a new ECU the same way the old one was damaged.

3. Never check connector terminals from the front, especially the main harness connector to the ECU. Excessive force can damage connector terminals and cause other faults. The correct testing method is to remove the connector cover and check the terminals from the holes provided in the side of the connector. Terminal numbers are usually stamped on the side of the connector.

4. When removing the control unit connector, release the lock tabs, then fold out the connector. Do not pull the ECU connector straight out. All electrical connectors should have some kind of lock device to keep the connectors from coming apart.

5. Remove any electronic control unit before subjecting the car to any temperature in excess of 176°F (80°C), such as when baking paint in an oven.

6. Cleanliness is extremely important when working on or around the fuel system. Do not allow dirt or grease to contaminate the fuel system. Always use new gaskets and seals during reassembly of components using them. Clean all fuel connections before removal, and prepare a clean work area.

7. Disconnect the ignition system when performing compression tests. Any arcing to the injectors or injector wiring can damage the control unit. Arcing to the ignition coil low tension side can damage vehicles equipped with Hall Effect distributors.

8. Never use a quick charger on the

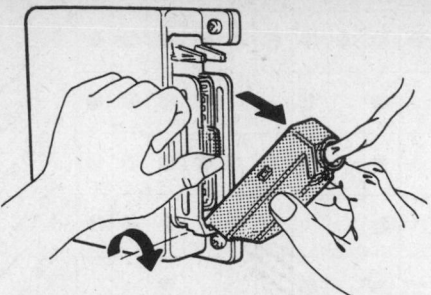

Release the locking clip and fold the control unit connector out as shown

battery or attempt to use a "hot shot" 24 volt starting aid. Maximum charging current should not exceed 15 amps.

9. Always depressurize the fuel system before attempting to disconnect any fuel lines or components.

10. Harsh chemicals such as carburetor cleaner should not be used to find vacuum leaks. The oxygen sensor is easily contaminated and ruined by certain chemicals and fuel additives commonly used on carbureted engines.

Troubleshooting

WATER IN FUEL

Water is one of the biggest killers of electronic fuel injection (EFI) system components, regardless of the type of system. The high pressures generated by the fuel pump can and will push water and fuel right through the fuel filter into the rest of the system.

Water problems can be minimized by changing filters regularly, using water absorbing fuel additives (especially in colder weather), and by installing a water filter.

Several companies manufacture water separation/filtration systems which electronically detect the presence of water in the fuel. They can be used in all environments under the hood, with all fuels, and packaged with all fittings, brackets and hardware for easy installation.

PRELIMINARY CHECKS

Before assuming the EFI system is at fault, make the standard preliminary checks of ignition system and engine conditions before going any further. Check the battery.

Check the electrical connections; EFI electrical systems won't tolerate corrosion or sloppy connections. Clean connections with one of the electrical cleaners available and be absolutely certain that spaded terminals snap tightly into their plastic connector bodies. Carefully crimp these where necessary with needlenose pliers. Also, check the main harness connector that plugs into the ECU for dirt, corrosion, or bent or spread-out terminals. This check alone has solved many intermittent EFI performance problems.

NOTE: Sealing electrical connections against moisture is important. Make sure all connectors snap tightly together and no bare wire protrudes from the back of the connector body. Replace any rubber protector caps removed during testing.

A bad set of ignition wires will cause the same symptoms as a bad pressure regulator, so check the ignition system first. Steady vacuum that's within specs is a must on these cars. A vacuum leak unbalances the system thoughout its entire operating range. A leaky engine will start, idle, and run poorly.

NOTE: L-Jetronic systems tend to be so "mixture sensitive" that crankcase air leaks will upset them. If the sealing ring around the oil filter cap is broken or missing, a VW for instance, with L-Jetronic just won't perform.

Fuel Pump

Fuel is drawn from the fuel tank into the fuel pump, from which it is discharged under pressure. As it flows through the mechanical fuel damper (if so equipped), pulsation in the fuel flow is damped. Then, the fuel is filtered in the fuel filter, goes through the fuel line, and is injected into the intake port. Surplus fuel is bled through the pressure regulator and is returned to the fuel tank. The pressure regulator controls the injection pressure in such a manner that the pressure difference between the fuel pressure and the intake manifold vacuum is always approximately 36 psi.

The fuel pump is a wet type pump where the vane rollers are directly coupled to a motor which is filled with fuel. The fuel cools and lubricates the pump internal components as it flows through, so the fuel pump should never be allowed to run dry. A relief

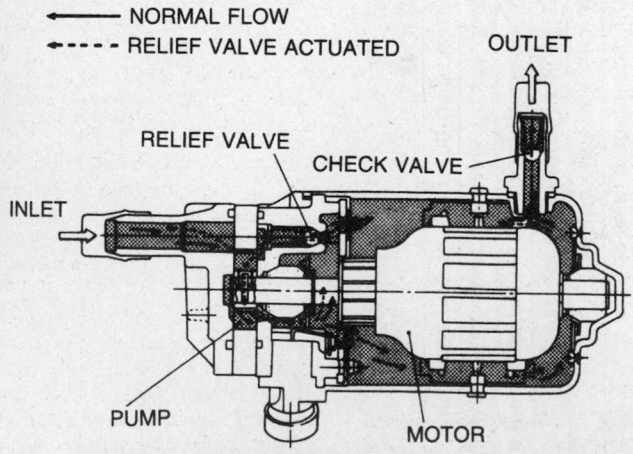

← — NORMAL FLOW
◄----- RELIEF VALVE ACTUATED

OUTLET

RELIEF VALVE

CHECK VALVE

INLET

PUMP

MOTOR

Typical fuel pump used on L–Jetronic systems

valve in the pump is designed to open when the pressure in the fuel lines rises over 43-64 psi due to a malfunction in the pressure system. A check valve prevents abrupt drop of pressure in the fuel pipe when stopping the engine.

NOTE: For fuel pump removal and installation procedures, please refer to individual car sections.

—— CAUTION ——
Operating the fuel pump dry for more than a few seconds can cause pump seizure.

RELIEVING FUEL SYSTEM PRESSURE

—— CAUTION ——
Fire hazard. Relieve fuel system pressure before attempting to disconnect any fuel injection system components.

1. Remove the vacuum hose from the fuel pressure regulator.
2. Connect a hand vacuum pump to the regulator and pump vacuum up to 20 in. Hg.

—— CAUTION ——
This procedure allows the fuel system pressure to vent into the tank, it does not however, remove all fuel from the lines.

3. Wrap a clean rag around a fuel connection to catch any fuel while carefully loosening connection. Listen for sound of venting into fuel tank.

Alternate Methods for Relieving Fuel Pressure

1. Disconnect the battery ground cable.
2. Disconnect the wiring harness to the cold start valve.

—— CAUTION ——
Do not disconnect any components with the engine running on later LH, LH II, LU and Motronic systems. Removing the battery cable will clear the trouble code memory on self-diagnosing injection systems.

3. Using two jumper wires from the battery, energize the cold start valve for two or three seconds to relieve pressure in the fuel system. Be careful not to short the jumpers together.
4. If an early L-Jet system is used, start the engine, then remove the fuel pump relay or unplug the pump connector and allow the engine to stall.
5. Carefully loosen the fuel line as in primary method.

FUEL PUMP POWER CHECK

If an AFC equipped car doesn't start, there's a good chance it might be the fuel pump

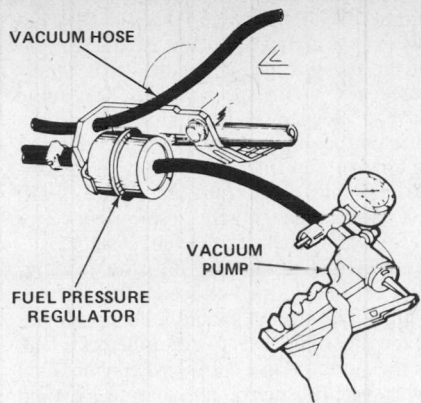

Relieving fuel system pressure on the L-Jetronic system

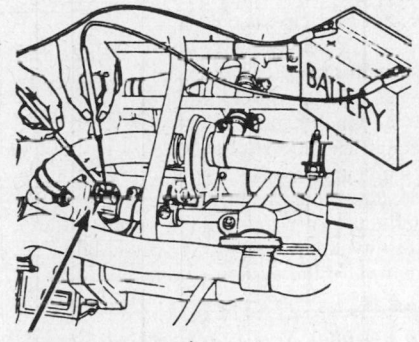

Alternate method for relieving fuel pressure

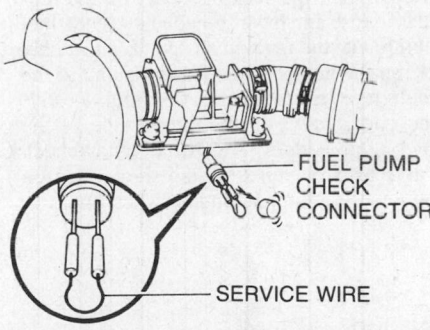

Testing the fuel pump on the L-Jetronic. Not all models have the test connector

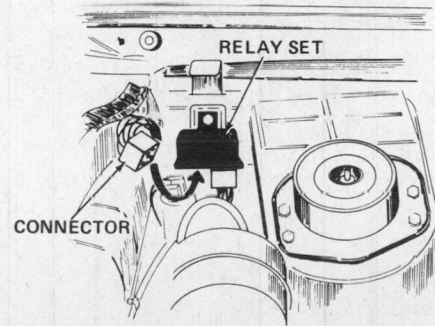

Typical L-Jetronic dual relay set, usually mounted somewhere in the engine compartment

or its circuit. First, visually check all the pump and relay wiring, as it could be nothing more than a bad connection. Be sure that the pump is grounded. Corrosion can break the ground circuit. Check the pump fuse and look to see if the fusible link in the system is burned. Don't forget to clean the battery cables—the pump calls for 12 volts. If the link or fuse is burned, it could be a seized or worn out pump. Or it could be watered gas, which will freeze the pump in winter. The last item to try is bypassing the relay with a jumper wire. If it works, then the relay's bad. Some models have a convenient fuel pump check connector under the air flow meter or fuel rail. Pry the cap off and, with a jumper wire, you can run the pump without starting the engine. If you can feel fuel pressure at the cold start valve and hear fuel returning through the regulator, the pump's working.

Exercise caution with the dual relays used in L-Jetronic cars. Refer to a wiring diagram of the particular vehicle because the main relay side and the pump relay side of the dual relay are seldom labeled by the manufacturer. Make sure the correct terminals connect the jumper across the *pump relay* side of the dual relay. Remember, too, that all AFC electric fuel pumps use a separate ground wire. So don't neglect to ground check during pump troubleshooting. As is the case with the fuse, these relays could be anywhere. Datsun hides a dual relay inside the kick panel; VW may have it under the dashboard; and others may have their pump relays under the hood. Some AFC systems use a single, main relay on later models.

FUEL PRESSURE CHECK

NOTE: Use this check to determine if the fuel pump is operating properly and to check for restrictions in fuel lines.

To test the L-Jetronic systems, you must have an extremely accurate pressure gauge that reads 0–50 psi in 0.5-psi increments. Also, remember that high operating pressures mean that connections must be tight. 30–40 psi pressures won't tolerate any haphazard connections. Don't risk a fire—use a reinforced fuel line hose that'll withstand 30–40 psi and use worm gear type clamps to secure the hose. Keep an eye out for leakage in the fuel plumbing and check the braided hose used as OEM equipment.

—— CAUTION ——
The fuel system must be depressurized before disconnecting any fuel system components. The cold start valve body is plastic, use care in removing the fuel hose.

Connect the pressure gauge to the cold start injector connection on the fuel rail, or that line between the fuel rail and filter. Banjo fittings are used throughout the Toyota AFC system. An adapter with a banjo fitting at one end will be needed to hook up the gauge. Take a good look at the hoses

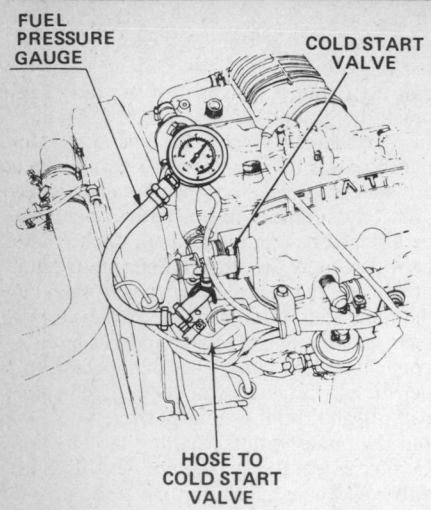

Checking the fuel pressure on L–Jetronic systems—typical

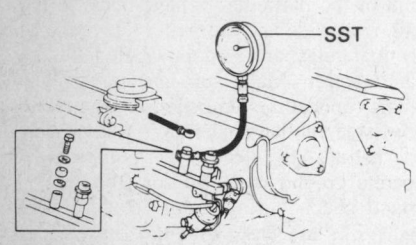

Typical fuel pressure gauge hook–up on Japanese L–Jetronic systems—note banjo fittings used for fuel connections

on these cars. Hoses must be in decent shape and fittings or clamps should be tight.

Start the engine and disconnect and plug the vacuum line to the pressure regulator. Pressure at idle should be approximately 33–38 psi (34–45 psi on later models). A bad pressure regulator is indicated by pressure that's too high. Look for kinked fuel lines, restrictive fuel filter, or a faulty pump or pump check valve, if the pressure is too low.

Connect the vacuum hose to the pressure regulator. Watch the gauge. Pressure should drop to 28 psi. A reading over 33 psi means the regulator's bad. Check pressure at full throttle. Pressure should climb to 37 psi as soon as the throttle is wide open. On all L-Jetronic systems, pressure should hold when the engine is shut off. An immediate pressure drop means an internally leaking injector(s), pressure regulator, or fuel pump.

NOTE: The pressure reading may slowly drop through the regulator valve seating or the pump non-return valve. A slow, steady drop is permissable, a rapid fall is not.

When taking a fuel pressure reading at idle, normal injector pulsation will cause the gauge to fluctuate. This pulsation is most pronounced on 4 cylinder engines. Watch the needle carefully and take the *average* pressure value. At idle, simply take your

pressure reading as being the mid-point between the highest and lowest fluctuations of the pressure gauge needle. If fuel pressure isn't within specs at idle, you could have a clogged fuel filter or either a restricted fuel line or fuel return line. Be sure to change fuel filters at least every 7,500–10,000 miles. Make sure any additives will not damage the oxygen sensor or converter before using them in the fuel system.

After taking the idle pressure reading, shut off the engine and watch the pressure gauge. The system should hold 17–20 psi. If the pressure drops to zero, there's a leak in the system. On a car with a conventional fuel system, such a pressure loss would suggest that either the fuel pump or the carburetor inlet valve were leaking. But assuming that they're not leaking fuel *externally*, there are four places an L-Jetronic system can leak *internally*:

1. The check valve in the output side of the electric fuel pump.
2. The pressure regulator.
3. One or more injectors.
4. The cold start valve.

To begin isolating a leak, crimp the hose connecting the fuel pressure regulator to the fuel tank. Turn the ignition switch off and on to cycle the fuel pump so you build up pressure in the system again.

--- CAUTION ---

Do not allow fuel system pressure to exceed 85 psi.

If the system now holds pressure, then the regulator is leaking. If the pressure still drops, keep the locking pliers on the regulator hose and have someone cycle the fuel pump with the ignition switch. Then quickly crimp the hose connecting the pump to the main fuel rail. If the pressure holds steady, the check valve in the output side of the fuel pump is defective. A bad pump check valve usually causes a hard start condition on an EFI equipped engine when hot.

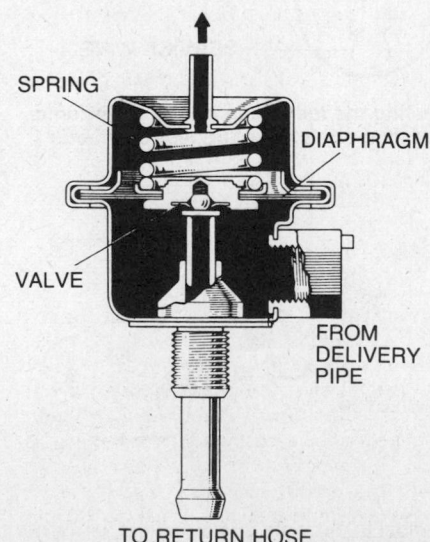

L–Jetronic fuel pressure regulator—typical

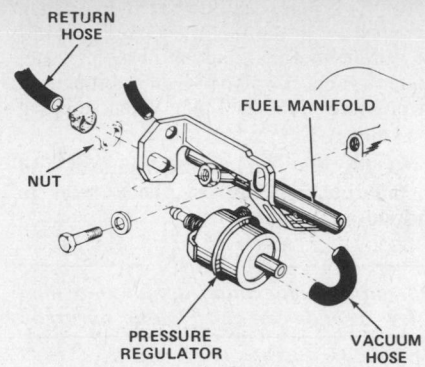

Typical pressure regulator mounting on L–Jetronic. Bracket fasteners and fuel connections will vary

VOLUME TEST

A pressure test alone won't reveal trouble with an EFI fuel pump. It's important to also perform a volume test as well as a pressure test. With 12 volts at the pump and at least half a tank of gas in the car, a typical L-Jetronic pump should deliver about a quart (almost a liter) of fuel in 30 seconds.

--- CAUTION ---

Take precautions to avoid fire hazard when performing pressure and volume tests.

Fuel Pressure Regulator

REMOVAL & INSTALLATION

1. Relieve fuel system pressure.
2. Disengage the vacuum line connecting the regulator to the intake manifold from the pressure regulator.
3. Remove the bolt and washers securing the pressure regulator mounting bracket and carefully pull the regulator and bracket upward. Note the position of the regulator in the bracket.
4. Unfasten the hose clamps and disconnect the pressure regulator from the fuel hose. Inspect the hose for signs of wear, cracks or fuel leaks.

NOTE: Place a clean rag under the pressure regulator to catch any spilled fuel.

5. Remove the lock nut and remove the pressure regulator.
6. Installation is the reverse of removal.

NOTE: Torque the fuel delivery union bolt to 18–25 ft. lbs. Do not overtighten.

Fuel Injectors

Fuel in the L-Jetronic system is not injected directly into the cylinder. Fuel is injected into the intake port, where the air/fuel mix-

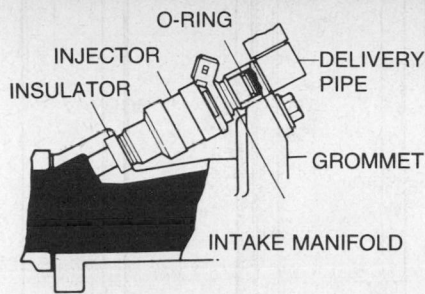

L—Jetronic fuel injector installation showing position of nozzle in the intake port

ture is drawn into the cylinder when the intake valve opens to start the intake stroke. An electrical signal from each engine sensor is introduced into the control unit for computation. The open valve time period of the injector is controlled by the duration of the pulse computed in the control unit.

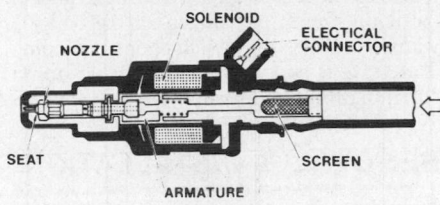

Sectional view of an L—Jetronic fuel injector

The injector operates on the solenoid valve principle. When an electric signal is applied to the coil built into the injector, the plunger is pulled into the solenoid, thereby opening the needle valve for fuel injection. The quantity of injected fuel is in proportion to the duration of the pulse applied from the control unit. The longer the pulse, the more fuel is delivered.

The fuel injectors are electrically connected, in parallel, in the control unit. All injectors receive the injection signal from the control unit at the same time. Therefore, injection is made independently of the engine stroke cycle (intake, combustion, and exhaust).

NOTE: For fuel injector removal and installation procedures, please refer to the individual car sections.

A bad injection valve can cause a number of problems:
1. Hot restart troubles.
2. Rough idle.
3. Hesitation.
4. Poor power.

Hot starting complaints can come from an injector or injectors that are leaking fuel droplets when they're supposed to be completely shut. The next three problems can be caused by a bad spray pattern from one or more of the injectors. Dribble patterns, fire hose shots, and uneven sprays will produce hesitation, stumbling and general lack of power. Replace any injector with a bad spray pattern.

TESTING THE FUEL INJECTOR

With the engine running or cranking, use an engine stethoscope to check that there is normal operating noise in proportion to engine rpm. Using a stethoscope or a screwdriver, you can listen to each injector. A regular clicking means it's working. The interval between clicks should shorten as engine speed is increased. If you don't hear an injector clicking, there may be a poor electrical connection at that injector. Try switching injector wires with an adjacent good injector. If swapping wires brings the dead injector to life, look for a corroded or loose connection or a broken injector wire. Early L-Jetronic systems apply 12 volts to the injectors, but later models usually use only 4 volts to energize the injectors. Check for voltage at the wire harness connector with a voltmeter.

NOTE: Be wary of smelling gasoline when starting a cold engine. Some EFI injectors have a bad habit of allowing fuel to gush out from the seam where the black plastic part of the injector mates with the colored plastic part. But as soon as they warm up, the leak stops.

Injector Winding Test

Use an ohmmeter to measure the resistance value of each injector by connecting the test leads to the terminals on the injector. Resistance should be 1.5–4.0 ohms. On LH II systems, connect ohmmeter between pump relay terminal 87 and control unit connector terminal 13. Resistance should be approximately 4 ohms. LH II injectors should read approximately 16 ohms across the injector terminals.

For continuity tests, remove the ground cable from the battery and disconnect the electrical connectors from the injectors. Check for continuity readings between the two injector terminals. If there is no indication, the injector is faulty.

––––––––––––– CAUTION –––––––––––––
Applying 12 volts directly to the fuel injector terminals can burn out the winding and ruin the injector. Do not apply battery voltage to fuel injectors under any circumstances.

Dead or Plugged Injectors

You can spot a dead or plugged injector several ways; perform a routine ignition and engine condition test on any EFI equipped engine before digging into its fuel system. If the ignition is sound and there is little or no rpm drop when you short a cylinder, there could be a vacuum leak at the nozzle seal. Injector O-rings are a potential vacuum leak on any EFI equipment engine.

To determine if there is a leaking O-ring, use the same technique for finding standard intake manifold leaks: spritz the O-ring with some carb and choke cleaner and watch for

a response on a vacuum gauge. Needle fluctuations indicate vacuum leaks.

Leaking Injectors

If the system doesn't hold pressure after crimping both the regulator and pump hoses, then an injector is leaking. Remove the entire fuel rail from the engine and switch the pump on and off again, then watch for the injector that's leaking fuel. The injector orifice may become wet, but no more than two drops should form on the valve (injector) per minute.

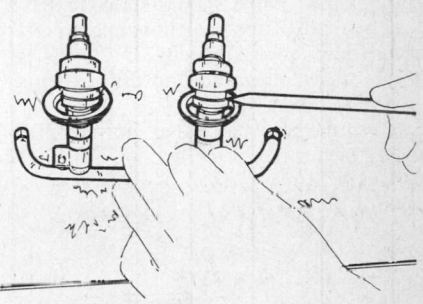

Pointer shows seam where leaks usually develop in fuel injectors

Cold Start Valve (Injector)

NOTE: Not all AFC fuel injection systems use a cold start valve.

To assist cold starting, a separate cold start valve sprays a fine jet of fuel against the air stream entering the plenum (air intake) chamber before fuel is added to it by the main injectors. The cold start valve is energized from the engine starter motor circuit through a thermo time switch. The purpose of the thermo–time switch is to ensure that the cold start valve will not be energized when the engine is at normal operating temperature or when the starter motor is used for prolonged periods when the engine is below operating temperature, preventing extra fuel being supplied to the engine when it is not needed. The thermo–time switch will isolate the cold start valve after 8 to 12 seconds.

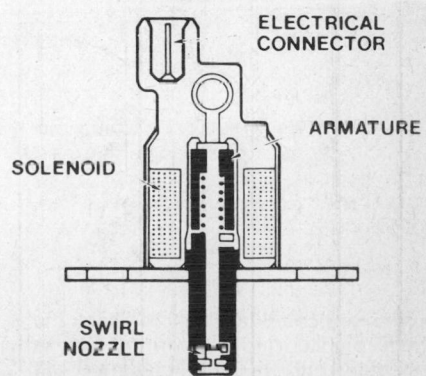

Sectional view of a cold start valve

Testing

CAUTION

Fire hazard. Take precautions when performing all tests.

1. Remove the screws holding the valve in the intake manifold. DO NOT disconnect the fuel lines or electrical connector.

2. Place the cold start valve in a container to catch fuel. Wrap a clean rag around the mouth of the container.

3. Operate the starter and note the injection time. Valve should spray fuel for 1–12 seconds if the coolant temperature is lower than approximately 35°C (95°F). Above this temperature, no drip or spray should be noted.

4. If the cold start valve sprays continuously or drips, replace it.

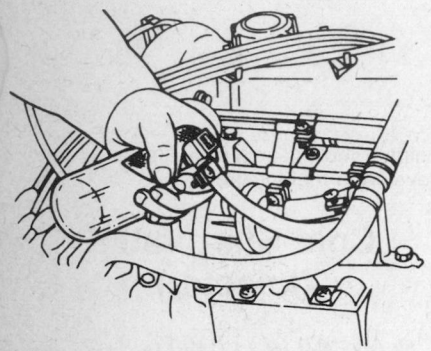

Place the cold start valve nozzle into a clear container when testing

5. If the cold start valve fails to function below 35°C (95°F), replace it.

NOTE: Perform this test as quickly as possible. Avoid energizing the injector for any length of time.

6. Disconnect the cold start valve and hook up a test light across its connector. Ground the No. 1 coil terminal and run the starter. The light should glow for several seconds and then go out. If not, replace the thermo-time switch. Measure the resistance of the cold start valve using an ohmmeter. Correct resistance is 3–5 ohms. Check continuity across the cold start valve terminals.

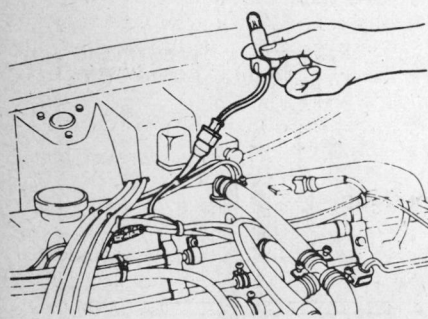

Using a fabricated test light to check the voltage signal from the wiring harness connector. Pulsed injector signals will cause the light to flash

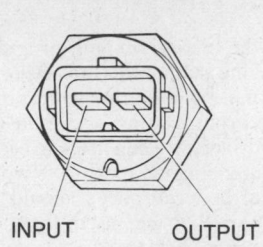

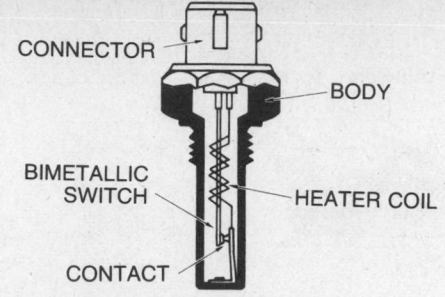

Typical thermo–time switch showing construction and wiring connector pins

NOTE: No starts or poor cold starting can be caused by a malfunctioning cold start valve. Cranking a cold engine with the coil wire grounded should produce a cone-shaped spray from the cold start valve. Cranking a warm engine should produce no fuel; if the injector dribbles gas, replace it.

REMOVAL & INSTALLATION

1. Relieve fuel system pressure as previously described.

2. Provide a container to catch any fuel, or wrap clean rags around connections. *Use care to prevent dirt from entering the fuel system, and take precautions to avoid the risk of fire.*

3. Disconnect the electrical connector from the cold start valve. Clean any dirt or grease.

4. Remove fuel line from the valve. Pull the fuel hose off of the valve. Inspect the hose condition.

CAUTION

The valve body is plastic. Use care in removing fuel hose.

5. Remove the two fasteners holding the cold start valve in the intake manifold, then remove the valve. Remove and discard O-ring or gasket.

6. Reinstall in reverse order, making sure the system is tight and free from leaks. Replace the rubber sealing ring, or gasket and hose clamp if questionable.

NOTE: Fuel injection systems are highly susceptible to dirt in the system. Take care that all components are clean and free from dirt before reinstalling them.

Thermo-Time Switch

NOTE: Not all AFC fuel injection systems use a thermo-time switch.

The thermo–time switch contains a bi–metallic switch and heater coil. The switch completes the circuit for the cold start valve. The harness is connected in series to the cold start valve from the thermo–time switch. The bi–metal contact in the thermo–time switch opens or closes depending on the cooling water temperature, and sends a signal to the cold start valve so that an additional amount of fuel can be injected for starting operation of the engine (mixture enrichment).

During starting, power is supplied to the heater coil which warms the bi–metallic switch. The switch opens within 15 seconds regardless of coolant temperature. The lower the temperature, the longer for the coil to warm up. When the switch opens, the cold start valve is no longer energized and stops enriching the fuel mixture.

REMOVAL & INSTALLATION

To remove the thermo–time switch, disconnect the electrical connector and unscrew the switch from its mounting. It may be necessary to drain the cooling system or replace lost coolant.

TESTING

CAUTION

Do not attempt to remove the thermo–time switch from a hot engine.

Primary Test

1. Remove the thermo–time switch and replace it with a plug to prevent loss of coolant liquid. Perform all tests on cold engine.

2. Cool the thermo–time switch by immersing it in cold water. Use a thermometer to check water temperature.

3. Connect the test wiring to the thermo–time switch as follows:

4. Connect one terminal to one of the wires of a test lamp. Connect the other end of the lamp to the postive (+) terminal of the battery.

5. Connect the negative (−) terminal of the battery to the body of thermo–time switch with a jumper wire. The lamp should light.

6. Place the thermo–time switch in a container of water and heat up the water while monitoring its temperature with a thermometer.

NOTE: Do not immerse test connections in water; just the lower end of the thermo–time switch should be submerged.

7. The lamp should go out between 31° and 39°C (88° and 102°F).

8. The nominal values of the thermo-time switch are marked on the six sides of the body (for example: 8 sec./35°C).

Secondary Test

Check the resistance values with an ohmmeter between terminals of the thermo-time switch connector and ground for temperatures lower than 30°C (86°F) and higher than 40°C (104°F). Resistance should be around 50–80 ohms on switches marked 95°F/85; and 25–40 ohms on switches marked 35°C/85.

Air Flow (Or Air Mass) Sensor

On L and LU injection systems, the air flow sensor measures the quantity of intake air, and sends a signal to the control unit so that the base pulse width (voltage signal) can be determined for correct fuel injection by the injector. The air flow sensor is provided with a flap in the air passage. As the air flows through the passage, the flap rotates and its angle of rotation electronically signals the control unit by means of a potentiometer.

The engine will draw in a certain volume of fresh air depending on the throttle valve position and engine speed. This air stream will cause the sensor plate inside the air flow sensor to move against the force of its return spring. The sensor plate is connected to the potentiometer, which sends a voltage signal to the control unit. The temperature sensor in the air flow sensor influences this signal. The control unit then sends out an opening signal to the fuel injectors to make sure that the volume of injected fuel is exactly right for the volume of intake air. A damping flap in the air flow sensor eliminates unwanted movement of the sensor plate. As the sensor plate moves, the damping flap moves into its damping chamber, acting like a shock absorber for the sensor plate. A small amount of intake air volume moves around the sensor plate via a bypass port. The air/fuel mixture for idling can be adjusted by changing the amount of air flowing through the bypass port with the adjusting screw.

If the sensor plate or its attached damper should become stuck inside the air flow sensor, excessive fuel consumption, marginal performance or a no-start condition could result. LH, LH II and Motronic injection systems incorporate an air mass sensor into the air box. On these systems, the flap valve is replaced with a heated platinum wire that is used to measure air mass without altitude influences.

NOTE: Because of the sensitivity of the air flow (or air mass) meter, there cannot be any air leaks in the ducts. Even the smallest leak could unbalance the system and affect the performance of the engine.

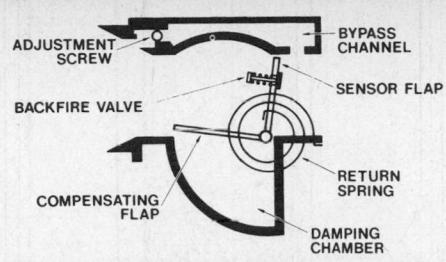

Schematic of an L–Jetronic air flow sensor. Note the sensor flap and idle air adjustment screw

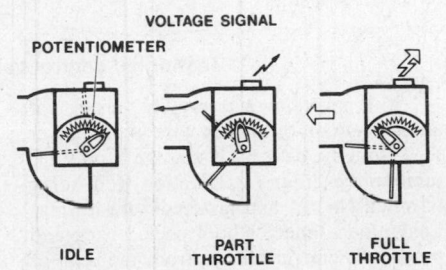

Potentiometer function on the air flow sensor. The voltage signal goes to the ECU

During every check, pay attention to hose connections, dipstick and oil filler cap for evidence of air leaks. Should you encounter any, take steps to correct the problem before proceeding with testing.

REMOVAL & INSTALLATION

1. Disconnect the air duct hoses from both sides of the air box.

2. Disconnect the electrical connector from the wire harness.

3. Remove all bolts, lockwashers, washers and bushings holding the air flow sensor to the bracket. Remove the unit assembly.

4. Reinstall in reverse order.

TESTING AIR FLOW SENSOR

1. Connect an ohmmeter to any terminal on the flow meter. Touch the flow

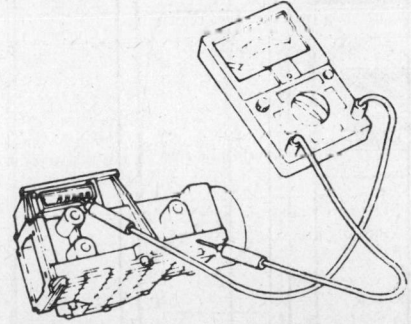

Checking the air flow meter insulation with an ohmmeter. Continuity indicates a problem

meter body with the other connector. If any continuity is indicated, the unit is defective and must be replaced.

2. Reach into the air flow meter and check the flap operation. If the flap opens and closes smoothly, without binding, the mechanical portion of the unit is working.

NOTE: If the air temperature sensor or potentiometer is malfunctioning, the entire air flow sensor must be replaced.

Auxiliary Air Regulator

The auxiliary air regulator allows more air to bypass the throttle plate when the engine is cold, triggering a richer fuel mixture for better cold starting.

A rotating metal disc inside the valve contains an opening that lines up with the bypass hoses when the engine is cold. As the engine heats up, a bi-metallic spring gradually closes the opening by rotating the disc. The bi-metallic spring is heated by coolant temperature and a heater coil which is energized through the ignition circuit.

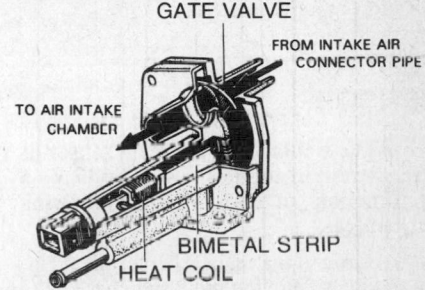

Typical auxiliary air regulator used on Japanese L–Jetronic systems

A double relay, usually located near the electronic control unit and grounded by a terminal of the control unit, controls the input to the fuel pump, the cold start valve, the injector positive feed, the control unit, and the auxiliary air regulator.

REMOVAL & INSTALLATION

1. Disconnect the air valve hoses.
2. Disconnect the air valve connector.
3. Disconnect the water bypass hose.
4. Remove the air valve attaching bolts and air valve.
5. Installation is the reverse of removal. Use a new gasket.

TESTING

With the whole assembly at a temperature of about 20°C (about 68°F) and the electrical connectors and air hoses disconnected, visually check through the inside of the air lines to make sure that the diaphragm is partly open.

1. Using an ohmmeter, measure the resistance between the air valve terminals.

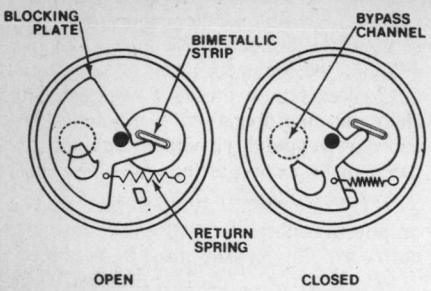

BLOCKING PLATE   BIMETALLIC STRIP   BYPASS CHANNEL   RETURN SPRING

OPEN   CLOSED

Operation of gate valve in auxiliary air regulator

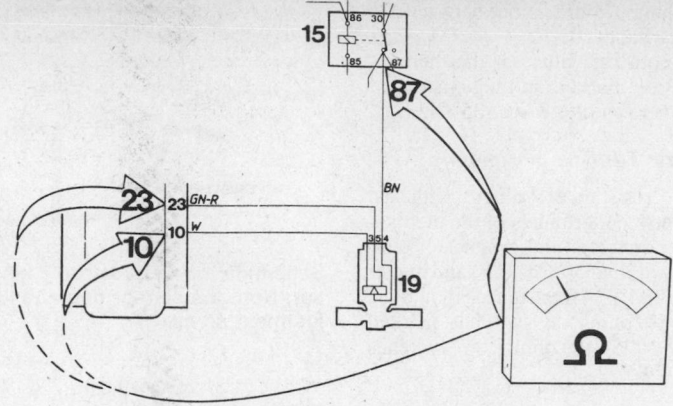

Testing air control valve with ohmmeter

Normal resistance is 29–49 ohms, depending on manufacturer's specifications.

2. Connect a voltmeter across the terminals of the connector and crank the engine.

3. If there is no voltage in the connector, look for a fault in the electrical system. If voltage is present, reconnect the valve and start the engine.

4. Check the engine rpm while pinching shut the air hose. At low temperature (below 140°F) the engine rpm should drop. After warm up, the engine speed should not drop more than 50 rpm.

TESTING AIR MASS SENSOR

NOTE: Replace the air mass sensor as an assembly if the test results indicate a malfunction in any of the following procedures.

1. Ground the main relay terminal No. 21 and make sure the relay switches ON (a slight click should be heard when grounding).

2. Peel back the rubber boot from around the air mass sensor harness connector, but leave it connected to the sensor assembly.

3. Connect a voltmeter between terminal 9 and ground. The voltmeter should ready battery voltage (12 volts). Probe all terminals from the rear of the connector.

4. Connect the voltmeter between terminals 9 and 36; the reading should again be 12 volts.

5. If no voltage is present, check for an open circuit or broken wire in the power feed from the battery. If voltage is present, remove the ground connection from relay terminal No. 21 and proceed with testing. Leave the connector boot peeled back and probe all wire terminals from the rear of the wiring harness connector for all tests.

CAUTION
Harness connectors can be damaged by test leads if probed from the front, causing a poor connection problem that didn't exist before testing. Exercise caution during all electrical test procedures and never use excessive force during probing, removal or installation of wire harness connectors or components.

---

6. Connect an ohmmeter between terminals 6 and 7 on the air mass meter. Resistance should be about 4 ohms.

7. Connect the ohmmeter between terminals 6 and 14 and read the resistance value. It should be between 0-1000 ohms (resistance varies depending on CO adjustment screw positioning). If values are as described, proceed with testing.

8. Connect a voltmeter between terminal 7 (+) and terminal 6 (−) on the air mass sensor connector.

9. Start the engine and note the voltage reading.

10. The voltage should increase with engine rpm. Slowly increase and decrease engine speed while watching the voltmeter and make sure the voltage changes up and down. Specific values are not as important as the fact that the needle (or digital readout) on the voltmeter swings back and forth as the rpm changes. If the readings change as described, proceed with testing.

11. Connect a voltmeter between terminals 8 (+) and 36 (−) to check the air mass sensor wire cleaning (burn-off) operation.

12. Start the engine and increase the engine speed to approximately 2500 rpm for a few seconds.

13. Switch off the engine. After about 5 seconds, the voltmeter should read approximately 1 volt for 1 second. Repeat this test a few times to verify the results.

14. If all tests are as described, remove the voltmeter and reposition the rubber boot cover around the air mass meter connector. Make sure the boot seals correctly to prevent moisture from corroding the electrical connectors.

Air Control Valve

On AFC systems with an air mass sensor, an air control valve is used to regulate the idle speed by bypassing air around the throttle valve. The amount of air bypassed is determined by a signal from the electronic control unit (ECU). Replacement of the air control valve is similar to the auxiliary air valve removal procedure.

TESTING

1. Connect an ohmmeter between the fuel pump relay terminal 87 and the control unit connector terminal 10. The reading should be approximately 20 ohms.

2. Connect the ohmmeter between relay terminal 87 and the control unit connector terminal 23. The resistance value should again be about 20 ohms.

3. Remove the ohmmeter and reconnect the harness connectors, if removed. Start and warm-up the engine.

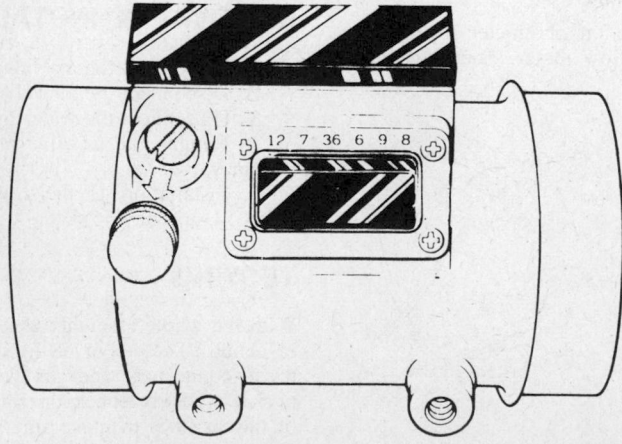

Air mass sensor showing connector pin numbers on housing. Note mixture adjustment screw located behind plug (arrow)

4. Check the idle speed with a tachometer and compare the test results with the idle specification listed on the underhood emission control sticker.

5. Switch on the air conditioner (if equipped) and verify that the idle speed increases when the compressor is energized. If the idle doesn't increase, check for a sticking air control valve or failure of the A/C power circuit (shorted or open wire or microswitch).

6. Switch the engine OFF, then remove the connector from the coolant temperature sensor to simulate a cold engine.

7. Start the engine and verify that the high idle specification is obtained with a tachometer. Turn the ignition OFF and reconnect the coolant temperature sensor if the high idle is correct, then restart the engine and make sure the idle speed is once again at the normal (warm) value.

NOTE: If the air control valve is suspected of malfunction, install a new valve and repeat the test procedures. Adjust idle speed as outlined in the individual car sections.

Throttle Switch

The throttle switch forms part of the control for the fuel injection system, providing the ECU with information on throttle operating conditions. The switch is grounded at the intake manifold.

The throttle valve switch is attached to the throttle chamber and actuates in response to accelerator pedal movement. This switch has two or three sets of contact points. One set monitors the idle position and the other set monitors full throttle position. Some use additional contacts for mid-range operation.

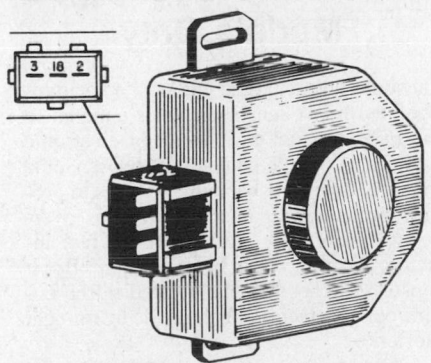

Typical throttle switch showing pin numbers

The idle contact closes when the throttle valve is positioned at idle and opens when it is at any other position. The idle contact compensates for after idle enrichment, and sends the fuel shut-off signal.

The full throttle contact closes only when the throttle valve is positioned at full throttle (more than 35 degree opening of the throttle valve). The contact is open while the throttle valve is at any other position. The full contact compensates for enrichment in full throttle.

On AFC systems with a Constant Idle Speed (CIS) feature incorporated into the injection circuit, a microswitch is used in place of the throttle switch. The microswitch is mounted so as to contact the throttle linkage at idle and signal the ECU as to what throttle position is being used. Some microswitches are set to be open at idle and some are closed. Use a test light to determine which type of microswitch is being used by checking for voltage while moving the throttle lever to open and close the contact lever. The microswitch is usually adjusted when setting the idle speed.

ADJUSTMENT

NOTE: A click should be heard when the throttle valve moves and the idle contact opens

1. Make sure that the idle speed is correct. Check the underhood sticker for correct specification.

2. Disconnect the connector from the switch. The center pin is usually the 12 volt input terminal.

3. Connect an ohmmeter between terminals 2 and 18 of the switch.

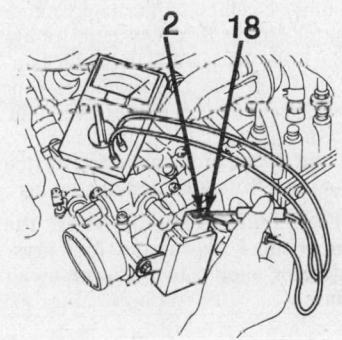

Checking the throttle switch adjustment with an ohmmeter

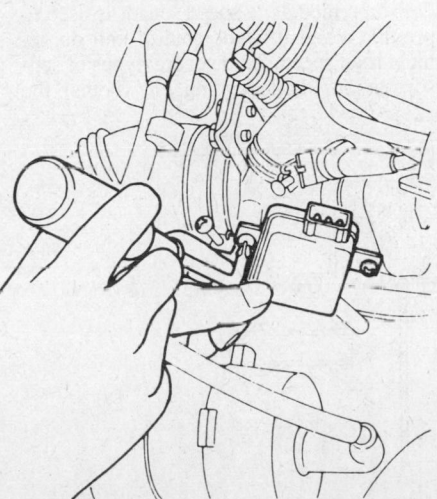

Adjust the throttle switch by loosening the fasteners

4. Loosen the two screws holding the throttle plate switch.

5. With the engine off, rotate the switch clockwise until the ohmmeter indicates a closed circuit (idle contact closes).

6. At the exact point that the ohmmeter indicates a closed circuit, tighten the two screws holding the switch.

7. Check the adjustment.

REMOVAL & INSTALLATION

1. Disconnect the electrical connector.

2. Remove the two screws and washers holding the switch to the intake manifold.

3. Remove the switch by slowly pulling it.

4. Reinstall in the reverse order and adjust the switch.

Vacuum Switch—LH-Jetronic System

On some applications, a vacuum switch takes the place of the throttle valve switch to indicate full load and idle (low ported vacuum signal) and part load (maximum vacuum signal) conditions to the electronic control unit. Instead of being mounted directly on the throttle shaft, the vacuum switch

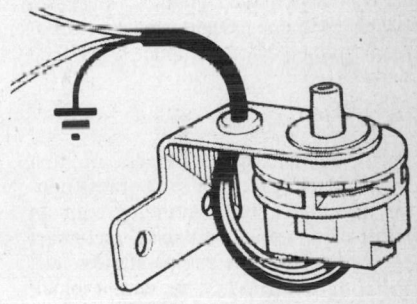

Typical vacuum switch

is usually located on the bulkhead or fender panel under the hood and is connected to a ported vacuum orifice in the throttle valve assembly by a vacuum hose.

TESTING

To test the vacuum switch, connect a hand vacuum pump to the vacuum fitting and connect an ohmmeter across terminals 3 and 5 at the control unit harness connector. With no vacuum applied to the switch, the resistance should be zero. When approximately 4 in. Hg is applied with the hand vacuum pump, the resistance should be infinite. A high resistance reading without vacuum indicates an open circuit and zero resistance when vacuum is applied indicates a short circuit. In either case, if incorrect resistance is noted, replace the vacuum switch and repeat the test.

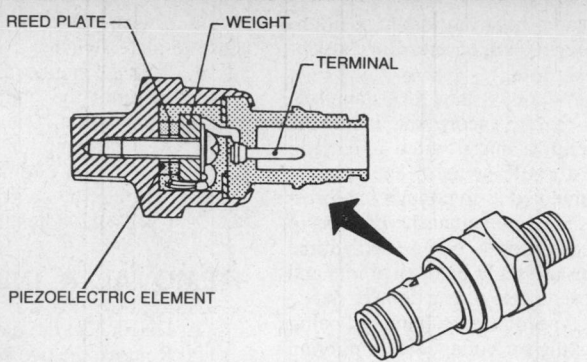

Cross section of detonation sensor used on ECCS injection system

Detonation Sensor

On some AFC installations, a detonation sensor is incorporated into the system to detect engine knock conditions. Engine knock (or ping) can be caused by using fuel with too low an octane rating or advanced timing. The detonations within the cylinder set up vibrations within the cylinder block that are detected by a piezoelectric element which converts vibrational pressure into an electrical signal (voltage impulse) which is used as an input signal to the control unit. The ECU uses the signal to measure detonatior and retard the timing to eliminate the problem. A detonation sensor is usually found on turbocharged engines, since serious engine damage can occur if turbocharged engines detonate under boost.

TESTING

To test the detonation sensor operation, first locate the sensor, remove the harness connector and check for continuity with an ohmmeter. If continuity exists, reconnect the sensor and start the engine after installing a timing light. When the engine block is tapped with a small hammer near the detonation sensor, the timing should change. Repeat the test several times and make sure the ignition timing changes (retards) when the block is tapped and returns to normal when the tapping stops. If no change in timing is noted and the sensor shows continuity, the problem is in the ECU, or the wiring harness.

Fuel Temperature Sensor

On some models, a fuel temperature sensor is built into the pressure regulator assembly to monitor fuel temperature. If the temperature rises beyond a preset value, the control unit enriches the mixture to compensate.

TESTING

The fuel temperature sensor is tested in the same manner as a coolant sensor. Connect an ohmmeter and check that the resistance value (ohms) changes as the temperature rises. On the Nissan ECCS system, for example, the resistance should fall as the temperature rises. If the temperature sensor checks out, perform a continuity test on the wiring harness connectors at the switch nd control unit. If no problem is found, the control unit itself may be malfunctioning.

NOTE: If found to be defective, the fuel temperature sensor and fuel pressure regulator should be replaced as an assembly.

Speed Sensor

On some models, a speed sensor is used to provide a signal to the control unit on vehicle road speed. Two general types of sensors are used, depending on whether the instrument cluster is an analog (needle) type or digital (LED) readout type of display. In the analog speedometer, the speed sensor is usually a reed switch which transforms vehicle speed into a pulse signal. On digital type instrument clusters the speed sensor consists of an LED (light emitting diode), photo diode, shutter and wave forming circuit (signal generator) whose operation closely resembles the crank angle sensor described under "ECCS Control Unit" later in the chapter.

TESTING

Regardless of instrument cluster type, the easiest method of checking the speed sensor opreation is to disconnect the speedometer cable at the transmission and connect an ohmmeter between the control unit harness connector terminal from the speed sensor (e.g. terminal No. 29 on Nissan 300 ZX models) to ground. Check for continuity while slowly rotating the speedometer cable. The ohmmeter should register the pulses from the speed sensor. If no reading is obtained, check the wiring harness to the speed sensor for continuity.

NOTE: Rotate the speedometer slowly and watch for meter changes. Most speed sensors send impulses about 24 times per revolution of the speedometer cable. If found to be defective, the speed sensor is usually replaced with the speedometer assembly as a unit, although some separate sensor assemblies are used in digital instrument cluster displays. Digital cluster speed sensors are checked with the key ON.

Boost Sensor Switch—Turbocharged Models Only

On some turbocharged engines, a vacuum-operated boost sensor provides a signal to the ECU for fuel enrichment or electronic wastegate controle while under boost. Some manufacturers use vacuum switches to provide protection against a dangerous over-boost situation by cutting off the fuel injectors above a certain boost pressure. Boost sensor switches may be located in the engine compartment, or behind the instrument cluster.

TESTING

To test vacuum actuated boost pressure switches, connect a hand-pumped vaccum gauge to the switch vacuum port and an ohmmeter to the terminals of the sensor connector. Pump the vacuum gauge and check for continuity between the terminals when the vacuum is applied. There should be no continuity when the vacuum is absent, and the resistance between the terminals should vary as the vacuum level ap-

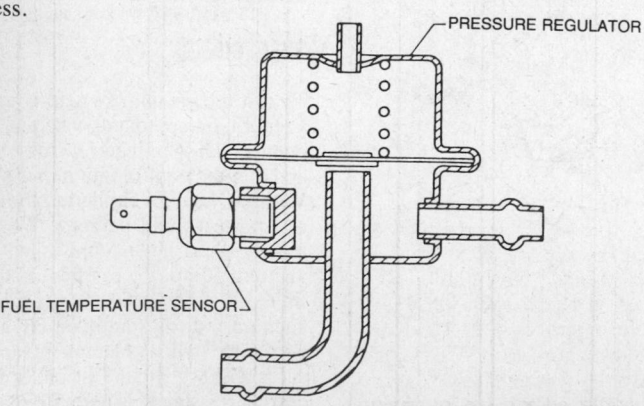

Location of fuel temperature sensor on pressure regulator

plied rises and falls. The switch can be inspected in the same manner by using a voltmeter and connecting battery voltage to one side of the switch. Voltage should vary just as resistance did, when the vacuum level changes. Look for changes rather than specific volt or ohm values to determine if the switch is functioning.

Coolant Temperature Sensor

NOTE: Most later models are equipped with cylinder head temperature sensors rather than water temperature sensors. However, the test is the same for both units.

The coolant temperature sensor is located near the cylinder head and provides a signal to the ECU that causes a longer injector open time when the engine is cold. The open time decreases as the engine reaches normal operating temperature. The coolant temperature sensor also completes the circuit for the extra air valve when the engine is cold. Typical resistance values at different temperatures are:

Temperature	Resistance (OHMS)
+80°C (175°F)	270–390
+20°C (68°F)	2100–2900
−10°C (14°F)	7000–116000

Note: Exact resistance values vary with manufacturer.

The cylinder head temperature sensor, built into the cylinder head, monitors change in cylinder head temperature and transmits a signal to increase the pulse duration (fuel delivery) during the warm-up period. The temperature sensing unit employs a thermistor which is very sensitive in the low temperature range. The electrical resistance of the thermistor decreases in response to the temperature rise.

REMOVAL & INSTALLATION

─────── CAUTION ───────
Allow the engine to cool before attempting this procedure.

Partially drain the cooling system. Then, disconnect the electrical terminal plug and unscrew the coolant temperature sensor. Install in reverse order, refilling and bleeding the cooling system.

TESTING

In general, coolant and cylinder head temperature sensors have a fairly high mortality rate on EFI systems. VW's, for example, use up cylinder head sensors often. On L-Jetronic systems, the intake air temperature sensor is incorporated into the air flow meter. If it fails, replace the air flow meter.

It's impossible to tune or adjust an EFI equipped engine if one of its sensors is bad. Check that the temperature sensor resistance, measured with an ohmmeter, changes when the sensor is checked cold, then after the engine is warmed up. Engine should be off for all tests. Extremely high test values indicates open circuit in temperature sensor or wiring (check temperature sensor ground at intake manifold). Zero resistance indicates short circuit.

Sensor Insulation Check

This check is done on the engine.
1. Disconnect the battery ground cable.
2. Disconnect the sensor harness connector.
3. Connect an ohmmeter to one of the terminals on the sensor and touch the engine block with the other. Any indication of continuity indicates a need to replace the unit.

Lambda (Oxygen) Sensor

The Lambda or Oxygen sensor is a probe with a ceramic body in a protective housing. It measures the oxygen concentration in the exhaust system and provides a feedback signal to the control unit.

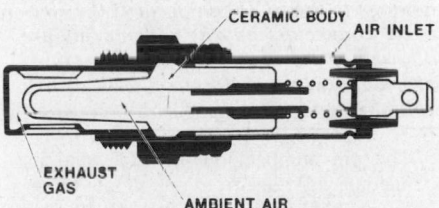

Sectional view of an oxygen sensor

The exhaust gas sensor produces a signal depending on air/fuel mixture ratio. The signal varies directly with the density of oxygen in exhaust gases. The fuel is burned at the best theoretically determined air/fuel ratio of the mixture; the oxygen sensor signal increases when there is a richer mixture, and decreases when there is a lean mixture. The signal from the sensor allows the ECU to fine tune the fuel mixture to allow the catalytic converter to operate at its peak efficiency.

NOTE: As with the catalytic converter, the use of leaded fuel will contaminate and ruin the Lambda sensor.

The idle switch will turn off the oxygen sensor when coasting due to the excessive oxygen present in the exhaust gas. The idle contact will open when the free play in the accelerator linkage is taken up, even though the throttle valve is still closed. The full throttle contact switches off the oxygen sensor if the throttle is opened more than 30° in order to lower exhaust gas temperature and protect the sensor and the cata-

lytic converter. The control unit will simultaneously switch to a 12% partial and full throttle enrichment.

NOTE: A service interval counter, much like the EGR and Catalytic Converter counters will light a dash warning light when the need for Oxygen Sensor replacement arises (around 30,000 miles). The service indicator must be reset after replacement of the Lambda sensor. Refer to the individual car sections for the warning light reset procedure, if equipped.

Since the oxygen sensor doesn't function until it reaches operating temperature, late models incorporate a heater circuit to warm up the sensor for quicker response and to keep the oxygen sensor at operating temperature during prolonged idle or low speed operation. Oxygen sensors with heaters are recognized by the third wire connector on the sensor body. Do not interchange old and new type sensors.

─────── CAUTION ───────
Testing the oxygen sensor output with a powered voltmeter can damage the sensor by drawing too much current through the sensor. The average oxygen sensor puts out about one volt in operation.

REMOVAL & INSTALLATION

1. Allow the exhaust system to cool.
2. Disconnect the cable from the oxygen sensor.
3. Remove the sensor from the exhaust manifold. It may be necessary to use penetrating oil or rust solvent.

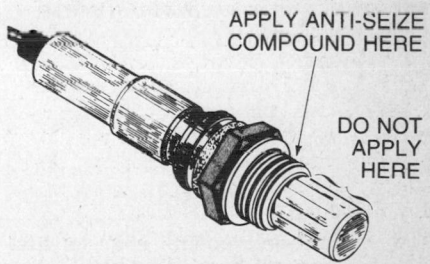

Use anti-seize compound when installing the oxygen sensor

4. Coat the threads of the sensor with anti-seize, anti-rust grease. Do not get grease on the sensor body itself.
5. Thread the sensor into the exhaust manifold and torque to 30–36 ft. lb.
6. Connect the electrical cable to the sensor and check the CO.

─────── CAUTION ───────
Do not allow grease to get on the sensor surface. This will contaminate and ruin the Lambda sensor. Exercise care when coating the threads with anti-seize compound. Check CO with suitable meter.

Electronic Control Unit (ECU)

The electronic control unit is the brain of the AFC fuel injection system. It controls various engine operating conditions by constantly measuring specific engine parameters (e.g. temperature, rpm, air mass or volume, etc.) and making adjustments by sending out appropriate voltage signals to components. Each ECU responds to its sensor inputs according to a specific design of its internal integrated circuits, or according to manufacturers instructions programmed into a PROM (Programmed Read Only Memory) microchip computer memory plugged into the solid state circuit board. The number and type of sensors employed by a particular ECU and the manner in which it responds to these sensor input signals is unique to each type of system and different from one manufacturer to another. For this reason, the ECU's are not interchangeable, even if the same type of injection system (L-Jetronic, for example) is used on two different models built by the same manufacturer. When replacing any ECU it is important to correctly identify not only the type of injection system and manufacturer, but also the year and model of car, engine and transmission. Carefully compare the part numbers of both old and new ECU to make sure the correct control unit is being installed or serious damage to the replacement part is likely.

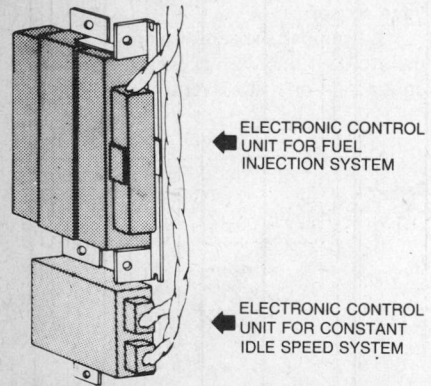

← ELECTRONIC CONTROL UNIT FOR FUEL INJECTION SYSTEM

← ELECTRONIC CONTROL UNIT FOR CONSTANT IDLE SPEED SYSTEM

Typical electronic control units for fuel injection and idle speed control

Depending on the type of fuel injection system, the ECU is designed to do different things. The basic L-Jetronic system is designed to control the fuel mixture under various engine load conditions and not much else. Later modifications incorporate other functions such as ignition timing control, EGR and other emission control device operation, idle speed, etc. Some ECU's operate with analog electrical signals while others use digital signals. The manner in which the AFC injection systems measures the intake air can vary from a counterbalanced air flap (L-Jetronic) to a heated platinum wire (LH-Jetronic) and the type and number of engine sensors will vary from one manufacturer to another. Some injec-

tion systems (Motronic and the E.C.C.S. system used on the Nissan 300ZX, for example) utilize sensors that measure the crankshaft angle to precisely control ignition timing and injection according to engine dynamometer data programmed into the control unit by the manufacturer. In addition, some injection systems are designed with a self-diagnosis capability that flashes a trouble code to indicate various malfunctions detected during operation. Before attempting any service or diagnosis procedures, familiarize yourself with the specific type of injection system used, as well as the various components, to determine what may be causing a problem and therefore what is in need of testing.

There are certain similarities common to most AFC systems that should be noted when testing. The service precautions outlined at the beginning of this section should be read and carefully followed to avoid causing damage to the control unit or electrical system during service. All ECU's are installed somewhere inside the passenger compartment and all use a large, multi-pin connector to tie the ECU into the wiring harness. This ECU connector is held in place with some form of locking device that must be released before the connector can be removed.

CAUTION

Never attempt to disconnect the ECU with the key ON or the engine running. Serious damage to the ECU can occur if the electrical connectors on any components are allowed to arc or the wrong connections are made when performing tests with a volt/ohmmeter or jumper wire.

The pin numbers on the ECU and its connector will vary from one model to another, so care must be taken to make sure the correct connections are being made before any test is attempted. These numbers are usually stamped on the side of the main connector. Do not probe the ECU connector terminals from the front, as test probes can damage the connectors. Probe all ECU connections from the rear of the connector, after removing the harness cover, in the test holes provided or with a thin paper clip carefully installed from the wire side to allow the use of small clips. Be careful not to damage any connector during test procedures and never use excessive force when dealing with any electrical component. The control unit should be handled with care when removed and protected from contact with any kind of solvents, water or direct contact with any electrical or magnetic devices. Never apply power directly to a control unit on the bench for any reason.

Most ECU's require special test equipment for pinpoint troubleshooting; however some simple pass/fail procedures are possible using an appropriate tach/dwell meter, volt/ohm meter and fabricating jumper wires and test bulbs with the correct terminal connections. Not all analog (meter) test equipment is compatible with all electronic con-

trol systems and a digital multimeter may be necessary for some procedures. Consult the manufacturer's instructions before connecting any powered test equipment to make sure it won't damage the ECU. When testing with an analog volt/ohm or tach/dwell remember that it is usually more important to look for needle movement (swing) than exact test values. Be sure to perform the preliminary checks on fuel, compression and ignition systems before assuming that the ECU is causing a problem. Experience usually shows that simple problems like loose or corroded connections, clogged air, fuel or emission control filters and vacuum or air leaks in the intake system cause most of the problems blamed on a faulty electronic control unit.

Because of their solid state construction and the fact that there are no moving parts, most ECU's are designed to last the life of the car in operation, and are maintenance-free. The ECU should be removed if any AFC-equipped vehicle is to be placed in a paint oven or exposed to any temperature exceeding approximately 176°F. Never attempt to disconnect any control unit with the ignition switch ON or the engine running, and inspect all connectors for damage before reconnecting the wiring harness.

ECU Diagnosis

QUICK TEST

By fabricating a small test light with an appropriate injector harness connector, the injector signal from the ECU can be checked. With the key OFF, connect the test lamp to the harness side of the fuel injector connector. Crank the engine and make sure the light flashes on and off. If the test lamp flashes, it indicates the control unit is supplying a pulse voltage to the injector and chances are it is operating properly.

NOTE: Because two different transistors are used in some AFC electronic control units, it may be necessary to test both the No. 1 and No. 4 cylinder injectors to determine if the control unit is supplying pulses to all of the injectors.

CIRCUIT TESTS

Individual control circuits within the ECU can be checked by performing resistance and continuity tests according to the following charts and connector pin locations illustrated. Read the service precautions concerning the ECU before attempting any tests and make sure the test equipment used will not damage the control unit. Make absolutely sure you are probing the correct terminals before making any connections, as serious ECU damage can occur if the wrong two pins are connected in a circuit.

— **CAUTION** —
On the Volvo LH-Jetronic system, the test point located behind the battery is NOT to be used in fault tracing the system. Unless special test equipment is used, using this test point can cause serious ECU damage. If equipped with a Constant Idle Speed system, there may be two test points.

Self-Diagnosing AFC Injection Systems

Some AFC fuel injection systems are equipped with a self-diagnosis capability to allow retrieval of stored trouble codes from the ECU memory. The number of codes stored and the meaning of the code numbers varies from one manufacturer to another. By activating the diagnostic mode and counting the number of flashes on the CHECK ENGINE or ECU lights, it is possible to ask the computer where the problem is (which circuit) and narrow down the number of pin connectors tested when diagnosing an AFC fuel injection problem.

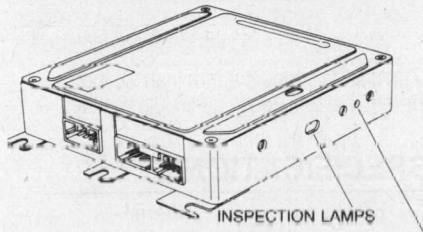

INSPECTION LAMPS
DIAGNOSIS MODE SELECTOR

Control unit used on ECCS fuel injection showing trouble code lamp and mode selector

NISSAN E.C.C.S. SYSTEM

On 1984 and later models, the E.C.C.S. control unit used on the 300ZX has a self-diagnosing capability. The E.C.C.S. control unit consists of a microcomputer, connectors for signal input and output and power supply, inspection lamps and a diagnostic mode selector. The control unit calculates basic injector pulse width (fuel delivery) by processing signals from the crank angle sensor and air flow meter. The crank angle sensor monitors engine speed and piston position and sends signals to the ECU for

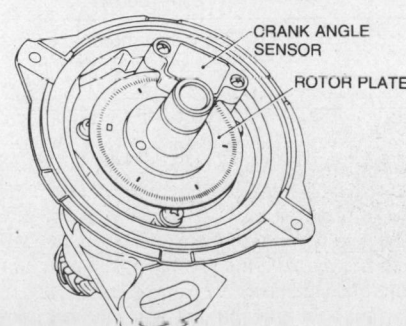

CRANK ANGLE SENSOR
ROTOR PLATE

Crankshaft angle sensor used on ECCS fuel injection

L–JETRONIC TROUBLESHOOTING GUIDE

Circuit Tested	Ohmmeter Terminal Connection	Correct Value (ohms)
Wire to coil terminal #1	1–Ground	Wire grounded–0 Coil disconnected–00
Idle circuit through throttle switch	2–18	Throttle closed–0 (Type IV only)
Full throttle enrichment through throttle switch	3–18	0 @ WOT ①
Ground circuit	5–Ground	0
Air sensor circuit	6–9	200–400
	6–8	130–260
	8–9	70–140
	6–7	40–300
	7–8	100–500
	6–27	2800 @ 68°F
Head sensor	13–Ground	2100–2900 @ 68°F 270–390 @ 176°F
Injector wire and resistor	14–10	7
	15–10	7
	32–10	7
	33–10	7
Ground circuit	16–Ground	0
	17–Ground	0
Auxiliary air regulator and wiring	34 @ ECU– 37 @ relay	30
VOLTMETER TESTS		
Signal from starter	4–Ground	12v–Cranking 0v–Otherwise
Voltage to ECU	10–Ground	12v–Key ON 0v–Key OFF
Fuel pump circuit	28–Ground	12v–Key ON and sensor flap open

① WOT—Wide Open Throttle

LH–JETRONIC TEST POINTS

Circuit Tested	Terminal Numbers	Test Results
Battery voltage from ignition switch to ECU	20–GND ①	ign ON–12 volts ign OFF–0 volts
System Relay test	34–GND ③ 10–GND ①	Voltmeter should indicate 12 volts
Fuel Pump Relay	28–GND ③	Fuel pump runs
Ground Check ④	5–GND ② 16–GND ② 17–GND ②	Resistance should be 0 ohms at all points

Note: Test connector located behind the battery is not to be used for fault tracing. Special test equipment must be used or system will be damaged.
GND–Ground
① Voltmeter connections
② Ohmmeter connections
③ Jumper wire connections
④ Ground circuits can be checked with 12v test light by connecting one end to the positive battery cable and probing connectors 5, 16 and 17. Test light should come on.

control of fuel injection, ignition timing, idle speed, fuel pump operation and EGR (emission control) operation.

The crank angle sensor consists of a rotor plate and wave forming circuit built into the distributor. The rotor plate has 360 slits for a 1° (engine speed) signal and 6 slits for a 120° signal (crankshaft angle). Light Emitting Diodes (LED's) and Photo Diodes are built into the wave forming circuit. When the rotor plate cuts the light which is sent to the photo diode from the LED, it causes an alternate voltage which is converted into an on-off pulse by the wave forming circuit and sent to the control unit. Enrichment rates are pre-programmed into the control unit for engine speed and basic injection pulse width.

NOTE: The ECU will shut off the injectors if the engine speed exceeds 6500 rpm, or road speed exceeds 137 mph, whichever comes first. The crank angle sensor is an important component in the E.C.C.S. system and a malfunctioning sensor is sometimes accompanied by a display which shows faults in other systems. Check the crank angle sensor first.

The self-diagnostic system determines the malfunctions of signal systems such as sensors, actuators and wire harness connectors based on the status of the input signals received by the E.C.C.S. control unit. Malfunction codes are displayed by two LED's (red and green) mounted on the side of the control unit. The self-diagnosis results are retained in the memory chip of the ECU and displayed only when the diagnosis mode selector (located on the left side of the ECU) is turned fully clockwise. The self-diagnosis system on the E.C.C.S. control unit is capable of displaying malfunctions being checked, as well as trouble codes stored in the memory. In this manner, an intermittent malfunction can be detected during service procedures.

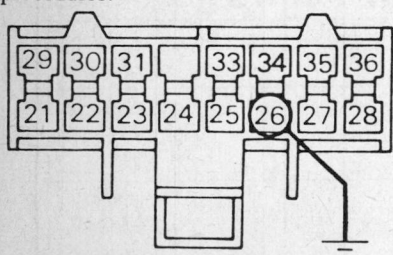

16-pin connector terminal numbers for ECCS control unit connector

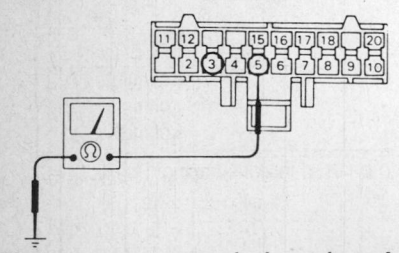

20-pin connector terminal numbers for ECCS control unit connector showing test connections to check ignition signal to control unit

LHII-JETRONIC ECU TEST POINTS

Circuit Tested	Terminal Numbers	Test Results
Battery voltage from ignition switch to ECU	18–GND ①	ign ON–12 volts ign OFF–0 volts
Fuel pump relay	17–GND ③	ign ON–pump runs
System Relay	9–GND① 21–GND③	Voltmeter should read 12 volts. Relay is on
Ground Check	11–GND② 25–GND②	0 ohms (no resistance) for both terminals
Ignition coil connection	1–GND ①	Meter should deflect when ignition is switched ON
Air Control Valve circuit	④	20 ohms

Note: Terminal numbers should be marked on connectors. Turn ignition OFF when removing or installing connectors.
GND–Ground
① Voltmeter connections
② Ohmmeter connections
③ Jumper wire connection
④ Connect ohmmeter between pump relay terminal 87 and ECU connector terminal 10; then between pump relay terminal 87 and ECU connector terminal 23. Readings should match.

PORSCHE 928 TEST SPECIFICATIONS

Circuit Tested	Terminal Test Connections	Normal Reading
OHMMETER TESTS		
Temperature sensor	5–13 ①	2–3 kΩ @ 68 deg. F 1.2–2.4 kΩ @ 83 deg. F
Idle microswitch A	2–18 ①	2–3 kΩ @ 68 deg. F 1.2–2.4 kΩ @ 83 deg. F
	2–18 ②	0Ω
Full throttle microswitch B	3–18 ①	0Ω
	3–18 ③	0 Ω @ 68 deg. F 0–10 Ω @ 83 deg. F
Air flow sensor④	6–9	400–800 Ω
	6–8	260–520 Ω
	8–9	140–280 Ω
	6–7	80–600 Ω
	7–8	200–1000 Ω
Air flow temperature sensor	27–6	2–3 kΩ @ 68 deg. F 1.2–2.4 kΩ @ 83 deg. F
Fuel injectors⑤		
1 + 5	10–15	1–1.5 Ω
4 + 8	10–14	1–1.5 Ω
3 + 7	10–32	1–1.5 Ω
2 + 6	10–33	1–1.5 Ω
Ground checks	16–GND	0Ω
	17–GND	0Ω
	35–GND	0Ω
	5–GND	0Ω

PORSCHE 928 TEST SPECIFICATIONS

Circuit Tested	Terminal Test Connections	Normal Reading
VOLTMETER TESTS		
Test conditions⑥		
IGN ON	1–GND	1 volt
IGN ON	10–GND	12 volts
IGN ON	29–GND	12 volts
Cranking	4–GND	8 volts (minimum)
Cranking	1–GND	2.5 volts

Note: When conducting tests, look for a change rather than specific values. All voltage values are approximate.

Ω–Ohms (kΩ-kilo-ohms)

GND–Ground

① Accelerator pedal released

② Throttle linkage play eliminated

③ Throttle open more than 1/3 (30 deg.)

④ As of production month 042 or later. For earlier production sensors, divide test values in half.

⑤ 2–3 ohms when each injector is checked separately.

⑥ All voltage values are approximate.

problem, it activates a CHECK ENGINE light on the dash to alert the driver. The computer will store trouble codes indicating problems in monitored systems including:

- Air flow sensor system
- Coolant temperature sensor
- Speed sensor
- Oxygen sensor
- Detonation sensor
- Injector system
- Electronic Control Unit (ECU)

NOTE: The self diagnosis system is only capable of troubleshooting the circuits in the I-TEC system, not in the components themselves. Malfunctions in a circuit may be caused by a variety of problems, including loose connections, failed components or damage to wiring.

Activating Diagnosis Mode

Locate the diagnosis lead near the control unit and connect the two leads with the ignition ON. The trouble codes stored in

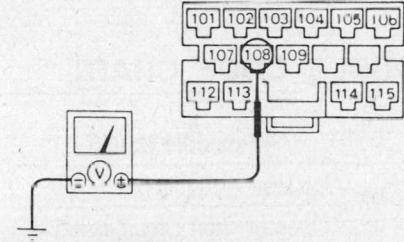

15-pin connector terminal numbers for ECCS control unit connector showing test connections for fuel pump power check

——— **CAUTION** ———

Turn the diagnostic mode selector carefully with a small screwdriver. Do not press hard to turn or the selector may be damaged.

Service codes are displayed as flashes of both the red and green LED. The red LED blinks first, followed by the green LED, and the two together indicate a code number. The red LED is the tenth digit, and the green LED is the unit digit. For example; when the red light blinks three times and the green light blinks twice, the code displayed is 32. All malfunctions are classified by code numbers. When all service procedures are complete, erase the memory by disconnecting the battery cable or the ECU harness connector. *Removing the power to the control unit automatically erases all trouble codes from the memory. Never erase the stored memory before performing self diagnosis tests.*

ISUZU I-TEC SYSTEM

The self diagnosis system is designed to monitor the input and output signals of the sensors and actuators and to store any malfunctions in its memory as a trouble code. When the electronic control unit detects a

NISSAN E.C.C.S. TROUBLE CODES

Code Number	ECU Circuit	Test Point Pin Numbers	Normal Test Results
11	Crank Angle Sensor	Check harness for open circuit	Continuity
12	Air Flow Meter	Ground terminal 26① connect VOM @ 26–31	IGN ON—1.5–1.7 volts
		Apply 12v @ E–D② connect VOM @ B–D	1.5–1.7 volts
		VOM @ 12–GND③	Continuity
		VOM @ C–F②	Continuity
13	Cylinder Head Temperature Sensor	VOM @ 23–26①	Above 68 deg F–2.9 kΩ Below 68 deg F–2.1 kΩ
14	Speed Sensor	VOM @ 29–GND④	Continuity
21	Ignition Signal	VOM @ 3–GND	Continuity
		VOM @ 5–GND	Continuity
		Check power transistor terminals to base plate	Continuity
22	Fuel Pump	VOM @ 108–GND⑤	IGN ON–12 volts
		Pump connectors	Continuity
		Pump relay:	Continuity
		VOM @ 1–2	[if]
		VOM @ 3–4	
		12v @ 1–2,	
		VOM @ 3–4	Continuity
23	Throttle Valve Switch	VOM @ 18–25⑥	Continuity
		VOM @ 18–GND	[if]
		VOM @ 25–GND	[if]
24	Neutral/Park Switch	VOM @ Switch terminals	Neutral–0Ω Drive–∞Ω
31	Air Conditioner	VOM @ 22–GND①	IGN ON–12 volts
32	Start Signal	VOM @ 9–GND③	12 volts with starter S terminal disconnected

NISSAN E.C.C.S. TROUBLE CODES

Code Number	ECU Circuit	Test Point Pin Numbers	Normal Test Results
34	Detonation Sensor	Disconnect sensor and check timing with engine running	Timing should retard 5 degrees above 2000 rpm
41	Fuel Temperature Sensor	VOM @ 15–GND③	Above 68 deg. F–2.9 kΩ Below 68 deg.F–2.1 kΩ
		VOM @ Sensor terminals	Resistance (ohms) should decrease as temperature rises
44	Normal Operation—no further testing required		

NOTE: Make sure test equipment will not damage the control unit before testing
VOM—Volt/ohm meter
GND—Ground
Ω—Ohms (kΩ = kilo-ohms)
∞—Infinite resistance
①16-pin harness connector
②6-pin air flow meter connection
③20-pin harness connector
④16-pin connector at ECU
⑤Throttle valve switch connector

20 POLE (BLACK)

9 POLE (WHITE)   13 POLE (WHITE)

Connector terminal numbers on Isuzu I-TEC control unit

--- CAUTION ---
Make sure of the terminal numbers and location when making test connections, since battery power is supplied to some terminals only when the ignition is ON. Do not probe connector terminals from the front as test probes can damage the pins and connectors. Use a pin to probe connectors from the rear.

the memory are displayed by the CHECK ENGINE light as flashes that indicate numbers (trouble codes). The I-TEC system ECU memory is capable of storing three different trouble codes which are displayed in numerical sequence no matter when the malfunctions occur. Each trouble code is repeated three times, then the next code is displayed. The ECU memory will display all stored trouble codes as long as the diagnosis lead is connected with the key ON. A code 12 indicates that the I-TEC system is functioning normally and that no further testing is necessary. After servicing, clear the trouble codes by disconnecting the No. 4 fuse in the fuse block.

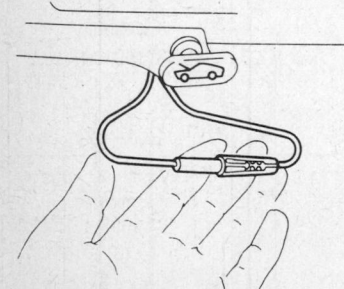

Under dash connector used to activate self-diagnosis mode on Isuzu I-TEC system

NOTE: All codes stored in the memory will be automatically cleared whenever the main harness connector is removed from the control unit.

Testing

The control unit wiring harness has three types of connectors with specifically numbered terminals. All inspection procedures refer to these numbers when describing terminal connections.

ISUZU I-TEC SYSTEM TROUBLE CODE CHART

Trouble Code	ECU Circuit	Possible Cause
12	Normal operation	No testing required
13	Oxygen sensor	Open or short circuit, failed sensor
44	Oxygen sensor	Low voltage signal
45	Oxygen sensor	High voltage signal
14	Coolant temperature sensor	Shorted with ground (no signal)
15	Coolant temperature sensor	Incorrect signal
16	Coolant temperture sensor	Excessive signal (harness open)
21	Throttle valve switch	Idle and WOT contacts closed at the same time
43	Throttle valve switch ①	Idle contact shorted
65	Throttle valve switch	Full throttle contact shorted
22	Starter signal	No signal
41	Crank angle sensor	No signal or wrong signal
61	Air flow sensor	Weak signal (harness shorted or open hot wire)
62	Air flow sensor	Excessive signal (open cold wire)
63	Speed sensor ①	No signal
66	Detonation sensor	Harness open or shorted to ground
51, 52, 55	ECU malfunction	Incorrect injection pulse or fixed timing

ISUZU I-TEC SYSTEM TROUBLE CODE CHART

Trouble Code	ECU Circuit	Possible Cause
23	Power transistor for ignition	Output terminal shorted to ground
35	Power transistor for ignition	Open harness wire
54	Power transistor for ignition	Faulty transistor or ground
25	Vacuum switching valve	Output terminal shorted to ground or open harness
53	Vacuum switching valve	Faulty transistor or ground
33	Fuel injector	Output terminal shorted to ground or open harness wire
64	Fuel injector	Faulty transistor or ground

①Not diagnosed when the air flow sensor is defective.

Location of connector to activate self-diagnosis mode on 1984 and later Toyota Celica models

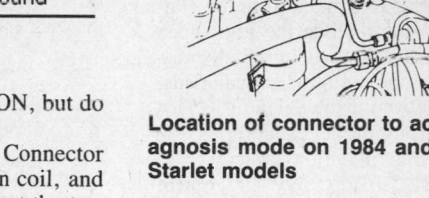

JUMPER WIRE

CHECK ENGINE CONNECTOR

Location of connector to activate self-diagnosis mode on 1984 and later Toyota Starlet models

TOYOTA EFI SYSTEM

NOTE: The Toyota ECU employs a dash-mounted CHECK ENGINE light that illuminates when the control unit detects a malfunction. The memory will store the trouble codes until the system is cleared by removing the EFI fuse with the engine off.

Activating Diagnosis Mode

To activate the trouble code readout and obtain the diagnostic codes stored in the memory, first check that the battery voltage is at least 11 volts, the throttle valve is fully closed, transmission is in neutral, the engine is at normal operating temperature and all accessories are turned off.

1. Turn the ignition switch ON, but do not start the engine.

2. Locate the Check Engine Connector under the hood, near the ignition coil, and use a short jumper wire to connect the terminals together.

3. Read the diagnostic code as indicated by the number of flashes of the CHECK ENGINE light. If normal system operation is occuring (no malfunctions), the light will blink once every 3 seconds (code 1).

4. The light will blink once every second to indicate a trouble code stored in the memory, with 3 second pauses between each code number. For example, three blinks, a pause, then three blinks indicates a code 3 (air flow meter malfunction) stored in the memory.

NOTE: The diagnostic code series will be repeated as long as the CHECK ENGINE terminals are connected by the jumper wire.

5. After all trouble codes are recorded, remove the jumper wire and replace the rubber cap on the connector.

6. Cancel the trouble codes in the memory after repairs by removing the STOP fuse for about 30 seconds (longer at lower ambient temperatures). If the diagnostic codes are not removed from the memory, they will be retained and reported as new problems the next time a malfunction oc-

STOP FUSE

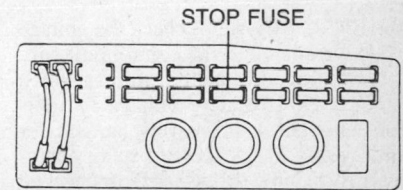

Clear the control unit trouble code memory by removing the fuse as shown on 1984 and later Toyota Celica models

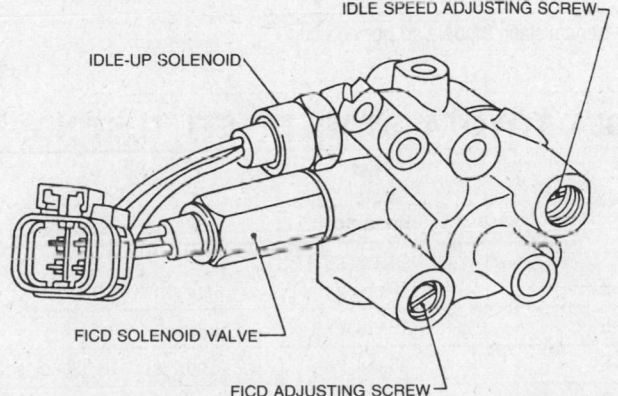

IDLE SPEED ADJUSTING SCREW

IDLE-UP SOLENOID

FICD SOLENOID VALVE

FICD ADJUSTING SCREW

Idle-up solenoid valve assembly showing adjustment screws

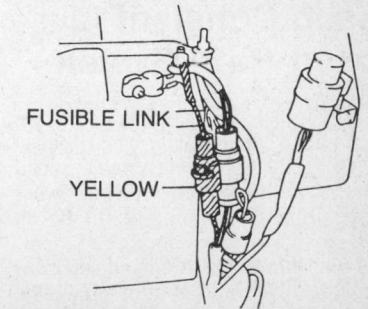

FUSIBLE LINK

YELLOW

On 1984 and later Toyota Starlet models, clear the trouble code memory by disconnecting the fusible link for 30 seconds

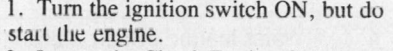

E₂	Vs	Vc	BATT	THA	B/K	STA		Ox	THW	IDL	VF	T	≠10	E₀₁
IG	E₃	W	+B			SPD			E₁	TL	Psw		≠20	E₀₂

Terminal identification on control unit connector for 1984 Toyota Starlet

curs in any other system. Repair success can be verified by clearing the memory and road testing the car to see if any malfunction codes appear. Code 1 should appear when the diagnostic connector is shorted with a jumper wire.

NOTE: Cancellation can also be done by removing the battery negative $(-)$ terminal, but in this case other memory systems (radio ETR, etc.) will also be cancelled out.

Idle Speed Control System

IDLE-UP SOLENOID VALVE

On the Nissan E.C.C.S. system, the idle-up solenoid valve is attached to the throttle body and responds to signals from the control unit (ECU) to stabilize the idle speed when the engine is loaded by accessories (A/C, power steering pump, electrical loads, etc.). The operation of the solenoid is part of the ECU's programmed capabilities. As with all AFC fuel injection systems, the solenoid controls an auxiliary air control valve that bypasses air around the throttle plate to raise the engine rpm. By regulating the amount of bypassed air, the ECU maintains the idle at a preset rpm value for the engine load sensed.

NOTE: Bosch LH and Motronic injection systems also have idle speed control as one of their programmed functions. On the LH system, an idle speed test point is provided that, when grounded, locks the air control valve in its minimum position for base idle setting.

TESTING

On the E.C.C.S. system, check the voltage between terminal 2 at the control unit connector and ground when the ignition switch is turned ON. If battery voltage (12v) is not present, check the wiring harness for continuity and check the EFI relay operation. The solenoid valve itself is checked by making sure continuity exists between the connector terminals on the switch.

Bosch Constant Idle Speed (CIS) System

Some AFC fuel injection systems are equipped with a separate idle speed control system designed to correct engine speed deviations very quickly, regardless of wear or changes in ignition timing. In the Bosch system, sensors read engine speed, temperature and throttle position and send impulses to an electronic control unit. The control unit continuously compares the sensor imputs with the ideal engine specifications programmed into the system mem-

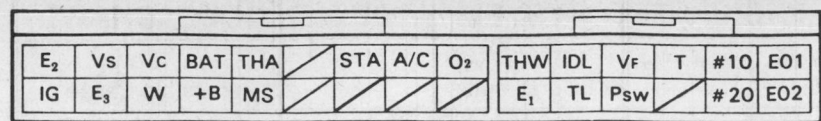

E₂	Vs	Vc	BAT	THA	/	/	STA	A/C	O₂	THW	IDL	VF	T	#10	E01
IG	E₃	W	+B	MS	/	/	/	/	/	E₁	TL	Psw	/	#20	E02

Terminal identification on control unit connector for 1984 Toyota Celica

TOYOTA EFI TROUBLE CODES

Code No.	ECU Circuit	Possible Cause	Diagnosis Testing
1	Normal operation	This appears when one of the other codes are stored in the memory	EFI system operating normally. No further testing required
2	Air flow meter signal (V_c)	Open circuit in V_C or V_C–V_S short circuited. Open circuit in V_B	Air flow meter circuit (V_C, V_S) Air flow meter EFI computer
3	Air flow meter signal (V_S)	Open circuit in V_S, or V_S–E_2 short circuited. Open circuit in V_B	Air flow meter circuit (V_B, V_C, V_S) Air flow meter EFI computer
4	Water thermo sensor signal (THW)	Open circuit in coolant temperature sensor signal.	Coolant temperature sensor circuit Coolant temperature sensor EFI computer
5	O_2 sensor signal	Open or short circuit in O_2 sensor signal (only lean or rich indication)	O_2 sensor circuit O_2 sensor EFI computer
6	Ignition signal	No ignition signal	Ignition system circuit Distributor Ignition coil and igniter EFI computer
7	Throttle position sensor signal	IDL-Psw short circuited	Throttle position sensor circuit Throttle position sensor EFI computer

NOTE: 5–speed transmission models do not use code 7

1984 TOYOTA STARLET EFI TESTING

ECU Terminal Connection	Test Meter Reading	Test Condition
	VOLTAGE TESTS	
+ B–E_1	10–14 V	Ignition switch ON
BATT–E_1	10–14 V	Ignition switch OFF
IDL–E_1	8–14 V	Throttle valve fully closed
P_{sw}–E_1	8–14 V	Throttle valve fully open
TL–E_1	8–14 V	Ignition switch OFF
IG–E_1	Above 3 V	Cranking and engine running
STA–E_1	6–12 V	Cranking
No. 10–E_1	9–14 V	Ignition switch ON
No. 20–E_1	9–14 V	Ignition switch ON
+ B–E_2	8–14 V	Ignition switch OFF

1984 TOYOTA STARLET EFI TESTING

ECU Terminal Connection	Test Meter Reading	Test Condition
V_c–E_2	4–9 V	Ignition switch OFF
V_s–E_2	0.5–2.5 V	Measuring plate fully closed
	5–8 V	Measuring plate fully open
	2.5–5.5 V	Idling
THA–E_2	2–6 V	Intake air temperature 20°C (68°F)
THW–E_2	0.5–2.5 V	Coolant temperature 80°C (176°F)
B/K–E_1	8–14 V	Stop light switch ON
RESISTANCE (OHM) TESTS		
TL–IDL	0	Throttle valve fully closed
TL–IDL	∞	Throttle valve fully open
TL–P_{sw}	∞	Throttle valve fully closed
TL–P_{sw}	0	Throttle valve fully open
IDL, TL, P_{sw}–Ground	∞	Ignition switch OFF
THW–E_2	200–400 Ω	Coolant temp. 80°C (176°F)
THA–E_2	2–3 kΩ	Intake air temp. 20°C (68°F)
THW, THA–Ground	∞	Ignition switch OFF
+B–E_2	200–400 Ω	Ignition switch OFF
V_c–E_2	100–300 Ω	Ignition switch OFF
V_s–E_2	20–100 Ω	Measuring plate fully closed
V_s–E_2	20–1,000 Ω	Measuring plate fully open
+B, V_c, V_s–Ground	∞	Ignition switch OFF
E_1, E_2, E_{01}, E_{02}–Ground	0	Ignition switch OFF

Note: Make sure test equipment will not damage control unit or components before testing
Ω–Ohms
V–Volts
∞–Infinity

ory by the manufacturer after dynamometer testing and tailored to every type of engine. The system is designed to be maintenance-free for the life of the engine.

The CIS system consists of the following components:

- Coolant Temperature Sensor
- Tachometer Connection (via ignition coil)
- Throttle Switch (position sensor)
- Air Control Valve (bypass air controls rpm)
- Electronic Control Unit (ECU)

NOTE: The ECU for idle speed control is a separate unit from the fuel injection control system. The CIS control unit is usually mounted near the fuel injection ECU. The two are very similar in appearance and care should be taken not to confuse one with the other during testing. The same service precautions apply as previously described for the fuel injection ECU.

The CIS system controls the idle speed by regulating an air control valve to bypass more air around the throttle valve, thereby raising the idle speed in the same manner as described under "Auxiliary Air Valve." A small electric motor rotates clockwise or counterclockwise, depending on the signal from the control unit, opening or closing the valve very quickly and precisely to regulate the air flow. There are three basic air flow modes; the low flow or deceleration mode reduces the air flow when the throttle switch circuit is closed during deceleration. The high or driving mode increases the air bypass flow at normal road speeds with the accelerator depressed. The regulated or idle flow mode maintains a steady idle speed

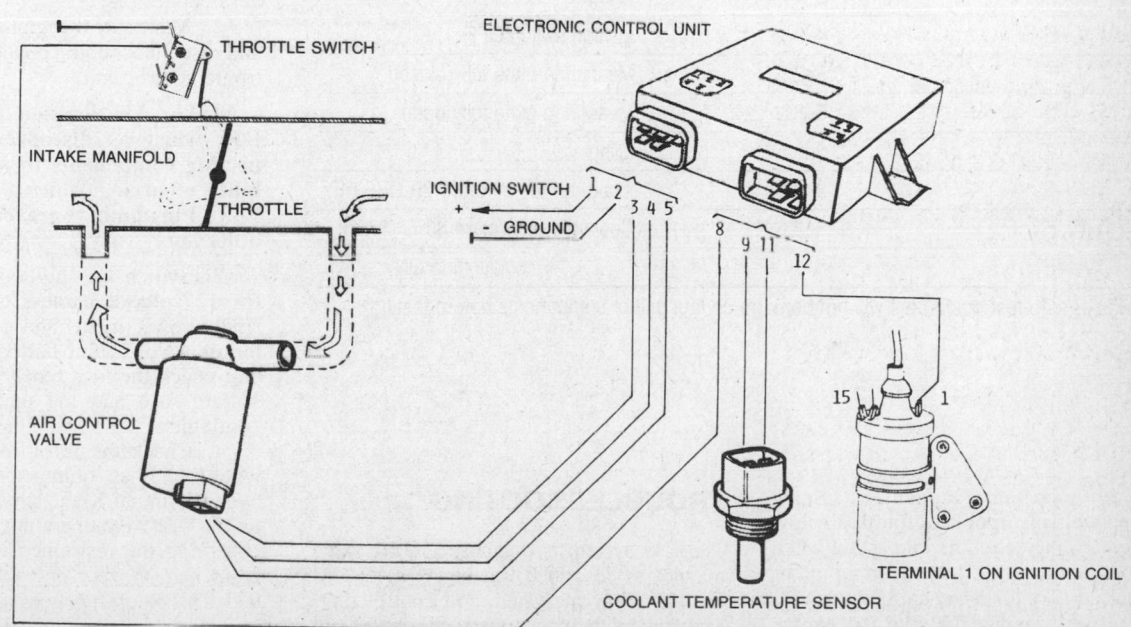

Schematic of Bosch Idle Speed Control System

1984 TOYOTA CELICA EFI TESTING

ECU Terminal Connection	Test Meter Reading	Test Condition
RESISTANCE (OHM) TESTS		
TL–IDL	0	Throttle valve fully closed
TL–IDL	∞	Throttle valve fully open
TL–P_{sw}	∞	Throttle valve fully closed
TL–P_{sw}	0	Throttle valve fully open
IDL, TL, P_{sw}–Ground	∞	Ignition switch OFF
THW–E_2	200–400 Ω	Coolant temp. 80°C (176°F)
THA–E_2	2– 3 kΩ	Intake air temp. 20°C (68°F)
THW, THA–Ground	∞	Ignition switch OFF
V_B–E_2	200– 400 Ω	Ignition switch OFF
V_C–E_2	100– 300 Ω	Ignition switch OFF
V_S–E_2	20– 400 Ω	Measuring plate fully closed
V_S–E_2	20–1,000 Ω	Measuring plate fully open
V_B, V_C, V_S–Ground	∞	Ignition switch OFF
E_1, E_{01}, E_{02}–Ground	0	Ignition switch OFF
VOLTAGE TESTS		
+ B–E_1	10–14 V	Ignition switch ON
BAT–E_1	10–14 V	Ignition switch OFF
IDL–E_1	8–14 V	Throttle valve fully closed
P_{sw}–E_1	8–14 V	Throttle valve fully open
TL–E_1	8–14 V	Ignition switch OFF
IG–E_1	Above 3 V	Cranking and engine running
STA–E_1	6–12 V	Cranking
No. 10–E_1	9–14 V	Ignition ON
No. 20–E_1	9–14 V	Ignition ON
W–E_1	8–14 V	No trouble and engine running
MS–E_1	8–14 V	Idling
V_c–E_2	4–9 V	Ignition switch OFF
V_s–E_2	0.5–2.5 V	Measuring plate fully closed
	5–8 V	Measuring plate fully open
	2.5–5.5 V	Idling
THA–E_2	2–6 V	Intake air temperature 20°C (68°F)
THW–E_2	0.5–2.5 V	Coolant temperature 80°C (176°F)
A/C–E_1	8–14 V	Air conditioning ON

Note: Make sure test equipment will not damage control unit or components before testing
Ω–Ohms
V–Volts
∞–Infinity

under all temperature conditions. Some newer models incorporate a fourth air flow mode which increases the idle speed when the air conditioner is turned on or other engine accessory loads are applied, providing improved cooling for both the engine and passenger compartment.

TROUBLESHOOTING

The CIS system is diagnosed in the same manner as described for the AFC fuel injection electrical system and control unit. Make all of the preliminary checks for obvious problems such as loose or corroded connectors and broken wires. Bad contacts cause many problems. On Volvo models, there are two connectors on the firewall and at the control unit. This dual wiring harness connection at the control unit differs from the standard single harness connector common to fuel injection ECU assemblies. If there is a problem with the engine idle speed on models equipped with a Bosch CIS system, check the air hoses for obstruction and the air control valve for sticking due to deposits from the PCV (positive crankcase ventilation) system. If there is a problem with periodic buildup of crankcase deposits in the air control valve, more frequent oil change intervals may be all that is necessary to correct the problem.

If the CIS system is suspected of causing a problem, most testing can be done with a good quality volt/ohmmeter and a 12V test light. The test light uses more current than a volt meter and sometimes is better at finding bad connections. The most common faults are poor or corroded contacts at the multipin connectors on the control unit, firewall and sensors.

—— **CAUTION** ——
Do not force the test probes directly into the wire harness connectors from the front. Test probes can spread the terminal contacts and cause a bad connection where none existed. Always test ECU connectors from the rear, using a pin to provide an accessible connection for test clips, if necessary. DO NOT pierce any wires with probes.

TESTING

1. Locate the CIS system electronic control unit and remove any cover panels as necessary to gain access to the wire harness connectors.

2. Make sure the ignition switch is OFF and disconnect both connectors at the electronic control unit.

NOTE: The ignition switch must be OFF whenever disconnecting or reconnecting components to avoid the possibility of arcing which can damage the ECU. Pin numbers are for Volvo models; others may vary.

3. Switch the ignition ON and check for 12 volts at harness connector No. 1 (ECU power input) and a good ground at terminal No. 2. If no battery voltage is present, check the fuse block for a blown CIS system fuse and the ignition switch for continuity.

4. Check the throttle switch (microswitch) with an ohmmeter connected between terminal 8 and ground with the ignition OFF. By operating the throttle and observing the resistance valve of the microswitch, correct operation can be verified. This on/off function can also be checked using a test light connected between harness terminals 1 and 8.

NOTE: It is important to determine how (open or closed) the throttle switch is indicating idle position to the control unit before any adjustment or testing is possible.

VOLVO CIS THROTTLE SWITCH OPERATION

Year/ Model	Throttle Position	Resistance (ohms)	Test Light
1981 B21F	idle	∞	OFF
	above idle	0	ON
B28F	idle	0	ON
	above idle	∞	OFF
1982 B21F	idle	∞	OFF
	above idle	0	ON
B28F	idle	∞	OFF
	above idle	0	ON

Note: Make sure of correct microswitch operation before attempting any adjustments.

5. Check the coolant temperature sensor by connecting an ohmmeter across terminals 9 and 11 and measuring the resistance change at various engine temperatures. Look for a change rather than a specific value; if the resistance changes as the temperature rises, the sensor is operating properly.

6. Connect a tachometer between terminal 12 and ground, then start the engine and note the tach reading. The engine speed as measured by the tachometer should match the actual rpm at idle. If an obviously wrong value is indicated, or no reading at all is obtained, check the firewall connectors. There should be a tach signal from the ignition switch.

7. To check the air control valve, fabricate two appropriate jumper wires and connect one across terminals 1 and 4; and the other across terminals 2 and 5. Start the engine and note the idle speed. It should be 1600–2400 rpm. If not, the idle air control valve is malfunctioning.

THROTTLE BODY FUEL INJECTION (TBI)
Operation

RENAULT MODELS
The Throttle Body Fuel Injection (TBI) system is a "pulse time" system that injects fuel into the throttle body above the throttle blade. Fuel is metered to the engine by one or more electronically controlled fuel injector(s). The Electronic Control Unit (ECU) controls injection according to input provided from sensors that detect exhaust gas oxygen content, coolant temperature, manifold absolute pressure, crankshaft position and throttle position. The sensors provide an electronic signal usually modulated by varying resistance within the sensor itself.

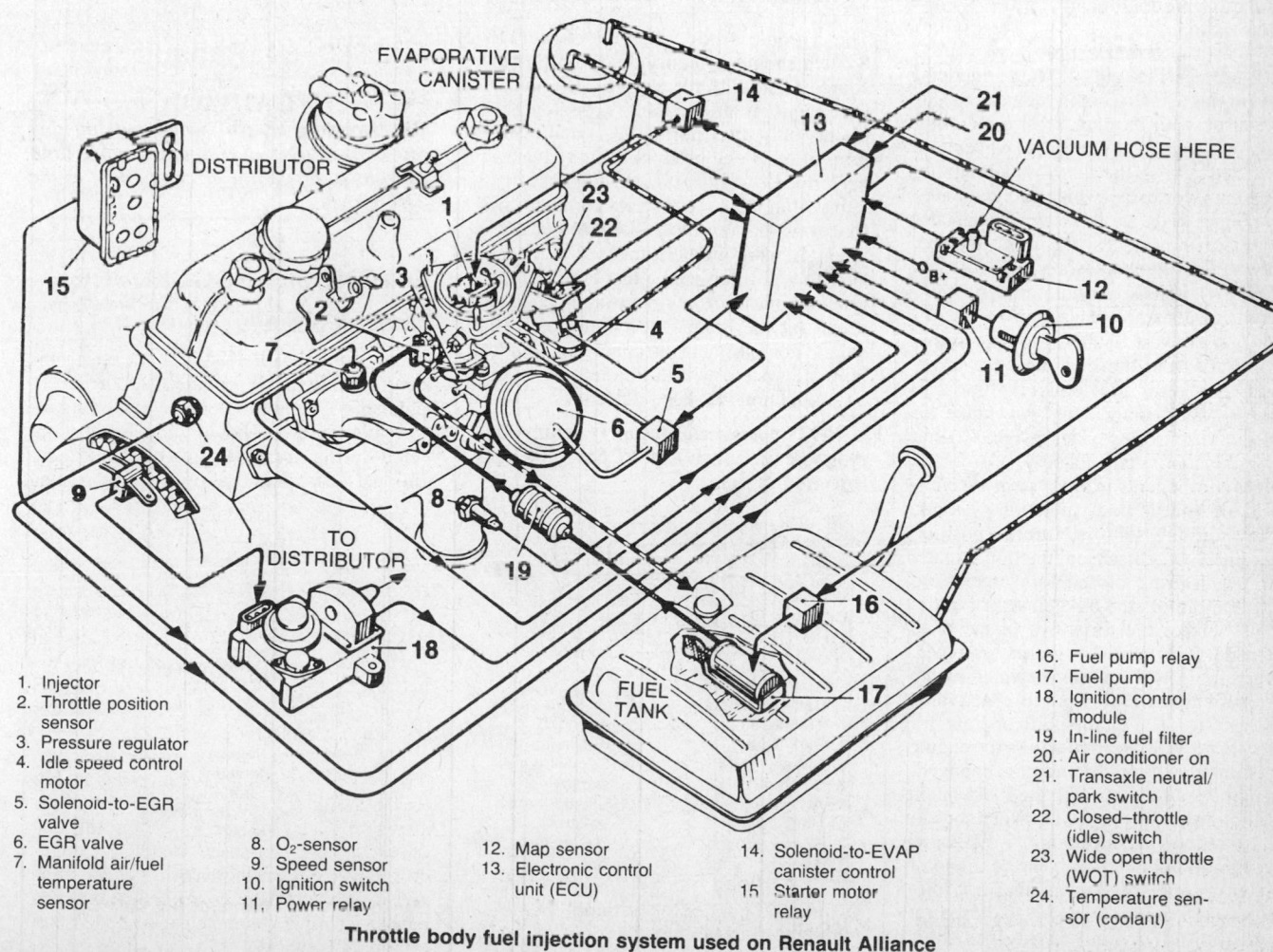

1. Injector
2. Throttle position sensor
3. Pressure regulator
4. Idle speed control motor
5. Solenoid-to-EGR valve
6. EGR valve
7. Manifold air/fuel temperature sensor
8. O₂-sensor
9. Speed sensor
10. Ignition switch
11. Power relay
12. Map sensor
13. Electronic control unit (ECU)
14. Solenoid-to-EVAP canister control
15. Starter motor relay
16. Fuel pump relay
17. Fuel pump
18. Ignition control module
19. In-line fuel filter
20. Air conditioner on
21. Transaxle neutral/park switch
22. Closed–throttle (idle) switch
23. Wide open throttle (WOT) switch
24. Temperature sensor (coolant)

Throttle body fuel injection system used on Renault Alliance

TBI fuel injection has two main sub-systems. The fuel system consists of an electric fuel pump (in tank), a fuel filter, a pressure regulator and a fuel injector. The control system consists of a manifold air/fuel mixture temperature (MAT) sensor, a coolant temperature sensor (CTS), a manifold absolute pressure (MAP) sensor, a wide open throttle (WOT) switch, a closed throttle (idle) switch, an exhaust oxygen (O_2) sensor, an electronic control unit (ECU), a gear position indicator (automatic transmission models only), a throttle position sensor and an idle speed control (ISC) motor. There may be more than one fuel injector used.

MITSUBISHI MODELS

The Mitsubishi Electronically Controlled Injection (ECI) system is basically a standard throttle body setup with some variations in operation and components. The fuel control system consists of an electronic control unit (ECU), two solenoid-type fuel injectors, an air flow sensor and several engine sensors. The ECU receives voltage signals from the engine sensors on operating conditions, then sends out impulses to the injectors to constantly adjust the fuel mixture. In addition, the ECU controls:

- Starting enrichment
- After-start enrichment
- Warm-up enrichment
- Fast idle
- Deceleration fuel cut-off
- Overboost fuel cut-off (turbo models)

One of the primary components is the air flow sensor with its device for generating Karman vortexes. Ultrasonic waves are transmitted across the air flow containing the Karman vortexes, which are generated in proportion to the air flow rate. The greater the number of vortices, the more the frequency of the ultrasonic waves are changed (modulated). These modulated (changed) ultrasonic waves are picked up by the receiver and converted into a voltage signal for the ECU, and the ECU uses the information to control fuel delivery time and secondary air management. An intake air temperature sensor provides a signal so that air density can be calculated.

Other components in the system are common to all throttle body injection systems. The temperature sensors, throttle position sensor and oxygen sensor function as later described. During closed loop operation, the ECU monitors the oxygen sensor to determine correct fuel mixture. In the open loop mode, fuel delivery is pre-programmed.

When the TBI System is activated by the ignition switch, the fuel pump is activated by the ECU. The pump will operate for approximately one second unless the engine is operating or the starter motor is engaged. All engine sensors are activated and begin providing input for the ECU. When the engine is started, the fuel pump is activated for continuous operation. The ISC motor will control idle speed (including fast idle) if the throttle position switch is closed (at idle position). The ignition advance shifts from base timing to the ECU programmed advance curve. The fuel pressure regulator maintains fuel pressure at approximately 14.5 psi (1 bar) by returning excess fuel to the tank.

The ECU provides a ground for the injector to precisely control the opening and closing time (pulse width) to deliver precise amounts of fuel to the engine, continuously adjusting the air/fuel mixture while monitoring signals from various engine sensors including:

- Engine Coolant Temperature
- Intake Manifold Air Temperature and Volume
- Barometric Pressure
- Intake Manifold Absolute Pressure
- Engine Speed (rpm)
- Idle Speed
- Detonation
- Boost Pressure (turbo models only)
- Throttle Position
- Exhaust Gas Content (oxygen level)

NOTE: The Bosch Mono-Jetronic TBI system uses an airflow meter, similar to the L-Jetronic, to measure intake air volume. Later models use air mass sensors.

Troubleshooting

PRELIMINARY CHECKS

The Throttle Body Fuel Injection (TBI) System should be considered as a possible source of trouble for engine performance, fuel economy and exhaust emission complaints only after normal tests and inspections of other engine components have been performed. An integral self-diagnostic system within the ECU detects common malfunctions that are most likely to occur.

On Renault models the self-diagnostic system will illuminate a test bulb if a malfunction exists. When the trouble code terminal (at the diagnostic connector in the engine compartment) is connected to a test bulb the system will flash a trouble code if a malfunction has been detected.

NOTE: A special tester is required to diagnose the Mitsubishi ECI throttle body injection system.

Before performing any test, make sure that the malfunction is not caused by a component other than the fuel injection system (e.g., spark plugs, distributor, advance timing, etc.); that no air is entering the intake and exhaust system above the catalytic converter and, finally, that fuel is actually reaching the injector (test the pressure in the circuit).

TBI SERVICE PRECAUTIONS

1. Never connect or disconnect any electrical component without turning off the ignition switch.
2. With the engine stopped and the ignition on, the fuel pump should not be operative. The fuel pump is controlled by the electronic control unit (ECU).
3. Disconnect the battery cables before charging.
4. If the temperature is likely to exceed 80°C (176°F), as in a paint shop bake oven, remove the electronic control unit (ECU).
5. Misconnections should be carefully avoided because even momentary contact may cause serious ECU or system damage.

1983–84 Renault TBI

--- CAUTION ---
Be extremely careful when making any test connections. Never apply more than 12 volts to any point or component in the TBI system.

DIAGNOSIS PROCEDURE

Renault Models

The self-diagnostic feature of the electronic control unit (ECU) provides support for diagnosing system problems by recording six possible failures should they be encountered during normal engine operation. Additional tests should allow specific tracing

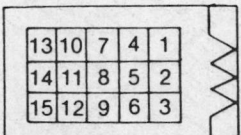

CONNECTOR D2

1. Battery (memory)
2. Trouble code
3. Park/Neutral Switch
4. B+ (power relay)
5. AC on
6. WOT switch
7. Sensor ground
8. Air temp. sensor
9. EGR solenoid
10. Canister purge solenoid
11. ISC motor forward
12. Coolant temp. sensor
13. Closed throttle switch
14. ISC motor reverse
15. Auto trans potentiometer

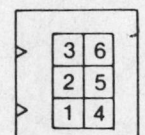

CONNECTOR D1

1. Tach (rpm) voltage
2. Ignition
3. Ground
4. Starter motor relay
5. Battery
6. Fuel pump

Diagnostic connector terminal identification. Make sure you connect the correct terminals during testing

TBI TROUBLE DIAGNOSIS

Condition or Trouble Code	Possible Cause	Correction
CODE 1 (poor low air temp. engine performance).	Manifold air/fuel temperature (MAT) sensor resistance is not less than 1000 ohms (HOT) or more than 100 kohms (VERY COLD).	Replace MAT sensor if not within specifications. Refer to MAT sensor test procedure.
CODE 2 (poor warm temp. engine performance-engine lacks power).	Coolant temperature sensor resistance is less than 300 ohms or more than 300 kohms (10 kohms at room temp.).	Replace coolant temperature sensor. Test MAT sensor. Refer to coolant temp. sensor test and MAT sensor test procedures.
CODE 3 (poor fuel economy, hard cold engine starting, stalling, and rough idle).	Defective wide open throttle (WOT) switch or closed (idle) throttle switch or both, and/or associated wire harness.	Test WOT switch operation and associated circuit. Refer to WOT switch test procedure. Test closed throttle switch operation and associated circuit. Refer to closed throttle switch test procedure.
CODE 4 (poor engine acceleration, sluggish performance, poor fuel economy).	Simultaneous closed throttle switch and manifold absolute pressure (MAP) sensor failure.	Test closed throttle switch and repair/replace as necessary. Refer to closed throttle switch test procedure. Test MAP sensor and associated hoses and wire harness. Repair or replace as necessary. Refer to MAP sensor test procedure.
CODE 5 (poor acceleration, sluggish performance).	Simultaneous WOT switch and manifold absolute pressure (MAP) sensor failure.	Test WOT switch and repair or replace as necessary. Refer to WOT switch test procedure. Test MAP sensor and associated hoses and wire harness. Repair or replace as necessary. Refer to MAP sensor test procedure.
CODE 6 (poor fuel economy, bad driveability, poor idle, black smoke from tailpipe).	Inoperative oxygen sensor.	Test oxygen sensor operation and replace if necessary. Test the fuel system for correct pressure. Test the EGR solenoid control. Test canister purge. Test secondary ignition circuit. Test PCV circuit. Refer to individual component test procedure.
No test bulb flash.	No battery voltage at ECU (J1-A with key on). No ground at ECU (J1-F). Simultaneous WOT and CTS switch contact (Ground at both D2 Pin 6 and D2 Pin 13). No battery voltage at test bulb (D2 Pin 4). Defective test bulb. Battery voltage low (less than 11.5V).	Repair or replace wire harness, connectors or relays. Repair or replace WOT switch, CTS switch, harness or connectors. Repair wire harness or connector. Replace test bulb. Charge or replace battery, repair vehicle wire harness.

ECU PIN (And Diagnostic Connector Pin)	SHOULD NEVER MAKE THIS CONNECTION
J1-E	12V or GND
J2-8 (D2, Pin 1)	12V
J2-18	12V
J2-17	12V
J1-B	12V
J1-C (D2, Pin 11)	12V or GND
J1-D (D2, Pin 14)	12V or GND
J1-K	12V
J1-H (D2, Pin 10)	12V
J1-G (D2, Pin 2)	12V
J1-J (D2, Pin 9)	12V
J2-2	12V or GND
J2-12	12V
J2-13 (D2, Pin 7)	12V
J2-4 (D1, Pin 1)	12V or GND
J2-1 (D1, Pin 5)	GND
J2-24 (D1, Pin 5)	GND
J1-A (D2, Pin 4)	GND
J1-F (D1, Pin 3)	12V
D1, Pin 6	GND

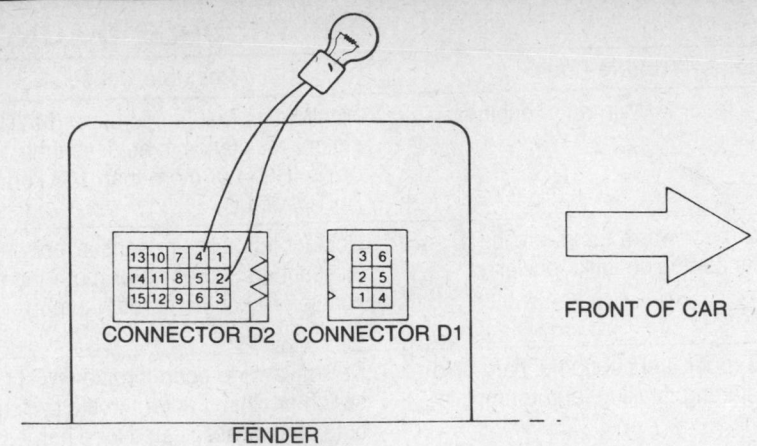

Trouble code test lamp connections

of a failure to a single-component source. Multiple disassociated failures must be diagnosed separately. It is possible that the test procedures can cause false interpretations of certain irregularities and consider them as ECU failures.

NOTE: In the following procedures, no specialized service equipment is necessary. It is necessary, however, to have available a volt/ohmmeter, a 12V test lamp, and an assortment of jumper wires and probes.

Trouble Code Test Lamp

Poor fuel economy, erratic idle speed, power surging and excessive engine stalling are typical symptoms when the fuel system has a component failure. If the ECU is functional, service diagnostic codes can be obtained by connecting a No. 158 test bulb (or equivalent) to pins D2-2 and D2-4 of the large diagnostic connector. With the test bulb installed, push the WOT switch lever on the throttle body and with the ISC motor plunger (closed throttle switch) also closed, have a helper turn on the ignition switch while observing the test bulb.

NOTE: IF the ECU is functioning normally, the test bulb should light for a moment then go out. This will always occur regardless of the failure condition, and serves as an indication that the ECU is functional.

After the initial illumination the ECU will cycle through and flash a single digit code

if any system malfunctions have been detected by the ECU during engine operation.

The ECU is capable of storing various trouble codes in memory. The initial trouble detected will be flashed first and then, followed by a short pause, the second trouble detected will be flashed. There will be a somewhat longer pause between the second code and the repeat cycle of the first code again. This provides distinction between codes 3 − 6 and 6 − 3. While both codes indicate the same two failures, the first digit indicates the initial trouble while the last digit indicates the most recent failure.

Renault TBI Trouble Codes

TBI TROUBLE CODES
1 Flash —Manifold Air/Fuel Temperature (MAT) Sensor Failure.
2 Flashes—Coolant Temperature Sensor Failure
3 Flashes—Simultaneous WOT and Closed Throttle Switch input.
4 Flashes—Simultaneous Closed Throttle Switch and High Air Flow
5 Flashes—Simultaneous WOT and Low Air Flow
6 Flashes—Oxygen Sensor Failure

In a given situation where further testing indicates no apparent cause for the failure indicated by the ECU self-diagnostic system, an intermittent failure, except that marginal components must be more closely examined. If the trouble code is erased and quickly returns with no other symptoms, the ECU should be suspected. However, in the absence of other negative symptoms, replacement of the ECU can be suspected. Again, because of the cost involved and the relative reliability of the ECU, the ECU should never be replaced without testing with dealer test equipment. If the ECU is

determined to be defective, it must be replaced. There are no dealer serviceable parts in the ECU. No repairs should be attempted.

It is important to note that the trouble memory is erased if the ECU power is interrupted by disconnecting the wire harness from the ECU, disconnecting either battery cable terminal, or allowing the engine to remain unstarted in excess of five days.

It is equally important to erase the trouble memory when a defective component is replaced. This can be done by any one of the actions listed above.

NOTE: On Mitsubishi models, a special ECU Checker with adapter connectors is necessary to read the trouble codes stored in the memory of the ECU.

Fuel Pump

The fuel pump is a roller type with a permanent magnet electric motor that is immersed in fuel. The check valve is designed to maintain the fuel pressure after the engine has stopped. The pump has two electric wire terminals marked + and − to ensure that it rotates in the correct direction.

The ECU controls the fuel pump, which is usually located inside the fuel tank and is attached to the fuel gauge sending unit assembly. Fuel pump power is supplied through two relays, located in the engine compartment.

NOTE: For Fuel pump removal and installation procedures, please refer to the individual car sections.

Pressure Regulator

The fuel pressure regulator (overflow-type) is integral with the throttle body. The valve is a diaphragm-operated relief valve in which one side of the valve is exposed to fuel pressure and the other side is exposed to air horn pressure. Nominal pressure is established by a calibrated spring.

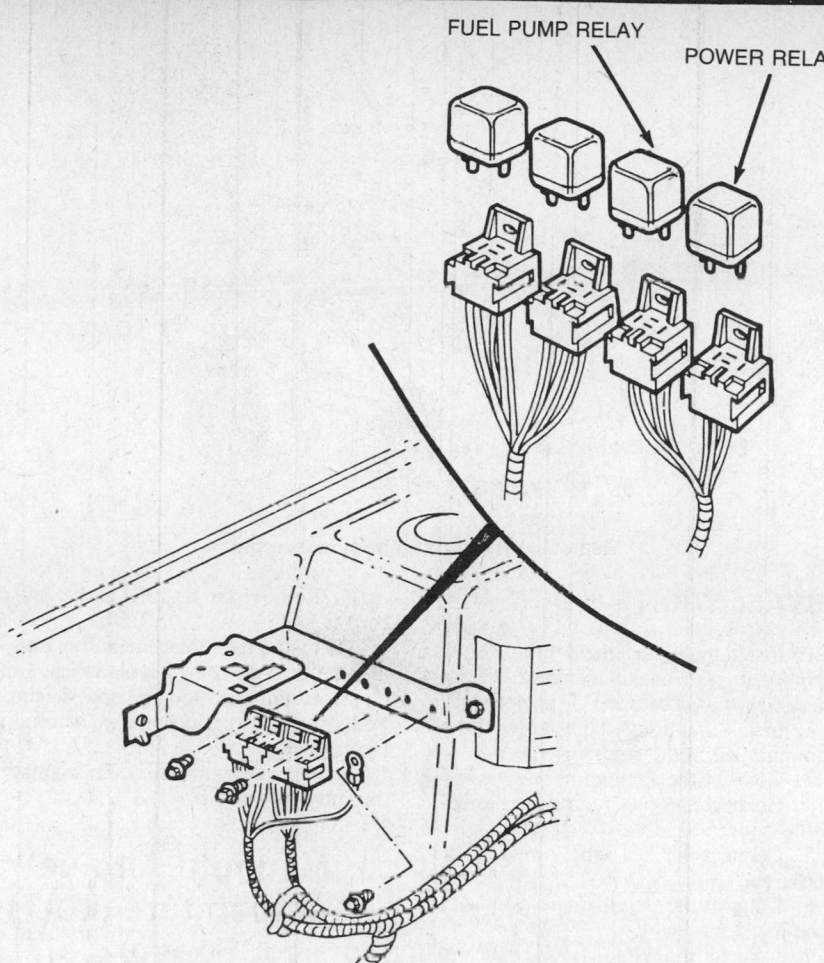

Relay block connector and bracket

on the bottom of the regulator to obtain 1 bar (14.5 psi) of pressure.

NOTE: Turning the screw inward increases the pressure and turning the screw outward decreases the pressure.

6. Install a lead seal ball to cover the regulator adjustment screw after adjusting the pressure to specification.

7. Turn the ignition off, then disconnect the tachometer.

8. Disconnect the fuel pressure gauge and install the cap on the test fitting. Install the air filter.

REMOVAL & INSTALLATION

1. Remove the three retaining screws that secure the pressure regulator to the throttle body.

2. Remove the pressure regulator assembly. Note the location of the components for assembly reference.

3. Discard the gasket.

4. Position the pressure regulator assembly with a replacement gasket.

5. Install the three retaining screws to secure the pressure regulator to the throttle body.

6. Start the engine and inspect for leaks.

Fuel Injector

The injector body contains a solenoid with a plunger or core piece that is pulled upward by the solenoid armature allowing the spring loaded ball valve to come off the valve seat. This allows fuel to pass through to the atomizer/spray nozzle. During engine operation, the fuel injector is energized by the ECU and serves to meter and direct atomized fuel into the throttle bore above the

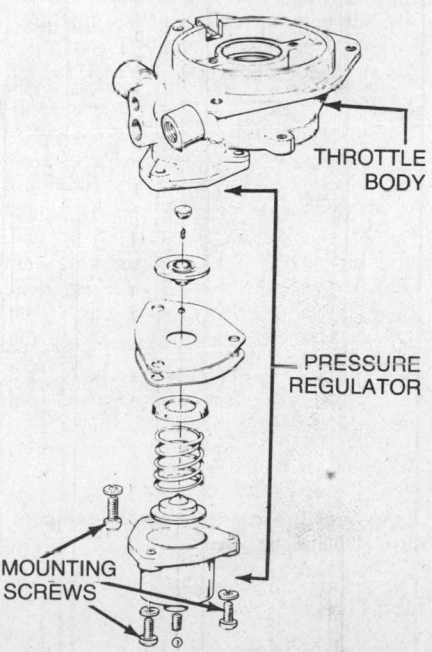

Exploded view of the pressure regulator assembly

The pressure regulator has a spring chamber that is vented to the same pressure as the tip of the injector. Because the differential pressure between the injector nozzle and the spring chamber is the same, the volume of fuel injected is dependent only on the length of time the injector is energized. The pump delivers fuel in excess of the maximum required by the engine and the excess fuel flows back to the fuel tank from the pressure regulator via the fuel return hose.

ADJUSTMENT

Renault Models

Adjustment of the fuel pressure regulator is necessary only to establish the correct pressure after a replacement has been installed.

1. Remove the air filter.

2. Connect a tachometer to the diagnostic connector terminals D1-1 and D1-3.

3. Connect an accurate fuel pressure gauge to the fuel body pressure test fitting. Exercise caution when removing fuel lines.

4. Start the engine and accelerate to approximately 2000 rpm.

5. Turn the allen head adjustment screw

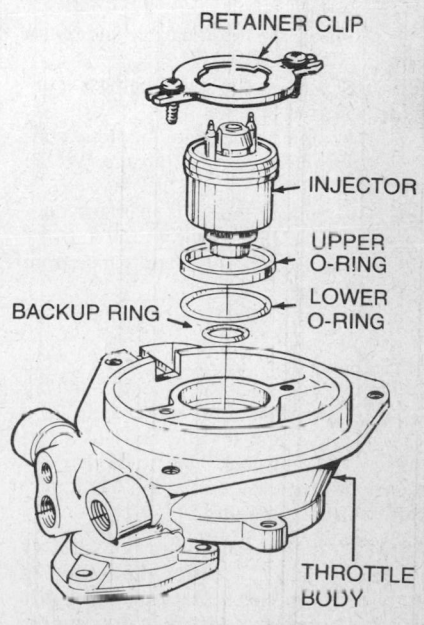

TBI fuel injector installation

throttle blade. During engine start-up the injector is energized to deliver a predetermined volume of fuel to aid starting.

NOTE: More than one injector may be used. Mitsubishi models use two.

REMOVAL & INSTALLATION

1. Remove the air filter.
2. Remove the injector wire connector.
3. Remove the injector retainer clip screws.
4. Remove the injector retainer clip.
5. Using a small pair of pliers, gently grasp the center collar of the injector (between electrical terminals) and carefully remove the injector with a lifting/twisting motion.
6. Discard the upper and lower O-rings. Note that the back-up ring fits over the upper O-ring.
7. To install the injector, proceed as follows: Lubricate with light oil and install a replacement lower O-ring in the housing bore.
8. Lubricate with light oil and install a replacement upper O-ring into housing bore.
9. Install the back-up ring over the upper O-ring.
10. Position the replacement injector in the throttle body and center the nozzle in the lower housing bore. Seat the injector using a pushing/twisting motion.
11. Align the wire terminals.
12. Install the retainer clip and screws.
13. Install the injector wire connector.
14. Install the air filter.

Throttle Body

NOTE: The following is a general procedure for all systems.

INSTALLATION

1. Remove the throttle cable and return spring.
2. Disconnect the wire harness connector from the injector.
3. Disconnect the wire harness connector from the wide open throttle (WOT) switch.
4. Disconnect the wire harness connector from the ISC motor.
5. Disconnect the fuel supply pipe from the throttle body.
6. Disconnect the fuel return pipe from the throttle body.
7. Disconnect the vacuum hoses from the throttle body assembly. Identify and tag the hoses for installation reference.
8. Remove the throttle body-to-manifold retaining nuts from the studs.
9. Remove the throttle body assembly from the intake manifold.

NOTE: If the throttle body assembly is being replaced, transfer the following components to the replacement throttle body; idle speed control (ISC) motor/ WOT switch and bracket assembly.

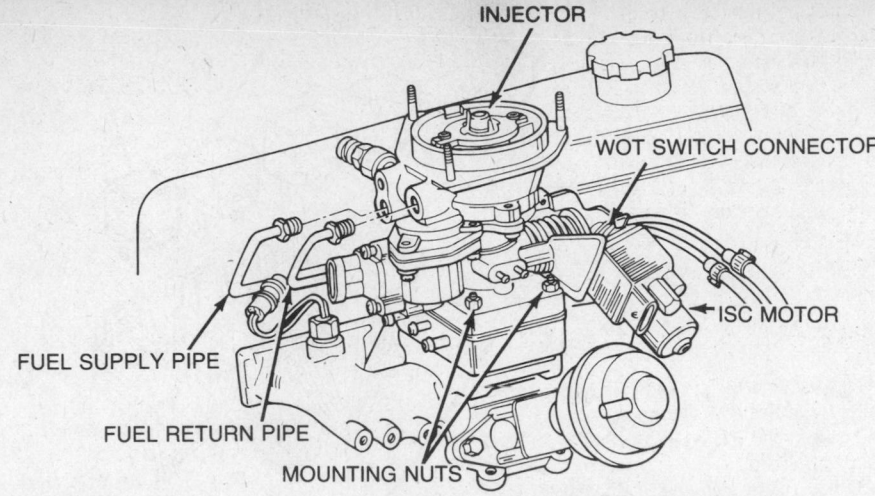

Removing the throttle body assembly

INSTALLATION

1. Install the replacement throttle body assembly on the intake manifold. Use a replacement gasket between the components.
2. Install the throttle body-to-manifold retaining nuts on the studs.
3. Connect the vacuum hoses.
4. Connect the fuel return pipe to the throttle body.
5. Connect the fuel supply pipe to the throttle body.
6. Connect the wire harness connector to the injector.
7. Connect the wire harness connector to the WOT switch.
8. Connect the wire harness connector to the ISC motor.
9. Install the throttle cable and return spring.

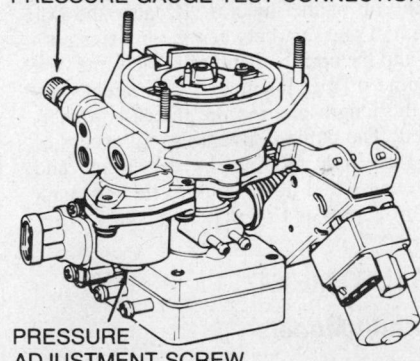

Throttle body assembly. Note testing and adjustment points for fuel pressure

Fuel Body Assembly

REMOVAL & INSTALLATION

1. Remove the throttle body assembly from the intake manifold.
2. Remove the three Torx® screws that retain the fuel body to the throttle body.

3. Remove the original gasket and discard it.
4. Install the replacement fuel body on the throttle body using a replacement gasket.
5. Install the three fuel body-to-throttle body retaining Torx® head screws and tighten securely.
6. Install the throttle body assembly on the intake manifold.

Manifold Air/Fuel Temperature (MAT) Sensor

The manifold air/fuel temperature (MAT) sensor is installed in the intake manifold in front of an intake port. This sensor reacts to the temperature of the air/fuel mixture (charge) in the intake manifold and provides an analog voltage for the ECU.

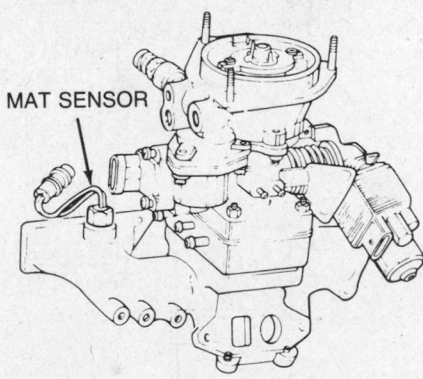

Location of the manifold air/fuel temperature (MAT) sensor

TESTING

Renault Models

1. Disconnect the wire harness connector from the MAT sensor.
2. Test the resistance of the sensor with

a high input impedance (digital) ohmmeter. Resistance ranges from 300 ohms to 300K ohms (10K ohms at room temperature).

3. Replace the sensor if it is not within the range of resistance specified above.

4. Test the resistance of the wire harness between the ECU harness connector J2-13 and the sensor connector, and J2-11 to sensor connector. Repair as necessary if the resistance is greater than 1 ohm.

NOTE: J2-13 and J2-11 are at ECU harness conductor.

REMOVAL & INSTALLATION

1. Disconnect the wire harness connector from the MAT sensor.
2. Remove the MAT sensor from the intake manifold.
3. Clean the threads in the manifold.
4. Install the replacement MAT sensor in the intake manifold.
5. Connect the wire harness connector to the MAT sensor.

Coolant Temperature Sensor (CTS)

The coolant temperature sensor is installed in the engine water jacket. This sensor provides an analog voltage for the ECU. The ECU will enrich the fuel mixture delivered by the injector as long as the engine is cold.

TESTING

Renault Models

1. Disconnect the harness from the coolant temperature sensor.
2. Disconnect the wire harness connector.
3. Test the resistance of the sensor with a high input impedance (digital) ohmmeter. The resistance ranges from 300 ohms to more than 300K ohms (10K ohms at room temperature).

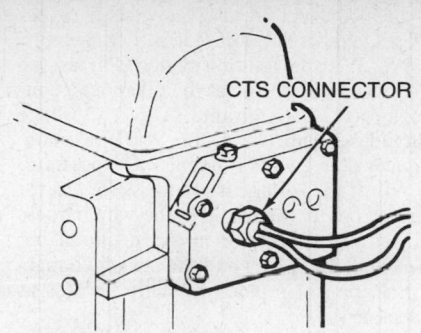

Coolant temperature sensor (CTS) installation

4. Replace the sensor if not within the range of resistance specified above.
5. Test the resistance of the wire harness between J2-14 and the sensor connector, and J2-11 to the sensor connector. Find and repair open wire in harness, if indicated.

NOTE: J2-14 and J2-11 are at the ECU connector.

REMOVAL & INSTALLATION

1. Remove the wire harness connector from the coolant temperature sensor (CTS).
2. Remove the CTS from the cylinder head and rapidly plug the hole to prevent loss of coolant. Installation is the reverse of removal.

--- CAUTION ---
DO NOT remove the CTS with the cooling system hot and under pressure. Serious burns from coolant can result.

Manifold Absolute Pressure (MAP) Sensor

The MAP sensor reacts to absolute pressure in the intake manifold and provides an analog voltage for the ECU. Manifold pres-

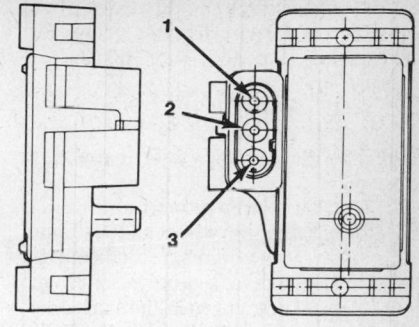

1. Ground
2. Output voltage
3. 5 volts

Manifold absolute pressure (MAP) sensor

sure is used to supply mixture density information and ambient barometric pressure information to the ECU. The sensor is remote mounted and a tube from the throttle body provides its input pressure.

TESTING

Renault Models

1. Inspect the MAP sensor vacuum hose connections at the throttle body and sensor. Repair as necessary.
2. Test the MAP sensor output voltage at the MAP sensor connector pin B (as marked on the sensor body) with the ig-

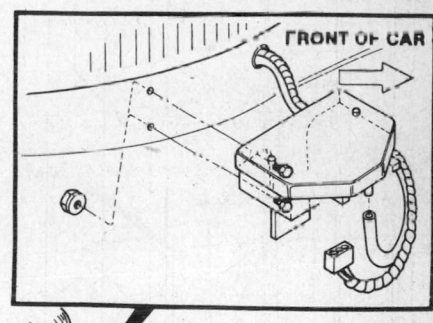

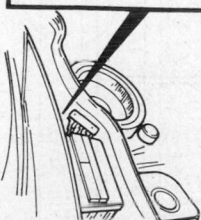

Replacement of the pressure sensor assembly—typical

nition switch ON and the engine OFF. Output voltage should be 4–5 volts.

NOTE: The voltage should drop 0.5–1.5 volts with a hot neutral idle speed condition.

3. Test ECU pin J2-12 for the same voltage described above to verify the wire harness condition. Repair as necessary.
4. Test the MAP sensor supply voltage at the sensor connector pin C with the ignition ON. The voltage should be 5 volts

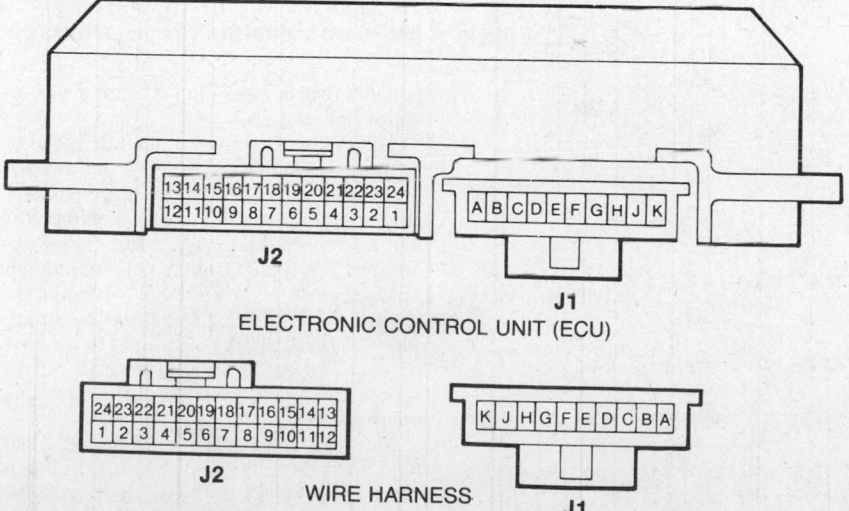

J2

ELECTRONIC CONTROL UNIT (ECU)

J1

J2

WIRE HARNESS

J1

Location of test pins on the ECU and wiring harness

(± 0.5V). The voltage should also be at pin J2-2 of the ECU wire harness connector. Repair or replace the wire harness as necessary.

5. Test the MAP sensor ground at sensor connector pin A and ECU connector pin J2-13. Repair the wire harness if necessary.

6. Test the sensor ground at the ECU connector between pin J2-13 and J1-F with an ohmmeter. If the ohmmeter indicates an open circuit, inspect for a good sensor ground on the flywheel housing near the starter motor. If the ground is good, replace the ECU. If J2-13 is shorted to 12 volts, correct this condition before replacing the ECU.

REMOVAL & INSTALLATION

1. Disconnect the electrical connector.
2. Disconnect the vacuum hose.
3. Remove the retaining nuts.
4. Remove the MAP sensor from the cowl panel.
5. Installation is the reverse of removal.

Wide Open Throttle (WOT) Switch

The WOT switch is mounted on the side of the throttle body. This switch provides a digital voltage for the ECU, which in turn

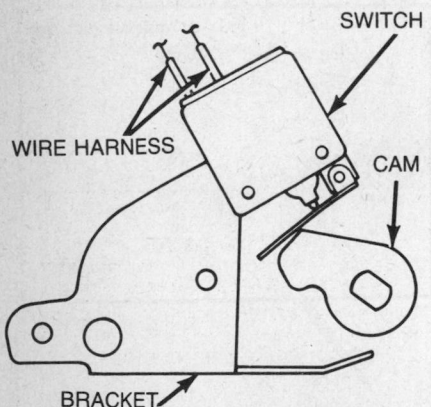

Wide open throttle (WOT) switch mounted on throttle body

enriches the fuel mixture delivered by the injector that is necessary for the increased air flow.

TESTING

Renault Models

1. Disconnect the wire harness from the WOT switch.
2. Test the operation of the WOT switch with a high input impedance ohmmeter. Open and close the switch manually.
3. Resistance should be infinite when the throttle is closed. A low resistance should be indicated at the WOT position. Test the switch operation several times.

4. Replace the WOT switch if defective. Connect the wire harness connector.

5. With the ignition switch ON, test the WOT switch voltage at the diagnostic connector (D2-6 to ground, D2-7). Voltage should be zero (0) at the WOT position; greater than 2 volts if not at WOT position.

6. If the voltage is always zero, test for a short circuit to ground in the wire harness or switch. Check for an open circuit between J2-19 (ECU) and the switch connector. Repair or replace the wire harness as necessary.

7. If the voltage is always greater than 2 volts, test for an open wire or connector between the switch and ground. Repair as necessary.

ADJUSTMENT

Renault Models

NOTE: Adjustment of the WOT switch is necessary only to establish the initial position of the switch after it has been replaced.

1. With the throttle body assembly removed from the engine, loosen the two retaining screws that attach the WOT switch to the bracket.
2. Open the throttle to wide open position.
3. Attach the alignment gauge J-26701 or equivalent on the flat surface of the throttle lever.
4. Rotate the degree scale of the gauge until the 15 degree mark is aligned with the pointer.
5. Adjust the bubble until it is centered.
6. Rotate the degree scale to align zero degrees with the pointer.
7. Close the throttle slightly to center the bubble on the gauge. The throttle is now at 15 degrees before WOT position.
8. Position the WOT switch lever on the throttle cam so that the switch plunger is just closed at 15 degrees before WOT position.

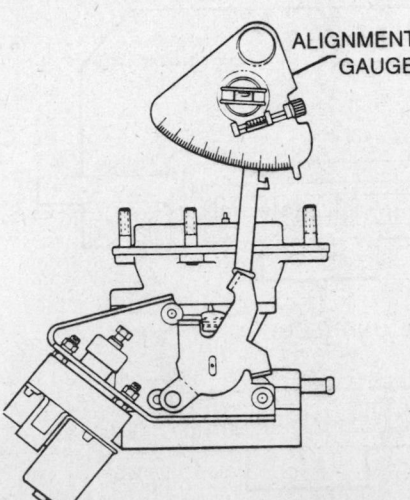

Wide open throttle switch adjustment

9. Tighten the WOT switch retaining screws.
10. Remove the alignment bubble gauge.

REMOVAL & INSTALLATION

1. Remove the air filter.
2. Disconnect the throttle return spring.
3. Disconnect the throttle cable.
4. Remove the ISC motor bracket-to-throttle body screws.
5. Disconnect the wire connectors from the WOT switch and ISC motor.
6. Remove the bracket, ISC motor and WOT switch assembly from the throttle body.
7. Remove the ISC motor.
8. Remove the two WOT switch-to-bracket screws.
9. Remove the WOT switch.
10. Installation is the reverse of removal.

Idle Speed Control (ISC) Motor

Engine idle speed and engine deceleration throttle stop angle are controlled by an electric motor driven actuator that changes the throttle stop angle by being a movable idle stop. The ECU controls the ISC motor actuator by providing the appropriate voltage outputs to produce the idle speed or throttle stop angle required for the particular engine operating condition. The electronic com-

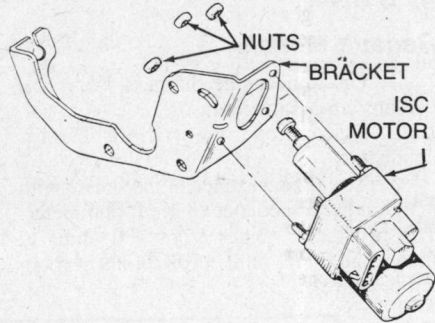

Idle speed control (ISC) motor replacement

ponents that control the ISC motor are integral with the ECU.

The system controls engine idle speed or throttle stop angle as would a dashpot for deceleration, as would a fast idle device for cold engine operation, and as would a normal idle speed device for warm engine operation. The inputs from the air conditioner compressor (ON/OFF), transaxle (PARK, NEUTRAL), and throttle extremities (OPEN/CLOSED) are used to increase or decrease the throttle stop angle in response to particular engine operating conditions.

For engine starting, the throttle is either held open for a longer period (COLD) or a short time (HOT) to provide adequate engine warm-up prior to normal engine operation. With normal engine idle speed operation, the idle speed is maintained at a programmed rpm and varies slightly according to engine operating conditions. Additionally, with certain engine deceleration conditions, the throttle is held slightly open.

ADJUSTMENT

Renault Models

NOTE: Adjustment is necessary only to establish the initial position of the plunger after the ISC motor has been replaced.

1. Remove the air cleaner.
2. Start the engine and allow it to reach normal operating temperature. Make sure that the air conditioning is turned off.
3. Connect a tachometer to terminal D1-1 and D1-3 of the diagnostic connector.
4. Turn the ignition off. The ISC motor plunger should move to the fully extended position.
5. Disconnect the ISC motor wire and start the engine. The engine idle should be 3300–3700 rpm. If not, turn the hex screw on the end of the plunger to achieve a 3500 rpm reading.
6. Fully retract the plunger by holding the closed throttle switch plunger in while the throttle is open. If the closed throttle switch plunger touches the throttle lever when the throttle is closed, check the throttle linkage for binding or damage and correct as required.
7. Connect the ISC motor wire.
8. Turn the ignition off for 10 seconds. The ISC plunger should fully extend.
9. Start the engine. The idle should be 3500 rpm for a short period, then gradually reduce to the specified idle speed.
10. Turn off the ignition and disconnect the tachometer.

NOTE: Holding the closed throttle switch plunger as described above may activate an intermittant trouble code in the ECU memory. To erase the code, disconnect the battery for at least 10 seconds.

CLOSED THROTTLE SWITCH TEST

Renault Models

NOTE: It is important that all testing be done with the idle speed control motor plunger in the fully extended position, as it would be after a normal engine shut down. If it is necessary to extend the motor plunger to test the switch an ISC motor failure can be suspected. Refer to ISC motor test if necessary.

1. With the ignition switch ON, test the switch voltage at the diagnostic connector (D2-13 and D2-7, ground). Voltage should be close to zero at closed throttle and greater than 2 volts off the closed throttle position.
2. If the voltage is always zero, test for a short circuit to ground in the wire harness

or switch. Test for an open circuit between J2-20 (ECU connector) and the switch.
3. If voltage is always more than 2 volts, test for an open circuit in the wire harness between the ECU and the switch connector, and between the switch connector, and ground. Repair or replace the wire harness as necessary.

REMOVAL & INSTALLATION

NOTE: The closed throttle (idle) switch is integral with the motor.

1. Disconnect the throttle return spring.
2. Disconnect the wire connector from the motor.
3. Remove the motor-to-bracket retaining nuts.
4. Remove the motor from its bracket.
5. Installation is the reverse of removal.

Oxygen (O₂) Sensor

The oxygen sensor is located in the exhaust pipe adaptor. The analog voltage output from this sensor, which varies with the oxygen content of the exhaust gas, is supplied to the ECU. The ECU utilizes it as a reference voltage.

TESTING

Renault models

1. Test the continuity of the harness between the O_2 sensor connector and J2-9

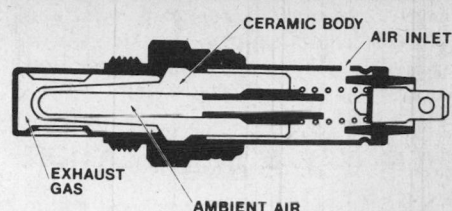

Schematic of a typical oxygen sensor

on the ECU wire harness connector with an ohmmeter. Ensure that the wire harness is not shorted to ground. Repair or replace the wire harness as necessary.
2. Test the continuity between the sensor ground (exhaust manifold) and Pin J2-13 on the ECU wire harness connector. Repair the wire harness if necessary.
3. Test the fuel system for the correct pressure. Pressure should be approximately 1 bar (14–15 psi) with the engine at idle speed. Refer to the fuel system pressure test. Repair the fuel system if necessary.
4. Check the sensor operation by driving the vehicle with a test lamp (No. 158 bulb) connected between the diagnostic connector D2-2 and D2-4.
5. Bulb lighted at start is normal operation for test circuit. If the bulb does not light after warm up, the O_2 sensor is functioning normally. If the bulb stays lit or lights after the engine warms up, replace the O_2 sensor.

NOTE: Additional testing may be required to locate the cause of an oxygen sensor failure. Other system failures that

MITSUBISHI ECI TROUBLE CODES

Trouble Code	ECU Circuit	Possible Cause
1	Oxygen sensor	Open circuit in wire harness, faulty oxygen sensor or connector
2	Ignition signal	Open or shorted wire harness, faulty igniter
3	Air flow sensor	Open or shorted wire harness, loose connector, defective air flow sensor
4	Boost pressure sensor	Defective boost sensor, open or shorted wire harness or connector
5	Throttle position sensor	Sensor contacts shorted, open or shorted wire harness or connector
6	ISC motor position sensor	Defective throttle sensor open or shorted wire harness or connector, defective ISC servo
7	Coolant temperature sensor	Defective sensor, open or shorted wire harness or connector
8	Speed sensor	Malfunction in speed sensor circuit, open or shorted wire harness or connector

could cause an O_2 sensor failure include EGR solenoid control, canister purge control, PCV system, secondary ignition circuit and fuel delivery system.

REMOVAL & INSTALLATION

1. Disconnect the wire connector from the O_2 sensor.
2. Remove the O_2 sensor from the exhaust pipe adaptor.
3. Clean the threads in the adaptor.
4. Apply anti–seize sealer to the threads on the O_2 sensor.

——— CAUTION ———
Apply anti-seize sealer only to the threads and not to any other part of the sensor.

5. Hand thread the sensor into the exhaust pipe adaptor.
6. Tighten the sensor with 27–34 Nm (20–25 ft. lbs.) torque.
7. Connect the wire connector.

——— CAUTION ———
Make sure that the wire terminal ends are properly seated in the connector prior to joining the connectors. Do not push the rubber boot down on the sensor body beyond 13 mm (0.5 in.) above the base. Also, the Oxygen Sensor pigtail wires cannot be spliced or soldered. If broken, replace the sensor.

ELECTRONIC CONTROL UNIT (ECU)

The Electronic Control Unit (ECU) is located below the glove box adjacent to the fuse panel. The ECU controls the injector fuel delivery time and changes the injected flow according to inputs received from sensors that react to exhaust gas oxygen, air temperature, coolant temperature, manifold absolute pressure, and crankshaft and throttle positions. The ECU is powered by the vehicle battery and, when the ignition is turned to the ON or START position, the voltage inputs are received from the sensors and switches. The desired air/fuel mixtures for various driving and atmospheric conditions are programmed into the ECU. As inputs are received from the sensors and switches, the ECU processes the inputs and computes the engine fuel requirements. The ECU energizes the injector for a specific time duration. The duration of pulse varies as engine operating conditions change.

TESTING

The only accurate and safe way to test the ECU is by using the self–diagnosis feature described earlier.

REMOVAL & INSTALLATION

1. Remove the retaining screws and

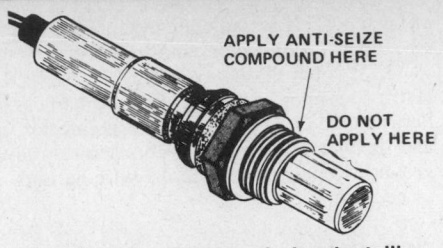

APPLY ANTI-SEIZE COMPOUND HERE

DO NOT APPLY HERE

Use anti–seize compound when installing the oxygen sensor

bracket that support the ECU below the glove box.
2. Remove the ECU.
3. Disconnect the wire harness connectors from the ECU.
4. Installation is the reverse of removal.

NOTE: It should be understood that the ECU is extremely reliable and must be the final component to be replaced if a doubt exists concerning the cause of an injection system failure.

MITSUBISHI ECI TEST SPECIFICATIONS

Circuit Tested	ECU Terminal Location	Normal Reading
Power supply	B-1	IGN OFF- 0 volts IGN ON- 11–13 volts
Secondary air control valve	A-10	Reading should change from 0.2–15 volts within 30 seconds at warm idle
Throttle position switch	A-1	IGN ON- 0.4–1.5 volts (4.5–5.0 volts @ WOT)
Coolant temperature sensor	A-3	3.5 volts @ 32 deg. F 0.5 volts @ 176 deg. F
Air temperature sensor	A-4	3.5 volts @ 32 deg. F 0.6 volts @ 176 deg. F
Idle position switch	A-5	IGN ON- 0–0.4 volts @ idle 11–13 volts @ WOT
ISC motor position switch	A-14	IGN ON- 11–13 volts ①
EGR control valve solenoid	B-4	0–0.5 volts above 3000 rpm 13–15 volts @ idle ②
Speed sensor	A-15	0.2–5 volts with transmission in gear and slowly accelerating
Cranking signal	A-13	Over 8 volts
Control relay	B-5	0–1 volts @ idle
Ignition pulse signal	A-8	12–15 volts @ idle 11–13 volts @ 3000 rpm
Air flow sensor signal	A-7	2.7–3.2 volts between idle and 3000 rpm
Injector No. 1	B-9	13–15 volts @ idle 12–13 volts @ 3000 rpm
Injector No. 2	B-10	13–15 volts @ idle 12–13 volts @ 3000 rpm
Oxygen sensor	A-6	0–2.7 volts ③
Pressure sensor	A-17	1.5–2.6 volts

NOTE: Turn ignition OFF between tests when making connections. All testing done with ignition ON unless noted otherwise. Make sure test equipment is compatible with injection system before making any voltage checks.

① If ignition switch is turned on for 15 seconds or more, the reading drops to 1 volt or less momentarily, then returns to 6–13 volts
② Engine warmed up to operating temperature
③ Do not use a powered voltmeter to test oxygen sensor. The sensor can be damaged by the voltage draw

WOT = Wide Open Throttle

Turbocharging

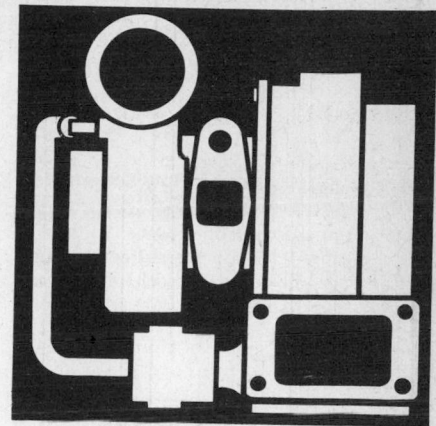

DESCRIPTION

A turbocharger is an exhaust-driven turbine which drives a centrifugal compressor wheel. The compressor is usually located between the air cleaner and the engine's intake manifold, while the turbine is located between the exhaust manifold and the muffler. Primarily, the turbocharger compresses the air entering the engine, forcing more air into the cylinders. This allows the engine to efficiently burn more fuel, thereby producing more horsepower.

All of the exhaust gases pass through the turbine housing. The expansion of these gases, acting on the turbine wheel, causes it to turn. After passing through the turbine the exhaust gases are routed to the atmosphere through the exhaust system. On some non-automotive applications, the turbocharger provides sufficient muffling of the exhaust noises to eliminate the need for a muffler.

1. V-band coupling
2. Compressor housing
3. Bolt, turbine
4. Lockplate, turbine
5. Clamp, turbine
6. Turbine housing
7. Nut, shaft
8. Turbine shaft wheel

9. Compressor wheel
10. Lockplate, backplate
11. Bolt, backplate
12. Backplate (vaneless on some models)
13. O-ring (used on vaned backplate)
14. Seal ring
15. Seal spacer
16. Piston ring
17. Thrust collar
18. Inboard thrust washer
19. Bearing retainer
20. Bearing washer
21. Bearing
22. Center housing
23. Shroud, turbine
24. Drive screw
25. Nameplate
26. Piston ring, turbine
27. Pin

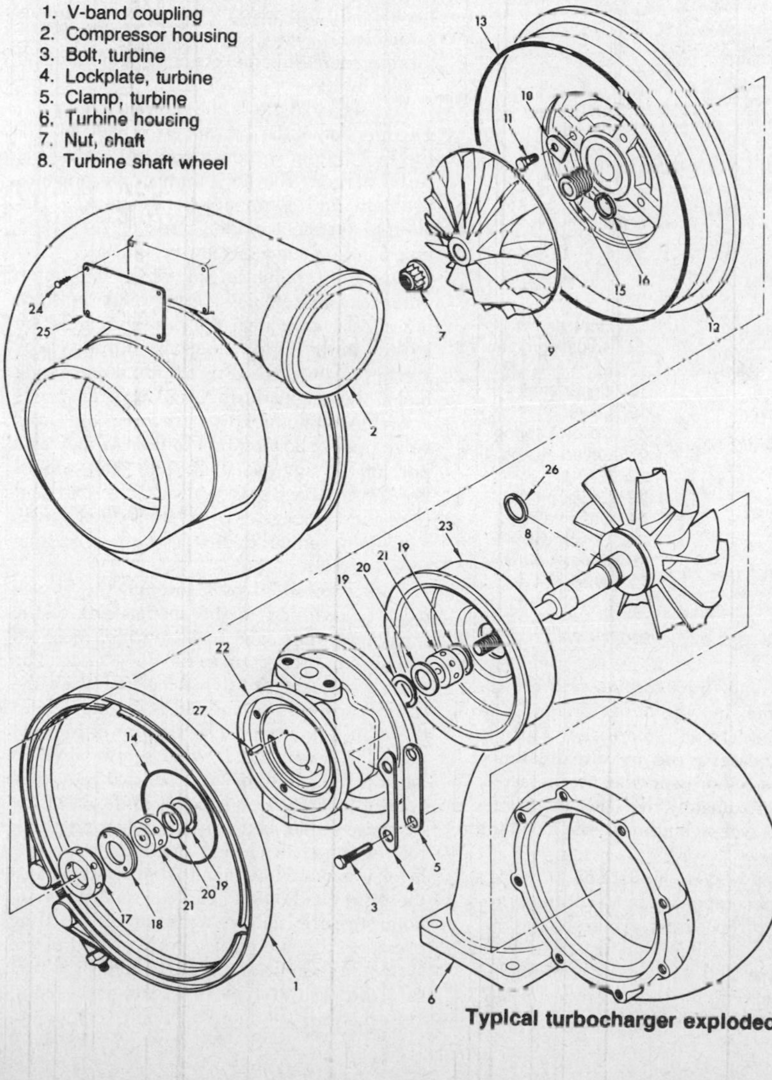

Typical turbocharger exploded view

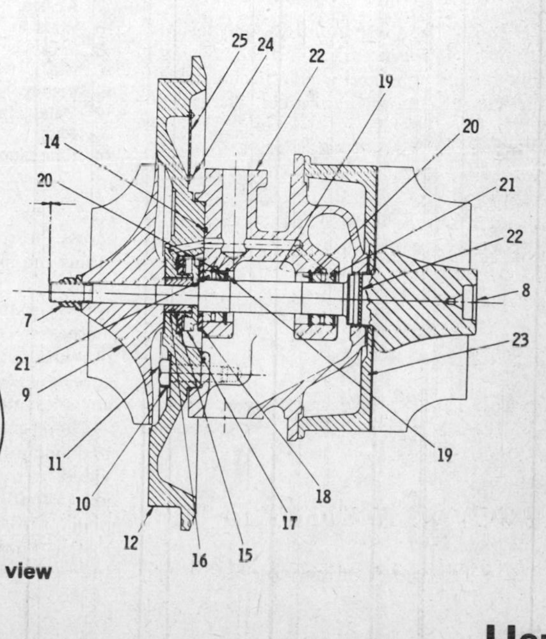

TURBOCHARGING

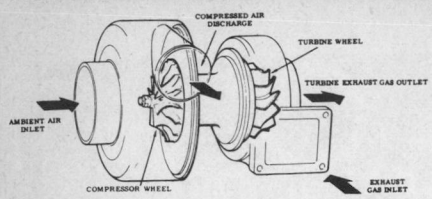

Typical turbocharger air flow schematic

The turbine also functions as a spark arrester. For example, the US Department of Agriculture recognizes the turbocharger as an adequate spark arrester for forestry operations.

OPERATION

The compressor and turbine are each enclosed in their own housings and are directly connected by a shaft. The housings are constructed of light alloy and are designed for maximum heat dissipation. The only power loss from the turbine to the compressor is the slight friction of the shaft journal bearings. Air is drawn in through the filtered intake system, compressed by the compressor wheel and discharged into the intake manifold. The extra charge of air provided by the turbocharger allows more fuel to be burned, providing more power.

As engine speed increases, the length of time the intake valves are open decreases, giving the air less time to fill the cylinders. On an engine running at 2500 rpm, the intake valves are open less than 0.017 second. The air drawn into a naturally aspirated engine's cylinder is less than atmospheric pressure. Turbochargers pack air into the cylinder at greater than atmospheric pressure at all speeds. The flow of exhaust gas from each cylinder occurs intermittantly as the exhaust valve opens. This results in fluctuating gas pressures, also known as pulse energy, at the turbine inlet. With a conventional turbine housing, only a small amount of pulse energy is used.

To better utilize these impulses, one design has an internal division in the turbine housing and the exhaust manifold which directs these exhaust gases to the turbine wheel. There is a

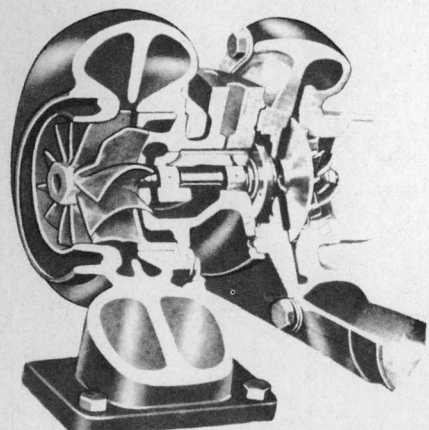

Altitude compensator

separate passage for each half of the engine cylinder exhaust.

On some four and six cylinder engines built to accommodate turbochargers, there is a separate passage for the front two or three cylinders and another for the rear half.

By using a fully divided exhaust system combined with a dual scroll turbine housing, the result is a highly effective nozzle velocity. This produces higher turbine speeds and manifold pressures than can be obtained with an undivided system.

At high altitudes, a naturally aspirated engine drops 3% in horsepower per 1000 feet elevation due to a 3% decrease in air density per 1000 feet.

With a turbocharged engine, an increase in altitude also increases the pressure drop

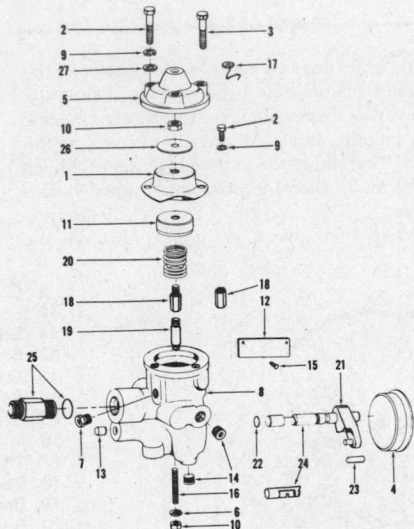

1. Bellows	15. Drive screw
2. Capscrew	16. Adjusting screw
3. Capscrew, seal type	17. Lead seal
4. Side cover	18. Upper shaft
5. Bellows cover	19. Lower shaft
6. Screw seal	20. Bellows spring
7. Air filter	21. Lever
8. Housing	22. O-ring
9. Lockwasher	23. Lever, pin
10. Nut	24. Shaft valve
11. Piston	25. Check valve
12. Dataplate	26. Bellows washer
13. Plug	27. Washer
14. Pipe plugs	

Aneroid exploded view

across the turbine. Inlet turbine pressure remains the same, but the outlet pressure decreases as the altitude increases. Turbine speed also increases as the pressure difference increases. The compressor wheel turns faster, providing approximately the same inlet pressure as at sea level, even though the incoming air is less dense.

There are, however, limitations to the actual amount of compensation for altitude provided by the turbocharger. These limitations are primarily a result of varying amounts of boost pressure and turbocharger-to-engine match. To make up for the difference in altitude compensation, an altitude compensator

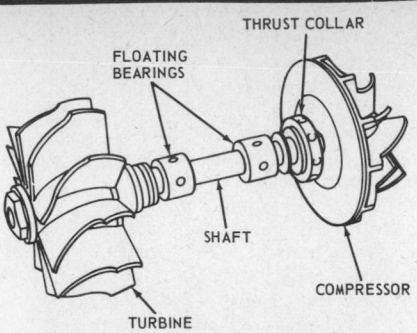

Basic parts of the turbocharger

is added to the system. During rapid acceleration or rapid engine load changes, the turbocharger speed, reflected in manifold pressure, inherently lags behind the power or fuel demand exercised by the opening of the throttle. This lag does not exist in the fuel system, so an overly rich mixture accompanied by heavy smoke occurs until the turbocharger catches up.

On diesel engines, two types of altitude compensators are used. One is a compressed air type which is very similar in appearance to the turbocharger. This type supplies compressed air to the intake manifold at a pressure about equal to sea level pressure. There is no increase of fuel for combustion and consequently no horsepower increase. However, the extra air provided by the altitude compensator usually increases combustion efficiency, thereby increasing fuel economy and reducing smoke levels.

The second type is the aneroid type unit. The function of the aneroid is to create a lag in the fuel system response equal to that of the turbocharger, thereby control the mixture problem and eliminating the smoke. The aneroid system is widely used on diesel engines and on some gasoline engines.

Fuel from the outlet side of the fuel pump enters the aneroid and goes through the starting check valve area. On others, it must be located in the supply line. The starting check valve prevents the aneroid from bypassing fuel at the engine during cranking. For speeds above cranking, fuel pressure forces the check valve open, allowing fuel to flow to the valve port of the aneroid shaft. The shaft and its bore form the bypass valve. This shaft and bore allow passage or restriction of fuel flow in a manner similar to that of a pressure/time type injection pump.

Fuel allowed to pass through the bypass valve is returned to the suction side of the injection pump. The bypassed fuel manifold pressure in proportion to the bypass rate. The shaft and sleeve are bypassing fuel when the control arm on the aneroid is resting against the adjusting screw. The amount of fuel bypassed is regulated by this screw which is located at the bottom of the aneroid body. The control lever, which is connected to a piston in the aneroid body by an actuating shaft, rotates the shaft closing the valve port. The lever is actuated by manifold pressure against the piston and diaphragm. Anytime the manifold pressure is above a present air actuating pressure, the aneroid is effectively out of the system. When pressure drops below the preset figure, the aneroid comes into the system.

In modern automotive gasoline engine applications with their stricter emission control standards, turbocharger lag is compensated for by means of modified spark control and/or an enrichment vacuum regulator system. The spark control system changes the ignition timing on demand and the vacuum regulator system regulates vacuum flow at the carburetor through a remote power enrichment port.

Some engines, particularly passenger car applications, in which boost pressure must be held at low levels, utilize a wastegate unit. Since turbocharger operation is self-perpetuating, unchecked operation will increase boost pressure beyond the operating capabilities of these engines. Some method of limiting this boost increases must be used. The principle means is by the inclusion of a wastegate in the system. The wastegate, usually located in the outlet elbow assembly, is activated when boost pressure reaches a predetermined level (usually 3-7 psi depending on application). The wastegate opens and bypasses exhaust flow around the turbine.

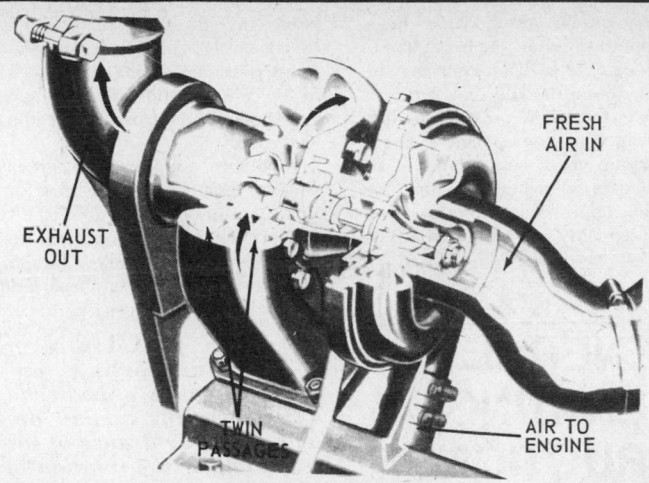

Twin passage turbine

LUBRICATION

Since turbine speeds routinely reach 140,000 rpm, adequate lubrication is vitally important. Turbochargers are lubricated by engine oil. Depending on the application, the lubrication may be either pressure-fed or gravity-fed. In areas of very heavy load or when shut-down after peak operation is routine, pressure feeding, sometimes with a separate oil pump, is used. In cases where a separate oil pump is used, the pump continues operating during spin-down. Since all parts of the rotating assemblies are protected by a film of oil, no metal-to-metal contact occurs. Consequently, no appreciable wear should occur. If a constant supply of clean engine oil is maintained, bearing life should be indefinite. If the unit has floating sleeve type bearings, they provide oil clearance between the bearing and housing as well as between the bearing and shaft. When the turbocharger is operating, this allows the bearing

to turn as the shaft turns. All clearances in the turbocharger are closely controlled and carefully machined. Any dirt in the oil will adversely affect service life of the working parts. Oil and filter changes should occur regularly. Some manufacturers recommend more frequent oil changes for turbocharged engines. In any case, on turbocharged engines, the oil filter(s) should ALWAYS be changed with the engine oil. ALWAYS use oil of the recommended viscosity for that particular engine application. Check the owner's manual for your engine or vehicle for recommended intervals and proper viscosity.

TWO-CYCLE APPLICATIONS

Turbochargers may be used in addition to the regular scavenging process. In these cases, the air is drawn into the blower or scavenging pump and then transferred to the turbocharger where it is compressed and forced into the engine.

At light loads, there is little energy available to drive the turbocharger. The mechanically driven blower alone supplies scavenging air to cylinders. At increased loads, the turbocharger speeds up and takes in a sufficient amount of additional air to allow the inlet

pressure to drop to atmospheric levels, causing the blower check valve to open. At this engine speed, the blower becomes unloaded, saving engine power, and the turbocharger enters the load range where it alone can provide scavenging and turbocharging. Under ideal conditions, the engine starting air contains enough energy to start the turbocharger and also supply enough air for combustion. In some applications, however, turbochargers can be equipped with additional methods for supplying necessary scavenging air while the engine is being started. This can be accomplished either mechanically by coupling the turbocharger to the crankshaft in such a manner that it is mechanically driven during starting and automatically disconnects when exhaust pressure is high enough or by jet air starting, where air is blown through jets into the turbocharger turbine or compressor. The air passing through the compressor also aids in scavenging during starting.

INTERCOOLERS

When the air passing through the compressor is compressed it becomes heated and expands. Expanding air is less dense, therefore less air is forced into the engine. This helps defeat the turbocharging process. To overcome this condition, some engine applications use a heat exchanger, also known as an inter-

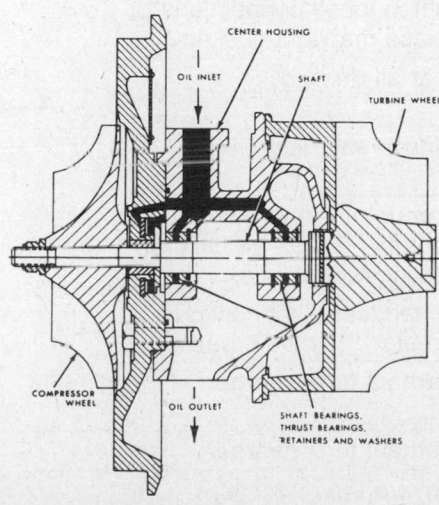

Turbocharger oil flow

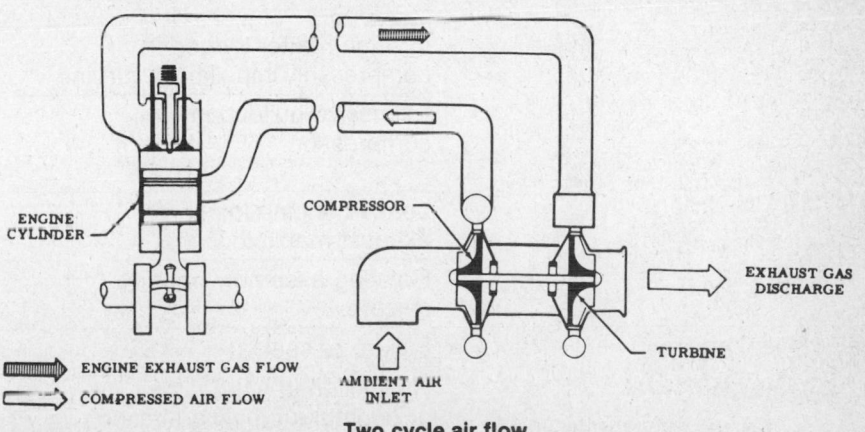

Two cycle air flow

cooler or after cooler. The intercooler reduces intake air temperature by as much as 90° F.

Located between the turbocharger and the intake manifold, the intercooler is a series of connected tubes, finned to provide dissipation, through which engine coolant is circulated. The carrying off of heat from the air makes the air denser, allowing more air to be forced into the engine. This provides more power, greater economy and quieter combustion.

GENERAL OPERATING INSTRUCTIONS FOR TURBOCHARGED ENGINES

1. After starting the engine, make sure there is sufficient oil pressure before accelerating or applying load.
2. When starting in cold weather, allow the engine to run a sufficient length of time (up to five minutes for diesel engines in extreme cold) before applying load or accelerating. This will insure adequate lubrication.
3. Should the engine stall at normal operating temperature, restart it immediately. This will prevent a rapid rise in the turbocharger

known as "temperature soaking". Also, the turbocharger, running hot during operation, may experience coking due to hot oil build-up in the center section. This coking will cause a blockage of the oil passages leading to failure of the unit.

4. Before stopping the engine, allow it to run a short length of time (up to two or three minutes for some diesels) to allow internal engine temperatures to normalize or equalize. Failure to allow temperature normalization can lead to heat fatique and/or blockage of oil passages due to coking.

— CAUTION —
When transporting an engine equipped with a turbocharger, always cover the exhaust outlet. This will prevent entrance of foreign material and/or the rotation of the turbine. Turbine rotation on a stopped engine could lead to bearing failure since no lubricating oil will be provided.

PREVENTIVE MAINTENANCE

1. Inspect all mountings and connections regularly to make sure they are secure and no leakage is present.
2. Make certain that there is no restriction in air flow at the crankcase ventilation system.

3. Run the engine at various, normal operating speeds and listen for unusual noises at the turbocharger.

Turbochargers normally emit a shrill whistle or whine. Bearings about to fail also emit a shrill whine, somewhat different from normal turbocharger noise. Try to distinguish between the two.

NOTE: After engine shut-off, the turbocharger will whine during rundown. Don't confuse this with bearing failure noise. Grating or scraping noises could indicate improper turbine or compressor wheel-to-housing clearances. If any such noises are heard, the unit should be removed for inspection.

4. Check the unit for unusual vibrations during operation.
5. Check for unusual smoking under load conditions. Excessive smoke means an incorrect air/fuel ratio.
6. Inspect and replace the air filter according to your owner's manual recommendations.

TROUBLE-SHOOTING

The turbocharger is a relatively simple unit. Most problems occur in other parts of the engine such as the lubrication system or the fuel system. With proper routine maintenance, the unit should give troublefree operation.

TURBOCHARGER TROUBLESHOOTING CHART

Trouble	Possible Cause	Remedy
Noisy operation or vibration.	Bearings not being lubricated.	Supply required oil pressure. Clean or replace oil line. If trouble persists, overhaul the turbocharger.
	Leak in engine intake or exhaust manifold.	Tighten loose connections or replace manifold gaskets.
Engine will not deliver rated power.	Clogged manifold system.	Clear all ducting.
	Foreign matter lodged in compressor, impeller, or turbine.	Disassemble and clean.
	Excessive buildup in compressor.	Thoroughly clean compressor assembly. Clean air cleaner and check for leaks.
	Leak in engine intake or exhaust manifold.	Tighten loose connections or replace manifold gaskets.
	Rotating assembly bearing seizure.	Overhaul turbocharger.
Oil seal leakage.	Failure of seal.	Overhaul turbocharger.
	Restriction in air cleaner or air intake creating suction.	Remove the restriction.

Engine Rebuilding

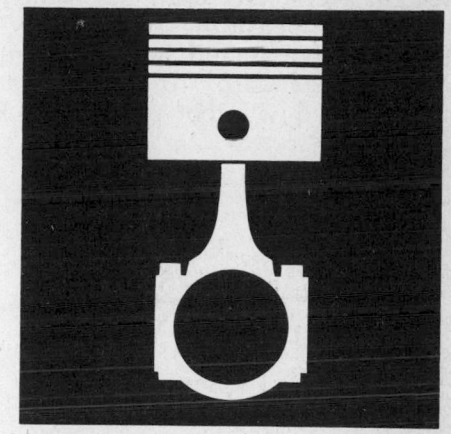

This section describes, in detail, the procedures involved in rebuilding a typical engine. The procedures are basically identical to those used in rebuilding engines of nearly all design and configurations.

The section is divided into two parts. The first, Cylinder Head Reconditioning, assumes that the cylinder head is removed from the engine, all manifolds are removed, and the cylinder head is on a workbench. The camshaft should be removed from overhead cam cylinder heads. The second section, Cylinder Block Reconditioning, covers the block, pistons, connecting rods and crankshaft. It is assumed that the engine is mounted on a work stand, and the cylinder head and all accessories are removed.

Procedures are identified as follows:

Unmarked—Basic procedures that must be performed in order to successfully complete the rebuilding process.

Starred(*)—Procedures that should be performed to ensure maximum performance and engine life.

Double starred (**)—Procedures that may be performed to increase engine performance and reliability.

In many cases, a choice of methods is also provided. Methods are identified in the same manner as procedures. The choice of method for a procedure is at the discretion of the user.

The tools required for the basic rebuilding procedure should, with minor exceptions, be those included in a mechanic's tool kit. An accurate torque wrench, and a dial indicator (reading in thousandths) mounted on a universal base should be available. Special tools, where required, all are readily available from the major tool suppliers. The services of a competent automotive machine shop must also be readily available.

When assembling the engine, any parts that will be in frictional contact must be pre-lubricated, to provide protection on initial start-up. Any product specifically formulated for this purpose may be used. NOTE: *Do not use engine oil.* Where semi-permanent (locked but removable) installation of bolts or nuts is desired, threads should be cleaned and coated with Loctite® or a similar product (non-hardening).

Aluminum has become increasingly popular for use in engines, due to its low weight and excellent heat transfer characteristics. The following precautions must be observed when handling aluminum engine parts:

—Never hot-tank aluminum parts.

—Remove all aluminum parts (identification tags, etc.) from engine parts before hot-tanking (otherwise they will be removed during the process).

—Always coat threads lightly with engine oil or anti-seize compounds before installation, to prevent seizure.

—Never over-torque bolts or spark plugs in aluminum threads. Should stripping occur, threads can be restored using any of a number of thread repair kits available (see next section).

Magnaflux and Zyglo are inspection techniques used to locate material flaws, such as stress cracks. Magnafluxing coats the part with fine magnetic particles, and subjects the part to a magnetic field. Cracks cause breaks in the magnetic field, which are outlined by the particles. Since Magnaflux is a magnetic process, it is applicable only to ferrous materials. The Zyglo process coats the material with a fluorescent dye penetrant, and then subjects it to blacklight inspection, under which cracks glow brightly. Parts made of any material may be tested using Zyglo. While Magnaflux and Zyglo are excellent for general inspection, and locating hidden defects, specific checks of suspected cracks may be made at lower cost and more readily using spot check dye. The dye is sprayed onto the suspected area, wiped off, and the area is then sprayed with a developer. Cracks then will show up brightly. Spot check dyes will only indicate surface cracks; therefore, structural cracks below the surface may escape detection. When questionable, the part should be tested using Magnaflux or Zyglo.

REPAIRING DAMAGED THREADS

Several methods of repairing damaged threads are available. Heli-Coil® (shown here), Keenserts® and Microdot® are among the most widely used. All involve basically

the same principle—drilling out stripped threads, tapping the hole and installing a pre-wound insert— making welding, plugging and oversize fasteners unnecessary.

Two types of thread repair inserts are usually supplied—a standard type for most Inch Coarse, Inch Fine, Metric Coarse and Metric Fine thread sizes and a spark plug type to fit most spark plug port sizes. Consult the individual manufacturer's catalog to determine exact applications. Typical thread repair kits will contain a selection of prewound threaded inserts, a tap (corresponding to the outside diameter threads of the insert) and an installation tool. Most manufacturers also supply blister-packed thread repair inserts separately and a master kit with a variety of taps and inserts plus installation tools.

Before effecting a repair to a threaded hole, remove any snapped, broken or damaged bolts or studs. Penetrating oil can be used to free frozen threads; the offending item can be removed with locking pliers or with a screw or stud extractor. After the hole is clear, the thread can be repaired as follows.

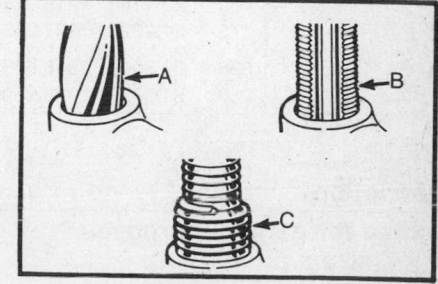

A. Drill out the damaged threads with the specified drill. Drill completely through the hole or to the bottom of a blind hole.

B. With the tap supplied tap the hole to receive the threaded insert. Keep the tap well oiled and back it out frequently to avoid clogging the threads.

C. Screw the threaded insert onto the installation tool until the tang engages the slot. Screw the insert into the tapped hole until it is ¼–½ turn below the top surface. After installation, break the tang off with a hammer and punch.

STANDARD TORQUE SPECIFICATIONS AND CAPSCREW MARKINGS

Newton-Meter has been designated as the world standard for measuring torque and will gradually replace the foot-pound and kilogram-meter torque measuring standard. Torquing tools are still being manufactured with foot-pounds and kilogram-meter scales, along with the new Newton-Meter standard. To assist the repairman, foot-pounds, kilogram-meter and Newton-Meter are listed in the following charts, and should be followed as applicable.

U.S. BOLTS

SAE Grade Number	1 or 2			5			6 or 7			8		
Capscrew Head Markings (Manufacturer's marks may vary. Three-line markings on heads below indicate SAE Grade 5.)	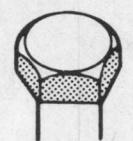						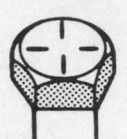					
Usage	Used Frequently			Used Frequently			Used at Times			Used at Times		
Quality of Material	Indeterminate			Minimum Commercial			Medium Commercial			Best Commercial		
Capacity Body Size	Torque			Torque			Torque			Torque		
(inches) – (thread)	Ft-Lb	kgm	Nm	Ft-Lb	kgm	Nm	Ft-Lb	kgm	Nm	Ft-Lb	kgm	Nm
1/4–20	5	0.6915	6.7791	8	1.1064	10.8465	10	1.3630	13.5582	12	1.6596	16.2698
–28	6	0.8298	8.1349	10	1.3830	13.5582				14	1.9362	18.9815
5/16–18	11	1.5213	14.9140	17	2.3511	23.0489	19	2.6277	25.7605	24	3.3192	32.5396
–24	13	1.7979	17.6256	19	2.6277	25.7605				27	3.7341	36.6071
3/8–16	18	2.4894	24.4047	31	4.2873	42.0304	34	4.7022	46.0978	44	6.0852	59.6560
–24	20	2.7660	27.1164	35	4.8405	47.4536				49	6.7767	66.4351
7/16–14	28	3.8132	37.9629	49	6.7767	66.4351	55	7.6065	74.5700	70	9.6810	94.9073
–20	30	4.1490	40.6745	55	7.6065	74.5700				78	10.7874	105.7538
1/2–13	39	5.3937	52.8769	75	10.3725	101.6863	85	11.7555	115.2445	105	14.5215	142.3609
–20	41	5.6703	55.5885	85	11.7555	115.2445				120	16.5860	162.6960
9/16–12	51	7.0533	69.1467	110	15.2130	149.1380	120	16.5960	162.6960	155	21.4365	210.1490
–18	55	7.6065	74.5700	120	16.5960	162.6960				170	23.5110	230.4860
5/8–11	83	11.4789	112.5329	150	20.7450	203.3700	167	23.0961	226.4186	210	29.0430	284.7180
–18	95	13.1385	128.8027	170	23.5110	230.4860				240	33.1920	325.3920
3/4–10	105	14.5215	142.3609	270	37.3410	366.0660	280	38.7240	379.6240	375	51.8625	508.4250
–16	115	15.9045	155.9170	295	40.7985	399.9610				420	58.0860	568.4360
7/8–9	160	22.1280	216.9280	395	54.6285	535.5410	440	60.8520	596.5520	605	83.6715	820.2590
–14	175	24.2025	237.2650	435	60.1605	589.7730				675	93.3525	915.1650
1–8	236	32.5005	318.6130	590	81.5970	799.9220	660	91.2780	894.8280	910	125.8530	1233.7780
–14	250	34.5750	338.9500	660	91.2780	849.8280				990	136.9170	1342.2420

METRIC BOLTS

Description	Torque ft-lbs. (Nm)			
Thread for general purposes (size x pitch (mm))	Head Mark 4		Head Mark 7	
6 x 1.0	2.2 to 2.9	(3.0 to 3.9)	3.6 to 5.8	(4.9 to 7.8)
8 x 1.25	5.8 to 8.7	(7.9 to 12)	9.4 to 14	(13 to 19)
10 x 1.25	12 to 17	(16 to 23)	20 to 29	(27 to 39)
12 x 1.25	21 to 32	(29 to 43)	35 to 53	(47 to 72)
14 x 1.5	35 to 52	(48 to 70)	57 to 85	(77 to 110)
16 x 1.5	51 to 77	(67 to 100)	90 to 120	(130 to 160)
18 x 1.5	74 to 110	(100 to 150)	130 to 170	(180 to 230)
20 x 1.5	110 to 140	(150 to 190)	190 to 240	(160 to 320)
22 x 1.5	150 to 190	(200 to 260)	250 to 320	(340 to 430)
24 x 1.5	190 to 240	(260 to 320)	310 to 410	(420 to 550)

CAUTION: Bolts threaded into aluminum require much less torque

NOTE: This engine rebuilding section is a guide to accepted rebuilding procedures. Typical examples of standard rebuilding procedures are illustrated.

CYLINDER HEAD RECONDITIONING

Procedure	Method
Identify the valves:	Invert the cylinder head, and number the valve faces front to rear, using a permanent felt-tip marker.
Remove the rocker arms (OHV engines only):	Remove the rocker arms with shaft(s) or balls and nuts. Wire the sets of rockers, balls and nuts together, and identify according to the corresponding valve.
Remove the camshaft (OHC engines only):	See the engine service procedures earlier in this book for details concerning specific engines.
Remove the valves and springs:	Using an appropriate valve spring compressor (depending on the configuration of the cylinder head), compress the valve springs. Lift out the keepers with needlenose pliers, release the compressor, and remove the valve, spring, and spring retainer.
Remove glow plugs and fuel injectors (Diesel engines only):	Label and remove all fuel injectors and glow plugs from the head. Glow plugs unscrew. See the appropriate car section for injector removal. Inspect glow plugs for bulges, cracks or signs of melting. Clean injector tips with a steel brush, then inspect for evidence of melting.
**Remove pre-combustion chamber inserts (Diesel engines only): 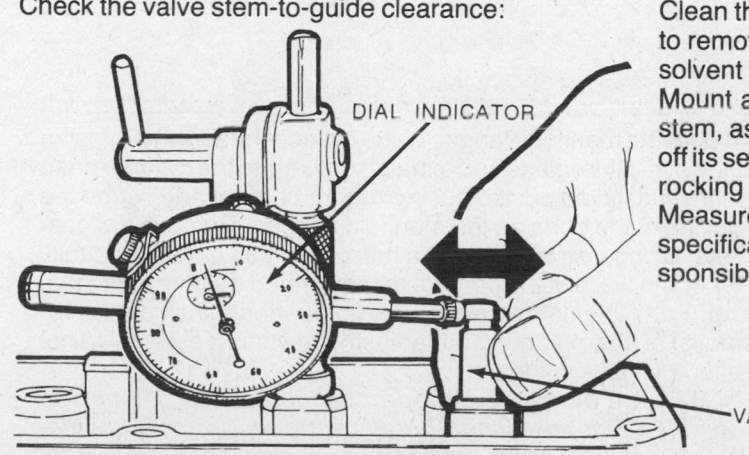	**Remove the pre-combustion chambers using a hammer and a thin, blunt brass drift, inserted through the injector hole (or glow plug hole, whichever is more convenient). If chamber is to be reused, carefully remove all carbon from it. NOTE: *Remove chamber only if being replaced, if a glow plug tip has broken off and must be removed, or if chamber is obviously damaged or loose.*

Removing pre-combustion chamber with a drift (© G.M. Corp.)

| Check the valve stem-to-guide clearance: | Clean the valve stem with lacquer thinner or a similar solvent to remove all gum and varnish. Clean the valve guides using solvent and an expanding wire-type valve guide cleaner. Mount a dial indicator so that the stem is at 90° to the valve stem, as close to the valve guide as possible. Move the valve off its seat, and measure the valve guide-to-stem clearance by rocking the stem back and forth to actuate the dial indicator. Measure the valve stems using a micrometer, and compare to specifications, to determine whether stem or guide wear is responsible for excessive clearance. |

DIAL INDICATOR

VALVE STEM

Checking the valve stem-to-guide clearance

CYLINDER HEAD RECONDITIONING

Procedure	Method

De-carbon the cylinder head and valves:

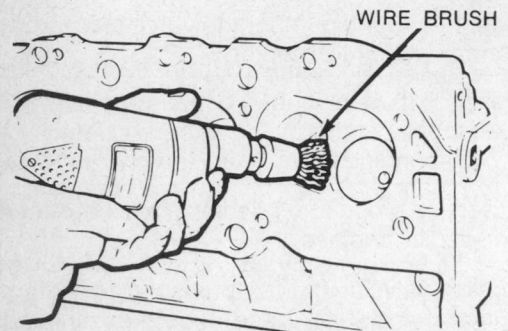

Removing carbon from the cylinder head

Chip carbon away from the valve heads, combustion chambers, and ports, using a chisel made of hardwood. Remove the remaining deposits with a stiff wire brush.
NOTE: *Ensure that the deposits are actually removed, rather than burnished.*

Hot-tank the cylinder head (cast iron heads only):
CAUTION: *Do not hot-tank aluminum parts.*

Have the cylinder head hot-tanked to remove grease, corrosion, and scale from the water passages.
NOTE: *In the case of overhead cam cylinder heads, consult the operator to determine whether the camshaft bearings will be damaged by the caustic solution.*

Degrease the remaining cylinder head parts:

Using solvent (i.e., Gunk), clean the rockers, rocker shaft(s) (where applicable), rocker balls and nuts, springs, spring retainers, and keepers. Do not remove the protective coating from the springs.

Check the cylinder head for warpage:

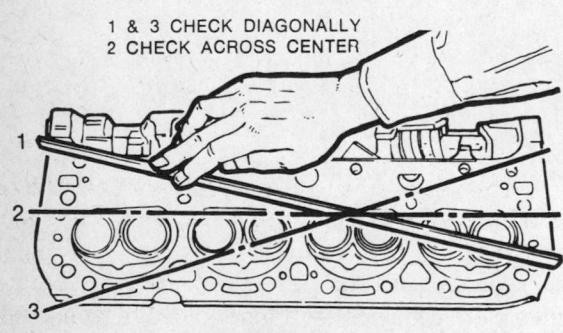

1 & 3 CHECK DIAGONALLY
2 CHECK ACROSS CENTER

Checking cylinder head for warpage

Place a straight-edge across the gasket surface of the cylinder head. Using feeler gauges, determine the clearance at the center of the straight-edge. Measure across both diagonals, along the longitudinal centerline, and across the cylinder head at several points. If warpage exceeds .003′ in a 6′ span, or .006′ over the total length, the cylinder head must be resurfaced.
NOTE: *If warpage exceeds the manufacturer's maximum tolerance for material removal, the cylinder head must be replaced.*
When milling the cylinder heads of V-type engines, the intake manifold mounting position is altered, and must be corrected by milling the manifold flange a proportionate amount.

**Porting and gasket matching:

**Coat the manifold flanges of the cylinder head with Prussian blue dye. Glue intake and exhaust gaskets to the cylinder head in their installed position using rubber cement and scribe the outline of the ports on the manifold flanges. Remove the gaskets. Using a small cutter in a hand-held power tool gradually taper the walls of the port out to the scribed outline of the gasket. Further enlargement of the ports should include the removal of sharp edges and radiusing of sharp corners. Do not alter the valve guides.
NOTE: *The most efficient port configuration is determined only by extensive testing. Therefore, it is best to consult someone experienced with the head in question to determine the optimum alterations.*

CYLINDER HEAD RECONDITIONING

Procedure	Method

*Knurling the valve guides:

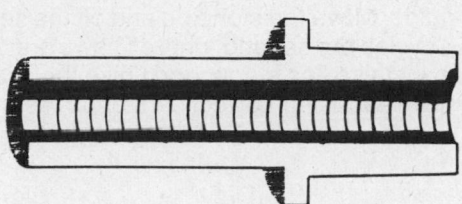

Cut-away view of a knurled valve guide

*Valve guides which are not excessively worn or distorted may, in some cases, be knurled rather than replaced. Knurling is a process in which metal is displaced and raised, thereby reducing clearance. Knurling also provides excellent oil control. The possibility of knurling rather than replacing valve guides should be discussed with a machinist.

Replacing the valve guides:
NOTE: *Valve guides should only be replaced if damaged or if an oversize valve stem is not available.*

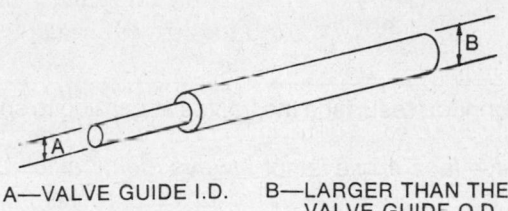

A—VALVE GUIDE I.D.   B—LARGER THAN THE VALVE GUIDE O.D.
Valve guide removal tool

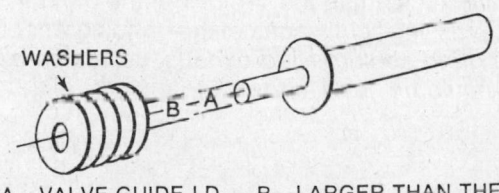

WASHERS

A—VALVE GUIDE I.D.   B—LARGER THAN THE VALVE GUIDE O.D.

Valve guide installation tool (with washers used for installation)

Depending on the type of cylinder head, valve guides may be pressed, hammered, or shrunk in. In cases where the guides are shrunk into the head, replacement should be left to an equipped machine shop. In other cases, the guides are replaced as follows: Press or tap the valve guides out of the head using a stepped drift (see illustration). Determine the height above the boss that the guide must extend, and obtain a stack of washers, their I.D. similar to the guide's O.D., of that height. Place the stack of washers on the guide, and insert the guide into the boss.
NOTE: *Valve guides are often tapered or beveled for installation.*
Using the stepped installation tool (see illustration), press or tap the guides into position. Ream the guides according to the size of the valve stem.

Replacing valve seat inserts:

Replacement of valve seat inserts which are worn beyond resurfacing or broken, if feasible, must be done by a machine shop.

Resurfacing the valve seats using reamers:

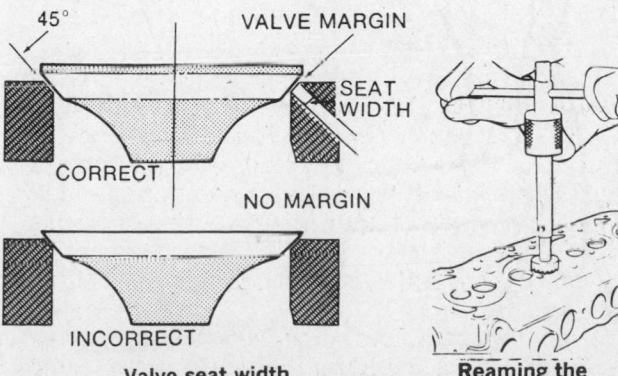

45°   VALVE MARGIN

SEAT WIDTH

CORRECT

NO MARGIN

INCORRECT

Valve seat width and centering

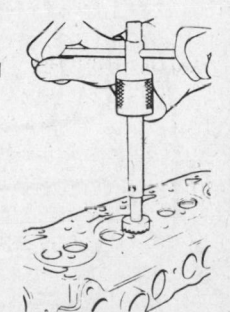

Reaming the valve seat

Select a reamer of the correct seat angle, slightly larger than the diameter of the valve seat, and assemble it with a pilot of the correct size. Install the pilot into the valve guide, and using steady pressure, turn the reamer clockwise.
CAUTION: *Do not turn the reamer counterclockwise.*
Remove only as much material as necessary to clean the seat. Check the concentricity of the seat (see below). If the dye method is not used, coat the valve face with Prussian blue dye, install and rotate it on the valve seat. Using the dye marked area as a centering guide, center and narrow the valve seat to specifications with correction cutters.
NOTE: *When no specifications are available, minimum seat width for exhaust valves should be 5/64", intake valves 1/16".*
After making correction cuts, check the position of the valve seat on the valve face using Prussian blue dye.
NOTE: *Do not cut induction hardened seats; they must be ground.*

CYLINDER HEAD RECONDITIONING

Procedure	Method

*Resurfacing the valve seats using a grinder:

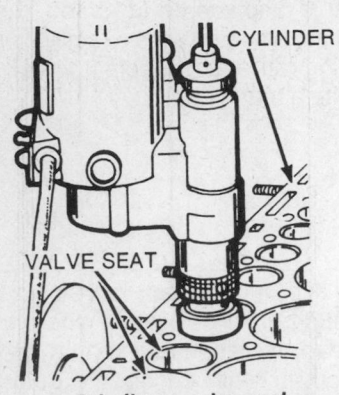

Grinding a valve seat

*Select a pilot of the correct size, and a coarse stone of the correct seat angle. Lubricate the pilot if necessary, and install the tool in the valve guide. Move the stone on and off the seat at approximately two cycles per second, until all flaws are removed from the seat. Install a fine stone, and finish the seat. Center and narrow the seat using correction stones, as described above.

Resurfacing (grinding) the valve face:

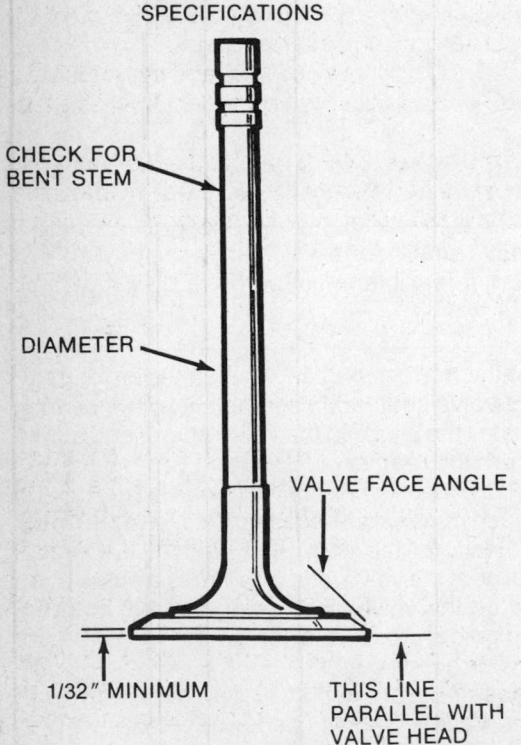

Critical valve dimensions

Using a valve grinder, resurface the valves according to specifications.
CAUTION: *Valve face angle is not always identical to valve seat angle.*
A minimum margin of 1/32" should remain after grinding the valve. The valve stem top should also be squared and resurfaced, by placing the stem in the V-block of the grinder, and turning it while pressing lightly against the grinding wheel.
NOTE: *Do not grind sodium filled exhaust valves on a machine. These should be hand lapped.*

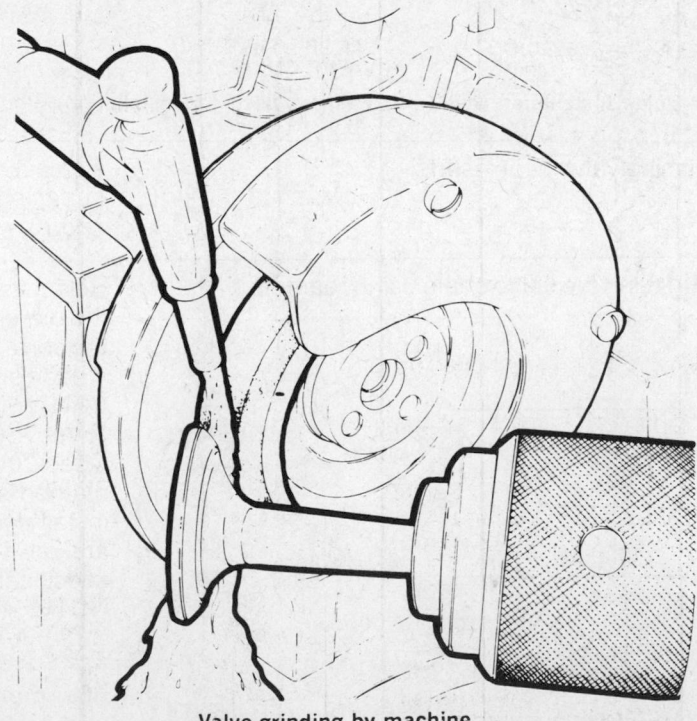

Valve grinding by machine

CYLINDER HEAD RECONDITIONING

Procedure	Method

Checking the valve seat concentricity:

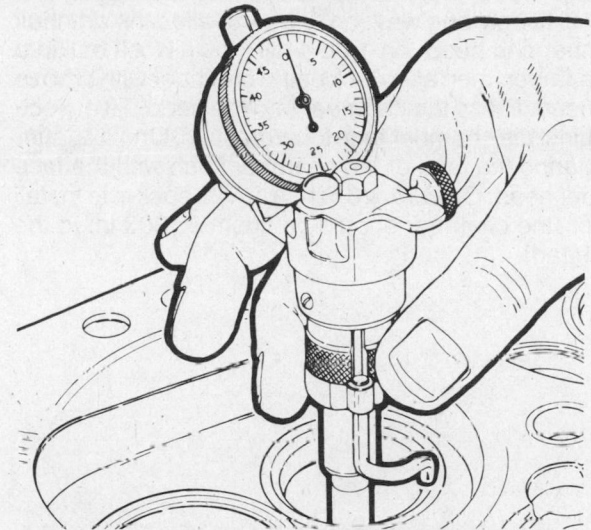

Checking valve seat concentricity using a dial gauge

Coat the valve face with Prussian blue dye, install the valve, and rotate it on the valve seat. If the entire seat becomes coated, and the valve is known to be concentric, the seat is concentric.

*Install the dial gauge pilot into the guide, and rest the arm on the valve seat. Zero the gauge, and rotate the arm around the seat. Run-out should not exceed .002″.

---

*Lapping the valves:
NOTE: *Valve lapping is done to ensure efficient sealing of resurfaced valves and seats.*

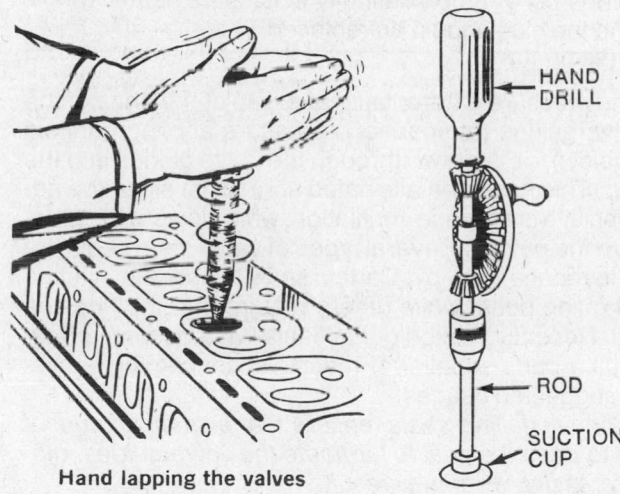

HAND DRILL

ROD

SUCTION CUP

Hand lapping the valves

Home made mechanical valve lapping tool

*Invert the cylinder head, lightly lubricate the valve stems, and install the valves in the head as numbered. Coat valve seats with fine grinding compound, and attach the lapping tool suction cup to a valve head.
NOTE: *Moisten the suction cup.*
Rotate the tool between the palms, changing position and lifting the tool often to prevent grooving. Lap the valve until a smooth, polished seat is evident. Remove the valve and tool, and rinse away all traces of grinding compound.
**Fasten a suction cup to a piece of drill rod, and mount the rod in a hand drill. Proceed as above, using the hand drill as a lapping tool.
CAUTION: *Due to the higher speeds involved when using the hand drill, care must be exercised to avoid grooving the seat.* Lift the tool and change direction of rotation often.

Check the valve springs:

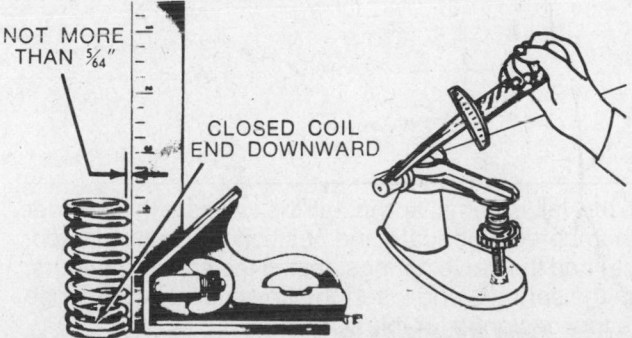

NOT MORE THAN 5/64″

CLOSED COIL END DOWNWARD

Checking valve spring free length and squareness

Measuring valve spring test pressure

Place the spring on a flat surface next to a square. Measure the height of the spring, and rotate it against the edge of the square to measure distortion. If spring height varies (by comparison) by more than 1/16″ or if distortion exceeds 1/16″, replace the spring.
**In addition to evaluating the spring as above, test the spring pressure at the installed and compressed (installed height minus valve lift) height using a valve spring tester. Springs used on small displacement engines (up to 3 liters) should be ∓ 1 lb. of all other springs in either position. A tolerance of ∓ 5 lbs. is permissible on larger engines.

CYLINDER HEAD RECONDITIONING

Procedure	Method

Install pre-combustion chambers (Diesel engines only)

Pre-combustion chambers are press-fit into the head. The chambers will fit only one way: on G.M. V8, align the notches in the chamber and head; on 1.8L 4 cyl., install lock ball into groove in chamber, then align lock ball in chamber with groove in cylinder head. Press the chamber into the head. Fit a piece of metal against the chamber face for protection. On 1.8L, after installation, grind the face of the chamber flush with the face of the cylinder head. On G.M. V8, use a 1¼ in. socket to install the chamber (the chamber should be flush ± .003 in. to the face of the head).

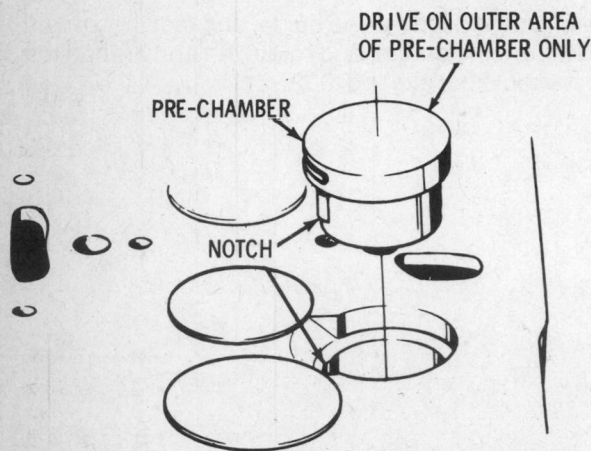

DRIVE ON OUTER AREA OF PRE-CHAMBER ONLY

PRE-CHAMBER

NOTCH

Align the notches to install the pre-combustion chamber (© G.M. Corp.)

Install fuel injectors and glow plugs (Diesel engines)

Before installing glow plugs, check for continuity across plug terminals and body. If no continuity exists, the heater wire is broken and the plug should be replaced.

---

*Install valve stem seals:

*Due to the pressure differential that exists at the ends of the intake valve guides (atmospheric pressure above, manifold vacuum below), oil is drawn through the valve guides into the intake port. This has been alleviated somewhat since the addition of positive crankcase ventilation, which lowers the pressure above the guides. Several types of valve stem seals are available to reduce blow-by. Certain seals simply slip over the stem and guide boss, while others require that the boss be machined. Recently, Teflon guide seals have become popular. Consult a parts supplier or machinist concerning availability and suggested usages.

NOTE: *When installing seals, ensure that a small amount of oil is able to pass the seal to lubricate the valve guides; otherwise, excessive wear may result.*

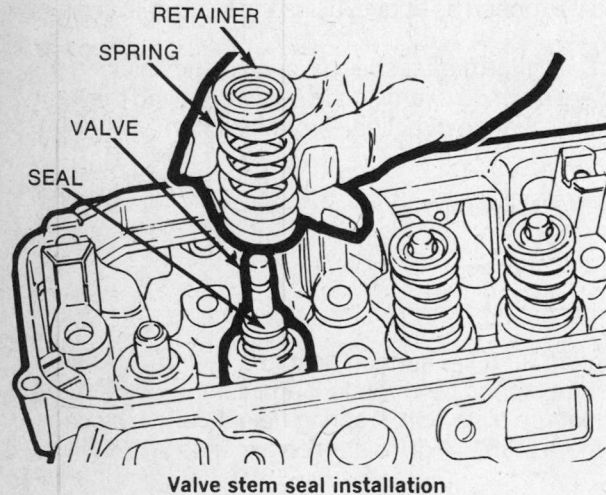

RETAINER

SPRING

VALVE

SEAL

Valve stem seal installation

Install the valves:

Lubricate the valve stems, and install the valves in the cylinder head as numbered. Lubricate and position the seals (if used, see above) and the valve springs. Install the spring retainers, compress the springs, and insert the keys using needlenose pliers or a tool designed for this purpose.

NOTE: *Retain the keys with wheel bearing grease during installation.*

CYLINDER HEAD RECONDITIONING

Procedure	Method

Check valve spring installed height:

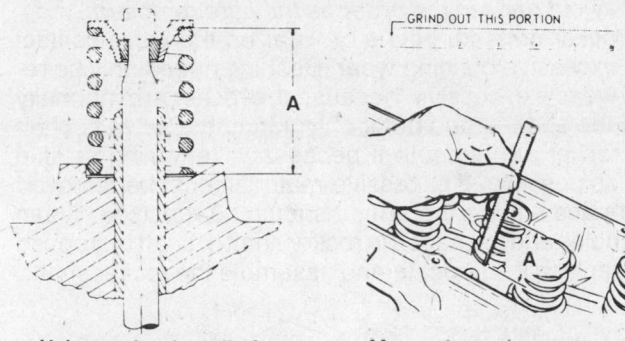

Valve spring installed
height dimension

Measuring valve spring
installed height

Measure the distance between the spring pad and the lower edge of the spring retainer, and compare to specifications. If the installed height is incorrect, add shim washers between the spring pad and the spring.
CAUTION: *Use only washers designed for this purpose.*

Install the camshaft (OHC engines only) and check end play:

See the engine service procedures earlier in this book for details concerning specific engines.

Inspect the rocker arms, balls, studs, and nuts (OHV engines only):

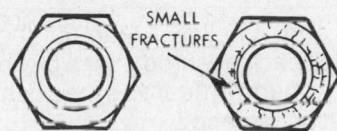

Stress cracks in the rocker nuts

Visually inspect the rocker arms, balls, studs, and nuts for cracks, galling, burning, scoring or wear. If all parts are intact, liberally lubricate the rocker arms and balls, and install them on the cylinder head. If wear is noted on a rocker arm at the point of valve contact, grind it smooth and square, removing as little material as possible. Replace the rocker arm if excessively worn. If a rocker stud shows signs of wear, it must be replaced (see below). If a rocker nut shows stress cracks, replace it. If an exhaust ball is galled or burned, substitute the intake ball from the same cylinder (if it is intact), and install a new intake ball.
NOTE: *Avoid using new rocker balls on exhaust valves.*

Replacing rocker studs (OHV engines only):

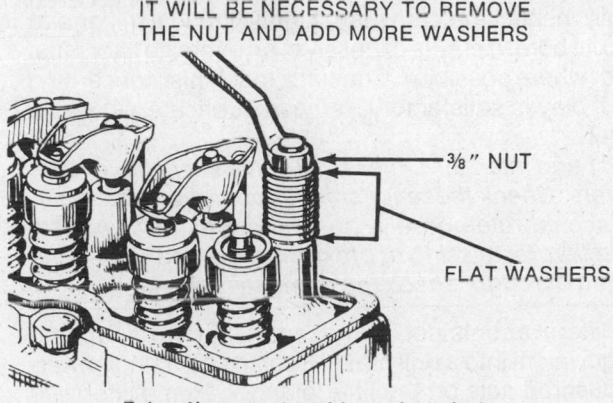

AS STUB BEGINS TO PULL UP, IT WILL BE NECESSARY TO REMOVE THE NUT AND ADD MORE WASHERS

3/8″ NUT

FLAT WASHERS

Extracting a pressed-in rocker stud

In order to remove a threaded stud, lock two nuts on the stud, and unscrew the stud using the lower nut. Coat the lower threads of the new stud with Loctite®, and install.
Two alternative methods are available for replacing pressed in studs. Remove the damaged stud using a stack of washers and a nut (see illustration). In the first, the boss is reamed .005–.006″ oversize, and an oversize stud pressed in. Control the stud extension over the boss using washers, in the same manner as valve guides. Before installing the stud, coat it with white lead and grease. To retain the stud more positively drill a hole through the stud and boss, and install a roll pin. In the second method, the boss is tapped, and a threaded stud installed. Retain the stud using Loctite® Stud and Bearing Mount.

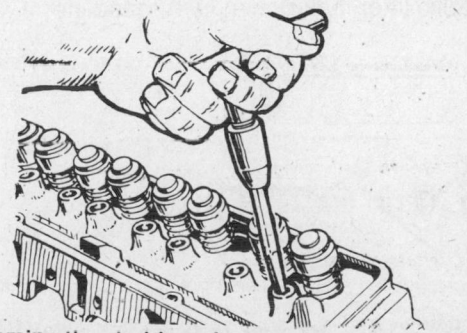

Reaming the stud bore for oversize rocker studs

CYLINDER HEAD RECONDITIONING

Procedure	Method

Inspect the rocker shaft(s) and rocker arms (OHV engines only):

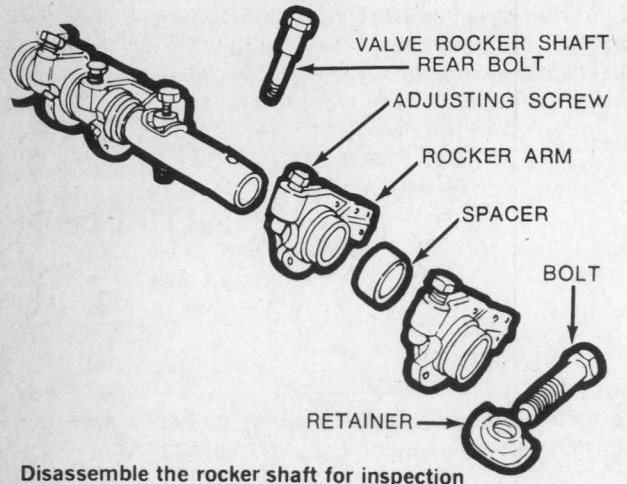

VALVE ROCKER SHAFT REAR BOLT
ADJUSTING SCREW
ROCKER ARM
SPACER
BOLT
RETAINER

Disassemble the rocker shaft for inspection

Remove rocker arms, springs and washers from rocker shaft. NOTE: *Lay out parts in the order as they are removed.* Inspect rocker arms for pitting or wear on the valve contact point, or excessive bushing wear. Bushings need only be replaced if wear is excessive, because the rocker arm normally contacts the shaft at one point only. Grind the valve contact point of rocker arm smooth if necessary, removing as little material as possible. If excessive material must be removed to smooth and square the arm, it should be replaced. Clean out all oil holes and passages in rocker shaft. If shaft is grooved or worn, replace it. Lubricate and assemble the rocker shaft.

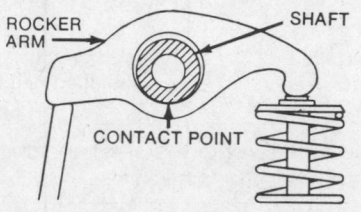

ROCKER ARM
SHAFT
CONTACT POINT

Rocker arm-to-rocker shaft contact area

Inspect the camshaft bushings and the camshaft (OHC engines):

See next section.

Inspect the pushrods (OHV engines only):

Remove the pushrods, and, if hollow, clean out the oil passages using fine wire. Roll each pushrod over a piece of clean glass. If a distinct clicking sound is heard as the pushrod rolls, the rod is bent, and must be replaced.

*The length of all pushrods must be equal. Measure the length of the pushrods, compare to specifications, and replace as necessary.

Inspect the valve lifters (OHV engines only):

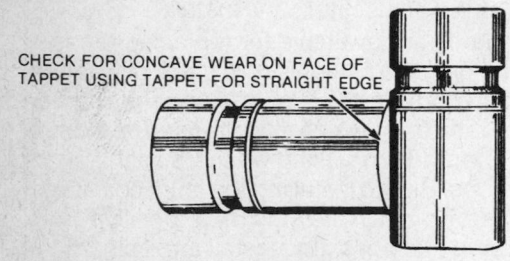

CHECK FOR CONCAVE WEAR ON FACE OF TAPPET USING TAPPET FOR STRAIGHT EDGE

Checking the lifter face

Remove lifters from their bores, and remove gum and varnish, using solvent. Clean walls of lifter bores. Check lifters for concave wear as illustrated. If face is worn concave, replace lifter, and carefully inspect the camshaft. Lightly lubricate lifter and insert it into its bore. If play is excessive, an oversize lifter must be installed (where possible). Consult a machinist concerning feasibility. If play is satisfactory, remove, lubricate, and reinstall the lifter.
NOTE: *1981 and later G.M. diesel V8 valve lifters have roller cam followers. Check these for smooth operation and wear. The roller should rotate freely, but without excessive play. Check the rollers for missing or broken needle bearings. If the roller is pitted or rough, check the camshaft lobe for wear.*

*Testing hydraulic lifter leak down (OHV gasoline engines only):

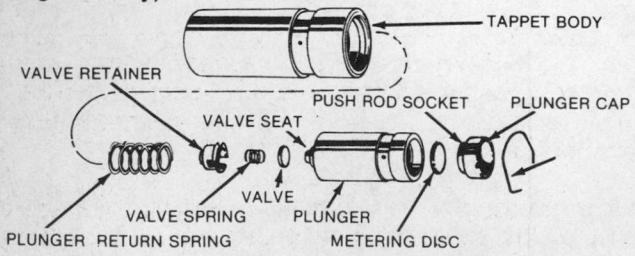

TAPPET BODY
VALVE RETAINER
PUSH ROD SOCKET
PLUNGER CAP
VALVE SEAT
VALVE
PLUNGER
PLUNGER RETURN SPRING
VALVE SPRING
METERING DISC

Typical exploded view of hydraulic valve lifter

Submerge lifter in a container of kerosene. Chuck a used pushrod or its equivalent into a drill press. Position container of kerosene so pushrod acts on the lifter plunger. Pump lifter with the drill press, until resistance increases. Pump several more times to bleed any air out of lifter. Apply very firm, constant pressure to the lifter, and observe rate at which fluid bleeds out of lifter. If the fluid bleeds very quickly (less than 15 seconds), lifter is defective. If the time exceeds 60 seconds, lifter is sticking. In either case, recondition or replace lifter. If lifter is operating properly (leak down time 15–60 seconds), lubricate and install it.

CYLINDER HEAD RECONDITIONING

Procedure	Method
Bleed the hydraulic lifters (diesel engines only):	After the cylinder heads are installed on G.M. V8 diesels, the valve lifters must be bled down before the crankshaft is turned. Failure to bleed down the lifters will cause damage to the valve train. See diesel engine rocker arm replacement procedure in Oldsmobile 88, 98, etc. car section for procedures. NOTE: *When installing new lifters, prime by working the lifter plunger while submerged in clean kerosene or diesel fuel.*

CYLINDER BLOCK RECONDITIONING

Procedure	Method
Checking the main bearing clearance: 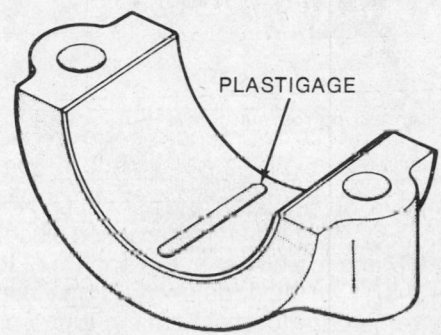 Plastigage® installed on the lower bearing shell  Measuring Plastigage® to determine bearing clearance	Invert engine, and remove cap from the bearing to be checked. Using a clean, dry rag, thoroughly clean all oil from crankshaft journal and bearing insert. NOTE: *Plastigage is soluble in oil; therefore, oil on the journal or bearing could result in erroneous readings.* Place a piece of Plastigage along the full length of journal, reinstall cap, and torque to specifications. Remove bearing cap, and determine bearing clearance by comparing width of Plastigage to the scale on Plastigage envelope. Journal taper is determined by comparing width of the Plastigage strip near its ends. Rotate crankshaft 90° and retest, to determine journal eccentricity. NOTE: *Do not rotate crankshaft with Plastigage installed.* If bearing insert and journal appear intact, and are within tolerances, no further main bearing service is required. If bearing or journal appear defective, cause of failure should be determined before replacement. *Remove crankshaft from block (see below). Measure the main bearing journals at each end twice (90° apart) using a micrometer, to determine diameter, journal taper and eccentricity. If journals are within tolerances, reinstall bearing caps at their specified torque. Using a telescope gauge and micrometer, measure bearing I.D. parallel to piston axis and at 30° on each side of piston axis. Subtract journal O.D. from bearing I.D. to determine oil clearance. If crankshaft journals appear defective, or do no meet tolerances, there is no need to measure bearings; for the crankshaft will require grinding and/or undersize bearings will be required. If bearing appears defective, cause for failure should be determined prior to replacement.
Checking the connecting rod bearing clearance:	Connecting rod bearing clearance is checked in the same manner as main bearing clearance, using Plastigage. Before removing the crankshaft, connecting rod side clearance also should be measured and recorded. *Checking connecting rod bearing clearance, using a micrometer, is identical to checking main bearing clearance. If no other service is required, the piston and rod assemblies need not be removed.

CYLINDER BLOCK RECONDITIONING

Procedure	Method

Removing the crankshaft:

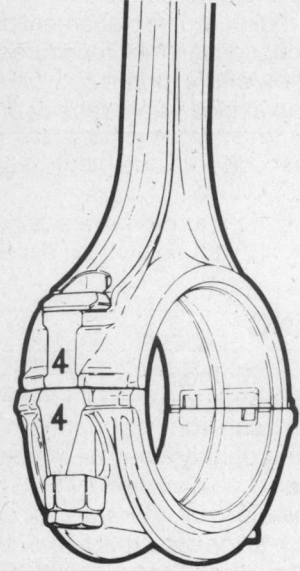

Connecting rod matched to cylinder with a number stamp

Using a punch, mark the corresponding main bearing caps and saddles according to position (i.e., one punch on the front main cap and saddle, two on the second, three on the third, etc.). Using number stamps, identify the corresponding connecting rods and caps, according to cylinder (if no numbers are present). Remove the main and connecting rod caps, and place sleeves of plastic tubing over the connecting rod bolts, to protect the journals as the crankshaft is removed. Lift the crankshaft out of the block.

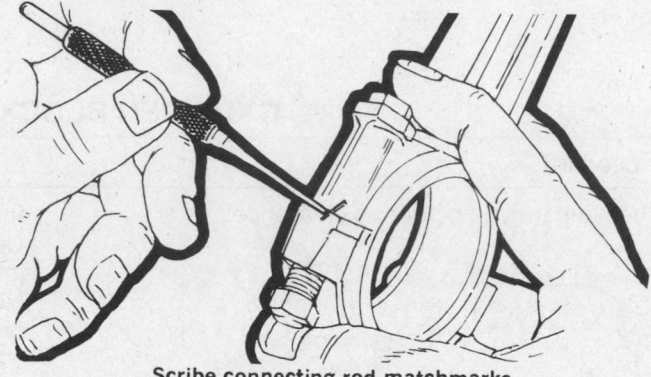

Scribe connecting rod matchmarks

Remove the ridge from the top of the cylinder:

RIDGE CAUSED BY CYLINDER WEAR

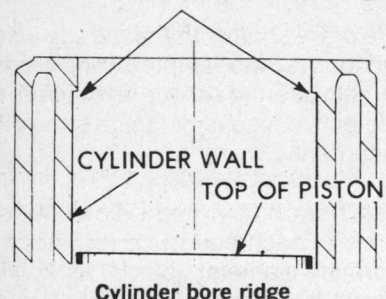

CYLINDER WALL
TOP OF PISTON

Cylinder bore ridge

In order to facilitate removal of the piston and connecting rod, the ridge at the top of the cylinder (unworn area; see illustration) must be removed. Place the piston at the bottom of the bore, and cover it with a rag. Cut the ridge away using a ridge reamer, exercising extreme care to avoid cutting to deeply. Remove the rag, and remove cuttings that remain on the piston.

CAUTION: *If the ridge is not removed, and new rings are installed, damage to rings will result.*

Removing the piston and connecting rod:

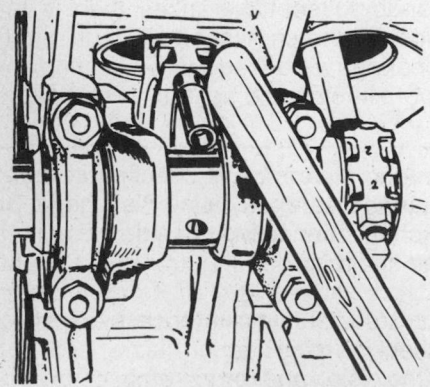

Removing the piston

Invert the engine, and push the pistons and connecting rods out of the cylinders. If necessary, tap the connecting rod boss with a wooden hammer handle, to force the piston out.

CAUTION: *Do not attempt to force the piston past the cylinder ridge* (see above).

CYLINDER BLOCK RECONDITIONING

Procedure	Method
Service the crankshaft:	Ensure that all oil holes and passages in the crankshaft are open and free of sludge. If necessary, have the crankshaft ground to the largest possible undersize. **Have the crankshaft Magnafluxed, to locate stress cracks. Consult a machinist concerning additional service procedures, such as surface hardening (e.g., nitriding, Tuftriding) to improve wear characteristics, cross drilling and chamfering the oil holes to improve lubrication, and balancing.
Removing freeze plugs:	Drill a small hole in the middle of the freeze plugs. Thread a large sheet metal screw into the hole and remove the plug with a slide hammer.
Remove the oil gallery plugs:	Threaded plugs should be removed using an appropriate (usually square) wrench. To remove soft, pressed in plugs, drill a hole in the plug, and thread in a sheet metal screw. Pull the plug out by the screw using pliers.
Hot-tank the block: NOTE: *Do not hot-tank aluminum parts.*	Have the block hot-tanked to remove grease, corrosion, and scale from the water jackets. NOTE: *Consult the operator to determine whether the camshaft bearings will be damaged during the hot-tank process.*

Check the block for cracks:	Visually inspect the block for cracks or chips. The most common locations are as follows:
	    Adjacent to freeze plugs.
	    Between the cylinders and water jackets.
	    Adjacent to the main bearing saddles.
	    At the extreme bottom of the cylinders.
	Check only suspected cracks using spot check dye (see introduction). If a crack is located, consult a machinist concerning possible repairs.
	
	**Magnaflux the block to locate hidden cracks. If cracks are located, consult a machinist about feasibility of repair.

Install the oil gallery plugs and freeze plugs:	Coat freeze plugs with sealer and tap into position using a piece of pipe, slightly smaller than the plug, as a driver. To ensure retention, stake the edges of the plugs. Coat threaded oil gallery plugs with sealer and install. Drive replacement soft plugs into block using a large drift as a driver. *Rather than reinstalling lead plugs, drill and tap the holes, and install threaded plugs.
*Check the deck height:	*The deck height is the distance from the crankshaft centerline to the block deck. To measure, invert the engine, and install the crankshaft, retaining it with the center main cap. Measure the distance from the crankshaft journal to the block deck, parallel to the cylinder centerline. Measure the diameter of the end (front and rear) main journals, parallel to the centerline of the cylinders, divide the diameter in half, and subtract it from the previous measurement. The results of the front and rear measurements should be identical. If the difference exceeds .005", the deck height should be corrected. NOTE: *Block deck height and warpage should be corrected at the same time.*

CYLINDER BLOCK RECONDITIONING

Procedure	Method
Check the block deck for warpage:	Using a straightedge and feeler gauges, check the block deck for warpage in the same manner that the cylinder head is checked (see Cylinder Head Reconditioning). If warpage exceeds specifications, have the deck resurfaced. NOTE: *In certain cases a specification for total material removal (Cylinder head and block deck) is provided. This specification must not be exceeded.*

Procedure	Method
Check the bore diameter and surface:	Visually inspect the cylinder bores for roughness, scoring, or scuffing. If evident, the cylinder bore must be bored or honed oversize to eliminate imperfections, and the smallest possible oversize piston used. The new pistons should be given to the machinist with the block, so that the cylinders can be bored or honed exactly to the piston size (plus clearance). If no flaws are evident, measure the bore diameter using a telescope gauge and micrometer, or dial guage, parallel and perpendicular to the engine centerline, at the top (below the ridge) and bottom of the bore. Subtract the bottom measurements from the top to determine taper, and the parallel to the centerline measurements from the perpendicular measurements to determine eccentricity. If the measurements are not within specifications, the cylinder must be bored or honed, and an oversize piston installed. If the measurements are within specifications the cylinder may be used as is, with only finish honing (see below). NOTE: *Prior to boring, check the block deck warpage, height and bearing alignment.* CAUTION: *The 4 cyl. 140 G.M. engine cylinder walls are impregnated with silicone. Boring or honing can be done only by a shop with the proper equipment.*

Measuring the cylinder bore with a dial gauge

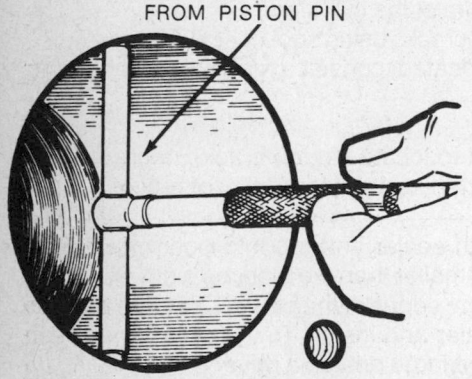

TELESCOPE GAUGE 90° FROM PISTON PIN

Measuring cylinder bore with a telescope gauge

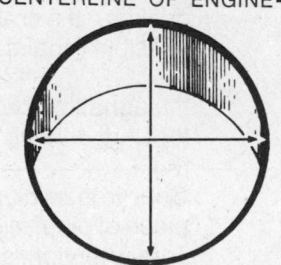

← CENTERLINE OF ENGINE →

A—AT RIGHT ANGLE TO CENTERLINE OF ENGINE
B—PARALLEL TO CENTERLINE OF ENGINE

Cylinder bore measuring points

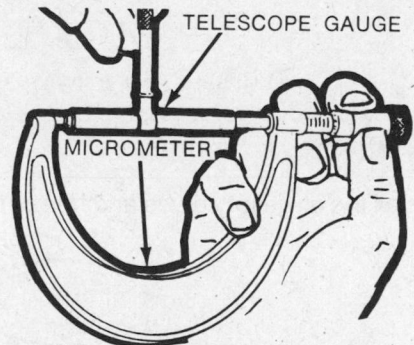

TELESCOPE GAUGE

MICROMETER

Determining cylinder bore by measuring telescope gauge with a micrometer

Procedure	Method
Check the cylinder block bearing alignment:	Remove the upper bearing inserts. Place a straightedge in the bearing saddles along the centerline of the crankshaft. If clearance exists between the straightedge and the center saddle, the block must be alignbored.

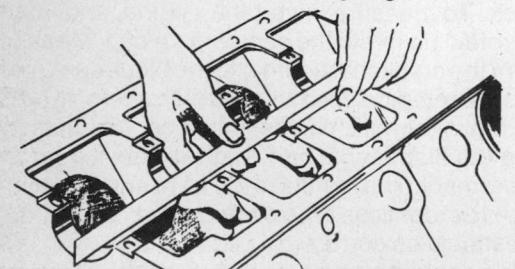

Checking main bearing saddle alignment

CYLINDER BLOCK RECONDITIONING

Procedure	Method
Clean and inspect the pistons and connecting rods:	Using a ring expander, remove the rings from the piston. Remove the retaining rings (if so equipped) and remove piston pin.

Clean and inspect the pistons and connecting rods:

Using a ring expander, remove the rings from the piston. Remove the retaining rings (if so equipped) and remove piston pin.
NOTE: *If the piston pin must be pressed out, determine the proper method and use the proper tools; otherwise the piston will distort.*
Clean the ring grooves using an appropriate tool, exercising care to avoid cutting too deeply. Thoroughly clean all carbon and varnish from the piston with solvent.
CAUTION: *Do not use a wire brush or caustic solvent on pistons.*
Inspect the pistons for scuffing, scoring, cracks, pitting, or excessive ring groove wear. If wear is evident, the piston must be replaced. Check the connecting rod length by measuring the rod from the inside of the large end to the inside of the small end using calipers (see illustration). All connecting rods should be equal length. Replace any rod that differs from the others in the engine.

*Have the connecting rod alignment checked in an alignment fixture by a machinist. Replace any twisted or bent rods.

*Magnaflux the connecting rods to locate stress cracks. If cracks are found, replace the connecting rod.

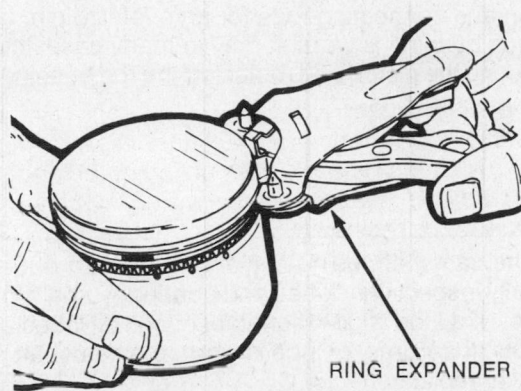

Removing the piston rings

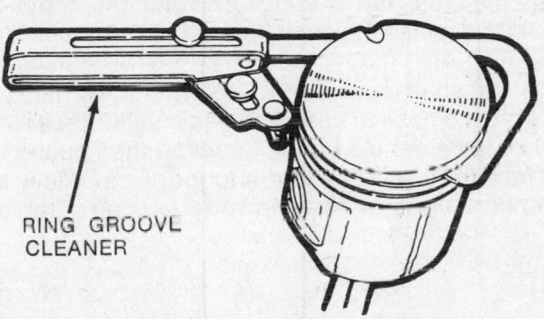

Cleaning the piston ring grooves

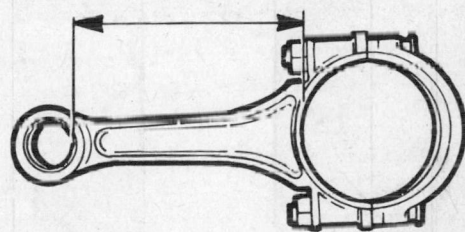

Check the connecting rod length (arrow)

Fit the pistons to the cylinders:

Using a telescope gauge and micrometer, or a dial gauge, measure the cylinder bore diameter perpendicular to the piston pin, 2½° below the deck. Measure the piston perpendicular to its pin on the skirt. The difference between the two measurements is the piston clearance. If the clearance is within specifications or slightly below (after boring or honing), finish honing is all that is required. If the clearance is excessive, try to obtain a slightly larger piston to bring clearance within specifications. Where this is not possible, obtain the first oversize piston, and hone (or if necessary, bore) the cylinder to size.

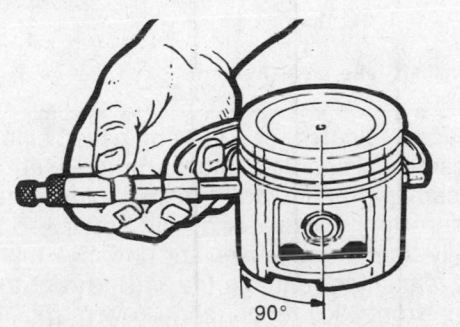

90°

Measuring the piston prior to fitting

Assemble the pistons and connecting rods:

Inspect piston pin, connecting rod small end bushing, and piston bore for galling, scoring, or excessive wear. If evident, replace defective part(s). Measure the I.D. of the piston boss and connecting rod small end, and the O.D. of the piston pin. If within specifications, assemble piston pin and rod.
CAUTION: *If piston pin must be pressed in, determine the proper method and use the proper tools; otherwise the piston will distort.*

CYLINDER BLOCK RECONDITIONING

Procedure	Method

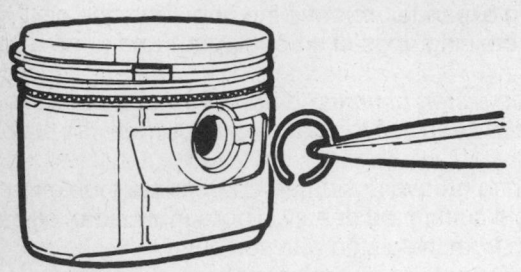

Installing piston pin lock rings

Install the lock rings; ensure that they seat properly. If the parts are not within specifications, determine the service method for the type of engine. In some cases, piston and pin are serviced as an assembly when either is defective. Others specify reaming the piston and connecting rods for an oversize pin. If the connecting rod bushing is worn, it may in many cases be replaced. Reaming the piston and replacing the rod bushing are machine shop operations.

Clean and inspect the camshaft:

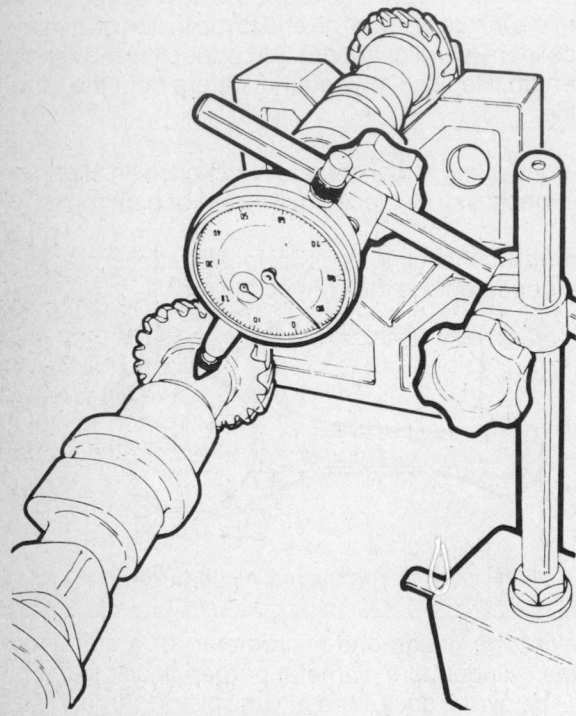

Checking the camshaft for straightness

Degrease the camshaft, using solvent, and clean out all oil holes. Visually inspect cam lobes and bearing journals for excessive wear. If a lobe is questionable, check all lobes as indicated below. If a journal or lobe is worn, the camshaft must be reground or replaced.

NOTE: *If a journal is worn, there is a good chance that the bushings are worn.*

If lobes and journals appear intact, place the front and rear journals in V-blocks, and rest a dial indicator on the center journal. Rotate the camshaft to check straightness. If deviation exceeds .001°, replace the camshaft.

*Check the camshaft lobes with a micrometer, by measuring the lobes from the nose to base and again at 90° (see illustration). The lift is determined by subtracting the second measurement from the first. If all exhaust lobes and all intake lobes are not identical, the camshaft must be reground or replaced.

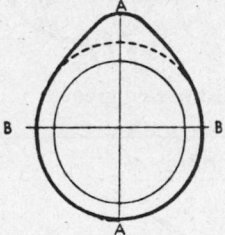

Camshaft lobe measurement

Replace the camshaft bearings (OHV engines only):

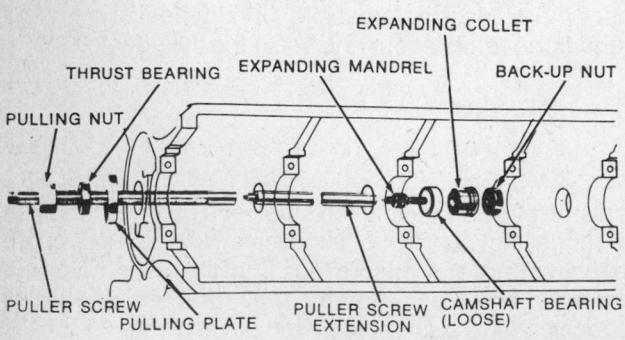

Camshaft removal and installation tool (typical)

If excessive wear is indicated, or if the engine is being completely rebuilt, camshaft bearings should be replaced as follows: Drive the camshaft rear plug from the block. Assemble the removal puller with its shoulder on the bearing to be removed. Gradually tighten the puller nut until bearing is removed. Remove remaining bearings, leaving the front and rear for last. To remove front and rear bearings, reverse position of the tool, so as to pull the bearings in toward the center of the block. Leave the tool in this position, pilot the new front and rear bearings on the installer, and pull them into position: Return the tool to its original position and pull remaining bearings into postion.

NOTE: *Ensure that oil holes align when installing bearings.*

Replace camshaft rear plug, and stake it into position to aid retention.

CYLINDER BLOCK RECONDITIONING

Procedure	Method

Finish hone the cylinders:

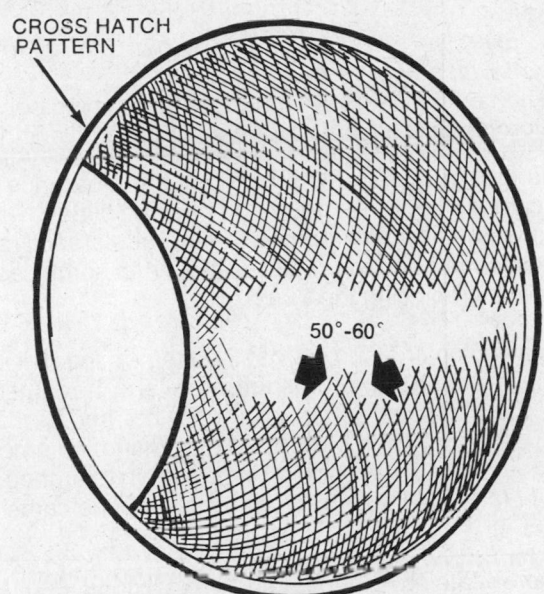

Chuck a flexible drive hone into a power drill, and insert it into the cylinder. Start the hone, and move it up and down the cylinder at a rate which will produce approximately a 60° cross-hatch pattern (see illustration).

NOTE: *Do not extend the hone below the cylinder bore.*

After developing the pattern, remove the hone and recheck piston fit. Wash the cylinders with a detergent and water solution to remove abrasive dust, dry, and wipe several times with a rag soaked in engine oil.

Check piston ring end-gap:

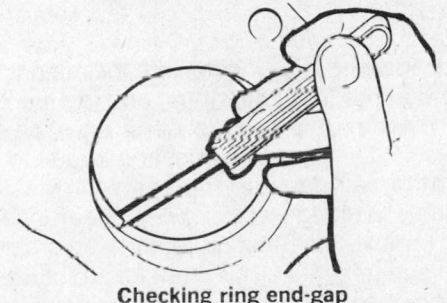

Checking ring end-gap

Compress the piston rings to be used in a cylinder, one at a time, into that cylinder, and press them approximately 1″ below the deck with an inverted piston. Using feeler gauges, measure the ring end-gap, and compare to specifications. Pull the ring out of the cylinder and file the ends with a fine file to obtain proper clearance.

CAUTION: *If inadequate ring end-gap is utilized, ring breakage will result.*

Install the piston rings:

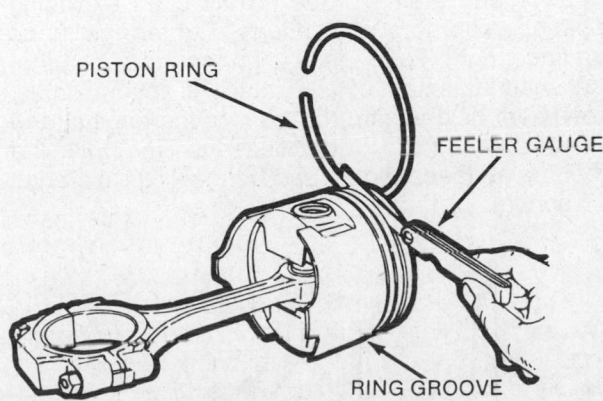

Checking ring side clearance

Inspect the ring grooves in the piston for excessive wear or taper. If necessary, recut the groove(s) for use with an overwidth ring or a standard ring and spacer. If the groove is worn uniformly, overwidth rings, or standard rings and spacers may be installed without recutting. Roll the outside of the ring around the groove to check for burrs or deposits. If any are found, remove with a fine file. Hold the ring in the groove, and measure side clearance. If necessary, correct as indicated above.

NOTE: *Always install any additional spacers above the piston ring.*

The ring groove must be deep enough to allow the ring to seat below the lands (see illustration). In many cases, a "go-no-go" depth gauge will be provided with the piston rings. Shallow grooves may be corrected by recutting, while deep grooves require some type of filler or expander behind the piston. Consult the piston ring supplier concerning the suggested method. Install the rings on the piston, lowest ring first, using a ring expander.

NOTE: *Position the ring markings as specified by the manufacturer (see car section).*

CYLINDER BLOCK RECONDITIONING

Procedure	Method
Install the camshaft (OHV engines only):	Liberally lubricate the camshaft lobes and journals, and install the camshaft. CAUTION: *Exercise extreme care to avoid damaging the bearings when inserting the camshaft.* Install and tighten the camshaft thrust plate retaining bolts. See the appropriate procedures for each individual engine.

Check camshaft end-play (OHV engines only):

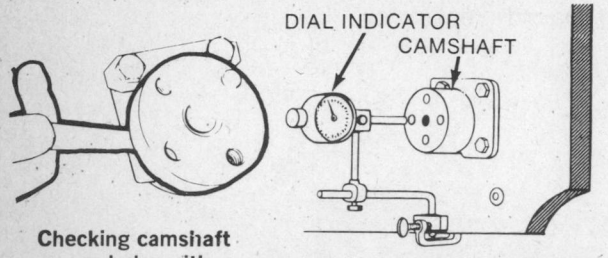

DIAL INDICATOR
CAMSHAFT

Checking camshaft end-play with a feeler gauge

Checking camshaft end-play with a dial indicator

Using feeler gauges, determine whether the clearance between the camshaft boss (or gear) and backing plate is within specifications. Install shims behind the thrust plate, or reposition the camshaft gear and retest end-play. In some cases, adjustment is by replacing the thrust plate.

*Mount a dial indicator stand so that the stem of the dial indicator rests on the nose of the camshaft, parallel to the camshaft axis. Push the camshaft as far in as possible and zero the gauge. Move the camshaft outward to determine the amount of camshaft endplay. If the endplay is not within tolerance, install shims behind the thrust plate, or reposition the camshaft gear and retest.

Install the rear main seal (where applicable):	See the appropriate procedures for each individual engine.

Install the crankshaft:

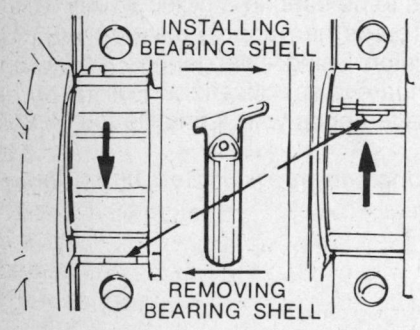

INSTALLING BEARING SHELL

REMOVING BEARING SHELL

Removal and installation of upper bearing insert using a roll-out pin

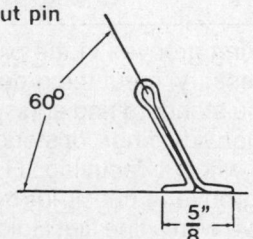

60°

$\frac{5}{8}$"

Home-made bearing roll-out pin

Thoroughly clean the main bearing saddles and caps. Place the upper halves of the bearing inserts on the saddles and press into position.
NOTE: *Ensure that the oil holes align.*
Press the corresponding bearing inserts into the main bearing caps. Lubricate the upper main bearings, and lay the crankshaft in position. Place a strip of Plastigage on each of the crankshaft journals, install the main caps, and torque to specifications. Remove the main caps, and compare the Plastigage to the scale on the Plastigage envelope. If clearances are within tolerances, remove the Plastigage, turn the crankshaft 90°, wipe off all oil and retest. If all clearances are correct, remove all Plastigage, thoroughly lubricate the main caps and bearing journals, and install the main caps. If clearances are not within tolerance, the upper bearing inserts may be removed, without removing the crankshaft, using a bearing roll out pin (see illustration). Roll in a bearing that will provide proper clearance, and retest. Torque all main caps, excluding the thrust bearing cap, to specifications. Tighten the thrust bearing cap finger tight. To properly align the thrust bearing, pry the crankshaft the extent of its axial travel several times, the last movement held toward the front of the engine, and torque the thrust bearing cap to specifications. Determine the crankshaft end-play (see below), and bring within tolerance with thrust washers.

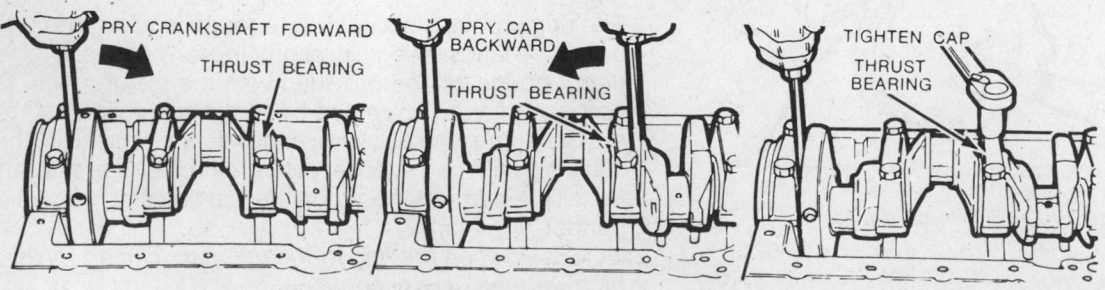

PRY CRANKSHAFT FORWARD
THRUST BEARING

PRY CAP BACKWARD
THRUST BEARING

TIGHTEN CAP
THRUST BEARING

Aligning the thrust bearing

CYLINDER BLOCK RECONDITIONING

Procedure	Method

Measure crankshaft end-play:

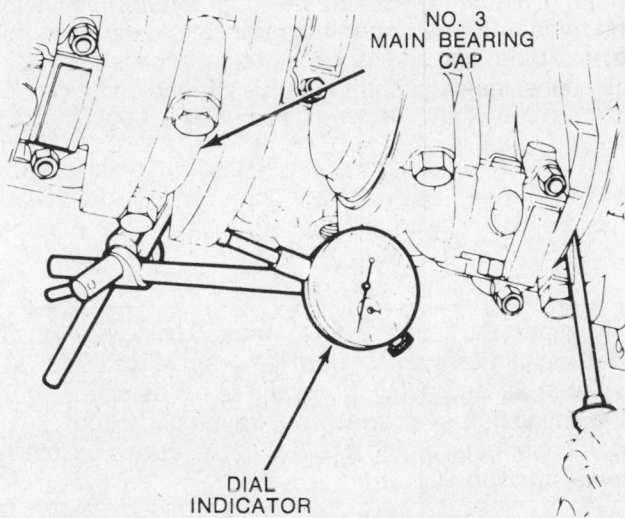

Checking crankshaft end-play with a dial indicator

Mount a dial indicator stand on the front of the block, with the dial indicator stem resting on the nose of the crankshaft, parallel to the crankshaft axis. Pry the crankshaft the extent of its travel rearward, and zero the indicator. Pry the crankshaft forward and record crankshaft end-play.

NOTE: *Crankshaft end-play also may be measured at the thrust bearing, using feeler gauges* (see illustration).

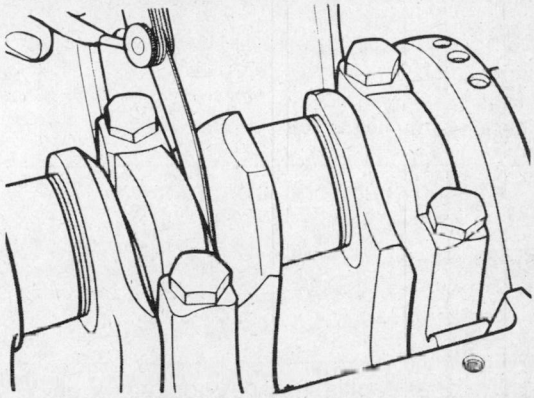

Checking crankshaft end-play with a feeler gauge

Install the pistons:

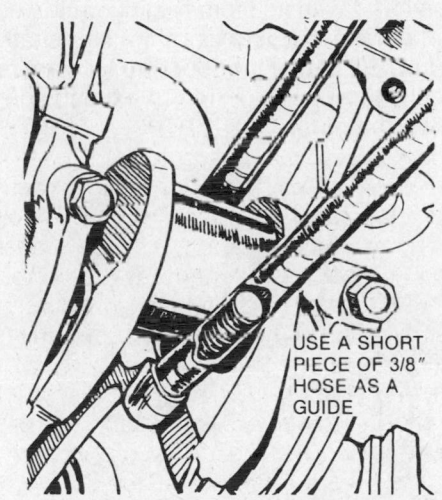

Tubing used to protect crankshaft journals and cylinder walls during piston installation

Press the upper connecting rod bearing halves into the connecting rods, and the lower halves into the connecting rod caps. Position the piston ring gaps according to specifications (see car section), and lubricate the pistons. Install a ring compressor on a piston, and press two long (8″) pieces of plastic tubing over the rod bolts. Using the tubes as a guide, press the pistons into the bores and onto the crankshaft with a wooden hammer handle. After seating the rod on the crankshaft journal, remove the tubes and install the cap finger tight. Install the remaining pistons in the same manner. Invert the engine and check the bearing clearance at two points (90° apart) on each journal with Plastigage.

NOTE: *Do not turn the crankshaft with Plastigage installed.*
If clearance is within tolerances, remove *all* Plastigage, thoroughly lubricate the journals, and torque the rod caps to specifications. If clearance is not within specifications, install different thickness bearing inserts and recheck.

CAUTION: *Never shim or file the connecting rods or caps.*
Always install plastic tube sleeves over the rod bolts when the caps are not installed, to protect the crankshaft journals.

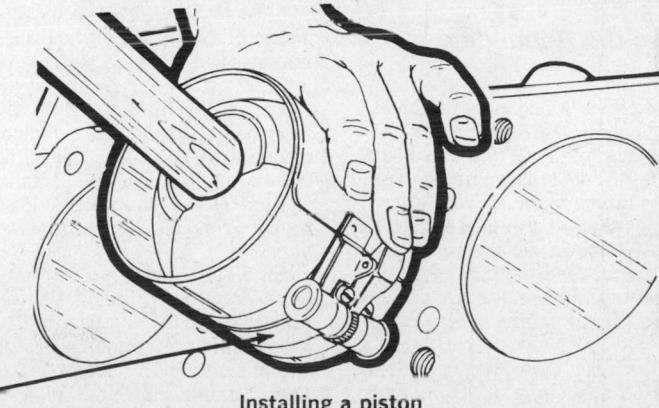

Installing a piston

CYLINDER BLOCK RECONDITIONING

Procedure	Method

Check connecting rod side clearance:

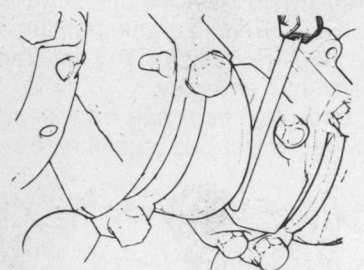

Checking connecting rod side clearance

Determine the clearance between the sides of the connecting rods and the crankshaft, using feeler gauges. If clearance is below the minimum tolerance, the rod may be machined to provide adequate clearance. If clearance is excessive, substitute an unworn rod, and recheck. If clearance is still outside specifications, the crankshaft must be welded and reground, or replaced.

Inspect the timing chain (or belt):

Visually inspect the timing chain for broken or loose links, and replace the chain if any are found. If the chain will flex sideways, it must be replaced. Install the timing chain as specified. Be sure the timing belt is not stretched, frayed or broken.
NOTE: *If the original timing chain is to be reused, install it in its original position.*

Check timing gear backlash and runout (OHV engines):

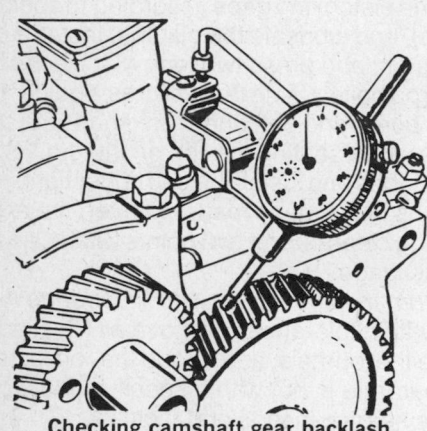

Checking camshaft gear backlash

Mount a dial indicator with its stem resting on a tooth of the camshaft gear (as illustrated). Rotate the gear until all slack is removed, and zero the indicator. Rotate the gear in the opposite direction until slack is removed, and record gear backlash. Mount the indicator with its stem resting on the edge of the camshaft gear, parallel to the axis of the camshaft. Zero the indicator, and turn the camshaft gear one full turn, recording the runout. If either backlash or runout exceed specifications, replace the worn gear(s).

Checking camshaft gear runout

Completing the Rebuilding Process

Following the above procedures, complete the rebuilding process as follows:

Fill the oil pump with oil, to prevent cavitating (sucking air) on initial engine start up. Install the oil pump and the pickup tube on the engine. Coat the oil pan gasket as necessary, and install the gasket and the oil pan. Mount the flywheel and the crankshaft vibration damper or pulley on the crankshaft. NOTE: *Always use new bolts when installing the flywheel.*
Inspect the clutch shaft pilot bushing in the crankshaft. If the bushing is excessively worn, remove it with an expanding puller and a slide hammer, and tap a new bushing into place.

Position the engine, cylinder head side up. Lubricate the lifters, and install them into their bores. Install the cylinder head, and torque it as specified. Insert the pushrods (where applicable), and install the rocker shaft(s) (if so equipped) or position the rocker arms on the pushrods. Adjust the valves.

Install the intake and exhaust manifolds, the carburetor(s), the distributor and spark plugs. Adjust the point gap and the static ignition timing. Mount all accessories and install the engine in the car. Fill the radiator with coolant, and the crankcase with high quality engine oil.

Break-in Procedure

Start the engine, and allow it to run at low speed for a few minutes, while checking for leaks. Stop the engine, check the oil level, and fill as necessary. Restart the engine, and fill the cooling system to capacity. Check the point dwell angle and adjust the ignition timing and the valves. Run the engine at low to medium speed (800–2500 rpm) for approximately ½ hour, and retorque the cylinder head bolts. Road test the car, and check again for leaks.

Follow the manufacturer's recommended engine break-in procedure and maintenance schedule for new engines.

U-Joint/CV-Joint Overhaul

UNIVERSAL JOINTS

U-joint is mechanic's jargon for universal joint. U-joints should not be confused with U-bolts, which are U-shaped bolts used to connect U-joints to the differential pinion flange.

Universal joints provide flexibility between the driveshaft and axle housing to accommodate changes in the angle between them (changes of length are accommodated by the sliding splined yoke between the driveshaft and transmission). The engine and transmission are mounted rigidly on the car frame, while the driving wheels are free to move up and down in relation to the frame. The angles between the transmission, driveshaft and axle change constantly as the car responds to various road conditions.

To give flexibility and still transmit power as smoothly as possible, several types of universal joints are used.

The most common type of universal joint is the cross and yoke type. Yokes are used on the ends of the driveshaft with the yoke arms opposite each other. Another yoke is used opposite the driveshaft and when placed together, both yokes engage a center member, or cross, with four arms spaced 90° apart (the U-joint cross is alternately referred to as a spider, and the arms are called trunnions). A bearing cup (or cap) is used on each arm of the cross to accommodate movement as the driveshaft rotates. The bearings used are needle bearings.

A conventional universal joint will cause the driveshaft to speed up and slow down through each revolution and cause a corresponding change in the velocity of the driven shaft. This change in speed causes

natural vibrations to occur through the driveline, necessitating a third type of universal joint: the constant velocity joint. A rolling ball moves in a curved groove, located between two yoke-and-cross universal joints, connected to each other by a coupling yoke. The result is a uniform motion as the driveshaft rotates, avoiding the fluctuations in driveshaft speed. This type of joint is found in cars with sharp driveline angles, or where the extra measure of isolation is desirable.

CROSS AND YOKE U-JOINT OVERHAUL

There are two types of cross and yoke U-joints. One type retains the cross within the

yoke with C-shaped snap rings. The second type of joint is held together by injection molded plastic retainer rings. The second type cannot be reassembled with the same parts, once disassembled. However, repair kits are available.

Snap-Ring Type

1. Remove the driveshaft. For the correct procedure, see the car section for the model you are working on.

2. If the front yoke is to be disassembled, matchmark the driveshaft and sliding splined yoke (transmission yoke) so that driveline balance is preserved upon reassembly. Remove the snap rings which retain the bearing caps.

3. Select two sockets, one small enough

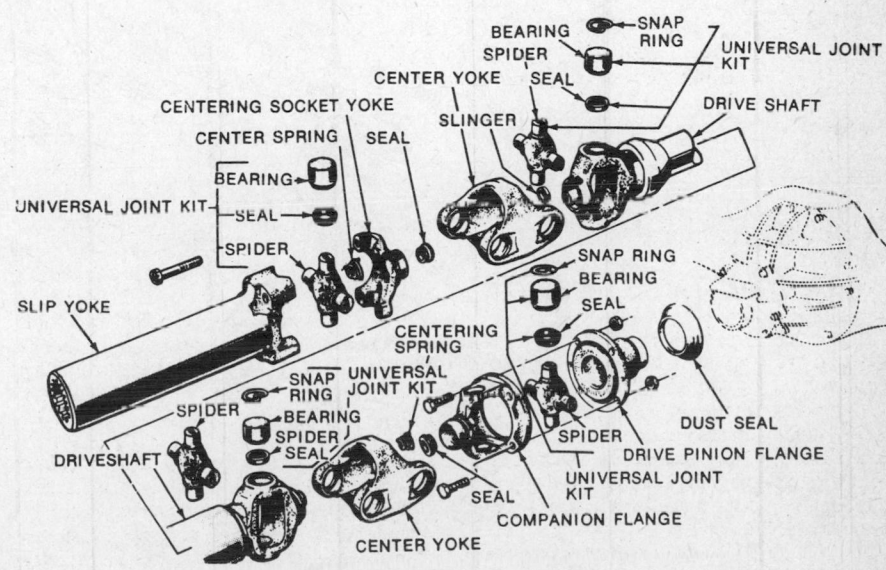

Typical driveshaft with cardan type U–joints

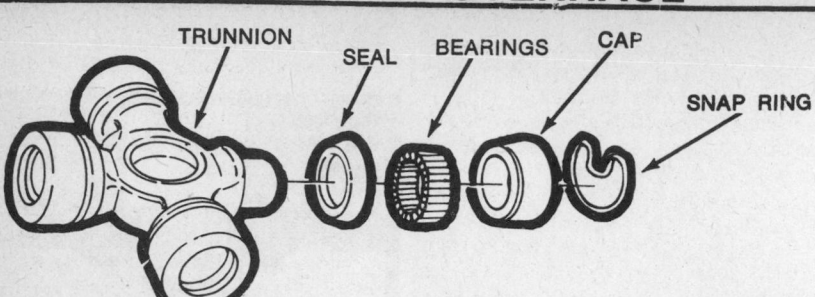

TRUNNION SEAL BEARINGS CAP SNAP RING

Snap ring type universal joint

to pass through the yoke holes for the bearing caps, the other large enough to receive the bearing cap.

4. Using a vise or a press, position the small and large sockets on either side of the U-joint. Press in on the smaller socket so that it presses the opposite bearing cap out of the yoke and into the larger socket. If the cap does not come all the way out, grasp it with a pair of pliers and work it out.

5. Reverse the position of the sockets so that the smaller socket presses on the cross. Press the other bearing cap out of the yoke.

6. Repeat the procedure on the other bearings.

7. To install, grease the bearing caps and needles thoroughly if they are not pregreased. Start a new bearing cap into one side of the yoke. Position the cross in the yoke.

8. Select two sockets small enough to pass through the yoke holes. Put the sockets against the cross and the cap, and press the bearing cap ¼ inch below the surface of the yoke. If there is a sudden increase in the force needed to press the cap into place,

or if the cross starts to bind, the bearings are cocked. They must be removed and restarted in the yoke. Failure to do so will greatly reduce the life of the bearing.

9. Install a new snap ring.

10. Start a new bearing into the opposite side. Place a socket on it and press in until the opposite bearing contacts the snap ring.

11. Install a new snap ring. It may be necessary to grind the facing surface of the snap ring slightly to permit easier installation.

12. Install the other bearings in the same manner.

13. Check the joint for free movement. If binding exists, smack the yoke ears with a brass or plastic faced hammer to seat the bearing needles. Do not strike the bearings, and support the shaft firmly. Do not install the driveshaft until free movement exists at all joints.

Plastic Retainer Type

Remove and install the bearing caps and trunnion (cross) as described for the snapring type universal joints. On an original universal joint, however, the bearing caps will be secured in the yokes with injected

plastic. The plastic will shear when the bearing caps are pressed. Service snap-rings are installed in the groove on the inside (of yoke) of the installed caps.

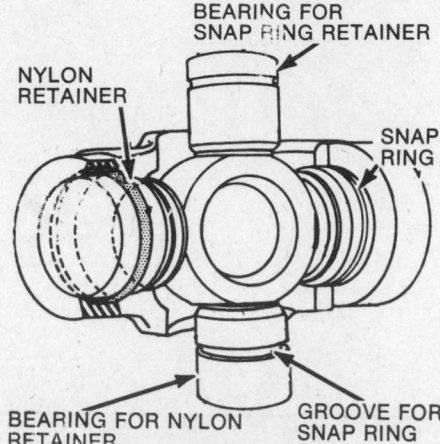

NYLON RETAINER BEARING FOR SNAP RING RETAINER SNAP RING BEARING FOR NYLON RETAINER GROOVE FOR SNAP RING

U-joint locking methods
(© Pontiac Div., G.M. Corp)

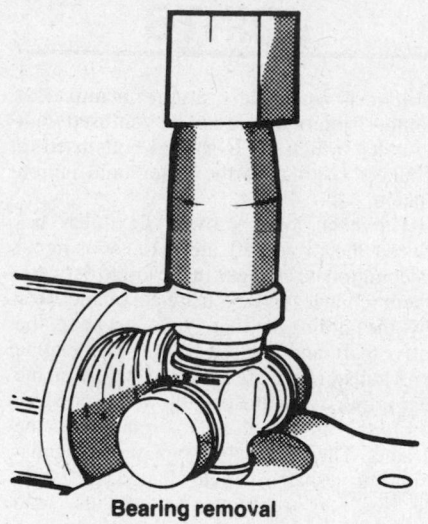

Bearing removal

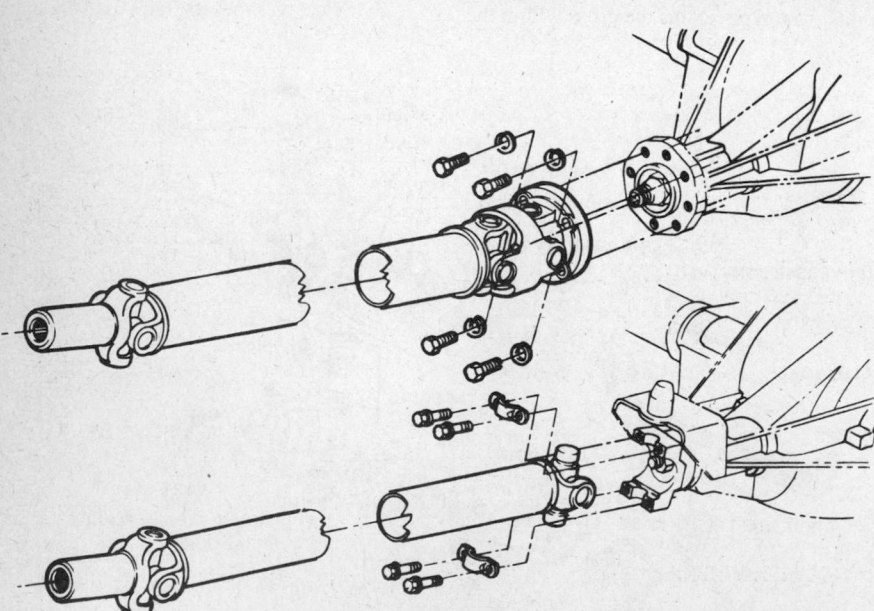

The driveshaft may be retained to the differential pinion by a flange (top) or by U-bolts or straps (bottom) (© Pontiac Div., G.M. Corp.)

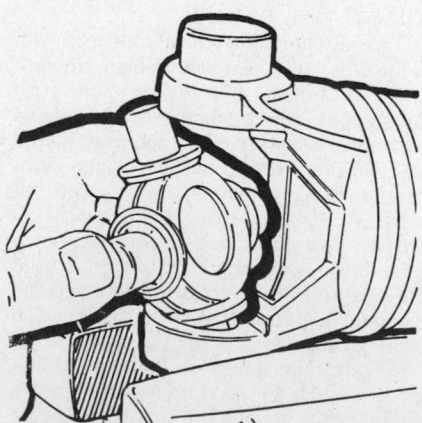

Press a bearing cap into the yoke, then install the cross

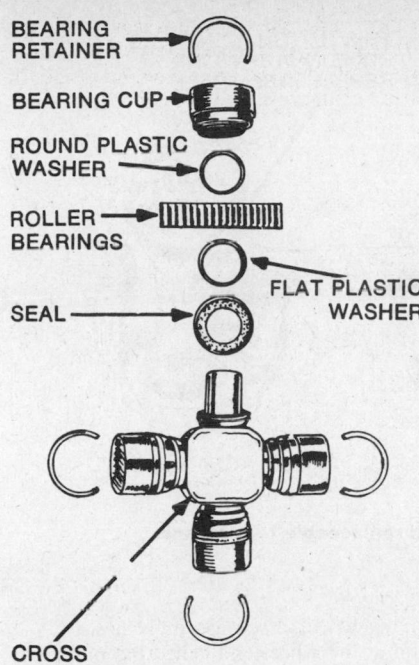

- BEARING RETAINER
- BEARING CUP
- ROUND PLASTIC WASHER
- ROLLER BEARINGS
- SEAL
- FLAT PLASTIC WASHER
- CROSS

Plastic retainer U-joint repair kit components

NOTE: The plastic which retains the bearing will be sheared when the bearing cup is pressed out. Be sure to remove the remains of the plastic retainer from the ears of the yoke. It is easier to remove the remains if a small pin or punch is first driven through the injection holes in the yoke. Failure to remove all of the plastic remains may prevent the bearing cups from being pressed into place and the bearing retainers from being properly seated.

CARDAN TYPE U-JOINT OVERHAUL

Some with Cardan type U-joints use snap rings to retain the bearing cups in the yokes. Other cars have plastic retainers. Be sure to obtain the correct rebuilding kit.

1. Use a punch to mark the coupling yoke and the adjoining yokes before disassembly, to ensure proper reassembly and driveline balance.

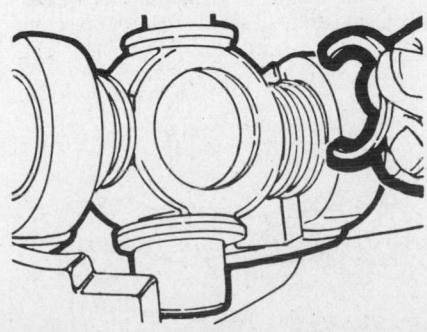

Service snap rings are installed inside the yoke

2. It is easiest to remove the bearings from the coupling yoke first. Follow the order indicated in the illustration.

3. Support the driveshaft horizontally on a press stand, or on the workbench if a vise is being used.

4. If snap rings are used to retain the bearing cups, remove them. Place the rear ear of the coupling yoke over a socket large enough to receive the cup. Place a smaller socket, or a cross press made for the purpose, over the opposite cup. Press the bearing cup out of the coupling yoke ear. If the cup is not completely removed, insert a spacer and complete the operation, or grasp the cup with a pair of slip joint pliers and work it out. If the cups are retained by plastic, this will shear the retainers. Remove any bits of plastic.

5. Rotate the driveshaft and repeat the operation on the opposite cup.

6. Disengage the trunnions of the spider, still attached to the flanged yoke, from the coupling yoke, and pull the flanged yoke and spider from the center ball on the ball support tube yoke.

NOTE: The joint between the shaft and coupling yoke can be serviced without disassembly of the joint between the coupling yoke and flanged yoke.

7. Pry the seal from the ball cavity, remove the washers, spring and three seats. Examine the ball stud seat and the ball stud for scores or wear. Worn parts can be replaced with a kit. Clean the ball seat cavity and fill it with grease. Install the spring, washer, ball seats, and spacer (washer) over the ball.

8. To assemble, insert one bearing cup

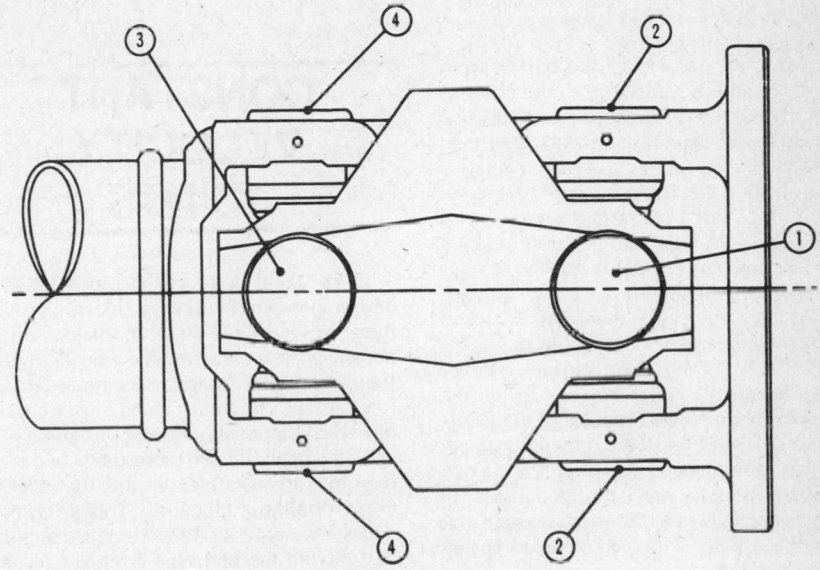

Cardan joint disassembly sequence

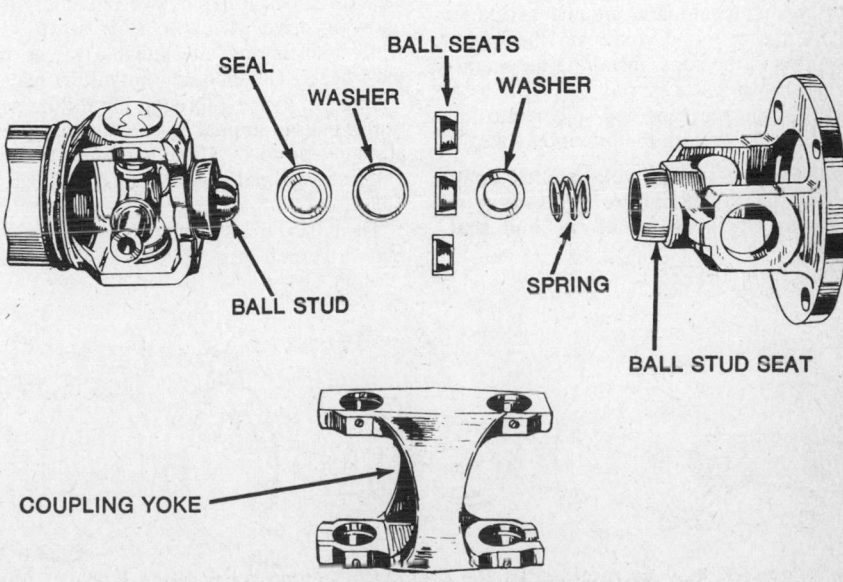

- SEAL
- WASHER
- BALL SEATS
- WASHER
- SPRING
- BALL STUD
- BALL STUD SEAT
- COUPLING YOKE

Cardan type joint

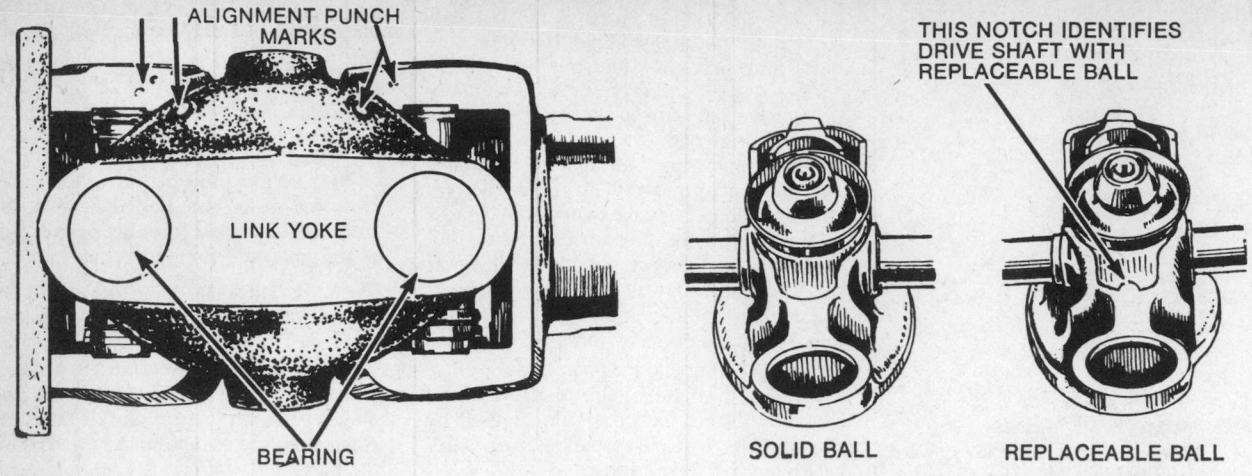

ALIGNMENT PUNCH MARKS

THIS NOTCH IDENTIFIES DRIVE SHAFT WITH REPLACEABLE BALL

LINK YOKE

BEARING

SOLID BALL

REPLACEABLE BALL

Match marks for double cardan joint

Solid and replaceable U-joint balls

part way into one ear of the ball support tube yoke and turn this cup to the bottom.

9. Insert the spider (cross) into the tube yoke so that the trunnion (arm) seats freely in the cup.

10. Install the opposite cup part way, making sure that both cups are straight.

11. Press the cups into position, making sure that both cups squarely engage the spider. Back off if there is a sudden increase in resistance, indicating that a cup is cocked or a needle bearing is out of place.

12. As soon as one bearing retainer groove clears the yoke, stop and install the retainer (plastic retainer models). On models with snap rings, press the cups into place, then install the snap rings over the cups.

13. If difficulty is encountered installing the plastic retainers or the snap rings, smack the yoke sharply with a hammer to spring the ears slightly.

14. Install one bearing cup part way into the ear of the coupling yoke. Make sure that the alignment marks are matched, then engage the coupling yoke over the spider and press in the cups, installing the retainers or snap rings as before.

15. Install the cups and spider into the flanged yoke as with the previous yoke.

NOTE: The flange yoke should snap over center to the right or left and up or down by the pressure of the ball seat spring.

CONSTANT VELOCITY JOINTS

Front wheel drive vehicles present several unique problems to engineers because the driveshaft must do three things, simultaneously. It must allow the wheels to turn for steering, telescope to compensate for road surface vibrations, and it must transmit torque continuously without vibration.

To compensate for these three factors a two-joint driveshaft allows the front wheels to perform these functions. This driveshaft mates disc type straight groove ball joint design with the bell type Rzeppa CV universal joint.

The Rzeppa joint on the outboard end of each driveshaft provides steering ability by allowing drive wheels to steer up to 43° while transmitting all available torque to the wheels. The inboard joint allows telescoping (up to 1½″) through the rolling action of balls in straight grooves and operates at angles up to 20°. The combined action of these two ball type u-joints eliminates vibration.

The typical front wheel drive vehicle uses two driveshaft assemblies—one to each

driving wheel. Each assembly has a CV–joint at the wheel end called the outboard joint. A second joint on each shaft located at the transaxle end is called the inboard joint. This joint may be either the ball or tripode type. It allows the slip motion required when the driveshaft must shorten or lengthen in response to suspension action when traveling over an irregular surface.

Constant velocity joints are precision machined parts that have difficult jobs to perform in a hostile environment. They are exposed to heat, shock, torque, and many thousands of miles of service. For this reason, the lubricants used are specially formulated to be compatible with the rubber boot and give proper lubrication. Most CV-joint repair kits have this special lubricant included.

NOTE: Wear pattern in a used ball or tripode CV-joint are impossible to match during reassembly. If there are any signs of wear, abnormal operating noise, corrosion, heat discoloration, the joint must be replaced.

TROUBLESHOOTING

Noises from the engine, drive axles, suspension and steering in the front drive cars can be misleading to the untrained ear. Ideally a smooth road serves best for detecting

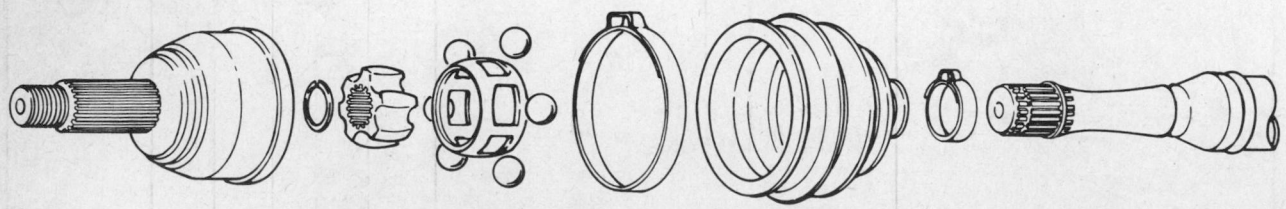

Fixed CV joint

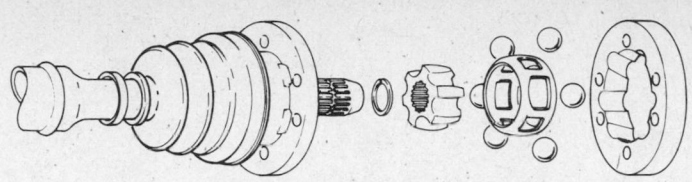

Ball style (Rzeppa) plunging CV joint

SHAFT REMOVAL

1. Remove the hub nut and discard it.
2. Drain the lubricant from the trans-axle.

CAUTION

The lubricant may be hot.

---

operating condition(s) that cause noise.
- A humming noise could indicate that early stage of insufficient or incorrect lubricant.
- Worn driveshaft joints will cause a continuous knock at low speeds.
- A popping or clicking sound on sharp turns indicates trouble in the outer or wheel end joint.
- The clunk noise at acceleration from coasting or deceleration from a load pull indicates two possibilities—damaged inner or transaxle joint or differential problem(s).
- An inner joint will create a vibration during acceleration due to plunging action hanging up and releasing repeatedly. Probable cause would be foreign particles or lack of lubrication, or improper assembly.

- Remember that tires, suspension, engine, and exhaust system are all up front to add their noises.
- Make a check with front wheels elevated off ground. Spin the wheels by hand to determine if wheel bearing could be noisy or if out of round tires are causing vibration. Many wheel bearings are prelubed and sealed at the factory.

CAUTION

Personal injury can occur from spinning wheels by engine power. Spinning a wheel at excess speed may cause damage to CV-joints that could be operating at angles too steep when wheels are allowed to hang. Over speeding might also cause damage to tires and the differential.

---

3. The speedometer pinion gear assembly must be removed before the right drive shaft can be removed. (Automatic transaxles only).
4. Rotate the driveshaft to view the circlip.
5. Compress the circlip tangs with needle nose pliers as you pry into the side gear. This compresses the circlip in position for shaft removal later. Keep an awl between the differential pinion shaft and the end face of the shaft to prevent circlip reentry to the groove.

NOTE: This applies to Chrysler only.

6. Remove the ball joint clamp bolt. Drop the lower arm too allow clearance. This will permit the front wheel to swing free.

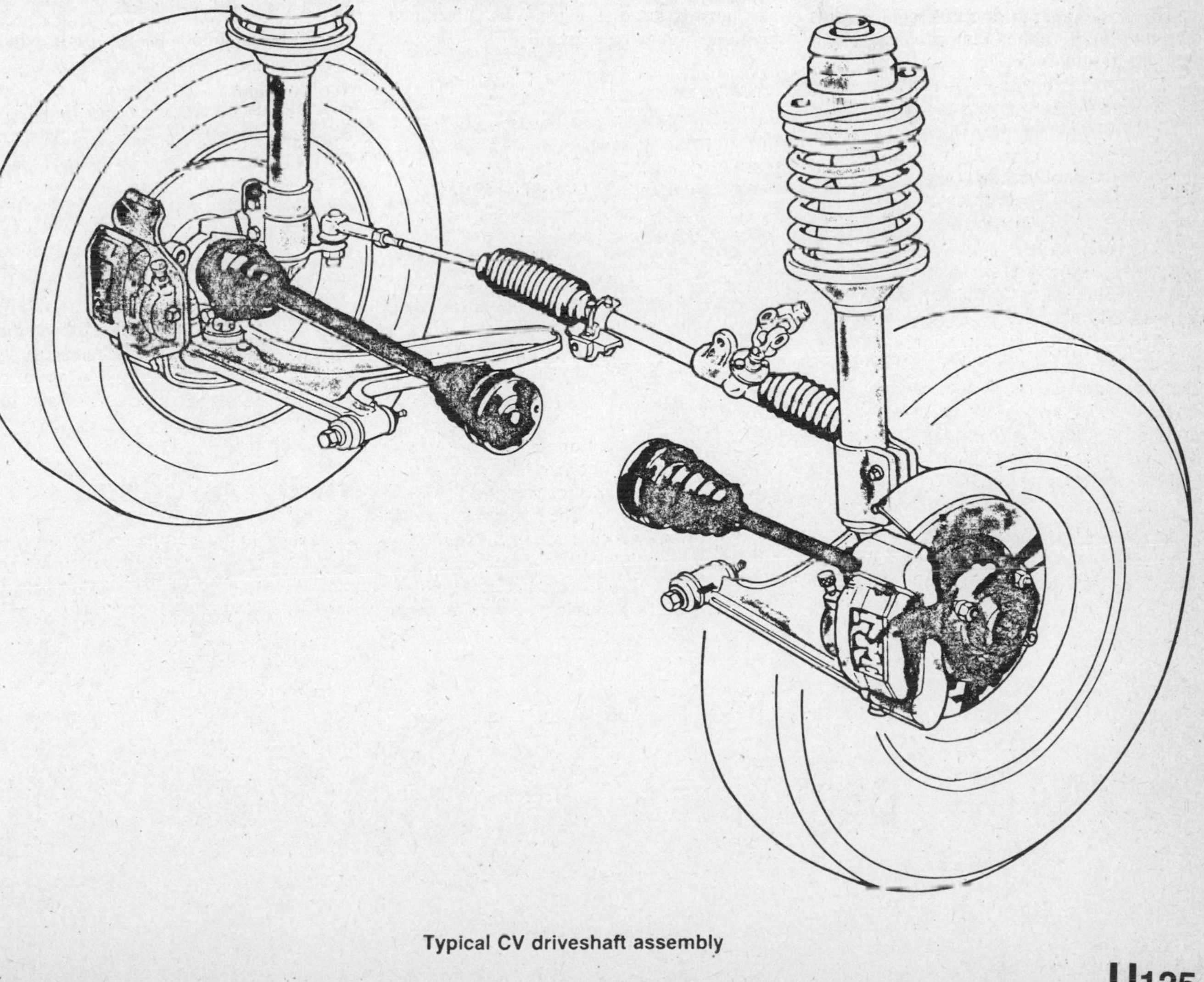

Typical CV driveshaft assembly

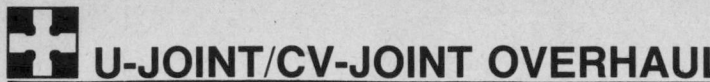

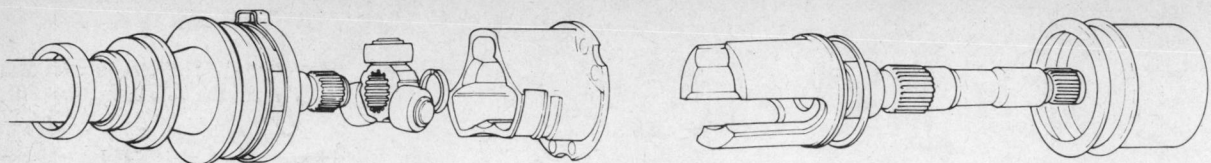

Closed tulip plunging CV joint　　　　　**Open tulip plunging CV joint**

7. Pull the outer splined shaft from the wheel hub, when swinging wheel hub away. Do not pull on the shaft. Grasp the joint housing.

8. Remove the inner joint by pulling outward on the inner joint housing. Do not pull the shaft.

NOTE: Do not allow the assembly to hang at either end. This can jam the CV-joint and cause vibration during operation. If necessary, support the shaft at either end by rope or wire.

INNER JOINT/BOOT

9. Place the assembly in a vise. Care must be taken not the crush the tubular shafts. Some shafts are solid steel.

10. If the inner joint needs replacement, cut the small rubber clamp, large metal clamp, and remove the rubber boot. These items must be discarded.

11. Inspect for internal wear and/or damage.

12. Clean the grease by hand from inside the joint housing and around the 3 ball trunnion assembly to inspect. Mark the tripod and housing for proper reassembly, if it is to be reinstalled.

13. To replace the boot, CV-joint, or both, remove the snap ring from the groove and tap the trunnion lightly with a brass drift pin. Leave the tripode bearings on the trunnion. Care must be taken to support the bearings as they may fall off.

14. Installation is the reverse of removal with the following recommendations: When reinstalling the tripode on the shaft place the chamfer face toward the retainer groove. The grease provided with the repair kit must be used. It can not be substituted with any other type grease.

OUTER JOINT/BOOT

1. Place the shaft in a vise. Be careful not to over tighten the vise thereby damaging the shaft.

2. Remove the boot and clamps. Discard these parts.

3. Using a soft hammer rap sharply on the housing. This forces the inner race over the internal circlip. Never remove the slinger from the housing.

4. Remove and discard the circlip. A new one is included with the boot kit. Leave the lock ring in place.

NOTE: Never disassemble the cage and balls from the housing. Reuse the joint assembly with a new boot kit, unless the grease is contaminated and prior diagnosis indicated trouble. In that case replace the joint and boot.

5. Installation is the reverse of removal.

Drive Axles

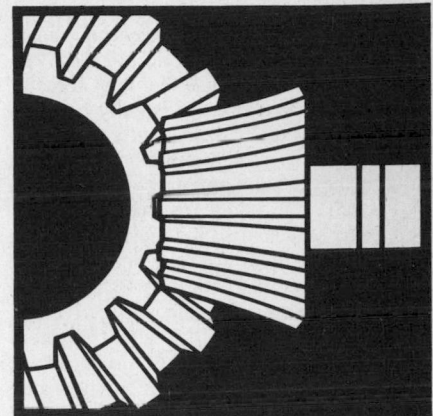

FRONT WHEEL DRIVE

Front wheel drive cars do not have conventional rear axles or drive shafts. Instead, power is transmitted from the engine to a transaxle, or a combination of transmission and drive axle, in one unit. Both the transmission and drive axle accomplish the same function as their counterparts in a front-engine/rear-drive axle design. The difference is in the location of the components.

In place of a conventional driveshaft, a front-wheel-drive design uses two driveshafts, sometimes called halfshafts, which couple the drive axle portion of the transaxle to the wheels. Universal joints or constant velocity joints are used just as they would in a rear wheel drive design.

REAR WHEEL DRIVE

The rear axle must transmit power through 90°. To accomplish this, straight cut bevel gears or spiral bevel gears were used. This type of gear is satisfactory for differential side gears, but since the centerline of the gears must intersect, they rapidly became unsuited for ring and pinion gears. The lowering of the driveshaft brought about a variation of the bevel gear, which is called the hypoid gear. This type of gear does not require a metting of the gear centerlines and can therefore be underslung, relative to the centerline of the ring gear.

Gear Ratios

The drive axle of a vehicle is said to have a certain axle ratio. This number (usually a whole number and a decimal fraction) is actually a comparison of the number of gear teeth on the ring gear and the pinion gear. For example, a 4.11 rear means that theoretically, there are 4.11 teeth on the ring gear and one tooth on the pinion. Actually, on a 4.11 rear, there are 37 teeth on the ring gear and nine teeth on the pinion gear. By dividing the number of teeth on the pinion gear into the number of teeth on the ring gear, the numerical axle ratio (4.11) is obtained. This also provides a good method of ascertaining exactly which axle ratio one is dealing with.

Differential Operation

The differential is an arrangement of gears that permits the rear wheels to turn at different speeds when cornering and divides the torque between the axle shafts. The differential gears are mounted on a pinion shaft and the gears are free to rotate on this shaft. The pinion shaft is fitted in a bore in the differential case and is at right angles to the axle shafts.

Power flow through the differential is as follows. The drive pinion, which is turned by the driveshaft, turns the ring gear. The

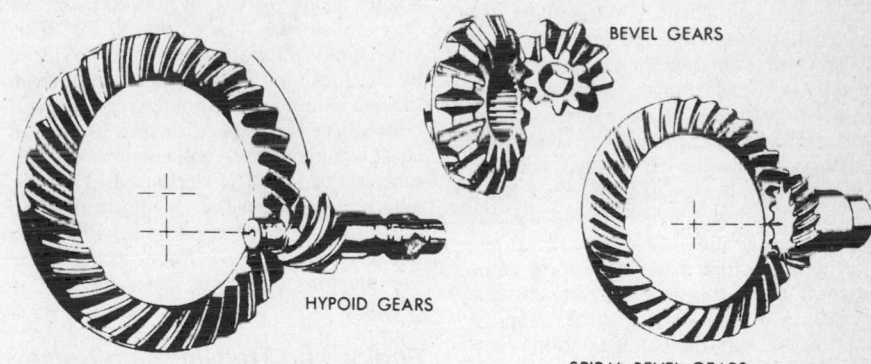

Hypoid gear application

Bevel gear application

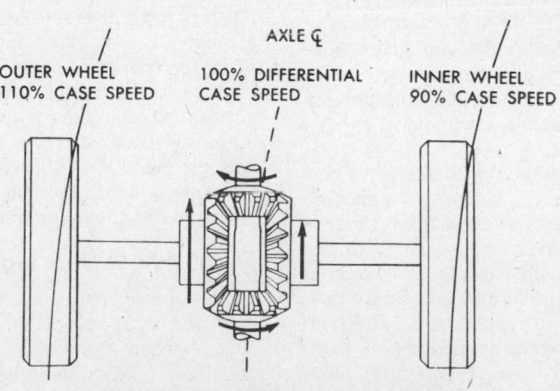

Differential action during cornering

ring gear, which is bolted to the differential case, rotates the case. The differential pinion forces the pinion gears against the side gears. In cases where both wheels have equal traction, the pinion gears do not rotate on the pinion shaft, because the input force of the pinion gear is divided equally between the two side gears. Consequently the pinion gears revolve with the pinion shaft, although they do not revolve on the pinion shaft itself. The side gears, which are splined to the axle shafts, and meshed with the pinion gears, rotate the axle shafts.

When it becomes necessary to turn a corner, the differential becomes effective and allows the axle shafts to rotate at different speeds. As the inner wheel slows down, the side gear splined to the inner wheel axle shaft also slows down. The pinion gears act as balancing levers by maintaining equal tooth loads to both gears while allowing unequal speeds of rotation at the axle shafts. If the vehicle speed remains constant, and the inner wheel slows down to 90% of vehicle speeds, the outer wheel will speed up to 110%.

Limited-Slip Differential Operation

Limited-slip differentials provide driving force to the wheel with the best traction before the other wheel begins to spin. This is accomplished through clutch plates or cones. The clutch plates (or cones) are located between the side gears and inner wall of the differential case. When they are squeezed together through spring tension and outward force from the side gears, three reactions occur. Resistance on the side gears causes more torque to be exerted on the clutch packs or cones. Rapid one-wheel spin cannot occur, because the side gear is forced to turn at the same speed as the case. Most important, with the side gear and the differential case turning at the same speed, the other wheel is forced to rotate in the same direction and at the same speed as the differential case. Thus driving force is applied to the wheel with the better traction.

DIFFERENTIAL DIAGNOSIS

The most essential part of rear axle service is proper diagnosis of the problem. Bent or broken axle shafts or broken gears pose little problem, but isolating an axle noise and correctly interpreting the problem can be extremely difficult, even for an experienced mechanic.

Any gear-driven unit will produce a certain amount of noise, therefore, a specific diagnosis for each individual unit is the best practice. Acceptable or normal noise can be classified as a slight noise heard only at certain speeds or under unusual conditions. This noise tends to reach a peak at 40–60 mph, depending on the road condition, load, gear ratio and tire size. Frequently, other noises are mistakenly diagnosed as coming from the rear axle. Vehicle noises from tires, transmission, driveshaft, U-joints and front and rear wheel bearings will often be mistaken as emanating from the rear axle. Raising the tire pressure to eliminate tire noise (although this will not silence mud or snow treads), listening for noise at varying speeds and road conditions and listening for noise at drive and coast conditions will aid in diagnosing alleged rear axle noises.

External Noise Elimination

It is advisable to make a thorough road test to determine whether the noise originates in the rear axle or whether it originates from the tires, engine transmission, wheel bearings or road surface. Noise originating from other places cannot be corrected by overhauling the rear axle.

Road Noise

Brick roads or rough surfaced concrete, may cause a noise which can be mistaken as coming from the rear axle. Driving on a different type of road (smooth asphalt or dirt) will determine whether the road is the cause of the noise. Road noise is usually the same on drive or coast conditions.

Tire Noise

Tire noise can be mistaken as rear axle noises, even though the tires on the front are at fault. Snow tread and mud tread tires or tires worn unevenly will frequently cause vibrations which seem to originate elsewhere; temporarily, and for test purposes only, inflate the tires to 40–50 lbs. This will significantly alter the noise produced by the tires, but will not alter noise from the rear axle. Noises from the rear axle will normally cease at speeds below 30 mph on coast, while tire noise will continue at lower tone as car speed is decreased. The rear axle noise will usually change from drive conditions to coast conditions, while tire noise will not. Do not forget to lower the tire pressure to normal after the test is complete.

Engine and Transmission Noise

Engine and transmission noises also seem to originate in the rear axle. Road test the vehicle and determine at which speeds the noise is most pronounced. Stop the car in a quiet place to avoid interfering noises. With the transmission in neutral, run the engine slowly through the engine speeds corresponding to the car speed at which the noise was most noticeable. If a similar noise was produced with the car standing still, the noise is not in the rear axle, but somewhere in the engine or transmission.

Front Wheel Bearing Noise

Front wheel bearing noises, sometimes confused with rear axle noises, will not change when comparing drive and coast conditions. While holding the car speed steady, lightly apply the footbrake. This will often cause wheel bearing noise to lessen, as some of the weight is taken off the bearing. Front wheel bearings are easily checked by jacking up the vehicle and spinning the wheels. Shaking the wheels will also determine if the wheel bearings are excessively loose.

Rear Axle Noises

If a logical test of the vehicle shows that the noise is not caused by external items, it can be assumed that the noise originates from the rear axle. The rear axle should be tested on a smooth level road to avoid road noise. It is not advisable to test the axle by jacking up the rear wheels and running the car.

True rear axle noises generally fall into two classes—gear noise and bearing noises, and can be caused by a faulty driveshaft, faulty wheel bearings, worn differential or pinion shaft bearings, U-joint misalignment, worn differential side gears and pinions, or mismatched, improperly adjusted, or scored ring and pinion gears.

REAR WHEEL BEARING NOISE

A rough rear wheel bearing causes a vibration or growl which will continue with the car coasting or in neutral. A brinelled rear wheel bearing will also cause a knock or click approximately every two revolutions of the rear wheel, due to the fact that the bearing rollers do not travel at the same speed as the rear wheel and axle. Jack up the rear wheels and spin the wheel slowly, listening for signs of a rough or brinelled wheel bearing.

DIFFERENTIAL SIDE GEAR AND PINION NOISE

Differential side gears and pinions seldom cause noise since their movement is relatively slight on straight ahead driving. Noise produced by these gears will be more noticeable on turns.

PINION BEARING NOISE

Pinion bearing failures can be distinguished by their speed of rotation, which is higher than side bearings or axle bearings. Rough or brinelled pinion bearings cause a continuous low pitch whirring or scraping noise beginning at low speeds.

SIDE BEARING NOISE

Side bearings produce a constant rough noise, which is slower than the pinion bearing noise. Side bearing noise may also fluctuate in the above rear wheel bearing test.

GEAR NOISE

Two basic types of gear noise exist. First is the type produced by bent or broken gear teeth which have been forcibly damaged. The noise from this type of damage is audible over the entire speed range. Scoring or damage to the hypoid gear teeth generally results from insufficient lubricant, improper lubricant, improper break-in, insufficient gear backlash, improper ring and pinion gear alignment or loss of torque on

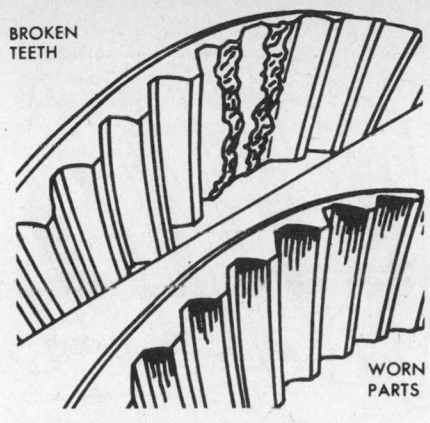

BROKEN TEETH

WORN PARTS

Two types of damage which cause gear noise

the drive pinion nut. If not corrected, the scoring will lead to eventual erosion or fracture of the gear teeth. Hypoid gear tooth fracture can also be caused by extended overloading of the gear set (fatigue fracture) or by shock overloading (sudden failure). Differential and side gears rarely give trouble, but common causes of differential failure are shock loading, extended overloading and differential pinion seizure at the cross-shaft, resulting from excessive wheel spin and consequent lubricant breakdown.

The second type of gear noise pertains to the mesh pattern between the ring and pinion gears. This type of abnormal gear noise can be recognized as a cycling pitch or whine audible in either drive, float or coast conditions. Gear noises can be recognized as they tend to peak out in a narrow speed range and remain constant in pitch, whereas bearing noises tend to vary in pitch with vehicle speeds. Noises produced by the ring and pinion gears will generally follow the pattern below.

A. Drive Noise:	Produced under vehicle acceleration.
B. Coast Noise:	Produced while the car coasts with a closed throttle.
C. Float Noise:	Occurs while maintaining constant car speed (just enough to keep speed constant) on a level road.
D. Drive, Coast and Float Noise:	These noises will vary in tone with speed and be very rough or irregular if the differential or pinion shaft bearings are worn.

Bearing Diagnosis

This section will help in the diagnosis of bearing failure and the causes. Bearing diagnosis can be very helpful in determining the cause of rear axle failure.

When disassembling a rear axle, the general condition of all bearings should be noted and classified where possible. Proper rec-

ognition of the cause will help in correcting the problem and avoiding a repetition of the failure.

Some of the common causes of bearing failure are:

    a. Abuse during assembly or disassembly.
    b. Improper assembly methods.
    c. Improper or inadequate lubrication.
    d. Bearing contact with dirt or water.
    e. Wear caused by dirt or metal chips.
    f. Corrosion or rust.
    g. Seizing due to overloading.
    h. Overheating.
    i. Frettage of the bearing seats.
    j. Brinelling from impact or shock loading.
    k. Manufacturing defects.
    l. Pitting due to fatigue.

To avoid damage to the bearing from improper handling, it is best to treat a used bearing the same as a new bearing. Always work in a clean area with clean tools. Remove all outside dirt from the housing before exposing a bearing and clean all bearing seats before installing a bearing.

CAUTION

Never spin a bearing, either by hand or with compressed air, as this will lead to almost certain bearing failure.

LIMITED-SLIP DIFFERENTIAL DIAGNOSIS

Lubrication

The use of proper lubricant is very important in limited-slip type drive axles. The forces applied when cornering tend to apply the clutch pack or clutch cones. The use of the wrong lubricant can cause the clutch surfaces to grab and chatter while turning. Always follow the manufacturer's recommendations regarding drive axle lubrication. When chatter is encountered, the differential lubricant should be drained and refilled with the specified lubricant.

General Diagnosis

Improper operation of a limited-slip type rear axle is generally indicated by clutch slippage or grabbing, which will sometimes produce a whirring or chatter sound. Occasionally, this condition is induced by improper lubrication. Check the unit for the wrong type of lubricant or lubricant which has broken down or become contaminated. Replace the lubricant with the type specified by the manufacturer.

During normal operation, i.e., straight-ahead driving, both wheels are rotating at equal speeds, and the driving force is distributed equally between both wheels. When cornering, the inside wheel delivers extra driving force, causing slippage in both clutch packs. Therefore, if the wheel rotation of both rear wheels is not equal, the unit will

constantly be functioning as if the car were cornering. This will cause constant slippage and lead to eventual failure of the unit. It is important that there be no excessive differences in wheel and tire size, wear pattern, or tire pressures between both rear wheels. Swerving on acceleration is an indication of one or more of the above conditions. Before attempting an overhaul or replacement operation, check both rear wheels for identical tire sizes, tire pressure, tire tread depth, and wear pattern.

DRIVE AXLE DISASSEMBLY ANALYSIS

Testing the Gear Tooth Contact Pattern

Once it has been established that the differential is indeed in need of service, the worst procedure is to simply plunge ahead and remove the differential and disassemble the parts. Prior to disassembly, a tooth contact pattern test should be made. However, it is worthwhile to first know the nomenclature associated with hypoid gear teeth.

The thick end of the tooth is called the heel and the thin end of the tooth is called the toe. The base half of the tooth is called the flank and the other end of the tooth is known as the face. The imaginary line at the halfway point between the face and flank is known as the pitch line. The space between the meshed pinion and ring gear tooth is known as backlash.

A gear tooth contact pattern can be made with the carrier in or out of the housing depending on the type of carrier. On integral carrier models, the lubricant must be drained and the rear cover removed. The ring gear will now be exposed and the test can be made with the carrier still in the housing. On removable carrier models, drain the lubricant and remove the carrier from the housing. The test can be made on the bench.

Unlike simple spur gears, hypoid gear teeth leave a complex pattern on the ring gear. When hypoid gears turn, the line contact between pinion and ring gear teeth has the same wiping motion as with spur gear teeth. Because of the complicated movement of hypoid gear teeth, the contact area takes an oval shape as opposed to the rectangular shape left by spur gear teeth. Actually, the tooth contact test shows where each gear tooth has been wiped by the movement of the contact line, so that you can tell whether the gears are set correctly. With a properly adjusted ring and pinion (with properly adjusted pinion depth and backlash) the tooth contact will be close to center. In this case, the load is borne by the strongest part of the tooth. If the gear setting is off, the contact line may reach any part of the edge of a tooth, and the metal will be overloaded at that point. When overload occurs, rapid deterioration of the gears will follow.

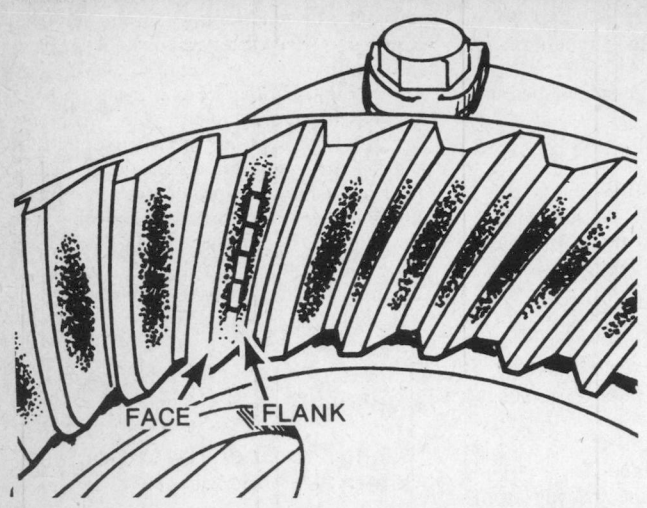

Gear tooth face and flank showing oval gear tooth contact pattern

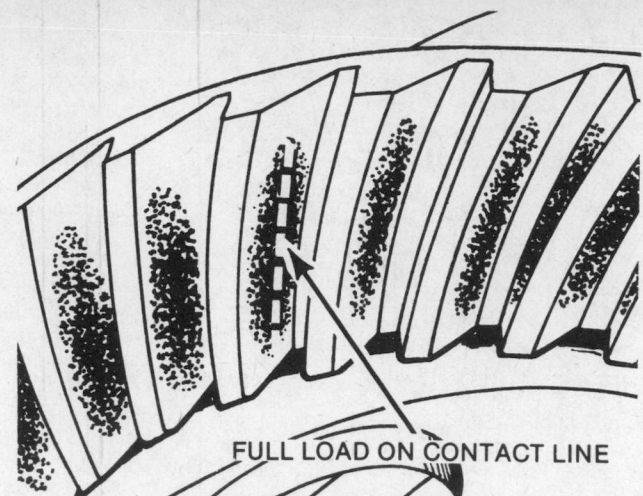

Gear tooth contact pattern showing load centered on gear tooth

PREPARING THE TEST

Coat the drive gear teeth with a metallic base artists' oil color such as zinc white or titanium white. The tooth coating material must be smooth and firm enough to spread without running. A consistency somewhat like toothpaste works well. If it is necessary to thicken the material, add a small amount of cup grease.

NOTE: Prussian blue dye does not work well, since the blue tends to smear the pattern.

Thoroughly clean the ring gear and pinion before applying the testing material. Any gear lube left on the teeth will make the pattern quite unreadable. Coat the drive and coast sides of all the ring gear teeth, but leave the pinion gear teeth clean. Do not apply the coating too thickly as the pattern will be smeared.

Because the axle gears are normally easy to rotate, turning resistance must be applied to produce pressure between the pinion and ring gear teeth to make a legible pattern. On a removable carrier type axle, insert a large prybar between the carrier housing and the differential case rim. Apply the load squarely against the case rim while prying out against the upper or lower section of the carrier housing. On integral carrier models, apply the parking brake to a point where it requires approximately 50 ft lbs to turn the pinion with a torque wrench. Since the shape and position of the contact pattern will vary, depending on the load, try to use the same load for each test or the results can be misleading. This is especially true when testing after an overhaul.

Once the gears have a load applied, obtain a tooth contact pattern by rotating the ring gear and pinion one complete turn in each direction. This will produce a constant pattern on the coast and drive side of each tooth. Do not rotate the ring gear more than one revolution in each direction as this will tend to obscure the pattern.

NOTE: If the pattern does not look right on the first try, try again.

Making a good gear tooth test takes a little practice; so if it is not right, try again.

INTERPRETING GEAR TOOTH CONTACT PATTERNS

The tooth contact pattern should be the same on every tooth. If the pattern shows heavy and light areas on different teeth, check the ring gear and differential case for excessive run-out.

NOTE: Run-out can be cured in many cases by removing the ring gear from the case, rotating it 90° or 180°, and remounting it.

Since you can only apply test load pressure to the gears, the contact pattern will be less distinct toward the tooth ends. But, when the ring gear and pinion are under operating loads in the vehicle, the tooth contact area spreads out, especially towards

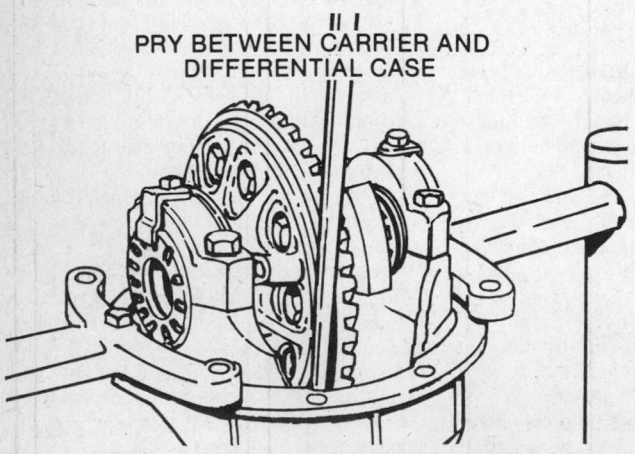

Applying a load to the differential case

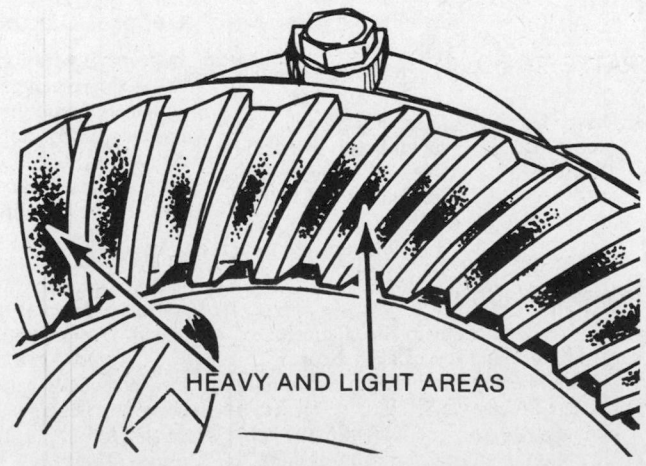

Excessive run-out will cause an uneven pattern

THICKER SPACER NEEDED

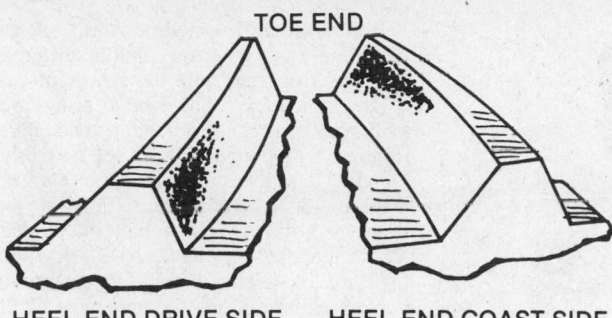

HEEL END-DRIVE SIDE (CONVEX)   HEEL END-COAST SIDE (CONCAVE)

Tooth contact patterns high on the tooth side

THINNER SPACER NEEDED

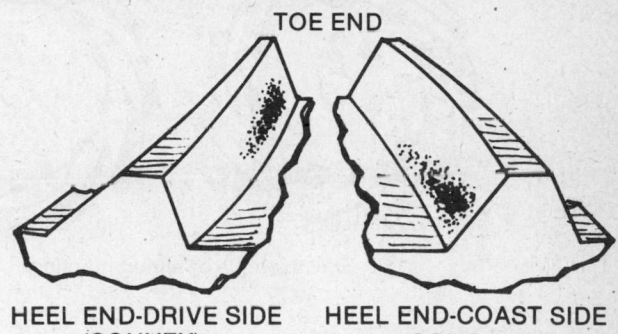

HEEL END-DRIVE SIDE (CONVEX)   HEEL END-COAST SIDE (CONCAVE)

Gear contact pattern low on tooth side

the heel end of the tooth. For this reason, do not try to "get by" with a tooth contact pattern that is centered, but favors the heel end of the teeth. This will only lead to overloading at the heel ends of the gear teeth. On the other hand, a contact pattern which is reasonably centered, but favors the toe end of the teeth, is acceptable.

Assuming that the tooth contact pattern is even on all teeth, the main problem is to get the most distinct part of the pattern centered on both the teeth. The contact patterns should be nearly opposite each other on both sides of each tooth. In some cases, the pattern will be centered on the drive side and off center on the coast side, or vice versa. The off center pattern can be moved to a more acceptable position by slightly altering the backlash. This procedure will not seriously affect the other pattern. More often, however, the pattern will be off center on both sides of the teeth. The basic cause of this condition is an improperly adjusted pinion.

ADJUSTING PINION DEPTH

It is necessary to understand that an incorrect pinion depth setting moves the contact pattern away from the center on both sides of the tooth in opposite directions. This

means that when you install a thicker or thinner washer under the pinion head, you bring the pattern into the center of the tooth from opposite ends.

When the contact pattern is high on the heel end of the drive side and low on the toe end of the coast side, a thicker washer is needed to bring the pinion in, toward the center of the drive gear. Increasing the thickness of the spacer washer will bring the pattern in, toward the center of the drive gear teeth, and also will move the pattern down from the tooth face. However, this movement is less than the in-or-out movement.

When tooth contact is low on the toe end of the drive side and high on the heel end of the coast side, the pinion must be moved out, by installing a thinner washer under the pinion head. This will move the pattern inward toward the center, and will also result in slight movement of the pattern up from the tooth flank.

A factory service facility will use special tools and gauge blocks to determine the thickness of the spacer under the pinion head. In the absence of such specialized equipment, the following procedure may be used. Bear in mind that with the "hit-or-miss" method, each time you are wrong

with the pinion depth, the unit must be disassembled, the spacer thickness changed, and the unit must be completely set up again.

Gather a handful of spacers to cover any thickness and several collapsible pinion spacers (if the unit uses them). Assemble the unit. If the original gear set is being reused, and the tooth contact pattern is reasonably correct, install a new spacer of the same thickness as the old one. This will provide a reasonable starting point. If the gear contact pattern test indicates a need for movement of the pinion, use a new spacer 0.001–0.002 in. thicker or thinner, depending on the direction the pinion must go. If a new gear set is being used, the thickness of the spacer will have to be determined in the following manner. Compare the markings on the old and new pinion. It will usually be marked with a number preceded by a plus (+) or minus (−) sign. This number indicates the production deviation from the nominal pinion, which are known as "zero pinions." In service, zero pinions are rare. Assume that the old pinion is marked with a plus two (+2). Assume that the new pinion is marked with a +3. By comparing the pinion markings, find the numerical difference between the two pinions, in this case +1. With a micrometer,

PATTERN MOVES TOWARD CENTER AND DOWN

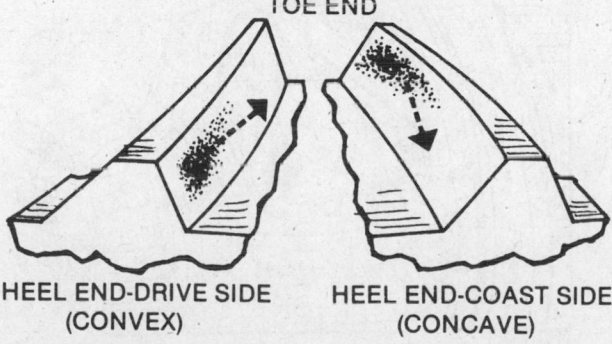

HEEL END-DRIVE SIDE (CONVEX)   HEEL END-COAST SIDE (CONCAVE)

A thicker spacer moves the pattern in and down

PATTERN MOVES INWARD AND UP

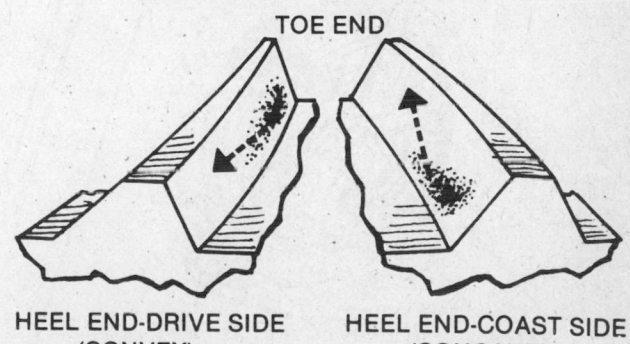

HEEL END-DRIVE SIDE (CONVEX)   HEEL END-COAST SIDE (CONCAVE)

A thinner spacer will move the pattern up and inward

One example of pinion markings

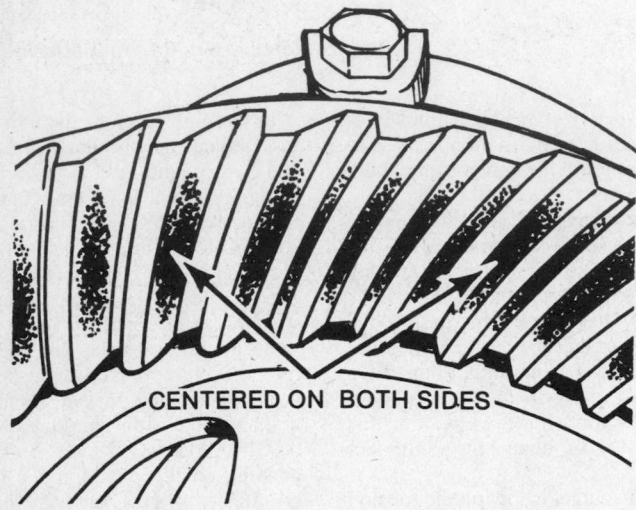

CENTERED ON BOTH SIDES

Gear tooth contact pattern showing load centered on gear tooth

increased by 0.001 in., to 0.031 in. total. This will only provide a reasonable beginning point.

It is rare that this method works out the first time. Assemble the pinion, differential, and ring gear with the spacer of calculated thickness. The side bearing preload, backlash, pinion nut torque, and pinion rotating torque must all be set correctly. Obtain a gear tooth pattern on the ring gear teeth and analyze the results. Small deviations from the acceptable pattern can usually be made by varying the backlash within the limits of specifications. If the gear tooth contact pattern is off, the unit must be disassembled and another spacer installed. This spacer must be of suitable thickness to compensate for the contact pattern test.

NOTE: Without special tools, there is absolutely no way of determining exactly how much to increase or decrease the thickness of the pinion shim; it must be estimated.

After estimating the thickness of the new shim, assemble the unit again, setting all preloads and backlash. Check the contact pattern again and act accordingly. If the unit uses a collapsible spacer, be sure a new one is installed each time it is disassembled. Crushed spacers can not be used again. It is well to note that the unit may have to be assembled and disassembled several times before an acceptable contact pattern is obtained.

Adjusting Backlash

The tooth contact pattern can be altered slightly, by varying the backlash adjustment within the limits of the specifications. The backlash adjustment can be used to alter a pattern which is slightly off center on either side of the tooth, but should not be used as a substitute for pinion depth adjustment. This adjustment must always be made after the pinion depth has been adjusted.

measure the thickness of the original spacer. We will assume that the old spacer is 0.030 in. thick. If the numerical difference between pinions is a positive number (+1) the spacer should be 0.001 in. thinner than the original spacer, or 0.029 in. total. If the numerical difference is a negative number (say, −1) then the spacer should be

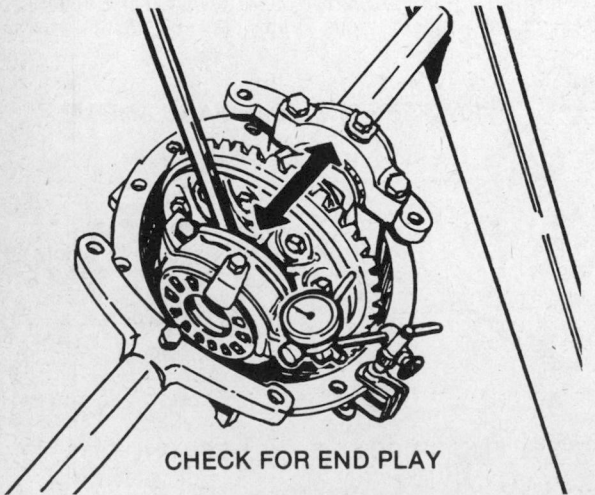

CHECK FOR END PLAY

Checking differential bearing end-play

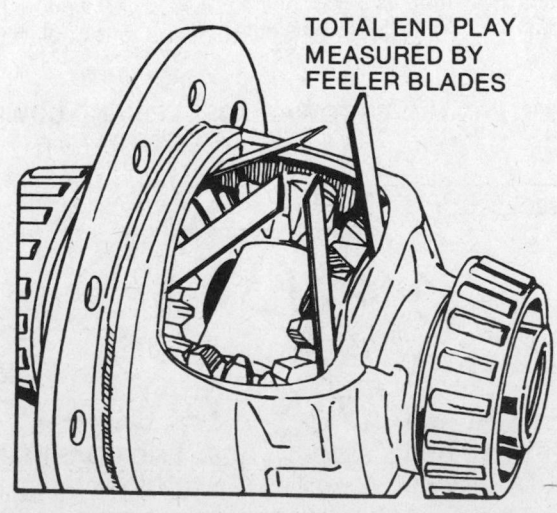

TOTAL END PLAY MEASURED BY FEELER BLADES

Checking total differential end-play

Manual Transmission Overhaul

MANUAL TRANSMISSIONS APPLICATION CHART

Make	Year	Vehicle Model	Transmission Model	Speeds	Reference Type No.	Page
BMW	'78–'83	320i	242/9, 18, 18.50	4	5	U144
			265/6	5	6	U147
	'78–'85	528i, 530i	262/8, 9, 9.2	4	4	U141
		630CSi, 633CSi	262/8, 9, 9.20, 9.90 ①	4	4	U141
		733i	262/8, 9, 9.10, 9.30, 9.35	4	4	U141
			265/6	5	6	U147
	'82–'85	528e	265/6	5	6	U147
Chrysler Corp./	'78	Arrow	KM110	4	1	U135
Mitsubishi	'78–'80	Arrow	KM119	5	2	U138
			KM132	5	3	U140
	'78	Colt/Champ	KM110	4	1	U135
	'78–'79	Colt/Champ	KM119	5	2	U138
			KM132	5	3	U140
	'78–'80	Colt/Champ Wagon	KM110	4	1	U135
			KM119	5	3	U140
			KM132	5	3	U140
	'78–'85	Challenger/Sapporo Starion, Conquest	KM119	5	2	U138
			KM132	5	3	U140
Datsun/Nissan	'78	B210	F4W60L	4	15	U170
	'82	210	F4W60L	4	15	U170
			F4W56A	4	11	U156
			FS5W60A,L	5	14	U166
	'78–'81	510	F4W63L	4	8,13 ②	U151, U162
			FS5W63A	5	12	U158
	'78–'85	810, Maxima	F4W71B	4	9	U153
			FS5W71B	5	10	U156
	'78–'79	200SX	FS5W63A	5	12	U158
	'80–'85	200SX	FS5W71B	5	10	U156

MANUAL TRANSMISSIONS APPLICATION CHART

Make	Year	Vehicle Model	Transmission Model	Speeds	Reference Type No.	Page
	'78–'83	280Z,ZX, Turbo	F4W71B	4	9	U153
			FS5W71B	5	10	U156
			FS5R90A	5	7	U149
	'84–'85	300ZX, Turbo	FS5W71C	5	10	U156
			FS5R90A	5	7	U149
Fiat	'78–'85	124, Spider	—	4 & 5	16	U173
	'78–'81	131, Brava	—	5	17	U175
Isuzu	'81–'85	All	—	4	22	U186
			—	5	23	U188
Mazda	'78	Cosmo	—	5	20	U182
	'78–'80	GLC	—	4 & 5	19	U180
	'78	RX-3	—	4	18	U177
	'78	RX-4	—	4	18	U177
			—	5	20	U182
	'79–'85	RX-7	—	5	20	U182
	'79–'82	626	—	4 & 5	19	U180
	'78	808	—	4	18	U177
			—	5	20	U182
Mercedes-Benz		All	—	4	21	U185
Peugeot	'78–'83	504	BA-7, BA-10, BA-10/4	4	24	U189
	'80–'85	505	BA-7, BA-10, BA-10/4	4	24	U189
			BA-10/5	5	30	U211
	'78–'80	604	BA-7, BA-10, BA-10/4	4	24	U189
	'82–'85	604	BA-10/5	5	30	U211
Toyota	'78–'85	Celica, Supra, Cressida	W40	4	27	U202
			W50, P51, W55, W58③	5	28	U203
	'78–'79	Corolla	K40, K50	4 & 5	25	U197
	'80–'84	Corolla	T40, T41, T50	4 & 5	26	U200
	'78–'82	Corona	W40	4	27	U202
			W50, P51	5	28	U203
	'81–'85	Starlet	K40, K50, K51	4 & 5	25	U197
Volvo	'78–'85	All	M45,M46	4	29	U209

NOTE: Although certain late model transmissions may differ slightly from the earlier models; certain basic similarities will usually exist, thus enabling overhaul of the newest models with the guidelines given within the text.

① 262/9.90 is the model designation for 1982-83 Calif. transmissions

② Two different versions of the same model were imported; see the illustrations to identify the transmission being overhauled

③ The W55 and W58 transmissions used in 1981 and later models are similar to the W50 and P51

TYPE 1

4 Speed Transmission—Model KM 110

Chrysler Corp./ Mitsubishi

DISASSEMBLY

1. Using a 3/16 in. punch, drive out the clutch spring pins. Remove the clutch shaft with release fork and springs.

2. Remove the speedometer gear assembly and the lockplate. Remove the clutch and the back-up light switches.

3. The extension housing can be removed by tapping lightly with a hammer.

4. With the transmission inverted, remove the bottom cover.

5. Remove the speedometer drive snap-rings, and gear. Remove the main drive gear retainer. Remove the countershaft stopper.

6. Remove the countershaft rearward. Remove the countergear, 40 roller bearings, spacers, and front and rear washers.

7. Lift out the thrust washer, rear idler gear, needle bearings, and spacer located on the reverse idler gear shaft.

8. Withdraw the gear shaft bolt and pull the shaft from the case: Remove the front idler gear.

9. Locate the three plugs on the left case side. Remove them and the poppet springs and balls.

10. Loosen the reverse shift bar and reverse locking bolt. Pull out the reverse shift bar. Remove the reverse shaft fork and spacer.

11. Using a 3/16 in. punch, drive the fork spring pins and shift bar from the mount. Remove the shift bar and the shaft fork. Do not disassemble the shift bar.

12. Remove the reverse gear from the case.

13. Remove the mainshaft and the main drive gear synchronizer ring.

14. Pull the main drive gear assembly from the case front. Remove all snap-rings.

15. Remove the shifter assembly.

TRANSMISSION SPECIFICATIONS:

Helical gear backlash: 0.002–0.006 in.
Shift fork to sleeve clearance: 0.004–0.008 in.
Spur gear backlash: 0.004–0.008 in.
Gear change lever-selector groove clearance: 0.004–0.012 in.
Reverse shift fork-reverse gear groove clearance: 0.004–0.012 in.

ASSEMBLY

1. Press the bearing onto the main drive gear.

2. Secure it with the snap-ring of appropriate thickness to give an end-play of 0.002 in.

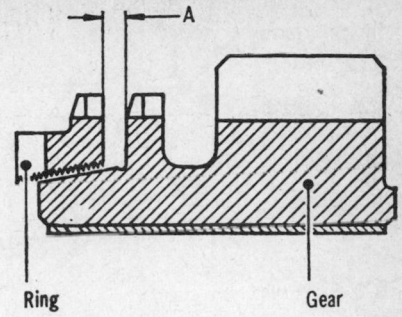

Synchronizer inspection—Dimension A = 0.059 in.

Snap-Ring Code (in.):
White 0.091
None 0.093
Red 0.094
Yellow 0.098

3. Assemble the hub and synchronizer ring.

4. Place the front and rear springs on the shaft in opposite directions.

5. Assemble the second gear synchronizer hub with the stepped gear end (narrow toothed side) rearward.

6. Assemble the needle bearings and third gear onto the mainshaft from the front end.

7. Install the synchronizer assembly.

8. Assemble the first-second synchronizer in the same direction it was removed.

9. Fit the snap-rings to give a proper end-play of 0.0012–0.0075 in. Third-fourth gear hub end-play is 0.00–0.0043 in.

1. Flywheel
2. Transmission case
3. Main drive gear
4. Synchronizer sleeve (for third-fourth speed)
5. Third-speed gear
6. Second-speed gear
7. Synchronizer sleeve (for first-second speeds)
8. First-speed gear
9. Rear bearing retainer
10. Reverse gear
11. Control shaft
12. Gearshift lever assembly
13. Pressure plate assembly
14. Counter gear
15. Under cover
16. Mainshaft
17. Reverse idler gear
18. Extension housing
19. Shift fork (reverse)
20. Speedometer drive gear

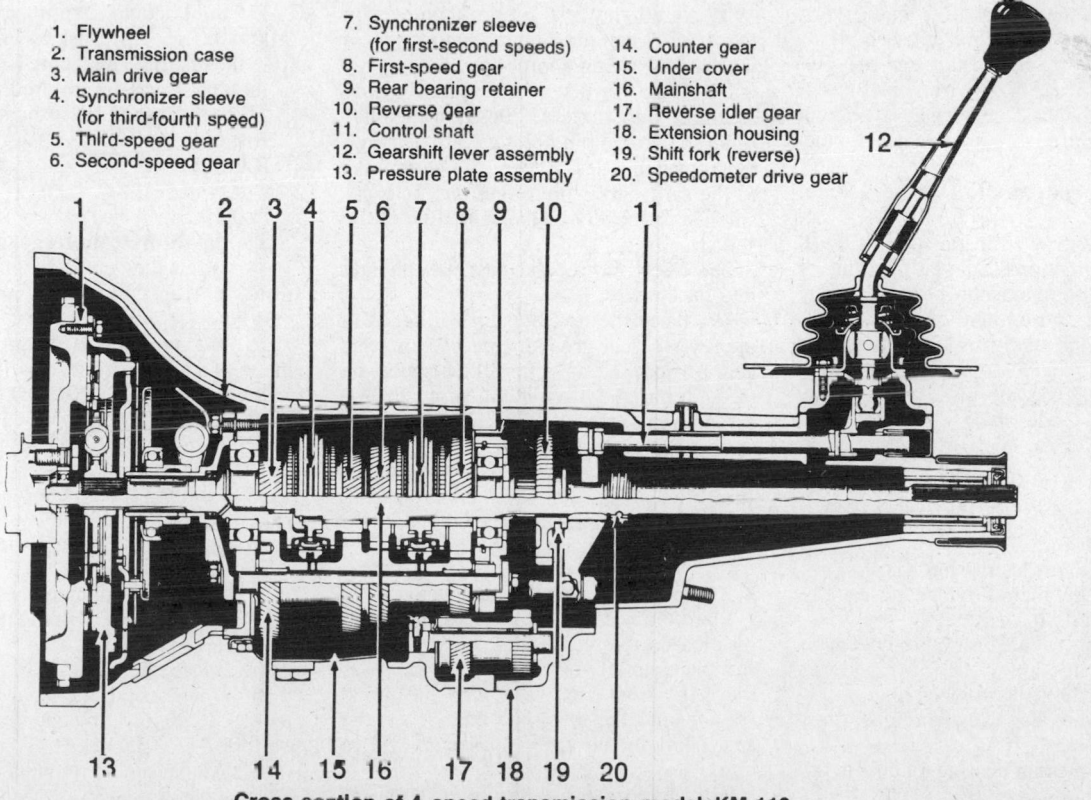

Cross section of 4-speed transmission model, KM 110

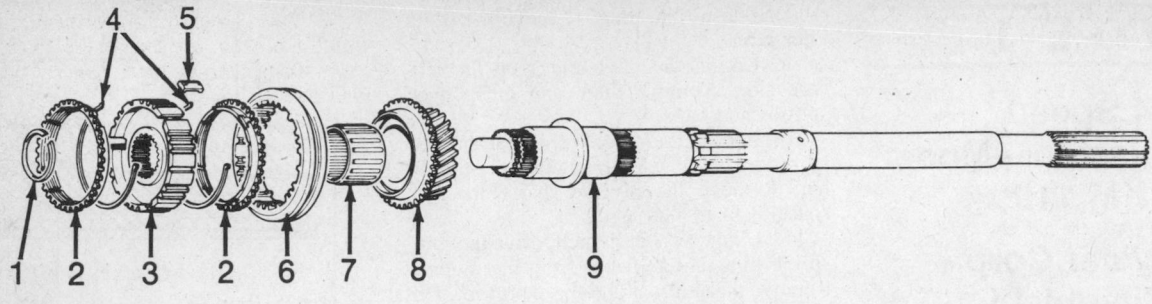

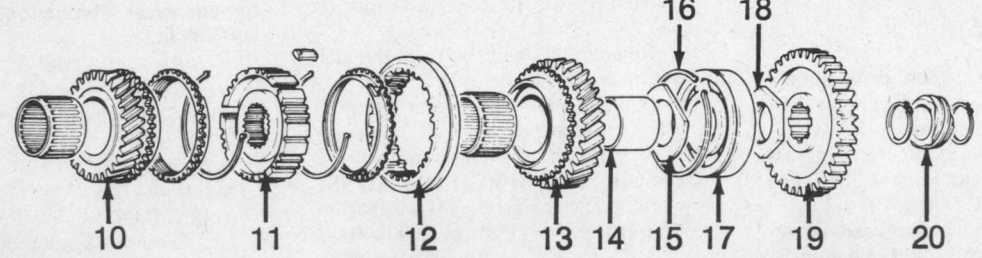

1. Snap-ring
2. Synchronizer ring
3. Synchronizer hub (3rd-4th speeds)
4. Synchronizer spring
5. Synchronizer piece
6. Synchronizer sleeve (3rd-4th speeds)
7. Needle bearing

8. 3rd-speed gear
9. Mainshaft
10. 2nd-speed gear
11. Synchronizer hub (1st-2nd speeds)
12. Synchronizer sleeve (1st-2nd speeds)
13. Low-speed gear
14. Spacer bushing

15. Spacer
16. Snap-ring
17. Ball bearing
18. Locknut
19. Reverse gear
20. Speedometer drive gear

Exploded view of mainshaft components

Snap-Ring Code (in.):
None 0.085
Yellow 0.087
Green 0.090
Blue 0.093

10. Place the needle bearings and the second gear on the mainshaft from the rear.

11. Install the synchronizer assembly.

12. Check and adjust the end-play to 0.0012–0.0075 in.

13. Place the first gear spacer, middle bearings, synchronizer, and first gear on the shaft.

14. Adjust end-play to 0.0012–0.0075 in.

15. Spacer must be installed with the I mark in the direction of the ball bearing.

16. Install the mainshaft bearing with a suitable driver and tighten the locknut.

17. Install the snap-ring and retainer.

18. Adjust to give a mainshaft bearing end-play of 0.00–0.006 in.

Snap-Ring Code (in.):
None 0.057
Red 0.060
White 0.064
Yellow 0.067
Blue 0.071

19. Invert the transmission case.

20. Install the main drive gear assembly into the transmission case.

21. Place the needle bearings on the main drive gear front end.

22. Install the synchronizer ring.

23. Be certain that all synchronizer rings are in proper mesh.

24. Install the rear bearing retainer in the case.

25. Place the reverse gear in position on the mainshaft. Install the shift fork into the shift fork groove in the synchronizer sleeve. While holding the forks, place the third-fourth shift bar assembly into the case through the lower rear hole.

26. Insert the first interlock plunger in the case; drive the plunger into position with the use of an appropriate driver.

27. Place the first-second gear shift bar assembly into the case. Position the shift forks so that the pin holes are aligned with the shift bar holes. Secure the shift forks to the shift bars with spring pins into position with the slot of the centerline of the shift bar.

28. Insert the second interlock plunger into the case.

29. Place the reverse shift fork ends in the reverse gear groove. Insert the reverse gear bar into the fork. Install the spacer on the shift bar and place the reverse shift bar assembly into the case. Secure the fork to the bar with a locking bolt.

30. Position the poppet balls and springs. Insert the plugs with commercial sealant. Be certain to install the tapered end of the poppet spring toward the poppet balls.

To install the reverse idler gear:
Place the needle bearings and spacers in position on the rear reverse idler gear. Insert the assembly into the rear of the case. Place the front idler gear with the thrust washer onto the rear shaft end. Insert the gear shaft in the case and secure with a bolt.

31. Measure the size from the rear sur-face of the transmission case to the rear of the reverse idler gear.

32. Measure the depth from the extension housing end to the idler gear shaft end. Add 0.004 in. This figure is the extension housing packing thickness.

33. Subtract No. 2 from No. 1. Subtract 0.009–0.012 in. (thrust washer clearance) from the result. (This figure is the thickness of the thrust washer required.)

Thrust Washer Identification (in.):
A-0.078
B-0.085
C-0.093
D-0.100

To install the countergear:

34. Insert the needle roller bearings (20 front, 20 rear) and spacers in the front and rear holes of the countergear.

35. Be sure the spacers are installed on the outside of the roller bearings.

36. Install a 1.378 in. OD thrust washer on the rear end.

37. Install a 1.181 in. ID thrust washer on the rear end.

38. Holding the countergear cluster inside the case, install the countergear shaft from the rear and properly mesh the gears.

39. Select a tear thrust washer to give 0.002–0.007 in. countergear end-play.

40. Secure the rear shaft end with a stopper plate.

41. Place the front bearing retainer in position and install the front bearing.

42. Bearing-to-retainer clearance should be 0.002–0.0012 in.

43. Place the speedometer drive gear on the mainshaft.

44. There should be no clearance between the speedometer gear and the snapring.

45. Shim if necessary.

46. Connect the extension housing to the transmission case.

47. When installing the washers, install with the bulged side toward the bolt head.

48. Install the transmission and backup light switch.

49. Next, install the locking plate and the transmission driven gear.

50. Finally, secure the under-cover to the transmission.

51. Place the gear lever in the first gear gate.

52. Be sure the nylon bushing is in the vertical position.

53. With the transmission in the car, apply sealant to the packings and grease bushings.

54. Insert the clutch control shaft into the transmission from the left-hand side.

55. Assemble the shift fork and springs onto the shaft.

56. Align the shift fork with the clutch control shaft.

57. Drive the spring pin into the pin hole and set the spring.

58. Be certain that the spring pin has its slot on the centerline of the clutch control shaft.

1. Shift rail (3rd-4th speed)
2. Shift rail (1st-2nd speed)
3. Shift fork (3rd-4th speed)
4. Shift fork (1st-2nd speed)
5. Spring pin
6. Selector (3rd-4th speed)

7. Selector (1st-2nd speed)
8. Shift fork (Reverse)
9. Shift rail (Reverse)
10. Distance piece
11. Interlock plunger

Exploded view of shift rail components

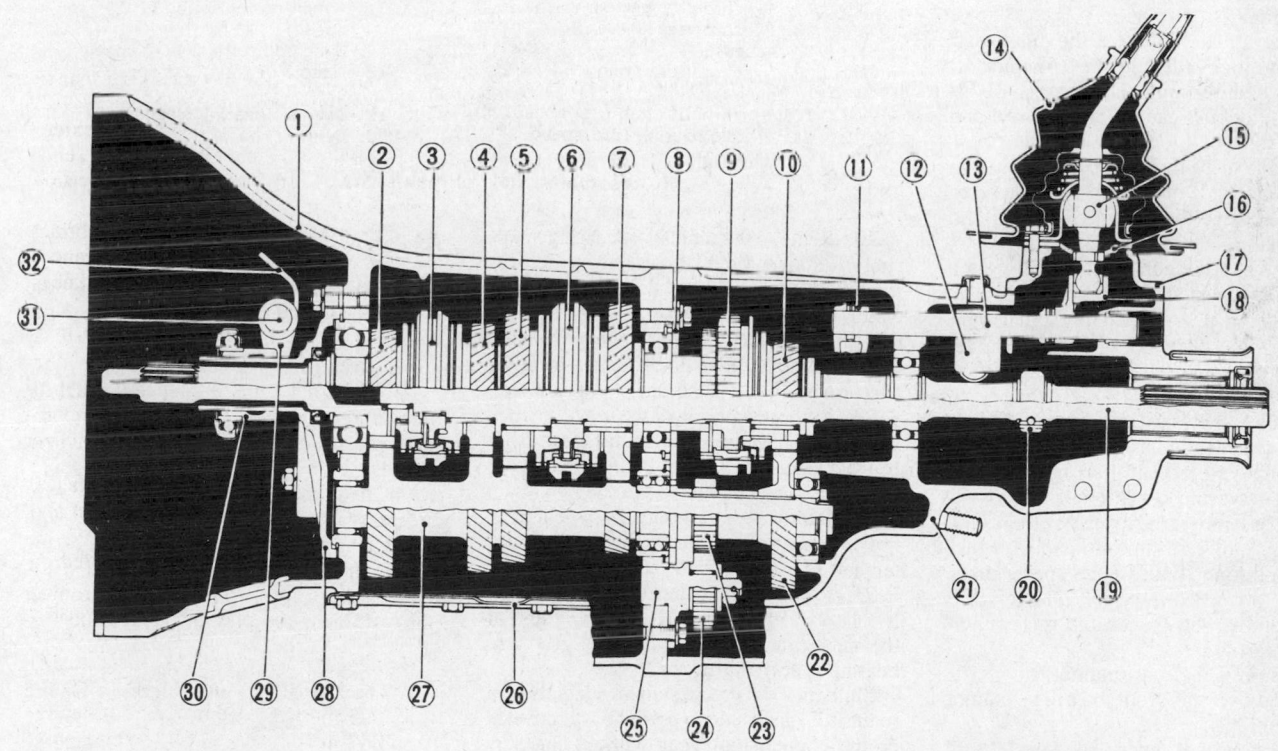

1. Transmission case
2. Main drive pinion
3. Synchronizer assy (3-4 speed)
4. 3rd speed gear
5. 2nd speed gear
6. Synchronizer assy (1-2 speed)
7. 1st speed gear
8. Rear bearing retainer
9. Synchronizer assy (overdrive)
10. Overdrive gear
11. Control finger
12. Neutral return finger
13. Control shaft
14. Control level cover
15. Control lever assy
16. Stopper plate
17. Control housing
18. Change shifter
19. Mainshaft
20. Speedometer drive gear
21. Extension housing
22. Counter overdrive gear
23. Counter reverse gear
24. Reverse idler gear
25. Reverse idler gear shaft
26. Under cover
27. Counter gear
28. Front bearing retainer
29. Clutch shift arm
30. Release bearing carrier
31. Clutch control shaft
32. Return spring

Cross section of 5-speed transmission, model KM 119

TYPE 2

5 Speed Transmission—Model KM 119

Chrysler Corp./ Mitsubishi

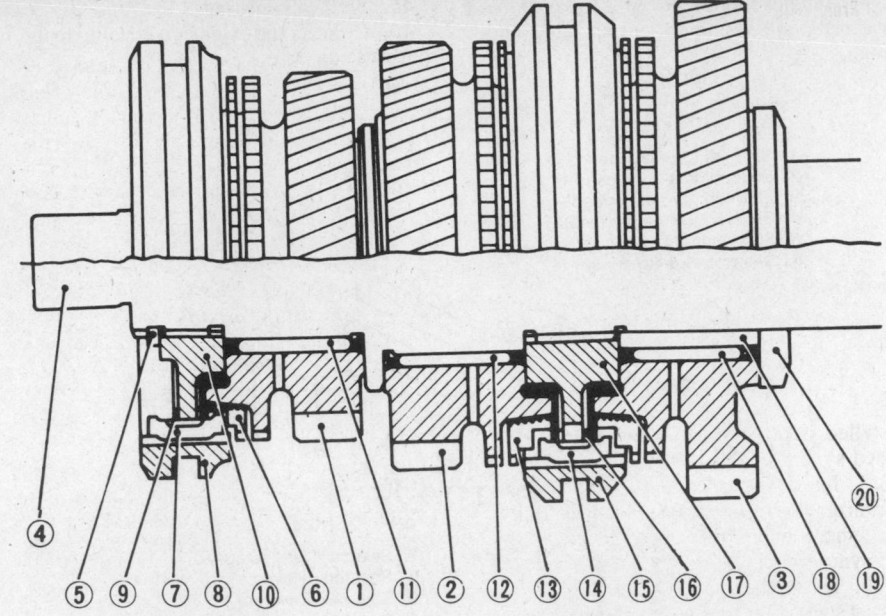

DISASSEMBLY

1. Remove the clutch assembly.
2. Remove the under cover.
3. Remove the back-up lamp switch. Remove the steel ball from the extension housing.
4. Remove the extension housing assembly, with the gearshift lever placed in the reverse and overtop position.
5. Remove the snap-ring. Remove the speedometer drive gear and the steel ball. Also remove the gear front snap-ring.
6. Remove the mainshaft rear bearing. Remove the bearing front snap-ring.
7. Remove the reverse idler gear and related parts.
8. Loosen and remove the mainshaft intermediate locknut and the countershaft gear rear end locknut. The mainshaft intermediate locknut cannot be removed and therefore is to be loosened only.
9. Remove the three poppet springs from the right-hand side of the transmission case, and then remove three poppet springs and three balls.
10. Remove the cotter pin retaining the 1-2 and 3-4 speed shift forks.
11. Pull the 1-2 speed shift rail toward the rear of the case. Remove the counter overdrive gear and the ball bearing simultaneously with the rail.
12. Pull the 3-4 speed shift rail out toward the rear of the case.
13. Remove the mainshaft nut.
14. Remove the overdrive-reverse synchronizer assembly, the overdrive gear, and the overdrive-reverse shift rail and shift fork at the same time. Pull off the spacer also.
15. Remove two interlock plungers.
16. Remove the spacer and the counter reverse gear.
17. Remove the rear retainer.
18. Remove the front bearing retainer and spacer.
19. Insert rear stopper plate special tool between the clutch gear and synchronizer ring of the 3rd speed gear, and the front stopper plate between the clutch gear and the synchronizer ring of the main drive gear.

NOTE: The front and rear stopper plates inserted are special tools used to prevent the 3-4 speed synchronizer from damage by the main drive gear bearing when these bearings are removed or installed.

1. 3rd speed gear
2. 2nd speed gear
3. 1st speed gear
4. Mainshaft
5. Snap ring
6. Synchronizer ring (3-4 speed)
7. Synchronizer piece
8. Synchronizer sleeve (3-4 speed)
9. Synchronizer spring (3-4 speed)
10. Synchronizer hub (3-4 speed)
11. Needle bearing (3rd speed gear)
12. Needle bearing (2nd speed gear)
13. Synchronizer ring (1-2 speed)
14. Synchronizer piece
15. Synchronizer sleeve (1-2 speed)
16. Synchronizer spring (1-2 speed)
17. Synchronizer hub (1-2 speed)
18. Needle bearing (1st speed gear)
19. 1st gear bearing sleeve
20. Bearing spacer

Assembled view of mainshaft

20. Remove the mainshaft bearing snap-ring. Remove the ball bearing. After removal of the bearing, slide special tool Mainshaft Support in place of the bearing over the mainshaft to support the mainshaft.
21. Remove the main drive gear bearing snap-rings. Pull off the bearing.
22. Remove special tools.
23. Remove the countershift gear front bearing snap-ring, of the countershaft gear front bearing.
24. Remove the countershaft gear rear bearing snap-ring, and remove the countershaft rear bearing.
25. Remove mainshaft adapter special tool. Lower the mainshaft assembly and at the same time take the 1st speed gear rear bearing spacer out of the case.

Shift the 3-4 speed synchronizer sleeve to the 3rd speed side to permit easy removal of the countershaft gear without interference with the sleeve.
26. Remove the countershaft gear.
27. Remove the 1-2 speed and 3-4 speed shift forks.
28. Remove the main drive gear.
29. Remove the mainshaft. Disassemble the mainshaft related parts. The synchronizer hub, sleeve, piece and spring, and the bearings for the 3-4 speed should be so laid as to prevent confusion with the 1-2 speed parts.

ASSEMBLY

1. Slide the 3rd speed gear and the needle bearing over the mainshaft from the front.
2. Install the synchronizer ring.
3. Assemble the 3-4 speed synchronizer hub and sleeve. Insert the synchronizer pieces, then install the synchronizer springs.
4. Install the assembled 3-4 speed synchronizer assembly on the mainshaft, with the synchronizer piece fitted into the ring groove in the synchronizer. Install a selected snap-ring so that the synchronizer hub will have end-play of 0–.003 in.

Thickness:	Identification Color:
.085 in.	Blue
.087 in.	None
.090 in.	Brown
.093 in.	White

5. Slide the 2nd speed gear and needle bearing over the mainshaft from the rear end.
6. Install the synchronizer ring.
7. Assemble the 1-2 speed synchronizer hub and sleeve. Insert the synchronizer piece and install the synchronizer spring. The synchronizer spring should be

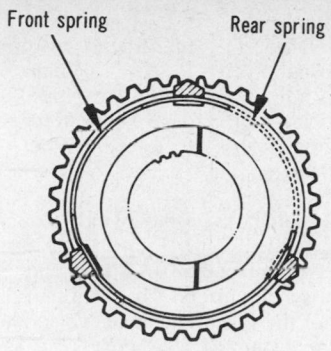

Spring installation

installed in the same manner as the 3-4 speed synchronizer spring.

8. Install the assembled 1-2 speed synchronizer assembly on the mainshaft, fitting the synchronizer piece into the groove in the synchronizer.

9. Install the synchronizer ring. Install the 1st speed gear, needle bearing and sleeve.

10. Install the bearing spacer. Check to see if, when the bearing spacer is pressed firmly forward, the 1st and 2nd speed gears have an end-play in excess of 0.001–0.007 in. Check the gear and hub ends for wear.

11. Install the mainshaft.

12. Install the synchronizer ring and the needle bearing to the main drive gear, and install the main drive gear.

13. Install the 1-2 speed and 3-4 speed shift forks. Shift the 3-4 speed synchronizer sleeve to 3rd speed side until the 1st speed gear rear bearing spacer is out of the case.

14. Install the countershaft gear.

15. Insert countershaft gear support special tool into the case to support the countergear.

16. After installing the snap-ring, install the countershaft gear bearing.

17. To install the countershaft gear front bearing, first install the outer race only into the transmission case and then install the needle bearing. The outer race and needle bearing, if assembled before installation, will damage the countershaft at the time of installation. To install the countershaft gear bearing, attach the snap-ring to the outer race and, using an aluminum rod, drive the bearing into place while tapping the circumference of the outer race evenly. Do not attempt to force the outer race into position.

18. Support the rear of the mainshaft.

19. Insert front stopper plate tool between the main drive gear and the synchronizer ring and insert the rear stopper plate tool between the 3rd speed gear and the synchronizer ring, with the stamped tool number on the tools directed to the front of the transmission.

20. To install the main drive gear bearing, first install the snap-ring to the bearing, and then using a bearing installer, drive the bearing into position. Subsequently, install the snap-ring (small) on the main drive gear. This snap-ring must be selected and installed to obtain 0–.002 in. clearance between the bearing inner race and the snap-ring.

Thickness:	Identification Color:
.087 in.	Dark Blue
.089 in.	Brown
.090 in.	Orange
.092 in.	Blue
.093 in.	Green

21. Install the snap-ring to the mainshaft bearing. Drive the bearing into proper position. Remove front and rear stopper plates.

22. Install the oil seal in the front bearing retainer.

23. Before installing the front bearing retainer, check the clearance between front bearing retainer and main drive gear. Select and install a spacer to obtain 0–0.004 in. To measure the clearance, check the amount of bearing projection (A) from the front end of the case and the depth (B) of the retainer. The thickness of the spacer to be installed

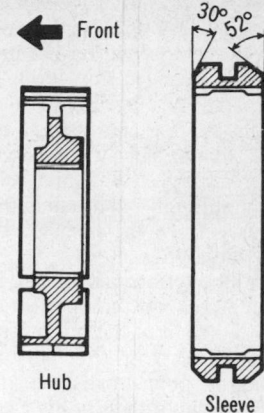

3-4-speed synchronizer

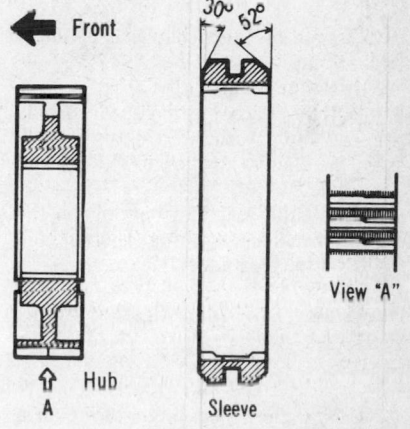

1-2-speed synchronizer

can be obtained from the formula (B + .3 (thickness of gasket) − A = Clearance). (0–.004 in.)

Thickness:	Identification Color:
.033 in.	Black
.037 in.	None
.040 in.	Red
.044 in.	White
.047 in.	Yellow
.051 in.	Blue
.054 in.	Green

24. Install the front bearing retainer in the transmission case.

25. Install the rear retainer.

26. Install the counter reverse gear and the spacer with the relieved side toward the bearing.

27. Install two interlock plungers.

28. Assemble the overdrive-reverse synchronizer.

NOTE: The synchronizer spring should be installed in the same manner as the 3–4 speed synchronizer.

29. Install the spacer on the mainshaft from the rear. Install the synchronizer ring, overdrive gear, needle bearing and sleeve to the synchronizer assembly assembled above.

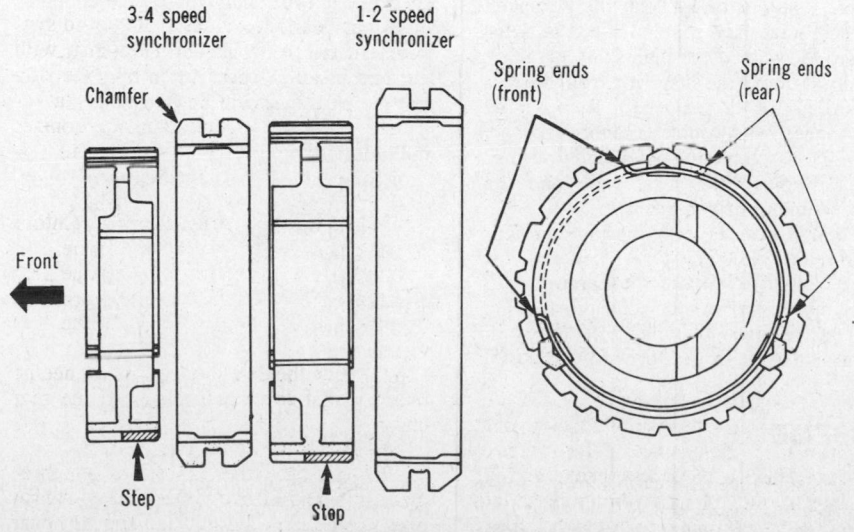

Assembled view of synchronizers

30. Install the mainshaft locknut.

31. Insert the 3-4 speed shift rail into the case from the rear and further into the 1-2 speed and 3-4 speed shift forks.

32. Insert the 1-2 speed shift rail into the case from the rear and further into the shift forks. At the same time, align the counter-overdrive gear with the relieved portion of the shift rail and install both parts simultaneously since they cannot be installed individually.

33. Install the spring pins into the holes. In this case the pin must not project out of the fork, and the slit of the pin must be in the direction of the axis of the shift rail.

34. Install the poppet balls and springs. Install the plugs until their heads are flush with the case surface and then apply sealant to them. The springs must be installed with their tapered ends directed inside (on the ball side).

35. Tighten the mainshaft and countershaft gear nuts.

36. Insert the reverse idler shaft into the case. Install the spacer bushing, gear, needle bearing and thrust washer. The thrust washer must be installed with the ground side on the gear side.

37. Install the rear ball bearing on the mainshaft. Install the snap-ring. There should be 0–0.007 in. clearance.

Thickness:	Identification Color:
.0591 in.	Red
.0630 in.	White

38. Install the speedometer drive gear and snap-ring.

39. Assemble the extension housing.

40. Install the extension housing assembly in the case.

When installing the extension housing, tilt the change shifter fully down to the left and install the change lever in the groove provided in the selector. Install the back-up light switch.

41. Install neutral return plungers A and B, springs and steel ball, and spring.

42. Install the under cover and gasket.

43. Install the transmission control lever.

TYPE 3

5 Speed Transmission—Model KM 132

Chrysler Corp./ Mitsubishi

DISASSEMBLY

1. Remove the clutch release bearing and carrier.

2. Remove the spring pin and the clutch control shaft. Remove the felt, return spring and clutch shift arm.

3. Remove the case cover.

4. Remove the back-up light switch.

5. Remove the extension housing.

6. Remove the speedometer drive gear.

7. Remove the ball bearing from the mainshaft rear end.

8. Loosen three poppet spring plugs, then remove three poppet springs and three balls.

9. Remove the 3-4 and 1-2 speed shift fork spring pins. Pull off each shift rail toward the rear of the transmission case, then remove the shift fork. Remove the interlock plunger.

10. Remove the overdrive and reverse shift forks spring pins, shift rails and forks.

11. Loosen the locknuts (mainshaft and countershaft rear ends).

12. Pull off the counter overdrive gear and the ball bearing at the same time using a puller. Remove the spacer and the counter reverse gear.

13. Remove the overdrive gear and sleeve from the mainshaft. Remove the overtop synchronizer assembly and spacer.

14. Remove the reverse idler gear.

15. Remove the rear bearing retainer.

16. Drive the reverse idler gear shaft from inside the case.

17. Remove the front bearing retainer.

18. With the countergear pressed to the rear, remove the rear bearing snap-ring. Remove the counter rear bearing.

19. Remove the counter front bearing.

20. Remove the countergear from the inside of the case.

21. Remove the main drive pinion from the front of the case. Remove the main drive pinion bearing.

22. Remove the mainshaft bearing snapring. Remove the ball bearing.

23. Pull the mainshaft assembly from the case.

24. Disassemble the mainshaft in the following order:

a. Remove the 1st gear, the 1-2 speed synchronizer and the 2nd speed gear toward the rear of the mainshaft.

b. Remove the snap-ring from the forward end of the mainshaft. Remove the 3-4 speed synchronizer and the 3rd gear.

25. Disassemble the extension housing.

a. Remove the lock plate and the speedometer driven gear.

b. Remove the plug, spring and neutral return plunger.

c. When removing the control shaft assembly, pull off the lock pin locking the gear shifter. To remove the lock pin, press the gear shifter forward and pull it off.

ASSEMBLY

1. Install the ball bearing on the main drive pinion. Install a selective snap-ring so that there will be 0–0.002 in. clearance between the snap-ring and the bearing.

Thickness of Snap-Ring:	Identification Color:
.0906 in.	White
.0925 in.	None
.0945 in.	Red
.0965 in.	Blue
.0984 in.	Yellow

2. Install the mainshaft in the following order.

a. Assemble the 3-4 speed and 1-2 speed synchronizers. The front and rear ends of the synchronizer sleeve and hub can be identified as shown. The synchronizer spring can be installed as shown.

b. Install the needle bearing, the 3rd speed gear, the synchronizer ring, and the 3-4 speed synchronizer assembly on to the mainshaft from the front end. Select and install a snap-ring of proper size so that the 3-4 speed synchronizer hub end-play will be 0–0.003 in.

Thickness of Snap-Ring:	Identification Color:
.0846 in.	None
.0874 in.	Yellow
.0902 in.	Green
.0929 in.	White

c. Check the 3rd gear end-play (.0016–.0079 in.).

d. Install the needle bearing, the 2nd speed gear, the synchronizer assembly, the bearing sleeve, the needle bearing, the 1st speed gear, and the bearing spacer on the mainshaft from the rear. With the bearing spacer pressed forward, check the 2nd and 1st gear end-play (0.0016–0.0079 in.).

3. Install the mainshaft into the transmission case and drive in the mainshaft center bearing.

4. Install the needle bearing and the synchronizer ring. Install the main drive pinion assembly into the case from the front.

5. Install the countershaft gear into the case. Drive the front bearing into the case.

6. Install the snap-ring on the countershaft rear bearing.

7. Install the front bearing retainer. Select and install a spacer of proper size so that the clearance will be 0–0.0039 in.

Thickness of Spacer:	Identification Color:
.0030 in.	Black
.0366 in.	None
.0402 in.	Red
.0437 in.	White
.0472 in.	Yellow
.0508 in.	Blue
.0543 in.	Green

Replace the front bearing retainer oil seal.

8. Install the rear bearing retainer.

9. Install the reverse idler gear shaft.

10. Install the needle bearing, the reverse idler gear and the thrust washer. Check the reverse idler gear end-play (.0047–.0110 in.). Install the thrust washer with the ground side toward the gear side.

1. Transmission case
2. Main drive pinion
3. Synchronizer assy (3-4 speed)
4. 3rd speed gear
5. 2nd speed gear
6. Synchronizer assy (1-2 speed)
7. 1st speed gear
8. Rear bearing retainer
9. Synchronizer assy (overtop)
10. Overtop gear
11. Control finger
12. Neutral return finger
13. Control shaft
14. Control lever cover
15. Control lever assy
16. Stopper plate
17. Control housing
18. Change shifter
19. Mainshaft
20. Speedometer drive gear
21. Extension housing
22. Counter overtop gear
23. Counter reverse gear
24. Reverse idler gear
25. Reverse idler gear shaft
26. Case cover
27. Counter gear
28. Front bearing retainer
29. Clutch shift arm
30. Release bearing carrier
31. Clutch control shaft
32. Return spring

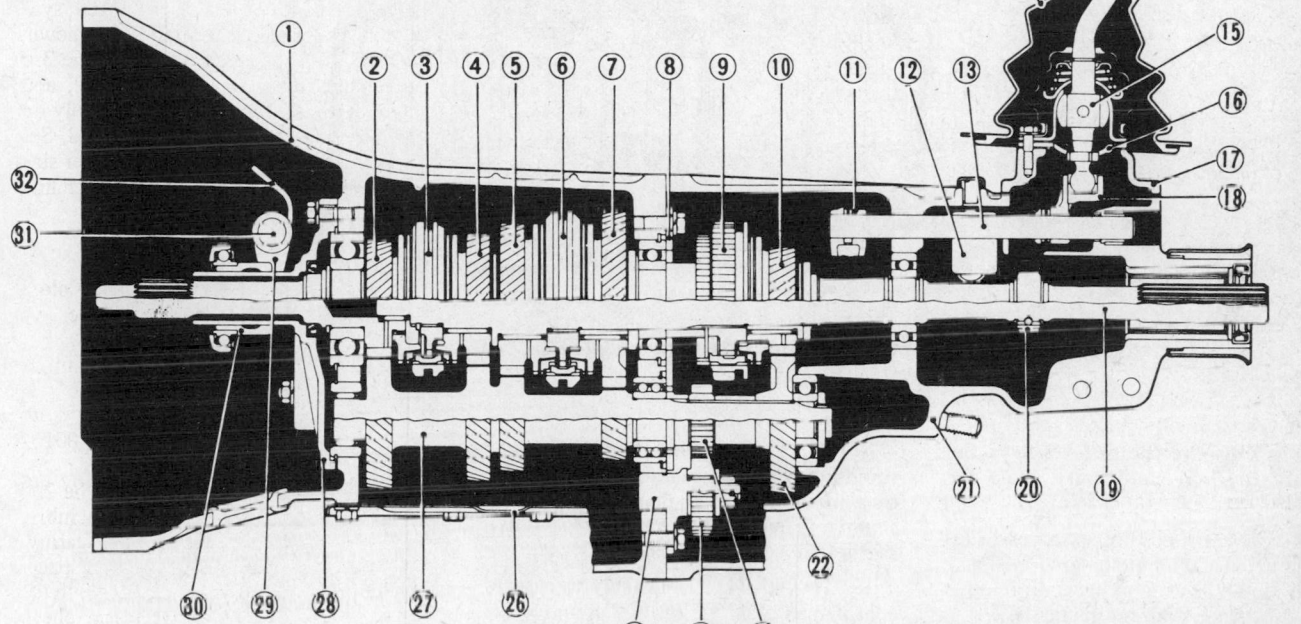

Cross section of 5-speed transmission, model KM 132

11. Assemble the overdrive synchronizer.

12. Install the spacer, the stop plate, the overdrive synchronizer assembly, the overdrive gear bearing sleeve, the needle bearing, the synchronizer ring and the overdrive gear in the written order on to the mainshaft from the rear end. Check the overdrive gear end-play.

13. Install the spacer, the counter reverse gear, the spacer, the counter overdrive gear and the ball bearing on to the countershaft gear from the rear end.

14. Insert the 3-4 and 1-2 speed shift forks into respective synchronizer sleeves. Insert each shift rail from the rear of the case. Lock the shift forks and rails with spring pins. Install an interlock plunger between shift rails. The pin should be installed with the slit in the axial direction of the shift rail.

15. Insert the ball and poppet spring into each shift rail. Install the poppet spring with the small end on the ball side.

16. Install the ball bearing on to the rear end of the mainshaft.

17. Install the speedometer drive gear.

18. Install the extension housing. Turn the change shifter fully down to the left. Make sure the forward end of the control finger is snugly fitted in the slot of the shift lug.

19. Install the neutral return plungers (A) and (B), the spring, and resistance spring and ball. Tighten each plug till its top is flush with the boss top surface.

20. Install the speedometer driven gear sleeve into the extension housing and into mesh with the drive gear.

21. Install the back-up light switch. Remember the steel ball.

22. Install the under cover.

23. Insert the clutch control shaft. Install the packing (felt), the return spring and the clutch shift arm. The spring pin should be installed in such a manner that the slip will be at right angles with the axis of the control shaft.

24. Install the transmission control level assembly. Fill the gear shifter area with grease.

25. After reassembly, rotate the drive pinion to see if it rotates smoothly.

TYPE 4

4 Speed Transmission—Models 262/8,9

BMW

DISASSEMBLY

1. Remove the console bracket from the rear of the transmission housing.

2. Remove the rear crossmember and the exhaust system bracket.

3. Slide the spring sleeve cover from the selector rod connector and drive the round pin from the coupler. Remove the selector rod connector.

4. Mount the transmission securely and drain the lubricating oil.

5. Remove the front cover retaining bolts and remove the cover with shims.

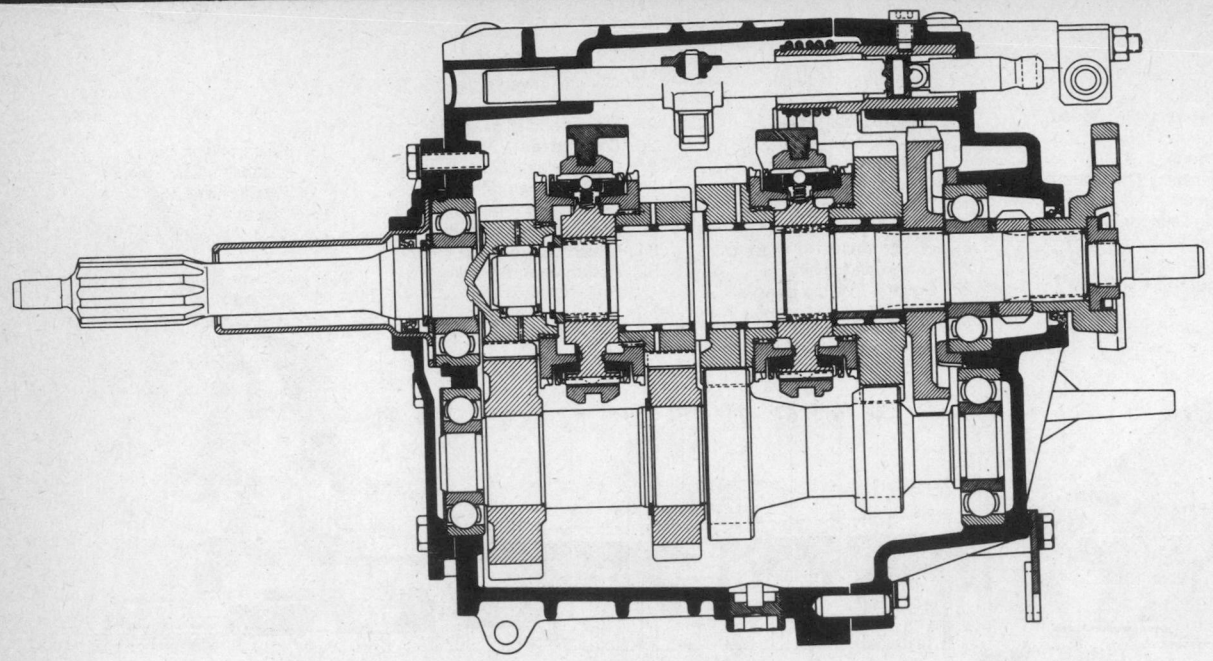

Cross section of 4-speed transmission, model 262/8, 9 (Getrag)

NOTE: Observe the difference in the length of the bolts and mark them for assembly.

6. Remove the circlip, spacer and support disc from the input shaft.

7. Using a bearing puller tool, remove the front bearing from the input shaft.

8. Using a bearing puller tool, remove the countershaft bearing.

9. Remove the selector lever lockpin cover, the lockpin and spring from the upper front side of the transmission case.

10. Remove the back-up light switch from the left front side of the transmission case.

11. Remove the front transmission case retaining bolts and remove the case from over the gear train.

12. Loosen the reverse gear selector lever holding bolt from outside the rear surface of the case, far enough so that the lever can be removed.

13. Using a pin punch, remove the lockpins from the 3rd-4th and reverse selector rods and forks.

14. Pull the reverse gear selector rod from the rear case. Do not lose the detent balls.

15. Turn the selector shaft so that the 3rd-4th gear selector rod can be pulled from the rear case. Do not lose the detent balls.

16. Install an output flange holding tool or equivalent on the output shaft flange, straighten the retaining nut lock-washer and remove the retaining nut from the shaft.

NOTE: Certain transmissions will have a collared nut without a lock washer and will require the use of a thread-lock compound.

17. Remove the rear bearing cover retaining bolts and remove the cover.

NOTE: The speedometer driven gear should have been removed during the transmission R & R procedure. If not, remove it before the rear bearing housing is taken from the case.

18. Heat the rear transmission case to approximately 175°F (80°C). Remove the input shaft, countershaft, reverse gear, 1st-2nd gear selector rod and the selector forks from the case.

NOTE: The use of wet hot towels placed over the case is recommended, rather than the use of open heat. Do not lose the balls and spring from the selector rod detents.

19. Remove the rollers from the selector shaft and remove the shaft from the case.

20. Remove all selector rod sealing covers from the case.

21. Remove the input shaft and its needle bearing cage. Remove the circlip, support disc, synchronizer assembly with the synchronizer (baulk) rings attached, the needle bearing cage and the 3rd gear.

22. Place the output shaft in a press or equivalent tool and remove the 2nd gear, synchronizer assembly with the synchronizer (baulk) rings, 1st gear, support ring, ball bearing, support disc and the speedometer drive gear from the shaft.

--- CAUTION ---
Mark the synchronizer assemblies so that they can be reassembled with their respective gears.

23. The 4th and 3rd gears can be pressed from the countergear assembly. A circlip must be removed before the 3rd gear can be pressed off.

--- CAUTION ---
Note the direction of the gears during the removal.

24. Remove the sliding sleeve from the synchronizer hub. Do not lose the balls, springs and pressure pads from the hub.

25. The seals, gaskets, necessary replacement parts should be renewed in preparation for assembly.

ASSEMBLY

1. Assemble the synchronizer sliding sleeve to the synchronizer hub, halfway, and install the springs, pressure pads and the balls in their positions on the hub. Press the balls in until the sleeve can be slid over the hub completely.

NOTE: The convex face of the pressure pads must face the sliding sleeve.

2. Install the synchronizer (baulk) rings in place on the synchronizer assembly and measure the distance between the ring and the body, in the area of the ring stops. The clearance should not be less than 0.031 inch (0.8 mm) for used rings, nor less than 0.039 inch (1.0 mm) for new rings.

3. Assemble the countergear assembly by pressing the 3rd gear in place, after heating the gear to approximately 250–300°F (120–150°C). Install the circlip in place on the shaft.

4. Press the 4th gear in place on the shaft after heating the gear to the same temperatures as the 3rd gear.

NOTE: Both the 3rd and 4th gears must be installed with the raised collar on the gear bore, facing the 2nd gear.

1. Input shaft
2. Needle bearing cage
3. Circlip
4. Support disc
5. Synchronizer ring
6. Hub with sliding sleeve
7. Synchronizer ring
8. Needle bearing cage
9. Gear wheel
10. 2nd gear
11. Needle bearing cage
12. Synchronizer ring
13. Hub with sliding sleeve
14. Synchronizer ring
15. 1st gear
16. Needle bearing cage
17. Spacer
18. Reverse gear
19. Support ring
20. Ball bearing
21. Support disc
22. Speedometer drive gear

Input and mainshaft components

5. Install the 2nd speed gear and needle cage on the rear of the output shaft and press into place. Position the 1st/2nd synchronizer assembly in place on the shaft and press into place.

NOTE: Assemble the synchronizer (baulk) rings so that they are reused with the same gears.

6. Install the 1st gear, the needle cage, spacer, reverse gear, support ring, ball bearing, support disc and the speedometer gear in place on the shaft.

7. Install the 3rd gear, needle cage, synchronizer assembly, support disc and circlip in place on the front of the output shaft.

NOTE: Assemble the synchronizer (baulk) rings so that they are reused with the same gears.

8. Install the needle bearing in the bore of the input shaft and install the input shaft onto the front of the output shaft.

The rear bearing shim size must be determined before the transmission is reassembled. The following procedure should be followed:
   a. Measure the case depth to the bearing seat with a depth gauge.
   b. Measure the bearing seat depth of the bearing bracket with a depth gauge.
   c. Measure the bearing outer race thickness in width.

   d. Add the results of the case and bracket together and subtract the thickness of the bearing race from the results to obtain the desired thickness of the shim.

9. Install two guide pins into the rear bearing holder and with the use of both hands, install the output shaft, countershaft and reverse gear assemblies into the transmission rear case. Heat the case to 175°F (80°C).

— CAUTION —
Do not drop the gear assemblies during the installation.

10. Install the remaining bolts into the rear bearing holder and tighten securely. Remove the guide pins.

11. Mount the reverse gear selector lever to the selector rod and secure with the rolled pin.

12. Install the selector rod into the transmission case. Install the rollers on the selector shaft.

13. Place the selector forks on their respective sliding sleeves.

NOTE: The high selector fork is the 3rd-4th.

14. Install the detent balls as the selector rods are installed.

15. Turn the selector shaft to the reverse position and install the 1st-2nd gear selector shaft.

16. Install the 3rd-4th selector rod. Secure the selector rods to the shifting forks with the rolled pins.

17. Install the shifting rod covers in the case and seal with a sealing compound.

18. Install and secure the selector lever for the reverse gear arm. Install the bolt into the lever and do not cross thread.

19. Install the output shaft flange, the nut and tighten securely. Lock the washer, if so equipped.

20. Install a new gasket and install the transmission front case. Secure the case to the rear case with the retaining bolts and tighten securely.

21. Install the back-up light switch and the lockpin and spring.

22. Heat the grooved inner races of the countershaft and input shaft bearings and install them on their respective shafts with a bearing installing tool.

NOTE: Heat the inner races to approximately 175°F (80°C).

— CAUTION —
Be sure the bearings are seated to the shafts tightly.

23. Install the support disc, spacer and circlip on the input shaft. Be sure the circlip is engaged in its groove on the shaft.

24. To find the proper shims to be used on the front bearings, measure as outlined:

a. Measure the distance from the front of the transmission case to the outer surface of the bearing race on the input shaft and record the reading.

b. Measure the distance from the front of the transmission case to the outer surface of the bearing race on the countershaft. Record the reading.

c. Attach the gasket to the front bearing housing and measure with a depth gauge, the distance from the surface of the gasket and the inner surface of the front bearing housing seat, for both the input shaft bearing and the countershaft bearing. Record each measurement.

d. Subtract the measurement reading of the transmission case to bearing results from the results of the depth measurement of the bearing seats in the front bearing housing.

e. The difference is the size of the shims needed to properly control the end-play of the input and countershaft bearings.

25. Install the shims and retain with a coating of grease, in the front bearing cover. Install the cover on the front case and secure with the retaining bolts.

NOTE: Be sure the guide flange is installed with the front cover.

— **CAUTION** —
Install the bolts in their original positions.

26. Install the selector rod connector and install the round pin into the coupler. Slide the spring sleeve cover into its place on the coupler.

27. Install the exhaust system bracket and the rear crossmember to the transmission case.

28. Install the console bracket to the rear of the transmission case.

TYPE 5

4 Speed Transmission—Models 242/9, 18, 18.50

BMW

DISASSEMBLY

1. Remove the crossmember and exhaust system bracket from the rear of the transmission.

2. Mount the transmission securely and drain the lubricating oil from the unit. Remove the console from the transmission.

3. Remove the clutch release bearing assembly and release lever from the front of the transmission.

4. Remove the front guide sleeve and retaining bolts. Do not lose the shims.

5. Remove the circlip and shim from the input shaft.

6. Remove the case cover mounting bolts and drive the two dowel pins from the case cover.

7. Using a special case puller or equivalent, remove the case cover from the transmission case.

NOTE: The input shaft bearing will remain with the case cover as the cover is removed from the transmission case.

8. Remove the front bearing from the case cover by driving it from the rear to the front. Do not lose the accompanying shim.

9. Remove the lockpin and spring from the case.

NOTE: The lockpin maintains the selector shaft positioning.

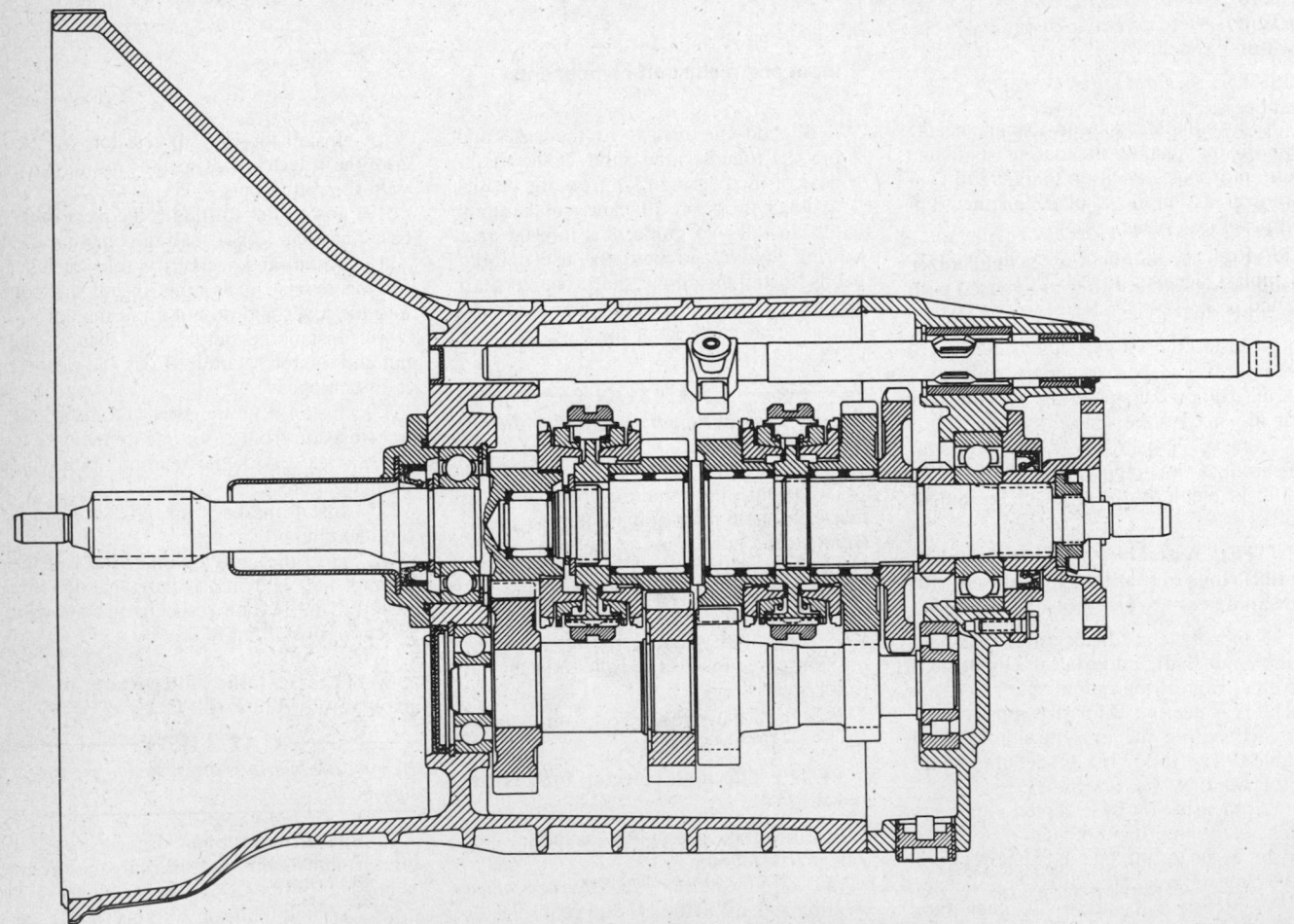

Cross section of 4-speed transmission, model 242/9 (Getrag)

10. Move the 3rd/4th selector lever and rod to the third speed position. Drive the fork retaining pin downward very carefully until the rod can be pulled out.

— CAUTION —

The fork retaining pin must be driven downward between the teeth of the synchronizer body. The pin should remain in the lower part of the selector fork.

11. Slide the locking sleeve away from the pin of the selector shaft coupler and drive the pin from the coupler.

12. Remove the selector rod by pulling it forward and out of the shifting fork.

13. Move the gear sleeve back to the neutral position and remove the selector fork.

14. Remove the bushing and the speedometer driven gear.

15. Straighten the bend in the lockplate on the output flange retaining nut. Install a flange holding tool and remove the locknut. Pull the flange from the output shaft.

16. Remove the rear bearing support ring and shims.

17. Using a special bearing puller or equivalent, remove the rear bearing from the transmission cover.

NOTE: A 0.078 inch (2.0 mm) metal strip must be placed between the 2nd and 3rd gears to prevent the pressing off of the 2nd gear synchronizer body during the removal of the rear bearing from the shaft and cover.

18. Lift the input and output shaft assemblies slightly and remove the countergear assembly from the end bearing and out of the cover.

19. Pull the selector fork, the reverse gear and the selector rod from the transmission cover. Do not lose the detent balls.

20. Remove the input and output shaft assemblies, along with the 1st/2nd selector rod and fork, from the transmission cover.

Do not lose the detent balls.

21. Remove the back-up lamp switch and the end cap for the 1st/2nd selector shaft.

22. Remove the input shaft from the output shaft and remove the 4th speed synchronizer (baulk) ring.

23. Remove the circlip from the front of the output shaft and remove the support disc, synchronizer body assembly, 3rd gear synchronizer (baulk) ring, needle bearing race and the 3rd gear from the shaft.

24. Place the output shaft into a press or equivalent, and remove the speedometer drive gear, washer, reverse gear, spacer, needle bearing race, 1st gear, synchronizer (baulk) ring, synchronizer body with the sliding sleeve, synchronizer (baulk) ring, needle bearing race and the 2nd speed gear from the shaft.

25. The 3rd and 4th gears can be pressed from the countershaft gear assembly, along with the roller bearing.

26. The pilot bearing can be removed from the bore of the input shaft.

27. The synchronizer unit can be disassembled by sliding the sleeve off the hub. The pressure pads will drop from the unit as the sleeve is removed.

28. Replace all worn, damaged or broken parts, along with new gaskets and seals.

ASSEMBLY

1. Install the synchronizer springs onto the hub with the hooked ends of the springs in different pressure pads.

2. Install the pressure pads in place and slide the sleeve, with the flat teeth locations, over the pressure pads.

3. If the 3rd and 4th gears have been removed from the countershaft, reinstall or replace the gears back on to the shaft. Heat the gears to 250 to 300°F (120 to 150°C) and install. The high collar on the bore of the 3rd and 4th gears should face the 2nd

gear. Install the bearing and race onto the shaft.

4. Place the output shaft in an upright position with the rear of the shaft up. Place the 2nd speed gear and needle bearing assembly onto the shaft. Install the 1st/2nd synchronizer assembly with the two synchronizer (baulk) rings onto the shaft, followed by the 1st speed gear, needle bearing, spacer, reverse gear wheel, washer and complete the assembly by pressing the speedometer gear onto the shaft.

NOTE: The end-play of the gear train should be 0.003 inch (0.09 mm). Adjust by changing the selective washer between the speedometer gear and the reverse gear.

5. Invert the output shaft and install the 3rd gear onto the shaft. Install the synchronizer assembly less the 4th speed synchronizer (baulk) ring onto the shaft and retain with the support disc and circlip.

Measurements Prior to Transmission Assembly

Washer type shims are used to control the end-play of the shafts and gears, while maintaining gear positioning, so that tooth contact is in proper relationship with each other. It is most important to inspect, measure and correct the shim packs to obtain the necessary preloads and clearances.

INPUT SHAFT

1. Install a 0.039 inch (1.0 mm) shim and the ball bearing into the case bore.

2. With a depth gauge, measure the distance, A, from the sealing surface of the case to the surface of the bearing race.

3. A numerical figure is electrically engraved on the input shaft and represents column B in the accompanying chart.

4. The thickness of the shim, X, needed on the input shaft can be determined by

1. Synchronizer ring
2. Circlip
3. Support disc
4. Hub and sliding sleeve
5. 3rd gear synchronizer ring
6. Needle bearing cage
7. 3rd gear

8. Speedometer drive gear
9. Washer
10. Reverse gear
11. Spacer
12. Needle bearing cage
13. 1st gear

14. Synchronizer ring
15. Hub and sliding sleeve
16. Synchronizer ring
17. Needle bearing cage
18. 2nd gear
19. Output shaft

Output shaft components

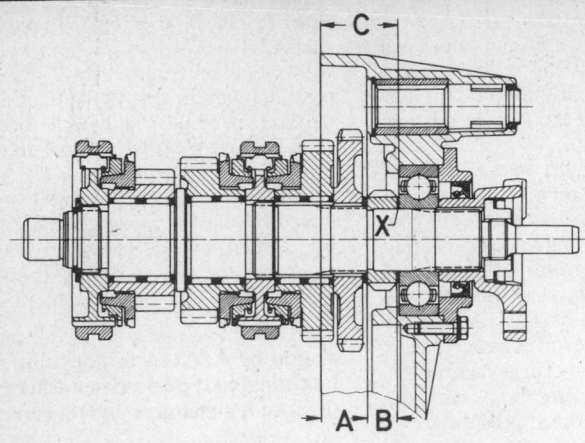

Measurement of extension case and gear assembly to determine shim "X" thickness

SPEEDOMETER GEAR–TO– TRANSMISSION CASE

1. Measure the thickness, B, of the speedometer gear.
2. Press the ball bearing into the transmission case and measure the distance, C, from the sealing surface of the case to the race of the bearing, without the gasket installed.
3. The nominal distance, A, is a predetermined distance and is used to arrive at the proper sized shim.
4. Subtract distance B from the nominal distance A. Subtract the result of A minus B from distance C, which is the proper sized shim, X, to be used between the speedometer gear and the ball bearing of the case.
5. An example is as follows;

Example:

A	22.0 mm (0.866″)	nominal distance
+ B	14.8 mm (0.582″)	

	36.8 mm (1.488″)	
C	37.0 mm (1.456″)	
−	36.8 mm (1.448″)	

X   0.2 mm (0.008″)

corresponding the measurements A and B to the chart and locating the proper shim from column X.

COUNTERSHAFT ASSEMBLY

1. Measure the distance, A, from the sealing surface of the case housing to the circlip in the bottom of the housing.
2. Install the countershaft into the transmission case bearing and measure the distance, B, from the top of the large bearing race to the sealing surface of the case, with the gasket installed.
3. Determine the thickness of the shim, C, by subtracting distance B from distance A. The result is shim C.

NOTE: The "C" shims can be used to change tooth engagement.

Transmission Assembly After Basic Measurements

1. Have the transmission case in a secure support.
2. Insert the selector rod detent balls and springs. Install the reverse gear selector rod with the reverse gear, into the case until the 1st lock is engaged.
3. Install the countershaft into the roller bearing, mounted in the case.
4. Install the input shaft on the output shaft and install the assembly into its position on the transmission case.
5. Install the predetermined shim between the speedometer gear and the ball bearing. Install the bearing into the case, but do not seat completely.
6. Using a special bearing installer tool or equivalent, seat the bearing on the output shaft and into the transmission case.
7. Check the tooth engagement of the input, output and countergear assemblies. Tooth engagement can be changed by movement of shims.
8. Install the speedometer bushing and driven gear.
9. Set the transmission assembly in the upright position with the output shaft pointing upward. Measure the distance A, from the case to the ball bearing race.
10. Measure the distance B, from the shoulder height of the sealing cover, to the surface of the gasket on the cover.
11. Subtract distance B from distance A and the result is the thickness of the needed shim between the ball bearing and the sealing cover.

"A"	"B"	"X"
153.9 mm 6.059″	45 . . . 50 mm 1.772 . . . 1.968″	0.5 mm / 0.020″
	35 . . . 40 mm 1.378 . . . 1.575″	0.6 mm / 0.024″
	25 . . . 30 mm 0.984 . . . 1.181″	0.7 mm / 0.027″
153.8 mm 6.055″	45 . . . 50 mm 1.772 . . . 1.968″	0.4 mm / 0.016″
	35 . . . 40 mm 1.378 . . . 1.575″	0.5 mm / 0.020″
	25 . . . 30 mm 0.984 . . . 1.181″	0.6 mm / 0.024″
153.7 mm 6.051″	45 . . . 50 mm 1.772 . . . 1.968″	0.3 mm / 0.012″
	35 . . . 40 mm 1.378 . . . 1.575″	0.4 mm / 0.016″
	25 . . . 30 mm 0.984 . . . 1.181″	0.5 mm / 0.020″
153.6 mm 6.047″	45 . . . 50 mm 1.722 . . . 1.968″	0.2 mm / 0.008″
	35 . . . 40 mm 1.378 . . . 1.575″	0.3 mm / 0.012″
	25 . . . 30 mm 0.984 . . . 1.181″	0.4 mm / 0.016″

Location of shim "X" and engraved measurement "B".

TYPE 6

5 Speed Transmission—Model 265/6

BMW

DISASSEMBLY

1. Remove the transmission from the vehicle and mount it on a transmission stand.
2. Drain the lubricant and then remove the console.
3. Engage 3rd gear, pull back on the spring sleeve and knock out the dowel pin. Pull off the selector rod.
4. Disconnect the extension bracket and the crossmember (with the rubber mount). Unscrew the back-up light switch.
5. Unscrew the seven mounting bolts and remove the guide flange.

NOTE: Be careful not to lose any shims upon removal of the guide flange.

6. Remove the circlip and slotted washer from around the input shaft.
7. Remove the cover, spring and lockpin.

—— CAUTION ——

There should be no end-play between the ball bearing race and the sealing cover. Remeasure and remove play with shims.

12. Secure the sealing cover and install the output flange. Install the locknut and washer. Jam the lockplate washer into the groove of the flange.
13. Install the 1st-2nd gear selector rod and fork into place. Insert the locking detent balls and springs. Secure the fork to the rod with the rolled pin.
14. Install the 3rd-4th selector fork into place on the sliding sleeve. Install the main selector rod. Install the lockpin and spring into the tapered bushing. Install the locking detent balls and springs.
15. Install the 3rd-4th gear selector rod and secure to the fork with the rolled pin. (Remove pin and reinstall from the top of the fork.)
16. Install the back-up lamp switch and the selector rod cap.
17. Install the gasket on the mating surfaces of the transmission case and housing. Install the predetermined shims on their respective locations and install the transmission housing over the gear assembly.
18. Bolt the housing to the case securely.

NOTE: It may be necessary to heat the transmission area of the input shaft to install the front bearing.

19. Install the shim and bearing onto the input shaft and housing. Install washer and circlip.
20. Install the clutch release guide sleeve and install a shim to eliminate any existing play between the guide and the bearing.
21. Measure the distance between the case and the ball bearing. This distance is A. Measure the distance from the top of the shoulder of the guide sleeve to the mating surface, with the gasket installed. This distance is B.
22. Subtract distance B from distance A and the result is the thickness of shim needed to remove the existing play between the guide and the bearing.
23. Install the selector rod coupler and

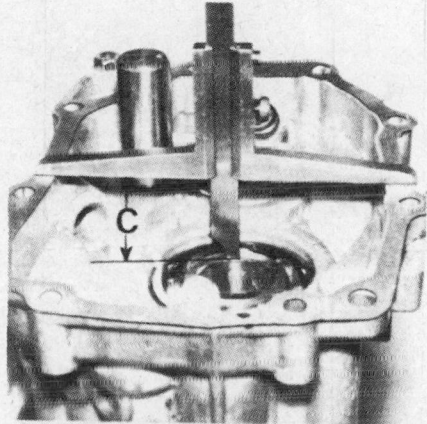

Measurement of distance between extension case edge and ball bearing. "C" equals distance.

Measurement of case edge to ball bearing ... "A" equals distance.

secure with the pin. Slide the sleeve over the pin location.
24. Install the console onto the transmission case.
25. Fill the unit with the proper level of lubricating oil.
26. Install the clutch release bearing assembly and the operating lever.
27. Install the crossmember and the exhaust system bracket.

Removing the lockpin

8. Knock out the guide pin aligning the front case and then unscrew the mounting bolts.
9. Separate the front case from the transmission.
10. Remove the lock plate from the rear case.
11. While holding the output flange with the special tool, remove the collar nut. Pull off the output flange.
12. Swing the selector shaft against its left stop and push forward; this will engage 2nd gear.
13. Unscrew the rear mounting bolts and pull off the rear case.

—— CAUTION ——

Always make sure that 2nd gear is engaged before removing the rear transmission case.

14. Remove the radial oil seal.

15. Swing down the output shaft and pull 5th gear off of the layshaft with a gear puller.

NOTE: The bearing inner race will be removed with the gear.

—————— CAUTION ——————

To avoid damage to 3rd gear when removing 5th, make sure that there is always play between 3rd gear and the layshaft. If possible, push up on the output shaft.

16. Using a puller, remove the bearing inner race from the output shaft.

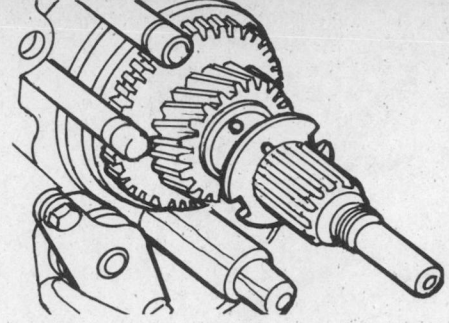

Remove the bearing inner race

17. Remove the washer and ball and then pull off 5th gear with the synchromesh ring and split needle bearing.

18. Remove the needle bearings from the selector shaft.

19. Knock the centerhold pin out of the selector shaft, pull the shaft backward and remove the selector arm.

20. Engage 2nd gear and knock out the centerhold pin.

21. Pull off and remove the rotary lock on the reversing lever, pull the selector rail forward and out and then take out 2nd gear again.

22. With the selector fork and operating

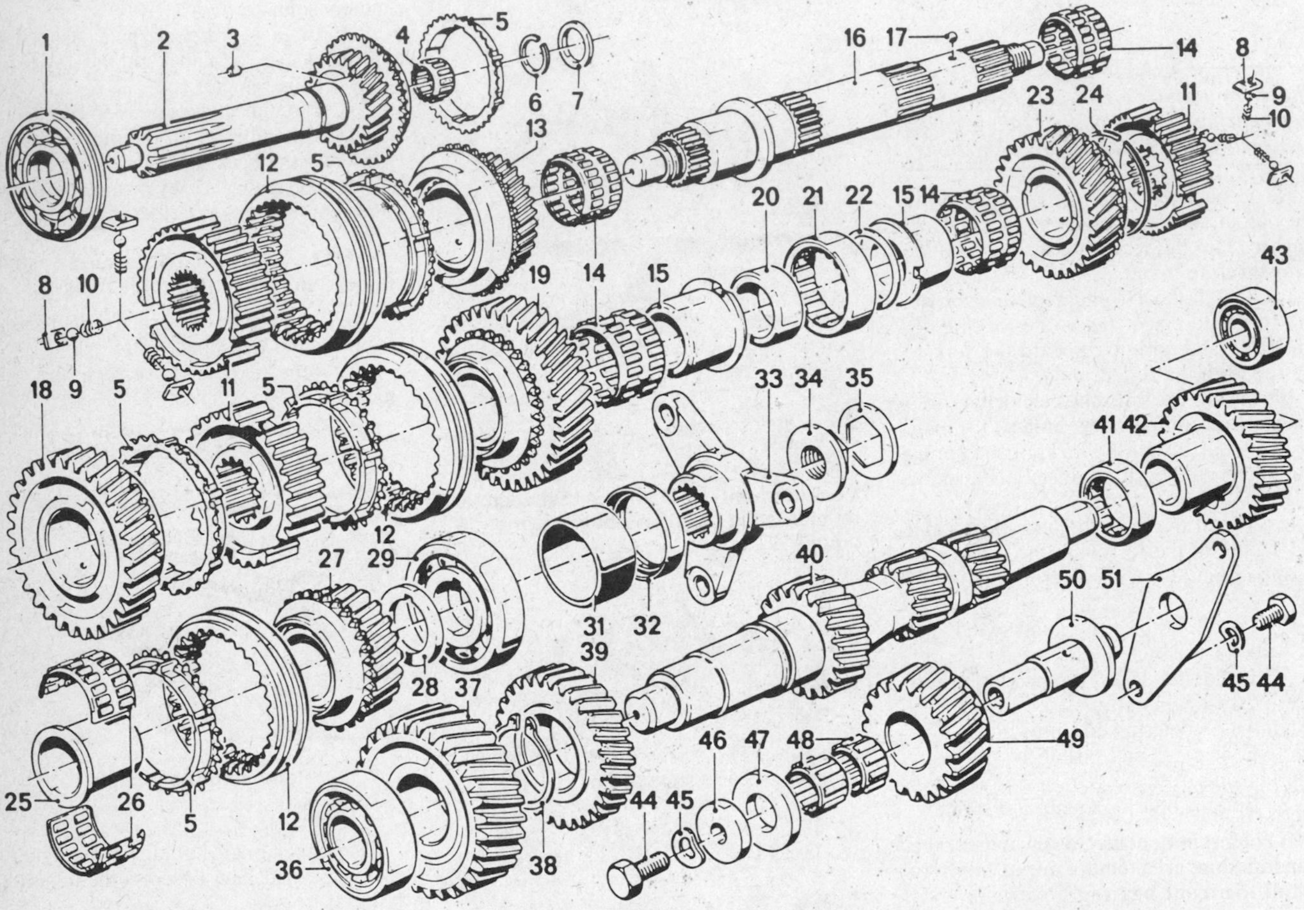

1 Ball bearing	**18** 2nd gear	**35** Lockplate
2 Input shaft with 4th gear	**19** 1st gear	**36** Roller bearing
3 Rotary lock	**20** Bearing race	**37** 4th gear
4 Needle bearing	**21** Roller bearing	**38** Circlip
5 Synchromesh ring	**22** Shim X	**39** 3rd gear
6 Circlip	**23** Reverse gear	**40** Layshaft
7 Washer	**24** Circlip	**41** Roller bearing
8 Pressure piece	**25** Bearing bush	**42** 5th gear
9 Ball	**26** Split needle bearing	**43** Roller bearing
10 Spring	**27** 5th gear	**44** Bolt
11 Guide sleeve	**28** Washer	**45** Washer
12 Sliding sleeve	**29** Ball bearing	**46** Plain washer
13 3rd gear	**31** Spacer	**47** Thrust washer
14 Needle bearing	**32** Radial oil seal	**48** Needle bearing
15 Bearing bush	**33** Output flange	**49** Reverse gear
16 Output shaft	**34** Collar nut	**50** Bearing pin
17 Ball		**51** Bearing bracket

Exploded view of the gear and shaft assembly—Type 6

sleeve toward the rear, pull out the 5th gear selector rod far enough so the centerhold pin can be knocked out.

23. Pull off the sliding sleeve and the 5th gear selector fork. Pull out the selector rod forward.

24. Pull the guide sleeve and bearing inner race off of the output shaft.

25. Remove the synchromesh ring. Pull off the reverse gear and needle bearing.

26. Engage 3rd gear and then knock out the pin.

NOTE: Knock the pin onto the tooth of 3rd gear until the selector rod can be pulled out forward. Remove the 3rd/4th gear selector rod.

27. Pull the output shaft toward the rear far enough so that the bearing inner race can be pulled off. Remove the shim.

28. Pull the input shaft, output shaft, layshaft and 1st/2nd gear selector rod out of the intermediate case.

29. Disconnect the holder and remove the reverse gear.

30. Unscrew the bolt and thrust washer holding the front end of the reverse gear shaft and remove the shaft.

ASSEMBLY

1. Install the reverse gear and holder.

NOTE: The shouldered collar of the reverse gear faces the holder.

2. Install the input/output shaft assembly into the intermediate case.

3. Install the output shaft shim. Heat the bearing bush to about 175°F and press it onto the shaft.

4. Position the needle bearing and reverse gear and then mount the synchromesh ring.

5. Knock the pin out of the 1st/2nd gear selector rod. Install the 1st/2nd gear selector fork. Push the 1st/2nd gear selector rod in against the spring. Insert the detent ball and while pushing down, push the selector rod in against the stop. Install a new centerhold pin (6 × 32mm).

6. Install the 3rd/4th gear selector fork and then repeat Step 5.

7. Insert the guide sleeve in the sliding sleeve so that the tab on the locking lever aligns with the opening in the sliding sleeve. Push the balls in far enough so that the guide sleeve slides into the sliding sleeve.

NOTE: The shouldered end of the sliding sleeve must be opposite the centering pin.

8. Install the guide sleeve so that the centering pin faces 5th gear.

9. Install the 5th/reverse gear selector fork. Insert the locking ball and push the selector rod in against the spring. Insert the detent ball and while pushing down, turn the selector rod while pushing in so that the openings are opposite the detent balls.

10. Push the selector rod in far enough so that a new centerhold pin (6 × 26mm)

can be pressed in. Push the rod and guide sleeve in against the stop.

11. Install the reverse lever with the smooth sides facing down.

12. Install the selector rail, push on the rotary lock and then press in a new pin (6 × 26mm).

13. Place a small rod in the centering pin, heat the bearing bush to about 175°F and then press it onto the output shaft.

14. Install the split needle bearing, synchromesh ring and 5th gear.

15. Mount the transmission on a press and lubricate the contact surface of the layshaft with oil. Heat 5th gear to about 300°F, mount it on the layshaft and then press it on.

NOTE: Lift and turn 5th gear until the teeth mesh.

16. Knock the bearing inner race onto the layshaft so that the collar faces the gear.

17. Insert the ball with grease and press on the washer.

18. Heat the ball bearing inner race to about 175°F and then press it onto the output shaft.

NOTE: The opening in the inner race (rotary lock) must engage with the ball in the output in the output shaft. Make a reference line to facilitate installation of the bearing race.

Make a reference line to facilitate installation of the bearing race

19. Install the selector shaft while pushing on the selector arm with the long arm facing the 3rd/4th gear selector rod. Install a new centerhold pin (6 × 32mm).

NOTE: The stop on the selector shaft must face the selector rail.

20. Hold the four needles on the selector shaft with grease.

21. Swing up the output shaft so that 2nd gear is engaged. Slide the 5th/reverse gear selector rod in until the opening is aligned with the end of the 1st/2nd gear selector rod.

22. Clean the sealing surfaces of the rear and intermediate cases thoroughly and then apply Loctite®.

NOTE: The lockpin must move easily and touch the bottom.

23. Hold the needles with grease. Position the rear transmission case making sure

that the spring of the selector arm engages on the lever.

24. Using an awl, push the lockpin into the opening of the 1st/2nd gear selector rod.

25. Bolt down the rear transmission case and then press on the bearing inner race.

26. Install the spacer over the output shaft and then press in the radial oil seal.

27. Clean the sealing surfaces of the front and intermediate cases, coat with Loctite® and then attach the front case.

28. Install the back-up light switch and the lockpin.

29. Heat the bearing inner race to 175°F, pull out the input shaft and press on the bearing race.

30. Install the slotted washer and circlip on the input shaft.

NOTE: Play between the washer and circlip should be 0–0.0035 in. Adjustment is made with different thickness circlips.

31. Check that the grooved ball bearing play of the input shaft and layshaft to the guide flange is 0.307 in. (input shaft) and 0.169 in. (layshaft)

32. Position the shims and install the guide flange.

33. Installation of the remaining components is in the reverse order of removal.

TYPE 7

5 Speed Transmission—Model FS5R90A

Datsun

DISASSEMBLY

1. Remove the transmission from the vehicle and attach it to a stand.

2. Drain the oil and then remove the shift lever assembly and damper sleeve.

3. Remove the pin from the offset lever.

4. Unscrew the mounting bolts and separate the extension housing from the transmission case. The offset lever, detent spring and ball will be removed with it.

NOTE: When removing the extension housing, be careful not to lose the thrust race and funnel.

5. Unscrew the transmission case cover bolts and then tap the cover *lightly* with a rubber mallet. Slide the cover toward the right side of the case and remove it.

6. Pull the shifter shaft to the rear and remove the striking lever-to-shifter shaft roll pin. Remove the shaft through the rear of the cover.

7. Remove the selector plates from the shift fork assemblies.

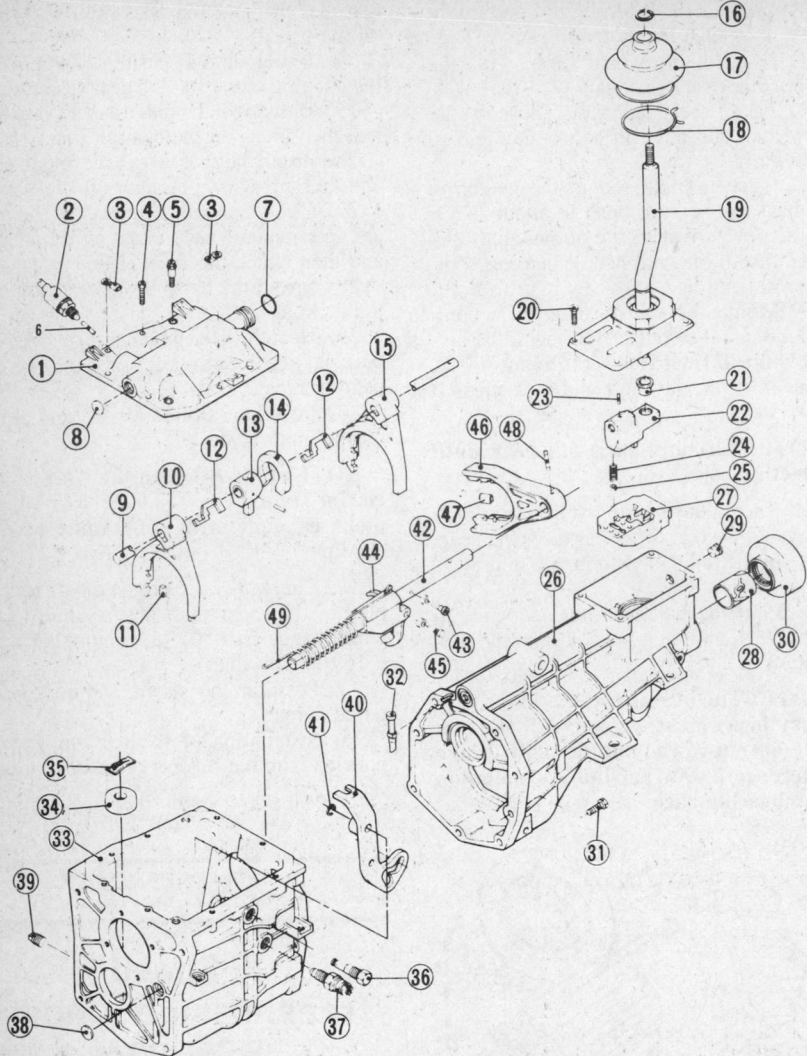

8. Remove the back–up light switch.

9. Remove the retainer ring and pivot pin.

10. Remove the funnel, thrust race and the needle thrust bearing.

11. Remove the snap-ring and thrust race from the back of the 5th gear synchronizer hub.

12. Remove the pin from the 5th gear shift fork. Remove the fork, synchronizer and counter gear.

13. Remove the front bearing retainer.

14. Remove the input shaft and main drive gear assembly. Position the flat area of the main drive gear toward the counter gear and remove it through the front of the case.

15. Remove the rear bearing race from the front of the mainshaft and then lift the mainshaft assembly out through the top of the case.

16. Remove the 5th gear shift rail, the reverse fork with 5th and the reverse relay lever and spring.

17. Remove the pin from the reverse idler shaft and then remove the shaft and gear.

18. Remove the snap-ring and spacer from the rear of the counter gear bearing. Press the gear toward the rear of the case until the bearing is free and then remove it.

—— **CAUTION** ——

When pressing out the bearing, do not let it drop into the case.

19. Remove the counter gear and the front thrust washer. Press the bearing from the case.

NOTE: This bearing should not be removed unless replacement is absolutely necessary.

20. Remove the speedometer gear and drive ball from the main shaft.

21. Press the 3rd/4th gear synchronizer from the mainshaft. Remove 3rd gear.

22. Press 5th gear from the mainshaft.

23. Slip the bearing off of the shaft and then remove the thrust washer.

24. Remove the pin and then press 1st gear from the mainshaft.

25. Remove the snap-ring, thrust washer and 2nd gear.

26. Remove the 1st/2nd gear synchronizer sleeve, inserts and springs.

ASSEMBLY

1. Install the 1st/2nd gear synchronizer sleeve, inserts and springs on the synchronizer hub.

2. Install 2nd gear, its thrust washer and snap-ring. Install 1st gear.

3. Position the thrust washer positioning pin so that it projects 0.12 in. above the bearing surface.

4. Install the thrust washer against 1st gear so that the slot in the washer aligns with the pin.

5. Install the rear bearing and then press 5th gear onto the mainshaft.

1	Case cover	
2	Neutral switch	
3	Wiring clip	
4	Hex head bolt	
5	Hex head shoulder bolt	
6	Pin	
7	O-ring	
8	Welsh plug	
9	Shifter shaft	
10	3–4 shift fork	
11	Shift fork insert	
12	Selector plate	
13	Control selector arm	
14	Interlock plate	
15	1–2 shift fork	
16	Boot retainer	
17	Boot	
18	Boot retainer	
19	Control lever/housing assembly	
20	Control housing screw	
21	Damper sleeve	
22	Offset lever	
23	Spring-pin	
24	Detent spring	
25	Ball	
26	Extension housing	Not serviced separately
27	Detent & guide plate	
28	Bushing	
29	Cup plug	
30	Oil seal	
31	Hex head flanged bolt	
32	Breather	
33	Case	
34	Magnet	
35	Clip	
36	Pivot pin	
37	Back-up lamp switch	
38	Welsh plug	
39	Pipe plug	
40	5th and reverse relay lever	
41	Retaining ring	
42	5th and reverse shift rail	Not serviced separately
43	Roller cam and pin	
44	Reverse shift fork	Not serviced separately
45	Roller cam and pin	
46	5th gear shift fork	
47	Insert	
48	Spring-pin	
49	Spring	

Exploded view of the transmission assembly—Type 7

6. Install 3rd gear and then press the 3rd/4th gear synchronizer onto the front of the mainshaft.

NOTE: Be sure that the portion of the hub with the extended hose faces forward.

7. Install the speedometer drive, ball, gear and snap-ring.

8. Install the front counter gear bearing:

a. Apply a *small* bead of adhesive to the outside diameter of the bearing.

b. Press the bearing into the case until the edge is flush with the case.

9. Position the counter gear thrust washer into the case so that the tang is aligned with the notch in the case.

NOTE: The washer may be held in position with a light coating of petroleum jelly.

10. Install the counter gear into the case and engage its front journal with the front bearing.

11. Install the rear counter gear bearing as follows:

a. Position the spacer at the rear of the counter gear.

b. Install a bearing protector on the counter gear.

c. Install the bearing over the protector and then press it into the case. When properly installed, the bearing race should protrude from the case 0.1228–0.1268 in.

d. Install a spacer and snap-ring behind the bearing.

12. Position the reverse idler gear into the case with the shift fork groove facing the rear. Install the reverse idler shaft, O-ring and retaining pin.

13. Install the reverse fork with 5th gear and reverse relay lever, 5th gear shift rail and the spring.

14. Install the back-up light switch.

15. Place the mainshaft assembly into the case and install the mainshaft rear bearing race.

16. Position the roller bearing into the main drive gear and hold them in position with a light coating of petroleum jelly.

17. Install the input shaft and main drive gear assembly, needle thrust bearing, thrust bearing race and locking ring into the case.

NOTE: Be sure that the flat area of the main drive gear is aligned with the counter gear. Be careful not to dislodge the roller bearings during installation.

18. Remove at least 0.0059 in. from under the front bearing race in the retainer. Install the remaining shims and race into the retainer.

19. Install the front bearing retainer to the case so that the oil collector groove is facing up. Tighten the bolts to 11–20 ft. lbs.

20. Install the 5th gear shift fork, counter gear and synchronizer as a unit. Install the retaining pin with the pin holes in the shift fork and rail in alignment.

Checking the preload—Type 7

21. Install the thrust race and snap-ring to the rear of the 5th gear synchronizer hub.

22. Locate the selector plates on the fork assemblies.

23. Slide the shifter shaft through the hole in the rear of the case cover and then assemble the 1st/2nd gear shift fork, interlock plate, striking lever and the 3rd/4th gear shift fork. Install the shifter shaft roll pin in the striking lever.

24. Apply a continuous bead of sealant to the cover–to–case mating surface and then install the cover.

25. Apply sealant to the threads of the two cover alignment dowels and install them. Apply sealant to the remaining bolt threads and tighten them to 6.0–12.8 ft. lbs.

26. Clean the mating surfaces of the case-to–rear extension housing and apply sealant to the mating surface of the case.

27. Using a light coating of petroleum jelly to retain them, locate the needle thrust bearing, race and funnel on the rear of the counter shaft.

28. Place the detent ball, spring and off-set lever into position on the guide plate and then connect the extension housing to the case.

29. Align the holes in the shifter shaft and offset lever and then install the retaining pin.

30. Insert the mounting bolts and tighten them to 20–46 ft. lbs.

31. Apply sealant to the shift cover hole in the extension housing. Assemble the damper sleeve into the offset lever and then install the shift lever. Tighten the mounting bolts to 11–20 ft. lbs.

32. Install the drain plug and fill with lubricant.

33. Push the input shaft to the rear and mount a dial indicator so the stem rests against the front end of the shaft. Zero the indicator.

34. Push the output shaft forward and note the indicator reading. Remove the indicator.

35. Remove the bearing retainer and race. Select the proper thickness shim to provide 0.0051–0.0098 in. preload.

NOTE: To get the desired shim thickness, add the dial indicator reading from Step 34 to the desired preload. The resulting total is the proper shim thickness.

36. Apply sealant to the bearing retainer mating surface and the bolt threads. Install the shims and race into the retainer as in Step 19.

37. Install the transmission into the vehicle.

TYPE 8

4 Speed Transmission—Model F4W63L

Datsun

DISASSEMBLY

The reverse and reverse idler drive gears are contained in the extension housing of this transmission. On late units, the cast, ribbed bottom cover is replaced by a stamped steel cover. Virtually all of these transmissions imported to the U.S. have a modified extension housing incorporating a floorshift mechanism.

1. Drain the transmission.

2. Remove the clutch throw-out lever and release bearing.

3. Remove the clevis pin which connects the striker rod to the shift lever.

4. Remove the speedometer drive pinion assembly.

5. Unbolt and remove the extension housing, disengaging the striker rod from the shift rod gates.

6. Remove the bottom and front covers.

7. Remove the three detent plugs, springs and balls.

8. Drive out the shift fork retaining pins. Remove the rods and forks.

9. Move the first/second and third/fourth coupling sleeves into gear at the same time to lock the mainshaft.

10. Pull out the countershaft and countergear with the two needle roller bearings and spacers.

11. Remove the snap-ring, reverse idler gears, and shaft.

12. Unbolt the mainshaft rear bearing retainer.

13. Pull out the mainshaft assembly to the rear. Pull out the clutch shaft to the front.

14. To disassemble the mainshaft, remove the snap-ring, third/fourth synchronizer hub and coupling sleeve. Remove third gear, with the roller bearing. Remove the mainshaft nut, lock-plate, speedometer drive gear, and steel ball. Take off reverse gear, and the hub. Press off the bearing and retainer.

ASSEMBLY

1. Assembly procedures are generally

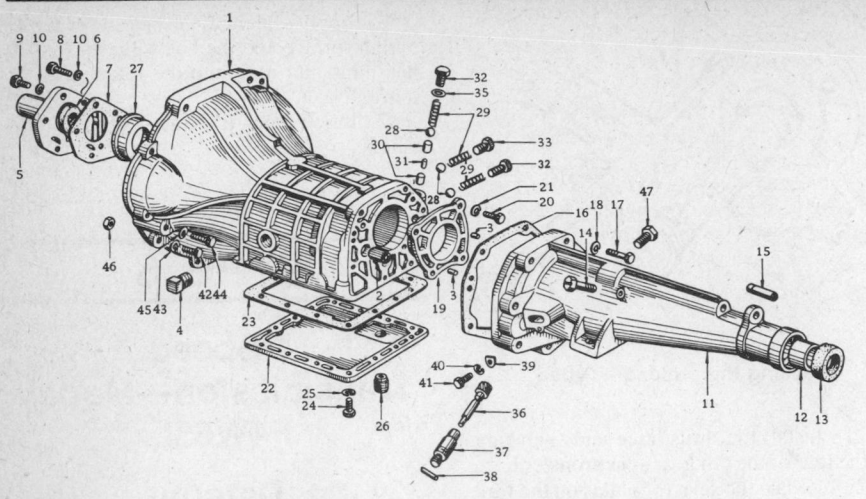

1. Case
2. Needle bearing
3. Dowel pin
4. Plug assembly
5. Front cover
6. Oil seal
7. Gasket
8. Bolt
9. Bolt
10. Lockwasher
11. Extension housing
12. Bushing
13. Oil seal
14. Breather
15. Striker bushing
16. Gasket
17. Bolt
18. Lockwasher
19. Bearing retainer
20. Bolt
21. Lockwasher
22. Bottom cover
23. Gasket
24. Bolt
25. Lockwasher
26. Drain plug
27. Bearing retainer
28. Detent ball
29. Detent spring
30. Interlock plunger
31. Interlock pin
32. Detent plug
33. Detent plug
34. Not used
35. Washer
36. Speedometer pinion
37. Pinion sleeve
38. Pin
39. Lockplate
40. Lockwasher
41. Bolt
42. Bolt
43. Lockwasher
44. Bolt
45. Lockwasher
46. Nut
47. Plug for backup light switch

Transmission case components, model F4W63L

the reverse of disassembly, however the following special instructions are required.

2. On the clutch shaft, there should be no end-play between the bearing and the snap-ring. Snap-rings are available in sizes from 0.0598 in. (1.52 mm) to 0.0697 in. (1.77 mm).

3. Some of these transmissions use a servo type synchronizer which utilizes brake bands. To assemble these synchronizers, place each gear on a flat surface. Install the synchronizer ring into the clutch gear. Place the thrust block and anchor block and install the circlip into the groove.

4. Third gear should be adjusted to give an end-play of 0.0020–0.0059 in. Snap-rings for adjustment are available in sizes from 0.0551 in. to 0.0630 in.

5. Install the reverse idler driving gear on the reverse shaft and fasten with a snap-ring. Install the shaft and gear into the case, placing a thrust washer between the gear and case. Place a thrust washer, idler gear, and snap-ring on the inside end of the shaft. Idler gear end-play should be 0.0039–0.0118 in. Snap-rings are available in sizes from 0.0433 in. to 0.0591 in.

6. Countergear end-play should be 0.0020–0.0059 in. Thrust washers for adjustment are available from 0.0945 in. to 0.1024 in.

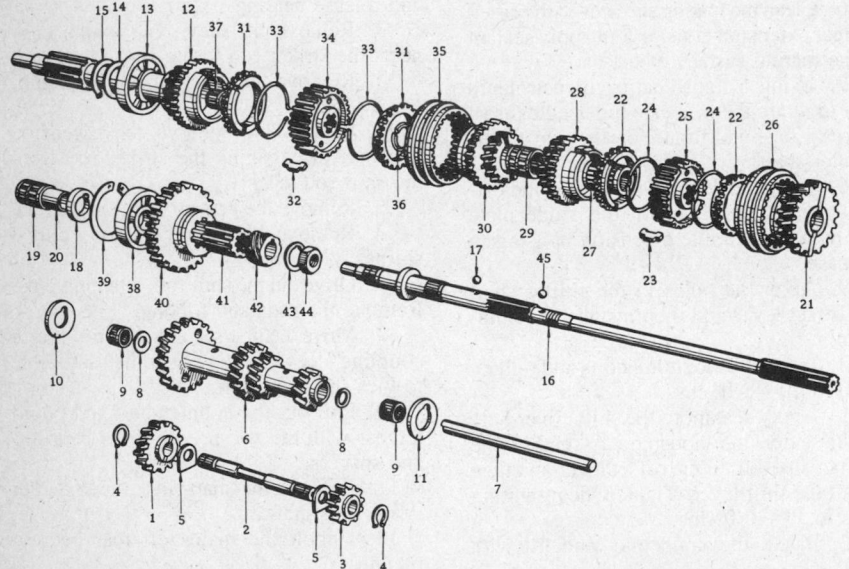

1. Reverse idler gear
2. Reverse idler shaft
3. Main reverse idler gear
4. Snap-ring
5. Thrust washer
6. Countergear
7. Countershaft
8. Spacer
9. Needle bearing
10. Front countershaft thrust washer
11. Rear countershaft thrust washer
12. Main drive gear
13. Main drive gear bearing
14. Washer
15. Snap-ring
16. Mainshaft
17. 5/32" steel ball
18. Thrust washer
19. Needle bearing
20. First gear bushing
21. First gear
22. Baulk ring
23. Shifting insert
24. Spreader ring
25. First/second synchro hub
26. Coupling sleeve
27. Needle bearing
28. Second gear
29. Needle bearing
30. Third gear
31. Baulk ring
32. Shifting insert
33. Spreader ring
34. Third/fourth synchro hub
35. Coupling sleeve
36. Snap-ring
37. Pilot bearing
38. Bearing
39. Snap-ring
40. Reverse gear
41. Reverse gear hub
42. Speedometer drive gear
43. Lockwasher
44. Nut
45. Steel ball

Exploded view of gear train components

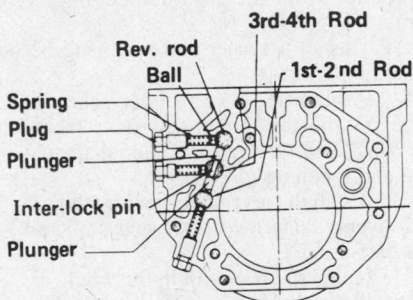

Shift rod interlock details for four speed bottom cover transmission

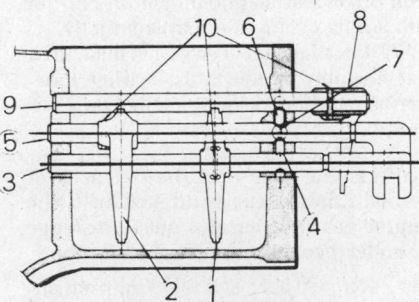

1. First/second shift fork
2. Third/fourth shift fork
3. First/second shift rod
4. Interlock plunger
5. Third/fourth shift rod
6. Interlock plunger
7. Interlock pin
8. Reverse shift fork
9. Reverse shift rod
10. Fork retaining pin

Shift rod and fork details, four speed bottom cover transmission

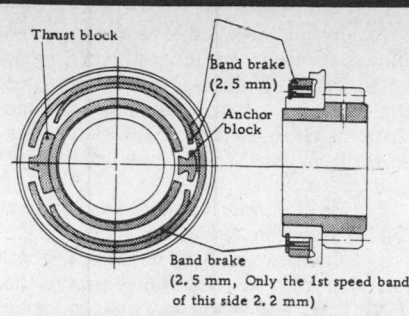

Thrust block
Band brake (2.5 mm)
Anchor block
Band brake
(2.5 mm, Only the 1st speed band of this side 2.2 mm)

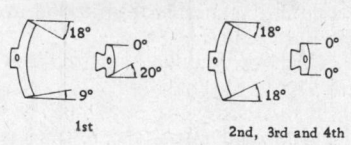

1st   2nd, 3rd and 4th

Servo type synchronizer assembly details

7. To assemble the shift mechanism, place the first/second and third/fourth forks onto their sleeves. Insert the first/second shift rod. Install an interlock plunger and then the third/forth shift rod with the interlock pin. Install the other interlock plunger and then the reverse shift fork and rod. Place a detent ball and spring into each detent hole. Use sealant on the plug threads.

8. Install the extension housing, engaging the striker rod with the shift rod.

TYPE 9

4 Speed Transmission—Model F4W71B

Datsun

DISASSEMBLY

This transmission is constructed in three sections: clutch housing, transmission housing and extension housing. There are no case cover plates. There is a cast iron adapter plate between the transmission and extension housings.

1. Remove the clutch housing dust cover. Remove the retaining spring, release bearing sleeve, and throw-out lever.

2. Remove the back-up light/neutral safety switch.

3. Unbolt and remove the clutch housing, rapping with a soft hammer if necessary. Remove the gasket, mainshaft bearing shim, and countershaft bearing shim.

4. Remove the speedometer pinion sleeve.

5. Remove the striker rod pin from the rod. Separate the striker rod from the shift lever bracket.

6. Unbolt and remove the rear exten

sion. It may be necessary to rap the housing with a soft hammer.

7. Remove the mainshaft bearing snap-ring.

8. Remove the adapter plate and gear assembly from the transmission case.

9. Punch out the shift fork retaining pins. Remove the shift rod snap-rings. Remove the detent plugs, springs and balls from the adapter plate. Remove the shift rods, being careful not to lose the interlock balls.

10. Remove the snap-ring speedometer drive gear and locating ball.

11. Remove the nut, lockwasher, thrust washer, reverse hub and reverse gear.

12. Remove the snap-ring and counter-

shaft reverse gear. Remove the snap-ring, reverse idler gear, thrust washer and needle bearing.

13. Support the gear assembly while rapping on the rear of the mainshaft with a soft hammer.

14. Remove the setscrew from the adapter plate. Remove the shaft nut, spring washer, plain washer and reverse idler shaft.

15. Remove the bearing retainer and the mainshaft rear bushing.

16. To disassemble the mainshaft (rear section), remove the front snap-ring, third/fourth synchronizer assembly, third gear and needle bearing. Fom the rear, remove the thrust washer, locating ball, first gear, needle bearing, first gear bushing, first/second

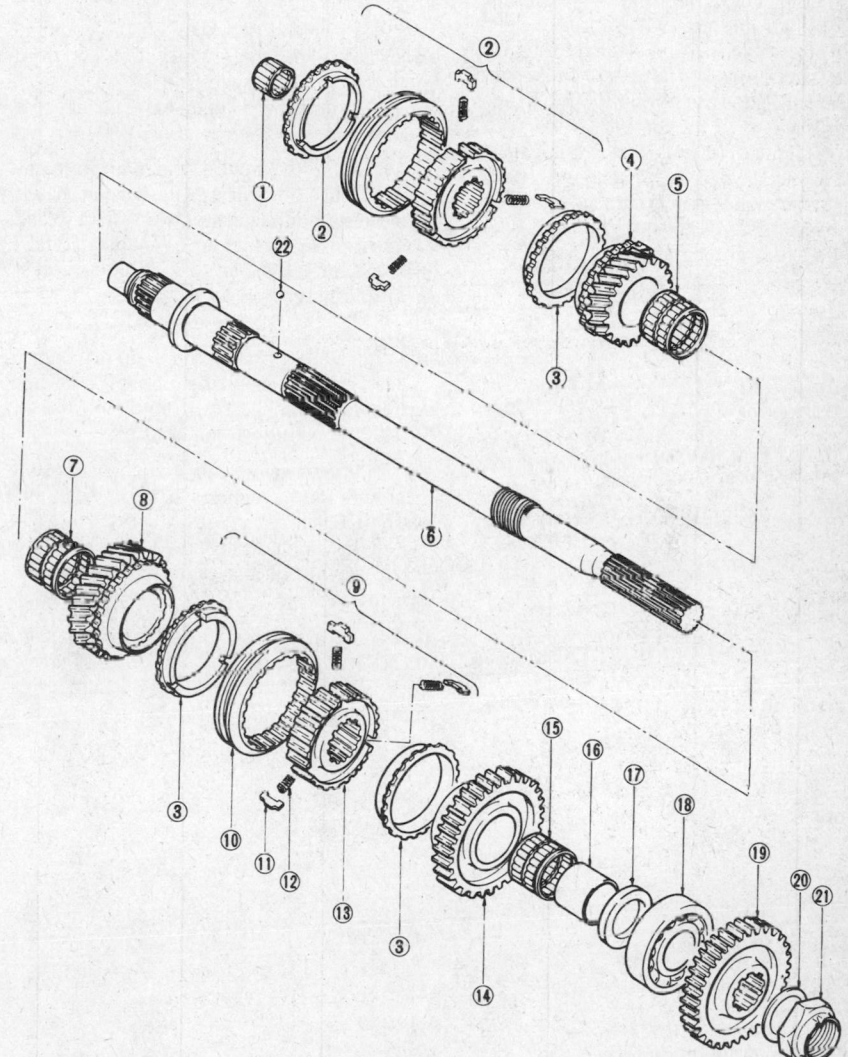

1. Pilot bearing	8. 2nd gear, mainshaft	15. Needle bearing
2. 3rd & 4th synchromesh assembly	9. 1st & 2nd synchromesh assembly	16. Bushing, 1st gear
3. Baulk ring	10. Coupling sleeve	17. Thrust washer, mainshaft
4. 3rd gear, mainshaft	11. Shifting insert	18. Mainshaft bearing
5. Needle bearing	12. Spread spring	19. Reverse gear, mainshaft
6. Mainshaft	13. Synchronizer hub	10. Thrust washer
7. Needle bearing	14. 1st gear, mainshaft	21. Nut
		22. Steel ball

Mainshaft—280Z

synchronizer assembly, second gear, and needle bearing.

17. To disassemble the clutch shaft, remove the snap-ring and bearing spacer and press off the bearing.

18. To dissassemble the countershaft, press off the front bearing. Press off the rear bearing, press off the gears and remove the keys.

19. Remove the retaining pin, control arm pin and shift control arm from the rear of the extension housing.

ASSEMBLY

1. Place the O-ring in the front cover. Install the front cover to the clutch housing with a press. Put in the front cover oil seal.

2. Install the rear extension oil seal.

3. Assemble the first/second and third/fourth synchronizer assemblies. Make sure that the ring gaps are not both on the same side of the unit.

4. On the rear end of the mainshaft, install the needle bearing, second gear, baulk ring, first/second synchronizer assembly, baulk ring, first gear bushing, needle bearing, first gear, locating ball and thrust washer.

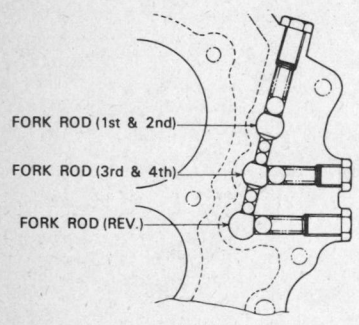

FORK ROD (1st & 2nd)
FORK ROD (3rd & 4th)
FORK ROD (REV.)

Interlock and detent plunger—F4W71B

5. Drive or press on the mainshaft rear bearing.

6. Install the countershaft rear bearing to the adapter plate. Drive or press the mainshaft rear bearing into the adapter plate until the bearing snap-ring groove comes through the rear side of the plate. Install the snap-ring. If it is not tight against the plate, press the bearing back in slightly.

7. Insert the countershaft bearing ring between the countershaft rear bearing and bearing retainer. Install the bearing retainer to the adapter plate. Stake both ends of the screws.

8. Insert the reverse idler shaft from the rear of the adapter plate. Install the spring washer and plain washer to the idler shaft.

9. Place the two keys on the countershaft and oil the shaft lightly. Press on third gear and install a snap-ring.

10. Install the countershaft into its rear bearing.

11. From the front of the mainshaft, install the needle bearing, third gear, baulk ring, third/fourth synchronizer assembly and snap-ring. Snap-rings are available in thicknesses from 0.0561 in. to 0.102 in. to adjust gear end-play.

12. Press the main drive bearing onto the clutch shaft. Install the main drive gear spacer and a snap-ring. Snap-rings are available in thicknesses from 0.0710 in. to 0.0820 in. to adjust gear end-play.

13. Insert a key into the countershaft drive gear with fourth gear and drive on the countershaft fourth gear with a drift. The rear end of the countershaft should be held steady while driving on the gear, to prevent rear bearing damage.

14. Install the reverse hub, reverse gear, thrust washer, and lock tab on the rear of the mainshaft. Install the shaft nut temporarily.

15. Install the needle bearing, reverse idler gear, thrust washer, and snap-ring.

16. Place the countershaft reverse gear and snap-ring on the rear of the countershaft. Snap-rings are available in thicknesses from 0.0433 in. to 0.063 in. to adjust gear end-play.

17. Engage both first and second gears to lock the shaft.

18. On the rear of the mainshaft, install the snap-ring, locating ball, speedometer drive gear, and snap-ring. Snap-rings are available in thicknesses from 0.063 in. to 0.0590 in.

19. Recheck end-play and backlash of all gears.

20. Place the reverse shift fork on the reverse gear and install the reverse shift rod. Install the detent ball, spring and plug. Install the fork retaining pin. Place two interlock balls between the reverse shift rod and the third/fourth shift rod location. Install the third/fourth shift fork and rod. Install the detent ball, spring and plug. This plug is shorter than the other two. Install the fork retaining pin. Place two interlock balls between the first/second shift rod location and the third/fourth shift rod. Install the first/second shift fork and rod. Install the detent ball, spring and plug.

21. Install the shift rod snap-rings.

22. Apply sealant sparingly to the adapter plate and transmission housing. Install the transmission housing to the adapter plate and bolt it down temporarily.

23. Drive in the countershaft front bearing with a drift. Place the snap-ring in the mainshaft front bearing.

24. Apply sealant sparingly to the adapter plate and extension housing. Align the shift rods in the neutral positions. Position the striker rod to the shift rods and bolt down the extension housing.

25. Insert the striker rod pin, connect the rod to the shift lever bracket and install the striker rod pin retaining ring. Replace the shift control arm.

26. To select the proper mainshaft bearing shim, first measure the amount the bearing protrudes from the front of the transmission case. This is measurement (B). Then measure the depth of the bearing recess in the rear of the clutch housing. This is measurement (A). Required shim thickness is found by subtracting (B) from (A). Shims are available in thicknesses of 0.0551 in. and 0.0630 in.

27. To select the proper countershaft front bearing shim, measure the amount that the bearing is recessed into the transmission case. Shim thickness should equal this measurement. Shims are available in thicknesses from 0.0157 in. (.4mm) to 0.0394 in. (1.0mm).

28. Apply sealant sparingly to the clutch and transmission housing mating surfaces.

29. Replace the clutch operating mechanism.

30. Install the shift lever temporarily and check shifting action.

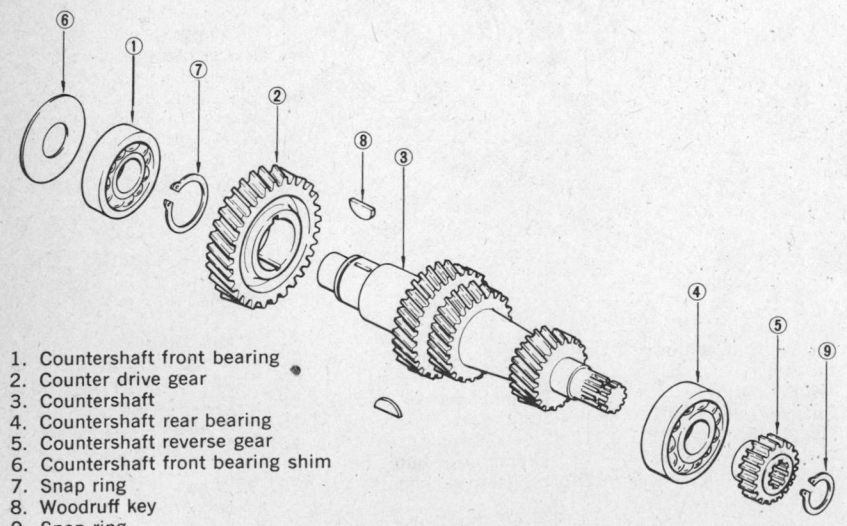

1. Countershaft front bearing
2. Counter drive gear
3. Countershaft
4. Countershaft rear bearing
5. Countershaft reverse gear
6. Countershaft front bearing shim
7. Snap ring
8. Woodruff key
9. Snap ring

Countershaft—F4W71B

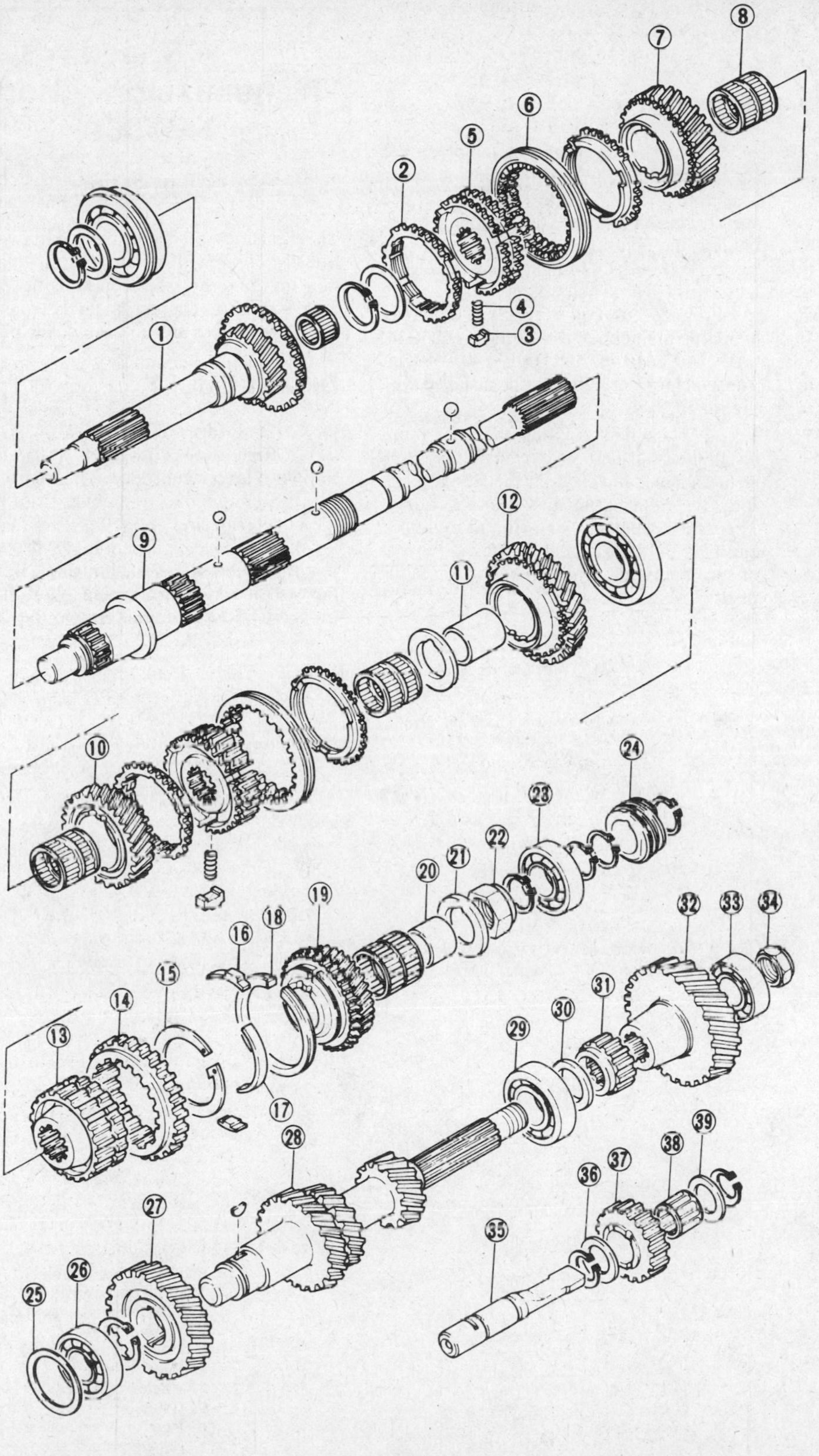

1. Main drive gear
2. Baulk ring
3. Shifting insert
4. Shifting insert spring
5. Synchronizer hub
6. Coupling sleeve
7. 3rd main gear
8. Needle bearing
9. Mainshaft
10. 2nd main gear
11. Bushing
12. 1st main gear
13. OD-reverse synchronizer hub
14. Reverse gear
15. Circlip
16. Thrust block
17. Brake band
18. Synchronizer ring
19. Overdrive main gear
20. Overdrive gear bushing
21. Washer
22. Mainshaft nut
23. Overdrive mainshaft bearing
24. Speedometer drive gear
25. Countershaft front bearing shim
26. Countershaft front bearing
27. Countershaft drive gear
28. Countershaft
29. Countershaft bearing
30. Reverse counter gear spacer
31. Reverse counter gear
32. Overdrive counter gear
33. Countershaft rear bearing
34. Countershaft nut
35. Reverse idler shaft
36. Reverse idler thrust washer
37. Reverse idler gear
38. Reverse idler gear bearing
39. Reverse idler thrust washer

Exploded view of the gear train—FS5W71B and FS5W71C

TYPE 10

5 Speed Transmission—Model FS5W71B and FS5W71C Datsun

These transmissions are similar to the 4 speed transmission, model F4W71B and the overhaul can be accomplished by following the outline for the disassembly and assembly of the model F4W71B transmission.

Servo type synchromesh is used, instead of the Borg-Warner type in the four speed. Shift linkage and interlock arrangements are the same, except the reverse shift rod also operates fifth gear. Most service procedures are identical to those for the four speed unit. Those unique to the five-speed follow.

DISASSEMBLY

To disassemble the synchronizers, remove the circlip, synchronizer ring, thrust block, brake band, and anchor block. Be careful not to mix parts of the different synchronizer assemblies.

ASSEMBLY

1. The synchronizer assemblies for second, third, and fourth are identical. When assembling the first gear synchronizer, be sure to install the 0.0866 in. thick brake band at the bottom.

2. When assembling the mainshaft, select a third gear synchronizer hub snap-ring to minimize hub end-play. Snap-rings are available in thicknesses of 0.061–0.630 in. 0.0591–0.0610 in. and 0.0571–0.0591 in. The synchronizer hub must be installed with the longer boss to the rear.

3. When reassembling the gear train, install the mainshaft, countershaft, and gears to the adapter plate. Hold the rear nut and force the front nut against it to a torque of 217 ft. lbs. Select a snap-ring to minimize end-play of the fifth gear bearing at the rear of the mainshaft. Snap-rings are available in thicknesses from 0.0433 in. to 0.0551 in.

TYPE 11

4 Speed Transmission—Model F4W56A Datsun

This transmission is constructed in two sections: a combined clutch and transmission housing, and an extension housing. There is a cast iron adapter plate between the housings. There are no case cover plates.

DISASSEMBLY

1. Drain the oil.
2. Remove the dust cover, spring, clutch throwout lever, and release bearing.
3. Remove the front cover from inside the clutch housing.
4. Remove the speedometer drive pinion from the extension housing. Remove the striker rod return spring plug, spring, plunger, and bushing. Remove the striker

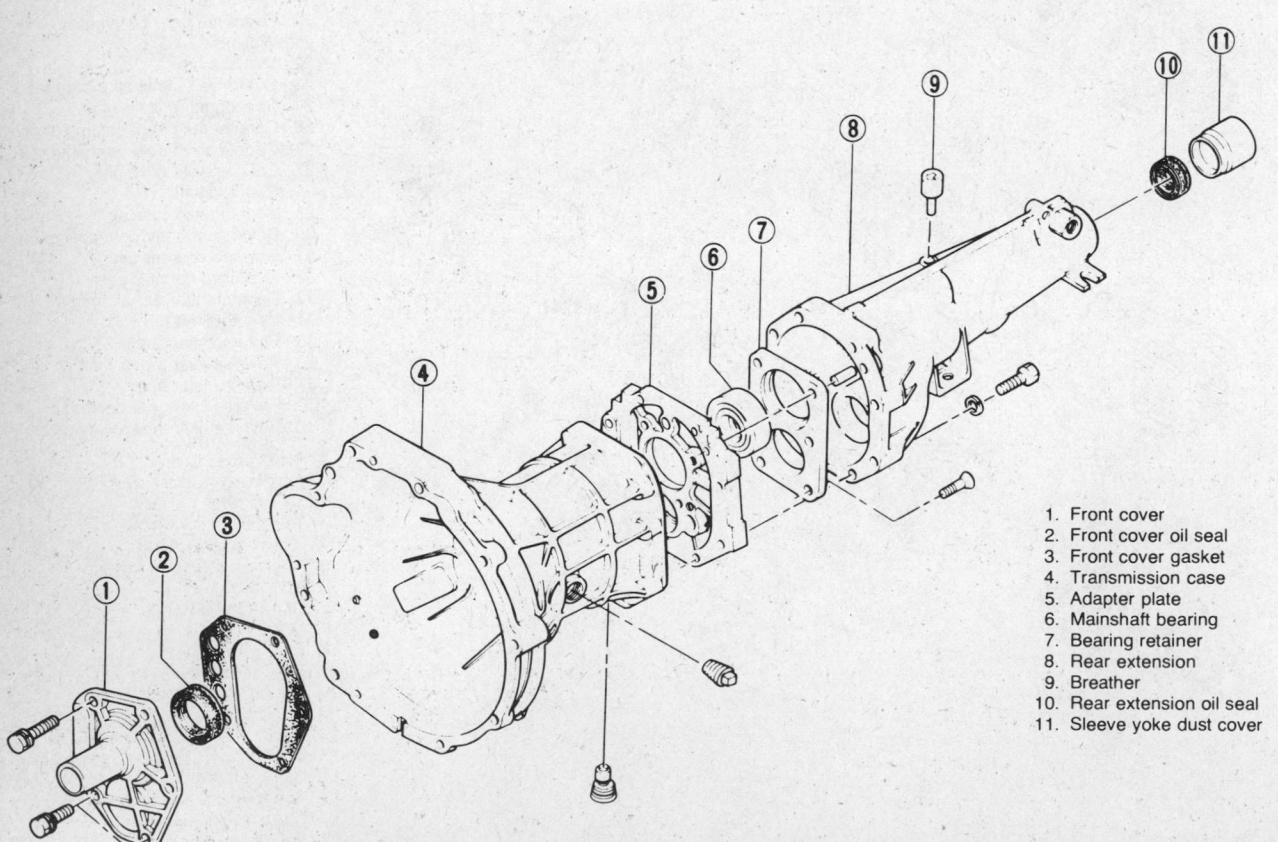

1. Front cover
2. Front cover oil seal
3. Front cover gasket
4. Transmission case
5. Adapter plate
6. Mainshaft bearing
7. Bearing retainer
8. Rear extension
9. Breather
10. Rear extension oil seal
11. Sleeve yoke dust cover

Component parts of the FS5W71B and FS5W71C transmission case

rod pin and separate the striker rod from the shift lever bracket.

5. Remove the extension housing. Tap it with a soft hammer, if necessary.

6. Separate the adapter plate from the transmission case, being careful not to lose the countershaft bearing washer.

7. Clamp the adapter plate in a vise with the reverse idler gear up.

8. Drive out the retaining pin and remove the reverse shift fork and reverse idler gear.

9. Remove the mainshaft rear snap-ring, washer, and reverse gear.

10. Drive out the remaining shift fork retaining pins. Remove all three detent plugs, springs, and balls. Remove the forks and shift rods. Be careful not to lose the interlock plungers.

11. Tap the rear of the mainshaft with a soft hammer to separate the mainshaft and countershaft from the adapter plate. Be careful not to drop the shafts. Separate the clutch shaft from the mainshaft.

12. From the front of the mainshaft, remove the needle bearing, synchronizer hub thrust washer, steel locating ball, third/fourth synchronizer, baulk ring, third gear, and needle bearing.

13. Press off the mainshaft bearing to the rear. Remove the thrust washer, first gear, needle bearing, baulk ring, first/second synchronizer, snap-ring and bearing.

ASSEMBLY

1. Press on the countershaft bearings. Install the countershaft assembly to the transmission case and replace the adapter plate temporarily. Countershaft end-play should be 0-0.0079 in. Front bearing shims are available for adjustment in thicknesses from 0.0315 in. to 0.0512 in. Remove the countershaft assembly from the case.

2. Install the coupling sleeve, shifting inserts, and spring on the synchronizer hub. Be careful not to hook the front and rear ends of the spring to the same insert.

3. Install the needle bearing from the rear of the mainshaft. Install second gear, the baulk ring, and synchronizer hub assembly. Align the shifting insert to the baulk ring groove. Install the first gear side needle bearing, baulk ring, and first gear. Install the mainshaft thrust washer and press on the rear bearing.

On the mainshaft front end, replace the needle bearing, third gear, baulk ring, synchronizer hub assembly, steel locating ball, thrust washer, and pilot bearing. Be sure to grease the sliding surface of the steel ball and thrust washer. The dimpled side of the thrust washer must face to the front and the oil grooved side to the rear.

4. Replace the main bearing, washer, and snap-ring onto the clutch shaft. The web side of the washer must face the bear-

ing. Place the baulk ring on the clutch shaft and assemble the clutch shaft to the mainshaft.

5. Align the mainshaft assembly with the countershaft assembly and install them to the adapter plate by lightly tapping on the clutch shaft with a soft hammer.

6. Place the first/second and third/fourth shift forks on the shift rods, being careful that the forks are not reversed. Install all three shift rods and the detent and interlock parts. Apply locking agent to the detent plug threads and screw the plugs in flush. Make sure the shift forks are in their grooves and drive in the retaining pins.

7. Install the mainshaft reverse gear, thrust washer, and snap-ring. Face the web side of the thrust washer to the gear.

8. Replace the reverse idler gear and pin on the reverse shift fork. Check interlock action by attempting to shift two shift rods at once.

9. Install the adapter plate to the transmission case. Make sure to install the countergear front shim selected in Step 1. Use sealant on the joint and seat the plate by tapping with a soft hammer.

10. Align the striker lever and install the extension housing. Use sealant on the joint. Install the bushing, plunger, return spring, and plug. Use sealant on the plug threads. Install the striker rod pin and the speedometer drive pinion.

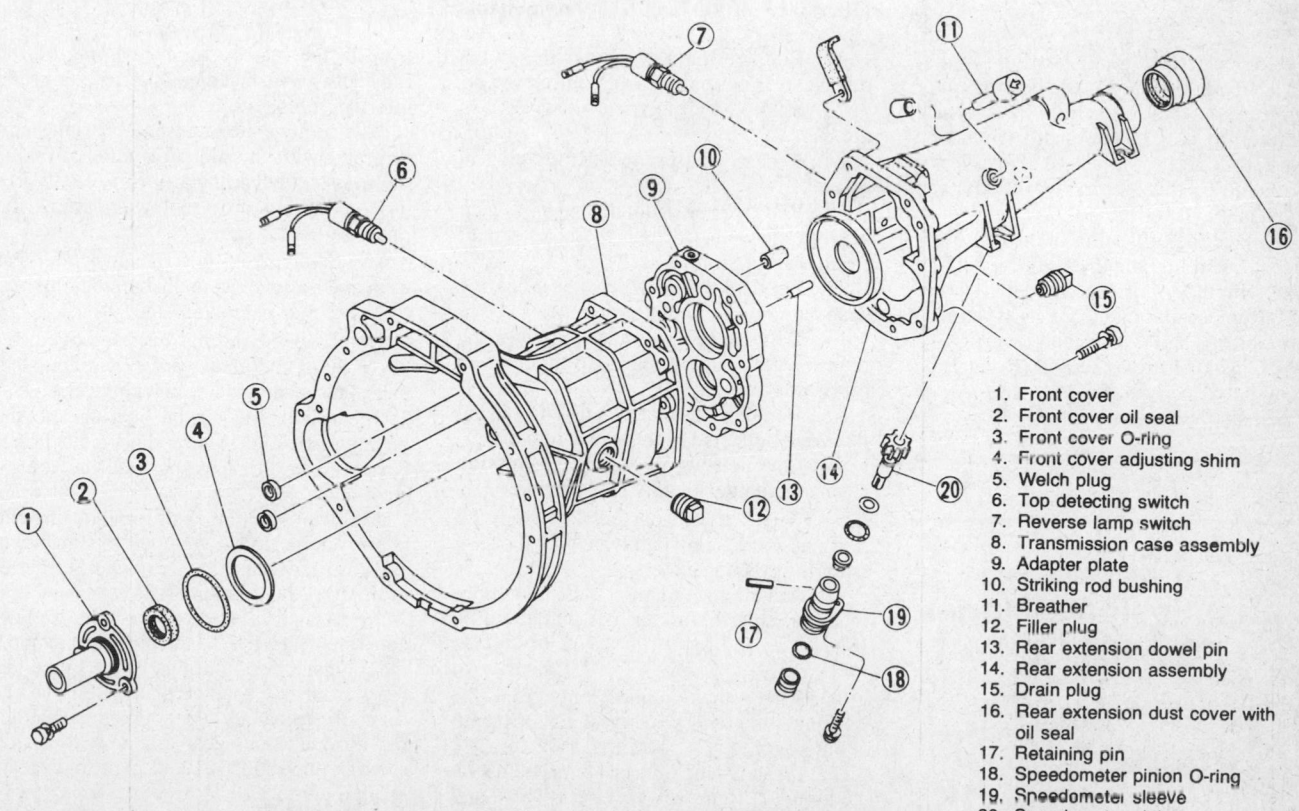

1. Front cover
2. Front cover oil seal
3. Front cover O-ring
4. Front cover adjusting shim
5. Welch plug
6. Top detecting switch
7. Reverse lamp switch
8. Transmission case assembly
9. Adapter plate
10. Striking rod bushing
11. Breather
12. Filler plug
13. Rear extension dowel pin
14. Rear extension assembly
15. Drain plug
16. Rear extension dust cover with oil seal
17. Retaining pin
18. Speedometer pinion O-ring
19. Speedometer sleeve
20. Speedometer pinion

Transmission case components—model F4W56A

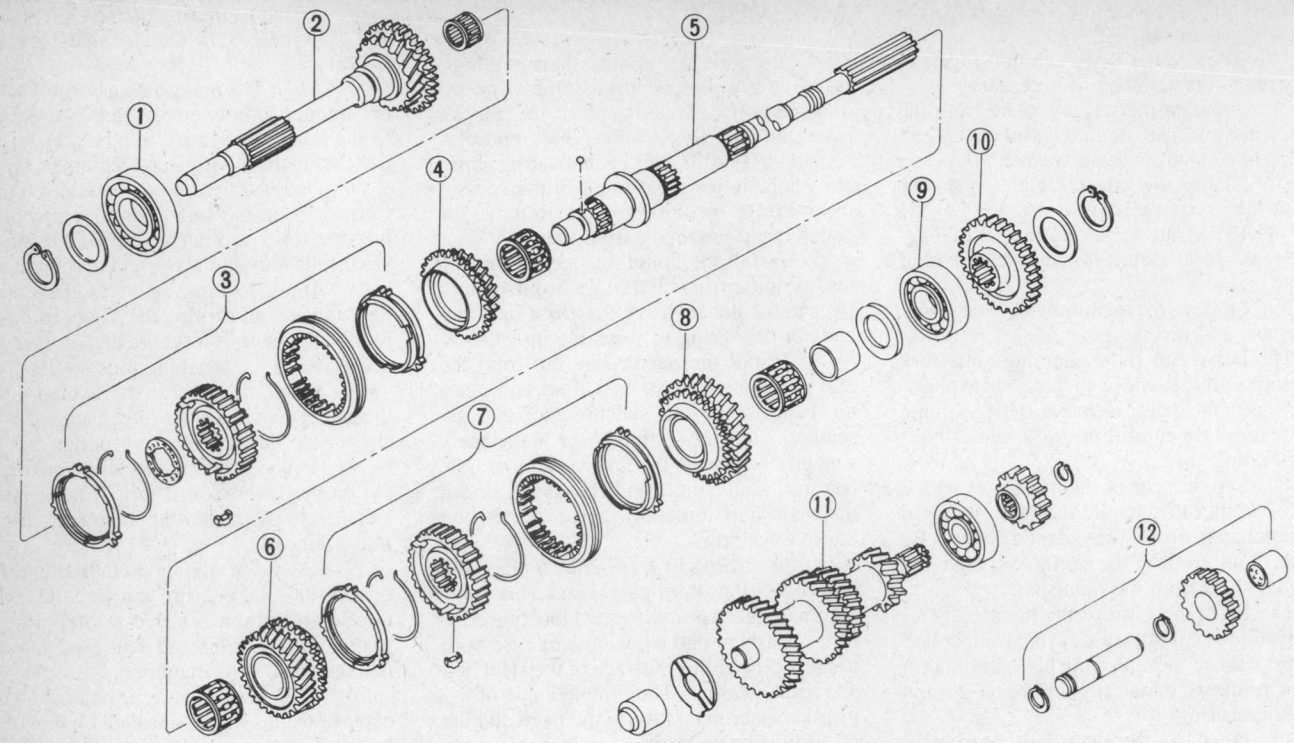

1. Main drive bearing
2. Main drive gear
3. 3rd & top synchronizer
4. 3rd gear, mainshaft
5. Mainshaft
6. 2nd gear, mainshaft
7. 1st & 2nd synchronizer
8. 1st gear, mainshaft
9. Mainshaft bearing
10. Reverse gear, mainshaft
11. Counter gear assembly
12. Idler gear assembly

Exploded view of the gear train components

11. Select clutch shaft bearing shim(s) by measuring the amount the bearing outer race is recessed below the machined surface for the front cover. The depth should be 0.1969–0.2028 in. Shims are available for adjustment in thicknesses of 0.0039 in., 0.0079 in., and 0.0197 in.

12. Place the oil seal in the front cover, grease the seal lip, and install the cover and O-ring with the shim(s) selected in Step 11.

13. Replace the clutch release bearing, return spring, and withdrawal lever.

14. Check shifting action. Rotate the clutch shaft slowly in neutral. The rear of the mainshaft should not turn.

TYPE 12

5 Speed Transmission—Model FS5W63A,L

Datsun

DISASSEMBLY

1. Secure the transmission and drain the lubricant.

2. Remove the dust cover, the clutch release bearing and the operating lever.

3. Remove the electrical switches from the case.

4. Remove the speedometer driven gear assembly.

5. Remove the front main drive gear bearing cover and detach the countershaft front bearing shim.

6. Remove the main drive gear bearing snap-ring from the outer race.

7. Remove the return spring plug, the return spring and plunger from the rear extension.

8. Remove the rear extension housing retaining bolts and with the use of a puller, remove the housing from the transmission case and adapter plate.

9. Separate the adapter plate from the transmission case by lightly tapping the case from the adapter plate.

10. Mount the adapter plate assembly into a holding fixture, either purchased or fabricated, and mount in a vise or similar tool.

11. Drive the retaining pins from the shifting forks and selector shaft rods with a pin punch.

12. Remove the three selector rod check ball plugs. Remove the check balls and springs.

13. Remove the selector rods from the

front to the rear by lightly tapping on the rods with a soft-faced hammer. Remove the interlock plungers.

14. Remove the mainshaft bearing snap-ring and with the aid of a puller, remove the mainshaft bearing from the shaft. Remove the second snap-ring from the mainshaft.

15. Engage two gears to lock the gear train and remove the mainshaft locking nut, from the rear extension side.

16. After the nut has been removed, remove the speedometer drive gear and steel ball, the synchronizer hub with reverse gear, 1st gear with the needle bearing and the bushing, the idler gear and needle bearing. Remove the thrust washer and the second steel ball.

17. From the rear extension housing end of the adapter plate, remove the snap-ring and thrust washer, 1st gear using a puller tool, from the countershaft.

18. Attach a special pushing tool or equivalent, to the adapter plate and push the mainshaft approximately 0.39 inch (10 mm) from the adapter plate. Remove the main drive gear and the countergear. Holding the mainshaft gear assembly by hand, remove the mainshaft and mainshaft gears as an assembly.

19. After the mainshaft has been removed, take the thrust washer, the steel

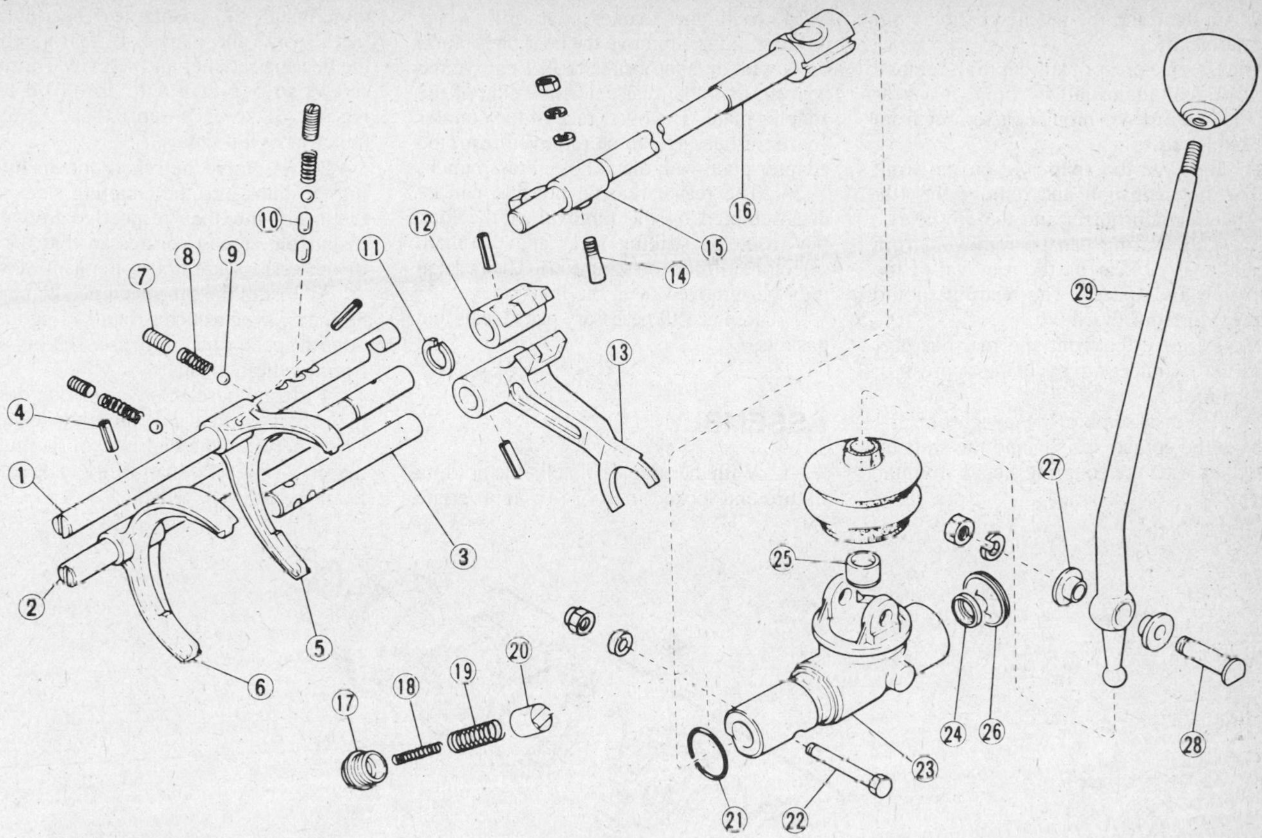

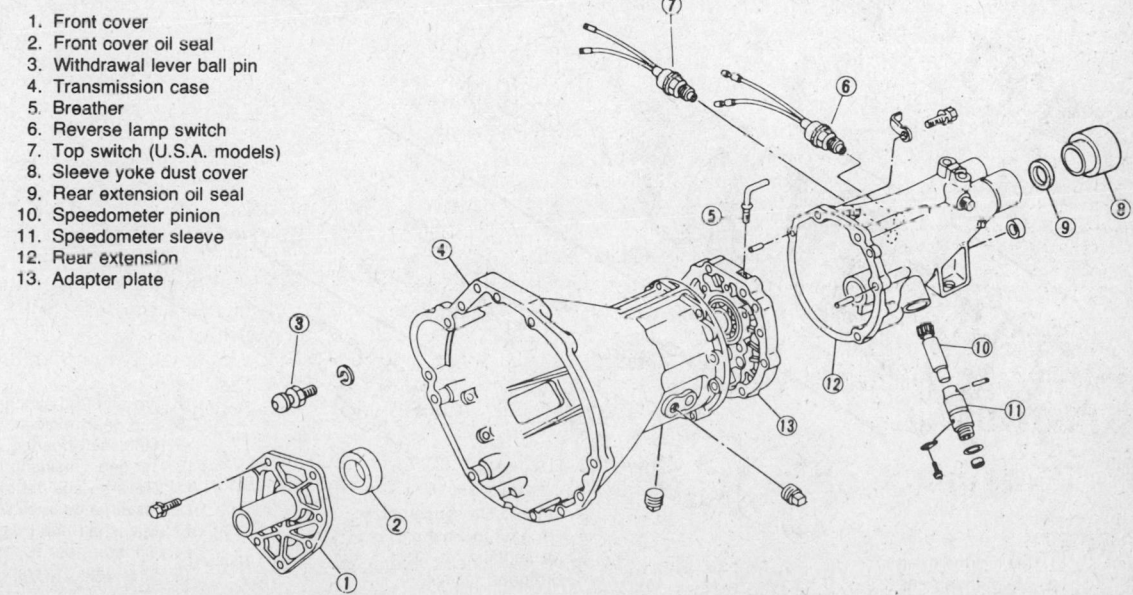

1. 1st & 2nd fork rod
2. 3rd & top fork rod
3. Reverse fork rod
4. Retaining pin
5. 1st & 2nd shift fork
6. 3rd & top shift fork
7. Checking ball plug
8. Check ball spring
9. Check ball
10. Interlock plunger

11. Stopper ring
12. Shift rod A bracket
13. Reverse shift fork
14. Lock pin
15. Striking lever
16. Striking rod
17. Return spring plug
18. Reverse check spring
19. Return spring
20. Plunger

21. O-ring
22. Stopper pin bolt
23. Striking guide assembly
24. Striking guide oil seal
25. Control lever bushing
26. Expansion plug
27. Control pin bushing
28. Control arm pin
29. Control lever

Exploded view of shift selector rod and fork components

1. Front cover
2. Front cover oil seal
3. Withdrawal lever ball pin
4. Transmission case
5. Breather
6. Reverse lamp switch
7. Top switch (U.S.A. models)
8. Sleeve yoke dust cover
9. Rear extension oil seal
10. Speedometer pinion
11. Speedometer sleeve
12. Rear extension
13. Adapter plate

Transmission case components, model FS5W63A

ball, 2nd gear and the needle bearing from the mainshaft.

20. Using a press or similar tool, remove the 2nd gear mainshaft bushing, 3rd gear and the 2nd/3rd synchronizer assembly from the mainshaft.

21. Remove the snap-ring on the front end of the mainshaft and remove the 4th/5th speed synchronizer and the 5th gear.

22. The bearing can be removed from the main drive gear by the removal of the snap-ring and spacer. The bearing should be pressed from the shaft.

23. Remove the front and rear bearings from the countergear by using a press or similar tool.

24. To disassemble the synchronizers, remove the spread springs and the shift inserts. Separate the coupling sleeve from the hub.

25. With the adapter plate still in the holding fixture, remove the bearing retainer bolts with an appropriate tool. Remove the bearing from the rear extension side of the adapter plate. The outer race of the counter gear rear bearing can be removed from the adapter plate with the aid of a brass punch.

26. The rear extension housing can be disassembled by the removal of the lock pin from the striking lever and the main selector shift rod (striking rod). The rod can then be removed from the housing.

27. Replace all necessary parts, seals and gaskets.

ASSEMBLY

1. With the adapter plate in the holding fixture and locked in a vise or appropriate tool, install the countergear bearing outer race. Install the mainshaft bearing. Install the bearing retainer and screws. Torque the screws to 5.8 to 9.4 ft. lbs. (0.8 to 1.3 Kg-m). Stake each screw head to the retainer at two points.

2. Assemble the synchronizers by placing the hubs into the coupling sleeves. Fit the inserts into their respective grooves and install the spread springs so that the ends of the springs are not in the same insert.

3. Install the 5th speed needle bearing, 5th gear, synchronizer (baulk) ring and the 4th/5th speed synchronizer assembly on the front of the mainshaft.

4. Install a selective snap-ring onto the mainshaft so that the minimum clearance exists between the end face of the hub and the snap-ring. The snap-ring can be selected from the following list:

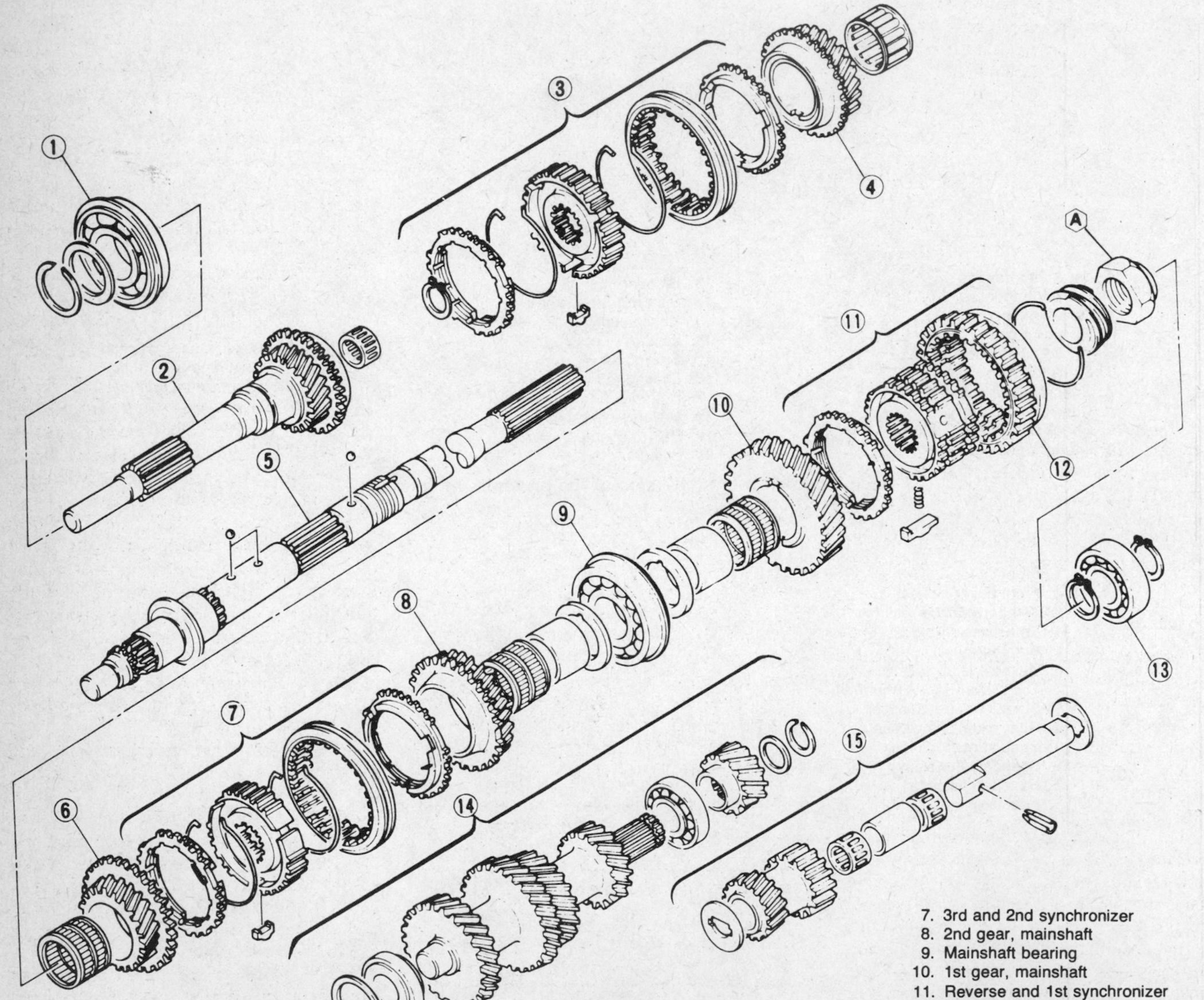

1. Main drive bearing
2. Main drive gear
3. 4th and 5th synchronizer
4. 5th gear, mainshaft
5. Mainshaft
6. 3rd gear, mainshaft
7. 3rd and 2nd synchronizer
8. 2nd gear, mainshaft
9. Mainshaft bearing
10. 1st gear, mainshaft
11. Reverse and 1st synchronizer
12. Reverse gear, mainshaft
13. Mainshaft end bearing
14. Counter gear assembly
15. Idler gear assembly

Exploded view of gear train components

No.	Thickness	
---	mm	(in.)
1	1.40 to 1.45	(0.0551 to 0.0571)
2	1.45 to 1.50	(0.0571 to 0.0591)
3	1.50 to 1.55	(0.0591 to 0.0610)
4	1.55 to 1.60	(0.0610 to 0.0630)
5	1.60 to 1.65	(0.0630 to 0.0650)

5. Install the 3rd gear needle bearing, 3rd gear, 3rd gear synchronizer (baulk) ring, 2nd/3rd gear synchronizer, fit the 2nd gear bushing to the mainshaft, along with the mainshaft bearing thrust washer.

6. Install the 2nd speed synchronizer (baulk) ring, needle bearing, 2nd gear, steel ball and the thrust washer.

7. Press the main drive gear bearing on to the main drive gear and install the spacer and secure with a snap-ring that will eliminate end-play between the spacer and the snap-ring. A selective snap-ring can be selected from the following list:

No.	Thickness	
---	mm	(in.)
1	1.49 to 1.55	(0.0587 to 0.0610)
2	1.56 to 1.62	(0.0614 to 0.0638)
3	1.62 to 1.68	(0.0638 to 0.0661)
4	1.68 to 1.74	(0.0661 to 0.0685)
5	1.74 to 1.80	(0.0685 to 0.0709)
6	1.80 to 1.86	(0.0709 to 0.0732)
7	1.86 to 1.92	(0.0732 to 0.0756)

8. Press the front and rear bearings onto the countergear with appropriate tools.

9. Place the mainshaft assembly into the adapter plate and place the mainshaft nut onto the shaft.

10. Using a puller type tool, move the mainshaft into the adapter plate until the thrust washer to bearing clearance is approximately 0.39 inch (10. mm).

11. Install the pilot bearing into the main drive gear bore and install the main drive gear and the synchronizer (baulk) ring onto the mainshaft assembly.

12. Assemble the countergear assembly to the mainshaft gear assembly.

13. Continuing the pulling effort, move the mainshaft and countergear assemblies into the adapter plate.

14. Place the 1st countergear on the countergear assembly and press into position. Install the spacer on the rear of the 1st countergear and secure it with a new snap-ring.

15. Install the steel ball and the thick thrust washer on the end of the mainshaft, install the synchronizer with the reverse gear, 1st gear along with the needle bearing and bushing, the idler gear and the needle bearing.

16. Install the mainshaft nut and tighten it snugly. Lock two gears at the same time

to lock the gear train, and tighten the locknut to 101 to 123 ft. lbs. (14 to 17 Kg-m). Stake the nut to the groove of the mainshaft with a punch.

17. Check the gear end-play, which should conform to the following specifications:

1st gear
0.27 to 0.37 mm
(0.0106 to 0.0146 in.)

2nd gear
0.20 to 0.30 mm
(0.0079 to 0.0118 in.)

3rd gear
0.05 to 0.15 mm
(0.0020 to 0.0059 in.)

5th gear
0.05 to 0.20 mm
(0.0020 to 0.0079 in.)

Reverse idler gear
0.15 to 0.40 mm
(0.0059 to 0.0157 in.)

18. Fit a 0.043 inch (1.1 mm) thick snap-ring to the front side of the mainshaft end bearing. Install the mainshaft end bearing and fit another snap-ring to the mainshaft on the rear side of the bearing, to eliminate end-play. A list of selective snap-rings are available as follows:

No.	Thickness	
---	mm	(in)
1	1.1	(0.043)
2	1.2	(0.047)
3	1.3	(0.051)
4	1.4	(0.055)

19. Place the 1st/reverse selector rod into the adapter plate, position the 1st/reverse fork into its gear position, and slide the selector rod into the fork.

20. Place the 1st/reverse selector rod in

the neutral position and install the interlock plunger into the adapter plate.

21. Insert the 2nd/3rd selector rod into the adapter plate, position the 2nd/3rd and 4th/5th forks in their respective gear grooves and slide the 2nd/3rd selector rod through the 2nd/3rd and 4th/5th forks.

22. Place the 2nd/3rd selector rod in the neutral position and insert the interlock plunger in the adapter plate.

23. Install the 4th/5th selector rod into the adapter plate and through the 4th/5th fork.

24. Secure the forks to the selector rods with the retaining pins.

25. Install the check balls and springs in their respective bores of the adapter plate.

26. Apply sealer to the check ball plugs and install the plugs in the adapter plate.

NOTE: The check ball plug for the 1st/ reverse selector rod is longer than the other plugs.

27. To insure that the interlock plungers are operating properly, slide the 2nd/3rd selector rod into gear and attempt to move the other selector rods into gear. The gears should not mesh. Continue to check the remaining selector rods.

28. Remove the adapter plate from the holder tool. Apply sealer to the mating surfaces of the transmission case and the adapter plate.

29. Slide the transmission case onto the adapter plate by lightly tapping on the case with a soft hammer until the case and the adapter plate meet. Be sure the dowel pin is properly aligned.

30. As the case is being installed to the adapter plate, the front drive gear bearing and the countergear front bearing must be aligned to the transmission case.

31. Install the front drive gear bearing snap-ring into the bearing groove.

32. Assemble the main selector rod to the rear extension housing in the reverse of its removal. Apply sealer to the mating surfaces of the extension housing and the transmission case. Place the transmission gear train in the 5th gear and install the rear extension into place.

33. During the installation of the rear extension housing, align the striking lever into the selector rods.

34. Install the rear extension bolts and torque to 9 to 13 ft. lbs. (1.3 to 1.8 Kg-m).

35. Install the plunger into the rear extension. Install the reverse check spring and the return spring. Apply sealer to the return spring plug and install the plug in place.

36. Support the transmission assembly with its front side up. Rotate the main drive gear until the bearings are settled.

37. Using a special measuring tool or equivalent, measure the clearance between the measuring tool, mounted on the countergear, and the transmission case, using a thickness gauge.

38. When the correct shim is selected, install the front cover. Apply sealant to the

No.	"H" mm	(in)	Thickness of countershaft front bearing shim mm	(in)
1	1.200 to 1.225	(0.0472 to 0.0482)	1.350	(0.0531)
2	1.225 to 1.250	(0.0482 to 0.0492)	1.375	(0.0541)
3	1.250 to 1.275	(0.0492 to 0.0502)	1.400	(0.0551)
4	1.275 to 1.300	(0.0502 to 0.0512)	1.425	(0.0561)
5	1.300 to 1.325	(0.0512 to 0.0522)	1.450	(0.0571)
6	1.325 to 1.350	(0.0522 to 0.0531)	1.475	(0.0581)
7	1.350 to 1.375	(0.0531 to 0.0541)	1.500	(0.0591)
8	1.375 to 1.400	(0.0541 to 0.0551)	1.525	(0.0600)
9	1.400 to 1.425	(0.0551 to 0.0561)	1.550	(0.0610)
10	1.425 to 1.450	(0.0561 to 0.0571)	1.575	(0.0620)
11	1.450 to 1.475	(0.0571 to 0.0581)	1.600	(0.0630)
12	1.475 to 1.500	(0.0581 to 0.0591)	1.625	(0.0640)
13	1.500 to 1.525	(0.0591 to 0.0600)	1.650	(0.0650)
14	1.525 to 1.550	(0.0600 to 0.0610)	1.675	(0.0659)
15	1.550 to 1.575	(0.0610 to 0.0620)	1.700	(0.0669)
16	1.575 to 1.600	(0.0620 to 0.0630)	1.725	(0.0679)
17	1.600 to 1.625	(0.0630 to 0.0640)	1.750	(0.0689)
18	1.625 to 1.650	(0.0640 to 0.0650)	1.775	(0.0699)

threads of the bolts and torque to 9 to 13 ft. lbs. (1.3 to 0.8 Kg-m).

39. Install the speedometer driven gear assembly, install the electrical switches that were removed during the disassembly.

40. Install the operating lever, the clutch release bearing and the return spring.

41. Install the dust cover, fill the transmission to the proper level with lubricant.

TYPE 13

4 Speed Transmission—Model F4W63L

Datsun

DISASSEMBLY

1. Secure the transmission and drain the lubricant.

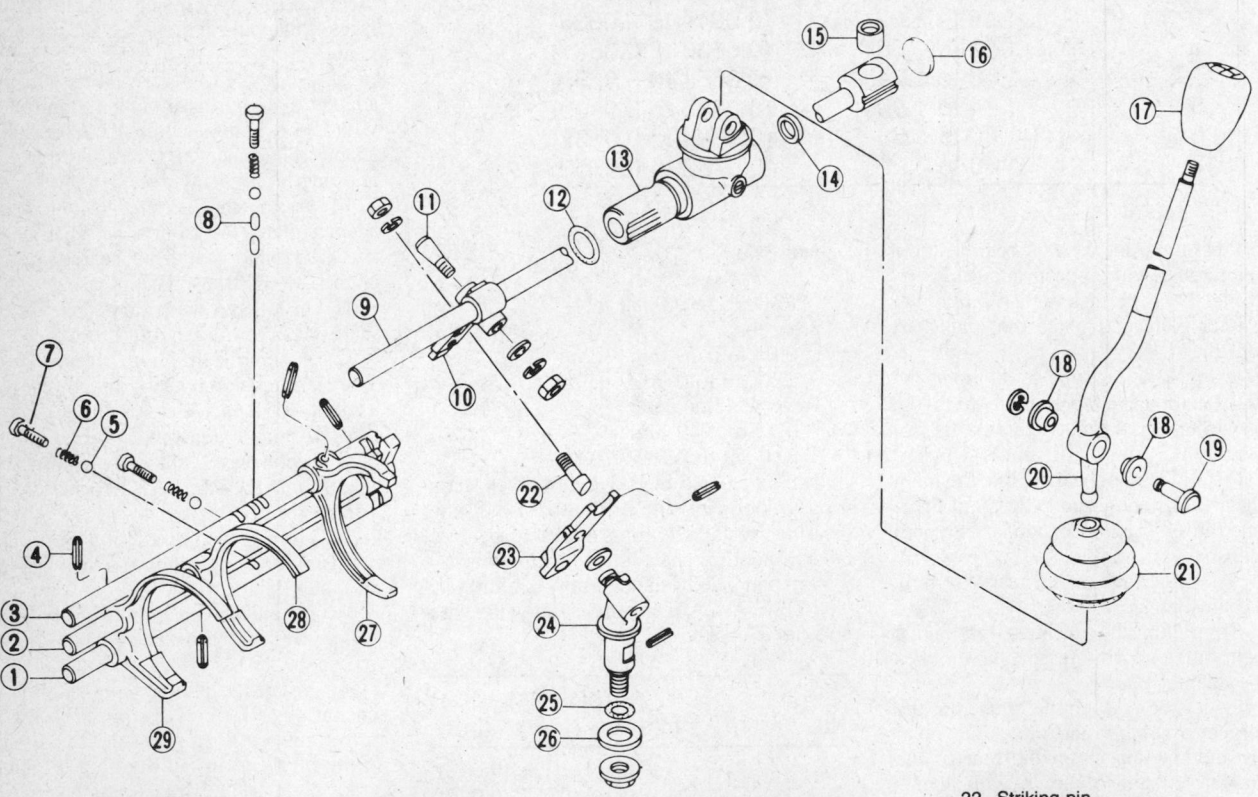

1. 4th and 5th fork rod	8. Interlock plunger	15. Control lever bushing
2. 2nd and 3rd fork rod	9. Striking rod	16. Expansion plug
3. 1st and reverse fork rod	10. Striking lever	17. Control lever knob
4. Retaining pin	11. Lock pin	18. Control pin bushing
5. Checking ball	12. O-ring	19. Control arm pin
6. Check ball spring	13. Striking guide	20. Control lever
7. Check ball plug	14. Striking guide oil seal	21. Control lever boot

22. Striking pin	
23. Shift arm	
24. Shift arm bracket	
25. Arm bracket O-ring	
26. Arm bracket plain washer	
27. 1st and reverse shift fork	
28. 2nd and 3rd shift fork	
29. 4th and 5th shift fork	

Exploded view of shift selector rod and fork components

2. Remove the dust cover from the transmission case.

3. Remove the release bearing and the operating lever. Remove the electrical switches from the case.

4. Remove the speedometer driven gear assembly.

5. Remove the front cover and the bottom cover from the transmission assembly.

6. Position the gearshift into the neutral position and pull out the striking rod (main shift control rod) pin bolt.

7. Remove the rear extension housing retaining bolts and tap the housing with a soft hammer to remove it from the transmission case.

8. Remove the striking rod (main shift control rod).

9. Drive the shifting fork retaining pins from the forks and selector shafts.

10. Remove the three check ball plugs. Do not lose the check balls and springs. Remove the two interlock plungers.

11. Remove the selector rods and shifting forks from the transmission. Keep in their proper order for installation.

12. Lock the gear train by meshing two gears at the same time. Straighten the lock washer and loosen the nut on the mainshaft. Place the gear train back in the neutral position.

13. Use a dummy countershaft tool or equivalent, and push the countershaft from the transmission case, from the rear to the front. Do not drop the needle bearings or thrust washers into the transmission.

14. Remove the counter gear assembly from the case.

15. Remove the snap-ring retaining the reverse idler counter gear in place and remove the shaft from the rear of the case. Do not remove the needle bearing.

16. Remove the mainshaft bearing retainer and bolts. Remove the mainshaft assembly from the rear of the transmission case. Remove the loose synchronizer (baulk) ring from the front of the mainshaft.

17. Remove the pilot bearing located between the main drive gear and the mainshaft.

18. Using a wooden shaft, drive the main drive gear and bearing from the transmission case. Do not allow the gear to drop.

19. The main drive gear bearing can be removed after the retaining snap-ring is removed. A press or bearing puller should be used.

20. Remove the front retaining snap-ring from the mainshaft and remove the 3rd/4th synchronizer assembly, the 3rd gear and mainshaft needle bearing from the shaft.

21. Remove the locknut from the mainshaft and remove the reverse gear, reverse gear hub and the speedometer drive gear.

NOTE: Do not lose the steel ball locating the speedometer drive gear to the mainshaft.

22. Install a suitable puller or set in a press and remove the 1st speed gear, along with the bearing and retainer.

--- **CAUTION** ---

Do not attach pulling or press tool to the 2nd gear as damage to the 1st gear mainshaft bushing can result. Do not remove the needle bearing with the 1st gear bearing as the needle bearing could be damaged by the second steel ball on the mainshaft.

23. Remove the second steel ball on the mainshaft and install a puller or set in a press and remove the 1st gear bushing, along with the 1st/2nd synchronizer assembly and the 2nd gear.

24. To disassemble the synchronizers, remove the spread springs and take out the shifting inserts. Separate the coupling sleeve from the synchronizer hub.

25. Clean the assemblies, replace the necessary parts and replace the necessary seals and gaskets.

ASSEMBLY

1. Install the synchronizer hub into the coupling sleeve and fit the three shift inserts in their respective grooves.

2. Install the spread springs on each side of the coupling sleeve and hook into the shift inserts.

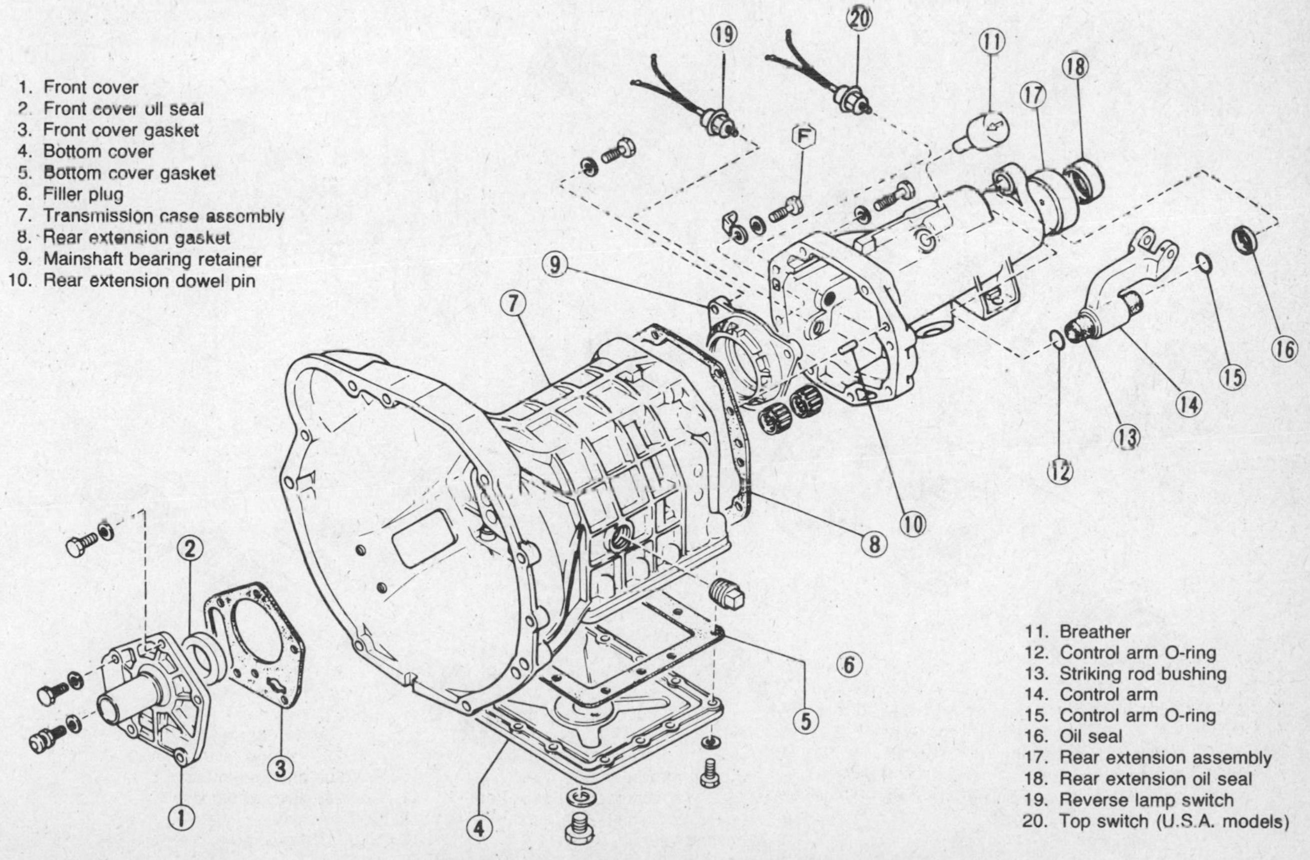

1. Front cover
2. Front cover oil seal
3. Front cover gasket
4. Bottom cover
5. Bottom cover gasket
6. Filler plug
7. Transmission case assembly
8. Rear extension gasket
9. Mainshaft bearing retainer
10. Rear extension dowel pin

11. Breather
12. Control arm O-ring
13. Striking rod bushing
14. Control arm
15. Control arm O-ring
16. Oil seal
17. Rear extension assembly
18. Rear extension oil seal
19. Reverse lamp switch
20. Top switch (U.S.A. models)

Transmission case components, model F4W63L

NOTE: Do not hook the spread spring ends in the same shift insert.

3. Assemble the 2nd gear needle bearing, 2nd gear, 2nd gear synchronizer (baulk) ring and the 1st/2nd speed synchronizer assembly onto the mainshaft.

4. Install the 1st gear bushing onto the mainshaft by using a brass drift. Install the 1st gear synchronizer (baulk) ring, needle bearing, steel ball and the thrust washer onto the mainshaft.

5. Press the mainshaft bearing and the reverse hub onto the mainshaft.

6. Install the 3rd gear needle roller bearing, 3rd synchronizer (baulk) ring, 3rd/4th speed synchronizer assembly onto the mainshaft.

7. Install a new snap-ring onto the mainshaft so that a minimum of clearance exists between the face of the hub and the snap-ring groove.

8. Install the reverse gear, the steel ball, the speedometer gear, lock plate and the nut onto the mainshaft.

9. Install the mainshaft assembly into the rear of the transmission case and install the mainshaft bearing retainer plate and bolts.

Torque to 5.8 to 7.2 ft. lbs. (7.8 to 9.8 Nm).

10. Install the main drive gear bearing in place, using a press or bearing installer.

Install the spacer and the retaining selector snap-ring, so that a minimum of clearance exists between the spacer and the snap-ring. Available selections are as follows:

No.	Thickness	
	mm	(in.)
1	1.15 to 1.25	(0.0453 to 0.0492)
2	1.35 to 1.45	(0.0531 to 0.0571)
3	1.25 to 1.35	(0.0492 to 0.0531)
4	1.45 to 1.55	(0.0571 to 0.0610)
5	1.05 to 1.15	(0.0413 to 0.0453)

No.	Thickness	
	mm	(in.)
1	2.35 to 2.40	(0.0925 to 0.0945)
2	2.40 to 2.45	(0.0945 to 0.0965)
3	2.45 to 2.50	(0.0965 to 0.0984)
4	2.50 to 2.55	(0.0984 to 0.1004)
5	2.55 to 2.60	(0.1004 to 0.1024)

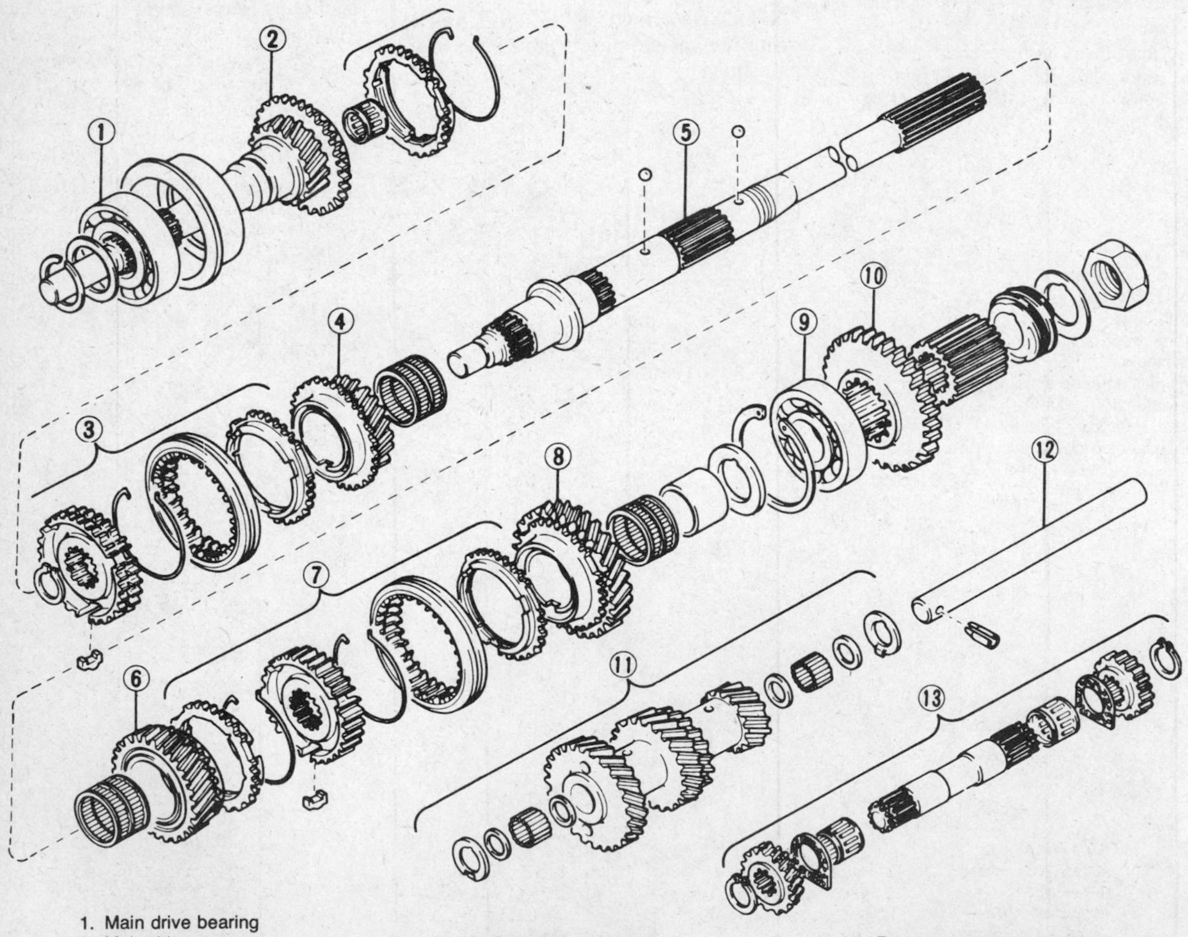

1. Main drive bearing
2. Main drive gear
3. 3rd & 4th synchronizer
4. 3rd gear, mainshaft
5. Mainshaft
6. 2nd gear, mainshaft
7. 1st & 2nd synchronizer
8. 1st gear, mainshaft
9. Mainshaft bearing
10. Reverse gear, mainshaft
11. Counter gear assembly
12. Countershaft
13. Idler gear assembly

Exploded view of gear train components

No.	Thickness mm	(in.)
1	1.40 to 1.45	(0.0551 to 0.0571)
2	1.45 to 1.50	(0.0571 to 0.0591)
3	1.50 to 1.55	(0.0591 to 0.0610)
4	1.55 to 1.60	(0.0610 to 0.0630)
5	1.60 to 1.65	(0.0630 to 0.0650)

No.	Thickness mm	(in.)
1	1.49 to 1.55	(0.0587 to 0.0610)
2	1.56 to 1.62	(0.0614 to 0.0638)
3	1.62 to 1.68	(0.0638 to 0.0661)
4	1.68 to 1.74	(0.0661 to 0.0685)
5	1.74 to 1.80	(0.0685 to 0.0709)
6	1.80 to 1.86	(0.0709 to 0.0732)
7	1.86 to 1.92	(0.0732 to 0.0756)

11. Install the pilot bearing into the bore of the main drive gear. Install the main drive gear assembly into the transmission case front.

12. Install the reverse idler shaft into the transmission case from the rear, with the identification mark facing towards the rear.

13. Assemble the thrust washer and the reverse idler (helical) gear and seat the snap-ring in its groove in the top of the reverse idler shaft.

14. Insert a 0.004 inch (0.1 mm) feeler gauge blade between the gear and the thrust washer. With the shaft pushed fully to the rear, install the thrust washer and the spur gear and fit the snap-ring, selected to obtain the proper end-play for the reverse idler gear.

15. The reverse idler gear end-play is 0.0039 to 0.0118 inch (0.10 to 0.30 mm).

NOTE: Install the thrust washers so that the grooved sides are facing towards the gears.

16. Install a dummy shaft or equivalent into the countergear and install the inner washers into the gear. Apply grease to the

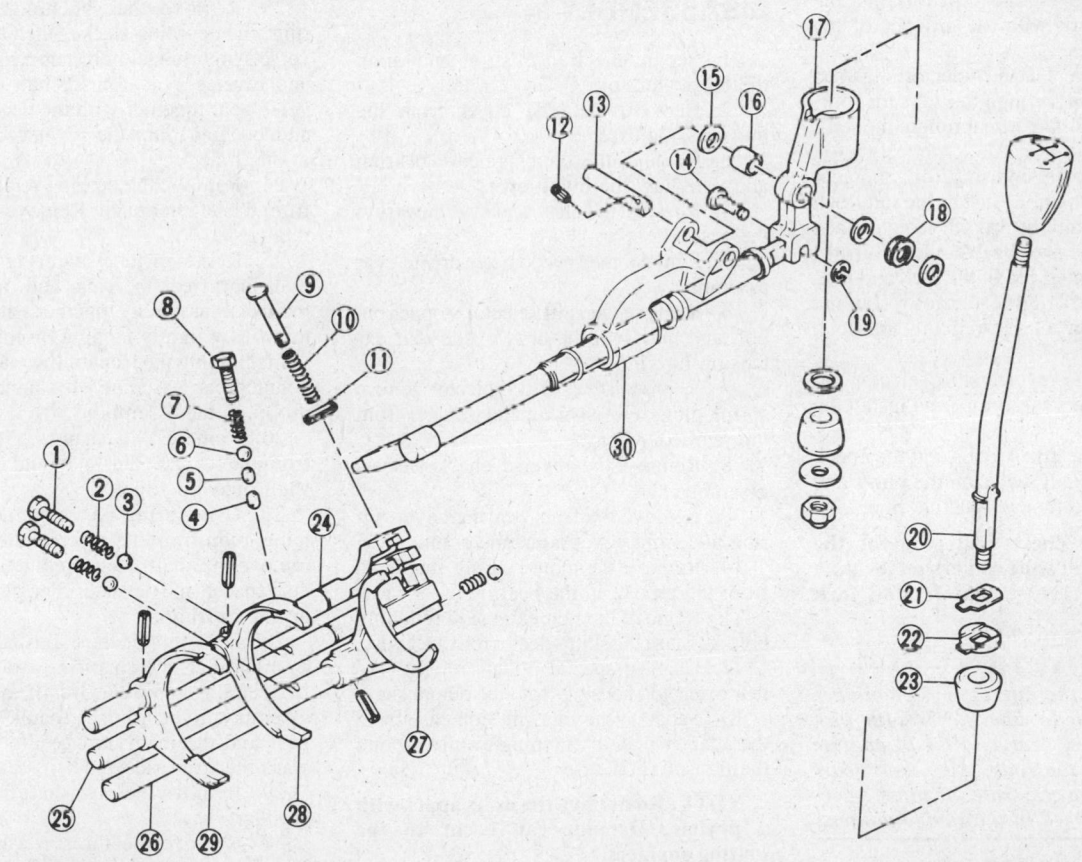

1. Check ball plug
2. Check ball spring
3. Check ball
4. Interlock plunger
5. Interlock plunger
6. Check ball
7. Check ball spring
8. Check ball plug
9. Reverse fork pin
10. Reverse pin return spring
11. Roller pin
12. Retaining pin
13. Control arm pin
14. Striking rod pin
15. Thrust washer
16. Control bushing
17. Control lever bracket
18. Control spring
19. Striking pin C-ring
20. Control lever
21. Control lever upper washer
22. Control lever upper washer
23. Control lever rubber
24. 1st and 2nd fork rod
25. 3rd and 4th fork rod
26. Reverse fork rod
27. Reverse shift fork
28. 1st and 2nd shift fork
29. 3rd and 4th fork rod
30. Control arm

Exploded view of shift selector rod and fork components

needle bearings and install 21 bearings on each end of the gear. Install the outer washers and the thrust washers in place on the gear assembly. Place the gear assembly into the transmission case.

NOTE: If a dummy countershaft is used, the shaft should only be as long as the gear assembly and the diameter smaller than the original countershaft.

17. Install the retaining pin in the front of the countershaft and push the shaft into the transmission case, from the front to the rear, engaging the thrust washer, the countergear and forcing the dummy shaft (if used) out through the hole in the back of the case.

18. The rear thrust washer is used to determine the countergear end-play. The end-play is 0.0020 to 0.0059 inch (0.05 to 0.15 mm).

19. After the end-play has been determined, locate the countershaft pin in its indent at the front of the transmission case.

20. Mesh two gears so that the transmission gear train is locked. Tighten the mainshaft locknut to 58 to 80 ft. lbs. (8.0 to 11.0 Kg-m). Secure the mainshaft locknut washer by bending over the nut.

21. Align the 1st/2nd shift fork and the 3rd/4th shift fork with the grooves of the coupling sleeves.

22. Install the 1st/2nd selector shift rod into the case and through the selector fork. Install the retaining pin through the fork and rod.

23. Place the 1st/2nd shift fork and gear in the Neutral position. Install the interlock plunger and install the 3rd/4th selector shift rod into the case and the 3rd/4th shift fork. Install the retaining pin in the fork and rod.

24. Place the 3rd/4th selector rod in the Neutral position and install the interlock plunger.

25. Install the reverse shift selector rod through the reverse shift fork and install the retaining pin.

26. Install the check balls and the check ball springs. Install sealer on the plugs and install them into their respective bores.

NOTE: The check ball plug for the 3rd/4th fork and shift rod is shorter than those for the reverse and 1st/2nd fork and shift rods.

—————— CAUTION ——————
To insure that the interlock plungers are properly installed, slide the 3rd/4th fork selector rod into gear and try to operate the other selector rods. All other gears should not mesh. Operate the other selector rods and check in the same manner.

27. Place all gears in the Neutral position and install the rear extension to the transmission case, using sealer on the mating surfaces.

28. As the rear extension housing is being installed, align the striking lever to the shift rod brackets.

29. Install the front main shaft cover.

Apply sealer to the threads of the bolts and torque to 5.8 to 7.2 ft. lbs. (0.8 to 1.0 Kg-m).

30. Install the clutch release bearing and the operating shaft to the front of the case. Install the dust cover.

31. Install the electrical switches that were removed during the disassembly.

32. Install the speedometer driven gear assembly.

33. Install the bottom cover to the case and fill the unit with the proper level of lubricant.

TYPE 14

5 Speed Transmission—Model FS5W60A, L

Datsun

DISASSEMBLY

1. Secure the transmission and drain the lubricating oil.

2. Remove the dust cover from the transmission case.

3. Remove the clutch release bearing and withdraw the pivot lever.

4. Remove the electrical switches from the case.

5. Remove the speedometer driven gear assembly.

6. Remove the shift selector stopper pin bolt and nut from the boss of the rear extension housing.

7. Remove the shift selector return spring plug, return spring and plunger from the rear extension.

8. Remove the reverse check sleeves assembly.

9. Remove the front bearing cover, O-ring and front cover adjusting shim.

10. Remove the main bearing snap-ring from the groove in the bearing outer race.

11. Remove the rear extension retaining bolts and turn the shift selector rod clockwise.

12. Using a special puller, remove the rear extension housing from the output shaft.

13. Separate the transmission case from the adapter plate by tapping evenly around the transmission case.

NOTE: Do not pry the units apart with a prybar. Damage can occur to the mating surfaces.

14. A special type holding tool should be used to hold the adapter plate so that it can be held in a vise or other holding tool. This plate can be purchased or fabricated.

15. Mount the unit in the holding tool and remove the countergear thrust washer.

16. Using a pin punch, remove the retaining pins from the forks and selector rods.

17. Remove the check ball plugs (3).

18. Remove the selector rods from the adapter plate and detach the forks from the rods.

—————— CAUTION ——————
Do not lose the check balls, springs and the two interlock plungers.

NOTE: Each gear and shaft can be removed from the adapter plate independently of the other shaft and without the removal of the selector rods and forks.

19. Remove the outer snap-ring of the mainshaft end bearing with a bearing puller. Remove the second bearing snap-ring from the shaft.

20. Engage the 1st and reverse speeds so that the gear train is locked in two gears at the same time. Remove the countergear nut after releasing the staking.

21. From the rear extension side of the adapter plate, remove the mainshaft holding snap-ring, C-ring holder, C-ring and the thrust washer.

22. Remove the O.D. main gear with the needle bearings and the O.D. countergear together.

23. Remove the synchronizer (baulk) ring, the coupling sleeve, the O.D. and reverse synchronizer hub snap-ring, the O.D. and reverse synchronizer hub and the reverse gear together with the needle bearing and bushing, and the reverse countergear at one time.

24. Remove the bearing retainer screws from the adapter plate. Remove the bearing retainer.

25. Remove the snap-ring from the mainshaft rear bearing and remove the mainshaft assembly together with the countergear by lightly tapping on the rear shaft while holding the front of the mainshaft and countergear assembly by hand to avoid dropping the assembly.

26. Remove the snap-ring and spacer from the reverse idler shaft and tap the idler shaft outward slightly.

27. Using a pin punch, remove the retaining pin from the reverse idler shaft and remove the shaft. Remove the thrust washers, spacer and reverse idler gear with the needle bearing.

28. Disassemble the mainshaft assembly by removing the snap-ring from the shaft front end. Remove the 3rd/4th synchronizer assembly, synchronizer (baulk) rings, 3rd gear and the mainshaft needle bearing toward the front side.

29. Remove the mainshaft bearing with a puller.

30. Remove the thrust washer and 1st gear, together with the needle bearing and bushing, synchronizer (baulk) rings, coupling sleeve, 1st/2nd synchronizer hub and the 2nd gear with the needle bearing.

31. Remove the snap-ring and spacer from the maindrive gear and remove the bearing with a press or puller.

32. The countershaft rear bearing can be removed with the use of a press.

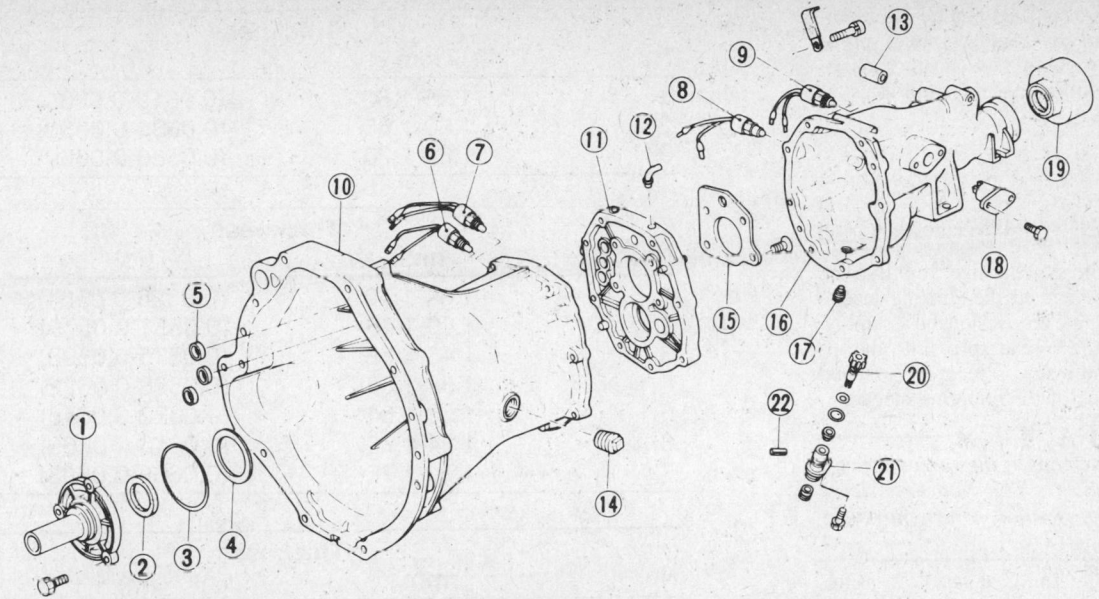

1. Front cover
2. Front cover oil seal
3. Front cover O-ring
4. Front cover adjusting shim
5. Welch plug
6. Top gear switch
7. O.D. gear switch
8. Reverse lamp switch

9. Neutral switch
10. Transmission case assembly
11. Adapter plate
12. Breather
13. Return spring bushing
14. Filler plug
15. Bearing retainer
16. Rear extension assembly

17. Drain plug
18. Reverse check sleeve
19. Rear extension dust cover with oil seal
20. Speedometer pinion
21. Speedometer sleeve
22. Retaining pin

Transmission case components, model FS5W60A

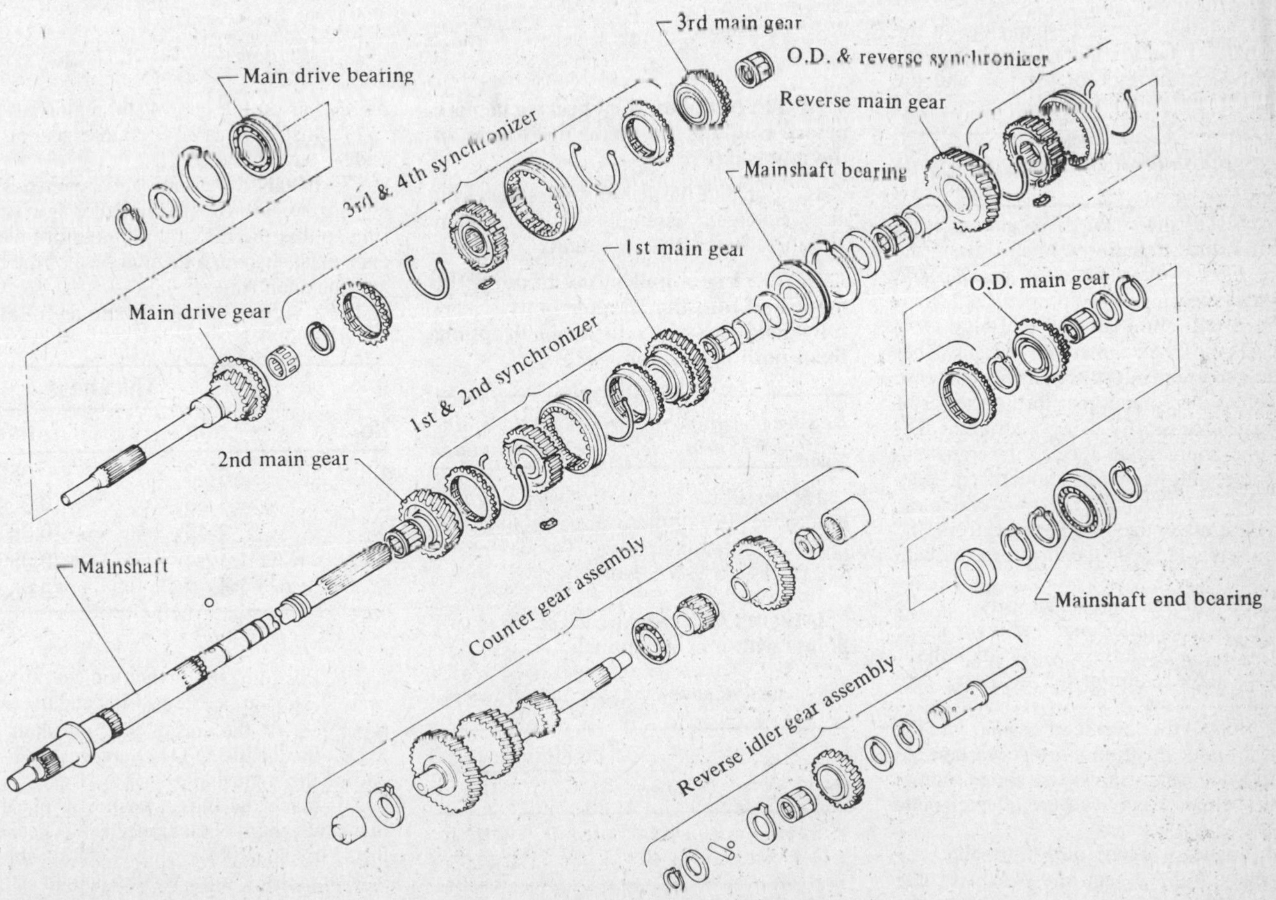

Exploded view of gear train components

33. The synchronizers can be disassembled for repairs by removing the spread spring and removing the shifting insert. Separate the coupling sleeve from the synchronizer hub.

ASSEMBLY

1. Replace any bearings, seals or worn parts as required.
2. Install the synchronizer hub into the coupling sleeve and fit the shifting inserts into their respective grooves on the assembly.
3. Install the spread springs to the inserts so that the insert is securely attached to the inner side of the coupling sleeve.

─────── CAUTION ───────
Do not hook the ends of the spread springs to the same insert. The hub and sleeve should operate smoothly when moved by hand.

4. Install the 2nd gear needle bearing, 2nd gear, synchronizer (baulk) ring, 1st/2nd speed synchronizer assembly, 1st gear synchronizer (baulk) ring, 1st gear bushing, needle bearing, 1st gear and thrust washer onto the mainshaft.
5. Press the bearing onto the mainshaft, using a press or bearing installer.
6. Install the 3rd gear needle bearing, 3rd gear, synchronizer (baulk) ring, 3rd/4th synchronizer assembly on the front side of the mainshaft.
7. Install a selective snap-ring on the mainshaft so that a minimum clearance exists between the face of the hub and the ring.

─────── CAUTION ───────
Be sure the snap-ring is fully seated in its groove.

8. Install the main drive gear bearing onto the shaft. Install the main drive bearing spacer on the main drive bearing and secure the bearing with a proper sized snapring that will eliminate any end-play.
9. Install the countergear thrust washer and countergear into the transmission case and select the countergear thrust washer of proper thickness, by using a straightedge, from the countergear face to the transmission case, allowing for standard end-play of 0.0039–0.0079 inch (0.10 mm–0.20 mm).
10. Remove the countergear from the transmission and keep the thrust washer with the gear.
11. Install the thrust washers, needle bearing, reverse idler gear and inner thrust washer in place on the reverse idler shaft. Install a new retaining pin in the reverse idler shaft.
12. Install the reverse idler shaft into the adapter plate. Position a thrust washer and install a new snap-ring so that the minimum clearance exists between the adapter plate and the thrust washer.
13. Install a synchronizer (baulk) ring on the main drive gear and place with the mainshaft to complete this portion of the assembly.

No.	Thickness	
	mm	(in)
1	1.55-1.60	(0.0610-0.0630)
2	1.60-1.65	(0.0630-0.0650)
3	1.65-1.70	(0.0650-0.0669)

No.	Thickness	
	mm	(in)
1	1.34-1.40	(0.0528-0.0551)
2	1.40-1.46	(0.0551-0.0575)
3	1.46-1.52	(0.0575-0.0598)
4	1.52-1.58	(0.0598-0.0622)
5	1.58-1.64	(0.0622-0.0646)
6	1.64-1.70	(0.0646-0.0669)
7	1.70-1.76	(0.0669-0.0693)

No.	Thickness	
	mm	(in)
1	2.20-2.25	(0.0866-0.0886)
2	2.25-2.30	(0.0886-0.0906)
3	2.30-2.35	(0.0906-0.0925)
4	2.35-2.40	(0.0925-0.0945)
5	2.40-2.45	(0.0945-0.0965)
6	2.45-2.50	(0.0965-0.0984)
7	2.50-2.55	(0.0984-0.1004)
8	2.55-2.60	(0.1004-0.1024)

NOTE: Install the pilot bearing in place before coupling the main drive gear to the mainshaft.

14. Combine the mainshaft assembly with the countergear assembly and place them into the adapter plate as a unit.

NOTE: Use a puller tool to move the mainshaft into the adapter plate. Carefully hold the gears to avoid dropping them until in position.

─────── CAUTION ───────
Be sure the snap-ring groove on the mainshaft rear bearing clears the adapter plate.

15. Install the rear bearing snap-ring into its groove. Install the bearing retainer and install the retaining screws. Torque to 5.1–7.2 ft. lbs. (6.9–9.8 Nm).

IMPORTANT: Stake each screw at two points with a center punch.

The selective snap-rings are as follows:

No.	Thickness	
	mm	(in)
1	1.1	(0.043)
2	1.2	(0.047)

16. Place the thrust washer, reverse gear bushing, needle bearing and the reverse main drive gear on the end of the mainshaft.
17. Install the reverse countergear on the end of the countershaft.
18. Install the O.D. and reverse synchronizer assembly and install a new snapring so that the minimum amount of clearance exists between the end face of the hub and the snap-ring.

The selective snap-rings are as follows:

No.	Thickness	
	mm	(in)
1	1.32	(0.0520)
2	1.38	(0.0543)
3	1.46	(0.0575)
4	1.54	(0.0606)
5	1.62	(0.0638)

19. Position the synchronizer (baulk) ring, O.D. gear needle bearing and the O.D. main gear on the end of the mainshaft.
20. Install the O.D. countergear on the end of the mainshaft.
21. Place the thrust washer in place so that a minimum of clearance exists between the C-holder and the ring. Position the C-ring and the C-ring holder and fit a new mainshaft holder snap-ring.

The selective snap-rings are as follows:

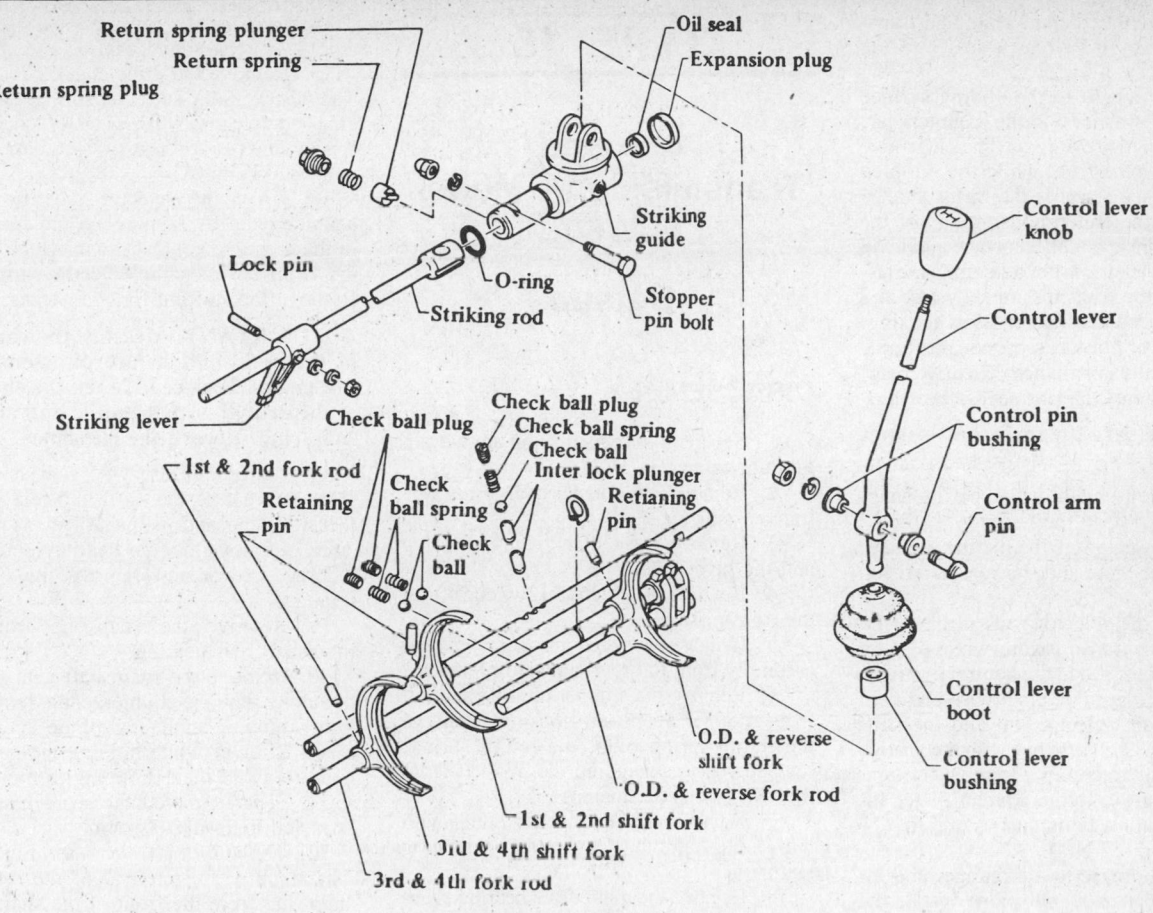

Exploded view of shift selector rod and fork components

No.	Thickness	
	mm	(in.)
1	7.87	(0.3098)
2	7.94	(0.3126)
3	8.01	(0.3154)
4	8.08	(0.3181)
5	8.15	(0.3209)
6	8.22	(0.3236)

22. Engage the 1st and reverse gears and tighten the countershaft nut to 36–43 ft. lbs. (49–59 Nm).

23. Stake the countershaft nut to the groove in the countershaft with a punch.

24. Measure the gear end-play. The measurements are as follows:

1st main gear
0.15–0.25mm
(0.0059–0.0098 in.)
2nd main gear
0.30–0.40 mm
(0.0118–0.0157 in.)
3rd main gear
0.15–0.35 mm
(0.0059–0.0138 in.)
O.D. (5th) main gear
0.30–0.40 mm
(0.0118–0.0157 in.)

Reverse main gear
0.30–0.55 mm
(0.0118–0.0217 in.)
Countergear
0.10–0.20 mm
(0.0039–0.0079 in.)
Reverse idler gear
0–0.20 mm
(0–0.0079 in.)

25. Place a snap-ring to the front of the mainshaft end bearing, measuring 0.0453 inch (1.15 mm).

26. Install the mainshaft end bearing using a bearing installer. Fit a snap-ring to the rear side of the bearing to eliminate any end-play. The available snap-rings are as follows:

No.	Thickness	
	mm	(in.)
1	1.15	(0.0453)
2	1.02	(0.047)

27. Install the O.D. and reverse fork and selector rod into the adapter plate. Place the rod in the neutral position and install the interlock plunger into its bore in the adapter plate.

28. Install the 3rd/4th selector rod into the fork and install a new snap-ring. Install the selector rod and fork into the adapter plate.

29. Insert the interlock plunger into the adapter plate with the selector rods in the neutral position.

30. Install the 1st/2nd selector rod into the fork and install both into the adapter plate.

31. Secure all the selector rods and forks with new retaining pins.

IMPORTANT: Properly align the groove in the assembled selector rod with the interlock plunger, during the assembly. Align the shift forks with their respective coupling sleeves before installing.

32. Install the check balls and springs into the proper bores. Seal and install the check ball plugs.

33. Align the center notch in each fork selector rod with the check balls, as required.

NOTE: The selector rod for the 1st/2nd gear is longer than the 3rd/4th or the O.D./Reverse selector rods.

───── CAUTION ─────

To make sure the interlock plunger is installed properly, slide the 1st/2nd selector rod into gear and operate the other selector rods. All other gears should not mesh. Check all other rods in the same manner.

34. Prepare the adapter plate and transmission case by installing a sealer to the mating surfaces.

35. Apply grease to the sliding surface of the thrust washer for the countergear, that was selected previously. The oil groove should face to the front while the dimpled side should face towards the thrust side.

36. Place the clutch housing end of the transmission case flat on a surface and level the housing. Position the adapter plate assembly into the transmission housing and tap the plate into the transmission housing. Line the dowel pin to its proper position.

37. Carefully install the main drive bearing and countergear front needle bearing.

NOTE: Be sure the mainshaft rotates freely.

38. Install the main drive bearing snap-ring in its groove in the bearing.

39. Apply sealant to the mating surfaces of the adapter plate and the rear extension housing.

40. Place the selector rods in the O.D. position on the transmission, while placing the main selector rod in the neutral position. Turn the striking guide clockwise and then adjust the main selector rod and the shift arm. Align the shift arm pin with the groove in the selector rods and assemble the rear extension housing to the adapter plate. Install the retaining bolts and torque to 12–16 ft. lbs. (16–22 Nm).

41. Install grease to the plunger and install it into the rear extension. Install the return spring, apply sealer to the return spring plug and install it.

42. Turn the transmission assembly so that the front is up. Measure the distance from the front end of the transmission case to the main drive bearing outer race with a depth gauge. Select a shim to correspond to the dimension or thickness "A". The front cover adjusting shim can be one of seven shims.

No.	"A"		Adjusting shim	
	mm	(in.)	mm	(in.)
1	6.05-6.09	(0.2382-0.2398)	0.50	(0.0197)
2	6.10-6.14	(0.2402-0.2417)	0.55	(0.0217)
3	6.15-6.19	(0.2421-0.2437)	0.60	(0.0236)
4	6.20-6.24	(0.2441-0.2457)	0.65	(0.0256)
5	6.25-6.29	(0.2461-0.2476)	0.70	(0.0276)
6	6.30-6.34	(0.2480-0.2496)	0.75	(0.0295)
7	6.35-6.39	(0.2500-0.2516)	0.80	(0.0315)

43. Install the front cover with the adjusting shim and the O-ring in place.

44. Install the speedometer driven gear and install the securing bolt and nut.

45. Install a new O-ring in the groove of the reverse check sleeve and tighten the bolts.

46. Replace the electrical switches that were removed during the disassembly.

47. Install the pivot lever, the release bearing and sleeve. Connect the holding spring and install the dust cover.

TYPE 15

4 Speed Transmission—Model F4W60L

Datsun

DISASSEMBLY

1. Secure the transmission and drain the lubricating oil.

2. Remove the dust cover from the transmission case.

3. Remove the clutch release bearing and the pivot lever.

4. Remove the electrical switches from the transmission case.

5. Remove the speedometer driven gear assembly from the rear extension housing.

6. Remove the stopper pin bolt and nut from the rear extension housing. Remove the return spring plug, the return spring, reverse check spring and the plunger from the rear extension housing.

7. Remove the front cover along with the O-ring and the front cover adjusting shim.

8. Remove the main drive bearing snap-ring from the bearing groove.

9. Remove the rear extension housing retaining bolts and rotate the striking rod (main shift control shaft) clockwise.

10. Drive the rear extension housing rearward by lightly tapping on the housing to separate the housing from the transmission.

11. Separate the transmission case from the adapter plate by lightly tapping the case from the plate.

---— **CAUTION** ———
Do not pry the transmission assembly apart with a pry bar. The mating surfaces can be damaged.
---

12. A special type holding tool should be used to hold the adapter plate so that it can be held in a vise or other holding tool. The plate can be purchased or fabricated.

13. Remove the countergear thrust washer and drive the shift fork retaining pins from the selector shafts.

14. Remove the reverse gear shift fork and the reverse idler gear.

15. Remove the three check ball plugs. The check balls and the springs will be exposed for removal. Visually check the spring lengths for proper installation and mark accordingly.

16. Drive the selector rods from the adapter plate by tapping on the front end of the rods. Do not lose the interlock plungers from between the selector shift rods. Remove the shifting forks as necessary.

IMPORTANT: Measure the end-play of the mainshaft before disassembly of the shaft. Measure between the end face of the 3rd/4th synchronizer hub and the snap-ring. Record the clearance.

17. Remove the reverse gear snap-ring from the rear of the shaft and remove the thrust washer and mainshaft reverse gear.

18. Remove the four bearing retainer attaching screws and remove the bearing retainer.

19. Remove the snap-ring from the mainshaft rear bearing.

20. Remove the mainshaft gear assembly along with the countergear assembly by lightly tapping on the rear of the shafts with a soft hammer while holding the gears by hand to avoid their dropping to the floor.

21. Separate the countergear, main drive gear and mainshaft assembly.

22. The mainshaft gear assembly can be disassembled by removal of the retaining snap-ring from the front of the shaft.

23. The mainshaft bearing must be pressed from the shaft and the remaining gears and hubs can be removed.

IMPORTANT: Observe the sequence and direction of the gear and hubs during the disassembly. Mark as required.

24. The main drive gear bearing can be pressed from the shaft after the removal of the retaining snap-ring. The pilot bearing can be removed from the shaft bore.

25. Remove the snap-ring from the rear of the countershaft and press out the counter reverse gear, using a suitable puller.

26. Remove the countergear rear bearing by the use of the bearing puller.

27. The synchronizers can be disassembled by removing the spread springs and removing the shifting inserts. Remove the coupling sleeves from the synchronizer hubs.

IMPORTANT: Note the direction of the coupling sleeves in relation to the hubs.

28. The reverse idler shaft snap-ring is removed and the shaft is removed from the adapter plate by lightly tapping on the shaft with a soft hammer.

29. The rear extension housing can be disassembled by removing the lock pin nut and lock pin from the striking lever (main shift control shaft). Remove the lever and the shaft can be removed from the housing.

30. Replace the necessary parts, clean the assembly, install new seal and prepare to reassemble.

1. Front cover
2. Front cover oil seal
3. Front cover O-ring
4. Front cover adjusting shim
5. Welch plug
6. Transmission case assembly
7. Filler plug
8. Adapter plate
9. Breather
10. Bearing retainer
11. Rear extension dowel pin
12. Reverse lamp switch
13. Rear extension assembly
14. Drain plug
15. Return spring bushing
16. Rear extension dust cover with oil seal
17. Top detecting switch

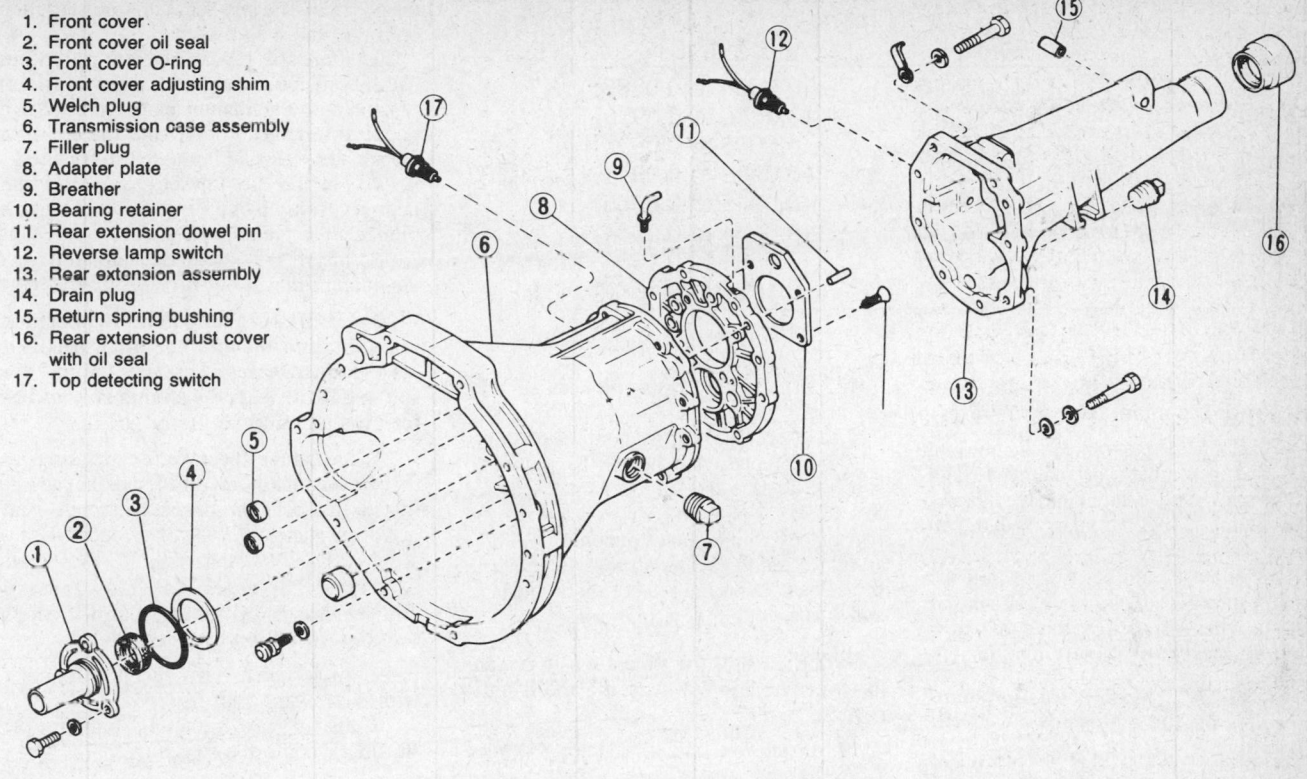

Transmission case components, model F4W60L

ASSEMBLY

1. Assemble the rear extension housing by installing the striking lever shaft (mainshaft control shaft) into the housing. Fit the striking lever to the shaft and install the retaining pin.

2. Install the reverse idler shaft into the adapter plate and install the retaining snapring.

3. Assemble the synchronizers by installing the coupling sleeves over the synchronizer hubs. Install the shifting inserts and the spread springs, being careful not to connect the spread spring ends to the same insert.

4. Assemble the mainshaft by installing the 2nd gear needle bearing, 2nd gear, the synchronizer (baulk) ring, 1st-2nd speed synchronizer assembly, the 1st gear synchronizer (baulk) ring, 1st gear bushing, needle bearing, 1st gear and the thrust washer.

5. Press the mainshaft bearing in place with a bearing installer.

6. Position the 3rd gear needle bearing, 3rd gear, synchronizer (baulk) ring and the 3rd-4th synchronizer assembly onto the front side of the mainshaft.

7. Fit a new snap-ring in place on the shaft so that a minimum of clearance exists between the end face of the hub and the snap-ring.

8. Install the main drive gear bearing in place on the shaft by the use of a bearing installer tool or press. Install the bearing spacer and a snap-ring to provide a mini-

mum of clearance between the snap-ring and the bearing spacer.

9. Using a bearing press, install the countergear bearing onto the countergear.

10. Install a countergear thrust washer and the countergear with bearing into the transmission case and with a special height gauge or equivalent, select a thrust washer from the accompanying chart to provide a standard end-play of 0.0039–0.0079 inch (0.10–0.20 mm).

11. Remove the countergear assembly from the transmission and press the counter reverse gear onto the countergear assembly, using a press or equivalent tool.

12. Install a new snap-ring into the groove at the end of the countergear.

13. Install a synchronizer (baulk) ring on the main drive gear and install it onto the mainshaft to complete the mainshaft assembly.

No.	Thickness	
	mm	(in.)
1	1.55 to 1.60	(0.0610 to 0.0630)
2	1.60 to 1.65	(0.0630 to 0.0650)
3	1.65 to 1.70	(0.0650 to 0.0669)

No.	Thickness	
	mm	(in.)
1	1.34 to 1.40	(0.0528 to 0.0551)
2	1.40 to 1.46	(0.0551 to 0.0575)
3	1.46 to 1.52	(0.0575 to 0.0598)
4	1.52 to 1.58	(0.0598 to 0.0622)
5	1.58 to 1.64	(0.0622 to 0.0646)
6	1.64 to 1.70	(0.0646 to 0.0669)
7	1.70 to 1.76	(0.0669 to 0.0693)

No.	Thickness	
	mm	(in.)
1	2.20 to 2.25	(0.0866 to 0.0886)
2	2.25 to 2.30	(0.0886 to 0.0906)
3	2.30 to 2.35	(0.0906 to 0.0925)
4	2.35 to 2.40	(0.0925 to 0.0945)
5	2.40 to 2.45	(0.0945 to 0.0965)
6	2.45 to 2.50	(0.0965 to 0.0984)
7	2.50 to 2.55	(0.0984 to 0.1004)
8	2.55 to 2.60	(0.1004 to 0.1024)

NOTE: Be sure to install the pilot bearing into the main drive gear bore.

14. Place the adapter plate in the holding device and assemble the mainshaft and countershaft and place them into the adapter plate as a unit. Hold the gears by hand so as not to drop them.

15. A puller should be used to pull the mainshaft into the adapter plate. The countershaft can be installed at the same time by tapping lightly with a soft hammer.

IMPORTANT: Make sure the snap-ring groove on the mainshaft clears the adapter plate.

16. Install the snap-ring on to the mainshaft.

17. Install the bearing retainer plate on the adapter plate and install the retaining screws. Torque the screws to 5.1–7.2 ft. lbs. (6.9–9.8 Nm) and stake each screw in two places with a center punch.

18. Install the mainshaft reverse gear and thrust washer on the rear of the mainshaft and secure with a new snap-ring.

NOTE: Install the thrust washer with its concave side towards the mainshaft reverse gear.

19. Install the 1st/2nd selector rod into the adapter plate and install the shifting fork onto the rod.

20. Place the 1st/2nd selector rod in the neutral position and install the interlock plunger into the adapter plate.

21. Insert the 3rd/4th selector rod into the adapter plate and install the shifting fork.

22. Set the 3rd/4th selector rod in the neutral position and install the interlock plunger into the adapter plate.

23. Install the reverse selector rod into the adapter plate.

NOTE: Be sure to install the interlock plungers into the adapter plate between each adjacent selector rod. Align the shifting forks with the sliding sleeves before installation.

24. Install the check balls and springs in their respective bores in the adapter plate. Install sealer to the check ball plugs and install in place.

NOTE: The check ball plug for 1st/ 2nd selector rod is longer than the plugs for the 3rd/4th and reverse rods.

25. Install the reverse idler gear together with the reverse shift fork.

26. Install new retaining pins in the shifting forks to the selector rods.

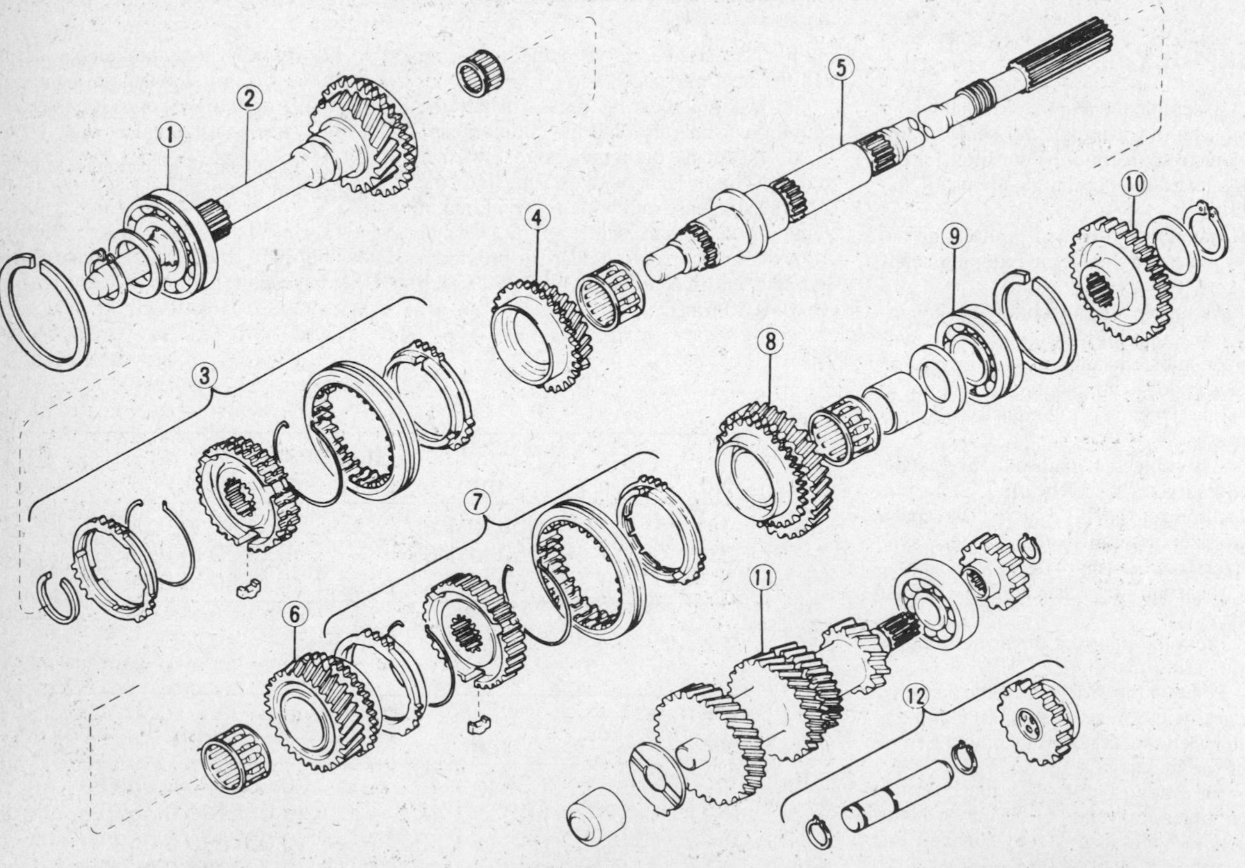

Exploded view of gear train components

1. Main drive bearing
2. Main drive gear
3. 3rd & top synchronizer
4. 3rd gear, mainshaft
5. Mainshaft
6. 2nd gear, mainshaft
7. 1st & 2nd synchronizer
8. 1st gear, mainshaft
9. Mainshaft bearing
10. Reverse gear, mainshaft
11. Counter gear assembly
12. Idler gear assembly

NOTE: To insure the interlock plunger is installed properly, slide the 3rd/4th fork and selector rod into gear and try to operate the other rods. Only the 3rd/4th gears should mesh. Operate the remaining selector rods in the same manner.

27. With all the gears assembled to the adapter plate, remove the assembly from the vise and remove the holder.

28. Clean all the mating surfaces of the transmission assembly. Install sealer to the surfaces of the adapter plate and the transmission surfaces.

29. Install the previously selected countergear thrust washer into the transmission case.

NOTE: The smooth side with the oil groove goes to the front of the transmission case, while the dimpled side goes towards the gear side.

30. Slide the transmission case onto the adapter plate assembly by lightly tapping the adapter plate with a soft hammer. Be sure the dowel pin is properly lined up.

31. Carefully install the main drive bearing and the front countergear needle bearing. Be sure the mainshaft rotates.

32. Install the main drive bearing snap-ring into its groove on the bearing outer race.

33. Apply sealant to the rear extension housing and the adapter plate. Place the selector rods in the neutral position and turn the striking rod (main shift selector rod) clockwise and gradually slide the rear extension onto the adapter plate, being sure the striking lever engages the fork rod brackets correctly.

34. Install the retaining bolts and tighten to 12–16 ft. lbs. (16–22 Nm).

35. Install the stopper pin bolt into the rear extension and tighten to 3.6–5.8 ft. lbs. (4.9–7.8 Nm).

36. Lubricate the plunger and install it into the rear extension. Install the reverse check spring and return spring. Apply sealer to the return spring plug and install it in place.

37. Turn the transmission assembly so that the front is up. Measure the distance from the front end of the transmission case to the main drive bearing outer race with a depth gauge. Select a shim to correspond to the dimension or thickness "A". The front cover adjusting shim can be one of seven shims.

38. Install the front cover to the transmission case with the O-ring and the shim in place.

39. Install the speedometer driven gear and install the securing bolt.

40. Install the electrical switches onto the case assembly.

41. Install the operating lever, the clutch release bearing and the dust cover. Install the proper level of lubricant to the transmission.

TYPE 16

4 and 5 Speed Transmissions

Fiat

DISASSEMBLY

1. Remove the oil filler plug.

2. Place the transmission upside down and remove the lower cover and gasket.

3. Remove the clutch release fork and slide the thrust bearing and control sleeve from the central support.

4. Remove the bellhousing and gasket. At the same time remove the center cover of the direct driveshaft with the oil seal and spring washer.

5. It may be necessary to remove the seal on the bench.

6. Remove the bolts which secure the 3rd and 4th gear selector forks.

NOTE: When the bolts have been removed, the fork can be removed along the bar and the two gears can be engaged simultaneously.

7. Slide the rubber dust cover from the end of the mainshaft.

8. Remove the snap-ring and flexible coupling ring.

9. Lock the mainshaft by proceeding according to the note above, and remove the spider from the mainshaft.

10. Remove the speedometer drive support and gasket from the rear transmission cover.

11. Remove the selector rod detent ball spring cover plate from the main casing.

12. Remove the springs from the recesses, followed by the detent balls.

NOTE: The reverse gear selector rod ball spring is not of the same compression as the other two springs. Keep this one separate from the other two.

13. Remove the rear cover complete with gear lever, by proceeding as follows:

14. Remove the stop screw which limits the side movement of the lever.

15. Remove the nuts which retain the cover to the main body.

16. Move the gear lever to the left to disengage it from the selector rods and remove the rear cover.

17. Remove the gear lever from the rear cover.

18. Slide the rear ball bearing and speedometer drive gear from the mainshaft.

19. Slide the reverse gear selector rod, complete with fork, from its seat in the main case and, at the same time, remove reverse gear from its spindle.

20. Remove the snap-ring which retains the reverse driving gear and remove the gear from the end of the layshaft.

21. Remove the snap-ring which retains the driven gear from the reverse gear train.

22. Remove the spring washers, driven gear of the reverse gear train, and remove the Woodruff key from its seat.

NOTE: Before removing the retaining clip of the reverse gear driven train, the spring washer must be compressed.

23. Engage the two gears to prevent the shafts from turning and remove the retaining bolt and front ball bearing from the layshaft.

24. Tilt the layshaft and remove it from the main case.

25. Remove the 3rd and 4th gear selector rods from the case and remove the bolt and spring washer holding the 1st and 2nd gear selector forks to the rod.

26. Remove the rod, followed by the 1st/2nd and 3rd/4th gear forks. The three safety rollers will be released as the selector rods are removed.

27. Remove the plate which retains the mainshaft intermediate ball bearing.

28. Withdraw the bearing from its housing.

29. Withdraw the reverse gear spindle from the main case.

30. Remove the direct drive and 4th gear shaft from the mainshaft, complete with ball bearing and 4th gear synchronizing ring.

31. Tilt the mainshaft and remove it from the case, complete with gears, hubs, sliding sleeves, and synchronizing rings.

32. Remove the following parts from the mainshaft: 1st gear with synchronizer and bushing. 1st and 2nd gear hub and sliding sleeve, 2d gear and synchronizer assembly.

33. Remove the snap-ring from its seat in the front end of the mainshaft and remove the following parts: spring washer, 3rd/4th

No.	"A" mm	(in.)	Adjusting shim mm	(in.)
1	6.05 to 6.09	(0.2382 to 0.2398)	0.50	(0.0197)
2	6.10 to 6.14	(0.2402 to 0.2417)	0.55	(0.0271)
3	6.15 to 6.19	(0.2421 to 0.2437)	0.60	(0.0236)
4	6.20 to 6.24	(0.2441 to 0.2457)	0.65	(0.0256)
5	6.25 to 6.29	(0.2461 to 0.2476)	0.70	(0.0276)
6	6.30 to 6.34	(0.2480 to 0.2496)	0.75	(0.0205)
7	6.35 to 0.39	(0.2500 to 0.2516)	0.80	(0.0315)

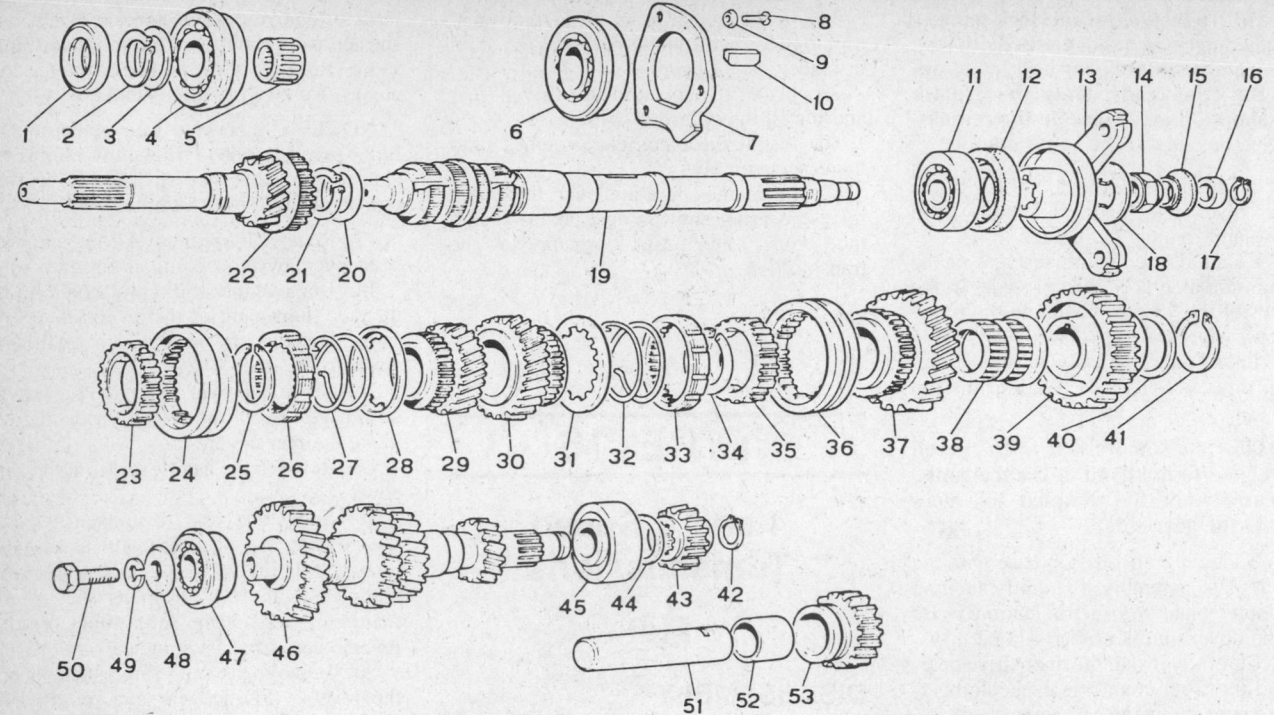

1. Inner cover seal
2. Bearing snap-ring
3. Spring washer
4. Direct drive shaft bearing
5. Needle roller bearing
6. Mainshaft intermediate bearing
7. Bearing retaining plate
8. Retaining screw
9. Retaining screw washer
10. Key
11. Mainshaft rear bearing
12. Rear cover oil seal
13. Flexible coupling
14. Retaining nut
15. Sealing ring
16. Centering ring
17. Snap-ring
18. Lock washer

19. Mainshaft
20. Spring washer
21. Retaining snap-ring
22. Direct drive and 4th gear shaft
23. 3rd/4th gear sliding sleeve hub
24. Sliding sleeve
25. Lock ring
26. Synchronizer ring
27. Synchronizer spring
28. Cup
29. 3rd speed driven gear
30. 2nd speed driven gear
31. Cup
32. Synchronizer spring
33. Synchronizer ring
34. Lock ring
35. 1st/2nd gear sliding sleeve hub
36. Sliding sleeve

37. 1st speed driven gear
38. 1st gear bushing
39. Reverse driven gear
40. Spring washer
41. Retaining snap-ring
42. Snap-ring
43. Reverse driving gear
44. Spring washer
45. Countershaft rear roller bearing
46. Countershaft with 1st, 2nd and 3rd speed gears
47. Countershaft front double row bearing
48. Flat washer
49. Spring washer
50. Countershaft front bearing
51. Reverse idler gear spindle
52. Reverse idler gear bushing
53. Reverse idler gear

Exploded view of gear train components, 4-speed transmission without intermediate housing

gear hub, 3rd gear, and synchronizer assembly.

34. Remove the snap-ring from the direct drive and 4th gear shaft and remove the spring washer and ball bearing.

ASSEMBLY

1. Assemble the following parts on the front of the mainshaft, in the order given: 3rd gear and synchronizing ring, 3rd/4th

gears and spring washer.

2. Insert the snap-ring in the groove, securing the parts listed above to the front of the mainshaft.

3. Slide the 2nd gear and synchronizing ring, 1st/2nd gear sliding sleeve and hub and 1st speed synchronizing ring and gear with bushing onto the rear end of the shaft.

4. Tilt the mainshaft and insert it into the transmission case.

5. Working from the rear end of the mainshaft, use a driver and insert the intermediate ball bearing.

6. Install the reverse idler gear shaft, then fit the shaft and bearing retaining plate.

7. Secure the plate to the main case and stake the nuts in place.

8. Fit the ball bearing and spring washer to the direct driveshaft and 4th gear shaft, and insert the spring retaining clip of the bearing in the groove.

9. Install the direct drive roller bearing onto the mainshaft.

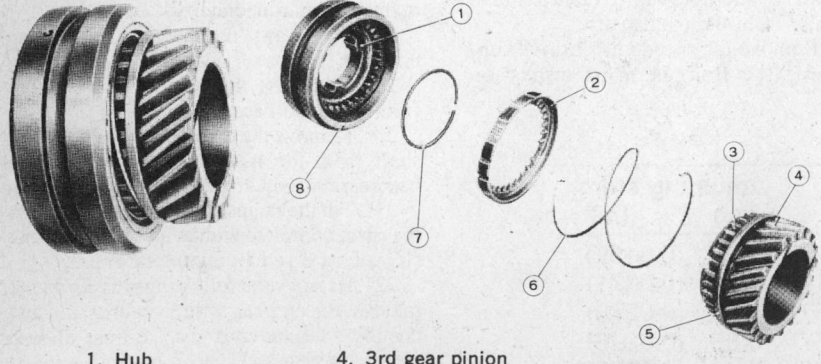

1. Hub
2. Synchronizing ring
3. Blocker ring
4. 3rd gear pinion
5. Cup ring
6. Spring
7. Circlip
8. Sliding sleeve

Third gear trynchronizer—4 and 5-speed

10. Insert the direct driveshaft in the main case and slide it onto the end of the mainshaft.

11. Install the 1st and 2nd gear selector fork to the sliding sleeve and slide the corresponding selector rod into the fork from outside.

12. Replace the locating roller of this bar to its seat and secure the fork to the rod.

13. Install the 3rd/4th gear selector fork and rod in the same manner.

NOTE: Do not lock the fork to the rod at this point, since it will be necessary to use this fork to lock the transmission at a later time.

14. Insert the layshaft into the main case.

15. Replace the front ball bearing and rear ball bearing of the layshaft.

16. Lock the shafts by engaging two gears at the same time.

17. Use the flat washer, spring washer and bolt to secure the front bearing to the layshaft.

18. Fit the key to the mainshaft and install the reverse driving gear and spring washer.

19. Retain these with a snap-ring.

NOTE: When installing the reverse driven gear snap-ring, center the spring washer so that the snap-ring cannot snap into the groove of the shaft. Fit the spring washer and reverse driving gear to the rear end of the layshaft and secure them with a snap-ring.

20. Insert the reverse selector rod locating roller in its seating, and fit the selector fork to the rod.

21. Retain this with a bolt and spring washer.

22. Install the selector rod in its guide and at the same time, fit the reverse idler gear to its spindle.

23. Install the speedometer drive gear and rear ball bearing on the mainshaft.

24. Fit the gear shifting assembly to the rear transmission cover, as follows.

25. Drive a new oil seal with inner spring into place.

26. Fit the gear shifting lever to the cover.

27. Attach the gear lever return spring to the lever and replace the screw in the cover.

28. Mount the lever assembly on the rear cover and fit the rear cover to the main transmission case. Be sure to fit a gasket between the two cases. Install the back-up light switch.

29. Replace the speedometer drive support with a gasket under it. It is held in place by a nut on a stud in the cover.

30. Install the flexible spider and flat washer on the tail of the mainshaft.

31. Lock the gears and tighten the nut, bending up the tab washer.

32. Install the dust cover on the mainshaft and drive the coupling centering ring into place and insert the snap-ring in the groove.

33. Drive an oil seal into the cover of the direct drive and 4th gear shaft and attach this cover to the front of the transmission body (bellhousing).

34. Insert a sealing ring between them.

35. Install the spring washer of the cover and fit the bellhousing to the main case, with a gasket.

36. Fit the 3rd and 4th gear selector fork to the selector rod and secure with a bolt and washer.

37. Replace the three selector rod detent balls and springs in their proper bores. Note that the reverse spring is different from the other two.

38. Fit the lower cover and gasket to the main case.

39. Install the oil drain plug.

40. Fit the clutch release sleeve and thrust bearing to the cover of the direct driveshaft and install the fork lever.

41. Turn the transmission right side up, and fill with 2.75 pints of oil. The oil must come to the brim of the filler hole.

42. Replace the filler plug.

124 (5–Speed)

This transmission is used on 124 Spider and 2000 Spider Coupe models. Basically, it is the same unit as the 4-speed, with the addition of a fifth gear or overdrive. The transmission is in three parts. The front body is bolted to the crankcase and houses the clutch and withdrawal sleeve, with a thrust bearing. The center body is bolted to the front body and contains the 1st, 2nd, 3rd and 4th gears. The rear cover is bolted to the center body and carries 5th and reverse gears, along with the selector bars. It also contains the mainshaft roller bearing and countershaft ball bearing. The upper part of the rear cover holds the gearshift extension mechanism which is slightly different from the 4-speed unit.

Disassembly and assembly are basically the same procedures as those outlined for the 124 (4 speed). Specifications remain identical to those for the 4-speed unit.

When assembling a synchronizer, be sure that the returned ends of the spring are inserted in the slots in the blocker ring, without distorting the normal diameter of the spring. This should be done before the circlip is fitted.

TYPE 17

5 Speed Transmission

Fiat

DISASSEMBLY

1. Pull the output yoke off of the output shaft.

2. Remove the speedometer driven gear retainer and gasket.

3. Remove the gearshift support and gasket from the rear housing.

4. Remove the seven bolts and washers retaining the rear housing to the main case. Tap lightly with wooden or plastic hammer and pull off to the rear.

5. Disconnect clutch release lever from ball joint pivot. Remove release bearing support and release lever.

6. Inside bellhousing, remove the seven bolts retaining bellhousing to main case. Tap lightly and remove bellhousing.

7. Remove snap-ring for speedometer drive gear and slide gear off output shaft.

8. Remove snap-ring in front of input shaft bearing.

9. Apply pressure to spring washer behind snap-ring at rear of output shaft and remove snap-ring. Remove spring washer.

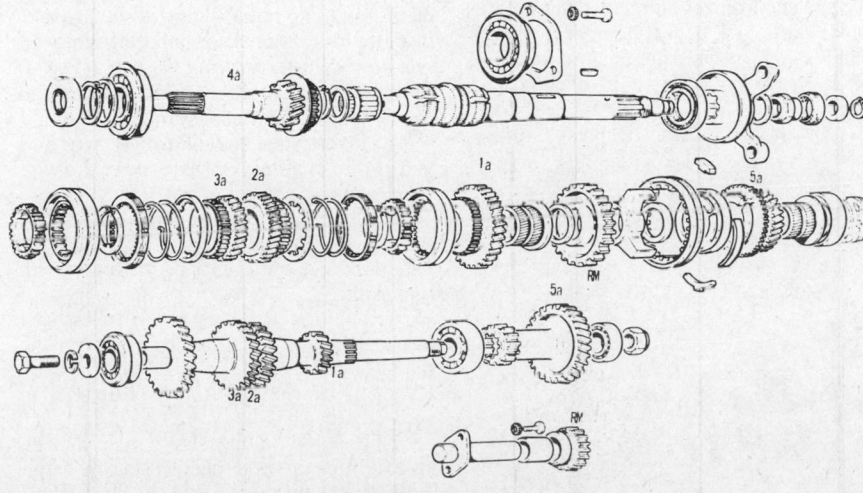

1A. 1st gear	3A. 3rd gear	5A. 5th gear
2A. 2nd gear	4A. 4th gear	RM. Reverse gear

Fifth speed gear train

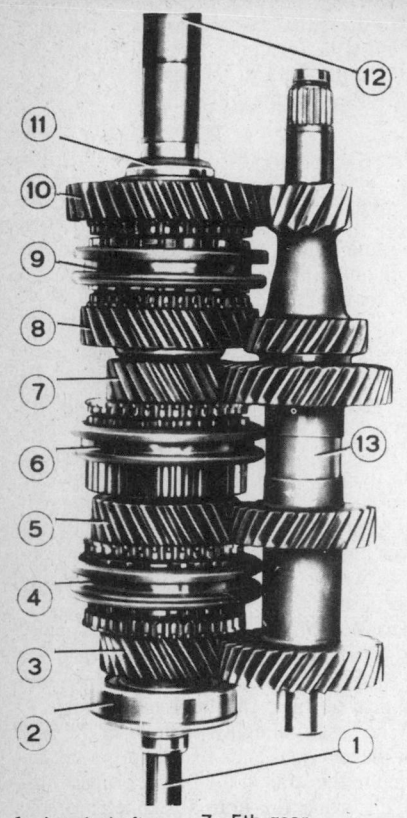

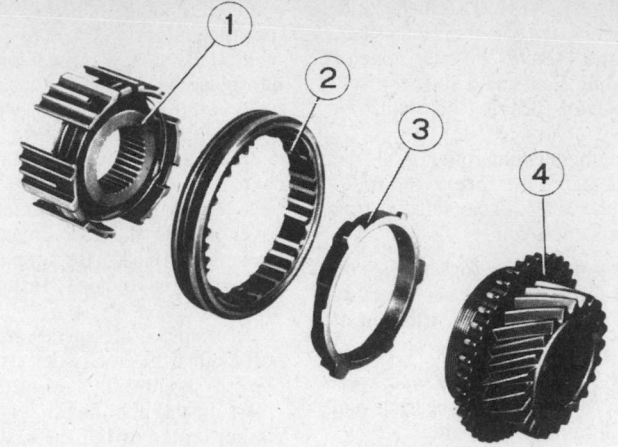

1. Hub
2. Sliding sleeve

3. Synchronizer ring
4. 5th gear

Third gear and synchronizer—131 and Brava

1. Input shaft
2. Bearing
3. 4th gear
4. 3rd and 4th gear synchronizer
5. 3rd gear
6. 5th gear synchronizer

7. 5th gear
8. 2nd gear
9. 1st and 2nd gear synchronizer
10. 1st gear
11. Bearing outer race
12. Main shaft
13. Auxiliary shaft

Main and auxiliary shafts—131 and Brava 5-speed transmission

10. Remove bolt retaining reverse shifting fork to shifting rod, and remove fork and reverse idler gear. Remove shifting rod spacer. Remove reverse gear from the mainshaft.

11. Remove bolt retaining extension for 3rd and 4th gear shifting rod. Remove extension.

12. Remove snap-ring retaining reverse drive gear onto auxiliary shaft, and remove the gear.

13. Remove two bolts retaining detent ball cover. Remove cover, springs and balls.

14. Remove Woodruff key from output shaft. Slide main case off of shafts. Remove magnet for front housing slot.

15. Remove bolt retaining fork to shifting rod, and remove rod. Assemble fork to rod for reference. Repeat for other shifting rods.

16. Remove mainshaft and auxiliary shaft from housing.

17. Disconnect input shaft from mainshaft. Remove bearing from inside input shaft.

18. Position mainshaft in vise with protective jaws. Using two screwdrivers, pry outer bearing race off of shaft. Then, slide 1st gear, outer race for thrust bearing, thrust bearing, inner race, and thrust washer off of mainshaft.

19. Remove roller bearing (122 rollers) and separator for bearings.

20. Remove snap-ring retaining 1st and 2nd gear synchronizer hub. Place mainshaft in press with block beneath 2nd gear. Press off hub, synchronizer ring, gear, and washers. Remove roller bearing (134 rollers) from shaft.

21. Invert mainshaft. Depress spring washer and remove snap-ring and washer from other end. Pull the 3rd and 4th gear synchronizer hub from shaft. Remove 3rd gear.

22. Remove snap-ring retaining 5th gear synchronizer hub. Pull off hub. Remove 5th gear.

23. Depress spring washer and remove snap-ring. Pull bearing from mainshaft.

ASSEMBLY

1. Press bearing on input shaft. Position spring washer and snap-ring on shaft. Depress spring washer and install snap-ring in groove.

2. Place 5th gear and synchronizer ring on mainshaft. Tap hub for 5th gear synchronizer down with brass drift until ring seats correctly in hub. Secure with snap-ring. Position sliding sleeve on hub with beveled teeth facing 5th gear.

3. Place 3rd gear and synchronizer on mainshaft. Tap hub down with brass drift. Install sliding sleeve on hub with grooved side down. Position spring washer and snap-ring on shaft. Depress spring washer and install snap-ring in groove.

4. Invert mainshaft. Position two rows of 67 roller bearings on shaft and retain with clean wheel bearing grease.

5. Place 2nd gear and synchronizer ring and hub for 1st and 2nd gear on mainshaft. Tap hub down with brass drift. Retain with snap-ring.

6. Position flat washer on mainshaft. Place a row of 61 roller bearings on the shaft, install a spacer, and then a second row of 61 bearings, forming a ring. Retain with grease.

7. Position sliding sleeve on hub with grooved side down. Place 1st gear on mainshaft, then install thrust washer, thrust bearing and washer.

8. Press bearing onto input shaft. Position flat washer and outer bearing race on shaft. Tap outer race down with brass drift.

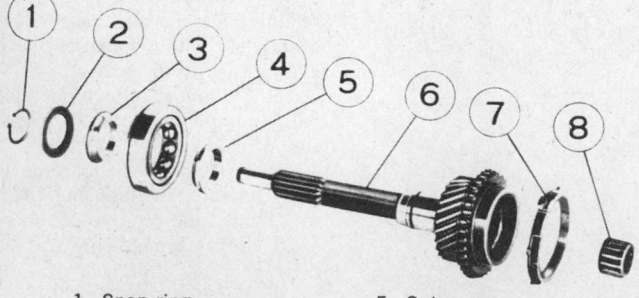

1. Snap ring
2. Spring washer
3. Outer race
4. Bearing

5. Outer race
6. Input shaft
7. Synchronizer ring
8. Bearing

Input shaft—131 and Brava

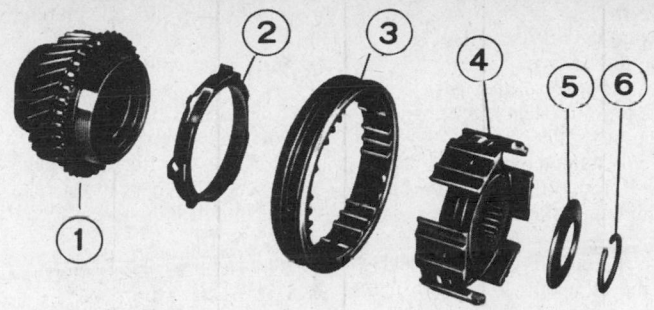

1. 3rd gear
2. Synchronizer ring
3. Sliding sleeve
4. Hub
5. Spring washer
6. Snap ring

Fifth gear synchronizer—131 and Brava

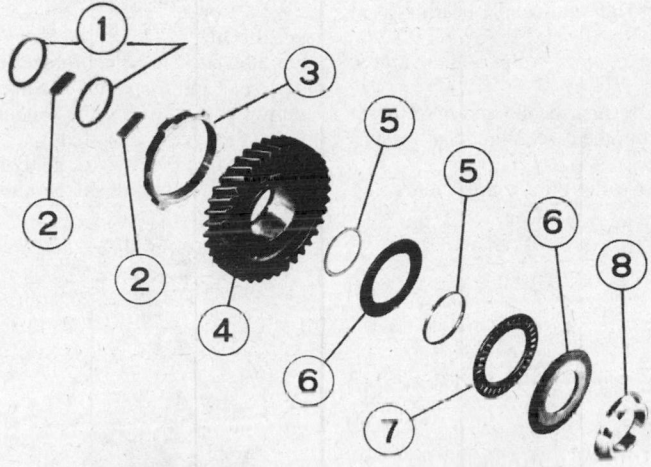

1. Spacer
2. Roller bearings
3. Synchronizer ring
4. 1st gear
5. Flat washer
6. Thrust washer
7. Thrust bearing
8. Outer race

First gear and synchronizer—131 and Brava

case, and retain plate with 2 bolts. Tighten to 18 ft. lbs.

18. Install reverse drive gear on auxiliary shaft with washer and secure with snap-ring.

19. Position 3rd and 4th gear shifting rod extension on rod. Install extension retaining bolt and lockwasher and tighten.

20. Install Woodruff key in mainshaft.

21. Install reverse gear on mainshaft. Place spacer on reverse shifting rod. Position shifting fork with reverse idler gear on shifting rod and idler shaft. Secure fork to rod with bolt and lockwasher.

22. Position spring washer and snap-ring on mainshaft. Depress spring washer and install snap-ring in groove.

23. Install speedometer drive gear on mainshaft and secure with snap-ring.

24. Install input shaft outer bearing retaining snap-ring.

25. Position bellhousing with gasket to main case, and secure with seven bolts and washers. Install clutch release lever and release bearing on input shaft and connect lever to ball joint pivot.

26. Position rear housing with gasket to main case and secure with seven bolts and washers.

27. Place both ends of shifter spring in rear housing slotted plate. Then, flip spring over and install over spring support boss.

28. Install gearshift support with gasket on rear housing. Install retaining bolts and check shifting action.

29. Install speedometer driven gear housing and gasket.

30. Slide output shaft yoke onto shaft.

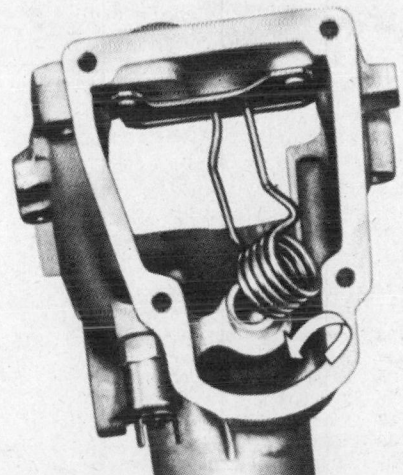

Installing shifter spring—131 and Brava

9. Place lockwasher on bearing in front housing for auxiliary shaft. Position magnet in case with magnetic face toward gears.

10. Install input shaft in mainshaft. Mesh together mainshaft and auxiliary shaft gears and install in front housing.

11. Remove Allen bolt from front housing. Position 5th gear shifting fork on rod in case with fork on 5th gear sliding sleeve. Install detent ball in front housing adjacent to 5th gear shifting rod.

12. Position 3rd and 4th gear shifting fork on rod. Install rod in case with fork on 3rd and 4th gear sliding sleeve. Install detent ball in front housing adjacent to 3rd and 4th gear shifting rod.

13. Position 1st and 3rd gear shifting fork on rod. Install rod in case with fork on 1st and 2nd gear sliding sleeve. Install Allen bolt. Tighten shifting fork bolts to 14.5 ft. lbs.

14. Coat auxiliary shaft bearing retainer with grease. Position retainer on bearing in case with grooved surface facing away from bearing.

15. Install main case and gasket over shafts and shifting rods. Position outer race for mainshaft bearing on shaft, and tap down with brass drift. Position washer and retainer plate on shaft.

16. Place reverse gear idle shaft in case. Position retainer plate tab in shaft groove. Secure with 4 bolts.

17. Position detent balls and springs in

TYPE 18

4 Speed Transmission

Mazda

DISASSEMBLY

1. Install the transmission on a workstand.

2. Drain the oil.

3. Remove the fork and throwout bearing from the housing.

4. Remove the bellhousing.

5. Remove the adjusting shim from the bellhousing bearing bore.

6. Remove the shift lever tower and gasket.

7. Remove the extension housing. Set the control lever end in the neutral position, press the control lever end as far left as possible, and slide the extension housing off the transmission.

8. Remove the neutral switch from the transmission (models with seat belt interlock).

9. Remove the gearshift yoke from the central lever.

10. Remove the speedometer sleeve and driven gear. Remove the back-up light switch.

11. Unfasten the speedometer drive gear snap-ring, slide the drive gear off of the output shaft, and remove the lockball.

12. Remove the bottom cover and gasket.

13. Remove the cap bolts, the detent springs, and detent balls.

14. Remove the blind covers and gaskets from the transmission case.

15. Remove the reverse shift rod and idler gear from the rear of the transmission case. Remove the reverse shift fork.

16. Unfasten third/fourth shift fork securing bolt and remove the third/fourth shift rod from the rear of the case.

17. Repeat Step 16 for the first/second shift rod.

18. Straighten out the output shaft lockwasher. Hold the output shaft to keep it from turning, and loosen the locknut. Slide the reverse gear and key off the end of the output shaft.

19. Remove the countershaft snap-ring (rear) and remove the reverse countergear.

20. Remove the bearing cover.

21. Remove the reverse idler gear.

22. Hold the fourth synchronizer ring and gear on the output shaft.

23. Remove the countershaft front bearing snap-ring. Remove the front bearing. Remove the adjusting shim from the case bearing bore.

24. Remove the countershaft rear bearing. Remove the adjusting shim from the case bearing bore.

25. Remove the input shaft bearing snap-ring and remove the bearing with the puller.

26. Lift the countershaft out.

27. Separate the input and output shafts. Remove the input shaft. Remove the fourth synchronizer ring and needle bearing from the input shaft.

28. Remove the output shaft gear assembly.

29. Remove first/second and third/fourth shift forks from the case. Withdraw the shift interlock pins.

30. Remove the third/fourth clutch hub snap-ring, then slide the clutch hub sleeve, third synchronizer ring and third gear off the front of the output shaft. Be careful not to mix up the synchronizer rings.

31. Slide the first gear and synchronizer ring off the rear of the output shaft.

32. Slide the first gear sleeve, second gear, second synchronizer ring and first/second clutch hub/sleeve assembly off the output shaft.

ASSEMBLY

1. Install the first/second clutch hub on its sleeve, place the three shift keys in the clutch hub key slots, and install the key springs. Be sure to keep the open ends of the key springs 120° apart.

2. Repeat Step 1 for the third/fourth synchronizer assembly.

3. Place the synchronizer ring on second gear and then slide second gear on the output shaft, so that the synchronizer ring faces the rear of the shaft.

4. Slide the first/second clutch hub and sleeve on the output shaft so that the clutch

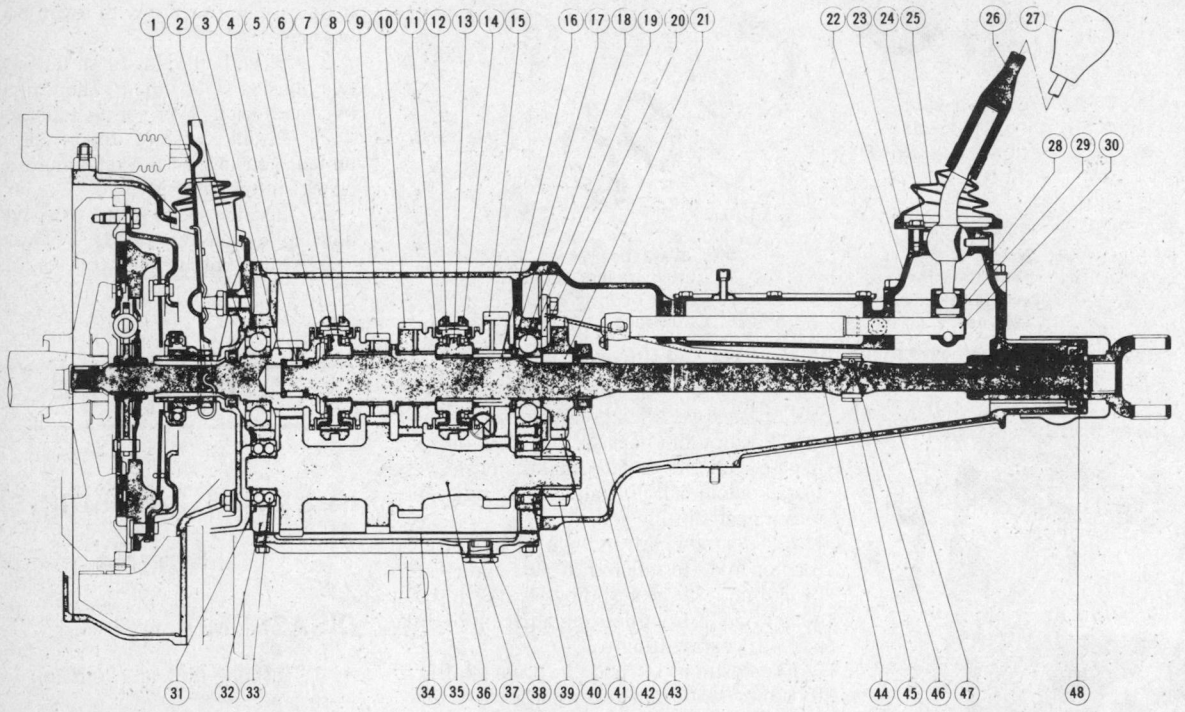

1. Adjusting shim
2. Main driveshaft bearing
3. Main driveshaft and gear
4. Needle bearing
5. Synchronizer ring
6. Third-and-fourth clutch hub
7. Synchronizer key
8. Clutch sleeve
9. Third gear
10. Second gear
11. Synchronizer ring
12. Synchronizer key
13. First-and-second clutch hub
14. Clutch sleeve
15. First gear
16. First gear sleeve
17. Thrust washer
18. Mainshaft bearing
19. Adjusting shim
20. Bearing cover plate
21. Key
22. Gearshift lever retainer
23. Cover
24. Shim
25. Boot
26. Gearshift lever
27. Gearshift lever knob
28. Bush
29. Control lever end
30. Gearshift control lever
31. Adjusting shim
32. Transmission case
33. Countershaft front bearing
34. Gasket
35. Transmission under cover
36. Countershaft
37. Drain plug
38. Gasket
39. Countershaft rear bearing
40. Counter reverse gear
41. Reverse gear
42. Lock washer
43. Locknut
44. Mainshaft
45. Speedometer drive gear
46. Lock ball
47. Extension housing
48. Mainshaft oil seal

Cross section of Mazda 4-speed transmission without intermediate housing

oil grooves face forward. Be sure that the three synchronizer keys engage the notches on the second gear synchronizer ring.

5. Install the first gear sleeve in the output shaft.

6. Install the synchronizer ring in the first gear and install the gear on the output shaft so that the ring faces the front of the shaft.

7. Install the same thrust washer on the output shaft that was removed.

8. Repeat Step 6 for third gear.

9. Install the third/fourth clutch hub and sleeve on the output shaft, being sure to engage the three synchronizer keys with the notches in the ring.

NOTE: The larger boss on the third/ fourth clutch hub goes toward the front.

10. Install the snap-ring on the front of the output shaft. Install the output shaft/ gear set assembly in the case. Fit the needle bearing on the front of the output shaft.

11. Place the synchronizer ring on the input shaft gear (fourth) and install the gear on the front of the output shaft. Be sure that the synchronizer keys engage the notches in the synchronizer ring.

12. Position the first/second and third/ fourth shift forks in groove on the clutch hub/sleeve assembly.

13. Install the countergear assembly in the case, being careful to engage each countergear with its respective output shift gear.

14. Check the output shaft bearing end-play as follows:

   a. Measure the depth of the transmission case output shaft bearing bore.

   b. Measure the height of the bearing.

   c. The difference between these two measurements indicates the correct thickness of the adjusting shim to be used The amount of end-play permitted is 0– 0.0039 in.

   d. Shims are available in thicknesses of 0.0039 or 0.0118 in.

15. Hold the fourth synchronizer ring off the input shaft synchronizer gear.

16. Install the input and output shaft bearings in their respective bores with a press.

17. Install the input shaft bearing snap-ring.

18. Check the countershaft bearing end-play, as outlined in Step 14 for the input shaft. The amount of end-play allowed and available shim size are the same for both bearings.

19. Repeat Step 15.

20. Press the countershaft front and rear bearings into their respective bores. Install the snap-ring on the front bearing.

21. Install the reverse countergear on the rear of the countershaft.

22. Install the reverse gear idler shaft in the transmission case.

23. Install the bearing cover on the case.

24. Secure the reverse gear on the output shaft with its key.

25. Hold the output shaft to keep it from turning and tighten to 150–180 ft. lbs.

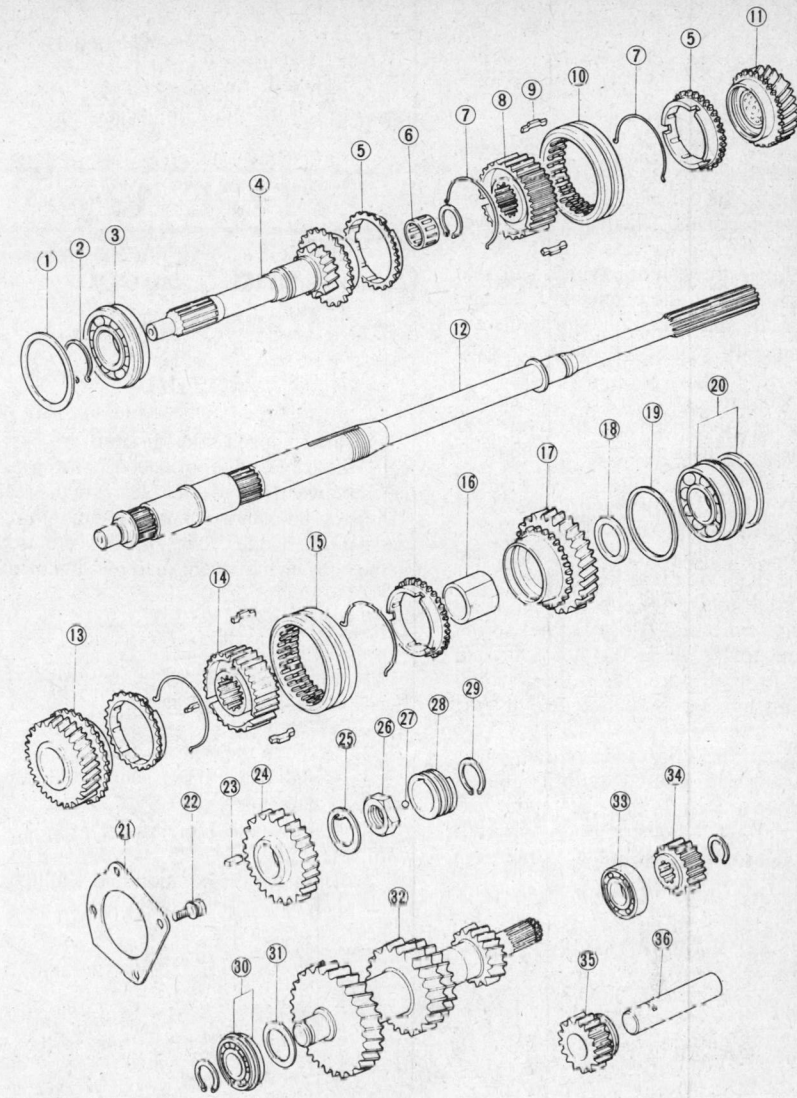

1. Adjusting shim	13. Second gear	25. Lockwasher
2. Snap-ring	14. First-and-Second clutch hub	26. Locknut
3. Input shaft bearing	15. Clutch hub sleeve	27. Steel ball
4. Input shaft	16. Gear sleeve	28. Speedometer drive gear
5. Synchronizer ring	17. First gear	29. Snap-ring
6. Needle bearing	18. Thrust washer	30. Ball bearing and clip
7. Synchronizer key spring	19. Adjust shim	31. Adjusting shim
8. Third-and-Fourth clutch hub	20. Ball bearing and clip	32. Countershaft
9. Synchronizer key	21. Bearing stop	33. Needle bearing
10. Clutch hub sleeve	22. Bolt	34. Reverse countergear
11. Third gear	23. Key	35. Reverse idler gear
12. Output shaft	24. Reverse gear	36. Reverse idler gear shaft

Exploded view of gear train components—Mazda 4-speed transmission without intermediate housing

26. Install the first/second shift rod into the case and secure it to the shift fork with the lockbolt. Place the shift rod in Neutral. Drive the interlock pin into its bore.

27. Repeat Step 26 for the third/fourth shift rod.

28. Slide the reverse shift rod, complete with the reverse idler gear, in from the rear of the case. Secure the shift rod to the reverse fork with its lockbolt.

29. Install the detent balls and springs in their bores and secure them with their cap bolts.

30. Check the synchronizer key-to-exposed edge of the synchronizer ring clearance with a feeler gauge; it should be 0.026– 0.079 in. If the clearance is greater, the synchronizer key could pop out. If the clearance is greater than specified, replace the selective-fit thrust washer with one of

the three available sizes.

31. Install the blind covers over their gaskets.

32. Install the lockball, speedometer drive gear, and snap-ring, in that order, on the rear of the output shaft.

33. Install the gearshift control lever through the holes in the front of the extension housing. Install the Woodruff key on the control lever and install the yoke over it. Secure the yoke with its setbolt.

34. Thread the Neutral switch (for seat belt interlock) into the extension housing.

35. Fit the spring and plunger in the extension housing and secure them with the capbolt.

36. Install the back-up light switch.

37. Secure the speedometer driven gear in its extension housing bore with the lockplate and bolt.

38. Push the gearshift control lever over to the left as far as possible. Place a gasket on the rear of the transmission case and install the extension housing over it.

39. Install the bottom cover.

40. Insert the select lockpin and spring in the shift tower. Align the slot in the pin with the lockball bore. Drop the lockball and spring into the bore; secure with the capbolt.

41. Install the shift tower on the extension housing and secure it with its bolts.

42. Repeat Step 14 for the input shaft bearing and clutch housing bore. The end-play and shim thickness are the same as in Step 14.

43. Lubricate the lip of the bellhousing oil seal.

44. Put a gasket on the front of the transmission case, and install the bellhousing.

45. Install the throwout bearing, release fork and boot in the bellhousing.

TYPE 19

4 and 5 Speed Transmission

Mazda

The 4 and 5 speed transmissions are basically the same, with an added housing located between the adapter plate and the rear extension housing, to carry the 5th and reverse gears. Added roller bearings are used in the housing to prevent shaft misalignment.

DISASSEMBLY

1. Remove the throw-out bearing return spring, throw-out bearing, and the release fork.

2. Remove the bearing housing.

3. Remove the input shaft and countershaft snap-rings.

4. Remove the floorshift lever retainer, complete with gasket.

5. Unfasten the cap bolt and withdraw the spring, steel ball, select lock pin and spring from the retainer.

6. Remove the extension housing. Turn the control lever as far left as it will go and slide the extension housing off the output shaft.

7. Remove the spring seat and spring from the end of the shift control lever.

8. Loosen the spring cap and withdraw the spring and plunger from their bore.

9. Remove the control rod and boss from the extension housing.

10. Remove the speedometer driven gear. Remove the back-up light switch.

11. Remove the speedometer drive gear.

12. Tap the front ends of the input shaft and countershaft with a plastic hammer; then remove the intermediate housing assembly from the transmission case.

13. Remove the three cap bolts; then withdraw the springs and lockballs.

14. Remove the reverse shift rod, reverse idler gear, and shift lever.

15. Remove the setscrews from all the shift forks and push the shift rods rearward to remove them. Remove the shift forks.

16. Withdraw the reverse shift rod lockball, spring, and interlock pins from the intermediate housing.

17. Remove reverse gear and key from the output shaft.

18. Remove the reverse countergear.

19. Remove the countershaft and output shaft from the intermediate housing.

20. Remove the bearings from the intermediate housing and transmission case.

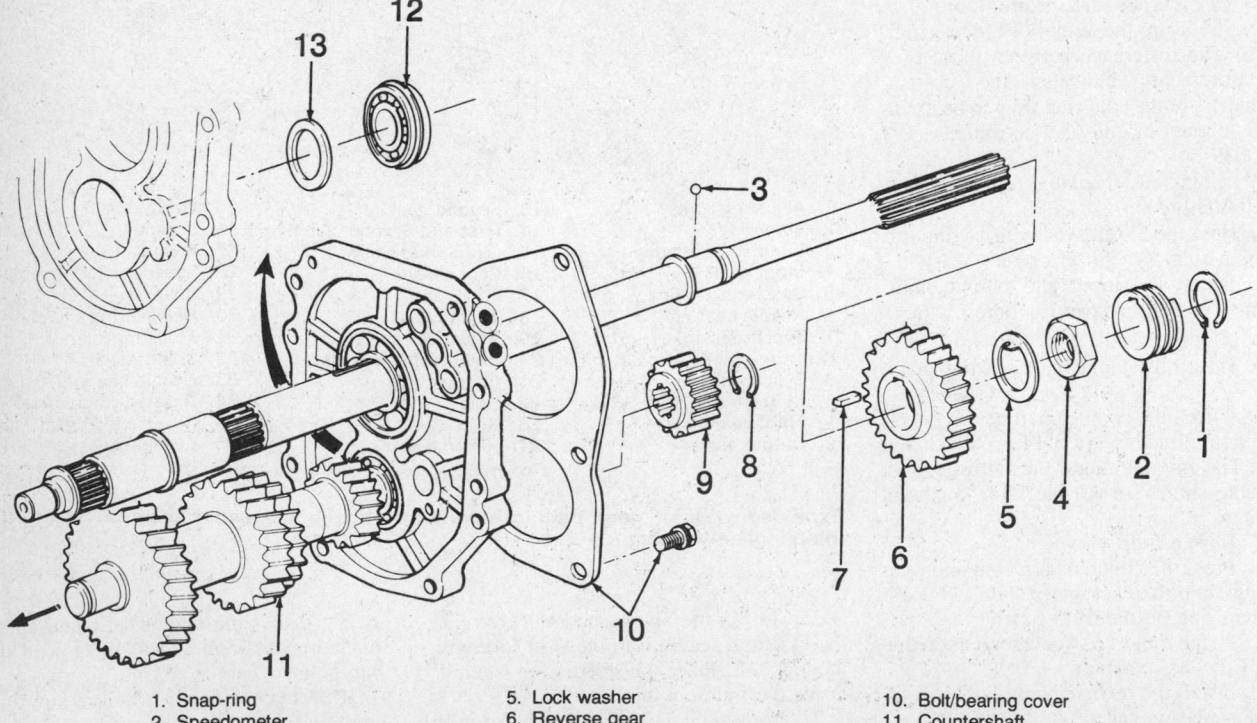

1. Snap-ring	5. Lock washer	10. Bolt/bearing cover
2. Speedometer drive gear	6. Reverse gear	11. Countershaft
3. Ball	7. Key	12. Countershaft rear bearing
4. Locknut	8. Snap-ring	13. Shim
	9. Counter reverse gear	

Gear train position in 4-speed transmission with intermediate housing

21. Remove the snap-ring from the output shaft.

22. Slide the third/fourth clutch hub, sleeve, synchronizer ring, and third gear off the output shaft.

23. Remove the thrust washer, first gear, sleeve, synchronizer ring, and second gear from the rear of the output shaft.

ASSEMBLY

1. Install the third/fourth synchronizer clutch hub on the sleeve. Place the three synchronizer keys in the clutch hub key slots. Install the key springs with their open ends 120° apart.

2. Install third gear and the synchronizer ring on the front of the output shaft. Install the third/fourth clutch hub assembly on the output shaft. Be sure that the larger boss faces the front of the shaft.

3. Secure the gear and synchronizer with the snap-ring.

4. Repeat Step 1 for the first/second synchronizer assembly.

5. Position the synchronizer ring on second gear. Slide second gear on the output shaft so that the synchronizer ring faces the rear of the shaft.

6. Install the first/second clutch hub assembly on the output shaft so that its oil grooves face the front of the shaft. Engage the keys in the notches on the second gear synchronizer ring.

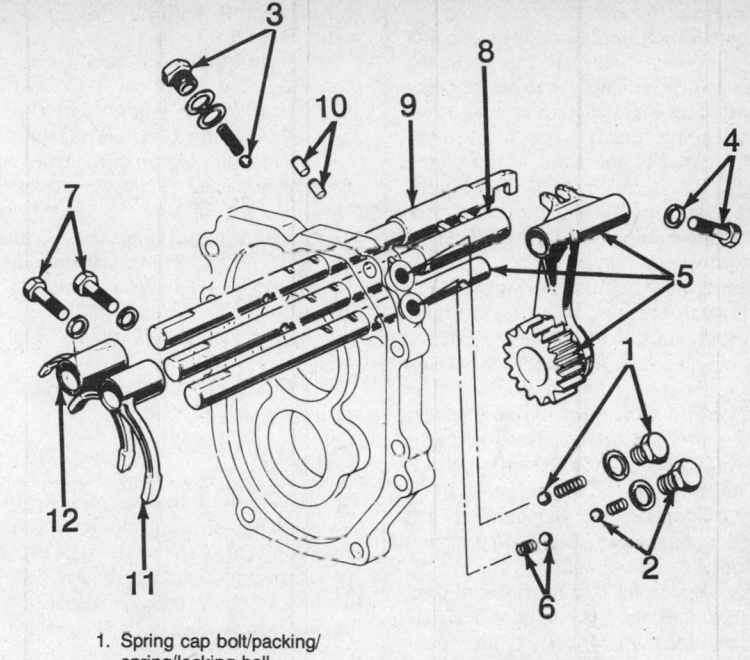

1. Spring cap bolt/packing/ spring/locking ball
2. Spring cap bolt/packing/ spring/locking ball
3. Spring cap bolt/packing/ spring/locking ball
4. Bolt/washer
5. Shift fork (Reverse)/rod/ reverse idler gear
6. Spring/locking ball
7. Bolt/washer
8. Shift rod (3rd & 4th)
9. Shift rod (1st & 2nd)
10. Interlock pin
11. Shift fork (3rd & 4th)
12. Shift fork (1st & 2nd)

Exploded view of shift selector rods and forks, 4-speed with intermediate housing

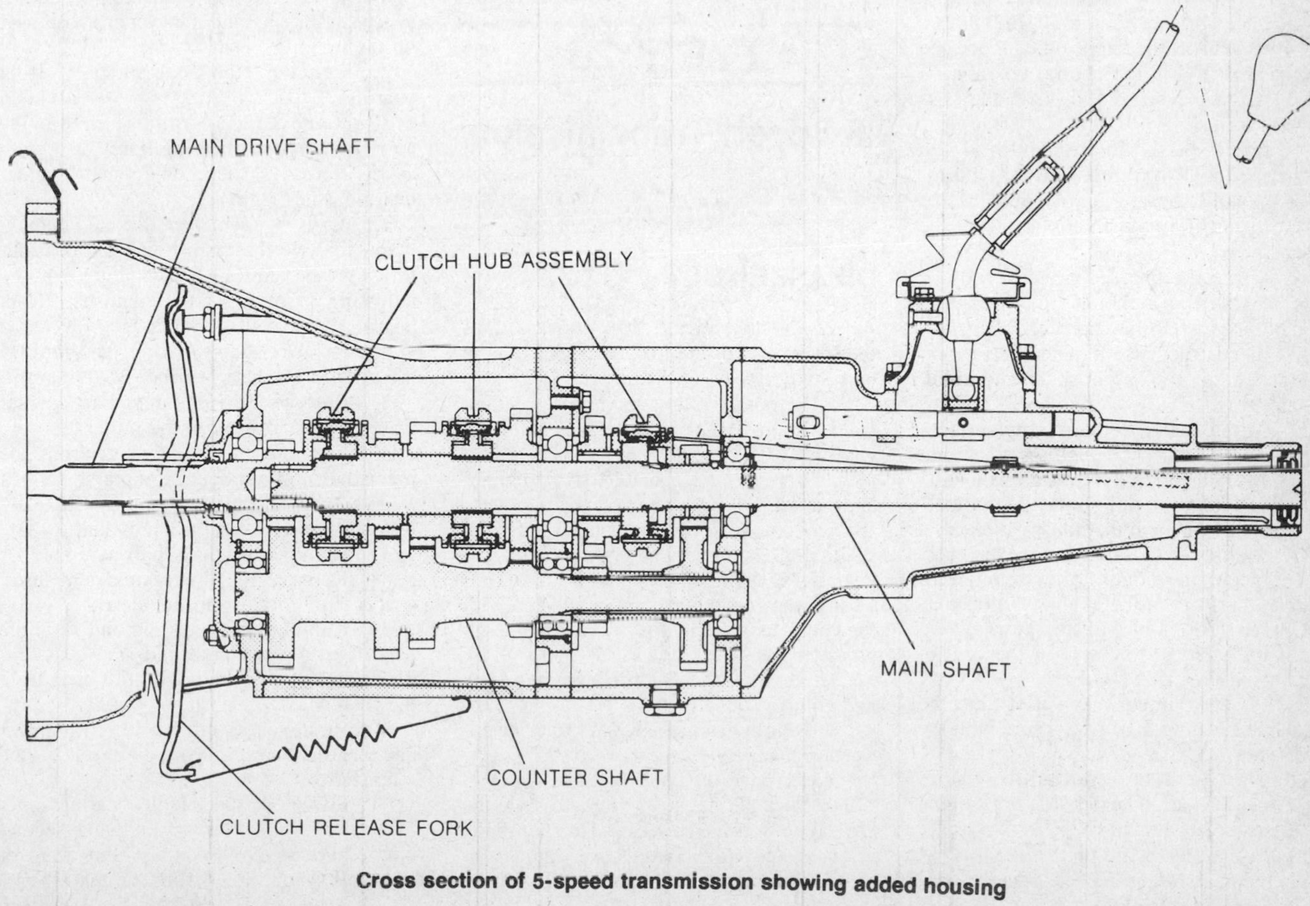

MAIN DRIVE SHAFT

CLUTCH HUB ASSEMBLY

MAIN SHAFT

COUNTER SHAFT

CLUTCH RELEASE FORK

Cross section of 5-speed transmission showing added housing

7. Slide the first gear sleeve onto the output shaft. Position the synchronizer ring on first gear. Install the first gear on the output shaft so that the synchronizer ring faces frontward. Rotate the first gear as required to engage the notches in the synchronizer ring with the keys in the clutch hub.

8. Slip the thrust washer on the rear of the output shaft. Install the needle bearing on the front of the output shaft.

9. Install the synchronizer ring on fourth gear and install the input shaft on the front of the output shaft.

10. Press the countershaft rear bearing and shim into the intermediate housing, then press the countershaft into the rear bearing.

11. Keep the thrust washer and first gear from falling off the output shaft by supporting the shaft. Install the output shaft on the intermediate housing. Be sure that each output shaft gear engages with its opposite number on the countershaft.

12. Tap the output shaft bearing and shim into the intermediate housing with a plastic hammer. Install the cover.

13. Install reverse gear on the output shaft and secure it with its key.

NOTE: The chamfer on the teeth of both the reverse gear and the reverse countergear should face rearward.

14. Install the reverse countergear.

15. Install the lockball and spring into the bore in the intermediate housing. Depress the ball with a screwdriver.

16. Install the reverse shift rod, lever, and idler gear at the same time. Place the reverse shift rod in the neutral position.

17. Align the bores and insert the shift interlock pin.

18. Install the third/fourth shift rod into the intermediate housing and shift bores. Place the shift rod in Neutral.

19. Install the next interlock pin in the bore.

20. Install the first/second shift rod.

21. Install the lockballs and springs in their bores. Install the cap bolt.

22. Install the speedometer drive gear and lockball on the output shaft, and install its snap-ring.

23. Apply sealer to the mating surfaces of the intermediate housing. Install the intermediate housing in the transmission case.

24. Install the input shaft and countershaft front bearings in the transmission case.

25. Secure the speedometer driven gear.

26. Install the control rod through the holes in the front of the extension housing.

27. Align the key with the keyway and install the yoke on the end of the control rod. Install the yoke lockbolt.

28. Fit the plunger and spring into the extension housing bore and secure with the spring cap.

29. Turn the control rod all the way to the left and install the extension housing on the intermediate housing.

30. Insert the spring and select lockpin inside the gearshift retainer. Align the steel ball and spring with the lockpin slot, and secure it with the spring cap.

31. Install the spring and spring seat in the control rod yoke.

32. Install the gearshift lever retainer over its gasket on the extension housing.

33. Lubricate the lip of the front bearing cover oil seal and secure the cover on the transmission case.

34. Check the clearance between the front bearing cover and bearing. It should be less than 0.006 in. If it is not within specifications insert additional adjusting shims. The shims are available in 0.006 in. or 0.012 in. sizes.

35. Install the throwout bearing, return spring and release fork.

5 Speed

The disassembly and assembly of the rear extension housing, selector levers and forks are completed in the same manner as the 4 speed transmission. After this has been done, the added housing can be removed by taking out the retaining bolts. The housing will have to be lightly tapped with a soft-faced hammer. The removal of the housing exposes the 5th/reverse synchronizer assembly, the reverse countergear, the countershaft and mainshaft bearings. The bearings are pulled from the shafts and then the gears can be removed. The assembly is in the reverse of the removal procedure.

TYPE 20

5 Speed Transmission

Mazda

DISASSEMBLY

1. Pull the release fork outward until the spring clip of the fork releases from the ball pivot.

2. Remove the fork and release bearing.

3. Remove the clutch housing shim and gasket.

4. Remove the gearshift lever retainer and gasket.

5. Remove the spring and steel ball, select lock spindle and spring from the gearshift lever retainer.

6. Remove the extension housing with the control lever end down to the left as far as it will go.

7. Remove the control lever end, key and control rod.

8. Remove the lock plate and speedometer gear.

9. Remove the back-up light switch.

10. Remove the snap-ring and slide the speedometer drive gear from the mainshaft.

11. Remove the bottom cover and gasket.

12. Remove the shift rod ends.

13. Remove the rear bearing housing.

14. Remove the snap-ring and remove the mainshaft rear bearing, thrust washer and race.

15. Using the puller, remove the washer and countershaft rear bearing.

16. Remove the counter fifth gear.

17. Remove the intermediate housing.

18. Remove the springs and shift locking balls.

19. Remove the two blind covers and gaskets from the case.

20. Remove the reverse/fifth shift rod, fork and interlock pin.

21. Remove the first/second and third/fourth shift forks, rods and interlock pins.

22. Remove the snap-ring and slide the washer, fifth gear and synchronizer ring from the mainshaft. Also, remove the steel ball and needle bearing.

23. Lock the rotation of the mainshaft with second and reverse.

24. Remove the locknut and slide the reverse/fifth clutch hub and sleeve assembly, synchronizer ring, reverse gear and needle bearing from the mainshaft.

25. Remove the spacer and counter reverse gear from the countershaft.

26. Remove the reverse idler gear, thrust washers and shaft from the transmission case.

27. Remove the bearing rear cover plate.

28. Remove the snap-ring from the front end of the countershaft and install Mazda tool number 49 0839 445 synchronizer ring holder or its equivalent between the fourth synchronizer ring and the synchromesh gear on the main driveshaft.

29. Remove the countershaft front bearing.

30. Remove the adjusting shim from the countershaft front bearing bore.

31. Remove the countershaft center bearing outer race.

32. With a special puller and attachment, remove the mainshaft front bearing, thrust washer and inner race along with the adjusting shim from the mainshaft front bearing bore.

33. Remove the snap-ring, and remove the main driveshaft bearing.

34. Remove the countershaft center bearing inner race with the puller.

35. Separate the input shaft from the mainshaft and remove the input shaft.

36. Remove the synchronizer ring and needle bearing from the input shaft.

37. Remove the mainshaft assembly.

38. Remove the first/second and third/fourth shift forks from the case.

39. Remove the snap-ring and slide the third/fourth clutch hub and sleeve assembly, synchronizer ring and third gear from the mainshaft.

40. Remove the thrust washer, first gear and needle bearing from the rear of the mainshaft.

41. Press out the needle bearing inner race, synchronizer ring, first and second clutch hub, sleeve assembly, synchronizer ring and second gear from the mainshaft.

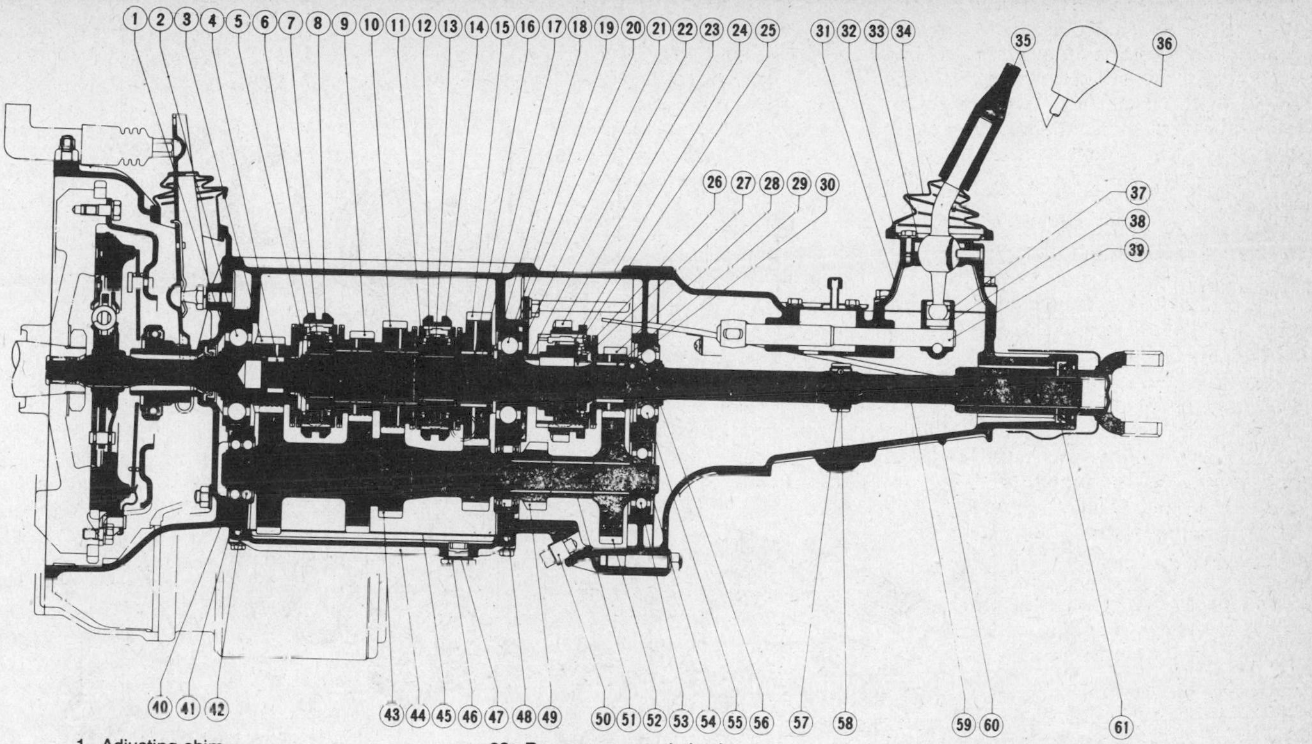

Cross section of Mazda 5-speed transmission

1. Adjusting shim
2. Main driveshaft bearing
3. Main driveshaft gear
4. Needle bearing
5. Synchronizer ring
6. Synchronizer key
7. 3rd-and 4th clutch hub
8. Clutch sleeve
9. 3rd gear
10. 2nd gear
11. Synchronizer ring
12. Synchronizer key
13. 1st-and-2nd clutch hub
14. Clutch sleeve
15. 1st gear
16. Needle bearing
17. Needle bearing inner race
18. Thrust washer
19. Mainshaft front bearing
20. Adjusting shim
21. Bearing cover plate
22. Spacer
23. Reverse gear and clutch sleeve assembly
24. Synchronizer key
25. Synchronizer ring
26. Lock washer
27. Locknut
28. 5th gear
29. Needle bearing
30. Thrust washer
31. Gearshift lever retainer
32. Cover
33. Gasket
34. Boot
35. Gearshift lever
36. Gearshift lever knob
37. Bush
38. Gearshift control lever end
39. Gearshift control lever
40. Adjusting shim
41. Transmission case
42. Countershaft front bearing
43. Countershaft
44. Transmission under cover
45. Gasket
46. Drain plug
47. Gasket
48. Countershaft center bearing
49. Counter reverse gear
50. Drain plug
51. Spacer
52. Counter 5th gear
53. Countershaft rear bearing
54. Thrust washer
55. Mainshaft rear bearing
56. Thrust washer
57. Speedometer drive gear
58. Lock ball
59. Mainshaft
60. Extension housing
61. Mainshaft oil seal

ASSEMBLY

1. Install the third/fourth clutch hub into the sleeve, place the three keys into the clutch hub slots and install the springs onto the hub.

2. Assemble the first/second and reverse/fifth clutch hub and sleeve as described in Step 1.

3. Install the needle bearing, second gear, synchronizer ring, and first/second clutch assembly on the rear section of the mainshaft.

4. Press on the first gear needle bearing inner race.

5. Install the third gear and synchronizer ring onto the front section of the mainshaft.

6. Install the third/fourth clutch assembly onto the mainshaft.

7. Install the snap-ring on the mainshaft.

8. Install the needle bearing, synchronizer ring, first gear and thrust washer on the mainshaft.

9. Install the mainshaft assembly.

10. Install the needle bearing on the front end of the mainshaft.

11. Install the first/second and third/fourth shift forks in their respective clutch sleeves.

12. Check the mainshaft bearing end-play. Check the depth of the mainshaft bearing bore in the case. Measure the mainshaft bearing height. The difference indicates the required adjusting shim to give a total end-play of less than 0.0039 in.

13. Install the synchronizer ring holder tool between the fourth synchronizer ring and the synchromesh gear on the input shaft.

14. Position the shims and mainshaft bearing in the bore and install with a press.

15. Install the input shaft bearing in the same way.

16. Check the countershaft front bearing end-play in the same way as the mainshaft bearing end-play.

17. Install the front bearing snap-ring.

18. Press the countershaft center bearing into position.

19. Install the bearing cover plate.

20. Install the reverse idler gearshaft, thrust washers and reverse idler gear.

21. Install the counter reverse gear and spacer on the rear end on the countershaft.

22. Install the thrust washer and press the needle bearing inner race of the reverse gear on the mainshaft.

23. Install the needle bearing, reverse gear, synchronizer ring, reverse/fifth clutch assembly and new mainshaft locknut on the mainshaft.

24. Lock the mainshaft with the second and reverse gears. Tighten the locknut.

25. Install the needle bearing, synchro-

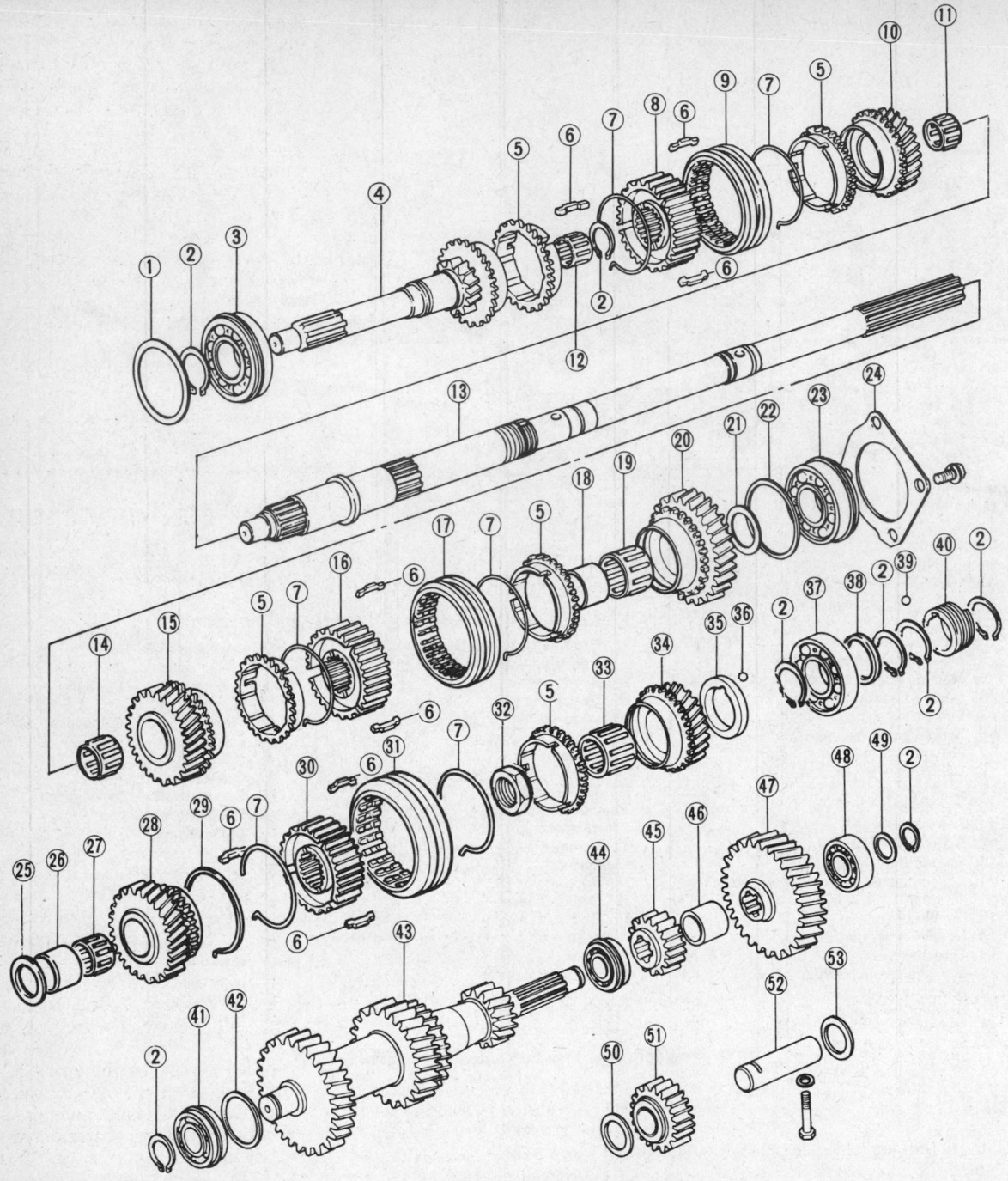

1. Shim	15. 2nd gear
2. Snap ring	16. 1st-and-2nd clutch hub
3. Main drive shaft bearing	17. Clutch sleeve
4. Main drive shaft gear	18. Bearing inner race
5. Synchronizer ring	19. Needle bearing
6. Synchronizer key	20. 1st gear
7. Synchronizer key spring	21. Thrust washer
8. 3rd-and-4th clutch hub	22. Shim
9. Clutch sleeve	23. Main shaft front bearing
10. 3rd gear	24. Bearing cover
11. Needle bearing	25. Thrust washer
12. Needle bearing	26. Bearing inner race
13. Main shaft	27. Needle bearing
14. Needle bearing	28. Reverse gear

29. Stop ring	43. Counter shaft
30. Rev.-and-5th clutch hub	44. Counter shaft center bearing
31. Clutch sleeve	45. Counter reverse gear
32. Main shaft lock nut	46. Spacer
33. Needle bearing	47. Reverse gear
34. 5th gear	48. Counter shaft rear bearing
35. Thrust washer	49. Thrust washer
36. Lock ball	50. Thrust washer
37. Main shaft rear bearing	51. Reverse idler gear
38. Thrust washer	52. Idler gear shaft
39. Lock ball	53. Thrust washer
40. Speedometer drive gear	
41. Counter shaft front bearing	
42. Shim	

Mazda 5-speed gear train

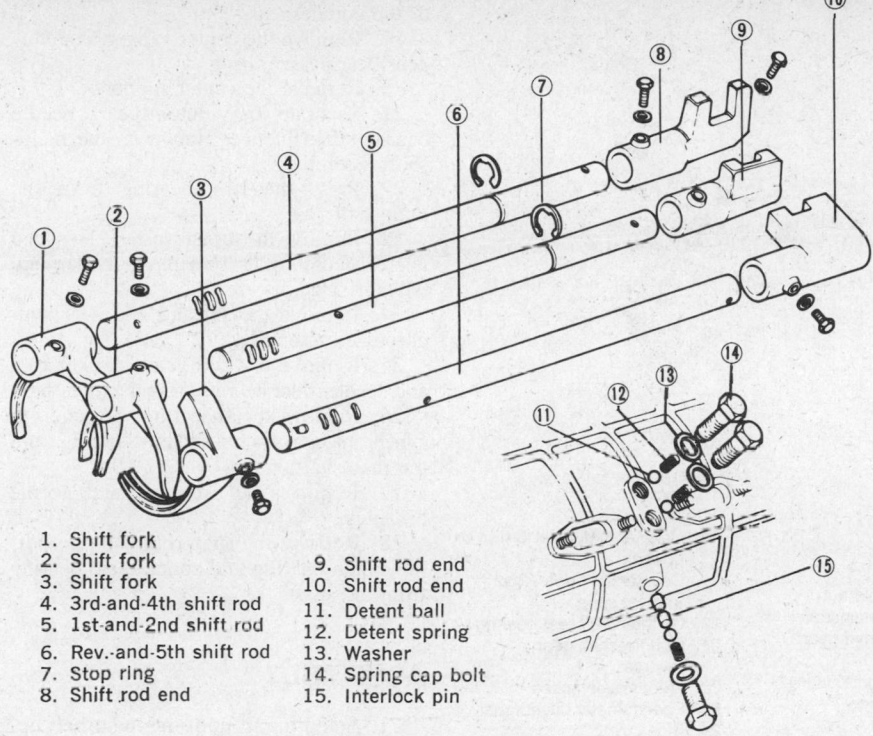

1. Shift fork
2. Shift fork
3. Shift fork
4. 3rd-and-4th shift rod
5. 1st-and-2nd shift rod
6. Rev.-and-5th shift rod
7. Stop ring
8. Shift rod end
9. Shift rod end
10. Shift rod end
11. Detent ball
12. Detent spring
13. Washer
14. Spring cap bolt
15. Interlock pin

Mazda 5-speed shift rod and forks

nizer ring and fifth gear on the mainshaft.

26. Install the thrust washer, steel ball and snap-ring on the mainshaft.

27. Check the thrust washer-to-snap-ring clearance. It should be 0.0039–0.0118 in.

28. Install the first/second shift rod through the holes in the case and fork.

29. Install the interlock pin with a special installer and guide.

30. Install the third/fourth shift rod through the holes in the case and fork.

31. Align the holes and install the lock bolts of each shift fork and rod.

32. Install the interlock pin as above.

33. Position the reverse/fifth shift fork on the clutch sleeve and install the shift rod.

34. Tighten the lockbolt.

35. Install the three shift locking balls, springs and cap bolts.

36. Place the third/fourth clutch sleeve in third gear.

37. Check the clearance between the synchronizer key and the exposed edge of the synchronizer ring with a feeler gauge. The gap should be 0.026–0.079 in. Adjust by varying thrust washers.

38. Install the two blind covers and gaskets.

39. Install the undercover and gasket.

40. Apply a thin coat of sealer to the mating edges and install the intermediate housing on the transmission case. Align the lockbolt holes of the housing and reverse idler gearshaft, install and tighten the lockbolt.

41. Position the counter fifth gear and bearing to the rear end of the countershaft and install with a press.

42. Install the thrust washer and snap-ring.

43. Check the clearance between the washer and snap-ring. Clearance should be less than 0.0039 in.

44. Install the mainshaft rear bearing.

45. Install the thrust washer and snap-ring.

46. Check the thrust washer-to-snap-ring clearance. Clearance should be less than 0.0059 in.

47. Apply a thin coat of sealing agent to the mating surfaces and install the bearing housing on the intermediate housing.

48. Install the shift rod ends on their respective rods.

49. Install the speedometer drive gear and steel ball on the mainshaft. Secure it with a snap-ring.

50. Install a speedometer driven gear assembly on the extension housing and secure it with the bolt and lock plate.

51. Insert the control rod through the holes from the front side of the extension housing.

52. Align the key and insert the control lever end in the control rod.

53. Install the bolt and tighten it to 20–30 ft. lbs.

54. Install the back-up light switch.

55. Place the gasket on the case and install the extension housing with the control lever end down and as far to the left as it will go.

56. Insert the select lock spindle and spring from the underside of the shift lever retainer.

57. Install the steel ball and spring in

alignment with the spindle groove and install the spring cap bolt.

58. Install the gearshift lever retainer and gasket on the extension housing.

59. Check the bearing end-play. Measure the depth of the bearing bore in the housing. Measure the height of the bearing protrusion. The difference indicates the thickness of the shim needed. The end-play should be less than 0.0039 in.

60. Place the gasket on the front side of the case. Apply lubricant to the lip of the oil seal and install the clutch housing on the case.

61. Install the release bearing and fork on the clutch housing.

TYPE 21

4. Speed Transmission

Mercedes–Benz

DISASSEMBLY AND ASSEMBLY

The G 76/18, G 76/18A, G 76/18B, G 76/27 and G 76/27A 4-speed manual transmissions are all very much alike. Overhaul is predominantly given for the G 76/18C since only minor modifications have been made.

1. Remove the throwout bearing and fork.

2. Remove the clutch housing with the slave cylinder.

3. Remove the reverse shift lever clamp.

4. Remove the reverse shift lever.

5. Remove the side cover.

6. Remove the shift forks.

7. Disassemble the side cover and forks.

8. Unbolt and remove the transmission front cover.

9. Remove the bearing housing.

10. Remove the rear transmission cover.

11. Press out the speedometer drive gear.

12. Remove the tachometer drive seal.

13. Remove the reverse gear from the mainshaft.

14. Remove the reverse sliding gear shaft from the housing while holding the sliding gear.

15. Unlock the nut on the rear of the countershaft.

16. Remove reverse gear from the countershaft.

17. Knock the pin from reverse shifter shaft and move the shaft as far forward as possible.

18. Remove the shift rod from the housing.

19. Unlock the slotted nut.

20. Remove the front countershaft bearing. On G 76/27A transmissions, the bearing is beveled and is removed toward the inside of the case.

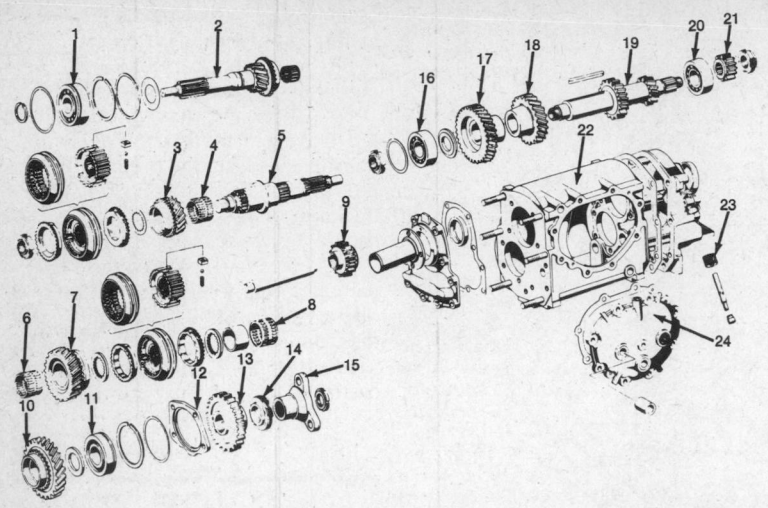

1. Input shaft bearing
2. Input shaft
3. 3rd gear
4. 3rd gear needle bearing
5. Mainshaft
6. 2nd gear needle bearing
7. 2nd gear
8. 1st gear needle bearing
9. Reverse slide gear
10. 1st gear
11. Rear bearing
12. Rear bearing holder
13. Reverse gear, mainshaft
14. Speedometer drive gear
15. Drive flange
16. Countershaft front bearing
17. Countershaft gear, constant speed
18. Countershaft gear, 3rd speed
19. Countershaft gear, 2nd and 1st speed
20. Countershaft rear bearing
21. Countershaft gear, reverse
22. Transmission case
23. Speedometer driven gear
24. Side cover

Exploded view of typical Mercedes-Benz 4-speed

21. Remove the rear countershaft bearing.

22. Lift the mainshaft at the rear and pull the input shaft out of the housing.

23. Push the mainshaft completely rearward and remove it at an angle.

24. Remove the countershaft from the housing.

25. Disassemble the mainshaft, if necessary.

26. If necessary, disassemble the countershaft.

27. Assembly is basically the reverse of disassembly. Try to obtain 0 end-play on the main and input shafts.

TYPE 22

4 Speed Transmission

Isuzu

DISASSEMBLY

1. Remove the boot, clutch fork and throwout bearing.

2. Remove bearing retainer, gasket and spring washer.

3. Remove the speedometer gear and bushing.

4. Remove the shifter cover and gasket.

5. Remove the back-up switch on California vehicles and both back-up and CRS switches on all others.

6. Remove the rear extension and gasket.

7. Remove the thrust washers and reverse idler gear.

8. Remove the snap-rings, speedometer drive gear and key from the mainshaft.

9. Remove the spring pin from the reverse shifter fork and reverse gear.

10. Remove the snap-ring from the outer circumference of the clutch gear shaft ball bearing.

11. Remove the center support assembly from the transmission case.

12. Drive out the spring pins from the third and fourth and first and second shift forks.

NOTE: When removing the spring pin, hold a round bar against the end of the shifter rods to prevent damage.

13. Remove the detent spring plate from the center support, then remove the detent springs and balls.

14. Remove the first and second and the third and fourth shifter rods from the center support, then remove the shifter forks.

15. Remove the reverse shifter rod forward as it is fitted with a stopper pin.

NOTE: Be careful not to lose the detent interlock plugs located between the shifter rods in the center support.

16. Move both synchronizers rearward to prevent turning of the mainshaft.

NOTE: It may be necessary to tap the synchronizers with the hammer handle to get them engaged.

17. Remove the locknut and washer from the mainshaft.

18. Remove the nut, washer, counter-shaft reverse gear and collar from the rear of the countergear.

19. Remove the center support counter-gear bearing snap-ring.

20. Remove the center support.

21. Separate the clutch gear, needle bearings and blocker ring from the mainshaft assembly.

22. Press the rear bearing from the mainshaft.

23. Remove the thrust washer, 1st speed gear, needle roller bearing, a collar and blocker ring.

24. Remove the 1st and 2nd gear synchronizer assembly.

25. Remove the 2nd gear, blocker ring and needle roller bearing from the mainshaft.

26. Remove the snap-ring, 3rd and 4th synchronizer assembly and blocker ring from the mainshaft.

27. Remove the 3rd gear and needle bearings.

28. Remove the snap-ring and press off the clutch bearing and countergear bearing from the shaft.

ASSEMBLY

1. Stand the front of the mainshaft upward and install the 3rd speed gear and needle roller bearing with the tapered side of the gear facing the front of the mainshaft.

2. Install a blocker ring with the clutching teeth upward over the synchronizing surface of the 3rd speed gear.

3. If it is necessary to reassemble the synchronizer assembly turn the face of the synchronizer hub with the heavy boss to the face of the sleeve with the light chamfering on the outer rim.

4. Fit the keys into the key groove and position the synchronizer springs into the hole in the side face of the hub.

5. Install the 3rd and 4th synchronizer assembly on the mainshaft with the face of the sleeve with the light chamfer rearward.

6. Turn the rear of the mainshaft upward and install the 2nd speed gear and needle roller bearing on the mainshaft with the tapered surface of the gear facing the rear of the mainshaft.

7. Install a blocker ring with the clutching teeth downward over the synchronizing surface of the 2nd speed gear.

8. Install the 1st and 2nd synchronizer assembly with the chamfer on the sleeve facing the front of the mainshaft.

9. Install a blocker ring with the clutching teeth rearward.

10. Install the collar, needle roller bearing and 1st speed gear on the mainshaft.

NOTE: The tapered side of the gear should be facing the front of the mainshaft.

11. Install the 1st speed gear thrust washer on the mainshaft with the grooved side facing 1st gear.

12. Press the rear bearing on the mainshaft with the snap-ring groove facing the front of the mainshaft.

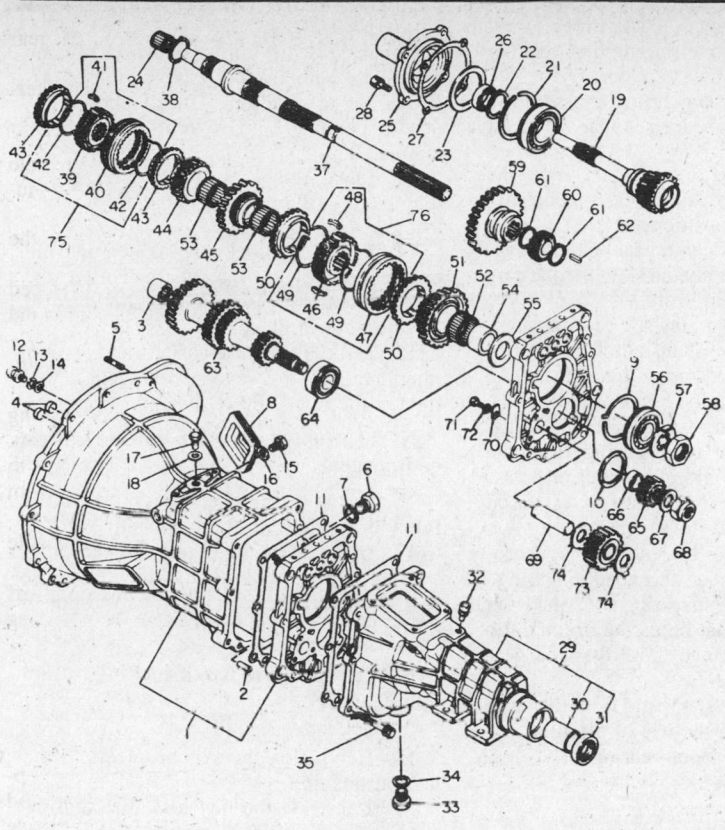

1. Case, w/center support
2. Pin, guide
3. Bearing, needle
4. Plug, shift rod
5. Stud
6. Plug, oil filler
7. O-ring, oil filler
8. Dust cover, shift fork
9. Ring, snap, mainshaft
10. Ring, snap counter gear
11. Gasket, case and rear cover
12. Ball stud
13. Washer, lock
14. Washer, plain
15. Plug, screw
16. Gasket, plug (Calif. spec.)
17. Plug, screw (Calif. spec.)
18. Gasket, plug (Calif. spec.)
19. Shaft, clutch gear
20. Bearing, ball
21. Ring, snap
22. Ring, snap
23. Spring, belleville
24. Bearing, needle
25. Bearing retainer
26. Seal, oil, bearing retainer
27. Gasket, bearing retainer
28. Bolt
29. Extension Assy., rear, w/bushing and seal
30. Bushing
31. Seal, oil, rear extension
32. Breather assy.
33. Plug, oil drain
34. O-ring, oil drain
35. Bolt
37. Shaft main
38. Ring, snap

39. Hub, synchronizer, 3rd-4th
40. Sleeve, synchronizer
41. Key, synchronizer
42. Spring, synchronizer
43. Ring, blocker
44. Gear assy., 3rd
45. Gear assy., 2nd
46. Hub, synchronizer, 1st-2nd
47. Sleeve, synchronizer
48. Key, synchronizer
49. Spring, synchronizer
50. Ring blocker
51. Gear assy., 1st
52. Bearing, needle, 1st
53. Bearing, needle, 2nd
54. Collar, needle bearing
55. Washer, thrust, 1st
56. Bearing, mainshaft
57. Washer, lock, mainshaft
58. Nut, mainshaft
59. Gear, reverse
60. Gear, speed drive
61. Ring, snap, drive gear
62. Key
63. Gear, counter
64. Bearing, angular ball
65. Gear, counter reverse
66. Spacer
67. Washer, plain
68. Nut, self lock
69. Shaft, reverse idle
70. Plate, lock
71. Bolt, lock
72. Washer, spring
73. Gear, reverse idle
74. Washer, thrust
75. Synchronizer assy., 3rd-4th
76. Synchronizer assy., 1st-2nd

Isuzu 4-speed manual transmission

13. If removed, press the ball bearing on the clutch gearshaft with the snap-ring groove on the bearing facing the front of the transmission. Install the snap-ring on the clutch gear shaft.

14. Assemble the needle roller bearing, blocker ring and clutch gear to the front of the mainshaft.

15. If removed, press on the countergear ball bearing with the snap-ring groove facing the rear of the transmission.

16. If removed, install the snap-rings in the inner circumference of the mainshaft and countergear holes of the center support.

17. If removed, insert the idler gear shaft with the lock plate groove side into the center support from the rear, then install the lock plate.

18. Mesh the countergear with the mainshaft assembly and install a holding tool on the mainshaft and countergear.

19. Install the center support.

20. Press the center support onto the shaft until the countergear bearing is brought into contact with its snap-ring.

21. Expand the countergear bearing snap-ring and press the center support further until the mainshaft and countergear snap-rings are fitted into their grooves.

22. Remove the holding tool from the mainshaft and countergear.

23. Move both synchronizers rearward to prevent turning of the mainshaft.

24. Install the collar, countershaft reverse gear, washer and nut on the rear of the countergear.

NOTE: Install the locknut so that the chamfered side if facing the lockwasher.

25. Install the locknut and lockwasher on the mainshaft.

NOTE: Install the locknut so that the chamfered side is facing the lockwasher.

26. Apply grease to the two detent plugs and insert them into their detent holes from the middle hole of the center support.

27. Install the 1st and 2nd shifter forks and the 3rd and 4th into their grooves in the synchronizer assembly.

28. Install 3rd and 4th shifter rod from the rear of the center support through the middle hole and into the 1st and 2nd, 3rd and 4th shifter forks. Align the spring pin hole in the shifter fork with the hole in the shifter rod.

NOTE: Identify the 3rd and 4th shifter rod by the two detent grooves on the side of the rod.

29. Install the 1st and 2nd shifter rod from the rear of the center support through the 1st and 2nd shifter fork and align the hole in the rod to the hole in the shifter fork.

30. If removed, install the stopper pin in the reverse shifter rod and the front of the center support.

31. Install the two spring pins in the 1st/2nd and 3rd/4th shifter forks.

32. Install the detent balls, spring, gasket and retainer on the center support.

33. Install the center support assembly and gasket.

34. Assemble the reverse shifter fork to the reverse gear and install these parts into position from the rear side of the mainshift, then connect them to the reverse shifter rod.

35. Install the spring pin in the reverse shifter fork.

36. Install the thrust washer and reverse idler gear on the idler shaft.

NOTE: The reverse idler gear should be installed with undercut teeth forward.

37. Install the speedometer drive gear snap-ring and key on the mainshaft.

38. Install a new oil seal in the rear extension.

39. Apply grease to the outer thrust washer of the reverse idler shaft and insert it in the rear extensions.

40. Install the rear extension and gasket.

41. Install the back-up lamp switch and CRS switch.

42. Install the shifter cover and gasket.

43. Install the oil O-ring to the speedometer drive gear and install the gear.

44. Install the front bearing retainer seal.

45. Install a snap-ring in the outer circumference of the clutch gear bearing.

46. Apply grease to the bearing retainer spring washer and place it in the bearing retainer with the dished face turned to the bearing outer race.

47. Install the bearing retainer to the front of the transmission case.

NOTE: The shorter bolts are used on

countergear front bearing side of the bearing retainer.

48. Install the ball stud to the bearing retainer.

49. Install the boot clutch fork and throwout bearing, then install the retaining spring.

TYPE 23

5 Speed Transmission

Isuzu

DISASSEMBLY

1. Drain the gear box of lubrication.

2. Remove the clutch release bearing and yoke assembly from the bell housing. Remove the clutch fork ball stud, if necessary, for removal clearance of the front bearing retainer.

3. Remove the front bearing retainer and Belleville spring.

4. Remove the speedometer driven gear and shift lever quadrant from the extension housing.

NOTE: Remove the Coasting Richer System switch from the quadrant on California models.

5. Remove the back-up lamp switch and the extension housing from the gear box.

6. Remove the snap-rings, speedometer drive gear, key, spacer and bearing from the mainshaft.

7. Remove the snap-ring, thrust washer and lock ball from the fifth gear on the mainshaft.

8. Remove the large snap-ring from the front bearing.

9. Remove the center support plate from the transmission case, with the mainshaft, countergear and drive gear as an assembly.

10. Support the ends of the 1st and 2nd, 3rd and 4th and 5th and reverse shift forks and drive the retaining pins from the forks.

11. Remove the detent spring plate from the center support plate and remove the three springs and balls.

12. Remove the shifter shafts from the center support plate and remove the shift forks and interlock pins.

13. To prevent the turning of the mainshaft and countergear while removing the locking nuts from the gear assembly, engage the synchronizers in 1st and 3rd gears.

14. Remove the nut and washer retaining the countergear and by using a puller, remove the ball bearing and the fifth gear from the rear of the countershaft.

15. Remove the fifth gear, blocker ring and needle bearing from the mainshaft.

16. Remove the nut from the reverse idler gearshaft and remove the thrust washers and gear from the idler gearshaft.

17. Straighten the mainshaft locking retainer tab and remove the nut and retainer from the mainshaft.

18. Remove the synchronizer assembly, reverse gear, needle bearing, collar and thrust washer.

19. Remove the reverse gear from the countergear and reposition the synchronizers to the neutral position.

20. Expand the countergear bearing snap-ring and move the center support plate by gently tapping on its front.

21. Expand the mainshaft bearing snap-ring and move the mainshaft inward. Remove the mainshaft and countergear.

22. Remove the drive gear, needle bearing and blocker ring from the mainshaft.

23. Remove the rear bearing from the mainshaft with the aid of a puller or press.

24. Remove the thrust washer, 1st speed gear, needle bearings and spacer.

25. Remove the 1st and 2nd synchronizer, 2nd speed gear and needle bearing.

26. Remove the snap-ring from the front of the mainshaft that holds the 3rd and 4th synchronizer. Remove the 3rd speed gear and needle bearing.

27. Remove the snap-ring from the drive gearshaft and with the use of a puller or a press, remove the front bearing.

ASSEMBLY

1. Place the coned side of the 3rd speed gear towards the front of the transmission and install it and the needle bearing on the front of the mainshaft.

2. Install the 3rd and 4th synchronizer on the mainshaft with the chamfered end towards the front of the transmission. Retain with a snap-ring.

3. Install the 2nd speed gear and needle bearing on the rear of the mainshaft with the coned end of the gear towards the rear of the transmission.

4. Install the 1st and 2nd synchronizer on the mainshaft with the large chamfered end towards the rear on the transmission.

5. Install the spacer, needle bearings and 1st speed gear on the mainshaft, with the coned end of the gear towards the front of the transmission.

6. Install the first gear thrust washer with the slots towards the gear.

7. Press the rear bearing onto the mainshaft with the snap-ring groove towards the front of the transmission.

8. Install the center support plate snap-rings and reverse idler shaft. Torque bolts to 14 ft. lbs.

9. Install the drive gear on the front of the mainshaft and engage with the countergear to install the center support plate.

10. Install countergear and mainshaft bearings into the center support plate and while expanding the snap-rings, move the bearings into place on the support plate and engage the snap-rings in the bearing grooves.

11. Engage the gears in 1st and 3rd to prevent turning and install the reverse gear

on the countergear.

12. Install the thrust washer on the mainshaft with the oil grooves turned towards the reverse gear. Install the collar, needle bearings and reverse gear on the mainshaft.

13. Install the synchronizer assembly so that the face of the clutch hub boss is turned to the reverse gear side.

14. Install the locking retainer and nut on the front of the mainshaft. Torque the nut to 94 ft. lbs. Bend the retainer tab to lock the nut in place.

15. Install the thrust washers and reverse idler gear on the reverse idler shaft and tighten the nut to 80 ft. lbs.

NOTE: Install new self-locking nut on countergear.

16. Install the blocker ring, needle bearing and 5th gear on the mainshaft.

17. Install the countergear 5th gear, ball bearing, washer and self-locking nut on the rear of the countergear. Torque the nut to 80 ft. lbs.

NOTE: Install new self-locking nut on countergear.

18. Reposition the synchronizers to the neutral position.

19. Lubricate the interlock pins and install in the center support plate.

20. Place the shift forks on the synchronizer sleeves and install the 3rd and 4th shifter shaft through the center support plate and into the shift fork for 3rd and 4th gear.

21. Install the 1st and 2nd shifter shaft through the center support plate and through the 1st and 2nd shift fork.

22. Install the reverse and 5th shifter shaft through the center support plate and into the reverse and 5th shifter fork.

23. Install the three detent balls and springs in the center support plate and retain with the detent plate and gasket. Torque the bolts to 14 ft. lbs.

24. Install the retaining pins in the shifter forks to the shifter shafts while supporting the ends of the shaft with a bar or block of wood.

25. Install the countergear needle bearing in the front of the transmission case.

26. Install a new gasket on the transmission case and install the center support plate assembly into the transmission case.

27. Install the large snap-ring on the front bearing of the mainshaft.

28. Install the lock ball and thrust washer on the mainshaft and retain with a snap-ring.

29. Measure the clearance between the 5th gear and the thrust washer on the mainshaft. The clearance should be 0.010–0.016 in.

30. If the clearance is out of specifications, replace the thrust washer with one of the following:

31. Install the speedometer drive gear front snap-ring, ball bearing and key onto the mainshaft.

1. Drive gear
2. Release bearing
3. Drive gear bearing retainer
4. Shift fork
5. Drive gear bearing
6. Shifter shaft
7. 3rd & 4th shift fork
8. 1st & 2nd shift fork
9. Mainshaft bearing
10. Center support
11. Shift lever quadrant
12. Shift lever
13. 5th & reverse shift fork
14. Mainshaft rear bearing
15. Extension housing
16. Rear seal
17. Speedometer drive gear
18. 5th gear assy
19. Counter gear rear bearing
20. 5th counter gear
21. Needle bearing
22. Reverse counter gear
23. Reverse idler shaft
24. Reverse idler gear
25. Counter gear bearing
26. Needle bearing
27. Counter gear
28. Mainshaft
29. Counter gear front bearing
30. Needle gearing

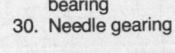

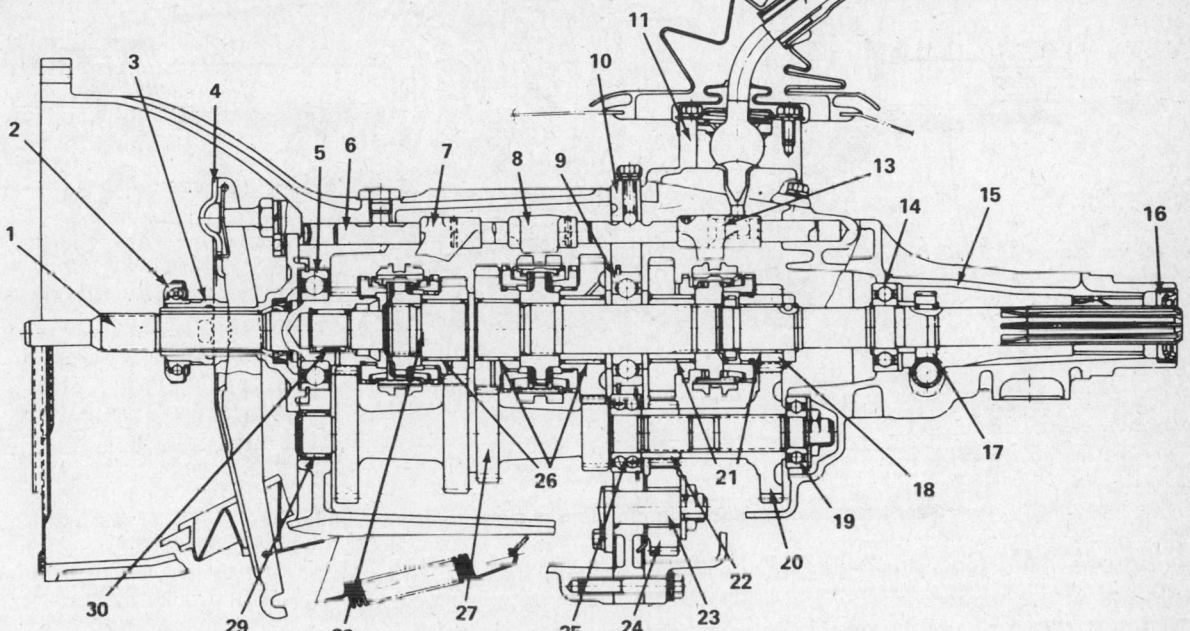

Cross section of Opel Isuzu 5-speed transmission

Part Number	Thickness (inches)	(Millimeters)
94025579	0.3014	7.656
94025580	0.3073	7.805
94025581	0.3132	7.955
94025582	0.3191	8.105

32. Align the groove in the speedometer drive gear with the key on the mainshaft and install the gear. Retain with a snap-ring.

33. Install the rear extension housing with a new gasket on to the center support plate. Torque the bolts to 27 ft. lbs.

34. Install the shift lever quadrant with gasket on the extension housing. Torque the bolts to 14 ft. lbs.

35. Install the speedometer driven gear and torque the retaining bolt to 14 ft. lbs.

36. California Models only: Install the CRS switch on the extension housing.

37. Install the Belleview washer with the dished side towards the drive gear bearing and install the bearing retainer and gasket. Torque the bolts to 14 ft. lbs.

NOTE: Seal the lower left bolt with a non-hardening sealer or equivalent.

38. Install the clutch release bearing and yoke assembly on the bell housing.

NOTE: The gearshift lever is installed when the transmission is in the vehicle.

TYPE 24

4 Speed Transmission—Models BA–7, BA–10, BA–10/4

Peugeot

DISASSEMBLY

BA–7

1. Drain the lubricating oil from the gear box and mount the assembly upside down in the support tool or its equivalent.

2. Remove the clutch release fork, the clutch housing and the back-up lamp switch.

3. Remove the speedometer drive gear socket bushing and the retaining screw from the rear extension.

NOTE: To pull the socket bushing from the housing, an expanding set of pliers

will be needed.

4. Invert the transmission on the support tool or its equivalent and secure.

5. Move the control lever to the neutral position and pull the selector lever fully to the rear.

6. Remove the rear extension housing retaining bolts and separate the rear housing from the transmission case.

NOTE: A rubber mallet may be needed to loosen the rear extension housing from the transmission case.

7. Remove the four Allen screws from the rear bearing lock plate.

8. Remove the eight half housing retaining bolts and remove the upper half housing from the lower half housing, with the gear train remaining in the lower housing.

9. Lift the gear train assembly from the lower half housing as a unit.

BA–10, BA–10/4

1. Mount the gear box by its left housing in the support tool or its equivalent and drain the lubricating oil, if not previously done.

2. Remove the set screw and the speedometer driven socket bushing from the rear extension housing.

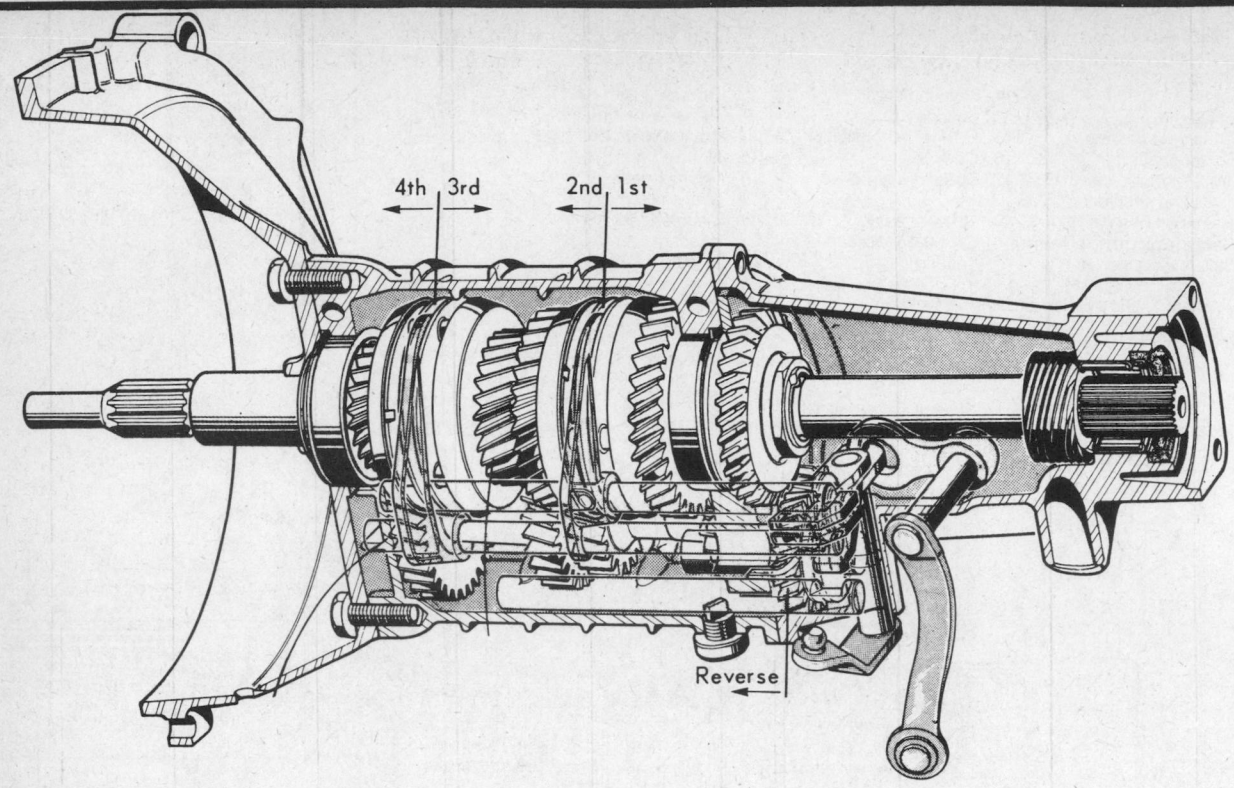

Gear train position and shift direction of synchronizers—Model BA-7

Gear train position in half housing and shift direction of synchronizers—Model BA-10

NOTE: An expanding set of pliers will be needed to pull the socket bushing from the housing.

3. Move the selector and control levers into the neutral position.

BA–7

Remove the return spring and its support from the extension housing.

NOTE: The return spring support is mounted on a rear extension housing bolt.

BA–10, BA–10/4

Remove the return spring and the reverse gear plunger from the rear extension housing.

NOTE: The return spring support is bolted to the rear of the extension housing.

4. Remove the retaining bolts and loosen the rear extension housing with a rubber mallet. Remove the housing from the transmission.

5. Engage the 4th gear and place an output shaft holding tool or its equivalent on the output shaft splines.

6. Hold the output shaft securely and remove the nut from the countershaft. Remove the reverse idling pinion gear.

7. Remove the clutch release bearing fork rubber protection cover, the clutch release fork and the clutch release bearing. Remove the retaining bolts from the clutch housing and remove the housing from the transmission case.

8. Engage the reverse gear and remove the rear bearing thrust plate retaining screws.

9. Remove the retaining bolts from the half housings and separate the two halfs by the removal of the right hand housing.

10. Lift the countershaft assembly from the left half housing. Mark the bearing outer races, in case they are to be reused.

11. Remove the input and mainshaft assembly from the half housing as a unit. Do not separate.

12. Set the reverse semi-synchronizer to the neutral position.

Countershaft

BA–7

1. Place the countershaft in a holding tool or vise and remove the snap-ring from the reverse idler gear. Remove the washer and the gear from the countershaft.

2. Remove the outer race from the bearing and with the use of a press, remove the front and rear bearings.

NOTE: Do not lose the adjusting shim located behind the front bearing.

BA–10, BA–10/4

1. Place the countershaft in a press and remove the front bearing and adjusting shim.

2. Invert the countershaft and press the rear bearing from the shaft.

Separation of Input and Mainshaft—All Models

1. Place the 3rd/4th synchronizer assembly in the 3rd speed position and pull the input shaft from the mainshaft. Do not lose the needle bearing from the input shaft bore.

Mainshaft

BA–7

1. Remove the grease from the 3rd/4th synchronizer assembly. Place the mainshaft assembly in a holding tool or vise.

2. Mark the position of the 3rd/4th sliding gear on the 3rd/4th hub, using a sharp brass rod or its equivalent. Remove the sliding gear.

3. Remove the snap-ring and spring washer retaining the 3rd/4th speed hub to the mainshaft.

4. While holding the reverse pinion with a holding tool or equivalent, and the mainshaft still in the vise or holding tool, fully unscrew the reverse pinion retaining nut from the mainshaft threads.

NOTE: The nut is retained on the shaft by the speedometer gear.

5. Remove the 3rd/4th synchronizer hub and 3rd speed gear from the mainshaft. A puller or a press may have to be used.

6. Place the mainshaft assembly into a press and press the mainshaft downward to free the rear bearing from its seat on the mainshaft.

— CAUTION —

Be sure the retaining nut is free of its threads on the mainshaft, before the press pressure is applied.

7. Continue the downward pressure on the mainshaft and remove the speedometer drive gear from the mainshaft.

8. Remove the assembly from the press and remove the parts from the mainshaft in the following order:
 a. Speedometer drive gear
 b. Nut
 c. Reverse pinion gear
 d. Rear bearing and retainer plate

Position of gear train in half housing and the shift direction of the synchronizers—Model BA-10/4

e. Rear bearing and adjusting shims
f. 1st speed gear spacer bushing
g. Needle bearing cage
h. 1st speed gear
i. 1st/2nd speed gear synchronizer and hub
j. 2nd speed gear

NOTE: Observe the direction of gear position on the mainshaft.

BA–10, BA–10/4

1. Degrease the 3rd/4th synchronizer assembly and mark the positioning of the sliding gear to the hub assembly with a sharp piece of brass welding rod.

2. Remove the sliding gear from the mainshaft.

3. Remove the circlip and spring washer from the front end of the mainshaft, holding the 3rd/4th synchronizer hub in place.

4. Holding the mainshaft in a vise or other holding fixture, remove the reverse gear nut from its threads on the mainshaft, while holding the reverse gear stationary.

5. Using a press or a puller, remove the 3rd gear synchronizer hub and the 3rd gear from the mainshaft.

6. Place the mainshaft assembly into a press with the rear of the mainshaft pointing upward. Using press pressure, force the mainshaft downward to unseat the rear bearing from its seat on the mainshaft.

------ CAUTION ------

Be sure the nut is free of its threads on the mainshaft, before the press pressure is applied.

7. Continue the downward pressure of the press on the mainshaft and remove the speedometer drive gear from the mainshaft.

8. Remove the assembly from the press and remove the parts from the mainshaft in the following order:
a. Speedometer drive gear
b. Retaining nut
c. Reverse gear driven pinion
d. Rear bearing thrust plate
e. Rear bearing and adjusting shims
f. 1st gear spacer collar
g. Needle bearing
h. 1st gear driven pinion
i. 1st/2nd synchronizer assembly with hub.
j. 2nd gear driven pinion
k. Needle bearing

NOTE: Observe the direction of gear position on the mainshaft.

Input Shaft
ALL MODELS

1. Remove the large and small circlips from the bearing and the shaft. Remove the spring washer from under the small circlip.

2. Using a press, force the input shaft from the bearing. Do not lose the oil defector or the adjusting shims.

Shifting Rails and Forks
BA–7

1. Place the 1st/2nd shifting mechanism in the 2nd speed position.

2. Using a drift of proper size, remove the roll pin from the 1st/2nd gear shift fork.

3. Return the 1st/2nd shift mechanism to the neutral position, and position the 3rd/4th shift rail to the 4th speed location. Remove the roll pin from 3rd/4th shifting fork.

4. Return the 3rd/4th shift rail to neutral position.

5. Remove the detent ball locking plug from the outside of the transmission case. An Allen key type tool is used.

6. Remove the 1st/2nd gear shift rail and the 3rd/4th gear shift rail from the transmission case.

7. Invert the transmission case and remove the reverse shifting detent ball locking plug with the Allen key tool.

8. Remove the shift rail and fork with the countershaft pinion from the transmission case.

9. Locate and remove from the case, the three locking springs, four balls and the one locking finger.

NOTE: If the balls are stuck in the passages, use a long rod to free them.

10. Remove the locking needle from the 3rd/4th speed shifting rail.

11. Using a drift, remove the roll pin from the reverse pinion shaft and move the shaft towards the inside of the case and remove.

BA–10

1. Place the 1st/2nd shift fork in the neutral position and remove the roll pin with a proper sized drift.

2. Move the 3rd/4th shift rail into the 4th speed position and remove the roll pin from the fork.

3. Remove the 1st/2nd locking spring

plug and remove the spring and ball from the outside of the transmission case.

4. Remove the shift rail and the shift fork.

5. Remove the reverse detent spring plug, the spring and the ball. If not done previously, remove the back-up light switch.

6. Remove the reverse shift fork and idler gear assembly. Remove the indent and spring (operating spigot).

7. Remove the 3rd/4th detent plug, spring and ball from the outside of the transmission case.

8. Remove the 3rd/4th shift rail. Remove the fork, the interlock pin, the detent ball and interlock finger from the bearing block.

9. Using a drift, remove the roll pin from the reverse shaft and push the shaft towards the outside of the housing.

BA–10/4

1. Remove the 3rd/4th detent spring from the hole in the bearing seat at the rear of the transmission half housing.

2. Place the selector rail into 4th gear and remove the roll pins from the 1st/2nd and 3rd/4th rails and forks.

3. If not done previously, remove the back-up light switch from the case.

4. Remove the 1st/2nd detent ball plug and spring from the outside of the case.

5. Remove the 1st/2nd shift rail and the 1st/2nd shift fork.

6. Remove the 3rd/4th shift rail and fork. Remove the detent balls and recover the interlock pins.

7. Remove the roll pin from the reverse gearshaft.

8. Remove the remaining detent plugs and springs from the outside of the case.

9. Remove the reverse gear assembly, consisting of the gear, shaft, fork and shifting rail and the semi-synchronizer bushing.

10. Obtain the detent balls and the interlock pins from the passages in the transmission case.

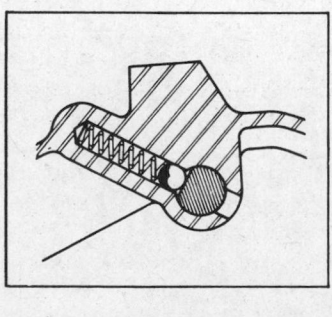
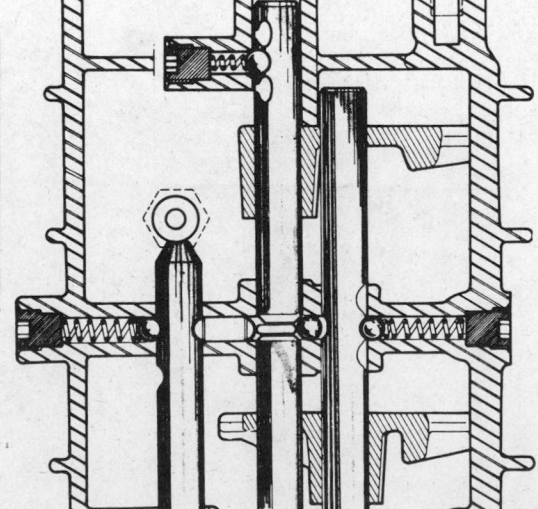

Diagram of detent and interlock components—Model BA-7

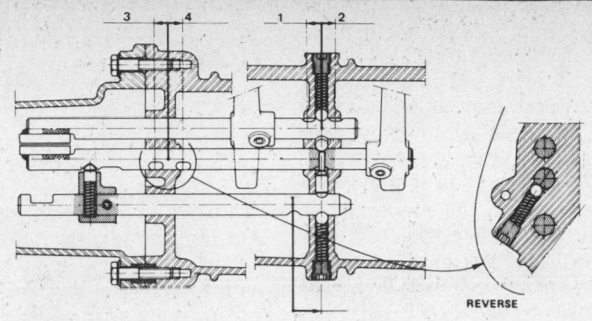

Diagram of detent and interlock components—Model BA-10

Neutral Ball Detent—Rear Extension Housing
ALL MODELS

1. Check the operation of the neutral position ball detent by pushing and pulling the selector lever in and out of the housing.

2. If the detent is found to be defective, remove the detent plug and check the condition of the spring and ball. Replace the necessary parts.

ASSEMBLY

General

1. When reassembling the gearboxes, replace the following parts as standard procedure.
   a. Shaft circlips
   b. Spring washers
   c. Roll pins
   d. Mainshaft nut
   e. Output shaft oil seal
   f. Input shaft oil seal
   g. Speedometer driven socket bushing
   h. Thrust washers

2. Oil the various gears, shafts and components before installation.

3. When joining the housings, apply a thin coat of jointing compound to seal the units.

4. Inspect the clutch housing to be sure the front and rear surfaces are parallel to each other. If a difference of more than 0.004 inch (0.10 mm) exists, the housing should be replaced.

5. Replace the thrust guide in the clutch housing by removing the oil seal, the circlip and pressing the guide from the housing.

6. Replace the thrust guide by applying grease to the tube and pressing it into place in the housing. Install the circlip and the oil seal.

NOTE: To avoid damage to the seal, do not install it into the clutch housing until the adjustment operations are made during the assembly of the unit.

7. Remove the rear oil seal in the extension housing by prying it from the housing bore. Remove the needle bearing with the aid of a press.

8. Install the needle bearing with the aid of a press and install the seal in its bore.

NOTE: The needle bearing assembly and seal should be replaced any time the transmission is disassembled.

When installing the needle bearing, position the bearings with the markings on it towards the outside.

Installation of Shift Rails, Forks and Detents
BA-7

1. Place the left hand transmission housing in the holding tool or equivalent.

2. Install the reverse pinion shaft and align the roll pin holes. Install the roll pin into the pre-aligned holes.

3. Turn the housing on its side so that the drain plug is upward and install the reverse gear along with the shifting fork.

NOTE: The shift fork collar on the gear should be towards the rear.

4. Install the ball and the spring detent into its passage, from the outside of the

case. Install a sealer on the plug threads and install the plug into the case. Torque to 9.4 ft. lb. Locate the reverse shift rail to the neutral position.

5. Rotate the housing to the opposite side to expose the locking passage and install the 3rd/4th locking finger (indent) into the passage.

6. Install the locking needle on the 3rd/4th shifting rail and hold with grease. Install the rail into its respective bore.

7. Rotate the housing until it is in its upright position and install the 1st/2nd shift fork into the case and 3rd/4th shift fork onto the shift rail. Push the rail inward until it is flush with the ball lock hole in the front of the case.

NOTE: The 1st/2nd shift fork will be along side the shift rail.

8. Insert a ball and spring into the hole and compress the spring and ball. Push the rail forward and over the ball and spring.

9. Set the shaft into the neutral position and secure the 3rd/4th shifting fork to the shift rail with a new roll pin.

10. Rest the housing on it side and install a locking ball into the passage to rest against the 3rd/4th shift rail.

11. Install the 1st/2nd shift rail into its respective bore until the neutral position is reached, and entering the 1st/2nd shift fork.

12. Install the locking ball and spring into its bore sealing the plug and installing it into the housing. Torque to 9.4 ft. lb. Secure the 1st/2nd shifting fork with a new roll pin.

BA–10

1. Install the reverse gear shaft and align the pin holes. Install a new roll pin into the pre-aligned holes.

2. Install the reverse gear, the shift fork and the shifting rail into the transmission case.

NOTE: The shifting fork collar of the reverse gear should face to the rear.

3. Install the ball and spring into the reverse lock hole and install the locking plug, after coating it with a sealer, into the transmission case.

4. Position the shifting shaft into the neutral position.

5. Place the 3rd/4th and reverse indent pin into the passage to contact the reverse shift rail.

6. Lubricate the interlock pin and place it in its position on the 3rd/4th shift rail.

7. Place the operating indent and spring on the reverse shift fork.

NOTE: The indent is commonly called "spigot".

8. Position the 3rd/4th shift fork rail into the case with the operating clevis horizontal and pointing to the left. Engage the rail by compressing the drive interlock pin (spigot) until the locking flat is opposite the indent.

9. Place the 3rd/4th shift fork in po-

Diagram of detent and interlock components—Model BA-10/4

sition with its collar towards the rear and engage the rail into the fork. Secure the shifting fork to the rail with a new roll pin.

IMPORTANT: Be assured that the interlock pin is in its proper position in the passage, located in the strut of the case.

10. Rotate the transmission case and install the detent ball in the passage to locate the ball between the 3rd/4th and the 1st/2nd shift rails.

11. Install the 1st/2nd shift rail and the 1st/2nd shift fork into the transmission case, with the shift collar of the gear towards the front. Engage the shift rail into the shift fork and install a new roll pin.

12. Install a ball and spring into the 1st/2nd speed detent passage and after coating the plug with sealer, install the plug into the passageway. Torque to 9.4 ft. lb.

13. Install the ball and spring into the 3rd/4th detent passage.

14. Coat the plug with a sealer and install into the transmission case. Torque to 9.4 ft. lbs.

BA–10/4

1. Install the reverse gear assembly consisting of the gear, shaft, fork and rail and the semi-synchronizer ring, into the transmission housing.

2. Align the holes in the reverse gear shaft and the transmission case strut and install a new roll pin.

3. Install the detent balls and springs into the detent passages in the following order. Rear passage—A detent ball and the 50 mm long spring. Intermediate passage—A detent ball and a 30 mm long spring.

4. Coat the plugs with a sealer and install in the case. Torque to 9.4 ft. lbs. Set the reverse rail to neutral position.

5. Install the interlock pin into the passage towards the front of the case.

6. Install the interlock pin into the hole in the 3rd/4th shift rail and hold in position with grease.

7. Place the 3rd/4th shifting fork in the case with the boss to the rear. Slide the 3rd/

4th shifting rail into position, through the case and into the shifting fork.

8. Install a detent ball into the open passage, towards the front of the case.

9. Install the 1st/2nd shifting fork with the boss towards the front of the case. Install the 1st/2nd shifting rail into the case and the fork.

10. Install a detent ball and a 30 mm long spring into the open detent passage, closest to the front, and coat the plug with sealer and install it into the case. Torque to 9.4 ft. lbs.

11. Align the holes in the 1st/2nd and 3rd/4th shifting forks and rails and install new roll pins to secure them.

Adjustment Prior to Assembly

Three major adjustments should be made prior to the assembly of the gear box components. The adjustments are as follows.

a. Position of the 4th speed synchronizer cone.

b. Position of the 2nd speed synchronizer cone.

c. Countershaft taper roller bearing preload.

Special tools are needed for the adjustments and should be attained prior to transmission repairs.

An explanation of the adjustments are outlined, with the use of the special tools included in the outline.

ADJUSTMENT OF THE 4TH SPEED SYNCHRONIZER CONE

1. Install the input shaft and bearing, less shims and oil deflector, into the clutch housing, inverted on a flat surface.

2. Install the right hand half of the transmission housing to the clutch housing and install two bolts. Torque the bolts to 14.5 ft. lbs.

--- **CAUTION** ---
Be sure the bearing is properly seated in the clutch housing bore and in the right transmission housing bore.

Position of dial indicator, input shaft and bearing, clutch housing and half housing during 4th speed synchronizer cone measurement

3. Seat the special tool gauge block (8.0314 G or equivalent) countershaft front bearing bore of the right transmission housing and the clutch housing.

4. Install the dial indictor (8.0310 FZ or equivalent), into the hole on its block base. Retain the dial indicator with the thumb screw.

5. Align the dial indicator stem with the edge of the 4th synchronizer cone. Rotate the shaft and cone, one turn, and obtain an average reading. Adjust the dial indicator to zero at the average reading height of the cone.

6. Reposition the dial indicator base to the tool gauge block so that the stem is resting on the gauge block surface. Record the measurement.

7. The measurement result represents the thickness of the shim or shims needed to be inserted between the input shaft and the front bearing. The measured value should be rounded off to the nearest 0.05 mm. Shims are available from 0.15 to 0.50 mm, in increments of 0.05 mm.

NOTE: Model BA–7, shims available—0.15 to 0.35 mm.

Prepare the shim stacks as follows:
Model BA–7

Example	
Dial indicator reading	0.58mm
Total shim pack needed (rounded off)	0.60 mm
Use—Oil deflector washer (constant size)	0.15 mm
Shim	0.20 mm
Shim	0.25 mm
Total	0.60 mm

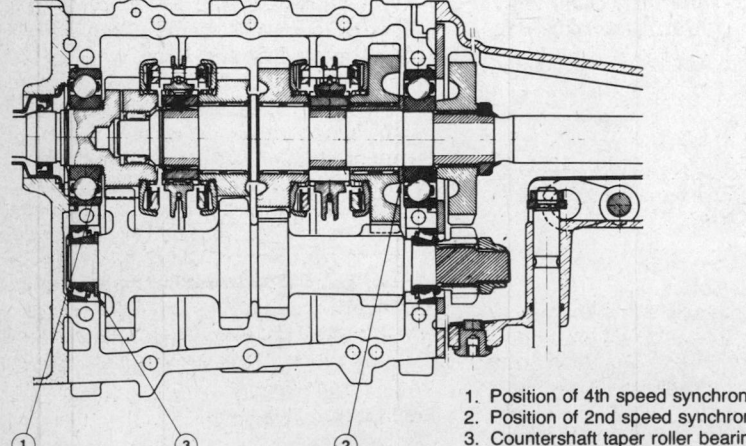

1. Position of 4th speed synchronizer cone
2. Position of 2nd speed synchronizer cone
3. Countershaft taper roller bearing preload

Location of adjusting shims needed during the transmission assembly—Models BA–7, BA–10, BA–10/4

Model BA–10 (Synchronizer cone diameter—91. mm)

Example

Dial indicator reading	0.43 mm
Total shim thickness needed (rounded off)	0.45 mm

NOTE: Remove the oil deflector washer and discard. Do not include it in the shim pact measurement.

Model BA–10/4 (Synchronizer cone diameter—96. mm)

Example

Dial indicator reading	0.87 mm
Subtract from obtained reading (constant)	0.50 mm
Result	0.37 mm
Shim required (rounded off)	0.35 mm

NOTE: Remove the oil deflector washer and discard. Do not include it in the shim pack measurement.

ADJUSTMENT OF THE 2ND SPEED SYNCHRONIZER CONE

1. With the input shaft and bearing in the same position as in the 1st measurement procedure, install a needle bearing into the bore of the input shaft.

2. Install the mainshaft, with the 2nd speed gear and needle bearing, the 1st/2nd speed synchronizer hub and the spacer. Be sure the 2nd speed gear is seated properly.

3. Install the rear bearing temporarily to steady the mainshaft.

4. Install the tool gauge block, (8.0314 K or equivalent) in the countershaft front bearing bore.

5. Place the dial indicator and block base, on the upper part of the transmission half case housing. Using a long dial indicator stem, place the end on the surface of the tool gauge block and set the dial indicator to zero.

6. Position the long dial indicator stem on the rim of the 2nd speed synchronizer cone and record the measurement.

7. The dial indicator reading represents the thickness of the shim or shims needed between the spacer and the rear bearing. Round the results off to the nearest 0.05 mm. Prepare the shim pack as follows:

Model BA–7

Example

Dial indicator reading	0.47 mm
Shims required (rounded off)	0.45 mm

NOTE: Shim available from 0.15 to 0.50 mm in increments of 0.05 mm.

Model BA–10

Example

Dial indicator reading	2.82 mm
Shim required (rounded off)	2.80 mm

Model BA–10/4

Example

Dial indicator reading	2.91 mm
Add to obtained reading (constant)	0.50 mm
Result	3.41 mm
Shim required (rounded off)	3.40 mm

NOTE: Shims are available for models BA–10 and BA–10/4 in steps of 0.05 mm, from 2.35 to 3.65 mm.

8. Remove the dial indicator unit, the mainshaft, the right hand housing and the input shaft.

ADJUSTMENT OF THE COUNTERSHAFT TAPERED ROLLER BEARING PRELOAD

1. Place the left hand housing in the holding stand or its equivalent.

2. Install the countershaft with its bearings and the thrust plate into the housing. Engage the reverse position.

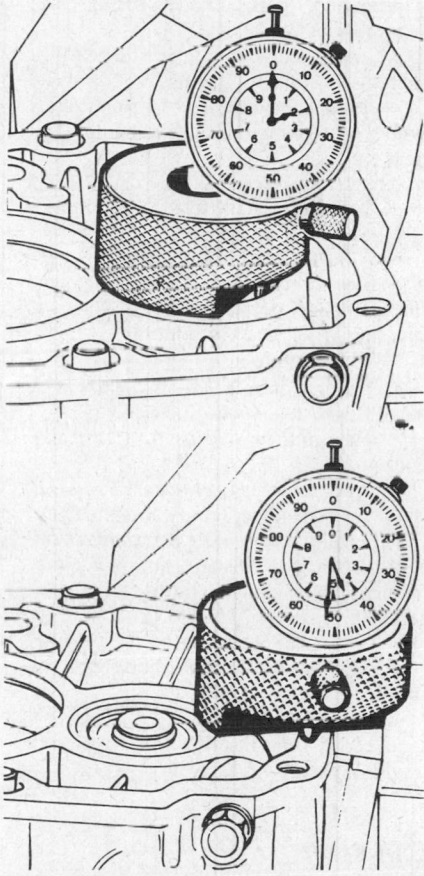

Position of dial indicator and base for measuring preload of countershaft tapered roller bearing

3. Place the right hand half housing on the left housing, with the dowel pins in position, and install two bearing center bolts and four thrust plate bolts. Hand-tighten only.

4. Position the gearbox housing in an upright position, with the front pointing up.

5. With tool number 8.0314 or equivalent, apply pressure to the countershaft

bearings. Rotate the shaft to seat the bearings properly.

6. Tighten the previously hand-tightened bolts to a torque of 7.2 ft. lb. (Bearing center bolts and the thrust plate bolts.)

7. Place the dial indicator and its base on the countershaft end with the indicator stem contacting the front bearing outer race. Turn the indicator and base in a complete circle and record the average measurement.

8. Move the dial indicator and base to have the stem contact the face of the half housing and again turn the indicator and base in a complete circle. Record the average measurement.

9. The difference between the two measurements is the run-out between the outer race and the front of the half housings. This measurement should not exceed 0.003 mm.

10. Should the measurement of the run-out exceed specifications, tap gently with a mallet on the outer bearing race, be sure the effort to turn the countershaft has not increased, and recheck the run-out.

11. If necessary, loosen and retighten the front bearing center bolt.

12. Position the dial indicator on the countershaft end with the stem resting on the bearing race. Set the dial indicator hands on 2 and 0.

13. Move the dial indicator so that the stem moves from the race to the front face of the housings. Note and record the dial indicator movement.

14. Add 0.10 mm to this measurement to provide for the bearing preload, and round off to the nearest 0.05 mm.

Example

Measurement to housing	4.27 mm
Preset measurement on race	2.00 mm
Difference	2.27 mm
Add preload	0.10 mm
Necessary shim	2.37 mm
Round off to nearest 0.05 mm	2.35 mm

NOTE: Available shims for the Model BA–7 range from 2.25 to 3.25 mm in increments of 0.05 mm. Available shims for the models BA–10 and BA–10/4 range from 2.15 to 3.30 mm in increments of 0.05 mm.

15. Remove the retaining bolts from the thrust plate and the bearing areas of the half housings and separate the two housings. Remove the countershaft and bearings.

16. Remove the front bearing from the countershaft and install the shim of proper thickness, as determined in the previous adjustment procedure, between the bearing and the gear. The shim chamfer should be facing the gear. Press the bearing in place on the countershaft.

Mainshaft Assembly
BA-7

1. Install the following components in order, aligning the previously marked ref-

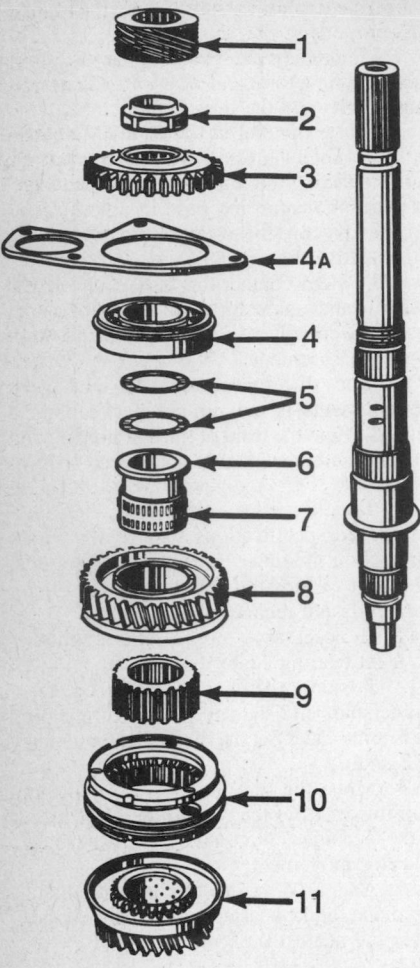

1. Speedometer drive gear
2. Nut
3. Reverse gear
4A. Rear bearing thrust plate
4. Rear bearing
5. Adjusting shim pack
6. 1st speed spacer bushing
7. Needle bearing
8. 1st speed gear
9. Synchronizer cage
10. Synchronizer hub
11. 2nd speed gear

Main shaft components—Model BA-7

erence points, made during the disassembly, on the mainshaft, from rear to front.

    a. 2nd gear
    b. Synchronizer hub and sliding sleeve
    c. 1st gear
    d. Needle bearing
    e. Spacer
    f. Adjusting shims
    g. Rear bearing with snap-ring groove towards the rear

NOTE: The bearing should be pressed on the shaft, not to exceed 3 tons with the parts bottomed.

    h. The thrust plate with the machined surface towards bearing.
    i. Reverse gear with chamfered edge of teeth towards the rear

---

    j. A new nut. Tighten to 40 ft. lbs. and lock
    k. Press speedometer drive gear onto mainshaft
  2. Install the following components in order, onto the mainshaft from front to rear, following the reference marks made previously.
    a. 3rd gear
    b. 3rd/4th gear synchronizer hub (press if necessary)
    c. Spring washer
    d. Snap-ring
    e. 3rd/4th sliding gear and engage 3rd gear.

BA-10, BA-10/4

  1. Install the following components on the mainshaft from rear to front, following the reference marks made during the disassembly.
    a. 2nd speed gear with needle bearing (length—31 mm)
    b. 1st/2nd synchronizer hub and cage, with the marking groove towards the 1st gear
    c. 1st speed gear
    d. Needle bearing (length—29 mm)
    e. Spacer ring
    f. Adjustment shims
    g. Rear bearing. Press the bearing onto the shaft and do not exceed 3 tons of pressure when bearing bottoms
    h. Thrust plate
    i. Reverse drive gear with the flat face towards the rear
    j. New nut, torque to 39 ft. lbs. and lock in place
    k. Speedometer drive gear. Press on shaft with the undercut towards the front
  2. Install the following components on the front of the mainshaft, following the reference marks made during the disassembly.
    a. 3rd speed gear and needle bearing
    b. 3rd/4th synchronizer hub. Press on if necessary
    c. Spring washer
    d. Snap-ring (Install with components under pressure, if necessary)

Input Shaft
ALL MODELS

  1. Install the predetermined shims (with oil deflector on model BA-7) on the input shaft.
  2. Position the bearing with the outer snap-ring groove facing the front of the shaft, and press the bearing into place on the shaft.
  3. Install a new spring washer and snapring while the pressure is on the bearing.
  4. Install the outer snap-ring in the outer bearing race groove.
  5. Install the needle bearing in the bore of the input shaft.
  6. Position the 3rd/4th synchronizer cage to the reference marks, made during the disassembly, on the mainshaft.

---

  7. Install the input shaft to the mainshaft, again aligning the reference marks made during the disassembly.
  8. Set both synchronizers to the neutral position.

Assembly of Components to the Half Housings
BA-7

  1. Secure the half housing with the shifting forks to the support base or equivalent.
  2. Install the countershaft assembly to the mainshaft/input shaft assembly by passing the reverse gear on the countershaft through the opening in the thrust plate. Mesh the gear teeth together and install the assembly into the left hand housing, aligning the shifting forks to the synchronizer sliding sleeves.
  3. Install the countershaft front bearing outer race to the bearing.
  4. Apply sealer to the housing mating surfaces and install the right housing to the left housing.
  5. Install the four housing retaining bolts and torque to 3.6 ft. lbs. (Two bolts at the rear and two bolts at the front.)
  6. Apply sealer to the rear face of the clutch housing and install on the transmission case.
  7. Secure the housing with the six bolts and torque to 20 ft. lbs.
  8. Install the four Allen screws and secure the rear bearing thrust plate. Torque to 7.2 ft. lbs.
  9. Loosen the four housing retaining bolts and strike the housings with a rubber mallet while turning the mainshaft. Retighten and torque the bolts to 11 ft. lbs.
  10. Use a dial indicator and base block to check the "out of flush" of the two half housings at their rear mating surfaces. The housings should not be out of flush more than 0.02 mm.
  11. Install the four assembly bolts and nuts to the half housings and torque to 7.2 ft. lbs.
  12. Apply sealer to the rear housing mating surface and install the housing to the transmission.
  13. Tighten the seven studs and bolts to 11 ft. lbs. after pulling the selector lever fully rearward.
  14. Install the speedometer drive socket bushing with a lubricated O-ring. Install the stop screw and locknut.
  15. Install the clutch release bearing and fork. Install the back-up lamp and fill with lubricant.

BA-10, BA-10/4

  1. Place the left hand housing in the support tool or equivalent.
  2. BA-10/4—Install a detent ball and a 30 mm long spring in the detent passage of the rear bearing seat.

3. Set the reverse gear semi-synchronizer to the neutral position. Set the assembled input and mainshaft synchronizers to the neutral position.

4. Install the gear trains into the half housing while engaging the shifting forks to their respective synchronizer sleeves.

5. Install the outer races to the countershaft bearings and install the countershaft into the housing. Mate the gears of the countershaft and the mainshaft.

6. Coat the half housing mating surfaces with sealer and install the right housing to the left, being sure the dowel pins are properly located.

7. Install the six end housing retaining bolts and torque to 3.5 ft. lbs.

8. Engage the reverse gear and install the four thrust plate bolts. Torque to 9.4 ft. lbs.

9. Fit the reverse idler gear to the countershaft with the boss of the gear to the front. Install a new nut.

10. Engage 4th gear, hold the mainshaft with a special holding tool or equivalent, and tighten the nut to 18 ft. lbs.

11. Lock the skirt of the nut to the countershaft by crimping the skirt with a pair of lock pliers.

--- CAUTION ---
Never hammer the nut to lock the skirt.

12. Install the oil seal in the clutch housing if not previously done. Coat the clutch housing mating surface with sealer and install on the transmission case. Tighten the seven securing nuts to a torque of 20 ft. lbs.

NOTE: Turn the mainshaft while tightening the clutch housing bolts.

13. Loosen the six bolts at the front and the rear of the transmission case. Tap the housing with a rubber mallet while turning the mainshaft. Retighten the six bearing bolts to a torque of 10 ft. lbs.

14. Install the remaining six bolts in the flanges of the assembled housings. Tighten to a torque of 7 ft. lbs.

15. Reset the reverse gear synchronizer to the neutral position. Apply sealer to the rear extension housing mating surface.

16. Turn the selector lever to the left (counterclockwise) as far as it will go and fit the rear housing to the transmission assembly. Tighten the bolts and nut to 10 ft. lbs.

17. Install the shift control return spring bracket and attach the spring.

18. BA-10/4—Install special tool 8.0310 V or equivalent between the jack lever and the housing. Install the reverse gear plunger until it touches the selector lever. Tighten the two bolts and connect the spring. Remove the gauge tool.

19. Install the speedometer driven gear socket bushing and a lubricated O-ring. Install the set screw and tighten.

20. Install the clutch release fork and bearing assembly, along with the rubber protector.

21. Install the back-up light switch and fill the transmission with lubricant.

TYPE 25

4 and 5 Speed Transmissions— Models K40, K50, K51

Toyota

DISASSEMBLY

1. Secure the transmission and drain the lubricant from the unit.

2. Remove the clutch release bearing, fork, boot and spring.

3. Remove the countershaft cover from the front of the transmission (K40).

4. Remove the front bearing retainer and bolts (K40).

5. Remove the shifting locking ball and spring retainer on top of the transmission case (K40).

6. Remove the back-up light switch.

7. Remove the speedometer driven gear assembly.

8. Remove the restricting pins from the shift control opening and the shift lever retainer.

9. Remove the rear extension housing bolts and the extension housing. Disengage the selector shaft from the shift fork shafts by moving the housing towards the bottom of the case.

10. Locate and retain the countergear thrust washer when the extension housing is removed (K50).

11. Remove the lower pan from the case assembly.

Case Disassembly, K40

1. Remove the lockbolt and remove the reverse idler gear and shaft.

2. Remove the countershaft by driving it from the front to the rear.

3. Remove the countergear, bearings and thrust washers from the case.

4. Shift the number one shift fork shaft to the neutral position and using a pin punch, remove the slotted spring pins from the shift forks and shafts.

5. Set each fork shaft to the neutral position and pull the shaft from the case.

6. Shift the number one clutch hub sleeve into 2nd gear and remove the shift fork from inside the case.

7. Arrange the three interlock pins and slotted spring pins and lay aside for the assembly.

8. Remove the output shaft from the

rear of the transmission with the gear intact. Remove the input shaft and gear.

9. Remove the snap-rings at the speedometer drive gear and remove the gear from the shaft.

10. Release the staked parts of the locknut on the mainshaft and remove the nut from the shaft with a holding tool and special wrench.

11. Remove the rear bearing and housing from the mainshaft.

12. Remove the 1st gear, bushing, needle bearing and locking ball from the shaft.

13. Remove the synchronizer (baulk) ring, 1st/2nd clutch hub and sleeve, synchronizer (baulk) ring and the 2nd speed gear from the shaft.

14. Remove the snap-ring from the front of the shaft and remove the 3rd/4th synchronizer assembly and the 3rd speed gear, with spacer.

Case Disassembly, K50

1. Remove the snap-rings and speedometer drive gear from the output or mainshaft.

2. Remove the 5th gearshift arm bracket, arm and the number 3 shift fork.

3. Remove the snap-ring and the shifting key retainer from the mainshaft.

4. Remove the number three clutch hub and sleeve, the synchronizer (baulk) ring and the 5th gear with its needle roller bearings.

5. Remove the snap-ring from the countergear and remove the counter 5th gear, the countergear rear bearing and sleeve. The sleeve is retained with a snap-ring.

6. Remove the locking bolt and pull the reverse idler shaft from the case. Remove the reverse idler gear.

7. Remove the countergear, thrust washer and the front bearing from the case as a unit.

8. Remove the locking balls and springs cover from the top of the transmission case. Remove the springs and balls.

9. Using a pin punch, drive the slotted spring pins from the forks and shafts.

10. Place each shaft into the neutral position and remove from the case.

11. Arrange the slotted spring pins, the interlock pins, and locking ball for easier assembly.

12. Shift the number one clutch into 2nd gear and remove the shift fork from inside the case.

13. Remove the input shaft and front bearing retainer from the front of the case.

14. Secure the pilot bearing rollers and the 4th speed synchronizer (baulk) ring.

15. Spread the expanding snap-ring on the rear bearing and remove the output shaft assembly from the front of the transmission case.

16. Disassemble the mainshaft by removing the rear snap-ring and removing the rear bearing, bushing, needle roller bearing and locating ball. Continue by removing the 1st gear, synchronizer (baulk) ring,

MANUAL TRANSMISSION OVERHAUL

number one clutch hub, sleeve, synchronizer (baulk) ring and the second gear.

17. Remove the front snap-ring, the number two clutch hub, sleeve, synchronizer (baulk) ring and the second gear.

NOTE: During the disassembly and assembly of the K40 and K50 transmissions, the need to press bearings or gears from and back onto the shafts will exist. Govern the disassembly and assembly procedures accordingly.

INSPECTION

Inspect the gears, shafts, bearings and other internal components and replace or repair the necessary parts. Install new seals and gaskets during the reassembly.

ASSEMBLY

Case Assembly, K40

1. Place the mainshaft in an upright position with the rear of the shaft pointing up. Place the 2nd speed gear and the synchronizer (baulk) ring onto the shaft, followed by the number one clutch hub and sleeve. Ring identification: Narrow insert gap for 1st gear and wide insert gap for 2nd gear.

2. Install the second synchronizer (baulk) ring, the 1st gear, the locking ball, the needle roller bearing and the bushing.

3. Install the rear bearing and housing onto the shaft and retain it with a washer and locknut. Tighten the locknut to a torque of 33–72 ft. lbs. (4.5–10.0 Kg-m) with the special wrench and the shaft holding tool. Stake the nut to the shaft.

4. Measure the thrust clearance of the 1st and 2nd speed gears:

1st gear—0.0071–0.0110 inch (0.18–0.28 mm)

2nd gear—0.0039–0.0098 inch (0.10–0.25 mm)

5. Install the 3rd gear on the front of the shaft. Line up the shifting key inserts with the insert slots in the synchronizer (baulk) ring and install the number two clutch hub and sleeve.

6. Push the number two clutch hub inward as far as it will go and measure the 3rd gear thrust clearance:

3rd gear—0.0020–0.0079 inch (0.05–0.20 mm)

Limit—0.0018 inch (0.30 mm)

7. When the 3rd gear thrust clearance is not within specifications, select a spacer from the following list;

Thickness	
mm	(in.)
4.30–4.35	(0.1693–0.1713)
4.35–4.40	(0.1713–0.1732)
4.40–4.45	(0.1732–0.1752)

8. Select a snap-ring that will control the clearance to zero between the snap-ring and the clutch hub, from the following list:

Thickness	
mm	(in.)
2.05–2.10	(0.0807–0.0827)
2.10–2.15	(0.0827–0.0846)
2.15–2.20	(0.0846–0.0866)
2.20–2.25	(0.0866–0.0886)
2.25–2.30	(0.0886–0.0906)
2.30–2.35	(0.0906–0.0925)
2.35–2.40	(0.0925–0.0945)
2.40–2.45	(0.0945–0.0965)

9. Install the snap-ring in place on the mainshaft.

10. If not previously done, install the front bearing on the input shaft. Install the needle roller bearings into the bore of the mainshaft and hold in place with grease.

11. Install the input shaft into the transmission case and select a front bearing retainer gasket in the following manner.

a. If the bearing face extends outside of the case machined surface, use a bearing retainer gasket of 0.020 inch (0.5 mm) in thickness.

b. If the bearing face is below the case machined surface, use a bearing retainer gasket of 0.012 inch (0.3 mm) in thickness.

12. Lubricate the front bearing retainer oil seal and install the retainer to the case. Torque the bolts 11–15 ft. lbs. (1.5–2.2 Kg-m).

13. Set the transmission case upright with the input shaft on the bottom. Be sure the needle bearings remain in their proper position in the input shaft bore.

14. Carefully insert the mainshaft assembly into the transmission case and align the shifting key inserts with the slots in the synchronizer (baulk) ring.

15. Align the pin on the rear bearing housing with the groove in the transmission case. Be sure the mainshaft and the input shaft rotate freely.

16. Temporarily, install a holding tool over the rear bearing retainer so that the gear train is held securely. Place the transmission with the bottom up.

17. Shift the synchronizer assembly sleeve into the 2nd speed position. Install the reverse shift fork, the 1st/2nd shift fork and the 3rd/4th shift fork in their respective sleeve grooves.

18. Insert the shift shafts into the transmission case and through their respective shifting forks. Place the center shaft in the neutral position, along with the reverse shifting shaft in the neutral position.

19. Install the 1st-2nd shifting shaft to the point where the shaft dummy hole and the case hole line up.

20. Insert a probe into the case hole and be sure the outer two shaft holes line up and the probe touches the inner shaft.

21. Install the interlock pins and push

the inner shaft to the neutral position. Move the center shift shaft to the third speed position. The other shafts should not move.

22. Align the forks to the holes in the shafts and install the slotted spring pins.

23. Coat the countergear thrust washers with grease and place them on the inner walls of the transmission case. Insert the countershaft from the rear of the case until the shaft end is even with the rear thrust washer.

24. Carefully install the countergear and push the countershaft into the transmission case and the countergear bearings. Measure the thrust clearance and correct by selecting a proper sized thrust washer. The thrust clearance should be 0.0020–0.0098 inch (0.05–0.25 mm).

25. Install the reverse idler gear and shaft. An adjustment can be made to prevent the gear from contacting the case surface. A spacer can be installed between the gear and the case. A clearance of 0.039–0.079 inch (1.0–2.0 mm) should exist between the teeth of the reverse gear and the teeth of the countergear. A pivot screw and locknut are provided on the case to help in the adjustment of the reverse gear clearance.

Thickness	
mm	(in.)
1.30–1.35	(0.0512–0.0531)
1.40–1.45	(0.0551–0.0571)
1.50–1.55	(0.0591–0.0610)
1.60–1.65	(0.0630–0.0650)

26. Set the transmission upright with the output shaft in the horizontal position and the pan opening down.

27. Install the three balls and springs into the holes in the case top and install the locking ball and spring cover.

28. Install the countergear shaft cover on the front of the transmission case.

29. Shift the fork shafts and be sure the shifting of the gear sleeves, forks and linkage is proper.

Case Assembly, K50

1. Position the mainshaft with the rear of the shaft pointing upward. Install the 2nd speed gear and the synchronizer (baulk) ring onto the shaft, followed by the number one clutch hub and sleeve.

Ring identification: Narrow insert gap for 1st gear and the wide insert gap for the 2nd gear.

2. Install the second synchronizer (baulk) ring, the 1st gear, the locking ball, the needle roller bearing and the bushing.

3. Install the rear bearing and select a selective snap-ring that will allow zero thrust clearance. The snap-ring thicknesses are as follows:

Thickness	
mm	(in.)
2.05–2.10	(0.0807–0.0827)
2.10–2.15	(0.0827–0.0846)
2.15–2.20	(0.0846–0.0866)
2.20–2.25	(0.0866–0.0886)
2.25–2.30	(0.0886–0.0906)
2.30–2.35	(0.0906–0.0925)
2.35–2.40	(0.0925–0.0945)
2.40–2.45	(0.0945–0.0965)
2.45–2.50	(0.0965–0.0984)
2.50–2.55	(0.0984–0.1004)

Install the snap-ring on the mainshaft in its groove.

4. Check the thrust clearances of the 1st and 2nd gears. The clearances should be as follows:

1st gear—0.0071–0.0110 inch (0.18–0.28 mm)

2nd gear—0.0039–0.0098 inch (0.10–0.25 mm)

Limit—0.0118 inch (0.30 mm)

5. Install the 3rd gear onto the front of the shaft and install the synchronizer hub and sleeve, along with the inner synchronizer (baulk) ring in place on the gear unit.

6. Push inward on the number two clutch hub and measure the 3rd gear thrust clearance. The clearance should be as follows:

3rd gear—0.0020–0.0079 inch (0.05–0.20 mm)

Limit—0.0118 inch (0.30 mm)

Install one of the following spacers as required:

Thickness	
mm	(in.)
4.30–4.35	(0.1693–0.1713)
4.35–4.40	(0.1713–0.1732)
4.40–4.45	(0.1732–0.1752)

7. Select a snap-ring of proper thickness to provide zero clearance between the snap-ring and the clutch hub, and install on the shaft. A list of available snap-rings are as follows:

Thickness	
mm	(in.)
2.05–2.10	(0.0807–0.0827)
2.10–2.15	(0.0827–0.0846)
2.15–2.20	(0.0846–0.0866)
2.20–2.25	(0.0866–0.0886)
2.25–2.30	(0.0886–0.0906)
2.30–2.35	(0.0906–0.0925)
2.35–2.40	(0.0925–0.0945)
2.40–2.45	(0.0945–0.0965)

8. Install the mainshaft assembly into the transmission case from the front. Stand the case assembly upright and pull the mainshaft assembly upward, seating the bearing into the case bore, while having the bearing snap-ring expanded in the case. Secure the bearing in the case with the snap-ring.

9. Install the roller bearing and housing on the input shaft, if not previously done. Install the needle bearings in the bore of the input shaft, holding them in place with grease. Place the synchronizer (baulk) ring on the input shaft and install the shaft assembly into the front of the case. Align the shifting key insert slots properly during the installation.

10. Install the front bearing retainer bolts and torque to 11–15 ft. lbs.

11. Shift the transmission gear train into the 2nd gear. Install the shift forks in their respective sleeve grooves.

12. Install the reverse shift shaft and fork. Install the interlock ball (coated with grease) into the hole in the reverse shift fork. Push it into position into the shaft groove.

13. Position the three shafts into their respective bores in the transmission case and position in the neutral mode, having entered the bores of the shifting forks. Move the 1st/2nd speed shaft until the dummy hole on the shaft is lined up with the case hole. Insert a probe in the hole to be sure the shafts are aligned.

14. Install the grease coated interlock pins and push them into position with a probe. Move the three fork shafts in the neutral position. Shift the number two or center shaft into the 3rd gear position and check that the remaining shafts do not move.

15. Align the pin holes in the shift forks and shift fork shafts and secure with the slotted spring pins.

16. Assemble the countergear and shaft with the thrust washer oil groove facing the countergear side, and install into the transmission case. Install the rear bearing and outer race into position in the case. The outer snap-ring must be expanded during this operation.

17. Install the reverse idler gear and shaft. Have the shift arm engaged with the hub of the reverse idler gear.

18. Install the 5th gear on the countershaft with the stepped side of the gear hub facing the case. Secure the gear to the shaft with a snap-ring of a selected size to provide zero clearance, as taken from the following list:

Thickness	
mm	(in.)
2.25–2.35	(0.0886–0.0925)
2.35–2.45	(0.0925–0.0965)
2.45–2.55	(0.0965–0.1004)

19. Select a countergear thrust washer by installing a thrust washer in place on the

countergear and installing the rear extension housing and torquing the retaining bolts 22–32 ft. lbs. (3.0–4.5 Kg-m) and measuring the thrust clearance of the countergear to case.

NOTE: Position the thrust washer with the oil groove facing the 5th gear.

20. The thrust clearance should be 0.0031–0.0157 inch (0.08–0.40 mm). Select the proper sized thrust washer from the following list:

Thickness	
mm	(in.)
1.71–1.81	(0.0673–0.0713)
1.83–1.93	(0.0720–0.0760)
1.95–2.05	(0.0768–0.0807)

21. Remove the extension housing and install the proper thrust washer in place on the counter 5th gear.

22. Align the shifting key insert slots and install the 5th gear and the 5th synchronizer assembly onto the output shaft. Tap the output shaft to the front of the transmission and with a snap-ring retainer pressed against the hub, select a snap-ring to provide a thrust clearance of 0.008–0.012 inch (0.2–0.3 mm) between the 5th gear hub and the rear bearing face.

23. Install the snap-ring and recheck the thrust clearance. Push up on the reverse idler gear until the fork shaft is in a position with the groove above the case.

24. Install the 5th gearshift arm bracket in place on the rear of the case and engage the bracket in the reverse shaft fork. Position the fork claw in the hub sleeve groove and the shift arm shaft in the gearshift head 1st groove.

Thickness	
mm	(in.)
2.05–2.10	(0.0807–0.0827)
2.10–2.15	(0.0827–0.0846)
2.15–2.20	(0.0846–0.0866)
2.20–2.25	(0.0866–0.0886)
2.25–2.30	(0.0886–0.0906)
2.30–2.35	(0.0906–0.0925)
2.35–2.40	(0.0925–0.0945)
2.40–2.45	(0.0945–0.0965)
2.45–2.50	(0.0965–0.0984)
2.50–2.55	(0.0984–0.1004)
2.55–2.60	(0.1004–0.1024)
2.60–2.65	(0.1024–0.1043)
2.65–2.70	(0.1043–0.1063)
2.70–2.75	(0.1063–0.1083)
2.75–2.80	(0.1083–0.1102)

25. Install the three locking balls and springs in the bores of the case. Install the cover and the retaining bolts.

26. Install the inner snap-ring, the speedometer drive gear and the outer snap-ring on the mainshaft. Be sure the locking ball is placed between the gear and the shaft.

27. Adjust the reverse idler gear position so that a clearance of 0.039–0.079 inch (1.0–2.0 mm) exists between the gear teeth of the countergear and the reverse idler gear teeth by the adjustment of the pivot bolt and locknut, located on the outside of the case.

28. Adjust the 5th speed synchronizer sleeve position so that the bottom of the sleeve groove is 0.039–0.059 inch (1.0–1.5 mm) above the rear face of the counter 5th gear.

K40, K50

1. Install the thrust washer on the counter 5th gear with the oil groove towards the gear side. (K50). Install the rear gaskets.

2. Align the shifting fork shafts in the neutral position and install the rear extension housing. Engage the selector shaft to the shift fork shafts. Install the housing retaining bolts and torque to 22–32 ft. lbs.

3. Install the shift control restricting pins and torque to the following values:
K40—Black = 1st and 2nd
    White = Reverse
K50—Black = 1st and 2nd
    White = 5th and Reverse
All—27–31 ft. lbs. (3.7–4.3 Kg-m)

4. Install the speedometer driven gear assembly.

5. Install the back-up light switch.

6. Install the clutch release bearing, fork, boot and spring.

7. Install the bottom cover and gasket. Fill the transmission with lubricant to its proper level.

8. Attach the shift lever and make sure the shifting of the gear train is proper.

TYPE 26

4 and 5 Speed Transmissions— Models T40, T41, T50

Toyota

DISASSEMBLY

CAUTION
The clutch housing, split transmission cage, and extension housing are all made of aluminum.

1. Drain the oil.

2. Remove the clutch housing, bearing retainer, release bearing, and release fork.

3. Remove the speedometer shaft sleeve and driven gear.

4. Remove the extension housing.

5. Remove the back-up light switch.

6. Separate the case halves. Do not pry apart.

7. Measure gear backlash. The backlash for all gears should be 0.004–0.008 in.

8. Remove the countergear set from the right-hand half of the case.

9. Use a magnet to remove the ball from the second countergear bearing.

10. Withdraw the input and the output shafts as a unit.

11. Use a punch to drive the three slotted spring pins out of the shift forks and shift fork shafts.

NOTE: The slotted pin cannot always be fully removed from the first/second shift fork; however, the shift fork can still be withdrawn. Do not try to force the pin out, as damage to the transmission case could result.

12. Remove the case cover and the three detent balls and springs.

13. Remove the shift fork shafts in the following order:
a. First/second shaft
b. Pin
c. Reverse shift fork shaft
d. Third/fourth shaft
e. Pin

14. Measure the thrust clearance of the reverse idler gear. The specified clearance is 0.002–0.020 in.

15. Remove the idler shaft. Remove the gear and washer.

16. Measure the thrust clearance of the gears on the output shaft.

1st, 2nd, 5th	0.006–0.010 in.
3rd	0.006–0.012 in.
Reverse	0.008–0.012 in.

5th gear is optional

17. Disassemble the components of the output shaft. Five-speed transmissions have an extra gearset and related parts.

Replace the front bearing if it is rough or noisy. Use a drift and a press. Remove the snap-ring first.

For bearing installing, replacement snap-rings are available in a range of sizes (0.0925–0.1024 in.) to obtain *minimum* axial play between the input shaft and the bearing.

ASSEMBLY

1. Assemble the components of the synchronizer hubs, and the output shaft.

2. Install the rear bushing on the output shaft, being careful to install it in the proper direction.

3. Install the ball into the groove of the bushing and slide the bushing over the shaft.

4. Install the needle roller bearing, reverse gear, the ball and the reverse gear synchronizer hub.

5. Install the following items on the output shaft of the four-speed transmission, in the order indicated:

4-Speed (T40)

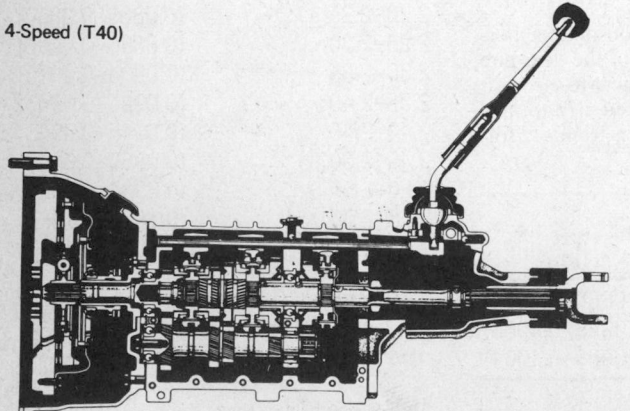

5-Speed (T50)

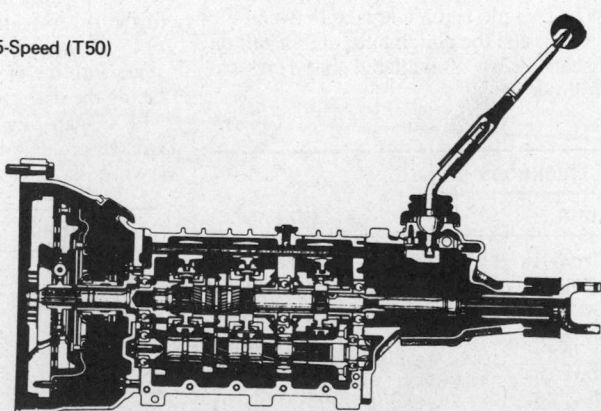

Cross section of models T 40 and T 50 transmissions

a. Large-diameter reverse gear spacer
b. Long spacer
c. Shims

6. Install the following items on the output shaft of the five-speed transmission in the order indicated:

a. Ball
b. Fifth gear synchronizer ring
c. Fifth gear
d. Needle roller bearing
e. Bushing
f. Rear support ball bearing.

7. Install the shims and the nut on the end of the output shaft.

NOTE: If the original nut is being used, change the number of shims to alter the locking portion of the nut.

8. Check the thrust clearance of each gear.

9. Working from the rear of the output shaft, install 3rd gear, synchronizer, spacer, and 3rd/4th synchronizer hub (should face forward).

10. Select a snap-ring to obtain a thrust clearance of less than 0.002 in. for the 3rd/4th synchronizer hub.

11. Assemble the following from the rear of the output shaft:

a. Snap-ring
b. Key
c. Speedometer drive gear
d. Snap-ring

12. Check thrust clearance of gears.

13. Install the fork and shaft assembly in the transmission case.

14. Insert the straight pins in the grooves on either side of the third/fourth shaft.

15. Assemble the first/second gear shaft and fork.

16. Perform Step 11 for the reverse shift fork shaft.

17. Insert the three detent balls, followed by their springs.

18. Place the cover gasket on the case and install the cover.

19. Use a punch to drive a slotted spring pin into each shift fork to secure it.

20. Assemble the input and output shafts.

21. Install the shift forks into their respective grooves on the input/output shaft assembly.

22. Install the shaft assembly in the righthand half of the transmission case, so that the snap-ring is positioned firmly against the front surface of the transmission case.

23. Apply grease to the countergear rear bearing lockball. Insert the ball into the hole in the rear bearing outer race.

24. Place the countergear assembly into the right-hand half of the transmission case. Mate the lockball with the hole in the transmission case. Place the bearing snap-ring

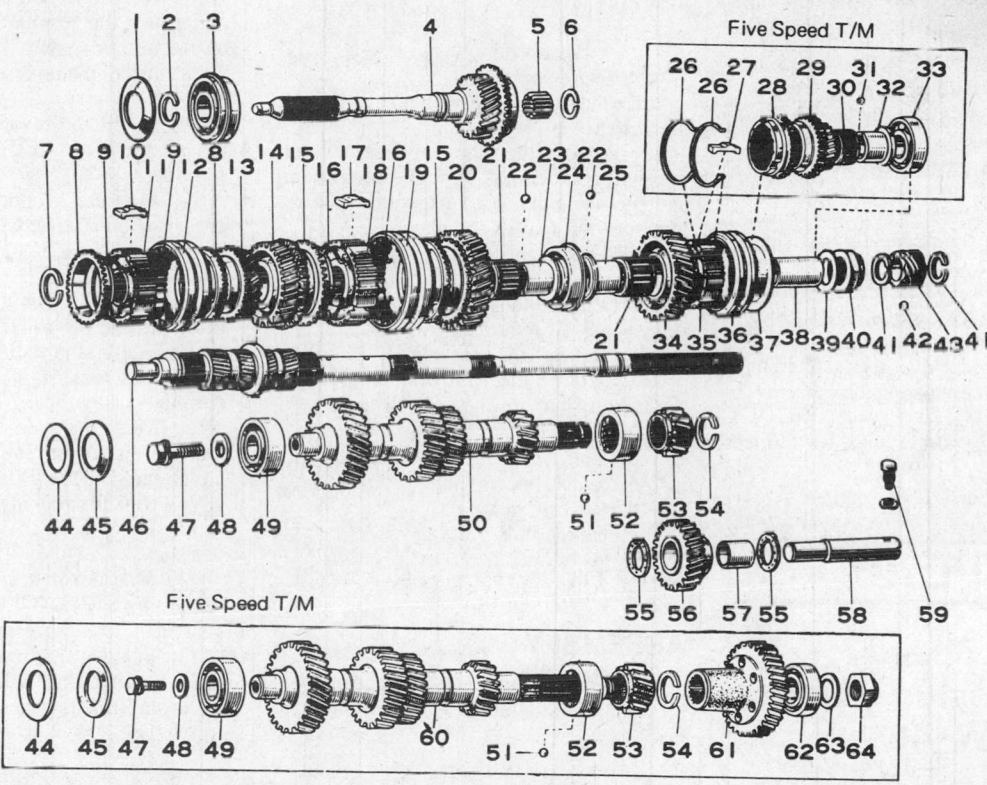

1. Conical spring	18. Clutch hub	34. Reverse gear	51. Ball
2. Shaft snap-ring	19. Hub sleeve	35. Clutch hub	52. Roller bearing
3. Ball bearing	20. First gear assembly	36. Hub sleeve	53. Reverse countergear
4. Input shaft	21. Needle roller bearing	37. Spacer	54. Snap-ring
5. Roller	22. Ball	38. Spacer (long)	55. Thrust washer—reverse idler gear
6. Snap-ring	23. First gear bushing	39. Shim	56. Reverse idler gear
7. Shaft snap-ring	24. Ball bearing	40. Nut	57. Bushing
8. Synchronizer ring	25. Reverse gear bushing	41. Shaft snap-ring	58. Reverse idler gear shaft
9. Shift-key spring	26. Shift-key spring*	42. Ball	59. Shaft retaining bolt
10. Shift-key	27. Shift-key*	43. Speedometer drive gear	60. Countergear*
11. Clutch hub	28. Synchronizer ring*	44. Shim	61. Fifth-speed countergear*
12. Hub sleeve	29. Fifth gear assembly*	45. Conical spring	62. Ball bearing*
13. Third gear assembly	30. Needle roller bearing*	46. Output shaft	63. Shim*
14. Second gear assembly	31. Ball*	47. Bolt and washer	64. Nut*
15. Synchronizer ring	32. Fifth gear bushing*	48. Plate washer	
16. Shift-key spring	33. Ball bearing*	49. Ball bearing	* Five-speed transmission only
17. Shift-key		50. Countergear	

Corolla and Carina 4 and 5-speed transmission components

firmly against the front surface of the transmission case.

25. Install the reverse idler gear.

26. Install the washers, so that their protrusions align with the grooves in the transmission case.

27. Install the shaft into the case and through the gears and washers.

28. Align the grooves in the idler shaft with the hole in the shaft boss. Install the retaining bolt and washer into the boss.

29. Apply a light coating of liquid sealer over the joint surfaces of the transmission case halves.

─── CAUTION ───

Do not apply sealer to the ½ in. hole for the back-up light switch.

30. Align the transmission case locating pins with their holes and assemble the halves of the case.

NOTE: There are four different bolt lengths, do not install the wrong bolt in the wrong hole.

31. Insert the ball, spring, and washer in the back-up light switch hole. Screw in the switch assembly.

32. Install the gasket and bolt the extension housing to the rear of the transmission.

33. Install the speedometer shaft sleeve and drive gear.

34. Apply grease to the conical springs. Install one spring over the input shaft bearing and the other over the countershaft bearing. Install the spacer over the countershaft bearing spring., after coating the spacer with grease.

35. Install the gasket and the clutch housing.

TYPE 27

4 Speed Transmission—Model W–40

Toyota

DISASSEMBLY

1. Drain the oil.

2. Remove the clutch housing, with the release fork, bearing and hub still attached.

3. Remove the back-up light switch.

4. Remove the gearshift lever retainer.

5. Rotate the shift rod housing counterclockwise (viewed from behind) and then disconnect the rod from the shift fork shafts.

6. Unbolt and remove the extension housing.

7. Drive out the slotted pin and separate the shift rod, housing and spring.

8. Remove the front bearing retainer.

9. Take off both of the front countershaft covers and the spacer.

10. Remove the snap-rings from the input and countershaft bearings.

11. Remove the intermediate plate.

12. When removing the intermediate plate, leave all of the gears and other parts attached.

13. Remove the speedometer driven gear.

14. Punch the slotted pin out of the reverse shift arm bracket bolt and remove the bracket, complete with the shift arm.

15. Remove the reverse idler shaft stop and withdraw the idler gear and shaft assembly away from the intermediate plate.

16. Remove the output shaft rear bearing retainer.

17. Remove the screw plug and spring from each shift fork and shaft.

18. Drive the slotted interlock pins out of each shaft.

19. Remove the shift fork shafts in the following order:

    a. Revese

    b. First/second

    c. Third/fourth

Once the shafts have been removed, slide the shift forks off them.

20. Remove the snap-ring from the output shaft rear bearing. Push the output shaft and countershaft out as an assembly, working from the rear of the plate.

21. Separate the input shaft and the front synchronizer ring from the output shaft.

22. Remove the hub and synchronizer ring, followed by third gear.

23. Press off the rear bearing.

24. Remove the following items from the output shaft, in the order listed:

    a. First gear

    b. Roller bearing with inner race

    c. Synchronizer ring

    d. Reverse gear

    e. Clutch hub

    f. Second gear

    g. Synchronizer ring

ASSEMBLY

1. Apply a thin coating of gear oil to all rotating or sliding surfaces, prior to assembly.

2. Assemble the 3rd/4th synchronizer hub:

    a. Install key springs in the hub.

    b. Pace the 3 keys in the hub slots.

    c. Install the 2nd clutch hub in the sleeve.

To maintain uniform spring pressure, keep the open end of the key springs 120° apart.

3. Assemble the synchronizer ring to third gear, and fit both of them on the output shaft.

4. Insert the third/fourth synchronizer hub on the output shaft, until it contacts the shoulder of the shaft.

5. Select a snap-ring to provide 0.002 in. axial play for the synchronizer hub and fit it onto the shaft. Snap-rings are available in a range of sizes.

6. Measure third gear thrust clearance with a feeler gauge. The clearance should be 0.004–0.010 in. Replace third gear if the clearance exceeds the limit of 0.012 in.

7. Install the synchronizer ring for second gear to the gear and install the assembly on the output shaft.

8. Install the reverse gear over its clutch hub.

9. Install the reverse gear and hub on the output shaft so that they contact the shoulder.

10. Measure second gear thrust clearance; it should be between 0.004–0.010 in. Replace the gear if the clearance is more than 0.012 in.

11. Coat the locking ball with grease. Insert it, and the roller bearing inner race, on the output shaft.

12. Assemble first gear with its synchronizer ring, bearing and bearing inner race. Install them on the output shaft, so that the end of the inner race contacts the clutch hub and the groove on the inner race aligns with the locking ball.

13. Press the rear bearing onto the output shaft.

14. Measure first gear thrust clearance; it should be 0.004–0.010 in. Replace the gear if the clearance exceeds 0.012 in.

15. Select a snap-ring for the rear output shaft bearing that will provide 0.002 in. axial play for it.

16. Use a press to insert the straight pin

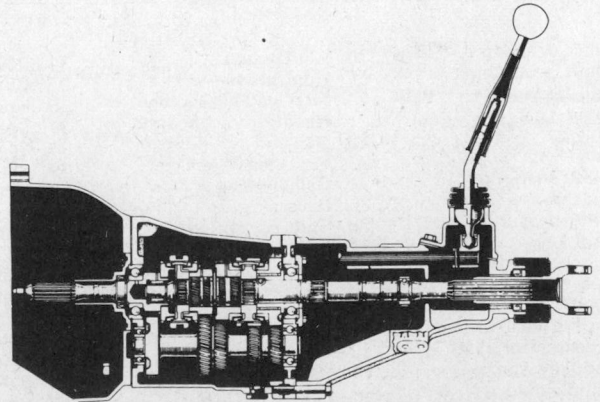

Cross section of model W 40 transmission

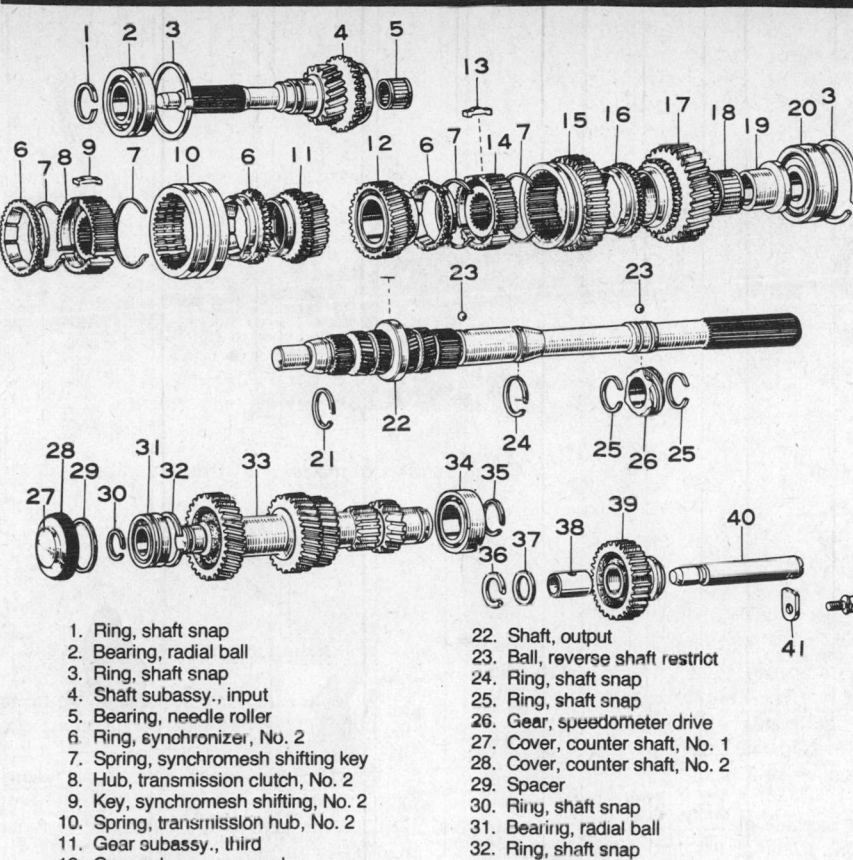

1. Ring, shaft snap
2. Bearing, radial ball
3. Ring, shaft snap
4. Shaft subassy., input
5. Bearing, needle roller
6. Ring, synchronizer, No. 2
7. Spring, synchromesh shifting key
8. Hub, transmission clutch, No. 2
9. Key, synchromesh shifting, No. 2
10. Spring, transmission hub, No. 2
11. Gear subassy., third
12. Gear subassy., second
13. Key, synchromesh shifting, No. 1
14. Hub, transmission clutch, No. 1
15. Gear, reverse
16. Ring, synchronizer, No. 1
17. Gear subassy., first
18. Bearing, needle roller
19. Race, first gear bearing inner
20. Bearing, radial ball
21. Ring, shaft snap

22. Shaft, output
23. Ball, reverse shaft restrict
24. Ring, shaft snap
25. Ring, shaft snap
26. Gear, speedometer drive
27. Cover, counter shaft, No. 1
28. Cover, counter shaft, No. 2
29. Spacer
30. Ring, shaft snap
31. Bearing, radial ball
32. Ring, shaft snap
33. Gear, counter
34. Bearing, radial ball
35. Ring, shaft snap
36. Ring, shaft snap
37. Spacer
38. Bushing, bimetal formed
39. Gear, reverse idler
40. Shaft, reverse idler
41. Stopper, reverse idler gear shaft

Exploded view of model W 40 gear train

into the intermediate plate, until it protrudes ¼–⁵⁄₁₆ in. from the cover front side.

17. Coat the roller bearing with grease and install it over the input shaft.

18. Apply gear oil to the front synchronizer ring on the output shaft.

19. Assemble the output shaft and the input shaft.

20. Assemble the output shaft and countergear, then fit them through the holes in the intermediate plate. Push them in until th snap-ring sticks out beyond the plate. Install the snap-ring and then push the shafts back until the snap-ring is flush with the intermediate plate.

21. Install the shaft through the reverse idler gear. Insert the end of the shaft into the end of the intermediate plate.

22. Install the spacer on the idler shaft and secure it with a snap-ring.

23. Install the idler shaft stop.

24. Install the first/second and third/fourth shift forks into the grooves on the hub sleeves, so that the longer parts of their bosses face each other.

25. Assemble the ends of the three shift fork shafts and insert them into the intermediate plate. Install the interlock pins, after coating them with grease.

26. Install the shafts through the forks and drive in the slotted spring pins to secure them.

27. Insert the lockballs, followed by their springs.

28. Install the output shaft rear bearing retainer.

NOTE: There should be zero clearance between the rear bearing snap-ring and the surface of the intermediate plate.

29. Assemble the reverse shift arm to its bracket. Install on the intermediate cover.

30. Drive the slotted mounting pin in, so that it protrudes 0.08–0.16 in. beyond the intermediate cover.

31. Shift the gears so that reverse is selected. Check the gear contact. If the gears are meshing properly, the front face of the idler gear will align with the front face of the reverse gear.

32. If necessary, adjust the gear mesh at the pivot.

NOTE: When the gears are meshing properly, the slot in the pivot should be perpendicular to the intermediate plate.

33. Tighten the pivot nut and install the lockpin. Be careful not to change gear contact.

34. Install the shift rod from the front end of the extension housing. Install the spring and housing onto the end of the shift rod.

35. Clean the gasket surfaces of the rear cover and transmission case. Install the intermediate plate.

36. Install the input shaft and countergear front bearing snap-rings.

37. Install the extension housing and gasket over the intermediate cover, after cleaning both gasket mounting surfaces.

38. Screw the securing bolts through the extension housing, the intermediate cover and into the transmission case.

39. Install the reverse restrictor pin and gasket.

40. Push the countergear rearward, as far as it will go and measure the distance (E) in the illustration. Select a spacer to yield the *minimum* clearance which is closest to the measurement obtained.

41. Install the spacer and then the countershaft end covers.

42. Align the front bearing retainer gasket with the oil holes. Install the bearing retainer over the gasket.

43. Bolt the clutch housing onto the front of the transmission case.

44. Attach the shift lever retainer to the extension housing.

45. Install the speedometer driven gear.

46. Install the back-up light switch.

TYPE 28

5 Speed Transmissions— Models W50, P51, W55, W58

Toyota

DISASSEMBLY

NOTE: The Model P-51 transmission disassembly and assembly, is basically the same as the W-50 transmission, with only minor variations.

1. Drain the oil.
2. Remove the clutch housing, with the release fork, bearing and hub still attached.
3. Remove the back-up light switch.
4. Remove the gearshift lever retainer.

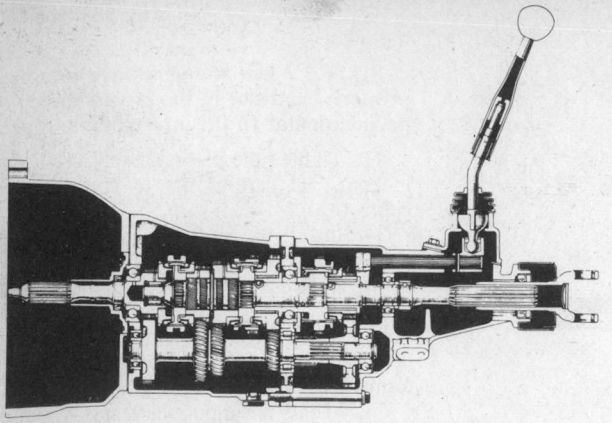

Cross section of model W 50 transmission

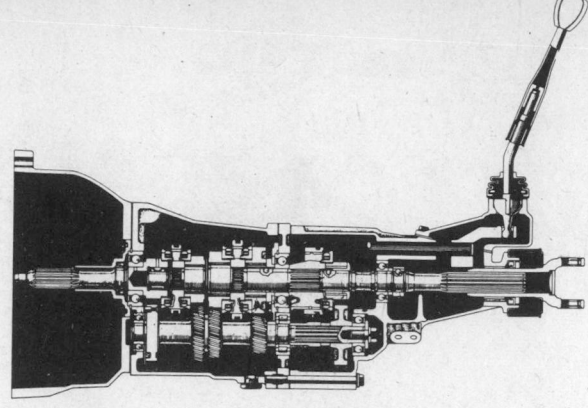

Cross section of model P-51 transmission

5. Rotate the shift rod housing counterclockwise (viewed from behind) and then disconnect the rod from the shift fork shafts.

6. Unbolt and remove the extension housing.

7. Drive out the slotted pin and separate the shift rod, housing and spring.

8. Remove the front bearing retainer.

9. Take off both of the front countershaft covers, and the spacer.

10. Remove the snap-rings from the input and countershaft bearings.

11. Remove the intermediate plate.

12. When removing the intermediate plate, leave all the gears and other parts attached.

13. Remove the speedometer driven gear.

NOTE: There are two reverse restrictor pins. The pins are located underneath plugs on the extension housing.

14. Remove the straight screw plugs from the shift forks and withdraw the springs.

15. Drive the slotted spring pins out of each shift fork.

16. Slide the gear shift fork shafts back and remove the forks.

17. Remove the speedometer drive gear snap-ring and remove the drive gear.

18. Remove the output shaft bearing.

19. Remove the countershaft bearing.

20. Remove the fifth and reverse gears from the countershaft.

21. Remove the snap-ring, fifth gear, its synchronizer ring, needle roller bearing, and fifth gear bearing inner race from the output shaft.

22. Remove the reverse gear and clutch hub from the output shaft.

23. Loosen the bolt and remove the reverse idler gear stop from the rear cover. Withdraw the reverse idler shaft from the rear; remove the reverse idler gear and spacer.

24. Remove the output shaft rear bearing retainer. Remove the rear bearing snap-ring.

25. Push the countergear bearing outer race rearward, and remove the bearing. Separate the countergear from the intermediate plate.

26. Separate the input shaft and synchronizer ring from the output shaft.

27. Remove the output shaft from the intermediate plate.

28. Remove the hub and synchronizer ring, followed by third gear.

29. Press off the rear bearing.

30. Remove the following items from the output shaft, in the order listed:
    a. First gear
    b. Roller bearing with inner race
    c. Synchronizer ring
    d. Reverse gear
    e. Clutch hub
    f. Second gear
    g. Synchronizer ring

ASSEMBLY

1. Install the sleeve over the third gear synchronizer hub. Insert the three shift keys into the hub and sleeve keyways install the two hub springs.

2. Assemble the synchronizer ring to third gear, and fit both of them on the output shaft.

3. Insert the third/fourth synchronizer hub on the output shaft, until it contacts the shoulder of the shaft.

4. Select a snap-ring to provide 0.002 in. axial play for the synchronizer hub and fit it onto the shaft. Snap-rings are available in a range of sizes.

5. Measure third gear thrust clearance with a feeler gauge. The clearance should be 0.004–0.010 in. Replace third gear if the clearance exceeds the limit of 0.010 in.

6. Install the synchronizer ring for second gear to the gear and install the assembly on the output shaft.

7. Install the reverse gear over its clutch hub.

8. Install the reverse gear and hub on the output shaft so that they contact the shoulder.

9. Measure second gear thrust clearance; it should be between 0.004–0.010 in. Replace the gear if the clearance is more than 0.010 in.

10. Coat the locking ball with grease. Insert it, and the roller bearing inner race, on the output shaft.

11. Assemble first gear with its synchronizer ring, bearing and bearing inner race. Install them on the output shaft, so that the end of the inner race contacts the clutch hub and the groove on the inner race aligns with the locking ball.

12. Press the rear bearing onto the output shaft.

13. Measure first gear thrust clearance.

NOTE: The thrust clearance of all gears in the W-50 5-speed transmission should be between 0.006–0.010 in.; the thrust clearance limit for all gears is 0.012 in.

14. Use a press to insert the straight pin into the intermediate plate, until it protrudes ¼–⁵⁄₁₆ in. from the cover front side.

15. Install the output shaft on the intermediate plate.

16. Coat the roller bearing with grease and install it over the input shaft.

17. Apply gear oil to the front synchronizer ring on the output shaft.

18. Assemble the output shaft and input shaft.

19. Install the countergear on the intermediate plate.

20. Install the cylindrical roller bearing into the intermediate plate, and then install the spacer.

21. Assemble the output shaft and countergear, then fit them through the holes in the intermediate plate. Push them in until the snap-ring sticks out beyond the inter-

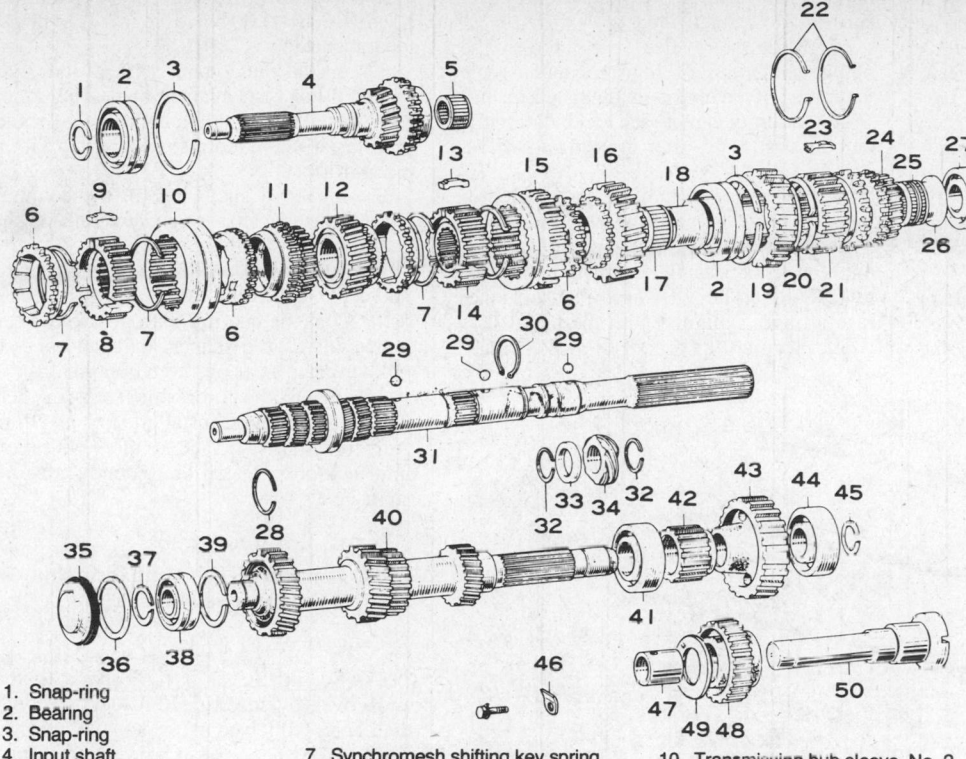

1. Snap-ring
2. Bearing
3. Snap-ring
4. Input shaft
5. Bearing
6. Synchronizer ring, No. 2

7. Synchromesh shifting key spring
8. Transmission clutch hub, No. 2
9. Synchromesh shifting key, No. 2

10. Transmission hub sleeve, No. 2
11. Third gear
12. Second gear sub-assembly

13. Synchromesh shifting key, No. 1
14. Transmission clutch hub, No. 1
15. Reverse gear
16. First gear
17. Bearing
18. First gear bearing inner race
19. Reverse gear
20. Snap-ring
21. Transmission clutch hub, No. 3
22. Synchromesh shifting key spring
23. Synchromesh shifting key, No. 3
24. Fifth gear
25. Bearing
26. Fifth gear bushing
27. Bearing
28. Snap-ring
29. Ball
30. Snap-ring
31. Output shaft
32. Snap-ring
33. Spacer
34. Speedometer drive gear
35. Countershaft cover
36. Spacer
37. Snap-ring
38. Bearing
39. Snap-ring
40. Counter gear
41. Bearing
42. Countershaft reverse gear
43. Countershaft fifth gear
44. Bearing
45. Snap-ring
46. Stopper
47. Bimetal formed bushing
48. Reverse idler gear
49. Reverse idler gear shaft spacer
50. Reverse idler gear shaft

Exploded view of gear train, model W 50 transmission

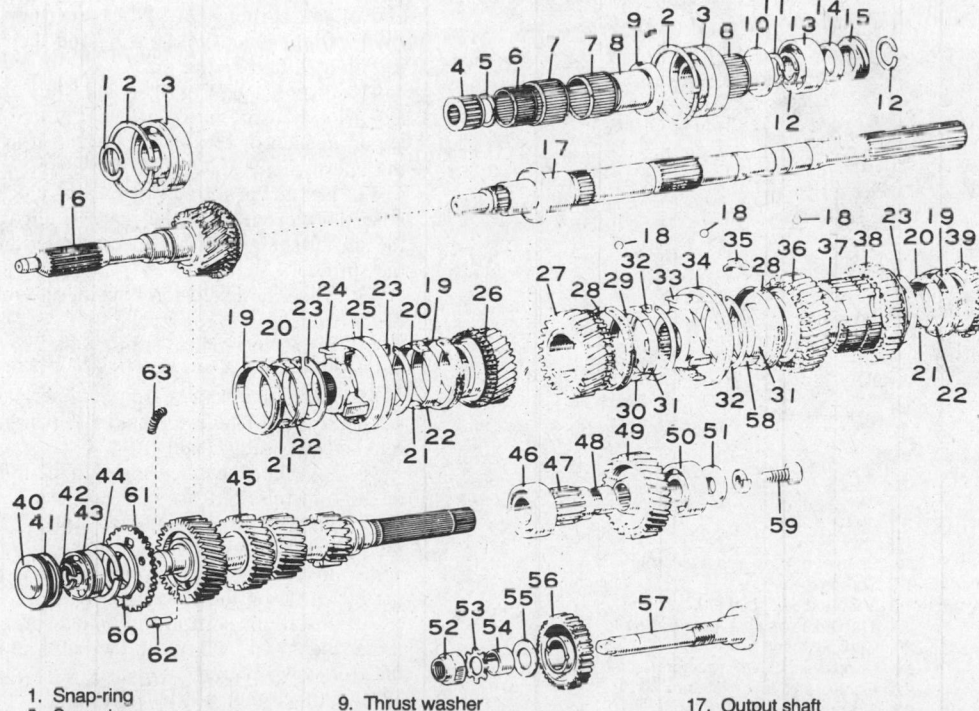

1. Snap-ring
2. Snap-ring
3. Bearing
4. Needle roller bearing
5. Snap-ring
6. Needle roller bearing
7. Needle roller bearing
8. Bearing inner race

9. Thrust washer
10. Bearing inner race
11. Snap-ring
12. Snap-ring
13. Bearing
14. Spacer
15. Speedometer drive gear
16. Input shaft

17. Output shaft
18. Ball
19. Synchronizer ring No. 2
20. Thrust block No. 3
21. Anchor block No. 3
22. Brake band No. 2
23. Snap-ring
24. Clutch hub No. 2

25. Hub sleeve No. 2
26. Third gear
27. Second gear
28. Synchronizer ring No. 1
29. Thrust block No. 2
30. Anchor block No. 2
31. Brake band No. 1
32. Snap-ring
33. Clutch hub No. 1
34. Hub sleeve No. 1
35. Thrust block No. 1
36. First gear
37. Clutch hub No. 3
38. Reverse gear
39. Fifth gear
40. Countershaft cover
41. Spacer
42. Snap-ring
43. Bearing
44. Snap-ring
45. Counter gear
46. Roller bearing
47. Countershaft reverse gear
48. Spacer
49. Countershaft fifth gear
50. Bearing
51. Spacer
52. Nut
53. Lock washer
54. Bushing
55. Spacer
56. Reverse idler gear
57. Reverse idler gear shaft
58. Anchor block No. 1
59. Bolt
60. Spacer
61. Counter gear plate
62. Pin
63. Spring

Exploded view of gear train, model P-51 transmission

mediate plate. Install the snap-ring and then push the shafts back until the snap-ring is flush with the intermediate plate surface.

22. Install the shaft through the reverse idler gear. Insert the end of the shaft into the end of the intermediate plate.

23. Install the spacer on the idler shaft and secure it with a snap-ring.

24. Lock the reverse idler shaft on the intermediate plate with its stop. Check the reverse idler gear thrust clearance, it should be 0.006–0.010 in.

25. Install the reverse clutch hub on the reverse gear.

26. Install the three shift keys into the hub keyways and secure them with the two springs and a snap-ring.

27. Slide the reverse gear hub over the output shaft until it registers against the inner race of the intermediate plate bearing.

28. Insert the inner race lockball into the output shaft bore, after greasing it so that it can't fall out.

29. Assemble fifth gear, its synchronizer ring, needle roller bearing, and race. Slide the assembly onto the output shaft until the inner bearing face rests against the reverse clutch hub. Be sure that the inner race groove is aligned with the lockball.

30. Secure fifth gear with a snap-ring.

31. Measure fifth gear thrust clearance; it should be 0.004–0.010 in. The thrust clearance limit is 0.012 in.

32. Install the countershaft reverse gear so that it just rests against the bearing inner race. Install the countershaft fifth gear and then install the countershaft bearing with a brass drift.

33. Install a snap-ring on the countershaft; select a snap-ring from one of the four available sizes.

34. Install a snap-ring on the output shaft, and drive its bearing into place with a brass drift. Coat the bearing with grease first.

35. Install the spacer, ball, and speedometer drive gear on the output shaft.

36. Install the three shift forks in their hub sleeve grooves. Install the first and third shift fork shafts and secure them with their interlock pins. Install the second shift fork shaft next.

NOTE: Place each shift fork shaft in Neutral during assembly.

37. Secure the shift fork shafts to the end cover by inserting the lockballs into their bores, followed by the lockball springs.

38. Use a new gasket between the transmission case and the intermediate plate. Slide the case into place.

39. Fit snap-rings on the input shaft and countershaft front bearings.

40. Install the shift lever housing on the end of the shifter shaft. Slide the shifter shaft into the extension housing and secure it with a slotted spring pin.

41. Install a new gasket and slide the extension housing into place, until there is about an inch of clearance between it and the intermediate plate.

42. Rotate the shift lever housing clockwise (as viewed from the rear) to engage the shifter shaft with the selector lever and the shift fork shaft.

43. Slide the extension housing the rest of the way.

44. Install the spacer and then the countershaft end covers.

45. Align the front bearing retainer gasket with the oil holes. Install the bearing retainer over the gasket.

46. Bolt the clutch housing onto the front of the transmission case.

47. Fit the restrictor pins and springs into their extension housing bores.

48. Install the shift lever retainer over the oil baffle on the extension housing.

49. Install the shift lever conical spring, large side down, and install the ball seat in the shift lever retainer.

50. Attach the shift lever retainer to the extension housing.

51. Install the speedometer driven gear.

52. Install the back-up light switch.

53. Check to see that the input shaft has no more than 0.020 in. end-play. Put the transmission in Neutral and see if the output shaft can be rotated freely by hand.

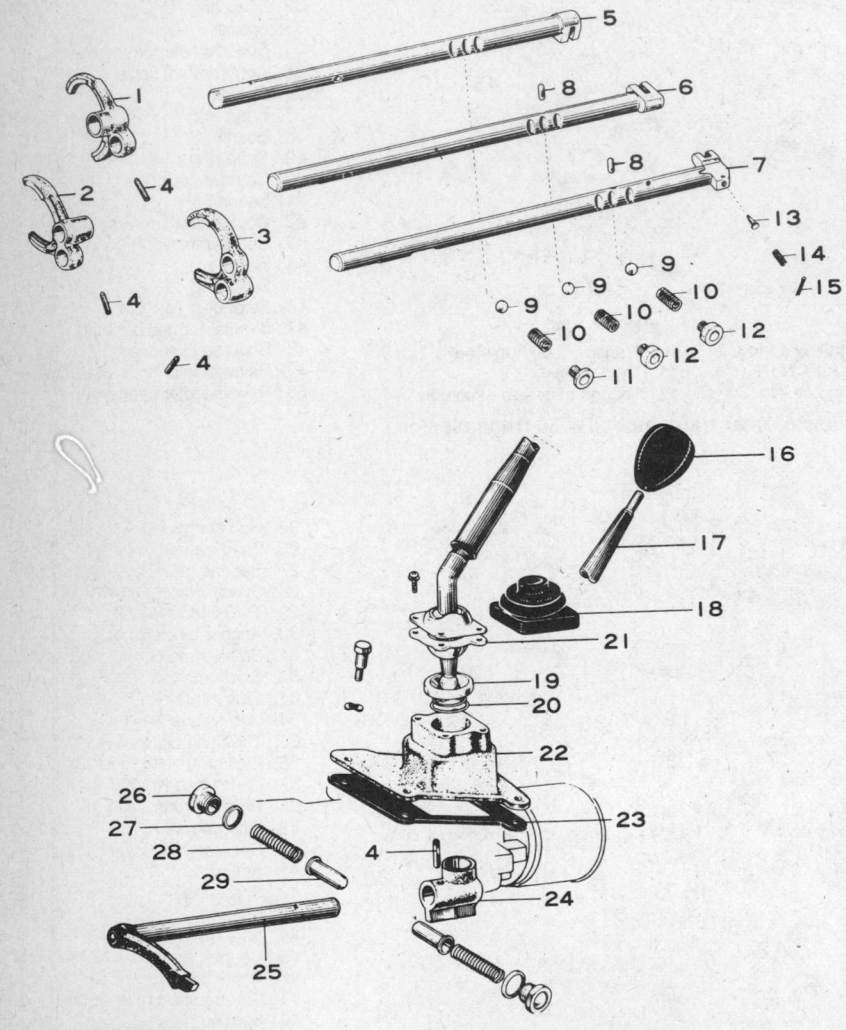

1. Gear shift fork, No. 2	16. Shift lever knob sub-assembly
2. Gear shift fork, No. 1	17. Shift lever
3. Gear shift fork, No. 3	18. Shift and select lever boot
4. Slotted spring pin	19. Transmission shift lever ball seat
5. Gear shift fork shaft, No. 1	20. Conical spring
6. Gear shift fork shaft, No. 2	21. Control shift lever retainer gasket, No. 2
7. Gear shift fork shaft, No. 3	22. Control shift lever retainer
8. Shift interlock pin	23. Extension housing oil baffle
9. Ball	24. Shift lever housing
10. Compression spring	25. Shift lever shaft, No. 1
11. Plug	26. Plug
12. Plug	27. Gasket
13. Reverse restrict pin	28. Compression spring
14. Compression spring	29. Restrict pin
15. Cotter pin	

Exploded view of model W 50 shift linkage—typical of model P-51

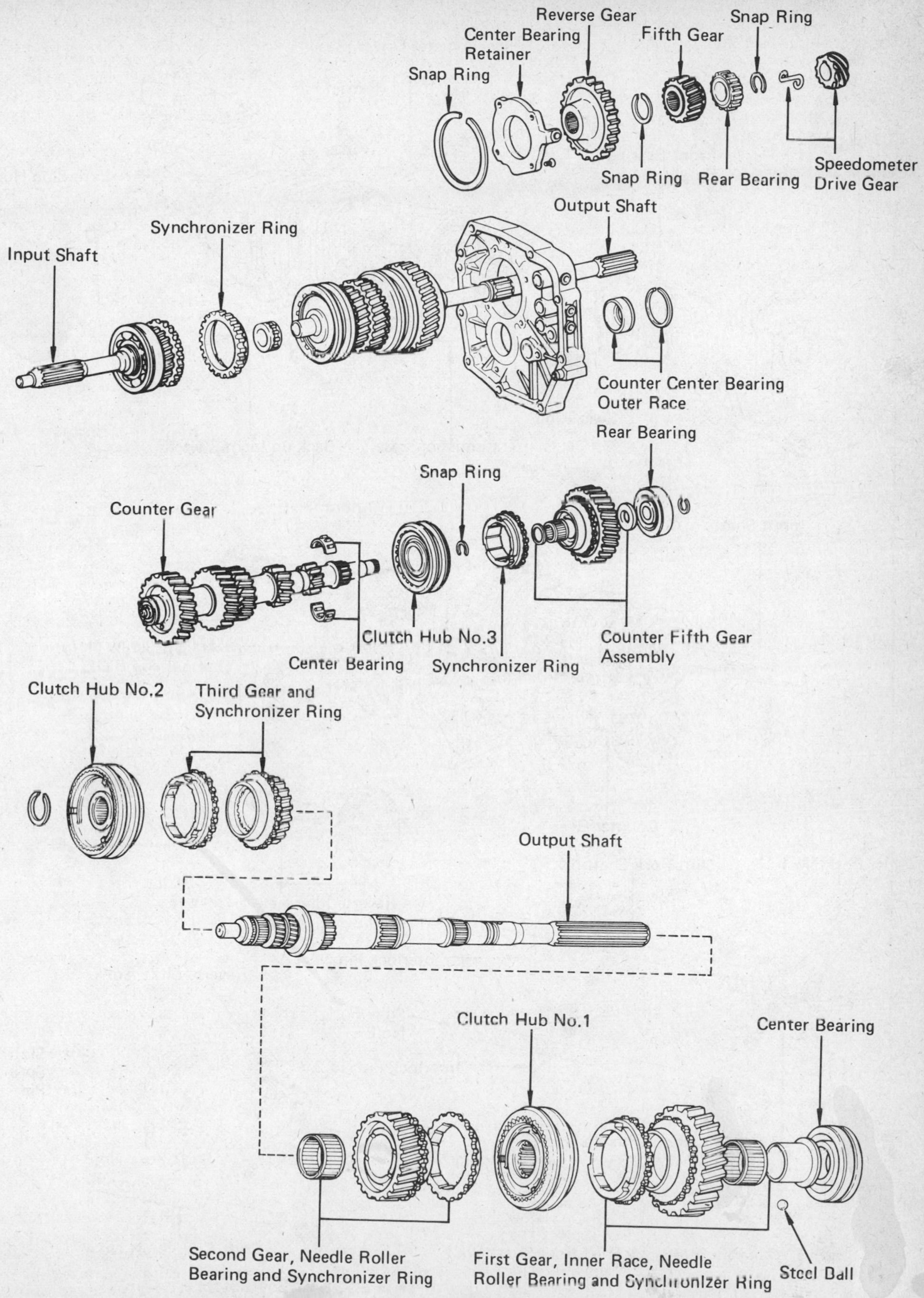

Snap Ring

Center Bearing
Retainer

Reverse Gear

Fifth Gear

Snap Ring

Snap Ring

Rear Bearing

Speedometer
Drive Gear

Input Shaft

Synchronizer Ring

Output Shaft

Counter Center Bearing
Outer Race

Rear Bearing

Counter Gear

Snap Ring

Clutch Hub No.3

Center Bearing

Synchronizer Ring

Counter Fifth Gear
Assembly

Clutch Hub No.2

Third Gear and
Synchronizer Ring

Output Shaft

Clutch Hub No.1

Center Bearing

Second Gear, Needle Roller
Bearing and Synchronizer Ring

First Gear, Inner Race, Needle
Roller Bearing and Synchronizer Ring

Steel Ball

Exploded view of the gear train—model W55 transmission

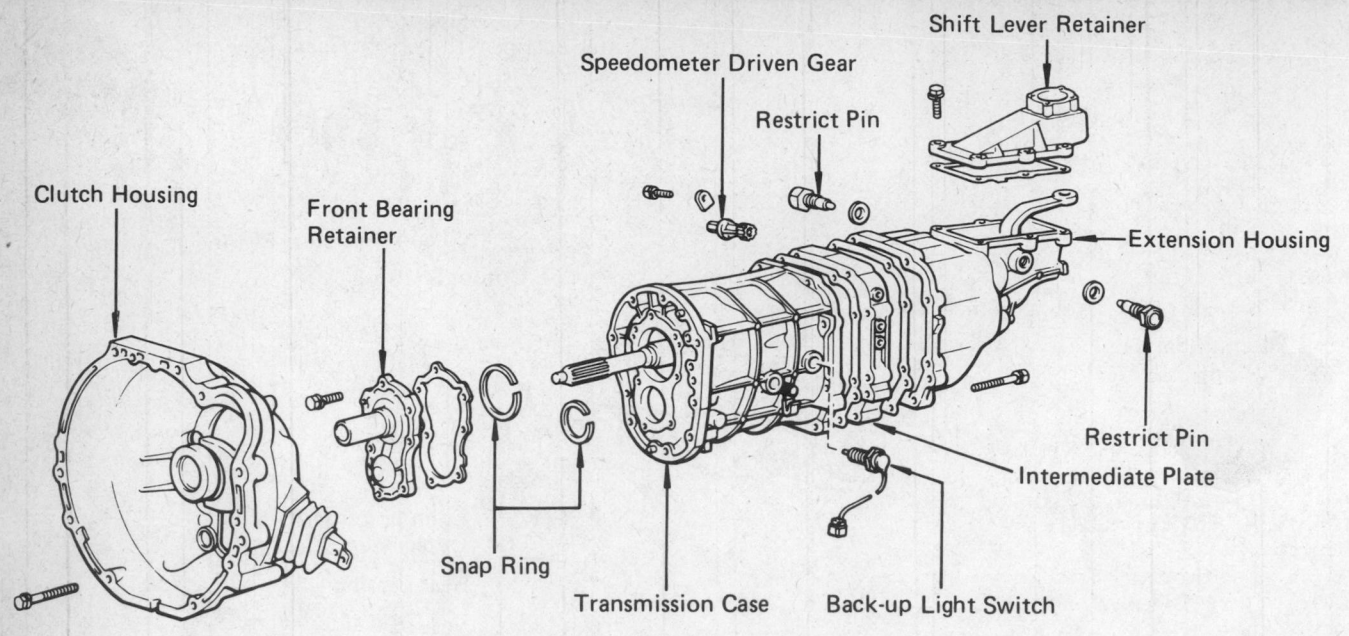

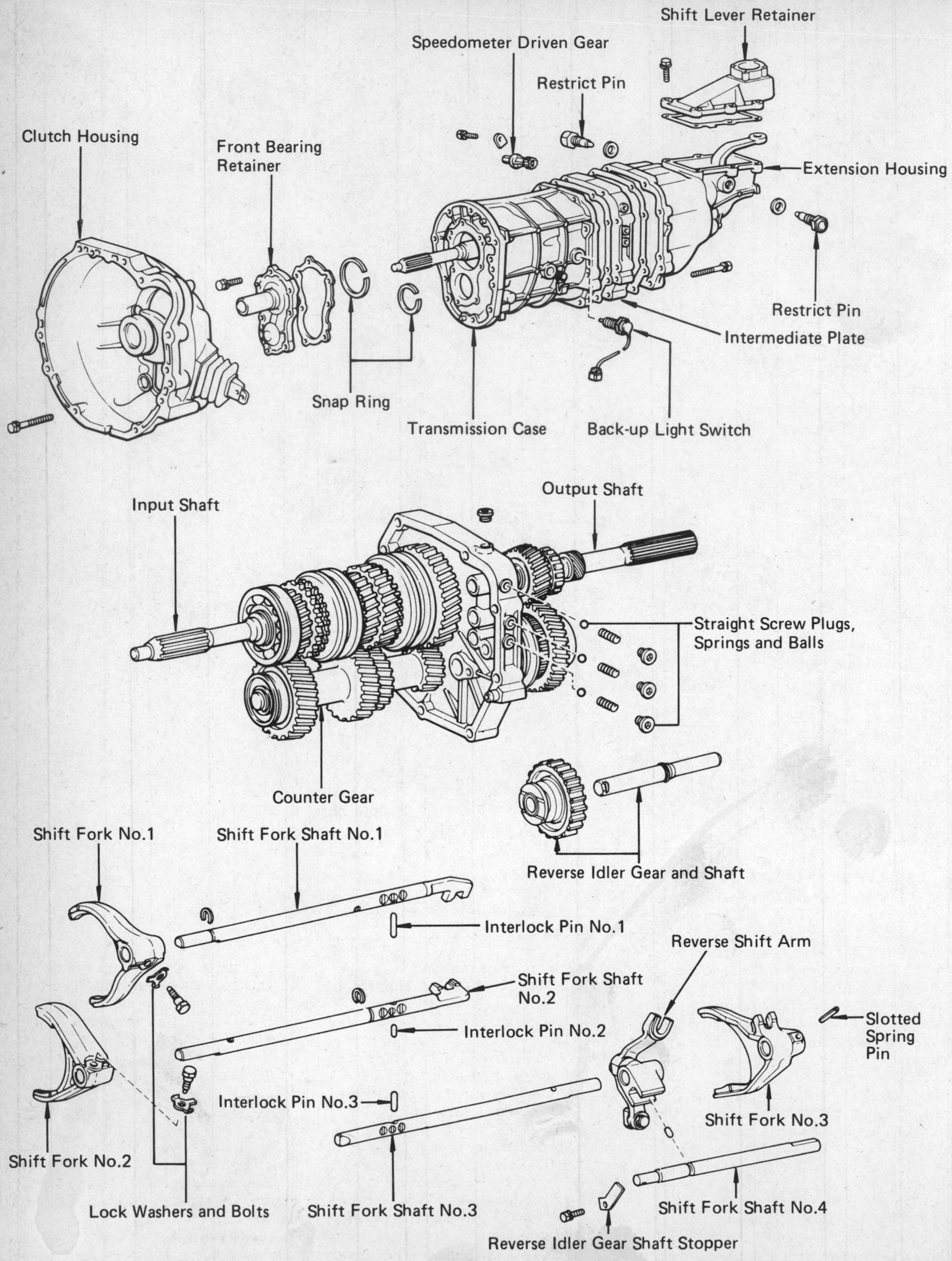

Detailed view of the W58 transmission

TYPE 29

4 Speed Transmission—Models M-45 (4 spd.), M-46 (4 spd. w/OD)

Volvo

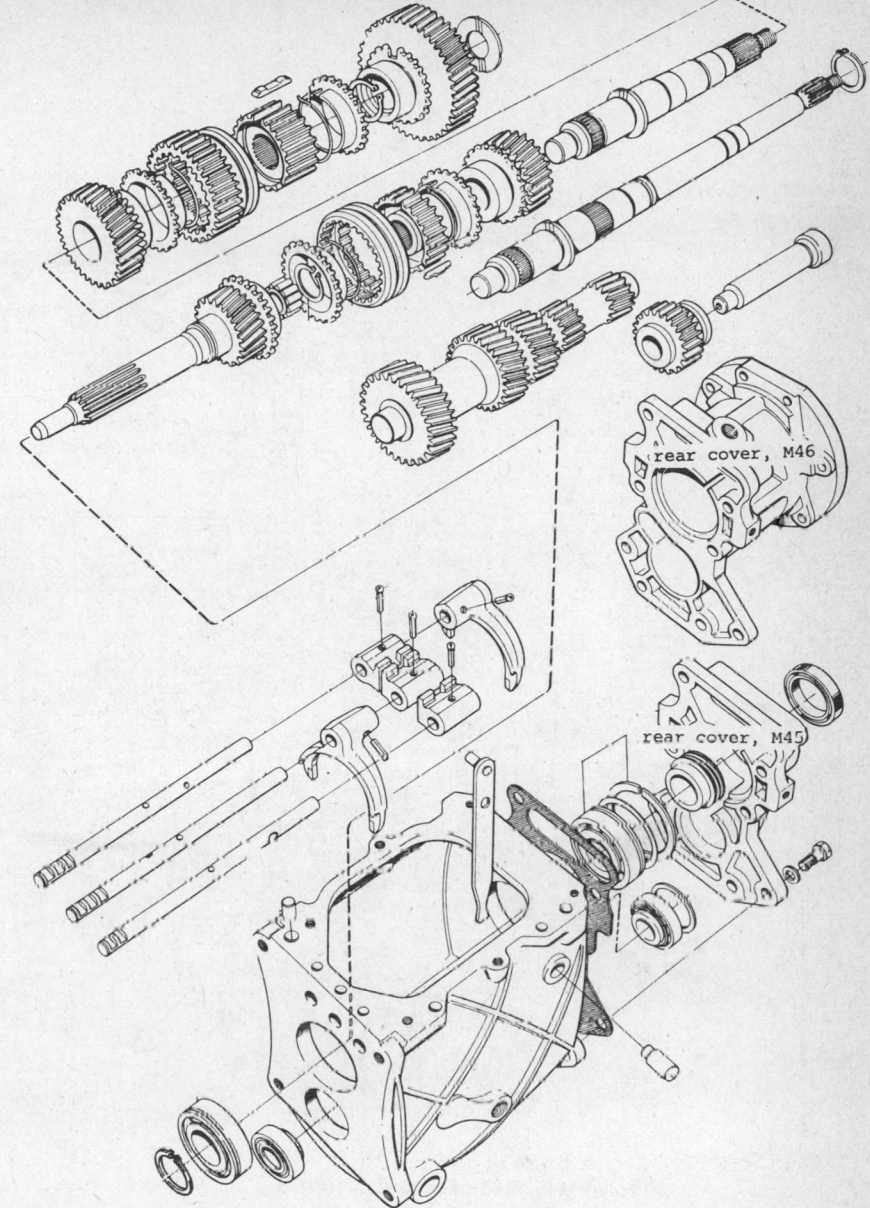

Volvo M45, M46 gear train

DISASSEMBLY

1. Remove the transmission.
2. Remove the gearshift bracket extension assembly. Remove the gearshift joint sleeve. Drive out the front pin for the gearshift joint and remove the rear gearshift extension rod.
3. On the M-45, block the output shaft flange from turning, and remove the rear flange.
4. On the M46, unbolt the overdrive unit. Attach a slide hammer to the output shaft of the overdrive unit and disconnect and remove the overdrive. Unbolt the intermediate housing.
5. On the M45, remove the speedometer driven gear. Remove the transmission rear cover, noting placement of bearing shims (if so equipped). Remove the speedometer drive gear.
6. Remove the back-up light switch.
7. Remove the top cover and gasket. Use a magnet to remove the spring detent balls.
8. Knock out the lockpins for the shift forks and shift rails.

NOTE: The forward gear shifters should be separated so that the pins do not damage the gears when driven out.

9. Remove the shift rails, shift forks and shifters for all forward speeds.
10. On the M46, remove the snap-ring and oil pump eccentric for the overdrive from the output shaft. Remove the eccentric retaining key.
11. Remove the mainshaft (output shaft) bearing inner and outer snap-rings. Before removing the mainshaft bearing, place a metal spacer (guard plate Volvo #2985) between the input shaft and the front synchronizer ring to prevent damage to the ring during bearing removal. Remove the mainshaft bearing ring and pull off the bearing. Remove the bearing thrust washer.
12. Remove the flywheel (bell) housing.
13. Remove the snap-ring and spacer rings retaining the input shaft bearing. With the front synchronizer ring protective spacer still in place, pull out the input shaft bearing. Remove the protective plate.
14. Knock the intermediate shaft back and remove the rear outer race for the intermediate shaft. Then, knock the shaft forward and remove the front intermediate shaft outer race.

15. Remove the input shaft.
16. Lift out the 4th gear synchronizer ring.
17. Lift out the mainshaft.
18. Lift out the intermediate shaft.
19. Drive back the reverse gear sliding shaft and remove the gear shift rail, unhook and remove the reverse gear shift fork. Remove the reverse gear shift rail.
20. Pull off the intermediate shaft bearing.
21. Remove 1st gear and its synchronizer ring from the mainshaft. Remove the snap-ring for the 1-2 synchronizer hub. Press off the synchronizer hub and gear. Remove the 3-4 synchronizer hub snap-ring and press off that gear and hub.
22. If the shift mechanism needs repair, unhook the detent plate spring, remove the

three retaining bolts, and remove the detent plate. Remove the shift shaft. If necessary, remove the shaft seal at the rear of the cover.
23. If leaking, remove the bell housing seal and the rear cover seal.
24. Push the two synchronizer hubs out of their sleeves and inspect for wear.

ASSEMBLY

1. Install new seals in the bell housing, shift cover and rear cover as required. Install the shifter assembly in the cover. The detent plate is installed with the flat washers between the plate and C-clips.
2. Connect the 3rd and 4th gear synchronizer hubs. The dogs must be positioned in the grounded slots in the hub. The

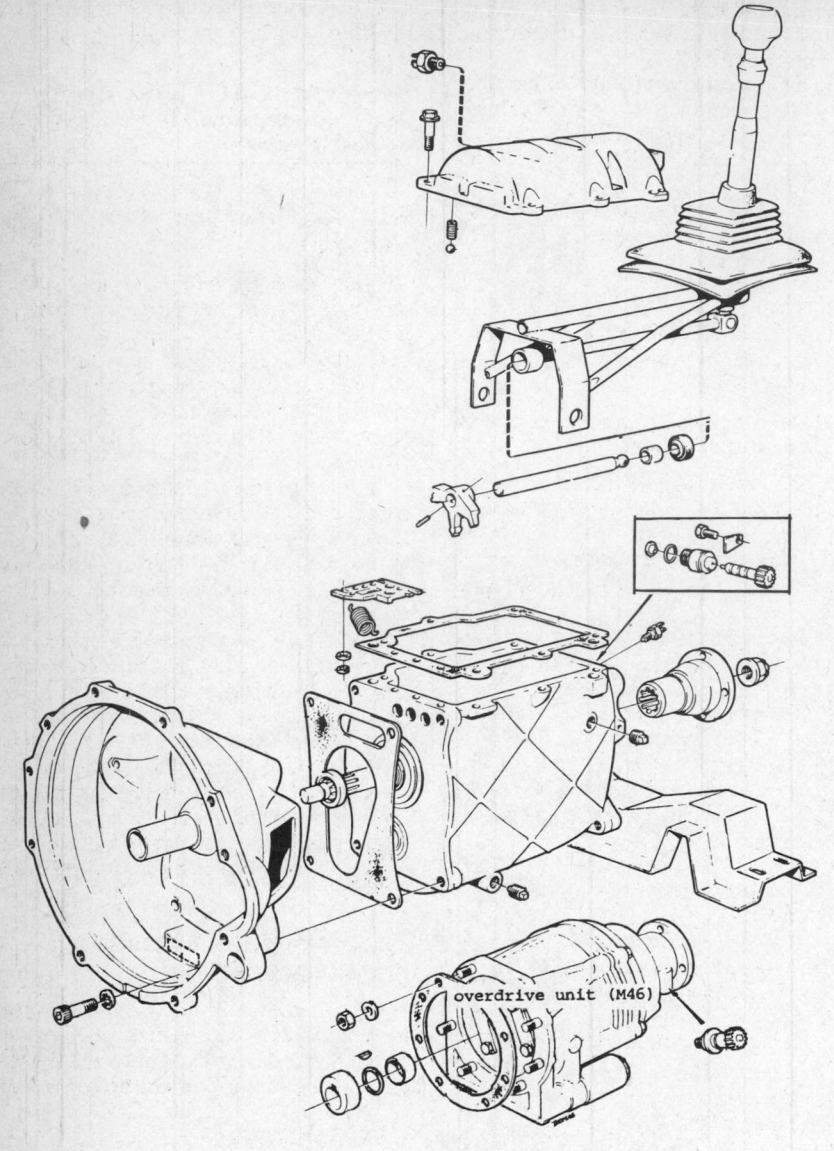

Volvo M45, M46 case and overdrive

the way, so it makes contact with the mainshaft.

12. Lift up the intermediate shaft so that both bearings locate in the case.

13. Pull out the input shaft slightly to install the spacer ring. Then push the input shaft back in so that the spacer rings contact the case.

14. Install the intermediate shaft outer bearing races.

15. Determine the shim thickness required between the bell housing and the input shaft bearing. Measure how much the input shaft bearing protrudes from the case, and measure the depth of the bearing seat in the bell housing. Subtract bell housing seat depth and bell housing gasket thickness (0.25 mm) from the input shaft bearing protrusion height, and then subtract from this the allowable clearance (0.01-0.15 mm), and you have your required shim clearance. Shims come in 0.10, 0.15 and 0.20 mm sizes.

16. Install the bell housing.

17. Install the shift forks on the synchronizer hubs (the forks are identical). Install the forward shift rails and shifters (not interchangeable) and secure with the lock pins. Drive in the pins until flush.

18. Determine the shim thickness required between the rear cover and the intermediate shaft outer race, and the shim thickness between the rear cover and the mainshaft bearing. Allowable clearance is 1.98 mm for the intermediate shaft outer race, and 0.24 mm for the mainshaft bearing. Gasket thickness is 0.25 mm. When measuring, turn the transmission case vertical with the input shaft facing down, to take any slack out of the intermediate or mainshafts.

19. On the M45, install the speedometer drive gear.

20. Install the rear cover (or intermediate housing on the M46) with shims and a new gasket.

21. On the M45, install the output shaft flange. Install the speedometer driven gear and new O-ring. Install the gear retainer and bolt.

22. Position the top cover gasket with shifter detent balls and springs. Install the cover. Install the back-up light switch. Check gear operation by inserting a punch through the shift rod eye and rotating the mainshaft.

23. On the M46, install the overdrive assembly.

24. Install a new rubber O-ring in the gearshift rod joint. Connect the gearshift rod and drive in the locking pin. Install the cover sleeve.

25. Install the gearshift bracket extension assembly with the spacers, rubber washers, and flat washers as shown to eliminate vibration. First install the two upper bolts flush with the spacer sleever, and then the two lower bolts. Then, tighten all four bolts to 15–18 lbs.

26. Fill the transmission with 0.8 qts. (2.4 qts. with overdrive M46) of 80W/90 hypoid gear oil. Install the plug(s).

sleeve end with the turned groove must face in the same direction as the hub flat end.

3. Assemble the mainshaft: install the 3rd gear and synchronizer ring, 3rd/4th synchronizer hubs, and snap-ring; install the 2nd gear and synchronizer ring, 1st/2nd synchronizer hubs, and snap-ring; install the 1st gear and synchronizer ring.

4. Press on the two intermediate shaft bearings.

5. Press on the input shaft bearing, and install its snap-ring.

NOTE: Do not install the spacer ring yet.

6. Install the reverse gear shift rail (without lockpin), shift fork and shifter. Install the reverse gear and shaft. Check that the reverse gear shaft aligns flush with the outside of the case. Also, check that

the clearance between the reverse gear and shift fork is 0.004 0.08 in. Adjust as necessary by knocking the shift fork pivot in axially with a punch.

7. Lay the intermediate shaft at the bottom of the case. Slip the thrust washer, ball bearing and positioning ring over the output end of the mainshaft. Press the mainshaft bearing into place, taking care not to damage the reverse gear. When the bearing seats properly, the positioning ring will butt against the case.

8. Grease and install the input shaft inner roller bearing.

9. On the M46, install the snap-ring for the mainshaft bearing. Install the Woodruff key, overdrive oil pump eccentric and snapring on the mainshaft extension.

10. Position the 4th gear synchronizer ring in its hub.

11. Push the input shaft into the case all

TYPE 30

5 Speed Transmission—Model BA–10/5

Peugeot

DISASSEMBLY

1. Mount the transmission in a holding fixture or equivalent and drain the lubricant.

2. Remove the speedometer driven gear socket set screw and remove the driven gear socket from the rear extension housing.

3. Position the transmission in the vertical position with the rear upward. Set the gear selectors in the neutral position. Remove the selection lever return spring.

4. Remove the 5th gear cover plate and its gasket. Remove the extension housing bolts.

5. Place an extractor plate tool or equivalent to the rear housing, using the three bolts of the cover plate. Remove the rear housing from the transmission.

6. Remove the 5th speed gear from the mainshaft with an appropriate puller. The rear bearing will be removed as part of the 5th speed gear.

7. Remove the 5th speed drive gear shim washer, the spacer washer, the 5th gear and its needle bearing from the 5th gear stub shaft.

8. Mark the direction of rotation of the 5th/reverse synchronizer and the position of the cage and hub, in relation to each other.

9. Engage the 5th gear and drive the 5th/reverse selector fork roll pin from the fork and rail.

—— CAUTION ——
Do not damage the mating surface of the housing.

10. Reset the rail to the neutral position and remove the 5th/reverse synchronizer cage and selector fork assembly, the synchronizer hub and the 5th gear subshaft.

11. Disengage the selection lever finger from the selector forks spindles. Remove the intermediate housing and retaining bolts.

12. Place the transmission in a horizontal position with the right side up. Remove the clutch fork and release bearing assembly from the front of the transmission. Remove the clutch housing and bolts.

13. Remove the six Allen headed screws from the rear bearing thrust plate. Remove the right hand housing retaining bolts and the housing.

14. Remove the countershaft from the exposed left hand housing.

NOTE: Mark and set aside the bearing races, if to be used again.

15. Lift the input and mainshaft assembly from the case as a unit. Do not separate while removing.

16. Separate the input and the mainshaft when the assembly is on a work bench. Remove the needle bearing from the bore of the input shaft. Hold the mainshaft in the 3rd gear position.

17. To disassemble the input shaft, remove the circlips, the spring washer and press the bearing from the shaft. Do not lose the adjusting shims.

18. To disassemble the mainshaft, mark the direction of rotation of the 3rd/4th synchronizer cage in relation to the synchronizer hub.

NOTE: Mark the components with a sharp piece of brass welding rod.

19. Remove the front synchronizer ring, the circlip and the spring washer from the front of the mainshaft.

20. Remove the 3rd/4th gear synchronizer hub and 3rd gear with an appropriate puller.

21. Invert the mainshaft and lock in a holding device such as a vise. Unscrew the reverse driven gear locknut from the mainshaft. Remove the reverse gear from the shaft.

22. Position the mainshaft and the remaining gears on a press bench and press the mainshaft through the rear bearing. Remove the gear components from the mainshaft in the following order;
   a. Rear bearing
   b. Bearing spacer
   c. Adjustment shim washer
   d. 1st speed driven gear
   e. Needle bearing
   f. 1st gear bushing
   g. 1st/2nd gear synchronizer and hub
   h. 2nd speed driven gear
   i. Needle bearing

23. Using a press, remove the front bearing and the shim adjusting washers. Remove the rear bearing.

24. To disassemble the rear housing, the ball bearing, the oil seal and the bearing race is pressed from the housing. Locate the shim washer in the race bore.

—— CAUTION ——
The press ram should be no bigger than 24 mm in diameter.

Selector Forks and Shift Rail Removal

1. Remove the spring and the 4th speed locking ball from the rear bearing bore of the half case.

2. Move the 4th gear fork and rail to the engaged position and drive the roll pins from the 1st/2nd and 3rd/4th selector forks. Return the 3rd/4th shift rail to the neutral position.

3. Remove the 1st/2nd locking ball plug, spring and ball from the passage on the center of the outer side of the case.

4. Pivot the 3rd/4th selector rail and remove the 1st/2nd rail from the case. Remove the fork.

5. Remove the reverse gear locking ball plug, spring and ball from the opposite side from the 3rd/4th locking ball passage.

6. Disengage the reverse fork and rail assembly and withdraw it from the case.

7. Remove the 3rd/4th shifting rail and remove the fork, interlock pin, the ball and the interlock plunger from the bearing bore.

8. Remove the roll pin from the reverse fork and rail. Push the shifting rail outward. Remove the fork.

Engagement Lever in the Intermediate Cover

Remove the circlip and washer. Remove the engagement lever spindle and recover the washer, spring, thrust plate and the operating fingers from the inside of the housing.

Clutch Housing

The thrust guide sleeve can be pressed from the housing after the oil seal has been removed.

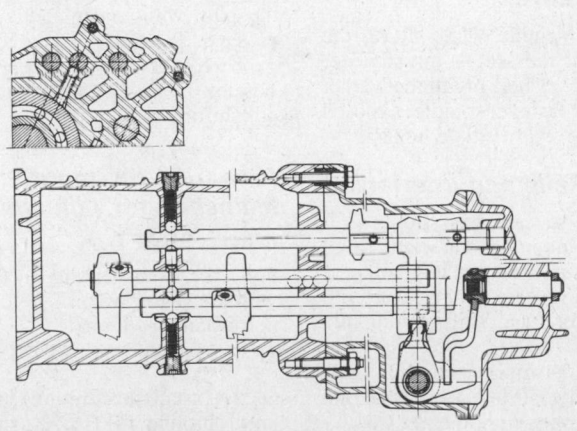

Diagram of the detent and interlock components—model BA-10/5

Position of the gear train in the half housing and the shift direction of the synchronizers—Model BA-10/5

ASSEMBLY

General

Always replace the following components when overahuling the transmission:
  a. Shaft circlips
  b. Spring washers
  c. Roll pins
  d. Mainshaft nut
  e. Output and input seals
  f. O-ring on speedometer driven bushing
  g. Thrust washers
  h. Necessary gaskets
  i. Sealing compound to mating surfaces

Engagement Levers

Install the lever spindle while fitting the operating fingers, the spring thrust plate, the spring and the washer. Install the washer and the circlip on the lever spindle, exposed on the side of the intermediate housing.

Forks, Shift Rails and Interlocks

1. Install the reverse gear sliding shift rail into the case and into the bracket. Align the roll pin holes and install a new roll pin.
2. Install the reverse sliding gear with the 5th/reverse fork and shifting rail into the case.
3. Install in the reverse interlock passage on the outside of the case, a ball and spring. Coat the plug with a sealer and install it into the passage. Torque to 9.5 ft. lbs. Move the shift rail to the neutral position.

4. Install the 3rd/4th and 5th/reverse interlock plunger into its passage in the case.
5. Install an interlock pin in the 3rd/4th shift rail and retain with grease. Install the shifting rail into the case. Align the holes in the fork and the rail. Be sure the interlock pin is in the correct position and install a new roll pin.
6. Install an interlock ball in the passage between the 3rd/4th and the 1st/2nd fork rails. Install the 1st/2nd gear fork in the case with the boss towards the front. Install the shifting rail and engage the shifting fork. Align the holes in the fork and the shifting rail and install a new roll pin.
7. Install an interlock ball and spring in the 3rd/4th/2nd/1st interlock passage. Coat the plug with sealer and install it in the passage. Torque to 9.5 ft. lbs.
8. Install the ball and spring in the passage of the rear bearing bore, for the 3rd/4th shifting rail.

Preparing the Input Shaft and Mainshaft for Adjustment

INPUT SHAFT

Press the front bearing on the input shaft with the snap-ring groove to the front. Do not install any shims.

MAINSHAFT

1. Install the 2nd speed gear and its needle bearing, the 1st/2nd synchronizer hub, the 1st speed gear spacer and washer. Install the rear bearing along with a new circlip.

NOTE: The bearing will have to be pressed on the shaft.

Do not exceed 3 meteric tons pressure after the bearing is seated.
2. Install the adjustment shim removed during the disassembly, the spacer and a new nut on the shaft following the rear bearing. Tighten the nut to 39 ft. lbs.

COUNTERSHAFT

Press the new bearings onto the countershaft, beginning with the rear bearing and then the front.

CLUTCH HOUSING

1. Install the thrust guide sleeve and new circlip in its groove.

NOTE: Do not install an oil seal in the housing until all adjustments are completed.

2. Verify the front and rear faces of the clutch housing are parallel with the use of a dial indicator. If out of parallel more than 0.10 mm, replace the housing.

Adjustments Prior to Assembly

Five adjustments are necessary, prior to the complete assembly of the transmission. The adjustments are as follows.
1. Position of the 4th gear synchronizer cone (prior to assembly).
2. Position of the 2nd gear synchronizer cone (prior to assembly).
3. Preload of the countershaft tapered roller bearings (prior to assembly).

4. Preload of the mainshaft tapered roller bearings (during assembly).

5. End play of the 5th/reverse sub-shaft (during assembly).

Special tools are available through the manufacturer and other sources for the measurement procedures needed during the adjustment phases. References will be made to the special tools needed.

Position of the 4th Gear Synchronizer Cone

1. Place the clutch housing, front down on a flat surface, and install the input shaft and bearing.

2. Install the right housing onto the clutch housing and secure with two bolts. Tighten to 14 ft. lbs.

---------- CAUTION ----------

Be sure the bearing fits into the bore of the clutch housing and the half housing.

3. Install the special setting gauge tool, 80314G or equivalent, into the clutch housing, in place of the countershaft front bearing.

4. Place the dial indicator and the special tool base, 80310FZ or equivalent, on the top of the setting tool.

5. Align the dial indicator stem on the edge of the synchronizer cone and rotate the input shaft one complete turn and obtain an average reading. Adjust the indicator to zero at the average reading point on the cone edge.

6. Reposition the dial indicator and base on the setting gauge block and record the measurement.

7. The measurement obtained represents the thickness of shims needed between the input shaft and the front bearing, minus 0.5 mm and rounded off to the nearest 0.05 mm.

Example:

Indicator reading	1.12 mm
Minus	0.50 mm
Result	0.62 mm
Rounded off to nearest 0.05 mm	0.60 mm

Therefore, a shim pack of 0.60 mm is needed between the input shaft and the front bearing, to properly position the 4th speed synchronizer cone, in this hypothetical example.

NOTE: Shims are available in steps of 0.05 mm, from 0.15 to 0.50 mm.

Position of the 2nd Gear Synchronizer Cone

1. Install the needle bearing into the bore of the input shaft. Install the mainshaft and prepared components into the input shaft, with the rear bearing seated in its bore on the right hand housing.

NOTE: Be sure the bearing circlip is installed in the half housing groove.

2. Install the larger setting tool, 80314K or equivalent, into the countershaft front bearing bore of the clutch housing.

Position of dial indicator and special tools for the measurements of the 4th gear synchronizer cone

3. Install a longer stem, 80310 J or equivalent, onto the dial indicator. Place the dial indicator and special base on the top of the right hand half housing, in a position to touch both the setting tool and the 2nd synchronizer cone.

4. With the dial indicator set to zero, position the stem on the top of the setting tool.

5. Reposition the indicator stem to the edge of the 2nd synchronizer cone and record the measurement reading. The amount of movement noted, represents the thickness of shims needed between the 1st gear spacer and the rear bearing, plus 0.50 mm, rounded off to the nearest 0.05 mm.

Example:

Indicator reading	2.51 mm
Plus	0.50 mm
Result	3.01 mm
Rounded off to nearest 0.05 mm	3.00 mm

6. Remove the input and mainshaft assemblies. Separate the clutch housing and the half housing.

Preload of the Countershaft Tapered Roller Bearings

1. Place the left half housing in the support stand or equivalent. Install the countershaft and its bearings into the housing.

2. Place the right housing in place on the left housing, making sure the dowel pins are in position.

3. Install two bearing center bolts into the housings and hand tighten the bolts. Install bolts into the rear bearing thrust plate and hand tighten the bolts.

4. Position the transmission with the front of the housings upward. Apply a downward pressure to the countershaft front bearing while rotating the countershaft, in order to seat the bearings.

5. Tighten the bearing center bolts and the bearing thrust plate bolts to 7 ft. lb.

6. By placing the dial indicator on the end of the countershaft and rotating it one complete turn with the stem contacting the housings, the run-out between the outer race and the face of the half housings must not exceed 0.03 mm.

7. Should the run-out exceed the specifications, the race must be realigned by tapping with a mallet. Should the countershaft be difficult to turn, the bearing center bolts and the bearing thrust plate bolts must be loosened and retightened and the run-out rechecked.

8. If the run-out is within specifications, set the dial indicator with a short stem, to number 2 and zero, with the stem resting on the side of the outer race. Move the indicator until the stem is contacting the face of the housing and record the measurement of the movement. Add 0.10 mm to the results for the preload of the bearings and round the results to the nearest 0.05 mm.

Example:

Housing reading	4.27 mm
Bearing reading (preset)	2.00 mm
Result	2.27 mm
Plus preload	0.10 mm
Shim pack needed	2.37 mm
Rounded off to nearest 0.05 mm	2.35 mm

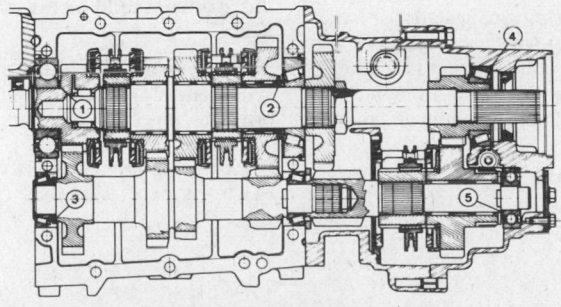

1. Position of 4th gear synchro cone
2. Position of 2nd gear synchro cone
3. Preloading of countershaft taper roller bearings
4. Preloading of mainshaft taper roller bearings
5. End float of 5th/R sub-shaft

Location of the adjustment shims needed during the assembly

NOTE: Shims are available from 2.15 to 3.30 mm, in increments of 0.05 mm.

9. Remove the countershaft and the front bearing from the countershaft. Install the predetermined shim with the chamfer facing the gear, between the gear and the bearing. Press the bearing in place.

NOTE: The 4th and 5th adjustments are made during the assembly of the transmission as noted in the adjustment list.

Final Assembly
INPUT SHAFT

1. Remove the bearing from the shaft and install the predetermined shim pack between the shaft and the bearing.

2. Reinstall the bearing, with the groove for the large circlip to the front. Press the bearing into position and install the spring washer and circlip on the input shaft. Be sure the circlip engages the groove completely.

MAINSHAFT

1. Remove the rear bearing and shims from the mainshaft, used in the measurement check.

2. Install in the following order, from the rear to the front of the shaft, the components as listed;

   a. The second gear and its needle bearing (31 mm wide).

   b. The synchronizer hub and cage.

   c. The 1st gear and needle bearing (29 mm wide).

   d. The spacer and adjusting shim (from measurement check).

   e. The bearing spacer.

   f. Press the bearing onto the shaft with the circlip to the rear.

   g. Install the reverse driven gear with the plain face to the rear.

   h. Install a new nut and tighten to 39 ft. lbs. and lock the collar to the shaft.

3. Invert the mainshaft and install the following in order.

   a. 3rd gear along with its needle bearing (31 mm wide).

   b. 3rd-4th synchronizer hub.

4. Install a new spring washer and circlip on the end of the mainshaft. Be sure circlip is in the groove.

5. Insert the needle bearing in the bore of the input shaft, fit the 3rd-4th synchronizer cage and assemble the input and mainshaft together. Set the synchronizers to neutral positions.

Installing Gear Trains Into Transmission Cases

1. Be sure the reverse synchronizer is in the neutral position and the 3rd-4th gear locking ball and spring is in position in the bearing bore.

2. Install the input and mainshaft assembly into the left half housing, engaging the selector forks with the synchronizer cages.

3. Install the outer races to the countershaft and install the countershaft into the housing. Be sure the teeth of both gear trains mate properly.

4. Be sure the alignment dowel pins are in place. Coat the mating surfaces of the half housings with sealer and position the right hand housing onto the left. Position the rear bearing thrust plate.

5. Install the six bearing bolts and tighten to 3 ft. lbs. Install the two thrust plate bolts and tighten to 7 ft. lbs.

6. Be sure the oil seal is installed in the clutch cover and install the clutch cover in place on the transmission housing.

7. Tighten the seven securing bolts to 19 ft. lbs. Rotate the input shaft during the clutch cover retaining bolt tightening.

8. Loosen the six bearing bolts in the housings and tap the half housings with a rubber mallet while rotating the input shaft. Retighten the six bearing bolts to 11 ft. lbs.

9. Install the six assembly bolts in the housing and torque to 7 ft. lbs.

10. Invert the transmission with the rear of the mainshaft upward. Be sure the alignment dowels are in place, coat the mating surfaces of the transmission housing and the intermediate housing with sealing compound and install the intermediate housing in place, while engaging the finger in the selector fork detents.

11. Tighten the five nuts and two bolts to 13 ft. lbs. Place the 5th/reverse spindle to the 5th gear position.

12. Install the 5th/reverse stub shaft and the 5th/reverse synchronizer hub.

NOTE: If a new hub is used, the marking groove should be towards the reverse gear.

13. As a unit, install the 5th/reverse synchronizer cage and the selector fork, bringing together the marks on the synchronizer hub and the cage.

14. Align the holes and install a new roll pin. Set the unit to the neutral position.

15. Install the 5th gear and needle bearing, along with the spacer.

5th Gear Assembly and Preparation for Measurements 4th and 5th

1. Press the bearing on to the gear pinion.

— CAUTION —
When new parts are used, match the pinion gear to the mainshaft by green or yellow color.

2. Place the 5th gear pinion with the bearing fitted, on a hot plate and place a small piece of solder on the pinion. When the solder melts, place the pinion gear onto the shaft.

NOTE: A drift may have to be used to seat the gear.

3. Remove the alignment dowels from the rear housing and set them aside for later use. Install a shim pack, 4.0 mm thick and the bearing race, into the rear housing.

Preload of the Mainshaft Tapered Roller Bearing (Number 4 Measurement)

1. Place the rear housing in position on the transmission case. Fit three bolts to hold housing and hand tighten.

2. Rotate the mainshaft, loosen the three bolts of the rear housing and retighten hand tight only.

3. A gap will exist between the two housings. Measure the gap to check for parallelism and to calculate the shim thickness needed to preload the mainshaft bearing.

Example

Thickness of basic shim	4.00 mm
Measurement of gap	1.85 mm
Difference	2.15 mm
Plus preload	0.10 mm
Shim thickness required	2.25 mm

NOTE: Shims are available in increments of 0.05 mm from 1.5 mm to 2.95 mm.

4. Remove the rear housing and remove the rear bearing outer race and the basic 4.00 mm shim pack.

Manual Transaxle Overhaul

MANUAL TRANSAXLE APPLICATION CHART

Make	Year	Vehicle Model	Transmission Model	Speeds	Reference Type No.	Page
Audi	'78–'79	Fox	—	4	2	U219
	'80–'85	4000	—	4	2	U219
			—	5	19	U250
	'78–'85	5000	—	4	1	U216
			—	5	21	U271
Chrysler Corp./ Mitsubishi	'80–'85	Colt, Champ, Tredia, Cordia①	K1160	4	3	U223
			KM165	4 (twinstick)	3	U223
			K1162	5	③	
Datsun/Nissan	'78–'81	F10, 310	F4WF60A	4	4	U227
			F5WF60A	5	4	U227
	'82–'85	310, Stanza Sentra, Pulsar	RN4F30A	4	6	U231
			RS5F30A	5	6	U231
			RS5F31A	5	6	U231
Fiat	'78–'85	128, X1/9, Strada	—	4 & 5	5	U229
Honda	'78–'85	All	—	4 & 5	7	U233
Mazda	'81–'85	GLC, 626	—	4 & 5	22	U276
Porsche	'78–'85	911,930	—	4 & 5	8	U235
	'78–'85	924, 944②	—	4	2	U219
	'78–'85	928	G 28.03	5	9	U238
Renault	'78–'83	Le Car	—	4	10	U241
	'81–'83	18i	—	4	11	U243
SAAB	'78–'85	All	—	4	12	U245
			—	5	13	U247
Subaru	'78–'84	All ex. 4WD	—	4	14	U248
			—	5	15	U251
	'78–'84	All 4WD	—	4	16	U252
Toyota	'80–'81	Tercel	Z40	4	17	U256
			Z50	5	17	U256
	'82–'85	Tercel	—	4 & 5	18	U260

MANUAL TRANSAXLE APPLICATION CHART

Make	Year	Vehicle Model	Transmission Model	Speeds	Reference Type No.	Page
Volkswagen	'78–'84	Types 1 & 2	002, 091	4	20	U266
	'78–'85	Rabbit, Scirocco, Jetta, Quantum	—	4 & 5	19	U262
	'78–'81	Dasher	—	4	2	U219

NOTE: Although certain late model transaxles may differ slightly from their predecessors, certain basic similarities continue to exist; thus enabling overhaul procedures for these newer models to be compatible with those given within the text.
① Cordia: twinstick only through 1984
② Information on the 1979 and later 924 and 944 with 5 speed transaxle was not available at the time of publication
③ Information on the new 5 speed models not available at the time of publication

TYPE 1

4 Speed Transaxle

Audi

DISASSEMBLY

1. Mount the transaxle in a holding fixture.
2. Block the drive flange with a drift and remove the center bolt. Remove both drive flanges.
3. Remove the differential cover and O-ring. Remove the differential.

— **CAUTION** —

If the tapered roller bearings on the pinion shaft are to be replaced, it is necessary to measure the pinion position before the transaxle is disassembled. Both pinion shaft bearings must be replaced at the same time with bearings of the same make. The pinion must be set to its original position when the transaxle is assembled.

4. Remove the bolts holding the gear carrier to the final drive housing.
5. Remove the dowel pin from the gear carrier.
6. Remove the selector shaft spring and cap. Push the selector shaft into the final drive housing.
7. Separate the gear carrier and the final drive housing.
8. Remove the end cap from the gear carrier. Remove the mainshaft bolt and washer.
9. Remove the shift rod stop-screws, spring, and interlock plungers.
10. Drive the spring pin out of the third/fourth gear shaft fork.
11. Pull the third/fourth gear selector rod out of the gear carrier. The shift fork will stay on the mainshaft.
12. Press the mainshaft out of the bearing. Guide the mainshaft and pinion shaft with the selector rod and fork for first/second gear.
13. Remove the main and pinion shafts together with the selector rod and shift forks. Swing the pinion shaft slightly to clear the reverse sliding gear.
14. Remove the speedometer drive gear.
15. Pry the oil seal from the differential cover.
16. Remove the bearing race from the differential cover. Remove the shim and record the size.
17. Remove the drive flange oil seal.
18. Pull the differential bearing outer race out of the final drive housing. Remove the shim and record the size.
19. Remove the selector shaft and oil seal.
20. Remove the clutch release shaft, bearing springs, and bushings. Remove the clutch bearing guide sleeve.
21. Remove the mainshaft oil seal.
22. Remove the pinion shaft needle bearings from the final drive housing.
23. Remove the mainshaft needle bearings.
24. Remove the reverse gear relay lever and the reverse selector rod.
25. Remove the reverse shaft and gear.
26. Press the synchronizer assembly (with third gear) off the mainshaft. Remove the needle bearings.
27. Remove the pinion shaft bolt.
28. Press the bearing (along with first gear and the synchronizer ring) off the pinion shaft. Remove the needle bearings.
29. Remove the circlip from the synchronizer.
30. Press the synchronizer assembly (along with second gear and the synchronizer ring) off the pinion shaft. Remove the needle bearings.

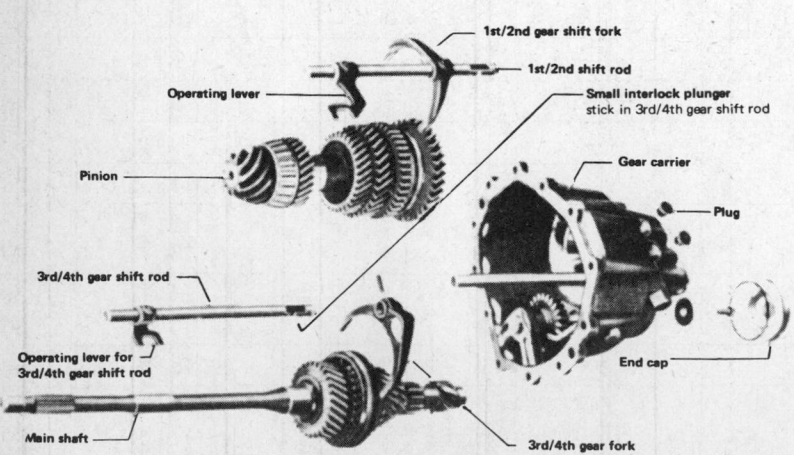

Gear carrier with gear train and selector components

31. Remove the third gear circlip and press third gear off the pinion shaft.

32. Remove the circlip from fourth gear and press it off the pinion shaft.

33. Press the large tapered roller bearing off the pinion shaft.

34. Remove the spring pin from the pinion gear shaft in the differential housing and drive the shaft out. Remove the thrust washers and pinion gears.

35. Remove the side gears, threaded washers, and shims. Record the shim size.

36. Remove the differential bearings and speedometer drive gear.

37. Remove the ring gear.

ASSEMBLY

1. Heat the ring gear to 212° F. and install it.

2. Heat the differential housing bearings to 212° F. and press them on. Install the speedometer drive gear.

3. Install the side gears with a 0.5 mm shim. Install the pinion gears and thrust washers.

4. Press the small gears outward and check the side gear play. Insert shims for the side gears until the play does not exceed 0.003 in. Install the threaded washers.

NOTE: The adjustment is correct when no play can be felt and the gears turn easily by hand without jamming.

5. Install the pinion gear shaft.

6. Press the large tapered roller bearing onto the pinion shaft.

7. Heat the fourth gear to 250° F. and press it onto the pinion shaft. The shoulder on the gear faces third gear.

NOTE: The pinion shaft and fourth gear must be absolutely free of oil and grease.

8. Install the circlip on fourth gear and measure the end-play. Play should be 0–0.0007 in. with the lower limit preferred.

9. Install the third gear needle bearings.

10. Heat third gear to 250° F. and press onto the pinion shaft.

NOTE: The pinion shaft and third gear must be absolutely free of grease and oil.

11. Install the third gear circlip. Measure the end-play with a feeler gauge and install a circlip that will give a play between 0–0.001 in. The lower limit is preferred.

12. Press the synchronizer rings on the first and second gears. Check the gap between the gears and synchronizer rings. On new parts the gap should be 0.039–0.066 in. The wear limit is 0.019 in.

13. Install the keys on the synchronizer hub. Install the synchronizer sleeve over the hub aligning the matchmarks. Install the springs on the synchronizer assembly 120° offset from each other. The angled spring end is hooked in the key hollow.

14. Press the synchronizer assembly onto the pinion shaft. Turn the synchronizing ring of the second gear so that the grooves align with the keys in the synchronizer hub. Install the circlip on the synchronizer assembly and measure the end-play with a feeler gauge. Play should be 0–0.0007 in. with the lower limit preferred.

15. Press the small tapered roller bearing onto the pinion shaft. Install the washer and bolt.

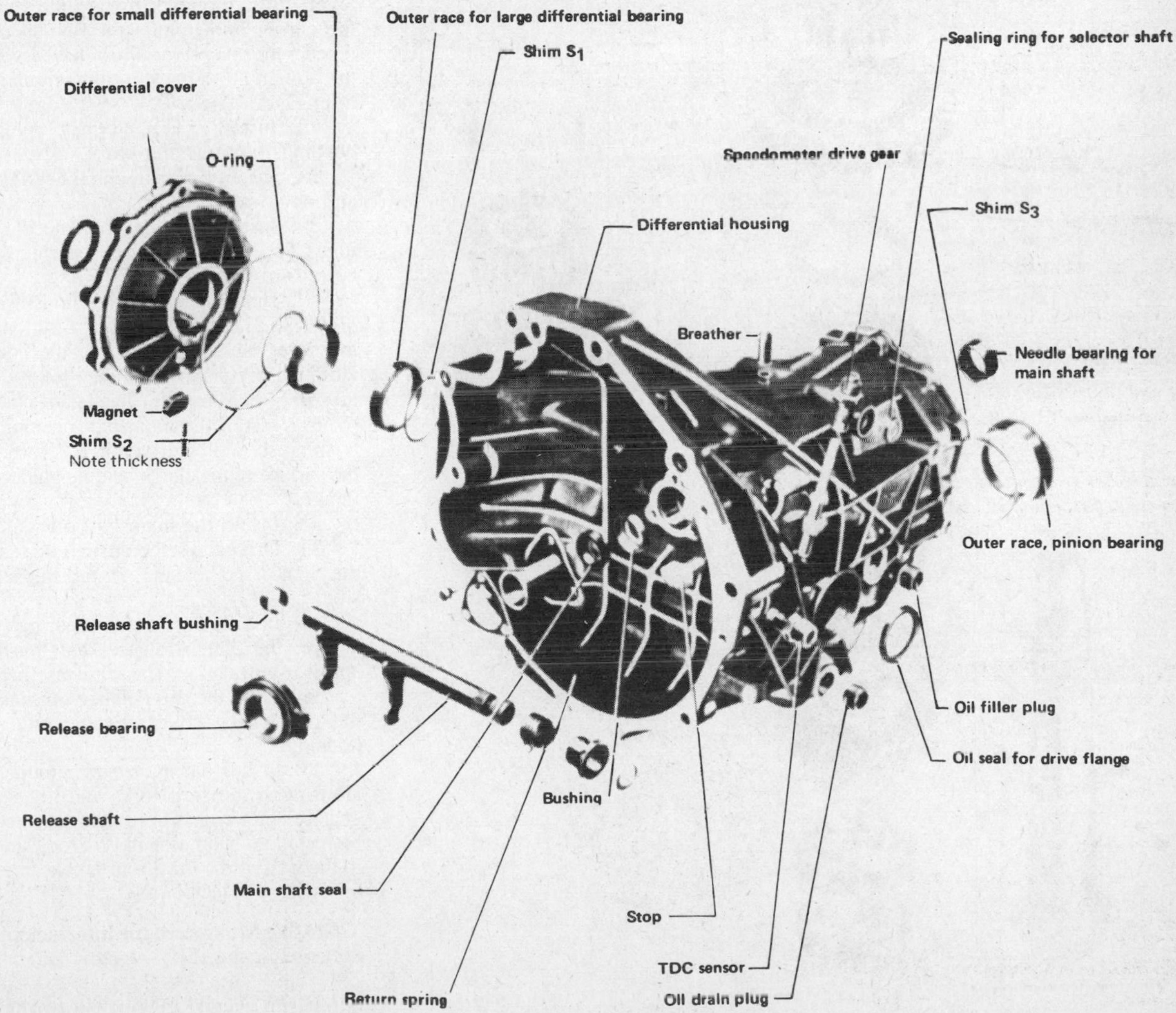

Outer race for small differential bearing

Differential cover

O-ring

Magnet

Shim S₂
Note thickness

Outer race for large differential bearing

Shim S₁

Speedometer drive gear

Differential housing

Breather

Sealing ring for selector shaft

Shim S₃

Needle bearing for main shaft

Outer race, pinion bearing

Release shaft bushing

Release bearing

Release shaft

Main shaft seal

Return spring

Bushing

Stop

TDC sensor

Oil drain plug

Oil filler plug

Oil seal for drive flange

Components of the final drive housing

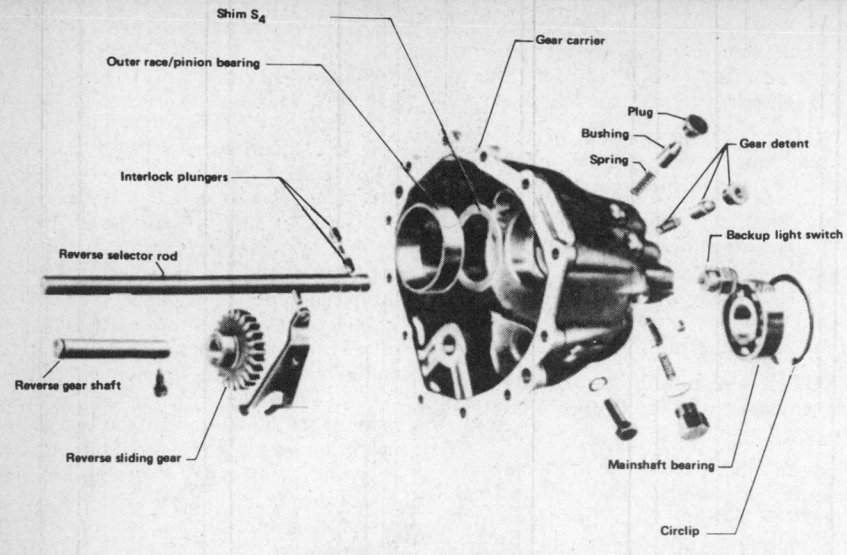

Gear carrier housing

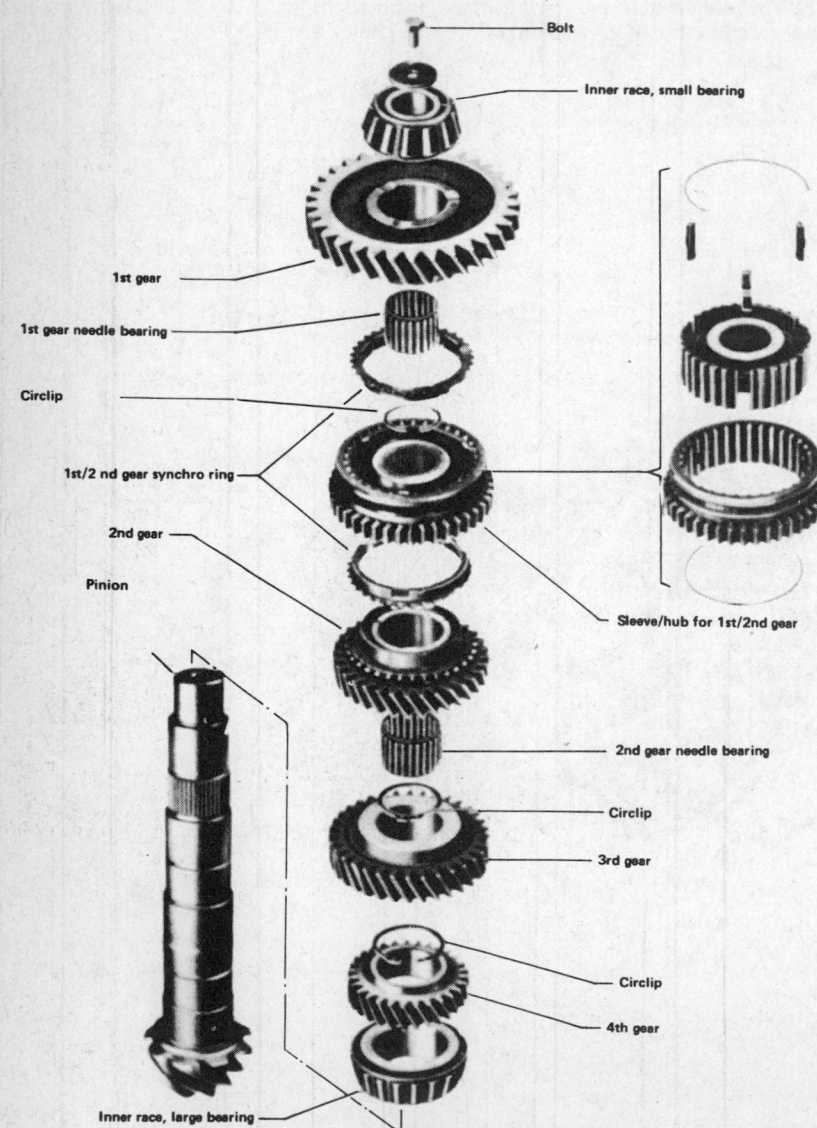

Pinion shaft assembly

16. Install the third gear needle bearings.

17. Install the synchronizer rings on third and fourth gears. The gap between new gears should be 0.039–0.066 in.

18. Assemble the third/fourth synchronizer.

19. Align the grooves in the synchronizer ring for third gear with the keys in the synchronizer hub. Press the synchronizer assembly, synchronizer ring, and third gear onto the mainshaft.

20. Install the synchronizer assembly circlip and measure the end-play. End-play should be 0–0.001 in.

21. Install the fourth gear bearings.

22. Install fourth gear and its thrust washer on the mainshaft. Play should be 0.007–0.013 in.

23. Drive the mainshaft bearing into the gear carrier (closed side out).

24. Install the shim and pinion bearing outer race.

25. Install reverse gear shaft and reverse gear.

26. Install the interlock plungers in the gear carrier. Install the reverse selector shaft. Install the reverse relay lever through the gear and into the threaded portion of the lever. Press the lever toward the center of the carrier and tighten the bolt in until it touches the relay lever. Press the lever against the bolt and turn back until the thread starts to engage.

27. Install the interlock plungers, bushings, springs and plugs.

28. Install the differential bearing shim and outer race.

29. Install the mainshaft needle bearings. The lettering on the bearing should be toward the drift.

30. Heat the final drive housing *completely* to 212° F. and press the pinion bearing outer race and shim into the housing. Hold the pressure on the race for 1–2 minutes until heat transfer has taken place.

31. Install the mainshaft bushing. The bushing should be driven in 0.452 in. from the surface of the clutch bearing guide sleeve flange.

32. Install the mainshaft oil seal.

33. Drive the selector shaft oil seal into the final drive housing. Install the selector shaft.

34. Install the clutch bearing guide sleeve, the clutch release shaft bushings, spring, shaft, oil seal, and release bearing.

35. Press the drive flange oil seals into the differential cover and the final drive housing.

36. Install the main and pinion shafts along with the shift forks and first/second gear selector rod. These components must be installed as an assembly. Hook the hole in the web of the third/fourth gear fork over the reverse selector rod.

NOTE: Make sure the interlock plungers engage the shift selector rod.

37. Pull the mainshaft into the bearing with an 8 mm bolt. When fully seated, install the mainshaft bolt.

38. Move the selector rods for first/second and reverse into neutral.

39. Slide the third/fourth selector rod into the shift fork and gear carrier. Make sure that the interlock plungers engage. Secure the shift fork to the rod with a new spring pin.

40. Install the shift rod stop screws.

41. Press the mainshaft cap and O ring into the gear carrier. The recess in the cap points towards the oil drilling in the gear carrier.

42. Install the gear carrier.

43. Assemble the measuring bar and measure the pinion location.

If the measurement is not the same as previously recorded, proceed as follows:

    a. If the reading is smaller, a thinner shim must be installed between the pinion shaft outer race and final drive housing.

    b. If the reading is the same or very close to the original reading, proceed to the next step.

    c. If the reading is larger, a thicker shim must be installed between the final drive housing. Install a new shim if necessary.

44. Install the dowel pin between the final drive housing and gear carrier.

45. Install the differential.

46. Install the differential cover.

47. Install the drive flanges.

48. Install the selector shaft spring and cover.

TYPE 2

4 Speed Transaxle

VW, Porsche and Audi

DISASSEMBLY

Certain variations are used in the application of this basic transaxle. The gear arrangement remains the same, the shifting mechanism differs in the shaping of various fingers and forks. The case is modified to adapt to the various vehicles in which it is used. Roller bearings are used in the majority of applications, while tapered bearings are used in the remainder. Needle caged bearings may be found as split, one piece or with a foldable cage. A pinion nut is used on varied models, while a bolt and washer are used on others.

A completely new five speed transaxle assembly is available for the 924 models, beginning with the 1980 model year. No service information is available at time of printing on this transaxle model. A modified version of this transaxle is used on the 1980 and later 924 Turbo models.

1. Mount the transaxle in a holding fixture.

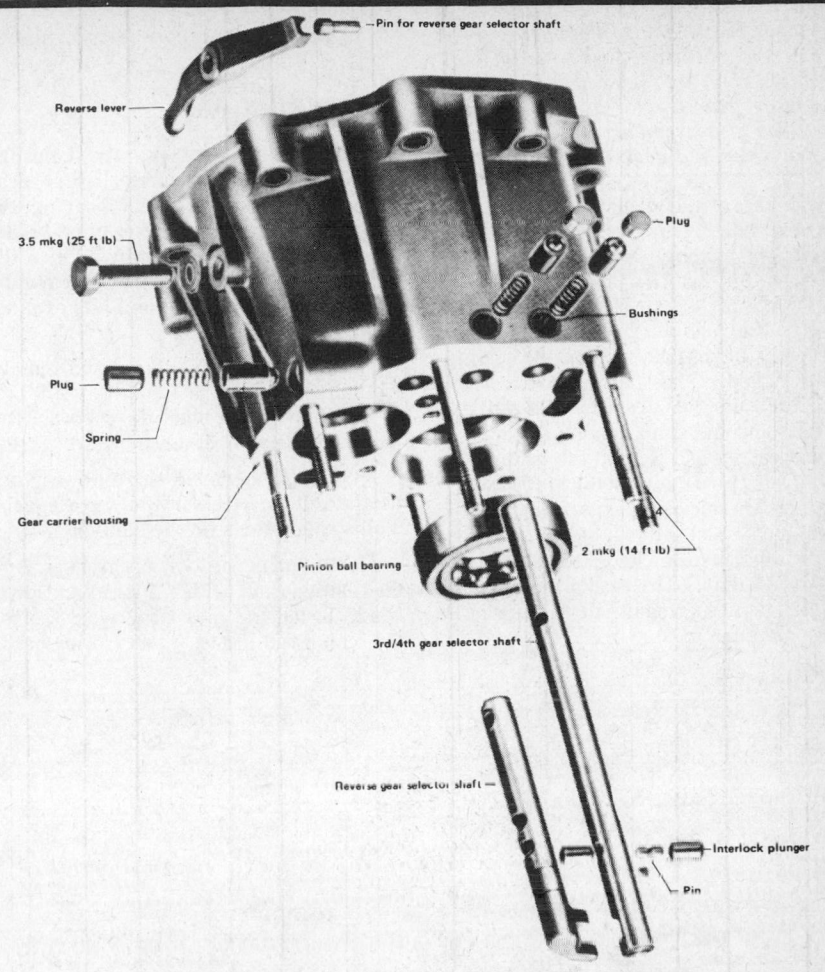

Gear carrier housing and shift rod interlock components

2. Separate the shift housing from the transaxle.

3. Mount a dial gauge and zero the gauge with a 3 mm preload.

─── **CAUTION** ───

The greatest care must be taken when determining the thickness of the gasket and shim used between the shift housing and the gear carrier. The thickness of these

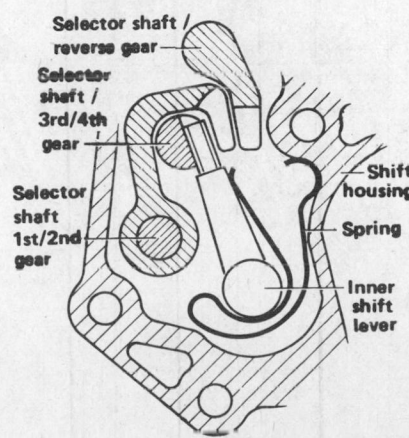

Spring loaded inner shift lever

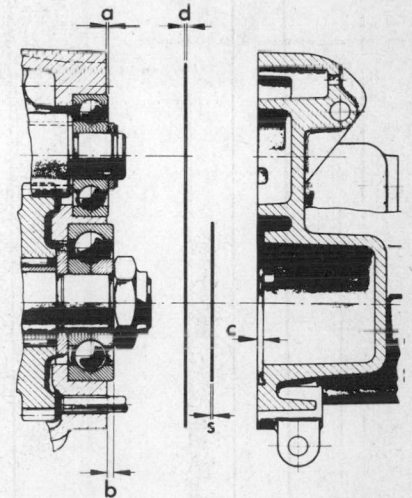

End cover gasket and shim dimensions

a — between main shaft bearing and gear carrier

b — between pinion bearing and gear carrier

c — between end face of gearshift housing and shim contact in gearshift housing

d — gasket thickness

s — shim thickness

two parts influence the position of the drive pinion. If the bearings for the mainshaft and pinion shaft are replaced or if the shift housing or gear carrier housing are replaced, the measurements must be remade and new shim and gasket sizes selected.

4. Measure the distance between the main shaft bearing and the gear carrier (a). Record this reading. Make sure that the bearing is fully seated.

5. Measure the distance between the pinion bearing and the gear carrier (b). Record the reading. Make sure that the bearing is fully seated.

6. Measure the distance between the end face and the shim contact surface on the gear carrier (c). Record the reading.

7. Determine the shim thickness as follows; add the measurements from Step 4 (a) and 6 (c), then subtract Step 5 (b). This will give the shim thickness required.

8. (Fox only.) The gasket thickness is determined by the mainshaft bearing projection obtained in Step 4.

Bearing projection (mm)	Gasket size (mm)
0.20–0.26	0.30
0.27–0.32	0.40

NOTE: When replacing the transmission housing, gear carrier, first gear needle bearing or the pinion bearing, the exact location of the pinion must be determined before disassembly. Once the new parts have been installed, it will be necessary to set the pinion to its original position.

9. Block the drive flange and remove the bolt.

10. Remove the final drive cover. Remove the differential assembly.

NOTE: To perform the following operation, it is necessary to have special Volkswagen tools or the equivalent.

11. Assemble the tool universal bar. Zero the dial indicator with a 2 mm preload.

12. Install the measuring plate tool on the pinion and install the measuring bar in the final drive housing.

13. Install the final drive cover and tighten the retaining nuts to 18 ft. lbs.

14. Move the second centering disc outward with the movable setting ring until the measuring bar can be turned by hand.

15. Turn the measuring bar until the measuring pin extension touches the plate on the pinion. Note the indicator needle at the point of maximum deflection. Record the reading.

NOTE: After parts have been replaced, this setting must be reproduced as closely as possible.

16. Separate the gear carrier from the final drive housing.

17. Drive the spring pin out of the 3rd/4th shift fork in the direction of the pinion.

18. Move the shift fork along the selector shaft and engage 3rd gear. *Do not move the shaft.*

19. Engage reverse gear. Place the gear carrier in the final drive housing. Loosen the pinion nut. Remove the gear carrier from

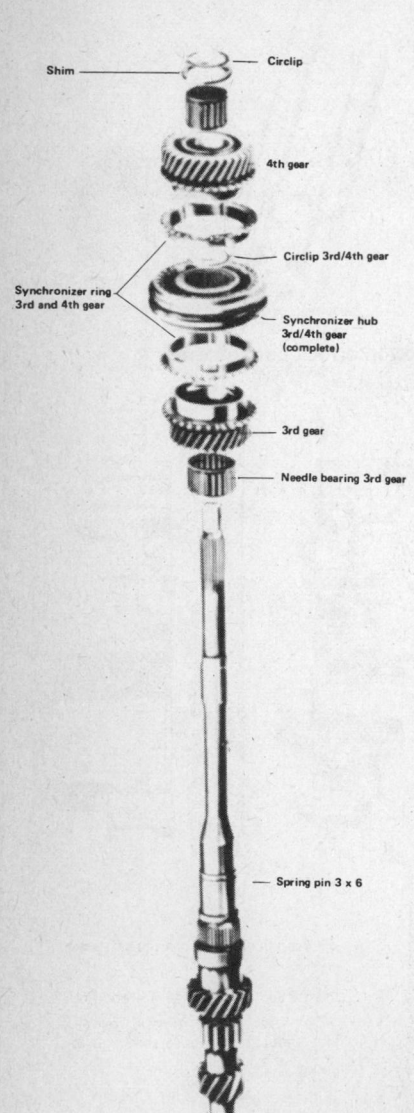

Mainshaft assembly

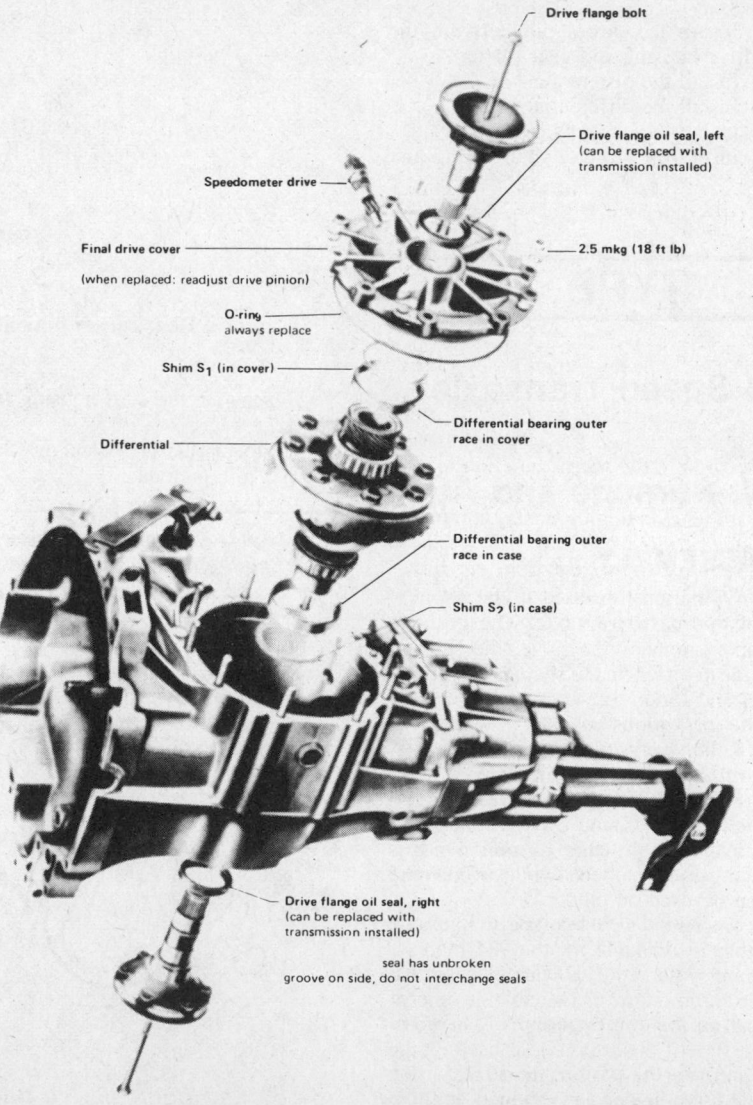

Components of differential housing

the final drive housing. Remove the 3rd/
4th shift fork.

20. Remove the mainshaft bearing using
a suitable bearing puller. Remove the
mainshaft.

21. Drive the reverse gear shaft out of
the gear carrier.

22. Place the remaining gears in neutral
and press the pinion shaft out of the gear
carrier along with the 1st/2nd selector shaft
and shift fork.

23. Remove the inner shift lever spring
from the shift housing, remove the shift
lever.

24. Press the transmission rear mount
off the shift housing.

25. Pry the inner shift lever oil seal out
of the shift housing.

26. Drive the inner shift lever rear bushing out of the shift housing.

27. Press the inner shift lever front bushing out of the shift housing.

28. Pry the mainshaft oil seal out of the
final drive housing.

29. Drive the mainshaft sleeve out of the
final drive housing from the gear carrier
end.

30. Drive the mainshaft needle bearings
out of the final drive housing from the front
(flywheel side).

31. Remove the dowel pin from the pinion bearing and drive it out of the final drive
housing.

32. Using a slide hammer, pull the clutch
release shaft bushing out of the final drive
housing.

33. Pull the starter bushing out of the
final drive housing.

34. Drive the pinion bearing out of the
gear carrier.

35. Remove the pin from the reverse gear
selector shaft.

36. Drive the 1st/2nd and 3rd/4th interlock plungers through the gear carrier and
remove through the access hole in the rear
of the gear carrier.

37. Tap the remaining interlock plunger
plug out.

38. Remove the circlip from the mainshaft which holds the 4th gear and the synchronizer ring. Remove the parts from the
shaft.

39. Remove the circlip retaining the
synchronizer hub, synchronizer ring, and
third gear from the main shaft.

40. Press the synchronizer hub and third
gear off the mainshaft.

41. Press the pinion bearing inner race
along with the first gear off the pinion shaft.

42. Press the synchronizer hub for 1st/
2nd gear along with second gear off the
pinion shaft.

43. Remove the third gear circlip from
the pinion shaft.

44. Press the third gear off the pinion
shaft.

45. Press the fourth gear off the pinion
shaft.

46. Remove the drive flange oil seal from
the final drive housing by prying.

47. Drive the differential outer bearing

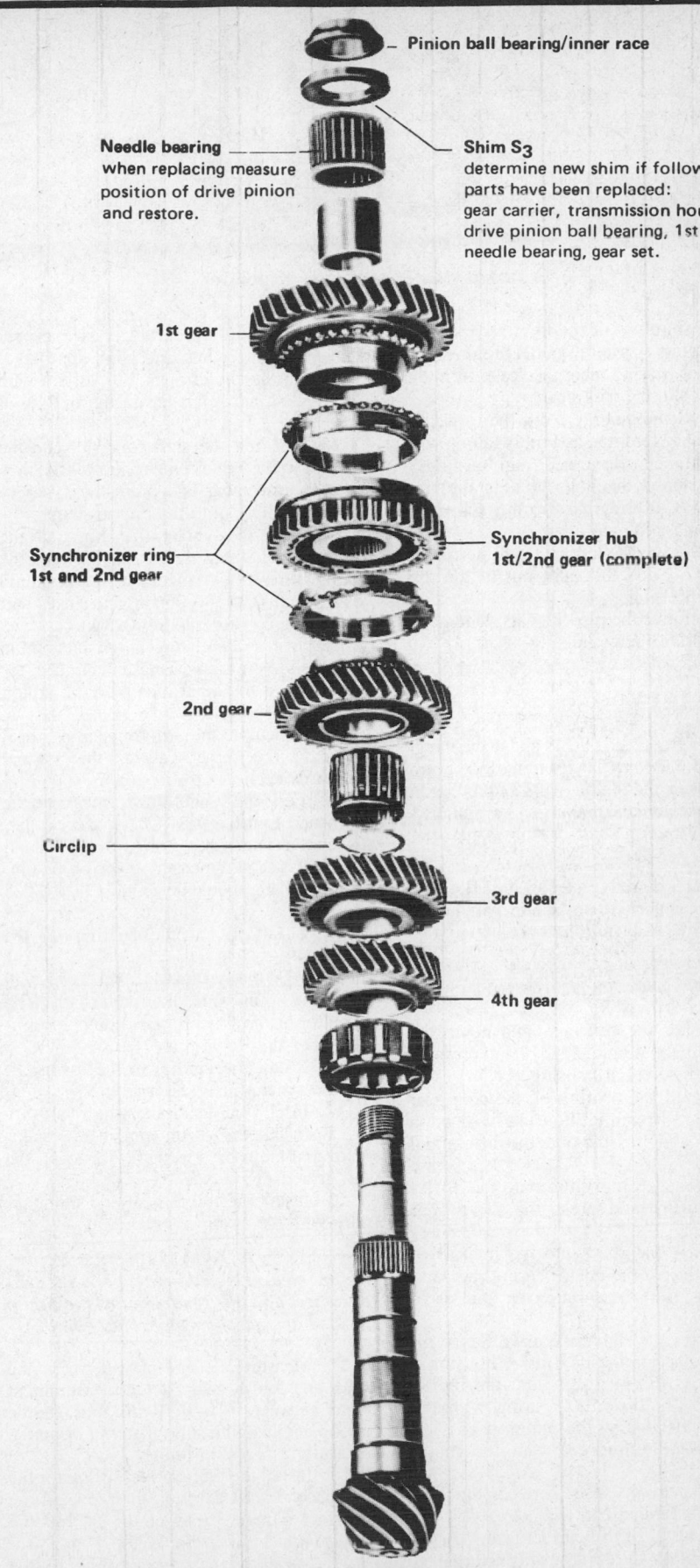

Pinion shaft assembly

Exploded view of 1st/2nd synchronizer

race and shim out of the final drive cover.

48. Using a suitable puller, remove the differential bearing inner race/cage from the side opposite the ring gear.

49. Pull the bearing from the ring gear side of the differential assembly, along with the speedometer drive gear and bushing.

50. Remove the bolts holding the ring gear to the differential housing and drive the housing and gear apart.

51. Remove the circlip from the pinion gear shaft. Slide the shaft out of the differential housing.

52. Remove the pinion gears, side gears and the drive flange nuts.

ASSEMBLY

1. Insert the side gears and drive flange nuts. Bolt the drive flanges to the side gears.

2. Insert the pinion gears and move the drive flange until the pinion gears are aligned. Install the pinion shaft. Remove the drive flanges.

NOTE: The drive pinion and the ring gears are matched units and can be replaced only as a matched set.

3. Heat the ring gear to approximately 212° F. and center on the differential housing with a drift.

4. Install the bearing opposite to the ring gear by heating to 212° F. and pressing onto the differential housing.

5. Install the bearing on the ring gear side of the differential housing by heating to 212° F. and pressing onto the differential housing.

6. Insert 1.8 mm shim onto the differential housing and press the drive gear bushing on.

7. Insert the shim into the final drive cover and drive the outer bearing race into place and insert the shim in the final drive housing.

8. Drive the right side drive flange oil seal into place in the final drive housing.

9. Press the 4th gear onto the pinion shaft while holding the bearing with the wide shoulder facing the pinion head.

10. Press the third gear onto the pinion shaft.

11. Measure the space between the third gear and the pinion shaft with a feeler gauge. Install a circlip of the correct size.

12. Position the three keys in the slots in the 1st/2nd gear synchronizer hub.

13. Place the synchronizer sleeve over the synchronizer hub and align the marks.

14. Install the springs 120° offset with the angled ends engaged in the hollow of a key.

15. Position the shift fork slot and the groove in the synchronizer hub so that they face the first gear and press the synchronizer assembly onto the pinion shaft.

16. Press the synchronizer ring onto the first gear and measure the gap between the parts with a feeler gauge. New parts should be between 0.042–0.066 in. and a used part should be no more than 0.023 in.

17. Install the first gear on the pinion shaft, slide on the bearing and shim.

18. Press the inner race onto the pinion shaft.

19. Assemble the 3rd/4th gear synchronizer in the same way as the 1st/2nd synchronizer.

20. Press the synchronizer rings onto the third and fourth gears. Check the gap between the synchronizer rings and the gears. New parts should measure 0.053–0.075 in. and used parts should be no more than 0.023 in.

21. Install the needle bearing on the mainshaft.

22. Press the synchronizer hub along with the third gear onto the mainshaft. The chamfer on the synchronizer hub inner splines faces third gear.

23. Install the circlip on the mainshaft for the synchronizer assembly.

24. Install the needle bearing.

25. Install the spring pin in the mainshaft and align the pin with the slot in the 4th gear.

26. Install the fourth gear and shim, secure with the circlip.

——— CAUTION ———
Before measuring end-play, press the synchronizer and third gear against the circlip located against the synchronizer hub.

27. Measure the end-play between the shim and fourth gear. If the measurement is not between 0.10–0.40 mm, remove the circlip and install a shim that will bring the measurement within limits.

28. Install the plunger and spring for the first/second shift selector shaft. Install interlock plunger (between the 1st/2nd and the 3rd/4th shafts) from the top of the case.

29. Install the plunger and spring for the 3rd/4th selector shaft. Hold down the plunger and install the 3rd/4th shift selector shaft.

30. Install the pin for the reverse gear selector shaft.

31. Install the second interlock plunger from the top of the gear carrier.

32. Install the reverse gear selector shaft. Install the remaining spring and plunger. Install the reverse lever pin in the selector shaft.

NOTE: The first/second selector shaft is not installed until the gear train is in place.

33. Install the plugs in the interlock plunger bores.

34. Install the reverse sliding gear. Insert the reverse lever with the shift segment.

35. Install the bolt and washer and press the reverse lever toward the center of the gear carrier.

36. Turn the bolt in until it touches the reverse lever. Press the lever against the bolt and make certain that the threads engage smoothly. Continue until the bolt is seated in the gear carrier. Tighten the bolt to 25 ft. lbs.

37. Check the operation of the reverse selector several times. Make sure that the lever moves easily in all positions. Remove the reverse sliding gear.

38. Press the pinion bearing into the gear carrier.

39. Drive a new starter bushing into the final drive housing.

40. Drive a new clutch release shaft bushing into the final drive housing.

41. Align the pinion bearing outer race with the hole in the final drive housing drive into place. The groove on the side must be toward the gear carrier. Install the dowel pin.

42. Drive the mainshaft needle bearings into place in the final drive housing.

43. Drive the mainshaft sleeve into position in the final drive housing.

44. Drive the mainshaft oil seal into position.

45. Install the clutch bearing guide sleeve, the clutch release shaft and spring and the clutch release bearing.

46. Press the inner shift lever rear bushing into the shift lever housing until it is flush with the shoulder.

47. Press the shift lever oil seal into the shift lever housing until it is flush with the housing.

48. Press the transmission rear mount onto the shift housing.

49. Press the inner shift lever front bushing into the housing until it is flush.

50. Install the inner shift lever and install the spring.

51. Press the pinion shaft assembly into the ball bearing in the gear carrier.

52. Drive the mainshaft bearing into the gear carrier assembly.

53. Position the 1st/2nd selector shaft and fork on the assembled pinion shaft assembly.

54. Press the pinion shaft assembly into the gear carrier assembly. Guide the shift

selector shaft into the operating sleeve. Make sure that the selector shaft does not jam.

55. Place the pinion shaft in a vise and tighten the pinion nut to 14–21 ft. lbs. Install the gear carrier in the final drive housing and secure with four nuts.

56. Repeat the measurements from Steps 11–15 of disassembly. If the measurements are not the same as previously recorded, proceed as follows:

   a. If the second measurement is smaller, a thinner shim must be installed (between the pinion shaft inner bearing race and needle bearing on the pinion shaft).

   b. If the measurement is the same or very close to the original reading, proceed to the next step.

   c. If the measurement is larger, a thicker shim must be installed.

57. Remove the gear carrier from the final drive housing, install a new shim if needed.

58. Place the mainshaft assembly in the gear carrier. Install the shim and circlip.

59. Install the 3rd/4th shift fork with the wider shoulder facing toward fourth gear. Secure the shift fork with a new spring pin.

60. Block the gear train and tighten the pinion nut to 72 ft. lbs.

61. Install the first/second gear selector dog.

62. Install the gear carrier assembly on the final drive housing. Install the dowel pins before tightening the nuts or bolts.

63. Install the differential assembly into the final drive housing.

64. Install the final drive cover.

65. Install the drive flanges and block with suitable drift.

66. Repeat the measurements from Steps 3–8 of disassembly. Select the proper shim and gasket to be installed between the gear carrier and shift housing.

67. Install the shift housing on the gear carrier assembly.

TYPE 3

4 Speed Transaxle— Model KM 160, 4 Speed Transaxle w/ Twin Stick—Model KM 165

Chrysler Corp./ Mitsubishi

DISASSEMBLY

1. Mount the transaxle securely and drain the lubricating oil.

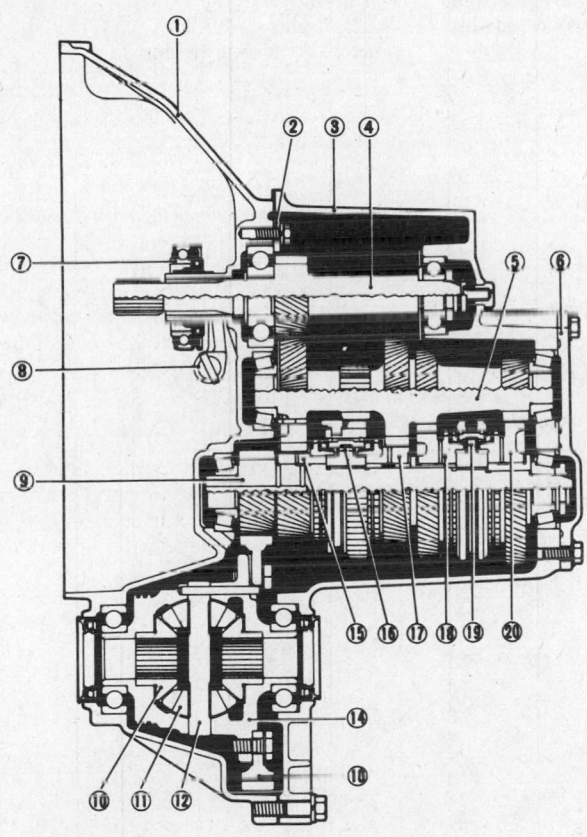

1. Clutch housing	12. Pinion shaft
2. Bearing retainer	13. Differential drive gear
3. Transaxle	14. Differential case
4. Input shaft	15. 4th speed gear
5. Intermediate gear	16. 3rd and 4th speed
6. Rear cover	synchronizer assembly
7. Clutch release bearing	17. 3rd speed gear
8. Clutch release fork	18. 2nd speed gear
9. Output shaft	19. 1st and 2nd speed
10. Differential side gear	synchronizer assembly
11. Differential pinion	20. 1st speed gear

Cross section of model KM 160 transaxle

1. Clutch housing	14. Differential pinion
2. Input shaft	15. Pinion shaft
3. Bearing retainer	16. Differential drive gear
4. Input low gear	17. Differential case
5. Synchronizer assembly	18. 4th speed gear
6. Input high gear	19. 3rd and 4th speed
7. Transaxle case	synchronizer assembly
8. Intermediate gear	20. 3rd speed gear
9. Rear cover	21. 2nd speed gear
10. Clutch release bearing	22. 1st and 2nd speed
11. Clutch release fork	synchronizer assembly
12. Output shaft	23. 1st speed gear
13. Differential side gear	

Cross section of model KM 165 transaxle (twin-stick)

2. Remove the clutch operating bracket and the transaxle mounting bracket.

3. Remove the back–up lamp switch and the steel ball from inside the transaxle case.

4. Remove the rear cover from the transaxle case. Remove the two spacers from the rear of the tapered roller bearings.

5. Remove the transaxle case, exposing the gear train assembly.

6. Locate all the shift rails in the neutral position.

NOTE: The shift rails would be locked if any one of the shift rails are in a position other than neutral.

7. Remove the three poppet plugs and remove the springs and balls (three each).

8. Remove the reverse idler shaft and the reverse idler gear.

NOTE: The reverse idler shaft sometimes will come off with the removal of the transaxle case.

9. Remove the reverse shift lever assembly.

10. Remove the reverse shift rail and the 3rd/4th speed shift rail spacer collar.

11. Using a pin punch and light hammer, remove the spring pins from the 1st/2nd and 3rd/4th speed shift forks.

— **CAUTION** —
Support the shift forks before attempting to remove the spring pins.

12. Pull the 1st/2nd speed shift rail upward from the case, sliding the rail through the fork.

NOTE: The 1st/2nd speed shift rail and fork cannot be removed until after Step 13.

13. Pull the 3rd/4th speed shift rail from the case and remove the 1st/2nd and 3rd/4th speed shift rails and forks together.

14. Move the 3rd/4th speed synchronizer into the 4th speed position and remove the output shaft assembly.

15. Remove the differential assembly from the case.

16. **KM 165 models**—Remove the plug, poppet and spring for the two-speed shift rail and fork.

17. Remove the bolts from the input shaft bearing retainer and remove the input shaft assembly.

18. **KM 165 models**—Remove the shift rail and fork, along with the intermediate shaft assembly, when the input shaft is removed.

19. Remove the shift shaft spring retainer and pull out the spring pin with pliers.

20. Move the shift shaft towards the outside of the case by using a pin punch in the pin hole. Pull the shaft from the case and remove the control finger, two springs, spacer collar poppet spring and ball.

— **CAUTION** —
During removal of the shift shaft from the case, the poppet ball will jump out of the control finger hole. Close the hole with an object or finger tip to prevent loss of the ball.

21. Put an identifying mark on the tapered roller bearing outer race and remove it from the case.

22. Remove the lock and the speedometer driven gear assembly.

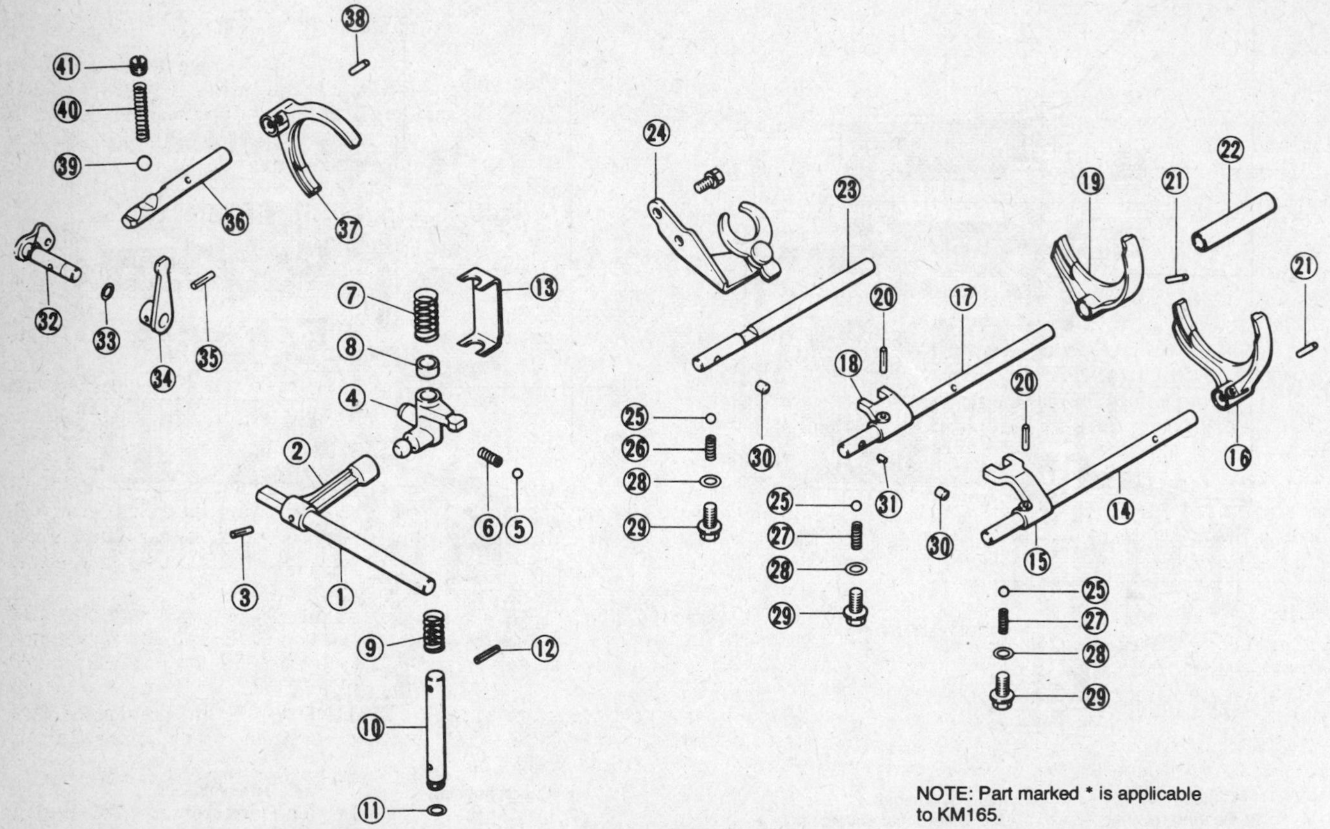

NOTE: Part marked * is applicable to KM165.

1. Control shaft	9. Reverse restrict spring	18. Shift lug	26. Reverse spring
2. Control lug	10. Shift shaft	19. Shift fork	[Length; 16.6 mm (.65 in.)]
3. Lock pin	11. O-ring	20. Lock pin	27. Spring
4. Control finger	12. Spring pin	21. Spring pin	[Length; 18.9 mm (.74 in.)]
5. Steel ball	13. Spring retainer	22. Spacer collar	28. Gasket
6. Spring	14. 1st and 2nd speed shift rail	23. Reverse shift rail	29. Plug
[Length; 18.9 mm (.74 in.)]	15. Shift lug	24. Reverse shift lever	30. Interlock plunger A
7. Neutral return spring	16. Shift fork	assembly	31. Interlock plunger B
8. Spacer collar	17. 3rd and 4th speed shift rail	25. Steel ball	*32. Selector shaft

*33. O-ring
*34. Selector finger
*35. Lock pin
*36. Shift rail
*37. Shift fork
*38. Lock pin
*39. Steel ball
*40. Spring
*41. Plug

Exploded view of shift mechanism

Input Shaft

DISASSEMBLY

KM 160

1. Remove the front bearing snap-ring and using a special puller, remove the front bearing from the input shaft.
2. Straighten the locking washer and remove the locknut at the rear of the input shaft.
3. Using a press or a special puller, remove the rear bearing from the shaft.

KM 165

1. Remove the front bearing snap-ring and remove the front bearing with a special puller.
2. Straighten the locking washer and remove the locknut at the rear of the input shaft.
3. Using a press and supporting the low gear of the input shaft, press on the rear of the input shaft and remove the input high gear, gear sleeve, synchronizer assembly, input low gear and the rear bearing.

NOTE: To remove the rear bearing only, use a special puller. The input high gear will come off with the rear bearing.

ASSEMBLY

KM 160

1. Install the front bearing on the input shaft using a bearing installer tool.
2. Install the front bearing selective snap-ring into the snap-ring groove.
3. Install a spacer to the rear of the input shaft, with the stepped side towards the rear bearing.
4. Install the rear bearing on the input shaft, using a bearing installer tool.
5. Install the locknut to the end of the input shaft and tighten to 66–79 ft. lbs (89–107 Nm). Stake the locknut into the notch of the input shaft only. Lock the lock plate, if reused.

── CAUTION ──

The shaft end will interfere with the breather if it is deformed by staking, resulting in breakage.

KM 165

1. Install the front bearing on the input shaft using a bearing installer.
2. Install the front bearing selective snap-ring into the snap-ring groove.
3. Install the synchronizer hub with the 0.16 inch (4 mm) diameter slot in the oil groove, facing the clutch or engine side.
4. The synchronizer sleeve must be installed with the 30° chamfer on the clutch or engine side.

NOTE: The opposite side of the synchronizer sleeve is machined at a 45° angle.

5. Install the synchronizer spring with its stepped part positioned on the synchronizer key. Alternate the stepped parts of the front and rear springs to avoid having the stepped parts on the same key.

6. Install the sub-gear to the input high gear and lubricate the entire surface.
7. Install the cone spring and install a new snap-ring, making sure the inner side of the cone spring is not in the snap-ring groove.
8. Install the input low gear and the needle bearing on the input shaft.
9. Install the synchronizer ring.
10. Using a special installer tool, press-fit the synchronizer assembly onto the input shaft with the synchronizer key correctly aligned with the synchronizer ring keyway.
11. Install the input high gear sleeve with a special installer tool. The input low gear should rotate smoothly. Install the synchronizer ring, the input high gear and needle bearing.
12. Install the spacer with the stepped side facing the rear bearing side.
13. Install the rear bearing with a special installer tool.
14. Install and tighten the input shaft rear nut to 66–79 ft. lbs. (89–107 Nm.) and stake in place into the notch on the input shaft. Should the lockplate be reused, bend the plate over a shoulder of the locknut.

Output Shaft

DISASSEMBLY

1. Unlock the rear locknut plate and remove the locknut from the shaft.
2. Remove the front and rear tapered bearings from the output shaft, using special bearing puller tools.
3. Using a puller tool, remove the 1st speed gear, gear sleeve, 1st and 2nd speed synchronizer assembly and the 2nd speed gear.
4. Remove the 2nd speed gear sleeve, 3rd speed gear, 3rd speed gear sleeve, 3rd/4th speed synchronizer assembly and the 4th speed gear.

ASSEMBLY

1. Assemble the synchronizers in the following manner:
    a. 3rd/4th synchronizer: Position the sleeve over the hub with the fork groove on the same side as the 0.160 inch (4.mm) oil groove on the hub.
    b. 1st/2nd synchronizer: Position the sleeve over the hub with the 30° chamfer on the same side as the 0.160 inch (4.mm) oil groove on the hub.
    c. Install the synchronizer springs into the 3rd/4th and 1st/2nd synchronizer unit with the stepped part of the springs on the synchronizer key.

NOTE: Do not have the stepped part of the front and rear springs on the same key. Alternate between keys.

2. Assemble the 4th speed gear onto the output shaft and install the synchronizer ring.

NOTE: Lubricate the contact surfaces with gear oil.

3. Press fit the 3rd/4th synchronizer unit to the output shaft with the oil grooves on

the hub and the fork groove in the sleeve facing towards the clutch (engine) side. Align the synchronizer ring keyway with the synchronizer ring key. After the installation, be sure the 4th speed gear rotates freely.
4. Install the 3rd speed gear sleeve by pressing into place. Install the 3rd speed gear assembly.
5. Install the 2nd speed gear sleeve by pressing into place. Be sure the 3rd speed gear rotates freely.
6. Install the 2nd speed gear and the 1st/2nd synchronizer ring.
7. Install the 1st/2nd speed synchronizer assembly onto the output shaft by pressing with the proper tools. Be sure the 2nd speed gear rotates freely.
8. Install the 1st/2nd synchronizer ring. Press the 1st/2nd speed synchronizer assembly into place on the output shaft. Be sure the 2nd speed gear rotates freely.
9. Install the 1st/2nd speed synchronizer ring with the keyways properly aligned with the keys.
10. Install 1st gear to the gear sleeve and press the unit onto the output shaft. Be sure the 1st speed gear rotates freely.
11. Install the front and rear tapered bearings on the front and the rear of the shaft.
12. Install the locknut on the rear of the shaft and torque to 66–79 ft. lbs. (89–107 Nm). Lock the locking plate to the nut, if used. Stake the locknut securely to the output shaft.

Intermediate Shaft

DISASSEMBLY

1. Remove the front tapered bearing with a press unit.
2. Remove the sub-gear and the spring assembly.
3. Remove the rear tapered bearing with the use of a press.

ASSEMBLY

1. Assemble the sub-gear spring assembly to the intermediate shaft gear with the longer end of the spring fitted to the 0.160 inch (4. mm) diameter hole in the sub-gear.
2. Install the sub-gear and insert the remaining end of the sub-gear spring into the smallest hole in the sub-gear, 0.160 inch (4. mm).
3. Install the front and rear tapered roller bearings on the shaft with a press tool.

Speedometer Driven Gear

NOTE: The speedometer driven gear assembly cannot be removed without disassembly of the transaxle.

DISASSEMBLY

1. Using a pin punch, remove the spring pin from the sleeve and driven gear shaft.
2. Separate the driven gear from the sleeve and remove the O-rings.

ASSEMBLY

1. Install new O-rings and lubricate the

driven gearshaft.

2. Insert the driven gearshaft into the sleeve.

3. Align the sleeve hole with the pin slot in the driven gear.

4. Install the spring pin in such a manner so as not to contact the gearshaft with the slit in the spring pin.

Control Shaft or Control Lug
REMOVAL

1. A centering hole is located on a 16 mm boss on the engine side of the lower part of the clutch housing.

2. Drill through the centering hole with a drill with a diameter of 0.470 inch (12. mm).

3. Remove the lock pin from the control shaft and lug. Remove the control shaft and lug.

INSTALLATION

1. Install the control shaft and lug. Install a new lock pin through the control lug and shaft.

2. Install a 0.470 inch (12. mm) cup plug in the drilled hole and seal the plug with a bonding sealant.

Differential

The overhaul of the differential assembly is confined to the replacement of the side bearings, ring gear and the differential and pinion gears. The replacement is done in the conventional manner. Necessary measurements during the assembly are given in the transaxle assembly procedures.

ASSEMBLY OF TRANSAXLE

NOTE: Lubricate all seals and O-rings during the assembly.

1. Prepare the transaxle case for component assembly by replacing all oil seals and case internal small parts that were removed during the disassembly.

2. Install the speedometer driven gear assembly into the clutch housing. Install the locking plate into the groove cut into the sleeve.

3. **Model KM 165**—Install an O-ring onto the selector shaft and lubricate the ring and the bore in the case. Install the shaft into the case and install the selector finger. Install the lock pin so that it is flush on the clutch housing side of the selector finger.

4. Install the poppet spring and steel ball into the control finger and with the use of a special tool, force the poppet ball into its bore. Leave the tool in position.

5. Install a new O-ring onto the shift shaft and install the shaft into the clutch housing and engage the reverse restrict spring and the control finger.

6. Press the shift shaft inward until the special tool, used to hold the poppet ball and spring, is forced out. Recover and lay aside. Install the spacer collar and the neutral return spring and force the shift shaft

to its bore in the opposite side of the case opening.

7. Align the spring pin holes and install the spring pins.

8. Install the spring retainer in place over the control finger assembly.

9. Install the differential gear assembly into the clutch housing. Adjust the differential case end-play as follows:

a. Place two pieces of plastic type gauge material, approximately ¾ inch in length, on the differential ball bearing outer race, 180° apart.

b. Install the transaxle case and gasket. Tighten the mounting bolts to 26–30 ft. lbs. (35–41 Nm). Remove the bolts and the transaxle case. Lay the case aside for later installation.

c. Measure the thickness of the plastic type gauge material and select a spacer of the proper thickness to provide the standard end-play. The end-play should range between 0.000–0.0059 inch (0.0–0.15 mm).

d. Spacer thicknesses are as follows:

Inch	MM	I.D. Mark
0.0516	1.31	E
0.0551	1.40	None
0.0587	1.49	C
0.0622	1.58	B
0.0657	1.67	A
0.0693	1.76	F

10. Turn the sub–gear in the direction of the embossed arrow to align the 0.310 inch (8 mm) hole in the intermediate gear with that in the sub-gear. Insert a bar or bolt in the holes to maintain alignment.

11. Install the input shaft assembly and the intermediate shaft assembly into the clutch housing as a unit.

NOTE: KM 165 models—Install the selector shift rail and fork assembly at the same time.

12. Install the selector shaft poppet ball, poppet spring and plug. Apply sealer to the plug and seat it flush with the housing surface.

13. Install the input shaft bearing retainer and remove the bar or bolt used to retain the alignment of the sub-gear to the intermediate gear.

14. Install the output shaft assembly.

15. Install the interlock plungers into the housing. Reassemble the 1st/2nd and 3rd/4th speed shift rails and forks in the reverse order of removal, into the housing.

16. Align the holes in the shift rail and the shift fork and install the pin. The pin must have its slit on the shift rail center line. Even the spring pin protrusion on both sides.

17. Install the reverse shift rail and install the three poppet balls, springs and plugs.

NOTE: The poppet spring with the white paint I.D. must be installed in the

poppet hole of the reverse shift rail. Install the small diameter ends of the springs towards the steel balls.

18. Install the reverse shift lever assembly, the reverse idler gear and shaft and apply lubricate to the gear and shaft.

19. Measure the height of the reverse idler gear. The height from the face of the case to the upper flat of the gear should be 1.4429–1.5374 inch (37.85 ± 1.2 mm). If less than specified, replace the reverse shift lever assembly.

20. Apply sealer to the gasket and install on to the clutch housing.

21. Install the selected spacer on the differential side bearing and install the transaxle case. Install the bolts and torque to 26–30 ft. lbs. (35–41 Nm).

22. Install the intermediate and output shaft rear tapered bearing outer races and press them in by hand.

23. Install the oil seal into the axle output shaft case hole, if not previously done.

NOTE: The oil seal hole must be chamfered before the seal is installed into the case, to prevent periphery damage to the seal and subsequent leakage.

24. To select the outer race end spacer, use the following procedure:

a. Seat the outer races properly and measure the depths of the transaxle case to the races, using a depth micrometer.

b. Select a spacer for each race 0.004 inch (0.4 mm) thicker than the measured value.

c. Install the spacers in their respective bores and install the rear cover. Torque the bolts to 14–16 ft. lbs. (19–22 Nm).

d. Using the special tool seal installer or equivalent, shift the transaxle to any desired gear, while rotating the input shaft.

NOTE: The input shaft may turn hard and the installation of the clutch plate may be necessary to assist in turning the shaft.

e. Remove the rear cover after setting the transaxle in a position with the rear cover up.

f. Remove the spacers and remeasure the depth as was done in Step a.

g. Reselect spacers of proper thickness so that an end-play of 0.000–0.0020 inch (0.0–0.05 mm) exists at the tapered roller bearing outer races.

h. Spacer thicknesses are as follows:

Inch	MN	I.D. Mark
.0724	1.84	84
.0736	1.87	87
.0748	1.90	90
.0760	1.93	93
.0772	1.96	96
.0783	1.99	99
.0795	2.02	02
.0807	2.05	05

Inch	MN	I.D. Mark
.0819	2.08	08
.0831	2.11	11
.0843	2.14	14
.0854	2.17	17
.0866	2.20	20
.0878	2.23	23
.0890	2.26	26
.0902	2.29	29
.0913	2.32	32
.0925	2.35	35
.0937	2.38	38
.0949	2.41	41
.0961	2.44	44
.0972	2.47	47
.0984	2.50	50
.0996	2.53	53
.1008	2.56	56
.1020	2.59	59
.1031	2.62	62
.1043	2.65	65
.1055	2.68	68

25. Apply sealer to the gasket and reinstall the rear cover. Torque the bolts to 14–16 ft. lbs. (19–22 Nm).

26. Install the back-up lamp switch with washer and steel ball in place.

27. Verify that the transaxle shifts and the internal gear rotate smoothly.

TYPE 4

4 and 5 Speed Transaxle—Models F4WF60A, F5WF60A

Datsun

DISASSEMBLY

1. Remove the reverse light switch and drain the transmission.

2. Remove the bearing housing and primary gear as a unit.

3. Remove the primary gear cover.

4. Take the bottom cover off the transmission. Put reverse and 1st gears into position (to keep the shaft from turning) and remove the main gear locknut.

5. Remove the primary gear cover.

6. Remove the clutch housing.

7. If necessary, drive out the drive and idler bearing with a puller. Then press the bearing out of the main drive input gear.

8. Remove the differential side flanges.

9. Remove the speedometer pinion gear.

10. Remove the differential case as a unit.

11. Pull the differential side bearings and remove the ring gear mounting bolts.

12. Remove the differential case and withdraw the pinion shaft and remove the side gear and pinion mate.

13. Loosen bolts D1 and D2 and remove the reverse fork lever and bracket. Loosen double nuts E1 and bolts D3 and remove the bearing retainer.

NOTE: Double nuts E1 should be loosened before bolts D3.

14. Remove the reverse idler gear and shaft and drive out the countergear and countershaft guide.

NOTE: The needle bearing on the countergear is not a retainer type. When removing the gear, do not allow the bearing to come off.

15. Remove the transmission case service plug. This will allow access to the roll pin on the 1st/2nd shift fork.

Using a punch, drive the roll pins out of the shift forks. Withdraw the fork rods and remove the shift forks.

NOTE: When driving out the roll pin from the 3rd/4th shift fork, shift the rod to 3rd gear before starting. Also be careful of the placement of the interlock plungers.

1. Primary drive gear
2. Primary idler gear
3. Sub gear
4. Main drive input gear
5. Main drive gear
6. Baulk ring
7. Spread spring
8. Coupling sleeve
9. Shifting insert
10. Synchronizer hub
11. 3rd main gear
12. Main gear bushing
13. Main gear spacer
14. 2nd main gear
15. 1st main gear
16. Reverse main gear
17. Main shaft
18. Final gear
19. Counter gear
20. Thrust washer
21. Thrust spring
22. Counter shaft
23. Reverse idler gear
24. Reverse idler shaft
25. Bearing retainer

4-speed gear components

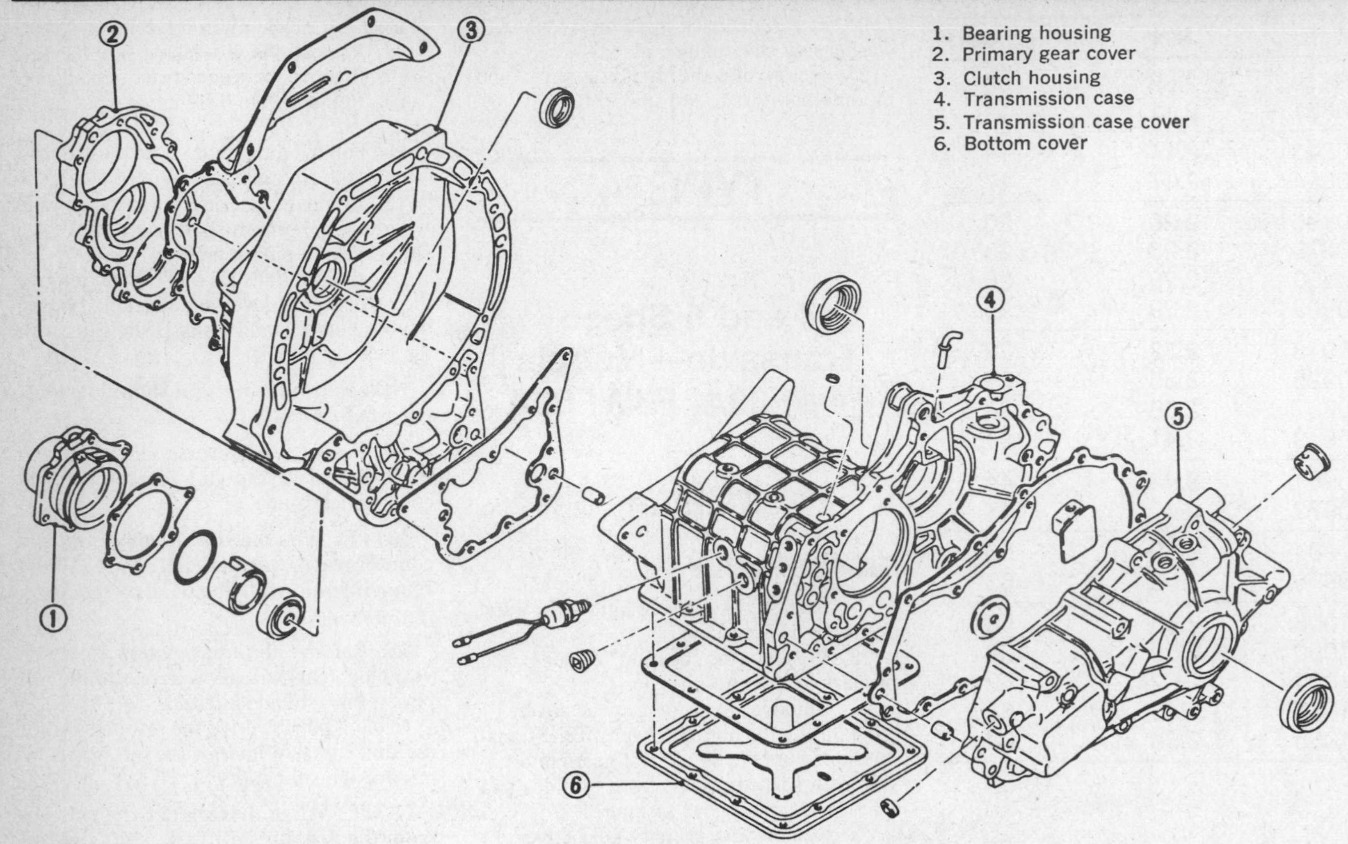

1. Bearing housing
2. Primary gear cover
3. Clutch housing
4. Transmission case
5. Transmission case cover
6. Bottom cover

Transaxle case components

16. Remove the mainshaft gear assembly and the main drive gear toward the final drive gear side.

NOTE: The locknut is caulked, but you do not have to remove the caulking for loosening.

17. Remove the mainshaft components in this order: 3rd/4th synchronizer, 3rd gear, main gear bushing, main gear spacer, 2nd gear, main gear bushing, 1st/2nd synchronizer, 1st gear, main gear bushing and reverse gear.

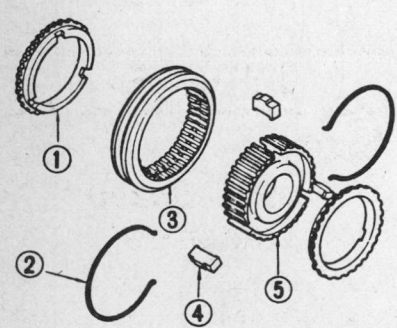

1. Baulk ring
2. Spread spring
3. Coupling sleeve
4. Shifting insert
5. Synchronizer hub

Exploded view of synchronizer unit

NOTE: The 3rd main gear bushing and mainshaft are press–fit. Remove the bushing with the main gear spacer and the 2nd main gear with a puller.

18. Press out the bearing from the mainshaft.

19. To disassemble a synchronizer, remove the spread springs and the shifting inserts, then separate the coupling sleeve from the synchro-hub.

ASSEMBLY

Generally, the procedures for assembly are the reverse of removal. However, there are certain steps you must observe.

1. Slide the synchro-hub into the coupling sleeve and fit the shifting inserts into their grooves.

2. Put one spread spring on the lower side of the shifting inserts to hold them to the inner side of the coupling sleeve. Put the other spread spring on the opposite side of the synchro-hub.

NOTE: Make sure the spread springs are opposite each other.

3. Press the ball bearing onto the mainshaft and assemble the reverse gear. Assemble the main gear bushing and 1st gear.

NOTE: Be sure to align the oil hole in the bushing with the one on the mainshaft.

4. Assemble baulk ring, synchronizer, main gear bushing, baulk ring, 2nd gear,

main gear spacer, main gear bushing, 3rd gear, baulk ring, synchronizer and locknut on the mainshaft.

5. Put the spacers and needles into both sides of the countergear. Be sure to grease the needles before inserting.

6. Insert a countershaft guide into the countergear.

7. Press the differential side bearing into the differential case.

8. Put the pinion mates, side gears, thrust washers and pinion shaft in the case.

9. Select the proper thrust washer to adjust side gear end-play to 0.008 in., then apply oil to the gear teeth and thrust surfaces.

10. Put the ring gear onto the differential case.

11. Press in the differential side flange oil seals after lubricating their lips with grease.

12. Assemble the main drive gear and mainshaft in the transmission case.

13. Put in the 1st/2nd shift fork and the 3rd/4th fork. Make sure they are into their grooves in the coupling sleeves.

14. Slide the 3rd/4th fork rod through the transmission case and the 3rd/4th shift fork. Secure it with a new retaining pin.

15. Assemble the check ball, spring and check ball plug. Before tightening, apply sealer to the plug. Be sure to align the notch in the 3rd/4th rod with the check ball. Place the unit in Neutral. Assemble the 1st/2nd and reverse fork rod similarly.

16. With the countershaft guide in place

1. Primary drive gear
2. Primary idler gear
3. Sub gear
4. Main drive input gear
5. Main drive gear
6. Baulk ring
7. Spread spring
8. Coupling sleeve
9. Shifting insert
10. Synchronizer hub
11. 4th main gear
12. 4th gear bushing

13. Main gear spacer
14. 3rd main gear
15. 2nd main gear
16. Reverse main gear
17. Main shaft
18. Final gear
19. 1st main gear
20. Counter gear
21. 1st-reverse counter gear
22. Reverse idler gear
23. Reverse idler input gear

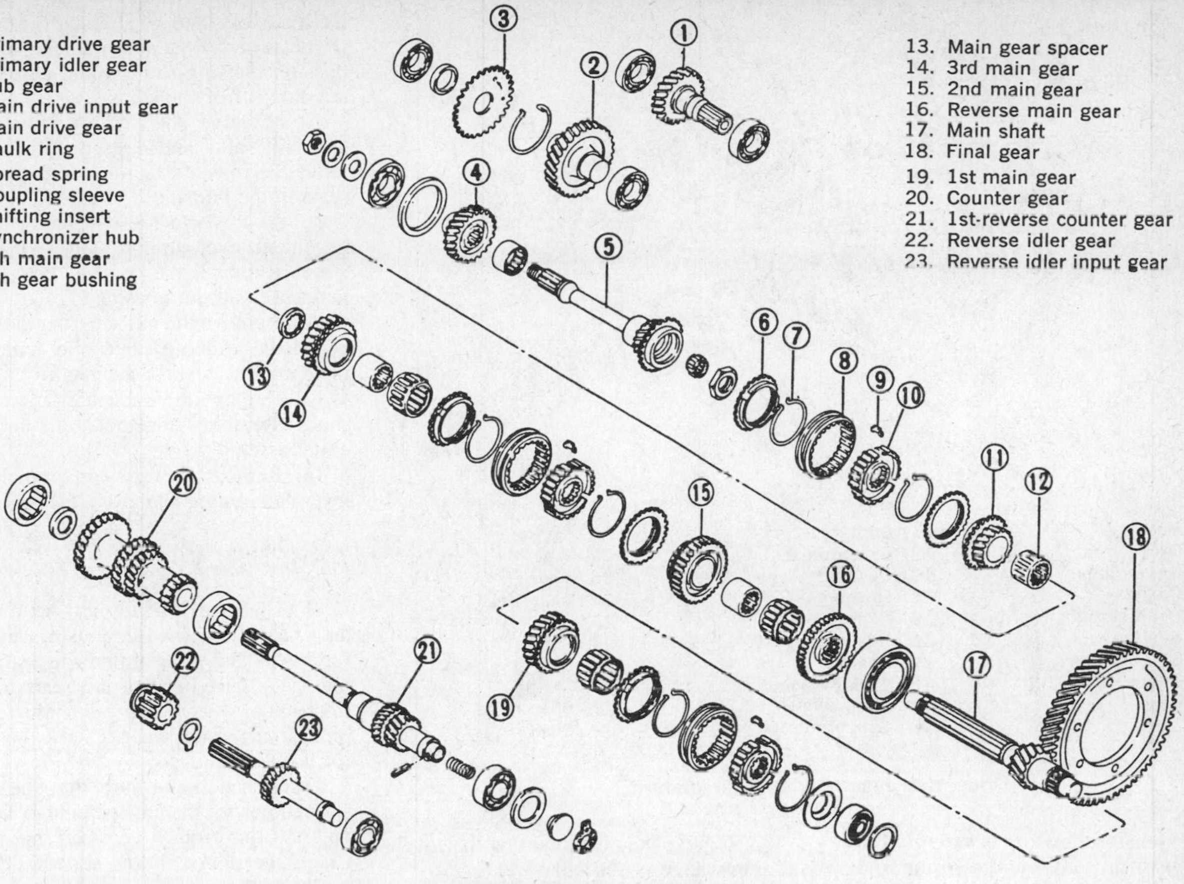

5-speed gear components

in the countergear, install the countergear, thrust washers and thrust spring on the transmission case. Insert the countershaft into the countergear and drive out the guide.

NOTE: Pay attention to the direction of thrust washer assembly. Align the cut out portion of the countershaft with the bearing retainer.

17. Assemble the reverse idler shaft, reverse idler gear, bearing retainer, reverse fork and fork bracket with the cutout portion of the reverse idler shaft aligned with the bearing retainer.
18. Before installing the differential case, measure bearing height "H".
If it is 4.720–4.730 in., a shim is not needed.
If it is 4.715–4.719 in., use a 0.0078 shim.
If it is 4.710–4.714 in., use a 0.0118 shim.
19. With the fork rods in Neutral, put the case cover onto the transmission.

NOTE: Make sure the shifter engages with the fork rod brackets correctly. If the resin-coating comes off the bolt threads, the bolt should not be reused.

20. Assemble the differential side flanges.
21. Put the clutch housing on the transmission case and press the bearings onto the primary and main drive input gears. Assemble the sub-gear on the idler gear.

a. Insert both ends of the ring spring into the 0.197 in. hole on the primary idler gear and sub-gear. Install the spacer and press the bearing onto the idler gear.

NOTE: Select a spacer that will insure that the sub-gear end-play is less than 0.004 in.

22. Put the idler gear into the clutch housing and assemble the main drive gear, setting the idler sub-gear by inserting a bar into the hole in the idler gear through the sub-gear.
23. Put the thrust washer, lock washer and drive gear together in that order.

NOTE: As in removal, mesh two gears to keep the mainshaft from turning while tightening.

24. Assemble the primary gear cover and install the bearing housing assembly and drive gear. Rotate the drive gear while assembling.
25. Assemble the bottom cover, speedometer gear, reverse light switch, drain plug and service hole plug.

5-Speed Transaxle

Most of the procedures described in the 4-speed section apply to the 5-speed, with the following exceptions:

When removing the mainshaft and drive gear, you may have to tap the end of the mainshaft with a hammer.

When assembling the 3rd main gear bushing, make sure the claw is lined up with the main gear spacer and that the thinner spline tooth side of the 2nd/3rd synchro-hub must point towards 3rd gear.

When installing the main gear spacer, make sure that the uneven side is pointed toward 4th gear. The 4th gear bushing is the same as the 4-speed main gear bushing.

TYPE 5

4 and 5 Speed Transaxle

Fiat

DISASSEMBLY

**NOTE: The five speed transaxle case and gear arrangement is basically the same as the four speed transaxle, except

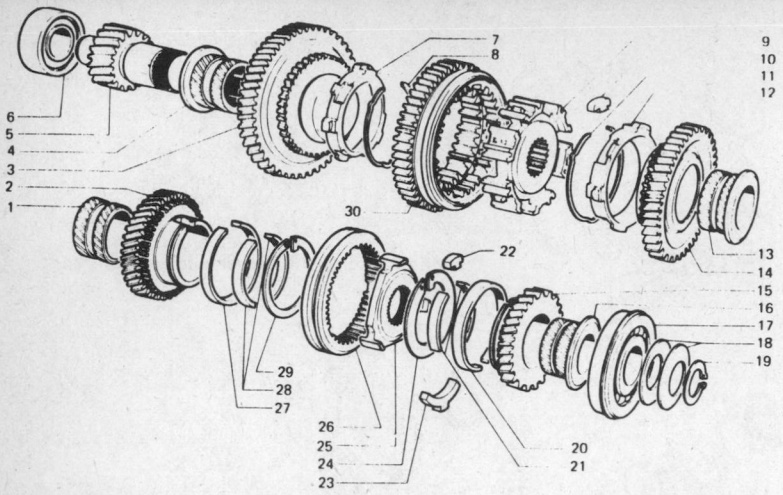

1. Bushing
2. Driven gear
3. Driven gear
4. Bushing
5. Countershaft
6. Bearing
7. Synchronizer
8. Spring
9. Hub
10. Pad
11. Spring
12. Synchronizer
13. Bushing
14. Driven gear
15. Gear
16. Bushing
17. Bearing
18. Spring washer
19. Snap ring
20. Synchronizer
21. Spring
22. Pad
23. Pad
24. Snap ring
25. Hub
26. Sleeve
27. Synchronizer
28. Spring
29. Snap ring
30. Sleeve

Drive gear assembly on countershaft

the rear extension housing is extended to include the fifth gear on the input and output shafts and shift forks are controlled by the fifth and reverse selector rail.

1. Remove the drain plug and drain the lubricant from the transmission/differential.

2. Remove the screws securing the oil boots and remove the axle shafts together with the oil boots.

3. Remove the nuts retaining the cover and remove the cover and gasket.

4. Remove the snap-ring from the mainshaft bearing.

5. Compress the spring washer in the countershaft and remove the snap-ring from the countershaft.

6. Remove the detent ball spring cover and gasket for the shift control rods. Remove the three ball springs and balls.

7. Remove the two ball bearings from the mainshaft and countershaft.

8. Remove the nuts attaching the transmission housing to the main case and lift the case off of the studs.

9. Remove the screws retaining the gearshift forks and dogs to the rods. Remove the rods, forks, and dogs from their seats in the housing.

10. Remove the gear selector and engagement lever support.

11. Remove the gasket between the maincase and the housing.

12. Remove the nut securing the reverse gearshaft retaining plate and remove the plate and the reverse gearshaft.

13. Remove the mainshaft and countershaft assemblies together with the differential assembly.

14. Remove the screw retaining the shift lever and remove the gear shift control rod.

ASSEMBLY

1. Clean all of the parts with solvent and check the maincase, housing, and cover for cracks and wear or damage to the bearing seats. Check all of the seals for deterioration or wear. Check all shafts for chipping or excessive wear. Check the splines for wear or damage.

Check and make sure that the sliding sleeve hubs for the engagement of first/second and third/fourth gears are not nicked. Check the sleeve sliding surface.

Check the synchronizer rings for signs of deterioration on the inside surface and on the teeth that mesh with the sliding sleeves. The rings must not be loose in their gear seat.

If splined parts do not slide easily and smoothly, remove the cause with a very fine file or replace the defective parts.

2. Install the bearing for the countershaft into the clutch cover end of the transmission case.

3. Install the outer bearing race for the differential bearing onto the case.

4. Install the gear shift control rod in the housing with the spring, gasket, cover, and boot. Next install the control lever.

5. Install the differential assembly in the housing.

6. Install the countershaft assembly in the housing.

7. Install the mainshaft assembly in the housing.

8. Install the reverse gearshaft with its gasket in the housing. Secure the reverse gearshaft assembly with the plate and nut.

9. Install the gasket onto the housing mating surface.

10. Make sure that the gear selector and engagement lever is sealed on the control lever attached to the gear control rod. Install the support for the selector and engagement lever on the housing. Secure the support with the nut.

11. Install the rod detent rollers in their seats on the support.

12. Install the gear selector rods, forks, and dogs.

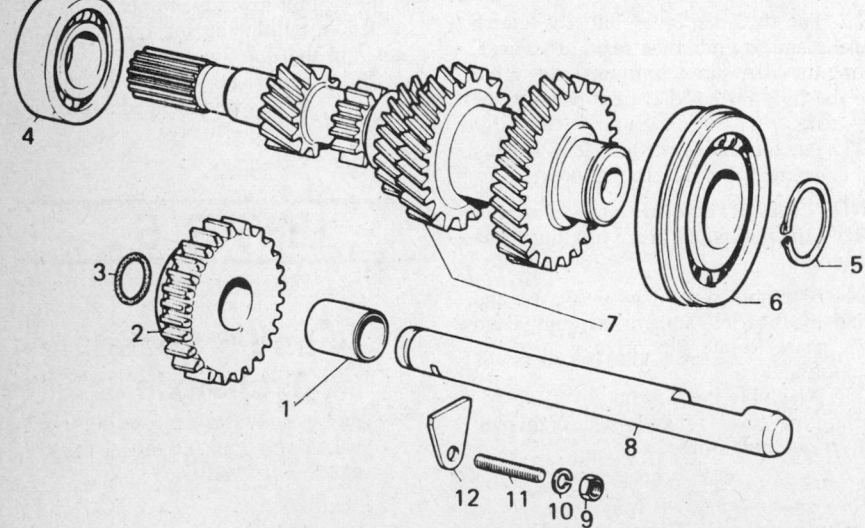

1. Bushing
2. Gear
3. Seal
4. Bearing
5. Snap ring
6. Bearing
7. Mainshaft
8. Shaft
9. Nut
10. Lockwasher
11. Stud
12. Plate

Mainshaft trand reverse and reverse idler gear

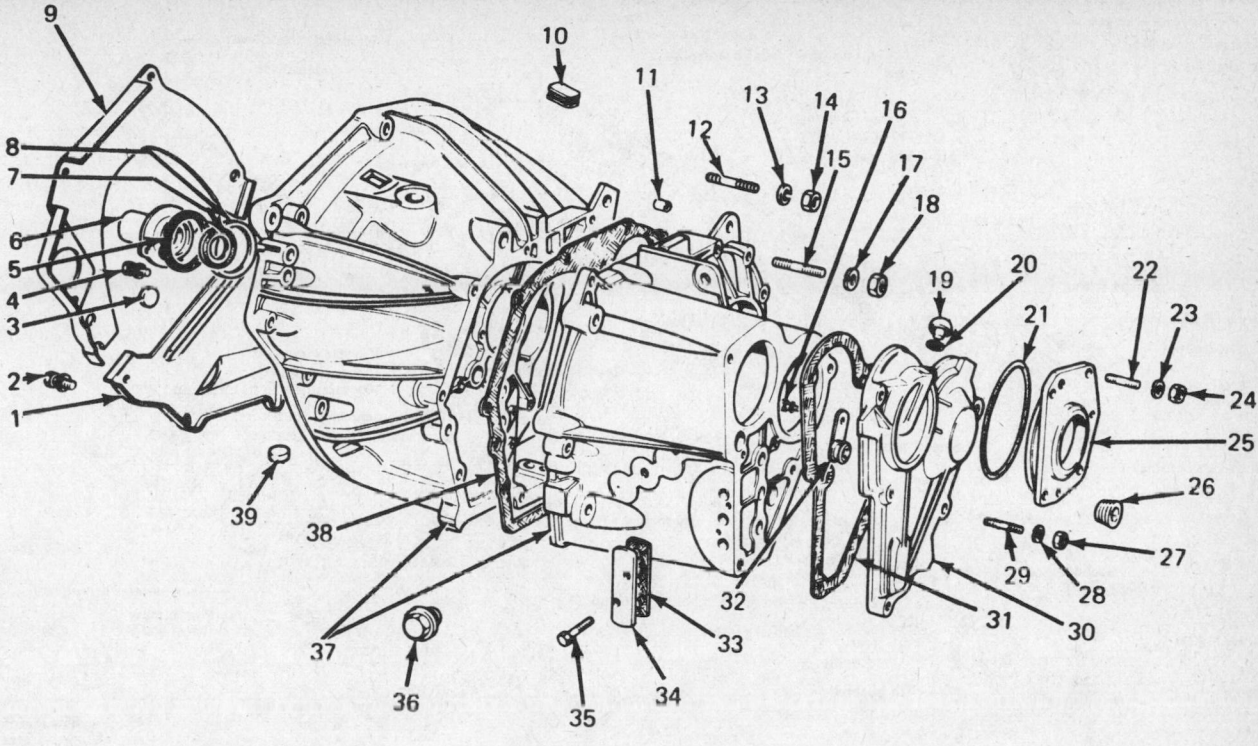

1. Cover	6. Cover	11. Dowel	16. Bolt and washer	21. Seal	26. Plug	31. Gasket	36. Plug
2. Bolt and washer	7. Seal	12. Stud	17. Lockwasher	22. Stud	27. Nut	32. Magnet	37. Case
3. Plug	8. Plug	13. Lockwasher	18. Nut	23. Lockwasher	28. Lockwasher	33. Gasket	38. Gasket
4. Bolt and washer	9. Cover	14. Nut	19. Vent	24. Nut	29. Stud	34. Cover	39. Plug
5. Gasket	10. Plug	15. Stud	20. Gasket	25. Flange	30. Cover	35. Bolt	

13. Install the transmission case on the housing.

14. Secure the two halves of the transmission case together with the washers and nuts.

15. Install the three detent balls and springs in the transmission case.

16. Install the gasket and spring retainer cover. Secure the cover with the two bolts.

17. Install the bearing on the countershaft. Install the two spring washers and snap-ring on the countershaft. Install the snap-ring on the mainshaft.

18. Install the gasket and cover on the transmission.

19. Set the differential bearing.

20. Install the clutch release fork lever and sliding sleeve.

TYPE 6

4 and 5 Speed Transaxle—Models RN4F30A, RS5F30A and RS5F31A

Datsun/Nissan

TRANSMISSION CASE

Transaxle case assembly

Disassembly

1. Drain the oil from the transmission case.

2. Remove the mounting bolts, tap the case lightly with a rubber mallet and then lift off the transmission case.

NOTE: When removing the transmission case, tilt it slightly to prevent interference from the 5th gear shift fork.

3. Disconnect the back-up light switch and then remove the oil gutter.

4. Remove the input shaft bearing.

5. Remove the case cover, the mainshaft bearing adjusting shim and the spacer.

6. Remove the mainshaft bearing rear outer race and the differential side bearing outer race.

7. Draw out the reverse idler spacer.

Assembly

1. Press fit the differential side bearing outer race and the mainshaft rear bearing outer race.

2. Install the input shaft needle bearing. Apply sealant to the welch plug and then install it on the transmission case.

3. Install the oil gutter. Apply sealant to the back-up light switch and install it.

4. If the transmission case has been replaced, adjust the differential side bearing and the mainshaft rotary frictional force by means of shims.

5. Apply an even coating of sealant to

the mating surfaces of the transmission case and the clutch housing. Mount the case on the clutch housing and tighten the mounting bolts to 12–15 ft. lbs.

6. Remove the transmission case cover. Clean the mating surfaces and apply sealant to the transmission case.

7. Install the case cover with the convex side facing outward. Tighten the mounting bolts to 4.6–6.1 ft. lbs.

8. Check that the gears move freely and then install the drain plug (with sealant) and fill with lubricant.

CLUTCH HOUSING

Disassembly

1. Drain the oil and then remove the transmission case.

2. Draw out the reverse idler spacer and fork shaft, then remove the 5th/3rd/4th shift fork.

NOTE: Do not lose the shifter caps.

3. Remove the control bracket with the 1st and 2nd gear shift fork.

NOTE: Be careful not to lose the select check ball, spring and the shifter caps (5 spd only).

On Stanza:

4. Remove the mainshaft and final drive assembly. Be sure to pull the mainshaft straight out.

5. Remove the bearing retainer securing bolts.

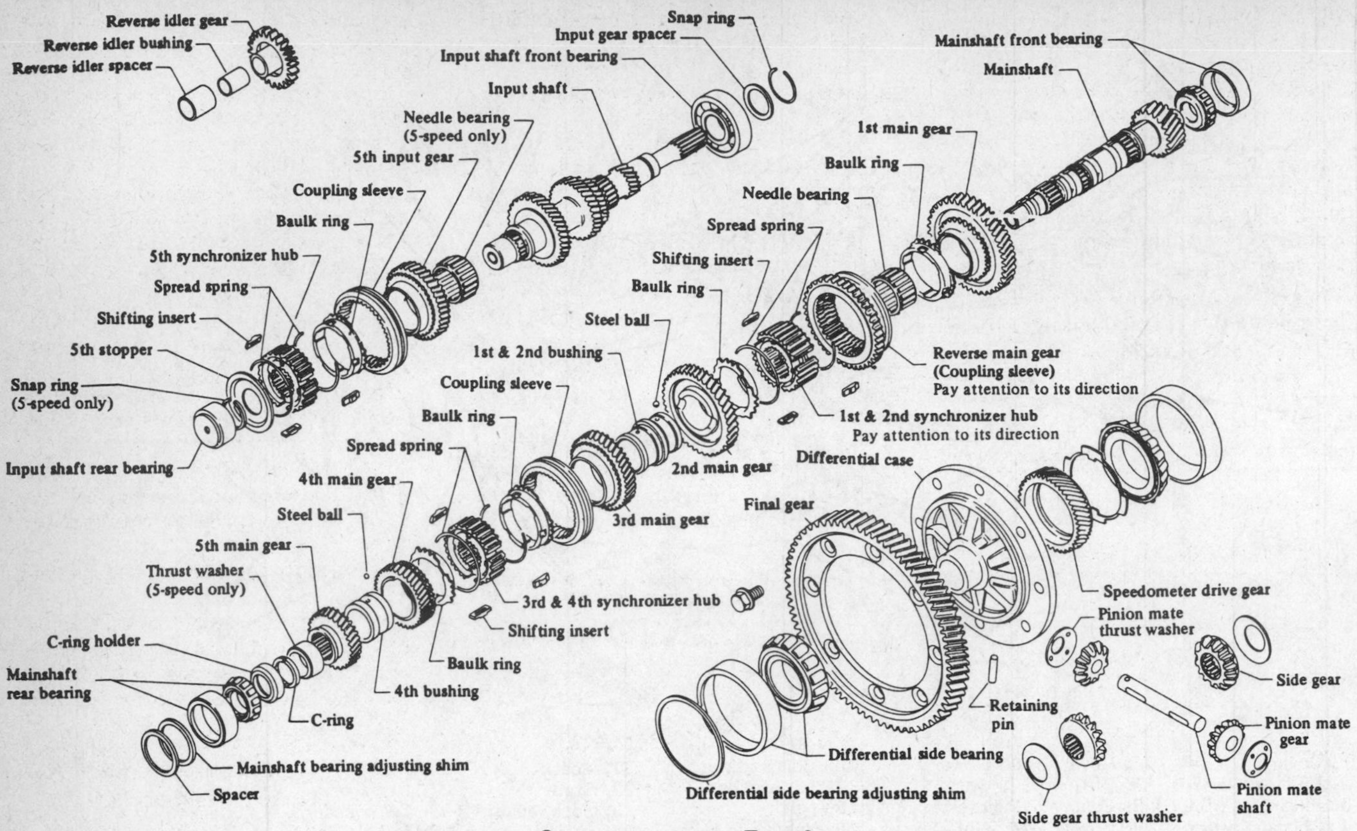

Reverse idler gear
Reverse idler bushing
Reverse idler spacer
Snap ring
Input gear spacer
Input shaft front bearing
Input shaft
Mainshaft front bearing
Mainshaft
Needle bearing (5-speed only)
5th input gear
Coupling sleeve
Baulk ring
5th synchronizer hub
Spread spring
Shifting insert
5th stopper
Snap ring (5-speed only)
Input shaft rear bearing
1st main gear
Baulk ring
Needle bearing
Spread spring
Shifting insert
Baulk ring
Steel ball
1st & 2nd bushing
Coupling sleeve
Baulk ring
Spread spring
4th main gear
Steel ball
5th main gear
Thrust washer (5-speed only)
C-ring holder
Mainshaft rear bearing
C-ring
Mainshaft bearing adjusting shim
Spacer
3rd main gear
2nd main gear
3rd & 4th synchronizer hub
Shifting insert
Baulk ring
4th bushing
Reverse main gear (Coupling sleeve) Pay attention to its direction
1st & 2nd synchronizer hub Pay attention to its direction
Differential case
Final gear
Differential side bearing
Differential side bearing adjusting shim
Speedometer drive gear
Pinion mate thrust washer
Side gear
Retaining pin
Pinion mate gear
Side gear thrust washer
Pinion mate shaft

Gear components—Type 6

Oil pocket
Oil seal
Clutch housing
Bearing retainer
Filler plug
Torx screw
* Switch plug
Speedometer pinion assembly
Oil seal
* Neutral switch
* Switch plug
Welch plug
Oil seal
Oil channel
Oil gutter
* Switch plug
Dust cover
Transmission case
Case cover
* Reverse lamp switch
Oil seal
Drain plug

* Apply locking sealer to threads of switches.

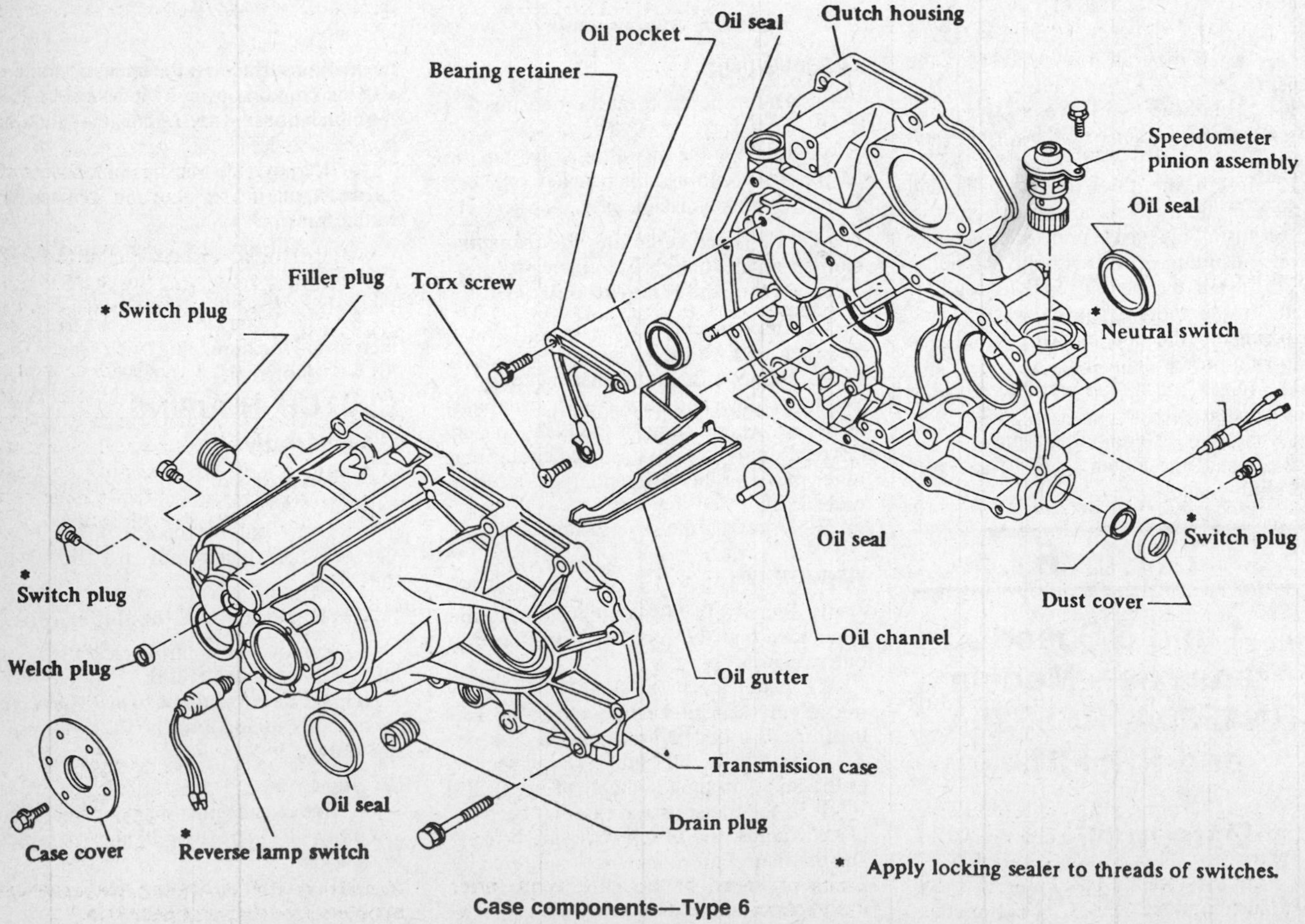

Case components—Type 6

All Other Models:

6. Remove the three screws and detach the bearing retainer. One of the screws is a special torx–type and should be removed using a special torx–head allen wrench.

7. Turn the clutch housing so that its side is facing down. Lightly tap the end of the input shaft (on the engine side) with a rubber mallet and then remove the input shaft along with the bearing retainer and reverse idler gear.

NOTE: Don't remove the reverse idler shaft from the clutch housing because these fittings will be loose.

--- **CAUTION** ---

Do not scratch the oil seal lip with the input shaft spline while removing the shaft.

8. Remove the reverse idler gear and final drive assembly.

9. Remove the oil pocket, shift check ball and springs and then the check ball plugs.

10. Drive the retaining pin out of the striking lever. Remove the striking rod, lever and interlock.

   a. Select a position where the pin doesn't interfere with the clutch housing when removing it.

   b. When removing the striking rod, be careful not to damage the oil seal lip. It may be a good idea to tape the edges of the striking rod when removing it.

11. Remove the reverse and 5th gear check plug and then detach the check spring and balls. Remove the reverse and 5th gear check assembly.

12. Remove the clutch control shaft, release bearing and clutch lever.

13. Remove the mainshaft bearing outer race. Remove the differential side bearing outer race.

14. Remove the oil channel.

Assembly

1. Install a new oil channel so that the oil groove in the channel faces the oil pocket.

2. Install the mainshaft bearing and differential side bearing outer races.

3. Install the clutch control shaft, release bearing and clutch lever.

4. Install the oil pocket.

NOTE: Make sure that oil flows from the oil pocket to the oil channel.

5. Install the reverse and 5th gear check assembly. The smaller check ball is inserted first and then the larger one.

NOTE: When installing the clutch housing and reverse and 5th gear check assembly, it is necessary to adjust the reverse check force.

   a. Install a used check plug and tighten it to 14–18 ft. lbs.

   b. Use a spring gauge to measure the spring check force (139–200 in. lbs.—4 spd; 195–239 in lbs.—5 spd).

   c. If the reverse check force is not within the above ranges, select another

check plug of a different length until the specifications can be met.

6. Installation of the remaining components is in the reverse order of removal. Please note the following:

   a. Follow all NOTES and CAUTIONS listed under the Disassembly procedures.

   b. Apply a locking sealer to the threads of the torx screw and tighten it to 12–15 ft. lbs. Use a punch and stake the head of the screw at two points.

   c. Tighten the bearing retainer bolts to 12–15 ft. lbs.

   d. Coat the select check ball (5 spd) and shifter caps with grease before installing.

   e. Coat the support spring with grease before installing it. This will prevent the spring from falling into the hole for the fork shaft in the clutch housing.

TYPE 7

4 and 5 Speed Transaxle

Honda

DISASSEMBLY

1. Remove the transmission end cover. Check the transmission mainshaft and countershaft end-play. End-play should be between 0.002–0.003 in. If the clearance is excessive, inspect the ball bearings after transmission disassembly.

2. Remove the locking tab from the mainshaft locknut. *The mainshaft locknut has left hand threads.* Place the transmission in gear and place the proper size wrench on the countershaft to keep it from moving. Remove the mainshaft locknut.

3. Remove the mainshaft bearing and the large snap-ring.

4. Loosen the three shift detent lock ball screws. Remove the screws, springs and balls.

5. Remove the transmission case bolts. Lightly tap the case with a hammer and drift and separate the case. *Do not pry the case apart with a screwdriver.*

6. Remove the reverse idler gear and shaft. Remove the reverse shift fork.

7. Remove the shift selector assembly. If repair to the shift selector is necessary, disassemble as follows:

   a. Remove the two screws and retaining plate. Stake the screws when reinstalling.

   b. Push the shift arm into the reverse position (towards the large spring). Then release it.

   c. The pivot shaft holds a spring loaded detent. Do not lose the detent ball and spring when removing. Remove the pivot shaft.

   d. Remove the interlock bar and shift arms.

   e. During reassembly, insert a screwdriver into the reverse side (large spring end) of the arm assembly to hold down the detent ball, while inserting the pivot shaft.

8. Remove the shift fork retaining bolts and pull the shift shafts up until they clear the case. Remove the forks and shafts.

NOTE: When reinstalling the fork retaining bolts turn the shaft so the threaded portion of the hole is facing away from the bolt.

9. Remove the mainshaft and countershaft at the same time by holding the two shafts and lightly tapping the flywheel end of the mainshaft.

10. Remove the shift rod boot, shift arm, lock washer and bolt. Remove the shift rod and shift arm.

NOTE: During installation of the shift arm retaining bolt, turn the shaft so that the threaded portion of the hole is facing away from the bolt.

11. Measure the side clearance of the low gear with a feeler gauge, if the clearance is excessive, replace the thrust plate. Perform the same measurement on the remaining gears, if the clearance is beyond the service limit, replace the bearing race (spacer). See chart for specifications.

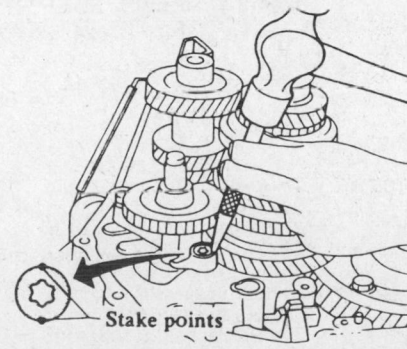

Stake the head of the Torx screw after installation—Type 6

Stake points

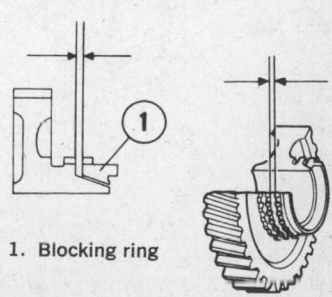

1. Blocking ring

Measuring the clearance between the synchronizer ring and gear hub

1. Needle roller bearing set plate
2. Needle roller bearing
3. Clutch case
4. Reverse gear shaft
5. Reverse idle gear
6. Reverse shift fork
7. Shift selector assembly
8. Countershaft gear assembly
9. Main shaft
10. First/second fork shaft
11. Reverse fork shaft
12. Third/fourth fork shaft
13. Steel ball
14. Ball set spring
15. Drain plug washer
16. Set ball spring screw
17. Ball bearing
18. Needle roller bearing
19. 48 mm snap ring
20. Ball bearing
21. 62 mm snap ring
22. 23 mm lock nut
23. 20 mm lock nut
24. Transmission rear cover
25. Speedometer gear

Exploded view of typical Honda manual transmission

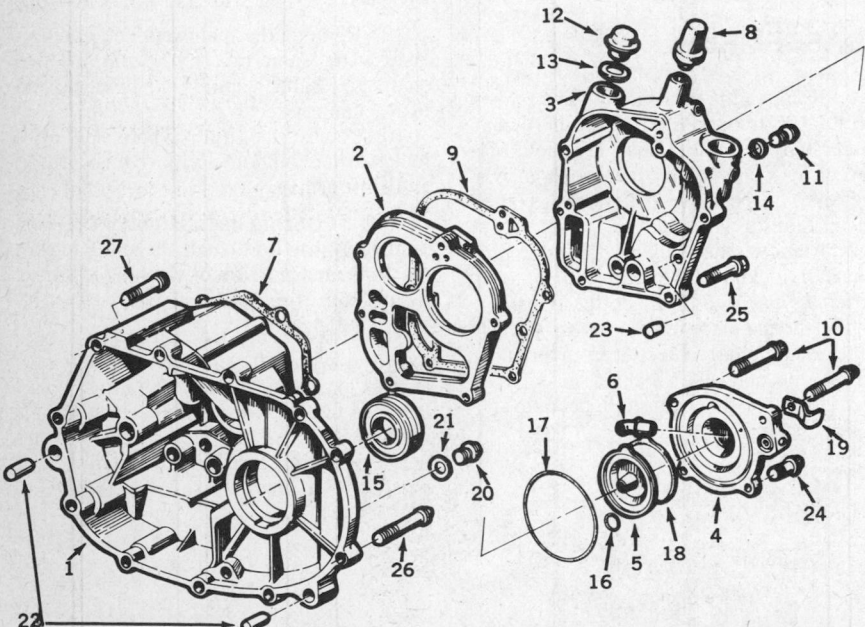

1 Housing, transmission
2 Spacer, transmission housing
3 Cover, transmission
4 Cover, right side
5 Plate, oil barrier
6 Tube, breather
7 Gasket, transmission housing
8 Cap, breather
9 Gasket, transmission case
10 Bolt, flanged, 6 x 85 mm
11 Bolt, oil check
12 Bolt, plug 25 mm
13 Washer, sealing, 25 mm
14 Washer, 8 mm
15 Oil seal, 35 x 56 x 9 mm
16 O-ring, 9.4 x 2.4
17 O-ring, 64.5 x 3
18 O-ring, 42 x 2.4
19 Bracket, wire harness
20 Bolt, drain plug, 14 mm
21 Washer, drain plug, 14 mm
22 Pin, dowel, 14 x 20 mm
23 Pin, dowel, 8 x 14 mm
24 Bolt, flanged, 6 x 20 mm
25 Bolt, flanged, 6 x 45 mm
26 Bolt, flanged, 8 x 40 mm
27 Bolt, flanged, 8 x 45 mm

Exploded view of housing and cover assemblies

12. If the countershaft must be disassembled to adjust the clearances, or replace gears, remove the locknut by installing the shaft in the case and holding the differential securely.

NOTE: Place the end lugs of the holder in the case and center the lug in the hole of the differential carrier.

13. Remove the two screws and retaining plate which hold the countershaft bearing. Remove the countershaft bearing with a bearing puller.

14. Clean all component parts thoroughly in the proper solvent.

15. Inspect the surfaces of each gear and blocking ring for roughness or damage. Apply a thin coat of oil to the tapered surfaces of each gear and push them together with a rotating motion. Measure the distance between the ring and gear. Replace all necessary parts. Clearance should be between 0.120-0.139 in.

16. Measure the clearance between the shift forks and synchronizer sleeves. The clearance should be between 0.039-0.018. If clearances are excessive, replace the shift forks, synchronizers or both.

17. Ensure that there are no restrictions in the oil holes on the countershaft. Check the splines for wear.

18. Inspect the condition of the main-shaft and countershaft bearing surfaces. Check run-out, gear tooth and spline condition.

19. Check the condition of all the gears. Check the condition of all bearing surfaces.

20. Inspect the bearing race (spacer) of each gear.

21. Replace all questionable parts.

ASSEMBLY

1. The transmission should be assembled in the reverse order of disassembly. During assembly, note the following points:

2. Check the differential bearing clearance.

3. Apply a thin coat of oil to all parts before they are installed.

4. Be certain that hub and synchronizer teeth match when they are assembled.

5. The mainshaft and countershaft must be installed at the same time. Next, install the third/fourth shift fork and shaft, first/second shift fork and shaft, and then the reverse shaft.

6. When the shift selector assembly is installed, there are two special bolts which must be inserted first. These bolts locate the assembly.

7. Lock the mainshaft and countershaft locknuts with a punch.

8. Make sure that the mainshaft and countershaft turn smoothly and that all gears engage freely. Check and be certain that all bolts are properly torqued.

TYPE 8

4 and 5 Speed Transaxle

Porsche

NOTE: Turbo (930) transaxle similar.

When disassembling and assembling a four speed transaxle, the procedures described in the five speed overhaul should be followed. The gear arrangement, 1st through 4th, on the pinion shaft in the four speed transaxle, it same as the gear arrangement, 2nd through 5th, in the five speed unit, with the front cover housing only the reverse gear.

Because of the reverse action of the 1st speed synchronizer in the four speed unit, as compared to the five speed unit, the synchronizer components have to be installed directly opposite each other. When installing the synchronizer components for the 1st speed in the four speed transaxle, it should be remembered to insert only one brake band.

The sportomatic transaxle unit is not covered in the manual transaxle section.

External shifting controls have been relocated from the front of the transaxle to the side on one model and the case has been modified from a tunnel type to a removable gear housing type on an other model. The gear trains remain basically the same in all models.

DISASSEMBLY

1. Mount the transaxle securely and drain the lubricating fluid.

2. Remove the starter assembly and the center caps from the drive flanges.

3. Remove the retaining bolts from the drive flanges and remove the flanges from the inner axle stub shafts.

NOTE: Place the transaxle in gear and block the input shaft to prevent turning.

4. Remove the side cover assembly and withdraw the differential assembly.

5. Remove the crossmember from the front cover, if not previously done, and remove the front cover assembly.

— CAUTION —
During the front cover removal, the reverse gear components may drop. Prevent from falling to the floor.

6. Remove the 1st/reverse selector fork retaining screw and remove the gear with the fork.

7. Remove the retaining bolt from the pinion shaft.

8. Remove the roll pin from the castled nut on the input shaft. Remove the castle nut and the 1st speed gear.

9. Place the transaxle gears in the neutral position and remove the retaining nut from the plate of the inner shift rod guide fork and remove the guide fork.

10. Remove the inner shift rod through the rear access hole. Shift the gears into the 5th speed position with a suitable bar and remove the intermediate plate with the gear clusters.

NOTE: A plastic hammer may be needed to lightly tap the plate loose.

— CAUTION —
The gear cluster can be installed or removed from the housing only when the transaxle gears are in the 5th speed gear position.

Intermediate Plate and Gear Cluster

DISASSEMBLY

1. Install the intermediate plate assembly in a vise or similar holder and remove the 1st/reverse hub gear, using two suitable prybars.

2. Remove the gear Number two of the 1st speed, along with the needle bearing cage.

3. Shift the gear assembly into neutral position. Remove the selector shaft detent plug and remove the detent spring.

4. Remove the 1st/reverse selector shaft, along with the detent ball.

NOTE: Mark all selector forks and rails during the disassembly to avoid assembly problems.

5. Remove the 2nd/3rd selector fork retaining screw. Remove the selector shaft, fork and detent.

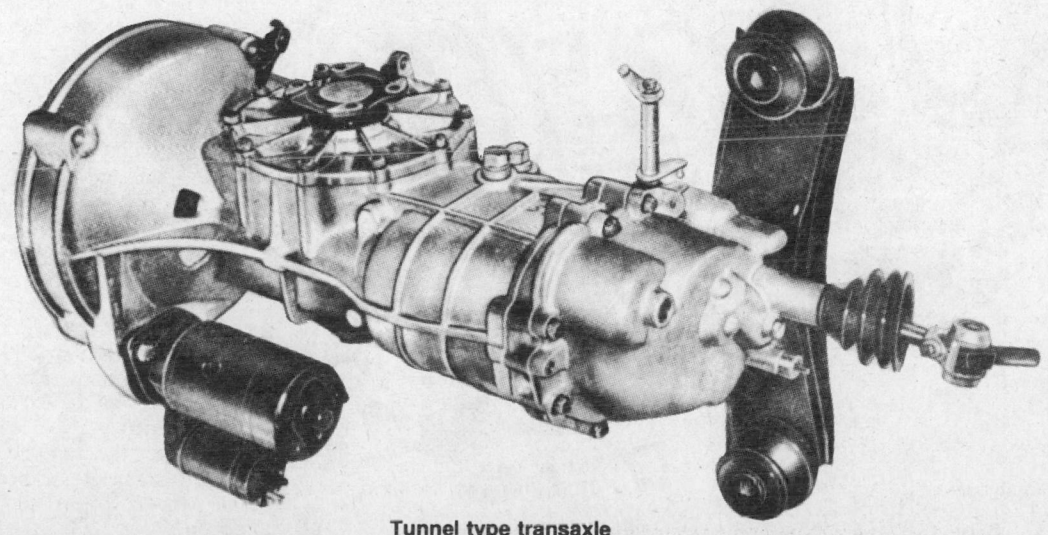

Tunnel type transaxle

6. Remove the 4th and 5th selector fork retaining screw. Remove the selector shaft, fork and detent ball.

7. Remove the detent ball, spring and detent.

8. The input and pinion shafts must be pressed from the intermediate plate.

NOTE: To allow the intermediate plate to lay flat on the press, drive the aligning dowels into the plate and remove the throttle linkage.

9. Remove the bearing plate assembly. Heat the intermediate plate to 248° F. (120° C.) and press the bearings from the plate.

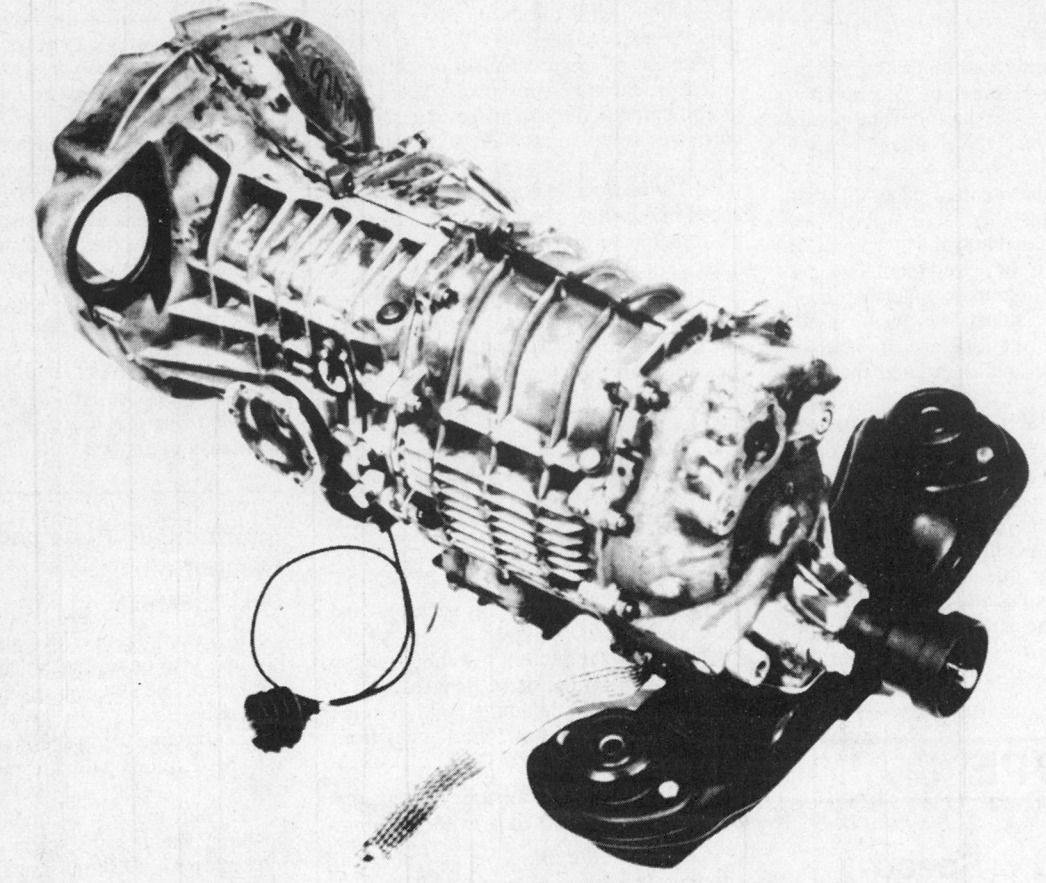

Non-tunnel type transaxle

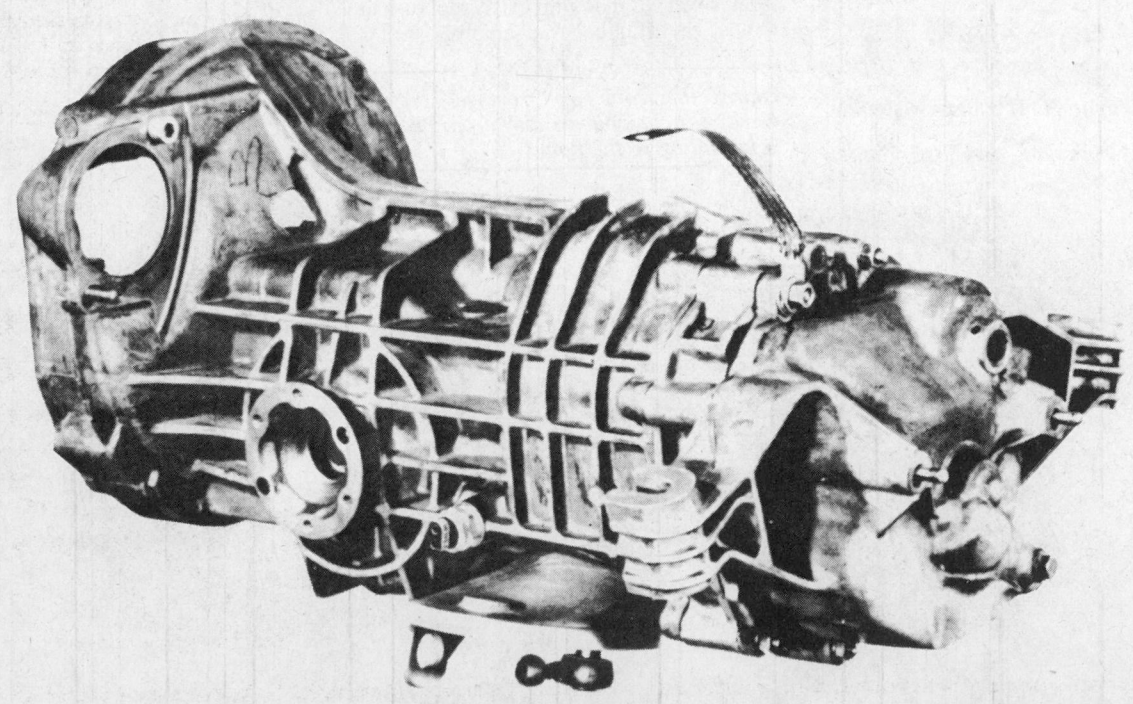

Side shift type transaxle

Remove the detent bushings as necessary.

ASSEMBLY

1. Install the detent bushings, if removed.

— CAUTION —

Do not allow the bushings to protrude into the selector shaft bores.

2. Heat the intermediate plate to 248° F. (120° C.) and press the two bearings into place.

3. Install the bearing brace plate assembly. Torque the retaining bolts to 18 ft. lbs. (2.5 Mkp) and lock the bolt heads in place with the lock plates.

4. Insert the input shaft and pinion shaft assemblies into the intermediate plate assembly.

5. Reposition the aligning dowels and the throttle linkage.

Housing Assembly
DISASSEMBLY AND ASSEMBLY

1. Before any attempt is made to install the bearing races, heat the housing to 248° F. (120° C.).

2. The bearing races can be installed with installer tools and a hammer. Replace the necessary seal or seals.

3. To prevent damages to the housing, install the bearing races squarely in to the housing.

Pinion Shaft
DISASSEMBLY AND ASSEMBLY

1. Remove the retaining bolt with the speedometer gear attached, from the pinion shaft.

2. The gear assemblies are removed by pressing the shaft from the gears.

3. Mark and identify all components so

as to maintain proper assembly sequence.

— CAUTION —

Note the number and thickness of spacers between the roller bearings and thick spacers to avoid recomputing spacer thickness during reassembly.

NOTE: Later transaxles have the thrust washer and spacer replaced with a single, beveled thrust washer.

Input Shaft
DISASSEMBLY AND ASSEMBLY

1. Straighten the locking tabs from the hex nut. Remove the retaining hex nut from the shaft, using the necessary special tools.

2. Press the roller bearing from the shaft, using special tools as necessary.

3. Remove the gears and components from the input shaft.

NOTE: Mark the needle bearing cages to properly install them during the installation procedure.

4. To remove the inner half of the ball bearing race from the stub end of the shaft, drive the race away from its seat with a drift punch or similar tool, and remove with a puller.

5. The reassembly of the shaft and components should be done in the reverse of the removal procedure.

6. The locknut should be torqued to 72–86 ft. lbs. (10–12 Mkp). Be sure to secure the nut with the locking tabs of the lock plate edge.

Differential Assembly

The differential assembly is overhauled in the conventional manner. Special measuring tools are needed to measure the preload, tooth contact and to determine the thickness of necessary shims and spacers.

L. Four point ballbearing
1. Gear II for 1st speed (Freewheeling)
2. Spider
3. Brake band
4. Gear II for 2nd speed (Freewheeling)
5. Gear II for 3rd speed (Fixed)
6. Gear II for 4th speed (Fixed)
7. Spacer
8. Roller bearing
9. Pinion shaft
10. Thrust washer (6.6 mm thickness)
11. Needle bearing inner race (gear speeds 1 thru 4)
12. Needle bearing cage (gear speeds 1 thru 4)
13. Sliding sleeve
14. Synchronizing ring
15. Needle bearing inner race
16. Needle bearing cage
17. Spacers
18. Retaining ring

Cross section of 4-speed pinion shaft assembly

Correct assembly of 1st speed synchronizer for the 5-speed gear train

Correct assembly of 1st speed synchronizer for the 4-speed gear train

Location of 1st/reverse sliding gear with selector fork in place—5-speed

Gear train assembled in the intermediate plate—typical

TRANSAXLE REASSEMBLY

1. Having the transaxle case overhauled as required and the intermediate plate assembled, place the gears in the 5th speed and prepare to install the assembly into the case.

2. Guide the intermediate plate assembly into the case and lightly tighten at four housing studs.

3. Install gear one of 1st speed on the input shaft. Install the spacer and tighten the castellated nut to a torque of 43–47 ft. lbs. (6.0–6.5 Mkp). Secure the nut with a spiral pin.

4. Install the thrust washer on the pinion shaft with the small collar facing the bearing. Guide the needle bearing in place with a suitable tool.

5. Install the needle bearing and gear two of 1st speed. Install the spider wheel of the 1st/reverse gear.

6. Tighten the pinion shaft bolt (with extension for tachometer) to 80–86 ft. lbs. (11–12 Mkp). Block the gear train to prevent turning.

7. Remove the intermediate plate assembly from the case assembly. Place the intermediate plate assembly into a holder so that the selector shafts can be installed.

8. Install the shafts in the following order:

   a. Place the selector sleeve of the 4th/5th speed selector shaft through the fork and through the intermediate plate. Tighten the fork retaining screw.

   b. Install into the detent bore, one ball, detent pin, one long spring and one more ball.

   c. Place the selector fork of 2nd/3rd speeds onto the respective sliding sleeve and push the selector shaft through the fork and into the intermediate plate.

NOTE: The 4th/5th selector shaft must be in the neutral position and the detent ball pressed down.

   d. Tighten the fork retaining screw and move the selector lever to the neutral position. Insert the detent.

   e. Install the 1st/reverse selector shaft into the intermediate plate and install the detent ball and short spring. Tighten the detent cap screw to 18 ft. lbs. (2.5 Mkp).

   f. Slide the selector fork and the sliding gear for the 1st/reverse speed together onto the spider wheel and selector shaft. Install and tighten the fork retaining screw.

NOTE: The sliding sleeves must be adjusted to a position in the exact center in relation to the synchronizer rings when in the neutral position. The forks can be moved by loosening the retaining bolts. A special gauge block is available for this operation, but normally not available to the average repair shop.

   g. When the adjustment of the forks are completed, torque the retaining bolts to 18 ft. lbs. (2.5 Mkp).

9. Install the inner shift rod into the transaxle housing, after having installed the shift finger onto the shaft and securing it with the retaining pin and cotter pin.

10. Guide the intermediate plate assembly into the transaxle housing with gaskets attached, carefully to avoid damage to the input shaft seal.

NOTE: The gear train assembly must be in the 5th speed position.

11. Shift the gear train into Neutral. Guide the inner shift rod into its proper position at the selector shaft tabs and into the rear rod bore.

12. Install the guide fork of the inner shift rod, using a new gasket and be sure the inner shift rod enters the guide fork.

13. Assemble the front cover and install on the transaxle assembly.

   a. Install the bearing cages and the spacer bushings.

   b. Install the reverse gear, axial thrust needle bearing and the thrust washer.

   c. Install the tachometer elbow unit drive unit into the cover and align the indent for the set screw with the hole in the cover.

   d. Install a new gasket and install the front cover. Pull the reverse gear and its axial thrust needle bearing with the thrust washer as far to the end of the shaft as possible to clear the sliding gear of the 1st/reverse speed gear.

NOTE: The machined recess in the thrust washer must align with the outer collar of the pinion shaft bearing.

14. Install the retaining nuts and torque to 15.2–16.6 ft. lbs. (2.1–2.8 Mkp).

15. Install the transaxle support.

TYPE 9

5 Speed Transaxle (Model G 28.03)

Porsche

DISASSEMBLY

1. Mount the transaxle assembly securely and drain the lubricating oil.

2. Remove the rear cover and top cover from the transaxle case.

3. Remove the right and left axle flange retaining bolts and remove the axle flanges.

4. Remove the right and left side cover retaining bolts and carefully separate the side covers, with shims, from the transaxle case. Carefully remove the differential carrier assembly.

5. Drive the main shift rod pin from the shift finger with a pin punch or other suitable tool. Remove the lockout spring and pin from the shaft. Remove the shaft from the transaxle case.

6. Remove the shift shaft interlock mechanism by removing the screw plugs, located on the left and right sides of the case, near the front upper sides.

7. Drive the pins from the shift fingers

and shift forks with a pin punch or other suitable tool. Remove the shafts to the rear of the transaxle case, being careful not to exert undue force. Remove the interlock detents and springs as the shafts are removed. Remove the shift fingers and forks from the case.

8. Remove the input shaft oil seal holder by pulling outward while turning.

9. Remove the countershaft retaining circlip from the transaxle case. From the rear of the case, tap the countershaft forward and out of the case.

NOTE: The pinion shaft bearing plate may have to be loosened.

───── CAUTION ─────
To avoid damage to the case or gears, hold the countergears from falling into the case with wire as a support.

10. With the use of a special puller to maintain straightness, remove the input shaft from the case.

11. Remove the pinion shaft bearing retainer plate bolts and remove the pinion shaft assembly by using a puller.

12. Lift the countergear assembly from the case.

13. Using an appropriate driver, remove the reverse idler shaft from the gear and case.

14. Remove the shift shaft oil seals from the case.

Input Shaft
DISASSEMBLY

1. Remove the synchronizer ring, shift band, stop and thrust block from the input shaft.

2. Remove the front ball bearing circlip and press the bearing from the input shaft.

3. With an appropriate puller, remove the two needle bearings and spacer from the input shaft.

ASSEMBLY

1. Install one needle bearing into the input shaft, followed by the spacer and the second needle bearing.

2. Heat the ball bearing assembly to 212° F. (100° C.) and drive it on to the input shaft. Install the retaining circlip.

3. Install the thrust block, stop, shift band and secure with the synchronizer ring on the input shaft.

Mainshaft
DISASSEMBLY

1. Remove the circlip and shims from the front of the mainshaft. Note the number and thickness of the shims for reassembly.

2. Using a press, remove the gears, bearings and races from the mainshaft, noting the direction of each gear and component for reassembly. Mark the disassembled parts as required. Note the location of all shims for reassembly.

3. Remove the locknut from the mainshaft with the appropriate tools and remove the reverse gear. Press the front tapered bearing and bearing retaining plate from the mainshaft. Press the rear tapered bearing from the mainshaft.

ASSEMBLY

1. Heat the rear tapered bearing to 212° F. (100° C.) and drive it on to the mainshaft.

2. Place the bearing retaining plate on the mainshaft and heat the front tapered bearing as was done to the rear bearing, and drive the front bearing on to the mainshaft.

3. Install the reverse gear with the small depression on the hub towards the front of the mainshaft. Install the locknut and torque to 109–130 ft. lbs. (15–18 Mkg). Stake the locknut collar to the small depression in the reverse gear hub.

4. To properly position the gears on the mainshaft, selective shims must be used in conjunction with the locknut. To obtain the proper specification, the following formula must be used.

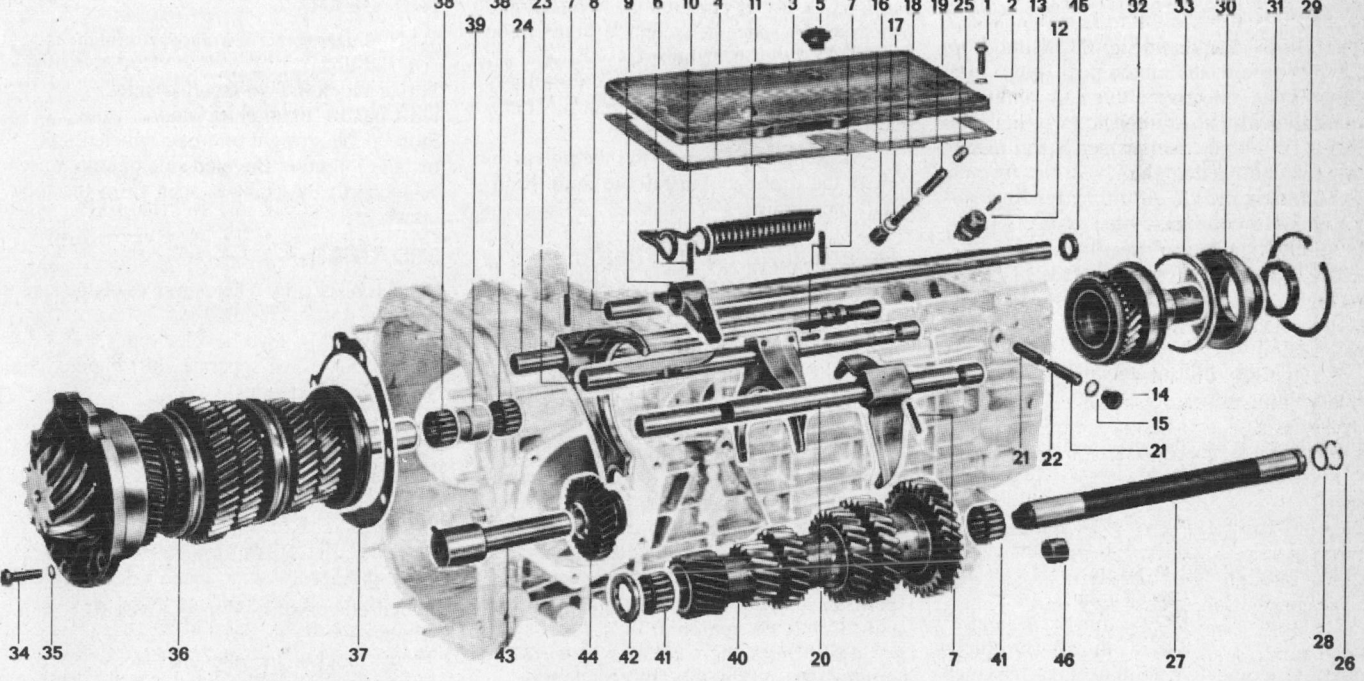

1. Bolt
2. Washer
3. Upper cover
4. Gasket
5. Vent
6. Roll pin
7. Split pin
8. Main shift rod
9. Shift finger
10. U-spring
11. Lockout spring
12. Backup light switch
13. Plunger
14. Plug
15. Seal
16. Plug
17. Seal
18. Spring
19. Detent plunger
20. Shift rod with shift fork for 4th and 5th gear
21. Detent/interlock plungers
22. Spring
23. Shift rod with shift fork for 2nd and 3rd gear
24. Shift rod with shift fork for 1st and reverse gear
25. Interlock pin
26. Circlip
27. Countershaft
28. O-ring
29. Circlip
30. Input shaft oil seal holder
31. Oil seal
32. Input shaft
33. O-ring
34. Bolt
35. Serrated lock washer
36. Pinion shaft assembly
37. Shim
38. Needle bearing
39. Spacer
40. Countershaft hub/gears
41. Needle bearing
42. Thrust washer
43. Reverse idler shaft
44. Reverse idler gear
45. Oil seal
46. Magnetic drain plug

Exploded view of shifting mechanism and gear train—928

Exploded view of pinion shaft gear assembly—928

1. Circlip
2. Shim (distance y)
3. Shift sleeve
4. Hub
5. Needle bearing
6. Inner race
7. Gear, 4th speed
8. Thrust washer
9. Needle bearing
10. Inner race
11. Gear, 3rd speed
12. Shift sleeve
13. Hub
14. Needle bearing
15. Inner race
16. Gear, 2nd speed
17. Thrust washer
18. Needle bearing
19. Inner race
20. Gear, 1st speed
21. Shift sleeve
22. Hub
23. Shim (distance x)
24. Locknut
25. Reverse gear
26. Tapered roller bearing inner race
27. Shim
28. Bearing retaining plate
29. Tapered roller bearing inner race
30. Pinion shaft

Measuring Formula

The design specification is 108.80 mm from the rear face of the pinion gear to the front face of the selective shim and should be measured with a sliding caliper or micrometer. To obtain the proper specification without the needed shim, use the formula by substituting the resulting readings, as illustrated by the example.

108.80 = Design specifications
A = Distance from rear face of pinion to the locknut bearing surface.
B = Distance $A + r$
X = Shim thickness required
r = Pinion shaft and gear deviation during manufacture

Example

Distance A = 106.90 mm
Distance $B = A + r$
    A = 106.90 mm
    r = +0.12 mm
    B = $\overline{107.02}$ mm
Distance X = 108.80 mm—B
    108.80 mm
    $\underline{107.02}$ mm
    $\overline{178.00}$ mm is the thickness of the selective shim needed (Distance X)

5. Following the disassembly order, replace the gears, spacers, bearings and circlips on the mainshaft.

NOTE: The inner races for the needle bearing have to be heated to 212° F. (100° C.) before installation on the mainshaft.

Determining Shim Thickness

1. Place the gear train of the trainshaft in a press, under approximately 5 ton, and measure the space between the front circlip and the 4th/5th gear hub.

2. Select a shim with maximum thickness to remove all play between the circlip and the gear hub.

3. Remove the unit from the press, remove the circlip and install the shim. Reinstall the circlip.

Determining Input Shaft Clearance (During Assembly)

1. The clearance between the input shaft and the 4th/5th gear hub can be determined by inserting a feeler gauge between the shaft end and the gear hub. The clearance should be 0.2–0.3 mm.

2. Should this clearance not be obtained, the mainshaft will have to be disassembled and the shim thickness at the locknut be rechecked and corrected.

3. Reassemble the mainshaft and recheck the clearance, again under pressure, between the circlip and the 4th/5th gear hub. Correct as required.

4. Recheck the clearance between the input shaft and the 4th/5th gear hub.

Synchronizer Component Identification

1ST GEAR

Synchronizer ring—One groove on face.
Thrust block—Two beveled sides.
Shift band—Uneven shift bands.
Stop—Two straight sides.
Installation note: Short side of shift band must be to the right of the thrust block.

2ND GEAR

Synchronizer ring—Two grooves on the face or a red dot
Thrust block—Two beveled sides.
Shift band—Even shift bands.
Stop—One straight and one beveled side.
Installation note: Beveled side of stop must be faced to the right as seen from the top view.

3RD GEAR

Synchronizer ring—Two grooves on the face or a red dot.
Thrust block—Two beveled sides.
Shift band—Two separate shift bands.
Stop—Beveled sides.

4TH GEAR

Synchronizer ring—No grooves.
Thrust block—Two beveled sides.
Shift band—Two separate shift bands.
Stop—Beveled sides.

5TH GEAR

Synchronizer ring—No grooves (0.6 mm wider)
Thrust block—Two beveled sides.
Shift band—Two separate shift bands.
Stop—Beveled sides.

NOTE: All synchronizers should have an installed diameter of 86.0 ± 0.24 mm, measured at the highest point of the ring.

Countershaft
DISASSEMBLY

1. Remove the circlip from the countershaft hub.

2. Press the 3rd, 4th and 5th gears from the countershaft hub.

INSTALLATION

1. Heat the gears to approximately 212° F. (100° C.) and press them into their proper position.

2. Install the circlip on the countershaft hub.

TRANSMISSION ASSEMBLY

1. Place the assembled countershaft assembly into the transmission case with lift wires attached.

2. Install the mainshaft into the case and install the bolts in the bearing retaining plate to case.

3. Install the input shaft assembly in the front of the transmission case.

4. With the lifting wire, raise the countershaft hub assembly in place and insert the countershaft from the front of the transmission case and towards the rear, engaging the notched portion of the shaft into the slot provided by the installation of the mainshaft bearing retainer plate.

NOTE: The bearing retaining plate may have to be loosened to allow the entry of the countershaft into its position in the rear of the case. Retighten the bearing retaining plate.

5. Check the gear train for freeness of rotation and proper clearances.

6. Install the shift rods, forks and finger in their proper locations and install the retaining pins through the forks and fingers to engage the shift rods. Install the necessary detent plungers and springs during the shift rod installation.

7. Install the detent plugs, necessary circlips and the input shaft oil seal holder.

8. Install the main shift rod and shift finger. Install the retaining pin into the finger and through the shaft.

9. Install the differential carrier assembly and the side covers with the removed shims.

NOTE: Should the differential need to be adjusted, refer to the individual car section.

10. Install the left and right axle flanges and retain with the retaining bolts.

11. Install the top and rear cover, using new gaskets.

12. Fill the transmission and the differential with hypoid type oil, 90 weight. Each must be filled separately.

TYPE 10

4 Speed Transaxle

Renault

DISASSEMBLY

1. Mount the transaxle assembly securely and drain the lubricating oil.

2. Remove the clutch housing assembly.

3. Remove the locking washers and bolts from the differential adjusting ring nuts and with the use of a special wrench or equivalent, remove the adjusting ring nuts.

4. Release the clutch shaft roll pin retaining spring and remove the pin. Remove the clutch shaft and the differential assembly.

5. Remove the top cover retaining bolts and the cover.

6. Remove the selector fork shaft springs and the locking balls.

7. Remove the front cover retaining bolts and the top cover.

8. Remove the primary shaft adjusting shims.

9. Remove the primary shaft rear bearing retaining plate and bolts.

10. Using a pin punch, remove the two roll pins holding the reverse gear pinion shaft. Remove the reverse gear selector shaft and the locking disc between the shifting shafts.

11. Engage the gears in one speed, unlock and remove the speedometer end nut from the final drive pinion, along with the rubber washer.

12. Move the gears to the neutral position, move the final drive pinion in towards the differential and remove the tapered bearing. Remove the final drive pinion.

13. Push the primary shaft towards the differential and free the rear bearing cage.

14. Remove the front bearing (freefitting), the primary shaft, the reverse gear shaft and the reverse gear.

15. Remove the 1st/2nd and 3rd/4th gear fork roll pins, using a pin punch. Remove the shafts and selector forks.

16. Remove the lock plate for the secondary bearing adjusting nut and remove the nut.

17. Remove the 4th speed gear thrust washer and push out the primary shaft front bearing assembly.

18. Lift the secondary shaft and the synchronizer assembly from the transaxle.

Differential

The differential assembly is overhauled in the conventional manner. Special tools are needed to measure the bearing preload, tooth contact and to determine the thickness of various shims, when used. To aid the repairman when differential repairs do not need to be done, all necessary measurements should be made of the differential assembly before disassembly and providing no internal parts were installed that would affect the differential measurements, reassemble to the original measurements.

Bearings and Races
REMOVAL AND INSTALLATION

A press and puller are needed to remove and replace the transaxle bearings and races from the case, adjusting ring nuts and the shafts. Caution must be exercised when removing the races because of a lip on varied races. Do not press in the wrong direction. Replace all seals during the overhaul of the transaxle assembly.

Primary Shaft

The disassembly and assembly of the primary shaft is limited to the replacement of the bearings, which should be pressed on and off as necessary.

Secondary Shaft (Pinion)
DISASSEMBLY

1. Mark the position of each sliding gear in relation to its hub, before disassembly.

2. Move each gear, hub and bearing

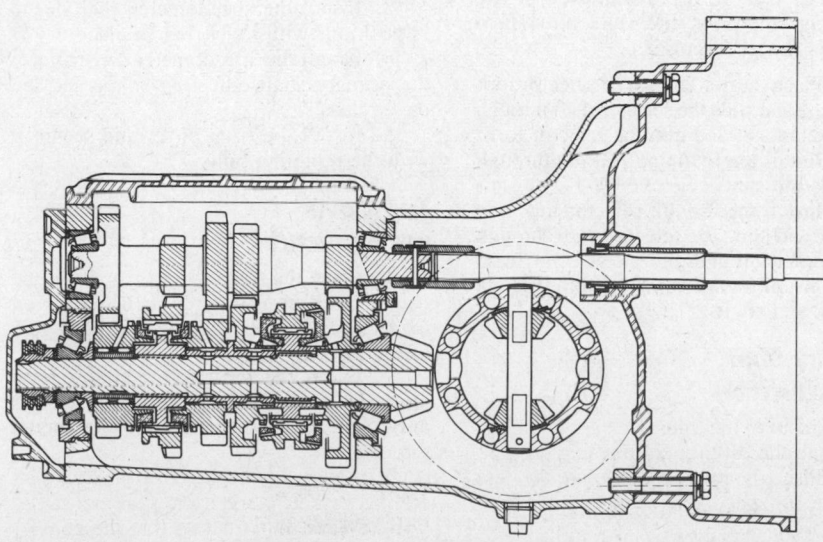

Cross section of Renault 4-speed transaxle

from the shaft, keeping each in its proper order.

3. Remove the pinion gear end bearing by pressing the shaft from the bearing.

ASSEMBLY

1. Install the pinion gear end bearing onto the shaft.

2. Install the gears, hubs and bearings onto the shaft in the order of their removal.

Top Cover

DISASSEMBLY

1. Remove the reverse gear selector and the two roll pins securing the selector finger.

2. Remove the control shaft assembly. Mark the location of the springs, stops and bellows.

3. If necessary, remove the bushing and the seal from the cover.

ASSEMBLY

1. Install the bushing and the seal, if removed.

2. Install the control shaft assembly. Position the spring, spring stops and the bellows.

3. Install the roll pins securing the selector finger.

4. Install the reverse gear selector and retaining bolt.

Synchronizers

When new synchronizers are installed, match the sliding sleeve over the hub assembly until a free fit is felt. Mark the assembly and install on the shaft in its proper turn.

1ST/2ND SYNCHRONIZER

1. Place the springs so that the three slots are covered on the hub assembly.

3RD/4TH SYNCHRONIZER

1. Place the springs into the hub so that the two springs are approximately 180° apart on each side of the hub.

2. Install the three keys and push the sliding sleeve over the hub, with the grooves on the sleeve facing towards the low part of the hub with the biggest offset.

3. Mark the unit for installation.

REASSEMBLY OF THE TRANSAXLE

Secondary (Pinion) Shaft

1. Have the case assembly in a vertical position and place the secondary gear stack, less the 4th speed driven gear, in the transaxle case.

2. Slide the final drive pinion shaft into the casing, mating the shaft splines to the 1st/2nd and 3rd/4th speed synchronizer hubs.

NOTE: A block can be used to hold the pinion shaft in the upright position while completing the assembly of the gear train.

3. Install the 4th speed gear and gear ring onto the shaft. Install the caged two

needle bearing and the 4th gear sleeve.

4. Place the 4th speed thrust washer with the large diameter facing the gear and screw the bearing ring adjusting nut into place until snug.

5. Install the tapered roller bearing on the final drive pinion, hand tight.

6. Hold the sliding gear in place with a special wrench or equivalent tool and tighten the speedometer drive pinion with a properly fitted wrench, so that the tapered roller bearing is drawn into position.

7. Remove the speedometer drive pinion and insert the spring washer. Reinstall the drive pinion and torque to 75–90 ft. lbs. (10–12 N · m). Lock the pinion into position.

Pinion Shaft Bearing Adjustment

1. Unscrew the adjusting ring nut until the race touches the rollers.

2. When using original bearings, no end-play should exist between the rollers and the race and no preload is required. When adjusted, install the lock plate.

3. When installing new bearings, a preload must be obtained. Perform the following operation:

   a. Unscrew the ring nut while turning the secondary (pinion) shaft by hand.

   b. When the shaft becomes hard to turn, preload has developed. Continue to rotate the shaft several times to seat the bearings.

   c. Tie a piece of string around the 3rd/4th sliding sleeve groove and wrap it several times around the sleeve.

   d. Using a spring scale, pull the string and measure the rotating force. The torque preload should be 1–3 lbs (0.5–1.7 N).

   e. Adjust the ring nut as necessary to obtain the proper preload.

   f. When the preload is correct, lock the ring nut with the lock plate.

Installation of Selector Forks

NOTE: During the installation of the retaining roll pins, the slots must face towards the differential.

1. Place the 1st/2nd speed selector fork in the case and slide the selector shaft through the case bracket and into the selector fork.

2. Install the retaining roll pin through the fork and shaft.

3. Install the 3rd/4th selector fork into the case and slide the selector shaft through the case bracket and into the selector fork.

4. Install the retaining roll pin through the fork and shaft.

Primary Shaft

INSTALLATION

1. Position the transaxle case in the upright with the differential housing on top.

2. Place the primary shaft into the case with the 4th speed gear setting on the transaxle case.

3. From the differential side, install the tapered roller bearing, using a length of

pipe stock, fitted to the inner race of the bearing.

4. Position the reverse gear in the case, with the groove facing towards the differential housing. Install the reverse shaft and secure with a roll pin.

NOTE: The roll pin should protrude equally from both sides of the shaft.

5. Install the primary shaft bearing race onto the rear of the shaft and install the race retaining plate and lockplate.

6. Tighten the lockplate bolts and bend the lockplate tabs over the bolt heads.

7. Install the primary shaft front bearing. The bearing should slide onto the shaft.

8. Install the outer race onto the shaft until it is flush with the case.

Primary Shaft Bearing Adjustment

NOTE: The end-play of the primary shaft should be adjusted to 0.001–0.005 inch (0.02–0.12 mm). Shims are used to adjust the end-play.

1. Mount a dial indicator gauge on the speedometer drive pinion end of the case. Push the bearing race inward to reduce the end-play of the shaft, measured by the dial indicator on the shaft end.

2. When the proper amount of end-play has been obtained, place the adjusting shims in position on the bearing race, so that the last shim extends beyond the gasket face by 0.012 inch (0.30 mm).

Front Cover

INSTALLATION

1. Install the locking disc between the selector shafts and slide the reverse gear shaft in place.

2. Install the lock balls and springs into the bores in the transaxle case.

NOTE: The longest spring is for the 1st/2nd gear selector shaft.

3. Install the speedometer gear sleeve in position, with its O-ring in place.

4. Install the speedometer driven gear, the primary shaft adjusting shims and the paper gasket.

5. Install the front cover and secure it with the retaining bolts.

Top Cover

INSTALLATION

1. Place the transaxle gear train in the neutral position. Slide the reverse gear on the shaft until it rests on the 4th speed gear of the primary shaft.

2. Invert the top cover and space the long end of the selector lever ⅜ inch (10 mm) from the center line of the stop on the top cover.

3. Again, invert the cover and with its sealing gasket, place it onto the transaxle.

4. Move the cover so that the ends of the gear lever engages in the selector fork notches and the ends of the reverse selector

lever engages the notch on the selector shaft and the groove in the gear.

5. Secure the cover with the retaining bolts.

Differential
INSTALLATION

1. Install the differential assembly into the housing. Install the clutch shaft and secure with a roll pin. Install the retaining spring.

2. Seal the threads of the differential adjusting nuts and install into the housing, matching the disassembly marks.

3. The backlash is adjusted by the movement of the adjusting ring nuts and should measure 0.005–0.010 inch (0.12–0.25 mm).

4. Install the lock plates to lock the adjusting rings.

Clutch Housing
INSTALLATION

1. Install the oil seal in the clutch housing and install the gasket.

2. Install a seal protector tool over the clutch shaft and install the clutch housing.

3. Install the retaining bolts for the clutch housing. Torque to 30 ft. lbs. (4 N · m).

4. Remove the seal protector tool from the clutch shaft.

TYPE 11

4 Speed Transaxle

Renault

DISASSEMBLY

NOTE: The shifting control linkage arm can be located at either the top or bottom of the front cover, depending upon the transaxle model.

1. Mount the transaxle securely and drain the lubricating oil.

2. Remove the clutch housing retaining bolts and remove the cover assembly.

3. Remove the back-up light switch and the front cover assembly. Remove the spacer and the primary shaft bearing adjusting shims. Measure the ring and pinion backlash and mark the differential adjusting locknuts for installation purposes.

4. Remove the right and left differential bearing adjusting locknuts, using the appropriate tools.

5. Remove the half housing assembly retaining bolts and separate the half housings.

6. Lift the pinion shaft assembly from the half housing, along with the stop peg which is used to lock the double tapered roller bearing outer cage.

7. Lift the primary shaft and the differential from the half housing.

8. Using a drift, remove the roll pin from the 3rd/4th speed fork. Remove the fork and shaft, while retaining the locking ball and spring. Remove the locking disc located between the shafts.

9. Move the selector lever into the 1st gear position and slide the reverse gear shaft as far as possible back on the control rod side.

10. Using a drift, remove the roll pin from the 1st/2nd gear fork. Remove the fork and shaft while retaining the locking ball and spring.

11. Unscrew the reverse gear swivel lever bolt and remove the swivel lever.

12. Using a drift, remove the reverse gear positioning shaft roll pin. Remove the shaft and fork.

NOTE: The roll pin will touch the housing and must be turned and the pin removed completely with a pair of pliers.

13. Remove the circlip from the reverse idler gear and shaft. Remove the shaft, the gear, thrust washer and the guide. Retain the locking ball and spring.

14. Necessary replacement of half housing parts and seals can now be accomplished.

Primary Shaft
DISASSEMBLY

1. Separate the clutch shaft from the primary shaft by removal of the roll pin with a drift.

2. Remove the bearings from the shaft, using appropriate pullers.

ASSEMBLY

1. Using a press or its equivalent, install the tapered bearing onto the primary shaft.

2. Install the clutch shaft onto the primary shaft, using a new roll pin.

Pinion Shaft (Secondary)
DISASSEMBLY

1. Place the pinion shaft assembly in a vise and secure on the 1st speed gear. Place the 1st/2nd synchronizer in the 1st speed position.

2. Release the speedometer drive gear locking tabs and unscrew the gear from the shaft.

3. Remove the double tapered roller bearing, the adjusting washer, the 4th speed gear and ring, along with the 3rd/4th speed synchronizer sliding sleeve and keys.

--- **CAUTION** ---
Mark the position of the sliding sleeve with reference to its position on the hub.

4. Using a press and appropriate tools, remove the 3rd/4th speed synchronizer hub from the shaft.

5. Remove the 3rd gear stop washer and retaining key. Remove the 3rd gear and synchronizer ring.

6. Remove the 2nd speed gear stop washer, the 2nd speed gear and synchronizer ring. Remove the 1st/2nd synchronizer sliding gear.

--- **CAUTION** ---
Mark the position of the sliding sleeve with reference to its position on the hub.

7. Remove the stop washer from the shaft for the 1st/2nd synchronizer hub.

8. Using a press or equivalent tool, remove the 1st/2nd gear synchronizer hub from the shaft.

9. Remove the 1st gear synchronizer ring, the stop washer and the 1st speed gear.

10. Install a retaining clip onto the strengthen crown wheel and pinion assemblies to prevent the tapered roller bearing from falling out. This clip is supplied with new crown wheel and pinion assemblies.

NOTE: The bearing inner track (race) is bonded to the final drive pinion shaft and cannot be replaced.

ASSEMBLY

1. Install a new crown wheel and pinion assembly, if required.

2. Install the 1st speed gear, the stop washer and the 1st speed gear onto the shaft.

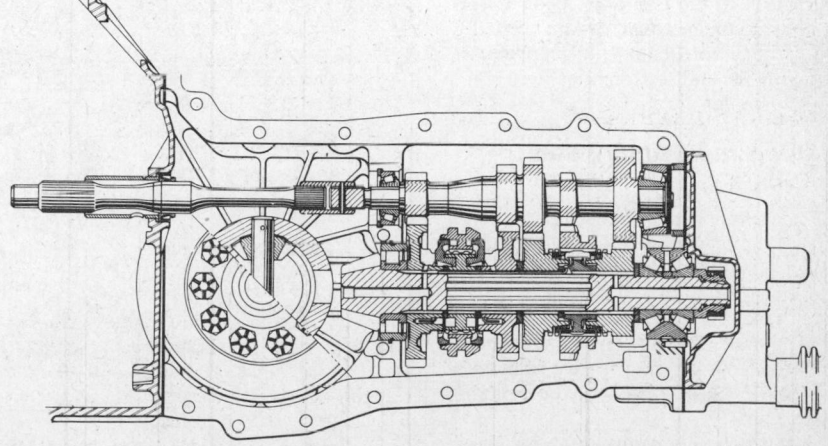

Cross section of Renault split case transaxle

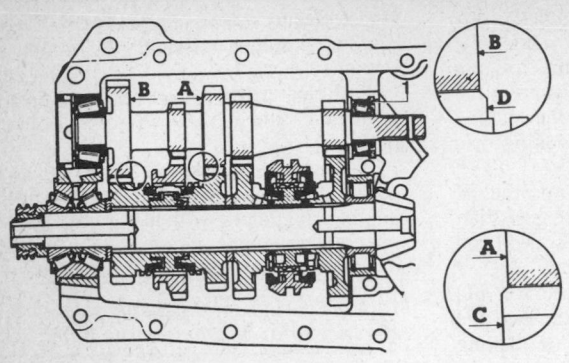

Positioning of the gears on the primary shaft

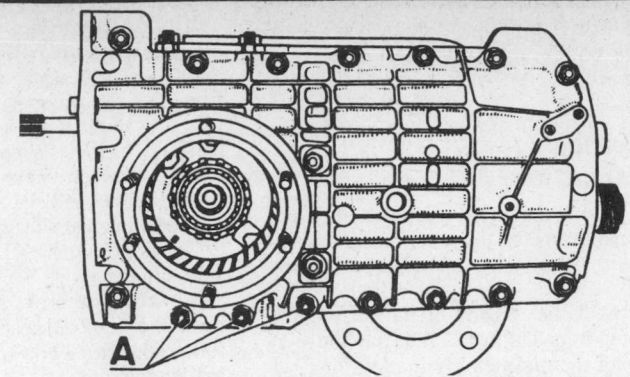

Position (A) of the three reversed nuts for clutch control clearance

3. The 1st/2nd synchronizer hub should be heated to 482° F. (250° C.) maximum, when installed on the pinion shaft.

4. Install the 1st/2nd gear synchronizer stop washer, the 1st/2nd synchronizer sliding gear and its ring and the 2nd speed gear stop washer.

5. Install the 3rd speed gear and synchronizer ring, the 3rd speed gear stop washer and the stop washer retaining key.

6. Install the 3rd/4th speed synchronizer hub.

NOTE: The hub can be heated or pressed onto the shaft.

7. Install the 3rd/4th speed synchronizer sliding gear and keys to their original positions as per the previous marks.

8. Install the 4th speed gear and synchronizer ring, the pinion sleeve adjusting washer and the double tapered roller bearing.

9. Install the speedometer drive gear and screw it on to the shaft. Place the pinion shaft in a vise, and secure the 1st speed gear. Place the synchronizer sliding sleeve into the 1st speed position.

10. Tighten the speedometer drive gear to 75–85 ft. lbs. Lock the tabs of the locking ring unless the pinion depth adjustment is to be made.

Differential

The differential assembly is overhauled in the conventional manner. Refer to the general instruction in the rear axle repair unit section. Special measuring tools are needed to measure the pinion depth, ring gear backlash adjustment and differential bearing preload adjustment.

Positioning the Primary and Pinion Shaft

1. Place the primary and the pinion (secondary) shafts into the left half housing.

2. The position of the 3rd speed gear on the primary shaft should be offset with reference to the 3rd speed gear of the pinion (secondary) shaft, by the same amount as the 4th speed gear on the primary shaft in reference to the 4th speed gear on the pinion (secondary) shaft.

3. To achieve the proper distance, the positioning is accomplished by using adjusting washers in selective sizes on the primary shaft.

Adjusting Primary Shaft Bearings

1. Place the primary shaft assembly into the left half housing and fit the right half housing in place, but do not secure it.

2. Fit the spacer and shim pack into the 4th gear side bearing bore.

3. The shaft should turn freely, without any end-play and the spacer should project past the housing 0.008 inch (0.2 mm), which represents the thickness of the front housing paper gasket.

4. Should the clearance be wrong, increase or decrease the shim sizes by selecting one of proper size.

5. Upon obtaining the proper clearance, remove the right half housing and the primary shaft.

TRANSAXLE ASSEMBLY

1. Install the reverse shaft and position the fork on the shaft. Retain the fork to the shaft by the roll pin.

2. Place the reverse shaft swivel lever in position and retain with the bolt. Torque to 20 ft. lbs.

3. Install the 1st/2nd shaft locking ball and spring. Insert the 1st/2nd speed selector shaft. Fit the reverse end fitting and retain it with a roll pin. Install the 1st/2nd speed gear fork and retain it with a roll pin.

4. Position the locking disc in place between the shafts and install the 3rd/4th selector shaft locking ball and spring.

5. Install the shaft and fit the 3rd/4th gear fork with the hub towards the differential end and retain it with a roll pin.

6. Install the locking ball and spring, the reverse idler shaft and gear, (with the hub towards the differential end) and the thrust washer into the right half housing. The thrust washer bronze face should be against the gear.

7. Install the guide from inside the bore and push the shaft fully into place. Install the gear retaining circlip.

8. Place the differential, the primary shaft with the clutch shaft in place and the secondary shaft assembly into the left half housing.

9. Install a sealing compound on the joint faces of the half housings and fit the right housing to the left housing, being sure the end of the reverse idler lever enters the slot in the reverse gear shaft.

10. Install the retaining bolts and nuts.

NOTE: The nuts are located on the right half housing, except three under the differential assembly, reversed to allow clearance for the clutch controls.

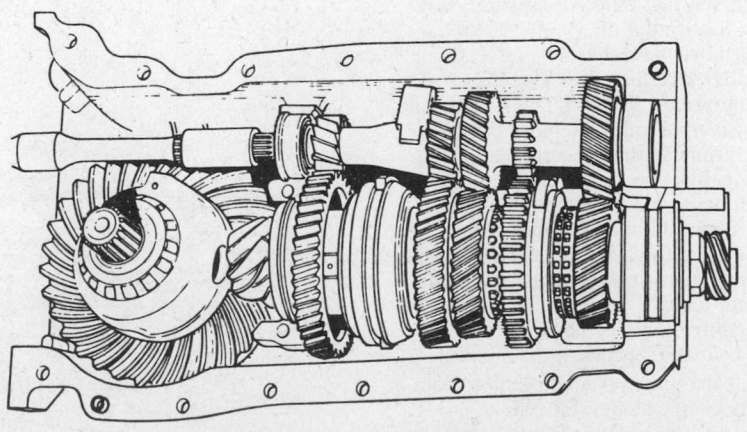

Positioning of gear train in the half case

11. Fit the primary shaft bearing adjusting shims and the spacer.

12. Install the shift fork shaft control lever.

13. Install a new gasket on the front housing and install in place on the transaxle, while engaging the shaft into the control lever.

14. Install the retaining pin with a drift. Install the cover retaining nuts but do not tighten.

15. Tighten the half housing bolts to the following torque;0.276 inch (7 mm)—15 ft. lbs.

0.315 inch (8 mm)—20 ft. lbs.

16. Tighten the front cover nuts.

17. Install the differential carriers and tighten to the original positions as marked during the disassembly.

18. Install a new gasket on the clutch housing and install the housing. Fill the transaxle with lubricating oil after the unit is installed in the vehicle.

TYPE 12

4 Speed Transaxle

SAAB

DISASSEMBLY

NOTE: The disassembly and assembly of the transaxle gear train can be accomplished without separating the engine and gearbox. However, the engine flywheel must be removed.

—— CAUTION ——

Before the transaxle disassembly is begun, measure the backlash of the differential ring and pinion gears, so that the same backlash is obtained during the reassembly, providing no affected components for the differential are replaced. Upon removal of the differential bearing seats, measure and mark the shims for later installation.

1. Secure the transaxle and drain the lubricating oil. Remove the side and end plates from the case.

2. Remove the differential bearing seat retaining bolts and with the aid of a puller type tool, remove the left and right seats. Remove the spring and plunger on each end of the inner driveshaft, along with the adjusting shims.

NOTE: The inner driveshafts will be removed with the seats as an assembly.

3. Remove the differential assembly from the housing.

4. Remove the lock plate that holds the intermediate and reverse gear shafts in place.

5. Using a special pulling tool or the equivalent, pull the intermediate gear shaft from the housing and allow the intermediate gear set to drop downward.

6. Remove the primary gear housing retaining bolts and separate the primary gear housing from the transaxle housing.

7. With the primary gear housing separated from the transaxle housing, the intermediate gear set can be removed from the transaxle.

8. Remove the transaxle side cover, if not already removed, and take out the spring and ball catch for the gear selector rod.

9. Remove the reverse gear selector shaft retaining screw, turn the gear selector rod so the driver is detached from the reverse gear shift and pull out the shaft.

10. Remove the shift shaft for the 1st/2nd gear, 3rd top gear and shift forks. Remove the shift fork and the sliding sleeve for the 3rd speed gear.

NOTE: The reverse lever does not need to be removed from the gear shift shaft when the shaft is removed.

11. Remove the reverse gear shaft and lift the reverse idler gear from the housing.

12. Remove the needle bearing from the pinion shaft and install a special holding tool or equivalent, as a lock on the reverse gear of the pinion shaft. Remove the pinion nut from the shaft.

13. Remove the gear holding tool and remove the 3rd/4th gear synchronizer hub and 3rd gear.

14. Remove the four pinion shaft bearing housing screws. Install a special pushing tool or equivalent, and remove the pinion shaft from the housing. Remove the gears, sleeves, washers and shims from the housing, noting each component's location.

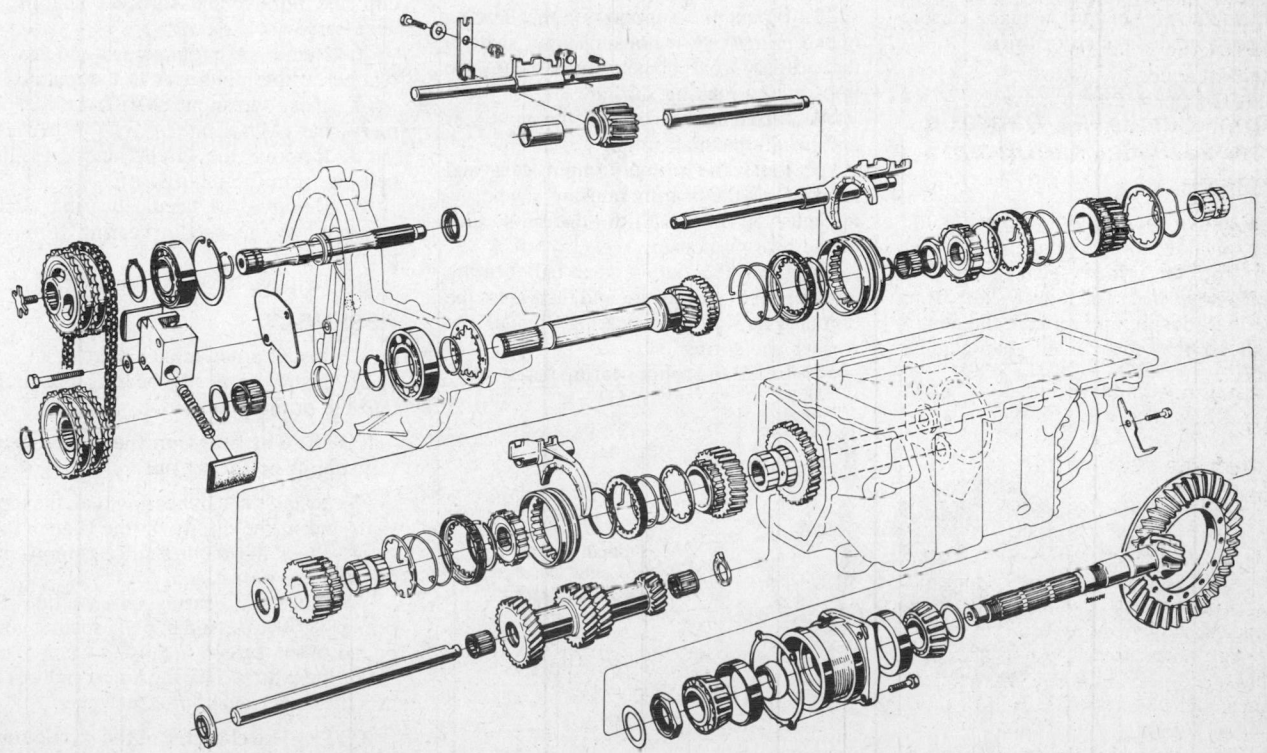

Exploded view of transaxle, chain driven primary gear train

Pinion Shaft and Housing
DISASSEMBLY

1. To remove the pinion shaft from the pinion shaft housing, the pinion bearing nut must be removed. The pinion shaft can then be pressed from the housing and the front bearing removed.

2. Place the pinion shaft and rear bearing in a press and remove the rear bearing from the shaft.

3. Remove the outer races from the pinion shaft housing as required, with a press and the necessary special tools.

ASSEMBLY

1. Install the outer races in the pinion shaft housing and seat firmly.

2. Press the rear bearing onto the pinion shaft. Fit the spacer and bearing housing onto the shaft.

NOTE: The bearings should be lightly oiled before assembly.

3. Place the shaft assembly in a press or equivalent tool, install the front bearing and force it into place on the shaft, while turning the housing until a resistance is felt.

4. Install a "locking" substance on the shaft threads and install the locking nut.

5. Wrap a cord around the pinion housing and attach a pull scale to the cord.

6. Tighten the locking nut until a pull torque of 10–15 lbs. (47–71 N—4.7–7.0 kp) is attained for new bearings, or a pull torque of 4.2–9.2 lbs. (19–43 N—1.9–4.3 kp) is reached for bearings having more than 1200 miles (2,000 KM), considered to be used bearings.

7. When the bearing pull torque is correct, lock the pinion nut in place on the shaft with a center punch or drift.

Primary Gear Case
(UP to and including Transaxle Number 817000, Gear Driven)
DISASSEMBLY

1. Remove the retaining bolts for the bearing housing and separate the bearing housing from the primary gear case.

2. Remove the center gear shaft from the bearing housing and remove the center gear nut so that the center gear can be removed.

3. The roller bearings and races can be pressed from the center gear as required.

4. Remove the cap from the bearing housing for the output shaft and press the output shaft from the housing, after removal of the shaft.

5. Press the input gear assembly from the bearing housing, complete with the bearing.

6. Remove the snap-ring and press the bearing from the input shaft.

7. Remove the bearing support that retains the 4th speed input gear with the bearing.

8. Press the primary gear housing 4th speed input gear out of the housing. Remove the snap-ring and remove the bearing from the shaft.

9. If necessary, remove the oil collector and the needle bearing from the primary gear housing.

NOTE: The needle bearing in the primary gear housing has been discontinued from the 1976 and later models and need not be replaced during the overhaul of early designed gearboxes. When gears in the primary gear assembly of earlier designed transaxles are to be replaced, the needle bearing must be removed and discarded because the replacement shaft has not been machined for it.

ASSEMBLY

1. Position the oil collector into the primary gear housing, if removed.

2. Install the bearing on the primary gear housing 4th speed gear. Install the snap-ring and press the 4th speed gear assembly into the primary gear housing.

3. Mount the support for the bearing of the primary gear housing input shaft to the primary gear housing and secure the bolts with a locking substance.

4. Install the bearing into the input gear and install the snap-ring.

5. Press the primary input gear and bearing into the bearing housing. The bearing must be flush with the mating surface of the bearing housing.

6. Press the output gear ball bearing into the bearing housing, and then press the output gear into the bearing. Install the washer and spring.

7. Install the roller bearing races, bearings and the shaft into the center gear. Install the locknut and snug.

8. Position the gear in a holding device and wrap a cord around the gear teeth so that the gear can be rotated on the bearings.

9. Pull the cord and cause the gear to rotate with a spring scale attached to the cord. A turning torque reading of 1.3–1.8 lbs. (6–8 N—0.6–0.8 kp). Obtain the correct reading by adjusting the locknut. Secure the locknut to the shaft with a center punch or drift.

10. Fit the center gear into the bearing housing and secure with the attaching bolt.

11. Install the primary input gear bearing into the primary housing, if previously removed.

12. Install the bearing housing onto the primary gear housing and secure with the retaining bolts.

Primary Gear Case (From Transaxle Numbers 900001 and S00001, Chain Driven)
DISASSEMBLY

1. Remove the retaining bolts and separate the cover from the primary gear housing.

2. Remove the chain tensioner assembly.

3. Remove the circlip from the lower gear sprocket and the circlip from the upper gear, through the opening in the gear sprocket.

4. Remove the gear sprockets and the chain at the same time. It may be necessary to apply pressure to the sprockets to remove.

5. Remove the upper gear sprocket circlip and remove the sprocket bearing, if necessary.

6. Remove the four screws and bearing retainer at the input gear to the gearbox.

7. Press the input shaft from the primary gear case.

8. Remove the circlip and press the bearing from the input shaft.

9. Remove the needle bearing circlip and remove the needle bearing from the primary gear case.

10. Remove the clutch shaft seal.

ASSEMBLY

1. Install a new clutch shaft seal.

2. Install the needle bearing and circlip into the primary gear case.

NOTE: The mark on the needle bearing should be facing out.

3. Install the ball bearing onto the input shaft and fit the circlip on the shaft.

4. Press the input shaft assembly into the primary gear case.

5. Place the bearing retainer onto the primary gear case and apply a sealing compound to the screw threads.

6. Install the bearing, race and circlip into the upper gear sprocket.

NOTE: The chamfer of the circlip must face outward when the gear is installed.

7. Install the chain on the sprocket gears

1. Input gear
2. Center wheel
3. Output gear

Primary gear train using gears to drive transaxle

and install onto the splines and stud in the primary gear case. Install the two circlips.

8. Install the chain tensioner with the oil passage at the top and place the backing plate so that its top edge is in line with the top edge of the chain tensioner housing. Apply thread sealant to the chain tensioner bolts and install.

9. Install the primary gear cover and new gasket.

ASSEMBLY OF TRANSAXLE

1. Install the guide studs into the transaxle housing and install the pinion assembly into the case, with the original shims between the bearing housing and the transaxle housing.

NOTE: Should new components be installed that would change the pinion depth, special tools would have to be used to correct the components to the proper pinion depth setting.

2. Remove the guide studs and install the four retaining bolts into the bearing housing.

NOTE: Any measurement operations and adjustments must be done before the bolts are secured with a "locking" substance.

3. The distance between the connecting surface for the primary gear housing and the pinion shaft nut should be checked before installing the reverse gear on the pinion shaft. The distance should be 7.677–7.681 inches (195.0–195.1 mm). Adjust a depth gauge to the measurement and measure the clearance with a feeler gauge. Install the necessary shims to close the clearance between the pinion nut and the reverse gear.

NOTE: If the pinion shaft depth was not changed, the original shims can be reused.

4. After the necessary shims have been selected and installed on the pinion shaft, install the reverse gear on the shaft.

NOTE: The gears will have to be driven on the pinion shaft with a sleeve and a plastic tipped hammer.

5. Install the 1st gear on the bearing sleeve of the reverse gear.

6. Install the 1st/2nd synchronizer hub in place on the pinion shaft. Place the 1st/2nd gear shift fork into the sliding sleeve and mount on the synchronizer hub.

7. Install the 2nd gear sleeve and mount the 2nd gear onto the sleeve.

8. Install the spacer and sleeve for the 3rd gear. Install the 3rd gear on the sleeve.

9. Install the 3rd/4th synchronizer hub. Place the 3rd/4th shifting fork into the sliding sleeve of the 3rd/4th gear and install on the synchronizer hub.

10. Lock the reverse gear so that the pinion shaft does not turn. Install and torque the pinion shaft nut to 30–45 ft. lbs. (40–60 Nm—4–6 KPM).

11. Secure the nut to the pinion shaft.

12. Install the pinion shaft needle bearing and its locking ring. Remove the shaft locking tool.

13. Locate the sliding sleeves in the neutral position and install the shift shaft for the 1st, 2nd, 3rd and 4th gear shift forks.

14. Turn the gear selector shaft clockwise to gain clearance to install the reverse gear shift shaft. Install the shaft and lock with the stop screw.

15. Mount the needle bearings into the intermediate gear assembly, using grease to hold them in place. Install the gear set into the bottom of the gear box housing.

16. Have the thrust washer located in the correct position for the intermediate gear assembly, on the primary gear housing. Be sure the connecting tube is fitted to the output shaft of the primary gear.

17. Seal the mating surface of the primary gear housing and mount it to the transaxle case.

NOTE: Do not tighten the primary gear housing screws until the intermediate gear shaft is installed.

18. Insert the intermediate gear shaft into position. Move the intermediate gear assembly in order that the shaft can be installed. Align the thrust washer so the shaft can be installed through it. Tighten the primary gear housing retaining screws.

19. Install the reverse gear and shaft. Be sure the reverse lever is fitted into the groove on the reverse gear. Install the lock plate over the reverse gear and the intermediate gear shaft ends. Secure the screw.

20. Install the spring and lock ball for the gear selector rod and fit the housing cover in place and secure with the retaining bolts.

21. Install the differential assembly into the housing.

22. Using the shims that were removed during the disassembly, install the inner drive shaft assemblies in place on the housing. Measure the differential gear backlash and adjust to the measurements obtained before the disassembly.

23. Complete the assembly by installing the cover onto the housing and filling the unit with lubricating oil to the specified level.

TYPE 13

5 Speed Transaxle

SAAB

DISASSEMBLY

1. Follow Steps 1–3 of the 4 speed transaxle procedure. Pay attention to all "NOTES" and "CAUTIONS."

2. Remove the dowel pin in the gear shift fork for 5th gear.

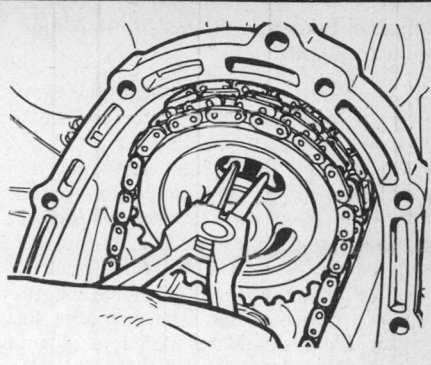

Remove the circlip through the hole in the sprocket—Type 13

3. Move the gear wheel for reverse into the reverse position and then select 5th gear.

4. Free the shaft (lower sprocket) tab washer from the input shaft and then remove the nut.

5. Remove the chain tensioner.

6. Working through the hole on the upper sprocket, remove the circlip from in front of the sprocket bearing.

7. Remove the sprockets and chains together as one unit.

NOTE: A slide hammer and/or a gear pulley may be necessary to remove the sprocket and chain assembly.

8. Separate the pinion on the input shaft from the gear wheel on the input layshaft by removing the circlip from the groove and sliding the synchromesh sleeve toward the pinion.

9. Remove the locking plate for the layshaft and reverse gear shaft. Using special tools 83 90 049 and 83 90 270, pull out the layshaft gear cluster and then remove the pinion from the input layshaft. The pinion should be removed through the side of the transmission case along with the synchromesh sleeve and thrust washer.

10. Remove the bolts and oil catcher from the input shaft bearing case. Remove the bearing case by means of a slide hammer.

11. Slide the gear selector for 5th gear through the full extent of its travel and then remove the selector fork and the synchromesh sleeve.

12. Up to and including gearbox No. 436500, remove the circlip and shims from the 5th gear synchrohub. Also remove the adjacent spacer from the pinion shaft.

13. On models having a gearbox number higher than 436500, remove the reverse gear and shaft. Lock the reverse gearwheel, remove the circlip and then unscrew the nut securing the synchrohub for 5th gear. Retain the hub and spacer.

14. Remove all primary gear case retaining bolts and then drift in the dowel pins so that the case can be separated from the gearbox housing.

NOTE: The 5th gear selector will remain in the housing and can be removed later. File away any burrs around the hole in the shaft so that the aperature in

the gear housing will not be damaged upon reassembly.

15. Remove the layshaft and layshaft gear cluster. Save the needle bearings and thrust washer for re-use.

16. Remove the selector shafts and the selectors. Remove the selectors for 1st and 2nd gears along with their synchromesh units. Remove the reverse selector together with the shaft for 5th and reverse gear.

17. The selector shafts should be removed from the front. The aperature for the taper pin should be filed free of any burrs. The selector, double lockout and the spring can be removed later. *Don't lose the selector ball and guide pin.*

18. Remove the four bolts for the pinion shaft bearing housing and then press out the shaft. Be sure to keep the gear wheels, sleeves, washers and shims in order.

Pinion Shaft and Housing

For all pinion shaft and housing disassembly and assembly procedures, please refer to the steps in the Type 12 section.

ASSEMBLY

1. Screw two locating studs into the transmission case and then shim and position the pinion shaft assembly into the case. Use a rubber mallet and a drift and gently tap the assembly into position. Install the retaining bolts for the bearing housing and tighten them to 15–18.5 ft. lbs.

2. Before installing the reverse gear onto the pinion shaft, check that the distance between the primary gear housing mating surface and the pinion shaft nut is 7.677–7.681 in. If it is not, shims must be placed between the nut and the reverse gear. Shims are available in thicknesses of 0.018, 0.0157, and 0.0197 in. If the distance is correct, the shims used earlier may be replaced.

3. Using a rubber mallet and a sleeve. install the reverse gear.

4. Install 1st gear on the bearing sleeve of reverse gear.

5. Install the 1st/2nd gear synchromesh hub. Position the 1st/2nd gear shift fork into the 1st/2nd gear synchromesh sleeve and then install it on the hub.

6. Press the 2nd gear sleeve onto the shaft and then install 2nd gear onto the sleeve.

7. Repeat Step 6 for the 3rd gear assembly.

8. Repeat Step 5 for 3rd/4th gear. Fit the bushing for 4th gear onto the shaft and then install the gear over it. Install the ball bearing bushing.

9. If the selector shaft was removed, install it together with the double lockout guide pin.

10. Slide the synchromesh sleeves onto the pinion shaft while in the neutral position and then install the 1st/2nd gear shift shaft and the 3rd/4th gear shift forks.

11. Install the reverse selector shaft with the selector. Seal the shaft stop bolt with Loctite® and tighten it.

12. Install the 5th gear selector on the reverse selector shaft.

13. Fit the needle bearing into the layshaft gear cluster and then position the whole assembly inside the gearbox housing.

14. Position the layshaft and raise the layshaft gear cluster so that it lines up with the shaft. Insert the shaft far enough into the cluster so that it holds the gears in position. The thrust washer can be installed later.

15. Slide the spacer, along with the 5th gear synchrohub and the circlip onto the pinion shaft. Insert shims between the hub and the sleeve so that there is no play between any of the parts on the pinion shaft. After all play has been removed, the spacer, hub and circlip should be removed.

16. Apply sealing compound to the mating surface of the primary gear casing and then bolt the casing to the gearbox housing.

17. Reinstall the spacer and the synchrohub on the pinion shaft.

18. Fit the shims which were used in Step 15 to the hub so that once the circlip is installed there will be no axial play. Install a locking tool (special tool 87 90 503) on the reverse gear and tighten the nut to 37 ± 7 ft. lbs.

19. Using a drift with a rounded nose, upset the flange of the nut in the groove in the hub.

20. Install the input shaft along with the bearing housing, oil catcher and connecting pipes. Using three guide pins for alignment and the sprocket as a spacer between the adapter and the bearing housing, insert bearing housing far enough for the shaft to meet the synchromesh sleeve. Use a slide hammer and drive the bearing housing into place.

NOTE: Check the compression of the bearing before installation.

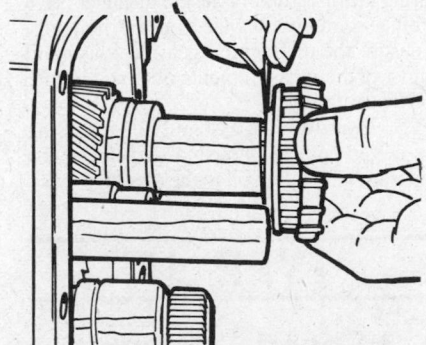

Use shims to remove the play between the synchrohub and sleeve—Type 13

Pinion shaft gear assembly—Type 13

21. Up to and including gearbox No. 437802 (1982 models), install the thrust washer for the constant–mesh gear on the input layshaft. Grease the washer and position it so that the locating tab is in the special recess.

On gearboxes No. 437803 and later (1982 models), install a new bearing without a thrust washer.

22. Install the input layshaft gear along with the sleeve, circlip and bearing rollers. Slide the layshaft back so that the input layshaft gear can be fitted.

23. Push the synchromesh sleeve onto the layshaft and fit the circlip in the groove.

24. Install the layshaft thrust washer. Withdraw the layshaft and slide the washer into position. Insert the shaft so that it locks into position.

25. Install the reverse gear wheel and shaft. Adjust the shaft until it locks in position.

NOTE: Make sure that the reverse lever engages the groove in the reverse gear.

26. Slide the locking plate over the shaft ends and install the bolt with Loctite.®

27. Install the primary gear sprockets and chains. Make sure that the hole for the tab washer on the lower sprocket is facing outward.

28. Install the chain tensioner using Loctite® on the mounting bolts.

29. Screw the nut onto the input shaft. Pull reverse and 5th gears at the same time so as to lock the input shaft and then tighten the nut. Using a round drift, knock one of the nut tabs into the recess in the gear wheel.

30. Install the dowel in the gear selector fork for 5th gear.

31. Install the differential.

32. Check and replace the shaft seals in the bearing retaining housings if necessary. Adjust the crownwheel backlash if necessary. Install the two driveshafts and inner joints—make sure that the seals are not damaged. Install the selector ball and spring and then install the gearbox top cover assembly and gasket.

33. Install the final drive unit, cover and gasket. Install the primary gear housing and the chain cover and gaskets.

34. Install the transaxle (if removed) and refill with the proper gear lubricant.

TYPE 14

4 Speed Transaxle

Subaru

DISASSEMBLY

1. Disconnect the return springs from

the release bearing holder and remove the clutch fork and release bearing holder.

2. Remove the transmission cover.

3. Wind vinyl tape on the spline of the right and left axle drive shafts to prevent the oil seals from being damaged when separating the case.

4. Separate the transmission case by removing the seventeen bolts.

NOTE: The case will separate easily if the two areas around the knock pins are tapped upward with a plastic hammer.

5. Use the shank of a hammer and remove the drive pinion.

6. Remove the transmission mainshaft.

7. Remove the differential.

8. Remove the three shifter rail spring plugs.

9. Remove the shifter forks and rails.

NOTE: When pulling out a rail, keep the other rails placed in Neutral. Pull the rail for the 4th/3rd by turning 90°.

10. Remove the one screw on the right and left side of the transmission case and remove the oil seal holder lock plate. Using a special oil seal holder wrench remove the oil seal holder and O-rings.

11. Remove the speedometer driven gear. Knock the speedometer shaft outside the case by tapping lightly.

12. Pull the knock pins out and then pull out the reverse idler gear shaft, reverse idler

gear and shifter lever.

13. Disassemble the transmission mainshaft.

a. Remove the snap-ring.

b. Press off the ball bearing, main shaft collar, 4th drive gear, synchronizer hub, 4th drive gear bushing and the 3rd drive gear.

NOTE: The 3rd drive gear bushing may be left installed but if replacement is necessary, cut a groove with a grinder and drive it off with a chisel. When the bushing moves a little remove it with a press.

14. Disassemble the drive pinion.

a. Unscrew the drive pinion locknut.

b. Remove the ball bearing and the 4th/3rd driven gear with a press then remove the 2nd gear and needle bearing by hand.

c. Remove the 1st driven gear, needle bearing race, synchronizer hub and needle bearing by using a press.

d. Remove the needle bearing race, drive pinion spacer and roller bearing by using a press.

15. Disassemble the transmission cover.

a. Remove the back-up light switch and remove the reverse accent spring, ball and straight pin.

b. Remove the plug in the upper part of the cover and then remove the reverse accent shaft and reverse return spring.

16. Disassemble the differential assembly.

a. Remove the right and left snap-rings and then remove the two axle driveshafts.

b. Remove the ring gear.

c. Drive out the straight pin toward the ring gear.

d. Pull out the differential pinion shaft, and then remove the differential pinion, side gear and washer.

e. Remove the roller bearing by using a puller.

ASSEMBLY

1. Reassemble the transmission mainshaft.

NOTE: Install the hub so that the end of the spline having the narrower tooth width is on the 3rd gear side. The shorter insert is for the 4th/3rd synchronizer and the longer insert is for the 1st/2nd synchronizer.

2. Reassemble the drive pinion.

a. Install the roller bearing in the drive pinion and press on the spacer.

b. Install the three synchronizer inserts, reverse driven gear and the two springs on the hub.

NOTE: Install the reverse driven gear so that its toothed side and the side of the synchronizer hub has its lower boss face in the same direction.

1. Reverse idle gear complete
2. Reverse idler gear bushing
3. Reverse idler gear shaft
4. Knock pin
5. Reverse shifter rail
6. Shifter fork rail
7. Shifter fork rail 2
8. Shifter rail plunger 2
9. Shifter rail plunger
10. Shifter fork
11. Shifter fork set screw
12. Reverse shifter rail arm
13. Reverse shifter lever complete
14. Shifter fork 2
15. Transmission main shaft collar 2
16. Snap-ring (outer)
17. Ball bearing
18. Transmission main shaft collar
19. Gear set
20. Synchronizer ring
21. 4th drive gear bushing
22. Synchronizer sleeve
23. Synchronizer hub spring
24. Synchronizer hub
25. Synchronizer hub insert
26. Third drive gear bushing
27. Transmission main shaft
28. Needle bearing
29. Oil seal
30. Drive pinion lock nut
31. Drive pinion lock washer
32. Ball bearing
33. Bolt
34. Spring washer
35. Drive pinion shim
36. Second driven gear
37. Synchronizer ring 2
38. Needle bearing
39. Needle bearing inner race
40. Reverse driven gear
41. Synchronizer hub spring 2
42. Synchronizer hub 2
43. Synchronizer hub insert 2
44. Low (1st) driven gear
45. Drive pinion spacer
46. Roller bearing
47. Key

Exploded view of 4-speed transaxle gear assemblies

c. Install the needle bearing race with a press.

d. Install the needle bearing. 1st driven gear, synchronizer rings and hub which was sub-assembled in (c).

e. Install the needle bearing race with a press.

f. Install the 2nd driven gear and insert a key into the groove on the drive pinion.

g. Install the 4th/3rd driven gear with a press.

h. Install the ball bearings with a press.

i. Install the drive pinion lockwasher.

NOTE: Stake the locknut in two places.

3. Reassemble the differential.

a. Install the side and pinion gears on the case and then insert the pinion shaft.

b. Measure the backlash between the gear and pinion and make adjustment using the proper washers.

c. Align the differential pinion shaft with the holes on the differential case and drive the straight pin in from the ring gear side. Drive it in until it falls in about 0.039 in. then stake the pin.

d. Press on the roller bearing on the differential case.

e. Using new lockwashers, clamp the ring gear on the case.

f. Install the axle driveshafts and lock it with snap-rings.

g. Measure the clearance between the pinion shaft and the tip of the axle driveshaft. Clearance should be 0–0.0079 in. Make adjustment by selecting the proper snap-ring.

NOTE: The figure of the lower three

digits marked on the drive pinion end face is the match number for combining it with the ring gear. The upper figure is for the shim adjustment. The first three digits on the ring gear indicates a number for combination with the drive pinion. The following digits indicate a value of appropriate backlash.

h. Adjust the drive pinion shim, place the drive pinion on the transmission case without a shim and tighten the pinion.

i. Press on the oil seal into the axle shaft oil seal holder.

4. Position the transmission case on the stand and screw the axle shaft oil seal holder into the case using the special wrench.

NOTE: Make sure the holder marked "R" is installed on the right side and holder marked "L" is installed on the left side.

5. Install the outer snap-ring and washer on the speedometer shaft, then install them into the transmission case. Install the speedometer driven gear on the shaft. Install the oil seal.

NOTE: Install the outer snap-ring on the speedometer driveshaft from the driven gear side.

6. Install the reverse shifter lever into the transmission case. Install the reverse idler gear and shaft.

7. Install the reverse shifter rail arm to the end of the reverse shifter lever. Install the reverse shifter rail.

8. Install the shifter fork rail spring, ball and gasket in the case and tighten the shifter rail spring plug.

9. Shifter the reverse shifter rail and select the reverse shifter rail arm so that the clearance between the reverse idler gear and the wall of the case is 0.059–0.079 in.

10. Install the shifter rail plunger into the hold of the case.

11. Wind tape around the splines of the axle driveshafts of the differential assembly to prevent damage to the oil seals.

12. Install the differential on the axle shaft oil seal holder.

13. Install the needle bearing on the transmission mainshaft and install the case.

NOTE: Make sure the knock pin of the case is fitted into the hole in the needle bearing outer race. To prevent damage to the roller bearing place the open end of the roving plunger on the bearing.

14. Install the shifter fork. Install the shifter rail plunger in the shifter fork rail.

15. Install the shims in the drive pinion selected in Step "k" under reassembling the differential assembly, and then install into the transmission case.

16. When installing the roller bearing outer race knock hole to the knock pin of the case, position the knock hole to the edge of the transmission case and put a mark on top of the outer race. Turn the outer race so that the mark comes to the edge of the transmission case while slightly up the drive pinion, then slightly move the outer race right and left and front and rear until the knock pin fits into the knock hole.

17. Install the shifter rail plunger.

18. Install the shifter fork and shifter fork rail.

19. Install the shifter fork rail spring,

1. Roller bearing
2. Bolt
3. Crown gear lock washer
4. Differential pinion shaft
5. Differential case
6. Straight pin
7. Axle drive shaft
8. Axle shaft oil seal holder
9. O-ring
10. Oil seal (RH)
11. Pinion & crown gear set (AT)
12. Pinion & crown gear set (4WD)
13-1. Pinion & crown gear set (4-speed)
13-2. Pinion & crown gear set (5-speed)
14. Washer
15. Differential side gear
16. Differential pinion
17. Snap-ring
18. Oil seal (LH)

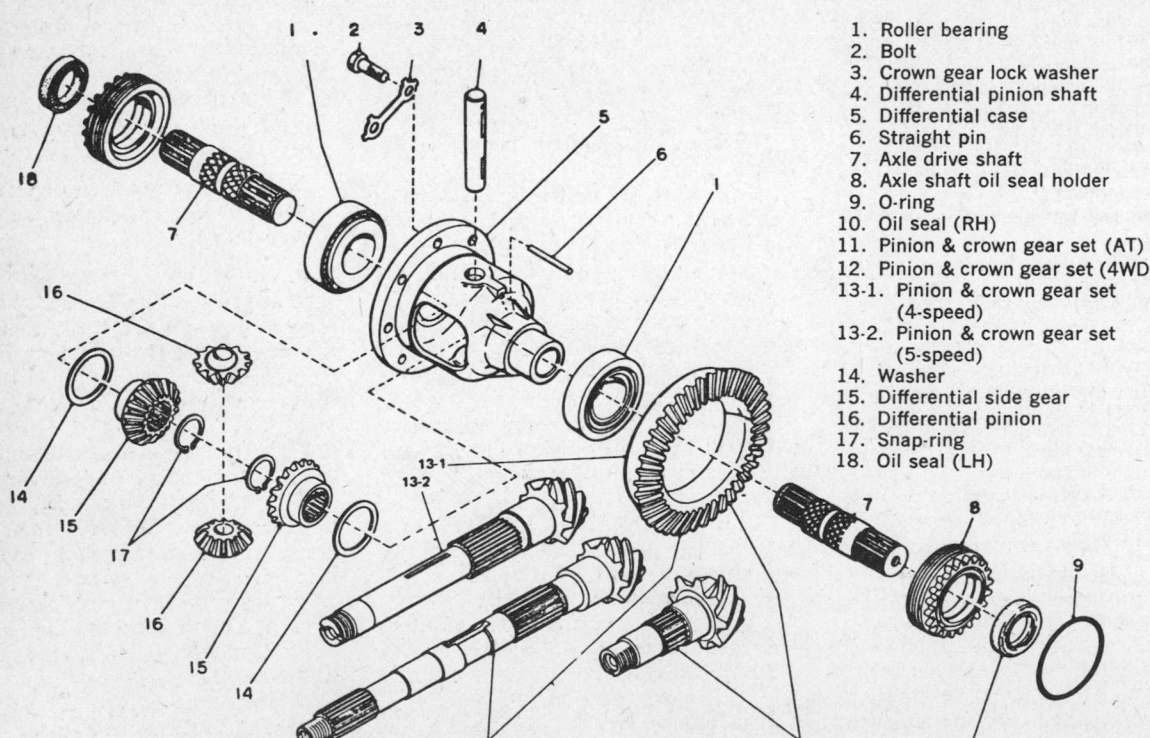

Exploded view of differential assembly and the three pinion gear lengths

ball and gasket into the case.

20. Select the shifter forks so that the synchronizer sleeve and reverse driven gear come to the center of the gears when the mainshaft and drive pinion are placed in the normal position (both the shaft and drive pinion are forced against the forward side without any clearance).

21. Check clearance A at the end of each rail. If dimension A is not within the range of 0.012–0.063 in., replace the rail, fork and set screw so that the proper dimension is obtained.

22. Install the mainshaft oil seal with its end surface A as shown in the illustration.

NOTE: When joining the case from above, be careful not to let the oil seal tilt. Apply liquid gasket to the case surfaces, remove the outer race of the roller bearings and make sure the speedometer gear tooth is meshed.

23. Clamp the clutch cable bracket, and back-up lamp wire clip together.

24. Install the drive pinion onto the case.

25. Install the outer race of the roller bearing.

26. Check and adjust the backlash of the ring gear and check the adjustment of pre-load on the roller bearing. Special tools are necessary unless it is done by trial-and-error. Backlash is as specified between 0.0039–0.0059 in.

27. Check the tooth contact of the hypoid gear as follows. To reduce backlash, loosen the holder on the upper case side and turn in the holder on the lower case side by the same amount. To increase backlash, loosen the lower and turn in the upper.

The drive pinion shim selected earlier may be too thick or thin. Increase or reduce its thickness.

28. Remove the lock plate (driveshaft holder). Loosen the driveshaft holder until the O-ring groove appears, install the O-ring into the groove and tighten the holder into position where the holder has been tightened in. Do this on both upper and lower heads.

29. Tighten the lock plate. Remove the protective vinyl tape wound on the axle shafts.

30. Reassemble the transmission cover.

31. Install the transmission cover.

a. Adjust the bearing side clearance 0–0.0118 in. using collar (transmission main shaft). For adjustment, insert collar if required.

b. Install the shifter arm in the cover (and install the cover to the transmission).

c. Adjust the transmission cover by inserting a bar through the hole of the shifter arm and shift the gear into 4th. Move the shifter arm from 4th position to 2nd and reverse position. The arm will move lightly toward 2nd side but heavy to reverse side because of the function of the return spring, and the arm will come into contact with the stopper at the end. To adjust, remove the plug on the cover and change the thickness of the

aluminum gasket, so that the light stroke and heavy stroke become the same.

32. Install the clutch release fork and release bearing holder and secure them with return springs.

NOTE: Fill the internal groove of the holder with grease.

TYPE 15

5 Speed Transaxle

Subaru

DISASSEMBLY

1. Remove the transmission.
2. Remove the clutch release fork and release bearing holder.
3. Remove the transmission rear cover.
4. Drive out the spring pin on the shifter fork.
5. Shift the gears into first gear, install the mainshaft stopper (special tool), release the staking on the drive pinion locknut and remove the nut.
6. Remove the synchronizer hub and shifter fork together.
7. Remove the 5th driven gear, needle bearing inner race, needle bearing and drive pinion spacer.
8. Remove the three bolts retaining the drive pinion assembly to the case.
9. Separate the left and right sections of the transmission case.
10. Remove the drive pinion assembly mainshaft assembly and differential assembly.
11. Remove the three shifter rail spring plugs.
12. Remove the shifter fork setscrew, shifter fork and shifter fork rail of 3rd/4th and 1st/2nd.

a. To remove the shifter fork rail, position the rest of the rails in neutral.

b. To remove the 3rd and 4th rails, turn them 90 degrees and let the shifter rail plunger fall in the groove of the reverse shifter rail.

13. Take out the lock pin and the reverse idler gear shaft, then remove the reverse idler gear and the reverse shifter lever as a unit.
14. Remove the outer snap-ring and take out the reverse shifter rail arm from the rail then remove the ball and spring.
15. Disassemble the mainshaft.

a. Using the special wrench and holder, remove the locknut and remove the 5th drive gear with a press.

b. Remove the Woodruff key.

c. Remove the ball bearing and 4th drive gear using a press.

d. Disassemble the synchronizer hub, third drive gear and 4th drive gear bush-

ing using a press.

e. Remove the outer snap-ring, 1st driven gear washer, 1st driven gear spring and 2nd driven gear spring, from the 1st driven gear and 2nd driven gear which were removed from the drive pinion.

16. The procedure for disassembling the main shaft differential gear, shifter fork, etc., is the same as the 4 speed transmission disassembly Steps 14–16.

ASSEMBLY

NOTE: Since some assembly procedures are the same as the 4-speed transmission, refer to that section where noted.

1. Reassemble the drive pinion component parts following the procedure in the four speed transmission section until the ball bearing, then install the spacer, needle bearing race, needle bearing, fifth driven gear, synchronizer hub, stopper, lock-washer and nut. Tighten the locknut to 60 ft. lbs.

2. Select a drive pinion shim (see Step 3—4 speed assembly procedures).

3. Put the shifter rail spring and ball in the reverse shifter rail arm. Insert the reverse shifter rail.

4. Install the outer snap-ring.

5. Put the shifter fork rail spring, ball and gasket in the case.

6. Select the reverse shifter lever so that the gap between the reverse idler gear and the case wall becomes 0.06–0.118 in. by shifting the reverse shifter rail.

7. Shift it to the neutral position, then select the right size washer so that the gap between the case wall becomes 0–0.002 in.

8. Put the shifter rail plunger into the grooves of the case and the reverse shifter rail arm.

9. Install the 1st driven gear spring (subgear) with the outer snap-ring and 1st driven gear washer to the 2nd driven gear.

NOTE: The clearance between the tooth tops of the gear and spring (subgear) is 0.0039–0.0197 in.

10. Reassemble the transmission mainshaft as given in Step 1 under assembly of 4 speed transmission. Then, install a key, 5th drive gear, lock washer and locknut to the mainshaft.

11. Fit the differential assembly into the case.

12. Attach the mainshaft assembly.

13. Insert a shifter rail plunger and install a shifter fork and rail.

14. Install the adjustment shim selected before with the drive pinion assembly and then install them to the case.

15. Insert the shifter rail plunger.

16. Install the shifter fork and shifter rail.

17. Install the shifter fork rail spring and ball in the case.

18. Select the shifter fork so that the synchronizer sleeve comes to the center of the 3rd and 4th drive gears.

19. Select the next shifter fork so that the reverse driven gear comes to the center

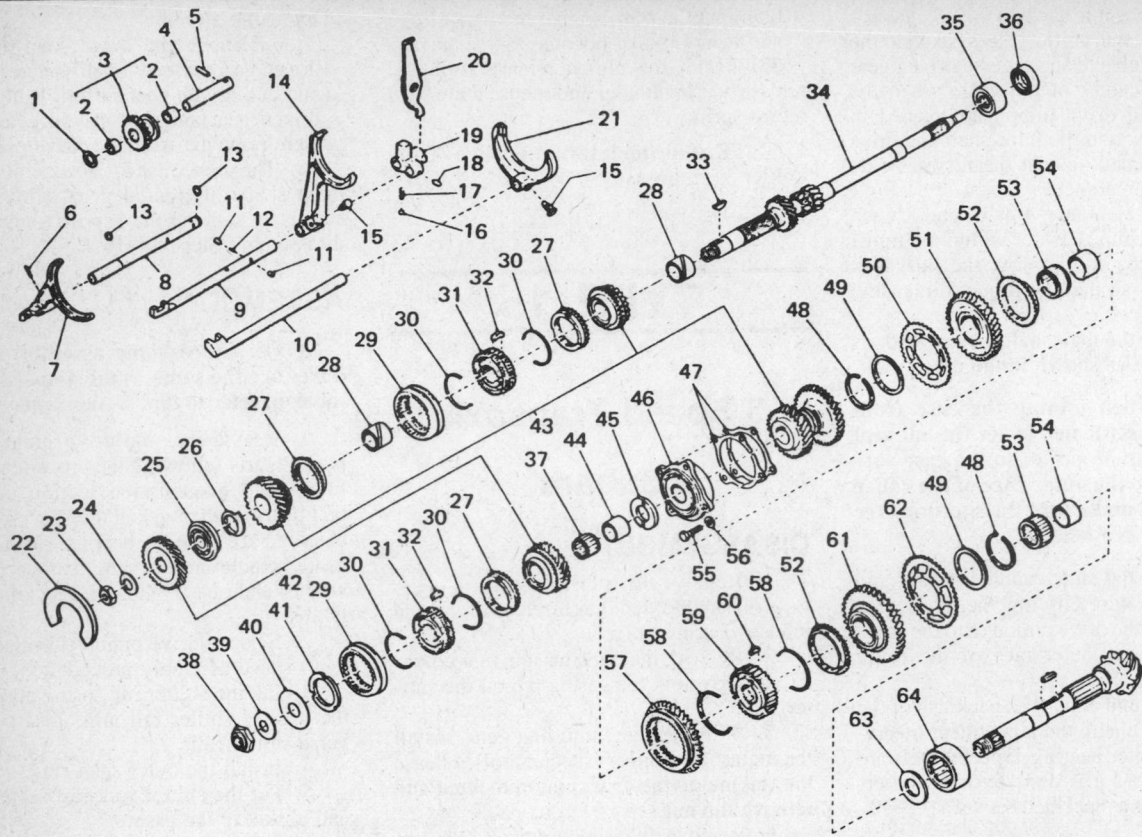

Exploded view of 5-speed transaxle gear assemblies

1. Washer
2. Reverse idler gear bushing
3. Reverse idler gear complete
4. Reverse idler gear shaft
5. Knock pin
6. Spring pin
7. Shifter fork 3
8. Reverse shifter rail
9. Shifter fork rail
10. Shifter fork rail 2
11. Shifter rail plunger 2
12. Shifter rail plunger
13. Snap ring (outer)
14. Shifter fork
15. Shifter fork set screw
16. Ball
17. Shifter fork rail spring 2

18. Shifter rail plunger 2
19. Reverse shifter rail arm
20. Reverse shifter lever complete
21. Shifter fork 2
22. Transmission main shaft collar 2
23. Transmission main shaft lock nut
24. Transmission main shaft lock washer
25. Ball bearing
26. Transmission main shaft collar
27. Synchronizer ring
28. 4th drive gear bushing
28. 3rd drive gear bushing
29. Synchronizer sleeve

30. Synchronizer hub spring
31. Synchronizer hub
32. Synchronizer hub insert
33. Woodruff key
34. Transmission main shaft
35. Needle bearing
36. Oil seal
37. Needle bearing
38. Drive pinion lock nut
39. Drive pinion lock washer
40. Synchronizer stopper 2
41. Synchronizer stopper
42. Fifth gear set
43. Third and fourth gear set
44. Needle bearing inner race 5
45. Drive pinion spacer 2
46. Ball bearing

47. Drive pinion shim
48. Snap ring
49. Low (1st) driven gear washer
50. Second driven spring gear
51. Second driven gear
52. Synchronizer ring 2
53. Needle bearing
54. Needle bearing inner race
55. Bolt
56. Spring washer
57. Reverse driven gear
58. Synchronizer hub spring 2
59. Synchronizer hub 2
60. Synchronizer hub insert 2
61. Low (1st) driven gear
62. Low (1st) driven spring gear
63. Drive pinion spacer
64. Roller bearing

of the 1st and 2nd driven gears.

20. Apply a liquid gasket to the mating surfaces of the case halves and put them together.

21. Tighten the drive pinion on to the transmission case.

22. Inspect the ring gear backlash and the tooth contact as described under 4 speed transmission assembly Steps 26 and 27.

23. Remove the locknut of the drive pinion assembly to remove the lockwasher, stoppers and hub.

24. Install the hub, fork and rail using the spring pin.

25. Install the synchronizer stoppers and drive pinion lockwasher. Using the main-shaft stopper tool, tighten the pinion locknut to 58 ft. lbs.

NOTE: Shift the gear to 1st position when tightening the drive pinion locknut.

26. Select the last shifter fork so that the clearance between the sleeve and the 5th driven gear becomes 0.008–0.020 when the gear is in the 5th position.

27. Stake the drive pinion locknut.

28. Check the clearance between the edges of each rail. If the clearance is not within 0.012–0.063 in., replace the rail, fork and setscrew as necessary.

29. Select the correct mainshaft collar.

30. Install the rear cover.

TYPE 16

4 Speed Transaxle

Subaru with 4/WD

DISASSEMBLY

NOTE: Since some of the overhaul procedures are the same as the 4 speed transmission refer to that section (Type 14) when noted.

1. Shifter fork rail 2
2. Shifter fork rail
3. Reverse shifter rail
4. Transmission main shaft lock nut
5. Transmission main shaft lock washer
6. Ball bearing
7. Transmission main shaft collar
8. Rear shaft driven gear
9. Synchronizer ring
10. Rear shaft driven gear bushing
11. Synchronizer sleeve
12. Synchronizer hub spring
13. Synchronizer hub
14. Synchronizer hub insert
15. Rear drive spacer
16. Snap ring
17. Ball bearing
18. Rear drive shaft
19. Washer
20. Drive pinion collar
21. Needle bearing race 5
22. Rear shaft drive gear

Exploded view of added gears and shafts for the 4 wheel drive unit

1. Remove the transmission.

2. Drive out the straight pin and pull out the shifter fork rail, fork, ball and spring.

3. Remove the case assembly.

4. Shift the gear to the 1st position, release the staked part of the nut, then using a main shaft stopper, remove the locknut and take out the rear shaft drive gear from the drive pinion.

5. Remove the case assembly.

6. Remove the race, needle bearing collar and washer from the drive pinion.

7. Shift the sleeve into the drive position and using a holder, remove the mainshaft locknut.

8. Remove the ball bearing assembly.

9. Remove the mainshaft spacer, rearshaft driven gear, sleeve, synchronizer hub and rear drive spacer from the rear driveshaft.

10. Remove the snap-ring from the case.

11. Punch out the rear driveshaft and using a press, remove the ball bearing.

12. Take out the O-ring from the shifter arm and remove the shifter arm.

13. Remove the back-up lamp switch from the case and the reverse accent spring ball and straight pin.

14. Remove the plug from the case and take out the reverse accent shaft and turn spring.

15. Remove the needle bearing from the case.

16. Remove the rear extension oil seal.

17. For the remainder of the transmission disassembly procedures refer to the 4 speed transaxle section (Type 14).

ASSEMBLY

1. Assemble the main transmission unit.
   a. The drive pinion assembly is assembled by fitting the ball bearing, washer collar, needle bearing inner race, rear drive shaft gear, lockwasher and locknut.

Do not stake the nut at this time.

2. Assemble the transmission case without the transfer system.

NOTE: After assembling, remove the locknut, lockwasher and rear shaft drive gear from the drive pinion.

3. Press fit the needle bearing into the case.

4. Insert the reverse return spring and the reverse accent shaft into the case. Install an adjusting aluminum gasket on the plug.

5. Set the ball reverse accent spring, straight pin and aluminum washer on the back-up lamp switch.

6. Install the shifter arm onto the transmission case.

7. Assemble the three synchronizer inserts, sleeve and two springs on the synchronizer hub.

NOTE: Make sure the hub is installed so that the spline with the smaller width is on the rear drive spacer side.

8. Press fit the ball bearing to the rear driveshaft.

9. Hammer the rear driveshaft into the transmission case and install the inner snapring.

10. Install the snap-ring rear drive spacer, synchronizer hub, rear shaft driven gear sleeve, synchronizer ring, rear shaft driven gear and mainshaft spacer to the shaft.

11. Press fit the ball bearing to the rear driveshaft.

12. Shift the sleeve to be fitted with a transmission mainshaft lockwasher to the drive position.

13. Adjust the bearing side clearance to 0–0.012 in. using a mainshaft collar.

14. Mount the case assembly on the main transmission unit.

15. Install the washer, drive pinion collar and needle bearing race to the drive

pinion. Shift the gear into 1st and then tighten the locknut.

16. Install the O-ring into the groove of the shifter arm.

17. Mount the case assembly and tighten the bolts.

NOTE: When installing, the rear shift drive and 4th drive gears should engage each other. Before tightening each bolt, make sure that the shifter arm shifts smoothly in each direction.

18. Install the 3rd shifter fork, spring, ball and rail into the case.

NOTE: To install the ball, press it down by using the end of the shifter fork rail while forcing the rail into the case with the round side down. Rotate the rail by 180° to its proper position.

19. Drive in the straight pin, then move the shifter fork rail and check the accent.

20. Install the transmission case cover.

21. Adjust the selecting direction and position of the shifter arm shaft.
   a. Install the gear shift system.
   b. Shift the gear into 4th.
   c. Shift the shifter arm from the 4th/3rd position to the 1st and reverse position.
   d. The arm moves lightly to the 1st position while it moves heavily to the reverse position and hits the stopper as the force of the return spring is applied.
   e. Adjust so that the light travel becomes the same as the heavy travel by removing the plug on the top of the transmission case and change the thickness of aluminum gasket.

22. When mounting the transmission on the car body, the gearshift system should be removed first.

23. For reassembly of the remaining transmission parts, please refer to the 4 speed transmission section (Type 14).

* Selective parts

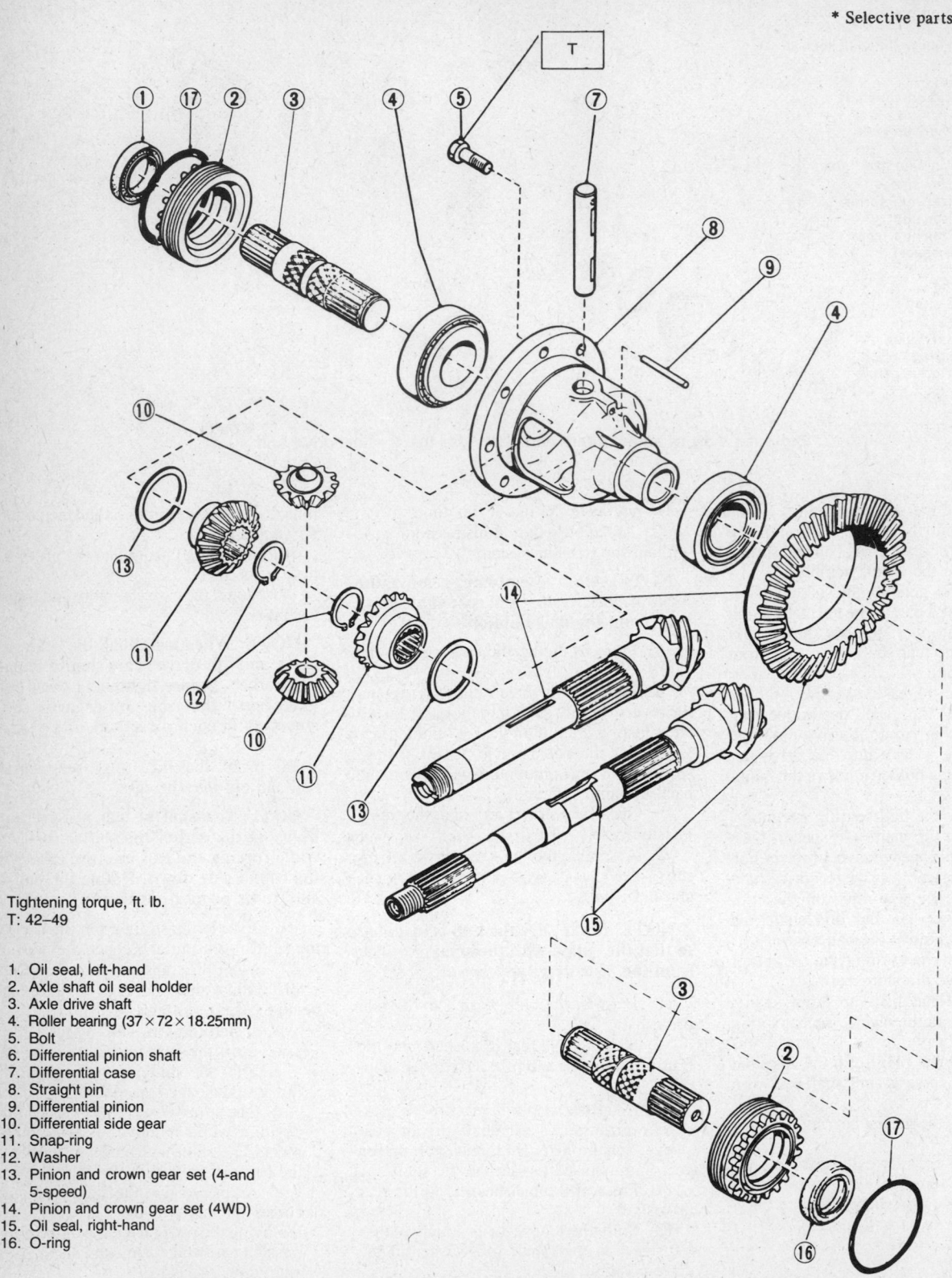

Tightening torque, ft. lb.
T: 42–49

1. Oil seal, left-hand
2. Axle shaft oil seal holder
3. Axle drive shaft
4. Roller bearing (37 × 72 × 18.25mm)
5. Bolt
6. Differential pinion shaft
7. Differential case
8. Straight pin
9. Differential pinion
10. Differential side gear
11. Snap-ring
12. Washer
13. Pinion and crown gear set (4-and 5-speed)
14. Pinion and crown gear set (4WD)
15. Oil seal, right-hand
16. O-ring

Exploded view of the Subaru differential unit

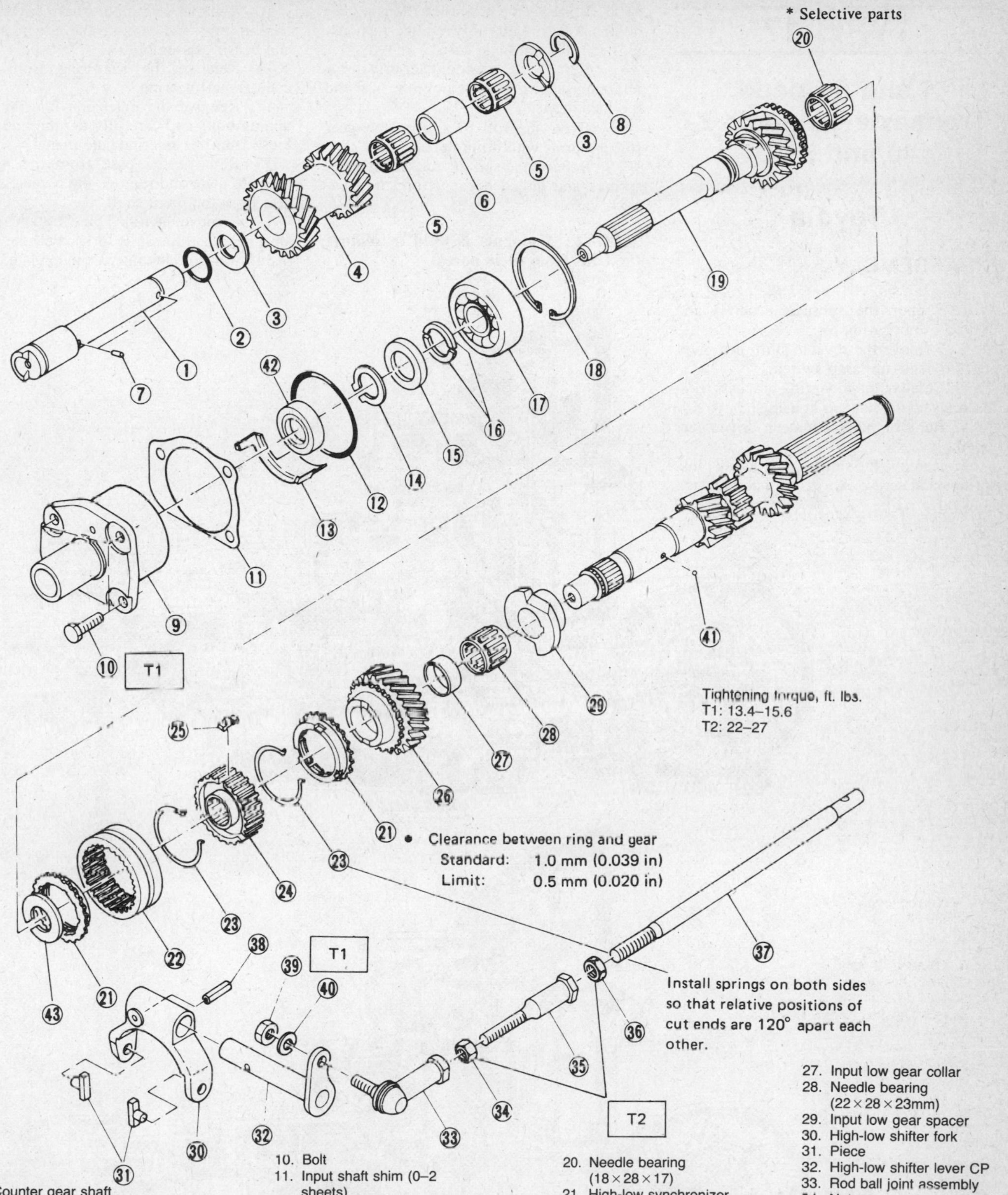

* Selective parts

Tightening torque, ft. lbs.
T1: 13.4–15.6
T2: 22–27

● Clearance between ring and gear
Standard: 1.0 mm (0.039 in)
Limit: 0.5 mm (0.020 in)

Install springs on both sides
so that relative positions of
cut ends are 120° apart each
other.

1. Counter gear shaft
2. O-ring
3. Counter gear washer
4. Counter gear
5. Needle bearing
   (18 × 25 × 22mm)
6. Counter gear collar
7. Knock pin
8. Clip
9. Input shaft holder

10. Bolt
11. Input shaft shim (0–2
    sheets)
12. O-ring (55.7 × 2.4mm)
13. Oil guide
14. Snap-ring (outer)
15. Input shaft retainer
16. Input shaft cotter
17. Ball bearing
    (22 × 56 × 16mm)
18. Snap-ring (inner-56)
19. Input shaft

20. Needle bearing
    (18 × 28 × 17)
21. High-low synchronizer
    ring
22. High-low synchronizer
    sleeve
23. Spring
24. High-low synchronizer
    hub
25. High-low synchronizer
    insert
26. Input low gear

27. Input low gear collar
28. Needle bearing
    (22 × 28 × 23mm)
29. Input low gear spacer
30. High-low shifter fork
31. Piece
32. High-low shifter lever CP
33. Rod ball joint assembly
34. Nut
35. Rod adjusting screw
36. Nut (left handed thread)
37. High-low shifter rod
38. Straight pin (5 × 22mm)
39. Nut
40. Spring washer
41. 3.9688 ball
42. Oil seal (22 × 40 × 10mm)
43. Snap-ring (outer-22)

Auxiliary transmission and High-Low shift linkage—Subaru 4-wheel drive

TYPE 17

4 and 5 Speed Transaxle—Models Z-40 and Z-50

Toyota

DISASSEMBLY

1. Support the transaxle securely and drain the lubricating oil.

2. Remove the reverse shift arm pivot and the back–up lamp switch.

3. Remove the mounting brackets from the transaxle extension housing.

4. Remove the speedometer driven gear assembly.

5. Remove the shifting restricting pins, springs and screw caps from the extension housing.

6. Remove the extension housing retaining bolts and carefully remove the housing from the transaxle case.

7. Remove the speedometer drive gear retaining snap-ring and remove the gear and the locating ball.

8. Drive the roll pins from the gear shifting arms with a pin punch.

9. Remove the shifting rod detent balls, springs and threaded caps from the transaxle case.

NOTE: A magnet is used to remove the balls from their bores.

10. Remove the input shaft cover retaining bolts and remove the cover, shaft and bearing assemblies.

11. Remove the snap-ring from the countershaft bearing.

12. Remove the extension housing retaining bolts and carefully tap the housing loose from the intermediate plate.

13. Remove the case from the intermediate plate and remove the reverse shift arm from the pivot shaft.

14. Remove the rolled pins from the gear shift head and the shift forks. Pull the No. 3 shift rod from the intermediate plate. Re-

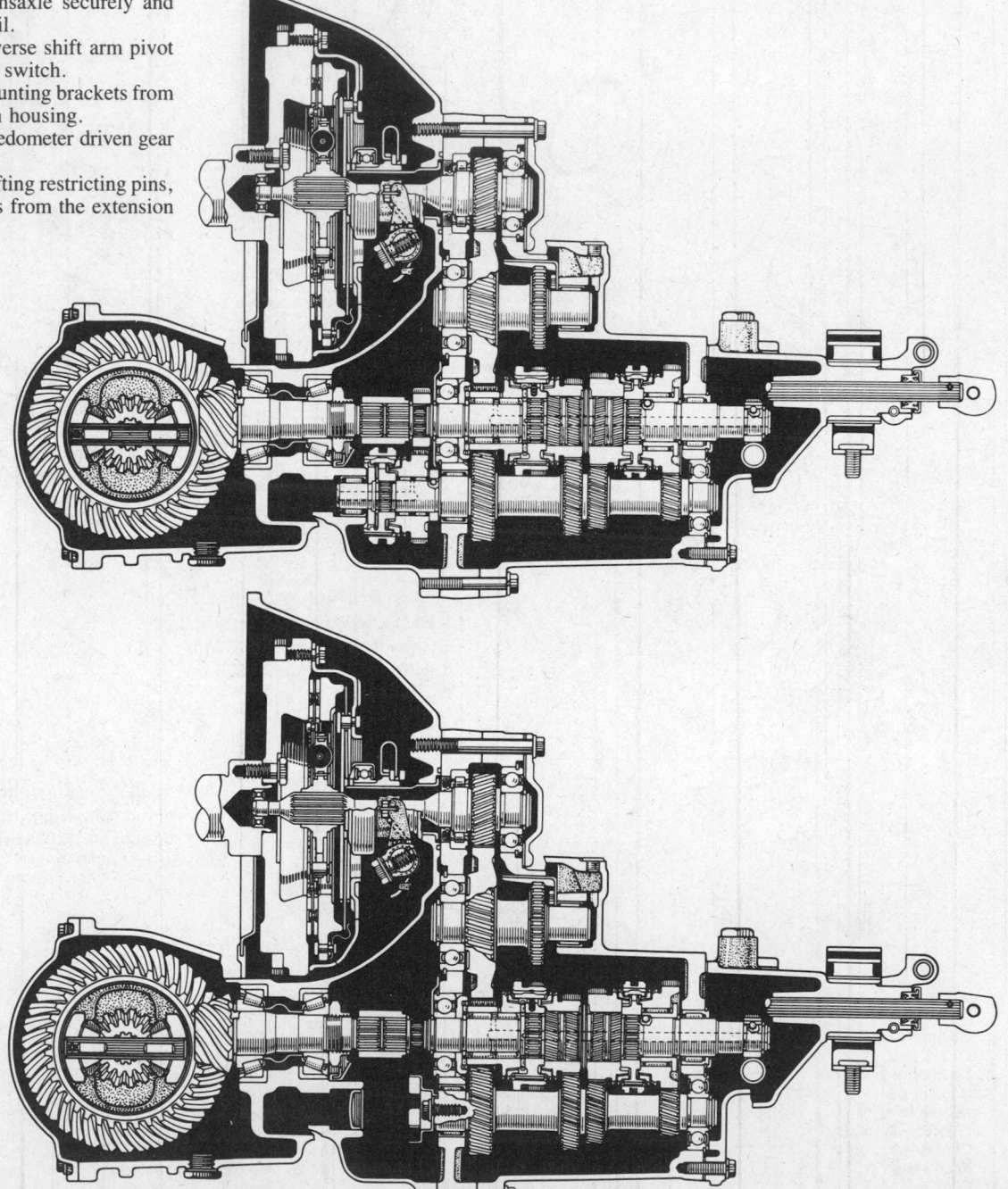

Z50

Z40

Cross section of models Z50 and Z40 transaxles

move the No. 3 shift fork from the coupling sleeve.

15. Remove the interlock pin and pull the No. 2 shift rod from the intermediate plate. Remove the shift fork from the coupling sleeve.

16. Remove the interlock pin and pull the No. 1 rod from the intermediate plate. Remove the No. 1 shift fork from the coupling sleeve. Remove the reverse shift fork.

17. To remove the gear assemblies from the intermediate plate, perform the following procedures as applies to each transaxle.

a. Z-50—Measure the 5th gear thrust clearance which should be 0.0059–0.0128 inch (0.15–0.325 mm), and with a service limit of 0.016 inch (0.4 mm). Remove the retaining snap-ring and remove the 5th gear, clutch hub and synchronizer ring with a puller type tool. Remove the roller bearing cage, the spacer and the steel locater ball.

b. Z-40—Remove the countergear plate, bolt and lock washer.

18. Remove the output shaft bearing retainer and bolts from the intermediate plate. Remove the two ball bearing snap-rings and with a plastic hammer or equivalent, force the output shaft, the reverse gearshaft and idler gear halfway out from the plate.

CAUTION
Support the shafts by hand.

19. Remove the idler gear and the reverse gearshaft as an assembly.

20. Remove the countergear and the output shaft together.

21. Measure the thrust clearance of the 1st, 2nd, 3rd and 4th gears before disassembly of the output shaft. Record the clearances for reference during the assembly.

22. Using a puller type tool, remove the sleeve yoke from the end of the output shaft.

23. Z-50—Remove the snap-ring from the shaft and remove the 5th gear with the puller type tool. Remove the ball bearing snap-ring.

24. Z-40—Remove the snap-ring from the shaft that locates the sleeve yoke and the snap-ring that retains the ball bearing in position on the shaft.

25. Using the puller type tool, remove the ball bearing from the shaft. Remove the spacer from the shaft, along with the thrust bearing.

CAUTION
Do not drop the thrust bearing.

26. Remove the 4th gear and the half needle bearing cages from the shaft.

27. Remove the snap-ring from the shaft and remove the No. 2 clutch hub, synchronizer ring and the 3rd speed gear from the shaft with the puller type tool.

28. Remove the snap-ring from the front of the shaft and remove the bushing needle bearing, 1st gear and the synchronizer ring. Using a magnet, remove the locating locking ball from the shaft.

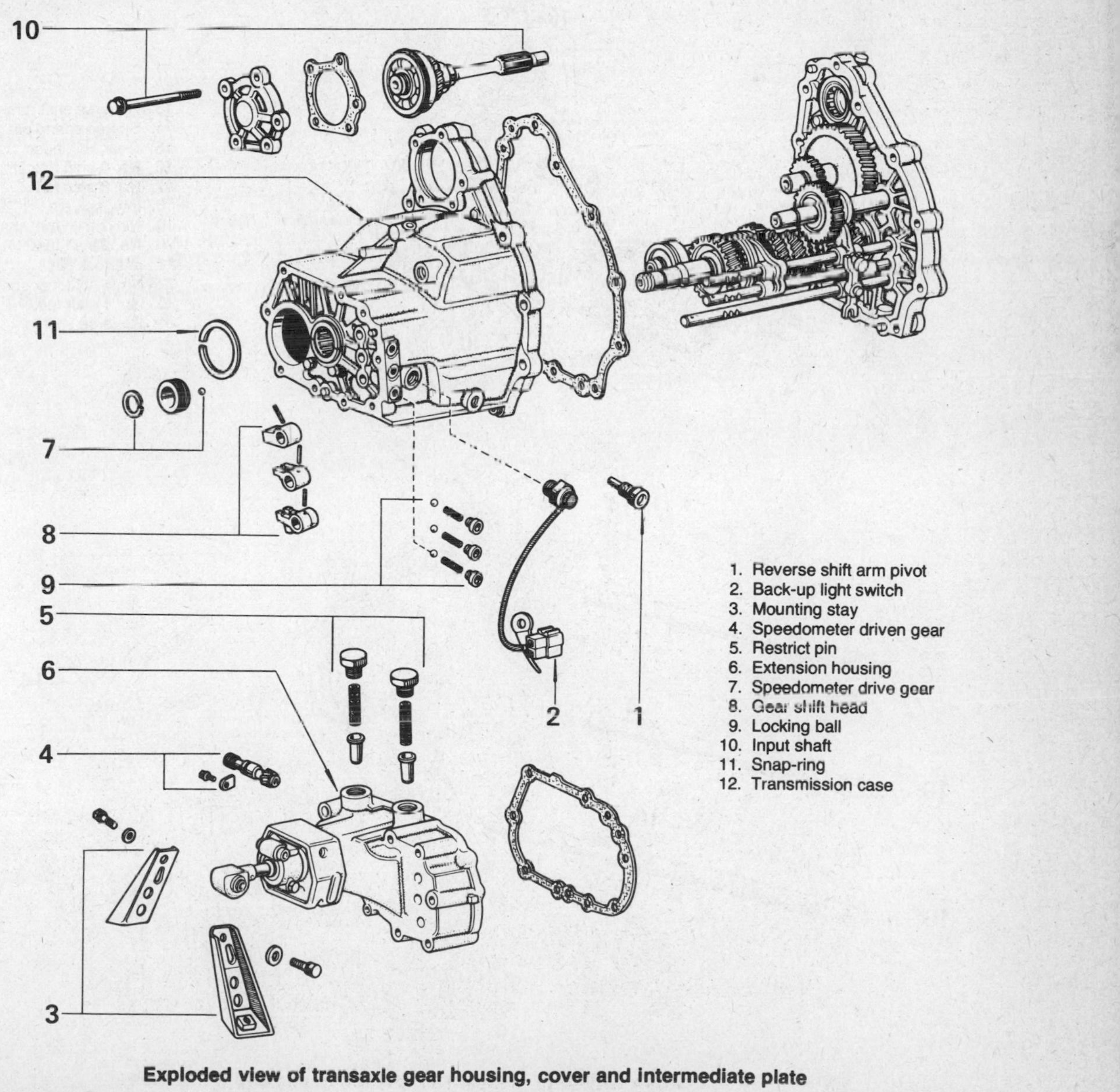

1. Reverse shift arm pivot
2. Back-up light switch
3. Mounting stay
4. Speedometer driven gear
5. Restrict pin
6. Extension housing
7. Speedometer drive gear
8. Gear shift head
9. Locking ball
10. Input shaft
11. Snap-ring
12. Transmission case

Exploded view of transaxle gear housing, cover trand intermediate plate

29. Remove the No. 1 clutch hub, synchronizer ring and the second gear from the shaft.

30. Inspect the gears, bearings, case, housing, plate, synchronizers, shafts and the remaining parts of the transaxle for wear and damage. Replace the necessary parts before the assembly.

ASSEMBLY

1. Begin the assembly by placing the 2nd gear on the output shaft, followed by the synchronizer ring and the Number one clutch hub. Install the locking ball in place on the shaft and install the synchronizer ring, the 1st gear, bearing and the bushing. Install the snap-ring of a thickness to obtain a thrust clearance of zero. The following snap-rings are available:

SNAP-RING SIZES

Mark	Thickness	
	mm	(in.)
1	2.15–2.20	(0.0846–0.0866)
2	2.20–2.25	(0.0866–0.0886)
3	2.25–2.30	(0.0886–0.0906)
4	2.30–2.35	(0.0906–0.0925)
5	2.35–2.40	(0.0925–0.0945)
6	2.40–2.45	(0.0945–0.0965)
7	2.45–2.50	(0.0965–0.0984)
8	2.50–2.55	(0.0984–0.1004)
9	2.55–2.60	(0.1004–0.1024)

2. Check the thrust clearances of the 1st and 2nd gears. The clearances should be as listed:

1st gears—0.0059–0.0108 inch (0.15–0.275 mm)

Service limit—0.0118 inch (0.30 mm)
2nd gears—0.0059–0.0004 inch (0.15–0.25 mm)
Service limit—0.0118 inch (0.30 mm)

3. Install the No. 2 clutch hub on the shaft and align the shifting keys with the key slots in the synchronizer rings.

4. Install the widest thrust bearing against the No. 2 clutch hub. Install the half needle bearing cages, synchronizer ring and the 4th speed gear.

5. Install the spacer and the snap-ring to the front side of the 4th gear.

6. Install the smaller thrust washer into the spacer and install the assembly onto the shaft with the thrust washer facing the 4th speed gear.

NOTE: The spacer will have to be pressed onto the shaft.

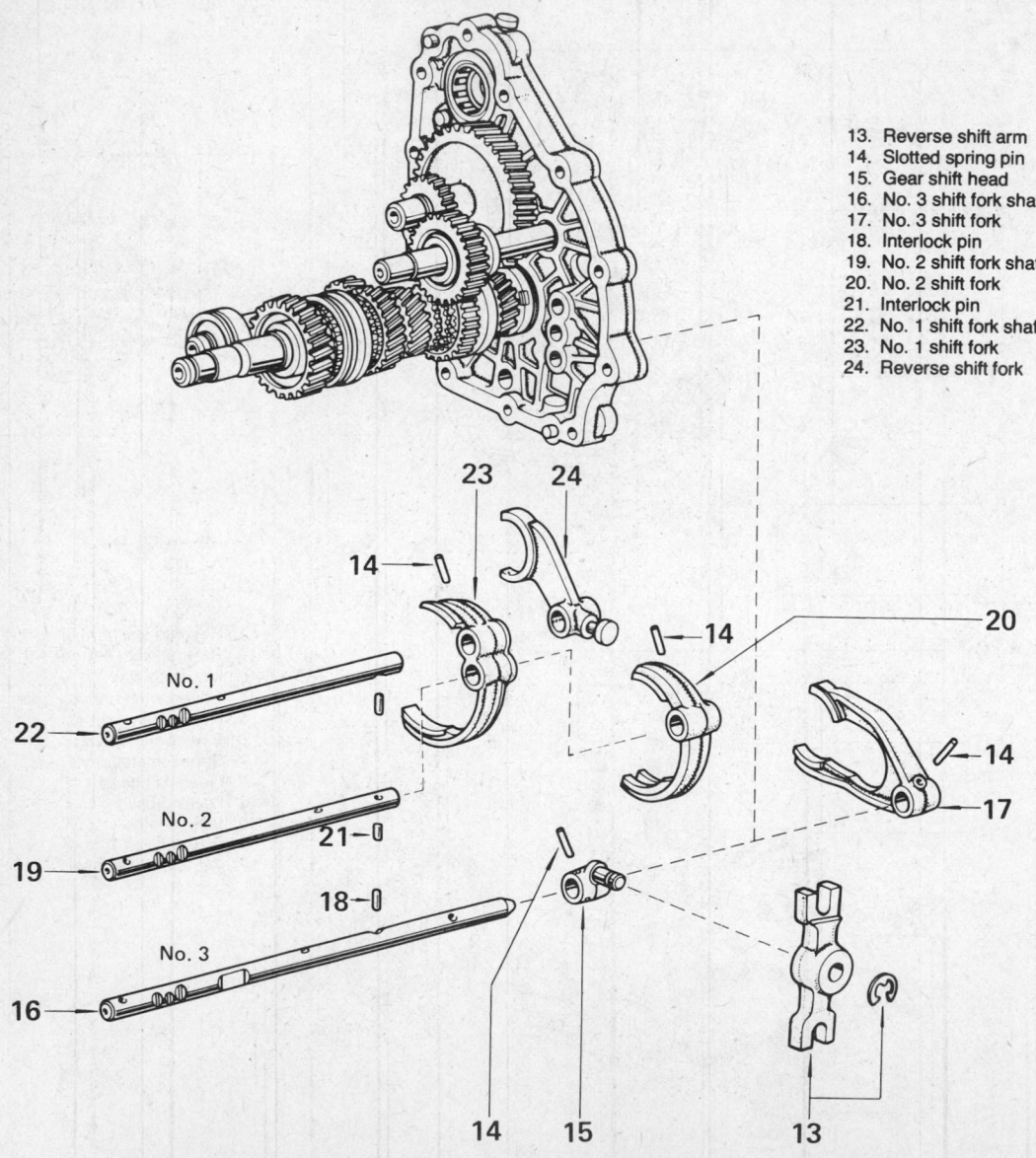

13. Reverse shift arm
14. Slotted spring pin
15. Gear shift head
16. No. 3 shift fork shaft
17. No. 3 shift fork
18. Interlock pin
19. No. 2 shift fork shaft
20. No. 2 shift fork
21. Interlock pin
22. No. 1 shift fork shaft
23. No. 1 shift fork
24. Reverse shift fork

Exploded view of shift mechanism, typical of models Z50 and Z40 transaxles

7. Press the ball bearing onto the shaft with the groove on the bearing facing towards the front.

8. Select a snap-ring of a thickness to obtain a thrust clearance of zero from the following list of available snap-rings.

SNAP-RING SIZES

| Mark | Thickness | |
	mm	(in.)
2	2.10–2.15	(0.0827–0.0846)
3	2.15–2.20	(0.0846–0.0866)
4	2.20–2.25	(0.0866–0.0886)
5	2.25–2.30	(0.0886–0.0906)
6	2.30–2.35	(0.0906–0.0925)
7	2.35–2.40	(0.0925–0.0945)
8	2.40–2.45	(0.0945–0.0965)
9	2.45–2.50	(0.0965–0.0984)
10	2.50–2.55	(0.0984–0.1004)

9. With the selected snap-ring installed, measure the thrust clearance of the 3rd and 4th gears.

The clearance should be as follows:

3rd gear—0.0059–0.0098 inch (0.15–0.25 mm)

Service limit—0.0118 inch (0.30 mm)

4th gear—0.008–0.0094 inch (0.02–0.24 mm)

Service limit—0.0118 inch (0.30 mm)

10. Z-50—Install the 5th gear and select a snap-ring of a thickness to obtain a clearance of zero from the following list of snap-rings.

SNAP-RING SIZES

| Mark | Thickness | |
	mm	(in.)
2	2.10–2.15	(0.0827–0.0846)
3	2.15–2.20	(0.0846–0.0866)
4	2.20–2.25	(0.0866–0.0886)
5	2.25–2.30	(0.0886–0.0906)
6	2.30–2.35	(0.0906–0.0925)

11. Z-40—Install the snap-ring in the groove on the shaft near the end.

12. Press the sleeve yoke onto the shaft until the yoke touches the first snap-ring and that zero clearance exists between the snap-ring and the shaft groove.

13. Place the intermediate plate in a holder and place the assembled output shaft and the countershaft gear assembly into the intermediate plate, approximately half-way.

14. Align the idler gear with the notched portion of the reverse idler gearshaft. Tap the idler gearshaft bearing approximately half way into the intermediate plate.

NOTE: Be sure the idler gear and the output shaft spacers are not in contact with each other.

15. Tap each gearshaft until the bearings are seated in the intermediate plate. Install the retaining snap-rings on the bearings.

16. Install the bearing retainer and secure the retaining bolts.

17. a. Z-40—Align the countergear plate with the countershaft protrusion and install the bolt and lockwasher. Torque to 8–11 ft. lbs. (1.0–1.6 Kg-m).

NOTE: Mesh the gears to lock the shaft.

b. Z-50—Align the synchronizer shifting slots and keys on the synchronizer ring and install the No. 3 clutch hub. Install a selective snap-ring of a thickness that will reduce the thrust clearance to zero, selected from the following chart.

SNAP-RING SIZES

| Thickness | |
mm	(In.)
1.80–1.85	(0.0709–0.0728)
1.85–1.90	(0.0728–0.0748)
1.90–1.95	(0.0748–0.0768)
1.95–2.00	(0.0768–0.0787)
2.00–2.05	(0.0787–0.0807)
2.05–2.10	(0.0807–0.0827)
2.10–2.15	(0.0827–0.0846)

18. Measure the 5th gear thrust clearance. The clearance should be 0.0059–0.0128 inch (0.5–0.325 mm), with a service limit of 0.0157 inch (0.40 mm).

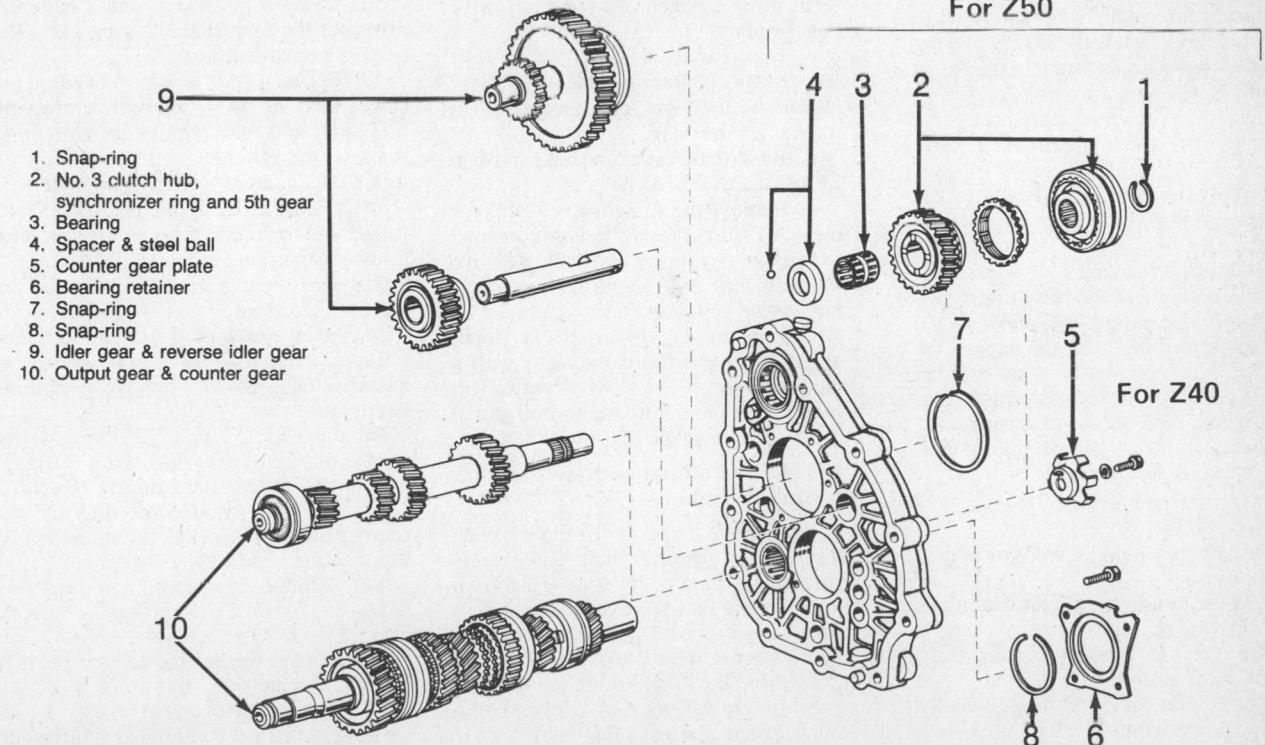

1. Snap-ring
2. No. 3 clutch hub, synchronizer ring and 5th gear
3. Bearing
4. Spacer & steel ball
5. Counter gear plate
6. Bearing retainer
7. Snap-ring
8. Snap-ring
9. Idler gear & reverse idler gear
10. Output gear & counter gear

For Z50

For Z40

Exploded view of intermediate plate and gears—model Z40 and Z50 parts illustrated

19. Fit the shifting forks into their respective coupling sleeves. Insert the number one shift rod into the No. 1 shifting fork, the reverse shift fork and into the intermediate plate bore.

20. Install the No. 2 shift rod into the lower hole of the No. 1 shift fork and through the No. 2 shift fork, and on into the intermediate plate bore.

21. Install the No. 3 shift rod into the No. 4 gear shift head and into the No. 3 shift fork. Continue inward with the shifting rod until the pin hole of the No. 3 shift fork is aligned with the interlock pin hole.

22. Insert a piece of wire into the interlock pin hole to a length of 4.7 inches (120 mm) from the outside of the intermediate plate.

23. Assemble the interlock pins so that a long pin is inserted first, followed by the small pin and then the same sized pin as the first one, for a total of three. Push the pins inward with a piece of wire and verify that the distance is 3.1 inches (80 mm) from the outside of the intermediate plate.

24. In the transaxle of the Z-50, install the number three shaft into the fork controlling the 5th speed synchronizer.

25. Place the shift rods in the neutral position. Move the No. 2 shift rod into the 3rd gear position and the number one and two shafts should not move.

26. Apply sealer to the plug for the interlocks and tighten into place.

27. Align the pin holes in the shift forks and shift fork shafts. Drive the roll pins into place and secure the forks to the shafts.

28. Install the gasket to the intermediate plate and carefully install the case to the plate.

29. Install the countershaft snap-ring to the ball bearing. Install the detent locking balls and springs. Apply sealer to the detent plugs and install.

30. Install the reverse shift arm pivot bolt through the under side of the reverse shift arm.

31. Install the gear shift heads to the shift rods and install the roll pins to retain the heads.

32. Install the locating ball, the speedometer drive gear and the snap-ring.

33. Apply the gasket and sealer to the mating surface of the case and engage the end of the shift lever shaft and the number two shift head, on the extension housing. Install the retaining bolts and secure.

34. Install the restricting pins in their proper positions as follows.

    Green—1st and 2nd gears
    Red—5th and reverse

35. Install the mounting brackets to their marked positions.

36. Fill the transaxle with lubricating oil to its proper level.

37. Be sure the transaxle gear shifts smoothly in all positions.

38. Install the input shaft, gasket and retainer. Secure with the retaining bolts.

39. Install the speedometer driven gear assembly and electrical switch.

TYPE 18

4 and 5 Speed Transaxle—Z41, 42, 44, 51, 52 and 52F (4 × 4)

Toyota

DISASSEMBLY

NOTE: The Type 18 transaxle is similar to the Type 17—illustrations are compatible with either section.

1. Support and drain the transaxle.

2. Remove the pivot from the reverse shifter arm. Remove the back-up light switch. Remove the 4 × 4 switch (Z52F only).

3. Remove the speedometer driven gear.

4. Remove the rear mounting stay and then the restrict pins.

5. Remove the retaining bolts and then remove the extension housing from the transmission case (all but Z52F).

6. On the Z52F only:

    a. Remove the transmission case cover, the spring and ball.

NOTE: Use a magnet to remove the ball from its seating.

    b. Remove the straight screw plug and then, using a punch and hammer, drive out the pin.

    c. Unscrew the six bolts for the shift lever retainer. Remove the shift lever housing set bolt and lock plate and then remove the housing.

    d. Remove the mounting bolts and then lift off the extension housing.

    e. Remove the straight screw plug for the 4 × 4 shift fork shaft. Use a magnet to remove the spring and ball. Remove the shift fork shaft along with the hub, hub sleeve and shift fork.

    f. Temporarily re-install the input shaft, cover the tip of the shaft with a cloth and secure the shaft in place with a pair of pliers. Remove the oil pump drive shaft and then the input shaft.

NOTE: The oil pump drive shaft has left-hand threads.

    g. Remove the set bolt and lock plate for the No. 4 gear shift shaft. Using snap-ring pliers, remove the snap-ring from the shaft and then remove the No. 4 shift fork along with the No. 4 shift fork shaft. Use a magnet and remove the inter-lock pin which should still be in its seating.

    h. Unscrew the nine transfer case-to-transmission case mounting bolts. Swivel the selector lever and remove the tip from the shift head groove and then pull off

the transfer case along with the selector lever and the extra low gear.

    i. Remove the output shaft and the oil pump gear from the extension housing.

7. Remove the speedometer drive gear.

8. Remove the gear shift head as follows:

    a. On all models but the Z52F, use a pin punch and a hammer and drive out the slotted spring pins. Remove the gear shift heads.

    b. On the Z52F, remove the C washer from the No. 1 and 2 shift fork shafts.

9. Using a special hexagon wrench, remove the straight screw plugs. Using a magnet, lift out the springs and balls.

10. Using snap-ring pliers, remove the bearing snap-ring.

11. Remove the transmission case cover and then pull out the input shaft.

12. Using a rubber mallet, lightly tap on the transmission case protrusion to break the seal between it and the intermediate plate. Remove the case from the intermediate plate.

13. Mount the intermediate plate in a soft-jawed vise.

CAUTION
Use the protrusion on the lower part of the intermediate plate to secure it in the vise.

14. On the Z41, 42 and 51, remove the E-ring that retains the reverse shift arm and then remove the arm.

15. On the Z44, 52 and 52F, remove the straight screw plug, spring and ball as detailed previously in this section.

16. Using a pin punch and a hammer, drive out the four slotted spring pins. Remove the gearshift head.

17. Set each shift fork to the neutral position, hold the shift fork, pull out the shift fork shaft and then remove the shift fork. Remove the interlock pins from the shift fork shafts and the intermediate plate.

18. On the Z51, 52 and 52F, use a feeler gauge and measure the counter 5th gear thrust clearance.

    Standard clearance: 0.0059–0.0157 in. (0.15–0.325 mm)

    Maximum clearance: 0.0157 in. (0.4 mm)

19. On the Z52 and 52F, remove the hole snap-ring and then remove the shifting key retainer.

    On the Z51, 52 and 52F, remove the snap-ring with snap-ring pliers. Using a two-armed gear puller, remove the No. 3 clutch hub, the sychronizer ring and the counter 5th gear together as an assembly. Remove the needle roller bearing.

20. Remove the spacer and steel ball (Z51, 52 and 52F). Remove the counter gear plate (Z41, 42 and 44).

21. Remove the bearing retainer and then the two bearing snap-rings.

22. Use a rubber mallet to tap the reverse gear shaft, the idler gear and the output shaft halfway out from the intermediate plate.

— **CAUTION** —
Support the gear shaft by hand.

23. Remove the idler gear and the reverse gear shaft together and then use a rubber mallet to tap out the counter gear and output shaft together.

— **CAUTION** —
Support the gear and shaft by hand.

24. Using a dial indicator, measure the 1st and 4th gear thrust clearance.
Standard clearance:
1st gear 0.0059–0.0108 in. (0.150–0.275mm)

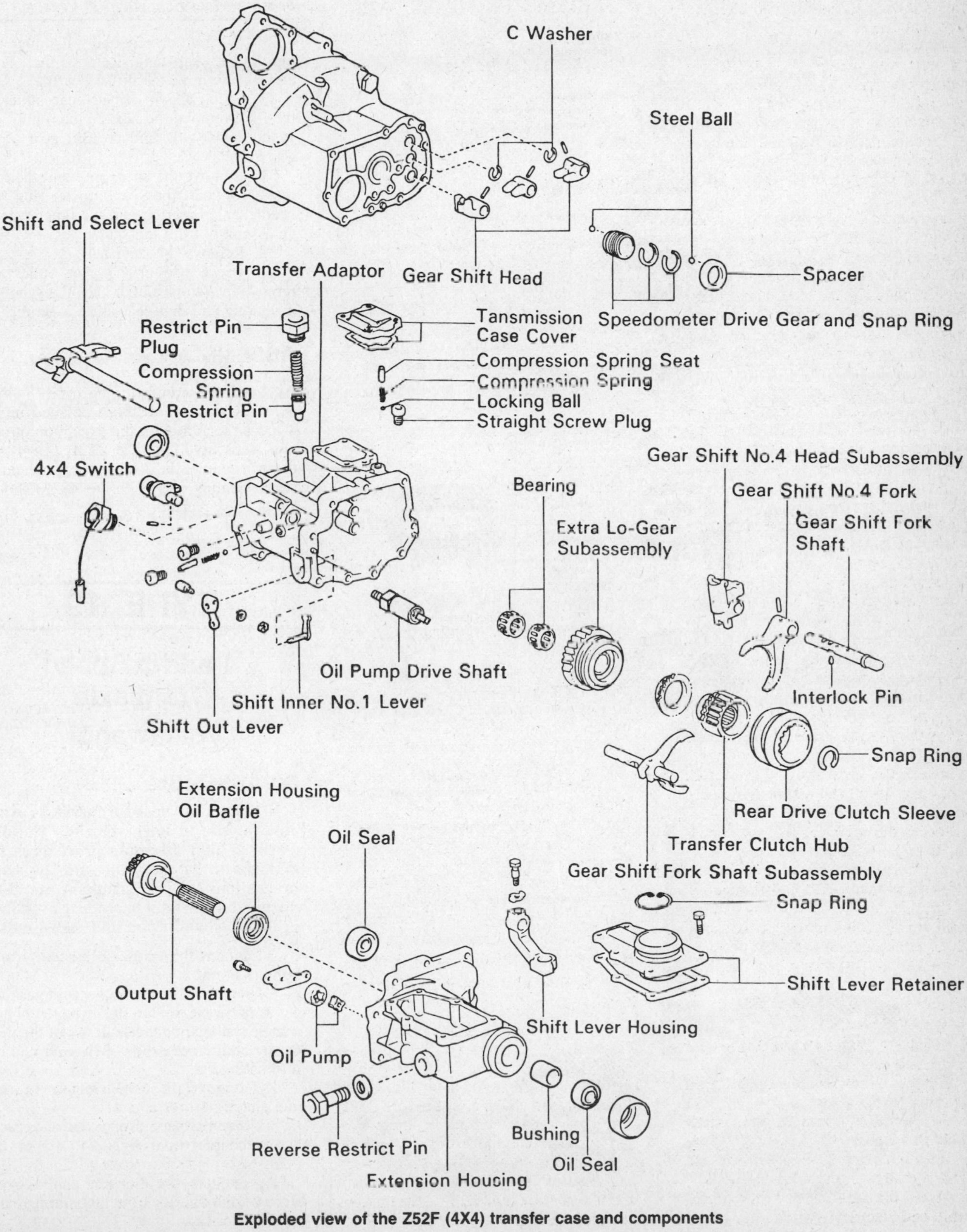

C Washer

Steel Ball

Spacer

Shift and Select Lever

Transfer Adaptor   Gear Shift Head

Speedometer Drive Gear and Snap Ring

Restrict Pin Plug

Compression Spring

Restrict Pin

Tansmission Case Cover

Compression Spring Seat

Compression Spring

Locking Ball

Straight Screw Plug

4x4 Switch

Bearing

Extra Lo-Gear Subassembly

Gear Shift No.4 Head Subassembly

Gear Shift No.4 Fork

Gear Shift Fork Shaft

Interlock Pin

Oil Pump Drive Shaft

Shift Inner No.1 Lever

Shift Out Lever

Snap Ring

Rear Drive Clutch Sleeve

Transfer Clutch Hub

Gear Shift Fork Shaft Subassembly

Extension Housing Oil Baffle

Oil Seal

Snap Ring

Output Shaft

Shift Lever Retainer

Oil Pump

Shift Lever Housing

Reverse Restrict Pin

Bushing

Oil Seal

Extension Housing

Exploded view of the Z52F (4X4) transfer case and components

4th gear 0.0008–0.0094 in. (0.02–0.24mm)

Maxium clearance; 0.0118 in. (0.3mm)

25. Using a feeler gauge, measure the 2nd and 3rd gear thrust clearance.

Standard clearance: 0.0059–0.0098 in. (0.15–0.25mm)

Maximum clearance: 0.0118 in. (0.3mm)

26. Press out the sleeve yoke. Remove the snap–ring and then press off 5th gear (Z51, 52 and 52F only).

27. Remove the output shaft front bearing snap–ring and then press out the bearing. Press out the spacer and then remove

the thrust bearing.

28. Remove 4th gear, the synchronizer ring and the needle roller bearing from the shaft as an assembly.

— CAUTION —
Be careful not to drop the needle roller bearing when removing 4th gear.

29. Use two drivers and a hammer and tap out the snap–ring. Remove the spacer and then remove the thrust bearing.

30. Using a two–armed gear puller or the like, remove the No. 2 clutch hub, the synchronizer ring and the 3rd gear as an assembly.

31. Remove the snap–ring and then remove 1st gear, the synchronizer ring, the needle roller bearing and the inner race as an assembly from the shaft.

32. Remove the steel ball.

33. Use a two–armed gear puller and remove the No. 1 clutch hub, the synchronizer ring and 2nd gear as an assembly.

ASSEMBLY

Assembly procedures for the Type 18 transaxle are identical to those detailed in the Type 17 section with the exception of certain steps involving the Z52F (4×4). In these instances, the disassembly procedures (those dealing only with the Z52F) should simply be reversed.

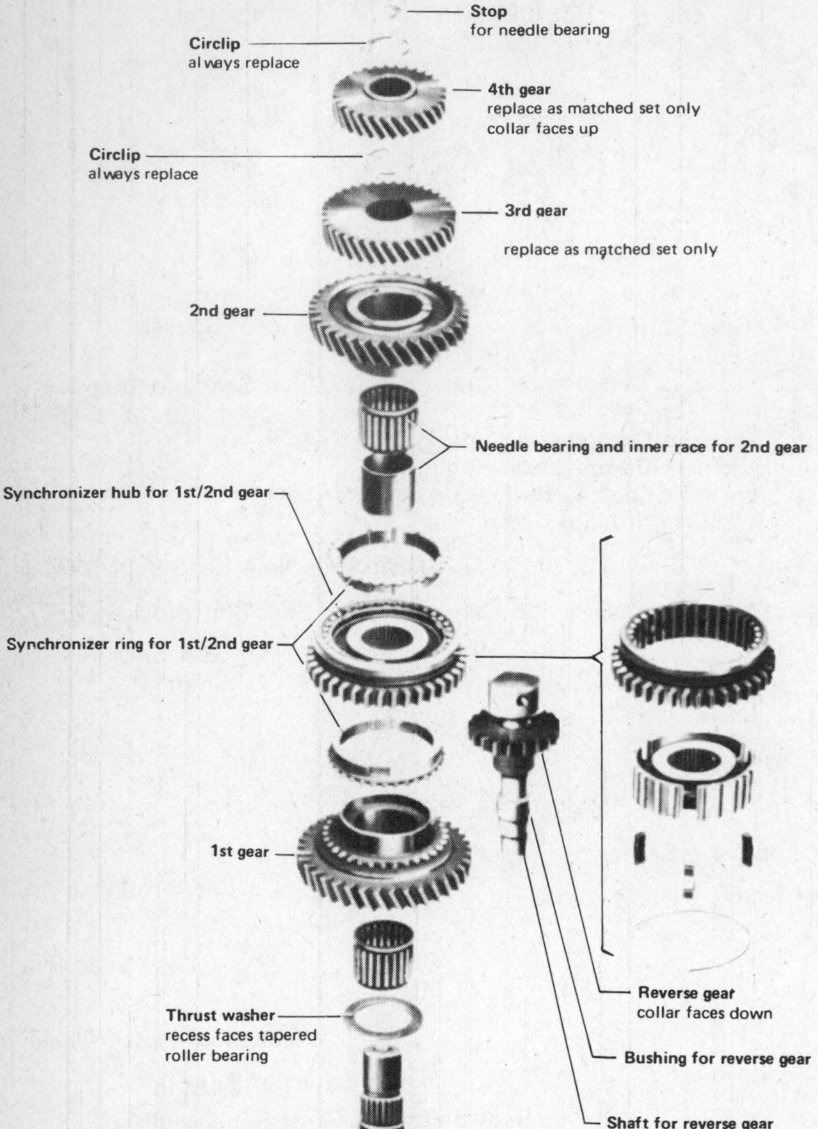

TYPE 19

4 and 5 Speed Transaxle Volkswagon

DISASSEMBLY

NOTE: A five speed transaxle is available for use in later vehicles. The disassembly and assembly procedures remain basically the same and the same precautions and care should be exercised during the overhaul procedure as is done in the overhaul of the four speed unit.

1. Mount the transaxle assembly in a holding fixture.

2. Remove the end cover and gasket.

3. Remove the circlips from the clutch release shaft. Slide the shaft out of the gear carrier and remove the clutch lever and return spring.

4. Remove the clutch release bearing and clutch pushrod.

5. Mount a bar with a locknut and spacer across the final drive housing to support the mainshaft.

6. Remove the selector shaft cover. Remove the interlock plunger springs, and the selector shaft.

Circlip
always replace

Circlip
always replace

Synchronizer hub for 1st/2nd gear

Synchronizer ring for 1st/2nd gear

1st gear

Thrust washer
recess faces tapered
roller bearing

Stop
for needle bearing

4th gear
replace as matched set only
collar faces up

3rd gear
replace as matched set only

2nd gear

Needle bearing and inner race for 2nd gear

Reverse gear
collar faces down

Bushing for reverse gear

Shaft for reverse gear

Exploded view of pinion shaft gear assembly

7. Remove the circlip from the gear carrier side drive flange. Install the special tool with two bolts on the drive flange. Remove the drive flange.

8. Remove the plastic caps covering the clamping screws. Remove the clamping screw nuts.

9. Remove the reverse shaft retaining bolt.

10. Mount the special tool on the gear carrier assembly and lift the gear carrier off the final drive assembly while threading the special tool bolt in.

11. Drive the drive flange oil seal out of the gear carrier housing.

12. Pry the clutch operating shaft oil seal out of the carrier housing.

13. Pull the pinion shaft needle bearing out of the gear carrier.

14. Remove the shift fork assembly and the mainshaft from the final drive housing.

15. Remove the remaining drive flange as outlined in Step 7.

16. Remove the needle bearing stop and the first circlip from the pinion shaft. Lift fourth gear off the shaft.

17. Remove the second circlip from the pinion shaft. Lift third gear, second gear, second gear inner race and the needle bearing off the shaft.

18. Remove the reverse shaft and gear.

19. Using a gear puller, remove the synchronizer hub and first/second gear from the pinion shaft.

20. Remove the pinion bearing cover and outer bearing race. Remove the pinion shaft.

21. Remove the differential assembly.

22. Pry the mainshaft oil seal out of the final drive housing.

23. Drive the drive flange oil seal out of the final drive housing.

24. Pull the starter bushing out of the final drive housing.

25. Pull the pinion outer bearing race out of the final drive housing.

26. Drive the differential outer bearing race out of the final drive housing.

27. Pull the mainshaft needle bearing out of the final drive housing.

28. Remove the two circlips from the shift fork shaft and slide the components off the shaft.

29. Remove the first circlip from the mainshaft and discard. Press the bearing off the shaft.

30. Mount the separator assembly on fourth gear and press the gear off the mainshaft. Remove the needle bearings.

31. Remove the second circlip from the mainshaft and discard. Press third gear and the synchronizer assembly off the shaft. Remove the needle bearings.

32. Slide a ⅜ in. rod in the mainshaft and drive the clutch pushrod out.

33. Press the two tapered roller bearings off the pinion shaft.

34. Remove the circlips from the differential pinion shaft and drive out.

35. Remove the differential pinion gears and thrust washers.

36. Remove the circlips from the drive

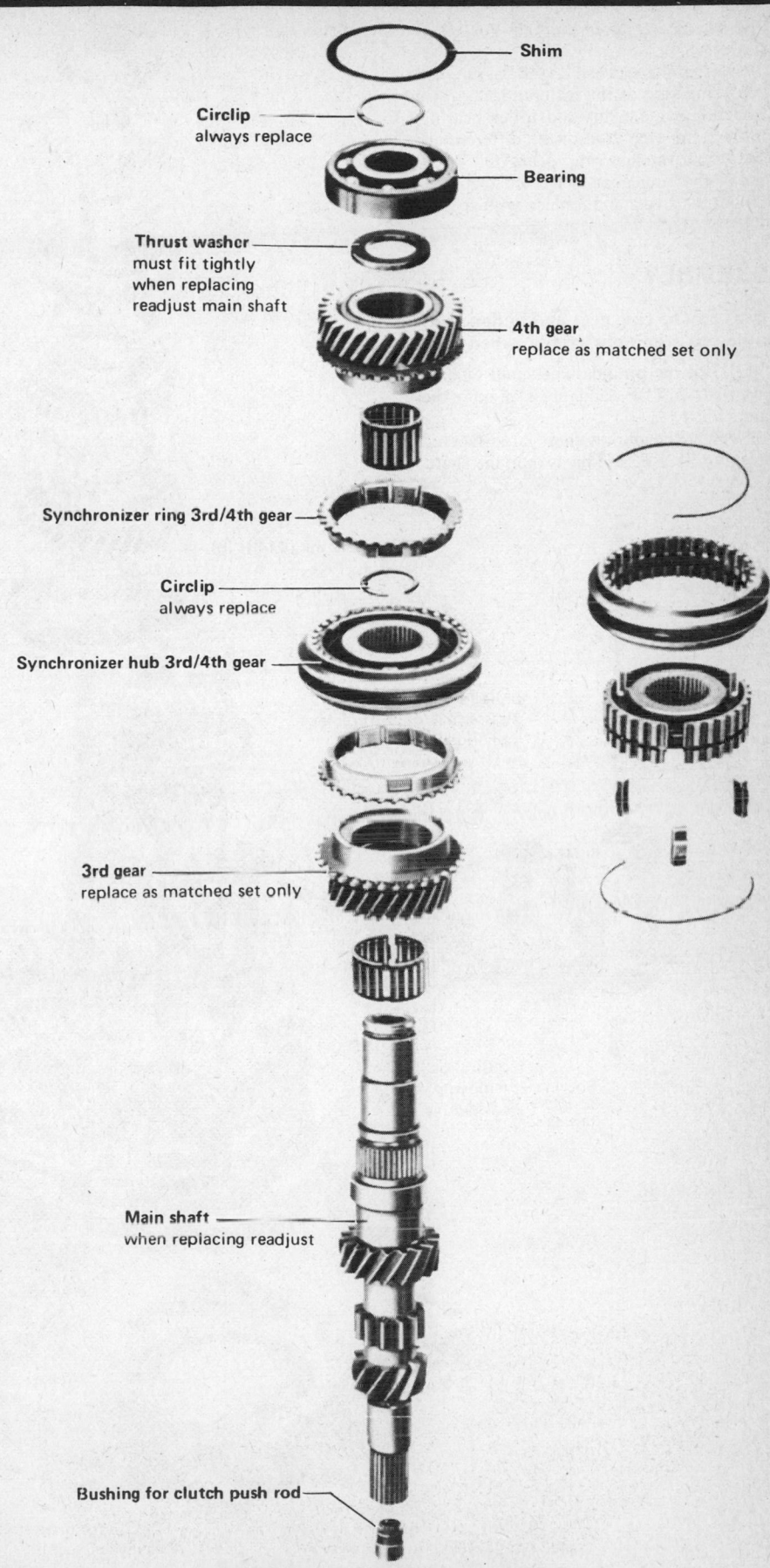

- Shim
- Circlip
  always replace
- Bearing
- Thrust washer
  must fit tightly
  when replacing
  readjust main shaft
- 4th gear
  replace as matched set only
- Synchronizer ring 3rd/4th gear
- Circlip
  always replace
- Synchronizer hub 3rd/4th gear
- 3rd gear
  replace as matched set only
- Main shaft
  when replacing readjust
- Bushing for clutch push rod

Exploded view of mainshaft assembly

flange shafts. Remove the side gears and thrust washers.

37. Press the tapered roller bearing off the housing side of the differential.

38. Remove the tapered roller bearing from the ring gear side of the differential.

39. Remove the ring gear. On 1977 models, the ring gear is riveted in place. Drill out the rivets and replace with special bolts.

ASSEMBLY

NOTE: The ring gear and pinion shaft can be replaced only as a matched set.

1. Heat the pinion shaft small tapered bearing to 212° F. and press it onto the shaft.

2. Heat the pinion shaft large tapered bearing to 212° F. and press onto the shaft.

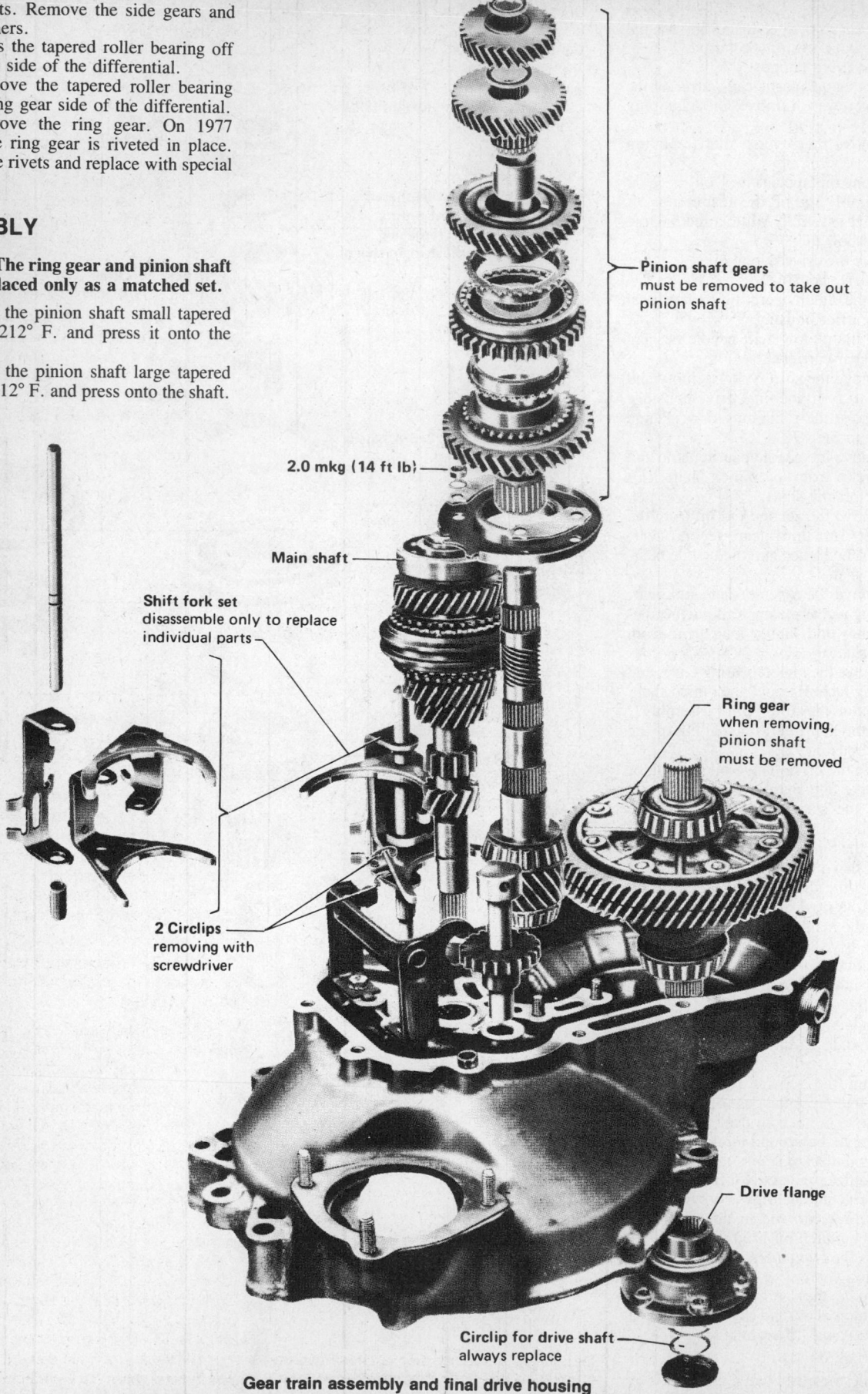

Pinion shaft gears
must be removed to take out
pinion shaft

2.0 mkg (14 ft lb)

Main shaft

Shift fork set
disassemble only to replace
individual parts

Ring gear
when removing,
pinion shaft
must be removed

2 Circlips
removing with
screwdriver

Drive flange

Circlip for drive shaft
always replace

Gear train assembly and final drive housing

3. Place a 0.75 mm shim in the pinion bore in the final drive housing and press the small bearing outer position.

4. Install the pinion shaft and cover.

5. Assemble the pinion adjustment fixture tools. Place the end plate on the pinion shaft. Attach the dial indicator and zero with a 1 mm preload.

— CAUTION —

Do not turn the pinion shaft while measuring because the bearings will settle and give an incorrect reading.

---

6. Move the pinion shaft up and down and note the reading.

7. Specified bearing preload is obtained by adding the constant figure of 0.20 mm to the measured reading and the shim thickness (0.75 mm).

Example:

Shim installed	0.75 mm
reading	0.30 mm
preload (constant figure)	+ 0.20 mm
shim size	1.25 mm

8. Remove the pinion shaft cover and the pinion shaft. Pull the pinion shaft small bearing outer race of the final drive housing.

9. Install the correct shim and press the pinion shaft small bearing outer race into the final drive housing.

NOTE: If new bearings have been installed on the pinion shaft, check the pinion shaft turning torque. The reading should be 4.4–13.1 in. lbs.

10. Install the side gears and thrust washers in the differential housing.

11. Install the pinion gears and thrust washers. Drive the pinion shaft into the differential housing.

12. Install centering pins on the differential housing. Heat the ring gear to 212° F. and press onto the differential housing.

13. Heat the housing side differential bearing to 212° F. and press the bearing into place.

14. Heat the ring gear side bearing to 212° F. and press the bearing into place.

NOTE: If new bearings have been installed, the differential must be adjusted.

15. Slide the drive flange shafts into the side gears. Determine the thickness of the circlip by pressing the drive flange shaft against the pinion gearshaft, while pressing the side gears against the housing. Insert the thickest possible circlip. The circlip should not be jammed sideways.

— CAUTION —

The differential inner and outer bearing races are matched to their bearings and cannot be interchanged.

---

16. If new differential bearings have been installed, proceed as follows:

a. Install the race in the final drive housing with a 1 mm shim.

b. Install the race in the gear carrier without a shim.

c. Place the differential assembly in the final drive housing. Install the gear carrier on the final drive housing, with the gasket.

d. Install the dial indicator fixture on the gear carrier tool and place the end plate on the drive flange. Install the dial indicator with a 1 mm preload.

— CAUTION —

Do not turn the differential when making the measurements because the bearings will settle and give incorrect readings.

---

e. Move the differential up and down and note the reading.

f. The correct bearing preload is determined by adding a constant figure or .40 mm to the measured reading.

Example:

measured reading	0.90 mm
preload (constant figure)	+ 0.40 mm
shim (for gear carrier side)	1.30 mm

g. Remove the gear carrier from the final drive housing.

h. Pull the bearing race out of the gear carrier housing with a suitable extractor.

i. Install the shims (determined in Step f) in the gear carrier starting with the thickest. Install the bearing race.

17. With the differential in the final drive housing, install the pinion shaft and tighten the nuts on the cover plate to 14 ft. lbs.

NOTE: Synchronizers can be replaced only as a matched unit.

18. Position the keys in the slots in the synchronizer hub. Place the synchronizer sleeve over the hub and align the marks. Install the springs 120° offset with the angled ends engaged in the hollow of a key.

19. Press the synchronizer rings onto the first and second gears. Check the gap between the ring and gear with a feeler gauge. The gap on new parts should be between 0.042–0.066 in. and no less than 0.019 in. on used parts.

20. Install the thrust washer and needle bearing for first gear on the pinion shaft. The recess in the thrust washer faces the roller bearing.

21. Align the grooves in the first gear synchronizer ring with the synchronizer shift keys. Position the shift fork slot in the operating sleeve toward second gear. The groove on the synchronizer hub should face toward first gear.

22. Heat the first gear and synchronizer

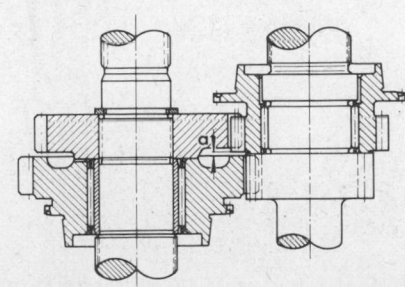

Measuring clearance (A) between pinion shaft third gear and mainshaft third gear

as an assembly to 250° F. and press onto the pinion shaft.

23. Drive the second gear needle bearing race onto the pinion shaft.

24. Install the second gear needle bearings and second gear.

25. Install third gear on the pinion shaft with the collar facing toward second gear. Secure third gear with the selective circlip which will give an axial play between 0.00–0.20 mm. Measure the play with a feeler gauge between the circlip and third gear.

26. Warm the reverse gear bushing and press it on the reverse shaft until the top of the bushing is 41 mm (1.614 in.) from the bottom of the shaft.

27. Install the reverse gear shaft retaining bolt in the shaft. Center the shaft and drive it in until the collar makes contact with the final drive housing. Remove the retaining bolt.

28. Assemble the third/fourth synchronizer in the same way outlined in Step 57.

29. Press the synchronizer rings onto third and fourth gear. The gap between the gear and synchronizer ring should be as follows.

New Part in. (mm)		Wear Limit in. (mm)
Third	0.045–0.068	0.019
	(1.15–1.75)	(0.5)
Fourth	0.051–0.074	0.19
	(1.3–1.9)	(0.5)

30. Press the clutch pushrod bushing into the mainshaft until it is flush.

31. Install the third gear needle bearings on the mainshaft.

32. Turn the synchronizer ring on third gear until the grooves align with the shift keys in the synchronizer hub. The chamfer on the synchronizer hub inner splines must face toward third gear.

33. Press the third gear and synchronizer onto the mainshaft as a unit. Install the circlip.

NOTE: If the mainshaft thrust washer is replaced, the mainshaft position must be re-adjusted.

34. Install the fourth gear needle bearings on the mainshaft. Install fourth gear.

35. Press the mainshaft thrust washer on until it contacts fourth gear.

36. Drive the mainshaft oil seal into the final drive housing. Drive the mainshaft needle bearings into the final drive housing.

37. Make sure that the mainshaft support bar, locknut and spacer are in place. Insert the mainshaft. Install the shift fork assembly and secure with the circlips. Make sure that the gears are in Neutral.

38. Lift the shaft with the spindle until the play between second gear on the pinion shaft and third gear on the mainshaft can be checked. Measure the end-play with a feeler gauge. Measurement should be 0.039 in. (1.0 mm). Lock the spindle at the support bar and check the measurement to make

sure it has not changed.

39. Install the measuring sleeve tool on the mainshaft. Place a new gasket on the final drive housing and install the gear carrier. Tighten the bolts to 14 ft. lbs.

40. Mount a dial indicator in a holding assembly and zero the indicator with a 3 mm preload. Move the measuring sleeve up and down, and record the indicator reading.

Mainshaft Play (mm)	Shim Size (mm)
0.00–0.46	No Shim Used
0.47–0.75	0.30
0.76–1.04	0.60
1.05–1.45	0.90

41. Remove the gear carrier from the final drive housing.

42. Install the shim (determined in Step 40) in the mainshaft bearing bore. Press the mainshaft bearing into the gear carrier, and secure with the clamping screws and nuts. Tighten the nuts to 11 ft. lbs.

43. Drive the drive flange oil seal into the final drive housing until it bottoms against the bearing race.

44. Install the drive flange on the final drive housing side, with the special tool (VW391), secure with a new circlip.

45. Drive the starter bushing into the final drive housing.

46. Drive the selector shaft oil seal into the gear carrier.

47. Drive the clutch operating lever oil seal into the gear carrier.

48. Drive the pinion shaft needle bearings into the gear carrier.

49. Drive the drive flange oil seal into the gear carrier cover until it bottoms on the differential bearing race.

50. Position the gasket on the final drive housing. Install the gear carrier housing on the final drive housing. Make sure that the reverse gear shaft is aligned with the hole in the gear carrier, install the reverse shaft retaining screw.

51. Install the gear carrier–to–final drive housing bolts and tighten to 14 ft. lbs.

52. Install the mainshaft circlip through the clutch release bearing opening in the gear carrier.

53. Install the remaining driveshaft flange and circlip using special tools.

54. Remove the mainshaft support bar. Insert the clutch pushrod.

55. Insert the clutch release bearing assembly. Insert the clutch operating lever through the spring and clutch bearing lever. The bent end of the spring must contact the gear carrier. The center part of the spring is hooked over the end of the clutch bearing lever. Install the two circlips. Install the gasket and cover.

56. Insert the selector shaft and springs into the selector opening in the gear carrier

assembly. Lubricate the selector with a multi-purpose grease before assembly. Install the selector shaft cover.

57. Install the interlock plunger assembly in the gear carrier assembly. Adjust the interlock plunger as follows:

    a. Turn the slotted screw (interlock plunger) in until the nut starts to move out (bottoms).

    b. Back the slotted screw out ¼ turn.

    c. Install the plastic cap.

58. Install the plastic caps over the bearing clamping screws.

TYPE 20

4 Speed Transaxle— Models 002 and 091

Volkswagen

NOTE: Many special tools are required in the overhaul procedures of these

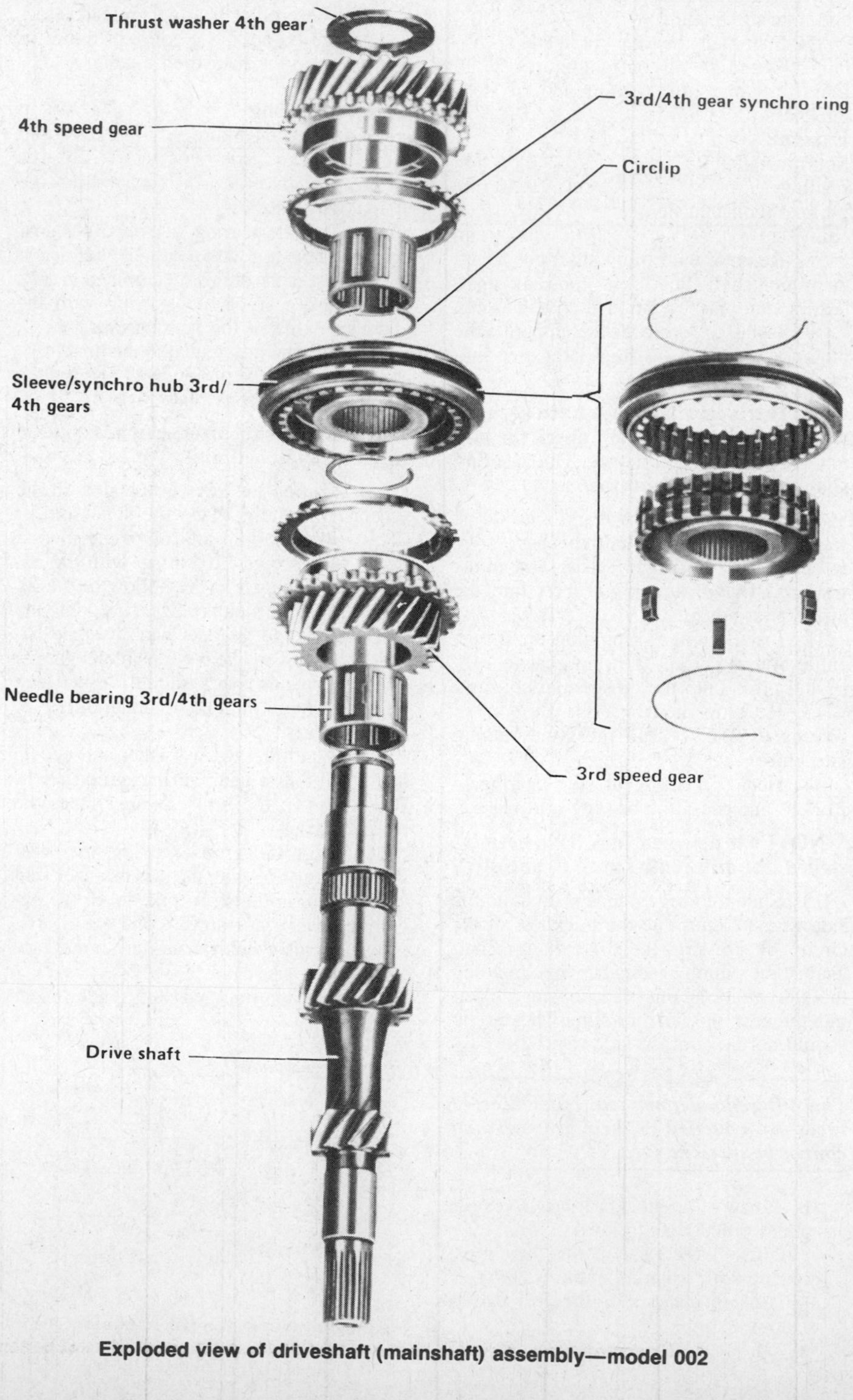

Thrust washer 4th gear

4th speed gear

3rd/4th gear synchro ring

Circlip

Sleeve/synchro hub 3rd/4th gears

Needle bearing 3rd/4th gears

3rd speed gear

Drive shaft

Exploded view of driveshaft (mainshaft) assembly—model 002

transaxles. Use only recommended or equivalent tools to prevent personal injury or damage to the units.

DISASSEMBLY

1. Mount the transaxle securely and drain the lubricating oil from the unit.

2. Pry the caps from the center of the left and right drive flanges and remove the circlips from the stub axles. Using a puller, remove the drive flanges.

3. Mark the positions of the differential adjusting rings and measure the distance or depth to which the rings are screwed into the transaxle case. Record the readings for the assembly references.

4. Loosen the left differential adjusting ring to relieve the tension within the transaxle housing and remove the clutch housing assembly. Remove the rear driveshaft by unscrewing the shaft from the front drive or mainshaft. Remove the reverse drive gear.

5. Remove the left and right differential adjusting rings and lift the differential assembly from the case.

6. Remove the pinion gear assembly retaining ring from the differential side of the transaxle case.

NOTE: The retaining ring is peened, so that extra effort must be used to remove the ring.

7. Remove the gear shift housing from the gear carrier housing carefully to avoid damaging the housing mating surfaces.

8. Remove the gear carrier housing from the transaxle case and press the gear train from the transaxle case.

NOTE: Locate the shims from between the tapered roller bearing and the transaxle case for reuse during the reassembly.

9. The pinion and mainshaft must be pressed from the gear carrier housing.

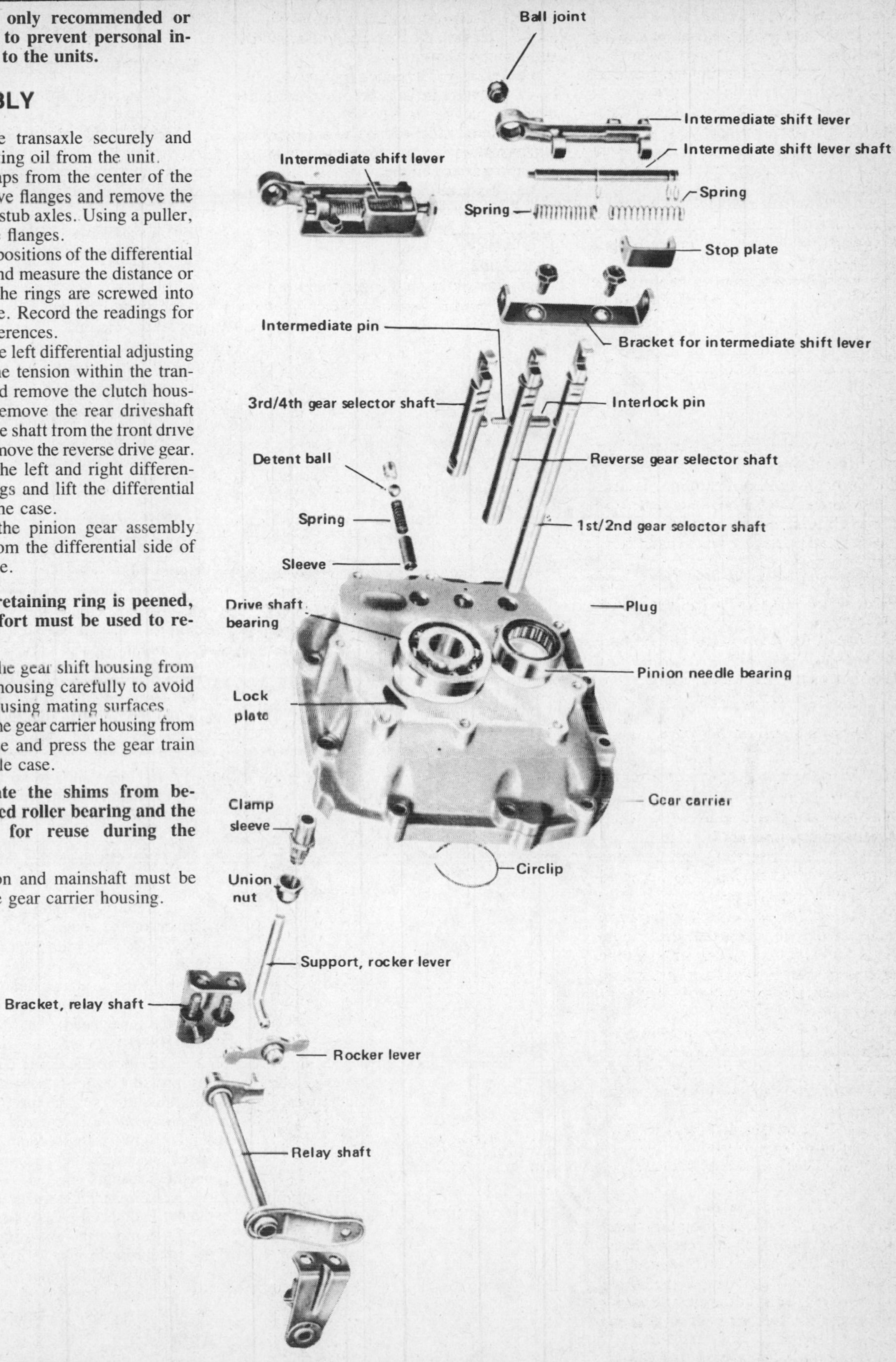

Exploded view of model 091 gear carrier housing and shift mechanism—typical of model 002

─────── **CAUTION** ───────
Remove the circlips before attempting any press work.

Mainshaft (Driveshaft)
DISASSEMBLY
Model 002

1. Press the 4th gear and thrust washer from the mainshaft.
2. Remove the caged roller bearing and the circlip.
3. Press the synchronizer hub from the shaft and remove the lower circlip.
4. Remove the 3rd speed gear and the split caged bearing.

Model 091

1. Remove the 4th speed gear and roller bearing.
2. Remove the circlip and press the 3rd/4th synchronizer hub from the shaft. Remove the lower circlip.
3. Remove the 3rd speed gear and the caged needle bearing from the shaft.

ASSEMBLY
Model 002

1. Install the split caged roller bearing and the 3rd speed gear.

NOTE: Use only the split caged bearings with the needle bearings in pairs.

2. Install the lower circlip in its groove on the shaft.
3. Press the 3rd/4th gear assembly into position on the shaft. Install the upper circlip.
4. Install the roller bearing and the 4th speed gear on the shaft.
5. Heat the thrust washer to 212°F. (100°C.) and press it on to the shaft with the oil grooves towards the 4th gear.

Model 091

1. Install the caged needle bearing on to the shaft and install the 3rd speed gear. Install the circlip.
2. Install the sleeve and hub for the 3rd and 4th gears. Install the second circlip.

NOTE: The identifying groove on the synchronizer ring should be towards the 4th speed gear.

3. Install the roller bearing and the 4th speed gear assembly.

Pinion Shaft
DISASSEMBLY

Model 002

1. Remove the upper circlip by applying pressure against the 4th speed gear to compress the spacer spring. Remove the gear and the spacer spring.

─────── **CAUTION** ───────
The pressure tool should be firmly seated on the 4th gear to avoid personal injury due to the spacer spring tension.

2. Remove the circlip holding the 3rd gear in place and remove the 3rd gear, 2nd gear and 1st gear assemblies from the pinion shaft.

NOTE: Observe the location and direction of the gear train components.

3. Remove the shim from the bearing surface of the round nut. Using a special tool, remove the round nut from the pinion shaft.
4. Using a press, remove the tapered roller bearing assembly from the shaft, along with the inner needle bearing race.

Model 091

1. Remove the upper circlip by applying pressure against the 4th speed gear to compress the spacer spring. *Remove the pressure cautiously to avoid personal injury.*
2. Remove the second circlip, the 3rd speed gear and the 2nd speed gear with needle bearing.
3. Remove the third circlip and remove the 1st/2nd speed gear assembly.
4. Remove the anti-rotation ring from the synchronizer hub with a punch.
5. Unscrew the inner race from the pinion shaft with a special tool. Press the tapered bearing assembly from the pinion shaft.

ASSEMBLY

NOTE: Should the pinion shaft or the tapered bearing be replaced, the pinion

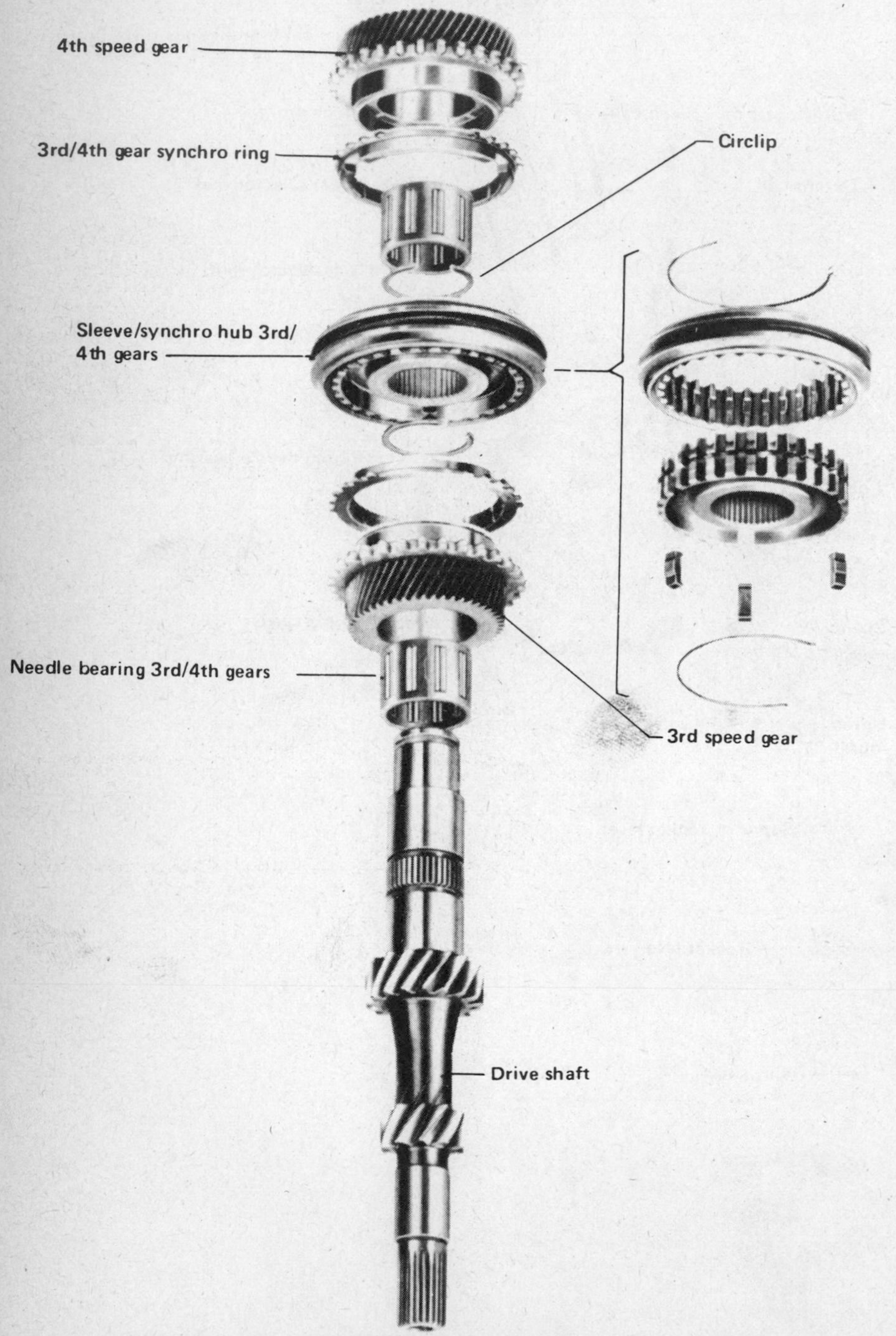

4th speed gear —

3rd/4th gear synchro ring —

Sleeve/synchro hub 3rd/ 4th gears —

Needle bearing 3rd/4th gears —

— Circlip

— 3rd speed gear

— Drive shaft

Exploded view of driveshaft (mainshaft) assembly—model 091

depth should be checked before total assembly is completed. Special tools are needed for the measurements.

Model 002

1. Heat the tapered bearing assembly to 212°F. (100° C.) and press into place on the pinion shaft.

2. Oil the bearing with hypoid oil and install the pinion and bearing assembly into the transaxle case. Install the retaining ring and torque to 159 ft. lbs. (22 mkg).

3. Install an inch/pound torque wrench or equivalent on to the end of the pinion shaft and turn the shaft in both directions, approximately 15–20 turns and read the turning torque. The torque should be between 2.7–18.2 in. lbs. (3.0–21.0 cmkg) for new bearings and 2.7–6.1 in. lbs. (2.7–7.0 cmkg) for used bearings or for bearings that have been run at least 30 miles (50 km).

4. Remove the tapered bearing assembly and pinion shaft from the case and continue the assembly.

5. Install the needle bearing inner race and the needle bearing assembly. Install the round nut and torque it to 144 ft. lbs. (20 mkg). Peen the locking shoulder into the spline.

6. Install the shim and the 1st gear and preassembled synchronizer as a unit, on the shaft and measure the axial play with a feeler gauge between the tapered bearing and the gear. The play should be 0.004–0.010 inch (0.10–0.25 mm). Adjust with selective shims.

7. Assemble the 2nd and 3rd speed gears to the shaft and install the circlip. Measure the clearance between the 3rd gear and the circlip. The clearance should be 0.004–0.010 inch (0.10–0.25 mm). Adjust by installing selective sized circlips.

8. Install the spacer spring, 4th gear and securely press downward with a press.

9. Heat the inner race to 212°F. (100° C.) and install on the shaft. Install the circlip on the shaft end.

Model 091

1. Heat the tapered bearing assembly to 212°F. (100° C.) and press into position on the pinion shaft.

2. Oil the bearing with hypoid oil and install the pinion and bearing assembly into the transaxle case. Install the retaining ring and torque to 159 ft. lbs. (22 mkg).

3. Install an inch/pound torque wrench or equivalent on to the end of the pinion shaft and turn the shaft in both directions, approximately 15–20 turns and read the turning torque. The torque should be between 2.7–18.2 in. lbs. (3.0–21.0 cmkg) for new bearings and 2.7–6.1 in. lbs. (2.7–7.0 cmkg) for used bearings or for bearings that have been run at least 30 miles (50 km).

4. Remove the tapered bearing assembly and pinion shaft from the case and continue the assembly.

5. Install the inner race and torque to 144 ft. lbs. (20 mkg). Peen the locking shoulder into the gear spline.

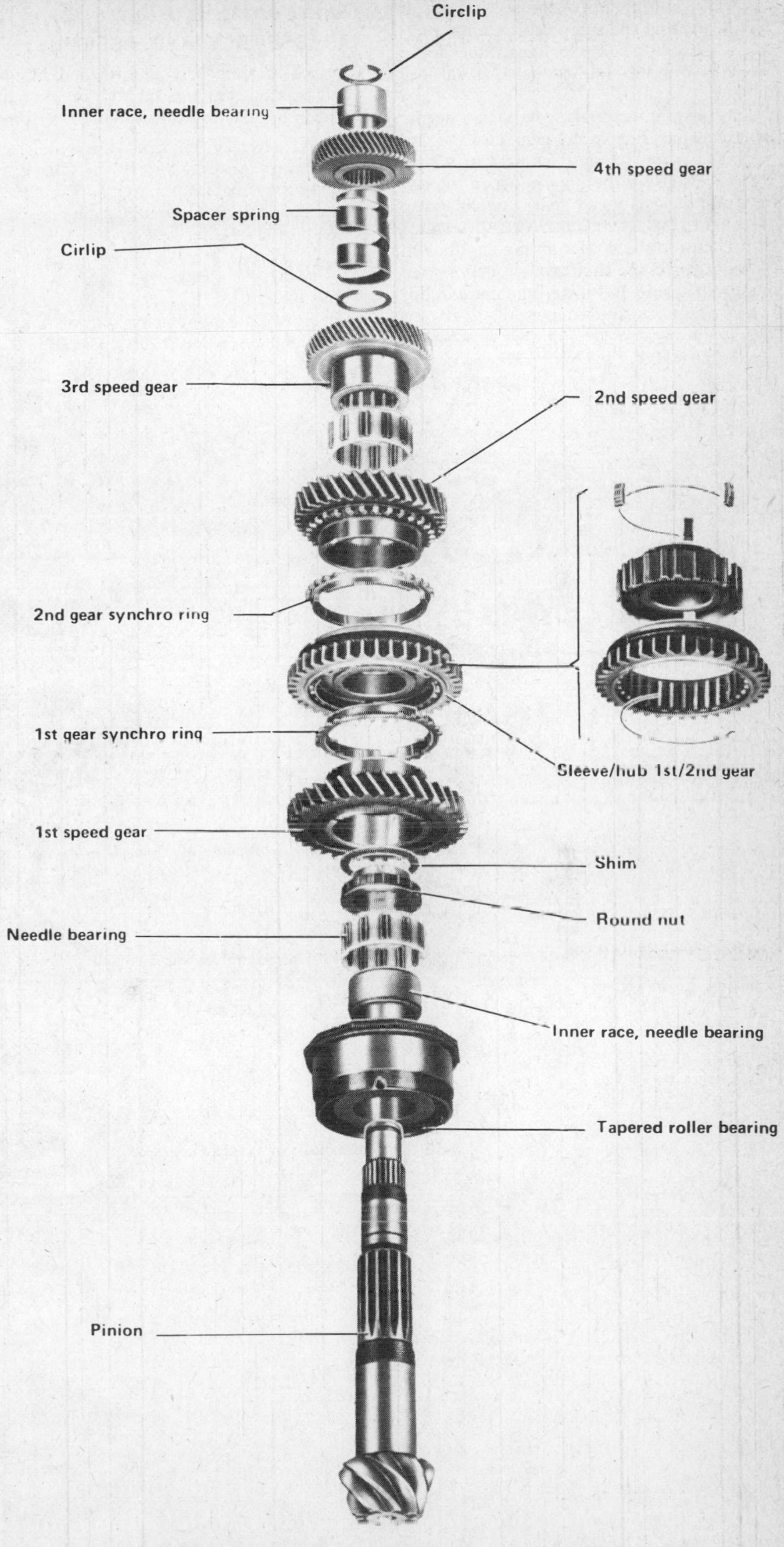

Exploded view of pinion shaft assembly—model 002

Circlip

Inner race, needle bearing

4th speed gear

Spacer spring

Cirlip

3rd speed gear

2nd speed gear

2nd gear synchro ring

1st gear synchro ring

Sleeve/hub 1st/2nd gear

1st speed gear

Shim

Round nut

Needle bearing

Inner race, needle bearing

Tapered roller bearing

Pinion

6. Install the inner race of the 1st gear needle bearing and a new anti-rotation ring.

7. Install the 1st speed gear, the sleeve and hub for the 1st/2nd gear. Install the retaining circlip.

8. Install the 2nd speed gear needle bearing, the 2nd speed gear and the 3rd speed gear on the shaft and retain with a circlip. Measure the play between the circlip and the 3rd speed gear. The clearance should be 0.002–0.008 inch (0.5–0.20 mm).

9. Install the spacer spring and the 4th speed gear on the shaft. Safely depress the gear and spring and install the end circlip.

Gear Carrier Housing
DISASSEMBLY AND ASSEMBLY

1. The mainshaft bearing and pinion shaft bearings are pressed both in and out.

2. The detent springs and interlock pins must be removed before the shift rods can be removed.

3. The bracket for the intermediate shift lever is removable by removing attaching bolts.

4. The relay rod, rocker lever, relay

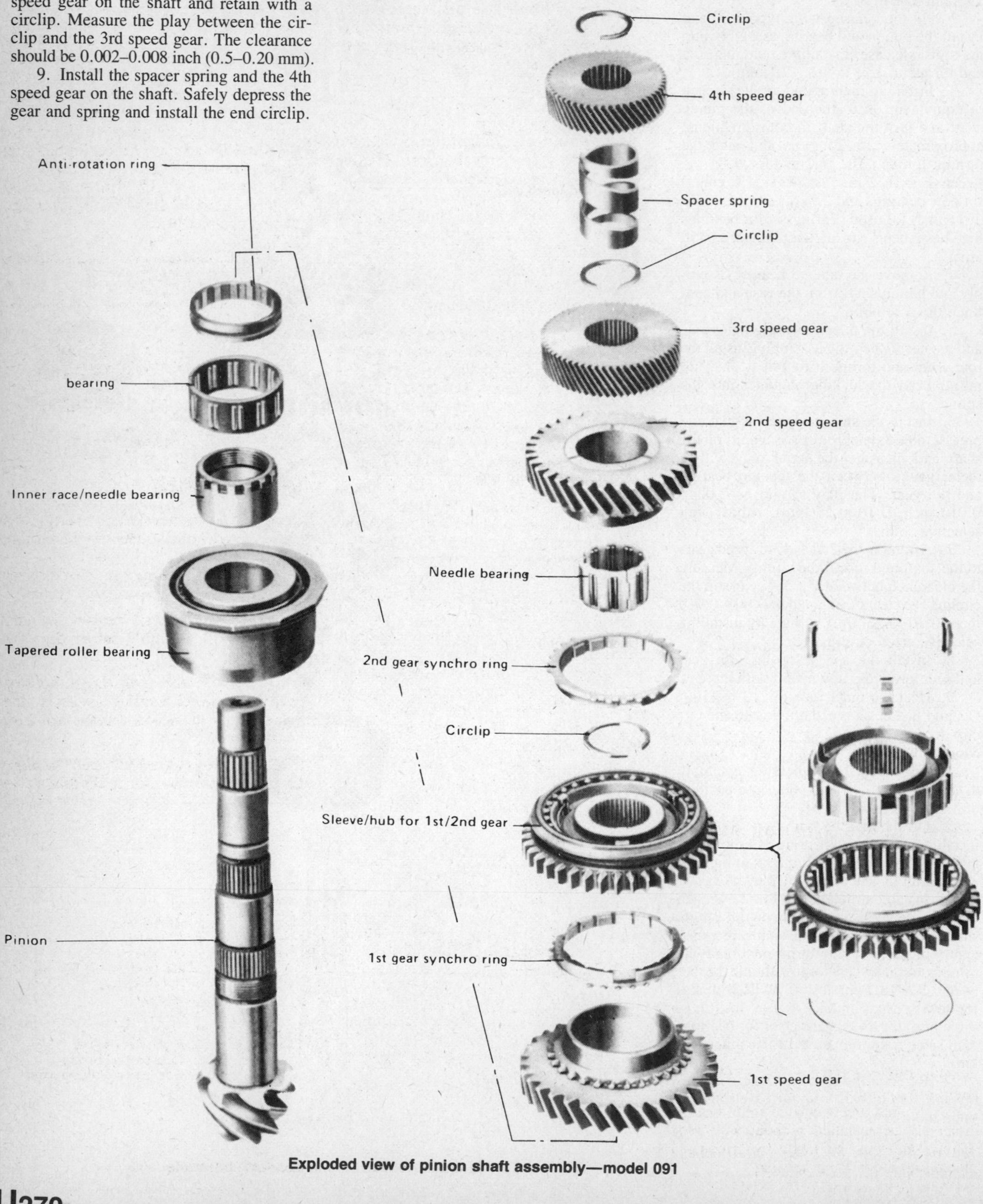

Anti-rotation ring

bearing

Inner race/needle bearing

Tapered roller bearing

Pinion

Circlip

4th speed gear

Spacer spring

Circlip

3rd speed gear

2nd speed gear

Needle bearing

2nd gear synchro ring

Circlip

Sleeve/hub for 1st/2nd gear

1st gear synchro ring

1st speed gear

Exploded view of pinion shaft assembly—model 091

shaft bracket and small components are removable. Note the location and direction of the individual parts for ease of reassembly.

Synchronizer Rings
MARKINGS ON RINGS
Model 002

1. 1st gear ring has no notch on the outer surface.

2. 2nd gear ring has three notches on the outer surface.

3. No identification on 3rd/4th gear rings.

4. Clearance between the ring and cone of the gear under pressure should be:

1st and 2nd gears—0.042 to 0.070 inch (1.1 to 1.8 mm).

3rd and 4th gears—0.039 to 0.074 inch (1.0 to 1.9 mm).

5. The sleeves and hubs are not matched and may be renewed separately. They should slide smoothly and have minimum backlash. The springs should be fitted with the end offset at 120° with the angled ends fitted over the keys.

Model 091

1. 1st gear ring has no notch on the outer surface, it is made of brass and the friction surface is treated with molybdenum.

2. The 2nd, 3rd and 4th gear rings have three notches on the outer surface or three depressions on the end face of the rings.

3. The 2nd gear ring is made of brass and has the friction surface coated with molybdenum.

4. The 3rd gear ring is steel and the friction surface is treated with molybdenum.

5. The 4th gear ring is made of brass and has no special coating.

6. The clearance between the ring and gear cone while under pressure is:

1st and 2nd gear—0.040 to 0.064 inch (1.0 to 1.6 mm).

3rd and 4th gear—0.040 to 0.066 inch (1.0 to 1.7 mm).

7. The sleeves and the hubs are not matched and may be replaced separately. They must slide smoothly and have minimum backlash.

Reverse Drive Gear and Shaft
Models 002 and 091

The reverse gear and shaft assemblies are removed and installed as a unit. The disassembly can be accomplished with the gear and shaft assemblies out of the case. Both the 002 and 091 model transaxles use basically the same gear and shaft arrangement with differences in gear teeth and shaft splines.

ASSEMBLY
Models 002 and 091
Before Assembly:

1. Should a new tapered roller bearing assembly be installed without a peening notch, one must be made by grinding a notch into the bearing housing.

———— CAUTION ————
Prevent metal particles from entering the bearings by using standard safety precautions.

---

2. Replacement of the transaxle housing, tapered roller bearing, ring and pinion or differential side bearings necessitate the measuring of the pinion depth and carrier adjustment. Special tools must be used for these operations.

ASSEMBLY

1. Press the mainshaft (driveshaft) and pinion shaft into the gear carrier housing bearings and secure as required. Locate the shift forks and shift fingers properly.

2. Place the removed shims into place on the transaxle housing. Using a new gasket, install the gear carrier housing assembly into the transaxle housing. Position the assembly into place by tapping on the pinion shaft with a plastic hammer.

NOTE: A special tool jig is used to adjust the shift forks and fingers before the gear train is installed. Since this type of tool is not always available, caution must be exercised so that the shift forks do not rub or exert pressure, but have clearance on the sides of the grooves in the operating sleeves, when in Neutral or while engaged in gear.

3. Install the tapered bearing retaining ring and torque to 159 ft. lbs. (22 mkg), back off and retighten to 159 ft. lbs.

4. Peen the retaining ring into the notch on the tapered bearing housing.

5. Using a new gasket, install the gearshift housing by guiding the inner shift lever into the ball joint on the intermediate lever.

6. Install the differential into the case and install the adjusting rings and necessary spacers with new seals and O-rings.

7. Using the disassembly marks and depth measurements, adjust the left and right adjusting rings and check for proper gear backlash and tooth contact.

---

8. Install the rear driveshaft and the reverse gear. Tighten the rear driveshaft stud into the forward driveshaft (mainshaft) snugly and back off one spline. Install the reverse drive gear.

NOTE: Lengths of the rear driveshafts differ with certain engine usage.

9. Loosen the left adjusting ring and carefully install the clutch housing assembly into place and install the retaining washers or nuts. Some units will use bolts with washers. Retighten the left adjusting ring to the previously marked position.

10. Install the drive flanges on the axle stubs and install the circlips. Install new center plugs in the drive flange centers.

11. Fill the unit with lubricating oil and rotate by hand to allow oil to cover the internal components.

TYPE 21

5 Speed Transaxle

Audi

DISASSEMBLY

1. Mount the transaxle assembly into a holder securely and drain the lubricating oil.

2. Mark and remove the gear selector lever and the gear selector shaft assembly.

NOTE: If necessary, replace the gear selector shaft assembly rather than repairing it.

3. Remove the gear carrier housing cover/gear carrier housing assembly, the mainshaft and the pinion from the final drive housing.

NOTE: Dowel pins are used to align the gear carrier housing to the final drive

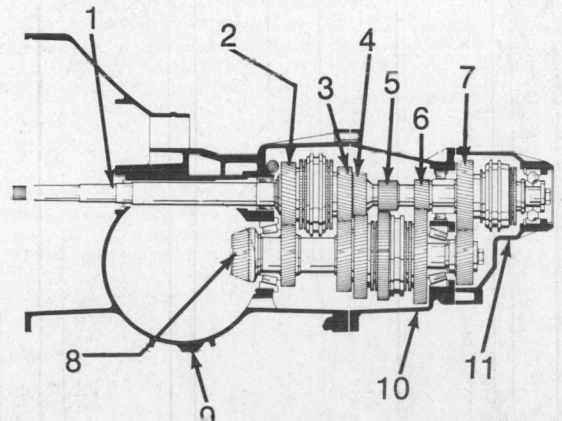

1. Main shaft
2. 4th gear
3. 3rd gear
4. 2nd gear
5. Reverse gear
6. 1st gear
7. 5th gear
8. Pinion
9. Final drive housing
10. Gear carrier housing
11. Gear carrier housing cover

Cross section of 5-speed Audi transaxle

housing. If the dowel pins are to be removed, drive them from the gear carrier.

4. Remove the gear carrier housing end plug with a sharp ended tool, by driving the tool into the center of the plug and prying the cover outward.

5. Place the mainshaft into a vise with soft jaw covers and remove the bolt from the mainshaft, in the cover cap opening.

6. Reposition the gear carrier housing so that the vise soft jaws are holding the housing instead of the mainshaft.

7. Remove the twelve retaining bolts from the gear carrier housing cover and separate the cover from the gear housing.

8. Remove the mainshaft bearing inner race from the gear carrier housing.

9. Remove the 5th gear clutch hub and mainshaft bearing inner race from the cover end of the mainshaft.

10. Remove the 5th gear synchronizer ring.

11. Drive the 5th gear shift fork roll pin from the fork with a pin punch.

── CAUTION ──
Support the selector rod and fork to avoid damage to the gear carrier housing.

12. Remove the circlip, the 5th speed gear with the synchronizer hub, needle bearing and the 5th speed gear shift fork.

NOTE: The 5th/reverse gear selector rod will remain in the gear carrier housing.

13. Remove the selector rod stop screws from the outside of the gear carrier housing.

14. Reposition the gear carrier housing assembly in the jaws of the vise, with the soft jaw covers, and clamp the 4th speed gear in the vise.

15. Remove the bolt from the pinion shaft and remove the 5th gear and the adjustment shim.

16. Reposition the gear carrier housing in the soft jawed vise and drive the 1st/2nd

gear selector fork roll pin from the fork.

── CAUTION ──
Support the selector rod and fork to avoid damage to the gear carrier housing.

17. Remove the 3rd/4th gear selector fork roll pin.

── CAUTION ──
Support the selector rod and fork to avoid damage to the gear carrier housing.

18. Remove the 3rd/4th selector rod from the gear carrier housing. The shifting fork should remain in the synchronizer hub.

NOTE: Do not lose the indent or interlock pin.

19. Remove the relay lever bolt from the reverse gear relay lever.

20. Pull the pinion and mainshaft partially from the gear carrier housing and remove the mainshaft with the 3rd/4th shift fork on the synchronizer hub.

21. Pull the pinion from the housing, far enough so that the selector rod and shift fork of the 1st/2nd gears can be removed, after the reverse gear spring clip on the pinion side is unhooked and turned.

22. Remove the pinion from the housing.

23. Inspect the transaxle components, replace all seals and gaskets, gears that are damaged or worn, and bearings, both needle and ball.

Mainshaft and Pinion Shaft

The mainshaft and pinion shaft gears can be disassembled by the removal of the end bearings or circlips. Certain gears will have to be removed either with a puller or a press. Mark the gears before the removal to avoid backward installation. The synchronizers are of the Borg Warner type and should be matchmarked before disassembly.

During the reassembly of the shafts, the following clearances should be observed.

MAINSHAFT
3rd/4th Synchronizer Rings–to–Hub Clearance
New rings—0.039–0.067 inch (1.0–1.7 mm)
    Wear limit—0.20 inch (0.5 mm)
5th Gear Synchronizer Ring–to–Hub Clearance
New ring—0.039–0.075 inch (1.0–1.9 mm)
    Wear limit—0.020 inch (0.5 mm)
3rd/4th Synchronizer Hub End-Play
0.000–0.002 inch (0.00–0.05 mm)
    Correct by selective circlips
4th Gear End-Play
0.008–0.013 inch (0.20–0.35 mm)

PINION SHAFT
4th Gear End-Play
Limit—0.0008 (0.02 mm)
    Correct by selective circlip
3rd Gear End-Play
0.000–0.0016 inch (0.00–0.04 mm)
1st/2nd Synchronizer Rings–to–Hub Clearance
New rings—0.039–0.067 inch (1.0–1.7 mm)
    Wear limit—0.020 inch (0.5 mm)
1st/2nd Synchronizer Hub End-Play
0.000–0.0016 inch (0.00–0.04 mm)
    Correct by selective circlip
Reverse Gear Synchronizer Clearance
New ring—0.029–0.090 inch (0.75–2.3 mm)
    Wear limit—0.007 inch (0.2 mm)

Differential Assembly

The different assembly is removed from the final drive housing after removal of the drive flange and the final drive cover. Methods of repairs are found in the Unit Overhaul section.

ASSEMBLY

1. Have the reverse gear engaged and the spring clip is unhooked on the one side and turned away from the pinion bore.

2. Install the pinion shaft assembly partially into the carrier housing. Install the 1st/2nd gear shift rod and press the pinion into the housing until it is fully seated.

3. Connect the unhooked spring clip and disengage the reverse gear.

4. Install the 3rd/4th gearshift fork with the slot into the 5th/reverse gearshift rod.

5. If the mainshaft bearing inner race is on the mainshaft, it must be removed before the shaft is installed into the gear carrier.

6. Install the mainshaft partially into the housing and insert the 3rd/4th shift fork into the sliding sleeve and install the mainshaft until fully seated.

7. Move all the shifting rods to the neutral position and check for the correct position of the interlock pins.

8. Install the 3rd/4th gear shift rod into the gear carrier housing and the shift fork. Install the interlock pin and secure the fork to the rod with the roll pin.

── CAUTION ──
Support the shift rod and fork when installing the roll pin.

1. 5th and reverse gear selector rod
2. Selector shaft assembly
3. Reverse gear shift fork
4. Relay lever
5. Reverse gear interlock
6. 5th gear synchronizer ring
7. 5th gear clutch sleeve
8. Main shaft
9. Selector shaft
10. Final drive housing
11. Mounting plate
12. Reverse gear synchronizer
13. Reverse gear
14. Gear carrier housing
15. 5th gear
16. 5th gear shift fork
17. 5th gear synchronizer hub

5th and reverse shift linkage viewed from the top

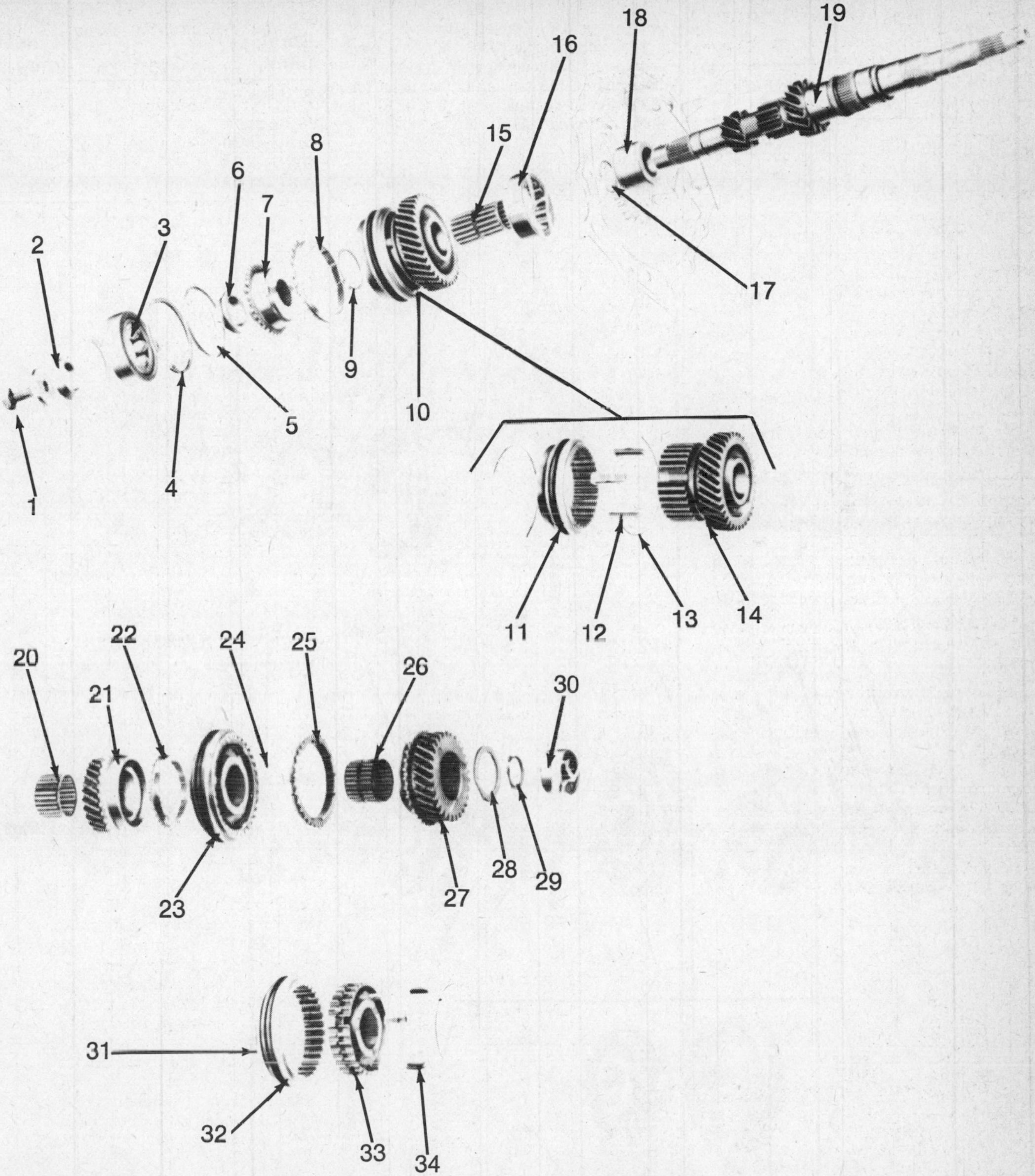

Exploded view of mainshaft assembly

1. Bolt
2. Main shaft bearing outer race
3. Main shaft bearing
4. Circlip
5. Baffle plate
6. Main shaft bearing inner race
7. 5th gear clutch hub
8. 5th gear synchronizer ring
9. Circlip

10. 5th gear with synchronizer hub and sleeve
11. Sleeve
12. Hollow key
13. Spring
14. 5th gear with synchronizer hub
15. 5th gear needle bearing
16. Main shaft bearing
17. Circlip
18. Mainshaft bearing inner race

19. Mainshaft
20. 3rd gear needle bearing
21. 3rd gear
22. 3rd gear synchronizer ring
23. 3rd & 4th gear synchronizer hub
24. Circlip
25. 4th gear synchronizer ring
26. 4th gear needle bearing
27. 4th gear

28. 4th gear thrust washer
29. Circlip
30. Main shaft needle bearing
31. Spring
32. Sleeve
33. Hub
34. Hollow key

9. Install the roll pin into the 1st/2nd gear selector rod and fork.

───── **CAUTION** ─────
Support the shift rod and fork when installing the roll pin.

10. Install the detent balls and springs. Place new gaskets on the stop screws and install them into the housing.

11. Clamp the 4th gear of the pinion shaft into a vise with soft jaw covers.

12. With the gear carrier housing/cover mating surface facing upward, measure the distance from the housing surface to the top of the pinion bearing outer race or to the shim. Selective shims are available as follows.

NOTE: Measurements are in mm. Convert to inches as required.

Depth (mm)	Shim Thickness (mm)
8.35—8.64	1.1
8.65—8.94	1.4
8.95—9.24	1.7
9.25—9.54	2.0
9.55—9.84	2.3

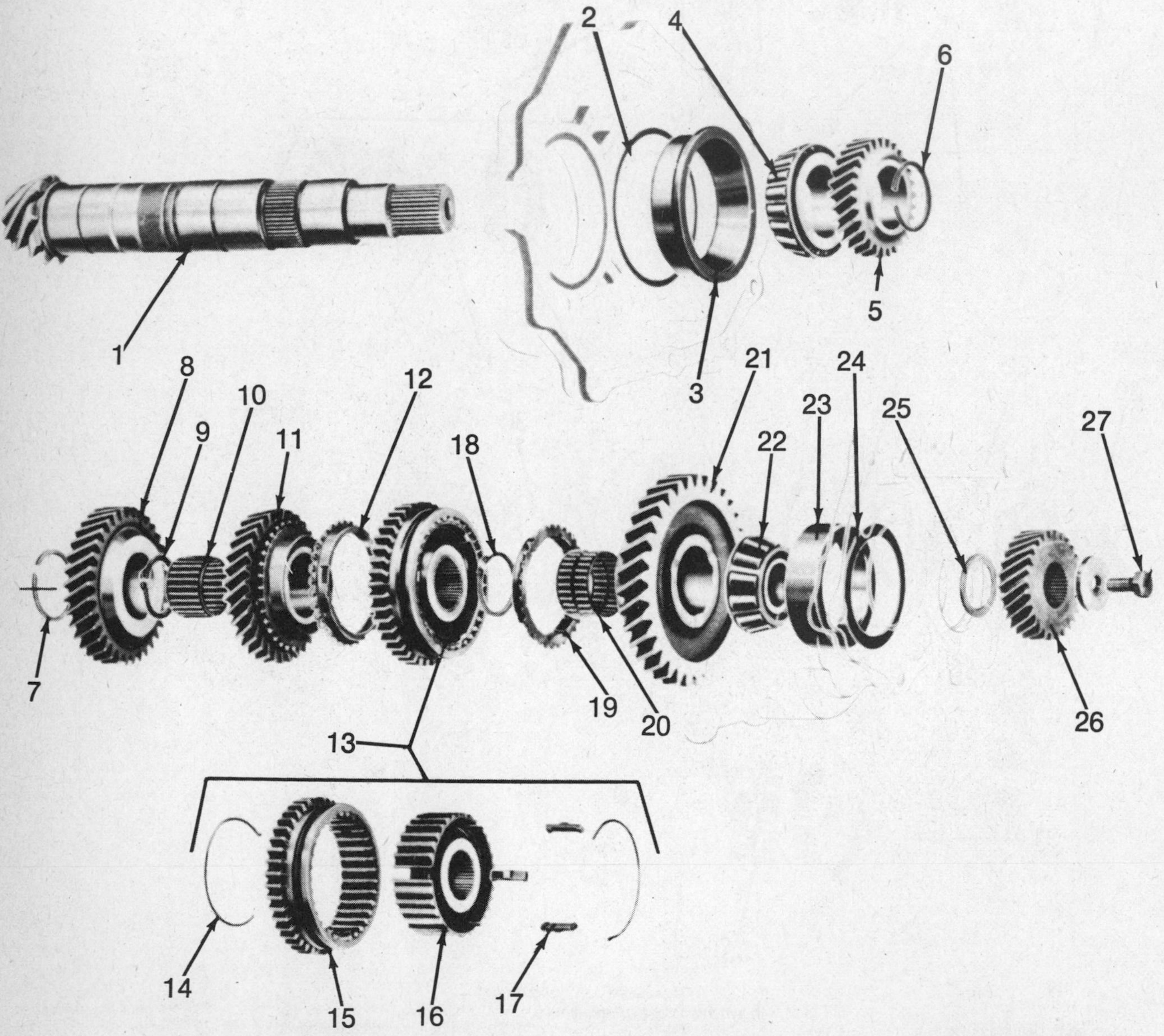

1. Pinion
2. Shim
3. Pinion bearing outer race
4. Pinion bearing
5. 4th gear
6. Circlip
7. Circlip
8. 3rd gear
9. Circlip
10. 2nd gear needle bearing
11. 2nd gear
12. 2nd gear synchronizer ring
13. Synchronizer sleeve/hub for 1st and 2nd gears
14. Spring
15. Synchronizer sleeve
16. Synchronizer hub
17. Hollow keys
18. Circlip
19. 1st gear synchronizer ring
20. 1st gear needle bearing
21. 1st gear
22. Pinion bearing
23. Pinion bearing outer race
24. Shim
25. Shim for 5th gear
26. 5th gear
27. Bolt

Exploded view of pinion shaft assembly

13. Heat the 5th gear to 250°F. (120° C.) and drive on the pinion shaft until seated on the selected shim.

NOTE: Be sure the collar of the gear faces the pinion head.

14. Install the washer and bolt and torque to 36 ft. lbs. (50 Nm).

15. Heat the main bearing inner race to 250° V. (120° C.) and drive on the mainshaft. Select a circlip of the proper thickness to fit tightly in the groove on the mainshaft.

16. Install the 5th gear with synchronizer hub, needle bearing and shift rod. Support the shift rod and install the roll pin.

17. Install the retaining circlip and install the 5th gear synchronizer ring.

18. Heat the 5th gear clutch hub to 250°F. (120° C.) and drive on the mainshaft. Drive on the mainshaft inner bearing race with a

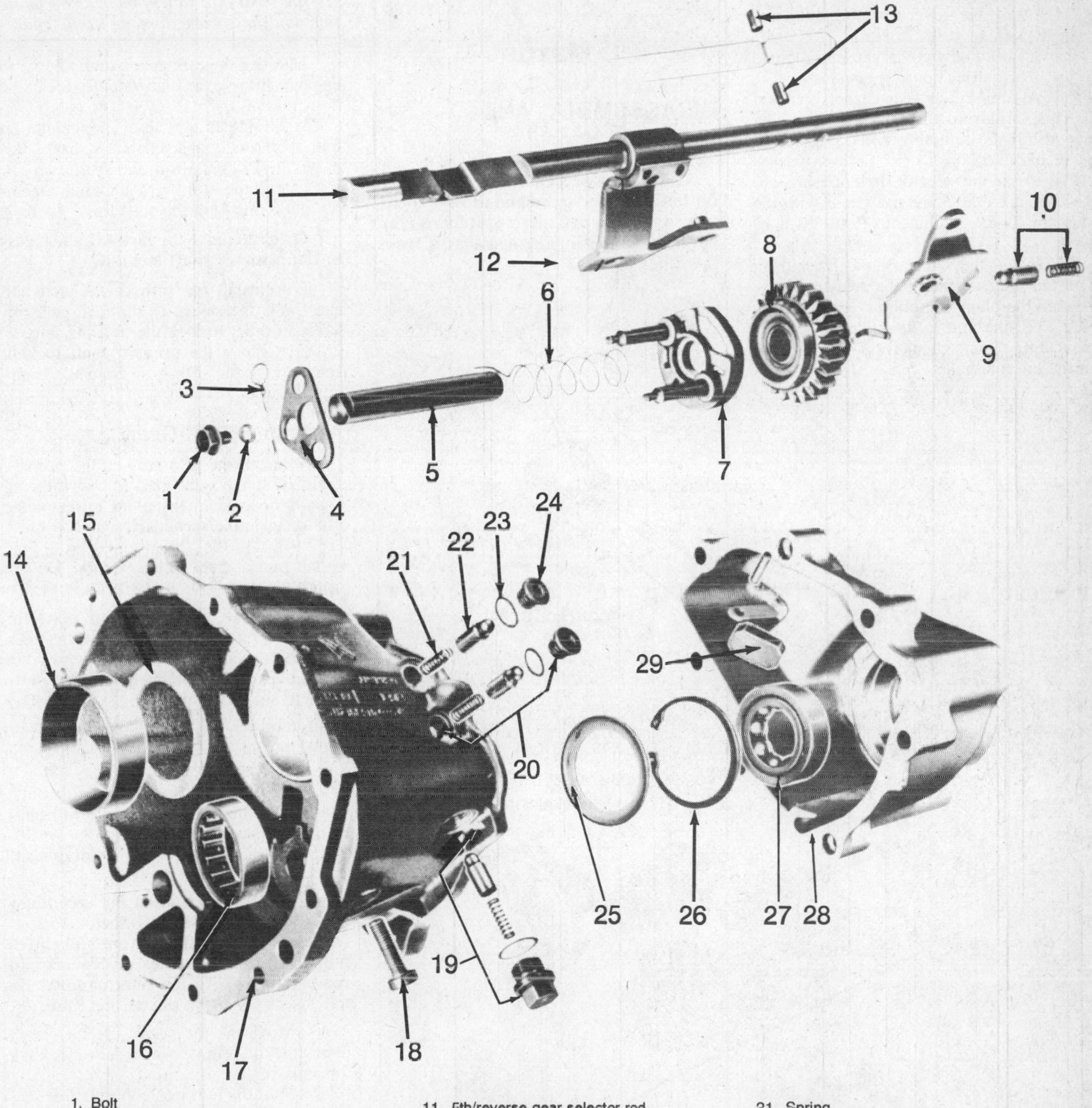

1. Bolt
2. Sleeve
3. Spring clip
4. Mounting plate
5. Reverse gear shaft
6. Spring
7. Reverse gear synchronizer
8. Reverse gear
9. Reverse gear relay lever
10. Reverse gear interlock plunger
11. 5th/reverse gear selector rod
12. Reverse gear shift fork
13. Plungers
14. Pinion bearing outer race
15. Shim
16. Main shaft bearing
17. Gear carrier housing
18. Relay lever bolt
19. 5th gear interlock mechanism
20. 1st to 4th gear interlock mechanism
21. Spring
22. Plunger
23. Gasket
24. Stop screw
25. Baffle plate
26. Circlip
27. Mainshaft bearing
28. Gear carrier housing cover
29. Magnet

Exploded view of gear carrier housing and cover components

driving sleeve type tool.

19. Install the dowel pins and a new gasket to the mating surface.

20. Carefully install the gear carrier housing cover, and drive the second mainshaft inner bearing race onto the shaft.

21. Install the washer and bolt onto the mainshaft and tighten to 36 ft. lbs. (50 Nm).

22. Install the cover retaining bolts and tighten to 18 ft. lbs. (25 Nm).

23. Install a new cover cap into the end of the gear carrier housing cover.

24. Assemble the gear carrier housing/cover assembly to the final drive housing and install the retaining bolts. Tighten to 18 ft. lbs. (25 Nm).

25. Install the selector shaft housing into the final drive housing and retain with the retaining bolts. Tighten to 7 ft. lbs. (10 Nm).

26. Install the selector shaft lever flush with the toothed end of the selector shaft. Tighten the clamping bolt.

27. Fill the unit to its proper level with lubricating oil and check for proper shifting on the internal gears.

TYPE 22

4 and 5 Speed Transaxle

Mazda

DISASSEMBLY AND ASSEMBLY

NOTE: The procedures described are for both the four speed and the five speed transaxle. The five speed unit has a rear cover which easily distinguishes it from the other unit.

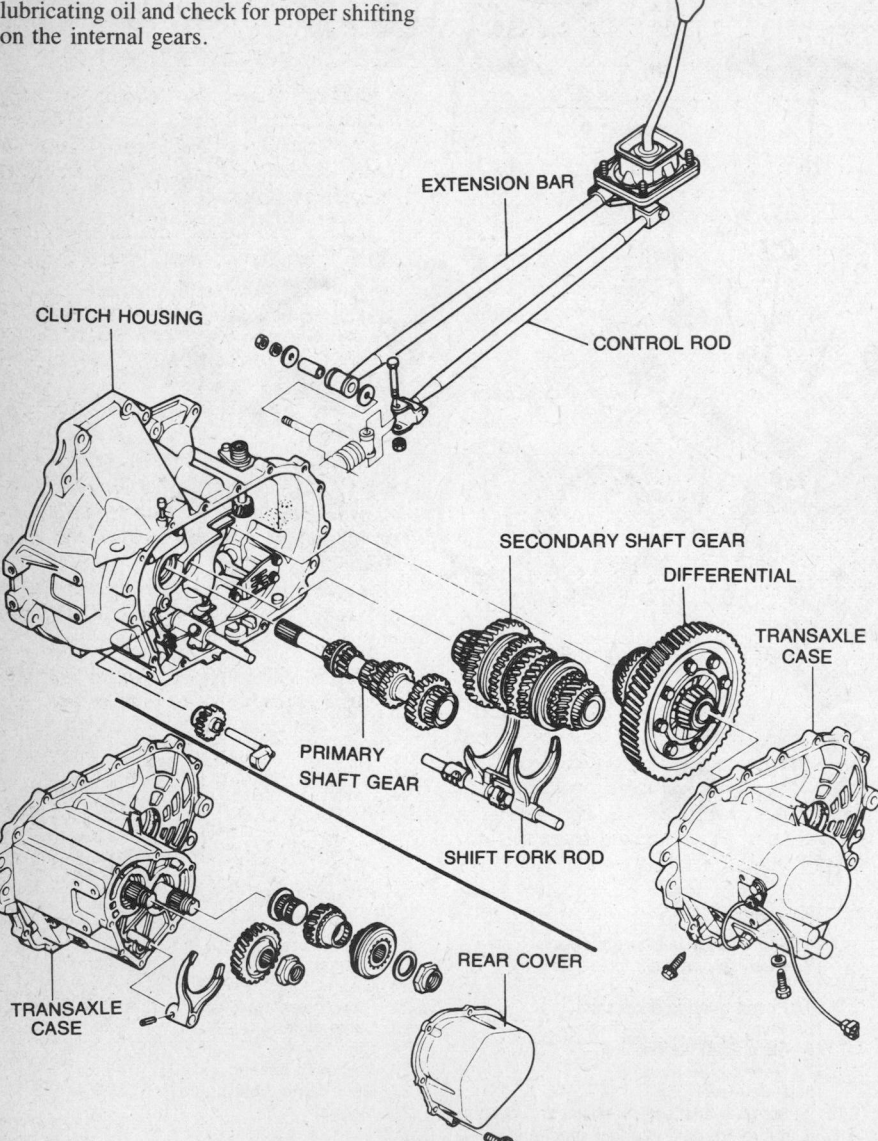

EXTENSION BAR

CONTROL ROD

CLUTCH HOUSING

SECONDARY SHAFT GEAR

DIFFERENTIAL

TRANSAXLE CASE

PRIMARY SHAFT GEAR

SHIFT FORK ROD

REAR COVER

TRANSAXLE CASE

Mazda GLC manual transaxle—exploded view

Disassembly (Fifth Gear)

1. Remove the rear cover. Remove the roll pin that secures the fifth gear shift fork to the selector shaft. Shift the transaxle unit into either first or second gear.

———— CAUTION ————
Do not shift into fourth gear as by doing this you may cause damage to the gears.

2. Move the fifth gear clutch sleeve, to engage fifth gear and double lock the transmission.

3. Straighten the tab of the locknut on both the primary and secondary shafts. Remove the locknuts from the shafts.

4. Pull the fifth gear clutch hub assembly out along with the shift fork.

NOTE: Remove the fork to gain access to the primary shaft locknut.

5. Reinstall the fifth gear clutch hub and move the sleeve to the fifth gear position in order to lock the transmission.

6. Remove the primary shaft locknut and remove the fifth gear from the transmission case.

Assembly (Fifth Gear)

1. Install the fifth gear on the primary shaft. Be sure that the marked boss is facing toward the locknut. Install the bush and the fifth gear on the secondary shaft.

2. Install the synchronizer ring and clutch hub and the selector fork. Do not install the shift fork pin.

NOTE: The stop washer or plate for the clutch hub must be installed between the locknut and clutch hub to prevent overtravel of the clutch when shifting into reverse gear to prevent the synchronizer keys from falling out.

3. Install the locknuts on both shafts and tighten them slightly

4. Shift into first or second gear only, using the control rod. Shift into fifth gear to double lock the transmission.

5. Tighten the primary shaft locknut and lock the hub.

NOTE: Do not tighten the secondary shaft locknut until the selector fork is installed. Remove the locknut and clutch hub from the secondary gear shaft and reassemble it with the selector fork. Do not insert the drive pin at this time.

6. Move the fifth gear selector clutch to engage the fifth gear in order to lock the transmission.

7. Shift the unit into either first or second gear.

8. Install the roll pin securing the fifth gear shift fork to the selector shaft. Install the cover.

Primary Shaft

The Mazda manual transaxle uses two types of primary shafts, one for the four speed transaxle and one for the five speed transaxle. Both shafts are made as a cluster with

Checking thrust clearance

Checking thrust clearance—fifth gear

reverse, first, second, third and fourth gears integral. The fifth gear (when equipped) is splined into the end of the shaft, thus distinguishing between the four and five speed unit.

Secondary Shaft

The secondary shaft assembly consists of the secondary shaft, gears, clutch hub and sleeve assemblies, synchro rings and bearings. The secondary shaft is manufactured integrally with the final drive gear.

There are three different types of secondary shafts used in the four speed transaxle and two different types used in the five speed transaxle. All of these shafts vary by the number of gear teeth on the final drive gears.

NOTE: The combination of the final drive gear on the secondary shaft and ring gear are identified by the groove provided in the construction of each individual gear.

Disassembly and Assembly (Secondary Gears)

1. Install a suitable bearing puller in the grooves between the gear and the gear spline of fourth gear. Remove the bearing and the fourth gear from the assembly.

2. Remove the snap-ring on the third and fourth clutch hub. Slide out the clutch hub and the sleeve assembly.

3. Remove the third gear, the thrust washer and the second gear.

4. Remove the snap-ring, and slide out the clutch hub and reverse gear assembly and first gear.

5. Install the bearing remover tool under the rollers and press out the shaft.

6. Assembly is the reverse of disassembly.

Synchronizer Rings

Bridge type synchronizer rings are used in the Mazda transaxle. There are three dif-

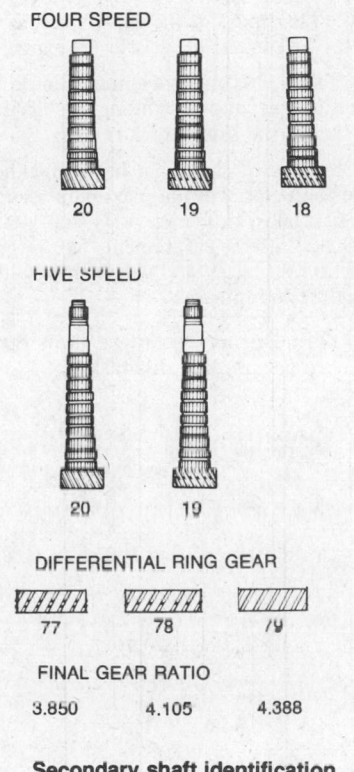

Secondary shaft identification

ferent synchronizer rings; one for second, third and fourth speed, another for first and third speed and one for fifth speed if the vehicle is so equipped. The first speed synchro ring can be identified from the other two because it has less teeth.

Thrust Clearance

The thrust clearance of each gear is checked by using a feeler gauge. The specification for thrust clearance is .5 mm (.020 in.).

Reverse Idler Shaft and Shift Rod

The reverse idler shaft has an integral mounting post which is secured to the case with a bolt. When installing the idler shaft, align the holes of the shaft with the notch

in the transaxle case. When installing the reverse shift rod to the shift gate, be sure that the screw holes are aligned and that the hole of the shift rod is not 180 degrees out of phase.

Bearing Preload Adjustment

NOTE: When the clutch housing, transaxle case, primary shaft, secondary shaft, bearings or differential case are replaced the bearing preload should be checked and adjusted.

1. Remove the oil seal and the differential bearing outer race. Adjust the shim from the transaxle case.

2. Remove the bearing outer races from the primary and secondary shafts. Adjust the shims from the transaxle case and the clutch housing.

3. Reinstall the outer races to the transaxle case.

4. Install the outer races (removed in Step 2) to their respective selectors. Install the selectors, primary shaft assembly and the secondary shaft assembly to the clutch housing.

5. Install the transaxle case and place the ten collars between the transaxle case and the clutch housing.

NOTE: The collars should be positioned as shown in the illustration.

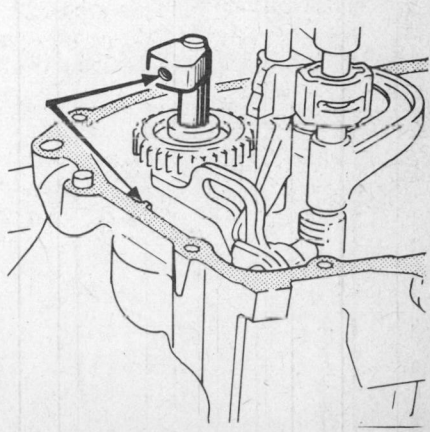

Reverse idler shaft alignment

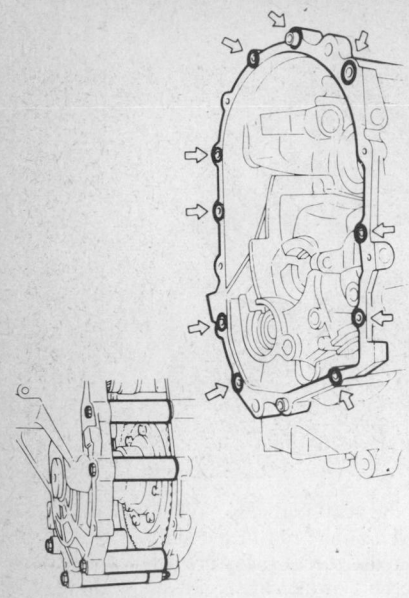

Collar positioning

6. To properly settle each bearing, using the tool turn the selector in a direction where the gap is widened until it cannot be turned by hand. Then turn the selector in the opposite direction until the gap is eliminated. Manually turn the selector to a direction where the gap becomes wider until the selector cannot be turned.

NOTE: Make sure that the shaft turns smoothly.

7. Measure the gap of the selector with a feeler gauge.

NOTE: This measurement should be taken at several places along the circumference of the selector.

8. Take the maximum reading and determine the shim to be used as follows.

9. For the primary shaft bearing, first subtract 1.00 mm (thickness of the diaphragm spring) from the gap (determined in Step 7).

EXAMPLE) Measurement 1.39 mm minus 1.00 mm equals .39 mm, select the next larger and closer shim which would be .40 mm.

NOTE: Do not use more than two shims.

10. For the secondary shaft bearing, select a shim which has a thickness that is larger and closer to the gap (determined in Step 7).

EXAMPLE) Measurement .42 mm, select the next larger and closer shim which would be .45 mm.

NOTE: Do not use more than two shims to accomplish this task.

11. For the differential bearing, set the preload adapters (tool # 49-0180-510A and # 49-FT01-515 or equivalent) to the pinion shaft through the hole for the driveshaft of the transaxle case. Hook a spring scale to the adapter and check the bearing preload.

NOTE: While checking the preload, turn the selector until the reading of the spring scale becomes 1.1–1.5 lb.

12. Then measure the gap of the selector on the differential using a feeler gauge.

NOTE: This measurement should be taken in several places along the circumference of the selector.

13. Select a shim that has a thickness larger and closer to the maximum reading that was taken in the previous step.

EXAMPLE) Measurement .54 mm, select the next larger and closer shim which would be .60 mm.

NOTE: Do not use more than three shims to accomplish this task.

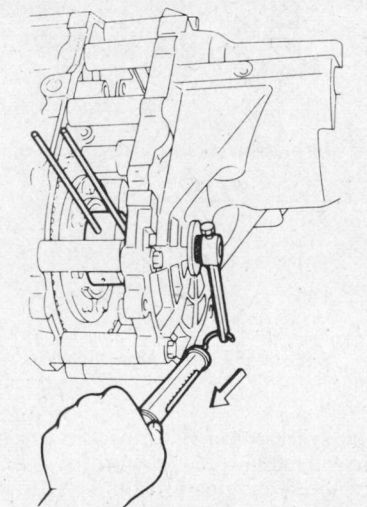

Checking differential bearing preload

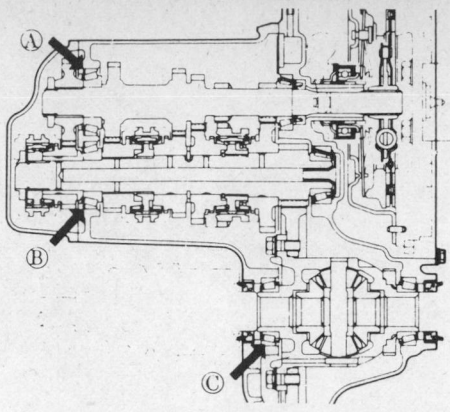

Selected shim installation

14. Remove the shim selectors and each bearing outer race. Install the shims selected in previous steps between the transaxle case and the bearing outer race.

15. A diaphragm spring is used to keep the bearing preload as specified and also to maintain low level gear noise. So when installing the diaphragm spring, be sure it is in the proper direction.

16. When installing the oil funnel on the clutch housing, be sure that it is in the proper position.

17. After assembling the transaxle, recheck the preloads of the differential bearing and the primary shaft bearing.

18. The differential bearing preload should be .3–6.6 in. lbs., and the reading on the spring scale should be .07–1.7 lb.

19. The primary shaft preload should be 1.7–3.5 in. lbs., and the reading on the spring scale should be .4–.9 lb.

Differential

The final gear is helical cut with the same tooth design as that used in the transmission. No adjustments are required.

There are three different ring gears in numbers of gear teeth on the manual transaxle. They are identified by the marks (grooves) provided on the gear outer surface.

The backlash between the differential side gear and pinion gear is adjusted by the thrust washer installed behind the side gear teeth. There are three different thicknesses of thrust washers available.

When checking the backlash, insert both driveshafts into the side gears.

Strut Overhaul

STRUT SERVICE AND REPAIR

MacPherson struts are appearing on the front (and rear) wheels of more and more cars. The strut design takes up less room in the engine compartment, compared to a conventional upper and lower arm with shock absorber arrangement. The trend toward smaller, lighter and more efficient packaging mandates the use of a strut suspension to permit more room for engine accessories and front wheel drive components.

Strut Suspension Design

In a conventional front suspension, the wheel is attached to a spindle, which is in turn, connected to upper and lower control arms through upper and lower ball joints. A coil spring between the control arms (sometimes on top of the upper arm) supports the weight of the vehicle and a shock absorber controls rebound and dampens oscillations.

In a strut type suspension, the strut performs a shock dampening function, like a shock absorber, but unlike a conventional shock absorber, the strut is a structural part of the vehicle's suspension.

The strut assembly usually contains a spring seat to retain the coil spring that supports the vehicle's weight. The shock absorber is built into the body of the strut housing. The strut is normally attached at the bottom to the lower control arm and at the top to the car body. The upper mount usually features a bearing that permits the coil spring to rotate as the wheels turn for smoother steering. The entire design eliminates the need for the upper control arm,

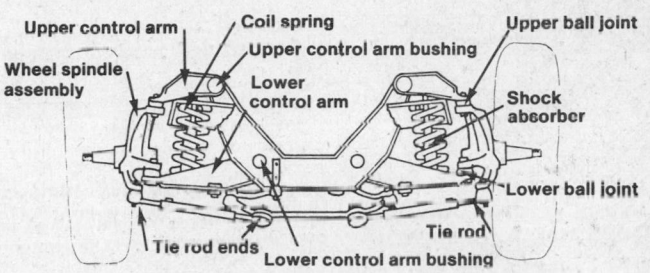

Conventional upper and lower arm suspension

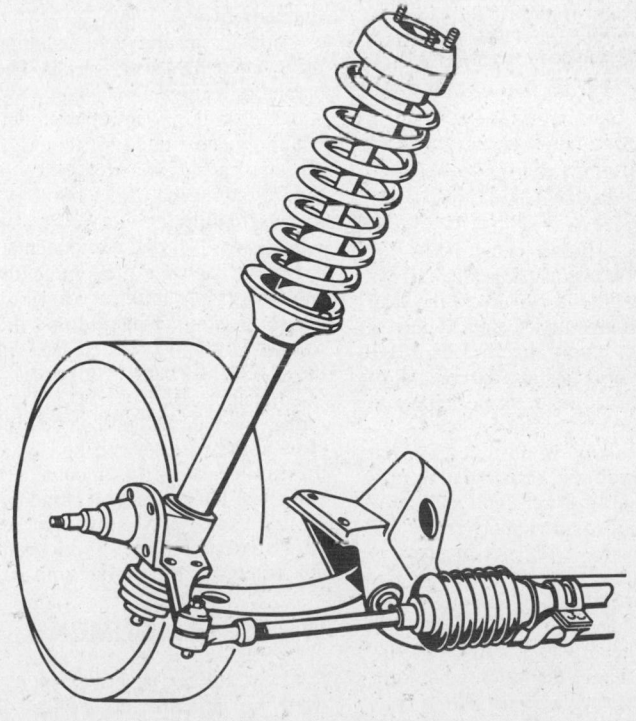

Strut with concentric coil spring (rear wheel drive)

U279

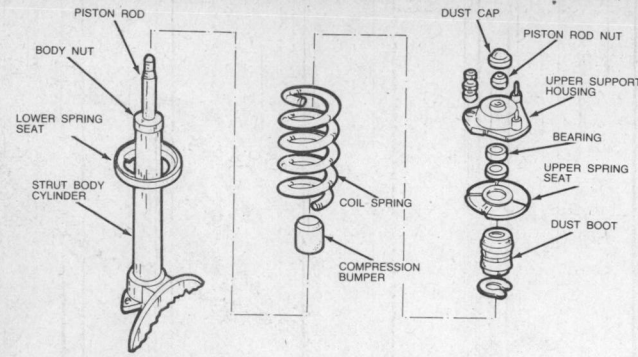

Exploded view of a typical strut

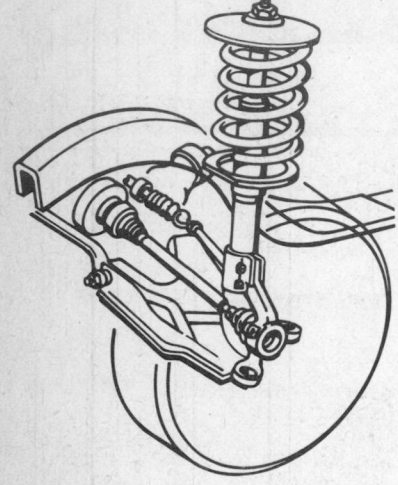

Strut with concentric coil spring (front wheel drive)

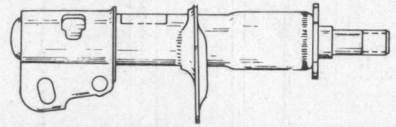

A sealed strut has no body nut and is serviceable by replacement

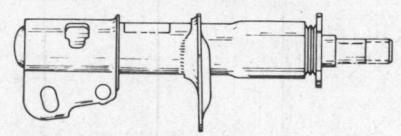

Serviceable struts have a removeable body nut to allow replacement of the strut cartridge

upper ball joint and many of the conventional suspension bushings. The lower ball joint is no longer a load carrying unit, because it is isolated from the weight of the vehicle.

Serviceability

Struts fall into 2 broad categories—serviceable and sealed units. A sealed strut is designed so that the top closure of the strut assembly is permanently sealed. There is no access to the shock absorber cartridge inside the strut housing and no means of replacing the cartridge. It is necessary to replace the entire strut unit.

A serviceable strut is designed so that the cartridge inside the housing, that provides the shock absorbing function, can be replaced with a new cartridge. Serviceable struts use a threaded body nut in place of a sealed cap to retain the cartridge.

The shock absorber device inside a serviceable strut is generally "wet". This means that the shock absorber contains oil that contacts and lubricates the inner wall of the strut body. The oil is sealed inside the strut by the body nut, O-ring and piston rod seal.

Servicing a "wet" strut with the equiv-

alent components involves a thorough cleaning of the inside of the strut body, absolute cleanliness and great care in reassembly.

Cartridge inserts were developed to simplify servicing "wet" struts. The insert is a factory sealed replacement for the strut shock absorber. The replacement cartridge is simply substituted for the original shock absorber cartridge and retained with the body nut, avoiding the near laboratory-like conditions required to service a "wet" strut with "wet" service components.

Import cars use predominantly concentric coil spring units and, for the most part are serviceable, meaning that they can be removed from the vehicle, disassembled and the shock absorber cartridge replaced in the old housing. Both OEM and aftermarket replacement cartridges can be used in these struts if they are serviceable. Exceptions to the serviceable struts include Ford Fiesta and some later Fiats and Hondas, but even on these cars OEM struts can be replaced with aftermarket units, which are serviceable once the aftermarket unit is installed.

WHEEL ALIGNMENT

It is not always necessary to re-align the wheels after struts are serviced. If care is taken matchmarking affected components and in reassembling, alignment may be un-

affected. However, if wheels were not in proper alignment prior to service, or if the entire strut assembly was replaced, a wheel alignment check should be made. Generally, only camber is adjustable, and then only within a narrow range.

Do not attempt to bend components to correct wheel alignment.

On most serviceable import struts, the position of the upper bearing plate or lower mount can be matchmarked and wheel alignment will be maintained during reassembly.

Tools

Without the right tools, a strut job will take longer than necessary and can be dangerous.

A normal selection of hand tools such as open end and box wrenches, sockets, pliers, screwdrivers and hammers are necessary to work on struts. Extensions and universal joints will help reach tight spots. Be sure to have both metric and inch-sized wrenches on hand. Two big time-savers are "crows-feet" and ratcheting box wrenches in assorted sizes. Torx fasteners are also showing up more and more in chassis fasteners.

In addition to the normal handtools, some sort of spanner is necessary to remove the body nut on serviceable struts. Sometimes a pipe wrench can be used successfully.

Strut and cartridge replacement requires a spring compressor.

Makeshift tools for compressing coil springs—threaded rod, chains, wire or other methods—should never be used. The coil spring is under tremendous compression and can fly off causing personal injury and damage to equipment. Use only a good quality spring compressor such as described below.

Economy, or manual, spring compressors are the least expensive but more time consuming to use. Angle hooks grasp the spring coils and must be compressed with a wrench. For those who service struts infrequently, this is probably the wisest investment for purchase.

Other manual spring compressors (jaws type) are faster to operate, have a more positive gripping action and can be used on or off the car. These types are probably not cost effective for the do-it-yourselfer, but can be rented from auto supply stores for single-time use.

For volume work, compressors that are pneumatically or hydraulically operated are best. Air operated compressors are suitable for all types of struts (through use of adaptors), are lightweight and can be used on or off the vehicle. Bench mounted hydraulically operated units are probably the safest, but are also the most expensive and require that the strut be removed from the vehicle, which means separating brake lines and other connections which can be time consuming.

There are also universal kits that fit all struts in either the manual or air operated types.

MAINTAINING WHEEL ALIGNMENT

The location and method of adjusting wheel alignment determines the components that must be match-marked to maintain wheel alignment. There are 4 basic methods of adjusting wheel alignment. Almost all cars use one of these or a slight variation.

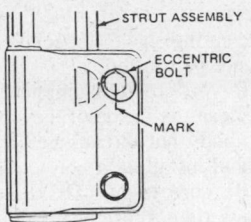

Mark the eccentric (camber adjusting bolt) relative to the clevis mounting bracket.

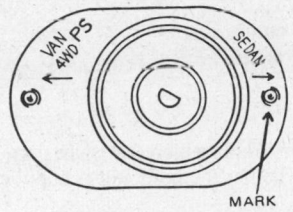

Mark the mounting stud that faces the front of the vehicle. This type of bracket is reversible for varying applications.

Mark the upper support housing relative to the inner fender before removing the strut from the upper mount.

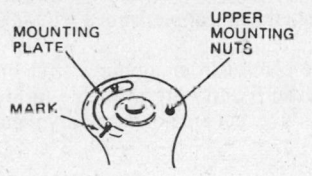

Mark the location of the mounting plate relative to the location on the inner fender.

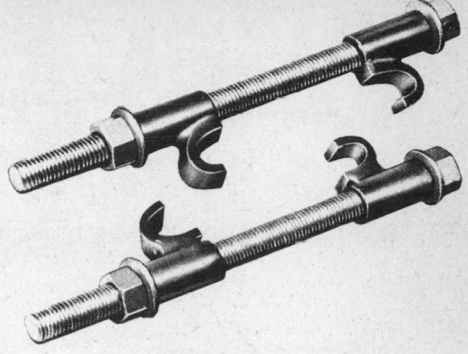

An economical manual spring compressor

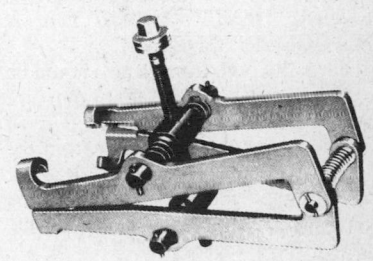

"Jaws" type spring compressor

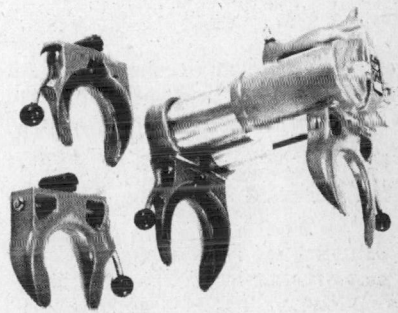

Lightweight, air operated, portable spring compressor can be used on or off the vehicle. Extra shoes are available to handle all strut applications

A simple spanner wrench designed for use with body nuts equipped with recessed lugs. A pipe wrench is a frequent substitute

Spanner wrench with adaptor inserts for various applications of body nuts. This type of spanner can be used with a torque wrench for retorqueing the body nut

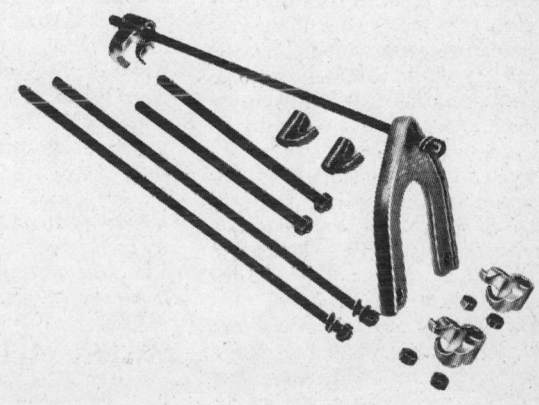

A manual spring compressor with plates or hooks for servicing virtually any strut

Stationary, universal pneumatic spring compressor

Repair Tips

1. Make sure you have all the tools you'll need. NEVER IMPROVISE A SPRING COMPRESSOR.

2. Normally both front struts should be repaired or replaced at the same time.

3. The easiest way to work on most struts is to remove the entire unit from the vehicle, unless you have access to an air operated spring compressor. Some struts, however, can, and should, be repaired while installed on the vehicle.

4. Always read the instructions packaged with any replacement parts. In particular, note whether the body nut is supplied new or re-used.

5. Mark the position(s) of any bearing plate nuts or cam bolts to assure proper alignment after installation.

6. Be sure to protect the rubber boot on the drive axle of front wheel drive cars.

7. If necessary to remove the brake caliper, do not let the caliper hang by the brake hose. Suspend the caliper from a wire hook or rope.

8. Be careful in clamping a strut in a vise. Special fixtures are available to hold struts in a vise, but are not necessary if care is used to be sure the housing is not crushed or dented. A block of soft wood on either side of the housing will prevent most damage.

9. Use a spring compressor to relieve tension from the spring. Be sure to clean and lubricate the screw threads, particularly on hand operated (manual) spring compressors.

Some springs have a special coating that should not be scuffed.

10. If you are replacing the strut cartridge, clean the inside of the strut housing and the body nut threads before replacing the oil and installing a new cartridge.

11. Be sure to use OEM quality fasteners any time a fastener is replaced.

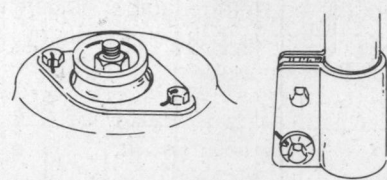

Mark the position of the attachments that control wheel alignment. See Maintaining Wheel Alignment earlier in this section

STRUT OVERHAUL (OFF-CAR)

Following is a typical overhaul procedure of a serviceable MacPherson strut, after having removed the strut from the vehicle. The vehicle should be firmly supported. If it is necessary, to separate the brake line from the strut for strut removal, the brakes will have to be bled after reinstallation. See the manufacturer's car section for specific MacPherson strut removal and installation procedures.

Photos Courtesy Gabriel Div., Maremont Corp.

Step 1. **Examine the strut assembly for damage, dented strut body, spring seat, broken or missing strut mounting parts. Any of these will require replacement of the complete assembly. Also inspect other suspension components for wear or damage**

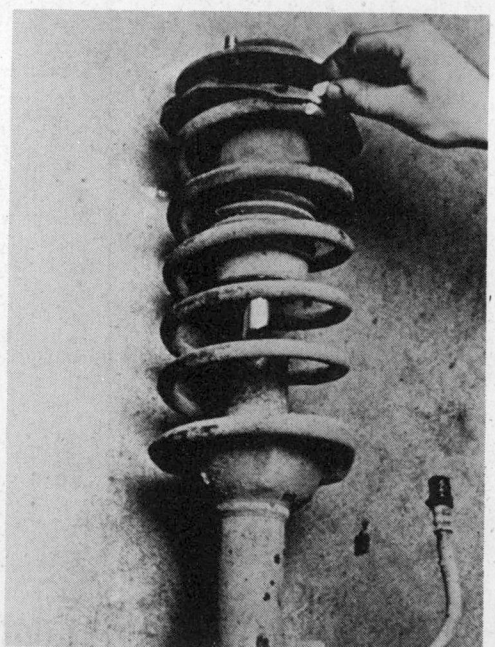

Step 2. **Matchmark the upper end of the coil spring and bearing plate to avoid confusion during reassembly**

Step 3. **To make servicing easier, clamp the strut in a strut vise. The strut vise is designed to clamp the strut tight without damage to strut cylinder. It is very handy for strut work and can be used in your shop vise or mounted to any bench**

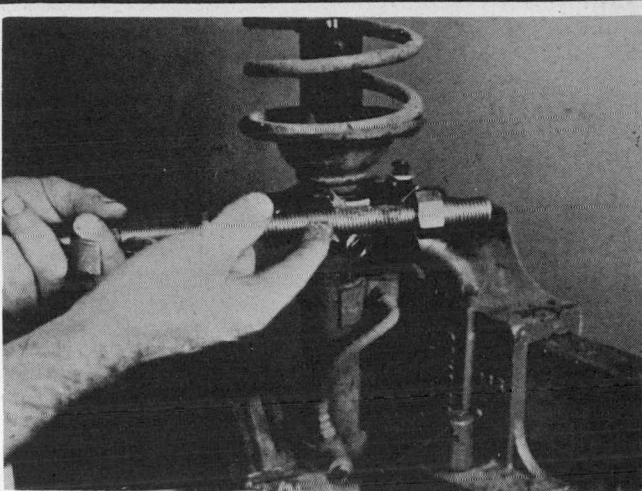

Step 4. **Before using the manual spring compressor, lubricate both sides of the thrust washers and the threads with a light coat of grease**

Step 5. **Install the compressor hooks on opposite sides of the coil spring with the hooks attached to the upper-most and lower-most spring coils. To avoid possible slippage, use tape or small hose clamps on either side of the compressor hooks**

Step 6. **Alternately tighten the bolts a few turns at a time until all tension is removed from the spring seat**

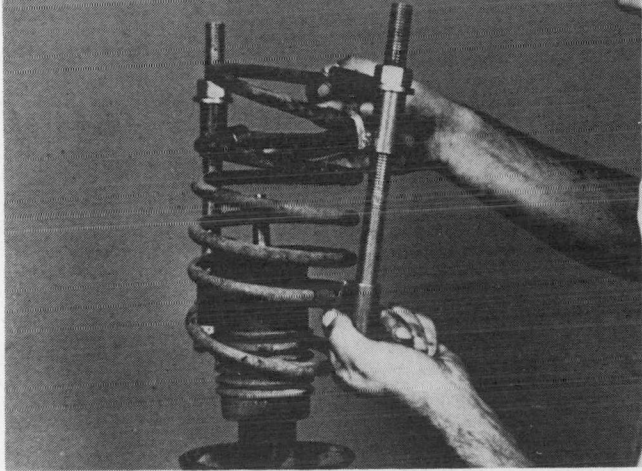

Step 7. **Remove the piston rod nut and disassemble the upper mounting parts, keeping them in order for reassembly. Remove the coil spring. There is no need to remove the compressor from the coil spring**

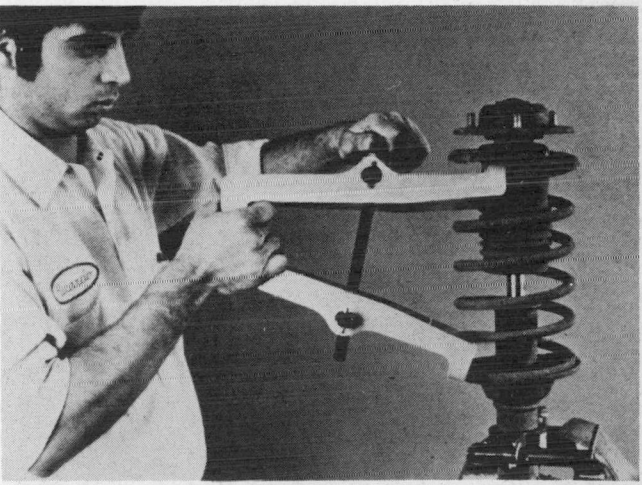

Step 8. **An alternative to the manual compressor is the "jaws" type. Turn the load screw to open or close the compressor until the maximum number of spring coils can be engaged**

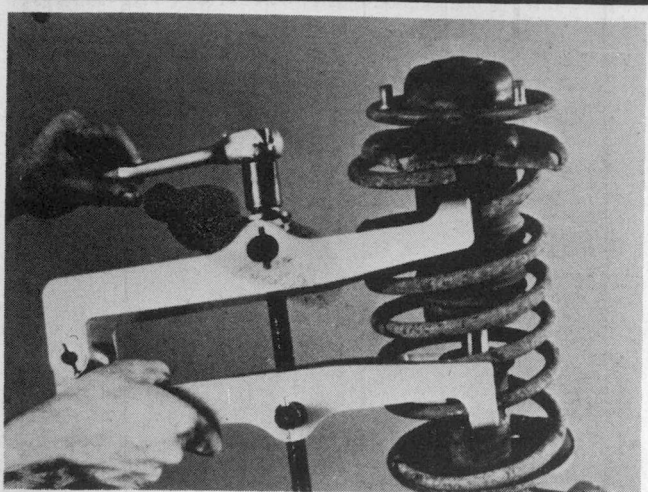

Step 9. **Tighten the load screw until the coil spring is loose from the spring seats. There is no need to compress the spring any further**

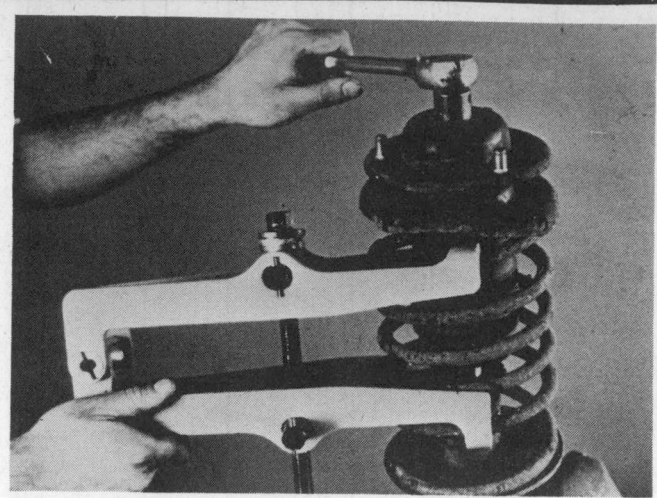

Step 10. **Remove the piston rod nut and disassemble the upper mounting parts**

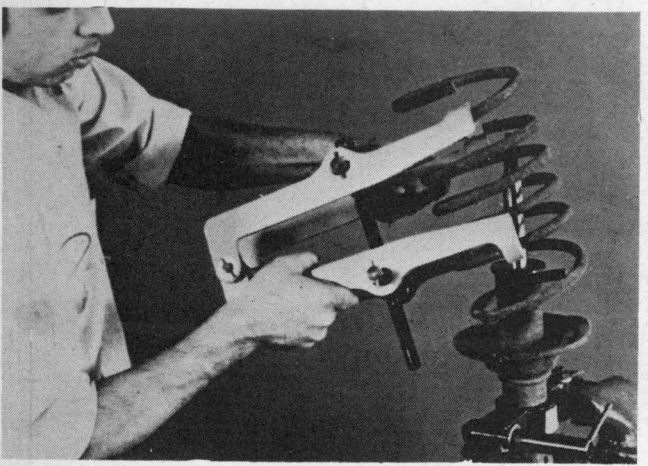

Step 11. **Like the manual compressor, there is no need to remove the compressor from the coil spring. Remove the coil spring and compressor**

Step 12. **Keep the upper mounting parts in order of their removal. They'll be re-assembled in reverse order**

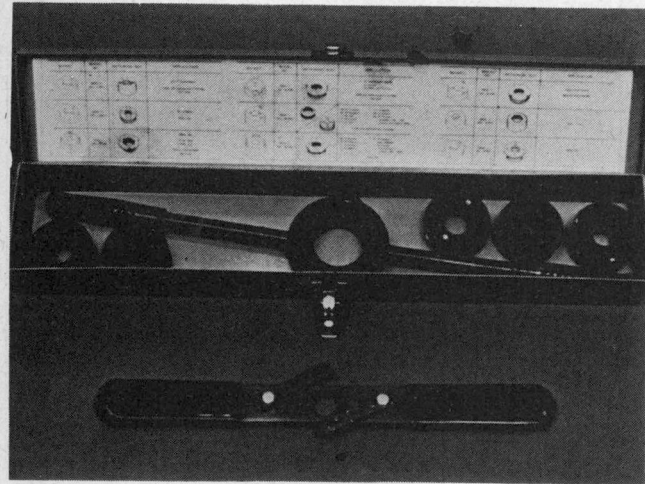

Step 13. **A spanner wrench is necessary to remove body nuts, although a pipe wrench will do the job**

Step 14. **Use the spanner wrench or pipe wrench to loosen the body nut**

Step 15. **Remove the body nut and discard if a new body nut came with the replacement cartridge. If not, save the body nut**

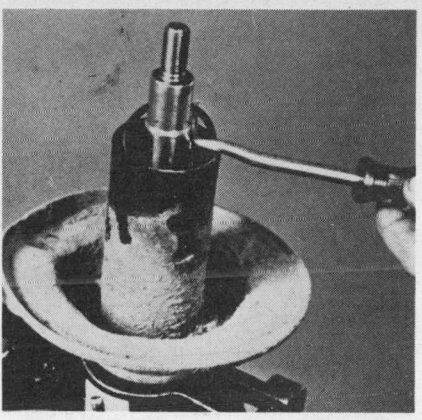

Step 16. **Use a scribe or suitable tool to remove the O—ring from the top of the housing**

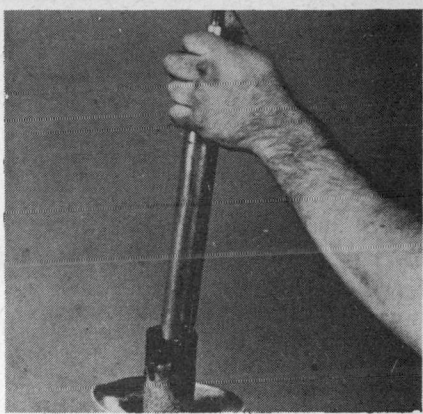

Step 17. **Grasp the piston rod and pull cartridge out of the housing. Remove it slowly to avoid splashing oil. Be sure all pieces come out of the housing**

Step 18. **Pour all of the strut fluid into a suitable container, clean the inside of the strut cylinder, and inspect the cylinder for dents and to insure that all loose parts have been removed from inside of strut body**

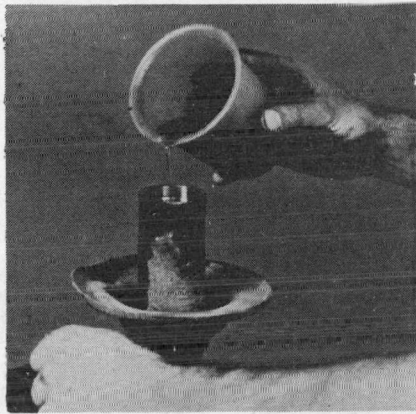

Step 19. **Refill the cylinder with one ounce (a shot glass) of the original oil or fresh oil. The oil helps dissipate internal cartridge heat during operation and results in a cooler running, longer lasting unit. Do not put too much oil in—otherwise the oil may leak at the body nut after it expands when heated**

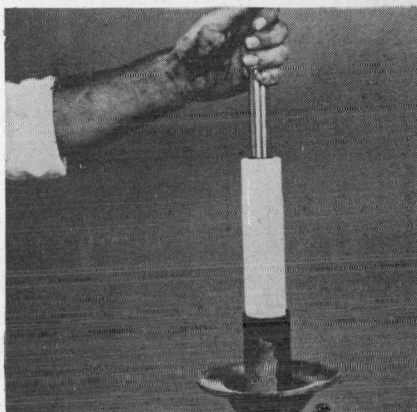

Step 20. **Insert the new replacement cartridge into the strut body**

Step 21. **Push the piston road *all* the way down, to avoid damage to the piston rod if the spanner wrench slips, and start the body nut by hand. Be sure it is not cross-threaded**

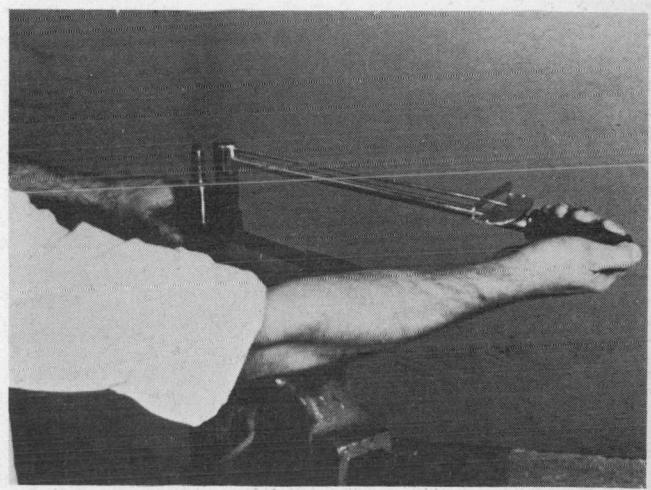

Step 22. **Tighten the body nut securely**

Step 23. Inspect the loose parts prior to re-assembly. Note the chalk mark location for proper seating of the upper spring seat

Step 24. Re-assemble the coil spring and upper mounting parts in reverse order. Tighten the piston rod nut and remove the spring compressor. Install the dust cap. Install the strut in the vehicle. See the car section for details

STRUT OVERHAUL (ON-CAR)

On some cars, it is best not to completely remove the strut for service. Removal or reassembly of some parts may be difficult without special equipment. Datsun Z-cars are among these. The service methods shown in the following procedure are typical of on-car strut overhaul, although parts or assembly sequences may vary. Refer to the individual manufacturer's car section for details of installations.

Photos Courtesy Gabriel Div., Maremont Corp.

Step 1. Raise the car to the desired working height and place jack stands under the crossmember, not under the lower control arm. Mark wheel rim and mating lug to assure that wheel balance is not disturbed

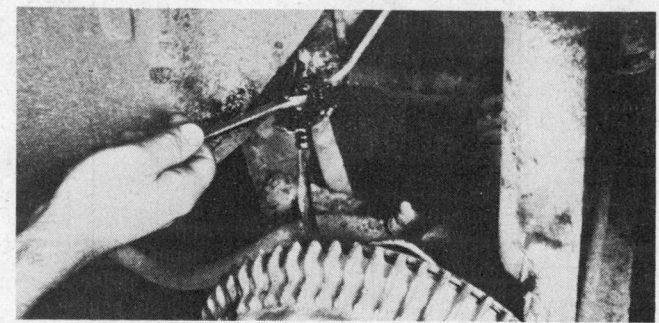

Step 2. Disconnect brake line at frame bracket

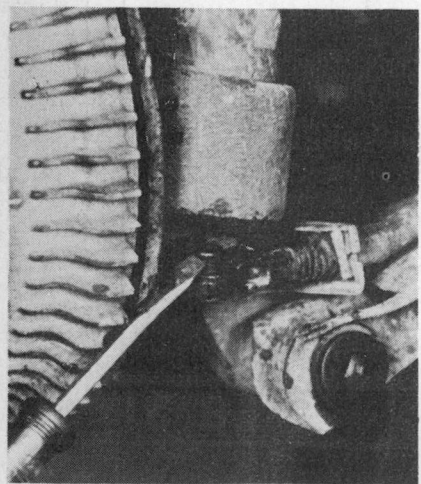

Step 3. Disconnect the emergency brake cable from actuator arm (Datsun uses a cotter key)

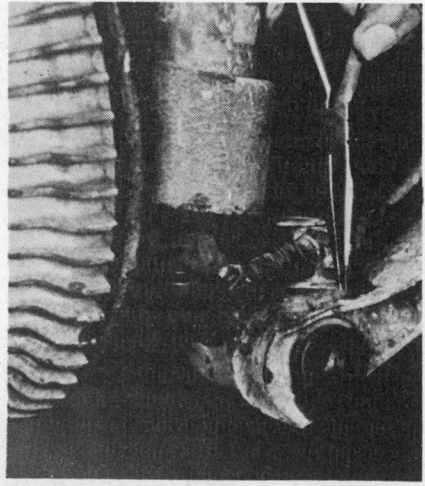

Step 4. Remove emergency brake cable from bracket by removing the spring clip

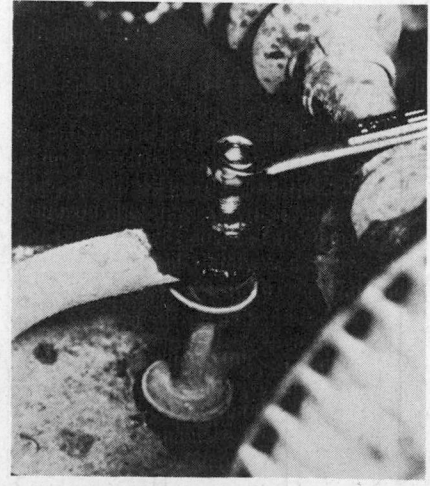

Step 5. Remove nut, retainer and bushing securing sway bar to its vertical link

Step 6. **Mark the driveshaft flange and hub to assure proper re-assembly. Remove the nuts, bolts, and lock washers securing the driveshaft to the hub**

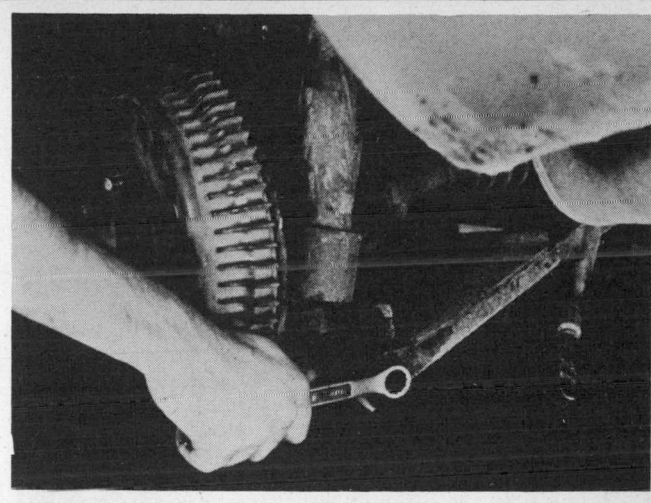

Step 7. **Loosen, but do not remove the nut securing the bottom of the strut to the lower control arm**

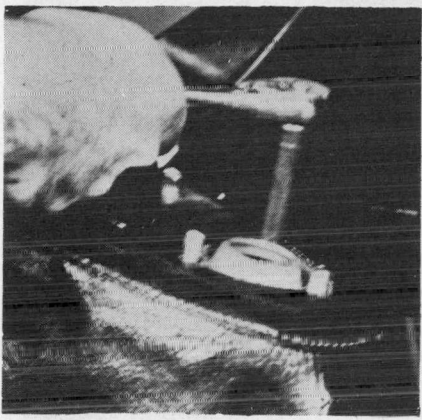

Step 8. **From inside the vehicle remove the nuts and lockwashers securing the upper support housing to vehicle fender**

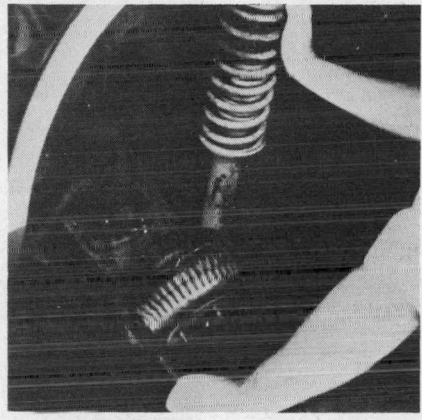

Step 9. **Press down on lower control arm with pry bar and swing strut from under fender. (Note:** *A slit hose can be used to protect wheel well fender edge)*

Step 10. **Either a manual or pneumatic spring compressor can be used to compress the spring. A pneumatic compressor is illustrated. Compress the spring and remove upper mounting parts. Remove the spring from the strut**

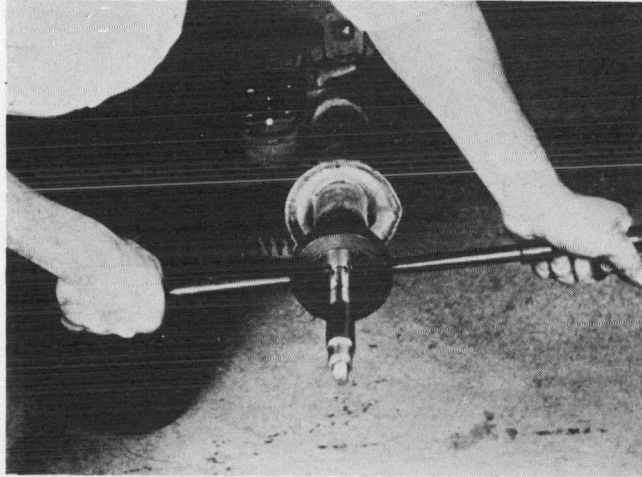

Step 11. **Remove body nut. For convenience, the strut can be propped up while removing body nut**

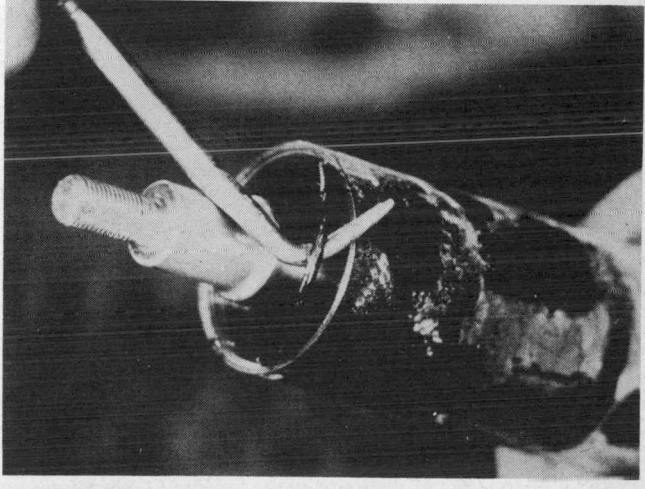

Step 12. **Remove O-ring using a small pick or an awl and remove the cartridge**

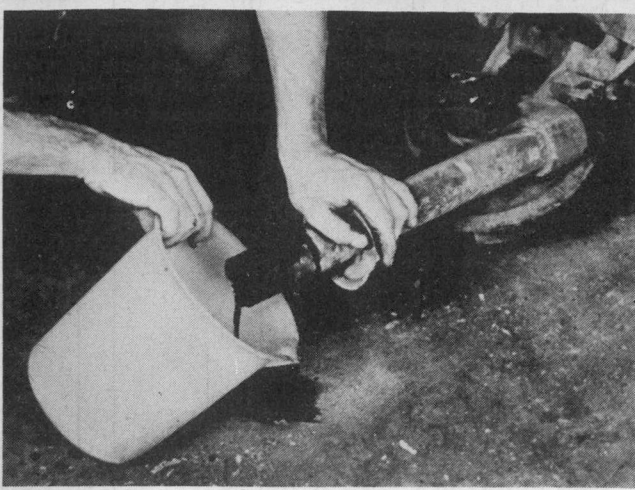

Step 13. Tilt strut down to allow all the oil to drain into a suitable container. Inspect cylinder for dents and to insure all loose parts have been removed from inside of strut body

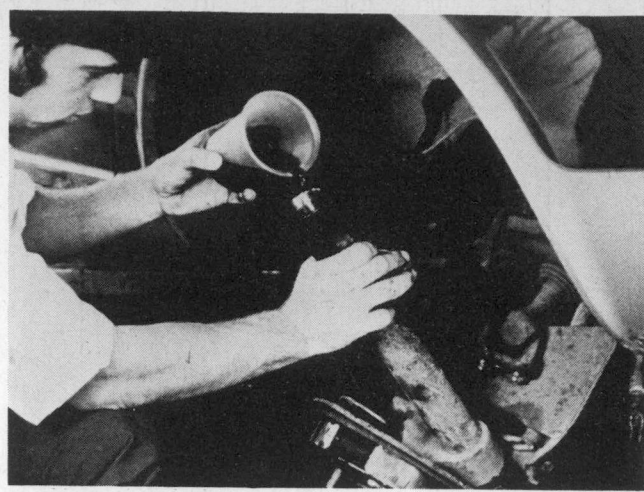

Step 14. Pour about one ounce (a shot glass) of oil back into the strut body for heat transfer. Avoid over-filling or the oil may leak past the body nut

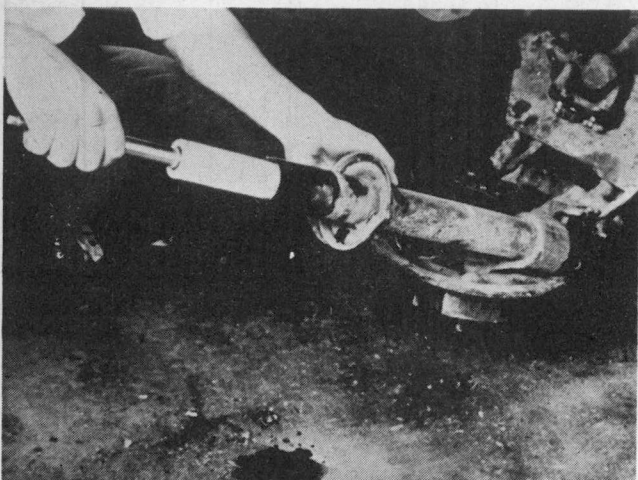

Step 15. Insert the new replacement cartridge into the strut body

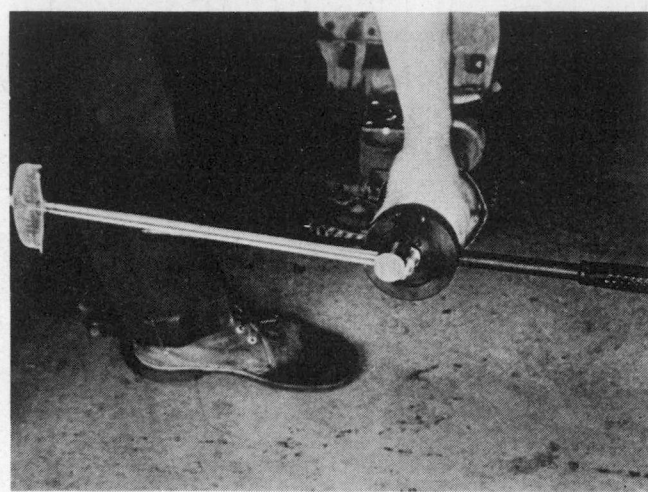

Step 16. Install the body nut and tighten securely

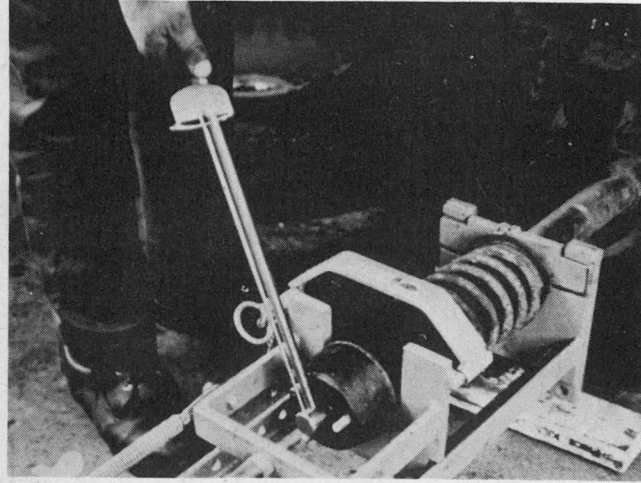

Step 17. Re-install compression bumper, coil spring, spring seat and upper support housing. Be sure to position the support housing studs relative to the holes in the vehicle's inner fender. Install the piston rod nut. Tighten securely. Relieve the spring tension

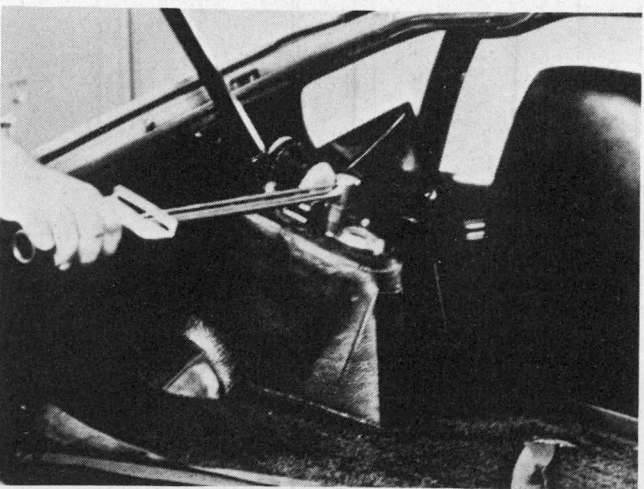

Step 18. Push the strut back under fender and install the nuts and lockwasher securing the upper support housing to the inner fender

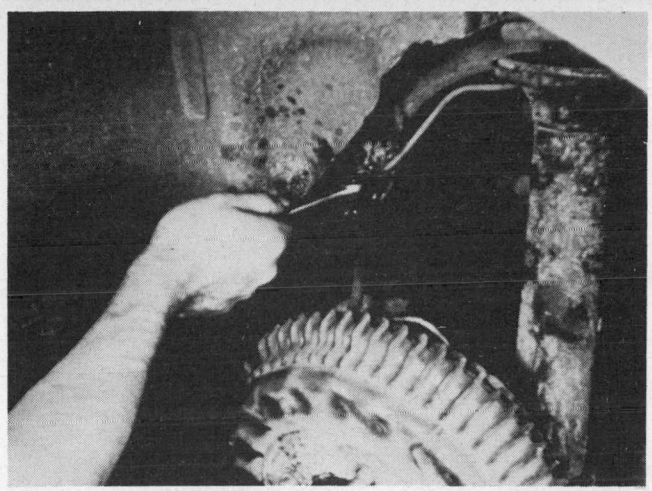

Step 19. Reconnect the brake line

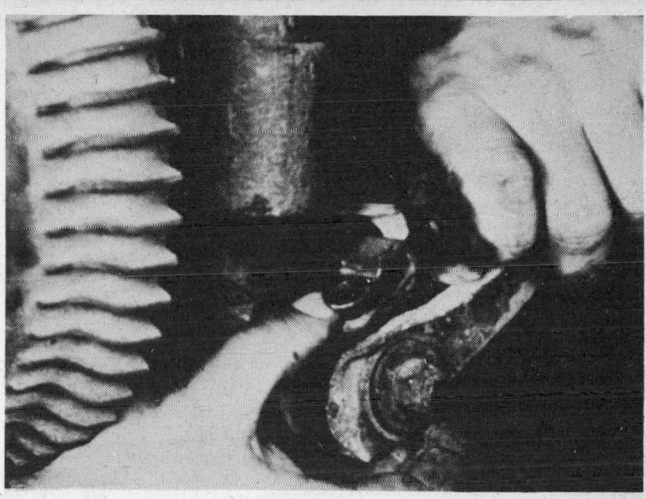

Step 20. Re–assemble the emergency brake cable in the bracket

Step 21. Re–assemble brake cable to actuator arm and install cotter pin

Step 22. Re–install the bushing retainer and nut on sway bar link

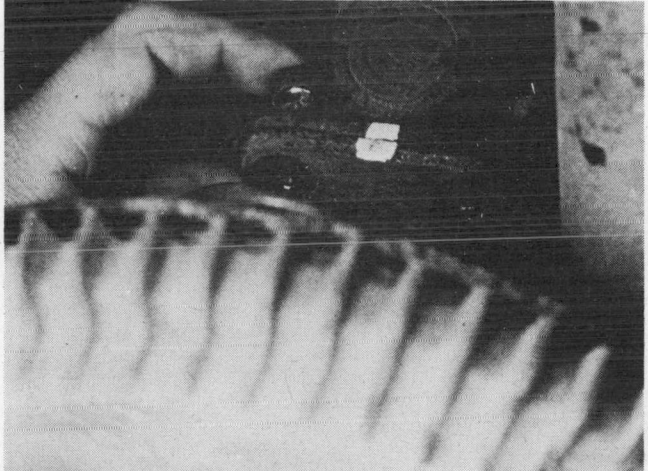

Step 23. Align marks made earlier, then install and tighten the four nuts and bolts that secure the driveshaft to the hub

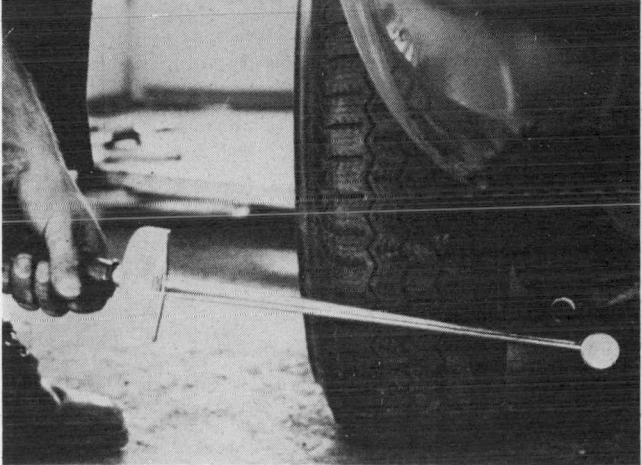

Step 24. Bleed the brakes and install the tire and lower the car to the ground. Tighten the two nuts securing the strut to the lower control arm. (Note: *Torqueing the nuts while the car is not on the ground can cause a hard, choppy ride due to incorrect bushing preload*)

— MACPHERSON STRUT PROBLEM DIAGNOSIS —

Problems with MacPherson struts generally fall into 3 main categories: suspension, tire wear and steering. In general, the symptoms encountered are not significantly different from those encountered on conventional suspensions.

Suspension

Sag

Vehicle "sag" is a visible tilt of the car from one side to the other or one end to the other while parked on a level surface.

Weak or damaged strut springs could cause this condition and should be repaired immediately.

Sag will also cause steering and tire wear problems to be more pronounced and vehicle instability on rough roads. Front wheel alignment will not solve the problem.

Weak strut springs increase vehicle sag. See "Tire Cupping".

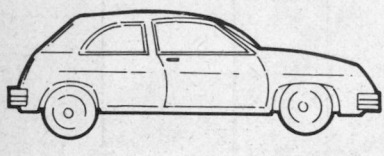

Cartridge Leaks

Strut cartridge leaks (not seepage) indicate the need for cartridge or strut replacement. Be sure the leakage is coming from the strut, and not from elsewhere on the vehicle.

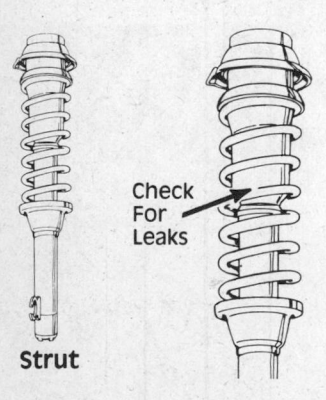

Check For Leaks

Strut

Abnormal Tire Wear

Wear on One Side

One sided tire wear indicates incorrect camber. Check the causes in the accompanying illustration and be sure the wheel alignment is correct.

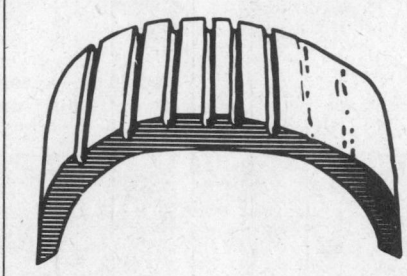

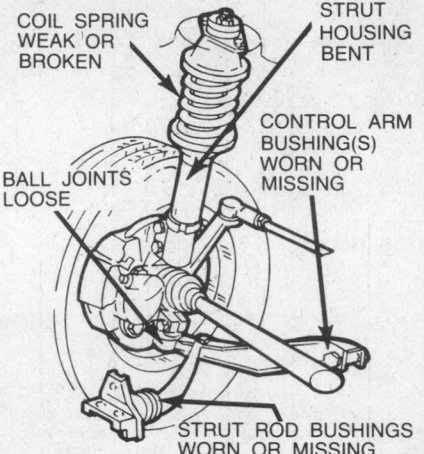

COIL SPRING WEAK OR BROKEN

STRUT HOUSING BENT

CONTROL ARM BUSHING(S) WORN OR MISSING

BALL JOINTS LOOSE

STRUT ROD BUSHINGS WORN OR MISSING

Tire "Cupping"

Cupped tires indicate any or all of the following problems.

1. A weak strut cartridge can be verified by bouncing each corner of the car vigorously and letting go. The car should not bounce more than once, if the shock absorber cartridges are good.

2. Weak strut springs allow sag to increase with only a slight amount of downward pressure. A visual inspection will reveal any broken springs or shiny spots.

3. Check for loose or worn wheel bearings with the weight of the car off of the wheel.

4. Check the wheel balance.

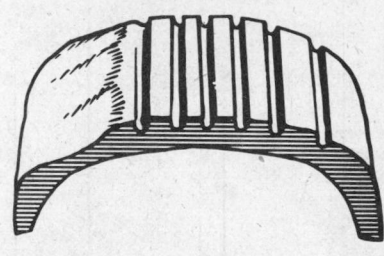

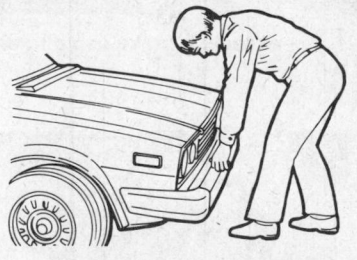

Tread Edge Wear

Wear along tread edges (feathering) indicates a suspension or steering system problem.

1. Strut rod bushings are worn or missing.

2. Tie rod end wear can be determined by grabbing the tie rod end firmly and forcing it up, down or sideways to check for lost motion.

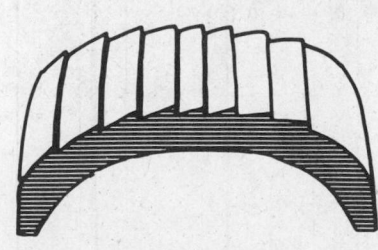

MACPHERSON STRUT PROBLEM DIAGNOSIS

Problems with MacPherson struts generally fall into 3 main categories: suspension, tire wear and steering. In general, the symptoms encountered are not significantly different from those encountered on conventional suspensions.

Tires

Both front tires should match and both rear tires should match. Be sure air pressure is correct.

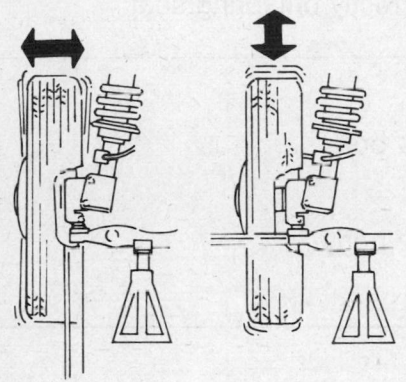

Strut Rod Bushings

Grasp the strut rod and shake it. Any noticeable play indicates excessive wear and need for parts replacement.

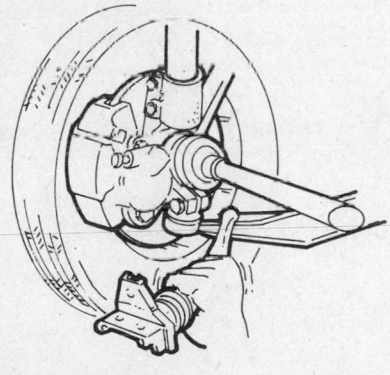

Steering

Ball Joints

Support the car under the frame or crossmember so that the jack does not interfere with the control arm. Rock the tire in and out and up and down. Excessive movement means that both ball joints should be replaced.

Struts with lower weight-carrying ball joints should be supported at the outer edge of the lower control arm. These vehicles usually have wear indicating ball joints that can be checked visually.

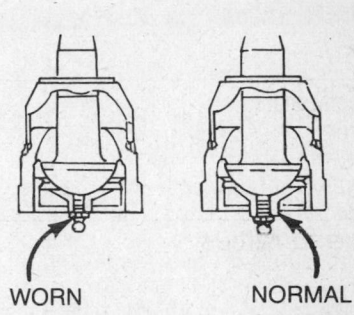

WORN   NORMAL

Stabilizer Bar Bushings

Check for worn bushings or lost motion with the vehicle level and the weight evenly distributed on all wheels.

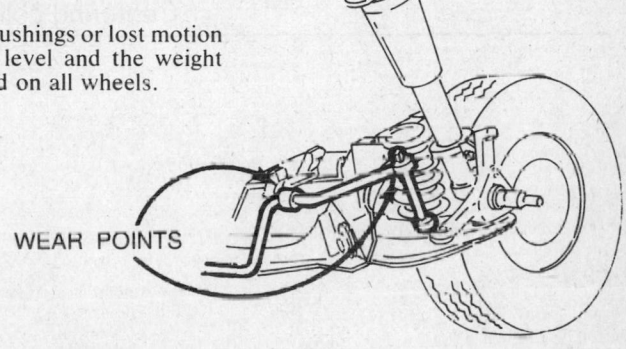

WEAR POINTS

Control Arm Bushings

Support the car under the frame or body and remove the weight from the wheel and control arm. Check for free-play in the bushings at the pivot point, using a pry bar.

NOTE: Some control arm bushings are serviceable only by replacing the entire arm.

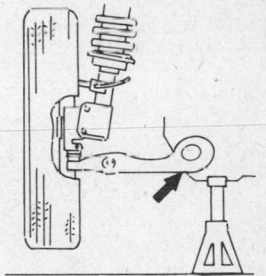

Strut Assembly

Check the strut assembly for cracks or dents in the housing. Look for worn, bent or loose piston rods or dents that will inhibit piston rod movement.

Steering Gear

Check for worn steering gear or loose or worn mounting bolts and bushings.

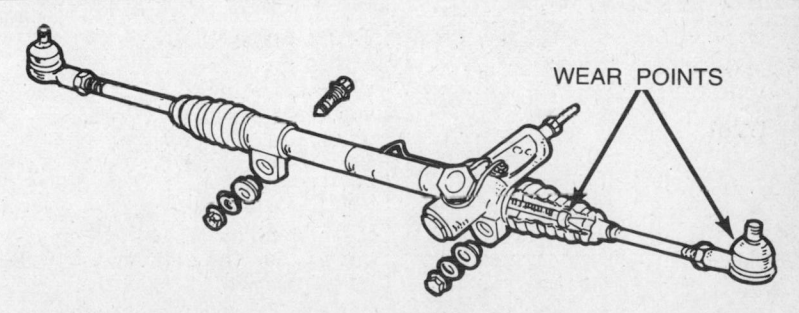

WEAR POINTS

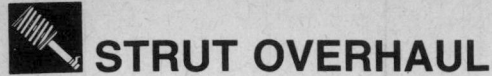

ROAD TEST TROUBLESHOOTING

Following are possible solutions to common potential problems which might be noticed during the road test after strut service is completed. Many are not exclusively strut service related.

Problem	Correction

Brake pedal low or soft	Bleed brakes
	Check for leaks
	  Brake lines
	  Wheel cylinder
	  Caliper piston seal

Erratic steering	Check upper support housing components for proper assembly Check spring assembly right side up Check for spring helix riding correctly on spring seat Check wheel alignment

Noises and rattles	Check torques
	  Piston rod nut
	  Upper support housing nuts & bolts
	  Lower mounting nuts & bolts
	  Body nut
	Check cartridge assembly in the body
	  Spacer used
	  Centering collar used

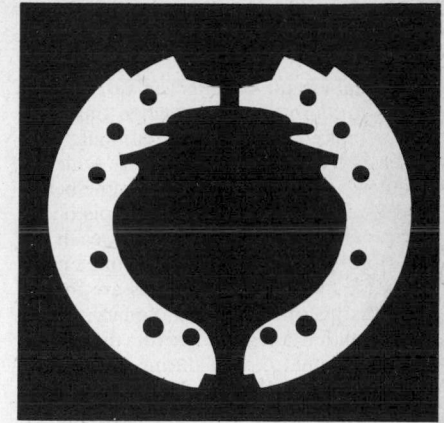

Brakes

BRAKE SYSTEM

Understanding the Brakes

HYDRAULIC SYSTEM
Basic Operating Principles

Hydraulic systems are used to actuate the brakes of all modern automobiles. The system transports the power required to force the frictional surfaces of the braking system together from the pedal to the individual brake units at each wheel. A hydraulic system is used for two reasons. First, fluid under pressure can be carried to all parts of an automobile by small hoses—some of which are flexible—without taking up a significant amount of room or posing routing problems. Second, a great mechanical advantage can be given to the brake pedal end of the system, and the foot pressure required to actuate the brakes can be reduced by making the surface area of the master cylinder pistons smaller than that of any of the pistons in the wheel cylinders or calipers.

The master cylinder consists of a fluid reservoir and either a single or double cylinder and piston assembly. Double type master cylinders are designed to separate two two-wheel braking systems hydrauli-

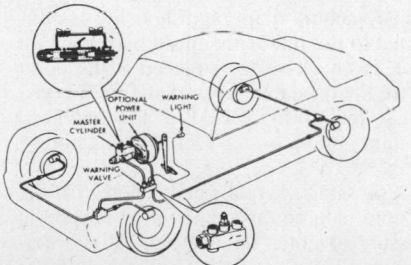

Dual braking system—front-to-rear split

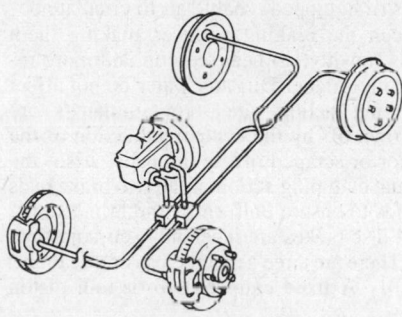

Dual braking system—diagonally split

cally in case of a leak. The standard approach has been to utilize two separate two-wheel circuits; one for the front wheels and another for the rear wheels.

Most newer models now use a diagonally split system; i.e. one front wheel and the opposite side rear wheel make up one braking circuit, while the remaining circuit consists of the other front wheel and its opposite side rear wheel.

Steel lines carry the brake fluid to a point on the vehicle's frame near each of the vehicle's wheels. The fluid is then carried to the slave cylinders by flexible tubes in order to allow for suspension and steering movements.

In drum brake systems, the slave cylinders are called wheel cylinders. Each wheel cylinder contains two pistons, one at either end, which push outward in opposite directions. In disc brake systems, the slave cylinders are part of the calipers. One, two or four cylinders are used to force the brake pads against the disc. All slave cylinder pistons employ some type of seal, usually made of rubber, to minimize the leakage of fluid around the piston. A rubber dust boot seals the outer end of the cylinder against dust and dirt. The boot fits around the outer end of the piston on disc brake calipers, and around the brake actuating rod on wheel cylinders.

The hydraulic system operates as follows: When at rest, the entire system, from the piston(s) in the master cylinder to those in the wheel cylinders or calipers, is full of brake fluid. Upon application of the brake pedal, fluid trapped in front of the master cylinder piston(s) is forced through the lines to the slave cylinders (wheel cylinders or calipers). Here, it forces the pistons outward, in the case of drum brakes, and inward toward the disc, in the case of disc brakes. The motion of the pistons is opposed by return springs mounted outside the cylinders in drum brakes, and by internal springs or spring seals, in disc brakes.

Upon release of the brake pedal, a spring located inside the master cylinder immediately returns the master cylinder pistons to the normal position. The pistons contain check valves and the master cylinder has compensating ports drilled in to it. These are uncovered as the pistons reach their normal position. The piston check valves allow fluid to flow toward the wheel cylinders or calipers as the pistons withdraw. Then, as the return springs force the brake pads or shoes into the released position, the excess fluid flows back to the reservoir through the compensating ports. It is during the time the pedal is in the released position that any fluid that has leaked out of the system will be replaced through the compensating ports.

Dual circuit master cylinders employ two pistons, located one behind the other, in the same cylinder. The primary piston is actuated directly by mechanical linkage from the brake pedal. The secondary piston is actuated by fluid trapped between the two pistons. If a leak develops in front of the secondary piston, it moves forward until it bottoms against the front of the master cylinder, and the fluid trapped between the pistons will operate one side of the split system. If the other side of the system develops a leak, the primary piston will move forward until direct contact with the secondary piston takes place, and it will force

the secondary piston to actuate the other side of the split system. In either case, the brake pedal moves farther when the brakes are applied, and less braking power is available.

All dual-circuit systems use a distributor switch to warn the driver when only half of the brake system is operational. This switch is located in a valve body which is mounted on the firewall or the frame below the master cylinder. A hydraulic piston receives pressure from both circuits, each circuit's pressure being applied to one end of the piston. When the pressures are in balance, the piston remains stationary. When one circuit has a leak, however, the greater pressure in that circuit during application of the brakes will push the piston to one side, closing the distributor switch and activating the brake warning light.

In disc brake systems, this valve body also contains a metering valve and, in some cases, a proportioning valve (or valves). The metering valve keeps pressure from traveling to the disc brakes on the front wheels until the brake shoes or pads on the rear wheels have contacted the drums or rotors, ensuring that the front brakes will never be used alone. The proportioning valve throttles the pressure to the rear brakes so as to avoid rear wheel lock-up during very hard braking.

These valves may be tested by removing the lines to the front and rear brake systems and installing special brake pressure testing gauges. Front and rear system pressures are then compared as the pedal is gradually depressed. Specifications vary with the manufacturer and design of the brake system.

Brake system warning lights may be tested by depressing the brake pedal and holding it while opening one of the wheel cylinder bleeder screws. If this does not cause the light to go on, substitute a new lamp, make continuity checks, and, finally, replace the switch as necessary.

The hydraulic system may be checked for leaks by applying pressure to the pedal gradually and steadily. If the pedal sinks very slowly to the floor, the system has a leak. This is not to be confused with a springy or spongy feel due to the compression of air within the lines. If the system leaks, there will be a gradual change in the position of the pedal with a constant pressure.

Check for leaks along all lines and at wheel cylinders. If no external leaks are apparent, the problem is inside the master cylinder.

DISC BRAKES
Basic Operating Principles

Instead of the traditional expanding brakes that press outward against a circular drum, disc brake systems utilize a cast iron disc with brake pads positioned on either side of it. Braking effect is achieved in a manner similar to the way you would squeeze a spinning phonograph record between your

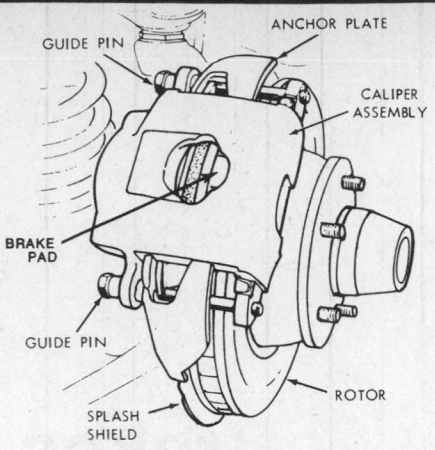

Typical disc brake assembly

fingers. The disc (rotor) is a one-piece casting which may be equipped with cooling fins between the two braking surfaces. The fins (if equipped) enable air to circulate between the braking surfaces making them less sensitive to heat buildup and more resistant to fade. Dirt and water do not affect braking action since contaminanats are thrown off by the centrifugal action of the rotor or scraped off by the pads. Also, the equal clamping action of the two brake pads tends to ensure uniform, straightline stops. All disc brakes are inherently self-adjusting.

There are three general types of disc brake:

1. A fixed caliper, two or four-piston type.

2. A floating caliper, single piston or double piston back–to–back type.

3. A sliding caliper, single piston or double piston back–to–back type.

The fixed caliper design uses one or two pistons mounted on either side of the rotor

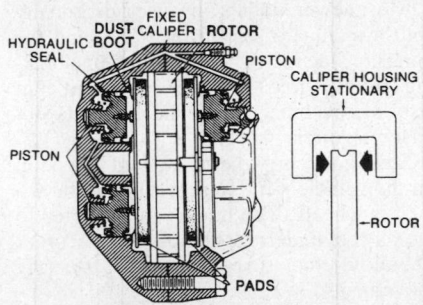

Typical fixed caliper disc brake (four piston shown)

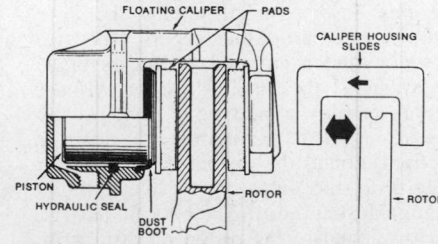

Typical floating caliper disc brake (sliding caliper similar)

(in each side of the caliper). The caliper is mounted rigidly and does not move.

The sliding and floating designs are quite similar. In fact, these two types are often lumped together. In both designs, the pad on the inside of the rotor is moved into contact with the rotor by hydraulic force. The caliper, which is not held in a fixed position, moves slightly, bringing the outside pad into contact with the rotor. There are various methods of attaching floating calipers. Some pivot at the bottom or top, and some slide on mounting bolts. In any event, the end result is the same.

DRUM BRAKES
Basic Operating Principles

Drum brakes employ two brake shoes mounted on a stationary backing plate. These shoes are positioned inside a circular cast iron (or aluminum) drum which rotates with the wheel assembly. The shoes are held in place by springs; this allows them to slide toward the drums (when they are applied) while keeping the linings and drums in alignment. The shoes are actuated by a wheel cylinder which is mounted at the top of the backing plate. When the brakes are applied, hydraulic pressure forces the wheel cylinder's two actuating links outward. Since these links bear directly against the top of the brake shoes, the tops of the shoes are then forced outward against the inner side of the drum. This action forces the bottoms of the two shoes to contact the brake drum by rotating the entire assembly slightly (known as servo action). When pressure within the wheel cylinder is relaxed, return springs pull the shoes back away from the drum.

Most modern drum brakes are designed to self-adjust themselves during application when the vehicle is moving in reverse. This motion causes both shoes to rotate very slightly with the drum, rocking an adjusting lever, thereby causing rotation of the adjusting screw by means of a star wheel.

POWER BRAKE BOOSTERS

Power brakes operate just as standard brake systems except in the actuation of the master cylinder pistons. A vacuum diaphragm is located on the front of the master cylinder and assists the driver in applying the brakes, reducing both the effort and travel he must put into moving the brake pedal.

The vacuum diaphragm housing is connected to the intake manifold by a vacuum hose. A check valve is placed at the point where the hose enters the diaphragm housing, so that during periods of low manifold vacuum, brake assist vacuum will not be lost.

Depressing the brake pedal closes off the vacuum source and allows atmospheric pressure to enter on one side of the diaphragm. This causes the master cylinder pistons to move and apply the brakes. When the brake pedal is released, vacuum is applied to both sides of the diaphragm, and return springs return the diaphragm and master cylinder pistons to the released position. If the vacuum fails, the brake pedal rod will butt against the end of the master cylinder actuating rod, and direct mechanical application will occur as the pedal is depressed.

HYDRAULIC CYLINDERS AND VALVES

Master Cylinders

The master cylinder is a type of hydraulic pump that is operated by a push rod attached to the brake pedal or by a push rod that is part of the power brake booster. The cylinder provides a means of converting mechanical force into hydraulic pressure. Two general types of master cylinders are in use on passenger cars; single system and dual system master cylinders.

SINGLE SYSTEM MASTER CYLINDER

This type master cylinder was used on many passenger car models. It has one fluid reservoir and one piston connected directly to the push rod. In a full pedal stroke, the single system pedal is stopped by the floorboard or other external stop before the cylinder can bottom-out. Fluid circulates between the single reservoir and the cylinder bore through the vent and replenishing ports. Fluid leakage past the secondary cup may be observed by pulling back the push rod boot or loosening the cylinder on its mount.

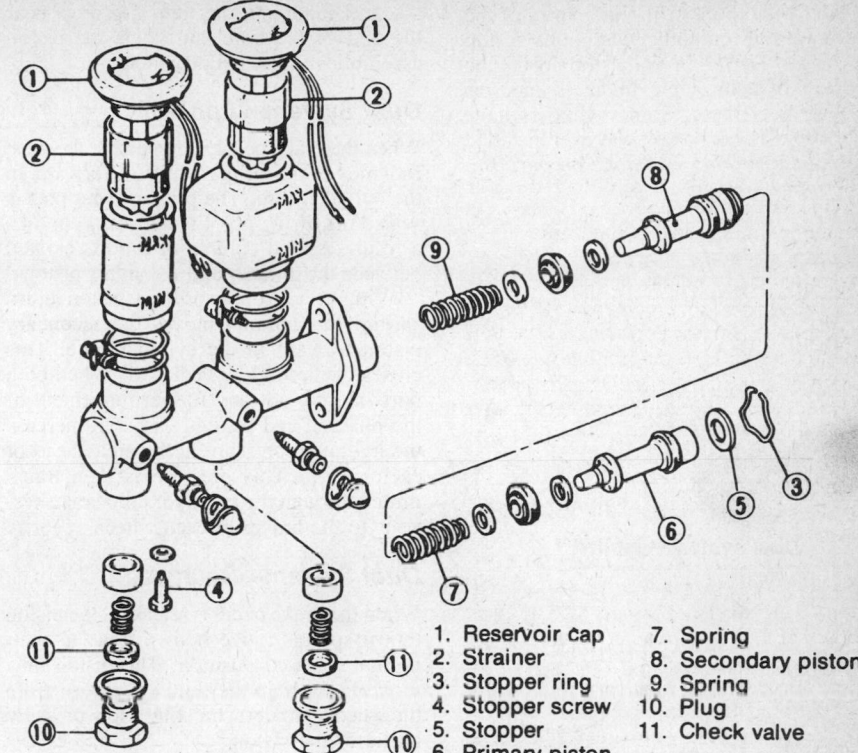

1. Reservoir cap
2. Strainer
3. Stopper ring
4. Stopper screw
5. Stopper
6. Primary piston
7. Spring
8. Secondary piston
9. Spring
10. Plug
11. Check valve

Exploded view of a dual system master cylinder

Some seepage (dampness) is not unusual but leaks affecting the fluid level require correction.

Single system master cylinders used on four wheel drum brake equipped cars usually contain a residual pressure check valve in the outlet port. This valve maintains a slight pressure in the line at all times to keep air from entering the system past the lips of the wheel cylinder cups when the pedal is released, and fluid returns from the wheel cylinder to the master cylinder.

Cars with front disc, rear drum brakes and a single system master cylinder may have the residual valve in the line leading to the rear brakes.

Single system master cylinder operation is the same as explained under tandem master cylinder operation, except movement of only the primary piston is involved.

DUAL SYSTEM TANDEM MASTER CYLINDER

In this type there are two separate hydraulic pressure systems. One of the hydraulic systems may be connected to the front brakes, and the other to the rear brakes, or the systems may connect diagonal wheels. If one system fails, the other system remains operational, thus providing an additional safety measure. There are two distinct fluid reservoirs and each has a vent and replenishing port that leads into the cylinder bore. These ports have been called compensating and inlet ports or bypass ports, and the terms have been used inconsistently causing confusion. The terms "vent" and "replenishing" ports are now standardized S.A.E. terms. An airtight seal for the reservoir is provided in the form of a rubber diaphragm, which is held in place by a metal cover. A bail type retainer or a bolt usually holds the cover on the reservoirs. The cover is vented to permit atmospheric pressure to enter above the diaphragm. The diaphragm prevents moisture and debris from contaminating the fluid. The cylinder bore contains the return springs, two pistons, and the seals. The piston stop bolt (if present) may be assembled in a threaded hole in the bottom of the cylinder.

Some master cylinders have the piston stop bolt assembled in a threaded hole in

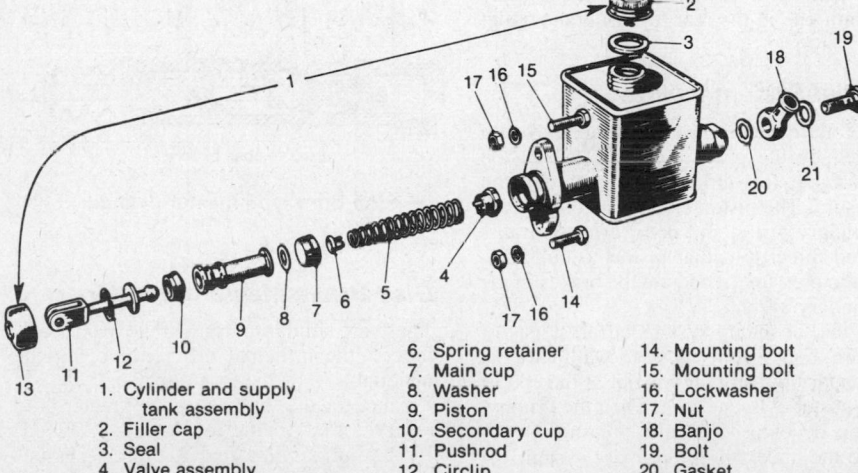

6. Spring retainer
7. Main cup
8. Washer
9. Piston
10. Secondary cup
11. Pushrod
12. Circlip
13. Boot

14. Mounting bolt
15. Mounting bolt
16. Lockwasher
17. Nut
18. Banjo
19. Bolt
20. Gasket
21. Gasket

1. Cylinder and supply tank assembly
2. Filler cap
3. Seal
4. Valve assembly
5. Spring

Exploded view of a single system master cylinder

the side of the bore or in the bottom of the front reservoir, and others do not have stop bolts at all. Do not install a stop bolt in the reservoir of a master cylinder if one was not originally there. Some cylinders have a tapped hole, but no bolt was ever installed in production. *This was done on purpose, and is not an error.*

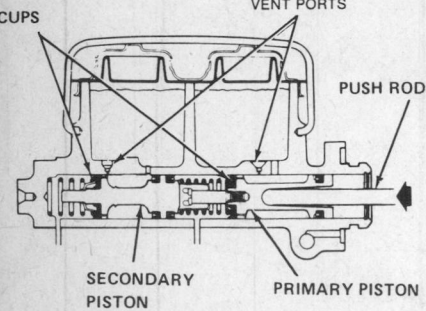

Dual system—applied

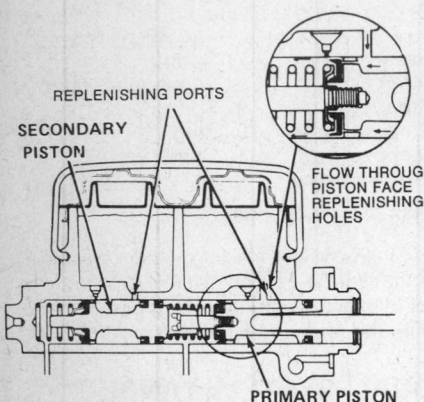

Dual system—released

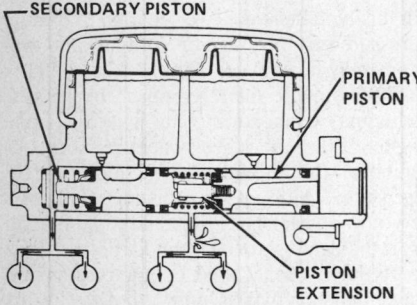

Primary system failure

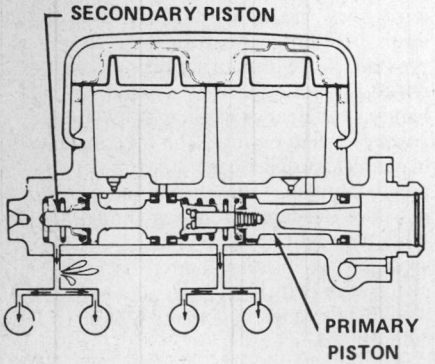

Secondary system failure

A retaining ring fits into a groove near the end of the bore and holds the piston assemblies in the cylinder bore.

Dual System—Applied

When the brake pedal is depressed, the push rod moves the primary piston forward in the cylinder bore. The primary vent port is sealed off by the lip of the primary cup. As a result, a solid column of fluid is created between the primary and secondary pistons.

With the help of the primary piston return spring, this column moves the secondary piston forward in the cylinder bore. This closes the secondary vent port. When both ports are closed, any further movement of the pushrod and pistons serves to increase the hydraulic pressure in the area ahead of each piston. This pressure is then transmitted through the two hydraulic brake systems to the brakes at each wheel.

Dual System—Released

When the brake pedal is released, the piston return springs move both pistons to their normal released position. The piston may move faster than the fluid can return from the wheel cylinders, creating a low pressure ahead of the piston.

To allow rapid pedal return, this low pressure must be relieved. Fluid flows from the reservoir through the replenishing port. It then flows around the outside of the piston and cup lips to the area ahead of the piston. Another design has this flow pass through small drilled holes in the piston face, then around the cup lips. This flow relieves the low pressure area ahead of the piston.

Due to this action, the area in the front of the pistons is kept full of brake fluid at all times. Any excess fluid is returned to the master cylinder reservoirs through the vent ports after the pistons reach their fully released positions. Tandem master cylinders on cars equipped with four wheel drum brakes may contain two residual check valves, one in each outlet port. Those on cars with front disc/rear drum brakes may contain one in the rear (drum) brake outlet port.

Partial System Failure

If a failure occurs in the hydraulic system served by the primary piston, this piston will move forward but will not develop pressure. The piston extension contacts the secondary piston and pedal effort is transmitted directly to that piston to build hydraulic pressure to operate the brakes in the secondary system.

If the secondary system suffers a leak or failure, both pistons move forward until the secondary piston bottoms out at the end of the master cylinder bore. Then the primary piston develops hydraulic pressure to operate the brakes in the primary system.

The loss of about half the pedal stroke is usually experienced when a half system failure occurs.

OTHER VARIATIONS
Dual Bore Type Master Cylinder

The housing of this type of master cylinder accomodates two cylinders side by side. Only one cylinder functions in the brake system, the other is used for hydraulic clutch actuation, and a common fluid reservoir with an internal partition is used. The clutch system does not have a residual pressure check valve. Each hydraulic system must be bled separately.

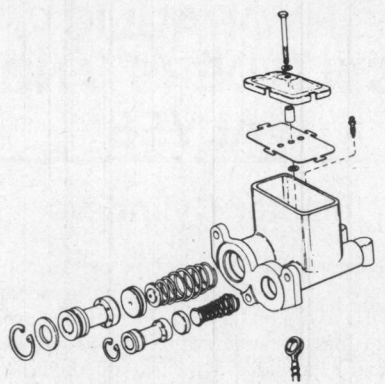

Dual bore type master cylinder

Step Bore Dual System Master Cylinder

This cylinder is the same as other cylinders except that the forward part of the bore is slightly smaller in diameter than the rear part. This difference contributes to correct brake balance.

Volvo has incorporated a step bore master cylinder into a sophisticated brake system which provides automatic brake proportioning, no pedal loss on half system failure, and automatically increases pressure on the remaining system during half system failure.

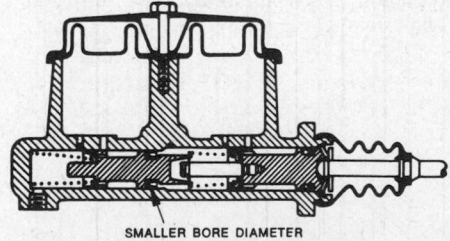

Step bore type master cylinder

Disc Brake Master Cylinder

These are similar to drum brake master cylinders, the principal difference being the unequal size of the two reservoirs.

Since the disc brakes require greater fluid reserve, a large fluid reservoir is provided.

The outlet connected to the disc brakes does not contain a residual pressure check valve, however the drum brake outlet may have one.

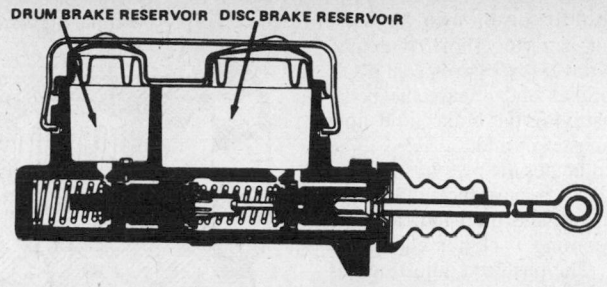

DRUM BRAKE RESERVOIR   DISC BRAKE RESERVOIR

Disc brake master cylinder

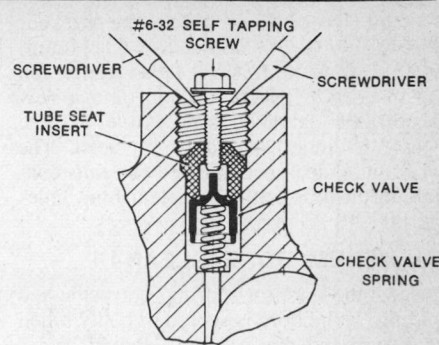

#6-32 SELF TAPPING SCREW
SCREWDRIVER
TUBE SEAT INSERT
SCREWDRIVER
CHECK VALVE
CHECK VALVE SPRING

Manual and Power Brake Master Cylinders

Both types are mostly the same except that manual brake cylinders normally include a dust boot, pushrod, and pushrod retainer. The pushrod used with power brake master cylinders is usually a part of the power brake booster.

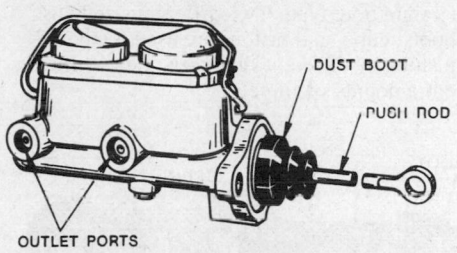

DUST BOOT
PUSH ROD
OUTLET PORTS

Manual brake master cylinder

Aluminum and Composite Tandem Master Cylinders.

Aluminum body master cylinders have been used on special applications for many years. Today its use is becoming more widespread due to the weight advantage over cast iron. The machined aluminum bore is usually anodized to resist corrosion, prevent galling, and provide better wear resistance. Aluminum master cylinder bores are not serviced if scored or pitted, but must be replaced. A "composite master cylinder" is a common phrase used to describe units with a plastic reservoir attached to a metal barrel. Composites offer reduced weight, lower material costs and greater application flexibility.

MASTER CYLINDER SERVICING

Just like any other brake parts, master cylinders require periodic service. The usual reason for a master cylinder failure is that the cups don't seal any more. Fluid leaks past cups internally, and sometimes shows up as an external leak as well. A common symptom is a "spongy" brake pedal that goes all the way to the floor when all other brake system components are in good shape. The rubber parts wear with usage or may deteriorate with age or fluid contamination. Corrosion or deposits formed in the bore

due to moisture or dirt in the hydraulic system may result in wear of the cylinder bore or the parts therein. Also, the fluid level in the reservoirs should be checked periodically. Whenever needed, clean brake fluid should be added to maintain the fluid level ¼" to ½" (6 to 13 mm) from the top of the reservoir.

Removal and Disassembly

1. Clean the area around the master cylinder to prevent dirt and grease from contaminating the cylinder or the hydraulic lines. Disconnect the tubes, remove nuts or bolts that secure the master cylinder to the fire wall or power brake, and remove the master cylinder from the car (for further details, refer to appropriate car section).

On cars with manual brakes, the push rod must be disconnected from the brake pedal before removing the master cylinder from the car.

2. Remove the reservoir cover, and drain the brake fluid from the reservoir. Then remove the piston stop bolt, if present, from the master cylinder. Remove the boot and snap ring, then slide the primary piston assembly out of the master cylinder. Next, remove the secondary piston assembly by tapping the master cylinder, or by using needle nose pliers to pull it from its bore, or by carefully using compressed air. Disassemble the secondary piston assembly.

3. Clamp the master cylinder in a vise with the outlet ports facing up. Test for the presence of a check valve by probing with wire through the hole in the tube seats. Replace tube seat(s) and check valve(s) only if a check valve is present and supplied in the rebuild kit. Remove the tube seat inserts, if required, by partially threading a self-tapping screw into each tube seat and using two screwdrivers to pry each seat out of the master cylinder. Remove the residual check valve and the spring from the outlet(s) (if present).

Plastic Reservoir Cleaning and Removal

Plastic reservoirs need to be removed only for the following reasons:

  a. Reservoir is damaged or the rubber grommet(s) between the reservoir and bore is leaking.

  b. Removal of the stop pin from Chrysler style plastic reservoir master

Removing the inserts from the master cylinder ports

cylinders to allow for the removal of pistons. Pin is located underneath front reservoir nipple.

The reservoir should be removed by first clamping the flange in a vice. Next remove the reservoir for the Chrysler style. Grasp the reservoir base on one end and pull away from the body. Some must be removed by prying between the reservoir and casting with a pry bar. Grommets can be reused if they are in good condition. Whether or not the reservoir is removed, it and the cover or caps should be thoroughly cleaned.

Cleaning and Inspection

Thoroughly clean the master cylinder and any other parts to be reused in clean alcohol. DO NOT USE PETROLEUM PRODUCTS FOR CLEANING. If the bore is not badly scored, rusted or corroded, it is possible to rebuild the master cylinder in some cases. A slight bit of honing is permissible to clean cups are facing.

—— **CAUTION** ——
Aluminum cylinder bores cannot be honed. The cylinder MUST be replaced if the bore is scored.

Lubricate all new rubber parts with brake fluid or brake system assembly lubricant.

CAST IRON BORE CLEAN-UP

Crocus cloth or an approved cylinder hone should be used to remove lightly pitted, scored, or corroded areas from the bore.

—— **CAUTION** ——
If an aluminum master cylinder has pits or scratches in the bore, it must be replaced.

Brake fluid can be used as a lubricant while honing lightly. The master cylinder should be replaced if it cannot be cleaned up readily. After using the crocus cloth or a hone, the master cylinder should be thoroughly washed in clean alcohol or brake fluid to remove all dust and grit. If alcohol is used, dry parts thoroughly before reinstalling.

—— **CAUTION** ——
Other solvents should not be used.

Then the clearance between the bore wall and the piston (primary piston of a dual

system master cylinder) should be checked. If a narrow (⅛″ (3.2 mm) to ¼″ (6.4 mm) wide) 0.006″ (0.15 mm) feeler gauge can be inserted between the wall and a new piston, the clearance is excessive, and the master cylinder should be replaced. The maximum clearance allowed for units containing pistons without replenishing holes is .009″ (0.23 mm).

ALUMINUM BORE CLEAN-UP

Inspect the bore for scoring, corrosion and pitting. If the bore is scored or badly pitted and corroded the assembly should be replaced. *Under no conditions should the bore be cleaned with an abrasive material.* This will remove the wear and corrosion resistant anodized surface. Clean the bore with a clean piece of cloth around a wooden dowel and wash thoroughly with alcohol. Do not confuse bore discoloration or staining with corrosion.

Reassembly and Installation

1. Carefully install the new cups or seals in the same positions and in reverse order of removal.

2. Use brake fluid or assembly fluid very generously to keep from damaging the seals.

3. Placing the small end of the pressure spring into the secondary piston retainer, slide the assembly into the cylinder bore, taking care not to nick or gouge any rubber part.

4. Place the spring retainer of the primary piston assembly over the secondary piston shoulder and push both assemblies into the bore.

5. Install and tighten the piston retaining screw and gasket, while holding the pistons in their seated positions. At the same time, reinstall any piston snap rings.

6. Install the residual check valve and spring in the proper master cylinder outlet (or both outlets, if originally present). If the tube seat inserts were removed, install new seats in both fluid outlets making sure that they are securely seated.

Bleeding and Checking

1. Bleed the hydraulic system as described later in this section.

NOTE: Be sure to bench bleed a rebuilt or new master cylinder before installation.

2. Check master cylinder vent port clearance by watching for a spurt of brake fluid in both reservoir vent holes when the brake pedal is slightly depressed, indicating proper port clearance.

Master Cylinder Push Rod Adjustment

After assembly of the master cylinder to the power section, the piston cup in the hydraulic cylinder should just clear the compensating port hole when the brake pedal is fully released. If the push rod is too

long, it will hold the piston over the port. A push rod that is too short, will give too much loose travel (excessive pedal play).

Apply the brakes and release the pedal all the way observing the brake fluid flow back into the master cylinder.

A full flow indicates the piston is coming back far enough to release the fluid.

A slow return of the fluid indicates the piston is not coming back far enough to clear the ports. The push rod adjustment is too tight, and should be shortened.

Wheel Cylinders

DRUM BRAKE WHEEL CYLINDER

The wheel cylinder performs in response to the master cylinder. It receives fluid from the hydraulic hose through its inlet port. As the pressure increases, the wheel cylinder cups and pistons are forced apart. As a result, the hydraulic pressure is converted into mechanical force acting on the brake shoes. The wheel cylinder size may vary from front to rear. The variation in wheel cylinder size (diameter) is one of the factors controlling the distribution of braking force in a vehicle. Larger diameter wheel cylinders are normally specified for the front brakes of front engine passenger cars equipped with drum brakes. Bleeder screws are provided to remove air or vapor trapped in the system.

Three types of wheel cylinders are normally used with drum brakes.

Single Piston or "Single-end" Type

A single piston wheel cylinder has only one cup, piston, and dust boot and spring. It may also contain a cup filler or cup expander.

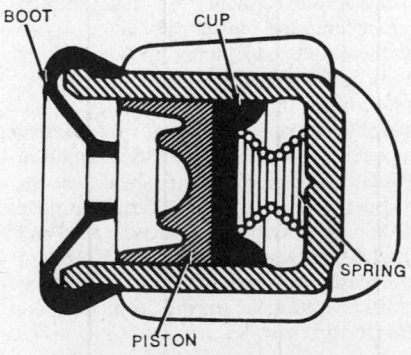

Single piston wheel cylinder

Double Piston or "Double-end" Straight Bore Type

This type is most commonly used on modern automobile brakes. It carries two opposed pistons, two cups and two boots.

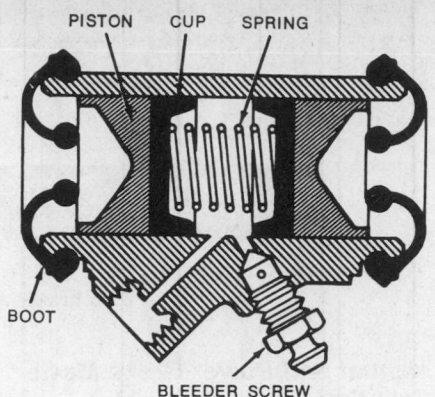

Double piston wheel cylinder

Double Piston or "Double-end" Step Bore Type

This type is used on some of the non-servo brakes and has the same components as the straight bore type. Two different sized dust boots, cups, and pistons are used. Opposed pistons of different diameters exert different amounts of force.

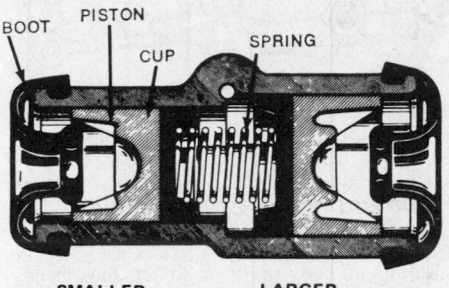

Step bore wheel cylinder

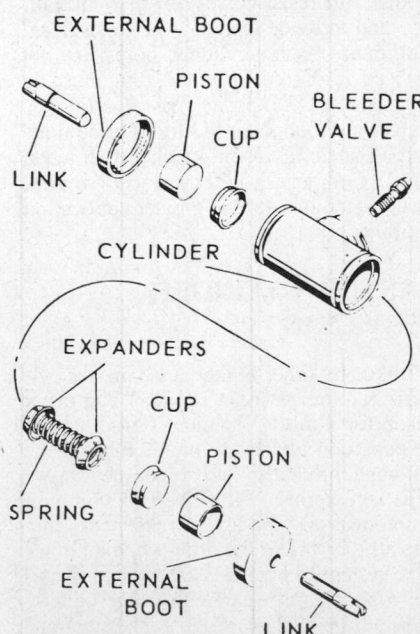

Typical wheel cylinder components

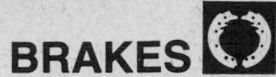
WHEEL CYLINDER OPERATION

The space between the cups in the cylinder bore must remain filled with fluid at all times. After depressing the brake pedal, additional brake fluid is forced into the cylinder bore. As a result of this, cups and pistons move outward in the cylinder bore pushing the shoe links and the brake shoes outward to contact the drum and apply the brakes.

On some designs, the end of the shoe web bears directly against the pistons and therefore, shoe links are not used.

SERVICE PROCEDURES

Wheel cylinders may need reconditioning or replacement whenever the brake shoes are replaced or when required to correct a leak condition. On many designs, the wheel cylinders can be disassembled without removing them from the backing plate. On some designs, however, the cylinder is mounted in an indention in the backing plate or a cylinder piston stop is welded to the backing plate. When servicing brakes of this type, the cylinder must be removed from the backing plate before being disassembled.

Diagnostic Inspection and Cleaning

Leaks which coat the boot and the cylinder with fluid, or result in a dropped reservoir fluid level, or dampen and stain the brake linings are dangerous. Such leaks can cause the brakes to "grab" or fail and should be immediately corrected. A leakage, not immediately apparent, can be detected by pulling back the cylinder boot. A small amount of fluid seepage dampening the interior of the boot is normal; a dripping boot is not. Unless other conditions causing a brake to pull, grab, or drag becomes obvious, the wheel cylinder is a suspect and should be included in general reconditioning.

Cylinder binding may be caused by rust, deposits, grime, or swollen cups due to fluid contamination, or by a cup wedged into an excessive piston clearance. If the clearance between the pistons and the bore wall exceeds allowable values, a condition called "heel drag" may exist. It can result in rapid cup wear and can cause the pistons to retract very slowly when the brakes are released.

A typical example of a scored, pitted or corroded cylinder bore is shown in the accompanying illustration. A ring of a hard, crystal-like substance is sometimes noticed in the cylinder bore where the piston stops after the brakes are released.

Light roughness or deposits can be removed with crocus cloth or an approved cylinder hone. While honing lightly, brake fluid can be used as a lubricant. If the bore cannot be cleaned up readily, the cylinder must be replaced.

NOTE: Aluminum wheel cylinders must not be honed.

Some front wheel cylinders have a baffle located between the opposed pistons. The baffle contains a small hole which causes the cylinder to act as a fluid shock absorber damping servo brake shoes as they become energized. These cylinders cannot be honed and should be replaced if the bore is pitted or corroded.

—————— CAUTION ——————
Hydraulic system parts should not be allowed to come in contact with oil or grease, neither should those be handled with greasy hands. Even a trace of any petroleum based product is sufficient to cause damage to the rubber parts.

Reconditioning Wheel Cylinders

It is a common practice to recondition a wheel cylinder without dismounting it, however some brakes are equipped with external piston stops which prevent disassembly unless the cylinder is removed. In order to dismount, remove the shoe springs and spread the shoes apart, disconnect the brake line, remove the mounting bolts or retaining clips, and pull the cylinder free.

Most wheel cylinders are attached to the backing plate with bolts and are easily removed for service or replacement. In recent years, some cars use a retaining clip for this purpose. To remove this type cylinder, use a special service tool, or this alternate method: Insert ⅛″ diameter or less awls or pins into the slots between the wheel cylinder pilot and the retainer locking tabs. Bend both tabs away at the same time until the tabs spring over the shoulder, releasing the cylinder. DISCARD old retainer.

To replace the cylinder, use a new retainer and the following procedure:

1. Hold the wheel cylinder against the backing plate by inserting a block between the wheel cylinder and axle shaft flange.

2. Position the wheel cylinder retainer clip so the tabs will be away from and in horizontal position with the backing plate when installing.

3. Press the new retaining clip over the wheel cylinder abutment and into position using a 1⅛ inch 12 point socket. The retainer is in place when the tabs are snapped under the retainer abutment. Examine closely to be sure both retainer tabs are properly engaged.

Another variation of retainer clip is used on some vehicles. The retainer usually consists of two or three separate pieces which when slid together will lock themselves and the wheel cylinder in place. The retainers can be carefully removed without incurring damage which allows them to be reused. If they are damaged or corroded, however, they must be replaced.

Pull the protective dust boots off the cylinder. Internal parts should slide out, or be picked out easily. Parts can be driven out with a wooden dowel, or blown out at low

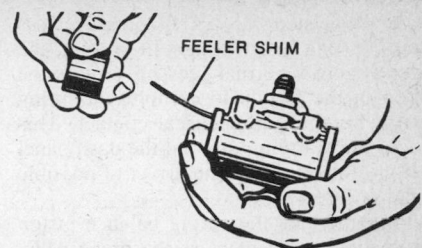
Checking the maximum piston clearance

pressure by applying compressed air to the fluid inlet port. Parts which cannot be removed easily indicate they are damaged beyond repair and the cylinder should be replaced.

Clean the cylinder and the parts in alcohol and/or brake fluid (do NOT use gasoline or other petroleum based products). Use only lint-free wiping cloths. Crocus cloth can be used to clean minute scratches, signs of rust, corrosion or discoloration from the cylinder bore and pistons. Slide the cloth in a circular rather than a lengthwise motion. A clean-up hone may be used. After a cylinder has been honed, inspect it for excessive piston clearance and remove any burrs formed on the edge of fluid intake or bleeder screw ports.

—————— CAUTION ——————
Do not rebuild aluminum cylinders.

To check the maximum piston clearance, place a ¼″ (6 mm) wide strip of feeler shim lengthwise in the cylinder bore.

If the piston can be inserted with the shim in place, the cylinder is oversize, and should be discarded. Depending upon the cylinder bore diameter, the shim (or the feeler gauge) thickness can vary as follows:

Cylinder Bore	Shim
¾″–1³⁄₁₆″ (19–30 mm)	.006″ (.15 mm)
1¼″–1⁷⁄₁₆″ (32–37 mm)	.007″ (.18 mm)
1½″ up (38 mm)	.008″ (.2 mm)

Assemble the cylinder with the internal parts, making sure that the cylinder wall is wet with brake fluid. Insert the cups and pistons from each end of a double-end cylinder; do not slide them through the cylinder. Cup lips should always face inward.

Hydraulic Control Valves

PRESSURE DIFFERENTIAL VALVE

The pressure differential valve activates a dash panel warning light if pressure loss in the brake system occurs. If pressure loss occurs in one half of the split system, the other system's normal pressure causes the piston in the switch to compress a spring until it touches an electrical contact. This causes the warning lamp on the dash panel to light, thus warning the driver of possible brake failure.

On some cars the spring balance piston automatically recenters as the brake pedal is released, warning the driver only upon brake application. On other cars, the light remains on until manually cancelled.

Valves may be located separately or as part of a combination valve. On certain front wheel drive cars, the valve and switch are usually incorporated into the master cylinder.

Re-setting Valves

On some cars, the valve piston(s) remain off center after failure, until necessary repairs are made. The valve will automatically reset itself (after repairs) when pressure is equal on both sides of the system.

If the light does not go out, bleed the brake system that is opposite the failed system. If front brakes failed, bleed the rear brakes, this should force the light control piston toward center.

If this fails, remove the terminal switch. If brake fluid is present in the electrical area, the seals are gone, replace the complete valve assembly.

METERING VALVE

The metering valve's function is to improve braking balance between the front and rear brakes, especially during light brake application.

The metering valve prevents application of the front disc brakes until the rear brakes overcome the return spring pressure. Thus, when the front disc pads contact the rotor, the rear shoes will contact the brake drum at the same time.

Inspect the metering valve each time the brakes are serviced. A slight amount of moisture inside the boot does not indicate a defective valve, however, fluid leakage indicates a damaged or worn valve. If fluid leakage is present, the valve must be replaced.

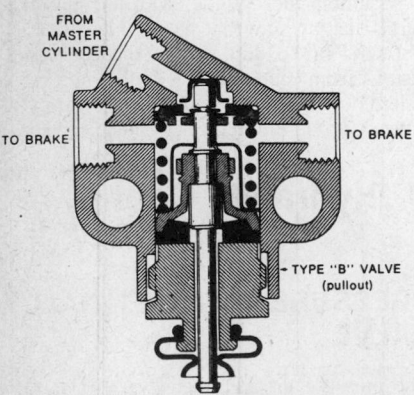

Typical pressure metering valve

The metering valve can be checked very simply. With the car stopped, gently apply the brakes. At about an inch of travel, a very small change in pedal effort (like a small bump) will be felt if the valve is operating properly. Metering valves are not serviceable, and must be replaced if defective.

PROPORTIONING VALVE

The proportioning (pressure control) valve is used, on some cars, to reduce the hydraulic pressure to the rear wheels to prevent skid during heavy brake application and to provide better brake balance. It is usually mounted in line to the rear wheels.

Whenever the brakes are serviced, the valve should be inspected for leakage. Premature rear brake application during light braking can mean a bad proportioning valve. Repair is by replacement of the valve. Make sure the valve port marked "R" is connected toward the rear wheels.

On some front wheel drive cars, the proportioning valve(s) is (are) screwed into the master cylinder. Since these cars usually have a diagonally split brake system, two valves are required. One rear brake line screws into each valve. The early type valves were steel, an occasional "clunking" noise was encountered on some early models, but does not affect brake efficiency. Replacement valves are now made of aluminum. Never mix an aluminum valve with a steel valve, always use two aluminum valves.

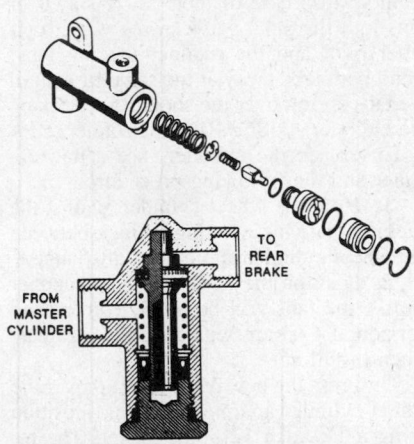

Typical proportioning valve

COMBINATION VALVE

The combination valve may perform two or three functions. They are; metering, proportioning and brake failure warning.

Variations of the two-way combination valve are; proportioning and brake failure warning or metering and brake failure warning.

A three-way combination valve directs the brake fluid to the appropriate wheel, performs necessary valving and contains a brake failure warning.

The combination valve is usually mounted

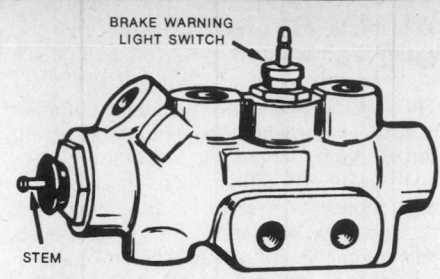

Two–way combination valve (metering and brake warning light switch)

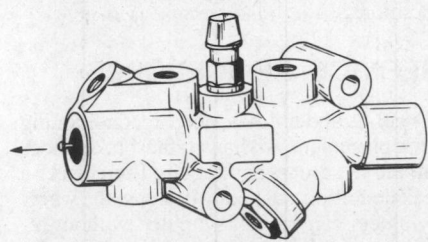

3–way combination valve

under the hood close to the master cylinder, where the brake lines can easily be connected and routed to the front or rear wheels.

The combination valve is nonserviceable and must be replaced if malfunctioning.

Brake Bleeding

The hydraulic brake system must be free of air to operate properly. Air can enter the system when hydraulic parts are disconnected for servicing or replacement, or when the fluid level in the master cylinder reservoir(s) is very low. Air in the system will give the brake pedal a spongy feeling upon application.

The quickest and easiest of the two ways for system bleeding is the pressure method, but special equipment is needed to externally pressurize the hydraulic system. The other, more commonly used method of brake bleeding is done manually.

BLEEDING SEQUENCE

Bleeding may be required at only one or two wheels or at the master cylinder, depending upon what point the system was opened to air. If after bleeding the cylinder/caliper that was rebuilt or replaced, the pedal still has a spongy feeling upon application, it will be necessary to bleed the entire system.

Bleed the system in the following order:

1. **Master cylinder:** If the cylinder is not equipped with bleeder screws, open the brake line(s) to the wheels slightly while pressure is applied to the brake pedal. Be sure to tighten the line before the brake pedal is released. The procedure for bench bleeding the master cylinder is in the following section.

2. **Power Brake Booster:** If the unit is equipped with bleeder screws, it should

be bled after the master cylinder. The car engine should be off and the brake pedal applied several times to exhaust any vacuum in the booster. If the unit is equipped with two bleeder screws, always bleed the higher one first.

3. **Combination Valve:** If equipped with a bleeder screw.

4. **Front/Back Split Systems:** Start with the wheel farthest away from the master cylinder, usually the right rear wheel. Bleed the other rear wheel, right front and then the left front.

NOTE: If you are unsuccessful in bleeding the front wheels, it may be necessary to deactivate the metering valve. This is accomplished by either pushing in, or pulling out a button or stem on the valve. The valve may be held by hand, with a special tool or taped, it should remain deactivated while the front brakes are bled.

5. **Diagonally Split System:** Start with the right rear then the left front. The left rear than the right front.

6. **Rear Disc Brakes:** If the car is equipped with rear disc brakes and the calipers have two bleeder screws, bleed the inner first and then the outer.

— CAUTION —
Do not allow brake fluid to spill on the car's finish, it will remove the paint. Flush the area with water.

MANUAL BLEEDING

1. Clean the bleeder screw at each wheel.

2. Start with the wheel farthest from the master cylinder (right rear).

3. Attach a small rubber hose to the bleeder screw and place the end in a clear container of brake fluid.

4. Fill the master cylinder with brake fluid (check often during bleeding). Have an assistant slowly pump up the brake pedal and hold pressure.

5. Open the bleed screw about one-quarter turn, press the brake pedal to the floor, close the bleed screw and slowly release the pedal. Continue until no more air bubbles are forced from the cylinder on application of the brake pedal.

6. Repeat the procedure on all remaining wheel cylinders and calipers.

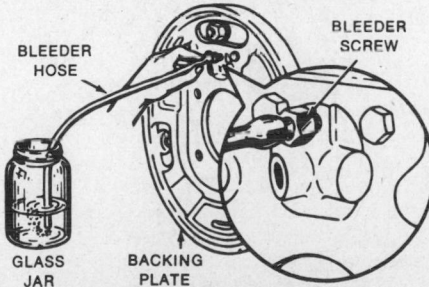

Manual bleeding drum brakes

Master cylinders equipped with bleed screws may be bled independently. When bleeding the Bendix-type dual master cylinder it is necessary to solidly cap one reservoir section while bleeding the other to prevent pressure loss through the cap vent hole.

NOTE: The disc should be rotated to make sure that the piston has returned to the unapplied position when bleeding is completed and the bleed screw closed.

— CAUTION —
The bleeder valve at the wheel cylinder must be closed at the end of each stroke, and before the brake pedal is released, to insure that no air can enter the system. It is also important that the brake pedal be returned to the full up position so the piston in the master cylinder moves back enough to clear the bypass outlets.

PRESSURE BLEEDING DISC BRAKES

Pressure bleeding disc brakes will close the metering valve and the front brakes will not bleed. For this reason it is necessary to manually hold the metering valve open during pressure bleeding. Never use a block or clamp to hold the valve open, and never force the valve stem beyond its normal position. Two different types of valves are used. The most common type requires the valve stem to be held in while bleeding the brakes, while the second type requires the valve stem to be held out (.060 in. minimum travel). Determine the type of valve by visual inspection.

— CAUTION —
Special adapters are required when pressure bleeding cylinders with plastic reservoirs.

Pressure bleeding equipment should be diaphragm type; placing a diaphragm between the pressurized air supply and the brake fluid. This prevents moisture and other contaminants from entering the hydraulic system.

NOTE: Front disc/rear drum equipped vehicles use a metering valve which closes off pressure to the front brakes under certain conditions. These systems contain manual release actuators which must be engaged to pressure bleed the front brakes.

1. Connect the tank hydraulic hose and adapter to the master cylinder.

2. Close the hydraulic valve on the bleeder equipment.

3. Apply air pressure to the bleeder equipment.

— CAUTION —
Follow the equipment manufacturer's recommendations for correct air pressure.

4. Open the valve to bleed air out of the pressure hose to the master cylinder.

NOTE: Never bleed this system using the secondary piston stopscrew on the bottom of many master cylinders.

5. Open the hydraulic valve and bleed each wheel cylinder and caliper. Bleed the rear brake system first when bleeding both front and rear systems.

FLUSHING HYDRAULIC BRAKE SYSTEMS

Hydraulic brake systems must be totally flushed if the fluid becomes contaminated with water, dirt or other corrosive chemicals. To flush, simply bleed the entire system until *all* fluid has been replaced with the correct type of new fluid.

BENCH BLEEDING MASTER CYLINDER

Bench bleeding the master cylinder before installing it on the car reduces the possibility of air getting into the lines.

1. Connect two short pieces of brake line to the outlet fittings, bend them until the free end is below the fluid level in the master cylinder reservoir(s).

2. Fill the reservoirs with fresh brake fluid. Pump the piston until no more air bubbles appear in the reservoir(s).

3. Disconnect the two short lines, refill the master cylinder and securely install the cylinder cap(s).

4. Install the master cylinder on the car. Attach the lines but do not completely tighten them. Force any air that might have been trapped in the connection by slowly depressing the brake pedal. Tighten the lines before releasing the brake pedal.

POWER BRAKES

Vacuum Operated Booster

Power brakes operate just as standard brake systems except in the actuation of the master cylinder pistons. A vacuum diaphragm is located on the front of the master cylinder and assists the driver in applying the brakes, reducing both the effort and travel he must put into moving the brake pedal.

The vacuum diaphragm housing is connected to the intake manifold by a vacuum hose. A check valve is placed at the point where the hose enters the diaphragm housing, so that during periods of low manifold vacuum brake assist vacuum will not be lost.

Depressing the brake pedal closes off the vacuum source and allows atmospheric pressure to enter on one side of the diaphragm. This causes the master cylinder pistons to move and apply the brakes. When

the brake pedal is released, vacuum is applied to both sides of the diaphragm, and return springs return the diaphragm and master cylinder pistons to the released position. If the vacuum fails, the brake pedal rod will butt against the end of the master cylinder actuating rod, and direct mechanical application will occur as the pedal is depressed.

The hydraulic and mechanical problems that apply to conventional brake systems also apply to power brakes, and should be checked for if the tests and chart below do not reveal the problem.

Tests for a system vacuum leak as described below:

1. Operate the engine at idle with the transmission in Neutral without touching the brake pedal for at least one minute.

2. Turn off the engine, and wait one minute.

3. Test for the presence of assist vacuum by depressing the brake pedal and releasing it several times. Light application will produce less and less pedal travel, if vacuum was present. If there is no vacuum, air is leaking into the system somewhere. Test for system operation as follows:

1. Pump the brake pedal (with engine off) until the supply vacuum is entirely gone.

2. Put a light, steady pressure on the pedal.

3. Start the engine, and operate it at idle with the transmission in Neutral. If the system is operating, the brake pedal should fall toward the floor if constant pressure is maintained on the pedal.

Power brake systems may be tested for hydraulic leaks just as ordinary systems are tested, except that the engine should be idling with the transmission in Neutral throughout the test.

POWER BRAKE BOOSTER TROUBLESHOOTING CHART

The following items are in addition to those listed in the General Troubleshooting Section. Check those items first.

Hard Pedal

1. Faulty vacuum check valve.
2. Vacuum hose kinked, collapsed, plugged, leaky, or improperly connected.
3. Internal leak in unit.
4. Damaged vacuum cylinder.
5. Damaged valve plunger.
6. Broken or faulty springs.
7. Broken plunger stem.

Grabbing Brakes

1. Damaged vacuum cylinder.
2. Faulty vacuum check valve.
3. Vacuum hose leaky or improperly connected.
4. Broken plunger stem.

Pedal Goes to Floor

Generally, when this problem occurs, it is not caused by the power brake booster. In rare cases, a broken plunger stem may be at fault.

Overhaul

Most power brake boosters are serviced by replacement only. In many cases, repair parts are not available. A good many special tools are required for rebuilding these units. For these reasons, it would be most practical to replace a failed booster with a new or remanufactured unit.

SERVICING DISC BRAKES

Disc Brake Caliper

An integral part of the caliper, the caliper bore(s) contains the piston(s) that direct thrust against the brake pads supported within the caliper. Since all braking forces (pad application force) are applied on each side of the rotor with no self energization, the cylinder and piston are large in comparison to a drum brake wheel cylinder.

Fixed–Type

A fixed type caliper is mounted solidly to the spindle bracket.

Pistons are located on both sides of the rotor, in inboard and outboard caliper halves. Fluid passes between caliper halves through an external crossover tube or through internal passages. A bleeder screw is located in the inboard caliper half. A dust boot protecting each cylinder fits in a circumferential groove on the piston.

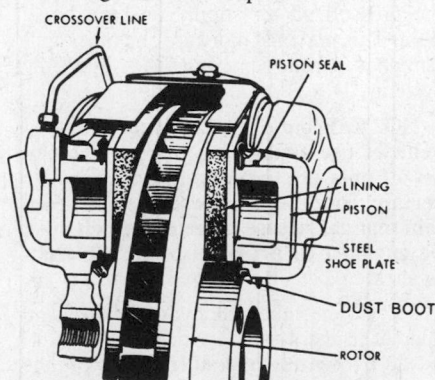

Fixed caliper disc brake

Floating–Type

Floating or sliding calipers are free to move in a fixed bracket or support.

The piston(s) is located only on the inboard side of the caliper housing, which straddles the rotor. The cylinder piston(s)

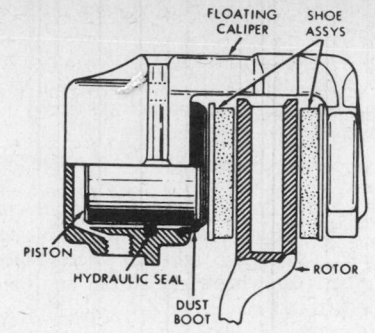

Floating caliper disc brake (sliding caliper similar)

applies the inboard brake shoe directly, and simultaneously hydraulic pressure slides the caliper in a clamping action which forces the caliper to apply the outboard brake shoe.

The actual applying movement is small. The unit merely grips during application, relaxes upon release, and the shoes do not retract an appreciable distance from the rotor. The fluid inlet port and the bleeder screw are located on the inboard side of the caliper. A dust boot is fitted into a circumferential groove on the piston and into a recess at or near the outer end of the cylinder bore.

A scratched piston, nicked seal, or a sludge or varnish deposit which limits the sealing edge away from the piston will cause a fluid leak. A serious leak could develop if calipers are not reconditioned when new pads are installed. Then dust and road grime, gradually accumulating behind the dust boot, could be carried into the seal when the piston is shoved inward to accommodate new thick linings. Old seals may have taken a "set," thus preventing proper seating in the retainer groove and on the piston. Therefore, when reconditioning calipers, new seals should be installed.

OVERHAUL PROCEDURES

Before servicing, syphon or syringe about ⅔ of the fluid from the master cylinder reservoir; do not, however, lower the fluid level below the cylinder intake port.

1. To prevent a gravity loss of fluid,

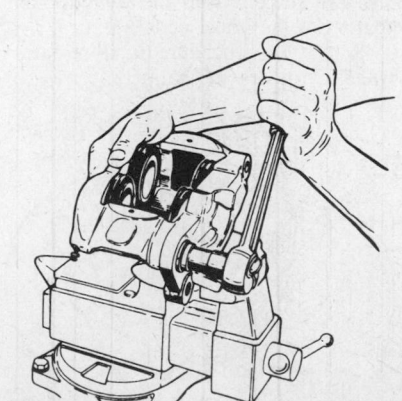

Removing the fixed caliper bridge bolts

plug the brake line after disconnecting it from the caliper.

2. To overhaul, remove the caliper from the vehicle, allow the unit to drain, and remove the brake shoes.

3. For benchwork, clamp the caliper housing in a soft jawed vice.

4. On fixed-caliper types, remove the bridge bolts and separate the caliper into halves. Remove the sealing O-rings at crossover points, if the unit has internal fluid passages across the halves.

5. Whenever required, use special tools to remove pistons, dust boots, and seals. If compressed air is used, apply it gradually, gently ease the pistons from the cylinders, and trap them in a clean cloth; do not allow them to pop out. *Take care to avoid pinching hands or fingers.*

6. While removing stroking type seals and boots, work the lip of the boot from the groove in the caliper. After the boot is free, pull the piston, and strip the seal and boot from the piston.

7. While removing fixed position (rectangular ring) seals and boots, pull the piston through the boot. *Do not use a metal tool which would scratch the piston.* Use a small pointed wooden or plastic tool to lift the boots and seals from the grooves in the cylinder bore.

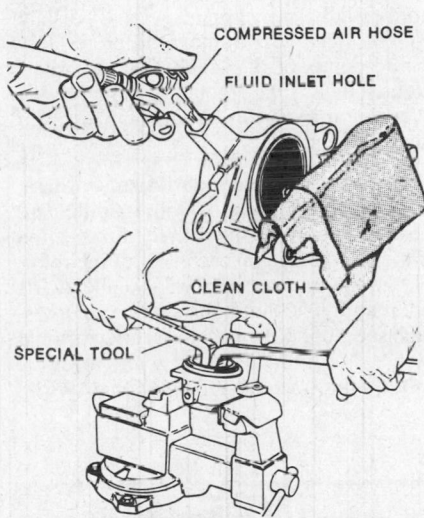

COMPRESSED AIR HOSE
FLUID INLET HOLE
CLEAN CLOTH
SPECIAL TOOL

Removing a hollow–end piston with compressed air (top) or the special tool (bottom)

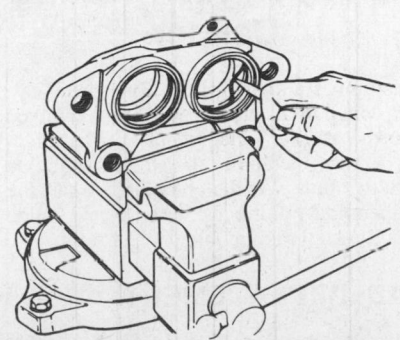

Removing a fixed position rectangular ring seal

Cleaning, Inspection, and Installation

Use only alcohol and/or brake fluid and a lint free wiping cloth to clean the caliper and parts.

—— CAUTION ——
Other solvents should not be used. Blow out passages with compressed air. Always wear eye protection when using compressed air or cleaning calipers.

1. To correct minor imperfections in the cylinder bore, polish with a fine grade of crocus cloth working in a circular rather than a lengthwise motion. Do not use any form of abrasive on a plated piston. Discard a piston which is pitted or has signs of plating wear.

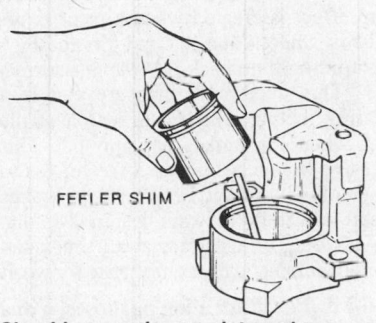

FEELER SHIM

Checking maximum piston clearance

2. Inspect the new seal. It should lie flat and be round. If it has suffered a distorted "set" during its shelf life, do not use it. Lubricate the cylinder wall and parts with brake fluid.

3. While installing stroking type seals and boots, stretch the boot and the seal over the piston and seat them in position.

4. Use special alignment tools for inserting lip culp seals.

5. Install the fixed position (rectangular ring) seals and be sure the ring does not twist or roll in the groove.

6. Where the boot lip is retained inside the cylinder bore, the following method works well:

a. Lubricate the bottom inside edge of the piston and brake seal in the caliper with brake fluid.

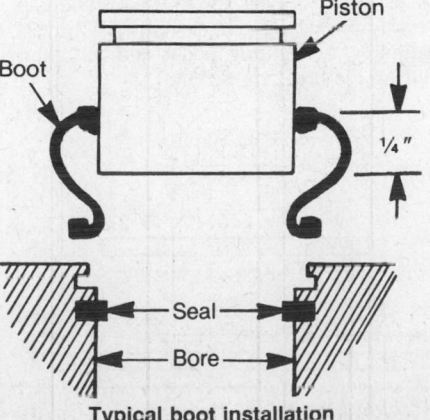

Boot
Piston
¼″
Seal
Bore

Typical boot installation

b. Pull the boot over the bottom end of the piston so that the boot is positioned on the bottom of the piston with the lip about ¼ inch up from bottom end.

c. Hold the piston suspended over bore.

d. Insert the back boot lip into the groove in the caliper.

e. Tuck the sides of the boot into the groove and work forward until only one bulge remains.

f. Tuck the final bulge into the front of the groove.

g. Push the piston carefully through the seal and boot to the bottom of the bore. The inside of the boot should slide on the piston and come to rest in the boot groove.

If the boot lip is retained outside the cylinder bore, first stretch the boot over the piston and seat it in its groove, then press the piston through the seal.

Fully depress the piston. You'll need 50 to 100 of pounds force to fasten the boot lip in place. On some designs, it is necessary to use a wooden drift or a special tool to seat the metal boot in the caliper counterbore below the face of the caliper.

Installing Fixed Caliper Bridge Bolts

If the caliper contains internal fluid crossover passages, be sure to install the new O-ring seals at the joints.

Install high tensile strength bridge bolts on the mated caliper halves.

Never replace the bridge bolts with ordinary standard hardware bolts; order the bolts by part numbers only. Tighten the bridge bolts, using a specified torque wrench as follows specified by the manufacturer.

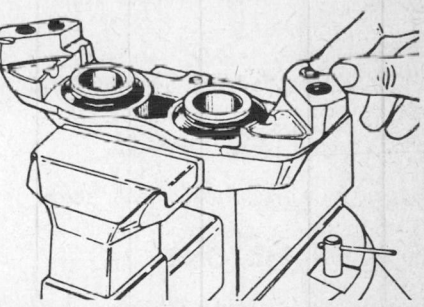

Replacing the O–rings in the internal cross–over passages

OVERHAUL NOTES

Field reports indicate that two factors determine whether to replace or rebuild calipers:

1. Can the piston or pistons be removed?

2. Will the bleed screw break off when removal is attempted? (Rebuilders will not accept a caliper with a broken bleed screw.) Since there is no way to predict how a bleed screw will react, follow this porcedure to attempt removal.

1. Insert a drill shank into the bleed screw hole (snug fit).

2. Tap the screw on all sides.

3. With a six point wrench apply pressure gently while working the drill up and down slightly.

4. If the drill starts to bind, the screw is beginning to collapse and cannot be removed intact.

Heating the caliper is another successful, but time consuming, bleed screw removal technique.

1. Remove the caliper from the car.

2. Heat the caliper.

3. Shrink the bleed screw by applying dry ice, and attempt removal.

BLEEDER SCREW REPLACEMENT

1. Using the existing hole in the bleeder screw for a pilot, drill ¼ in. hole completely through the existing bleeder.

2. Increase the hole to ⁷/₁₆ in.

3. Tap hole using a ¼ in. (18-national pipe tap) ½ in. deep-(full thread.)

4. Install bleeder repair kit.

5. Test for leaks and full brake pedal pressure.

Replacing a disc brake bleeder screw

FROZEN PISTONS

Sliding or Floating Caliper

1. **Hydraulic Removal:** remove the caliper assembly from the rotor.

2. Remove the brake pads and dust seal. With flexible brake line connected and the bleed screw closed, apply enough pedal pressure to move the piston most of the way out of the bore. (Brake fluid will begin to ooze past the piston inner seal.)

1. **Pneumatic Removal:** remove the caliper from the car.

2. With the bleed screw closed, apply air pressure to force the piston out.

--- CAUTION ---
Hydraulic and pneumatic methods of piston removal should be done carefully to prevent personal injury or piston damage.

Fixed Caliper

NOTE: The hydraulic or pneumatic methods which apply to the single piston type caliper will not work on the multiple type brake caliper.

1. Remove the caliper from the car with the two halves separated.

2. Mount in a vise and use a piston puller (many types available) to remove the pistons.

Brake Disc (Rotor)

ROTOR RUNOUT

Manufacturers differ widely on permissible runout, but too much can sometimes be felt as a pulsation at the brake pedal. A wobble pump effect is created when a rotor is not perfectly smooth and the pad hits the high spots forcing fluid back into the master cylinder. This alternating pressure causes a pulsating feeling which can be felt at the pedal when the brakes are applied. This excessive runout also causes the brakes to be out of adjustment because disc brakes are self-adjusting; they are designed so that the pads drag on the rotor at all times and therefore automatically compensate for wear.

NOTE: For illustration purposes, a dial gauge is shown making rotor measurements. There are several other more convenient types of measurement tools. (Disc illustrations are exaggerated views to more clearly emphasize the conditions.)

To check the actual runout of the rotor, first tighten the wheel spindle nut to a snug bearing adjustment, end-play removed. Fasten a dial indicator on the suspension at a convenient place so that the indicator stylus contacts the rotor face approximately one inch from its outer edge. Set the dial at zero. Check the total indicator reading while turning the rotor one full revolution. If the rotor is warped beyond the runout specification, it is likely that it can be successfully remachined.

Lateral Runout: A wobbly movement of the rotor from side to side as it rotates. Excessive lateral runout causes the rotor faces to knock back the disc pads and can result in chatter, excessive pedal travel, pumping or fighting pedal and vibration during the breaking action.

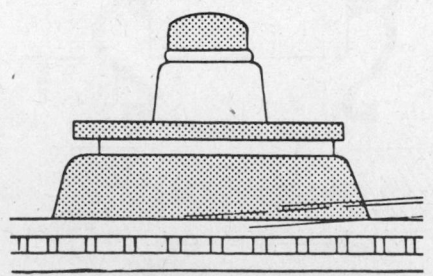

Excessive runout

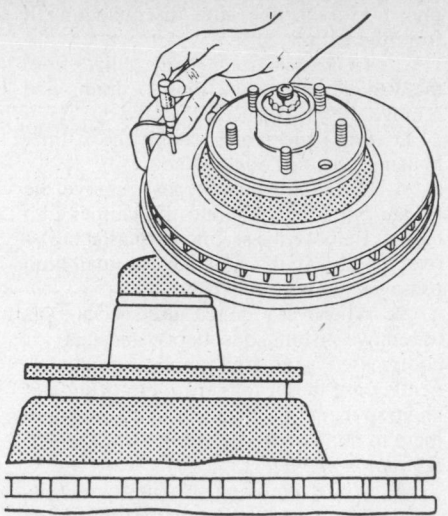

Parallelism

Parallelism (lack of): Refers to the amount of variation in the thickness of the rotor. Excessive variation can cause pedal vibration or fight, front end vibrations and possible "grab" during the braking action; a condition comparable to an "out-of-round brake drum." Check parallelism with a micrometer. "mike" the thickness at eight or more equally spaced points, equally distant from the outer edge of the rotor, preferrably at mid-points of the braking surface. Parallelism then is the amount of variation between maximum and minimum measurements.

Surface or Micro-inch finish, flatness, smoothness: Different from parallelism, these terms refer to the degree of perfection of the flat surface on each side of the rotor; that is, the minute hills, valleys and swirls inherent in machining the surface. In a visual inspection, the remachined surface should have a fine ground polish with, at most, only a faint trace of nondirectional swirls.

TYPE 1

Kelsey-Hayes Floating Caliper

This unit is a single piston, one-piece caliper which floats on two guide pins screwed into the adapter (anchor plate). The adaptor, in turn, is held to the steering knuckle with two bolts. As the brake pads wear, the caliper floats along the adapter and guide pins during braking.

PAD REPLACEMENT

1. Raise the front of the vehicle and support it with jackstands. Remove the wheel.

DISC BRAKE APPLICATION CHART

Make	Year/Model		Reference Number	Caliper Design
Audi	78–'79 Fox		6	Sliding Yoke
			4	Floating
	'80–'85 4000		4	Floating
	'78–'80 5000		6	Sliding Yoke
	'81–'85 5000		4	Floating
	'80–'85 Turbo	Front	4	Floating
		Rear	4	Floating
	'82–'85 Quattro	Front	4	Floating
		Rear	4	Floating
BMW	'78–'85, 528i, 530i, 630CSi, 633CSi, 733i	Front	2	Fixed
		Rear	2	Fixed
	'78–'83 320i		2	Fixed
	'84–'85 318i, 325e	Front	4	Floating
		Rear	4	Floating
	'82–'85 528e, 533i	Front	4	Floating
		Rear	4	Floating
Chrysler	'78–'84 Colt/Champ (ex. Sta. Wag.)		3	Floating
	(Sta. Wag.)		5	Sliding
	'78–'80 Arrow (w/Rear Drums)		3	Floating
	(w/Rear Discs)		5②	Sliding
	'78–'83 Challenger/Sapporo	Front	5	Sliding
		Rear	5	Sliding
	'84–'85 Conquest	Front	4	Floating
			9	Floating
Datsun/Nissan	'78–'82 B210, 210, 310, 510, 710, F10		7	Sliding Yoke
	'78–'81 200SX	Front	7	Sliding Yoke
		Rear	7	Sliding Yoke
	'82–'83 200SX	Front	7	Sliding Yoke
		Rear	4	Floating
	'84–'85 200SX	Front	4	Floating
		Rear	4	Floating
	'78–'80 810	Front	7	Sliding Yoke
		Rear	7	Sliding Yoke
	'81–'85 810, Maxima	Front	4	Floating
		Rear	4③	Floating
	'78 280Z		2	Fixed
	'79–'81 280ZX	Front	4	Floating
		Rear	7	Sliding Yoke
	'82–'83 280ZX	Front	4	Floating
		Rear	4	Floating
	'84–'85 300ZX	Front	4	Floating
		Rear	4	Floating
	'82–'85 Sentra, Stanza, Pulsar		4	Floating
Fiat	'78–'85 All		5②	Sliding

DISC BRAKE APPLICATION CHART

Make	Year/Model		Reference Number	Caliper Design
Honda	'78–'79 Civic (ex. Sta. Wag.)		7	Sliding Yoke
	(Sta. Wag.)		3	Floating
	'80–'85 Civic (ex. pre-'84 Sta. Wag.)		4	Floating
	(pre-'84 Sta. Wag.)		5	Sliding
	'78–'81 Accord		5	Sliding
	'82–'85 Accord		4	Floating
	'79–'85 Prelude	Front	4	Floating
		Rear	4	Floating
Isuzu	'81–'85 I-Mark		2	Fixed
	'83–'85 Impulse		4②	Floating
Mazda	'78–'79 808, RX-3		3	Floating
	'79–'85 626		4	Floating
	'78–'85 RX-4, Cosmo, GLC		5④	Sliding
	'79 RX-7		5	Sliding
	'80–'85 RX-7		4	Floating
Mercedes-Benz	'78–'84 All (ex. 300SEC)	Front	2	Fixed
		Rear	2	Fixed
	'82–'84 300SEC	Front	5	Sliding
		Rear	5	Sliding
Mitsubishi	'83–'85 Cordia, Tredia		4	Floating
	'83–'85 Starion	Front	4	Floating
		Rear	9	Floating
Peugeot	'78–'83 504		7	Floating
	'80–'85 505	Front	6	Sliding Yoke
		Rear	7	Sliding Yoke
	'78–'85 604	Front	7	Sliding Yoke
		Rear	6	Sliding Yoke
Porsche	'78–'85 911, 930	Front	2	Fixed
		Rear	2	Fixed
	'78–'82 924		6	Sliding Yoke
	'78–'85 928, 944	Front	6	Sliding Yoke
		Rear	6	Sliding Yoke
Renault	'78–'83 Le Car		5	Sliding
	'81–'85 18i, Fuego		8	Floating
	'83–'85 Alliance		4	Floating
SAAB	'78–'85 All	Front	7	Sliding
		Rear	2	Fixed
Subaru	'78–'79 All		5	Sliding
	'80–'85 All		9	Floating
Toyota	'78–'82 Corona		2	Fixed
	'78–'79 Corolla (ex. 1200)		5	Sliding
	(1200)		3	Floating
	'80–'85 Corolla		3	Floating
	'80–'85 Tercel, Starlet		4	Floating

DISC BRAKE APPLICATION CHART

Make	Year/Model		Reference Number	Caliper Design
	'78–'80 Cressida		2	Fixed
	'81 Cressida		5	Sliding
	'81–'85 Cressida	Front	4	Floating
		Rear	3	Floating
	'78–'81 Celica, Supra		5⑤	Sliding
	'82–'85 Celica, Supra		4⑤	Floating
Volkswagen	'78–'85 Types 1 & 2		2	Fixed
	'78 Dasher		6, 7	Sliding, Sliding Yoke
	'78–'81 Dasher		4	Floating
	'78–'85 Rabbit, Scirocco, Jetta, Quantum		1, 6, 7②	Floating, Sliding, Sliding Yoke
Volvo	'78–'85 All Exc. 760	Front	2②	Fixed
	'83–'85 760	Front	4	Floating

①All applications are for front discs only unless otherwise noted
②Applies to both front and rear
③1981: 7, Sliding Yoke
④Also applies to Cosmo w/rear discs
⑤Also applies to Supra w/rear discs

Kelsey–Hayes floating caliper disc brake assembly

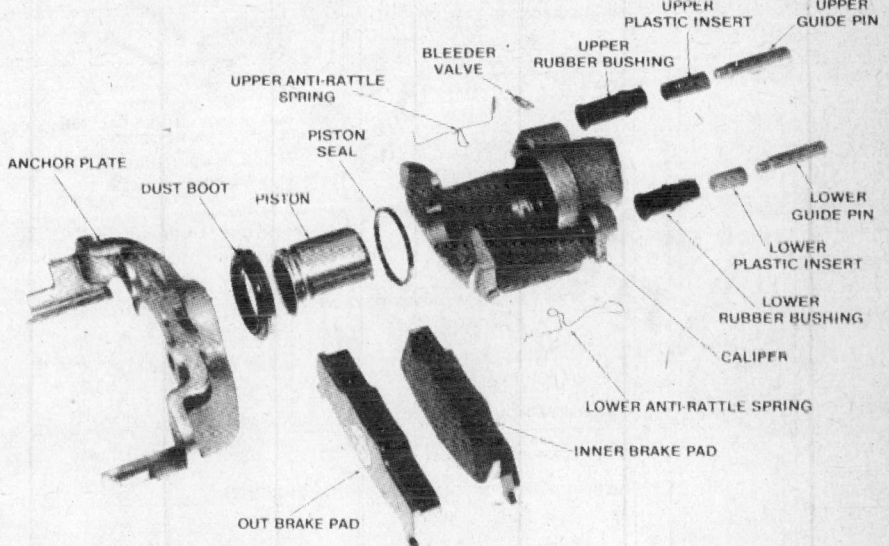

Exploded view of a Kelsey–Hayes floating caliper

2. Siphon some brake fluid from the master cylinder reservoir to prevent its overflowing when the piston is retracted into the cylinder bore.

3. Disconnect the brake pad warning indicator if so equipped.

4. Using a pair of needlenose pliers or the like, remove the anti-rattle springs.

5. Using an Allen wrench, back out the two guide pins that attach the caliper to the anchor plate.

NOTE: When replacing pads only, it is not necessary to remove the guide pins completely from the rubber bushings, as they may be difficult to reinstall.

6. Lift off the caliper and position it out of the way with some wire—you need not remove the brake lines.

——— CAUTION ———
Never allow the caliper to hang by its brake lines.

7. Slide the outer pad out of the anchor plate and then remove the inner pad. Check the rotor as detailed in the appropriate section. Check the caliper for fluid leaks or cracked boots. If any damage is found, the caliper will require overhauling or replacement.

8. Carefully clean the anchor plate with a wire brush or some other abrasive material. Install the new brake pads into position on the anchor plate. The inner pad usually has chamfered edges.

NOTE: When replacing brake pads, always replace both pads on both sides of the vehicle. Mixed pads will cause uneven braking.

9. Slowly and carefully push the piston into its bore until it's bottomed and then position the caliper onto the anchor plate. Install the guide pins and tighten them to 25–30 ft. lbs.

NOTE: The upper guide pin is usually longer than the lower one.

——— CAUTION ———
Use extreme care so as not to cross-thread the guide pins when tightening.

10. Install the anti-rattle springs between the anchor plate and brake pads ears. The loops on the springs should be positioned inboard.

11. Fill the reservoir with brake fluid and pump the brake pedal several times to set the piston. It should not be necessary to bleed the system; however, if a firm pedal cannot be obtained, the system must be bled (see "Bleeding the Brakes" in this section).

12. Install the wheel and lower the vehicle.

TYPE 2

ATE, Girling, Sumitomo Fixed Caliper

These units are either two or four piston, two-piece calipers that are fixed directly to the steering knuckle or spindle.

Brake pads may be changed without removing the caliper on all of these models. There may be some differences in retainers or anti-rattle springs from the illustrations, but all versions are basically the same. Before removing any parts, carefully note the position of any springs, retainers or clips. Change pads on one wheel at a time and use the other as a reference.

All pads on all models are held in position by either retaining pins or retainer plates. The retainer plates are bolted to the caliper housing and need only be loosened and rotated out of the way for pad removal.

PAD REPLACEMENT

1. Raise the front (or rear) of the vehicle and support it with jackstands. Remove the wheel.

2. Siphon a sufficient quantity of brake fluid from the master cylinder reservoir to prevent the brake fluid from overflowing the master cylinder when removing or installing new pads. This is necessary as the pistons must be forced into the cylinder bore to provide sufficient clearance to remove the pads.

3. Some models may use a cover plate over the access hole for the pads, if so,

Typical fixed caliper disc brake assembly

remove it. Disconnect the brake pad lining wear indicator wire on models so equipped.

4. Carefully clean the exterior of the caliper with a wire brush and note the position of any dampening shims or anti-rattle springs.

5. Remove the pad retaining pins and any retaining clips holding them. Remove the anti-rattle springs if so equipped. Some pads may be held in position by a plate with a retaining bolt. If so, loosen the bolt and swing the plate away. Lift out the spreader spring if so equipped.

NOTE: It is a good idea to remove one retaining spring or plate and then remove the anti-rattle springs or spreader spring. Remove the second retaining pin or plate last.

6. Force the old pads away from the rotor for easy withdrawal and remove the pads from the caliper.

7. If so equipped, remove the lower anti-rattle springs and dampening shims using needlenose pliers.

8. Check the brake disc (rotor) as detailed in the appropriate section.

9. Examine the dust boot for cracks or damage and push the pistons back into the

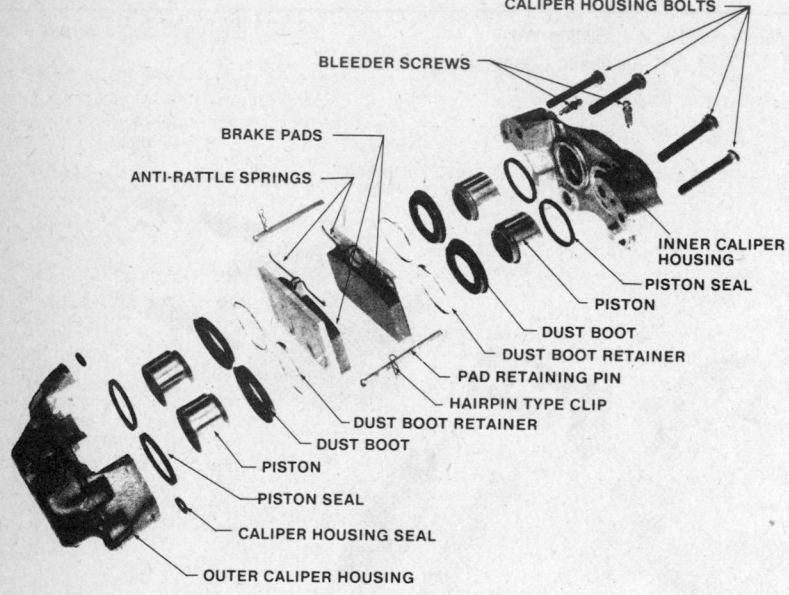

Exploded view of a four-piston fixed caliper

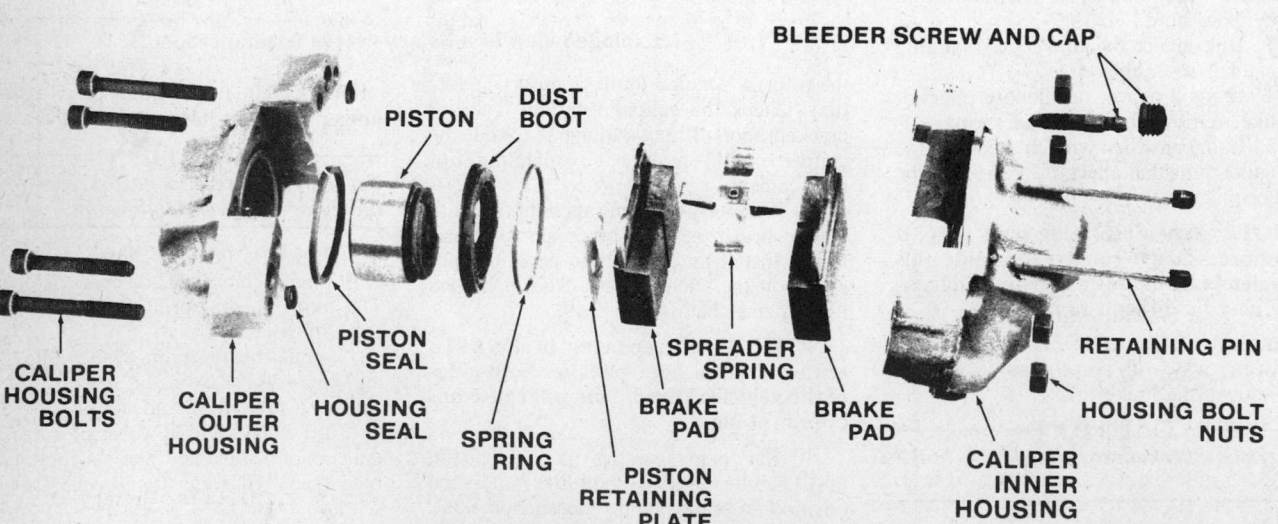

Exploded view of a two-piston fixed caliper

cylinder bores. If the pistons are frozen or if the caliper is leaking hydraulic fluid, it must be overhauled.

10. Install the anti–rattle spring or damping shims and slip the new pads into the caliper. If damping shims are used, be sure that the directional arrow on the shims face the forward rotation of the rotor.

11. Install one pad retaining pin and hairpin clip. Position the anti–rattle springs and/or spreader spring and then install the other pad retaining pin and clip.

12. Refill the master cylinder to the correct level with the proper brake fluid.

13. Replace the wheel and lower the vehicle. Pump the brake pedal several times to bring the pads into correct adjustment. Road test the vehicle.

NOTE: If a firm pedal cannot be obtained, the system will require bleeding (see "Bleeding the Brakes" in this section).

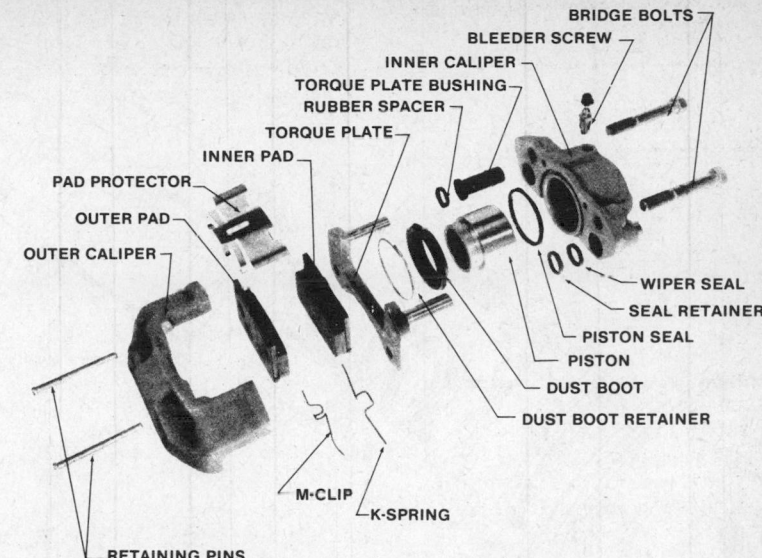

Exploded view of a Sumitomo Torque Plate floating caliper

TYPE 3

Sumitomo Torque Plate Floating Caliper

This unit is a single piston, two–piece caliper which floats on torque plate pins. The torque plate itself is bolted to the steering knuckle. The outer caliper half may be separated from the inner half although the caliper need not be separated or removed for pad replacement.

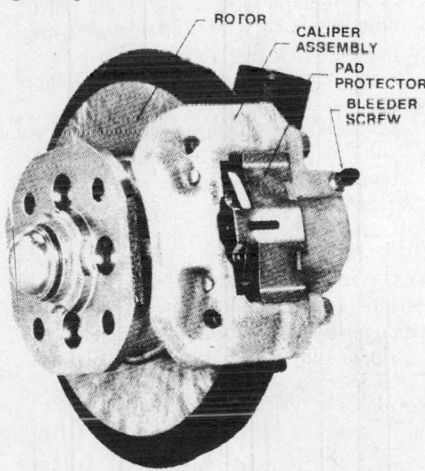

Typical Sumitomo Torque Plate floating caliper disc brake assembly

PAD REPLACEMENT

1. Raise the front of the vehicle and support it on jackstands. Remove the wheel.

2. Siphon a sufficient quantity of brake fluid from the master cylinder reservoir to prevent the brake fluid from overflowing the master cylinder when removing or in-

stalling new pads. This is necessary as the piston must be forced into the cylinder bore to provide sufficient clearance to remove the pads.

3. Use a small prybar or other suitable tool and pry the pad protector off of the retaining pins.

4. Remove the center of the 'M' clip from the hole in the outboard pad and its ends from the retaining pins.

NOTE: To facilitate the reassembly operation later on, note how the 'M' clip and the 'K' spring are positioned in the caliper.

5. Pull out the retaining pins and remove the 'K' spring from the inboard pad.

6. Remove the inner and outer pads.

7. Check the brake disc (rotor) as detailed in the appropriate section.

8. Examine the dust boot for cracks or damage and then push the piston back into the cylinder bore. Use a C-clamp or other suitable tool to bottom the piston. If the piston is frozen, or if the caliper is leaking hydraulic fluid, the caliper must be overhauled or replaced.

9. Install new pads into the caliper.

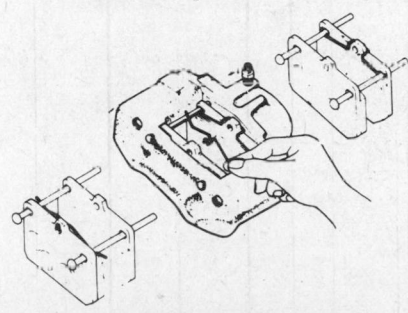

Spring and clip installation

10. Install one retaining pin.

11. Install the inboard pad 'K' spring. Hook one end of the 'K' spring under the retaining pin and the center of the 'K' spring

over the top of the inboard pad. Insert the other retaining pin through the outboard pad, over the 'K' spring and through the inboard pad.

12. Insert the ends of the 'M' clip into the holes in the retaining pins and press the center of the spring into the hole in the outboard pad.

13. Install the pad protector.

14. Refill the master cylinder with fresh brake fluid.

15. Install the tire and wheel assembly and then pump the brake pedal several times to bring the pads into adjustment. Road test the vehicle.

NOTE: If a firm pedal cannot be obtained, bleed the system as detailed in "Bleeding the Brakes".

TYPE 4

ATE, Girling, etc. Floating Caliper

Although similar in many respects to a sliding caliper, this single piston unit floats on guide pins and bushings which are threaded into a mounting bracket. The mounting bracket is bolted to the steering knuckle.

Variations in pad retainers, shims, anti–rattle and retaining springs will be encountered but the service procedures are all basically the same. Note the position of all springs, clips or shims when removing the pads. Work on one side at a time and use the other for reference.

PAD REPLACEMENT

1. Raise and support the front (or rear)

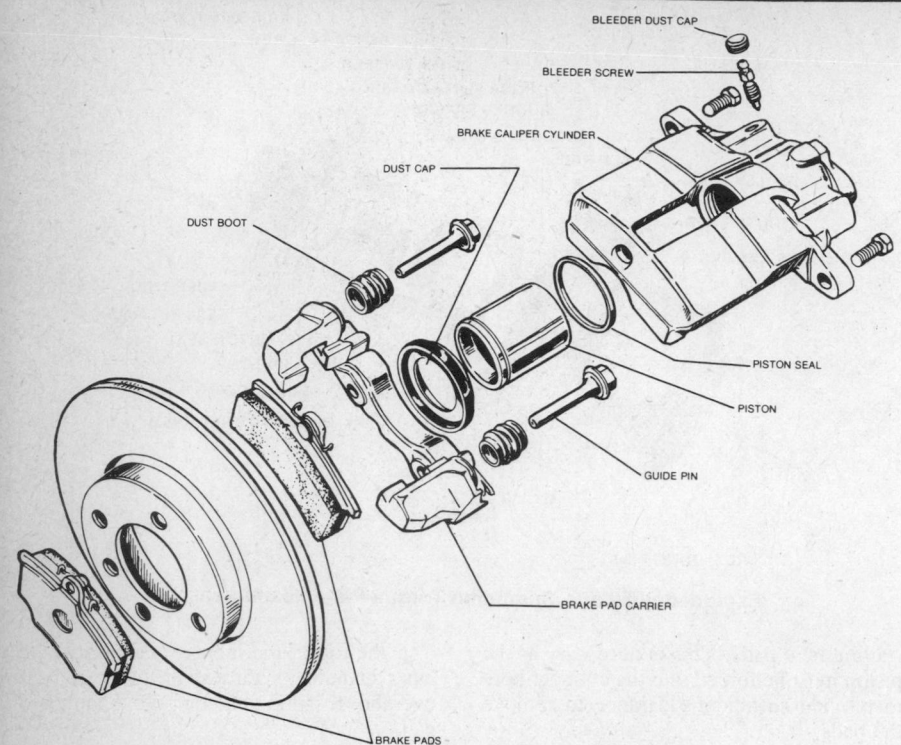

Exploded view of a typical Type 4 floating caliper

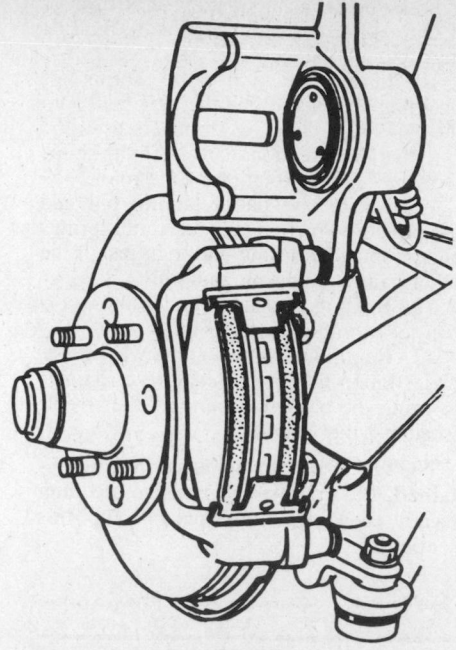

On some models, the caliper cylinder may be pivoted upwards to remove the pads

of the vehicle on jackstands. Remove the wheel.

2. Siphon a sufficient quantity of brake fluid from the master cylinder reservoir to prevent the brake fluid from overflowing the master cylinder when removing or installing new pads. This is necessary as the piston must be forced into the cylinder bore to provide sufficient clearance to remove the pads.

3. Grasp the cliper from behind and pull it toward you. This will push the piston back into the cylinder bore.

4. Disconnect the brake pad lining wear indicator if so equipped. Remove any anti–rattle springs or clips if so equipped.

NOTE: Depending on the model and year of the particular caliper, you may not have to remove it entirely to get at

the brake pads. If the caliper is the "swing" type, remove the lower guide bolt, pivot the caliper on the upper bolt and swing it upward exposing the brake pads. If this method is employed, skip to Step 7.

5. Remove the caliper guide pins.

6. Remove the caliper from the rotor by slowly sliding it out and away from the rotor. Position the caliper out of the way and support it with wire so that it doesn't hang by the brake line.

7. Slide the outboard pad out of the adapter.

8. Remove the inboard pad. Remove any shims or shields behind the pads and note their positions.

9. Install the anti–rattle hardware and then the pads (in their proper positions!).

10. On Audis (or Datsuns) with rear disc brakes, use an Allen wrench (or needle–nosed pliers) to turn the piston to the right and then push it back into the cylinder bore.

11. Install any pad shims or heat shields.

12. Reposition the caliper and install the guide pins.

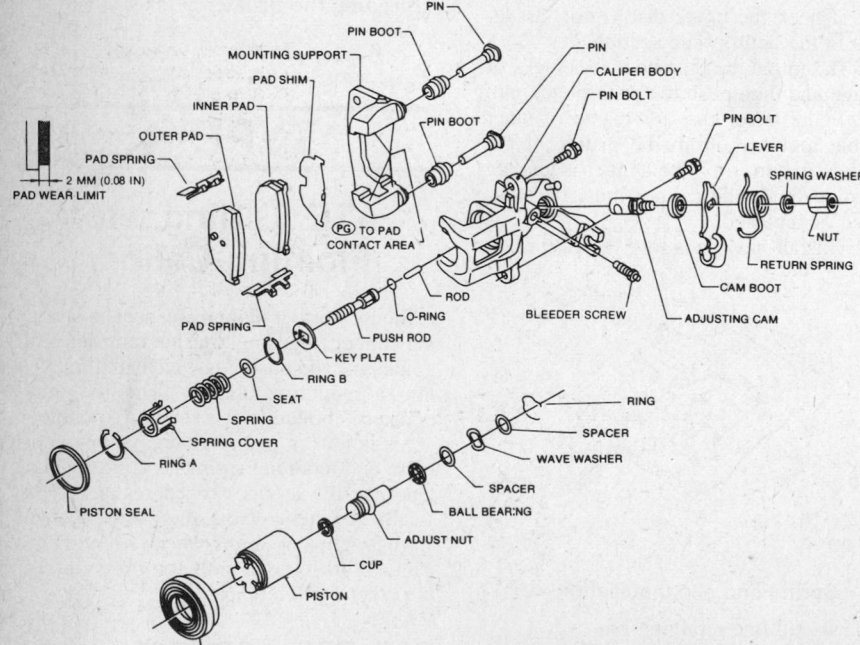

Exploded view of a Type 4 floating caliper with parking brake (Datsun shown, others similar)

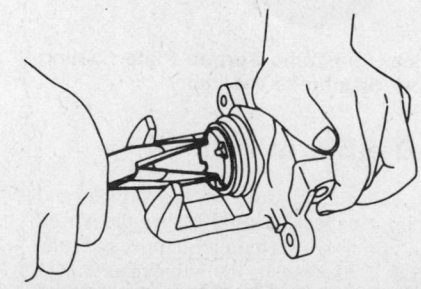

Using needle–nosed pliers to turn the piston before pushing it into the cylinder bore

NOTE: If the caliper is the "swing" type, you need only pivot it back into position and install the lower guide pin.

13. Refill the master cylinder with fresh brake fluid.

14. Install the tire and wheel assembly and then pump the brake pedal several times to bring the pads into adjustment. Road test the vehicle.

NOTE: After installing new pads on Audis with rear disc brakes, depress the brake pedal firmly, approximately 40 times with the engine turned off to permit automatic adjusting. Check the parking brake adjustment.

NOTE: If a firm pedal cannot be obtained, bleed the system as detailed in "Bleeding the Brakes".

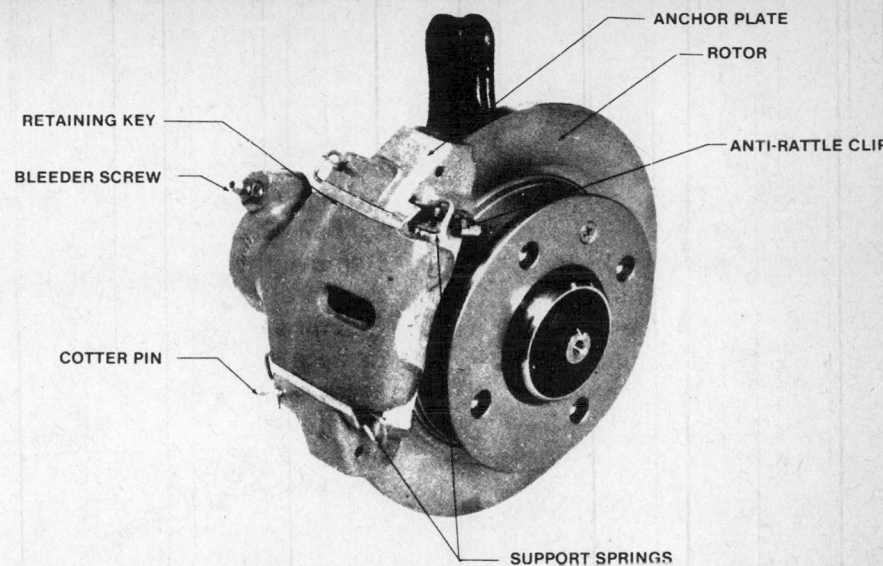

Typical sliding caliper disc brake assembly

TYPE 5

Akebono, Girling, etc. Sliding Caliper

This unit is a single piston, one–piece caliper that slides on a mounting bracket or frame which bolts to the steering knuckle. The caliper is retained in the mounting bracket by caliper guides (retaining keys) and support springs. Narrow support plates under each brake pad are utilized to eliminate rattle. One or two caliper guides may be used—it is imperative that they are replaced as originally found.

PAD REPLACEMENT

1. Raise and support the front (or rear) of the vehicle on jackstands. Remove the front wheel.

2. Siphon a sufficient quantity of brake fluid from the master cylinder reservoir to prevent the brake fluid from overflowing the master cylinder when removing or installing pads. This is necessary as the piston must be forced into the cylinder bore to provide sufficient clearance to remove the pads.

NOTE: On Subarus (and Fiats, Supras and Chryslers with rear disc brakes) only, remove the outer cable clip and then remove the parking brake cable.

3. Remove the clips or pins that hold the caliper guides in position.

4. Lightly tap out the guides—there may only be one, so remember the correct positioning.

5. Lift the caliper off of the mounting bracket.
It may be necessary to rock it back and forth a bit in order to seat the piston so it will clear the brake pads. Position the caliper out of the way and support it with wire so it doesn't hang by the brake lines.

6. Remove the brake pads from the mounting bracket. *Do not remove the support springs*.

7. A support plate is under each pad; they are not interchangeable and must be

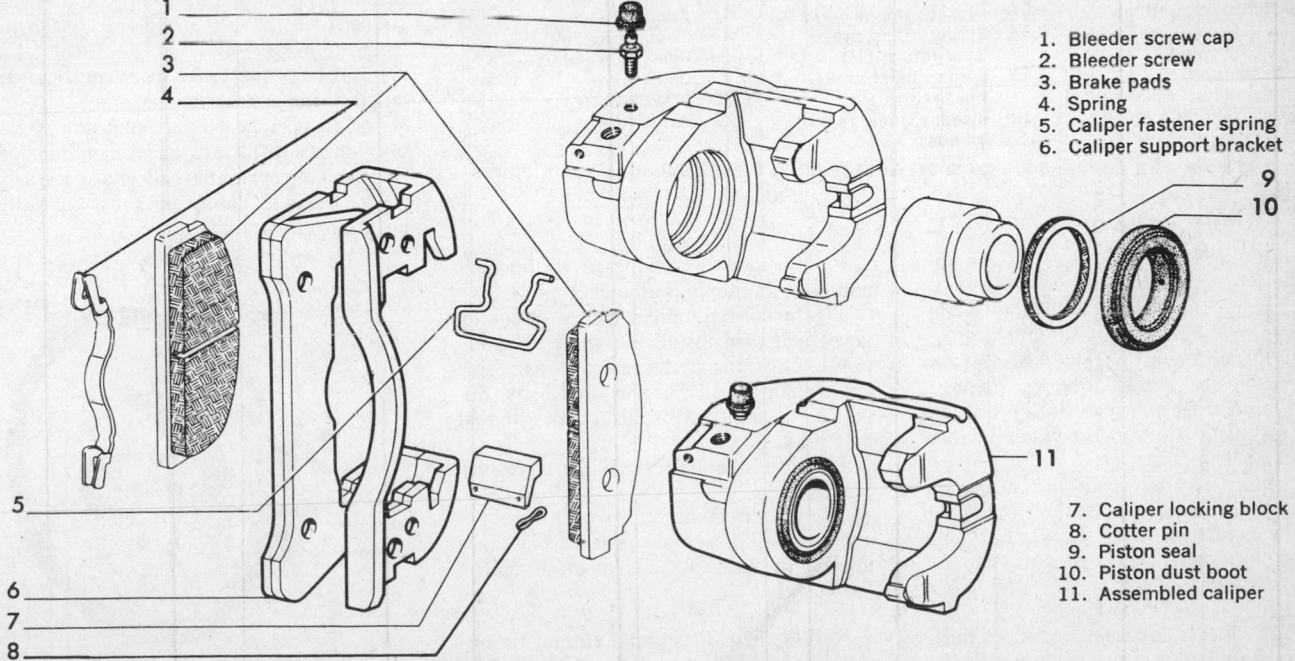

1. Bleeder screw cap
2. Bleeder screw
3. Brake pads
4. Spring
5. Caliper fastener spring
6. Caliper support bracket

7. Caliper locking block
8. Cotter pin
9. Piston seal
10. Piston dust boot
11. Assembled caliper

Exploded view of a Type 5 sliding caliper

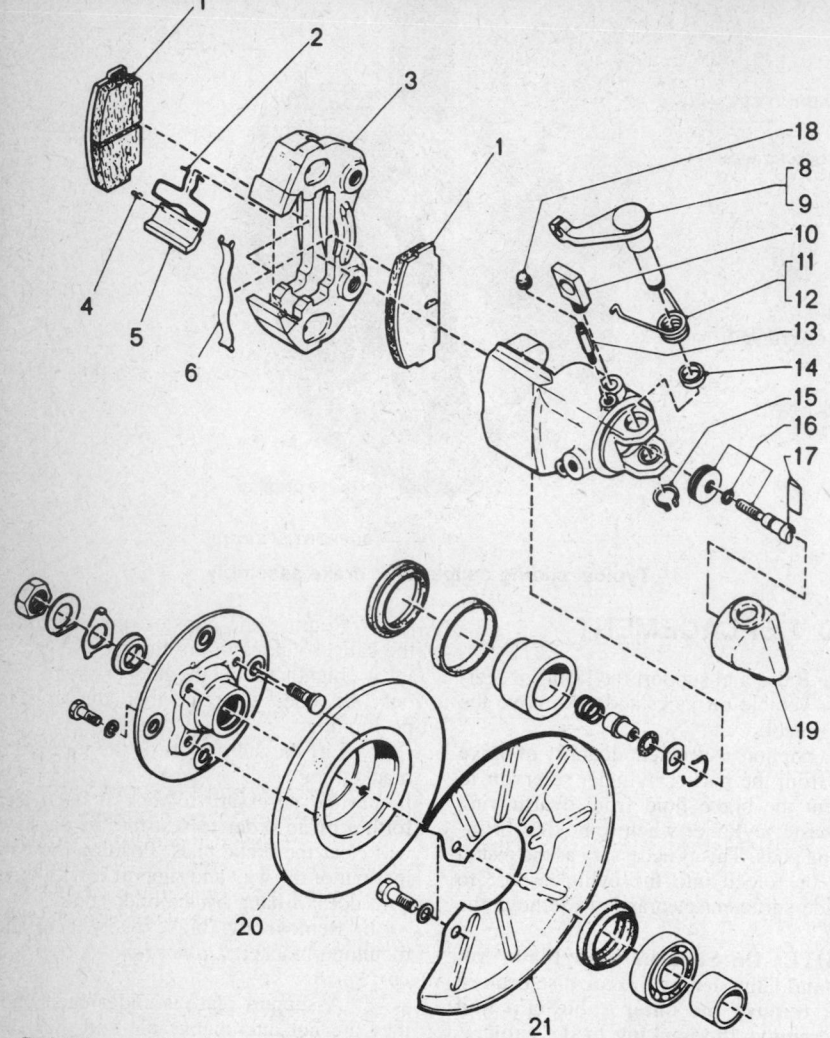

TYPE 6

ATE Sliding Yoke Caliper

This unit is a single piston, two–piece caliper. It has a fixed mounting frame which is bolted to the steering knuckle. The pads are retained in the fixed frame. A floating frame, or yoke, slides on the fixed frame. The cylinder attaches to this yoke, creating a caliper. Braking pressure forces tbe piston against the inner pad. The reaction causes the yoke to move in the opposite direction, applying pressure to the outer pad.

PAD REPLACEMENT

1. Raise the front (or rear) of the vehicle and support it with jackstands. Remove the wheel.

2. Siphon a sufficient quantity of brake fluid from the master cylinder reservoir to prevent the brake fluid from overflowing the master cylinder when removing or installing new pads. This is necessary as the piston must be forced into the cylinder bore to provide sufficient clearance to remove the pads.

3. Disconnect the wire connector leading to the brake pad wear indicator.

4. Remove the brake pad retaining clips on the inside of the caliper and then drive out the retaining pins. Don't lose the pad positioner (spreader) that is held down by the pins.

5. Pull out the inner brake pad.

6. The outer pads are secured by a notch at the top of the pad. Grasp the caliper assembly from the inside and pull it toward yourself. Remove the pad and detach the wear indicator.

7. Check the brake disc (rotor) as detailed in the appropriate section.

8. Inspect the caliper and piston assembly for breaks, cracks or other damage. Overhaul or replace the caliper as necessary.

9. Use a C–clamp and press the piston back into the cylinder bore.

1. Pad (disc brake F)
2. Spring (caliper)
3. Bracket (mounting)
4. Pin (caliper)
5. Stopper (plug)
6. Spring (pad)
7. Body caliper ass'y
8. Lever & spindle ass'y (LH)
9. Lever & spindle ass'y (RH)
10. Bracket (hand brake)
11. Spring (hand brake lever return LH)
12. Spring (hand brake lever return RH)
13. Bleeder screw (wheel cylinder)
14. Bushing (hand brake)
15. Retaining spring
16. Spindle ass'y
17. Connecting link
18. Cap (air bleeder)
19. Cap (lever)
20. Brake disc (F)
21. Cover (disc)

Exploded view of a Type 5 sliding caliper with parking brake (Subaru shown, others similar)

replaced correctly. Remove the support plates.

8. Inspect the brake disc (rotor) as detailed in the appropriate section.

9. Inspect the caliper and piston assembly for breaks, cracks or other damage. Overhaul or replace the caliper as necessary.

10. Replace the support plates in their original positions.

11. Place the new pads in the support bracket over the support springs.

12. Push the piston all the way back into its bore (a C–clamp may be necessary for this operation).

NOTE: The piston must be turned back into its seated position on certain models. Check piston type before seating.

13. Position the caliper over the pads and onto the mounting bracket.

14. Install the caliper guides (retaining keys) and then install the guide retaining pins or clips. Install the parking brake cable and its clip on all Subarus (and Fiats, Supras and Chrysler/Mitsubishi cars with rear disc brakes).

15. Refill the master cylinder with fresh brake fluid.

16. Install the tire and wheel assembly and then pump the brake pedal several times to bring the pads into adjustment. Road test the vehicle.

NOTE: If a firm pedal cannot be obtained, bleed the system as detailed in "Bleeding the Brakes".

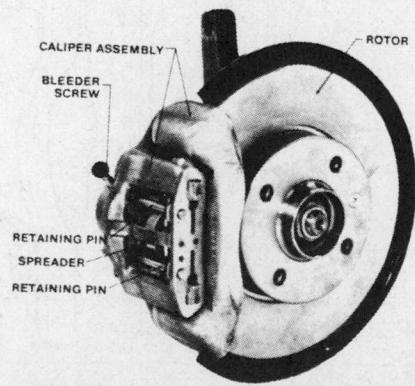

Typical ATE sliding yoke disc brake assembly

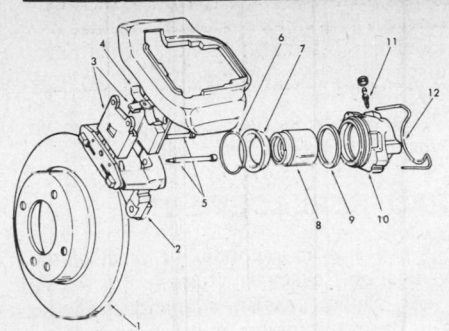

1. Brake disc
2. Caliper mounting frame
3. Pads
4. Cross spring
5. Retaining pins
6. Clamp ring
7. Boot
8. Piston
9. Seal
10. Cylinder
11. Bleeder nipple
12. Guide spring

Exploded view of an ATE sliding yoke caliper

10. Install the wear indicator on the outer pad and then install both pads.

11. Installation of the remaining components is the reverse order or removal.

12. Top off the master cylinder with fresh brake fluid.

13. Pump the brake pedal several times to bring the pads into adjustment. Road test the vehicle. If a firm pedal cannot be obtained, bleed the brakes as detailed in "Bleeding the Brakes".

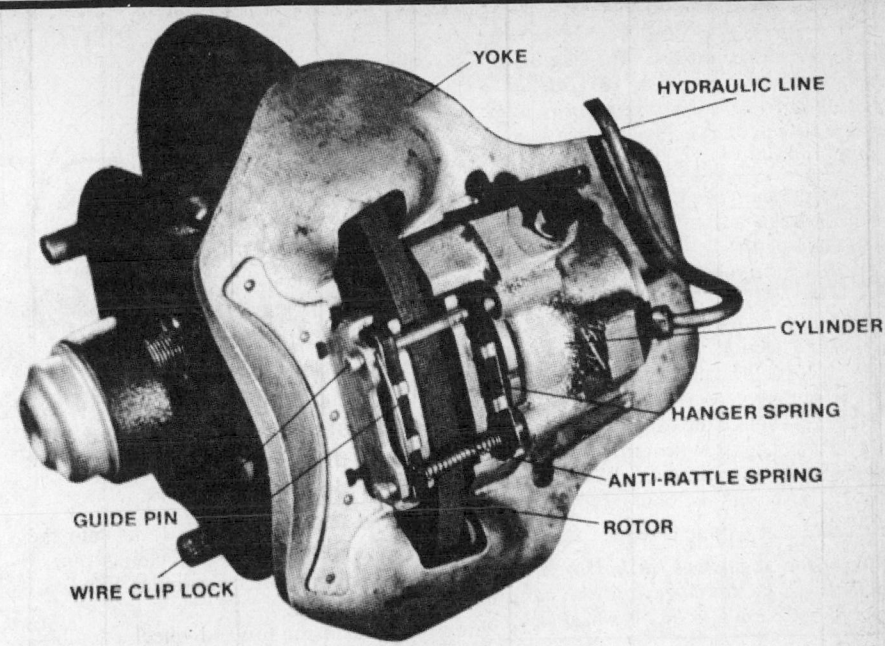

Typical Type 7 sliding yoke caliper disc brake assembly

PAD REPLACEMENT

1. Raise and support the front (or rear) of the vehicle on jackstands. Remove the wheel.

2. Siphon a sufficient quantity of brake fluid from the master cylinder reservoir to prevent the brake fluid from overflowing the master cylinder when removing or installing new pads. This is necessary as the piston must be forced into the cylinder bore to provide sufficient clearance to remove the pads.

3. Disconnect the brake pad lining wear indicator if so equipped.

4. Remove the dust cover and/or anti-rattle (damper) clip if so equipped.

5. Lift off the wire clip(s) which hold the guide pins or retaining pin in place.

6. Remove the upper guide pin and the two hanger springs. Carefully tap out the lower guide pin.

TYPE 7

Girling/Annette Sliding Yoke Caliper

This unit is a double piston, one-piece caliper. The cylinder body contains two pistons, back-to-back, in a thru-bore. The cylinder body is bolted to the steering knuckle, with both pistons inboard of the rotor. A yoke, which slides on the cylinder body, is installed over the rotor and the caliper.

When the brakes are applied, hydraulic pressure forces the pistons apart in the double ended bore. The piston closest to the rotor applies force directly to the inboard pad. The other piston applies force to the yoke, which transmitts the force to the outer pad, creating a friction force on each side of the rotor.

One variation has a yoke that floats on guide pins screwed into the cylinder body.

Some designs incorporate parking brake mechanisms which are actuated by a lever and cam working between the piston and the yoke.

The yokes do not have to be removed to replace the brake pads.

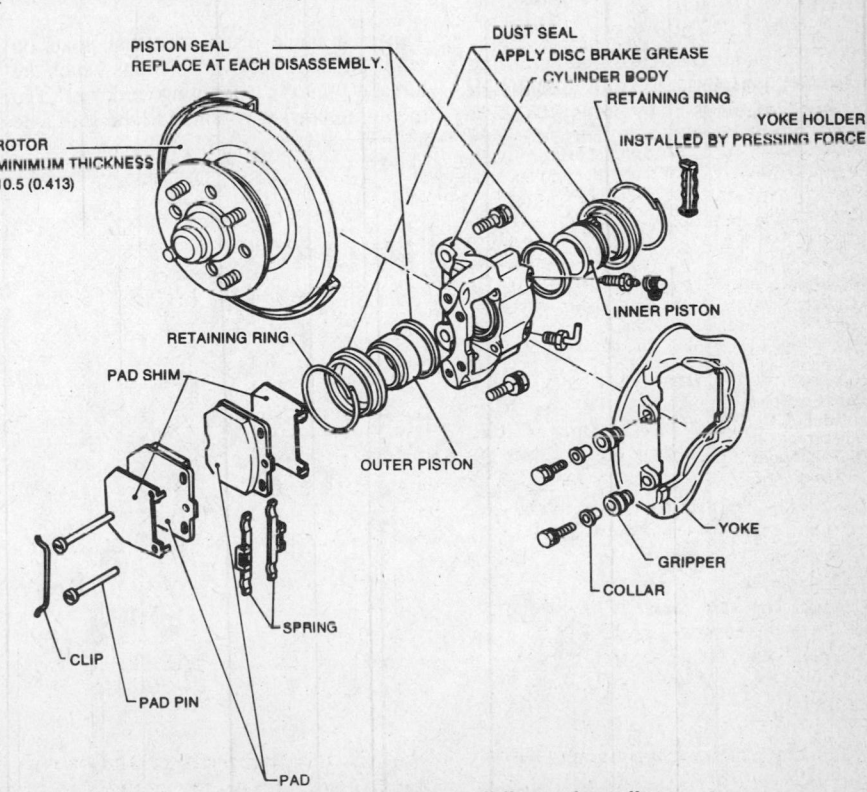

Exploded view of a Type 7 sliding yoke caliper

U313

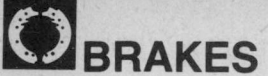

The lower guide pin usually contains an anti–rattle coil spring—be careful not to lose this spring. If a retaining pin is used, pull the pin out and remove the two hanger springs.

7. Slide the yoke outward and remove the outer brake pad and the anti–noise shim (if so equipped).

8. Slide the yoke inward and repeat Step 7.

9. Check the rotor as detailed in the appropriate section.

10. Inspect the caliper and piston assembly for breaks, cracks or other damage. Overhaul or replace the caliper as necessary.

11. Push the piston next to the rotor back into the cylinder bore until the end of the piston is flush with the boot retaining ring.

—————— CAUTION ——————

If the piston is pushed further than this, the seal will be damaged and the caliper assembly will have to be overhauled.

12. Retract the piston farthest from the rotor by pulling the yoke toward the outside of the vehicle.

13. Install the outboard pad. Anti–noise shims (if so equipped) must be located on the plate side of the pad with the triangular cutout pointing toward the top of the caliper.

14. Install the inboard pad with the shims (if so equipped) in the correct position.

15. Replace the lower guide pin and the anti–rattle coil spring.

16. Hook the hanger springs under the pin and over the brake pads.

17. Install the upper guide pin over the ends of the hanger springs.

NOTE: If a single two–sided retaining pin is used, install the pin and then install the hanger springs as in Steps 16–17.

1. Yoke	20. Spring cover
2. Yoke spring	21. Spring
3. Clip	22. Spring seat
4. Pad pin	23. Snap ring C
5. Anti–squeal spring	24. Key plate
6. Pad	25. Push rod
7. Retaining ring	26. O-ring
8. Dust seal	27. Strut
9. Outer piston	28. Inner piston
10. Oil seal	29. Cam
11. Adjusting nut	30. Toggle lever
12. Bearing	31. Spring
13. Spacer	32. Washer
14. Wave washer	33. Nut
15. Snap ring B	
16. Piston seal	
17. Cylinder body	
18. Retainer	
19. Snap ring A	

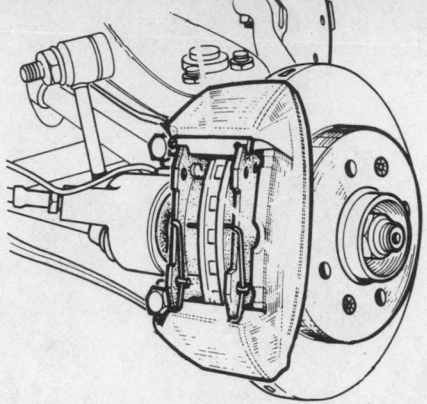

Typical Bendix floating caliper disc brake assembly

18. Insert the wire clip locks into the holes in the guide pins or retaining pin.

19. Refill the master cylinder with fresh brake fluid.

20. Install the tire and wheel assembly. Pump the brake pedal several times to bring the pads into adjustment. Road test the vehicle. If a firm pedal cannot be obtained, refer to "Bleeding the Brakes".

TYPE 8

Bendix Floating Caliper

This is a single piston unit that floats on guide pins and bellows bushings which are threaded into a mounting bracket. The mounting bracket is bolted to the stub axle

Exploded view of a Type 7 sliding yoke caliper with parking brake

carrier. This caliper is unique in that it is mounted on the leading edge of the brake disc, where most are mounted on the trailing edge.

The caliper does not have to be removed when replacing the brake pads.

PAD REPLACEMENT

1. Raise and support the front of the vehicle on jackstands. Remove the wheel.

2. Siphon a sufficient quantity of brake fluid from the master cylinder reservoir to prevent the brake fluid from overflowing the master cylinder when removing or installing new pads. This is necessary as the piston must be forced into the cylinder bore to provide sufficient clearance to remove the pads.

3. Grasp the cylinder from behind and carefully pull it toward you. This will push the piston back into the cylinder bore.

4. Disconnect the brake pad lining wear indicator wires. Remove the anti–rattle springs.

5. Remove the retaining key clip on the upper side of the caliper. Remove the retaining key.

6. Lift out the brake pads.

7. Inspect the brake disc (rotor) as detailed in the appropriate section.

8. Inspect the caliper and piston assembly for breaks, cracks or other damage. Overhaul or replace the caliper as necessary.

9. Push the piston all the way back into its bore (a C–clamp may be necessary for this operation).

10. Slide the new pads into their original positions.

11. Slide the retaining key into position and replace the clip.

12. Reinstall the anti–rattle springs and the wear indicator.

13. Refill the master cylinder with fresh brake fluid.

14. Install the tire and wheel assembly and then pump the brake pedal several times to bring the pads into adjustment. Road test the vehicle.

NOTE: If a firm pedal cannot be obtained, bleed the system as detailed in "Bleeding the Brakes".

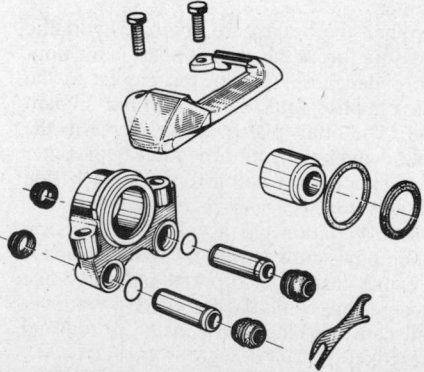

Exploded view of the Bendix floating caliper

TYPE 9

Akebono Floating Caliper W/Parking Brake

This is a single piston unit that floats on guide pins and bushings which are threaded into a mounting bracket. The mounting bracket is bolted to the steering knuckle. This unit also incorporates a parking brake into the caliper.

The caliper does not have to be removed completely in order to remove the brake pads.

PAD REPLACEMENT

1. Raise and support the front of the vehicle on jackstands. Remove the wheel.

2. Siphon a sufficient quantity of brake fluid from the master cylinder reservoir to prevent the brake fluid from overflowing the master cylinder when removing or installing new pads. This is necessary as the piston must be forced into the cylinder bore to provide sufficient clearance to remove the pads.

3. Release the parking brake and disconnect the cable from the caliper lever.

4. Remove the 6 mm lock pin bolt (lower front of the caliper). Loosen and remove the lock pin.

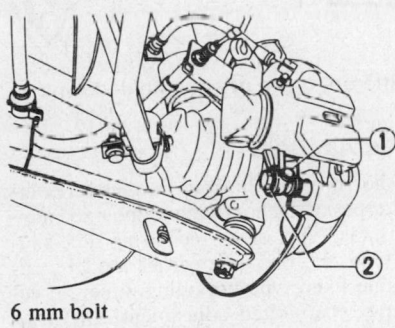

6 mm bolt
Lock pin

Removing the lock pin

NOTE: Do not pull out the lock pin until it is loosened to the position shown in the illustration.

5. The caliper will now pivot on its upper support, swing it up and out of the way.

6. Remove the pads. Note the positions of the pad shims and the inner and outer pad clips.

7. Inspect the brake disc (rotor) as detailed in the appropriate section.

8. Inspect the caliper and piston assembly for breaks, cracks or other damage. Overhaul or replace the caliper as necessary.

9. Turn the caliper piston clockwise into the cylinder bore and align the notches.

NOTE: Do not force the piston into the cylinder bore. The piston is mounted on a threaded spindle which will bend under pressure.

10. Insert the new pads making sure that all shims and clips are in their original positions.

11. Swing the caliper down into position and install the lock pin and the 6 mm bolt.

12. Reconnect the parking brake.

13. Refill the master cylinder with fresh brake fluid.

14. Install the tire and wheel assembly and then pump the brake pedal several times to bring the pads into adjustment. Road test the vehicle.

NOTE: If a firm pedal cannot be obtained, bleed the system as detailed in "Bleeding the Brakes".

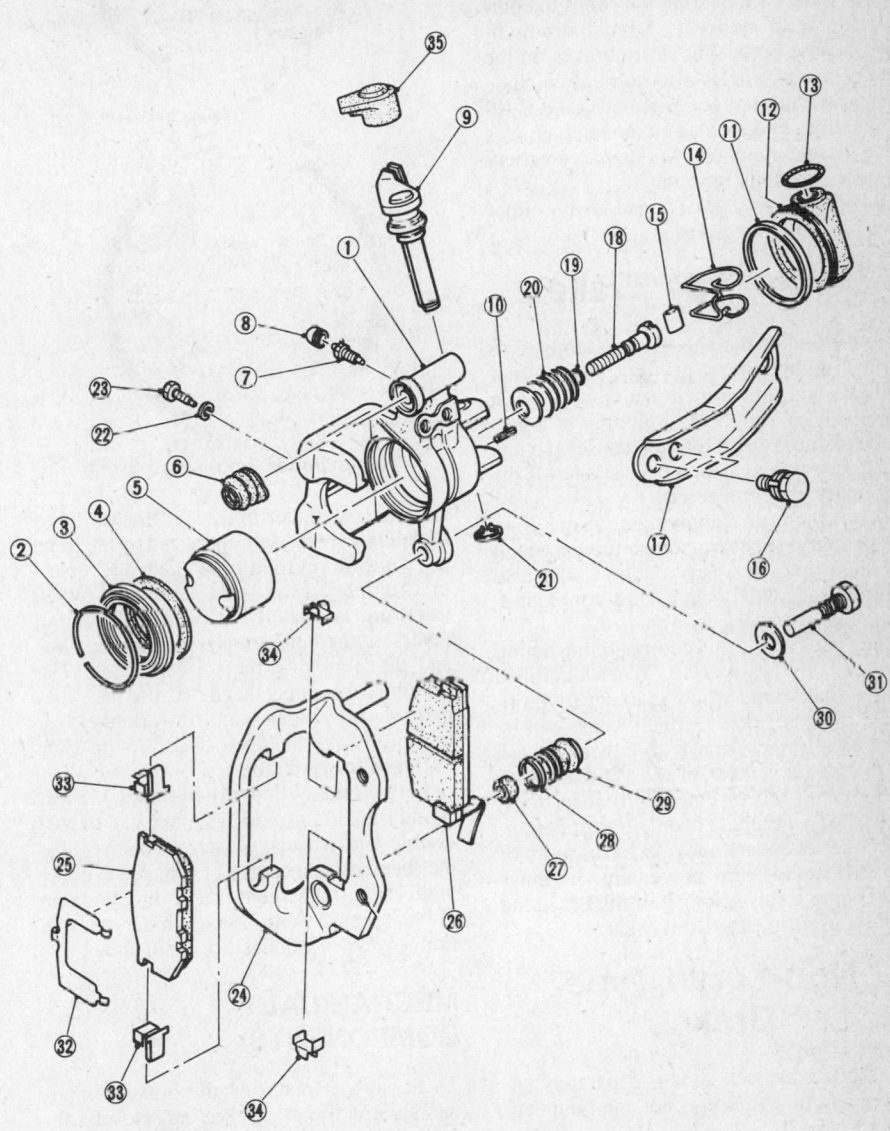

1 Caliper body	13 Gutter spring	25 Outer pad
2 Boot ring	14 Return spring	26 Inner pad
3 Piston boot	15 Connecting link	27 Rubber bushing
4 Piston seal	16 Bolt assembly	28 Retainer
5 Piston	17 Bracket	29 Lock pin boot
6 Guide pin boot	18 Spindle	30 Cone spring
7 Air bleeder screw	19 O-ring	31 Lock pin
8 Air bleeder cap	20 Cone spring	32 Shim
9 Lever & spindle	21 Snap ring	33 Outer pad clip
10 Spring pin	22 Spring washer	34 Inner pad clip
11 Cap ring	23 Bolt	35 Lever cap (upper)
12 Lever cap	24 Support	

Exploded view of the Type 9 floating caliper

SERVICING DRUM BRAKES

A typical drum brake assembly includes a backing or support plate, with one or two wheel cylinders attached to it. Mounted on the backing plate are two lined brake shoes with shoe return springs and hold-down parts, and a means of adjusting the shoes to compensate for lining wear. A brake drum encloses these parts. The drum brakes on the rear of most vehicles also normally include the parts required for parking brakes. All of the drum brakes used on modern vehicles have these components but there is a variety of configurations for each.

Drum brakes are designed to be either "servo" or "non-servo" acting.

Servo Type Brakes

In these brakes the shoes are assembled to form a compound, "primary" and "secondary" shoe unit joined at one end by an adjustable floating link. The drag of a normal (forward) drum rotation causes the primary shoe to leave its anchor and holds the secondary shoe anchored.

All of the forces applying and anchoring the primary shoe are transmitted through the shoe link, in a servo action, and also apply the secondary shoe, thus compounding its braking effect. When the drum is rotated backward, this compounding action of the shoes is reversed. When equipped with a double-end wheel cylinder (two opposed pistons), brake effectiveness can be substantially the same with either forward or reverse movement of the vehicle. With a single-end wheel cylinder (one piston), the brake is energized in only one direction. Since the secondary shoe performs more of the work in forward movement, it shows more lining wear. A longer or thicker lining is often used to offset this wear.

Non-Servo Type Brakes

In these brakes each shoe is separately anchored and their action is not compounded.

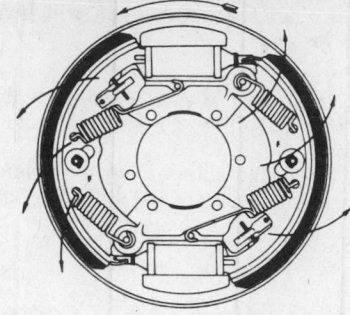

NON-DIRECTIONAL ACTING
Moving Forward

Moving Backward

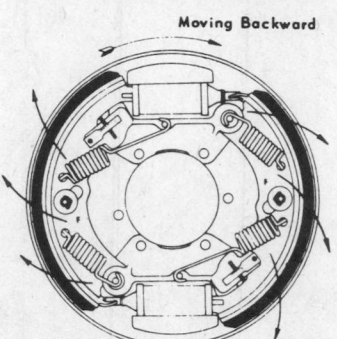

Two cylinder, non-servo brake

On single cylinder brakes a "forward" or "leading" shoe is self-energized by the usual (forward) drum rotation while a "reverse" or "trailing" shoe is de-energized. When the drum is rotated backward, this action reverses, thus energizing the reverse shoe and de-energizing the forward shoe. The lining wear is unbalanced because the shoes perform different amounts of work; the wear is more rapid on the forward acting shoe during a forward stop.

Large two cylinder non-servo brakes, found on certain models, make use of two double-end wheel cylinders which enable the shoes to be anchored or actuated at either end. This arrangement is non-directional in effectiveness. With two-cylinder brakes, lining wear is balanced on both shoes.

MECHANICAL COMPONENTS

To be sure of restoring the brake components correctly after servicing, closely observe the arrangement of shoe hook-up parts as the brake is disassembled. These arrangements may vary on different models. Usually the brake shoes are held in a sliding fit by spring tensions, at rest upon their anchor by the return springs, and against support pads by spring or clip type hold-downs. Opposite the anchor, a star wheel adjuster links the shoe webs and provides a threaded adjustment which permits the shoes to be expanded or contracted. Some rear brakes have adjustable links. The shoes are held against the adjuster by a spring.

Shoe Hold-Downs

Various shoe hold-downs are shown in the illustration.

To unlock or lock the straight pin hold-downs, depress the locking cup and coil spring, or the spring clip, and rotate the pin or lock 90 degrees. On certain lever type adjusters, the inner (bottom) cup has a sleeve which aligns the adjuster lever.

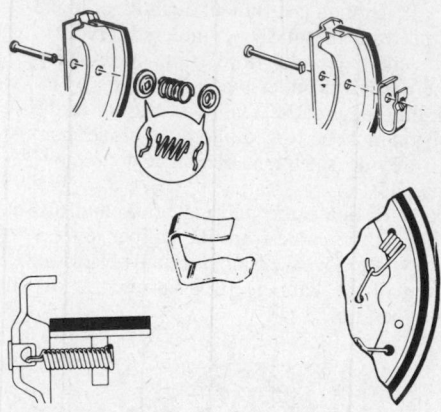

Different types of shoe hold-downs

Shoe Anchors

As shown in the illustration, there are various types of anchors such as the fixed non-adjustable type, or self-centering shoe sliding type, or, on some earlier models, adjustable fixed type providing either an eccentric or a slotted adjustment. On some front brakes, fixed anchors are threaded into or are bolted through the steering knuckle and also support the wheel cylinder.

On adjustable anchors, when necessary to re-center the shoes in the drum or drum

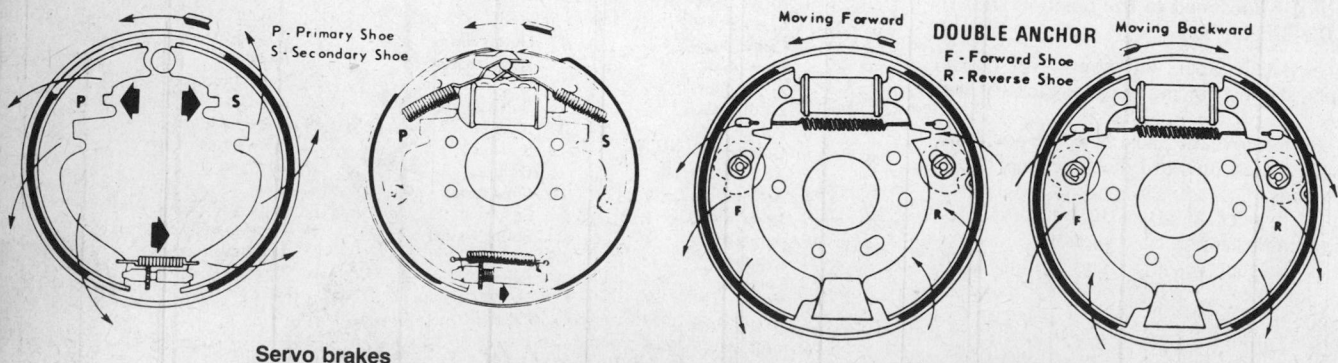

Servo brakes   Non-servo brakes

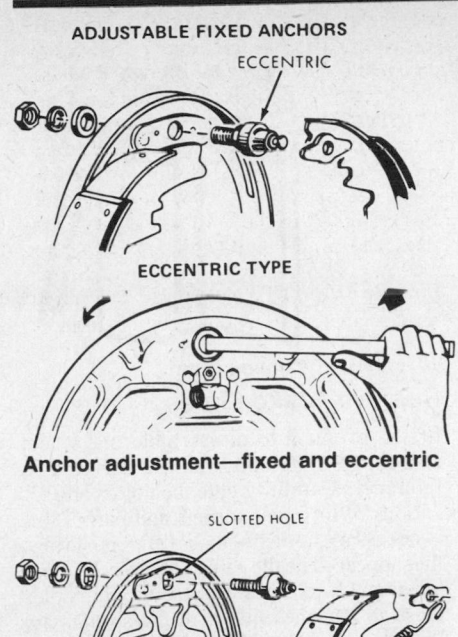

ADJUSTABLE FIXED ANCHORS
ECCENTRIC

ECCENTRIC TYPE

Anchor adjustment—fixed and eccentric

SLOTTED HOLE

SLOTTED TYPE

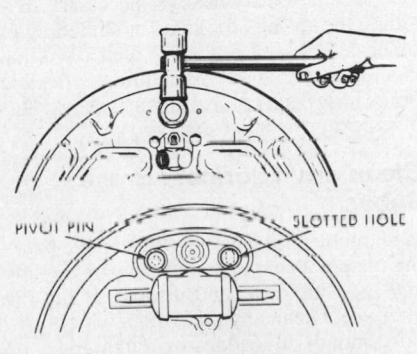

PIVOT PIN · SLOTTED HOLE

PIVOTED SLOTTED TYPE

Anchor adjustment—slotted type

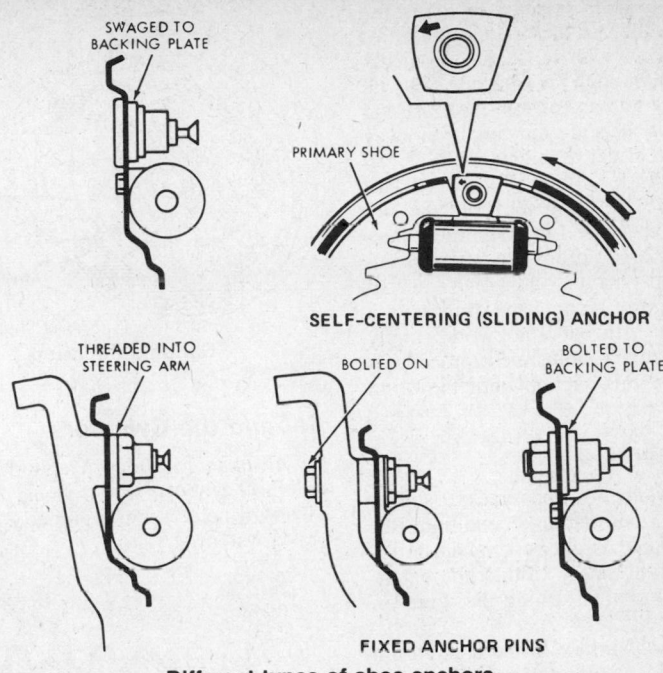

SWAGED TO BACKING PLATE

PRIMARY SHOE

SELF-CENTERING (SLIDING) ANCHOR

THREADED INTO STEERING ARM · BOLTED ON · BOLTED TO BACKING PLATE

FIXED ANCHOR PINS

Different types of shoe anchors

gauge, loosen the locknut enough to permit the anchor to slip out, but not so much that it can tilt.

On the eccentric type anchors, tighten the star wheel to heavy brake drag. Rotate the eccentric anchor in the direction which frees the brake until drag cannot be relieved. Tighten the anchor nut. Back off the star wheel to a normal manual adjustment.

On the slotted type anchor, tighten the star wheel to heavy drag. Tap the support plate until the anchor slips and frees the brake. Repeat this sequence until drag cannot be relieved. Tighten the locknut to the proper torque. Back off the star wheel to a normal manual adjustment.

Brake Shoes

In the same brake sizes, there can be differences in web thickness, shape of web cut-outs and positions of any reinforcements. Some vehicles require shoes made of higher tensile strength steels. Higher strength shoes usually are coded with a letter symbol stamped on the shoe web. Shoes with extra web holes or table nibs or tabs which do not cause interference generally are considered interchangeable with other shoes.

Stops

An eccentric stop under the primary or secondary shoe web on tilted front brakes prevents the shoes from bumping against the drum. Before adjusting the star wheel, loosen the lock nut on the support plate and rotate the eccentric in the forward direction until the shoe drags. Back-off until drag is relieved and tighten the lock nut.

PISTON STOPS

If the brake is equipped with piston stops, the wheel cylinder must be dismounted for reconditioning.

BASIC SERVICE

CAUTION

Do not blow the brake dust out of the drums with compressed air or lung power; always use a damp cloth and wipe it out. Brake linings contain asbestos, a known cancer causing substance. Dispose of the cloth after use.

NOTE: Never work on a car supported only on a jack. Use a hydraulic lift or jack stands to support the vehicle while working.

Raising both front or rear wheels at once and supporting them on jack stands also allows comparison of the brake being serviced to the brake on the opposite side.

Check for Leaks

Press the brake pedal to ensure that there are no leaks in the hydraulic system. If the pedal does not remain hard, and drops to the floor, it is an indication of a leak in the master cylinder, hoses, wheel cylinders, or disc brake calipers. When performing this test, the engine should be running if the car is equipped with power brakes. With power brakes it is normal for the pedal to drop slightly when the engine starts. If it continues to drop, start looking for a leak.

Drum Removal

Safely support the car and release the parking brake if working on the rear axle. Remove the lug nuts, the wheel/tire assembly and then pull off the drums. If the brake shoes have expanded too tightly against the drum, or have cut into the friction surface of the brake drum, the drums may be too

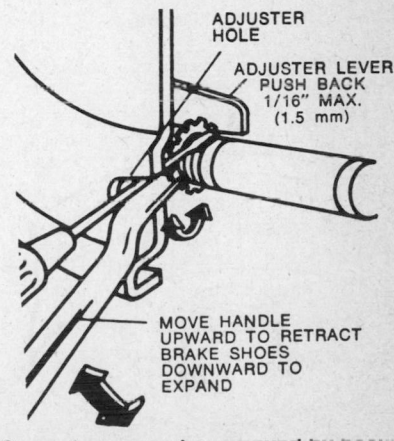

ADJUSTER HOLE

ADJUSTER LEVER PUSH BACK 1/16" MAX. (1.5 mm)

MOVE HANDLE UPWARD TO RETRACT BRAKE SHOES DOWNWARD TO EXPAND

Some drums can be removed by backing off the self-adjuster

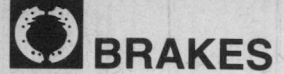
tight for removal. In such a case, adjust the shoes inward before the brake drum is removed. On cars with self-adjusting mechanisms, reach through the adjusting slot with a very small prybar (or similar tool) and carefully push the self-adjusting lever away from the star wheel by a maximum of 1/16″ (1.5 mm). While holding the lever back, insert a brake adjusting tool into the slot and turn the star wheel in the proper direction until the brake drum can be removed. On cars with manual adjusting mechanisms, try lightly tapping the drum with a rubber mallet. If this does not work, simply reverse the manual adjustment procedures given later in this section until the drum can be removed.

Drum Inspection

Check the drums for any cracks, scores, grooves, or an out-of-round condition. Replace if cracked. Slight scores can be removed with fine emery cloth while extensive scoring requires turning the drum on a lathe.

If the friction surface of the brake drum appears scored or otherwise damaged beyond repair, it will require reconditioning. After machining, the drum diameter must not exceed the diameter cast on the drum or 0.060″ (1.5 mm) over the original nominal diameter. Carefully look for signs of grease or oil at the center of the assembly. If any leak is noticed, the seal should be replaced.

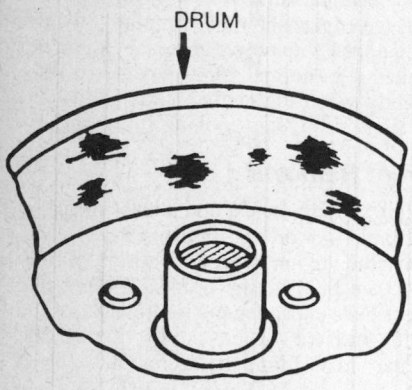

Hard or chill spots

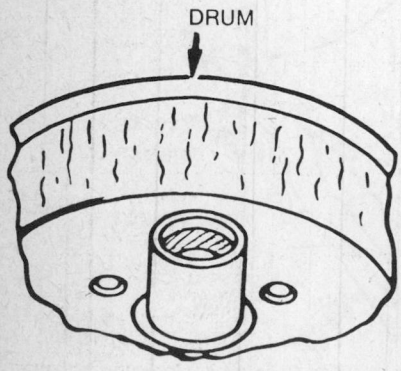

Heat checks

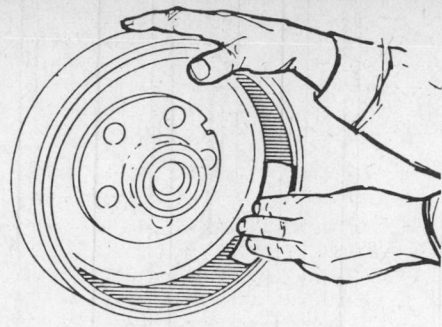

Sanding the drum

Rebuild the Cylinders

It is *always* a good idea to rebuild or replace the wheel cylinders when relining the brakes. This will help assure a properly operating brake system.

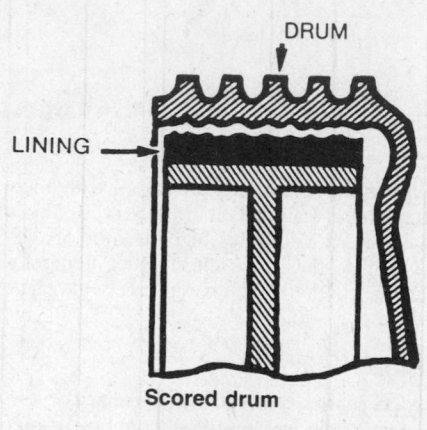

Scored drum

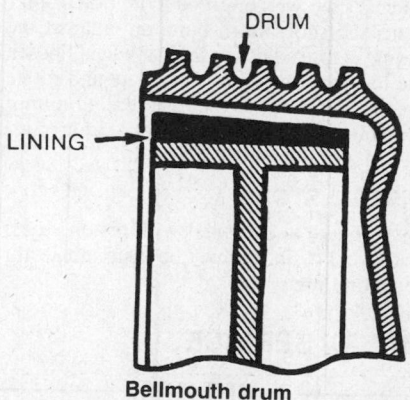

Bellmouth drum

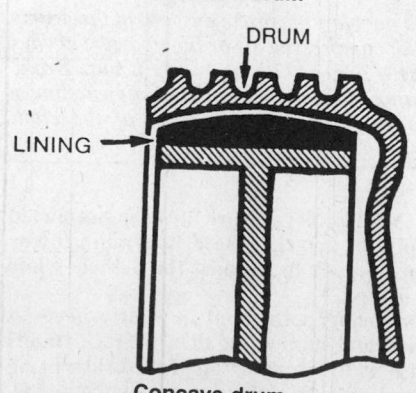

Concave drum

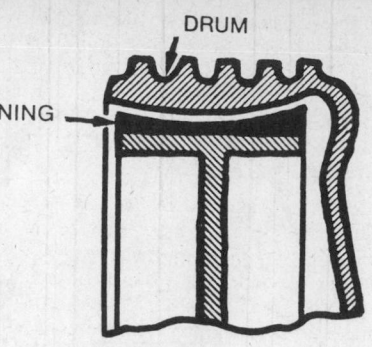

Convex drum

Remove Brake Shoes

It is convenient to disassemble one wheel at a time so the opposite side serves as a reference. Carefully note the colors and locations of different springs and parts. This is necessary to distinguish different springs that appear to be the same but have different tensions. If there are extra unused holes close to the ones in which the springs are located, use a dab of paint or other marking on the new shoes to identify the holes to be used. Replace any discolored springs and other parts found corroded or distorted. Use special tools whenever necessary. Examine the springs for signs of stretching or other defects and replace if their condition is at all questionable. Examine the flexible brake hoses and replace any that show signs of cracking or other damage.

Clean and Lubricate Brake Shoes

With all the brake parts off, clean the backing plate with a damp cloth to avoid raising any asbestos dust, and dispose of the rag after use. Clean any rust with a wire brush. File smooth any ridges or rough edges on the contact points on the backing plate, and lubricate with approved brake lubricant. Clean and lightly lubricate the adjuster threads, and screw the adjuster all the way together to facilitate reassembly later on. Wash the wheel bearings with solvent and repack them with the proper grease. Check backing plate bolts to make sure they are tight.

Reassemble and Install Brake Shoes

Reassemble the brakes in the reverse order of disassembly. Make sure all parts are in their proper locations and that both brake shoes are properly positioned in either end of the adjuster. Also, both brake shoes should correctly engage the wheel cylinder push rods and parking brake links, and should be centered on the backing plate. Parking brake links and levers should be in place on the rear brakes. With all the parts in place, try the fit of the brake drum over the new shoes. If not slightly snug, pull it off and turn the star wheel until a slight drag is felt when sliding the drum on. The use of a brake preset gauge will make this job easy. This makes final brake adjustment

simpler. Then install the brake drum, wheel bearings, spindle nuts, cotter pins, dust caps, and wheel/tire assemblies, and make final brake adjustments as specified. Torque the spindle and lug nuts to specifications.

Bleed and Road-Test

Bleed the brakes to make sure of a high, hard brake pedal, and road-test the car. Most self-adjusting mechanisms are activated only during the rearward motion of a car. So, whenever servicing self-adjusting brakes, make sure that the road test includes enough stops, traveling in reverse, to allow the self-

adjusters to perform the proper match-up of all wheels. Or, operate the parking brake several times if that activates the automatic adjuster.

CHILTON TIPS

- The primary brake shoe is the one toward the front of the car, and its lining is usually shorter than that on the secondary (rearward) shoe.
- Self-adjusting mechanisms are usually mounted on the secondary shoe.
- The star wheel part of an adjuster usually (but not always) goes toward the

rear of the car.
- Different color springs belong in different locations.
- Self-adjusters and related parts are not interchangeable from one side of a car to the other since the direction of adjuster rotation varies from one side of a car to the other. Most adjusters on one side of a car have right hand threads, and the adjusters on the other side have left hand threads.
- Never press the brake pedal when one or more brake drums are off, or a wheel cylinder will pop apart.

DRUM BRAKE APPLICATION CHART

Make	Year/Model	Reference Number	Adjuster Type
Audi	'78–'79 Fox '78 5000	13	Manual (star wheel)
	'80–'85 4000 '79–'84 5000	12	Automatic
BMW	'78–'83 320i	5	Manual (cam type)
Chrysler	'78–'84 Challenger/Sapporo, Arrow, Colt (rear wheel drive)	9	Automatic
	'79–'85 Colt/Champ (front wheel drive)	14	Automatic
Datsun/Nissan	'78 280Z	7	Automatic
	'82–'85 Sentra, Pulsar	14	Automatic
	'78–'85 All Others	15	Automatic
Fiat	'78–'82 128, 131, Strada	5, 6①	Manual (cam type), Automatic
Honda	'78–'79 Civic '80–'85 Civic	8 11	Manual (bolt type) Automatic
	'78–'81 Accord '82–'85 Accord	8 3	Manual (bolt type) Semi-Automatic
	'79–'82 Prelude '83 Prelude	11 3	Automatic Semi-Automatic
Isuzu	'81–'85 All	9	Automatic
Mazda	'78–'83 RX-3, RX-4, RX-7	13	Automatic
	'78–'80 808, GLC	1	Manual
	'81–'85 GLC	15	Automatic
	'82 626 '83–'85 626	13 11	Automatic Automatic
Mitsubishi	'83–'85 Cordia, Tredia	9	Automatic
Porsche	'78–'82 924	1	Manual
Renault	'81–'85 18i, Fuego, Sportwagon	9	Automatic
	'78–'83 Le Car '82–'85 Alliance	5 3	Manual (cam type) Semi-Automatic
Subaru	'78–'84 All	8	Manual (bolt type)

DRUM BRAKE APPLICATION CHART

Make	Year/Model	Reference Number	Adjuster Type
Toyota	'78–'85 Celica/Supra	3	Semi-Automatic
	'78–'85 All Others	3, 4, 5, 6, 14②	Semi-Automatic, Manual (star wheel), Manual (bolt type), Automatic, Automatic
Volkswagen	'78–'85 Types 1 & 2	1	Manual
	'78–'85 Rabbit, Scirocco, Jetta, Dasher, Quantum	10, 12②	Manual (star wheel), Automatic

① Due to the large number of different models covered in each section, slight differences in brake hardware and/or appearance may occur. The basic procedure as given, though, will apply to all models covered.

② When more than one reference number is given, compare the brake being serviced with those illustrated in each section until the correct one is found.

TYPE 1

Lockheed Non–Servo—Manual Adjuster

This brake consists of non-servo forward and reverse shoes with a double-end type wheel cylinder. The shoes anchor upon the slotted adjusting screws which permit them a sliding self centering action. Brakes are mounted with cylinder and adjuster hori-zontally (VW front), or with the cylinder at the top and the adjuster at the bottom.

REMOVAL & INSTALLATION

1. Raise the front/rear of the vehicle and support it on jackstands. Remove the tire and wheel.
2. Remove the drums (some vehicles may require special pullers).
3. Detach both retracting springs.
4. Remove the hold-down springs and lift the brake shoes from the backing plate. On the rear wheels, unhook the parking brake cable from parking brake lever before shoe removal.

5. Clean and lubricate the backing plate as detailed earlier.
6. Check the wheel cylinder for frozen pistons or fluid leaks. If any are found, rebuild or replace the cylinder. Disassemble the adjusters and clean and lubricate them.
7. Install the parking brake lever on a new reverse shoe (only on rear wheel brakes).
8. Place new brake shoes on the backing plate and attach the hold-down springs.

NOTE: Slots in the adjusting screws must be slanted toward the center of the assembly.

The ends of the shoes should engage the wheel cylinder piston slots, and the adjuster slots. If the adjuster screw ends have a slot with a bevel on one side. Make sure the bevel lines up with the bevel on the shoe web.

The end of the shoe with a slot for the parking strut should be installed near the wheel cylinder.

9. For rear wheels, hook the parking brake lever on the parking brake cable and then install the parking brake strut.
10. Install the heavier retracting spring between the toe or cylinder ends of the brake shoes.
11. Attach the lighter retracting spring to the heel or anchor ends of the shoes.
12. Replace the drums, bleed and adjust the assembly and road test the car.

ADJUSTMENT

Insert an adjusting spoon or a small screwdriver through the adjusting hole in the backing plate and expand the shoe assembly by revolving the notched adjusting wheel in a clockwise direction when facing the

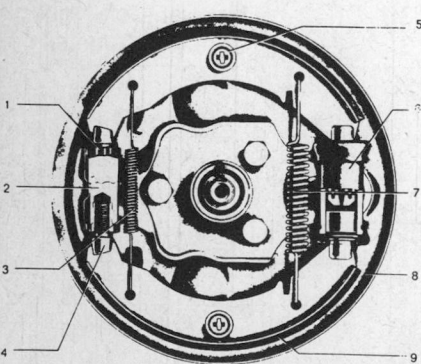

Front wheel brake

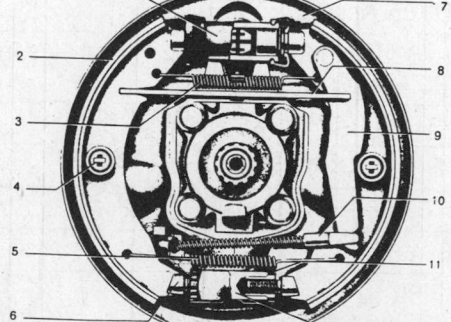

Rear wheel brake

FRONT
1. Adjusting screw
2. Anchor block
3. Front return spring
4. Adjusting nut
5. Guide spring with cup and pin
6. Cylinder
7. Rear return spring

8. Back plate
9. Brake shoe with lining

REAR
1. Cylinder
2. Brake shoe with lining
3. Upper return spring
4. Spring with cup and pin

5. Lower return spring
6. Adjusting screw
7. Back plate
8. Connecting link
9. Lever
10. Brake cable
11. Adjusting nut
12. Anchor block

Typical Lockhead non–servo drum brake assembly (left—front brakes; right—rear brakes)

Rear drum brake shoe adjusters are found behind the two lower rubber plugs on the backing plate. The two higher plugs (if so equipped) are removed to check brake shoe wear

end of the wheel cylinder. Adjust the shoe until a heavy drag is felt when turning the wheel and drum; then, back off the adjustment until the wheel spins freely. Adjust one shoe at a time and repeat this procedure at all brake shoes.

TYPE 2

Girling Non–Servo Sliding Cylinder— Manual Adjuster

This brake consists of non–servo forward and reverse shoes with a single–end type sliding wheel cylinder. The brakes are mounted with the cylinder at the bottom and the anchor plate/adjuster at the top.

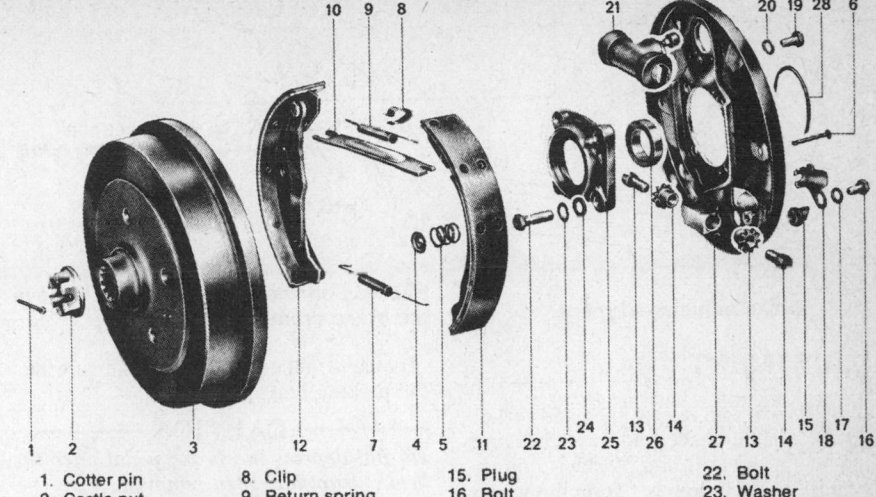

1. Cotter pin	8. Clip
2. Castle nut	9. Return spring
3. Brake drum	10. Pressure rod
4. Spring retainer	11. Brake shoe
5. Spring	12. Brake lever
6. Pin	13. Adjusting screw
7. Return spring	14. Adjusting nut

15. Plug	22. Bolt
16. Bolt	23. Washer
17. Lockwasher	24. Plain washer
18. Holder	25. Cover
19. Bolt	26. Spacer
20. Lockwasher	27. Brake carrier
21. Wheel brake cylinder	28. Seal

Exploded view of a Type 1 drum brake

REMOVAL & INSTALLATION

1. Raise the rear of the vehicle and support it with jackstands. Remove the tire and wheel.

2. Remove the brake drums.

3. Remove the brake shoes by prying one shoe out of the groove in the wheel cylinder (use a small prybar). Both shoes and retracting springs can now be removed from the backing plate.

4. Check the wheel cylinder for a frozen piston or leaks. If any are found, rebuild or replace the wheel cylinder.

5. Clean component parts and lubricate the backing plate.

6. To replace lined shoes on the backing plate, hook the retracting springs to the shoes and mount them in the adjuster and wheel cylinder slots.

7. Back off all adjustment on the adjusting mechanism.

8. Replace the drums. Center the brake shoes in the drum by depressing the brake pedal a few times.

9. Adjust and bleed brakes.

10. Road test the car.

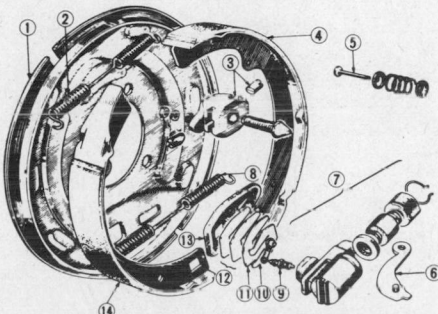

1. Brake disc	8. Return spring cylinder side
2. Return spring adjuster side	9. Bleeder
3. Brake shoe adjuster	10. Lock plate A
4. Brake shoe assembly-fore	11. Lock plate B
5. Anti-rattler pin	12. Lock plate C and D
6. Lever	13. Dust cover
7. Rear wheel cylinder	14. Brake shoe assembly-after

Exploded view of a Type 2 drum brake

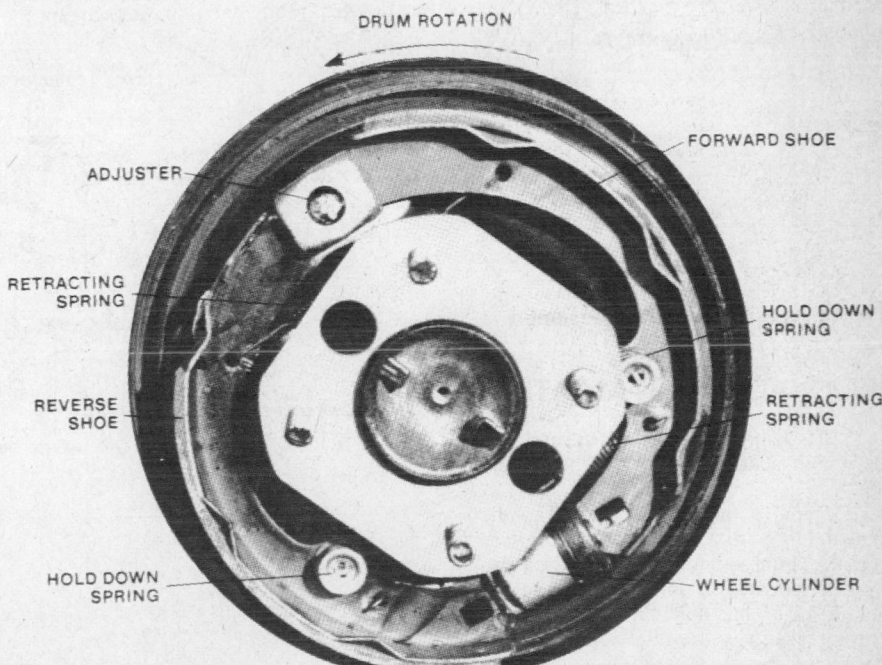

Typical Girling sliding cylinder brake assembly

Brake adjuster—Type 2

ADJUSTMENT

Jack up the car and release the hand brake. Turn the square-headed adjuster (backing plate side at the top) in a clockwise direction until a heavy drag is felt on the wheel and drum, then back off until the wheel spins freely.

TYPE 3

Non–Servo—Semi–Automatic Adjuster

This brake consists of non–servo forward and reverse shoes with a double–ended type wheel cylinder. The brake shoes are adjusted automatically whenever the parking brake is applied.

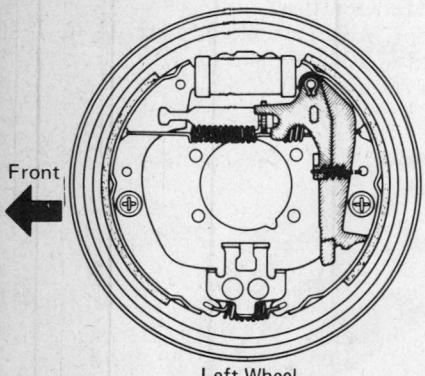

Left Wheel

Typical Type 3 drum brake assembly

REMOVAL & INSTALLATION

1. Raise the rear of the vehicle and support it with jackstands. Remove the tire and wheel.

2. Remove the brake drum. Tap the drum lightly with a mallet in order to free it. If the drum cannot be removed easily, insert a screwdriver into the hole in the backing plate and hold the automatic adjusting lever away from the adjusting bolt. Using another screwdriver, relieve the brake shoe tension by turning the adjusting bolt clockwise. If the drum still will not come

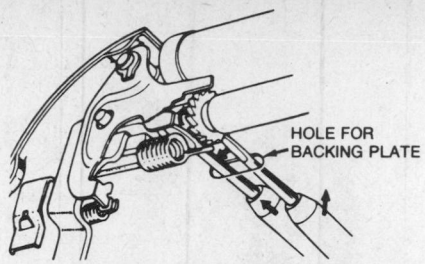

Backing off the brake shoes to remove the brake drum—Type 3

off, use a puller; but first make sure that the parking brake is released.

CAUTION
Do not depress the brake pedal once the brake drum has been removed.

---

3. Unhook the shoe tension springs from the shoes with the aid of a brake spring removing tool.

4. Remove the brake shoe securing springs.

5. Disconnect the parking brake cable at the parking brake shoe lever.

6. Withdraw the shoes, complete with the parking brake shoe lever.

7. Unfasten the C-clip and remove the adjuster assembly from the shoes.

8. Inspect the shoes for wear and scoring.

9. Check the wheel cylinder for frozen pistons or fluid leaks. If any are found, rebuild or replace the wheel cylinder.

10. Clean and inspect all parts. Lubricate the backing plate bosses and anchor plate.

11. Check the tension springs to see if they are weak, distorted or rusted.

12. Inspect the teeth on the automatic adjuster wheel for chipping or other damage.

Installation is performed in the following order:

NOTE: Grease the point of the shoe which slides against the backing plate. Do not get grease on the linings.

1. Attach the parking brake shoe lever and the automatic adjuster lever to the rear side of the shoe.

2. Fasten the parking brake cable to the lever on the brake shoe.

3. Install the automatic adjuster and fit the tension spring on the adjuster lever.

4. Install the securing spring on the *rear* shoe and then install the securing spring on the *front* shoe.

NOTE: The tension spring should be installed on the anchor, before performing Step 4.

5. Hook one end of the tension spring over the rear shoe with the tool used during removal; hook the other end over the front shoe.

CAUTION
Be sure that the wheel cylinder boots are not being pinched in the ends of the shoes.

---

6. Test the automatic adjuster by operating the parking brake shoe lever.

7. Install the drum and adjust the brakes.

ADJUSTMENT

These brakes are equipped with automatic adjusters actuated by the parking brake

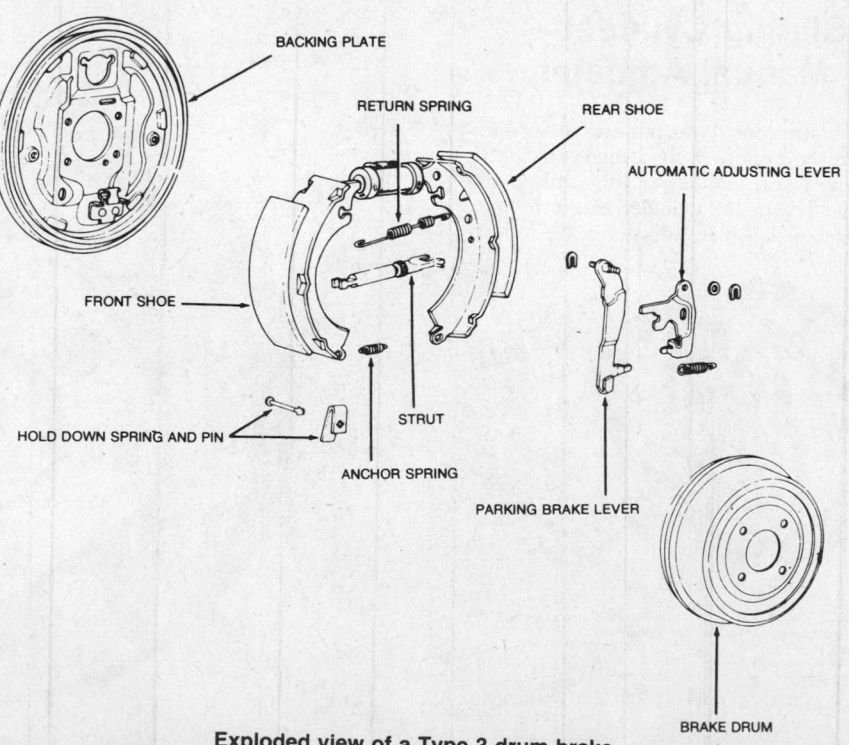

Exploded view of a Type 3 drum brake

mechanism. No periodic adjustment of the drum brakes is necessary if this mechanism is working properly. If the brake shoe to drum clearance is incorrect, and applying and releasing the parking brake a few times does not adjust it properly, the parts will have to be disassembled for repair.

TYPE 4

Non–Servo—Manual Adjuster

This brake is a non–servo unit with two single-piston wheel cylinders that act upon an individual shoe.

REMOVAL & INSTALLATION

1. Raise the rear of the vehicle and support it with jackstands. Remove the tire and wheel.
2. Remove the brake drum as previously detailed.
3. Remove the retracting springs and hold down spring clips.
4. Lift the shoes off of the backing plate.
5. Check the wheel cylinders for frozen pistons or leaks. If any are found, the wheel cylinder must be rebuilt or replaced.
6. Clean the backing plate and lubricate the bosses and bearing ends of the new shoes.
7. Place the new shoes in the slots of the wheel cylinders and the adjusters. Install the hold down spring clips.
8. Install the retracting springs. The blue, lighter weight spring is installed to the piston side of the shoe; the black, heavier weight spring to the adjuster side of shoe.
9. The shoes must slide freely in the slots.
10. Replace the drum and wheel; bleed and adjust the brake.
11. Road test the car.

ADJUSTMENT

Adjust each shoe individually by rotating the notched adjuster (backing plate side) until a heavy drag is felt when turning the wheel and drum in a forward direction. Back off the adjuster until the wheel spins freely.

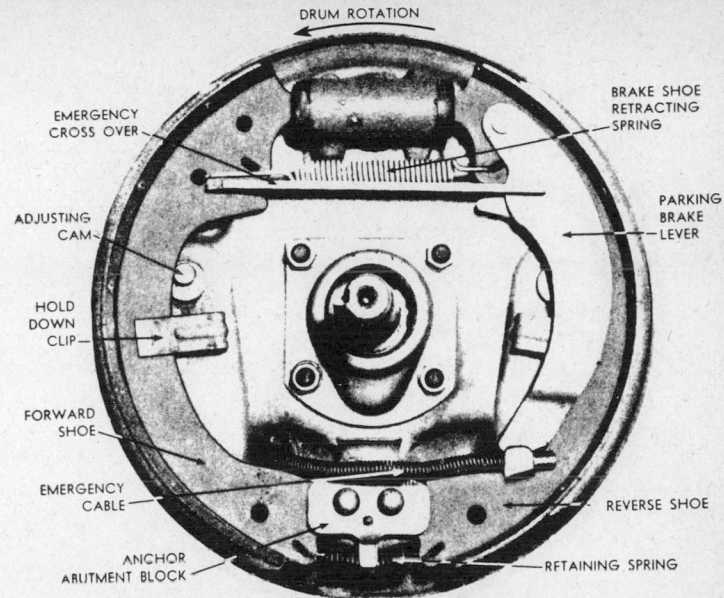

Typical Bendix drum brake assembly with self–centering shoes

TYPE 5

Bendix Non–Servo, Self–Centering— Manual Adjuster

This brake consists of non–servo forward and reverse shoes with a double–ended type wheel cylinder. The brake shoes are self–centering by means of an anchor block and two adjusting cams.

REMOVAL & INSTALLATION

1. Raise the rear of the vehicle and support it with jackstands. Remove the tire and wheel.
2. Remove the brake drums as previously detailed.
3. Remove the retracting spring (and hold-down springs, if used) and lift the shoe assembly from the backing plate. On the rear wheels, unhook the parking brake cable from the parking brake lever.
4. Separate the shoes by removing the connecting spring.
5. Check the wheel cylinder for frozen pistons or leaks. If any are found, rebuild or replace the cylinder.
6. Clean and lubricate the backing plate bosses and hold down clips.
7. Install the parking brake lever on the new reverse shoe.
8. Attach the connecting spring to the heel ends of the shoes.
9. Mount the shoes on the backing plate. For the rear wheels, hook the parking brake lever on the parking brake cable and install the parking brake strut.

Typical Type 4 drum brake assembly

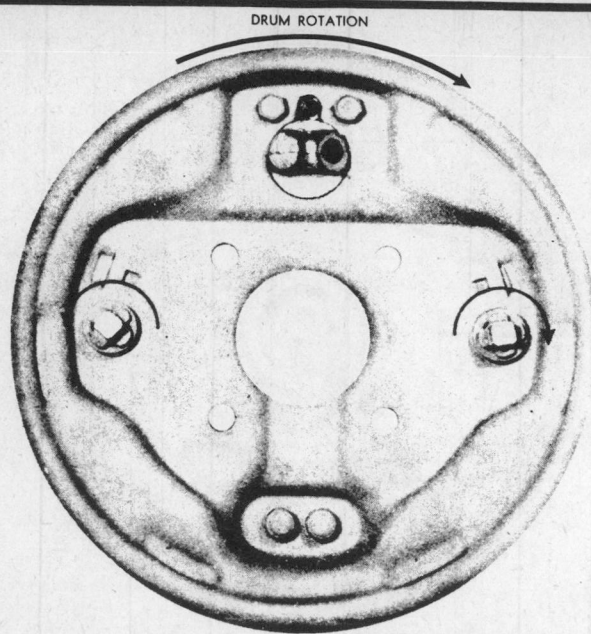

DRUM ROTATION

Adjustment of the Type 5 brake shoes is made by means of adjusting cams found on the backing plate

10. Attach the retracting spring to the toe ends of the shoes.

11. Replace the drums. Center the shoes in the drums by depressing the pedal.

12. Bleed and adjust the brakes.

13. Road test the car.

ADJUSTMENT

Because of the self-centering feature of this brake, only minor adjustments to compensate for lining wear are necessary.

1. Jack up the car and support it with jackstands.

2. See that the parking brake lever is in the fully released position. Check the rear brake shoes to make certain they have not been moved away from the adjusting cams (partially applied) by improper adjustment of the cable (or cables) or by a sticking cable. If the shoes are not resting against the adjusting cams, back off or disconnect the parking brake cable.

3. Expand the brake shoes by turning the adjusting cams. If the adjusting cams have lock nuts, loosen the lock nut. Spin the wheel, while turning the adjusting cam in the proper direction, until a heavy drag is reached and then back the cam off gradually in the opposite direction until the wheel spins freely. When adjusting the forward shoe, spin the wheel in the forward direction. When adjusting the reverse shoe, spin the wheel in the reverse direction.

4. Apply the brake pedal firmly a few times and check all wheels to be sure that they spin freely. If a brake drag is noticed at this point, readjust the brake in accordance with Step 3.

TYPE 6

Bendix Non–Servo–Automatic Adjuster

This brake consists of non–servo forward and reverse shoes with a double–ended type wheel cylinder. The shoes anchor to the slotted anchor plate permitting them a sliding self–centering action.

REMOVAL & INSTALLATION

1. Raise the rear of the vehicle and support it with jackstands, Remove the tire and wheel.

2. Before removing the brake drum, remove the rubber grommet from the adjustment release hole in the backing plate. Insert a small prybar and push down on the adjustment latch. This will allow the shoes to retract and will eliminate possible interference between the brake shoes and brake drum.

3. Remove the brake drum and disengage the automatic adjuster spring from the strut and the reverse shoe. Remove the anti-noise spring.

4. Remove the upper shoe-to-shoe spring.

5. Remove the strut and disengage the shoes from the hold down springs. Check the springs for cracks or fatigue.

6. Unhook the lower shoe-to-shoe spring. Remove the spring and forward shoe assembly.

7. Disconnect the parking brake cable and remove the parking brake lever from the reverse shoe.

8. Remove the adjusting latch and the automatic adjusting lever from the forward shoe. Check for worn or damaged teeth.

To install:

1. Clean and inspect all parts. Replace if necessary.

2. Lubricate the shoe guide pads on the backing plate and the curved edges of the anchor plate.

3. Lubricate the latch pin (long pin) and attach the latch to the outer surface of the forward shoe web.

4. Lubricate the adjustment lever pin (short pin) and attach the adjustment lever to the web of the forward shoe.

5. Lubricate the parking brake lever pin and attach the parking brake lever to the web of the reverse shoe. The reverse shoe has a short lining.

6. Attach the parking brake cable.

DRUM ROTATION

UPPER SHOE TO SHOE SPRING
WHEEL CYLINDER
AUTOMATIC ADJUSTING LEVER
PARKING BRAKE LEVER
PARKING BRAKE STRUT
AUTOMATIC ADJUSTMENT SPRING
FORWARD SHOE
REVERSE SHOE
HOLD DOWN CLIP
HOLD DOWN CLIP
ANTI-NOISE SPRING
ADJUSTMENT RELEASE HOLE
LATCH PIN
ANCHOR PLATE
AUTOMATIC ADJUSTMENT LATCH
LOWER SHOE TO SHOE SPRING
LATCH SPRING

Typical Type 6 drum brake assembly

7. Attach the lower shoe-to-shoe spring to the forward and reverse shoes.

8. Place the forward and reverse shoes in position on the backing plate and install the parking brake strut. Engage the tab on the strut in the slot of the adjustment lever and place the upper ends of the shoe webs against the wheel cylinder pistons.

9. Install the upper shoe-to-shoe spring.

10. Install the automatic adjustment spring. The spring must hold the strut tight against the parking brake lever.

11. Lubricate the inner surfaces of the shoe hold down springs and install the springs over the shoe webs.

12. Install the latch spring over the latch pivot pin. With the adjustment lever against the shoe rim, hook the spring over the latch.

13. Attach the anti-noise spring between the anchor plate and reverse shoe.

14. Install the drum and wheel. Bleed the system if necessary and then road test the vehicle.

ADJUSTMENT

An initial adjustment can be made after the brake drum has been removed and replaced by applying the handbrake several times. Aside from this initial adjustment, the brakes are self—adjusting and no further adjustment should ever be required.

TYPE 7

Non—Servo— Automatic Adjuster

This brake consists of non—servo forward and reverse shoes with a single—end type wheel cylinder. The anchor plate is mounted at the top of the brake plate while the wheel cylinder is at the bottom.

REMOVAL & INSTALLATION

1. Raise the rear of the vehicle and sup-port it with jackstands. Remove the tire and wheel assembly.

2. Remove the brake drum. If it is necessary to retract the shoes in order to remove a worn drum: disconnect the parking brake cable; remove the adjusting hole plug located in the drum; insert a small prybar and pry the adjusting lever away from the adjusting wheel. While holding the adjusting lever away from the adjusting wheel, turn the adjusting wheel with the suitable tool to retract the shoes.

3. Remove the upper shoe-to-shoe return spring.

4. Remove the brake shoe hold-down springs by compressing and rotating the spring 90° while holding the guide pin.

5. Pivot the shoes out of the slots in the upper anchor plate and remove the shoes along with the lower shoe-to-shoe return spring.

6. Check the wheel cylinder for frozen pistons or fluid leaks. If any are found, rebuild or replace the wheel cylinder.

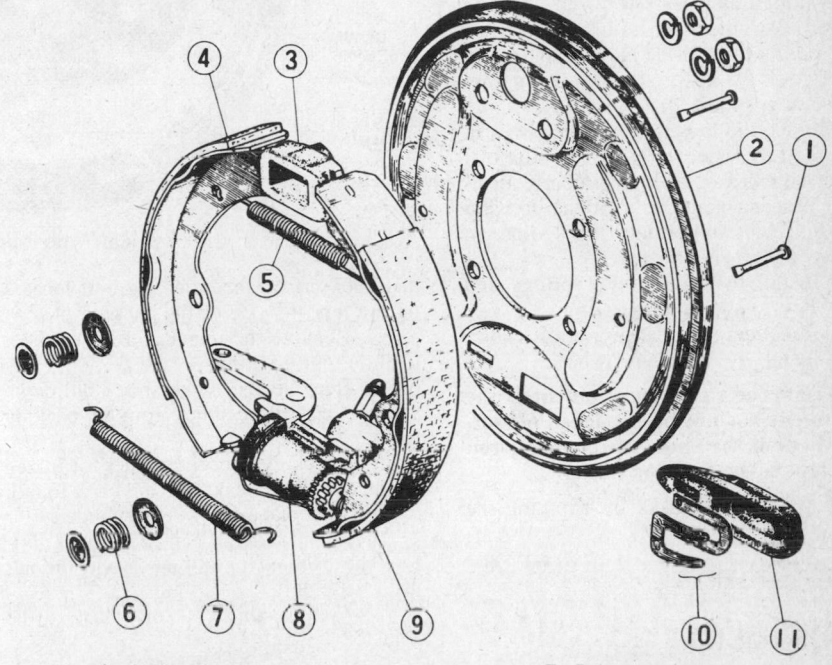

1. Anti-rattle pin
2. Brake backing plate
3. Anchor block
4. After shoe assembly
5. Return spring
6. Anti-rattle spring
7. Return spring
8. Wheel cylinder
9. Fore shoe assembly
10. Retaining shim
11. Dust cover

Exploded view of the Type 7 drum brake

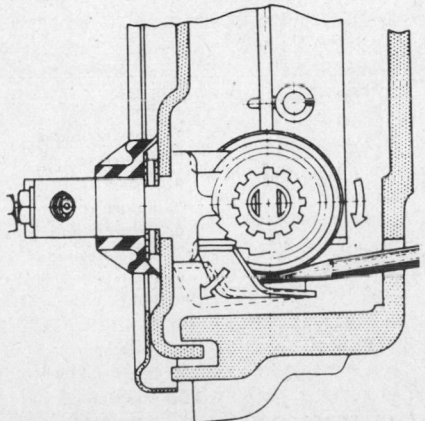

Backing off the adjusting wheel to remove the drum

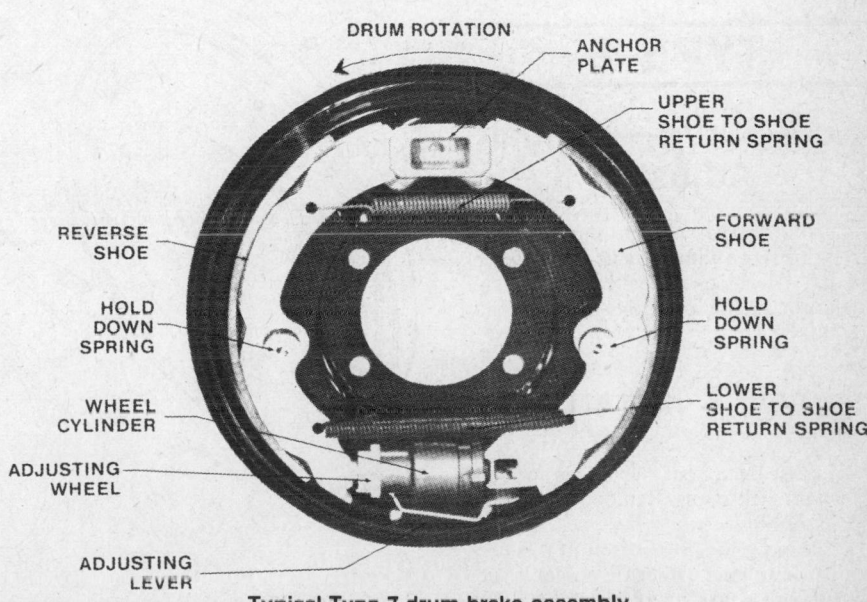

Typical Type 7 drum brake assembly

7. Inspect the old springs. If the old springs are damaged or have been overheated, they should be replaced. Indications of overheated springs are paint discoloration and distortion.

8. Inspect the drum and recondition or replace if necessary.

9. Clean and lubricate the bosses on the backing plate which make contact with the brake shoe. Apply a light coat of lubricant to the upper and lower web of the new shoes.

10. Back off all remaining adjustment on the slotted adjuster screw. Position the adjuster lever under the adjuster wheel, so that it points toward the backing plate.

11. Hook the lower shoe-to-shoe spring into the new shoes.

12. Place the lower end of the shoes in the slots of the wheel cylinder. Be sure that the parking brake lever is properly positioned in the square hole of the forward shoe. Place the upper end of the shoes in the slots of the anchor plate.

13. Install the hold-down springs and upper shoe-to-shoe return spring.

14. Reconnect the parking brake cable.

15. Install the drum and wheel.

NOTE: The drum may not fit if the adjustment has not been backed off sufficiently or if the shoes are not centered properly on the backing plate.

16. Adjust the brakes by applying the parking brake several times.

17. Bleed the system if necessary and road test the vehicle.

ADJUSTMENT

Other than the initial adjustment with the parking brake described previously, no further adjustments are either necessary or possible.

TYPE 8

Non–Servo—Manual Adjuster

This brake consists of non–servo forward and reverse shoes with a double–ended wheel cylinder. The shoes are held in position by an adjuster/anchor plate and are manually adjusted.

REMOVAL & INSTALLATION

1. Raise the rear of the vehicle and support it with jackstands. Remove the tire and wheel assembly.

2. Remove the brake drum. If it is necessary to retract the shoes in order to remove a worn drum, remove the dust cover

and back off on the adjusting bolt located on the inboard side of the backing plate.

3. Remove the upper and lower shoe-to-shoe return springs.

4. Remove the brake shoe hold-down springs and lift the shoes from the backing plate.

5. Check the wheel cylinder for frozen pistons or fluid leaks. If any are found, rebuild or replace the wheel cylinder.

6. Clean and inspect all parts. Lubricate the backing plate bosses and the adjuster assembly.

7. Apply a thin coat of grease to the adjuster.

8. Back off all adjustment on the adjusting bolt located behind the backing plate.

9. Mount the new shoes to the backing plate and install the brake shoe hold-down springs. Be sure that the webs of the shoes are properly engaged in the parking brake mechanism, adjuster assembly and wheel cylinder.

10. Install the upper and lower shoe-to-shoe return springs.

NOTE: The upper and lower shoe-to-shoe return springs are not interchangeable and must be installed in the proper direction. Use the other wheel for ref-

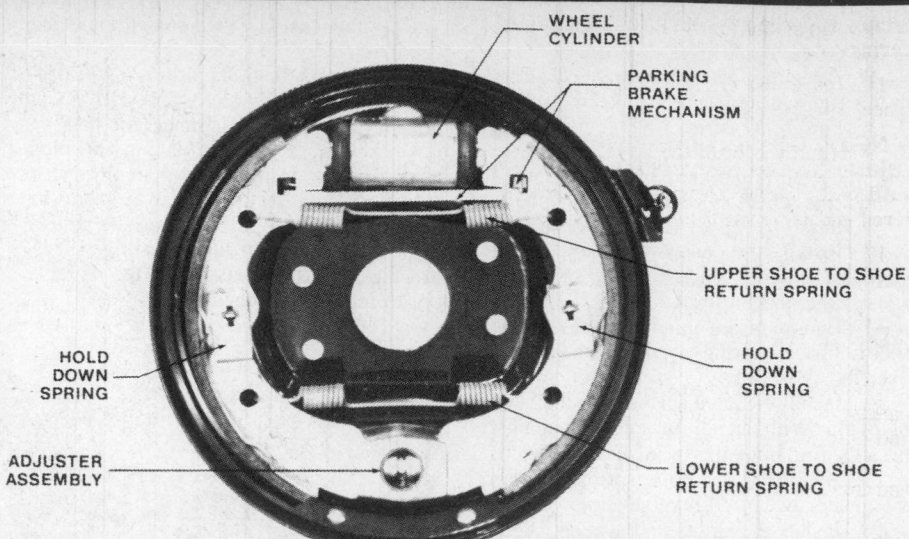

Typical Type 8 drum brake assembly

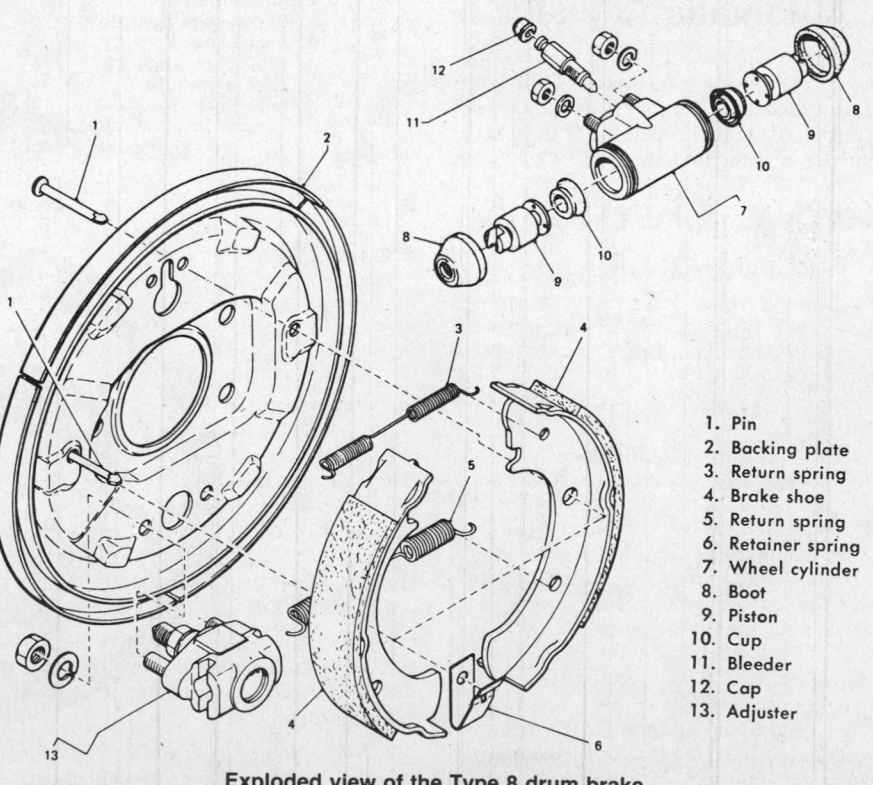

1. Pin
2. Backing plate
3. Return spring
4. Brake shoe
5. Return spring
6. Retainer spring
7. Wheel cylinder
8. Boot
9. Piston
10. Cup
11. Bleeder
12. Cap
13. Adjuster

Exploded view of the Type 8 drum brake

erence if necessary when installing these springs.

11. Install the drum and then install the wheel and tire assembly.

NOTE: The drum may not fit if the adjustment bolt has not been backed off sufficiently or if the shoes are not centered properly on the backing plate.

12. Bleed the system if necessary and then road test the vehicle.

ADJUSTMENT

1. Block the front wheels, release the parking brake, raise the rear of the vehicle and support it with jackstands.
2. Depress the brake pedal several times and then release it.
3. Locate the adjuster on the inboard side of the brake backing plate and turn it clockwise until the wheel will no longer spin.
4. Back off the adjuster (counterclockwise) approximately two (2) turns or until the wheel just begins to turn freely.

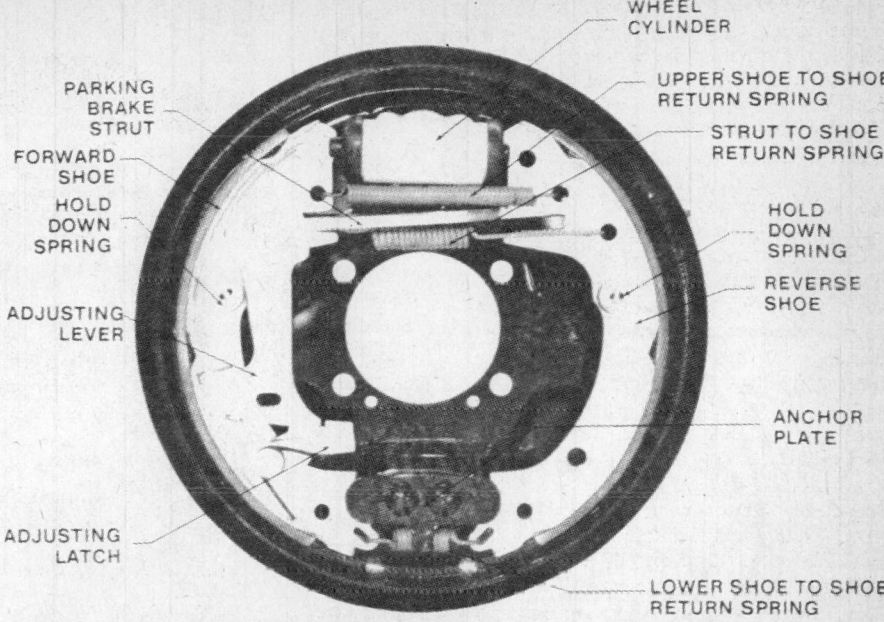

Typical Type 9 drum brake assembly

TYPE 9

Non–Servo— Automatic Adjuster

This brake consists of non–servo forward and reverse shoes with a double–ended wheel cylinder. The shoes are held in position by an anchor plate and are automatically adjusted.

REMOVAL & INSTALLATION

1. Raise the rear of the vehicle and support it with jackstands. Remove the tire and wheel assembly.
2. Remove the drum. If it is necessary to retract the shoes in order to remove a worn drum, insert a small prybar through the hole in the backing plate and press down on the adjusting latch.
3. Remove the brake shoe hold-down springs.
4. Remove the upper strut-to-shoe spring and the upper shoe-to-shoe return spring.
5. Remove the reverse shoe along with the lower shoe-to-shoe return spring.
6. Holding the adjusting latch on the forward shoe downward, pull the adjusting lever toward the center of the brake and then remove the leading shoe assembly.
7. Check the wheel cylinder for frozen pistons or leaks. If any are found, rebuild or replace the cylinder.
8. Inspect old springs. If old springs are damaged or have been overheated, they should be replaced. Indications of over-

heated springs are paint discoloration and distortion.

9. Inspect the drum and recondition or replace if necessary.
10. Check the adjusting lever and adjusting latch for wear and damage. Replace damaged parts.
11. Clean and lubricate the backing plate bosses.
12. Remove the adjusting lever and latch from the forward shoe and install them on a new forward shoe.
13. Before mounting the forward shoe, rotate the adjusting lever outward away from the rim of the new shoe. Engage the adjusting lever with the parking brake strut. Rotate the adjusting lever inward until it touches the rim of the shoe and place the shoe against the backing plate.
14. Install the brake shoe hold-down spring to the forward shoe. Be sure that the web of the shoe is engaged with the slot in the wheel cylinder piston.
15. Hook one end of the lower shoe-to-shoe spring to the forward shoe and the other end to a new reverse shoe. Place the lower part of the reverse shoe on the anchor. Using the lower anchor as a pivot, rotate the reverse shoe upward toward the wheel cylinder and secure it to the backing plate with the hold-down spring.
16. Install the upper shoe-to-shoe spring and the upper strut-to-shoe spring. Be sure that the web of the shoes is properly engaged with the slots in the wheel cylinder piston and parking brake lever.
17. Install the drum and wheel.

NOTE: The drum may not fit if the shoes are partially adjusted outward or if they are not centered properly on the backing plate.

18. Apply the brake pedal a few times to bring the brake shoes into adjustment.

19. Bleed the system and road test the vehicle.

ADJUSTMENT

This brake is automatically adjusted; no adjustment is either necessary or possible.

TYPE 10

Non–Servo—Manual Adjuster

This brake consists of non–servo forward and reverse shoes with a double–ended wheel cylinder. The shoes are held in position by an anchor plate and are manually adjusted.

REMOVAL & INSTALLATION

1. Raise the rear of the vehicle and support it with jackstands. Remove the tire and wheel assembly.
2. Remove the plug from the brake adjusting hole. Using a small prybar or other suitable tool, release the brake shoes by rotating the shoe adjuster downward on the right side of the vehicle and upward on the left side of the vehicle.
3. Remove the brake drum.
4. Remove the parking brake cable from the parking brake lever by compressing the cable return spring.
5. Remove the shoe-to-anchor springs located at the bottom.
6. Remove the brake shoe hold-down clips and pins.
7. Remove the adjuster screw assem-

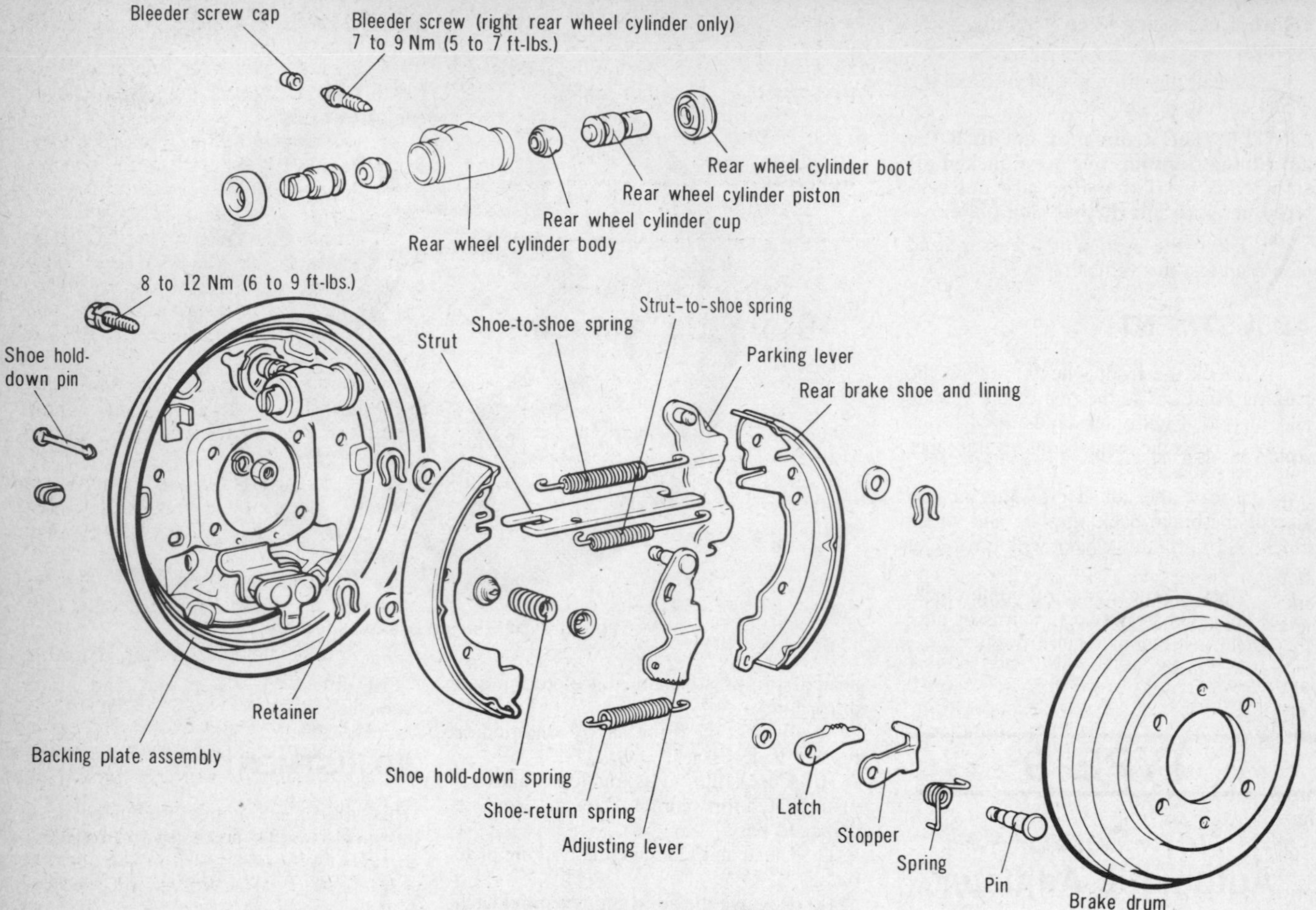

Bleeder screw cap

Bleeder screw (right rear wheel cylinder only)
7 to 9 Nm (5 to 7 ft-lbs.)

Rear wheel cylinder boot

Rear wheel cylinder piston

Rear wheel cylinder cup

Rear wheel cylinder body

8 to 12 Nm (6 to 9 ft-lbs.)

Strut

Shoe-to-shoe spring

Strut-to-shoe spring

Parking lever

Rear brake shoe and lining

Shoe hold-down pin

Backing plate assembly

Retainer

Shoe hold-down spring

Shoe-return spring

Adjusting lever

Latch

Stopper

Spring

Pin

Brake drum

Exploded view of a Type 9 drum brake

bly by spreading the shoes apart making sure that the adjuster screw is fully backed off.

8. Pull the reverse shoe away from the anchor plate to release the tension on the upper return spring. Disengage the shoe and remove the spring. To facilitate the reassembly operation, note how the upper return spring is positioned on the shoe and how it is connected to the hole in the anchor plate.

9. Remove the forward shoe in the same manner as above.

10. Inspect the wheel cylinder and recondition or replace if necessary.

11. Clean and inspect the adjuster screw assembly. Apply a thin coat of lubricant to the adjuster threads.

12. Inspect the old springs. If old springs are damaged or have been overheated, they should be replaced. Indications of overheated springs are paint discoloration or distortion.

13. Lubricate the bosses on the anchor plate which make contact with the brake shoe tabs.

To install:

1. Remove the parking brake lever and attach the parking brake lever to the web of a new reverse shoe.

2. Position the upper return spring on

the forward shoe and hook the other end of the spring into the hole in the backing plate.

3. Rotate the shoe outward with the upper part of the shoe against the wheel cylinder piston and insert the bottom part of the shoe under the anchor plate.

4. Repeat the above procedure for the reverse shoe.

5. With the adjuster screw fully retracted, position the straight forked end of the adjuster screw assembly on the parking brake lever. Make sure that the spring lock

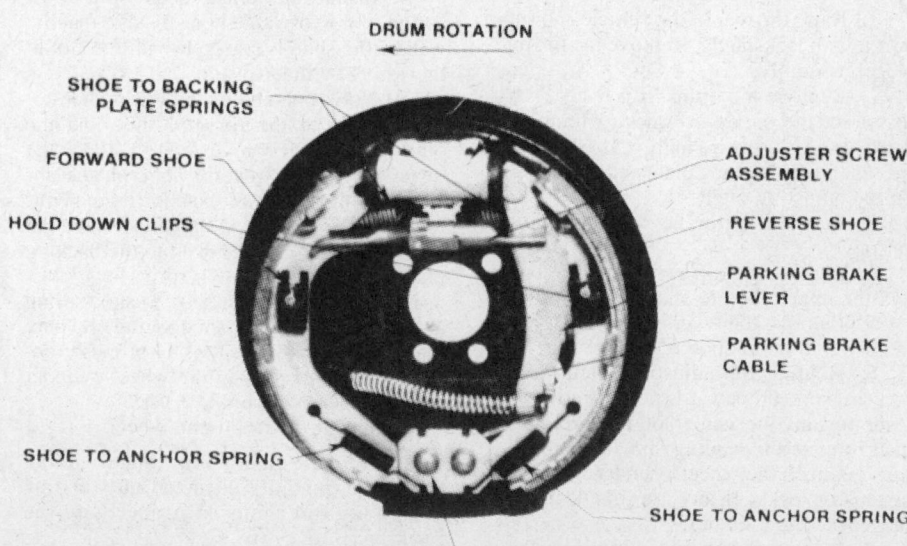

DRUM ROTATION

SHOE TO BACKING PLATE SPRINGS

FORWARD SHOE

HOLD DOWN CLIPS

ADJUSTER SCREW ASSEMBLY

REVERSE SHOE

PARKING BRAKE LEVER

PARKING BRAKE CABLE

SHOE TO ANCHOR SPRING

SHOE TO ANCHOR SPRING

ANCHOR PLATE

Typical Type 10 drum brake assembly

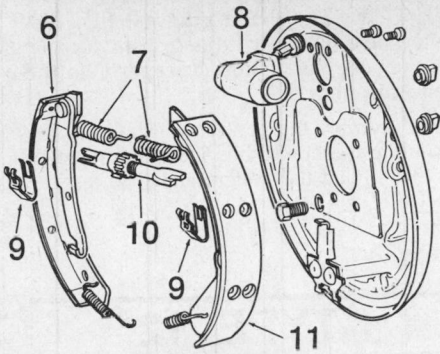

6. Brake shoe with parking brake lever
7. Return spring
8. Wheel cylinder
9. Hold-down spring
10. Adjuster
11. Brake shoe

Exploded view of a Type 10 drum brake

on the adjuster screw is on the outside and away from the adjusting hole.

6. Rotate the bottom of the forward shoe off the anchor plate and insert the curved fork end of the adjuster screw assembly into the web of the forward shoe.

NOTE: Make sure that the curved portion of the forked end is facing downward and that the spring lock is on the outside and away from the adjusting hole.

7. Insert the pins for the hold-down clips through the backing plate and web of the shoes. Install the hold-down clips.

8. Install the shoe-to-anchor springs.

9. Compress the brake cable return spring and attach the cable to the bottom of the parking brake lever.

10. Install the brake drum.

11. Install the wheel and tire assembly.

12. Adjust the brakes.

13. Bleed the system and road test the car.

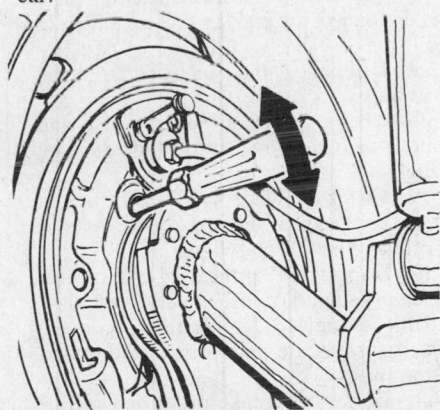

Adjusting the brake shoes—Type 10

ADJUSTMENT

Adjust the brakes through the adjusting hole located in the backing plate. Adjustment is made manually by spreading the adjuster screw assembly which is located directly under the wheel cylinder. Insert a small prybar or other suitable tool through the hole in the backing plate and rotate the adjuster wheel clockwise until the brakes drag

as you turn the wheel in a forward direction. Turn the adjuster in the opposite direction until you just pass the point of drag. Repeat the procedure on the other wheel.

TYPE 11

Non–Servo– Automatic Adjuster

These brakes are a leading-trailing shoe design with a ratchet type self-adjusting mechanism. The shoes are held against the anchors at the top by a shoe to shoe spring. At the bottom the shoe webs are held against the wheel cylinder piston ends by a return spring.

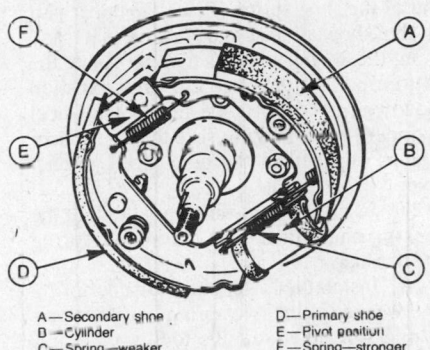

A—Secondary shoe
B—Cylinder
C—Spring—weaker
D—Primary shoe
E—Pivot position
F—Spring—stronger

Typical Type 11 drum brake assembly

The self-adjusting mechanism consists of a spacer strut and a pair of toothed ratchets attached to the primary brake shoe. The parking brake actuating lever is pivoted on the spacer strut.

The self-adjusting mechanism automatically senses the correct lining to drum clearance. As the linings wear, the clearance is adjusted by increasing the effective length of the spacer strut. This strut has projections to engage the inner edge of the secondary shoe via the handbrake lever and the inner edge of the large ratchet on the primary shoe. As wear on the linings increases, the movement of the shoes to bring them in contact with the drums becomes greater than the gap. The spacer strut, bearing on the shoe web, is moved together with the secondary shoe to close the gap. Further movement causes the large ratchet, behind the primary shoe, to rotate inwards against the spring-loaded small ratchet, and the serrations on the mating edges maintain this new setting until further wear on the shoes results in another readjustment. On releasing brake pedal pressure, the return springs cause the shoes to move into contact with the shoulders of the spacer strut/handbrake actuating lever, thus restoring the clearance between the linings and the drum proportionate to the gap shown.

REMOVAL & INSTALLATION

1. Raise the rear of the vehicle and support it with jackstands. Remove the wheel and tire assembly.

2. Disconnect the brake cable from the operating lever at the back of the backing plate. Remove the dust boot from the operating lever.

3. Remove the brake drum. If it is necessary to retract the shoes in order to remove a worn drum, insert a small prybar through the hole in the backing plate and lift the small ratchet lever on the adjuster assembly.

4. Remove the hold-down spring from the reverse shoe by depressing and rotating the washer. Remove the washer, spring and hold-down pin.

5. Twist the reverse shoe outwards and upwards away from the backing plate, taking care not to damage the wheel cylinder dust boot.

6. Unfasten the upper and lower shoe-to-shoe return springs and remove the shoe and springs.

7. Remove the hold-down spring from the forward shoe.

8. Lift the forward shoe along with the parking brake lever and spacer strut assembly away from the anchor plate. The operating lever should slide out of the hole in the backing plate.

NOTE: To facilitate the reassembly operation later on, note how the parking brake lever is attached to the forward shoe.

9. Disengage the parking brake lever and spacer strut assembly from the forward shoe by twisting inward to remove the tension on the spring.

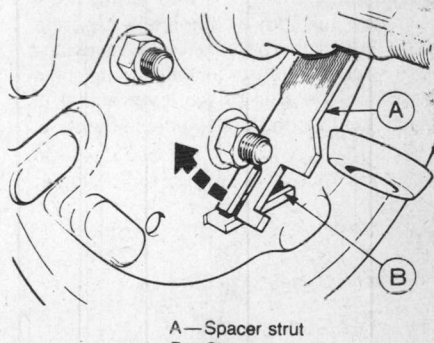

A—Spacer strut
B—Slot

Removing the spacer strut from the carrier plate

10. Disassemble the ratchet assembly from the reverse shoe by first removing the retaining washers. Note how the ratchet levers are assembled so that you can put them back on a new shoe in the same way.

11. Rotate the large ratchet lever outward from under the tension spring and remove the ratchet lever from the shoe.

12. Remove the pressure spring and the small ratchet lever.

13. Check the wheel cylinder for frozen

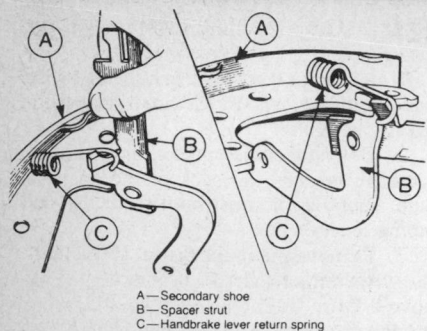

A—Secondary shoe
B—Spacer strut
C—Handbrake lever return spring

Assembling the secondary shoe components

pistons or leaks. If any are found, rebuild or replace the wheel cylinder.

14. Inspect the old springs. If the old springs are damaged or have been overheated, they should be replaced. Indications of overheated springs are paint discoloration and distortion.

15. Inspect the drum and recondition or replace if necessary.

16. Check the adjusting lever and adjusting latch for wear and damage. Replace damaged parts.

17. Clean and lubricate the backing plate bosses.

18. Install the large ratchet on a new reverse shoe and secure it with a new retaining washer.

19. Install the small ratchet and pressure spring on the pivot of the new reverse shoe and secure with a new retaining washer. Be sure that the ratchet rotates and returns freely with spring pressure.

20. Pull back the small ratchet and rotate the large ratchet inward toward the rim of the shoe. Release the small ratchet and slowly rotate the large ratchet lever outward until the hole in the brake shoe web for the hold-down spring becomes completely exposed.

21. Attach the parking brake lever and spacer strut assembly to a new forward shoe. Hook the short side of the lever and strut tension spring to the slotted hole in the shoe.

Hook the long end of the spring to the spacer strut part of the brake lever assembly and rotate the lever assembly until it is attached to the new shoe.

22. Place the forward shoe on the backing plate by inserting the operating lever through the hole in the backing plate. Insert the forked end of the spacer strut into the slotted carrier plate. Rest the upper part of the shoe against the anchor plate and the lower part against the wheel cylinder piston.

23. Insert the hold-down pin through the backing plate and web of the shoe. Install the hold-down spring and washer.

24. Before mounting the reverse shoe, note the slot in the long ratchet lever. The spacer strut must be engaged in the slotted hole in the long ratchet lever when the shoe is mounted to the backing plate.

25. Hook the stronger (thicker) shoe-to-shoe spring through the hole at the top of the already installed forward shoe.

26. Hook the reverse shoe to the other end of the shoe spring. Place the upper part of the shoe against the anchor plate and using the anchor plate as a pivot, rotate the bottom part of the shoe outward. Position the lower part of the shoe against the wheel cylinder piston making sure that the spacer strut is engaged in the hole in the ratchet lever.

27. Insert the hold-down pin through the backing plate. Install the hold-down spring and washer.

28. Install the lower shoe-to-shoe spring (the weaker of the two springs) using a pair of pliers or other suitable tool.

29. Before installing the brake drum, lift the small ratchet lever upwards against the spring. This will allow the long ratchet lever to rotate inward toward the rim of the shoe and provide the clearance needed to install the drum.

30. Replace the dust boot over the operating lever behind the backing plate.

31. Reconnect the brake cable to the operating lever.

32. Install the brake drum and wheel.

NOTE: The drum may not fit if the shoes are partially adjusted outward or if they are not centered properly on the backing plate.

33. Apply the brake pedal a few times to bring the brake shoe into adjustment.

34. Bleed the system and road test the vehicle.

TYPE 12

Non–Servo– Automatic Adjuster

This brake consists of non–servo forward and reverse shoes with a double–ended wheel cylinder. The shoes are mounted by means of hold-down springs and an anchor plate. Adjustment is performed automatically.

REMOVAL & INSTALLATION

1. Raise the rear of the vehicle and support it with jackstands. Remove the tire and wheel assembly.

2. Remove the brake drum.

NOTE: If it is necessary to retract the shoes in order to remove a worn drum, insert a small prybar through one of the stud holes in the brake drum. Retract the adjuster wedge upward by pressing down on the prybar.

3. Remove the adjusting wedge spring.

4. Remove the upper and lower return springs.

5. Remove the hold-down springs.

6. Lift the shoes from the backing plate and disconnect the parking brake cable from the lever.

7. Disconnect the rear shoe from the push bar.

8. Clamp the push bar in a vise and remove the tensioning spring and adjusting wedge.

9. Check the wheel cylinder for frozen pistons or leaks. If any are found, rebuild or replace the wheel cylinder.

10. Inspect old springs. If old springs are damaged or have been overheated, they should be replaced. Indications of overheated springs are paint discoloration and distortion.

11. Inspect the brake drum and recondition or replace if necessary.

12. Clean and lubricate all contact points on the backing plate.

13. Attach the push bar and tensioning spring to the new front shoe.

14. Insert the adjusting wedge so that its lug is pointing toward the backing plate.

15. Remove the parking brake lever from the old rear shoe and attach it onto the new rear brake shoe.

16. Install the push bar onto the rear brake shoe and parking brake lever assembly.

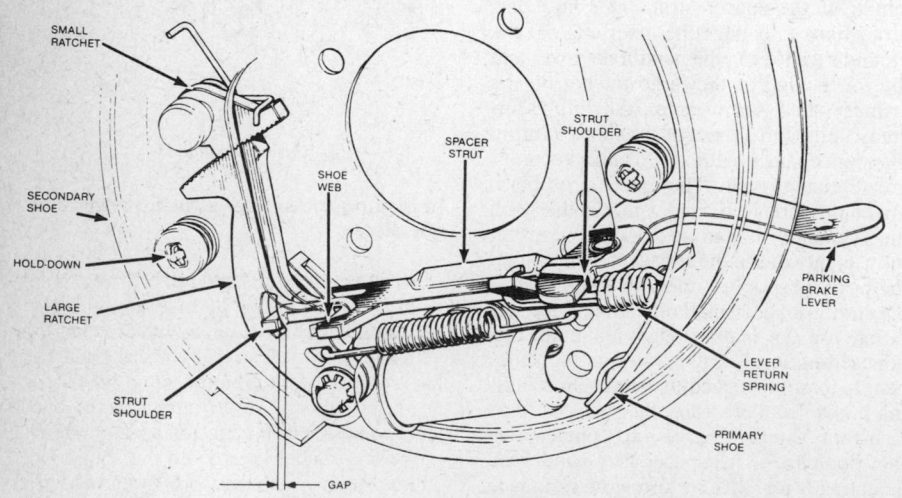

Self–adjusting mechanism

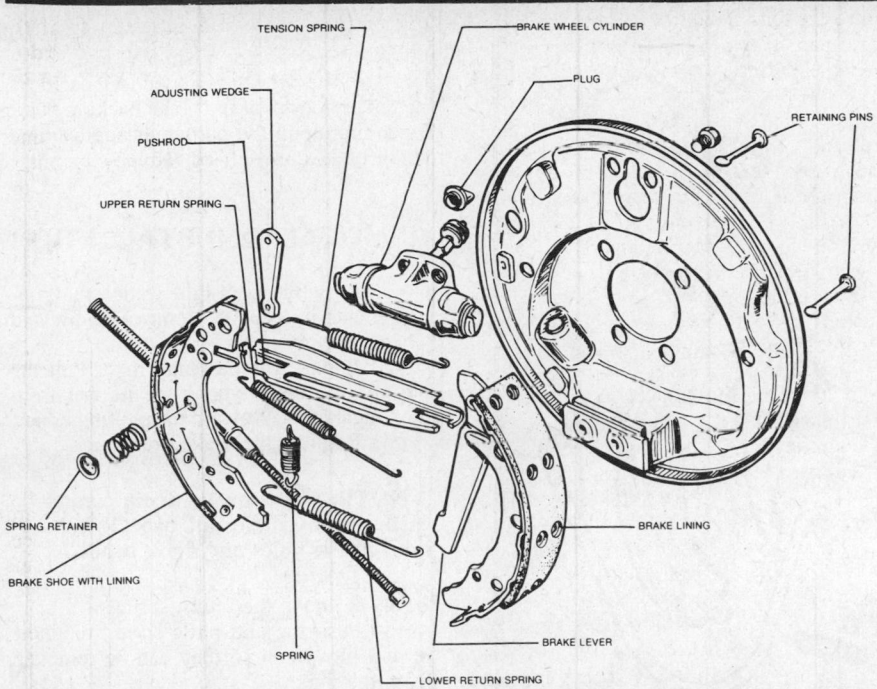

Exploded view of the Type 12 drum brake assembly

(Labels on diagram: TENSION SPRING, BRAKE WHEEL CYLINDER, ADJUSTING WEDGE, PLUG, PUSHROD, RETAINING PINS, UPPER RETURN SPRING, SPRING RETAINER, BRAKE SHOE WITH LINING, SPRING, LOWER RETURN SPRING, BRAKE LEVER, BRAKE LINING)

17. Connect the parking brake cable to the lever and place the whole assembly onto the backing plate.

18. Install the hold-down springs.

19. Install the upper and lower return springs.

20. Install the adjusting wedge spring.

21. Center the brake shoes on the backing plate making sure the adjusting wedge is fully released before installing the drum.

22. Install the drum and wheel assembly and torque the wheel lugs to the manufacturer's specifications.

23. Apply the brake pedal several times to bring the brake shoes into adjustment.

24. Bleed the system and road test the vehicle.

ADJUSTMENT

This brake adjusts itself automatically; aside from the initial adjustments given in the previous section, no adjustments are either necessary or possible.

TYPE 13

Non–Servo–Manual Adjuster

This brake consists of non–servo forward and reverse shoes with a double–ended wheel cylinder. The brake shoes are retained in position by an anchor plate and retaining springs.

REMOVAL & INSTALLATION

1. Raise the rear of the car and support it with jackstands.

2. Remove the wheels and then remove the brake drum.

NOTE: If the drum does not come off easily, the brakes will have to be backed off. First, push the lever on the proportioning valve toward the rear axle to relieve the residual brake pressure. Next remove the plug on the backing plate and turn the adjusting wheel to back off the brake shoes.

3. Use brake pliers to remove the upper and lower return springs.

4. Turn and remove the washers to release the brake shoe retaining springs.

5. Disconnect the parking brake cable by pressing the spring toward the front of the car and unhooking the cable from the brake lever.

6. Lift out the brake shoes. Make sure you take note of how the adjuster mechanism fits into the brake shoe web.

7. Check the wheel cylinder for frozen pistons or leaks. If any are found, rebuild or replace the wheel cylinder.

8. Inspect old springs. If old springs are damaged or have been overheated, they should be replaced. Indications of overheated springs are paint discoloration and distortion.

9. Inspect the brake drum and recondition or replace if necessary.

10. Clean and lubricate all contact points on the backing plate.

11. Fit the adjuster mechanism into the brake shoe web and then position the shoes onto the brake backing plate.

12. Push the retaining pin springs in and turn the washers onto the retaining pins.

13. Squeeze the spring and hook the parking brake cable to the parking brake lever.

14. Install the upper and lower retaining springs.

15. Install the brake drums and wheels and then lower the vehicle.

16. Bleed (if necessary) and adjust the brakes. Road test the vehicle.

ADJUSTMENT

1. Press the lever of the proportioning valve in the direction of the rear axle to relieve the residual brake pressure.

2. Remove the rubber plug from the brake backing plate.

3. Insert a small prybar into the hole and turn the adjusting wheel until the brake linings are just touching the drum.

4. Back off the adjusting wheel 6–8 teeth and replace the rubber plug.

Press the proportioning valve lever in the direction of the rear axle (Audi shown)

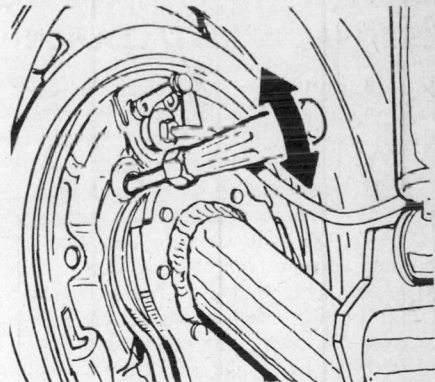

Adjusting the brake shoes—Type 13

TYPE 14

Non–Servo– Automatic Adjuster

This brake consists of non–servo forward and reverse shoes with a double–ended type wheel cylinder. The brake shoes are held

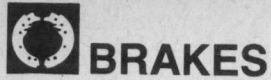
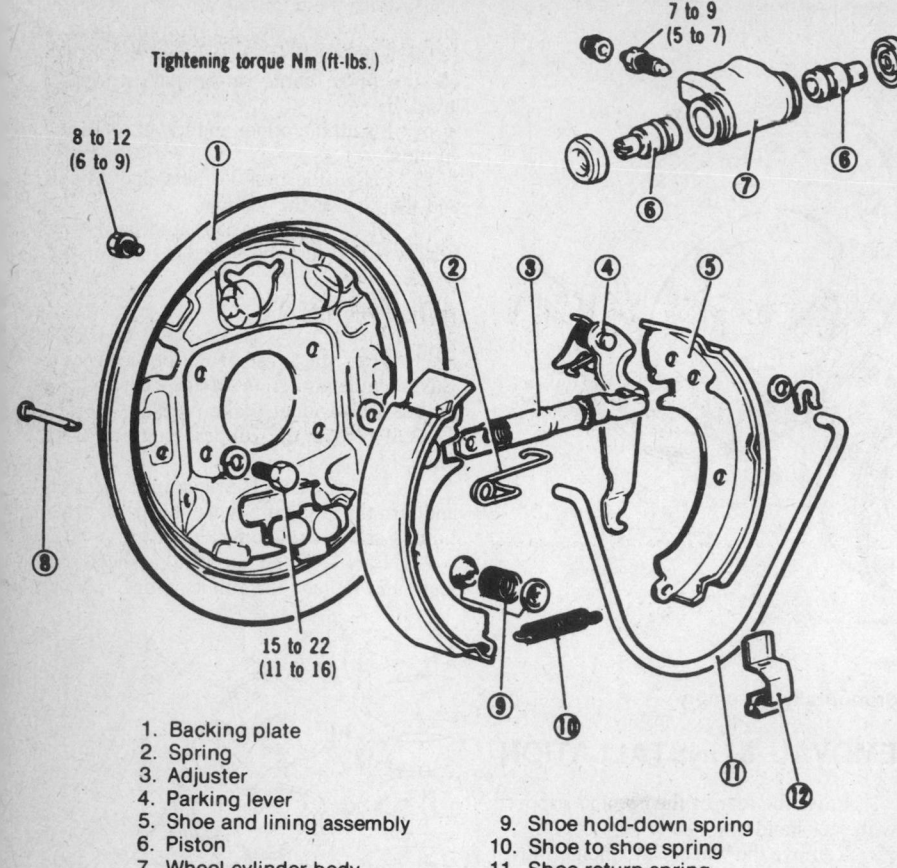

Tightening torque Nm (ft-lbs.)

8 to 12
(6 to 9)

7 to 9
(5 to 7)

15 to 22
(11 to 16)

1. Backing plate
2. Spring
3. Adjuster
4. Parking lever
5. Shoe and lining assembly
6. Piston
7. Wheel cylinder body
8. Shoe hold spring pin
9. Shoe hold-down spring
10. Shoe to shoe spring
11. Shoe return spring
12. Clip spring

Exploded view of the Type 14 drum brake

in position by an anchor plate and two hold down springs. The brakes are self–adjusting.

REMOVAL & INSTALLATION

1. Raise the rear of the vehicle and support it with jackstands. Remove the wheel and tire assembly.
2. Remove the brake drums.
3. Remove the lower pressed metal spring clip, the shoe return spring (the large one piece spring between the two shoes), and the two shoe hold-down springs.
4. Remove the shoes and adjuster as an assembly, Disconnect the parking brake cable from the lever, remove the spring between the shoes and the lever from the rear (trailing) shoe. Disconnect the adjuster retaining spring and remove the adjuster, turn the star wheel in to the adjuster body after cleaning and lubricating the threads.
5. The wheel cylinder may be removed for service or replacement, if necessary.
6. Clean the backing plate with a wire brush. Install the wheel cylinder if it was removed. Lubricate all contact points on the backing plate, anchor plate, wheel cylinder–to-shoe contact and parking brake strut joints and contacts. Installation of the brake shoes, from this point, is the reverse of removal after the lever has been transfered to the new rear (trailing) shoe.

7. Pre-adjustment of the brake shoe can be made by turning the adjuster star wheel out until the drum will just slide on over the brake shoes. Before installing the drum, make sure the parking brake is not adjusted too tightly, if it is, loosen, or the adjustment of the rear brakes will not be correct.
8. If the wheel cylinders were serviced, bleed the brake system. The brake shoes are then adjusted by pumping the brake pedal and applying and releasing the parking brake. Adjust the parking brake stroke. Road test the car.

ADJUSTMENT

The brakes are self-adjusting. Aside from the initial adjustments given in the "Removal and Installation" section, no adjustments are either necessary or possible.

TYPE 15

Non-Servo—Automatic Adjuster

This brake consists of non-servo forward and reverse shoes with a double-ended type wheel cylinder. The shoes are held in position by an anchor plate and anti-rattle springs. The wheel cylinder is located at the top or bottom of the brake backing plate depending upon the particular application. These brakes are self-adjusting.

REMOVAL & INSTALLATION

1. Raise the rear of the vehicle and support it with jackstands. Remove the tire and wheel assembly.
2. Engage the parking brake. Pull the pin out and then remove the stopper from the toggle lever. Release the parking brake.
3. Remove the brake drum.

NOTE: If the brake drum cannot be easily removed, install two (2) bolts (8 mm) in the holes and drive it out.

4. Remove the return springs.
5. Push the anti-rattle spring retainers in and turn them so they can be removed from the pins.
6. Remove the brake shoes.
7. Clean the brake backing plate and check the wheel cylinder for leaks or other damage; replace as necessary.
8. Hook the return springs into the new shoes. The springs should be between the shoes and the backing plate. The longer return spring must be adjacent to the wheel cylinder. A very thin film of grease may be applied to the pivot points at the ends of the brake shoes. Grease the shoe locating buttons on the backing plate, also. Be careful not to get grease on the linings or drums.
9. Place one shoe in the adjuster and piston slots, and pry the other shoe into position.
10. Press and turn the anti-rattle spring retainers onto the pins.
11. Replace the drums and wheels. Adjust the brakes. Bleed the hydraulic system if the brake lines were disconnected.
12. Reconnect the handbrake, making sure that it does not cause the shoes to drag when it is released.

ADJUSTMENT

These brakes adjust themselves automatically with each application of the brake pedal or the parking brake; other than this, no adjustments are either necessary or possible.

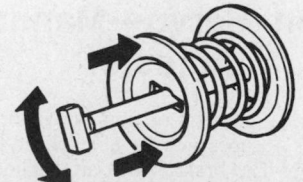

Removing the anti–rattle spring and pin

Troubleshooting and Diagnosis

ENGINE

Gasoline Engine Troubleshooting

See applicable Car or Unit Repair section for specific service procedures

INDEX TO PROBLEMS

Problem Symptom	Begin at Specific Diagnosis, Number
Engine Won't Start	
Starter doesn't turn	1.1, 2.1
Starter turns, engine doesn't	2.1
Starter turns engine very slowly	1.1, 2.4
Starter turns engine normally	3.1, 4.1
Starter turns engine very quickly	6.1
Engine fires intermittently	4.1
Engine fires consistently	5.1, 6.1
Engine Runs Poorly	
Hard starting	3.1, 4.1, 5.1, 8.1
Rough idle	4.1, 5.1, 8.1
Stalling	3.1, 4.1, 5.1, 8.1
Engine dies at high speeds	4.1, 5.1
Hesitation (on acceleration from standing stop)	5.1, 8.1
Poor pickup	4.1, 5.1, 8.1
Lack of power	3.1, 4.1, 5.1, 8.1
Backfire through the carburetor	4.1, 8.1, 9.1
Backfire through the exhaust	4.1, 8.1, 9.1
Blue exhaust gases	6.1, 7.1
Black exhaust gases	5.1
Running on (after the ignition is shut off)	3.1, 8.1
Susceptible to moisture	4.1
Engine misfires under load	4.1, 7.1, 8.4, 9.1
Engine misfires at speed	4.1, 8.4
Engine misfires at idle	3.1, 4.1, 5.1, 7.1, 8.4

SAMPLE SECTION

Test and Procedure	Results and Indications	Proceed to
4.1 Check for spark: Hold each spark plug wire approximately $\frac{1}{4}''$ from ground with gloves or a heavy, dry rag. Crank the engine and observe the spark.	If no spark is evident	4.2
	If spark is good in some cases	4.3
	If spark is good in all cases	4.6

SPECIFIC DIAGNOSIS

This section is arranged so that following each test, instructions are given to proceed to another, until a problem is diagnosed.

SECTION 1—BATTERY

Test and Procedure	Results and Indications	Proceed to
1.1 Inspect the battery visually for case condition (corrosion, cracks) and water level.	If case is cracked, replace battery.	1.4
	If the case is intact, remove corrosion with a solution of baking soda and water. **(CAUTION: Do not get the solution into the battery).** Fill with water.	1.2

DIRT ON TOP OF BATTERY
CORROSION
PLUGGED VENT
LOOSE CABLE OR POSTS
CRACKS
LOW WATER LEVEL

Inspect the battery case

1.2 Check the battery cable connections: Insert a screwdriver between the battery post and the cable clamp. Turn the headlights on high beam, and observe them as the screwdriver is gently twisted to ensure good metal to metal contact.	If the lights brighten, remove and clean the clamp and post; coat the post with petroleum jelly, install and tighten the clamp.	1.4
	If no improvement is noted	1.3

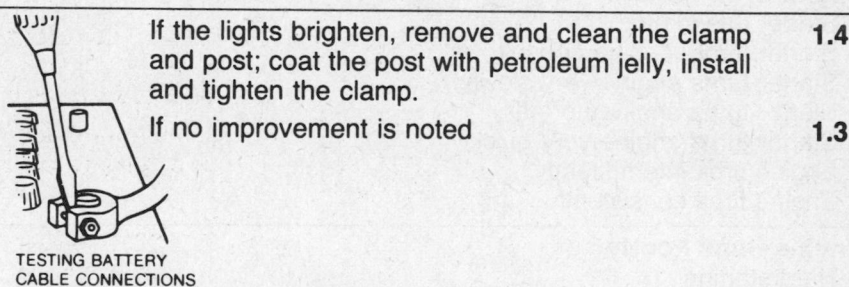

TESTING BATTERY CABLE CONNECTIONS USING A SCREWDRIVER

1.3 Test the state of charge of the battery using an individual cell tester or hydrometer.	If indicated, charge the battery. **NOTE: If no obvious reason exists for the low state of charge (i.e., battery age, prolonged storage), proceed to:**	1.4

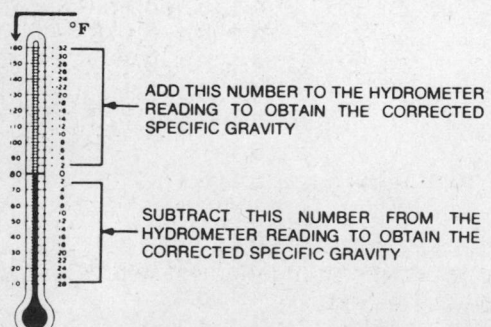

°F

ADD THIS NUMBER TO THE HYDROMETER READING TO OBTAIN THE CORRECTED SPECIFIC GRAVITY

SUBTRACT THIS NUMBER FROM THE HYDROMETER READING TO OBTAIN THE CORRECTED SPECIFIC GRAVITY

Specific Gravity (@ 80° F.)

Minimum	Battery Charge
1.260	100% Charged
1.230	75% Charged
1.200	50% Charged
1.170	25% Charged
1.140	Very Little Power Left
1.110	Completely Discharged

The effects of temperature on battery specific gravity (left) and amount of battery charge in relation to specific gravity (right)

Test and Procedure	Results and Indications	Proceed To
1.4 Visually inspect battery cables for cracking, bad connection to ground, or bad connection to starter.	If necessary, tighten connections or replace the cables.	2.1

SECTION 2—STARTING SYSTEM

Test and Procedure	Results and Indications	Proceed to

Note: Tests in Group 2 are performed with coil high tension lead disconnected to prevent accidental starting.

Test and Procedure	Results and Indications	Proceed to
2.1 Test the starter motor and solenoid: Connect a jumper from the battery post of the solenoid (or relay) to the starter post of the solenoid (or relay).	If starter turns the engine normally	2.2
	If the starter buzzes, or turns the engine very slowly	2.4
	If no response, replace the solenoid (or relay).	3.1
	If the starter turns, but the engine doesn't, ensure that the flywheel ring gear is intact. If the gear is undamaged, replace the starter drive.	3.1
2.2 Determine whether ignition override switches are functioning properly (clutch start switch, neutral safety switch), by connecting a jumper across the switch(es), and turning the ignition switch to "start".	If starter operates, adjust or replace switch.	3.1
	If the starter doesn't operate	2.3
2.3 Check the ignition switch "start" position: Connect a 12V test lamp or voltmeter between the starter post of the solenoid (or relay) and ground. Turn the ignition switch to the "start" position, and jiggle the key.	If the lamp doesn't light or the meter needle doesn't move when the switch is turned, check the ignition switch for loose connections, cracked insulation, or broken wires. Repair or replace as necessary.	3.1
	If the lamp flickers or needle moves when the key is jiggled, replace the ignition switch.	3.3

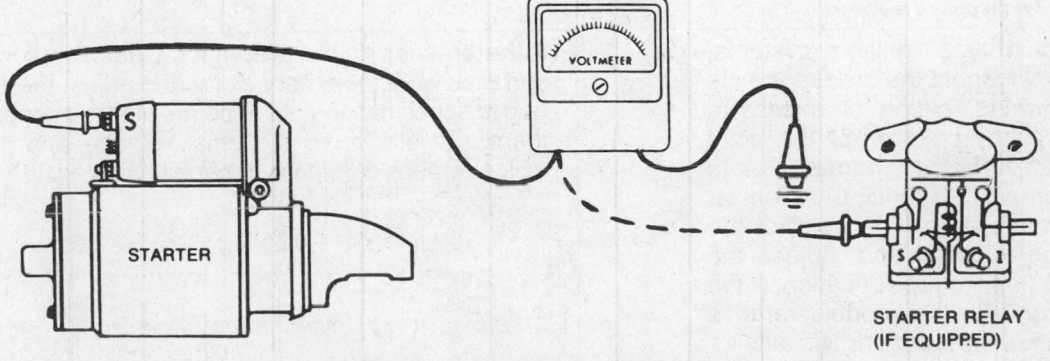

Checking the ignition switch "start" position

Test and Procedure	Results and Indications	Proceed to
2.4 Remove and bench test the starter, according to specifications in the car section.	If the starter does not meet specifications, repair or replace as needed	3.1
	If the starter is operating properly	2.5

Test and Procedure	Results and Indications	Proceed To
2.5 Determine whether the engine can turn freely: Remove the spark plugs, and check for water in the cylinders. Check for water on the dipstick, or oil in the radiator. Attempt to turn the engine using an 18″ flex drive and socket on the crankshaft pulley nut or bolt.	If the engine will turn freely only with the spark plugs out, and hydrostatic lock (water in the cylinders) is ruled out, check valve timing.	9.2
	If engine will not turn freely, and it is known that the clutch and transmission are free, the engine must be disassembled for further evaluation.	See Car Section

SECTION 3—PRIMARY ELECTRICAL SYSTEM

Test and Procedure	Results and Indications	Proceed to
3.1 Check the ignition switch "on" position: Connect a jumper wire between the distributor side of the coil and ground, and a 12V test lamp between the switch side of the coil and ground. Remove the high tension lead from the coil. Turn the ignition switch on and jiggle the key.	If the lamp lights	3.2
	If the lamp flickers when the key is jiggled, replace the ignition switch.	3.3
	If the lamp doesn't light, check for loose or open connections. If none are found, remove the ignition switch and check for continuity. If the switch is faulty, replace it.	3.3

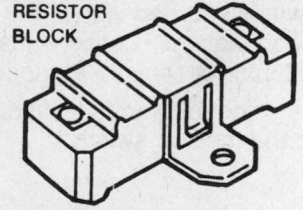

Checking the ignition switch "on" position

3.2 Check the ballast resistor or resistance wire for an open circuit, using an ohmmeter.	Replace the resistor or resistance wire if the resistance is zero. **NOTE: Some ignition systems have no ballast resistor.**	3.3

RESISTOR BLOCK

CALIBRATED RESISTANCE LEAD

Two types of resistors

3.3 On point-type ignition systems, visually inspect the breaker points for burning, pitting or excessive wear. Gray coloring of the point contact surfaces is normal. Rotate the crankshaft until the contact heel rests on a high point of the distributor cam and adjust the point gap to specifications. On electronic ignition models, remove the distributor cap and visually inspect the armature. Ensure that the armature pin is in place, and that the armature is on tight and rotates when the engine is cranked. Make sure there are no cracks, chips or rounded edges on the armature.	If the breaker points are intact, clean the contact surfaces with fine emery cloth, and adjust the point gap to specifications. If the points are worn, replace them. On electronic systems, replace any parts which appear defective. If condition persists	3.4

Test and Procedure	Results and Indications	Proceed To
3.4 On point-type ignition systems, connect a dwell-meter between the distributor primary lead and ground. Crank the engine and observe the point dwell angle. On electronic ignition systems, conduct a stator (magnetic pickup assembly) test. See Electronic Ignition Unit Repair Section.	On point-type systems, adjust the dwell angle if necessary. **NOTE: Increasing the point gap decreases the dwell angle and vice-versa.**	**3.6**
	If the dwell meter shows little or no reading	**3.5**
	On electronic ignition systems, if the stator is bad, replace the stator. If the stator is good, proceed to the other tests in The Electronic Ignition Unit Repair Section.	

Dwell is a function of point gap

3.5 On the point-type ignition systems, check the condenser for short: connect an ohmmeter across the condenser body and the pigtail lead.	If any reading other than infinite is noted, replace the condenser	**3.6**

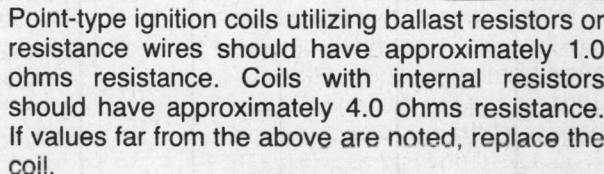

Checking the condenser for short

3.6 Test the coil primary resistance: On point-type ignition systems, connect an ohmmeter across the coil primary terminals, and read the resistance on the low scale. Note whether an external ballast resistor or resistance wire is used. On electronic ignition systems, test the coil primary resistance.	Point-type ignition coils utilizing ballast resistors or resistance wires should have approximately 1.0 ohms resistance. Coils with internal resistors should have approximately 4.0 ohms resistance. If values far from the above are noted, replace the coil.	**4.1**

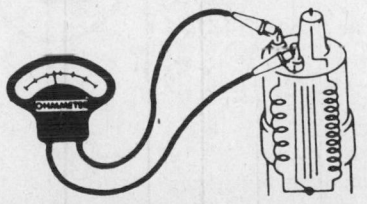

Checking the coil primary resistance

SECTION 4—SECONDARY ELECTRICAL SYSTEM

Test and Procedure	Results and Indications	Proceed to
4.1 Check for spark: Hold each spark plug wire approximately ¼″ from ground with gloves or heavy, dry rag. Crank the engine, and observe the spark.	If no spark is evident	**4.2**
	If spark is good in some cylinders	**4.3**
	If spark is good in all cylinders	**4.6**

Check for spark at the plugs

4.2 Check for spark at the coil high tension lead: Remove the coil high tension lead from the distributor and position it approximately ¼″ from ground. Crank the engine and observe spark. **CAUTION: This test should not be performed on engines equipped with electronic ignition.**	If the spark is good and consistent	**4.3**
	If the spark is good but intermittent, test the primary electrical system starting at 3.3.	**3.3**
	If the spark is weak or non-existent, replace the coil high tension lead, clean and tighten all connections and retest. If no improvement is noted	**4.4**

4.3 Visually inspect the distributor cap and rotor for burned or corroded contacts, cracks, carbon tracks, or moisture. Also check the fit of the rotor on the distributor shaft (where applicable).	If moisture is present, dry thoroughly, and retest per 4.1.	**4.1**
	If burned or excessively corroded contacts, cracks, or carbon tracks are noted, replace the defective part(s) and retest per 4.1.	**4.1**
	If the rotor and cap appear intact, or are only slightly corroded, clean the contacts thoroughly (including the cap towers and spark plug wire ends) and retest per 4.1.	
	If the spark is good in all cases	**4.6**
	If the spark is poor in all cases	**4.5**

CORRODED OR LOOSE WIRE

HIGH RESISTANCE CARBON

EXCESSIVE WEAR OF BUTTON

ROTOR TIP BURNED AWAY

Inspect the distributor cap and rotor

4.4 Check the coil secondary resistance: On point-type systems connect an ohmmeter across the distributor side of the coil and the coil tower. Read the resistance on the high scale of the ohmmeter. On electronic ignition systems, see The Electronic Ignition Unit Repair Section for specific tests.

The resistance of a satisfactory coil should be between 4,000 and 10,000 ohms. If resistance is considerably higher (i.e., 40,000 ohms) replace the coil and retest per 4.1.
NOTE: This does not apply to high performance coils.

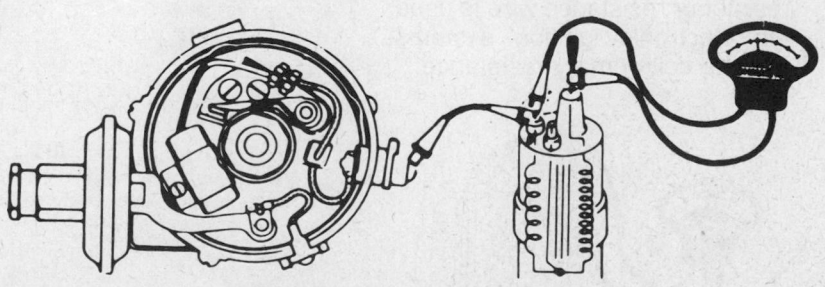

Testing the coil secondary resistance

Spark Plug Analysis

Normal

APPEARANCE

This plug is typical of one operating normally. The insulator nose varies from a light tan to grayish color with slight electrode wear. The presence of slight deposits is normal on used plugs and will have no adverse effect on engine performance. The spark plug heat range is correct for the engine and the engine is running normally.

CAUSE

Properly running engine

RECOMMENDATION

Before reinstalling this plug, the electrodes should be cleaned and filed square. Set the gap to specifications. If the plug has been in service for more than 10–12,000 miles, the entire set should probably be replaced with a fresh set of the same heat range.

Incorrect Heat Range

APPEARANCE

The effects of high temperature on a spark plug are indicated by clean white, often blistered insulator. This can also be accompanied by excessive wear of the electrode, and the absence of deposits.

CAUSE

Check for the correct spark plug heat range. A plug which is too hot for the engine can result in overheating. A car operated mostly at high speeds may require a colder plug. Also check ignition timing, cooling system level, fuel mixture and leaking intake manifold.

RECOMMENDATION

If all ignition and engine adjustments are known to be correct, and no other malfunction exists, install spark plugs one heat range colder.

Oil Deposits

APPEARANCE

The firing end of the plug is covered with a wet, oily coating.

CAUSE

The problem is poor oil control. On high mileage engines, oil is leaking past the rings or valve guides into the combustion chamber. A common cause is also a plugged PCV valve, and a ruptured fuel pump diaphragm can also cause this condition. Oil fouled plugs such as these are often found in new or recently overhauled engines, before normal oil control is achieved, and can be cleaned and reinstalled.

RECOMMENDATION

A hotter spark plug may temporarily relieve the problem, but the engine is probably in need of engine work.

Carbon Deposits

APPEARANCE

Carbon fouling is easily identified by the presence of dry, soft, black, sooty deposits.

CAUSE

Changing the heat range can often lead to carbon fouling, as can prolonged slow, stop-and-start driving. If the heat range is correct, carbon fouling can be attributed to a rich fuel mixture, sticking choke, clogged air cleaner, worn breaker points, retarded timing or low compression. If only one or two plugs are carbon fouled, check for corroded or cracked wires on the affected plugs. Also look for cracks in the distributor cap between the towers of affected cylinders.

RECOMMENDATION

After the problem is corrected, these plugs can be cleaned and reinstalled if not worn severely.

Ash Deposits

APPEARANCE

Ash deposits are characterized by light brown or white colored deposits crusted on the side or center electrodes. In some cases it may give the plug a rusty appearance.

CAUSE

Ash deposits are normally derived from oil or fuel additives burned during normal combustion. Normally they are harmless, though excessive amounts can cause misfiring. If deposits are excessive in short mileage, the valve guides may be worn. Reddish or rusty deposits are caused by manganese, an anti-knock compound replacing lead in unleaded gas. No engine malfunction is indicated.

RECOMMENDATION

Ash-fouled plugs can be cleaned, gapped and reinstalled.

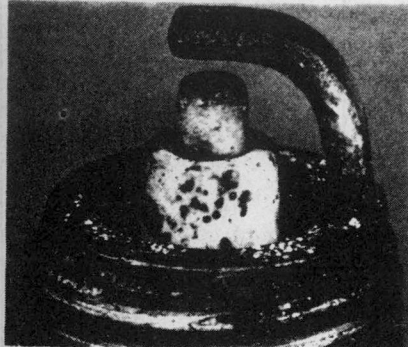

Splash Deposits

APPEARANCE

Splash deposits occur in varying degrees as spotty deposits on the insulator.

CAUSE

These usually occur after a long delayed tune-up. By-products of combustion have accumulated on pistons and valves because of a delayed tune-up. Following tune-up or during hard acceleration, the deposits loosen and are thrown against the hot surface of the plug. If the deposits accumulate sufficiently, misfiring can occur.

RECOMMENDATION

These plugs can be cleaned, gapped and reinstalled.

High Speed Glazing

APPEARANCE

Glazing appears as shiny coating on the plug, either yellow or tan in color.

CAUSE

During hard, fast acceleration, plug temperatures rise suddenly. Deposits from normal combustion have no chance to fluff-off; instead, they melt on the insulator forming an electrically conductive coating which causes misfiring.

RECOMMENDATION

Glazed plugs are not easily cleaned. They should be replaced with a fresh set of plugs of the correct heat range. If the condition recurs, using plugs with a heat range one step colder may cure the problem.

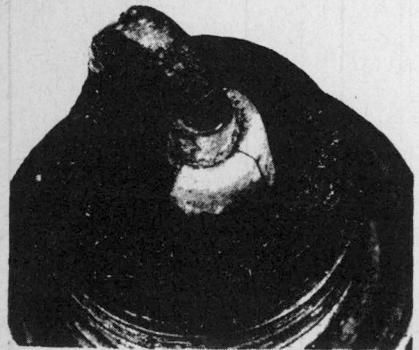

Detonation

APPEARANCE

Detonation is usually characterized by a broken plug insulator.

CAUSE

A portion of the fuel charge will begin to burn spontaneously, from the increased heat following ignition. The explosion that results applies extreme pressure to engine components, frequently damaging spark plugs and pistons.

Detonation can result by over-advanced ignition timing, inferior gasoline (low octane) lean air fuel mixture, poor carburetion, engine lugging or an increase in compression ratio due to combustion chamber deposits or engine modification.

RECOMMENDATION

Replace the plugs after correcting the problem.

Test and Procedure	Results and Indications	Proceed To
4.5 Visually inspect the spark plug wires for cracking or brittleness. Ensure that no two wires are positioned so as to cause induction firing (adjacent and parallel). Remove each wire, one by one, and check resistance with an ohmmeter.	Replace any cracked or brittle wires. If any of the wires are defective, replace the entire set. Replace any wires with excessive resistance (over 8000 Ω per foot for suppression wire), and separate any wires that might cause induction firing.	4.6

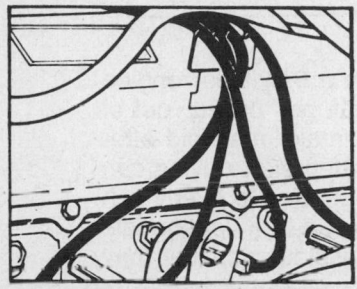

Misfiring can be the result of spark plug leads to adjacent, consecutively firing cylinders running parallel and too close together

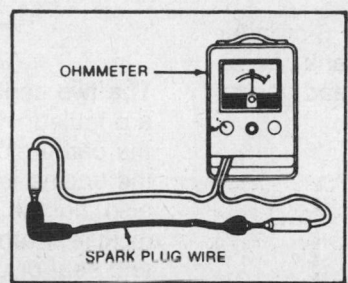

On point-type ignition systems, check the spark plug wires as shown. On electronic ignitions, do not remove the wire from the distributor cap terminal; instead, test through the cap

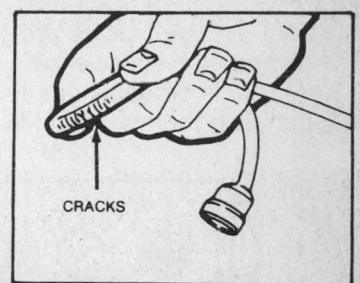

Spark plugs wires can be checked visually by bending them in a loop over your finger. This will reveal any cracks, burned or broken insulation. Any wire with cracked insulation should be replaced

Test and Procedure	Results and Indications	Proceed To
4.6 Remove the spark plugs, noting the cylinders from which they were removed, and evaluate according to the chart in this section.	See chart.	**See Chart**
4.7 Reinstall the spark plugs. **NOTE: Modern electronic ignition systems generate extremely high voltages and high heats. The spark plug boots can soften and actually fuse to the ceramic insulator of the spark plugs after long exposures to high temperature and voltage. If this happens, the boot (and possibly the wire) must be replaced.** To help alleviate this condition, many manufacturers are recommending new silicone compounds to slow the deterioration. The compounds are generally nonconductive, protective lubricants that will not dry out, harden, or melt away. They form a weather-tight seal between rubber or plastic and metal and are found in several typical locations: Inside the insulating boots of spark plug wires, inside primary ignition circuit cable connectors, on distributor and rotor cap electrodes, and under the control module.		4.8

Test and Procedure	Results and Indications	Proceed To

4.8 Examine the location of all the plugs.

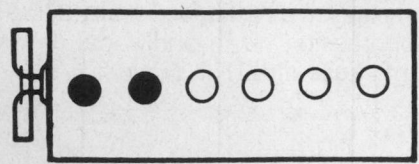

Two adjacent plugs are fouled in a 6-cylinder engine, 4-cylinder engine or either bank of a V-8. This is probably due to a blown head gasket between the two cylinders.

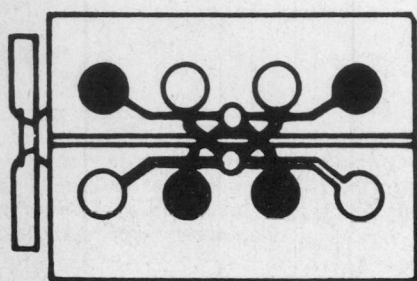

An unbalanced carburetor is indicated. Following the fuel flow on this particular design shows that the cylinders fed by the right-hand barrel are fouled from overly rich mixture, while the cylinders fed by the left-hand barrel are normal.

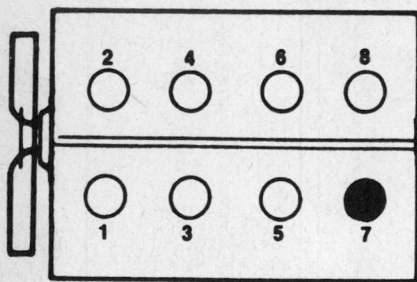

Finding one plug overheated may indicate an intake manifold leak near the affected cylinder. If the overheated plug is the second of two adjacent, consecutively firing plugs, it could be the result of ignition cross-firing. Separating the leads to these two plugs will eliminate cross-fire.

The following diagrams illustrate some of the conditions that the location of plugs will reveal.

4.9

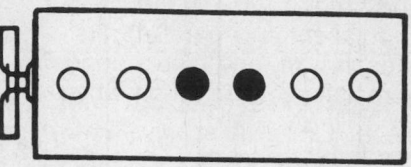

The two center plugs in a 6-cylinder engine are fouled. Raw fuel may be "boiled" out of the carburetor into the intake manifold after the engine is shut-off. Stop-start driving can also foul the center plugs, due to overly rich mixture. Proper float level, a new float needle and seat or use of an insulating spacer may help this problem.

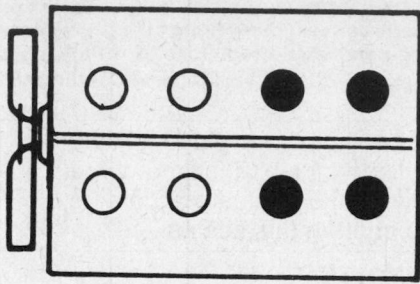

If the four rear plugs are overheated, a cooling system problem is suggested. A thorough cleaning of the cooling system may restore coolant circulation and cure the problem.

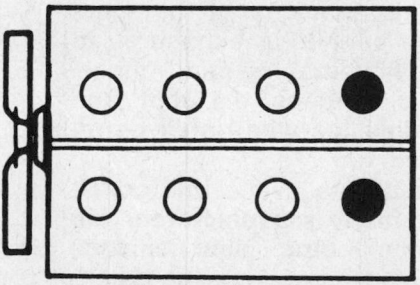

Occasionally, the two rear plugs in large, lightly used V-8's will become oil fouled. High oil consumption and smoky exhaust may also be noticed. It is probably due to plugged oil drain holes in the rear of the cylinder head, causing oil to be sucked in around the valve stems. This usually occurs in the rear cylinders first, because the engine slants that way.

Test and Procedure		Results and Indications	Proceed To
4.9	Determine the static ignition timing. Using the crankshaft pulley timing marks as a guide, locate top dead center on the compression stroke of the number one cylinder.	The rotor should be pointing toward the No. 1 tower in the distributor cap, and, on electronic ignitions, the armature spoke for that cylinder should be lined up with the stator.	4.10
4.10	Check coil polarity: Connect a voltmeter negative lead to the coil high tension lead, and the positive lead to ground. **NOTE: Reverse the hook-up for positive ground systems.** Crank the engine momentarily.	If the voltmeter reads up-scale, the polarity is correct.	5.1
		If the voltmeter reads down-scale, reverse the coil polarity (switch the primary leads).	5.1

Checking coil polarity

SECTION 5—FUEL SYSTEM

Test and Procedure		Results and Indications	Proceed to
5.1	Determine that the air filter is functioning efficiently: Hold paper elements up to a strong light, and attempt to see light through the filter.	Clean permanent air filters in solvent (or manufacturer's recommendation), and allow to dry. Replace paper elements through which light cannot be seen.	5.2
5.2	Determine whether a flooding condition exists: Flooding is identified by a strong gasoline odor, and excessive gasoline present in the throttle bore(s) of the carburetor.	If flooding is not evident	5.3
		If flooding is evident, permit the gasoline to dry for a few moments and restart.	
		If flooding doesn't recur	5.7
		If flooding is persistent	5.5

If the engine floods repeatedly, check the choke butterfly flap

5.3	Check that fuel is reaching the carburetor: Detach the fuel line at the carburetor inlet. Hold the end of the line in a cup (not styrofoam), and crank the engine.	If fuel flows smoothly	5.7
		If fuel doesn't flow	5.4
		If fuel flows erratically.	
		NOTE: Make sure that there is fuel in the tank	

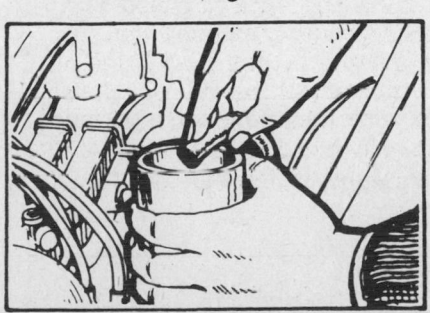

Check the fuel pump by disconnecting the output line (fuel pump-to-carburetor) at the carburetor and operating the starter briefly

Test and Procedure	Results and Indications	Proceed To
5.4 Test the fuel pump: Disconnect all fuel lines from the fuel pump. Hold a finger over the input fitting, crank the engine (with electric pump, turn the ignition or pump on); and feel for suction.	If suction is evident, blow out the fuel line to the tank with low pressure compressed air until bubbling is heard from the fuel filler neck. Also blow out the carburetor fuel line (both ends disconnected).	5.7
	If no suction is evident, replace or repair the fuel pump. **NOTE: Repeated oil fouling of the spark plugs, or a no-start condition, could be the result of a ruptured vacuum booster pump diaphragm, through which oil or gasoline is being drawn into the intake manifold (where applicable).**	5.7
5.5 Occasionally, small specks of dirt will clog the small jets and orifices in the carburetor. With the engine cold, hold a flat piece of wood or similar material over the carburetor, where possible, and crank the engine.	If the engine starts, but runs roughly the engine is probably not run enough.	
	If the engine won't start.	5.9
5.6 Check the needle and seat: Tap the carburetor in the area of the needle and seat.	If flooding stops, a gasoline additive (e.g., Gumout) will often cure the problem.	5.7
	If flooding continues, check the fuel pump for excessive pressure at the carburetor (according to specifications). If the pressure is normal, the needle and seat must be removed and checked, and/or the float level adjusted.	5.7
5.7 Test the accelerator pump by looking into the throttle bores while operating the throttle.	If the accelerator pump appears to be operating normally	5.8
	If the accelerator pump is not operating, the pump must be reconditioned. Where possible, service the pump with the carburetor(s) installed on the engine. If necessary, remove the carburetor. Prior to removal	5.8

Check for gas at the carburetor by looking down the carburetor throat while someone moves the accelerator

5.8 Determine whether the carburetor main fuel system is functioning: Spray a commercial starting fluid into the carburetor while attempting to start the engine.	If the engine starts, runs for a few seconds, and dies	5.9
	If the engine doesn't start	6.1
5.9 Uncommon fuel system malfunctions: See below:	If the problem is solved	6.1
	If the problem remains, remove and recondition the carburetor.	

Condition	Indication	Test	Prevailing Weather Conditions	Remedy
Vapor lock	Engine will not re-start shortly after running.	Cool the components of the fuel system until the engine starts. Vapor lock can be cured faster by draping a wet cloth over a mechanical fuel pump.	Hot to very hot	Ensure that the exhaust manifold heat control valve is operating. Check with the vehicle manufacturer for the recommended solution to vapor lock on the model in question.
Carburetor icing	Engine will not idle, stalls at low speeds.	Visually inspect the throttle plate area of the throttle bores for frost.	High humidity, 32–40° F.	Ensure that the exhaust manifold heat control valve is operating, and that the intake manifold heat riser is not blocked.
Water in the fuel	Engine sputters and stalls; may not start.	Pump a small amount of fuel into a glass jar. Allow to stand, and inspect for droplets of a layer of water.	High humidity, extreme temperature changes.	For droplets, use one or two cans of commercial gas line anti-freeze. For a layer of water, the tank must be drained, and the fuel lines blown out with compressed air.

SECTION 6—ENGINE COMPRESSION

Test and Procedure	Results and Indications	Proceed to
6.1 Test engine compression: Remove all spark plugs. Block the throttle wide open. Insert a compression gauge into a spark plug port, crank the engine to obtain the maximum reading, and record.	If compression is within limits on all cylinders	7.1
	If gauge reading is extremely low on all cylinders	6.2
	If gauge reading is low on one or two cylinders: (If gauge readings are identical and low on two or more adjacent cylinders, the head gasket must be replaced.)	6.2

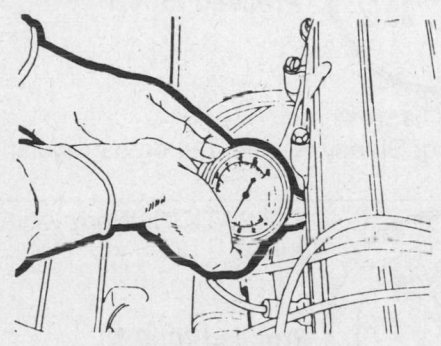

Checking compression

6.2 Test engine compression (wet): Squirt approximately 30 cc. of engine oil into each cylinder, and retest per 6.1.	If the readings improve, worn or cracked rings or broken pistons are indicated:	**See Car Section**
	If the readings do not improve, burned or excessively carboned valves or a jumped timing chain are indicated.	7.1
	NOTE: A jumped timing chain is often indicated by difficult cranking.	

SECTION 7—ENGINE VACUUM

Test and Procedure	Results and Indications	Proceed to
7.1 Attach a vacuum gauge to the intake manifold beyond the throttle plate. Start the engine, and observe the action of the needle over the range of engine speeds.	See below.	**See below**

INDICATION: Normal engine in good condition

Proceed to: 8.1

Normal engine

Gauge reading: Steady, from 17–22 in./Hg.

INDICATION: Sticking valves or ignition miss

Proceed to: 9.1, 8.3

Sticking valves

Gauge reading: Intermittent fluctuation at idle

INDICATION: Late ignition or valve timing, low compression, stuck throttle valve, leaking carburetor or manifold gasket

Proceed to: 6.1

Incorrect valve timing

Gauge reading: Low (10–15 in./Hg) but steady

INDICATION: Improper carburetor adjustment or minor intake leak.

Proceed to: 7.2

Carburetor requires adjustment

Gauge reading: Drifting needle

INDICATION: Ignition miss, blown cylinder head gasket, leaking valve or weak valve spring

Proceed to: 8.3, 6.1

Blown head gasket

Gauge reading: Needle fluctuates as engine speed increases

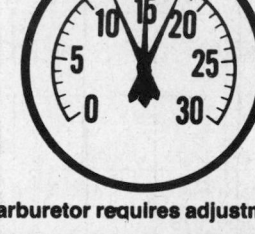

INDICATION: Burnt valve or faulty valve clearance: Needle will fall when defective valve operates

Proceed to: 9.1

Burnt or leaking valves

Gauge reading: Steady needle, but drops regularly

INDICATION: Choked muffler, excessive back pressure in system

Proceed to: 10.1

Clogged exhaust system

Gauge reading: Gradual drop in reading at idle

INDICATION: Worn valve guides

Proceed to: 9.1

Worn valve guides

Gauge reading: Needle vibrates excessively at idle, but steadies as engine speed increases

White pointer = steady gauge hand

Black pointer = fluctuating gauge hand

Test and Procedure	Results and Indications	Proceed To
7.2 Attach a vacuum gauge per 7.1, and test for an intake manifold leak. Squirt a small amount of oil around the intake manifold gaskets, carburetor gaskets, plugs and fittings. Observe the action of the vacuum gauge.	If the reading improves, replace the indicated gasket, or seal the indicated fitting or plug:	8.1
	If the reading remains low:	7.3
7.3 Test all vacuum hoses and accessories for leaks as described in 7.2. Also check the carburetor body (dashpots, automatic choke mechanism, throttle shafts) for leaks in the same manner.	If the reading improves, service or replace the offending part(s):	8.1
	If the reading remains low:	6.1

SECTION 8—SECONDARY ELECTRICAL SYSTEM

Test and Procedure	Results and Indications	Proceed to
8.1 Remove the distributor cap and check to make sure that the rotor turns when the engine is cranked. Visually inspect the distributor components.	Clean, tighten or replace any components which appear defective.	8.2
8.2 Connect a timing light (per manufacturer's recommendation) and check the dynamic ignition timing. Disconnect and plug the vacuum hose(s) to the distributor if specified, start the engine, and observe the timing marks at the specified engine speed.	If the timing is not correct, adjust to specifications by rotating the distributor in the engine: (Advance timing by rotating distributor opposite normal direction of rotor rotation, retard timing by rotating distributor in same direction as rotor rotation.)	8.3
8.3 Check the operation of the distributor advance mechanism(s): To test the mechanical advance, disconnect the vacuum lines from the distributor advance unit and observe the timing marks with a timing light as the engine speed is increased from idle. If the mark moves smoothly, without hesitation, it may be assumed that the mechanical advance is functioning properly. To test vacuum advance and/or retard systems, alternately crimp and release the vacuum line, and observe the timing mark for movement. If movement is noted, the system is operating.	If the systems are functioning	8.4
	If the systems are not functioning, remove the distributor, and test on a distributor tester.	8.4
8.4 Locate an ignition miss: With the engine running, remove each spark plug wire, one at a time, until one is found that doesn't cause the engine to roughen and slow down. **CAUTION: Do not pull on the wire to remove the boot from the plug. Be sure your hand is insulated from the wire.**	When the missing cylinder is identified	4.1

SECTION 9—VALVE TRAIN

Test and Procedure	Results and Indications	Proceed to
9.1 Evaluate the valve train: Remove the valve cover, and ensure that the valves are adjusted to specifications. A mechanic's stethoscope may be used to aid in the diagnosis of the valve train. By pushing the probe on or near push rods or rockers, valve noise often can be isolated. A timing light also may be used to diagnose valve problems. Connect the light according to manufacturer's recommendations, and start the engine. Vary the firing moment of the light by increasing the engine speed (and therefore the ignition advance), and moving the trigger from cylinder to cylinder. Observe the movement of each valve.	Sticking valves or erratic valve train motion can be observed with the timing light. The cylinder head must be disassembled for repairs.	**See Car Section**
9.2 Check the valve timing: Locate top dead center of the No. 1 piston, and install a degree wheel or tape on the crankshaft pulley or damper with zero corresponding to an index mark on the engine. Rotate the crankshaft in its direction of rotation, and observe the opening of the No. 1 cylinder intake valve. The opening should correspond with the correct mark on the degree wheel according to specifications.	If the timing is not correct, the timing cover must be removed for further investigation.	**See Car Section**

SECTION 10—EXHAUST SYSTEM

Test and Procedure	Results and Indications	Proceed to
10.1 Determine whether the exhaust manifold heat control valve is operating: Operate the valve by hand to determine whether it is free to move. If the valve is free, run the engine to operating temperature and observe the action of the valve, to ensure that it is opening.	If the valve sticks, spray it with a suitable solvent, open and close the valve to free it, and retest. If the valve functions properly	10.2
	If the valve does not free, or does not operate, replace the valve.	10.2
10.2 Ensure that there are no exhaust restrictions: Visually inspect the exhaust system for kinks, dents, or crushing. Also note that gases are flowing freely from the tailpipe at all engine speeds, indicating no restriction in the muffler or resonator.	Replace any damaged portion of the system.	11.1

SECTION 11—COOLING SYSTEM

Test and Procedure	Results and Indications	Proceed to
11.1 Visually inspect the fan belt for glazing, cracks, and fraying, and replace if necessary. Tighten the belt so that the longest span has approximately ½″ play at its midpoint under thumb pressure (see Maintenance Section).	Replace or tighten the fan belt as necessary.	**11.2**

Checking belt tension

Test and Procedure	Results and Indications	Proceed to
11.2 Check the fluid level of the cooling system.	If full or slightly low, fill as necessary.	**11.5**
	If extremely low	**11.3**
11.3 Visually inspect the external portions of the cooling system (radiator, radiator hoses, thermostat elbow, water pump seals, heater hoses, etc.) for leaks. If none are found, pressurize the cooling system to 14–15 psi.	If cooling system holds the pressure	**11.5**
	If cooling system loses pressure rapidly, reinspect external parts of the system for leaks under pressure. If none are found, check dipstick for coolant in crankcase. If no coolant is present, but pressure loss continues	**11.4**
	If coolant is evident in crankcase, remove cylinder head(s), and check gasket(s). If gaskets are intact, block and cylinder head(s) should be checked for cracks or holes.	
	If the gasket(s) is blown, replace, and purge the crankcase of coolant.	**12.6**
	NOTE: Occasionally, due to atmospheric and driving conditions, condensation of water can occur in the crankcase. This causes the oil to appear milky white. To remedy, run the engine until hot, and change the oil and oil filter.	
11.4 Check for combustion leaks into the cooling system: Pressurize the cooling system as above. Start the engine, and observe the pressure gauge. If the needle fluctuates, remove each spark plug wire, one at a time, noting which cylinder(s) reduce or eliminate the fluctuation.	Cylinders which reduce or eliminate the fluctuation, when the spark plug wire is removed, are leaking into the cooling system. Replace the head gasket on the affected cylinder bank(s).	**See Car Section**

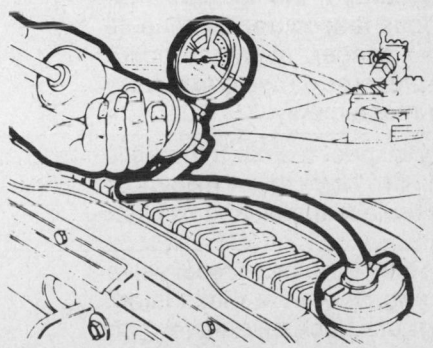

Pressurizing the cooling system

Test and Procedure	Results and Indications	Proceed To
11.5 Check the radiator pressure cap: Attach a radiator pressure tester to the radiator cap (wet the seal prior to installation). Quickly pump up the pressure, noting the point at which the cap releases.	If the cap releases within ±1 psi of the specified rating, it is operating properly.	**11.6**
	If the cap releases at more than ±1 psi of the specified rating, it should be replaced.	**11.6**

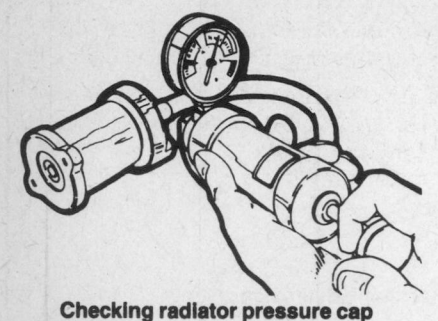
Checking radiator pressure cap

Test and Procedure	Results and Indications	Proceed To
11.6 Test the thermostat: Start the engine cold, remove the radiator cap, and insert a thermometer into the radiator. Allow the engine to idle. After a short while, there will be a sudden, rapid increase in coolant temperature. The temperature at which this sharp rise stops is the thermostat opening temperature.	If the thermostat opens at or about the specified temperature	**11.7**
	If the temperature doesn't increase (If the temperature increases slowly and gradually, replace the thermostat.)	**11.7**
11.7 Check the water pump: Remove the thermostat elbow and the thermostat, disconnect the coil high tension lead (to prevent starting), and crank the engine momentarily.	If coolant flows, replace the thermostat and retest per 11.6.	**11.6**
	If coolant doesn't flow, reverse flush the cooling system to alleviate any blockage that might exist. If system is not blocked, and coolant will not flow, replace the water pump.	**See Car Section**

SECTION 12—LUBRICATION

Test and Procedure	Results and Indications	Proceed to
12.1 Check the oil pressure gauge or warning light: If the gauge shows low pressure, or the light is on for no obvious reason, remove the oil pressure sender. Install an accurate oil pressure gauge and run the engine momentarily.	If oil pressure builds normally, run engine for a few moments to determine that it is functioning normally, and replace the sender.	—
	If the pressure remains low	**12.2**
	If the pressure surges	**12.3**
	If the oil pressure is zero	**12.3**
12.2 Visually inspect the oil: If the oil is watery or very thin, milky, or foamy, replace the oil and oil filter.	If the oil is normal	**12.3**
	If after replacing oil the pressure remains low	**12.3**
	If after replacing oil the pressure becomes normal	—
12.3 Inspect the oil pressure relief valve and spring, to ensure that it is not sticking or stuck. Remove and thoroughly clean the valve, spring, and the valve body.	If the oil pressure improves	—
	If no improvement is noted	**12.4**

Test and Procedure	Results and Indications	Proceed To
12.4 Check to ensure that the oil pump is not cavitating (sucking air instead of oil): See that the crankcase is neither over nor underfull, and that the pickup in the sump is in the proper position and free from sludge.	Fill or drain the crankcase to the proper capacity, and clean the pickup screen in solvent if necessary. If no improvement is noted	**12.5**
12.5 Inspect the oil pump drive and the oil pump:	If the pump drive or the oil pump appear to be defective, service as necessary and retest per 12.1. If the pump drive and pump appear to be operating normally, the engine should be disassembled to determine where blockage exists.	**12.1**
12.6 Purge the engine of ethylene glycol coolant: Competely drain the crankcase and the oil filter. Obtain a commercial butyl cellosolve base solvent, designated for this purpose, and follow the instructions precisely. Following this, install a new oil filter and refill the crankcase with the proper weight oil. The next oil and filter change should follow shortly thereafter (1000 miles).		

TROUBLESHOOTING AND DIAGNOSIS

Diesel Engine Troubleshooting

NOTE: The following troubleshooting procedures cover problems usually associated with diesel engines. Those problems common to both gasoline and diesel engines are covered in the gasoline engine troubleshooting procedures.

INDEX TO PROBLEMS

SECTION 1—Fuel System

Test and Procedure		Results and Indication	Proceed To
1.1a	Check for pressure at the outlet of the feed pump	If pressure exists, there is a clog in the supply line. Clean or replace it. If there is little or no pressure at the outlet, the filter is clogged. Clean or replace the filter. If the filter is clear, the feed pump piston is inoperative. Relace it.	1.1b
1.1b	Check the feed pump valves	If the inlet and outlet valves do not operate, the check valve or spring is broken. Replace it.	1.2a
1.2a	Check for fuel leakage at the overflow or return line	A clogged filter can result in high pressure causing leakage. Replace the filter.	1.2b
1.2b	Check for fuel in the filter leaking at the overflow valve	If leakage is found, the overflow valve is damaged. Replace it.	1.2c
1.2c	Check for leakage at the injection pump overflow valve	If leakage is found, it is caused by: damaged overflow valve, sticking plunger, or sticking delivery valve. Replace the defective part(s).	1.2d
1.2d	Check the injection pump plunger feed pressures.	If pressure at the plungers is low, replace the plunger(s).	1.2e

Test and Procedure		Results and Indication	Proceed To
1.2e	Check to make sure the injection pump is operating	An inoperative pump is caused by: a damaged or missing shaft key, or a damaged drive gear train.	1.3a
1.3a	Check that the pump timing marks are correctly aligned in the gear train	Incorrect timing marks alignment must be corrected.	1.3b
1.3b	Check that the injection pump is properly mounted	Remove and install the pump correctly	1.4a
1.4a	Install an injection nozzle on a tester and make sure that fuel is continuously ejected	A broken or intermittent stream is caused by a damaged spring or a sticking nozzle needle	1.4b
1.4b	With the nozzle on the tester as in 1.4a, check that shutoff is clean with no dribble or afterdrip	Dribble is caused by a defective nozzle valve seat. Replace the nozzle.	1.4c
1.4c	Using a tester, check injection pressure	Low pressure is a result of a weak spring. Replace the spring or adjust the initial injection pressure.	1.5a
1.5a	See 1.2a	Proceed as in 1.2a	1.5b
1.5b	Check for water in the fuel	Drain and clean the tank	1.5c
1.5c	Check for air in the fuel lines	Air can be introduced through a damaged fuel inlet line, a loose inlet line connector or a damaged gasket	1.5d
1.5d	Check for insufficient fuel feed	Insufficient fuel feed is caused by: a damaged feed pump, a clogged tank vent, or a clogged filter. Replace or repair as necessary.	1.6a
1.6a	Check the control rack action for smooth operation	Uneven control rack operation is caused by: a sticking plunger, improper meshing of the rack and pinion, poor seating of the plunger spring, insufficient clearance between the plunger and lower spring seat, or an overly tight delivery valve holder. Replace or adjust as necessary.	1.6b
1.6b	Check that the injection pump discharge is uniform	If the output is uneven, adjust as necessary	1.6c
1.6c	Check that the injection pump discharge volume is adequate	An inadequate discharge volume is caused by a worn plunger or a broken spring	1.6d
1.6d	Check for even low speed engine performance	If the engine performs unevenly or erratically at low speed only, a worn feed pump piston or defective feed pump valve is the cause.	1.6e
1.6e	Check for smooth engine operation throughout the operating range	This problem is usually caused by mechanical governor defects such as: a defective low speed spring, defective damper spring, or excessive friction among moving parts. Replace the defective parts.	1.6f
1.6f	Check the injectors on a tester	Improper nozzle operation should be corrected accordingly	1.7a
1.7a	Check the operating governor	A broken or weak spring in the governor will prevent full speed operation.	1.7b
1.7b	Check the injectors on a tester for a drop in injector output	A drop in output is caused by a sticking needle or a dirty nozzle. Replace or clean as necessary.	1.8a

Test and Procedure	Results and Indications	Proceed To
1.8a Check the injection pump for proper rack and pinion action	A catching or dirty rack and pinion will cause overspeeding.	1.8b
1.8b Check the governor adjustment	An improperly adjusted governor will cause overspeeding. Adjust.	1.9a
1.9a Check the injection pump output	Low output can be caused by: Incorrect adjustment—Adjust Loose delivery valve—Tighten Broken delivery valve seal—Replace Poor valve seat contact—Replace Broken/weak delivery valve spring—Replace	1.9b
1.9b Check for unusual noise at the injection pump	A noisy pump is an indication of a broken plunger spring	1.9c
1.9c Check plunger operation	A sticking injection pump plunger will cause power loss. Replace.	1.9d
1.9d Check the injection timer	A lag in injection timing is caused by large clearances in the timer due to wear. Replace.	1.9e
1.9e Check for air or water in the fuel	Bleed the air or drain the fuel and clean the tank and lines	1.9f
1.9f Check the injection timing	Readjust timing if necessary	1.10a
1.10a Check the initial injection timing	Adjust if necessary	1.10b
1.10b Check the injection pressure	High pressure will cause knock. Adjust as necessary	1.10c
1.10c Check the injector nozzle	A clogged nozzle causes knock. Clean or replace the nozzle.	1.11a
1.11a Check the injection pump output and timing	Excessive output, coupled with incorrect timing causes knock. Adjust as necessary	1.11b
1.11b Check the delivery valve seat	Replace a defective seat	1.11c
1.11c Check the pump plungers	Replace badly worn plungers	1.11d
1.11d Check injector opening pressure on a tester	Adjust as necessary	1.11e
1.11e Check the injector	Replace a broken nozzle spring or sticking needle.	

SECTION 2—ENGINE MECHANICAL

Test and Procedure		Results and Indications	Proceed To
2.1a	Check for piston seizing	Seized pistons are caused by low oil pressure, oil breakdown, or overheating. Replace the pistons and liners.	2.1b
2.1b	Check for a damaged flywheel ring gear	A damaged ring gear will cause poor meshing with the starter. Replace the ring gear.	2.1c
2.1c	Make a compression check	Low compression can be caused by: sticking rings, worn rings, worn liners. Replace the rings or liners.	2.2a
2.2a	A knocking noise at idle or during acceleration can be caused by a variety of wear problems.	Use a stethoscope or similar listening device to try to pinpoint the source of the noise. Among other reasons for knocking are: piston pins, rod bearings, loose rod caps, crankshaft journals and/or bearings, crankshaft thrust washer. Replace any worn parts.	2.2b
2.2b	An infrequently encountered noise is a continuous growl during acceleration	This problem is usually caused by problems in the engine timing gears. Poor contact, excessive backlash or loose gears are usually at fault.	2.2c
2.2c	Intermittent noises are the hardest to find. They are usually caused by broken moving parts.	Check the gear train for a chipped or cracked gear; the oil pan for broken parts or foreign objects or the cylinder head for a broken valve or valve spring.	2.3
2.3	Check for oil in the combustion chambers	Oil entering the combustion chambers will cause the engine to overspeed if the amount of oil is too great, or run unevenly. Check for broken or sticking rings, bad head gasket(s) or worn valve guides.	2.4
2.4	Check the compression	Low compression is the main cause of power loss. The main causes for low compression are: worn rings or liners, cracked valves, warped head or block, and bad head gasket.	2.5
2.5	A large amount of black exhaust is caused by low compression	See 2.4 above	2.6
2.6	If the engine stops suddenly during operation, the cause is usually sudden damage	Check the pistons, main bearings or rod bearings for lack of lubrication. A seized camshaft is also a result of low or no lubrication. Check the timing gears for damage.	2.7
2.7	Check for excessive clearance between the bearings and journals on both the mains and rod bearings. Check the oil pressure.	Replace as necessary. Replace the pump as necessary.	2.8
2.8	Aside from the usual leaking gasket problems, check the condition of the combustion chamber O-rings.	Replace as necessary	2.9
2.9	Compression leakage is usually caused by a seal defect between the head and the block	Check the head gasket; check for loose head bolts; check for head or block warpage. Replace or repair as necessary.	

Engine Overheating Troubleshooting

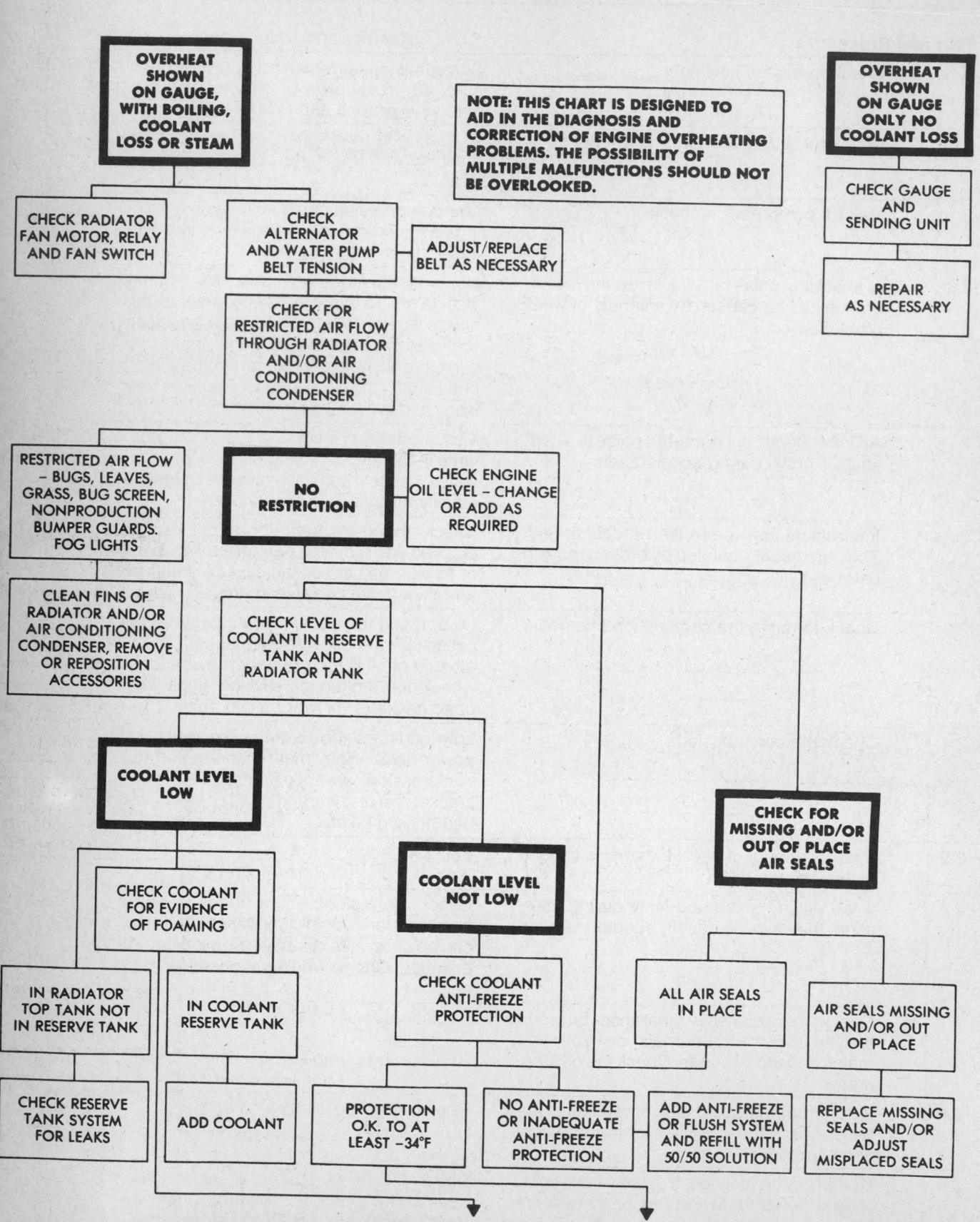

OVERHEAT SHOWN ON GAUGE, WITH BOILING, COOLANT LOSS OR STEAM

NOTE: THIS CHART IS DESIGNED TO AID IN THE DIAGNOSIS AND CORRECTION OF ENGINE OVERHEATING PROBLEMS. THE POSSIBILITY OF MULTIPLE MALFUNCTIONS SHOULD NOT BE OVERLOOKED.

OVERHEAT SHOWN ON GAUGE ONLY NO COOLANT LOSS

CHECK GAUGE AND SENDING UNIT

REPAIR AS NECESSARY

CHECK RADIATOR FAN MOTOR, RELAY AND FAN SWITCH

CHECK ALTERNATOR AND WATER PUMP BELT TENSION

ADJUST/REPLACE BELT AS NECESSARY

CHECK FOR RESTRICTED AIR FLOW THROUGH RADIATOR AND/OR AIR CONDITIONING CONDENSER

RESTRICTED AIR FLOW – BUGS, LEAVES, GRASS, BUG SCREEN, NONPRODUCTION BUMPER GUARDS. FOG LIGHTS

NO RESTRICTION

CHECK ENGINE OIL LEVEL – CHANGE OR ADD AS REQUIRED

CLEAN FINS OF RADIATOR AND/OR AIR CONDITIONING CONDENSER, REMOVE OR REPOSITION ACCESSORIES

CHECK LEVEL OF COOLANT IN RESERVE TANK AND RADIATOR TANK

COOLANT LEVEL LOW

CHECK COOLANT FOR EVIDENCE OF FOAMING

COOLANT LEVEL NOT LOW

CHECK FOR MISSING AND/OR OUT OF PLACE AIR SEALS

CHECK COOLANT ANTI-FREEZE PROTECTION

IN RADIATOR TOP TANK NOT IN RESERVE TANK

IN COOLANT RESERVE TANK

ALL AIR SEALS IN PLACE

AIR SEALS MISSING AND/OR OUT OF PLACE

CHECK RESERVE TANK SYSTEM FOR LEAKS

ADD COOLANT

PROTECTION O.K. TO AT LEAST –34°F

NO ANTI-FREEZE OR INADEQUATE ANTI-FREEZE PROTECTION

ADD ANTI-FREEZE OR FLUSH SYSTEM AND REFILL WITH 50/50 SOLUTION

REPLACE MISSING SEALS AND/OR ADJUST MISPLACED SEALS

Engine Overheating Troubleshooting

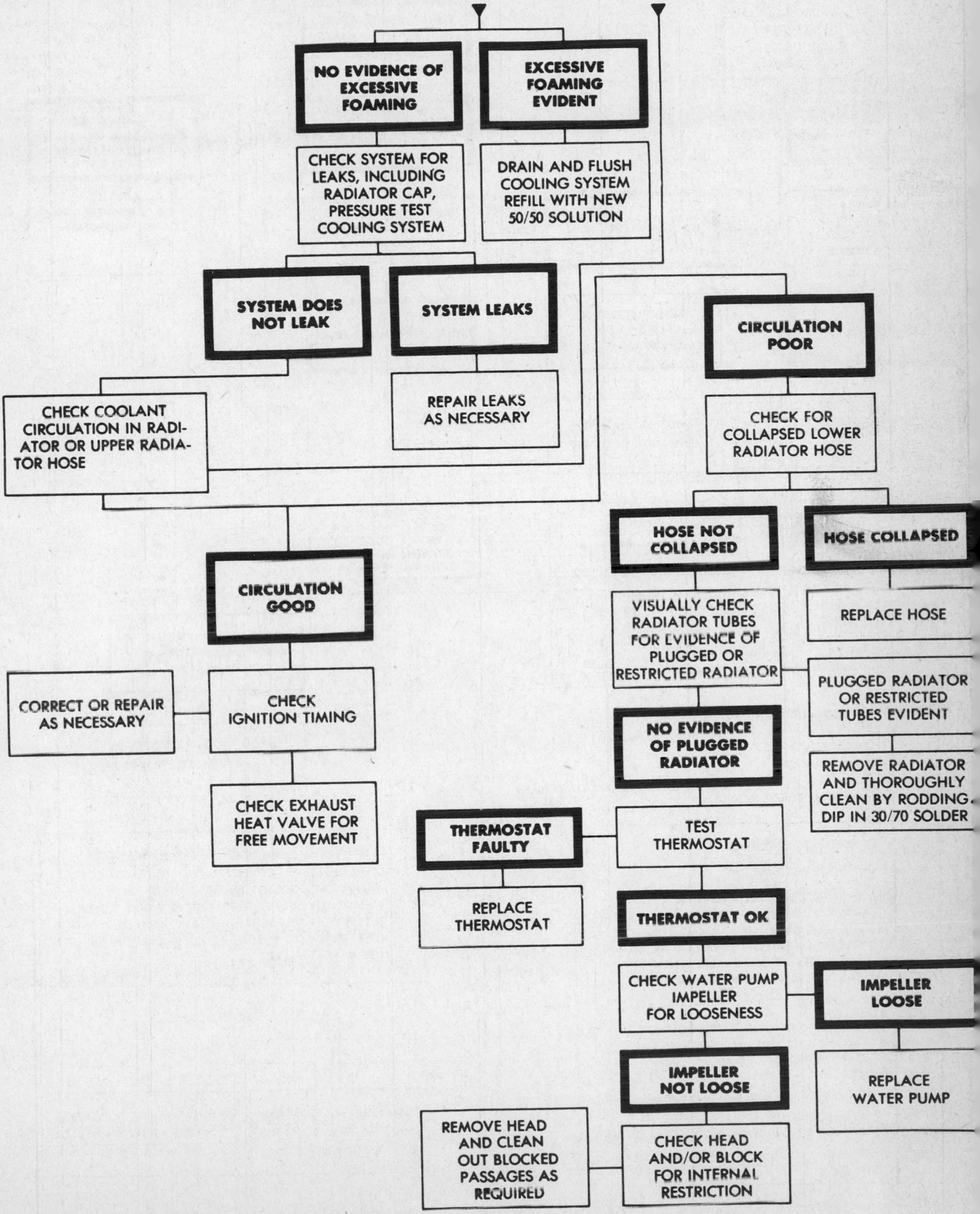

NO EVIDENCE OF EXCESSIVE FOAMING

CHECK SYSTEM FOR LEAKS, INCLUDING RADIATOR CAP, PRESSURE TEST COOLING SYSTEM

EXCESSIVE FOAMING EVIDENT

DRAIN AND FLUSH COOLING SYSTEM REFILL WITH NEW 50/50 SOLUTION

SYSTEM DOES NOT LEAK

SYSTEM LEAKS

REPAIR LEAKS AS NECESSARY

CIRCULATION POOR

CHECK FOR COLLAPSED LOWER RADIATOR HOSE

CHECK COOLANT CIRCULATION IN RADIATOR OR UPPER RADIATOR HOSE

HOSE NOT COLLAPSED

HOSE COLLAPSED

VISUALLY CHECK RADIATOR TUBES FOR EVIDENCE OF PLUGGED OR RESTRICTED RADIATOR

REPLACE HOSE

CIRCULATION GOOD

CORRECT OR REPAIR AS NECESSARY

CHECK IGNITION TIMING

NO EVIDENCE OF PLUGGED RADIATOR

PLUGGED RADIATOR OR RESTRICTED TUBES EVIDENT

REMOVE RADIATOR AND THOROUGHLY CLEAN BY RODDING. DIP IN 30/70 SOLDER

CHECK EXHAUST HEAT VALVE FOR FREE MOVEMENT

THERMOSTAT FAULTY

TEST THERMOSTAT

REPLACE THERMOSTAT

THERMOSTAT OK

CHECK WATER PUMP IMPELLER FOR LOOSENESS

IMPELLER LOOSE

IMPELLER NOT LOOSE

REPLACE WATER PUMP

REMOVE HEAD AND CLEAN OUT BLOCKED PASSAGES AS REQUIRED

CHECK HEAD AND/OR BLOCK FOR INTERNAL RESTRICTION

TROUBLESHOOTING AND DIAGNOSIS

Low Engine Temperature Troubleshooting

ENGINE TEMPERATURE LOW- OR SLOW ENGINE WARM-UP

NORMAL TEMPERATURE SHOWN ON GAUGE. LOW HEATER AIR TEMPERATURE

LOW TEMPERATURE SHOWN ON GAUGE AND LOW HEATER AIR TEMPERATURE

LOW TEMPERATURE SHOWN ON GAUGE AND NO HEATER AIR TEMPERATURE COMPLAINTS

CHECK COOLANT LEVEL IN THE RADIATOR AND COOLANT RESERVE BOTTLE

COOLANT LEVEL LOW

CHECK COOLANT LEVEL IN THE RADIATOR AND COOLANT RESERVE BOTTLE

CHECK TEMPERATURE GAUGE AND SENDING UNIT

PROPER COOLANT LEVEL

INSPECT COOLING SYSTEM AND HEATER CIRCUIT FOR LEAKS

PROPER COOLANT LEVEL

REPAIR LEAKS AND/OR REFILL WITH COOLANT

POSSIBLE HEATER SYSTEM MALFUNCTIONS

HEATER SYSTEM WORKING PROPERLY

CHECK THERMOSTAT HOUSING BOLTS FOR PROPER TORQUE (POSSIBLE INTERNAL COOLANT LEAKAGE)

THERMOSTAT HOUSING BOLTS PROPERLY TORQUED

THERMOSTAT HOUSING BOLTS NOT PROPERLY TORQUED

CHECK THERMOSTAT OPERATION

TORQUE HOUSING BOLTS

THERMOSTAT TESTING PROCEDURE

1. REMOVE RADIATOR PRESSURE CAP.

   CAUTION: IF VEHICLE HAS BEEN RUN RECENTLY, WAIT 15 MINUTES BEFORE REMOVING CAP, THEN PLACE A RAG OVER THE CAP AND TURN IT TO THE FIRST STOP. ALLOW PRESSURE TO ESCAPE THROUGH THE OVERFLOW TUBE AND WHEN THE SYSTEM STABILIZES REMOVE THE CAP COMPLETELY.

2. DRAIN ONE QUART OF COOLANT FROM THE RADIATOR.

3. WARM THE ENGINE TO OPERATING TEMPERATURE BY IDLING FOR 20 MINUTES, WITH THE PRESSURE CAP OFF. IDLE LONGER IF WORKING OUTDOORS IN COLD TEMPERATURES.

4. WITH THE ENGINE IDLING, PLACE A THERMOMETER INTO THE COOLANT IN THE RADIATOR FILLER NECK.

5. COOLANT TEMPERATURE SHOULD STABILIZE AT NO LOWER THAN 187°F. (86°C) (OR 8° BELOW THERMOSTAT OPENING TEMPERATURE.)

IF TEMPERATURE OF COOLANT FAILS TO REACH OPERATING LEVEL, COVER FRONT OF RADIATOR CORE AND ALLOW COOLANT TEMPERATURE TO REACH 210°F. THEN REMOVE COVER, REPEAT STEPS 3 THRU 5 OF THERMOSTAT TEST PROCEDURE. (THE PURPOSE OF THIS OPERATION IS TO PURGE DIRT ACCUMULATION ON THERMOSTAT VALVE.)

IF TEMPERATURE STABILIZES ABOVE 187°F. (86°C) DO NOT REPLACE THE THERMOSTAT.

IF TEMPERATURE DOES NOT STABILIZE AT 187°F. (86°C) OR ABOVE, REPLACE THERMOSTAT.

DRIVELINE
Clutch System Troubleshooting

Condition	Possible Cause	Corrective Action
Clutch chatter	1. Grease on driven plate (disc) facing. 2. Binding clutch linkage. 3. Loose, damaged facings on driven plate (disc). 4. Engine mounts loose. 5. Incorrect height adjustment of pressure plate release levers. 6. Clutch housing or housing to transmission adapter misalignment. 7. Loose driven plate hub.	1. Replace plate. 2. Check for worn, bent, broken parts. Replace as required. Lube linkage. 3. Replace driven plate. 4. Tighten mounts. Replace if damaged. 5. Adjust release lever height. 6. Check bore and face run out. Correct as required. 7. Replace driven plate.
Clutch grabbing	1. Oil, grease on driven plate (disc) facing. 2. Broken pressure plate. 3. Warped or binding driven plate. Driven plate binding on clutch shaft.	1. Replace driven plate. 2. Replace pressure plate. 3. Replace warped driven plate. Replace clutch shaft if defective, scored, worn.
Clutch slips	1. Lack of lubrication in clutch linkage (linkage binds, causes incomplete engagement. 2. Incorrect pedal, or linkage adjustment. 3. Broken pressure plate springs. 4. Weak pressure plate springs. 5. Grease on driven plate facings (disc).	1. Lubricate linkage. 2. Adjust as required. 3. Replace pressure plate. 4. Replace pressure plate. 5. Replace driven plate.
Incomplete clutch release	1. Incorrect pedal or linkage adjustment or linkage binding. 2. Incorrect height adjustment on pressure plate release levers. 3. Loose, broken facings on driven plate (disc). 4. Bent, dished, warped driven plate caused by overheating.	1. Adjust as required. Lubricate linkage. 2. Adjust release lever height. 3. Replace driven plate. 4. Replace driven plate.
Grinding, whirring grating noise when pedal is depressed	1. Worn or defective throwout bearing. 2. Starter drive teeth contacting flywheel ring gear teeth.	1. Replace throwout bearing. 2. Look for milled or polished teeth on ring gear. Align clutch housing, replace starter drive or drive spring as required.
Squeal, howl, trumpeting noise when pedal is being released (occurs during first inch to inch and one-half of pedal travel)	1. Pilot bushing worn or lack of lubricant.	1. Replace worn bushing. If bushing appears OK, polish bushing with emery, soak lube wick in oil, lube bushing with oil, apply film of chassis grease to clutch shaft pilot hub, reassemble. **NOTE:** Bushing wear may be due to misalignment of clutch housing or housing to transmission adapter.
Vibration or clutch pedal pulsation with clutch disengaged (pedal fully depressed)	1. Worn or defective engine transmission mounts. 2. Flywheel run out, or damaged or defective clutch components.	1. Inspect and replace as required. 2. Replace components as required. (Flywheel run out at face not to exceed 0.005″).

Manual Transmission Troubleshooting

Condition	Probable Cause
Jumping out of high gear	1. Misalignment of transmission case or clutch housing. 2. Worn pilot bearing in crankshaft. 3. Bent transmission shaft. 4. Worn high speed sliding gear. 5. Worn teeth in clutch shaft. 6. Insufficient spring tension on shifter rail plunger. 7. Bent or loose shifter fork. 8. End-play in clutch shaft. 9. Gears not engaging completely. 10. Loose or worn bearings on clutch shaft or mainshaft.
Sticking in high gear	1. Clutch not releasing fully. 2. Burred or battered teeth on clutch shaft. 3. Burred or battered transmission mainshaft. 4. Frozen synchronizing clutch. 5. Stuck shifter rail plunger. 6. Gearshift lever twisting and binding shifter rail. 7. Battered teeth on high speed sliding gear or on sleeve. 8. Lack of lubrication. 9. Improper lubrication. 10. Corroded transmission parts. 11. Defective mainshaft pilot bearing.
Jumping out of second gear	1. Insufficient spring tension on shifter rail plunger. 2. Bent or loose shifter fork. 3. Gears not engaging completely. 4. End-play in transmission mainshaft. 5. Loose transmission gear bearing. 6. Defective mainshaft pilot bearing. 7. Bent transmission shaft. 8. Worn teeth on second speed sliding gear or sleeve. 9. Loose or worn bearings on transmission mainshaft. 10. End-play in countershaft.
Sticking in second gear	1. Clutch not releasing fully. 2. Burred or battered teeth on sliding sleeve. 3. Burred or battered transmission mainshaft. 4. Frozen synchronizing clutch. 5. Stuck shifter rail plunger. 6. Gearshift lever twisting and binding shifter rail. 7. Lack of lubrication. 8. Second speed transmission gear bearings locked will give same effect as gears stuck in second. 9. Improper lubrication. 10. Corroded transmission parts.
Jumping out of low gear	1. Gears not engaging completely. 2. Bent or loose shifter fork. 3. End-play in transmission mainshaft. 4. End-play in countershaft. 5. Loose or worn bearings on transmission mainshaft. 6. Loose or worn bearings in countershaft. 7. Defective mainshaft pilot bearing.
Sticking in low gear	1. Clutch not releasing fully. 2. Burred or battered transmission mainshaft. 3. Stuck shifter rail plunger. 4. Gearshift lever twisting and binding shifter rail. 5. Lack of lubrication. 6. Improper lubrication. 7. Corroded transmission parts.

Condition	Probable Cause
Jumping out of reverse gear	1. Insufficient spring tension on shifter rail plunger. 2. Bent or loose shifter fork. 3. Badly worn gear teeth. 4. Gears not engaging completely. 5. End-play in transmission mainshaft. 6. Idler gear bushings loose or worn. 7. Loose or worn bearings on transmission mainshaft. 8. Defective mainshaft pilot bearing.
Sticking in reverse gear	1. Clutch not releasing fully. 2. Burred or battered transmission mainshaft. 3. Stuck shifter rail plunger. 4. Gearshift lever twisting and binding shifter rail. 5. Lack of lubrication. 6. Improper lubrication. 7. Corroded transmission parts.
Failure of gears to synchronize	1. Binding pilot bearing on mainshaft, will synchronize in high gear only. 2. Clutch not releasing fully. 3. Detent spring weak or broken. 4. Weak or broken springs under balls in sliding gear sleeve. 5. Binding bearing on clutch shaft. 6. Binding countershaft. 7. Binding pilot bearing in crankshaft 8. Badly worn gear teeth. 9. Scored or worn cones. 10. Improper lubrication. 11. Constant mesh gear not turning freely on transmission mainshaft. Will synchronize in that gear only.
Gears spinning when shifting into gear from neutral	1. Clutch not releasing fully. 2. In some cases an extremely light lubricant in transmission will cause gears to continue to spin for a short time after clutch is released. 3. Binding pilot bearing in crankshaft.
Noisy in all gears	1. Insufficient lubricant. 2. Worn countergear bearings. 3. Worn or damaged main drive gear or countergear. 4. Damaged main drive gear or mainshaft bearings. 5. Worn or damaged countergear anti-lash plate.
Noisy in high gear	1. Damaged main drive gear bearing. 2. Damaged mainshaft bearing. 3. Damaged high speed gear synchronizer.
Noisy in neutral	1. Damaged main drive gear bearing. 2. Damaged or loose mainshaft pilot bearing. 3. Worn or damaged countergear anti-lash plate. 4. Worn countergear bearings.
Noisy in all reduction gears	1. Insufficient lubricant. 2. Worn or damaged drive gear or countergear.
Noisy in second only	1. Damaged or worn second gear constant mesh gears. 2. Worn or damaged countergear rear bearings. 3. Damaged or worn second gear synchronizer.
Noisy in second only	1. Damaged or worn second gear constant mesh gears. 2. Worn or damaged countergear rear bearings. 3. Damaged or worn second gear synchronizer.
Noisy in third only (four speed)	1. Damaged or worn third gear constant mesh gears. 2. Worn or damaged countergear bearings.

TROUBLESHOOTING AND DIAGNOSIS

Condition	Probable Cause
Noisy in reverse only	1. Worn or damaged reverse idler gear or idler bushing. 2. Worn or damaged mainshaft reverse gear. 3. Worn or damaged reverse countergear. 4. Damaged shift mechanism.
Excessive backlash in all reduction gears	1. Worn countergear bearings. 2. Excessive end–play in countergear.

Automatic Transmission Troubleshooting

Keeping alert to changes in the operating characteristics of the transmission (changing shift points, noises, etc.) can prevent small problems from becoming large ones. If the problem cannot be traced to loose bolts, fluid level, misadjusted linkage, clogged filters or similar problems, you should probably seek professional service.

TRANSMISSION FLUID INDICATIONS

The appearance and odor of the transmission fluid can give valuable clues to the overall condition of the transmission. Always note the appearance of the fluid when you check the fluid level or change the fluid. Rub a small amount of fluid between your fingers to feel for grit and smell the fluid on the dipstick.

If The Fluid Appears	It Indicates
Clear and red colored	Normal operation
Discolored (extremely dark red or brownish) or smells burned	Band or clutch pack failure, usually caused by an overheated transmission. Hauling very heavy loads with insufficient power or failure to change the fluid often results in overheating. Do not confuse this appearance with newer fluids that have a darker red color and a strong odor (though not a burned odor).
Foamy or aerated (light in color and full of bubbles)	The level is too high (gear train is churning oil) An internal air leak (air is mixing with the fluid). Have the transmission checked professionally.
Solid residue in the fluid	Defective bands, clutch pack or bearings. Bits of band material or metal abrasives are clinging to the dipstick. Have the transmission checked professionally.
Varnish coating on the dipstick	The transmission fluid is overheating

Problem	Possible Cause	Correction
Slow initial engagement	1. Improper fluid level. 2. Damaged or improperly adjusted linkage. 3. Contaminated fluid. 4. Faulty clutch and band application, or oil control pressure system.	1. Add fluid as required. 2. Repair or adjust linkage. 3. Perform fluid level check. 4. Perform control pressure test.
Rough initial engagement in either forward or reverse	1. Improper fluid level. 2. High engine idle. 3. Looseness in the driveshaft, U-joints or engine mounts. 4. Incorrect linkage adjustment. 5. Faulty clutch or band application, or oil control pressure system. 6. Sticking or dirty valve body.	1. Perform fluid level check. 2. Adjust idle to specifications. 3. Repair as required. 4. Repair or adjust linkage. 5. Perform control pressure test. 6. Clean, repair or replace valve body.

Problem	Possible Cause	Correction
No drive, slips or chatters in first gear in D. All other gears normal.	1. Faulty one-way clutch.	1. Repair or replace one-way clutch.
No drive, slips or chatters in second gear.	1. Improper fluid level. 2. Damaged or improperly adjusted linkage. 3. Intermediate band out of adjustment. 4. Faulty band or clutch application, or oil pressure control system. 5. Faulty servo and/or internal leaks. 6. Dirty or sticking valve body. 7. Polished, glazed intermediate band or drum.	1. Perform fluid level check. 2. Repair or adjust linkage. 3. Adjust intermediate band. 4. Perform control pressure test. 5. Perform air pressure test. 6. Clean, repair or replace valve body. 7. Replace or repair as required.
No drive in any gear.	1. Improper fluid level. 2. Damaged or improperly adjusted linkage. 3. Faulty clutch or band application, or oil control pressure system. 4. Internal leakage. 5. Valve body loose. 6. Faulty clutches. 7. Sticking or dirty valve body.	1. Perform fluid level check. 2. Repair or adjust linkage. 3. Perform control pressure test. 4. Check and repair as required. 5. Tighten to specification. 6. Perform air pressure test. 7. Clean, repair or replace valve body.
No drive forward—reverse OK.	1. Improper fluid level 2. Damaged or improperly adjusted linkage. 3. Faulty clutch or band application, or oil pressure control system. 4. Faulty forward clutch or governor. 5. Valve body loose 6. Dirty or sticking valve body.	1. Perform fluid level check. 2. Repair or adjust linkage. 3. Perform control pressure test. 4. Perform air pressure test. 5. Tighten to specification. 6. Clean, repair or replace valve body.
No drive, slips or chatters in reverse—forward OK.	1. Improper fluid level 2. Damaged or improperly adjusted linkage. 3. Looseness in the drivehsaft, U-joints or engine mounts. 4. Bands or clutches out of adjustment. 5. Faulty oil pressure control system. 6. Faulty reverse clutch or servo. 7. Valve body loose. 8. Dirty or sticking valve body.	1. Perform fluid level check. 2. Repair or adjust linkage. 3. Repair as required. 4. Adjust as necessary. 5. Perform control pressure test. 6. Perform air pressure test. 7. Tighten to specifications. 8. Clean, repair or replace valve body.
Starts in high—in D drag or lockup at 1–2 shift point or in 2 or 1.	1. Improper fluid level. 2. Damaged or improperly adjusted linkage. 3. Faulty governor. 4. Faulty clutches and/or internal leaks. 5. Valve body loose. 6. Dirty, sticking valve body. 7. Poor mating of valve body to case mounting surfaces.	1. Perform fluid level check. 2. Repair or adjust linkage. 3. Repair or replace governor, clean screen. 4. Perform air pressure test. 5. Tighten to specifications. 6. Clean, repair or replace valve body. 7. Replace valve body or case.

TROUBLESHOOTING AND DIAGNOSIS

Problem	Possible Cause	Correction
Starts up in 2nd or 3rd but no lockup at 1-2 shift points.	1. Improper fluid level. 2. Damaged or improperly adjusted linkage. 3. Improper band and/or clutch application, or oil pressure control system. 4. Faulty governor. 5. Valve body loose. 6. Dirty or sticking valve body. 7. Cross leaks between valve body and case mating surface.	1. Perform fluid level check. 2. Repair or adjust linkage. 3. Perform control pressure test. 4. Perform governor check. Replace or repair governor, clean screen. 5. Tighten to specification. 6. Clean, repair or replace valve body. 7. Replace valve body and/or case as required.
Shift points incorrect.	1. Improper fluid level. 2. Improper vacuum hose routing or leaks. 3. Improper operation of EGR system. 4. Linkage out of adjustment. 5. Improper speedometer gear installed. 6. Improper clutch or band application, or oil pressure control system. 7. Faulty governor. 8. Dirty or sticking valve body.	1. Perform fluid level check. 2. Correct hose routing. 3. Repair or replace as required. 4. Repair or adjust linkage. 5. Replace gear. 6. Perform shift test and control pressure test. 7. Repair or replace governor—clean screen. 8. Clean, repair or replace valve body.
No upshift at any speed in D.	1. Improper fluid level. 2. Vacuum leak to diaphragm unit. 3. Linkage out of adjustment. 4. Improper band or clutch application, or oil pressure control system. 5. Faulty governor. 6. Dirty or sticking valve bdy.	1. Perform fluid level check. 2. Repair vacuum line or hose. 3. Repair or adjust linkage. 4. Perform control pressure test. 5. Repair or replace governor, clean screen. 6. Clean, repair or replace valve body.
Shifts 1-3 in D.	1. Improper fluid level. 2. Intermediate band out of adjustment. 3. Faulty front servo and/or internal leaks. 4. Polished, glazed band or drum. 5. Improper band or clutch application, or oil pressure control system. 6. Dirty or sticking valve body.	1. Perform fluid level check. 2. Adjust band. 3. Perform air pressure test. Repair front servo and/or internal leaks. 4. Repair or replace band or drum. 5. Perform control pressure test. 6. Clean, repair or replace valve body.
Engine over-speeds on 2-3 shift.	1. Improper fluid level. 2. Linkage out of adjustment. 3. Improper band or clutch application, or oil pressure control system. 4. Faulty high clutch and/or intermediate servo. 5. Dirty or sticking valve body.	1. Perform fluid level check. 2. Repair or adjust linkage. 3. Perform control pressure test. 4. Perform air pressure test. Repair as required. 5. Clean repair or replace valve body.
Mushy 1-2 shift.	1. Improper fluid level 2. Incorrect engine idle and/or performance. 3. Improper linkage adjustment. 4. Intermediate band out of adjustment.	1. Perform fluid level check. 2. Tune, adjust engine idle as required. 3. Repair or adjust linkage. 4. Adjust intermediate band. 5. Perform control pressure test.

Problem	Possible Cause	Correction
Mushy 1-2 shift.	5. Improper band or clutch application, or oil pressure control system. 6. Faulty high clutch and/or intermediate servo release. 7. Polished, glazed band or drum. 8. Dirty or sticking valve body.	6. Perform air pressure test. Repair as required. 7. Repair or replace as required. 8. Clean, repair or replace valve body.
Rough 1-2 shift.	1. Improper fluid level. 2. Incorrect engine idle or performance. 3. Intermediate band out of adjustment. 4. Improper band or clutch application, or oil pressure control system. 5. Faulty intermediate servo. 6. Dirty or sticking valve body.	1. Perform fluid level check. 2. Tune, and adjust engine idle. 3. Adjust intermediate band. 4. Perform control pressure test. 5. Air pressure check intermediate servo. 6. Clean, repair or replace valve body.
Rough 2-3 shift	1. Improper fluid level. 2. Incorrect engine idle or performance. 3. Improper band or clutch application, or oil control pressure system. 4. Faulty intermediate servo apply and release and high clutch piston check ball. 5. Dirty or sticking valve body.	1. Perform fluid level check. 2. Tune and adjust engine idle. 3. Perform control pressure test. 4. Air pressure test the intermediate servo apply and release and the high clutch piston check ball. Repair as required. 5. Clean, repair or replace valve body.
Rough 3-1 shift at closed throttle in D.	1. Improper fluid level. 2. Incorrect engine idle or performance. 3. Improper linkage adjustment. 4. Improper clutch or band application or oil pressure control system. 5. Faulty governor operation. 6. Dirty or sticking valve body.	1. Perform fluid level check. 2. Tune, and adjust engine idle. 3. Repair or adjust linkage. 4. Perform control pressure test. 5. Perform governor test. Repair as required. 6. Clean, repair or replace valve body.
No forced downshifts.	1. Improper fluid level. 2. Linkage out of adjustment. 3. Improper clutch or band application, or oil pressure control system. 4. Faulty internal kickdown linkage. 5. Dirty or sticking valve body.	1. Perform fluid level check. 2. Repair or adjust linkage. 3. Perform control pressure test. 4. Repair internal kickdown linkage. 5. Clean, repair or replace valve body.
No 3-1 shift in D.	1. Improper fluid level. 2. Incorrect engine idle, or performance. 3. Faulty governor. 4. Dirty or sticking valve body.	1. Perform fluid level check. 2. Tune, and adjust engine idle. 3. Perform govenor check. Repair as required. 4. Clean, repair or replace valve body.
Runaway engine on 3-2 downshift.	1. Improper fluid level. 2. Linkage out of adjustment. 3. Intermediate band out of adjustment. 4. Improper band or clutch application, or oil pressure control system.	1. Perform fluid level check. 2. Repair or adjust linkage. 3. Adjust intermediate band. 4. Perform control pressure test. 5. Air pressure test check the intermediate servo. Repair servo and/or seals.

Problem	Possible Cause	Correction
Runaway engine on 3-2 downshift.	5. Faulty intermediate servo. 6. Polished, glazed band or drum. 7. Dirty or sticking valve body.	6. Repair or replace as required. 7. Clean, repair or replace valve body.
No engine braking in manual first gear.	1. Improper fluid level. 2. Linkage out of adjustment. 3. Bands or clutches out of adjustment. 4. Faulty oil pressure control system. 5. Faulty reverse servo. 6. Polished, glazed band or drum.	1. Perform fluid level check. 2. Repair or adjust linkage. 3. Adjust as necessary. 4. Perform control pressure test. 5. Perform air pressure test of reverse servo. Repair reverse clutch or rear servo as required. 6. Repair or replace as required.
No engine braking in manual second gear.	1. Improper fluid level. 2. Linkage out of adjustment. 3. Intermediate band out of adjustment. 4. Improper band or clutch application, or oil pressure control system. 5. Intermediate servo leaking. 6. Polished or glazed band or drum.	1. Perform fluid level check. 2. Repair or adjust linkage. 3. Adjust intermediate band. 4. Perform control pressure test. 5. Perform air pressure test of intermediate servo for leakage. Repair as required. 6. Repair or replace as required.
Transmission noisy—valve resonance.	1. Improper fluid level. 2. Linkage out of adjustment. 3. Improper band or clutch application, or oil pressure control system. 4. Cooler lines grounding. 5. Dirty sticking valve body. 6. Internal leakage or pump cavitation.	1. Perform fluid level check. 2. Repair or adjust linkage. 3. Perform control pressure test. 4. Free up cooler lines. 5. Clean, repair or replace valve body. 6. Repair as required.
Transmission overheats.	1. Improper fluid level. 2. Incorrect engine idle, or performance. 3. Improper clutch or band application, or oil pressure control system. 4. Restriction in cooler or lines. 5. Seized one-way clutch. 6. Dirty or sticking valve body.	1. Perform fluid level check. 2. Tune, or adjust engine idle. 3. Perform control pressure test. 4. Repair restriction. 5. Replace one-way clutch. 6. Clean, repair or replace valve body.
Transmission fluid leaks.	1. Improper fluid level. 2. Leakage at gasket, seals, etc. 3. Vacuum diaphragm unit leaking.	1. Perform fluid level check. 2. Remove all traces of lube on exposed surfaces of transmission. Check the vent for free breathing. Operate transmission at normal temperatures and inspect for leakage. Repair as required. 3. Replace diaphragm.

Automatic Transmission Troubleshooting

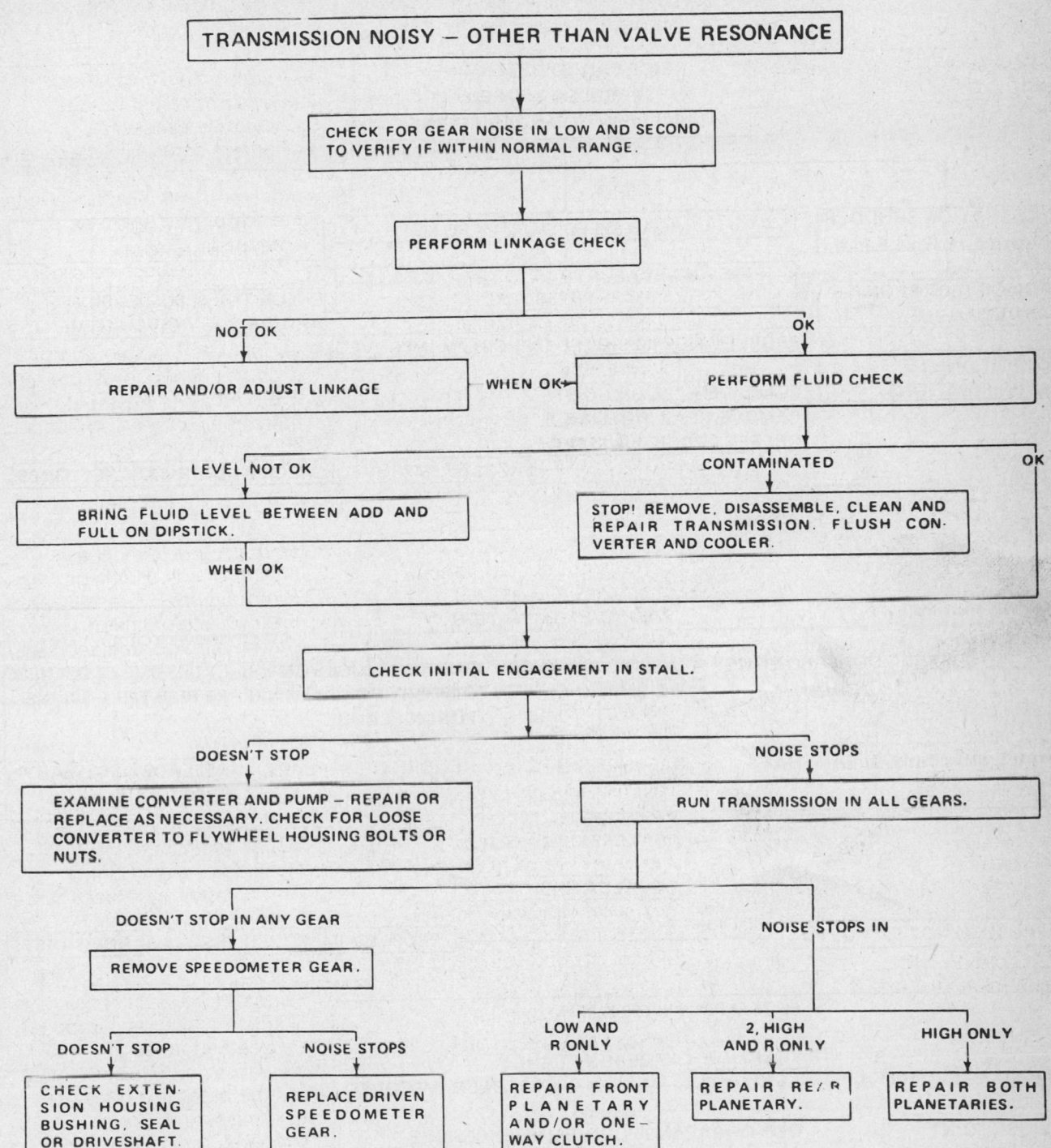

TRANSMISSION NOISY — OTHER THAN VALVE RESONANCE

CHECK FOR GEAR NOISE IN LOW AND SECOND TO VERIFY IF WITHIN NORMAL RANGE.

PERFORM LINKAGE CHECK

NOT OK — REPAIR AND/OR ADJUST LINKAGE

OK — PERFORM FLUID CHECK

WHEN OK →

LEVEL NOT OK — BRING FLUID LEVEL BETWEEN ADD AND FULL ON DIPSTICK.

WHEN OK

CONTAMINATED — STOP! REMOVE, DISASSEMBLE, CLEAN AND REPAIR TRANSMISSION. FLUSH CONVERTER AND COOLER.

OK

CHECK INITIAL ENGAGEMENT IN STALL.

DOESN'T STOP — EXAMINE CONVERTER AND PUMP — REPAIR OR REPLACE AS NECESSARY. CHECK FOR LOOSE CONVERTER TO FLYWHEEL HOUSING BOLTS OR NUTS.

NOISE STOPS — RUN TRANSMISSION IN ALL GEARS.

DOESN'T STOP IN ANY GEAR — REMOVE SPEEDOMETER GEAR.

DOESN'T STOP — CHECK EXTENSION HOUSING BUSHING, SEAL OR DRIVESHAFT.

NOISE STOPS — REPLACE DRIVEN SPEEDOMETER GEAR.

NOISE STOPS IN

LOW AND R ONLY — REPAIR FRONT PLANETARY AND/OR ONE-WAY CLUTCH.

2, HIGH AND R ONLY — REPAIR REAR PLANETARY.

HIGH ONLY — REPAIR BOTH PLANETARIES.

Driveshaft Troubleshooting
Vibration, Roughness, Rumble and/or Boom

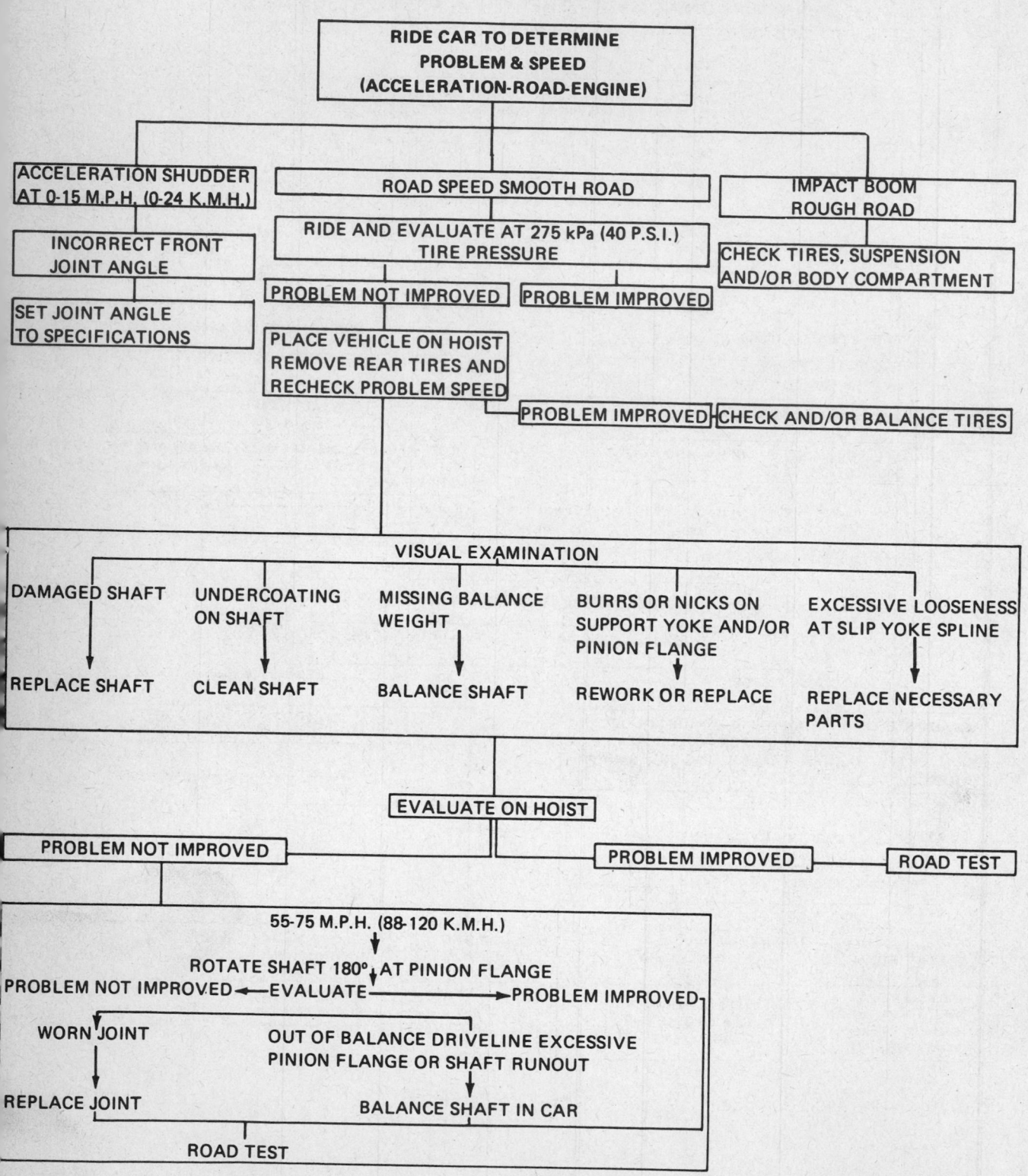

Universal Joint Troubleshooting

Problem	Possible Cause	Correction
Leak at front slip yoke. **NOTE:** An occasional drop of lubricant leaking from splined yoke is normal and requires no attention.	1. Rough outside surface on splined yoke. 2. Defective transmission rear oil seal.	1. Replace seal if cut by burrs on yoke. Minor burrs can be smoothed by careful use of crocus cloth or honing with a fine stone. Replace yoke if outside surface is rough or burred badly. 2. Replace transmission rear oil seal. 3. Bring transmission oil up to proper level after correction.
Knock in drive line, clunking noise when car is operated under floating condition at 10 mph in high gear or neutral.	1. Worn or damaged universal joints. 2. Side gear hub counterbore in differential worn oversize.	1. Disassemble universal joints, inspect and replace worn or damaged parts. 2. Replace differential case and/or side gears as required.
Ping, snap or click in drive line. **NOTE:** Usually occurs on initial load application after transmission has been put into gear, either forward or reverse.	1. Loose upper or lower control arm bushing bolts. 2. Loose companion flange.	1. Tighten bolts to specified torque. 2. Remove companion flange, turn 180° from its original position, apply white lead to splines and reinstall. Tighten pinion nut to specified torque.

Front Wheel Drive Halfshaft Troubleshooting

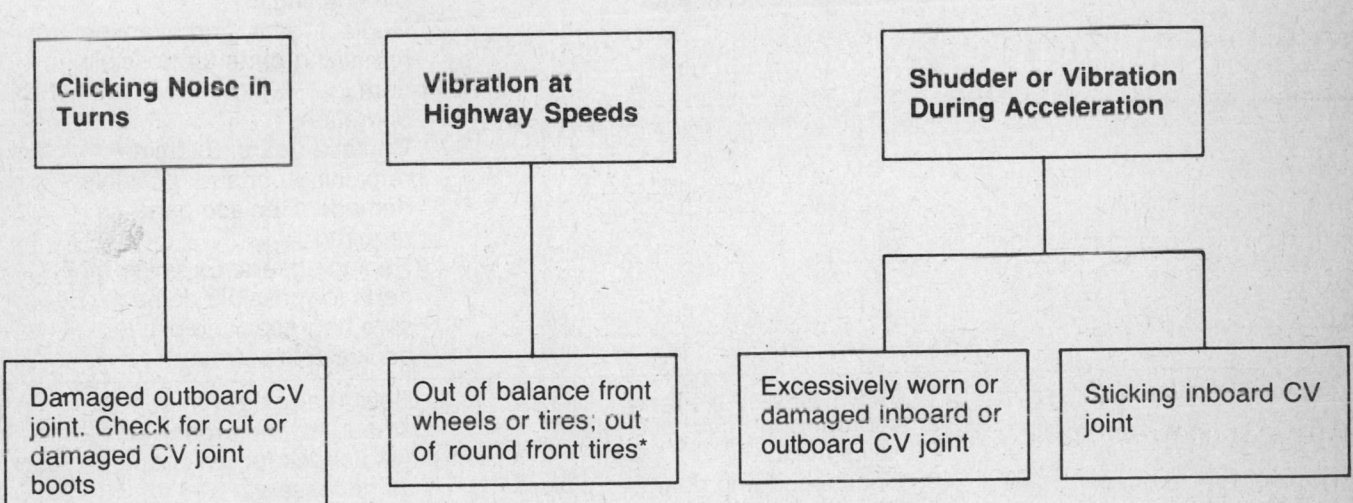

*Halfshafts do not usually contribute to rotational vibrations.

Drive Axle Troubleshooting

Condition	Possible Cause	Correction
Rear wheel noise	1. Loose wheel. 2. Spalled wheel bearing cup or cone. 3. Defective or brinelled wheel bearing. 4. Excessive axle shaft endplay. 5. Bent or sprng axle shaft flange.	1. Tighten loose wheel nuts. 2. Check rear wheel bearings. If spalled or worn, replace. 3. Defective or brinelled bearings must be replaced. Check rear axle shaft end play. 4. Readjust axle shaft end play. 5. Replace bent or sprung axle shaft.
Scoring of differential gears and pinions	1. Insufficient lubrication. 2. Improper grade of lubricant. 3. Excessive spinning of one wheel.	1. Replace scored gears. Scoring marks on the pressure face of gear teeth or in the bore are caused by instantaneous fusing of the mating surfaces. Scored gears should be replaced. Fill rear axle to required capacity with proper lubricant. 2. Replace scored gears. Inspect all gears and bearings for possible damage. Clean and refill axle to required capacity with proper lubricant. 3. Replace scored gears. Inspect all gears, pinion bores and shaft for scoring, or bearings for possible damage.
Tooth breakage (ring gear and pinion)	1. Overloading. 2. Erratic clutch operation. 3. Ice-spotted pavements. 4. Improper adjustments.	1. Replace gear. Examine other gears and bearings for possible damage. Avoid future overloading. 2. Replace gear, and examine remaining parts for possible damage. Avoid erratic clutch operation. 3. Replace gears. Examine remaining parts for possible damage. Replace parts as required. 4. Replace gears. Examine other parts for possible damage. Be sure ring gear and pinion backlash is correct.
Rear axle noise	1. Insufficient lubricant. 2. Improper ring gear and pinion adjustment. 3. Unmatched ring gear and pinion. 4. Worn teeth on ring gear or pinion. 5. End-play in drive pinion bearings. 6. Side play in differential bearings. 7. Incorrect drive gearlash. 8. Limited-slip differential—moan and chatter.	1. Refill rear axle with correct amount of the proper lubricant. Also check for leaks and correct as necessary. 2. Check ring gear and pinion tooth contact. 3. Remove unmatched ring gear and pinion. Replace with a new matched gear and pinion set. 4. Check teeth on ring gear and pinion for contact. If necessary, replace with new matched set. 5. Adjust drive pinion bearing preload.

Problem	Possible Cause	Correction
Rear axle noise		6. Adjust differential bearing preload. 7. Correct drive gear lash. 8. Drain and flush lubricant. Refill with proper lubricant.
Loss of lubricant	1. Lubricant level too high. 2. Worn axle shaft oil seals. 3. Cracked rear axle housing. 4. Worn drive pinion oil seal. 5. Scored and worn companion flange. 6. Clogged vent. 7. Loose carrier housing bolts or housing cover screws.	1. Drain excess lubricant. 2. Replace worn oil seals with new ones. Prepare new seals before replacement. 3. Repair or replace housing as required. 4. Replace worn drive pinion oil seal with a new one. 5. Replace worn or scored companion flange and oil seal. 6. Remove obstructions. 7. Tighten bolts or cover screws to specifications and fill to correct level with proper lubricant.
Overheating of unit	1. Lubricant level too low. 2. Incorrect grade of lubricant. 3. Bearing adjusted too tightly. 4. Excessive wear in gears. 5. Insufficient ring gear-to-pinion clearance.	1. Refill rear axle. 2. Drain, flush and refill rear axle with correct amount of the proper lubricant. 3. Readjust bearings. 4. Check gears for excessive wear or scoring. Replace as necessary. 5. Readjust ring gear and pinion backlash and check gears for possible scoring.

CHASSIS

Shock Absorber and Rear Spring Troubleshooting

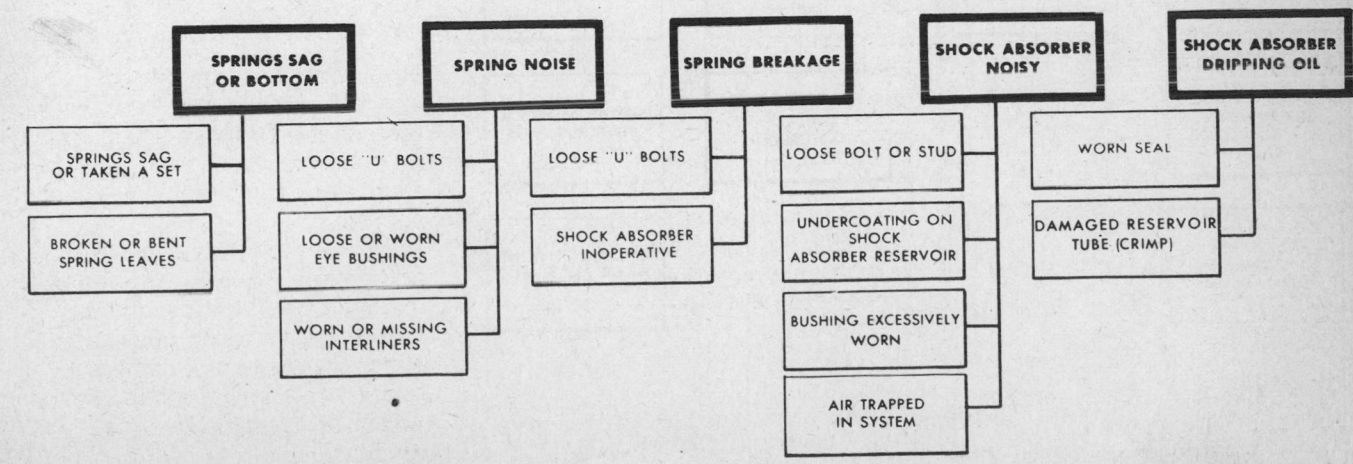

Front Suspension and Steering Linkage
Troubleshooting—Rear Wheel Drive

FRONT END NOISE	EXCESSIVE PLAY IN STEERING	FRONT WHEEL SHIMMY	INSTABILITY	HARD STEERING	CAR PULLS TO ONE SIDE
LOOSE OR WORN FRONT WHEEL BEARINGS	LOOSE OR WORN FRONT WHEEL BEARINGS	LOOSE OR WORN WHEEL BEARINGS	LOW OR UNEVEN TIRE PRESSURE	LOW OR UNEVEN TIRE PRESSURE	BROKEN REAR SPRING
LOOSE OR WORN SHOCK ABSORBER MOUNTING OR SHOCK ABSORBER	LOOSE OR WORN STEERING SHAFT COUPLING	TIRE, WHEEL OUT OF BALANCE	LOOSE WHEEL BEARINGS	LACK OF ASSIST OF POWER STEERING SYSTEM	POWER STEERING CONTROL VALVE OUT OF ADJUSTMENT
LOOSE STEERING GEAR TO FRAME MOUNTING BOLTS	LOOSE STEERING GEAR TO FRAME MOUNTING BOLTS	UNEVEN TIRE WEAR, OR EXCESSIVELY WORN TIRES	BROKEN REAR SPRING	STEERING GEAR NOT ADJUSTED	LOOSE OR WORN STRUT BUSHINGS
STEERING KNUCKLE ARM CONTACTING THE LOWER CONTROL ARM WHEEL STOP	WORN TIE ROD ENDS	WORN TIE ROD ENDS	SHOCK ABSORBER INOPERATIVE	INCORRECT FRONT WHEEL ALIGNMENT (PARTICULARLY CASTER)	INCORRECT FRONT WHEEL ALIGNMENT (PARTICULARLY CASTER)
WORN UPPER CONTROL ARM BUSHINGS	WORN IDLER ARM BUSHING	LOOSE OR WORN STRUT BUSHINGS	IMPROPER STEERING CROSS SHAFT ADJUSTMENT		
WORN LOWER CONTROL ARM SHAFT BUSHINGS	WORN STEERING GEAR PARTS	LOOSE OR WORN UPPER CONTROL ARM BALL JOINTS	STEERING GEAR NOT CENTERED		
LOOSE OR WORN STRUT BUSHINGS	INCORRECT STEERING GEAR ADJUSTMENT	INCORRECT FRONT WHEEL ALIGNMENT (PARTICULARLY CASTER)	WORN IDLER ARM BUSHING		
LOOSE STRUTS OR LOWER CONTROL ARM		WORN SHOCK ABSORBER	LOOSE OR WORN STRUT BUSHINGS		
BALL JOINTS REQUIRE LUBRICATION			INCORRECT FRONT WHEEL ALIGNMENT		

Suspension and Steering Linkage
Troubleshooting— Front Wheel Drive

NOISE	INSTABILITY	EXCESSIVE PLAY IN STEERING	HARD STEERING	CAR PULLS TO ONE SIDE
(DRIVE OR COAST) ROAD/TIRE NOISE	LOW OR UNEVEN TIRE PRESSURE	LOOSE OR WORN HUB BEARINGS	LOW OR UNEVEN TIRE PRESSURE	LOW OR UNEVEN TIRE PRESSURE
(PRONOUNCED ON TURNS) FRONT HUB BEARINGS	LOOSE OR WORN HUB BEARINGS	LOOSE OR WORN STEERING SHAFT COUPLING	LACK OF ASSIST OF POWER STEERING SYSTEM	WHILE BRAKING BRAKE SERVICE
(ON ACCELERATION OR DECELERATION) FRONT WHEEL BEARINGS TRANSAXLE GEARS	BROKEN SPRING OR BENT REAR SUSPENSION	LOOSE STEERING GEAR MOUNTING BOLTS	STEERING GEAR LOW ON LUBRICANT	BROKEN FRONT OR REAR SPRING OR BENT REAR SUSPENSION
(CLUNK-ON ACCELERATION OR DECELERATION) TRANSAXLE BEARINGS OR GEARS	INOPERATIVE SHOCK ABSORBING (STRUTS)	WORN TIE ROD ENDS	INCORRECT WHEEL ALIGNMENT	LOOSE LOWER CONTROL ARM
(CLICKING NOISE ON TURNS) EXCESSIVE WEAR OR BROKEN C.V. JOINT	IMPROPER STEERING GEAR ADJUSTMENT			INCORRECT WHEEL ALIGNMENT
	LOOSE OR WORN STRUT			UNBALANCED STEERING GEAR VALVE (POWER)
	INCORRECT WHEEL ALIGNMENT FRONT OR REAR			

Tapered Wheel Bearing Troubleshooting

CONSIDER THE FOLLOWING FACTORS WHEN DIAGNOSING BEARING CONDITION:

1. GENERAL CONDITION OF ALL PARTS DURING DISASSEMBLY AND INSPECTION.

2. CLASSIFY THE FAILURE WITH THE AID OF THE ILLUSTRATIONS.

3. DETERMINE THE CAUSE.

4. MAKE ALL REPAIRS FOLLOWING RECOMMENDED PROCEDURES.

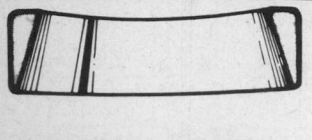 **GOOD BEARING**	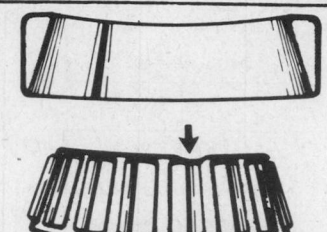 **BENT CAGE** CAGE DAMAGE DUE TO IMPROPER HANDLING OR TOOL USAGE. REPLACE BEARING.	 **BENT CAGE** CAGE DAMAGE DUE TO IMPROPER HANDLING OR TOOL USAGE. REPLACE BEARING.
 **GALLING** METAL SMEARS ON ROLLER ENDS DUE TO OVERHEAT, LUBRICANT FAILURE OR OVERLOAD. REPLACE BEARING — CHECK SEALS AND CHECK FOR PROPER LUBRICATION.	 **ABRASIVE STEP WEAR** PATTERN ON ROLLER ENDS CAUSED BY FINE ABRASIVES. CLEAN ALL PARTS AND HOUSINGS, CHECK SEALS AND BEARINGS AND REPLACE IF LEAKING, ROUGH OR NOISY.	 **ETCHING** BEARING SURFACES APPEAR GRAY OR GRAYISH BLACK IN COLOR WITH RELATED ETCHING AWAY OF MATERIAL USUALLY AT ROLLER SPACING. REPLACE BEARINGS — CHECK SEALS AND CHECK FOR PROPER LUBRICATION.
 **MISALIGNMENT** OUTER RACE MISALIGNMENT DUE TO FOREIGN OBJECT. CLEAN RELATED PARTS AND REPLACE BEARING. MAKE SURE RACES ARE PROPERLY SEATED.	 **INDENTATIONS** SURFACE DEPRESSIONS ON RACE AND ROLLERS CAUSED BY HARD PARTICLES OF FOREIGN MATERIAL. CLEAN ALL PARTS AND HOUSINGS, CHECK SEALS AND REPLACE BEARINGS IF ROUGH OR NOISY.	 **FATIGUE SPALLING** FLAKING OF SURFACE METAL RESULTING FROM FATIGUE. REPLACE BEARING — CLEAN ALL RELATED PARTS.

Tapered Wheel Bearing Troubleshooting

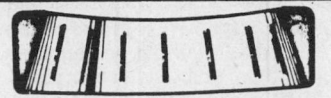

BRINELLING

SURFACE INDENTATIONS IN RACEWAY CAUSED BY ROLLERS EITHER UNDER IMPACT LOADING OR VIBRATION WHILE THE BEARING IS NOT ROTATING.

REPLACE BEARING IF ROUGH OR NOISY.

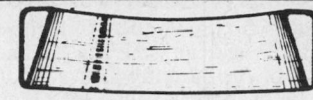

CAGE WEAR

WEAR AROUND OUTSIDE DIAMETER OF CAGE AND ROLLER POCKETS CAUSED BY ABRASIVE MATERIAL AND INEFFICIENT LUBRICATION. CHECK SEALS AND REPLACE BEARINGS.

ABRASIVE ROLLER WEAR

PATTERN ON RACES AND ROLLERS CAUSED BY FINE ABRASIVES.

CLEAN ALL PARTS AND HOUSINGS, CHECK SEALS AND BEARINGS AND REPLACE IF LEAKING, ROUGH OR NOISY.

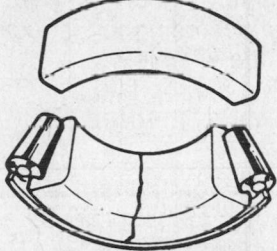

CRACKED INNER RACE

RACE CRACKED DUE TO IMPROPER FIT, COCKING, OR POOR BEARING SEATS.

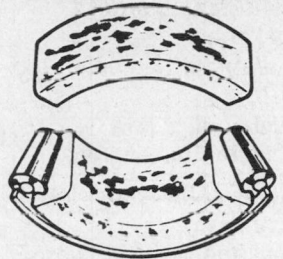

SMEARS

SMEARING OF METAL DUE TO SLIPPAGE. SLIPPAGE CAN BE CAUSED BY POOR FITS, LUBRICATION, OVERHEATING, OVERLOADS OR HANDLING DAMAGE.

REPLACE BEARINGS, CLEAN RELATED PARTS AND CHECK FOR PROPER FIT AND LUBRICATION.

REPLACE SHAFT IF DAMAGED.

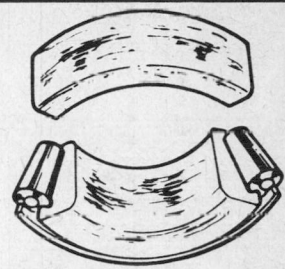

FRETTAGE

CORROSION SET UP BY SMALL RELATIVE MOVEMENT OF PARTS WITH NO LUBRICATION.

REPLACE BEARING. CLEAN RELATED PARTS. CHECK SEALS AND CHECK FOR PROPER LUBRICATION.

HEAT DISCOLORATION

HEAT DISCOLORATION CAN RANGE FROM FAINT YELLOW TO DARK BLUE RESULTING FROM OVERLOAD OR INCORRECT LUBRICANT.

EXCESSIVE HEAT CAN CAUSE SOFTENING OF RACES OR ROLLERS.

TO CHECK FOR LOSS OF TEMPER ON RACES OR ROLLERS A SIMPLE FILE TEST MAY BE MADE. A FILE DRAWN OVER A TEMPERED PART WILL GRAB AND CUT META, WHEREAS, A FILE DRAWN OVER A HARD PART WILL GLIDE READILY WITH NO METAL CUTTING.

REPLACE BEARINGS IF OVER HEATING DAMAGE IS INDICATED. CHECK SEALS AND OTHER PARTS

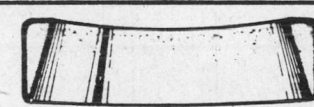

STAIN DISCOLORATION

DISCOLORATION CAN RANGE FROM LIGHT BROWN TO BLACK CAUSED BY INCORRECT LUBRICANT OR MOISTURE.

RE-USE BEARINGS IF STAINS CAN BE REMOVED BY LIGHT POLISHING OR IF NO EVIDENCE OF OVERHEATING IS OBSERVED.

CHECK SEALS AND RELATED PARTS FOR DAMAGE.

Manual Steering Troubleshooting

INSPECTION AND ALIGNMENT

Before any steering gear adjustments are made, it is recommended that the front end of the car be raised and a thorough inspection be made for stiffness or lost motion in steering gear, steering linkage and front suspension. Worn or damaged parts should be replaced, since a satisfactory adjustment of the steering gear cannot be obtained if bent or badly worn parts exist.

It is also very important that the steering gear be properly aligned in the car. Misalignment of the gear places a stress on the steering worm shaft, therefore a proper adjustment is impossible. To align the steering gear, loosen the mounting bolts to permit the gear to align itself. Check the steering gear mounting seat, and if there is a gap at any of the mounting bolts, proper alignment may be obtained by placing shims where excessive gap appears. Tighten the steering gear bolts. Alignment of the gear in the car is very important and should be done carefully so that a satisfactory, trouble-free gear adjustment may be obtained.

Condition	Possible Cause	Corrective Action
Hard steering	1. Low or uneven tire pressure. 2. Insufficient lubricant in the steering gear housing or in steering linkage. 3. Steering gear shaft adjusted too tight. 4. Front wheels out of line. 5. Steering column misaligned.	1. Inflate tires to recommended pressures. 2. Lubricate as necessary. 3. Adjust according to instructions. 4. Align the wheels. 5. See the appropriate Car Section for alignment procedures.
Excessive play or looseness in the steering wheel	1. Steering gear shaft adjust too loose or badly worn. 2. Steering linkage loose or worn. 3. Front wheel bearings improperly adjusted. 4. Steering arm loose on steering gear shaft. 5. Steering gear housing attaching bolts loose. 6. Steering arms loose at steering knuckles. 7. Worn ball joints. 8. Worm shaft bearing adjustment too loose.	1. Replace worn parts and adjust according to instructions. 2. Replace worn parts. 3. Adjust according to instructions. 4. Inspect for damage to the gear shaft and steering arm, replace parts as necessary. 5. Tighten attaching bolts to specifications. 6. Tighten according to specifications. 7. Replace the ball joints as necessary. 8. Adjust worm bearing preload according to instructions.

Power Steering Systems Troubleshooting

Condition	Possible Cause	Corrective Action
Hard steering	1. Improper tire pressure. 2. Loose pump drive belt. 3. Low or incorrect fluid. 4. Loose, bent or poorly lubricated front end parts. 5. Improper front end alignment. 6. Bind in steering column or linkage.	1. Inflate tires to recommended pressures. 2. Tighten or replace belt. 3. Refill reservoir with proper fluid; check for leaks; 4. Tighten or replace parts; lubricate at all fittings. 5. Align front end.

Condition	Possible Cause	Correction Action
Hard steering	7. Air in hydraulic system. 8. Low pump output or leaks in system. 9. Obstruction in lines. 10. Pump valves sticking or out of adjustment.	6. Disassemble and inspect component parts. Repair or replace as necessary. 7. Bleed system, refill and check for leaks. 8. Disassemble pump, check for worn or damaged parts. Check for leaks in the system. 9. Clean or replace lines. 10. Replace or adjust valves.
Loose steering	1. Loose wheel bearings 2. Faulty shocks. 3. Worn linkage components. 4. Loose steering gear mounting or linkage points. 5. Steering mechanism worn or improperly adjusted. 6. Valve spool improperly adjusted	1. Adjust wheel bearings. 2. Relace shocks. 3. Replace worn components. 4. Tighten mountings or linkage. 5. Replace and/or adjust mechanism. 6. Adjust valve spool.
Veer or wander	1. Improper tire pressure. 2. Improper front end alignment. 3. Dragging brakes. 4. Bent frame. 5. Improper rear end alignment. 6. Faulty shocks or springs. 7. Loose or bent front end components. 8. Play in Pitman arm 9. Loose wheel bearings. 10. Binding Pitman arm. 11. Spool valve sticking or improperly adjusted.	1. Inflate tires to recommended pressures. 2. Align front end. 3. Inspect, replace and/or adjust brakes. 4. Straighten frame. 5. Inspect shocks and control arm torque. Replace and/or adjust as necessary. 6. Replace as necessary. 7. Replace as necessary. 8. Inspect bushings and arm. Replace as necessary. 9. Adjust to specifications. 10. Replace arm. 11. Adjust or replace as necessary.
Wheel oscillation	1. Improper tire pressure. 2. Loose wheel bearings. 3. Improper front end alignment. 4. Bent spindle. 5. Worn, bent or broken front end components. 6. Tires out of round or out of balance. 7. Excessive lateral runout in disc brake rotor.	1. Inflate tires to recommended pressures. 2. Adjust to specifications. 3. Align front end. 4. Replace spindle. 5. Inspect, repair or replace as necessary. 6. Replace or balance tires. 7. Reface or replace rotor.
Noises	1. Loose belts. 2. Low fluid, air in system. 3. Foreign matter in system. 4. Improper lubrication. 5. Interference or chafing in linkage. 6. Steering gear mountings loose. 7. Incorrect adjustment or wear in gear box. 8. Faulty valves or wear in pump.	1. Replace and/or adjust belts. 2. Refill and check for leaks. 3. Disassemble and clean system. 4. Lubricate all fittings. 5. Disassemble, inspect, replace or adjust components. 6. Tighten mountings. 7. Disassemble, inspect, repair, replace and/or adjust parts. 8. Replace parts as necessary.

How To Read Tire Wear

The way your tires wear is a good indicator of other parts of the suspension. Abnormal wear patterns are often caused by the need for simple tire maintenance, or for front end alignment.

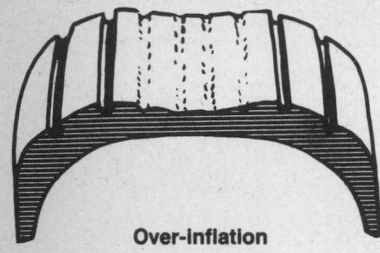

Over-inflation

Excessive wear at the center of the tread indicates that the air pressure in the tire is consistently too high. The tire is riding on the center of the tread and wearing it prematurely. Occasionally, this wear pattern can result from outrageously wide tires on narrow rims. The cure for this is to replace either the tires or the wheels.

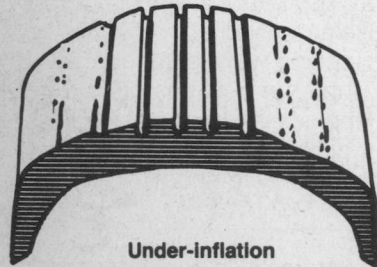

Under-inflation

This type of wear usually results from consistent under-inflation. When a tire is under-inflated, there is too much contact with the road by the outer treads, which wear prematurely. When this type of wear occurs, and the tire pressure is known to be consistently correct, a bent or worn steering component or the need for wheel alignment could be indicated.

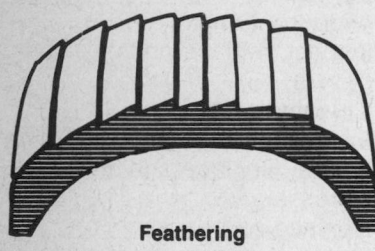

Feathering

Feathering is a condition when the edge of each tread rib develops a slightly rounded edge on one side and a sharp edge on the other. By running your hand over the tire, you can usually feel the sharper edges before you'll be able to see them. The most common causes of feathering are incorrect toe-in setting or deteriorated bushings in the front suspension.

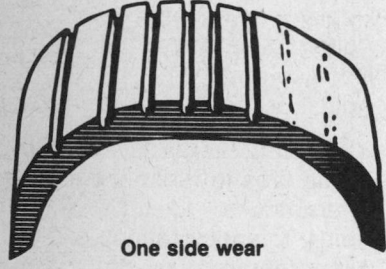

One side wear

When an inner or outer rib wears faster than the rest of the tire, the need for wheel alignment is indicated. There is excessive camber in the front suspension, causing the wheel to lean too much putting excessive load on one side of the tire. Misalignment could also be due to sagging springs, worn ball joints, or worn control arm bushings. Be sure the vehicle is loaded the way it's normally driven when you have the wheels aligned.

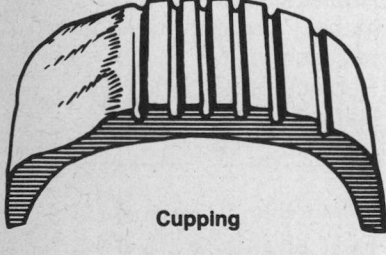

Cupping

Cups or scalloped dips appearing around the edge of the tread almost always indicate worn (sometimes bent) suspension parts. Adjustment of wheel alignment alone will seldom cure the problem. Any worn component that connects the wheel to the suspension can cause this type of wear. Occasionally, wheels that are out of balance will wear like this, but wheel imbalance usually shows up as bald spots between the outside edges and center of the tread.

Second-rib wear

Second-rib wear is usually found only in radial tires, and appears where the steel belts end in relation to the tread. It can be kept to a minimum by paying careful attention to tire pressure and frequently rotating the tires. This is often considered normal wear but excessive amounts indicate that the tires are too wide for the wheels.

Drum Brake Troubleshooting

Condition	Possible Cause	Correction Action
Pedal goes to floor	1. Fluid low in reservoir. 2. Air in hydraulic brake system. 3. Improperly adjusted brake. 4. Leaking wheel cylinders. 5. Loose or broken brake lines. 6. Leaking or worn master cylinder. 7. Excessively worn brake lining.	1. Fill and bleed master cylinder. 2. Fill and bleed hydraulic brake system. 3. Repair or replace self-adjuster as required. 4. Recondition or replace wheel cylinder and replace both brake shoes. 5. Tighten all brake fittings or replace brake line. 6. Recondition or replace master cylinder and bleed hydraulic system. 7. Reline and adjust brakes.
Spongy brake pedal	1. Air in hydraulic system. 2. Improper brake fluid (low boiling point). 3. Excessively worn or cracked brake drums. 4. Broken pedal pivot bushing.	1. Fill master cylinder and bleed hydraulic system. 2. Drain, flush and refill with brake fluid. 3. Replace all faulty brake drums. 4. Replace nylon pivot bushing.
Brakes pulling	1. Contaminated lining. 2. Front end out of alignment. 3. Incorrect brake adjustment. 4. Unmatched brake lining. 5. Brake drums out of round. 6. Brake shoes distorted. 7. Restricted brake hose or line. 8. Broken rear spring.	1. Replace contaminated brake lining. 2. Align front end. 3. Adjust brakes and check fluid. 4. Match primary, secondary with same type of lining on all wheels. 5. Grind or replace brake drums. 6. Replace faulty brake shoes. 7. Replace plugged hose or brake line. 8. Replace broken spring.
Squealing brakes	1. Glazed brake lining. 2. Saturated brake lining. 3. Weak or broken brake shoe retaining spring. 4. Broken or weak brake shoe return spring. 5. Incorrect brake lining. 6. Distorted brake shoes. 7. Bent support plate. 8. Dust in brakes or scored brake drums.	1. Cam grind or replace brake lining. 2. Replace saturated lining. 3. Replace retaining spring. 4. Replace return spring. 5. Install matched brake lining. 6. Replace brake shoes. 7. Replace support plate. 8. Blow out brake assembly with compressed air and grind brake drums.
Chirping brakes	1. Out of round drum or eccentric axle flange pilot.	1. Repair as necessary, and lubricate support plate contact areas (6 places).
Dragging brakes	1. Incorrect wheel or parking brake adjustment. 2. Parking brakes engaged. 3. Weak or broken brake shoe return spring. 4. Brake pedal binding. 5. Master cylinder cup sticking. 6. Obstructed master cylinder relief port. 7. Saturated brake lining. 8. Bent or out of round brake drum.	1. Adjust brake and check fluid. 2. Release parking brakes. 3. Replace brake shoe return spring. 4. Free up and lubricate brake pedal and linkage. 5. Recondition master cylinder. 6. Use compressed air and blow out relief port. 7. Replace brake lining. 8. Grind or replace faulty brake drum.

TROUBLESHOOTING AND DIAGNOSIS

Condition	Possible Cause	Corrective Action
Hard pedal	1. Brake booster inoperative. 2. Incorrect brake lining. 3. Restricted brake line or hose. 4. Frozen brake pedal linkage.	1. Replace brake booster. 2. Install matched brake lining. 3. Clean out or replace brake line or hose. 4. Free up and lubricate brake linkage.
Wheel locks	1. Contaminated brake lining. 2. Loose or torn brake lining. 3. Wheel cylinder cups sticking. 4. Incorrect wheel bearing adjustment.	1. Reline both front or rear of all four brakes. 2. Replace brake lining. 3. Recondition or replace wheel cylinder. 4. Clean, pack and adjust wheel bearings.
Brakes fade (high speed)	1. Incorrect lining. 2. Overheated brake drums. 3. Incorrect brake fluid (low boiling temperature) 4. Saturated brake lining.	1. Replace lining. 2. Inspect for dragging brakes. 3. Drain, flush, refill and bleed hydraulic brake system. 4. Reline both front or rear or all four brakes.
Pedal pulsates	1. Bent or out of round brake drum.	1. Grind or replace brake drums.
Brake chatter and shoe knock	1. Out of round brake drum. 2. Loose support plate. 3. Bent support plate. 4. Distorted brake shoes. 5. Machine grooves in contact face of brake drum. (Shoe Knock). 6. Contaminated brake lining.	1. Grind or replace brake drums. 2. Tighten support plate bolts to proper specifications. 3. Replace support plate. 4. Replace brake shoes. 5. Grind or replace brake drum. 6. Replace either front or rear or all four linings.
Brakes do not self adjust	1. Adjuster screw frozen in thread. 2. Adjuster screw corroded at thrust washer. 3. Adjuster level does not engage star wheel. 4. Adjuster installed on wrong wheel.	1. Clean and free-up all thread areas. 2. Clean threads and replace thrust washer if necessary. 3. Repair, free up or replace adjusters as required. 4. Install correct adjuster parts.

Disc Brake Troubleshooting

Condition	Possible Cause	Correction Action
Noise—Groan—Brake noise emanating when slowly releasing brakes (creep-groan).	1. Not detrimental to function of disc brakes—no corrective action required. (Indicate to operator this noise may be eliminated by slightly increasing or decreasing brake pedal efforts.)	
Rattle—Brake noise or rattle emanating at low speeds on rough roads, (front wheels only).	1. Shoe anti-rattle spring missing or not properly positioned. 2. Excessive clearance between shoe and caliper.	1. Install new anti-rattle spring or position properly. 2. Install new shoe and lining assemblies.

Condition	Possible Cause	Corrective Action
Scraping	1. Mounting bolts too long. 2. Loose wheel bearings.	1. Install mounting bolts of correct length. 2. Readjust wheel bearings to correct specifications.
Front brakes heat up during driving and fail to release	1. Operator riding brake pedal. 2. Stop light switch improperly adjusted. 3. Sticking pedal linkage. 4. Frozen or seized piston. 5. Residual pressure valve in master cylinder. 6. Power brake malfunction.	1. Instruct owner how to drive with disc brakes. 2. Adjust stop light to allow full return of pedal. 3. Free up sticking pedal linkage. 4. Disassemble caliper and free up piston. 5. Remove valve. 6. Replace.
Leaky wheel cylinder	1. Damaged or worn caliper piston seal. 2. Scores or corrosion on surface of cylinder bore.	1. Disassemble caliper and install new seal. 2. Disassemble caliper and hone cylinder bore. Install new seal.
Grabbing or uneven brake action	1. Causes listed under "Pull." 2. Power brake malfunction.	1. Corrections listed under "Pull". 2. Replace.
Brake pedal can be depressed without braking effect	1. Air in hydraulic system or improper bleeding procedure. 2. Leak past primary cup in master cylinder. 3. Leak in system. 4. Rear brakes out of adjustment. 5. Bleeder screw open.	1. Bleed system. 2. Recondition master cylinder. 3. Check for leak and repair as required. 4. Adjust rear brakes. 5. Close bleeder screw and bleed entire system.
Excessive pedal travel	1. Air, leak, or insufficient fluid in system or caliper. 2. Warped or excessively tapered shoe and lining assembly. 3. Excessive disc runout. 4. Rear brake adjustment required. 5. Loose wheel bearing adjustment. 6. Damaged caliper piston seal. 7. Improper brake fluid (boil). 8. Power brake malfunction.	1. Check system for leaks and bleed. 2. Install new shoe and linings. 3. Check disc for runout with dial indicator. Install new or refinished disc. 4. Check and adjust rear brakes. 5. Readjust wheel bearing to specified torque. 6. Install new piston seal. 7. Drain and install correct fluid. 8. Replace.
Brake roughness or chatter (pedal pumping)	1. Excessive thickness variation of braking disc. 2. Excessive lateral runout of braking disc. 3. Rear brake drums out-of-round. 4. Excessive front bearing clearance.	1. Check disc for thickness variation using a micrometer. 2. Check disc for lateral runout with dial indicator. Install new or refinished disc. 3. Reface rear drums and check for out-of-round. 4. Readjust wheel bearings to specified torque.
Excessive pedal effort	1. Brake fluid, oil or grease on linings. 2. Incorrect lining. 3. Frozen or seized pistons. 4. Power brake malfunction.	1. Install new shoe linings as required. 2. Remove lining and install correct lining. 3. Disassemble caliper and free up pistons. 4. Replace.

Condition	Possible Cause	Corrective Action
Pull	1. Brake fluid, oil or grease on linings. 2. Unmatched linings. 3. Distorted brake shoes. 4. Frozen or seized pistons. 5. Incorrect tire pressure. 6. Front end out of alignment. 7. Broken rear spring. 8. Rear brake pistons sticking. 9. Restricted hose or line. 10. Caliper not in proper alignment to braking disc.	1. Install new shoe and linings. 2. Install correct lining. 3. Install new brake shoes. 4. Disassemble caliper and free up pistons. 5. Inflate tires to recommended pressures. 6. Align front end and check. 7. Install new rear spring. 8. Free up rear brake pistons. 9. Check hoses and lines and correct as necessary. 10. Remove caliper and reinstall. Check alignment.

ELECTRICAL

Turn Signal and Flasher Troubleshooting

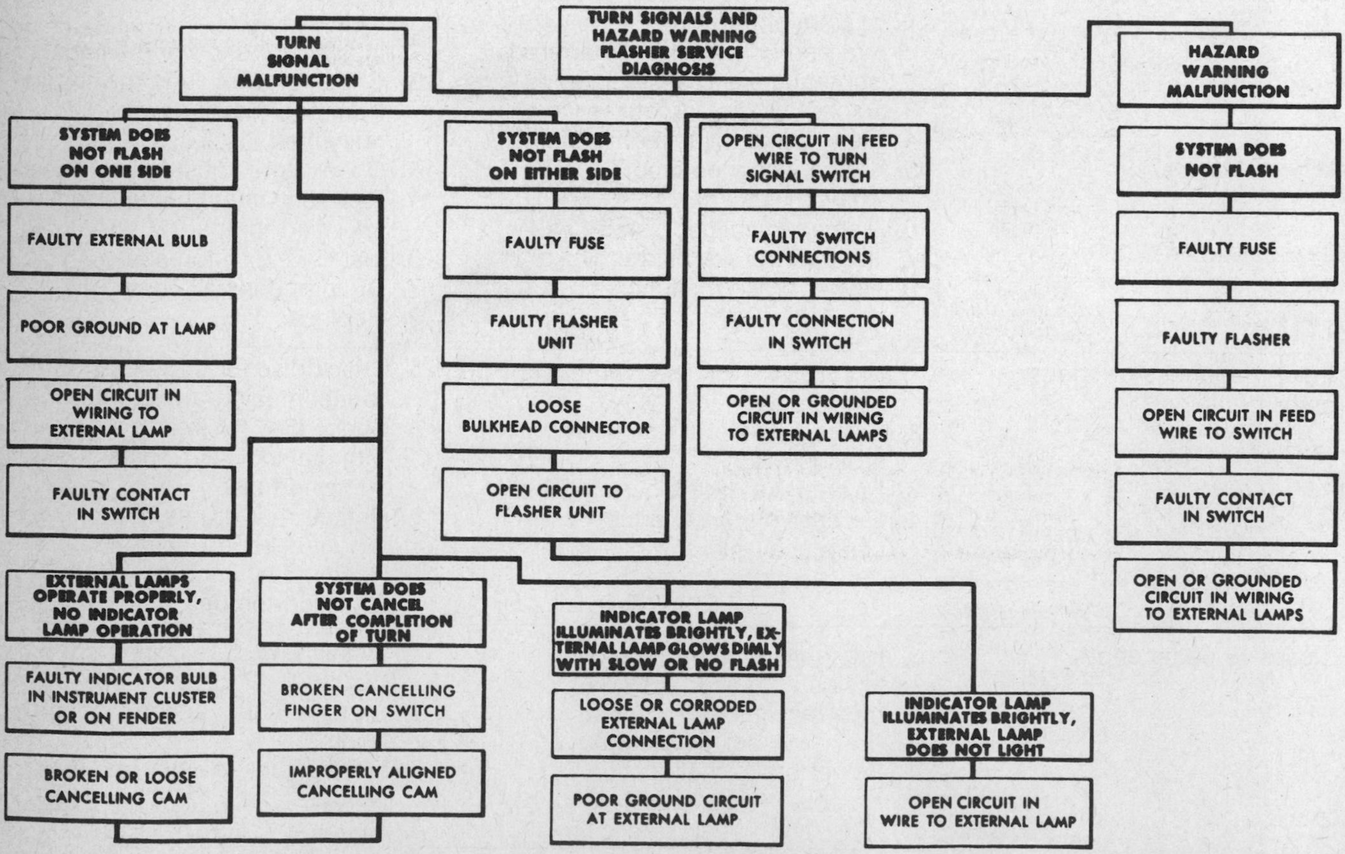

TURN SIGNALS AND HAZARD WARNING FLASHER SERVICE DIAGNOSIS

TURN SIGNAL MALFUNCTION
- SYSTEM DOES NOT FLASH ON ONE SIDE
  - FAULTY EXTERNAL BULB
  - POOR GROUND AT LAMP
  - OPEN CIRCUIT IN WIRING TO EXTERNAL LAMP
  - FAULTY CONTACT IN SWITCH
- EXTERNAL LAMPS OPERATE PROPERLY, NO INDICATOR LAMP OPERATION
  - FAULTY INDICATOR BULB IN INSTRUMENT CLUSTER OR ON FENDER
  - BROKEN OR LOOSE CANCELLING CAM

- SYSTEM DOES NOT CANCEL AFTER COMPLETION OF TURN
  - BROKEN CANCELLING FINGER ON SWITCH
  - IMPROPERLY ALIGNED CANCELLING CAM

- SYSTEM DOES NOT FLASH ON EITHER SIDE
  - FAULTY FUSE
  - FAULTY FLASHER UNIT
  - LOOSE BULKHEAD CONNECTOR
  - OPEN CIRCUIT TO FLASHER UNIT

- INDICATOR LAMP ILLUMINATES BRIGHTLY, EXTERNAL LAMP GLOWS DIMLY WITH SLOW OR NO FLASH
  - LOOSE OR CORRODED EXTERNAL LAMP CONNECTION
  - POOR GROUND CIRCUIT AT EXTERNAL LAMP

- OPEN CIRCUIT IN FEED WIRE TO TURN SIGNAL SWITCH
  - FAULTY SWITCH CONNECTIONS
  - FAULTY CONNECTION IN SWITCH
  - OPEN OR GROUNDED CIRCUIT IN WIRING TO EXTERNAL LAMPS

- INDICATOR LAMP ILLUMINATES BRIGHTLY, EXTERNAL LAMP DOES NOT LIGHT
  - OPEN CIRCUIT IN WIRE TO EXTERNAL LAMP

HAZARD WARNING MALFUNCTION
- SYSTEM DOES NOT FLASH
  - FAULTY FUSE
  - FAULTY FLASHER
  - OPEN CIRCUIT IN FEED WIRE TO SWITCH
  - FAULTY CONTACT IN SWITCH
  - OPEN OR GROUNDED CIRCUIT IN WIRING TO EXTERNAL LAMPS

Windshield Wiper Troubleshooting

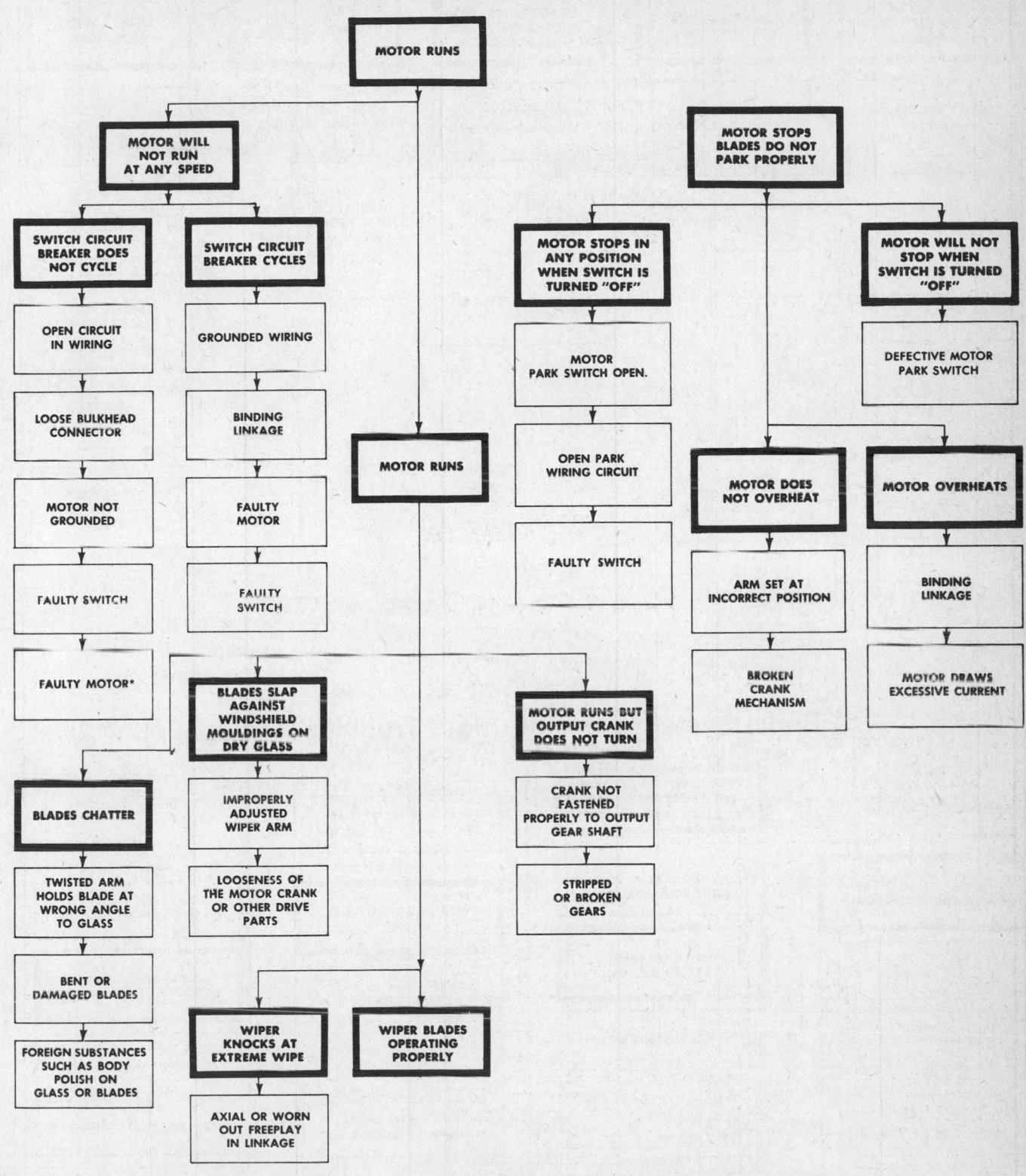

Headlamp Troubleshooting

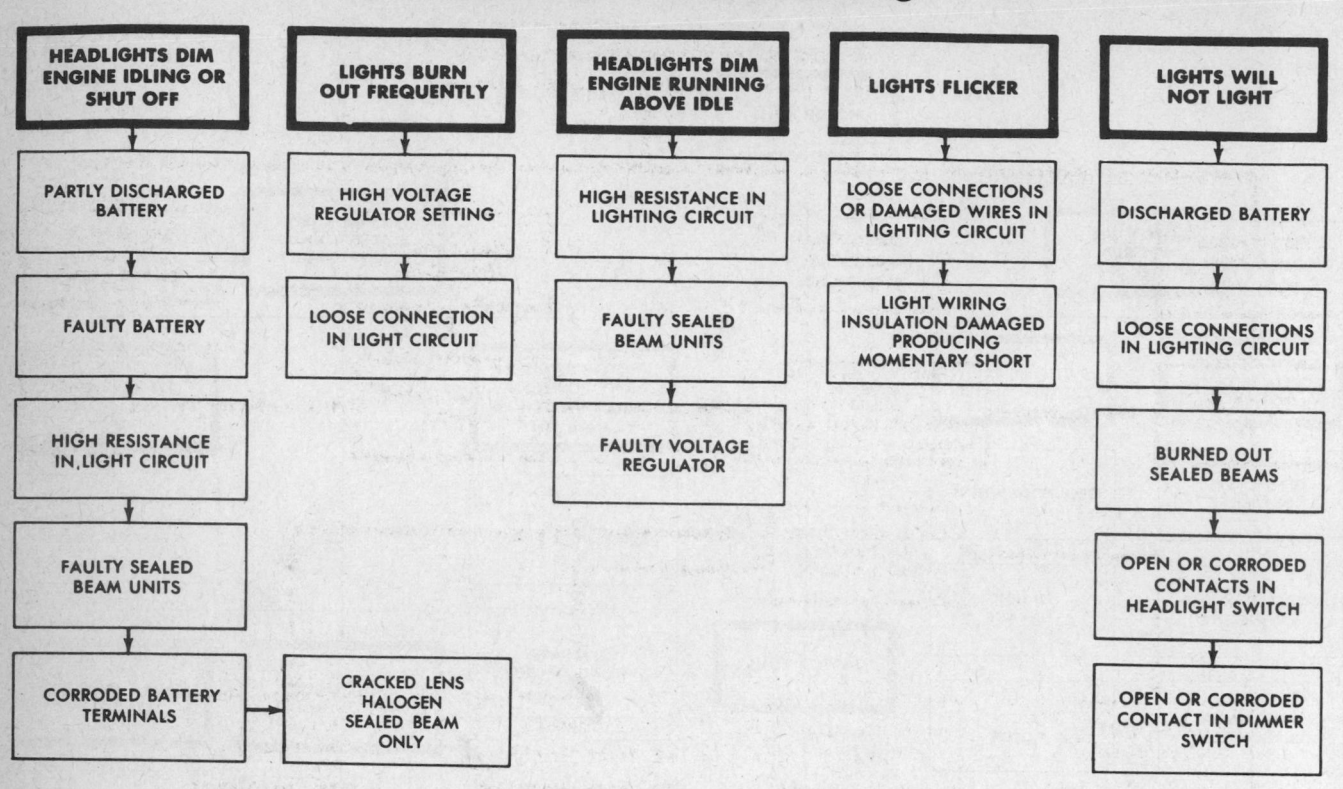

Brake System Warning Light Troubleshooting

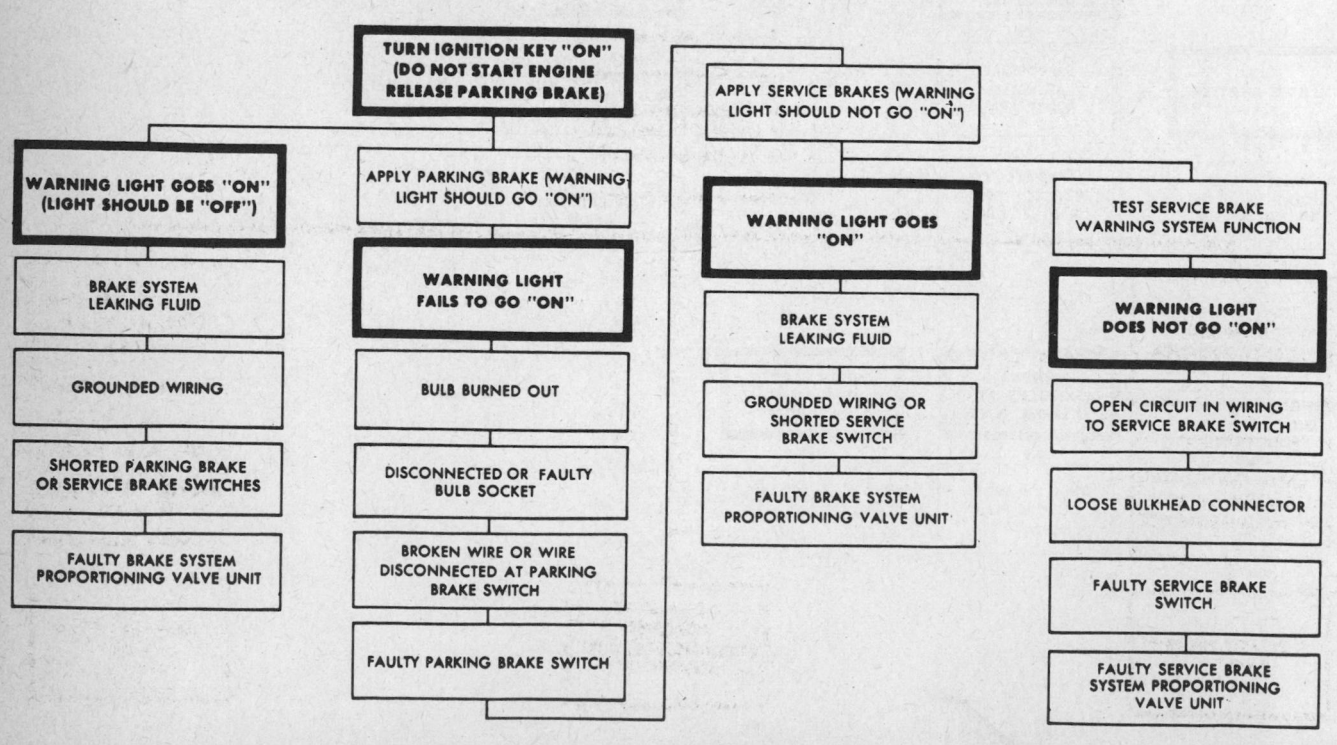

Fuel Gauge System Troubleshooting

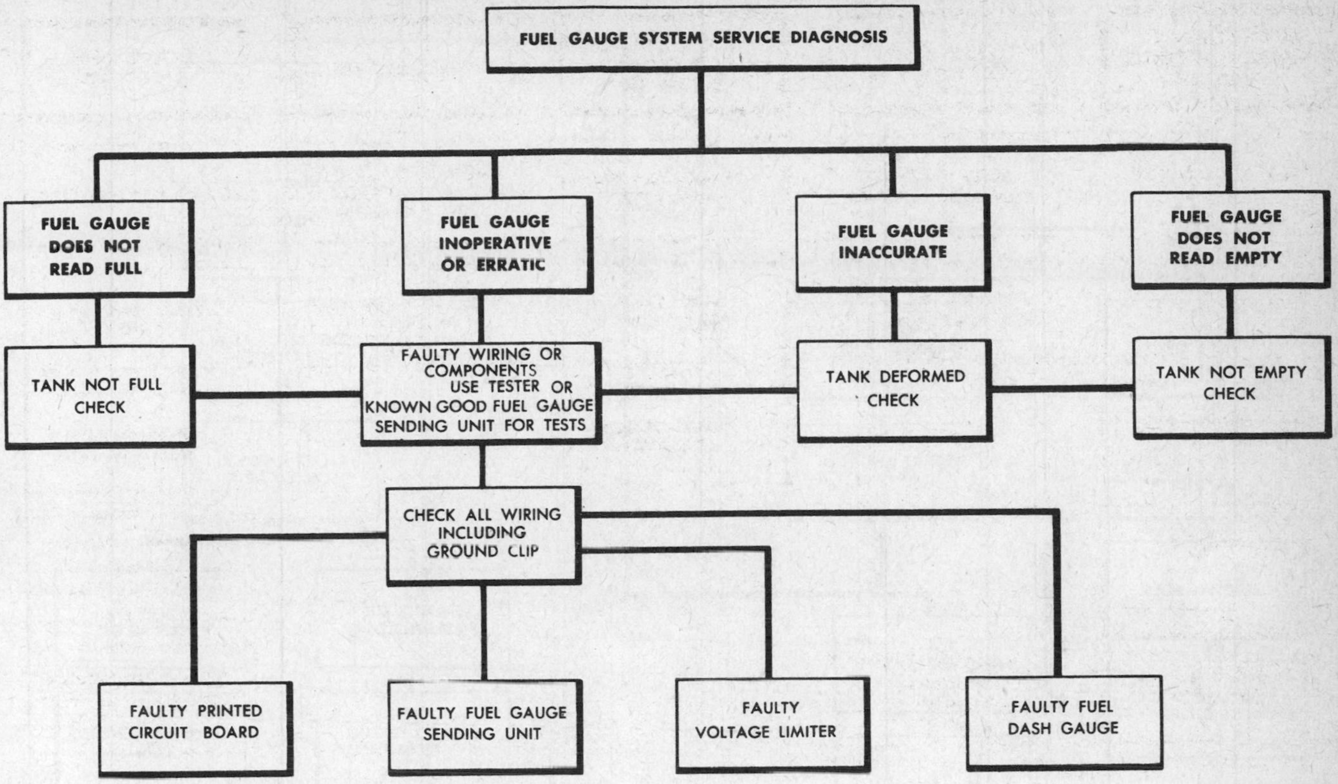

```
                    ┌─────────────────────────────────┐
                    │  FUEL GAUGE SYSTEM SERVICE       │
                    │         DIAGNOSIS                │
                    └─────────────────────────────────┘
```

FUEL GAUGE DOES NOT READ FULL	FUEL GAUGE INOPERATIVE OR ERRATIC	FUEL GAUGE INACCURATE	FUEL GAUGE DOES NOT READ EMPTY
TANK NOT FULL CHECK	FAULTY WIRING OR COMPONENTS USE TESTER OR KNOWN GOOD FUEL GAUGE SENDING UNIT FOR TESTS	TANK DEFORMED CHECK	TANK NOT EMPTY CHECK

```
                    ┌─────────────────────────────────┐
                    │  CHECK ALL WIRING INCLUDING      │
                    │         GROUND CLIP              │
                    └─────────────────────────────────┘
```

FAULTY PRINTED CIRCUIT BOARD	FAULTY FUEL GAUGE SENDING UNIT	FAULTY VOLTAGE LIMITER	FAULTY FUEL DASH GAUGE

Voltage Limiter Troubleshooting

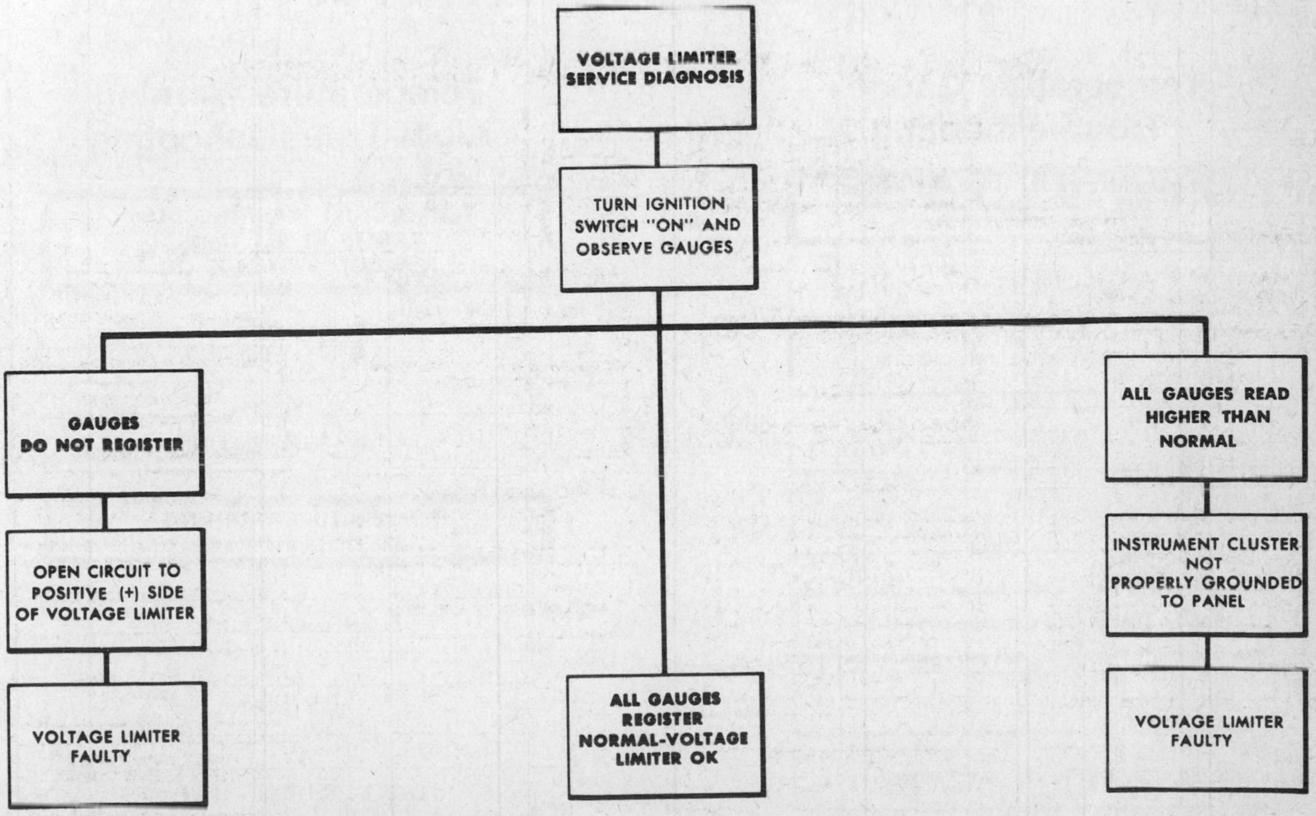

```
                    ┌─────────────────────────────────┐
                    │  VOLTAGE LIMITER SERVICE         │
                    │         DIAGNOSIS                │
                    └─────────────────────────────────┘

                    ┌─────────────────────────────────┐
                    │  TURN IGNITION SWITCH "ON" AND   │
                    │        OBSERVE GAUGES            │
                    └─────────────────────────────────┘
```

GAUGES DO NOT REGISTER	ALL GAUGES REGISTER NORMAL-VOLTAGE LIMITER OK	ALL GAUGES READ HIGHER THAN NORMAL
OPEN CIRCUIT TO POSITIVE (+) SIDE OF VOLTAGE LIMITER		INSTRUMENT CLUSTER NOT PROPERLY GROUNDED TO PANEL
VOLTAGE LIMITER FAULTY		VOLTAGE LIMITER FAULTY

TROUBLESHOOTING AND DIAGNOSIS

Low Oil Pressure Warning Light Troubleshooting

```
         LOW OIL PRESSURE
         WARNING LIGHT
         SERVICE DIAGNOSIS
                │
                ▼
         TURN IGNITION
         SWITCH "ON"
    (DO NOT START ENGINE)
                │
        ┌───────┴───────┐
        ▼               ▼
    LIGHT "OFF"     LIGHT "ON"
        │               │
        ▼               ▼
    DEFECTIVE       START AND IDLE
    SENDING UNIT    ENGINE
        │               │
        ▼               ▼
    DEFECTIVE       LIGHT GOES "OFF"
    BULB                │
        │               ▼
        ▼           WARNING LIGHT OK
    BULB SOCKET OR
    WIRING OPEN


    LIGHT STAYS "ON"
          │
          ▼
    CHECK FOR
    GROUNDED WIRING
          │
          ▼
    CHECK FOR LOW
    OIL LEVEL
          │
          ▼
    TEST ENGINE
    OIL PRESSURE
          │
    ┌─────┴─────┐
    ▼           ▼
ENGINE OIL   ENGINE OIL
PRESSURE LOW PRESSURE OK
    │           │
    ▼           ▼
REFER TO     DEFECTIVE
ENGINE       SENDING UNIT
SERVICE
DIAGNOSIS
```

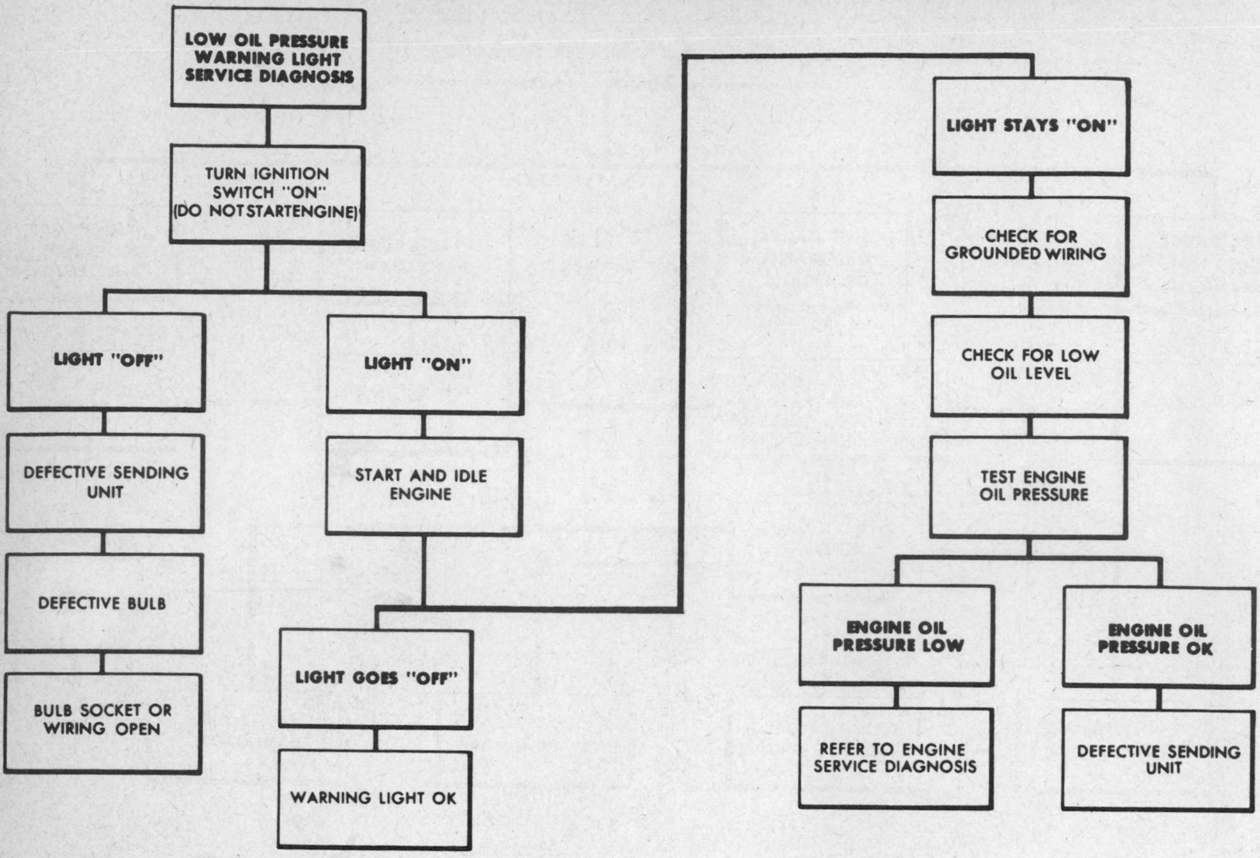

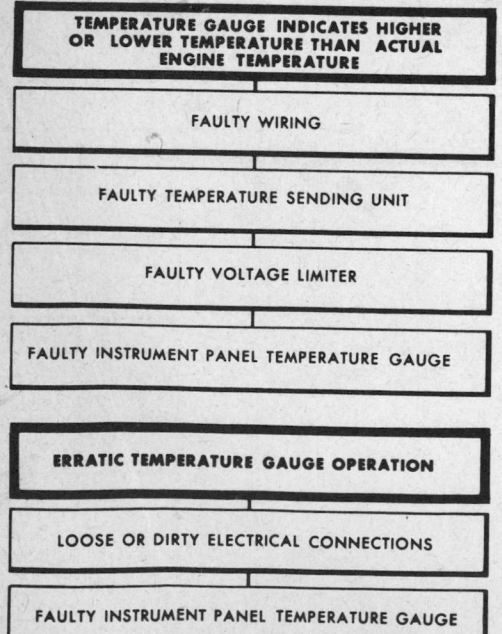

Temperature Gauge Troubleshooting

- **TEMPERATURE GAUGE INDICATES HIGHER OR LOWER TEMPERATURE THAN ACTUAL ENGINE TEMPERATURE**
- FAULTY WIRING
- FAULTY TEMPERATURE SENDING UNIT
- FAULTY VOLTAGE LIMITER
- FAULTY INSTRUMENT PANEL TEMPERATURE GAUGE

- **ERRATIC TEMPERATURE GAUGE OPERATION**
- LOOSE OR DIRTY ELECTRICAL CONNECTIONS
- FAULTY INSTRUMENT PANEL TEMPERATURE GAUGE

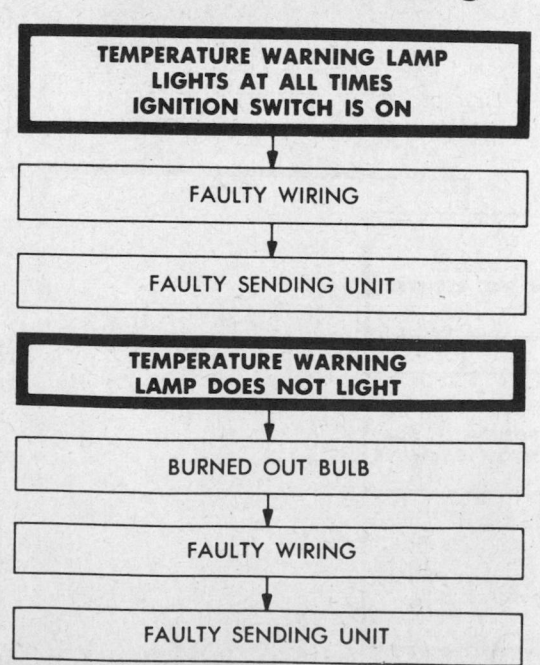

Temperature Warning Light Troubleshooting

- **TEMPERATURE WARNING LAMP LIGHTS AT ALL TIMES IGNITION SWITCH IS ON**
- FAULTY WIRING
- FAULTY SENDING UNIT

- **TEMPERATURE WARNING LAMP DOES NOT LIGHT**
- BURNED OUT BULB
- FAULTY WIRING
- FAULTY SENDING UNIT

GENERAL CONVERSION TABLE

Multiply By	To Convert	To	
		Length	—
2.54	Inches	Centimeters	.3937
25.4	Inches	Millimeters	.03937
30.48	Feet	Centimeters	.0328
.304	Feet	Meters	3.28
.914	Yards	Meters	1.094
1.609	Miles	Kilometers	.621
		Volume	
.473	Pints	Liters	2.11
.946	Quarts	Liters	1.06
3.785	Gallons	Liters	.264
.016	Cubic inches	Liters	61.02
16.39	Cubic inches	Cubic cms.	.061
28.3	Cubic feet	Liters	.0353
		Mass (Weight)	
28.35	Ounces	Grams	.035
.4536	Pounds	Kilograms	2.20
		Area	
.645	Square inches	Square cms.	.155
.836	Square yds.	Square meters	1.196
		Force	
4.448	Pounds	Newtons	.225
.138	Ft./lbs.	Kilogram/meters	7.23
1.36	Ft./lbs.	Newton-meters	.737
.112	In./lbs.	Newton-meters	8.844
		Pressure	
.068	Psi	Atmospheres	14.7
6.89	Psi	Kilopascals	.145
		Other	
1.104	Horsepower (DIN)	Horsepower (SAE)	.9861
.746	Horsepower (SAE)	Kilowatts (KW)	1.34
1.60	Mph	Km/h	.625
.425	Mpg	Km/1	2.35
—	To obtain	From	Multiply by

TAP DRILL SIZES

NATIONAL COARSE OR U.S.S.						NATIONAL FINE OR S.A.E.					
Screw & Tap Size	Threads Per Inch	Use Drill Number	Screw & Tap Size	Threads Per Inch	Use Drill Number	Screw & Tap Size	Threads Per Inch	Use Drill Number	Screw & Tap Size	Threads Per Inch	Use Drill Number
No. 5	40	39	1/2	13	27/64	No. 5	44	37	1/2	20	29/64
No. 6	32	36	9/16	12	31/64	No. 6	40	33	9/16	18	33/64
No. 8	32	29	5/8	11	17/32	No. 8	36	29	5/8	18	37/64
No. 10	24	25	3/4	10	21/32	No. 10	32	21	3/4	16	11/16
No. 12	24	17	7/8	9	49/64	No. 12	28	15	7/8	14	13/16
1/4	20	8	1	8	7/8	1/4	28	3	1 1/8	12	1 3/64
5/16	18	F	1 1/8	7	63/64	5/16	24	1	1 1/4	12	1 11/64
3/8	16	5/16	1 1/4	7	1 7/64	3/8	24	Q	1 1/2	12	1 27/64
7/16	14	U	1 1/2	6	1 11/32	7/16	20	W			

MECHANIC'S DATA

DRILL SIZES IN DECIMAL EQUIVALENTS

Inch	Decimal	Wire	mm
1/64	.0156		.39
	.0157		.4
	.0160	78	
	.0165		.42
	.0173		.44
	.0177		.45
	.0180	77	
	.0181		.46
	.0189		.48
	.0197		.5
	.0200	76	
	.0210	75	
	.0217		.55
	.0225	74	
	.0236		.6
	.0240	73	
	.0250	72	
	.0256		.65
	.0260	71	
	.0276		.7
	.0280	70	
	.0292	69	
	.0295		.75
	.0310	68	
1/32	.0312		.79
	.0315		.8
	.0320	67	
	.0330	66	
	.0335		.85
	.0350	65	
	.0354		.9
	.0360	64	
	.0370	63	
	.0374		.95
	.0380	62	
	.0390	61	
	.0394		1.0
	.0400	60	
	.0410	59	
	.0413		1.05
	.0420	58	
	.0430	57	
	.0433		1.1
	.0453		1.15
	.0465	56	
3/64	.0469		1.19
	.0472		1.2
	.0492		1.25
	.0512		1.3
	.0520	55	
	.0531		1.35
	.0550	54	
	.0551		1.4
	.0571		1.45
	.0591		1.5
	.0595	53	

Inch	Decimal	Wire	mm
	.0610		1.55
1/16	.0625		1.59
	.0630		1.6
	.0635	52	
	.0650		1.65
	.0669		1.7
	.0670	51	
	.0689		1.75
	.0700	50	
	.0709		1.8
	.0728		1.85
	.0730	49	
	.0748		1.9
	.0760	48	
	.0768		1.95
5/64	.0781		1.98
	.0785	47	
	.0787		2.0
	.0807		2.05
	.0810	46	
	.0820	45	
	.0827		2.1
	.0846		2.15
	.0860	44	
	.0866		2.2
	.0886		2.25
	.0890	43	
	.0906		2.3
	.0925		2.35
	.0935	42	
3/32	.0938		2.38
	.0945		2.4
	.0960	41	
	.0965		2.45
	.0980	40	
	.0981		2.5
	.0995	39	
	.1015	38	
	.1024		2.6
	.1040	37	
	.1063		2.7
	.1065	36	
	.1083		2.75
7/64	.1094		2.77
	.1100	35	
	.1102		2.8
	.1110	34	
	.1130	33	
	.1142		2.9
	.1160	32	
	.1181		3.0
	.1200	31	
	.1220		3.1
1/8	.1250		3.17
	.1260		3.2
	.1280		3.25

Inch	Decimal	Wire	mm
	.1285	30	
	.1299		3.3
	.1339		3.4
	.1360	29	
	.1378		3.5
	.1405	28	
9/64	.1406		3.57
	.1417		3.6
	.1440	27	
	.1457		3.7
	.1470	26	
	.1476		3.75
	.1495	25	
	.1496		3.8
	.1520	24	
	.1535		3.9
	.1540	23	
5/32	.1562		3.96
	.1570	22	
	.1575		4.0
	.1590	21	
	.1610	20	
	.1614		4.1
	.1654		4.2
	.1660	19	
	.1673		4.25
	.1693		4.3
	.1695	18	
11/64	.1719		4.36
	.1730	17	
	.1732		4.4
	.1770	16	
	.1772		4.5
	.1800	15	
	.1811		4.6
	.1820	14	
	.1850	13	
	.1850		4.7
	.1870		4.75
3/16	.1875		4.76
	.1890		4.8
	.1890	12	
	.1910	11	
	.1929		4.9
	.1935	10	
	.1960	9	
	.1969		5.0
	.1990	8	
	.2008		5.1
	.2010	7	
13/64	.2031		5.16
	.2040	6	
	.2047		5.2
	.2055	5	
	.2067		5.25
	.2087		5.3

Inch	Decimal	Wire & Letter	mm
	.2090	4	
	.2126		5.4
	.2130	3	
	.2165		5.5
7/32	.2188		5.55
	.2205		5.6
	.2210	2	
	.2244		5.7
	.2264		5.75
	.2280	1	
	.2283		5.8
	.2323		5.9
	.2340	A	
15/64	.2344		5.95
	.2362		6.0
	.2380	B	
	.2402		6.1
	.2420	C	
	.2441		6.2
	.2460	D	
	.2461		6.25
	.2480		6.3
1/4	.2500	E	6.35
	.2520		6.4
	.2559		6.5
	.2570	F	
	.2598		6.6
	.2610	G	
	.2638		6.7
17/64	.2656		6.74
	.2657		6.75
	.2660	H	
	.2677		6.8
	.2717		6.9
	.2720	I	
	.2756		7.0
	.2770	J	
	.2795		7.1
	.2810	K	
9/32	.2812		7.14
	.2835		7.2
	.2854		7.25
	.2874		7.3
	.2900	L	
	.2913		7.4
	.2950	M	
	.2953		7.5
19/64	.2969		7.54
	.2992		7.6
	.3020	N	
	.3031		7.7
	.3051		7.75
	.3071		7.8
	.3110		7.9
5/16	.3125		7.93
	.3150		8.0

Inch	Decimal	Letter	mm
	.3160	O	
	.3189		8.1
	.3228		8.2
	.3230	P	
	.3248		8.25
	.3268		8.3
21/64	.3281		8.33
	.3307		8.4
	.3320	Q	
	.3346		8.5
	.3386		8.6
	.3390	R	
	.3425		8.7
11/32	.3438		8.73
	.3445		8.75
	.3465		8.8
	.3480	S	
	.3504		8.9
	.3543		9.0
	.3580	T	
	.3583		9.1
23/64	.3594		9.12
	.3622		9.2
	.3642		9.25
	.3661		9.3
	.3680	U	
	.3701		9.4
	.3740		9.5
3/8	.3750		9.52
	.3770	V	
	.3780		9.6
	.3819		9.7
	.3839		9.75
	.3858		9.8
	.3860	W	
	.3898		9.9
25/64	.3906		9.92
	.3937		10.0
	.3970	X	
	.4040	Y	
13/32	.4062		10.31
	.4130	Z	
	.4134		10.5
27/64	.4219		10.71
	.4331		11.0
7/16	.4375		11.11
	.4528		11.5
29/64	.4531		11.51
15/32	.4688		11.90
	.4724		12.0
31/64	.4844		12.30
	.4921		12.5
1/2	.5000		12.70
	.5118		13.0
33/64	.5156		13.09
17/32	.5312		13.49

Inch	Decimal	mm
	.5315	13.5
35/64	.5469	13.89
	.5512	14.0
9/16	.5625	14.28
	.5709	14.5
37/64	.5781	14.68
	.5906	15.0
19/32	.5938	15.08
39/64	.6094	15.47
	.6102	15.5
5/8	.6250	15.87
	.6299	16.0
41/64	.6406	16.27
	.6496	16.5
21/32	.6562	16.66
	.6693	17.0
43/64	.6719	17.06
11/16	.6875	17.46
	.6890	17.5
45/64	.7031	17.85
	.7087	18.0
23/32	.7188	18.25
	.7283	18.5
47/64	.7344	18.65
	.7480	19.0
3/4	.7500	19.05
49/64	.7656	19.44
	.7677	19.5
25/32	.7812	19.84
	.7874	20.0
51/64	.7969	20.24
	.8071	20.5
13/16	.8125	20.63
	.8268	21.0
53/64	.8281	21.03
27/32	.8438	21.43
	.8465	21.5
55/64	.8594	21.82
	.8661	22.0
7/8	.8750	22.22
	.8858	22.5
57/64	.8906	22.62
	.9055	23.0
29/32	.9062	23.01
59/64	.9219	23.41
	.9252	23.5
15/16	.9375	23.81
	.9449	24.0
61/64	.9531	24.2
	.9646	24.5
31/32	.9688	24.6
	.9843	25.0
63/64	.9844	25.0
1	1.0000	25.4